**2016** *Standard Catalog of®*

# WORLD COINS

## *2001-Date*

**10th Edition**


**George S. Cuhaj**, Editor • **Thomas Michael**, Market Analyst • **Harry Miller**, U.S. Market Analyst

**Deborah McCue**, Database Specialist • **Kay Sanders**, Editorial Assistant

## *Special Contributors*

**Mahdi Bseiso**

**Melvyn Kassenoff**

**Gerhard Schön**



**Bullion Value (BV) Market Valuations**

Valuations for all platinum, gold, palladium and silver coins of the more common, basically bullion types, or those possessing only modest numismatic premiums are presented in this edition based on market spot prices of:

**$1,120 - $1,285** per ounce for **platinum**
**$1,150 - $1,300** per ounce for **gold**
**$730 - $830** per ounce for **palladium**
**$15.40 - $18.50** per ounce for **silver**

Published by

Krause Publications, a division of F+W Media, Inc.
700 East State Street • Iola, WI 54990-0001
715-445-2214 • 888-457-2873
www.krausebooks.com

To order books or other products call toll-free 1-800-258-0929
or visit us online at www.shopnumismaster.com

ISSN 1935-4339
ISBN-13: 978-1-4402-4410-0
ISBN-10: 1-4402-4410-3

Designed by Jana Tappa
Edited by Arlyn G. Sieber

Printed in the United States of America

# INTRODUCTION

Welcome to the 10th edition of the 21st Century Standard Catalog of World Coins. The most recent annual version of our ever growing series of comprehensive reference catalogs is designed to meet the needs of those whose interest in coins exceeds the casual jingle of those in your pants pocket or purse. Perhaps you have traveled overseas and still have some coins that came home with you, maybe you read in the news about the Euro circulating commemoratives or issues from recently formed nations, or you are a long-term collector who wants to wade out into the most current of numismatic trends. In all cases, this book is for you.

Arranged in alphabetical order by country and with groupings for political structure, coinage type and denomination this catalog offers an easy-to-follow flow of data. You will find many illustrations, complete listings of metal content, descriptions of the designs and events depicted on the coins as well as date, mint mark varieties and values in multiple grades of preservation. In short, just about all of the information you could want on the most modern coins of the world.

With the information presented in these listings, one can marvel at the ingenuity of today's most inventive world mints, which are striking coins in a variety of shapes, sizes, colors and textures. Enjoy the practicality of coins designed for serious circulation in durable metals. Celebrate the advent of coins made of acrylic materials, those which house precious stones, display selective gold overlays or are pad-printed in colorful designs. All are here in this 21st Century edition.

The accuracy of the information offered in this volume is assured through the assistance of a vast number of contributing coin dealers, collectors, manufacturers and researchers who have lent their knowledge to the compiling of this reference by providing our staff with information on new issues, new dates to existing types, accurate mintages and expanded up-to-date pricing. To them all, we offer a heartfelt "Thank You" for their generosity and dedication to the advancement of our shared field of coin collecting.

In addition to the traditional printed catalog we also offer our database information in smaller geographic digital downloads. CD's and DVD's of full catalogs, fixed information from the past on our website www.NumisMaster.com and as licensed material for use with many other websites you may currently be using. To discover our full media line and purchase these materials go to www.shopNumisMaster.com,

Finally, to you the reader, we extend our wishes that you may enjoy using this catalog as much as we have enjoyed its production. Look it over, put it to good use and please let us know if you have any comments or questions.

Best Wishes,
Thomas Michael
Editorial Staff - Standard Catalog of World Coins

# ACKNOWLEDGMENTS

**Many individuals have contributed countless changes, which have been incorporated into the current edition. While all may not be acknowledged, special appreciation is extended to the following who have exhibited a special enthusiasm for this edition.**

Dylan Arthur
Esko Ahlroth
Thomas Augustsson
Oksana Bandrivska
Albert Beck
Anton Belcev
Jan Bendix
Richard Benson
Shamik Biswas
Gunta Bluke
Joseph E. Boling
Richard Borek jun.
Al Boulanger
Mark A. Brown
Maruta Brûkle
Mahdi Bseiso
Chris Budesa
John T. Bucek
Beth Caspar
Adolpho Cayón
Clemente Cayón
Juan Cayón
Fred Colombo
James Douglas
Wilhelm R. Eglseer
Esko Ekman
Makeila Ellis
Andrzej Fischer
Dagmar Flachén
Eugene Freeman
Peter Frei
Arthur Friedburg
Tom Galway
Hans-Henning Goehrum
Francesco Guerriero
Flemming Lyngbeck Hansen
David Harrison
Istvan Hegedus
Frans Hellendall
Emmanuel Henry
Geraldine Herneman
Jennifer Hird
Katriina Holm
Teréz Horváth
Serge Huard
Sadhir Humnabadkar
Nelva G. Icaza
Hector Carlos Janson
Alex Kaglyan
Henna Karjalainen
Melvyn Kassenoff
Craig Keplinger
Sebastian Krämer
Rodolphe Krempp
Alex Lazarovici
Ma Tak Wo
Jenny Manders
Ranko Mandic
Miguel Angel Pratt Mayans
Bernhard H. Mayer
Sabine Meyer
Dimitar Mihov
Auli Mikkonen
Juozas Minikevicius
Andy Mirski
Ing. Benjamin M. Mizrachi R.
Paul Montz
Joanna Mould
Horst-Dieter Müller
Victoria Newman
Michael G. Nielsen
Bill Noyes
José L. Orozco
Alberto Paashaus
Frank Passic
Martin Peeters
Kirsten F. Petersen
Andreas Pitsillides
Taya Pobjoy
Gastone Polacco
Juri Pschegorlinski
Jordi Puigdemasa
Kitty Quan
Yahya Qureshi
Dr. Dennis G. Rainey
Ivan Rakitin
Pilar Rodríguez
Sarah Roe
William M. Rosenblum
Egon Conti Rossini
Pabitra K. Saha
Remy Said
Leon Saryan
Erwin Schäffer
Jacco Scheper
Dr. Andreas Schikora
Gerhard Schön
George Schumacher
Alexander Shapiro
Ole Sjoelund
Mira Spijker
Heimo Steriti
Abu Shamin Mohammad Talha
Mehmet Tolga Taner
Rivka Toledano
Amelia Travaglini
Anthony Tumonis
Erik J. Van Loon
Natanya van Niekerk
Neil Vance
Carmen Viciedo
Wakim Wakim
Paul Welz
J. Brix Westergaard
J. Hugh Witherow
Joseph Zaffern

## AUCTION HOUSES

Dix-Noonan-Webb
Heritage World Coin Auctions
Fritz Rudolf Künker
Marudhar Arts
MPO Auctions
Münzenhandlung Harald Möller, GmbH
Noble Numismatics, Pty. Ltd.
Stack's, Bowers and Ponterio
Stephen Album Rare Coins
St. James's Auctions
Teutoburger Münzauktion & Handel GmbH
World Wide Coins of California

## WORLD MINTS, CENTRAL BANKS AND DISTRIBUTORS

Austrian Mint
Banco de Mexico
Banque Centrale Du Luxembourg
Bank du Liban
Black Mountain Coins
Casa de la Moneda de Cuba
Casa da Moeda do Brasil
Central Bank of D.P.R. Korea - Kumbyol Trading Corp.
Central Bank of the Russian Federation
CIT
Czech National Bank
Downies
East India Company
Educational Coin Company
Faude & Huguenin
Global Coins & Medals Ltd. - Official Sales Company of the Bulgarian Mint
Helvetic Mint
Imprensa Nacional - Casa da Moeda, S.A.
Israel Coins & Medals Corp.
Istituto Poligrafico e Zecca dello Stato I.p.A.
Jablonex Group - Division of Czech Mint
Japan Mint
JVP Investment Coins
Kazakhstan Mint
KOMSCO - South Korea
Latvijas Banka
Lietuvos Bankas
Lithuanian Mint
Magyar Penzvero Zrt.
Mayer's Mint GmbH
MDM
Mennica Polska
Mincovna Kremnica
Mint of Finland, Ltd.
Mint of Norway
Monnaie de Paris
Moscow Mint
National Bank of the Republic of Belarus
National Bank of Ukraine
New Zealand Mint
Numiscom
Numistrade Gmbh & Co. kg.
PAMP
PandaAmerica
Perth Mint
Pobjoy Mint
Real Casa de la Moneda – Spain
Romanian Mint
Royal Mint
Royal Australian Mint
Royal Belgian Mint
Royal Canadian Mint
Royal Dutch Mint
Royal Thai Mint
Servei D'Emissions Principat D'Andorra
Singapore Mint
South African Mint
Staatliche Munze Berlin
Staatliche Munze Baden-Wurttemberg
Talisman Coins
Thailand Treasury Department
Ufficio Filatelico e Numismatico - Vatican
United States Mint

# COUNTRY INDEX

# HOW TO USE THIS CATALOG

This catalog is designed to serve the needs of both the novice and advanced collectors. It provides a comprehensive guide to world coins struck in the 21st century (2001 to present). It is arranged so that persons with a basic knowledge of world history and a casual acquaintance with coin collecting can consult it with confidence and ease. The following explanations summarize the general practices used in preparing the catalog listings. However, because of specialized requirements, which may vary by country and political era within a country, these should not be considered ironclad.

## ARRANGEMENT

Countries are arranged alphabetically. Political changes within a country are arranged chronologically. In countries where Rulers are the single most significant political entity, a chronological arrangement by Ruler has been employed. Distinctive sub-geographic regions are listed alphabetically following the country's main listings. A few exceptions to these rules may exist. If a location is in question, please refer to the Country Index.

Diverse coinage types relating to fabrication methods, revaluations and change in denomination systems have been identified, separated and arranged in a logical fashion. Chronological arrangement is employed for most circulating coinage. Monetary system reforms will flow in order of their institution. Special non-circulating types such as Essais, Piedforts, Patterns, Trial Strikes, Mint and Proof sets follow at the end of the individual county's listings.

Within a coinage type, coins will be listed by denomination, from smallest to largest. Numbered types within a denomination will be ordered by their first date of issue.

## IDENTIFICATION

The most important step in the identification of a coin is the determination of the nation of origin. This is generally easily accomplished where the country name appears in easy to read characters; if in doubt, use the country index. The coins of Great Britain do not have the county name, just the name and image of the ruler.

The coins of many countries beyond the English-language realm, such as those of French, Italian or Spanish heritage, are also quite easy to identify through reference to their legends, which appear in the national languages based on Western alphabets. In many instances the name is spelled exactly the same in English as in the national language; while in other cases it varies only slightly, like Italia for Italy, Belgique or Belgie for Belgium, Brasil for Brazil and Danmark for Denmark.

This is not always the case, however, as in Soumi for Finland, Norge for Norway, Espana for Spain, Slovensko for Slovakia, Sverige for Sweden and Helvetia for Switzerland. Some other examples include: Empire Cherifin Maroc for Morocco, Estados Unidos Mexicanos for United Mexican States (Mexico) and Etat du Grand Liban - State of Great Lebanon (Lebanon).

With the introduction of the Euro Coinage, some member nations have identified their coin with only country initials, such as BE for Belgium, IR for Italy, RF for France.

Thus it can be seen there are instances in which a little effort in the rudiments of foreign languages can be most helpful. In general, colonial possessions of countries using the Western alphabet are similarly identifiable as they often carry portraits of their current rulers, the familiar lettering, sometimes in combination with a companion designation in the local language.

Collectors have the greatest difficulty with coins that do not bear legends or dates in the Western systems. These include coins bearing Cyrillic lettering attributable to Bulgaria, Russia, the Slavic states and Mongolia; the Greek script peculiar to Greece, Crete and the Ionian Islands; the Amharic characters of Ethiopia; or Hebrew in the case of Israel. Dragons and sunbursts along with the distinctive word characters attribute a coin to the Oriental countries of China, Japan, Korea, Tibet, Viet Nam and their component parts.

The most difficult coins to identify are those bearing only Persian or Arabic script and its derivatives, found on the issues of nations stretching in a wide swath across North Africa and East Asia, from Morocco to Indonesia, and the Indian subcontinent, although the task of identification on the more modern issues of these lands is often eased by the added presence of Western alphabet legends.

Certain characteristics and symbols featured in addition to the prominent legends are typical on coins from a given country or group of countries. For instance, a predominant design feature on the coins of Nepal is the trident; while neighboring Tibet features a lotus blossom or lion on many of their issues.

We also suggest reference to the comprehensive Country Index and Denomination Index.

## DENOMINATIONS

The second basic consideration to be met in the attribution of a coin is the determination of denomination. Since denominations are usually expressed in numeric rather than word form on a coin, this is usually quite easily accomplished on coins from nations which use Western numerals, except in those instances where issues are devoid of any mention of face value, and denomination must be attributed by size, metallic composition or weight. Coins illustrated in this volume are generally illustrated in actual size up to 55mm in diameter. Illustrations of coins larger than 55mm are reduced to 55mm, and the actual size is indicated in the listing of the type.

The sphere of countries stretching from North Africa through the Orient, on which numeric symbols generally unfamiliar to Westerners are employed, provide the collector with a challenge. This is particularly true on nearly all pre-20th Century issues. In many cases as the years progressed, Western-style numerals are often presented in combination with the local numeric systems on these coins.

Determination of a coin's currency system can also be valuable in attributing the issue to its country of origin. The table of Standard International Numeral Systems presents lists of the basic numeric designations found on coins of non-Western origin. Although denomination numerals are generally prominently displayed on coins, it must be remembered that these are general representations of characters, which individual coin designers may have rendered in a wide variety of engraving styles. Where numeric or script denominations designation forms peculiar to a given coin or country apply, such as the script used on some Persian (Iranian) issues, they are so indicated or illustrated in conjunction with the appropriate listings.

## DATING

Coin dating is the final basic attribution consideration. Here, the problem can be more difficult because the reading of a coin date is subject not only to the vagaries of numeric styling, but to calendar variations caused by the observance of various religious eras or regal periods from country to country, or even within a country. Here again, with the exception of the sphere from North Africa through the Orient, it will be found that most countries rely on Western date numerals and Christian (AD) era reckoning, although in a few instances, coin dating has been tied to the year of a reign or government. The Vatican, for example dates its coinage according to the year of reign of the current pope, in addition to the Christian-era date.

Countries in the Arabic sphere generally date their coins to the Muslim era (AH), which commenced on July 16, 622 AD (Julian calendar), when the prophet Mohammed fled from Mecca to Medina. As their calendar is reckoned by the lunar year of 354 days, which is about three percent (precisely 2.98%) shorter than the Christian year, a formula is required to convert AH dating to its Western equivalent. To convert an AH date to the approximate AD date, subtract three percent of the AH date (round to the closest whole number) from the AH date and add 622. A chart converting all AH years from 1010 (July 2, 1601) to 1450 (May 25, 2028) may be found elsewhere in this catalog under the name Hejira Date Chart.

The Muslim calendar is not always based on the lunar year (AH), however, causing some confusion, particularly in Afghanistan and Iran, where a calendar based on the solar year (SH) was introduced around 1920. These dates can be converted to AD by simply adding 621. In 1976 the government of Iran implemented a new solar calendar based on the foundation of the Iranian monarchy in 559 BC. The first year observed on the new calendar was 2535 (MS), which commenced March 20, 1976. A reversion to the traditional SH dating standard occurred a few years later.

Several different eras of reckoning, including Christian and Muslim (AH), have been used to date coins of the Indian subcontinent. The two basic systems are the Vikrama Samvat (VS), which dates from Oct. 18, 58 BC, and the Saka era, the origin of which is reckoned from March 3, 78 AD. Dating according to both eras appears on various coins of the area.

Coins of Thailand (Siam) are found dated by three different eras. The most predominant is the Buddhist era (BE), which originated in 543 BC. Next is the Bangkok or Ratanakosindsok (RS) era, dating from 1781 AD; followed by the Chula-Sakarat (CS) era, dating from 638 AD. The latter era originated in Burma and is used on that country's coins.

Other calendars include that of the Ethiopian era (EE), which commenced seven years, eight months after AD dating; and that of the Jewish people, which commenced on Oct. 7, 3761 BC. Korea claims a legendary dating from 2333 BC, which is acknowledged in some of its coin dating. Some coin issues of the Indonesian area carry dates determined by the Javanese Aji Saka era (AS), a calendar of 354 days (100 Javanese years equal 97 Christian or Gregorian calendar years), which can be matched to AD dating by comparing it to AH dating.

The following table indicates the year dating for the various eras, which correspond to 2014 in Christian calendar reckoning, but it must be remembered that there are overlaps between the eras in some instances.

|  | |  |
|---|---|---|
| Christian era (AD) | - | 2015 |
| Muslim era (AH) | - | AH1436 |
| Solar year (SH) | - | SH1393 |
| Monarchic Solar era (MS) | - | MS2574 |
| Vikrama Samvat (VS) | - | VS2072 |
| Saka era (SE) | - | SE1937 |
| Buddhist era (BE) | - | BE2558 |
| Bangkok era (RS) | - | RS234 |
| Chula-Sakarat era (CS) | - | CS1377 |
| Ethiopian era (EE) | - | EE2008 |
| Korean era | - | 4348 |
| Javanese Aji Saka era (AS) | - | AS1948 |
| Fasli era (FE) | - | FE1425 |
| Jewish era (JE) | - | JE5775 |
| Roman | - | MMXV |

Coins of Asian origin - principally Japan, Korea, China, Turkestan and Tibet and some modern gold issues of Turkey - are generally dated to the year of the government, dynasty, reign or cyclic eras, with the dates indicated in Asian characters which usually read from right to left. In recent years, however, some dating has been according to the Christian calendar and in Western numerals. In Japan, Asian character dating was reversed to read from left to right in Showa year 23 (1948 AD).

More detailed guides to less prevalent coin dating systems, which are strictly local in nature, are presented with the appropriate listings.

Some coins carry dates according to both locally observed and Christian eras. This is particularly true in the Arabic world, where the Hejira date may be indicated in Arabic numerals and the Christian date in Western numerals, or both dates in either form.

The date actually carried on a given coin is generally cataloged here in the first column (Date). If this date is in a non-Christian dating system, such as 'AH' (Muslim), the Christian equivalent date will appear in parentheses(), for example AH1336(1917). Dates listed alone in the date column which do not actually appear on a given coin, or dates which are known, but do not appear on the coin, are generally enclosed by parentheses with 'ND' at the left, for example ND(1926).

Timing differentials between some era of reckoning, particularly the 354-day Mohammedan and 365-day Christian years, cause situations whereby coins which carry dates for both eras exist bearing two year dates from one calendar combined with a single date from another.

Countermarked Coinage is presented with both 'Countermark Date' and 'Host Coin' date for each type. Actual date representation follows the rules outlined above.

For a more detailed information on coin dating see the *Illustrated Coin Dating Guide for the Eastern World* by Albert Galloway, Krause Publications, F+W Media, 2012.

## NUMBERING SYSTEM

Some catalog numbers assigned in this volume are based on other established references. This practice has been observed for two reasons: First, when world coins are listed chronologically they are basically self-cataloging;

second, there was no need to confuse collectors with totally new numeric designations where appropriate systems already existed. As time progressed we found many of these established systems incomplete and inadequate and many have now been replaced with KM numbers. If numbers have changed, appropriate cross-referencing has been provided.

Some of these references used in this catalog are (Y#) identified assigned by R.S. Yeoman, or slight adaptations thereof, in his *Modern World Coins*, and *Current Coins of the World.*

## MINTAGES

Quantities minted of each date are indicated where that information is available; the uncirculated mintages numbers include those inserted into annual uncirculated sets. For combined mintage figures the abbreviation "Inc. Above" means Included Above, while "Inc. Below" means Included Below. "Est." beside a mintage figure indicates the number given is an estimate of the intended mintage or an advertised mintage limit when the final (actual) mintage figure is not known.

## MINT AND PRIVY MARKS

The presence of distinctive, but frequently inconspicuously placed, mintmarks indicates the mint of issue for many of the coins listed in this catalog. An appropriate designation in the date listing note the presence, if any, of a mint mark on a particular coin type by incorporating the letter or letters of the mint mark adjoining the date, i.e., 2010D or 2005R.

The presence of mint and/or mintmaster's privy marks on a coin in non-letter form is indicated by incorporating a letter in lower case within parentheses adjoining the date; i.e. 2010(sm). The corresponding mark is illustrated or identified in the introduction of the country.

In countries where privy marks are used, such as Australia, Canada and Isle of Man, a letter in (a) may be employed or a descriptive word may be used to describe it in the listing or in reference to the chart at the beginning of that country's listings.

## METALS

Each numbered type listing will contain a description of the coins metallic content. The traditional coinage metals and their symbolic chemical abbreviations are:

| | |
|---|---|
| Platinum - (PT) | Copper - (Cu) |
| Gold - (Au) | Silver - (Ag) |
| Copper-Nickel- (CN) | Lead - (Pb) |
| Nickel - (Ni) | Zinc - (Zn) |
| Tin - (Sn) | Bronze - (Ae) |
| | Aluminum - (Al) |

During the 18th and 19th centuries, most of the world's coins were struck of copper or bronze, silver, and gold. Commencing in the early years of the 20th century, however, numerous new coinage metals, primarily non-precious metal alloys, were introduced. Gold has not been widely used for circulation coinages since World War I, although silver remained a popular coinage metal in most parts of the world until after World War II. With the disappearance of silver for circulation coinage, numerous additional compositions were introduced to circulating coinage applications.

Most recent is the development of clad or plated planchets in order to maintain circulation life and extend the life of a set of production dies as used in the production of the copper-nickel clad copper 50 centesimos of Panama or in the latter case to reduce production costs of the planchets and yet provide a coin quite similar in appearance to its predecessor as in the case of the copper plated zinc core United States 1983 cent.

Modern commemorative coins have employed still more unusual methods such as bimetallic coins, color applications and precious metal or gem inlays.

## OFF-METAL STRIKES

Off-metal strikes previously designated by "OMS" which also included the wide range of error coinage struck in other than their officially authorized compositions have been incorporated into Pattern listings along with special issues, which were struck for presentation or other reasons.

## PRECIOUS METAL WEIGHTS

Listings of weight, fineness and actual silver (ASW), gold (AGW), platinum or palladium (APW) content of most machine-struck silver, gold, platinum and palladium coins are provided in this edition. This information will be found at the start of a type description, followed by other information related to the coin.

The ASW, AGW and APW figures were determined by multiplying the gross weight of a given coin by its officially known standard or tested fineness and converting the resulting gram or grain weight into troy ounces, rounded to the nearest hundredth of an ounce. A silver coin with a 24.25-gram weight and .875 fineness for example, would have a fine weight of approximately 21.22 grams, or a .6822 ASW, a factor that can be used to accurately determine the intrinsic value for multiple examples.

The ASW, AGW or APW figure can be multiplied by the spot price of each precious metal to determine the current intrinsic value of any coin accompanied by these designations.

Coin weights are indicated in grams (abbreviated "g") along with fineness where the information is of value in differentiating between types. These weights are based on 31.103 grams per troy (scientific) ounce, as opposed to the avoirdupois (commercial) standard of 28.35 grams. Actual coin weights are generally shown in hundredths of a gram; i.e., 0.500 SILVER 2.92g.

## WEIGHTS AND FINENESSES

As the silver and gold bullion markets have advanced and declined sharply over the years, the fineness and total precious metal content of coins has become especially significant where bullion coins - issues which trade on the basis of their intrinsic metallic content rather than numismatic value - are concerned. In many instances, such issues have become worth more in bullion form than their nominal collector values or denominations indicate.

Establishing the weight of a coin can also be valuable for determining its denomination. Actual weight is also necessary to ascertain the specific gravity of the coin's metallic content, an important factor in determining authenticity.

### TROY WEIGHT STANDARDS

24 Grains = 1 Pennyweight
480 Grains = 1 Ounce
31.103 Grams = 1 Ounce

### UNIFORM WEIGHTS

15.432 Grains = 1 Gram
0.0648 Gram = 1 Grain

## AVOIRDUPOIS STANDARDS

27-11/32 Grains = 11 Dram
437-1/2 Grains = 1 Ounce
28.350 Grams = 1 Ounce

## BULLION VALUE

The simplest method for determining the bullion value of a precious metal coin is to multiply the actual precious metal weight by the current spot price for that metal. Using the example above, a silver coin with a .6822 actual silver weight (ASW) would have an intrinsic value of $12.25 when the spot price of silver is $17.95. If the spot price of silver would increase to $22.50, that same coins' intrinsic value would rise to $15.35.

## PHOTOGRAPHS

To assist the reader in coin identification, every effort has been made to use actual size images of each type listed. When available both sides are illustrated. When the coin has a diameter of 39mm or larger, usually the side required for identification of the type is illustrated. All coins up to 55mm are illustrated actual size, to the nearest 1/2mm up to 25mm, and to the nearest 1mm thereafter. Coins larger than 55mm diameter are illustrated in reduced size, with the actual size noted in the descriptive text of the listing. Where slight change in size is important to coin type identification, actual millimeter measurements are stated in the listing.

## TRADE COINS

From approximately 1750-1940, a number of nations, particularly European colonial powers and commercial traders, minted trade coins to facilitate commerce with the local populace of Africa, the Arab countries, the Indian subcontinent, Southeast Asia and the Far East. Such coins generally circulated at a value based on the weight and fineness of their silver or gold content, rather than their stated denomination. Examples include the sovereigns of Great Britain and the gold ducat issues of Austria, Hungary and the Netherlands. These coins will be segregated into a Trade coinage section near the end of the domestic issues.

## VALUATIONS

Values quoted in this catalog represent the current retail market and are compiled from recommendations provided and verified through various source documents and specialized consultants. It should be stressed, however, that this book is intended to serve only as an aid for evaluating coins, actual market conditions are constantly changing and additional influences, such as particularly strong local demand for certain coin series, fluctuation of international exchange rates, changes in spot price of precious metals and worldwide collecting patterns must also be considered. Publication of this catalog is not intended as a solicitation by the publisher, editors or contributors to buy or sell the coins listed at the prices indicated.

All valuations are stated in U.S. dollars, based on careful assessment of the varied international collector markets. Valuations for coins priced below $100.00 are generally stated in full amounts, i.e. 37.50 or 95.00, while valuations at or above that $100.00 are rounded off in even dollars - i.e. $125.00 is expressed 125. A comma is added to indicate thousands of dollars in value (12,500.)

A dash (-) to the left of given values in a specific value field indicates a lack of a collectible premium. A coin in these lower grades would be worth only its face or intrinsic value. A dash (-) to the right of given values may mean very few or no examples of that grade exist for the type.

For coins which trade close to their bullion value (BV) autocalculations have been determined and instituted in this edition. These formulas will calculate a value based on the BV value of a coin, plus an acceptable premium. Unusual figures in the value column are an indication of this autocalculation function. To determine a current BV value in shifting spot metal conditions, simply multiply the actual precious metal weight by the current spot metal price.

For the convenience of overseas collectors and for U.S. collectors doing business with overseas dealers, the exchange rate for current currencies is presented in the Foreign Exchange Table.

## MEDALLIC ISSUES

Medallic issues are similar to coin-type issues and can generally be identified as commemoratives produced to the country's established coinage standards but without the usual indicator of denomination. These pieces sometimes feature designs adapted from the country's regular issue or commemorative coinage, and occasionally have been issued in conjunction with related coinage issues.

Medallic issues, though bearing these similarities to coinage issues, are not coins and therefore are not listed in this catalog but can be found in the companion catalog *Unusual World Coins*. These Medallic issues are also listed on our searchable web catalog at www.NumisMaster.com.

## RESTRIKES, COUNTERFEITS

Deceptive restrike and counterfeit (both contemporary and modern) examples exist of some coin issues. Where possible, the existence of official restrikes is noted. Warnings are also incorporated in instances where particularly deceptive counterfeits are known to exist. If you are uncertain about the authenticity of a coin held in your collection, or being offered for sale, one should take the precaution of having it authenticated by one of the recognized third party grading services. Their services are reasonably priced, and their products are widely accepted by collectors and dealers alike.

## NON-CIRCULATING LEGAL TENDER COINS

Coins of non-circulating legal tender (NCLT) origin are individually listed and integrated by denomination into the regular listings for each country, excepting where large, established serialized categories exist. These coins fall outside the customary definitions of coin-of-the-realm issues, but where created and sold by, or under authorization of, agencies of sovereign governments expressly for collectors. These are primarily individual coins and sets of a commemorative nature, marketed at prices substantially in excess of both face and intrinsic value, and usually do not have counterparts released for circulation. If you are only interested in coins which circulate in commerce we offer a catalog titled *Collecting World Coins*, which lists world issues since 1901. The current edition is available at www.shopnumismaster.com.

## EDGE VARIETIES

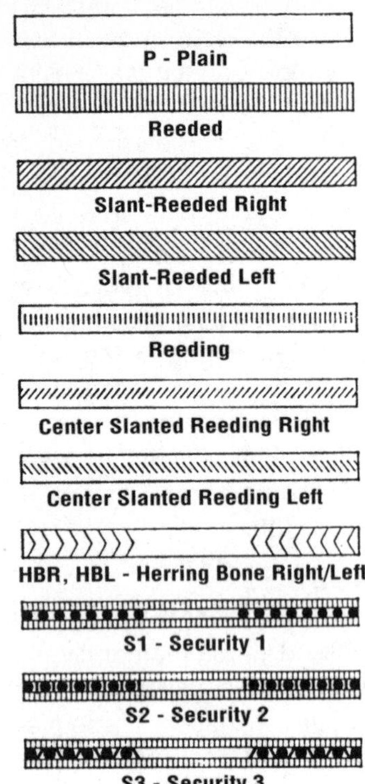


## NEW ISSUES

All coins dated from 2001 to present that have been physically observed by our staff or confirmed by our reliable sources have been incorporated into this edition. Exceptions exist in some countries where current date coin production lags far behind or information on current issues is less accessible.

## SETS

Listings in this catalog for specimen, proof and mint sets are for official, government-produced sets. In many instances privately packaged sets also exist, these are not listed.

**Mint Sets / Fleur de Coin Sets:** Specially prepared by worldwide mints to provide banks, collectors and government dignitaries with examples of current coinage. These coins are often subjected to rigorous inspection to insure that top quality specimens of selected business strikes are provided. One of the most popular mint set is that given out by the monarch of Great Britain each year on Maundy Thursday. This set contains four special coins in denominations of 1, 2, 3 and 4 pence, struck in silver and contained in a little pouch. They have been given away in a special ceremony for the poor for more than two centuries.

The Paris Mint introduced polyvinyl plastic cases packed within a cardboard box for homeland and colonial Fleur de Coin sets of the 1960s. British colonial sets were issued in velvet-lined metal cases similar to those used for proof sets. For its client nations, the Franklin Mint introduced a sealed composition of cardboard and specially molded hard clear plastic protective container inserted in a soft plastic wallet. Discovery that soft polyvinyl packaging has proved hazardous to coins has resulted in a change to the use of hard, inert plastics for virtually all mint sets.

Some of the highest quality mint sets ever produced were those struck by the Franklin Mint during 1972-74. In many cases matte finish dies were used to strike a polished proof planchet. Later on, from 1975, sets contained highly polished, glassy-looking coins (similar to those struck by the Bombay Mint) for collectors over a period of twelve years.

**Specimen Sets:** Forerunners of today's proof sets. In most cases the coins were specially struck, perhaps even double struck, to produce a very soft or matte finish on the effigies and fields, along with high, sharp, "wire" rims. The finish is rather dull to the naked eye.

The original purpose of these sets was to provide VIPs, monarchs and mintmasters around the world with samples of the highest quality workmanship of a particular mint. These were usually housed in elaborate velvet-lined leather and metal cases.

**Proof-like Sets** are relatively new to the field of numismatics. During the mid-1950s the Royal Canadian Mint furnished the hobby with specially selected early business strike coins that exhibited some qualities similar to proof coinage. However, the "proof-like" fields are generally flawed and the edges are rounded. These pieces are not double struck. These are commonly encountered in cardboard holders, later in soft plastic or pliofilm packaging. Of late, the Royal Canadian Mint packages such sets in rigid plastic cases.

Many worldwide officially issued proof sets would in reality fall into this category upon careful examination of the quality of the coin's finish.

Another term encountered in this category is "Special Select," used to describe the crowns of the Union of South Africa and 100-schilling coins produced for collectors in the late 1970s by the Austrian Mint.

**Proof Sets:** This is undoubtedly among the most misused terms in the hobby, not only by collectors and dealers, but also by many of the world mints.

A true proof set must be comprised of coins which are at least double-struck on specially prepared polished planchets and struck using dies (which are also often polished) of the highest quality under greater than normal pressure. Modern-day proof quality coins often consist of frosted portraits or design elements surrounded by absolute mirror-like fields. A reverse-proof has frosted portraits or design elements surrounded by frosted fields.

Listings for proof sets in this catalog are for officially issued proof sets so designated by the issuing authority, and depending on country of origin, may or may not possess what are considered modern proof quality standards.

It is necessary for collectors to acquire the knowledge to allow them to differentiate true proof sets from would-be proof sets and proof-like sets which are encountered.

## CONDITIONS / GRADING

Wherever possible, coin valuations are presented in five grades of preservation. In this catalog we have adopted the use of the 70-point numerical grading system employed in the United States. For modern commemoratives, which do not circulate, only Mint State prices are sufficient. Proof issues are indicated by the prefix PF-60, PF-63 or PF-65 next to the valuation following the mintage. Coins which are proof in quality but not yet priced, have the notation of Proof next to the date and no price information. For very recent circulating coins and coins of limited value only one, two or three grade values are presented with lower grade fields containing a dash (-) value indicating no collector premium above face or intrinsic value.

There are almost no grading guides for world coins. What follows is an attempt to help bridge that gap until a detailed, illustrated guide becomes available.

In grading world coins, there are two elements to look for: 1) Overall wear, and 2) loss of design details, such as strands of hair, feathers on eagles, design elements on the coat-of-arms, etc.

The age, rarity or type of a coin should not be a consideration in grading.

Grade each coin by the weaker of the two sides. This method appears to give results most nearly consistent with the American Numismatic Association standards for U.S. coins. Split grades, i.e., F/VF for obverse and reverse, respectively, are normally no more than one grade apart. If the two sides are more than one grade apart, the series of coins probably wears differently on each side and should then be graded by the weaker side alone.

Grade a coin by the amount of overall wear and loss of design detail evident on each side of the coin. On coins with a moderately small design element (which is prone to early wear) grade by that design alone. For example, the 5-ore (KM#554) of Sweden has a crown above the monogram on which the beads on the arches show wear most clearly. So, grade by the crown alone.

For **MS-65 (Gem Brilliant Uncirculated, GemBU)** grade there will be no visible signs of wear or handling, even under a 10-power loop. Full mint luster will be present. No bag or adjustment marks will be present. Sharp rims and bold detail are characteristic of this grade.

For **MS-63 (Choice Brilliant Uncirculated, ChoiceBU)** grade there will be no visible signs of wear or handling, even under a 10-power loop. Mint luster will be present. Ideally no bags marks will be evident, light adjustment marks may be present.

For **MS-60 (Uncirculated, Unc.)** grade there will be no visible signs of wear or handling, even under a 10-power loop. Adjustment marks and bag marks may be present.

For **AU-50 (Almost Uncirculated, AU)** all details will be visible. There will be the slightest of wear only on the highest point of the coin. There will often be half or more of the original mint luster present.

On the **XF-40 (Extremely Fine, XF or EF)** coin, there will be about 95% of the original detail visible. Or, on a coin with a design with no inner detail to wear down, there will be a light wear over nearly all the coin. If a small design is used as the grading area, about 90% of the original detail will be visible. This latter rule stems from the logic that a smaller amount of detail needs to be present because a small area is being used to grade the whole coin.

The **VF-20 (Very Fine, VF)** coin will have about 75% of the original detail visible. Or, on a coin with no inner detail, there will be moderate wear over the entire coin. Corners of letters and numbers may be weak. A small grading area will have about 66% of the original detail.

For **F-12 (Fine, F)**, there will be about 50% of the original detail visible. Or, on a coin with no inner detail, there will be fairly heavy wear over all of the coin. Sides of letters will be weak. A coin which has not been cleaned will often appear as dirty or dull. A small amount of the grading area will have just about 50% of the original detail.

On the **VG-8 (Very Good, VG)** coin, there will be about 25% of the original detail visible. There will be heavy wear on all of the coin.

The **G-4 (Good, G)** coin's design will be clearly outlined but with substantial wear. Some of the larger detail may be visible. The rim may have a few weak spots of wear.

Strong or weak strikes, partially weak strikes, damage, corrosion, attractive or unattractive toning, rim bumps, dipping or cleaning should be described along with the above grades. These factors affect the quality of the coin just as do wear and loss of detail, but are easier to describe.

As the proof designation is a method of manufacture and not a grade, the price listings of PF-60, PF-63 and PF-65 are employed in these listings. At these levels, it is often the quality of strike and not actual wear, which is judged. In order to buy and sell proof coins at these designated grades, normally third-party grading and encapsulation is required. As the 21st century dawned, mints and distributors have employed special clean-room manufacturing processes which have virtually eliminated problems and imperfections in proof coins. The modern low mintage proof coin is often only available in sealed multi-coin sets, or encased within individual plastic holders within a larger fitted display case.

**Coin Alignment**

**Medal Alignment**

## COIN vs MEDAL ALIGNMENT

Some coins are struck with obverse and reverse aligned at a rotation of 180° from each other. When a coin is held for vertical viewing with the obverse design aligned upright and the index finger and thumb at the top and bottom, upon rotation from left to right for viewing the reverse, the latter will be upside down. Such alignment is called "coin rotation." Other coins are struck with the obverse and reverse designs mated on an alignment of zero or 360°. If such an example is held and rotated as described, the reverse will appear upright. This is the alignment, which is generally observed in the striking of medals, and for that reason coins produced in this manner are considered struck in "medal rotation". In some instances, often through error, certain coin issues have been struck to both alignment standards, creating interesting collectible varieties, which will be found noted in some listings. In addition, some countries are now producing coins with other designated obverse to reverse alignments which are considered standard for this type.

# STANDARD INTERNATIONAL GRADING TERMINOLOGY AND ABBREVIATIONS

| U.S. and ENGLISH SPEAKING LANDS | UNCIRCULATED | EXTREMELY FINE | VERY FINE | FINE | VERY GOOD | GOOD | POOR |
|---|---|---|---|---|---|---|---|
| Abbreviation | UNC | EF or XF | VF | FF | VG | G | PR |
| BRAZIL | (1) DW | (3) S | (5) MBC | (7) BC | (8) | (9) R | UTGeG |
| DENMARK | O | 01 | 1+ | 1 | 1÷ | 2 | 3 |
| FINLAND | 0 | 01 | 1+ | 1 | 1? | 2 | 3 |
| FRANCE | NEUF | SUP | TTB or TB | TB or TB | B | TBC | BC |
| GERMANY | KFR | II / VZGL | III / SS | IV / S | V / S.g.E. | VI / G.e. | G.e.s. |
| ITALY | FdS | SPL | BB | MB | B | M | — |
| JAPAN | 未使用 | 極美品 | 美品 | 並品 | — | — | — |
| NETHERLANDS | FDC | Pr. | Z.F. | Fr. | Z.g. | G | — |
| NORWAY | 0 | 01 | 1+ | 1 | 1÷ | 2 | 3 |
| PORTUGAL | Novo | Soberbo | Muito bo | — | — | — | — |
| SPAIN | Lujo | SC, IC or EBC | MBC | BC | — | RC | MC |
| SWEDEN | 0 | 01 | 1+ | 1 | 1? | 2 | — |

## BRAZIL

FE — Flor de Estampa
S — Soberba
MBC — Muito Bem Conservada
BC — Bem Conservada
R — Regular
UTGeG — Um Tanto Gasto e Gasto

## DENMARK

O — Uncirkuleret
01 — Meget Paent Eksemplar
1+ — Paent Eksemplar
1 — Acceptabelt Eksemplar
1 —Noget Slidt Eksemplar
2 — Darlight Eksemplar
3 — Meget Darlight Eskemplar

## FINLAND

00 — Kiiltolyönti
0 — Lyöntiveres
01 — Erittäin Hyvä
1+ — Hyvä
1? — Heikko
2 — Huono

## FRANCE

NEUF — New
FDC — Fleur De Coin
SPL — Splendide
SUP — Superbe
TTB — Très Très Beau
TB — Très Beau
B — Beau
TBC — Tres Bien Conserve
BC — Bien Conserve

## GERMANY

VZGL — Vorzüglich
SS — Sehr schön
S — Schön
S.g.E. — Sehr gut erhalten
G.e. — Gut erhalten
G.e.S. — Gering erhalten Schlecht

## ITALY

Fds — Fior di Stampa
SPL — Splendid
BB — Bellissimo
MB — Molto Bello
B — Bello
M — Mediocre

## JAPAN

未使用 — Mishiyo
極美品 — Goku Bihin
美品 — Bihin
並品 — Futuhin

## NETHERLANDS

Pr. — Prachtig
Z.F. — Zeer Fraai
Fr. — Fraai
Z.g. — Zeer Goed
G — Goed

## NORWAY

0 — Usirkuleret eks
01 — Meget pent eks
1+ — Pent eks
1 — Fullgodt eks
1- — Ikke Fullgodt eks
2 — Darlig eks

## ROMANIA

NC — Necirculata (UNC)
FF — Foarte Frumoasa (VF)
F — Frumoasa (F)
FBC — Foarte Bine Conservata (VG)
BC — Bine Conservata (G)
M — Mediocru Conservata (POOR)

## SPAIN

EBC — Extraordinariamente Bien Conservada
SC — Sin Circular
IC — Incirculante
MBC — Muy Bien Conservada
BC — Bien Conservada
RC — Regular Conservada
MC — Mala Conservada

## SWEDEN

0 — Ocirkulerat
01 — Mycket Vackert
1+ — Vackert
1 — Fullgott
1? — Ej Fullgott
2 — Dalight

# STANDARD INTERNATIONAL NUMERAL SYSTEMS

Prepared especially for the *Standard Catalog of World Coins*© 2014 by Krause Publications

| Western | 0 | ½ | 1 | 2 | 3 | 4 | 5 | 6 | 7 | 8 | 9 | 10 | 50 | 100 | 500 | 1000 |
|---|---|---|---|---|---|---|---|---|---|---|---|---|---|---|---|---|
| Roman | | | I | II | III | IV | V | VI | VII | VIII | IX | X | L | C | D | M |
| Arabic-Turkish | ٠ | ١/٢ | ١ | ٢ | ٣ | ٤ | ٥ | ٦ | ٧ | ٨ | ٩ | ١٠ | ٥٠ | ١٠٠ | ٥٠٠ | ١٠٠٠ |
| Malay-Persian | ٠ | ١/٢ | ١ | ٢ | ٣ | ۴ | ۵ | ٦ or ۶ | ٧ | ٨ | ٩ | ١٠ | ۵٠ | ١٠٠ | ۵٠٠ | ١٠٠٠ |
| Eastern Arabic | 0 | 1/2 | 1 | ٢ | ٣ | ٤ | ٥ | ٦ | ٧ | ٨ | ٩ | 10 | ٥10 | 100 | ٥100 | 1000 |
| Hyderabad Arabic | 0 | ١/٢ | ١ | ٢ | ٣ | ۴ | ۵ | ۶ | ٧ | ٨ | ٩ | ١0 | ۵0 | ١00 | ۵00 | ١000 |
| Indian (Sanskrit) | ० | १/२ | १ | २ | ३ | ४ | ५ | ६ | ७ | ८ | ९ | १० | ५० | १०० | ५०० | १००० |
| Assamese | ০ | ১/২ | ১ | ২ | ৩ | ৪ | ৫ | ৬ | ৭ | ৮ | ৯ | ১০ | ৫০ | ১০০ | ৫০০ | ১০০০ |
| Bengali | ০ | ১/২ | ১ | ২ | ৩ | ৪ | ৫ | ৬ | ৭ | ৮ | ৯ | ১০ | ৫০ | ১০০ | ৫০০ | ১০০০ |
| Gujarati | ૦ | ૧/૨ | ૧ | ૨ | ૩ | ૪ | ૫ | ૬ | ૭ | ૮ | ૯ | ૧૦ | ૫૦ | ૧૦૦ | ૫૦૦ | ૧૦૦૦ |
| Kutch | ० | १/२ | १ | २ | ३ | ४ | ५ | ६ | ७ | ८ | ९ | १० | ५० | १०० | ५०० | १००० |
| Devavnagri | ० | १/२ | १ | २ | ३ | ४ | ५ | ६ or ६ | ७ | ८ | ९ or ९ | १० | ५० | १०० | ५०० | १००० |
| Nepalese | ० | १/२ | १ | २ | ३ | ४ | ५ | ६ | ७ | ८ | ९ | १० | ५० | १०० | ५०० | १००० |
| Tibetan | ༠ | ༡/༢ | ༡ | ༢ | ༣ | ༤ | ༥ | ༦ | ༧ | ༨ | ༩ | ༡༠ | ༥༠ | ༡༠༠ | ༥༠༠ | ༡༠༠༠ |
| Mongolian | ᠐ | ᠑/᠒ | ᠑ | ᠒ | ᠓ | ᠔ | ᠕ | ᠖ | ᠗ | ᠘ | ᠙ | ᠑᠐ | ᠕᠐ | ᠑᠐᠐ | ᠕᠐᠐ | ᠑᠐᠐᠐ |
| Burmese | ၀ | ၁/၂ | ၁ | ၂ | ၃ | ၄ | ၅ | ၆ | ၇ | ၈ | ၉ | ၁၀ | ၅၀ | ၁၀၀ | ၅၀၀ | ၁၀၀၀ |
| Thai-Lao | ๐ | ๑/๒ | ๑ | ๒ | ๓ | ๔ | ๕ | ๖ | ๗ | ๘ | ๙ | ๑๐ | ๕๐ | ๑๐๐ | ๕๐๐ | ๑๐๐๐ |
| Lao-Laotian | ໐ | | ໑ | ໒ | ໓ | ໔ | ໕ | ໖ | ໗ | ໘ | ໙ | ໑໐ | | | | |
| Javanese | ꧐ | | ꧑ | ꧒ | ꧓ | ꧔ | ꧕ | ꧖ | ꧗ | ꧘ | ꧙ | ꧑꧐ | ꧕꧐ | ꧑꧐꧐ | ꧕꧐꧐ | ꧑꧐꧐꧐ |
| Ordinary Chinese Japanese-Korean | 零 | 半 | 一 | 二 | 三 | 四 | 五 | 六 | 七 | 八 | 九 | 十 | 十五 | 百 | 百五 | 千 |
| Official Chinese | | | 壹 | 貳 | 叁 | 肆 | 伍 | 陸 | 柒 | 捌 | 玖 | 拾 | 拾伍 | 佰 | 佰伍 | 仟 |
| Commercial Chinese | | | 〡 | 〢 | 〣 | 〤 | 〥 | 〦 | 〧 | 〨 | 〩 | 十 | 〥十 | 〡百 | 〥百 | 〡千 |
| Korean | | 반 | 일 | 이 | 삼 | 사 | 오 | 육 | 칠 | 팔 | 구 | 십 | 오십 | 백 | 오백 | 천 |
| Georgian | | | ა | ბ | გ | დ | ე | ვ | ზ | ჱ | თ | ი | ნ | რ | ფ | ჩ |
| | | | 11 ლ | 20 კ | 30 ლ | 40 მ | 60 ჲ | 70 ო | 80 პ | 90 ჟ | 200 ს | 300 ტ | 400 უ | 600 ქ | 700 ღ | 800 ყ |
| Ethiopian | ◆ | | ፩ | ፪ | ፫ | ፬ | ፭ | ፮ | ፯ | ፰ | ፱ | ፲ | ፶ | ፻ | ፭፻ | ፲፻ |
| | | | | 20 ፳ | 30 ፴ | 40 ፵ | 60 ፷ | 70 ፸ | 80 ፹ | 90 ፺ | | | | | | |
| Hebrew | | | א | ב | ג | ד | ה | ו | ז | ח | ט | י | נ | ק | תק | |
| | | | | 20 כ | 30 ל | 40 מ | 60 ס | 70 ע | 80 פ | 90 צ | 200 ר | 300 ש | 400 ת | 600 תר | 700 תש | 800 תת |
| Greek | | | Α | Β | Γ | Δ | Ε | Τ | Ζ | Η | Θ | Ι | Ν | Ρ | Φ | Α |
| | | | | 20 Κ | 30 Λ | 40 Μ | 60 Ξ | 70 Ο | 80 Π | | 200 Σ | 300 Τ | 400 Υ | 600 Χ | 700 Ψ | 800 Ω |

# DENOMINATION INDEX

**Afghani** - Afghanistan
**Agorot** - Israel
**Angel** - Isle of Man
**Ariary** - Madagascar
**Asarphi** - Nepal
**Avo** - Macau
**Azadi** - Iran
**Baisa** - Oman
**Balboa** - Panama
**Ban** - Moldova, Romania
**Bhat** - Thailand
**Birr** - Ethiopia
**Bolivano** - Bolivia
**Bututs** - Gambia
**Cedi** - Ghana
**Cent** - Aruba, Australia, Bahamas, Barbados, Belize, Bermuda, Canada, Cayman Islands, Cook Islands, Cyprus, East Caribbean States, Ethiopia, Fiji, Jamaica, Kenya, Kiribati, Liberia, Malta, Mauritius, Namibia, Netherlands, Netherlands Antilles, New Zealand, Niue, Pitcairn Islands, Seychelles, Singapore, Solomon Islands, South Africa, Sri Lanka, Suriname, Swaziland, Trinidad & Tobago
**Centavo** - Argentina, Bolivia, Brazil, Cuba ,East Timor, Ecuador, Guatemala, Honduras, Mexico, Mozambique, Nicaragua
**Centesimo** - Panama
**Centim** - Andorra
**Centime** - Belgium, Congo Democratic Republic, France, Morocco
**Centimos** - Paraguay, Peru
**Centu** - Lithuania
**Chetrum** - Bhutan
**Chon** - North Korea
**Colon** - Costa Rica
**Cordoba** - Nicaragua
**Crown** - Falkland Islands, Gibraltar, Isle of Man, Tristan da Cunha, Gough Island, Stoltenhoff Island
**Dalasi** - Gambia
**Denar** - Macedonia
**Dinar** - Algeria, Iran, Iraq, Jordan, Libya, Serbia, Sudan, Tunisia
**Diner** - Andorra
**Diram** - Tajikistan
**Dirham** - Libya, Morocco, Qatar, United Arab Emirates
**Dollar** - Australia, Bahamas, Barbados, Belize, Bermuda, British Virgin Islands, Brunei, Canada, Cayman Islands, Cook Islands, Creek Nation, East Caribbean States, Fiji, Guyana, Hong Kong, Jamaica, Kiribati, Liberia, Namibia, Nauru, New Zealand, Niue, Palau, Pitcairn Islands, Shawnee Tribal Nation, Sierra Leone, Singapore, Solomon Islands, Suriname, Tokelau, Trinidad & Tobago
**Dram** - Armenia, Nagorno-Karabakh, Tajikistan
**Ducat** - Netherlands
**Emalangeni** - Swaziland
**Escudo** - Cape Verde, Portugal
**Euro** - Austria, Belgium, Cyprus, Estonia, Finland, France, Germany, Greece, Ireland, Italy, Latvia, Luxembourg, Malta, Monaco, Netherlands, Portugal, San Marino, Slovakia, Slovenia, Spain
**Fen** - China
**Feninga** - Bosnia-Herzegovina
**Fil** - Bahrain, Kuwait, United Arab Emirates
**Florin** - Aruba
**Forint** - Hungary
**Franc** - Belgium, Burundi, Central African States, Chad, Comoros, Congo Republic, Congo Democratic Republic, Djibouti, France, French Polynesia, Gabon, Guinea, Madagascar, New Caledonia, Rwanda, Switzerland, Togo, Benin, Cameroon, Ivory Coast, Niger
**Frank** - Belgium
**Franken** - Liechtenstein
**Gourde** - Haiti
**Gram** - Mexico
**Groschen** - Austria
**Grosz** - Poland
**Guarani** - Paraguay
**Gulden** - Netherlands, Netherlands Antilles
**Halala** - Saudi Arabia
**Haleru** - Czech Republic
**Halierov** - Slovakia
**Hryvnia** - Ukraine
**Jiao** - China
**Kilo** - Mexico
**Kina** - Papua New Guinea
**Kip** - Lao
**Kobo** - Nigeria
**Konvertible Marka** - Bosnia-Herzegovina
**Kopek** - Russia
**Kopiyka** - Ukraine
**Korun** - Slovakia
**Koruna** - Czech Republic
**Krona** - Iceland
**Krone** - Denmark, Norway
**Kronor** - Sweden
**Kroon** - Estonia
**Krugerrand** - South Africa
**Kuna** - Croatia
**Kune** - Croatia
**Kurush** - Turkey
**Kwacha** - Malawi
**Kwanza** - Angola
**Laari** - Maldive Islands
**Lari** - Georgia
**Lats** - Latvia
**Lei** - Moldova, Romania
**Lek** - Albania

## HEJIRA DATE CONVERSION CHART

HEJIRA (Hijira, Hegira), the name of the Muslim era (A.H. = Anno Hegirae) dates back to the Christian year 622 when Mohammed "fled" from Mecca, escaping to Medina to avoid persecution from the Koreish tribemen. Based on a lunar year the Muslim year is 11 days shorter.

*=Leap Year (Christian Calendar)

| AH Hejira | AD Christian Date |
|---|---|
| 1010 | 1601, July 2 |
| 1011 | 1602, June 21 |
| 1012 | 1603, June 11 |
| 1013 | 1604, May 30 |
| 1014 | 1605, May 19 |
| 1015 | 1606, May 9 |
| 1016 | 1607, April 28 |
| 1017 | 1608, April 17 |
| 1018 | 1609, April 6 |
| 1019 | 1610, March 26 |
| 1020 | 1611, March 16 |
| 1021 | 1612, March 4 |
| 1022 | 1613, February 21 |
| 1023 | 1614, February 11 |
| 1024 | 1615, January 31 |
| 1025 | 1616, January 20 |
| 1026 | 1617, January 9 |
| 1027 | 1617, December 29 |
| 1028 | 1618, December 19 |
| 1029 | 1619, December 8 |
| 1030 | 1620, November 26 |
| 1031 | 1621, November 16 |
| 1032 | 1622, November 5 |
| 1033 | 1623, October 25 |
| 1034 | 1624, October 14 |
| 1035 | 1625, October 3 |
| 1036 | 1626, September 22 |
| 1037 | 1627, September 12 |
| 1038 | 1628, August 31 |
| 1039 | 1629, August 21 |
| 1040 | 1630, August 10 |
| 1041 | 1631, July 30 |
| 1042 | 1632, July 19 |
| 1043 | 1633, July 8 |
| 1044 | 1634, June 27 |
| 1045 | 1635, June 17 |
| 1046 | 1636, June 5 |
| 1047 | 1637, May 26 |
| 1048 | 1638, May 15 |
| 1049 | 1639, May 4 |
| 1050 | 1640, April 23 |
| 1051 | 1641, April 12 |
| 1052 | 1642, April 1 |
| 1053 | 1643, March 22 |
| 1054 | 1644, March 10 |
| 1055 | 1645, February 27 |
| 1056 | 1646, February 17 |
| 1057 | 1647, February 6 |
| 1058 | 1648, January 27 |
| 1059 | 1649, January 15 |
| 1060 | 1650, January 4 |
| 1061 | 1650, December 25 |
| 1062 | 1651, December 14 |
| 1063 | 1652, December 2 |
| 1064 | 1653, November 22 |
| 1065 | 1654, November 11 |
| 1066 | 1655, October 31 |
| 1067 | 1656, October 20 |
| 1068 | 1657, October 9 |
| 1069 | 1658, September 29 |
| 1070 | 1659, September 18 |
| 1071 | 1660, September 6 |
| 1072 | 1661, August 27 |
| 1073 | 1662, August 16 |
| 1074 | 1663, August 5 |
| 1075 | 1664, July 25 |
| 1076 | 1665, July 14 |
| 1077 | 1666, July 4 |
| 1078 | 1667, June 23 |
| 1079 | 1668, June 11 |
| 1080 | 1669, June 1 |
| 1081 | 1670, May 21 |
| 1082 | 1671, May 10 |
| 1083 | 1672, April 29 |
| 1084 | 1673, April 18 |
| 1085 | 1674, April 7 |
| 1086 | 1675, March 28 |
| 1087 | 1676, March 16* |

| AH Hejira | AD Christian Date |
|---|---|
| 1088 | 1677, March 6 |
| 1089 | 1678, February 23 |
| 1090 | 1679, February 12 |
| 1091 | 1680, February 2* |
| 1092 | 1681, January 21 |
| 1093 | 1682, January 10 |
| 1094 | 1682, December 31 |
| 1095 | 1683, December 20 |
| 1096 | 1684, December 8* |
| 1097 | 1685, November 28 |
| 1098 | 1686, November 17 |
| 1099 | 1687, November 7 |
| 1100 | 1688, October 26* |
| 1101 | 1689, October 15 |
| 1102 | 1690, October 5 |
| 1103 | 1691, September 24 |
| 1104 | 1692, September 12* |
| 1105 | 1693, September 2 |
| 1106 | 1694, August 22 |
| 1107 | 1695, August 12 |
| 1108 | 1696, July 31* |
| 1109 | 1697, July 20 |
| 1110 | 1698, July 10 |
| 1111 | 1699, June 29 |
| 1112 | 1700, June 18 |
| 1113 | 1701, June 8 |
| 1114 | 1702, May 28 |
| 1115 | 1703, May 17 |
| 1116 | 1704, May 6* |
| 1117 | 1705, April 25 |
| 1118 | 1706, April 15 |
| 1119 | 1707, April 4 |
| 1120 | 1708, March 23* |
| 1121 | 1709, March 13 |
| 1122 | 1710, March 2 |
| 1123 | 1711, February 19 |
| 1124 | 1712, February 9* |
| 1125 | 1713, January 28 |
| 1126 | 1714, January 17 |
| 1127 | 1715, January 7 |
| 1128 | 1715, December 27 |
| 1129 | 1716, December 16* |
| 1130 | 1717, December 5 |
| 1131 | 1718, November 24 |
| 1132 | 1719, November 14 |
| 1133 | 1720, November 2* |
| 1134 | 1721, October 22 |
| 1135 | 1722, October 12 |
| 1136 | 1723, October 1 |
| 1137 | 1724, September 19 |
| 1138 | 1725, September 9 |
| 1139 | 1726, August 29 |
| 1140 | 1727, August 19 |
| 1141 | 1728, August 7* |
| 1142 | 1729, July 27 |
| 1143 | 1730, July 17 |
| 1144 | 1731, July 6 |
| 1145 | 1732, June 24* |
| 1146 | 1733, June 14 |
| 1147 | 1734, June 3 |
| 1148 | 1735, May 24 |
| 1149 | 1736, May 12* |
| 1150 | 1737, May 1 |
| 1151 | 1738, April 21 |
| 1152 | 1739, April 10 |
| 1153 | 1740, March 29* |
| 1154 | 1741, March 19 |
| 1155 | 1742, March 8 |
| 1156 | 1743, February 25 |
| 1157 | 1744, February 15* |
| 1158 | 1745, February 3 |
| 1159 | 1746, January 24 |
| 1160 | 1747, January 13 |
| 1161 | 1748, January 2 |
| 1162 | 1748, December 22* |
| 1163 | 1749, December 11 |
| 1164 | 1750, November 30 |
| 1165 | 1751, November 20 |
| 1166 | 1752, November 8* |
| 1167 | 1753, October 29 |
| 1168 | 1754, October 18 |
| 1169 | 1755, October 7 |
| 1170 | 1756, September 26* |
| 1171 | 1757, September 15 |
| 1172 | 1758, September 4 |
| 1173 | 1759, August 25 |
| 1174 | 1760, August 13* |
| 1175 | 1761, August 2 |
| 1176 | 1762, July 23 |
| 1177 | 1763, July 12 |
| 1178 | 1764, July 1* |

| AH Hejira | AD Christian Date |
|---|---|
| 1179 | 1765, June 20 |
| 1180 | 1766, June 9 |
| 1181 | 1767, May 30 |
| 1182 | 1768, May 18* |
| 1183 | 1769, May 7 |
| 1184 | 1770, April 27 |
| 1185 | 1771, April 16 |
| 1186 | 1772, April 4* |
| 1187 | 1773, March 25 |
| 1188 | 1774, March 14 |
| 1189 | 1775, March 4 |
| 1190 | 1776, February 21* |
| 1191 | 1777, February 1 |
| 1192 | 1778, January 30 |
| 1193 | 1779, January 19 |
| 1194 | 1780, January 8* |
| 1195 | 1780, December 28* |
| 1196 | 1781, December 17 |
| 1197 | 1782, December 7 |
| 1198 | 1783, November 26 |
| 1199 | 1784, November 14* |
| 1200 | 1785, November 4 |
| 1201 | 1786, October 24 |
| 1202 | 1787, October 13 |
| 1203 | 1788, October 2* |
| 1204 | 1789, September 21 |
| 1205 | 1790, September 10 |
| 1206 | 1791, August 31 |
| 1207 | 1792, August 19* |
| 1208 | 1793, August 9 |
| 1209 | 1794, July 29 |
| 1210 | 1795, July 18 |
| 1211 | 1796, July 7* |
| 1212 | 1797, June 26 |
| 1213 | 1798, June 15 |
| 1214 | 1799, June 5 |
| 1215 | 1800, May 25 |
| 1216 | 1801, May 14 |
| 1217 | 1802, May 4 |
| 1218 | 1803, April 23 |
| 1219 | 1804, April 12* |
| 1220 | 1805, April 1 |
| 1221 | 1806, March 21 |
| 1222 | 1807, March 11 |
| 1223 | 1808, February 28* |
| 1224 | 1809, February 16 |
| 1225 | 1810, February 6 |
| 1226 | 1811, January 26 |
| 1227 | 1812, January 16* |
| 1228 | 1813, January 6 |
| 1229 | 1813, December 24 |
| 1230 | 1814, December 14 |
| 1231 | 1815, December 3 |
| 1232 | 1816, November 21* |
| 1233 | 1817, November 11 |
| 1234 | 1818, October 31 |
| 1235 | 1819, October 20 |
| 1236 | 1820, October 9* |
| 1237 | 1821, September 28 |
| 1238 | 1822, September 18 |
| 1239 | 1823, September 8 |
| 1240 | 1824, August 26* |
| 1241 | 1825, August 16 |
| 1242 | 1826, August 5 |
| 1243 | 1827, July 25 |
| 1244 | 1828, July 14* |
| 1245 | 1829, July 3 |
| 1246 | 1830, June 22 |
| 1247 | 1831, June 12 |
| 1248 | 1832, May 31* |
| 1249 | 1833, May 21 |
| 1250 | 1834, May 10 |
| 1251 | 1835, April 29 |
| 1252 | 1836, April 18* |
| 1253 | 1837, April 7 |
| 1254 | 1838, March 27 |
| 1255 | 1839, March 17 |
| 1256 | 1840, March 5* |
| 1257 | 1841, February 23 |
| 1258 | 1842, February 12 |
| 1259 | 1843, February 1 |
| 1260 | 1844, January 22* |
| 1261 | 1845, January 10 |
| 1262 | 1845, December 30 |
| 1263 | 1846, December 20 |
| 1264 | 1847, December 9 |
| 1265 | 1848, November 27* |
| 1266 | 1849, November 17 |
| 1267 | 1850, November 6 |
| 1268 | 1851, October 27 |
| 1269 | 1852, October 15* |

| AH Hejira | AD Christian Date |
|---|---|
| 1270 | 1853, October 4 |
| 1271 | 1854, September 24 |
| 1272 | 1855, September 13 |
| 1273 | 1856, September 1* |
| 1274 | 1857, August 22 |
| 1275 | 1858, August 11 |
| 1276 | 1859, July 31 |
| 1277 | 1860, July 20* |
| 1278 | 1861, July 9 |
| 1279 | 1862, June 29 |
| 1280 | 1863, June 18 |
| 1281 | 1864, June 6* |
| 1282 | 1865, May 27 |
| 1283 | 1866, May 16 |
| 1284 | 1867, May 5 |
| 1285 | 1868, April 24* |
| 1286 | 1869, April 13 |
| 1287 | 1870, April 3 |
| 1288 | 1871, March 23 |
| 1289 | 1872, March 11* |
| 1290 | 1873, March 1 |
| 1291 | 1874, February 18 |
| 1292 | 1875, February 7 |
| 1293 | 1876, January 28* |
| 1294 | 1877, January 16 |
| 1295 | 1878, January 5 |
| 1296 | 1878, December 26 |
| 1297 | 1879, December 15 |
| 1298 | 1880, December 4* |
| 1299 | 1881, November 23 |
| 1300 | 1882, November 12 |
| 1301 | 1883, November 2 |
| 1302 | 1884, October 21* |
| 1303 | 1885, October 10 |
| 1304 | 1886, September 30 |
| 1305 | 1887, September 19 |
| 1306 | 1888, September 7* |
| 1307 | 1889, August 28 |
| 1308 | 1890, August 17 |
| 1309 | 1891, August 7 |
| 1310 | 1892, July 26* |
| 1311 | 1893, July 15 |
| 1312 | 1894, July 5 |
| 1313 | 1895, June 24 |
| 1314 | 1896, June 12* |
| 1315 | 1897, June 2 |
| 1316 | 1898, May 22 |
| 1317 | 1899, May 12 |
| 1318 | 1900, May 1 |
| 1319 | 1901, April 20 |
| 1320 | 1902, April 10 |
| 1321 | 1903, March 30 |
| 1322 | 1904, March 18* |
| 1323 | 1905, March 8 |
| 1324 | 1906, February 25 |
| 1325 | 1907, February 14 |
| 1326 | 1908, February 4* |
| 1327 | 1909, January 23 |
| 1328 | 1910, January 13 |
| 1329 | 1911, January 2 |
| 1330 | 1911, December 22 |
| 1331 | 1912, December 11 |
| 1332 | 1913, November 30 |
| 1333 | 1914, November 19 |
| 1334 | 1915, November 9 |
| 1335 | 1916, October 28* |
| 1336 | 1917, October 17 |
| 1337 | 1918, October 7 |
| 1338 | 1919, September 26 |
| 1339 | 1920, September 15* |
| 1340 | 1921, September 4 |
| 1341 | 1922, August 24 |
| 1342 | 1923, August 14 |
| 1343 | 1924, August 2* |
| 1344 | 1925, July 22 |
| 1345 | 1926, July 12 |
| 1346 | 1927, July 1 |
| 1347 | 1928, June 20* |
| 1348 | 1929, June 9 |
| 1349 | 1930, May 29 |
| 1350 | 1931, May 19 |
| 1351 | 1932, May 7* |
| 1352 | 1933, April 26 |
| 1353 | 1934, April 16 |
| 1354 | 1935, April 5 |
| 1355 | 1936, March 24* |
| 1356 | 1937, March 14 |
| 1357 | 1938, March 3 |
| 1358 | 1939, February 21 |
| 1359 | 1940, February 10* |
| 1360 | 1941, January 29 |

| AH Hejira | AD Christian Date |
|---|---|
| 1361 | 1942, January 19 |
| 1362 | 1943, January 8 |
| 1363 | 1943, December 28 |
| 1364 | 1944, December 17* |
| 1365 | 1945, December 6 |
| 1366 | 1946, November 25 |
| 1367 | 1947, November 15 |
| 1368 | 1948, November 3* |
| 1369 | 1949, October 24 |
| 1370 | 1950, October 13 |
| 1371 | 1951, October 2 |
| 1372 | 1952, September 21* |
| 1373 | 1953, September 10 |
| 1374 | 1954, August 30 |
| 1375 | 1955, August 20 |
| 1376 | 1956, August 8* |
| 1377 | 1957, July 29 |
| 1378 | 1958, July 18 |
| 1379 | 1959, July 7 |
| 1380 | 1960, June 25* |
| 1381 | 1961, June 14 |
| 1382 | 1962, June 4 |
| 1383 | 1963, May 25 |
| 1384 | 1964, May 13* |
| 1385 | 1965, May 2 |
| 1386 | 1966, April 22 |
| 1387 | 1967, April 11 |
| 1388 | 1968, March 31* |
| 1389 | 1969, March 20 |
| 1390 | 1970, March 9 |
| 1391 | 1971, February 27 |
| 1392 | 1972, February 16* |
| 1393 | 1973, February 4 |
| 1394 | 1974, January 25 |
| 1395 | 1975, January 14 |
| 1396 | 1976, January 3* |
| 1397 | 1976, December 23* |
| 1398 | 1977, December 12 |
| 1399 | 1978, December 2 |
| 1400 | 1979, November 21 |
| 1401 | 1980, November 9* |
| 1402 | 1981, October 30 |
| 1403 | 1982, October 19 |
| 1404 | 1983, October 6 |
| 1405 | 1984, September 27* |
| 1406 | 1985, September 16 |
| 1407 | 1986, September 6 |
| 1409 | 1987, August 26 |
| 1409 | 1988, August 14* |
| 1410 | 1989, August 3 |
| 1411 | 1990, July 24 |
| 1412 | 1991, July 13 |
| 1413 | 1992, July 2* |
| 1414 | 1993, June 21 |
| 1415 | 1994, June 10 |
| 1416 | 1995, May 31 |
| 1417 | 1996, May 19* |
| 1418 | 1997, May 9 |
| 1419 | 1998, April 28 |
| 1420 | 1999, April 17 |
| 1421 | 2000, April 6* |
| 1422 | 2001, March 26 |
| 1423 | 2002, March 15 |
| 1424 | 2003, March 5 |
| 1425 | 2004, February 22* |
| 1426 | 2005, February 10 |
| 1427 | 2006, January 31 |
| 1428 | 2007, January 20 |
| 1429 | 2008, January 10* |
| 1430 | 2008, December 29 |
| 1431 | 2009, December 18 |
| 1432 | 2010, December 8 |
| 1433 | 2011, November 27* |
| 1434 | 2012, November 15 |
| 1435 | 2013, November 5 |
| 1436 | 2014, October 25 |
| 1437 | 2015, October 15* |
| 1438 | 2016, October 3 |
| 1439 | 2017, September 22 |
| 1440 | 2018, September 12 |
| 1441 | 2019, September 1* |
| 1442 | 2020, August 20 |
| 1443 | 2021, August 10 |
| 1444 | 2022, July 30 |
| 1445 | 2023, July 19* |
| 1446 | 2024, July 8 |
| 1447 | 2025, June 27 |
| 1448 | 2026, June 17 |
| 1449 | 2027, June 6* |
| 1450 | 2028, May25 |

# AFGHANISTAN

The Islamic State of Afghanistan, which occupies a mountainous region of Southwest Asia, has an area of 251,825 sq. mi. (652,090 sq. km.) and a population of 25.59 million. Presently, about a fifth of the total population lives in exile as refugees, (mostly in Pakistan). Capital: Kabul. It is bordered by Iran, Pakistan, Turkmenistan, Uzbekistan, Tajikistan, and China's Sinkiang Province. Agriculture and herding are the principal industries; textile mills and cement factories add to the industrial sector. Cotton, wool, fruits, nuts, oil, sheepskin coats and hand-woven carpets are normally exported but foreign trade has been interrupted since 1979.

On September 11, 2001, a terrorist attack on the United States, supported by the Taliban, led to retaliatory strikes by the U.S. Military in coalition with Afghans of a Northern Alliance. The Taliban regime was deposed. During a UN-sponsored conference on Afghanistan that was held in Bonn, Germany, in early November 2001, an agreement was reached for an Interim Authority, under the leadership of Hamid Karzai, to be installed in Afghanistan on December 22, 2001 and to hold power for the following four to six months. A "loya jirga" (Grand Council) then established a Transitional Authority with Hamid Karzai as president to prepare for general elections and a new constitution.

The national symbol on most coins of the kingdom is a stylized mosque, within which is seen the *mihrab*, a niche indicating the direction of Mecca, and the *minbar*, the pulpit, with a flight of steps leading up to it. Inscriptions in Pashtu were first used under the rebel Habibullah, but did not become standard until 1950.

## ISLAMIC STATE

SH1373-1381 / 1994-2002AD

### STANDARD COINAGE

**KM# 1043 500 AFGHANIS**
19.87 g., 0.999 Silver 0.6382 oz. ASW, 37.9 mm. **Subject:** World Championship of Soccer - 2006 - Germany **Obv:** State Emblem **Rev:** Soccer ball on German map **Edge:** Reeded

| Date | Mintage | VF20 | XF40 | MS60 | MS63 | MS65 |
|---|---|---|---|---|---|---|
| 2001 | — | PF63 30.00 | PF65 35.00 | | | |

**KM# 1048 500 AFGHANIS**
15.00 g., Silver, 35.08 mm. **Subject:** 100th Anniversary Death of Giuseppe Verdi **Obv:** National arms **Rev:** Bust of Verdi 3/4 left, music score below **Edge:** Plain

| Date | Mintage | VF20 | XF40 | MS60 | MS63 | MS65 |
|---|---|---|---|---|---|---|
| SH1380 | — | PF63 20.00 | PF65 25.00 | | | |

## REPUBLIC

SH1381- / 2002- AD

### DECIMAL COINAGE

100 Pul = 1 Afghani; 20 Afghani = 1 Amani

**KM# 1044 AFGHANI**
3.28 g., Copper Plated Steel, 20 mm. **Obv:** Value, legend above, legend and date below **Rev:** Mosque with flags in wreath

| Date | Mintage | VF20 | XF40 | MS60 | MS63 | MS65 |
|---|---|---|---|---|---|---|
| SH1383(2004) | — | — | — | 0.15 | 0.25 | 1.00 |
| SH1384(2005) | — | — | — | 0.15 | 0.25 | 1.00 |

**KM# 1045 2 AFGHANIS**
4.10 g., Stainless Steel, 22 mm. **Obv:** Value, legend above, legend and date below **Rev:** Mosque with flags in wreath

| Date | Mintage | VF20 | XF40 | MS60 | MS63 | MS65 |
|---|---|---|---|---|---|---|
| SH1383(2004) | — | — | — | 0.25 | 0.50 | 1.00 |
| SH1384(2005) | — | — | — | 0.25 | 0.50 | 1.00 |

**KM# 1046 5 AFGHANIS**
5.08 g., Brass, 24 mm. **Obv:** Value, legend above, legend and date below **Rev:** Mosque with flags in wreath

| Date | Mintage | VF20 | XF40 | MS60 | MS63 | MS65 |
|---|---|---|---|---|---|---|
| SH1383(2004) | — | — | — | 0.25 | 0.50 | 1.00 |
| SH1384(2005) | — | — | — | 0.25 | 0.50 | 1.00 |

# ALBANIA

The Republic of Albania, a Balkan republic bounded by Macedonia, Greece, Montenegro, and the Adriatic Sea, has an area of 11,100 sq. mi. (28,748 sq. km.) and a population of 3.49 million. Capital: Tirane. The country is predominantly agricultural, although recent progress has been made in the manufacturing and mining sectors. Petroleum, chrome, iron, copper, cotton textiles, tobacco and wood products are exported.

## REPUBLIC

### STANDARD COINAGE

**KM# 75 LEK**
3.00 g., Bronze, 18.1 mm. **Obv:** Dalmatian pelican **Rev:** Denomination **Edge:** Plain

| Date | Mintage | VF20 | XF40 | MS60 | MS63 | MS65 |
|---|---|---|---|---|---|---|
| 2008 | — | — | — | 0.40 | 1.50 | 2.00 |

**KM# 76 5 LEKE**
3.12 g., Nickel Plated Steel, 20 mm. **Obv:** Imperial eagle **Rev:** Olive branch, denomination

| Date | Mintage | VF20 | XF40 | MS60 | MS63 | MS65 |
|---|---|---|---|---|---|---|
| 2011 | — | — | — | — | 1.00 | 1.25 |

**KM# 93 10 LEKE**
3.60 g., Aluminum-Bronze, 21.25 mm. **Subject:** 85th Anniversary Tirana as capital **Obv:** Archaic Tomb **Obv. Legend:** SHQIPERI • ALBANIA **Rev:** Outlined bird above value **Edge:** Reeded

| Date | Mintage | VF20 | XF40 | MS60 | MS63 | MS65 |
|---|---|---|---|---|---|---|
| 2005 | — | — | — | — | 2.00 | 3.00 |

**KM# 94 10 LEKE**
3.60 g., Aluminum-Bronze, 21.25 mm. **Subject:** Culture **Obv:** Ornate vest **Obv. Legend:** SHQIPERI • ALBANIA **Rev:** Ornate value **Rev. Legend:** OBJEKTE TE TRASHEGIMISE KULTURORE **Edge:** Reeded

| Date | Mintage | VF20 | XF40 | MS60 | MS63 | MS65 |
|---|---|---|---|---|---|---|
| 2005 | — | — | — | — | 2.00 | 3.00 |

**KM# 87 20 LEKE**
8.54 g., Brass, 26.1 mm. **Subject:** Prehistoric art **Obv:** Horseman **Rev:** Ancient coin design with Apollo portrait **Edge:** Reeded

| Date | Mintage | VF20 | XF40 | MS60 | MS63 | MS65 |
|---|---|---|---|---|---|---|
| 2002 | — | — | — | — | 3.00 | 4.00 |

**KM# 81 50 LEKE**
7.50 g., Copper-Nickel, 28 mm. **Subject:** Michaelangelo's "David", 500th Anniversary **Obv:** Towered building **Rev:** Statue's head and denomination **Edge:** Plain

| Date | Mintage | VF20 | XF40 | MS60 | MS63 | MS65 |
|---|---|---|---|---|---|---|
| 2001 | 3,000 | — | — | — | 6.50 | 8.00 |

**KM# 88 50 LEKE**
12.00 g., Brass, 28 mm. **Subject:** Declaration of Independence, 90th Anniversary **Obv:** Value within circle **Rev:** Bust facing, dates below **Edge:** Reeded

| Date | Mintage | VF20 | XF40 | MS60 | MS63 | MS65 |
|---|---|---|---|---|---|---|
| 2002 | 20,000 | — | — | — | 3.00 | 4.00 |

**KM# 86 50 LEKE**
5.50 g., Copper-Nickel, 24.25 mm. **Obv:** Value and legend **Rev:** Ancient Illyrian helmet **Edge:** Reeded

| Date | Mintage | VF20 | XF40 | MS60 | MS63 | MS65 |
|---|---|---|---|---|---|---|
| 2003 | 200,000 | — | — | — | 6.00 | 7.50 |

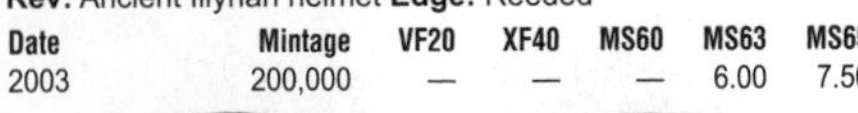

**KM# 89 50 LEKE**
12.00 g., Brass, 28 mm. **Subject:** Jeronim de Rada, 100th Anniversary of Death **Obv:** Bust 3/4 facing, dates below, circle surrounds **Rev:** Value within box within circle **Edge:** Plain

| Date | Mintage | VF20 | XF40 | MS60 | MS63 | MS65 |
|---|---|---|---|---|---|---|
| 2003 | — | — | — | — | 3.00 | 4.00 |

**KM# 90 50 LEKE**
5.50 g., Copper-Nickel, 24.25 mm. **Subject:** The Beauty of Durrës **Obv:** Wheel design **Rev:** Ancient bust above value within circle **Edge:** Reeded

| Date | Mintage | VF20 | XF40 | MS60 | MS63 | MS65 |
|---|---|---|---|---|---|---|
| 2004 | 200,000 | — | — | — | 3.00 | 4.00 |

**KM# 91 50 LEKE**
5.50 g., Copper-Nickel, 24.25 mm. **Obv:** Soldier within circle **Rev:** Value within circle **Edge:** Reeded

| Date | Mintage | VF20 | XF40 | MS60 | MS63 | MS65 |
|---|---|---|---|---|---|---|
| 2004 | 200,000 | — | — | — | 3.00 | 4.00 |

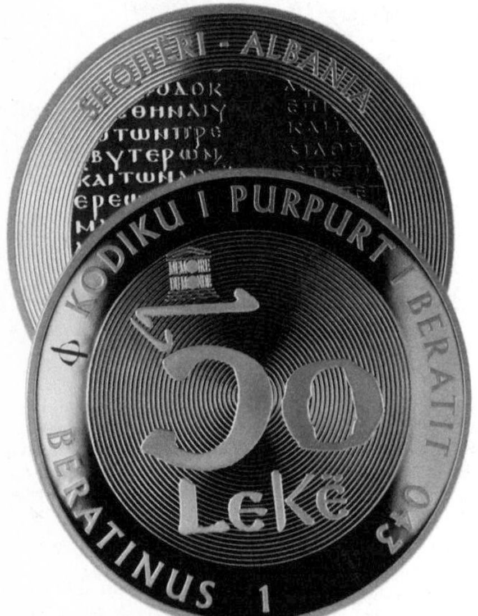

**KM# 95 50 LEKE**
90.00 g., 0.925 Silver 2.6765 oz. ASW, 60 mm. **Subject:** Codex Breatinus **Obv:** Bible page **Rev:** Large 50 on circles

| Date | Mintage | VF20 | XF40 | MS60 | MS63 | MS65 |
|---|---|---|---|---|---|---|
| 2011 | 1,000 | PF65 200 | | | | |

**KM# 96 50 LEKE**
12.00 g., Aluminum-Bronze, 28 mm. **Subject:** Albanian Independence, 100th Anniversary **Obv:** Two clasped hands **Rev:** Double headed eagle, dates above

| Date | Mintage | VF20 | XF40 | MS60 | MS63 | MS65 |
|---|---|---|---|---|---|---|
| 2012 | 10,000 | PF65 20.00 | | | | |

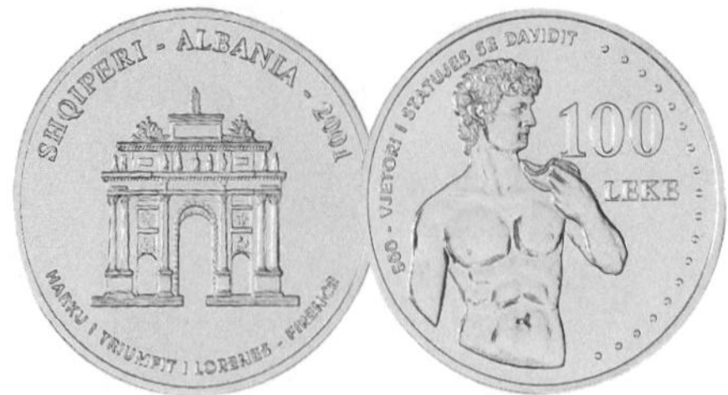

**KM# 82 100 LEKE**
15.70 g., 0.925 Silver 0.4669 oz. ASW, 32.65 mm. **Subject:** Michaelangelo's "David", 500th Anniversary **Obv:** Arch of Triumph **Rev:** Statue's upper half and denomination **Edge:** Plain

| Date | Mintage | VF20 | XF40 | MS60 | MS63 | MS65 |
|---|---|---|---|---|---|---|
| 2001 | 3,000 | — | — | — | 32.00 | 35.00 |

**KM# 84 100 LEKE**
15.00 g., 0.925 Silver 0.4461 oz. ASW, 32 mm. **Subject:** Albanian-European Integration **Obv:** Dove in flight, stars encircle **Rev:** European and Albanian maps, stars encircle **Edge:** Plain

| Date | Mintage | VF20 | XF40 | MS60 | MS63 | MS65 |
|---|---|---|---|---|---|---|
| 2001 | 3,000 | — | — | — | 30.00 | 32.50 |

**KM# 92 100 LEKE**
30.00 g., 0.925 Silver 0.8922 oz. ASW, 38 mm. **Subject:** Declaration of Independence, 90th Anniversary **Obv:** Crossed rifle and pistol on manuscript, quill pen **Obv. Legend:** SHQIPERI - ALBANIA **Rev:** Bust of Qemali 3/4 right

| Date | Mintage | VF20 | XF40 | MS60 | MS63 | MS65 |
|---|---|---|---|---|---|---|
| 2002 | 7,000 | PF65 50.00 | | | | |

**KM# 97 100 LEKE**
30.00 g., 0.925 Silver 0.8922 oz. ASW, 38 mm. **Subject:** Independence, 100th Anniversary **Obv:** Independence document **Rev:** Double headed eagle

| Date | Mintage | VF20 | XF40 | MS60 | MS63 | MS65 |
|---|---|---|---|---|---|---|
| 2012 | 1,000 | PF65 75.00 | | | | |

**KM# 83 200 LEKE**
7.65 g., 0.900 Gold 0.2214 oz. AGW, 25.45 mm. **Subject:** Michaelangelo's "David", 500th Anniversary **Obv:** City plaza **Rev:** Statue of "David" and denomination **Edge:** Plain

| Date | Mintage | VF20 | XF40 | MS60 | MS63 | MS65 |
|---|---|---|---|---|---|---|
| 2001 | 1,000 | — | — | — | 400 | 425 |

**KM# 85 200 LEKE**
15.00 g., 0.925 Silver 0.4461 oz. ASW, 32 mm. **Subject:** Albanian-European Integration **Obv:** Dove in flight within inner circle, stars encircle **Rev:** Adult and infant hand within inner circle, stars encircle **Edge:** Plain

| Date | Mintage | VF20 | XF40 | MS60 | MS63 | MS65 |
|---|---|---|---|---|---|---|
| 2001 | 1,000 | — | — | — | 37.50 | 40.00 |

**KM# 98 200 LEKE**
15.50 g., 0.900 Gold 0.4485 oz. AGW, 25.45 mm. **Subject:** Ismail Qemali, first President of the National Assembly **Obv:** Bust right **Rev:** Double headed eagle

| Date | Mintage | VF20 | XF40 | MS60 | MS63 | MS65 |
|---|---|---|---|---|---|---|
| 2012 | 1,000 | PF65 800 | | | | |

**KM# 99 200 LEKE**
15.55 g., 0.900 Gold 0.4499 oz. AGW, 25.45 mm. **Subject:** Mother Teresa **Obv:** Bust right **Rev:** Dove in color

| Date | Mintage | VF20 | XF40 | MS60 | MS63 | MS65 |
|---|---|---|---|---|---|---|
| 2012 | PF65 800 | | | | | |

## MINT SETS

| KM# | Date | Mintage | Identification | Issue Price | Mkt Val |
|---|---|---|---|---|---|
| MS3 | 2002-03 (4) | — | KM86, 89 (2003), 87, 88 (2002) | — | 22.50 |

# ALDERNEY

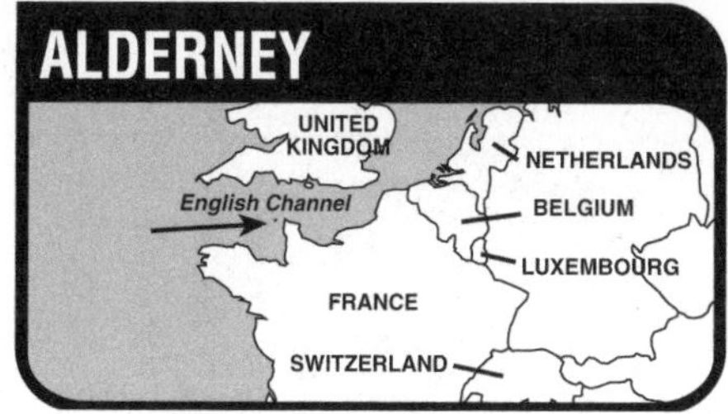


Alderney, the northernmost and third largest of the Channel Islands, separated from the coast of France by the dangerous 8-mile-wide tidal channel, has an area of 3 sq. mi. (8 km.) and a population of 1,686. It is a dependency of the British island of Guernsey, to the southwest. Capital: St. Anne. Principal industries are agriculture and raising cattle. The Channel Islands have never been subject to the British Parliament and are self-governing units under the direct rule of the Crown acting through the Privy Council. Alderney is one of the nine Channel Islands, the only part of the Duchy of Normandy still belonging to the British Crown, and has been a British possession since the Norman Conquest of 1066. Legislation was only recently introduced for the issue of its own coinage, a right it now shares with Jersey and Guernsey.

**RULER**
British

**MONETARY SYSTEM**
100 Pence = 1 Pound Sterling

## DEPENDENCY

### STANDARD COINAGE

**KM# 75 50 PENCE**
8.00 g., 0.925 Silver 0.2379 oz. ASW **Ruler:** Elizabeth II **Subject:** 50th Anniversary of Coronation **Obv:** Crowned head right **Rev:** Royal coach **Edge:** Plain **Shape:** 7-sided

| Date | Mintage | VF20 | XF40 | MS60 | MS63 | MS65 |
|---|---|---|---|---|---|---|
| 2003 | — | PF63 17.00 | PF65 20.00 | | | |

**KM# 76 50 PENCE**
8.00 g., 0.925 Silver 0.2379 oz. ASW **Ruler:** Elizabeth II **Subject:** 50th Anniversary of Coronation **Obv:** Crowned head right **Rev:** St. Edward's crown **Edge:** Plain **Shape:** 7-sided

| Date | Mintage | VF20 | XF40 | MS60 | MS63 | MS65 |
|---|---|---|---|---|---|---|
| 2003 | — | PF63 17.00 | PF65 20.00 | | | |

**KM# 77 50 PENCE**
8.00 g., 0.925 Silver 0.2379 oz. ASW **Ruler:** Elizabeth II **Subject:** 50th Anniversary of Coronation **Obv:** Crowned head right **Rev:** Elizabeth II horseback **Edge:** Plain **Shape:** 7-sided

| Date | Mintage | VF20 | XF40 | MS60 | MS63 | MS65 |
|---|---|---|---|---|---|---|
| 2003 | — | PF63 17.00 | PF65 20.00 | | | |

**KM# 78 50 PENCE**
8.00 g., 0.925 Silver 0.2379 oz. ASW **Ruler:** Elizabeth II **Subject:** 50th Anniversary of Coronation **Obv:** Crowned head right **Rev:** Elizabeth II seated on throne **Edge:** Plain **Shape:** 7-sided

| Date | Mintage | VF20 | XF40 | MS60 | MS63 | MS65 |
|---|---|---|---|---|---|---|
| 2003 | — | PF63 17.00 | PF65 20.00 | | | |

**KM# 73 POUND**
9.50 g., 0.925 Silver 0.2825 oz. ASW **Ruler:** Elizabeth II **Subject:** Queen's 75th Birthday **Obv:** Crowned head right

| Date | Mintage | VF20 | XF40 | MS60 | MS63 | MS65 |
|---|---|---|---|---|---|---|
| 2001 | — | PF63 17.00 | PF65 20.00 | | | |

**KM# 91 POUND**
1.24 g., 0.999 Gold 0.0398 oz. AGW, 13.92 mm. **Ruler:** Elizabeth II **Rev:** State arms

| Date | Mintage | VF20 | XF40 | MS60 | MS63 | MS65 |
|---|---|---|---|---|---|---|
| 2002 | — | PF63 70.00 | PF65 80.00 | | | |

**KM# 119 POUND**
1.24 g., 0.999 Gold 0.0398 oz. AGW, 13.92 mm. **Ruler:** Elizabeth II **Subject:** Trafalgar - Horatio Nelson **Obv:** Head crowned right **Rev:** Bust right in Navy uniform

| Date | Mintage | VF20 | XF40 | MS60 | MS63 | MS65 |
|---|---|---|---|---|---|---|
| 2005 | Est. 20000 | PF63 75.00 | PF65 85.00 | | | |

**KM# 122 POUND**
1.24 g., 0.999 Gold 0.0398 oz. AGW, 13.92 mm. **Ruler:** Elizabeth II **Rev:** Queen Elizabeth I

| Date | Mintage | VF20 | XF40 | MS60 | MS63 | MS65 |
|---|---|---|---|---|---|---|
| 2006 | Est. 20000 | PF63 75.00 | PF65 85.00 | | | |

**KM# 123 POUND**
1.24 g., 0.999 Gold 0.0398 oz. AGW, 13.92 mm. **Ruler:** Elizabeth II **Rev:** Sir Isaac Newton

| Date | Mintage | VF20 | XF40 | MS60 | MS63 | MS65 |
|---|---|---|---|---|---|---|
| 2006 | Est. 20000 | PF63 75.00 | PF65 85.00 | | | |

**KM# 124 POUND**
1.24 g., 0.999 Gold 0.0398 oz. AGW, 13.92 mm. **Ruler:** Elizabeth II **Rev:** William Shakespeare

| Date | Mintage | VF20 | XF40 | MS60 | MS63 | MS65 |
|---|---|---|---|---|---|---|
| 2006 | 20,000 | PF63 75.00 | PF65 85.00 | | | |

**KM# 125 POUND**
1.24 g., 0.999 Gold 0.0398 oz. AGW, 13.92 mm. **Ruler:** Elizabeth II **Rev:** Charles Dickens

| Date | Mintage | VF20 | XF40 | MS60 | MS63 | MS65 |
|---|---|---|---|---|---|---|
| 2006 | Est. 20000 | PF63 75.00 | PF65 85.00 | | | |

**KM# 130 POUND**
1.24 g., 0.999 Gold 0.0398 oz. AGW, 13.92 mm. **Ruler:** Elizabeth II **Rev:** Sir Winston Churchill

| Date | Mintage | VF20 | XF40 | MS60 | MS63 | MS65 |
|---|---|---|---|---|---|---|
| 2006 | — | PF63 75.00 | PF65 85.00 | | | |

**KM# 131 POUND**
1.24 g., 0.999 Gold 0.0398 oz. AGW, 13.92 mm. **Ruler:** Elizabeth II **Rev:** Elizabeth II corronation

| Date | Mintage | VF20 | XF40 | MS60 | MS63 | MS65 |
|---|---|---|---|---|---|---|
| 2006 | — | PF63 75.00 | PF65 85.00 | | | |

**KM# 154 POUND**
1.24 g., 0.999 Gold 0.0398 oz. AGW, 13.92 mm. **Ruler:** Elizabeth II **Rev:** Capt. James Cook

| Date | Mintage | VF20 | XF40 | MS60 | MS63 | MS65 |
|---|---|---|---|---|---|---|
| 2007 | Est. 20000 | PF63 75.00 | PF65 85.00 | | | |

**KM# 155 POUND**
1.24 g., 0.999 Gold 0.0398 oz. AGW, 13.92 mm. **Ruler:** Elizabeth II **Rev:** Sir Edward Elgar

| Date | Mintage | VF20 | XF40 | MS60 | MS63 | MS65 |
|---|---|---|---|---|---|---|
| 2007 | Est. 20000 | PF63 75.00 | PF65 85.00 | | | |

**KM# 156 POUND**
1.24 g., 0.999 Gold 0.0398 oz. AGW, 13.92 mm. **Ruler:** Elizabeth II **Rev:** Sir Francis Drake

| Date | Mintage | VF20 | XF40 | MS60 | MS63 | MS65 |
|---|---|---|---|---|---|---|
| 2007 | 20,000 | PF63 75.00 | PF65 85.00 | | | |

**KM# 157 POUND**
1.24 g., 0.999 Gold 0.0398 oz. AGW, 13.92 mm. **Ruler:** Elizabeth II **Rev:** John Constable

| Date | Mintage | VF20 | XF40 | MS60 | MS63 | MS65 |
|---|---|---|---|---|---|---|
| 2007 | Est. 20000 | PF63 75.00 | PF65 85.00 | | | |

**KM# 174 POUND**
1.24 g., 0.999 Gold 0.0398 oz. AGW, 13.92 mm. **Ruler:** Elizabeth II **Subject:** Princess Diana, 10th Anniversary of Death **Rev:** Bust 3/4 facing left

| Date | Mintage | VF20 | XF40 | MS60 | MS63 | MS65 |
|---|---|---|---|---|---|---|
| 2007 | Est. 20000 | PF63 75.00 | PF65 85.00 | | | |

**KM# 175a POUND**
28.28 g., 0.925 Silver 0.841 oz. ASW, 38.61 mm. **Ruler:** Elizabeth II

| Date | Mintage | VF20 | XF40 | MS60 | MS63 | MS65 |
|---|---|---|---|---|---|---|
| 2007 | Est. 10000 | PF63 50.00 | PF65 55.00 | | | |

**KM# 175b POUND**
39.94 g., 0.916 Gold 1.1762 oz. AGW, 38.61 mm. **Ruler:** Elizabeth II **Subject:** Princess Diana, 10th Anniversary of Death

| Date | Mintage | VF20 | XF40 | MS60 | MS63 | MS65 |
|---|---|---|---|---|---|---|
| 2007 | — | PF65 1,708 | | | | |

**KM# 189 POUND**
1.24 g., 0.999 Gold 0.0398 oz. AGW, 13.92 mm. **Ruler:** Elizabeth II **Rev:** Concord

| Date | Mintage | VF20 | XF40 | MS60 | MS63 | MS65 |
|---|---|---|---|---|---|---|
| 2008 | Est. 1000 | PF63 75.00 | PF65 85.00 | | | |

**KM# 84 POUND**
1.24 g., 0.999 Gold 0.0398 oz. AGW, 13.92 mm. **Ruler:** Elizabeth II **Subject:** Mini Cooper 50th Anniversary **Rev:** Mini Cooper on tiled floor

| Date | Mintage | VF20 | XF40 | MS60 | MS63 | MS65 |
|---|---|---|---|---|---|---|
| 2009 | 5,000 | PF63 100 | PF65 120 | | | |

**KM# 59 5 POUNDS**
28.28 g., 0.925 Silver 0.841 oz. ASW, 38.6 mm. **Ruler:** Elizabeth II **Subject:** Queen's 75th Birthday **Obv:** Queen's portrait right **Rev:** Queen in casual dress surrounded by rose, thistle, daffodil and pimper nickel

| Date | Mintage | VF20 | XF40 | MS60 | MS63 | MS65 |
|---|---|---|---|---|---|---|
| 2001 | — | PF63 45.00 | PF65 50.00 | | | |

**KM# 60 5 POUNDS**
28.28 g., Copper-Nickel, 38.6 mm. **Ruler:** Elizabeth II **Subject:** Queen's 75th Birrthday **Obv:** Queen's portrait right **Rev:** Queen in casual dress surrounded by rose, thistle, daffodil and primper nickel

| Date | Mintage | VF20 | XF40 | MS60 | MS63 | MS65 |
|---|---|---|---|---|---|---|
| 2001 | — | — | — | — | 13.00 | 15.00 |

**KM# 24 5 POUNDS**
28.28 g., Copper-Nickel, 38.6 mm. **Ruler:** Elizabeth II **Subject:** Queen Elizabeth II - 50 Years of Reigh **Obv:** Queen's head right **Rev:** Sword hilt and denomination with royal arms background **Edge:** Reeded

| Date | Mintage | VF20 | XF40 | MS60 | MS63 | MS65 |
|---|---|---|---|---|---|---|
| 2002 | 15,000 | PF63 12.00 | PF65 15.00 | | | |

**KM# 24a 5 POUNDS**
28.28 g., 0.925 Silver 0.841 oz. ASW, 38.6 mm. **Ruler:** Elizabeth II **Subject:** Queen Elizabeth II - 50 Years of Reign **Obv:** Queen's head right **Rev:** Sword hilt and denomination with royal arms background **Edge:** Reeded

| Date | Mintage | VF20 | XF40 | MS60 | MS63 | MS65 |
|---|---|---|---|---|---|---|
| 2002 | 15,000 | PF63 40.00 | PF65 45.00 | | | |

**KM# 25 5 POUNDS**
28.28 g., 0.925 Silver 0.841 oz. ASW, 38.6 mm. **Ruler:** Elizabeth II **Subject:** Queen's Golden Jubilee **Obv:** Queen's portrait **Rev:** Honor guard and trumpets **Edge:** Reeded

| Date | Mintage | VF20 | XF40 | MS60 | MS63 | MS65 |
|---|---|---|---|---|---|---|
| 2002 | 15,000 | PF63 40.00 | PF65 45.00 | | | |

**KM# 27 5 POUNDS**
28.28 g., Copper-Nickel, 38.6 mm. **Ruler:** Elizabeth II **Subject:** 5th Anniversary Death of Princess Diana **Obv:** Crowned head right **Rev:** Diana accepting flowers from girl **Edge:** Reeded

| Date | Mintage | VF20 | XF40 | MS60 | MS63 | MS65 |
|---|---|---|---|---|---|---|
| 2002 | — | — | — | — | 13.00 | 15.00 |

**KM# 27a 5 POUNDS**
28.28 g., 0.925 Silver 0.841 oz. ASW, 38.6 mm. **Ruler:** Elizabeth II **Subject:** 5th Anniversary Death of Princess Diana **Obv:** Crowned head right **Rev:** Diana accepting flowers from girl **Edge:** Reeded

| Date | Mintage | VF20 | XF40 | MS60 | MS63 | MS65 |
|---|---|---|---|---|---|---|
| 2002 | 20,000 | PF63 40.00 | PF65 45.00 | | | |

**KM# 27b 5 POUNDS**
39.94 g., 0.9167 Gold 1.1771 oz. AGW, 38.6 mm. **Ruler:** Elizabeth II **Subject:** 5th Anniversary Death of Princess Diana **Obv:** Crowned head right **Rev:** Diana accepting flowers from girl **Edge:** Reeded

| Date | Mintage | VF20 | XF40 | MS60 | MS63 | MS65 |
|---|---|---|---|---|---|---|
| 2002 | 100 | PF65 1,709 | | | | |

**KM# 29 5 POUNDS**
28.28 g., Copper-Nickel, 38.6 mm. **Ruler:** Elizabeth II **Subject:** 150th Anniversary Death of the Duke of Wellington **Obv:** Queen's portrait **Rev:** Coat of arms, castle and portrait **Edge:** Reeded

| Date | Mintage | VF20 | XF40 | MS60 | MS63 | MS65 |
|---|---|---|---|---|---|---|
| 2002 | — | — | — | — | 13.00 | 15.00 |

**KM# 29a 5 POUNDS**
28.28 g., 0.925 Silver 0.841 oz. ASW, 38.6 mm. **Ruler:** Elizabeth II **Subject:** 150th Anniversary Death of the Duke of Wellington **Obv:** Queen's portrait **Rev:** Multicolor coat of arms, portrait and castle **Edge:** Reeded

| Date | Mintage | VF20 | XF40 | MS60 | MS63 | MS65 |
|---|---|---|---|---|---|---|
| 2002 | 15,000 | PF63 50.00 | PF65 55.00 | | | |

**KM# 29b 5 POUNDS**
39.94 g., 0.9167 Gold 1.1771 oz. AGW, 38.6 mm. **Ruler:** Elizabeth II **Subject:** 150th Anniversary Death of the Duke of Wellington **Obv:** Queen's portrait **Rev:** Coat of arms, castle and portrait **Edge:** Reeded

| Date | Mintage | VF20 | XF40 | MS60 | MS63 | MS65 |
|---|---|---|---|---|---|---|
| 2002 | 200 | PF65 1,709 | | | | |

**KM# 31 5 POUNDS**
28.28 g., Copper-Nickel, 38.6 mm. **Ruler:** Elizabeth II **Subject:** Prince William **Obv:** Queen's portrait **Rev:** Portrait with open shirt collar **Edge:** Reeded

| Date | Mintage | VF20 | XF40 | MS60 | MS63 | MS65 |
|---|---|---|---|---|---|---|
| 2003 | — | — | — | — | 16.00 | 18.00 |

**KM# 31a 5 POUNDS**
28.28 g., 0.925 Silver 0.841 oz. ASW, 38.6 mm. **Ruler:** Elizabeth II **Subject:** Prince William **Obv:** Queen's portrait **Rev:** Portrait with open shirt collar **Edge:** Reeded

| Date | Mintage | VF20 | XF40 | MS60 | MS63 | MS65 |
|---|---|---|---|---|---|---|
| 2003 | — | PF63 42.50 | PF65 47.50 | | | |

**KM# 31b 5 POUNDS**
39.94 g., 0.9166 Gold 1.177 oz. AGW, 38.6 mm. **Ruler:** Elizabeth II **Subject:** Prince Willliam **Obv:** Queen's portrait **Rev:** Portrait with open shirt collar **Edge:** Reeded

| Date | Mintage | VF20 | XF40 | MS60 | MS63 | MS65 |
|---|---|---|---|---|---|---|
| 2003 | 200 | PF65 1,709 | | | | |

**KM# 35 5 POUNDS**
28.28 g., Copper-Nickel, 38.61 mm. **Ruler:** Elizabeth II **Subject:** Last Flight of the Concorde, October 24, 2003 **Obv:** Crowned bust right **Obv. Legend:** ELIZABETH II - ALDERNEY **Rev:** Concorde in flight **Rev. Legend:** CONCORDE 1969 - 2003 **Edge:** Reeded

| Date | Mintage | VF20 | XF40 | MS60 | MS63 | MS65 |
|---|---|---|---|---|---|---|
| 2003 | 5,000 | — | — | — | 12.00 | 15.00 |

**KM# 35a 5 POUNDS**
28.28 g., 0.925 Silver 0.841 oz. ASW, 38.61 mm. **Ruler:** Elizabeth II **Subject:** Last Flight of the Concorde, October 24, 2003 **Obv:** Crowned bust right **Obv. Legend:** ELIZABETH II - ALDERNEY **Rev:** Concorde in flight **Rev. Legend:** CONCORDE 1969 - 2003 **Edge:** Reeded

| Date | Mintage | VF20 | XF40 | MS60 | MS63 | MS65 |
|---|---|---|---|---|---|---|
| 2003 | 5,000 | PF63 45.00 | PF65 50.00 | | | |

**KM# 35b 5 POUNDS**
39.94 g., 0.9166 Gold 1.177 oz. AGW, 38.6 mm. **Ruler:** Elizabeth II **Obv:** Queen's portrait **Rev:** Concorde in flight, October 24, 2003 **Edge:** Reeded

| Date | Mintage | VF20 | XF40 | MS60 | MS63 | MS65 |
|---|---|---|---|---|---|---|
| 2003 | 500 | PF65 1,709 | | | | |

**KM# 44 5 POUNDS**
28.28 g., Copper-Nickel, 38.6 mm. **Ruler:** Elizabeth II **Obv:** Queen's portrait **Rev:** HMS Mary Rose **Edge:** Reeded

| Date | Mintage | VF20 | XF40 | MS60 | MS63 | MS65 |
|---|---|---|---|---|---|---|
| 2003 | — | — | — | — | 12.00 | 14.00 |

**KM# 44a 5 POUNDS**
28.28 g., 0.925 Silver 0.841 oz. ASW, 38.6 mm. **Ruler:** Elizabeth II **Obv:** Queen's portrait **Rev:** HMS Mary Rose below multicolor flag **Edge:** Reeded

| Date | Mintage | VF20 | XF40 | MS60 | MS63 | MS65 |
|---|---|---|---|---|---|---|
| 2003 | 15,000 | PF63 55.00 | PF65 60.00 | | | |

**KM# 45 5 POUNDS**
28.28 g., Copper-Nickel, 38.6 mm. **Ruler:** Elizabeth II **Obv:** Queen's portrait **Rev:** Alfred the Great on ship **Edge:** Reeded

| Date | Mintage | VF20 | XF40 | MS60 | MS63 | MS65 |
|---|---|---|---|---|---|---|
| 2003 | — | — | — | — | 12.00 | 14.00 |

**KM# 45a 5 POUNDS**
28.28 g., 0.925 Silver 0.841 oz. ASW, 38.6 mm. **Ruler:** Elizabeth II **Obv:** Queen's portrait **Rev:** Alfred the Great on ship below multicolor flag **Edge:** Reeded

| Date | Mintage | VF20 | XF40 | MS60 | MS63 | MS65 |
|---|---|---|---|---|---|---|
| 2003 | 15,000 | PF63 55.00 | PF65 60.00 | | | |

**KM# 45b 5 POUNDS**
39.94 g., 0.9167 Gold 1.1771 oz. AGW, 38.6 mm. **Ruler:** Elizabeth II **Obv:** Queen's portrait **Rev:** Alfred the Great on ship **Edge:** Reeded

| Date | Mintage | VF20 | XF40 | MS60 | MS63 | MS65 |
|---|---|---|---|---|---|---|
| 2003 | 500 | PF65 1,709 | | | | |

**KM# 38 5 POUNDS**
28.28 g., Copper-Nickel, 38.6 mm. **Ruler:** Elizabeth II **Obv:** Queen's portrait **Rev:** Battleship and transports, HMS Belfast **Edge:** Reeded **Note:** D-Day

| Date | Mintage | VF20 | XF40 | MS60 | MS63 | MS65 |
|---|---|---|---|---|---|---|
| 2004 | — | — | — | — | 15.00 | 18.00 |

**KM# 38a 5 POUNDS**
28.28 g., 0.925 Silver 0.841 oz. ASW, 38.6 mm. **Ruler:** Elizabeth II **Obv:** Queen's portrait **Rev:** Battleship and transports

| Date | Mintage | VF20 | XF40 | MS60 | MS63 | MS65 |
|---|---|---|---|---|---|---|
| 2004 | 10,000 | PF63 75.00 | PF65 85.00 | | | |

**KM# 38b 5 POUNDS**
39.94 g., 0.9167 Gold 1.1771 oz. AGW, 38.6 mm. **Ruler:** Elizabeth II **Obv:** Queen's portrait **Rev:** Battleship and transports

| Date | Mintage | VF20 | XF40 | MS60 | MS63 | MS65 |
|---|---|---|---|---|---|---|
| 2004 | 500 | PF65 1,709 | | | | |

**KM# 42 5 POUNDS**
28.28 g., Copper-Nickel, 38.6 mm. **Ruler:** Elizabeth II **Obv:** Crowned head right **Rev:** Florence Nightingale **Edge:** Reeded

| Date | Mintage | VF20 | XF40 | MS60 | MS63 | MS65 |
|---|---|---|---|---|---|---|
| 2004 | — | — | — | — | 18.00 | 20.00 |

**KM# 42a 5 POUNDS**
28.28 g., 0.925 Silver 0.841 oz. ASW, 38.6 mm. **Ruler:** Elizabeth II **Obv:** Queen's portrait **Rev:** Florence Nightingale **Edge:** Reeded

| Date | Mintage | VF20 | XF40 | MS60 | MS63 | MS65 |
|---|---|---|---|---|---|---|
| 2004 | 25,000 | PF63 60.00 | PF65 70.00 | | | |

**KM# 43 5 POUNDS**
28.28 g., Copper-Nickel, 38.6 mm. **Ruler:** Elizabeth II **Subject:** 150th Anniversary of the Crimean War **Obv:** Crowned head right **Rev:** Florence Nightingale head above the Battle of Inkerman scene with one soldier in color **Edge:** Reeded

| Date | Mintage | VF20 | XF40 | MS60 | MS63 | MS65 |
|---|---|---|---|---|---|---|
| 2004 plain | — | — | — | — | 25.00 | 28.00 |
| 2004 partial color | — | — | — | — | 25.00 | 28.00 |

**KM# 43a 5 POUNDS**
28.28 g., 0.925 Silver 0.841 oz. ASW, 38.6 mm. **Ruler:** Elizabeth II **Subject:** 150th Anniversary Crimean War **Obv:** Crowned head right **Rev:** Florence Nightingale head above Battle of Inkerman scene with one multicolor soldier **Edge:** Reeded

| Date | Mintage | VF20 | XF40 | MS60 | MS63 | MS65 |
|---|---|---|---|---|---|---|
| 2004 | 10,000 | PF63 75.00 | PF65 85.00 | | | |

**KM# 43b 5 POUNDS**
39.94 g., 0.9166 Gold 1.177 oz. AGW, 38.6 mm. **Ruler:** Elizabeth II **Subject:** 150th Anniversary Crimean War **Obv:** Crowned head right **Rev:** Florence Nightingale head above Battle of Inkerman scene with one multicolor soldier **Edge:** Reeded

| Date | Mintage | VF20 | XF40 | MS60 | MS63 | MS65 |
|---|---|---|---|---|---|---|
| 2004 | 500 | PF65 1,709 | | | | |

**KM# 47 5 POUNDS**
28.28 g., Copper-Nickel, 38.6 mm. **Ruler:** Elizabeth II **Obv:** Queen's portrait **Rev:** Locomotive, The Rocket **Edge:** Reeded

| Date | Mintage | VF20 | XF40 | MS60 | MS63 | MS65 |
|---|---|---|---|---|---|---|
| 2004 | — | — | — | — | 16.00 | 18.00 |

**KM# 47a 5 POUNDS**
28.28 g., 0.925 Silver 0.841 oz. ASW, 38.6 mm. **Ruler:** Elizabeth II **Obv:** Queen's portrait **Rev:** Locomotive, The Rocket **Edge:** Reeded

| Date | Mintage | VF20 | XF40 | MS60 | MS63 | MS65 |
|---|---|---|---|---|---|---|
| 2004 | 20,000 | PF63 55.00 | PF65 60.00 | | | |

**KM# 47b 5 POUNDS**
39.94 g., 0.9167 Gold 1.1771 oz. AGW, 38.6 mm. **Ruler:** Elizabeth II **Obv:** Queen's portrait **Rev:** Locomotive, The Rocket **Edge:** Reeded

| Date | Mintage | VF20 | XF40 | MS60 | MS63 | MS65 |
|---|---|---|---|---|---|---|
| 2004 | 500 | PF65 1,709 | | | | |

**KM# 48 5 POUNDS**
28.28 g., Copper-Nickel, 38.6 mm. **Ruler:** Elizabeth II **Obv:** Queen's portrait **Rev:** Locomotive, The Royal Scot **Edge:** Reeded

| Date | Mintage | VF20 | XF40 | MS60 | MS63 | MS65 |
|---|---|---|---|---|---|---|
| 2004 | — | — | — | — | 16.00 | 18.00 |

**KM# 48a 5 POUNDS**
28.28 g., 0.925 Silver 0.841 oz. ASW, 38.6 mm. **Ruler:** Elizabeth II **Obv:** Queen's portrait **Rev:** Locomotive, The Royal Scot **Edge:** Reeded

| Date | Mintage | VF20 | XF40 | MS60 | MS63 | MS65 |
|---|---|---|---|---|---|---|
| 2004 | 10,000 | PF63 55.00 | PF65 60.00 | | | |

**KM# 49 5 POUNDS**
28.28 g., Copper-Nickel, 38.6 mm. **Ruler:** Elizabeth II **Obv:** Queen's portrait **Rev:** Locomotive, The Merchant Navy 21C1 **Edge:** Reeded

| Date | Mintage | VF20 | XF40 | MS60 | MS63 | MS65 |
|---|---|---|---|---|---|---|
| 2004 | — | — | — | — | 16.00 | 18.00 |

### KM# 49a 5 POUNDS

28.28 g., 0.925 Silver 0.841 oz. ASW, 38.6 mm. **Ruler:** Elizabeth II **Obv:** Queen's portrait **Rev:** Locomotive, The Merchant Navy 21C1 **Edge:** Reeded

| Date | Mintage | VF20 | XF40 | MS60 | MS63 | MS65 |
|---|---|---|---|---|---|---|
| 2004 | 10,000 | PF63 55.00 | PF65 60.00 | | | |

### KM# 94 5 POUNDS

28.28 g., 0.925 Silver 0.841 oz. ASW, 38.61 mm. **Ruler:** Elizabeth II **Subject:** David Beckham **Rev:** Soccer player and ball as background

| Date | Mintage | VF20 | XF40 | MS60 | MS63 | MS65 |
|---|---|---|---|---|---|---|
| 2004 | — | PF63 40.00 | PF65 45.00 | | | |

### KM# 95 5 POUNDS

28.28 g., 0.925 Silver 0.841 oz. ASW, 38.61 mm. **Ruler:** Elizabeth II **Subject:** Michael Owen **Rev:** Soccer player and ball as background

| Date | Mintage | VF20 | XF40 | MS60 | MS63 | MS65 |
|---|---|---|---|---|---|---|
| 2004 | — | PF63 40.00 | PF65 45.00 | | | |

### KM# 53 5 POUNDS

Copper-Nickel, 38.61 mm. **Ruler:** Elizabeth II **Subject:** End of World War II, 60th Anniversary

| Date | Mintage | VF20 | XF40 | MS60 | MS63 | MS65 |
|---|---|---|---|---|---|---|
| 2005 | — | — | — | — | 14.00 | 16.00 |

### KM# 53a 5 POUNDS

28.28 g., 0.925 Silver 0.841 oz. ASW, 38.6 mm. **Ruler:** Elizabeth II **Subject:** End of WWII **Obv:** Elizabeth II by Maklouf **Rev:** Flag waving crowd **Edge:** Reeded

| Date | Mintage | VF20 | XF40 | MS60 | MS63 | MS65 |
|---|---|---|---|---|---|---|
| 2005 | 5,000 | PF63 75.00 | PF65 85.00 | | | |

### KM# 53b 5 POUNDS

39.94 g., 0.9167 Gold 1.1771 oz. AGW, 38.6 mm. **Ruler:** Elizabeth II **Subject:** 60th Anniversary - End of WWII **Obv:** Elizabeth II by Maklouf **Rev:** Flag waving crowd **Edge:** Reeded

| Date | Mintage | VF20 | XF40 | MS60 | MS63 | MS65 |
|---|---|---|---|---|---|---|
| 2005 | 150 | PF65 1,709 | | | | |

### KM# 54 5 POUNDS

28.28 g., Copper-Nickel, 38.61 mm. **Ruler:** Elizabeth II **Subject:** Winston Churchill

| Date | Mintage | VF20 | XF40 | MS60 | MS63 | MS65 |
|---|---|---|---|---|---|---|
| 2005 | Est. 5000 | — | — | — | 14.00 | 16.00 |

### KM# 54a 5 POUNDS

39.94 g., 0.916 Silver 1.1762 oz. ASW, 38.61 mm. **Ruler:** Elizabeth II **Subject:** Sir Winston Churchill

| Date | Mintage | VF20 | XF40 | MS60 | MS63 | MS65 |
|---|---|---|---|---|---|---|
| 2005 | — | PF63 60.00 | PF65 65.00 | | | |

### KM# 54b 5 POUNDS

39.94 g., 0.9167 Gold 1.1771 oz. AGW, 38.6 mm. **Ruler:** Elizabeth II **Subject:** WWII Liberation **Obv:** Elizabeth II by Maklouf **Rev:** Churchill flashing the "V" sign **Edge:** Reeded

| Date | Mintage | VF20 | XF40 | MS60 | MS63 | MS65 |
|---|---|---|---|---|---|---|
| 2005 | 150 | PF65 1,709 | | | | |

### KM# 66 5 POUNDS

28.28 g., Copper-Nickel, 38.6 mm. **Ruler:** Elizabeth II **Subject:** Viscount Samuel Hood on his flagship after the Battle of Saints Passage in 1782 **Obv:** Queen's portrait

| Date | Mintage | VF20 | XF40 | MS60 | MS63 | MS65 |
|---|---|---|---|---|---|---|
| 2005 | — | — | — | — | 13.00 | 15.00 |

### KM# 66a 5 POUNDS

28.28 g., 0.925 Silver 0.841 oz. ASW, 38.6 mm. **Ruler:** Elizabeth II **Subject:** Viscount Samuel Hood on his flagship after the Battle of Saints Passage in 1782 **Obv:** Queen's portrait **Note:** Ensign is colored.

| Date | Mintage | VF20 | XF40 | MS60 | MS63 | MS65 |
|---|---|---|---|---|---|---|
| 2005 | — | PF63 45.00 | PF65 50.00 | | | |

### KM# 68 5 POUNDS

28.28 g., Copper-Nickel, 38.6 mm. **Ruler:** Elizabeth II **Obv:** Crowned head right **Rev:** HMS Revenge fighting at Azores, 1591

| Date | Mintage | VF20 | XF40 | MS60 | MS63 | MS65 |
|---|---|---|---|---|---|---|
| 2005 | — | — | — | — | 12.00 | 14.00 |

### KM# 68a 5 POUNDS

28.28 g., 0.925 Silver 0.841 oz. ASW, 38.6 mm. **Ruler:** Elizabeth II **Obv:** Crowned head right **Rev:** HMS Revenge fighting at Azores, 1591 **Note:** Ensign is colorized.

| Date | Mintage | VF20 | XF40 | MS60 | MS63 | MS65 |
|---|---|---|---|---|---|---|
| 2005 | — | PF63 55.00 | PF65 60.00 | | | |

### KM# 79 5 POUNDS

28.28 g., Copper-Nickel, 38.61 mm. **Ruler:** Elizabeth II **Subject:** 200th Anniversary Battle of Trafalgar **Obv:** Crowned head right

| Date | Mintage | VF20 | XF40 | MS60 | MS63 | MS65 |
|---|---|---|---|---|---|---|
| 2005 | — | — | — | — | 16.00 | 18.00 |

### KM# 79a 5 POUNDS

28.28 g., 0.925 Silver 0.841 oz. ASW **Ruler:** Elizabeth II **Subject:** 200th Anniversary Battle of Trafalgar **Obv:** Crowned head right

| Date | Mintage | VF20 | XF40 | MS60 | MS63 | MS65 |
|---|---|---|---|---|---|---|
| 2005 | — | PF63 55.00 | PF65 60.00 | | | |

### KM# 83 5 POUNDS

28.28 g., Copper-Nickel, 38.61 mm. **Ruler:** Elizabeth II **Subject:** Royal Navy - Admiral Sir John Foster Woodward

| Date | Mintage | VF20 | XF40 | MS60 | MS63 | MS65 |
|---|---|---|---|---|---|---|
| 2005 | — | — | — | — | 13.00 | 15.00 |

### KM# 83a 5 POUNDS

28.28 g., 0.925 Silver 0.841 oz. ASW, 38.61 mm. **Ruler:** Elizabeth II **Subject:** History of the Royal Navy **Obv:** Heraldic shield **Rev:** Admiral John Woodward, partially colored

| Date | Mintage | VF20 | XF40 | MS60 | MS63 | MS65 |
|---|---|---|---|---|---|---|
| 2005 | — | PF63 40.00 | PF65 45.00 | | | |

### KM# 96 5 POUNDS

28.28 g., 0.925 Silver 0.841 oz. ASW **Ruler:** Elizabeth II **Subject:** Locomotives, 200th Anniversary **Rev:** Train station on a branch line

| Date | Mintage | VF20 | XF40 | MS60 | MS63 | MS65 |
|---|---|---|---|---|---|---|
| 2005 | Est. 10000 | PF63 55.00 | PF65 60.00 | | | |
| 2006 | Est. 25000 | PF63 50.00 | PF65 55.00 | | | |

### KM# 97 5 POUNDS

28.28 g., 0.925 Silver 0.841 oz. ASW **Ruler:** Elizabeth II **Subject:** Locomotives, 200th Anniversary **Rev:** Locomotive Shop

| Date | Mintage | VF20 | XF40 | MS60 | MS63 | MS65 |
|---|---|---|---|---|---|---|
| 2005 | Est. 10000 | PF63 55.00 | PF65 60.00 | | | |
| 2006 proof | — | PF63 50.00 | PF65 55.00 | | | |

### KM# 98 5 POUNDS

28.28 g., 0.925 Silver 0.841 oz. ASW **Ruler:** Elizabeth II **Subject:** Locomotives, 200th Anniversary **Rev:** Viaduct

| Date | Mintage | VF20 | XF40 | MS60 | MS63 | MS65 |
|---|---|---|---|---|---|---|
| 2005 | Est. 10000 | PF63 55.00 | PF65 60.00 | | | |
| 2006 | Est. 25000 | PF63 50.00 | PF65 55.00 | | | |

### KM# 99 5 POUNDS

28.28 g., 0.925 Silver 0.841 oz. ASW, 38.61 mm. **Ruler:** Elizabeth II **Subject:** Wayne Rooney **Obv:** Shield **Rev:** Soccer player and ball design

| Date | Mintage | VF20 | XF40 | MS60 | MS63 | MS65 |
|---|---|---|---|---|---|---|
| 2005 | — | PF63 40.00 | PF65 45.00 | | | |

### KM# 100 5 POUNDS

28.28 g., 0.925 Silver 0.841 oz. ASW, 38.61 mm. **Ruler:** Elizabeth II **Subject:** Frank Lampard **Obv:** Shield **Rev:** Soccer player and ball design

| Date | Mintage | VF20 | XF40 | MS60 | MS63 | MS65 |
|---|---|---|---|---|---|---|
| 2005 | — | PF63 40.00 | PF65 45.00 | | | |

### KM# 101 5 POUNDS

28.28 g., 0.925 Silver 0.841 oz. ASW, 38.61 mm. **Ruler:** Elizabeth II **Obv:** Shield **Rev:** Soccer player and ball design

| Date | Mintage | VF20 | XF40 | MS60 | MS63 | MS65 |
|---|---|---|---|---|---|---|
| 2005 | — | PF63 40.00 | PF65 45.00 | | | |

### KM# 102 5 POUNDS

28.28 g., 0.925 Silver 0.841 oz. ASW, 38.61 mm. **Ruler:** Elizabeth II **Subject:** Steven Gerrard **Obv:** Shield **Rev:** Soccer player and ball design

| Date | Mintage | VF20 | XF40 | MS60 | MS63 | MS65 |
|---|---|---|---|---|---|---|
| 2005 | — | PF63 40.00 | PF65 45.00 | | | |

### KM# 103 5 POUNDS

28.28 g., 0.925 Silver 0.841 oz. ASW, 38.61 mm. **Ruler:** Elizabeth II **Obv:** Shield **Rev:** Soccer player and ball design

| Date | Mintage | VF20 | XF40 | MS60 | MS63 | MS65 |
|---|---|---|---|---|---|---|
| 2005 | — | PF63 40.00 | PF65 45.00 | | | |

### KM# 104 5 POUNDS

28.28 g., 0.925 Silver 0.841 oz. ASW, 38.61 mm. **Ruler:** Elizabeth II **Obv:** Shield **Rev:** Soccer player and ball design

| Date | Mintage | VF20 | XF40 | MS60 | MS63 | MS65 |
|---|---|---|---|---|---|---|
| 2005 | — | PF63 40.00 | PF65 45.00 | | | |

### KM# 105 5 POUNDS

28.28 g., 0.925 Silver 0.841 oz. ASW, 38.61 mm. **Ruler:** Elizabeth II **Obv:** Shield **Rev:** Soccer player and ball design

| Date | Mintage | VF20 | XF40 | MS60 | MS63 | MS65 |
|---|---|---|---|---|---|---|
| 2005 | — | PF63 40.00 | PF65 45.00 | | | |

### KM# 106 5 POUNDS

28.28 g., 0.925 Silver 0.841 oz. ASW, 38.61 mm. **Ruler:** Elizabeth II **Obv:** Shield **Rev:** Soccer player and ball design

| Date | Mintage | VF20 | XF40 | MS60 | MS63 | MS65 |
|---|---|---|---|---|---|---|
| 2005 | — | PF63 40.00 | PF65 45.00 | | | |

### KM# 107 5 POUNDS

28.28 g., 0.925 Silver 0.841 oz. ASW, 38.61 mm. **Ruler:** Elizabeth II **Obv:** Shield **Rev:** Soccer player and ball design

| Date | Mintage | VF20 | XF40 | MS60 | MS63 | MS65 |
|---|---|---|---|---|---|---|
| 2005 | — | PF63 40.00 | PF65 45.00 | | | |

### KM# 108 5 POUNDS

28.25 g., 0.925 Silver 0.8401 oz. ASW, 38.61 mm. **Ruler:** Elizabeth II **Obv:** Shield **Rev:** Soccer player and ball design

| Date | Mintage | VF20 | XF40 | MS60 | MS63 | MS65 |
|---|---|---|---|---|---|---|
| 2005 | — | PF63 40.00 | PF65 45.00 | | | |

### KM# 113 5 POUNDS

28.28 g., Copper-Nickel, 38.61 mm. **Ruler:** Elizabeth II **Subject:** Prince William, 21st Birthday

| Date | Mintage | VF20 | XF40 | MS60 | MS63 | MS65 |
|---|---|---|---|---|---|---|
| 2005 | — | — | — | — | 13.00 | 15.00 |

### KM# 113a 5 POUNDS

28.28 g., 0.925 Silver 0.841 oz. ASW, 38.61 mm. **Ruler:** Elizabeth II **Subject:** Prince William, 21st Birthday

| Date | Mintage | VF20 | XF40 | MS60 | MS63 | MS65 |
|---|---|---|---|---|---|---|
| 2005 | Est. 2500 | PF63 55.00 | PF65 60.00 | | | |

### KM# 113b 5 POUNDS

39.94 g., 0.9167 Gold 1.1771 oz. AGW, 38.61 mm. **Ruler:** Elizabeth II **Subject:** Prince William, 21st Birthday

| Date | Mintage | VF20 | XF40 | MS60 | MS63 | MS65 |
|---|---|---|---|---|---|---|
| 2005 | Est. 150 | PF65 1,709 | | | | |

### KM# 116 5 POUNDS

28.28 g., Copper-Nickel, 38.61 mm. **Ruler:** Elizabeth II **Subject:** Royal Navy - H.M.S. Warspite

| Date | Mintage | VF20 | XF40 | MS60 | MS63 | MS65 |
|---|---|---|---|---|---|---|
| 2005 | — | — | — | — | 13.00 | 15.00 |

**KM# 116a 5 POUNDS**
28.28 g., 0.925 Silver 0.841 oz. ASW, 38.61 mm. **Ruler:** Elizabeth II **Subject:** British Navy - H.M.S. Warspite **Rev:** Multicolor flag

| Date | Mintage | VF20 | XF40 | MS60 | MS63 | MS65 |
|---|---|---|---|---|---|---|
| 2005 | Est. 15000 | PF63 50.00 | PF65 55.00 | | | |

**KM# 70 5 POUNDS**
28.28 g., 0.925 Silver 0.841 oz. ASW, 38.6 mm. **Ruler:** Elizabeth II **Subject:** Queen's 80th Birthday **Obv:** Crowned bust right - gilt **Obv. Legend:** ELIZABETH II - ALDERNEY **Rev:** 1/2 length figures of Queen mother and daughter hugging, facing

| Date | Mintage | VF20 | XF40 | MS60 | MS63 | MS65 |
|---|---|---|---|---|---|---|
| 2006 | — | PF63 40.00 | PF65 45.00 | | | |

**KM# 126 5 POUNDS**
28.28 g., Copper-Nickel, 38.61 mm. **Ruler:** Elizabeth II **Rev:** Elizabeth I

| Date | Mintage | VF20 | XF40 | MS60 | MS63 | MS65 |
|---|---|---|---|---|---|---|
| 2006 | — | — | — | — | 12.00 | 14.00 |

**KM# 126a 5 POUNDS**
28.28 g., 0.925 Silver 0.841 oz. ASW, 38.61 mm. **Ruler:** Elizabeth II **Rev:** Queen Elizabeth I

| Date | Mintage | VF20 | XF40 | MS60 | MS63 | MS65 |
|---|---|---|---|---|---|---|
| 2006 | Est. 25000 | PF63 45.00 | PF65 55.00 | | | |

**KM# 126b 5 POUNDS**
39.94 g., 0.916 Gold 1.1762 oz. AGW, 38.61 mm. **Ruler:** Elizabeth II **Rev:** Queen Elizabeth I

| Date | Mintage | VF20 | XF40 | MS60 | MS63 | MS65 |
|---|---|---|---|---|---|---|
| 2006 | — | PF65 1,708 | | | | |

**KM# 127 5 POUNDS**
28.28 g., Copper-Nickel, 38.61 mm. **Ruler:** Elizabeth II **Rev:** Sir Isaac Newton

| Date | Mintage | VF20 | XF40 | MS60 | MS63 | MS65 |
|---|---|---|---|---|---|---|
| 2006 | — | — | — | — | 13.00 | 15.00 |

**KM# 127a 5 POUNDS**
28.28 g., 0.925 Silver 0.841 oz. ASW, 38.61 mm. **Ruler:** Elizabeth II **Rev:** Sir Isaac Newton

| Date | Mintage | VF20 | XF40 | MS60 | MS63 | MS65 |
|---|---|---|---|---|---|---|
| 2006 | — | PF63 50.00 | PF65 55.00 | | | |

**KM# 127b 5 POUNDS**
39.94 g., 0.9167 Gold 1.1771 oz. AGW, 38.61 mm. **Ruler:** Elizabeth II **Rev:** Sir Isaac Newton

| Date | Mintage | VF20 | XF40 | MS60 | MS63 | MS65 |
|---|---|---|---|---|---|---|
| 2006 | — | PF65 1,709 | | | | |

**KM# 128 5 POUNDS**
28.28 g., Copper-Nickel, 38.61 mm. **Ruler:** Elizabeth II **Rev:** William Shakespeare

| Date | Mintage | VF20 | XF40 | MS60 | MS63 | MS65 |
|---|---|---|---|---|---|---|
| 2006 | — | — | — | — | 13.00 | 15.00 |

**KM# 128a 5 POUNDS**
28.28 g., 0.925 Silver 0.841 oz. ASW, 38.61 mm. **Ruler:** Elizabeth II **Rev:** William Shakespeare

| Date | Mintage | VF20 | XF40 | MS60 | MS63 | MS65 |
|---|---|---|---|---|---|---|
| 2006 | — | PF63 50.00 | PF65 55.00 | | | |

**KM# 128b 5 POUNDS**
39.94 g., 0.916 Gold 1.1762 oz. AGW, 38.61 mm. **Ruler:** Elizabeth II **Rev:** William Shakespeare

| Date | Mintage | VF20 | XF40 | MS60 | MS63 | MS65 |
|---|---|---|---|---|---|---|
| 2006 | — | PF65 1,708 | | | | |

**KM# 129 5 POUNDS**
28.28 g., Copper-Nickel, 38.61 mm. **Ruler:** Elizabeth II **Rev:** Charles Dickens

| Date | Mintage | VF20 | XF40 | MS60 | MS63 | MS65 |
|---|---|---|---|---|---|---|
| 2006 | — | — | — | — | 13.00 | 15.00 |

**KM# 129a 5 POUNDS**
28.28 g., 0.925 Silver 0.841 oz. ASW, 38.61 mm. **Ruler:** Elizabeth II **Rev:** Charles Dickens

| Date | Mintage | VF20 | XF40 | MS60 | MS63 | MS65 |
|---|---|---|---|---|---|---|
| 2006 | — | PF63 50.00 | PF65 55.00 | | | |

**KM# 129b 5 POUNDS**
39.94 g., 0.916 Gold 1.1762 oz. AGW, 38.61 mm. **Ruler:** Elizabeth II **Rev:** Charles Dickens

| Date | Mintage | VF20 | XF40 | MS60 | MS63 | MS65 |
|---|---|---|---|---|---|---|
| 2006 | — | PF65 1,708 | | | | |

**KM# 132 5 POUNDS**
28.28 g., Copper-Nickel, 38.61 mm. **Ruler:** Elizabeth II **Rev:** Elizabeth II Coronation

| Date | Mintage | VF20 | XF40 | MS60 | MS63 | MS65 |
|---|---|---|---|---|---|---|
| 2006 | — | — | — | — | 13.00 | 15.00 |

**KM# 132a 5 POUNDS**
28.28 g., 0.925 Silver 0.841 oz. ASW, 38.61 mm. **Ruler:** Elizabeth II **Rev:** Elizabeth II Corronation

| Date | Mintage | VF20 | XF40 | MS60 | MS63 | MS65 |
|---|---|---|---|---|---|---|
| 2006 | Est. 25000 | PF63 50.00 | PF65 55.00 | | | |

**KM# 133 5 POUNDS**
28.28 g., Copper-Nickel, 38.61 mm. **Ruler:** Elizabeth II **Obv:** Head in tiara right **Rev:** Bust in tiara right

| Date | Mintage | VF20 | XF40 | MS60 | MS63 | MS65 |
|---|---|---|---|---|---|---|
| 2006 | — | — | — | — | 13.00 | 15.00 |

**KM# 133a 5 POUNDS**
28.28 g., 0.925 Silver 0.841 oz. ASW, 38.61 mm. **Ruler:** Elizabeth II **Obv:** Head in tiara right **Rev:** Bust in tiara right

| Date | Mintage | VF20 | XF40 | MS60 | MS63 | MS65 |
|---|---|---|---|---|---|---|
| 2006 | — | PF63 50.00 | PF65 55.00 | | | |

**KM# 133b.1 5 POUNDS**
39.94 g., 0.9167 Gold 1.1771 oz. AGW with diamonds, 38.61 mm. **Ruler:** Elizabeth II **Obv:** Head in tiara right **Rev:** Bust in tiara right

| Date | Mintage | VF20 | XF40 | MS60 | MS63 | MS65 |
|---|---|---|---|---|---|---|
| 2006 | — | PF65 1,734 | | | | |

**KM# 133b 5 POUNDS**
39.94 g., 0.9167 Gold 1.1771 oz. AGW, 38.61 mm. **Ruler:** Elizabeth II **Obv:** Head in tiara right **Rev:** Bust in tiara right

| Date | Mintage | VF20 | XF40 | MS60 | MS63 | MS65 |
|---|---|---|---|---|---|---|
| 2006 | — | PF65 1,709 | | | | |

**KM# 138 5 POUNDS**
28.28 g., 0.925 Silver 0.841 oz. ASW, 38.61 mm. **Ruler:** Elizabeth II **Obv:** Shield **Rev:** Soccer player

| Date | Mintage | VF20 | XF40 | MS60 | MS63 | MS65 |
|---|---|---|---|---|---|---|
| 2006 | — | PF63 45.00 | PF65 55.00 | | | |

**KM# 139 5 POUNDS**
28.28 g., 0.925 Silver 0.841 oz. ASW, 38.61 mm. **Ruler:** Elizabeth II **Obv:** Shield **Rev:** Soccer player

| Date | Mintage | VF20 | XF40 | MS60 | MS63 | MS65 |
|---|---|---|---|---|---|---|
| 2006 | — | PF63 45.00 | PF65 55.00 | | | |

**KM# 140 5 POUNDS**
28.28 g., 0.925 Silver 0.841 oz. ASW, 38.61 mm. **Ruler:** Elizabeth II **Obv:** Shield **Rev:** Soccer player

| Date | Mintage | VF20 | XF40 | MS60 | MS63 | MS65 |
|---|---|---|---|---|---|---|
| 2006 | — | PF63 45.00 | PF65 55.00 | | | |

**KM# 141 5 POUNDS**
28.28 g., 0.925 Silver 0.841 oz. ASW, 38.61 mm. **Ruler:** Elizabeth II **Obv:** Shield **Rev:** Soccer player

| Date | Mintage | VF20 | XF40 | MS60 | MS63 | MS65 |
|---|---|---|---|---|---|---|
| 2006 | — | PF63 45.00 | PF65 55.00 | | | |

**KM# 142 5 POUNDS**
28.28 g., 0.925 Silver 0.841 oz. ASW, 38.61 mm. **Ruler:** Elizabeth II **Obv:** Shield **Rev:** Soccer player

| Date | Mintage | VF20 | XF40 | MS60 | MS63 | MS65 |
|---|---|---|---|---|---|---|
| 2006 | — | PF63 45.00 | PF65 55.00 | | | |

**KM# 143 5 POUNDS**
28.28 g., 0.925 Silver 0.841 oz. ASW, 38.61 mm. **Ruler:** Elizabeth II **Obv:** Shield **Rev:** Soccer player

| Date | Mintage | VF20 | XF40 | MS60 | MS63 | MS65 |
|---|---|---|---|---|---|---|
| 2006 | — | PF63 45.00 | PF65 55.00 | | | |

**KM# 144 5 POUNDS**
28.28 g., 0.925 Silver 0.841 oz. ASW, 38.61 mm. **Ruler:** Elizabeth II **Obv:** Shield **Rev:** Soccer player

| Date | Mintage | VF20 | XF40 | MS60 | MS63 | MS65 |
|---|---|---|---|---|---|---|
| 2006 | — | PF63 45.00 | PF65 55.00 | | | |

**KM# 145 5 POUNDS**
28.28 g., 0.925 Silver 0.841 oz. ASW, 38.61 mm. **Ruler:** Elizabeth II **Obv:** Shield **Rev:** Soccer player

| Date | Mintage | VF20 | XF40 | MS60 | MS63 | MS65 |
|---|---|---|---|---|---|---|
| 2006 | — | PF63 45.00 | PF65 55.00 | | | |

**KM# 146 5 POUNDS**
28.28 g., 0.925 Silver 0.841 oz. ASW, 38.61 mm. **Ruler:** Elizabeth II **Obv:** Shield **Rev:** Soccer player

| Date | Mintage | VF20 | XF40 | MS60 | MS63 | MS65 |
|---|---|---|---|---|---|---|
| 2006 | — | PF63 45.00 | PF65 55.00 | | | |

**KM# 147 5 POUNDS**
28.28 g., 0.925 Silver 0.841 oz. ASW, 38.61 mm. **Ruler:** Elizabeth II **Obv:** Shield **Rev:** Soccer player

| Date | Mintage | VF20 | XF40 | MS60 | MS63 | MS65 |
|---|---|---|---|---|---|---|
| 2006 | — | PF63 45.00 | PF65 55.00 | | | |

**KM# 148 5 POUNDS**
28.28 g., Copper-Nickel, 38.61 mm. **Ruler:** Elizabeth II **Subject:** Victoria Cross, 150th Anniversary **Rev:** Henry Ramage and Victoria Cross medal

| Date | Mintage | VF20 | XF40 | MS60 | MS63 | MS65 |
|---|---|---|---|---|---|---|
| 2006 | — | — | — | — | 13.00 | 15.00 |

**KM# 148a 5 POUNDS**
28.28 g., 0.925 Silver 0.841 oz. ASW, 38.61 mm. **Ruler:** Elizabeth II **Subject:** Victoria Cross, 150th Anniversary **Rev:** Henry Ramage and Victoria Cross medal

| Date | Mintage | VF20 | XF40 | MS60 | MS63 | MS65 |
|---|---|---|---|---|---|---|
| 2006 | Est. 30000 | PF63 45.00 | PF65 55.00 | | | |

**KM# 149 5 POUNDS**
28.28 g., 0.925 Silver 0.841 oz. ASW, 38.61 mm. **Ruler:** Elizabeth II **Subject:** Victoria Cross, 150th Anniversary **Rev:** Charles Lucas, Victoria Cross medal

| Date | Mintage | VF20 | XF40 | MS60 | MS63 | MS65 |
|---|---|---|---|---|---|---|
| 2006 | Est. 30000 | PF63 45.00 | PF65 55.00 | | | |

**KM# 150 5 POUNDS**
28.28 g., 0.925 Silver 0.841 oz. ASW, 38.61 mm. **Ruler:** Elizabeth II **Subject:** Victoria Cross, 150th Anniversary **Rev:** Ernest Smith, Victoria Cross medal

| Date | Mintage | VF20 | XF40 | MS60 | MS63 | MS65 |
|---|---|---|---|---|---|---|
| 2006 | Est. 30000 | PF63 45.00 | PF65 55.00 | | | |

**KM# 151 5 POUNDS**
28.28 g., 0.925 Silver 0.841 oz. ASW, 38.61 mm. **Ruler:** Elizabeth II **Subject:** Victoria Cross, 150th Anniversary **Rev:** Stanley Hollis, Victoria Cross medal

| Date | Mintage | VF20 | XF40 | MS60 | MS63 | MS65 |
|---|---|---|---|---|---|---|
| 2006 | — | PF63 45.00 | PF65 55.00 | | | |

**KM# 152 5 POUNDS**
28.28 g., 0.925 Silver 0.841 oz. ASW, 38.61 mm. **Ruler:** Elizabeth II **Subject:** Victoria Cross, 150th Anniversary **Rev:** Geoffrey Keyes, Victoria Cross medal

| Date | Mintage | VF20 | XF40 | MS60 | MS63 | MS65 |
|---|---|---|---|---|---|---|
| 2006 | Est. 30000 | PF63 45.00 | PF65 55.00 | | | |

**KM# 153 5 POUNDS**
28.28 g., 0.925 Silver 0.841 oz. ASW, 38.61 mm. **Ruler:** Elizabeth II **Subject:** Victoria Cross, 150th Anniversary **Rev:** Daniel Laidlow, Victoria Cross medal

| Date | Mintage | VF20 | XF40 | MS60 | MS63 | MS65 |
|---|---|---|---|---|---|---|
| 2006 | Est. 30000 | PF63 45.00 | PF65 55.00 | | | |

**KM# 158 5 POUNDS**
28.28 g., Copper-Nickel, 38.61 mm. **Ruler:** Elizabeth II **Rev:** Capt. James Cook

| Date | Mintage | VF20 | XF40 | MS60 | MS63 | MS65 |
|---|---|---|---|---|---|---|
| 2007 | — | — | — | — | 13.00 | 15.00 |

**KM# 158a 5 POUNDS**
28.28 g., 0.925 Silver 0.841 oz. ASW, 38.61 mm. **Ruler:** Elizabeth II **Rev:** Capt. Jmes Cook

| Date | Mintage | VF20 | XF40 | MS60 | MS63 | MS65 |
|---|---|---|---|---|---|---|
| 2007 | — | PF63 50.00 | PF65 55.00 | | | |

**KM# 158b 5 POUNDS**
39.94 g., 0.916 Gold 1.1762 oz. AGW, 38.61 mm. **Ruler:** Elizabeth II **Rev:** Capt. James Cook

| Date | Mintage | VF20 | XF40 | MS60 | MS63 | MS65 |
|---|---|---|---|---|---|---|
| 2007 | — | PF65 1,708 | | | | |

**KM# 159 5 POUNDS**
28.28 g., Copper-Nickel, 38.61 mm. **Ruler:** Elizabeth II **Rev:** Sir Edward Elgar

| Date | Mintage | VF20 | XF40 | MS60 | MS63 | MS65 |
|---|---|---|---|---|---|---|
| 2007 | — | — | — | — | 13.00 | 15.00 |

**KM# 159a 5 POUNDS**
28.28 g., 0.925 Silver 0.841 oz. ASW, 38.61 mm. **Ruler:** Elizabeth II **Rev:** Sir Edward Elgar

| Date | Mintage | VF20 | XF40 | MS60 | MS63 | MS65 |
|---|---|---|---|---|---|---|
| 2007 | Est. 25000 | PF63 45.00 | PF65 55.00 | | | |

**KM# 159b 5 POUNDS**
39.94 g., 0.9167 Gold 1.1771 oz. AGW, 38.61 mm. **Ruler:** Elizabeth II **Rev:** Sir Edward Elgar

| Date | Mintage | VF20 | XF40 | MS60 | MS63 | MS65 |
|---|---|---|---|---|---|---|
| 2007 | — | PF65 1,709 | | | | |

**KM# 160 5 POUNDS**
28.28 g., Copper-Nickel, 38.61 mm. **Ruler:** Elizabeth II **Rev:** Sir Francis Drake

| Date | Mintage | VF20 | XF40 | MS60 | MS63 | MS65 |
|---|---|---|---|---|---|---|
| 2007 | — | PF63 13.00 | PF65 15.00 | | | |

**KM# 160a 5 POUNDS**
28.28 g., 0.925 Silver 0.841 oz. ASW, 38.61 mm. **Ruler:** Elizabeth II **Rev:** Sir Francis Drake

| Date | Mintage | VF20 | XF40 | MS60 | MS63 | MS65 |
|---|---|---|---|---|---|---|
| 2007 | Est. 25000 | PF63 45.00 | PF65 55.00 | | | |

**KM# 160b 5 POUNDS**
39.94 g., 0.9167 Gold 1.1771 oz. AGW, 38.61 mm. **Ruler:** Elizabeth II **Rev:** Sir Francis Drake

| Date | Mintage | VF20 | XF40 | MS60 | MS63 | MS65 |
|---|---|---|---|---|---|---|
| 2007 | — | PF65 1,709 | | | | |

**KM# 161 5 POUNDS**
28.28 g., Copper-Nickel, 38.61 mm. **Ruler:** Elizabeth II **Rev:** John Constable

| Date | Mintage | VF20 | XF40 | MS60 | MS63 | MS65 |
|---|---|---|---|---|---|---|
| 2007 | — | — | — | — | 13.00 | 15.00 |

**KM# 161a 5 POUNDS**
28.28 g., 0.925 Silver 0.841 oz. ASW, 38.61 mm. **Ruler:** Elizabeth II **Rev:** John Constable

| Date | Mintage | VF20 | XF40 | MS60 | MS63 | MS65 |
|---|---|---|---|---|---|---|
| 2007 | Est. 25000 | **PF63** 45.00 | **PF65** 55.00 | | | |

**KM# 161b 5 POUNDS**
39.94 g., 0.9167 Gold 1.1771 oz. AGW, 39.94 mm. **Ruler:** Elizabeth II **Rev:** John Constable

| Date | Mintage | VF20 | XF40 | MS60 | MS63 | MS65 |
|---|---|---|---|---|---|---|
| 2007 | — | **PF65** 1,709 | | | | |

**KM# 162 5 POUNDS**
28.28 g., 0.925 Silver 0.841 oz. ASW partially gilt, 38.61 mm. **Ruler:** Elizabeth II **Rev:** Henry VII

| Date | Mintage | VF20 | XF40 | MS60 | MS63 | MS65 |
|---|---|---|---|---|---|---|
| 2007 | — | **PF63** 45.00 | **PF65** 55.00 | | | |

**KM# 163 5 POUNDS**
28.28 g., 0.925 Silver 0.841 oz. ASW partially gilt, 38.61 mm. **Ruler:** Elizabeth II **Rev:** Henry VIII

| Date | Mintage | VF20 | XF40 | MS60 | MS63 | MS65 |
|---|---|---|---|---|---|---|
| 2007 | Est. 37500 | **PF63** 45.00 | **PF65** 55.00 | | | |

**KM# 164 5 POUNDS**
28.28 g., 0.925 Silver 0.841 oz. ASW partially gilt, 38.61 mm. **Ruler:** Elizabeth II **Rev:** Edward VI

| Date | Mintage | VF20 | XF40 | MS60 | MS63 | MS65 |
|---|---|---|---|---|---|---|
| 2007 | Est. 37500 | **PF63** 45.00 | **PF65** 55.00 | | | |

**KM# 165 5 POUNDS**
28.28 g., 0.925 Silver 0.841 oz. ASW partially gilt, 38.61 mm. **Ruler:** Elizabeth II **Rev:** Mary I

| Date | Mintage | VF20 | XF40 | MS60 | MS63 | MS65 |
|---|---|---|---|---|---|---|
| 2007 | Est. 37500 | **PF63** 45.00 | **PF65** 55.00 | | | |

**KM# 166 5 POUNDS**
28.28 g., 0.925 Silver 0.841 oz. ASW, 38.61 mm. **Ruler:** Elizabeth II **Rev:** Elizabeth I

| Date | Mintage | VF20 | XF40 | MS60 | MS63 | MS65 |
|---|---|---|---|---|---|---|
| 2007 | — | **PF63** 45.00 | **PF65** 55.00 | | | |

**KM# 167 5 POUNDS**
28.28 g., 0.925 Silver 0.841 oz. ASW partially gilt, 38.61 mm. **Ruler:** Elizabeth II **Rev:** James I

| Date | Mintage | VF20 | XF40 | MS60 | MS63 | MS65 |
|---|---|---|---|---|---|---|
| 2007 | Est. 37500 | **PF63** 45.00 | **PF65** 55.00 | | | |

**KM# 168 5 POUNDS**
28.28 g., 0.925 Silver 0.841 oz. ASW, 38.61 mm. **Ruler:** Elizabeth II **Rev:** Charles I

| Date | Mintage | VF20 | XF40 | MS60 | MS63 | MS65 |
|---|---|---|---|---|---|---|
| 2007 | Est. 37500 | **PF63** 45.00 | **PF65** 55.00 | | | |

**KM# 169 5 POUNDS**
28.28 g., 0.925 Silver 0.841 oz. ASW partially gilt, 38.61 mm. **Ruler:** Elizabeth II **Rev:** Charles II

| Date | Mintage | VF20 | XF40 | MS60 | MS63 | MS65 |
|---|---|---|---|---|---|---|
| 2007 | Est. 37500 | **PF63** 45.00 | **PF65** 55.00 | | | |

**KM# 170 5 POUNDS**
28.28 g., 0.916 Silver 0.8328 oz. ASW partially gilt, 38.61 mm. **Ruler:** Elizabeth II **Rev:** James II

| Date | Mintage | VF20 | XF40 | MS60 | MS63 | MS65 |
|---|---|---|---|---|---|---|
| 2007 | Est. 37500 | **PF63** 45.00 | **PF65** 55.00 | | | |

**KM# 171 5 POUNDS**
28.28 g., 0.925 Silver 0.841 oz. ASW partially gilt, 38.61 mm. **Ruler:** Elizabeth II **Rev:** William and Mary

| Date | Mintage | VF20 | XF40 | MS60 | MS63 | MS65 |
|---|---|---|---|---|---|---|
| 2007 | Est. 37500 | **PF63** 45.00 | **PF65** 55.00 | | | |

**KM# 172 5 POUNDS**
28.28 g., 0.925 Silver 0.841 oz. ASW partially gilt, 38.61 mm. **Ruler:** Elizabeth II **Rev:** William III

| Date | Mintage | VF20 | XF40 | MS60 | MS63 | MS65 |
|---|---|---|---|---|---|---|
| 2007 | 37,500 | **PF63** 45.00 | **PF65** 55.00 | | | |

**KM# 173 5 POUNDS**
28.28 g., 0.925 Silver 0.841 oz. ASW, 38.61 mm. **Ruler:** Elizabeth II **Rev:** Anne

| Date | Mintage | VF20 | XF40 | MS60 | MS63 | MS65 |
|---|---|---|---|---|---|---|
| 2007 | Est. 37500 | **PF63** 45.00 | **PF65** 55.00 | | | |

**KM# 175 5 POUNDS**
28.28 g., Copper-Nickel, 38.61 mm. **Ruler:** Elizabeth II **Subject:** Princess Diana, 10th Anniversary of Death

| Date | Mintage | VF20 | XF40 | MS60 | MS63 | MS65 |
|---|---|---|---|---|---|---|
| 2007 | — | — | — | — | 13.00 | 15.00 |

**KM# 177 5 POUNDS**
28.28 g., Copper-Nickel, 38.61 mm. **Ruler:** Elizabeth II **Subject:** Elizabeth II & Prince Philip, 60th Wedding Anniversary **Rev:** 1947 Wedding Portrait

| Date | Mintage | VF20 | XF40 | MS60 | MS63 | MS65 |
|---|---|---|---|---|---|---|
| 2007 | — | — | — | — | 13.00 | 15.00 |

**KM# 177a 5 POUNDS**
28.28 g., 0.925 Silver 0.841 oz. ASW, 38.61 mm. **Ruler:** Elizabeth II **Subject:** Elizabeth II and Prince Philip, 60th Wedding Anniversary **Rev:** 1947 Wedding Portrait

| Date | Mintage | VF20 | XF40 | MS60 | MS63 | MS65 |
|---|---|---|---|---|---|---|
| 2007 | — | **PF63** 50.00 | **PF65** 55.00 | | | |

**KM# 178 5 POUNDS**
28.28 g., Copper-Nickel, 38.61 mm. **Ruler:** Elizabeth II **Subject:** Elizabeth II and Prince Philip, 60th Wedding Anniversary **Rev:** State Carriage

| Date | Mintage | VF20 | XF40 | MS60 | MS63 | MS65 |
|---|---|---|---|---|---|---|
| 2007 | — | — | — | — | 13.00 | 15.00 |

**KM# 178a 5 POUNDS**
28.28 g., 0.925 Silver 0.841 oz. ASW, 38.61 mm. **Ruler:** Elizabeth II **Subject:** Elizabeth II and Prince Philip, 60th Wedding Anniversary **Rev:** State Carriage

| Date | Mintage | VF20 | XF40 | MS60 | MS63 | MS65 |
|---|---|---|---|---|---|---|
| 2007 | — | **PF63** 50.00 | **PF65** 55.00 | | | |

**KM# 179 5 POUNDS**
28.28 g., Copper-Nickel, 38.61 mm. **Ruler:** Elizabeth II **Subject:** Elizabeth II and Prince Philip, 60th Wedding Anniversary **Rev:** Honeymoon departure

| Date | Mintage | VF20 | XF40 | MS60 | MS63 | MS65 |
|---|---|---|---|---|---|---|
| 2007 | — | — | — | — | 13.00 | 15.00 |

**KM# 179a 5 POUNDS**
28.28 g., 0.925 Silver 0.841 oz. ASW, 38.61 mm. **Ruler:** Elizabeth II **Subject:** Elizabeth II and Prince Philip, 60th Wedding Anniversary **Rev:** Honeymoon departure

| Date | Mintage | VF20 | XF40 | MS60 | MS63 | MS65 |
|---|---|---|---|---|---|---|
| 2007 | — | **PF63** 50.00 | **PF65** 55.00 | | | |

**KM# 180 5 POUNDS**
28.28 g., Copper-Nickel, 38.61 mm. **Ruler:** Elizabeth II **Subject:** Elizabeth II and Prince Philip, 60th Wedding Anniversary **Rev:** Portraits

| Date | Mintage | VF20 | XF40 | MS60 | MS63 | MS65 |
|---|---|---|---|---|---|---|
| 2007 | — | — | — | — | 13.00 | 15.00 |

**KM# 180a 5 POUNDS**
28.28 g., 0.925 Silver 0.841 oz. ASW, 38.61 mm. **Ruler:** Elizabeth II **Subject:** Elizabeth II and Prince Philip, 60th Wedding Anniversary **Rev:** Elizabeth II and Philip portraits

| Date | Mintage | VF20 | XF40 | MS60 | MS63 | MS65 |
|---|---|---|---|---|---|---|
| 2007 | — | **PF63** 50.00 | **PF65** 55.00 | | | |

**KM# 181 5 POUNDS**
28.28 g., 0.925 Silver 0.841 oz. ASW, 38.61 mm. **Ruler:** Elizabeth II **Subject:** Elizabeth II and Prince Philip, 60th Wedding Anniversary **Rev:** Bridal couple outside Westminster Abbey

| Date | Mintage | VF20 | XF40 | MS60 | MS63 | MS65 |
|---|---|---|---|---|---|---|
| 2007 | Est. 30000 | **PF63** 45.00 | **PF65** 55.00 | | | |

**KM# 182 5 POUNDS**
28.28 g., 0.925 Silver 0.841 oz. ASW, 38.61 mm. **Ruler:** Elizabeth II **Subject:** Elizabeth II and Prince Philip, 60th Wedding Anniversary **Rev:** Birth of Prince Charles

| Date | Mintage | VF20 | XF40 | MS60 | MS63 | MS65 |
|---|---|---|---|---|---|---|
| 2007 | Est. 30000 | **PF63** 45.00 | **PF65** 55.00 | | | |

**KM# 183 5 POUNDS**
28.28 g., 0.925 Silver 0.841 oz. ASW, 38.61 mm. **Ruler:** Elizabeth II **Subject:** Elizabeth II and Prince Philip, 60th Wedding Anniversary **Rev:** Modern portrait of Elizabeth and Philip

| Date | Mintage | VF20 | XF40 | MS60 | MS63 | MS65 |
|---|---|---|---|---|---|---|
| 2007 | Est. 30000 | **PF63** 45.00 | **PF65** 55.00 | | | |

**KM# 222 5 POUNDS**
28.28 g., 0.925 Silver 0.841 oz. ASW, 38.61 mm. **Ruler:** Elizabeth II **Subject:** Elizabeth II 50th Wedding Anniversary **Shape:** 7-sided

| Date | Mintage | VF20 | XF40 | MS60 | MS63 | MS65 |
|---|---|---|---|---|---|---|
| 2007 | Est. 130000 | **PF63** 35.00 | **PF65** 40.00 | | | |

**KM# 223 5 POUNDS**
28.28 g., 0.925 Silver 0.841 oz. ASW, 38.61 mm. **Ruler:** Elizabeth II **Subject:** Queen Elizabeth II 50th Wedding Anniversary **Shape:** 7-Sided

| Date | Mintage | VF20 | XF40 | MS60 | MS63 | MS65 |
|---|---|---|---|---|---|---|
| 2007 | Est. 30000 | **PF63** 35.00 | **PF65** 40.00 | | | |

**KM# 224 5 POUNDS**
28.28 g., 0.925 Silver 0.841 oz. ASW, 38.61 mm. **Ruler:** Elizabeth II **Subject:** Birth of Prince Charles **Shape:** 7-Sided

| Date | Mintage | VF20 | XF40 | MS60 | MS63 | MS65 |
|---|---|---|---|---|---|---|
| 2004 | Est. 30000 | **PF63** 35.00 | **PF65** 40.00 | | | |

**KM# 184 5 POUNDS**
28.28 g., 0.925 Silver 0.841 oz. ASW, 38.61 mm. **Ruler:** Elizabeth II **Subject:** End of World War I, 90th Anniversary **Rev:** Soldiers and workers, flag in background

| Date | Mintage | VF20 | XF40 | MS60 | MS63 | MS65 |
|---|---|---|---|---|---|---|
| 2008 | Est. 15000 | **PF63** 50.00 | **PF65** 55.00 | | | |

**KM# 184a 5 POUNDS**
39.94 g., 0.9167 Gold 1.1771 oz. AGW, 38.61 mm. **Ruler:** Elizabeth II **Subject:** End of World War I, 90th Anniversary **Rev:** Soldiers and workers, flag in background

| Date | Mintage | VF20 | XF40 | MS60 | MS63 | MS65 |
|---|---|---|---|---|---|---|
| 2008 | Est. 250 | **PF65** 1,709 | | | | |

**KM# 185 5 POUNDS**
28.28 g., 0.925 Silver 0.841 oz. ASW, 38.61 mm. **Ruler:** Elizabeth II **Subject:** End of World War I, 90th Anniversary **Rev:** Tank and soldier

| Date | Mintage | VF20 | XF40 | MS60 | MS63 | MS65 |
|---|---|---|---|---|---|---|
| 2008 | Est. 15000 | **PF63** 50.00 | **PF65** 55.00 | | | |

**KM# 185a 5 POUNDS**
39.94 g., 0.9167 Gold 1.1771 oz. AGW, 38.61 mm. **Ruler:** Elizabeth II **Subject:** End of World War I, 90th Anniversary **Rev:** Tank and soldier

| Date | Mintage | VF20 | XF40 | MS60 | MS63 | MS65 |
|---|---|---|---|---|---|---|
| 2008 | Est. 250 | **PF65** 1,709 | | | | |

**KM# 186 5 POUNDS**
28.28 g., 0.925 Silver 0.841 oz. ASW, 38.61 mm. **Ruler:** Elizabeth II **Subject:** End of World War I, 90th Anniversary **Rev:** Soldiers and gravesites

| Date | Mintage | VF20 | XF40 | MS60 | MS63 | MS65 |
|---|---|---|---|---|---|---|
| 2008 | Est. 15000 | **PF63** 50.00 | **PF65** 55.00 | | | |

**KM# 186a 5 POUNDS**
39.94 g., 0.9167 Gold 1.1771 oz. AGW, 38.61 mm. **Ruler:** Elizabeth II **Subject:** End of World War I, 90th Anniversary **Rev:** Soldiers and gravesites

| Date | Mintage | VF20 | XF40 | MS60 | MS63 | MS65 |
|---|---|---|---|---|---|---|
| 2008 | Est. 250 | **PF65** 1,709 | | | | |

**KM# 187 5 POUNDS**
28.28 g., 0.925 Silver 0.841 oz. ASW, 38.61 mm. **Ruler:** Elizabeth II **Subject:** End of World War I, 90th Anniversary **Rev:** Propaganda

| Date | Mintage | VF20 | XF40 | MS60 | MS63 | MS65 |
|---|---|---|---|---|---|---|
| 2008 | Est. 15000 | **PF63** 50.00 | **PF65** 55.00 | | | |

**KM# 190 5 POUNDS**
28.28 g., Copper-Nickel, 38.61 mm. **Ruler:** Elizabeth II **Rev:** Concorde

| Date | Mintage | VF20 | XF40 | MS60 | MS63 | MS65 |
|---|---|---|---|---|---|---|
| 2008 | — | — | — | — | 13.00 | 15.00 |

**KM# 190a 5 POUNDS**
28.28 g., 0.925 Silver 0.841 oz. ASW, 38.61 mm. **Ruler:** Elizabeth II **Rev:** Concorde

| Date | Mintage | VF20 | XF40 | MS60 | MS63 | MS65 |
|---|---|---|---|---|---|---|
| 2008 | — | PF63 50.00 | PF65 55.00 | | | |

**KM# 190b 5 POUNDS**
39.94 g., 0.916 Gold 1.1762 oz. AGW, 38.61 mm. **Ruler:** Elizabeth II **Rev:** Concorde

| Date | Mintage | VF20 | XF40 | MS60 | MS63 | MS65 |
|---|---|---|---|---|---|---|
| 2008 | Est. 250 | PF65 60,000 | | | | |

**KM# 85 5 POUNDS**
28.28 g., Copper-Nickel, 38.61 mm. **Ruler:** Elizabeth II **Subject:** Mini Cooper 50th Anniversary **Rev:** 1959 Mini Cooper on tiled floor

| Date | Mintage | VF20 | XF40 | MS60 | MS63 | MS65 |
|---|---|---|---|---|---|---|
| 2009 | 50,000 | — | — | — | 16.00 | 18.00 |

**KM# 86 5 POUNDS**
28.28 g., 0.925 Silver 0.841 oz. ASW, 38.61 mm. **Ruler:** Elizabeth II **Subject:** Mini Cooper, 50th Anniversary **Rev:** 1959 Mini Cooper multicolor British flag on roof

| Date | Mintage | VF20 | XF40 | MS60 | MS63 | MS65 |
|---|---|---|---|---|---|---|
| 2009 | — | PF63 65.00 | PF65 75.00 | | | |

**KM# 87 5 POUNDS**
28.28 g., 0.925 Silver 0.841 oz. ASW, 38.61 mm. **Ruler:** Elizabeth II **Subject:** Mini Cooper, 50th Anniversary **Rev:** Mini Cooper, red and pink flowers

| Date | Mintage | VF20 | XF40 | MS60 | MS63 | MS65 |
|---|---|---|---|---|---|---|
| 2009 | 2,000 | PF63 65.00 | PF65 75.00 | | | |

**KM# 88 5 POUNDS**
28.28 g., 0.925 Silver 0.841 oz. ASW, 38.61 mm. **Ruler:** Elizabeth II **Subject:** Mini Cooper, 50th Anniversary **Rev:** Mini Cooper, 4 views

| Date | Mintage | VF20 | XF40 | MS60 | MS63 | MS65 |
|---|---|---|---|---|---|---|
| 2009 | 2,000 | PF63 65.00 | PF65 75.00 | | | |

**KM# 89 5 POUNDS**
28.28 g., 0.925 Silver 0.841 oz. ASW, 38.61 mm. **Ruler:** Elizabeth II **Subject:** Mini Cooper, 50th Anniversary **Rev:** Rally Minis

| Date | Mintage | VF20 | XF40 | MS60 | MS63 | MS65 |
|---|---|---|---|---|---|---|
| 2009 | 2,000 | PF63 65.00 | PF65 75.00 | | | |

**KM# 193 5 POUNDS**
28.28 g., 0.925 Silver 0.841 oz. ASW, 38.61 mm. **Ruler:** Elizabeth II **Subject:** British Automobiles **Rev:** Morris Minor

| Date | Mintage | VF20 | XF40 | MS60 | MS63 | MS65 |
|---|---|---|---|---|---|---|
| 2009 | 20,000 | PF63 45.00 | PF65 55.00 | | | |

**KM# 194 5 POUNDS**
28.28 g., 0.925 Silver 0.841 oz. ASW, 38.61 mm. **Ruler:** Elizabeth II **Subject:** British Automobiles **Rev:** Land Rover series 1

| Date | Mintage | VF20 | XF40 | MS60 | MS63 | MS65 |
|---|---|---|---|---|---|---|
| 2009 | Est. 20000 | PF63 45.00 | PF65 55.00 | | | |

**KM# 195 5 POUNDS**
28.28 g., 0.925 Silver 0.841 oz. ASW, 38.61 mm. **Ruler:** Elizabeth II **Subject:** British Automobiles **Rev:** Jaguar E type series 1

| Date | Mintage | VF20 | XF40 | MS60 | MS63 | MS65 |
|---|---|---|---|---|---|---|
| 2009 | Est. 20000 | PF63 45.00 | PF65 55.00 | | | |

**KM# 196 5 POUNDS**
28.28 g., 0.925 Silver 0.841 oz. ASW, 38.61 mm. **Ruler:** Elizabeth II **Subject:** British Automobiles **Rev:** Rolls Royce Silver Ghost

| Date | Mintage | VF20 | XF40 | MS60 | MS63 | MS65 |
|---|---|---|---|---|---|---|
| 2009 | Est. 20000 | PF63 45.00 | PF65 55.00 | | | |

**KM# 197 5 POUNDS**
28.28 g., 0.925 Silver 0.841 oz. ASW, 38.61 mm. **Ruler:** Elizabeth II **Subject:** British Automobiles **Rev:** Austrin Seven "Baby Austin

| Date | Mintage | VF20 | XF40 | MS60 | MS63 | MS65 |
|---|---|---|---|---|---|---|
| 2009 | Est. 20000 | PF63 45.00 | PF65 55.00 | | | |

**KM# 198 5 POUNDS**
28.28 g., 0.925 Silver 0.841 oz. ASW, 38.61 mm. **Ruler:** Elizabeth II **Subject:** British Automobiles **Rev:** Triumph Herald

| Date | Mintage | VF20 | XF40 | MS60 | MS63 | MS65 |
|---|---|---|---|---|---|---|
| 2009 | — | PF63 45.00 | PF65 55.00 | | | |

**KM# 199 5 POUNDS**
28.28 g., 0.925 Silver 0.841 oz. ASW **Ruler:** Elizabeth II **Subject:** British Automobiles **Rev:** Bentley R type Contiental

| Date | Mintage | VF20 | XF40 | MS60 | MS63 | MS65 |
|---|---|---|---|---|---|---|
| 2009 | — | PF63 45.00 | PF65 55.00 | | | |

**KM# 200 5 POUNDS**
28.28 g., 0.925 Silver 0.841 oz. ASW, 38.61 mm. **Ruler:** Elizabeth II **Subject:** British Automobiles **Rev:** Lotus Elite (1957)

| Date | Mintage | VF20 | XF40 | MS60 | MS63 | MS65 |
|---|---|---|---|---|---|---|
| 2009 | Est. 20000 | PF63 45.00 | PF65 55.00 | | | |

**KM# 201 5 POUNDS**
28.28 g., 0.925 Silver 0.841 oz. ASW, 38.61 mm. **Ruler:** Elizabeth II **Subject:** British Automobiles **Rev:** Aston Martin DB 5 (1963)

| Date | Mintage | VF20 | XF40 | MS60 | MS63 | MS65 |
|---|---|---|---|---|---|---|
| 2009 | Est. 20000 | PF63 45.00 | PF65 55.00 | | | |

**KM# 202 5 POUNDS**
28.28 g., 0.925 Silver 0.841 oz. ASW, 38.61 mm. **Ruler:** Elizabeth II **Subject:** British Automobiles **Rev:** Austin healey Sprint MK 1

| Date | Mintage | VF20 | XF40 | MS60 | MS63 | MS65 |
|---|---|---|---|---|---|---|
| 2009 | Est. 20000 | PF63 45.00 | PF65 55.00 | | | |

**KM# 203 5 POUNDS**
28.28 g., 0.925 Silver 0.841 oz. ASW, 38.61 mm. **Ruler:** Elizabeth II **Subject:** British Automobiles **Rev:** Bentley 4-1/2 Litre

| Date | Mintage | VF20 | XF40 | MS60 | MS63 | MS65 |
|---|---|---|---|---|---|---|
| 2009 | Est. 20000 | PF63 45.00 | PF65 55.00 | | | |

**KM# 204 5 POUNDS**
28.28 g., 0.925 Silver 0.841 oz. ASW, 38.61 mm. **Ruler:** Elizabeth II **Subject:** British Automobiles **Rev:** Hillman Imp

| Date | Mintage | VF20 | XF40 | MS60 | MS63 | MS65 |
|---|---|---|---|---|---|---|
| 2009 | Est. 20000 | PF63 45.00 | PF65 55.00 | | | |

**KM# 205 5 POUNDS**
28.28 g., 0.925 Silver 0.841 oz. ASW, 38.61 mm. **Ruler:** Elizabeth II **Subject:** British Automobiles **Rev:** MGB Roadster MK 1

| Date | Mintage | VF20 | XF40 | MS60 | MS63 | MS65 |
|---|---|---|---|---|---|---|
| 2009 | Est. 20000 | PF63 45.00 | PF65 55.00 | | | |

**KM# 206 5 POUNDS**
28.28 g., 0.925 Silver 0.841 oz. ASW, 38.61 mm. **Ruler:** Elizabeth II **Subject:** British Automobiles **Rev:** MG TC Midget

| Date | Mintage | VF20 | XF40 | MS60 | MS63 | MS65 |
|---|---|---|---|---|---|---|
| 2009 | Est. 20000 | PF63 45.00 | PF65 55.00 | | | |

**KM# 207 5 POUNDS**
28.28 g., 0.925 Silver 0.841 oz. ASW, 38.61 mm. **Ruler:** Elizabeth II **Subject:** British Automobiles **Rev:** BMC Mini

| Date | Mintage | VF20 | XF40 | MS60 | MS63 | MS65 |
|---|---|---|---|---|---|---|
| 2009 | Est. 20000 | PF63 45.00 | PF65 55.00 | | | |

**KM# 208 5 POUNDS**
28.28 g., 0.925 Silver 0.841 oz. ASW, 38.61 mm. **Ruler:** Elizabeth II **Subject:** British Automobiles **Rev:** Morgan Plus Four

| Date | Mintage | VF20 | XF40 | MS60 | MS63 | MS65 |
|---|---|---|---|---|---|---|
| 2009 | Est. 20000 | PF63 45.00 | PF65 55.00 | | | |

**KM# 209 5 POUNDS**
28.28 g., 0.925 Silver 0.841 oz. ASW, 38.61 mm. **Ruler:** Elizabeth II **Subject:** British Automobiles **Rev:** Rover P5B

| Date | Mintage | VF20 | XF40 | MS60 | MS63 | MS65 |
|---|---|---|---|---|---|---|
| 2009 | Est. 20000 | PF63 45.00 | PF65 55.00 | | | |

**KM# 210 5 POUNDS**
28.28 g., 0.925 Silver 0.841 oz. ASW, 38.61 mm. **Ruler:** Elizabeth II **Subject:** British Automobiles **Rev:** Vauhall - Prince Henry

| Date | Mintage | VF20 | XF40 | MS60 | MS63 | MS65 |
|---|---|---|---|---|---|---|
| 2009 | Est. 20000 | PF63 45.00 | PF65 55.00 | | | |

**KM# 211 5 POUNDS**
28.28 g., Copper-Nickel, 38.61 mm. **Ruler:** Elizabeth II **Subject:** Engagement - Prince William and Catherine Middleton **Obv:** Head in tiara right **Rev:** Conjoined busts left

| Date | Mintage | VF20 | XF40 | MS60 | MS63 | MS65 |
|---|---|---|---|---|---|---|
| 2010 | 100,000 | — | — | — | 18.00 | 20.00 |

**KM# 211a 5 POUNDS**
28.28 g., 0.925 Silver 0.841 oz. ASW, 38.61 mm. **Ruler:** Elizabeth II **Subject:** Engagement - Prince William and Catherine Middleton **Obv:** Head in tiara right **Rev:** Conjoined busts left

| Date | Mintage | VF20 | XF40 | MS60 | MS63 | MS65 |
|---|---|---|---|---|---|---|
| 2010 | 1,500 | PF63 100 | PF65 120 | | | |

**KM# 211b 5 POUNDS**
39.94 g., 0.9167 Gold 1.1771 oz. AGW, 38.61 mm. **Ruler:** Elizabeth II **Subject:** Engagement of Prince William and Catherine Middleton **Obv:** Head in tiara right **Rev:** Conjoined busts left

| Date | Mintage | VF20 | XF40 | MS60 | MS63 | MS65 |
|---|---|---|---|---|---|---|
| 2010 | 1,000 | PF65 1,709 | | | | |

**KM# 218 5 POUNDS**
28.28 g., Copper-Nickel, 38.6 mm. **Ruler:** Elizabeth II **Subject:** Battle of Britain, 1940 **Obv:** Head in tiara right **Rev:** Fighter planes

| Date | Mintage | VF20 | XF40 | MS60 | MS63 | MS65 |
|---|---|---|---|---|---|---|
| 2010 | — | PF63 17.00 | PF65 20.00 | | | |

**KM# 212 5 POUNDS**
28.28 g., Copper-Nickel, 38.61 mm. **Ruler:** Elizabeth II **Subject:** Royal Wedding **Obv:** Head with tiara right **Rev:** Catherine and William busts left

| Date | Mintage | VF20 | XF40 | MS60 | MS63 | MS65 |
|---|---|---|---|---|---|---|
| 2011 | — | — | — | — | 16.00 | 18.00 |

**KM# 212a 5 POUNDS**
28.28 g., 0.925 Silver 0.841 oz. ASW, 38.61 mm. **Ruler:** Elizabeth II **Subject:** Royal Wedding **Obv:** Head with tiara right **Rev:** Catherine and William busts left

| Date | Mintage | VF20 | XF40 | MS60 | MS63 | MS65 |
|---|---|---|---|---|---|---|
| 2011 | — | PF63 65.00 | PF65 75.00 | | | |

**KM# 219 5 POUNDS**
28.28 g., Copper-Nickel, 38.61 mm. **Ruler:** Elizabeth II **Subject:** Remembrance Day **Obv:** Head in tiara right **Rev:** Large poppy in color at left, legend at right **Rev. Legend:** THE ELEVENTH HOUR OF THE ELEVENTH DAY OF THE ELEVENTH MONTH

| Date | Mintage | VF20 | XF40 | MS60 | MS63 | MS65 |
|---|---|---|---|---|---|---|
| 2012 | — | — | — | — | 18.00 | 20.00 |

**KM# 220 5 POUNDS**
28.28 g., Copper-Nickel, 38.61 mm. **Ruler:** Elizabeth II **Subject:** Titanic, 100th Anniversary **Obv:** Head with tiara right **Rev:** Female statue from titanic memorial at top left, Ship sailing to left, at right

| Date | Mintage | VF20 | XF40 | MS60 | MS63 | MS65 |
|---|---|---|---|---|---|---|
| 2012 | — | — | — | — | 22.00 | 25.00 |

**KM# 220a 5 POUNDS**
28.28 g., 0.925 Silver 0.841 oz. ASW, 38.61 mm. **Ruler:** Elizabeth II **Subject:** Titanic, 100th Anniversary **Obv:** Head with tiara right **Rev:** Part of Titanic memorial at left, ship sailing left, at right

| Date | Mintage | VF20 | XF40 | MS60 | MS63 | MS65 |
|---|---|---|---|---|---|---|
| 2012 | — | PF63 65.00 | PF65 75.00 | | | |

**KM# 225 5 POUNDS**
0.925 Silver, 38.61 mm. **Ruler:** Elizabeth II **Subject:** Royal Duties - Parliament **Obv:** Head with tiara right **Rev:** Royal standard above, outline of Parliament buildings

| Date | Mintage | VF20 | XF40 | MS60 | MS63 | MS65 |
|---|---|---|---|---|---|---|
| 2012 | — | PF65 75.00 | | | | |

**KM# 227 5 POUNDS**
Silver, 38.61 mm. **Ruler:** Elizabeth II **Subject:** Royal Duties - Air Force **Obv:** Jets in formation

| Date | Mintage | VF20 | XF40 | MS60 | MS63 | MS65 |
|---|---|---|---|---|---|---|
| 2012 | — | PF65 75.00 | | | | |

**KM# 219a 5 POUNDS**
28.28 g., 0.925 Silver 0.841 oz. ASW, 38.61 mm. **Ruler:** Elizabeth II **Obv:** Head with tiara right **Rev:** Large poppy in red at left

| Date | Mintage | VF20 | XF40 | MS60 | MS63 | MS65 |
|---|---|---|---|---|---|---|
| 2013 | — | PF65 50.00 | | | | |

**KM# 36 10 POUNDS**
155.52 g., 0.925 Silver 4.625 oz. ASW, 65.06 mm. **Ruler:** Elizabeth II **Subject:** Last Flight of the Concorde **Obv:** Crowned bust right **Obv. Legend:** ELIIZABETH II - ALDERNEY **Rev:** Concorde in flight **Rev. Legend:** CONCORDE 1969 - 2003 **Edge:** Reeded **Note:** Illustration reduced.

| Date | Mintage | VF20 | XF40 | MS60 | MS63 | MS65 |
|---|---|---|---|---|---|---|
| 2003 | 1,969 | PF63 175 | PF65 200 | | | |

**KM# 55 10 POUNDS**
155.51 g., 0.925 Silver 4.6248 oz. ASW, 65 mm. **Ruler:** Elizabeth II **Subject:** WWII Liberation **Obv:** Elizabeth II by Maklouf sign **Rev:** Churchill flashing the "V **Edge:** Reeded

| Date | Mintage | VF20 | XF40 | MS60 | MS63 | MS65 |
|---|---|---|---|---|---|---|
| 2005 | 1,945 | PF63 275 | PF65 325 | | | |

**KM# 120 10 POUNDS**
155.50 g., 0.925 Silver 4.6245 oz. ASW, 65 mm. **Ruler:** Elizabeth II **Subject:** Trafalgar - England espects that every man will do his duty

| Date | Mintage | VF20 | XF40 | MS60 | MS63 | MS65 |
|---|---|---|---|---|---|---|
| 2005 | — | PF65 275 | | | | |

**KM# 82 10 POUNDS**
155.52 g., 0.925 Silver 4.625 oz. ASW, 65 mm. **Ruler:** Elizabeth II **Obv:** Crowned bust right **Obv. Legend:** ELIZABETH II - ALDERNEY **Rev:** Four small gilt coinage busts in ornate quadralobe **Rev. Legend:** + HER MAJESTY QUEEN ELIZABETH II + EIGHTIETH BIRTHDAY + **Edge:** Reeded, gilt

| Date | Mintage | VF20 | XF40 | MS60 | MS63 | MS65 |
|---|---|---|---|---|---|---|
| 2006 | 1,926 | PF63 175 | PF65 200 | | | |

**KM# 135 10 POUNDS**
155.50 g., 0.925 Silver 4.6245 oz. ASW with diamonds, 65 mm. **Ruler:** Elizabeth II **Obv:** Head in tiara right **Rev:** Bust in tiara right

| Date | Mintage | VF20 | XF40 | MS60 | MS63 | MS65 |
|---|---|---|---|---|---|---|
| 2006 | Est. 1000 | PF65 250 | | | | |

**KM# 176 10 POUNDS**
155.50 g., 0.925 Silver 4.6245 oz. ASW, 65 mm. **Ruler:** Elizabeth II **Subject:** Princess Diana, 10th Anniversary of Death

| Date | Mintage | VF20 | XF40 | MS60 | MS63 | MS65 |
|---|---|---|---|---|---|---|
| 2007 | Est. 1500 | PF63 245 | PF65 275 | | | |

**KM# 188 10 POUNDS**
155.50 g., 0.925 Silver 4.6245 oz. ASW, 65 mm. **Ruler:** Elizabeth II **Subject:** End of World War I, 90th Anniversary

| Date | Mintage | VF20 | XF40 | MS60 | MS63 | MS65 |
|---|---|---|---|---|---|---|
| 2008 | Est. 150 | PF65 350 | | | | |

**KM# 191 10 POUNDS**
155.50 g., 0.925 Silver 4.6245 oz. ASW, 65 mm. **Ruler:** Elizabeth II **Rev:** Corcorde

| Date | Mintage | VF20 | XF40 | MS60 | MS63 | MS65 |
|---|---|---|---|---|---|---|
| 2008 | Est. 750 | PF65 275 | | | | |

**KM# 213 10 POUNDS**
155.50 g., 0.925 Silver 4.6245 oz. ASW, 65 mm. **Ruler:** Elizabeth II **Subject:** Royal Wedding - Prince William and Catherine Middleton **Obv:** Head in tiara right **Rev:** Conjoined busts left, rose window in background

| Date | Mintage | VF20 | XF40 | MS60 | MS63 | MS65 |
|---|---|---|---|---|---|---|
| 2011 | 500 | PF65 200 | | | | |

**KM# 61 25 POUNDS**
7.98 g., 0.9167 Gold 0.2352 oz. AGW, 22 mm. **Ruler:** Elizabeth II **Subject:** Queen's 75th Birthday **Obv:** Queen's portrait right **Rev:** Queen in casual dress surrounded by rose, thistle, daffodil and pimpernel

| Date | Mintage | VF20 | XF40 | MS60 | MS63 | MS65 |
|---|---|---|---|---|---|---|
| 2001 | — | PF63 425 | PF65 450 | | | |

**KM# 28 25 POUNDS**
7.98 g., 0.9167 Gold 0.2352 oz. AGW, 22.05 mm. **Ruler:** Elizabeth II **Subject:** 5th Anniversary Death of Princess Diana **Obv:** Queen's portrait **Rev:** Diana's cameo portrait left above denomination **Edge:** Reeded

| Date | Mintage | VF20 | XF40 | MS60 | MS63 | MS65 |
|---|---|---|---|---|---|---|
| 2002 | 2,500 | PF63 425 | PF65 450 | | | |

**KM# 30 25 POUNDS**
7.98 g., 0.9166 Gold 0.2352 oz. AGW, 22 mm. **Ruler:** Elizabeth II **Subject:** 150th Anniversary Death of the Duke of Wellington **Obv:** Queen's portrait **Rev:** Coat of arms, castle and portrait **Edge:** Reeded

| Date | Mintage | VF20 | XF40 | MS60 | MS63 | MS65 |
|---|---|---|---|---|---|---|
| 2002 | 2,500 | PF63 425 | PF65 450 | | | |

**KM# 58 25 POUNDS**
7.98 g., 0.9166 Gold 0.2352 oz. AGW, 22 mm. **Ruler:** Elizabeth II **Subject:** Queen Elizabeth II - Golden Jubilee of Reign **Obv:** Crowned head right **Rev:** Sword hilt and denomination with royal arms in background

| Date | Mintage | VF20 | XF40 | MS60 | MS63 | MS65 |
|---|---|---|---|---|---|---|
| 2002 | 2,500 | PF63 425 | PF65 450 | | | |

**KM# 74 25 POUNDS**
7.98 g., 0.9166 Gold 0.2352 oz. AGW **Ruler:** Elizabeth II **Subject:** Queen Elizabet II - Golden Jubilee of Reign **Obv:** Crowned head right **Rev:** Honor guard and trumpets

| Date | Mintage | VF20 | XF40 | MS60 | MS63 | MS65 |
|---|---|---|---|---|---|---|
| 2002 | — | PF63 425 | PF65 450 | | | |

**KM# 32 25 POUNDS**
7.98 g., 0.9166 Gold 0.2352 oz. AGW, 22 mm. **Ruler:** Elizabeth II **Subject:** Prince William **Obv:** Queen's portrait **Rev:** Portrait with open shirt collar **Edge:** Reeded

| Date | Mintage | VF20 | XF40 | MS60 | MS63 | MS65 |
|---|---|---|---|---|---|---|
| 2003 | 1,500 | PF63 425 | PF65 450 | | | |

**KM# 46 25 POUNDS**
7.98 g., 0.9167 Gold 0.2352 oz. AGW, 22 mm. **Ruler:** Elizabeth II **Obv:** Queen's portrait **Rev:** HMS Mary Rose **Edge:** Reeded

| Date | Mintage | VF20 | XF40 | MS60 | MS63 | MS65 |
|---|---|---|---|---|---|---|
| 2003 | 2,500 | PF63 450 | PF65 475 | | | |

**KM# 93 25 POUNDS**
7.98 g., 0.916 Gold 0.235 oz. AGW **Ruler:** Elizabeth II **Subject:** Royal navy - Alfred the Great

| Date | Mintage | VF20 | XF40 | MS60 | MS63 | MS65 |
|---|---|---|---|---|---|---|
| 2003 | Est. 1000 | PF63 475 | PF65 500 | | | |

**KM# 39 25 POUNDS**
7.98 g., 0.9167 Gold 0.2352 oz. AGW, 22 mm. **Ruler:** Elizabeth II **Subject:** D-Day **Obv:** Queen's portrait **Rev:** Battleship and transports **Edge:** Reeded

| Date | Mintage | VF20 | XF40 | MS60 | MS63 | MS65 |
|---|---|---|---|---|---|---|
| 2004 | 500 | PF63 450 | PF65 475 | | | |

**KM# 50 25 POUNDS**
7.98 g., 0.9167 Gold 0.2352 oz. AGW, 22 mm. **Ruler:** Elizabeth II **Obv:** Queen's portrait **Rev:** Locomotive, The Rocket **Edge:** Reeded

| Date | Mintage | VF20 | XF40 | MS60 | MS63 | MS65 |
|---|---|---|---|---|---|---|
| 2004 | 2,500 | PF63 450 | PF65 475 | | | |

**KM# 51 25 POUNDS**
7.98 g., 0.9167 Gold 0.2352 oz. AGW, 22 mm. **Ruler:** Elizabeth II **Obv:** Queen's portrait **Rev:** Locomotive, The Merchant Navy 21C1 **Edge:** Reeded

| Date | Mintage | VF20 | XF40 | MS60 | MS63 | MS65 |
|---|---|---|---|---|---|---|
| 2004 | 1,500 | PF63 450 | PF65 475 | | | |

**KM# 67 25 POUNDS**
7.98 g., 0.9167 Gold 0.2352 oz. AGW, 22 mm. **Ruler:** Elizabeth II **Subject:** Viscount Samuel Hood on his flagship after the Battle of Saints Passage in 1782 **Obv:** Queen's portrait

| Date | Mintage | VF20 | XF40 | MS60 | MS63 | MS65 |
|---|---|---|---|---|---|---|
| 2005 | — | PF63 425 | PF65 450 | | | |

**KM# 69 25 POUNDS**
7.98 g., 0.9167 Gold 0.2352 oz. AGW, 22 mm. **Ruler:** Elizabeth II **Obv:** Queen's portrait right **Rev:** HMS Revenge fighting at Azores, 1591

| Date | Mintage | VF20 | XF40 | MS60 | MS63 | MS65 |
|---|---|---|---|---|---|---|
| 2005 | — | PF63 450 | PF65 475 | | | |

**KM# 109 25 POUNDS**
7.98 g., 0.916 Gold 0.235 oz. AGW **Ruler:** Elizabeth II **Subject:** David Beckham **Obv:** Shield **Rev:** Soccer player and ball design

| Date | Mintage | VF20 | XF40 | MS60 | MS63 | MS65 |
|---|---|---|---|---|---|---|
| 2005 | Est. 5000 | PF63 475 | PF65 500 | | | |

**KM# 110 25 POUNDS**
7.98 g., 0.916 Gold 0.235 oz. AGW **Ruler:** Elizabeth II **Subject:** Michael Owen **Obv:** Shield **Rev:** Soccer player and ball design

| Date | Mintage | VF20 | XF40 | MS60 | MS63 | MS65 |
|---|---|---|---|---|---|---|
| 2005 | Est. 5000 | PF63 475 | PF65 500 | | | |

**KM# 111 25 POUNDS**
7.98 g., 0.916 Gold 0.235 oz. AGW **Ruler:** Elizabeth II **Subject:** Lrank Lampard **Obv:** Shield **Rev:** Soccer player and ball design

| Date | Mintage | VF20 | XF40 | MS60 | MS63 | MS65 |
|---|---|---|---|---|---|---|
| 2005 | — | PF63 475 | PF65 500 | | | |

**KM# 112 25 POUNDS**
7.98 g., 0.916 Gold 0.235 oz. AGW **Ruler:** Elizabeth II **Subject:** Jeremiah Campbell **Obv:** Shield **Rev:** Soccer player and ball design.

| Date | Mintage | VF20 | XF40 | MS60 | MS63 | MS65 |
|---|---|---|---|---|---|---|
| 2005 | Est. 5000 | PF63 475 | PF65 500 | | | |

**KM# 117 25 POUNDS**
7.98 g., 0.916 Gold 0.235 oz. AGW **Ruler:** Elizabeth II **Subject:** Royal Navy - H.M.S. Warspite

| Date | Mintage | VF20 | XF40 | MS60 | MS63 | MS65 |
|---|---|---|---|---|---|---|
| 2005 | Est. 1500 | PF63 475 | PF65 500 | | | |

**KM# 118 25 POUNDS**
7.98 g., 0.916 Gold 0.235 oz. AGW **Ruler:** Elizabeth II **Subject:** Royal Navy - Admiral Sir John Foster Woodward

| Date | Mintage | VF20 | XF40 | MS60 | MS63 | MS65 |
|---|---|---|---|---|---|---|
| 2005 | Est. 1500 | PF63 475 | PF65 500 | | | |

**KM# 121 25 POUNDS**
7.98 g., 0.916 Gold 0.235 oz. AGW **Ruler:** Elizabeth II **Series:** Trafalgar - England expects that every man will do his duty

| Date | Mintage | VF20 | XF40 | MS60 | MS63 | MS65 |
|---|---|---|---|---|---|---|
| 2005 | — | PF63 475 | PF65 500 | | | |

**KM# 92 50 POUNDS**
1000.00 g., Bi-Metallic .925 Silver center in .917 Gold ring, 100 mm. **Ruler:** Elizabeth II **Rev:** Coronation at Westminster

| Date | Mintage | VF20 | XF40 | MS60 | MS63 | MS65 |
|---|---|---|---|---|---|---|
| 2002 | Est. 2002 | PF65 1,250 | | | | |

**KM# 33 50 POUNDS**
1000.00 g., 0.925 Silver 29.7394 oz. ASW, 100 mm. **Ruler:** Elizabeth II **Subject:** Prince William **Obv:** Queen's portrait **Rev:** Portrait with open shirt collar **Edge:** Reeded

| Date | Mintage | VF20 | XF40 | MS60 | MS63 | MS65 |
|---|---|---|---|---|---|---|
| 2003 | 500 | PF65 1,200 | | | | |

**KM# 62 50 POUNDS**
1000.00 g., 0.925 Silver 29.7394 oz. ASW, 100 mm. **Ruler:** Elizabeth II **Subject:** 50th Anniversary of Coronation **Obv:** Queen's portrait right **Rev:** State coach in which the Queen travelled to and from her coronation

| Date | Mintage | VF20 | XF40 | MS60 | MS63 | MS65 |
|---|---|---|---|---|---|---|
| 2003 | — | PF65 1,150 | | | | |

**KM# 63 50 POUNDS**
1000.00 g., 0.925 Silver 29.7394 oz. ASW, 100 mm. **Ruler:** Elizabeth II **Subject:** 50th Anniversary of Coronation **Obv:** Queen's portrait right **Rev:** St. Edward's crown, royal scepter, orb of England

| Date | Mintage | VF20 | XF40 | MS60 | MS63 | MS65 |
|---|---|---|---|---|---|---|
| 2003 | — | PF65 1,150 | | | | |

**KM# 64 50 POUNDS**
1000.00 g., 0.925 Silver 29.7394 oz. ASW, 100 mm. **Ruler:** Elizabeth II **Subject:** 50th Anniversary of Coronation **Obv:** Queen's portrait right **Rev:** Queen on horseback dressed in the ceremonial uniform of the Colonel in Chief of the Household Brigade

| Date | Mintage | VF20 | XF40 | MS60 | MS63 | MS65 |
|---|---|---|---|---|---|---|
| 2003 | — | PF65 1,150 | | | | |

**KM# 65 50 POUNDS**
1000.00 g., 0.925 Silver 29.7394 oz. ASW, 100 mm. **Ruler:** Elizabeth II **Subject:** 50th Anniversary of Coronation **Obv:** Queen's portrait right **Rev:** The Queen crowned, seated, holding the orb and scepter

| Date | Mintage | VF20 | XF40 | MS60 | MS63 | MS65 |
|---|---|---|---|---|---|---|
| 2003 | — | PF65 1,150 | | | | |

**KM# 40 50 POUNDS**
1000.00 g., 0.925 Silver 29.7394 oz. ASW, 100 mm. **Ruler:** Elizabeth II **Subject:** D-Day **Obv:** Queen's portrait **Rev:** US and British troops wading ashore **Edge:** Reeded

| Date | Mintage | VF20 | XF40 | MS60 | MS63 | MS65 |
|---|---|---|---|---|---|---|
| 2004 | 600 | PF65 1,200 | | | | |

**KM# 80 50 POUNDS**
1000.00 g., 0.925 Silver 29.7394 oz. ASW **Ruler:** Elizabeth II **Subject:** 200th Anniversary Battle of Trafalgar **Obv:** Crowned head right

| Date | Mintage | VF20 | XF40 | MS60 | MS63 | MS65 |
|---|---|---|---|---|---|---|
| 2005 | — | PF65 1,200 | | | | |

**KM# 114 50 POUNDS**
1000.00 g., 0.925 Silver 29.7394 oz. ASW, 100 mm. **Ruler:** Elizabeth II **Subject:** Prince William, 21st Birthday

| Date | Mintage | VF20 | XF40 | MS60 | MS63 | MS65 |
|---|---|---|---|---|---|---|
| 2005 | Est. 100 | PF65 1,200 | | | | |

**KM# 136 50 POUNDS**
1000.00 g., 0.925 Silver 29.7394 oz. ASW partially gilt, 100 mm. **Ruler:** Elizabeth II **Rev:** Portraits of Elizabeth II and cross of 8 floral emblems

| Date | Mintage | VF20 | XF40 | MS60 | MS63 | MS65 |
|---|---|---|---|---|---|---|
| 2006 | Est. 250 | PF65 1,150 | | | | |

**KM# 214 50 POUNDS**
1000.00 g., 0.925 Silver 29.7394 oz. ASW, 100 mm. **Ruler:** Elizabeth II **Subject:** Royal Wedding - Prince William and Catherine Middleton **Obv:** Head in tiara right **Rev:** Conjoined busts left, roase window in background

| Date | Mintage | VF20 | XF40 | MS60 | MS63 | MS65 |
|---|---|---|---|---|---|---|
| 2011 | — | PF65 1,150 | | | | |

**KM# 34 100 POUNDS**
1000.00 g., 0.9166 Gold 29.4694 oz. AGW, 100 mm. **Ruler:** Elizabeth II **Subject:** Prince William **Obv:** Queen's portrait **Rev:** Portrait with open shirt collar **Edge:** Reeded

| Date | Mintage | VF20 | XF40 | MS60 | MS63 | MS65 |
|---|---|---|---|---|---|---|
| 2003 | — | PF65 55,000 | | | | |

**KM# 81 100 POUNDS**
1000.00 g., 0.9166 Gold 29.4694 oz. AGW **Ruler:** Elizabeth II **Subject:** 200th Anniversary Battle of Trafalgar **Obv:** Crowned head right

| Date | Mintage | VF20 | XF40 | MS60 | MS63 | MS65 |
|---|---|---|---|---|---|---|
| 2005 | — | PF65 55,000 | | | | |

**KM# 37 1000 POUNDS**
1090.86 g., 0.9166 Gold 32.1469 oz. AGW, 100 mm. **Ruler:** Elizabeth II **Subject:** Last Flight of the Concorde **Obv:** Queen's portrait **Rev:** Concorde in flight **Edge:** Reeded

| Date | Mintage | VF20 | XF40 | MS60 | MS63 | MS65 |
|---|---|---|---|---|---|---|
| 2003 | 34 | PF65 60,000 | | | | |

**KM# 41 1000 POUNDS**
1000.00 g., 0.9167 Gold 29.4726 oz. AGW, 100 mm. **Ruler:** Elizabeth II **Subject:** D-Day **Obv:** Queen's portrait **Rev:** US and British troops wading ashore **Edge:** Reeded

| Date | Mintage | VF20 | XF40 | MS60 | MS63 | MS65 |
|---|---|---|---|---|---|---|
| 2004 | 60 | PF65 55,000 | | | | |

**KM# 115 1000 POUNDS**
1098.86 g., 0.916 Gold 32.3615 oz. AGW, 38.61 mm. **Ruler:** Elizabeth II **Subject:** Prince William, 21st Birthday

| Date | Mintage | VF20 | XF40 | MS60 | MS63 | MS65 |
|---|---|---|---|---|---|---|
| 2005 | Est. 21 | PF65 60,000 | | | | |

**KM# 216 1000 POUNDS**
1090.00 g., 0.9167 Gold 32.1251 oz. AGW, 11 mm. **Ruler:** Elizabeth II **Subject:** Trafalgar, 200th Anniversary

| Date | Mintage | VF20 | XF40 | MS60 | MS63 | MS65 |
|---|---|---|---|---|---|---|
| 2005 | — | PF65 60,000 | | | | |

**KM# 137 1000 POUNDS**
1090.86 g., 0.916 Gold 32.1259 oz. AGW, 100 mm. **Ruler:** Elizabeth II **Rev:** Portraits of Elizabeth II and cross of 8 floral emblems

| Date | Mintage | VF20 | XF40 | MS60 | MS63 | MS65 |
|---|---|---|---|---|---|---|
| 2006 | — | PF65 60,000 | | | | |

**KM# 192 1000 POUNDS**
1090.86 g., 0.916 Gold 32.1259 oz. AGW, 100 mm. **Ruler:** Elizabeth II **Subject:** Prince Charles, 60th Birthday

| Date | Mintage | VF20 | XF40 | MS60 | MS63 | MS65 |
|---|---|---|---|---|---|---|
| 2008 | Est. 30 | PF65 60,000 | | | | |

**KM# 215 1000 POUNDS**
1000.00 g., 0.916 Gold 29.4501 oz. AGW, 100 mm. **Ruler:** Elizabeth II **Subject:** Royal Wedding - Prince William and Catherine Middleton **Obv:** Head in tiara right **Rev:** Conjoined busts left, rose window in background

| Date | Mintage | VF20 | XF40 | MS60 | MS63 | MS65 |
|---|---|---|---|---|---|---|
| 2011 | — | PF65 57,500 | | | | |

## MINT SETS

| KM# | Date | Mintage | Identification | Issue Price | Mkt Val |
|---|---|---|---|---|---|
| MS1 | 2004 | (1) — | Alderney KM#43, Guernsey KM#155, Jersey KM#126, 150th Anniversary of the Crimean War | — | 95.00 |

## ALGERIA

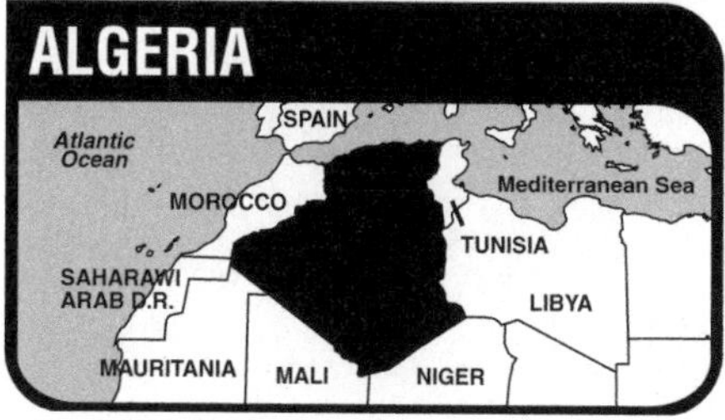


The People's Democratic Republic of Algeria, a North African country fronting on the Mediterranean Sea between Tunisia and Morocco, has an area of 919,595 sq. mi. (2,381,740 sq. km.) and a population of 31.6 million. Capital: Algiers (Alger). Most of the country's working population is engaged in agriculture although a recent industrial diversification, financed by oil revenues, is making steady progress. Wines, fruits, iron and zinc ores, phosphates, tobacco products, liquified natural gas, and petroleum are exported.

**MONETARY SYSTEM**
100 Centimes = 1 Franc

## REPUBLIC
### STANDARD COINAGE

**KM# 127 1/4 DINAR**
1.15 g., Aluminum, 16.5 mm. **Subject:** Fennec Fox **Obv:** Value in small circle **Rev:** Head facing

| Date | Mintage | VF20 | XF40 | MS60 | MS63 | MS65 |
|---|---|---|---|---|---|---|
| AH1423-2003 | — | — | 1.50 | 3.00 | 4.50 | 5.50 |

**KM# 129 DINAR**
4.24 g., Stainless Steel, 20.6 mm. **Obv:** Value on silhouette of country, within circle **Rev:** African buffalo's head 3/4 left, ancient drawings above **Edge:** Plain

| Date | Mintage | VF20 | XF40 | MS60 | MS63 | MS65 |
|---|---|---|---|---|---|---|
| AH1422-2002 | — | — | 1.00 | 2.00 | 3.50 | 6.00 |
| AH1423-2002 | — | — | 1.00 | 2.00 | 3.50 | 6.00 |
| AH1423-2003 | — | — | 1.00 | 2.00 | 3.50 | 6.00 |
| AH1424-2003 | — | — | 1.00 | 2.00 | 3.50 | 6.00 |
| AH1424-2004 | — | — | 1.00 | 2.00 | 3.50 | 6.00 |
| AH1426-2005 | — | — | 1.00 | 2.00 | 3.50 | 6.00 |
| AH1427-2006 | — | — | 1.00 | 2.00 | 3.50 | 6.00 |
| AH1428-2007 | — | — | 1.00 | 2.00 | 3.50 | 6.00 |
| AH1430-2009 | — | — | 1.00 | 2.00 | 3.50 | 6.00 |
| AH1431-2010 | — | — | 1.00 | 2.00 | 3.50 | 6.00 |

**KM# 130 2 DINARS**
5.13 g., Stainless Steel, 22.5 mm. **Obv:** Value on silhouette of country **Rev:** Dromedary camel's head right **Edge:** Plain

| Date | Mintage | VF20 | XF40 | MS60 | MS63 | MS65 |
|---|---|---|---|---|---|---|
| AH1422-2001 | — | — | 1.00 | 2.00 | 4.00 | 7.00 |
| AH1422-2002 | — | — | 1.00 | 2.00 | 4.00 | 7.00 |
| AH1423-2002 | — | — | 1.00 | 2.00 | 4.00 | 7.00 |
| AH1424-2003 | — | — | 1.00 | 2.00 | 4.00 | 7.00 |
| AH1424-2004 | — | — | 1.00 | 2.00 | 4.00 | 7.00 |
| AH1426-2005 | — | — | 1.00 | 2.00 | 4.00 | 7.00 |
| AH1427-2006 | — | — | 1.00 | 2.00 | 4.00 | 7.00 |
| AH1428-2007 | — | — | 1.00 | 2.00 | 4.00 | 7.00 |
| AH1430-2009 | — | — | 1.00 | 2.00 | 4.00 | 7.00 |
| AH1431-2010 | — | — | 1.00 | 2.00 | 4.00 | 7.00 |

**KM# 123 5 DINARS**
6.20 g., Stainless Steel, 24.5 mm. **Obv:** Denomination within circle **Rev:** Forepart of African elephant right **Edge:** Plain

| Date | Mintage | VF20 | XF40 | MS60 | MS63 | MS65 |
|---|---|---|---|---|---|---|
| AH1422-2003 | — | — | 1.25 | 3.00 | 5.50 | 9.50 |
| AH1423-2003 | — | — | 1.00 | 3.00 | 5.50 | 9.50 |
| AH1424-2003 | — | — | 1.00 | 3.00 | 5.00 | 8.00 |
| AH1424-2004 | — | — | 1.00 | 3.00 | 5.50 | 9.50 |
| AH1426-2005 | — | — | 1.00 | 3.00 | 5.00 | 8.00 |
| AH1426-2006 | — | — | 1.00 | 3.00 | 5.50 | 9.50 |
| AH1427-2006 | — | — | 1.00 | 3.00 | 5.00 | 8.00 |
| AH1428-2007 | — | — | 1.00 | 3.00 | 5.00 | 8.00 |
| AH1429-2008 | — | — | 1.00 | 3.00 | 5.00 | 8.00 |
| AH1430-2009 | — | — | 1.00 | 3.00 | 5.00 | 8.00 |
| AH1431-2010 | — | — | 1.00 | 3.00 | 5.00 | 8.00 |
| AH1432-2011 | — | — | 1.00 | 3.00 | 5.00 | 8.00 |
| AH1433-2012 | — | — | 1.00 | 3.00 | 5.00 | 8.00 |
| AH1434-2013 | — | — | 1.00 | 3.00 | 5.00 | 8.00 |

**KM# 124 10 DINARS**
4.95 g., Bi-Metallic Aluminum center in Stainless Steel ring, 26.5 mm. **Obv:** Denomination **Rev:** Barbary falcon's head right **Edge:** Plain

| Date | Mintage | VF20 | XF40 | MS60 | MS63 | MS65 |
|---|---|---|---|---|---|---|
| AH1422-2002 | — | — | 1.50 | 3.50 | 9.00 | — |
| AH1423-2002 | — | — | 1.50 | 3.50 | 9.00 | — |
| AH1424-2003 | — | — | 1.50 | 3.50 | 9.00 | — |
| AH1425-2004 | — | — | 1.50 | 3.50 | 9.00 | — |
| AH1426-2005 | — | — | 1.50 | 3.50 | 9.00 | — |
| AH1427-2006 | — | — | 1.50 | 3.50 | 9.00 | — |
| AH1428-2007 | — | — | 1.50 | 3.50 | 9.00 | — |
| AH1429-2008 | — | — | 1.50 | 3.50 | 9.00 | — |
| AH1430-2009 | — | — | 1.50 | 3.50 | 9.00 | — |
| AH1431-2010 | — | — | 1.50 | 3.50 | 9.00 | — |
| AH1432-2011 | — | — | 1.50 | 3.50 | 9.00 | — |
| AH1433-2012 | — | — | 1.50 | 3.50 | 9.00 | — |
| AH1434-2013 | — | — | 1.50 | 3.50 | 9.00 | — |

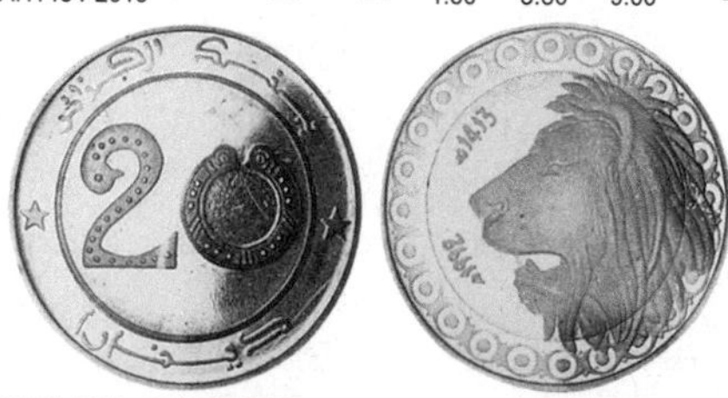

**KM# 125 20 DINARS**
8.62 g., Bi-Metallic Aluminum-Bronze center in Stainless Steel ring, 27.5 mm. **Subject:** Lion **Obv:** Denomination **Rev:** Head left

| Date | Mintage | VF20 | XF40 | MS60 | MS63 | MS65 |
|---|---|---|---|---|---|---|
| AH1424-2004 | — | — | 3.50 | 7.50 | 16.00 | 20.00 |
| AH1426-2005 | — | — | 3.50 | 7.50 | 16.00 | 20.00 |
| AH1427-2006 | — | — | 3.50 | 7.50 | 16.00 | 20.00 |
| AH1428-2007 | — | — | 3.50 | 7.50 | 16.00 | 20.00 |
| AH1430-2009 | — | — | 3.50 | 7.50 | 16.00 | 20.00 |
| AH1431-2010 | — | — | 3.50 | 7.50 | 16.00 | 20.00 |
| AH1432-2011 | — | — | 3.50 | 7.50 | 16.00 | 20.00 |
| AM1433-2012 | — | — | 3.50 | 7.50 | 16.00 | 20.00 |
| AM1434-2013 | — | — | 3.50 | 7.50 | 16.00 | 20.00 |

**KM# 126 50 DINARS**
9.27 g., Bi-Metallic Stainless Steel center in Aluminum-Bronze ring, 28.5 mm. **Obv:** Denomination **Rev:** Dama gazelle with head left

| Date | Mintage | VF20 | XF40 | MS60 | MS63 | MS65 |
|---|---|---|---|---|---|---|
| AH1424-2003 | — | — | 3.50 | 7.50 | 16.50 | — |
| AH1425-2004 | — | — | 3.50 | 7.50 | 16.50 | — |
| AH1428-2007 | — | — | 3.50 | 7.50 | 16.50 | — |
| AH1429-2008 | — | — | 3.50 | 7.50 | 16.50 | — |
| AH1430-2009 | — | — | 3.50 | 7.50 | 16.50 | — |
| AH1432-2011 | — | — | 3.50 | 7.50 | 16.50 | — |
| AM1434-2013 | — | — | 3.50 | 7.50 | 16.50 | — |

**KM# 138 50 DINARS**
9.27 g., Bi-Metallic Stainless Steel center in Aluminum-Bronze ring, 28.5 mm. **Subject:** 50th Anniversary of Liberation **Obv:** Large value **Rev:** Stylized flag and two Moudjahid (revolutionaries)

| Date | Mintage | VF20 | XF40 | MS60 | MS63 | MS65 |
|---|---|---|---|---|---|---|
| AH1425-2004 | 3,000,000 | — | — | 5.50 | 12.50 | 15.00 |
| AH1429-2008 | — | — | — | 5.50 | 12.50 | 15.00 |
| AH1434-2013 | — | — | — | 5.50 | 12.50 | 15.00 |

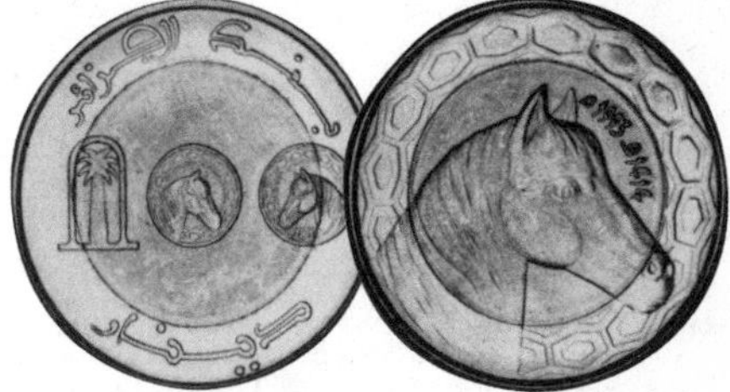

**KM# 132 100 DINARS**
11.00 g., Bi-Metallic Copper-Nickel center in Stainless Steel ring, 29.5 mm. **Obv:** Denomination stylized with reverse design **Rev:** Horse head right **Edge:** Reeded

| Date | Mintage | VF20 | XF40 | MS60 | MS63 | MS65 |
|---|---|---|---|---|---|---|
| AH1422-2002 | — | — | 5.00 | 10.00 | 20.00 | 25.00 |
| AH1423-2002 | — | — | 5.00 | 10.00 | 20.00 | 25.00 |
| AH1423-2003 | — | — | 5.00 | 10.00 | 20.00 | 25.00 |
| AH1425-2004 | — | — | 5.00 | 10.00 | 20.00 | 25.00 |
| AH1428-2007 | — | — | 5.00 | 10.00 | 20.00 | 25.00 |
| AH1430-2009 | — | — | 5.00 | 10.00 | 20.00 | 25.00 |
| AH1431-2010 | — | — | 5.00 | 10.00 | 20.00 | 25.00 |
| AH1432-2011 | — | — | 5.00 | 10.00 | 20.00 | 25.00 |
| AM1434-2013 | — | — | 5.00 | 10.00 | 20.00 | 25.00 |

**KM# 137 100 DINARS**
11.00 g., Bi-Metallic Aluminum-Bronze center in Stainless Steel ring, 29.5 mm. **Subject:** 40th Anniversary of Independence **Obv:** Stylized value using palm tree in doorway and two coins depicting horses' heads **Rev:** Number 40 and stylized face **Edge:** Reeded

| Date | Mintage | VF20 | XF40 | MS60 | MS63 | MS65 |
|---|---|---|---|---|---|---|
| AH1422-2002 | — | — | — | — | 25.00 | 28.00 |

ANDORRA

Bay of Biscay
FRANCE
SPAIN
Mediterranean Sea

Principality of Andorra (Principat d'Andorra), situated on the southern slopes of the Pyrenees Mountains between France and Spain, has an area of 181 sq. mi. (453 sq. km.) and a population of 80,000. Capital: Andorra la Vella. Tourism is the chief source of income. Timber, cattle and derivatives, and furniture are exported.

**RULER**
Joan D.M. Bisbe D'Urgell I

**MONETARY SYSTEM**
100 Centims = 1 Diner

**NOTE**: The Diners have been struck for collectors while the Euro is used in everyday commerce.

# PRINCIPALITY

## DECIMAL COINAGE

### KM# 176 CENTIM

2.10 g., Aluminum, 27 mm. **Subject:** Charlemagne **Obv:** National arms, date below **Rev:** Crowned head facing, denomination below **Edge:** Plain

| Date | Mintage | VF20 | XF40 | MS60 | MS63 | MS65 |
|---|---|---|---|---|---|---|
| 2002 | — | — | — | — | 1.50 | 2.00 |

### KM# 177 CENTIM

2.13 g., Aluminum, 27 mm. **Subject:** Isard **Obv:** National arms, date below **Rev:** Chamois left facing, denomination at right **Edge:** Plain

| Date | Mintage | VF20 | XF40 | MS60 | MS63 | MS65 |
|---|---|---|---|---|---|---|
| 2002 | — | — | — | — | 1.50 | 2.00 |

### KM# 178 CENTIM

2.14 g., Aluminum, 27 mm. **Subject:** Agnus Dei **Obv:** National arms **Rev:** Lamb of God **Edge:** Plain

| Date | Mintage | VF20 | XF40 | MS60 | MS63 | MS65 |
|---|---|---|---|---|---|---|
| 2002 | — | — | — | — | 1.00 | 1.50 |

### KM# 198 CENTIM

Aluminum-Magnesium, 27 mm. **Obv:** National arms **Rev:** A piece of the wall paintings belonging to the 12th century Romanesque church of St. Marti de la Cortinado

| Date | Mintage | VF20 | XF40 | MS60 | MS63 | MS65 |
|---|---|---|---|---|---|---|
| 2003 | — | — | — | — | 1.25 | 1.75 |

### KM# 199 CENTIM

Aluminum-Magnesium, 27 mm. **Obv:** National arms **Rev:** Pont de la Margineda, reproduction of the bridge

| Date | Mintage | VF20 | XF40 | MS60 | MS63 | MS65 |
|---|---|---|---|---|---|---|
| 2003 | — | — | — | — | 1.25 | 1.75 |

### KM# 200 CENTIM

Aluminum-Magnesium, 27 mm. **Obv:** National arms **Rev:** Image of the 12th century Romanesque church of St. Miquel d'Engolasters with its bell tower, the Romanesque apse, the small portico and the large Lombard windows

| Date | Mintage | VF20 | XF40 | MS60 | MS63 | MS65 |
|---|---|---|---|---|---|---|
| 2003 | — | — | — | — | 1.25 | 1.75 |

### KM# 229 CENTIM

Aluminum **Obv:** Crowned arms **Rev:** Santa Coloma

| Date | Mintage | VF20 | XF40 | MS60 | MS63 | MS65 |
|---|---|---|---|---|---|---|
| 2004 | — | — | — | — | 0.90 | 1.20 |

### KM# 230 CENTIM

Aluminum **Obv:** Crowned arms **Rev:** Sant Martí de la Cortinada

| Date | Mintage | VF20 | XF40 | MS60 | MS63 | MS65 |
|---|---|---|---|---|---|---|
| 2004 | — | — | — | — | 0.90 | 1.20 |

### KM# 231 CENTIM

Aluminum **Obv:** Crowned arms **Rev:** Altar at Santa Coloma

| Date | Mintage | VF20 | XF40 | MS60 | MS63 | MS65 |
|---|---|---|---|---|---|---|
| 2004 | — | — | — | — | 0.90 | 1.20 |

### KM# 236 CENTIM

2.80 g., Brass, 18 mm. **Subject:** Death of Pope John Paul II **Obv:** National arms **Rev:** Karol Wojtyla as priest **Edge:** Reeded

| Date | Mintage | VF20 | XF40 | MS60 | MS63 | MS65 |
|---|---|---|---|---|---|---|
| 2005 | 15,000 | — | 0.30 | 0.50 | 0.80 | 1.20 |

### KM# 245 CENTIM

2.80 g., Brass, 18 mm. **Obv:** National arms **Rev:** Findern flower - Poet's Daffodil

| Date | Mintage | VF20 | XF40 | MS60 | MS63 | MS65 |
|---|---|---|---|---|---|---|
| 2005 | 15,000 | — | — | — | 0.80 | 1.20 |
| 2006 | 10,000 | — | — | — | 0.80 | 1.20 |
| 2007 | 10,000 | — | — | — | 0.80 | 1.20 |
| 2008 | 5,000 | — | — | — | 0.80 | 1.20 |

### KM# 290 CENTIM

2.80 g., Brass, 18 mm. **Obv:** National Arms **Rev:** Portrait of Joseph Ratzinger as priest **Edge:** Reeded

| Date | Mintage | VF20 | XF40 | MS60 | MS63 | MS65 |
|---|---|---|---|---|---|---|
| 2006 | 15,000 | — | — | — | — | 1.20 |

### KM# 306 CENTIM

2.80 g., Brass, 18 mm. **Subject:** Popes of the 20th Century **Obv:** National arms **Rev:** Pope Leo XIII **Edge:** Reeded

| Date | Mintage | VF20 | XF40 | MS60 | MS63 | MS65 |
|---|---|---|---|---|---|---|
| 2007 | 5,000 | — | — | — | — | 1.20 |

### KM# 179 2 CENTIMS

Brass, 18 mm. **Subject:** Grandalla **Obv:** National arms **Rev:** Edelweiss flower **Edge:** Plain

| Date | Mintage | VF20 | XF40 | MS60 | MS63 | MS65 |
|---|---|---|---|---|---|---|
| 2002 | — | — | — | — | 1.50 | 2.00 |

### KM# 201 2 CENTIMS

Copper-Nickel-Zinc, 18.15 mm. **Obv:** National arms **Rev:** Clavell Deltoide, a flower found in Andorra

| Date | Mintage | VF20 | XF40 | MS60 | MS63 | MS65 |
|---|---|---|---|---|---|---|
| 2003 | — | — | — | — | 1.75 | 2.50 |

### KM# 232 2 CENTIMS

Brass **Obv:** Crowned arms **Rev:** West Gothic robe

| Date | Mintage | VF20 | XF40 | MS60 | MS63 | MS65 |
|---|---|---|---|---|---|---|
| 2004 | — | — | — | — | 1.20 | 1.60 |

### KM# 237 2 CENTIMS

4.00 g., Brass, 21.3 mm. **Subject:** Death of Pope John-Paul II **Obv:** National arms **Rev:** Karol Wojtyla as priest

| Date | Mintage | VF20 | XF40 | MS60 | MS63 | MS65 |
|---|---|---|---|---|---|---|
| 2005 | 15,000 | — | 0.50 | 0.70 | 1.20 | 1.60 |

### KM# 246 2 CENTIMS

4.00 g., Brass, 21.3 mm. **Obv:** National arms **Rev:** Pyrenean Chamois **Edge:** Reeded

| Date | Mintage | VF20 | XF40 | MS60 | MS63 | MS65 |
|---|---|---|---|---|---|---|
| 2005 | 15,000 | — | — | — | 1.20 | 1.60 |
| 2006 | 10,000 | — | — | — | 1.20 | 1.60 |
| 2007 | 10,000 | — | — | — | 1.20 | 1.60 |
| 2008 | 5,000 | — | — | — | 1.20 | 1.60 |

### KM# 291 2 CENTIMS

4.00 g., Brass, 21.3 mm. **Obv:** National Arms **Rev:** Portrait of Joseph Ratzinger as priest

| Date | Mintage | VF20 | XF40 | MS60 | MS63 | MS65 |
|---|---|---|---|---|---|---|
| 2006 | 15,000 | — | — | — | — | 1.60 |

### KM# 307 2 CENTIMS

4.00 g., Brass, 21.3 mm. **Subject:** Popes of the 20th Century **Obv:** National Arms **Rev:** Pope Pius X

| Date | Mintage | VF20 | XF40 | MS60 | MS63 | MS65 |
|---|---|---|---|---|---|---|
| 2007 | 5,000 | — | — | — | — | 1.60 |

### KM# 282 2 CENTIMS

0.73 g., 0.999 Gold, 11 mm. **Subject:** Berlin Wall, 20th anniversary **Obv:** Shield **Rev:** Brandenburg Gate and brick wall **Edge:** Reeded

| Date | Mintage | VF20 | XF40 | MS60 | MS63 | MS65 |
|---|---|---|---|---|---|---|
| 2009 | 5,000 | PF63 70.00 | PF65 75.00 | | | |

### KM# 180 5 CENTIMS

Brass, 21.8 mm. **Subject:** Squirrel **Obv:** National arms **Rev:** Red Squirrel on tree stump **Edge:** Plain

| Date | Mintage | VF20 | XF40 | MS60 | MS63 | MS65 |
|---|---|---|---|---|---|---|
| 2002 | — | — | — | — | 2.00 | 2.50 |

**KM# 181 5 CENTIMS**

Brass, 21.8 mm. **Subject:** Gall Fer **Obv:** National arms **Rev:** Male Eurasian Capercaillie (grouse) displaying plumage **Edge:** Plain

| Date | Mintage | VF20 | XF40 | MS60 | MS63 | MS65 |
|---|---|---|---|---|---|---|
| 2002 | — | — | — | — | 2.00 | 2.50 |

**KM# 202 5 CENTIMS**

Brass, 21.8 mm. **Obv:** National arms **Rev:** The cross of Seven Arms, traditional Gothic cross

| Date | Mintage | VF20 | XF40 | MS60 | MS63 | MS65 |
|---|---|---|---|---|---|---|
| 2003 | — | — | — | — | 2.25 | 2.75 |

**KM# 203 5 CENTIMS**

Brass, 21.8 mm. **Obv:** National arms **Rev:** Wall painting from the 11th century church of Sant Serni de Nagol showing an eagle

| Date | Mintage | VF20 | XF40 | MS60 | MS63 | MS65 |
|---|---|---|---|---|---|---|
| 2003 | — | — | — | — | 2.25 | 2.75 |

**KM# 233 5 CENTIMS**

Brass **Obv:** Crowned arms **Rev:** Gothic cross

| Date | Mintage | VF20 | XF40 | MS60 | MS63 | MS65 |
|---|---|---|---|---|---|---|
| 2004 | — | — | — | — | 1.80 | 2.40 |

**KM# 234 5 CENTIMS**

Brass **Obv:** Crowned arms **Rev:** Lady of Canolic

| Date | Mintage | VF20 | XF40 | MS60 | MS63 | MS65 |
|---|---|---|---|---|---|---|
| 2004 | — | — | — | — | 1.80 | 2.40 |

**KM# 238 5 CENTIMS**

5.50 g., Brass, 24.5 mm. **Subject:** Death of Pope John-Paul II **Obv:** National arms **Rev:** Karol Wojtyla as bishop **Edge:** Reeded

| Date | Mintage | VF20 | XF40 | MS60 | MS63 | MS65 |
|---|---|---|---|---|---|---|
| 2005 | 15,000 | — | 0.70 | 1.00 | 1.80 | 2.40 |

**KM# 247 5 CENTIMS**

5.50 g., Brass, 24.5 mm. **Obv:** National arms **Rev:** Wall painting from Santa Coloma church **Edge:** Reeded

| Date | Mintage | VF20 | XF40 | MS60 | MS63 | MS65 |
|---|---|---|---|---|---|---|
| 2005 | 15,000 | — | — | — | 1.80 | 2.40 |
| 2006 | 10,000 | — | — | — | 1.80 | 2.40 |
| 2007 | 10,000 | — | — | — | 1.80 | 2.40 |
| 2008 | 5,000 | — | — | — | 1.80 | 2.40 |

**KM# 292 5 CENTIMS**

5.50 g., Brass, 24.5 mm. **Obv:** National Arms **Rev:** Portrait of Joseph Ratzinger as archbishop

| Date | Mintage | VF20 | XF40 | MS60 | MS63 | MS65 |
|---|---|---|---|---|---|---|
| 2006 | 15,000 | — | — | — | — | 2.50 |

**KM# 308 5 CENTIMS**

5.50 g., Brass, 24.5 mm. **Subject:** Popes of the 20th Century **Obv:** National Arms **Rev:** Pope Benedict XV

| Date | Mintage | VF20 | XF40 | MS60 | MS63 | MS65 |
|---|---|---|---|---|---|---|
| 2007 | 5,000 | — | — | — | — | 2.40 |

**KM# 182 10 CENTIMS**

Brass **Subject:** St. Joan de Caselles **Obv:** National arms **Rev:** Tower and building **Edge:** Plain

| Date | Mintage | VF20 | XF40 | MS60 | MS63 | MS65 |
|---|---|---|---|---|---|---|
| 2002 | — | — | — | — | 3.00 | 4.00 |

**KM# 204 10 CENTIMS**

Nickel Plated Steel, 27.8 mm. **Obv:** National arms **Rev:** 12th century wood carving image from Our Lady of Meritxell

| Date | Mintage | VF20 | XF40 | MS60 | MS63 | MS65 |
|---|---|---|---|---|---|---|
| 2003 | — | — | — | — | 3.50 | 4.50 |

**KM# 235 10 CENTIMS**

Nickel Plated Steel **Obv:** Crowned arms **Rev:** Casa de la Vall

| Date | Mintage | VF20 | XF40 | MS60 | MS63 | MS65 |
|---|---|---|---|---|---|---|
| 2004 | — | — | — | — | 3.00 | 4.00 |

**KM# 239 10 CENTIMS**

6.50 g., Copper-Nickel, 22.2 mm. **Subject:** Death of Pope John-Paul II **Obv:** National arms **Rev:** Karol Wojtyla as archbishop **Edge:** Reeded

| Date | Mintage | VF20 | XF40 | MS60 | MS63 | MS65 |
|---|---|---|---|---|---|---|
| 2005 | 15,000 | — | 1.00 | 1.75 | 2.40 | 3.20 |

**KM# 248 10 CENTIMS**

6.50 g., Copper-Nickel, 22.2 mm. **Obv:** National arms **Rev:** Saint Vicenç d'Enclar church

| Date | Mintage | VF20 | XF40 | MS60 | MS63 | MS65 |
|---|---|---|---|---|---|---|
| 2005 | 15,000 | — | — | — | 2.40 | 3.20 |
| 2006 | 10,000 | — | — | — | 2.40 | 3.20 |
| 2007 | 10,000 | — | — | — | 2.40 | 3.20 |
| 2008 | 5,000 | — | — | — | 2.40 | 3.20 |

**KM# 293 10 CENTIMS**

6.50 g., Copper-Nickel, 22.2 mm. **Obv:** National Arms **Rev:** Portrait of Joseph Ratzinger as archbishop

| Date | Mintage | VF20 | XF40 | MS60 | MS63 | MS65 |
|---|---|---|---|---|---|---|
| 2006 | 15,000 | — | — | — | — | 4.00 |

**KM# 309 10 CENTIMS**

6.50 g., Copper-Nickel, 22.2 mm. **Subject:** Popes of the 20th Century **Obv:** National Arms **Rev:** Pope Pius XI

| Date | Mintage | VF20 | XF40 | MS60 | MS63 | MS65 |
|---|---|---|---|---|---|---|
| 2007 | 5,000 | — | — | — | — | 3.40 |

**KM# 240 25 CENTIMS**

7.75 g., Copper-Nickel, 24.2 mm. **Subject:** Death of Pope John-Paul II **Obv:** National arms **Rev:** Karol Wojtyla as cardinal

| Date | Mintage | VF20 | XF40 | MS60 | MS63 | MS65 |
|---|---|---|---|---|---|---|
| 2005 | 15,000 | — | 1.20 | 2.00 | 3.00 | 4.00 |

**KM# 249 25 CENTIMS**

7.75 g., Copper-Nickel, 24.2 mm. **Obv:** National arms **Rev:** Our Lady of Meritxell sanctuary

| Date | Mintage | VF20 | XF40 | MS60 | MS63 | MS65 |
|---|---|---|---|---|---|---|
| 2005 | 15,000 | — | — | — | 3.00 | 4.00 |
| 2006 | 10,000 | — | — | — | 3.00 | 4.00 |
| 2007 | 10,000 | — | — | — | 3.00 | 4.00 |
| 2008 | 5,000 | — | — | — | 3.00 | 4.00 |

**KM# 294 25 CENTIMS**

7.75 g., Copper-Nickel, 24.2 mm. **Obv:** National Arms **Rev:** Portrait of Joseph Ratzinger as cardinal

| Date | Mintage | VF20 | XF40 | MS60 | MS63 | MS65 |
|---|---|---|---|---|---|---|
| 2006 | 15,000 | — | — | — | — | 4.00 |

**KM# 310 25 CENTIMS**

7.75 g., Copper-Nickel, 24.2 mm. **Subject:** Popes of the 20th Century **Obv:** National Arms **Rev:** Pope Pius XII

| Date | Mintage | VF20 | XF40 | MS60 | MS63 | MS65 |
|---|---|---|---|---|---|---|
| 2007 | 5,000 | — | — | — | — | 4.00 |

**KM# 417 25 CENTIMS**

7.78 g., 0.999 Silver 0.2499 oz. ASW, 20.18 mm. **Obv:** Round National shield **Rev:** Bald Eagle vignette

| Date | Mintage | VF20 | XF40 | MS60 | MS63 | MS65 |
|---|---|---|---|---|---|---|
| 2013 | — | — | — | — | — | 20.00 |

**KM# 241 50 CENTIMS**

9.00 g., Copper-Nickel, 25.9 mm. **Subject:** Death of Pope John-Paul II **Obv:** National arms **Rev:** Karol Wojtyla as cardinal

| Date | Mintage | VF20 | XF40 | MS60 | MS63 | MS65 |
|---|---|---|---|---|---|---|
| 2005 | 15,000 | — | 2.25 | 2.75 | 3.60 | 4.80 |

**KM# 250 50 CENTIMS**

9.00 g., Copper-Nickel, 25.9 mm. **Obv:** National arms **Rev:** Map of Andorra, 7 towns highlighted

| Date | Mintage | VF20 | XF40 | MS60 | MS63 | MS65 |
|---|---|---|---|---|---|---|
| 2005 | 15,000 | — | — | — | 4.00 | 5.00 |
| 2006 | 10,000 | — | — | — | 4.00 | 5.00 |
| 2007 | 10,000 | — | — | — | 4.00 | 5.00 |
| 2008 | 5,000 | — | — | — | 4.00 | 5.00 |

**KM# 295 50 CENTIMS**

9.00 g., Copper-Nickel, 25.9 mm. **Obv:** National Arms **Rev:** Portrait of Joseph Ratzinger as cardinal

| Date | Mintage | VF20 | XF40 | MS60 | MS63 | MS65 |
|---|---|---|---|---|---|---|
| 2006 | 15,000 | — | — | — | — | 4.80 |

**KM# 311 50 CENTIMS**

9.00 g., Copper-Nickel, 25.9 mm. **Subject:** Popes of the 20th Century **Obv:** National Arms **Rev:** Pope John XXIII

| Date | Mintage | VF20 | XF40 | MS60 | MS63 | MS65 |
|---|---|---|---|---|---|---|
| 2007 | 5,000 | — | — | — | — | 6.00 |

**KM# 418 50 CENTIMS**

15.55 g., 0.999 Silver 0.4994 oz. ASW, 27.66 mm. **Obv:** Round National shield **Rev:** Bank Eagle from vignette

| Date | Mintage | VF20 | XF40 | MS60 | MS63 | MS65 |
|---|---|---|---|---|---|---|
| 2013 | — | — | — | — | — | 20.00 |

**KM# 362 .5 DINER**

0.50 g., 0.585 Gold AGW with 24Kt plating, 11 mm. **Subject:** Napoleon

| Date | Mintage | VF20 | XF40 | MS60 | MS63 | MS65 |
|---|---|---|---|---|---|---|
| 2013 | Est. 7500 | PF63 35.00 | PF65 40.00 | | | |

**KM# 242 DINER**

8.50 g., Bi-Metallic Brass center in Copper-Nickel ring, 24.5 mm. **Subject:** Death of Pope John-Paul II **Obv:** National arms **Rev:** Karol Wojtyla as pope **Edge:** Reeded

| Date | Mintage | VF20 | XF40 | MS60 | MS63 | MS65 |
|---|---|---|---|---|---|---|
| 2005 | 15,000 | — | 1.60 | 2.50 | 4.00 | 6.00 |

**KM# 251 DINER**

8.50 g., Bi-Metallic Brass center in Copper-Nickel ring, 24.5 mm. **Obv:** National arms **Rev:** Our Lady of Meritxell **Edge:** Reeded

| Date | Mintage | VF20 | XF40 | MS60 | MS63 | MS65 |
|---|---|---|---|---|---|---|
| 2005 | 15,000 | — | — | — | 4.50 | 6.00 |
| 2006 | 10,000 | — | — | — | 4.50 | 6.00 |
| 2007 | 10,000 | — | — | — | 4.50 | 6.00 |
| 2008 | 5,000 | — | — | — | 4.50 | 6.00 |

**KM# 296 DINER**

8.50 g., Bi-Metallic Brass center in Copper-Nickel ring, 24.5 mm. **Obv:** National Arms **Rev:** Portrait of Joseph Ratzinger as Pope Benedict XVI

| Date | Mintage | VF20 | XF40 | MS60 | MS63 | MS65 |
|---|---|---|---|---|---|---|
| 2006 | 15,000 | — | — | — | — | 6.00 |

**KM# 299 DINER**

11.00 g., Nickel, 25x25 mm. **Subject:** Chess Set **Obv:** National Arms **Rev:** Pawn **Shape:** Square

| Date | Mintage | VF20 | XF40 | MS60 | MS63 | MS65 |
|---|---|---|---|---|---|---|
| 2006 | 40,000 | — | — | — | — | 6.00 |

**KM# 299a DINER**

11.00 g., Brass Gilt, 25x25 mm. **Subject:** Chess Set **Obv:** National Arms **Rev:** Pawn **Shape:** Square

| Date | Mintage | VF20 | XF40 | MS60 | MS63 | MS65 |
|---|---|---|---|---|---|---|
| 2006 | 40,000 | — | — | — | — | 6.00 |

**KM# 300 DINER**

11.00 g., Nickel, 25x25 mm. **Subject:** Chess Set **Obv:** National arms **Rev:** Rook **Shape:** Square

| Date | Mintage | VF20 | XF40 | MS60 | MS63 | MS65 |
|---|---|---|---|---|---|---|
| 2006 | 10,000 | — | — | — | — | 12.00 |

**KM# 300a DINER**

11.00 g., Brass Gilt, 25x25 mm. **Subject:** Chess Set **Obv:** National Arms **Rev:** Rook **Shape:** Square

| Date | Mintage | VF20 | XF40 | MS60 | MS63 | MS65 |
|---|---|---|---|---|---|---|
| 2006 | 10,000 | — | — | — | — | 12.00 |

**KM# 301 DINER**

11.00 g., Nickel, 25x25 mm. **Subject:** Chess Set **Obv:** National Arms **Rev:** Knight **Shape:** Square

| Date | Mintage | VF20 | XF40 | MS60 | MS63 | MS65 |
|---|---|---|---|---|---|---|
| 2006 | 10,000 | — | — | — | — | 12.00 |

**KM# 301a DINER**

11.00 g., Brass Gilt, 25x25 mm. **Subject:** Chess Set **Obv:** National Arms **Rev:** Knight **Shape:** Square

| Date | Mintage | VF20 | XF40 | MS60 | MS63 | MS65 |
|---|---|---|---|---|---|---|
| 2006 | 10,000 | — | — | — | — | 12.00 |

**KM# 302 DINER**

11.00 g., Nickel, 25x25 mm. **Subject:** Chess Set **Obv:** National Arms **Rev:** Bishop **Shape:** Square

| Date | Mintage | VF20 | XF40 | MS60 | MS63 | MS65 |
|---|---|---|---|---|---|---|
| 2006 | 10,000 | — | — | — | — | 12.00 |

**KM# 302a DINER**

11.00 g., Brass Gilt, 25x25 mm. **Subject:** Chess Set **Obv:** National Arms **Rev:** Bishop **Shape:** Square

| Date | Mintage | VF20 | XF40 | MS60 | MS63 | MS65 |
|---|---|---|---|---|---|---|
| 2006 | 10,000 | — | — | — | — | 12.00 |

**KM# 303 DINER**

11.00 g., Nickel, 25x25 mm. **Subject:** Chess Set **Obv:** National Arms **Rev:** Queen **Shape:** Square

| Date | Mintage | VF20 | XF40 | MS60 | MS63 | MS65 |
|---|---|---|---|---|---|---|
| 2006 | 5,000 | — | — | — | — | 18.00 |

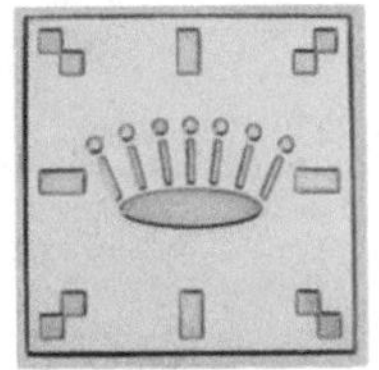

**KM# 303a DINER**

11.00 g., Brass Gilt, 25x25 mm. **Subject:** Chess Set **Obv:** National Arms **Rev:** Queen **Shape:** Square

| Date | Mintage | VF20 | XF40 | MS60 | MS63 | MS65 |
|---|---|---|---|---|---|---|
| 2006 | 5,000 | — | — | — | — | 18.00 |

**KM# 304 DINER**

11.00 g., Nickel, 25x25 mm. **Subject:** Chess Set **Obv:** National Arms **Rev:** King **Shape:** Square

| Date | Mintage | VF20 | XF40 | MS60 | MS63 | MS65 |
|---|---|---|---|---|---|---|
| 2006 | 5,000 | — | — | — | — | 18.00 |

**KM# 304a DINER**

11.00 g., Brass Gilt, 25x25 mm. **Subject:** Chess Set **Obv:** National Arms **Rev:** King **Shape:** Square

| Date | Mintage | VF20 | XF40 | MS60 | MS63 | MS65 |
|---|---|---|---|---|---|---|
| 2006 | 5,000 | — | — | — | — | 18.00 |

**KM# 312 DINER**

8.50 g., Bi-Metallic Brass center in Copper-Nickel ring, 24.5 mm. **Subject:** Popes of the 20th Century **Obv:** National Arms **Rev:** Pope Paul VI

| Date | Mintage | VF20 | XF40 | MS60 | MS63 | MS65 |
|---|---|---|---|---|---|---|
| 2007 | 5,000 | — | — | — | — | 8.00 |

**KM# 410 DINER**

0.50 g., 0.999 Gold AGW, 11 mm. **Rev:** Venus de Milo facing right

| Date | Mintage | VF20 | XF40 | MS60 | MS63 | MS65 |
|---|---|---|---|---|---|---|
| 2008 | Est. 10000 | PF65 40.00 | | | | |

**KM# 411 DINER**

0.50 g., 0.999 Gold AGW, 11 mm. **Rev:** St. Peter's Basilica

| Date | Mintage | VF20 | XF40 | MS60 | MS63 | MS65 |
|---|---|---|---|---|---|---|
| 2008 | Est. 10000 | PF65 50.00 | | | | |

**KM# 412 DINER**

1.00 g., 0.999 Gold 0.0321 oz. AGW, 13.92 mm. **Rev:** Michelangelo's Pieta

| Date | Mintage | VF20 | XF40 | MS60 | MS63 | MS65 |
|---|---|---|---|---|---|---|
| 2008 | Est. 15000 | PF65 75.00 | | | | |

**KM# 421 DINER**

0.50 g., 0.999 Gold AGW, 11 mm. **Obv:** Meritxell Sanctuary **Rev:** Sacred Architecture

| Date | Mintage | VF20 | XF40 | MS60 | MS63 | MS65 |
|---|---|---|---|---|---|---|
| 2009 | Est. 10000 | PF65 40.00 | | | | |

**KM# 422 DINER**

0.50 g., 0.999 Gold AGW, 11 mm. **Subject:** Johannes Kepler, 400th Anniversary of the Astronomia Nova

| Date | Mintage | VF20 | XF40 | MS60 | MS63 | MS65 |
|---|---|---|---|---|---|---|
| 2009 | Est. 10000 | PF65 40.00 | | | | |

**KM# 435 DINER**

0.50 g., 0.999 Gold AGW, 11 mm. **Subject:** 2012 Summer Olympics, London **Rev:** Tennis

| Date | Mintage | VF20 | XF40 | MS60 | MS63 | MS65 |
|---|---|---|---|---|---|---|
| 2010 | PF65 40.00 | | | | | |

**KM# 436 DINER**

0.50 g., 0.999 Gold AGW, 11 mm. **Rev:** Church of St. Coloma

| Date | Mintage | VF20 | XF40 | MS60 | MS63 | MS65 |
|---|---|---|---|---|---|---|
| 2010 | Est. 10000 | PF65 40.00 | | | | |

**KM# 437 DINER**

0.50 g., 0.999 Gold AGW, 11 mm. **Subject:** Mother Teresa of Calcutta, 100th Anniversary of Birth

| Date | Mintage | VF20 | XF40 | MS60 | MS63 | MS65 |
|---|---|---|---|---|---|---|
| 2010 | Est. 5000 | PF65 35.00 | | | | |

**KM# 438 DINER**

0.50 g., 0.585 Gold AGW, 11 mm. **Rev:** Statue of Liberty in NY Harbor

| Date | Mintage | VF20 | XF40 | MS60 | MS63 | MS65 |
|---|---|---|---|---|---|---|
| 2010 | Est. 5000 | PF65 35.00 | | | | |

**KM# 439 DINER**

0.50 g., 0.585 Gold AGW, 11 mm. **Rev:** Cathedral of Santiago de Compostela

| Date | Mintage | VF20 | XF40 | MS60 | MS63 | MS65 |
|---|---|---|---|---|---|---|
| 2010 | Est. 5000 | PF65 35.00 | | | | |

**KM# 331 DINER**

1.24 g., 0.999 Gold 0.0398 oz. AGW, 13.92 mm. **Obv:** National arms **Rev:** John Paul II with cross croizer

| Date | Mintage | VF20 | XF40 | MS60 | MS63 | MS65 |
|---|---|---|---|---|---|---|
| 2011 | — | PF63 115 | PF65 125 | | | |

**KM# 443 DINER**

0.50 g., 0.999 Gold AGW, 11 mm. **Subject:** Napoleon Bonaparte, 190th Anniversary of Death **Rev:** Napoleon

| Date | Mintage | VF20 | XF40 | MS60 | MS63 | MS65 |
|---|---|---|---|---|---|---|
| 2011 | Est. 15000 | PF65 40.00 | | | | |
| 2011 | Est. 15000 | PF65 40.00 | | | | |

**KM# 349 DINER**

0.50 g., 0.9999 Gold, 11 mm. **Subject:** Joan d'Arc

| Date | Mintage | VF20 | XF40 | MS60 | MS63 | MS65 |
|---|---|---|---|---|---|---|
| 2012 | Est. 15000 | PF63 30.00 | PF65 35.00 | | | |

**KM# 350 DINER**
0.50 g., 0.9999 Gold, 11 mm. **Subject:** Venus de Milo

| Date | Mintage | VF20 | XF40 | MS60 | MS63 | MS65 |
|---|---|---|---|---|---|---|
| 2012 | Est. 5000 | PF63 35.00 | PF65 40.00 | | | |

**KM# 452 DINER**
27.00 g., Copper-Nickel, 38.61 mm. **Obv:** National shield **Rev:** Robin as a prism insert

| Date | Mintage | VF20 | XF40 | MS60 | MS63 | MS65 |
|---|---|---|---|---|---|---|
| 2012 | Est. 2500 | PF65 30.00 | | | | |

**KM# 453 DINER**
27.00 g., Copper-Nickel, 38.61 mm. **Obv:** National shield **Rev:** Duck as prism insert

| Date | Mintage | VF20 | XF40 | MS60 | MS63 | MS65 |
|---|---|---|---|---|---|---|
| 2012 | Est. 2500 | PF65 30.00 | | | | |

**KM# 454 DINER**
27.00 g., Copper-Nickel, 38.61 mm. **Obv:** National shield **Rev:** Capercaillie as prism insert

| Date | Mintage | VF20 | XF40 | MS60 | MS63 | MS65 |
|---|---|---|---|---|---|---|
| 2012 | Est. 2500 | PF65 30.00 | | | | |

**KM# 459 DINER**
0.50 g., 0.999 Gold AGW, 11 mm. **Subject:** Padre Pio, 125th Anniversary of Birth

| Date | Mintage | VF20 | XF40 | MS60 | MS63 | MS65 |
|---|---|---|---|---|---|---|
| 2012 | Est. 5000 | PF65 40.00 | | | | |

**KM# 460 DINER**
1.24 g., 0.999 Gold 0.0398 oz. AGW, 13.92 mm. **Subject:** Padre Pio, 125th Anniversary of Birth

| Date | Mintage | VF20 | XF40 | MS60 | MS63 | MS65 |
|---|---|---|---|---|---|---|
| 2012 | Est. 5000 | PF65 80.00 | | | | |

**KM# 461 DINER**
0.999 Silver ASW, 20 mm. **Subject:** 20th Century Popes **Rev:** Pope Leo XIII

| Date | Mintage | VF20 | XF40 | MS60 | MS63 | MS65 |
|---|---|---|---|---|---|---|
| 2012 | Est. 2500 | PF65 20.00 | | | | |

**KM# 462 DINER**
0.999 Silver ASW, 20 mm. **Subject:** 20th Century Popes **Rev:** Pope Pius X

| Date | Mintage | VF20 | XF40 | MS60 | MS63 | MS65 |
|---|---|---|---|---|---|---|
| 2012 | Est. 2500 | PF65 20.00 | | | | |

**KM# 463 DINER**
0.999 Silver ASW, 20 mm. **Subject:** 20th Century Popes **Rev:** Pope Benedict XV

| Date | Mintage | VF20 | XF40 | MS60 | MS63 | MS65 |
|---|---|---|---|---|---|---|
| 2012 | Est. 2500 | PF65 20.00 | | | | |

**KM# 464 DINER**
0.999 Silver ASW, 20 mm. **Subject:** 20th Century Popes **Rev:** Pope Pius XI

| Date | Mintage | VF20 | XF40 | MS60 | MS63 | MS65 |
|---|---|---|---|---|---|---|
| 2012 | Est. 2500 | PF65 20.00 | | | | |

**KM# 465 DINER**
0.999 Silver ASW, 20 mm. **Subject:** 20th Century Popes **Rev:** Pope Pius XII

| Date | Mintage | VF20 | XF40 | MS60 | MS63 | MS65 |
|---|---|---|---|---|---|---|
| 2012 | Est. 2500 | PF65 20.00 | | | | |

**KM# 466 DINER**
0.999 Silver ASW, 20 mm. **Subject:** 20th Century Popes **Rev:** Pope John XXIII

| Date | Mintage | VF20 | XF40 | MS60 | MS63 | MS65 |
|---|---|---|---|---|---|---|
| 2012 | Est. 2500 | PF65 20.00 | | | | |

**KM# 467 DINER**
0.999 Silver ASW, 20 mm. **Subject:** 20th Century Popes **Rev:** Pope Paul VI

| Date | Mintage | VF20 | XF40 | MS60 | MS63 | MS65 |
|---|---|---|---|---|---|---|
| 2012 | Est. 2500 | PF65 20.00 | | | | |

**KM# 468 DINER**
0.999 Silver ASW, 20 mm. **Subject:** 20th Century Popes **Rev:** Pope John Paul I

| Date | Mintage | VF20 | XF40 | MS60 | MS63 | MS65 |
|---|---|---|---|---|---|---|
| 2012 | Est. 2500 | PF65 20.00 | | | | |

**KM# 361 DINER**
0.50 g., 0.999 Gold AGW, 11 mm. **Subject:** Henry IV

| Date | Mintage | VF20 | XF40 | MS60 | MS63 | MS65 |
|---|---|---|---|---|---|---|
| 2013 | Est. 10000 | PF63 45.00 | PF65 50.00 | | | |

**KM# 363 DINER**
0.50 g., 0.999 Gold AGW, 11 mm. **Subject:** St. Peter's Basilica, Rome

| Date | Mintage | VF20 | XF40 | MS60 | MS63 | MS65 |
|---|---|---|---|---|---|---|
| 2013 | Est. 5000 | PF63 45.00 | PF65 50.00 | | | |

**KM# 243 2 DINERS**
11.25 g., Bi-Metallic Copper-Nickel center in Brass ring, 28.4 mm. **Subject:** Death of Pope John-Paul II **Obv:** National arms **Rev:** Karol Wojtyla as pope **Edge:** Reeded

| Date | Mintage | VF20 | XF40 | MS60 | MS63 | MS65 |
|---|---|---|---|---|---|---|
| 2005 | 15,000 | — | 2.40 | 3.50 | 6.00 | 8.00 |

**KM# 252 2 DINERS**
11.25 g., Bi-Metallic Copper-Nickel center in Brass ring, 28.4 mm. **Obv:** National arms **Rev:** Signing of the Umpirage between the Bishop of Urgell and Count of Foix **Edge:** Reeded

| Date | Mintage | VF20 | XF40 | MS60 | MS63 | MS65 |
|---|---|---|---|---|---|---|
| 2005 | 15,000 | — | — | — | 6.00 | 8.00 |
| 2006 | 10,000 | — | — | — | 6.00 | 8.00 |
| 2007 | 10,000 | — | — | — | 6.00 | 8.00 |
| 2008 | 5,000 | — | — | — | 6.00 | 8.00 |

**KM# 297 2 DINERS**
11.25 g., Bi-Metallic Copper-Nickel center in Brass ring, 28.4 mm. **Obv:** National Arms **Rev:** Portrait of Joseph Ratzinger as Pope Benedict XVI

| Date | Mintage | VF20 | XF40 | MS60 | MS63 | MS65 |
|---|---|---|---|---|---|---|
| 2006 | 15,000 | — | — | — | — | 8.00 |

**KM# 313 2 DINERS**
6.00 g., Bi-Metallic Copper-Nickel center in Brass ring, 28.4 mm. **Subject:** Popes of the 20th Century **Obv:** National Arms **Rev:** Pope John Paul I

| Date | Mintage | VF20 | XF40 | MS60 | MS63 | MS65 |
|---|---|---|---|---|---|---|
| 2007 | 5,000 | — | — | — | — | 10.00 |

**KM# 269 2 DINERS**
0.73 g., 0.999 Gold, 11 mm. **Subject:** von Beethoven **Obv:** National arms **Rev:** Beethoven seated at desk

| Date | Mintage | VF20 | XF40 | MS60 | MS63 | MS65 |
|---|---|---|---|---|---|---|
| 2008 | 5,000 | PF63 75.00 | PF65 80.00 | | | |

**KM# 413 2 DINERS**
0.73 g., 0.999 Gold AGW, 11 mm. **Subject:** Lourdes visions, 150th Anniversary **Rev:** Statue of Mary with wreath of stars

| Date | Mintage | VF20 | XF40 | MS60 | MS63 | MS65 |
|---|---|---|---|---|---|---|
| 2008 | PF65 60.00 | | | | | |

**KM# 414 2 DINERS**
0.73 g., 0.999 Gold AGW, 11 mm. **Subject:** Napoleon Bonaparte, 240th Anniversary of Birth **Rev:** Napoleon

| Date | Mintage | VF20 | XF40 | MS60 | MS63 | MS65 |
|---|---|---|---|---|---|---|
| 2008 | Est. 5000 | PF65 60.00 | | | | |

**KM# 281 2 DINERS**
0.73 g., 0.999 Gold, 11 mm. **Obv:** Shield **Rev:** Charlemagne **Edge:** Reeded

| Date | Mintage | VF20 | XF40 | MS60 | MS63 | MS65 |
|---|---|---|---|---|---|---|
| 2009 | 5,000 | PF63 75.00 | PF65 80.00 | | | |

**KM# 423 2 DINERS**
0.73 g., 0.999 Gold AGW, 11 mm. **Subject:** Apollo 11 Moon landing, 40th Anniversary **Rev:** Neil Armstrong and moon

| Date | Mintage | VF20 | XF40 | MS60 | MS63 | MS65 |
|---|---|---|---|---|---|---|
| 2009 | Est. 5000 | PF65 60.00 | | | | |

**KM# 426 2 DINERS**
0.73 g., 0.999 Gold AGW, 11 mm. **Rev:** Pope John Paul II

| Date | Mintage | VF20 | XF40 | MS60 | MS63 | MS65 |
|---|---|---|---|---|---|---|
| 2009 | Est. 5000 | PF65 60.00 | | | | |

**KM# 441 2 DINERS**
1.00 g., 0.900 Gold 0.0289 oz. AGW, 12 mm. **Rev:** Pope John Paul II

| Date | Mintage | VF20 | XF40 | MS60 | MS63 | MS65 |
|---|---|---|---|---|---|---|
| 2010 | Est. 10000 | PF65 70.00 | | | | |

**KM# 419a 2 DINERS**
1.00 g., 0.9999 Gold 0.0321 oz. AGW, 13.92 mm. **Obv:** Round National arms **Rev:** Bald eagle from vignette

| Date | Mintage | VF20 | XF40 | MS60 | MS63 | MS65 |
|---|---|---|---|---|---|---|
| 2012 | — | — | — | — | — | 75.00 |
| 2013 | — | — | — | — | — | 75.00 |

**KM# 419 2 DINERS**
1.00 g., 0.999 Gold 0.0321 oz. AGW, 13.92 mm. **Obv:** Round National shield **Rev:** Bald Eagle from vignette

| Date | Mintage | VF20 | XF40 | MS60 | MS63 | MS65 |
|---|---|---|---|---|---|---|
| 2013 | — | — | — | — | — | 75.00 |

**KM# 193 5 DINERS**
1.24 g., 0.999 Gold 0.0398 oz. AGW, 13.92 mm. **Obv:** National arms **Rev:** The Escorial Palace in Madrid **Edge:** Reeded

| Date | Mintage | VF20 | XF40 | MS60 | MS63 | MS65 |
|---|---|---|---|---|---|---|
| 2004 | 3,000 | PF63 65.00 | PF65 75.00 | | | |

**KM# 194 5 DINERS**
1.24 g., 0.999 Gold 0.0398 oz. AGW, 13.92 mm. **Obv:** National arms **Rev:** Eiffel Tower **Edge:** Reeded

| Date | Mintage | VF20 | XF40 | MS60 | MS63 | MS65 |
|---|---|---|---|---|---|---|
| 2004 | 3,000 | PF63 65.00 | PF65 75.00 | | | |

**KM# 195 5 DINERS**
1.24 g., 0.999 Gold 0.0398 oz. AGW, 13.92 mm. **Obv:** National arms **Rev:** Atomic model monument **Edge:** Reeded

| Date | Mintage | VF20 | XF40 | MS60 | MS63 | MS65 |
|---|---|---|---|---|---|---|
| 2004 | 3,000 | PF63 65.00 | PF65 75.00 | | | |

**KM# 196 5 DINERS**
1.24 g., 0.999 Gold 0.0398 oz. AGW, 13.92 mm. **Subject:** Andorran membership in the United Nations **Obv:** National arms **Rev:** Seated woman, world globe and UN logo **Edge:** Reeded

| Date | Mintage | VF20 | XF40 | MS60 | MS63 | MS65 |
|---|---|---|---|---|---|---|
| 2004 | 3,000 | PF63 70.00 | PF65 80.00 | | | |

**KM# 315 5 DINERS**
15.60 g., 0.999 Silver 0.501 oz. ASW, 35 mm. **Rev:** Bear facing

| Date | Mintage | VF20 | XF40 | MS60 | MS63 | MS65 |
|---|---|---|---|---|---|---|
| 2010 | 3,000 | PF63 65.00 | PF65 75.00 | | | |

**KM# 324 5 DINERS**
20.00 g., 0.925 Silver 0.5948 oz. ASW, 38.6 mm. **Subject:** Beautification of Pope John Paul II **Rev:** Hologram with image of John Paul II at left, St. Peter's facade at right

| Date | Mintage | VF20 | XF40 | MS60 | MS63 | MS65 |
|---|---|---|---|---|---|---|
| 2011 | 2,500 | PF65 135 | | | | |

**KM# 326 5 DINERS**
15.50 g., 0.925 Silver 0.461 oz. ASW, 35 mm. **Subject:** Wildlife of the Pyrenees - Golden Eagle **Obv:** National Arms **Rev:** Eagle in flight, eagle on nest

| Date | Mintage | VF20 | XF40 | MS60 | MS63 | MS65 |
|---|---|---|---|---|---|---|
| 2011 | 3,000 | PF63 115 | PF65 125 | | | |

**KM# 329 5 DINERS**
15.60 g., 0.999 Silver 0.501 oz. ASW, 35 mm. **Subject:** Christmas **Obv:** National arms **Rev:** Star over stable with Holy Family, color

| Date | Mintage | VF20 | XF40 | MS60 | MS63 | MS65 |
|---|---|---|---|---|---|---|
| 2011 | — | PF65 90.00 | | | | |

**KM# 333 5 DINERS**
20.00 g., 0.925 Silver 0.5948 oz. ASW, 38.6 mm. **Subject:** Birds of Andorra **Obv:** National arms **Rev:** Cappercaillie bird left, prism color

| Date | Mintage | VF20 | XF40 | MS60 | MS63 | MS65 |
|---|---|---|---|---|---|---|
| 2012 | 2,500 | — | — | — | — | 50.00 |

**KM# 334 5 DINERS**
20.00 g., 0.925 Silver 0.5948 oz. ASW, 38.61 mm. **Subject:** Birds of Andorra **Obv:** National arms **Rev:** Northern Shoveler in flight right, prism color

| Date | Mintage | VF20 | XF40 | MS60 | MS63 | MS65 |
|---|---|---|---|---|---|---|
| 2012 | 2,500 | — | — | — | — | 50.00 |

**KM# 335 5 DINERS**
20.00 g., 0.925 Silver 0.5948 oz. ASW, 38.6 mm. **Subject:** Birds of Andorra **Obv:** National arms **Rev:** Robin facing left, prism color

| Date | Mintage | VF20 | XF40 | MS60 | MS63 | MS65 |
|---|---|---|---|---|---|---|
| 2012 | 2,500 | — | — | — | — | 50.00 |

**KM# 337 5 DINERS**
0.925 Silver **Obv:** National arms at center **Rev:** DaVinci's Last supper in color

| Date | Mintage | VF20 | XF40 | MS60 | MS63 | MS65 |
|---|---|---|---|---|---|---|
| 2012 | — | PF63 90.00 | PF65 100 | | | |

**KM# 348 5 DINERS**
20.00 g., 0.925 Silver 0.5948 oz. ASW, 38.61 mm. **Subject:** 2014 FIFA World Cup - Brazil

| Date | Mintage | VF20 | XF40 | MS60 | MS63 | MS65 |
|---|---|---|---|---|---|---|
| 2012 | Est. 10000 | PF63 65.00 | PF65 75.00 | | | |

**KM# 351 5 DINERS**
20.00 g., 0.999 Silver 0.6424 oz. ASW, 38.6 mm. **Subject:** Aquila Daurada

| Date | Mintage | VF20 | XF40 | MS60 | MS63 | MS65 |
|---|---|---|---|---|---|---|
| 2012 | Est. 10000 | PF63 60.00 | PF65 65.00 | | | |

**KM# 365 5 DINERS**
20.00 g., 0.999 Silver 0.6424 oz. ASW, 34 mm. **Subject:** Spring **Obv:** National arms **Rev:** Female head left, flowers around and in hair

| Date | Mintage | VF20 | XF40 | MS60 | MS63 | MS65 |
|---|---|---|---|---|---|---|
| 2012 Antique patina | 2,000 | — | — | — | — | 50.00 |

**KM# 366 5 DINERS**
20.00 g., 0.999 Silver 0.6424 oz. ASW, 34 mm. **Subject:** Summer **Obv:** National arms **Rev:** Female bust with butterfly on shoulder

| Date | Mintage | VF20 | XF40 | MS60 | MS63 | MS65 |
|---|---|---|---|---|---|---|
| 2012 Antique patina | 2,000 | — | — | — | — | 50.00 |

**KM# 367 5 DINERS**
20.00 g., 0.999 Silver 0.6424 oz. ASW, 34 mm. **Subject:** Autumn **Obv:** National arms **Rev:** Bearded portrait facing within wreath of harvest bounty

| Date | Mintage | VF20 | XF40 | MS60 | MS63 | MS65 |
|---|---|---|---|---|---|---|
| 2012 Antique patina | 2,000 | — | — | — | — | 50.00 |

**KM# 368 5 DINERS**
0.999 Silver ASW 20, 34 mm. **Subject:** Winter **Obv:** National arms **Rev:** Bearded portrait facing

| Date | Mintage | VF20 | XF40 | MS60 | MS63 | MS65 |
|---|---|---|---|---|---|---|
| 2012 Antique patina | 2,000 | — | — | — | — | 50.00 |

**KM# 352 5 DINERS**
14.14 g., 0.925 Silver 0.4205 oz. ASW, 22.4 x 32 mm. **Subject:** Wonders of Jesus Christ **Rev:** Wedding at Canna

| Date | Mintage | VF20 | XF40 | MS60 | MS63 | MS65 |
|---|---|---|---|---|---|---|
| 2013 | Est. 6000 | PF63 55.00 | PF65 60.00 | | | |

**KM# 353 5 DINERS**
14.14 g., 0.925 Silver 0.4205 oz. ASW, 22.4 x 32 mm. **Subject:** Wonders of Jesus Christ **Rev:** Feeding the Multitude

| Date | Mintage | VF20 | XF40 | MS60 | MS63 | MS65 |
|---|---|---|---|---|---|---|
| 2013 | Est. 6000 | PF63 55.00 | PF65 60.00 | | | |

**KM# 354 5 DINERS**
14.14 g., 0.925 Silver 0.4205 oz. ASW, 22.4 x 32 mm. **Subject:** The Wonders of Jesus Christ **Obv:** Healing the Blind

| Date | Mintage | VF20 | XF40 | MS60 | MS63 | MS65 |
|---|---|---|---|---|---|---|
| 2013 | Est. 6000 | PF63 55.00 | PF65 60.00 | | | |

**KM# 355 5 DINERS**
14.14 g., 0.925 Silver 0.4205 oz. ASW, 22.4 x 32 mm. **Subject:** The Wonders of Jesus Christ **Obv:** Jesus Walking on Water

| Date | Mintage | VF20 | XF40 | MS60 | MS63 | MS65 |
|---|---|---|---|---|---|---|
| 2013 | Est. 6000 | PF63 55.00 | PF65 60.00 | | | |

**KM# 356 5 DINERS**
14.14 g., 0.925 Silver 0.4205 oz. ASW, 22.4 x 32 mm. **Subject:** The Wonders of Jesus **Obv:** The Transfiguration

| Date | Mintage | VF20 | XF40 | MS60 | MS63 | MS65 |
|---|---|---|---|---|---|---|
| 2013 | Est. 6000 | PF63 55.00 | PF65 60.00 | | | |

**KM# 357 5 DINERS**
14.14 g., 0.925 Silver 0.4205 oz. ASW, 22.4 x 32 mm. **Subject:** The Wonders of Jesus **Obv:** Raising of Lazarus

| Date | Mintage | VF20 | XF40 | MS60 | MS63 | MS65 |
|---|---|---|---|---|---|---|
| 2013 | Est. 6000 | PF63 55.00 | PF65 60.00 | | | |

**KM# 358 5 DINERS**
14.14 g., 0.925 Silver 0.4205 oz. ASW, 22.4 x 32 mm. **Subject:** The Wonders of Jesus **Obv:** Last Supper in color

| Date | Mintage | VF20 | XF40 | MS60 | MS63 | MS65 |
|---|---|---|---|---|---|---|
| 2013 | Est. 6000 | PF63 55.00 | PF65 60.00 | | | |

**KM# 359 5 DINERS**
14.14 g., 0.925 Silver 0.4205 oz. ASW, 22.4 x 32 mm. **Subject:** The Wonders of Jesus Christ **Obv:** Resurrection of Christ

| Date | Mintage | VF20 | XF40 | MS60 | MS63 | MS65 |
|---|---|---|---|---|---|---|
| 2013 | Est. 6000 | PF63 55.00 | PF65 60.00 | | | |

**KM# 360 5 DINERS**
20.00 g., 0.925 Silver 0.5948 oz. ASW, 38.61 mm. **Subject:** 2016 Olympics - Badminton

| Date | Mintage | VF20 | XF40 | MS60 | MS63 | MS65 |
|---|---|---|---|---|---|---|
| 2013 | Est. 10000 | PF63 65.00 | PF65 75.00 | | | |

**KM# 364 5 DINERS**
20.00 g., 0.999 Silver 0.6424 oz. ASW, 38.61 mm. **Subject:** Aguila Daurada

| Date | Mintage | VF20 | XF40 | MS60 | MS63 | MS65 |
|---|---|---|---|---|---|---|
| 2013 | Est. 10000 | PF63 65.00 | PF65 75.00 | | | |

**KM# 486 5 DINERS**
20.00 g., 0.925 Silver 0.5948 oz. ASW, 38.61 mm. **Subject:** Equestrian Federation, 92nd Anniversary **Rev:** Dressage in color

| Date | Mintage | VF20 | XF40 | MS60 | MS63 | MS65 |
|---|---|---|---|---|---|---|
| 2013 | Est. 2000 | PF65 70.00 | | | | |

**KM# 487 5 DINERS**
20.00 g., 0.925 Silver 0.5948 oz. ASW, 38.61 mm. **Subject:** Equestrian Federation, 92nd Anniversary **Rev:** Reining in color

| Date | Mintage | VF20 | XF40 | MS60 | MS63 | MS65 |
|---|---|---|---|---|---|---|
| 2013 | Est. 2000 | PF65 70.00 | | | | |

**KM# 488 5 DINERS**
20.00 g., 0.925 Silver 0.5948 oz. ASW, 38.61 mm. **Subject:** Equestrian Federation, 92nd Anniversary **Rev:** Horse in color

| Date | Mintage | VF20 | XF40 | MS60 | MS63 | MS65 |
|---|---|---|---|---|---|---|
| 2013 | Est. 70 | PF65 70.00 | | | | |

**KM# 172 10 DINERS**
31.47 g., 0.925 Silver 0.9359 oz. ASW, 38.6 mm. **Subject:** Europa **Obv:** National arms **Rev:** Europa in chariot **Edge:** Reeded

| Date | Mintage | VF20 | XF40 | MS60 | MS63 | MS65 |
|---|---|---|---|---|---|---|
| 2001 | 15,000 | PF63 40.00 | PF65 45.00 | | | |

**KM# 173 10 DINERS**
31.47 g., 0.925 Silver 0.9359 oz. ASW, 38.6 mm. **Subject:** Concordia Europea **Obv:** National arms **Rev:** Two crowned women holding hands **Edge:** Reeded

| Date | Mintage | VF20 | XF40 | MS60 | MS63 | MS65 |
|---|---|---|---|---|---|---|
| 2001 | 15,000 | PF63 40.00 | PF65 45.00 | | | |

**KM# 175 10 DINERS**
31.47 g., 0.925 Silver 0.9359 oz. ASW, 38.6 mm. **Subject:** Olympics **Obv:** National arms **Rev:** Snowboarder **Edge:** Reeded

| Date | Mintage | VF20 | XF40 | MS60 | MS63 | MS65 |
|---|---|---|---|---|---|---|
| 2002 | 15,000 | PF63 40.00 | PF65 45.00 | | | |

**KM# 183 10 DINERS**
31.47 g., 0.925 Silver 0.9359 oz. ASW, 38.6 mm. **Subject:** Mouflon **Obv:** National arms **Rev:** Mouflon ram **Edge:** Reeded

| Date | Mintage | VF20 | XF40 | MS60 | MS63 | MS65 |
|---|---|---|---|---|---|---|
| 2002 | 15,000 | PF63 45.00 | PF65 50.00 | | | |

**KM# 289 10 DINERS**
31.47 g., 0.925 Silver 0.9359 oz. ASW, 38.61 mm. **Subject:** FIFA World Cup **Obv:** National Arms **Rev:** Soccer ball, names and years of previous World Cup host countries **Edge:** Reeded

| Date | Mintage | VF20 | XF40 | MS60 | MS63 | MS65 |
|---|---|---|---|---|---|---|
| 2003 | 50,000 | PF63 75.00 | PF65 85.00 | | | |

**KM# 188 10 DINERS**
31.10 g., 0.925 Silver 0.925 oz. ASW, 38.6 mm. **Obv:** National arms **Rev:** Pope with doves **Edge:** Reeded

| Date | Mintage | VF20 | XF40 | MS60 | MS63 | MS65 |
|---|---|---|---|---|---|---|
| 2004 | 9,999 | PF63 60.00 | PF65 70.00 | | | |

**KM# 189 10 DINERS**
31.10 g., 0.925 Silver 0.925 oz. ASW, 38.6 mm. **Obv:** National arms **Rev:** Pope holding staff with 2 hands **Edge:** Reeded

| Date | Mintage | VF20 | XF40 | MS60 | MS63 | MS65 |
|---|---|---|---|---|---|---|
| 2004 | 9,999 | PF63 60.00 | PF65 70.00 | | | |

**KM# 190 10 DINERS**
31.10 g., 0.925 Silver 0.925 oz. ASW, 38.6 mm. **Obv:** National arms **Rev:** Pope raising a chalice **Edge:** Reeded

| Date | Mintage | VF20 | XF40 | MS60 | MS63 | MS65 |
|---|---|---|---|---|---|---|
| 2004 | 9,999 | PF63 60.00 | PF65 70.00 | | | |

**KM# 191 10 DINERS**
31.10 g., 0.925 Silver 0.925 oz. ASW, 38.6 mm. **Obv:** National arms **Rev:** Pope with hammer **Edge:** Reeded

| Date | Mintage | VF20 | XF40 | MS60 | MS63 | MS65 |
|---|---|---|---|---|---|---|
| 2004 | 9,999 | PF63 60.00 | PF65 70.00 | | | |

**KM# 192 10 DINERS**
31.10 g., 0.925 Silver 0.925 oz. ASW, 38.6 mm. **Obv:** National arms **Rev:** Gold-plated Pope writing **Edge:** Reeded

| Date | Mintage | VF20 | XF40 | MS60 | MS63 | MS65 |
|---|---|---|---|---|---|---|
| 2004 | 9,999 | PF63 60.00 | PF65 70.00 | | | |

**KM# 205 10 DINERS**
31.10 g., 0.925 Silver 0.9249 oz. ASW, 38.6 mm. **Rev:** Gold plated Pope John Paul II wearing mitre and holding crucifix staff **Edge:** Reeded

| Date | Mintage | VF20 | XF40 | MS60 | MS63 | MS65 |
|---|---|---|---|---|---|---|
| 2005 | 9,999 | PF63 60.00 | PF65 70.00 | | | |

**KM# 206 10 DINERS**
31.10 g., 0.925 Silver 0.9249 oz. ASW, 38.6 mm. **Obv:** National arms **Rev:** Pope John Paul II with the Holy Virgin in background **Edge:** Reeded

| Date | Mintage | VF20 | XF40 | MS60 | MS63 | MS65 |
|---|---|---|---|---|---|---|
| 2005 | 9,999 | PF63 60.00 | PF65 70.00 | | | |

**KM# 207 10 DINERS**
31.10 g., 0.925 Silver 0.9249 oz. ASW, 38.6 mm. **Obv:** National arms **Rev:** Pope John Paul II in prayer with crucifix at right **Edge:** Reeded

| Date | Mintage | VF20 | XF40 | MS60 | MS63 | MS65 |
|---|---|---|---|---|---|---|
| 2005 | 9,999 | PF63 60.00 | PF65 70.00 | | | |

**KM# 208 10 DINERS**
31.10 g., 0.925 Silver 0.9249 oz. ASW, 38.6 mm. **Obv:** National arms **Rev:** Pope John Paul II blessing Vatican crowd **Edge:** Reeded

| Date | Mintage | VF20 | XF40 | MS60 | MS63 | MS65 |
|---|---|---|---|---|---|---|
| 2005 | 9,999 | PF63 60.00 | PF65 70.00 | | | |

**KM# 209 10 DINERS**
31.10 g., 0.925 Silver 0.9249 oz. ASW, 38.6 mm. **Obv:** National arms **Rev:** Pope John Paul II and Mother Teresa **Edge:** Reeded

| Date | Mintage | VF20 | XF40 | MS60 | MS63 | MS65 |
|---|---|---|---|---|---|---|
| 2005 | 9,999 | PF63 60.00 | PF65 70.00 | | | |

**KM# 210 10 DINERS**
31.10 g., 0.925 Silver 0.9249 oz. ASW, 38.6 mm. **Obv:** National arms **Rev:** Bearded man above Vatican City **Edge:** Reeded

| Date | Mintage | VF20 | XF40 | MS60 | MS63 | MS65 |
|---|---|---|---|---|---|---|
| 2005 | 9,999 | PF63 50.00 | PF65 60.00 | | | |

**KM# 211 10 DINERS**
31.10 g., 0.925 Silver 0.9249 oz. ASW, 38.6 mm. **Obv:** National arms **Rev:** Sad woman above Fatima **Edge:** Reeded

| Date | Mintage | VF20 | XF40 | MS60 | MS63 | MS65 |
|---|---|---|---|---|---|---|
| 2005 | 9,999 | PF63 50.00 | PF65 60.00 | | | |

**KM# 212 10 DINERS**
31.10 g., 0.925 Silver 0.9249 oz. ASW, 38.6 mm. **Obv:** National arms **Rev:** Radiant woman above Guadalupe Cathedral **Edge:** Reeded

| Date | Mintage | VF20 | XF40 | MS60 | MS63 | MS65 |
|---|---|---|---|---|---|---|
| 2005 | 9,999 | PF63 50.00 | PF65 60.00 | | | |

**KM# 213 10 DINERS**
31.10 g., 0.925 Silver 0.9249 oz. ASW, 38.6 mm. **Obv:** National arms **Rev:** Sea shell above Santiago De Compostel-la Cathedral **Edge:** Reeded

| Date | Mintage | VF20 | XF40 | MS60 | MS63 | MS65 |
|---|---|---|---|---|---|---|
| 2005 | 9,999 | PF63 50.00 | PF65 60.00 | | | |

**KM# 214 10 DINERS**
31.10 g., 0.925 Silver 0.9249 oz. ASW, 38.6 mm. **Obv:** National arms **Rev:** Dead man's face with Church of the Holy Sepulchure in the background **Edge:** Reeded

| Date | Mintage | VF20 | XF40 | MS60 | MS63 | MS65 |
|---|---|---|---|---|---|---|
| 2005 | 9,999 | PF63 50.00 | PF65 60.00 | | | |

**KM# 215 10 DINERS**
28.80 g., 0.925 Silver 0.8565 oz. ASW, 38.61 mm. **Obv:** National arms **Rev:** 2006 Olympics freestyle skier **Edge:** Reeded

| Date | Mintage | VF20 | XF40 | MS60 | MS63 | MS65 |
|---|---|---|---|---|---|---|
| 2005 | 15,000 | PF63 40.00 | PF65 50.00 | | | |

**KM# 338 10 DINERS**
28.28 g., 0.925 Silver 0.841 oz. ASW, 38.61 mm. **Subject:** Benedict XVI election **Obv:** Naitonal arms **Rev:** Benedict XVI with hands raised, gilt; Crystal cross at right

| Date | Mintage | VF20 | XF40 | MS60 | MS63 | MS65 |
|---|---|---|---|---|---|---|
| 2005 | — | — | — | — | — | 75.00 |

**KM# 217 10 DINERS**
3.11 g., 0.9999 Gold 0.100 oz. AGW, 20 mm. **Obv:** National arms **Rev:** Jesus carrying the cross **Edge:** Reeded

| Date | Mintage | VF20 | XF40 | MS60 | MS63 | MS65 |
|---|---|---|---|---|---|---|
| 2006 | 9,999 | PF63 175 | PF65 185 | | | |

**KM# 218 10 DINERS**
31.10 g., 0.925 Silver 0.925 oz. ASW, 38.6 mm. **Obv:** National arms **Rev:** Birth of Jesus **Edge:** Reeded

| Date | Mintage | VF20 | XF40 | MS60 | MS63 | MS65 |
|---|---|---|---|---|---|---|
| 2006 | 9,999 | PF63 50.00 | PF65 60.00 | | | |

**KM# 219 10 DINERS**
31.10 g., 0.925 Silver 0.925 oz. ASW, 38.6 mm. **Obv:** National arms **Rev:** The Last Supper **Edge:** Reeded

| Date | Mintage | VF20 | XF40 | MS60 | MS63 | MS65 |
|---|---|---|---|---|---|---|
| 2006 | 9,999 | PF63 50.00 | PF65 60.00 | | | |

**KM# 404 10 DINERS**
31.47 g., 0.925 Silver 0.9359 oz. ASW, 38.61 mm. **Subject:** 18th World Soccer championship 2006, Germany **Rev:** Soccer players

| Date | Mintage | VF20 | XF40 | MS60 | MS63 | MS65 |
|---|---|---|---|---|---|---|
| 2006 | Est. 10000 | PF65 50.00 | | | | |

**KM# 276 10 DINERS**
28.28 g., 0.925 Silver 0.841 oz. ASW, 38.6 mm. **Subject:** Extreme Sports - Mountain Bike **Obv:** Arms **Rev:** Multicolor biker

| Date | Mintage | VF20 | XF40 | MS60 | MS63 | MS65 |
|---|---|---|---|---|---|---|
| 2007 | 5,000 | PF63 60.00 | PF65 65.00 | | | |

**KM# 277 10 DINERS**
28.28 g., 0.925 Silver 0.841 oz. ASW, 38.6 mm. **Subject:** Extreme Sports - Snowboarding **Obv:** Arms **Rev:** Multicolor snowboarder

| Date | Mintage | VF20 | XF40 | MS60 | MS63 | MS65 |
|---|---|---|---|---|---|---|
| 2007 | 5,000 | PF63 60.00 | PF65 65.00 | | | |

**KM# 278 10 DINERS**
28.28 g., 0.925 Silver 0.841 oz. ASW, 38.6 mm. **Subject:** Extreme Sports - Heliskiing **Obv:** Arms **Rev:** Multicolor heliskier

| Date | Mintage | VF20 | XF40 | MS60 | MS63 | MS65 |
|---|---|---|---|---|---|---|
| 2007 | 5,000 | PF63 60.00 | PF65 65.00 | | | |

**KM# 405 10 DINERS**
28.28 g., 0.925 Silver 0.841 oz. ASW, 38.61 mm. **Subject:** 2008 Summer Olympics, Beijing **Rev:** Ribbon dancers

| Date | Mintage | VF20 | XF40 | MS60 | MS63 | MS65 |
|---|---|---|---|---|---|---|
| 2007 | — | PF65 50.00 | | | | |

**KM# 406 10 DINERS**
25.00 g., 0.925 Silver 0.7435 oz. ASW **Subject:** Christmas **Rev:** Manger scene

| Date | Mintage | VF20 | XF40 | MS60 | MS63 | MS65 |
|---|---|---|---|---|---|---|
| 2007 | Est. 5000 | PF65 80.00 | | | | |

**KM# 244 10 DINERS**
28.28 g., 0.925 Silver 0.841 oz. ASW, 28x40 mm. **Subject:** Great Painters of the World **Obv:** Mona lisa, national arms at lower left, multicolor **Rev:** Head of Leonardo daVinci at lower left, study of man in background, multicolor **Edge:** Plain **Shape:** Vertical rectangular

| Date | Mintage | VF20 | XF40 | MS60 | MS63 | MS65 |
|---|---|---|---|---|---|---|
| 2008 | 15,000 | — | — | — | — | 60.00 |

**KM# 271 10 DINERS**
28.28 g., 0.925 Silver 0.841 oz. ASW, 28x40 mm. **Obv:** National arms at left, color painting of ladies at a piano **Rev:** Renoir facing, female portrait in color in artist's pallet shape **Shape:** Vertical rectangle

| Date | Mintage | VF20 | XF40 | MS60 | MS63 | MS65 |
|---|---|---|---|---|---|---|
| 2008 | 20,000 | PF63 60.00 | PF65 65.00 | | | |

**KM# 272 10 DINERS**
33.00 g., 0.925 Silver 0.9814 oz. ASW parially gilt, 38.6 mm. **Subject:** Vikings

| Date | Mintage | VF20 | XF40 | MS60 | MS63 | MS65 |
|---|---|---|---|---|---|---|
| 2008 | 15,000 | — | — | — | — | 60.00 |

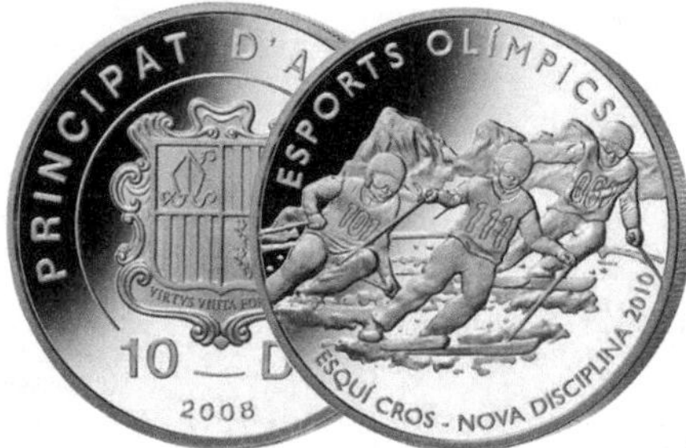


**KM# 273 10 DINERS**
28.28 g., 0.925 Silver 0.841 oz. ASW, 38.6 mm. **Subject:** Cross-country Skiing

| Date | Mintage | VF20 | XF40 | MS60 | MS63 | MS65 |
|---|---|---|---|---|---|---|
| 2008 | 10,000 | PF63 35.00 | PF65 45.00 | | | |

**KM# 407 10 DINERS**
33.00 g., 0.925 Silver 0.9814 oz. ASW, 38.61 mm. **Obv:** National shield **Rev:** Thor wielding hammer in color

| Date | Mintage | VF20 | XF40 | MS60 | MS63 | MS65 |
|---|---|---|---|---|---|---|
| 2008 | Est. 7500 | PF65 100 | | | | |

**KM# 408 10 DINERS**
33.00 g., 0.925 Silver 0.9814 oz. ASW, 38.61 mm. **Obv:** National shield **Rev:** Ship in color

| Date | Mintage | VF20 | XF40 | MS60 | MS63 | MS65 |
|---|---|---|---|---|---|---|
| 2007 | Est. 7500 | PF65 100 | | | | |

**KM# 409 10 DINERS**
33.00 g., 0.925 Silver 0.9814 oz. ASW, 38.61 mm. **Obv:** National shield **Rev:** Female in color

| Date | Mintage | VF20 | XF40 | MS60 | MS63 | MS65 |
|---|---|---|---|---|---|---|
| 2008 | 7,500 | PF65 100 | | | | |

**KM# 415 10 DINERS**
28.28 g., 0.925 Silver 0.841 oz. ASW, 38.61 mm. **Subject:** Extreme sports **Rev:** Kite boarding in color

| Date | Mintage | VF20 | XF40 | MS60 | MS63 | MS65 |
|---|---|---|---|---|---|---|
| 2008 | Est. 5000 | PF65 60.00 | | | | |

**KM# 280 10 DINERS**
28.28 g., 0.925 Silver 0.841 oz. ASW, 38.61 mm. **Subject:** World Cup Football, 2010 **Obv:** Shield **Rev:** Linear and shaded player skicking ball **Edge:** Reeded

| Date | Mintage | VF20 | XF40 | MS60 | MS63 | MS65 |
|---|---|---|---|---|---|---|
| 2009 | 10,000 | PF63 40.00 | PF65 50.00 | | | |

**KM# 316 10 DINERS**
28.28 g., 0.925 Silver 0.841 oz. ASW, 38.61 mm. **Subject:** Chopin **Rev:** Hand and autograph

| Date | Mintage | VF20 | XF40 | MS60 | MS63 | MS65 |
|---|---|---|---|---|---|---|
| 2009 | — | PF63 35.00 | PF65 45.00 | | | |

**KM# 317 10 DINERS**
28.28 g., 0.925 Silver 0.841 oz. ASW **Subject:** Chopin - Vienna **Rev:** Bust at left, house at right

| Date | Mintage | VF20 | XF40 | MS60 | MS63 | MS65 |
|---|---|---|---|---|---|---|
| 2009 | — | PF63 35.00 | PF65 45.00 | | | |

**KM# 318 10 DINERS**
28.28 g., 0.925 Silver 0.841 oz. ASW, 38.61 mm. **Subject:** Chopin - Paris **Rev:** Party scene, Paris

| Date | Mintage | VF20 | XF40 | MS60 | MS63 | MS65 |
|---|---|---|---|---|---|---|
| 2009 | — | PF63 35.00 | PF65 45.00 | | | |

**KM# 319 10 DINERS**
28.28 g., 0.925 Silver 0.841 oz. ASW, 38.6 mm. **Subject:** Chopin **Rev:** Bust at left, memorial stone at right

| Date | Mintage | VF20 | XF40 | MS60 | MS63 | MS65 |
|---|---|---|---|---|---|---|
| 2009 | — | PF63 35.00 | PF65 45.00 | | | |

**KM# 320 10 DINERS**
28.28 g., 0.925 Silver 0.841 oz. ASW, 38.6 mm. **Subject:** Chopin **Rev:** Portrait pair in ovals, Mallorca

| Date | Mintage | VF20 | XF40 | MS60 | MS63 | MS65 |
|---|---|---|---|---|---|---|
| 2009 | — | PF63 35.00 | PF65 45.00 | | | |

**KM# 321 10 DINERS**
28.28 g., 0.925 Silver 0.841 oz. ASW, 38.61 mm. **Subject:** Chopin **Rev:** Portrait pair in ovals, Dresden

| Date | Mintage | VF20 | XF40 | MS60 | MS63 | MS65 |
|---|---|---|---|---|---|---|
| 2009 | — | PF63 35.00 | PF65 45.00 | | | |

**KM# 322 10 DINERS**
28.28 g., 0.925 Silver 0.841 oz. ASW partially gilt, 38.61 mm. **Subject:** Chopin **Rev:** Chopin at piano left, Gilt profile head at right

| Date | Mintage | VF20 | XF40 | MS60 | MS63 | MS65 |
|---|---|---|---|---|---|---|
| 2009 | — | PF63 35.00 | PF65 45.00 | | | |

**KM# 323 10 DINERS**
28.28 g., 0.925 Silver 0.841 oz. ASW, 38.61 mm. **Subject:** Chopin **Rev:** Two portraits, one in color - Wausau

| Date | Mintage | VF20 | XF40 | MS60 | MS63 | MS65 |
|---|---|---|---|---|---|---|
| 2009 | — | PF63 35.00 | PF65 45.00 | | | |

**KM# 420 10 DINERS**
28.28 g., 0.925 Silver 0.841 oz. ASW, 38.61 mm. **Obv:** National shield **Rev:** Mountain Biking

| Date | Mintage | VF20 | XF40 | MS60 | MS63 | MS65 |
|---|---|---|---|---|---|---|
| 2009 | Est. 10000 | PF65 60.00 | | | | |

**KM# 427 10 DINERS**
28.28 g., 0.925 Silver 0.841 oz. ASW, 38.61 mm. **Subject:** Wonders of the Modern World **Obv:** National shield on world map **Rev:** Great Wall of China in color

| Date | Mintage | VF20 | XF40 | MS60 | MS63 | MS65 |
|---|---|---|---|---|---|---|
| 2009 | Est. 10000 | PF65 60.00 | | | | |

**KM# 428 10 DINERS**
28.28 g., 0.925 Silver 0.841 oz. ASW, 38.61 mm. **Subject:** Wonders of the World **Obv:** National shield on world map **Rev:** Treasury at Petra in color

| Date | Mintage | VF20 | XF40 | MS60 | MS63 | MS65 |
|---|---|---|---|---|---|---|
| 2009 | Est. 10000 | PF65 60.00 | | | | |

**KM# 429 10 DINERS**
28.28 g., 0.925 Silver 0.841 oz. ASW, 38.61 mm. **Subject:** Wonders of the World **Obv:** National shield on world map **Rev:** Christ statue at Rio de Janeiro in color

| Date | Mintage | VF20 | XF40 | MS60 | MS63 | MS65 |
|---|---|---|---|---|---|---|
| 2009 | Est. 10000 | PF65 60.00 | | | | |

**KM# 430 10 DINERS**
28.28 g., 0.925 Silver 0.841 oz. ASW, 38.61 mm. **Subject:** Wonders of the World **Obv:** National shield on world map **Rev:** Machu Picchu in color

| Date | Mintage | VF20 | XF40 | MS60 | MS63 | MS65 |
|---|---|---|---|---|---|---|
| 2009 | Est. 10000 | PF65 60.00 | | | | |

**KM# 431 10 DINERS**
28.28 g., 0.925 Silver 0.841 oz. ASW, 38.61 mm. **Subject:** Wonders of the World **Obv:** National shield on world map **Rev:** Chichen Itza in color

| Date | Mintage | VF20 | XF40 | MS60 | MS63 | MS65 |
|---|---|---|---|---|---|---|
| 2009 | Est. 10000 | PF65 60.00 | | | | |

**KM# 432 10 DINERS**
28.28 g., 0.925 Silver 0.841 oz. ASW, 38.61 mm. **Subject:** Wonders of the World **Obv:** National shield on world map **Rev:** Coliseum in Rome

| Date | Mintage | VF20 | XF40 | MS60 | MS63 | MS65 |
|---|---|---|---|---|---|---|
| 2009 | Est. 10000 | PF65 60.00 | | | | |

**KM# 433 10 DINERS**
28.28 g., 0.925 Silver 0.841 oz. ASW, 38.61 mm. **Subject:** Wonders of the World **Obv:** National shield on world map **Rev:** Taj Mahal in color

| Date | Mintage | VF20 | XF40 | MS60 | MS63 | MS65 |
|---|---|---|---|---|---|---|
| 2009 | Est. 10000 | PF65 60.00 | | | | |

**KM# 283 10 DINERS**
28.28 g., 0.925 Silver 0.841 oz. ASW, 40x28 mm. **Subject:** Albrecht Durer **Obv:** Adama dn even engraving and shield **Rev:** Durer's Adoration of the Holy Trinity

| Date | Mintage | VF20 | XF40 | MS60 | MS63 | MS65 |
|---|---|---|---|---|---|---|
| 2010 | 15,000 | PF63 40.00 | PF65 50.00 | | | |

**KM# 284 10 DINERS**
28.28 g., 0.925 Silver 0.841 oz. ASW, 38.61 mm. **Obv:** Shield **Rev:** St. Christopher

| Date | Mintage | VF20 | XF40 | MS60 | MS63 | MS65 |
|---|---|---|---|---|---|---|
| 2010 | 5,000 | PF63 60.00 | PF65 65.00 | | | |

**KM# 285 10 DINERS**
28.28 g., 0.925 Silver 0.841 oz. ASW, 38.61 mm. **Obv:** Shield **Rev:** St. George **Edge:** Reeded

| Date | Mintage | VF20 | XF40 | MS60 | MS63 | MS65 |
|---|---|---|---|---|---|---|
| 2010 | 5,000 | PF63 60.00 | PF65 65.00 | | | |

**KM# 286 10 DINERS**
28.28 g., 0.925 Silver 0.841 oz. ASW, 38.61 mm. **Obv:** Shield **Rev:** St. Catherine **Edge:** Reeded

| Date | Mintage | VF20 | XF40 | MS60 | MS63 | MS65 |
|---|---|---|---|---|---|---|
| 2010 | 5,000 | PF63 60.00 | PF65 65.00 | | | |

**KM# 287 10 DINERS**
28.28 g., 0.925 Silver 0.841 oz. ASW, 38.61 mm. **Obv:** Shield **Rev:** St. Barbara **Edge:** Reeded

| Date | Mintage | VF20 | XF40 | MS60 | MS63 | MS65 |
|---|---|---|---|---|---|---|
| 2010 | 5,000 | PF63 60.00 | PF65 65.00 | | | |

**KM# 434 10 DINERS**
28.28 g., 0.925 Silver 0.841 oz. ASW, 38.61 mm. **Obv:** Tennis **Rev:** 2012 Summer Olympics, London

| Date | Mintage | VF20 | XF40 | MS60 | MS63 | MS65 |
|---|---|---|---|---|---|---|
| 2010 | Est. 6000 | PF65 60.00 | | | | |

**KM# 440 10 DINERS**
28.28 g., 0.925 Silver 0.841 oz. ASW, 28x40 mm. **Rev:** Pope John Paul II in kinegram

| Date | Mintage | VF20 | XF40 | MS60 | MS63 | MS65 |
|---|---|---|---|---|---|---|
| 2010 | Est. 15000 | PF65 60.00 | | | | |

**KM# 332 10 DINERS**
31.10 g., 0.999 Silver 0.999 oz. ASW, 38.6 mm. **Obv:** National arms **Rev:** St. Margaret and dragon

| Date | Mintage | VF20 | XF40 | MS60 | MS63 | MS65 |
|---|---|---|---|---|---|---|
| 2011 | — | PF63 90.00 | PF65 100 | | | |

**KM# 442 10 DINERS**
28.28 g., 0.925 Silver 0.841 oz. ASW, 38.61 mm. **Subject:** 2014 Winter Olympics, Sochi **Rev:** Downhill skier

| Date | Mintage | VF20 | XF40 | MS60 | MS63 | MS65 |
|---|---|---|---|---|---|---|
| 2011 | Est. 5000 | PF65 60.00 | | | | |

**KM# 444 10 DINERS**
30.00 g., 0.999 Silver 0.9636 oz. ASW, 38.61 mm. **Obv:** National shield on world map **Rev:** Mohandas Gandhi and Equatorial Guinea

| Date | Mintage | VF20 | XF40 | MS60 | MS63 | MS65 |
|---|---|---|---|---|---|---|
| 2011 | Est. 10000 | PF65 60.00 | | | | |

**KM# 445 10 DINERS**
30.00 g., 0.999 Silver 0.9636 oz. ASW, 30 mm. **Obv:** National shield on world map **Rev:** Mother Teresa in color

| Date | Mintage | VF20 | XF40 | MS60 | MS63 | MS65 |
|---|---|---|---|---|---|---|
| 2011 | Est. 10000 | PF65 60.00 | | | | |

**KM# 339 10 DINERS**
31.11 g., 0.999 Silver 0.999 oz. ASW, 30x45 mm. **Subject:** Seven Virtures by Pierodel and Antonio Pollaiulo **Obv:** National arms and value **Rev:** Caritas in color **Shape:** Vertical

| Date | Mintage | VF20 | XF40 | MS60 | MS63 | MS65 |
|---|---|---|---|---|---|---|
| 2012 | 4,000 | PF65 120 | | | | |

**KM# 340 10 DINERS**
31.11 g., 0.999 Silver 0.999 oz. ASW, 30x45 mm. **Subject:** Seven Virtures by Pierodel and Antonio Pollaiulo **Obv:** National arms and value **Rev:** Temperantia in color **Shape:** Vertical

| Date | Mintage | VF20 | XF40 | MS60 | MS63 | MS65 |
|---|---|---|---|---|---|---|
| 2012 | 4,000 | PF65 120 | | | | |

**KM# 341 10 DINERS**
31.11 g., 0.999 Silver 0.999 oz. ASW, 30x45 mm. **Subject:** Seven Virtures by Pierodel and Antonio Pollaiulo **Obv:** National arms and value **Rev:** Fides in color **Shape:** Vertical

| Date | Mintage | VF20 | XF40 | MS60 | MS63 | MS65 |
|---|---|---|---|---|---|---|
| 2012 | 4,000 | PF65 120 | | | | |

**KM# 342 10 DINERS**
31.11 g., 0.999 Silver 0.999 oz. ASW, 30x45 mm. **Subject:** Seven Virtures by Pierodel and Antonio Pollaiulo **Obv:** National arms and value **Rev:** Fortitudo in color **Shape:** Vertical

| Date | Mintage | VF20 | XF40 | MS60 | MS63 | MS65 |
|---|---|---|---|---|---|---|
| 2012 | 4,000 | PF65 120 | | | | |

**KM# 343 10 DINERS**
31.11 g., 0.999 Silver 0.999 oz. ASW, 30x45 mm. **Subject:** Seven Virtures by Pierodel and Antonio Pollaiulo **Obv:** National arms and value **Rev:** Iustitia in color **Shape:** Vertical

| Date | Mintage | VF20 | XF40 | MS60 | MS63 | MS65 |
|---|---|---|---|---|---|---|
| 2012 | 4,000 | PF65 120 | | | | |

**KM# 344 10 DINERS**
31.11 g., 0.999 Silver 0.999 oz. ASW, 30x45 mm. **Subject:** Seven Virtures by Pierodel and Antonio Pollaiulo **Obv:** National arms and value **Rev:** Prudentia in color **Shape:** Vertical

| Date | Mintage | VF20 | XF40 | MS60 | MS63 | MS65 |
|---|---|---|---|---|---|---|
| 2012 | 4,000 | PF65 120 | | | | |

**KM# 345 10 DINERS**
31.11 g., 0.999 Silver 0.999 oz. ASW, 30x45 mm. **Subject:** Seven Virtures by Pierodel and Antonio Pollaiulo **Obv:** Naitonal arms and value **Rev:** Spes in color **Shape:** Vertical

| Date | Mintage | VF20 | XF40 | MS60 | MS63 | MS65 |
|---|---|---|---|---|---|---|
| 2012 | 4,000 | PF65 120 | | | | |

**KM# 471 10 DINERS**
31.11 g., 0.999 Silver 0.999 oz. ASW, 30x45 mm. **Rev:** Aphrodite gilt

| Date | Mintage | VF20 | XF40 | MS60 | MS63 | MS65 |
|---|---|---|---|---|---|---|
| 2012 | Est. 3000 | PF65 75.00 | | | | |

**KM# 472 10 DINERS**
31.11 g., 0.999 Silver 0.999 oz. ASW, 30x45 mm. **Rev:** Venus gilt

| Date | Mintage | VF20 | XF40 | MS60 | MS63 | MS65 |
|---|---|---|---|---|---|---|
| 2012 | Est. 3000 | PF65 75.00 | | | | |

**KM# 473 10 DINERS**
31.11 g., 0.999 Silver 0.999 oz. ASW, 30x45 mm. **Rev:** Guanyin gilt

| Date | Mintage | VF20 | XF40 | MS60 | MS63 | MS65 |
|---|---|---|---|---|---|---|
| 2012 | Est. 3000 | PF65 75.00 | | | | |

**KM# 474 10 DINERS**
31.11 g., 0.999 Silver 0.999 oz. ASW, 30x45 mm. **Rev:** Benten gilt

| Date | Mintage | VF20 | XF40 | MS60 | MS63 | MS65 |
|---|---|---|---|---|---|---|
| 2012 | Est. 3000 | PF65 75.00 | | | | |

**KM# 475 10 DINERS**
31.11 g., 0.999 Silver 0.999 oz. ASW, 30x45 mm. **Rev:** Freedom gilt

| Date | Mintage | VF20 | XF40 | MS60 | MS63 | MS65 |
|---|---|---|---|---|---|---|
| 2012 | Est. 3000 | PF65 75.00 | | | | |

**KM# 476 10 DINERS**
31.11 g., 0.999 Silver 0.999 oz. ASW, 30x45 mm. **Rev:** Xochiquetzal gilt

| Date | Mintage | VF20 | XF40 | MS60 | MS63 | MS65 |
|---|---|---|---|---|---|---|
| 2012 | Est. 3000 | PF65 75.00 | | | | |

**KM# 477 10 DINERS**
31.11 g., 0.999 Silver 0.999 oz. ASW, 30x45 mm. **Rev:** Hathor gilt

| Date | Mintage | VF20 | XF40 | MS60 | MS63 | MS65 |
|---|---|---|---|---|---|---|
| 2012 | Est. 3000 | PF65 75.00 | | | | |

**KM# 478 10 DINERS**
28.28 g., 0.925 Silver 0.841 oz. ASW, 28x40 mm. **Rev:** Moses and Mt. Sinai

| Date | Mintage | VF20 | XF40 | MS60 | MS63 | MS65 |
|---|---|---|---|---|---|---|
| 2012 | Est. 2000 | **PF65** 75.00 | | | | |

**KM# 479 10 DINERS**
28.28 g., 0.925 Silver 0.841 oz. ASW, 28x40 mm. **Rev:** Baptism in the Jordan

| Date | Mintage | VF20 | XF40 | MS60 | MS63 | MS65 |
|---|---|---|---|---|---|---|
| 2012 | Est. 2000 | **PF65** 75.00 | | | | |

**KM# 506 10 DINERS**
31.105 Silver-Bronze .999, 40 mm. **Rev:** Golden eagle in flight in color **Shape:** Country shape

| Date | Mintage | VF20 | XF40 | MS60 | MS63 | MS65 |
|---|---|---|---|---|---|---|
| 2013 | Est. 3000 | **PF65** 75.00 | | | | |

**KM# 507 10 DINERS**
31.11 g., 0.999 Silver 0.999 oz. ASW, 40 mm. **Rev:** Animal in color **Shape:** Country shape

| Date | Mintage | VF20 | XF40 | MS60 | MS63 | MS65 |
|---|---|---|---|---|---|---|
| 2013 | Est. 3000 | **PF65** 75.00 | | | | |

**KM# 508 10 DINERS**
31.11 g., 0.999 Silver 0.999 oz. ASW, 40 mm. **Rev:** Alpine marmot in color **Shape:** Country shape

| Date | Mintage | VF20 | XF40 | MS60 | MS63 | MS65 |
|---|---|---|---|---|---|---|
| 2013 | Est. 3000 | **PF65** 75.00 | | | | |

**KM# 509 10 DINERS**
31.11 g., 0.999 Silver 0.999 oz. ASW, 40 mm. **Rev:** Animal in color **Shape:** Country shape

| Date | Mintage | VF20 | XF40 | MS60 | MS63 | MS65 |
|---|---|---|---|---|---|---|
| 2013 | Est. 3000 | **PF65** 75.00 | | | | |

**KM# 510 10 DINERS**
31.11 g., 0.999 Silver 0.999 oz. ASW, 40 mm. **Rev:** Squirrel in color **Shape:** Country shape

| Date | Mintage | VF20 | XF40 | MS60 | MS63 | MS65 |
|---|---|---|---|---|---|---|
| 2013 | Est. 3000 | **PF65** 75.00 | | | | |

**KM# 327 15 DINERS**
Silver **Subject:** Leonardo daVinci painting **Rev:** Madonna **Shape:** Vertical rectangle

| Date | Mintage | VF20 | XF40 | MS60 | MS63 | MS65 |
|---|---|---|---|---|---|---|
| 2011 | — | **PF65** 150 | | | | |

**KM# 328 15 DINERS**
Silver **Subject:** Botticelli painting **Shape:** Vertical rectangle

| Date | Mintage | VF20 | XF40 | MS60 | MS63 | MS65 |
|---|---|---|---|---|---|---|
| 2011 | — | **PF65** 125 | | | | |

**KM# 346 15 DINERS**
50.00 g., 0.999 Silver 1.6059 oz. ASW **Subject:** Painting by Lucas Cranche **Rev:** Madonna and Child in color

| Date | Mintage | VF20 | XF40 | MS60 | MS63 | MS65 |
|---|---|---|---|---|---|---|
| 2012 | — | **PF65** 200 | | | | |

**KM# 470 15 DINERS**
50.00 g., 0.999 Silver 1.6059 oz. ASW, 40x60 mm. **Subject:** Raffaello Sanzio painting **Rev:** Madonna and Child with two angels in color

| Date | Mintage | VF20 | XF40 | MS60 | MS63 | MS65 |
|---|---|---|---|---|---|---|
| 2012 | Est. 3000 | **PF65** 100 | | | | |

**KM# 489 15 DINERS**
50.00 g., 0.999 Silver 1.6059 oz. ASW, 40x60 mm. **Rev:** Madonna and child with two angels

| Date | Mintage | VF20 | XF40 | MS60 | MS63 | MS65 |
|---|---|---|---|---|---|---|
| 2013 | Est. 3000 | **PF65** 100 | | | | |

**KM# 490 15 DINERS**
50.00 g., 0.999 Silver 1.6059 oz. ASW, 40x60 mm. **Rev:** Madonna and Child under fir

| Date | Mintage | VF20 | XF40 | MS60 | MS63 | MS65 |
|---|---|---|---|---|---|---|
| 2013 | Est. 3000 | **PF65** 100 | | | | |

**KM# 174 25 DINERS**
12.44 g., 0.999 Gold 0.3996 oz. AGW, 26 mm. **Subject:** Christmas **Obv:** National arms **Rev:** Nativity scene **Edge:** Reeded

| Date | Mintage | VF20 | XF40 | MS60 | MS63 | MS65 |
|---|---|---|---|---|---|---|
| 2001 | 3,000 | **PF63** 700 | **PF65** 725 | | | |

**KM# 184 25 DINERS**
10.00 g., 0.9999 Gold 0.3215 oz. AGW, 26 mm. **Subject:** Christmas **Obv:** National arms **Rev:** Standing Christ child **Edge:** Reeded

| Date | Mintage | VF20 | XF40 | MS60 | MS63 | MS65 |
|---|---|---|---|---|---|---|
| 2002 | 2,000 | **PF63** 600 | **PF65** 625 | | | |

**KM# 185 25 DINERS**
7.78 g., 0.999 Gold 0.2498 oz. AGW, 26 mm. **Subject:** Christmas **Obv:** National arms **Rev:** Madonna-like mother and child **Edge:** Reeded

| Date | Mintage | VF20 | XF40 | MS60 | MS63 | MS65 |
|---|---|---|---|---|---|---|
| 2003 | 3,000 | **PF63** 450 | **PF65** 475 | | | |

**KM# 197 25 DINERS**
8.00 g., 0.999 Gold 0.2569 oz. AGW, 26 mm. **Subject:** Christmas **Obv:** National arms **Rev:** Nativity scene **Edge:** Reeded

| Date | Mintage | VF20 | XF40 | MS60 | MS63 | MS65 |
|---|---|---|---|---|---|---|
| 2004 | 5,000 | **PF63** 450 | **PF65** 475 | | | |

**KM# 216 25 DINERS**
6.00 g., 0.9999 Gold 0.1929 oz. AGW, 26 mm. **Obv:** National arms **Rev:** St. Joseph holding infant Jesus **Edge:** Reeded

| Date | Mintage | VF20 | XF40 | MS60 | MS63 | MS65 |
|---|---|---|---|---|---|---|
| 2005 | 9,999 | **PF63** 365 | **PF65** 385 | | | |

**KM# 305 25 DINERS**
6.00 g., 0.999 Gold 0.1927 oz. AGW, 26 mm. **Subject:** Christmas - the Holy Family **Obv:** National Arms **Rev:** St. Joseph, Mary and Jesus

| Date | Mintage | VF20 | XF40 | MS60 | MS63 | MS65 |
|---|---|---|---|---|---|---|
| 2006 | 5,000 | **PF63** 350 | **PF65** 400 | | | |

**KM# 314 25 DINERS**
6.00 g., 0.999 Gold 0.1927 oz. AGW, 26 mm. **Subject:** Christmas **Obv:** National Arms **Rev:** Angels playing musical instruments

| Date | Mintage | VF20 | XF40 | MS60 | MS63 | MS65 |
|---|---|---|---|---|---|---|
| 2007 | 2,000 | **PF63** 525 | **PF65** 575 | | | |

**KM# 274 25 DINERS**
6.00 g., 0.999 Gold 0.1927 oz. AGW, 26 mm. **Subject:** Constitution

| Date | Mintage | VF20 | XF40 | MS60 | MS63 | MS65 |
|---|---|---|---|---|---|---|
| 2008 | 2,000 | **PF63** 400 | **PF65** 425 | | | |

**KM# 275 25 DINERS**
6.00 g., 0.999 Gold 0.1927 oz. AGW, 26 mm. **Subject:** Three Kings **Rev:** Magi following star

| Date | Mintage | VF20 | XF40 | MS60 | MS63 | MS65 |
|---|---|---|---|---|---|---|
| 2008 | 2,000 | **PF63** 375 | **PF65** 400 | | | |

**KM# 279 25 DINERS**
6.00 g., 0.999 Gold 0.1927 oz. AGW, 26 mm. **Obv:** Shield **Rev:** Madonna and child, star of Bethlehem in backgorund **Edge:** Reeded

| Date | Mintage | VF20 | XF40 | MS60 | MS63 | MS65 |
|---|---|---|---|---|---|---|
| 2009 | 1,200 | PF63 375 | PF65 400 | | | |

**KM# 288 25 DINERS**
6.00 g., 0.999 Gold 0.1927 oz. AGW, 26 mm. **Subject:** Christmas **Obv:** Shield **Rev:** Archangel Gabriel telling the good news to Mary

| Date | Mintage | VF20 | XF40 | MS60 | MS63 | MS65 |
|---|---|---|---|---|---|---|
| 2010 | 1,200 | PF63 375 | PF65 400 | | | |

**KM# 330 25 DINERS**
6.00 g., 0.999 Gold 0.1927 oz. AGW, 26 mm. **Obv:** National arms **Rev:** Holy family

| Date | Mintage | VF20 | XF40 | MS60 | MS63 | MS65 |
|---|---|---|---|---|---|---|
| 2011 | — | PF63 400 | PF65 425 | | | |

**KM# 186 50 DINERS**
159.50 g., 0.999 Bi-Metallic 5.1229 oz. .999 Silver 155.5g coin with .999 Gold 4g, 20x50mm insert, 65 mm. **Subject:** 10th Anniversary of Constitution **Obv:** National arms **Rev:** Seated allegorical woman holding scrolled constitution **Edge:** Reeded **Note:** Illustration reduced.

| Date | Mintage | VF20 | XF40 | MS60 | MS63 | MS65 |
|---|---|---|---|---|---|---|
| 2003 | 3,000 | — | — | — | 325 | 375 |

**KM# 512 50 DINERS**
15.55 g., 0.999 Gold 0.4994 oz. AGW, 25 mm. **Obv:** National shield **Rev:** Eagle

| Date | Mintage | VF20 | XF40 | MS60 | MS63 | MS65 |
|---|---|---|---|---|---|---|
| 2013 | — | — | — | — | — | 681 |

**KM# 347 100 DINERS**
1000.00 g., 0.999 Silver 32.1186 oz. ASW, 166x240 mm. **Subject:** Painting by Raffaello **Rev:** Madonna **Shape:** Vertical

| Date | Mintage | VF20 | XF40 | MS60 | MS63 | MS65 |
|---|---|---|---|---|---|---|
| 2012 | — | PF65 1,300 | | | | |

**KM# 491 100 DINERS**
62.20 g., 0.999 Silver 1.9978 oz. ASW, 52.5x50 mm. **Subject:** Trevi Fountain, 250th Anniversary **Rev:** Angel

| Date | Mintage | VF20 | XF40 | MS60 | MS63 | MS65 |
|---|---|---|---|---|---|---|
| 2013 | Est. 250 | PF65 100 | | | | |

**KM# 492 100 DINERS**
62.20 g., 0.999 Silver 1.9978 oz. ASW, 52.5x50 mm. **Subject:** Trevi Fountain, 250th Anniversary **Rev:** Papal Arms of Clement XII

| Date | Mintage | VF20 | XF40 | MS60 | MS63 | MS65 |
|---|---|---|---|---|---|---|
| 2013 | Est. 250 | PF65 100 | | | | |

**KM# 493 100 DINERS**
62.20 g., 0.999 Silver 1.9978 oz. ASW, 52.5x50 mm. **Subject:** Trevi Fountain, 250th Anniversary **Rev:** Angel

| Date | Mintage | VF20 | XF40 | MS60 | MS63 | MS65 |
|---|---|---|---|---|---|---|
| 2013 | Est. 250 | PF65 100 | | | | |

**KM# 494 100 DINERS**
62.20 g., 0.999 Silver 1.9978 oz. ASW, 52.5x50 mm. **Subject:** Trevi Fountain, 250th Anniversary

| Date | Mintage | VF20 | XF40 | MS60 | MS63 | MS65 |
|---|---|---|---|---|---|---|
| 2013 | Est. 250 | PF65 100 | | | | |

**KM# 495 100 DINERS**
62.20 g., 0.999 Silver 1.9978 oz. ASW, 52.5x50 mm. **Subject:** Trevi Fountain, 250th Anniversary

| Date | Mintage | VF20 | XF40 | MS60 | MS63 | MS65 |
|---|---|---|---|---|---|---|
| 2013 | Est. 250 | PF65 100 | | | | |

**KM# 496 100 DINERS**
62.20 g., 0.999 Silver 1.9978 oz. ASW, 52.5x50 mm. **Subject:** Trevi Fountain, 250th Anniversary

| Date | Mintage | VF20 | XF40 | MS60 | MS63 | MS65 |
|---|---|---|---|---|---|---|
| 2013 | Est. 250 | PF65 100 | | | | |

**KM# 497 100 DINERS**
62.20 g., 0.999 Silver 1.9978 oz. ASW, 62.5x50 mm. **Subject:** Trevi Fountain, 250th Anniversary

| Date | Mintage | VF20 | XF40 | MS60 | MS63 | MS65 |
|---|---|---|---|---|---|---|
| 2013 | Est. 250 | PF65 100 | | | | |

**KM# 498 100 DINERS**
62.20 g., 0.999 Silver 1.9978 oz. ASW, 52.5x50 mm. **Subject:** Trevi Fountain, 250th Anniversary

| Date | Mintage | VF20 | XF40 | MS60 | MS63 | MS65 |
|---|---|---|---|---|---|---|
| 2013 | Est. 250 | PF65 100 | | | | |

**KM# 499 100 DINERS**
62.20 g., 0.999 Silver 1.9978 oz. ASW, 52.5x50 mm. **Subject:** Trevi Fountain, 250th Anniversary

| Date | Mintage | VF20 | XF40 | MS60 | MS63 | MS65 |
|---|---|---|---|---|---|---|
| 2013 | Est. 250 | PF65 100 | | | | |

**KM# 500 100 DINERS**
62.20 g., 0.999 Silver 1.9978 oz. ASW, 52.5x50 mm. **Subject:** Trevi Fountain, 250th Anniversary

| Date | Mintage | VF20 | XF40 | MS60 | MS63 | MS65 |
|---|---|---|---|---|---|---|
| 2013 | Est. 250 | PF65 100 | | | | |

**KM# 501 100 DINERS**
62.20 g., 0.999 Silver 1.9978 oz. ASW, 52.5x50 mm. **Subject:** Trevi Fountain, 250th Anniversary

| Date | Mintage | VF20 | XF40 | MS60 | MS63 | MS65 |
|---|---|---|---|---|---|---|
| 2013 | Est. 250 | PF65 100 | | | | |

**KM# 502 100 DINERS**
62.20 g., 0.999 Silver 1.9978 oz. ASW, 52.5x50 mm. **Subject:** Trevi Fountain, 250th Anniversary **Rev:** Inscription

| Date | Mintage | VF20 | XF40 | MS60 | MS63 | MS65 |
|---|---|---|---|---|---|---|
| 2013 | Est. 250 | PF65 100 | | | | |

**KM# 503 100 DINERS**
84.53 g., 0.999 Silver 2.715 oz. ASW, 52.5x68 mm. **Subject:** Trevi Fountain, 250th Anniversary **Rev:** Ocean statues

| Date | Mintage | VF20 | XF40 | MS60 | MS63 | MS65 |
|---|---|---|---|---|---|---|
| 2013 | Est. 250 | PF65 120 | | | | |

**KM# 504 100 DINERS**
84.53 g., 0.999 Silver 2.715 oz. ASW, 52.5x68 mm. **Subject:** Trevi Fountain, 250th Anniversary **Rev:** Oceans statue group

| Date | Mintage | VF20 | XF40 | MS60 | MS63 | MS65 |
|---|---|---|---|---|---|---|
| 2013 | Est. 250 | PF65 120 | | | | |

**KM# 505 100 DINERS**
84.53 g., 0.999 Silver 2.715 oz. ASW, 52.5x68 mm. **Subject:** Trevi Fountain, 250th Anniversary **Rev:** Oceans statue group

| Date | Mintage | VF20 | XF40 | MS60 | MS63 | MS65 |
|---|---|---|---|---|---|---|
| 2013 | Est. 250 | PF65 120 | | | | |

**KM# 513 100 DINERS**
31.11 g., 0.999 Gold 0.999 oz. AGW, 30 mm. **Obv:** National shield **Rev:** Eagle

| Date | Mintage | VF20 | XF40 | MS60 | MS63 | MS65 |
|---|---|---|---|---|---|---|
| 2013 | — | — | — | — | — | 1,324 |

**KM# 336 1000 DINERS**
1000.00 g., 0.999 Gold 32.1186 oz. AGW **Subject:** Pope John Paul II Beautification **Obv:** John Paul II with arms raised, National arms at right **Rev:** Profile at right, looking left

| Date | Mintage | VF20 | XF40 | MS60 | MS63 | MS65 |
|---|---|---|---|---|---|---|
| 2011 | — | PF65 45,000 | | | | |

## BULLION COINAGE

**KM# 268 DINER**
31.11 g., 0.999 Silver 0.999 oz. ASW, 38.6 mm. **Obv:** Eagle with wings outstretched **Rev:** National Arms **Edge:** Reeded

| Date | Mintage | VF20 | XF40 | MS60 | MS63 | MS65 |
|---|---|---|---|---|---|---|
| 2008 | — | — | — | — | — | 37.50 |
| 2009 | — | — | — | — | — | 37.50 |
| 2010 | — | — | — | — | — | 37.50 |
| 2011 | — | — | — | — | — | 37.50 |

**KM# 257 5 DINERS**
1.55 g., 0.999 Gold 0.0498 oz. AGW, 13.92 mm. **Obv:** Eagle with wings outstretched **Rev:** National Arms

| Date | Mintage | VF20 | XF40 | MS60 | MS63 | MS65 |
|---|---|---|---|---|---|---|
| 2009 | — | — | — | — | — | 100 |
| 2010 | — | — | — | — | — | 100 |

**KM# 258 10 DINERS**
3.11 g., 0.999 Gold 0.0999 oz. AGW, 16.46 mm. **Obv:** Eagle with wings outstretched **Rev:** National Arms

| Date | Mintage | VF20 | XF40 | MS60 | MS63 | MS65 |
|---|---|---|---|---|---|---|
| 2009 | — | — | — | — | — | 200 |
| 2010 | — | — | — | — | — | 200 |

**KM# 446 10 DINERS**
250.00 g., 0.999 Silver 8.0296 oz. ASW, 29x59x16 mm.

| Date | Mintage | VF20 | XF40 | MS60 | MS63 | MS65 |
|---|---|---|---|---|---|---|
| 2011 | — | — | — | — | — | 175 |

**KM# 451 10 DINERS**
3.11 g., 0.999 Gold 0.0999 oz. AGW, 18 mm. **Obv:** National shield **Rev:** Eagle in flight right

| Date | Mintage | VF20 | XF40 | MS60 | MS63 | MS65 |
|---|---|---|---|---|---|---|
| 2012 | Est. 2000 | PF65 225 | | | | |

**KM# 447 15 DINERS**
500.00 g., 0.999 Silver 16.0593 oz. ASW, 40x69x20 mm.

| Date | Mintage | VF20 | XF40 | MS60 | MS63 | MS65 |
|---|---|---|---|---|---|---|
| 2011 | — | PF65 350 | | | | |

**KM# 259 25 DINERS**
7.77 g., 0.999 Gold 0.2496 oz. AGW, 22.5 mm. **Obv:** Eagle with wings outstretched **Rev:** National Arms

| Date | Mintage | VF20 | XF40 | MS60 | MS63 | MS65 |
|---|---|---|---|---|---|---|
| 2009 | — | — | — | — | — | 450 |
| 2010 | — | — | — | — | — | 450 |

**KM# 511 25 DINERS**
7.78 g., 0.999 Gold 0.2499 oz. AGW, 20 mm. **Obv:** National shield **Rev:** Eagle

| Date | Mintage | VF20 | XF40 | MS60 | MS63 | MS65 |
|---|---|---|---|---|---|---|
| 2013 | — | — | — | — | — | 347 |

**KM# 448 30 DINERS**
1000.00 g., Silver, 40x90x26 mm.

| Date | Mintage | VF20 | XF40 | MS60 | MS63 | MS65 |
|---|---|---|---|---|---|---|
| 2011 | — | — | — | — | — | 500 |

**KM# 260 50 DINERS**
15.55 g., 0.999 Gold 0.4994 oz. AGW, 26 mm. **Obv:** Eagle with wings outstretched **Rev:** National Arms

| Date | Mintage | VF20 | XF40 | MS60 | MS63 | MS65 |
|---|---|---|---|---|---|---|
| 2009 | — | — | — | — | — | 875 |
| 2010 | — | — | — | — | — | 875 |

**KM# 254 50 DINERS**
1000.00 g., 0.999 Silver 32.1186 oz. ASW, 100 mm. **Obv:** Eagle with wings outstretched **Rev:** National Arms

| Date | Mintage | VF20 | XF40 | MS60 | MS63 | MS65 |
|---|---|---|---|---|---|---|
| 2010 | — | — | — | — | — | 1,200 |

**KM# 298 100 DINERS**
31.10 g., 0.999 Gold 0.999 oz. AGW, 35 mm. **Obv:** Eagle with open wings **Rev:** Details of National Arms **Edge:** Reeded

| Date | Mintage | VF20 | XF40 | MS60 | MS63 | MS65 |
|---|---|---|---|---|---|---|
| 2006 | 1,500 | — | — | — | — | 2,000 |

**KM# 261 100 DINERS**
31.11 g., 0.999 Gold 0.999 oz. AGW, 33 mm. **Obv:** Eagle with wings outstretched **Rev:** National Arms

| Date | Mintage | VF20 | XF40 | MS60 | MS63 | MS65 |
|---|---|---|---|---|---|---|
| 2009 | — | — | — | — | — | 1,750 |
| 2010 | — | — | — | — | — | 1,750 |

**KM# 255 100 DINERS**
3110.50 g., 0.999 Silver 99.9048 oz. ASW, 120 mm. **Obv:** Eagle with wings outstretched **Rev:** National Arms **Note:** 29mm thick.

| Date | Mintage | VF20 | XF40 | MS60 | MS63 | MS65 |
|---|---|---|---|---|---|---|
| 2010 | — | — | — | — | — | 5,000 |

**KM# 449 100 DINERS**
5000.00 g., 0.999 Silver 160.5929 oz. ASW, 75x165x51 mm.

| Date | Mintage | VF20 | XF40 | MS60 | MS63 | MS65 |
|---|---|---|---|---|---|---|
| 2011 | — | — | — | — | — | 3,000 |

**KM# 450 100 DINERS**
15000.00 g., 0.999 Silver 481.7786 oz. ASW, 100x235x75 mm.

| Date | Mintage | VF20 | XF40 | MS60 | MS63 | MS65 |
|---|---|---|---|---|---|---|
| 2011 | — | — | — | — | — | 5,000 |

**KM# 256 200 DINERS**
6221.00 g., 0.999 Silver 199.8096 oz. ASW, 140 mm. **Obv:** Eagle with wings outstretched **Rev:** National Arms **Note:** 42mm thick

| Date | Mintage | VF20 | XF40 | MS60 | MS63 | MS65 |
|---|---|---|---|---|---|---|
| 2010 | — | — | — | — | — | 10,000 |

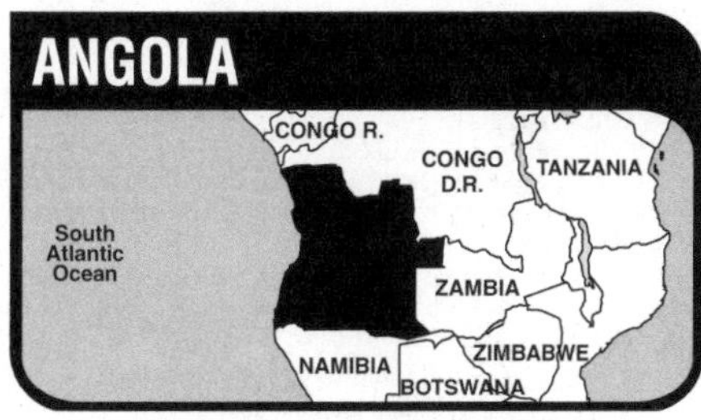


# PEOPLES REPUBLIC

## REFORM COINAGE

1999 -

**KM# 107 50 CENTIMOS**
Copper-Nickel, 20.6 mm. **Obv:** BNA logo within textile pattern border **Rev:** Large value within textile pattern border

| Date | Mintage | VF20 | XF40 | MS60 | MS63 | MS65 |
|---|---|---|---|---|---|---|
| 2012 | — | — | — | 1.00 | 1.50 | 1.75 |

**KM# 105 KWANZA**
23.00 g., Bi-Metallic Silver center in Gold ring, 35 mm. **Obv:** Large value **Rev:** Central Bank building

| Date | Mintage | VF20 | XF40 | MS60 | MS63 | MS65 |
|---|---|---|---|---|---|---|
| 2006 | 2,500 | PF65 100 | | | | |

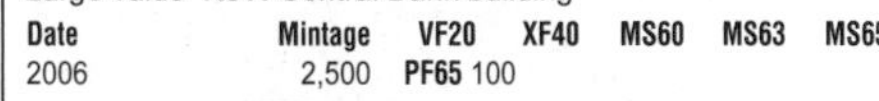

**KM# 108 KWANZA**
Nickel-Brass, 22.1 mm. **Obv:** BNA logo within textile border **Rev:** Value within textile border

| Date | Mintage | VF20 | XF40 | MS60 | MS63 | MS65 |
|---|---|---|---|---|---|---|
| 2012 | — | — | — | 1.50 | 1.75 | 2.00 |

**KM# 109 5 KWANZAS**
Bi-Metallic Copper-Nickel center in Nickel-Brass ring, 25 mm. **Obv:** National arms within textile border **Rev:** Large value within textile border

| Date | Mintage | VF20 | XF40 | MS60 | MS63 | MS65 |
|---|---|---|---|---|---|---|
| 2012 | — | — | — | 4.00 | 6.00 | 7.00 |

**KM# 110 10 KWANZAS**
Bi-Metallic Nickel-Brass center in Copper-Nickel ring, 27 mm. **Obv:** National arms within textile border **Rev:** Large value within textile border

| Date | Mintage | VF20 | XF40 | MS60 | MS63 | MS65 |
|---|---|---|---|---|---|---|
| 2012 | — | — | — | 5.00 | 7.00 | 8.00 |

**KM# 106 20 KWANZAS**
Silver ASW, 35 mm. **Subject:** Central Bank, 35th Anniversary **Obv:** National arms **Rev:** Linear logo

| Date | Mintage | VF20 | XF40 | MS60 | MS63 | MS65 |
|---|---|---|---|---|---|---|
| 2011 | — | PF65 75.00 | | | | |

The Argentine Republic, located in southern South America, has an area of 1,073,518 sq. mi. (3,761,274 sq. km.) and an estimated population of 37.03 million. Capital: Buenos Aires. Its varied topography ranges from the subtropical lowlands of the north to the towering Andean Mountains in the west and the wind-swept Patagonian steppe in the south. The rolling, fertile pampas of central Argentina are ideal for agriculture and grazing, and support most of the republic's population. Meatpacking, flour milling, textiles, sugar refining and dairy products are the principal industries. Oil is found in Patagonia, but most mineral requirements must be imported.

# REPUBLIC

## REFORM COINAGE

1992

100 Centavos = 1 Peso

**KM# 109 5 CENTAVOS**
2.02 g., Aluminum-Bronze, 17.2 mm. **Obv:** Radiant sunface **Rev:** Large value, date below **Edge:** Reeded **Note:** Prev. KM#84.

| Date | Mintage | VF20 | XF40 | MS60 | MS63 | MS65 |
|---|---|---|---|---|---|---|
| 2004 | 30,000,000 | — | — | — | 0.45 | 0.60 |
| 2005 | 76,000,000 | — | — | — | 0.45 | 0.60 |

**KM# 109b 5 CENTAVOS**

2.00 g., Brass Plated Steel, 17.2 mm. **Obv:** Radiant Sunface **Rev:** Large value, date below **Edge:** Plain

| Date | Mintage | VF20 | XF40 | MS60 | MS63 | MS65 |
|---|---|---|---|---|---|---|
| 2006 | 23,800,000 | — | — | — | 0.45 | 0.60 |
| 2007 | 183,000,000 | — | — | — | 0.45 | 0.60 |
| 2008 | 114,000,000 | — | — | — | 0.45 | 0.60 |
| 2009 | — | — | — | — | 0.45 | 0.60 |
| 2010 | — | — | — | — | 0.45 | 0.60 |
| 2011 | — | — | — | — | 0.45 | 0.60 |

**KM# 107 10 CENTAVOS**

2.25 g., Aluminum-Bronze, 18.2 mm. **Obv:** Argentine arms **Rev:** Value, date below **Edge:** Reeded **Note:** Prev. KM#82.

| Date | Mintage | VF20 | XF40 | MS60 | MS63 | MS65 |
|---|---|---|---|---|---|---|
| 2004 | 190,000,000 | — | — | — | 0.65 | 0.85 |
| 2005 | 114,400,000 | — | — | — | 0.65 | 0.85 |

**KM# 107a 10 CENTAVOS**

2.20 g., Brass Plated Steel, 18.2 mm. **Obv:** Argentine arms **Rev:** Large value, date below **Edge:** Plain

| Date | Mintage | VF20 | XF40 | MS60 | MS63 | MS65 |
|---|---|---|---|---|---|---|
| 2006 | 99,600,000 | — | — | — | 0.65 | 0.85 |
| 2007 | 204,000,000 | — | — | — | 0.65 | 0.85 |
| 2008 | 317,000,000 | — | — | — | 0.65 | 0.85 |
| 2009 | — | — | — | — | 0.65 | 0.85 |
| 2010 | — | — | — | — | 0.65 | 0.85 |
| 2011 | — | — | — | — | 0.65 | 0.85 |

**KM# 110.1 25 CENTAVOS**

5.40 g., Aluminum-Bronze, 24.2 mm. **Obv:** Buenos Aires City Hall, fine lettering **Rev:** Large value, date below **Edge:** Reeded **Note:** Prev. KM#85.1.

| Date | Mintage | VF20 | XF40 | MS60 | MS63 | MS65 |
|---|---|---|---|---|---|---|
| 2009 | — | — | — | — | 0.50 | 1.00 |
| 2010 | — | — | — | — | 0.50 | 1.00 |

**KM# 110a 25 CENTAVOS**

6.10 g., Copper-Nickel, 24.2 mm. **Obv:** Buenos Aires City Hall, bold lettering **Rev:** Large value, date below **Edge:** Reeded **Note:** Prev. KM#85a.

| Date | Mintage | VF20 | XF40 | MS60 | MS63 | MS65 |
|---|---|---|---|---|---|---|
| 2009 | — | — | — | — | 0.50 | 1.00 |

**KM# 111.1 50 CENTAVOS**

5.80 g., Aluminum-Bronze, 25.2 mm. **Obv:** Tucuman's house where the independence was signed; fine lettering **Rev:** Large value, date below **Edge:** Reeded **Note:** Prev. KM#86.1.

| Date | Mintage | VF20 | XF40 | MS60 | MS63 | MS65 |
|---|---|---|---|---|---|---|
| 2009 | — | — | — | — | 1.00 | 1.50 |
| 2010 | — | — | — | — | 1.00 | 1.50 |

**KM# 111.2 50 CENTAVOS**

5.80 g., Aluminum-Bronze, 25.2 mm. **Obv:** Tucuman's House where the independence was signed; bold lettering **Rev:** Large value, date below **Edge:** Reeded **Note:** Prev. KM#86.2.

| Date | Mintage | VF20 | XF40 | MS60 | MS63 | MS65 |
|---|---|---|---|---|---|---|
| 2009 | — | — | — | — | 1.00 | 1.50 |

**KM# 112.1 PESO**

6.35 g., Bi-Metallic Aluminum-Bronze center in Copper-Nickel ring, 23 mm. **Obv:** Argentine arms in circle **Rev:** Design of first Argentine coin in center **Edge:** Plain **Note:** Prev. KM#87.1.

| Date | Mintage | VF20 | XF40 | MS60 | MS63 | MS65 |
|---|---|---|---|---|---|---|
| 2006 | 30,000,000 | — | — | 0.50 | 1.20 | 1.60 |
| 2007 | 33,000,000 | — | — | 0.50 | 1.20 | 1.60 |
| 2008 | 89,600,000 | — | — | 0.50 | 1.20 | 1.60 |
| 2009 D | — | — | — | 0.50 | 1.20 | 1.60 |
| 2010 E | — | — | — | 0.50 | 1.20 | 1.60 |

**KM# 132.1 PESO**

6.35 g., Bi-Metallic Aluninum-Bronze center in Copper-Nickel ring, 23 mm. **Subject:** General Urquiza **Obv:** Stylized portrait facing **Rev:** Urquiza's house at San Jose and denomination **Edge:** Reeded

| Date | Mintage | VF20 | XF40 | MS60 | MS63 | MS65 |
|---|---|---|---|---|---|---|
| 2001 | 995,000 | — | — | — | 3.50 | 4.50 |

**KM# 132.2 PESO**

6.35 g., Bi-Metallic Aluminum-Bronze center in Copper-Nickel ring, 23 mm. **Subject:** General Urquiza **Obv:** Stylized portrait facing **Rev:** Urquiza's house at San Jose and denomination **Edge:** Plain

| Date | Mintage | VF20 | XF40 | MS60 | MS63 | MS65 |
|---|---|---|---|---|---|---|
| 2001 | 5,000 | — | — | — | 6.00 | 7.00 |

**KM# 141 PESO**

25.00 g., 0.900 Silver 0.7234 oz. ASW, 37 mm. **Obv:** Maria Eva Duarte de Peron **Rev:** EVITA" audience **Edge:** Reeded

| Date | Mintage | VF20 | XF40 | MS60 | MS63 | MS65 |
|---|---|---|---|---|---|---|
| ND (2004) | 5,000 | PF65 65.00 | | | | |

**KM# 140 PESO**

25.00 g., 0.900 Silver 0.7234 oz. ASW, 37 mm. **Subject:** 70th Anniversary of Central Bank **Obv:** Bank building **Rev:** Liberty head in wreath **Edge:** Reeded

| Date | Mintage | VF20 | XF40 | MS60 | MS63 | MS65 |
|---|---|---|---|---|---|---|
| 2005 | 2,000 | PF65 70.00 | | | | |

**KM# 155 PESO**

25.00 g., 0.900 Silver 0.7234 oz. ASW, 37 mm. **Subject:** Jorge Luis Borges **Obv:** Stylized bust facing **Rev:** Man walking at street corner

| Date | Mintage | VF20 | XF40 | MS60 | MS63 | MS65 |
|---|---|---|---|---|---|---|
| 2006 A | — | — | — | — | — | 42.50 |

**KM# 153 PESO**

25.00 g., 0.900 Silver 0.7234 oz. ASW, 37 mm. **Subject:** 25th Anniversary Malvinas Islands Occupation - Heroes **Obv:** Soldier's bust facing **Obv. Legend:** REPUBLICA ARGENTINA -1982 - 2007 - LA NACIÓN A SUS HÉROES **Rev:** Outlined map of islands **Rev. Legend:** MALVINAS ARGENTINAS **Rev. Inscription:** 2 DE APRIL / 1982 **Edge:** Reeded

| Date | Mintage | VF20 | XF40 | MS60 | MS63 | MS65 |
|---|---|---|---|---|---|---|
| 2007 | 3,000 | PF65 75.00 | | | | |

**KM# 156 PESO**

6.35 g., Bi-Metallic Aluminum-Bronze center in Copper-Nickel ring, 23 mm. **Subject:** Bicentennial - El Palmar **Obv:** Stylized radiant sun **Rev:** Palm trees

| Date | Mintage | VF20 | XF40 | MS60 | MS63 | MS65 |
|---|---|---|---|---|---|---|
| 2010 | — | — | — | — | 1.20 | 1.60 |

**KM# 157 PESO**

6.35 g., Bi-Metallic Aluminum-Bronze center in Copper-Nickel ring, 23 mm. **Subject:** Bicentennial - Aconcagua **Obv:** Stylized radiant run **Rev:** Mountains

| Date | Mintage | VF20 | XF40 | MS60 | MS63 | MS65 |
|---|---|---|---|---|---|---|
| 2010 | — | — | — | — | 1.20 | 1.60 |

**KM# 158 PESO**
6.35 g., Bi-Metallic Aluminum-Bronze center in Copper-Nickel ring, 23 mm. **Subject:** Bicentennial - Mar del Plata **Obv:** Stylized radiant sun **Rev:** Elephant seal and fishing boat

| Date | Mintage | VF20 | XF40 | MS60 | MS63 | MS65 |
|---|---|---|---|---|---|---|
| 2010 | — | — | — | — | 1.20 | 1.60 |

**KM# 159 PESO**
6.35 g., Bi-Metallic Aluminum-Bronze center in Copper-Nickel ring, 23 mm. **Subject:** Bicentennial - Pucara de Tilcara **Obv:** Stylized radiant sun **Rev:** Cactus and mountains

| Date | Mintage | VF20 | XF40 | MS60 | MS63 | MS65 |
|---|---|---|---|---|---|---|
| 2010 | — | — | — | — | 1.20 | 1.60 |

**KM# 160 PESO**
6.35 g., Bi-Metallic Aluminum-Bronze center in Copper-Nickel ring, 23 mm. **Subject:** Bicentennial - Glaciar Perito Moreno **Obv:** Stylized radiant sun **Rev:** Glaciar ice bridge and sea

| Date | Mintage | VF20 | XF40 | MS60 | MS63 | MS65 |
|---|---|---|---|---|---|---|
| 2010 | — | — | — | — | 1.20 | 1.60 |

**KM# 164 PESO**
25.00 g., 0.900 Silver 0.7234 oz. ASW, 37 mm. **Subject:** Revolution anniversary - Aconcagua **Rev:** Mountains

| Date | Mintage | VF20 | XF40 | MS60 | MS63 | MS65 |
|---|---|---|---|---|---|---|
| 2010 | 1,000 | PF65 75.00 | | | | |

**KM# 135.1 2 PESOS**
10.40 g., Copper-Nickel, 30 mm. **Subject:** Eva Peron **Obv:** Head left **Rev:** Stylized crowd scene, value **Rev. Inscription:** EVITA **Edge:** Reeded

| Date | Mintage | VF20 | XF40 | MS60 | MS63 | MS65 |
|---|---|---|---|---|---|---|
| 2002 | 1,995,000 | — | — | 0.85 | 1.85 | 2.50 |

**KM# 135.2 2 PESOS**
10.40 g., Copper-Nickel, 30 mm. **Subject:** Eva Peron **Obv:** Head left **Rev:** Stylized crowd scene, value **Rev. Inscription:** EVITA **Edge:** Plain

| Date | Mintage | VF20 | XF40 | MS60 | MS63 | MS65 |
|---|---|---|---|---|---|---|
| 2002 | 5,000 | — | — | — | 5.00 | 7.00 |

**KM# 161.1 2 PESOS**
10.47 g., Copper-Nickel, 30.35 mm. **Subject:** Declaration of Human Rights **Obv:** Legend **Rev:** Female's scarf **Edge:** Reeded

| Date | Mintage | VF20 | XF40 | MS60 | MS63 | MS65 |
|---|---|---|---|---|---|---|
| 2006 | — | — | — | — | 1.85 | 2.50 |

**KM# 161.2 2 PESOS**
10.40 g., Copper-Nickel, 30.35 mm. **Subject:** Declaration of Human Rights **Edge:** Plain

| Date | Mintage | VF20 | XF40 | MS60 | MS63 | MS65 |
|---|---|---|---|---|---|---|
| 2006 Sets only | — | — | — | — | — | 9.00 |

**KM# 144.1 2 PESOS**
10.40 g., Copper-Nickel, 30 mm. **Subject:** Malvinas Islands War, 25th Anniversary **Obv:** Soldier's bust facing **Obv. Legend:** REPUBLICA ARGENTINA - 1982 - 2007 - LA NACIÓN A SUS HÉROES **Rev:** Outlined map of islands **Rev. Legend:** MALVINAS ARGENTINAS **Rev. Inscription:** 2 DE APRIL / 1982 **Edge:** Reeded

| Date | Mintage | VF20 | XF40 | MS60 | MS63 | MS65 |
|---|---|---|---|---|---|---|
| 2007 | 1,995,000 | — | — | 0.85 | 1.85 | 2.50 |

**KM# 144.2 2 PESOS**
10.40 g., Copper-Nickel, 30 mm. **Subject:** Malvinas Islands War, 25th Anniversary **Obv:** Soldier's bust facing **Obv. Legend:** REPUBLICA ARGENTINA - 1982 - 2007 - LA NACIÓN A SUS HÉROES **Rev:** Outlined map of islands **Rev. Legend:** MALVINAS ARGENTINAS **Rev. Inscription:** 2 DE APRIL / 1982 **Edge:** Plain

| Date | Mintage | VF20 | XF40 | MS60 | MS63 | MS65 |
|---|---|---|---|---|---|---|
| 2007 | 5,000 | — | — | — | — | 8.00 |

**KM# 145.1 2 PESOS**
Copper-Nickel, 30.35 mm. **Subject:** 100th Anniversary First Oil Well **Obv:** Oil well **Obv. Legend:** REPÚBLICA ARGENTINA - DESCUBRIMIENTO DEL PETRÓLEO **Rev:** Modern pump **Rev. Inscription:** CHUBUT **Edge:** Reeded

| Date | Mintage | VF20 | XF40 | MS60 | MS63 | MS65 |
|---|---|---|---|---|---|---|
| 2007 | 995,000 | — | — | — | 6.00 | 7.50 |

**KM# 145.2 2 PESOS**
10.40 g., Copper-Nickel, 30.35 mm. **Subject:** 100th Anniversary First Oil Well **Obv:** Oil well **Rev:** Modern pump **Edge:** Plain

| Date | Mintage | VF20 | XF40 | MS60 | MS63 | MS65 |
|---|---|---|---|---|---|---|
| 2007 Sets only | — | — | — | — | — | 9.00 |

**KM# 162.1 2 PESOS**
10.47 g., Copper-Nickel, 30.35 mm. **Subject:** Central Bank, 75th Anniversary **Obv:** Bank's main doors **Rev:** Head at right, facing left **Edge:** Reeded

| Date | Mintage | VF20 | XF40 | MS60 | MS63 | MS65 |
|---|---|---|---|---|---|---|
| 2010 | — | — | — | — | 1.85 | 2.50 |

**KM# 162.2 2 PESOS**
10.40 g., Copper-Nickel, 30.35 mm. **Subject:** Central Bank, 75th Anniversary **Obv:** Bank's main doors **Rev:** Head at right facing left **Edge:** Plain

| Date | Mintage | VF20 | XF40 | MS60 | MS63 | MS65 |
|---|---|---|---|---|---|---|
| 2010 Sets only | — | — | — | — | — | 9.00 |

**KM# 165 2 PESOS**
7.20 g., Bi-Metallic Copper-Nickel center in Aluminum-Bronze ring, 24.5 mm. **Subject:** 1810 Revolution, 200th Anniversary **Obv:** Sunburst at center of wreath **Rev:** Value at center of wreath **Edge:** Segmented reeding

| Date | Mintage | VF20 | XF40 | MS60 | MS63 | MS65 |
|---|---|---|---|---|---|---|
| 2010 | 100,000,000 | — | — | — | 3.00 | 5.00 |
| 2011 | — | — | — | — | 3.00 | 5.00 |

**KM# 133 5 PESOS**
8.06 g., 0.900 Gold 0.2333 oz. AGW, 22 mm. **Subject:** Gral. Justo Jose de Urquiza **Obv:** Stylized portrait facing **Rev:** Urquiza's house at San Jose and denomination **Edge:** Reeded

| Date | Mintage | VF20 | XF40 | MS60 | MS63 | MS65 |
|---|---|---|---|---|---|---|
| 2001 | 1,000 | PF63 425 | PF65 450 | | | |

**KM# 149 5 PESOS**
8.06 g., 0.900 Gold 0.2333 oz. AGW **Subject:** 100th Anniversary City of Comodoro Rivadavia

| Date | Mintage | VF20 | XF40 | MS60 | MS63 | MS65 |
|---|---|---|---|---|---|---|
| 2001 | 750 | PF63 450 | PF65 475 | | | |

**KM# 143 5 PESOS**
27.00 g., 0.925 Silver 0.803 oz. ASW, 40 mm. **Subject:** FIFA - XVIII World Championship Football - Germany 2006 **Obv:** Football at right on grass, chaff in background **Obv. Legend:** REPÚBLICA ARGENTINA **Rev:** Logo **Rev. Legend:** COPA MUNDIAL DE LA FIFA **Rev. Inscription:** ALEMANIA **Edge:** Reeded

| Date | Mintage | VF20 | XF40 | MS60 | MS63 | MS65 |
|---|---|---|---|---|---|---|
| 2003 | 50,000 | PF63 50.00 | PF65 55.00 | | | |

**KM# 142 5 PESOS**
8.06 g., 0.900 Gold 0.2333 oz. AGW, 22 mm. **Obv:** Maria Eva Duarte de Peron **Rev:** EVITA" and audience

| Date | Mintage | VF20 | XF40 | MS60 | MS63 | MS65 |
|---|---|---|---|---|---|---|
| ND (2004) | 1,000 | PF63 425 | PF65 450 | | | |

**KM# 146 5 PESOS**
27.00 g., 0.925 Silver 0.803 oz. ASW **Subject:** FIFA - XVIII World Football Championship - Germany 2006 **Obv. Legend:** REPÚBLICA ARGENTINA **Rev:** Logo **Edge:** Reeded

| Date | Mintage | VF20 | XF40 | MS60 | MS63 | MS65 |
|---|---|---|---|---|---|---|
| 2004 | 50,000 | PF63 50.00 | PF65 55.00 | | | |

KM# 150 5 PESOS
27.00 g., 0.925 Silver 0.803 oz. ASW **Subject:** FIFA - XVIII World Championship Football - Germany 2006 **Obv:** Forward player **Rev:** Logo

| Date | Mintage | VF20 | XF40 | MS60 | MS63 | MS65 |
|---|---|---|---|---|---|---|
| 2005 | — | PF63 60.00 | PF65 65.00 | | | |

KM# 154 5 PESOS
8.06 g., 0.900 Gold 0.2333 oz. AGW, 22 mm. **Subject:** 25th Anniversary Malvinas Islands Occupation - Heroes **Obv:** Soldier's bust facing **Obv. Legend:** REPUBLICA ARGENTINA - 1982 - 2007 - LA NACIÓN A SUS HÉROES **Rev:** Outlined map of islands **Rev. Legend:** MALVINAS ISLANDS **Rev. Inscription:** 2 DE APRIL / 1982 **Edge:** Reeded

| Date | Mintage | VF20 | XF40 | MS60 | MS63 | MS65 |
|---|---|---|---|---|---|---|
| 2007 | 1,000 | PF63 425 | PF65 450 | | | |

KM# 147 10 PESOS
6.75 g., 0.999 Gold 0.2168 oz. AGW **Subject:** FIFA - XVIII World Football Championship - Germany 2006 **Obv. Legend:** REPÚBLICA ARGENTINA **Edge:** Reeded

| Date | Mintage | VF20 | XF40 | MS60 | MS63 | MS65 |
|---|---|---|---|---|---|---|
| 2004 | 25,000 | PF63 375 | PF65 400 | | | |

KM# 151 10 PESOS
6.75 g., 0.999 Gold 0.2168 oz. AGW **Subject:** FIFA - XVIII World Championship Football - Germany 2006 **Obv:** Forward player **Rev:** Logo

| Date | Mintage | VF20 | XF40 | MS60 | MS63 | MS65 |
|---|---|---|---|---|---|---|
| 2005 | — | PF63 375 | PF65 400 | | | |

KM# 138 25 PESOS
27.00 g., 0.925 Silver 0.803 oz. ASW, 40 mm. **Subject:** IBERO-AMERICA Series **Obv:** Coats of arms **Rev:** Tall ship "Presidente Sarmiento **Edge:** Reeded

| Date | Mintage | VF20 | XF40 | MS60 | MS63 | MS65 |
|---|---|---|---|---|---|---|
| 2002 | — | PF63 60.00 | PF65 65.00 | | | |

KM# 139 25 PESOS
27.00 g., 0.925 Silver 0.803 oz. ASW, 40 mm. **Subject:** Ibero-America **Obv:** National arms in circle of arms **Rev:** Colon Theater building **Edge:** Reeded

| Date | Mintage | VF20 | XF40 | MS60 | MS63 | MS65 |
|---|---|---|---|---|---|---|
| 2005 | 15,500 | PF63 50.00 | PF65 55.00 | | | |

KM# 167 25 PESOS
27.00 g., 0.925 Silver 0.803 oz. ASW, 40 mm. **Obv:** Arms within other national arms **Rev:** Arm dunking basketball

| Date | Mintage | VF20 | XF40 | MS60 | MS63 | MS65 |
|---|---|---|---|---|---|---|
| 2007 | — | PF63 70.00 | PF65 75.00 | | | |

KM# 166 25 PESOS
27.00 g., 0.925 Silver 0.803 oz. ASW, 40 mm. **Obv:** National arms within circle of other country's arms **Rev:** 1881 Argentinian coin design at center

| Date | Mintage | VF20 | XF40 | MS60 | MS63 | MS65 |
|---|---|---|---|---|---|---|
| 2010 | — | PF63 70.00 | PF65 75.00 | | | |

## PROOF SETS

| KM# | Date | Mintage | Identification | Issue Price | Mkt Val |
|---|---|---|---|---|---|
| PS6 | 2007 (2) | 300 | KM#153, 154 | 475 | 525 |

Rioja. Total area of the province is 35,649 sq. mi. and the main industries are centered around agriculture and include olive trees, grapes and wine production.

# ARMENIA

The Republic of Armenia, formerly Armenian S.S.R., is bordered to the north by Georgia, the east by Azerbaijan and the south and west by Turkey and Iran. It has an area of 11,506 sq. mi. (29,800 sq. km) and an estimated population of 3.66 million. Capital: Yerevan. Agriculture including cotton, vineyards and orchards, hydroelectricity, chemicals - primarily synthetic rubber and fertilizers, vast mineral deposits of copper, zinc and aluminum, and production of steel and paper are major industries.

Fighting between Christians in Armenia and Muslim forces of Azerbaijan escalated in 1992 and continued through early 1994. Each country claimed the Nagorno-Karabakh, an Armenian ethnic enclave, in Azerbaijan. A temporary cease-fire was announced in May 1994.

**MONETARY SYSTEM**
100 Luma = 1 Dram

**MINT NAME**
Revan, (Erevan, now Yerevan)

## REPUBLIC

### STANDARD COINAGE

KM# 112 10 DRAM
1.30 g., Aluminum, 20 mm. **Obv:** National arms **Rev:** Value **Edge:** Plain

| Date | Mintage | VF20 | XF40 | MS60 | MS63 | MS65 |
|---|---|---|---|---|---|---|
| 2004 | — | — | — | — | 1.00 | 1.50 |

KM# 93 20 DRAM
2.75 g., Copper Plated Steel, 20.5 mm. **Obv:** National arms **Rev:** Denomination **Edge:** Plain

| Date | Mintage | VF20 | XF40 | MS60 | MS63 | MS65 |
|---|---|---|---|---|---|---|
| 2003 | — | — | — | — | 1.00 | 1.50 |

KM# 94 50 DRAM
3.50 g., Brass Plated Steel, 21.5 mm. **Obv:** National arms **Rev:** Value **Edge:** Reeded

| Date | Mintage | VF20 | XF40 | MS60 | MS63 | MS65 |
|---|---|---|---|---|---|---|
| 2003 | — | — | — | — | 1.25 | 1.50 |

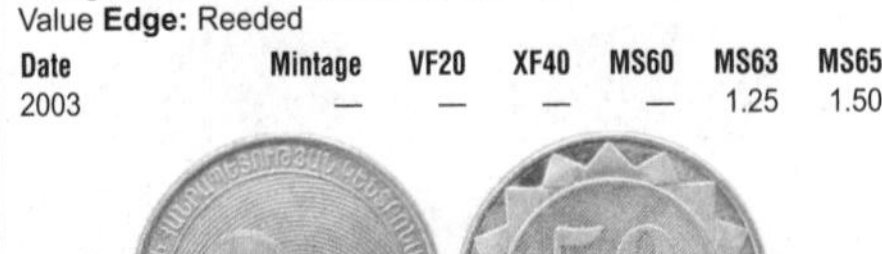

KM# 212 50 DRAM
3.50 g., Brass Plated Steel, 21.5 mm. **Subject:** Aragatsotn region **Edge:** Reeded

| Date | Mintage | VF20 | XF40 | MS60 | MS63 | MS65 |
|---|---|---|---|---|---|---|
| 2012 | 60,000 | — | — | — | 1.50 | 2.50 |

**KM# 213 50 DRAM**
3.50 g., Brass Plated Steel, 21.5 mm. **Subject:** Ararat region **Edge:** Reeded

| Date | Mintage | VF20 | XF40 | MS60 | MS63 | MS65 |
|---|---|---|---|---|---|---|
| 2012 | 60,000 | — | — | — | 1.50 | 2.50 |

**KM# 214 50 DRAM**
3.50 g., Brass Plated Steel, 21.5 mm. **Subject:** Armavir region **Edge:** Reeded

| Date | Mintage | VF20 | XF40 | MS60 | MS63 | MS65 |
|---|---|---|---|---|---|---|
| 2012 | — | — | — | — | 1.50 | 2.50 |

**KM# 215 50 DRAM**
3.50 g., Brass Plated Steel, 21.5 mm. **Subject:** Gegharkunik region **Edge:** Reeded

| Date | Mintage | VF20 | XF40 | MS60 | MS63 | MS65 |
|---|---|---|---|---|---|---|
| 2012 | 60,000 | — | — | — | 1.50 | 2.50 |

**KM# 216 50 DRAM**
3.50 g., Brass Plated Steel, 21.5 mm. **Subject:** Kotayk region **Edge:** Reeded

| Date | Mintage | VF20 | XF40 | MS60 | MS63 | MS65 |
|---|---|---|---|---|---|---|
| 2012 | 60,000 | — | — | — | 1.50 | 2.50 |

**KM# 217 50 DRAM**
3.50 g., Brass Plated Steel, 21.5 mm. **Subject:** Lori region **Edge:** Reeded

| Date | Mintage | VF20 | XF40 | MS60 | MS63 | MS65 |
|---|---|---|---|---|---|---|
| 2012 | 60,000 | — | — | — | 1.50 | 2.50 |

**KM# 218 50 DRAM**
3.50 g., Brass Plated Steel, 21.5 mm. **Subject:** Shirak region **Edge:** Reeded

| Date | Mintage | VF20 | XF40 | MS60 | MS63 | MS65 |
|---|---|---|---|---|---|---|
| 2012 | 60,000 | — | — | — | 1.50 | 2.50 |

**KM# 219 50 DRAM**
3.50 g., Brass Plated Steel, 21.5 mm. **Subject:** Syunik region **Edge:** Reeded

| Date | Mintage | VF20 | XF40 | MS60 | MS63 | MS65 |
|---|---|---|---|---|---|---|
| 2012 | 60,000 | — | — | — | 1.50 | 2.50 |

**KM# 220 50 DRAM**
3.50 g., Brass Plated Steel, 21.5 mm. **Subject:** Tavush region **Edge:** Reeded

| Date | Mintage | VF20 | XF40 | MS60 | MS63 | MS65 |
|---|---|---|---|---|---|---|
| 2012 | 60,000 | — | — | — | 1.50 | 2.50 |

**KM# 221 50 DRAM**
3.50 g., Brass Plated Steel, 21.5 mm. **Subject:** Vayots Dzor region **Edge:** Reeded

| Date | Mintage | VF20 | XF40 | MS60 | MS63 | MS65 |
|---|---|---|---|---|---|---|
| 2012 | 60,000 | — | — | — | 1.50 | 2.50 |

**KM# 222 50 DRAM**
3.50 g., Brass Plated Steel, 21.5 mm. **Subject:** Yerevan region **Edge:** Reeded

| Date | Mintage | VF20 | XF40 | MS60 | MS63 | MS65 |
|---|---|---|---|---|---|---|
| 2012 | 60,000 | — | — | — | 1.50 | 2.50 |

**KM# 86 100 DRAM**
31.10 g., 0.999 Silver 0.9989 oz. ASW, 38 mm. **Obv:** National arms **Rev:** Bust of General Garegin Nzhdeh facing at right **Edge:** Plain **Edge Lettering:** Serial number

| Date | Mintage | VF20 | XF40 | MS60 | MS63 | MS65 |
|---|---|---|---|---|---|---|
| 2001 | 170 | PF63 2,200 | PF65 2,500 | | | |

**KM# 86a 100 DRAM**
31.10 g., 0.999 Silver Gilt 0.9989 oz., 38 mm. **Obv:** National arms **Obv. Inscription:** Bust of General Garegin Nzhdeh facing at right **Edge:** Plain **Edge Lettering:** Serial number

| Date | Mintage | VF20 | XF40 | MS60 | MS63 | MS65 |
|---|---|---|---|---|---|---|
| 2001 | 30 | PF65 10,000 | | | | |

**KM# 87 100 DRAM**
31.04 g., 0.999 Silver 0.997 oz. ASW, 38 mm. **Subject:** Armenian Membership in the Council of Europe joined January 1, 2001 **Obv:** National arms **Rev:** Spiral design with star circle **Edge:** Plain **Edge Lettering:** Serial number

| Date | Mintage | VF20 | XF40 | MS60 | MS63 | MS65 |
|---|---|---|---|---|---|---|
| 2001 | 200 | PF63 450 | PF65 500 | | | |

**KM# 98 100 DRAM**
31.10 g., 0.925 Silver 0.9249 oz. ASW, 40 mm. **Obv:** National arms **Rev:** Aram Khachatryan, Birth Centennial **Edge:** Reeded

| Date | Mintage | VF20 | XF40 | MS60 | MS63 | MS65 |
|---|---|---|---|---|---|---|
| 2002 | 300 | — | — | — | — | 120 |

Note: Issued in blister pack only

**KM# 99 100 DRAM**
31.10 g., 0.925 Silver 0.9249 oz. ASW, 40 mm. **Obv:** The Book of Sadness **Rev:** Saint Grigor Narekatsi with book and quill millennium of his poem "The Book of Sadness **Edge:** Reeded

| Date | Mintage | VF20 | XF40 | MS60 | MS63 | MS65 |
|---|---|---|---|---|---|---|
| 2002 | 500 | PF63 90.00 | PF65 100 | | | |

**KM# 95 100 DRAM**
4.00 g., Nickel Plated Steel, 22.5 mm. **Obv:** National arms **Rev:** Value **Edge:** Reeded

| Date | Mintage | VF20 | XF40 | MS60 | MS63 | MS65 |
|---|---|---|---|---|---|---|
| 2003 | — | — | — | — | 1.50 | 2.00 |

**KM# 110 100 DRAM**
33.92 g., 0.925 Silver 1.0088 oz. ASW, 39 mm. **Subject:** 110th Anniversary of State Banking in Armenia and 10th Year of National Currency October 7 1893 - November 22, 1993 **Obv:** Building above value **Rev:** State Bank emblem **Edge:** Reeded

| Date | Mintage | VF20 | XF40 | MS60 | MS63 | MS65 |
|---|---|---|---|---|---|---|
| 2003 | 300 | PF63 185 | PF65 200 | | | |

**KM# 111 100 DRAM**
28.28 g., 0.925 Silver 0.841 oz. ASW, 38.6 mm. **Subject:** FIFA World Cup Soccer Games - Germany **Obv:** National arms **Rev:** Three soccer players

| Date | Mintage | VF20 | XF40 | MS60 | MS63 | MS65 |
|---|---|---|---|---|---|---|
| 2004 | 300 | PF63 130 | PF65 150 | | | |

**KM# 113 100 DRAM**
31.10 g., 0.999 Silver 0.9989 oz. ASW, 38 mm. **Subject:** Gandzasar Monastery **Obv:** Monastery **Rev:** Folk art crucifix and denomination

| Date | Mintage | VF20 | XF40 | MS60 | MS63 | MS65 |
|---|---|---|---|---|---|---|
| 2004 | 500 | PF63 90.00 | PF65 100 | | | |

**KM# 115 100 DRAM**
31.10 g., 0.925 Silver 0.9249 oz. ASW, 40 mm. **Subject:** Anania Shirakatsi 1400 Anniversary, Scientist **Obv:** Profile of Shirakatsi, deep in thought **Rev:** Planets and stars, denomination

| Date | Mintage | VF20 | XF40 | MS60 | MS63 | MS65 |
|---|---|---|---|---|---|---|
| 2005 | 500 | PF63 90.00 | PF65 100 | | | |

**KM# 123 100 DRAM**
31.10 g., 0.925 Silver 0.9249 oz. ASW, 40.00 mm. **Subject:** Creation of the Armenian alphabet **Obv:** National arms **Rev:** King Vramshapuh standing at left, alphabet at right

| Date | Mintage | VF20 | XF40 | MS60 | MS63 | MS65 |
|---|---|---|---|---|---|---|
| 2005 | 500 | PF63 130 | PF65 150 | | | |

**KM# 124 100 DRAM**
31.10 g., 0.925 Silver 0.9249 oz. ASW, 40.00 mm. **Subject:** Creation of the Armenian alphabet **Obv:** National arms **Rev:** Sahak Partev standing at left, alphabet at right

| Date | Mintage | VF20 | XF40 | MS60 | MS63 | MS65 |
|---|---|---|---|---|---|---|
| 2005 | 500 | PF63 130 | PF65 150 | | | |

**KM# 125 100 DRAM**
31.10 g., 0.925 Silver 0.9249 oz. ASW, 40.00 mm. **Subject:** 100th Anniversary - Birth of Artem Mikoyan - Inventor of MIG Jet **Obv:** Three jet airplanes **Rev:** Bust of Mikoyan 3/4 left

| Date | Mintage | VF20 | XF40 | MS60 | MS63 | MS65 |
|---|---|---|---|---|---|---|
| 2005 | 500 | PF63 125 | PF65 145 | | | |

**KM# 119 100 DRAM**
28.28 g., 0.925 Silver 0.841 oz. ASW, 38.61 mm. **Obv:** National arms **Rev:** Brown bear and two red lines **Edge:** Plain

| Date | Mintage | VF20 | XF40 | MS60 | MS63 | MS65 |
|---|---|---|---|---|---|---|
| 2006 | 3,000 | PF63 150 | PF65 165 | | | |

**KM# 120 100 DRAM**
28.28 g., 0.925 Silver 0.841 oz. ASW, 38.61 mm. **Obv:** National arms **Rev:** Long-eared Hedgehog and two red lines **Edge:** Plain

| Date | Mintage | VF20 | XF40 | MS60 | MS63 | MS65 |
|---|---|---|---|---|---|---|
| 2006 | 3,000 | PF63 150 | PF65 165 | | | |

**KM# 121 100 DRAM**
28.28 g., 0.925 Silver 0.841 oz. ASW, 38.6 mm. **Obv:** National arms, date and value **Rev:** Caucasian Forest Cat **Edge:** Plain

| Date | Mintage | VF20 | XF40 | MS60 | MS63 | MS65 |
|---|---|---|---|---|---|---|
| 2006 | 3,000 | PF63 90.00 | PF65 100 | | | |

**KM# 122 100 DRAM**
28.28 g., 0.925 Silver 0.841 oz. ASW, 38.6 mm. **Obv:** National arms, date and value **Rev:** Armenian Tortoise **Edge:** Plain

| Date | Mintage | VF20 | XF40 | MS60 | MS63 | MS65 |
|---|---|---|---|---|---|---|
| 2006 | 3,000 | PF63 110 | PF65 120 | | | |

**KM# 127 100 DRAM**
28.28 g., 0.925 Silver 0.841 oz. ASW, 38.61 mm. **Subject:** International Polar Year **Obv:** National arms **Obv. Legend:** REPUBLIC OF ARMENIA **Rev:** Bust of Fridtjof Nansen right at left, ship stuck in ice at lower right, multicolor emblem above

| Date | Mintage | VF20 | XF40 | MS60 | MS63 | MS65 |
|---|---|---|---|---|---|---|
| 2006 | 10,000 | PF63 40.00 | PF65 50.00 | | | |

**KM# 129 100 DRAM**
28.28 g., 0.925 Silver 0.841 oz. ASW **Subject:** Hovhannes Aivazovsky **Obv:** National arms at lower left, sailing ship listing at center right multicolor **Rev:** Bust of Aivazovsky 3/4 left at lower left, sailing ships at center right **Shape:** Rectangular, 40 x 28 mm

| Date | Mintage | VF20 | XF40 | MS60 | MS63 | MS65 |
|---|---|---|---|---|---|---|
| 2006 | 5,000 | PF63 350 | PF65 400 | | | |

**KM# 135 100 DRAM**
28.24 g., 0.925 Silver 0.8398 oz. ASW, 38.53 mm. **Subject:** Caucasian Leopard **Obv:** National arms **Obv. Legend:** REPUBLIC OF ARMENIA **Rev:** Leopard walking left **Edge:** Plain

| Date | Mintage | VF20 | XF40 | MS60 | MS63 | MS65 |
|---|---|---|---|---|---|---|
| 2007 | 3,000 | PF63 90.00 | PF65 100 | | | |

**KM# 136 100 DRAM**
28.24 g., 0.925 Silver 0.8398 oz. ASW, 38.5 mm. **Subject:** Northern Shoveler duck **Obv:** National arms **Obv. Legend:** REPUBLIC OF ARMENIA **Rev:** Duck standing left **Edge:** Plain

| Date | Mintage | VF20 | XF40 | MS60 | MS63 | MS65 |
|---|---|---|---|---|---|---|
| 2007 | 3,000 | PF63 75.00 | PF65 85.00 | | | |

**KM# 141 100 DRAM**
28.28 g., 0.925 Silver 0.841 oz. ASW Zircon crystal attached., 38.5 mm. **Series:** Signs of the Zodiac **Obv:** National arms within ring of signs of the Zodiac **Obv. Legend:** REPUBLIC OF ARMENIA **Rev:** Capricorn with jeweled star at left, multicolor **Edge:** Plain

| Date | Mintage | VF20 | XF40 | MS60 | MS63 | MS65 |
|---|---|---|---|---|---|---|
| 2007 | 12,000 | PF63 70.00 | PF65 80.00 | | | |

**KM# 153 100 DRAM**
28.28 g., 0.925 Silver 0.841 oz. ASW, 38.6 mm. **Obv:** National arms **Obv. Legend:** REPUBLIC OF ARMENIA **Rev:** Lake Sevan Salmon

| Date | Mintage | VF20 | XF40 | MS60 | MS63 | MS65 |
|---|---|---|---|---|---|---|
| 2007 | 3,000 | PF63 70.00 | PF65 80.00 | | | |

**KM# 154 100 DRAM**
28.28 g., 0.925 Silver 0.841 oz. ASW, 38.6 mm. **Obv:** National arms **Obv. Legend:** REPUBLIC OF ARMENIA **Rev:** Armenian viper

| Date | Mintage | VF20 | XF40 | MS60 | MS63 | MS65 |
|---|---|---|---|---|---|---|
| 2007 | 3,000 | PF63 75.00 | PF65 85.00 | | | |

**KM# 157 100 DRAM**
28.28 g., 0.925 Silver 0.841 oz. ASW, 38.6 mm. **Subject:** Aquarius

| Date | Mintage | VF20 | XF40 | MS60 | MS63 | MS65 |
|---|---|---|---|---|---|---|
| 2007 | — | PF63 70.00 | PF65 80.00 | | | |

**KM# 158 100 DRAM**
28.28 g., 0.925 Silver 0.841 oz. ASW, 38.6 mm. **Subject:** Pisces

| Date | Mintage | VF20 | XF40 | MS60 | MS63 | MS65 |
|---|---|---|---|---|---|---|
| 2007 | — | PF63 70.00 | PF65 80.00 | | | |

**KM# 155 100 DRAM**
28.28 g., 0.925 Silver 0.841 oz. ASW, 39 mm. **Obv:** National Arms **Rev:** Caucasian owl on branch, (Aegolius Funereus Caucasious) red arcs at top and bottom

| Date | Mintage | VF20 | XF40 | MS60 | MS63 | MS65 |
|---|---|---|---|---|---|---|
| 2008 | 3,000 | PF63 70.00 | PF65 80.00 | | | |

**KM# 159 100 DRAM**
28.28 g., 0.925 Silver 0.841 oz. ASW, 38.6 mm. **Subject:** Aries

| Date | Mintage | VF20 | XF40 | MS60 | MS63 | MS65 |
|---|---|---|---|---|---|---|
| 2008 | — | PF63 70.00 | PF65 80.00 | | | |

**KM# 160 100 DRAM**
28.28 g., 0.925 Silver 0.841 oz. ASW, 38.6 mm. **Subject:** Taurus

| Date | Mintage | VF20 | XF40 | MS60 | MS63 | MS65 |
|---|---|---|---|---|---|---|
| 2008 | — | PF63 70.00 | PF65 80.00 | | | |

**KM# 161 100 DRAM**
28.28 g., 0.925 Silver 0.841 oz. ASW, 38.6 mm. **Subject:** Gemini

| Date | Mintage | VF20 | XF40 | MS60 | MS63 | MS65 |
|---|---|---|---|---|---|---|
| 2008 | — | PF63 70.00 | PF65 80.00 | | | |

**KM# 162 100 DRAM**
28.28 g., 0.925 Silver 0.841 oz. ASW **Subject:** Cancer

| Date | Mintage | VF20 | XF40 | MS60 | MS63 | MS65 |
|---|---|---|---|---|---|---|
| 2008 | — | PF63 70.00 | PF65 80.00 | | | |

**KM# 163 100 DRAM**
28.28 g., 0.925 Silver 0.841 oz. ASW, 38.6 mm. **Subject:** Leo

| Date | Mintage | VF20 | XF40 | MS60 | MS63 | MS65 |
|---|---|---|---|---|---|---|
| 2008 | — | PF63 70.00 | PF65 80.00 | | | |

**KM# 164 100 DRAM**
28.28 g., 0.925 Silver 0.841 oz. ASW, 38.6 mm. **Subject:** Virgo

| Date | Mintage | VF20 | XF40 | MS60 | MS63 | MS65 |
|---|---|---|---|---|---|---|
| 2008 | — | PF63 70.00 | PF65 80.00 | | | |

**KM# 165 100 DRAM**
28.28 g., 0.925 Silver 0.841 oz. ASW, 38.6 mm. **Subject:** Libra

| Date | Mintage | VF20 | XF40 | MS60 | MS63 | MS65 |
|---|---|---|---|---|---|---|
| 2008 | — | PF63 70.00 | PF65 80.00 | | | |

**KM# 167 100 DRAM**
28.28 g., 0.925 Silver 0.841 oz. ASW, 38.6 mm. **Subject:** Bezoar goat

| Date | Mintage | VF20 | XF40 | MS60 | MS63 | MS65 |
|---|---|---|---|---|---|---|
| 2008 | — | PF63 70.00 | PF65 80.00 | | | |

**KM# 172 100 DRAM**
28.28 g., 0.925 Silver 0.841 oz. ASW, 38.6 mm. **Subject:** Scorpio

| Date | Mintage | VF20 | XF40 | MS60 | MS63 | MS65 |
|---|---|---|---|---|---|---|
| 2008 | — | PF63 70.00 | PF65 80.00 | | | |

**KM# 174 100 DRAM**
28.28 g., 0.925 Silver 0.841 oz. ASW, 38.6 mm. **Subject:** Sagittarius

| Date | Mintage | VF20 | XF40 | MS60 | MS63 | MS65 |
|---|---|---|---|---|---|---|
| 2008 | — | PF63 70.00 | PF65 80.00 | | | |

**KM# 177 100 DRAM**
28.28 g., 0.925 Silver 0.841 oz. ASW, 38.6 mm. **Subject:** Armenian Moufflon

| Date | Mintage | VF20 | XF40 | MS60 | MS63 | MS65 |
|---|---|---|---|---|---|---|
| 2008 | — | PF63 65.00 | PF65 75.00 | | | |

**KM# 178 100 DRAM**
28.28 g., 0.925 Silver 0.841 oz. ASW, 38.6 mm. **Subject:** Toad Agama

| Date | Mintage | VF20 | XF40 | MS60 | MS63 | MS65 |
|---|---|---|---|---|---|---|
| 2008 | — | PF63 65.00 | PF65 75.00 | | | |

**KM# 182 100 DRAM**
28.28 g., 0.925 Silver 0.841 oz. ASW, 38.6 mm. **Subject:** Pele

| Date | Mintage | VF20 | XF40 | MS60 | MS63 | MS65 |
|---|---|---|---|---|---|---|
| 2008 | — | PF63 50.00 | PF65 60.00 | | | |

**KM# 183 100 DRAM**
28.28 g., 0.925 Silver 0.841 oz. ASW, 38.6 mm. **Subject:** Eusebio

| Date | Mintage | VF20 | XF40 | MS60 | MS63 | MS65 |
|---|---|---|---|---|---|---|
| 2008 | — | PF63 50.00 | PF65 60.00 | | | |

**KM# 184 100 DRAM**
28.28 g., 0.925 Silver 0.841 oz. ASW, 38.6 mm. **Subject:** Lev Jashin

| Date | Mintage | VF20 | XF40 | MS60 | MS63 | MS65 |
|---|---|---|---|---|---|---|
| 2008 | — | PF63 50.00 | PF65 60.00 | | | |

**KM# 187 100 DRAM**
28.28 g., 0.925 Silver 0.841 oz. ASW, 38.6 mm. **Subject:** Franz Beckenbauer

| Date | Mintage | VF20 | XF40 | MS60 | MS63 | MS65 |
|---|---|---|---|---|---|---|
| 2008 | — | PF63 45.00 | PF65 55.00 | | | |

**KM# 156 100 DRAM**
28.28 g., 0.925 Silver 0.841 oz. ASW, 38.6 mm. **Subject:** Zbigniew Boniek **Rev:** Portrait facing, multicolor flag

| Date | Mintage | VF20 | XF40 | MS60 | MS63 | MS65 |
|---|---|---|---|---|---|---|
| 2009 | 50,000 | PF63 45.00 | PF65 55.00 | | | |

**KM# 260 100 DRAM**
28.28 g., 0.925 Silver 0.841 oz. ASW, 28 x 40 mm. **Subject:** Vardgez Sureniants

| Date | Mintage | VF20 | XF40 | MS60 | MS63 | MS65 |
|---|---|---|---|---|---|---|
| 2010 | Est. 500 | PF63 140 | PF65 150 | | | |

**KM# 271 100 DRAM**
28.28 g., 0.925 Silver 0.841 oz. ASW, 40x28 mm. **Subject:** Teodor Axentowicz

| Date | Mintage | VF20 | XF40 | MS60 | MS63 | MS65 |
|---|---|---|---|---|---|---|
| 2010 | Est. 4000 | PF63 50.00 | PF65 60.00 | | | |

**KM# 209 100 DRAM**
33.62 g., 0.925 Silver 0.9998 oz. ASW, 38.61 mm. **Obv:** Arms with lion supporters **Rev:** Michael Platini, soccer ball and flag in color

| Date | Mintage | VF20 | XF40 | MS60 | MS63 | MS65 |
|---|---|---|---|---|---|---|
| 2011 | — | PF63 60.00 | PF65 70.00 | | | |

**KM# 223 100 DRAM**
28.28 g., 0.925 Silver 0.841 oz. ASW, 28x40 mm. **Subject:** Sergei Parajanov **Obv:** Artist in studio, painting in color **Rev:** Self portrait **Shape:** Vertical rectangle

| Date | Mintage | VF20 | XF40 | MS60 | MS63 | MS65 |
|---|---|---|---|---|---|---|
| 2012 | Est. 5555 | PF65 60.00 | | | | |

**KM# 251 100 DRAM**
28.28 g., 0.925 Silver 0.841 oz. ASW, 28 x 40 mm. **Subject:** Stephan Aghajanian

| Date | Mintage | VF20 | XF40 | MS60 | MS63 | MS65 |
|---|---|---|---|---|---|---|
| 2013 | Est. 500 | PF63 90.00 | PF65 100 | | | |

**KM# 254 100 DRAM**
28.28 g., 0.925 Silver 0.841 oz. ASW, 28 x 40 mm. **Subject:** Ara Baqaryan

| Date | Mintage | VF20 | XF40 | MS60 | MS63 | MS65 |
|---|---|---|---|---|---|---|
| 2013 | Est. 500 | PF63 90.00 | PF65 100 | | | |

**KM# 96 200 DRAM**
4.50 g., Brass, 24 mm. **Obv:** National arms **Rev:** Value **Edge:** Reeded

| Date | Mintage | VF20 | XF40 | MS60 | MS63 | MS65 |
|---|---|---|---|---|---|---|
| 2003 | — | — | — | — | 3.00 | 4.00 |

**KM# 106 500 DRAM**
155.50 g., 0.925 Silver 4.6245 oz. ASW, 63 mm. **Subject:** 10th Anniversary of Independence **Obv:** National arms **Rev:** Tower with flag, logo at right 9-21-91

| Date | Mintage | VF20 | XF40 | MS60 | MS63 | MS65 |
|---|---|---|---|---|---|---|
| 2001 | 200 | PF63 375 | PF65 425 | | | |

**KM# 97 500 DRAM**
5.00 g., Bi-Metallic Copper-Nickel center in a Brass ring, 22 mm. **Obv:** National arms **Rev:** Value **Edge:** Segmented reeding

| Date | Mintage | VF20 | XF40 | MS60 | MS63 | MS65 |
|---|---|---|---|---|---|---|
| 2003 | — | — | — | — | 6.00 | 8.00 |
| 2004 | — | — | — | — | — | — |

Note: Requires confirmation.

**KM# 210 500 DRAM**
1.24 g., 0.999 Gold 0.0398 oz. AGW, 13.92 mm. **Obv:** National arms, value below **Rev:** Pomegranate

| Date | Mintage | VF20 | XF40 | MS60 | MS63 | MS65 |
|---|---|---|---|---|---|---|
| 2011 | — | PF63 130 | PF65 150 | | | |

**KM# 109 1000 DRAM**
15.55 g., 0.585 Gold 0.2925 oz. AGW, 26 mm. **Obv:** National arms on ancient coin design **Rev:** Tigran the Great ancient coin portrait

| Date | Mintage | VF20 | XF40 | MS60 | MS63 | MS65 |
|---|---|---|---|---|---|---|
| 2003 | 500 | — | — | — | — | 800 |

**KM# 128 1000 DRAM**
33.60 g., 0.925 Silver 0.9992 oz. ASW, 38 mm. **Subject:** 100th Anniversary Birth of Marshal Babajanian **Obv:** National arms **Rev:** Bust of Babajanian 3/4 right

| Date | Mintage | VF20 | XF40 | MS60 | MS63 | MS65 |
|---|---|---|---|---|---|---|
| 2006 | 500 | PF63 130 | PF65 150 | | | |

**KM# 133 1000 DRAM**
33.60 g., 0.925 Silver 0.9992 oz. ASW, 40 mm. **Subject:** Armenian grapes **Obv:** National arms **Rev:** Large bunch of grapes at left

| Date | Mintage | VF20 | XF40 | MS60 | MS63 | MS65 |
|---|---|---|---|---|---|---|
| 2007 | 5,000 | PF63 115 | PF65 125 | | | |

**KM# 169 1000 DRAM**
33.60 g., 0.925 Silver 0.9992 oz. ASW, 40 mm. **Subject:** Viktor Ambartsumian, 100th Anniversary of Birth **Edge:** Reeded

| Date | Mintage | VF20 | XF40 | MS60 | MS63 | MS65 |
|---|---|---|---|---|---|---|
| 2008 | 500 | PF63 120 | PF65 180 | | | |

**KM# 171 1000 DRAM**
33.60 g., 0.925 Silver 0.9992 oz. ASW, 40 mm. **Subject:** A. Spendiaryan Theater of Ballet and Opera, 75th Anniversary

| Date | Mintage | VF20 | XF40 | MS60 | MS63 | MS65 |
|---|---|---|---|---|---|---|
| 2008 | — | PF63 90.00 | PF65 100 | | | |

**KM# 192 1000 DRAM**
33.60 g., 0.925 Silver 0.9992 oz. ASW, 40 mm. **Subject:** Mkhitar Gosh - The Codex **Edge:** Reeded

| Date | Mintage | VF20 | XF40 | MS60 | MS63 | MS65 |
|---|---|---|---|---|---|---|
| 2009 | 500 | PF63 90.00 | PF65 100 | | | |

**KM# 193 1000 DRAM**
31.10 g., 0.999 Silver 0.9989 oz. ASW, 38 mm. **Subject:** Gladzor University, 750th Anniversary

| Date | Mintage | VF20 | XF40 | MS60 | MS63 | MS65 |
|---|---|---|---|---|---|---|
| 2009 | — | PF63 90.00 | PF65 100 | | | |

**KM# 259 1000 DRAM**
33.60 g., 0.925 Silver 0.9992 oz. ASW, 40 mm. **Subject:** Movses Khorenatsi

| Date | Mintage | VF20 | XF40 | MS60 | MS63 | MS65 |
|---|---|---|---|---|---|---|
| 2010 | Est. 500 | PF63 90.00 | PF65 100 | | | |

**KM# 262 1000 DRAM**
33.60 g., 0.925 Silver 0.9992 oz. ASW, 40 mm. **Subject:** Leonid Engibarov

| Date | Mintage | VF20 | XF40 | MS60 | MS63 | MS65 |
|---|---|---|---|---|---|---|
| 2010 | Est. 500 | PF63 100 | PF65 110 | | | |

**KM# 264 1000 DRAM**
33.60 g., 0.925 Silver 0.9992 oz. ASW, 40 mm. **Subject:** Leo

| Date | Mintage | VF20 | XF40 | MS60 | MS63 | MS65 |
|---|---|---|---|---|---|---|
| 2010 | Est. 500 | PF63 90.00 | PF65 100 | | | |

**KM# 266 1000 DRAM**
31.10 g., 0.999 Silver 0.9989 oz. ASW, 32 x 32 mm. **Series:** Gospel Scenes in Armenian Miniatures: Annunciation

| Date | Mintage | VF20 | XF40 | MS60 | MS63 | MS65 |
|---|---|---|---|---|---|---|
| 2010 | 6,000 | PF63 90.00 | PF65 100 | | | |

**KM# 267 1000 DRAM**
31.10 g., 0.999 Silver 0.9989 oz. ASW, 32 x 32 mm. **Series:** Gospel Scenes in Armenian Miniatures: Adoration of the Magi

| Date | Mintage | VF20 | XF40 | MS60 | MS63 | MS65 |
|---|---|---|---|---|---|---|
| 2010 | Est. 6000 | PF63 90.00 | PF65 100 | | | |

**KM# 268 1000 DRAM**
31.10 g., 0.999 Silver 0.9989 oz. ASW, 32 x 32 mm. **Subject:** Gospel Scenes in Armenian Miniatures: Entry into Jerusalem

| Date | Mintage | VF20 | XF40 | MS60 | MS63 | MS65 |
|---|---|---|---|---|---|---|
| 2010 | Est. 6000 | PF63 100 | PF65 110 | | | |

**KM# 269 1000 DRAM**
31.10 g., 0.999 Silver 0.9989 oz. ASW, 32 x 32 mm. **Subject:** Gospel Scenes in Armenian Miniatures: Ascension

| Date | Mintage | VF20 | XF40 | MS60 | MS63 | MS65 |
|---|---|---|---|---|---|---|
| 2010 | Est. 6000 | PF63 100 | PF65 110 | | | |

**KM# 270 1000 DRAM**
28.28 g., 0.925 Silver 0.841 oz. ASW, 38.61 mm. **Subject:** Jazz **Obv:** Band performing **Rev:** Montage of instruments

| Date | Mintage | VF20 | XF40 | MS60 | MS63 | MS65 |
|---|---|---|---|---|---|---|
| 2010 | Est. 10000 | PF63 65.00 | PF65 75.00 | | | |

**KM# 199 1000 DRAM**
33.60 g., 0.925 Silver 0.9992 oz. ASW, 40 mm. **Rev:** Poppy plant and flower in color

| Date | Mintage | VF20 | XF40 | MS60 | MS63 | MS65 |
|---|---|---|---|---|---|---|
| 2011 | — | PF63 65.00 | PF65 75.00 | | | |

**KM# 201 1000 DRAM**
28.28 g., 0.925 Silver 0.841 oz. ASW, 38.61 mm. **Obv:** Berries and flower in color **Rev:** Sorbus Hajastana in color

| Date | Mintage | VF20 | XF40 | MS60 | MS63 | MS65 |
|---|---|---|---|---|---|---|
| 2011 | 10,000 | PF63 65.00 | PF65 75.00 | | | |

**KM# 202 1000 DRAM**
28.28 g., 0.925 Silver 0.841 oz. ASW, 38.61 mm. **Obv:** Two crocus flowers in color **Rev:** Crocus flower open

| Date | Mintage | VF20 | XF40 | MS60 | MS63 | MS65 |
|---|---|---|---|---|---|---|
| 2011 | 10,000 | PF63 65.00 | PF65 75.00 | | | |

**KM# 203 1000 DRAM**
28.28 g., 0.925 Silver 0.841 oz. ASW, 38.61 mm. **Subject:** WuSu **Obv:** Shaolin Monastery and dragons **Rev:** Three sportsmen

| Date | Mintage | VF20 | XF40 | MS60 | MS63 | MS65 |
|---|---|---|---|---|---|---|
| 2011 | 5,000 | PF63 70.00 | PF65 80.00 | | | |

**KM# 204 1000 DRAM**
28.28 g., 0.925 Silver 0.841 oz. ASW, 38.61 mm. **Subject:** Judo **Obv:** Eishoji Tempole in Kamakura and lake reflection **Rev:** Two pair of Judo sportsmen, Mt. Fuji and cherry blossom

| Date | Mintage | VF20 | XF40 | MS60 | MS63 | MS65 |
|---|---|---|---|---|---|---|
| 2011 | 5,000 | PF63 70.00 | PF65 80.00 | | | |

**KM# 206 1000 DRAM**
33.60 g., 0.925 Silver 0.9992 oz. ASW, 40 mm. **Subject:** Treaty of Vienna, 200th Anniversary **Obv:** Two partial building façades **Rev:** Treaty with seal, building tower

| Date | Mintage | VF20 | XF40 | MS60 | MS63 | MS65 |
|---|---|---|---|---|---|---|
| 2011 | — | PF63 90.00 | PF65 100 | | | |

**KM# 207 1000 DRAM**
15.60 g., 0.585 Gold 0.2934 oz. AGW, 26 mm. **Subject:** Artashat, 2200th Anniversary of Founding **Obv:** Ancient coin at center, Tyche head right **Rev:** Ancient coin at center, Figure standing

| Date | Mintage | VF20 | XF40 | MS60 | MS63 | MS65 |
|---|---|---|---|---|---|---|
| 2011 Antique patina | 1,000 | — | — | — | — | 600 |

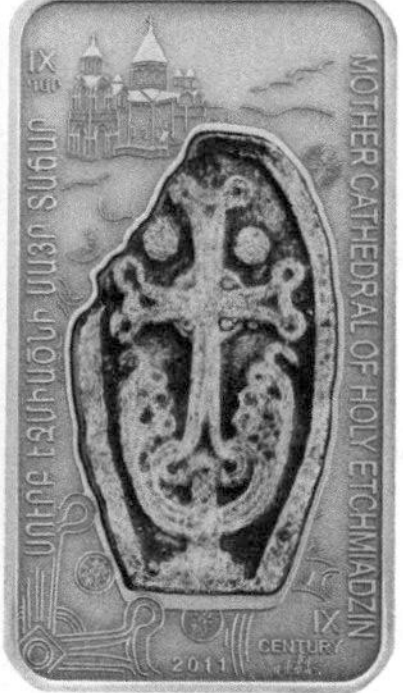


**KM# 208 1000 DRAM**
Silver, 27x47 mm. **Obv:** National arms, value below **Rev:** Historic fragment and church **Shape:** Vertical rectangle

| Date | Mintage | VF20 | XF40 | MS60 | MS63 | MS65 |
|---|---|---|---|---|---|---|
| 2011 Antique patina | — | — | — | — | — | 150 |

**KM# 265 1000 DRAM**
15.60 g., 0.585 Gold 0.2934 oz. AGW, 26 mm. **Subject:** Ani

| Date | Mintage | VF20 | XF40 | MS60 | MS63 | MS65 |
|---|---|---|---|---|---|---|
| 2011 Antique Patina | Est. 1000 | — | — | — | — | 700 |

**KM# 272 1000 DRAM**
28.28 g., 0.925 Silver 0.841 oz. ASW, 38.61 mm. **Subject:** The Art of Fighting

| Date | Mintage | VF20 | XF40 | MS60 | MS63 | MS65 |
|---|---|---|---|---|---|---|
| 2011 | Est. 5000 | **PF63** 75.00 | **PF65** 80.00 | | | |

**KM# 228 1000 DRAM**
33.60 g., 0.925 Silver 0.9992 oz. ASW, 40 mm. **Subject:** Army, 20th Anniversary **Rev:** Emblem of the Army and the 8-sided Order of the Motherland

| Date | Mintage | VF20 | XF40 | MS60 | MS63 | MS65 |
|---|---|---|---|---|---|---|
| 2012 | 500 | **PF65** 200 | | | | |

**KM# 249 1000 DRAM**
0.93 g., 0.925 Silver, 40 mm. **Subject:** Hovsep Orbeli

| Date | Mintage | VF20 | XF40 | MS60 | MS63 | MS65 |
|---|---|---|---|---|---|---|
| 2012 | — | **PF63** 90.00 | **PF65** 100 | | | |

**KM# 250 1000 DRAM**
33.60 g., 0.925 Silver 0.9992 oz. ASW, 40 mm. **Subject:** Armenian Book Printing

| Date | Mintage | VF20 | XF40 | MS60 | MS63 | MS65 |
|---|---|---|---|---|---|---|
| 2012 | Est. 500 | **PF63** 90.00 | **PF65** 100 | | | |

**KM# 255 1000 DRAM**
28.28 g., 0.925 Silver 0.841 oz. ASW, 38.61 mm. **Subject:** Art of Fighting: Karate

| Date | Mintage | VF20 | XF40 | MS60 | MS63 | MS65 |
|---|---|---|---|---|---|---|
| 2012 | Est. 5000 | **PF63** 70.00 | **PF65** 80.00 | | | |

**KM# 256 1000 DRAM**
31.10 g., 0.925 Silver 0.9249 oz. ASW, 38 mm. **Subject:** Anniversaries of the Treaty on Collective Security

| Date | Mintage | VF20 | XF40 | MS60 | MS63 | MS65 |
|---|---|---|---|---|---|---|
| 2012 | Est. 200 | **PF63** 90.00 | **PF65** 100 | | | |

**KM# 258 1000 DRAM**
Silver, 38.61 mm. **Rev:** Tree

| Date | Mintage | VF20 | XF40 | MS60 | MS63 | MS65 |
|---|---|---|---|---|---|---|
| 2012 | — | **PF63** 65.00 | **PF65** 75.00 | | | |

**KM# 277 1000 DRAM**
25.00 g., 0.925 Silver 0.7435 oz. ASW Partially colorized, 27 x 47 mm. **Subject:** Armenian Monasteries and Churches **Obv:** Noravank Monastery **Rev:** Coat of arms **Shape:** Rectangular

| Date | Mintage | VF20 | XF40 | MS60 | MS63 | MS65 |
|---|---|---|---|---|---|---|
| 2012 | Est. 2500 | **PF63** 90.00 | **PF65** 100 | | | |

**KM# 278 1000 DRAM**
25.00 g., 0.925 Silver 0.7435 oz. ASW Partially colorized, 27 x 47 mm. **Subject:** Armenian Monasteries and Churches **Obv:** Mother Cathedral of Holy Etchmiadzin **Shape:** Rectangular

| Date | Mintage | VF20 | XF40 | MS60 | MS63 | MS65 |
|---|---|---|---|---|---|---|
| 2012 | Est. 2500 | **PF63** 90.00 | **PF65** 100 | | | |

**KM# 279 1000 DRAM**
28.28 g., 0.925 Silver 0.841 oz. ASW Partially colorized, 38.61 mm. **Subject:** Art of Fighting **Obv:** Kokh **Rev:** Coat of arms

| Date | Mintage | VF20 | XF40 | MS60 | MS63 | MS65 |
|---|---|---|---|---|---|---|
| 2012 | Est. 5000 | **PF63** 90.00 | **PF65** 100 | | | |

**KM# 281 1000 DRAM**
25.00 g., 0.925 Silver 0.7435 oz. ASW, 27 x 47 mm. **Subject:** Armenian Monasteries and Churches **Obv:** Gndevank **Rev:** Coat of Arms **Shape:** Rectangular

| Date | Mintage | VF20 | XF40 | MS60 | MS63 | MS65 |
|---|---|---|---|---|---|---|
| 2012 | Est. 2500 | **PF63** 90.00 | **PF65** 100 | | | |

**KM# 253 1000 DRAM**
33.60 g., 0.925 Silver 0.9992 oz. ASW, 40 mm. **Subject:** Beniamin Margaryan

| Date | Mintage | VF20 | XF40 | MS60 | MS63 | MS65 |
|---|---|---|---|---|---|---|
| 2013 | Est. 500 | **PF63** 145 | **PF65** 200 | | | |

**KM# 257 1000 DRAM**
31.10 g., 0.999 Silver 0.9989 oz. ASW, 38 mm. **Subject:** 20th Anniversary of Armenian Dram (1933-2013)

| Date | Mintage | VF20 | XF40 | MS60 | MS63 | MS65 |
|---|---|---|---|---|---|---|
| 2013 | Est. 500 | **PF63** 145 | **PF65** 200 | | | |

**KM# 282 1000 DRAM**
33.60 g., 0.925 Silver 0.9992 oz. ASW, 40 mm. **Subject:** National Currency, 20th Anniversary **Obv:** National arms, 20 in color

| Date | Mintage | VF20 | XF40 | MS60 | MS63 | MS65 |
|---|---|---|---|---|---|---|
| 2013 | — | **PF63** 65.00 | **PF65** 75.00 | | | |

**KM# 134 1957 DRAM**
33.60 g., 0.925 Silver 0.9992 oz. ASW, 40 mm. **Subject:** 50th Anniversay of Matenadaran **Obv:** Small national arms at center surrounded by intricate pattern **Rev:** Building at left center

| Date | Mintage | VF20 | XF40 | MS60 | MS63 | MS65 |
|---|---|---|---|---|---|---|
| 2007 | 500 | **PF63** 125 | **PF65** 145 | | | |

**KM# 117 5000 DRAM**
31.10 g., 0.925 Silver 0.9249 oz. ASW, 38 mm. **Subject:** Armenian Armed Forces **Obv:** Order of the Combat Cross of the Second Degree and the Emblem of the Ministry of Defense of the Republic of Armenia **Rev:** Arms, date and denomination **Shape:** Octagonal

| Date | Mintage | VF20 | XF40 | MS60 | MS63 | MS65 |
|---|---|---|---|---|---|---|
| 2005 | 500 | **PF63** 130 | **PF65** 150 | | | |

**KM# 126 5000 DRAM**
168.10 g., 0.925 Silver 4.9992 oz. ASW, 63 mm. **Subject:** 15th Anniversary of Independence **Obv:** National arms **Rev:** Building at center left, multicolor emblem above, mountains in background

| Date | Mintage | VF20 | XF40 | MS60 | MS63 | MS65 |
|---|---|---|---|---|---|---|
| 2006 | 300 | **PF63** 350 | **PF65** 400 | | | |

**KM# 139 5000 DRAM**
4.30 g., 0.900 Gold 0.1244 oz. AGW, 18 mm. **Subject:** Haik Nahapet **Obv:** Small national arms at upper left, Orion constellation at right **Rev:** 3/4 length classical Archer right

| Date | Mintage | VF20 | XF40 | MS60 | MS63 | MS65 |
|---|---|---|---|---|---|---|
| 2007 | 3,000 | **PF63** 350 | **PF65** 400 | | | |

**KM# 179 5000 DRAM**
168.10 g., 0.925 Silver 4.9992 oz. ASW partially gold plated, 63 mm. **Subject:** National Currency, 15th Anniversary

| Date | Mintage | VF20 | XF40 | MS60 | MS63 | MS65 |
|---|---|---|---|---|---|---|
| 2008 | — | **PF63** 160 | **PF65** 190 | | | |

**KM# 195 5000 DRAM**
4.30 g., 0.900 Gold 0.1244 oz. AGW, 18 mm. **Subject:** St. Sargis the Commander

| Date | Mintage | VF20 | XF40 | MS60 | MS63 | MS65 |
|---|---|---|---|---|---|---|
| 2009 | — | **PF63** 350 | **PF65** 400 | | | |

**KM# 205 5000 DRAM**
168.10 g., 0.925 Silver 4.9992 oz. ASW, 63 mm. **Subject:** 20th Anniversary of the Republic **Obv:** National arms **Rev:** Two birds in flight, date in color

| Date | Mintage | VF20 | XF40 | MS60 | MS63 | MS65 |
|---|---|---|---|---|---|---|
| 2011 | — | **PF63** 325 | **PF65** 350 | | | |

**KM# 107 10000 DRAM**
8.60 g., 0.999 Gold 0.2762 oz. AGW, 22 mm. **Obv:** Mesrop Mashtots, creator of the Armenian alphabet **Rev:** Armenian alphabet

| Date | Mintage | VF20 | XF40 | MS60 | MS63 | MS65 |
|---|---|---|---|---|---|---|
| 2002 | 1,000 | **PF63** 750 | **PF65** 800 | | | |

**KM# 108 10000 DRAM**
8.60 g., 0.999 Gold 0.2762 oz. AGW, 22 mm. **Obv:** Building above value **Rev:** Aram Khachatryan left birth centennial

| Date | Mintage | VF20 | XF40 | MS60 | MS63 | MS65 |
|---|---|---|---|---|---|---|
| 2002 | 500 | PF63 750 | PF65 800 | | | |

**KM# 114 10000 DRAM**
8.60 g., 0.999 Gold 0.2762 oz. AGW, 22 mm. **Subject:** Arshile Gorky birth April 15, 1904 **Obv:** Bust of Gorky **Rev:** Denomination

| Date | Mintage | VF20 | XF40 | MS60 | MS63 | MS65 |
|---|---|---|---|---|---|---|
| 2004 | 1,000 | PF63 750 | PF65 800 | | | |

**KM# 116 10000 DRAM**
8.60 g., 0.999 Gold 0.2762 oz. AGW, 22 mm. **Subject:** Martiros Saryan 125th Anniversary of Birth **Obv:** Bust of Saryan **Rev:** Landscape, denomination

| Date | Mintage | VF20 | XF40 | MS60 | MS63 | MS65 |
|---|---|---|---|---|---|---|
| 2005 | 1,000 | PF63 750 | PF65 800 | | | |

**KM# 130 10000 DRAM**
8.60 g., 0.999 Gold 0.2762 oz. AGW, 22 mm. **Subject:** Komitas Vardapet **Obv:** Musical notations and score **Rev:** Bust of Vardapet 3/4 right

| Date | Mintage | VF20 | XF40 | MS60 | MS63 | MS65 |
|---|---|---|---|---|---|---|
| 2006 | 1,000 | PF63 750 | PF65 800 | | | |

**KM# 131 10000 DRAM**
8.60 g., 0.900 Gold 0.2488 oz. AGW, 22 mm. **Subject:** 37th Chess Olympiad **Obv:** Chess piece at right **Rev:** National arms within 6 chess pieces in circle

| Date | Mintage | VF20 | XF40 | MS60 | MS63 | MS65 |
|---|---|---|---|---|---|---|
| 2006 | 1,000 | PF63 750 | PF65 800 | | | |

**KM# 132 10000 DRAM**
8.60 g., 0.900 Gold 0.2488 oz. AGW, 22 mm. **Subject:** Hakob Gurjian **Obv:** Seated female sculpture **Rev:** Head 3/4 right

| Date | Mintage | VF20 | XF40 | MS60 | MS63 | MS65 |
|---|---|---|---|---|---|---|
| 2006 | 1,000 | PF63 750 | PF65 800 | | | |

**KM# 137 10000 DRAM**
8.60 g., 0.900 Gold 0.2488 oz. AGW, 22 mm. **Subject:** Jean Carzou **Obv:** National arms with stylized view of shopping bourse **Rev:** Bust of Carzou 3/4 right at laft center

| Date | Mintage | VF20 | XF40 | MS60 | MS63 | MS65 |
|---|---|---|---|---|---|---|
| 2007 | 1,000 | PF63 750 | PF65 800 | | | |

**KM# 138 10000 DRAM**
8.60 g., 0.900 Gold 0.2488 oz. AGW, 22 mm. **Subject:** 15th Anniversary of Armenian Army **Obv:** National arms **Rev:** Military badge

| Date | Mintage | VF20 | XF40 | MS60 | MS63 | MS65 |
|---|---|---|---|---|---|---|
| 2007 | 1,000 | PF63 750 | PF65 800 | | | |

**KM# 140 10000 DRAM**
8.60 g., 0.900 Gold 0.2488 oz. AGW, 22 mm. **Subject:** 15th Anniversary Liberation of Shushi **Obv:** Bird with wings outspread above two shields **Rev:** Swirl in background

| Date | Mintage | VF20 | XF40 | MS60 | MS63 | MS65 |
|---|---|---|---|---|---|---|
| 2007 | 1,000 | PF63 750 | PF65 800 | | | |

**KM# 166 10000 DRAM**
8.60 g., 0.900 Gold 0.2488 oz. AGW, 22 mm. **Subject:** Libra

| Date | Mintage | VF20 | XF40 | MS60 | MS63 | MS65 |
|---|---|---|---|---|---|---|
| 2008 | — | PF63 650 | PF65 700 | | | |

**KM# 168 10000 DRAM**
8.60 g., 0.900 Gold 0.2488 oz. AGW, 22 mm. **Subject:** Court, 10th Anniversary

| Date | Mintage | VF20 | XF40 | MS60 | MS63 | MS65 |
|---|---|---|---|---|---|---|
| 2008 | — | PF63 650 | PF65 700 | | | |

**KM# 170 10000 DRAM**
8.60 g., 0.900 Gold 0.2488 oz. AGW, 22 mm. **Subject:** William Saroyan, 100th Anniversary of Birth

| Date | Mintage | VF20 | XF40 | MS60 | MS63 | MS65 |
|---|---|---|---|---|---|---|
| 2008 | — | PF63 650 | PF65 700 | | | |

**KM# 173 10000 DRAM**
8.60 g., 0.900 Gold 0.2488 oz. AGW, 22 mm. **Subject:** Scorpio

| Date | Mintage | VF20 | XF40 | MS60 | MS63 | MS65 |
|---|---|---|---|---|---|---|
| 2008 | — | PF63 650 | PF65 700 | | | |

**KM# 175 10000 DRAM**
8.60 g., 0.900 Gold 0.2488 oz. AGW, 22 mm. **Subject:** Sagittarius

| Date | Mintage | VF20 | XF40 | MS60 | MS63 | MS65 |
|---|---|---|---|---|---|---|
| 2008 | — | PF63 650 | PF65 700 | | | |

**KM# 176 10000 DRAM**
8.60 g., 0.900 Gold 0.2488 oz. AGW, 22 mm. **Subject:** Capricorn

| Date | Mintage | VF20 | XF40 | MS60 | MS63 | MS65 |
|---|---|---|---|---|---|---|
| 2008 | — | PF63 650 | PF65 700 | | | |

**KM# 180 10000 DRAM**
8.60 g., 0.900 Gold 0.2488 oz. AGW, 22 mm. **Subject:** Aquarius

| Date | Mintage | VF20 | XF40 | MS60 | MS63 | MS65 |
|---|---|---|---|---|---|---|
| 2008 | — | PF63 650 | PF65 700 | | | |

**KM# 181 10000 DRAM**
8.60 g., 0.900 Gold 0.2488 oz. AGW, 22 mm. **Subject:** Pisces

| Date | Mintage | VF20 | XF40 | MS60 | MS63 | MS65 |
|---|---|---|---|---|---|---|
| 2008 | — | PF63 650 | PF65 700 | | | |

**KM# 185 10000 DRAM**
8.60 g., 0.900 Gold 0.2488 oz. AGW, 22 mm. **Subject:** Aries

| Date | Mintage | VF20 | XF40 | MS60 | MS63 | MS65 |
|---|---|---|---|---|---|---|
| 2008 | — | PF63 650 | PF65 700 | | | |

**KM# 186 10000 DRAM**
8.60 g., 0.900 Gold 0.2488 oz. AGW, 22 mm. **Subject:** Taurus

| Date | Mintage | VF20 | XF40 | MS60 | MS63 | MS65 |
|---|---|---|---|---|---|---|
| 2008 | — | PF63 650 | PF65 700 | | | |

**KM# 188 10000 DRAM**
8.60 g., 0.900 Gold 0.2488 oz. AGW, 22 mm. **Subject:** Gemini

| Date | Mintage | VF20 | XF40 | MS60 | MS63 | MS65 |
|---|---|---|---|---|---|---|
| 2008 | — | PF63 650 | PF65 700 | | | |

**KM# 189 10000 DRAM**
8.60 g., 0.900 Gold 0.2488 oz. AGW, 22 mm. **Subject:** Cancer

| Date | Mintage | VF20 | XF40 | MS60 | MS63 | MS65 |
|---|---|---|---|---|---|---|
| 2008 | — | PF63 650 | PF65 700 | | | |

**KM# 190 10000 DRAM**
8.60 g., 0.900 Gold 0.2488 oz. AGW, 22 mm. **Subject:** Leo

| Date | Mintage | VF20 | XF40 | MS60 | MS63 | MS65 |
|---|---|---|---|---|---|---|
| 2008 | — | PF63 650 | PF65 700 | | | |

**KM# 191 10000 DRAM**
8.60 g., 0.900 Gold 0.2488 oz. AGW, 22 mm. **Subject:** Virgo

| Date | Mintage | VF20 | XF40 | MS60 | MS63 | MS65 |
|---|---|---|---|---|---|---|
| 2009 | — | PF63 650 | PF65 700 | | | |

**KM# 194 10000 DRAM**
8.60 g., 0.900 Gold 0.2488 oz. AGW, 22 mm. **Subject:** Khachatour Aboryan, 200th Anniversary of Birth

| Date | Mintage | VF20 | XF40 | MS60 | MS63 | MS65 |
|---|---|---|---|---|---|---|
| 2009 | — | PF63 750 | PF65 800 | | | |

**KM# 261 10000 DRAM**
8.60 g., 0.900 Gold 0.2488 oz. AGW, 22 mm. **Subject:** Vahan Teryan

| Date | Mintage | VF20 | XF40 | MS60 | MS63 | MS65 |
|---|---|---|---|---|---|---|
| 2010 | Est. 1000 | PF63 750 | PF65 800 | | | |

**KM# 263 10000 DRAM**
8.60 g., 0.900 Gold 0.2488 oz. AGW, 22 mm. **Subject:** Raffi

| Date | Mintage | VF20 | XF40 | MS60 | MS63 | MS65 |
|---|---|---|---|---|---|---|
| 2010 | Est. 1000 | PF63 750 | PF65 800 | | | |

**KM# 200 10000 DRAM**
8.60 g., 0.900 Gold 0.2488 oz. AGW, 22 mm. **Subject:** Misaq Metsarents, poet, 125th Anniversary of Birth **Edge:** Reeded

| Date | Mintage | VF20 | XF40 | MS60 | MS63 | MS65 |
|---|---|---|---|---|---|---|
| 2011 | 1,000 | PF63 650 | PF65 700 | | | |

**KM# 211 10000 DRAM**
8.60 g., 0.900 Gold 0.2488 oz. AGW, 22 mm. **Subject:** Toros Roslin, 800th Anniversary **Edge:** Reeded

| Date | Mintage | VF20 | XF40 | MS60 | MS63 | MS65 |
|---|---|---|---|---|---|---|
| 2011 | 1,000 | PF63 650 | PF65 700 | | | |

**KM# 229 10000 DRAM**
8.60 g., 0.900 Gold 0.2488 oz. AGW, 20 mm. **Subject:** Army, 20th Anniversary **Rev:** Army emblem and Order of the Motherland

| Date | Mintage | VF20 | XF40 | MS60 | MS63 | MS65 |
|---|---|---|---|---|---|---|
| 2012 | 500 | PF65 750 | | | | |

**KM# 247 10000 DRAM**
8.60 g., 0.900 Gold 0.2488 oz. AGW, 22 mm. **Subject:** Sayat-Nova

| Date | Mintage | VF20 | XF40 | MS60 | MS63 | MS65 |
|---|---|---|---|---|---|---|
| 2012 | Est. 1000 | PF63 650 | PF65 700 | | | |

**KM# 248 10000 DRAM**
8.60 g., 0.900 Gold 0.2488 oz. AGW, 22 mm. **Subject:** 20th Anniversary of the Liberation of Shushi

| Date | Mintage | VF20 | XF40 | MS60 | MS63 | MS65 |
|---|---|---|---|---|---|---|
| 2012 | Est. 1000 | PF63 650 | PF65 700 | | | |

**KM# 280 10000 DRAM**
8.60 g., 0.900 Gold 0.2488 oz. AGW, 22 mm. **Subject:** 20th Anniversary of the Liberation of Sushi

| Date | Mintage | VF20 | XF40 | MS60 | MS63 | MS65 |
|---|---|---|---|---|---|---|
| 2012 | 500 | PF65 700 | | | | |

**KM# 252 10000 DRAM**
8.60 g., 0.900 Gold 0.2488 oz. AGW, 22 mm. **Subject:** Vahram Papazyan

| Date | Mintage | VF20 | XF40 | MS60 | MS63 | MS65 |
|---|---|---|---|---|---|---|
| 2013 | Est. 1000 | PF63 650 | PF65 700 | | | |

**KM# 118 50000 DRAM**
8.60 g., 0.999 Gold 0.2762 oz. AGW, 22 mm. **Subject:** Armenian Armed Forces **Obv:** Order of the Combat Cross of the Second Degree and the Emblem of the Ministry of Defense of the Republic of Armenia **Rev:** Arms, date and denomination

| Date | Mintage | VF20 | XF40 | MS60 | MS63 | MS65 |
|---|---|---|---|---|---|---|
| 2005 | 1,000 | PF63 750 | PF65 800 | | | |

## BULLION COINAGE

**KM# 198 100 DRAM**
7.77 g., 0.999 Silver 0.2496 oz. ASW **Obv:** National arms **Rev:** Noah's Ark

| Date | Mintage | VF20 | XF40 | MS60 | MS63 | MS65 |
|---|---|---|---|---|---|---|
| 2011 LEV | — | — | — | — | — | 15.00 |
| 2012 LEV | — | — | — | — | — | 15.00 |
| 2013 | — | — | — | — | — | 15.00 |

**KM# 197 200 DRAM**
15.55 g., 0.999 Silver 0.4994 oz. ASW **Obv:** National arms **Rev:** Noah's Ark

| Date | Mintage | VF20 | XF40 | MS60 | MS63 | MS65 |
|---|---|---|---|---|---|---|
| 2011 LEV | — | — | — | — | — | 25.00 |
| 2012 LEV | — | — | — | — | — | 25.00 |
| 2013 | — | — | — | — | — | 25.00 |

**KM# 196 500 DRAM**
31.11 g., 0.999 Silver 0.999 oz. ASW, 38.6 mm. **Obv:** National arms **Rev:** Dove, Noah's Ark and sun rise over Mt. Ararat

| Date | Mintage | VF20 | XF40 | MS60 | MS63 | MS65 |
|---|---|---|---|---|---|---|
| 2011 LEV | — | — | — | — | — | 50.00 |
| 2012 LEV | — | — | — | — | — | 50.00 |
| 2013 | — | — | — | — | — | 35.00 |

**KM# 227 1000 DRAM**
155.50 g., 0.999 Silver 4.9944 oz. ASW, 62.2 mm. **Obv:** National arms **Rev:** Noah's Ark

| Date | Mintage | VF20 | XF40 | MS60 | MS63 | MS65 |
|---|---|---|---|---|---|---|
| 2012 LEV | — | — | — | — | — | 200 |

**KM# 226 5000 DRAM**
311.05 g., 0.999 Silver 9.9905 oz. ASW, 75.5 mm. **Obv:** National arms **Rev:** Noah's Ark **Note:** 7.4mm thick.

| Date | Mintage | VF20 | XF40 | MS60 | MS63 | MS65 |
|---|---|---|---|---|---|---|
| 2012 LEV | — | — | — | — | — | 400 |

## KM# 225 10000 DRAM

1000.00 g., 0.999 Silver 32.1186 oz. ASW, 100 mm. **Obv:** National arms **Rev:** Noah's Ark **Note:** 14mm thick.

| Date | Mintage | VF20 | XF40 | MS60 | MS63 | MS65 |
|---|---|---|---|---|---|---|
| 2012 LEV | — | — | — | — | — | 1,200 |

## KM# 224 20000 DRAM

5000.00 g., 0.999 Silver 160.5929 oz. ASW, 164.6 mm. **Obv:** National arms **Rev:** Noah's Ark **Note:** 29mm thick

| Date | Mintage | VF20 | XF40 | MS60 | MS63 | MS65 |
|---|---|---|---|---|---|---|
| 2012 LEV | — | — | — | — | — | 6,000 |

# ARUBA

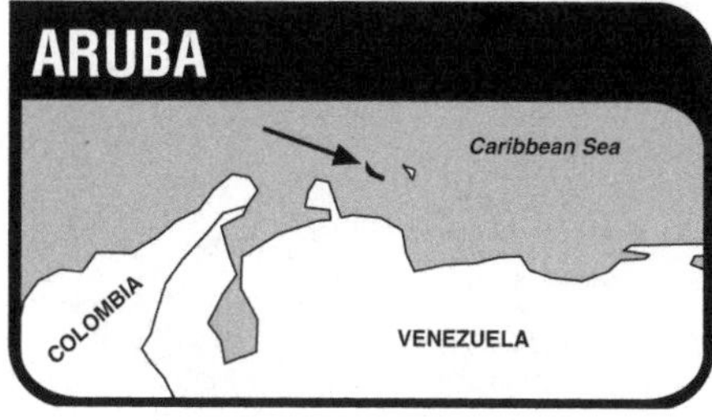


The second largest island of the former Netherlands Antilles, Aruba is situated near the Venezuelan coast. The island has an area of 74-1/2 sq. mi. (193 sq. km.) and a population of 105,000. Capital: Oranjestad, named after the Dutch royal family. Aruba was important in the processing and transportation of petroleum products in the first part of the twentieth century, but today the chief industry is tourism.

For earlier issues see Curacao and the Netherlands Antilles.

**RULER**

Dutch

**MINT MARKS**

(u) Utrecht - Privy marks only Wine tendril with grapes 2001-
Wine tendril with grapes plus star, 2002-
Sails of a clipper, 2003-

**MONETARY SYSTEM**

100 Cents = 1 Florin

# DUTCH STATE

Status Aparte

## DECIMAL COINAGE

### KM# 1 5 CENTS

2.00 g., Nickel Bonded Steel, 16 mm. **Ruler:** Beatrix **Obv:** National arms **Rev:** Geometric design with value **Edge:** Plain

| Date | Mintage | VF20 | XF40 | MS60 | MS63 | MS65 |
|---|---|---|---|---|---|---|
| 2001 (u) | 946,900 | — | 0.10 | 0.25 | 0.50 | 1.00 |
| 2002 (u) | 1,006,000 | — | 0.10 | 0.25 | 0.50 | 1.00 |
| 2003 (u) | 1,104,100 | — | 0.10 | 0.25 | 0.50 | 1.00 |
| 2004 (u) | 502,500 | — | 0.10 | 0.25 | 0.50 | 1.00 |
| 2005 (u) | 602,500 | — | 0.10 | 0.25 | 0.50 | 1.00 |
| 2006 (u) | 602,000 | — | 0.10 | 0.25 | 0.50 | 1.00 |
| 2007 (u) | 1,152,000 | — | 0.10 | 0.25 | 0.50 | 1.00 |
| 2008 (u) | 1,152,000 | — | 0.10 | 0.25 | 0.50 | 1.00 |
| 2009 (u) | — | — | 0.10 | 0.25 | 0.50 | 1.00 |
| 2010 (u) | — | — | 0.10 | 0.25 | 0.50 | 1.00 |
| 2011 (u) | — | — | 0.10 | 0.25 | 0.50 | 1.00 |
| 2012 (u) | — | — | 0.10 | 0.25 | 0.50 | 1.00 |
| 2013 (u) | — | — | 0.10 | 0.25 | 0.60 | 1.10 |

### KM# 2 10 CENTS

3.00 g., Nickel Bonded Steel, 18 mm. **Ruler:** Beatrix **Obv:** National arms **Rev:** Geometric design with value **Edge:** Reeded

| Date | Mintage | VF20 | XF40 | MS60 | MS63 | MS65 |
|---|---|---|---|---|---|---|
| 2001 (u) | 1,006,900 | — | 0.20 | 0.35 | 0.60 | 1.10 |
| 2002 (u) | 1,006,000 | — | 0.20 | 0.35 | 0.60 | 1.10 |
| 2003 (u) | 1,004,000 | — | 0.20 | 0.35 | 0.60 | 1.10 |
| 2004 (u) | 402,500 | — | 0.20 | 0.35 | 0.60 | 1.10 |
| 2005 (u) | 402,500 | — | 0.20 | 0.35 | 0.60 | 1.10 |
| 2006 (u) | 452,500 | — | 0.20 | 0.35 | 0.60 | 1.10 |
| 2007 (u) | 1,102,000 | — | 0.20 | 0.35 | 0.60 | 1.10 |
| 2008 (u) | 1,442,000 | — | 0.20 | 0.35 | 0.60 | 1.10 |
| 2009 (u) | — | — | 0.20 | 0.35 | 0.60 | 1.10 |
| 2009 (u) | — | — | 0.20 | 0.35 | 0.60 | 1.10 |
| 2010 (u) | — | — | 0.20 | 0.35 | 0.60 | 1.10 |
| 2011 | — | — | 0.20 | 0.35 | 0.60 | 1.10 |
| 2012 (u) | — | — | 0.20 | 0.35 | 0.60 | 1.10 |
| 2013 (u) | — | — | 0.20 | 0.35 | 0.60 | 1.10 |

### KM# 3 25 CENTS

3.50 g., Nickel Bonded Steel, 20 mm. **Ruler:** Beatrix **Obv:** National arms **Rev:** Geometric design with value **Edge:** Plain

| Date | Mintage | VF20 | XF40 | MS60 | MS63 | MS65 |
|---|---|---|---|---|---|---|
| 2001 (u) | 716,900 | — | 0.20 | 0.40 | 0.75 | 1.50 |
| 2002 (u) | 806,000 | — | 0.20 | 0.40 | 0.75 | 1.50 |
| 2003 (u) | 804,000 | — | 0.20 | 0.40 | 0.75 | 1.50 |
| 2004 (u) | 362,500 | — | 0.20 | 0.40 | 0.75 | 1.50 |
| 2005 (u) | 302,500 | — | 0.20 | 0.40 | 0.75 | 1.50 |
| 2006 (u) | 302,000 | — | 0.20 | 0.40 | 0.75 | 1.50 |
| 2007 (u) | 202,000 | — | 0.20 | 0.40 | 0.75 | 1.50 |
| 2008 (u) | 202,000 | — | 0.20 | 0.40 | 0.75 | 1.50 |
| 2009 (u) | — | — | 0.20 | 0.40 | 0.75 | 1.50 |
| 2010 (u) | — | — | 0.20 | 0.40 | 0.75 | 1.50 |
| 2011 (u) | — | — | 0.20 | 0.40 | 0.75 | 1.50 |
| 2012 (u) | — | — | 0.20 | 0.40 | 0.75 | 1.50 |
| 2013 (u) | — | — | 0.20 | 0.40 | 0.75 | 1.50 |

### KM# 4 50 CENTS

5.00 g., Nickel Bonded Steel, 20 mm. **Ruler:** Beatrix **Obv:** National arms **Rev:** Geometric design with value **Edge:** Plain **Shape:** 4-sided

| Date | Mintage | VF20 | XF40 | MS60 | MS63 | MS65 |
|---|---|---|---|---|---|---|
| 2001 (u) | 506,900 | — | 0.30 | 0.50 | 1.00 | 1.50 |
| 2002 (u) | 306,000 | — | 0.30 | 0.50 | 1.00 | 1.50 |
| 2003 (u) | 279,000 | — | 0.30 | 0.50 | 1.00 | 1.50 |
| 2004 (u) | 402,500 | — | 0.30 | 0.50 | 1.00 | 1.50 |
| 2005 (u) | 102,500 | — | 0.30 | 0.50 | 1.00 | 1.50 |
| 2006 (u) | 102,500 | — | 0.30 | 0.50 | 1.00 | 1.50 |
| 2007 (u) | 32,000 | — | 0.30 | 0.60 | 1.50 | 2.50 |
| 2008 (u) | 302,000 | — | 0.30 | 0.60 | 1.50 | 2.50 |
| 2009 (u) | — | — | 0.30 | 0.60 | 1.50 | 2.50 |
| 2010 (u) | — | — | 0.30 | 0.60 | 1.50 | 2.50 |
| 2011 (u) | — | — | 0.30 | 0.60 | 1.50 | 2.50 |
| 2012 (u) | — | — | 0.30 | 0.60 | 1.50 | 2.50 |
| 2013 (u) | — | — | 0.30 | 0.60 | 1.50 | 2.50 |

### KM# 5 FLORIN

8.50 g., Nickel Bonded Steel, 26 mm. **Ruler:** Beatrix **Obv:** Head left **Rev:** National arms and value **Edge:** Lettered **Edge Lettering:** GOD * ZIJ * MET * ONS *

| Date | Mintage | VF20 | XF40 | MS60 | MS63 | MS65 |
|---|---|---|---|---|---|---|
| 2001 (u) | 406,900 | — | 0.60 | 1.00 | 2.00 | 3.00 |
| 2002 (u) | 206,000 | — | 0.60 | 1.00 | 2.00 | 3.00 |
| 2003 (u) | 179,000 | — | 0.60 | 1.00 | 2.00 | 3.00 |
| 2004 (u) | 410,000 | — | 0.60 | 1.00 | 2.00 | 3.00 |
| 2005 (u) | 352,500 | — | 0.60 | 1.00 | 2.00 | 3.00 |
| 2006 (u) | 402,000 | — | 0.60 | 1.00 | 2.00 | 3.00 |
| 2007 (u) | 502,000 | — | 0.60 | 1.00 | 2.00 | 3.00 |
| 2008 (u) | 289,000 | — | 0.60 | 1.00 | 2.00 | 3.00 |
| 2009 (u) | — | — | 0.60 | 1.00 | 2.00 | 3.00 |
| 2010 (u) | — | — | 0.60 | 1.00 | 2.00 | 3.00 |
| 2011 (u) | — | — | 0.60 | 1.00 | 2.00 | 3.00 |
| 2012 (u) | — | — | 0.60 | 1.00 | 2.00 | 3.00 |
| 2013 (u) | — | — | 0.60 | 1.00 | 2.00 | 3.00 |

### KM# 6 2-1/2 FLORIN

10.30 g., Nickel Bonded Steel, 30 mm. **Ruler:** Beatrix **Obv:** Head left **Rev:** National arms with value **Edge:** Lettered **Edge Lettering:** GOD * ZIJ * MET * ONS *

| Date | Mintage | VF20 | XF40 | MS60 | MS63 | MS65 |
|---|---|---|---|---|---|---|
| 2001 (u) Sets only | 6,900 | — | — | — | 3.00 | 7.00 |
| 2002 (u) Sets only | 6,000 | — | — | — | 3.00 | 7.00 |
| 2003 (u) Sets only | 4,000 | — | — | — | 3.00 | 7.00 |
| 2004 (u) Sets only | 2,500 | — | — | — | 3.00 | 7.00 |
| 2005 (u) Sets only | 2,500 | — | — | — | 3.00 | 7.00 |
| 2006 (u) Sets only | 2,000 | — | — | — | 3.00 | 7.00 |
| 2007 (u) Sets only | 2,000 | — | — | — | 3.00 | 7.00 |
| 2008 (u) Sets only | 2,000 | — | — | — | 3.00 | 7.00 |
| 2009 (u) Sets only | 2,000 | — | — | — | 3.00 | 7.00 |
| 2010 (u) Sets only | — | — | — | — | 3.00 | 7.00 |
| 2011 (u) | — | — | — | 2.00 | 3.00 | 7.00 |
| 2012 (u) | — | — | — | 2.00 | 3.00 | 7.00 |
| 2013 (u) | — | — | — | 2.00 | 3.00 | 7.00 |

### KM# 12 5 FLORIN

8.64 g., Nickel Bonded Steel, 26 mm. **Ruler:** Beatrix **Obv:** Head left **Rev:** National arms with value **Edge:** Plain **Shape:** 4-sided

| Date | Mintage | VF20 | XF40 | MS60 | MS63 | MS65 |
|---|---|---|---|---|---|---|
| 2001 (u) Sets only | 6,900 | — | — | 3.00 | 7.00 | 9.00 |
| 2002 (u) Sets only | 6,000 | — | — | 3.00 | 7.00 | 9.00 |
| 2003 (u) Sets only | 4,000 | — | — | 3.00 | 7.00 | 9.00 |
| 2004 (u) Sets only | 2,500 | — | — | 3.00 | 7.00 | 9.00 |
| 2005 (u) Sets only | 2,500 | — | — | 3.00 | 7.00 | 9.00 |

### KM# 25 5 FLORIN

11.90 g., 0.925 Silver 0.3539 oz. ASW, 29 mm. **Ruler:** Beatrix **Subject:** 50th Anniversary Charter for the Kingdom of the Netherlands including Netherlands Antilles **Obv:** Head left **Rev:** Royal seal **Edge Lettering:** GOD * ZIJ * MET * ONS *

| Date | Mintage | VF20 | XF40 | MS60 | MS63 | MS65 |
|---|---|---|---|---|---|---|
| 2004 (u) | 4,000 | PF63 35.00 | PF65 40.00 | | | |

### KM# 34 5 FLORIN

11.90 g., 0.925 Silver 0.3539 oz. ASW, 29 mm. **Ruler:** Beatrix **Subject:** Queen's Silver Jubilee **Obv:** Head left **Rev:** Flag **Edge Lettering:** GOD * ZIJ * MET * ONS

| Date | Mintage | VF20 | XF40 | MS60 | MS63 | MS65 |
|---|---|---|---|---|---|---|
| 2005 (u) | 3,100 | PF63 28.00 | PF65 32.00 | | | |

**KM# 38 5 FLORIN**
8.40 g., Aluminum-Bronze, 22.5 mm. **Ruler:** Beatrix **Obv:** Queen with a half crown on face **Rev:** Value and arms **Edge Lettering:** GOD * ZIJ * MET * ONS *

| Date | Mintage | VF20 | XF40 | MS60 | MS63 | MS65 |
|---|---|---|---|---|---|---|
| 2005 (u) | 827,500 | — | — | — | 5.00 | 8.00 |
| 2006 (u) | 102,000 | — | — | — | 7.00 | 10.00 |
| 2007 (u) | 52,000 | — | — | — | 7.00 | 10.00 |
| 2008 (u) | 22,000 | — | — | — | 7.00 | 15.00 |
| 2009 (u) | — | — | — | — | 7.00 | 15.00 |
| 2010 (u) | — | — | — | — | 7.00 | 15.00 |
| 2011 (u) | — | — | — | — | 7.00 | 15.00 |
| 2012 (u) | — | — | — | — | 7.00 | 15.00 |
| 2013 | — | — | — | — | 7.00 | 15.00 |

**KM# 41 5 FLORIN**
11.90 g., 0.925 Silver 0.3539 oz. ASW, 29 mm. **Ruler:** Beatrix **Subject:** Year of the dolphin **Obv:** Head left **Rev:** Two dolphins bounding out of the water **Edge Lettering:** GOD * ZIJ * MET * ONS *

| Date | Mintage | VF20 | XF40 | MS60 | MS63 | MS65 |
|---|---|---|---|---|---|---|
| 2007 (u) | 1,250 | PF63 30.00 | PF65 35.00 | | | |

**KM# 42 5 FLORIN**
11.90 g., 0.925 Silver 0.3539 oz. ASW, 29 mm. **Ruler:** Beatrix **Subject:** Fiesta de San Juan **Obv:** Head left **Rev:** Harvesting farmer **Edge Lettering:** GOD * ZIJ * MET * ONS

| Date | Mintage | VF20 | XF40 | MS60 | MS63 | MS65 |
|---|---|---|---|---|---|---|
| 2008 (u) | 1,250 | PF63 35.00 | PF65 40.00 | | | |

**KM# 43 5 FLORIN**
11.90 g., 0.925 Silver 0.3539 oz. ASW, 29 mm. **Ruler:** Beatrix **Subject:** Dante at New Year's **Obv:** Head left **Rev:** Dance at New Year's, Hand dropping coins into hat **Edge Lettering:** GOD * ZIJ * MET * ONS

| Date | Mintage | VF20 | XF40 | MS60 | MS63 | MS65 |
|---|---|---|---|---|---|---|
| 2009 (u) | 1,250 | PF63 35.00 | PF65 40.00 | | | |

**KM# 45 5 FLORIN**
11.90 g., 0.925 Silver 0.3539 oz. ASW, 29 mm. **Ruler:** Beatrix **Subject:** Olympic Games 2012 **Obv:** Queen Beatrix **Rev:** Two judoka fight men in action **Edge Lettering:** GOD * ZIJ * MET * ONS *

| Date | Mintage | VF20 | XF40 | MS60 | MS63 | MS65 |
|---|---|---|---|---|---|---|
| 2010 | 5,000 | PF63 30.00 | PF65 35.00 | | | |

**KM# 46 5 FLORIN**
11.90 g., 0.925 Silver 0.3539 oz. ASW, 29 mm. **Ruler:** Beatrix **Obv:** Head left **Rev:** California lighthouse and waves **Edge Lettering:** GOD * ZIJ * MET * ONS *

| Date | Mintage | VF20 | XF40 | MS60 | MS63 | MS65 |
|---|---|---|---|---|---|---|
| 2010 (u) | 1,250 | PF63 35.00 | PF65 40.00 | | | |

**KM# 47 5 FLORIN**
11.90 g., 0.925 Silver 0.3539 oz. ASW, 29 mm. **Ruler:** Beatrix **Obv:** Shield in wreath above mintmarks **Rev:** 25 years Status Aparte with Parliament building **Edge Lettering:** GOD * ZIJ * MET * ONS *

| Date | Mintage | VF20 | XF40 | MS60 | MS63 | MS65 |
|---|---|---|---|---|---|---|
| 2011 (u) | 1,250 | PF63 40.00 | PF65 45.00 | | | |

**KM# 48 5 FLORIN**
11.90 g., 0.925 Silver 0.3539 oz. ASW, 29 mm. **Ruler:** Beatrix **Subject:** Royal Vista **Obv:** Shield in wreath above mintmarks **Rev:** Queen Beatrix, Prince Willem-Alexander and Princess Maxima looking left, orange top stripe, blue bottom stripe **Edge Lettering:** GOD * ZIJ * MET * ONS *

| Date | Mintage | VF20 | XF40 | MS60 | MS63 | MS65 |
|---|---|---|---|---|---|---|
| 2011 (u) | 1,250 | PF63 45.00 | PF65 50.00 | | | |

**KM# 50 5 FLORIN**
11.90 g., 0.925 Silver 0.3539 oz. ASW, 29 mm. **Ruler:** Beatrix **Subject:** Alternative reality

| Date | Mintage | VF20 | XF40 | MS60 | MS63 | MS65 |
|---|---|---|---|---|---|---|
| 2012 | — | PF63 30.00 | PF65 35.00 | | | |

**KM# 51 5 FLORIN**
11.90 g., 0.925 Silver 0.3539 oz. ASW, 29 mm. **Ruler:** Beatrix **Obv:** National arms **Rev:** Shoco (owl) in color **Edge Lettering:** GOD * ZIJ * MET * ONS *

| Date | Mintage | VF20 | XF40 | MS60 | MS63 | MS65 |
|---|---|---|---|---|---|---|
| 2012 (u) Proof | 2,500 | — | — | — | 55.00 | 65.00 |

**KM# 52 5 FLORIN**
8.40 g., Aluminum-Bronze, 23.5 mm. **Ruler:** Beatrix **Subject:** Abdication of Beatrix **Obv:** National arms **Rev:** Beatrix and Willem Alexander; colored flag **Edge Lettering:** GOD * ZIJ * MET * ONS *

| Date | Mintage | VF20 | XF40 | MS60 | MS63 | MS65 |
|---|---|---|---|---|---|---|
| 2013 (u) | 11,000 | — | — | — | 15.00 | 18.00 |

**KM# 53 5 FLORIN**
25.00 g., 0.925 Silver 0.7435 oz. ASW, 38 mm. **Ruler:** Willem-Alexander **Subject:** Aruba welcomes Willem Alexander **Obv:** National arms and crown **Rev:** Willem Alexander right **Edge Lettering:** GOD * ZIJ * MET * ONS *

| Date | Mintage | VF20 | XF40 | MS60 | MS63 | MS65 |
|---|---|---|---|---|---|---|
| 2013 (u) | 2,000 | PF65 75.00 | | | | |

**KM# 54 5 FLORIN**
25.00 g., 0.925 Silver 0.7435 oz. ASW, 38 mm. **Ruler:** Willem-Alexander **Subject:** Royal visit **Obv:** National arms within wreath **Rev:** Willem Alexander and Maxima right **Edge Lettering:** GOD * ZIJ * MET * ONS *

| Date | Mintage | VF20 | XF40 | MS60 | MS63 | MS65 |
|---|---|---|---|---|---|---|
| 2013 | 1,250 | PF65 75.00 | | | | |

**KM# 20 10 FLORIN**
25.00 g., 0.925 Silver 0.7435 oz. ASW, 38 mm. **Ruler:** Beatrix **Subject:** Green Sea Turtles **Obv:** Head left **Rev:** Seven sea turtles **Edge:** Plain

| Date | Mintage | VF20 | XF40 | MS60 | MS63 | MS65 |
|---|---|---|---|---|---|---|
| 2001 (u) Prooflike | 2,000 | — | — | — | 60.00 | 65.00 |

**KM# 24 10 FLORIN**
17.80 g., 0.925 Silver 0.5294 oz. ASW, 33 mm. **Ruler:** Beatrix **Subject:** Crown Prince's Wedding **Obv:** Head left **Rev:** Conjoined busts of prince and princess Maxima, right **Edge Lettering:** GOD ZIJ MET ONS

| Date | Mintage | VF20 | XF40 | MS60 | MS63 | MS65 |
|---|---|---|---|---|---|---|
| ND(2002) (u) Prooflike | 5,000 | — | — | — | 40.00 | 45.00 |

**KM# 27 10 FLORIN**
25.00 g., 0.925 Silver 0.7435 oz. ASW, 38 mm. **Ruler:** Beatrix **Obv:** Head left **Rev:** Sea shell **Edge:** Plain

| Date | Mintage | VF20 | XF40 | MS60 | MS63 | MS65 |
|---|---|---|---|---|---|---|
| 2003 (u) | 2,000 | PF63 55.00 | PF65 60.00 | | | |

**KM# 28 10 FLORIN**
25.00 g., 0.925 Silver 0.7435 oz. ASW, 38 mm. **Ruler:** Beatrix **Obv:** Head left **Rev:** Arubia Rattlesnake (Crotalus unicolor). **Edge:** Plain

| Date | Mintage | VF20 | XF40 | MS60 | MS63 | MS65 |
|---|---|---|---|---|---|---|
| 2003 (u) | 2,000 | PF63 55.00 | PF65 60.00 | | | |

**KM# 29 10 FLORIN**
25.00 g., 0.925 Silver 0.7435 oz. ASW, 38 mm. **Ruler:** Beatrix **Obv:** Head left **Rev:** Burrowing Owl (Athena cunicularia). **Edge:** Plain

| Date | Mintage | VF20 | XF40 | MS60 | MS63 | MS65 |
|---|---|---|---|---|---|---|
| 2003 (u) | 1,000 | PF63 55.00 | PF65 60.00 | | | |

**KM# 26 10 FLORIN**
6.72 g., 0.900 Gold 0.1944 oz. AGW, 22.5 mm. **Ruler:** Beatrix **Subject:** 20th Anniversary of Autonomy **Obv:** Head left **Rev:** Royal seal **Edge:** Reeded

| Date | Mintage | VF20 | XF40 | MS60 | MS63 | MS65 |
|---|---|---|---|---|---|---|
| 2004 (u) | 1,000 | PF63 325 | PF65 375 | | | |

**KM# 30 10 FLORIN**
25.00 g., 0.925 Silver 0.7435 oz. ASW, 38 mm. **Ruler:** Beatrix **Obv:** Head left **Rev:** Cuban Tree Frog (Osteopilus septentrionalis). **Edge:** Plain

| Date | Mintage | VF20 | XF40 | MS60 | MS63 | MS65 |
|---|---|---|---|---|---|---|
| 2004 (u) | 1,000 | PF63 45.00 | PF65 50.00 | | | |

**KM# 31 10 FLORIN**
25.00 g., 0.925 Silver 0.7435 oz. ASW, 38 mm. **Ruler:** Beatrix **Obv:** Head left **Rev:** Fish right **Edge:** Plain

| Date | Mintage | VF20 | XF40 | MS60 | MS63 | MS65 |
|---|---|---|---|---|---|---|
| 2004 (u) | 1,000 | PF63 45.00 | PF65 50.00 | | | |

**KM# 33 10 FLORIN**
1.24 g., 0.999 Gold 0.040 oz. AGW, 13.9 mm. **Ruler:** Beatrix **Subject:** Death of Juliana **Obv:** Head left **Rev:** Juliana in center **Edge:** Reeded

| Date | Mintage | VF20 | XF40 | MS60 | MS63 | MS65 |
|---|---|---|---|---|---|---|
| ND (2005) (u) | 10,000 | PF63 70.00 | PF65 75.00 | | | |

**KM# 35 10 FLORIN**
6.72 g., 0.900 Gold 0.1944 oz. AGW, 22.5 mm. **Ruler:** Beatrix **Subject:** Queen's Silver Jubilee **Obv:** Head left **Rev:** Flag **Edge:** Reeded

| Date | Mintage | VF20 | XF40 | MS60 | MS63 | MS65 |
|---|---|---|---|---|---|---|
| 2005 (u) | 750 | PF63 325 | PF65 375 | | | |

**KM# 36 10 FLORIN**
25.00 g., 0.925 Silver 0.7435 oz. ASW, 38 mm. **Ruler:** Beatrix **Subject:** Status Aparte 20th Anniversary - Flag 30th Anniversary **Obv:** Queen's portrait **Rev:** Queen standing next to value and country name **Edge Lettering:** DIOS * TA * CU * NOS *

| Date | Mintage | VF20 | XF40 | MS60 | MS63 | MS65 |
|---|---|---|---|---|---|---|
| 2006 (u) | 1,250 | PF63 40.00 | PF65 45.00 | | | |

**KM# 44 10 FLORIN**
1.24 g., 0.999 Gold 0.040 oz. AGW, 13.9 mm. **Ruler:** Beatrix **Subject:** Carnival **Obv:** Head left **Rev:** Carnival feathered facemask

| Date | Mintage | VF20 | XF40 | MS60 | MS63 | MS65 |
|---|---|---|---|---|---|---|
| 2009 | 5,000 | PF63 70.00 | PF65 75.00 | | | |

**KM# 49 10 FLORIN**
3.36 g., 0.900 Gold 0.0974 oz. AGW, 18.5 mm. **Ruler:** Beatrix **Subject:** Status Aparte **Obv:** Shield in wreath above mintmarks **Rev:** 25 years Status Aparte with Parliament building **Edge:** Reeded

| Date | Mintage | VF20 | XF40 | MS60 | MS63 | MS65 |
|---|---|---|---|---|---|---|
| 2011 (u) | 1,000 | PF63 220 | PF65 250 | | | |

**KM# 55 10 FLORIN**
1.24 g., 0.999 Gold 0.0398 oz. AGW, 13.92 mm. **Ruler:** Willem-Alexander **Subject:** Aruba welcomes Willem Alexander **Obv:** National arms and crown **Rev:** Willem Alexander right **Edge:** Reeded

| Date | Mintage | VF20 | XF40 | MS60 | MS63 | MS65 |
|---|---|---|---|---|---|---|
| 2013 (u) | 750 | PF65 130 | | | | |

**KM# 22 25 FLORIN**
25.00 g., 0.925 Silver 0.7435 oz. ASW, 38 mm. **Ruler:** Beatrix **Subject:** 15th Anniversary of Autonomy **Obv:** Head left **Rev:** National arms and inscription **Edge:** Plain

| Date | Mintage | VF20 | XF40 | MS60 | MS63 | MS65 |
|---|---|---|---|---|---|---|
| 2001 (u) | 3,000 | PF63 40.00 | PF65 45.00 | | | |

**KM# 37 25 FLORIN**
6.72 g., 0.900 Gold 0.1944 oz. AGW, 22.5 mm. **Ruler:** Beatrix **Subject:** Status Aparte 20th Anniversary - Flag 30th Anniversary **Obv:** Queen's portrait **Rev:** Queen standing next to value and country name **Edge:** Reeded **Note:** Status Aparte

| Date | Mintage | VF20 | XF40 | MS60 | MS63 | MS65 |
|---|---|---|---|---|---|---|
| 2006 (u) | 1,000 | PF63 325 | PF65 375 | | | |

**KM# 23 100 FLORIN**
6.72 g., Gold, 22.5 mm. **Ruler:** Beatrix **Subject:** Independence **Obv:** Arms, treaty name, dates **Rev:** Head left **Edge:** Grained

| Date | Mintage | VF20 | XF40 | MS60 | MS63 | MS65 |
|---|---|---|---|---|---|---|
| 2001 (u) | 1,000 | PF63 350 | PF65 400 | | | |

## PATTERNS

| KM# | Date | Mintage | Identification | Mkt Val |
|---|---|---|---|---|
| Pn1 | 2002(u) | — | 5 Florin Brass KM#38 | 700 |
| Pn3 | 2002(u) | | 5 Florin Nickel Bonded Steel KM#38 with SPECIMEN added | 700 |

## MINT SETS

| KM# | Date | Mintage | Identification | Issue Price | Mkt Val |
|---|---|---|---|---|---|
| MS19 | 2001 (7) | 6,900 | KM#1-6, 12 | 13.25 | 18.00 |
| MS20 | 2002 (6) | 6,000 | KM# 1-6, 12 | 15.00 | 20.00 |
| MS21 | 2003 (7) | 4,000 | KM# 1-6, 12 | 15.00 | 20.00 |
| MS22 | 2004 (7) | 2,500 | KM# 1-6, 12 | 15.00 | 30.00 |
| MS23 | 2005 (7) | 2,500 | KM# 1-6, 12 | 15.00 | 30.00 |
| MS24 | 2006 (7) | 2,000 | KM# 1-6, 38 | 15.00 | 30.00 |
| MS25 | 2007 (7) | 2,500 | KM#1-6, 38 | 20.00 | 30.00 |
| MS26 | 2008 (7) | 2,000 | KM#1-6, 38 | 26.00 | 30.00 |
| MS27 | 2009 (7) | 2,000 | KM#1-6, 38 | 26.00 | 30.00 |
| MS28 | 2010 (7) | 2,000 | KM#1-6, 38 | 26.00 | 30.00 |
| MS29 | 2011 (7) | 2,000 | KM#1-6, 38 | 26.00 | 30.00 |
| MS30 | 2012 (7) | 2,000 | KM#1-6, 38 | 28.00 | 30.00 |

# ASCENSION ISLAND

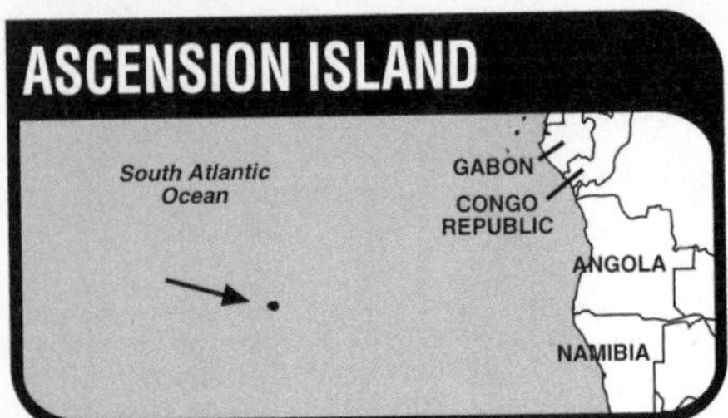


An island of volcanic origin, Ascension Island lies in the South Atlantic, 700 miles (1,100 km.) northwest of St. Helena. It has an area of 34 sq. mi. (88 sq. km.) on an island 9 miles (14 km.) long and 6 miles (10 km.) wide. Approximate population: 1,146. Although having little vegetation and scant rainfall, the island has a very healthy climate. The island is the nesting place for a large number of sea turtles and sooty terns. Phosphates and guano are the chief natural sources of income. Ascension is a dependency of the British Colony of St. Helena.

**RULER**
British

**MINT MARK**
PM - Pobjoy Mint

## BRITISH ADMINISTRATION

### STANDARD COINAGE

**KM# 13 50 PENCE**
28.63 g., Copper-Nickel, 38.6 mm. **Subject:** 75th Birthday of Queen Elizabeth **Obv:** Crowned bust right, denomination below **Rev:** Crowned monogram above flowers within circle, date below **Edge:** Reeded

| Date | Mintage | VF20 | XF40 | MS60 | MS63 | MS65 |
|---|---|---|---|---|---|---|
| 2001 | — | — | — | — | 7.00 | 8.00 |

**KM# 13a 50 PENCE**
28.28 g., 0.925 Silver 0.841 oz. ASW, 38.6 mm. **Subject:** Queen Elizabeth II's 75th Birthday **Obv:** Crowned bust right, denomination below **Rev:** Crowned monogram above roses within circle, date below **Edge:** Reeded

| Date | Mintage | VF20 | XF40 | MS60 | MS63 | MS65 |
|---|---|---|---|---|---|---|
| 2001 | 10,000 | PF63 40.00 | PF65 45.00 | | | |

**KM# 13b 50 PENCE**
47.54 g., 0.9166 Gold 1.401 oz. AGW, 38.6 mm. **Subject:** Queen Elizabeth II's 75th Birthday **Obv:** Crowned bust right, denomination below **Rev:** Crowned monogram above roses within circle, date below **Edge:** Reeded

| Date | Mintage | VF20 | XF40 | MS60 | MS63 | MS65 |
|---|---|---|---|---|---|---|
| 2001 | 75 | PF65 2,200 | | | | |

**KM# 14 50 PENCE**
28.63 g., Copper-Nickel, 38.6 mm. **Subject:** Centennial - Queen Victoria's Death **Obv:** Crowned bust right, denomination below **Rev:** Crowned bust left, three dates **Edge:** Reeded

| Date | Mintage | VF20 | XF40 | MS60 | MS63 | MS65 |
|---|---|---|---|---|---|---|
| 2001 | — | — | — | — | 7.00 | 8.00 |

**KM# 14a 50 PENCE**
28.28 g., 0.925 Silver 0.841 oz. ASW, 38.6 mm. **Subject:** Centennial of Queen Victoria's Death **Obv:** Crowned bust right, denomination below **Rev:** Crowned bust left, three dates **Edge:** Reeded

| Date | Mintage | VF20 | XF40 | MS60 | MS63 | MS65 |
|---|---|---|---|---|---|---|
| 2001 | 10,000 | PF63 40.00 | PF65 45.00 | | | |

**KM# 14b 50 PENCE**
47.54 g., 0.9166 Gold 1.401 oz. AGW, 38.6 mm. **Subject:** Centennial of Queen Victoria's Death **Obv:** Crowned bust right, denomination below **Rev:** Crowned bust left, three dates **Edge:** Reeded

| Date | Mintage | VF20 | XF40 | MS60 | MS63 | MS65 |
|---|---|---|---|---|---|---|
| 2001 | 100 | PF65 2,500 | | | | |

**KM# 15 50 PENCE**
28.35 g., Copper-Nickel, 38.6 mm. **Subject:** Queen's Golden Jubilee **Obv:** Crowned bust right, denomination below **Rev:** Westminster Abby, monogram at left, circle surrounds, two dates below **Edge:** Reeded

| Date | Mintage | VF20 | XF40 | MS60 | MS63 | MS65 |
|---|---|---|---|---|---|---|
| ND(2002) | — | — | — | — | 7.00 | 8.00 |

**KM# 15a 50 PENCE**
28.28 g., 0.925 Silver 0.841 oz. ASW, 38.6 mm. **Subject:** Queen Elizabeth II's Golden Jubilee **Obv:** Gold-plated crowned bust right, denomination below **Rev:** Monogram and Westminster Abbey within circle, dates below **Edge:** Reeded

| Date | Mintage | VF20 | XF40 | MS60 | MS63 | MS65 |
|---|---|---|---|---|---|---|
| ND(2002) | 10,000 | PF63 40.00 | PF65 45.00 | | | |

**KM# 18 50 PENCE**

28.28 g., Copper-Nickel, 38.6 mm. **Subject:** Death of Queen Mother **Obv:** Crowned bust right, denomination below **Rev:** Queen Mother bust right, between her life dates **Edge:** Reeded

| Date | Mintage | VF20 | XF40 | MS60 | MS63 | MS65 |
|---|---|---|---|---|---|---|
| ND(2002) | — | — | — | — | 9.00 | 10.00 |

**KM# 18a 50 PENCE**

28.28 g., 0.925 Silver 0.841 oz. ASW, 38.6 mm. **Subject:** Death of Queen Mother **Obv:** Crowned bust right, denomination below **Rev:** Queen Mother bust right, between her life dates **Edge:** Reeded

| Date | Mintage | VF20 | XF40 | MS60 | MS63 | MS65 |
|---|---|---|---|---|---|---|
| ND(2002) | 10,000 | PF63 40.00 | PF65 45.00 | | | |

**KM# 16 50 PENCE**

28.36 g., Copper-Nickel, 38.6 mm. **Subject:** Coronation Jubilee **Obv:** Crowned bust right, denomination below **Rev:** Crown, two scepters and the ampula **Edge:** Reeded

| Date | Mintage | VF20 | XF40 | MS60 | MS63 | MS65 |
|---|---|---|---|---|---|---|
| ND (2003) Prooflike | — | — | — | — | 9.00 | 10.00 |

**KM# 16a 50 PENCE**

28.28 g., 0.925 Silver 0.841 oz. ASW, 38.6 mm. **Subject:** Queen Elizabeth II's - 50th Anniversary of Coronation **Obv:** Crowned bust right, denomination below **Rev:** Crown, two scepters and the ampula **Edge:** Reeded

| Date | Mintage | VF20 | XF40 | MS60 | MS63 | MS65 |
|---|---|---|---|---|---|---|
| ND(2003) | 5,000 | PF63 45.00 | PF65 50.00 | | | |

**KM# 16b 50 PENCE**

39.94 g., 0.9166 Gold 1.177 oz. AGW, 38.6 mm. **Subject:** Queen Elizabeth II's - 50th Anniversary of Coronation **Obv:** Crowned bust right, denomination below **Rev:** Crown, two scepters and the ampula **Edge:** Reeded

| Date | Mintage | VF20 | XF40 | MS60 | MS63 | MS65 |
|---|---|---|---|---|---|---|
| ND(2003) | 50 | PF65 2,450 | | | | |

**KM# 17 50 PENCE**

28.28 g., Copper-Nickel, 38.6 mm. **Subject:** Queen Elizabeth II's- 50th Anniversary of Coronation **Obv:** Crowned head right, denomination below **Rev:** Crowned monogram **Edge:** Reeded

| Date | Mintage | VF20 | XF40 | MS60 | MS63 | MS65 |
|---|---|---|---|---|---|---|
| ND(2003) | — | — | — | — | 9.00 | 10.00 |

**KM# 17a 50 PENCE**

28.28 g., 0.925 Silver 0.841 oz. ASW, 38.6 mm. **Subject:** Queen Elizabeth II's- 50th Anniversary of Coronation **Obv:** Crowned head right, denomination below **Rev:** Crowned monogram **Edge:** Reeded

| Date | Mintage | VF20 | XF40 | MS60 | MS63 | MS65 |
|---|---|---|---|---|---|---|
| ND(2003) | 5,000 | PF63 45.00 | PF65 50.00 | | | |

**KM# 17b 50 PENCE**

39.94 g., 0.9166 Gold 1.177 oz. AGW, 38.6 mm. **Subject:** Queen Elizabeth II's - 50th Anniversary of Coronation **Obv:** Crowned bust right, denomination below **Rev:** Crowned monogram **Edge:** Reeded

| Date | Mintage | VF20 | XF40 | MS60 | MS63 | MS65 |
|---|---|---|---|---|---|---|
| ND(2003) | 50 | PF65 2,450 | | | | |

**KM# 19 2 POUNDS**

28.28 g., Copper-Nickel, 38.6 mm. **Subject:** Royal Wedding, Prince William and Catherine Middleton **Obv:** Bust in tiara right **Rev:** Two bells and two doves

| Date | Mintage | VF20 | XF40 | MS60 | MS63 | MS65 |
|---|---|---|---|---|---|---|
| 2011 PM | — | — | — | — | 9.00 | 10.00 |

**KM# 19a 2 POUNDS**

28.28 g., 0.925 Silver 0.841 oz. ASW **Subject:** Royal Wedding of Prince William and Catherine Middleton **Obv:** Bust in tiara right **Rev:** Two bells and two doves

| Date | Mintage | VF20 | XF40 | MS60 | MS63 | MS65 |
|---|---|---|---|---|---|---|
| 2011 PM | — | PF63 55.00 | PF65 65.00 | | | |

**KM# 20 2 POUNDS**

28.28 g., Copper-Nickel, 38.61 mm. **Subject:** Royal Wedding of Prince William and Catherine Middleton **Obv:** Bust with tiara right **Rev:** Westminster Abbey, profiel portraits conjoined in oval at right

| Date | Mintage | VF20 | XF40 | MS60 | MS63 | MS65 |
|---|---|---|---|---|---|---|
| 2011 PM | — | — | — | — | 9.00 | 10.00 |

**KM# 20a 2 POUNDS**

28.28 g., 0.925 Silver 0.841 oz. ASW, 38.61 mm. **Subject:** Royal Wedding of Prince William and Catherine Middleton **Obv:** Bust in tiara right **Rev:** Westminster Abbey, portraits in oval at right

| Date | Mintage | VF20 | XF40 | MS60 | MS63 | MS65 |
|---|---|---|---|---|---|---|
| 2011 PM | — | PF63 55.00 | PF65 65.00 | | | |

**KM# 21 2 POUNDS**

28.28 g., Copper-Nickel, 38.61 mm. **Obv:** Conjoined busts right of 1952 and 2012 portraits **Rev:** 1952 era portrait of Elizabeth II **Rev. Legend:** Life of Queen Elizabeth II

| Date | Mintage | VF20 | XF40 | MS60 | MS63 | MS65 |
|---|---|---|---|---|---|---|
| 2012 PM | — | — | — | — | — | 20.00 |

**KM# 22 2 POUNDS**

28.28 g., Copper-Nickel, 38.61 mm. **Subject:** Life of Queen Elizabeth II **Obv:** Conjoined busts right **Rev:** Elizabeth nursing Prince Charles

| Date | Mintage | VF20 | XF40 | MS60 | MS63 | MS65 |
|---|---|---|---|---|---|---|
| 2012 PM | — | — | — | — | — | 15.00 |

**KM# 26 2 POUNDS**

Copper-Nickel **Subject:** New coat of arms **Obv:** Bust in tiara right **Rev:** Shield with turtle

| Date | Mintage | VF20 | XF40 | MS60 | MS63 | MS65 |
|---|---|---|---|---|---|---|
| 2013 | — | PF65 25.00 | | | | |

**KM# 23 5 POUNDS**

62.21 g., 0.999 Silver 1.9981 oz. ASW, 38.61 mm. **Subject:** Elizabeth II 60th Anniversary **Obv:** Conjoined busts of 2012 and 1952 portraits **Rev:** Young postrait wearing state crown in ultra high relief

| Date | Mintage | VF20 | XF40 | MS60 | MS63 | MS65 |
|---|---|---|---|---|---|---|
| 2012 PM | — | PF65 90.00 | | | | |

**KM# 23a 5 POUNDS**

31.11 g., 0.999 Gold 0.999 oz. AGW **Obv:** Conjoined busts right of 2012 and 1952 portraits **Rev:** Youthful Elizabeth II wearing state crown in ultra-high relief

| Date | Mintage | VF20 | XF40 | MS60 | MS63 | MS65 |
|---|---|---|---|---|---|---|
| 2012 PM | — | PF65 2,000 | | | | |

**KM# 25 60 CROWNS**

1866.30 g., 0.999 Silver 59.9429 oz. ASW **Obv:** Conjoined busts right of 2012 and 1952 portratis **Rev:** Youthful Elizabeth II wearing gilt state crown inset with 60 diamond chips **Note:** Diamond chip inserts total 1 karat in weight.

| Date | Mintage | VF20 | XF40 | MS60 | MS63 | MS65 |
|---|---|---|---|---|---|---|
| 2012 PM | — | PF65 3,000 | | | | |

# AUSTRALIA

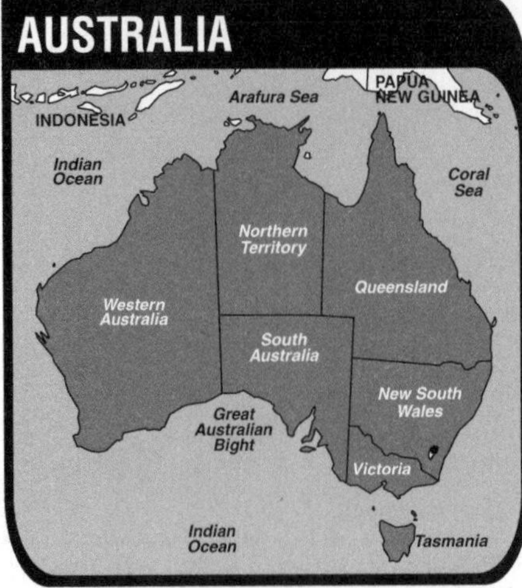


The Commonwealth of Australia, the smallest continent in the world, is located south of Indonesia between the Indian and Pacific oceans. It has an area of 2,967,893 sq. mi. (7,686,850 sq. km.) and an estimated population of 18.84 million. Capital: Canberra. Due to its early and sustained isolation, Australia is the habitat of such curious and unique fauna as the kangaroo, koala, platypus, wombat, echidna and frilled-necked lizard. The continent possesses extensive mineral deposits, the most important of which are iron ore, coal, gold, silver, nickel, uranium, lead and zinc. Raising livestock, mining and manufacturing are the principal industries. Chief exports are wool, meat, wheat, iron ore, coal and nonferrous metals.

Australia is a founding member of the Commonwealth of Nations. Elizabeth II is the Head of State as Queen of Australia; the Prime Minister is Head of Government.

NOTE: Home market grading of Australian coinage is generally stricter than USA practiced standards. The pricing in this catalog reflects strict home market grading standard.

**RULER**

British until 1942

**MONETARY SYSTEM**

Decimal Coinage (Commencing 1966)100 Cents = 1 Dollar

## COMMONWEALTH OF AUSTRALIA

### DECIMAL COINAGE

**KM# 62a CENT**

2.60 g., 0.999 Silver 0.0835 oz. ASW, 17.53 mm. **Ruler:** Elizabeth II **Obv:** Young bust right **Rev:** Feather-tailed glider and value **Edge:** Plain

| Date | Mintage | VF20 | XF40 | MS60 | MS63 | MS65 |
|---|---|---|---|---|---|---|
| 2006 | 6,500 | PF65 15.00 | | | | |

**KM# 767 CENT**

2.60 g., Bronze, 17.65 mm. **Ruler:** Elizabeth II **Obv:** Head with tiara right **Rev:** Feather-tailed glider and value **Edge:** Plain

| Date | Mintage | VF20 | XF40 | MS60 | MS63 | MS65 |
|---|---|---|---|---|---|---|
| 2006 B Sets only | — | — | — | — | — | 15.00 |
| 2006 B | — | PF65 18.00 | | | | |

**KM# 767b CENT**

5.61 g., 0.999 Gold 0.1802 oz. AGW, 17.53 mm. **Ruler:** Elizabeth II **Obv:** Head with tiara right **Rev:** Feather-tailed glider **Edge:** Plain

| Date | Mintage | VF20 | XF40 | MS60 | MS63 | MS65 |
|---|---|---|---|---|---|---|
| 2006 | 300 | PF65 650 | | | | |

**KM# 1249 CENT**

2.43 g., 0.999 Silver 0.078 oz. ASW, 17.6 mm. **Ruler:** Elizabeth II **Subject:** 1966 Decimal Pattern **Obv:** Head right **Rev:** Waratah, flower of New South Wales

| Date | Mintage | VF20 | XF40 | MS60 | MS63 | MS65 |
|---|---|---|---|---|---|---|
| 2009 P | 3,344 | PF65 15.00 | | | | |

**KM# 767a CENT**

2.93 g., 0.999 Silver 0.0941 oz. ASW, 17.53 mm. **Ruler:** Elizabeth II **Obv:** Head with tiara right **Rev:** Feather-tailed glider and value

| Date | Mintage | VF20 | XF40 | MS60 | MS63 | MS65 |
|---|---|---|---|---|---|---|
| 2011 | 6,000 | PF65 50.00 | | | | |

**KM# 2032 CENT**

0.50 g., 0.9999 Gold, 11.15 mm. **Ruler:** Elizabeth II **Subject:** Australian Miniature Money

| Date | Mintage | VF20 | XF40 | MS60 | MS63 | MS65 |
|---|---|---|---|---|---|---|
| 2012 | — | PF65 75.00 | | | | |

**KM# 63a 2 CENTS**

5.18 g., 0.999 Silver 0.1664 oz. ASW, 21.6 mm. **Ruler:** Elizabeth II **Obv:** Young bust right **Rev:** Frill-necked lizard and value **Edge:** Plain

| Date | Mintage | VF20 | XF40 | MS60 | MS63 | MS65 |
|---|---|---|---|---|---|---|
| 2006 | 6,500 | PF65 15.00 | | | | |

**KM# 768 2 CENTS**

5.20 g., Bronze, 21.59 mm. **Ruler:** Elizabeth II **Obv:** Head with tiara right **Rev:** Frill-necked lizard and value

| Date | Mintage | VF20 | XF40 | MS60 | MS63 | MS65 |
|---|---|---|---|---|---|---|
| 2006 B | — | — | — | — | — | 15.00 |
| 2006 B | — | PF65 5.00 | | | | |

**KM# 768b 2 CENTS**

11.31 g., 0.999 Gold 0.3633 oz. AGW, 21.6 mm. **Ruler:** Elizabeth II **Obv:** Head with tiara right **Rev:** Frill-necked Lizard and value **Edge:** Plain

| Date | Mintage | VF20 | XF40 | MS60 | MS63 | MS65 |
|---|---|---|---|---|---|---|
| 2006 | 300 | PF65 700 | | | | |

**KM# 1250 2 CENTS**

5.53 g., 0.999 Silver 0.1776 oz. ASW, 21.6 mm. **Ruler:** Elizabeth II **Subject:** 1966 Decimal Pattern **Obv:** Head right **Rev:** Wattle, national flower

| Date | Mintage | VF20 | XF40 | MS60 | MS63 | MS65 |
|---|---|---|---|---|---|---|
| 2009 P | 3,344 | PF65 20.00 | | | | |

**KM# 768a 2 CENTS**

6.03 g., 0.999 Silver 0.1937 oz. ASW, 21.6 mm. **Ruler:** Elizabeth II **Obv:** Head with tiara right **Rev:** Frill-necked lizard and value

| Date | Mintage | VF20 | XF40 | MS60 | MS63 | MS65 |
|---|---|---|---|---|---|---|
| 2011 | 6,000 | PF65 100 | | | | |

**KM# 2033 2 CENTS**

0.50 g., 0.9999 Gold, 11.15 mm. **Ruler:** Elizabeth II **Subject:** Australian Miniature Money

| Date | Mintage | VF20 | XF40 | MS60 | MS63 | MS65 |
|---|---|---|---|---|---|---|
| 2012 | Est. 2000 | PF65 75.00 | | | | |

### KM# 401 5 CENTS

2.83 g., Copper-Nickel, 19.41 mm. **Ruler:** Elizabeth II **Obv:** Head with tiara right **Rev:** Echidna and value **Edge:** Reeded

| Date | Mintage | VF20 | XF40 | MS60 | MS63 | MS65 |
|---|---|---|---|---|---|---|
| 2001 | 174,579,000 | — | — | 1.00 | 2.00 | 3.00 |
| Note: Large obverse head, IRB spaced | | | | | | |
| 2001 | Inc. above | — | — | 1.00 | 2.00 | 3.00 |
| Note: Smaller obverse head, RB joined | | | | | | |
| 2001 | 59,569 | PF65 15.00 | | | | |
| 2002 | 148,812,000 | — | — | 1.00 | 2.00 | 3.00 |
| 2002 | 39,514 | PF65 15.00 | | | | |
| 2003 | 115,470,000 | — | — | 1.00 | 2.00 | 3.00 |
| 2003 | 39,090 | PF65 5.00 | | | | |
| 2004 | 147,658,000 | — | — | 1.00 | 2.00 | 3.00 |
| Note: Normal sized SD | | | | | | |
| 2004 | Inc. above | — | — | 1.00 | 2.00 | 3.00 |
| Note: Smaller SD | | | | | | |
| 2004 | 50,000 | PF65 5.00 | | | | |
| 2005 | 194,300,000 | — | — | 1.00 | 2.00 | 3.00 |
| Note: Normal sized SD | | | | | | |
| 2005 | Inc. above | — | — | 1.00 | 2.00 | 3.00 |
| Note: Smaller SD | | | | | | |
| 2005 | 33,520 | PF65 5.00 | | | | |
| 2006 | — | — | — | 1.00 | 2.00 | 3.00 |
| 2006 | — | PF65 5.00 | | | | |
| 2007 | — | — | — | 1.00 | 2.00 | 3.00 |
| 2007 | — | PF65 5.00 | | | | |
| 2008 | — | — | — | 1.00 | 2.00 | 3.00 |
| 2008 | — | PF65 5.00 | | | | |
| 2009 | — | — | — | 1.00 | 2.00 | 3.00 |
| 2009 | — | PF65 5.00 | | | | |
| 2010 | — | — | — | 1.00 | 2.00 | 3.00 |
| 2010 | — | PF65 5.00 | | | | |
| 2011 | — | — | — | 1.00 | 2.00 | 3.00 |
| 2011 | — | PF65 5.00 | | | | |
| 2012 | — | — | — | 1.00 | 2.00 | 3.00 |
| 2012 | — | PF65 5.00 | | | | |
| 2013 | — | — | — | 2.00 | 3.00 | — |
| 2013 | — | PF65 5.00 | | | | |
| 2014 | — | — | — | 2.00 | 3.00 | — |
| 2014 | — | PF65 5.00 | | | | |
| 2015 | — | — | — | 2.00 | 3.00 | — |
| 2015 | — | PF65 5.00 | | | | |

### KM# 401a 5 CENTS

6.03 g., 0.999 Gold 0.1937 oz. AGW, 19.41 mm. **Ruler:** Elizabeth II **Subject:** Federation Centennial **Obv:** Head with tiara right **Rev:** Echidna and value

| Date | Mintage | VF20 | XF40 | MS60 | MS63 | MS65 |
|---|---|---|---|---|---|---|
| 2001 B | 650 | PF65 650 | | | | |
| 2005 B | 650 | PF65 450 | | | | |
| 2006 B | 300 | PF65 700 | | | | |
| 2013 B | 500 | PF65 450 | | | | |

### KM# 401b 5 CENTS

3.24 g., 0.9999 Silver 0.1042 oz. ASW, 19.41 mm. **Ruler:** Elizabeth II **Obv:** Head with tiara right **Rev:** Echidna and value **Edge:** Reeded

| Date | Mintage | VF20 | XF40 | MS60 | MS63 | MS65 |
|---|---|---|---|---|---|---|
| 2003 B | 6,500 | PF65 30.00 | | | | |
| 2004 B | 6,500 | PF65 20.00 | | | | |
| 2005 B | 6,500 | PF65 20.00 | | | | |
| 2006 B | — | PF65 20.00 | | | | |
| 2007 B | — | PF65 20.00 | | | | |
| 2008 B | — | PF65 20.00 | | | | |
| 2009 B | — | PF65 20.00 | | | | |
| 2010 B | — | PF65 20.00 | | | | |
| 2011 B | 6,000 | PF65 20.00 | | | | |
| 2013 B | 5,000 | PF65 25.00 | | | | |

### KM# 64a 5 CENTS

3.24 g., 0.999 Silver 0.1041 oz. ASW, 19.41 mm. **Ruler:** Elizabeth II **Obv:** Young bust right **Rev:** Echidna **Edge:** Reeded

| Date | Mintage | VF20 | XF40 | MS60 | MS63 | MS65 |
|---|---|---|---|---|---|---|
| 2006 | 6,500 | PF65 20.00 | | | | |

### KM# 1251 5 CENTS

2.74 g., 0.999 Silver 0.088 oz. ASW, 19.6 mm. **Ruler:** Elizabeth II **Subject:** 1966 Decimal Pattern **Obv:** Head right **Rev:** Platypus and yabbie

| Date | Mintage | VF20 | XF40 | MS60 | MS63 | MS65 |
|---|---|---|---|---|---|---|
| 2009 P | 3,344 | PF65 35.00 | | | | |

### KM# 2034 5 CENTS

0.50 g., 0.9999 Gold, 11.15 mm. **Ruler:** Elizabeth II **Subject:** Australian Miniature Money

| Date | Mintage | VF20 | XF40 | MS60 | MS63 | MS65 |
|---|---|---|---|---|---|---|
| 2012 | Est. 2000 | PF65 75.00 | | | | |

### KM# 402 10 CENTS

5.65 g., Copper-Nickel, 23.6 mm. **Ruler:** Elizabeth II **Obv:** Head with tiara right **Rev:** Lyrebird and value **Edge:** Reeded

| Date | Mintage | VF20 | XF40 | MS60 | MS63 | MS65 |
|---|---|---|---|---|---|---|
| 2001 | 109,357,000 | — | — | 2.00 | 3.00 | 4.00 |
| Note: Large obverse head, IRB spaced | | | | | | |
| 2001 | Inc. above | — | — | — | 3.00 | 4.00 |
| Note: Smaller obverse head, RB joined | | | | | | |
| 2001 | 59,569 | PF65 15.00 | | | | |
| 2002 | 70,329,000 | — | — | 2.00 | 3.00 | 4.00 |
| 2002 | 39,514 | PF65 5.00 | | | | |
| 2003 | 53,635,000 | — | — | 1.00 | 2.00 | 3.00 |
| 2003 | 39,090 | PF65 5.00 | | | | |
| 2004 | 89,000,000 | — | — | 2.00 | 3.00 | 4.00 |
| 2004 | 50,000 | PF65 5.00 | | | | |
| 2005 | 116,700,000 | — | — | 1.00 | 2.00 | 3.00 |
| 2005 | 33,520 | PF65 5.00 | | | | |
| 2006 | 157,087,000 | — | — | 1.00 | 2.00 | 3.00 |
| 2006 | — | PF65 5.00 | | | | |
| 2007 | 61,096,000 | — | — | 2.00 | 3.00 | 4.00 |
| 2007 | — | PF65 4.00 | | | | |
| 2008 | 82,860,000 | — | — | 2.00 | 3.00 | 4.00 |
| 2008 | — | PF65 5.00 | | | | |
| 2009 | — | — | — | 2.00 | 3.00 | 4.00 |
| 2009 | — | PF65 5.00 | | | | |
| 2010 | — | — | — | 2.00 | 3.00 | 4.00 |
| 2010 | — | PF65 5.00 | | | | |
| 2011 | — | — | — | 2.00 | 3.00 | 4.00 |
| 2011 | — | PF65 5.00 | | | | |
| 2012 | — | — | — | 2.00 | 3.00 | 4.00 |
| 2012 | — | PF65 5.00 | | | | |
| 2013 | — | PF65 5.00 | | | | |
| 2013 | — | — | — | 3.00 | 4.00 | — |
| 2014 | — | — | — | 3.00 | 4.00 | — |
| 2014 | — | PF65 5.00 | | | | |
| 2015 | — | — | — | 3.00 | 4.00 | — |
| 2015 | — | PF65 5.00 | | | | |

### KM# 402a 10 CENTS

12.14 g., 0.9999 Gold 0.3903 oz. AGW, 23.6 mm. **Ruler:** Elizabeth II **Obv:** Head with tiara right **Rev:** Lyrebird and value **Edge:** Reeded

| Date | Mintage | VF20 | XF40 | MS60 | MS63 | MS65 |
|---|---|---|---|---|---|---|
| 2001 B | 650 | PF65 750 | | | | |
| 2005 B | 650 | PF65 700 | | | | |
| 2006 B | 300 | PF65 850 | | | | |
| 2013 B | 500 | PF65 700 | | | | |

### KM# 402b 10 CENTS

6.57 g., 0.9999 Silver 0.2112 oz. ASW, 23.6 mm. **Ruler:** Elizabeth II **Obv:** Head with tiara right **Rev:** Lyrebird and value **Edge:** Reeded

| Date | Mintage | VF20 | XF40 | MS60 | MS63 | MS65 |
|---|---|---|---|---|---|---|
| 2003 B | 6,500 | PF65 20.00 | | | | |
| 2004 B | 6,500 | PF65 15.00 | | | | |
| 2005 B | 6,500 | PF65 15.00 | | | | |
| 2006 B | — | PF65 15.00 | | | | |
| 2007 B | — | PF65 15.00 | | | | |
| 2008 B | — | PF65 15.00 | | | | |
| 2009 B | — | PF65 15.00 | | | | |
| 2010 B | — | PF65 15.00 | | | | |
| 2011 B | 6,000 | PF65 15.00 | | | | |
| 2013 B | 5,000 | PF65 35.00 | | | | |

### KM# 65a 10 CENTS

6.57 g., 0.999 Silver 0.211 oz. ASW, 23.6 mm. **Ruler:** Elizabeth II **Obv:** Young bust right **Rev:** Superb Lyrebird **Edge:** Reeded

| Date | Mintage | VF20 | XF40 | MS60 | MS63 | MS65 |
|---|---|---|---|---|---|---|
| 2006 | 6,500 | PF65 15.00 | | | | |

### KM# 1252 10 CENTS

6.07 g., 0.999 Silver 0.195 oz. ASW, 23.6 mm. **Ruler:** Elizabeth II **Subject:** 1966 Decimal Pattern **Obv:** Head right **Rev:** Kookabura eating snake

| Date | Mintage | VF20 | XF40 | MS60 | MS63 | MS65 |
|---|---|---|---|---|---|---|
| 2009 P | 3,344 | PF65 45.00 | | | | |

### KM# 1789 10 CENTS

3.12 g., 0.999 Silver 0.1002 oz. ASW, 21 mm. **Ruler:** Elizabeth II **Obv:** Head with tiara right **Rev:** Koala leaning on and hugging branch

| Date | Mintage | VF20 | XF40 | MS60 | MS63 | MS65 |
|---|---|---|---|---|---|---|
| 2012 P | — | — | — | — | — | 15.00 |

### KM# 2035 10 CENTS

0.50 g., 0.9999 Gold, 11.15 mm. **Ruler:** Elizabeth II **Subject:** Australian Miniature Money

| Date | Mintage | VF20 | XF40 | MS60 | MS63 | MS65 |
|---|---|---|---|---|---|---|
| 2012 | Est. 2000 | PF65 75.00 | | | | |

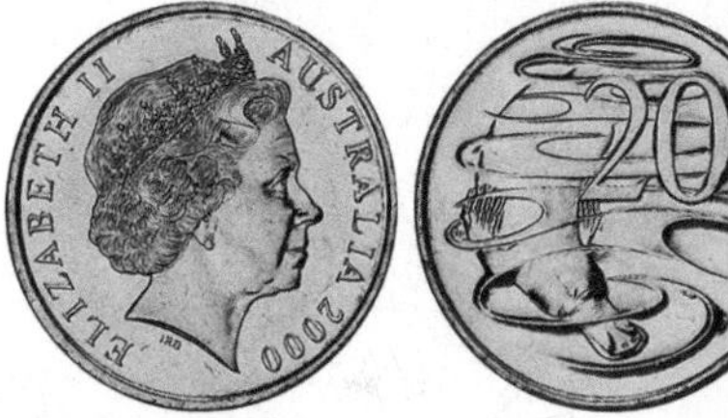

### KM# 403 20 CENTS

11.30 g., Copper-Nickel, 28.65 mm. **Ruler:** Elizabeth II **Obv:** Head with tiara right **Rev:** Duckbill Platypus **Edge:** Reeded

| Date | Mintage | VF20 | XF40 | MS60 | MS63 | MS65 |
|---|---|---|---|---|---|---|
| 2001 | 81,967,000 | — | — | 2.00 | 3.00 | 4.00 |
| Note: IRB spaced | | | | | | |
| 2001 | Inc. above | — | — | 2.00 | 3.00 | 4.00 |
| Note: RB joined | | | | | | |
| 2001 | Inc. above | — | — | 2.00 | 3.00 | 4.00 |
| Note: IRB joined | | | | | | |
| 2001 | 59,569 | PF65 25.00 | | | | |
| 2002 | 27,244,000 | — | — | 2.00 | 3.00 | 4.00 |
| 2002 | 39,514 | PF65 2.00 | | | | |
| 2004 | 74,609,000 | — | — | 2.00 | 3.00 | 4.00 |
| Note: Small obverse head, flat top A | | | | | | |
| 2004 | Est. 400000 | — | — | 12.00 | 15.00 | 20.00 |
| Note: Large obverse head, pointed A | | | | | | |
| 2004 | 50,000 | PF65 10.00 | | | | |
| Note: Large obverse head, pointed top A | | | | | | |
| 2004 | Inc. above | PF65 10.00 | | | | |
| Note: Small obverse head, flat top A | | | | | | |
| 2005 | 58,600,000 | — | — | 7.00 | 9.00 | 10.00 |
| 2005 | — | PF65 25.00 | | | | |
| 2006 | 102,462,000 | — | — | 2.00 | 3.00 | 4.00 |
| 2006 | — | PF65 6.00 | | | | |
| 2007 | 42,712,000 | — | — | 2.00 | 3.00 | 4.00 |
| 2007 | — | PF65 25.00 | | | | |
| 2008 | 106,220,000 | — | — | 0.50 | 1.00 | 2.00 |
| 2008 | — | PF65 12.00 | | | | |
| 2009 | — | — | — | 0.50 | 1.00 | 2.00 |
| 2009 | — | PF65 12.00 | | | | |
| 2010 | — | — | — | 0.50 | 1.00 | 2.00 |
| 2010 | — | PF65 12.00 | | | | |
| 2011 | — | — | — | 0.50 | 1.00 | 2.00 |
| 2011 | — | PF65 12.00 | | | | |
| 2012 | — | — | — | 0.50 | 1.00 | 2.00 |
| 2012 | — | PF65 12.00 | | | | |
| 2013 | — | — | — | 1.00 | 2.00 | — |
| 2013 | — | PF65 12.00 | | | | |
| 2014 | — | — | — | 1.00 | 2.00 | — |

| Date | Mintage | VF20 | XF40 | MS60 | MS63 | MS65 |
|---|---|---|---|---|---|---|
| 2014 | — | PF65 12.00 | | | | |
| 2015 | — | — | — | 7.00 | 8.00 | — |
| 2015 | — | PF65 10.00 | | | | |

## KM# 532 20 CENTS

11.30 g., Copper-Nickel, 28.65 mm. **Ruler:** Elizabeth II **Subject:** Centenary of Federation - Norfolk Island **Obv:** Head with tiara right **Rev:** Norfolk Pine over map of island **Edge:** Reeded

| Date | Mintage | VF20 | XF40 | MS60 | MS63 | MS65 |
|---|---|---|---|---|---|---|
| 2001 B | 2,000,000 | — | — | 2.00 | 3.50 | 5.00 |
| 2001 B | — | PF65 10.00 | | | | |

## KM# 550 20 CENTS

11.30 g., Copper-Nickel, 28.65 mm. **Ruler:** Elizabeth II **Series:** Centenary of Federation - New South Wales **Obv:** Head with tiara right **Rev:** Waratah on state map **Edge:** Reeded

| Date | Mintage | VF20 | XF40 | MS60 | MS63 | MS65 |
|---|---|---|---|---|---|---|
| 2001 | 2,000,000 | — | — | 2.00 | 3.50 | 5.00 |
| 2001 | — | PF65 10.00 | | | | |

## KM# 552 20 CENTS

11.30 g., Copper-Nickel, 28.65 mm. **Ruler:** Elizabeth II **Series:** Centenary of Federation - Australian Capital Territory **Obv:** Head with tiara right **Rev:** Parliament House, map, flowers **Edge:** Reeded **Note:** Prev. KM#551.

| Date | Mintage | VF20 | XF40 | MS60 | MS63 | MS65 |
|---|---|---|---|---|---|---|
| 2001 | 2,000,000 | — | — | 3.00 | 5.00 | 6.00 |
| 2001 | — | PF65 20.00 | | | | |

## KM# 554 20 CENTS

11.30 g., Copper-Nickel, 28.65 mm. **Ruler:** Elizabeth II **Series:** Centenary of Federation - Queensland **Obv:** Head with tiara right **Rev:** Jennifer Gray **Edge:** Reeded

| Date | Mintage | VF20 | XF40 | MS60 | MS63 | MS65 |
|---|---|---|---|---|---|---|
| 2001 | 2,320,000 | — | — | 4.00 | 6.00 | 8.00 |
| 2001 | — | PF65 20.00 | | | | |

## KM# 556 20 CENTS

11.30 g., Copper-Nickel, 28.65 mm. **Ruler:** Elizabeth II **Series:** Centenary of Federation - Victoria **Obv:** Head with tiara right **Rev:** Capital building **Edge:** Reeded

| Date | Mintage | VF20 | XF40 | MS60 | MS63 | MS65 |
|---|---|---|---|---|---|---|
| 2001 | 2,000,000 | — | — | 4.00 | 6.00 | 8.00 |
| 2001 | — | PF65 20.00 | | | | |

## KM# 558 20 CENTS

11.30 g., Copper-Nickel, 28.65 mm. **Ruler:** Elizabeth II **Series:** Centenary of Federation - Northern Territory **Obv:** Head with tiara right **Rev:** Two brolga cranes in ritual dance **Edge:** Reeded

| Date | Mintage | VF20 | XF40 | MS60 | MS63 | MS65 |
|---|---|---|---|---|---|---|
| 2001 | 2,100,000 | — | — | 4.00 | 6.00 | 9.00 |
| 2001 | — | PF65 20.00 | | | | |

## KM# 560 20 CENTS

11.30 g., Copper-Nickel, 28.65 mm. **Ruler:** Elizabeth II **Series:** Centenary of Federation - South Australia **Obv:** Head with tiara right **Rev:** Sturt's Desert Pea, landscape and southern cross **Edge:** Reeded

| Date | Mintage | VF20 | XF40 | MS60 | MS63 | MS65 |
|---|---|---|---|---|---|---|
| 2001 | 2,320,000 | — | — | 4.00 | 6.00 | 8.00 |
| 2001 | — | PF65 20.00 | | | | |

## KM# 562 20 CENTS

11.30 g., Copper-Nickel, 28.65 mm. **Ruler:** Elizabeth II **Series:** Centenary of Federation - Western Australia **Obv:** Head with tiara right **Rev:** Rabbit-eared Bandicoot (bilby), plant and map **Edge:** Reeded

| Date | Mintage | VF20 | XF40 | MS60 | MS63 | MS65 |
|---|---|---|---|---|---|---|
| 2001 | 2,000,000 | — | — | 4.00 | 6.00 | 10.00 |
| 2001 | — | PF65 20.00 | | | | |

## KM# 564 20 CENTS

11.30 g., Copper-Nickel, 28.65 mm. **Ruler:** Elizabeth II **Series:** Centenary of Federation - Tasmania **Obv:** Head with tiara right **Rev:** Tasmanian Tiger on map **Edge:** Reeded

| Date | Mintage | VF20 | XF40 | MS60 | MS63 | MS65 |
|---|---|---|---|---|---|---|
| 2001 | 2,000,000 | — | — | 4.00 | 6.00 | 10.00 |
| 2001 | — | PF65 20.00 | | | | |

## KM# 589 20 CENTS

11.30 g., Copper-Nickel, 28.65 mm. **Ruler:** Elizabeth II **Subject:** Sir Donald Bradman **Obv:** Head with tiara right **Rev:** Sir Donald Bradman **Edge:** Reeded

| Date | Mintage | VF20 | XF40 | MS60 | MS63 | MS65 |
|---|---|---|---|---|---|---|
| 2001 B | 10,000,000 | — | — | 28.00 | 35.00 | 40.00 |

## KM# 819 20 CENTS

24.36 g., 0.999 Gold 0.7824 oz. AGW, 28.52 mm. **Ruler:** Elizabeth II **Obv:** Head with tiara right **Rev:** Platypus with Federation Star **Edge:** Reeded

| Date | Mintage | VF20 | XF40 | MS60 | MS63 | MS65 |
|---|---|---|---|---|---|---|
| 2001 | 650 | PF65 1,450 | | | | |

## KM# 403a 20 CENTS

13.36 g., 0.9999 Silver 0.4295 oz. ASW, 28.52 mm. **Ruler:** Elizabeth II **Obv:** Head with tiara right **Rev:** Platypus and value **Edge:** Reeded

| Date | Mintage | VF20 | XF40 | MS60 | MS63 | MS65 |
|---|---|---|---|---|---|---|
| 2003 B | 6,500 | PF65 30.00 | | | | |
| 2004 B | 6,500 | PF65 25.00 | | | | |
| 2006 B | 6,500 | PF65 25.00 | | | | |
| 2007 B | — | PF65 25.00 | | | | |
| 2008 B | — | PF65 25.00 | | | | |
| 2009 B | — | PF65 25.00 | | | | |
| 2010 B | — | PF65 25.00 | | | | |
| 2011 B | 6,000 | PF65 25.00 | | | | |
| 2013 B | 5,000 | PF65 50.00 | | | | |

## KM# 688 20 CENTS

11.30 g., Copper-Nickel, 28.65 mm. **Ruler:** Elizabeth II **Obv:** Head with tiara right **Rev:** Group of Australian Volunteers **Edge:** Reeded

| Date | Mintage | VF20 | XF40 | MS60 | MS63 | MS65 |
|---|---|---|---|---|---|---|
| 2003 B | 7,600,000 | — | — | 2.00 | 3.00 | 4.00 |
| 2003 B | — | PF65 15.00 | | | | |

## KM# 688A 20 CENTS

11.30 g., 0.999 Silver 0.3629 oz. ASW, 28.65 mm. **Ruler:** Elizabeth II **Obv:** Head right **Rev:** Group of Australian Volunteers **Edge:** Reeded

| Date | Mintage | VF20 | XF40 | MS60 | MS63 | MS65 |
|---|---|---|---|---|---|---|
| 2003 B | 6,500 | PF65 35.00 | | | | |

## KM# 688b 20 CENTS

24.36 g., 0.999 Gold 0.7824 oz. AGW, 28.65 mm. **Ruler:** Elizabeth II **Obv:** Head with tiara right **Rev:** Group of Australian Volunteers **Edge:** Reeded

| Date | Mintage | VF20 | XF40 | MS60 | MS63 | MS65 |
|---|---|---|---|---|---|---|
| 2003 B | 650 | PF65 1,450 | | | | |

## KM# 745 20 CENTS

11.30 g., Copper-Nickel, 28.65 mm. **Ruler:** Elizabeth II **Subject:** 60th Anniversary - End of WWII **Obv:** Head right **Rev:** Soldier with wife and child **Edge:** Reeded

| Date | Mintage | VF20 | XF40 | MS60 | MS63 | MS65 |
|---|---|---|---|---|---|---|
| 2005 B | 33,500,000 | — | — | 1.00 | 2.00 | 3.00 |
| 2005 B | — | PF65 10.00 | | | | |

## KM# 745A 20 CENTS

13.36 g., 0.999 Silver 0.4291 oz. ASW, 28.65 mm. **Ruler:** Elizabeth II **Obv:** Head right **Rev:** Soldier with wife and child **Edge:** Reeded

| Date | Mintage | VF20 | XF40 | MS60 | MS63 | MS65 |
|---|---|---|---|---|---|---|
| 2005 B | 6,500 | PF65 35.00 | | | | |

## KM# 745B 20 CENTS

24.36 g., 0.9999 Gold 0.7831 oz. AGW, 28.65 mm. **Ruler:** Elizabeth II **Obv:** Head right **Rev:** Soldier with wife and child **Edge:** Reeded

| Date | Mintage | VF20 | XF40 | MS60 | MS63 | MS65 |
|---|---|---|---|---|---|---|
| 2005 B | 650 | PF65 1,450 | | | | |

**KM# 66a 20 CENTS**
13.36 g., 0.999 Silver 0.4291 oz. ASW, 28.52 mm. **Ruler:** Elizabeth II **Obv:** Young bust right **Rev:** Platypus **Edge:** Reeded

| Date | Mintage | VF20 | XF40 | MS60 | MS63 | MS65 |
|---|---|---|---|---|---|---|
| 2006 | 6,500 | PF65 28.00 | | | | |

**KM# 403b 20 CENTS**
24.56 g., 0.9999 Gold 0.7895 oz. AGW, 28.52 mm. **Ruler:** Elizabeth II **Subject:** Federation Centennial **Obv:** Head with tiara right **Rev:** Duckbill Platyus and value **Edge:** Reeded

| Date | Mintage | VF20 | XF40 | MS60 | MS63 | MS65 |
|---|---|---|---|---|---|---|
| 2006 B | 300 | PF65 1,500 | | | | |
| 2013 B | 500 | PF65 1,450 | | | | |

**KM# 820 20 CENTS**
11.30 g., Copper-Nickel, 28.65 mm. **Ruler:** Elizabeth II **Subject:** Year of the Surf Lifesaver **Obv:** Head with tiara right **Rev:** Female lifesaver working line **Edge:** Reeded

| Date | Mintage | VF20 | XF40 | MS60 | MS63 | MS65 |
|---|---|---|---|---|---|---|
| 2007 | — | — | — | 5.00 | 7.00 | 10.00 |
| 2007 | — | PF65 20.00 | | | | |

**KM# 820a 20 CENTS**
13.36 g., 0.999 Silver 0.4291 oz. ASW, 28.52 mm. **Ruler:** Elizabeth II **Subject:** Year of the Surfer Lifesaver **Rev:** Female with rope line

| Date | Mintage | VF20 | XF40 | MS60 | MS63 | MS65 |
|---|---|---|---|---|---|---|
| 2007 B | — | PF65 25.00 | | | | |

**KM# 1058 20 CENTS**
11.30 g., Copper-Nickel, 28.65 mm. **Ruler:** Elizabeth II **Subject:** Planet earth **Rev:** Map of Australia with water and rocks around

| Date | Mintage | VF20 | XF40 | MS60 | MS63 | MS65 |
|---|---|---|---|---|---|---|
| 2008 | — | PF65 12.00 | | | | |
| 2008 | — | — | — | 8.00 | 10.00 | 12.00 |

**KM# 1075 20 CENTS**
15.55 g., Copper-Nickel, 28.52 mm. **Ruler:** Elizabeth II **Subject:** Year of Astronomy **Rev:** Star gazers

| Date | Mintage | VF20 | XF40 | MS60 | MS63 | MS65 |
|---|---|---|---|---|---|---|
| 2009 | — | PF65 25.00 | | | | |
| 2009 | — | — | — | 8.00 | 10.00 | 12.00 |

**KM# 1088 20 CENTS**
15.55 g., Copper-Nickel, 28.52 mm. **Ruler:** Elizabeth II **Rev:** Poppy

| Date | Mintage | VF20 | XF40 | MS60 | MS63 | MS65 |
|---|---|---|---|---|---|---|
| 2009 | — | — | — | 8.00 | 10.00 | 12.00 |

**KM# 1253 20 CENTS**
12.86 g., 0.999 Silver 0.413 oz. ASW, 28.6 mm. **Ruler:** Elizabeth II **Subject:** 1966 Decimal Pattern **Obv:** Head right **Rev:** Black swan in flight

| Date | Mintage | VF20 | XF40 | MS60 | MS63 | MS65 |
|---|---|---|---|---|---|---|
| 2009 P | 5,459 | PF65 200 | | | | |

**KM# 1433 20 CENTS**
11.30 g., Copper-Nickel, 28.65 mm. **Ruler:** Elizabeth II **Subject:** Nurses **Rev:** Nurse looking over serviceman

| Date | Mintage | VF20 | XF40 | MS60 | MS63 | MS65 |
|---|---|---|---|---|---|---|
| 2009 C | — | — | — | 3.00 | 5.00 | 7.00 |

**KM# 1430 20 CENTS**
11.30 g., Copper-Nickel, 28.65 mm. **Ruler:** Elizabeth II **Subject:** Burke & Wills, 150th Anniversary **Rev:** Burke and Wills on camels

| Date | Mintage | VF20 | XF40 | MS60 | MS63 | MS65 |
|---|---|---|---|---|---|---|
| 2010 C | — | — | — | 3.00 | 5.00 | 7.00 |
| 2010 C | — | PF65 10.00 | | | | |

**KM# 1502 20 CENTS**
11.30 g., Copper-Nickel, 28.65 mm. **Ruler:** Elizabeth II **Subject:** Wool Industry **Rev:** Wheel with sheep industry design in spoke wedges

| Date | Mintage | VF20 | XF40 | MS60 | MS63 | MS65 |
|---|---|---|---|---|---|---|
| 2010 C | — | PF65 12.00 | | | | |
| 2010 C | — | — | — | 1.00 | 2.00 | 4.00 |

**KM# 1513 20 CENTS**
11.30 g., Copper-Nickel, 28.65 mm. **Ruler:** Elizabeth II **Subject:** Taxation office, 100th Anniversary

| Date | Mintage | VF20 | XF40 | MS60 | MS63 | MS65 |
|---|---|---|---|---|---|---|
| 2010 | — | — | — | 0.75 | 1.50 | 2.50 |

**KM# 1518 20 CENTS**
11.30 g., Copper-Nickel, 28.65 mm. **Ruler:** Elizabeth II **Subject:** Lost Soldiers of Promelles **Rev:** Soldier carrying another on his shoulder

| Date | Mintage | VF20 | XF40 | MS60 | MS63 | MS65 |
|---|---|---|---|---|---|---|
| 2010 | — | — | — | 0.75 | 1.50 | 2.50 |

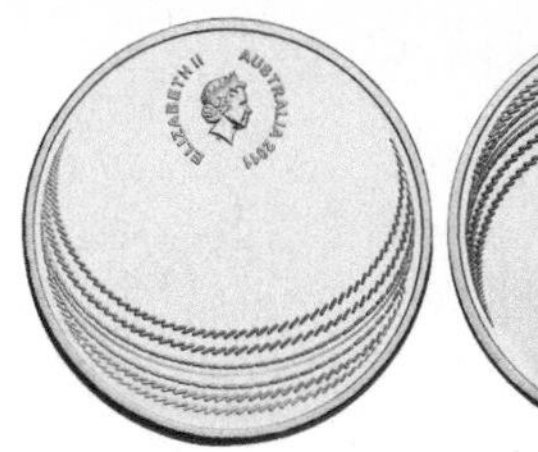

**KM# 1517 20 CENTS**
11.30 g., Copper-Nickel, 28.65 mm. **Ruler:** Elizabeth II **Subject:** Ashes Cricket tournament

| Date | Mintage | VF20 | XF40 | MS60 | MS63 | MS65 |
|---|---|---|---|---|---|---|
| 2011 | — | — | — | 0.75 | 1.50 | 2.50 |

**KM# 1566 20 CENTS**
11.30 g., Copper-Nickel, 28.65 mm. **Ruler:** Elizabeth II **Subject:** Royal Wedding **Rev:** Catherine Middleton and Prince William busts left

| Date | Mintage | VF20 | XF40 | MS60 | MS63 | MS65 |
|---|---|---|---|---|---|---|
| 2011 | — | — | — | 2.00 | 4.00 | 6.00 |

**KM# 1634 20 CENTS**
11.30 g., Copper-Nickel, 28.65 mm. **Ruler:** Elizabeth II **Subject:** Year of the Volunteer **Obv:** Head with tiara right **Rev:** Logo within wreath

| Date | Mintage | VF20 | XF40 | MS60 | MS63 | MS65 |
|---|---|---|---|---|---|---|
| 2011 | — | — | — | 1.50 | 3.00 | 4.00 |

**KM# 1642 20 CENTS**
11.30 g., Copper-Nickel, 28.65 mm. **Ruler:** Elizabeth II **Subject:** International Womens Day, 100th Anniversary **Obv:** Head with tiara right **Rev:** Three stylized joyful figures

| Date | Mintage | VF20 | XF40 | MS60 | MS63 | MS65 |
|---|---|---|---|---|---|---|
| 2011 | — | — | — | 1.50 | 3.00 | 4.00 |

**KM# 1648 20 CENTS**
11.30 g., Copper-Nickel, 28.65 mm. **Ruler:** Elizabeth II **Subject:** War Historians **Obv:** Head with tiara right **Rev:** Man with tripod taking photograph from atop tank

| Date | Mintage | VF20 | XF40 | MS60 | MS63 | MS65 |
|---|---|---|---|---|---|---|
| 2011 | — | — | — | 1.50 | 3.00 | 4.00 |

**KM# 1625 20 CENTS**
11.30 g., Copper-Nickel, 28.65 mm. **Ruler:** Elizabeth II **Subject:** Australian Wheat **Obv:** Head with tiara right **Rev:** Wheat ear upright

| Date | Mintage | VF20 | XF40 | MS60 | MS63 | MS65 |
|---|---|---|---|---|---|---|
| 2012 | — | PF65 15.00 | | | | |
| 2012 | — | — | — | 1.00 | 2.00 | 2.50 |

**KM# 1742 20 CENTS**
11.30 g., Copper-Nickel, 28.65 mm. **Ruler:** Elizabeth II **Subject:** World War II, Bombing of Australia **Obv:** Head with tiara right **Rev:** People entering air raid shelter

| Date | Mintage | VF20 | XF40 | MS60 | MS63 | MS65 |
|---|---|---|---|---|---|---|
| 2012 | — | — | — | 1.50 | 3.00 | 4.00 |

**KM# 1743 20 CENTS**
11.30 g., Copper-Nickel, 28.65 mm. **Ruler:** Elizabeth II **Obv:** Head with tiara right **Rev:** Military lookout

| Date | Mintage | VF20 | XF40 | MS60 | MS63 | MS65 |
|---|---|---|---|---|---|---|
| 2012 | — | — | — | 1.50 | 3.00 | 5.00 |

**KM# 1743a 20 CENTS**
13.36 g., 0.999 Silver 0.4291 oz. ASW, 28.65 mm. **Ruler:** Elizabeth II **Subject:** Bombing of Australia - World War II **Obv:** Head with tiara right **Rev:** Military lookout

| Date | Mintage | VF20 | XF40 | MS60 | MS63 | MS65 |
|---|---|---|---|---|---|---|
| 2012 | — | PF65 35.00 | | | | |

**KM# 1857 20 CENTS**
11.30 g., Copper-Nickel, 28.65 mm. **Ruler:** Elizabeth II **Subject:** Merchant Navy **Rev:** WWII Freighter sailing left

| Date | Mintage | VF20 | XF40 | MS60 | MS63 | MS65 |
|---|---|---|---|---|---|---|
| 2012 | — | — | — | 2.00 | 4.00 | 5.00 |

**KM# 2036 20 CENTS**
0.50 g., 0.9999 Gold, 11.15 mm. **Ruler:** Elizabeth II **Subject:** Australian Miniature Money

| Date | Mintage | VF20 | XF40 | MS60 | MS63 | MS65 |
|---|---|---|---|---|---|---|
| 2012 | Est. 2000 | PF65 75.00 | | | | |

**KM# 403a.1 20 CENTS**
Silver ASW partially gilt, 28.65 mm. **Ruler:** Elizabeth II **Obv:** Head with tiara right **Rev:** Duckbill Platypus gilt

| Date | Mintage | VF20 | XF40 | MS60 | MS63 | MS65 |
|---|---|---|---|---|---|---|
| 2013 | — | PF65 25.00 | | | | |

**KM# 403c 20 CENTS**
11.30 g., Copper-Nickel with color, 28.65 mm. **Ruler:** Elizabeth II **Rev:** Platypus in color

| Date | Mintage | VF20 | XF40 | MS60 | MS63 | MS65 |
|---|---|---|---|---|---|---|
| 2013 | — | — | — | — | — | 15.00 |

**KM# 403D 20 CENTS**
13.36 g., Silver gilt, 28.65 mm. **Ruler:** Elizabeth II **Rev:** Platypus gilt

| Date | Mintage | VF20 | XF40 | MS60 | MS63 | MS65 |
|---|---|---|---|---|---|---|
| 2013 | — | PF65 35.00 | | | | |

**KM# 1961 20 CENTS**
11.30 g., Copper-Nickel, 28.52 mm. **Ruler:** Elizabeth II **Subject:** Centenary of Australian Banknotes

| Date | Mintage | VF20 | XF40 | MS60 | MS63 | MS65 |
|---|---|---|---|---|---|---|
| 2013 | — | — | — | 2.00 | 4.00 | 5.00 |

**KM# 1962 20 CENTS**
11.30 g., Copper-Nickel, 28.52 mm. **Ruler:** Elizabeth II **Subject:** Centenary of Australian Banknotes

| Date | Mintage | VF20 | XF40 | MS60 | MS63 | MS65 |
|---|---|---|---|---|---|---|
| 2013 | — | — | — | 2.00 | 4.00 | 5.00 |

**KM# 1966 20 CENTS**
11.30 g., Copper-Nickel, 28.52 mm. **Ruler:** Elizabeth II **Subject:** 25th Anniversary of Australian Parliament House

| Date | Mintage | VF20 | XF40 | MS60 | MS63 | MS65 |
|---|---|---|---|---|---|---|
| 2013 | — | — | — | 2.00 | 4.00 | 5.00 |

**KM# 1967 20 CENTS**
11.30 g., Copper-Nickel, 28.52 mm. **Ruler:** Elizabeth II **Subject:** Royal Australian Army Chaplains

| Date | Mintage | VF20 | XF40 | MS60 | MS63 | MS65 |
|---|---|---|---|---|---|---|
| 2013 | — | — | — | 2.00 | 4.00 | 5.00 |

**KM# 2010 20 CENTS**
11.30 g., Copper-Nickel, 28.65 mm. **Ruler:** Elizabeth II **Subject:** Mining **Rev:** Mechanisms of mining

| Date | Mintage | VF20 | XF40 | MS60 | MS63 | MS65 |
|---|---|---|---|---|---|---|
| 2013 | 40,000 | — | — | 2.00 | 4.00 | 5.00 |
| 2013 | 25,000 | PF65 25.00 | | | | |

**KM# 2080 20 CENTS**
11.30 g., Copper-Nickel, 28.65 mm. **Ruler:** Elizabeth II **Subject:** Canberra, 100th Anniversary **Rev:** Map of city

| Date | Mintage | VF20 | XF40 | MS60 | MS63 | MS65 |
|---|---|---|---|---|---|---|
| 2013 | — | — | — | — | — | 8.00 |

**KM# 2144 20 CENTS**
11.30 g., Copper-Nickel **Ruler:** Elizabeth II **Subject:** Ashes **Obv:** Head with tiara right **Rev:** Cricket player

| Date | Mintage | VF20 | XF40 | MS60 | MS63 | MS65 |
|---|---|---|---|---|---|---|
| 2013 | — | — | — | — | — | 4.00 |

**KM# 599 25 CENTS**
7.78 g., 0.999 Silver 0.2497 oz. ASW, 24.8 mm. **Ruler:** Elizabeth II **Obv:** Head with tiara right **Rev:** Parliament House **Edge:** Plain **Shape:** 7-pointed star **Note:** The Dump" portion of the "Holey Dollar" KM#598.

| Date | Mintage | VF20 | XF40 | MS60 | MS63 | MS65 |
|---|---|---|---|---|---|---|
| 2001 Prooflike | 21,668 | — | — | — | — | 28.00 |

**KM# 1881 25 CENTS**
Silver gilt, 18 mm. **Ruler:** Elizabeth II **Subject:** Good Fortune and Prosperity

| Date | Mintage | VF20 | XF40 | MS60 | MS63 | MS65 |
|---|---|---|---|---|---|---|
| 2007 P | 5,994 | PF65 15.00 | | | | |

**KM# 1917 25 CENTS**
5.95 g., 0.999 Silver 0.191 oz. ASW, 17.6 mm. **Ruler:** Elizabeth II **Subject:** 200th Anniversary of the Australian Holey Dollar & Dump

| Date | Mintage | VF20 | XF40 | MS60 | MS63 | MS65 |
|---|---|---|---|---|---|---|
| 2013 Proof | Est. 4000 | — | — | — | — | 10.00 |

### KM# 404 50 CENTS

15.55 g., Copper-Nickel, 31.65 mm. **Ruler:** Elizabeth II **Obv:** Head with tiara right **Rev:** Australian coat of arms with kangaroo and emu supporters **Edge:** Plain **Shape:** 12-sided

| Date | Mintage | VF20 | XF40 | MS60 | MS63 | MS65 |
|---|---|---|---|---|---|---|
| 2004 | 17,918,000 | — | — | 7.00 | 9.00 | 10.00 |
| 2004 | — | PF65 25.00 | | | | |
| 2005 | 30,000 | — | — | 20.00 | 25.00 | 40.00 |
| Note: Issued as part of a PNC only | | | | | | |
| 2005 | — | PF65 10.00 | | | | |
| 2006 | — | — | — | 7.00 | 9.00 | 10.00 |
| 2006 | — | PF65 25.00 | | | | |
| 2007 | — | — | — | 5.00 | 7.00 | 8.00 |
| 2007 | — | PF65 10.00 | | | | |
| 2008 | — | — | — | 5.00 | 7.00 | 8.00 |
| 2008 | — | PF65 10.00 | | | | |
| 2009 | — | — | — | 5.00 | 7.00 | 8.00 |
| 2009 | — | PF65 10.00 | | | | |
| 2010 | — | — | — | 5.00 | 7.00 | 8.00 |
| 2010 | — | PF65 10.00 | | | | |
| 2011 | — | — | — | 5.00 | 7.00 | 8.00 |
| 2011 | — | PF65 10.00 | | | | |
| 2012 | — | — | — | 5.00 | 7.00 | 8.00 |

### KM# 491.1 50 CENTS

15.55 g., Copper-Nickel, 31.65 mm. **Ruler:** Elizabeth II **Subject:** Centenary of Federation, 1901-2001 **Obv:** Head with tiara right **Rev:** Commonwealth coat of arms **Edge:** Plain **Shape:** 12-sided **Note:** Prev. KM#491.

| Date | Mintage | VF20 | XF40 | MS60 | MS63 | MS65 |
|---|---|---|---|---|---|---|
| 2001 B | 43,149,600 | — | — | 4.00 | 5.00 | 6.00 |
| 2001 B | — | PF65 40.00 | | | | |

### KM# 491.1A 50 CENTS

33.88 g., 0.9999 Gold 1.0892 oz. AGW, 31.65 mm. **Ruler:** Elizabeth II **Subject:** Federation Centennial **Obv:** Elizabeth II **Rev:** Commonwealth arms above value

| Date | Mintage | VF20 | XF40 | MS60 | MS63 | MS65 |
|---|---|---|---|---|---|---|
| 2001 B | 650 | PF65 1,950 | | | | |

### KM# 491.2 50 CENTS

15.55 g., Copper-Nickel, 31.65 mm. **Ruler:** Elizabeth II **Subject:** Federation Centennial **Obv:** Elizabeth II right **Rev:** Multicolor arms above value **Edge:** Plain **Shape:** 12-sided

| Date | Mintage | VF20 | XF40 | MS60 | MS63 | MS65 |
|---|---|---|---|---|---|---|
| 2001 B | 60,000 | PF65 50.00 | | | | |

### KM# 491.2a 50 CENTS

15.55 g., Copper-Nickel, 31.65 mm. **Ruler:** Elizabeth II **Subject:** Centenary of Federation, 1901-2001 **Obv:** Head with tiara right **Rev:** Multicolored Commonwealth coat of arms **Edge:** Plain **Shape:** 12-sided **Note:** Prev. KM#491a.

| Date | Mintage | VF20 | XF40 | MS60 | MS63 | MS65 |
|---|---|---|---|---|---|---|
| 2001 B | — | PF65 50.00 | | | | |

### KM# 533 50 CENTS

15.55 g., Copper-Nickel, 31.65 mm. **Ruler:** Elizabeth II **Subject:** Centennial - Norfolk Island Federation **Obv:** Head with tiara right **Rev:** Norfolk Island coat of arms **Edge:** Plain **Shape:** 12-sided

| Date | Mintage | VF20 | XF40 | MS60 | MS63 | MS65 |
|---|---|---|---|---|---|---|
| 2001 B | 2,000,000 | — | — | 5.00 | 7.00 | 15.00 |
| 2001 B | — | PF65 70.00 | | | | |

### KM# 535 50 CENTS

16.89 g., 0.999 Silver 0.5424 oz. ASW, 32.1 mm. **Ruler:** Elizabeth II **Subject:** Year of the Snake **Obv:** Head right **Rev:** Snake with eggs **Edge:** Plain

| Date | Mintage | VF20 | XF40 | MS60 | MS63 | MS65 |
|---|---|---|---|---|---|---|
| 2001 | 500,000 | — | — | — | — | 22.00 |
| 2001 P | 5,000 | PF65 65.00 | | | | |

### KM# 551 50 CENTS

15.55 g., Copper-Nickel, 31.65 mm. **Ruler:** Elizabeth II **Series:** Centenary of Federation - New South Wales **Obv:** Head with tiara right **Rev:** New South Wales state arms **Edge:** Plain **Shape:** 12-sided

| Date | Mintage | VF20 | XF40 | MS60 | MS63 | MS65 |
|---|---|---|---|---|---|---|
| 2001 | 3,000,000 | — | — | 4.00 | 6.00 | 7.00 |
| 2001 | — | PF65 40.00 | | | | |

### KM# 553 50 CENTS

15.55 g., Copper-Nickel, 31.65 mm. **Ruler:** Elizabeth II **Series:** Centenary of Federation - Australian Capital Territory **Obv:** Head right **Rev:** Australian Capital Territory arms **Edge:** Plain **Shape:** 12-sided

| Date | Mintage | VF20 | XF40 | MS60 | MS63 | MS65 |
|---|---|---|---|---|---|---|
| 2001 | 2,000,000 | — | — | 4.00 | 6.00 | 9.00 |
| 2001 | — | PF65 40.00 | | | | |

### KM# 555 50 CENTS

15.55 g., Copper-Nickel, 31.65 mm. **Ruler:** Elizabeth II **Series:** Centenary of Federation - Queensland **Obv:** Head with tiara right **Rev:** Queensland state arms **Edge:** Plain **Shape:** 12-sided

| Date | Mintage | VF20 | XF40 | MS60 | MS63 | MS65 |
|---|---|---|---|---|---|---|
| 2001 | 2,300,000 | — | — | 4.00 | 6.00 | 9.00 |
| 2001 | — | PF65 40.00 | | | | |

### KM# 557 50 CENTS

15.55 g., Copper-Nickel, 31.65 mm. **Ruler:** Elizabeth II **Series:** Centenary of Federation - Victoria **Obv:** Head with tiara right **Rev:** Victoria state arms **Edge:** Plain **Shape:** 12-sided

| Date | Mintage | VF20 | XF40 | MS60 | MS63 | MS65 |
|---|---|---|---|---|---|---|
| 2001 | 2,800,000 | — | — | 4.00 | 6.00 | 8.00 |
| 2001 | — | PF65 40.00 | | | | |

### KM# 559 50 CENTS

15.55 g., Copper-Nickel, 31.65 mm. **Ruler:** Elizabeth II **Series:** Centenary of Federation - Northern Territory **Obv:** Head with tiara right **Rev:** Northern Territory state arms **Edge:** Plain **Shape:** 12-sided

| Date | Mintage | VF20 | XF40 | MS60 | MS63 | MS65 |
|---|---|---|---|---|---|---|
| 2001 | 2,100,000 | — | — | 4.00 | 6.00 | 10.00 |
| 2001 | — | PF65 50.00 | | | | |

### KM# 561 50 CENTS

15.55 g., Copper-Nickel, 31.65 mm. **Ruler:** Elizabeth II **Series:** Centenary of Federation - South Australia **Obv:** Head with tiara right **Rev:** South Australia state arms **Edge:** Plain **Shape:** 12-sided

| Date | Mintage | VF20 | XF40 | MS60 | MS63 | MS65 |
|---|---|---|---|---|---|---|
| 2001 | 2,400,000 | — | — | 5.00 | 10.00 | 20.00 |
| 2001 | — | PF65 60.00 | | | | |

### KM# 563 50 CENTS

15.55 g., Copper-Nickel, 31.65 mm. **Ruler:** Elizabeth II **Series:** Centenary of Federation - Western Australia **Obv:** Head with tiara right **Rev:** Western Australia state arms **Edge:** Plain **Shape:** 12-sided

| Date | Mintage | VF20 | XF40 | MS60 | MS63 | MS65 |
|---|---|---|---|---|---|---|
| 2001 | 2,400,000 | — | — | 4.00 | 7.00 | 15.00 |
| 2001 | — | PF65 50.00 | | | | |

### KM# 565 50 CENTS

15.55 g., Copper-Nickel, 31.65 mm. **Ruler:** Elizabeth II **Series:** Centenary of Federation - Tasmania **Obv:** Head with tiara right **Rev:** Tasmania state arms **Edge:** Plain **Shape:** 12-sided

| Date | Mintage | VF20 | XF40 | MS60 | MS63 | MS65 |
|---|---|---|---|---|---|---|
| 2001 | 2,200,000 | — | — | 4.00 | 6.00 | 10.00 |
| 2001 | — | PF65 50.00 | | | | |

## KM# 694 50 CENTS

15.55 g., Copper-Nickel, 31.65 mm. **Ruler:** Elizabeth II **Obv:** Head with tiara right **Rev:** Koala, Lorikeet (bird) and Wombat **Edge:** Plain **Shape:** 12-sided

| Date | Mintage | VF20 | XF40 | MS60 | MS63 | MS65 |
|---|---|---|---|---|---|---|
| 2001 | — | PF65 9.00 | | | | |
| 2004 B | 10,577,000 | — | — | 2.00 | 3.00 | 5.00 |

## KM# 602 50 CENTS

15.55 g., Copper-Nickel, 31.65 mm. **Ruler:** Elizabeth II **Subject:** The Outback Region **Obv:** Head right **Rev:** Windmill **Edge:** Plain **Shape:** 12-sided

| Date | Mintage | VF20 | XF40 | MS60 | MS63 | MS65 |
|---|---|---|---|---|---|---|
| 2002 B | 11,507,000 | — | — | 4.00 | 6.00 | 7.00 |
| 2002 B | 39,000 | PF65 25.00 | | | | |

## KM# 645 50 CENTS

15.55 g., Copper-Nickel, 31.65 mm. **Ruler:** Elizabeth II **Subject:** Queen's 50th Anniversary of Accession **Obv:** Head right **Rev:** Crown and star **Shape:** 12-sided

| Date | Mintage | VF20 | XF40 | MS60 | MS63 | MS65 |
|---|---|---|---|---|---|---|
| 2002 B | 32,102 | — | — | — | — | 60.00 |

Note: Issued only in PNC cover

## KM# 645a 50 CENTS

18.24 g., 0.999 Silver 0.5858 oz. ASW, 31.65 mm. **Ruler:** Elizabeth II **Subject:** Queen's 50th Anniversary of Accession **Obv:** Head right **Rev:** Crown and star **Shape:** 12-sided

| Date | Mintage | VF20 | XF40 | MS60 | MS63 | MS65 |
|---|---|---|---|---|---|---|
| 2002 B | 13,500 | PF65 60.00 | | | | |

## KM# 404a 50 CENTS

18.24 g., 0.9999 Silver 0.5864 oz. ASW, 31.65 mm. **Ruler:** Elizabeth II **Obv:** Head with tiara right **Rev:** Arms and value **Edge:** Plain **Shape:** 12-sided

| Date | Mintage | VF20 | XF40 | MS60 | MS63 | MS65 |
|---|---|---|---|---|---|---|
| 2003 B | 6,500 | PF65 35.00 | | | | |
| 2004 B | 6,500 | PF65 35.00 | | | | |
| 2005 B | 6,500 | PF65 35.00 | | | | |
| 2006 B | — | PF65 35.00 | | | | |
| 2007 B | — | PF65 35.00 | | | | |
| 2008 B | — | PF65 35.00 | | | | |
| 2009 B | — | PF65 35.00 | | | | |
| 2010 B | — | PF65 35.00 | | | | |
| 2011 B | 6,000 | PF65 35.00 | | | | |
| 2013 B | 5,000 | PF65 70.00 | | | | |

## KM# 689 50 CENTS

15.55 g., Copper-Nickel, 31.65 mm. **Ruler:** Elizabeth II **Obv:** Head right **Rev:** Value within circle of volunteer activities **Edge:** Plain **Shape:** 12-sided

| Date | Mintage | VF20 | XF40 | MS60 | MS63 | MS65 |
|---|---|---|---|---|---|---|
| 2003 B | 13,927,000 | — | — | 3.50 | 4.50 | 5.00 |
| 2003 B | — | PF65 20.00 | | | | |

## KM# 689a 50 CENTS

15.55 g., 0.999 Silver 0.4994 oz. ASW, 31.65 mm. **Ruler:** Elizabeth II **Obv:** Head right **Rev:** Value within circle of volunteer activities

| Date | Mintage | VF20 | XF40 | MS60 | MS63 | MS65 |
|---|---|---|---|---|---|---|
| 2003 B | 6,500 | PF65 45.00 | | | | |

## KM# 799 50 CENTS

14.09 g., Aluminum-Bronze, 31.51 mm. **Ruler:** Elizabeth II **Subject:** 50th Anniversary of the Coronation of Elizabeth II **Obv:** Head with tiara right **Rev:** Crown, Federation star, dates **Edge:** Plain **Shape:** 12-sided

| Date | Mintage | VF20 | XF40 | MS60 | MS63 | MS65 |
|---|---|---|---|---|---|---|
| 2003 | 65,003 | — | — | — | 35.00 | 40.00 |

## KM# 799a 50 CENTS

18.24 g., 0.999 Silver 0.5858 oz. ASW, 31.51 mm. **Ruler:** Elizabeth II **Subject:** 50th Anniversary of the Coronation of Elizabeth II **Obv:** Head with tiara right **Rev:** Crown, Federation star, dates **Edge:** Plain **Shape:** 12-sided

| Date | Mintage | VF20 | XF40 | MS60 | MS63 | MS65 |
|---|---|---|---|---|---|---|
| 2003 | 6,967 | PF65 60.00 | | | | |

## KM# 694a 50 CENTS

18.24 g., 0.999 Silver 0.5858 oz. ASW, 31.65 mm. **Ruler:** Elizabeth II **Obv:** Head with tiara right **Rev:** Wombat, lorikeet and koala **Edge:** Plain **Shape:** 12-sided

| Date | Mintage | VF20 | XF40 | MS60 | MS63 | MS65 |
|---|---|---|---|---|---|---|
| 2004 B | 8,203 | PF65 75.00 | | | | |

## KM# 746 50 CENTS

15.55 g., Copper-Nickel, 31.65 mm. **Ruler:** Elizabeth II **Obv:** Head with tiara right **Rev:** Military cemetery scene **Edge:** Plain **Shape:** 12-sided

| Date | Mintage | VF20 | XF40 | MS60 | MS63 | MS65 |
|---|---|---|---|---|---|---|
| 2005 B | 11,033,000 | — | — | 2.00 | 3.00 | 4.00 |
| 2005 B | — | PF65 20.00 | | | | |

## KM# 746a 50 CENTS

18.24 g., 0.999 Silver 0.5858 oz. ASW, 31.65 mm. **Ruler:** Elizabeth II **Obv:** Head with tiara right **Rev:** Military cemetery scene **Edge:** Plain **Shape:** 12-sided

| Date | Mintage | VF20 | XF40 | MS60 | MS63 | MS65 |
|---|---|---|---|---|---|---|
| 2005 B | 6,500 | PF65 38.00 | | | | |

## KM# 746b 50 CENTS

33.63 g., 0.9999 Gold 1.0811 oz. AGW, 31.65 mm. **Ruler:** Elizabeth II **Obv:** Head with tiara right **Rev:** Military cemetery scene **Edge:** Plain **Shape:** 12-sided

| Date | Mintage | VF20 | XF40 | MS60 | MS63 | MS65 |
|---|---|---|---|---|---|---|
| 2005 B | 650 | PF65 1,950 | | | | |

## KM# 769 50 CENTS

15.55 g., Copper-Nickel, 31.65 mm. **Ruler:** Elizabeth II **Subject:** Commonwealth Games, Secondary School Design Competition **Obv:** Head with tiara right **Rev:** Athletes

| Date | Mintage | VF20 | XF40 | MS60 | MS63 | MS65 |
|---|---|---|---|---|---|---|
| 2005 | 20,500,000 | — | — | 1.50 | 2.50 | 3.50 |
| 2005 | — | PF65 65.00 | | | | |

## KM# 67a 50 CENTS

18.24 g., 0.999 Silver 0.5858 oz. ASW, 31.51 mm. **Ruler:** Elizabeth II **Obv:** Young bust right **Rev:** Australian coat of arms **Edge:** Reeded

| Date | Mintage | VF20 | XF40 | MS60 | MS63 | MS65 |
|---|---|---|---|---|---|---|
| 2006 | 6,500 | PF65 65.00 | | | | |

## KM# 770 50 CENTS

15.55 g., Copper-Nickel, 31.65 mm. **Ruler:** Elizabeth II **Subject:** Basketball **Obv:** Head with tiara right **Obv. Legend:** ELIZABETH II - AUSTRALIA **Rev:** Basketball player shooting basket, Melbourne 2006 logo at left **Rev. Legend:** XVIII COMMONWEALTH GAMES **Shape:** 12-sided

| Date | Mintage | VF20 | XF40 | MS60 | MS63 | MS65 |
|---|---|---|---|---|---|---|
| 2006 | 5,002 | — | — | 7.00 | 8.50 | 10.00 |

**KM# 771 50 CENTS**
15.55 g., Copper-Nickel, 31.65 mm. **Ruler:** Elizabeth II **Subject:** Hockey **Obv:** Head with tiara right **Obv. Legend:** ELIZABETH II - AUSTRALIA **Rev:** Hockey player hitting puck, Melboune 2006 logo at upper left **Rev. Legend:** XVIII COMMONWEALTH GAMES **Shape:** 12-sided

| Date | Mintage | VF20 | XF40 | MS60 | MS63 | MS65 |
|---|---|---|---|---|---|---|
| 2006 | 4,082 | — | — | 7.00 | 8.50 | 10.00 |

**KM# 772 50 CENTS**
15.55 g., Copper-Nickel, 31.65 mm. **Ruler:** Elizabeth II **Subject:** Shooting **Obv:** Head with tiara right **Obv. Legend:** ELIZABETH II - AUSTRALIA **Rev:** Shooter, Melbourne 2006 logo at upper right **Rev. Legend:** XVIII COMMONWEALTH GAMES **Shape:** 12-sided

| Date | Mintage | VF20 | XF40 | MS60 | MS63 | MS65 |
|---|---|---|---|---|---|---|
| 2006 | 21,070 | — | — | 7.00 | 8.50 | 10.00 |

**KM# 773 50 CENTS**
15.55 g., Copper-Nickel, 31.65 mm. **Ruler:** Elizabeth II **Subject:** Weightlifting **Obv:** Head with tiara right **Obv. Legend:** ELIZABETH II - AUSTRALIA **Rev:** Weightlifter holding barbells above head, Melbourne 2006 logo at left **Rev. Legend:** XVIII COMMONWEALTH GAMES **Shape:** 12-sided

| Date | Mintage | VF20 | XF40 | MS60 | MS63 | MS65 |
|---|---|---|---|---|---|---|
| 2006 | 22,332 | — | — | 7.00 | 8.50 | 10.00 |

**KM# 774 50 CENTS**
15.55 g., Copper-Nickel, 31.65 mm. **Ruler:** Elizabeth II **Subject:** Gymnastics **Obv:** Head with tiara right **Obv. Legend:** ELIZABETH II - AUSTRALIA **Rev:** Gymnast standing with right leg up, Melbourne 2006 logo at left **Rev. Legend:** XVIII COMMONWEALTH GAMES **Edge:** Plain **Shape:** 12-sided

| Date | Mintage | VF20 | XF40 | MS60 | MS63 | MS65 |
|---|---|---|---|---|---|---|
| 2006 | 3,000 | — | — | 7.00 | 8.50 | 10.00 |

**KM# 775 50 CENTS**
15.55 g., Copper-Nickel, 31.65 mm. **Ruler:** Elizabeth II **Subject:** Rugby 7's **Obv:** Head with tiara right **Obv. Legend:** ELIZABETH II - AUSTRALIA **Rev:** Rugby player running right, Melbourne 2006 logo at upper left **Rev. Legend:** XVIII COMMONWEALTH GAMES **Shape:** 12-sided

| Date | Mintage | VF20 | XF40 | MS60 | MS63 | MS65 |
|---|---|---|---|---|---|---|
| 2006 | 24,427 | — | — | 7.00 | 8.50 | 10.00 |

**KM# 776 50 CENTS**
15.55 g., Copper-Nickel, 31.65 mm. **Ruler:** Elizabeth II **Subject:** Cycling **Obv:** Head with tiara right **Obv. Legend:** ELIZABETH II - AUSTRALIA **Rev:** Cyclist heading right, Melbourne 2006 logo at upper right **Rev. Legend:** XVIII COMMONWEALTH GAMES **Shape:** 12-sided

| Date | Mintage | VF20 | XF40 | MS60 | MS63 | MS65 |
|---|---|---|---|---|---|---|
| 2006 | 22,861 | — | — | 7.00 | 8.50 | 10.00 |

**KM# 777 50 CENTS**
15.55 g., Copper-Nickel, 31.65 mm. **Ruler:** Elizabeth II **Subject:** Athletics **Obv:** Head with tiara right **Obv. Legend:** ELIZABETH II - AUSTRALIA **Rev:** Runner right, Melbourne 2006 logo at lower right **Rev. Legend:** XVIII COMMONWEALTH GAMES **Shape:** 12-sided

| Date | Mintage | VF20 | XF40 | MS60 | MS63 | MS65 |
|---|---|---|---|---|---|---|
| 2006 | 22,475 | — | — | 7.00 | 8.50 | 10.00 |

**KM# 778 50 CENTS**
15.55 g., Copper-Nickel, 31.65 mm. **Ruler:** Elizabeth II **Subject:** Triathlon **Obv:** Head with tiara right **Obv. Legend:** ELIZABETH II - AUSRALIA **Rev:** Bicycle, runner, Melbourne 2006 logo below **Rev. Legend:** XVIII COMMONWEALTH GAMES **Shape:** 12-sided

| Date | Mintage | VF20 | XF40 | MS60 | MS63 | MS65 |
|---|---|---|---|---|---|---|
| 2006 | 22,302 | — | — | 7.00 | 8.50 | 10.00 |

**KM# 779 50 CENTS**
15.55 g., Copper-Nickel, 31.65 mm. **Ruler:** Elizabeth II **Subject:** Netball **Obv:** Head with tiara right **Obv. Legend:** ELIZABETH II - AUSTRALIA **Rev:** Player shooting basket, Melbourne 2006 logo at upper left **Rev. Legend:** XVIII COMMONWEALTH GAMES **Shape:** 12-sided

| Date | Mintage | VF20 | XF40 | MS60 | MS63 | MS65 |
|---|---|---|---|---|---|---|
| 2006 | 22,432 | — | — | 7.00 | 8.50 | 10.00 |

**KM# 780 50 CENTS**
15.55 g., Copper-Nickel, 31.65 mm. **Ruler:** Elizabeth II **Subject:** Table tennis **Obv:** Head with tiara right **Obv. Legend:** ELIZABETH II - AUSTRALIA **Rev:** Player hitting ball, Melbourne 2006 logo below **Rev. Legend:** XVIII COMMONWEALTH GAMES **Shape:** 12-sided

| Date | Mintage | VF20 | XF40 | MS60 | MS63 | MS65 |
|---|---|---|---|---|---|---|
| 2006 | 22,070 | — | — | 7.00 | 8.50 | 10.00 |

**KM# 781 50 CENTS**
15.55 g., Copper-Nickel, 31.65 mm. **Ruler:** Elizabeth II **Subject:** Aquatics **Obv:** Head with tiara right **Obv. Legend:** ELIZABETH II - AUSTRALIA **Rev:** Swimmer, Melbourne 2006 logo **Rev. Legend:** XVIII COMMONWEALTH GAMES **Shape:** 12-sided

| Date | Mintage | VF20 | XF40 | MS60 | MS63 | MS65 |
|---|---|---|---|---|---|---|
| 2006 | 31,702 | — | — | 7.00 | 8.50 | 10.00 |

**KM# 801 50 CENTS**
15.55 g., Copper-Nickel, 31.65 mm. **Ruler:** Elizabeth II **Subject:** 80th Birthday of Queen Elizabeth II **Obv:** Head with tiara right **Rev:** Royal Cipher **Shape:** 12-sided

| Date | Mintage | VF20 | XF40 | MS60 | MS63 | MS65 |
|---|---|---|---|---|---|---|
| 2006 | 28,191 | — | — | — | 45.00 | 60.00 |

**KM# 801a 50 CENTS**
18.24 g., 0.999 Silver 0.5858 oz. ASW partially gilt, 31.65 mm. **Ruler:** Elizabeth II **Subject:** 80th Birthday of Queen Elizabeth II **Obv:** Head with tiara right **Rev:** Crowned Royal Cipher on large 80, border of alternating British and Australian flags **Shape:** 12-sided

| Date | Mintage | VF20 | XF40 | MS60 | MS63 | MS65 |
|---|---|---|---|---|---|---|
| 2006 | 7,500 | **PF65** 85.00 | | | | |

**KM# 802 50 CENTS**
15.55 g., Copper-Nickel, 31.65 mm. **Ruler:** Elizabeth II **Subject:** Visit of Queen Elizabeth II **Obv:** Head with tiara right **Rev:** Australian map and world globe **Shape:** 12-sided

| Date | Mintage | VF20 | XF40 | MS60 | MS63 | MS65 |
|---|---|---|---|---|---|---|
| 2006 | — | — | — | — | 30.00 | 45.00 |

**KM# 802a 50 CENTS**
18.24 g., 0.999 Silver 0.5858 oz. ASW partially gilt, 31.65 mm. **Ruler:** Elizabeth II **Subject:** Visit of Queen Elizabeth II **Obv:** Head with tiara right **Rev:** Australian map and world globe **Shape:** 12-sided

| Date | Mintage | VF20 | XF40 | MS60 | MS63 | MS65 |
|---|---|---|---|---|---|---|
| 2006 | 7,500 | **PF65** 90.00 | | | | |

**KM# 821 50 CENTS**
13.28 g., 0.800 Silver 0.3416 oz. ASW, 31.51 mm. **Ruler:** Elizabeth II **Obv:** Head with tiara right **Rev:** Australian coat of arms **Edge:** Reeded

| Date | Mintage | VF20 | XF40 | MS60 | MS63 | MS65 |
|---|---|---|---|---|---|---|
| 2006 | — | **PF65** 70.00 | | | | |

**KM# 821a 50 CENTS**
25.30 g., 0.999 Gold 0.8126 oz. AGW, 31.51 mm. **Ruler:** Elizabeth II **Obv:** Head with tiara right **Rev:** Australian coat of arms **Edge:** Reeded

| Date | Mintage | VF20 | XF40 | MS60 | MS63 | MS65 |
|---|---|---|---|---|---|---|
| 2006 | 300 | **PF65** 1,500 | | | | |

**KM# 1001 50 CENTS**
15.55 g., Copper-Nickel, 31.65 mm. **Ruler:** Elizabeth II **Subject:** XVIII COMMONWEALTH GAMES **Obv:** Head with tiara right **Obv. Legend:** ELIZABETH II - AUSTRALIA **Rev:** Squash player, Melbourne 2006 logo **Edge:** Plain **Shape:** 12-sided

| Date | Mintage | VF20 | XF40 | MS60 | MS63 | MS65 |
|---|---|---|---|---|---|---|
| 2006 | — | — | — | 10.00 | 12.50 | 15.00 |

**KM# 1002 50 CENTS**
15.55 g., Copper-Nickel, 31.65 mm. Ruler: Elizabeth II Subject: XVIII COMMONWEALTH GAMES Obv: Head with tiara right Obv. Legend: ELIZABETH II - AUSTRALIA Rev: Lawn bowler, Melbourne 2006 logo Edge: Plain Shape: 12-sided

| Date | Mintage | VF20 | XF40 | MS60 | MS63 | MS65 |
|---|---|---|---|---|---|---|
| 2006 | 22,602 | — | — | 10.00 | 12.50 | 15.00 |

**KM# 1003 50 CENTS**
15.55 g., Copper-Nickel, 31.65 mm. **Ruler:** Elizabeth II **Subject:** XVIII COMMONWEALTH GAMES **Obv:** Head with tiara right **Obv. Legend:** ELIZABETH II - AUSTRALIA **Rev:** Boxer, Melbourne 2006 logo **Edge:** Plain **Shape:** 12-sided

| Date | Mintage | VF20 | XF40 | MS60 | MS63 | MS65 |
|---|---|---|---|---|---|---|
| 2006 | — | — | — | 10.00 | 12.50 | 15.00 |

**KM# 1004 50 CENTS**
Aluminum-Bronze, 30 mm. **Ruler:** Elizabeth II **Obv:** Head with tiara right **Obv. Legend:** ELIZABETH II - AUSTRALIA **Rev:** Everage head facing, multicolor **Rev. Legend:** DAME EDNA EVERAGE - 50TH ANNIVERSARY

| Date | Mintage | VF20 | XF40 | MS60 | MS63 | MS65 |
|---|---|---|---|---|---|---|
| ND-2006 P | — | — | — | 15.00 | 20.00 | 25.00 |

**KM# 1570 50 CENTS**
15.55 g., Copper-Nickel, 31.65 mm. **Ruler:** Elizabeth II **Subject:** Commonwealth Games **Rev:** Badminton

| Date | Mintage | VF20 | XF40 | MS60 | MS63 | MS65 |
|---|---|---|---|---|---|---|
| 2006 | — | — | — | 7.00 | 8.50 | 10.00 |

**KM# 1041 50 CENTS**
15.55 g., Copper-Nickel, 31.65 mm. **Ruler:** Elizabeth II **Subject:** Elizabeth and Philip Wedding Anniversary **Rev:** Profile portraits and diamond at center of circle of trumpets

| Date | Mintage | VF20 | XF40 | MS60 | MS63 | MS65 |
|---|---|---|---|---|---|---|
| 2007 B | 60,030 | — | — | 12.00 | 15.00 | 18.00 |

**KM# 1049 50 CENTS**
15.55 g., Copper-Nickel, 31.65 mm. **Ruler:** Elizabeth II **Subject:** Scouting Centennial in Australia **Rev:** Australian Scout Emblem

| Date | Mintage | VF20 | XF40 | MS60 | MS63 | MS65 |
|---|---|---|---|---|---|---|
| 2008 | 49,517 | — | — | 8.00 | 10.00 | 12.00 |

**KM# 1062 50 CENTS**
15.55 g., Copper-Nickel, 31.65 mm. **Ruler:** Elizabeth II **Subject:** 25th Anniversary Australia's Win of the America's Cup **Rev:** Yacht Australia II sailing left **Shape:** 12-sided

| Date | Mintage | VF20 | XF40 | MS60 | MS63 | MS65 |
|---|---|---|---|---|---|---|
| 2008 | 32,916 | — | — | 12.00 | 15.00 | 18.00 |

**KM# 1100 50 CENTS**
15.55 g., 0.999 Silver 0.4994 oz. ASW, 36.6 mm. **Ruler:** Elizabeth II **Subject:** Great Barrier Reef **Obv:** Head right **Rev:** Lion fish, multicolor **Edge:** reeded

| Date | Mintage | VF20 | XF40 | MS60 | MS63 | MS65 |
|---|---|---|---|---|---|---|
| 2009 P | 10,000 | **PF65** 75.00 | | | | |

**KM# 1101 50 CENTS**
15.55 g., 0.999 Silver 0.4994 oz. ASW, 36.6 mm. **Ruler:** Elizabeth II **Subject:** Great Barrier Reef **Obv:** Head right **Rev:** Leafy Sea Dragon, multicolor **Edge:** Reeded

| Date | Mintage | VF20 | XF40 | MS60 | MS63 | MS65 |
|---|---|---|---|---|---|---|
| 2009 P | 10,000 | **PF65** 75.00 | | | | |

**KM# 1102 50 CENTS**
15.55 g., 0.999 Silver 0.4994 oz. ASW, 36.6 mm. **Ruler:** Elizabeth II **Subject:** Great Barrier Reef **Rev:** Sea turtle, multicolor

| Date | Mintage | VF20 | XF40 | MS60 | MS63 | MS65 |
|---|---|---|---|---|---|---|
| 2009 P | — | **PF65** 75.00 | | | | |

**KM# 1432 50 CENTS**
15.55 g., Copper-Nickel, 31.65 mm. **Ruler:** Elizabeth II **Subject:** Moon Landing 40th Anniversary **Rev:** Earth, moon and orbiter

| Date | Mintage | VF20 | XF40 | MS60 | MS63 | MS65 |
|---|---|---|---|---|---|---|
| 2009 C | — | — | — | — | — | 10.00 |

**KM# 1328 50 CENTS**
15.55 g., 0.999 Silver 0.4994 oz. ASW, 36.6 mm. **Ruler:** Elizabeth II **Subject:** Great Barrier Reef **Obv:** Head right **Rev:** Clownfish, multicolor

| Date | Mintage | VF20 | XF40 | MS60 | MS63 | MS65 |
|---|---|---|---|---|---|---|
| 2010 P | — | **PF65** 60.00 | | | | |

**KM# 1329 50 CENTS**
15.57 g., 0.999 Silver 0.5002 oz. ASW, 36.6 mm. **Ruler:** Elizabeth II **Subject:** Great Barrier Reef **Rev:** Big belly sea horse in multicolor

| Date | Mintage | VF20 | XF40 | MS60 | MS63 | MS65 |
|---|---|---|---|---|---|---|
| 2010 P | — | PF65 75.00 | | | | |

**KM# 1389 50 CENTS**
15.55 g., 0.999 Silver 0.4994 oz. ASW, 36.6 mm. **Ruler:** Elizabeth II **Subject:** Great Barrier Reef - Morey Eel **Obv:** Hear right **Rev:** Tessellate Moray Eel, multicolor

| Date | Mintage | VF20 | XF40 | MS60 | MS63 | MS65 |
|---|---|---|---|---|---|---|
| 2010 P | — | PF65 86.00 | | | | |

**KM# 1450 50 CENTS**
15.56 g., 0.999 Silver 0.4998 oz. ASW **Ruler:** Elizabeth II **Rev:** Australian Sugar Glider, multicolor

| Date | Mintage | VF20 | XF40 | MS60 | MS63 | MS65 |
|---|---|---|---|---|---|---|
| 2010 P | — | PF65 45.00 | | | | |

**KM# 1456 50 CENTS**
15.56 g., 0.999 Silver 0.4998 oz. ASW **Ruler:** Elizabeth II **Rev:** Australian kangaroo, multicolor

| Date | Mintage | VF20 | XF40 | MS60 | MS63 | MS65 |
|---|---|---|---|---|---|---|
| 2010 P | — | PF65 30.00 | | | | |

**KM# 1493 50 CENTS**
15.50 g., 0.999 Silver 0.4978 oz. ASW, 36.6 mm. **Ruler:** Elizabeth II **Rev:** Dingo

| Date | Mintage | VF20 | XF40 | MS60 | MS63 | MS65 |
|---|---|---|---|---|---|---|
| 2010 | — | PF65 50.00 | | | | |

**KM# 1500 50 CENTS**
15.55 g., Copper-Nickel, 31.65 mm. **Ruler:** Elizabeth II **Subject:** Australia Day **Shape:** 12-sided

| Date | Mintage | VF20 | XF40 | MS60 | MS63 | MS65 |
|---|---|---|---|---|---|---|
| 2010 | — | — | — | 1.50 | 2.50 | 4.50 |

**KM# 1501 50 CENTS**
15.55 g., Copper-Nickel, 31.65 mm. **Ruler:** Elizabeth II **Subject:** Melbourne Cup, 150th Anniversary **Rev:** Horses racing right passing finish pole **Shape:** 12-sided

| Date | Mintage | VF20 | XF40 | MS60 | MS63 | MS65 |
|---|---|---|---|---|---|---|
| 2010 | — | — | — | 1.50 | 2.50 | 4.50 |

**KM# 1519 50 CENTS**
18.24 g., 0.999 Silver 0.5858 oz. ASW, 31.5 mm. **Ruler:** Elizabeth II **Subject:** Melbourne Cup, 150th race **Rev:** Trophy, partially gilt **Shape:** 12-sided

| Date | Mintage | VF20 | XF40 | MS60 | MS63 | MS65 |
|---|---|---|---|---|---|---|
| 2010 | — | PF65 80.00 | | | | |

**KM# 1520 50 CENTS**
18.24 g., 0.999 Silver 0.5858 oz. ASW, 31.5 mm. **Ruler:** Elizabeth II **Subject:** Melbourne Cup **Rev:** Horse and rider, partially gilt **Shape:** 12-sided

| Date | Mintage | VF20 | XF40 | MS60 | MS63 | MS65 |
|---|---|---|---|---|---|---|
| 2010 | — | PF65 80.00 | | | | |

**KM# 1525 50 CENTS**
15.55 g., Copper-Nickel, 31.5 mm. **Ruler:** Elizabeth II **Subject:** Australia Day **Rev:** Circle of people clasping hands

| Date | Mintage | VF20 | XF40 | MS60 | MS63 | MS65 |
|---|---|---|---|---|---|---|
| 2010 | — | — | — | 3.00 | 4.00 | 5.00 |

**KM# 1525a 50 CENTS**
18.24 g., Silver, 31.5 mm. **Ruler:** Elizabeth II **Subject:** Australia day **Rev:** Circle of people clasping hands, partially gilt **Shape:** 12-sided

| Date | Mintage | VF20 | XF40 | MS60 | MS63 | MS65 |
|---|---|---|---|---|---|---|
| 2010 | — | PF65 40.00 | | | | |

**KM# 1571 50 CENTS**
15.55 g., Copper-Nickel, 31.65 mm. **Ruler:** Elizabeth II **Subject:** Prince William and Catherine Middelton engagement **Rev:** Bundle of roses, Royal arms of Prince William below **Shape:** 12-sided

| Date | Mintage | VF20 | XF40 | MS60 | MS63 | MS65 |
|---|---|---|---|---|---|---|
| 2010 | — | — | — | 3.00 | 4.00 | 5.00 |

**KM# 1571a 50 CENTS**
18.24 g., 0.999 Silver 0.5858 oz. ASW partially gilt, 31.65 mm. **Ruler:** Elizabeth II **Subject:** Prince William and Catherine Middelton engagement **Rev:** Bunch of roses, gilt; Royal arms of Prince William below **Shape:** 12-sided

| Date | Mintage | VF20 | XF40 | MS60 | MS63 | MS65 |
|---|---|---|---|---|---|---|
| 2010 | — | PF65 60.00 | | | | |

**KM# 1521 50 CENTS**
15.55 g., Copper-Nickel, 31.65 mm. **Ruler:** Elizabeth II **Subject:** National Service, 60th Anniversary **Shape:** 12-sided

| Date | Mintage | VF20 | XF40 | MS60 | MS63 | MS65 |
|---|---|---|---|---|---|---|
| 2011 | — | — | — | 3.00 | 4.00 | 5.00 |

**KM# 1532 50 CENTS**
15.55 g., 0.999 Silver 0.4994 oz. ASW, 36.6 mm. **Ruler:** Elizabeth II **Subject:** Bush Baby **Rev:** Koala in color

| Date | Mintage | VF20 | XF40 | MS60 | MS63 | MS65 |
|---|---|---|---|---|---|---|
| 2011 P | — | PF65 65.00 | | | | |

### KM# 1533 50 CENTS

15.55 g., 0.999 Silver 0.4994 oz. ASW **Ruler:** Elizabeth II **Subject:** Bush Babies **Rev:** Bilby in color

| Date | Mintage | VF20 | XF40 | MS60 | MS63 | MS65 |
|---|---|---|---|---|---|---|
| 2011 P | — | PF65 65.00 | | | | |

### KM# 1567 50 CENTS

15.55 g., Copper-Nickel, 31.65 mm. **Ruler:** Elizabeth II **Subject:** Royal Wedding **Rev:** Catherine and William busts left **Shape:** 12-sided

| Date | Mintage | VF20 | XF40 | MS60 | MS63 | MS65 |
|---|---|---|---|---|---|---|
| 2011 | — | — | — | 2.50 | 3.50 | 5.00 |

### KM# 1567a 50 CENTS

18.24 g., 0.999 Silver 0.5858 oz. ASW partially gilt, 31.65 mm. **Ruler:** Elizabeth II **Subject:** Royal Wedding **Rev:** Catherine and William busts left, gilt flower at bottom **Shape:** 12-sided

| Date | Mintage | VF20 | XF40 | MS60 | MS63 | MS65 |
|---|---|---|---|---|---|---|
| 2011 | — | PF65 60.00 | | | | |

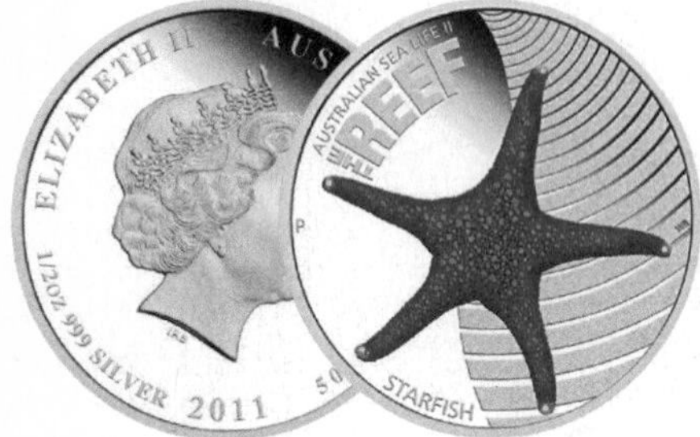


### KM# 1577 50 CENTS

15.59 g., 0.999 Silver 0.5008 oz. ASW, 36.6 mm. **Ruler:** Elizabeth II **Subject:** Australian Sea Life - Starfish **Rev:** Starfish in color

| Date | Mintage | VF20 | XF40 | MS60 | MS63 | MS65 |
|---|---|---|---|---|---|---|
| 2011 P | 10,000 | PF65 75.00 | | | | |

### KM# 1579 50 CENTS

15.59 g., 0.999 Silver 0.5008 oz. ASW, 36.6 mm. **Ruler:** Elizabeth II **Subject:** Australian sea life - Hawksbill Turtle **Rev:** Color turtle swimming right

| Date | Mintage | VF20 | XF40 | MS60 | MS63 | MS65 |
|---|---|---|---|---|---|---|
| 2011 P | 10,000 | PF65 70.00 | | | | |

### KM# 1624 50 CENTS

15.55 g., Copper-Nickel, 31.65 mm. **Ruler:** Elizabeth II **Subject:** Triple Zero Code for Emergency, 50th Anniversary **Obv:** Head with tiara right **Rev:** Telephone handset and 000, in color **Shape:** 12-sided

| Date | Mintage | VF20 | XF40 | MS60 | MS63 | MS65 |
|---|---|---|---|---|---|---|
| 2011 | — | — | — | — | — | 20.00 |

### KM# 404b 50 CENTS

15.55 g., Copper-Nickel with color, 31.65 mm. **Ruler:** Elizabeth II **Obv:** Head with tiara right **Rev:** Australian coat-of-arms with Kangaroo and Emu supporters all in color **Shape:** 12-sided

| Date | Mintage | VF20 | XF40 | MS60 | MS63 | MS65 |
|---|---|---|---|---|---|---|
| 2012 | — | — | — | — | — | 25.00 |

### KM# 404c 50 CENTS

18.24 g., 0.999 Silver 0.5858 oz. ASW partially gilt, 31.65 mm. **Ruler:** Elizabeth II **Obv:** Head with tiara right **Rev:** Australian coat-of-arms with Kangaroo and Emu supporters all gilt **Shape:** 12-sided

| Date | Mintage | VF20 | XF40 | MS60 | MS63 | MS65 |
|---|---|---|---|---|---|---|
| 2012 | — | PF65 75.00 | | | | |

### KM# 1578 50 CENTS

15.59 g., 0.999 Silver 0.5008 oz. ASW, 36.6 mm. **Ruler:** Elizabeth II **Subject:** Australian sea life - Surgeonfish **Rev:** Surgeonfish in blue, black and yellow colors

| Date | Mintage | VF20 | XF40 | MS60 | MS63 | MS65 |
|---|---|---|---|---|---|---|
| 2012 P | 10,000 | PF65 75.00 | | | | |

### KM# 1697 50 CENTS

15.59 g., Silver, 36.6 mm. **Ruler:** Elizabeth II **Subject:** Australian 2012 London Olympic Team **Obv:** Head with tiara right **Rev:** Male runner, Syndey Harbor Birdge, Tower of London images

| Date | Mintage | VF20 | XF40 | MS60 | MS63 | MS65 |
|---|---|---|---|---|---|---|
| 2012 P | 750 | PF65 45.00 | | | | |

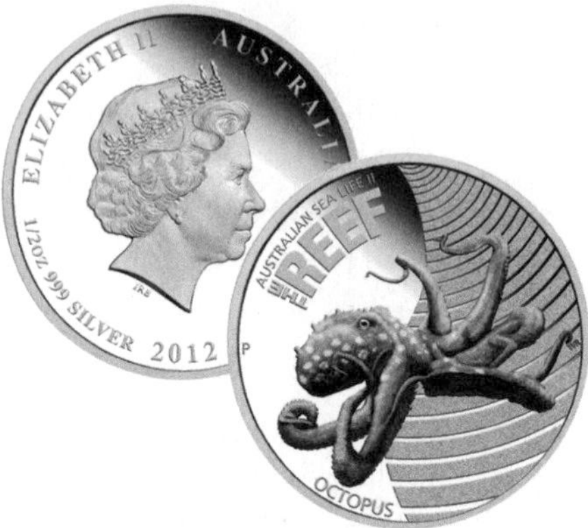


### KM# 1712 50 CENTS

15.59 g., 0.999 Silver 0.5008 oz. ASW, 36.6 mm. **Ruler:** Elizabeth II **Obv:** Head with tiara right **Rev:** Reef Octopus in color

| Date | Mintage | VF20 | XF40 | MS60 | MS63 | MS65 |
|---|---|---|---|---|---|---|
| 2012 P | 10,000 | PF65 50.00 | | | | |

### KM# 1741 50 CENTS

15.55 g., Copper-Nickel, 31.65 mm. **Ruler:** Elizabeth II **Subject:** Elizabeth II, 60th Anniversary **Obv:** Head with tiara right **Rev:** State Crown and floral design **Shape:** 12-sided

| Date | Mintage | VF20 | XF40 | MS60 | MS63 | MS65 |
|---|---|---|---|---|---|---|
| 2012 | — | — | — | 8.00 | 10.00 | 15.00 |

### KM# 1741a 50 CENTS

18.24 g., 0.999 Silver 0.5858 oz. ASW, 31.65 mm. **Ruler:** Elizabeth II **Subject:** Elizabeth II, 60th Anniversary **Obv:** Head with tiara right **Rev:** State Crown and floral **Shape:** 12-sided

| Date | Mintage | VF20 | XF40 | MS60 | MS63 | MS65 |
|---|---|---|---|---|---|---|
| 2012 | — | PF65 75.00 | | | | |

### KM# 1744 50 CENTS

15.55 g., Copper-Nickel, 31.65 mm. **Ruler:** Elizabeth II **Subject:** World War II, Bombing of Australia **Obv:** Head with tiara right **Rev:** Map of Astralia with bombed sites highlighted **Shape:** 12-sided

| Date | Mintage | VF20 | XF40 | MS60 | MS63 | MS65 |
|---|---|---|---|---|---|---|
| 2012 | — | — | — | 6.00 | 7.50 | 15.00 |

### KM# 1795 50 CENTS

15.55 g., 0.999 Silver 0.4994 oz. ASW, 36.6 mm. **Ruler:** Elizabeth II **Subject:** Love Koala **Rev:** Two koalas seated in color heart shape

| Date | Mintage | VF20 | XF40 | MS60 | MS63 | MS65 |
|---|---|---|---|---|---|---|
| 2012 P | 7,500 | PF65 150 | | | | |

### KM# 1801 50 CENTS

15.50 g., 0.999 Silver 0.4978 oz. ASW, 36.6 mm. **Ruler:** Elizabeth II **Subject:** FIFA **Rev:** Soccer player in native costume

| Date | Mintage | VF20 | XF40 | MS60 | MS63 | MS65 |
|---|---|---|---|---|---|---|
| 2012 P | — | PF65 60.00 | | | | |

### KM# 1816 50 CENTS

15.55 g., 0.999 Silver 0.4994 oz. ASW, 36.6 mm. **Ruler:** Elizabeth II **Subject:** Bush Babies - Lemur

| Date | Mintage | VF20 | XF40 | MS60 | MS63 | MS65 |
|---|---|---|---|---|---|---|
| 2012 P | — | PF65 50.00 | | | | |

## KM# 1847 50 CENTS

15.56 g., 0.999 Silver 0.4998 oz. ASW, 36.6 mm. **Ruler:** Elizabeth II **Subject:** Australian Sea Life II, The Reef **Rev:** Manta Ray in color

| Date | Mintage | VF20 | XF40 | MS60 | MS63 | MS65 |
|---|---|---|---|---|---|---|
| 2012 P | — | PF65 45.00 | | | | |

## KM# 1854 50 CENTS

15.55 g., Copper-Nickel, 31.5 mm. **Ruler:** Elizabeth II **Subject:** Australian Ballet, 50th Anniversary **Rev:** Two dancers **Shape:** 12-sided

| Date | Mintage | VF20 | XF40 | MS60 | MS63 | MS65 |
|---|---|---|---|---|---|---|
| 2012 | — | — | — | 3.00 | 4.00 | 5.00 |

## KM# 1854a 50 CENTS

18.24 g., 0.999 Silver 0.5858 oz. ASW, 31.5 mm. **Ruler:** Elizabeth II **Subject:** Australian Ballet, 50th Anniversary **Rev:** Two dancers **Shape:** 12-sided

| Date | Mintage | VF20 | XF40 | MS60 | MS63 | MS65 |
|---|---|---|---|---|---|---|
| 2012 | — | PF65 50.00 | | | | |

## KM# 1855 50 CENTS

15.50 g., Copper-Nickel, 31.5 mm. **Ruler:** Elizabeth II **Rev:** Kokoda Campaign monument **Shape:** 12-sided

| Date | Mintage | VF20 | XF40 | MS60 | MS63 | MS65 |
|---|---|---|---|---|---|---|
| 2012 | — | — | — | 3.00 | 4.00 | 5.00 |

## KM# 1856 50 CENTS

15.50 g., Copper-Nickel, 31.5 mm. **Ruler:** Elizabeth II **Subject:** Bathurst Endurance Race **Rev:** Racecar and landscape

| Date | Mintage | VF20 | XF40 | MS60 | MS63 | MS65 |
|---|---|---|---|---|---|---|
| 2012 | — | — | — | 3.00 | 4.00 | 5.00 |

## KM# 2020 50 CENTS

15.37 g., Copper-Nickel, 31.5 mm. **Ruler:** Elizabeth II **Subject:** Year of the Dragon **Rev:** Dragon

| Date | Mintage | VF20 | XF40 | MS60 | MS63 | MS65 |
|---|---|---|---|---|---|---|
| 2012 | — | — | — | — | — | 12.50 |

## KM# 2037 50 CENTS

0.50 g., 0.9999 Gold, 11.15 mm. **Ruler:** Elizabeth II **Subject:** Australian Miniature Money

| Date | Mintage | VF20 | XF40 | MS60 | MS63 | MS65 |
|---|---|---|---|---|---|---|
| 2012 | Est. 2000 | PF65 75.00 | | | | |

## KM# 404d 50 CENTS

33.63 g., 0.9999 Gold 1.0811 oz. AGW, 31.51 mm. **Ruler:** Elizabeth II **Obv:** Head with tiara right **Rev:** Arms with supporters, value below

| Date | Mintage | VF20 | XF40 | MS60 | MS63 | MS65 |
|---|---|---|---|---|---|---|
| 2013 | 500 | PF65 1,950 | | | | |

## KM# 1815 50 CENTS

15.55 g., 0.999 Silver 0.4994 oz. ASW, 36.6 mm. **Ruler:** Elizabeth II **Subject:** Birds - Cockatoo

| Date | Mintage | VF20 | XF40 | MS60 | MS63 | MS65 |
|---|---|---|---|---|---|---|
| 2013 P | — | PF65 50.00 | | | | |

## KM# 1817 50 CENTS

15.50 g., 0.999 Silver 0.4978 oz. ASW, 36.6 mm. **Ruler:** Elizabeth II **Subject:** Bush Babies - Kookaburra

| Date | Mintage | VF20 | XF40 | MS60 | MS63 | MS65 |
|---|---|---|---|---|---|---|
| 2013 P | — | PF65 50.00 | | | | |

## KM# 1818 50 CENTS

15.55 g., Copper-Nickel, 31.65 mm. **Ruler:** Elizabeth II **Subject:** Alesandra Stokic **Rev:** Surfer in wave

| Date | Mintage | VF20 | XF40 | MS60 | MS63 | MS65 |
|---|---|---|---|---|---|---|
| 2013 | — | — | — | — | — | 9.00 |

## KM# 1914 50 CENTS

15.50 g., 0.999 Silver 0.4978 oz. ASW, 36.6 mm. **Ruler:** Elizabeth II **Subject:** Australian Bush Babies II - Wombat

| Date | Mintage | VF20 | XF40 | MS60 | MS63 | MS65 |
|---|---|---|---|---|---|---|
| 2013 | Est. 10000 | PF65 50.00 | | | | |

## KM# 1915 50 CENTS

15.50 g., 0.999 Silver 0.4978 oz. ASW, 36.6 mm. **Ruler:** Elizabeth II **Subject:** Australian Bush Babies II - Platypus

| Date | Mintage | VF20 | XF40 | MS60 | MS63 | MS65 |
|---|---|---|---|---|---|---|
| 2013 | Est. 10000 | PF65 50.00 | | | | |

## KM# 1923 50 CENTS

15.50 g., 0.999 Silver 0.4978 oz. ASW, 36.6 mm. **Ruler:** Elizabeth II **Subject:** Birds of Australia - Budgerigar

| Date | Mintage | VF20 | XF40 | MS60 | MS63 | MS65 |
|---|---|---|---|---|---|---|
| 2013 Proof | Est. 10000 | — | — | — | — | — |

## KM# 1924 50 CENTS

15.50 g., 0.999 Silver 0.4978 oz. ASW, 36.6 mm. **Ruler:** Elizabeth II **Subject:** Birds of Australia - Regent Bowerbird

| Date | Mintage | VF20 | XF40 | MS60 | MS63 | MS65 |
|---|---|---|---|---|---|---|
| 2013 P Proof | Est. 10000 | — | — | — | — | 35.00 |

## KM# 1925 50 CENTS

15.50 g., 0.999 Silver 0.4978 oz. ASW, 36.6 mm. **Ruler:** Elizabeth II **Subject:** Birds of Australia - Rainbow Lorikeet

| Date | Mintage | VF20 | XF40 | MS60 | MS63 | MS65 |
|---|---|---|---|---|---|---|
| 2013 | Est. 10000 | PF65 50.00 | | | | |

**KM# 1926 50 CENTS**
15.50 g., 0.999 Silver 0.4978 oz. ASW, 36.6 mm. **Ruler:** Elizabeth II **Subject:** Newborn Baby

| Date | Mintage | VF20 | XF40 | MS60 | MS63 | MS65 |
|---|---|---|---|---|---|---|
| 2013 | — | PF65 35.00 | | | | |

**KM# 1960 50 CENTS**
15.55 g., Copper-Nickel, 31.51 mm. **Ruler:** Elizabeth II **Subject:** 100 Years of Commonwealth

| Date | Mintage | VF20 | XF40 | MS60 | MS63 | MS65 |
|---|---|---|---|---|---|---|
| 2013 | — | — | — | 3.00 | 4.00 | 5.00 |

**KM# 1963 50 CENTS**
15.55 g., Copper-Nickel, 31.51 mm. **Ruler:** Elizabeth II **Subject:** Centenary of Australian Banknotes

| Date | Mintage | VF20 | XF40 | MS60 | MS63 | MS65 |
|---|---|---|---|---|---|---|
| 2013 | — | — | — | 3.00 | 4.00 | 5.00 |

**KM# 2011 50 CENTS**
15.55 g., Copper-Nickel, 31.65 mm. **Ruler:** Elizabeth II **Subject:** Year of the Snake **Edge:** Snake **Shape:** 12 sided

| Date | Mintage | VF20 | XF40 | MS60 | MS63 | MS65 |
|---|---|---|---|---|---|---|
| 2013 | — | — | — | 3.00 | 4.00 | 5.00 |

**KM# 2057 50 CENTS**
15.59 g., 0.999 Silver 0.5008 oz. ASW, 36.6 mm. **Ruler:** Elizabeth II **Obv:** Head with tiara right **Rev:** Splendid Fairy-Wren in color

| Date | Mintage | VF20 | XF40 | MS60 | MS63 | MS65 |
|---|---|---|---|---|---|---|
| 2013 P | Est. 10000 | PF65 50.00 | | | | |

**KM# 2064 50 CENTS**
15.59 g., 0.999 Silver 0.5008 oz. ASW, 36.6 mm. **Ruler:** Elizabeth II **Obv:** Head with tiara right **Rev:** Christmas tree in color, stars

| Date | Mintage | VF20 | XF40 | MS60 | MS63 | MS65 |
|---|---|---|---|---|---|---|
| 2013 P | 5,000 | PF65 50.00 | | | | |

**KM# 2073 50 CENTS**
15.55 g., 0.999 Silver 0.4994 oz. ASW, 36.6 mm. **Ruler:** Elizabeth II **Subject:** Australian-American WWII memorial **Rev:** Eagle monument, flags in background

| Date | Mintage | VF20 | XF40 | MS60 | MS63 | MS65 |
|---|---|---|---|---|---|---|
| 2013 P | — | PF65 35.00 | | | | |

**KM# 2094 50 CENTS**
15.55 g., Copper-Nickel, 31.65 mm. **Ruler:** Elizabeth II **Subject:** Elizabeth II, 60th Anniversary of Coronation **Rev:** Sixty stylized crowns in circle **Shape:** 12-sided

| Date | Mintage | VF20 | XF40 | MS60 | MS63 | MS65 |
|---|---|---|---|---|---|---|
| 2013 | — | — | — | 3.00 | 4.00 | 5.00 |

**KM# 2094a 50 CENTS**
15.55 g., 0.999 Silver 0.4994 oz. ASW, 31.5 mm. **Ruler:** Elizabeth II **Subject:** Elizabeth II, 60th Anniversary of reign **Rev:** Sixty stylized crowns in circle **Shape:** 12-sided

| Date | Mintage | VF20 | XF40 | MS60 | MS63 | MS65 |
|---|---|---|---|---|---|---|
| 2013 Proof | — | — | — | — | — | 15.00 |

**KM# 2094b 50 CENTS**
33.63 g., 0.999 Gold 1.0801 oz. AGW, 31.5 mm. **Ruler:** Elizabeth II **Subject:** Elizabeth II, 60th Anniversary of Reign **Rev:** Sixty stylized crowns in circle **Shape:** 12-sided

| Date | Mintage | VF20 | XF40 | MS60 | MS63 | MS65 |
|---|---|---|---|---|---|---|
| 2013 | — | PF65 1,950 | | | | |

**KM# 2140 50 CENTS**
15.55 g., 0.999 Silver 0.4994 oz. ASW **Ruler:** Elizabeth II **Obv:** Head with tiara right **Rev:** Regent Bowerbird in color

| Date | Mintage | VF20 | XF40 | MS60 | MS63 | MS65 |
|---|---|---|---|---|---|---|
| 2013 | — | PF65 30.00 | | | | |

**KM# 2141 50 CENTS**
Silver ASW **Ruler:** Elizabeth II **Obv:** Head with tiara right **Rev:** Australian red one penny stamp - Kangaroo on map **Shape:** Vertical rectangle

| Date | Mintage | VF20 | XF40 | MS60 | MS63 | MS65 |
|---|---|---|---|---|---|---|
| 2013 | — | PF65 40.00 | | | | |

**KM# 2145 50 CENTS**
15.55 g., Copper-Nickel, 31.65 mm. **Ruler:** Elizabeth II **Subject:** Elizabeth II coronation, 60th Anniversary **Obv:** Head with tiara right **Rev:** Sixty crowns **Shape:** 12-sided

| Date | Mintage | VF20 | XF40 | MS60 | MS63 | MS65 |
|---|---|---|---|---|---|---|
| 2013 | — | — | — | — | — | 5.00 |

**KM# 2146 50 CENTS**
15.55 g., Copper-Nickel, 31.65 mm. **Ruler:** Elizabeth II **Subject:** Birth of Prince George **Obv:** Head with tiara right **Rev:** Crowned W and C in vines **Shape:** 12-sided

| Date | Mintage | VF20 | XF40 | MS60 | MS63 | MS65 |
|---|---|---|---|---|---|---|
| 2013 | — | — | — | — | — | 5.00 |

### KM# 2146a 50 CENTS

18.24 g., 0.999 Silver 0.5858 oz. ASW, 31.65 mm. **Ruler:** Elizabeth II **Subject:** Birth of Prince George **Obv:** Head with tiara right **Rev:** Crowned W and C in vines

| Date | Mintage | VF20 | XF40 | MS60 | MS63 | MS65 |
|---|---|---|---|---|---|---|
| 2013 | — | PF65 60.00 | | | | |

### KM# 1254 55 CENTS

15.55 g., 0.999 Silver 0.4994 oz. ASW, 26x38 mm. **Ruler:** Elizabeth II **Subject:** Postal Service, 200th Anniversary **Obv:** Head right **Rev:** Early post box **Edge:** Irregular as with a stamp **Shape:** Vertical rectangle

| Date | Mintage | VF20 | XF40 | MS60 | MS63 | MS65 |
|---|---|---|---|---|---|---|
| 2009 P | 8,700 | PF65 90.00 | | | | |

### KM# 1255 55 CENTS

15.55 g., 0.999 Silver 0.4994 oz. ASW, 26x38 mm. **Ruler:** Elizabeth II **Subject:** Postal Service, 200th Anniversary **Obv:** Head right **Rev:** Home delivery **Edge:** Irregular as with a stamp **Shape:** Vertical rectangle

| Date | Mintage | VF20 | XF40 | MS60 | MS63 | MS65 |
|---|---|---|---|---|---|---|
| 2009 P | 8,700 | PF65 90.00 | | | | |

### KM# 1803 60 CENTS

Silver **Ruler:** Elizabeth II **Subject:** London Olympics **Rev:** Scenes of London - Double decker bus; Big Ben; St. Paul's Cathedral, Wheel **Shape:** Vertical rectangle

| Date | Mintage | VF20 | XF40 | MS60 | MS63 | MS65 |
|---|---|---|---|---|---|---|
| 2012 P | — | PF65 100 | | | | |

### KM# 489 DOLLAR

9.00 g., Aluminum-Bronze, 25 mm. **Ruler:** Elizabeth II **Obv:** Head with tiara right **Rev:** Circle of 5 kangaroos **Edge:** Segmented reeding

| Date | Mintage | VF20 | XF40 | MS60 | MS63 | MS65 |
|---|---|---|---|---|---|---|
| 2001 B | 1,001,000 | PF65 55.00 | | | | |
| 2004 B | 8,800,000 | — | — | 5.00 | 6.00 | 7.00 |
| 2004 B | 50,000 | PF65 75.00 | | | | |
| 2005 B | 5,792,000 | — | — | 5.00 | 6.00 | 7.00 |
| 2005 B | 33,520 | PF65 85.00 | | | | |
| 2006 B | 38,691,000 | — | — | 3.00 | 4.00 | 5.00 |
| 2006 B | — | PF65 45.00 | | | | |
| 2006 B Special Proof | — | PF65 3,500 | | | | |
| Note: Mintage of 25-35 pieces | | | | | | |
| 2007 B | — | — | — | 18.00 | 20.00 | 25.00 |
| 2007 B | — | PF65 45.00 | | | | |
| 2008 B | 30,106,000 | — | — | 2.00 | 3.00 | 5.00 |
| 2008 B | — | PF65 45.00 | | | | |
| 2009 B | 4,682,000 | — | — | 3.00 | 4.00 | 6.00 |
| 2009 C Mintmaster mark | — | — | — | — | — | 25.00 |
| 2009 B | — | PF65 45.00 | | | | |
| 2010 B | — | — | — | — | — | 5.00 |
| 2010 B | — | PF65 45.00 | | | | |
| 2011 B | — | — | — | — | — | 5.00 |
| 2011 B | — | PF65 45.00 | | | | |
| 2012 B | — | — | — | — | — | 5.00 |
| 2012 B | — | PF65 45.00 | | | | |
| 2013 | — | — | — | — | 5.00 | — |
| 2013 | — | PF65 45.00 | | | | |
| 2014 | — | — | — | — | 5.00 | — |
| 2014 Proof | — | — | — | — | — | — |
| 2015 | — | PF63 5.00 | | | | |
| 2015 | — | PF65 45.00 | | | | |

### KM# 530 DOLLAR

9.00 g., Aluminum-Bronze, 25 mm. **Ruler:** Elizabeth II **Subject:** Army Centennial **Obv:** Head with tiara right **Rev:** Army crest **Edge:** Segmented reeding

| Date | Mintage | VF20 | XF40 | MS60 | MS63 | MS65 |
|---|---|---|---|---|---|---|
| 2001 C | 125,186 | — | — | — | 18.00 | 20.00 |
| Note: Large head, IRB spaced | | | | | | |
| 2001 C | Inc. above | — | — | — | 18.00 | 20.00 |
| Note: Small head, IRB joined | | | | | | |
| 2001 S | 38,095 | — | — | — | 25.00 | 30.00 |

### KM# 530a DOLLAR

11.66 g., 0.999 Silver 0.3745 oz. ASW, 24.9 mm. **Ruler:** Elizabeth II **Subject:** Army Centennial **Obv:** Head with tiara right **Rev:** Army crest **Edge:** Segmented reeding

| Date | Mintage | VF20 | XF40 | MS60 | MS63 | MS65 |
|---|---|---|---|---|---|---|
| 2001 | 17,839 | PF65 50.00 | | | | |

### KM# 531 DOLLAR

9.00 g., Aluminum-Bronze, 25 mm. **Ruler:** Elizabeth II **Subject:** 80th Anniversary Royal Australian Air Force **Obv:** Head with tiara right **Rev:** Air Force crest **Edge:** Segmented reeding

| Date | Mintage | VF20 | XF40 | MS60 | MS63 | MS65 |
|---|---|---|---|---|---|---|
| 2001 B | 99,281 | — | — | — | 18.00 | 20.00 |
| Note: IRB spaced | | | | | | |
| 2001 B | Inc. above | — | — | — | 25.00 | 30.00 |
| Note: IRB joined | | | | | | |

### KM# 534.1 DOLLAR

9.00 g., Aluminum-Bronze, 25 mm. **Ruler:** Elizabeth II **Subject:** Australian Centenary of Federation - Norfolk Island **Obv:** Head with tiara right **Rev:** Stylized ribbon map of Australia with star **Edge:** Segmented reeding **Note:** Reverse design raised above field. Prev. KM#534.

| Date | Mintage | VF20 | XF40 | MS60 | MS63 | MS65 |
|---|---|---|---|---|---|---|
| 2001 B | 6,781,200 | — | — | — | 50.00 | 55.00 |
| Note: IRB joined | | | | | | |
| 2001 B | Inc. above | — | — | — | 50.00 | 55.00 |
| Note: IRB spaced | | | | | | |
| 2001 B | — | PF65 5.00 | | | | |

### KM# 534.1a DOLLAR

21.70 g., 0.9999 Gold 0.6976 oz. AGW, 25 mm. **Ruler:** Elizabeth II **Subject:** Federation Centennial **Obv:** Elizabeth II **Rev:** Federation logo

| Date | Mintage | VF20 | XF40 | MS60 | MS63 | MS65 |
|---|---|---|---|---|---|---|
| 2001 B | 650 | PF65 1,300 | | | | |

### KM# 534.2 DOLLAR

9.00 g., Aluminum-Bronze, 25 mm. **Ruler:** Elizabeth II **Subject:** Australian Centenary of Federation - Norfolk Island **Obv:** Head with tiara right **Rev:** Multicolor ribbon design of Australia with star, printed on the surface. **Edge:** Segmented reeding

| Date | Mintage | VF20 | XF40 | MS60 | MS63 | MS65 |
|---|---|---|---|---|---|---|
| 2001 | 27,905,000 | — | — | 4.00 | 5.00 | 7.00 |
| 2001 | — | PF65 12.50 | | | | |

### KM# 588 DOLLAR

9.00 g., Aluminum-Bronze, 25 mm. **Ruler:** Elizabeth II **Subject:** 90th Anniversary Royal Australian Navy **Obv:** Head with tiara right **Rev:** Navy crest **Edge:** Segmented reeding

| Date | Mintage | VF20 | XF40 | MS60 | MS63 | MS65 |
|---|---|---|---|---|---|---|
| 2001 | 62,429 | — | — | — | 60.00 | 65.00 |

### KM# 594 DOLLAR

31.10 g., 0.999 Silver 0.999 oz. ASW partially gilt, 40 mm. **Ruler:** Elizabeth II **Subject:** Millennium **Obv:** Head with tiara right **Rev:** Gold inset sun on multicolor earth above Egyptian obelisk **Edge:** Reeded

| Date | Mintage | VF20 | XF40 | MS60 | MS63 | MS65 |
|---|---|---|---|---|---|---|
| 2001 Prooflike | 30,000 | — | — | — | 37.00 | 42.00 |

### KM# 598 DOLLAR

31.10 g., 0.999 Silver 0.9989 oz. ASW, 40.4 mm. **Ruler:** Elizabeth II **Subject:** Centenary of Federation "Holey Dollar **Obv:** Legend around star-shaped center hole **Rev:** Seven coats of arms around star-shaped hole **Edge:** Reeded

| Date | Mintage | VF20 | XF40 | MS60 | MS63 | MS65 |
|---|---|---|---|---|---|---|
| ND(2001) Prooflike | 21,668 | — | — | — | 35.00 | 40.00 |

### KM# 682 DOLLAR

9.00 g., Aluminum-Bronze, 25 mm. **Ruler:** Elizabeth II **Subject:** International Year of Volunteers **Rev:** Volunteers in wreath **Edge:** Segmented reeding

| Date | Mintage | VF20 | XF40 | MS60 | MS63 | MS65 |
|---|---|---|---|---|---|---|
| 2001 B | 6,000,000 | — | — | — | 12.00 | 15.00 |

### KM# 600.1 DOLLAR

9.00 g., Aluminum-Bronze, 25 mm. **Ruler:** Elizabeth II **Subject:** Year of the Outback **Obv:** Head with tiara right **Rev:** Stylized map of Australia **Edge:** Segmented reeding **Note:** Prev. KM#600.

| Date | Mintage | VF20 | XF40 | MS60 | MS63 | MS65 |
|---|---|---|---|---|---|---|
| 2002 | 34,074,000 | — | — | 4.00 | 5.00 | 7.00 |
| 2002 | — | PF65 10.00 | | | | |
| 2002 C | 68,447 | — | — | 5.00 | 7.00 | 9.00 |
| 2002 B | 32,698 | — | — | 5.00 | 7.00 | 9.00 |
| 2002 M | 31,694 | — | — | 5.00 | 7.00 | 9.00 |
| 2002 S | 36,931 | — | — | 5.00 | 7.00 | 9.00 |

### KM# 600.1a DOLLAR

11.66 g., 0.990 Silver 0.3711 oz. ASW, 25 mm. **Ruler:** Elizabeth II **Subject:** Year of the Outback **Obv:** Head with tiara right **Rev:** Stylized map of Australia **Edge:** Segmented reeding

| Date | Mintage | VF20 | XF40 | MS60 | MS63 | MS65 |
|---|---|---|---|---|---|---|
| 2002 B | 12,500 | PF65 65.00 | | | | |

**KM# 600.2 DOLLAR**
9.00 g., Aluminum-Bronze, 25 mm. **Ruler:** Elizabeth II **Subject:** Year of the Outback **Obv:** Head with tiara right **Rev:** Multicolor stylized map of Australia **Edge:** Segmented reeding

| Date | Mintage | VF20 | XF40 | MS60 | MS63 | MS65 |
|---|---|---|---|---|---|---|
| 2002 B | 39,514 | PF65 15.00 | | | | |

**KM# 632 DOLLAR**
31.10 g., 0.999 Silver 0.999 oz. ASW, 40 mm. **Ruler:** Elizabeth II **Subject:** Queen's Golden Jubilee **Obv:** Head right **Rev:** Queen on horse with multicolor flag background **Edge:** Reeded

| Date | Mintage | VF20 | XF40 | MS60 | MS63 | MS65 |
|---|---|---|---|---|---|---|
| 2002 | 34,074,000 | — | — | — | — | 50.00 |
| 2002 P | 26,782 | PF65 65.00 | | | | |

**KM# 660 DOLLAR**
31.10 g., 0.999 Silver 0.999 oz. ASW partially gilt, 40 mm. **Ruler:** Elizabeth II **Subject:** Melbourne Mint **Obv:** Head with tiara right **Rev:** Mint entrance between two gold foil inserts replicating gold sovereign reverse designs **Edge:** Reeded

| Date | Mintage | VF20 | XF40 | MS60 | MS63 | MS65 |
|---|---|---|---|---|---|---|
| 2002 B | 13,328 | PF65 58.00 | | | | |

**KM# 489a DOLLAR**
11.66 g., 0.999 Silver 0.3745 oz. ASW, 25 mm. **Ruler:** Elizabeth II **Obv:** Head with tiara right **Rev:** Five kangaroos and value **Edge:** Segmented reeding

| Date | Mintage | VF20 | XF40 | MS60 | MS63 | MS65 |
|---|---|---|---|---|---|---|
| 2003 B | 6,500 | PF65 40.00 | | | | |
| 2004 B | 6,500 | PF65 40.00 | | | | |
| 2005 B | 6,500 | PF65 40.00 | | | | |
| 2006 B | — | PF65 40.00 | | | | |
| 2007 B | — | PF65 40.00 | | | | |
| 2008 B | — | PF65 40.00 | | | | |
| 2009 B | — | PF65 40.00 | | | | |
| 2010 B | — | PF65 40.00 | | | | |
| 2011 B | 6,000 | PF65 40.00 | | | | |
| 2013 B | 5,000 | PF65 50.00 | | | | |

**KM# 663 DOLLAR**
9.00 g., Aluminum-Bronze, 25 mm. **Ruler:** Elizabeth II **Subject:** 50th Anniversary - End of Korean War **Obv:** Head with tiara right **Rev:** Dove of Peace **Edge:** Segmented reeding

| Date | Mintage | VF20 | XF40 | MS60 | MS63 | MS65 |
|---|---|---|---|---|---|---|
| 2003 B | 34,949 | — | — | 4.00 | 6.00 | 8.00 |
| 2003 C | 93,572 | — | — | 4.00 | 6.00 | 8.00 |
| 2003 M | 36,142 | — | — | 4.00 | 6.00 | 8.00 |
| 2003 S | 36,091 | — | — | 4.00 | 6.00 | 8.00 |

**KM# 663a DOLLAR**
11.66 g., 0.999 Silver 0.3745 oz. ASW, 25 mm. **Ruler:** Elizabeth II **Subject:** Korean War **Obv:** Queens head right **Rev:** Dove of Peace **Edge:** Segmented reeding

| Date | Mintage | VF20 | XF40 | MS60 | MS63 | MS65 |
|---|---|---|---|---|---|---|
| 2003 B | 15,000 | PF65 55.00 | | | | |

**KM# 685 DOLLAR**
31.10 g., 0.999 Silver 0.999 oz. ASW, 40.6 mm. **Ruler:** Elizabeth II **Subject:** 21st Birthday of William **Obv:** Head right **Rev:** Multicolor Prince William **Edge:** Segmented reeding

| Date | Mintage | VF20 | XF40 | MS60 | MS63 | MS65 |
|---|---|---|---|---|---|---|
| ND(2003) P | 12,500 | PF65 45.00 | | | | |

**KM# 690.1 DOLLAR**
9.00 g., Aluminum-Bronze, 25 mm. **Ruler:** Elizabeth II **Subject:** Australia's Volunteers **Obv:** Elizabeth II **Rev:** Multicolor Australia's Volunteers logo **Edge:** Segmented reeding

| Date | Mintage | VF20 | XF40 | MS60 | MS63 | MS65 |
|---|---|---|---|---|---|---|
| 2003 B | 39,090 | PF65 15.00 | | | | |

**KM# 690 DOLLAR**
9.00 g., Aluminum-Bronze, 25 mm. **Ruler:** Elizabeth II **Obv:** Queens head right **Rev:** Australia Volunteers logo **Edge:** Segmented reeding

| Date | Mintage | VF20 | XF40 | MS60 | MS63 | MS65 |
|---|---|---|---|---|---|---|
| 2003 B | 4,149,000 | — | — | — | 15.00 | 17.00 |

**KM# 690a DOLLAR**
9.00 g., 0.999 Silver 0.2891 oz. ASW, 25 mm. **Ruler:** Elizabeth II **Obv:** Queens head right **Rev:** Australia Volunteers logo

| Date | Mintage | VF20 | XF40 | MS60 | MS63 | MS65 |
|---|---|---|---|---|---|---|
| 2003 B | 6,500 | PF65 30.00 | | | | |

**KM# 754 DOLLAR**
9.00 g., Aluminum-Bronze, 25 mm. **Ruler:** Elizabeth II **Subject:** Womens Suffrage **Obv:** Queens head right **Rev:** Suffragette talking to Britannia **Edge:** Segmented reeding

| Date | Mintage | VF20 | XF40 | MS60 | MS63 | MS65 |
|---|---|---|---|---|---|---|
| 2003 B | 10,007,000 | — | — | 4.00 | 5.00 | 7.00 |

**KM# 763 DOLLAR**
13.36 g., 0.999 Silver 0.4291 oz. ASW, 28.5 mm. **Ruler:** Elizabeth II **Series:** Masterpieces in Silver - Port Phillip Patterns **Obv:** 1/4 Ounce design **Rev:** Kangaroo design **Edge:** Reeded

| Date | Mintage | VF20 | XF40 | MS60 | MS63 | MS65 |
|---|---|---|---|---|---|---|
| 2003 B | 10,000 | PF65 80.00 | | | | |

**KM# 803 DOLLAR**
9.00 g., Aluminum-Bronze, 25 mm. **Ruler:** Elizabeth II **Subject:** Vietnam War Veterans 1962-1973 **Obv:** Head with tiara right **Rev:** Australian Vietnam Forces National Memorial

| Date | Mintage | VF20 | XF40 | MS60 | MS63 | MS65 |
|---|---|---|---|---|---|---|
| 2003 | 57,000 | — | — | — | 45.00 | 50.00 |

**KM# 822 DOLLAR**
54.30 g., 0.999 Silver 1.744 oz. ASW, 50 mm. **Ruler:** Elizabeth II **Obv:** Superimposed head above replica of Holey Dollar **Rev:** Replica of Holey Dollar **Edge:** Reeded **Note:** Holey Dollar replica is embedded in silver collar and comes with replica Dump also in 0.999 silver.

| Date | Mintage | VF20 | XF40 | MS60 | MS63 | MS65 |
|---|---|---|---|---|---|---|
| 2003 | 11,000 | PF65 90.00 | | | | |

**KM# 823 DOLLAR**
31.10 g., 0.999 Silver 0.999 oz. ASW, 40 mm. **Ruler:** Elizabeth II **Subject:** 50th Anniversary - Coronation Elizabeth II **Obv:** Head with tiara right **Rev:** Crown in lettered garland **Note:** Colored design.

| Date | Mintage | VF20 | XF40 | MS60 | MS63 | MS65 |
|---|---|---|---|---|---|---|
| 2003 P | 40,400 | PF65 45.00 | | | | |

**KM# 824 DOLLAR**
31.10 g., 0.999 Silver 0.999 oz. ASW, 40 mm. **Ruler:** Elizabeth II **Subject:** Golden Pipeline **Obv:** Head with tiara right **Rev:** Charles Yelverton O'Connor, innovative engineer, multicolor

| Date | Mintage | VF20 | XF40 | MS60 | MS63 | MS65 |
|---|---|---|---|---|---|---|
| 2003 P | 5,000 | PF65 130 | | | | |

**KM# 725 DOLLAR**
56.23 g., 0.999 Bi-Metallic 1.806 oz. Copper center in Silver ring, 50 mm. **Ruler:** Elizabeth II **Subject:** The Last Penny **Obv:** 1964 dated penny obverse **Rev:** 1964 date penny reverse **Edge:** Reeded

| Date | Mintage | VF20 | XF40 | MS60 | MS63 | MS65 |
|---|---|---|---|---|---|---|
| 2004 B | 16,437 | PF65 85.00 | | | | |

**KM# 726 DOLLAR**
9.00 g., Aluminum-Bronze, 25 mm. **Ruler:** Elizabeth II **Subject:** Eureka Stockade 1854-2004 **Obv:** Head with tiara right **Rev:** Stockade and stylized soldiers **Edge:** Segmented reeding

| Date | Mintage | VF20 | XF40 | MS60 | MS63 | MS65 |
|---|---|---|---|---|---|---|
| 2004 E | 95,948 | — | — | 3.00 | 5.00 | 6.00 |
| 2004 B | 33,835 | — | — | 3.00 | 5.00 | 6.00 |
| 2004 C | 70,913 | — | — | 3.00 | 5.00 | 6.00 |
| 2004 S | 45,098 | — | — | 3.00 | 5.00 | 6.00 |
| 2004 M | 37,526 | — | — | 3.00 | 5.00 | 6.00 |
| 2004 3 known | — | — | — | — | — | 1,000 |
| 2004 | — | — | — | 6.00 | 8.00 | 10.00 |

**KM# 726a DOLLAR**
11.66 g., 0.999 Silver 0.3745 oz. ASW, 25 mm. **Ruler:** Elizabeth II **Subject:** Eureka Stockade **Obv:** Head with tiara right **Rev:** Stockade and stylized soldiers **Edge:** Segmented reeding

| Date | Mintage | VF20 | XF40 | MS60 | MS63 | MS65 |
|---|---|---|---|---|---|---|
| 2004 B | 17,697 | PF65 38.00 | | | | |

**KM# 733.1 DOLLAR**
9.00 g., Aluminum-Bronze, 25 mm. **Ruler:** Elizabeth II **Rev:** Five kangaroos **Edge:** Segmented reeding

| Date | Mintage | VF20 | XF40 | MS60 | MS63 | MS65 |
|---|---|---|---|---|---|---|
| 2004 B | — | — | — | — | — | 4.50 |

**KM# 733.1a DOLLAR**
11.66 g., 0.9999 Silver 0.3748 oz. ASW, 25 mm. **Ruler:** Elizabeth II **Rev:** Five Kangaroos

| Date | Mintage | VF20 | XF40 | MS60 | MS63 | MS65 |
|---|---|---|---|---|---|---|
| 2004 B | 6,500 | PF65 35.00 | | | | |

**KM# 733 DOLLAR**
9.00 g., Aluminum-Bronze, 25 mm. **Ruler:** Elizabeth II **Obv:** Head with tiara right **Rev:** Multicolor holographic five kangaroos design **Edge:** Segmented reeding

| Date | Mintage | VF20 | XF40 | MS60 | MS63 | MS65 |
|---|---|---|---|---|---|---|
| 2004 B | — | PF65 25.00 | | | | |

**KM# 734 DOLLAR**
31.10 g., 0.999 Silver 0.999 oz. ASW, 40 mm. **Ruler:** Elizabeth II **Subject:** First Moon Walk **Obv:** Head with tiara right **Rev:** Multicolor rocket in flight **Edge:** Reeded

| Date | Mintage | VF20 | XF40 | MS60 | MS63 | MS65 |
|---|---|---|---|---|---|---|
| 2004 P | 18,415 | PF65 100 | | | | |

**KM# 735 DOLLAR**
31.10 g., 0.999 Silver 0.999 oz. ASW, 40 mm. **Ruler:** Elizabeth II **Subject:** First Moon Walk **Obv:** Head with tiara right **Rev:** Multicolor scene of astronauts planting flag on moon **Edge:** Reeded

| Date | Mintage | VF20 | XF40 | MS60 | MS63 | MS65 |
|---|---|---|---|---|---|---|
| 2004 P | 18,415 | PF65 110 | | | | |

**KM# 736 DOLLAR**
31.10 g., 0.999 Silver 0.999 oz. ASW, 40 mm. **Ruler:** Elizabeth II **Subject:** First Moon Walk **Obv:** Head with tiara right **Rev:** Multicolor close up of astronaut on moon **Edge:** Reeded

| Date | Mintage | VF20 | XF40 | MS60 | MS63 | MS65 |
|---|---|---|---|---|---|---|
| 2004 P | 18,415 | PF65 95.00 | | | | |

**KM# 737 DOLLAR**
31.10 g., 0.999 Silver 0.999 oz. ASW, 40 mm. **Ruler:** Elizabeth II **Obv:** Head with tiara right **Rev:** Multicolor Antarctic view of Mawson Station and penguins **Edge:** Reeded

| Date | Mintage | VF20 | XF40 | MS60 | MS63 | MS65 |
|---|---|---|---|---|---|---|
| 2004 P | 7,500 | PF65 60.00 | | | | |

**KM# 738 DOLLAR**
31.10 g., 0.999 Silver 0.999 oz. ASW partially gilt, 40 mm. **Ruler:** Elizabeth II **Subject:** 50th Anniversary of Royal Visit **Obv:** Queens head right **Rev:** Gilt lion and kangaroo **Edge:** Reeded

| Date | Mintage | VF20 | XF40 | MS60 | MS63 | MS65 |
|---|---|---|---|---|---|---|
| ND (2004) | 12,500 | PF65 85.00 | | | | |

**KM# 740 DOLLAR**
24.38 g., 0.999 Silver 0.7829 oz. ASW Encapsulated gold nuggets in center, 40.6 mm. **Ruler:** Elizabeth II **Obv:** Crowned head right **Rev:** Eureka Stockade leader, miners and flag **Edge:** Reeded

| Date | Mintage | VF20 | XF40 | MS60 | MS63 | MS65 |
|---|---|---|---|---|---|---|
| 2004 | 12,500 | PF65 145 | | | | |

**KM# A797 DOLLAR**
31.64 g., 0.999 Silver 1.0161 oz. ASW, 40 mm. **Subject:** 60th Anniversary of the End of WWII **Obv:** Bust right **Rev:** Moving image of Dancing Man

| Date | Mintage | VF20 | XF40 | MS60 | MS63 | MS65 |
|---|---|---|---|---|---|---|
| 2005 | 25,000 | PF65 85.00 | | | | |

**KM# 747 DOLLAR**
9.00 g., Aluminum-Bronze, 25 mm. **Ruler:** Elizabeth II **Subject:** 60th Anniversary World War II **Obv:** Head with tiara right **Rev:** Rejoicing serviceman **Edge:** Segmented reeding

| Date | Mintage | VF20 | XF40 | MS60 | MS63 | MS65 |
|---|---|---|---|---|---|---|
| 2005 B | 31,788,000 | — | — | 2.00 | 3.00 | 4.00 |
| 2005 B | — | PF65 35.00 | | | | |

**KM# 747a DOLLAR**
11.66 g., 0.999 Silver 0.3745 oz. ASW, 25 mm. **Ruler:** Elizabeth II **Obv:** Queen's head right **Rev:** Rejoicing servicemen **Edge:** Segmented reeding

| Date | Mintage | VF20 | XF40 | MS60 | MS63 | MS65 |
|---|---|---|---|---|---|---|
| 2005 B | 6,500 | PF65 45.00 | | | | |

**KM# 747b DOLLAR**
21.52 g., 0.9999 Gold 0.6918 oz. AGW, 25 mm. **Ruler:** Elizabeth II **Obv:** Queen's head right **Rev:** Rejoicing servicemen **Edge:** Segmented reeding

| Date | Mintage | VF20 | XF40 | MS60 | MS63 | MS65 |
|---|---|---|---|---|---|---|
| 2005 B | 629 | PF65 1,300 | | | | |

**KM# 748 DOLLAR**
9.00 g., Aluminum-Bronze, 25 mm. **Ruler:** Elizabeth II **Subject:** 90th Anniversary Gallipoli Landing 1915-2005 **Obv:** Head with tiara right **Rev:** Bugler silhouette **Edge:** Segmented reeding

| Date | Mintage | VF20 | XF40 | MS60 | MS63 | MS65 |
|---|---|---|---|---|---|---|
| 2005 | 15,000 | — | — | — | 25.00 | 30.00 |
| 2005 B | 36,108 | — | — | 3.00 | 5.00 | 6.00 |
| 2005 C | 76,173 | — | — | 3.00 | 5.00 | 6.00 |
| 2005 G | 35,452 | — | — | — | 35.00 | 40.00 |
| 2005 M | 38,727 | — | — | 3.00 | 5.00 | 6.00 |
| 2005 S | 39,569 | — | — | 4.00 | 6.00 | 7.00 |

**KM# 748a DOLLAR**
11.66 g., 0.999 Silver 0.3745 oz. ASW, 25 mm. **Ruler:** Elizabeth II **Subject:** Gallipoli **Obv:** Queen's head right **Rev:** Bugler silhouette **Edge:** Segmented reeding

| Date | Mintage | VF20 | XF40 | MS60 | MS63 | MS65 |
|---|---|---|---|---|---|---|
| 2005 B | 17,749 | PF65 45.00 | | | | |
| 2005 B Proof, 2 known | — | PF65 1,500 | | | | |

**KM# 825 DOLLAR**
56.45 g., 0.999 Silver 1.8131 oz. ASW partially gilt, 50 mm. **Ruler:** Elizabeth II **Obv:** Small head with tiara right superimposed above replica of Sydney Mint Sovereign **Rev:** Replica of Sydney Mint Sovereign **Edge:** Reeded

| Date | Mintage | VF20 | XF40 | MS60 | MS63 | MS65 |
|---|---|---|---|---|---|---|
| 2005 | 11,845 | PF65 90.00 | | | | |

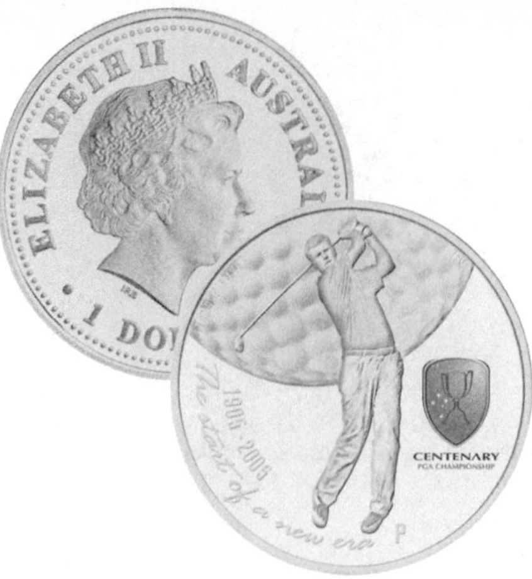

**KM# 830 DOLLAR**
31.60 g., 0.999 Silver 1.0149 oz. ASW, 40 mm. **Ruler:** Elizabeth II **Subject:** Centenary Australian Tennis Open 1905-2005 **Obv:** Head with tiara right **Rev:** Tennis players

| Date | Mintage | VF20 | XF40 | MS60 | MS63 | MS65 |
|---|---|---|---|---|---|---|
| 2005 | 7,500 | PF65 50.00 | | | | |

**KM# 831 DOLLAR**
31.60 g., 0.999 Silver 1.0149 oz. ASW, 40 mm. **Ruler:** Elizabeth II **Subject:** Centenary Australian PGA Gold Open 1905-2005 **Obv:** Head with tiara right **Rev:** Golfer

| Date | Mintage | VF20 | XF40 | MS60 | MS63 | MS65 |
|---|---|---|---|---|---|---|
| 2005 | 10,000 | PF65 85.00 | | | | |

**KM# 832 DOLLAR**
31.60 g., 0.999 Silver 1.0149 oz. ASW, 40 mm. **Ruler:** Elizabeth II **Subject:** Rotary International, 100th Anniversary **Obv:** Head with tiara right **Rev:** Rotary International Logo in color

| Date | Mintage | VF20 | XF40 | MS60 | MS63 | MS65 |
|---|---|---|---|---|---|---|
| 2005 | 10,870 | PF65 90.00 | | | | |

**KM# 833 DOLLAR**
31.10 g., 0.999 Silver 0.999 oz. ASW, 40 mm. **Ruler:** Elizabeth II **Subject:** 90th Anniversary Gallipoli Landings **Obv:** Head with tiara right **Rev:** Multicolor Australian and New Zealand soldiers beneath Australian flag

| Date | Mintage | VF20 | XF40 | MS60 | MS63 | MS65 |
|---|---|---|---|---|---|---|
| 2005 | 15,000 | PF65 185 | | | | |

**KM# 835 DOLLAR**
Aluminum-Bronze, 38.74 mm. **Ruler:** Elizabeth II **Subject:** Living Icons of Australia and New Zealand **Obv:** Head with tiara right **Rev:** Indigenous image of kangaroo

| Date | Mintage | VF20 | XF40 | MS60 | MS63 | MS65 |
|---|---|---|---|---|---|---|
| 2005 | 16,547 | — | — | — | 15.00 | 20.00 |

**KM# 836 DOLLAR**
31.10 g., 0.999 Silver 0.999 oz. ASW, 40 mm. **Ruler:** Elizabeth II **Subject:** Prince Harry, 21st Birthday **Obv:** Head with tiara right **Rev:** Prince Harry in color

| Date | Mintage | VF20 | XF40 | MS60 | MS63 | MS65 |
|---|---|---|---|---|---|---|
| 2005 | 6,088 | PF65 80.00 | | | | |

**KM# 1015 DOLLAR**
31.60 g., 0.999 Silver 1.0149 oz. ASW, 40.5 mm. **Ruler:** Elizabeth II **Subject:** 50th Anniversary Australian Territory **Obv:** Head with tiara right **Obv. Legend:** ELIZABETH II • AUSTRALIA **Rev:** Red-footed Booby perched on a branch, multicolor **Rev. Legend:** COCOS (KEELING) ISLANDS **Edge:** Reeded

| Date | Mintage | VF20 | XF40 | MS60 | MS63 | MS65 |
|---|---|---|---|---|---|---|
| 2005 P | 6,436 | PF65 70.00 | | | | |

**KM# 1018 DOLLAR**
31.75 g., 0.999 Silver 1.0198 oz. ASW, 40.5 mm. **Ruler:** Elizabeth II **Obv:** Head with tiara right **Obv. Legend:** ELIZABETH II - AUSTRALIA **Rev:** Leopard seal with pup on ice, multicolor **Rev. Legend:** Australian Antarctic Territory **Edge:** Reeded

| Date | Mintage | VF20 | XF40 | MS60 | MS63 | MS65 |
|---|---|---|---|---|---|---|
| 2005 P | 7,500 | PF65 60.00 | | | | |

**KM# 77a DOLLAR**
11.66 g., 0.999 Silver 0.3745 oz. ASW, 25 mm. **Ruler:** Elizabeth II **Obv:** Young bust right **Rev:** Kangaroos **Edge:** Segmented reeding

| Date | Mintage | VF20 | XF40 | MS60 | MS63 | MS65 |
|---|---|---|---|---|---|---|
| 2006 | 6,500 | PF65 40.00 | | | | |

**KM# 489b DOLLAR**
21.52 g., 0.999 Gold 0.6912 oz. AGW, 25 mm. **Ruler:** Elizabeth II **Obv:** Head with tiara right **Rev:** Five kangaroos and value **Edge:** Segmented reeding

| Date | Mintage | VF20 | XF40 | MS60 | MS63 | MS65 |
|---|---|---|---|---|---|---|
| 2006 | 300 | PF65 1,300 | | | | |
| 2013 | 500 | PF65 1,250 | | | | |

**KM# 804 DOLLAR**
9.00 g., Aluminum-Bronze, 25 mm. **Ruler:** Elizabeth II **Subject:** XVIII Commonwealth Games **Obv:** Head with tiara right **Rev:** Graphic at left, logo at right

| Date | Mintage | VF20 | XF40 | MS60 | MS63 | MS65 |
|---|---|---|---|---|---|---|
| 2006 | — | — | — | 2.50 | 3.50 | 5.00 |

## KM# 805 DOLLAR

9.00 g., Aluminum-Bronze, 25 mm. **Ruler:** Elizabeth II **Subject:** 50 Years of Television **Obv:** Head with tiara right **Rev:** TV mast and camera **Edge:** Segmented reeding

| Date | Mintage | VF20 | XF40 | MS60 | MS63 | MS65 |
|---|---|---|---|---|---|---|
| 2006 B | 47,228 | — | — | 3.00 | 5.00 | 6.00 |
| 2006 C | 135,221 | — | — | 3.00 | 5.00 | 6.00 |
| 2006 M | 39,600 | — | — | 3.00 | 5.00 | 6.00 |
| 2006 S | 48,490 | — | — | 3.00 | 5.00 | 6.00 |
| 2006 TV | 46,370 | — | — | — | 15.00 | 17.00 |
| 2006 Without mint mark, 4 known | — | — | — | — | — | 1,000 |

## KM# 805A DOLLAR

11.66 g., 0.999 Silver 0.3745 oz. ASW, 25 mm. **Ruler:** Elizabeth II **Subject:** 50 Years of Television **Obv:** Head with tiara right **Rev:** TV mast and camera **Edge:** Segmented reeding

| Date | Mintage | VF20 | XF40 | MS60 | MS63 | MS65 |
|---|---|---|---|---|---|---|
| 2006 | 10,790 | PF65 45.00 | | | | |
| 2006 A | 3,859 | PF65 60.00 | | | | |

## KM# 806 DOLLAR

9.00 g., Aluminum-Bronze Issued in folder., 25 mm. **Ruler:** Elizabeth II **Series:** Colored Oceans **Obv:** Head with tiara right **Rev:** Multicolor jumping Bottlenose dolphins **Edge:** Segmented reeding

| Date | Mintage | VF20 | XF40 | MS60 | MS63 | MS65 |
|---|---|---|---|---|---|---|
| 2006 | 29,310 | — | — | — | — | 35.00 |

## KM# 807 DOLLAR

9.00 g., Aluminum-Bronze, 25 mm. **Ruler:** Elizabeth II **Series:** Colored Oceans **Obv:** Head with tiara right **Rev:** Multicolor clown fish **Edge:** Segmented reeding **Note:** Issued in folder.

| Date | Mintage | VF20 | XF40 | MS60 | MS63 | MS65 |
|---|---|---|---|---|---|---|
| 2006 | 29,310 | — | — | 22.00 | 25.00 | 30.00 |

## KM# 826 DOLLAR

60.50 g., 0.999 Silver 1.9432 oz. ASW, 50 mm. **Ruler:** Elizabeth II **Obv:** Replica of 1758 Mexico City Mint 8 Reales **Obv. Legend:** ELIZABETH II (small head right) AUSTRALIA **Rev:** Replica of 1758 Mexico City Mint 8 Reales **Rev. Legend:** PILLAR DOLLAR **Edge:** Reeded

| Date | Mintage | VF20 | XF40 | MS60 | MS63 | MS65 |
|---|---|---|---|---|---|---|
| 2006 | 9,846 | — | — | — | — | 115 |

## KM# 838 DOLLAR

31.10 g., 0.999 Silver 0.999 oz. ASW, 40 mm. **Ruler:** Elizabeth II **Subject:** Australain-Japan Year of Exchange **Obv:** Head with tiara right **Rev:** Kangaroo leaping with kangaroo rim decoration

| Date | Mintage | VF20 | XF40 | MS60 | MS63 | MS65 |
|---|---|---|---|---|---|---|
| 2006 | 48,279 | PF65 50.00 | | | | |

## KM# 841 DOLLAR

31.10 g., 0.999 Silver 0.999 oz. ASW Colorized lenticular display. **Ruler:** Elizabeth II **Subject:** Australia Television, 50th Anniversary **Obv:** Head with tiara right **Rev:** Lenticular display of six historic TV show images **Shape:** Square

| Date | Mintage | VF20 | XF40 | MS60 | MS63 | MS65 |
|---|---|---|---|---|---|---|
| 2006 | 9,470 | PF65 95.00 | | | | |

## KM# 842 DOLLAR

31.10 g., 0.999 Silver 0.999 oz. ASW, 40 mm. **Ruler:** Elizabeth II **Subject:** End of Pre-Decimal Coinage, 40th Anniversary **Obv:** Head with tiara right above transparent locket containing small replicas of pre-decimal currency **Rev:** Rim legend about locket

| Date | Mintage | VF20 | XF40 | MS60 | MS63 | MS65 |
|---|---|---|---|---|---|---|
| 2006 P | 5,401 | PF65 150 | | | | |

## KM# 843 DOLLAR

31.10 g., 0.999 Silver 0.999 oz. ASW, 40 mm. **Ruler:** Elizabeth II **Subject:** 80th Birthday of Queen Elizabeth II **Obv:** Head with tiara right **Rev:** Queen Elizabeth II

| Date | Mintage | VF20 | XF40 | MS60 | MS63 | MS65 |
|---|---|---|---|---|---|---|
| 2006 P | 5,823 | PF65 85.00 | | | | |

## KM# 844 DOLLAR

31.10 g., 0.999 Silver 0.999 oz. ASW, 40 mm. **Ruler:** Elizabeth II **Subject:** Figures of Note **Obv:** Head with tiara right **Rev:** Queen Elizabeth as portrayed on Australia 1 dollar banknote

| Date | Mintage | VF20 | XF40 | MS60 | MS63 | MS65 |
|---|---|---|---|---|---|---|
| 2006 P | 2,409 | PF65 175 | | | | |

## KM# 845 DOLLAR

31.10 g., 0.999 Silver 0.999 oz. ASW, 40 mm. **Ruler:** Elizabeth II **Subject:** Figures of Note **Obv:** Head with tiara right **Rev:** MacArthur and Farrer as portrayed on Australia 2 dollar banknote

| Date | Mintage | VF20 | XF40 | MS60 | MS63 | MS65 |
|---|---|---|---|---|---|---|
| 2006 P | 2,409 | PF65 95.00 | | | | |

## KM# 846 DOLLAR

31.10 g., 0.999 Silver 0.999 oz. ASW, 40 mm. **Ruler:** Elizabeth II **Subject:** Figures of Note **Obv:** Head with tiara right **Rev:** Banks and Chisholm as portrayed on Australia 5 dollar banknote

| Date | Mintage | VF20 | XF40 | MS60 | MS63 | MS65 |
|---|---|---|---|---|---|---|
| 2006 P | 2,271 | PF65 95.00 | | | | |

## KM# 847 DOLLAR

31.10 g., 0.999 Silver 0.999 oz. ASW, 40 mm. **Ruler:** Elizabeth II **Subject:** Figures of Note **Obv:** Head with tiara right **Rev:** Greenway and Lawson as portrayed on Australia 10 dollar banknote

| Date | Mintage | VF20 | XF40 | MS60 | MS63 | MS65 |
|---|---|---|---|---|---|---|
| 2006 P | 2,209 | PF65 95.00 | | | | |

## KM# 848 DOLLAR

31.10 g., 0.999 Silver 0.999 oz. ASW, 40 mm. **Ruler:** Elizabeth II **Subject:** Figures of Note **Obv:** Head with tiara right **Rev:** Kingsford-Smith and Hargrave as portrayed on Australia 20 dollar banknote

| Date | Mintage | VF20 | XF40 | MS60 | MS63 | MS65 |
|---|---|---|---|---|---|---|
| 2006 P | 2,198 | PF65 95.00 | | | | |

## KM# 849 DOLLAR

31.10 g., 0.999 Silver 0.999 oz. ASW, 40 mm. **Ruler:** Elizabeth II **Obv:** Head with tiara right **Obv. Legend:** ELIZABETH II - AUSTRALIA **Rev:** Everage head facing, multicolor **Rev. Legend:** DAME EDNA EVERAGE - 50TH ANNIVERSARY

| Date | Mintage | VF20 | XF40 | MS60 | MS63 | MS65 |
|---|---|---|---|---|---|---|
| ND-2006 P | 4,512 | PF65 60.00 | | | | |

## KM# 940 DOLLAR

31.10 g., 0.999 Silver 0.999 oz. ASW **Ruler:** Elizabeth II **Subject:** Australian Landmarks **Obv:** Head with tiara right **Rev:** Melbourne

| Date | Mintage | VF20 | XF40 | MS60 | MS63 | MS65 |
|---|---|---|---|---|---|---|
| 2006 P | 5,923 | PF65 50.00 | | | | |

## KM# 941 DOLLAR

31.10 g., 0.999 Silver 0.999 oz. ASW **Ruler:** Elizabeth II **Subject:** Australian Landmarks **Obv:** Head with tiara right **Rev:** Uluru

| Date | Mintage | VF20 | XF40 | MS60 | MS63 | MS65 |
|---|---|---|---|---|---|---|
| 2006 P | 5,938 | PF65 50.00 | | | | |

## KM# 942 DOLLAR

31.10 g., 0.999 Silver 0.999 oz. ASW **Ruler:** Elizabeth II **Subject:** Australian Landmarks **Obv:** Head with tiara right **Rev:** Canberra

| Date | Mintage | VF20 | XF40 | MS60 | MS63 | MS65 |
|---|---|---|---|---|---|---|
| 2006 P | 4,926 | PF65 50.00 | | | | |

## KM# 943 DOLLAR

31.10 g., 0.999 Silver 0.999 oz. ASW, 40.6 mm. **Ruler:** Elizabeth II **Subject:** Australian Landmarks **Obv:** Head with tiara right **Rev:** Perth

| Date | Mintage | VF20 | XF40 | MS60 | MS63 | MS65 |
|---|---|---|---|---|---|---|
| 2006 P | 7,500 | PF65 50.00 | | | | |

### KM# 944 DOLLAR

31.10 g., 0.999 Silver 0.999 oz. ASW **Ruler:** Elizabeth II **Subject:** Australian Landmarks **Obv:** Head with tiara right **Rev:** Great Barrier Reef

| Date | Mintage | VF20 | XF40 | MS60 | MS63 | MS65 |
|---|---|---|---|---|---|---|
| 2006 P | 5,751 | **PF65** 50.00 | | | | |

### KM# 1008 DOLLAR

31.10 g., 0.999 Silver 0.999 oz. ASW, 40.5 mm. **Ruler:** Elizabeth II **Subject:** 400th Anniversary **Obv:** Head with tiara right **Obv. Legend:** ELIZABETH II - AUSTRALIA **Rev:** Sailing ship at left, early map at right in color **Rev. Legend:** 1606-2006 / Australia on the Map

| Date | Mintage | VF20 | XF40 | MS60 | MS63 | MS65 |
|---|---|---|---|---|---|---|
| 2006 P | 9,941 | **PF65** 55.00 | | | | |

### KM# 1019 DOLLAR

31.30 g., 0.999 Silver 1.0053 oz. ASW, 40.5 mm. **Ruler:** Elizabeth II **Subject:** 20th Anniversary of base **Obv:** Head with tiara right **Obv. Legend:** ELIZABETH II - AUSTRALIA **Rev:** Plane above Albatross and chick on ice, multicolor **Rev. Legend:** Australian Antarctic Territory - EDGEWORTH DAVID BASE **Edge:** Reeded

| Date | Mintage | VF20 | XF40 | MS60 | MS63 | MS65 |
|---|---|---|---|---|---|---|
| 2006 P | 7,500 | **PF65** 60.00 | | | | |

### KM# 808 DOLLAR

9.00 g., Aluminum-Bronze, 25 mm. **Ruler:** Elizabeth II **Subject:** Ashes Cricket Series 1882-2007 **Obv:** Head with tiara right **Rev:** Urn with supporters **Edge:** Segmented reeding

| Date | Mintage | VF20 | XF40 | MS60 | MS63 | MS65 |
|---|---|---|---|---|---|---|
| 2007 | — | — | — | 2.00 | 3.00 | 4.00 |

### KM# 809 DOLLAR

9.00 g., Aluminum-Bronze, 25 mm. **Ruler:** Elizabeth II **Subject:** Year of the Pig **Obv:** Head with tiara right **Rev:** Pig **Edge:** Segmented reeding

| Date | Mintage | VF20 | XF40 | MS60 | MS63 | MS65 |
|---|---|---|---|---|---|---|
| 2007 | 7,500 | — | — | — | — | 95.00 |

### KM# 809a DOLLAR

11.66 g., 0.999 Silver 0.3745 oz. ASW, 25 mm. **Ruler:** Elizabeth II **Subject:** Year of the Pig **Obv:** Head with tiara right **Rev:** Pig **Edge:** Segmented reeding

| Date | Mintage | VF20 | XF40 | MS60 | MS63 | MS65 |
|---|---|---|---|---|---|---|
| 2007 | — | **PF65** 28.00 | | | | |

### KM# 828 DOLLAR

9.00 g., Aluminum-Bronze, 25 mm. **Ruler:** Elizabeth II **Subject:** Year of the Surf Lifesaver **Obv:** Head with tiara right **Rev:** Three lifesavers carrying rescued person **Edge:** Segmented reeding

| Date | Mintage | VF20 | XF40 | MS60 | MS63 | MS65 |
|---|---|---|---|---|---|---|
| 2007 | 34,500 | **PF65** 20.00 | | | | |

### KM# 828a DOLLAR

11.66 g., 0.999 Silver 0.3745 oz. ASW, 25 mm. **Ruler:** Elizabeth II **Subject:** Year of the Surfer Lifesaver **Rev:** Three men saving fourth

| Date | Mintage | VF20 | XF40 | MS60 | MS63 | MS65 |
|---|---|---|---|---|---|---|
| 2007 B | — | **PF65** 40.00 | | | | |

### KM# 829 DOLLAR

9.00 g., Aluminum-Bronze, 25 mm. **Ruler:** Elizabeth II **Subject:** Norman Lindsay and his Magic Pudding **Obv:** Head with tiara right **Rev:** Lindsay and Pudding characters **Edge:** Segmented reeding

| Date | Mintage | VF20 | XF40 | MS60 | MS63 | MS65 |
|---|---|---|---|---|---|---|
| 2007 | 33,690 | — | — | — | — | 65.00 |

### KM# 850 DOLLAR

27.22 g., Copper-Nickel, 38.74 mm. **Ruler:** Elizabeth II **Obv:** Head with tiara right **Rev:** Kangaroo mother and joey **Edge:** Reeded

| Date | Mintage | VF20 | XF40 | MS60 | MS63 | MS65 |
|---|---|---|---|---|---|---|
| 2007 | 5,000 | — | — | — | 275 | 300 |

### KM# 945 DOLLAR

31.10 g., 0.999 Silver 0.999 oz. ASW **Ruler:** Elizabeth II **Subject:** Australian Landmarks **Obv:** Head with tiara right **Rev:** Gold Coast

| Date | Mintage | VF20 | XF40 | MS60 | MS63 | MS65 |
|---|---|---|---|---|---|---|
| 2007 P | 4,558 | **PF65** 60.00 | | | | |

### KM# 946 DOLLAR

31.10 g., 0.999 Silver 0.999 oz. ASW **Ruler:** Elizabeth II **Subject:** Australian Landmarks **Obv:** Head with tiara right **Rev:** Phillip Island

| Date | Mintage | VF20 | XF40 | MS60 | MS63 | MS65 |
|---|---|---|---|---|---|---|
| 2007 P | 4,668 | **PF65** 60.00 | | | | |

### KM# 947 DOLLAR

31.10 g., 0.999 Silver 0.999 oz. ASW **Ruler:** Elizabeth II **Subject:** Australian Landmarks **Obv:** Head with tiara right **Rev:** Port Arthur

| Date | Mintage | VF20 | XF40 | MS60 | MS63 | MS65 |
|---|---|---|---|---|---|---|
| 2007 P | 6,105 | **PF65** 60.00 | | | | |

### KM# 948 DOLLAR

31.10 g., 0.999 Silver 0.999 oz. ASW **Ruler:** Elizabeth II **Subject:** Australian Landmarks **Obv:** Head with tiara right **Rev:** Adelaide

| Date | Mintage | VF20 | XF40 | MS60 | MS63 | MS65 |
|---|---|---|---|---|---|---|
| 2007 P | 6,376 | **PF65** 60.00 | | | | |

### KM# 949 DOLLAR

31.10 g., 0.999 Silver 0.999 oz. ASW **Ruler:** Elizabeth II **Subject:** Australian Landmarks **Obv:** Head with tiara right **Rev:** Sydney

| Date | Mintage | VF20 | XF40 | MS60 | MS63 | MS65 |
|---|---|---|---|---|---|---|
| 2007 P | 5,945 | **PF65** 60.00 | | | | |

### KM# 1009 DOLLAR

31.10 g., 0.999 Silver 0.999 oz. ASW, 40 mm. **Ruler:** Elizabeth II **Subject:** Phar Lap, 75th Anniversary death **Obv:** Head with tiara right **Obv. Legend:** ELIZABETH II - AUSTRALIA **Rev:** Horse and rider racing right

| Date | Mintage | VF20 | XF40 | MS60 | MS63 | MS65 |
|---|---|---|---|---|---|---|
| ND-2007 P | 5,055 | **PF65** 95.00 | | | | |

**KM# 1011 DOLLAR**
31.11 g., 0.999 Silver 0.999 oz. ASW, 40 mm. **Ruler:** Elizabeth II **Obv:** Crowned bust right at top **Obv. Legend:** ELIZABETH II - AUSTRALIA **Rev:** 12 Lunar figures

| Date | Mintage | VF20 | XF40 | MS60 | MS63 | MS65 |
|---|---|---|---|---|---|---|
| 2007 | 5,994 | PF65 90.00 | | | | |

**KM# 1012 DOLLAR**
31.10 g., 0.999 Silver 0.999 oz. ASW, 40 mm. **Ruler:** Elizabeth II **Obv:** Bust with tiara right **Obv. Legend:** ELIZABETH II - AUSTRALIA **Rev:** Bridge, multicolor fireworks above **Rev. Legend:** 75th ANNIVERSARY - SYDNEY HARBOUR BRIDGE

| Date | Mintage | VF20 | XF40 | MS60 | MS63 | MS65 |
|---|---|---|---|---|---|---|
| ND-2007 P | 8,433 | PF65 85.00 | | | | |

**KM# 1016 DOLLAR**
11.66 g., 0.999 Silver 0.3745 oz. ASW, 25 mm. **Ruler:** Elizabeth II **Subject:** 75th Anniversary - Sydney Harbor Bridge **Obv:** Head with tiara right **Obv. Legend:** ELIZABETH II _ AUSTRALIA **Rev:** Three men standing at bridge joint **Edge:** Segmented reeding

| Date | Mintage | VF20 | XF40 | MS60 | MS63 | MS65 |
|---|---|---|---|---|---|---|
| 2007 B | 12,500 | PF65 35.00 | | | | |

**KM# 1016A DOLLAR**
9.00 g., Aluminum-Bronze, 25 mm. **Ruler:** Elizabeth II **Subject:** Sydney Harbor Bridge, 75th Anniversary **Obv:** Head with tiara right **Rev:** Three men standing at bridge joint

| Date | Mintage | VF20 | XF40 | MS60 | MS63 | MS65 |
|---|---|---|---|---|---|---|
| 2007 S | — | — | — | 2.00 | 3.00 | 4.00 |

**KM# 1020 DOLLAR**
31.48 g., 0.999 Silver 1.0111 oz. ASW, 40.5 mm. **Ruler:** Elizabeth II **Subject:** 50th Anniversary of Station **Obv:** Head with tiara right **Obv. Legend:** ELIZABETH II - AUSTRALIA **Rev:** Ship "Kista Dan", multicolor **Rev. Legend:** Australian Antarctic Territory - DAVIS STATION **Edge:** Reeded

| Date | Mintage | VF20 | XF40 | MS60 | MS63 | MS65 |
|---|---|---|---|---|---|---|
| 2007 P | 7,500 | PF65 60.00 | | | | |

**KM# 1024 DOLLAR**
9.00 g., Aluminum-Bronze, 25 mm. **Ruler:** Elizabeth II **Series:** Colored Oceans **Obv:** Head with tiara right **Rev:** Biscuit Star, multicolor **Edge:** Segmented reeding **Note:** Issued in folder.

| Date | Mintage | VF20 | XF40 | MS60 | MS63 | MS65 |
|---|---|---|---|---|---|---|
| 2007 | — | — | — | — | — | 22.00 |

**KM# 1025 DOLLAR**
9.00 g., Aluminum-Bronze, 25 mm. **Ruler:** Elizabeth II **Series:** Colored Oceans **Obv:** Head with tiara right **Rev:** Longfin Banner fish, multicolor **Edge:** Segmented reeding

| Date | Mintage | VF20 | XF40 | MS60 | MS63 | MS65 |
|---|---|---|---|---|---|---|
| 2007 | 25,930 | — | — | — | — | 22.00 |

**KM# 1026 DOLLAR**
9.00 g., Aluminum-Bronze, 25 mm. **Ruler:** Elizabeth II **Series:** Colored Oceans **Obv:** Head with tiara right **Rev:** White Shark, multicolor **Edge:** Segmented reeding **Note:** Issued in folder.

| Date | Mintage | VF20 | XF40 | MS60 | MS63 | MS65 |
|---|---|---|---|---|---|---|
| 2007 | 30,416 | — | — | — | — | 22.00 |

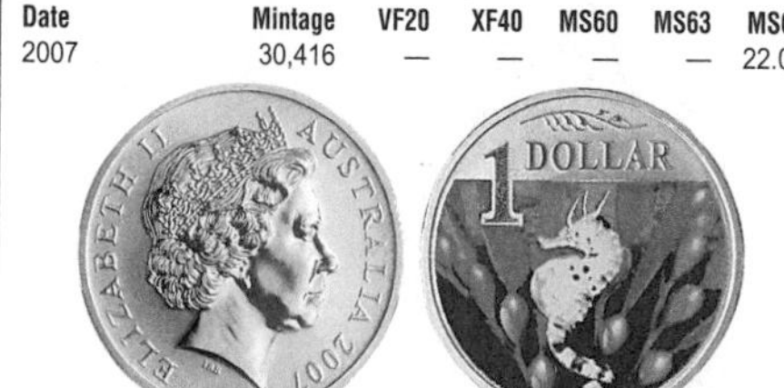


**KM# 1027 DOLLAR**
9.00 g., Aluminum-Bronze, 25 mm. **Ruler:** Elizabeth II **Series:** Colored Oceans **Obv:** Head with tiara right **Rev:** Big Belly seahorse **Edge:** Segmented reeding

| Date | Mintage | VF20 | XF40 | MS60 | MS63 | MS65 |
|---|---|---|---|---|---|---|
| 2007 | — | — | — | — | — | 22.00 |

**KM# 1040 DOLLAR**
9.00 g., Aluminum-Bronze, 25 mm. **Ruler:** Elizabeth II **Subject:** APEC **Rev:** Multiple stars

| Date | Mintage | VF20 | XF40 | MS60 | MS63 | MS65 |
|---|---|---|---|---|---|---|
| 2007 B | 20,108,000 | — | — | 2.00 | 3.00 | 4.00 |

**KM# 1042 DOLLAR**
9.00 g., Aluminum-Bronze, 25 mm. **Ruler:** Elizabeth II **Subject:** 60th Anniversary - Peacekeepers **Rev:** Hand holding globe within wreath, dove above

| Date | Mintage | VF20 | XF40 | MS60 | MS63 | MS65 |
|---|---|---|---|---|---|---|
| 2007 B | 31,028 | — | — | — | — | 15.00 |

**KM# 1437 DOLLAR**
Silver partially gilt **Ruler:** Elizabeth II **Subject:** Lunar dollar

| Date | Mintage | VF20 | XF40 | MS60 | MS63 | MS65 |
|---|---|---|---|---|---|---|
| 2007 | — | PF65 50.00 | | | | |

**KM# 1438 DOLLAR**
Silver partially gilt **Ruler:** Elizabeth II **Subject:** One Johanna

| Date | Mintage | VF20 | XF40 | MS60 | MS63 | MS65 |
|---|---|---|---|---|---|---|
| 2007 | — | PF65 50.00 | | | | |

**KM# 1653 DOLLAR**
9.00 g., Aluminum-Bronze, 25 mm. **Ruler:** Elizabeth II **Subject:** International Polar Year **Obv:** Head with tiara right **Rev:** Sailing ship in ice

| Date | Mintage | VF20 | XF40 | MS60 | MS63 | MS65 |
|---|---|---|---|---|---|---|
| 2007 | — | — | — | 4.00 | 6.00 | 8.00 |

**KM# 1021 DOLLAR**
31.11 g., 0.999 Silver 0.999 oz. ASW, 40 mm. **Ruler:** Elizabeth II **Subject:** Hobart **Rev:** Buildings and harbor **Rev. Legend:** DISCOVER AUSTRALIA

| Date | Mintage | VF20 | XF40 | MS60 | MS63 | MS65 |
|---|---|---|---|---|---|---|
| 2008 P | 7,277 | PF65 80.00 | | | | |

**KM# 1039 DOLLAR**
9.00 g., Aluminum-Bronze, 25 mm. **Ruler:** Elizabeth II **Subject:** Boy Scouts, 100th Anniversary

| Date | Mintage | VF20 | XF40 | MS60 | MS63 | MS65 |
|---|---|---|---|---|---|---|
| 2008 | — | — | — | 4.00 | 6.00 | 7.00 |

**KM# 1047 DOLLAR**
9.00 g., Aluminum-Bronze, 25 mm. **Ruler:** Elizabeth II **Rev:** First coat of arms

| Date | Mintage | VF20 | XF40 | MS60 | MS63 | MS65 |
|---|---|---|---|---|---|---|
| 2008 M | 25,202 | — | — | 3.00 | 5.00 | 6.00 |
| 2008 B | 32,500 | — | — | 3.00 | 5.00 | 6.00 |
| 2008 C | 104,689 | — | — | — | 15.00 | 17.00 |
| 2008 S | 32,500 | — | — | 3.00 | 5.00 | 6.00 |

**KM# 1047a DOLLAR**
11.60 g., 0.999 Silver 0.3726 oz. ASW, 25 mm. **Ruler:** Elizabeth II **Rev:** First coat of arms

| Date | Mintage | VF20 | XF40 | MS60 | MS63 | MS65 |
|---|---|---|---|---|---|---|
| 2008 C | 12,500 | PF65 45.00 | | | | |

**KM# 1052 DOLLAR**
9.00 g., Aluminum-Bronze, 25 mm. **Ruler:** Elizabeth II **Subject:** Rugby League Centennial **Rev:** Rugby anniversary logo

| Date | Mintage | VF20 | XF40 | MS60 | MS63 | MS65 |
|---|---|---|---|---|---|---|
| 2008 | 60,400 | — | — | — | 15.00 | 17.00 |

**KM# 1056 DOLLAR**
9.00 g., Aluminum-Bronze, 25 mm. **Ruler:** Elizabeth II **Subject:** Year of the Rat

| Date | Mintage | VF20 | XF40 | MS60 | MS63 | MS65 |
|---|---|---|---|---|---|---|
| 2008 | — | — | — | — | 13.00 | 15.00 |

**KM# 1056a DOLLAR**
11.66 g., 0.999 Silver 0.3745 oz. ASW, 25 mm. **Ruler:** Elizabeth II **Subject:** Year of the Rat **Rev:** Mouse at center, flora in arches

| Date | Mintage | VF20 | XF40 | MS60 | MS63 | MS65 |
|---|---|---|---|---|---|---|
| 2008 | 10,000 | PF65 45.00 | | | | |

**KM# 1059 DOLLAR**
9.00 g., Aluminum-Bronze, 25 mm. **Ruler:** Elizabeth II **Subject:** Planet Earth **Rev:** Four hands and elements

| Date | Mintage | VF20 | XF40 | MS60 | MS63 | MS65 |
|---|---|---|---|---|---|---|
| 2008 | — | PF65 25.00 | | | | |
| 2008 | 28,399 | — | — | — | 20.00 | 22.00 |

**KM# 1063 DOLLAR**
9.00 g., Aluminum-Bronze, 25 mm. **Ruler:** Elizabeth II **Subject:** Saint Sister Mary Mackillop **Rev:** Nun and three children, world map in background

| Date | Mintage | VF20 | XF40 | MS60 | MS63 | MS65 |
|---|---|---|---|---|---|---|
| 2008 | 29,800 | — | — | — | 15.00 | 17.00 |

**KM# 1064 DOLLAR**
9.00 g., Aluminum-Bronze, 25 mm. **Ruler:** Elizabeth II **Subject:** Centennial of Quarantine **Rev:** Beagle and suitcase like map of Australia

| Date | Mintage | VF20 | XF40 | MS60 | MS63 | MS65 |
|---|---|---|---|---|---|---|
| 2008 | 30,094 | — | — | — | 15.00 | 17.00 |

**KM# 1068 DOLLAR**
9.00 g., Aluminum-Bronze, 25 mm. **Ruler:** Elizabeth II **Rev:** Multicolor Echidna

| Date | Mintage | VF20 | XF40 | MS60 | MS63 | MS65 |
|---|---|---|---|---|---|---|
| 2008 | 20,589 | — | — | — | 18.00 | 22.00 |

**KM# 1069 DOLLAR**
9.00 g., Aluminum-Bronze, 25 mm. **Ruler:** Elizabeth II **Rev:** Multicolor Rock Wallaby

| Date | Mintage | VF20 | XF40 | MS60 | MS63 | MS65 |
|---|---|---|---|---|---|---|
| 2008 | 24,863 | — | — | — | 18.00 | 22.00 |

**KM# 1070 DOLLAR**
9.00 g., Aluminum-Bronze, 25 mm. **Ruler:** Elizabeth II **Rev:** Multicolor koala

| Date | Mintage | VF20 | XF40 | MS60 | MS63 | MS65 |
|---|---|---|---|---|---|---|
| 2008 | 27,045 | — | — | — | 18.00 | 22.00 |

**KM# 1071 DOLLAR**
9.00 g., Aluminum-Bronze, 25 mm. **Ruler:** Elizabeth II **Rev:** Multicolor wombat

| Date | Mintage | VF20 | XF40 | MS60 | MS63 | MS65 |
|---|---|---|---|---|---|---|
| 2008 | 22,295 | — | — | — | 18.00 | 22.00 |

**KM# 1076 DOLLAR**
9.00 g., Aluminum-Bronze, 25 mm. **Ruler:** Elizabeth II **Subject:** Year of Astronomy **Rev:** Parkes Telescope

| Date | Mintage | VF20 | XF40 | MS60 | MS63 | MS65 |
|---|---|---|---|---|---|---|
| 2008 | — | PF65 25.00 | | | | |
| 2008 | — | — | — | — | 12.00 | 14.00 |

**KM# 1090 DOLLAR**
13.50 g., Aluminum-Bronze, 29.5 mm. **Ruler:** Elizabeth II **Subject:** Ghost Bat **Obv:** Head right **Rev:** Ghost bat against night sky **Edge:** Reeded

| Date | Mintage | VF20 | XF40 | MS60 | MS63 | MS65 |
|---|---|---|---|---|---|---|
| 2008 | 11,914 | — | — | — | — | 14.00 |

**KM# 1091 DOLLAR**
31.11 g., 0.999 Silver 0.999 oz. ASW, 40.6 mm. **Ruler:** Elizabeth II **Subject:** UNESCO Heritage site - Kakadu National Park **Rev:** Saltwater crocodile and multicolor swamp

| Date | Mintage | VF20 | XF40 | MS60 | MS63 | MS65 |
|---|---|---|---|---|---|---|
| 2008 P | 7,500 | PF65 75.00 | | | | |

**KM# 1168 DOLLAR**
13.50 g., Aluminum-Bronze, 29.5 mm. **Ruler:** Elizabeth II **Obv:** Head right **Rev:** Common wombat

| Date | Mintage | VF20 | XF40 | MS60 | MS63 | MS65 |
|---|---|---|---|---|---|---|
| 2008 P | 11,908 | — | — | — | — | 14.00 |

**KM# 1169 DOLLAR**
13.50 g., Aluminum-Bronze, 29.5 mm. **Ruler:** Elizabeth II **Obv:** Head right **Rev:** Echidna

| Date | Mintage | VF20 | XF40 | MS60 | MS63 | MS65 |
|---|---|---|---|---|---|---|
| 2008 P | 11,850 | — | — | — | — | 14.00 |

**KM# 1170 DOLLAR**
13.50 g., Aluminum-Bronze, 29.5 mm. **Ruler:** Elizabeth II **Obv:** Head right **Rev:** Frilled-neck lizard

| Date | Mintage | VF20 | XF40 | MS60 | MS63 | MS65 |
|---|---|---|---|---|---|---|
| 2008 P | 11,864 | — | — | — | — | 14.00 |

**KM# 1171 DOLLAR**
13.50 g., Aluminum-Bronze, 29.5 mm. **Ruler:** Elizabeth II **Obv:** Head right **Rev:** Grey kangaroo

| Date | Mintage | VF20 | XF40 | MS60 | MS63 | MS65 |
|---|---|---|---|---|---|---|
| 2008 P | 14,385 | — | — | — | — | 14.00 |

**KM# 1172 DOLLAR**
13.50 g., Aluminum-Bronze, 29.5 mm. **Ruler:** Elizabeth II **Obv:** Head right **Rev:** Splendid wren

| Date | Mintage | VF20 | XF40 | MS60 | MS63 | MS65 |
|---|---|---|---|---|---|---|
| 2008 P | 11,796 | — | — | — | — | 14.00 |

**KM# 1173 DOLLAR**
13.50 g., Aluminum-Bronze, 29.5 mm. **Ruler:** Elizabeth II **Obv:** Head right **Rev:** Palm cockatoo

| Date | Mintage | VF20 | XF40 | MS60 | MS63 | MS65 |
|---|---|---|---|---|---|---|
| 2008 P | 11,759 | — | — | — | — | 14.00 |

**KM# 1174 DOLLAR**
13.50 g., Aluminum-Bronze, 29.5 mm. **Ruler:** Elizabeth II **Obv:** Head right **Rev:** Wedge-tailed eagle

| Date | Mintage | VF20 | XF40 | MS60 | MS63 | MS65 |
|---|---|---|---|---|---|---|
| 2008 P | 14,034 | — | — | — | — | 14.00 |

**KM# 1175 DOLLAR**
13.50 g., Aluminum-Bronze, 29.5 mm. **Ruler:** Elizabeth II **Obv:** Head right **Rev:** Whale shark

| Date | Mintage | VF20 | XF40 | MS60 | MS63 | MS65 |
|---|---|---|---|---|---|---|
| 2008 P | 11,943 | — | — | — | — | 14.00 |

**KM# 1176 DOLLAR**
13.50 g., Aluminum-Bronze, 29.5 mm. **Ruler:** Elizabeth II **Obv:** Head right **Rev:** Green sea turtle

| Date | Mintage | VF20 | XF40 | MS60 | MS63 | MS65 |
|---|---|---|---|---|---|---|
| 2008 P | 11,881 | — | — | — | — | 14.00 |

**KM# 1177 DOLLAR**
13.50 g., Aluminum-Bronze, 29.5 mm. **Ruler:** Elizabeth II **Obv:** Head right **Rev:** Platypus

| Date | Mintage | VF20 | XF40 | MS60 | MS63 | MS65 |
|---|---|---|---|---|---|---|
| 2008 P | 11,960 | — | — | — | — | 14.00 |

**KM# 1178 DOLLAR**
13.50 g., Aluminum-Bronze, 29.5 mm. **Ruler:** Elizabeth II **Obv:** Head right **Rev:** Australian sea lion

| Date | Mintage | VF20 | XF40 | MS60 | MS63 | MS65 |
|---|---|---|---|---|---|---|
| 2008 P | 13,884 | — | — | — | — | 14.00 |

**KM# 1179 DOLLAR**
31.11 g., 0.999 Silver 0.999 oz. ASW, 40.6 mm. **Ruler:** Elizabeth II **Subject:** 90th Anniversary - End of WWI **Obv:** Head right **Rev:** Silhouette of bugler, multicolor poppies below

| Date | Mintage | VF20 | XF40 | MS60 | MS63 | MS65 |
|---|---|---|---|---|---|---|
| 2008 P | 7,554 | **PF65** 90.00 | | | | |

**KM# 1181 DOLLAR**
31.11 g., 0.999 Silver 0.999 oz. ASW, 40 mm. **Ruler:** Elizabeth II **Subject:** Darwin **Obv:** Head right **Rev:** Harbor, multicolor **Rev. Legend:** DISCOVER AUSTRALIA

| Date | Mintage | VF20 | XF40 | MS60 | MS63 | MS65 |
|---|---|---|---|---|---|---|
| 2008 P | 7,319 | **PF65** 80.00 | | | | |

**KM# 1182 DOLLAR**
31.11 g., 0.999 Silver 0.999 oz. ASW, 40 mm. **Ruler:** Elizabeth II **Subject:** Kakadu **Obv:** Head right **Rev:** Crocodile, multicolor **Rev. Legend:** DISCOVER AUSTRALIA

| Date | Mintage | VF20 | XF40 | MS60 | MS63 | MS65 |
|---|---|---|---|---|---|---|
| 2008 P | 7,252 | **PF65** 80.00 | | | | |

**KM# 1183 DOLLAR**
31.11 g., 0.999 Silver 0.999 oz. ASW **Ruler:** Elizabeth II **Subject:** Brisbane **Obv:** Head right **Rev:** Bridge and view **Rev. Legend:** DISCOVER AUSTRALIA

| Date | Mintage | VF20 | XF40 | MS60 | MS63 | MS65 |
|---|---|---|---|---|---|---|
| 2008 P | 7,500 | **PF65** 80.00 | | | | |

**KM# 1184 DOLLAR**
31.11 g., 0.999 Silver 0.999 oz. ASW **Ruler:** Elizabeth II **Subject:** Broome **Obv:** Head right **Rev:** Seascape, pearls, multicolor **Rev. Legend:** DISCOVER AUSTRALIA

| Date | Mintage | VF20 | XF40 | MS60 | MS63 | MS65 |
|---|---|---|---|---|---|---|
| 2008 P | 7,252 | **PF65** 80.00 | | | | |

**KM# 1185 DOLLAR**
31.11 g., 0.999 Silver 0.999 oz. ASW **Ruler:** Elizabeth II **Subject:** Sydney **Obv:** Head right **Rev:** Opera House, Harbor Bridge, multicolor **Rev. Legend:** DISCOVER AUSTRALIA

| Date | Mintage | VF20 | XF40 | MS60 | MS63 | MS65 |
|---|---|---|---|---|---|---|
| 2008 P | 7,500 | **PF65** 80.00 | | | | |

**KM# 1654 DOLLAR**
31.11 g., 0.999 Silver 0.999 oz. ASW, 40.6 mm. **Ruler:** Elizabeth II **Subject:** HMAS Sydney II

| Date | Mintage | VF20 | XF40 | MS60 | MS63 | MS65 |
|---|---|---|---|---|---|---|
| 2008 | 7,430 | **PF65** 90.00 | | | | |

**KM# 1682 DOLLAR**
13.80 g., Aluminum-Bronze, 30.6 mm. **Ruler:** Elizabeth II **Subject:** World Youth Day **Rev:** Pope Benedict XVI and WYD logo in color

| Date | Mintage | VF20 | XF40 | MS60 | MS63 | MS65 |
|---|---|---|---|---|---|---|
| 2008 | 42,369 | — | — | — | — | 15.00 |

**KM# 1749 DOLLAR**
31.11 g., 0.999 Silver 0.999 oz. ASW, 40.6 mm. **Ruler:** Elizabeth II **Subject:** Treasurers of Australia, Opals **Obv:** Small head above container of five opals **Rev:** landscape above container

| Date | Mintage | VF20 | XF40 | MS60 | MS63 | MS65 |
|---|---|---|---|---|---|---|
| 2008 P | 7,500 | PF65 75.00 | | | | |

**KM# 1867 DOLLAR**
31.11 g., 0.999 Silver 0.999 oz. ASW, 40.5 mm. **Ruler:** Elizabeth II **Subject:** World Youth Day

| Date | Mintage | VF20 | XF40 | MS60 | MS63 | MS65 |
|---|---|---|---|---|---|---|
| 2008 P | 5,054 | PF65 60.00 | | | | |

**KM# 1077 DOLLAR**
9.00 g., Aluminum-Bronze, 25 mm. **Ruler:** Elizabeth II **Subject:** Dorothy Wall **Rev:** Portrait and four characters to right

| Date | Mintage | VF20 | XF40 | MS60 | MS63 | MS65 |
|---|---|---|---|---|---|---|
| 2009 | — | — | — | — | — | 12.00 |

**KM# 1078 DOLLAR**
9.00 g., Aluminum-Bronze, 25 mm. **Ruler:** Elizabeth II **Subject:** Year of the Ox **Rev:** V. Gottwald

| Date | Mintage | VF20 | XF40 | MS60 | MS63 | MS65 |
|---|---|---|---|---|---|---|
| 2009 | — | — | — | — | 12.00 | 13.00 |

**KM# 1078a DOLLAR**
11.66 g., 0.999 Silver 0.3745 oz. ASW, 25 mm. **Ruler:** Elizabeth II **Subject:** Year of the Ox

| Date | Mintage | VF20 | XF40 | MS60 | MS63 | MS65 |
|---|---|---|---|---|---|---|
| 2009 | 10,000 | PF65 45.00 | | | | |

**KM# 1082 DOLLAR**
27.22 g., Copper-Nickel, 38.74 mm. **Ruler:** Elizabeth II **Rev:** Kangaroo

| Date | Mintage | VF20 | XF40 | MS60 | MS63 | MS65 |
|---|---|---|---|---|---|---|
| 2009 | — | — | — | — | — | 25.00 |

**KM# 1087 DOLLAR**
9.00 g., Aluminum-Bronze, 25 mm. **Ruler:** Elizabeth II **Subject:** 60th Anniversary - Citizenship **Obv:** Head right **Rev:** Portraits around globe

| Date | Mintage | VF20 | XF40 | MS60 | MS63 | MS65 |
|---|---|---|---|---|---|---|
| 2009 C | — | PF65 28.00 | | | | |

**KM# 1087a DOLLAR**
11.90 g., 0.999 Silver 0.3822 oz. ASW, 25 mm. **Ruler:** Elizabeth II **Subject:** 60th Anniversary - Citizenship **Rev:** Portraits around globe

| Date | Mintage | VF20 | XF40 | MS60 | MS63 | MS65 |
|---|---|---|---|---|---|---|
| 2009 C | — | PF65 40.00 | | | | |

**KM# 1089 DOLLAR**
Aluminum-Bronze **Ruler:** Elizabeth II **Subject:** Postal Service, 200th Anniversary **Obv:** Head with tiara right **Rev:** Isaac Nichols, first postman

| Date | Mintage | VF20 | XF40 | MS60 | MS63 | MS65 |
|---|---|---|---|---|---|---|
| 2009 | — | — | — | — | — | 13.00 |

**KM# 1092 DOLLAR**
13.30 g., Aluminum-Bronze, 30.6 mm. **Ruler:** Elizabeth II **Subject:** Celebrate Australia - Western Australia **Rev:** Kangaroo and multicolor Perth city view

| Date | Mintage | VF20 | XF40 | MS60 | MS63 | MS65 |
|---|---|---|---|---|---|---|
| 2009 | 13,067 | — | — | — | — | 13.00 |

**KM# 1093 DOLLAR**
13.30 g., Aluminum-Bronze, 30.6 mm. **Ruler:** Elizabeth II **Series:** Celebrate Australia - Victoria **Rev:** Little Penguin and multicolor Melbourne city view

| Date | Mintage | VF20 | XF40 | MS60 | MS63 | MS65 |
|---|---|---|---|---|---|---|
| 2009 | 9,499 | — | — | — | — | 13.00 |

**KM# 1094 DOLLAR**
13.30 g., Aluminum-Bronze, 30.6 mm. **Ruler:** Elizabeth II **Subject:** Celebrate Australia - Tasmania **Rev:** Tasmanian Devil and multicolor Cradle Mountain National Park

| Date | Mintage | VF20 | XF40 | MS60 | MS63 | MS65 |
|---|---|---|---|---|---|---|
| 2009 P | 9,689 | — | — | — | — | 13.00 |

**KM# 1095 DOLLAR**
13.30 g., Aluminum-Bronze, 30.6 mm. **Ruler:** Elizabeth II **Subject:** Celebrate Australia - South Australia **Rev:** Wombat and multicolor cathedral

| Date | Mintage | VF20 | XF40 | MS60 | MS63 | MS65 |
|---|---|---|---|---|---|---|
| 2009 P | 8,591 | — | — | — | — | 13.00 |

**KM# 1096 DOLLAR**
13.30 g., Aluminum-Bronze, 30.6 mm. **Ruler:** Elizabeth II **Subject:** Celebrate Australia - Queensland **Rev:** Sea Turtle with multicolor skyline of Brisbane

| Date | Mintage | VF20 | XF40 | MS60 | MS63 | MS65 |
|---|---|---|---|---|---|---|
| 2009 P | 9,666 | — | — | — | — | 13.00 |

**KM# 1097 DOLLAR**
13.30 g., Aluminum-Bronze, 30.6 mm. **Ruler:** Elizabeth II **Subject:** Celebrate Australia - Northern Territoty **Rev:** Saltwater crocodile and multicolor Kakadu National Park

| Date | Mintage | VF20 | XF40 | MS60 | MS63 | MS65 |
|---|---|---|---|---|---|---|
| 2009 P | 9,813 | — | — | — | — | 13.00 |

**KM# 1098 DOLLAR**
13.30 g., Aluminum-Bronze, 30.6 mm. **Ruler:** Elizabeth II **Subject:** Celebrate Australia - New South Wales **Rev:** Koala, multicolor Sydney Opera House and Harbor Bridge

| Date | Mintage | VF20 | XF40 | MS60 | MS63 | MS65 |
|---|---|---|---|---|---|---|
| 2009 P | 13,657 | — | — | — | — | 13.00 |

**KM# 1099 DOLLAR**
13.30 g., Aluminum-Bronze, 30.6 mm. **Ruler:** Elizabeth II **Subject:** Celebrate Australia - Capital Territory, Canberra **Rev:** Cockatoo and multicolor design

| Date | Mintage | VF20 | XF40 | MS60 | MS63 | MS65 |
|---|---|---|---|---|---|---|
| 2009 P | 9,735 | — | — | — | — | 13.00 |

**KM# 1103 DOLLAR**
31.11 g., 0.999 Silver 0.999 oz. ASW, 27x47 mm. **Ruler:** Elizabeth II **Rev:** Turtle Dreaming **Shape:** Rectangle

| Date | Mintage | VF20 | XF40 | MS60 | MS63 | MS65 |
|---|---|---|---|---|---|---|
| 2009 | — | PF65 75.00 | | | | |

**KM# 1107 DOLLAR**
31.11 g., 0.9999 Silver 0.9999 oz. ASW, 27x47 mm. **Ruler:** Elizabeth II **Rev:** Kangaroo dreaming **Shape:** Vertical rectangle

| Date | Mintage | VF20 | XF40 | MS60 | MS63 | MS65 |
|---|---|---|---|---|---|---|
| 2009 | — | PF65 75.00 | | | | |

**KM# 1211 DOLLAR**
31.11 g., 0.999 Silver 0.999 oz. ASW, 40.6 mm. **Ruler:** Elizabeth II **Subject:** Antarctic Territory **Obv:** Head right **Rev:** Douglas Mawson, one of two men standing on magnetic South Pole

| Date | Mintage | VF20 | XF40 | MS60 | MS63 | MS65 |
|---|---|---|---|---|---|---|
| 2009 P | 6,703 | PF65 85.00 | | | | |

**KM# 1212 DOLLAR**
31.11 g., 0.999 Silver 0.999 oz. ASW, 40.6 mm. **Ruler:** Elizabeth II **Obv:** Head right **Rev:** Dreaming kangaroo, multicolor **Rev. Legend:** DISCOVER AUSTRALIA

| Date | Mintage | VF20 | XF40 | MS60 | MS63 | MS65 |
|---|---|---|---|---|---|---|
| 2009 P | 10,000 | PF63 80.00 | PF65 90.00 | | | |

**KM# 1213 DOLLAR**
31.11 g., 0.999 Silver 0.999 oz. ASW **Ruler:** Elizabeth II **Obv:** Head right **Rev:** Dreaming dolphin, multicolor **Rev. Legend:** DISCOVER AUSTRALIA **Shape:** 40.6

| Date | Mintage | VF20 | XF40 | MS60 | MS63 | MS65 |
|---|---|---|---|---|---|---|
| 2009 P | 10,000 | PF63 80.00 | PF65 90.00 | | | |

**KM# 1214 DOLLAR**
31.11 g., 0.999 Silver 0.999 oz. ASW, 40.6 mm. **Ruler:** Elizabeth II **Obv:** Head right **Rev:** Dreaming king brown snake, multicolor **Rev. Legend:** DISCOVER AUSTRALIA

| Date | Mintage | VF20 | XF40 | MS60 | MS63 | MS65 |
|---|---|---|---|---|---|---|
| 2009 P | 10,000 | PF63 80.00 | PF65 90.00 | | | |

**KM# 1215 DOLLAR**
31.11 g., 0.999 Silver 0.999 oz. ASW, 40.6 mm. **Ruler:** Elizabeth II **Obv:** Head right **Rev:** Dreaming brolga, multicolor

| Date | Mintage | VF20 | XF40 | MS60 | MS63 | MS65 |
|---|---|---|---|---|---|---|
| 2009 P | 10,000 | PF63 80.00 | PF65 90.00 | | | |

**KM# 1216 DOLLAR**
31.11 g., 0.999 Silver 0.999 oz. ASW, 40.6 mm. **Ruler:** Elizabeth II **Obv:** Head right **Rev:** Dreaming echidna, multicolor

| Date | Mintage | VF20 | XF40 | MS60 | MS63 | MS65 |
|---|---|---|---|---|---|---|
| 2009 P | 10,000 | PF63 80.00 | PF65 90.00 | | | |

**KM# 1222 DOLLAR**
3.11 g., 0.999 Gold 0.0999 oz. AGW, 16 mm. **Ruler:** Elizabeth II **Obv:** Head right **Rev:** Dreaming kangaroo

| Date | Mintage | VF20 | XF40 | MS60 | MS63 | MS65 |
|---|---|---|---|---|---|---|
| 2009 P | 2,500 | PF65 175 | | | | |

**KM# 1242 DOLLAR**
31.11 g., 0.999 Silver 0.999 oz. ASW, 40.6 mm. **Ruler:** Elizabeth II **Subject:** Treasures of Australia **Obv:** Head right **Rev:** Mountains **Note:** Insert container with 1 carat of diamonds.

| Date | Mintage | VF20 | XF40 | MS60 | MS63 | MS65 |
|---|---|---|---|---|---|---|
| 2009 P | 7,500 | PF63 110 | PF65 120 | | | |

**KM# 1245 DOLLAR**
31.11 g., 0.999 Silver 0.999 oz. ASW **Ruler:** Elizabeth II **Subject:** 2010 FIFA World Cup, South Africa **Obv:** Head right **Rev:** Soccer player and kangaroo in background

| Date | Mintage | VF20 | XF40 | MS60 | MS63 | MS65 |
|---|---|---|---|---|---|---|
| 2009 P | 15,000 | PF63 90.00 | PF65 100 | | | |

**KM# 1248 DOLLAR**
31.11 g., 0.999 Silver 0.999 oz. ASW, 40.6 mm. **Ruler:** Elizabeth II **Subject:** World Masters Games **Obv:** Head right **Rev:** Sydney Harbor Bridge, multicolor logo

| Date | Mintage | VF20 | XF40 | MS60 | MS63 | MS65 |
|---|---|---|---|---|---|---|
| 2009 P | 1,742 | PF65 100 | | | | |

**KM# 1256 DOLLAR**
13.80 g., Aluminum-Bronze, 31 mm. **Ruler:** Elizabeth II **Subject:** Space Topics - Astronomers **Obv:** Head right **Rev:** Galileo Galilei and telescope

| Date | Mintage | VF20 | XF40 | MS60 | MS63 | MS65 |
|---|---|---|---|---|---|---|
| 2009 P | 5,316 | — | — | — | — | 12.00 |

**KM# 1257 DOLLAR**
Aluminum-Bronze, 31 mm. **Ruler:** Elizabeth II **Subject:** Space Topics - Craters **Obv:** Head right **Rev:** Moon crater Daedalus

| Date | Mintage | VF20 | XF40 | MS60 | MS63 | MS65 |
|---|---|---|---|---|---|---|
| 2009 P | 5,316 | — | — | — | — | 12.00 |

**KM# 1258 DOLLAR**
Aluminum-Bronze, 31 mm. **Ruler:** Elizabeth II **Subject:** Space Topics - Moons **Obv:** Head right **Rev:** Apollo astronaut on moon walk

| Date | Mintage | VF20 | XF40 | MS60 | MS63 | MS65 |
|---|---|---|---|---|---|---|
| 2009 P | 5,316 | — | — | — | — | 12.00 |

**KM# 1259 DOLLAR**
Aluminum-Bronze, 31 mm. **Ruler:** Elizabeth II **Subject:** Space Topics - Observatories **Obv:** Head right **Rev:** Parkes Observatory, New South Wales

| Date | Mintage | VF20 | XF40 | MS60 | MS63 | MS65 |
|---|---|---|---|---|---|---|
| 2009 P | 5,316 | — | — | — | — | 12.00 |

**KM# 1260 DOLLAR**
Aluminum-Bronze, 31 mm. **Ruler:** Elizabeth II **Subject:** Space Topics - Rockets **Obv:** Head right **Rev:** Saturn V rocket on launch pad

| Date | Mintage | VF20 | XF40 | MS60 | MS63 | MS65 |
|---|---|---|---|---|---|---|
| 2009 P | 5,316 | — | — | — | — | 12.00 |

**KM# 1261 DOLLAR**
Aluminum-Bronze, 31 mm. **Ruler:** Elizabeth II **Subject:** Space Topics - Rovers **Obv:** Head right **Rev:** Mars rover - Spirit and Opportunity

| Date | Mintage | VF20 | XF40 | MS60 | MS63 | MS65 |
|---|---|---|---|---|---|---|
| 2009 P | 5,316 | — | — | — | — | 12.00 |

**KM# 1262 DOLLAR**
Aluminum-Bronze, 31 mm. **Ruler:** Elizabeth II **Subject:** Space Topics - Space Shuttles **Obv:** Head right **Rev:** Shuttle Discovery and Space Exploration

| Date | Mintage | VF20 | XF40 | MS60 | MS63 | MS65 |
|---|---|---|---|---|---|---|
| 2009 P | 5,316 | — | — | — | — | 12.00 |

**KM# 1263 DOLLAR**
Aluminum-Bronze, 31 mm. **Ruler:** Elizabeth II **Subject:** Space Topics - Probes **Obv:** Head right **Rev:** Deep Space Probes - Pioneer 11 and 11

| Date | Mintage | VF20 | XF40 | MS60 | MS63 | MS65 |
|---|---|---|---|---|---|---|
| 2009 P | 5,316 | — | — | — | — | 12.00 |

**KM# 1264 DOLLAR**
Aluminum-Bronze, 31 mm. **Ruler:** Elizabeth II **Subject:** Space Topics - Space Telescope **Obv:** Head right **Rev:** Hubble Space Telescope

| Date | Mintage | VF20 | XF40 | MS60 | MS63 | MS65 |
|---|---|---|---|---|---|---|
| 2009 P | 5,316 | — | — | — | — | 12.00 |

**KM# 1265 DOLLAR**
31.11 g., 0.999 Silver 0.999 oz. ASW, 27x48 mm. **Ruler:** Elizabeth II **Subject:** Chinese Mythological Character - Wealth **Obv:** Head right **Rev:** Man standing, multicolor **Shape:** Vertical rectangle

| Date | Mintage | VF20 | XF40 | MS60 | MS63 | MS65 |
|---|---|---|---|---|---|---|
| 2009 P | — | — | — | — | — | 65.00 |

**KM# 1266 DOLLAR**
31.11 g., 0.999 Silver 0.999 oz. ASW, 27x48 mm. **Ruler:** Elizabeth II **Subject:** Chinese Mythological Character - Longevity **Obv:** Head right **Rev:** Man standing with staff, multicolor **Edge Lettering:** Vertical rectangle

| Date | Mintage | VF20 | XF40 | MS60 | MS63 | MS65 |
|---|---|---|---|---|---|---|
| 2009 P | — | — | — | — | — | 65.00 |

**KM# 1267 DOLLAR**
31.11 g., 0.999 Silver 0.999 oz. ASW, 27x48 mm. **Ruler:** Elizabeth II **Subject:** Chinese Mythological Character - Success **Obv:** Head right **Rev:** Man standing with deer, multicolor **Shape:** Vertical rectangle

| Date | Mintage | VF20 | XF40 | MS60 | MS63 | MS65 |
|---|---|---|---|---|---|---|
| 2009 P | — | — | — | — | — | 65.00 |

**KM# 1268 DOLLAR**
31.11 g., 0.999 Silver 0.999 oz. ASW, 27x48 mm. **Ruler:** Elizabeth II **Subject:** Chinese Mythological Character - Fortune **Obv:** Head right **Rev:** Man standing with scroll, multicolor **Shape:** Vertical rectangle

| Date | Mintage | VF20 | XF40 | MS60 | MS63 | MS65 |
|---|---|---|---|---|---|---|
| 2009 P | — | — | — | — | — | 65.00 |

**KM# 1357 DOLLAR**
31.14 g., 0.999 Silver 1.000 oz. ASW, 40.6 mm. **Ruler:** Elizabeth II **Subject:** International Year of Astronomy **Obv:** Head right **Rev:** Youth looking through telescope, pointing at universe

| Date | Mintage | VF20 | XF40 | MS60 | MS63 | MS65 |
|---|---|---|---|---|---|---|
| 2009 P | 6,814 | PF65 60.00 | | | | |

## KM# 1358 DOLLAR

30.60 g., Aluminum-Bronze, 30.6 mm. **Ruler:** Elizabeth II **Subject:** Swimming **Obv:** Head light **Rev:** Swimmer

| Date | Mintage | VF20 | XF40 | MS60 | MS63 | MS65 |
|---|---|---|---|---|---|---|
| 2009 (p) | 8,467 | — | — | 5.50 | 7.50 | 10.00 |

## KM# 1359 DOLLAR

32.14 g., 0.999 Silver 1.0321 oz. ASW, 40 mm. **Ruler:** Elizabeth II **Subject:** Swimming **Obv:** Head right **Rev:** Swimmer with hologram effect added

| Date | Mintage | VF20 | XF40 | MS60 | MS63 | MS65 |
|---|---|---|---|---|---|---|
| 2009 (p) | 1,993 | PF65 70.00 | | | | |

## KM# 1428 DOLLAR

13.80 g., Aluminum-Bronze, 30.6 mm. **Ruler:** Elizabeth II **Subject:** Citizenship **Obv:** Head in tiara right **Rev:** National arms

| Date | Mintage | VF20 | XF40 | MS60 | MS63 | MS65 |
|---|---|---|---|---|---|---|
| 2009 P | — | — | — | — | — | 14.00 |
| 2010 P | — | — | — | — | — | 14.00 |
| 2011 P | — | — | — | — | — | 14.00 |
| 2012 P | — | — | — | — | — | 14.00 |
| 2013 (p) | — | — | — | — | 14.00 | — |
| 2014 P | — | — | — | — | 14.00 | — |
| 2015 P | — | — | — | — | 14.00 | — |

## KM# 1429 DOLLAR

9.00 g., Aluminum-Bronze, 25 mm. **Ruler:** Elizabeth II **Subject:** Steve Irwin **Rev:** Steve Irwin and animal montage

| Date | Mintage | VF20 | XF40 | MS60 | MS63 | MS65 |
|---|---|---|---|---|---|---|
| 2009 (p) | — | — | — | — | — | 12.00 |

## KM# 1497 DOLLAR

13.80 g., Aluminum-Bronze, 30.6 mm. **Ruler:** Elizabeth II **Subject:** ANZAC **Rev:** Child on lap of grandfather, bugler in background

| Date | Mintage | VF20 | XF40 | MS60 | MS63 | MS65 |
|---|---|---|---|---|---|---|
| 2009 | 18,561 | — | — | 5.50 | 7.50 | 10.00 |

## KM# 1498 DOLLAR

9.00 g., Aluminum-Bronze, 25 mm. **Ruler:** Elizabeth II **Subject:** Age pensions, 100th Anniversary **Rev:** Extended family portrait, elder members seated at front center in detail

| Date | Mintage | VF20 | XF40 | MS60 | MS63 | MS65 |
|---|---|---|---|---|---|---|
| 2009 | — | — | — | 5.50 | 7.50 | 10.00 |

## KM# 1499 DOLLAR

9.00 g., Aluminum-Bronze, 25 mm. **Ruler:** Elizabeth II **Subject:** Girl Guides, 100th Anniversary

| Date | Mintage | VF20 | XF40 | MS60 | MS63 | MS65 |
|---|---|---|---|---|---|---|
| 2010 | — | — | — | 5.50 | 7.50 | 10.00 |

## KM# 1655 DOLLAR

9.00 g., Aluminum-Bronze, 25 mm. **Ruler:** Elizabeth II **Obv:** Head with tiara right **Rev:** Baby bilby in color right

| Date | Mintage | VF20 | XF40 | MS60 | MS63 | MS65 |
|---|---|---|---|---|---|---|
| 2009 | — | — | — | — | — | 10.00 |

## KM# 1656 DOLLAR

9.00 g., Aluminum-Bronze, 25 mm. **Ruler:** Elizabeth II **Obv:** Head with tiara right **Rev:** Frilly lizard in color right

| Date | Mintage | VF20 | XF40 | MS60 | MS63 | MS65 |
|---|---|---|---|---|---|---|
| 2009 | — | — | — | — | — | 10.00 |

## KM# 1657 DOLLAR

9.00 g., Aluminum-Bronze, 25 mm. **Ruler:** Elizabeth II **Subject:** World Masters Games **Obv:** Head with tiara right **Rev:** Sydney Harbor Bridge, games logo above

| Date | Mintage | VF20 | XF40 | MS60 | MS63 | MS65 |
|---|---|---|---|---|---|---|
| 2009 | — | — | — | 5.00 | 7.00 | 10.00 |

## KM# 1324 DOLLAR

31.11 g., 0.999 Silver 0.999 oz. ASW, 41 mm. **Ruler:** Elizabeth II **Subject:** Lachen Macquarie, Governor of New South Wales **Obv:** Head right **Rev:** Macquarie, Sydney's "Rum" Hospital, Holey Dollar

| Date | Mintage | VF20 | XF40 | MS60 | MS63 | MS65 |
|---|---|---|---|---|---|---|
| 2010 P | 7,500 | PF63 80.00 | PF65 90.00 | | | |

## KM# 1325 DOLLAR

31.11 g., 0.999 Silver 0.999 oz. ASW, 41 mm. **Ruler:** Elizabeth II **Subject:** 2010 Australian Olympic Team **Obv:** Head right **Rev:** Downhill skier, multicolor Australian flag

| Date | Mintage | VF20 | XF40 | MS60 | MS63 | MS65 |
|---|---|---|---|---|---|---|
| 2010 P | 5,000 | PF63 90.00 | PF65 100 | | | |

## KM# 1326 DOLLAR

31.11 g., 0.999 Silver 0.999 oz. ASW, 41 mm. **Ruler:** Elizabeth II **Subject:** Century of Flight in Australia **Obv:** Head right **Rev:** Bi-plane, multicolor

| Date | Mintage | VF20 | XF40 | MS60 | MS63 | MS65 |
|---|---|---|---|---|---|---|
| 2010 P | 7,500 | PF63 80.00 | PF65 90.00 | | | |

## KM# 1380 DOLLAR

13.80 g., Aluminum-Bronze, 30.6 mm. **Ruler:** Elizabeth II **Subject:** Anzac Navy **Obv:** Head right **Rev:** Naval crew member and ship

| Date | Mintage | VF20 | XF40 | MS60 | MS63 | MS65 |
|---|---|---|---|---|---|---|
| 2010 (p) | — | — | — | — | — | 12.00 |

## KM# 1381 DOLLAR

31.10 g., 0.999 Silver 0.999 oz. ASW, 40.5 mm. **Ruler:** Elizabeth II **Subject:** Antarctic - Huskey **Obv:** Head right **Rev:** Huskey in multicolor

| Date | Mintage | VF20 | XF40 | MS60 | MS63 | MS65 |
|---|---|---|---|---|---|---|
| 2010 (p) | 7,500 | PF65 60.00 | | | | |

## KM# 1382 DOLLAR

13.80 g., Aluminum-Bronze, 30.6 mm. **Ruler:** Elizabeth II **Subject:** Flight Centennial **Obv:** Head right **Rev:** Bi-plane flying right

| Date | Mintage | VF20 | XF40 | MS60 | MS63 | MS65 |
|---|---|---|---|---|---|---|
| 2010 (p) | — | — | — | — | — | 13.00 |

**KM# 1383 DOLLAR**
31.10 g., 0.999 Silver 0.999 oz. ASW, 40 mm. **Ruler:** Elizabeth II **Subject:** Edward VII Coinage **Obv:** Head right **Rev:** Coin designs and Edward VII in multicolor

| Date | Mintage | VF20 | XF40 | MS60 | MS63 | MS65 |
|---|---|---|---|---|---|---|
| 2010 (p) | — | — | — | — | — | 60.00 |

**KM# 1384 DOLLAR**
13.80 g., Aluminum-Bronze, 30.6 mm. **Ruler:** Elizabeth II **Subject:** Celebrate Australia - Barrier Reef **Obv:** Head right **Rev:** Sea Turtle and multicolor background

| Date | Mintage | VF20 | XF40 | MS60 | MS63 | MS65 |
|---|---|---|---|---|---|---|
| 2010 P | — | — | — | — | — | 15.00 |

**KM# 1385 DOLLAR**
13.80 g., Aluminum-Bronze, 30.6 mm. **Ruler:** Elizabeth II **Subject:** Celebrate Australia - Blue Mountain **Obv:** Head right **Rev:** Frog and multicolor background

| Date | Mintage | VF20 | XF40 | MS60 | MS63 | MS65 |
|---|---|---|---|---|---|---|
| 2010 P | — | — | — | — | — | 15.00 |

**KM# 1386 DOLLAR**
13.80 g., Aluminum-Bronze, 30.6 mm. **Ruler:** Elizabeth II **Subject:** Celebrate Australia - Heard Island **Obv:** Head right **Rev:** Penguins and multicolor background

| Date | Mintage | VF20 | XF40 | MS60 | MS63 | MS65 |
|---|---|---|---|---|---|---|
| 2010 P | — | — | — | — | — | 15.00 |

**KM# 1387 DOLLAR**
13.80 g., Aluminum-Bronze, 30.6 mm. **Ruler:** Elizabeth II **Subject:** Celebrate Australia - Shark Bay **Obv:** Head right

| Date | Mintage | VF20 | XF40 | MS60 | MS63 | MS65 |
|---|---|---|---|---|---|---|
| 2010 P | — | — | — | — | — | 15.00 |

**KM# 1388 DOLLAR**
13.80 g., Aluminum-Bronze, 30.6 mm. **Ruler:** Elizabeth II **Subject:** Celebrate Australia - Tasmanian Wilderness **Obv:** Head right **Rev:** Animal before multicolor waterfall background

| Date | Mintage | VF20 | XF40 | MS60 | MS63 | MS65 |
|---|---|---|---|---|---|---|
| 2010 P | — | — | — | — | — | 15.00 |

**KM# 1391 DOLLAR**
31.11 g., 0.999 Silver 0.999 oz. ASW **Ruler:** Elizabeth II **Obv:** Head right **Rev:** Panda and koala

| Date | Mintage | VF20 | XF40 | MS60 | MS63 | MS65 |
|---|---|---|---|---|---|---|
| 2010 (p) | — | — | — | — | — | 45.00 |

**KM# 1392 DOLLAR**
31.11 g., 0.999 Silver 0.999 oz. ASW **Ruler:** Elizabeth II **Subject:** World Expo **Obv:** Head right **Rev:** Austrlian Panham

| Date | Mintage | VF20 | XF40 | MS60 | MS63 | MS65 |
|---|---|---|---|---|---|---|
| 2010 (p) | — | — | — | — | — | 50.00 |

**KM# 1393 DOLLAR**
31.11 g., 0.999 Silver 0.999 oz. ASW **Ruler:** Elizabeth II **Obv:** Head right **Rev:** Kookaburra mascot

| Date | Mintage | VF20 | XF40 | MS60 | MS63 | MS65 |
|---|---|---|---|---|---|---|
| 2010 (p) | — | — | — | — | — | 45.00 |

**KM# 1394 DOLLAR**
31.11 g., 0.999 Silver 0.999 oz. ASW **Ruler:** Elizabeth II **Obv:** Head right **Rev:** City scape

| Date | Mintage | VF20 | XF40 | MS60 | MS63 | MS65 |
|---|---|---|---|---|---|---|
| 2010 (p) | — | — | — | — | — | 45.00 |

**KM# 1395 DOLLAR**
Silver, 40x60 mm. **Ruler:** Elizabeth II **Series:** World Expo **Obv:** Head right **Shape:** Australian outline

| Date | Mintage | VF20 | XF40 | MS60 | MS63 | MS65 |
|---|---|---|---|---|---|---|
| 2010 (p) | — | — | — | — | — | 70.00 |

**KM# 1396 DOLLAR**
13.80 g., Aluminum-Bronze, 30.6 mm. **Ruler:** Elizabeth II **Subject:** 2010 Shanghai World Expo **Obv:** Head with tiara right **Rev:** Artistic tiger seen from above, advancing forward

| Date | Mintage | VF20 | XF40 | MS60 | MS63 | MS65 |
|---|---|---|---|---|---|---|
| 2010 P | — | — | — | — | — | 14.00 |

**KM# 1403 DOLLAR**
31.11 g., 0.999 Silver 0.999 oz. ASW, 40.6 mm. **Ruler:** Elizabeth II **Obv:** Head right **Rev:** Frill-neck lizard, multicolor

| Date | Mintage | VF20 | XF40 | MS60 | MS63 | MS65 |
|---|---|---|---|---|---|---|
| 2010 (p) | — | PF63 80.00 | PF65 90.00 | | | |

**KM# 1409 DOLLAR**
31.11 g., 0.999 Silver 0.999 oz. ASW, 40.6 mm. **Ruler:** Elizabeth II **Obv:** Head right **Rev:** Koala and multicolor

| Date | Mintage | VF20 | XF40 | MS60 | MS63 | MS65 |
|---|---|---|---|---|---|---|
| 2010 (p) | — | PF63 80.00 | PF65 90.00 | | | |

**KM# 1415 DOLLAR**
31.11 g., 0.999 Silver 0.999 oz. ASW, 40.6 mm. **Ruler:** Elizabeth II **Obv:** Head right **Rev:** Multicolor platypus

| Date | Mintage | VF20 | XF40 | MS60 | MS63 | MS65 |
|---|---|---|---|---|---|---|
| 2010 (p) | — | PF63 80.00 | PF65 90.00 | | | |

**KM# 1421 DOLLAR**
31.11 g., 0.999 Silver 0.999 oz. ASW, 40.6 mm. **Ruler:** Elizabeth II **Obv:** Head right **Rev:** Multicolor salt water crocodile

| Date | Mintage | VF20 | XF40 | MS60 | MS63 | MS65 |
|---|---|---|---|---|---|---|
| 2010 (p) | — | PF63 80.00 | PF65 90.00 | | | |

**KM# 1427 DOLLAR**
31.11 g., 0.999 Silver 0.999 oz. ASW, 40.6 mm. **Ruler:** Elizabeth II **Obv:** Head right **Rev:** Multicolor wombat

| Date | Mintage | VF20 | XF40 | MS60 | MS63 | MS65 |
|---|---|---|---|---|---|---|
| 2010 (p) | — | PF63 80.00 | PF65 90.00 | | | |

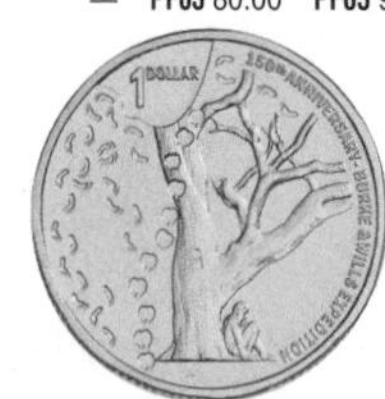

**KM# 1431 DOLLAR**
9.00 g., Aluminum-Bronze, 25 mm. **Ruler:** Elizabeth II **Subject:** Burke and Wills 150th Anniversary **Obv:** Head with tiara right **Rev:** King seated under dig tree

| Date | Mintage | VF20 | XF40 | MS60 | MS63 | MS65 |
|---|---|---|---|---|---|---|
| 2010 C | — | — | — | — | — | 12.50 |
| 2010 C | — | PF65 17.50 | | | | |

**KM# 1434 DOLLAR**
31.14 g., 0.999 Silver 1.000 oz. ASW **Ruler:** Elizabeth II **Subject:** Burke & Wills expedition **Rev:** Multicolor scene of explorers

| Date | Mintage | VF20 | XF40 | MS60 | MS63 | MS65 |
|---|---|---|---|---|---|---|
| 2010 P | 7,500 | PF65 80.00 | | | | |

**KM# 1435 DOLLAR**
31.14 g., 0.999 Silver 1.000 oz. ASW, 40.6 mm. **Ruler:** Elizabeth II **Subject:** Treasures of Australia - Gold **Rev:** Three gold nuggets within insert

| Date | Mintage | VF20 | XF40 | MS60 | MS63 | MS65 |
|---|---|---|---|---|---|---|
| 2010 P | — | PF65 135 | | | | |

**KM# 1440 DOLLAR**
13.30 g., Aluminum-Bronze, 30.6 mm. **Ruler:** Elizabeth II **Rev:** Blowfly

| Date | Mintage | VF20 | XF40 | MS60 | MS63 | MS65 |
|---|---|---|---|---|---|---|
| 2010 P | — | — | — | — | — | 12.00 |

**KM# 1441 DOLLAR**
13.30 g., Aluminum-Bronze, 30.6 mm. **Ruler:** Elizabeth II **Rev:** Bull Ant

| Date | Mintage | VF20 | XF40 | MS60 | MS63 | MS65 |
|---|---|---|---|---|---|---|
| 2010 P | — | — | — | — | — | 12.00 |

**KM# 1442 DOLLAR**
13.30 g., Aluminum-Bronze, 30.6 mm. **Ruler:** Elizabeth II **Rev:** Burlwing Buttlerfly

| Date | Mintage | VF20 | XF40 | MS60 | MS63 | MS65 |
|---|---|---|---|---|---|---|
| 2010 P | — | — | — | — | — | 12.00 |

**KM# 1443 DOLLAR**
13.30 g., Aluminum-Bronze, 30.6 mm. **Ruler:** Elizabeth II **Rev:** Cicada

| Date | Mintage | VF20 | XF40 | MS60 | MS63 | MS65 |
|---|---|---|---|---|---|---|
| 2010 P | — | — | — | — | — | 12.00 |

**KM# 1444 DOLLAR**
13.30 g., Aluminum-Bronze, 30.6 mm. **Ruler:** Elizabeth II **Rev:** Dragonfly

| Date | Mintage | VF20 | XF40 | MS60 | MS63 | MS65 |
|---|---|---|---|---|---|---|
| 2010 P | — | — | — | — | — | 12.00 |

### KM# 1445 DOLLAR

13.30 g., Aluminum-Bronze, 30.6 mm. **Ruler:** Elizabeth II **Rev:** Grasshopper

| Date | Mintage | VF20 | XF40 | MS60 | MS63 | MS65 |
|---|---|---|---|---|---|---|
| 2010 P | — | — | — | — | — | 12.00 |

### KM# 1446 DOLLAR

13.30 g., Aluminum-Bronze, 30.6 mm. **Ruler:** Elizabeth II **Rev:** Ladybug

| Date | Mintage | VF20 | XF40 | MS60 | MS63 | MS65 |
|---|---|---|---|---|---|---|
| 2010 P | — | — | — | — | — | 12.00 |

### KM# 1447 DOLLAR

13.30 g., Aluminum-Bronze, 30.6 mm. **Ruler:** Elizabeth II **Rev:** Praying mantis

| Date | Mintage | VF20 | XF40 | MS60 | MS63 | MS65 |
|---|---|---|---|---|---|---|
| 2010 P | — | — | — | — | — | 12.00 |

### KM# 1448 DOLLAR

13.30 g., Aluminum-Bronze, 30.6 mm. **Ruler:** Elizabeth II **Rev:** Red-backed spider

| Date | Mintage | VF20 | XF40 | MS60 | MS63 | MS65 |
|---|---|---|---|---|---|---|
| 2010 P | — | — | — | — | — | 12.00 |

### KM# 1451 DOLLAR

31.11 g., 0.999 Silver 0.999 oz. ASW **Ruler:** Elizabeth II **Subject:** New South Wales - Sidney Coin Show **Rev:** Koala and multicolor opera house and harbor bridge views

| Date | Mintage | VF20 | XF40 | MS60 | MS63 | MS65 |
|---|---|---|---|---|---|---|
| 2010 P | — | PF65 45.00 | | | | |

### KM# 1452 DOLLAR

31.11 g., 0.999 Silver 0.999 oz. ASW **Ruler:** Elizabeth II **Subject:** Victoria - Melbourne Coin Show **Rev:** Penguin and multicolor tram and building

| Date | Mintage | VF20 | XF40 | MS60 | MS63 | MS65 |
|---|---|---|---|---|---|---|
| 2010 P | — | PF65 45.00 | | | | |

### KM# 1453 DOLLAR

31.11 g., 0.999 Silver 0.999 oz. ASW, 27x47 mm. **Ruler:** Elizabeth II **Rev:** Dreaming dolphin **Shape:** Vertical rectangle

| Date | Mintage | VF20 | XF40 | MS60 | MS63 | MS65 |
|---|---|---|---|---|---|---|
| 2010 P Proof | — | — | — | — | — | 80.00 |

### KM# 1490 DOLLAR

13.30 g., Aluminum-Bronze, 30.6 mm. **Ruler:** Elizabeth II **Rev:** Burke & Willis statue

| Date | Mintage | VF20 | XF40 | MS60 | MS63 | MS65 |
|---|---|---|---|---|---|---|
| 2010 P | — | — | — | — | — | 12.00 |

### KM# 1491 DOLLAR

31.11 g., 0.999 Silver 0.999 oz. ASW, 40.6 mm. **Ruler:** Elizabeth II **Obv:** Head with tiara right **Rev:** Saint Mary Mackillop in color

| Date | Mintage | VF20 | XF40 | MS60 | MS63 | MS65 |
|---|---|---|---|---|---|---|
| 2010 | — | PF65 60.00 | | | | |

### KM# 1494 DOLLAR

31.11 g., 0.999 Silver 0.999 oz. ASW **Ruler:** Elizabeth II **Subject:** New South Wales

| Date | Mintage | VF20 | XF40 | MS60 | MS63 | MS65 |
|---|---|---|---|---|---|---|
| 2010 | — | PF65 50.00 | | | | |

### KM# 1495 DOLLAR

9.00 g., Aluminum-Bronze, 25 mm. **Ruler:** Elizabeth II **Subject:** Australian coinage, 100th Anniversary **Obv:** Head with tiara right **Rev:** Coinage portraits of Elizabeth II, George VI, George V and Edward VII

| Date | Mintage | VF20 | XF40 | MS60 | MS63 | MS65 |
|---|---|---|---|---|---|---|
| 2010 C | — | — | — | 3.00 | 4.00 | 5.00 |
| 2010 B | — | — | — | 3.00 | 4.00 | 5.00 |
| 2010 M | — | — | — | 3.00 | 4.00 | 5.00 |
| 2010 S | — | — | — | 3.00 | 4.00 | 5.00 |

### KM# 1495A DOLLAR

11.66 g., 0.999 Silver 0.3745 oz. ASW, 25 mm. **Ruler:** Elizabeth II **Subject:** Centennial of Commonwealth Coins **Obv:** Head in tiara right **Rev:** Four portraits

| Date | Mintage | VF20 | XF40 | MS60 | MS63 | MS65 |
|---|---|---|---|---|---|---|
| 2010 | 12,500 | PF65 50.00 | | | | |

### KM# 1496 DOLLAR

9.00 g., Aluminum-Bronze, 25 mm. **Ruler:** Elizabeth II **Subject:** Fred Hollows - Inspirational Australians

| Date | Mintage | VF20 | XF40 | MS60 | MS63 | MS65 |
|---|---|---|---|---|---|---|
| 2010 | — | — | — | 2.50 | 3.50 | 5.00 |

### KM# 1503 DOLLAR

9.00 g., Aluminum-Bronze, 25 mm. **Ruler:** Elizabeth II **Subject:** Wool Industry **Rev:** Sheep sheering and map of Australia

| Date | Mintage | VF20 | XF40 | MS60 | MS63 | MS65 |
|---|---|---|---|---|---|---|
| 2010 | — | — | — | 4.00 | 5.00 | 6.00 |
| 2010 | — | PF65 25.00 | | | | |

### KM# 1505 DOLLAR

31.11 g., 0.999 Silver 0.999 oz. ASW, 40.6 mm. **Ruler:** Elizabeth II **Subject:** Perth-ANDA Bridge **Rev:** City view

| Date | Mintage | VF20 | XF40 | MS60 | MS63 | MS65 |
|---|---|---|---|---|---|---|
| 2010 | — | PF63 60.00 | PF65 65.00 | | | |

**KM# 1568 DOLLAR**
31.11 g., 0.999 Silver 0.999 oz. ASW, 32.6 mm. **Ruler:** Elizabeth II **Subject:** Sidney Cove Medallion, Wedgewood theme **Obv:** Head with tiara right **Rev:** One female standing on rock facing three others, seascape in backgorund **Edge:** Reeded **Note:** High relief

| Date | Mintage | VF20 | XF40 | MS60 | MS63 | MS65 |
|---|---|---|---|---|---|---|
| 2010 P | Est. 5000 | PF65 85.00 | | | | |

**KM# 1659 DOLLAR**
9.00 g., Aluminum-Bronze, 25 mm. **Ruler:** Elizabeth II **Subject:** Year of the Tiger **Rev:** Tiger head at center in circle, floral around

| Date | Mintage | VF20 | XF40 | MS60 | MS63 | MS65 |
|---|---|---|---|---|---|---|
| 2010 | — | — | — | — | — | 10.00 |

**KM# 1659a DOLLAR**
11.66 g., 0.999 Silver 0.3745 oz. ASW, 25 mm. **Ruler:** Elizabeth II **Subject:** Year of the Tiger **Obv:** Head with tiara right **Rev:** Tiger head in circle, floral around

| Date | Mintage | VF20 | XF40 | MS60 | MS63 | MS65 |
|---|---|---|---|---|---|---|
| 2010 | — | PF65 30.00 | | | | |

**KM# 1504 DOLLAR**
9.00 g., Aluminum-Bronze, 25 mm. **Ruler:** Elizabeth II **Subject:** Historical coin designs **Rev:** Sheep head

| Date | Mintage | VF20 | XF40 | MS60 | MS63 | MS65 |
|---|---|---|---|---|---|---|
| 2011 C | — | — | — | 4.00 | 5.00 | 6.00 |

**KM# 1523 DOLLAR**
31.10 g., 0.999 Silver 0.999 oz. ASW, 40.6 mm. **Ruler:** Elizabeth II **Subject:** Australia's Bronze Coinagae, 100th Anniversary **Obv:** Head with tiara right **Rev:** George V and coins, in color

| Date | Mintage | VF20 | XF40 | MS60 | MS63 | MS65 |
|---|---|---|---|---|---|---|
| 2011 | — | PF65 75.00 | | | | |

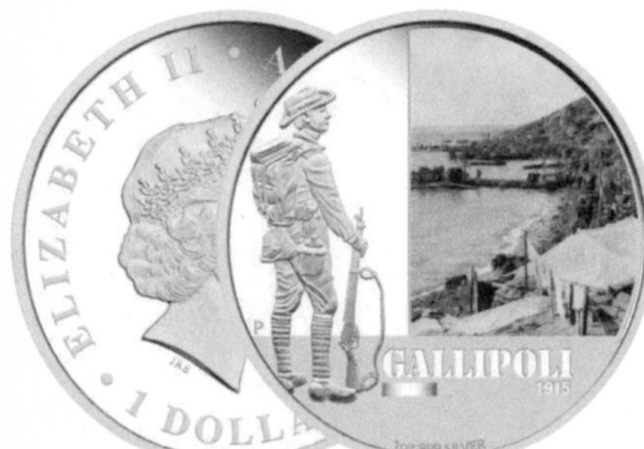


**KM# 1528 DOLLAR**
31.11 g., 0.999 Silver 0.999 oz. ASW, 40.6 mm. **Ruler:** Elizabeth II **Subject:** Famous Battles in Australian History **Rev:** Soldier standing at left, view of Gallipoli, 1915 at right

| Date | Mintage | VF20 | XF40 | MS60 | MS63 | MS65 |
|---|---|---|---|---|---|---|
| 2011 P | 5,000 | PF65 110 | | | | |

**KM# 1529 DOLLAR**
13.30 g., Aluminum-Bronze, 30.6 mm. **Ruler:** Elizabeth II **Subject:** ANZAC Day, RAAF **Rev:** Bugler and plane, two airmen at lower right

| Date | Mintage | VF20 | XF40 | MS60 | MS63 | MS65 |
|---|---|---|---|---|---|---|
| 2011 P | — | — | — | — | — | 13.00 |

**KM# 1530 DOLLAR**
31.11 g., 0.999 Silver 0.999 oz. ASW **Ruler:** Elizabeth II **Subject:** Royal Wedding **Rev:** Catherine Middleton and Prince William in color, Westminster Abbey at left

| Date | Mintage | VF20 | XF40 | MS60 | MS63 | MS65 |
|---|---|---|---|---|---|---|
| 2011 P | 12,500 | PF65 110 | | | | |

**KM# 1531 DOLLAR**
31.11 g., 0.999 Silver 0.999 oz. ASW **Ruler:** Elizabeth II **Subject:** Naval Battles **Rev:** Battle of Midway

| Date | Mintage | VF20 | XF40 | MS60 | MS63 | MS65 |
|---|---|---|---|---|---|---|
| 2011 P | 5,000 | PF65 110 | | | | |

**KM# 1534 DOLLAR**
31.11 g., 0.999 Silver 0.999 oz. ASW **Ruler:** Elizabeth II **Subject:** Dreaming Emu **Rev:** Linear emu in color

| Date | Mintage | VF20 | XF40 | MS60 | MS63 | MS65 |
|---|---|---|---|---|---|---|
| 2011 P | — | PF65 105 | | | | |

**KM# 1540 DOLLAR**
31.11 g., 0.999 Silver 0.999 oz. ASW **Ruler:** Elizabeth II **Subject:** Dreaming Tasmanian Devil **Rev:** Linear tasmanian devil in color

| Date | Mintage | VF20 | XF40 | MS60 | MS63 | MS65 |
|---|---|---|---|---|---|---|
| 2011 P | — | PF65 105 | | | | |

**KM# 1546 DOLLAR**
31.11 g., 0.999 Silver 0.999 oz. ASW **Ruler:** Elizabeth II **Rev:** Linear Kookaburra in color

| Date | Mintage | VF20 | XF40 | MS60 | MS63 | MS65 |
|---|---|---|---|---|---|---|
| 2011 P | — | PF65 115 | | | | |

**KM# 1552 DOLLAR**
31.11 g., 0.999 Silver 0.999 oz. ASW **Ruler:** Elizabeth II **Subject:** Dreaming Shark **Rev:** Linear shark in color

| Date | Mintage | VF20 | XF40 | MS60 | MS63 | MS65 |
|---|---|---|---|---|---|---|
| 2011 P | — | PF65 105 | | | | |

**KM# 1558 DOLLAR**
31.11 g., 0.999 Silver 0.999 oz. ASW **Ruler:** Elizabeth II **Subject:** Dreaming Dingo **Rev:** Linear dingo in color

| Date | Mintage | VF20 | XF40 | MS60 | MS63 | MS65 |
|---|---|---|---|---|---|---|
| 2011 P | — | PF65 105 | | | | |

**KM# 1564 DOLLAR**
31.11 g., 0.999 Silver 0.999 oz. ASW **Ruler:** Elizabeth II **Subject:** Treasures of Australia **Rev:** Keshi pearl engased in mother of pearl locket

| Date | Mintage | VF20 | XF40 | MS60 | MS63 | MS65 |
|---|---|---|---|---|---|---|
| 2011 P | — | **PF65** 185 | | | | |

**KM# 1565 DOLLAR**
31.11 g., 0.999 Silver 0.999 oz. ASW, 40.6 mm. **Ruler:** Elizabeth II **Subject:** Antartica **Obv:** Head with tiara right **Rev:** Killer whale in color

| Date | Mintage | VF20 | XF40 | MS60 | MS63 | MS65 |
|---|---|---|---|---|---|---|
| 2011 P | 7,500 | **PF65** 115 | | | | |

**KM# 1572 DOLLAR**
13.00 g., Aluminum-Bronze, 30.6 mm. **Ruler:** Elizabeth II **Subject:** Bush Babies - Koala **Rev:** Koala lounging at left

| Date | Mintage | VF20 | XF40 | MS60 | MS63 | MS65 |
|---|---|---|---|---|---|---|
| 2011 (p) | — | — | — | — | — | 15.00 |

**KM# 1573 DOLLAR**
13.00 g., Aluminum-Bronze, 30.6 mm. **Ruler:** Elizabeth II **Subject:** Bush babies - Dingo **Rev:** Dingo seated at left

| Date | Mintage | VF20 | XF40 | MS60 | MS63 | MS65 |
|---|---|---|---|---|---|---|
| 2011 (p) | — | — | — | — | — | 15.00 |

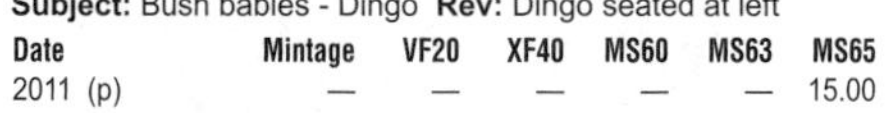

**KM# 1574 DOLLAR**
13.00 g., Aluminum-Bronze, 30.6 mm. **Ruler:** Elizabeth II **Subject:** Bush babies - Bilby **Rev:** Bilby at left

| Date | Mintage | VF20 | XF40 | MS60 | MS63 | MS65 |
|---|---|---|---|---|---|---|
| 2011 (p) | — | — | — | — | — | 15.00 |

**KM# 1575 DOLLAR**
13.00 g., Aluminum-Bronze, 30.6 mm. **Ruler:** Elizabeth II **Subject:** Bush babies - Sugar Glider **Rev:** Sugar Glider at left

| Date | Mintage | VF20 | XF40 | MS60 | MS63 | MS65 |
|---|---|---|---|---|---|---|
| 2011 (p) | — | — | — | — | — | 15.00 |

**KM# 1576 DOLLAR**
13.00 g., Aluminum-Bronze, 30.6 mm. **Ruler:** Elizabeth II **Subject:** Bush babies - Kangaroo **Rev:** Kangaroo seated at left

| Date | Mintage | VF20 | XF40 | MS60 | MS63 | MS65 |
|---|---|---|---|---|---|---|
| 2011 (p) | — | — | — | — | — | 15.00 |

**KM# 1580 DOLLAR**
13.80 g., Aluminum-Bronze, 30.6 mm. **Ruler:** Elizabeth II **Subject:** Mythical creatures - Dragon

| Date | Mintage | VF20 | XF40 | MS60 | MS63 | MS65 |
|---|---|---|---|---|---|---|
| 2011 P | — | — | — | — | — | 12.50 |

**KM# 1581 DOLLAR**
13.80 g., Aluminum-Bronze, 30.6 mm. **Ruler:** Elizabeth II **Subject:** Mythical creatures - Fairy

| Date | Mintage | VF20 | XF40 | MS60 | MS63 | MS65 |
|---|---|---|---|---|---|---|
| 2011 P | — | — | — | — | — | 12.50 |

**KM# 1582 DOLLAR**
13.80 g., Aluminum-Bronze, 30.6 mm. **Ruler:** Elizabeth II **Subject:** Mythical creatures - Goblin

| Date | Mintage | VF20 | XF40 | MS60 | MS63 | MS65 |
|---|---|---|---|---|---|---|
| 2011 P | — | — | — | — | — | 12.50 |

**KM# 1583 DOLLAR**
13.80 g., Aluminum-Bronze, 30.6 mm. **Ruler:** Elizabeth II **Subject:** Mythical creatures - Griffin

| Date | Mintage | VF20 | XF40 | MS60 | MS63 | MS65 |
|---|---|---|---|---|---|---|
| 2011 P | — | — | — | — | — | 12.50 |

**KM# 1584 DOLLAR**
13.80 g., Aluminum-Bronze, 30.6 mm. **Ruler:** Elizabeth II **Subject:** Mythical creatures - Mermaid

| Date | Mintage | VF20 | XF40 | MS60 | MS63 | MS65 |
|---|---|---|---|---|---|---|
| 2011 P | — | — | — | — | — | 12.50 |

**KM# 1585 DOLLAR**
13.80 g., Aluminum-Bronze, 30.6 mm. **Ruler:** Elizabeth II **Subject:** Mythical creatures - Tree ent

| Date | Mintage | VF20 | XF40 | MS60 | MS63 | MS65 |
|---|---|---|---|---|---|---|
| 2011 P | — | — | — | — | — | 12.50 |

**KM# 1586 DOLLAR**
13.80 g., Aluminum-Bronze, 30.6 mm. **Ruler:** Elizabeth II **Subject:** Mythical creatures - Ogre

| Date | Mintage | VF20 | XF40 | MS60 | MS63 | MS65 |
|---|---|---|---|---|---|---|
| 2011 P | — | — | — | — | — | 12.50 |

**KM# 1587 DOLLAR**
13.80 g., Aluminum-Bronze, 30.6 mm. **Ruler:** Elizabeth II **Subject:** Mythical creatures - Phoenix

| Date | Mintage | VF20 | XF40 | MS60 | MS63 | MS65 |
|---|---|---|---|---|---|---|
| 2011 P | — | — | — | — | — | 12.50 |

### KM# 1588 DOLLAR

13.80 g., Aluminum-Bronze, 30.6 mm. **Ruler:** Elizabeth II **Subject:** Mythical creatures - Unicorn

| Date | Mintage | VF20 | XF40 | MS60 | MS63 | MS65 |
|---|---|---|---|---|---|---|
| 2011 P | — | — | — | — | — | 12.50 |

### KM# 1589 DOLLAR

13.80 g., Aluminum-Bronze, 30.6 mm. **Ruler:** Elizabeth II **Obv:** Head in tiara right **Rev:** Christmas tree decorated in color, presents below, stars around, holly at bottom flanking **Rev. Legend:** WISHING YOU A MERRY CHRISTMAS / 2011

| Date | Mintage | VF20 | XF40 | MS60 | MS63 | MS65 |
|---|---|---|---|---|---|---|
| 2011 P | — | — | — | — | — | 12.50 |

### KM# 1590 DOLLAR

31.10 g., 0.999 Silver 0.999 oz. ASW, 40 mm. **Ruler:** Elizabeth II **Subject:** Dame Nellie Melba **Obv:** Head with tiara right **Rev:** Colored bust right, musical notes below, flowers at left

| Date | Mintage | VF20 | XF40 | MS60 | MS63 | MS65 |
|---|---|---|---|---|---|---|
| 2011 P | Est. 5000 | PF65 100 | | | | |

### KM# 1591 DOLLAR

13.80 g., Aluminum-Bronze, 30.6 mm. **Ruler:** Elizabeth II **Subject:** Dame Nellie Melba **Obv:** Head with tiara right **Rev:** Bust at left facing right, flowers at right

| Date | Mintage | VF20 | XF40 | MS60 | MS63 | MS65 |
|---|---|---|---|---|---|---|
| 2011 P | — | — | — | — | — | 12.50 |

### KM# 1592 DOLLAR

31.11 g., 0.999 Silver 0.999 oz. ASW, 40 mm. **Ruler:** Elizabeth II **Subject:** Royal Military College - Duntroon; 100th Anniversary **Obv:** Head with tiara right **Rev:** College emblem gilt above images of soldiers

| Date | Mintage | VF20 | XF40 | MS60 | MS63 | MS65 |
|---|---|---|---|---|---|---|
| 2011 P | Est. 7500 | PF65 100 | | | | |

### KM# 1593 DOLLAR

13.80 g., Aluminum-Bronze, 30.6 mm. **Ruler:** Elizabeth II **Subject:** Royal Military College - Duntroon; 100th Anniversary **Obv:** Head with tiara right **Rev:** Military hat badge

| Date | Mintage | VF20 | XF40 | MS60 | MS63 | MS65 |
|---|---|---|---|---|---|---|
| 2011 P | — | — | — | — | — | 12.50 |

### KM# 1594 DOLLAR

31.11 g., 0.999 Silver 0.999 oz. ASW, 40 mm. **Ruler:** Elizabeth II **Subject:** Australian Antartic Territory, Killer Whale **Obv:** Head with tiara right **Rev:** Killer whale, jumping, and in the water with a calf

| Date | Mintage | VF20 | XF40 | MS60 | MS63 | MS65 |
|---|---|---|---|---|---|---|
| 2011 P | Est. 7500 | PF65 100 | | | | |

### KM# 1597 DOLLAR

Aluminum-Bronze, 40 mm. **Ruler:** Elizabeth II **Subject:** Wiggles, 20th Anniversary **Obv:** Head with tiara right **Rev:** Wiggles characters in Big Red car **Edge:** Reeded

| Date | Mintage | VF20 | XF40 | MS60 | MS63 | MS65 |
|---|---|---|---|---|---|---|
| 2011 P | — | — | — | — | — | 17.50 |

### KM# 1598 DOLLAR

Aluminum-Bronze, 40 mm. **Ruler:** Elizabeth II **Subject:** Wiggles, 20th Anniversary **Obv:** Head in tiara right **Rev:** Wiggles four band members at instruments **Edge:** Reeded

| Date | Mintage | VF20 | XF40 | MS60 | MS63 | MS65 |
|---|---|---|---|---|---|---|
| 2011 P | — | — | — | — | — | 17.50 |

### KM# 1599 DOLLAR

Aluminum-Bronze, 40 mm. **Ruler:** Elizabeth II **Subject:** Wiggles, 20th Anniversary **Obv:** Head with tiara right **Rev:** Wiggles Pirate and animal characters

| Date | Mintage | VF20 | XF40 | MS60 | MS63 | MS65 |
|---|---|---|---|---|---|---|
| 2011 P | — | — | — | — | — | 17.50 |

### KM# 1600 DOLLAR

Aluminum-Bronze, 40 mm. **Ruler:** Elizabeth II **Subject:** Wiggles, 20th Anniversary **Obv:** Head with tiara right **Rev:** Wiggles charactes in starburst

| Date | Mintage | VF20 | XF40 | MS60 | MS63 | MS65 |
|---|---|---|---|---|---|---|
| 2011 P | — | — | — | — | — | 17.50 |

### KM# 1601 DOLLAR

31.11 g., 0.999 Silver 0.999 oz. ASW, 40 mm. **Ruler:** Elizabeth II **Subject:** Royal Australian Navy, 100th Anniversary **Obv:** Head with tiara right **Rev:** HMAS Yarra, HMAS Anzac and sailors **Edge:** Reeded

| Date | Mintage | VF20 | XF40 | MS60 | MS63 | MS65 |
|---|---|---|---|---|---|---|
| 2011 P | — | PF65 120 | | | | |

### KM# 1602 DOLLAR

13.80 g., Aluminum-Bronze, 30.6 mm. **Ruler:** Elizabeth II **Subject:** Royal Australian Navy, 100th Anniversary **Obv:** Head with tiara right **Rev:** Navy cap badge

| Date | Mintage | VF20 | XF40 | MS60 | MS63 | MS65 |
|---|---|---|---|---|---|---|
| 2011 P | — | — | — | — | — | 15.00 |

### KM# 1603 DOLLAR

13.80 g., Aluminum-Bronze, 30.6 mm. **Ruler:** Elizabeth II **Subject:** Elizabeth II's 85th Birthday **Obv:** Head with tiara right **Rev:** Elizabeth II in hat at left, birthday legend and emblem below **Edge:** Reeded

| Date | Mintage | VF20 | XF40 | MS60 | MS63 | MS65 |
|---|---|---|---|---|---|---|
| 2011 P | — | — | — | — | — | 15.00 |

### KM# 1604 DOLLAR

31.11 g., 0.999 Silver 0.999 oz. ASW, 40 mm. **Ruler:** Elizabeth II **Subject:** Wallabies Rugby team **Obv:** Head with tiara right **Rev:** Wallabies logo in color at left, rugby player at right **Edge:** Reeded

| Date | Mintage | VF20 | XF40 | MS60 | MS63 | MS65 |
|---|---|---|---|---|---|---|
| 2011 P | — | PF65 100 | | | | |

### KM# 1606 DOLLAR

31.11 g., 0.999 Silver 0.999 oz. ASW, 40 mm. **Ruler:** Elizabeth II **Subject:** World War II - Siege of Tobruk **Obv:** Head with tiara right **Rev:** Soldier standing at left, image of solder carried on stretcher at right; Campaign ribbon below **Edge:** Reeded

| Date | Mintage | VF20 | XF40 | MS60 | MS63 | MS65 |
|---|---|---|---|---|---|---|
| 2011 P | Est. 5000 | PF65 100 | | | | |

### KM# 1607 DOLLAR

31.11 g., 0.999 Silver 0.999 oz. ASW, 40 mm. **Ruler:** Elizabeth II **Subject:** Ginger Meggs, 90th Birthday **Obv:** Head with tiara right **Rev:** Cartoon boy riding kangaroo right **Edge:** Reeded

| Date | Mintage | VF20 | XF40 | MS60 | MS63 | MS65 |
|---|---|---|---|---|---|---|
| 2011 P | Est. 3000 | PF65 100 | | | | |

**KM# 1609 DOLLAR**
31.11 g., 0.999 Silver 0.999 oz. ASW, 27x47 mm. **Ruler:** Elizabeth II **Obv:** Head with tiara right **Rev:** Dearming Platypus **Shape:** Vertical rectangle

| Date | Mintage | VF20 | XF40 | MS60 | MS63 | MS65 |
|---|---|---|---|---|---|---|
| 2011 P | — | — | — | — | — | 80.00 |

**KM# 1612 DOLLAR**
13.80 g., Aluminum-Bronze, 30.6 mm. Ruler: Elizabeth II Subject: Wet Tropics of Queensland Obv: Head with tiara right Rev: Bird walking right and color fauna background Edge: Reeded

| Date | Mintage | VF20 | XF40 | MS60 | MS63 | MS65 |
|---|---|---|---|---|---|---|
| 2011 P | — | — | — | — | — | 15.00 |

**KM# 1613 DOLLAR**
13.80 g., Aluminum-Bronze, 30.6 mm. **Ruler:** Elizabeth II **Subject:** Macquarie Island **Obv:** Bust with tiara right **Rev:** Sea lion and color background **Edge:** Reeded

| Date | Mintage | VF20 | XF40 | MS60 | MS63 | MS65 |
|---|---|---|---|---|---|---|
| 2011 P | — | — | — | — | — | 15.00 |

**KM# 1614 DOLLAR**
13.80 g., Aluminum-Bronze, 30.6 mm. **Ruler:** Elizabeth II **Subject:** Goondwana Rainforests **Obv:** Head with tiara right **Rev:** Bird left with color fauna background **Edge:** Reeded

| Date | Mintage | VF20 | XF40 | MS60 | MS63 | MS65 |
|---|---|---|---|---|---|---|
| 2011 P | — | — | — | — | — | 15.00 |

**KM# 1615 DOLLAR**
13.80 g., Aluminum-Bronze, 30.6 mm. **Ruler:** Elizabeth II **Subject:** Australian Fossil Mammal Sites **Obv:** Head with tiara right **Rev:** Dingo left with color landscape in background **Edge:** Reeded

| Date | Mintage | VF20 | XF40 | MS60 | MS63 | MS65 |
|---|---|---|---|---|---|---|
| 2011 P | — | — | — | — | — | 15.00 |

**KM# 1616 DOLLAR**
13.80 g., Aluminum-Bronze, 30.6 mm. **Ruler:** Elizabeth II **Subject:** Purnululu National Park **Obv:** Head with tiara right **Rev:** Kangaroo right with color background **Edge:** Reeded

| Date | Mintage | VF20 | XF40 | MS60 | MS63 | MS65 |
|---|---|---|---|---|---|---|
| 2011 P | — | — | — | — | — | 15.00 |

**KM# 1617 DOLLAR**
9.00 g., Aluminum-Bronze, 25 mm. **Ruler:** Elizabeth II **Obv:** Head with tiara right **Rev:** Crimson Rosella in color

| Date | Mintage | VF20 | XF40 | MS60 | MS63 | MS65 |
|---|---|---|---|---|---|---|
| 2011 | — | — | — | — | — | 15.00 |

**KM# 1618 DOLLAR**
9.00 g., Aluminum-Bronze, 25 mm. **Ruler:** Elizabeth II **Obv:** Head with tiara right **Rev:** Kookaburra in color

| Date | Mintage | VF20 | XF40 | MS60 | MS63 | MS65 |
|---|---|---|---|---|---|---|
| 2011 | — | — | — | — | — | 15.00 |

**KM# 1619 DOLLAR**
9.00 g., Aluminum-Bronze, 25 mm. **Ruler:** Elizabeth II **Subject:** CHOGM meeting, Perth **Obv:** Head with tiara right **Rev:** Flags around globe

| Date | Mintage | VF20 | XF40 | MS60 | MS63 | MS65 |
|---|---|---|---|---|---|---|
| 2011 | — | — | — | — | — | 10.00 |

**KM# 1620 DOLLAR**
9.00 g., Aluminum-Bronze, 25 mm. **Ruler:** Elizabeth II **Subject:** President's Cup **Obv:** Head with tiara right **Rev:** Golfer talking swing

| Date | Mintage | VF20 | XF40 | MS60 | MS63 | MS65 |
|---|---|---|---|---|---|---|
| 2011 | — | — | — | — | — | 10.00 |

**KM# 1620a DOLLAR**
11.90 g., 0.999 Silver 0.3822 oz. ASW, 25 mm. **Ruler:** Elizabeth II **Subject:** President's Cup **Obv:** Head with tiara right **Rev:** Golfer taking swing

| Date | Mintage | VF20 | XF40 | MS60 | MS63 | MS65 |
|---|---|---|---|---|---|---|
| 2011 | — | PF65 40.00 | | | | |

**KM# 1621 DOLLAR**
31.11 g., 0.999 Silver 0.999 oz. ASW, 40 mm. **Ruler:** Elizabeth II **Subject:** President's Cup **Obv:** Head with tiara right **Rev:** Golf Ball and color trophy and logo, players around edge

| Date | Mintage | VF20 | XF40 | MS60 | MS63 | MS65 |
|---|---|---|---|---|---|---|
| 2011 | — | PF65 100 | | | | |

**KM# 1635 DOLLAR**
9.00 g., Aluminum-Bronze, 25 mm. **Ruler:** Elizabeth II **Subject:** Census, 100th Anniversary **Obv:** Head with tiara right **Rev:** Multiple stylized heads at left, geometric Australia outline at right

| Date | Mintage | VF20 | XF40 | MS60 | MS63 | MS65 |
|---|---|---|---|---|---|---|
| 2011 | — | — | — | 5.00 | 7.00 | 8.00 |

**KM# 1643 DOLLAR**
9.00 g., Aluminum-Bronze, 25 mm. **Ruler:** Elizabeth II **Obv:** Head with tiara right **Rev:** Mitchell Cockatoo in color

| Date | Mintage | VF20 | XF40 | MS60 | MS63 | MS65 |
|---|---|---|---|---|---|---|
| 2011 | — | — | — | — | — | 10.00 |

**KM# 1644 DOLLAR**
9.00 g., Aluminum-Bronze, 25 mm. **Ruler:** Elizabeth II **Obv:** Head with tiara right **Rev:** Kingfisher in color

| Date | Mintage | VF20 | XF40 | MS60 | MS63 | MS65 |
|---|---|---|---|---|---|---|
| 2011 | — | — | — | — | — | 10.00 |

**KM# 1645 DOLLAR**
9.00 g., Aluminum-Bronze, 25 mm. **Ruler:** Elizabeth II **Subject:** Dame Joan Sutherland **Obv:** Head with tiara right **Rev:** Sutherland in opera role facing right

| Date | Mintage | VF20 | XF40 | MS60 | MS63 | MS65 |
|---|---|---|---|---|---|---|
| 2011 | — | — | — | 3.00 | 5.00 | 7.00 |

**KM# 1646 DOLLAR**
9.00 g., Aluminum-Bronze, 25 mm. **Ruler:** Elizabeth II **Obv:** Head with tiara right **Rev:** Birdwing Butterfly in color

| Date | Mintage | VF20 | XF40 | MS60 | MS63 | MS65 |
|---|---|---|---|---|---|---|
| 2011 | — | — | — | — | — | 10.00 |

**KM# 1647 DOLLAR**
9.00 g., Aluminum-Bronze, 25 mm. **Ruler:** Elizabeth II **Obv:** Head with tiara right **Rev:** Flying Fox Bat in color

| Date | Mintage | VF20 | XF40 | MS60 | MS63 | MS65 |
|---|---|---|---|---|---|---|
| 2011 | — | — | — | — | — | 10.00 |

**KM# 1661 DOLLAR**
9.00 g., Aluminum-Bronze, 25 mm. **Ruler:** Elizabeth II **Subject:** Year of the Rabbit **Obv:** Head with tiara right **Rev:** Rabbit in circle, floral around

| Date | Mintage | VF20 | XF40 | MS60 | MS63 | MS65 |
|---|---|---|---|---|---|---|
| 2011 | — | — | — | — | — | 10.00 |

**KM# 1661a DOLLAR**
11.66 g., 0.999 Silver 0.3745 oz. ASW, 25 mm. **Ruler:** Elizabeth II **Subject:** Year of the rabbit **Obv:** Head with tiara right **Rev:** Rabbit in circle, floral around

| Date | Mintage | VF20 | XF40 | MS60 | MS63 | MS65 |
|---|---|---|---|---|---|---|
| 2011 | — | **PF65** 30.00 | | | | |

**KM# 1626 DOLLAR**
9.00 g., Aluminum-Bronze, 25 mm. **Ruler:** Elizabeth II **Subject:** Australian Wheat **Obv:** Head with tiara right **Rev:** Stylized wheat field and combine harvester

| Date | Mintage | VF20 | XF40 | MS60 | MS63 | MS65 |
|---|---|---|---|---|---|---|
| 2012 | — | **PF65** 40.00 | | | | |
| 2012 | — | — | — | 4.00 | 6.00 | 10.00 |

**KM# 1680 DOLLAR**
9.00 g., Aluminum-Bronze, 25 mm. **Ruler:** Elizabeth II **Subject:** Year of the Dragon **Rev:** Dragon head within circle, floral around

| Date | Mintage | VF20 | XF40 | MS60 | MS63 | MS65 |
|---|---|---|---|---|---|---|
| 2012 | — | — | — | — | — | 10.00 |

**KM# 1680a DOLLAR**
11.90 g., 0.999 Silver 0.3822 oz. ASW, 25 mm. **Ruler:** Elizabeth II **Subject:** Year of the Dragon **Rev:** Dragon head within circle, floral around

| Date | Mintage | VF20 | XF40 | MS60 | MS63 | MS65 |
|---|---|---|---|---|---|---|
| 2012 | — | **PF65** 40.00 | | | | |

**KM# 1680b DOLLAR**
0.999 Gold, 25 mm. **Ruler:** Elizabeth II **Subject:** Year of the Dragon **Rev:** Dragon at center

| Date | Mintage | VF20 | XF40 | MS60 | MS63 | MS65 |
|---|---|---|---|---|---|---|
| 2012 Proof | — | — | — | — | — | — |

**KM# 1699 DOLLAR**
31.14 g., 0.999 Silver 1.000 oz. ASW, 40.6 mm. **Ruler:** Elizabeth II **Subject:** Battle of Kapyong, Korean War **Obv:** Head with tiara right **Rev:** Soldier walking at left, image of soldiers seated at right **Edge:** Reeded

| Date | Mintage | VF20 | XF40 | MS60 | MS63 | MS65 |
|---|---|---|---|---|---|---|
| 2012 P | Est. 5000 | **PF65** 100 | | | | |

**KM# 1700 DOLLAR**
31.11 g., 0.999 Silver 0.999 oz. ASW, 40.6 mm. **Ruler:** Elizabeth II **Subject:** Battle of Kokoda, World War II **Obv:** Head with tiara right **Rev:** Soldier standing at left, image of soldiers walking over bridge at right **Edge:** Reeded

| Date | Mintage | VF20 | XF40 | MS60 | MS63 | MS65 |
|---|---|---|---|---|---|---|
| 2012 P | Est. 5000 | **PF65** 100 | | | | |

**KM# 1701 DOLLAR**
31.14 g., 0.999 Silver 1.000 oz. ASW, 40.5 mm. **Ruler:** Elizabeth II **Subject:** Elizabeth II, 60th Anniversary **Obv:** Head with tiara right **Rev:** Dargie's "wattle painting" of Elizabeth II at left, emblem and signature at right **Edge:** Reeded

| Date | Mintage | VF20 | XF40 | MS60 | MS63 | MS65 |
|---|---|---|---|---|---|---|
| 2012 P | 7,500 | **PF65** 100 | | | | |

**KM# 1704 DOLLAR**
13.80 g., Aluminum-Bronze, 30.6 mm. **Ruler:** Elizabeth II **Subject:** Year of the Dragon

| Date | Mintage | VF20 | XF40 | MS60 | MS63 | MS65 |
|---|---|---|---|---|---|---|
| 2012 P | — | — | — | — | — | 15.00 |

**KM# 1705 DOLLAR**
31.14 g., 0.999 Silver 1.000 oz. ASW, 36.6 mm. **Ruler:** Elizabeth II **Obv:** Head with tiara right **Rev:** Koala in a gum tree detailed in an opal at center

| Date | Mintage | VF20 | XF40 | MS60 | MS63 | MS65 |
|---|---|---|---|---|---|---|
| 2012 P | 8,000 | **PF65** 100 | | | | |

**KM# 1706 DOLLAR**
31.14 g., Silver, 40.6 mm. **Ruler:** Elizabeth II **Obv:** Head with tiara right **Rev:** Green gold bellfrog, background in color **Edge:** Reeded

| Date | Mintage | VF20 | XF40 | MS60 | MS63 | MS65 |
|---|---|---|---|---|---|---|
| 2012 P | 7,500 | **PF65** 100 | | | | |

**KM# 1707 DOLLAR**
31.14 g., 0.999 Silver 1.000 oz. ASW, 40.6 mm. **Ruler:** Elizabeth II **Obv:** Head with tiara right **Rev:** Red kangaroo and color background

| Date | Mintage | VF20 | XF40 | MS60 | MS63 | MS65 |
|---|---|---|---|---|---|---|
| 2012 P | 7,500 | **PF65** 100 | | | | |

**KM# 1708 DOLLAR**

31.14 g., 0.999 Silver 1.000 oz. ASW, 40.6 mm. **Ruler:** Elizabeth II **Obv:** Head with tiara right **Rev:** Kookaburra with color background

| Date | Mintage | VF20 | XF40 | MS60 | MS63 | MS65 |
|---|---|---|---|---|---|---|
| 2012 P | 7,500 | PF65 100 | | | | |

**KM# 1709 DOLLAR**

31.14 g., 0.999 Silver 1.000 oz. ASW, 40.6 mm. **Ruler:** Elizabeth II **Obv:** Head with tiara right **Rev:** Goanna on color background

| Date | Mintage | VF20 | XF40 | MS60 | MS63 | MS65 |
|---|---|---|---|---|---|---|
| 2012 P | 7,500 | PF65 100 | | | | |

**KM# 1710 DOLLAR**

31.14 g., 0.999 Silver 1.000 oz. ASW, 40.6 mm. **Ruler:** Elizabeth II **Obv:** Head with tiara right **Rev:** Whale shark on color background

| Date | Mintage | VF20 | XF40 | MS60 | MS63 | MS65 |
|---|---|---|---|---|---|---|
| 2012 P | — | PF65 100 | | | | |

**KM# 1711 DOLLAR**

9.00 g., Aluminum-Bronze, 25 mm. **Ruler:** Elizabeth II **Subject:** Ethel C. Pedley **Rev:** Bust facing at left, ncharacters Dot and the Kangaroo at right

| Date | Mintage | VF20 | XF40 | MS60 | MS63 | MS65 |
|---|---|---|---|---|---|---|
| 2012 | — | — | — | — | — | 12.50 |

**KM# 1714 DOLLAR**

13.80 g., Aluminum-Bronze, 30.6 mm. **Ruler:** Elizabeth II **Subject:** ANZAC Day - Nurses **Obv:** Head with tiara right **Rev:** Nurse tending to soldier

| Date | Mintage | VF20 | XF40 | MS60 | MS63 | MS65 |
|---|---|---|---|---|---|---|
| 2012 P | — | — | — | — | — | 13.50 |

**KM# 1732 DOLLAR**

9.00 g., Aluminum-Bronze, 25 mm. **Ruler:** Elizabeth II **Obv:** Head with tiara right **Rev:** Three wheat ears

| Date | Mintage | VF20 | XF40 | MS60 | MS63 | MS65 |
|---|---|---|---|---|---|---|
| 2012 B | — | — | — | — | — | 5.00 |
| 2012 C | — | — | — | 2.00 | 3.00 | 5.00 |
| 2012 C bluebell | — | — | — | — | — | 20.00 |
| 2012 M | — | — | — | — | — | 5.00 |
| 2012 S | — | — | — | — | — | 5.00 |

**KM# 1732a DOLLAR**

11.60 g., 0.999 Silver 0.3726 oz. ASW, 25 mm. **Ruler:** Elizabeth II **Obv:** Head with tiara right **Rev:** Three wheat ears

| Date | Mintage | VF20 | XF40 | MS60 | MS63 | MS65 |
|---|---|---|---|---|---|---|
| 2012 | — | PF65 40.00 | | | | |

**KM# 1734 DOLLAR**

9.00 g., Aluminum-Bronze, 25 mm. **Ruler:** Elizabeth II **Subject:** Australian Open **Obv:** Head with tiara right **Rev:** Men's Trophy

| Date | Mintage | VF20 | XF40 | MS60 | MS63 | MS65 |
|---|---|---|---|---|---|---|
| 2012 | — | — | — | — | — | 15.00 |

**KM# 1735 DOLLAR**

9.00 g., Aluminum-Bronze, 25 mm. **Ruler:** Elizabeth II **Subject:** Australian Open **Obv:** Head with tiara right **Rev:** Women's Trophy

| Date | Mintage | VF20 | XF40 | MS60 | MS63 | MS65 |
|---|---|---|---|---|---|---|
| 2012 | — | — | — | — | — | 15.00 |

**KM# 1736 DOLLAR**

9.00 g., Aluminum-Bronze, 25 mm. **Ruler:** Elizabeth II **Subject:** International Year of Cooperatives **Obv:** Head with tiara right **Rev:** Stick figures moving blocks into position

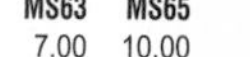

| Date | Mintage | VF20 | XF40 | MS60 | MS63 | MS65 |
|---|---|---|---|---|---|---|
| 2012 | — | — | — | 5.00 | 7.00 | 10.00 |

**KM# 1738 DOLLAR**

9.00 g., Aluminum-Bronze, 25 mm. **Ruler:** Elizabeth II **Subject:** Year of the Farmer **Obv:** Head with tiara right **Rev:** Stylized farm layout with produce and animals

| Date | Mintage | VF20 | XF40 | MS60 | MS63 | MS65 |
|---|---|---|---|---|---|---|
| 2012 | — | — | — | 5.00 | 7.00 | 10.00 |

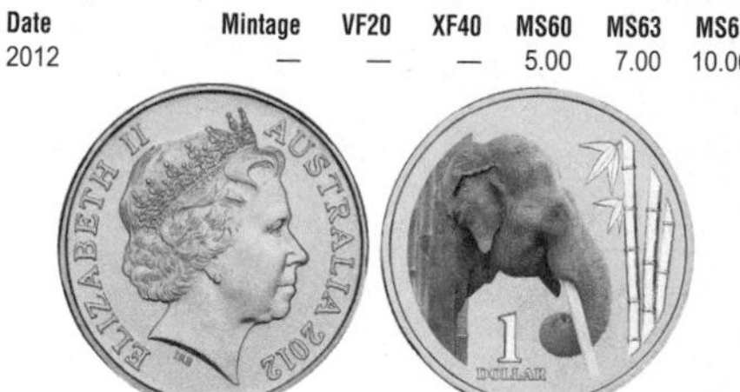


**KM# 1745 DOLLAR**

9.00 g., Aluminum-Bronze, 25 mm. **Ruler:** Elizabeth II **Obv:** Head with tiara right **Rev:** Asian Elephant at left in color

| Date | Mintage | VF20 | XF40 | MS60 | MS63 | MS65 |
|---|---|---|---|---|---|---|
| 2012 | — | — | — | — | — | 15.00 |

**KM# 1746 DOLLAR**

9.00 g., Aluminum-Bronze, 25 mm. **Ruler:** Elizabeth II **Obv:** Head with tiara right **Rev:** Western Lowland Gorilla at right in color

| Date | Mintage | VF20 | XF40 | MS60 | MS63 | MS65 |
|---|---|---|---|---|---|---|
| 2012 | — | — | — | — | — | 15.00 |

**KM# 1748 DOLLAR**

31.14 g., 0.999 Silver 1.000 oz. ASW, 40.6 mm. **Ruler:** Elizabeth II **Subject:** Australian Olympic Team, 2012 London Games **Obv:** Head with tiara right **Rev:** Runner with Big Ben and Sydney Harbor Bridge in color

| Date | Mintage | VF20 | XF40 | MS60 | MS63 | MS65 |
|---|---|---|---|---|---|---|
| 2012 P | 7,500 | PF65 100 | | | | |

**KM# 1787 DOLLAR**

31.14 g., 0.999 Silver 1.000 oz. ASW, 40.6 mm. **Ruler:** Elizabeth II **Subject:** Elizabeth II's Diamond Jubilee **Obv:** Head with tiara right **Rev:** Elizabeth half-length adjusting shall, gilt royal shield below **Edge:** Reeded

| Date | Mintage | VF20 | XF40 | MS60 | MS63 | MS65 |
|---|---|---|---|---|---|---|
| 2012 P | 1,000 | PF65 100 | | | | |

**KM# 1788 DOLLAR**

31.14 g., 0.999 Silver 1.000 oz. ASW, 40.6 mm. **Ruler:** Elizabeth II **Subject:** Elizabeth II's Diamond Jubilee **Obv:** Head with tiara right **Rev:** Elizabeth half-length facing at left, royal trumphants at right **Edge:** Reeded

| Date | Mintage | VF20 | XF40 | MS60 | MS63 | MS65 |
|---|---|---|---|---|---|---|
| 2012 P | 1,000 | PF65 100 | | | | |

**KM# 1791 DOLLAR**

31.11 g., 0.999 Silver 0.999 oz. ASW, 40.6 mm. **Ruler:** Elizabeth II **Rev:** Kookaburra in color **Shape:** Irregular, Map of Australia

| Date | Mintage | VF20 | XF40 | MS60 | MS63 | MS65 |
|---|---|---|---|---|---|---|
| 2012 P | 6,000 | PF65 150 | | | | |

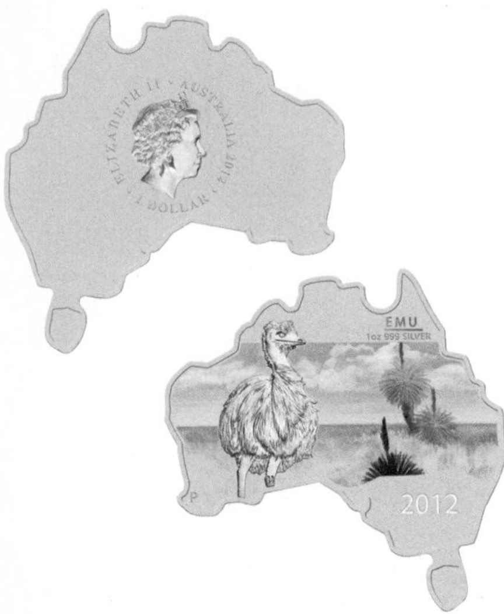


**KM# 1792 DOLLAR**

31.11 g., 0.999 Silver 0.999 oz. ASW, 40.6 mm. **Ruler:** Elizabeth II **Rev:** Emu in color **Shape:** Irregular, Map of Australia

| Date | Mintage | VF20 | XF40 | MS60 | MS63 | MS65 |
|---|---|---|---|---|---|---|
| 2012 P | 6,000 | PF65 120 | | | | |

**KM# 1796 DOLLAR**

31.11 g., 0.999 Silver 0.999 oz. ASW **Ruler:** Elizabeth II **Rev:** Wombat with opal

| Date | Mintage | VF20 | XF40 | MS60 | MS63 | MS65 |
|---|---|---|---|---|---|---|
| 2012 P | Est. 8000 | PF65 100 | | | | |

**KM# 1800 DOLLAR**

31.11 g., 0.999 Silver 0.999 oz. ASW, 40.6 mm. **Ruler:** Elizabeth II **Subject:** Australia-China Friendship, 40th Anniversary **Rev:** kangaroo and Panda under national flags in color

| Date | Mintage | VF20 | XF40 | MS60 | MS63 | MS65 |
|---|---|---|---|---|---|---|
| 2012 P | — | PF65 125 | | | | |

**KM# 1804 DOLLAR**

13.50 g., Aluminum-Bronze, 30 mm. **Ruler:** Elizabeth II **Subject:** London Olympics, 2012 **Rev:** Faster - Runner

| Date | Mintage | VF20 | XF40 | MS60 | MS63 | MS65 |
|---|---|---|---|---|---|---|
| 2012 P | — | — | — | — | — | 14.00 |

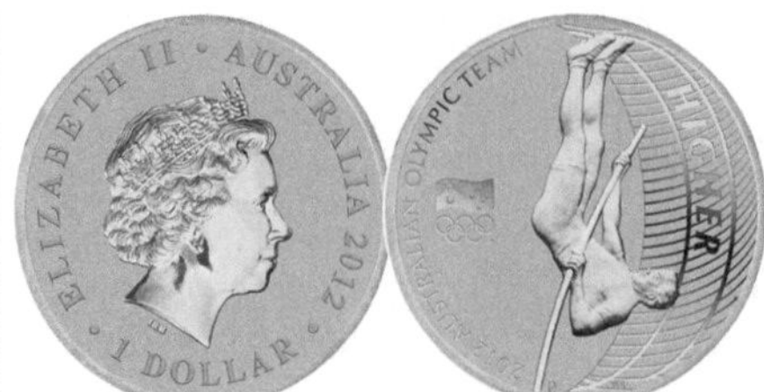


**KM# 1805 DOLLAR**

13.50 g., Aluminum-Bronze, 30 mm. **Ruler:** Elizabeth II **Subject:** London Olympics, 2012 **Rev:** Higher - Pole Vaulter

| Date | Mintage | VF20 | XF40 | MS60 | MS63 | MS65 |
|---|---|---|---|---|---|---|
| 2012 P | — | — | — | — | — | 14.00 |

**KM# 1806 DOLLAR**

13.50 g., Aluminum-Bronze, 30 mm. **Ruler:** Elizabeth II **Subject:** London Olympics, 2012 **Rev:** Stronger - Weight Lifter

| Date | Mintage | VF20 | XF40 | MS60 | MS63 | MS65 |
|---|---|---|---|---|---|---|
| 2012 P | — | — | — | — | — | 14.00 |

**KM# 1807 DOLLAR**

13.50 g., Aluminum-Bronze, 30 mm. **Ruler:** Elizabeth II **Subject:** London Olympics, 2012 **Rev:** Victory - Swimmer, hands raised

| Date | Mintage | VF20 | XF40 | MS60 | MS63 | MS65 |
|---|---|---|---|---|---|---|
| 2012 P | — | — | — | — | — | 14.00 |

**KM# 1808 DOLLAR**

13.80 g., Aluminum-Bronze, 30.6 mm. **Ruler:** Elizabeth II **Subject:** Australian 2012 London Olympic Team **Obv:** Head with tiara right **Rev:** Kangaroo with boxing gloves raised

| Date | Mintage | VF20 | XF40 | MS60 | MS63 | MS65 |
|---|---|---|---|---|---|---|
| 2012 P | 750 | — | — | — | — | 15.00 |

**KM# 1809 DOLLAR**

13.30 g., Aluminum-Bronze, 30.6 mm. **Ruler:** Elizabeth II **Subject:** Animal Athletics - Cheetah

| Date | Mintage | VF20 | XF40 | MS60 | MS63 | MS65 |
|---|---|---|---|---|---|---|
| 2012 P | — | — | — | — | — | 14.00 |

**KM# 1810 DOLLAR**

13.30 g., Aluminum-Bronze, 30.6 mm. **Ruler:** Elizabeth II **Subject:** Animal Athletics - Monarch Butterfly

| Date | Mintage | VF20 | XF40 | MS60 | MS63 | MS65 |
|---|---|---|---|---|---|---|
| 2012 P | — | — | — | — | — | 14.00 |

**KM# 1811 DOLLAR**
13.80 g., Aluminum-Bronze, 30.6 mm. **Ruler:** Elizabeth II **Obv:** Head with tiara right **Rev:** Two boxing kangaroos on color backgorund

| Date | Mintage | VF20 | XF40 | MS60 | MS63 | MS65 |
|---|---|---|---|---|---|---|
| 2012 P | 7,500 | — | — | — | — | 15.00 |

**KM# 1812 DOLLAR**
13.30 g., Aluminum-Bronze, 30.6 mm. **Ruler:** Elizabeth II **Subject:** Animal Athletics - Sailfish

| Date | Mintage | VF20 | XF40 | MS60 | MS63 | MS65 |
|---|---|---|---|---|---|---|
| 2012 P | — | — | — | — | — | 14.00 |

**KM# 1813 DOLLAR**
13.30 g., Aluminum-Bronze, 30.6 mm. **Ruler:** Elizabeth II **Subject:** Animal Athletics - Rhino Beetle

| Date | Mintage | VF20 | XF40 | MS60 | MS63 | MS65 |
|---|---|---|---|---|---|---|
| 2012 P | — | — | — | — | — | 14.00 |

**KM# 1814 DOLLAR**
13.30 g., Aluminum-Bronze, 30.6 mm. **Ruler:** Elizabeth II **Subject:** Animal Athletics - Rocket Frog

| Date | Mintage | VF20 | XF40 | MS60 | MS63 | MS65 |
|---|---|---|---|---|---|---|
| 2012 P | — | — | — | — | — | 14.00 |

**KM# 1819 DOLLAR**
31.11 g., 0.999 Silver 0.999 oz. ASW, 40.6 mm. **Ruler:** Elizabeth II **Subject:** Famous Battles - Long Tan

| Date | Mintage | VF20 | XF40 | MS60 | MS63 | MS65 |
|---|---|---|---|---|---|---|
| 2012 P | — | **PF65** 100 | | | | |

**KM# 1820 DOLLAR**
13.80 g., Aluminum-Bronze, 30.6 mm. **Ruler:** Elizabeth II **Subject:** Lord Howe Island Group **Rev:** Pair of sparrows in flight, color background

| Date | Mintage | VF20 | XF40 | MS60 | MS63 | MS65 |
|---|---|---|---|---|---|---|
| 2012 P | — | — | — | — | — | 15.00 |

**KM# 1821 DOLLAR**
13.80 g., Aluminum-Bronze, 30.6 mm. **Ruler:** Elizabeth II **Subject:** Uluru Kata Tyuta National Park **Rev:** Lizard, color background

| Date | Mintage | VF20 | XF40 | MS60 | MS63 | MS65 |
|---|---|---|---|---|---|---|
| 2012 P | — | — | — | — | — | 15.00 |

**KM# 1822 DOLLAR**
13.80 g., Aluminum-Bronze, 30.6 mm. **Ruler:** Elizabeth II **Subject:** Fraser Island **Rev:** Dingo, color background

| Date | Mintage | VF20 | XF40 | MS60 | MS63 | MS65 |
|---|---|---|---|---|---|---|
| 2012 P | — | — | — | — | — | 15.00 |

**KM# 1823 DOLLAR**
13.80 g., Aluminum-Bronze, 30.6 mm. **Ruler:** Elizabeth II **Subject:** Kakadu National Park **Rev:** Two storks, color background

| Date | Mintage | VF20 | XF40 | MS60 | MS63 | MS65 |
|---|---|---|---|---|---|---|
| 2012 P | — | — | — | — | — | 15.00 |

**KM# 1824 DOLLAR**
13.80 g., Aluminum-Bronze, 30.6 mm. **Ruler:** Elizabeth II **Subject:** Willandra Lakes Region **Rev:** Eagle, color background

| Date | Mintage | VF20 | XF40 | MS60 | MS63 | MS65 |
|---|---|---|---|---|---|---|
| 2012 P | — | — | — | — | — | 15.00 |

**KM# 1826 DOLLAR**
31.11 g., 0.999 Silver 0.999 oz. ASW, 40.6 mm. **Ruler:** Elizabeth II **Subject:** Antartic Territories **Rev:** Penguins

| Date | Mintage | VF20 | XF40 | MS60 | MS63 | MS65 |
|---|---|---|---|---|---|---|
| 2012 P | — | **PF65** 100 | | | | |

**KM# 1858 DOLLAR**
9.00 g., Aluminum-Bronze, 25 mm. **Ruler:** Elizabeth II **Subject:** Southern Corrobreee Frog

| Date | Mintage | VF20 | XF40 | MS60 | MS63 | MS65 |
|---|---|---|---|---|---|---|
| 2012 | — | — | — | — | — | 10.00 |

**KM# 1859 DOLLAR**
9.00 g., Aluminum-Bronze, 25 mm. **Ruler:** Elizabeth II **Subject:** Sumatran Tiger

| Date | Mintage | VF20 | XF40 | MS60 | MS63 | MS65 |
|---|---|---|---|---|---|---|
| 2012 | — | — | — | — | — | 10.00 |

**KM# 1860 DOLLAR**
9.00 g., Aluminum-Bronze, 25 mm. **Ruler:** Elizabeth II **Rev:** Monkey in tree

| Date | Mintage | VF20 | XF40 | MS60 | MS63 | MS65 |
|---|---|---|---|---|---|---|
| 2012 | — | — | — | — | — | 10.00 |

**KM# 1861 DOLLAR**
9.00 g., Aluminum-Bronze, 25 mm. **Ruler:** Elizabeth II **Subject:** Sir Douglas Mawson, explorer

| Date | Mintage | VF20 | XF40 | MS60 | MS63 | MS65 |
|---|---|---|---|---|---|---|
| 2012 | — | — | — | 3.00 | 4.00 | 5.00 |

**KM# 1865 DOLLAR**
31.11 g., 0.999 Silver 0.999 oz. ASW, 40 mm. **Ruler:** Elizabeth II **Subject:** Saltwater Crocodile - Bindi

| Date | Mintage | VF20 | XF40 | MS60 | MS63 | MS65 |
|---|---|---|---|---|---|---|
| 2012 | — | PF65 75.00 | | | | |

**KM# 1866 DOLLAR**
31.10 g., 0.999 Silver 0.999 oz. ASW, 40.6 mm. **Ruler:** Elizabeth II **Obv:** Crystal insert above head with tiara right **Rev:** Large snowflakes, crystal insert at top

| Date | Mintage | VF20 | XF40 | MS60 | MS63 | MS65 |
|---|---|---|---|---|---|---|
| 2012 P | Est. 5000 | PF65 125 | | | | |

**KM# 2008 DOLLAR**
13.80 g., Aluminum-Bronze, 30.6 mm. **Ruler:** Elizabeth II **Subject:** Christmas **Rev:** Two bells and evergreen in color

| Date | Mintage | VF20 | XF40 | MS60 | MS63 | MS65 |
|---|---|---|---|---|---|---|
| 2012 | — | — | — | — | — | 15.00 |

**KM# 2009 DOLLAR**
Aluminum-Bronze, 30.8 mm. **Ruler:** Elizabeth II **Series:** First Banknote 100th Anniversary **Rev:** 10 Shilling design

| Date | Mintage | VF20 | XF40 | MS60 | MS63 | MS65 |
|---|---|---|---|---|---|---|
| 2012 P | — | — | — | — | — | 15.00 |

**KM# 2022 DOLLAR**
9.00 g., Aluminum-Bronze, 25 mm. **Ruler:** Elizabeth II **Subject:** AFL Premiers **Rev:** Cup

| Date | Mintage | VF20 | XF40 | MS60 | MS63 | MS65 |
|---|---|---|---|---|---|---|
| 2012 | — | — | — | — | — | 20.00 |

**KM# 1824a DOLLAR**
31.11 g., 0.999 Silver 0.999 oz. ASW, 40.6 mm. **Ruler:** Elizabeth II **Subject:** ANDA Show **Obv:** Head with tiara right **Rev:** Wilandra Lakes, Eagle, colored background

| Date | Mintage | VF20 | XF40 | MS60 | MS63 | MS65 |
|---|---|---|---|---|---|---|
| 2013 P | — | PF65 75.00 | | | | |

**KM# 1909 DOLLAR**
31.10 g., 0.999 Silver 0.9989 oz. ASW, 33.2 x 33.2 mm. **Ruler:** Elizabeth II **Subject:** Australian Seasons - Summer

| Date | Mintage | VF20 | XF40 | MS60 | MS63 | MS65 |
|---|---|---|---|---|---|---|
| 2013 | Est. 5000 | PF65 75.00 | | | | |

**KM# 1910 DOLLAR**
31.14 g., 0.999 Silver 1.000 oz. ASW, 33.2 x 33.2 mm. **Ruler:** Elizabeth II **Subject:** Australian Seasons - Autumn

| Date | Mintage | VF20 | XF40 | MS60 | MS63 | MS65 |
|---|---|---|---|---|---|---|
| 2013 | Est. 5000 | PF65 75.00 | | | | |

**KM# 1911 DOLLAR**
31.14 g., 0.999 Silver 1.000 oz. ASW, 33.2 x 33.2 mm. **Ruler:** Elizabeth II **Subject:** Australian Seasons - Winter **Rev:** Green Tree Frog, color background **Edge:** Reeded

| Date | Mintage | VF20 | XF40 | MS60 | MS63 | MS65 |
|---|---|---|---|---|---|---|
| 2013 P | Est. 5000 | PF65 60.00 | | | | |

**KM# 1912 DOLLAR**
31.14 g., 0.999 Silver 1.000 oz. ASW, 33.2 x 33.2 mm. **Ruler:** Elizabeth II **Subject:** Australian Seasons - Spring **Obv:** Head with tiara right **Rev:** Two White Cockatoos, color background **Edge:** Reeded

| Date | Mintage | VF20 | XF40 | MS60 | MS63 | MS65 |
|---|---|---|---|---|---|---|
| 2013 P | Est. 5000 | PF65 75.00 | | | | |

**KM# 1913 DOLLAR**
15.50 g., 0.999 Silver 0.4978 oz. ASW, 36.6 mm. **Ruler:** Elizabeth II **Subject:** Australian Bush Babies II - Echidna

| Date | Mintage | VF20 | XF40 | MS60 | MS63 | MS65 |
|---|---|---|---|---|---|---|
| 2013 | — | PF65 50.00 | | | | |

**KM# 1916 DOLLAR**
25.19 g., 0.999 Silver 0.809 oz. ASW, 40.6 mm. **Ruler:** Elizabeth II **Subject:** 200th Anniversary of the Australian Holey Dollar & Dump

| Date | Mintage | VF20 | XF40 | MS60 | MS63 | MS65 |
|---|---|---|---|---|---|---|
| 2013 | Est. 4000 | PF65 75.00 | | | | |

**KM# 1918 DOLLAR**
31.14 g., 0.999 Silver 1.000 oz. ASW, 40.6 mm. **Ruler:** Elizabeth II **Subject:** 2013 The Land Down Under - Sydney Opera House

| Date | Mintage | VF20 | XF40 | MS60 | MS63 | MS65 |
|---|---|---|---|---|---|---|
| 2013 | Est. 5000 | PF65 75.00 | | | | |

**KM# 1920 DOLLAR**
31.14 g., 0.999 Silver 1.000 oz. ASW, 40.6 mm. **Ruler:** Elizabeth II **Subject:** The Land Down Under - Didgeridoo

| Date | Mintage | VF20 | XF40 | MS60 | MS63 | MS65 |
|---|---|---|---|---|---|---|
| 2013 | Est. 5000 | PF65 75.00 | | | | |

**KM# 1927 DOLLAR**
31.14 g., 0.999 Silver 1.000 oz. ASW, 40.6 mm. **Ruler:** Elizabeth II **Subject:** HM Queen Elizabeth II - 60th Anniversary of Coronation

| Date | Mintage | VF20 | XF40 | MS60 | MS63 | MS65 |
|---|---|---|---|---|---|---|
| 2013 P | Est. 7500 | PF65 75.00 | | | | |

**KM# 1929 DOLLAR**
31.14 g., 0.999 Silver 1.000 oz. ASW, 40.6 mm. **Ruler:** Elizabeth II **Subject:** Australia Map Shaped Coin - Kangaroo **Shape:** Australia continent

| Date | Mintage | VF20 | XF40 | MS60 | MS63 | MS65 |
|---|---|---|---|---|---|---|
| 2013 P | Est. 6000 | PF65 100 | | | | |

**KM# 1930 DOLLAR**
31.14 g., 0.999 Silver 1.000 oz. ASW, 40.6 mm. **Ruler:** Elizabeth II **Subject:** Queen VIctoria 175th Anniversary of Coronation

| Date | Mintage | VF20 | XF40 | MS60 | MS63 | MS65 |
|---|---|---|---|---|---|---|
| 2013 P | Est. 5000 | PF65 75.00 | | | | |

**KM# 1932 DOLLAR**
31.14 g., 0.999 Silver 1.000 oz. ASW, 40.6 mm. **Ruler:** Elizabeth II **Subject:** Treasures of the World - Europe - Garnet **Obv:** Head with tiara right **Rev:** Mountainside challet and ferns

| Date | Mintage | VF20 | XF40 | MS60 | MS63 | MS65 |
|---|---|---|---|---|---|---|
| 2013 P | Est. 7500 | PF65 100 | | | | |

**KM# 1936 DOLLAR**
31.14 g., 0.999 Silver 1.000 oz. ASW, 40.6 mm. **Ruler:** Elizabeth II **Subject:** Discover Australia - Kangaroo **Rev. Legend:** Ing Ing Jong

| Date | Mintage | VF20 | XF40 | MS60 | MS63 | MS65 |
|---|---|---|---|---|---|---|
| 2013 P | Est. 5000 | PF65 75.00 | | | | |

**KM# 1937 DOLLAR**
31.14 g., 0.999 Silver 1.000 oz. ASW, 40.6 mm. **Ruler:** Elizabeth II **Subject:** Discover Australia - Koala **Rev. Legend:** Ing Ing Jong

| Date | Mintage | VF20 | XF40 | MS60 | MS63 | MS65 |
|---|---|---|---|---|---|---|
| 2013 P | Est. 5000 | PF65 70.00 | | | | |

**KM# 1938 DOLLAR**
31.14 g., 0.999 Silver 1.000 oz. ASW, 40.6 mm. **Ruler:** Elizabeth II **Subject:** Discover Australia - Emu

| Date | Mintage | VF20 | XF40 | MS60 | MS63 | MS65 |
|---|---|---|---|---|---|---|
| 2013 P | Est. 5000 | PF65 70.00 | | | | |

**KM# 1939 DOLLAR**
31.14 g., 0.999 Silver 1.000 oz. ASW, 40.6 mm. **Ruler:** Elizabeth II **Subject:** Discover Australia - Kookaburra

| Date | Mintage | VF20 | XF40 | MS60 | MS63 | MS65 |
|---|---|---|---|---|---|---|
| 2013 | Est. 5000 | PF65 70.00 | | | | |

**KM# 1940 DOLLAR**
31.14 g., 0.999 Silver 1.000 oz. ASW, 40.6 mm. **Ruler:** Elizabeth II **Subject:** Discover Australia - Platypus

| Date | Mintage | VF20 | XF40 | MS60 | MS63 | MS65 |
|---|---|---|---|---|---|---|
| 2013 | Est. 5000 | PF65 70.00 | | | | |

**KM# 1941 DOLLAR**
31.13 g., 0.999 Silver 0.9999 oz. ASW, 40.6 mm. **Ruler:** Elizabeth II **Subject:** The Land Down Under - Captan James Cook

| Date | Mintage | VF20 | XF40 | MS60 | MS63 | MS65 |
|---|---|---|---|---|---|---|
| 2013 P | Est. 5000 | PF65 70.00 | | | | |

**KM# 1943 DOLLAR**
13.80 g., Aluminum-Bronze, 30.2 mm. **Ruler:** Elizabeth II **Subject:** Experience It Series - Surfing **Obv:** Head in tiara right **Rev:** Surfer, color waves

| Date | Mintage | VF20 | XF40 | MS60 | MS63 | MS65 |
|---|---|---|---|---|---|---|
| 2013 | — | — | — | — | — | 15.00 |

**KM# 1944 DOLLAR**
13.00 g., Aluminum-Bronze, 30.6 mm. **Ruler:** Elizabeth II **Subject:** Elizabeth II, 60th Anniversary of Coronation **Rev:** Coronation crown

| Date | Mintage | VF20 | XF40 | MS60 | MS63 | MS65 |
|---|---|---|---|---|---|---|
| 2013 | — | — | — | — | — | 15.00 |

**KM# 1945 DOLLAR**
13.00 g., Aluminum-Bronze, 30.6 mm. **Ruler:** Elizabeth II **Subject:** Victoria, 175th Anniversary of Coronation **Rev:** Coronation crown

| Date | Mintage | VF20 | XF40 | MS60 | MS63 | MS65 |
|---|---|---|---|---|---|---|
| 2013 | — | — | — | — | — | 15.00 |

**KM# 1946 DOLLAR**
31.10 g., Silver, 40 mm. **Ruler:** Elizabeth II **Subject:** Kangaroos of the World

| Date | Mintage | VF20 | XF40 | MS60 | MS63 | MS65 |
|---|---|---|---|---|---|---|
| 2013 | Est. 10000 | PF65 75.00 | | | | |

**KM# 1947 DOLLAR**
9.00 g., Aluminum-Bronze, 25 mm. **Ruler:** Elizabeth II **Subject:** Polar Animals - Polar Bear

| Date | Mintage | VF20 | XF40 | MS60 | MS63 | MS65 |
|---|---|---|---|---|---|---|
| 2013 | — | — | — | — | — | 15.00 |

**KM# 1948 DOLLAR**
Aluminum-Bronze, 25 mm. **Ruler:** Elizabeth II **Subject:** Polar Animals - Walarus

| Date | Mintage | VF20 | XF40 | MS60 | MS63 | MS65 |
|---|---|---|---|---|---|---|
| 2013 | — | — | — | — | — | 15.00 |

**KM# 1949 DOLLAR**
9.00 g., Aluminum-Bronze, 25 mm. **Ruler:** Elizabeth II **Subject:** Polar Animals - Humpback Whale

| Date | Mintage | VF20 | XF40 | MS60 | MS63 | MS65 |
|---|---|---|---|---|---|---|
| 2013 | — | — | — | — | — | 15.00 |

**KM# 1950 DOLLAR**
9.00 g., Aluminum-Bronze, 25 mm. **Ruler:** Elizabeth II **Subject:** Polar Animals - Atlantic Puffin

| Date | Mintage | VF20 | XF40 | MS60 | MS63 | MS65 |
|---|---|---|---|---|---|---|
| 2013 | — | — | — | — | — | 15.00 |

**KM# 1951 DOLLAR**
9.00 g., Aluminum-Bronze, 25 mm. **Ruler:** Elizabeth II **Subject:** Polar Animals - Weddell Seal

| Date | Mintage | VF20 | XF40 | MS60 | MS63 | MS65 |
|---|---|---|---|---|---|---|
| 2013 | — | — | — | — | — | 15.00 |

**KM# 1952 DOLLAR**
36.31 g., 0.999 Silver 1.1662 oz. ASW, 38.74 mm. **Ruler:** Elizabeth II **Subject:** Centenary of Canberra

| Date | Mintage | VF20 | XF40 | MS60 | MS63 | MS65 |
|---|---|---|---|---|---|---|
| 2013 | Est. 5000 | PF65 75.00 | | | | |

**KM# 1953 DOLLAR**
31.10 g., 0.999 Silver 0.9989 oz. ASW, 40 mm. **Ruler:** Elizabeth II **Subject:** Kangaroo Road Sign

| Date | Mintage | VF20 | XF40 | MS60 | MS63 | MS65 |
|---|---|---|---|---|---|---|
| 2013 | Est. 40000 | PF65 40.00 | | | | |

**KM# 1968 DOLLAR**
9.00 g., Aluminum-Bronze, 25 mm. **Ruler:** Elizabeth II **Subject:** 200 Years of the Benevolent Society

| Date | Mintage | VF20 | XF40 | MS60 | MS63 | MS65 |
|---|---|---|---|---|---|---|
| 2013 | — | — | — | — | — | 15.00 |

**KM# 1976 DOLLAR**
9.00 g., Aluminum-Nickel-Bronze, 25 mm. **Ruler:** Elizabeth II **Subject:** Polar Animals - Penguin

| Date | Mintage | VF20 | XF40 | MS60 | MS63 | MS65 |
|---|---|---|---|---|---|---|
| 2013 | — | — | — | — | — | 15.00 |

**KM# 2004 DOLLAR**
13.80 g., Aluminum-Bronze, 30.6 mm. **Ruler:** Elizabeth II **Subject:** Year of the Snake

| Date | Mintage | VF20 | XF40 | MS60 | MS63 | MS65 |
|---|---|---|---|---|---|---|
| 2013 P | — | — | — | — | — | 15.00 |

**KM# 2013 DOLLAR**
31.11 g., 0.999 Silver 0.999 oz. ASW **Ruler:** Elizabeth II **Subject:** Bindi **Rev:** Crocodile

| Date | Mintage | VF20 | XF40 | MS60 | MS63 | MS65 |
|---|---|---|---|---|---|---|
| 2013 P | — | — | — | — | — | 32.00 |

**KM# 2014 DOLLAR**
9.00 g., Aluminum-Bronze, 25 mm. **Ruler:** Elizabeth II **Subject:** Slim Dusty

| Date | Mintage | VF20 | XF40 | MS60 | MS63 | MS65 |
|---|---|---|---|---|---|---|
| 2013 | — | — | — | — | — | 15.00 |

**KM# 2015 DOLLAR**
9.00 g., Aluminum-Bronze, 25 mm. **Ruler:** Elizabeth II **Subject:** Year of the Snake **Rev:** Snake at center

| Date | Mintage | VF20 | XF40 | MS60 | MS63 | MS65 |
|---|---|---|---|---|---|---|
| 2013 | — | — | — | — | — | 10.00 |

**KM# 2015a DOLLAR**
Silver, 25 mm. **Ruler:** Elizabeth II **Subject:** Year of the Snake **Rev:** Snake at center

| Date | Mintage | VF20 | XF40 | MS60 | MS63 | MS65 |
|---|---|---|---|---|---|---|
| 2013 | — | PF65 40.00 | | | | |

**KM# 2015b DOLLAR**
Gold, 25 mm. **Ruler:** Elizabeth II **Subject:** Year of the Snake **Rev:** Snake at center

| Date | Mintage | VF20 | XF40 | MS60 | MS63 | MS65 |
|---|---|---|---|---|---|---|
| 2013 Proof | — | — | — | — | — | — |

**KM# 2016 DOLLAR**
9.00 g., Aluminum-Bronze, 25 mm. **Ruler:** Elizabeth II **Subject:** Discovery of Gold **Rev:** Prospector panning in stream bed

| Date | Mintage | VF20 | XF40 | MS60 | MS63 | MS65 |
|---|---|---|---|---|---|---|
| 2013 | Est. 40000 | — | — | — | — | 15.00 |
| 2013 | Est. 25000 | PF65 30.00 | | | | |

**KM# 2017 DOLLAR**
9.00 g., Aluminum-Bronze, 25 mm. **Ruler:** Elizabeth II **Subject:** Black Caviar **Rev:** Horse and jockey right, owners colors

| Date | Mintage | VF20 | XF40 | MS60 | MS63 | MS65 |
|---|---|---|---|---|---|---|
| 2013 | — | — | — | — | — | 15.00 |

### KM# 2018 DOLLAR

31.10 g., 0.999 Silver 0.999 oz. ASW **Ruler:** Elizabeth II **Subject:** Black Caviar **Rev:** Horse and jockey advancing left **Shape:** 40

| Date | Mintage | VF20 | XF40 | MS60 | MS63 | MS65 |
|---|---|---|---|---|---|---|
| 2013 | — | PF63 75.00 | PF65 85.00 | | | |

### KM# 2021 DOLLAR

31.11 g., 0.999 Silver 0.999 oz. ASW, 40 mm. **Ruler:** Elizabeth II **Subject:** AFL Premiers - Sidney Swans **Rev:** Cup

| Date | Mintage | VF20 | XF40 | MS60 | MS63 | MS65 |
|---|---|---|---|---|---|---|
| 2013 | — | PF65 115 | | | | |

### KM# 2028 DOLLAR

9.00 g., Aluminum-Bronze, 25 mm. **Ruler:** Elizabeth II **Subject:** Holey Dollar **Rev:** NSW coin and Spanish 8 real reverse

| Date | Mintage | VF20 | XF40 | MS60 | MS63 | MS65 |
|---|---|---|---|---|---|---|
| 2013 B | — | — | — | — | — | 6.00 |
| 2013 C | — | — | — | — | — | 6.00 |
| 2013 M | — | — | — | — | — | 6.00 |
| 2013 S | — | — | — | — | — | 6.00 |

### KM# 2028a DOLLAR

9.00 g., Aluminum-Bronze, 25 mm. **Ruler:** Elizabeth II **Subject:** Holey Dollar **Rev:** NSW coin and Spansih 8 real reverse

| Date | Mintage | VF20 | XF40 | MS60 | MS63 | MS65 |
|---|---|---|---|---|---|---|
| 2013 B | — | — | — | — | — | 6.00 |

### KM# 2029 DOLLAR

31.11 g., 0.999 Silver 0.999 oz. ASW, 40.6 mm. **Ruler:** Elizabeth II **Subject:** Bindi - Saltwater Crocodile **Rev:** Crocodile head in color

| Date | Mintage | VF20 | XF40 | MS60 | MS63 | MS65 |
|---|---|---|---|---|---|---|
| 2013 | Est. 5000 | PF65 110 | | | | |

### KM# 2038 DOLLAR

0.50 g., 0.9999 Gold, 11.15 mm. **Ruler:** Elizabeth II **Subject:** Australian Miniature Money

| Date | Mintage | VF20 | XF40 | MS60 | MS63 | MS65 |
|---|---|---|---|---|---|---|
| 2013 | Est. 2000 | PF65 75.00 | | | | |

### KM# 2043 DOLLAR

31.14 g., 0.999 Silver 1.000 oz. ASW, 36.6 mm. **Ruler:** Elizabeth II **Rev:** Kangaroo in opal at center

| Date | Mintage | VF20 | XF40 | MS60 | MS63 | MS65 |
|---|---|---|---|---|---|---|
| 2013 | Est. 8000 | PF65 100 | | | | |

### KM# 2045 DOLLAR

13.80 g., Aluminum-Bronze, 30.60 mm. **Ruler:** Elizabeth II **Subject:** Anzac Day - Engineers

| Date | Mintage | VF20 | XF40 | MS60 | MS63 | MS65 |
|---|---|---|---|---|---|---|
| 2013 P | — | — | — | — | — | 15.00 |

### KM# 2046 DOLLAR

31.14 g., 0.999 Silver 1.000 oz. ASW, 40.6 mm. **Ruler:** Elizabeth II **Subject:** Antarctic Territory - Aurora Australis **Obv:** Head with tiara right **Rev:** Researcher and colored Aurora, Antarctic map shape

| Date | Mintage | VF20 | XF40 | MS60 | MS63 | MS65 |
|---|---|---|---|---|---|---|
| 2013 P | Est. 7500 | PF65 75.00 | | | | |

### KM# 2051 DOLLAR

31.14 g., 0.999 Silver 1.000 oz. ASW, 40.6 mm. **Ruler:** Elizabeth II **Subject:** Land Down Under - Surfing **Obv:** Head with tiara right **Rev:** Surfer standing holding vertical surfboard, watching waves roll in

| Date | Mintage | VF20 | XF40 | MS60 | MS63 | MS65 |
|---|---|---|---|---|---|---|
| 2013 P | Est. 5000 | PF63 75.00 | PF65 80.00 | | | |

### KM# 2058 DOLLAR

13.80 g., Aluminum-Bronze, 30.2 mm. **Ruler:** Elizabeth II **Obv:** Head with tiara right **Rev:** Downhill skier left

| Date | Mintage | VF20 | XF40 | MS60 | MS63 | MS65 |
|---|---|---|---|---|---|---|
| 2013 P | — | — | — | — | — | 15.00 |

### KM# 2059 DOLLAR

13.20 g., Aluminum-Bronze, 30.6 mm. **Ruler:** Elizabeth II **Obv:** Head with tiara right **Rev:** Baby Wombat

| Date | Mintage | VF20 | XF40 | MS60 | MS63 | MS65 |
|---|---|---|---|---|---|---|
| 2013 P | — | — | — | — | — | 15.00 |

### KM# 2060 DOLLAR

31.14 g., 0.999 Silver 1.000 oz. ASW, 40.6 mm. **Ruler:** Elizabeth II **Subject:** H.R.H. Prince George, Birth **Obv:** Head with tiara right **Rev:** Prince William and Catherine holding infant

| Date | Mintage | VF20 | XF40 | MS60 | MS63 | MS65 |
|---|---|---|---|---|---|---|
| 2013 P | Est. 10000 | PF63 75.00 | PF65 85.00 | | | |

### KM# 2062 DOLLAR

31.14 g., 0.999 Silver 1.000 oz. ASW, 36.6 mm. **Ruler:** Elizabeth II **Rev:** Pygmy Possum in center opal insert

| Date | Mintage | VF20 | XF40 | MS60 | MS63 | MS65 |
|---|---|---|---|---|---|---|
| 2013 P | Est. 8000 | PF65 100 | | | | |

**KM# 2063 DOLLAR**
13.80 g., Aluminum-Bronze, 30.2 mm. **Ruler:** Elizabeth II **Obv:** Head with tiara right **Rev:** Horse and rider

| Date | Mintage | VF20 | XF40 | MS60 | MS63 | MS65 |
|---|---|---|---|---|---|---|
| 2013 P | — | — | — | — | — | 15.00 |

**KM# 2065 DOLLAR**
31.14 g., 0.999 Silver 1.000 oz. ASW, 40.6 mm. **Ruler:** Elizabeth II **Subject:** A. B. Banjo Paterson, 150th Anniversary of Birth **Obv:** Head with tiara right **Rev:** Paterson in color

| Date | Mintage | VF20 | XF40 | MS60 | MS63 | MS65 |
|---|---|---|---|---|---|---|
| 2013 P | 4,000 | PF65 80.00 | | | | |

**KM# 2068 DOLLAR**
13.80 g., Aluminum-Bronze, 30.2 mm. **Ruler:** Elizabeth II **Obv:** Head with tiara right **Rev:** Skateboarder

| Date | Mintage | VF20 | XF40 | MS60 | MS63 | MS65 |
|---|---|---|---|---|---|---|
| 2013 P | — | — | — | — | — | 15.00 |

**KM# 2069 DOLLAR**
13.80 g., Aluminum-Bronze, 30.2 mm. **Ruler:** Elizabeth II **Subject:** Ludwig Leichhardt, explorer **Obv:** Head with tiara right **Rev:** Leichhardt and expedition map

| Date | Mintage | VF20 | XF40 | MS60 | MS63 | MS65 |
|---|---|---|---|---|---|---|
| 2013 P | — | — | — | — | — | 15.00 |

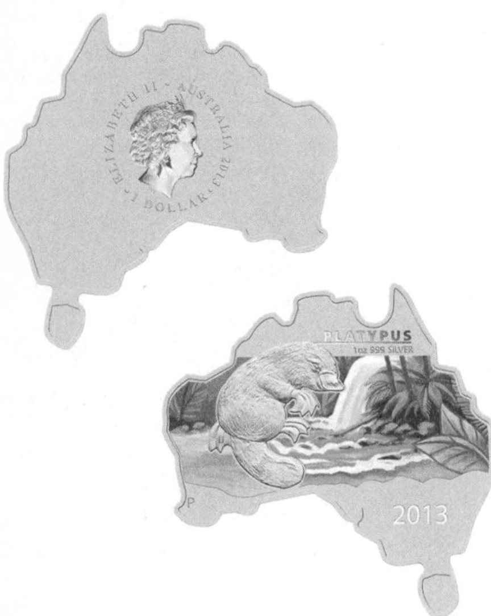

**KM# 2070 DOLLAR**
31.14 g., 0.999 Silver 1.000 oz. ASW, 40.6 mm. **Ruler:** Elizabeth II **Obv:** Head with tiara right **Rev:** Platypus along stream in color **Shape:** Irregular

| Date | Mintage | VF20 | XF40 | MS60 | MS63 | MS65 |
|---|---|---|---|---|---|---|
| 2013 P | Est. 6000 | PF65 90.00 | | | | |

**KM# 2071 DOLLAR**
13.80 g., Aluminum-Bronze, 30.2 mm. **Ruler:** Elizabeth II **Obv:** Head with tiara right **Rev:** Platypus

| Date | Mintage | VF20 | XF40 | MS60 | MS63 | MS65 |
|---|---|---|---|---|---|---|
| 2013 P | — | — | — | — | — | 15.00 |

**KM# 2075 DOLLAR**
13.80 g., Aluminum-Bronze, 30.6 mm. **Ruler:** Elizabeth II **Subject:** Bush babies **Rev:** Possum

| Date | Mintage | VF20 | XF40 | MS60 | MS63 | MS65 |
|---|---|---|---|---|---|---|
| 2013 P | — | — | — | — | — | 15.00 |

**KM# 2076 DOLLAR**
13.80 g., Aluminum-Bronze, 30.6 mm. **Ruler:** Elizabeth II **Subject:** Bush babies **Rev:** Kookaburra

| Date | Mintage | VF20 | XF40 | MS60 | MS63 | MS65 |
|---|---|---|---|---|---|---|
| 2013 P | — | — | — | — | — | 15.00 |

**KM# 2077 DOLLAR**
13.80 g., Aluminum-Bronze, 30.6 mm. **Ruler:** Elizabeth II **Subject:** Bush babies **Rev:** Echidna

| Date | Mintage | VF20 | XF40 | MS60 | MS63 | MS65 |
|---|---|---|---|---|---|---|
| 2013 P | — | — | — | — | — | 15.00 |

**KM# 2092 DOLLAR**
31.11 g., 0.999 Silver 0.999 oz. ASW **Ruler:** Elizabeth II **Subject:** National Currency, 100th Anniversary **Rev:** 1913 10 Shilling Bank Note in color **Shape:** Rectangle

| Date | Mintage | VF20 | XF40 | MS60 | MS63 | MS65 |
|---|---|---|---|---|---|---|
| 2013 P | — | PF65 100 | | | | |

**KM# 2136 DOLLAR**
13.80 g., Aluminum-Bronze, 30.6 mm. **Ruler:** Elizabeth II **Obv:** Head with tiara right **Rev:** BMX riding in color

| Date | Mintage | VF20 | XF40 | MS60 | MS63 | MS65 |
|---|---|---|---|---|---|---|
| 2013 | — | — | — | — | — | 15.00 |

**KM# 2137 DOLLAR**
13.80 g., Aluminum-Bronze, 30.6 mm. **Ruler:** Elizabeth II **Obv:** Head with tiara right **Rev:** Snorkeling in color

| Date | Mintage | VF20 | XF40 | MS60 | MS63 | MS65 |
|---|---|---|---|---|---|---|
| 2013 | — | — | — | — | — | 15.00 |

**KM# 2138 DOLLAR**
13.80 g., Aluminum-Bronze, 30.6 mm. **Ruler:** Elizabeth II **Subject:** Christmas **Obv:** Head with tiara right **Rev:** Two candles and greens

| Date | Mintage | VF20 | XF40 | MS60 | MS63 | MS65 |
|---|---|---|---|---|---|---|
| 2013 | — | — | — | — | — | 15.00 |

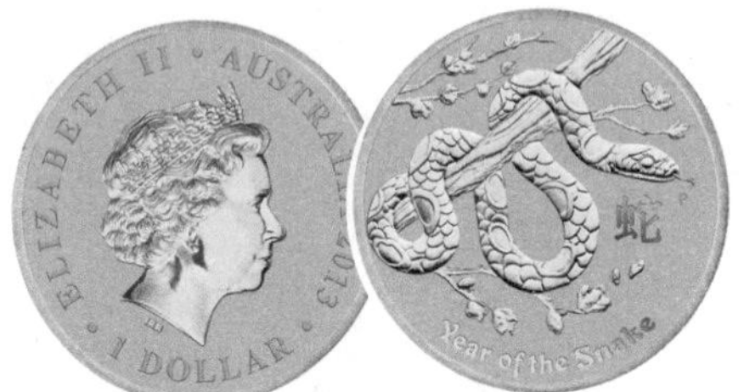

**KM# 2139 DOLLAR**
13.80 g., Aluminum-Bronze, 30.6 mm. **Ruler:** Elizabeth II **Subject:** Year of the Snake **Obv:** Head with tiara right **Rev:** Snake coiled on branch

| Date | Mintage | VF20 | XF40 | MS60 | MS63 | MS65 |
|---|---|---|---|---|---|---|
| 2013 | — | — | — | — | — | 15.00 |

**KM# 2142 DOLLAR**
31.11 g., 0.999 Silver 0.999 oz. ASW, 40.6 mm. **Ruler:** Elizabeth II **Subject:** Sister Cities **Obv:** Head with tiara right **Rev:** Lenticular views of St. Petersburg switching to Melbourne view

| Date | Mintage | VF20 | XF40 | MS60 | MS63 | MS65 |
|---|---|---|---|---|---|---|
| 2013 | — | PF65 50.00 | | | | |

### KM# 2143 DOLLAR

31.11 g., 0.999 Silver 0.999 oz. ASW, 40.6 mm. **Ruler:** Elizabeth II **Obv:** Head with tiara right **Rev:** Kangaroo and joey in color

| Date | Mintage | VF20 | XF40 | MS60 | MS63 | MS65 |
|---|---|---|---|---|---|---|
| 2013 | — | **PF65** 50.00 | | | | |

### KM# 2147 DOLLAR

9.00 g., Aluminum-Bronze, 25 mm. **Ruler:** Elizabeth II **Subject:** Korean War, 60th Anniversary **Obv:** Head with tiara right **Rev:** Dove in flight

| Date | Mintage | VF20 | XF40 | MS60 | MS63 | MS65 |
|---|---|---|---|---|---|---|
| 2013 | — | — | — | — | — | 15.00 |

### KM# 2148 DOLLAR

31.11 g., 0.999 Silver 0.999 oz. ASW, 40 mm. **Ruler:** Elizabeth II **Subject:** Korean War, 60th Anniversary **Obv:** Head with tiara right **Rev:** Dove in flight

| Date | Mintage | VF20 | XF40 | MS60 | MS63 | MS65 |
|---|---|---|---|---|---|---|
| 2013 | — | **PF63** 70.00 | **PF65** 75.00 | | | |

### KM# 2149 DOLLAR

9.00 g., Aluminum-Bronze, 25 mm. **Ruler:** Elizabeth II **Subject:** 40th Anniversary **Obv:** Head with tiara right **Rev:** Sydney Opera House

| Date | Mintage | VF20 | XF40 | MS60 | MS63 | MS65 |
|---|---|---|---|---|---|---|
| 2013 | — | — | — | — | — | 15.00 |

### KM# 2150 DOLLAR

31.11 g., 0.999 Silver 0.999 oz. ASW, 40 mm. **Ruler:** Elizabeth II **Subject:** 40th Anniversary **Obv:** Head with tiara right **Rev:** Sydney Opera House

| Date | Mintage | VF20 | XF40 | MS60 | MS63 | MS65 |
|---|---|---|---|---|---|---|
| 2013 | 5,000 | **PF63** 90.00 | **PF65** 100 | | | |

### KM# 2151 DOLLAR

9.00 g., Aluminum-Bronze, 25 mm. **Ruler:** Elizabeth II **Subject:** AFL Trophy **Obv:** Head with tiara right **Rev:** Premiers Cup

| Date | Mintage | VF20 | XF40 | MS60 | MS63 | MS65 |
|---|---|---|---|---|---|---|
| 2013 | — | — | — | — | — | 15.00 |

### KM# 2152 DOLLAR

9.00 g., Aluminum-Bronze, 25 mm. **Ruler:** Elizabeth II **Obv:** Head with tiara right **Rev:** Ethel Pedley bust facing

| Date | Mintage | VF20 | XF40 | MS60 | MS63 | MS65 |
|---|---|---|---|---|---|---|
| 2013 | — | — | — | — | — | 15.00 |

### KM# 2134 DOLLAR

31.11 g., 0.999 Silver 0.999 oz. ASW **Ruler:** Elizabeth II **Subject:** New Year **Obv:** Head right **Rev:** Sydney Harbor bridge, holographic fireworks above, eye on bridge

| Date | Mintage | VF20 | XF40 | MS60 | MS63 | MS65 |
|---|---|---|---|---|---|---|
| 2014 | — | **PF63** 70.00 | **PF65** 75.00 | | | |

### KM# 406 2 DOLLARS

6.60 g., Aluminum-Bronze, 20.5 mm. **Ruler:** Elizabeth II **Obv:** Head with tiara right **Rev:** Aboriginal elder at left, stars above at right **Edge:** Segmented reeding

| Date | Mintage | VF20 | XF40 | MS60 | MS63 | MS65 |
|---|---|---|---|---|---|---|
| 2001 | 35,650,000 | — | — | — | 5.00 | 6.00 |
| Note: Large obverse head, IRB spaced | | | | | | |
| 2001 | Inc. above | — | — | — | — | — |
| Note: Smaller obverse head, IRB joined | | | | | | |
| 2001 | 59,569 | **PF65** 8.00 | | | | |
| 2002 | 29,689,000 | — | — | — | 4.00 | 6.00 |
| 2002 | 39,514 | **PF65** 8.00 | | | | |
| 2003 | 13,656,000 | — | — | — | 4.00 | 6.00 |
| 2003 | 39,090 | **PF65** 8.00 | | | | |
| 2004 | 20,084,000 | — | — | — | 3.50 | 5.00 |
| 2004 | 50,000 | **PF65** 7.00 | | | | |
| 2005 | — | — | — | — | 3.50 | 5.00 |
| 2005 | 33,520 | **PF65** 7.00 | | | | |
| 2006 | — | — | — | — | 3.50 | 5.00 |
| 2006 | — | **PF65** 7.00 | | | | |
| 2007 | — | — | — | — | 3.00 | 4.50 |
| 2007 | — | **PF65** 6.00 | | | | |
| 2008 | — | — | — | — | 3.00 | 4.50 |
| 2008 | — | **PF65** 6.00 | | | | |
| 2009 | — | — | — | — | 3.00 | 4.50 |
| 2009 | — | **PF65** 6.00 | | | | |
| 2010 | — | — | — | — | 3.00 | 4.50 |
| 2010 | — | **PF65** 6.00 | | | | |
| 2011 | — | — | — | — | 3.00 | 4.50 |
| 2011 | — | **PF65** 6.00 | | | | |
| 2012 | — | — | — | — | 3.00 | 4.50 |
| 2012 | — | **PF65** 6.00 | | | | |
| 2013 | — | — | — | 3.00 | 4.50 | — |
| 2013 | — | **PF65** 6.00 | | | | |
| 2014 | — | — | — | 3.00 | 4.50 | — |
| 2014 | — | **PF60** 6.00 | | | | |
| 2015 | — | — | — | 3.00 | 4.50 | — |
| 2015 | — | **PF65** 6.00 | | | | |

### KM# 406a 2 DOLLARS

15.88 g., 0.9999 Gold 0.5105 oz. AGW, 20.5 mm. **Ruler:** Elizabeth II **Obv:** Head with tiara right **Rev:** Aboriginal elder and value **Edge:** Segmented reeding

| Date | Mintage | VF20 | XF40 | MS60 | MS63 | MS65 |
|---|---|---|---|---|---|---|
| 2001 B | 350 | **PF65** 925 | | | | |
| 2005 B | 650 | **PF65** 900 | | | | |
| 2006 B | 300 | **PF65** 950 | | | | |
| 2013 B | 500 | **PF65** 925 | | | | |

### KM# 406b 2 DOLLARS

8.55 g., 0.9999 Silver 0.2749 oz. ASW, 20.5 mm. **Ruler:** Elizabeth II **Obv:** Head with tiara right **Rev:** Aboriginal elder and value **Edge:** Segmented reeding

| Date | Mintage | VF20 | XF40 | MS60 | MS63 | MS65 |
|---|---|---|---|---|---|---|
| 2003 B | 6,500 | **PF65** 22.00 | | | | |
| 2004 B | 6,500 | **PF65** 22.00 | | | | |
| 2005 B | 6,500 | **PF65** 22.00 | | | | |
| 2013 B | 5,000 | **PF65** 40.00 | | | | |

### KM# 764 2 DOLLARS

18.22 g., 0.999 Silver 0.5852 oz. ASW, 32.5 mm. **Ruler:** Elizabeth II **Series:** Masterpieces in Silver - Port Phillip Patterns **Obv:** 1/2 ounce design **Rev:** Kangaroo design **Edge:** Reeded

| Date | Mintage | VF20 | XF40 | MS60 | MS63 | MS65 |
|---|---|---|---|---|---|---|
| 2003 B | 10,000 | **PF65** 35.00 | | | | |

### KM# 755 2 DOLLARS

62.27 g., 0.999 Silver 2.000 oz. ASW, 50 mm. **Ruler:** Elizabeth II **Series:** Australian Peacekeepers **Obv:** Queen's head right **Rev:** Australian army and color insignia **Edge:** Reeded

| Date | Mintage | VF20 | XF40 | MS60 | MS63 | MS65 |
|---|---|---|---|---|---|---|
| 2005 P | 2,500 | **PF65** 90.00 | | | | |

**KM# 756 2 DOLLARS**

62.27 g., 0.999 Silver 2.000 oz. ASW, 50.3 mm. **Ruler:** Elizabeth II **Series:** Australian Peacekeepers **Obv:** Queen's head right **Rev:** Australian navy and color insignia **Edge:** Reeded

| Date | Mintage | VF20 | XF40 | MS60 | MS63 | MS65 |
|---|---|---|---|---|---|---|
| 2005 P | 2,500 | PF65 90.00 | | | | |

**KM# 757 2 DOLLARS**

62.27 g., 0.999 Silver 2.000 oz. ASW, 50.3 mm. **Ruler:** Elizabeth II **Subject:** Australian Peacekeepers Set **Obv:** Queen's head right **Rev:** Australian airforce and color insignia **Edge:** Reeded

| Date | Mintage | VF20 | XF40 | MS60 | MS63 | MS65 |
|---|---|---|---|---|---|---|
| 2005 P | 2,500 | PF65 90.00 | | | | |

**KM# 758 2 DOLLARS**

62.27 g., 0.999 Silver 2.000 oz. ASW, 50.3 mm. **Ruler:** Elizabeth II **Series:** Australian Peacekeepers **Obv:** Queen's head right **Rev:** Australian federal police and color insignia **Edge:** Reeded

| Date | Mintage | VF20 | XF40 | MS60 | MS63 | MS65 |
|---|---|---|---|---|---|---|
| 2005 P | 2,500 | PF65 90.00 | | | | |

**KM# 759 2 DOLLARS**

62.27 g., 0.999 Silver 2.000 oz. ASW, 50.3 mm. **Ruler:** Elizabeth II **Series:** Australian Peacekeepers **Obv:** Queen's head right **Rev:** Australian Agency for International Development and color insignia **Edge:** Reeded

| Date | Mintage | VF20 | XF40 | MS60 | MS63 | MS65 |
|---|---|---|---|---|---|---|
| 2005 P | 2,500 | PF65 90.00 | | | | |

**KM# 852 2 DOLLARS**

8.85 g., 0.999 Silver 0.2842 oz. ASW, 20.5 mm. **Ruler:** Elizabeth II **Obv:** Young bust right **Rev:** Aboriginal elder **Edge:** Segmented reeding

| Date | Mintage | VF20 | XF40 | MS60 | MS63 | MS65 |
|---|---|---|---|---|---|---|
| 2006 | 6,500 | PF65 22.00 | | | | |

**KM# 853 2 DOLLARS**

1.24 g., 0.999 Gold 0.040 oz. AGW **Ruler:** Elizabeth II **Obv:** Head with tiara right **Rev:** FIFA World Cup

| Date | Mintage | VF20 | XF40 | MS60 | MS63 | MS65 |
|---|---|---|---|---|---|---|
| 2006 P | 50,000 | PF65 80.00 | | | | |

**KM# 1246 2 DOLLARS**

0.50 g., 0.999 Gold, 12 mm. **Ruler:** Elizabeth II **Subject:** 2010 FIFA World Cup, South Africa **Obv:** Head right **Rev:** Dream kangaroo and soccer ball

| Date | Mintage | VF20 | XF40 | MS60 | MS63 | MS65 |
|---|---|---|---|---|---|---|
| 2009 P | 7,500 | PF65 85.00 | | | | |

**KM# 1627 2 DOLLARS**

31.11 g., 0.999 Silver 0.999 oz. ASW, 40.6 mm. **Ruler:** Elizabeth II **Subject:** Royal Austrailian Navy, 100th Anniversary **Obv:** Head with tiara right **Rev:** HMAS AE 2 submarine

| Date | Mintage | VF20 | XF40 | MS60 | MS63 | MS65 |
|---|---|---|---|---|---|---|
| 2011 | — | PF65 100 | | | | |

**KM# 1628 2 DOLLARS**

31.11 g., 0.999 Silver 0.999 oz. ASW, 40.6 mm. **Ruler:** Elizabeth II **Subject:** Royal Australian Navy, 100th Anniversary **Obv:** Head with tiara right **Rev:** HMAS Australia II

| Date | Mintage | VF20 | XF40 | MS60 | MS63 | MS65 |
|---|---|---|---|---|---|---|
| 2011 | — | PF65 100 | | | | |

**KM# 1629 2 DOLLARS**

31.11 g., 0.999 Silver 0.999 oz. ASW, 40.6 mm. **Ruler:** Elizabeth II **Subject:** Royal Australian Navy, 100th Anniversary **Obv:** Head with tiara right **Rev:** HMAS Hobart II

| Date | Mintage | VF20 | XF40 | MS60 | MS63 | MS65 |
|---|---|---|---|---|---|---|
| 2011 | — | PF65 100 | | | | |

**KM# 1630 2 DOLLARS**

31.11 g., 0.999 Silver 0.999 oz. ASW, 40.6 mm. **Ruler:** Elizabeth II **Subject:** Royal Australian Navy, 100th Anniversary **Obv:** Head with tiara right **Rev:** HMAS Yarra III

| Date | Mintage | VF20 | XF40 | MS60 | MS63 | MS65 |
|---|---|---|---|---|---|---|
| 2011 | — | PF65 100 | | | | |

**KM# 1631 2 DOLLARS**

31.11 g., 0.999 Silver 0.999 oz. ASW, 40.6 mm. **Ruler:** Elizabeth II **Subject:** Royal Australian Navy, 100th Anniversary **Obv:** Head with tiara right **Rev:** HMAS Sydney III

| Date | Mintage | VF20 | XF40 | MS60 | MS63 | MS65 |
|---|---|---|---|---|---|---|
| 2011 | — | PF65 100 | | | | |

**KM# 1632 2 DOLLARS**

31.11 g., 0.999 Silver 0.999 oz. ASW, 40.6 mm. **Ruler:** Elizabeth II **Subject:** Royal Australian Navy, 100th Anniversary **Obv:** Head with tiara right **Rev:** HMAS Armidale II

| Date | Mintage | VF20 | XF40 | MS60 | MS63 | MS65 |
|---|---|---|---|---|---|---|
| 2011 | — | PF65 100 | | | | |

**KM# 1740 2 DOLLARS**

20.00 g., 0.999 Silver 0.6424 oz. ASW partially gilt, 34 mm. **Ruler:** Elizabeth II **Subject:** Australian Open **Obv:** Small Queen's portrait above tennis ball **Rev:** Player serving

| Date | Mintage | VF20 | XF40 | MS60 | MS63 | MS65 |
|---|---|---|---|---|---|---|
| 2012 | 10,000 | PF65 100 | | | | |

**KM# 1802 2 DOLLARS**

0.50 g., 0.999 Gold, 11.6 mm. **Ruler:** Elizabeth II **Subject:** FIFA **Rev:** Scoccer player and Australia map

| Date | Mintage | VF20 | XF40 | MS60 | MS63 | MS65 |
|---|---|---|---|---|---|---|
| 2012 P | — | PF65 75.00 | | | | |

W

**KM# 1825 2 DOLLARS**

0.50 g., 0.999 Gold, 11.6 mm. **Ruler:** Elizabeth II **Subject:** Mini-Roo **Rev:** Kangaroo

| Date | Mintage | VF20 | XF40 | MS60 | MS63 | MS65 |
|---|---|---|---|---|---|---|
| 2012 P | — | PF65 50.00 | | | | |

**KM# 1864 2 DOLLARS**
Silver **Ruler:** Elizabeth II **Subject:** Remembrance Day **Rev:** Poppy in color at center

| Date | Mintage | VF20 | XF40 | MS60 | MS63 | MS65 |
|---|---|---|---|---|---|---|
| 2012 | — | PF65 100 | | | | |

**KM# 2007 2 DOLLARS**
6.60 g., Aluminum-Bronze, 20.5 mm. **Ruler:** Elizabeth II **Subject:** Remembrance Day **Rev:** Poppy at center

| Date | Mintage | VF20 | XF40 | MS60 | MS63 | MS65 |
|---|---|---|---|---|---|---|
| 2012 | — | — | — | — | — | 5.00 |

**KM# 2007A 2 DOLLARS**
6.60 g., Aluminum-Bronze, 20.5 mm. **Ruler:** Elizabeth II **Subject:** Remembrance Day **Rev:** Red and black poppy at center

| Date | Mintage | VF20 | XF40 | MS60 | MS63 | MS65 |
|---|---|---|---|---|---|---|
| 2012 C | — | — | — | — | — | 15.00 |
| 2012 | — | — | — | — | — | 15.00 |

**KM# 1922 2 DOLLARS**
62.20 g., 0.999 Silver 1.9978 oz. ASW, 55.6 mm. **Ruler:** Elizabeth II **Subject:** Ludwig Leichhardt

| Date | Mintage | VF20 | XF40 | MS60 | MS63 | MS65 |
|---|---|---|---|---|---|---|
| 2013 P | Est. 2013 | PF65 150 | | | | |

**KM# 1959 2 DOLLARS**
0.50 g., 0.9999 Gold, 11 mm. **Ruler:** Elizabeth II **Subject:** Frilled Neck Lizard

| Date | Mintage | VF20 | XF40 | MS60 | MS63 | MS65 |
|---|---|---|---|---|---|---|
| 2013 | — | PF65 45.00 | | | | |

**KM# 2039 2 DOLLARS**
0.50 g., 0.9999 Gold, 11.15 mm. **Ruler:** Elizabeth II **Subject:** Australian Miniature Money

| Date | Mintage | VF20 | XF40 | MS60 | MS63 | MS65 |
|---|---|---|---|---|---|---|
| 2013 | Est. 2000 | PF65 75.00 | | | | |

**KM# 2153 2 DOLLARS**
6.60 g., Aluminum-Bronze, 20.5 mm. **Ruler:** Elizabeth II **Subject:** Elizabeth's Coronation, 60th Anniversary **Obv:** Head with tiara right **Rev:** Crown within purple ring

| Date | Mintage | VF20 | XF40 | MS60 | MS63 | MS65 |
|---|---|---|---|---|---|---|
| 2013 | — | — | — | — | — | 15.00 |

**KM# 591 5 DOLLARS**
36.31 g., 0.999 Silver 1.1662 oz. ASW, 38.74 mm. **Ruler:** Elizabeth II **Subject:** Centennial of Federation Series Finale **Obv:** Queen's head right **Rev:** Multicolor dual hologram: map and rotunda **Edge:** Reeded

| Date | Mintage | VF20 | XF40 | MS60 | MS63 | MS65 |
|---|---|---|---|---|---|---|
| 2001 B | — | PF65 55.00 | | | | |

**KM# 592 5 DOLLARS**
36.31 g., 0.999 Silver 1.1662 oz. ASW, 38.74 mm. **Ruler:** Elizabeth II **Subject:** Barton and Reid **Obv:** Queen's head right **Rev:** Portraits of Dame Flora Reid and Lady Jean Barton **Edge:** Reeded

| Date | Mintage | VF20 | XF40 | MS60 | MS63 | MS65 |
|---|---|---|---|---|---|---|
| 2001 B | 5,000 | PF65 60.00 | | | | |

**KM# 637 5 DOLLARS**
36.31 g., 0.999 Silver 1.1662 oz. ASW, 38.74 mm. **Ruler:** Elizabeth II **Subject:** Kingston, Barton and Deakin **Obv:** Queen's head right **Rev:** Three rectangular portraits and value **Edge:** Reeded

| Date | Mintage | VF20 | XF40 | MS60 | MS63 | MS65 |
|---|---|---|---|---|---|---|
| 2001 B | 5,000 | PF65 60.00 | | | | |

**KM# 638 5 DOLLARS**
36.31 g., 0.999 Silver 1.1662 oz. ASW, 38.74 mm. **Ruler:** Elizabeth II **Subject:** Clark, Parkes and Griffith **Obv:** Queen's head right **Rev:** Three rectangular portraits and value **Edge:** Reeded

| Date | Mintage | VF20 | XF40 | MS60 | MS63 | MS65 |
|---|---|---|---|---|---|---|
| 2001 B | 5,000 | PF65 60.00 | | | | |

**KM# 639 5 DOLLARS**
36.31 g., 0.999 Silver 1.1662 oz. ASW, 38.74 mm. **Ruler:** Elizabeth II **Subject:** Spence, Nicholls and Anderson **Obv:** Queen's head right **Rev:** Three circular portraits and value **Edge:** Reeded

| Date | Mintage | VF20 | XF40 | MS60 | MS63 | MS65 |
|---|---|---|---|---|---|---|
| 2001 B | 5,000 | PF65 60.00 | | | | |

**KM# 640 5 DOLLARS**
36.31 g., 0.999 Silver 1.1662 oz. ASW, 38.74 mm. **Ruler:** Elizabeth II **Subject:** Reid, Forrest and Quick **Obv:** Queen's head right **Rev:** Three rectangular portraits and value **Edge:** Reeded

| Date | Mintage | VF20 | XF40 | MS60 | MS63 | MS65 |
|---|---|---|---|---|---|---|
| 2001 B | 5,000 | PF65 60.00 | | | | |

**KM# 641 5 DOLLARS**
36.31 g., 0.999 Silver 1.1662 oz. ASW, 38.74 mm. **Ruler:** Elizabeth II **Subject:** Bathurst Ladies Organizing Committee **Obv:** Queen's head right **Rev:** Circular design with names above value **Edge:** Reeded

| Date | Mintage | VF20 | XF40 | MS60 | MS63 | MS65 |
|---|---|---|---|---|---|---|
| 2001 B | 5,000 | PF65 60.00 | | | | |

**KM# 662 5 DOLLARS**
36.31 g., 0.999 Silver 1.1662 oz. ASW, 38.74 mm. **Ruler:** Elizabeth II **Subject:** Year of the Outback **Obv:** Queen's head right **Rev:** Multicolor holographic landscape **Edge:** Reeded

| Date | Mintage | VF20 | XF40 | MS60 | MS63 | MS65 |
|---|---|---|---|---|---|---|
| 2002 B | 15,000 | PF65 100 | | | | |

**KM# 761 5 DOLLARS**
36.31 g., 0.999 Silver 1.1662 oz. ASW **Ruler:** Elizabeth II **Obv:** Queen's head right **Rev:** Sir Donald Bradman

| Date | Mintage | VF20 | XF40 | MS60 | MS63 | MS65 |
|---|---|---|---|---|---|---|
| 2001 | — | PF65 55.00 | | | | |

**KM# 762 5 DOLLARS**
20.00 g., Aluminum-Bronze, 38.74 mm. **Ruler:** Elizabeth II **Obv:** Queen's head right **Rev:** Sir Donald Bradman

| Date | Mintage | VF20 | XF40 | MS60 | MS63 | MS65 |
|---|---|---|---|---|---|---|
| 2001 | — | — | — | — | 8.50 | 9.50 |

**KM# 601 5 DOLLARS**
10.52 g., Bi-Metallic Aluminumn-Bronze center in Stainless Steel ring, 27.8 mm. **Ruler:** Elizabeth II **Subject:** Battle of Sunda Strait **Obv:** Head with tiara right **Rev:** Ships bell from the "USS Houston", denomination below **Shape:** 24-sided **Note:** Demagnetized.

| Date | Mintage | VF20 | XF40 | MS60 | MS63 | MS65 |
|---|---|---|---|---|---|---|
| 2002 B | — | — | — | — | 7.50 | 9.50 |

**KM# 647 5 DOLLARS**
28.00 g., Aluminum-Bronze, 38.74 mm. **Ruler:** Elizabeth II **Subject:** Battle of Sunda Strait **Obv:** Queen's head right **Rev:** Two ships; USS Houston and HMS Perth **Edge:** Reeded

| Date | Mintage | VF20 | XF40 | MS60 | MS63 | MS65 |
|---|---|---|---|---|---|---|
| 2002 B | 15,000 | PF65 25.00 | | | | |

**KM# 649 5 DOLLARS**
20.00 g., Aluminum-Bronze, 38.74 mm. **Ruler:** Elizabeth II **Subject:** Commonwealth Games **Obv:** Head with tiara right, denomination below **Rev:** Eight arms, each represents an event of the games **Edge:** Reeded

| Date | Mintage | VF20 | XF40 | MS60 | MS63 | MS65 |
|---|---|---|---|---|---|---|
| 2002 B | 11,145 | — | — | — | 8.50 | 9.50 |

**KM# 650 5 DOLLARS**
20.00 g., Aluminum-Bronze, 38.74 mm. **Ruler:** Elizabeth II **Subject:** Commonwealth Games **Obv:** Head with tiara right, denomination below **Rev:** Eight arms, each represents an event at the games **Edge:** Reeded

| Date | Mintage | VF20 | XF40 | MS60 | MS63 | MS65 |
|---|---|---|---|---|---|---|
| 2002 B | 11,145 | — | — | — | 8.50 | 9.50 |

**KM# 651 5 DOLLARS**
20.00 g., Aluminum-Bronze, 38.74 mm. **Ruler:** Elizabeth II **Subject:** Commonwealth Games **Obv:** Head with tiara right, denomination below **Rev:** Blue games logo; star above tail of stylized kangaroo and torch **Edge:** Reeded

| Date | Mintage | VF20 | XF40 | MS60 | MS63 | MS65 |
|---|---|---|---|---|---|---|
| 2002 B | 11,145 | — | — | — | 8.50 | 9.50 |

**KM# 652 5 DOLLARS**
36.31 g., 0.999 Silver 1.1662 oz. ASW, 38.74 mm. **Ruler:** Elizabeth II **Subject:** Commonwealth Games **Obv:** Head with tiara right, denomination below **Rev:** Victorious athletes **Edge:** Reeded

| Date | Mintage | VF20 | XF40 | MS60 | MS63 | MS65 |
|---|---|---|---|---|---|---|
| 2002 B | 7,581 | PF65 50.00 | | | | |

**KM# 653 5 DOLLARS**
36.31 g., 0.999 Silver 1.1662 oz. ASW, 38.74 mm. **Ruler:** Elizabeth II **Obv:** Queen's head right **Rev:** Dutch sailing ship, The Duyfken **Edge:** Reeded

| Date | Mintage | VF20 | XF40 | MS60 | MS63 | MS65 |
|---|---|---|---|---|---|---|
| 2002 B | 9,096 | PF65 47.00 | | | | |

**KM# 654 5 DOLLARS**
36.31 g., 0.999 Silver 1.1662 oz. ASW, 38.74 mm. **Ruler:** Elizabeth II **Obv:** Queen's head right **Rev:** HMS Endeavour sailing ship **Edge:** Reeded

| Date | Mintage | VF20 | XF40 | MS60 | MS63 | MS65 |
|---|---|---|---|---|---|---|
| 2002 B | 9,096 | PF65 47.00 | | | | |

**KM# 655 5 DOLLARS**
36.31 g., 0.999 Silver 1.1662 oz. ASW, 38.74 mm. **Ruler:** Elizabeth II **Obv:** Queen's head right **Rev:** HMS Sirius sailing ship **Edge:** Reeded

| Date | Mintage | VF20 | XF40 | MS60 | MS63 | MS65 |
|---|---|---|---|---|---|---|
| 2002 B | 9,096 | PF65 47.00 | | | | |

**KM# 656 5 DOLLARS**
36.31 g., 0.999 Silver 1.1662 oz. ASW, 38.74 mm. **Ruler:** Elizabeth II **Obv:** Queen's head right **Rev:** HMS Investigator sailing ship **Edge:** Reeded

| Date | Mintage | VF20 | XF40 | MS60 | MS63 | MS65 |
|---|---|---|---|---|---|---|
| 2002 B | 9,096 | PF65 47.00 | | | | |

**KM# 659 5 DOLLARS**
31.10 g., 0.999 Silver 0.999 oz. ASW, 40 mm. **Ruler:** Elizabeth II **Subject:** Queen Mother **Obv:** Queen's head right **Rev:** Queen Mother circa 1927 within wreath of roses **Edge:** Reeded

| Date | Mintage | VF20 | XF40 | MS60 | MS63 | MS65 |
|---|---|---|---|---|---|---|
| 2002 B | 30,000 | PF65 40.00 | | | | |

**KM# 765 5 DOLLARS**
36.31 g., 0.999 Silver 1.1662 oz. ASW, 38.7 mm. **Ruler:** Elizabeth II **Series:** Masterpieces in Silver - Port Phillip Patterns **Obv:** One ounce design **Rev:** Kangaroo design **Edge:** Reeded

| Date | Mintage | VF20 | XF40 | MS60 | MS63 | MS65 |
|---|---|---|---|---|---|---|
| 2003 B | 10,000 | PF65 45.00 | | | | |

**KM# 810 5 DOLLARS**
36.31 g., 0.995 Silver 1.1616 oz. ASW partially gilt, 40 mm. **Ruler:** Elizabeth II **Subject:** Rugby World Cup **Obv:** Head with tiara right **Rev:** Rugby World Cup and official logos **Edge:** Reeded

| Date | Mintage | VF20 | XF40 | MS60 | MS63 | MS65 |
|---|---|---|---|---|---|---|
| 2003 | 20,501 | PF65 85.00 | | | | |

**KM# 854 5 DOLLARS**
20.00 g., Aluminum-Bronze, 38.74 mm. **Ruler:** Elizabeth II **Subject:** Rugby World Cup **Obv:** Head with tiara right **Rev:** Player kicking ball at posts, official logo **Edge:** Reeded

| Date | Mintage | VF20 | XF40 | MS60 | MS63 | MS65 |
|---|---|---|---|---|---|---|
| 2003 | 43,802 | — | — | — | 15.00 | 16.50 |

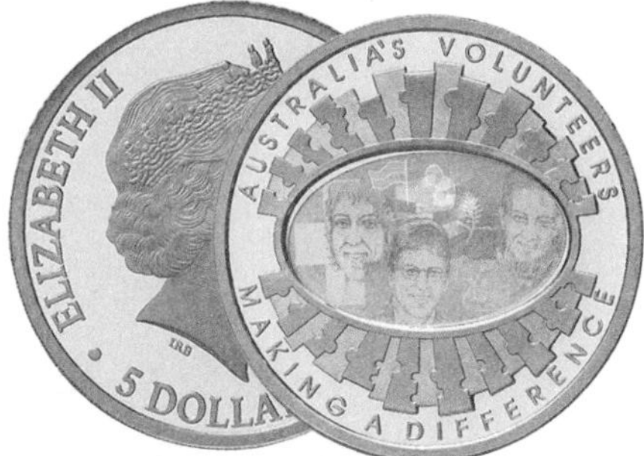


**KM# 1017 5 DOLLARS**
36.21 g., 0.999 Silver 1.163 oz. ASW, 38.7 mm. **Ruler:** Elizabeth II **Obv:** Head with tiara right **Obv. Legend:** ELIZABETH II - AUSTRALIA **Rev:** Faces in oval hologram in ornate frame **Rev. Legend:** AUSTRALIA'S VOLUNTEERS - MAKING A DIFFERENCE **Edge:** Reeded

| Date | Mintage | VF20 | XF40 | MS60 | MS63 | MS65 |
|---|---|---|---|---|---|---|
| 2003 B | 15,000 | PF65 45.00 | | | | |

**KM# 727 5 DOLLARS**
36.31 g., 0.999 Silver 1.1662 oz. ASW, 38.74 mm. **Ruler:** Elizabeth II **Subject:** Olympics **Obv:** Queen's head right **Rev:** Parthenon, Sydney Opera House and shield with multicolor flag and rings **Edge:** Reeded

| Date | Mintage | VF20 | XF40 | MS60 | MS63 | MS65 |
|---|---|---|---|---|---|---|
| 2004 B | 17,500 | PF65 40.00 | | | | |

**KM# 728 5 DOLLARS**
36.31 g., 0.999 Silver 1.1662 oz. ASW, 38.74 mm. **Ruler:** Elizabeth II **Subject:** Tasmania **Obv:** Queen's head right **Rev:** Ship on island map **Edge:** Reeded

| Date | Mintage | VF20 | XF40 | MS60 | MS63 | MS65 |
|---|---|---|---|---|---|---|
| 2004 B | 7,500 | PF65 47.00 | | | | |

**KM# 728a 5 DOLLARS**
20.00 g., Aluminum-Bronze, 38.74 mm. **Ruler:** Elizabeth II **Subject:** Tasmanian Bicentennial **Obv:** Head with tiara right **Rev:** Ship, map, state flower **Edge:** Reeded

| Date | Mintage | VF20 | XF40 | MS60 | MS63 | MS65 |
|---|---|---|---|---|---|---|
| 2004 | 18,561 | — | — | — | 12.00 | 14.00 |
| 2004 H | 2,841 | — | — | — | 17.50 | 20.00 |

**KM# 729 5 DOLLARS**
31.10 g., 0.999 Silver 0.999 oz. ASW, 40 mm. **Ruler:** Elizabeth II **Subject:** Adelaide to Darwin Railroad **Obv:** Queen's head right **Rev:** Train, tracks and outline map **Edge:** Reeded

| Date | Mintage | VF20 | XF40 | MS60 | MS63 | MS65 |
|---|---|---|---|---|---|---|
| 2004 B | 12,500 | PF65 40.00 | | | | |

**KM# 730 5 DOLLARS**
31.10 g., 0.999 Silver 0.999 oz. ASW, 40 mm. **Ruler:** Elizabeth II **Subject:** 150 Years of Australian Steam Railways **Obv:** Queen's head right **Rev:** Old steam train **Edge:** Reeded

| Date | Mintage | VF20 | XF40 | MS60 | MS63 | MS65 |
|---|---|---|---|---|---|---|
| 2004 B | 15,000 | PF65 37.50 | | | | |

**KM# 812 5 DOLLARS**
Aluminum-Bronze, 38.74 mm. **Ruler:** Elizabeth II **Subject:** Olympic Games 2000-2004 **Obv:** Head with tiara right

| Date | Mintage | VF20 | XF40 | MS60 | MS63 | MS65 |
|---|---|---|---|---|---|---|
| 2004 | — | — | — | — | 15.00 | 16.50 |

**KM# 855 5 DOLLARS**
27.25 g., Copper-Nickel partially gilt, 38.74 mm. **Ruler:** Elizabeth II **Subject:** Australia's Own Game **Obv:** Head with tiara right **Rev:** Cup and logos **Edge:** Reeded

| Date | Mintage | VF20 | XF40 | MS60 | MS63 | MS65 |
|---|---|---|---|---|---|---|
| 2004 | 16,163 | PF65 45.00 | | | | |

**KM# 856 5 DOLLARS**
20.00 g., Aluminum-Bronze, 38.74 mm. **Ruler:** Elizabeth II **Subject:** Olympic Games - Sydney To Athens **Obv:** Head with tiara right **Rev:** Silhouettes ancient Greek athlete and Aboriginal **Edge:** Reeded

| Date | Mintage | VF20 | XF40 | MS60 | MS63 | MS65 |
|---|---|---|---|---|---|---|
| 2004 | 24,376 | — | — | — | 15.00 | 16.50 |

**KM# 750 5 DOLLARS**
20.00 g., Aluminum-Bronze, 38.74 mm. **Ruler:** Elizabeth II **Obv:** Queen's head right **Rev:** Tennis player **Edge:** Reeded

| Date | Mintage | VF20 | XF40 | MS60 | MS63 | MS65 |
|---|---|---|---|---|---|---|
| 2005 B | — | — | — | — | 7.50 | 8.50 |

**KM# 782 5 DOLLARS**
36.31 g., 0.9999 Silver 1.1673 oz. ASW, 38.74 mm. **Ruler:** Elizabeth II **Subject:** XVIII Commonwealth Games City of Sport **Obv:** Head with tiara right, denomination below **Rev:** City skyline alongside river

| Date | Mintage | VF20 | XF40 | MS60 | MS63 | MS65 |
|---|---|---|---|---|---|---|
| 2006 | 10,000 | PF63 50.00 | PF65 55.00 | | | |

**KM# 783 5 DOLLARS**
20.00 g., Aluminum-Bronze, 38.74 mm. **Ruler:** Elizabeth II **Subject:** XVIII Commonwealth Games in Melbourne **Obv:** Head with tiara right, denomination below **Rev:** Games logo and crown surrounded by stylized athletes **Edge:** Reeded

| Date | Mintage | VF20 | XF40 | MS60 | MS63 | MS65 |
|---|---|---|---|---|---|---|
| 2006 | — | — | — | — | 15.00 | 16.50 |

### KM# 786 5 DOLLARS

20.00 g., Aluminum-Bronze, 38.74 mm. **Ruler:** Elizabeth II **Subject:** XVIII Commonwealth Games Queen's Baton Relay **Obv:** Head with tiara right **Rev:** Stylized baton runner **Edge:** Reeded

| Date | Mintage | VF20 | XF40 | MS60 | MS63 | MS65 |
|---|---|---|---|---|---|---|
| 2006 | 20,488 | — | — | — | 15.00 | 16.50 |

### KM# 786a 5 DOLLARS

36.31 g., 0.999 Silver 1.1662 oz. ASW, 38.74 mm. **Ruler:** Elizabeth II **Subject:** XVIII Commonwealth Games Queen's Baton Relay **Obv:** Head with tiara right **Rev:** Stylized baton runner **Edge:** Reeded

| Date | Mintage | VF20 | XF40 | MS60 | MS63 | MS65 |
|---|---|---|---|---|---|---|
| 2006 | 9,100 | PF65 75.00 | | | | |

### KM# 787 5 DOLLARS

36.31 g., 0.999 Silver 1.1662 oz. ASW, 38.74 mm. **Ruler:** Elizabeth II **Subject:** Masterpieces in Silver: Australia's Artists **Obv:** Head with tiara right **Rev:** Sidney Nolan: Burke & Wills

| Date | Mintage | VF20 | XF40 | MS60 | MS63 | MS65 |
|---|---|---|---|---|---|---|
| 2006 | 10,000 | PF63 55.00 | PF65 60.00 | | | |

### KM# 788 5 DOLLARS

36.31 g., 0.999 Silver 1.1662 oz. ASW, 38.74 mm. **Ruler:** Elizabeth II **Subject:** Masters in Art - Siding

| Date | Mintage | VF20 | XF40 | MS60 | MS63 | MS65 |
|---|---|---|---|---|---|---|
| 2006 | 10,000 | PF63 50.00 | PF65 55.00 | | | |

### KM# 789 5 DOLLARS

36.31 g., 0.999 Silver 1.1662 oz. ASW, 38.74 mm. **Ruler:** Elizabeth II **Subject:** Masterpieces in Silver: Australia's Artists **Obv:** Head with tiara right **Rev:** Brett Whitley: Self Portrait in the Studio

| Date | Mintage | VF20 | XF40 | MS60 | MS63 | MS65 |
|---|---|---|---|---|---|---|
| 2006 | 10,000 | PF63 55.00 | PF65 60.00 | | | |

### KM# 790 5 DOLLARS

36.31 g., 0.999 Silver 1.1662 oz. ASW, 38.74 mm. **Ruler:** Elizabeth II **Subject:** Masterpieces in Silver: Australia's Artists **Obv:** Head with tiara right **Rev:** Russell Drysdale: The Drover's Wife

| Date | Mintage | VF20 | XF40 | MS60 | MS63 | MS65 |
|---|---|---|---|---|---|---|
| 2006 | 10,000 | PF63 55.00 | PF65 60.00 | | | |

### KM# 813 5 DOLLARS

20.00 g., Aluminum-Bronze, 38.74 mm. **Ruler:** Elizabeth II **Subject:** Voyage of Discovery 1606 **Obv:** Head with tiara right **Rev:** Dutch yacht Duyfken **Edge:** Reeded **Note:** Mint mark: G.

| Date | Mintage | VF20 | XF40 | MS60 | MS63 | MS65 |
|---|---|---|---|---|---|---|
| 2006 | — | — | — | — | 15.00 | 16.50 |

### KM# 813a 5 DOLLARS

36.31 g., 0.999 Silver 1.1662 oz. ASW, 38.74 mm. **Ruler:** Elizabeth II **Subject:** Voyage of Discovery 1606 **Obv:** Head with tiara right **Rev:** Dutch yacht Duyfken **Edge:** Reeded **Note:** Mint mark: Tulip.

| Date | Mintage | VF20 | XF40 | MS60 | MS63 | MS65 |
|---|---|---|---|---|---|---|
| 2006 P | 8,500 | PF65 125 | | | | |

### KM# 857 5 DOLLARS

36.31 g., 0.9999 Silver 1.1673 oz. ASW, 38.74 mm. **Ruler:** Elizabeth II **Subject:** 150 Year of State Government **Obv:** Head with tiara right **Rev:** Outline map of State of New South Wales **Edge:** Reeded

| Date | Mintage | VF20 | XF40 | MS60 | MS63 | MS65 |
|---|---|---|---|---|---|---|
| 2006 | 12,500 | PF65 85.00 | | | | |

### KM# 858 5 DOLLARS

36.31 g., 0.999 Silver 1.1662 oz. ASW, 38.74 mm. **Ruler:** Elizabeth II **Subject:** 150 Year of State Government **Obv:** Head with tiara right **Rev:** Outline map of State of Tasmania **Edge:** Reeded

| Date | Mintage | VF20 | XF40 | MS60 | MS63 | MS65 |
|---|---|---|---|---|---|---|
| 2006 | 12,500 | PF65 85.00 | | | | |

### KM# 859 5 DOLLARS

36.31 g., 0.999 Silver 1.1662 oz. ASW, 38.74 mm. **Ruler:** Elizabeth II **Subject:** 150 Year of State Government **Obv:** Head with tiara right **Rev:** Outline map of State of Victoria **Edge:** Reeded

| Date | Mintage | VF20 | XF40 | MS60 | MS63 | MS65 |
|---|---|---|---|---|---|---|
| 2006 | 12,500 | PF65 85.00 | | | | |

### KM# 860 5 DOLLARS

36.31 g., 0.999 Silver 1.1662 oz. ASW, 38.74 mm. **Ruler:** Elizabeth II **Subject:** Masterpieces in Silver: Australia's Artists **Obv:** Ian Rank-Broadley **Rev:** Jeffrey Smart: Keswick Siding

| Date | Mintage | VF20 | XF40 | MS60 | MS63 | MS65 |
|---|---|---|---|---|---|---|
| 2006 | 10,000 | PF63 55.00 | PF65 60.00 | | | |

### KM# 950 5 DOLLARS

1.24 g., 0.999 Gold 0.040 oz. AGW **Ruler:** Elizabeth II **Subject:** Australian Fauna **Obv:** Head with tiara right **Rev:** Salt water crocodile

| Date | Mintage | VF20 | XF40 | MS60 | MS63 | MS65 |
|---|---|---|---|---|---|---|
| 2006 | 4,812 | PF65 100 | | | | |

### KM# 953 5 DOLLARS

1.24 g., 0.999 Gold 0.040 oz. AGW **Ruler:** Elizabeth II **Subject:** Australian Fauna **Obv:** Head with tiara right **Rev:** Grey kangaroo

| Date | Mintage | VF20 | XF40 | MS60 | MS63 | MS65 |
|---|---|---|---|---|---|---|
| 2006 | 2,096 | PF65 100 | | | | |

### KM# 956 5 DOLLARS

1.24 g., 0.999 Gold 0.040 oz. AGW **Ruler:** Elizabeth II **Subject:** Australian Fauna **Obv:** Head with tiara right **Rev:** Emu

| Date | Mintage | VF20 | XF40 | MS60 | MS63 | MS65 |
|---|---|---|---|---|---|---|
| 2006 | 1,655 | PF65 85.00 | | | | |

### KM# 959 5 DOLLARS

1.24 g., 0.999 Gold 0.040 oz. AGW **Ruler:** Elizabeth II **Subject:** Australian Fauna **Obv:** Head with tiara right **Rev:** Koala

| Date | Mintage | VF20 | XF40 | MS60 | MS63 | MS65 |
|---|---|---|---|---|---|---|
| 2006 | 2,519 | PF65 100 | | | | |

### KM# 962 5 DOLLARS

1.24 g., 0.999 Gold 0.040 oz. AGW **Ruler:** Elizabeth II **Subject:** Australian Fauna **Obv:** Head with tiara right **Rev:** Kookaburra

| Date | Mintage | VF20 | XF40 | MS60 | MS63 | MS65 |
|---|---|---|---|---|---|---|
| 2006 | 1,697 | PF65 100 | | | | |

### KM# 1014 5 DOLLARS

1.24 g., 0.9999 Gold 0.040 oz. AGW, 19 mm. **Ruler:** Elizabeth II **Obv:** Bust with tiara right **Obv. Legend:** ELIZABETH II - AUSTRALIA **Rev:** Sydney Opera House

| Date | Mintage | VF20 | XF40 | MS60 | MS63 | MS65 |
|---|---|---|---|---|---|---|
| 2006 P | 100,000 | PF65 75.00 | | | | |

## KM# 861 5 DOLLARS

36.31 g., 0.999 Silver 1.1662 oz. ASW, 38.74 mm. **Ruler:** Elizabeth II **Subject:** Masterpieces in Silver: Australia's Artists **Obv:** Head with tiara right **Rev:** Grace Cossington-Smith: Curve of the Bridge

| Date | Mintage | VF20 | XF40 | MS60 | MS63 | MS65 |
|---|---|---|---|---|---|---|
| 2007 | 10,000 | **PF63** 50.00 | **PF65** 55.00 | | | |

## KM# 862 5 DOLLARS

36.31 g., 0.999 Silver 1.1662 oz. ASW, 38.74 mm. **Ruler:** Elizabeth II **Subject:** Masterpieces in Silver: Australia's Artists **Obv:** Head with tiara right **Rev:** Clifford Possum Tjpaltjarri: Yuelamu Honey Ant Dreaming

| Date | Mintage | VF20 | XF40 | MS60 | MS63 | MS65 |
|---|---|---|---|---|---|---|
| 2007 | 10,000 | **PF63** 50.00 | **PF65** 55.00 | | | |

## KM# 863 5 DOLLARS

36.31 g., 0.999 Silver 1.1662 oz. ASW, 38.74 mm. **Ruler:** Elizabeth II **Subject:** Masterpieces in Silver: Australia's Artists **Obv:** Head with tiara right **Rev:** William Dobell: Margaret Olley

| Date | Mintage | VF20 | XF40 | MS60 | MS63 | MS65 |
|---|---|---|---|---|---|---|
| 2007 | 10,000 | **PF63** 50.00 | **PF65** 55.00 | | | |

## KM# 864 5 DOLLARS

36.31 g., 0.999 Silver 1.1662 oz. ASW, 38.74 mm. **Ruler:** Elizabeth II **Subject:** Masterpieces in Silver: Australia's Artists **Obv:** Ian Rank-Broadley **Rev:** Margaret Preston: Implement Blue

| Date | Mintage | VF20 | XF40 | MS60 | MS63 | MS65 |
|---|---|---|---|---|---|---|
| 2007 | 10,000 | **PF63** 50.00 | **PF65** 55.00 | | | |

## KM# 865 5 DOLLARS

36.31 g., 0.999 Silver 1.1662 oz. ASW, 38.74 mm. **Ruler:** Elizabeth II **Subject:** Ashes Cricket Series 1882-2007 **Obv:** Head with tiara right **Rev:** Urn with supporters **Edge:** Reeded

| Date | Mintage | VF20 | XF40 | MS60 | MS63 | MS65 |
|---|---|---|---|---|---|---|
| 2007 | 12,500 | **PF63** 45.00 | **PF65** 50.00 | | | |

## KM# 965 5 DOLLARS

1.24 g., 0.999 Gold 0.040 oz. AGW **Ruler:** Elizabeth II **Subject:** Australian Fauna **Obv:** Head with tiara right **Rev:** Echidna

| Date | Mintage | VF20 | XF40 | MS60 | MS63 | MS65 |
|---|---|---|---|---|---|---|
| 2007 | 1,269 | **PF65** 100 | | | | |

## KM# 968 5 DOLLARS

1.24 g., 0.999 Gold 0.040 oz. AGW **Ruler:** Elizabeth II **Subject:** Australian Fauna **Obv:** Head with tiara right **Rev:** Common wombat

| Date | Mintage | VF20 | XF40 | MS60 | MS63 | MS65 |
|---|---|---|---|---|---|---|
| 2007 | 1,242 | **PF65** 100 | | | | |

## KM# 971 5 DOLLARS

1.24 g., 0.999 Gold 0.040 oz. AGW **Ruler:** Elizabeth II **Subject:** Australian Fauna **Obv:** Head with tiara right **Rev:** Tasmanian devil

| Date | Mintage | VF20 | XF40 | MS60 | MS63 | MS65 |
|---|---|---|---|---|---|---|
| 2007 | 1,274 | **PF65** 95.00 | | | | |

## KM# 974 5 DOLLARS

1.24 g., 0.999 Gold 0.040 oz. AGW **Ruler:** Elizabeth II **Subject:** Australian Fauna **Obv:** Head with tiara right **Rev:** Great white shark

| Date | Mintage | VF20 | XF40 | MS60 | MS63 | MS65 |
|---|---|---|---|---|---|---|
| 2007 | 1,656 | **PF65** 100 | | | | |

## KM# 977 5 DOLLARS

1.24 g., 0.999 Gold 0.040 oz. AGW **Ruler:** Elizabeth II **Subject:** Australian Fauna **Obv:** Head with tiara right **Rev:** Platypus

| Date | Mintage | VF20 | XF40 | MS60 | MS63 | MS65 |
|---|---|---|---|---|---|---|
| 2007 | 1,188 | **PF65** 100 | | | | |

## KM# 1013 5 DOLLARS

36.31 g., 0.999 Silver 1.1662 oz. ASW, 38.74 mm. **Ruler:** Elizabeth II **Subject:** Sydney Harbour Bridge, 75th Anniversary **Obv:** Bust with tiara right **Obv. Legend:** ELIZABETH II - AUSTRALIA **Rev:** Bridge **Rev. Inscription:** SYDNEY / HARBOUR / BRIDGE

| Date | Mintage | VF20 | XF40 | MS60 | MS63 | MS65 |
|---|---|---|---|---|---|---|
| 2007 | 12,500 | **PF65** 50.00 | | | | |

## KM# 1045 5 DOLLARS

36.31 g., 0.999 Silver 1.1662 oz. ASW, 38.74 mm. **Ruler:** Elizabeth II **Subject:** Year of the surfer lifesaver **Rev:** Rowboat in rough seas

| Date | Mintage | VF20 | XF40 | MS60 | MS63 | MS65 |
|---|---|---|---|---|---|---|
| 2007 B | 12,500 | **PF65** 65.00 | | | | |

## KM# 1046 5 DOLLARS

36.31 g., 0.999 Silver 1.1662 oz. ASW, 38.74 mm. **Ruler:** Elizabeth II **Subject:** South Australia State Government **Rev:** Australia map and state enlarged

| Date | Mintage | VF20 | XF40 | MS60 | MS63 | MS65 |
|---|---|---|---|---|---|---|
| 2007 B | 12,500 | **PF65** 65.00 | | | | |

## KM# 1117 5 DOLLARS

1.24 g., 0.999 Gold 0.0398 oz. AGW, 14 mm. **Ruler:** Elizabeth II **Subject:** Sydney Harbor Bridge **Obv:** Head right **Rev:** Bridge view

| Date | Mintage | VF20 | XF40 | MS60 | MS63 | MS65 |
|---|---|---|---|---|---|---|
| 2007 P | 100,000 | **PF63** 100 | **PF65** 110 | | | |

## KM# 1050 5 DOLLARS

31.11 g., 0.999 Silver 0.999 oz. ASW, 38.74 mm. **Ruler:** Elizabeth II **Subject:** Scouting Centennial in Australia **Rev:** Scout sign and map

| Date | Mintage | VF20 | XF40 | MS60 | MS63 | MS65 |
|---|---|---|---|---|---|---|
| 2008 | 5,000 | **PF65** 65.00 | | | | |

### KM# 1053 5 DOLLARS

36.31 g., 0.999 Silver 1.1662 oz. ASW, 38.74 mm. **Ruler:** Elizabeth II **Subject:** Rugby League **Rev:** Two players

| Date | Mintage | VF20 | XF40 | MS60 | MS63 | MS65 |
|---|---|---|---|---|---|---|
| 2008 | 10,000 | PF65 65.00 | | | | |

### KM# 1055 5 DOLLARS

31.11 g., 0.999 Silver 0.999 oz. ASW, 38.74 mm. **Ruler:** Elizabeth II **Rev:** Antarctic skua in flight over map

| Date | Mintage | VF20 | XF40 | MS60 | MS63 | MS65 |
|---|---|---|---|---|---|---|
| 2008 | 12,500 | PF65 65.00 | | | | |

### KM# 1065 5 DOLLARS

36.31 g., 0.999 Silver 1.1662 oz. ASW, 38.74 mm. **Ruler:** Elizabeth II **Subject:** 30th Anniversary - Northern Territorial Government **Rev:** Territory map and Australia map

| Date | Mintage | VF20 | XF40 | MS60 | MS63 | MS65 |
|---|---|---|---|---|---|---|
| 2008 | 12,500 | PF65 65.00 | | | | |

### KM# 1066 5 DOLLARS

1.15 g., 0.999 Gold 0.0369 oz. AGW, 14 mm. **Ruler:** Elizabeth II **Rev:** Kisp Koala

| Date | Mintage | VF20 | XF40 | MS60 | MS63 | MS65 |
|---|---|---|---|---|---|---|
| 2008 | 10,000 | PF63 100 | PF65 110 | | | |

### KM# 1067 5 DOLLARS

1.15 g., 0.999 Gold 0.0369 oz. AGW, 14 mm. **Ruler:** Elizabeth II **Rev:** Binny Bilby

| Date | Mintage | VF20 | XF40 | MS60 | MS63 | MS65 |
|---|---|---|---|---|---|---|
| 2008 | 10,000 | PF63 100 | PF65 110 | | | |

### KM# 1072 5 DOLLARS

36.31 g., 0.999 Silver 1.1662 oz. ASW, 38.74 mm. **Ruler:** Elizabeth II **Rev:** Avro 504K airplane

| Date | Mintage | VF20 | XF40 | MS60 | MS63 | MS65 |
|---|---|---|---|---|---|---|
| 2008 | 10,000 | PF63 60.00 | PF65 65.00 | | | |

### KM# 1073 5 DOLLARS

36.31 g., 0.999 Silver 1.1662 oz. ASW, 38.74 mm. **Ruler:** Elizabeth II **Rev:** Airbus A380 airplane

| Date | Mintage | VF20 | XF40 | MS60 | MS63 | MS65 |
|---|---|---|---|---|---|---|
| 2008 | 10,000 | PF63 60.00 | PF65 65.00 | | | |

### KM# 1084 5 DOLLARS

Aluminum-Bronze, 38.74 mm. **Ruler:** Elizabeth II **Subject:** Sir Donald Bradman 100th Anniversary of Birth **Rev:** Player with cricket bat

| Date | Mintage | VF20 | XF40 | MS60 | MS63 | MS65 |
|---|---|---|---|---|---|---|
| 2008 | — | — | — | — | — | 10.00 |

### KM# 1080 5 DOLLARS

36.31 g., 0.999 Silver 1.1662 oz. ASW, 38.74 mm. **Ruler:** Elizabeth II **Rev:** Three arctic explorers on map

| Date | Mintage | VF20 | XF40 | MS60 | MS63 | MS65 |
|---|---|---|---|---|---|---|
| 2009 | 12,500 | PF65 65.00 | | | | |

### KM# 1081 5 DOLLARS

36.31 g., 0.999 Silver 1.1662 oz. ASW, 38.74 mm. **Ruler:** Elizabeth II **Subject:** Aurora Australis **Obv:** Head right **Rev:** Sailing ship in Antartic ice in hologram

| Date | Mintage | VF20 | XF40 | MS60 | MS63 | MS65 |
|---|---|---|---|---|---|---|
| 2009 | 12,500 | PF63 55.00 | PF65 60.00 | | | |

### KM# 1085 5 DOLLARS

1.20 g., 0.999 Gold 0.0385 oz. AGW, 14 mm. **Ruler:** Elizabeth II **Obv:** Head right **Rev:** Lilly Pilly full-neck lizard

| Date | Mintage | VF20 | XF40 | MS60 | MS63 | MS65 |
|---|---|---|---|---|---|---|
| 2009 | 10,000 | PF63 70.00 | PF65 75.00 | | | |

### KM# 1086 5 DOLLARS

1.20 g., 0.999 Gold 0.0385 oz. AGW, 14 mm. **Ruler:** Elizabeth II **Obv:** Head right **Rev:** Petey Platypus

| Date | Mintage | VF20 | XF40 | MS60 | MS63 | MS65 |
|---|---|---|---|---|---|---|
| 2009 | 10,000 | PF63 70.00 | PF65 75.00 | | | |

### KM# 1217 5 DOLLARS

1.25 g., 0.999 Gold 0.0401 oz. AGW, 14 mm. **Ruler:** Elizabeth II **Obv:** Head right **Rev:** Dreaming kangaroo

| Date | Mintage | VF20 | XF40 | MS60 | MS63 | MS65 |
|---|---|---|---|---|---|---|
| 2009 P | 25,000 | PF63 115 | PF65 125 | | | |

### KM# 1218 5 DOLLARS

1.25 g., 0.999 Gold 0.0401 oz. AGW, 14 mm. **Ruler:** Elizabeth II **Obv:** Head right **Rev:** Dreaming dolphin

| Date | Mintage | VF20 | XF40 | MS60 | MS63 | MS65 |
|---|---|---|---|---|---|---|
| 2009 P | 25,000 | PF63 115 | PF65 125 | | | |

### KM# 1219 5 DOLLARS

1.25 g., 0.999 Gold 0.0401 oz. AGW, 14 mm. **Ruler:** Elizabeth II **Obv:** Head right **Rev:** Dreaming king brown snake

| Date | Mintage | VF20 | XF40 | MS60 | MS63 | MS65 |
|---|---|---|---|---|---|---|
| 2009 P | 25,000 | PF63 115 | PF65 125 | | | |

### KM# 1220 5 DOLLARS

1.25 g., 0.999 Gold 0.0401 oz. AGW, 14 mm. **Ruler:** Elizabeth II **Obv:** Head right **Rev:** Dreaming brolga

| Date | Mintage | VF20 | XF40 | MS60 | MS63 | MS65 |
|---|---|---|---|---|---|---|
| 2009 P | 25,000 | PF63 115 | PF65 125 | | | |

### KM# 1221 5 DOLLARS

1.25 g., 0.999 Gold 0.0401 oz. AGW, 14 mm. **Ruler:** Elizabeth II **Obv:** Head right **Rev:** Dreaming echidna

| Date | Mintage | VF20 | XF40 | MS60 | MS63 | MS65 |
|---|---|---|---|---|---|---|
| 2009 P | 25,000 | PF63 115 | PF65 125 | | | |

### KM# 1224 5 DOLLARS

3.11 g., 0.999 Gold 0.0999 oz. AGW, 14 mm. **Ruler:** Elizabeth II **Obv:** Head right **Rev:** Dreaming brown snake

| Date | Mintage | VF20 | XF40 | MS60 | MS63 | MS65 |
|---|---|---|---|---|---|---|
| 2009 P | 2,500 | PF65 175 | | | | |

### KM# 1658 5 DOLLARS

36.31 g., 0.999 Silver 1.1662 oz. ASW, 38.74 mm. **Ruler:** Elizabeth II **Subject:** Queensland Government **Rev:** Map of Australian states, Queensland highlighted

| Date | Mintage | VF20 | XF40 | MS60 | MS63 | MS65 |
|---|---|---|---|---|---|---|
| 2009 | — | PF65 85.00 | | | | |

### KM# 1402 5 DOLLARS

1.24 g., 0.999 Gold 0.0398 oz. AGW, 14 mm. **Ruler:** Elizabeth II **Obv:** Head right **Rev:** Frill-neck lizard

| Date | Mintage | VF20 | XF40 | MS60 | MS63 | MS65 |
|---|---|---|---|---|---|---|
| 2010 P | 25,000 | PF63 120 | PF65 130 | | | |

**KM# 1408 5 DOLLARS**
1.24 g., 0.999 Gold 0.0398 oz. AGW, 14 mm. **Ruler:** Elizabeth II **Obv:** Head right **Rev:** Koala

| Date | Mintage | VF20 | XF40 | MS60 | MS63 | MS65 |
|---|---|---|---|---|---|---|
| 2010 P | 25,000 | PF63 120 | PF65 130 | | | |

**KM# 1414 5 DOLLARS**
1.24 g., 0.999 Gold 0.0398 oz. AGW, 14 mm. **Ruler:** Elizabeth II **Obv:** Head right **Rev:** Platypus

| Date | Mintage | VF20 | XF40 | MS60 | MS63 | MS65 |
|---|---|---|---|---|---|---|
| 2010 P | 25,000 | PF63 120 | PF65 130 | | | |

**KM# 1420 5 DOLLARS**
1.24 g., 0.999 Gold 0.0398 oz. AGW, 14 mm. **Ruler:** Elizabeth II **Obv:** Head right **Rev:** Salt water crocodile

| Date | Mintage | VF20 | XF40 | MS60 | MS63 | MS65 |
|---|---|---|---|---|---|---|
| 2010 P | 25,000 | PF63 120 | PF65 130 | | | |

**KM# 1426 5 DOLLARS**
1.24 g., 0.999 Gold 0.0398 oz. AGW, 14 mm. **Ruler:** Elizabeth II **Obv:** Head right **Rev:** Wombat

| Date | Mintage | VF20 | XF40 | MS60 | MS63 | MS65 |
|---|---|---|---|---|---|---|
| 2010 P | 25,000 | PF63 120 | PF65 130 | | | |

**KM# 1509 5 DOLLARS**
36.31 g., 0.999 Silver 1.1662 oz. ASW, 38.74 mm. **Ruler:** Elizabeth II **Subject:** Aviation - Constellation L749

| Date | Mintage | VF20 | XF40 | MS60 | MS63 | MS65 |
|---|---|---|---|---|---|---|
| 2010 | — | PF63 60.00 | PF65 65.00 | | | |

**KM# 1510 5 DOLLARS**
36.31 g., 0.999 Silver 1.1662 oz. ASW, 37.84 mm. **Ruler:** Elizabeth II **Subject:** Aviation - De Havilland DH 86

| Date | Mintage | VF20 | XF40 | MS60 | MS63 | MS65 |
|---|---|---|---|---|---|---|
| 2010 | — | PF63 60.00 | PF65 65.00 | | | |

**KM# 1511 5 DOLLARS**
36.31 g., 0.999 Silver 1.1662 oz. ASW, 38.74 mm. **Ruler:** Elizabeth II **Subject:** Aviation - S.25 Sandringham

| Date | Mintage | VF20 | XF40 | MS60 | MS63 | MS65 |
|---|---|---|---|---|---|---|
| 2010 | — | PF63 60.00 | PF65 65.00 | | | |

**KM# 1512 5 DOLLARS**
36.31 g., 0.999 Silver 1.1662 oz. ASW, 38.74 mm. **Ruler:** Elizabeth II **Subject:** Aviation - Boeing 747

| Date | Mintage | VF20 | XF40 | MS60 | MS63 | MS65 |
|---|---|---|---|---|---|---|
| 2010 | — | PF63 60.00 | PF65 65.00 | | | |

**KM# 1535 5 DOLLARS**
1.24 g., 0.999 Gold 0.0398 oz. AGW **Ruler:** Elizabeth II **Subject:** Dreaming Emu **Rev:** Linear emu in color

| Date | Mintage | VF20 | XF40 | MS60 | MS63 | MS65 |
|---|---|---|---|---|---|---|
| 2011 P | 25,000 | PF63 115 | PF65 125 | | | |

**KM# 1541 5 DOLLARS**
1.24 g., 0.999 Gold 0.0398 oz. AGW **Ruler:** Elizabeth II **Subject:** Dreaming Tasmanian Devil **Rev:** Linear tasmanian devil in color

| Date | Mintage | VF20 | XF40 | MS60 | MS63 | MS65 |
|---|---|---|---|---|---|---|
| 2011 P | 25,000 | PF63 115 | PF65 125 | | | |

**KM# 1547 5 DOLLARS**
1.24 g., 0.999 Gold 0.0398 oz. AGW **Ruler:** Elizabeth II **Obv:** Dreaming Kookaburra **Edge:** Linear Kookaburra in color

| Date | Mintage | VF20 | XF40 | MS60 | MS63 | MS65 |
|---|---|---|---|---|---|---|
| 2011 P | 250,000 | PF63 115 | PF65 125 | | | |

**KM# 1553 5 DOLLARS**
1.24 g., 0.999 Gold 0.0398 oz. AGW **Ruler:** Elizabeth II **Subject:** Dreaming shark **Rev:** Linear shark in color

| Date | Mintage | VF20 | XF40 | MS60 | MS63 | MS65 |
|---|---|---|---|---|---|---|
| 2011 P | 25,000 | PF63 115 | PF65 125 | | | |

**KM# 1559 5 DOLLARS**
1.24 g., 0.999 Gold 0.0398 oz. AGW **Ruler:** Elizabeth II **Subject:** Dreaming Dingo **Rev:** Linear dingo in color

| Date | Mintage | VF20 | XF40 | MS60 | MS63 | MS65 |
|---|---|---|---|---|---|---|
| 2011 P | 25,000 | PF63 115 | PF65 125 | | | |

**KM# 1633 5 DOLLARS**
20.00 g., Aluminum-Bronze, 38.74 mm. **Ruler:** Elizabeth II **Subject:** Royal Visit **Obv:** Head with tiara right **Rev:** Sixteen crowns

| Date | Mintage | VF20 | XF40 | MS60 | MS63 | MS65 |
|---|---|---|---|---|---|---|
| 2011 | — | — | — | — | — | 15.00 |

**KM# 1636 5 DOLLARS**
1.24 g., 0.999 Gold 0.0398 oz. AGW, 14 mm. **Ruler:** Elizabeth II **Subject:** Historic Convict Past - Hyde Park Barracks

| Date | Mintage | VF20 | XF40 | MS60 | MS63 | MS65 |
|---|---|---|---|---|---|---|
| 2011 | 3,000 | PF63 115 | PF65 125 | | | |

**KM# 1637 5 DOLLARS**
1.24 g., 0.999 Gold 0.0398 oz. AGW, 14 mm. **Ruler:** Elizabeth II **Subject:** Historic Convict Past - Port Arthur Historic Site

| Date | Mintage | VF20 | XF40 | MS60 | MS63 | MS65 |
|---|---|---|---|---|---|---|
| 2011 | 3,000 | PF63 115 | PF65 125 | | | |

**KM# 1638 5 DOLLARS**
1.24 g., 0.999 Gold 0.0398 oz. AGW, 14 mm. **Ruler:** Elizabeth II **Subject:** Historic Convict Past - Cascades Female Factory

| Date | Mintage | VF20 | XF40 | MS60 | MS63 | MS65 |
|---|---|---|---|---|---|---|
| 2011 | 3,000 | PF63 115 | PF65 125 | | | |

**KM# 1639 5 DOLLARS**
1.24 g., 0.999 Gold 0.0398 oz. AGW, 14 mm. **Ruler:** Elizabeth II **Subject:** Historic Convict Past - Fremantle Prison

| Date | Mintage | VF20 | XF40 | MS60 | MS63 | MS65 |
|---|---|---|---|---|---|---|
| 2011 | 3,000 | PF63 115 | PF65 125 | | | |

**KM# 1640 5 DOLLARS**
1.24 g., 0.999 Gold 0.0398 oz. AGW, 14 mm. **Ruler:** Elizabeth II **Subject:** Historic Convict Past - Coal Mines Historic Site

| Date | Mintage | VF20 | XF40 | MS60 | MS63 | MS65 |
|---|---|---|---|---|---|---|
| 2011 | 3,000 | PF63 115 | PF65 125 | | | |

**KM# 1641 5 DOLLARS**
1.24 g., 0.999 Gold 0.0398 oz. AGW, 14 mm. **Ruler:** Elizabeth II **Subject:** Historic Convict Past - Old Government House and Domain

| Date | Mintage | VF20 | XF40 | MS60 | MS63 | MS65 |
|---|---|---|---|---|---|---|
| 2011 | 3,000 | PF63 115 | PF65 125 | | | |

**KM# 1652 5 DOLLARS**
20.00 g., Aluminum-Bronze, 38.74 mm. **Ruler:** Elizabeth II **Subject:** Remembrance Day, 11.11.11 **Obv:** Head with tiara right **Rev:** Poppy in multicolor

| Date | Mintage | VF20 | XF40 | MS60 | MS63 | MS65 |
|---|---|---|---|---|---|---|
| 2011 | — | — | — | — | — | 17.50 |

**KM# 1716 5 DOLLARS**
1.24 g., 0.999 Gold 0.040 oz. AGW, 14.6 mm. **Ruler:** Elizabeth II **Rev:** Green and Gold Bell Frog in greass

| Date | Mintage | VF20 | XF40 | MS60 | MS63 | MS65 |
|---|---|---|---|---|---|---|
| 2012 P | 2,500 | PF63 100 | PF65 115 | | | |

**KM# 1717 5 DOLLARS**
1.24 g., 0.999 Gold 0.040 oz. AGW, 14.6 mm. **Ruler:** Elizabeth II **Rev:** Kookaburra facing right

| Date | Mintage | VF20 | XF40 | MS60 | MS63 | MS65 |
|---|---|---|---|---|---|---|
| 2012 P | 2,500 | PF63 100 | PF65 115 | | | |

**KM# 1718 5 DOLLARS**
1.24 g., 0.999 Gold 0.040 oz. AGW, 14.1 mm. **Ruler:** Elizabeth II **Rev:** Whale shark swimming right

| Date | Mintage | VF20 | XF40 | MS60 | MS63 | MS65 |
|---|---|---|---|---|---|---|
| 2012 P | 2,500 | PF63 100 | PF65 115 | | | |

**KM# 1719 5 DOLLARS**
1.24 g., 0.999 Gold 0.040 oz. AGW, 14.6 mm. **Ruler:** Elizabeth II **Rev:** Kangaroo bounding right

| Date | Mintage | VF20 | XF40 | MS60 | MS63 | MS65 |
|---|---|---|---|---|---|---|
| 2012 P | 2,500 | PF63 100 | PF65 115 | | | |

**KM# 1720 5 DOLLARS**
1.24 g., 0.999 Gold 0.040 oz. AGW, 14.6 mm. **Ruler:** Elizabeth II **Rev:** Goanna lizard right

| Date | Mintage | VF20 | XF40 | MS60 | MS63 | MS65 |
|---|---|---|---|---|---|---|
| 2012 P | 2,500 | PF63 100 | PF65 115 | | | |

**KM# 1739 5 DOLLARS**
20.00 g., Aluminum-Bronze, 38.74 mm. **Ruler:** Elizabeth II **Subject:** Australian Open **Obv:** Small Queen's head above tennis ball **Rev:** Player serving

| Date | Mintage | VF20 | XF40 | MS60 | MS63 | MS65 |
|---|---|---|---|---|---|---|
| 2012 | — | — | — | — | — | 20.00 |

**KM# 1747 5 DOLLARS**
20.00 g., Aluminum-Bronze, 38.74 mm. **Ruler:** Elizabeth II **Obv:** Gead with tiara right **Rev:** Perth Town Hall

| Date | Mintage | VF20 | XF40 | MS60 | MS63 | MS65 |
|---|---|---|---|---|---|---|
| 2012 Antique patina | — | — | — | — | 20.00 | — |

**KM# 1853 5 DOLLARS**
36.31 g., 0.999 Silver 1.1662 oz. ASW, 38.74 mm. **Ruler:** Elizabeth II **Rev:** Southen Cross in blue sky **Note:** Concave planchet

| Date | Mintage | VF20 | XF40 | MS60 | MS63 | MS65 |
|---|---|---|---|---|---|---|
| 2012 P | — | PF65 125 | | | | |

**KM# 1965 5 DOLLARS**
0.999 Silver **Ruler:** Elizabeth II **Subject:** 25th Anniversary of Australian Parliament House **Shape:** Triangle

| Date | Mintage | VF20 | XF40 | MS60 | MS63 | MS65 |
|---|---|---|---|---|---|---|
| 2013 | Est. 10000 | PF65 125 | | | | |

**KM# 1969 5 DOLLARS**
31.10 g., 0.999 Silver 0.9989 oz. ASW, 39.62 mm. **Ruler:** Elizabeth II **Subject:** Southern Sky - Pavo **Rev:** Constellation in color **Note:** Concave

| Date | Mintage | VF20 | XF40 | MS60 | MS63 | MS65 |
|---|---|---|---|---|---|---|
| 2013 | Est. 10000 | PF65 125 | | | | |

**KM# 2154 5 DOLLARS**
36.31 g., 0.999 Silver 1.1662 oz. ASW, 38.74 mm. **Ruler:** Elizabeth II **Subject:** Canberra, 100th Anniversary **Obv:** Head with tiara right **Rev:** Canberra views, old and new

| Date | Mintage | VF20 | XF40 | MS60 | MS63 | MS65 |
|---|---|---|---|---|---|---|
| 2013 | — | PF63 70.00 | PF65 75.00 | | | |

**KM# 1269 8 DOLLARS**
5.00 g., 0.999 Gold 0.1606 oz. AGW, 14x23 mm. **Ruler:** Elizabeth II **Subject:** Chinese Mythological Character **Obv:** Head right **Rev:** Man standing, multicolor **Shape:** Vertical rectangle

| Date | Mintage | VF20 | XF40 | MS60 | MS63 | MS65 |
|---|---|---|---|---|---|---|
| 2008 P | 1,168 | — | — | — | — | 435 |

**KM# 1270 8 DOLLARS**
5.00 g., 0.999 Gold 0.1606 oz. AGW, 14x23 mm. **Ruler:** Elizabeth II **Subject:** Chinese Mythological Character - Longevity **Obv:** Head right **Rev:** Nam standing with staff, multicolor **Shape:** Vertical rectangle

| Date | Mintage | VF20 | XF40 | MS60 | MS63 | MS65 |
|---|---|---|---|---|---|---|
| 2008 P | 1,187 | — | — | — | — | 435 |

**KM# 1271 8 DOLLARS**
5.00 g., 0.999 Gold 0.1606 oz. AGW, 14x23 mm. **Ruler:** Elizabeth II **Subject:** Chinese Mythological Character - Success **Obv:** Hand right **Rev:** Man standing with deer, multicolor **Shape:** Vertical rectangle

| Date | Mintage | VF20 | XF40 | MS60 | MS63 | MS65 |
|---|---|---|---|---|---|---|
| 2008 P | 1,181 | — | — | — | — | 435 |

**KM# 1272 8 DOLLARS**
5.00 g., 0.999 Gold 0.1606 oz. AGW, 14x23 mm. **Ruler:** Elizabeth II **Subject:** Mythological Chinese Character - Fortune **Obv:** Head right **Rev:** Man standing with scroll, multicolor **Shape:** Vertical rectangle

| Date | Mintage | VF20 | XF40 | MS60 | MS63 | MS65 |
|---|---|---|---|---|---|---|
| 2008 P | 1,181 | — | — | — | — | 435 |

**KM# 2066 8 DOLLARS**
155.67 g., 0.999 Silver 4.9999 oz. ASW, 60.6 mm. **Ruler:** Elizabeth II **Subject:** A.B. Banjo Paterson, 150th Anniversary of Birth **Obv:** Head with tiara right **Rev:** Paterson in color

| Date | Mintage | VF20 | XF40 | MS60 | MS63 | MS65 |
|---|---|---|---|---|---|---|
| 2013 P | 250 | PF65 600 | | | | |

**KM# 593 10 DOLLARS**
33.15 g., Bi-Metallic Gold plated .999 Silver center in Copper ring, 38.74 mm. **Ruler:** Elizabeth II **Subject:** The Future **Obv:** Queen's portrait **Rev:** Tree, map and denomination **Edge:** Reeded

| Date | Mintage | VF20 | XF40 | MS60 | MS63 | MS65 |
|---|---|---|---|---|---|---|
| 2001 B | — | PF65 55.00 | | | | |

**KM# 596 10 DOLLARS**
311.04 g., 0.999 Silver 9.990 oz. ASW, 75.5 mm. **Ruler:** Elizabeth II **Subject:** Calendar Evolution **Obv:** Head with tiara right, denomination below **Rev:** Multicolor solar system in center, zodiac symbols in outer circle **Edge:** Segmented reeding **Note:** Illustration reduced.

| Date | Mintage | VF20 | XF40 | MS60 | MS63 | MS65 |
|---|---|---|---|---|---|---|
| ND(2001) | 1,802 | PF65 375 | | | | |

**KM# 633 10 DOLLARS**
311.04 g., 0.999 Silver 9.990 oz. ASW, 75.5 mm. **Ruler:** Elizabeth II **Subject:** Evolution of Time **Obv:** Queen's portrait right **Rev:** Various time keeping devices **Edge:** Segmented reeding

| Date | Mintage | VF20 | XF40 | MS60 | MS63 | MS65 |
|---|---|---|---|---|---|---|
| 2002 P | 1,533 | PF65 425 | | | | |

**KM# 661 10 DOLLARS**
60.50 g., 0.999 Silver 1.9432 oz. ASW, 50 mm. **Ruler:** Elizabeth II **Subject:** The Adelaide Pound **Obv:** Queen's portrait above gold-plated coin design **Rev:** Legend around gold-plated coin design **Edge:** Reeded

| Date | Mintage | VF20 | XF40 | MS60 | MS63 | MS65 |
|---|---|---|---|---|---|---|
| 2002 B | 10,000 | PF65 95.00 | | | | |

**KM# 686 10 DOLLARS**
311.00 g., 0.999 Silver 9.9889 oz. ASW, 75.5 mm. **Ruler:** Elizabeth II **Obv:** Queen's head right **Rev:** Alphabet evolution design **Edge:** Reeded

| Date | Mintage | VF20 | XF40 | MS60 | MS63 | MS65 |
|---|---|---|---|---|---|---|
| 2003 P | 1,041 | PF65 425 | | | | |

**KM# 751 10 DOLLARS**
60.50 g., 0.999 Silver 1.9432 oz. ASW Partially gilt, 50 mm. **Ruler:** Elizabeth II **Subject:** 150th Anniversary - Sydney Mint **Obv:** Head with tiara right above gilt 1853 Sovereign Pattern of Queen Victoria facing left **Rev:** Gilt reverse of Sovereign Pattern **Edge:** Reeded

| Date | Mintage | VF20 | XF40 | MS60 | MS63 | MS65 |
|---|---|---|---|---|---|---|
| 2003 B | 10,000 | PF65 100 | | | | |
| ND(2005) B | 10,000 | PF65 80.00 | | | | |

**KM# 766 10 DOLLARS**
36.31 g., 0.999 Silver 1.1662 oz. ASW, 38.7 mm. **Ruler:** Elizabeth II **Series:** Masterpieces in Silver - Port Phillip Patterns **Obv:** Queen's head right **Rev:** Kangaroo design **Edge:** Reeded

| Date | Mintage | VF20 | XF40 | MS60 | MS63 | MS65 |
|---|---|---|---|---|---|---|
| 2003 B | 10,000 | PF65 90.00 | | | | |

**KM# 1439 10 DOLLARS**
Silver partially gilt **Ruler:** Elizabeth II **Subject:** Sydney Mint, 100th Anniversary

| Date | Mintage | VF20 | XF40 | MS60 | MS63 | MS65 |
|---|---|---|---|---|---|---|
| 2003 | 10,000 | PF63 75.00 PF65 85.00 | | | | |

**KM# 739 10 DOLLARS**
311.04 g., 0.999 Silver 9.990 oz. ASW, 75.5 mm. **Ruler:** Elizabeth II **Subject:** Evolution of Numbers **Obv:** Queen's head right **Rev:** Numbers, symbols, abacus and calculator **Edge:** Reeded

| Date | Mintage | VF20 | XF40 | MS60 | MS63 | MS65 |
|---|---|---|---|---|---|---|
| 2004 | 1,051 | PF65 425 | | | | |

**KM# 744 10 DOLLARS**
311.35 g., 0.999 Silver 10.000 oz. ASW, 75.5 mm. **Ruler:** Elizabeth II **Obv:** Queen's head right **Rev:** Multicolor symbolic design **Edge:** Reeded

| Date | Mintage | VF20 | XF40 | MS60 | MS63 | MS65 |
|---|---|---|---|---|---|---|
| 2005 | 1,314 | PF65 425 | | | | |

**KM# 866 10 DOLLARS**
7.75 g., 0.999 Gold 0.2489 oz. AGW, 17.53 mm. **Ruler:** Elizabeth II **Subject:** 90th Anniversary Gallipoli Landings **Obv:** Head with tiara right **Rev:** Australian slouch hat on inverted rifle before memorial

| Date | Mintage | VF20 | XF40 | MS60 | MS63 | MS65 |
|---|---|---|---|---|---|---|
| 2005 | 1,000 | PF65 750 | | | | |

**KM# 869 10 DOLLARS**
7.78 g., 0.999 Gold 0.2498 oz. AGW, 17.53 mm. **Ruler:** Elizabeth II **Subject:** FIFA World Cup **Obv:** Head with tiara right **Rev:** Kangaroo and players on football

| Date | Mintage | VF20 | XF40 | MS60 | MS63 | MS65 |
|---|---|---|---|---|---|---|
| 2006 P | 25,000 | PF65 475 | | | | |

**KM# 1118 10 DOLLARS**
1.24 g., 0.999 Gold 0.0398 oz. AGW, 14 mm. **Ruler:** Elizabeth II **Obv:** Bust right **Rev:** Salt water crocodile **Rev. Legend:** DISCOVER AUSTRALIA

| Date | Mintage | VF20 | XF40 | MS60 | MS63 | MS65 |
|---|---|---|---|---|---|---|
| 2006 P | 25,000 | **PF63** 100 | **PF65** 110 | | | |

**KM# 1119 10 DOLLARS**
1.24 g., 0.999 Gold 0.0398 oz. AGW, 14 mm. **Ruler:** Elizabeth II **Obv:** Head right **Rev:** Grey kangaroo **Rev. Legend:** DISCOVER AUSTRALIA

| Date | Mintage | VF20 | XF40 | MS60 | MS63 | MS65 |
|---|---|---|---|---|---|---|
| 2006 P | 25,000 | **PF63** 100 | **PF65** 110 | | | |

**KM# 1120 10 DOLLARS**
1.24 g., 0.999 Gold 0.0398 oz. AGW, 14 mm. **Ruler:** Elizabeth II **Obv:** Head right **Rev:** Emu **Rev. Legend:** DISCOVER AUSTRALIA

| Date | Mintage | VF20 | XF40 | MS60 | MS63 | MS65 |
|---|---|---|---|---|---|---|
| 2006 P | 25,000 | **PF63** 100 | **PF65** 110 | | | |

**KM# 1121 10 DOLLARS**
1.24 g., 0.999 Gold 0.0398 oz. AGW, 14 mm. **Ruler:** Elizabeth II **Obv:** Head right **Rev:** Koala **Rev. Legend:** DISCOVER AUSTRALIA

| Date | Mintage | VF20 | XF40 | MS60 | MS63 | MS65 |
|---|---|---|---|---|---|---|
| 2006 P | 25,000 | **PF63** 100 | **PF65** 110 | | | |

**KM# 1122 10 DOLLARS**
1.24 g., 0.999 Gold 0.0398 oz. AGW, 14 mm. **Ruler:** Elizabeth II **Obv:** Head right **Rev:** Kookaburra **Rev. Legend:** DISCOVER AUSTRALIA

| Date | Mintage | VF20 | XF40 | MS60 | MS63 | MS65 |
|---|---|---|---|---|---|---|
| 2006 P | 25,000 | **PF63** 100 | **PF65** 110 | | | |

**KM# 1133 10 DOLLARS**
3.10 g., 0.999 Platinum 0.0996 oz. APW, 16 mm. **Ruler:** Elizabeth II **Obv:** Head right **Rev:** Cooktown orchid, multicolor **Rev. Legend:** DISCOVER AUSTRALIA

| Date | Mintage | VF20 | XF40 | MS60 | MS63 | MS65 |
|---|---|---|---|---|---|---|
| 2006 P | 2,500 | **PF65** 300 | | | | |

**KM# 1134 10 DOLLARS**
3.10 g., 0.999 Platinum 0.0996 oz. APW, 16 mm. **Ruler:** Elizabeth II **Obv:** Head right **Rev:** Sturt's desert rose, multicolor **Rev. Legend:** DISCOVER AUSTRALIA

| Date | Mintage | VF20 | XF40 | MS60 | MS63 | MS65 |
|---|---|---|---|---|---|---|
| 2006 P | 2,500 | **PF65** 300 | | | | |

**KM# 1135 10 DOLLARS**
3.10 g., 0.999 Platinum 0.0996 oz. APW, 16 mm. **Ruler:** Elizabeth II **Obv:** Head right **Rev:** Royal Bluebell, multicolor **Rev. Legend:** DISCOVER AUSTRALIA

| Date | Mintage | VF20 | XF40 | MS60 | MS63 | MS65 |
|---|---|---|---|---|---|---|
| 2006 P | 2,500 | **PF65** 300 | | | | |

**KM# 1136 10 DOLLARS**
3.10 g., 0.999 Platinum 0.0996 oz. APW, 16 mm. **Ruler:** Elizabeth II **Obv:** Head right **Rev:** Red and green kangaroo paw, multicolor **Rev. Legend:** DISCOVER AUSTRALIA

| Date | Mintage | VF20 | XF40 | MS60 | MS63 | MS65 |
|---|---|---|---|---|---|---|
| 2006 P | 2,500 | **PF65** 300 | | | | |

**KM# 1137 10 DOLLARS**
3.10 g., 0.999 Platinum 0.0996 oz. APW, 16 mm. **Ruler:** Elizabeth II **Obv:** Head right **Rev:** Common pink heath, multicolor **Rev. Legend:** DISCOVER AUSTRALIA

| Date | Mintage | VF20 | XF40 | MS60 | MS63 | MS65 |
|---|---|---|---|---|---|---|
| 2006 P | 2,500 | **PF65** 300 | | | | |

**KM# 867 10 DOLLARS**
3.11 g., 0.999 Gold 0.0999 oz. AGW **Ruler:** Elizabeth II **Subject:** Ashes Cricket Series 1882-2007 **Obv:** Head with tiara right **Rev:** Urn and supporters **Edge:** Reeded

| Date | Mintage | VF20 | XF40 | MS60 | MS63 | MS65 |
|---|---|---|---|---|---|---|
| 2007 | — | **PF65** 195 | | | | |

**KM# 1000 10 DOLLARS**
3.11 g., 0.999 Gold 0.0999 oz. AGW, 17.53 mm. **Ruler:** Elizabeth II **Subject:** Year of the Pig **Obv:** Head with tiara right **Rev:** Mother kangaroo with joey **Edge:** Reeded

| Date | Mintage | VF20 | XF40 | MS60 | MS63 | MS65 |
|---|---|---|---|---|---|---|
| 2007 | — | **PF65** 210 | | | | |

**KM# 1143 10 DOLLARS**
1.24 g., 0.999 Gold 0.0398 oz. AGW, 14 mm. **Ruler:** Elizabeth II **Obv:** Head right **Rev:** Echidna **Rev. Legend:** DISCOVER AUSTRALIA

| Date | Mintage | VF20 | XF40 | MS60 | MS63 | MS65 |
|---|---|---|---|---|---|---|
| 2007 P | 25,000 | **PF63** 100 | **PF65** 110 | | | |

**KM# 1144 10 DOLLARS**
1.24 g., 0.999 Gold 0.0398 oz. AGW, 14 mm. **Ruler:** Elizabeth II **Obv:** Head right **Rev:** Common wombat **Rev. Legend:** DISCOVER AUSTRALIA

| Date | Mintage | VF20 | XF40 | MS60 | MS63 | MS65 |
|---|---|---|---|---|---|---|
| 2007 P | 25,000 | **PF63** 100 | **PF65** 110 | | | |

**KM# 1145 10 DOLLARS**
1.24 g., 0.999 Gold 0.0398 oz. AGW, 14 mm. **Ruler:** Elizabeth II **Obv:** Head right **Rev:** Tasmanian devil **Rev. Legend:** DISCOVER AUSTRALIA

| Date | Mintage | VF20 | XF40 | MS60 | MS63 | MS65 |
|---|---|---|---|---|---|---|
| 2007 P | 25,000 | **PF63** 100 | **PF65** 110 | | | |

**KM# 1146 10 DOLLARS**
1.24 g., 0.999 Gold 0.0398 oz. AGW, 14 mm. **Ruler:** Elizabeth II **Obv:** Head right **Rev:** Great white shark **Rev. Legend:** DISCOVER AUSTRALIA

| Date | Mintage | VF20 | XF40 | MS60 | MS63 | MS65 |
|---|---|---|---|---|---|---|
| 2007 P | 25,000 | **PF63** 100 | **PF65** 110 | | | |

**KM# 1147 10 DOLLARS**
1.24 g., 0.999 Gold 0.0398 oz. AGW, 14 mm. **Ruler:** Elizabeth II **Obv:** Head right **Rev:** Platypus **Rev. Legend:** DISCOVER AUSTRALIA

| Date | Mintage | VF20 | XF40 | MS60 | MS63 | MS65 |
|---|---|---|---|---|---|---|
| 2007 P | 25,000 | **PF63** 100 | **PF65** 110 | | | |

**KM# 1159 10 DOLLARS**
3.10 g., 0.999 Platinum 0.0996 oz. APW, 16 mm. **Ruler:** Elizabeth II **Obv:** Head right **Rev:** Sturt's desert pea, multicolor **Rev. Legend:** DISCOVER AUSTRALIA

| Date | Mintage | VF20 | XF40 | MS60 | MS63 | MS65 |
|---|---|---|---|---|---|---|
| 2007 P | 2,500 | **PF65** 300 | | | | |

**KM# 1160 10 DOLLARS**
3.10 g., 0.999 Platinum 0.0996 oz. APW, 16 mm. **Ruler:** Elizabeth II **Obv:** Head right **Rev:** Tasmanian bluegum, multicolor **Rev. Legend:** DISCOVER AUSTRALIA

| Date | Mintage | VF20 | XF40 | MS60 | MS63 | MS65 |
|---|---|---|---|---|---|---|
| 2007 P | 2,500 | **PF65** 300 | | | | |

**KM# 1161 10 DOLLARS**
3.10 g., 0.999 Platinum 0.0996 oz. APW, 16 mm. **Ruler:** Elizabeth II **Obv:** Head right **Rev:** Waratah, multicolor **Rev. Legend:** DISCOVER AUSTRALIA

| Date | Mintage | VF20 | XF40 | MS60 | MS63 | MS65 |
|---|---|---|---|---|---|---|
| 2007 P | 2,500 | **PF65** 300 | | | | |

**KM# 1162 10 DOLLARS**
3.10 g., 0.999 Platinum 0.0996 oz. APW, 16 mm. **Ruler:** Elizabeth II **Obv:** Head right **Rev:** Golden wattle, multicolor **Rev. Legend:** DISCOVER AUSTRALIA

| Date | Mintage | VF20 | XF40 | MS60 | MS63 | MS65 |
|---|---|---|---|---|---|---|
| 2007 P | 2,500 | **PF65** 300 | | | | |

**KM# 1051 10 DOLLARS**
3.10 g., 0.999 Gold 0.0996 oz. AGW, 17.5 mm. **Ruler:** Elizabeth II **Subject:** Scouting Centennial in Australia **Rev:** Shadow linear portrait of Baden-Powell

| Date | Mintage | VF20 | XF40 | MS60 | MS63 | MS65 |
|---|---|---|---|---|---|---|
| 2008 | 1,500 | **PF65** 335 | | | | |

**KM# 1054 10 DOLLARS**
3.11 g., 0.999 Gold 0.0999 oz. AGW, 17.53 mm. **Ruler:** Elizabeth II **Subject:** Rugby League

| Date | Mintage | VF20 | XF40 | MS60 | MS63 | MS65 |
|---|---|---|---|---|---|---|
| 2008 | 3,000 | **PF65** 235 | | | | |

**KM# 1622 10 DOLLARS**
31.11 g., 0.999 Silver 0.999 oz. ASW partially gilt, 40 mm. **Ruler:** Elizabeth II **Subject:** President's Cup **Obv:** Head with tiara right **Rev:** Trophy, gilt

| Date | Mintage | VF20 | XF40 | MS60 | MS63 | MS65 |
|---|---|---|---|---|---|---|
| 2011 | — | **PF65** 120 | | | | |

**KM# 1662 10 DOLLARS**
3.11 g., 0.999 Gold 0.0999 oz. AGW, 17.53 mm. **Ruler:** Elizabeth II **Subject:** Year of the Rabbit **Rev:** Rabbit seated left within circle, floral around

| Date | Mintage | VF20 | XF40 | MS60 | MS63 | MS65 |
|---|---|---|---|---|---|---|
| 2011 | — | **PF65** 200 | | | | |

**KM# 1660 10 DOLLARS**
3.11 g., 0.999 Gold 0.0999 oz. AGW, 17.53 mm. **Ruler:** Elizabeth II **Subject:** Year of the Tiger **Rev:** Tiger head within circle, floral around

| Date | Mintage | VF20 | XF40 | MS60 | MS63 | MS65 |
|---|---|---|---|---|---|---|
| 2012 | — | **PF65** 200 | | | | |

**KM# 1681 10 DOLLARS**
3.11 g., 0.999 Gold 0.0999 oz. AGW, 17.53 mm. **Ruler:** Elizabeth II **Subject:** Year of the Dragon **Rev:** Dragon head within circle, floral around

| Date | Mintage | VF20 | XF40 | MS60 | MS63 | MS65 |
|---|---|---|---|---|---|---|
| 2012 | — | **PF65** 200 | | | | |

**KM# 2019 10 DOLLARS**
3.11 g., 0.999 Gold 0.0999 oz. AGW, 17.53 mm. **Ruler:** Elizabeth II **Rev:** Three sheafs of wheat

| Date | Mintage | VF20 | XF40 | MS60 | MS63 | MS65 |
|---|---|---|---|---|---|---|
| 2012 C | Est. 2500 | **PF65** 360 | | | | |

**KM# 1954 10 DOLLARS**
155.50 g., 0.999 Silver 4.9944 oz. ASW, 65 mm. **Ruler:** Elizabeth II **Subject:** Kangaroo Road Sign

| Date | Mintage | VF20 | XF40 | MS60 | MS63 | MS65 |
|---|---|---|---|---|---|---|
| 2013 | Est. 5000 | **PF65** 175 | | | | |

### KM# 1964 10 DOLLARS

0.999 Silver **Ruler:** Elizabeth II **Subject:** Bicentenary of the Crossing of the Blue Mountains

| Date | Mintage | VF20 | XF40 | MS60 | MS63 | MS65 |
|---|---|---|---|---|---|---|
| 2013 | Est. 5000 | PF65 200 | | | | |

### KM# 2027 10 DOLLARS

31.11 g., 0.999 Gold 0.9992 oz. AGW, 17.53 mm. **Ruler:** Elizabeth II **Subject:** Holey Dollar **Rev:** NSW coin and 8 real reverse

| Date | Mintage | VF20 | XF40 | MS60 | MS63 | MS65 |
|---|---|---|---|---|---|---|
| 2013 | Est. 2500 | PF65 360 | | | | |

### KM# 2031 10 DOLLARS

3.11 g., 0.999 Gold 0.0999 oz. AGW, 17.53 mm. **Ruler:** Elizabeth II **Rev:** Kangaroo standing on rock at left

| Date | Mintage | VF20 | XF40 | MS60 | MS63 | MS65 |
|---|---|---|---|---|---|---|
| 2013 | Est. 1500 | PF65 360 | | | | |

### KM# 2041 10 DOLLARS

311.35 g., 0.999 Silver 10.000 oz. ASW, 75.6 mm. **Ruler:** Elizabeth II **Subject:** Sydney Opera House

| Date | Mintage | VF20 | XF40 | MS60 | MS63 | MS65 |
|---|---|---|---|---|---|---|
| 2013 | 750 | PF65 885 | | | | |

### KM# 951 15 DOLLARS

3.11 g., 0.999 Gold 0.0999 oz. AGW **Ruler:** Elizabeth II **Subject:** Australian Fauna **Obv:** Head with tiara right **Rev:** Saltwater crocodile

| Date | Mintage | VF20 | XF40 | MS60 | MS63 | MS65 |
|---|---|---|---|---|---|---|
| 2006 | 2,500 | PF65 195 | | | | |

### KM# 954 15 DOLLARS

3.11 g., 0.999 Gold 0.0999 oz. AGW **Ruler:** Elizabeth II **Subject:** Australian Fauna **Obv:** Head with tiara right **Rev:** Grey kangaroo

| Date | Mintage | VF20 | XF40 | MS60 | MS63 | MS65 |
|---|---|---|---|---|---|---|
| 2006 | 1,999 | PF65 195 | | | | |

### KM# 957 15 DOLLARS

3.11 g., 0.999 Gold 0.0999 oz. AGW **Ruler:** Elizabeth II **Subject:** Australian Fauna **Obv:** Head with tiara right **Rev:** Emu

| Date | Mintage | VF20 | XF40 | MS60 | MS63 | MS65 |
|---|---|---|---|---|---|---|
| 2006 | 896 | PF65 195 | | | | |

### KM# 960 15 DOLLARS

3.11 g., 0.999 Gold 0.0999 oz. AGW **Ruler:** Elizabeth II **Subject:** Australian Fauna **Obv:** Head with tiara right **Rev:** Koala

| Date | Mintage | VF20 | XF40 | MS60 | MS63 | MS65 |
|---|---|---|---|---|---|---|
| 2006 | 2,257 | PF65 195 | | | | |

### KM# 963 15 DOLLARS

3.11 g., 0.999 Gold 0.0999 oz. AGW **Ruler:** Elizabeth II **Subject:** Australian Fauna **Obv:** Head with tiara right **Rev:** Kookaburra

| Date | Mintage | VF20 | XF40 | MS60 | MS63 | MS65 |
|---|---|---|---|---|---|---|
| 2006 | 1,184 | PF65 195 | | | | |

### KM# 980 15 DOLLARS

3.11 g., 0.999 Platinum 0.0999 oz. APW **Ruler:** Elizabeth II **Subject:** Australian Flora **Obv:** Head with tiara right **Rev:** Cooktown orchid

| Date | Mintage | VF20 | XF40 | MS60 | MS63 | MS65 |
|---|---|---|---|---|---|---|
| 2006 | 1,891 | PF65 220 | | | | |

### KM# 982 15 DOLLARS

3.11 g., 0.999 Platinum 0.0999 oz. APW **Ruler:** Elizabeth II **Subject:** Australian Flora **Obv:** Head with tiara right **Rev:** Sturt's desert rose

| Date | Mintage | VF20 | XF40 | MS60 | MS63 | MS65 |
|---|---|---|---|---|---|---|
| 2006 | 1,713 | PF65 220 | | | | |

### KM# 984 15 DOLLARS

3.11 g., 0.999 Platinum 0.0999 oz. APW **Ruler:** Elizabeth II **Subject:** Australian Flora **Obv:** Head with tiara right **Rev:** Royal bluebell

| Date | Mintage | VF20 | XF40 | MS60 | MS63 | MS65 |
|---|---|---|---|---|---|---|
| 2006 | 615 | PF65 220 | | | | |

### KM# 986 15 DOLLARS

3.11 g., 0.999 Platinum 0.0999 oz. APW **Ruler:** Elizabeth II **Subject:** Australian Flora **Obv:** Head with tiara right **Rev:** Kangaroo paw

| Date | Mintage | VF20 | XF40 | MS60 | MS63 | MS65 |
|---|---|---|---|---|---|---|
| 2006 | 1,606 | PF65 220 | | | | |

### KM# 988 15 DOLLARS

3.11 g., 0.999 Platinum 0.0999 oz. APW **Ruler:** Elizabeth II **Subject:** Australian Flora **Obv:** Head with tiara right **Rev:** Common pink heath

| Date | Mintage | VF20 | XF40 | MS60 | MS63 | MS65 |
|---|---|---|---|---|---|---|
| 2006 | 500 | PF65 220 | | | | |

### KM# 966 15 DOLLARS

3.11 g., 0.999 Gold 0.0999 oz. AGW **Ruler:** Elizabeth II **Subject:** Australian Fauna **Obv:** Head with tiara right **Rev:** Echidna

| Date | Mintage | VF20 | XF40 | MS60 | MS63 | MS65 |
|---|---|---|---|---|---|---|
| 2007 | 1,664 | PF65 195 | | | | |

### KM# 969 15 DOLLARS

3.11 g., 0.999 Gold 0.0999 oz. AGW **Ruler:** Elizabeth II **Subject:** Australian Fauna **Obv:** Head with tiara right **Rev:** Common wombat

| Date | Mintage | VF20 | XF40 | MS60 | MS63 | MS65 |
|---|---|---|---|---|---|---|
| 2007 | 1,678 | PF65 195 | | | | |

### KM# 972 15 DOLLARS

3.11 g., 0.999 Gold 0.0999 oz. AGW **Ruler:** Elizabeth II **Subject:** Australian Fauna **Obv:** Head with tiara right **Rev:** Tasmanian devil

| Date | Mintage | VF20 | XF40 | MS60 | MS63 | MS65 |
|---|---|---|---|---|---|---|
| 2007 | 1,687 | PF65 195 | | | | |

### KM# 975 15 DOLLARS

3.11 g., 0.999 Gold 0.0999 oz. AGW **Ruler:** Elizabeth II **Subject:** Australian Fauna **Obv:** Head with tiara right **Rev:** Great white shark

| Date | Mintage | VF20 | XF40 | MS60 | MS63 | MS65 |
|---|---|---|---|---|---|---|
| 2007 | 2,119 | PF65 195 | | | | |

### KM# 978 15 DOLLARS

3.11 g., 0.999 Gold 0.0999 oz. AGW **Ruler:** Elizabeth II **Subject:** Australian Fauna **Obv:** Head with tiara right **Rev:** Platypus

| Date | Mintage | VF20 | XF40 | MS60 | MS63 | MS65 |
|---|---|---|---|---|---|---|
| 2007 | 1,632 | PF65 195 | | | | |

### KM# 990 15 DOLLARS

3.11 g., 0.999 Platinum 0.0999 oz. APW **Ruler:** Elizabeth II **Subject:** Australian Flora **Obv:** Head with tiara right **Rev:** Anemone buttercup

| Date | Mintage | VF20 | XF40 | MS60 | MS63 | MS65 |
|---|---|---|---|---|---|---|
| 2007 | 404 | PF65 220 | | | | |

### KM# 992 15 DOLLARS

3.11 g., 0.999 Platinum 0.0999 oz. APW **Ruler:** Elizabeth II **Subject:** Australian Flora **Obv:** Head with tiara right **Rev:** Sturt's desert pea

| Date | Mintage | VF20 | XF40 | MS60 | MS63 | MS65 |
|---|---|---|---|---|---|---|
| 2007 | 359 | PF65 220 | | | | |

### KM# 994 15 DOLLARS

3.11 g., 0.999 Platinum 0.0999 oz. APW **Ruler:** Elizabeth II **Subject:** Australian Flora **Obv:** Head with tiara right **Rev:** Tasmanian bluegum

| Date | Mintage | VF20 | XF40 | MS60 | MS63 | MS65 |
|---|---|---|---|---|---|---|
| 2007 | 348 | PF65 220 | | | | |

### KM# 996 15 DOLLARS

3.11 g., 0.999 Platinum 0.0999 oz. APW **Ruler:** Elizabeth II **Subject:** Australian Flora **Obv:** Head with tiara right **Rev:** Waratah

| Date | Mintage | VF20 | XF40 | MS60 | MS63 | MS65 |
|---|---|---|---|---|---|---|
| 2007 | 364 | PF65 220 | | | | |

### KM# 998 15 DOLLARS

3.11 g., 0.999 Platinum 0.0999 oz. APW **Ruler:** Elizabeth II **Subject:** Australian Flora **Obv:** Head with tiara right **Rev:** Golden wattle

| Date | Mintage | VF20 | XF40 | MS60 | MS63 | MS65 |
|---|---|---|---|---|---|---|
| 2007 | 414 | PF65 220 | | | | |

### KM# 1186 15 DOLLARS

3.11 g., 0.999 Gold 0.0999 oz. AGW, 14 mm. **Ruler:** Elizabeth II **Obv:** Head right **Rev:** Dolphin **Rev. Legend:** DISCOVER AUSTRALIA

| Date | Mintage | VF20 | XF40 | MS60 | MS63 | MS65 |
|---|---|---|---|---|---|---|
| 2008 P | 1,857 | PF65 110 | | | | |

### KM# 1187 15 DOLLARS

3.11 g., 0.999 Gold 0.0999 oz. AGW, 14 mm. **Ruler:** Elizabeth II **Obv:** Head right **Rev:** King brown snake **Rev. Legend:** DISCOVER AUSTRALIA

| Date | Mintage | VF20 | XF40 | MS60 | MS63 | MS65 |
|---|---|---|---|---|---|---|
| 2008 P | 1,308 | PF65 110 | | | | |

### KM# 1188 15 DOLLARS

3.11 g., 0.999 Gold 0.0999 oz. AGW, 14 mm. **Ruler:** Elizabeth II **Obv:** Head right **Rev:** Brolga **Rev. Legend:** DISCOVER AUSTRALIA

| Date | Mintage | VF20 | XF40 | MS60 | MS63 | MS65 |
|---|---|---|---|---|---|---|
| 2008 P | 1,475 | PF65 100 | | | | |

### KM# 1189 15 DOLLARS

3.11 g., 0.999 Gold 0.0999 oz. AGW, 14 mm. **Ruler:** Elizabeth II **Obv:** Head right **Rev:** Dingo **Rev. Legend:** DISCOVER AUSTRALIA

| Date | Mintage | VF20 | XF40 | MS60 | MS63 | MS65 |
|---|---|---|---|---|---|---|
| 2008 P | 1,494 | PF65 110 | | | | |

### KM# 1190 15 DOLLARS

3.11 g., 0.999 Gold 0.0999 oz. AGW, 14 mm. **Ruler:** Elizabeth II **Obv:** Head right **Rev:** Frill-neck lizard **Rev. Legend:** DISCOVER AUSTRALIA

| Date | Mintage | VF20 | XF40 | MS60 | MS63 | MS65 |
|---|---|---|---|---|---|---|
| 2008 P | 1,788 | PF65 110 | | | | |

### KM# 1201 15 DOLLARS

3.10 g., 0.999 Platinum 0.0996 oz. APW, 16 mm. **Ruler:** Elizabeth II **Obv:** Head right **Rev:** Black anther fax lilly, multicolor **Rev. Legend:** DISCOVER AUSTRALIA

| Date | Mintage | VF20 | XF40 | MS60 | MS63 | MS65 |
|---|---|---|---|---|---|---|
| 2008 P | 352 | PF65 300 | | | | |

**KM# 1202 15 DOLLARS**
3.10 g., 0.999 Platinum 0.0996 oz. APW, 16 mm. **Ruler:** Elizabeth II **Obv:** Head right **Rev:** Native frangipani, multicolor **Rev. Legend:** DISCOVER AUSTRALIA

| Date | Mintage | VF20 | XF40 | MS60 | MS63 | MS65 |
|---|---|---|---|---|---|---|
| 2008 P | 356 | PF65 300 | | | | |

**KM# 1203 15 DOLLARS**
3.10 g., 0.999 Platinum 0.0996 oz. APW, 16 mm. **Ruler:** Elizabeth II **Obv:** Head right **Rev:** Geraldton wax, multicolor

| Date | Mintage | VF20 | XF40 | MS60 | MS63 | MS65 |
|---|---|---|---|---|---|---|
| 2008 P | 373 | PF65 300 | | | | |

**KM# 1204 15 DOLLARS**
3.10 g., 0.999 Platinum 0.0996 oz. APW, 16 mm. **Ruler:** Elizabeth II **Obv:** Head right **Rev:** Red-flowered kurrajong, multicolor **Rev. Legend:** DISCOVER AUSTRALIA

| Date | Mintage | VF20 | XF40 | MS60 | MS63 | MS65 |
|---|---|---|---|---|---|---|
| 2008 P | 338 | PF65 300 | | | | |

**KM# 1205 15 DOLLARS**
3.10 g., 0.999 Platinum 0.0996 oz. APW, 16 mm. **Ruler:** Elizabeth II **Obv:** Head right **Rev:** Small-leaf lily pilly, multicolor **Rev. Legend:** DISCOVER AUSTRALIA

| Date | Mintage | VF20 | XF40 | MS60 | MS63 | MS65 |
|---|---|---|---|---|---|---|
| 2008 P | 380 | PF65 300 | | | | |

**KM# 1104 15 DOLLARS**
2.50 g., 0.9999 Gold 0.0804 oz. AGW, 13x22 mm. **Ruler:** Elizabeth II **Rev:** Turtle Dreaming **Shape:** Rectangle

| Date | Mintage | VF20 | XF40 | MS60 | MS63 | MS65 |
|---|---|---|---|---|---|---|
| 2009 | — | PF65 175 | | | | |

**KM# 1108 15 DOLLARS**
2.50 g., 0.9999 Gold 0.0804 oz. AGW, 13x22 mm. **Ruler:** Elizabeth II **Rev:** Kangaroo Dreaming **Shape:** Vertical rectangle

| Date | Mintage | VF20 | XF40 | MS60 | MS63 | MS65 |
|---|---|---|---|---|---|---|
| 2009 | — | PF65 175 | | | | |

**KM# 1223 15 DOLLARS**
3.11 g., 0.999 Gold 0.0999 oz. AGW, 16 mm. **Ruler:** Elizabeth II **Obv:** Head right **Rev:** Dreaming dolphin

| Date | Mintage | VF20 | XF40 | MS60 | MS63 | MS65 |
|---|---|---|---|---|---|---|
| 2009 P | 2,500 | PF65 195 | | | | |

**KM# 1225 15 DOLLARS**
3.11 g., 0.999 Gold 0.0999 oz. AGW, 16 mm. **Ruler:** Elizabeth II **Obv:** Head right **Rev:** Dreaming brolga

| Date | Mintage | VF20 | XF40 | MS60 | MS63 | MS65 |
|---|---|---|---|---|---|---|
| 2009 P | 2,500 | PF65 195 | | | | |

**KM# 1226 15 DOLLARS**
3.11 g., 0.999 Gold 0.0999 oz. AGW, 16 mm. **Ruler:** Elizabeth II **Obv:** Head right **Rev:** Dreaming echidna

| Date | Mintage | VF20 | XF40 | MS60 | MS63 | MS65 |
|---|---|---|---|---|---|---|
| 2009 P | 2,500 | PF65 195 | | | | |

**KM# 1228 15 DOLLARS**
15.55 g., 0.999 Gold 0.4994 oz. AGW, 25 mm. **Ruler:** Elizabeth II **Obv:** Head right **Rev:** Dreaming dolphin

| Date | Mintage | VF20 | XF40 | MS60 | MS63 | MS65 |
|---|---|---|---|---|---|---|
| 2009 P | 1,000 | PF65 1,100 | | | | |

**KM# 1232 15 DOLLARS**
3.11 g., 0.999 Platinum 0.0999 oz. APW, 16 mm. **Ruler:** Elizabeth II **Obv:** Head right **Rev:** Dreaming kangaroo, multicolor

| Date | Mintage | VF20 | XF40 | MS60 | MS63 | MS65 |
|---|---|---|---|---|---|---|
| 2009 P | 2,500 | PF65 400 | | | | |

**KM# 1233 15 DOLLARS**
3.11 g., 0.999 Platinum 0.0999 oz. APW, 16 mm. **Ruler:** Elizabeth II **Obv:** Head right **Rev:** Dreaming dolphin, multicolor

| Date | Mintage | VF20 | XF40 | MS60 | MS63 | MS65 |
|---|---|---|---|---|---|---|
| 2009 P | 2,500 | PF65 400 | | | | |

**KM# 1234 15 DOLLARS**
3.11 g., 0.999 Platinum 0.0999 oz. APW, 16 mm. **Ruler:** Elizabeth II **Obv:** Head right **Rev:** Dreaming king brown snake, multicolor

| Date | Mintage | VF20 | XF40 | MS60 | MS63 | MS65 |
|---|---|---|---|---|---|---|
| 2009 P | 2,500 | PF65 400 | | | | |

**KM# 1235 15 DOLLARS**
3.11 g., 0.999 Platinum 0.0999 oz. APW, 16 mm. **Ruler:** Elizabeth II **Obv:** Head right **Rev:** Dreaming brolga

| Date | Mintage | VF20 | XF40 | MS60 | MS63 | MS65 |
|---|---|---|---|---|---|---|
| 2009 P | 2,500 | PF65 400 | | | | |

**KM# 1236 15 DOLLARS**
3.11 g., 0.999 Platinum 0.0999 oz. APW, 16 mm. **Ruler:** Elizabeth II **Obv:** Head right **Rev:** Dreaming echidna, multicolor

| Date | Mintage | VF20 | XF40 | MS60 | MS63 | MS65 |
|---|---|---|---|---|---|---|
| 2009 P | 2,500 | PF65 400 | | | | |

**KM# 1401 15 DOLLARS**
3.11 g., 0.999 Gold 0.0999 oz. AGW, 17 mm. **Ruler:** Elizabeth II **Obv:** Head right **Rev:** Frill-neck lizard

| Date | Mintage | VF20 | XF40 | MS60 | MS63 | MS65 |
|---|---|---|---|---|---|---|
| 2010 (p) | 2,500 | PF65 260 | | | | |

**KM# 1405 15 DOLLARS**
3.11 g., 0.999 Platinum 0.0999 oz. APW, 17 mm. **Ruler:** Elizabeth II **Obv:** Head right **Rev:** Multicolor koala

| Date | Mintage | VF20 | XF40 | MS60 | MS63 | MS65 |
|---|---|---|---|---|---|---|
| 2010 (p) | 2,500 | PF65 335 | | | | |

**KM# 1407 15 DOLLARS**
3.11 g., 0.999 Gold 0.0999 oz. AGW, 16 mm. **Ruler:** Elizabeth II **Obv:** Head right **Rev:** Koala

| Date | Mintage | VF20 | XF40 | MS60 | MS63 | MS65 |
|---|---|---|---|---|---|---|
| 2010 (p) | 2,500 | PF65 260 | | | | |

**KM# 1411 15 DOLLARS**
3.11 g., 0.999 Platinum 0.0999 oz. APW, 17 mm. **Ruler:** Elizabeth II **Obv:** Head right **Rev:** Multicolor platypus

| Date | Mintage | VF20 | XF40 | MS60 | MS63 | MS65 |
|---|---|---|---|---|---|---|
| 2010 (p) | 2,500 | PF65 335 | | | | |

**KM# 1413 15 DOLLARS**
0.999 Gold, 16 mm. **Ruler:** Elizabeth II **Obv:** Head right **Rev:** Platypus

| Date | Mintage | VF20 | XF40 | MS60 | MS63 | MS65 |
|---|---|---|---|---|---|---|
| 2010 (p) | 2,500 | PF65 260 | | | | |

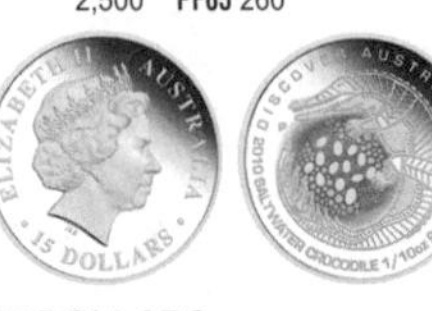

**KM# 1417 15 DOLLARS**
0.999 Platinum APW, 17 mm. **Ruler:** Elizabeth II **Obv:** Head right **Rev:** Muticolor saltwater crocodile

| Date | Mintage | VF20 | XF40 | MS60 | MS63 | MS65 |
|---|---|---|---|---|---|---|
| 2010 (p) | 2,500 | PF65 335 | | | | |

**KM# 1419 15 DOLLARS**
3.11 g., 0.999 Gold 0.0999 oz. AGW, 16 mm. **Ruler:** Elizabeth II **Obv:** Head right **Rev:** Saltwater crocodile

| Date | Mintage | VF20 | XF40 | MS60 | MS63 | MS65 |
|---|---|---|---|---|---|---|
| 2010 (p) | 2,500 | PF65 260 | | | | |

**KM# 1423 15 DOLLARS**
3.11 g., 0.999 Platinum 0.0999 oz. APW, 17 mm. **Ruler:** Elizabeth II **Obv:** Head right **Rev:** Multicolor wombat

| Date | Mintage | VF20 | XF40 | MS60 | MS63 | MS65 |
|---|---|---|---|---|---|---|
| 2010 (p) | 2,500 | PF65 335 | | | | |

**KM# 1425 15 DOLLARS**
0.999 Gold, 16 mm. **Ruler:** Elizabeth II **Obv:** Head right **Rev:** Wombat

| Date | Mintage | VF20 | XF40 | MS60 | MS63 | MS65 |
|---|---|---|---|---|---|---|
| 2010 (p) | 2,500 | PF65 260 | | | | |

**KM# 1454 15 DOLLARS**
2.50 g., 0.999 Gold 0.0803 oz. AGW, 13x22 mm. **Ruler:** Elizabeth II **Rev:** Dolphin dreaming **Shape:** Vertical rectangle

| Date | Mintage | VF20 | XF40 | MS60 | MS63 | MS65 |
|---|---|---|---|---|---|---|
| 2010 P | — | PF65 175 | | | | |

**KM# 1492 15 DOLLARS**
3.11 g., 0.999 Gold 0.0999 oz. AGW, 17.53 mm. **Ruler:** Elizabeth II **Obv:** Head with tiara right **Rev:** Saint Mary Mackillup in color

| Date | Mintage | VF20 | XF40 | MS60 | MS63 | MS65 |
|---|---|---|---|---|---|---|
| 2010 | 2,010 | PF65 215 | | | | |

**KM# 1536 15 DOLLARS**
3.11 g., 0.999 Gold 0.0999 oz. AGW **Ruler:** Elizabeth II **Subject:** Dreaming Emu **Rev:** Linear emu in color

| Date | Mintage | VF20 | XF40 | MS60 | MS63 | MS65 |
|---|---|---|---|---|---|---|
| 2011 P | 2,500 | PF65 250 | | | | |

**KM# 1538 15 DOLLARS**
3.11 g., 0.999 Platinum 0.0999 oz. APW **Ruler:** Elizabeth II **Subject:** Dreaming Emu **Rev:** Linear emu in color

| Date | Mintage | VF20 | XF40 | MS60 | MS63 | MS65 |
|---|---|---|---|---|---|---|
| 2011 P | 2,500 | PF65 375 | | | | |

**KM# 1542 15 DOLLARS**
3.11 g., 0.999 Gold 0.0999 oz. AGW **Ruler:** Elizabeth II **Subject:** Dreaming Tasmanian Devil **Rev:** Linear tasmanian devil in color

| Date | Mintage | VF20 | XF40 | MS60 | MS63 | MS65 |
|---|---|---|---|---|---|---|
| 2011 P | 2,500 | PF65 250 | | | | |

**KM# 1544 15 DOLLARS**
3.11 g., 0.999 Platinum 0.0999 oz. APW **Ruler:** Elizabeth II **Subject:** Dreaming Tasmanian Devil **Rev:** Linear tasmanian devil in color

| Date | Mintage | VF20 | XF40 | MS60 | MS63 | MS65 |
|---|---|---|---|---|---|---|
| 2011 P | 2,500 | PF65 375 | | | | |

**KM# 1548 15 DOLLARS**
3.11 g., 0.999 Gold 0.0999 oz. AGW **Ruler:** Elizabeth II **Subject:** Dreaming Kookaburra **Rev:** Linear kookaburra in color

| Date | Mintage | VF20 | XF40 | MS60 | MS63 | MS65 |
|---|---|---|---|---|---|---|
| 2011 P | 2,500 | PF65 250 | | | | |

**KM# 1550 15 DOLLARS**
3.11 g., 0.999 Platinum 0.0999 oz. APW **Ruler:** Elizabeth II **Subject:** Dreaming Kookaburra **Rev:** Linear kookaburra in color

| Date | Mintage | VF20 | XF40 | MS60 | MS63 | MS65 |
|---|---|---|---|---|---|---|
| 2011 P | 2,500 | PF65 375 | | | | |

**KM# 1554 15 DOLLARS**
3.11 g., 0.999 Gold 0.0999 oz. AGW **Ruler:** Elizabeth II **Subject:** Dreaming Shark **Rev:** Linear shark in color

| Date | Mintage | VF20 | XF40 | MS60 | MS63 | MS65 |
|---|---|---|---|---|---|---|
| 2011 P | 2,500 | PF65 250 | | | | |

**KM# 1556 15 DOLLARS**
3.11 g., 0.999 Platinum 0.0999 oz. APW **Ruler:** Elizabeth II **Subject:** Dreaming Shark **Rev:** Linear shark in color

| Date | Mintage | VF20 | XF40 | MS60 | MS63 | MS65 |
|---|---|---|---|---|---|---|
| 2011 P | 2,500 | PF65 375 | | | | |

**KM# 1560 15 DOLLARS**
3.11 g., 0.999 Gold 0.0999 oz. AGW **Ruler:** Elizabeth II **Subject:** Dreaming Dingo **Rev:** Linear dingo in color

| Date | Mintage | VF20 | XF40 | MS60 | MS63 | MS65 |
|---|---|---|---|---|---|---|
| 2011 P | 2,500 | PF65 250 | | | | |

**KM# 1562 15 DOLLARS**
3.11 g., 0.999 Platinum 0.0999 oz. APW **Ruler:** Elizabeth II **Subject:** Dreaming Dingo **Rev:** Linear dingo in color

| Date | Mintage | VF20 | XF40 | MS60 | MS63 | MS65 |
|---|---|---|---|---|---|---|
| 2011 P | 2,500 | PF65 375 | | | | |

**KM# 1610 15 DOLLARS**
2.50 g., 0.999 Gold 0.0803 oz. AGW, 13x22 mm. **Ruler:** Elizabeth II **Obv:** Head with tiara right **Rev:** Platypus dreaming **Shape:** Vertical rectangle

| Date | Mintage | VF20 | XF40 | MS60 | MS63 | MS65 |
|---|---|---|---|---|---|---|
| 2011 P | — | PF65 175 | | | | |

**KM# 1721 15 DOLLARS**
3.11 g., 0.999 Gold 0.0999 oz. AGW, 16.6 mm. **Ruler:** Elizabeth II **Rev:** Green and Gold Bell Frog in grass

| Date | Mintage | VF20 | XF40 | MS60 | MS63 | MS65 |
|---|---|---|---|---|---|---|
| 2012 P | 1,000 | PF65 225 | | | | |

**KM# 1722 15 DOLLARS**
3.11 g., 0.999 Gold 0.0999 oz. AGW, 16.6 mm. **Ruler:** Elizabeth II **Rev:** Kookaburra standing right

| Date | Mintage | VF20 | XF40 | MS60 | MS63 | MS65 |
|---|---|---|---|---|---|---|
| 2012 P | 1,000 | PF65 225 | | | | |

**KM# 1723 15 DOLLARS**
3.11 g., 0.999 Gold 0.0999 oz. AGW, 16.6 mm. **Ruler:** Elizabeth II **Rev:** Whale Shark swimming right

| Date | Mintage | VF20 | XF40 | MS60 | MS63 | MS65 |
|---|---|---|---|---|---|---|
| 2012 P | 1,000 | PF65 225 | | | | |

**KM# 1724 15 DOLLARS**
3.11 g., 0.999 Gold 0.0999 oz. AGW, 16.6 mm. **Ruler:** Elizabeth II **Rev:** Kangaroo bounding right

| Date | Mintage | VF20 | XF40 | MS60 | MS63 | MS65 |
|---|---|---|---|---|---|---|
| 2012 P | 1,000 | PF65 225 | | | | |

**KM# 1725 15 DOLLARS**
3.11 g., 0.999 Gold 0.0999 oz. AGW, 16.6 mm. **Ruler:** Elizabeth II **Rev:** Goanna lizard right

| Date | Mintage | VF20 | XF40 | MS60 | MS63 | MS65 |
|---|---|---|---|---|---|---|
| 2012 P | 1,000 | PF65 225 | | | | |

**KM# 1848 15 DOLLARS**
3.11 g., 0.999 Platinum 0.0999 oz. APW, 16.6 mm. **Ruler:** Elizabeth II **Rev:** Bell Frog and color background

| Date | Mintage | VF20 | XF40 | MS60 | MS63 | MS65 |
|---|---|---|---|---|---|---|
| 2012 P | 1,000 | PF65 325 | | | | |

**KM# 1849 15 DOLLARS**
3.11 g., 0.999 Platinum 0.0999 oz. APW, 16.6 mm. **Ruler:** Elizabeth II **Rev:** Kookaburra with color background

| Date | Mintage | VF20 | XF40 | MS60 | MS63 | MS65 |
|---|---|---|---|---|---|---|
| 2012 P | 1,000 | PF65 325 | | | | |

**KM# 1850 15 DOLLARS**
3.11 g., 0.999 Platinum 0.0999 oz. APW, 16.1 mm. **Ruler:** Elizabeth II **Rev:** Whale shark on color background

| Date | Mintage | VF20 | XF40 | MS60 | MS63 | MS65 |
|---|---|---|---|---|---|---|
| 2012 P | 1,000 | PF65 325 | | | | |

**KM# 1851 15 DOLLARS**
3.11 g., 0.999 Platinum 0.0999 oz. APW, 16.1 mm. **Ruler:** Elizabeth II **Rev:** Kangaroo on color background

| Date | Mintage | VF20 | XF40 | MS60 | MS63 | MS65 |
|---|---|---|---|---|---|---|
| 2012 P | 1,000 | PF65 325 | | | | |

**KM# 1852 15 DOLLARS**
3.11 g., 0.999 Platinum 0.0999 oz. APW, 16.1 mm. **Ruler:** Elizabeth II **Rev:** Goanna on color background

| Date | Mintage | VF20 | XF40 | MS60 | MS63 | MS65 |
|---|---|---|---|---|---|---|
| 2012 P | 1,000 | PF65 325 | | | | |

**KM# 2074 15 DOLLARS**
3.11 g., 0.9999 Gold 0.100 oz. AGW, 17.53 mm. **Ruler:** Elizabeth II **Subject:** Australian - American WWII memorial **Rev:** Eagle monument before US and Australian

| Date | Mintage | VF20 | XF40 | MS60 | MS63 | MS65 |
|---|---|---|---|---|---|---|
| 2013 P | — | PF65 215 | | | | |

**KM# 595 20 DOLLARS**
14.03 g., Bi-Metallic .999 4.5287 Silver center in .9999 9.499 Gold ring, 32.1 mm. **Ruler:** Elizabeth II **Subject:** Gregorian Millennium **Obv:** Head with tiara right **Rev:** Chronograph watch face with observatory in center and three depictions of the earth's rotation **Edge:** Reeded

| Date | Mintage | VF20 | XF40 | MS60 | MS63 | MS65 |
|---|---|---|---|---|---|---|
| 2001 Prooflike | 7,500 | — | — | — | — | 475 |

**KM# 597 20 DOLLARS**
19.63 g., Bi-Metallic .9999 8.8645 Gold center in .9999 10.7618 Silver ring, 32.1 mm. **Ruler:** Elizabeth II **Subject:** Centenary of Federation **Obv:** Head with tiara right within star design **Rev:** National arms on a flowery background **Edge:** Reeded

| Date | Mintage | VF20 | XF40 | MS60 | MS63 | MS65 |
|---|---|---|---|---|---|---|
| ND(2001) Prooflike | 7,635 | — | — | — | — | 475 |

**KM# 760 20 DOLLARS**
Bi-Metallic Gold center in Silver ring **Ruler:** Elizabeth II **Rev:** Sir Donald Bradman portrait

| Date | Mintage | VF20 | XF40 | MS60 | MS63 | MS65 |
|---|---|---|---|---|---|---|
| 2001 | 8,589 | PF65 500 | | | | |

**KM# 634 20 DOLLARS**
18.35 g., Bi-Metallic .999 Silver, 4.6655g, breast star shaped center in a .9999 Gold ,13.6855g outer ring, 32.1 mm. **Ruler:** Elizabeth II **Subject:** Queen's Golden Jubilee **Obv:** Queen's head right **Rev:** Queen before Buckingham Palace **Edge:** Reeded

| Date | Mintage | VF20 | XF40 | MS60 | MS63 | MS65 |
|---|---|---|---|---|---|---|
| 2002 P | 7,500 | PF65 675 | | | | |

**KM# 687 20 DOLLARS**
13.41 g., Bi-Metallic .999 Gold 8.3979g Center in a .999 Silver 5.0077g Ring, 32 mm. **Ruler:** Elizabeth II **Subject:** Golden Jubilee of Coronation **Obv:** Head with tiara right **Rev:** Four different coinage portraits of Queen Elizabeth II **Edge:** Reeded

| Date | Mintage | VF20 | XF40 | MS60 | MS63 | MS65 |
|---|---|---|---|---|---|---|
| 2003 P | 1,338 | PF65 625 | | | | |

**KM# 1105 20 DOLLARS**
5.00 g., 0.9999 Gold 0.1607 oz. AGW, 14x23.2 mm. **Ruler:** Elizabeth II **Rev:** Turtle Dreaming **Shape:** Rectangle

| Date | Mintage | VF20 | XF40 | MS60 | MS63 | MS65 |
|---|---|---|---|---|---|---|
| 2009 | — | PF65 325 | | | | |

**KM# 1109 20 DOLLARS**
5.00 g., 0.9999 Gold 0.1607 oz. AGW, 14x23.2 mm. **Ruler:** Elizabeth II **Rev:** Kangaroo dreaming **Shape:** Vertical rectangle

| Date | Mintage | VF20 | XF40 | MS60 | MS63 | MS65 |
|---|---|---|---|---|---|---|
| 2009 | — | PF65 325 | | | | |

**KM# 868 25 DOLLARS**
7.99 g., 0.9167 Gold 0.2354 oz. AGW **Ruler:** Elizabeth II **Subject:** 150th Anniversary First Australian Sovereign **Obv:** Head with tiara right

| Date | Mintage | VF20 | XF40 | MS60 | MS63 | MS65 |
|---|---|---|---|---|---|---|
| 2005 | 7,500 | PF65 475 | | | | |

**KM# 1123 25 DOLLARS**
3.10 g., 0.999 Gold 0.0996 oz. AGW, 15.5 mm. **Ruler:** Elizabeth II **Obv:** Head right **Rev:** Saltwater crocodile **Rev. Legend:** DISCOVER AUSTRALIA

| Date | Mintage | VF20 | XF40 | MS60 | MS63 | MS65 |
|---|---|---|---|---|---|---|
| 2006 P | 2,500 | PF65 195 | | | | |

**KM# 1124 25 DOLLARS**
3.10 g., 0.999 Gold 0.0996 oz. AGW, 15.5 mm. **Ruler:** Elizabeth II **Obv:** Head right **Rev:** Grey kangaroo **Rev. Legend:** DISCOVER AUSTRALIA

| Date | Mintage | VF20 | XF40 | MS60 | MS63 | MS65 |
|---|---|---|---|---|---|---|
| 2006 P | 2,500 | PF65 195 | | | | |

**KM# 1125 25 DOLLARS**

3.10 g., 0.999 Gold 0.0996 oz. AGW, 15.5 mm. **Ruler:** Elizabeth II **Obv:** Head right **Rev:** Emu **Rev. Legend:** DISCOVER AUSTRALIA

| Date | Mintage | VF20 | XF40 | MS60 | MS63 | MS65 |
|---|---|---|---|---|---|---|
| 2006 P | 2,500 | **PF65** 195 | | | | |

**KM# 1126 25 DOLLARS**

3.10 g., 0.999 Gold 0.0996 oz. AGW, 15.5 mm. **Ruler:** Elizabeth II **Obv:** Head right **Rev:** Koala **Rev. Legend:** DISCOVER AUSTRALIA

| Date | Mintage | VF20 | XF40 | MS60 | MS63 | MS65 |
|---|---|---|---|---|---|---|
| 2006 P | 2,500 | **PF65** 195 | | | | |

**KM# 1127 25 DOLLARS**

3.10 g., 0.999 Gold 0.0996 oz. AGW, 15.5 mm. **Ruler:** Elizabeth II **Obv:** Head right **Rev:** Kookaburra **Rev. Legend:** DISCOVER AUSTRALIA

| Date | Mintage | VF20 | XF40 | MS60 | MS63 | MS65 |
|---|---|---|---|---|---|---|
| 2006 P | 2,500 | **PF65** 195 | | | | |

**KM# 1148 25 DOLLARS**

3.10 g., 0.999 Gold 0.0996 oz. AGW, 15.5 mm. **Ruler:** Elizabeth II **Obv:** Head right **Rev:** Echinda **Rev. Legend:** DISCOVER AUSTRALIA

| Date | Mintage | VF20 | XF40 | MS60 | MS63 | MS65 |
|---|---|---|---|---|---|---|
| 2007 P | 2,500 | **PF65** 195 | | | | |

**KM# 1149 25 DOLLARS**

3.10 g., 0.999 Gold 0.0996 oz. AGW, 15.5 mm. **Ruler:** Elizabeth II **Obv:** Head right **Rev:** Common wombat **Rev. Legend:** DISCOVER AUSTRALIA

| Date | Mintage | VF20 | XF40 | MS60 | MS63 | MS65 |
|---|---|---|---|---|---|---|
| 2007 P | 2,500 | **PF65** 195 | | | | |

**KM# 1150 25 DOLLARS**

3.10 g., 0.999 Gold 0.0996 oz. AGW, 15.5 mm. **Ruler:** Elizabeth II **Obv:** Head right **Rev:** Tasmanian devil **Rev. Legend:** DISCOVER AUSTRALIA

| Date | Mintage | VF20 | XF40 | MS60 | MS63 | MS65 |
|---|---|---|---|---|---|---|
| 2007 P | 2,500 | **PF65** 195 | | | | |

**KM# 1151 25 DOLLARS**

3.10 g., 0.999 Gold 0.0996 oz. AGW, 15.5 mm. **Ruler:** Elizabeth II **Obv:** Head right **Rev:** Great white shark **Rev. Legend:** DISCOVER AUSTRALIA

| Date | Mintage | VF20 | XF40 | MS60 | MS63 | MS65 |
|---|---|---|---|---|---|---|
| 2007 P | 2,500 | **PF65** 195 | | | | |

**KM# 1152 25 DOLLARS**

3.10 g., 0.999 Gold 0.0996 oz. AGW, 15.5 mm. **Ruler:** Elizabeth II **Obv:** Head right **Rev:** Platypus **Rev. Legend:** DISCOVER AUSTRALIA

| Date | Mintage | VF20 | XF40 | MS60 | MS63 | MS65 |
|---|---|---|---|---|---|---|
| 2007 P | 2,500 | **PF65** 195 | | | | |

**KM# 1158 25 DOLLARS**

3.10 g., 0.999 Platinum 0.0996 oz. APW, 16 mm. **Ruler:** Elizabeth II **Obv:** Head right **Rev:** Anemone buttercup, multicolor **Rev. Legend:** DISCOVER AUSTRALIA

| Date | Mintage | VF20 | XF40 | MS60 | MS63 | MS65 |
|---|---|---|---|---|---|---|
| 2007 P | 2,500 | **PF65** 325 | | | | |

**KM# 1180 25 DOLLARS**

7.77 g., 0.999 Gold 0.2496 oz. AGW, 20 mm. **Ruler:** Elizabeth II **Subject:** End of WWI, 90th Anniversary **Obv:** Head right **Rev:** Field cross, multicolor poppies **Rev. Legend:** Ian Rank-Broadley **Edge:** Reeded

| Date | Mintage | VF20 | XF40 | MS60 | MS63 | MS65 |
|---|---|---|---|---|---|---|
| 2008 P | 1,918 | **PF65** 675 | | | | |

**KM# 1191 25 DOLLARS**

3.10 g., 0.999 Gold 0.0996 oz. AGW, 15.5 mm. **Ruler:** Elizabeth II **Obv:** Head right **Rev:** Dolphin **Rev. Legend:** DISCOVER AUSTRALIA

| Date | Mintage | VF20 | XF40 | MS60 | MS63 | MS65 |
|---|---|---|---|---|---|---|
| 2008 P | 2,500 | **PF65** 195 | | | | |

**KM# 1192 25 DOLLARS**

3.10 g., 0.999 Gold 0.0996 oz. AGW, 15.5 mm. **Ruler:** Elizabeth II **Obv:** Head right **Rev:** King brown snake **Rev. Legend:** DISCOVER AUSTRALIA

| Date | Mintage | VF20 | XF40 | MS60 | MS63 | MS65 |
|---|---|---|---|---|---|---|
| 2008 P | 2,500 | **PF65** 195 | | | | |

**KM# 1193 25 DOLLARS**

3.10 g., 0.999 Gold 0.0996 oz. AGW, 15.5 mm. **Ruler:** Elizabeth II **Obv:** Head right **Rev:** Brolga **Rev. Legend:** DISCOVER AUSTRALIA

| Date | Mintage | VF20 | XF40 | MS60 | MS63 | MS65 |
|---|---|---|---|---|---|---|
| 2008 P | 2,500 | **PF65** 195 | | | | |

**KM# 1194 25 DOLLARS**

3.10 g., 0.999 Gold 0.0996 oz. AGW, 15.5 mm. **Ruler:** Elizabeth II **Obv:** Head right **Rev:** Dingo **Rev. Legend:** DISCOVER AUSTRALIA

| Date | Mintage | VF20 | XF40 | MS60 | MS63 | MS65 |
|---|---|---|---|---|---|---|
| 2008 P | 2,500 | **PF65** 195 | | | | |

**KM# 1195 25 DOLLARS**

3.10 g., 0.999 Gold 0.0996 oz. AGW, 15.5 mm. **Ruler:** Elizabeth II **Obv:** Head right **Rev:** Frill-neck lizard **Rev. Legend:** DISCOVER AUSTRALIA

| Date | Mintage | VF20 | XF40 | MS60 | MS63 | MS65 |
|---|---|---|---|---|---|---|
| 2008 P | 2,500 | **PF65** 195 | | | | |

**KM# 1273 25 DOLLARS**

10.00 g., 0.999 Gold 0.3212 oz. AGW, 15x25 mm. **Ruler:** Elizabeth II **Subject:** Mythological Chinese Character - Wealth **Obv:** Head right **Rev:** Man standing **Shape:** Vertical rectangle

| Date | Mintage | VF20 | XF40 | MS60 | MS63 | MS65 |
|---|---|---|---|---|---|---|
| 2008 P | 376 | — | — | — | — | 800 |

**KM# 1274 25 DOLLARS**

10.00 g., 0.999 Gold 0.3212 oz. AGW, 15x25 mm. **Ruler:** Elizabeth II **Subject:** Mythological Chinese Character - Longivity **Obv:** Head right **Rev:** Man standing with staff **Shape:** Vertical rectangle

| Date | Mintage | VF20 | XF40 | MS60 | MS63 | MS65 |
|---|---|---|---|---|---|---|
| 2008 P | 383 | — | — | — | — | 825 |

**KM# 1275 25 DOLLARS**

10.00 g., 0.999 Gold 0.3212 oz. AGW, 15x25 mm. **Ruler:** Elizabeth II **Subject:** Mythological Chinese Character - Success **Obv:** Head right **Rev:** Man standing with deer **Shape:** Vertical rectangle

| Date | Mintage | VF20 | XF40 | MS60 | MS63 | MS65 |
|---|---|---|---|---|---|---|
| 2008 P | 376 | — | — | — | — | 800 |

**KM# 1276 25 DOLLARS**

10.00 g., 0.999 Gold 0.3212 oz. AGW, 15x25 mm. **Ruler:** Elizabeth II **Subject:** Mythological Chinese Character - Fortune **Obv:** Head right **Rev:** Man standing with scroll **Shape:** Vertical rectangle

| Date | Mintage | VF20 | XF40 | MS60 | MS63 | MS65 |
|---|---|---|---|---|---|---|
| 2008 P | 374 | — | — | — | — | 825 |

**KM# 1106 25 DOLLARS**

10.00 g., 0.9999 Gold 0.3215 oz. AGW, 15.4x25.4 mm. **Ruler:** Elizabeth II **Rev:** Turtle dreaming **Shape:** Verticle rectangle

| Date | Mintage | VF20 | XF40 | MS60 | MS63 | MS65 |
|---|---|---|---|---|---|---|
| 2009 | — | **PF65** 625 | | | | |

**KM# 1110 25 DOLLARS**

10.00 g., 0.9999 Gold 0.3215 oz. AGW, 15.4x25.4 mm. **Ruler:** Elizabeth II **Rev:** Kangaroo dreaming **Shape:** Vertical rectangle

| Date | Mintage | VF20 | XF40 | MS60 | MS63 | MS65 |
|---|---|---|---|---|---|---|
| 2009 | — | **PF65** 650 | | | | |

**KM# 1247 25 DOLLARS**

7.77 g., 0.999 Gold 0.2496 oz. AGW, 21 mm. **Ruler:** Elizabeth II **Subject:** 2010 FIFA World Cup, South Africa **Obv:** Head right **Rev:** Soccer player and kangaroo

| Date | Mintage | VF20 | XF40 | MS60 | MS63 | MS65 |
|---|---|---|---|---|---|---|
| 2009 P | 7,500 | **PF65** 775 | | | | |

**KM# 1397 25 DOLLARS**

7.99 g., 0.9167 Gold 0.2354 oz. AGW, 22.6 mm. **Ruler:** Elizabeth II **Subject:** Sovereign **Obv:** Head in tiara right **Rev:** National Arms with supporters and flora

| Date | Mintage | VF20 | XF40 | MS60 | MS63 | MS65 |
|---|---|---|---|---|---|---|
| 2009 P | 2,500 | **PF65** 825 | | | | |
| 2010 P | — | **PF65** 825 | | | | |
| 2011 P | — | **PF65** 825 | | | | |
| 2012 P | — | **PF65** 825 | | | | |

**KM# 1455 25 DOLLARS**

10.00 g., 0.999 Gold 0.3212 oz. AGW, 15.4x25.4 mm. **Ruler:** Elizabeth II **Rev:** Dolphin dreaming **Shape:** Vertical rectangle

| Date | Mintage | VF20 | XF40 | MS60 | MS63 | MS65 |
|---|---|---|---|---|---|---|
| 2010 P | — | **PF65** 600 | | | | |

**KM# 1611 25 DOLLARS**

10.00 g., 0.999 Gold 0.3212 oz. AGW, 15.4x25.4 mm. **Ruler:** Elizabeth II **Obv:** Head with tiara right **Rev:** Platypus dreaming **Shape:** Vertical rectangle

| Date | Mintage | VF20 | XF40 | MS60 | MS63 | MS65 |
|---|---|---|---|---|---|---|
| 2011 P | — | **PF65** 625 | | | | |

**KM# 1623 25 DOLLARS**

7.77 g., 0.999 Gold 0.2496 oz. AGW, 21 mm. **Ruler:** Elizabeth II **Subject:** President's Cup **Obv:** Head with tiara right **Rev:** Golfer taking swing

| Date | Mintage | VF20 | XF40 | MS60 | MS63 | MS65 |
|---|---|---|---|---|---|---|
| 2011 | — | **PF65** 600 | | | | |

**KM# 1703 25 DOLLARS**

7.77 g., 0.9999 Gold 0.2498 oz. AGW, 20.6 mm. **Ruler:** Elizabeth II **Subject:** Elizabeth II, 60th Anniversary **Obv:** Head with tiara right **Rev:** Young bust right **Edge:** Reeded

| Date | Mintage | VF20 | XF40 | MS60 | MS63 | MS65 |
|---|---|---|---|---|---|---|
| 2012 P | Est. 1000 | **PF65** 550 | | | | |

**KM# 1919 25 DOLLARS**

7.77 g., 0.9999 Gold 0.2498 oz. AGW, 20.6 mm. **Ruler:** Elizabeth II **Subject:** The Land Down Under - Sydney Opera House

| Date | Mintage | VF20 | XF40 | MS60 | MS63 | MS65 |
|---|---|---|---|---|---|---|
| 2013 P | Est. 1000 | **PF65** 500 | | | | |

**KM# 1921 25 DOLLARS**

7.77 g., 0.9999 Gold 0.2498 oz. AGW, 20.6 mm. **Ruler:** Elizabeth II **Subject:** The Land Down Under - Digeridoo

| Date | Mintage | VF20 | XF40 | MS60 | MS63 | MS65 |
|---|---|---|---|---|---|---|
| 2013 P | Est. 1000 | **PF65** 500 | | | | |

**KM# 1928 25 DOLLARS**
7.77 g., 0.9999 Gold 0.2498 oz. AGW, 20.6 mm. **Ruler:** Elizabeth II **Subject:** HM Queen Elizabeth II - 60th Anniversary of Coronation

| Date | Mintage | VF20 | XF40 | MS60 | MS63 | MS65 |
|---|---|---|---|---|---|---|
| 2013 P | Est. 1000 | PF65 500 | | | | |

**KM# 1933 25 DOLLARS**
7.77 g., 0.9999 Gold 0.2498 oz. AGW, 22.6 mm. **Ruler:** Elizabeth II **Subject:** 2014 FIFA World Cup Brazil **Obv:** Head with tiara right **Rev:** Linear abroiginal figure superimposed on map of Australia **Edge:** Reeded

| Date | Mintage | VF20 | XF40 | MS60 | MS63 | MS65 |
|---|---|---|---|---|---|---|
| 2013 P | — | PF65 500 | | | | |

**KM# 1934 25 DOLLARS**
7.99 g., 0.916 Gold 0.2353 oz. AGW, 22.6 mm. **Ruler:** Elizabeth II **Subject:** Australian Sovereign - Perth Mint **Rev:** Country name within crowned wreath **Edge:** Reeded

| Date | Mintage | VF20 | XF40 | MS60 | MS63 | MS65 |
|---|---|---|---|---|---|---|
| 2013 P | Est. 1750 | PF65 500 | | | | |

**KM# 1942 25 DOLLARS**
7.77 g., 0.9999 Gold 0.2498 oz. AGW, 20.6 mm. **Ruler:** Elizabeth II **Subject:** The Land Down Under - Captain James Cook

| Date | Mintage | VF20 | XF40 | MS60 | MS63 | MS65 |
|---|---|---|---|---|---|---|
| 2013 | Est. 1000 | PF65 450 | | | | |

**KM# 2052 25 DOLLARS**
7.78 g., 0.9999 Gold 0.250 oz. AGW, 20.6 mm. **Ruler:** Elizabeth II **Subject:** Land Down Under - Surfing **Obv:** Head with tiara right **Rev:** Female surfer riding wave

| Date | Mintage | VF20 | XF40 | MS60 | MS63 | MS65 |
|---|---|---|---|---|---|---|
| 2013 P | 1,000 | PF65 600 | | | | |

**KM# 2061 25 DOLLARS**
7.78 g., 0.9999 Gold 0.250 oz. AGW, 20.6 mm. **Ruler:** Elizabeth II **Subject:** H.R.H. Prince George, Birth **Obv:** Head with tiara right **Rev:** Prince William and Catherine holding infant

| Date | Mintage | VF20 | XF40 | MS60 | MS63 | MS65 |
|---|---|---|---|---|---|---|
| 2013 P | Est. 1000 | PF65 600 | | | | |

**KM# 2067 25 DOLLARS**
7.84 g., 0.9999 Gold 0.2519 oz. AGW, 20.6 mm. **Ruler:** Elizabeth II **Subject:** A.B. Banjo Paterson, 150th Anniversary of Birth **Obv:** Head with tiara right **Rev:** Paterson in color

| Date | Mintage | VF20 | XF40 | MS60 | MS63 | MS65 |
|---|---|---|---|---|---|---|
| 2013 P | 5,000 | PF65 600 | | | | |

**KM# 784 30 DOLLARS**
1000.00 g., 0.999 Silver 32.1186 oz. ASW **Ruler:** Elizabeth II **Subject:** Commonwealth Games **Obv:** Head with tiara right **Rev:** Two figures within circle of all the sports

| Date | Mintage | VF20 | XF40 | MS60 | MS63 | MS65 |
|---|---|---|---|---|---|---|
| 2006 | — | PF65 1,250 | | | | |

**KM# 1955 30 DOLLARS**
1000.00 g., 0.999 Silver 32.1186 oz. ASW, 100 mm. **Ruler:** Elizabeth II **Subject:** Kangaroo Road Sign

| Date | Mintage | VF20 | XF40 | MS60 | MS63 | MS65 |
|---|---|---|---|---|---|---|
| 2013 | Est. 1500 | PF65 900 | | | | |

**KM# 648 50 DOLLARS**
36.51 g., Tri-Metallic .9999 Gold 7.8g, 13.1 mm center in .999 Silver 13.39g, 26.85mm inner ring within a copper 15.32g, 3, 38.74 mm. **Ruler:** Elizabeth II **Subject:** Commonwealth Games **Obv:** Head with tiara right **Rev:** Victorious athletes within inscriptions and runners **Edge:** Reeded

| Date | Mintage | VF20 | XF40 | MS60 | MS63 | MS65 |
|---|---|---|---|---|---|---|
| 2002 B | 5,000 | PF65 600 | | | | |

**KM# 724 50 DOLLARS**
36.51 g., Tri-Metallic .999 Gold 7.8g center in .999 Silver 13.39g ring within .999 Copper 15.32g outer ring, 38.74 mm. **Ruler:** Elizabeth II **Subject:** Olympics - Sydney to Athens **Obv:** Head with tiara right, denomination below **Rev:** Crossed olive and wattle branches about Australian flag and Olympic ring logo **Edge:** Reeded

| Date | Mintage | VF20 | XF40 | MS60 | MS63 | MS65 |
|---|---|---|---|---|---|---|
| 2004 B | 2,500 | PF65 625 | | | | |

**KM# 785 50 DOLLARS**
Tri-Metallic Gold center within Silver ring within Copper outer ring, 38.74 mm. **Ruler:** Elizabeth II **Subject:** Melbourne Commonwealth Games **Obv:** Head with tiara right, denomination below **Rev:** Two stylized athletes on central plug surrounded by Games legend and circle of athletes

| Date | Mintage | VF20 | XF40 | MS60 | MS63 | MS65 |
|---|---|---|---|---|---|---|
| 2006 | — | PF65 550 | | | | |

**KM# 952 50 DOLLARS**
15.50 g., 0.999 Gold 0.4979 oz. AGW, 25 mm. **Ruler:** Elizabeth II **Subject:** Australian Fauna **Obv:** Head with tiara right **Rev:** Saltwater crocodile

| Date | Mintage | VF20 | XF40 | MS60 | MS63 | MS65 |
|---|---|---|---|---|---|---|
| 2006 P | 588 | PF65 900 | | | | |

**KM# 955 50 DOLLARS**
15.50 g., 0.999 Gold 0.4979 oz. AGW, 25 mm. **Ruler:** Elizabeth II **Subject:** Australian Fauna **Obv:** Head with tiara right **Rev:** Grey kangaroo

| Date | Mintage | VF20 | XF40 | MS60 | MS63 | MS65 |
|---|---|---|---|---|---|---|
| 2006 P | 714 | PF65 900 | | | | |

**KM# 958 50 DOLLARS**
15.50 g., 0.999 Gold 0.4979 oz. AGW, 25 mm. **Ruler:** Elizabeth II **Subject:** Australian Fauna **Obv:** Head with tiara right **Rev:** Emu

| Date | Mintage | VF20 | XF40 | MS60 | MS63 | MS65 |
|---|---|---|---|---|---|---|
| 2006 P | 446 | PF65 900 | | | | |

**KM# 961 50 DOLLARS**
15.50 g., 0.999 Gold 0.4979 oz. AGW, 25 mm. **Ruler:** Elizabeth II **Subject:** Australian Fauna **Obv:** Head with tiara right **Rev:** Koala

| Date | Mintage | VF20 | XF40 | MS60 | MS63 | MS65 |
|---|---|---|---|---|---|---|
| 2006 P | 1,000 | PF65 900 | | | | |

**KM# 964 50 DOLLARS**
15.50 g., 0.999 Gold 0.4979 oz. AGW, 25 mm. **Ruler:** Elizabeth II **Subject:** Australian Fauna **Obv:** Head with tiara right **Rev:** Kookaburra

| Date | Mintage | VF20 | XF40 | MS60 | MS63 | MS65 |
|---|---|---|---|---|---|---|
| 2006 P | 738 | PF65 900 | | | | |

**KM# 981 50 DOLLARS**
15.50 g., 0.999 Platinum 0.4979 oz. APW **Ruler:** Elizabeth II **Subject:** Australian Flora **Obv:** Head with tiara right **Rev:** Cooktown orchid

| Date | Mintage | VF20 | XF40 | MS60 | MS63 | MS65 |
|---|---|---|---|---|---|---|
| 2006 P | 169 | PF65 975 | | | | |

**KM# 983 50 DOLLARS**
15.50 g., 0.999 Platinum 0.4979 oz. APW **Ruler:** Elizabeth II **Subject:** Australian Flora **Obv:** Head with tiara right **Rev:** Sturt's desert rose

| Date | Mintage | VF20 | XF40 | MS60 | MS63 | MS65 |
|---|---|---|---|---|---|---|
| 2006 P | 171 | PF65 975 | | | | |

**KM# 985 50 DOLLARS**
15.50 g., 0.999 Platinum 0.4979 oz. APW **Ruler:** Elizabeth II **Subject:** Australian Flora **Obv:** Head with tiara right **Rev:** Royal bluebell

| Date | Mintage | VF20 | XF40 | MS60 | MS63 | MS65 |
|---|---|---|---|---|---|---|
| 2006 P | 153 | PF65 975 | | | | |

**KM# 987 50 DOLLARS**
15.50 g., 0.999 Platinum 0.4979 oz. APW **Ruler:** Elizabeth II **Subject:** Australian Flora **Obv:** Head with tiara right **Rev:** Kangaroo paw

| Date | Mintage | VF20 | XF40 | MS60 | MS63 | MS65 |
|---|---|---|---|---|---|---|
| 2006 P | 155 | **PF65** 975 | | | | |

**KM# 989 50 DOLLARS**
15.50 g., 0.999 Platinum 0.4979 oz. APW **Ruler:** Elizabeth II **Subject:** Australian Flora **Obv:** Head with tiara right **Rev:** Common pink heath

| Date | Mintage | VF20 | XF40 | MS60 | MS63 | MS65 |
|---|---|---|---|---|---|---|
| 2006 P | 138 | **PF65** 975 | | | | |

**KM# 967 50 DOLLARS**
15.50 g., 0.999 Gold 0.4979 oz. AGW, 25 mm. **Ruler:** Elizabeth II **Subject:** Australian Fauna **Obv:** Head with tiara right **Rev:** Echidna

| Date | Mintage | VF20 | XF40 | MS60 | MS63 | MS65 |
|---|---|---|---|---|---|---|
| 2007 P | 269 | **PF65** 900 | | | | |

**KM# 970 50 DOLLARS**
15.50 g., 0.999 Gold 0.4979 oz. AGW, 25 mm. **Ruler:** Elizabeth II **Subject:** Australian Fauna **Obv:** Head with tiara right **Rev:** Common wombat

| Date | Mintage | VF20 | XF40 | MS60 | MS63 | MS65 |
|---|---|---|---|---|---|---|
| 2007 P | 253 | **PF65** 900 | | | | |

**KM# 973 50 DOLLARS**
15.50 g., 0.999 Gold 0.4979 oz. AGW, 25 mm. **Ruler:** Elizabeth II **Subject:** Australian Fauna **Obv:** Head with tiara right **Rev:** Tasmanian devil

| Date | Mintage | VF20 | XF40 | MS60 | MS63 | MS65 |
|---|---|---|---|---|---|---|
| 2007 P | 284 | **PF65** 900 | | | | |

**KM# 976 50 DOLLARS**
15.50 g., 0.999 Gold 0.4979 oz. AGW, 25 mm. **Ruler:** Elizabeth II **Subject:** Australian Fauna **Obv:** Head with tiara right **Rev:** Great white shark

| Date | Mintage | VF20 | XF40 | MS60 | MS63 | MS65 |
|---|---|---|---|---|---|---|
| 2007 P | 706 | **PF65** 900 | | | | |

**KM# 979 50 DOLLARS**
15.50 g., 0.999 Gold 0.4979 oz. AGW, 25 mm. **Ruler:** Elizabeth II **Subject:** Australian Fauna **Obv:** Head with tiara right **Rev:** Platypus

| Date | Mintage | VF20 | XF40 | MS60 | MS63 | MS65 |
|---|---|---|---|---|---|---|
| 2007 P | 257 | **PF65** 900 | | | | |

**KM# 991 50 DOLLARS**
15.50 g., 0.999 Platinum 0.4979 oz. APW, 24 mm. **Ruler:** Elizabeth II **Subject:** Australian Flora **Obv:** Head with tiara right **Rev:** Anemone buttercup

| Date | Mintage | VF20 | XF40 | MS60 | MS63 | MS65 |
|---|---|---|---|---|---|---|
| 2007 P | 78 | **PF65** 975 | | | | |

**KM# 993 50 DOLLARS**
15.50 g., 0.999 Platinum 0.4979 oz. APW **Ruler:** Elizabeth II **Subject:** Australian Flora **Obv:** Head with tiara right **Rev:** Sturt's desert pea

| Date | Mintage | VF20 | XF40 | MS60 | MS63 | MS65 |
|---|---|---|---|---|---|---|
| 2007 P | 78 | **PF65** 975 | | | | |

**KM# 995 50 DOLLARS**
15.50 g., 0.999 Platinum 0.4979 oz. APW, 24 mm. **Ruler:** Elizabeth II **Subject:** Australian Flora **Obv:** Head with tiara right **Rev:** Tasmanian Bluegum

| Date | Mintage | VF20 | XF40 | MS60 | MS63 | MS65 |
|---|---|---|---|---|---|---|
| 2007 P | 79 | **PF65** 975 | | | | |

**KM# 997 50 DOLLARS**
15.50 g., 0.999 Platinum 0.4979 oz. APW **Ruler:** Elizabeth II **Subject:** Australian Flora **Obv:** Head with tiara right **Rev:** Waratah

| Date | Mintage | VF20 | XF40 | MS60 | MS63 | MS65 |
|---|---|---|---|---|---|---|
| 2007 P | 83 | **PF65** 975 | | | | |

**KM# 999 50 DOLLARS**
15.50 g., 0.999 Platinum 0.4979 oz. APW **Ruler:** Elizabeth II **Subject:** Australian Flora **Obv:** Head with tiara right **Rev:** Golden wattle

| Date | Mintage | VF20 | XF40 | MS60 | MS63 | MS65 |
|---|---|---|---|---|---|---|
| 2007 P | 80 | **PF65** 975 | | | | |

**KM# 1167 50 DOLLARS**
15.55 g., 0.999 Platinum 0.4994 oz. APW, 25 mm. **Ruler:** Elizabeth II **Subject:** Australian Flora **Rev:** Black-anther flax lily **Rev. Legend:** DISCOVER AUSTRALIA

| Date | Mintage | VF20 | XF40 | MS60 | MS63 | MS65 |
|---|---|---|---|---|---|---|
| 2008 | — | **PF65** 975 | | | | |

**KM# 1196 50 DOLLARS**
15.55 g., 0.999 Gold 0.4994 oz. AGW, 25 mm. **Ruler:** Elizabeth II **Obv:** Head right **Rev:** Dolphin **Rev. Legend:** DISCOVER AUSTRALIA

| Date | Mintage | VF20 | XF40 | MS60 | MS63 | MS65 |
|---|---|---|---|---|---|---|
| 2008 P | 673 | **PF65** 900 | | | | |

**KM# 1197 50 DOLLARS**
15.55 g., 0.999 Gold 0.4994 oz. AGW, 25 mm. **Ruler:** Elizabeth II **Obv:** Head right **Rev:** King brown snake **Rev. Legend:** DISCOVER AUSTRALIA

| Date | Mintage | VF20 | XF40 | MS60 | MS63 | MS65 |
|---|---|---|---|---|---|---|
| 2008 P | 255 | **PF65** 900 | | | | |

**KM# 1198 50 DOLLARS**
15.55 g., 0.999 Gold 0.4994 oz. AGW, 25 mm. **Ruler:** Elizabeth II **Obv:** Head right **Rev:** Brogla **Rev. Legend:** DISCOVER AUSTRALIA

| Date | Mintage | VF20 | XF40 | MS60 | MS63 | MS65 |
|---|---|---|---|---|---|---|
| 2008 P | 211 | **PF65** 900 | | | | |

**KM# 1199 50 DOLLARS**
15.55 g., 0.999 Gold 0.4994 oz. AGW, 25 mm. **Ruler:** Elizabeth II **Obv:** Head right **Rev:** Dingo **Rev. Legend:** DISCOVER AUSTRALIA

| Date | Mintage | VF20 | XF40 | MS60 | MS63 | MS65 |
|---|---|---|---|---|---|---|
| 2008 P | 221 | **PF65** 900 | | | | |

**KM# 1200 50 DOLLARS**
15.55 g., 0.999 Gold 0.4994 oz. AGW, 25 mm. **Ruler:** Elizabeth II **Obv:** Head right **Rev:** Frill-neck lizard **Rev. Legend:** DISCOVER AUSTRALIA

| Date | Mintage | VF20 | XF40 | MS60 | MS63 | MS65 |
|---|---|---|---|---|---|---|
| 2008 P | 219 | **PF65** 900 | | | | |

**KM# 1206 50 DOLLARS**
15.55 g., 0.999 Platinum 0.4994 oz. APW, 26 mm. **Ruler:** Elizabeth II **Obv:** Head right **Rev:** Black anther flax lily, multicolor **Rev. Legend:** DISCOVER AUSTRALIA

| Date | Mintage | VF20 | XF40 | MS60 | MS63 | MS65 |
|---|---|---|---|---|---|---|
| 2008 P | 104 | PF65 1,500 | | | | |

**KM# 1207 50 DOLLARS**
15.55 g., 0.999 Platinum 0.4994 oz. APW, 26 mm. **Ruler:** Elizabeth II **Obv:** Head right **Rev:** Native fragipan, multicolor **Rev. Legend:** DISCOVER AUSTRALIA

| Date | Mintage | VF20 | XF40 | MS60 | MS63 | MS65 |
|---|---|---|---|---|---|---|
| 2008 P | 105 | PF65 1,500 | | | | |

**KM# 1208 50 DOLLARS**
15.55 g., 0.999 Platinum 0.4994 oz. APW, 26 mm. **Ruler:** Elizabeth II **Obv:** Head right **Rev:** Geraldton wax, multicolor **Rev. Legend:** DISCOVER AUSTRALIA

| Date | Mintage | VF20 | XF40 | MS60 | MS63 | MS65 |
|---|---|---|---|---|---|---|
| 2008 P | 101 | PF65 1,500 | | | | |

**KM# 1209 50 DOLLARS**
15.55 g., 0.999 Platinum 0.4994 oz. APW, 26 mm. **Ruler:** Elizabeth II **Obv:** Head right **Rev:** Red-flowered kurrajong, multicolor **Rev. Legend:** DISCOVER AUSTRALIA

| Date | Mintage | VF20 | XF40 | MS60 | MS63 | MS65 |
|---|---|---|---|---|---|---|
| 2008 P | 101 | PF65 1,500 | | | | |

**KM# 1210 50 DOLLARS**
15.55 g., 0.999 Platinum 0.4994 oz. APW **Ruler:** Elizabeth II **Obv:** Head right **Rev:** Small-leaf lilly pilly, multicolor **Rev. Legend:** DISCOVER AUSTRALIA

| Date | Mintage | VF20 | XF40 | MS60 | MS63 | MS65 |
|---|---|---|---|---|---|---|
| 2008 P | 99 | PF65 1,500 | | | | |

**KM# 1227 50 DOLLARS**
15.55 g., 0.999 Gold 0.4994 oz. AGW, 25 mm. **Ruler:** Elizabeth II **Obv:** Head right **Rev:** Dreaming kangaroo

| Date | Mintage | VF20 | XF40 | MS60 | MS63 | MS65 |
|---|---|---|---|---|---|---|
| 2009 P | 1,000 | PF65 1,100 | | | | |

**KM# 1229 50 DOLLARS**
15.55 g., 0.999 Gold 0.4994 oz. AGW, 25 mm. **Ruler:** Elizabeth II **Obv:** Head right **Rev:** Dreaming king brown snake

| Date | Mintage | VF20 | XF40 | MS60 | MS63 | MS65 |
|---|---|---|---|---|---|---|
| 2009 P | 1,000 | PF65 1,100 | | | | |

**KM# 1230 50 DOLLARS**
15.55 g., 0.999 Gold 0.4994 oz. AGW, 25 mm. **Ruler:** Elizabeth II **Obv:** Head right **Rev:** Dreaming brolga

| Date | Mintage | VF20 | XF40 | MS60 | MS63 | MS65 |
|---|---|---|---|---|---|---|
| 2009 P | 1,000 | PF65 1,100 | | | | |

**KM# 1231 50 DOLLARS**
15.55 g., 0.999 Gold 0.4994 oz. AGW, 25 mm. **Ruler:** Elizabeth II **Obv:** Head right **Rev:** Dreaming echidna

| Date | Mintage | VF20 | XF40 | MS60 | MS63 | MS65 |
|---|---|---|---|---|---|---|
| 2009 P | 1,000 | PF65 1,100 | | | | |

**KM# 1237 50 DOLLARS**
15.55 g., 0.999 Platinum 0.4994 oz. APW, 25 mm. **Ruler:** Elizabeth II **Obv:** Head right **Rev:** Dreaming kangaroo, multicolor

| Date | Mintage | VF20 | XF40 | MS60 | MS63 | MS65 |
|---|---|---|---|---|---|---|
| 2009 P | 1,000 | PF65 1,500 | | | | |

**KM# 1238 50 DOLLARS**
15.55 g., 0.999 Platinum 0.4994 oz. APW, 25 mm. **Ruler:** Elizabeth II **Obv:** Head right **Rev:** Dreaming dolphin, multicolor

| Date | Mintage | VF20 | XF40 | MS60 | MS63 | MS65 |
|---|---|---|---|---|---|---|
| 2009 P | 1,000 | PF65 1,500 | | | | |

**KM# 1239 50 DOLLARS**
15.55 g., 0.999 Platinum 0.4994 oz. APW, 25 mm. **Ruler:** Elizabeth II **Obv:** Head right **Rev:** Dreaming king brown snake, multicolor

| Date | Mintage | VF20 | XF40 | MS60 | MS63 | MS65 |
|---|---|---|---|---|---|---|
| 2009 P | 1,000 | PF65 1,500 | | | | |

**KM# 1240 50 DOLLARS**
15.55 g., 0.999 Platinum 0.4994 oz. APW, 25 mm. **Ruler:** Elizabeth II **Obv:** Head right **Rev:** Dreaming brolga, multicolor

| Date | Mintage | VF20 | XF40 | MS60 | MS63 | MS65 |
|---|---|---|---|---|---|---|
| 2009 P | 1,000 | PF65 1,500 | | | | |

**KM# 1241 50 DOLLARS**
15.55 g., 0.999 Platinum 0.4994 oz. APW, 25 mm. **Ruler:** Elizabeth II **Obv:** Head right **Rev:** Dreaming echidna, multicolor

| Date | Mintage | VF20 | XF40 | MS60 | MS63 | MS65 |
|---|---|---|---|---|---|---|
| 2009 P | 1,000 | PF65 1,500 | | | | |

**KM# 1398 50 DOLLARS**
15.50 g., 0.999 Platinum 0.4978 oz. APW, 26 mm. **Ruler:** Elizabeth II **Obv:** Head right **Rev:** Multicolor frill-neck lizard

| Date | Mintage | VF20 | XF40 | MS60 | MS63 | MS65 |
|---|---|---|---|---|---|---|
| 2010 P | 1,000 | PF65 1,550 | | | | |

**KM# 1400 50 DOLLARS**
15.50 g., 0.999 Gold 0.4978 oz. AGW, 26 mm. **Ruler:** Elizabeth II **Obv:** Head right **Rev:** Frill-neck lizard

| Date | Mintage | VF20 | XF40 | MS60 | MS63 | MS65 |
|---|---|---|---|---|---|---|
| 2010 P | 1,000 | PF65 1,250 | | | | |

**KM# 1404 50 DOLLARS**
15.50 g., 0.999 Platinum 0.4978 oz. APW, 26 mm. **Ruler:** Elizabeth II **Obv:** Head right **Rev:** Multicolor koala

| Date | Mintage | VF20 | XF40 | MS60 | MS63 | MS65 |
|---|---|---|---|---|---|---|
| 2010 P | 1,000 | PF65 1,550 | | | | |

**KM# 1406 50 DOLLARS**
15.50 g., 0.999 Gold 0.4978 oz. AGW, 26 mm. **Ruler:** Elizabeth II **Obv:** Head right **Rev:** Koala

| Date | Mintage | VF20 | XF40 | MS60 | MS63 | MS65 |
|---|---|---|---|---|---|---|
| 2010 P | 1,000 | PF65 1,250 | | | | |

**KM# 1410 50 DOLLARS**
15.50 g., 0.999 Platinum 0.4978 oz. APW, 26 mm. **Ruler:** Elizabeth II **Obv:** Head right **Rev:** Multicolor platypus

| Date | Mintage | VF20 | XF40 | MS60 | MS63 | MS65 |
|---|---|---|---|---|---|---|
| 2010 P | 1,000 | PF65 1,550 | | | | |

**KM# 1412 50 DOLLARS**
15.50 g., 0.999 Gold 0.4978 oz. AGW **Ruler:** Elizabeth II **Obv:** Head right **Rev:** Platypus

| Date | Mintage | VF20 | XF40 | MS60 | MS63 | MS65 |
|---|---|---|---|---|---|---|
| 2010 P | 1,000 | PF65 1,250 | | | | |

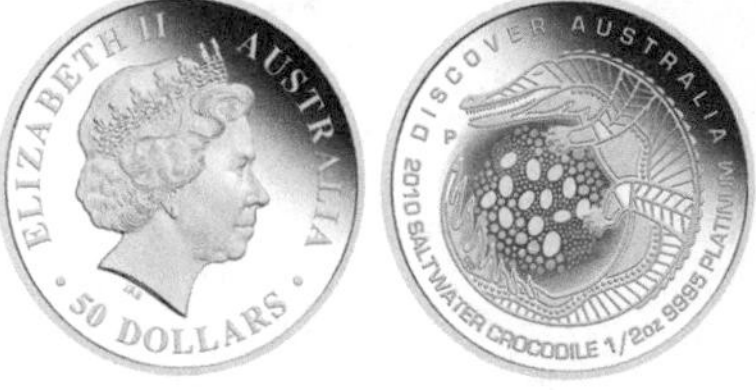


**KM# 1416 50 DOLLARS**
15.50 g., 0.999 Platinum 0.4978 oz. APW, 26 mm. **Ruler:** Elizabeth II **Obv:** Head right **Rev:** Multicolor saltwater crocodile

| Date | Mintage | VF20 | XF40 | MS60 | MS63 | MS65 |
|---|---|---|---|---|---|---|
| 2010 P | 1,000 | PF65 1,550 | | | | |

**KM# 1418 50 DOLLARS**
15.50 g., 0.999 Gold 0.4978 oz. AGW, 26 mm. **Ruler:** Elizabeth II **Obv:** Head right **Rev:** Saltwater crocodile

| Date | Mintage | VF20 | XF40 | MS60 | MS63 | MS65 |
|---|---|---|---|---|---|---|
| 2010 P | 1,000 | PF65 1,250 | | | | |

**KM# 1422 50 DOLLARS**
15.50 g., 0.999 Platinum 0.4978 oz. APW, 26 mm. **Ruler:** Elizabeth II **Obv:** Head right **Rev:** Multicolor wombat

| Date | Mintage | VF20 | XF40 | MS60 | MS63 | MS65 |
|---|---|---|---|---|---|---|
| 2010 P | 1,000 | PF65 1,100 | | | | |

**KM# 1424 50 DOLLARS**
15.50 g., 0.999 Gold 0.4978 oz. AGW, 26 mm. **Ruler:** Elizabeth II **Obv:** Head right **Rev:** Wombat

| Date | Mintage | VF20 | XF40 | MS60 | MS63 | MS65 |
|---|---|---|---|---|---|---|
| 2010 P | 2,500 | PF65 1,250 | | | | |

### KM# 1537 50 DOLLARS

15.55 g., 0.999 Gold 0.4994 oz. AGW **Ruler:** Elizabeth II **Subject:** Dreaming Emu **Rev:** Linear emu in color

| Date | Mintage | VF20 | XF40 | MS60 | MS63 | MS65 |
|---|---|---|---|---|---|---|
| 2011 P | — | PF65 1,250 | | | | |

### KM# 1539 50 DOLLARS

15.55 g., 0.999 Platinum 0.4994 oz. APW **Ruler:** Elizabeth II **Subject:** Dreaming Emu **Rev:** Linear emu in color

| Date | Mintage | VF20 | XF40 | MS60 | MS63 | MS65 |
|---|---|---|---|---|---|---|
| 2011 P | 1,000 | PF65 1,800 | | | | |

### KM# 1543 50 DOLLARS

15.55 g., 0.999 Gold 0.4994 oz. AGW **Ruler:** Elizabeth II **Subject:** Dreaming Tasmanian Devil **Rev:** Linear tasmanian devil in color

| Date | Mintage | VF20 | XF40 | MS60 | MS63 | MS65 |
|---|---|---|---|---|---|---|
| 2011 P | — | PF65 1,250 | | | | |

### KM# 1545 50 DOLLARS

15.55 g., 0.999 Platinum 0.4994 oz. APW **Ruler:** Elizabeth II **Subject:** Dreaming Tasmanian Devil **Rev:** Linear tasmanian devil in color

| Date | Mintage | VF20 | XF40 | MS60 | MS63 | MS65 |
|---|---|---|---|---|---|---|
| 2011 P | — | PF65 1,800 | | | | |

### KM# 1549 50 DOLLARS

15.55 g., 0.999 Gold 0.4994 oz. AGW **Ruler:** Elizabeth II **Series:** Dreaming Kookaburra **Rev:** Linear kookaburra in color

| Date | Mintage | VF20 | XF40 | MS60 | MS63 | MS65 |
|---|---|---|---|---|---|---|
| 2011 P | — | PF65 1,250 | | | | |

### KM# 1551 50 DOLLARS

15.55 g., 0.999 Platinum 0.4994 oz. APW **Ruler:** Elizabeth II **Subject:** Dreaming Kookaburra **Rev:** Linear kookaburra in color

| Date | Mintage | VF20 | XF40 | MS60 | MS63 | MS65 |
|---|---|---|---|---|---|---|
| 2011 P | 1,000 | PF65 1,800 | | | | |

### KM# 1555 50 DOLLARS

15.55 g., 0.999 Gold 0.4994 oz. AGW **Ruler:** Elizabeth II **Subject:** Dreaming shark **Rev:** Linear shark in color

| Date | Mintage | VF20 | XF40 | MS60 | MS63 | MS65 |
|---|---|---|---|---|---|---|
| 2011 P | — | PF65 1,250 | | | | |

### KM# 1557 50 DOLLARS

15.55 g., 0.999 Platinum 0.4994 oz. APW **Ruler:** Elizabeth II **Subject:** Dreaming shark **Rev:** Linear shark in color

| Date | Mintage | VF20 | XF40 | MS60 | MS63 | MS65 |
|---|---|---|---|---|---|---|
| 2011 P | 1,000 | PF65 1,800 | | | | |

### KM# 1561 50 DOLLARS

15.55 g., 0.999 Gold 0.4994 oz. AGW **Ruler:** Elizabeth II **Subject:** Dreaming Dingo **Rev:** Linear dingo in color

| Date | Mintage | VF20 | XF40 | MS60 | MS63 | MS65 |
|---|---|---|---|---|---|---|
| 2011 P | — | PF65 1,250 | | | | |

### KM# 1563 50 DOLLARS

15.55 g., 0.999 Platinum 0.4994 oz. APW **Ruler:** Elizabeth II **Subject:** Dreaming Dingo **Rev:** Linear dingo in color

| Date | Mintage | VF20 | XF40 | MS60 | MS63 | MS65 |
|---|---|---|---|---|---|---|
| 2011 P | 1,000 | PF65 1,800 | | | | |

### KM# 1726 50 DOLLARS

15.55 g., 0.999 Gold 0.4996 oz. AGW, 25.6 mm. **Ruler:** Elizabeth II **Rev:** Green and Gold Bell Frog in grass

| Date | Mintage | VF20 | XF40 | MS60 | MS63 | MS65 |
|---|---|---|---|---|---|---|
| 2012 P | 500 | PF65 950 | | | | |

### KM# 1727 50 DOLLARS

15.55 g., 0.999 Gold 0.4996 oz. AGW, 25.6 mm. **Ruler:** Elizabeth II **Rev:** Kookaburra standing right

| Date | Mintage | VF20 | XF40 | MS60 | MS63 | MS65 |
|---|---|---|---|---|---|---|
| 2012 P | 500 | PF65 950 | | | | |

### KM# 1728 50 DOLLARS

15.55 g., 0.999 Gold 0.4996 oz. AGW, 25.6 mm. **Ruler:** Elizabeth II **Rev:** Whale Shark swimming right

| Date | Mintage | VF20 | XF40 | MS60 | MS63 | MS65 |
|---|---|---|---|---|---|---|
| 2012 P | 500 | PF65 950 | | | | |

### KM# 1729 50 DOLLARS

15.55 g., 0.999 Gold 0.4996 oz. AGW, 25.6 mm. **Ruler:** Elizabeth II **Rev:** Kangaroo bounding right

| Date | Mintage | VF20 | XF40 | MS60 | MS63 | MS65 |
|---|---|---|---|---|---|---|
| 2012 P | 500 | PF65 950 | | | | |

### KM# 1730 50 DOLLARS

15.55 g., 0.999 Gold 0.4996 oz. AGW, 25.6 mm. **Ruler:** Elizabeth II **Rev:** Goanna lizard right

| Date | Mintage | VF20 | XF40 | MS60 | MS63 | MS65 |
|---|---|---|---|---|---|---|
| 2012 P | 500 | PF65 950 | | | | |

### KM# 2053 50 DOLLARS

15.55 g., 0.9999 Gold 0.500 oz. AGW, 25.6 mm. **Ruler:** Elizabeth II **Obv:** Head with tiara right **Rev:** Kangaroo, road landscape

| Date | Mintage | VF20 | XF40 | MS60 | MS63 | MS65 |
|---|---|---|---|---|---|---|
| 2013 P | Est. 550 | PF65 1,000 | | | | |

### KM# 1696 60 DOLLARS

10.00 g., 0.999 Gold 0.3212 oz. AGW, 22.5 mm. **Ruler:** Elizabeth II **Subject:** Australian 2012 London Olympic Team **Obv:** Head with tiara right **Rev:** Athlete standing on platform with flag

| Date | Mintage | VF20 | XF40 | MS60 | MS63 | MS65 |
|---|---|---|---|---|---|---|
| 2012 P | 2,012 | PF65 675 | | | | |

### KM# 643 100 DOLLARS

10.37 g., 0.9999 Gold 0.3333 oz. AGW, 25 mm. **Ruler:** Elizabeth II **Subject:** Golden Wattle Flower **Obv:** Queen's head right **Rev:** Flower and denomination **Edge:** Reeded

| Date | Mintage | VF20 | XF40 | MS60 | MS63 | MS65 |
|---|---|---|---|---|---|---|
| 2001 B | 3,000 | — | — | — | 600 | 625 |
| 2001 B | 2,500 | PF65 650 | | | | |

### KM# 636 100 DOLLARS

31.10 g., 0.9995 Platinum 0.9995 oz. APW, 32.1 mm. **Ruler:** Elizabeth II **Subject:** Multiculturalism **Obv:** Head with tiara right **Rev:** Six racially diverse portraits against a blue background **Edge:** Reeded

| Date | Mintage | VF20 | XF40 | MS60 | MS63 | MS65 |
|---|---|---|---|---|---|---|
| 2002 | 1,000 | PF65 1,850 | | | | |

### KM# 646 100 DOLLARS

31.40 g., 0.9999 Gold 1.0094 oz. AGW, 34.1 mm. **Ruler:** Elizabeth II **Subject:** Queen's 50th Anniversary of Accession **Obv:** Queen's head right **Rev:** Silhouette of George VI, queen's portrait and denomination **Edge:** Reeded

| Date | Mintage | VF20 | XF40 | MS60 | MS63 | MS65 |
|---|---|---|---|---|---|---|
| 2002 B | 2,002 | PF65 1,775 | | | | |

### KM# 657 100 DOLLARS

10.37 g., 0.9999 Gold 0.3333 oz. AGW, 25 mm. **Ruler:** Elizabeth II **Obv:** Queen's head right **Rev:** Sturt's Desert Rose **Edge:** Reeded

| Date | Mintage | VF20 | XF40 | MS60 | MS63 | MS65 |
|---|---|---|---|---|---|---|
| 2002 B | 2,500 | PF65 650 | | | | |
| 2002 B | 3,000 | — | — | — | 600 | 625 |

### KM# 800 100 DOLLARS

31.10 g., 0.999 Gold 0.999 oz. AGW, 34 mm. **Ruler:** Elizabeth II **Subject:** 50th Anniversary of the Coronation of Elizabeth II **Obv:** Head with tiara right **Rev:** Young portrait of Queen Elizabeth facing left, royal cipher, crown **Edge:** Plain

| Date | Mintage | VF20 | XF40 | MS60 | MS63 | MS65 |
|---|---|---|---|---|---|---|
| 2003 | 660 | PF65 1,800 | | | | |

### KM# 870 100 DOLLARS

10.37 g., 0.999 Gold 0.333 oz. AGW, 25 mm. **Ruler:** Elizabeth II **Subject:** State Floral Emblems **Obv:** Head with tiara right **Rev:** Royal Blue Bell flowers **Edge:** Reeded

| Date | Mintage | VF20 | XF40 | MS60 | MS63 | MS65 |
|---|---|---|---|---|---|---|
| 2003 | 1,383 | PF65 650 | | | | |

### KM# 797 100 DOLLARS

31.11 g., 0.999 Gold 0.9991 oz. AGW, 25.1 mm. **Ruler:** Elizabeth II **Subject:** 60th Anniversary of end of World War II **Obv:** Head with tiara right **Rev:** Latent news real photographic images of a dancing man celebrating the end of WWII

| Date | Mintage | VF20 | XF40 | MS60 | MS63 | MS65 |
|---|---|---|---|---|---|---|
| 2005 P | 750 | PF65 1,800 | | | | |

### KM# 1243 100 DOLLARS

31.11 g., 0.999 Gold 0.999 oz. AGW, 36 mm. **Ruler:** Elizabeth II **Subject:** Treasures of Australia **Obv:** Head right **Rev:** Mountains **Note:** Insert container with 1 carat of diamonds.

| Date | Mintage | VF20 | XF40 | MS60 | MS63 | MS65 |
|---|---|---|---|---|---|---|
| 2009 P | 715 | PF65 2,150 | | | | |

### KM# 1436 100 DOLLARS

Gold **Ruler:** Elizabeth II

| Date | Mintage | VF20 | XF40 | MS60 | MS63 | MS65 |
|---|---|---|---|---|---|---|
| 2010 | — | PF65 1,800 | | | | |

**KM# 1595 100 DOLLARS**
31.11 g., 0.999 Gold 0.999 oz. AGW, 36 mm. **Ruler:** Elizabeth II **Subject:** Treasures of Australia **Obv:** Head above pearl container **Rev:** Landscape above pearl container **Edge:** Reeded

| Date | Mintage | VF20 | XF40 | MS60 | MS63 | MS65 |
|---|---|---|---|---|---|---|
| 2011 P | Est. 1000 | PF65 2,250 | | | | |

**KM# 1596 100 DOLLARS**
31.11 g., 0.999 Gold 0.999 oz. AGW, 32 mm. **Ruler:** Elizabeth II **Subject:** Gold Coin Program, 25th Anniversary **Obv:** Head with tiara right **Rev:** Nugget

| Date | Mintage | VF20 | XF40 | MS60 | MS63 | MS65 |
|---|---|---|---|---|---|---|
| 2011 P | Est. 1500 | PF65 1,850 | | | | |

**KM# 2096 100 DOLLARS**
1000.00 g., 0.999 Silver 32.1186 oz. ASW **Ruler:** Elizabeth II **Subject:** Elizabeth II, 60th Anniversary of Reign **Rev:** St. Edward's Crown edged by 60 diamond motifs

| Date | Mintage | VF20 | XF40 | MS60 | MS63 | MS65 |
|---|---|---|---|---|---|---|
| 2012 P | 600 | PF65 2,000 | | | | |

**KM# 1956 100 DOLLARS**
31.10 g., 0.9999 Gold 0.9998 oz. AGW, 38 mm. **Ruler:** Elizabeth II **Subject:** Kangaroo Road Sign

| Date | Mintage | VF20 | XF40 | MS60 | MS63 | MS65 |
|---|---|---|---|---|---|---|
| 2013 | Est. 5000 | PF65 1,650 | | | | |

**KM# 2079 100 DOLLARS**
31.11 g., 0.999 Gold 0.999 oz. AGW **Ruler:** Elizabeth II **Subject:** Treasures of Europe - Garnet **Rev:** Alpine house and mountain

| Date | Mintage | VF20 | XF40 | MS60 | MS63 | MS65 |
|---|---|---|---|---|---|---|
| 2013 P | — | PF65 1,750 | | | | |

**KM# 2135 100 DOLLARS**
13.80 g., Aluminum-Bronze, 30.6 mm. **Ruler:** Elizabeth II **Subject:** Birth of Prince George **Obv:** Head with tiara right **Rev:** Prince William and Katherine with Prince George

| Date | Mintage | VF20 | XF40 | MS60 | MS63 | MS65 |
|---|---|---|---|---|---|---|
| 2013 | — | — | — | — | — | 15.00 |

**KM# 644 150 DOLLARS**
15.55 g., 0.9999 Gold 0.4999 oz. AGW, 30 mm. **Ruler:** Elizabeth II **Obv:** Queen's head right **Rev:** Golden Wattle flower, value **Edge:** Reeded

| Date | Mintage | VF20 | XF40 | MS60 | MS63 | MS65 |
|---|---|---|---|---|---|---|
| 2001 B | 1,500 | PF65 900 | | | | |

**KM# 658 150 DOLLARS**
15.55 g., 0.9999 Gold 0.4999 oz. AGW, 30 mm. **Ruler:** Elizabeth II **Subject:** State Floral Emblems **Obv:** Queen's head right **Rev:** Sturt's Desert Rose **Edge:** Reeded

| Date | Mintage | VF20 | XF40 | MS60 | MS63 | MS65 |
|---|---|---|---|---|---|---|
| 2002 B | 1,500 | PF65 900 | | | | |

**KM# 872 150 DOLLARS**
15.55 g., 0.999 Gold 0.4995 oz. AGW, 30 mm. **Ruler:** Elizabeth II **Subject:** State Floral Emblems **Obv:** Head with tiara right **Rev:** Royal Blue Bell flowers **Edge:** Reeded

| Date | Mintage | VF20 | XF40 | MS60 | MS63 | MS65 |
|---|---|---|---|---|---|---|
| 2003 | 1,105 | PF65 900 | | | | |

**KM# 874 150 DOLLARS**
15.55 g., 0.999 Gold 0.4995 oz. AGW, 30 mm. **Ruler:** Elizabeth II **Subject:** Rare Australian Birds **Obv:** Head with tiara right **Rev:** Red-tailed black cockatoo **Edge:** Reeded

| Date | Mintage | VF20 | XF40 | MS60 | MS63 | MS65 |
|---|---|---|---|---|---|---|
| 2003 | 2,500 | PF65 900 | | | | |

**KM# 731 150 DOLLARS**
10.37 g., 0.999 Gold 0.333 oz. AGW, 25 mm. **Ruler:** Elizabeth II **Obv:** Queen's head right **Rev:** Cassowary bird **Edge:** Reeded

| Date | Mintage | VF20 | XF40 | MS60 | MS63 | MS65 |
|---|---|---|---|---|---|---|
| 2004 B | 2,500 | PF65 625 | | | | |

**KM# 752 150 DOLLARS**
10.37 g., 0.9999 Gold 0.3333 oz. AGW, 25 mm. **Ruler:** Elizabeth II **Obv:** Queen's head right **Rev:** Malleefowl bird **Edge:** Reeded

| Date | Mintage | VF20 | XF40 | MS60 | MS63 | MS65 |
|---|---|---|---|---|---|---|
| 2005 B | 2,500 | PF65 625 | | | | |

**KM# 873 150 DOLLARS**
10.37 g., 0.999 Gold 0.333 oz. AGW, 25 mm. **Ruler:** Elizabeth II **Subject:** Rare Australian Birds **Obv:** Head with tiara right **Rev:** Red-tailed black cockatoo **Edge:** Reeded

| Date | Mintage | VF20 | XF40 | MS60 | MS63 | MS65 |
|---|---|---|---|---|---|---|
| 2006 | 2,500 | PF65 625 | | | | |

**KM# 732 200 DOLLARS**
15.55 g., 0.999 Gold 0.4995 oz. AGW, 30 mm. **Ruler:** Elizabeth II **Obv:** Queen's head right **Rev:** Cassowary bird **Edge:** Reeded

| Date | Mintage | VF20 | XF40 | MS60 | MS63 | MS65 |
|---|---|---|---|---|---|---|
| 2004 B | 2,500 | PF65 900 | | | | |

**KM# 753 200 DOLLARS**
15.55 g., 0.9999 Gold 0.500 oz. AGW, 30 mm. **Ruler:** Elizabeth II **Obv:** Queen's head right **Rev:** Malleefowl bird **Edge:** Reeded

| Date | Mintage | VF20 | XF40 | MS60 | MS63 | MS65 |
|---|---|---|---|---|---|---|
| 2005 B | 2,500 | PF65 900 | | | | |

**KM# 2006 200 DOLLARS**
Gold, 30 mm. **Ruler:** Elizabeth II **Rev:** Bird's head right

| Date | Mintage | VF20 | XF40 | MS60 | MS63 | MS65 |
|---|---|---|---|---|---|---|
| 2006 | — | PF65 900 | | | | |

**KM# 1695 200 DOLLARS**
62.21 g., 0.999 Gold 1.9982 oz. AGW **Ruler:** Elizabeth II **Subject:** Australian 2012 London Olympic Team

| Date | Mintage | VF20 | XF40 | MS60 | MS63 | MS65 |
|---|---|---|---|---|---|---|
| 2012 | — | PF65 3,750 | | | | |

**KM# 1702 200 DOLLARS**
62.22 g., 0.999 Gold 1.9983 oz. AGW, 41.1 mm. **Ruler:** Elizabeth II **Subject:** Elizabeth II, 60th Anniversary **Obv:** Head with tiara right **Rev:** Young head portrait right

| Date | Mintage | VF20 | XF40 | MS60 | MS63 | MS65 |
|---|---|---|---|---|---|---|
| 2012 P | 60 | PF65 4,500 | | | | |

**KM# 1931 200 DOLLARS**
62.21 g., 0.9999 Gold 2.000 oz. AGW, 41 mm. **Ruler:** Elizabeth II **Subject:** Queen Victoria 175th Anniversary of Coronation

| Date | Mintage | VF20 | XF40 | MS60 | MS63 | MS65 |
|---|---|---|---|---|---|---|
| 2013 P | Est. 150 | PF65 3,000 | | | | |

**KM# 2042 200 DOLLARS**
62.22 g., 0.9999 Gold 2.0001 oz. AGW, 41.1 mm. **Ruler:** Elizabeth II **Subject:** Sydney Opera House

| Date | Mintage | VF20 | XF40 | MS60 | MS63 | MS65 |
|---|---|---|---|---|---|---|
| 2013 | 200 | PF65 5,120 | | | | |

**KM# 1957 500 DOLLARS**
155.50 g., 0.9999 Gold 4.9989 oz. AGW, 60 mm. **Ruler:** Elizabeth II **Subject:** Kangaroo Road Sign

| Date | Mintage | VF20 | XF40 | MS60 | MS63 | MS65 |
|---|---|---|---|---|---|---|
| 2013 | — | PF65 7,500 | | | | |

**KM# 2095 1000 DOLLARS**
1000.00 g., 0.999 Gold 32.1186 oz. AGW **Ruler:** Elizabeth II **Subject:** Elizabeth II, 60th Anniversary of Reign **Rev:** St. Edward's Crown edged by 60 diamond motifs

| Date | Mintage | VF20 | XF40 | MS60 | MS63 | MS65 |
|---|---|---|---|---|---|---|
| 2012 P | 60 | PF65 63,000 | | | | |

**KM# 1958 3000 DOLLARS**
1000.00 g., 0.9999 Gold 32.1475 oz. AGW, 75 mm. **Ruler:** Elizabeth II **Subject:** Kangaroo Road Sign

| Date | Mintage | VF20 | XF40 | MS60 | MS63 | MS65 |
|---|---|---|---|---|---|---|
| 2013 | Est. 100 | PF65 47,500 | | | | |

## BULLION - KANGAROO

**KM# 1797 50 CENTS**
15.50 g., 0.999 Silver 0.4978 oz. ASW, 36.6 mm. **Ruler:** Elizabeth II **Rev:** Kangaroo in color

| Date | Mintage | VF20 | XF40 | MS60 | MS63 | MS65 |
|---|---|---|---|---|---|---|
| 2012 P | — | PF65 50.00 | | | | |

**KM# 2087 50 CENTS**
15.55 g., 0.9999 Silver 0.4999 oz. ASW, 36.6 mm. **Ruler:** Elizabeth II **Rev:** Kangaroo standing right, color background

| Date | Mintage | VF20 | XF40 | MS60 | MS63 | MS65 |
|---|---|---|---|---|---|---|
| 2013 P | — | PF65 50.00 | | | | |

**KM# 590 DOLLAR**
31.10 g., 0.999 Silver 0.999 oz. ASW, 40 mm. **Ruler:** Elizabeth II **Obv:** Queen's portrait **Rev:** Aboriginal-kangaroo design with dots **Edge:** Reeded

| Date | Mintage | VF20 | XF40 | MS60 | MS63 | MS65 |
|---|---|---|---|---|---|---|
| 2001 B Frosted Unc | — | — | — | — | — | 35.00 |
| 2001 B | — | PF65 40.00 | | | | |

**KM# 642 DOLLAR**
31.10 g., 0.999 Silver 0.999 oz. ASW, 40 mm. **Ruler:** Elizabeth II **Obv:** Head with tiara right, denomination below **Rev:** Aboriginal-style kangaroo with wavy line background **Edge:** Reeded

| Date | Mintage | VF20 | XF40 | MS60 | MS63 | MS65 |
|---|---|---|---|---|---|---|
| 2002 B | — | — | — | — | 35.00 | 42.00 |
| 2002 B | — | PF65 50.00 | | | | |

**KM# 798 DOLLAR**
31.10 g., 0.999 Silver 0.999 oz. ASW, 40 mm. **Ruler:** Elizabeth II **Obv:** Head with tiara right **Rev:** Aboriginal-style kangaroo design **Edge:** Reeded

| Date | Mintage | VF20 | XF40 | MS60 | MS63 | MS65 |
|---|---|---|---|---|---|---|
| 2003 | 35,230 | — | — | — | — | 40.00 |
| 2003 | 20,400 | PF65 45.00 | | | | |

**KM# 798a DOLLAR**
31.10 g., 0.999 Silver 0.999 oz. ASW partially gilt, 40 mm. **Ruler:** Elizabeth II **Obv:** Head with tiara right **Rev:** Aboriginal-style kangaroo design **Edge:** Reeded

| Date | Mintage | VF20 | XF40 | MS60 | MS63 | MS65 |
|---|---|---|---|---|---|---|
| 2003 | 7,450 | — | — | — | — | 125 |

**KM# 723 DOLLAR**
31.10 g., 0.999 Silver 0.999 oz. ASW, 40 mm. **Ruler:** Elizabeth II **Obv:** Head with tiara right, denomination below **Rev:** Kangaroo with semi-circle background **Edge:** Reeded

| Date | Mintage | VF20 | XF40 | MS60 | MS63 | MS65 |
|---|---|---|---|---|---|---|
| 2004 B | 12,500 | PF65 42.00 | | | | |
| 2004 B Frosted Unc | — | — | — | — | — | 37.00 |

**KM# 723a DOLLAR**
31.10 g., 0.999 Silver 0.999 oz. ASW partially gilt, 40 mm. **Ruler:** Elizabeth II **Obv:** Head with tiara right, denomination below **Rev:** Kangaroo with semi-circle background **Edge:** Reeded

| Date | Mintage | VF20 | XF40 | MS60 | MS63 | MS65 |
|---|---|---|---|---|---|---|
| 2004 B Frosted Unc | — | — | — | — | — | 65.00 |

**KM# 749 DOLLAR**
31.60 g., 0.999 Silver 1.0149 oz. ASW, 40 mm. **Ruler:** Elizabeth II **Obv:** Head with tiara right **Rev:** Kangaroo bounding under Southern Cross and above Federation Star **Edge:** Reeded

| Date | Mintage | VF20 | XF40 | MS60 | MS63 | MS65 |
|---|---|---|---|---|---|---|
| 2005 | — | — | — | — | 35.00 | 45.00 |
| 2005 | 12,500 | PF65 50.00 | | | | |

**KM# 749a DOLLAR**
31.10 g., 0.999 Silver 0.999 oz. ASW Partially Gold Plated, 40 mm. **Ruler:** Elizabeth II **Obv:** Head with tiara right **Rev:** Kangaroo bounding under Southern Cross and above Federation Star **Edge:** Reeded

| Date | Mintage | VF20 | XF40 | MS60 | MS63 | MS65 |
|---|---|---|---|---|---|---|
| 2005 | 12,500 | PF65 60.00 | | | | |

**KM# 837 DOLLAR**
31.60 g., 0.999 Silver 1.0149 oz. ASW, 40 mm. **Ruler:** Elizabeth II **Obv:** Head with tiara right **Rev:** Kangaroo bounding under Australian sun **Edge:** Reeded

| Date | Mintage | VF20 | XF40 | MS60 | MS63 | MS65 |
|---|---|---|---|---|---|---|
| 2006 | — | — | — | — | — | 35.00 |
| 2006 | 12,500 | PF65 42.00 | | | | |

**KM# 837a DOLLAR**
31.60 g., 0.999 Silver 1.0149 oz. ASW partially gilt, 40 mm. **Ruler:** Elizabeth II **Obv:** Head with tiara right **Rev:** Kangaroo bounding under Australian sun **Edge:** Reeded

| Date | Mintage | VF20 | XF40 | MS60 | MS63 | MS65 |
|---|---|---|---|---|---|---|
| 2006 | 7,500 | — | — | — | — | 55.00 |

**KM# 851 DOLLAR**
31.60 g., 0.999 Silver 1.0149 oz. ASW, 40 mm. **Ruler:** Elizabeth II **Obv:** Head with tiara right **Rev:** Kangaroo mother and joey **Edge:** Reeded

| Date | Mintage | VF20 | XF40 | MS60 | MS63 | MS65 |
|---|---|---|---|---|---|---|
| 2007 | 15,000 | — | — | — | — | 45.00 |
| 2007 | 12,500 | PF65 50.00 | | | | |

**KM# 1061 DOLLAR**
27.22 g., Copper-Nickel, 38.74 mm. **Ruler:** Elizabeth II **Rev:** Kangaroo holding football

| Date | Mintage | VF20 | XF40 | MS60 | MS63 | MS65 |
|---|---|---|---|---|---|---|
| 2008 | 9,234 | — | — | — | — | 25.00 |

**KM# 1061a DOLLAR**
31.11 g., 0.999 Silver 0.999 oz. ASW, 40 mm. **Ruler:** Elizabeth II **Rev:** Kangaroo holding football

| Date | Mintage | VF20 | XF40 | MS60 | MS63 | MS65 |
|---|---|---|---|---|---|---|
| 2008 | 7,500 | — | — | — | — | 65.00 |
| 2008 | 10,000 | PF65 50.00 | | | | |

**KM# 1061b DOLLAR**
31.11 g., 0.999 Silver 0.999 oz. ASW, 40 mm. **Ruler:** Elizabeth II **Rev:** Kangaroo holding football in color

| Date | Mintage | VF20 | XF40 | MS60 | MS63 | MS65 |
|---|---|---|---|---|---|---|
| 2008 | 12,500 | PF65 95.00 | | | | |

**KM# 1083 DOLLAR**
31.11 g., 0.999 Silver 0.999 oz. ASW, 40 mm. **Ruler:** Elizabeth II **Rev:** Kangaroo

| Date | Mintage | VF20 | XF40 | MS60 | MS63 | MS65 |
|---|---|---|---|---|---|---|
| 2009 | 20,000 | PF65 65.00 | | | | |
| 2009 | 20,000 | — | — | — | — | 50.00 |

**KM# 1083a DOLLAR**
31.11 g., 0.999 Silver 0.999 oz. ASW Partially gilt, 40 mm. **Ruler:** Elizabeth II **Rev:** Kangaroo

| Date | Mintage | VF20 | XF40 | MS60 | MS63 | MS65 |
|---|---|---|---|---|---|---|
| 2009 | — | — | — | — | — | 90.00 |

**KM# 1083b DOLLAR**
31.10 g., 0.999 Silver 0.999 oz. ASW, 40 mm. **Ruler:** Elizabeth II **Rev:** Kangaroo in color

| Date | Mintage | VF20 | XF40 | MS60 | MS63 | MS65 |
|---|---|---|---|---|---|---|
| 2009 | — | PF65 75.00 | | | | |

**KM# 1457 DOLLAR**
31.11 g., 0.999 Silver 0.999 oz. ASW, 40 mm. **Ruler:** Elizabeth II **Rev:** Two kangaroos playing

| Date | Mintage | VF20 | XF40 | MS60 | MS63 | MS65 |
|---|---|---|---|---|---|---|
| 2010 P | — | PF65 42.00 | | | | |

**KM# 1514 DOLLAR**
31.11 g., 0.999 Silver 0.999 oz. ASW, 40. mm. **Ruler:** Elizabeth II **Rev:** Kangaroo in color

| Date | Mintage | VF20 | XF40 | MS60 | MS63 | MS65 |
|---|---|---|---|---|---|---|
| 2010 | — | PF65 60.00 | | | | |

**KM# 1515 DOLLAR**
31.11 g., 0.999 Silver 0.999 oz. ASW, 40 mm. **Ruler:** Elizabeth II **Rev:** Kangaroo in color

| Date | Mintage | VF20 | XF40 | MS60 | MS63 | MS65 |
|---|---|---|---|---|---|---|
| 2010 | — | PF65 60.00 | | | | |

**KM# 1516 DOLLAR**
31.11 g., 0.999 Silver 0.999 oz. ASW, 40 mm. **Ruler:** Elizabeth II **Rev:** Kangaroo in color

| Date | Mintage | VF20 | XF40 | MS60 | MS63 | MS65 |
|---|---|---|---|---|---|---|
| 2010 | — | PF65 60.00 | | | | |

**KM# 1758 DOLLAR**
31.11 g., 0.999 Silver 0.999 oz. ASW, 40.6 mm. **Ruler:** Elizabeth II **Obv:** Head with tiara right **Rev:** Kangaroo right on rocks

| Date | Mintage | VF20 | XF40 | MS60 | MS63 | MS65 |
|---|---|---|---|---|---|---|
| 2010 P | — | PF65 85.00 | | | | |
| 2010 P | — | — | — | — | — | 75.00 |

**KM# 1762 DOLLAR**
31.11 g., 0.999 Silver 0.999 oz. ASW, 40.6 mm. **Ruler:** Elizabeth II **Obv:** Head with tiara right **Rev:** Kangaroo bounding left at sunset

| Date | Mintage | VF20 | XF40 | MS60 | MS63 | MS65 |
|---|---|---|---|---|---|---|
| 2010 F15 | 5,000 | PF65 125 | | | | |
| 2010 F15 | 7,000 | — | — | — | — | 125 |

**KM# 1605 DOLLAR**
31.11 g., 0.999 Silver 0.999 oz. ASW, 33 mm. **Ruler:** Elizabeth II **Obv:** Head with tiara right **Rev:** Kangaroo left, sun rays in background **Edge:** Reeded **Note:** Ultra High Relief

| Date | Mintage | VF20 | XF40 | MS60 | MS63 | MS65 |
|---|---|---|---|---|---|---|
| 2011 P | Est. 20000 | PF65 110 | | | | |

**KM# 1759 DOLLAR**
31.11 g., 0.999 Silver 0.999 oz. ASW, 40.6 mm. **Ruler:** Elizabeth II **Obv:** Head with tiara right **Rev:** Kangaroo and joey

| Date | Mintage | VF20 | XF40 | MS60 | MS63 | MS65 |
|---|---|---|---|---|---|---|
| 2011 P | — | PF65 85.00 | | | | |
| 2011 P | — | — | — | — | — | 75.00 |

## KM# 1737 DOLLAR

31.14 g., 0.999 Silver 1.000 oz. ASW, 40 mm. **Ruler:** Elizabeth II **Obv:** Head with tiara right **Rev:** Mareeba Rock Wallaby

| Date | Mintage | VF20 | XF40 | MS60 | MS63 | MS65 |
|---|---|---|---|---|---|---|
| 2012 | 20,000 | PF65 100 | | | | |
| 2012 | 20,000 | — | — | — | — | 75.00 |

## KM# 1830 DOLLAR

31.11 g., 0.999 Silver 0.999 oz. ASW, 33 mm. **Ruler:** Elizabeth II **Rev:** Kangaroo **Note:** Ultra High Relief

| Date | Mintage | VF20 | XF40 | MS60 | MS63 | MS65 |
|---|---|---|---|---|---|---|
| 2012 P | — | PF65 110 | | | | |

## KM# 1862 DOLLAR

31.11 g., 0.999 Silver 0.999 oz. ASW, 40 mm. **Ruler:** Elizabeth II **Obv:** Head in tiara right **Rev:** Kangaroo bounding right

| Date | Mintage | VF20 | XF40 | MS60 | MS63 | MS65 |
|---|---|---|---|---|---|---|
| 2012 | — | PF65 100 | | | | |

## KM# 1863 DOLLAR

31.11 g., 0.999 Silver 0.999 oz. ASW, 40 mm. **Ruler:** Elizabeth II **Obv:** Head in tiara right **Rev:** Kangaroo bounding right

| Date | Mintage | VF20 | XF40 | MS60 | MS63 | MS65 |
|---|---|---|---|---|---|---|
| 2013 | Est. 5000 | PF65 60.00 | | | | |

## KM# 2005 DOLLAR

6.03 g., 0.999 Silver 0.1937 oz. ASW, 21.69 mm. **Ruler:** Elizabeth II **Subject:** Kangaroo at Sunset

| Date | Mintage | VF20 | XF40 | MS60 | MS63 | MS65 |
|---|---|---|---|---|---|---|
| 2013 | Est. 5000 | PF63 20.00 | PF65 25.00 | | | |

## KM# 2023 DOLLAR

31.10 g., 0.999 Silver 0.999 oz. ASW, 40 mm. **Ruler:** Elizabeth II **Subject:** Kangaroo Series 20th Anniversary **Rev:** Kangaroo bounding right

| Date | Mintage | VF20 | XF40 | MS60 | MS63 | MS65 |
|---|---|---|---|---|---|---|
| 2013 | Est. 5000 | PF65 100 | | | | |

## KM# 2030 DOLLAR

31.11 g., 0.999 Silver 0.999 oz. ASW, 40 mm. **Ruler:** Elizabeth II **Rev:** Kangaroo standing on rock at left

| Date | Mintage | VF20 | XF40 | MS60 | MS63 | MS65 |
|---|---|---|---|---|---|---|
| 2013 | Est. 20000 | PF65 100 | | | | |
| 2013 | Est. 20000 | — | — | — | — | 80.00 |

## KM# 2085 DOLLAR

31.11 g., 0.9999 Silver 0.9999 oz. ASW, 40.6 mm. **Ruler:** Elizabeth II **Rev:** Kangaroo standing right **Note:** High relief

| Date | Mintage | VF20 | XF40 | MS60 | MS63 | MS65 |
|---|---|---|---|---|---|---|
| 2013 P | — | PF65 75.00 | | | | |

## KM# 1390 2 DOLLARS

0.50 g., 0.999 Gold **Ruler:** Elizabeth II **Obv:** Head right **Rev:** Kangaroo

| Date | Mintage | VF20 | XF40 | MS60 | MS63 | MS65 |
|---|---|---|---|---|---|---|
| 2010 (p) | — | — | — | — | 32.00 | 35.00 |

## KM# 1527 2 DOLLARS

0.50 g., 0.999 Gold, 11.6 mm. **Ruler:** Elizabeth II **Obv:** Head in tiara right **Rev:** Kangaroo bounding left

| Date | Mintage | VF20 | XF40 | MS60 | MS63 | MS65 |
|---|---|---|---|---|---|---|
| 2010 P | — | — | — | — | — | 50.00 |

## KM# 1649 2 DOLLARS

0.50 g., 0.999 Gold, 11.6 mm. **Ruler:** Elizabeth II **Obv:** Head with tiara right **Rev:** Kangaroo left

| Date | Mintage | VF20 | XF40 | MS60 | MS63 | MS65 |
|---|---|---|---|---|---|---|
| 2011 | — | PF65 50.00 | | | | |

## KM# 1790 2 DOLLARS

0.50 g., 0.999 Gold, 12 mm. **Ruler:** Elizabeth II **Obv:** Head in tiara right **Rev:** Kangaroo standing right, wind water pump at left

| Date | Mintage | VF20 | XF40 | MS60 | MS63 | MS65 |
|---|---|---|---|---|---|---|
| 2012 P | — | — | — | — | — | 50.00 |

## KM# 2072 2 DOLLARS

0.50 g., 0.9999 Gold, 14.1 mm. **Ruler:** Elizabeth II **Rev:** Kangaroo standing right

| Date | Mintage | VF20 | XF40 | MS60 | MS63 | MS65 |
|---|---|---|---|---|---|---|
| 2013 P | — | PF65 100 | | | | |

## KM# 893 5 DOLLARS

1.57 g., 0.999 Gold 0.0505 oz. AGW **Ruler:** Elizabeth II **Obv:** Head with tiara right **Rev:** Two kangaroos on map of Australia

| Date | Mintage | VF20 | XF40 | MS60 | MS63 | MS65 |
|---|---|---|---|---|---|---|
| 2001 | 10,000 | — | — | — | — | 93.00 |

## KM# 1776 10 DOLLARS

3.11 g., 0.999 Gold 0.0999 oz. AGW, 17.53 mm. **Ruler:** Elizabeth II **Rev:** Kangaroo bounding left at sunset

| Date | Mintage | VF20 | XF40 | MS60 | MS63 | MS65 |
|---|---|---|---|---|---|---|
| 2007 P | — | — | — | — | — | 225 |

## KM# 1772 10 DOLLARS

3.11 g., 0.999 Gold 0.0999 oz. AGW, 17.53 mm. **Ruler:** Elizabeth II **Rev:** Kangaroo bounding right in grassland

| Date | Mintage | VF20 | XF40 | MS60 | MS63 | MS65 |
|---|---|---|---|---|---|---|
| 2008 P | — | — | — | — | — | 225 |

## KM# 1764 10 DOLLARS

3.11 g., 0.999 Gold 0.0999 oz. AGW, 17.53 mm. **Ruler:** Elizabeth II **Obv:** Head with tiara right **Rev:** Kangaroo left, constellation in background

| Date | Mintage | VF20 | XF40 | MS60 | MS63 | MS65 |
|---|---|---|---|---|---|---|
| 2009 P | — | PF65 250 | | | | |

## KM# 1763 10 DOLLARS

3.11 g., 0.999 Gold 0.0999 oz. AGW, 17.53 mm. **Ruler:** Elizabeth II **Obv:** Head with tiara right **Rev:** Kangaroo right on rocks

| Date | Mintage | VF20 | XF40 | MS60 | MS63 | MS65 |
|---|---|---|---|---|---|---|
| 2010 P | 1,500 | PF65 250 | | | | |

## KM# 1768 10 DOLLARS

3.11 g., 0.999 Gold 0.0999 oz. AGW, 17.53 mm. **Ruler:** Elizabeth II **Rev:** Kangaroo

| Date | Mintage | VF20 | XF40 | MS60 | MS63 | MS65 |
|---|---|---|---|---|---|---|
| 2010 P | — | — | — | — | — | 225 |

## KM# 1522 10 DOLLARS

3.11 g., 0.999 Gold 0.0999 oz. AGW, 17.53 mm. **Ruler:** Elizabeth II **Rev:** Two kangaroos

| Date | Mintage | VF20 | XF40 | MS60 | MS63 | MS65 |
|---|---|---|---|---|---|---|
| 2011 | 1,500 | PF65 265 | | | | |

## KM# 1683 10 DOLLARS

3.11 g., 0.999 Gold 0.0999 oz. AGW, 17.53 mm. **Ruler:** Elizabeth II **Rev:** Kangaroo

| Date | Mintage | VF20 | XF40 | MS60 | MS63 | MS65 |
|---|---|---|---|---|---|---|
| 2012 P | — | PF65 200 | | | | |

## KM# 894 15 DOLLARS

3.11 g., 0.999 Gold 0.0999 oz. AGW **Ruler:** Elizabeth II **Obv:** Head with tiara right **Rev:** Two kangaroos on map of Australia

| Date | Mintage | VF20 | XF40 | MS60 | MS63 | MS65 |
|---|---|---|---|---|---|---|
| 2001 | 800 | — | — | — | — | 159 |

## KM# 897 15 DOLLARS

3.11 g., 0.999 Gold 0.0999 oz. AGW **Ruler:** Elizabeth II **Obv:** Head with tiara right **Rev:** Kangaroo browsing

| Date | Mintage | VF20 | XF40 | MS60 | MS63 | MS65 |
|---|---|---|---|---|---|---|
| 2002 | 800 | — | — | — | — | 159 |

## KM# 902 15 DOLLARS

3.11 g., 0.999 Gold 0.0999 oz. AGW **Ruler:** Elizabeth II **Obv:** Head with tiara right **Rev:** Two kangaroos hopping

| Date | Mintage | VF20 | XF40 | MS60 | MS63 | MS65 |
|---|---|---|---|---|---|---|
| 2003 | 500 | — | — | — | — | 159 |

## KM# 907 15 DOLLARS

3.11 g., 0.999 Gold 0.0999 oz. AGW **Ruler:** Elizabeth II **Obv:** Head with tiara right **Rev:** Crouching kangaroos facing left, Grass tree plant at right

| Date | Mintage | VF20 | XF40 | MS60 | MS63 | MS65 |
|---|---|---|---|---|---|---|
| 2004 | 500 | — | — | — | — | 159 |

## KM# 911 15 DOLLARS

3.11 g., 0.999 Gold 0.0999 oz. AGW **Ruler:** Elizabeth II **Obv:** Head with tiara right **Rev:** Kangaroo in bush

| Date | Mintage | VF20 | XF40 | MS60 | MS63 | MS65 |
|---|---|---|---|---|---|---|
| 2005 | 500 | — | — | — | — | 159 |

## KM# 1362 15 DOLLARS

3.11 g., 0.999 Gold 0.0999 oz. AGW **Ruler:** Elizabeth II **Obv:** Head right **Rev:** Kangaroo

| Date | Mintage | VF20 | XF40 | MS60 | MS63 | MS65 |
|---|---|---|---|---|---|---|
| 2010 (p) | — | — | — | — | — | 159 |

## KM# 1989 15 DOLLARS

3.11 g., 0.9999 Gold 0.100 oz. AGW, 16.6 mm. **Ruler:** Elizabeth II **Subject:** Australian Kangaroo

| Date | Mintage | VF20 | XF40 | MS60 | MS63 | MS65 |
|---|---|---|---|---|---|---|
| 2013 | Est. 200000 | PF65 159 | | | | |

## KM# 2081 15 DOLLARS

3.11 g., 0.9999 Gold 0.100 oz. AGW, 17.53 mm. **Ruler:** Elizabeth II **Rev:** Kangaroo standing right

| Date | Mintage | VF20 | XF40 | MS60 | MS63 | MS65 |
|---|---|---|---|---|---|---|
| 2013 P | — | PF65 159 | | | | |

**KM# 895 25 DOLLARS**
7.75 g., 0.999 Gold 0.2489 oz. AGW **Ruler:** Elizabeth II **Obv:** Head with tiara right **Rev:** Two kangaroos on map of Australia

| Date | Mintage | VF20 | XF40 | MS60 | MS63 | MS65 |
|---|---|---|---|---|---|---|
| 2001 | 500 | — | — | — | — | 379 |

**KM# 898 25 DOLLARS**
7.75 g., 0.999 Gold 0.2489 oz. AGW **Ruler:** Elizabeth II **Obv:** Head with tiara right **Rev:** Kangaroo browsing

| Date | Mintage | VF20 | XF40 | MS60 | MS63 | MS65 |
|---|---|---|---|---|---|---|
| 2002 | 500 | — | — | — | — | 379 |

**KM# 903 25 DOLLARS**
7.75 g., 0.999 Gold 0.2489 oz. AGW **Ruler:** Elizabeth II **Obv:** Head with tiara right **Rev:** Two kangaroos hopping

| Date | Mintage | VF20 | XF40 | MS60 | MS63 | MS65 |
|---|---|---|---|---|---|---|
| 2003 | 250 | — | — | — | — | 384 |

**KM# 908 25 DOLLARS**
7.75 g., 0.999 Gold 0.2489 oz. AGW **Ruler:** Elizabeth II **Obv:** Head with tiara right **Rev:** Crouching kangaroos facing left, Grass tree plant at right

| Date | Mintage | VF20 | XF40 | MS60 | MS63 | MS65 |
|---|---|---|---|---|---|---|
| 2004 | 250 | — | — | — | — | 384 |

**KM# 912 25 DOLLARS**
7.75 g., 0.999 Gold 0.2489 oz. AGW **Ruler:** Elizabeth II **Obv:** Head with tiara right **Rev:** Kangaroo in bush

| Date | Mintage | VF20 | XF40 | MS60 | MS63 | MS65 |
|---|---|---|---|---|---|---|
| 2005 | 250 | — | — | — | — | 384 |

**KM# 1777 25 DOLLARS**
7.77 g., 0.999 Gold 0.2496 oz. AGW **Ruler:** Elizabeth II **Rev:** Kangaroo bounding left at sunset

| Date | Mintage | VF20 | XF40 | MS60 | MS63 | MS65 |
|---|---|---|---|---|---|---|
| 2007 P | — | — | — | — | — | 385 |

**KM# 1773 25 DOLLARS**
7.77 g., 0.999 Gold 0.2496 oz. AGW **Ruler:** Elizabeth II **Rev:** Kangaroo bounding right in grassland

| Date | Mintage | VF20 | XF40 | MS60 | MS63 | MS65 |
|---|---|---|---|---|---|---|
| 2008 P | — | — | — | — | — | 385 |

**KM# 1765 25 DOLLARS**
7.77 g., 0.999 Gold 0.2496 oz. AGW, 22 mm. **Ruler:** Elizabeth II **Obv:** Head with tiara right **Rev:** Kangaroo left, constellation in background

| Date | Mintage | VF20 | XF40 | MS60 | MS63 | MS65 |
|---|---|---|---|---|---|---|
| 2009 P | — | PF65 385 | | | | |

**KM# 1363 25 DOLLARS**
7.75 g., 0.999 Gold 0.2489 oz. AGW **Ruler:** Elizabeth II **Rev:** Two kangaroos playing

| Date | Mintage | VF20 | XF40 | MS60 | MS63 | MS65 |
|---|---|---|---|---|---|---|
| 2010 P | — | — | — | — | — | 379 |

**KM# 1506 25 DOLLARS**
6.22 g., 0.999 Gold 0.1998 oz. AGW, 21.69 mm. **Ruler:** Elizabeth II **Obv:** Head with tiara right **Rev:** Kangaroo in outback, windmill at right

| Date | Mintage | VF20 | XF40 | MS60 | MS63 | MS65 |
|---|---|---|---|---|---|---|
| 2010 | 1,000 | PF65 825 | | | | |

**KM# 1507 25 DOLLARS**
6.22 g., 0.999 Gold 0.1998 oz. AGW, 21.69 mm. **Ruler:** Elizabeth II **Obv:** Head in tiara right **Rev:** Kangaroo in outback, windmill at center

| Date | Mintage | VF20 | XF40 | MS60 | MS63 | MS65 |
|---|---|---|---|---|---|---|
| 2010 | 1,000 | PF65 825 | | | | |

**KM# 1508 25 DOLLARS**
6.22 g., 0.999 Gold 0.1998 oz. AGW, 21.69 mm. **Ruler:** Elizabeth II **Obv:** Head in tiara right **Rev:** Kangaroo in outback, windmill at left

| Date | Mintage | VF20 | XF40 | MS60 | MS63 | MS65 |
|---|---|---|---|---|---|---|
| 2010 | 1,000 | PF65 825 | | | | |

**KM# 1769 25 DOLLARS**
7.77 g., 0.999 Gold 0.2496 oz. AGW **Ruler:** Elizabeth II **Rev:** Kangaroo

| Date | Mintage | VF20 | XF40 | MS60 | MS63 | MS65 |
|---|---|---|---|---|---|---|
| 2010 P | — | — | — | — | — | 385 |

**KM# 1684 25 DOLLARS**
7.77 g., 0.999 Gold 0.2496 oz. AGW **Ruler:** Elizabeth II **Rev:** Kangaroo

| Date | Mintage | VF20 | XF40 | MS60 | MS63 | MS65 |
|---|---|---|---|---|---|---|
| 2012 P | — | PF65 475 | | | | |

**KM# 1990 25 DOLLARS**
7.78 g., 0.9999 Gold 0.250 oz. AGW, 20.6 mm. **Ruler:** Elizabeth II **Subject:** Australian Kangaroo

| Date | Mintage | VF20 | XF40 | MS60 | MS63 | MS65 |
|---|---|---|---|---|---|---|
| 2013 | Est. 150000 | PF65 475 | | | | |

**KM# 2025 25 DOLLARS**
6.22 g., 0.999 Gold 0.1998 oz. AGW, 21.7 mm. **Ruler:** Elizabeth II **Rev:** Kangaroo bounding left at sunset

| Date | Mintage | VF20 | XF40 | MS60 | MS63 | MS65 |
|---|---|---|---|---|---|---|
| 2013 | Est. 1000 | PF65 650 | | | | |

**KM# 2082 25 DOLLARS**
7.77 g., 0.9999 Gold 0.2498 oz. AGW, 21.7 mm. **Ruler:** Elizabeth II **Rev:** Kangaroo standing right

| Date | Mintage | VF20 | XF40 | MS60 | MS63 | MS65 |
|---|---|---|---|---|---|---|
| 2013 P | — | PF65 500 | | | | |

**KM# 2124 25 DOLLARS**
7.78 g., 0.9999 Gold 0.250 oz. AGW, 20.6 mm. **Ruler:** Elizabeth II **Rev:** Kangaroo set against rural vista

| Date | Mintage | VF20 | XF40 | MS60 | MS63 | MS65 |
|---|---|---|---|---|---|---|
| 2014 P | 150,000 | — | — | — | — | 349 |

**KM# 899 50 DOLLARS**
15.50 g., 0.999 Gold 0.4979 oz. AGW **Ruler:** Elizabeth II **Obv:** Head with tiara right **Rev:** Kangaroo browsing

| Date | Mintage | VF20 | XF40 | MS60 | MS63 | MS65 |
|---|---|---|---|---|---|---|
| 2002 | 650 | — | — | — | — | 727 |

**KM# 904 50 DOLLARS**
15.50 g., 0.999 Gold 0.4979 oz. AGW **Ruler:** Elizabeth II **Obv:** Head with tiara right **Rev:** Two kangaroos hopping

| Date | Mintage | VF20 | XF40 | MS60 | MS63 | MS65 |
|---|---|---|---|---|---|---|
| 2003 | 500 | — | — | — | — | 727 |

**KM# 909 50 DOLLARS**
15.50 g., 0.999 Gold 0.4979 oz. AGW **Ruler:** Elizabeth II **Obv:** Head with tiara right **Rev:** Crouching kangaroos facing left, Grass tree plant at right

| Date | Mintage | VF20 | XF40 | MS60 | MS63 | MS65 |
|---|---|---|---|---|---|---|
| 2004 | 500 | — | — | — | — | 727 |

Note: Sets only

**KM# 913 50 DOLLARS**
15.50 g., 0.999 Gold 0.4979 oz. AGW **Ruler:** Elizabeth II **Obv:** Head with tiara right **Rev:** Kangaroo in bush

| Date | Mintage | VF20 | XF40 | MS60 | MS63 | MS65 |
|---|---|---|---|---|---|---|
| 2005 | 500 | — | — | — | — | 727 |

**KM# 1778 50 DOLLARS**
15.55 g., 0.999 Gold 0.4994 oz. AGW **Ruler:** Elizabeth II **Rev:** Kangaroo bounding left in sunset

| Date | Mintage | VF20 | XF40 | MS60 | MS63 | MS65 |
|---|---|---|---|---|---|---|
| 2007 P | — | — | — | — | — | 744 |

**KM# 1774 50 DOLLARS**
15.55 g., 0.999 Gold 0.4994 oz. AGW **Ruler:** Elizabeth II **Rev:** Kangaroo bounding right in grassland

| Date | Mintage | VF20 | XF40 | MS60 | MS63 | MS65 |
|---|---|---|---|---|---|---|
| 2008 P | — | — | — | — | — | 744 |

**KM# 1766 50 DOLLARS**
15.55 g., 0.999 Gold 0.4994 oz. AGW, 25 mm. **Ruler:** Elizabeth II **Obv:** Head with tiara right **Rev:** Kangaroo left, constellation in background

| Date | Mintage | VF20 | XF40 | MS60 | MS63 | MS65 |
|---|---|---|---|---|---|---|
| 2009 P | — | PF65 759 | | | | |

**KM# 1364 50 DOLLARS**
15.56 g., 0.999 Gold 0.4998 oz. AGW, 25 mm. **Ruler:** Elizabeth II **Obv:** Head right **Rev:** Two kangaroos playing

| Date | Mintage | VF20 | XF40 | MS60 | MS63 | MS65 |
|---|---|---|---|---|---|---|
| 2010 (p) | — | — | — | — | — | 730 |

**KM# 1770 50 DOLLARS**
15.55 g., 0.999 Gold 0.4994 oz. AGW, 25 mm. **Ruler:** Elizabeth II **Rev:** Kangaroo

| Date | Mintage | VF20 | XF40 | MS60 | MS63 | MS65 |
|---|---|---|---|---|---|---|
| 2010 P | — | — | — | — | — | 744 |

**KM# 1685 50 DOLLARS**
15.55 g., 0.999 Gold 0.4994 oz. AGW, 25 mm. **Ruler:** Elizabeth II **Rev:** Kangaroo

| Date | Mintage | VF20 | XF40 | MS60 | MS63 | MS65 |
|---|---|---|---|---|---|---|
| 2012 P | — | PF65 759 | | | | |

**KM# 1991 50 DOLLARS**
15.55 g., 0.9999 Gold 0.500 oz. AGW, 25.6 mm. **Ruler:** Elizabeth II **Subject:** Australian Kangaroo

| Date | Mintage | VF20 | XF40 | MS60 | MS63 | MS65 |
|---|---|---|---|---|---|---|
| 2013 | Est. 100000 | PF65 730 | | | | |

**KM# 2083 50 DOLLARS**
15.55 g., 0.9999 Gold 0.4999 oz. AGW, 25 mm. **Ruler:** Elizabeth II **Rev:** Kangaroo standing right

| Date | Mintage | VF20 | XF40 | MS60 | MS63 | MS65 |
|---|---|---|---|---|---|---|
| 2013 P | — | PF65 760 | | | | |

**KM# 1779 100 DOLLARS**
31.11 g., 0.999 Gold 0.999 oz. AGW, 32 mm. **Ruler:** Elizabeth II **Rev:** Kangaroo bounding left at sunset

| Date | Mintage | VF20 | XF40 | MS60 | MS63 | MS65 |
|---|---|---|---|---|---|---|
| 2007 P | — | — | — | — | — | 1,405 |

**KM# 1775 100 DOLLARS**
31.11 g., 0.999 Gold 0.999 oz. AGW, 32 mm. **Ruler:** Elizabeth II **Rev:** Kangaroo bounding right in grassland

| Date | Mintage | VF20 | XF40 | MS60 | MS63 | MS65 |
|---|---|---|---|---|---|---|
| 2008 P | — | — | — | — | — | 1,405 |

**KM# 1767 100 DOLLARS**
31.11 g., 0.999 Gold 0.999 oz. AGW, 32 mm. **Ruler:** Elizabeth II **Obv:** Head with tiara right **Rev:** Kangaroo left, constellation in background

| Date | Mintage | VF20 | XF40 | MS60 | MS63 | MS65 |
|---|---|---|---|---|---|---|
| 2009 P | — | PF65 1,405 | | | | |

**KM# 1365 100 DOLLARS**
31.10 g., 0.999 Gold 0.999 oz. AGW, 32 mm. **Ruler:** Elizabeth II **Obv:** Head right **Rev:** Kangaroo

| Date | Mintage | VF20 | XF40 | MS60 | MS63 | MS65 |
|---|---|---|---|---|---|---|
| 2010 (p) | — | — | — | — | — | 1,405 |

**KM# 1771 100 DOLLARS**
31.11 g., 0.999 Gold 0.999 oz. AGW, 32 mm. **Ruler:** Elizabeth II **Rev:** Kangaroo

| Date | Mintage | VF20 | XF40 | MS60 | MS63 | MS65 |
|---|---|---|---|---|---|---|
| 2010 P | — | — | — | — | — | 1,405 |

**KM# 1686 100 DOLLARS**
31.11 g., 0.999 Gold 0.999 oz. AGW, 32 mm. **Ruler:** Elizabeth II **Rev:** Kangaroo

| Date | Mintage | VF20 | XF40 | MS60 | MS63 | MS65 |
|---|---|---|---|---|---|---|
| 2012 P | — | PF65 1,405 | | | | |

**KM# 1992 100 DOLLARS**
31.11 g., 0.9999 Gold 1.0002 oz. AGW, 32.6 mm. **Ruler:** Elizabeth II **Subject:** Australian Kangaroo

| Date | Mintage | VF20 | XF40 | MS60 | MS63 | MS65 |
|---|---|---|---|---|---|---|
| 2013 | Est. 350000 | PF65 1,372 | | | | |

**KM# 2024 100 DOLLARS**
31.10 g., 0.999 Gold 0.999 oz. AGW, 38.74 mm. **Ruler:** Elizabeth II **Subject:** Kangaroo Series 20th Anniversary **Rev:** Kangaroo bounding right

| Date | Mintage | VF20 | XF40 | MS60 | MS63 | MS65 |
|---|---|---|---|---|---|---|
| 2013 | Est. 500 | PF65 2,600 | | | | |

**KM# 2084 100 DOLLARS**
31.11 g., 0.9999 Gold 0.9999 oz. AGW, 32 mm. **Ruler:** Elizabeth II **Rev:** Kangaroo standing right

| Date | Mintage | VF20 | XF40 | MS60 | MS63 | MS65 |
|---|---|---|---|---|---|---|
| 2013 P | — | PF65 1,407 | | | | |

**KM# 896 200 DOLLARS**
62.21 g., 0.999 Gold 1.9982 oz. AGW, 41 mm. **Ruler:** Elizabeth II **Obv:** Head with tiara right **Rev:** Two kangaroos on map of Australia

| Date | Mintage | VF20 | XF40 | MS60 | MS63 | MS65 |
|---|---|---|---|---|---|---|
| 2001 | 300 | — | — | — | — | 3,500 |

**KM# 901 200 DOLLARS**
62.21 g., 0.999 Gold 1.9982 oz. AGW, 41 mm. **Ruler:** Elizabeth II **Obv:** Head with tiara right **Rev:** Kangaroo browsing

| Date | Mintage | VF20 | XF40 | MS60 | MS63 | MS65 |
|---|---|---|---|---|---|---|
| 2002 | 300 | — | — | — | — | 3,500 |

**KM# 905 200 DOLLARS**
62.21 g., 0.999 Gold 1.9982 oz. AGW, 41 mm. **Ruler:** Elizabeth II **Obv:** Head with tiara right **Rev:** Two kangaroos hopping

| Date | Mintage | VF20 | XF40 | MS60 | MS63 | MS65 |
|---|---|---|---|---|---|---|
| 2003 | 200 | PF65 3,500 | | | | |

**KM# 910 200 DOLLARS**
62.21 g., 0.999 Gold 1.9982 oz. AGW, 41 mm. **Ruler:** Elizabeth II **Obv:** Head with tiara right **Rev:** Crouching kangaroos facing left, Grass tree plant at right

| Date | Mintage | VF20 | XF40 | MS60 | MS63 | MS65 |
|---|---|---|---|---|---|---|
| 2004 | 200 | PF65 3,500 | | | | |

**KM# 1462 300 DOLLARS**
1000.00 g., 0.999 Gold 32.1186 oz. AGW **Ruler:** Elizabeth II **Obv:** Head with tiara right **Rev:** Two kangaroos playing

| Date | Mintage | VF20 | XF40 | MS60 | MS63 | MS65 |
|---|---|---|---|---|---|---|
| 2010 P | — | — | — | — | — | 55,500 |

**KM# 1687 3000 DOLLARS**
1000.00 g., 0.9999 Gold 32.1475 oz. AGW, 75.6 mm. **Ruler:** Elizabeth II **Rev:** Red Kangaroo bounding left within circle of rays

| Date | Mintage | VF20 | XF40 | MS60 | MS63 | MS65 |
|---|---|---|---|---|---|---|
| 2012 P | — | — | — | — | — | 41,644 |
| 2013 P | — | — | — | — | — | 41,644 |
| 2014 P | — | — | — | — | — | 41,644 |

**KM# 1993 3000 DOLLARS**
1000.00 g., 0.9999 Gold 32.1475 oz. AGW, 75.6 mm. **Ruler:** Elizabeth II **Subject:** Australian Kangaroo

| Date | Mintage | VF20 | XF40 | MS60 | MS63 | MS65 |
|---|---|---|---|---|---|---|
| 2013 | — | PF65 46,500 | | | | |

**KM# 1569 1000000 DOLLARS**
1000000.00 g., 0.9999 Gold 32147.5075 oz. AGW, 800 mm. **Ruler:** Elizabeth II **Obv:** Head with tiara right **Rev:** Red Kangaroo bounding left **Note:** Cast. 120mm thick.

| Date | Mintage | VF20 | XF40 | MS60 | MS63 | MS65 |
|---|---|---|---|---|---|---|
| 2012 P Rare | 1 | — | — | — | — | — |

## BULLION - KOOKABURRA

**KM# 875 50 CENTS**
15.55 g., 0.999 Silver 0.4994 oz. ASW, 38.74 mm. **Ruler:** Elizabeth II **Obv:** Head with tiara right **Rev:** Kookaburra on branch, tail above, two leaves **Edge:** Reeded **Shape:** Square **Note:** Lenticular technology makes kookaburra appear to move.

| Date | Mintage | VF20 | XF40 | MS60 | MS63 | MS65 |
|---|---|---|---|---|---|---|
| 2002 P | 35,788 | PF65 35.00 | | | | |

**KM# 684 50 CENTS**
15.55 g., 0.999 Silver 0.4994 oz. ASW, 32.1x32.1 mm. **Ruler:** Elizabeth II **Obv:** Head with tiara right, denomination below **Rev:** Two kookaburras, one in flight **Edge:** Reeded **Shape:** Square

| Date | Mintage | VF20 | XF40 | MS60 | MS63 | MS65 |
|---|---|---|---|---|---|---|
| 2003 P | 11,585 | PF65 32.00 | | | | |

**KM# 876 50 CENTS**
15.55 g., 0.999 Silver 0.4994 oz. ASW, 38.74 mm. **Ruler:** Elizabeth II **Obv:** Head with tiara right **Rev:** Kookaburra perched on branch, tail below, four leaves **Edge:** Reeded **Shape:** Square

| Date | Mintage | VF20 | XF40 | MS60 | MS63 | MS65 |
|---|---|---|---|---|---|---|
| 2004 P | 9,839 | PF65 32.00 | | | | |

**KM# 877 50 CENTS**
15.55 g., 0.999 Silver 0.4994 oz. ASW, 25x25 mm. **Ruler:** Elizabeth II **Obv:** Head with tiara right **Rev:** Two kookaburras on branch, one laughing **Edge:** Reeded **Shape:** Square

| Date | Mintage | VF20 | XF40 | MS60 | MS63 | MS65 |
|---|---|---|---|---|---|---|
| 2005 P | 8,433 | PF65 32.00 | | | | |

**KM# 1799 50 CENTS**
15.50 g., 0.999 Silver 0.4978 oz. ASW, 36.6 mm. **Ruler:** Elizabeth II **Rev:** Kookaburra in color

| Date | Mintage | VF20 | XF40 | MS60 | MS63 | MS65 |
|---|---|---|---|---|---|---|
| 2012 P | — | PF65 50.00 | | | | |

**KM# 2086 50 CENTS**
15.55 g., 0.9999 Silver 0.4999 oz. ASW, 36.6 mm. **Ruler:** Elizabeth II **Rev:** Two kookaburra on branches, color background

| Date | Mintage | VF20 | XF40 | MS60 | MS63 | MS65 |
|---|---|---|---|---|---|---|
| 2013 P | — | PF65 50.00 | | | | |

## KM# 479 DOLLAR

31.97 g., 0.999 Silver 1.0268 oz. ASW **Ruler:** Elizabeth II **Obv:** Head with tiara right, denomination below **Rev:** Two kookaburras back-to-back on branch

| Date | Mintage | VF20 | XF40 | MS60 | MS63 | MS65 |
|---|---|---|---|---|---|---|
| 2001 | — | — | — | — | 35.00 | — |
| 2001 | 10,000 | — | — | — | 45.00 | — |
| Note: Federation star privy mark | | | | | | |
| 2001 | 50,000 | — | — | — | 35.00 | — |
| Note: Santa Claus privy mark | | | | | | |
| 2001 | 1,000 | — | — | — | 125 | — |
| Note: Love token personal message | | | | | | |
| 2001 | 75,000 | — | — | — | 42.00 | — |
| Note: New York State Quarter privy mark | | | | | | |
| 2001 | 75,000 | — | — | — | 42.00 | — |
| Note: North Carolina State Quarter privy mark | | | | | | |
| 2001 | 75,000 | — | — | — | 42.00 | — |
| Note: Rhode Island State Quarter privy mark | | | | | | |
| 2001 | 75,000 | — | — | — | 42.00 | — |
| Note: Vermont State Quarter privy mark | | | | | | |
| 2001 | 75,000 | — | — | — | 42.00 | — |
| Note: Kentucky State Quarter privy mark | | | | | | |

## KM# 691.1 DOLLAR

31.10 g., 0.999 Silver 0.999 oz. ASW, 40 mm. **Ruler:** Elizabeth II **Obv:** Head with tiara right, denomination below **Rev:** Kookaburra flying over map of Australia **Edge:** Reeded

| Date | Mintage | VF20 | XF40 | MS60 | MS63 | MS65 |
|---|---|---|---|---|---|---|
| 2001 P | 4,097 | PF65 42.00 | | | | |
| 2002 P | — | — | — | — | 35.00 | 37.00 |

## KM# 625 DOLLAR

31.10 g., 0.999 Silver 0.999 oz. ASW, 40.4 mm. **Ruler:** Elizabeth II **Subject:** U.S. State Quarter

| Date | Mintage | VF20 | XF40 | MS60 | MS63 | MS65 |
|---|---|---|---|---|---|---|
| 2002 | 75,000 | — | — | — | 45.00 | — |
| Note: Tennessee State Quarter privy mark | | | | | | |
| 2002 | 75,000 | — | — | — | 45.00 | — |
| Note: Ohio State Quarter privy mark | | | | | | |
| 2002 | 75,000 | — | — | — | 45.00 | — |
| Note: Louisiana State Quarter privy mark | | | | | | |
| 2002 | 75,000 | — | — | — | 45.00 | — |
| Note: Indiana State Quarter privy mark | | | | | | |
| 2002 | 75,000 | — | — | — | 45.00 | — |
| Note: Mississippi State Quarter privy mark | | | | | | |

## KM# 666 DOLLAR

31.62 g., 0.999 Silver 1.0156 oz. ASW, 40.3 mm. **Ruler:** Elizabeth II **Obv:** Head with tiara right, denomination below **Rev:** Kookaburra perched on branch **Edge:** Reeded

| Date | Mintage | VF20 | XF40 | MS60 | MS63 | MS65 |
|---|---|---|---|---|---|---|
| 2002 | 2,498 | PF65 37.00 | | | | |

## KM# 691.2 DOLLAR

31.62 g., 0.999 Silver 1.0156 oz. ASW, 40.5 mm. **Ruler:** Elizabeth II **Obv:** Head with tiara right, denomination below **Rev:** Multicolor US flag above a kookaburra in flight over Australian map **Edge:** Reeded

| Date | Mintage | VF20 | XF40 | MS60 | MS63 | MS65 |
|---|---|---|---|---|---|---|
| 2002 | 18,500 | — | — | — | 35.00 | 40.00 |

## KM# 683 DOLLAR

31.10 g., 0.999 Silver 0.999 oz. ASW, 40 mm. **Ruler:** Elizabeth II **Obv:** Head with tiara right, denomination below **Rev:** Two kookaburras, one in flight **Edge:** Reeded **Note:** Gilded.

| Date | Mintage | VF20 | XF40 | MS60 | MS63 | MS65 |
|---|---|---|---|---|---|---|
| 2003 P | 2,065 | PF65 37.00 | | | | |
| 2004 | 10,000 | — | — | — | — | 35.00 |
| 2004 | 15,000 | PF65 45.00 | | | | |

## KM# 1761 DOLLAR

31.11 g., 0.999 Silver 0.999 oz. ASW, 40.6 mm. **Ruler:** Elizabeth II **Obv:** Head with tiara right **Rev:** Kookaburra right on branch

| Date | Mintage | VF20 | XF40 | MS60 | MS63 | MS65 |
|---|---|---|---|---|---|---|
| 2003 P | — | — | — | — | — | 75.00 |

## KM# 883 DOLLAR

31.11 g., 0.999 Silver 0.999 oz. ASW, 40.5 mm. **Ruler:** Elizabeth II **Obv:** Head with tiara right **Rev:** Kookaburra perched on branch with four leaves **Edge:** Reeded

| Date | Mintage | VF20 | XF40 | MS60 | MS63 | MS65 |
|---|---|---|---|---|---|---|
| 2004 P | 2,156 | PF65 35.00 | | | | |
| 2005 | 5,000 | — | — | — | 45.00 | — |
| Note: Gemini privy mark | | | | | | |
| 2005 | 5,000 | — | — | — | 45.00 | — |
| Note: Aquarius privy mark | | | | | | |
| 2005 | 5,000 | — | — | — | 45.00 | — |
| Note: Pisces privy mark | | | | | | |
| 2005 | 5,000 | — | — | — | 45.00 | — |
| Note: Aries privy mark | | | | | | |
| 2005 | 5,000 | — | — | — | 45.00 | — |
| Note: Taurus privy mark | | | | | | |
| 2005 | 5,000 | — | — | — | 45.00 | — |
| Note: Cancer privy mark | | | | | | |
| 2005 | 5,000 | — | — | — | 45.00 | — |
| Note: Leo privy mark | | | | | | |
| 2005 | 5,000 | — | — | — | 45.00 | — |
| Note: Virgo privy mark | | | | | | |
| 2005 | 5,000 | — | — | — | 45.00 | — |
| Note: Libra privy mark | | | | | | |
| 2005 | 5,000 | — | — | — | 45.00 | — |
| Note: Scorpio privy mark | | | | | | |
| 2005 | 5,000 | — | — | — | 45.00 | — |
| Note: Sagittarius privy mark | | | | | | |
| 2005 | 5,000 | — | — | — | 45.00 | — |
| Note: Capricorn privy mark | | | | | | |

## KM# 883a DOLLAR

31.10 g., 0.999 Silver 0.999 oz. ASW partially gilt, 40 mm. **Ruler:** Elizabeth II **Obv:** Head with tiara right **Rev:** Kookaburra perched on branch with four leaves

| Date | Mintage | VF20 | XF40 | MS60 | MS63 | MS65 |
|---|---|---|---|---|---|---|
| 2004 | 10,000 | — | — | — | 55.00 | — |

## KM# 720 DOLLAR

1.04 g., 0.999 Silver 0.0332 oz. ASW partially gilt, 40 mm. **Ruler:** Elizabeth II **Obv:** Head with tiara right, denomination below **Rev:** Kookabarra, partially gilt **Edge:** Reeded

| Date | Mintage | VF20 | XF40 | MS60 | MS63 | MS65 |
|---|---|---|---|---|---|---|
| 2005 | — | PF65 65.00 | | | | |

### KM# 886 DOLLAR

31.56 g., 0.999 Silver 1.0137 oz. ASW, 40.5 mm. **Ruler:** Elizabeth II **Obv:** Head with tiara right **Rev:** Two kookaburras on branch, one laughing **Edge:** Reeded

| Date | Mintage | VF20 | XF40 | MS60 | MS63 | MS65 |
|---|---|---|---|---|---|---|
| 2005 P | 3,457 | **PF65** 40.00 | | | | |

### KM# 886a DOLLAR

31.56 g., 0.999 Silver 1.0137 oz. ASW partially gilt, 40.5 mm. **Ruler:** Elizabeth II **Obv:** Head with tiara right **Rev:** Two kookaburras on branch, one laughing **Edge:** Reeded

| Date | Mintage | VF20 | XF40 | MS60 | MS63 | MS65 |
|---|---|---|---|---|---|---|
| 2005 P | 9,170 | **PF65** 45.00 | | | | |

### KM# 889 DOLLAR

31.56 g., 0.999 Silver 1.0137 oz. ASW, 40.5 mm. **Ruler:** Elizabeth II **Obv:** Head with tiara right **Rev:** Kookaburra on branch, no leaves

| Date | Mintage | VF20 | XF40 | MS60 | MS63 | MS65 |
|---|---|---|---|---|---|---|
| 2007 | 300,000 | — | — | — | 35.00 | 38.00 |

### KM# 889a DOLLAR

31.56 g., 0.999 Silver 1.0137 oz. ASW partially gilt, 40.5 mm. **Ruler:** Elizabeth II **Obv:** Head with tiara right **Rev:** Kookaburra on branch, no leaves **Edge:** Reeded

| Date | Mintage | VF20 | XF40 | MS60 | MS63 | MS65 |
|---|---|---|---|---|---|---|
| 2008 P | 3,000 | **PF65** 45.00 | | | | |

### KM# 1760 DOLLAR

31.11 g., 0.999 Silver 0.999 oz. ASW, 40.6 mm. **Ruler:** Elizabeth II **Obv:** Head with tiara right **Rev:** Kookaburra on branch look at spider web at lower left

| Date | Mintage | VF20 | XF40 | MS60 | MS63 | MS65 |
|---|---|---|---|---|---|---|
| 2008 P | — | — | — | — | — | 75.00 |

### KM# 1277 DOLLAR

31.11 g., 0.999 Silver 0.999 oz. ASW, 40 mm. **Ruler:** Elizabeth II **Subject:** Kookaburra 20th Anniversary **Obv:** Head right **Rev:** Kookaburra standing right

| Date | Mintage | VF20 | XF40 | MS60 | MS63 | MS65 |
|---|---|---|---|---|---|---|
| 2009 P20 | 10,000 | **PF63** 45.00 | **PF65** 47.00 | | | |

### KM# 1278 DOLLAR

31.11 g., 0.999 Silver 0.999 oz. ASW, 40 mm. **Ruler:** Elizabeth II **Subject:** Kookaburra 20th Anniversary **Obv:** Head right **Rev:** Kookaburra on branch, head right

| Date | Mintage | VF20 | XF40 | MS60 | MS63 | MS65 |
|---|---|---|---|---|---|---|
| 2009 P20 | 10,000 | **PF63** 45.00 | **PF65** 47.00 | | | |

### KM# 1279 DOLLAR

31.11 g., 0.999 Silver 0.999 oz. ASW, 40 mm. **Ruler:** Elizabeth II **Subject:** Kookaburra 20th Anniversary **Obv:** Head right **Rev:** Kookaburra on branch left, head upwards

| Date | Mintage | VF20 | XF40 | MS60 | MS63 | MS65 |
|---|---|---|---|---|---|---|
| 2009 P20 | 10,000 | **PF63** 45.00 | **PF65** 47.00 | | | |

### KM# 1280 DOLLAR

31.11 g., 0.999 Silver 0.999 oz. ASW, 40 mm. **Ruler:** Elizabeth II **Subject:** Kookaburra 20th Anniversary **Obv:** Head right **Rev:** Kookaburra feeding young in nest at right

| Date | Mintage | VF20 | XF40 | MS60 | MS63 | MS65 |
|---|---|---|---|---|---|---|
| 2009 P20 | 10,000 | **PF63** 45.00 | **PF65** 47.00 | | | |

### KM# 1281 DOLLAR

31.11 g., 0.999 Silver 0.999 oz. ASW, 40 mm. **Ruler:** Elizabeth II **Subject:** Kookaburra 20th Anniversary **Obv:** Head right **Rev:** Kookaburra pair on branch

| Date | Mintage | VF20 | XF40 | MS60 | MS63 | MS65 |
|---|---|---|---|---|---|---|
| 2009 P20 | 10,000 | **PF63** 45.00 | **PF65** 47.00 | | | |

### KM# 1282 DOLLAR

31.11 g., 0.999 Silver 0.999 oz. ASW, 40 mm. **Ruler:** Elizabeth II **Obv:** Head right **Rev:** Kookaburra on branch, head left

| Date | Mintage | VF20 | XF40 | MS60 | MS63 | MS65 |
|---|---|---|---|---|---|---|
| 2009 P20 | 10,000 | **PF63** 45.00 | **PF65** 47.00 | | | |

### KM# 1283 DOLLAR

31.11 g., 0.999 Silver 0.999 oz. ASW, 40 mm. **Ruler:** Elizabeth II **Subject:** Kookaburra 20th Anniversary **Obv:** Head right **Rev:** Kookaburra in flight right

| Date | Mintage | VF20 | XF40 | MS60 | MS63 | MS65 |
|---|---|---|---|---|---|---|
| 2009 P20 | 10,000 | **PF63** 45.00 | **PF65** 47.00 | | | |

### KM# 1284 DOLLAR

31.11 g., 0.999 Silver 0.999 oz. ASW, 40 mm. **Ruler:** Elizabeth II **Subject:** Kookaburra 20th Anniversary **Obv:** Head right **Rev:** Kookaburra by nest at left

| Date | Mintage | VF20 | XF40 | MS60 | MS63 | MS65 |
|---|---|---|---|---|---|---|
| 2009 P20 | 10,000 | **PF63** 45.00 | **PF65** 47.00 | | | |

### KM# 1285 DOLLAR

31.11 g., 0.999 Silver 0.999 oz. ASW, 40 mm. **Ruler:** Elizabeth II **Subject:** Kookaburra 20th Anniversary **Obv:** Head right **Rev:** Kookaburra on fence post

| Date | Mintage | VF20 | XF40 | MS60 | MS63 | MS65 |
|---|---|---|---|---|---|---|
| 2009 P20 | 10,000 | **PF63** 45.00 | **PF65** 47.00 | | | |

### KM# 1286 DOLLAR

31.11 g., 0.999 Silver 0.999 oz. ASW, 40 mm. **Ruler:** Elizabeth II **Subject:** Kookaburra 20th Anniversary **Obv:** Head right **Rev:** Kookaburra pair on branch left

| Date | Mintage | VF20 | XF40 | MS60 | MS63 | MS65 |
|---|---|---|---|---|---|---|
| 2009 P20 | 10,000 | **PF63** 45.00 | **PF65** 47.00 | | | |

### KM# 1287 DOLLAR

31.11 g., 0.999 Silver 0.999 oz. ASW, 40 mm. **Ruler:** Elizabeth II **Subject:** Kookaburra 20th Anniversary **Obv:** Head right **Rev:** Kookaburra on leafy branch left

| Date | Mintage | VF20 | XF40 | MS60 | MS63 | MS65 |
|---|---|---|---|---|---|---|
| 2009 P20 | 10,000 | **PF63** 45.00 | **PF65** 47.00 | | | |

### KM# 1288 DOLLAR

31.11 g., 0.999 Silver 0.999 oz. ASW, 40 mm. **Ruler:** Elizabeth II **Subject:** Kookaburra 20th Anniversary **Obv:** Head right **Rev:** Kookaburra pair on branch, beaks upward

| Date | Mintage | VF20 | XF40 | MS60 | MS63 | MS65 |
|---|---|---|---|---|---|---|
| 2009 P20 | 10,000 | **PF63** 45.00 | **PF65** 47.00 | | | |

### KM# 1289 DOLLAR

31.11 g., 0.999 Silver 0.999 oz. ASW, 40 mm. **Ruler:** Elizabeth II **Subject:** Kookaburra 20th Anniversary **Obv:** Head right **Rev:** Kookaburra in flight on map of Australia

| Date | Mintage | VF20 | XF40 | MS60 | MS63 | MS65 |
|---|---|---|---|---|---|---|
| 2009 P20 | 10,000 | **PF63** 45.00 | **PF65** 47.00 | | | |

### KM# 1290 DOLLAR

31.11 g., 0.999 Silver 0.999 oz. ASW, 40 mm. **Ruler:** Elizabeth II **Subject:** Kookaburra 20th Anniversary **Obv:** Head right **Rev:** Kookaburra on branch right

| Date | Mintage | VF20 | XF40 | MS60 | MS63 | MS65 |
|---|---|---|---|---|---|---|
| 2009 P20 | 10,000 | **PF63** 45.00 | **PF65** 47.00 | | | |

### KM# 1291 DOLLAR

31.11 g., 0.999 Silver 0.999 oz. ASW, 40 mm. **Ruler:** Elizabeth II **Subject:** Kookaburra 20th Anniversary **Obv:** Head right **Rev:** Two kookaburras, one in flight, one on branch

| Date | Mintage | VF20 | XF40 | MS60 | MS63 | MS65 |
|---|---|---|---|---|---|---|
| 2009 P20 | 10,000 | **PF63** 45.00 | **PF65** 47.00 | | | |

### KM# 1292 DOLLAR

31.11 g., 0.999 Silver 0.999 oz. ASW, 40 mm. **Ruler:** Elizabeth II **Subject:** Kookaburra 20th Anniversary **Obv:** Head right **Rev:** Kookaburra on branch, head right

| Date | Mintage | VF20 | XF40 | MS60 | MS63 | MS65 |
|---|---|---|---|---|---|---|
| 2009 P20 | 10,000 | **PF63** 45.00 | **PF65** 47.00 | | | |

### KM# 1293 DOLLAR

31.11 g., 0.999 Silver 0.999 oz. ASW, 40 mm. **Ruler:** Elizabeth II **Subject:** Kookaburra 20th Anniversary **Obv:** Head right **Rev:** Kookaburra pair on branch left

| Date | Mintage | VF20 | XF40 | MS60 | MS63 | MS65 |
|---|---|---|---|---|---|---|
| 2009 P20 | 10,000 | **PF63** 45.00 | **PF65** 47.00 | | | |

### KM# 1294 DOLLAR

31.11 g., 0.999 Silver 0.999 oz. ASW, 40 mm. **Ruler:** Elizabeth II **Subject:** Kookaburra 20th Anniversary **Obv:** Head right **Rev:** Kookaburra on branch left

| Date | Mintage | VF20 | XF40 | MS60 | MS63 | MS65 |
|---|---|---|---|---|---|---|
| 2009 P20 | 10,000 | **PF63** 45.00 | **PF65** 47.00 | | | |

### KM# 1295 DOLLAR

31.11 g., 0.999 Silver 0.999 oz. ASW, 40 mm. **Ruler:** Elizabeth II **Subject:** Kookaburra 20th Anniversary **Obv:** Head right **Rev:** Kookaburra admiring spider web

| Date | Mintage | VF20 | XF40 | MS60 | MS63 | MS65 |
|---|---|---|---|---|---|---|
| 2009 P20 | 10,000 | **PF63** 45.00 | **PF65** 47.00 | | | |

### KM# 1296 DOLLAR

31.11 g., 0.999 Silver 0.999 oz. ASW, 40 mm. **Ruler:** Elizabeth II **Subject:** Kookaburra 20th Anniversary **Obv:** Head right **Rev:** Kookaburra on branch, sunburst in background

| Date | Mintage | VF20 | XF40 | MS60 | MS63 | MS65 |
|---|---|---|---|---|---|---|
| 2009 P20 | 10,000 | **PF63** 45.00 | **PF65** 47.00 | | | |

### KM# 1471 DOLLAR

31.11 g., 0.999 Silver 0.999 oz. ASW, 40 mm. **Ruler:** Elizabeth II **Rev:** Kookabburra on branch

| Date | Mintage | VF20 | XF40 | MS60 | MS63 | MS65 |
|---|---|---|---|---|---|---|
| 2010 P | — | — | — | — | — | 45.00 |

### KM# 1692 DOLLAR

31.11 g., 0.999 Silver 0.999 oz. ASW, 40.5 mm. **Ruler:** Elizabeth II **Rev:** Kookaburra

| Date | Mintage | VF20 | XF40 | MS60 | MS63 | MS65 |
|---|---|---|---|---|---|---|
| 2012 P | — | — | — | — | — | 45.00 |

### KM# 1829 DOLLAR

31.11 g., 0.999 Silver 0.999 oz. ASW, 33 mm. **Ruler:** Elizabeth II **Rev:** Kookaburra **Note:** Ultra High Relief

| Date | Mintage | VF20 | XF40 | MS60 | MS63 | MS65 |
|---|---|---|---|---|---|---|
| 2012 P | — | **PF65** 110 | | | | |

**KM# 1985 DOLLAR**
31.14 g., 0.999 Silver 1.000 oz. ASW, 40.6 mm. **Ruler:** Elizabeth II **Rev:** Kookaburra

| Date | Mintage | VF20 | XF40 | MS60 | MS63 | MS65 |
|---|---|---|---|---|---|---|
| 2013 P | Est. 1000000 | **PF63** 65.00 **PF65** 75.00 | | | | |

**KM# 1988 DOLLAR**
31.14 g., 0.999 Silver 1.000 oz. ASW, 32.6 mm. **Ruler:** Elizabeth II **Rev:** Kookaburra **Note:** High Releif.

| Date | Mintage | VF20 | XF40 | MS60 | MS63 | MS65 |
|---|---|---|---|---|---|---|
| 2013 P | Est. 10000 | **PF63** 70.00 **PF65** 75.00 | | | | |

**KM# 623.1 2 DOLLARS**
62.85 g., 0.999 Silver 2.0187 oz. ASW, 50 mm. **Ruler:** Elizabeth II **Obv:** Head with tiara right, denomination below **Rev:** Two kookaburras back to back **Edge:** Reeded

| Date | Mintage | VF20 | XF40 | MS60 | MS63 | MS65 |
|---|---|---|---|---|---|---|
| 2001 | — | — | — | — | 80.00 | 85.00 |

**KM# 623.2 2 DOLLARS**
62.21 g., 0.999 Silver 1.998 oz. ASW **Ruler:** Elizabeth II **Subject:** USA State Quarters - 2001 **Obv:** Head with tiara right, denomination below **Rev:** Two kookaburras on branch with five U.S. State Quarter designs added **Edge:** Segmented reeding **Note:** Prev. KM#623

| Date | Mintage | VF20 | XF40 | MS60 | MS63 | MS65 |
|---|---|---|---|---|---|---|
| 2001 | 10,000 | — | — | — | 145 | 160 |

**KM# 678 2 DOLLARS**
62.21 g., 0.999 Silver 1.998 oz. ASW, 40 mm. **Ruler:** Elizabeth II **Obv:** Head with tiara right, denomination below **Rev:** Kookaburra flying over Australian map **Edge:** Reeded

| Date | Mintage | VF20 | XF40 | MS60 | MS63 | MS65 |
|---|---|---|---|---|---|---|
| 2001 P | 1,261 | **PF65** 90.00 | | | | |
| 2002 | 1,500 | — | — | — | — | 82.00 |
| Note: 1661 Spanish cob privy mark | | | | | | |
| 2002 | 1,500 | — | — | — | — | 82.00 |
| Note: 1771 Spanish pillar dollar privy mark | | | | | | |
| 2002 | 1,500 | — | — | — | — | 82.00 |
| Note: 1881 Gold sovereign privy mark | | | | | | |
| 2002 | 1,500 | — | — | — | — | 82.00 |
| Note: 1991 Gold Australian nugget privy mark | | | | | | |

**KM# 879 2 DOLLARS**
62.85 g., 0.999 Silver 2.0187 oz. ASW, 40 mm. **Ruler:** Elizabeth II **Obv:** Head with tiara right **Rev:** Kookaburra on branch plus two leaves **Edge:** Reeded

| Date | Mintage | VF20 | XF40 | MS60 | MS63 | MS65 |
|---|---|---|---|---|---|---|
| 2002 P | 1,262 | **PF65** 90.00 | | | | |
| 2003 | 1,000 | — | — | — | — | 115 |
| Note: Boer War privy mark | | | | | | |
| 2003 | 1,000 | — | — | — | — | 115 |
| Note: World War I privy mark | | | | | | |
| 2003 | 1,000 | — | — | — | — | 115 |
| Note: World War II privy mark | | | | | | |
| 2003 | 1,000 | — | — | — | — | 115 |
| Note: Korean War privy mark | | | | | | |
| 2003 | 1,000 | — | — | — | — | 115 |
| Note: Vietnam War privy mark | | | | | | |

**KM# 881 2 DOLLARS**
62.21 g., 0.999 Silver 1.998 oz. ASW, 50 mm. **Ruler:** Elizabeth II **Obv:** Head with tiara right **Rev:** Two kookaburras, one in flight **Edge:** Reeded

| Date | Mintage | VF20 | XF40 | MS60 | MS63 | MS65 |
|---|---|---|---|---|---|---|
| 2003 P | 821 | **PF65** 90.00 | | | | |

**KM# 884 2 DOLLARS**
62.21 g., 0.999 Silver 1.998 oz. ASW, 50 mm. **Ruler:** Elizabeth II **Obv:** Head with tiara right **Rev:** Kookaburra perched on branch with four leaves **Edge:** Reeded

| Date | Mintage | VF20 | XF40 | MS60 | MS63 | MS65 |
|---|---|---|---|---|---|---|
| 2004 P | 800 | **PF65** 90.00 | | | | |

**KM# 887 2 DOLLARS**
62.21 g., 0.999 Silver 1.998 oz. ASW, 50 mm. **Ruler:** Elizabeth II **Obv:** Head with tiara right **Rev:** Two kookaburras on branch, one laughing **Edge:** Reeded

| Date | Mintage | VF20 | XF40 | MS60 | MS63 | MS65 |
|---|---|---|---|---|---|---|
| 2005 P | 795 | **PF65** 90.00 | | | | |

**KM# 890 2 DOLLARS**
62.21 g., 0.999 Silver 1.998 oz. ASW, 50 mm. **Ruler:** Elizabeth II **Obv:** Head with tiara right **Rev:** Kookaburra on branch, no leaves

| Date | Mintage | VF20 | XF40 | MS60 | MS63 | MS65 |
|---|---|---|---|---|---|---|
| 2007 | — | — | — | — | 85.00 | — |

**KM# 1297 5 DOLLARS**
1.55 g., 0.999 Gold 0.0498 oz. AGW, 14 mm. **Ruler:** Elizabeth II **Subject:** Kookaburra 20th Anniversary **Obv:** Head right **Rev:** Kookaburra standing on stump right

| Date | Mintage | VF20 | XF40 | MS60 | MS63 | MS65 |
|---|---|---|---|---|---|---|
| 2009 P20 | 2,009 | **PF63** 115 **PF65** 125 | | | | |

**KM# 1298 5 DOLLARS**
1.55 g., 0.999 Gold 0.0498 oz. AGW, 14 mm. **Ruler:** Elizabeth II **Subject:** Kookaburra 20th Anniversary **Obv:** Head right **Rev:** Kookaburra on branch, head right

| Date | Mintage | VF20 | XF40 | MS60 | MS63 | MS65 |
|---|---|---|---|---|---|---|
| 2009 P20 | 2,009 | **PF63** 115 **PF65** 125 | | | | |

**KM# 1299 5 DOLLARS**
1.55 g., 0.999 Gold 0.0498 oz. AGW, 14 mm. **Ruler:** Elizabeth II **Subject:** Kookaburra 20th Anniversary **Obv:** Head right **Rev:** Kookaburra on branch left

| Date | Mintage | VF20 | XF40 | MS60 | MS63 | MS65 |
|---|---|---|---|---|---|---|
| 2009 P20 | 2,009 | **PF63** 115 **PF65** 125 | | | | |

**KM# 1300 5 DOLLARS**
1.55 g., 0.999 Gold 0.0498 oz. AGW, 14 mm. **Ruler:** Elizabeth II **Subject:** Kookaburra 20th Anniversary **Obv:** Head right **Rev:** Kookaburra on branch feeding young at right

| Date | Mintage | VF20 | XF40 | MS60 | MS63 | MS65 |
|---|---|---|---|---|---|---|
| 2009 P20 | 2,009 | **PF63** 115 **PF65** 125 | | | | |

**KM# 1301 5 DOLLARS**
1.55 g., 0.999 Gold 0.0498 oz. AGW, 14 mm. **Ruler:** Elizabeth II **Subject:** Kookaburra 20th Anniversary **Obv:** Head right **Rev:** Kookaburra pair on branch, heads opposite

| Date | Mintage | VF20 | XF40 | MS60 | MS63 | MS65 |
|---|---|---|---|---|---|---|
| 2009 P20 | 2,009 | **PF63** 115 **PF65** 125 | | | | |

**KM# 1302 5 DOLLARS**
1.55 g., 0.999 Gold 0.0498 oz. AGW, 14 mm. **Ruler:** Elizabeth II **Subject:** Kookaburra 20th Anniversary **Obv:** Head right **Rev:** Kookaburra on branch, head left

| Date | Mintage | VF20 | XF40 | MS60 | MS63 | MS65 |
|---|---|---|---|---|---|---|
| 2009 P20 | 2,009 | **PF63** 115 **PF65** 125 | | | | |

**KM# 1303 5 DOLLARS**
1.55 g., 0.999 Gold 0.0498 oz. AGW, 14 mm. **Ruler:** Elizabeth II **Subject:** Kookaburra 20th Anniversary **Obv:** Head right **Rev:** Kookaburra in flight right

| Date | Mintage | VF20 | XF40 | MS60 | MS63 | MS65 |
|---|---|---|---|---|---|---|
| 2009 P20 | 2,009 | **PF63** 115 **PF65** 125 | | | | |

**KM# 1304 5 DOLLARS**
1.55 g., 0.999 Gold 0.0498 oz. AGW, 14 mm. **Ruler:** Elizabeth II **Subject:** Kookaburra 20th Anniversary **Obv:** Head right **Rev:** Kookaburra at nest left, head right

| Date | Mintage | VF20 | XF40 | MS60 | MS63 | MS65 |
|---|---|---|---|---|---|---|
| 2009 P20 | 2,009 | **PF63** 115 **PF65** 125 | | | | |

**KM# 1305 5 DOLLARS**
1.55 g., 0.999 Gold 0.0498 oz. AGW, 14 mm. **Ruler:** Elizabeth II **Subject:** Kookaburra 20th Anniversary **Obv:** Head right **Rev:** Kookaburra on fence post

| Date | Mintage | VF20 | XF40 | MS60 | MS63 | MS65 |
|---|---|---|---|---|---|---|
| 2009 P20 | 2,009 | **PF63** 115 **PF65** 125 | | | | |

**KM# 1306 5 DOLLARS**
1.55 g., 0.999 Gold 0.0498 oz. AGW, 14 mm. **Ruler:** Elizabeth II **Subject:** Kookaburra 20th Anniversary **Obv:** Head right **Rev:** Kookaburra pair left

| Date | Mintage | VF20 | XF40 | MS60 | MS63 | MS65 |
|---|---|---|---|---|---|---|
| 2009 P20 | 2,009 | **PF63** 115 **PF65** 125 | | | | |

**KM# 1307 5 DOLLARS**
1.55 g., 0.999 Gold 0.0498 oz. AGW, 14 mm. **Ruler:** Elizabeth II **Subject:** Kookaburra 20th Anniversary **Obv:** Head right **Rev:** Kookaburra left on leafy branch

| Date | Mintage | VF20 | XF40 | MS60 | MS63 | MS65 |
|---|---|---|---|---|---|---|
| 2009 P20 | 2,009 | **PF63** 115 **PF65** 125 | | | | |

**KM# 1308 5 DOLLARS**
1.55 g., 0.999 Gold 0.0498 oz. AGW, 14 mm. **Ruler:** Elizabeth II **Subject:** Kookaburra 20th Anniversary **Obv:** Head right **Rev:** Kookaburra pair facing opposite

| Date | Mintage | VF20 | XF40 | MS60 | MS63 | MS65 |
|---|---|---|---|---|---|---|
| 2009 P20 | 2,009 | **PF63** 115 **PF65** 125 | | | | |

**KM# 1309 5 DOLLARS**
1.55 g., 0.999 Gold 0.0498 oz. AGW, 14 mm. **Ruler:** Elizabeth II **Subject:** Kookaburra 20th Anniversary **Obv:** Head right **Rev:** Kookaburra in flight on map of Australia

| Date | Mintage | VF20 | XF40 | MS60 | MS63 | MS65 |
|---|---|---|---|---|---|---|
| 2009 P20 | 2,009 | **PF63** 115 **PF65** 125 | | | | |

**KM# 1310 5 DOLLARS**
1.55 g., 0.999 Gold 0.0498 oz. AGW, 14 mm. **Ruler:** Elizabeth II **Subject:** Kookaburra 20th Anniversary **Obv:** Head right **Rev:** Kookaburra on branch right

| Date | Mintage | VF20 | XF40 | MS60 | MS63 | MS65 |
|---|---|---|---|---|---|---|
| 2009 P20 | 2,009 | **PF63** 115 **PF65** 125 | | | | |

**KM# 1311 5 DOLLARS**
1.55 g., 0.999 Gold 0.0498 oz. AGW, 14 mm. **Ruler:** Elizabeth II **Subject:** Kookaburra 20th Anniversary **Obv:** Head right **Rev:** Kookaburras, one in flight, one on branch

| Date | Mintage | VF20 | XF40 | MS60 | MS63 | MS65 |
|---|---|---|---|---|---|---|
| 2009 P20 | 2,009 | **PF63** 115 **PF65** 125 | | | | |

**KM# 1312 5 DOLLARS**
1.55 g., 0.999 Gold 0.0498 oz. AGW, 14 mm. **Ruler:** Elizabeth II **Subject:** Kookaburra 20th Anniversary **Obv:** Head right **Rev:** Kookaburra on branch, head right

| Date | Mintage | VF20 | XF40 | MS60 | MS63 | MS65 |
|---|---|---|---|---|---|---|
| 2009 P20 | 2,009 | **PF63** 115 **PF65** 125 | | | | |

**KM# 1313 5 DOLLARS**
1.55 g., 0.999 Gold 0.0498 oz. AGW, 14 mm. **Ruler:** Elizabeth II **Subject:** Kookaburra 20th Anniversary **Obv:** Head right **Rev:** Kookaburra pair on branch, one with head upward

| Date | Mintage | VF20 | XF40 | MS60 | MS63 | MS65 |
|---|---|---|---|---|---|---|
| 2009 P20 | 2,009 | **PF63** 115 **PF65** 125 | | | | |

**KM# 1314 5 DOLLARS**
1.55 g., 0.999 Gold 0.0498 oz. AGW, 14 mm. **Ruler:** Elizabeth II **Subject:** Kookaburra 20th Anniversary **Obv:** Head right **Rev:** Kookaburra on branch left

| Date | Mintage | VF20 | XF40 | MS60 | MS63 | MS65 |
|---|---|---|---|---|---|---|
| 2009 P20 | 2,009 | **PF63** 115 **PF65** 125 | | | | |

**KM# 1315 5 DOLLARS**
1.55 g., 0.999 Gold 0.0498 oz. AGW, 14 mm. **Ruler:** Elizabeth II **Subject:** Kookaburra 20th Anniversary **Obv:** Head right **Rev:** Kookaburra on branch admiring spider web

| Date | Mintage | VF20 | XF40 | MS60 | MS63 | MS65 |
|---|---|---|---|---|---|---|
| 2009 P20 | 2,009 | **PF63** 115 **PF65** 125 | | | | |

**KM# 1316 5 DOLLARS**
1.55 g., 0.999 Gold 0.0498 oz. AGW, 14 mm. **Ruler:** Elizabeth II **Subject:** Kookaburra 20th Anniversary **Obv:** Head right **Rev:** Kookaburra on branch, sunburst in background

| Date | Mintage | VF20 | XF40 | MS60 | MS63 | MS65 |
|---|---|---|---|---|---|---|
| 2009 P20 | 2,009 | **PF63** 115 **PF65** 125 | | | | |

**KM# 603 10 DOLLARS**
311.04 g., 0.999 Silver 9.990 oz. ASW, 74.9 mm. **Ruler:** Elizabeth II **Subject:** Kookaburra **Obv:** Head with tiara right, denomination below **Rev:** Flying bird over map **Edge:** Reeded

| Date | Mintage | VF20 | XF40 | MS60 | MS63 | MS65 |
|---|---|---|---|---|---|---|
| 2002 | — | **PF65** 400 | | | | |

**KM# 891 10 DOLLARS**
311.04 g., 0.999 Silver 9.990 oz. ASW, 74.9 mm. **Ruler:** Elizabeth II **Obv:** Head with tiara right **Rev:** Kookaburra on branch, no leaves

| Date | Mintage | VF20 | XF40 | MS60 | MS63 | MS65 |
|---|---|---|---|---|---|---|
| 2007 | — | — | — | — | 400 | — |

**KM# 1360 10 DOLLARS**
311.04 g., 0.999 Silver 9.990 oz. ASW, 75.5 mm. **Ruler:** Elizabeth II **Obv:** Head right **Rev:** Kookaburra

| Date | Mintage | VF20 | XF40 | MS60 | MS63 | MS65 |
|---|---|---|---|---|---|---|
| 2010 (p) | — | PF65 425 | | | | |

**KM# 1693 10 DOLLARS**
311.04 g., 0.999 Silver 9.990 oz. ASW **Ruler:** Elizabeth II **Rev:** Kookaburra

| Date | Mintage | VF20 | XF40 | MS60 | MS63 | MS65 |
|---|---|---|---|---|---|---|
| 2012 P | — | PF65 400 | | | | |

**KM# 1986 10 DOLLARS**
311.35 g., 0.999 Silver 10.000 oz. ASW, 75.6 mm. **Ruler:** Elizabeth II **Rev:** Kookaburra

| Date | Mintage | VF20 | XF40 | MS60 | MS63 | MS65 |
|---|---|---|---|---|---|---|
| 2013 P | — | PF65 300 | | | | |

**KM# 630 20 DOLLARS**
62.21 g., 0.999 Silver 1.998 oz. ASW **Ruler:** Elizabeth II **Subject:** USA State Quarters - 2002 **Obv:** Head with tiara right, denomination below **Rev:** Kookaburra on branch with five state quarter designs added below **Edge:** Reeded and plain sections

| Date | Mintage | VF20 | XF40 | MS60 | MS63 | MS65 |
|---|---|---|---|---|---|---|
| 2002 | 10,000 | — | — | — | 82.00 | 85.00 |

**KM# 624 30 DOLLARS**
1002.50 g., 0.999 Silver 32.1989 oz. ASW, 101 mm. **Ruler:** Elizabeth II **Subject:** USA State Quarters - 2001 **Obv:** Head with tiara right, denomination below **Rev:** Two kookaburras on branch with five state quarter designs added below **Edge:** Reeded and plain sections

| Date | Mintage | VF20 | XF40 | MS60 | MS63 | MS65 |
|---|---|---|---|---|---|---|
| 2001 | 1,000 | — | — | — | — | 1,200 |

**KM# 680 30 DOLLARS**
1002.50 g., 0.999 Silver 32.1989 oz. ASW, 101 mm. **Ruler:** Elizabeth II **Obv:** Head with tiara right, denomination below **Rev:** Kookaburra in flight above Australian map **Edge:** Segmented reeding

| Date | Mintage | VF20 | XF40 | MS60 | MS63 | MS65 |
|---|---|---|---|---|---|---|
| 2001 P | 212 | PF65 1,200 | | | | |
| 2002 | — | — | — | — | — | 1,250 |

**KM# 631 30 DOLLARS**
1002.50 g., 0.999 Silver 32.1989 oz. ASW, 101 mm. **Ruler:** Elizabeth II **Subject:** USA State Quarters - 2002 **Obv:** Head with tiara right, denomination below **Rev:** Kookaburra on branch with five state quarter designs added in gold **Edge:** Reeded and plain sections

| Date | Mintage | VF20 | XF40 | MS60 | MS63 | MS65 |
|---|---|---|---|---|---|---|
| 2002 | 1,000 | — | — | — | — | 1,200 |

**KM# 880 30 DOLLARS**
1002.50 g., 0.999 Silver 32.1989 oz. ASW, 101 mm. **Ruler:** Elizabeth II **Obv:** Head with tiara right **Rev:** Kookaburra standing on branch **Edge:** Reeded

| Date | Mintage | VF20 | XF40 | MS60 | MS63 | MS65 |
|---|---|---|---|---|---|---|
| 2002 P | 198 | PF65 1,250 | | | | |

**KM# 882 30 DOLLARS**
1002.50 g., 0.999 Silver 32.1989 oz. ASW, 101 mm. **Ruler:** Elizabeth II **Obv:** Head with tiara right **Rev:** Two kookaburras, one in flight **Edge:** Reeded

| Date | Mintage | VF20 | XF40 | MS60 | MS63 | MS65 |
|---|---|---|---|---|---|---|
| 2003 P | 135 | PF65 1,250 | | | | |

**KM# 885 30 DOLLARS**
1002.50 g., 0.999 Silver 32.1989 oz. ASW, 101 mm. **Ruler:** Elizabeth II **Obv:** Head with tiara right **Rev:** Kookaburra perched on branch with four leaves **Edge:** Reeded

| Date | Mintage | VF20 | XF40 | MS60 | MS63 | MS65 |
|---|---|---|---|---|---|---|
| 2004 P | 165 | PF65 1,250 | | | | |

**KM# 888 30 DOLLARS**
1002.50 g., 0.999 Silver 32.1989 oz. ASW, 101 mm. **Ruler:** Elizabeth II **Obv:** Head with tiara right **Rev:** Two kookaburras on branch, one laughing **Edge:** Reeded

| Date | Mintage | VF20 | XF40 | MS60 | MS63 | MS65 |
|---|---|---|---|---|---|---|
| 2005 P | 316 | PF65 1,250 | | | | |

**KM# 892 30 DOLLARS**
1002.50 g., 0.999 Silver 32.1989 oz. ASW, 101 mm. **Ruler:** Elizabeth II **Obv:** Head with tiara right **Rev:** Kookaburras on branch, no leaves

| Date | Mintage | VF20 | XF40 | MS60 | MS63 | MS65 |
|---|---|---|---|---|---|---|
| 2007 | — | — | — | — | 1,200 | — |

**KM# 1115 30 DOLLARS**
1000.00 g., 0.999 Silver 32.1186 oz. ASW, 101 mm. **Ruler:** Elizabeth II **Rev:** Kookaburra on branch, sunburst background

| Date | Mintage | VF20 | XF40 | MS60 | MS63 | MS65 |
|---|---|---|---|---|---|---|
| 2009 P | — | PF65 1,300 | | | | |

**KM# 1361 30 DOLLARS**
1000.00 g., 0.999 Silver 32.1186 oz. ASW, 100 mm. **Ruler:** Elizabeth II **Obv:** Head right **Rev:** Kookaburra

| Date | Mintage | VF20 | XF40 | MS60 | MS63 | MS65 |
|---|---|---|---|---|---|---|
| 2010 (p) | — | — | — | — | — | 1,200 |

**KM# 1694 30 DOLLARS**
1000.00 g., 0.999 Silver 32.1186 oz. ASW **Ruler:** Elizabeth II **Rev:** Kookaburra

| Date | Mintage | VF20 | XF40 | MS60 | MS63 | MS65 |
|---|---|---|---|---|---|---|
| 2012 P | — | — | — | — | — | 1,200 |

**KM# 1987 30 DOLLARS**
1001.00 g., 0.999 Silver 32.1508 oz. ASW, 100.6 mm. **Ruler:** Elizabeth II **Rev:** Kookaburra

| Date | Mintage | VF20 | XF40 | MS60 | MS63 | MS65 |
|---|---|---|---|---|---|---|
| 2013 P | — | PF65 900 | | | | |

**KM# 2054 50 DOLLARS**
15.55 g., 0.9999 Gold 0.500 oz. AGW, 25.6 mm. **Ruler:** Elizabeth II **Obv:** Head with tiara right **Rev:** Kookaburra seated on branch

| Date | Mintage | VF20 | XF40 | MS60 | MS63 | MS65 |
|---|---|---|---|---|---|---|
| 2013 P | 550 | PF65 1,000 | | | | |

**KM# 878 200 DOLLARS**
31.60 g., 0.999 Silver 1.0149 oz. ASW, 40 mm. **Ruler:** Elizabeth II **Obv:** Head with tiara right with denomination **Rev:** Kookaburra in flight over map of Australia **Note:** Mule.

| Date | Mintage | VF20 | XF40 | MS60 | MS63 | MS65 |
|---|---|---|---|---|---|---|
| ND-2001 | Est. 20 | PF65 2,500 | | | | |

## BULLION - NUGGET

**KM# 692 50 DOLLARS**
15.50 g., 0.9999 Gold 0.4983 oz. AGW, 25.1 mm. **Ruler:** Elizabeth II **Subject:** Tribute to Liberty **Obv:** Head with tiara right, denomination below **Rev:** Two kangaroos on map above silver Liberty Bell **Edge:** Reeded

| Date | Mintage | VF20 | XF40 | MS60 | MS63 | MS65 |
|---|---|---|---|---|---|---|
| 2001 | 419 | — | — | — | — | 875 |
| 2002 | 1,498 | — | — | — | — | 875 |
| 2002 | 515 | PF65 900 | | | | |

**KM# 693 100 DOLLARS**
31.10 g., 0.9999 Gold 0.9999 oz. AGW, 32.1 mm. **Ruler:** Elizabeth II **Subject:** Tribute to Liberty **Obv:** Head with tiara right, denomination below **Rev:** Two kangaroos on map above silver Liberty Bell **Edge:** Reeded

| Date | Mintage | VF20 | XF40 | MS60 | MS63 | MS65 |
|---|---|---|---|---|---|---|
| 2001 | 1,498 | — | — | — | — | 1,735 |
| 2002 | — | — | — | — | — | 1,735 |

### KM# 635 100 DOLLARS

31.10 g., 0.9999 Gold 0.9999 oz. AGW, 32.1 mm. **Ruler:** Elizabeth II **Subject:** Gold Panning **Obv:** Queen's head right **Rev:** Two prospectors dry panning for gold with color highlighted pans and dust **Edge:** Reeded

| Date | Mintage | VF20 | XF40 | MS60 | MS63 | MS65 |
|---|---|---|---|---|---|---|
| 2002 P | 1,500 | PF65 1,775 | | | | |

### KM# 900 100 DOLLARS

31.10 g., 0.9999 Gold 0.9999 oz. AGW, 32 mm. **Ruler:** Elizabeth II **Obv:** Head with tiara right **Rev:** Prospectors dry-blowing gold dust, colored image

| Date | Mintage | VF20 | XF40 | MS60 | MS63 | MS65 |
|---|---|---|---|---|---|---|
| 2002 | 940 | — | — | — | — | 1,735 |

### KM# 906 100 DOLLARS

31.10 g., 0.999 Gold 0.999 oz. AGW, 32 mm. **Ruler:** Elizabeth II **Obv:** Head with tiara right **Rev:** Prospectors camp, colored image

| Date | Mintage | VF20 | XF40 | MS60 | MS63 | MS65 |
|---|---|---|---|---|---|---|
| 2003 | 658 | — | — | — | — | 1,735 |

### KM# 741 100 DOLLARS

31.10 g., 0.9999 Gold 0.9999 oz. AGW, 32 mm. **Ruler:** Elizabeth II **Subject:** Eureka Stockade **Obv:** Head with tiara right, denomination below **Rev:** Eureka Stockade leader Peter Lalor and blue flag, colored image **Edge:** Reeded

| Date | Mintage | VF20 | XF40 | MS60 | MS63 | MS65 |
|---|---|---|---|---|---|---|
| 2004 | 1,500 | — | — | — | — | 1,735 |
| 2004 P | 1,500 | PF65 1,750 | | | | |

### KM# 915 100 DOLLARS

31.10 g., 0.999 Gold 0.999 oz. AGW, 32 mm. **Ruler:** Elizabeth II **Subject:** Welcome Stranger Nugget **Obv:** Head with tiara right **Rev:** Welcome Stranger Nugget surrounded by Outback setting, colored image

| Date | Mintage | VF20 | XF40 | MS60 | MS63 | MS65 |
|---|---|---|---|---|---|---|
| 2005 | 1,500 | — | — | — | — | 1,735 |

### KM# 914 200 DOLLARS

62.21 g., 0.999 Gold 1.9982 oz. AGW, 41 mm. **Ruler:** Elizabeth II **Obv:** Head with tiara right **Rev:** Kangaroo in multicolor bush

| Date | Mintage | VF20 | XF40 | MS60 | MS63 | MS65 |
|---|---|---|---|---|---|---|
| 2005 | 200 | — | — | — | — | 3,500 |

## BULLION - KOALA

### KM# 1838 10 CENTS

3.11 g., 0.999 Silver 0.0999 oz. ASW, 30 mm. **Ruler:** Elizabeth II **Rev:** Koala sleeping hugging branch

| Date | Mintage | VF20 | XF40 | MS60 | MS63 | MS65 |
|---|---|---|---|---|---|---|
| 2012 P | — | PF65 25.00 | | | | |

### KM# 1977 10 CENTS

3.14 g., 0.999 Silver 0.1007 oz. ASW, 20.6 mm. **Ruler:** Elizabeth II **Rev:** Koala seated in tree

| Date | Mintage | VF20 | XF40 | MS60 | MS63 | MS65 |
|---|---|---|---|---|---|---|
| 2013 P | — | PF65 20.00 | | | | |

### KM# 1366 50 CENTS

15.55 g., 0.999 Silver 0.4994 oz. ASW **Ruler:** Elizabeth II **Obv:** Head right **Rev:** Koala

| Date | Mintage | VF20 | XF40 | MS60 | MS63 | MS65 |
|---|---|---|---|---|---|---|
| 2010 (p) | — | — | — | — | — | 35.00 |

### KM# 1688 50 CENTS

15.50 g., 0.999 Silver 0.4978 oz. ASW, 32 mm. **Ruler:** Elizabeth II **Rev:** Koala

| Date | Mintage | VF20 | XF40 | MS60 | MS63 | MS65 |
|---|---|---|---|---|---|---|
| 2012 P | — | — | — | — | — | 20.00 |

### KM# 1798 50 CENTS

15.50 g., 0.999 Silver 0.4978 oz. ASW, 32 mm. **Ruler:** Elizabeth II **Rev:** Koala sleeping hugging branch

| Date | Mintage | VF20 | XF40 | MS60 | MS63 | MS65 |
|---|---|---|---|---|---|---|
| 2012 P | — | — | — | — | — | 40.00 |

### KM# 1798a 50 CENTS

15.50 g., 0.999 Silver 0.4978 oz. ASW, 36.6 mm. **Ruler:** Elizabeth II **Rev:** Koala in color

| Date | Mintage | VF20 | XF40 | MS60 | MS63 | MS65 |
|---|---|---|---|---|---|---|
| 2012 P | — | PF65 50.00 | | | | |

### KM# 1978 50 CENTS

15.59 g., 0.999 Silver 0.5008 oz. ASW, 36.6 mm. **Ruler:** Elizabeth II **Rev:** Koala seated in tree

| Date | Mintage | VF20 | XF40 | MS60 | MS63 | MS65 |
|---|---|---|---|---|---|---|
| 2013 P | — | PF65 40.00 | | | | |

### KM# 1978a 50 CENTS

15.55 g., 0.9999 Silver 0.4999 oz. ASW, 36.6 mm. **Ruler:** Elizabeth II **Rev:** Koala seated in tree, color

| Date | Mintage | VF20 | XF40 | MS60 | MS63 | MS65 |
|---|---|---|---|---|---|---|
| 2013 P | — | PF65 30.00 | | | | |

### KM# 1111 DOLLAR

31.11 g., 0.999 Silver 0.999 oz. ASW, 40.6 mm. **Ruler:** Elizabeth II **Rev:** Koala seated left on branch, shimmer background

| Date | Mintage | VF20 | XF40 | MS60 | MS63 | MS65 |
|---|---|---|---|---|---|---|
| 2009 P | — | — | — | — | — | 45.00 |

### KM# 1111a DOLLAR

31.11 g., 0.9999 Silver 0.9999 oz. ASW partially gilt, 40.6 mm. **Ruler:** Elizabeth II **Rev:** Koala seated left on branch, gilt

| Date | Mintage | VF20 | XF40 | MS60 | MS63 | MS65 |
|---|---|---|---|---|---|---|
| 2009 P | 10,000 | PF65 60.00 | | | | |

**KM# 1464 DOLLAR**
31.11 g., 0.999 Silver 0.999 oz. ASW, 40 mm. **Ruler:** Elizabeth II **Rev:** Koala on branch

| Date | Mintage | VF20 | XF40 | MS60 | MS63 | MS65 |
|---|---|---|---|---|---|---|
| 2010 P | — | — | — | — | — | 45.00 |

**KM# 1464a DOLLAR**
31.11 g., 0.9999 Silver 0.9999 oz. ASW partially gilt **Ruler:** Elizabeth II **Rev:** Koala on branch

| Date | Mintage | VF20 | XF40 | MS60 | MS63 | MS65 |
|---|---|---|---|---|---|---|
| 2010 P | — | PF65 60.00 | | | | |

**KM# 1689 DOLLAR**
31.11 g., 0.999 Silver 0.999 oz. ASW, 40.5 mm. **Ruler:** Elizabeth II **Rev:** Koala

| Date | Mintage | VF20 | XF40 | MS60 | MS63 | MS65 |
|---|---|---|---|---|---|---|
| 2012 P | — | — | — | — | — | 45.00 |

**KM# 1828 DOLLAR**
31.11 g., 0.999 Silver 0.999 oz. ASW, 33 mm. **Ruler:** Elizabeth II **Rev:** Koala **Note:** Ultra High Relief

| Date | Mintage | VF20 | XF40 | MS60 | MS63 | MS65 |
|---|---|---|---|---|---|---|
| 2012 P | — | PF65 110 | | | | |

**KM# 1840 DOLLAR**
31.11 g., 0.999 Silver 0.999 oz. ASW, 40.6 mm. **Ruler:** Elizabeth II **Rev:** Koala sleeping hugging branch

| Date | Mintage | VF20 | XF40 | MS60 | MS63 | MS65 |
|---|---|---|---|---|---|---|
| 2012 P Berlin privy mark | — | — | — | — | — | 75.00 |
| 2012 P | — | — | — | — | — | 55.00 |

**KM# 1840a DOLLAR**
31.11 g., 0.999 Silver 0.999 oz. ASW partially gilt, 40.6 mm. **Ruler:** Elizabeth II **Rev:** Gilt Koala sleeping hugging branch

| Date | Mintage | VF20 | XF40 | MS60 | MS63 | MS65 |
|---|---|---|---|---|---|---|
| 2012 P | — | — | — | — | — | 75.00 |

**KM# 1840b DOLLAR**
31.11 g., 0.999 Silver 0.999 oz. ASW, 40.6 mm. **Ruler:** Elizabeth II **Rev:** Koala sleeping hugging branch

| Date | Mintage | VF20 | XF40 | MS60 | MS63 | MS65 |
|---|---|---|---|---|---|---|
| 2012 P | — | PF65 70.00 | | | | |

**KM# 1979 DOLLAR**
31.14 g., 0.999 Silver 1.000 oz. ASW, 40.6 mm. **Ruler:** Elizabeth II **Rev:** Koala seated in tree

| Date | Mintage | VF20 | XF40 | MS60 | MS63 | MS65 |
|---|---|---|---|---|---|---|
| 2013 P | — | PF65 75.00 | | | | |

**KM# 1979a DOLLAR**
31.14 g., 0.999 Silver 1.000 oz. ASW Partially gilt, 40.6 mm. **Ruler:** Elizabeth II **Rev:** Koala seated in tree, gilt

| Date | Mintage | VF20 | XF40 | MS60 | MS63 | MS65 |
|---|---|---|---|---|---|---|
| 2013 P | Est. 10000 | PF65 50.00 | | | | |

**KM# 1979b DOLLAR**
31.14 g., 0.999 Silver 1.000 oz. ASW, 40.6 mm. **Ruler:** Elizabeth II **Rev:** Koala seated in tree, in color

| Date | Mintage | VF20 | XF40 | MS60 | MS63 | MS65 |
|---|---|---|---|---|---|---|
| 2013 | — | PF65 65.00 | | | | |

**KM# 2050 DOLLAR**
31.14 g., 0.999 Silver 1.000 oz. ASW, 32.6 mm. **Ruler:** Elizabeth II **Obv:** Head with tiara right **Rev:** Koala seated in tree **Note:** High relief.

| Date | Mintage | VF20 | XF40 | MS60 | MS63 | MS65 |
|---|---|---|---|---|---|---|
| 2013 P | Est. 10000 | PF65 90.00 | | | | |

**KM# 2078 2 DOLLARS**
0.50 g., 0.9999 Gold **Ruler:** Elizabeth II **Rev:** Seated Koala

| Date | Mintage | VF20 | XF40 | MS60 | MS63 | MS65 |
|---|---|---|---|---|---|---|
| 2013 P Proof | — | — | — | — | — | 50.00 |

**KM# 916 5 DOLLARS**
1.57 g., 0.999 Platinum 0.0505 oz. APW **Ruler:** Elizabeth II **Obv:** Head with tiara right **Rev:** Two koalas on branch

| Date | Mintage | VF20 | XF40 | MS60 | MS63 | MS65 |
|---|---|---|---|---|---|---|
| 2001 | 809 | PF65 125 | | | | |

**KM# 1868 5 DOLLARS**
1.24 g., 0.999 Platinum 0.0398 oz. APW, 14.1 mm. **Ruler:** Elizabeth II **Rev:** Koala

| Date | Mintage | VF20 | XF40 | MS60 | MS63 | MS65 |
|---|---|---|---|---|---|---|
| 2002 P | 714 | PF65 150 | | | | |

**KM# 1869 5 DOLLARS**
1.24 g., 0.999 Platinum 0.0398 oz. APW, 14.1 mm. **Ruler:** Elizabeth II **Rev:** Koala

| Date | Mintage | VF20 | XF40 | MS60 | MS63 | MS65 |
|---|---|---|---|---|---|---|
| 2003 P | 99 | PF65 150 | | | | |

**KM# 1870 5 DOLLARS**
1.24 g., 0.999 Platinum 0.0398 oz. APW, 14.1 mm. **Ruler:** Elizabeth II **Rev:** Koala

| Date | Mintage | VF20 | XF40 | MS60 | MS63 | MS65 |
|---|---|---|---|---|---|---|
| 2004 P | 65 | PF65 150 | | | | |

**KM# 1871 5 DOLLARS**
1.24 g., 0.999 Platinum 0.0398 oz. APW, 14.1 mm. **Ruler:** Elizabeth II **Rev:** Koala

| Date | Mintage | VF20 | XF40 | MS60 | MS63 | MS65 |
|---|---|---|---|---|---|---|
| 2005 P | 200 | PF65 150 | | | | |

**KM# 1872 5 DOLLARS**
1.24 g., 0.999 Gold 0.0398 oz. AGW, 14.1 mm. **Ruler:** Elizabeth II **Rev:** Koala

| Date | Mintage | VF20 | XF40 | MS60 | MS63 | MS65 |
|---|---|---|---|---|---|---|
| 2008 P | 8,957 | PF65 125 | | | | |

**KM# 1113 5 DOLLARS**
1.24 g., 0.9999 Gold 0.040 oz. AGW, 14.1 mm. **Ruler:** Elizabeth II **Rev:** Koala seated left on branch

| Date | Mintage | VF20 | XF40 | MS60 | MS63 | MS65 |
|---|---|---|---|---|---|---|
| 2009 P | 15,000 | PF65 95.00 | | | | |

**KM# 1467 5 DOLLARS**
1.24 g., 0.999 Gold 0.0398 oz. AGW **Ruler:** Elizabeth II **Rev:** Koala on branch

| Date | Mintage | VF20 | XF40 | MS60 | MS63 | MS65 |
|---|---|---|---|---|---|---|
| 2010 P | — | — | — | — | — | 90.00 |

**KM# 1843 5 DOLLARS**
1.24 g., 0.999 Gold 0.0398 oz. AGW, 14.1 mm. **Ruler:** Elizabeth II **Rev:** Koala sleeping hugging branch

| Date | Mintage | VF20 | XF40 | MS60 | MS63 | MS65 |
|---|---|---|---|---|---|---|
| 2012 P | — | PF65 150 | | | | |

**KM# 1841 8 DOLLARS**
155.50 g., 0.999 Silver 4.9944 oz. ASW, 101 mm. **Ruler:** Elizabeth II **Rev:** Koala sleeping hugging branch

| Date | Mintage | VF20 | XF40 | MS60 | MS63 | MS65 |
|---|---|---|---|---|---|---|
| 2012 P | — | — | — | — | — | 350 |

**KM# 2044 8 DOLLARS**
155.67 g., 0.999 Silver 5.000 oz. ASW, 50.6 mm. **Ruler:** Elizabeth II **Rev:** Koala seated in tree **Note:** Ultra High Relief

| Date | Mintage | VF20 | XF40 | MS60 | MS63 | MS65 |
|---|---|---|---|---|---|---|
| 2013 | Est. 5000 | PF65 250 | | | | |

**KM# 1368 10 DOLLARS**
311.35 g., 0.999 Silver 10.0001 oz. ASW **Ruler:** Elizabeth II **Obv:** Head right **Rev:** Koala

| Date | Mintage | VF20 | XF40 | MS60 | MS63 | MS65 |
|---|---|---|---|---|---|---|
| 2010 P | — | — | — | — | — | 400 |

**KM# 1690 10 DOLLARS**
311.35 g., 0.999 Silver 10.0001 oz. ASW **Ruler:** Elizabeth II **Rev:** Koala

| Date | Mintage | VF20 | XF40 | MS60 | MS63 | MS65 |
|---|---|---|---|---|---|---|
| 2012 P | — | — | — | — | — | 400 |

**KM# 1980 10 DOLLARS**
311.35 g., 0.999 Silver 10.000 oz. ASW, 75.6 mm. **Ruler:** Elizabeth II **Rev:** Koala seated in tree

| Date | Mintage | VF20 | XF40 | MS60 | MS63 | MS65 |
|---|---|---|---|---|---|---|
| 2013 P | — | PF65 300 | | | | |

**KM# 917 15 DOLLARS**
3.11 g., 0.999 Platinum 0.0999 oz. APW **Ruler:** Elizabeth II **Obv:** Head with tiara right **Rev:** Two koalas on a branch

| Date | Mintage | VF20 | XF40 | MS60 | MS63 | MS65 |
|---|---|---|---|---|---|---|
| 2001 | 407 | PF65 210 | | | | |

**KM# 922 15 DOLLARS**
3.11 g., 0.999 Platinum 0.0999 oz. APW **Ruler:** Elizabeth II **Obv:** Head with tiara right **Rev:** Koala up a gum tree

| Date | Mintage | VF20 | XF40 | MS60 | MS63 | MS65 |
|---|---|---|---|---|---|---|
| 2002 | 665 | PF65 210 | | | | |

**KM# 926 15 DOLLARS**
3.11 g., 0.999 Platinum 0.0999 oz. APW **Ruler:** Elizabeth II **Obv:** Head with tiara right **Rev:** Mother and baby koala

| Date | Mintage | VF20 | XF40 | MS60 | MS63 | MS65 |
|---|---|---|---|---|---|---|
| 2003 | 431 | PF65 210 | | | | |

**KM# 931 15 DOLLARS**
3.11 g., 0.999 Platinum 0.0999 oz. APW **Ruler:** Elizabeth II **Obv:** Head with tiara right **Rev:** Single koala on branch

| Date | Mintage | VF20 | XF40 | MS60 | MS63 | MS65 |
|---|---|---|---|---|---|---|
| 2004 | 302 | PF65 210 | | | | |

**KM# 935 15 DOLLARS**
3.11 g., 0.999 Platinum 0.0999 oz. APW **Ruler:** Elizabeth II **Obv:** Head with tiara right **Rev:** Single koala with gum leaves

| Date | Mintage | VF20 | XF40 | MS60 | MS63 | MS65 |
|---|---|---|---|---|---|---|
| 2005 | 700 | PF65 210 | | | | |

**KM# 1873 15 DOLLARS**
3.11 g., 0.999 Gold 0.0999 oz. AGW **Ruler:** Elizabeth II **Rev:** Koala

| Date | Mintage | VF20 | XF40 | MS60 | MS63 | MS65 |
|---|---|---|---|---|---|---|
| 2008 P | 5,030 | PF65 250 | | | | |

**KM# 1114 15 DOLLARS**
3.11 g., 0.9999 Gold 0.0999 oz. AGW, 16.1 mm. **Ruler:** Elizabeth II **Rev:** Koala seated left on tree branch

| Date | Mintage | VF20 | XF40 | MS60 | MS63 | MS65 |
|---|---|---|---|---|---|---|
| 2009 P | 5,000 | PF65 190 | | | | |

**KM# 1468 15 DOLLARS**
3.11 g., 0.999 Gold 0.0999 oz. AGW **Ruler:** Elizabeth II **Rev:** Koala on branch

| Date | Mintage | VF20 | XF40 | MS60 | MS63 | MS65 |
|---|---|---|---|---|---|---|
| 2010 P | — | — | — | — | — | 190 |

**KM# 1844 15 DOLLARS**
3.11 g., 0.999 Gold 0.0999 oz. AGW, 16.1 mm. **Ruler:** Elizabeth II **Rev:** Koala sleeping hugging branch

| Date | Mintage | VF20 | XF40 | MS60 | MS63 | MS65 |
|---|---|---|---|---|---|---|
| 2012 P | — | PF65 250 | | | | |

**KM# 1982 15 DOLLARS**
3.11 g., 0.9999 Gold 0.100 oz. AGW, 16.1 mm. **Ruler:** Elizabeth II **Subject:** Australian Koala **Rev:** Koala seated in tree

| Date | Mintage | VF20 | XF40 | MS60 | MS63 | MS65 |
|---|---|---|---|---|---|---|
| 2013 P | — | PF65 175 | | | | |

**KM# 2049 15 DOLLARS**
3.11 g., 0.9999 Gold 0.100 oz. AGW, 16.1 mm. **Ruler:** Elizabeth II **Obv:** Head with tiara right **Rev:** Koala seated in tree

| Date | Mintage | VF20 | XF40 | MS60 | MS63 | MS65 |
|---|---|---|---|---|---|---|
| 2013 P | — | PF65 225 | | | | |

**KM# 2056 15 DOLLARS**
3.11 g., 0.9999 Gold 0.100 oz. AGW, 16.6 mm. **Ruler:** Elizabeth II **Obv:** Head with tiara right **Rev:** Koala seated in tree

| Date | Mintage | VF20 | XF40 | MS60 | MS63 | MS65 |
|---|---|---|---|---|---|---|
| 2013 P | Est. 550 | PF65 225 | | | | |

**KM# 918 25 DOLLARS**
7.75 g., 0.999 Platinum 0.2489 oz. APW **Ruler:** Elizabeth II **Obv:** Head with tiara right **Rev:** Two koalas on a branch

| Date | Mintage | VF20 | XF40 | MS60 | MS63 | MS65 |
|---|---|---|---|---|---|---|
| 2001 | 171 | PF65 485 | | | | |

**KM# 923 25 DOLLARS**
7.75 g., 0.999 Platinum 0.2489 oz. APW **Ruler:** Elizabeth II **Obv:** Head with tiara right **Rev:** Koala up a gum tree

| Date | Mintage | VF20 | XF40 | MS60 | MS63 | MS65 |
|---|---|---|---|---|---|---|
| 2002 | 138 | PF65 485 | | | | |

**KM# 927 25 DOLLARS**
7.75 g., 0.999 Platinum 0.2489 oz. APW **Ruler:** Elizabeth II **Obv:** Head with tiara right **Rev:** Mother and baby koala

| Date | Mintage | VF20 | XF40 | MS60 | MS63 | MS65 |
|---|---|---|---|---|---|---|
| 2003 | 99 | PF65 485 | | | | |

**KM# 932 25 DOLLARS**
7.75 g., 0.999 Platinum 0.2489 oz. APW **Ruler:** Elizabeth II **Obv:** Head with tiara right **Rev:** Single koala on branch

| Date | Mintage | VF20 | XF40 | MS60 | MS63 | MS65 |
|---|---|---|---|---|---|---|
| 2004 | 65 | PF65 485 | | | | |

**KM# 936 25 DOLLARS**
7.75 g., 0.999 Platinum 0.2489 oz. APW **Ruler:** Elizabeth II **Obv:** Head with tiara right **Rev:** Single koala with gum leaves

| Date | Mintage | VF20 | XF40 | MS60 | MS63 | MS65 |
|---|---|---|---|---|---|---|
| 2005 | 200 | PF65 485 | | | | |

**KM# 1112 30 DOLLARS**
1000.00 g., 0.9999 Silver 32.1475 oz. ASW, 100.6 mm. **Ruler:** Elizabeth II **Rev:** Koala seated left on branch

| Date | Mintage | VF20 | XF40 | MS60 | MS63 | MS65 |
|---|---|---|---|---|---|---|
| 2009 P Prooflike | — | — | — | — | — | 1,150 |

**KM# 1369 30 DOLLARS**
1000.00 g., 0.999 Silver 32.1186 oz. ASW, 100.6 mm. **Ruler:** Elizabeth II **Obv:** Head light **Rev:** Koala

| Date | Mintage | VF20 | XF40 | MS60 | MS63 | MS65 |
|---|---|---|---|---|---|---|
| 2010 (p) | — | — | — | — | — | 1,150 |

**KM# 1466 30 DOLLARS**
1000.00 g., 0.999 Silver 32.1186 oz. ASW, 100.6 mm. **Ruler:** Elizabeth II **Rev:** Koala on branch

| Date | Mintage | VF20 | XF40 | MS60 | MS63 | MS65 |
|---|---|---|---|---|---|---|
| 2010 P | — | — | — | — | — | 1,200 |

**KM# 1691 30 DOLLARS**
1000.00 g., 0.999 Silver 32.1186 oz. ASW, 100.6 mm. **Ruler:** Elizabeth II **Rev:** Koala

| Date | Mintage | VF20 | XF40 | MS60 | MS63 | MS65 |
|---|---|---|---|---|---|---|
| 2012 P | — | — | — | — | — | 1,200 |

**KM# 1785 30 DOLLARS**
1000.00 g., 0.999 Silver 32.1186 oz. ASW, 100.6 mm. **Ruler:** Elizabeth II **Obv:** Head with tiara right **Rev:** Koala hugging and lying on branch **Edge:** Reeded

| Date | Mintage | VF20 | XF40 | MS60 | MS63 | MS65 |
|---|---|---|---|---|---|---|
| 2012 P | — | PF65 1,250 | | | | |

**KM# 1842 30 DOLLARS**
1000.00 g., 0.999 Silver 32.1186 oz. ASW, 101 mm. **Ruler:** Elizabeth II **Rev:** Koala sleeping hugging branch

| Date | Mintage | VF20 | XF40 | MS60 | MS63 | MS65 |
|---|---|---|---|---|---|---|
| 2012 P | — | — | — | — | — | 1,400 |

**KM# 1981 30 DOLLARS**
1001.00 g., 0.999 Silver 32.1508 oz. ASW, 100.6 mm. **Ruler:** Elizabeth II **Rev:** Koala seated in tree

| Date | Mintage | VF20 | XF40 | MS60 | MS63 | MS65 |
|---|---|---|---|---|---|---|
| 2013 P Proof | — | PF65 1,000 | | | | |
| Matte finish | | | | | | |
| 2013 P | — | PF65 1,000 | | | | |

**KM# 919 50 DOLLARS**
15.50 g., 0.999 Platinum 0.4979 oz. APW **Ruler:** Elizabeth II **Obv:** Head with tiara right **Rev:** Two koalas on a branch

| Date | Mintage | VF20 | XF40 | MS60 | MS63 | MS65 |
|---|---|---|---|---|---|---|
| 2001 | 238 | PF65 960 | | | | |

**KM# 924 50 DOLLARS**
15.50 g., 0.999 Platinum 0.4979 oz. APW **Ruler:** Elizabeth II **Obv:** Head with tiara right **Rev:** Koala up a gum tree

| Date | Mintage | VF20 | XF40 | MS60 | MS63 | MS65 |
|---|---|---|---|---|---|---|
| 2002 | 648 | PF65 960 | | | | |

**KM# 928 50 DOLLARS**
15.50 g., 0.999 Platinum 0.4979 oz. APW **Ruler:** Elizabeth II **Obv:** Head with tiara right **Rev:** Mother and baby koala

| Date | Mintage | VF20 | XF40 | MS60 | MS63 | MS65 |
|---|---|---|---|---|---|---|
| 2003 | 180 | PF65 960 | | | | |

**KM# 933 50 DOLLARS**
15.50 g., 0.999 Platinum 0.4979 oz. APW **Ruler:** Elizabeth II **Obv:** Head with tiara right **Rev:** Single koala on branch

| Date | Mintage | VF20 | XF40 | MS60 | MS63 | MS65 |
|---|---|---|---|---|---|---|
| 2004 | 148 | PF65 960 | | | | |

**KM# 937 50 DOLLARS**
15.50 g., 0.999 Platinum 0.4979 oz. APW **Ruler:** Elizabeth II **Obv:** Head with tiara right **Rev:** Single koala with gum leaves

| Date | Mintage | VF20 | XF40 | MS60 | MS63 | MS65 |
|---|---|---|---|---|---|---|
| 2005 | 297 | PF65 960 | | | | |

**KM# 2040 50 DOLLARS**
15.56 g., 0.9995 Platinum 0.500 oz. APW, 25.1 mm. **Ruler:** Elizabeth II **Rev:** Koala standing

| Date | Mintage | VF20 | XF40 | MS60 | MS63 | MS65 |
|---|---|---|---|---|---|---|
| 2013 | 1,200 | PF65 1,485 | | | | |

**KM# 2055 50 DOLLARS**
15.55 g., 0.9999 Gold 0.500 oz. AGW, 25.6 mm. **Ruler:** Elizabeth II **Obv:** Head with tiara right **Rev:** Koala seated in tree

| Date | Mintage | VF20 | XF40 | MS60 | MS63 | MS65 |
|---|---|---|---|---|---|---|
| 2013 P | Est. 550 | PF65 1,000 | | | | |

**KM# 921 100 DOLLARS**
31.10 g., 0.999 Platinum 0.999 oz. APW **Ruler:** Elizabeth II **Obv:** Head with tiara right **Rev:** Federation: Sir Henry Parkes, flag, parliament house, colored image

| Date | Mintage | VF20 | XF40 | MS60 | MS63 | MS65 |
|---|---|---|---|---|---|---|
| 2001 | 228 | PF65 1,875 | | | | |

**KM# 1874 100 DOLLARS**
31.11 g., 0.999 Platinum 0.999 oz. APW **Ruler:** Elizabeth II **Rev:** Koala

| Date | Mintage | VF20 | XF40 | MS60 | MS63 | MS65 |
|---|---|---|---|---|---|---|
| 2002 P | 1,650 | PF65 1,875 | | | | |

**KM# 930 100 DOLLARS**
31.10 g., 0.999 Platinum 0.999 oz. APW **Ruler:** Elizabeth II **Obv:** Head with tiara right **Rev:** The Arts: Dancers, paint brushes, opera house, colored image

| Date | Mintage | VF20 | XF40 | MS60 | MS63 | MS65 |
|---|---|---|---|---|---|---|
| 2003 | 1,000 | PF65 1,875 | | | | |

**KM# 742 100 DOLLARS**
31.10 g., 0.9995 Platinum 0.9995 oz. APW, 32.1 mm. **Ruler:** Elizabeth II **Obv:** Head with tiara right, denomination below **Rev:** Sports: Australian sportsmen and women, colored image **Edge:** Reeded

| Date | Mintage | VF20 | XF40 | MS60 | MS63 | MS65 |
|---|---|---|---|---|---|---|
| 2004 P | 109 | PF65 1,875 | | | | |

**KM# 939 100 DOLLARS**
31.10 g., 0.999 Platinum 0.999 oz. APW **Ruler:** Elizabeth II **Obv:** Head with tiara right **Rev:** Two workers and machine, colored image

| Date | Mintage | VF20 | XF40 | MS60 | MS63 | MS65 |
|---|---|---|---|---|---|---|
| 2005 | 247 | PF65 1,875 | | | | |

**KM# 1875 100 DOLLARS**
31.11 g., 0.999 Gold 0.999 oz. AGW, 32.1 mm. **Ruler:** Elizabeth II **Rev:** Koala

| Date | Mintage | VF20 | XF40 | MS60 | MS63 | MS65 |
|---|---|---|---|---|---|---|
| 2008 P | 1,860 | PF65 1,800 | | | | |

**KM# 1469 100 DOLLARS**
31.11 g., 0.999 Gold 0.999 oz. AGW, 32.1 mm. **Ruler:** Elizabeth II **Rev:** Koala on branch

| Date | Mintage | VF20 | XF40 | MS60 | MS63 | MS65 |
|---|---|---|---|---|---|---|
| 2010 P | — | — | — | — | — | 1,800 |

**KM# 1608 100 DOLLARS**
31.11 g., 0.999 Gold 0.999 oz. AGW, 28 mm. **Ruler:** Elizabeth II **Obv:** Head with tiara right **Rev:** Two pandas seated in fork of a eucalyptus tree **Edge:** Reeded **Note:** Ultra High Relief

| Date | Mintage | VF20 | XF40 | MS60 | MS63 | MS65 |
|---|---|---|---|---|---|---|
| 2011 P | 2,000 | PF65 1,950 | | | | |

**KM# 1845 100 DOLLARS**
31.11 g., 0.999 Gold 0.999 oz. AGW, 28 mm. **Ruler:** Elizabeth II **Rev:** Koala sleeping hugging branch **Note:** Ultra High Relief

| Date | Mintage | VF20 | XF40 | MS60 | MS63 | MS65 |
|---|---|---|---|---|---|---|
| 2012 P | — | PF65 1,900 | | | | |

**KM# 1983 100 DOLLARS**
31.11 g., 0.9999 Gold 1.000 oz. AGW, 27.3 mm. **Ruler:** Elizabeth II **Subject:** Australian Koala

| Date | Mintage | VF20 | XF40 | MS60 | MS63 | MS65 |
|---|---|---|---|---|---|---|
| 2013 | Est. 2000 | PF65 1,900 | | | | |

**KM# 2048 100 DOLLARS**
31.11 g., 0.9999 Gold 1.000 oz. AGW, 27.3 mm. **Ruler:** Elizabeth II **Obv:** Head with tiara right **Rev:** Koala seated in tree **Note:** High relief.

| Date | Mintage | VF20 | XF40 | MS60 | MS63 | MS65 |
|---|---|---|---|---|---|---|
| 2013 P | — | PF65 2,250 | | | | |

**KM# 920 200 DOLLARS**
62.21 g., 0.999 Platinum 1.9982 oz. APW, 41 mm. **Ruler:** Elizabeth II **Obv:** Head with tiara right **Rev:** Two koalas sitting on branch

| Date | Mintage | VF20 | XF40 | MS60 | MS63 | MS65 |
|---|---|---|---|---|---|---|
| 2001 | 305 | PF65 3,800 | | | | |

**KM# 925 200 DOLLARS**
62.21 g., 0.999 Platinum 1.9982 oz. APW, 41 mm. **Ruler:** Elizabeth II **Obv:** Head with tiara right **Rev:** Koala up a gum tree

| Date | Mintage | VF20 | XF40 | MS60 | MS63 | MS65 |
|---|---|---|---|---|---|---|
| 2002 | 117 | PF65 3,800 | | | | |

**KM# 929 200 DOLLARS**
62.21 g., 0.999 Platinum 1.9982 oz. APW, 41 mm. **Ruler:** Elizabeth II **Obv:** Head with tiara right **Rev:** Mother and baby koala

| Date | Mintage | VF20 | XF40 | MS60 | MS63 | MS65 |
|---|---|---|---|---|---|---|
| 2003 | 65 | PF65 3,800 | | | | |

**KM# 934 200 DOLLARS**
62.21 g., 0.999 Platinum 1.9982 oz. APW, 41 mm. **Ruler:** Elizabeth II **Obv:** Head with tiara right **Rev:** Single koala on branch

| Date | Mintage | VF20 | XF40 | MS60 | MS63 | MS65 |
|---|---|---|---|---|---|---|
| 2004 | 41 | PF65 3,800 | | | | |

**KM# 938 200 DOLLARS**
62.21 g., 0.999 Platinum 1.9982 oz. APW, 41 mm. **Ruler:** Elizabeth II **Obv:** Head with tiara right **Rev:** Single koala with gum leaves in color

| Date | Mintage | VF20 | XF40 | MS60 | MS63 | MS65 |
|---|---|---|---|---|---|---|
| 2005 | 91 | PF65 3,800 | | | | |

**KM# 1876 200 DOLLARS**
62.24 g., 0.999 Gold 1.9991 oz. AGW, 40.6 mm. **Ruler:** Elizabeth II **Rev:** Koala

| Date | Mintage | VF20 | XF40 | MS60 | MS63 | MS65 |
|---|---|---|---|---|---|---|
| 2008 P | 250 | PF65 3,750 | | | | |

**KM# 1470 200 DOLLARS**
62.24 g., 0.999 Gold 1.9991 oz. AGW, 41 mm. **Ruler:** Elizabeth II **Rev:** Koala on branch

| Date | Mintage | VF20 | XF40 | MS60 | MS63 | MS65 |
|---|---|---|---|---|---|---|
| 2010 P | — | — | — | — | — | 3,750 |

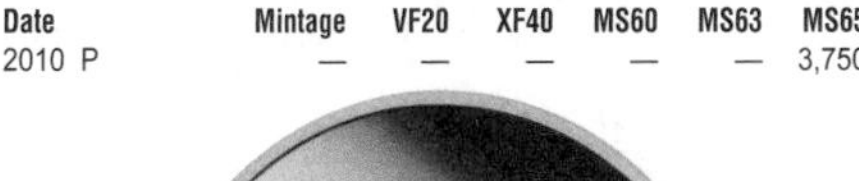

**KM# 1846 200 DOLLARS**
62.20 g., 0.999 Gold 1.9978 oz. AGW, 40.6 mm. **Ruler:** Elizabeth II **Rev:** Koala sleeping hugging branch

| Date | Mintage | VF20 | XF40 | MS60 | MS63 | MS65 |
|---|---|---|---|---|---|---|
| 2012 P | — | PF65 3,750 | | | | |

**KM# 1984 200 DOLLARS**
62.22 g., 0.9999 Gold 2.0001 oz. AGW, 36.6 mm. **Ruler:** Elizabeth II **Rev:** Koala seated in tree **Note:** High releif.

| Date | Mintage | VF20 | XF40 | MS60 | MS63 | MS65 |
|---|---|---|---|---|---|---|
| 2013 P | Est. 250 | PF65 3,250 | | | | |

## BULLION - PLATYPUS

**KM# 1731 100 DOLLARS**
31.12 g., 0.9995 Platinum 1.000 oz. APW, 32.6 mm. **Ruler:** Elizabeth II **Obv:** Head with tiara right **Rev:** Platypus swimming downward **Edge:** Reeded

| Date | Mintage | VF20 | XF40 | MS60 | MS63 | MS65 |
|---|---|---|---|---|---|---|
| 2012 P | 30,000 | — | — | — | — | 1,750 |
| 2013 P | — | — | — | — | — | 1,750 |
| 2014 P | — | — | — | — | — | 1,750 |

## BULLION - LUNAR YEAR

**KM# 1010 25 CENTS**
0.999 Silver Gilt, 17.8 mm. **Ruler:** Elizabeth II **Obv:** Bust with tiara right **Obv. Legend:** ELIZABETH II - AUSTRALIA **Rev:** 4 Chinese characters **Rev. Legend:** LUNAR NEW YEAR - GOOD FORTUNE & PROSPERITY

| Date | Mintage | VF20 | XF40 | MS60 | MS63 | MS65 |
|---|---|---|---|---|---|---|
| 2007 | 8,888 | PF65 45.00 | | | | |

**KM# 1880 50 CENTS**
15.55 g., 0.999 Silver 0.4994 oz. ASW, 32.1 mm. **Ruler:** Elizabeth II **Subject:** Year of the Snake

| Date | Mintage | VF20 | XF40 | MS60 | MS63 | MS65 |
|---|---|---|---|---|---|---|
| 2001 P | 2,023 | PF65 35.00 | | | | |

**KM# 579 50 CENTS**
15.55 g., 0.999 Silver 0.4995 oz. ASW, 32.1 mm. **Ruler:** Elizabeth II **Subject:** Year of the Horse **Obv:** Head with tiara right, denomination below **Rev:** Horse running left **Edge:** Reeded

| Date | Mintage | VF20 | XF40 | MS60 | MS63 | MS65 |
|---|---|---|---|---|---|---|
| 2002 P | 1,810 | PF65 35.00 | | | | |

**KM# 664 50 CENTS**
16.40 g., 0.999 Silver 0.5267 oz. ASW, 31.9 mm. **Ruler:** Elizabeth II **Subject:** Year of the Goat **Obv:** Head with tiara right, denomination below **Rev:** Two goats **Edge:** Reeded

| Date | Mintage | VF20 | XF40 | MS60 | MS63 | MS65 |
|---|---|---|---|---|---|---|
| 2003 | — | — | — | — | 20.00 | 25.00 |
| 2003 | 1,028 | PF65 35.00 | | | | |

**KM# 673 50 CENTS**
15.55 g., 0.999 Silver 0.4995 oz. ASW, 32.1 mm. **Ruler:** Elizabeth II **Subject:** Year of the Monkey **Obv:** Head with tiara right, denomination below **Rev:** Monkey sitting on branch **Edge:** Reeded

| Date | Mintage | VF20 | XF40 | MS60 | MS63 | MS65 |
|---|---|---|---|---|---|---|
| 2004 | — | — | — | — | — | 20.00 |
| 2004 | 930 | PF65 35.00 | | | | |

**KM# 791 50 CENTS**
15.57 g., 0.999 Silver 0.500 oz. ASW, 32.1 mm. **Ruler:** Elizabeth II **Subject:** Year of the Rooster **Obv:** Elizabeth II **Rev:** Standing Rooster looking backwards **Edge:** Reeded

| Date | Mintage | VF20 | XF40 | MS60 | MS63 | MS65 |
|---|---|---|---|---|---|---|
| 2005 P | — | — | — | — | — | 20.00 |
| 2005 P | 900 | PF65 50.00 | | | | |

**KM# 814 50 CENTS**
15.55 g., 0.999 Silver 0.4994 oz. ASW **Ruler:** Elizabeth II **Subject:** Bullion Lunar Year - Rooster **Obv:** Head with tiara right

| Date | Mintage | VF20 | XF40 | MS60 | MS63 | MS65 |
|---|---|---|---|---|---|---|
| 2005 | — | — | — | — | — | 20.00 |

**KM# 1877 50 CENTS**
15.55 g., 0.999 Silver 0.4994 oz. ASW, 32 mm. **Ruler:** Elizabeth II **Subject:** Year of the Dog

| Date | Mintage | VF20 | XF40 | MS60 | MS63 | MS65 |
|---|---|---|---|---|---|---|
| 2006 P | 1,668 | — | — | — | — | 30.00 |

**KM# 1878 50 CENTS**
15.55 g., 0.999 Silver 0.4994 oz. ASW, 32 mm. **Ruler:** Elizabeth II **Subject:** Year of the Pig

| Date | Mintage | VF20 | XF40 | MS60 | MS63 | MS65 |
|---|---|---|---|---|---|---|
| 2007 P | 1,339 | — | — | — | — | 30.00 |

**KM# 1879 50 CENTS**
15.55 g., 0.999 Silver 0.4994 oz. ASW, 32 mm. **Ruler:** Elizabeth II **Subject:** Year of the Rat

| Date | Mintage | VF20 | XF40 | MS60 | MS63 | MS65 |
|---|---|---|---|---|---|---|
| 2008 P | 366 | — | — | — | — | 30.00 |

**KM# 1750 50 CENTS**
15.55 g., 0.999 Silver 0.4994 oz. ASW, 32 mm. **Ruler:** Elizabeth II **Subject:** Year of the Ox **Obv:** Head with tiara right **Rev:** Two oxen standing

| Date | Mintage | VF20 | XF40 | MS60 | MS63 | MS65 |
|---|---|---|---|---|---|---|
| 2009 P | — | — | — | — | — | 85.00 |

**KM# 1750a 50 CENTS**
15.55 g., 0.999 Silver 0.4994 oz. ASW, 32 mm. **Ruler:** Elizabeth II **Subject:** Year of the Ox **Rev:** Two colored oxen standing

| Date | Mintage | VF20 | XF40 | MS60 | MS63 | MS65 |
|---|---|---|---|---|---|---|
| 2009 P | — | — | — | — | — | 100 |

**KM# 1370 50 CENTS**
15.55 g., 0.990 Silver 0.4949 oz. ASW, 32 mm. **Ruler:** Elizabeth II **Subject:** Year of the Tiger **Obv:** Head right **Rev:** Tiger at rest left

| Date | Mintage | VF20 | XF40 | MS60 | MS63 | MS65 |
|---|---|---|---|---|---|---|
| 2010 P | — | — | — | — | — | 20.00 |

**KM# 1474 50 CENTS**
15.56 g., 0.999 Silver 0.4998 oz. ASW, 32 mm. **Ruler:** Elizabeth II **Subject:** Year of the Rabbit **Rev:** Mother and baby rabbit nose to nose

| Date | Mintage | VF20 | XF40 | MS60 | MS63 | MS65 |
|---|---|---|---|---|---|---|
| 2011 P | — | PF65 30.00 | | | | |

**KM# 1663 50 CENTS**
15.55 g., 0.999 Silver 0.4995 oz. ASW, 31.9 mm. **Ruler:** Elizabeth II **Subject:** Year of the Dragon

| Date | Mintage | VF20 | XF40 | MS60 | MS63 | MS65 |
|---|---|---|---|---|---|---|
| 2012 P | — | PF65 25.00 | | | | |

**KM# 1663a 50 CENTS**
15.55 g., 0.999 Silver 0.4995 oz. ASW, 32.1 mm. **Ruler:** Elizabeth II **Subject:** Year of the Dragon **Rev:** Dragon in color

| Date | Mintage | VF20 | XF40 | MS60 | MS63 | MS65 |
|---|---|---|---|---|---|---|
| 2012 P | — | PF65 30.00 | | | | |

**KM# 1832 50 CENTS**
15.50 g., 0.999 Silver 0.4978 oz. ASW, 36.6 mm. **Ruler:** Elizabeth II **Subject:** Year of the Snake **Obv:** Head with tiara right **Rev:** Snake

| Date | Mintage | VF20 | XF40 | MS60 | MS63 | MS65 |
|---|---|---|---|---|---|---|
| 2013 P | — | PF65 40.00 | | | | |

**KM# 1832a 50 CENTS**
15.55 g., 0.999 Silver 0.4994 oz. ASW, 36.6 mm. **Ruler:** Elizabeth II **Subject:** Year of the Snake **Rev:** Snake in color

| Date | Mintage | VF20 | XF40 | MS60 | MS63 | MS65 |
|---|---|---|---|---|---|---|
| 2013 P | — | PF65 35.00 | | | | |

**KM# 536 DOLLAR**
31.10 g., 0.999 Silver 0.999 oz. ASW, 40.6 mm. **Ruler:** Elizabeth II **Subject:** Year of the Snake **Obv:** Head with tiara right, denomination below **Rev:** Snake with eggs **Edge:** Reeded

| Date | Mintage | VF20 | XF40 | MS60 | MS63 | MS65 |
|---|---|---|---|---|---|---|
| 2001 | 300,000 | — | — | — | 80.00 | 100 |
| 2001 P | 3,354 | PF65 100 | | | | |

**KM# 536a DOLLAR**
31.64 g., 0.999 Silver 1.0161 oz. ASW partially gilt, 40.6 mm. **Ruler:** Elizabeth II **Subject:** Year of the Snake **Obv:** Head with tiara right, denomination below **Rev:** Gold-plated snake **Edge:** Reeded

| Date | Mintage | VF20 | XF40 | MS60 | MS63 | MS65 |
|---|---|---|---|---|---|---|
| 2001 | 16,335 | — | — | — | 45.00 | 50.00 |

**KM# 580 DOLLAR**
31.10 g., 0.999 Silver 0.999 oz. ASW, 40.6 mm. **Ruler:** Elizabeth II **Subject:** Year of the Horse **Obv:** Head with tiara right, denomination below **Rev:** Horse running left **Edge:** Reeded

| Date | Mintage | VF20 | XF40 | MS60 | MS63 | MS65 |
|---|---|---|---|---|---|---|
| 2002 P | — | — | — | — | 75.00 | 80.00 |
| 2002 P | 2,011 | PF65 75.00 | | | | |

**KM# 580a DOLLAR**
31.64 g., 0.999 Silver 1.0161 oz. ASW partially gilt, 40.6 mm. **Ruler:** Elizabeth II **Obv:** Head with tiara right **Rev:** Gold-plated horse **Edge:** Reeded

| Date | Mintage | VF20 | XF40 | MS60 | MS63 | MS65 |
|---|---|---|---|---|---|---|
| 2002 | 16,859 | — | — | — | 40.00 | 45.00 |

**KM# 665 DOLLAR**
31.62 g., 0.999 Silver 1.0156 oz. ASW, 40.3 mm. **Ruler:** Elizabeth II **Subject:** Year of the Goat **Obv:** Head with tiara right, denomination below **Rev:** Two goats **Edge:** Reeded

| Date | Mintage | VF20 | XF40 | MS60 | MS63 | MS65 |
|---|---|---|---|---|---|---|
| 2003 | — | — | — | — | 50.00 | 75.00 |
| 2003 | 1,489 | PF65 75.00 | | | | |

**KM# 665a DOLLAR**
31.64 g., 0.999 Silver 1.0161 oz. ASW partially gilt, 40.6 mm. **Ruler:** Elizabeth II **Subject:** Year of the Goat **Obv:** Head with tiara right, denomination below **Rev:** Gold-plated goat **Edge:** Reeded

| Date | Mintage | VF20 | XF40 | MS60 | MS63 | MS65 |
|---|---|---|---|---|---|---|
| 2003 | 15,842 | — | — | — | 50.00 | 55.00 |

**KM# 674 DOLLAR**
31.10 g., 0.999 Silver 0.999 oz. ASW, 40.6 mm. **Ruler:** Elizabeth II **Subject:** Year of the Monkey **Obv:** Head with tiara right, denomination below **Rev:** Monkey sitting on branch **Edge:** Reeded

| Date | Mintage | VF20 | XF40 | MS60 | MS63 | MS65 |
|---|---|---|---|---|---|---|
| 2004 | — | — | — | — | 40.00 | 45.00 |
| 2004 | 1,187 | PF65 55.00 | | | | |

**KM# 674a DOLLAR**
31.64 g., 0.999 Silver 1.0161 oz. ASW partially gilt, 40.6 mm. **Ruler:** Elizabeth II **Subject:** Year of the Monkey **Obv:** Head with tiara right, denomination below **Rev:** Monkey, gilt **Edge:** Reeded

| Date | Mintage | VF20 | XF40 | MS60 | MS63 | MS65 |
|---|---|---|---|---|---|---|
| 2004 | 25,599 | — | — | — | 50.00 | 55.00 |

### KM# 674b DOLLAR

31.10 g., 0.999 Silver 0.999 oz. ASW, 40.6 mm. **Ruler:** Elizabeth II **Subject:** Year of the Monkey **Rev:** Monkey in color

| Date | Mintage | VF20 | XF40 | MS60 | MS63 | MS65 |
|---|---|---|---|---|---|---|
| 2004 P | 31,406 | — | — | — | — | 75.00 |

### KM# 695 DOLLAR

31.11 g., 0.999 Silver 0.999 oz. ASW, 40.5 mm. **Ruler:** Elizabeth II **Subject:** Year of the Rooster **Obv:** Head with tiara right, denomination below **Rev:** Rooster **Edge:** Reeded

| Date | Mintage | VF20 | XF40 | MS60 | MS63 | MS65 |
|---|---|---|---|---|---|---|
| 2005 | — | — | — | — | 75.00 | 65.00 |
| 2005 P | 1,734 | PF65 80.00 | | | | |

### KM# 695a DOLLAR

31.64 g., 0.999 Silver 1.0161 oz. ASW partially gilt, 40.5 mm. **Ruler:** Elizabeth II **Subject:** Year of the Rooster **Obv:** Head with tiara right, denomination below **Rev:** Gilt rooster **Edge:** Reeded

| Date | Mintage | VF20 | XF40 | MS60 | MS63 | MS65 |
|---|---|---|---|---|---|---|
| 2005 Polished fields | 28,960 | — | — | — | 45.00 | 50.00 |
| 2005 Matte fields | — | — | — | — | 175 | 185 |

### KM# 695b DOLLAR

31.11 g., 0.999 Silver 0.999 oz. ASW partially gilt and colored, 40.5 mm. **Ruler:** Elizabeth II **Subject:** Year of the Rooster **Rev:** Gilt field, colored Rooster

| Date | Mintage | VF20 | XF40 | MS60 | MS63 | MS65 |
|---|---|---|---|---|---|---|
| 2005 P | 8,832 | — | — | — | — | 60.00 |

### KM# 695c DOLLAR

31.11 g., 0.999 Silver 0.999 oz. ASW, 40.5 mm. **Ruler:** Elizabeth II **Subject:** Year of the Rooster **Rev:** Colored Rooster

| Date | Mintage | VF20 | XF40 | MS60 | MS63 | MS65 |
|---|---|---|---|---|---|---|
| 2005 P | 38,000 | — | — | — | — | 60.00 |

### KM# 1882 DOLLAR

31.11 g., 0.999 Silver 0.999 oz. ASW, 40 mm. **Ruler:** Elizabeth II **Subject:** Year of the Dog

| Date | Mintage | VF20 | XF40 | MS60 | MS63 | MS65 |
|---|---|---|---|---|---|---|
| 2006 P | 2,887 | PF65 50.00 | | | | |

### KM# 1883 DOLLAR

31.11 g., 0.999 Silver 0.999 oz. ASW, 40 mm. **Ruler:** Elizabeth II **Subject:** Year of the Pig

| Date | Mintage | VF20 | XF40 | MS60 | MS63 | MS65 |
|---|---|---|---|---|---|---|
| 2007 P | 2,833 | PF65 50.00 | | | | |

### KM# 1755 DOLLAR

31.11 g., 0.999 Silver 0.999 oz. ASW, 40 mm. **Ruler:** Elizabeth II **Subject:** Year of the Mouse **Obv:** Head with tiara right **Rev:** Mouse pair

| Date | Mintage | VF20 | XF40 | MS60 | MS63 | MS65 |
|---|---|---|---|---|---|---|
| 2008 P | 4,715 | — | — | — | — | 75.00 |

### KM# 1755a DOLLAR

31.11 g., 0.999 Silver 0.999 oz. ASW, 40 mm. **Ruler:** Elizabeth II **Subject:** Year of the Mouse **Obv:** Head with tiara right **Rev:** Mouse pair in color

| Date | Mintage | VF20 | XF40 | MS60 | MS63 | MS65 |
|---|---|---|---|---|---|---|
| 2008 P | — | — | — | — | — | 85.00 |

### KM# 1755b DOLLAR

31.11 g., 0.999 Silver 0.999 oz. ASW partially gilt, 40 mm. **Ruler:** Elizabeth II **Subject:** Year of the Rat **Rev:** Mouse gilt

| Date | Mintage | VF20 | XF40 | MS60 | MS63 | MS65 |
|---|---|---|---|---|---|---|
| 2008 P | — | — | — | — | — | 85.00 |

### KM# 1755c DOLLAR

31.11 g., 0.999 Silver 0.999 oz. ASW, 40.5 mm. **Ruler:** Elizabeth II **Subject:** Year of the Rat **Rev:** Mouse with diamond chip in eye

| Date | Mintage | VF20 | XF40 | MS60 | MS63 | MS65 |
|---|---|---|---|---|---|---|
| 2008 P | — | — | — | — | — | 85.00 |

### KM# 1317 DOLLAR

31.11 g., 0.999 Silver 0.999 oz. ASW, 40.6 mm. **Ruler:** Elizabeth II **Subject:** Year of the Tiger **Obv:** Head right **Rev:** Tiger at rest left

| Date | Mintage | VF20 | XF40 | MS60 | MS63 | MS65 |
|---|---|---|---|---|---|---|
| 2010 P | — | — | — | — | — | 50.00 |
| 2010 P | 1,000 | PF65 75.00 | | | | |

### KM# 1317a DOLLAR

31.11 g., 0.999 Silver 0.999 oz. ASW, 40.6 mm. **Ruler:** Elizabeth II **Subject:** Year of the Tiger **Obv:** Head right **Rev:** Tiger at rest left, partially gilt

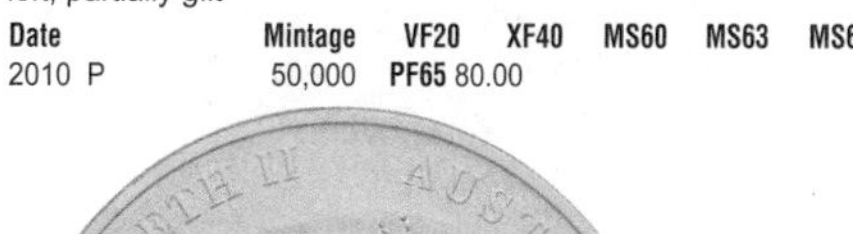

| Date | Mintage | VF20 | XF40 | MS60 | MS63 | MS65 |
|---|---|---|---|---|---|---|
| 2010 P | 50,000 | PF65 80.00 | | | | |

### KM# 1317b DOLLAR

31.11 g., 0.999 Silver 0.999 oz. ASW, 40.6 mm. **Ruler:** Elizabeth II **Subject:** Year of the Tiger **Obv:** Head right **Rev:** Multicolor tiger at rest left

| Date | Mintage | VF20 | XF40 | MS60 | MS63 | MS65 |
|---|---|---|---|---|---|---|
| 2010 P | 170,000 | PF65 75.00 | | | | |

### KM# 1475 DOLLAR

31.11 g., 0.999 Silver 0.999 oz. ASW, 40 mm. **Ruler:** Elizabeth II **Subject:** Year of the Rabbit **Rev:** Mother and baby rabbit nose to nose

| Date | Mintage | VF20 | XF40 | MS60 | MS63 | MS65 |
|---|---|---|---|---|---|---|
| 2011 P | — | PF65 50.00 | | | | |

### KM# 1475a DOLLAR

31.11 g., 0.999 Silver 0.999 oz. ASW, 40.5 mm. **Ruler:** Elizabeth II **Subject:** Year of the Rabbit **Rev:** Two rabbits, partially gilt

| Date | Mintage | VF20 | XF40 | MS60 | MS63 | MS65 |
|---|---|---|---|---|---|---|
| 2011 P | — | PF65 75.00 | | | | |

### KM# 1475b DOLLAR

31.11 g., 0.999 Silver 0.999 oz. ASW, 40.5 mm. **Ruler:** Elizabeth II **Subject:** Year of the Rabbit **Rev:** Two rabbits in color

| Date | Mintage | VF20 | XF40 | MS60 | MS63 | MS65 |
|---|---|---|---|---|---|---|
| 2011 P | — | PF65 75.00 | | | | |

## KM# 1664.1 DOLLAR

31.11 g., 0.999 Silver 0.999 oz. ASW partially gilt, 40.5 mm. **Ruler:** Elizabeth II **Subject:** Year of the Dragon **Rev:** Dragon gilt

| Date | Mintage | VF20 | XF40 | MS60 | MS63 | MS65 |
|---|---|---|---|---|---|---|
| 2012 P | — | PF65 75.00 | | | | |

## KM# 1664.2 DOLLAR

31.11 g., 0.999 Silver 0.999 oz. ASW, 40.5 mm. **Ruler:** Elizabeth II **Subject:** Year of the Dragon **Rev:** Dragon in black collor

| Date | Mintage | VF20 | XF40 | MS60 | MS63 | MS65 |
|---|---|---|---|---|---|---|
| 2012 P | — | — | — | — | — | 70.00 |
| 2012 P | — | PF65 75.00 | | | | |

## KM# 1664.3 DOLLAR

31.11 g., 0.999 Silver 0.999 oz. ASW, 40 mm. **Ruler:** Elizabeth II **Subject:** Year of the Dragon **Obv:** Head with tiara right **Rev:** Dragon colored red, brown and yellow

| Date | Mintage | VF20 | XF40 | MS60 | MS63 | MS65 |
|---|---|---|---|---|---|---|
| 2012 P | 20,000 | — | — | — | — | 100 |

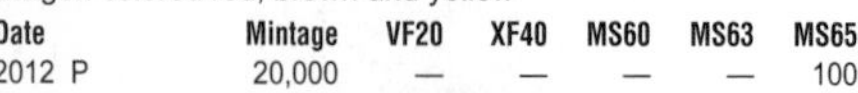

## KM# 1664.4 DOLLAR

31.11 g., 0.999 Silver 0.999 oz. ASW, 40 mm. **Ruler:** Elizabeth II **Subject:** Year of the Dragon **Obv:** Bust with tiara right **Rev:** Dragon colored black and red

| Date | Mintage | VF20 | XF40 | MS60 | MS63 | MS65 |
|---|---|---|---|---|---|---|
| 2012 P | — | — | — | — | — | 100 |

## KM# 1664.5 DOLLAR

31.11 g., 0.999 Silver 0.999 oz. ASW, 40 mm. **Ruler:** Elizabeth II **Subject:** Year of the Dragon **Obv:** Head with tiara right **Rev:** Dragon colored yellow and lavender

| Date | Mintage | VF20 | XF40 | MS60 | MS63 | MS65 |
|---|---|---|---|---|---|---|
| 2012 P | — | — | — | — | — | 100 |

## KM# 1664.6 DOLLAR

31.11 g., 0.999 Silver 0.999 oz. ASW, 40 mm. **Ruler:** Elizabeth II **Subject:** Year of the Dragon **Obv:** Head with tiara right **Rev:** Dragon colored blue and yellow

| Date | Mintage | VF20 | XF40 | MS60 | MS63 | MS65 |
|---|---|---|---|---|---|---|
| 2012 P | — | — | — | — | — | 100 |

## KM# 1664.7 DOLLAR

31.11 g., 0.999 Silver 0.999 oz. ASW, 40 mm. **Ruler:** Elizabeth II **Subject:** Year of the Dragon **Obv:** Head with tiara right **Rev:** Dragon colored purple and yellow

| Date | Mintage | VF20 | XF40 | MS60 | MS63 | MS65 |
|---|---|---|---|---|---|---|
| 2012 P | — | — | — | — | — | 100 |

## KM# 1664.8 DOLLAR

31.11 g., 0.999 Silver 0.999 oz. ASW, 40 mm. **Ruler:** Elizabeth II **Subject:** Year of the Dragon **Obv:** Head with tiara right **Rev:** Dragon colored orange, brown and yellow

| Date | Mintage | VF20 | XF40 | MS60 | MS63 | MS65 |
|---|---|---|---|---|---|---|
| 2012 P | — | — | — | — | — | 100 |

## KM# 1664.9 DOLLAR

31.11 g., 0.999 Silver 0.999 oz. ASW, 40 mm. **Ruler:** Elizabeth II **Subject:** Year of the Dragon **Obv:** Head with tiara right **Rev:** Dragon colored white and blue

| Date | Mintage | VF20 | XF40 | MS60 | MS63 | MS65 |
|---|---|---|---|---|---|---|
| 2012 P | — | — | — | — | — | 100 |

## KM# 1664.1 DOLLAR

31.11 g., 0.999 Silver 0.999 oz. ASW, 40 mm. **Ruler:** Elizabeth II **Subject:** Year of the Dragon **Obv:** Head with tiara right **Rev:** Dragon colored brown and orange

| Date | Mintage | VF20 | XF40 | MS60 | MS63 | MS65 |
|---|---|---|---|---|---|---|
| 2012 P | — | — | — | — | — | 100 |

## KM# 1664.11 DOLLAR

31.11 g., 0.999 Silver 0.999 oz. ASW, 40 mm. **Ruler:** Elizabeth II **Subject:** Year of the Dragon **Obv:** head with tiara right **Rev:** Dragon colored lavender and grey

| Date | Mintage | VF20 | XF40 | MS60 | MS63 | MS65 |
|---|---|---|---|---|---|---|
| 2012 P | — | — | — | — | — | 100 |

## KM# 1664 DOLLAR

31.11 g., 0.999 Silver 0.999 oz. ASW, 40.5 mm. **Ruler:** Elizabeth II **Subject:** Year of the Dragon **Rev:** Dragon

| Date | Mintage | VF20 | XF40 | MS60 | MS63 | MS65 |
|---|---|---|---|---|---|---|
| 2012 P | — | — | — | — | — | 40.00 |
| 2012 P Lion privy mark | — | — | — | — | — | 60.00 |
| 2012 P | — | PF65 45.00 | | | | |

## KM# 1713 DOLLAR

31.14 g., 0.999 Silver 1.000 oz. ASW, 32.6 mm. **Ruler:** Elizabeth II **Subject:** Year of the Dragon **Obv:** Head with tiara right **Rev:** Dragon **Edge:** Reeded **Note:** High Relief

| Date | Mintage | VF20 | XF40 | MS60 | MS63 | MS65 |
|---|---|---|---|---|---|---|
| 2012 P | 7,500 | PF65 100 | | | | |

## KM# 1793 DOLLAR

31.11 g., 0.999 Silver 0.999 oz. ASW **Ruler:** Elizabeth II **Subject:** Year of the Dragon **Note:** High releif

| Date | Mintage | VF20 | XF40 | MS60 | MS63 | MS65 |
|---|---|---|---|---|---|---|
| 2012 P | — | PF65 75.00 | | | | |

## KM# 1827 DOLLAR

31.11 g., 0.999 Silver 0.999 oz. ASW, 32.6 mm. **Ruler:** Elizabeth II **Subject:** Year of the Snake **Note:** Ultra high relief

| Date | Mintage | VF20 | XF40 | MS60 | MS63 | MS65 |
|---|---|---|---|---|---|---|
| 2013 P | 7,500 | PF65 110 | | | | |

## KM# 1831 DOLLAR

31.11 g., 0.999 Silver 0.999 oz. ASW, 40.6 mm. **Ruler:** Elizabeth II **Subject:** Year of the Snake

| Date | Mintage | VF20 | XF40 | MS60 | MS63 | MS65 |
|---|---|---|---|---|---|---|
| 2013 P | — | PF65 50.00 | | | | |
| 2013 P | — | — | — | — | — | 40.00 |

## KM# 1831a DOLLAR

31.11 g., 0.999 Silver 0.999 oz. ASW partially gilt, 40.6 mm. **Ruler:** Elizabeth II **Subject:** Year of the Snake **Rev:** Gilt snake

| Date | Mintage | VF20 | XF40 | MS60 | MS63 | MS65 |
|---|---|---|---|---|---|---|
| 2013 P | — | — | — | — | — | 60.00 |
| 2013 P | — | PF65 75.00 | | | | |

## KM# 1831b DOLLAR

31.11 g., 0.999 Silver 0.999 oz. ASW, 40.6 mm. **Ruler:** Elizabeth II **Subject:** Year of the Snake **Rev:** Snake in color

| Date | Mintage | VF20 | XF40 | MS60 | MS63 | MS65 |
|---|---|---|---|---|---|---|
| 2013 P | — | — | — | — | — | 65.00 |
| 2013 P | — | PF65 75.00 | | | | |

## KM# 1831c DOLLAR

31.14 g., 0.999 Silver 1.000 oz. ASW, 40.6 mm. **Ruler:** Elizabeth II **Subject:** Year of the Snake **Rev:** Snake in green **Note:** Sold at the Berlin World Money Fair.

| Date | Mintage | VF20 | XF40 | MS60 | MS63 | MS65 |
|---|---|---|---|---|---|---|
| 2013 P | — | PF65 100 | | | | |

## KM# 1970 DOLLAR

31.10 g., 0.999 Silver 0.9989 oz. ASW, 40 mm. **Ruler:** Elizabeth II **Subject:** Year of the Snake

| Date | Mintage | VF20 | XF40 | MS60 | MS63 | MS65 |
|---|---|---|---|---|---|---|
| 2013 Proof-like | Est. 10000 | — | — | — | — | 65.00 |

## KM# 2155 DOLLAR

31.11 g., 0.999 Silver 0.999 oz. ASW, 40 mm. **Ruler:** Elizabeth II **Subject:** Year of the Snake **Obv:** Head with tiara right **Rev:** Snake coiled upwards

| Date | Mintage | VF20 | XF40 | MS60 | MS63 | MS65 |
|---|---|---|---|---|---|---|
| 2013 | — | PF65 50.00 | | | | |

## KM# 537 2 DOLLARS

62.21 g., 0.999 Silver 1.998 oz. ASW, 50.3 mm. **Ruler:** Elizabeth II **Subject:** Year of the Snake **Obv:** Head with tiara right, denomination below **Rev:** Snake with eggs **Edge:** Segmented reeding

| Date | Mintage | VF20 | XF40 | MS60 | MS63 | MS65 |
|---|---|---|---|---|---|---|
| 2001 | — | — | — | — | 75.00 | 85.00 |
| 2001 P | 1,827 | PF65 110 | | | | |

## KM# 581 2 DOLLARS

62.21 g., 0.999 Silver 1.998 oz. ASW, 50 mm. **Ruler:** Elizabeth II **Subject:** Year of the Horse **Obv:** Head with tiara right, denomination below **Rev:** Horse running left **Edge:** Reeded

| Date | Mintage | VF20 | XF40 | MS60 | MS63 | MS65 |
|---|---|---|---|---|---|---|
| 2002 | — | — | — | — | 75.00 | 85.00 |
| 2002 P | 1,118 | PF65 110 | | | | |

## KM# 679 2 DOLLARS

62.85 g., 0.999 Silver 2.0187 oz. ASW, 50 mm. **Ruler:** Elizabeth II **Subject:** Year of the Goat **Obv:** Head with tiara right, denomination below **Rev:** Two goats **Edge:** Reeded

| Date | Mintage | VF20 | XF40 | MS60 | MS63 | MS65 |
|---|---|---|---|---|---|---|
| 2003 | — | — | — | — | 75.00 | 85.00 |
| 2003 P | 669 | PF65 110 | | | | |

## KM# 675 2 DOLLARS

62.21 g., 0.999 Silver 1.998 oz. ASW, 50 mm. **Ruler:** Elizabeth II **Subject:** Year of the Monkey **Obv:** Head with tiara right, denomination below **Rev:** Monkey sitting on branch **Edge:** Reeded

| Date | Mintage | VF20 | XF40 | MS60 | MS63 | MS65 |
|---|---|---|---|---|---|---|
| 2004 | — | — | — | — | 75.00 | 85.00 |
| 2004 | 520 | PF65 110 | | | | |

## KM# 793 2 DOLLARS

62.27 g., 0.999 Silver 2.000 oz. ASW, 50.3 mm. **Ruler:** Elizabeth II **Subject:** Year of the Rooster **Obv:** Elizabeth II **Rev:** Standing Rooster looking backwards **Edge:** Reeded

| Date | Mintage | VF20 | XF40 | MS60 | MS63 | MS65 |
|---|---|---|---|---|---|---|
| 2005 P | 555 | PF65 150 | | | | |

## KM# 1884 2 DOLLARS

62.27 g., 0.999 Silver 2.000 oz. ASW, 50.3 mm. **Ruler:** Elizabeth II **Subject:** Year of the Dog

| Date | Mintage | VF20 | XF40 | MS60 | MS63 | MS65 |
|---|---|---|---|---|---|---|
| 2006 P | 1,375 | — | — | — | — | 125 |

## KM# 1885 2 DOLLARS

62.27 g., 0.999 Silver 2.000 oz. ASW, 50.3 mm. **Ruler:** Elizabeth II **Subject:** Year of the Pig

| Date | Mintage | VF20 | XF40 | MS60 | MS63 | MS65 |
|---|---|---|---|---|---|---|
| 2007 P | 702 | — | — | — | — | 125 |

## KM# 1886 2 DOLLARS

62.27 g., 0.999 Silver 2.000 oz. ASW, 50.3 mm. **Ruler:** Elizabeth II **Subject:** Year of the Rat

| Date | Mintage | VF20 | XF40 | MS60 | MS63 | MS65 |
|---|---|---|---|---|---|---|
| 2008 P | 366 | — | — | — | — | 125 |

## KM# 1751 2 DOLLARS

62.27 g., 0.999 Silver 2.000 oz. ASW, 50 mm. **Ruler:** Elizabeth II **Subject:** Year of the Ox **Obv:** Head with tiara right **Rev:** Two oxen standing

| Date | Mintage | VF20 | XF40 | MS60 | MS63 | MS65 |
|---|---|---|---|---|---|---|
| 2009 P | — | — | — | — | — | 125 |

**KM# 1751a 2 DOLLARS**
62.27 g., 0.999 Silver 2.000 oz. ASW, 50 mm. **Ruler:** Elizabeth II **Subject:** Year of the Ox **Obv:** Head with tiara right **Rev:** Two colored oxen standing

| Date | Mintage | VF20 | XF40 | MS60 | MS63 | MS65 |
|---|---|---|---|---|---|---|
| 2009 P | — | — | — | — | — | 125 |

**KM# 1320 2 DOLLARS**
62.21 g., 0.999 Silver 1.9981 oz. ASW, 50 mm. **Ruler:** Elizabeth II **Subject:** Year of the Tiger **Obv:** Head right **Rev:** Tiger seated left

| Date | Mintage | VF20 | XF40 | MS60 | MS63 | MS65 |
|---|---|---|---|---|---|---|
| 2010 P | 1,000 | PF65 160 | | | | |

**KM# 1476 2 DOLLARS**
62.20 g., 0.999 Silver 1.9978 oz. ASW **Ruler:** Elizabeth II **Subject:** Year of the Rabbit **Rev:** Mother and baby rabbit nose to nose

| Date | Mintage | VF20 | XF40 | MS60 | MS63 | MS65 |
|---|---|---|---|---|---|---|
| 2011 P | — | PF65 110 | | | | |

**KM# 1665 2 DOLLARS**
62.27 g., 0.999 Silver 2.000 oz. ASW, 50.3 mm. **Ruler:** Elizabeth II **Subject:** Year of the Dragon

| Date | Mintage | VF20 | XF40 | MS60 | MS63 | MS65 |
|---|---|---|---|---|---|---|
| 2012 P | — | PF65 150 | | | | |

**KM# 1833 2 DOLLARS**
62.20 g., 0.999 Silver 1.9978 oz. ASW, 50.3 mm. **Ruler:** Elizabeth II **Subject:** Year of the Snake

| Date | Mintage | VF20 | XF40 | MS60 | MS63 | MS65 |
|---|---|---|---|---|---|---|
| 2013 P | — | PF65 150 | | | | |

**KM# 1833a 2 DOLLARS**
62.27 g., 0.999 Silver 2.000 oz. ASW, 50.3 mm. **Ruler:** Elizabeth II **Subject:** Year of the Snake **Rev:** Snake in color

| Date | Mintage | VF20 | XF40 | MS60 | MS63 | MS65 |
|---|---|---|---|---|---|---|
| 2013 P | — | — | — | — | — | 140 |
| 2013 P | — | PF65 150 | | | | |

**KM# 538 5 DOLLARS**
1.57 g., 0.999 Gold 0.0505 oz. AGW, 14.1 mm. **Ruler:** Elizabeth II **Subject:** Year of the Snake **Obv:** Head with tiara right, denomination below **Rev:** Snake in tree **Edge:** Reeded

| Date | Mintage | VF20 | XF40 | MS60 | MS63 | MS65 |
|---|---|---|---|---|---|---|
| 2001 | 100,000 | — | — | — | — | 95.00 |
| 2001 P | 100,000 | PF65 100 | | | | |

**KM# 582 5 DOLLARS**
1.56 g., 0.999 Gold 0.050 oz. AGW, 14.1 mm. **Ruler:** Elizabeth II **Subject:** Year of the Horse **Obv:** Head with tiara right, denomination below **Rev:** Horse galloping left **Edge:** Reeded

| Date | Mintage | VF20 | XF40 | MS60 | MS63 | MS65 |
|---|---|---|---|---|---|---|
| 2002 P | 100,000 | — | — | — | — | 95.00 |

**KM# 1887 5 DOLLARS**
1.57 g., 0.999 Gold 0.0504 oz. AGW, 14.1 mm. **Ruler:** Elizabeth II **Subject:** Year of the Goat

| Date | Mintage | VF20 | XF40 | MS60 | MS63 | MS65 |
|---|---|---|---|---|---|---|
| 2003 P | — | PF65 100 | | | | |

**KM# 668 5 DOLLARS**
1.57 g., 0.9999 Gold 0.0505 oz. AGW, 14.1 mm. **Ruler:** Elizabeth II **Subject:** Year of the Monkey **Obv:** Head with tiara right, denomination below **Rev:** Monkey **Edge:** Reeded

| Date | Mintage | VF20 | XF40 | MS60 | MS63 | MS65 |
|---|---|---|---|---|---|---|
| 2004 P | 100,000 | PF65 100 | | | | |

**KM# 1022 5 DOLLARS**
1.57 g., 0.9999 Gold 0.0505 oz. AGW, 13.93 mm. **Ruler:** Elizabeth II **Obv:** Head with tiara right **Rev:** Rooster standing right **Edge:** Reeded **Note:** Polished images with matte fields.

| Date | Mintage | VF20 | XF40 | MS60 | MS63 | MS65 |
|---|---|---|---|---|---|---|
| 2005 | 28,000 | PF65 110 | | | | |

**KM# 1022a 5 DOLLARS**
1.57 g., 0.9999 Gold 0.0505 oz. AGW, 13.93 mm. **Ruler:** Elizabeth II **Subject:** Year of the Rooster **Obv:** Head with tiara right **Rev:** Rooster standing right, mulwwticolor **Edge:** Reeded

| Date | Mintage | VF20 | XF40 | MS60 | MS63 | MS65 |
|---|---|---|---|---|---|---|
| 2005 | 22,564 | PF65 120 | | | | |

**KM# 1481 5 DOLLARS**
1.57 g., 0.9999 Gold 0.0505 oz. AGW, 14.1 mm. **Ruler:** Elizabeth II **Subject:** Year of the Rabbit

| Date | Mintage | VF20 | XF40 | MS60 | MS63 | MS65 |
|---|---|---|---|---|---|---|
| 2011 P | — | PF65 100 | | | | |

**KM# 1666 5 DOLLARS**
155.52 g., 0.999 Silver 4.995 oz. ASW, 65 mm. **Ruler:** Elizabeth II **Subject:** Year of the Dragon

| Date | Mintage | VF20 | XF40 | MS60 | MS63 | MS65 |
|---|---|---|---|---|---|---|
| 2012 P | — | PF65 225 | | | | |

### KM# 1670 5 DOLLARS

1.56 g., 0.999 Gold 0.050 oz. AGW, 14.1 mm. **Ruler:** Elizabeth II **Subject:** Year of the Dragon **Rev:** Dragon

| Date | Mintage | VF20 | XF40 | MS60 | MS63 | MS65 |
|---|---|---|---|---|---|---|
| 2012 P | — | PF65 110 | | | | |

### KM# 1679 5 DOLLARS

1.55 g., 0.999 Gold 0.0498 oz. AGW, 14.1 mm. **Ruler:** Elizabeth II **Subject:** Year of the Dragon **Rev:** Dragon head facing in color

| Date | Mintage | VF20 | XF40 | MS60 | MS63 | MS65 |
|---|---|---|---|---|---|---|
| 2012 P | — | PF65 125 | | | | |

### KM# 1997 5 DOLLARS

1.55 g., 0.9999 Gold 0.0498 oz. AGW, 14.8 mm. **Ruler:** Elizabeth II **Subject:** Year of the Snake

| Date | Mintage | VF20 | XF40 | MS60 | MS63 | MS65 |
|---|---|---|---|---|---|---|
| 2013 P | — | PF65 100 | | | | |

### KM# 2088 5 DOLLARS

1.55 g., 0.9999 Gold 0.0498 oz. AGW, 14.1 mm. **Ruler:** Elizabeth II **Subject:** Year of the Snake **Rev:** Snake in color

| Date | Mintage | VF20 | XF40 | MS60 | MS63 | MS65 |
|---|---|---|---|---|---|---|
| 2013 P | — | PF65 125 | | | | |

### KM# 1477 8 DOLLARS

155.52 g., 0.999 Silver 4.995 oz. ASW, 65 mm. **Ruler:** Elizabeth II **Subject:** Year of the Rabbit **Rev:** Two rabbits nestled under tree

| Date | Mintage | VF20 | XF40 | MS60 | MS63 | MS65 |
|---|---|---|---|---|---|---|
| 2011 P | — | PF60 225 | | | | |

### KM# 743 8 DOLLARS

155.52 g., 0.999 Silver 4.995 oz. ASW, 65 mm. **Ruler:** Elizabeth II **Subject:** Year of the Monkey **Obv:** Head with tiara right, denomination below **Rev:** Gold-plated seated monkey and multicolored ornamentation **Edge:** Reeded **Note:** Illustration reduced.

| Date | Mintage | VF20 | XF40 | MS60 | MS63 | MS65 |
|---|---|---|---|---|---|---|
| 2004 | 6,000 | — | — | — | — | 220 |

### KM# 1023 8 DOLLARS

155.52 g., 0.999 Silver 4.9949 oz. ASW partially gilt, 65 mm. **Ruler:** Elizabeth II **Subject:** Year of the Rooster **Obv:** Head with tiara right **Rev:** Rooster standing left gilt, floral in color **Edge:** Reeded

| Date | Mintage | VF20 | XF40 | MS60 | MS63 | MS65 |
|---|---|---|---|---|---|---|
| 2005 | 10,000 | PF65 300 | | | | |

### KM# 1754 8 DOLLARS

155.52 g., 0.999 Silver 4.9949 oz. ASW, 65 mm. **Ruler:** Elizabeth II **Subject:** Year of the Dog **Rev:** German shepard in color seated

| Date | Mintage | VF20 | XF40 | MS60 | MS63 | MS65 |
|---|---|---|---|---|---|---|
| 2006 P | — | — | — | — | — | 220 |

### KM# 1756 8 DOLLARS

155.58 g., 0.999 Silver 4.9968 oz. ASW, 65 mm. **Ruler:** Elizabeth II **Subject:** Year of the Pig **Obv:** Head with tiara right **Rev:** Pig in color

| Date | Mintage | VF20 | XF40 | MS60 | MS63 | MS65 |
|---|---|---|---|---|---|---|
| 2007 P | — | — | — | — | — | 225 |

### KM# 1757 8 DOLLARS

155.58 g., 0.999 Silver 4.9968 oz. ASW, 65 mm. **Ruler:** Elizabeth II **Subject:** Year of the Mouse **Obv:** Head with tiara right **Rev:** Two mice in color

| Date | Mintage | VF20 | XF40 | MS60 | MS63 | MS65 |
|---|---|---|---|---|---|---|
| 2008 P | — | — | — | — | — | 225 |

### KM# 1371 8 DOLLARS

155.52 g., 0.999 Silver 4.995 oz. ASW, 65 mm. **Ruler:** Elizabeth II **Subject:** Year of the Tiger **Obv:** Head right **Rev:** Tiger at rest left

| Date | Mintage | VF20 | XF40 | MS60 | MS63 | MS65 |
|---|---|---|---|---|---|---|
| 2010 P | — | — | — | — | — | 225 |

### KM# 1794 8 DOLLARS

155.50 g., 0.999 Silver 4.9944 oz. ASW, 65 mm. **Ruler:** Elizabeth II **Subject:** Year of the Dragon

| Date | Mintage | VF20 | XF40 | MS60 | MS63 | MS65 |
|---|---|---|---|---|---|---|
| 2012 P | — | PF65 250 | | | | |

**KM# 1994 8 DOLLARS**
155.67 g., 0.999 Silver 5.000 oz. ASW, 65.6 mm. **Ruler:** Elizabeth II **Subject:** Year of the Snake

| Date | Mintage | VF20 | XF40 | MS60 | MS63 | MS65 |
|---|---|---|---|---|---|---|
| 2013 | — | PF65 225 | | | | |

**KM# 2097 8 DOLLARS**
155.51 g., 0.9999 Silver 4.9993 oz. ASW, 65 mm. **Ruler:** Elizabeth II **Subject:** Year of the Snake **Rev:** Snake

| Date | Mintage | VF20 | XF40 | MS60 | MS63 | MS65 |
|---|---|---|---|---|---|---|
| 2013 P | — | — | — | — | — | 200 |

**KM# 539 10 DOLLARS**
311.04 g., 0.999 Silver 9.990 oz. ASW, 75.5 mm. **Ruler:** Elizabeth II **Subject:** Year of the Snake **Obv:** Head with tiara right, denomination below **Rev:** Snake with eggs **Edge:** Segmented reeding

| Date | Mintage | VF20 | XF40 | MS60 | MS63 | MS65 |
|---|---|---|---|---|---|---|
| 2001 | — | — | — | — | 375 | 400 |
| 2001 P | 289 | PF65 475 | | | | |

**KM# 583 10 DOLLARS**
311.04 g., 0.999 Silver 9.990 oz. ASW, 75.5 mm. **Ruler:** Elizabeth II **Subject:** Year of the Horse **Obv:** Head with tiara right, denomination below **Rev:** Horse running left **Edge:** Segmented reeding

| Date | Mintage | VF20 | XF40 | MS60 | MS63 | MS65 |
|---|---|---|---|---|---|---|
| 2002 | — | — | — | — | 375 | 400 |
| 2002 P | 68 | PF65 450 | | | | |

**KM# 710 10 DOLLARS**
311.04 g., 0.999 Silver 9.990 oz. ASW, 75.5 mm. **Ruler:** Elizabeth II **Subject:** Year of the Goat **Obv:** Head with tiara right, denomination below **Rev:** Goat

| Date | Mintage | VF20 | XF40 | MS60 | MS63 | MS65 |
|---|---|---|---|---|---|---|
| 2003 | — | — | — | — | 375 | 400 |
| 2003 | 78 | PF65 450 | | | | |

**KM# 1339 10 DOLLARS**
311.04 g., 0.999 Silver 9.990 oz. ASW, 75.5 mm. **Ruler:** Elizabeth II **Subject:** Year of the Goat **Obv:** Head right

| Date | Mintage | VF20 | XF40 | MS60 | MS63 | MS65 |
|---|---|---|---|---|---|---|
| 2003 P | — | PF65 475 | | | | |
| 2003 P | — | — | — | — | 400 | 375 |

**KM# 676 10 DOLLARS**
311.04 g., 0.999 Silver 9.990 oz. ASW, 75.5 mm. **Ruler:** Elizabeth II **Subject:** Year of the Monkey **Obv:** Head with tiara right, denomination below **Rev:** Monkey sitting on branch **Edge:** Segmented reeding

| Date | Mintage | VF20 | XF40 | MS60 | MS63 | MS65 |
|---|---|---|---|---|---|---|
| 2004 | — | — | — | — | 375 | 400 |
| 2004 | 84 | PF65 475 | | | | |

**KM# 696 10 DOLLARS**
311.04 g., 0.999 Silver 9.990 oz. ASW, 75.5 mm. **Ruler:** Elizabeth II **Subject:** Year of the Rooster **Obv:** Head with tiara right, denomination below **Rev:** Rooster

| Date | Mintage | VF20 | XF40 | MS60 | MS63 | MS65 |
|---|---|---|---|---|---|---|
| 2005 | — | — | — | — | 375 | 400 |
| 2005 | — | PF65 475 | | | | |

**KM# 1057 10 DOLLARS**
3.11 g., 0.999 Gold 0.0999 oz. AGW, 17.53 mm. **Ruler:** Elizabeth II **Subject:** Year of the Rat

| Date | Mintage | VF20 | XF40 | MS60 | MS63 | MS65 |
|---|---|---|---|---|---|---|
| 2008 | 2,500 | PF65 200 | | | | |

**KM# 1079 10 DOLLARS**
3.11 g., 0.999 Gold 0.0999 oz. AGW, 17.53 mm. **Ruler:** Elizabeth II **Subject:** Year of the Ox

| Date | Mintage | VF20 | XF40 | MS60 | MS63 | MS65 |
|---|---|---|---|---|---|---|
| 2009 | 2,500 | PF65 245 | | | | |

**KM# 1752 10 DOLLARS**
311.04 g., 0.999 Silver 9.990 oz. ASW, 75.5 mm. **Ruler:** Elizabeth II **Subject:** Year of the Ox **Obv:** Head with tiara right **Rev:** Two oxen standing

| Date | Mintage | VF20 | XF40 | MS60 | MS63 | MS65 |
|---|---|---|---|---|---|---|
| 2009 P | — | — | — | — | — | 350 |

**KM# 1752a 10 DOLLARS**
311.04 g., 0.999 Silver 9.990 oz. ASW, 75.5 mm. **Ruler:** Elizabeth II **Subject:** Year of the Ox **Obv:** Head with tiara right **Rev:** Two colored oxen standing

| Date | Mintage | VF20 | XF40 | MS60 | MS63 | MS65 |
|---|---|---|---|---|---|---|
| 2009 P | — | — | — | — | — | 365 |

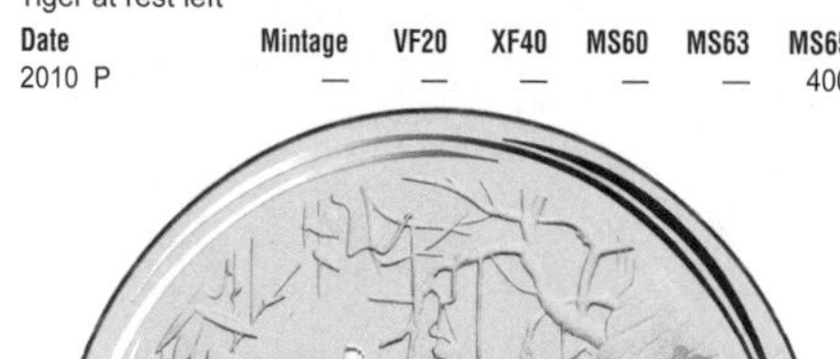

**KM# 1321 10 DOLLARS**
3.11 g., 0.999 Gold 0.0999 oz. AGW, 19 mm. **Ruler:** Elizabeth II **Subject:** Year of the Tiger **Obv:** Head right **Rev:** Tiger head facing

| Date | Mintage | VF20 | XF40 | MS60 | MS63 | MS65 |
|---|---|---|---|---|---|---|
| 2010 P | 8,000 | PF65 260 | | | | |

**KM# 1372 10 DOLLARS**
311.04 g., 0.999 Silver 9.990 oz. ASW, 75.5 mm. **Ruler:** Elizabeth II **Subject:** Year of the Tiger **Obv:** Head right **Rev:** Tiger at rest left

| Date | Mintage | VF20 | XF40 | MS60 | MS63 | MS65 |
|---|---|---|---|---|---|---|
| 2010 P | — | — | — | — | — | 400 |

**KM# 1478 10 DOLLARS**
311.05 g., 0.999 Silver 9.9905 oz. ASW, 75.5 mm. **Ruler:** Elizabeth II **Subject:** Year of the Rabbit **Rev:** Two rabbits nestled under tree

| Date | Mintage | VF20 | XF40 | MS60 | MS63 | MS65 |
|---|---|---|---|---|---|---|
| 2011 P | — | PF65 400 | | | | |

**KM# 1667 10 DOLLARS**
311.04 g., 0.999 Silver 9.990 oz. ASW, 75.5 mm. **Ruler:** Elizabeth II **Subject:** Year of the Dragon **Rev:** Dragon

| Date | Mintage | VF20 | XF40 | MS60 | MS63 | MS65 |
|---|---|---|---|---|---|---|
| 2012 P | — | PF65 400 | | | | |

**KM# 1971 10 DOLLARS**
155.50 g., 0.999 Silver 4.9944 oz. ASW, 65 mm. **Ruler:** Elizabeth II **Subject:** Year of the Snake

| Date | Mintage | VF20 | XF40 | MS60 | MS63 | MS65 |
|---|---|---|---|---|---|---|
| 2013 Proof-like | Est. 5000 | — | — | — | — | 200 |

**KM# 1995 10 DOLLARS**
311.35 g., 0.999 Silver 10.000 oz. ASW, 85.6 mm. **Ruler:** Elizabeth II **Series:** Year of the Snake

| Date | Mintage | VF20 | XF40 | MS60 | MS63 | MS65 |
|---|---|---|---|---|---|---|
| 2013 | — | PF65 350 | | | | |

**KM# 2098 10 DOLLARS**
311.10 g., 0.9999 Silver 10.0011 oz. ASW, 75.5 mm. **Ruler:** Elizabeth II **Subject:** Year of the Snake

| Date | Mintage | VF20 | XF40 | MS60 | MS63 | MS65 |
|---|---|---|---|---|---|---|
| 2013 P | — | — | — | — | — | 400 |

**KM# 2156 10 DOLLARS**
155.50 g., 0.999 Silver 4.9944 oz. ASW, 65 mm. **Ruler:** Elizabeth II **Subject:** Year of the Snake **Obv:** Head with tiara right **Rev:** Snake coiled upward

| Date | Mintage | VF20 | XF40 | MS60 | MS63 | MS65 |
|---|---|---|---|---|---|---|
| 2013 | — | PF65 225 | | | | |

**KM# 540 15 DOLLARS**

3.11 g., 0.999 Gold 0.0999 oz. AGW, 16.1 mm. **Ruler:** Elizabeth II **Subject:** Year of the Snake **Obv:** Head with tiara right, denomination below **Rev:** Snake in tree **Edge:** Reeded

| Date | Mintage | VF20 | XF40 | MS60 | MS63 | MS65 |
|---|---|---|---|---|---|---|
| 2001 | 80,000 | — | — | — | — | 175 |
| 2001 P | 3,083 | PF65 185 | | | | |

**KM# 584 15 DOLLARS**

3.11 g., 0.999 Gold 0.0999 oz. AGW, 16.1 mm. **Ruler:** Elizabeth II **Subject:** Year of the Horse **Obv:** Head with tiara right, denomination below **Rev:** Horse galloping half left **Edge:** Reeded

| Date | Mintage | VF20 | XF40 | MS60 | MS63 | MS65 |
|---|---|---|---|---|---|---|
| 2002 P | — | — | — | — | — | 175 |
| 2002 P | 2,812 | PF65 185 | | | | |

**KM# 711 15 DOLLARS**

3.11 g., 0.9999 Gold 0.100 oz. AGW, 16.1 mm. **Ruler:** Elizabeth II **Subject:** Year of the Goat **Obv:** Head with tiara right, denomination below **Rev:** Goat

| Date | Mintage | VF20 | XF40 | MS60 | MS63 | MS65 |
|---|---|---|---|---|---|---|
| 2003 | — | — | — | — | — | 175 |
| 2003 P | 3,003 | PF65 185 | | | | |

**KM# 669 15 DOLLARS**

3.11 g., 0.9999 Gold 0.100 oz. AGW, 16.1 mm. **Ruler:** Elizabeth II **Subject:** Year of the Monkey **Obv:** Head with tiara right, denomination below **Rev:** Monkey **Edge:** Reeded

| Date | Mintage | VF20 | XF40 | MS60 | MS63 | MS65 |
|---|---|---|---|---|---|---|
| 2004 P | — | — | — | — | — | 175 |
| 2004 P | 1,966 | PF65 185 | | | | |

**KM# 794 15 DOLLARS**

3.11 g., 0.9999 Gold 0.100 oz. AGW, 16.1 mm. **Ruler:** Elizabeth II **Subject:** Year of the Rooster **Obv:** Elizabeth II **Rev:** Standing rooster right **Edge:** Reeded

| Date | Mintage | VF20 | XF40 | MS60 | MS63 | MS65 |
|---|---|---|---|---|---|---|
| 2005 P | 1,388 | PF65 185 | | | | |

**KM# 794a.1 15 DOLLARS**

3.11 g., 0.750 Gold 0.075 oz. AGW **Ruler:** Elizabeth II **Subject:** Year of the Rooster **Obv:** Head with tiara right **Rev:** Rooster standing right in color **Edge:** Reeded

| Date | Mintage | VF20 | XF40 | MS60 | MS63 | MS65 |
|---|---|---|---|---|---|---|
| 2005 P | 16,700 | PF65 185 | | | | |

**KM# 794a.2 15 DOLLARS**

3.11 g., 0.999 Gold 0.0999 oz. AGW, 16.1 mm. **Ruler:** Elizabeth II **Subject:** Year of the Rooster **Rev:** Rooster in color, pad printed

| Date | Mintage | VF20 | XF40 | MS60 | MS63 | MS65 |
|---|---|---|---|---|---|---|
| 2005 P | 7,816 | PF65 185 | | | | |

**KM# 794b 15 DOLLARS**

3.11 g., 0.999 Gold 0.0999 oz. AGW, 16.1 mm. **Ruler:** Elizabeth II **Subject:** Year of the Rooster **Note:** Rose gold

| Date | Mintage | VF20 | XF40 | MS60 | MS63 | MS65 |
|---|---|---|---|---|---|---|
| 2005 P | 7,816 | PF65 185 | | | | |

**KM# 1888 15 DOLLARS**

3.11 g., 0.999 Gold 0.0999 oz. AGW, 16.1 mm. **Ruler:** Elizabeth II **Subject:** Year of the Dog

| Date | Mintage | VF20 | XF40 | MS60 | MS63 | MS65 |
|---|---|---|---|---|---|---|
| 2006 P | 2,894 | PF65 185 | | | | |

**KM# 1889 15 DOLLARS**

3.11 g., 0.999 Gold 0.0999 oz. AGW, 16.1 mm. **Ruler:** Elizabeth II **Subject:** Year of the Pig

| Date | Mintage | VF20 | XF40 | MS60 | MS63 | MS65 |
|---|---|---|---|---|---|---|
| 2007 P | 3,030 | PF65 185 | | | | |

**KM# 1890 15 DOLLARS**

3.11 g., 0.999 Gold 0.0999 oz. AGW, 16.1 mm. **Ruler:** Elizabeth II **Subject:** Year of the Rat

| Date | Mintage | VF20 | XF40 | MS60 | MS63 | MS65 |
|---|---|---|---|---|---|---|
| 2008 P | 2,863 | PF65 185 | | | | |

**KM# 1891 15 DOLLARS**

3.11 g., 0.999 Gold 0.0999 oz. AGW, 16.1 mm. **Ruler:** Elizabeth II **Subject:** Year of the Ox

| Date | Mintage | VF20 | XF40 | MS60 | MS63 | MS65 |
|---|---|---|---|---|---|---|
| 2009 P | — | PF65 185 | | | | |

**KM# 1373 15 DOLLARS**

500.00 g., 0.999 Silver 16.0593 oz. ASW **Ruler:** Elizabeth II **Subject:** Year of the Tiger **Obv:** Head right **Rev:** Tiger at rest left

| Date | Mintage | VF20 | XF40 | MS60 | MS63 | MS65 |
|---|---|---|---|---|---|---|
| 2010 P | — | — | — | — | — | 650 |

**KM# 1375 15 DOLLARS**

3.11 g., 0.999 Gold 0.0999 oz. AGW, 16.1 mm. **Ruler:** Elizabeth II **Subject:** Year of the Tiger **Obv:** Head right

| Date | Mintage | VF20 | XF40 | MS60 | MS63 | MS65 |
|---|---|---|---|---|---|---|
| 2010 P | — | — | — | — | — | 175 |

**KM# 1482 15 DOLLARS**

3.10 g., 0.999 Gold 0.0996 oz. AGW, 16.1 mm. **Ruler:** Elizabeth II **Subject:** Year of the Rabbit **Rev:** Rabbit left

| Date | Mintage | VF20 | XF40 | MS60 | MS63 | MS65 |
|---|---|---|---|---|---|---|
| 2011 P | — | PF65 185 | | | | |

**KM# 1671 15 DOLLARS**

3.11 g., 0.999 Gold 0.0999 oz. AGW, 16.1 mm. **Ruler:** Elizabeth II **Subject:** Year of the Dragon

| Date | Mintage | VF20 | XF40 | MS60 | MS63 | MS65 |
|---|---|---|---|---|---|---|
| 2012 P | — | PF65 225 | | | | |

**KM# 1671a 15 DOLLARS**

3.11 g., 0.999 Gold 0.0999 oz. AGW, 16.1 mm. **Ruler:** Elizabeth II **Subject:** Year of the Dragon **Rev:** Multicolor dragon

| Date | Mintage | VF20 | XF40 | MS60 | MS63 | MS65 |
|---|---|---|---|---|---|---|
| 2012 P | — | PF65 225 | | | | |

**KM# 1835 15 DOLLARS**

3.11 g., 0.999 Gold 0.0999 oz. AGW, 16.1 mm. **Ruler:** Elizabeth II **Subject:** Year of the Snake

| Date | Mintage | VF20 | XF40 | MS60 | MS63 | MS65 |
|---|---|---|---|---|---|---|
| 2013 P | — | PF65 250 | | | | |

**KM# 2089 15 DOLLARS**

3.11 g., 0.9999 Gold 0.100 oz. AGW, 16.1 mm. **Ruler:** Elizabeth II **Subject:** Year of the Snake **Rev:** Snake in color

| Date | Mintage | VF20 | XF40 | MS60 | MS63 | MS65 |
|---|---|---|---|---|---|---|
| 2013 P | — | PF65 175 | | | | |

**KM# 541 25 DOLLARS**

7.75 g., 0.999 Gold 0.2489 oz. AGW, 20.1 mm. **Ruler:** Elizabeth II **Subject:** Year of the Snake **Obv:** Head with tiara right, denomination below **Rev:** Snake in tree **Edge:** Reeded

| Date | Mintage | VF20 | XF40 | MS60 | MS63 | MS65 |
|---|---|---|---|---|---|---|
| 2001 | 60,000 | — | — | — | — | 450 |
| 2001 P | 2,710 | PF65 475 | | | | |

**KM# 585 25 DOLLARS**

7.78 g., 0.999 Gold 0.2498 oz. AGW, 20.1 mm. **Ruler:** Elizabeth II **Subject:** Year of the Horse **Obv:** Head with tiara right, denomination below **Rev:** Horse galloping half left **Edge:** Reeded

| Date | Mintage | VF20 | XF40 | MS60 | MS63 | MS65 |
|---|---|---|---|---|---|---|
| 2002 P | — | — | — | — | — | 450 |
| 2002 P | 2,195 | PF65 475 | | | | |

**KM# 712 25 DOLLARS**

7.75 g., 0.9999 Gold 0.2491 oz. AGW **Ruler:** Elizabeth II **Subject:** Year of the Goat **Obv:** Head with tiara right, denomination below **Rev:** Goat

| Date | Mintage | VF20 | XF40 | MS60 | MS63 | MS65 |
|---|---|---|---|---|---|---|
| 2003 | — | — | — | — | — | 450 |
| 2003 P | 1,969 | PF65 475 | | | | |

**KM# 670 25 DOLLARS**

7.75 g., 0.9999 Gold 0.2492 oz. AGW, 20.1 mm. **Ruler:** Elizabeth II **Subject:** Year of the Monkey **Obv:** Head with tiara right, denomination below **Rev:** Monkey **Edge:** Reeded

| Date | Mintage | VF20 | XF40 | MS60 | MS63 | MS65 |
|---|---|---|---|---|---|---|
| 2004 P | 1,401 | PF65 475 | | | | |
| 2004 P | — | — | — | — | — | 450 |

**KM# 795 25 DOLLARS**

7.78 g., 0.9999 Gold 0.250 oz. AGW, 20.1 mm. **Ruler:** Elizabeth II **Subject:** Year of the Rooster **Obv:** Elizabeth II **Rev:** Standing rooster right **Edge:** Reeded

| Date | Mintage | VF20 | XF40 | MS60 | MS63 | MS65 |
|---|---|---|---|---|---|---|
| 2005 P | 1,961 | PF65 475 | | | | |

**KM# 795a 25 DOLLARS**

7.78 g., 0.999 Gold 0.2498 oz. AGW, 20.1 mm. **Ruler:** Elizabeth II **Subject:** Year of the Rooster **Rev:** Rooster in color

| Date | Mintage | VF20 | XF40 | MS60 | MS63 | MS65 |
|---|---|---|---|---|---|---|
| 2005 P | 2,889 | PF65 475 | | | | |

**KM# 1892 25 DOLLARS**

7.78 g., 0.999 Gold 0.2498 oz. AGW, 20.1 mm. **Ruler:** Elizabeth II **Subject:** Year of the Dog

| Date | Mintage | VF20 | XF40 | MS60 | MS63 | MS65 |
|---|---|---|---|---|---|---|
| 2006 P | 2,051 | PF65 475 | | | | |

**KM# 1893 25 DOLLARS**

7.78 g., 0.999 Gold 0.2498 oz. AGW, 20.1 mm. **Ruler:** Elizabeth II **Subject:** Year of the Pig

| Date | Mintage | VF20 | XF40 | MS60 | MS63 | MS65 |
|---|---|---|---|---|---|---|
| 2007 P | 2,206 | PF65 475 | | | | |

**KM# 1894 25 DOLLARS**

7.78 g., 0.999 Gold 0.2498 oz. AGW, 20.1 mm. **Ruler:** Elizabeth II **Subject:** Year of the Rat

| Date | Mintage | VF20 | XF40 | MS60 | MS63 | MS65 |
|---|---|---|---|---|---|---|
| 2008 P | 2,088 | PF65 475 | | | | |

**KM# 1895 25 DOLLARS**

7.78 g., 0.999 Gold 0.2498 oz. AGW, 20.1 mm. **Ruler:** Elizabeth II **Subject:** Year of the Ox

| Date | Mintage | VF20 | XF40 | MS60 | MS63 | MS65 |
|---|---|---|---|---|---|---|
| 2009 P | — | PF65 475 | | | | |

**KM# 1322 25 DOLLARS**

7.77 g., 0.999 Gold 0.2496 oz. AGW, 22 mm. **Ruler:** Elizabeth II **Subject:** Year of the Tiger **Obv:** Head right **Rev:** Tiger head facing

| Date | Mintage | VF20 | XF40 | MS60 | MS63 | MS65 |
|---|---|---|---|---|---|---|
| 2010 P | 8,000 | PF65 650 | | | | |

**KM# 1483 25 DOLLARS**
7.77 g., 0.999 Gold 0.2496 oz. AGW **Ruler:** Elizabeth II **Subject:** Year of the Rabbit **Rev:** Rabbit left

| Date | Mintage | VF20 | XF40 | MS60 | MS63 | MS65 |
|---|---|---|---|---|---|---|
| 2011 P | — | PF65 475 | | | | |

**KM# 1672 25 DOLLARS**
7.77 g., 0.999 Gold 0.2496 oz. AGW, 22 mm. **Ruler:** Elizabeth II **Subject:** Year of the Dragon

| Date | Mintage | VF20 | XF40 | MS60 | MS63 | MS65 |
|---|---|---|---|---|---|---|
| 2012 P | — | PF65 475 | | | | |

**KM# 1672a 25 DOLLARS**
7.77 g., 0.999 Gold 0.2496 oz. AGW, 22 mm. **Ruler:** Elizabeth II **Subject:** Year of the Dragon **Rev:** Multicolor dragon

| Date | Mintage | VF20 | XF40 | MS60 | MS63 | MS65 |
|---|---|---|---|---|---|---|
| 2012 P | — | PF65 500 | | | | |

**KM# 1836 25 DOLLARS**
7.77 g., 0.999 Gold 0.2496 oz. AGW, 20 mm. **Ruler:** Elizabeth II **Subject:** Year of the Snake

| Date | Mintage | VF20 | XF40 | MS60 | MS63 | MS65 |
|---|---|---|---|---|---|---|
| 2013 P | — | PF65 550 | | | | |

**KM# 2090 25 DOLLARS**
7.77 g., 0.9999 Gold 0.2498 oz. AGW, 22 mm. **Ruler:** Elizabeth II **Subject:** Year of the Snake **Rev:** Snake in color

| Date | Mintage | VF20 | XF40 | MS60 | MS63 | MS65 |
|---|---|---|---|---|---|---|
| 2013 P | — | PF65 650 | | | | |

**KM# 542 30 DOLLARS**
1002.50 g., 0.999 Silver 32.1989 oz. ASW, 101 mm. **Ruler:** Elizabeth II **Subject:** Year of the Snake **Obv:** Head with tiara right, denomination below **Rev:** Snake with eggs **Edge:** Segmented reeding

| Date | Mintage | VF20 | XF40 | MS60 | MS63 | MS65 |
|---|---|---|---|---|---|---|
| 2001 | — | — | — | — | — | 1,150 |
| 2001 P | 490 | PF65 1,350 | | | | |

**KM# 586 30 DOLLARS**
1002.50 g., 0.999 Silver 32.1989 oz. ASW, 101 mm. **Ruler:** Elizabeth II **Subject:** Year of the Horse **Obv:** Head with tiara right, denomination below **Rev:** Horse running left **Edge:** Segmented reeding **Note:** Illustration reduced.

| Date | Mintage | VF20 | XF40 | MS60 | MS63 | MS65 |
|---|---|---|---|---|---|---|
| 2002 | — | — | — | — | — | 1,150 |
| 2002 P | 139 | PF65 1,350 | | | | |

**KM# 586a 30 DOLLARS**
1002.50 g., 0.999 Silver 32.1989 oz. ASW, 101 mm. **Ruler:** Elizabeth II **Subject:** Year of the Horse **Rev:** Horse prancing left, diamond eyes

| Date | Mintage | VF20 | XF40 | MS60 | MS63 | MS65 |
|---|---|---|---|---|---|---|
| 2002 P | 883 | PF65 1,350 | | | | |

**KM# 681 30 DOLLARS**
1000.00 g., 0.999 Silver 32.1186 oz. ASW, 101 mm. **Ruler:** Elizabeth II **Subject:** Year of the Goat **Obv:** Head with tiara right, denomination below **Rev:** Nanny goat and kid **Edge:** Segmented reeding

| Date | Mintage | VF20 | XF40 | MS60 | MS63 | MS65 |
|---|---|---|---|---|---|---|
| 2003 | — | — | — | — | — | 1,150 |
| 2003 P | 105 | PF65 1,350 | | | | |

**KM# 681a 30 DOLLARS**
1000.00 g., 0.999 Silver 32.1186 oz. ASW, 101 mm. **Ruler:** Elizabeth II **Subject:** Year of the Goat **Rev:** Goat with diamond eyes

| Date | Mintage | VF20 | XF40 | MS60 | MS63 | MS65 |
|---|---|---|---|---|---|---|
| 2003 P | 492 | PF65 1,350 | | | | |

**KM# 677.1 30 DOLLARS**
1000.00 g., 0.999 Silver 32.1186 oz. ASW, 101 mm. **Ruler:** Elizabeth II **Subject:** Year of the Monkey **Obv:** Head with tiara right, denomination below **Rev:** Monkey sitting on branch **Edge:** Segmented reeding

| Date | Mintage | VF20 | XF40 | MS60 | MS63 | MS65 |
|---|---|---|---|---|---|---|
| 2004 | — | — | — | — | — | 1,150 |
| 2004 | 5,250 | PF65 1,250 | | | | |

**KM# 677.2 30 DOLLARS**
1000.00 g., 0.999 Silver 32.1186 oz. ASW, 101 mm. **Ruler:** Elizabeth II **Subject:** Year of the Monkey **Obv:** Head with tiara right, denomination below **Rev:** Multicolor ornamentation and monkey with diamond chip eyes sitting on branch **Edge:** Segmented reeding **Note:** Illustration reduced.

| Date | Mintage | VF20 | XF40 | MS60 | MS63 | MS65 |
|---|---|---|---|---|---|---|
| 2004 | 5,000 | PF65 1,300 | | | | |

**KM# 697 30 DOLLARS**
1000.00 g., 0.999 Silver 32.1186 oz. ASW, 101 mm. **Ruler:** Elizabeth II **Subject:** Year of the Rooster **Obv:** Head with tiara right, denomination below **Rev:** Rooster, partially gilt and colored **Note:** Illustration reduced.

| Date | Mintage | VF20 | XF40 | MS60 | MS63 | MS65 |
|---|---|---|---|---|---|---|
| 2005 | 2,124 | PF65 1,300 | | | | |

**KM# 697a 30 DOLLARS**
1000.00 g., 0.999 Silver 32.1186 oz. ASW, 101 mm. **Ruler:** Elizabeth II **Subject:** Year of the Rooster **Rev:** Rooster wiht diamond eye

| Date | Mintage | VF20 | XF40 | MS60 | MS63 | MS65 |
|---|---|---|---|---|---|---|
| 2005 P | 588 | PF65 1,300 | | | | |

**KM# 1896 30 DOLLARS**
1000.00 g., 0.9999 Silver 32.1475 oz. ASW, 101 mm. **Ruler:** Elizabeth II **Subject:** Year of the Dog

| Date | Mintage | VF20 | XF40 | MS60 | MS63 | MS65 |
|---|---|---|---|---|---|---|
| 2006 P | 100 | PF65 1,300 | | | | |

**KM# 1897 30 DOLLARS**
1000.00 g., 0.999 Silver 32.1186 oz. ASW, 101 mm. **Ruler:** Elizabeth II **Subject:** Year of the Pig

| Date | Mintage | VF20 | XF40 | MS60 | MS63 | MS65 |
|---|---|---|---|---|---|---|
| 2007 P | 100 | PF65 1,300 | | | | |

**KM# 1898 30 DOLLARS**
1000.00 g., 0.999 Silver 32.1186 oz. ASW, 101 mm. **Ruler:** Elizabeth II **Subject:** Year of the Rat

| Date | Mintage | VF20 | XF40 | MS60 | MS63 | MS65 |
|---|---|---|---|---|---|---|
| 2008 P | 171 | PF65 1,300 | | | | |

**KM# 1899 30 DOLLARS**
1000.00 g., 0.999 Silver 32.1186 oz. ASW, 101 mm. **Ruler:** Elizabeth II **Subject:** Year of the Ox

| Date | Mintage | VF20 | XF40 | MS60 | MS63 | MS65 |
|---|---|---|---|---|---|---|
| 2009 P | — | PF65 1,300 | | | | |

**KM# 1319 30 DOLLARS**
1000.00 g., 0.999 Silver 32.1186 oz. ASW, 101 mm. **Ruler:** Elizabeth II **Subject:** Year of the Tiger **Obv:** Head right **Rev:** Tiger at rest left **Note:** Illustration reduced.

| Date | Mintage | VF20 | XF40 | MS60 | MS63 | MS65 |
|---|---|---|---|---|---|---|
| 2010 P | 5,000 | PF65 1,600 | | | | |

**KM# 1374 30 DOLLARS**
1000.00 g., 0.999 Silver 32.1186 oz. ASW, 101 mm. **Ruler:** Elizabeth II **Subject:** Year of the Tiger **Obv:** Head right

| Date | Mintage | VF20 | XF40 | MS60 | MS63 | MS65 |
|---|---|---|---|---|---|---|
| 2010 P | — | — | — | — | — | 1,150 |

**KM# 1479 30 DOLLARS**
1000.00 g., 0.999 Silver 32.1186 oz. ASW, 101 mm. **Ruler:** Elizabeth II **Subject:** Year of the Rabbit **Rev:** Mother and baby rabbit nose to nose **Note:** Illustration reduced.

| Date | Mintage | VF20 | XF40 | MS60 | MS63 | MS65 |
|---|---|---|---|---|---|---|
| 2010 P | — | PF65 1,300 | | | | |

**KM# 1668 30 DOLLARS**
1000.00 g., 0.999 Silver 32.1186 oz. ASW, 101 mm. **Ruler:** Elizabeth II **Subject:** Year of the Dragon **Rev:** Dragon

| Date | Mintage | VF20 | XF40 | MS60 | MS63 | MS65 |
|---|---|---|---|---|---|---|
| 2012 P | — | PF65 1,250 | | | | |

**KM# 1668a 30 DOLLARS**
1000.00 g., 0.999 Silver 32.1186 oz. ASW, 101 mm. **Ruler:** Elizabeth II **Obv:** Head with tiara right **Rev:** Dragon in color with gemstone

| Date | Mintage | VF20 | XF40 | MS60 | MS63 | MS65 |
|---|---|---|---|---|---|---|
| 2012 P | — | PF65 1,400 | | | | |

**KM# 1834 30 DOLLARS**
1000.00 g., 0.999 Silver 32.1186 oz. ASW, 101 mm. **Ruler:** Elizabeth II **Subject:** Year of the Snake

| Date | Mintage | VF20 | XF40 | MS60 | MS63 | MS65 |
|---|---|---|---|---|---|---|
| 2013 P | — | PF65 1,500 | | | | |

**KM# 1834a 30 DOLLARS**
1000.00 g., 0.999 Silver 32.1186 oz. ASW, 101 mm. **Ruler:** Elizabeth II **Subject:** Year of the Snake **Rev:** Snake in color with diamond chip as eye

| Date | Mintage | VF20 | XF40 | MS60 | MS63 | MS65 |
|---|---|---|---|---|---|---|
| 2013 P | — | PF65 1,750 | | | | |

**KM# 1972 30 DOLLARS**
1000.00 g., 0.999 Silver 32.1186 oz. ASW, 100 mm. **Ruler:** Elizabeth II **Subject:** Year of the Snake

| Date | Mintage | VF20 | XF40 | MS60 | MS63 | MS65 |
|---|---|---|---|---|---|---|
| 2013 Prooflike | Est. 1500 | — | — | — | — | 800 |

**KM# 2099 30 DOLLARS**
1000.00 g., 0.9999 Silver 32.1475 oz. ASW, 101 mm. **Ruler:** Elizabeth II **Subject:** Year of the Snake

| Date | Mintage | VF20 | XF40 | MS60 | MS63 | MS65 |
|---|---|---|---|---|---|---|
| 2013 P | — | — | — | — | — | 900 |

**KM# 671 50 DOLLARS**
15.59 g., 0.9999 Gold 0.5013 oz. AGW, 25.1 mm. **Ruler:** Elizabeth II **Subject:** Year of the Monkey **Obv:** Head with tiara right, denomination below **Rev:** Monkey **Edge:** Reeded

| Date | Mintage | VF20 | XF40 | MS60 | MS63 | MS65 |
|---|---|---|---|---|---|---|
| 2004 P | 40,000 | PF65 900 | | | | |

**KM# 1900 50 DOLLARS**
15.55 g., 0.999 Gold 0.4994 oz. AGW, 25 mm. **Ruler:** Elizabeth II **Subject:** Year of the Rooster

| Date | Mintage | VF20 | XF40 | MS60 | MS63 | MS65 |
|---|---|---|---|---|---|---|
| 2005 P | — | PF65 900 | | | | |

**KM# 1901 50 DOLLARS**
15.55 g., 0.999 Gold 0.4994 oz. AGW, 25 mm. **Ruler:** Elizabeth II **Subject:** Year of the Dog

| Date | Mintage | VF20 | XF40 | MS60 | MS63 | MS65 |
|---|---|---|---|---|---|---|
| 2006 P | — | PF65 900 | | | | |

**KM# 1902 50 DOLLARS**
15.55 g., 0.999 Gold 0.4994 oz. AGW, 25 mm. **Ruler:** Elizabeth II **Subject:** Year of the Pig

| Date | Mintage | VF20 | XF40 | MS60 | MS63 | MS65 |
|---|---|---|---|---|---|---|
| 2007 P | — | PF65 900 | | | | |

**KM# 1903 50 DOLLARS**
15.55 g., 0.999 Gold 0.4994 oz. AGW, 25 mm. **Ruler:** Elizabeth II **Subject:** Year of the Rat

| Date | Mintage | VF20 | XF40 | MS60 | MS63 | MS65 |
|---|---|---|---|---|---|---|
| 2008 P | — | PF65 900 | | | | |

**KM# 1904 50 DOLLARS**
15.55 g., 0.999 Gold 0.4994 oz. AGW, 25 mm. **Ruler:** Elizabeth II **Subject:** Year of the Ox

| Date | Mintage | VF20 | XF40 | MS60 | MS63 | MS65 |
|---|---|---|---|---|---|---|
| 2009 P | — | PF65 900 | | | | |

**KM# 1376 50 DOLLARS**
15.59 g., 0.999 Gold 0.5009 oz. AGW, 25 mm. **Ruler:** Elizabeth II **Subject:** Year of the Tiger **Obv:** Head right

| Date | Mintage | VF20 | XF40 | MS60 | MS63 | MS65 |
|---|---|---|---|---|---|---|
| 2010 P | — | PF65 900 | | | | |

**KM# 1484 50 DOLLARS**
15.59 g., 0.999 Gold 0.5009 oz. AGW, 25.1 mm. **Ruler:** Elizabeth II **Subject:** Year of the Rabbit

| Date | Mintage | VF20 | XF40 | MS60 | MS63 | MS65 |
|---|---|---|---|---|---|---|
| 2011 P | — | PF65 950 | | | | |

**KM# 1673 50 DOLLARS**
15.55 g., 0.999 Gold 0.4994 oz. AGW, 25 mm. **Ruler:** Elizabeth II **Subject:** Year of the dragon

| Date | Mintage | VF20 | XF40 | MS60 | MS63 | MS65 |
|---|---|---|---|---|---|---|
| 2012 P | — | PF65 950 | | | | |

**KM# 1998 50 DOLLARS**
15.55 g., 0.9999 Gold 0.500 oz. AGW, 30.6 mm. **Ruler:** Elizabeth II **Subject:** Year of the Snake

| Date | Mintage | VF20 | XF40 | MS60 | MS63 | MS65 |
|---|---|---|---|---|---|---|
| 2013 P | — | PF65 775 | | | | |

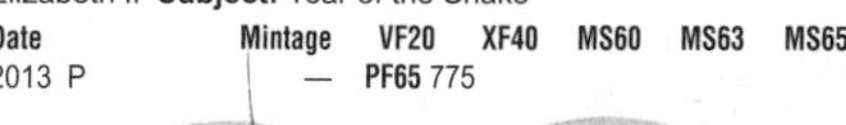

**KM# 543 100 DOLLARS**
31.10 g., 0.999 Gold 0.999 oz. AGW, 32.1 mm. **Ruler:** Elizabeth II **Subject:** Year of the Snake **Obv:** Head with tiara right, denomination below **Rev:** Snake in tree **Edge:** Reeded

| Date | Mintage | VF20 | XF40 | MS60 | MS63 | MS65 |
|---|---|---|---|---|---|---|
| 2001 | 30,000 | — | — | — | — | 1,750 |
| 2001 P | 1,223 | PF65 1,800 | | | | |

**KM# 587 100 DOLLARS**
31.10 g., 0.999 Gold 0.999 oz. AGW, 32.1 mm. **Ruler:** Elizabeth II **Subject:** Year of the Horse **Obv:** Head with tiara right, denomination below **Rev:** Horse running left **Edge:** Reeded

| Date | Mintage | VF20 | XF40 | MS60 | MS63 | MS65 |
|---|---|---|---|---|---|---|
| 2002 | — | — | — | — | — | 1,750 |
| 2002 P | 1,471 | PF65 1,800 | | | | |

**KM# 713 100 DOLLARS**
31.10 g., 0.9999 Gold 0.9999 oz. AGW, 32.1 mm. **Ruler:** Elizabeth II **Subject:** Year of the Goat **Obv:** Head with tiara right, denomination below **Rev:** Goat

| Date | Mintage | VF20 | XF40 | MS60 | MS63 | MS65 |
|---|---|---|---|---|---|---|
| 2003 P | — | — | — | — | — | 1,750 |
| 2003 P | 1,187 | PF65 1,800 | | | | |

**KM# 672 100 DOLLARS**
31.10 g., 0.9999 Gold 0.9999 oz. AGW, 32.1 mm. **Ruler:** Elizabeth II **Subject:** Year of the Monkey **Obv:** Head with tiara right, denomination below **Rev:** Monkey walking left on branch **Edge:** Reeded

| Date | Mintage | VF20 | XF40 | MS60 | MS63 | MS65 |
|---|---|---|---|---|---|---|
| 2004 | 30,000 | — | — | — | — | 1,750 |
| 2004 P | 999 | PF65 1,800 | | | | |

**KM# 796 100 DOLLARS**
31.10 g., 0.9999 Gold 0.9999 oz. AGW, 32.1 mm. **Ruler:** Elizabeth II **Subject:** Year of the Rooster **Obv:** Elizabeth II **Rev:** Standing rooster right **Edge:** Reeded

| Date | Mintage | VF20 | XF40 | MS60 | MS63 | MS65 |
|---|---|---|---|---|---|---|
| 2005 P | 1,388 | PF65 1,800 | | | | |

**KM# 1905 100 DOLLARS**
31.10 g., 0.9999 Gold 0.9999 oz. AGW, 32.1 mm. **Ruler:** Elizabeth II **Subject:** Year of the Dog

| Date | Mintage | VF20 | XF40 | MS60 | MS63 | MS65 |
|---|---|---|---|---|---|---|
| 2006 P | 1,274 | PF65 1,800 | | | | |

**KM# 1906 100 DOLLARS**
31.10 g., 0.999 Gold 0.999 oz. AGW, 32.1 mm. **Ruler:** Elizabeth II **Subject:** Year of the Pig

| Date | Mintage | VF20 | XF40 | MS60 | MS63 | MS65 |
|---|---|---|---|---|---|---|
| 2007 P | 1,556 | PF65 1,800 | | | | |

**KM# 1907 100 DOLLARS**
31.10 g., 0.999 Gold 0.999 oz. AGW, 32.1 mm. **Ruler:** Elizabeth II **Subject:** Year of the Rat

| Date | Mintage | VF20 | XF40 | MS60 | MS63 | MS65 |
|---|---|---|---|---|---|---|
| 2008 P | 1,748 | PF65 1,800 | | | | |

**KM# 1908 100 DOLLARS**
31.10 g., 0.999 Gold 0.999 oz. AGW, 32.1 mm. **Ruler:** Elizabeth II **Subject:** Year of the Ox

| Date | Mintage | VF20 | XF40 | MS60 | MS63 | MS65 |
|---|---|---|---|---|---|---|
| 2009 P | — | PF65 1,800 | | | | |

**KM# 1323 100 DOLLARS**
31.11 g., 0.999 Gold 0.999 oz. AGW, 39.34 mm. **Ruler:** Elizabeth II **Subject:** Year of the Tiger **Obv:** Head right **Rev:** Tiger head facing

| Date | Mintage | VF20 | XF40 | MS60 | MS63 | MS65 |
|---|---|---|---|---|---|---|
| 2010 P | 6,000 | PF65 2,650 | | | | |

**KM# 1485 100 DOLLARS**
31.11 g., 0.999 Gold 0.999 oz. AGW, 39.34 mm. **Ruler:** Elizabeth II **Subject:** Year of the Rabbit **Rev:** Rabbit seated left

| Date | Mintage | VF20 | XF40 | MS60 | MS63 | MS65 |
|---|---|---|---|---|---|---|
| 2011 P | — | PF65 1,800 | | | | |

**KM# 1674 100 DOLLARS**
31.11 g., 0.999 Gold 0.999 oz. AGW, 27.30 mm. **Ruler:** Elizabeth II **Subject:** Year of the Dragon **Note:** High relief

| Date | Mintage | VF20 | XF40 | MS60 | MS63 | MS65 |
|---|---|---|---|---|---|---|
| 2012 P | 38 | PF65 2,500 | | | | |

**KM# 1674a 100 DOLLARS**
31.11 g., 0.999 Gold 0.999 oz. AGW, 39.34 mm. **Ruler:** Elizabeth II **Subject:** Year of the Dragon **Rev:** Multicolor dragon

| Date | Mintage | VF20 | XF40 | MS60 | MS63 | MS65 |
|---|---|---|---|---|---|---|
| 2012 P | — | PF65 1,875 | | | | |

**KM# 1837 100 DOLLARS**
31.11 g., 0.999 Gold 0.999 oz. AGW, 32.1 mm. **Ruler:** Elizabeth II **Subject:** Year of the Snake

| Date | Mintage | VF20 | XF40 | MS60 | MS63 | MS65 |
|---|---|---|---|---|---|---|
| 2013 P | — | PF65 1,900 | | | | |

**KM# 1973 100 DOLLARS**
31.10 g., 0.9999 Gold 0.9998 oz. AGW, 38.74 mm. **Ruler:** Elizabeth II **Subject:** Year of the Snake

| Date | Mintage | VF20 | XF40 | MS60 | MS63 | MS65 |
|---|---|---|---|---|---|---|
| 2013 Proof-like | Est. 1500 | — | — | — | — | 1,500 |

**KM# 2003 100 DOLLARS**
31.11 g., 0.9999 Gold 1.000 oz. AGW, 27.3 mm. **Ruler:** Elizabeth II **Subject:** Year of the Snake **Note:** High Relief

| Date | Mintage | VF20 | XF40 | MS60 | MS63 | MS65 |
|---|---|---|---|---|---|---|
| 2013 P | Est. 388 | PF65 1,550 | | | | |

**KM# 2091 100 DOLLARS**
31.11 g., 0.9999 Gold 0.9999 oz. AGW, 32.1 mm. **Ruler:** Elizabeth II **Subject:** Year of the Snake **Rev:** Snake in color

| Date | Mintage | VF20 | XF40 | MS60 | MS63 | MS65 |
|---|---|---|---|---|---|---|
| 2013 P | — | PF65 1,850 | | | | |

**KM# 2157 100 DOLLARS**
31.11 g., 0.999 Gold 0.999 oz. AGW, 32.1 mm. **Ruler:** Elizabeth II **Subject:** Year of the Snake **Obv:** Head with tiara right **Rev:** Snake coiled upward

| Date | Mintage | VF20 | XF40 | MS60 | MS63 | MS65 |
|---|---|---|---|---|---|---|
| 2013 | — | PF65 1,450 | | | | |

**KM# 704 200 DOLLARS**
62.21 g., 0.9999 Gold 2.000 oz. AGW, 41.1 mm. **Ruler:** Elizabeth II **Subject:** Year of the Snake **Obv:** Head with tiara right, denomination below **Rev:** Snake

| Date | Mintage | VF20 | XF40 | MS60 | MS63 | MS65 |
|---|---|---|---|---|---|---|
| 2001 | — | PF65 3,500 | | | | |

**KM# 1333 200 DOLLARS**
62.21 g., 0.999 Gold 1.9981 oz. AGW, 41.1 mm. **Ruler:** Elizabeth II **Subject:** Year of the Snake **Obv:** Head right

| Date | Mintage | VF20 | XF40 | MS60 | MS63 | MS65 |
|---|---|---|---|---|---|---|
| 2001 P | — | PF65 3,500 | | | | |

**KM# 707 200 DOLLARS**
62.21 g., 0.9999 Gold 2.000 oz. AGW, 41.1 mm. **Ruler:** Elizabeth II **Subject:** Year of the Horse **Rev:** Horse

| Date | Mintage | VF20 | XF40 | MS60 | MS63 | MS65 |
|---|---|---|---|---|---|---|
| 2002 | — | PF65 3,500 | | | | |

**KM# 1336 200 DOLLARS**
62.21 g., 0.999 Gold 1.9981 oz. AGW, 41.1 mm. **Ruler:** Elizabeth II **Subject:** Year of the Horse

| Date | Mintage | VF20 | XF40 | MS60 | MS63 | MS65 |
|---|---|---|---|---|---|---|
| 2002 P | — | PF65 3,500 | | | | |

**KM# 714 200 DOLLARS**
62.21 g., 0.9999 Gold 2.000 oz. AGW, 41.1 mm. **Ruler:** Elizabeth II **Subject:** Year of the Goat **Obv:** Head with tiara right **Rev:** Goat

| Date | Mintage | VF20 | XF40 | MS60 | MS63 | MS65 |
|---|---|---|---|---|---|---|
| 2003 | — | PF65 3,500 | | | | |

**KM# 717 200 DOLLARS**
62.21 g., 0.9999 Gold 1.9999 oz. AGW, 41.1 mm. **Ruler:** Elizabeth II **Subject:** Year of the Monkey **Obv:** Head with tiara right **Rev:** Monkey

| Date | Mintage | VF20 | XF40 | MS60 | MS63 | MS65 |
|---|---|---|---|---|---|---|
| 2004 | — | PF65 3,500 | | | | |

**KM# 698 200 DOLLARS**
62.21 g., 0.9999 Gold 1.9999 oz. AGW, 41.1 mm. **Ruler:** Elizabeth II **Subject:** Year of the Rooster **Obv:** Head with tiara right **Rev:** Rooster

| Date | Mintage | VF20 | XF40 | MS60 | MS63 | MS65 |
|---|---|---|---|---|---|---|
| 2005 | — | PF65 3,500 | | | | |

**KM# 1377 200 DOLLARS**
62.21 g., 0.999 Gold 1.9981 oz. AGW, 41.1 mm. **Ruler:** Elizabeth II **Obv:** Year of the Tiger **Rev:** Tiger head facing

| Date | Mintage | VF20 | XF40 | MS60 | MS63 | MS65 |
|---|---|---|---|---|---|---|
| 2010 P | — | — | — | — | — | 3,600 |

**KM# 1486 200 DOLLARS**
62.21 g., 0.999 Gold 1.9981 oz. AGW, 41.1 mm. **Ruler:** Elizabeth II **Subject:** Year of the Rabbit

| Date | Mintage | VF20 | XF40 | MS60 | MS63 | MS65 |
|---|---|---|---|---|---|---|
| 2011 P | — | PF65 3,600 | | | | |

**KM# 1675 200 DOLLARS**
62.21 g., 0.999 Gold 1.9982 oz. AGW, 41.1 mm. **Ruler:** Elizabeth II **Subject:** Year of the Dragon

| Date | Mintage | VF20 | XF40 | MS60 | MS63 | MS65 |
|---|---|---|---|---|---|---|
| 2012 P | — | PF65 3,550 | | | | |

**KM# 1999 200 DOLLARS**
62.22 g., 0.9999 Gold 2.0001 oz. AGW, 41.1 mm. **Ruler:** Elizabeth II **Subject:** Year of the Snake

| Date | Mintage | VF20 | XF40 | MS60 | MS63 | MS65 |
|---|---|---|---|---|---|---|
| 2013 P | — | PF65 3,000 | | | | |

**KM# 1006 300 DOLLARS**
10000.00 g., 0.999 Silver 321.1857 oz. ASW **Ruler:** Elizabeth II **Series:** Lunar year **Subject:** Year of the Dog **Obv:** Head with tiara right **Obv. Legend:** ELIZABETH II - AUSTRALIA **Rev:** Dog sitting, facing right

| Date | Mintage | VF20 | XF40 | MS60 | MS63 | MS65 |
|---|---|---|---|---|---|---|
| 2006 | — | — | — | — | — | 11,500 |

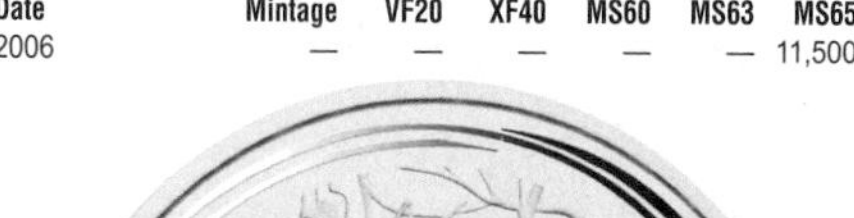

**KM# 1480 300 DOLLARS**
10000.00 g., 0.999 Silver 321.1857 oz. ASW **Ruler:** Elizabeth II **Subject:** Year of the Rabbit **Rev:** Two rabbits nestled under tree

| Date | Mintage | VF20 | XF40 | MS60 | MS63 | MS65 |
|---|---|---|---|---|---|---|
| 2011 P | — | PF65 11,750 | | | | |

**KM# 1669 300 DOLLARS**
10000.00 g., 0.999 Silver 321.1857 oz. ASW **Ruler:** Elizabeth II **Subject:** Year of the Dragon **Rev:** Dragon

| Date | Mintage | VF20 | XF40 | MS60 | MS63 | MS65 |
|---|---|---|---|---|---|---|
| 2012 P | — | PF65 11,500 | | | | |

**KM# 1996 300 DOLLARS**
10010.00 g., 0.999 Silver 321.5069 oz. ASW, 221 mm. **Ruler:** Elizabeth II **Subject:** Year of the Snake

| Date | Mintage | VF20 | XF40 | MS60 | MS63 | MS65 |
|---|---|---|---|---|---|---|
| 2013 | Est. 200 | PF65 11,500 | | | | |

**KM# 1974 500 DOLLARS**
155.50 g., 0.9999 Gold 4.9989 oz. AGW, 60 mm. **Ruler:** Elizabeth II **Subject:** Year of the Snake

| Date | Mintage | VF20 | XF40 | MS60 | MS63 | MS65 |
|---|---|---|---|---|---|---|
| 2013 Prooflike | Est. 1000 | — | — | — | — | 7,000 |

**KM# 705 1000 DOLLARS**
311.05 g., 0.9999 Gold 9.9994 oz. AGW, 75.6 mm. **Ruler:** Elizabeth II **Subject:** Year of the Snake **Obv:** Head with tiara right, denomination below **Rev:** Snake

| Date | Mintage | VF20 | XF40 | MS60 | MS63 | MS65 |
|---|---|---|---|---|---|---|
| 2001 | — | — | — | — | — | 18,000 |

**KM# 1334 1000 DOLLARS**
311.05 g., 0.999 Gold 9.9904 oz. AGW, 75.6 mm. **Ruler:** Elizabeth II **Subject:** Year of the Snake **Obv:** Head right

| Date | Mintage | VF20 | XF40 | MS60 | MS63 | MS65 |
|---|---|---|---|---|---|---|
| 2001 P | — | — | — | — | — | 18,000 |

**KM# 708 1000 DOLLARS**
311.05 g., 0.9999 Gold 9.9994 oz. AGW, 75.6 mm. **Ruler:** Elizabeth II **Subject:** Year of the Horse **Obv:** Head with tiara right, denomination below **Rev:** Horse

| Date | Mintage | VF20 | XF40 | MS60 | MS63 | MS65 |
|---|---|---|---|---|---|---|
| 2002 | — | — | — | — | — | 18,000 |

**KM# 1337 1000 DOLLARS**
311.05 g., 0.999 Gold 9.9904 oz. AGW, 75.6 mm. **Ruler:** Elizabeth II **Subject:** Year of the Horse **Obv:** Head right

| Date | Mintage | VF20 | XF40 | MS60 | MS63 | MS65 |
|---|---|---|---|---|---|---|
| 2002 P | — | — | — | — | — | 18,000 |

**KM# 715 1000 DOLLARS**
311.05 g., 0.9999 Gold 9.9994 oz. AGW, 75.6 mm. **Ruler:** Elizabeth II **Subject:** Year of the Goat **Obv:** Head with tiara right, denomination below **Rev:** Goat

| Date | Mintage | VF20 | XF40 | MS60 | MS63 | MS65 |
|---|---|---|---|---|---|---|
| 2003 | — | — | — | — | — | 18,000 |

**KM# 718 1000 DOLLARS**
311.05 g., 0.9999 Gold 9.9994 oz. AGW, 75.6 mm. **Ruler:** Elizabeth II **Subject:** Year of the Monkey **Obv:** Head with tiara right, denomination below **Rev:** Monkey

| Date | Mintage | VF20 | XF40 | MS60 | MS63 | MS65 |
|---|---|---|---|---|---|---|
| 2004 | — | — | — | — | — | 18,000 |

**KM# 699 1000 DOLLARS**
311.05 g., 0.9999 Gold 9.9994 oz. AGW, 75.6 mm. **Ruler:** Elizabeth II **Subject:** Year of the Rooster **Obv:** Head with tiara right, denomination below **Rev:** Rooster

| Date | Mintage | VF20 | XF40 | MS60 | MS63 | MS65 |
|---|---|---|---|---|---|---|
| 2005 | — | — | — | — | — | 18,000 |

**KM# 1378 1000 DOLLARS**
311.05 g., 0.999 Gold 9.9904 oz. AGW, 75.6 mm. **Ruler:** Elizabeth II **Subject:** Year of the Tiger **Obv:** Head right

| Date | Mintage | VF20 | XF40 | MS60 | MS63 | MS65 |
|---|---|---|---|---|---|---|
| 2010 (p) | — | — | — | — | — | 18,000 |

**KM# 1487 1000 DOLLARS**
311.05 g., 0.999 Gold 9.9904 oz. AGW, 75.6 mm. **Ruler:** Elizabeth II **Subject:** Year of the Rabbit

| Date | Mintage | VF20 | XF40 | MS60 | MS63 | MS65 |
|---|---|---|---|---|---|---|
| 2011 P | — | PF65 18,000 | | | | |

**KM# 1676 1000 DOLLARS**
311.05 g., 0.999 Gold 9.9905 oz. AGW, 75.6 mm. **Ruler:** Elizabeth II **Subject:** Year of the Dragon

| Date | Mintage | VF20 | XF40 | MS60 | MS63 | MS65 |
|---|---|---|---|---|---|---|
| 2012 P | — | PF65 18,000 | | | | |

**KM# 2000 1000 DOLLARS**
311.07 g., 0.9999 Gold 10.000 oz. AGW, 75.6 mm. **Ruler:** Elizabeth II **Subject:** Year of the Snake

| Date | Mintage | VF20 | XF40 | MS60 | MS63 | MS65 |
|---|---|---|---|---|---|---|
| 2013 P | — | PF65 15,000 | | | | |

**KM# 706 3000 DOLLARS**
1000.00 g., 0.9999 Gold 32.1475 oz. AGW, 100.6 mm. **Ruler:** Elizabeth II **Subject:** Year of the Snake **Obv:** Head with tiara right, denomination below **Rev:** Snake

| Date | Mintage | VF20 | XF40 | MS60 | MS63 | MS65 |
|---|---|---|---|---|---|---|
| 2001 | — | — | — | — | — | 42,052 |

**KM# 1335 3000 DOLLARS**
1000.00 g., 0.999 Gold 32.1186 oz. AGW, 100.6 mm. **Ruler:** Elizabeth II **Subject:** Year of the Snake **Obv:** Head right

| Date | Mintage | VF20 | XF40 | MS60 | MS63 | MS65 |
|---|---|---|---|---|---|---|
| 2001 P | — | — | — | — | — | 42,014 |

**KM# 709 3000 DOLLARS**
1000.00 g., 0.9999 Gold 32.1475 oz. AGW, 100.6 mm. **Ruler:** Elizabeth II **Subject:** Year of the Horse **Obv:** Head with tiara right, denomination below **Rev:** Horse

| Date | Mintage | VF20 | XF40 | MS60 | MS63 | MS65 |
|---|---|---|---|---|---|---|
| 2002 | — | — | — | — | — | 42,052 |

**KM# 1338 3000 DOLLARS**
1000.00 g., 0.999 Gold 32.1186 oz. AGW, 100.6 mm. **Ruler:** Elizabeth II **Subject:** Year of the Horse **Obv:** Head right

| Date | Mintage | VF20 | XF40 | MS60 | MS63 | MS65 |
|---|---|---|---|---|---|---|
| 2002 P | — | — | — | — | — | 42,014 |

**KM# 716 3000 DOLLARS**
1000.00 g., 0.9999 Gold 32.1475 oz. AGW, 100.6 mm. **Ruler:** Elizabeth II **Subject:** Year of the Goat **Obv:** Head with tiara right, denomination below **Rev:** Goat

| Date | Mintage | VF20 | XF40 | MS60 | MS63 | MS65 |
|---|---|---|---|---|---|---|
| 2003 | — | — | — | — | — | 42,052 |

**KM# 719 3000 DOLLARS**
1000.00 g., 0.9999 Gold 32.1475 oz. AGW, 100.6 mm. **Ruler:** Elizabeth II **Subject:** Year of the Monkey **Obv:** Head with tiara right, denomination below **Rev:** Monkey

| Date | Mintage | VF20 | XF40 | MS60 | MS63 | MS65 |
|---|---|---|---|---|---|---|
| 2004 | — | — | — | — | — | 42,052 |

**KM# 700 3000 DOLLARS**
1000.00 g., 0.9999 Gold 32.1475 oz. AGW, 100.6 mm. **Ruler:** Elizabeth II **Subject:** Year of the Rooster **Obv:** Head with tiara right, denomination below **Rev:** Rooster

| Date | Mintage | VF20 | XF40 | MS60 | MS63 | MS65 |
|---|---|---|---|---|---|---|
| 2005 | — | — | — | — | — | 42,052 |

**KM# 1379 3000 DOLLARS**
1000.00 g., 0.999 Gold 32.1186 oz. AGW, 100.6 mm. **Ruler:** Elizabeth II **Subject:** Year of the Tiger **Obv:** Head right

| Date | Mintage | VF20 | XF40 | MS60 | MS63 | MS65 |
|---|---|---|---|---|---|---|
| 2010 P | — | — | — | — | — | 42,014 |

**KM# 1488 3000 DOLLARS**
1000.00 g., 0.999 Gold 32.1186 oz. AGW, 100.6 mm. **Ruler:** Elizabeth II **Subject:** Year of the Rabbit

| Date | Mintage | VF20 | XF40 | MS60 | MS63 | MS65 |
|---|---|---|---|---|---|---|
| 2011 P | — | PF65 42,014 | | | | |

**KM# 1677 3000 DOLLARS**
1000.00 g., 0.999 Gold 32.1186 oz. AGW, 100.6 mm. **Ruler:** Elizabeth II **Subject:** Year of the Dragon

| Date | Mintage | VF20 | XF40 | MS60 | MS63 | MS65 |
|---|---|---|---|---|---|---|
| 2012 P | — | PF65 42,014 | | | | |

**KM# 1975 3000 DOLLARS**
1000.00 g., 0.9999 Gold 32.1475 oz. AGW, 75 mm. **Ruler:** Elizabeth II **Subject:** Year of the Snake

| Date | Mintage | VF20 | XF40 | MS60 | MS63 | MS65 |
|---|---|---|---|---|---|---|
| 2013 Proof-like | Est. 100 | — | — | — | — | 46,500 |

**KM# 2001 3000 DOLLARS**
1000.00 g., 0.9999 Gold 32.1475 oz. AGW, 100.6 mm. **Ruler:** Elizabeth II **Subject:** Year of the Snake

| Date | Mintage | VF20 | XF40 | MS60 | MS63 | MS65 |
|---|---|---|---|---|---|---|
| 2013 P | — | PF65 46,500 | | | | |

**KM# 1007 30000 DOLLARS**
10000.00 g., 0.9999 Gold 321.4751 oz. AGW, 180.6 mm. **Ruler:** Elizabeth II **Series:** Lunar year **Subject:** Year of the Dog **Obv:** Head with tiara right **Obv. Legend:** ELIZABETH II - AUSTRALIA **Rev:** Dog standing left

| Date | Mintage | VF20 | XF40 | MS60 | MS63 | MS65 |
|---|---|---|---|---|---|---|
| 2006 | 100 | PF65 416,439 | | | | |

**KM# 1489 30000 DOLLARS**
10000.00 g., 0.999 Gold 321.1857 oz. AGW, 180.6 mm. **Ruler:** Elizabeth II **Subject:** Year of the Rabbit

| Date | Mintage | VF20 | XF40 | MS60 | MS63 | MS65 |
|---|---|---|---|---|---|---|
| 2011 P | 100 | PF65 416,064 | | | | |

**KM# 1678 30000 DOLLARS**
10000.00 g., 0.999 Gold 321.1857 oz. AGW, 180.6 mm. **Ruler:** Elizabeth II **Subject:** Year of the Dragon

| Date | Mintage | VF20 | XF40 | MS60 | MS63 | MS65 |
|---|---|---|---|---|---|---|
| 2012 P | 100 | PF65 416,064 | | | | |

**KM# 2002 30000 DOLLARS**
10001.00 g., 0.9999 Gold 321.5072 oz. AGW, 180.6 mm. **Ruler:** Elizabeth II **Subject:** Year of the Snake

| Date | Mintage | VF20 | XF40 | MS60 | MS63 | MS65 |
|---|---|---|---|---|---|---|
| 2013 | Est. 100 | PF65 416,480 | | | | |

## BABY MINT SETS

| KM# | Date | Mintage | Identification | Issue Price | Mkt Val |
|---|---|---|---|---|---|
| BMS9 | 2001 (6) | 32,494 | KM#401-403, 406, 491.1, 534.1 plus bronze medal | — | 110 |
| BMS10 | 2002 (6) | 32,479 | KM#401-403, 406, 600.1, 602 plus bronze medal | — | 47.50 |
| BMS11 | 2003 (6) | 37,748 | KM#401-402, 406, 688-690 plus bronze medal | — | 40.00 |
| BMS12 | 2004 (6) | 31,000 | KM#401-404, 406, 733.1 plus bronze medal | — | 40.00 |
| BMS13 | 2005 (6) | 34,748 | KM#401-402, 406, 745-747 plus bronze medal | 24.00 | 27.50 |
| BMS14 | 2006 (6) | — | KM#401-404, 406, 489 plus bronze medal | 24.00 | 35.00 |

## BABY PROOF SETS

| KM# | Date | Mintage | Identification | Issue Price | Mkt Val |
|---|---|---|---|---|---|
| BPS7 | 2001 (6) | 15,011 | KM#401-403, 406, 491.1, 534.1 plus silver medal | — | 165 |
| BPS8 | 2002 (6) | 13,996 | KM#401, 403, 406, 600.2, 602 plus silver medal | — | 152 |
| BPS9 | 2003 (6) | 14,799 | KM#401-402, 406, 688-689, 690.1 plus silver medal | — | 125 |
| BPS10 | 2004 (6) | 13,996 | KM#401-404, 406, 733 plus silver medal | — | 110 |
| BPS11 | 2005 (6) | — | KM#401-402, 406, 745-747 plus silver medal | — | 100 |
| BPS12 | 2006 (6) | — | KM#401-404, 406, 489 plus silver medal | — | 120 |

## MINT SETS

| KM# | Date | Mintage | Identification | Issue Price | Mkt Val |
|---|---|---|---|---|---|
| MS39 | 2001 (3) | — | KM532, 533, 534.1 | 7.80 | 75.00 |
| MS40 | 2001 (3) | — | KM534.1, 550, 551 | 7.80 | 70.00 |
| MS41 | 2001 (3) | — | KM534.1, 552, 553 | 7.80 | 70.00 |
| MS42 | 2001 (3) | — | KM534.1, 554, 555 | 7.80 | 75.00 |
| MS43 | 2001 (3) | — | KM534.1, 556, 557 | 7.80 | 72.50 |
| MS44 | 2001 (3) | — | KM534.1, 558, 559 | 7.80 | 75.00 |
| MS45 | 2001 (3) | — | KM534.1, 560, 561 | 7.80 | 85.00 |
| MS46 | 2001 (3) | — | KM534.1, 562, 563 | 7.80 | 80.00 |
| MS47 | 2001 (3) | — | KM534.1, 564, 565 | 7.80 | 75.00 |
| MS48 | 2001 (20) | — | KM532-533, 534.1, 491.1, 550-565 | 43.68 | 235 |
| MS49 | 2001 (6) | — | KM#401-403, 406, 491.1, 534.1 | — | 80.00 |
| MS50 | 2002 (6) | — | KM#401-403, 406, 600.1, 602 | — | 65.00 |
| MS51 | 2002 (3) | — | KM#691.2, 692, 693 | — | 2,300 |
| MS52 | 2003 (5) | — | KM401, 402, 406, 689, 690 | — | 35.00 |
| MS53 | 2004 (6) | — | KM401-404, 406, 733.1 | — | 32.50 |
| MS54 | 2005 (6) | — | KM#401, 402, 406, 745-747 | — | 25.00 |
| MS55 | 2006 (8) | — | KM#401-404, 406, 489, 767-768 40 Years of Decimal Currency | 18.50 | 55.00 |
| MS56 | 2006 (15) | — | KM#770-781, 1001-1003 | 80.00 | 165 |

## PROOF SETS

| KM# | Date | Mintage | Identification | Issue Price | Mkt Val |
|---|---|---|---|---|---|
| PS107 | 2001 (3) | — | KM532, 533, 534.2 | 21.00 | 95.00 |
| PS108 | 2001 (3) | — | KM534.2, 550, 551 | 21.00 | 65.00 |
| PS109 | 2001 (3) | — | KM534.2, 552, 553 | 21.00 | 75.00 |
| PS110 | 2001 (3) | — | KM534.2, 554, 555 | 21.00 | 75.00 |
| PS111 | 2001 (3) | — | KM534.2, 556, 557 | 21.00 | 75.00 |
| PS112 | 2001 (3) | — | KM534.2, 558, 559 | 21.00 | 85.00 |
| PS113 | 2001 (3) | — | KM534.2, 560, 561 | 21.00 | 95.00 |
| PS114 | 2001 (3) | — | KM534.2, 562, 563 | 21.00 | 85.00 |
| PS115 | 2001 (3) | — | KM534.2, 564, 565 | 21.00 | 85.00 |
| PS116 | 2001 (20) | — | KM491.2, 532-533, 534.2, 549.2, 550-565 | 120 | 665 |
| PS117 | 2001 (6) | — | KM#401-403, 406, 491.1, 534.1 | — | 145 |
| PS118 | 2001 (1) | 650 | Federation Centennial Set | — | 6,000 |
| PS119 | 2002 (6) | 39,513 | KM#401-403, 406, 600.2, 602 | — | 95.00 |
| PS120 | 2006 (6) | 39,090 | KM#401-402, 406, 688-689, 690.1 | — | 70.00 |
| PS121 | 2003 (6) | 6,500 | KM#401b, 402b, 406b, 688a, 689a, 690a | — | 180 |
| PS122 | 2003 (4) | 10,000 | KM763-766 | 118 | 250 |
| PS123 | 2004 (6) | 50,000 | KM#401-404, 406, 733 | — | 80.00 |
| PS124 | 2004 (6) | 6,500 | KM#401b, 402b, 403b, 404a, 406b, 733.1a | — | 150 |
| PS125 | 2005 (6) | — | KM#401, 402, 406, 745-747 | — | 85.00 |
| PS126 | 2005 (6) | 6,500 | KM#401b, 402b, 406b, 745a, 746a, 747a | — | 175 |
| PS127 | 2005 (6) | 650 | KM#401a, 402a, 406a, 745b, 746b, 747b | — | 5,850 |
| PS128 | 2006 (8) | — | KM#401-404, 406, 489, 767-768 | 62.50 | 120 |
| PS129 | 2006 (8) | 6,500 | KM#62a, 63a, 64a, 65a, 66a, 77a, 852 | 180 | 220 |

## WEDDING SPECIMEN SETS

| KM# | Date | Mintage | Identification | Issue Price | Mkt Val |
|---|---|---|---|---|---|
| WSS1 | 2002 (6) | 3,322 | KM#401-403, 406, 600.1, 602 Plaque | — | 97.50 |
| WSS2 | 2003 (6) | 3,249 | KM#401-402, 406, 688-690 Plaque | — | 55.00 |
| WSS3 | 2004 (6) | 4,000 | KM#401-404, 406, 733.1 Plaque | — | 58.50 |
| WSS4 | 2005 (6) | — | KM#401-402, 406, 745-747 Plaque | 60.00 | 60.00 |
| WSS5 | 2006 (8) | — | KM#401-404, 406, 489, 767-768 Plaque | 60.00 | 60.00 |

# AUSTRIA

The Republic of Austria, a parliamentary democracy located in mountainous central Europe, has an area of 32,374 sq. mi. (83,850 sq. km.) and a population of 8.08 million. Capital: Wien (Vienna). Austria is primarily an industrial country. Machinery, iron, steel, textiles, yarns and timber are exported.

The territories later to be known as Austria were overrun in pre-Roman times by various tribes, including the Celts. Upon the fall of the Roman Empire, the country became a margravate of Charlemagne's Empire. Premysl II of Otakar, King of Bohemia, gained possession in 1252, only to lose the territory to Rudolf of Habsburg in 1276. Thereafter, until World War I, the story of Austria was conducted by the ruling Habsburgs.

During the 17th century, Austrian coinage reflected the geo-political strife of three wars. From 1618-1648, the Thirty Years' War between northern Protestants and southern Catholics produced low quality, "kipperwhipper" strikes of 12, 24, 30, 60, 75 and 150 Kreuzer. Later, during the Austrian-Turkish War, 1660-1664, coinages used to maintain soldier's salaries also reported the steady division of Hungarian territories. Finally, between 1683 and 1699, during the second Austrian-Turkish conflict, new issues of 3, 6 and 15 Kreuzers were struck, being necessary to help defray mounting expenses of the war effort.

During World War I, the Austro-Hungarian Empire was one of the Central Powers with Germany, Bulgaria and Turkey. At the end of the war, the Empire was dismembered and Austria established as an independent republic. In March 1938, Austria was incorporated into Hitler's short-lived Greater German Reich. Allied forces of both East and West occupied Austria in April 1945, and subsequently divided it into 4 zones of military occupation. On May 15, 1955, the 4 powers formally recognized Austria as a sovereign independent democratic state.

**NOTE:** During the **GERMAN OCCUPATION** (1938-1945), the German Reichsmark coins and banknotes were circulated.

**RULERS**
Franz Joseph I, 1848-1916
Karl I, 1916-1918

## REPUBLIC

### POST WWII DECIMAL COINAGE

100 Groschen - 1 Schilling

**KM# 2878 10 GROSCHEN**
1.10 g., Aluminum, 20 mm. **Obv:** Small Imperial Eagle with Austrian shield on breast, at top between numbers, scalloped rim, stylized inscription below **Rev:** Large value above date, scalloped rim **Edge:** Plain **Mint:** Vienna

| Date | Mintage | VF20 | XF40 | MS60 | MS63 | MS65 |
|---|---|---|---|---|---|---|
| 2001 Special Unc | 75,000 | — | — | — | — | 1.50 |

**KM# 2885 50 GROSCHEN**
3.00 g., Aluminum-Bronze, 19.5 mm. **Obv:** Austrian shield **Rev:** Large value above date **Edge:** Reeded

| Date | Mintage | VF20 | XF40 | MS60 | MS63 | MS65 |
|---|---|---|---|---|---|---|
| 2001 Special Unc | 75,000 | — | — | — | — | 1.50 |

**KM# 2886 SCHILLING**
4.20 g., Aluminum-Bronze, 22.5 mm. **Obv:** Large value above date **Rev:** Edelweiss flower **Edge:** Plain

| Date | Mintage | VF20 | XF40 | MS60 | MS63 | MS65 |
|---|---|---|---|---|---|---|
| 2001 Special Unc | 75,000 | — | — | — | — | 1.00 |

**KM# 2889a 5 SCHILLING**
4.80 g., Copper-Nickel, 23.5 mm. **Obv:** Lippizaner stallion with rider, rearing left **Rev:** Austrian shield divides date, value above, sprays below **Edge:** Plain

| Date | Mintage | VF20 | XF40 | MS60 | MS63 | MS65 |
|---|---|---|---|---|---|---|
| 2001 Special Unc | 75,000 | — | — | — | — | 1.50 |

**KM# 2918 10 SCHILLING**
6.20 g., Copper-Nickel Plated Nickel, 26 mm. **Obv:** Imperial Eagle with Austrian shield on breast, holding hammer and sickle **Rev:** Woman of Wachau left, value and date right of hat **Edge:** Reeded

| Date | Mintage | VF20 | XF40 | MS60 | MS63 | MS65 |
|---|---|---|---|---|---|---|
| 2001 Special Unc | 75,000 | — | — | — | — | 1.50 |

**KM# 3075 20 SCHILLING**
8.00 g., Copper-Aluminum-Nickel, 27.7 mm. **Subject:** Johann Nepomuk Nestroy **Obv:** Denomination within square **Rev:** Bust half left **Edge:** 19 incuse dots **Mint:** Vienna

| Date | Mintage | VF20 | XF40 | MS60 | MS63 | MS65 |
|---|---|---|---|---|---|---|
| 2001 | 225,000 | — | — | — | 2.00 | |
| 2001 Special Unc | 75,000 | — | — | — | — | 3.00 |

**KM# 3076 50 SCHILLING**
8.15 g., Bi-Metallic Copper-Nickel clad Nickel center in Aluminum-Bronze ring, 26.5 mm. **Subject:** The Schilling Era **Obv:** Denomination and shields **Rev:** Four old coin designs **Edge:** Plain **Mint:** Vienna

| Date | Mintage | VF20 | XF40 | MS60 | MS63 | MS65 |
|---|---|---|---|---|---|---|
| 2001 | 600,000 | — | — | — | 5.00 | — |
| 2001 Special Unc. | 100,000 | — | — | — | — | 5.00 |

**KM# 3073 100 SCHILLING**
13.70 g., Bi-Metallic Titanium center in 9.95g .900 silver ring 0.2879 oz. ASW, 34 mm. **Subject:** Transportation **Obv:** Automobile engine **Rev:** Car, train, truck, and plane **Edge:** Plain **Mint:** Vienna

| Date | Mintage | VF20 | XF40 | MS60 | MS63 | MS65 |
|---|---|---|---|---|---|---|
| 2001 | 50,000 | | | | | |

**KM# 3077 100 SCHILLING**
20.00 g., 0.900 Silver 0.5787 oz. ASW, 34 mm. **Subject:** Charlemagne **Obv:** Holy Roman Emperor's crown above denomination **Rev:** Bust 3/4 facing with scepter, two shields at right **Edge:** Reeded **Mint:** Vienna

| Date | Mintage | VF20 | XF40 | MS60 | MS63 | MS65 |
|---|---|---|---|---|---|---|
| 2001 | 50,000 | PF65 10.00 | | | | |

**KM# 3079 100 SCHILLING**
20.00 g., 0.900 Silver 0.5787 oz. ASW, 34 mm. **Subject:** Duke Rudolf IV **Obv:** University teaching scene **Rev:** Bust on right looking left, St. Stephen's Cathedral at left **Edge:** Reeded **Mint:** Vienna

| Date | Mintage | VF20 | XF40 | MS60 | MS63 | MS65 |
|---|---|---|---|---|---|---|
| 2001 | 50,000 | PF65 10.00 | | | | |

**KM# 3074 500 SCHILLING**
10.14 g., 0.986 Gold 0.3214 oz. AGW, 22 mm. **Subject:** 2000 Years of Christianity - Bible **Obv:** Bible and symbols of the saints: Matthew, Luke, Mark, and John **Rev:** St. Paul reading from a scroll to two listeners **Mint:** Vienna

| Date | Mintage | VF20 | XF40 | MS60 | MS63 | MS65 |
|---|---|---|---|---|---|---|
| 2001 | 50,000 | PF65 600 | | | | |

**KM# 3078 500 SCHILLING**
24.00 g., 0.925 Silver 0.7137 oz. ASW, 37 mm. **Subject:** Kufstein Castle **Obv:** Castle view above denomination **Rev:** Emperor Maximilian being shown one of his new cannons **Edge:** Plain with engraved lettering **Mint:** Vienna

| Date | Mintage | VF20 | XF40 | MS60 | MS63 | MS65 |
|---|---|---|---|---|---|---|
| 2001 | 50,000 | — | — | — | 45.00 | — |
| 2001 Special Unc. | 15,000 | — | — | — | — | 50.00 |
| 2001 | 30,000 | PF65 45.00 | | | | |

### KM# 3080 500 SCHILLING

24.00 g., 0.925 Silver 0.7137 oz. ASW, 37 mm. **Subject:** Schattenburg Castle **Obv:** Castle view **Rev:** Two medieval armourers at work **Edge:** Plain with engraved lettering **Mint:** Vienna

| Date | Mintage | VF20 | XF40 | MS60 | MS63 | MS65 |
|---|---|---|---|---|---|---|
| 2001 | 37,000 | — | — | — | 45.00 | — |
| 2001 Special Unc | 15,000 | — | — | — | — | 45.00 |
| 2001 | 43,000 | PF65 45.00 | | | | |

### KM# 3081 1000 SCHILLING

16.22 g., 0.986 Gold 0.5142 oz. AGW, 30 mm. **Subject:** Austrian National Library **Obv:** Archduke Maximilian as a student **Rev:** Library interior view **Edge:** Reeded **Mint:** Vienna

| Date | Mintage | VF20 | XF40 | MS60 | MS63 | MS65 |
|---|---|---|---|---|---|---|
| 2001 | 30,000 | PF65 850 | | | | |

## BULLION COINAGE

Philharmonic Issues

### KM# 3004 200 SCHILLING

3.12 g., 0.9999 Gold 0.1003 oz. AGW, 16 mm. **Series:** Vienna Philharmonic Orchestra **Obv:** The Golden Hall organ **Rev:** Wind and string instruments **Edge:** Reeded

| Date | Mintage | VF20 | XF40 | MS60 | MS63 | MS65 |
|---|---|---|---|---|---|---|
| 2001 | 26,400 | — | — | — | — | 144 |

### KM# 2989 500 SCHILLING

7.78 g., 0.9999 Gold 0.250 oz. AGW, 22 mm. **Series:** Vienna Philharmonic Orchestra **Obv:** The Golden Hall organ **Rev:** Wind and string instruments **Edge:** Reeded

| Date | Mintage | VF20 | XF40 | MS60 | MS63 | MS65 |
|---|---|---|---|---|---|---|
| 2001 | 25,800 | — | — | — | — | 349 |

### KM# 3031 1000 SCHILLING

15.55 g., 0.9999 Gold 0.500 oz. AGW, 28 mm. **Series:** Vienna Philharmonic Orchestra **Obv:** The Golden Hall organ **Rev:** Wind and string instruments **Edge:** Reeded

| Date | Mintage | VF20 | XF40 | MS60 | MS63 | MS65 |
|---|---|---|---|---|---|---|
| 2001 | 26,800 | — | — | — | — | 686 |

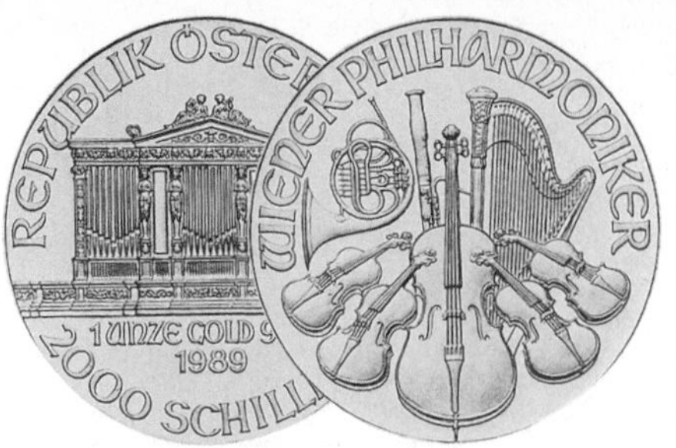

### KM# 2990 2000 SCHILLING

31.10 g., 0.9999 Gold 0.9999 oz. AGW, 37 mm. **Series:** Vienna Philharmonic Orchestra **Obv:** The Golden Hall organ **Rev:** Wind and string instruments **Edge:** Reeded

| Date | Mintage | VF20 | XF40 | MS60 | MS63 | MS65 |
|---|---|---|---|---|---|---|
| 2001 | 54,700 | — | — | — | — | 1,321 |

## EURO COINAGE

European Union Issues

### KM# 3082 EURO CENT

2.30 g., Copper Plated Steel, 16.25 mm. **Obv:** Gentian flower **Obv. Legend:** EIN EURO CENT **Rev:** Denomination and globe **Edge:** Plain **Mint:** Vienna

| Date | Mintage | VF20 | XF40 | MS60 | MS63 | MS65 |
|---|---|---|---|---|---|---|
| 2002 | 378,400,000 | — | — | — | 0.35 | — |
| 2002 Special Unc | 100,000 | — | — | — | — | 0.50 |
| 2002 | 10,000 | PF65 15.00 | | | | |
| 2003 | 10,800,000 | — | — | — | 0.35 | — |
| 2003 Special Unc | 125,000 | — | — | — | — | 0.50 |
| 2003 | 25,000 | PF65 3.00 | | | | |
| 2004 | 115,000,000 | — | — | — | 0.35 | — |
| 2004 Special Unc | 100,000 | — | — | — | — | 0.50 |
| 2004 | 20,000 | PF65 3.00 | | | | |
| 2005 | 122,900,000 | — | — | — | 0.35 | — |
| 2005 Special Unc | 100,000 | — | — | — | — | 0.50 |
| 2005 | 20,000 | PF65 4.00 | | | | |
| 2006 | 48,300,000 | — | — | — | 0.35 | — |
| 2006 Special Unc | 100,000 | — | — | — | — | 0.50 |
| 2006 | 20,000 | PF65 4.00 | | | | |
| 2007 | 111,900,000 | — | — | — | 0.35 | — |
| 2007 Special Unc | 75,000 | — | — | — | — | 0.50 |
| 2007 | 20,000 | PF65 4.00 | | | | |
| 2008 | 50,900,000 | — | — | — | 0.35 | — |
| 2008 Special Unc | 50,000 | — | — | — | — | 0.50 |
| 2008 | 15,000 | PF65 4.00 | | | | |
| 2009 | 158,900,000 | — | — | — | 0.35 | — |
| 2009 Special Unc | 75,000 | — | — | — | — | 0.50 |
| 2009 | 15,000 | PF65 4.00 | | | | |
| 2010 | 168,500,000 | — | — | — | 0.35 | — |
| 2010 Special Unc | 50,000 | — | — | — | — | 0.50 |
| 2010 | 15,000 | PF65 4.00 | | | | |
| 2011 | 189,600,000 | — | — | — | 0.35 | — |
| 2011 Special Unc | 50,000 | — | — | — | — | 0.50 |
| 2011 | 15,000 | PF65 4.00 | | | | |
| 2012 | 169,300,000 | — | — | — | 0.35 | — |
| 2012 Special Unc | 50,000 | — | — | — | — | 0.50 |
| 2012 | 10,000 | PF65 4.00 | | | | |
| 2013 Special Unc. | 50,000 | — | — | — | — | 0.75 |
| 2013 | 10,000 | PF65 4.00 | | | | |
| 2014 | — | — | — | — | 0.35 | — |
| 2014 Special Unc. | 50,000 | — | — | — | — | 0.75 |

### KM# 3083 2 EURO CENT

3.06 g., Copper Plated Steel, 18.75 mm. **Obv:** Edelweiss flower in inner circle, stars in outer circle **Obv. Legend:** ZWEI EURO CENT **Rev:** Denomination and globe **Edge:** Grooved **Mint:** Vienna

| Date | Mintage | VF20 | XF40 | MS60 | MS63 | MS65 |
|---|---|---|---|---|---|---|
| 2002 | 326,400,000 | — | — | — | 0.50 | — |
| 2002 Special Unc | 100,000 | — | — | — | — | 0.65 |
| 2002 | 10,000 | PF65 20.00 | | | | |
| 2003 | 118,500,000 | — | — | — | 0.50 | — |
| 2003 Special Unc | 125,000 | — | — | — | — | 0.65 |
| 2003 | 25,000 | PF65 5.00 | | | | |
| 2004 | 156,400,000 | — | — | — | 0.50 | — |
| 2004 Special Unc | 100,000 | — | — | — | — | 0.65 |
| 2004 | 20,000 | PF65 5.00 | | | | |
| 2005 | 113,000,000 | — | — | — | 0.50 | — |
| 2005 Special Unc | 100,000 | — | — | — | — | 0.65 |
| 2005 | 20,000 | PF65 6.00 | | | | |
| 2006 | 39,800,000 | — | — | — | 0.35 | — |
| 2006 Special Unc | 100,000 | — | — | — | — | 0.65 |
| 2006 | 20,000 | PF65 6.00 | | | | |
| 2007 | 72,200,000 | — | — | — | 0.35 | — |
| 2007 Special Unc | 75,000 | — | — | — | — | 0.65 |
| 2007 | 20,000 | PF65 6.00 | | | | |
| 2008 | 125,100,000 | — | — | — | 0.35 | — |
| 2008 Special Unc | 50,000 | — | — | — | — | 0.65 |
| 2008 | 15,000 | PF65 6.00 | | | | |
| 2009 | 120,400,000 | — | — | — | 0.35 | — |
| 2009 Special Unc | 75,000 | — | — | — | — | 0.65 |
| 2009 | 15,000 | PF65 6.00 | | | | |
| 2010 | 104,200,000 | — | — | — | 0.35 | — |
| 2010 Special Unc | 50,000 | — | — | — | — | 0.65 |
| 2010 | 15,000 | PF65 6.00 | | | | |
| 2011 | 148,600,000 | — | — | — | 0.35 | — |
| 2011 Special Unc | 50,000 | — | — | — | — | 0.65 |
| 2011 | 15,000 | PF65 6.00 | | | | |
| 2012 | 78,100,000 | — | — | — | 0.35 | — |
| 2012 Special Unc | 50,000 | — | — | — | — | 0.65 |
| 2012 | 10,000 | PF65 6.00 | | | | |
| 2013 Special Unc. | 50,000 | — | — | — | — | 0.75 |
| 2013 | 10,000 | PF65 6.00 | | | | |
| 2014 | — | — | — | — | 0.35 | — |
| 2014 Special Unc | 50,000 | — | — | — | — | 0.75 |

### KM# 3084 5 EURO CENT

3.92 g., Copper Plated Steel, 21.25 mm. **Obv:** Alpine prim rose flower in inner ring, stars in outer ring **Obv. Legend:** FUNF EURO CENT **Rev:** Denomination and globe **Edge:** Plain **Mint:** Vienna

| Date | Mintage | VF20 | XF40 | MS60 | MS63 | MS65 |
|---|---|---|---|---|---|---|
| 2002 | 217,000,000 | — | — | — | 0.75 | — |
| 2002 Special Unc | 100,000 | — | — | — | — | 1.00 |
| 2002 | 10,000 | PF65 30.00 | | | | |
| 2003 | 108,500,000 | — | — | — | 0.75 | — |
| 2003 Special Unc | 125,000 | — | — | — | — | 1.00 |
| 2003 | 25,000 | PF65 8.50 | | | | |
| 2004 | 89,300,000 | — | — | — | 0.75 | — |
| 2004 Special Unc | 100,000 | — | — | — | — | 1.00 |
| 2004 | 20,000 | PF65 9.00 | | | | |
| 2005 | 66,100,000 | — | — | — | 0.75 | — |
| 2005 Special Unc | 100,000 | — | — | — | — | 1.00 |
| 2005 | 20,000 | PF65 10.00 | | | | |
| 2006 | 5,600,000 | — | — | — | 0.75 | — |
| 2006 Special Unc | 100,000 | — | — | — | — | 1.00 |
| 2006 | 20,000 | PF65 10.00 | | | | |
| 2007 | 52,700,000 | — | — | — | 0.75 | — |
| 2007 Special Unc | 75,000 | — | — | — | — | 1.00 |
| 2007 | 20,000 | PF65 10.00 | | | | |
| 2008 | 96,700,000 | — | — | — | 0.75 | — |
| 2008 Special Unc | 50,000 | — | — | — | — | 1.00 |
| 2008 | 15,000 | PF65 10.00 | | | | |
| 2009 | 5,800,000 | — | — | — | 0.75 | — |
| 2009 Special Unc | 75,000 | — | — | — | — | 1.00 |
| 2009 | 15,000 | PF65 10.00 | | | | |
| 2010 | 63,700,000 | — | — | — | 0.75 | — |
| 2010 Special Unc | 50,000 | — | — | — | — | 1.00 |
| 2010 | 15,000 | PF65 10.00 | | | | |
| 2011 | 66,600,000 | — | — | — | 0.75 | — |
| 2011 Special Unc | 50,000 | — | — | — | — | 1.00 |
| 2011 | 15,000 | PF65 10.00 | | | | |
| 2012 | 35,300,000 | — | — | — | 0.75 | — |
| 2012 Special Unc | 50,000 | — | — | — | — | 1.00 |
| 2012 | 10,000 | PF65 10.00 | | | | |
| 2013 Special Unc | 50,000 | — | — | — | — | 1.00 |
| 2013 | 10,000 | PF65 10.00 | | | | |
| 2014 | — | — | — | — | 0.75 | — |
| 2014 Special Unc | 50,000 | — | — | — | — | 1.00 |

### KM# 3085 10 EURO CENT

4.10 g., Brass, 19.75 mm. **Obv:** St. Stephen's Cathedral spires **Rev:** Relief map of European Union at left, denomination at center right **Edge:** Reeded **Mint:** Vienna

| Date | Mintage | VF20 | XF40 | MS60 | MS63 | MS65 |
|---|---|---|---|---|---|---|
| 2002 | 441,600,000 | — | — | — | 0.75 | — |
| 2002 Special Unc | 100,000 | — | — | — | — | 1.00 |
| 2002 | 10,000 | PF65 45.00 | | | | |
| 2003 Special Unc | 125,000 | — | — | — | — | 4.00 |
| 2003 | 35,000 | PF65 8.50 | | | | |
| 2004 | 5,200,000 | — | — | — | 0.80 | — |

| Date | Mintage | VF20 | XF40 | MS60 | MS63 | MS65 |
|---|---|---|---|---|---|---|
| 2004 Special Unc | 100,000 | — | — | — | — | 1.00 |
| 2004 | 20,000 | PF65 9.00 | | | | |
| 2005 | 5,200,000 | — | — | — | 0.80 | — |
| 2005 Special Unc | 100,000 | — | — | — | — | 1.00 |
| 2005 | 20,000 | PF65 10.00 | | | | |
| 2006 | 40,000,000 | — | — | — | 0.75 | — |
| 2006 Special Unc | 100,000 | — | — | — | — | 1.00 |
| 2006 | 20,000 | PF65 10.00 | | | | |
| 2007 | 81,300,000 | — | — | — | 0.75 | — |
| 2007 Special Unc | 75,000 | — | — | — | — | 1.00 |
| 2007 | 20,000 | PF65 10.00 | | | | |

### KM# 3139 10 EURO CENT

4.10 g., Brass, 19.75 mm. **Obv:** St. Stephen's Cathedral spires **Rev:** Relief Map of Western Europe, stars, lines and value **Edge:** Reeded **Mint:** Vienna

| Date | Mintage | VF20 | XF40 | MS60 | MS63 | MS65 |
|---|---|---|---|---|---|---|
| 2008 | 70,200,000 | — | — | — | 0.75 | — |
| 2008 Special Unc | 50,000 | — | — | — | — | 1.00 |
| 2008 | 15,000 | PF65 10.00 | | | | |
| 2009 | 15,900,000 | — | — | — | 0.75 | — |
| 2009 Special Unc | 75,000 | — | — | — | — | 1.00 |
| 2009 | 15,000 | PF65 10.00 | | | | |
| 2010 | 42,800,000 | — | — | — | 0.75 | — |
| 2010 Special Unc | 50,000 | — | — | — | — | 1.00 |
| 2010 | 15,000 | PF65 10.00 | | | | |
| 2011 | 27,600,000 | — | — | — | 0.75 | — |
| 2011 Special Unc | 50,000 | — | — | — | — | 1.00 |
| 2011 | 15,000 | PF65 10.00 | | | | |
| 2012 | 25,000,000 | — | — | — | 0.75 | — |
| 2012 Special Unc | 50,000 | — | — | — | — | 1.00 |
| 2012 | 10,000 | PF65 10.00 | | | | |
| 2013 Special Unc | 50,000 | — | — | — | — | 1.00 |
| 2013 | 10,000 | PF65 1.00 | | | | |
| 2014 | — | — | — | — | — | 1.00 |
| 2014 Special Unc | 50,000 | — | — | — | 0.75 | — |

### KM# 3086 20 EURO CENT

5.74 g., Brass, 22.25 mm. **Obv:** Belvedere Palace gate **Rev:** Relief map of European Union at left, denomination at center right **Edge:** Notched **Mint:** Vienna

| Date | Mintage | VF20 | XF40 | MS60 | MS63 | MS65 |
|---|---|---|---|---|---|---|
| 2002 | 203,400,000 | — | — | — | 1.00 | — |
| 2002 Special Unc | 100,000 | — | — | — | — | 1.25 |
| 2002 | 10,000 | PF65 60.00 | | | | |
| 2003 | 50,900,000 | — | — | — | 1.00 | — |
| 2003 Special Unc | 125,000 | — | — | — | — | 1.25 |
| 2003 | 25,000 | PF65 10.00 | | | | |
| 2004 | 54,800,000 | — | — | — | 1.00 | — |
| 2004 Special Unc | 100,000 | — | — | — | — | 1.25 |
| 2004 | 20,000 | PF65 11.50 | | | | |
| 2005 | 4,100,000 | — | — | — | 1.10 | — |
| 2005 Special Unc | 100,000 | — | — | — | — | 1.25 |
| 2005 | 20,000 | PF65 12.50 | | | | |
| 2006 | 8,200,000 | — | — | — | 1.00 | — |
| 2006 Special Unc | 100,000 | — | — | — | — | 1.25 |
| 2006 | 20,000 | PF65 12.50 | | | | |
| 2007 | 45,000,000 | — | — | — | 1.00 | — |
| 2007 Special Unc | 75,000 | — | — | — | — | 1.25 |
| 2007 | 20,000 | PF65 12.50 | | | | |

### KM# 3140 20 EURO CENT

5.74 g., Brass, 22.25 mm. **Obv:** Belvedere Palace gate **Rev:** Expanded relief map of European Union at left, denomination at center right **Edge:** Notched **Mint:** Vienna

| Date | Mintage | VF20 | XF40 | MS60 | MS63 | MS65 |
|---|---|---|---|---|---|---|
| 2008 | 45,300,000 | — | — | — | 1.00 | — |
| 2008 Special Unc. | 50,000 | — | — | — | — | 1.50 |
| 2008 | 15,000 | PF65 12.50 | | | | |
| 2009 | 49,800,000 | — | — | — | 1.00 | — |
| 2009 Special Unc. | 75,000 | — | — | — | — | 1.50 |
| 2009 | 15,000 | PF65 12.50 | | | | |
| 2010 | 4,200,000 | — | — | — | 1.00 | — |

| Date | Mintage | VF20 | XF40 | MS60 | MS63 | MS65 |
|---|---|---|---|---|---|---|
| 2010 Special Unc. | 50,000 | — | — | — | — | 1.50 |
| 2010 | 15,000 | PF65 12.50 | | | | |
| 2011 | 21,300,000 | — | — | — | 1.00 | — |
| 2011 Special Unc. | 50,000 | — | — | — | — | 1.50 |
| 2011 | 15,000 | PF65 12.50 | | | | |
| 2012 | 10,800,000 | — | — | — | 1.00 | — |
| 2012 Special Unc. | 50,000 | — | — | — | — | 1.50 |
| 2012 | 10,000 | PF65 12.50 | | | | |
| 2013 Special Unc | 50,000 | — | — | — | 1.00 | — |
| 2013 | 10,000 | PF65 12.50 | | | | |
| 2014 | — | — | — | — | 1.00 | — |
| 2014 Special Unc | 5,000 | — | — | — | — | 1.50 |

### KM# 3087 50 EURO CENT

7.80 g., Brass, 24.25 mm. **Obv:** Secession building in Vienna **Rev:** Relief map of European Union at left, denomination at center right **Edge:** Reeded **Mint:** Vienna

| Date | Mintage | VF20 | XF40 | MS60 | MS63 | MS65 |
|---|---|---|---|---|---|---|
| 2002 | 169,100,000 | — | — | — | 1.25 | — |
| 2002 Special Unc | 100,000 | — | — | — | — | 1.50 |
| 2002 | 10,000 | PF65 75.00 | | | | |
| 2003 | 9,100,000 | — | — | — | 1.25 | — |
| 2003 Special Unc | 125,000 | — | — | — | — | 1.50 |
| 2003 | 25,000 | PF65 12.50 | | | | |
| 2004 | 3,100,000 | — | — | — | 1.25 | — |
| 2004 Special Unc | 100,000 | — | — | — | — | 1.50 |
| 2004 | 20,000 | PF65 13.50 | | | | |
| 2005 | 3,100,000 | — | — | — | 1.25 | — |
| 2005 Special Unc | 100,000 | — | — | — | — | 1.50 |
| 2005 | 20,000 | PF65 15.00 | | | | |
| 2006 | 3,200,000 | — | — | — | 1.25 | — |
| 2006 Special Unc | 100,000 | — | — | — | — | 1.50 |
| 2006 | 20,000 | PF65 15.00 | | | | |
| 2007 | 3,000,000 | — | — | — | 1.25 | — |
| 2007 Special Unc | 75,000 | — | — | — | — | 1.50 |
| 2007 | 20,000 | PF65 15.00 | | | | |

### KM# 3141 50 EURO CENT

7.80 g., Brass, 24.25 mm. **Obv:** Secession building in Vienna **Rev:** Expanded relief map of European Union at left, denomination at right **Edge:** Reeded **Mint:** Vienna

| Date | Mintage | VF20 | XF40 | MS60 | MS63 | MS65 |
|---|---|---|---|---|---|---|
| 2008 | 3,000,000 | — | — | — | 1.25 | — |
| 2008 Special Unc | 50,000 | — | — | — | — | 1.50 |
| 2008 | 15,000 | PF65 15.00 | | | | |
| 2009 | 14,700,000 | — | — | — | 1.25 | — |
| 2009 Special Unc | 75,000 | — | — | — | — | 1.50 |
| 2009 | 15,000 | PF65 15.00 | | | | |
| 2010 | 30,000,000 | — | — | — | 1.25 | — |
| 2010 Special Unc | 50,000 | — | — | — | — | 1.50 |
| 2010 | 15,000 | PF65 15.00 | | | | |
| 2011 | 6,000,000 | — | — | — | 1.25 | — |
| 2011 Special Unc | 50,000 | — | — | — | — | 1.50 |
| 2011 | 15,000 | PF65 15.00 | | | | |
| 2012 Special Unc. | 50,000 | — | — | — | — | 1.50 |
| 2012 | 10,000 | PF65 15.00 | | | | |
| 2013 Special Unc | 50,000 | — | — | — | — | 1.50 |
| 2013 | 10,000 | PF65 15.00 | | | | |
| 2014 | — | — | — | — | 1.25 | — |
| 2014 Special Unc | 50,000 | — | — | — | — | 1.50 |

### KM# 3088 EURO

7.50 g., Bi-Metallic Copper-Nickel center in Nickel-Brass ring, 23.25 mm. **Obv:** Bust of Mozart right within inner circle, stars in outer circle **Rev:** Value at left, relief map of European Union at right **Edge:** Segmented reeding **Mint:** Vienna

| Date | Mintage | VF20 | XF40 | MS60 | MS63 | MS65 |
|---|---|---|---|---|---|---|
| 2002 | 223,500,000 | — | — | — | 2.50 | — |
| 2002 Special Unc | 100,000 | — | — | — | — | 2.75 |
| 2002 | 10,000 | PF65 100 | | | | |
| 2003 Special Unc | 125,000 | — | — | — | — | 5.00 |

| Date | Mintage | VF20 | XF40 | MS60 | MS63 | MS65 |
|---|---|---|---|---|---|---|
| 2003 | 25,000 | PF65 16.50 | | | | |
| 2004 | 2,600,000 | — | — | — | 2.50 | — |
| 2004 Special Unc | 100,000 | — | — | — | — | 2.75 |
| 2004 | 20,000 | PF65 17.50 | | | | |
| 2005 | 2,600,000 | — | — | — | 2.50 | — |
| 2005 Special Unc | 100,000 | — | — | — | — | 2.75 |
| 2005 | 20,000 | PF65 18.50 | | | | |
| 2006 | 7,700,000 | — | — | — | 2.50 | — |
| 2006 Special Unc | 100,000 | — | — | — | — | 2.75 |
| 2006 | 20,000 | PF65 18.50 | | | | |
| 2007 | 41,100,000 | — | — | — | 2.50 | — |
| 2007 Special Unc | 75,000 | — | — | — | — | 2.75 |
| 2007 | 20,000 | PF65 18.50 | | | | |

### KM# 3142 EURO

7.50 g., Bi-Metallic Copper-Nickel center in Nickel-Brass ring, 23.25 mm. **Obv:** Bust of Mozart right within inner circle, stars in outer circle **Rev:** Value at left, expanded relief map of European Union at right **Edge:** Segmented reeding

| Date | Mintage | VF20 | XF40 | MS60 | MS63 | MS65 |
|---|---|---|---|---|---|---|
| 2008 | 65,500,000 | — | — | — | 2.00 | — |
| 2008 Special Unc | 50,000 | — | — | — | — | 2.75 |
| 2008 | 15,000 | PF65 15.00 | | | | |
| 2009 | 40,300,000 | — | — | — | 2.00 | — |
| 2009 Special Unc | 75,000 | — | — | — | — | 2.75 |
| 2009 | 15,000 | PF65 15.00 | | | | |
| 2010 | 11,200,000 | — | — | — | 2.00 | — |
| 2010 Special Unc | 50,000 | — | — | — | — | 2.75 |
| 2010 | 15,000 | PF65 15.00 | | | | |
| 2011 | 8,000,000 | — | — | — | 2.00 | — |
| 2011 Special Unc | 50,000 | — | — | — | — | 2.75 |
| 2011 | 15,000 | PF65 15.00 | | | | |
| 2012 Special Unc. | 50,000 | — | — | — | — | 2.75 |
| 2012 | 10,000 | PF65 15.00 | | | | |
| 2013 Special Unc | 50,000 | — | — | — | — | 2.75 |
| 2013 | 10,000 | PF65 15.00 | | | | |
| 2014 | — | — | — | — | 2.00 | — |
| 2014 Special Unc | 50,000 | — | — | — | — | 2.75 |

### KM# 3089 2 EURO

8.50 g., Bi-Metallic Nickel-Brass center in Copper-Nickel ring, 25.75 mm. **Obv:** Bust of Bertha von Suttner, Novelist and winner of 1905 Peace Prize, facing left within inner circle, stars in outer circle **Rev:** Value at left, relief map of European Union at right **Edge Lettering:** 2 EURO (star) (star) (star) (star) **Mint:** Vienna

| Date | Mintage | VF20 | XF40 | MS60 | MS63 | MS65 |
|---|---|---|---|---|---|---|
| 2002 | 196,400,000 | — | — | — | 3.75 | — |
| 2002 Special Unc | 100,000 | — | — | — | — | 4.00 |
| 2002 | 10,000 | PF65 125 | | | | |
| 2003 | 4,700,000 | — | — | — | 3.75 | — |
| 2003 Special Unc | 125,000 | — | — | — | — | 4.00 |
| 2003 | 25,000 | PF65 25.00 | | | | |
| 2004 | 2,500,000 | — | — | — | 3.75 | — |
| 2004 Special Unc | 100,000 | — | — | — | — | 4.00 |
| 2004 | 20,000 | PF65 27.50 | | | | |
| 2006 | 2,300,000 | — | — | — | 3.75 | — |
| 2006 Special Unc | 100,000 | — | — | — | — | 4.00 |
| 2006 | 20,000 | PF65 27.50 | | | | |

### KM# 3124 2 EURO

8.50 g., Bi-Metallic Nickel-Brass center in Copper-Nickel ring, 25.75 mm. **Subject:** 50th Anniversary of the State Treaty **Obv:** Treaty seals and signatures **Rev:** Denomination and map **Edge:** Reeding over lettering **Edge Lettering:** 2 EURO" and 3 stars repeated four times **Mint:** Vienna

| Date | Mintage | VF20 | XF40 | MS60 | MS63 | MS65 |
|---|---|---|---|---|---|---|
| 2005 | 6,880,000 | — | — | — | 5.00 | — |
| 2005 Special Unc | 100,000 | — | — | — | — | 6.00 |
| 2005 | 20,000 | PF65 27.50 | | | | |

**KM# 3150 2 EURO**
8.50 g., Bi-Metallic Nickel-Brass center in Copper-Nickel ring, 25.75 mm. **Subject:** 50th Anniversary - Treaty of Rome **Edge:** Reeded and lettered **Mint:** Vienna

| Date | Mintage | VF20 | XF40 | MS60 | MS63 | MS65 |
|---|---|---|---|---|---|---|
| 2007 | 8,905,000 | — | — | — | 4.00 | — |
| 2007 Special Unc | 75,000 | — | — | — | — | 5.00 |
| 2007 | 20,000 | PF65 27.50 | | | | |

**KM# 3143 2 EURO**
8.50 g., Bi-Metallic Nickel-Brass center in Copper-Nickel ring, 25.75 mm. **Obv:** Bust of Bertha von Suttner, Novelist and winner of 1905 Peace Prize, at right facing left in inner circle, stars in outer circle **Rev:** Value at left, expanded relief map of European Union at right **Edge Lettering:** 2 EURO ☐ Z ☐ Z ☐ Z **Mint:** Vienna

| Date | Mintage | VF20 | XF40 | MS60 | MS63 | MS65 |
|---|---|---|---|---|---|---|
| 2008 | 2,600,000 | — | — | — | 5.00 | — |
| 2008 Special Unc | 50,000 | — | — | — | — | 6.00 |
| 2008 | 15,000 | PF65 25.00 | | | | |
| 2010 | 17,000,000 | — | — | — | 5.00 | — |
| 2010 Special Unc | 50,000 | — | — | — | — | 6.00 |
| 2010 | 15,000 | PF65 25.00 | | | | |
| 2011 | 27,700,000 | — | — | — | 5.00 | — |
| 2011 Special Unc | 50,000 | — | — | — | — | 6.00 |
| 2011 | 15,000 | PF65 25.00 | | | | |
| 2012 | 21,200,000 | — | — | — | 4.50 | — |
| 2013 Special Unc | 50,000 | — | — | — | — | 6.00 |
| 2013 | 10,000 | PF65 25.00 | | | | |
| 2014 Special Unc | 50,000 | — | — | — | — | 6.00 |

**KM# 3175 2 EURO**
8.50 g., Bi-Metallic Nickel-Brass center in Copper-Nickel ring, 25.75 mm. **Subject:** 10th Anniversary - European Monetary Union **Edge:** Reeded and lettered

| Date | Mintage | VF20 | XF40 | MS60 | MS63 | MS65 |
|---|---|---|---|---|---|---|
| 2009 | 4,910,000 | — | — | — | 6.00 | — |
| 2009 Special Unc | 75,000 | — | — | — | — | 7.50 |
| 2009 | 15,000 | PF65 25.00 | | | | |

**KM# 3205 2 EURO**
8.50 g., Bi-Metallic Nickel-Brass center in Copper-Nickel ring, 25.75 mm. **Subject:** Euro Coinage, 10th Anniversary **Obv:** Euro symbol on globe at center, child-like rendering around **Mint:** Vienna

| Date | Mintage | VF20 | XF40 | MS60 | MS63 | MS65 |
|---|---|---|---|---|---|---|
| 2012 | 11,000,000 | — | — | — | 6.00 | 8.00 |
| 2012 Special Unc. | 50,000 | — | — | — | — | 15.00 |
| 2012 | 10,000 | PF65 25.00 | | | | |

**KM# 3091 5 EURO**
10.00 g., 0.800 Silver 0.2572 oz. ASW, 28.5 mm. **Subject:** Schoenbrunn Zoo **Obv:** Denomination within sun design at center, provincial arms surround **Rev:** Building and animals **Edge:** Plain **Shape:** 9-sided **Mint:** Vienna

| Date | Mintage | VF20 | XF40 | MS60 | MS63 | MS65 |
|---|---|---|---|---|---|---|
| ND(2002) | 500,000 | — | — | — | 12.50 | — |
| ND(2002) Special Unc | 100,000 | — | — | — | — | 22.50 |

**KM# 3105 5 EURO**
10.00 g., 0.800 Silver 0.2572 oz. ASW, 28.5 mm. **Subject:** Water Power **Obv:** Denomination within sun design at center, provincial arms surround **Rev:** Dam with turbine, electric power plant and fish **Edge:** Plain **Shape:** 9-sided **Mint:** Vienna

| Date | Mintage | VF20 | XF40 | MS60 | MS63 | MS65 |
|---|---|---|---|---|---|---|
| 2003 | 500,000 | — | — | — | 11.50 | — |
| 2003 Special Unc | 100,000 | — | — | — | — | 15.00 |

**KM# 3113 5 EURO**
10.00 g., 0.800 Silver 0.2572 oz. ASW, 28.5 mm. **Obv:** Denomination within sun design at center, provincial arms surround **Rev:** Soccer player scoring a goal **Edge:** Plain **Shape:** 9-sided **Mint:** Venice **Note:** Centennial of Austrian Soccer

| Date | Mintage | VF20 | XF40 | MS60 | MS63 | MS65 |
|---|---|---|---|---|---|---|
| 2004 | 600,000 | — | — | — | 10.00 | — |
| 2004 Special Unc | 100,000 | — | — | — | — | 12.50 |

**KM# 3122 5 EURO**
10.00 g., 0.800 Silver 0.2572 oz. ASW, 28.5 mm. **Subject:** Enlargement of the European Union **Obv:** Denomination within sun design at center, provincial arms surround **Rev:** Map of Europe above country names **Edge:** Plain **Shape:** 9-sided **Mint:** Vienna

| Date | Mintage | VF20 | XF40 | MS60 | MS63 | MS65 |
|---|---|---|---|---|---|---|
| 2004 | 275,000 | — | — | — | 10.00 | — |
| 2004 Special Unc | 125,000 | — | — | — | — | 12.50 |

**KM# 3117 5 EURO**
10.00 g., 0.800 Silver 0.2572 oz. ASW, 28.5 mm. **Subject:** Centennial of Sport Skiing **Obv:** Denomination within sun design at center, provincial arms surround **Rev:** Skier within snowflake design **Edge:** Plain **Shape:** 9-sided **Mint:** Vienna

| Date | Mintage | VF20 | XF40 | MS60 | MS63 | MS65 |
|---|---|---|---|---|---|---|
| 2005 | 500,000 | — | — | — | 10.00 | — |
| 2005 Special Unc | 100,000 | — | — | — | — | 14.50 |

**KM# 3120 5 EURO**
10.00 g., 0.800 Silver 0.2572 oz. ASW, 28.5 mm. **Subject:** 10th Anniversary of Austrian E U Membership **Obv:** Denomination within sun design at center, provincial arms surround **Rev:** Carinthian Gate Theater and Beethoven cameo portrait **Edge:** Plain **Shape:** 9-sided **Mint:** Vienna

| Date | Mintage | VF20 | XF40 | MS60 | MS63 | MS65 |
|---|---|---|---|---|---|---|
| 2005 | 275,000 | — | — | — | 12.50 | — |
| 2005 Special Unc | 125,000 | — | — | — | — | 14.50 |

**KM# 3131 5 EURO**
10.00 g., 0.800 Silver 0.2572 oz. ASW, 28.5 mm. **Subject:** Mozart **Obv:** Denomination within sun design at center, provincial arms surround **Rev:** Mozart and the Salzburg Cathedral **Edge:** Plain **Shape:** Nine sided **Mint:** Vienna

| Date | Mintage | VF20 | XF40 | MS60 | MS63 | MS65 |
|---|---|---|---|---|---|---|
| 2006 | 375,000 | — | — | — | 15.00 | — |
| 2006 Special Unc | 125,000 | — | — | — | — | 17.50 |

**KM# 3132 5 EURO**
10.00 g., 0.800 Silver 0.2572 oz. ASW, 28.5 mm. **Subject:** Austrian Presidency of the EU **Obv:** Value in circle of arms **Rev:** Vienna Hofburg and Josefsplatz view **Edge:** Plain **Shape:** Nine sided **Mint:** Vienna

| Date | Mintage | VF20 | XF40 | MS60 | MS63 | MS65 |
|---|---|---|---|---|---|---|
| 2006 | 250,000 | — | — | — | 12.50 | — |
| 2006 Special Unc | 100,000 | — | — | — | — | 14.50 |

**KM# 3144 5 EURO**
10.00 g., 0.800 Silver 0.2572 oz. ASW, 28.5 mm. **Subject:** Universal Male Suffrage Centennial **Obv:** Value in circle of shields **Rev:** Cameo portraits of Franz Joseph and von Beck on Reichsrat scene **Edge:** Plain **Shape:** 9-sided **Mint:** Vienna

| Date | Mintage | VF20 | XF40 | MS60 | MS63 | MS65 |
|---|---|---|---|---|---|---|
| 2007 | 150,000 | — | — | — | 13.00 | — |
| 2007 Special Unc | 100,000 | — | — | — | — | 15.00 |

**KM# 3145 5 EURO**
10.00 g., 0.800 Silver 0.2572 oz. ASW, 28.5 mm. **Obv:** Value in circle of shields **Rev:** Mariazell church **Edge:** Plain **Shape:** 9-sided **Mint:** Vienna

| Date | Mintage | VF20 | XF40 | MS60 | MS63 | MS65 |
|---|---|---|---|---|---|---|
| 2007 | 450,000 | — | — | — | 15.00 | — |
| 2007 Special Unc | 100,000 | — | — | — | — | 20.00 |

### KM# 3156 5 EURO

10.00 g., 0.800 Silver 0.2572 oz. ASW, 28.5 mm. **Subject:** Herbert Von Karajan, 100th Birth Anniversary **Obv:** Value and nine provincial shields **Rev:** Bust and notes of Beethoven's Ninth Symphony **Shape:** 9-sided

| Date | Mintage | VF20 | XF40 | MS60 | MS63 | MS65 |
|---|---|---|---|---|---|---|
| 2008 Special Unc | 100,000 | — | — | — | — | 20.00 |
| 2008 | 150,000 | — | — | — | 17.00 | — |

### KM# 3163 5 EURO

10.00 g., 0.800 Silver 0.2572 oz. ASW, 28.5 mm. **Obv:** Value within center of nine shields **Rev:** Two soccer players **Shape:** 9-sided **Mint:** Vienna

| Date | Mintage | VF20 | XF40 | MS60 | MS63 | MS65 |
|---|---|---|---|---|---|---|
| 2008 Special Unc | 100,000 | — | — | — | — | 20.00 |
| 2008 | 225,000 | — | — | — | 15.00 | — |

### KM# 3164 5 EURO

10.00 g., 0.800 Silver 0.2572 oz. ASW, 28.5 mm. **Obv:** Value within center of nine shields **Rev:** One soccer player **Shape:** 9-sided **Mint:** Vienna

| Date | Mintage | VF20 | XF40 | MS60 | MS63 | MS65 |
|---|---|---|---|---|---|---|
| 2008 Special Unc | 100,000 | — | — | — | — | 20.00 |
| 2008 | 225,000 | — | — | — | 15.00 | — |

### KM# 3170 5 EURO

10.00 g., 0.800 Silver 0.2572 oz. ASW, 28.5 mm. **Subject:** Joseph Haydn, 200th Anniversary of Death **Obv:** Value at center of nine shields **Rev:** Bust facing right at left, pair of violins at right **Shape:** 9-sided

| Date | Mintage | VF20 | XF40 | MS60 | MS63 | MS65 |
|---|---|---|---|---|---|---|
| 2009 | 450,000 | — | — | — | 15.00 | — |
| 2009 Special Unc | 100,000 | — | — | — | — | 20.00 |

### KM# 3177 5 EURO

10.00 g., 0.800 Silver 0.2572 oz. ASW, 28.5 mm. **Subject:** Tyrolean Resistance Fighters, 1809 **Shape:** 9-sided **Mint:** Vienna

| Date | Mintage | VF20 | XF40 | MS60 | MS63 | MS65 |
|---|---|---|---|---|---|---|
| 2009 Special Unc | 100,000 | — | — | — | — | 30.00 |
| 2009 | 250,000 | — | — | — | 20.00 | — |

### KM# 3184 5 EURO

10.00 g., 0.800 Silver 0.2572 oz. ASW, 28.5 mm. **Subject:** Grossglockner - High Alpine Road **Shape:** 9-sided **Mint:** Vienna

| Date | Mintage | VF20 | XF40 | MS60 | MS63 | MS65 |
|---|---|---|---|---|---|---|
| 2010 | 250,000 | — | — | — | 15.00 | — |
| 2010 Special Unc | 50,000 | — | — | — | — | 20.00 |

### KM# 3192 5 EURO

10.00 g., 0.800 Silver 0.2572 oz. ASW, 28.5 mm. **Subject:** Winter sports **Obv:** Nine provincial shields **Rev:** Snowboarding **Shape:** 9-sided **Mint:** Vienna

| Date | Mintage | VF20 | XF40 | MS60 | MS63 | MS65 |
|---|---|---|---|---|---|---|
| 2010 | 225,000 | — | — | — | 15.00 | — |
| 2010 Special Unc | 50,000 | — | — | — | — | 20.00 |

### KM# 3193 5 EURO

10.00 g., 0.800 Silver 0.2572 oz. ASW, 28.5 mm. **Subject:** Winter Sports **Obv:** Nine provincial shields **Rev:** Ski jumper **Shape:** 9-sided **Mint:** Vienna

| Date | Mintage | VF20 | XF40 | MS60 | MS63 | MS65 |
|---|---|---|---|---|---|---|
| 2010 | 225,000 | — | — | — | 15.00 | — |
| 2010 Special Unc | 50,000 | — | — | — | — | 20.00 |

### KM# 3195 5 EURO

10.00 g., 0.800 Silver 0.2572 oz. ASW, 28.5 mm. **Subject:** Pummerin, Bell, 1711-2011 **Obv:** Value within circle of shields **Rev:** Large bell **Shape:** 9-sided **Mint:** Vienna

| Date | Mintage | VF20 | XF40 | MS60 | MS63 | MS65 |
|---|---|---|---|---|---|---|
| 2011 Special Unc. | 50,000 | — | — | — | — | 20.00 |

### KM# 3196 5 EURO

10.00 g., 0.800 Silver 0.2572 oz. ASW, 28.5 mm. **Subject:** Land of Forests **Shape:** 9-sided **Mint:** Vienna

| Date | Mintage | VF20 | XF40 | MS60 | MS63 | MS65 |
|---|---|---|---|---|---|---|
| 2011 Special Unc. | 50,000 | — | — | — | — | 20.00 |

### KM# 3206 5 EURO

8.90 g., Copper, 28.5 mm. **Subject:** Society of Music Lovers, 200th Anniversary **Obv:** Value at center of circle of nine shields **Rev:** Interior of the "Golden Hall" in Vienna **Shape:** 9-sided **Mint:** Vienna

| Date | Mintage | VF20 | XF40 | MS60 | MS63 | MS65 |
|---|---|---|---|---|---|---|
| 2012 | 300,000 | — | — | — | 8.00 | — |

### KM# 3206a 5 EURO

10.00 g., 0.800 Silver 0.2572 oz. ASW, 28.5 mm. **Subject:** Society of Music Lovers, 200th Anniversary **Obv:** Value in circle of nine shields **Rev:** Interior of the "Golden Hall" in Vienna **Shape:** 9-sided **Mint:** Vienna

| Date | Mintage | VF20 | XF40 | MS60 | MS63 | MS65 |
|---|---|---|---|---|---|---|
| 2012 Special Unc. | 50,000 | — | — | — | — | 28.00 |

### KM# 3215 5 EURO

8.90 g., Copper, 28.5 mm. **Subject:** Schladming **Rev:** Downhill skier **Shape:** 9-sided **Mint:** Vienna

| Date | Mintage | VF20 | XF40 | MS60 | MS63 | MS65 |
|---|---|---|---|---|---|---|
| 2012 | 300,000 | — | — | — | — | 8.00 |

### KM# 3215a 5 EURO

10.00 g., 0.800 Silver 0.2572 oz. ASW, 28.5 mm. **Subject:** Schladming **Rev:** Downhill skier **Shape:** 9-sided **Mint:** Vienna

| Date | Mintage | VF20 | XF40 | MS60 | MS63 | MS65 |
|---|---|---|---|---|---|---|
| 2012 Special Unc | 50,000 | — | — | — | — | 25.00 |

### KM# 3216 5 EURO

8.90 g., Copper, 28.5 mm. **Subject:** Vienna Waltz **Rev:** Dancers **Shape:** 9-sided **Mint:** Vienna

| Date | Mintage | VF20 | XF40 | MS60 | MS63 | MS65 |
|---|---|---|---|---|---|---|
| 2012 | 200,000 | — | — | — | — | 8.00 |

### KM# 3216a 5 EURO

10.00 g., 0.800 Silver 0.2572 oz. ASW, 28.5 mm. **Subject:** Vienna Waltz **Rev:** Two dancers **Mint:** Vienna

| Date | Mintage | VF20 | XF40 | MS60 | MS63 | MS65 |
|---|---|---|---|---|---|---|
| 2012 Special Unc | 50,000 | — | — | — | — | 30.00 |

### KM# 3222 5 EURO

8.90 g., Copper, 28.5 mm. **Subject:** Land of Water, UNESCO Year of Water Cooperation, 2013 **Rev:** Heron in pond, kingfisher and flora **Rev. Legend:** LAND DES WASSERS **Mint:** Vienna

| Date | Mintage | VF20 | XF40 | MS60 | MS63 | MS65 |
|---|---|---|---|---|---|---|
| 2013 | 200,000 | — | — | — | — | 8.00 |

### KM# 3222a 5 EURO

10.00 g., 0.800 Silver 0.2572 oz. ASW, 28.5 mm. **Subject:** Land of Water **Obv:** Nine provincial shields **Rev:** Heron standing in pond, kingfisher and flora **Mint:** Vienna

| Date | Mintage | VF20 | XF40 | MS60 | MS63 | MS65 |
|---|---|---|---|---|---|---|
| 2013 Special Unc. | 50,000 | — | — | — | — | 30.00 |

### KM# 3237 5 EURO

8.90 g., Copper, 28.5 mm. **Subject:** New Year traditions **Rev:** Die Fledermaus opera **Shape:** 9-sided **Mint:** Vienna

| Date | Mintage | VF20 | XF40 | MS60 | MS63 | MS65 |
|---|---|---|---|---|---|---|
| 2015 | 200,000 | — | — | — | — | 8.00 |

### KM# 3237a 5 EURO

10.00 g., 0.800 Silver 0.2572 oz. ASW, 28.5 mm. **Subject:** New Year traditions **Rev:** Die Fledermaus opera **Mint:** Vienna

| Date | Mintage | VF20 | XF40 | MS60 | MS63 | MS65 |
|---|---|---|---|---|---|---|
| 2015 Special Unc. | 50,000 | — | — | — | — | 50.00 |

**KM# 3096 10 EURO**
17.30 g., 0.925 Silver 0.5145 oz. ASW, 32 mm. **Subject:** Ambras Palace **Obv:** Palace, denomination below **Rev:** Three strolling musicians **Edge:** Reeded **Mint:** Vienna

| Date | Mintage | VF20 | XF40 | MS60 | MS63 | MS65 |
|---|---|---|---|---|---|---|
| 2002 | 130,000 | — | — | — | 20.00 | — |
| 2002 Special Unc | 20,000 | — | — | — | — | 30.00 |
| 2002 | 50,000 | PF65 40.00 | | | | |

**KM# 3099 10 EURO**
17.30 g., 0.925 Silver 0.5145 oz. ASW, 32 mm. **Subject:** Eggenberg Palace and Johannes Kepler **Obv:** Palace, denomination below **Rev:** Half figure seated with tools **Edge:** Reeded **Mint:** Vienna

| Date | Mintage | VF20 | XF40 | MS60 | MS63 | MS65 |
|---|---|---|---|---|---|---|
| 2002 | 130,000 | — | — | — | 20.00 | — |
| 2002 Special Unc | 20,000 | — | — | — | — | 30.00 |
| 2002 | 50,000 | PF65 32.50 | | | | |

**KM# 3103 10 EURO**
17.30 g., 0.925 Silver 0.5145 oz. ASW, 32 mm. **Subject:** Castle of Schlosshof **Obv:** Baroque fountain and palace, denomination below **Rev:** Two gardeners at work **Mint:** Vienna

| Date | Mintage | VF20 | XF40 | MS60 | MS63 | MS65 |
|---|---|---|---|---|---|---|
| 2003 | 130,000 | — | — | — | 30.00 | — |
| 2003 Special Unc | 20,000 | — | — | — | — | 35.00 |
| 2003 | 50,000 | PF65 40.00 | | | | |

**KM# 3106 10 EURO**
17.30 g., 0.925 Silver 0.5145 oz. ASW, 32 mm. **Subject:** Schoenbrunn Palace **Obv:** Fountain with palace background, denomination below **Rev:** Palmenhaus greenhouse **Mint:** Vienna

| Date | Mintage | VF20 | XF40 | MS60 | MS63 | MS65 |
|---|---|---|---|---|---|---|
| 2003 | 100,000 | — | — | — | 30.00 | — |
| 2003 Special Unc | 40,000 | — | — | — | — | 35.00 |
| 2003 | 60,000 | PF65 40.00 | | | | |

**KM# 3111 10 EURO**
17.30 g., 0.925 Silver 0.5145 oz. ASW, 32 mm. **Obv:** Hellbrunn Castle, denomination below **Rev:** Archbishop Marcus Sitticus and Hellbrunn's "Roman Theatre **Edge:** Reeded **Mint:** Vienna

| Date | Mintage | VF20 | XF40 | MS60 | MS63 | MS65 |
|---|---|---|---|---|---|---|
| 2004 | 130,000 | — | — | — | 30.00 | — |
| 2004 Special Unc | 40,000 | — | — | — | — | 35.00 |
| 2004 | 60,000 | PF65 40.00 | | | | |

**KM# 3115 10 EURO**
17.30 g., 0.925 Silver 0.5145 oz. ASW, 32 mm. **Obv:** Artstetten Castle, denomination below **Rev:** Crypt entrance behind portraits of Franz Ferdinand and Sophie **Mint:** Vienna

| Date | Mintage | VF20 | XF40 | MS60 | MS63 | MS65 |
|---|---|---|---|---|---|---|
| 2004 | 130,000 | — | — | — | 30.00 | — |
| 2004 Special Unc | 40,000 | — | — | — | — | 35.00 |
| 2004 | 60,000 | PF65 40.00 | | | | |

**KM# 3121 10 EURO**
17.30 g., 0.925 Silver 0.5145 oz. ASW, 32 mm. **Subject:** 60th Anniversary of the Second Republic **Obv:** Statue of Athena, nine provincial shields and denomination at right **Rev:** Parliament building above broken chain, crowd below **Mint:** Vienna

| Date | Mintage | VF20 | XF40 | MS60 | MS63 | MS65 |
|---|---|---|---|---|---|---|
| 2005 | 130,000 | — | — | — | 30.00 | — |
| 2005 Special Unc | 40,000 | — | — | — | — | 35.00 |
| 2005 | 60,000 | PF65 40.00 | | | | |

**KM# 3125 10 EURO**
17.30 g., 0.925 Silver 0.5145 oz. ASW, 32 mm. **Subject:** Reopening of the Burg Theater and Opera **Obv:** Two large buildings, denomination at left **Rev:** Comedy and Tragedy Masks **Mint:** Vienna

| Date | Mintage | VF20 | XF40 | MS60 | MS63 | MS65 |
|---|---|---|---|---|---|---|
| 2005 | 130,000 | — | — | — | 30.00 | — |
| 2005 Special Unc | 40,000 | — | — | — | — | 35.00 |
| 2005 | 60,000 | PF65 40.00 | | | | |

**KM# 3129 10 EURO**
17.30 g., 0.925 Silver 0.5145 oz. ASW, 32 mm. **Subject:** Nonnenberg Abbey **Obv:** Abbey view, denomination below **Rev:** Statue of St. Erentrudis **Edge:** Reeded **Mint:** Vienna

| Date | Mintage | VF20 | XF40 | MS60 | MS63 | MS65 |
|---|---|---|---|---|---|---|
| 2006 | 130,000 | — | — | — | 30.00 | — |
| 2006 Special Unc | 40,000 | — | — | — | — | 35.00 |
| 2006 | 60,000 | PF65 40.00 | | | | |

**KM# 3137 10 EURO**
17.30 g., 0.925 Silver 0.5145 oz. ASW, 32 mm. **Obv:** Gottweig Abby above value **Rev:** Charles VI and staircase **Mint:** Vienna

| Date | Mintage | VF20 | XF40 | MS60 | MS63 | MS65 |
|---|---|---|---|---|---|---|
| 2006 | 130,000 | — | — | — | 30.00 | — |
| 2006 Special Unc | 40,000 | — | — | — | — | 35.00 |
| 2006 | 60,000 | PF65 40.00 | | | | |

**KM# 3146 10 EURO**
17.30 g., 0.925 Silver 0.5145 oz. ASW, 32 mm. **Obv:** Melk Abbey view **Rev:** Inner view of the Melk Abbey dome **Mint:** Vienna

| Date | Mintage | VF20 | XF40 | MS60 | MS63 | MS65 |
|---|---|---|---|---|---|---|
| 2007 | 130,000 | — | — | — | 30.00 | — |
| 2007 Special Unc | 40,000 | — | — | — | — | 35.00 |
| 2007 | 60,000 | PF65 40.00 | | | | |

**KM# 3148 10 EURO**
17.30 g., 0.925 Silver 0.5145 oz. ASW, 32 mm. **Obv:** St. Paul's Abbey complex **Obv. Legend:** ST. PAUL IM LAVANTTAL **Obv. Inscription:** REPUBLIK / ÖSTERREICH **Rev:** Entrance facade **Mint:** Vienna

| Date | Mintage | VF20 | XF40 | MS60 | MS63 | MS65 |
|---|---|---|---|---|---|---|
| 2007 | 130,000 | — | — | — | 30.00 | — |
| 2007 Special Unc | 60,000 | — | — | — | — | 35.00 |
| 2007 | 40,000 | PF65 40.00 | | | | |

**KM# 3157 10 EURO**
17.30 g., 0.925 Silver 0.5145 oz. ASW, 32 mm. **Subject:** Abby of Klosterneuburg **Obv:** Aerial exterior view of church complex **Rev:** Cloister

| Date | Mintage | VF20 | XF40 | MS60 | MS63 | MS65 |
|---|---|---|---|---|---|---|
| 2008 Special Unc | 40,000 | — | — | — | — | 35.00 |
| 2008 | 130,000 | — | — | — | 30.00 | — |
| 2008 | 60,000 | PF65 45.00 | | | | |

**KM# 3162 10 EURO**
17.30 g., 0.925 Silver 0.5145 oz. ASW, 32 mm. **Subject:** Seckau Benedictine Abbey **Obv:** Exterior of abby, value, date and inscriptions "BENEDIKTINERABTEI SECKAU" and "REPUBLIK OESTERREICH **Rev:** Interior of abbey

| Date | Mintage | VF20 | XF40 | MS60 | MS63 | MS65 |
|---|---|---|---|---|---|---|
| 2008 | 130,000 | — | — | — | 30.00 | — |
| 2008 Special Unc | 40,000 | — | — | — | — | 35.00 |
| 2008 | 60,000 | PF65 45.00 | | | | |

**KM# 3176 10 EURO**
17.30 g., 0.925 Silver 0.5145 oz. ASW, 32 mm. **Series:** Tales and Legends **Subject:** Basilisk of Vienna **Mint:** Vienna

| Date | Mintage | VF20 | XF40 | MS60 | MS63 | MS65 |
|---|---|---|---|---|---|---|
| 2009 Special Unc | 30,000 | — | — | — | — | 35.00 |
| 2009 | 130,000 | — | — | — | 30.00 | — |
| 2009 | 40,000 | PF65 45.00 | | | | |

**KM# 3180 10 EURO**
17.30 g., 0.925 Silver 0.5145 oz. ASW, 32 mm. **Series:** Tales and Legends **Subject:** Richard the Lionheart in Dürnstein **Mint:** Vienna

| Date | Mintage | VF20 | XF40 | MS60 | MS63 | MS65 |
|---|---|---|---|---|---|---|
| 2009 Special Unc | 30,000 | — | — | — | — | 35.00 |
| 2009 | 130,000 | — | — | — | 30.00 | — |
| 2009 | 40,000 | PF65 45.00 | | | | |

**KM# 3185 10 EURO**
17.30 g., 0.925 Silver 0.5145 oz. ASW, 32 mm. **Subject:** Erzberg in Styria **Obv:** Iron Mine **Rev:** Two mermen with cloak **Mint:** Vienna

| Date | Mintage | VF20 | XF40 | MS60 | MS63 | MS65 |
|---|---|---|---|---|---|---|
| 2010 | 130,000 | — | — | — | 30.00 | — |
| 2010 | 40,000 | PF65 45.00 | | | | |
| 2010 Special Unc | 30,000 | — | — | — | — | 35.00 |

**KM# 3186 10 EURO**
17.30 g., 0.925 Silver 0.5145 oz. ASW, 32 mm. **Subject:** Charlemagne in the Undersberg **Mint:** Vienna

| Date | Mintage | VF20 | XF40 | MS60 | MS63 | MS65 |
|---|---|---|---|---|---|---|
| 2010 (h) Special Unc | 30,000 | — | — | — | — | 45.00 |
| 2010 (h) | 130,000 | — | — | — | 30.00 | — |
| 2010 (h) | 40,000 | PF65 45.00 | | | | |

**KM# 3197 10 EURO**
17.30 g., 0.925 Silver 0.5145 oz. ASW, 32 mm. **Subject:** The Lindworm in Klagenfurt **Mint:** Vienna

| Date | Mintage | VF20 | XF40 | MS60 | MS63 | MS65 |
|---|---|---|---|---|---|---|
| 2011 Special Unc. | 30,000 | — | — | — | — | 45.00 |
| 2011 | 40,000 | PF65 55.00 | | | | |

**KM# 3198 10 EURO**
17.30 g., 0.925 Silver 0.5145 oz. ASW, 32 mm. **Subject:** My dear old Augustin **Mint:** Vienna

| Date | Mintage | VF20 | XF40 | MS60 | MS63 | MS65 |
|---|---|---|---|---|---|---|
| 2011 Special Unc. | 30,000 | — | — | — | — | 45.00 |
| 2011 | 40,000 | PF65 65.00 | | | | |

**KM# 3207 10 EURO**
15.00 g., Copper, 32 mm. **Subject:** Steiermark **Obv:** Graz town view **Rev:** Child's drawing of countryside **Mint:** Vienna

| Date | Mintage | VF20 | XF40 | MS60 | MS63 | MS65 |
|---|---|---|---|---|---|---|
| 2012 | 130,000 | — | — | — | 17.00 | — |

**KM# 3207a 10 EURO**
17.30 g., 0.925 Silver 0.5145 oz. ASW, 32 mm. **Subject:** Steiermark **Obv:** Graz town view **Rev:** Child's design of countryside **Mint:** Vienna

| Date | Mintage | VF20 | XF40 | MS60 | MS63 | MS65 |
|---|---|---|---|---|---|---|
| 2012 Special Unc | 40,000 | — | — | — | 50.00 | — |
| 2012 | 30,000 | PF65 60.00 | | | | |

**KM# 3208 10 EURO**
15.00 g., Copper, 32 mm. **Subject:** Carinthia **Obv:** Falconer with bird **Rev:** Child's drawing of countryside **Mint:** Vienna

| Date | Mintage | VF20 | XF40 | MS60 | MS63 | MS65 |
|---|---|---|---|---|---|---|
| 2012 | 130,000 | — | — | — | 17.00 | — |

**KM# 3208a 10 EURO**
17.30 g., 0.925 Silver 0.5145 oz. ASW, 32 mm. **Subject:** Carinthia **Obv:** Falconer and bird **Rev:** Child's drawing of countryside **Mint:** Vienna

| Date | Mintage | VF20 | XF40 | MS60 | MS63 | MS65 |
|---|---|---|---|---|---|---|
| 2012 Special Unc. | 40,000 | — | — | — | — | 50.00 |
| 2012 | 30,000 | PF65 55.00 | | | | |

**KM# 3211 10 EURO**
20.00 g., 0.900 Silver 0.5787 oz. ASW, 34 mm. **Series:** Rome on the Danube - Brigantium **Subject:** Brigantium **Mint:** Vienna

| Date | Mintage | VF20 | XF40 | MS60 | MS63 | MS65 |
|---|---|---|---|---|---|---|
| 2012 | 50,000 | PF65 70.00 | | | | |

**KM# 3221 10 EURO**
15.00 g., Copper **Subject:** Federal Provinces: Lower Austria **Mint:** Vienna

| Date | Mintage | VF20 | XF40 | MS60 | MS63 | MS65 |
|---|---|---|---|---|---|---|
| 2013 Special Unc. | 130,000 | — | — | — | — | 15.00 |

**KM# 3221a 10 EURO**
17.30 g., 0.925 Silver 0.5145 oz. ASW, 32 mm. **Subject:** Federal Provinces: Lower Austria **Mint:** Vienna

| Date | Mintage | VF20 | XF40 | MS60 | MS63 | MS65 |
|---|---|---|---|---|---|---|
| 2013 Special Unc. | 40,000 | — | — | — | — | 50.00 |
| 2013 | 30,000 | PF65 55.00 | | | | |

**KM# 3224 10 EURO**
15.00 g., Copper, 32 mm. **Subject:** Federal Provinces: Vorarlberg **Mint:** Vienna

| Date | Mintage | VF20 | XF40 | MS60 | MS63 | MS65 |
|---|---|---|---|---|---|---|
| 2013 | 130,000 | — | — | — | 17.00 | — |

**KM# 3224a 10 EURO**
17.30 g., 0.925 Silver 0.5145 oz. ASW, 32 mm. **Subject:** Federal Provinces: Vorarlberg **Mint:** Vienna

| Date | Mintage | VF20 | XF40 | MS60 | MS63 | MS65 |
|---|---|---|---|---|---|---|
| 2013 Special Unc. | 40,000 | — | — | — | — | 45.00 |
| 2013 | 30,000 | PF65 55.00 | | | | |

**KM# 3097 20 EURO**
20.00 g., 0.900 Silver 0.5787 oz. ASW, 34 mm. **Subject:** Ferdinand I - Renaissance **Obv:** Hofburg Palace "Swiss Gate" with two guards, denomination below **Rev:** Bust looking left, coat of arms at left, dates at right **Edge:** Reeded **Mint:** Vienna

| Date | Mintage | VF20 | XF40 | MS60 | MS63 | MS65 |
|---|---|---|---|---|---|---|
| 2002 | — | PF65 37.50 | | | | |

**KM# 3098 20 EURO**
20.00 g., 0.900 Silver 0.5787 oz. ASW, 34 mm. **Subject:** Prince Eugen - Baroque Period **Obv:** Baroque staircase with statues, denomination below **Rev:** Uniformed bust 1/4 left and dates at right, flags above cannons at left **Edge:** Reeded **Mint:** Vienna

| Date | Mintage | VF20 | XF40 | MS60 | MS63 | MS65 |
|---|---|---|---|---|---|---|
| 2002 | — | PF65 50.00 | | | | |

**KM# 3104 20 EURO**
20.00 g., 0.900 Silver 0.5787 oz. ASW, 34 mm. **Subject:** Prince Metternich **Obv:** Early steam locomotive, denomination below **Rev:** Portrait with map background **Edge:** Reeded **Mint:** Vienna

| Date | Mintage | VF20 | XF40 | MS60 | MS63 | MS65 |
|---|---|---|---|---|---|---|
| 2003 | 50,000 | PF65 50.00 | | | | |

**KM# 3107 20 EURO**
20.00 g., 0.900 Silver 0.5787 oz. ASW, 34 mm. **Obv:** Republic of Austria arms, denomination below **Rev:** Four men in a jeep **Edge:** Reeded **Mint:** Vienna **Note:** Post War Austrian Reconstruction

| Date | Mintage | VF20 | XF40 | MS60 | MS63 | MS65 |
|---|---|---|---|---|---|---|
| 2003 | 50,000 | PF65 50.00 | | | | |

**KM# 3112 20 EURO**
20.00 g., 0.900 Silver 0.5787 oz. ASW, 34 mm. **Obv:** S.M.S Novara under sail in Chinese waters, denomination below **Rev:** Standing figures behind table with globe and microscope **Edge:** Reeded **Mint:** Vienna **Note:** First Global Circumnavigation by an Austrian ship.

| Date | Mintage | VF20 | XF40 | MS60 | MS63 | MS65 |
|---|---|---|---|---|---|---|
| 2004 | 50,000 | PF65 50.00 | | | | |

**KM# 3114 20 EURO**
20.00 g., 0.900 Silver 0.5787 oz. ASW, 34 mm. **Obv:** SMS Erzherzog Ferdinand Max sailing to the Battle of Lissa, denomination below **Rev:** Sailors at the wheel with Admiral Tegetthof in background **Edge:** Reeded **Mint:** Vienna

| Date | Mintage | VF20 | XF40 | MS60 | MS63 | MS65 |
|---|---|---|---|---|---|---|
| 2004 | 50,000 | PF65 52.50 | | | | |

**KM# 3126 20 EURO**
20.00 g., 0.900 Silver 0.5787 oz. ASW, 34 mm. **Obv:** Ship, "Admiral Tegetthoff" in arctic waters, denomination below **Rev:** Expedition leaders, von Payer and Weyprecht with their icebound ship behind them **Edge:** Reeded **Mint:** Vienna

| Date | Mintage | VF20 | XF40 | MS60 | MS63 | MS65 |
|---|---|---|---|---|---|---|
| 2005 | 50,000 | PF65 50.00 | | | | |

**KM# 3127 20 EURO**
20.00 g., 0.900 Silver 0.5787 oz. ASW, 34 mm. **Obv:** SMS St. George sailing past the Statue of Liberty, denomination below **Rev:** Shipyard at Pola, boat on water **Edge:** Reeded **Mint:** Vienna

| Date | Mintage | VF20 | XF40 | MS60 | MS63 | MS65 |
|---|---|---|---|---|---|---|
| 2005 | 50,000 | PF65 50.00 | | | | |

**KM# 3133 20 EURO**
20.00 g., 0.900 Silver 0.5787 oz. ASW, 34 mm. **Subject:** Austrian Merchant Marine **Obv:** Two passing steam ships **Rev:** 19th Century Triest harbor view **Edge:** Reeded **Mint:** Vienna

| Date | Mintage | VF20 | XF40 | MS60 | MS63 | MS65 |
|---|---|---|---|---|---|---|
| 2006 | 50,000 | PF65 50.00 | | | | |

**KM# 3134 20 EURO**
20.00 g., 0.900 Silver 0.5787 oz. ASW, 34 mm. **Obv:** SMS Viribus Unitis, flag ship of the Austrian fleet, and other ships steaming left **Rev:** SMS Viribus Unitis, submarine conning tower and seaplane **Edge:** Reeded **Mint:** Vienna

| Date | Mintage | VF20 | XF40 | MS60 | MS63 | MS65 |
|---|---|---|---|---|---|---|
| 2006 | 50,000 | PF65 50.00 | | | | |

**KM# 3149 20 EURO**
20.00 g., 0.900 Silver 0.5787 oz. ASW, 34 mm. **Series:** Austrian Railways **Obv:** Steam locomotive 1837 with passenger wagons **Obv. Legend:** REPUBLIK ÖSTERREICH **Obv. Inscription:** DAMPFLOKOMOTIVE / AUSTRIA / 1837 **Rev:** People waving at passenger train crossing a trestle **Rev. Legend:** KAISER - FERDINANDS - NORDBAHN **Edge:** Reeded **Mint:** Vienna

| Date | Mintage | VF20 | XF40 | MS60 | MS63 | MS65 |
|---|---|---|---|---|---|---|
| 2007 | 50,000 | PF65 70.00 | | | | |

**KM# 3151 20 EURO**
20.00 g., 0.900 Silver 0.5787 oz. ASW, 34 mm. **Series:** Austrian Railways **Obv:** Steam locomotive 1848 standing still, viaduct in background **Obv. Legend:** REPUBLIK ÖSTERREICH **Obv. Inscription:** DAMPF-/ LOKOMOTIVE / STEINBRØCK / 1848 **Rev:** Steam train traveling right through city **Rev. Legend:** K.K. SÜDBAHN WIEN - TRIEST **Edge:** Reeded **Mint:** Vienna

| Date | Mintage | VF20 | XF40 | MS60 | MS63 | MS65 |
|---|---|---|---|---|---|---|
| 2007 | 50,000 | PF65 70.00 | | | | |

**KM# 3154 20 EURO**
20.00 g., 0.900 Silver 0.5787 oz. ASW, 34 mm. **Subject:** Southern Railways **Obv:** Steam Locomotive on iron railway bridge **Obv. Inscription:** KOK kkStB 306 **Rev:** Statue of Empress Elizabeth and train platform in Vienna's West Railway station **Rev. Inscription:** KAISERIN-/ ELIZABETH-/ WESTBAHN **Edge:** Reeded **Mint:** Vienna

| Date | Mintage | VF20 | XF40 | MS60 | MS63 | MS65 |
|---|---|---|---|---|---|---|
| 2008 | 50,000 | PF65 70.00 | | | | |

**KM# 3161 20 EURO**
20.00 g., 0.900 Silver 0.5787 oz. ASW, 34 mm. **Subject:** Imperal - Royal State Railway **Obv:** Locomotive steaming left **Obv. Legend:** Nordbahnhof/Wein **Rev:** Female on platform **Edge:** Reeded

| Date | Mintage | VF20 | XF40 | MS60 | MS63 | MS65 |
|---|---|---|---|---|---|---|
| 2008 | 50,000 | PF65 70.00 | | | | |

**KM# 3178 20 EURO**
20.00 g., 0.900 Silver 0.5787 oz. ASW, 34 mm. **Subject:** The Electric Railway **Obv:** Locomotive model 1189, the Crocodile **Rev:** Train on the Trisanna Bridge, Wiesburg Castle in background **Edge:** Reeded **Mint:** Vienna

| Date | Mintage | VF20 | XF40 | MS60 | MS63 | MS65 |
|---|---|---|---|---|---|---|
| 2009 | 50,000 | PF65 70.00 | | | | |

**KM# 3179 20 EURO**
20.00 g., 0.900 Silver 0.5787 oz. ASW, 34 mm. **Subject:** Railways of the Future **Obv:** Railjet highspeed OBB train **Rev:** Electric locomotive of the 1063 class in freight yard **Edge:** Reeded **Mint:** Vienna

| Date | Mintage | VF20 | XF40 | MS60 | MS63 | MS65 |
|---|---|---|---|---|---|---|
| 2009 | 50,000 | PF65 70.00 | | | | |

**KM# 3187 20 EURO**
20.00 g., 0.900 Silver 0.5787 oz. ASW, 34 mm. **Series:** Rome on the Danube **Subject:** Virunum **Obv:** Emperor Claudium, 2-horse wagon, gravestone **Rev:** Street scene, wagon and temple facade **Edge:** Reeded **Mint:** Vienna

| Date | Mintage | VF20 | XF40 | MS60 | MS63 | MS65 |
|---|---|---|---|---|---|---|
| 2010 | 50,000 | PF65 70.00 | | | | |

**KM# 3188 20 EURO**
20.00 g., 0.900 Silver 0.5787 oz. ASW, 34 mm. **Series:** Rome on the Danube **Subject:** Vindofona **Edge:** Reeded **Mint:** Vienna

| Date | Mintage | VF20 | XF40 | MS60 | MS63 | MS65 |
|---|---|---|---|---|---|---|
| 2010 | 50,000 | PF65 70.00 | | | | |

**KM# 3199 20 EURO**
20.00 g., 0.900 Silver 0.5787 oz. ASW, 34 mm. **Series:** Rome on the Danube **Subject:** Carnuntum **Edge:** Reeded **Mint:** Vienna

| Date | Mintage | VF20 | XF40 | MS60 | MS63 | MS65 |
|---|---|---|---|---|---|---|
| 2011 | 50,000 | PF65 70.00 | | | | |

**KM# 3200 20 EURO**
20.00 g., 0.900 Silver 0.5787 oz. ASW, 34 mm. **Series:** Rome on the Danube **Subject:** Aguntum **Mint:** Vienna

| Date | Mintage | VF20 | XF40 | MS60 | MS63 | MS65 |
|---|---|---|---|---|---|---|
| 2011 | 50,000 | PF65 70.00 | | | | |

**KM# 3201 20 EURO**
20.00 g., 0.900 Silver 0.5787 oz. ASW, 34 mm. **Subject:** Nikolaus Joseph von Jacquin **Obv:** Bust at left, flower at right **Rev:** Karibuk Expedition, Jacquin taking notes of plants in book **Mint:** Vienna

| Date | Mintage | VF20 | XF40 | MS60 | MS63 | MS65 |
|---|---|---|---|---|---|---|
| 2011 | 50,000 | PF65 70.00 | | | | |

**KM# 3209 20 EURO**
20.00 g., 0.900 Silver 0.5787 oz. ASW, 34 mm. **Series:** European Artists **Subject:** Egon Schiele **Obv:** Portrait of the artist **Rev:** Painting of a female **Mint:** Vienna

| Date | Mintage | VF20 | XF40 | MS60 | MS63 | MS65 |
|---|---|---|---|---|---|---|
| 2012 | 50,000 | PF65 70.00 | | | | |

**KM# 3210 20 EURO**
20.00 g., 0.900 Silver 0.5787 oz. ASW, 34 mm. **Series:** Rome on the Danube **Subject:** Lauriacum **Mint:** Vienna

| Date | Mintage | VF20 | XF40 | MS60 | MS63 | MS65 |
|---|---|---|---|---|---|---|
| 2012 | 50,000 | PF65 70.00 | | | | |

**KM# 3219 20 EURO**
20.00 g., 0.900 Silver 0.5787 oz. ASW, 34 mm. **Subject:** European Writers: Stefan Zweig **Mint:** Vienna

| Date | Mintage | VF20 | XF40 | MS60 | MS63 | MS65 |
|---|---|---|---|---|---|---|
| 2013 | 50,000 | PF65 70.00 | | | | |

**KM# 3220 20 EURO**
20.00 g., 0.900 Silver 0.5787 oz. ASW, 34 mm. **Series:** Prehistoric Life **Subject:** Trias - Life in the water **Mint:** Vienna

| Date | Mintage | VF20 | XF40 | MS60 | MS63 | MS65 |
|---|---|---|---|---|---|---|
| 2013 | 50,000 | PF65 70.00 | | | | |

**KM# 3223 20 EURO**

20.00 g., 0.900 Silver 0.5787 oz. ASW, 34 mm. **Series:** Prehistoric Life **Subject:** Jura - Life in the Air **Obv:** Rhamphorhynchus and Jurassic period timeline **Rev:** Two flying Rhamphorhynchus hunting large dragonfly. Lush tropical vegitation **Mint:** Vienna

| Date | Mintage | VF20 | XF40 | MS60 | MS63 | MS65 |
|---|---|---|---|---|---|---|
| 2013 | 50,000 | PF65 65.00 | | | | |

**KM# 3227 25 EURO**

16.50 g., Bi-Metallic, 34 mm. **Subject:** Evolution **Obv:** DNA and RNA stands **Rev:** Steps in evolution **Designer:** Helmut Andexlinger **Note:** Two colors of Niobium

| Date | Mintage | F12 | VF20 | XF40 | MS60 | MS63 |
|---|---|---|---|---|---|---|
| 2014 Special Unc | 65,000 | — | — | — | — | 80.00 |

**KM# 3239 20 EURO**

20.00 g., 0.900 Silver 0.5787 oz. ASW, 34 mm. **Subject:** Spanish Riding School, 450th Anniversary **Mint:** Vienna

| Date | Mintage | VF20 | XF40 | MS60 | MS63 | MS65 |
|---|---|---|---|---|---|---|
| 2015 | 50,000 | PF65 70.00 | | | | |

**KM# 3240 20 EURO**

20.00 g., 0.900 Silver 0.5787 oz. ASW, 34 mm. **Subject:** Quaternary Era - Life on the ground

| Date | Mintage | VF20 | XF40 | MS60 | MS63 | MS65 |
|---|---|---|---|---|---|---|
| 2015 | 50,000 | PF65 70.00 | | | | |

**KM# 3101 25 EURO**

17.15 g., Bi-Metallic 7.15g pure Niobium (Columbium) blue color center in a 10 g., 0.900 Silver ring, 34 mm. **Subject:** City of Hall in Tyrol **Obv:** Satellite mapping the city from outer space **Rev:** Depiction of the die face used to strike the 1486 guldiner coin **Edge:** Plain **Mint:** Vienna

| Date | Mintage | VF20 | XF40 | MS60 | MS63 | MS65 |
|---|---|---|---|---|---|---|
| 2003 Special Unc | 50,000 | — | — | — | — | 125 |

**KM# 3109 25 EURO**

17.15 g., Bi-Metallic 7.15g Niobium center in 10g, 0.900 Silver ring, 34 mm. **Subject:** Semmering Alpine Railway **Obv:** Modern and antique locomotives **Rev:** Steam train **Edge:** Plain **Mint:** Vienna

| Date | Mintage | VF20 | XF40 | MS60 | MS63 | MS65 |
|---|---|---|---|---|---|---|
| 2004 Special Unc | 50,000 | — | — | — | — | 100 |

**KM# 3119 25 EURO**

17.15 g., Bi-Metallic Purple color pure Niobium 7.15g center in 10g, 0.900 Silver ring, 34 mm. **Subject:** 50 Years Austrian Television **Obv:** The original test pattern of the 1950's **Rev:** World globe behind "rabbit ear" antenna; television developmental milestones from 7-1 o'clock **Edge:** Plain **Mint:** Vienna

| Date | Mintage | VF20 | XF40 | MS60 | MS63 | MS65 |
|---|---|---|---|---|---|---|
| 2005 Special Unc | 65,000 | — | — | — | — | 75.00 |

**KM# 3135 25 EURO**

17.15 g., Bi-Metallic Niobium 7.15g center in 10g, 0.900 Silver ring, 34 mm. **Subject:** European Satellite Navigation **Obv:** Austrian Mint's global location inscribed on a compass face **Rev:** Satellites in orbit around the world globe **Edge:** Plain **Mint:** Vienna

| Date | Mintage | VF20 | XF40 | MS60 | MS63 | MS65 |
|---|---|---|---|---|---|---|
| 2006 Special Unc | 65,000 | — | — | — | — | 75.00 |

**KM# 3147 25 EURO**

16.50 g., Bi-Metallic 6.5g Niobium center in 10g, 0.900 Silver ring, 34 mm. **Subject:** Austrian Aviation **Obv:** Interior view of modern cockpit **Rev:** Taube airplane flying above glider and pilot **Edge:** Plain **Mint:** Vienna

| Date | Mintage | VF20 | XF40 | MS60 | MS63 | MS65 |
|---|---|---|---|---|---|---|
| 2007 Special Unc | 65,000 | — | — | — | — | 75.00 |

**KM# 3158 25 EURO**

16.50 g., Bi-Metallic 6.5g Niobium center in 10g, 0.900 Silver ring, 34 mm. **Subject:** Carl Baron Auer von Welsbach, 150th Anniversary of Birth **Obv:** Lighting gas lamp before Vienna City Wall **Rev:** Head of Welsbach, development of light bulbs

| Date | Mintage | VF20 | XF40 | MS60 | MS63 | MS65 |
|---|---|---|---|---|---|---|
| 2008 Special Unc | 65,000 | — | — | — | — | 80.00 |

**KM# 3174 25 EURO**

16.50 g., Bi-Metallic 6.5g Niobium center in 10g, 0.900 silver ring, 34 mm. **Subject:** Year of Astronomy **Obv:** Galileo head and instruments **Rev:** Space exploration satellite **Mint:** Vienna

| Date | Mintage | VF20 | XF40 | MS60 | MS63 | MS65 |
|---|---|---|---|---|---|---|
| 2009 Special Unc | 65,000 | — | — | — | — | 80.00 |

**KM# 3189 25 EURO**

16.50 g., Bi-Metallic 6.5g Niobium center in 10g, 0.900 Silver ring, 34 mm. **Obv:** Tree and the 4 elements: earth, wind, water, and fire **Rev:** Solar panels, hydroelectric turbine, global thermal energy and wind turbine **Mint:** Vienna

| Date | Mintage | VF20 | XF40 | MS60 | MS63 | MS65 |
|---|---|---|---|---|---|---|
| 2010 Special Unc | 65,000 | — | — | — | — | 80.00 |

**KM# 3204 25 EURO**

16.50 g., Bi-Metallic 6.5g Niobium center in 10.0g, 0.900 Silver ring, 34 mm. **Subject:** Robotics **Rev:** Mars rover **Mint:** Vienna

| Date | Mintage | VF20 | XF40 | MS60 | MS63 | MS65 |
|---|---|---|---|---|---|---|
| 2011 Special Unc. | 65,000 | — | — | — | — | 80.00 |

**KM# 3212 25 EURO**

16.50 g., Bi-Metallic 6.5g Niobium center in 10.0g, 0.900 Silver ring., 34 mm. **Subject:** Bionics **Mint:** Vienna

| Date | Mintage | VF20 | XF40 | MS60 | MS63 | MS65 |
|---|---|---|---|---|---|---|
| 2012 Special Unc. | 65,000 | — | — | — | — | 75.00 |

**KM# 3217 25 EURO**

16.50 g., 0.900 Bi-Metallic 0.4774 oz. 6.5g Niobium center in 10.0g 0.900 Silver ring, 34 mm. **Subject:** Tunneling **Obv:** Tunnel boring machine and air vents **Rev:** 19th century tunnel worker and tunnel **Mint:** Vienna

| Date | Mintage | VF20 | XF40 | MS60 | MS63 | MS65 |
|---|---|---|---|---|---|---|
| 2013 Special Unc | 65,000 | — | — | — | — | 80.00 |

**KM# 3238 25 EURO**

16.50 g., Bi-Metallic Niobium center in .900 9g Silver ring, 34 mm. **Subject:** Cosmos **Mint:** Vienna

| Date | Mintage | VF20 | XF40 | MS60 | MS63 | MS65 |
|---|---|---|---|---|---|---|
| 2015 Special Unc. | 65,000 | — | — | — | — | 80.00 |

**KM# 3090 50 EURO**
10.14 g., 0.986 Gold 0.3214 oz. AGW, 22 mm. **Subject:** Saints Benedict and Scholastica **Obv:** St. Benedict and his sister St. Scholastica **Rev:** Monk copying a manuscript **Edge:** Reeded **Mint:** Vienna

| Date | Mintage | VF20 | XF40 | MS60 | MS63 | MS65 |
|---|---|---|---|---|---|---|
| 2002 | 50,000 | PF65 600 | | | | |

**KM# 3102 50 EURO**
10.14 g., 0.986 Gold 0.3214 oz. AGW, 22 mm. **Subject:** Christian Charity **Obv:** Nursing Sister with hospital patient **Rev:** The Good Samaritan **Edge:** Reeded **Mint:** Vienna

| Date | Mintage | VF20 | XF40 | MS60 | MS63 | MS65 |
|---|---|---|---|---|---|---|
| 2003 | 50,000 | PF65 600 | | | | |

**KM# 3110 50 EURO**
10.14 g., 0.986 Gold 0.3214 oz. AGW, 22 mm. **Subject:** Great Composers - Joseph Haydn (1732-1809) **Obv:** Esterhazy Palace **Rev:** Bust 3/4 right **Mint:** Vienna

| Date | Mintage | VF20 | XF40 | MS60 | MS63 | MS65 |
|---|---|---|---|---|---|---|
| 2004 | 50,000 | PF65 600 | | | | |

**KM# 3118 50 EURO**
10.14 g., 0.986 Gold 0.3214 oz. AGW, 22 mm. **Subject:** Great Composers - Ludwig Van Beethoven (1770-1827) **Obv:** Lobkowitz Palace above value and document **Rev:** Bust 3/4 facing, dates at left **Mint:** Vienna

| Date | Mintage | VF20 | XF40 | MS60 | MS63 | MS65 |
|---|---|---|---|---|---|---|
| 2005 | 50,000 | PF65 600 | | | | |

**KM# 3130 50 EURO**
10.14 g., 0.986 Gold 0.3214 oz. AGW, 22 mm. **Subject:** Great Composers - Mozart **Obv:** Mozart's birthplace, denomination below **Rev:** Leopold and Wolfgang Mozart **Mint:** Vienna

| Date | Mintage | VF20 | XF40 | MS60 | MS63 | MS65 |
|---|---|---|---|---|---|---|
| 2006 | 50,000 | PF65 600 | | | | |

**KM# 3138 50 EURO**
10.14 g., 0.986 Gold 0.3214 oz. AGW, 22 mm. **Obv:** Gerard Van Swieten holding book and facing left **Rev:** Akademie der Wissenschaften building **Mint:** Vienna

| Date | Mintage | VF20 | XF40 | MS60 | MS63 | MS65 |
|---|---|---|---|---|---|---|
| 2007 | 50,000 | PF65 600 | | | | |

**KM# 3153 50 EURO**
10.14 g., 0.986 Gold 0.3214 oz. AGW, 22 mm. **Subject:** Ignaz Philipp Sammelweis - Personal Hygiene **Obv:** Bust of Sammelweis 3/4 right, staff of Aesculapius at lower right **Obv. Legend:** REPUBLIK ÖSTERREICH **Rev:** Vienna General Hospital, Sammelweis helping patient wash at lower right **Rev. Legend:** ALLGEMEINES KRANKENHAUS WEIN **Mint:** Vienna

| Date | Mintage | VF20 | XF40 | MS60 | MS63 | MS65 |
|---|---|---|---|---|---|---|
| 2008 | 50,000 | PF65 600 | | | | |

**KM# 3171 50 EURO**
10.14 g., 0.986 Gold 0.3214 oz. AGW, 22 mm. **Subject:** Theodor Billroth **Obv:** Bust and Aesculapius staff **Rev:** Operation scene

| Date | Mintage | VF20 | XF40 | MS60 | MS63 | MS65 |
|---|---|---|---|---|---|---|
| 2009 | 50,000 | PF65 600 | | | | |

**KM# 3194 50 EURO**
10.14 g., 0.986 Gold 0.3214 oz. AGW, 22 mm. **Subject:** Baron Clemens von Pirquet **Obv:** Portrait of von Pirquet **Rev:** Facade of Children's Clinic of Vienna **Mint:** Vienna

| Date | Mintage | VF20 | XF40 | MS60 | MS63 | MS65 |
|---|---|---|---|---|---|---|
| 2010 | 50,000 | PF65 600 | | | | |

**KM# 3202 50 EURO**
10.14 g., 0.986 Gold 0.3214 oz. AGW, 22 mm. **Subject:** Joanneum Museum **Obv:** Exterior of Art Museum **Rev:** Armor display **Mint:** Vienna

| Date | Mintage | VF20 | XF40 | MS60 | MS63 | MS65 |
|---|---|---|---|---|---|---|
| 2011 | 50,000 | PF65 600 | | | | |

**KM# 3213 50 EURO**
10.14 g., 0.986 Gold 0.3214 oz. AGW, 22 mm. **Series:** Klimt and his woman **Subject:** Adele Bloch Bauer **Obv:** Portrait of artist **Rev:** Female subject from painting **Mint:** Vienna

| Date | Mintage | VF20 | XF40 | MS60 | MS63 | MS65 |
|---|---|---|---|---|---|---|
| 2012 | 30,000 | PF65 675 | | | | |

**KM# 3218 50 EURO**
10.11 g., 0.986 Gold 0.3205 oz. AGW, 22 mm. **Series:** Klimt and his Women **Subject:** The Expectation **Mint:** Vienna

| Date | Mintage | VF20 | XF40 | MS60 | MS63 | MS65 |
|---|---|---|---|---|---|---|
| 2013 | 30,000 | PF65 675 | | | | |

**KM# 3241 50 EURO**
10.14 g., 0.986 Gold 0.3214 oz. AGW, 22 mm. **Subject:** Klimt and his Women **Rev:** Medicine **Mint:** Vienna

| Date | Mintage | VF20 | XF40 | MS60 | MS63 | MS65 |
|---|---|---|---|---|---|---|
| 2015 | 30,000 | PF65 675 | | | | |

**KM# 3100 100 EURO**
16.23 g., 0.986 Gold 0.5144 oz. AGW, 30 mm. **Subject:** Raphael Donner **Obv:** Portrait in front of building **Rev:** Providentia Fountain **Edge:** Reeded **Mint:** Vienna

| Date | Mintage | VF20 | XF40 | MS60 | MS63 | MS65 |
|---|---|---|---|---|---|---|
| 2002 | 30,000 | PF65 900 | | | | |

**KM# 3108 100 EURO**
16.23 g., 0.986 Gold 0.5144 oz. AGW, 30 mm. **Obv:** Gustav Klimt standing **Rev:** Klimt's painting "The Kiss **Edge:** Reeded **Mint:** Vienna

| Date | Mintage | VF20 | XF40 | MS60 | MS63 | MS65 |
|---|---|---|---|---|---|---|
| 2003 | 30,000 | PF65 900 | | | | |

**KM# 3116 100 EURO**
16.23 g., 0.986 Gold 0.5144 oz. AGW, 30 mm. **Obv:** Secession Exhibit Hall in Vienna **Rev:** Knight in armor, "strength" with two women, "ambition and sympathy **Mint:** Vienna

| Date | Mintage | VF20 | XF40 | MS60 | MS63 | MS65 |
|---|---|---|---|---|---|---|
| 2004 | 30,000 | PF65 900 | | | | |

**KM# 3128 100 EURO**
16.23 g., 0.986 Gold 0.5144 oz. AGW, 30 mm. **Subject:** St. Leopold's Church at Steinhof **Obv:** Domed church building, denomination below **Rev:** Two angels flank stained glass portrait **Mint:** Vienna

| Date | Mintage | VF20 | XF40 | MS60 | MS63 | MS65 |
|---|---|---|---|---|---|---|
| 2005 | 30,000 | PF65 900 | | | | |

**KM# 3136 100 EURO**
16.23 g., 0.986 Gold 0.5144 oz. AGW, 30 mm. **Subject:** Vienna's River Gate Park **Obv:** Bridge over river scene **Rev:** One of two "sculpted ladies" flanking the park entrance **Mint:** Vienna

| Date | Mintage | VF20 | XF40 | MS60 | MS63 | MS65 |
|---|---|---|---|---|---|---|
| 2006 | 30,000 | PF65 900 | | | | |

**KM# 3155 100 EURO**
16.23 g., 0.986 Gold 0.5144 oz. AGW, 30 mm. **Obv:** Building at Linke Wienzeile Nr 38 by architect Otto Koloman Wagner **Rev:** Ornate elevator and stairwell

| Date | Mintage | VF20 | XF40 | MS60 | MS63 | MS65 |
|---|---|---|---|---|---|---|
| 2007 | 30,000 | **PF65** 900 | | | | |

**KM# 3160 100 EURO**
16.23 g., 0.986 Gold 0.5144 oz. AGW, 30 mm. **Series:** Crowns of the Habsburgs **Obv:** Crown of the Holy Roman Emperor set upon coronation robe **Rev:** Otto I seated facing and old St. Peter's Bastilica, Rome **Mint:** Vienna

| Date | Mintage | VF20 | XF40 | MS60 | MS63 | MS65 |
|---|---|---|---|---|---|---|
| 2008 | 30,000 | **PF65** 900 | | | | |

**KM# 3181 100 EURO**
16.23 g., 0.986 Gold 0.5144 oz. AGW, 30 mm. **Series:** Crowns of the Habsburgs **Subject:** Archducal crown of Austria **Obv:** Crown resting on pillow **Rev:** Procession of the crown, orb and sceptre, Plague memorial column in background **Mint:** Vienna

| Date | Mintage | VF20 | XF40 | MS60 | MS63 | MS65 |
|---|---|---|---|---|---|---|
| 2009 | 30,000 | **PF65** 800 | | | | |

**KM# 3191 100 EURO**
16.23 g., 0.986 Gold 0.5144 oz. AGW, 30 mm. **Series:** Crowns of the Habsburgs **Subject:** St. Stephen's Hungarian Crown **Obv:** Crown of St. Stephen **Rev:** Naria Theresa on horseback **Mint:** Vienna

| Date | Mintage | VF20 | XF40 | MS60 | MS63 | MS65 |
|---|---|---|---|---|---|---|
| 2010 | 30,000 | **PF65** 900 | | | | |

**KM# 3203 100 EURO**
16.23 g., 0.986 Gold 0.5144 oz. AGW, 30 mm. **Series:** Crowns of the Hapsburgs **Subject:** Crown of St. Wenceslas **Mint:** Vienna

| Date | Mintage | VF20 | XF40 | MS60 | MS63 | MS65 |
|---|---|---|---|---|---|---|
| 2011 | 30,000 | **PF65** 1,000 | | | | |

**KM# 3214 100 EURO**
16.23 g., 0.986 Gold 0.5144 oz. AGW, 30 mm. **Series:** Crowns of the hapsburgs **Obv:** Imperial Crown of Austria **Rev:** Emperor Franz Joseph I **Mint:** Vienna

| Date | Mintage | VF20 | XF40 | MS60 | MS63 | MS65 |
|---|---|---|---|---|---|---|
| 2012 | 30,000 | **PF65** 1,000 | | | | |

**KM# 3225 100 EURO**
16.23 g., 0.986 Gold 0.5144 oz. AGW, 30 mm. **Series:** Austrian Wildlife **Subject:** Red Deer **Mint:** Vienna

| Date | Mintage | VF20 | XF40 | MS60 | MS63 | MS65 |
|---|---|---|---|---|---|---|
| 2013 | 30,000 | **PF65** 900 | | | | |

## EURO BULLION COINAGE

Philharmonic Issues

**KM# 3159 1-1/2 EURO**
31.10 g., 0.999 Silver 0.999 oz. ASW, 37 mm. **Obv:** Golden Concert Hall **Rev:** Bouquet of Instruments **Edge:** Plain **Mint:** Vienna

| Date | Mintage | VF20 | XF40 | MS60 | MS63 | MS65 |
|---|---|---|---|---|---|---|
| 2008 | 7,800,000 | — | — | — | 19.00 | 21.00 |
| 2009 | 9,014,800 | — | — | — | 19.00 | 21.00 |
| 2010 | 11,358,200 | — | — | — | 19.00 | 21.00 |
| 2011 | 17,873,700 | — | — | — | 19.00 | 21.00 |
| 2012 | 8,769,200 | — | — | — | 19.00 | 21.00 |
| 2013 | — | — | — | — | 19.00 | 21.00 |

**KM# 3092 10 EURO**
3.12 g., 0.9999 Gold 0.1003 oz. AGW, 16 mm. **Subject:** Vienna Philharmonic **Obv:** The Golden Hall organ **Rev:** Musical instruments **Edge:** Segmented reeding **Mint:** Vienna

| Date | Mintage | VF20 | XF40 | MS60 | MS63 | MS65 |
|---|---|---|---|---|---|---|
| 2002 | 75,789 | — | — | — | — | 144 |
| 2003 | 59,654 | — | — | — | — | 144 |
| 2004 | 67,994 | — | — | — | — | 144 |
| 2005 | 62,071 | — | — | — | — | 144 |
| 2006 | 39,892 | — | — | — | — | 144 |
| 2007 | 76,325 | — | — | — | — | 144 |
| 2008 | 176,400 | — | — | — | — | 144 |
| 2009 | 437,700 | — | — | — | — | 144 |
| 2010 | 226,700 | — | — | — | — | 144 |
| 2011 | 268,200 | — | — | — | — | 144 |
| 2012 | 176,300 | — | — | — | — | 144 |
| 2013 | — | — | — | — | — | 144 |

**KM# 3093 25 EURO**
7.78 g., 0.9999 Gold 0.250 oz. AGW, 22 mm. **Subject:** Vienna Philharmonic **Obv:** The Golden Hall organ **Rev:** Musical instruments **Edge:** Segmented reeding **Mint:** Vienna

| Date | Mintage | VF20 | XF40 | MS60 | MS63 | MS65 |
|---|---|---|---|---|---|---|
| 2002 | 40,807 | — | — | — | — | 349 |
| 2003 | 34,019 | — | — | — | — | 349 |
| 2004 | 32,449 | — | — | — | — | 349 |
| 2005 | 32,817 | — | — | — | — | 349 |
| 2006 | 29,609 | — | — | — | — | 349 |
| 2007 | 34,631 | — | — | — | — | 349 |
| 2008 | 97,100 | — | — | — | — | 349 |
| 2009 | 172,000 | — | — | — | — | 349 |
| 2010 | 84,900 | — | — | — | — | 349 |
| 2011 | 102,000 | — | — | — | — | 349 |
| 2012 | 64,300 | — | — | — | — | 349 |
| 2013 | — | — | — | — | — | 349 |
| 2014 Proof sets only | 5,000 | **PF65** 349 | | | | |

**KM# 3094 50 EURO**
15.55 g., 0.9999 Gold 0.500 oz. AGW, 28 mm. **Subject:** Vienna Philharmonic **Obv:** The Golden Hall organ **Rev:** Musical instruments **Edge:** Segmented reeding **Mint:** Vienna

| Date | Mintage | VF20 | XF40 | MS60 | MS63 | MS65 |
|---|---|---|---|---|---|---|
| 2002 | 40,922 | — | — | — | — | 686 |
| 2003 | 26,848 | — | — | — | — | 686 |
| 2004 | 24,269 | — | — | — | — | 686 |
| 2005 | 21,049 | — | — | — | — | 686 |
| 2006 | 20,085 | — | — | — | — | 686 |
| 2007 | 25,091 | — | — | — | — | 686 |
| 2008 | 73,800 | — | — | — | — | 686 |
| 2009 | 92,300 | — | — | — | — | 686 |
| 2010 | 56,600 | — | — | — | — | 686 |
| 2011 | 77,500 | — | — | — | — | 686 |
| 2012 | 49,500 | — | — | — | — | 686 |
| 2013 | — | — | — | — | — | 686 |

**KM# 3095 100 EURO**
31.12 g., 0.9999 Gold 1.0004 oz. AGW, 37 mm. **Subject:** Vienna Philharmonic **Obv:** The Golden Hall organ **Rev:** Musical instruments **Edge:** Segmented reeding **Mint:** Vienna

| Date | Mintage | VF20 | XF40 | MS60 | MS63 | MS65 |
|---|---|---|---|---|---|---|
| 2002 | 164,105 | — | — | — | — | 1,321 |
| 2003 | 179,881 | — | — | — | — | 1,321 |
| 2004 | 176,319 | — | — | — | — | 1,321 |
| 2005 | 158,564 | — | — | — | — | 1,321 |
| 2006 | 82,174 | — | — | — | — | 1,321 |
| 2007 | 108,675 | — | — | — | — | 1,321 |
| 2008 | 715,800 | — | — | — | — | 1,321 |
| 2009 | 835,700 | — | — | — | — | 1,321 |
| 2010 | 501,800 | — | — | — | — | 1,321 |
| 2011 | 586,700 | — | — | — | — | 1,321 |
| 2012 | 341,400 | — | — | — | — | 1,321 |
| 2013 | — | — | — | — | — | 1,321 |
| 2013 | | | | | | |
| 2014 Proof set only | 5,000 | **PF65** 1,398 | | | | |

**KM# 3182 2000 EURO**
622.10 g., 0.9999 Gold 19.999 oz. AGW, 74 mm. **Subject:** Vienna Philharmonic **Obv:** The Golden Hall Organ **Rev:** Musical instruments **Edge:** Reeded **Mint:** Vienna

| Date | Mintage | VF20 | XF40 | MS60 | MS63 | MS65 |
|---|---|---|---|---|---|---|
| 2009 | 6,027 | — | — | — | — | 26,669 |

**KM# 3123 100000 EURO**
31103.50 g., 0.9999 Gold 999.900 oz. AGW, 370 mm. **Obv:** The Golden Hall organ **Rev:** Musical instruments **Edge:** Reeded **Mint:** Vienna

| Date | Mintage | VF20 | XF40 | MS60 | MS63 | MS65 |
|---|---|---|---|---|---|---|
| 2004 Proof | 15 | — | — | — | — | 1,333,367 |

## MINT SETS

| KM# | Date | Mintage | Identification | Issue Price | Mkt Val |
|---|---|---|---|---|---|
| MS10 | 2001 (6) | 75,000 | KM#2878, 2885, 2886, 2889a, 2918, 3075 | 25.00 | 40.00 |
| MS11 | 2002 (8) | 100,000 | KM#3082-3089, Euro | 22.50 | 25.00 |
| MS12 | 2003 (8) | 125,000 | KM#3082-3089, Mozart | 22.50 | 25.00 |
| MS13 | 2004 (8) | 100,000 | KM#3082-3089, von Suttner | — | 25.00 |
| MS14 | 2005 (8) | 100,000 | KM#3082-3088, 3124, State treaty | — | 25.00 |
| MS15 | 2006 (8) | 100,000 | KM#3082-3089, St. Stephan's Cathedral | — | 35.00 |
| MS16 | 2007 (8) | 75,000 | KM#3082-3088, 3150, Treaty of Rome | — | 25.00 |
| MS17 | 2008 (8) | 50,000 | KM#3082-3084, 3139-3143, European Map | — | 35.00 |
| MS18 | 2009 (8) | 75,000 | KM#3082-3084, 3139-3142, 3175 | — | 25.00 |
| MS19 | 2010 (8) | 50,000 | KM#3082-3084, 3139-3143 | — | 35.00 |
| MS20 | 2011 (8) | 50,000 | KM#3082-3084, 3139-3143 | — | 35.00 |
| MS21 | 2012 (8) | 50,000 | KM#3082-3084, 3139-3142, 3205 | — | 32.00 |
| MS22 | 2012 (8) | Inc. Above | KM#3082-3084, 3139-3142, 3205 (Baby Mint Set) | — | 35.00 |

## PROOF SETS

| KM# | Date | Mintage | Identification | Issue Price | Mkt Val |
|---|---|---|---|---|---|
| PS53 | 2002 (8) | 10,000 | KM#3082-3089 | 85.00 | 485 |
| PS54 | 2003 (8) | 25,000 | KM#3082-3089 | 85.00 | 95.00 |
| PS55 | 2004 (8) | 20,000 | KM#3082-3089 | — | 105 |
| PS56 | 2005 (8) | 20,000 | KM#3082-3088, 3124 | — | 110 |
| PS57 | 2006 (8) | 20,000 | KM#3082-3089 | — | 110 |
| PS58 | 2007 (8) | 20,000 | KM#3082-3088, 3150 | — | 110 |
| PS59 | 2008 (8) | 15,000 | KM#3082-3084, 3139-3143 | — | 120 |
| PS60 | 2009 (8) | 15,000 | KM#3082-3084, 3139-3142, 3175 | — | 120 |
| PS61 | 2010 (8) | 15,000 | KM#3082-3084, 3139-3143 | — | 110 |
| PS62 | 2011 (8) | 15,000 | KM#3082-3084, 3139-3143 | — | 110 |
| PS63 | 2012 (8) | 10,000 | KM#3082-3084, 3139-3142, 3205 | — | 110 |

# AZERBAIJAN

The Republic of Azerbaijan (formerly Azerbaijan S.S.R.) includes the Nakhichevan Autonomous Republic. Situated in the eastern area of Transcaucasia, it is bordered in the west by Armenia, in the north by Georgia and Dagestan, to the east by the Caspian Sea and to the south by Iran. It has an area of 33,430 sq. mi. (86,600 sq. km.) and a population of 7.8 million. Capital: Baku. The area is rich in mineral deposits of aluminum, copper, iron, lead, salt and zinc, with oil as its leading industry. Agriculture and livestock follow in importance.

**MONETARY SYSTEM**
100 Qapik = 1 Manat

## REPUBLIC

### DECIMAL COINAGE

**KM# 39 QAPIK**
2.80 g., Copper Plated Steel, 16.25 mm. **Obv:** Map above value **Rev:** Value and musical instruments **Edge:** Plain

| Date | Mintage | VF20 | XF40 | MS60 | MS63 | MS65 |
|---|---|---|---|---|---|---|
| ND (2006) | — | — | 0.60 | 1.00 | 1.20 | 2.00 |

**KM# 40 3 QAPIK**
3.45 g., Copper Plated Steel, 18 mm. **Obv:** Map above value **Rev:** Value above books **Edge:** Grooved

| Date | Mintage | VF20 | XF40 | MS60 | MS63 | MS65 |
|---|---|---|---|---|---|---|
| ND (2006) | — | — | 0.75 | 1.20 | 1.50 | 2.50 |

**KM# 41 5 QAPIK**
4.85 g., Copper Plated Steel, 19.75 mm. **Obv:** Map above value **Rev:** The Maiden Tower, Baku, above value **Edge:** Reeded

| Date | Mintage | VF20 | XF40 | MS60 | MS63 | MS65 |
|---|---|---|---|---|---|---|
| ND (2006) | — | — | 0.80 | 1.25 | 1.65 | 2.75 |

**KM# 42 10 QAPIK**
5.25 g., Brass Plated Steel, 22.25 mm. **Obv:** Map above value **Rev:** Value and Military Helmet, Symbolic of desire to regain Nagorno-Karabakh **Edge:** Notched

| Date | Mintage | VF20 | XF40 | MS60 | MS63 | MS65 |
|---|---|---|---|---|---|---|
| ND (2006) | — | — | 0.85 | 1.30 | 1.75 | 3.00 |
| 2010 | — | — | — | — | — | — |

**KM# 43 20 QAPIK**
6.60 g., Brass Plated Steel, 24.25 mm. **Obv:** Map above value **Rev:** Value and spiral staircase **Edge:** Segmented reeding

| Date | Mintage | VF20 | XF40 | MS60 | MS63 | MS65 |
|---|---|---|---|---|---|---|
| ND (2006) | — | — | 1.25 | 1.85 | 2.50 | 4.00 |

**KM# 44 50 QAPIK**
7.70 g., Bi-Metallic Brass plated Steel center in Stainless Steel ring, 25.5 mm. **Obv:** Map above value **Rev:** Two oil wells **Edge:** Reeded and lettered

| Date | Mintage | VF20 | XF40 | MS60 | MS63 | MS65 |
|---|---|---|---|---|---|---|
| ND (2006) | — | — | 1.50 | 2.25 | 3.00 | 5.00 |

**KM# 37 50 MANAT**
28.34 g., 0.925 Silver 0.8428 oz. ASW, 38.6 mm. **Subject:** Heydar Aliyev **Obv:** National map **Rev:** Bust 3/4 right **Edge:** Reeded

| Date | Mintage | VF20 | XF40 | MS60 | MS63 | MS65 |
|---|---|---|---|---|---|---|
| 2004 | 2,000 | PF65 100 | | | | |

**KM# 48 50 MANAT**
28.28 g., 0.925 Silver 0.841 oz. ASW, 38.6 mm. **Subject:** FIFA World Cup, 2006 **Edge:** Plain

| Date | Mintage | VF20 | XF40 | MS60 | MS63 | MS65 |
|---|---|---|---|---|---|---|
| 2004 | 200 | PF65 175 | | | | |

**KM# 46 100 MANAT**
39.94 g., 0.9167 Gold 1.1771 oz. AGW **Subject:** Heydar Aliyev **Obv:** National map **Rev:** Bust 3/4 right **Edge:** Reeded

| Date | Mintage | VF20 | XF40 | MS60 | MS63 | MS65 |
|---|---|---|---|---|---|---|
| 2004 | 1,000 | PF63 2,000 | PF65 2,250 | | | |

**KM# 47 500 MANAT**
50.00 g., 0.999 Platinum 1.6059 oz. APW **Subject:** Heydar Aliyev **Obv:** National map **Rev:** Bust 3/4 right **Edge:** Reeded

| Date | Mintage | VF20 | XF40 | MS60 | MS63 | MS65 |
|---|---|---|---|---|---|---|
| 2004 | 100 | PF65 3,500 | | | | |

## MINT SETS

| KM# | Date | Mintage | Identification | Issue Price | Mkt Val |
|---|---|---|---|---|---|
| MS1 | 2006 (6) | — | KM#39-44. | — | 150 |

# THE BAHAMAS

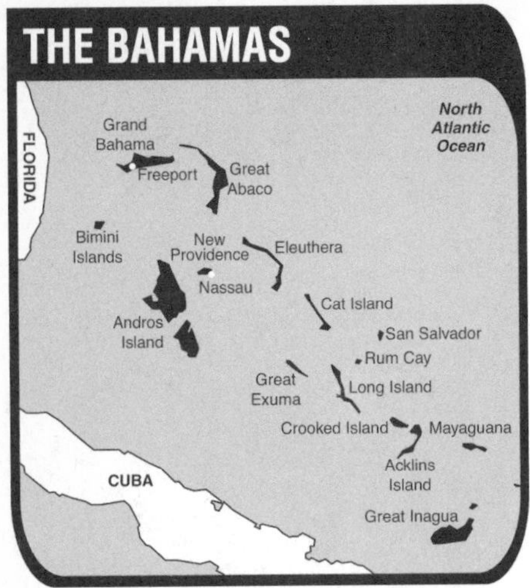


The Commonwealth of the Bahamas is an archipelago of about 3,000 islands, cays and rocks located in the Atlantic Ocean east of Florida and north of Cuba. The total land area of the 800 mile (1,287 km.) long chain of islands is 5,382 sq. mi. (13,935 sq. km.). They have a population of 302,000. Capital: Nassau. The Bahamas import most of their food and manufactured products and export cement, refined oil, pulpwood and lobsters. Tourism is the principal industry. The Bahamas is a member of the Commonwealth of Nations. Elizabeth II is Head of State as Queen of The Bahamas.

**RULER**
British

## COMMONWEALTH

### DECIMAL COINAGE

100 Cents = 1 Dollar

**KM# 59a CENT**
2.50 g., Copper Plated Zinc, 19 mm. **Ruler:** Elizabeth II **Obv:** National arms above date **Obv. Legend:** COMMONWEALTH OF THE BAHAMAS **Rev:** Starfish, value at top **Edge:** Plain

| Date | Mintage | VF20 | XF40 | MS60 | MS63 | MS65 |
|---|---|---|---|---|---|---|
| 2001 | — | — | — | 0.10 | 0.25 | 0.75 |
| 2004 | — | — | — | 0.10 | 0.25 | 0.75 |

**KM# 218.1 CENT**
2.50 g., Copper Plated Zinc, 19 mm. **Ruler:** Elizabeth II **Obv:** National arms, date below **Rev:** Three starfish

| Date | Mintage | VF20 | XF40 | MS60 | MS63 | MS65 |
|---|---|---|---|---|---|---|
| 2006 | — | — | — | — | 0.25 | 0.75 |
| 2007 | — | — | — | — | 0.25 | 0.75 |

**KM# 218.2 CENT**
1.75 g., Copper Plated Zinc, 17 mm. **Ruler:** Elizabeth II **Obv:** National arms, date below **Rev:** Three starfish

| Date | Mintage | VF20 | XF40 | MS60 | MS63 | MS65 |
|---|---|---|---|---|---|---|
| 2009 | — | — | — | — | 0.25 | 0.75 |
| 2014 | — | — | — | — | 0.25 | 0.75 |

**KM# 60 5 CENTS**
3.94 g., Copper-Nickel, 21 mm. **Ruler:** Elizabeth II **Obv:** National arms above date **Obv. Legend:** COMMONWEALTH OF THE BAHAMAS **Rev:** Pineapple above garland divides value at top **Edge:** Plain

| Date | Mintage | VF20 | XF40 | MS60 | MS63 | MS65 |
|---|---|---|---|---|---|---|
| 2004 | — | — | — | 0.10 | 0.25 | 0.75 |
| 2005 | — | — | — | 0.10 | 0.25 | 0.75 |
| 2006 | — | — | — | 0.10 | 0.25 | 0.75 |

**KM# 61 10 CENTS**
5.13 g., Copper-Nickel, 23.5 mm. **Ruler:** Elizabeth II **Obv:** National arms, date below, within beaded circle **Rev:** Two bonefish above denomination **Edge:** Plain **Shape:** Scalloped

| Date | Mintage | VF20 | XF40 | MS60 | MS63 | MS65 |
|---|---|---|---|---|---|---|
| 2005 | — | — | — | 0.25 | 0.60 | 0.80 |

**KM# 219 10 CENTS**
5.54 g., Copper-Nickel, 23.5 mm. **Ruler:** Elizabeth II **Obv:** National arms, date below **Rev:** Two fish, value above **Shape:** Scalloped

| Date | Mintage | VF20 | XF40 | MS60 | MS63 | MS65 |
|---|---|---|---|---|---|---|
| 2007 | — | — | — | 0.25 | 0.60 | 0.80 |

**KM# 62 15 CENTS**
6.50 g., Copper-Nickel, 25 mm. **Ruler:** Elizabeth II **Obv:** National arms above date **Rev:** Hibiscus, value divided at bottom **Edge:** Plain **Shape:** 4-sided

| Date | Mintage | VF20 | XF40 | MS60 | MS63 | MS65 |
|---|---|---|---|---|---|---|
| 2005 | — | — | — | 0.20 | 0.50 | 1.50 |

**KM# 63.2 25 CENTS**
5.75 g., Copper-Nickel, 24.26 mm. **Ruler:** Elizabeth II **Obv:** National arms, date below **Rev:** Bahamian Sloop, value above **Edge:** Reeded

| Date | Mintage | VF20 | XF40 | MS60 | MS63 | MS65 |
|---|---|---|---|---|---|---|
| 2005 | — | — | — | 0.30 | 0.50 | 1.50 |

**KM# 217 DOLLAR**
Silver and gold plated ring **Ruler:** Elizabeth II **Subject:** Queen Mother's 100th Birthday

| Date | Mintage | VF20 | XF40 | MS60 | MS63 | MS65 |
|---|---|---|---|---|---|---|
| 2002 | — | PF65 50.00 | | | | |

# BAHRAIN

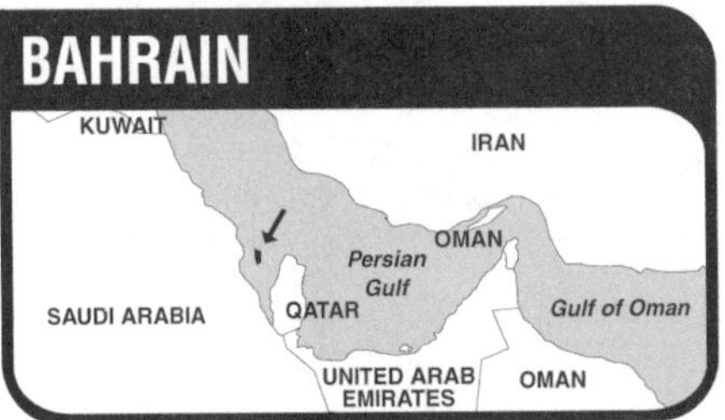


The Kingdom of Bahrain, a group of islands in the Persian Gulf off Saudi Arabia, has an area of 268 sq. mi. (622 sq. km.) and a population of 618,000. Capital: Manama. Prior to the depression of the 1930's, the economy was based on pearl fishing. Petroleum and aluminum industries and transit trade are the vital factors in the economy today.

**RULERS**

**Al Khalifa Dynasty**
Hamed Bin Isa, 1999-

**TITLES**

دولة البحرين

State of Bahrain

مملكة البحرين

Kingdom of Bahrain

## KINGDOM

### STANDARD COINAGE

**KM# 30 5 FILS**
2.50 g., Brass, 19 mm. **Ruler:** Hamed Bin Isa **Obv:** Palm tree **Obv. Legend:** KINGDOM OF BAHRAIN **Rev:** Denomination in chain link border **Edge:** Plain

| Date | Mintage | VF20 | XF40 | MS60 | MS63 | MS65 |
|---|---|---|---|---|---|---|
| AH1426-2005 | — | — | — | 0.50 | 0.75 | 1.25 |
| AH1428-2007 | — | — | — | 0.50 | 0.75 | 1.25 |
| AH1430-2009 | — | — | — | 0.50 | 0.75 | 1.25 |
| AH1431-2010 | — | — | — | 0.50 | 0.75 | 1.25 |

**KM# 30a 5 FILS**
2.50 g., 0.925 Silver 0.0743 oz. ASW, 19 mm. **Ruler:** Hamed Bin Isa **Obv:** Palm tree **Rev:** Denomination in chain link border

| Date | Mintage | VF20 | XF40 | MS60 | MS63 | MS65 |
|---|---|---|---|---|---|---|
| AH1431-2010 | 500 | PF65 15.00 | | | | |

**KM# 28 10 FILS**
3.35 g., Brass, 21 mm. **Ruler:** Hamed Bin Isa **Obv:** Palm tree **Obv. Legend:** KINGDOM OF BAHRAIN **Rev:** Denomination in chain link border **Edge:** Plain

| Date | Mintage | VF20 | XF40 | MS60 | MS63 | MS65 |
|---|---|---|---|---|---|---|
| AH1423-2002 | — | — | — | 1.00 | 1.50 | 2.50 |
| AH1424-2004 | — | — | — | 1.00 | 1.50 | 2.50 |
| AH1426-2005 | — | — | — | 1.00 | 1.50 | 2.50 |
| AH1428-2007 | — | — | — | 1.00 | 1.50 | 2.50 |
| AH1429-2008 | — | — | — | 1.00 | 1.50 | 2.50 |
| AH1430-2009 | — | — | — | 1.00 | 1.50 | 2.50 |
| AH1431-2010 | — | — | — | 1.00 | 1.50 | 2.50 |
| AH1432-2011 | — | — | — | 1.00 | 1.50 | 2.50 |

**KM# 28a 10 FILS**
3.35 g., 0.925 Silver 0.0996 oz. ASW, 21 mm. **Ruler:** Hamed Bin Isa **Obv:** Palm tree **Rev:** Denomination in chain link border

| Date | Mintage | VF20 | XF40 | MS60 | MS63 | MS65 |
|---|---|---|---|---|---|---|
| AH1431-2010 | 500 | PF65 25.00 | | | | |

**KM# 24 25 FILS**
3.50 g., Copper-Nickel, 20 mm. **Ruler:** Hamed Bin Isa **Obv:** Ancient painting **Obv. Legend:** KINGDOM OF BAHRAIN **Rev:** Denomination in chain link border **Edge:** Reeded

| Date | Mintage | VF20 | XF40 | MS60 | MS63 | MS65 |
|---|---|---|---|---|---|---|
| AH1423-2002 | — | — | — | 1.00 | 2.00 | 3.00 |
| AH1426-2005 | — | — | — | 1.00 | 2.00 | 3.00 |
| AH1428-2007 | — | — | — | 1.00 | 2.00 | 3.00 |
| AH1429-2008 | — | — | — | 1.00 | 2.00 | 3.00 |
| AH1430-2009 | — | — | — | 1.00 | 2.00 | 3.00 |

**KM# 24a 25 FILS**
3.50 g., 0.925 Silver 0.1041 oz. ASW, 20 mm. **Ruler:** Hamed Bin Isa **Obv:** Ancient painting **Rev:** Denomination in chain link border

| Date | Mintage | VF20 | XF40 | MS60 | MS63 | MS65 |
|---|---|---|---|---|---|---|
| AH1431-2010 | 500 | PF65 25.00 | | | | |

**KM# 25 50 FILS**
4.50 g., Copper-Nickel, 22 mm. **Ruler:** Hamed Bin Isa **Subject:** Kingdom **Obv:** Stylized sailboats **Obv. Legend:** KINGDOM OF BAHRAIN **Rev:** Denomination in chain link border **Edge:** Reeded

| Date | Mintage | VF20 | XF40 | MS60 | MS63 | MS65 |
|---|---|---|---|---|---|---|
| AH1423-2002 | — | — | — | 1.00 | 2.00 | 3.00 |
| AH1426-2005 | — | — | — | 1.00 | 2.00 | 3.00 |

| Date | Mintage | VF20 | XF40 | MS60 | MS63 | MS65 |
|---|---|---|---|---|---|---|
| AH1428-2007 | — | — | — | 1.00 | 2.00 | 3.00 |
| AH1429-2008 | — | — | — | 1.00 | 2.00 | 3.00 |
| AH1430-2009 | — | — | — | 1.00 | 2.00 | 3.00 |
| AH1431-2010 | — | — | — | 1.00 | 2.00 | 3.00 |

### KM# 25a 50 FILS
4.50 g., 0.925 Silver 0.1338 oz. ASW, 22 mm. **Ruler:** Hamed Bin Isa **Obv:** Stylized sailboats **Rev:** Denomination in chain link border

| Date | Mintage | VF20 | XF40 | MS60 | MS63 | MS65 |
|---|---|---|---|---|---|---|
| AH1431-2010 | 500 | **PF65** 25.00 | | | | |

### KM# 20 100 FILS
6.00 g., Bi-Metallic Copper-Nickel center in Brass ring, 24 mm. **Obv:** Coat of arms within circle, dates at either side **Obv. Legend:** STATE OF BAHRAIN **Rev:** Numeric denomination back of boxed denomination within circle, chain surrounds **Edge:** Reeded

| Date | Mintage | VF20 | XF40 | MS60 | MS63 | MS65 |
|---|---|---|---|---|---|---|
| AH1422-2001 | — | — | — | 1.50 | 2.50 | 5.00 |

### KM# 26 100 FILS
6.00 g., Bi-Metallic Copper-Nickel center in Brass ring, 24 mm. **Ruler:** Hamed Bin Isa **Subject:** Kingdom **Obv:** National arms **Obv. Legend:** KINGDOM OF BAHRAIN **Rev:** Denomination in chain link border **Edge:** Reeded

| Date | Mintage | VF20 | XF40 | MS60 | MS63 | MS65 |
|---|---|---|---|---|---|---|
| AH1423-2002 | — | — | — | 1.50 | 2.50 | 5.00 |
| AH1425-2004 | — | — | — | 1.50 | 2.50 | 5.00 |
| AH1426-2005 | — | — | — | 1.50 | 2.50 | 5.00 |
| AH1427-2006 | — | — | — | 1.50 | 2.50 | 5.00 |
| AH1428-2007 | — | — | — | 1.50 | 2.50 | 5.00 |
| AH1429-2008 | — | — | — | 1.50 | 2.50 | 5.00 |
| AH1430-2009 | — | — | — | 1.50 | 2.50 | 4.00 |
| AH1431-2010 | — | — | — | 1.50 | 2.50 | 4.00 |

### KM# 29 100 FILS
6.00 g., Bi-Metallic Copper-Nickel center in Brass ring, 24 mm. **Ruler:** Hamed Bin Isa **Subject:** 1st Bahrain Grand Prix **Obv:** Maze design within circle **Rev:** Numeric denomination back of boxed denomination within circle, chain surrounds **Edge:** Reeded

| Date | Mintage | VF20 | XF40 | MS60 | MS63 | MS65 |
|---|---|---|---|---|---|---|
| AH1425-2004 | 30,000 | — | — | — | 30.00 | 35.00 |

### KM# 26a 100 FILS
6.00 g., 0.925 Silver 0.1784 oz. ASW, 24 mm. **Ruler:** Hamed Bin Isa **Obv:** National arms **Rev:** Denomination in chain link border

| Date | Mintage | VF20 | XF40 | MS60 | MS63 | MS65 |
|---|---|---|---|---|---|---|
| AH1431-2010 | 500 | **PF65** 30.00 | | | | |

### KM# 22 500 FILS
9.00 g., Bi-Metallic Brass center in Copper-Nickel ring, 27 mm. **Ruler:** Hamed Bin Isa **Obv:** Monument and inscription **Obv. Inscription:** STATE OF BAHRAIN **Rev:** Denomination **Edge:** Reeded

| Date | Mintage | VF20 | XF40 | MS60 | MS63 | MS65 |
|---|---|---|---|---|---|---|
| 2001 | — | — | — | 3.00 | 5.00 | 9.00 |

### KM# 27 500 FILS
9.00 g., Bi-Metallic Brass center in Copper-Nickel ring, 27 mm. **Ruler:** Hamed Bin Isa **Subject:** Kingdom **Obv:** Monument and inscription **Obv. Legend:** KINGDOM OF BAHRAIN **Rev:** Denomination **Edge:** Reeded

| Date | Mintage | VF20 | XF40 | MS60 | MS63 | MS65 |
|---|---|---|---|---|---|---|
| 2002 | — | — | — | 4.00 | 6.00 | 10.00 |

### KM# 27a 500 FILS
9.00 g., 0.925 Silver 0.2677 oz. ASW, 27 mm. **Ruler:** Hamed Bin Isa **Obv:** Monument and inscription **Rev:** Denomination

| Date | Mintage | VF20 | XF40 | MS60 | MS63 | MS65 |
|---|---|---|---|---|---|---|
| AH1431-2010 | 500 | **PF63** 35.00 | **PF65** 45.00 | | | |

## PROOF SETS

| KM# | Date | Mintage | Identification | Issue Price | Mkt Val |
|---|---|---|---|---|---|
| PS4 | 2010 (6) | 500 | KM#30a, 28a, 24a, 25a, 26a, 27a | 160 | 160 |

# BANGLADESH

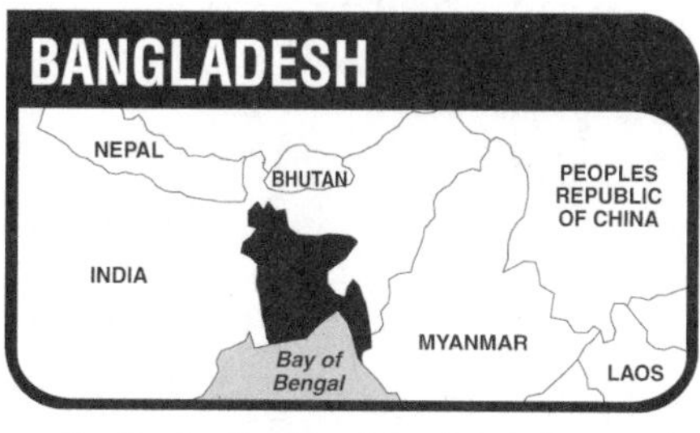


The Peoples Republic of Bangladesh (formerly East Pakistan), a parliamentary democracy located on the Bay of Bengal bordered by India and Burma, has an area of 55,598 sq. mi. (143,998 sq. km.) and a population of 128.1 million. Capital: Dhaka. The economy is predominantly agricultural. Jute products, jute and tea are exported.

Bangladesh is a member of the Commonwealth of Nations. The president is the Head of State and the Government.

**MONETARY SYSTEM**

100 Poisha = 1 Taka

**DATING**

Christian era using Bengali numerals.

## PEOPLES REPUBLIC

## STANDARD COINAGE

### KM# 24 50 POISHA
2.60 g., Stainless Steel, 19.3 mm. **Obv:** National emblem, Shapla (water lily) within wreath above water **Rev:** Fish, chicken and produce within inner circle **Edge:** Plain **Shape:** Octagonal

| Date | Mintage | VF20 | XF40 | MS60 | MS63 | MS65 |
|---|---|---|---|---|---|---|
| 2001 | — | 1.50 | 2.00 | 3.00 | — | — |

### KM# 9b TAKA
4.00 g., Brass, 25 mm. **Obv:** National emblem, Shapla (water lily) **Rev:** Stylized family, value at right **Edge:** Reeded **Note:** Prev. KM # 9.3.

| Date | Mintage | VF20 | XF40 | MS60 | MS63 | MS65 |
|---|---|---|---|---|---|---|
| 2003 | — | — | — | — | — | — |

### KM# 9c TAKA
4.25 g., Stainless Steel, 24.91 mm. **Obv:** National emblem, Shapla (water lily) within wreath above water in octagonal frame **Rev:** Stylized family, value at right within octagonal frame **Edge:** Reeded **Note:** Prev. KM # 9.5.

| Date | Mintage | VF20 | XF40 | MS60 | MS63 | MS65 |
|---|---|---|---|---|---|---|
| 2001 | — | — | — | — | — | — |
| 2002 | — | 1.25 | 1.75 | 2.25 | — | — |
| 2003 | — | 1.25 | 1.75 | 2.25 | — | — |
| 2007 | — | — | — | — | — | — |

### KM# 32 TAKA
3.25 g., Steel, 21.5 mm. **Obv:** Bank emblem **Rev:** Sheikh Mujibur Rahman facing

| Date | Mintage | VF20 | XF40 | MS60 | MS63 | MS65 |
|---|---|---|---|---|---|---|
| 2010 | 500,000 | — | 1.25 | 2.25 | 2.75 | 4.00 |

### KM# 25 2 TAKA
7.00 g., Stainless Steel, 26.03 mm. **Obv:** State emblem and "TWO 2 TAKA" within beaded border **Rev:** Two children reading, legend within beaded border **Edge:** Plain

| Date | Mintage | VF20 | XF40 | MS60 | MS63 | MS65 |
|---|---|---|---|---|---|---|
| 2004 | — | 1.75 | 2.25 | 3.00 | 4.00 | — |
| 2008 | — | 1.75 | 2.25 | 3.00 | 4.00 | — |

### KM# 31 2 TAKA
5.50 g., Stainless Steel, 24 mm. **Obv:** State emblem **Rev:** Bust facing

| Date | Mintage | VF20 | XF40 | MS60 | MS63 | MS65 |
|---|---|---|---|---|---|---|
| 2010 | — | — | 1.50 | 2.50 | 3.50 | — |

### KM# 26.1 5 TAKA
8.17 g., Steel, 26.8 mm. **Obv:** National emblem, Shapla (water lily) within wreath above water **Rev:** Bridge, date and denomination below, thick characters, limited clouds **Note:** Prev. KM#18.3. The 2006 date is non-magnetic, whereas the 2008 is magnetic. Die varieties exist.

| Date | Mintage | VF20 | XF40 | MS60 | MS63 | MS65 |
|---|---|---|---|---|---|---|
| 2006 | — | 1.50 | 2.25 | 3.25 | 4.25 | — |

**KM# 26.2 5 TAKA**
8.17 g., Steel, 26.8 mm. **Obv:** National emblem, Shapla (water lily) within wreath above water **Rev:** Bridge, date and denomination below, thin characters, extensive clouds above

| Date | Mintage | VF20 | XF40 | MS60 | MS63 | MS65 |
|---|---|---|---|---|---|---|
| 2008 | — | 1.50 | 2.25 | 3.25 | 4.25 | — |

**KM# 33 5 TAKA**
6.50 g., Steel, 25.5 mm. **Obv:** Urn within wreath **Rev:** Sheikh Mujibur Rahman

| Date | Mintage | VF20 | XF40 | MS60 | MS63 | MS65 |
|---|---|---|---|---|---|---|
| 2012 | 600,000 | — | 1.75 | 3.50 | 4.00 | 4.50 |

**KM# 27 10 TAKA**
0.925 Silver **Subject:** Cricket World Cup **Obv:** Cricket ball logo **Rev:** Trophy

| Date | Mintage | VF20 | XF40 | MS60 | MS63 | MS65 |
|---|---|---|---|---|---|---|
| 2011 | — | PF60 75.00 | PF63 90.00 | | | |

**KM# 28 10 TAKA**
22.10 g., 0.925 Silver 0.6572 oz. ASW, 38 mm. **Subject:** Rabindranath Tagore, 150th Anniversary of Birth **Obv:** Legend **Rev:** Bust right

| Date | Mintage | VF20 | XF40 | MS60 | MS63 | MS65 |
|---|---|---|---|---|---|---|
| 2011 | — | PF60 75.00 | PF63 90.00 | | | |

**KM# 29 10 TAKA**
25.00 g., 0.999 Silver 0.803 oz. ASW, 38 mm. **Subject:** Nationhood, 40th Anniversary **Obv:** Bangabandhu Sheikh Mujibur Rahman at center **Rev:** Six freedom fighters with hands raised

| Date | Mintage | VF20 | XF40 | MS60 | MS63 | MS65 |
|---|---|---|---|---|---|---|
| 2011 | — | PF60 75.00 | PF63 90.00 | | | |

**KM# 30 10 TAKA**
25.00 g., 0.999 Silver 0.803 oz. ASW, 38 mm. **Subject:** Poem: Bidrohi; 90th Anniversary **Obv:** Legend **Rev:** Kazi Nazrul Islam facing

| Date | Mintage | VF20 | XF40 | MS60 | MS63 | MS65 |
|---|---|---|---|---|---|---|
| 2011 | — | PF60 75.00 | PF63 90.00 | | | |

**KM# 34 100 TAKA**
22.00 g., 0.925 Silver 0.6543 oz. ASW, 38 mm. **Subject:** 100th Anniversary of Bangladesh National Museum (1913-2013) **Obv:** 18th century terracotta plaque with image of Horseman **Rev:** Bangladesh Bank monogram

| Date | Mintage | VF20 | XF40 | MS60 | MS63 | MS65 |
|---|---|---|---|---|---|---|
| 2013 | — | PF60 75.00 | PF63 90.00 | | | |

# BARBADOS

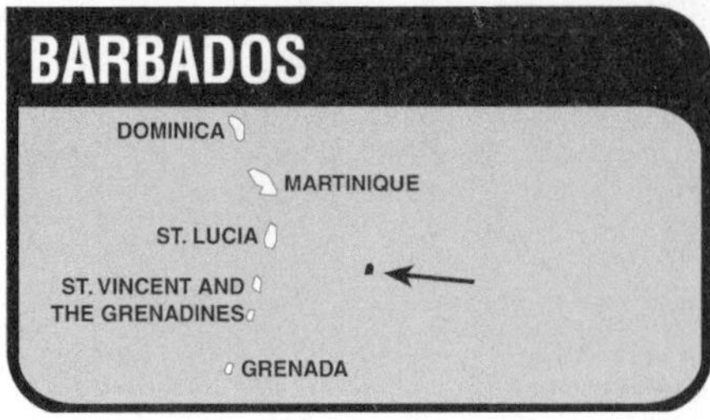


Barbados, a Constitutional Monarchy within the Commonwealth of Nations, is located in the Windward Islands of the West Indies east of St. Vincent. The coral island has an area of 166 sq. mi. (430 sq. km.) and a population of 269,000. Capital: Bridgetown. The economy is based on sugar and tourism. Sugar, petroleum products, molasses, and rum are exported.

**MONETARY SYSTEM**
100 Cents = 1 Dollar

**MINT MARKS**
(brm) – British Royal Mint
(O) – Ottawa Royal Canadian Mint
(v) - Valcambi

## COMMONWEALTH

### DECIMAL COINAGE

**KM# 10a CENT**
2.50 g., Copper Plated Zinc, 19 mm. **Obv:** National arms **Rev:** Trident above value **Edge:** Plain

| Date | Mintage | VF20 | XF40 | MS60 | MS63 | MS65 |
|---|---|---|---|---|---|---|
| 2001 | — | — | — | 0.10 | 0.25 | 0.75 |
| 2002 | — | — | — | — | 0.25 | 0.75 |
| 2003 | — | — | — | — | 0.25 | 0.75 |
| 2004 | — | — | — | — | 0.25 | 0.75 |
| 2005 | — | — | — | — | 0.25 | 0.75 |
| 2006 | — | — | — | — | 0.25 | 0.75 |
| 2007 | — | — | — | — | 0.25 | 0.75 |

**KM# 10b CENT**
2.78 g., Copper Plated Steel, 18.86 mm. **Obv:** National arms **Rev:** Trident above value

| Date | Mintage | VF20 | XF40 | MS60 | MS63 | MS65 |
|---|---|---|---|---|---|---|
| 2008 | — | — | — | — | 0.25 | 0.50 |
| 2009 | — | — | — | — | 0.25 | 0.50 |
| 2010 | — | — | — | — | 0.25 | 0.50 |
| 2011 | — | — | — | — | 0.25 | 0.50 |
| 2012 | — | — | — | — | 0.25 | 0.50 |

**KM# 11 5 CENTS**
3.75 g., Brass, 21 mm. **Obv:** National arms **Rev:** South Point Lighthouse, value below **Edge:** Plain

| Date | Mintage | VF20 | XF40 | MS60 | MS63 | MS65 |
|---|---|---|---|---|---|---|
| 2001 | — | — | — | — | 0.25 | 0.75 |
| 2002 | — | — | — | — | 0.25 | 0.75 |
| 2004 | — | — | — | — | 0.25 | 0.75 |
| 2005 | — | — | — | — | 0.25 | 0.75 |
| 2006 | — | — | — | — | 0.25 | 0.75 |
| 2007 | — | — | — | — | 0.25 | 0.75 |

**KM# 11a 5 CENTS**
3.46 g., Brass Plated Steel, 21 mm. **Obv:** National arms **Rev:** South Point Lighthouse, value below

| Date | Mintage | VF20 | XF40 | MS60 | MS63 | MS65 |
|---|---|---|---|---|---|---|
| 2008 | — | — | — | — | 0.25 | 0.75 |
| 2009 | — | — | — | — | 0.25 | 0.75 |
| 2010 | — | — | — | — | 0.25 | 0.75 |
| 2011 | — | — | — | — | 0.25 | 0.75 |

**KM# 12 10 CENTS**
2.29 g., Copper-Nickel, 17.77 mm. **Obv:** National arms **Rev:** Tern flying left, value below **Edge:** Reeded

| Date | Mintage | VF20 | XF40 | MS60 | MS63 | MS65 |
|---|---|---|---|---|---|---|
| 2001 | — | — | — | 0.25 | 0.50 | 1.50 |
| 2003 | — | — | — | 0.25 | 0.50 | 1.50 |
| 2004 | — | — | — | 0.25 | 0.50 | 1.50 |
| 2005 | — | — | — | 0.25 | 0.50 | 1.50 |

**KM# 12a 10 CENTS**
2.09 g., Nickel Plated Steel, 17.77 mm. **Obv:** National arms **Rev:** Tern flying left, value below **Edge:** Reeded

| Date | Mintage | VF20 | XF40 | MS60 | MS63 | MS65 |
|---|---|---|---|---|---|---|
| 2007 | — | — | — | — | 0.50 | 1.00 |
| 2008 | — | — | — | — | 0.50 | 1.00 |
| 2009 | — | — | — | — | 0.50 | 1.00 |
| 2012 | — | — | — | — | 0.50 | 1.00 |

**KM# 13 25 CENTS**
5.65 g., Copper-Nickel, 23.66 mm. **Obv:** National arms **Rev:** Morgan Lewis Windmill, value above **Edge:** Reeded

| Date | Mintage | VF20 | XF40 | MS60 | MS63 | MS65 |
|---|---|---|---|---|---|---|
| 2001 | — | — | — | 0.30 | 0.60 | 1.60 |
| 2003 | — | — | — | 0.30 | 0.60 | 1.60 |
| 2004 | — | — | — | 0.30 | 0.60 | 1.60 |
| 2005 | — | — | — | 0.30 | 0.60 | 1.60 |
| 2006 | — | — | — | 0.30 | 0.60 | 1.60 |

**KM# 13a 25 CENTS**
5.10 g., Nickel Plated Steel, 23.66 mm. **Obv:** National arms **Rev:** Morgan Lewis Windmill, value above **Edge:** Reeded

| Date | Mintage | VF20 | XF40 | MS60 | MS63 | MS65 |
|---|---|---|---|---|---|---|
| 2007 | — | — | — | 0.30 | 0.60 | 1.00 |
| 2008 | — | — | — | 0.30 | 0.60 | 1.00 |
| 2009 | — | — | — | 0.30 | 0.60 | 1.00 |
| 2011 | — | — | — | 0.30 | 0.60 | 1.00 |

**KM# 14.2 DOLLAR**
5.95 g., Copper-Nickel, 25.85 mm. **Obv:** National arms **Rev:** Flying fish left, value below **Shape:** 7-sided **Note:** Thinner planchet.

| Date | Mintage | VF20 | XF40 | MS60 | MS63 | MS65 |
|---|---|---|---|---|---|---|
| 2004 | — | — | — | — | 1.50 | 2.50 |
| 2005 | — | — | — | — | 1.50 | 2.50 |

**KM# 14.2a DOLLAR**
5.95 g., Nickel Plated Steel, 25.85 mm. **Obv:** National arms **Rev:** Flying fish left, value below

| Date | Mintage | VF20 | XF40 | MS60 | MS63 | MS65 |
|---|---|---|---|---|---|---|
| 2007 | — | — | — | — | 2.00 | 2.50 |
| 2008 | — | — | — | — | 2.25 | 3.00 |
| 2009 | — | — | — | — | 2.00 | 2.50 |
| 2012 | — | — | — | — | 2.00 | 2.50 |

**KM# 69 5 DOLLARS**
28.28 g., 0.925 Silver 0.841 oz. ASW, 38.6 mm. **Subject:** UNICEF **Obv:** National arms divide date, denomination below **Rev:** Three boys playing cricket **Edge:** Reeded

| Date | Mintage | VF20 | XF40 | MS60 | MS63 | MS65 |
|---|---|---|---|---|---|---|
| 2001 (v) | 100 | **PF63** 60.00 | **PF65** 65.00 | | | |

**KM# 73 5 DOLLARS**
28.28 g., 0.925 Silver 0.841 oz. ASW, 38.61 mm. **Subject:** 375th Anniversary of the City of Bridgetown **Obv:** Coat of Arms of Barbados **Rev:** Montefiore Fountain (Coleridge Street, Bridgetown)

| Date | Mintage | VF20 | XF40 | MS60 | MS63 | MS65 |
|---|---|---|---|---|---|---|
| 2003 (brm) | 200 | **PF63** 55.00 | **PF65** 60.00 | | | |

**KM# 76 5 DOLLARS**
28.28 g., 0.925 Silver 0.841 oz. ASW, 38.61 mm. **Subject:** 3 W's (Sirs Clyde Walcott, Everton Weekes and Frank Worrell) **Obv:** Coat of Arms of Barbados **Rev:** Sirs Clyde Walcott, Everton Weekes and Frank Worrell relaxing together on the cricket field with a cricket bat and ball beside them, legend, their nickname, circumferential legend, denomination **Rev. Legend:** Barbados - Home of the Masters

| Date | Mintage | VF20 | XF40 | MS60 | MS63 | MS65 |
|---|---|---|---|---|---|---|
| 2007 | 250 | **PF63** 90.00 | **PF65** 100 | | | |

**KM# 78 5 DOLLARS**
28.28 g., 0.925 Silver 0.841 oz. ASW, 38.61 mm. **Subject:** The Right Excellent Sir Garfield Sobers **Obv:** Coat of Arms of Barbados **Rev:** Sir Garfield Sobers in action playing a glorious cover drive, legend, circumferential legend, denomination **Rev. Legend:** The Right Excellent Sir Garfield Sobers; Barbados - Home of the Masters

| Date | Mintage | VF20 | XF40 | MS60 | MS63 | MS65 |
|---|---|---|---|---|---|---|
| 2007 (brm) | 250 | **PF63** 90.00 | **PF65** 100 | | | |

**KM# 74 50 DOLLARS**
15.97 g., 0.9167 Gold 0.4707 oz. AGW, 28.4 mm. **Subject:** 375th Anniversary of the City of Bridgetown **Obv:** Coat of Arms of Barbados **Rev:** Montefiore Fountain (Coleridge Street, Bridgetown)

| Date | Mintage | VF20 | XF40 | MS60 | MS63 | MS65 |
|---|---|---|---|---|---|---|
| 2003 | 50 | **PF63** 900 | **PF65** 950 | | | |

**KM# 75 50 DOLLARS**
15.97 g., 0.9167 Gold 0.4707 oz. AGW, 28.4 mm. **Subject:** 350th Anniversary of the Bridgetown Synagogue **Obv:** Coat of Arms of Barbados **Rev:** Rum barrel with the initials "mt" on its top (design based on 18th century token used as currency and minted by (and credited with its design) Joseph Tolanto, a Jewish merchant), legend, denomination **Rev. Legend:** 350th ANNIVERSARY OF THE BRIDGETOWN SYNAGOGUE

| Date | Mintage | VF20 | XF40 | MS60 | MS63 | MS65 |
|---|---|---|---|---|---|---|
| 2004 | 100 | **PF63** 850 | **PF65** 900 | | | |

**KM# 77 50 DOLLARS**
15.97 g., 0.9167 Gold 0.4707 oz. AGW, 28.4 mm. **Subject:** Sirs Clyde Walcott, Everton Weekes and Frank Worrell **Obv:** Coat of Arms of Barbados **Rev:** Sirs Clyde Walcott, Everton Weekes and Frank Worrell relaxing together on the cricket field with a cricket bat and ball beside them, legend, their nickname, circumferential legend, denomination **Rev. Legend:** Barbados - Home of the Masters

| Date | Mintage | VF20 | XF40 | MS60 | MS63 | MS65 |
|---|---|---|---|---|---|---|
| 2007 (brm) | 50 | **PF63** 950 | **PF65** 1,000 | | | |

**KM# 79 50 DOLLARS**
15.97 g., 0.9167 Gold 0.4707 oz. AGW, 28.4 mm. **Subject:** The Right Excellent Sir Garfield Sobers **Obv:** Coat of Arms of Barbados **Rev:** Sir Garfield Sobers in action playing a glorious cover drive, legend, circumferential legend, denomination **Rev. Legend:** The Right Excellent Sir Garfield Sobers; Barbados - Home of the Masters

| Date | Mintage | VF20 | XF40 | MS60 | MS63 | MS65 |
|---|---|---|---|---|---|---|
| 2007 (brm) | 50 | **PF63** 950 | **PF65** 1,000 | | | |

# BELARUS

Belarus (Byelorussia, Belorussia, or White Russia-formerly the Belorussian S.S.R.) is situated along the western Dvina and Dnieper Rivers, bounded in the west by Poland, to the north by Latvia and Lithuania, to the east by Russia and the south by the Ukraine. It has an area of 80,154 sq. mi. (207,600 sq. km.) and a population of 4.8 million. Capital: Minsk. Chief products: peat, salt, and agricultural products including flax, fodder and grasses for cattle breeding and dairy products.

**MONETARY SYSTEM**
100 Kapeek = 1 Rouble

## REPUBLIC

### STANDARD COINAGE

**KM# 47 ROUBLE**
13.14 g., Copper-Nickel, 31.9 mm. **Obv:** National arms **Rev:** European Bison **Edge:** Reeded

| Date | Mintage | VF20 | XF40 | MS60 | MS63 | MS65 |
|---|---|---|---|---|---|---|
| 2001 | 5,000 | **PF65** 40.00 | | | | |

**KM# 50 ROUBLE**
13.15 g., Copper-Nickel, 28.7 mm. **Subject:** 2002 Winter Olympics **Obv:** National arms **Rev:** Two freestyle skiers **Edge:** Reeded

| Date | Mintage | VF20 | XF40 | MS60 | MS63 | MS65 |
|---|---|---|---|---|---|---|
| 2001 Prooflike | 2,000 | — | — | — | — | 35.00 |

**KM# 110 ROUBLE**
Copper-Nickel, 32 mm. **Subject:** 900th Anniversary of Euphrasinta **Obv:** National arms **Rev:** Euphrasinta of Polatsk

| Date | Mintage | VF20 | XF40 | MS60 | MS63 | MS65 |
|---|---|---|---|---|---|---|
| 2001 | — | — | — | — | 50.00 | — |

**KM# 112 ROUBLE**
Copper-Nickel, 32 mm. **Subject:** Tower of Kamyantes **Obv:** National arms **Rev:** Kamyanets Tower, seal

| Date | Mintage | VF20 | XF40 | MS60 | MS63 | MS65 |
|---|---|---|---|---|---|---|
| 2001 | 2,000 | — | — | — | 40.00 | — |

**KM# 44 ROUBLE**
13.14 g., Copper-Nickel, 31.9 mm. **Obv:** National arms **Rev:** Eurasian Beaver and young **Edge:** Reeded

| Date | Mintage | VF20 | XF40 | MS60 | MS63 | MS65 |
|---|---|---|---|---|---|---|
| 2002 | 5,000 | **PF65** 25.00 | | | | |

**KM# 69 ROUBLE**
Copper-Nickel, 33 mm. **Subject:** 80th Anniversary of the Savings Bank **Obv:** Folk art design

| Date | Mintage | VF20 | XF40 | MS60 | MS63 | MS65 |
|---|---|---|---|---|---|---|
| 2002 Prooflike | 10,000 | — | — | — | 15.00 | — |

**KM# 106 ROUBLE**
Copper-Nickel, 31.9 mm. **Subject:** Jakub Kalas 1881-1956

| Date | Mintage | VF20 | XF40 | MS60 | MS63 | MS65 |
|---|---|---|---|---|---|---|
| 2002 | 2,000 | **PF65** 35.00 | | | | |

**KM# 114 ROUBLE**
Copper-Nickel, 32 mm. **Subject:** 200th Birthday of Ignatius Dameika **Obv:** National arms **Rev:** Ignatius Dameika, hammer

| Date | Mintage | VF20 | XF40 | MS60 | MS63 | MS65 |
|---|---|---|---|---|---|---|
| 2002 Prooflike | 2,000 | — | — | — | — | 40.00 |

**KM# 116 ROUBLE**
Copper-Nickel, 33 mm. **Subject:** 120th Birthday of Yanka Kupala **Obv:** National arms **Rev:** Yanka Kupala, 1882-1942

| Date | Mintage | VF20 | XF40 | MS60 | MS63 | MS65 |
|---|---|---|---|---|---|---|
| 2002 Prooflike | 2,000 | — | — | — | — | 40.00 |

**KM# 118 ROUBLE**
Copper-Nickel, 33 mm. **Subject:** 120th Birthday of Yakub Kolas **Obv:** National arms **Rev:** Yukab Kolas, 1882-1956

| Date | Mintage | VF20 | XF40 | MS60 | MS63 | MS65 |
|---|---|---|---|---|---|---|
| 2002 | 2,000 | — | — | — | 40.00 | — |

**KM# 54 ROUBLE**
13.12 g., Copper-Nickel, 31.9 mm. **Obv:** National arms **Rev:** Mute swans on water with reflections **Edge:** Reeded

| Date | Mintage | VF20 | XF40 | MS60 | MS63 | MS65 |
|---|---|---|---|---|---|---|
| 2003 | 5,000 | **PF65** 35.00 | | | | |

**KM# 55 ROUBLE**
13.10 g., Copper-Nickel, 31.9 mm. **Obv:** State arms **Rev:** Herring gull in flight **Edge:** Reeded

| Date | Mintage | VF20 | XF40 | MS60 | MS63 | MS65 |
|---|---|---|---|---|---|---|
| 2003 | 5,000 | **PF65** 25.00 | | | | |

**KM# 56 ROUBLE**
13.10 g., Copper-Nickel, 32 mm. **Obv:** National arms **Rev:** Church of the Savior and Transfiguration **Edge:** Reeded

| Date | Mintage | VF20 | XF40 | MS60 | MS63 | MS65 |
|---|---|---|---|---|---|---|
| 2003 | 2,000 | — | — | — | 35.00 | — |

**KM# 61 ROUBLE**
13.16 g., Copper-Nickel, 32 mm. **Obv:** National arms **Rev:** Wrestlers **Edge:** Reeded

| Date | Mintage | VF20 | XF40 | MS60 | MS63 | MS65 |
|---|---|---|---|---|---|---|
| 2003 Prooflike | 5,000 | — | — | — | — | 10.00 |

**KM# 292 ROUBLE**
13.16 g., Copper-Nickel, 32 mm. **Obv:** National arms **Rev:** Church

| Date | Mintage | VF20 | XF40 | MS60 | MS63 | MS65 |
|---|---|---|---|---|---|---|
| 2003 Prooflike | 2,000 | — | — | — | — | 100 |

**KM# 60 ROUBLE**
13.16 g., Copper-Nickel, 32 mm. **Obv:** National arms **Rev:** Two common cranes **Edge:** Reeded

| Date | Mintage | VF20 | XF40 | MS60 | MS63 | MS65 |
|---|---|---|---|---|---|---|
| 2004 | 5,000 | PF65 25.00 | | | | |

**KM# 62 ROUBLE**
Copper-Nickel, 31.9 mm. **Subject:** Sculling **Obv:** National arms **Rev:** Two rowers against a background of stylized oars

| Date | Mintage | VF20 | XF40 | MS60 | MS63 | MS65 |
|---|---|---|---|---|---|---|
| 2004 | 3,000 | — | — | — | 15.00 | — |

**KM# 75 ROUBLE**
15.92 g., Copper-Nickel Antiqued Finish, 33 mm. **Subject:** Kupalle **Obv:** Folk art cross design **Rev:** Flower above ferns **Edge:** Reeded

| Date | Mintage | VF20 | XF40 | MS60 | MS63 | MS65 |
|---|---|---|---|---|---|---|
| 2004 | 5,000 | — | — | — | 40.00 | — |

**KM# 76 ROUBLE**
15.92 g., Copper-Nickel, 33 mm. **Subject:** Kalyady **Obv:** Folk art cross design **Rev:** Stylized sunflower **Edge:** Reeded

| Date | Mintage | VF20 | XF40 | MS60 | MS63 | MS65 |
|---|---|---|---|---|---|---|
| 2004 | 5,000 | — | — | — | 35.00 | — |

**KM# 78 ROUBLE**
15.90 g., Copper-Nickel, 33 mm. **Obv:** National arms **Rev:** Radziwill's Castle in Neswizh **Edge:** Reeded

| Date | Mintage | VF20 | XF40 | MS60 | MS63 | MS65 |
|---|---|---|---|---|---|---|
| 2004 Prooflike | 2,000 | — | — | — | — | 40.00 |

**KM# 80 ROUBLE**
15.90 g., Copper-Nickel, 33 mm. **Subject:** Defenders of Brest **Obv:** Soviet Patriotic War Order **Rev:** Courage" monument **Edge:** Reeded

| Date | Mintage | VF20 | XF40 | MS60 | MS63 | MS65 |
|---|---|---|---|---|---|---|
| 2004 | 5,000 | — | — | — | 25.00 | — |

**KM# 83 ROUBLE**
Copper-Nickel, 33 mm. **Subject:** Memory of Facist Victims **Obv:** National arms **Rev:** Man holding dead

| Date | Mintage | VF20 | XF40 | MS60 | MS63 | MS65 |
|---|---|---|---|---|---|---|
| 2004 | 3,000 | — | — | — | 25.00 | — |

**KM# 85 ROUBLE**
Copper-Nickel, 33 mm. **Subject:** Soviet Warriors - Liberators **Obv:** Order of the Patriotric War **Rev:** Partisans with blown up railway track

| Date | Mintage | VF20 | XF40 | MS60 | MS63 | MS65 |
|---|---|---|---|---|---|---|
| 2004 | 3,000 | — | — | — | 25.00 | — |

**KM# 293 ROUBLE**
14.35 g., Copper-Nickel, 33 mm. **Subject:** Mogilev **Obv:** National arms **Rev:** Shield and town view

| Date | Mintage | VF20 | XF40 | MS60 | MS63 | MS65 |
|---|---|---|---|---|---|---|
| 2004 Prooflike | 2,000 | — | — | — | — | 40.00 |

**KM# 294 ROUBLE**
14.35 g., Copper-Nickel, 33 mm. **Subject:** WWII anniversary **Obv:** Order star **Rev:** Soldier and tank

| Date | Mintage | VF20 | XF40 | MS60 | MS63 | MS65 |
|---|---|---|---|---|---|---|
| 2004 Prooflike | 3,000 | — | — | — | — | 40.00 |

**KM# 81 ROUBLE**
Copper-Nickel, 33 mm. **Subject:** 60th Anniversary of Victory **Obv:** Order of the Victory **Rev:** Star and arrows

| Date | Mintage | VF20 | XF40 | MS60 | MS63 | MS65 |
|---|---|---|---|---|---|---|
| 2005 | 2,000 | — | — | — | 25.00 | — |

**KM# 97 ROUBLE**
14.50 g., Copper-Nickel, 33 mm. **Subject:** Almany Bogs **Obv:** Blooming plant on frosted design **Rev:** Great Grey Owl **Edge:** Lettered

| Date | Mintage | VF20 | XF40 | MS60 | MS63 | MS65 |
|---|---|---|---|---|---|---|
| 2005 | 5,000 | PF65 30.00 | | | | |

**KM# 104 ROUBLE**
Copper-Nickel, 33 mm. **Subject:** Christmas Egg **Obv:** National arms and folk art cross design **Rev:** Easter egg

| Date | Mintage | VF20 | XF40 | MS60 | MS63 | MS65 |
|---|---|---|---|---|---|---|
| 2005 | 5,000 | — | — | — | 35.00 | — |

**KM# 107 ROUBLE**
Copper-Nickel, 31.9 mm. **Subject:** Bagach - Candle in Basket **Obv:** National arms and solar symbol **Rev:** Basket of grain, candle, ear, table, tablecloth

| Date | Mintage | VF20 | XF40 | MS60 | MS63 | MS65 |
|---|---|---|---|---|---|---|
| 2005 | 5,000 | — | — | — | 35.00 | — |

**KM# 127 ROUBLE**
Copper-Nickel, 32 mm. **Subject:** 1000th Anniversary of Vaukavysk **Obv:** National arms **Rev:** National arms of Vaukavysk

| Date | Mintage | VF20 | XF40 | MS60 | MS63 | MS65 |
|---|---|---|---|---|---|---|
| 2005 | 2,000 | — | — | — | 40.00 | — |

**KM# 130 ROUBLE**
Copper-Nickel, 32 mm. **Subject:** Jesuit Roman Catholic Church **Obv:** National arms **Rev:** Jesuit Roman Catholic Church in Neswizh

| Date | Mintage | VF20 | XF40 | MS60 | MS63 | MS65 |
|---|---|---|---|---|---|---|
| 2005 | 2,000 | — | — | — | 40.00 | — |

**KM# 132 ROUBLE**
Copper-Nickel, 33 mm. **Subject:** Usyaslau of Polatsk **Obv:** Cathedral of St. Sophia **Rev:** Usyaslav of Polatsk, wolf on a solar disk

| Date | Mintage | VF20 | XF40 | MS60 | MS63 | MS65 |
|---|---|---|---|---|---|---|
| 2005 | 5,000 | PF65 15.00 | | | | |

**KM# 134 ROUBLE**
Copper-Nickel, 33 mm. **Subject:** Tennis **Obv:** National arms **Rev:** Tennis player against racket background

| Date | Mintage | VF20 | XF40 | MS60 | MS63 | MS65 |
|---|---|---|---|---|---|---|
| 2005 | 5,000 | — | — | — | 12.00 | — |

**KM# 295 ROUBLE**
14.35 g., Copper-Nickel, 33 mm. **Subject:** Grodno **Obv:** National arms **Rev:** Shield and city fortress

| Date | Mintage | VF20 | XF40 | MS60 | MS63 | MS65 |
|---|---|---|---|---|---|---|
| 2005 Prooflike | 2,000 | — | — | — | — | 40.00 |

**KM# 296 ROUBLE**
14.35 g., Copper-Nickel, 33 mm. **Subject:** Brest **Obv:** National arms **Rev:** Shield and city view

| Date | Mintage | VF20 | XF40 | MS60 | MS63 | MS65 |
|---|---|---|---|---|---|---|
| 2005 Prooflike | 2,000 | — | — | — | — | 40.00 |

**KM# 135 ROUBLE**
Copper-Nickel, 32 mm. **Subject:** Vtaselle Wedding **Obv:** National arms, birds, shamrock **Rev:** Loaf of bread, wedding rings, diadem of flowers, background of honeycomb

| Date | Mintage | VF20 | XF40 | MS60 | MS63 | MS65 |
|---|---|---|---|---|---|---|
| 2006 | 5,000 | — | — | — | 20.00 | 25.00 |

**KM# 138 ROUBLE**
Copper-Nickel, 33 mm. **Subject:** Sophia of Galshany 600th Anniversary **Obv:** Castle of Galshany **Rev:** National arms and Sophia of Galshany

| Date | Mintage | VF20 | XF40 | MS60 | MS63 | MS65 |
|---|---|---|---|---|---|---|
| 2006 | 5,000 | — | — | — | 20.00 | — |

**KM# 140 ROUBLE**
Copper-Nickel, 33 mm. **Subject:** Syomukha **Obv:** National arms, solar symbol **Rev:** Chalice, Chaplet of birch, maple, rowan sweet flag leaves

| Date | Mintage | VF20 | XF40 | MS60 | MS63 | MS65 |
|---|---|---|---|---|---|---|
| 2006 | 5,000 | — | — | — | 25.00 | — |

**KM# 146 ROUBLE**
Copper-Nickel, 33 mm. **Subject:** Chyrvomy Bar **Obv:** National arms, blooming plant **Rev:** European Mink

| Date | Mintage | VF20 | XF40 | MS60 | MS63 | MS65 |
|---|---|---|---|---|---|---|
| 2006 | 5,000 | PF65 17.50 | | | | |

**KM# 273 ROUBLE**
13.20 g., Copper-Nickel, 32 mm. **Subject:** Skiing **Edge:** Reeded

| Date | Mintage | VF20 | XF40 | MS60 | MS63 | MS65 |
|---|---|---|---|---|---|---|
| 2006 | 5,000 | — | — | — | — | 20.00 |

**KM# 274 ROUBLE**
15.50 g., Copper-Nickel, 33 mm. **Subject:** Rogwald

| Date | Mintage | VF20 | XF40 | MS60 | MS63 | MS65 |
|---|---|---|---|---|---|---|
| 2006 | 5,000 | — | — | — | — | 20.00 |

**KM# 275 ROUBLE**
13.16 g., Copper-Nickel, 32 mm. **Subject:** Commonwealth of Independent States, 15th Anniversary **Edge:** Reeded

| Date | Mintage | VF20 | XF40 | MS60 | MS63 | MS65 |
|---|---|---|---|---|---|---|
| 2006 Prooflike | 5,000 | — | — | — | — | 20.00 |

**KM# 276 ROUBLE**
13.20 g., Copper-Nickel, 32 mm. **Subject:** Cycling **Edge:** Plain

| Date | Mintage | VF20 | XF40 | MS60 | MS63 | MS65 |
|---|---|---|---|---|---|---|
| 2006 | 5,000 | — | — | — | — | 20.00 |

**KM# 297 ROUBLE**
14.35 g., Copper-Nickel, 33 mm. **Subject:** Gomel **Obv:** National arms **Rev:** Shield and city view

| Date | Mintage | VF20 | XF40 | MS60 | MS63 | MS65 |
|---|---|---|---|---|---|---|
| 2006 Prooflike | 2,000 | — | — | — | — | 75.00 |

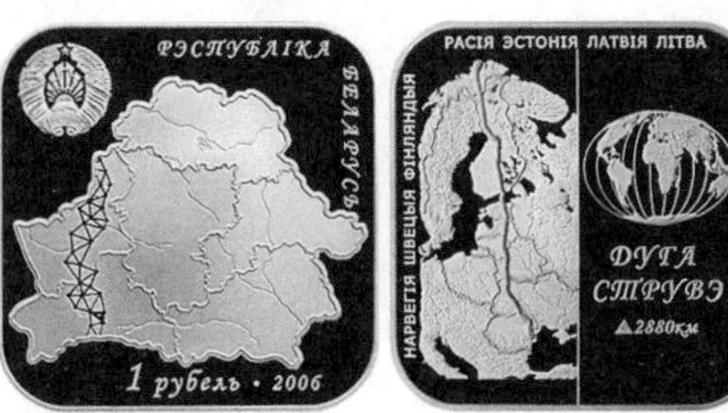


**KM# 298 ROUBLE**
15.50 g., Copper-Nickel, 29x29 mm. **Subject:** Struve-Bogen trail **Obv:** National arms and map **Rev:** Eastern Europe map **Shape:** Square

| Date | Mintage | VF20 | XF40 | MS60 | MS63 | MS65 |
|---|---|---|---|---|---|---|
| 2006 Prooflike | 5,000 | — | — | — | — | 25.00 |

**KM# 417 ROUBLE**
15.55 g., Copper-Nickel, 33 mm. **Subject:** Rogvold of Polotsk and Rogneda **Obv:** Ancient fortress of Izyaslavl **Rev:** Rogvold at left with female

| Date | Mintage | VF20 | XF40 | MS60 | MS63 | MS65 |
|---|---|---|---|---|---|---|
| 2006 Prooflike | 5,000 | — | — | — | — | 30.00 |

**KM# 150 ROUBLE**
16.00 g., Copper-Nickel, 33 mm. **Subject:** Holidays and Ceremonies **Obv:** Small arms above quilted star design **Rev:** Food, bowl with spoon - Maslenica

| Date | Mintage | VF20 | XF40 | MS60 | MS63 | MS65 |
|---|---|---|---|---|---|---|
| 2007 Antique | 5,000 | — | — | — | 35.00 | — |

**KM# 151 ROUBLE**
13.16 g., Copper-Nickel, 32 mm. **Obv:** Thrush Nightingale in hands in oval **Obv. Legend:** РЭСПУБЛІКА БЕЛАРУСЬ **Rev:** Thrush Nightingale perched on branch in oval **Edge:** Reeded

| Date | Mintage | VF20 | XF40 | MS60 | MS63 | MS65 |
|---|---|---|---|---|---|---|
| 2007 Prooflike | 5,000 | — | — | — | — | 17.50 |

**KM# 217 ROUBLE**
14.35 g., Copper-Nickel, 33 mm. **Rev:** Sturgeon

| Date | Mintage | VF20 | XF40 | MS60 | MS63 | MS65 |
|---|---|---|---|---|---|---|
| 2007 | 5,000 | PF65 15.00 | | | | |

**KM# 299 ROUBLE**
13.16 g., Copper-Nickel, 32 mm. **Subject:** Belarus-China relations, 15th anniversary **Obv:** National arms **Rev:** Two archways, with Belerus and China views

| Date | Mintage | VF20 | XF40 | MS60 | MS63 | MS65 |
|---|---|---|---|---|---|---|
| 2007 Prooflike | 3,000 | — | — | — | — | 25.00 |

**KM# 300 ROUBLE**
13.16 g., Copper-Nickel, 32 mm. **Subject:** Naoleon Orda, 200th Anniversary of Birth **Obv:** Three castle views **Rev:** Bust facing, musical notes and sytlized record

| Date | Mintage | VF20 | XF40 | MS60 | MS63 | MS65 |
|---|---|---|---|---|---|---|
| 2007 Prooflike | 7,000 | — | — | — | — | 25.00 |

**KM# 301 ROUBLE**
15.50 g., Copper-Nickel, 33 mm. **Subject:** Gleb Menski **Obv:** Wooden fortress **Rev:** Knight seated left

| Date | Mintage | VF20 | XF40 | MS60 | MS63 | MS65 |
|---|---|---|---|---|---|---|
| 2007 Prooflike | 5,000 | — | — | — | — | 25.00 |

**KM# 302 ROUBLE**
13.16 g., Copper-Nickel, 32 mm. **Subject:** A. Aladawa **Obv:** Building façade **Rev:** Bust and picture frame

| Date | Mintage | VF20 | XF40 | MS60 | MS63 | MS65 |
|---|---|---|---|---|---|---|
| 2007 Prooflike | 4,000 | — | — | — | — | 25.00 |

**KM# 303 ROUBLE**
15.50 g., Copper-Nickel, 33 mm. **Subject:** Legend of the Stork **Obv:** Five stylized storks **Rev:** Large stylized stork

| Date | Mintage | VF20 | XF40 | MS60 | MS63 | MS65 |
|---|---|---|---|---|---|---|
| 2007 Prooflike | 5,000 | — | — | — | — | 25.00 |

**KM# 215 ROUBLE**
13.18 g., Copper-Nickel, 33 mm. **Obv:** Sea chart and compose rose **Rev:** Sailing ship Sedov

| Date | Mintage | VF20 | XF40 | MS60 | MS63 | MS65 |
|---|---|---|---|---|---|---|
| 2008 | 7,000 | PF65 15.00 | | | | |

**KM# 304 ROUBLE**
13.16 g., Copper-Nickel, 32 mm. **Subject:** Zair Azgur **Obv:** Bust sculpture on pedestal **Rev:** Portrait right

| Date | Mintage | VF20 | XF40 | MS60 | MS63 | MS65 |
|---|---|---|---|---|---|---|
| 2008 Prooflike | 3,000 | — | — | — | — | 25.00 |

**KM# 305 ROUBLE**
13.16 g., Copper-Nickel, 32 mm. **Subject:** Vincent Dunin-Martsynkevich **Obv:** Open stage curtian **Rev:** Bust facing, play names at right

| Date | Mintage | VF20 | XF40 | MS60 | MS63 | MS65 |
|---|---|---|---|---|---|---|
| 2008 Prooflike | 3,000 | — | — | — | — | 25.00 |

**KM# 306 ROUBLE**
15.50 g., Copper-Nickel, 33 mm. **Subject:** Legend **Obv:** Five stylized birds **Rev:** Stylized bird

| Date | Mintage | VF20 | XF40 | MS60 | MS63 | MS65 |
|---|---|---|---|---|---|---|
| 2008 Prooflike | 5,000 | — | — | — | — | 25.00 |

**KM# 307 ROUBLE**
13.16 g., Copper-Nickel, 32 mm. **Subject:** House-warming **Obv:** Cat standing left **Rev:** Key in window, house façade **Edge:** Reeded

| Date | Mintage | VF20 | XF40 | MS60 | MS63 | MS65 |
|---|---|---|---|---|---|---|
| 2008 | 5,000 | — | — | — | — | 25.00 |

**KM# 308 ROUBLE**
13.16 g., Copper-Nickel, 32 mm. **Subject:** Great White Egret **Obv:** Bird in hand in horizontal oval **Rev:** Great White Egret standing in vertical oval **Edge:** Reeded

| Date | Mintage | VF20 | XF40 | MS60 | MS63 | MS65 |
|---|---|---|---|---|---|---|
| 2008 Prooflike | 5,000 | — | — | — | — | 30.00 |

**KM# 309 ROUBLE**
16.00 g., Copper-Nickel, 33 mm. **Obv:** Folk embroidery star pattern **Rev:** Two angles with candle above log home entrance with festive table set

| Date | Mintage | VF20 | XF40 | MS60 | MS63 | MS65 |
|---|---|---|---|---|---|---|
| 2008 Antique patina | 5,000 | — | — | — | — | 50.00 |

**KM# 310 ROUBLE**
14.35 g., Copper-Nickel, 33 mm. **Subject:** Minsk **Obv:** EurAsEC logo and graphic **Rev:** Old and new city views in two ovals

| Date | Mintage | VF20 | XF40 | MS60 | MS63 | MS65 |
|---|---|---|---|---|---|---|
| 2008 Prooflike | 7,000 | — | — | — | — | 20.00 |

**KM# 311 ROUBLE**
15.50 g., Copper-Nickel, 33 mm. **Subject:** Davyd of Garadzen **Obv:** Fortress **Rev:** Knight standing facing

| Date | Mintage | VF20 | XF40 | MS60 | MS63 | MS65 |
|---|---|---|---|---|---|---|
| 2008 Prooflike | 5,000 | — | — | — | — | 25.00 |

**KM# 312 ROUBLE**
13.16 g., Copper-Nickel, 32 mm. **Series:** Ministry of Finance, 90th Anniversary **Obv:** National arms **Rev:** Ministry of Finance arms

| Date | Mintage | VF20 | XF40 | MS60 | MS63 | MS65 |
|---|---|---|---|---|---|---|
| 2008 Prooflike | 3,000 | — | — | — | — | 20.00 |

**KM# 313 ROUBLE**
14.35 g., Copper-Nickel, 33 mm. **Subject:** Kingfisher **Obv:** Flower **Rev:** Kingfisher on grass near waterway

| Date | Mintage | VF20 | XF40 | MS60 | MS63 | MS65 |
|---|---|---|---|---|---|---|
| 2008 Prooflike | 5,000 | — | — | — | — | 25.00 |

**KM# 218 ROUBLE**
13.16 g., Copper-Nickel, 32 mm. **Subject:** Bialowieza Forest, 600th Anniversary **Obv:** Figures joining hands around tree trunk **Rev:** Stylized nature view **Edge:** Reeded

| Date | Mintage | VF20 | XF40 | MS60 | MS63 | MS65 |
|---|---|---|---|---|---|---|
| 2009 Prooflike | 5,000 | — | — | — | — | 25.00 |

**KM# 219 ROUBLE**
13.16 g., Copper-Nickel, 32 mm. **Subject:** Grey Goose **Obv:** Bird in hand **Rev:** Grey goose in oval **Edge:** Reeded

| Date | Mintage | VF20 | XF40 | MS60 | MS63 | MS65 |
|---|---|---|---|---|---|---|
| 2009 Prooflike | 5,000 | — | — | — | — | 20.00 |

**KM# 220 ROUBLE**
15.50 g., Copper-Nickel, 32 mm. **Subject:** Pakatigaroshak **Rev:** Man clubbing dragon

| Date | Mintage | VF20 | XF40 | MS60 | MS63 | MS65 |
|---|---|---|---|---|---|---|
| 2009 | 3,500 | PF65 17.50 | | | | |

**KM# 221 ROUBLE**
15.50 g., Copper-Nickel, 33 mm. **Subject:** Legend of the Skylark **Obv:** five stylized birds in flight **Rev:** Stylized skylark, head left

| Date | Mintage | VF20 | XF40 | MS60 | MS63 | MS65 |
|---|---|---|---|---|---|---|
| 2009 Prooflike | 5,000 | — | — | — | — | 13.00 |

**KM# 222 ROUBLE**
15.50 g., Copper-Nickel, 33 mm. **Subject:** Folk Art - Straw Weaving **Rev:** Horse

| Date | Mintage | VF20 | XF40 | MS60 | MS63 | MS65 |
|---|---|---|---|---|---|---|
| 2009 Prooflike | 5,000 | — | — | — | — | 13.00 |

**KM# 259 ROUBLE**
13.16 g., Copper-Nickel, 32 mm. **Obv:** Compass **Rev:** Dar Parmoza at sail

| Date | Mintage | VF20 | XF40 | MS60 | MS63 | MS65 |
|---|---|---|---|---|---|---|
| 2009 | 5,000 | — | — | — | — | 25.00 |

**KM# 314 ROUBLE**
13.16 g., Copper-Nickel, 32 mm. **Subject:** Academy of Science **Obv:** Earth and spaceship orbits **Rev:** Academy building

| Date | Mintage | VF20 | XF40 | MS60 | MS63 | MS65 |
|---|---|---|---|---|---|---|
| 2009 Prooflike | 4,000 | — | — | — | — | 20.00 |

**KM# 315 ROUBLE**
13.16 g., Copper-Nickel, 32 mm. **Subject:** Zodiac - Pisces **Obv:** Sun and moon **Rev:** Two fish **Edge:** Reeded

| Date | Mintage | VF20 | XF40 | MS60 | MS63 | MS65 |
|---|---|---|---|---|---|---|
| 2009 | 10,000 | — | — | — | — | 20.00 |

**KM# 316 ROUBLE**
13.16 g., Copper-Nickel, 32 mm. **Subject:** Zodiac - Aries **Obv:** Sun and moon **Rev:** Ram **Edge:** Reeded

| Date | Mintage | VF20 | XF40 | MS60 | MS63 | MS65 |
|---|---|---|---|---|---|---|
| 2009 | 10,000 | — | — | — | — | 20.00 |

**KM# 317 ROUBLE**
13.16 g., Copper-Nickel, 32 mm. **Subject:** Zodiac - Taurus **Obv:** Sun and moon **Rev:** Bull

| Date | Mintage | VF20 | XF40 | MS60 | MS63 | MS65 |
|---|---|---|---|---|---|---|
| 2009 Prooflike | 10,000 | — | — | — | — | 20.00 |

**KM# 318 ROUBLE**
13.16 g., Copper-Nickel, 32 mm. **Subject:** Zodiac - Gemini **Obv:** Sun and moon **Rev:** Twins

| Date | Mintage | VF20 | XF40 | MS60 | MS63 | MS65 |
|---|---|---|---|---|---|---|
| 2009 Prooflike | 10,000 | — | — | — | — | 20.00 |

**KM# 319 ROUBLE**
13.16 g., Copper-Nickel, 32 mm. **Subject:** Zodiac - Cancer **Obv:** Sun and moon **Rev:** Crab

| Date | Mintage | VF20 | XF40 | MS60 | MS63 | MS65 |
|---|---|---|---|---|---|---|
| 2009 Prooflike | 10,000 | — | — | — | — | 20.00 |

**KM# 320 ROUBLE**
13.16 g., Copper-Nickel, 32 mm. **Subject:** Christening **Obv:** Stylized stork **Rev:** Child in a baptism gown **Edge:** Reeded

| Date | Mintage | VF20 | XF40 | MS60 | MS63 | MS65 |
|---|---|---|---|---|---|---|
| 2009 | 5,000 | — | — | — | — | 20.00 |

**KM# 321 ROUBLE**
13.16 g., Copper-Nickel, 32 mm. **Subject:** Zodiac - Leo **Obv:** Sun and moon **Rev:** Lion standing left **Edge:** Reeded

| Date | Mintage | VF20 | XF40 | MS60 | MS63 | MS65 |
|---|---|---|---|---|---|---|
| 2009 | 10,000 | — | — | — | — | 20.00 |

**KM# 322 ROUBLE**
14.35 g., Copper-Nickel, 33 mm. **Series:** Liberationfrom the Nazis, 65th Anniversary **Rev:** Child looking upwards to birds in flight **Edge:** Reeded

| Date | Mintage | VF20 | XF40 | MS60 | MS63 | MS65 |
|---|---|---|---|---|---|---|
| 2009 Prooflike | 4,000 | — | — | — | — | 20.00 |

**KM# 323 ROUBLE**
13.16 g., Copper-Nickel, 32 mm. **Subject:** Zodiac - Virgo **Obv:** Sun and moon **Rev:** Little girl

| Date | Mintage | VF20 | XF40 | MS60 | MS63 | MS65 |
|---|---|---|---|---|---|---|
| 2009 Prooflike | 10,000 | — | — | — | — | 20.00 |

**KM# 324 ROUBLE**
13.16 g., Copper-Nickel, 32 mm. **Subject:** Zodiac - Libra **Obv:** Sun and moon **Rev:** Scales **Edge:** Reeded

| Date | Mintage | VF20 | XF40 | MS60 | MS63 | MS65 |
|---|---|---|---|---|---|---|
| 2009 | 10,000 | — | — | — | — | 20.00 |

**KM# 325 ROUBLE**
16.00 g., Copper-Nickel, 33 mm. **Subject:** Harvesttime **Obv:** Star embroidery pattern **Rev:** Apple, honey and grain harvest

| Date | Mintage | VF20 | XF40 | MS60 | MS63 | MS65 |
|---|---|---|---|---|---|---|
| 2009 Antique patina | 5,000 | — | — | — | — | 25.00 |

**KM# 326 ROUBLE**
13.16 g., Copper-Nickel, 32 mm. **Subject:** Zodiac - Scorpio **Obv:** Sun and moon **Rev:** Scorpion

| Date | Mintage | VF20 | XF40 | MS60 | MS63 | MS65 |
|---|---|---|---|---|---|---|
| 2009 Proofilke | 10,000 | — | — | — | — | 20.00 |

**KM# 327 ROUBLE**
14.35 g., Copper-Nickel, 33 mm. **Subject:** White Stork **Obv:** Stork footprint **Rev:** White Stork and nest

| Date | Mintage | VF20 | XF40 | MS60 | MS63 | MS65 |
|---|---|---|---|---|---|---|
| 2009 Prooflike | 5,000 | — | — | — | — | 25.00 |

**KM# 329 ROUBLE**
13.16 g., Copper-Nickel, 32 mm. **Subject:** Zodiac - Sagittarius **Obv:** Sun and moon **Rev:** Girl with bow and arrow

| Date | Mintage | VF20 | XF40 | MS60 | MS63 | MS65 |
|---|---|---|---|---|---|---|
| 2009 Prooflike | 10,000 | — | — | — | — | 20.00 |

**KM# 331 ROUBLE**
13.16 g., Copper-Nickel, 32 mm. **Subject:** Zodiac - Capricorn **Obv:** Sun and moon **Rev:** Ram

| Date | Mintage | VF20 | XF40 | MS60 | MS63 | MS65 |
|---|---|---|---|---|---|---|
| 2009 Prooflike | 10,000 | — | — | — | — | 20.00 |

**KM# 332 ROUBLE**
13.16 g., Copper-Nickel, 32 mm. **Subject:** Zodiac - Aquarius **Obv:** Sun and moon **Rev:** Child in bathtub **Edge:** Reeded

| Date | Mintage | VF20 | XF40 | MS60 | MS63 | MS65 |
|---|---|---|---|---|---|---|
| 2009 | 10,000 | — | — | — | — | 20.00 |

**KM# 223 ROUBLE**
14.35 g., Copper-Nickel, 33 mm. **Subject:** EURASEC, 10th Anniversary **Obv:** Folk embroidery pattern **Rev:** Six flags around globe

| Date | Mintage | VF20 | XF40 | MS60 | MS63 | MS65 |
|---|---|---|---|---|---|---|
| 2010 | 3,500 | PF65 13.00 | | | | |

**KM# 226 ROUBLE**
13.16 g., Copper-Nickel, 33 mm. **Subject:** 1st Belarus Front **Rev:** Gen. Konstantin Rokossovsky

| Date | Mintage | VF20 | XF40 | MS60 | MS63 | MS65 |
|---|---|---|---|---|---|---|
| 2010 | 3,000 | PF65 13.00 | | | | |

**KM# 227 ROUBLE**
13.16 g., Copper-Nickel, 33 mm. **Subject:** 2nd Belarus Front **Rev:** Col. Gen. G.F. Zaharov

| Date | Mintage | VF20 | XF40 | MS60 | MS63 | MS65 |
|---|---|---|---|---|---|---|
| 2010 | 3,000 | PF65 13.00 | | | | |

**KM# 228 ROUBLE**
13.16 g., Copper-Nickel, 33 mm. **Subject:** 3rd Belarus Front **Rev:** Col. Gen. Ivan Chernyakhovsky

| Date | Mintage | VF20 | XF40 | MS60 | MS63 | MS65 |
|---|---|---|---|---|---|---|
| 2010 | 3,000 | PF65 13.00 | | | | |

### KM# 229 ROUBLE

13.16 g., Copper-Nickel, 33 mm. **Subject:** 1st Baltic Forces **Rev:** Gen. Hovhannes Bagramayn

| Date | Mintage | VF20 | XF40 | MS60 | MS63 | MS65 |
|---|---|---|---|---|---|---|
| 2010 | 3,000 | PF65 13.00 | | | | |

### KM# 234 ROUBLE

13.16 g., Copper-Nickel, 32 mm. **Rev:** U.S. Frigate Constitution

| Date | Mintage | VF20 | XF40 | MS60 | MS63 | MS65 |
|---|---|---|---|---|---|---|
| 2010 | 3,000 | PF65 13.00 | | | | |

### KM# 236 ROUBLE

15.50 g., Copper-Nickel, 33 mm. **Subject:** Legend of the Tortoise **Obv:** Five stylized turtles **Rev:** Stylized turtle

| Date | Mintage | VF20 | XF40 | MS60 | MS63 | MS65 |
|---|---|---|---|---|---|---|
| 2010 Prooflike | 3,000 | — | — | — | — | 20.00 |

### KM# 240 ROUBLE

Copper-Nickel, 32 mm. **Subject:** Age of Majority **Rev:** Flowers and folk patterns

| Date | Mintage | VF20 | XF40 | MS60 | MS63 | MS65 |
|---|---|---|---|---|---|---|
| 2010 | 4,000 | PF65 13.00 | | | | |

### KM# 262 ROUBLE

14.35 g., Copper-Nickel, 33 mm. **Subject:** End of World War II, 65th Anniversary **Obv:** Broken clock face **Rev:** 5 doves in flight, kiting

| Date | Mintage | VF20 | XF40 | MS60 | MS63 | MS65 |
|---|---|---|---|---|---|---|
| 2010 Prooflike | 3,000 | — | — | — | — | 25.00 |

### KM# 263 ROUBLE

13.16 g., Copper-Nickel, 32 mm. **Obv:** Compass and chart **Rev:** Amergo Vespucci sailing ship

| Date | Mintage | VF20 | XF40 | MS60 | MS63 | MS65 |
|---|---|---|---|---|---|---|
| 2010 | 4,000 | PF65 17.50 | | | | |

### KM# 264 ROUBLE

15.50 g., Copper-Nickel, 33 mm. **Subject:** Metalsmith **Rev:** Horseshoe, house within, small horsemen flanking

| Date | Mintage | VF20 | XF40 | MS60 | MS63 | MS65 |
|---|---|---|---|---|---|---|
| 2010 | 3,500 | PF65 17.50 | | | | |

### KM# 265 ROUBLE

15.55 g., Copper-Nickel, 33 mm. **Subject:** Judaism **Rev:** Valozhyn Yeshiva façade, 1806 date

| Date | Mintage | VF20 | XF40 | MS60 | MS63 | MS65 |
|---|---|---|---|---|---|---|
| 2010 | 3,000 | PF65 15.00 | | | | |

### KM# 334 ROUBLE

15.50 g., Copper-Nickel, 33 mm. **Subject:** Battle of Grunwald, 600th Anniversary **Obv:** Figure in shape of cross **Rev:** Fingerprint **Edge:** Reeded

| Date | Mintage | VF20 | XF40 | MS60 | MS63 | MS65 |
|---|---|---|---|---|---|---|
| 2010 Prooflike | 3,000 | — | — | — | — | 25.00 |

### KM# 336 ROUBLE

13.16 g., Copper-Nickel, 32 mm. **Obv:** Bird in hand **Rev:** Kestrel in oval **Edge:** Reeded

| Date | Mintage | VF20 | XF40 | MS60 | MS63 | MS65 |
|---|---|---|---|---|---|---|
| 2010 Prooflike | 4,000 | — | — | — | — | 25.00 |

### KM# 337 ROUBLE

14.48 g., Copper-Nickel, 32 mm. **Subject:** Winter into Springtime **Obv:** Embroidery pattern **Rev:** Bird emerging from snow, into new fields and sunshine **Edge:** Reeded

| Date | Mintage | VF20 | XF40 | MS60 | MS63 | MS65 |
|---|---|---|---|---|---|---|
| 2010 Prooflike | 3,000 | — | — | — | — | 20.00 |

### KM# 338 ROUBLE

15.50 g., Copper-Nickel, 33 mm. **Subject:** Leu Sapieha **Obv:** Early document **Rev:** Standing figure in robes

| Date | Mintage | VF20 | XF40 | MS60 | MS63 | MS65 |
|---|---|---|---|---|---|---|
| 2010 Prooflike | 3,000 | — | — | — | — | 25.00 |

### KM# 270 ROUBLE

13.16 g., Copper-Nickel, 32 mm. **Obv:** Compass rose and chart **Rev:** Cutty Sark sailing right

| Date | Mintage | VF20 | XF40 | MS60 | MS63 | MS65 |
|---|---|---|---|---|---|---|
| 2011 | 3,000 | PF65 13.00 | | | | |

### KM# 287 ROUBLE

13.16 g., Copper-Nickel, 32 mm. **Subject:** M. Bogdanowicz **Obv:** Embroidery pattern **Rev:** Bust at left center

| Date | Mintage | VF20 | XF40 | MS60 | MS63 | MS65 |
|---|---|---|---|---|---|---|
| 2011 Prooflike | 2,000 | — | — | — | — | 20.00 |

### KM# 288 ROUBLE

20.00 g., Copper-Nickel, 37 mm. **Subject:** I. Bujnicki **Obv:** Scene of play **Rev:** Bust at left, scene of play

| Date | Mintage | VF20 | XF40 | MS60 | MS63 | MS65 |
|---|---|---|---|---|---|---|
| 2011 Prooflike | 2,000 | — | — | — | — | 25.00 |

### KM# 291 ROUBLE

13.16 g., Copper-Nickel, 32 mm. **Obv:** National arms **Rev:** Curlew bird standing left, oval background

| Date | Mintage | VF20 | XF40 | MS60 | MS63 | MS65 |
|---|---|---|---|---|---|---|
| 2011 Prooflike | 2,000 | — | — | — | — | 20.00 |

### KM# 339 ROUBLE

20.00 g., Copper-Nickel, 37 mm. **Subject:** Slavianski Bazaar in Vitebsk **Obv:** Stylized design **Rev:** Historic buildings and stylized designs **Edge:** Reeded

| Date | Mintage | VF20 | XF40 | MS60 | MS63 | MS65 |
|---|---|---|---|---|---|---|
| 2011 Prooflike | 2,500 | — | — | — | — | 25.00 |

### KM# 340 ROUBLE

13.16 g., Copper-Nickel, 32 mm. **Subject:** Motherhood **Obv:** Embroidery pattern **Rev:** Mother and baby

| Date | Mintage | VF20 | XF40 | MS60 | MS63 | MS65 |
|---|---|---|---|---|---|---|
| 2011 Prooflike | 2,000 | — | — | — | — | 20.00 |

### KM# 341 ROUBLE

13.16 g., Copper-Nickel, 32 mm. **Subject:** Kruzensztern **Obv:** Compass rose and nautical charts **Rev:** Square-rigged sailing ship

| Date | Mintage | VF20 | XF40 | MS60 | MS63 | MS65 |
|---|---|---|---|---|---|---|
| 2011 Prooflike | 2,000 | — | — | — | — | 50.00 |

**KM# 419 ROUBLE**
13.16 g., Copper-Nickel, 32 mm. **Subject:** Belarus-China Diplomatic Relations, 20th Anniversary **Obv:** National arms **Rev:** Hands clasped at center, national motifs around **Edge:** Reeded

| Date | Mintage | VF20 | XF40 | MS60 | MS63 | MS65 |
|---|---|---|---|---|---|---|
| 2012 | 2,000 | **PF65** 20.00 | | | | |

**KM# 427 ROUBLE**
15.50 g., Copper-Nickel, 33 mm. **Subject:** Belarus Bank, 90th Anniversary **Obv:** National arms **Rev:** Bank Building

| Date | Mintage | VF20 | XF40 | MS60 | MS63 | MS65 |
|---|---|---|---|---|---|---|
| 2012 Prooflike | 4,000 | — | — | — | — | 25.00 |

**KM# 428 ROUBLE**
20.00 g., Copper-Nickel, 37.1 mm. **Subject:** Belarus railways, 150th Anniversary **Obv:** National arms and modern trains **Rev:** Old locomotive at station

| Date | Mintage | VF20 | XF40 | MS60 | MS63 | MS65 |
|---|---|---|---|---|---|---|
| 2012 Prooflike | 2,000 | — | — | — | — | 25.00 |

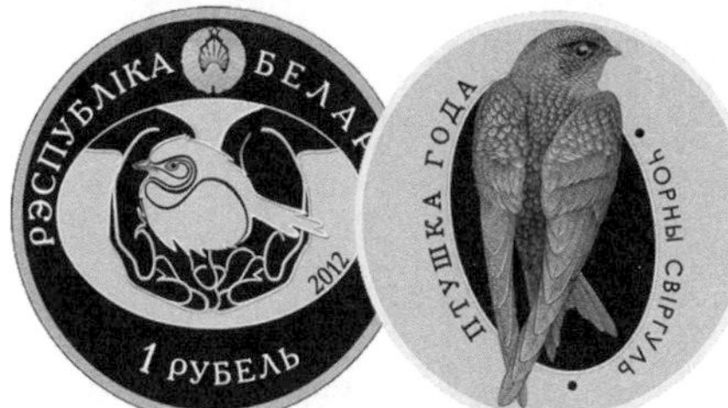


**KM# 429 ROUBLE**
13.16 g., Copper-Nickel, 32 mm. **Subject:** Birds of Belarus **Obv:** National arms and nesting bird **Rev:** Common Swift

| Date | Mintage | VF20 | XF40 | MS60 | MS63 | MS65 |
|---|---|---|---|---|---|---|
| 2012 Prooflike | 2,000 | — | — | — | — | 25.00 |

**KM# 430 ROUBLE**
13.10 g., Copper-Nickel, 32.1 mm. **Subject:** Fatherhood **Obv:** National arms and stylized DNA **Rev:** Stork carrying baby

| Date | Mintage | VF20 | XF40 | MS60 | MS63 | MS65 |
|---|---|---|---|---|---|---|
| 2012 Prooflike | 2,000 | — | — | — | — | 25.00 |

**KM# 431 ROUBLE**
19.50 g., Copper-Nickel, 37 mm. **Subject:** Maxim Tank, 100th Anniversary **Obv:** National arms and landscape **Rev:** Maxim tank and cranes

| Date | Mintage | VF20 | XF40 | MS60 | MS63 | MS65 |
|---|---|---|---|---|---|---|
| 2012 Prooflike | 2,000 | — | — | — | — | 25.00 |

**KM# 432 ROUBLE**
15.50 g., Copper-Nickel, 33 mm. **Subject:** Pottery **Obv:** National arms and wreath **Rev:** Pitcher filled with water

| Date | Mintage | VF20 | XF40 | MS60 | MS63 | MS65 |
|---|---|---|---|---|---|---|
| 2012 Prooflike | 25 | — | — | — | — | 3,000 |

**KM# 433 ROUBLE**
19.60 g., Copper-Nickel, 37.1 mm. **Subject:** War of 1812, 200th Anniversary **Obv:** National arms **Rev:** Memorial stone with inscription

| Date | Mintage | VF20 | XF40 | MS60 | MS63 | MS65 |
|---|---|---|---|---|---|---|
| 2012 Prooflike | 3,000 | — | — | — | — | 25.00 |

**KM# 434 ROUBLE**
27.03 g., Copper-Nickel, 38.61 mm. **Subject:** World Cup Soccer **Obv:** National arms **Rev:** Soccer player

| Date | Mintage | VF20 | XF40 | MS60 | MS63 | MS65 |
|---|---|---|---|---|---|---|
| 2013 Prooflike | 5,000 | — | — | — | — | 25.00 |

**KM# 435 ROUBLE**
19.50 g., Copper-Nickel, 37 mm. **Subject:** Belarus Ballet **Obv:** National arms and National Opera **Rev:** Ballerina

| Date | Mintage | VF20 | XF40 | MS60 | MS63 | MS65 |
|---|---|---|---|---|---|---|
| 2013 | 5,000 | **PF65** 20.00 | | | | |

**KM# 436 ROUBLE**
13.16 g., Copper-Nickel, 32 mm. **Subject:** BPS-Sberbank, 90th Anniversary **Obv:** National arms and geometric pattern **Rev:** Blossomed tree of life

| Date | Mintage | VF20 | XF40 | MS60 | MS63 | MS65 |
|---|---|---|---|---|---|---|
| 2013 Prooflike | 5,000 | — | — | — | — | 40.00 |

**KM# 437 ROUBLE**
15.50 g., Copper-Nickel, 33 mm. **Subject:** Christianization of the Rus, 1025th Anniversary **Obv:** National arms and stylized cross **Rev:** Dove and angels

| Date | Mintage | VF20 | XF40 | MS60 | MS63 | MS65 |
|---|---|---|---|---|---|---|
| 2013 Prooflike | 5,000 | — | — | — | — | 25.00 |

**KM# 438 ROUBLE**
19.50 g., Copper-Nickel, 37 mm. **Obv:** National arms and Budsalaus' Catholic Church **Rev:** Icon of Virgin Mary

| Date | Mintage | VF20 | XF40 | MS60 | MS63 | MS65 |
|---|---|---|---|---|---|---|
| 2013 | 5,000 | **PF65** 20.00 | | | | |

**KM# 448 ROUBLE**
27.00 g., Copper-Nickel, 38.61 mm. **Subject:** 2014 FIFA World Cup Brazil

| Date | Mintage | VF20 | XF40 | MS60 | MS63 | MS65 |
|---|---|---|---|---|---|---|
| 2013 | Est. 5000 | **PF65** 30.00 | | | | |

**KM# 454 ROUBLE**
19.50 g., Copper-Nickel, 37 mm. **Subject:** Belarusian Ballet

| Date | Mintage | VF20 | XF40 | MS60 | MS63 | MS65 |
|---|---|---|---|---|---|---|
| 2013 | Est. 5000 | **PF65** 25.00 | | | | |

**KM# 451 5 ROUBLE**
0.50 g., 0.999 Gold AGW, 11 mm. **Subject:** Belarusian Ballet

| Date | Mintage | VF20 | XF40 | MS60 | MS63 | MS65 |
|---|---|---|---|---|---|---|
| 2013 | Est. 10000 | **PF65** 50.00 | | | | |

**KM# 64 10 ROUBLES**
16.82 g., 0.925 Silver 0.5002 oz. ASW, 32.9 mm. **Obv:** National arms **Rev:** Jakub Kolas (1882-1956) **Edge:** Reeded

| Date | Mintage | VF20 | XF40 | MS60 | MS63 | MS65 |
|---|---|---|---|---|---|---|
| 2002 | 1,000 | **PF65** 150 | | | | |

**KM# 117 10 ROUBLES**
15.55 g., 0.925 Silver 0.4624 oz. ASW, 33 mm. **Subject:** 120th Birthday of Yanka Kupala **Obv:** National arms **Rev:** Yanka Kupala, 1882-1942

| Date | Mintage | VF20 | XF40 | MS60 | MS63 | MS65 |
|---|---|---|---|---|---|---|
| 2002 | 1,000 | **PF65** 150 | | | | |

**KM# 129 10 ROUBLES**
1.24 g., 0.999 Gold 0.0398 oz. AGW, 13.92 mm. **Subject:** Belarussian Ballet **Obv:** National arms **Rev:** Dancing ballerina

| Date | Mintage | VF20 | XF40 | MS60 | MS63 | MS65 |
|---|---|---|---|---|---|---|
| 2005 | 25,000 | — | — | — | 100 | 130 |

**KM# 342 10 ROUBLES**
1.24 g., 0.999 Gold 0.0398 oz. AGW, 13.92 mm. **Subject:** Ballet **Obv:** National arms **Rev:** Two ballet performers **Edge:** Reeded

| Date | Mintage | VF20 | XF40 | MS60 | MS63 | MS65 |
|---|---|---|---|---|---|---|
| 2006 | 25,000 | **PF65** 150 | | | | |

**KM# 156 10 ROUBLES**
16.81 g., 0.925 Silver 0.4999 oz. ASW, 32 mm. **Subject:** Alena Aladana **Rev:** Half-length figure facing, picture in background

| Date | Mintage | VF20 | XF40 | MS60 | MS63 | MS65 |
|---|---|---|---|---|---|---|
| 2007 | 4,000 | **PF65** 35.00 | | | | |

**KM# 157 10 ROUBLES**
16.81 g., 0.925 Silver 0.4999 oz. ASW, 32 mm. **Subject:** Thrush Nightingale **Rev:** Bird standing right on branch

| Date | Mintage | VF20 | XF40 | MS60 | MS63 | MS65 |
|---|---|---|---|---|---|---|
| 2007 | 5,000 | **PF65** 40.00 | | | | |

**KM# 343 10 ROUBLES**
1.24 g., 0.999 Gold 0.0398 oz. AGW, 13.92 mm. **Subject:** Ballet **Obv:** National arms **Rev:** Mirror image of ballerina **Edge:** Reeded

| Date | Mintage | VF20 | XF40 | MS60 | MS63 | MS65 |
|---|---|---|---|---|---|---|
| 2007 | 10,000 | **PF65** 150 | | | | |

**KM# 172 10 ROUBLES**
16.81 g., 0.925 Silver 0.4999 oz. ASW, 32 mm. **Subject:** Zair Azgur **Rev:** Profile right

| Date | Mintage | VF20 | XF40 | MS60 | MS63 | MS65 |
|---|---|---|---|---|---|---|
| 2008 | 3,000 | **PF65** 40.00 | | | | |

**KM# 173 10 ROUBLES**
16.81 g., 0.925 Silver 0.4999 oz. ASW, 32 mm. **Subject:** Great White Egret **Rev:** Bird standing left

| Date | Mintage | VF20 | XF40 | MS60 | MS63 | MS65 |
|---|---|---|---|---|---|---|
| 2008 | 5,000 | **PF65** 45.00 | | | | |

**KM# 174 10 ROUBLES**
16.81 g., 0.925 Silver 0.4999 oz. ASW, 32 mm. **Subject:** Vincent Dunin **Rev:** Bust facing

| Date | Mintage | VF20 | XF40 | MS60 | MS63 | MS65 |
|---|---|---|---|---|---|---|
| 2008 | 3,000 | **PF65** 35.00 | | | | |

**KM# 175 10 ROUBLES**
16.81 g., 0.925 Silver 0.4999 oz. ASW, 32 mm. **Subject:** St. Euphrosyne of Polotsk **Rev:** Half-length figure facing within frame

| Date | Mintage | VF20 | XF40 | MS60 | MS63 | MS65 |
|---|---|---|---|---|---|---|
| 2008 | 5,000 | **PF65** 40.00 | | | | |

**KM# 176 10 ROUBLES**
16.81 g., 0.925 Silver 0.4999 oz. ASW, 32 mm. **Subject:** St. Steraphin of Sarov **Rev:** Half-length figure standing within frame

| Date | Mintage | VF20 | XF40 | MS60 | MS63 | MS65 |
|---|---|---|---|---|---|---|
| 2008 | 5,000 | **PF65** 40.00 | | | | |

**KM# 177 10 ROUBLES**
16.81 g., 0.925 Silver 0.4999 oz. ASW, 32 mm. **Subject:** St. Sergii of Radonezh **Rev:** Half-length figure standing within frame

| Date | Mintage | VF20 | XF40 | MS60 | MS63 | MS65 |
|---|---|---|---|---|---|---|
| 2008 | 5,000 | **PF65** 40.00 | | | | |

**KM# 178 10 ROUBLES**
16.81 g., 0.925 Silver 0.4999 oz. ASW, 32 mm. **Subject:** St. Nicholas **Rev:** Half-length figure standing within frame

| Date | Mintage | VF20 | XF40 | MS60 | MS63 | MS65 |
|---|---|---|---|---|---|---|
| 2008 | 5,000 | **PF65** 40.00 | | | | |

**KM# 179 10 ROUBLES**
16.81 g., 0.925 Silver 0.4999 oz. ASW, 32 mm. **Subject:** St. Panteleimon **Rev:** Half-length figure standing within frame

| Date | Mintage | VF20 | XF40 | MS60 | MS63 | MS65 |
|---|---|---|---|---|---|---|
| 2008 | 5,000 | **PF65** 40.00 | | | | |

**KM# 194 10 ROUBLES**
16.81 g., 0.925 Silver 0.4999 oz. ASW, 32 mm. **Subject:** Academy of Science, 80th Anniversary **Rev:** Building

| Date | Mintage | VF20 | XF40 | MS60 | MS63 | MS65 |
|---|---|---|---|---|---|---|
| 2009 | 3,000 | **PF65** 40.00 | | | | |

**KM# 195 10 ROUBLES**
16.81 g., 0.925 Silver 0.4999 oz. ASW, 32 mm. **Subject:** Greylag goose **Rev:** Goose swimming left

| Date | Mintage | VF20 | XF40 | MS60 | MS63 | MS65 |
|---|---|---|---|---|---|---|
| 2009 | 5,000 | **PF65** 40.00 | | | | |

**KM# 344 10 ROUBLES**
16.81 g., 0.925 Silver 0.4999 oz. ASW, 33 mm. **Subject:** Establishment of the Federated State, 10th Anniversary **Obv:** National arms **Rev:** Document and ribbon **Edge:** Reeded

| Date | Mintage | VF20 | XF40 | MS60 | MS63 | MS65 |
|---|---|---|---|---|---|---|
| 2009 | 3,000 | PF65 50.00 | | | | |

**KM# 230 10 ROUBLES**
16.81 g., 0.925 Silver 0.4999 oz. ASW, 33 mm. **Subject:** 1st Belarus Front **Rev:** Gen. Konstantin Rokosovsky

| Date | Mintage | VF20 | XF40 | MS60 | MS63 | MS65 |
|---|---|---|---|---|---|---|
| 2010 | 2,500 | PF65 35.00 | | | | |

**KM# 231 10 ROUBLES**
16.81 g., 0.925 Silver 0.4999 oz. ASW, 33 mm. **Subject:** 2nd Belarus Front **Rev:** Col. Gen. G.F. Zakharov

| Date | Mintage | VF20 | XF40 | MS60 | MS63 | MS65 |
|---|---|---|---|---|---|---|
| 2010 | 2,500 | PF65 35.00 | | | | |

**KM# 232 10 ROUBLES**
16.55 g., 0.925 Silver 0.4922 oz. ASW, 33 mm. **Subject:** 3rd Belarus front **Rev:** Col. Gen. Ivan Chernyakovsky

| Date | Mintage | VF20 | XF40 | MS60 | MS63 | MS65 |
|---|---|---|---|---|---|---|
| 2010 | 2,500 | PF65 35.00 | | | | |

**KM# 233 10 ROUBLES**
16.55 g., 0.925 Silver 0.4922 oz. ASW, 33 mm. **Subject:** 1st Baltic Front **Rev:** Gen. Hovhannes Bagramgan

| Date | Mintage | VF20 | XF40 | MS60 | MS63 | MS65 |
|---|---|---|---|---|---|---|
| 2010 | 2,500 | PF65 35.00 | | | | |

**KM# 260 10 ROUBLES**
16.81 g., 0.925 Silver 0.4999 oz. ASW, 32 mm. **Obv:** Stylized kestrel in egg **Rev:** Common kestrel

| Date | Mintage | VF20 | XF40 | MS60 | MS63 | MS65 |
|---|---|---|---|---|---|---|
| 2010 | 2,500 | PF65 75.00 | | | | |

**KM# 345 10 ROUBLES**
16.81 g., 0.925 Silver 0.4999 oz. ASW, 33 mm. **Subject:** Talmudic School **Obv:** Menorah and writings **Rev:** School façade

| Date | Mintage | VF20 | XF40 | MS60 | MS63 | MS65 |
|---|---|---|---|---|---|---|
| 2010 | 300 | PF65 75.00 | | | | |

**KM# 284 10 ROUBLES**
16.81 g., 0.925 Silver 0.4999 oz. ASW, 37 mm. **Subject:** I. Bujnicki **Obv:** Play scene **Rev:** Bust at left, place scene

| Date | Mintage | VF20 | XF40 | MS60 | MS63 | MS65 |
|---|---|---|---|---|---|---|
| 2011 Prooflike | 2,000 | — | — | — | — | 75.00 |

**KM# 346 10 ROUBLES**
16.81 g., 0.925 Silver 0.4999 oz. ASW, 37 mm. **Subject:** Slavianski Bazaar **Obv:** Stylized design **Rev:** Historic buildings and stylized design **Edge:** Reeded

| Date | Mintage | VF20 | XF40 | MS60 | MS63 | MS65 |
|---|---|---|---|---|---|---|
| 2011 | 2,500 | PF65 75.00 | | | | |

**KM# 347 10 ROUBLES**
1.00 g., 0.900 Gold 0.0289 oz. AGW, 12 mm. **Subject:** M. Oginski **Obv:** National arms **Rev:** Bust facing

| Date | Mintage | VF20 | XF40 | MS60 | MS63 | MS65 |
|---|---|---|---|---|---|---|
| 2011 | 2,000 | PF65 150 | | | | |

**KM# 348 10 ROUBLES**
16.81 g., 0.925 Silver 0.4999 oz. ASW, 32 mm. **Subject:** Curlew bird **Obv:** Bird in hand **Rev:** Curlew bird in vertical oval

| Date | Mintage | VF20 | XF40 | MS60 | MS63 | MS65 |
|---|---|---|---|---|---|---|
| 2011 Prooflike | 2,000 | — | — | — | — | 75.00 |

**KM# 349 10 ROUBLES**
16.81 g., 0.925 Silver 0.4999 oz. ASW, 32 mm. **Subject:** M. Bogdanowicz **Obv:** Embroidery pattern **Rev:** Bust at left, pattern design

| Date | Mintage | VF20 | XF40 | MS60 | MS63 | MS65 |
|---|---|---|---|---|---|---|
| 2011 Prooflike | 2,000 | — | — | — | — | 75.00 |

**KM# 424 10 ROUBLES**
20.00 g., 0.925 Silver 0.5948 oz. ASW, 38.61 mm. **Obv:** National arms **Rev:** Centaurea Cyanus flower

| Date | Mintage | VF20 | XF40 | MS60 | MS63 | MS65 |
|---|---|---|---|---|---|---|
| 2012 | — | PF65 32.50 | | | | |

**KM# 425 10 ROUBLES**
0.925 Silver, 38.61 mm. **Subject:** Railways: 150th Anniversary **Obv:** Modern train and station **Rev:** Old time train and station

| Date | Mintage | VF20 | XF40 | MS60 | MS63 | MS65 |
|---|---|---|---|---|---|---|
| 2012 | — | — | — | — | 100 | 120 |

**KM# 446 10 ROUBLES**
20.00 g., 0.925 Silver 0.5948 oz. ASW, 38.61 mm. **Subject:** 2014 FFIA World Cup Brazil

| Date | Mintage | VF20 | XF40 | MS60 | MS63 | MS65 |
|---|---|---|---|---|---|---|
| 2013 | Est. 10000 | PF65 75.00 | | | | |

**KM# 46 20 ROUBLES**
33.73 g., 0.925 Silver 1.0031 oz. ASW, 38.6 mm. **Subject:** Wildlife **Obv:** National arms **Rev:** European Bison **Edge:** Reeded

| Date | Mintage | VF20 | XF40 | MS60 | MS63 | MS65 |
|---|---|---|---|---|---|---|
| 2001 | 2,000 | PF65 350 | | | | |

**KM# 49 20 ROUBLES**
28.32 g., 0.925 Silver 0.8422 oz. ASW, 38.6 mm. **Subject:** 2002 Winter Olympics **Obv:** National arms **Rev:** Marksman aiming at bullseye **Edge:** Reeded

| Date | Mintage | VF20 | XF40 | MS60 | MS63 | MS65 |
|---|---|---|---|---|---|---|
| 2001 | 15,000 | PF65 60.00 | | | | |

**KM# 51 20 ROUBLES**
33.65 g., 0.925 Silver 1.0007 oz. ASW, 38.6 mm. **Subject:** 2002 Winter Olympics **Obv:** National arms **Rev:** Two freestyle skiers **Edge:** Reeded

| Date | Mintage | VF20 | XF40 | MS60 | MS63 | MS65 |
|---|---|---|---|---|---|---|
| 2001 | 2,000 | PF65 70.00 | | | | |

**KM# 111 20 ROUBLES**
31.10 g., 0.925 Silver 0.9249 oz. ASW, 38.61 mm. **Subject:** 900th Anniversary of Euphrasinta **Obv:** National arms **Rev:** Euphrasinta of Polatsk, gold cross

| Date | Mintage | VF20 | XF40 | MS60 | MS63 | MS65 |
|---|---|---|---|---|---|---|
| 2001 | Est. 2000 | PF65 350 | | | | |

**KM# 113 20 ROUBLES**
31.10 g., 0.925 Silver 0.9249 oz. ASW, 38.61 mm. **Subject:** Tower of Kamyantes **Obv:** National arms **Rev:** Kamyanets Tower, seal

| Date | Mintage | VF20 | XF40 | MS60 | MS63 | MS65 |
|---|---|---|---|---|---|---|
| 2001 | 2,000 | PF65 110 | | | | |

**KM# 45 20 ROUBLES**
33.73 g., 0.925 Silver 1.0031 oz. ASW, 38.8 mm. **Obv:** National arms **Rev:** European beaver and young **Edge:** Reeded

| Date | Mintage | VF20 | XF40 | MS60 | MS63 | MS65 |
|---|---|---|---|---|---|---|
| 2002 | 2,000 | PF65 200 | | | | |

**KM# 59 20 ROUBLES**
28.63 g., 0.925 Silver 0.8514 oz. ASW, 38.6 mm. **Obv:** National arms **Rev:** Brown bear with two cubs **Edge:** Reeded

| Date | Mintage | VF20 | XF40 | MS60 | MS63 | MS65 |
|---|---|---|---|---|---|---|
| 2002 | 5,000 | PF65 120 | | | | |

**KM# 70 20 ROUBLES**
33.85 g., 0.925 Silver 1.0067 oz. ASW, 38.61 mm. **Obv:** National arms **Rev:** 80th Anniversary - National Savings Bank **Edge:** Reeded

| Date | Mintage | VF20 | XF40 | MS60 | MS63 | MS65 |
|---|---|---|---|---|---|---|
| 2002 | 1,000 | PF65 225 | | | | |

**KM# 115 20 ROUBLES**
31.10 g., 0.925 Silver 0.9249 oz. ASW, 38.61 mm. **Subject:** 200th Birthday of Ignatius Dameika **Obv:** National arms **Rev:** Ignatius Dameika, hammer and inset with a dameikit stone

| Date | Mintage | VF20 | XF40 | MS60 | MS63 | MS65 |
|---|---|---|---|---|---|---|
| 2002 | 1,000 | PF65 350 | | | | |

**KM# 119 20 ROUBLES**
28.28 g., 0.925 Silver 0.841 oz. ASW, 38.61 mm. **Subject:** 2006 World Cup Football **Obv:** National arms **Rev:** Stylized 2006, football

| Date | Mintage | VF20 | XF40 | MS60 | MS63 | MS65 |
|---|---|---|---|---|---|---|
| 2002 | 25,000 | PF65 75.00 | | | | |

**KM# 53 20 ROUBLES**
33.84 g., 0.925 Silver 1.0064 oz. ASW, 38.5 mm. **Obv:** State arms **Rev:** Two Mute swans on water with reflections **Edge:** Reeded

| Date | Mintage | VF20 | XF40 | MS60 | MS63 | MS65 |
|---|---|---|---|---|---|---|
| 2003 | 2,000 | PF65 250 | | | | |

**KM# 57 20 ROUBLES**
31.10 g., 0.925 Silver 0.9249 oz. ASW, 38.6 mm. **Obv:** National arms **Rev:** Church of the Savior and Transfiguration **Edge:** Reeded

| Date | Mintage | VF20 | XF40 | MS60 | MS63 | MS65 |
|---|---|---|---|---|---|---|
| 2003 | 2,000 | PF65 100 | | | | |

**KM# 120 20 ROUBLES**
31.10 g., 0.925 Silver 0.9249 oz. ASW, 38.61 mm. **Subject:** Freestyle Wrestling **Obv:** National arms **Rev:** Two wrestlers

| Date | Mintage | VF20 | XF40 | MS60 | MS63 | MS65 |
|---|---|---|---|---|---|---|
| 2003 | 3,000 | PF65 65.00 | | | | |

**KM# 122 20 ROUBLES**
31.10 g., 0.925 Silver 0.9249 oz. ASW, 38.61 mm. **Obv:** National arms **Rev:** Herring gull in flight

| Date | Mintage | VF20 | XF40 | MS60 | MS63 | MS65 |
|---|---|---|---|---|---|---|
| 2003 | 2,000 | PF65 200 | | | | |

**KM# 149 20 ROUBLES**
28.28 g., 0.925 Silver 0.841 oz. ASW, 38.61 mm. **Subject:** 2004 Olympic Games **Obv:** National arms **Rev:** Female shot-putter

| Date | Mintage | VF20 | XF40 | MS60 | MS63 | MS65 |
|---|---|---|---|---|---|---|
| 2003 | 25,000 | PF65 65.00 | | | | |

**KM# 71 20 ROUBLES**
31.10 g., 0.925 Silver 0.9249 oz. ASW, 38.6 mm. **Subject:** Kupalle **Obv:** Folk art design **Rev:** Fern flower with inset red synthetic crystal **Edge:** Reeded

| Date | Mintage | VF20 | XF40 | MS60 | MS63 | MS65 |
|---|---|---|---|---|---|---|
| 2004 Antique finish | 3,000 | — | — | — | 600 | — |

**KM# 72 20 ROUBLES**
31.10 g., 0.925 Silver 0.9249 oz. ASW, 38.6 mm. **Subject:** Defense of Brest **Obv:** Multicolor Soviet Order of the Patriotic War **Rev:** Courage" monument **Edge:** Reeded

| Date | Mintage | VF20 | XF40 | MS60 | MS63 | MS65 |
|---|---|---|---|---|---|---|
| 2004 | 3,000 | PF65 100 | | | | |

**KM# 73 20 ROUBLES**
31.10 g., 0.925 Silver 0.9249 oz. ASW, 38.6 mm. **Obv:** National arms **Rev:** Two common cranes **Edge:** Reeded

| Date | Mintage | VF20 | XF40 | MS60 | MS63 | MS65 |
|---|---|---|---|---|---|---|
| 2004 | 2,000 | PF65 170 | | | | |

**KM# 77 20 ROUBLES**
31.10 g., 0.925 Silver 0.9249 oz. ASW, 38.6 mm. **Subject:** Kalyady **Obv:** Folk art cross design **Rev:** Stylized sunflower with inset blue synthetic crystal **Edge:** Reeded

| Date | Mintage | VF20 | XF40 | MS60 | MS63 | MS65 |
|---|---|---|---|---|---|---|
| 2004 Antique finish | 5,000 | — | — | — | 350 | — |

**KM# 79 20 ROUBLES**
31.10 g., 0.925 Silver 0.9249 oz. ASW, 38.6 mm. **Obv:** National arms **Rev:** Radziwill's Castle in Neswizh **Edge:** Reeded

| Date | Mintage | VF20 | XF40 | MS60 | MS63 | MS65 |
|---|---|---|---|---|---|---|
| 2004 | 2,000 | PF65 100 | | | | |

**KM# 84 20 ROUBLES**
31.10 g., 0.925 Silver 0.9249 oz. ASW, 38.61 mm. **Subject:** Memory of Facist Victims **Obv:** Multicolored Order of the Patriotic War **Rev:** Man holding dead

| Date | Mintage | VF20 | XF40 | MS60 | MS63 | MS65 |
|---|---|---|---|---|---|---|
| 2004 | 2,000 | — | — | — | 100 | — |

**KM# 86 20 ROUBLES**
31.10 g., 0.925 Silver 0.9249 oz. ASW, 38.61 mm. **Subject:** Soviet Warriors - Liberators **Obv:** Multicolored Order of the Patriotic War **Rev:** Partisans with blown up railway track

| Date | Mintage | VF20 | XF40 | MS60 | MS63 | MS65 |
|---|---|---|---|---|---|---|
| 2004 | 2,000 | — | — | — | 100 | — |

**KM# 91 20 ROUBLES**
31.10 g., 0.925 Silver 0.9249 oz. ASW, 38.61 mm. **Subject:** Trade Union Movement Centennial **Obv:** National arms

| Date | Mintage | VF20 | XF40 | MS60 | MS63 | MS65 |
|---|---|---|---|---|---|---|
| 2004 | 1,500 | PF65 200 | | | | |

**KM# 124 20 ROUBLES**
31.10 g., 0.925 Silver 0.9249 oz. ASW, 38.61 mm. **Subject:** Sculling **Obv:** National arms **Rev:** Two rowers against a background of stylized oars

| Date | Mintage | VF20 | XF40 | MS60 | MS63 | MS65 |
|---|---|---|---|---|---|---|
| 2004 | 3,000 | — | — | — | 50.00 | — |

**KM# 350 20 ROUBLES**
33.62 g., 0.925 Silver 0.9998 oz. ASW, 38.61 mm. **Obv:** Russian Order star **Rev:** Soldier with rifle and tank

| Date | Mintage | VF20 | XF40 | MS60 | MS63 | MS65 |
|---|---|---|---|---|---|---|
| 2004 | 2,000 | PF65 150 | | | | |

**KM# 351 20 ROUBLES**
33.62 g., 0.925 Silver 0.9998 oz. ASW, 39 mm. **Subject:** Mogilev **Obv:** National arms **Rev:** Shield and city view

| Date | Mintage | VF20 | XF40 | MS60 | MS63 | MS65 |
|---|---|---|---|---|---|---|
| 2004 | 2,000 | PF65 200 | | | | |

**KM# 82 20 ROUBLES**
28.72 g., 0.925 Silver 0.8541 oz. ASW, 38.6 mm. **Subject:** WW II Victory **Obv:** Multicolor Soviet Order of Victory **Rev:** Soviet soldiers raising their flag in the Reichstag in Berlin **Edge:** Reeded

| Date | Mintage | VF20 | XF40 | MS60 | MS63 | MS65 |
|---|---|---|---|---|---|---|
| 2005 | 12,000 | PF65 60.00 | | | | |

**KM# 92 20 ROUBLES**
28.63 g., 0.925 Silver 0.8514 oz. ASW, 38.6 mm. **Obv:** Two children sitting on crescent moon **Rev:** Symon the Musician and inset orange color glass crystal **Edge:** Plain

| Date | Mintage | VF20 | XF40 | MS60 | MS63 | MS65 |
|---|---|---|---|---|---|---|
| 2005 Antique finish | 20,000 | — | — | — | 65.00 | — |

**KM# 93 20 ROUBLES**
28.28 g., 0.925 Silver 0.841 oz. ASW, 38.61 mm. **Subject:** Kalyady's star **Obv:** Two children sitting on a crescent moon **Rev:** Snow Queen, blue glass crystal inset on forehead, flower **Edge:** Plain

| Date | Mintage | VF20 | XF40 | MS60 | MS63 | MS65 |
|---|---|---|---|---|---|---|
| 2005 Antique finish | 20,000 | — | — | — | 65.00 | — |

**KM# 94 20 ROUBLES**
28.63 g., 0.925 Silver 0.8514 oz. ASW, 38.6 mm. **Obv:** Two children sitting on a crescent moon **Rev:** White glass crystal inset above landscape with fox, the Little Prince **Edge:** Plain

| Date | Mintage | VF20 | XF40 | MS60 | MS63 | MS65 |
|---|---|---|---|---|---|---|
| 2005 Antique finish | 20,000 | — | — | — | 65.00 | — |

**KM# 95 20 ROUBLES**
28.63 g., 0.925 Silver 0.8514 oz. ASW, 38.61 mm. **Obv:** Two children sitting on a crescent moon **Rev:** The Stone Flower, Yellow glass crystal inset in flower design, heads flank **Edge:** Plain

| Date | Mintage | VF20 | XF40 | MS60 | MS63 | MS65 |
|---|---|---|---|---|---|---|
| 2005 Antique finish | 20,000 | — | — | — | 65.00 | — |

**KM# 96 20 ROUBLES**
33.66 g., 0.925 Silver 1.001 oz. ASW, 38.6 mm. **Subject:** Festivals and Rites - Bogach **Obv:** Small national arms above quilted star design **Rev:** Yellow glass crystal inset in candle flame above basket **Edge:** Reeded

| Date | Mintage | VF20 | XF40 | MS60 | MS63 | MS65 |
|---|---|---|---|---|---|---|
| 2005 Antique patina | 5,000 | — | — | — | 170 | — |

**KM# 98 20 ROUBLES**
33.63 g., 0.925 Silver 1.0001 oz. ASW, 38.6 mm. **Subject:** Almany Bogs **Obv:** Blooming plant on frosted design **Rev:** Great grey owl in flight **Edge:** Reeded

| Date | Mintage | VF20 | XF40 | MS60 | MS63 | MS65 |
|---|---|---|---|---|---|---|
| 2005 | 5,000 | PF65 70.00 | | | | |

**KM# 99 20 ROUBLES**
31.10 g., 0.925 Silver 0.9249 oz. ASW, 38.6 mm. **Series:** Easter Egg **Obv:** Quilted cross design **Rev:** Decorated Easter egg with inset pink glass crystal

| Date | Mintage | VF20 | XF40 | MS60 | MS63 | MS65 |
|---|---|---|---|---|---|---|
| 2005 Antique finish | 5,000 | — | — | — | 250 | — |

**KM# 100 20 ROUBLES**
33.62 g., 0.925 Silver 0.9998 oz. ASW, 38.6 mm. **Obv:** Large church **Rev:** Usyaslau of Polatsk

| Date | Mintage | VF20 | XF40 | MS60 | MS63 | MS65 |
|---|---|---|---|---|---|---|
| 2005 | 5,000 | PF65 60.00 | | | | |

**KM# 101 20 ROUBLES**
25.00 g., 0.925 Silver 0.7435 oz. ASW, 38.6 mm. **Subject:** 2006 FIFA World Cup Germany **Obv:** National arms **Rev:** Multicolor Europe, Asia and African maps on soccer ball **Note:** 2006 World Cup Soccer

| Date | Mintage | VF20 | XF40 | MS60 | MS63 | MS65 |
|---|---|---|---|---|---|---|
| 2005 | 50,000 | PF65 55.00 | | | | |

### KM# 102 20 ROUBLES

33.94 g., 0.925 Silver 1.0094 oz. ASW, 39 mm. **Obv:** National arms **Rev:** Female tennis player

| Date | Mintage | VF20 | XF40 | MS60 | MS63 | MS65 |
|---|---|---|---|---|---|---|
| 2005 | 7,000 | PF65 60.00 | | | | |

### KM# 128 20 ROUBLES

31.10 g., 0.925 Silver 0.9249 oz. ASW, 38.61 mm. **Subject:** 1000th Anniversary of Vaukavysk **Obv:** National arms **Rev:** National arms of Vaukavysk

| Date | Mintage | VF20 | XF40 | MS60 | MS63 | MS65 |
|---|---|---|---|---|---|---|
| 2005 | 2,000 | PF65 100 | | | | |

### KM# 131 20 ROUBLES

31.10 g., 0.925 Silver 0.9249 oz. ASW, 38.61 mm. **Subject:** Jesuit Roman Catholic Church **Obv:** National arms **Rev:** Jesuit Roman Catholic Church in Niasvizh

| Date | Mintage | VF20 | XF40 | MS60 | MS63 | MS65 |
|---|---|---|---|---|---|---|
| 2005 | 2,000 | PF65 100 | | | | |

### KM# 133 20 ROUBLES

28.28 g., 0.925 Silver 0.841 oz. ASW, 38.61 mm. **Subject:** 2006 Olympic Games **Obv:** National arms **Rev:** Two hockey players

| Date | Mintage | VF20 | XF40 | MS60 | MS63 | MS65 |
|---|---|---|---|---|---|---|
| 2005 | 15,000 | PF65 60.00 | | | | |

### KM# 352 20 ROUBLES

33.62 g., 0.925 Silver 0.9998 oz. ASW, 39 mm. **Subject:** Grodno **Obv:** National arms **Rev:** Shield and fortress

| Date | Mintage | VF20 | XF40 | MS60 | MS63 | MS65 |
|---|---|---|---|---|---|---|
| 2005 | 2,000 | PF65 150 | | | | |

### KM# 353 20 ROUBLES

33.62 g., 0.925 Silver 0.9998 oz. ASW, 39 mm. **Subject:** Brest **Obv:** National arms **Rev:** Shield and fortress

| Date | Mintage | VF20 | XF40 | MS60 | MS63 | MS65 |
|---|---|---|---|---|---|---|
| 2005 | 2,000 | PF65 150 | | | | |

### KM# 136 20 ROUBLES

33.63 g., 0.925 Silver 1.0001 oz. ASW, 38.61 mm. **Subject:** Vtaselle Wedding **Obv:** National arms, birds, shamrock **Rev:** Loaf of bread, golden wedding rings, diadem of flowers, background of honeycomb

| Date | Mintage | VF20 | XF40 | MS60 | MS63 | MS65 |
|---|---|---|---|---|---|---|
| 2006 | 25,000 | — | — | — | 70.00 | — |

### KM# 139 20 ROUBLES

33.62 g., 0.925 Silver 0.9998 oz. ASW, 38.61 mm. **Subject:** Sophia of Galshany 600th Anniversary **Obv:** Castle of Galshany **Rev:** National arms and Sophia of Galshany

| Date | Mintage | VF20 | XF40 | MS60 | MS63 | MS65 |
|---|---|---|---|---|---|---|
| 2006 | 5,000 | PF65 70.00 | | | | |

### KM# 141 20 ROUBLES

33.62 g., 0.925 Silver 0.9998 oz. ASW, 38.61 mm. **Subject:** Festivals and Rites - Syomukha **Obv:** National arms, solar symbol **Rev:** Chalice, Chaplet of birch, maple, rowan, sweet flag leaves inserted in green crystal

| Date | Mintage | VF20 | XF40 | MS60 | MS63 | MS65 |
|---|---|---|---|---|---|---|
| 2006 Antique patina | 5,000 | — | — | — | 150 | — |

### KM# 147 20 ROUBLES

33.63 g., 0.925 Silver 1.0001 oz. ASW, 38.61 mm. **Subject:** Chyrvomy Bar **Obv:** National arms, blooming plant **Rev:** European mink

| Date | Mintage | VF20 | XF40 | MS60 | MS63 | MS65 |
|---|---|---|---|---|---|---|
| 2006 | 5,000 | PF65 100 | | | | |

### KM# 148 20 ROUBLES

28.28 g., 0.925 Silver 0.841 oz. ASW, 38.5 mm. **Subject:** Twelve Months **Obv:** Two children sitting on a crescent moon **Rev:** Campfire with inset amber in a circle of produce **Edge:** Plain **Note:** Antiqued finish. Prev. duplicate of KM #137.

| Date | Mintage | VF20 | XF40 | MS60 | MS63 | MS65 |
|---|---|---|---|---|---|---|
| 2006 | 20,000 | — | — | — | 65.00 | — |

### KM# 155 20 ROUBLES

33.62 g., 0.925 Silver 0.9998 oz. ASW, 36x36 mm. **Subject:** Struve Geodetric Arc **Rev:** Map of Eastern Europe **Shape:** Square

| Date | Mintage | VF20 | XF40 | MS60 | MS63 | MS65 |
|---|---|---|---|---|---|---|
| 2006 | 5,000 | PF65 60.00 | | | | |

### KM# 354 20 ROUBLES

33.62 g., 0.925 Silver 0.9998 oz. ASW, 39 mm. **Subject:** Homel **Obv:** National arms **Rev:** Shield and fortress

| Date | Mintage | VF20 | XF40 | MS60 | MS63 | MS65 |
|---|---|---|---|---|---|---|
| 2006 | 2,000 | PF65 350 | | | | |

### KM# 355 20 ROUBLES

33.62 g., 0.925 Silver 0.9998 oz. ASW, 38.61 mm. **Subject:** CIS, 15th Anniversary **Obv:** Building façade **Rev:** Emblem

| Date | Mintage | VF20 | XF40 | MS60 | MS63 | MS65 |
|---|---|---|---|---|---|---|
| 2006 | 5,000 | PF65 75.00 | | | | |

### KM# 356 20 ROUBLES

33.62 g., 0.925 Silver 0.9998 oz. ASW, 38.61 mm. **Subject:** Ski Center in Siliczy **Obv:** Skier **Rev:** Town view

| Date | Mintage | VF20 | XF40 | MS60 | MS63 | MS65 |
|---|---|---|---|---|---|---|
| 2006 | 5,000 | PF65 75.00 | | | | |

### KM# 357 20 ROUBLES

33.62 g., 0.925 Silver 0.9998 oz. ASW, 38.61 mm. **Subject:** Rogwold and Rogneda **Obv:** Fortified circular town **Rev:** Norseman and female, ship

| Date | Mintage | VF20 | XF40 | MS60 | MS63 | MS65 |
|---|---|---|---|---|---|---|
| 2006 | 5,000 | PF65 85.00 | | | | |

### KM# 358 20 ROUBLES

28.28 g., 0.925 Silver 0.841 oz. ASW, 38.61 mm. **Subject:** Tale of the Thousand and one nights **Obv:** Boy and girl sitting on crescent moon **Rev:** Arabic window frame and motif

| Date | Mintage | VF20 | XF40 | MS60 | MS63 | MS65 |
|---|---|---|---|---|---|---|
| 2006 Antique patina | 20,000 | — | — | — | — | 75.00 |

### KM# 359 20 ROUBLES

33.62 g., 0.925 Silver 0.9998 oz. ASW, 38.61 mm. **Subject:** Cycling **Obv:** National arms **Rev:** Two bikes on track

| Date | Mintage | VF20 | XF40 | MS60 | MS63 | MS65 |
|---|---|---|---|---|---|---|
| 2006 | 5,000 | PF65 80.00 | | | | |

### KM# 360 20 ROUBLES

28.28 g., 0.925 Silver 0.841 oz. ASW, 38.61 mm. **Subject:** Beijing Olympics, 2008 **Obv:** National arms **Rev:** Runners around center circle

| Date | Mintage | VF20 | XF40 | MS60 | MS63 | MS65 |
|---|---|---|---|---|---|---|
| 2006 | 20,000 | PF65 80.00 | | | | |

### KM# 158 20 ROUBLES

33.62 g., 0.925 Silver 0.9998 oz. ASW, 38.61 mm. **Subject:** Belarus - China diplomatic relations **Rev:** Double arches with country scene

| Date | Mintage | VF20 | XF40 | MS60 | MS63 | MS65 |
|---|---|---|---|---|---|---|
| 2007 | 2,000 | PF65 100 | | | | |

### KM# 159 20 ROUBLES

33.62 g., 0.925 Silver 0.9998 oz. ASW, 38.61 mm. **Subject:** Festivals and Rites - Maslenica **Rev:** Pancake and syrup

| Date | Mintage | VF20 | XF40 | MS60 | MS63 | MS65 |
|---|---|---|---|---|---|---|
| 2007 Antique Patina | 5,000 | — | — | — | 130 | — |

### KM# 160 20 ROUBLES

33.63 g., 0.925 Silver 1.0001 oz. ASW, 38.61 mm. **Subject:** Napoleon Orda **Rev:** Bust facing, record and musical notes in background

| Date | Mintage | VF20 | XF40 | MS60 | MS63 | MS65 |
|---|---|---|---|---|---|---|
| 2007 | 5,000 | PF65 60.00 | | | | |

**KM# 161 20 ROUBLES**
28.28 g., 0.925 Silver 0.841 oz. ASW, 38.61 mm. **Subject:** Alice in Wonderland **Obv:** Two children sitting on crescent moon reading book **Rev:** Alice and the March Hare

| Date | Mintage | VF20 | XF40 | MS60 | MS63 | MS65 |
|---|---|---|---|---|---|---|
| 2007 Matte Proof | 20,000 | PF65 60.00 | | | | |

**KM# 162 20 ROUBLES**
28.28 g., 0.925 Silver 0.841 oz. ASW, 38.61 mm. **Subject:** Alice Through the Looking Glass **Obv:** Two children sitting on crescent moon reading book **Rev:** Alice and chess board

| Date | Mintage | VF20 | XF40 | MS60 | MS63 | MS65 |
|---|---|---|---|---|---|---|
| 2007 Matte Proof | 20,000 | PF65 60.00 | | | | |

**KM# 163 20 ROUBLES**
31.11 g., 0.999 Silver 0.999 oz. ASW, 40 mm. **Subject:** Belarusian Ballet **Rev:** Ballerina and mirror view

| Date | Mintage | VF20 | XF40 | MS60 | MS63 | MS65 |
|---|---|---|---|---|---|---|
| 2007 | 10,000 | PF65 60.00 | | | | |

**KM# 164 20 ROUBLES**
31.10 g., 0.925 Silver 0.9249 oz. ASW, 38.61 mm. **Subject:** International Polar Year **Obv:** IPY logo **Rev:** Antartic map behind two penguins

| Date | Mintage | VF20 | XF40 | MS60 | MS63 | MS65 |
|---|---|---|---|---|---|---|
| 2007 | 10,000 | PF65 60.00 | | | | |

**KM# 165 20 ROUBLES**
33.62 g., 0.925 Silver 0.9998 oz. ASW, 38.61 mm. **Subject:** Prince Gleb of Mensk **Obv:** Wood log building **Rev:** Knight seated left

| Date | Mintage | VF20 | XF40 | MS60 | MS63 | MS65 |
|---|---|---|---|---|---|---|
| 2007 | 5,000 | PF65 60.00 | | | | |

**KM# 166 20 ROUBLES**
33.62 g., 0.925 Silver 0.9998 oz. ASW, 38.61 mm. **Subject:** Legend of the Stork **Obv:** Woven basket design **Rev:** Stylized bird

| Date | Mintage | VF20 | XF40 | MS60 | MS63 | MS65 |
|---|---|---|---|---|---|---|
| 2007 | 5,000 | PF65 65.00 | | | | |

**KM# 167 20 ROUBLES**
31.11 g., 0.999 Silver 0.999 oz. ASW, 38.61 mm. **Subject:** Wolf - Canis Lupus **Rev:** Wolf head facing

| Date | Mintage | VF20 | XF40 | MS60 | MS63 | MS65 |
|---|---|---|---|---|---|---|
| 2007 | 7,000 | PF65 90.00 | | | | |

**KM# 168 20 ROUBLES**
31.11 g., 0.999 Silver 0.999 oz. ASW, 38.61 mm. **Subject:** Wolf - Canis Lupis **Rev:** Wolf standing on rock ledge behind second wolf's head facing

| Date | Mintage | VF20 | XF40 | MS60 | MS63 | MS65 |
|---|---|---|---|---|---|---|
| 2007 | 7,000 | PF65 90.00 | | | | |

**KM# 169 20 ROUBLES**
33.63 g., 0.925 Silver 1.0001 oz. ASW, 38.61 mm. **Subject:** Dniepra - Sozhsky **Rev:** Sturgeon fish

| Date | Mintage | VF20 | XF40 | MS60 | MS63 | MS65 |
|---|---|---|---|---|---|---|
| 2007 | 5,000 | PF65 85.00 | | | | |

**KM# 180 20 ROUBLES**
33.63 g., 0.925 Silver 1.0001 oz. ASW, 38.61 mm. **Subject:** Minsk **Rev:** Old and new city views

| Date | Mintage | VF20 | XF40 | MS60 | MS63 | MS65 |
|---|---|---|---|---|---|---|
| 2008 | 7,000 | PF65 60.00 | | | | |

**KM# 181 20 ROUBLES**
33.63 g., 0.925 Silver 1.0001 oz. ASW, 38.61 mm. **Subject:** Financial System, 90th Anniversary **Rev:** Shield

| Date | Mintage | VF20 | XF40 | MS60 | MS63 | MS65 |
|---|---|---|---|---|---|---|
| 2008 | 3,000 | PF65 60.00 | | | | |

**KM# 182 20 ROUBLES**
33.63 g., 0.925 Silver 1.0001 oz. ASW, 38.61 mm. **Subject:** Lipichanskaya Pushcha **Rev:** Kingfisher seated on branch

| Date | Mintage | VF20 | XF40 | MS60 | MS63 | MS65 |
|---|---|---|---|---|---|---|
| 2008 | 5,000 | PF65 65.00 | | | | |

**KM# 183 20 ROUBLES**
33.62 g., 0.925 Silver 0.9998 oz. ASW, 38.61 mm. **Subject:** Festivala and Rites - Dzyady **Rev:** Two angels above table

| Date | Mintage | VF20 | XF40 | MS60 | MS63 | MS65 |
|---|---|---|---|---|---|---|
| 2008 Antique patina | 5,000 | — | — | — | 90.00 | — |

**KM# 184 20 ROUBLES**
33.62 g., 0.925 Silver 0.9998 oz. ASW, 38.61 mm. **Subject:** David of Garadzen **Rev:** Half-length figure of knight

| Date | Mintage | VF20 | XF40 | MS60 | MS63 | MS65 |
|---|---|---|---|---|---|---|
| 2008 | 5,000 | **PF65** 60.00 | | | | |

**KM# 185 20 ROUBLES**
31.11 g., 0.999 Silver 0.999 oz. ASW, 40 mm. **Rev:** Figure skater

| Date | Mintage | VF20 | XF40 | MS60 | MS63 | MS65 |
|---|---|---|---|---|---|---|
| 2008 | 10,000 | **PF65** 55.00 | | | | |

**KM# 186 20 ROUBLES**
31.11 g., 0.999 Silver 0.999 oz. ASW, 38.61 mm. **Subject:** Lynx **Rev:** Lynx head facing

| Date | Mintage | VF20 | XF40 | MS60 | MS63 | MS65 |
|---|---|---|---|---|---|---|
| 2008 | 8,000 | **PF65** 95.00 | | | | |

**KM# 187 20 ROUBLES**
31.11 g., 0.999 Silver 0.999 oz. ASW, 38.61 mm. **Subject:** Lynx **Rev:** Adult lynx with cub

| Date | Mintage | VF20 | XF40 | MS60 | MS63 | MS65 |
|---|---|---|---|---|---|---|
| 2008 | 8,000 | **PF65** 95.00 | | | | |

**KM# 188 20 ROUBLES**
33.62 g., 0.925 Silver 0.9998 oz. ASW, 38.61 mm. **Subject:** Cuckoo Legend **Rev:** Stylized cuckoo

| Date | Mintage | VF20 | XF40 | MS60 | MS63 | MS65 |
|---|---|---|---|---|---|---|
| 2008 | 5,000 | **PF65** 60.00 | | | | |

**KM# 189 20 ROUBLES**
28.28 g., 0.925 Silver 0.841 oz. ASW, 38.61 mm. **Subject:** Turandot **Rev:** Female opera character

| Date | Mintage | VF20 | XF40 | MS60 | MS63 | MS65 |
|---|---|---|---|---|---|---|
| 2008 Antique | — | — | — | — | 65.00 | — |

**KM# 190 20 ROUBLES**
33.63 g., 0.925 Silver 1.0002 oz. ASW, 38.61 mm. **Subject:** House Warming **Obv:** Cat **Rev:** Plated key within house facade

| Date | Mintage | VF20 | XF40 | MS60 | MS63 | MS65 |
|---|---|---|---|---|---|---|
| 2008 | 25,000 | **PF65** 60.00 | | | | |

**KM# 191 20 ROUBLES**
28.28 g., 0.925 Silver 0.841 oz. ASW, 38.61 mm. **Subject:** Sedov **Obv:** Compass star, multicolor **Rev:** Sailing ship

| Date | Mintage | VF20 | XF40 | MS60 | MS63 | MS65 |
|---|---|---|---|---|---|---|
| 2008 | 25,000 | **PF65** 70.00 | | | | |

**KM# 196 20 ROUBLES**
33.63 g., 0.925 Silver 1.0001 oz. ASW, 38.61 mm. **Subject:** 65th Anniversary of Liberation **Rev:** Child looking upward to freeded birds

| Date | Mintage | VF20 | XF40 | MS60 | MS63 | MS65 |
|---|---|---|---|---|---|---|
| 2009 | 4,000 | **PF65** 60.00 | | | | |

**KM# 197 20 ROUBLES**
28.28 g., 0.925 Silver 0.841 oz. ASW, 40x28 mm. **Subject:** Llya Repin **Rev:** Bust and house, artist's palet in corner **Shape:** Rectangle

| Date | Mintage | VF20 | XF40 | MS60 | MS63 | MS65 |
|---|---|---|---|---|---|---|
| 2009 | 1,500 | **PF65** 60.00 | | | | |

**KM# 198 20 ROUBLES**
28.28 g., 0.925 Silver 0.841 oz. ASW, 38.61 mm. **Subject:** Spasy **Rev:** Bee honey comb, apple tree, grain **Edge:** Reeded

| Date | Mintage | VF20 | XF40 | MS60 | MS63 | MS65 |
|---|---|---|---|---|---|---|
| 2009 Antique finish | 5,000 | — | — | — | — | 80.00 |

**KM# 199 20 ROUBLES**
33.63 g., 0.999 Silver 1.0801 oz. ASW, 38.61 mm. **Subject:** Christening **Rev:** Child in christening gown

| Date | Mintage | VF20 | XF40 | MS60 | MS63 | MS65 |
|---|---|---|---|---|---|---|
| 2009 | 5,000 | **PF65** 80.00 | | | | |

**KM# 200 20 ROUBLES**
28.28 g., 0.925 Silver 0.841 oz. ASW, 38.61 mm. **Subject:** Dar Pomorza **Rev:** Sail training vessel

| Date | Mintage | VF20 | XF40 | MS60 | MS63 | MS65 |
|---|---|---|---|---|---|---|
| 2009 | 25,000 | **PF65** 60.00 | | | | |

**KM# 201 20 ROUBLES**
33.63 g., 0.925 Silver 1.0001 oz. ASW, 38.61 mm. **Subject:** White stork **Rev:** Bird and nest

| Date | Mintage | VF20 | XF40 | MS60 | MS63 | MS65 |
|---|---|---|---|---|---|---|
| 2009 | 7,000 | **PF65** 70.00 | | | | |

**KM# 202 20 ROUBLES**
33.63 g., 0.925 Silver 1.0001 oz. ASW, 38.61 mm. **Subject:** Belavezhskaya Pushcha **Rev:** Range animals

| Date | Mintage | VF20 | XF40 | MS60 | MS63 | MS65 |
|---|---|---|---|---|---|---|
| 2009 | 8,000 | **PF65** 60.00 | | | | |

**KM# 203 20 ROUBLES**
28.28 g., 0.925 Silver 0.841 oz. ASW, 38.61 mm. **Series:** Zodiac - Pisces **Rev:** Two fish

| Date | Mintage | VF20 | XF40 | MS60 | MS63 | MS65 |
|---|---|---|---|---|---|---|
| 2009 Matte Proof | 25,000 | **PF65** 55.00 | | | | |

**KM# 204 20 ROUBLES**
28.28 g., 0.925 Silver 0.841 oz. ASW, 38.61 mm. **Subject:** Zodiac - Aries **Rev:** Ram

| Date | Mintage | VF20 | XF40 | MS60 | MS63 | MS65 |
|---|---|---|---|---|---|---|
| 2009 Matte Proof | 25,000 | **PF65** 55.00 | | | | |

**KM# 205 20 ROUBLES**
28.28 g., 0.925 Silver 0.841 oz. ASW, 38.61 mm. **Subject:** Zodiac - Taurus **Rev:** Bull

| Date | Mintage | VF20 | XF40 | MS60 | MS63 | MS65 |
|---|---|---|---|---|---|---|
| 2009 Matte Proof | 25,000 | **PF65** 55.00 | | | | |

**KM# 206 20 ROUBLES**
28.28 g., 0.925 Silver 0.841 oz. ASW, 38.61 mm. **Subject:** Zodiac - Gemini **Rev:** Twins

| Date | Mintage | VF20 | XF40 | MS60 | MS63 | MS65 |
|---|---|---|---|---|---|---|
| 2009 Matte Proof | 25,000 | **PF65** 55.00 | | | | |

**KM# 207 20 ROUBLES**
28.28 g., 0.925 Silver 0.841 oz. ASW, 38.61 mm. **Subject:** Zodiac - Cancer **Rev:** Crab

| Date | Mintage | VF20 | XF40 | MS60 | MS63 | MS65 |
|---|---|---|---|---|---|---|
| 2009 Matte Proof | 25,000 | **PF65** 55.00 | | | | |

**KM# 208 20 ROUBLES**
28.28 g., 0.925 Silver 0.841 oz. ASW, 38.61 mm. **Subject:** Zodiac - Leo **Rev:** Lion

| Date | Mintage | VF20 | XF40 | MS60 | MS63 | MS65 |
|---|---|---|---|---|---|---|
| 2009 Matte Proof | 25,000 | **PF65** 55.00 | | | | |

**KM# 209 20 ROUBLES**
28.28 g., 0.925 Silver 0.841 oz. ASW, 38.61 mm. **Subject:** Zodiac - Virgo **Rev:** Little girl

| Date | Mintage | VF20 | XF40 | MS60 | MS63 | MS65 |
|---|---|---|---|---|---|---|
| 2009 Matte Proof | 25,000 | **PF65** 55.00 | | | | |

**KM# 210 20 ROUBLES**
28.28 g., 0.925 Silver 0.841 oz. ASW, 38.61 mm. **Subject:** Zodiac - Libra **Rev:** Balance scales

| Date | Mintage | VF20 | XF40 | MS60 | MS63 | MS65 |
|---|---|---|---|---|---|---|
| 2009 Matte Proof | 25,000 | **PF65** 55.00 | | | | |

**KM# 211 20 ROUBLES**
28.28 g., 0.925 Silver 0.841 oz. ASW, 38.61 mm. **Rev:** Scorpion

| Date | Mintage | VF20 | XF40 | MS60 | MS63 | MS65 |
|---|---|---|---|---|---|---|
| 2009 Matte Proof | 25,000 | PF65 55.00 | | | | |

**KM# 242 20 ROUBLES**
28.28 g., 0.925 Silver 0.841 oz. ASW, 38.61 mm. **Subject:** 3 Musketeers **Rev:** D'Artagnan, with red stone insert

| Date | Mintage | VF20 | XF40 | MS60 | MS63 | MS65 |
|---|---|---|---|---|---|---|
| 2009 | 10,000 | PF65 85.00 | | | | |
| 2009 | 5,000 | — | — | — | — | 75.00 |

**KM# 243 20 ROUBLES**
28.28 g., 0.925 Silver 0.841 oz. ASW, 38.61 mm. **Subject:** The Three Musketeers **Rev:** Aramis, light blue stone insert

| Date | Mintage | VF20 | XF40 | MS60 | MS63 | MS65 |
|---|---|---|---|---|---|---|
| 2009 | 5,000 | — | — | — | — | 75.00 |
| 2009 | 10,000 | PF65 85.00 | | | | |

**KM# 244 20 ROUBLES**
28.28 g., 0.925 Silver 0.841 oz. ASW, 38.61 mm. **Subject:** The Three Musketeers **Rev:** Athos, blue stone insert

| Date | Mintage | VF20 | XF40 | MS60 | MS63 | MS65 |
|---|---|---|---|---|---|---|
| 2009 | 5,000 | PF65 85.00 | | | | |
| 2009 | 10,000 | — | — | — | — | 75.00 |

**KM# 245 20 ROUBLES**
28.28 g., 0.925 Silver 0.841 oz. ASW, 38.61 mm. **Subject:** The Three Musketeers **Rev:** Porthos, red stone insert

| Date | Mintage | VF20 | XF40 | MS60 | MS63 | MS65 |
|---|---|---|---|---|---|---|
| 2009 | 10,000 | PF65 85.00 | | | | |
| 2009 | 5,000 | — | — | — | — | 75.00 |

**KM# 254 20 ROUBLES**
28.28 g., 0.925 Silver 0.841 oz. ASW, 45.3x35.3 mm. **Subject:** Pushkin's stories **Rev:** Tale of Tsar Saltan **Shape:** Vertical oval

| Date | Mintage | VF20 | XF40 | MS60 | MS63 | MS65 |
|---|---|---|---|---|---|---|
| 2009 | 7,000 | PF65 85.00 | | | | |

**KM# 361 20 ROUBLES**
28.28 g., 0.925 Silver 0.841 oz. ASW, 38.61 mm. **Subject:** Zodiac - Sagittarius **Obv:** Sun and moon **Rev:** Girl with bow and arrow

| Date | Mintage | VF20 | XF40 | MS60 | MS63 | MS65 |
|---|---|---|---|---|---|---|
| 2009 Matte Proof | 25,000 | PF65 55.00 | | | | |

**KM# 362 20 ROUBLES**
28.28 g., 0.925 Silver 0.841 oz. ASW, 38.61 mm. **Subject:** Zodiac - Capricorn **Obv:** Sun and moon **Rev:** Capricorn

| Date | Mintage | VF20 | XF40 | MS60 | MS63 | MS65 |
|---|---|---|---|---|---|---|
| 2009 Matte Proof | 25,000 | PF65 55.00 | | | | |

**KM# 363 20 ROUBLES**
33.62 g., 0.925 Silver 0.9998 oz. ASW, 38.61 mm. **Subject:** Straw Plaiting **Obv:** National arms within floral wreath **Rev:** Straw horse figure **Edge:** Reeded

| Date | Mintage | VF20 | XF40 | MS60 | MS63 | MS65 |
|---|---|---|---|---|---|---|
| 2009 | 5,000 | PF65 75.00 | | | | |

**KM# 364 20 ROUBLES**
28.28 g., 0.925 Silver 0.841 oz. ASW, 38.61 mm. **Subject:** Nutcracker **Obv:** Boy and girl on crescent moon **Rev:** scenes from the Nutcracker ballet

| Date | Mintage | VF20 | XF40 | MS60 | MS63 | MS65 |
|---|---|---|---|---|---|---|
| 2009 Antique patina | 25,000 | — | — | — | — | 75.00 |

**KM# 365 20 ROUBLES**
28.28 g., 0.925 Silver 0.841 oz. ASW, 38.61 mm. **Subject:** Zodiac - Aquarius **Obv:** Sun and moon **Rev:** Boy in bathtub

| Date | Mintage | VF20 | XF40 | MS60 | MS63 | MS65 |
|---|---|---|---|---|---|---|
| 2009 Matte Proof | 25,000 | PF65 55.00 | | | | |

**KM# 366 20 ROUBLES**
33.63 g., 0.925 Silver 1.0001 oz. ASW, 38.61 mm. **Subject:** Legend of the skylark **Obv:** Five stylized birds in flight **Rev:** Stylized bird, head left

| Date | Mintage | VF20 | XF40 | MS60 | MS63 | MS65 |
|---|---|---|---|---|---|---|
| 2009 Prooflike | 5,000 | PF65 75.00 | | | | |

**KM# 367 20 ROUBLES**
33.63 g., 0.925 Silver 1.0001 oz. ASW, 38.61 mm. **Subject:** Pakatigaroshak - Tale of the Dragon **Obv:** Geometric pattern and EURASAC logo **Rev:** Man clubbing dragon

| Date | Mintage | VF20 | XF40 | MS60 | MS63 | MS65 |
|---|---|---|---|---|---|---|
| 2009 | 3,000 | PF65 75.00 | | | | |

**KM# 368 20 ROUBLES**
31.10 g., 0.999 Silver 0.9989 oz. ASW, 38.61 mm. **Obv:** National arms **Rev:** Squirrel right eating nut **Edge:** Reeded

| Date | Mintage | VF20 | XF40 | MS60 | MS63 | MS65 |
|---|---|---|---|---|---|---|
| 2009 | 5,000 | PF65 150 | | | | |

**KM# 369 20 ROUBLES**
31.10 g., 0.999 Silver 0.9989 oz. ASW, 38.61 mm. **Obv:** National arms **Rev:** Two squirrels on a branch, crystals in eyes **Edge:** Reeded

| Date | Mintage | VF20 | XF40 | MS60 | MS63 | MS65 |
|---|---|---|---|---|---|---|
| 2009 | 5,000 | PF65 150 | | | | |

**KM# 370 20 ROUBLES**
31.10 g., 0.925 Silver 0.9249 oz. ASW, 40 mm. **Subject:** London Olympics, 2012 **Obv:** Logo and National arms **Rev:** Two stylized players and Tower Bridge

| Date | Mintage | VF20 | XF40 | MS60 | MS63 | MS65 |
|---|---|---|---|---|---|---|
| 2009 | 6,000 | PF65 75.00 | | | | |

**KM# 224 20 ROUBLES**
33.63 g., 0.925 Silver 1.0001 oz. ASW, 38.61 mm. **Subject:** EURASEC, 10th Anniversary **Obv:** Folk embroidery pattern **Rev:** Six flags around multicolor globe

| Date | Mintage | VF20 | XF40 | MS60 | MS63 | MS65 |
|---|---|---|---|---|---|---|
| 2010 | 3,000 | PF65 60.00 | | | | |

**KM# 225 20 ROUBLES**
33.63 g., 0.925 Silver 1.0001 oz. ASW, 38.6 mm. **Subject:** Syarednaya Pripyat Reserve **Obv:** Eight ferns forming double cross **Rev:** Marsh turtle

| Date | Mintage | VF20 | XF40 | MS60 | MS63 | MS65 |
|---|---|---|---|---|---|---|
| 2010 | 3,000 | PF65 70.00 | | | | |

**KM# 235 20 ROUBLES**
28.28 g., 0.925 Silver 0.841 oz. ASW, 38.61 mm. **Rev:** U.S. Frigate Constitution

| Date | Mintage | VF20 | XF40 | MS60 | MS63 | MS65 |
|---|---|---|---|---|---|---|
| 2010 | 7,000 | PF65 75.00 | | | | |

**KM# 237 20 ROUBLES**
33.62 g., 0.925 Silver 0.9998 oz. ASW, 38.61 mm. **Subject:** Legend of the tortoise

| Date | Mintage | VF20 | XF40 | MS60 | MS63 | MS65 |
|---|---|---|---|---|---|---|
| 2010 | 3,000 | PF65 60.00 | | | | |

**KM# 239 20 ROUBLES**
28.28 g., 0.925 Silver 0.841 oz. ASW, 38.6 mm. **Subject:** Battle of Grunwald **Obv:** Figure with outstretched arms **Rev:** Legend within Fingerprint

| Date | Mintage | VF20 | XF40 | MS60 | MS63 | MS65 |
|---|---|---|---|---|---|---|
| 2010 | 2,500 | PF65 60.00 | | | | |

**KM# 241 20 ROUBLES**
33.63 g., 0.925 Silver 1.0001 oz. ASW, 38.61 mm. **Subject:** Age of Majority **Rev:** Multicolor flowers within folk patterns

| Date | Mintage | VF20 | XF40 | MS60 | MS63 | MS65 |
|---|---|---|---|---|---|---|
| 2010 | — | PF65 60.00 | | | | |

**KM# 246 20 ROUBLES**
28.28 g., 0.925 Silver 0.841 oz. ASW, 38.61 mm. **Subject:** Orthodox Churches **Rev:** Cathedral of the Assumption

| Date | Mintage | VF20 | XF40 | MS60 | MS63 | MS65 |
|---|---|---|---|---|---|---|
| 2010 | 3,000 | PF65 75.00 | | | | |

**KM# 247 20 ROUBLES**
28.28 g., 0.925 Silver 0.841 oz. ASW, 38.61 mm. **Subject:** Orthodox Churches **Rev:** Cathedral of SS Peter and Paul

| Date | Mintage | VF20 | XF40 | MS60 | MS63 | MS65 |
|---|---|---|---|---|---|---|
| 2010 | 3,000 | PF65 75.00 | | | | |

**KM# 248 20 ROUBLES**
28.28 g., 0.925 Silver 0.841 oz. ASW, 38.61 mm. **Subject:** Orthodox Churches **Rev:** Cathedral of Alexander Nevsky

| Date | Mintage | VF20 | XF40 | MS60 | MS63 | MS65 |
|---|---|---|---|---|---|---|
| 2010 | 3,000 | PF65 75.00 | | | | |

**KM# 249 20 ROUBLES**
28.28 g., 0.925 Silver 0.841 oz. ASW, 38.61 mm. **Subject:** Orthodox Churches **Rev:** Cathedral of St. Nicholas

| Date | Mintage | VF20 | XF40 | MS60 | MS63 | MS65 |
|---|---|---|---|---|---|---|
| 2010 | 3,000 | PF65 75.00 | | | | |

**KM# 250 20 ROUBLES**
28.28 g., 0.925 Silver 0.841 oz. ASW, 45.3x35.3 mm. **Subject:** Pushkin's stories **Rev:** Tale of the Golden Cockerel in multicolor **Shape:** Vertical oval

| Date | Mintage | VF20 | XF40 | MS60 | MS63 | MS65 |
|---|---|---|---|---|---|---|
| 2010 | 7,000 | PF65 85.00 | | | | |

**KM# 251 20 ROUBLES**
28.28 g., 0.925 Silver 0.841 oz. ASW, 45.3x35.3 mm. **Subject:** Pushkin's stories **Rev:** Tale of the fisherman and the fish **Shape:** Vertical oval

| Date | Mintage | VF20 | XF40 | MS60 | MS63 | MS65 |
|---|---|---|---|---|---|---|
| 2010 | 7,000 | PF65 85.00 | | | | |

**KM# 252 20 ROUBLES**
28.28 g., 0.925 Silver 0.841 oz. ASW, 45.3x35.3 mm. **Subject:** Pushkin's stories **Rev:** Tale of one Dead Princess and Seven Knights **Shape:** Vertical oval

| Date | Mintage | VF20 | XF40 | MS60 | MS63 | MS65 |
|---|---|---|---|---|---|---|
| 2010 | 7,000 | PF65 85.00 | | | | |

**KM# 253 20 ROUBLES**
28.28 g., 0.925 Silver 0.841 oz. ASW, 45.3x35.3 mm. **Subject:** Pushkin's stories **Rev:** Ruslan and Ludmila **Shape:** Vertical oval

| Date | Mintage | VF20 | XF40 | MS60 | MS63 | MS65 |
|---|---|---|---|---|---|---|
| 2010 | 7,000 | PF65 85.00 | | | | |

**KM# 256 20 ROUBLES**
31.10 g., 0.999 Silver 0.9989 oz. ASW, 38.61 mm. **Subject:** Slavic Woman **Rev:** Madonna and child

| Date | Mintage | VF20 | XF40 | MS60 | MS63 | MS65 |
|---|---|---|---|---|---|---|
| 2010 Proof | 7,000 | — | — | — | — | 75.00 |

**KM# 257 20 ROUBLES**
28.28 g., 0.925 Silver 0.841 oz. ASW, 28x40 mm. **Subject:** Ivan Khrutsky **Obv:** Color painting of female with fruit basket, arms at lower left **Rev:** Half-length figure of Khrutsky, flowers in vase on table **Shape:** Vertical rectangle

| Date | Mintage | VF20 | XF40 | MS60 | MS63 | MS65 |
|---|---|---|---|---|---|---|
| 2010 | 4,000 | — | — | — | — | 75.00 |

**KM# 258 20 ROUBLES**
33.62 g., 0.925 Silver 0.9998 oz. ASW, 38.61 mm. **Subject:** Expo 2010 **Obv:** Folk pattern **Rev:** Exposition buildings of the past

| Date | Mintage | VF20 | XF40 | MS60 | MS63 | MS65 |
|---|---|---|---|---|---|---|
| 2010 | 5,000 | PF65 100 | | | | |

**KM# 261 20 ROUBLES**
33.63 g., 0.925 Silver 1.0001 oz. ASW, 38.61 mm. **Subject:** End of World War II, 65th Anniversary **Rev:** Five doves in flight, kiting

| Date | Mintage | VF20 | XF40 | MS60 | MS63 | MS65 |
|---|---|---|---|---|---|---|
| 2010 | 2,000 | PF65 75.00 | | | | |

**KM# 266 20 ROUBLES**
28.28 g., 0.925 Silver 0.841 oz. ASW, 30x45 mm. **Subject:** Icon of the Most Holy Theotokos of Minsk **Rev:** Madonna icon, partially gilt **Shape:** Vertical rectangle

| Date | Mintage | VF20 | XF40 | MS60 | MS63 | MS65 |
|---|---|---|---|---|---|---|
| 2010 | 7,000 | PF65 200 | | | | |

**KM# 267 20 ROUBLES**
28.28 g., 0.925 Silver 0.841 oz. ASW, 30x45 mm. **Subject:** Icon of the Mold Holy Theotokos of Smolensk **Rev:** Madonna Icon, partially gilt **Shape:** Vertical rectangle

| Date | Mintage | VF20 | XF40 | MS60 | MS63 | MS65 |
|---|---|---|---|---|---|---|
| 2010 Prooflike | 7,000 | — | — | — | — | 150 |

**KM# 268 20 ROUBLES**
28.28 g., 0.925 Silver 0.841 oz. ASW, 28x40 mm. **Rev:** Nefertiti bust **Shape:** Vertical rectangle

| Date | Mintage | VF20 | XF40 | MS60 | MS63 | MS65 |
|---|---|---|---|---|---|---|
| 2010 | 7,000 | PF65 100 | | | | |

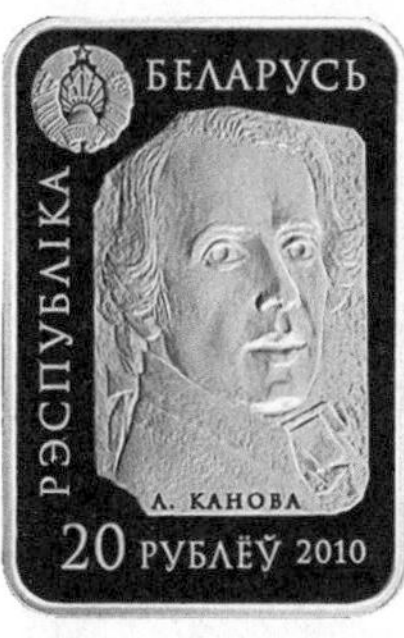

**KM# 269 20 ROUBLES**
28.28 g., 0.925 Silver 0.841 oz. ASW, 28x40 mm. **Rev:** Cupid & Psyche **Shape:** Vertical rectangle

| Date | Mintage | VF20 | XF40 | MS60 | MS63 | MS65 |
|---|---|---|---|---|---|---|
| 2010 | 7,000 | PF65 100 | | | | |

**KM# 271 20 ROUBLES**
28.28 g., 0.925 Silver 0.841 oz. ASW, 38.6 mm. **Obv:** Compass rose and chart **Rev:** Cutty Sark sailing right

| Date | Mintage | VF20 | XF40 | MS60 | MS63 | MS65 |
|---|---|---|---|---|---|---|
| 2010 | — | PF65 55.00 | | | | |

**KM# 272 20 ROUBLES**
28.28 g., 0.925 Silver 0.841 oz. ASW, 38.61 mm. **Obv:** Compass rose and chart **Rev:** Amerigo Vespucci sailing left

| Date | Mintage | VF20 | XF40 | MS60 | MS63 | MS65 |
|---|---|---|---|---|---|---|
| 2010 | — | PF65 75.00 | | | | |

**KM# 278 20 ROUBLES**
7.78 g., 0.999 Gold 0.2499 oz. AGW, 22 mm. **Subject:** Slavic Women **Obv:** Large lis, national arms at top **Rev:** Madonna and Child

| Date | Mintage | VF20 | XF40 | MS60 | MS63 | MS65 |
|---|---|---|---|---|---|---|
| 2010 | Est. 2500 | PF65 475 | | | | |

**KM# 279 20 ROUBLES**
31.10 g., 0.999 Silver 0.9989 oz. ASW, 38.61 mm. **Obv:** National arms **Rev:** Two eagle owls, crystals in eyes

| Date | Mintage | VF20 | XF40 | MS60 | MS63 | MS65 |
|---|---|---|---|---|---|---|
| 2010 | 5,000 | PF65 100 | | | | |

**KM# 371 20 ROUBLES**
28.28 g., 0.925 Silver 0.841 oz. ASW, 38.61 mm. **Obv:** Heart with butterflies within **Rev:** Heart with vine and crystal

| Date | Mintage | VF20 | XF40 | MS60 | MS63 | MS65 |
|---|---|---|---|---|---|---|
| 2010 | 10,000 | PF65 125 | | | | |

**KM# 372 20 ROUBLES**
5.76 g., 0.900 Gold 0.1667 oz. AGW, 19.8 mm. **Subject:** Battle of Grunwald, 600th Anniversary **Obv:** Standard head **Rev:** pellet cross within standard head

| Date | Mintage | VF20 | XF40 | MS60 | MS63 | MS65 |
|---|---|---|---|---|---|---|
| 2010 | 500 | PF65 400 | | | | |

**KM# 373 20 ROUBLES**
28.28 g., 0.925 Silver 0.841 oz. ASW, 28x40 mm. **Subject:** Rodin **Obv:** Portrait facing **Rev:** The Thinker statue

| Date | Mintage | VF20 | XF40 | MS60 | MS63 | MS65 |
|---|---|---|---|---|---|---|
| 2010 | 7,000 | PF65 125 | | | | |

**KM# 374 20 ROUBLES**
28.28 g., 0.925 Silver 0.841 oz. ASW, 28x40 mm. **Subject:** Bernini **Obv:** Portrait facing **Rev:** Ecstasy of St. Theresa

| Date | Mintage | VF20 | XF40 | MS60 | MS63 | MS65 |
|---|---|---|---|---|---|---|
| 2010 | 7,000 | PF65 125 | | | | |

**KM# 375 20 ROUBLES**
31.10 g., 0.999 Silver 0.9989 oz. ASW, 38.61 mm. **Obv:** National arms **Rev:** Owl head facing, crystal eyes

| Date | Mintage | VF20 | XF40 | MS60 | MS63 | MS65 |
|---|---|---|---|---|---|---|
| 2010 | 5,000 | PF65 125 | | | | |

**KM# 376 20 ROUBLES**
33.63 g., 0.925 Silver 1.0001 oz. ASW, 38.61 mm. **Subject:** Blacksmithing **Obv:** National arms within floral wreath **Rev:** Horseshoe and village church

| Date | Mintage | VF20 | XF40 | MS60 | MS63 | MS65 |
|---|---|---|---|---|---|---|
| 2010 | 3,000 | PF65 100 | | | | |

**KM# 377 20 ROUBLES**
33.63 g., 0.925 Silver 1.0001 oz. ASW, 38.61 mm. **Subject:** Candlemas **Obv:** Embroidery pattern **Rev:** Bird rising out of the snow to a flowered field and sunrise **Edge:** Reeded

| Date | Mintage | VF20 | XF40 | MS60 | MS63 | MS65 |
|---|---|---|---|---|---|---|
| 2010 | 2,500 | PF65 150 | | | | |

**KM# 378 20 ROUBLES**
33.63 g., 0.925 Silver 1.0001 oz. ASW, 38.61 mm. **Subject:** Lew Sapieha **Obv:** Ancient document **Rev:** Figure standing

| Date | Mintage | VF20 | XF40 | MS60 | MS63 | MS65 |
|---|---|---|---|---|---|---|
| 2010 | 3,000 | PF65 125 | | | | |

**KM# 255 20 ROUBLES**
28.28 g., 0.925 Silver 0.841 oz. ASW, 38.61 mm. **Subject:** My Love **Rev:** Two cats, red heart shaped crystal insert at top

| Date | Mintage | VF20 | XF40 | MS60 | MS63 | MS65 |
|---|---|---|---|---|---|---|
| 2011 | 15,000 | PF65 100 | | | | |

**KM# 280 20 ROUBLES**
28.28 g., 0.925 Silver 0.841 oz. ASW, 38.61 mm. **Subject:** Krusenstern **Obv:** Compass rose and charts, national arms at top **Rev:** Fully-rigged sailing ship left

| Date | Mintage | VF20 | XF40 | MS60 | MS63 | MS65 |
|---|---|---|---|---|---|---|
| 2011 | 7,000 | PF65 100 | | | | |

**KM# 281 20 ROUBLES**
33.63 g., 0.925 Silver 1.0001 oz. ASW, 38.61 mm. **Subject:** Motherhood **Obv:** Folk embroidery pattern **Rev:** Mother holding baby, bird

| Date | Mintage | VF20 | XF40 | MS60 | MS63 | MS65 |
|---|---|---|---|---|---|---|
| 2011 | 10,000 | PF65 90.00 | | | | |

**KM# 281a 20 ROUBLES**
33.63 g., 0.925 Silver 1.0001 oz. ASW partially gilt, 38.61 mm. **Obv:** Folk embroidery pattern **Rev:** Mother and child, gilt bird

| Date | Mintage | VF20 | XF40 | MS60 | MS63 | MS65 |
|---|---|---|---|---|---|---|
| 2011 | — | PF65 90.00 | | | | |

**KM# 282 20 ROUBLES**
31.10 g., 0.925 Silver 0.9249 oz. ASW, 30x45 mm. **Subject:** Madonna icon; Theotokos of Kazan **Obv:** Cross at center of design **Rev:** Icon image, ornate frame

| Date | Mintage | VF20 | XF40 | MS60 | MS63 | MS65 |
|---|---|---|---|---|---|---|
| 2011 | 10,000 | PF65 250 | | | | |

**KM# 283 20 ROUBLES**
31.10 g., 0.925 Silver 0.9249 oz. ASW, 30x45 mm. **Subject:** Madonna icon, Theotokos of Zhirovichy **Obv:** Cross within design **Rev:** Madonna icon, angellic corners

| Date | Mintage | VF20 | XF40 | MS60 | MS63 | MS65 |
|---|---|---|---|---|---|---|
| 2011 | 10,000 | PF65 250 | | | | |

**KM# 289 20 ROUBLES**
28.28 g., 0.925 Silver 0.841 oz. ASW **Subject:** Paleolithic Venus **Obv:** Cave drawing of steer **Rev:** Carved statue of pregnant female **Shape:** Vertical rectangle

| Date | Mintage | VF20 | XF40 | MS60 | MS63 | MS65 |
|---|---|---|---|---|---|---|
| 2011 | Est. 3500 | PF65 90.00 | | | | |

**KM# 290 20 ROUBLES**
28.28 g., 0.925 Silver 0.841 oz. ASW **Subject:** Voltaire **Obv:** Carved portrait bust **Rev:** Statue of seated Voltaire **Shape:** Vertical rectangle

| Date | Mintage | VF20 | XF40 | MS60 | MS63 | MS65 |
|---|---|---|---|---|---|---|
| 2011 | Est. 3500 | PF65 90.00 | | | | |

**KM# 379 20 ROUBLES**
28.28 g., 0.925 Silver 0.841 oz. ASW, 38.61 mm. **Subject:** Polotsk **Obv:** Map, ship and national arms **Rev:** Shield and city view

| Date | Mintage | VF20 | XF40 | MS60 | MS63 | MS65 |
|---|---|---|---|---|---|---|
| 2011 | 7,000 | PF65 110 | | | | |

**KM# 380 20 ROUBLES**
28.28 g., 0.925 Silver 0.841 oz. ASW, 38.61 mm. **Subject:** Arabic Dance

| Date | Mintage | VF20 | XF40 | MS60 | MS63 | MS65 |
|---|---|---|---|---|---|---|
| 2011 | 6,000 | PF65 110 | | | | |

**KM# 381 20 ROUBLES**
31.10 g., 0.999 Silver 0.9989 oz. ASW, 38.61 mm. **Subject:** Hedgehog **Obv:** National arms **Rev:** Hedgehog left, crystal eye

| Date | Mintage | VF20 | XF40 | MS60 | MS63 | MS65 |
|---|---|---|---|---|---|---|
| 2011 | 4,000 | PF65 125 | | | | |

**KM# 382 20 ROUBLES**
31.10 g., 0.999 Silver 0.9989 oz. ASW, 38.61 mm. **Subject:** Hedgehog **Obv:** National arms **Rev:** Hedgehog facing, crystal eyes

| Date | Mintage | VF20 | XF40 | MS60 | MS63 | MS65 |
|---|---|---|---|---|---|---|
| 2011 | 4,000 | PF65 125 | | | | |

**KM# 383 20 ROUBLES**
31.10 g., 0.925 Silver 0.9249 oz. ASW, 45x30 mm. **Subject:** Akhal-Teke Horses **Obv:** Two horses galloping thru low water right **Rev:** Ancient two-horse carriage, horse walking right **Shape:** Rectangle

| Date | Mintage | VF20 | XF40 | MS60 | MS63 | MS65 |
|---|---|---|---|---|---|---|
| 2011 | 6,000 | PF65 125 | | | | |

**KM# 413 20 ROUBLES**
31.11 g., 0.999 Silver 0.999 oz. ASW, 38.61 mm. **Obv:** National emblem **Rev:** Hedgehog family, Swarovski crystal in eyes

| Date | Mintage | VF20 | XF40 | MS60 | MS63 | MS65 |
|---|---|---|---|---|---|---|
| 2011 | 4,000 | PF65 100 | | | | |

**KM# 414 20 ROUBLES**
31.11 g., 0.999 Silver 0.999 oz. ASW, 38.61 mm. **Obv:** National emblem **Rev:** Hedgehog facing left, Swarovski crystal in eye

| Date | Mintage | VF20 | XF40 | MS60 | MS63 | MS65 |
|---|---|---|---|---|---|---|
| 2011 | 4,000 | PF65 100 | | | | |

**KM# 416 20 ROUBLES**
0.925 Silver, 30x45 mm. **Obv:** Stylized cross in ornaments **Rev:** Icon of Vladimir Madonna

| Date | Mintage | VF20 | XF40 | MS60 | MS63 | MS65 |
|---|---|---|---|---|---|---|
| 2012 | 10,000 | PF65 100 | | | | |

**KM# 418 20 ROUBLES**
0.925 Silver **Subject:** Reconstruction of Izyaslavl fortress **Rev:** Regvolod of Polotsk **Edge Lettering:** 38.61

| Date | Mintage | VF20 | XF40 | MS60 | MS63 | MS65 |
|---|---|---|---|---|---|---|
| 2012 | 5,000 | PF65 100 | | | | |

**KM# 420 20 ROUBLES**
31.11 g., 0.999 Silver 0.999 oz. ASW, 38.61 mm. **Obv:** National Arms **Rev:** Bison head facing, two crystal eyes

| Date | Mintage | VF20 | XF40 | MS60 | MS63 | MS65 |
|---|---|---|---|---|---|---|
| 2012 | — | PF63 50.00 | PF65 55.00 | | | |

**KM# 422 20 ROUBLES**
31.11 g., 0.999 Silver 0.999 oz. ASW, 38.61 mm. **Obv:** National arms **Rev:** Two bison butting heads

| Date | Mintage | VF20 | XF40 | MS60 | MS63 | MS65 |
|---|---|---|---|---|---|---|
| 2012 | Est. 5000 | PF63 50.00 | PF65 55.00 | | | |

**KM# 423 20 ROUBLES**
20.00 g., 0.925 Silver 0.5948 oz. ASW, 38.61 mm. **Obv:** National arms **Rev:** Nymphaea Alba - flower in color

| Date | Mintage | VF20 | XF40 | MS60 | MS63 | MS65 |
|---|---|---|---|---|---|---|
| 2012 | — | PF65 32.50 | | | | |

**KM# 426 20 ROUBLES**
28.28 g., 0.925 Silver 0.841 oz. ASW, 38.6 mm. **Subject:** Bear legend **Obv:** National arms and stylized pattern with bears **Rev:** Bear

| Date | Mintage | VF20 | XF40 | MS60 | MS63 | MS65 |
|---|---|---|---|---|---|---|
| 2012 | 2,000 | PF65 65.00 | | | | |

**KM# 439 20 ROUBLES**
0.925 Silver ASW, 30x45 mm. **Obv:** Stylized cross in ornaments **Rev:** Icon of Barkalabava Madonna

| Date | Mintage | VF20 | XF40 | MS60 | MS63 | MS65 |
|---|---|---|---|---|---|---|
| 2012 | 10,000 | PF65 100 | | | | |

**KM# 440 20 ROUBLES**
33.60 g., 0.925 Silver 0.9992 oz. ASW, 38.61 mm. **Subject:** Belarusbank, 90th Anniversary **Obv:** National arms **Rev:** Bank building

| Date | Mintage | VF20 | XF40 | MS60 | MS63 | MS65 |
|---|---|---|---|---|---|---|
| 2012 | 7,000 | PF65 65.00 | | | | |

**KM# 441 20 ROUBLES**
33.63 g., 0.925 Silver 1.0001 oz. ASW, 38.61 mm. **Subject:** Belarus-China relations, 20th Anniversary **Obv:** National arms **Rev:** Clasped hands

| Date | Mintage | VF20 | XF40 | MS60 | MS63 | MS65 |
|---|---|---|---|---|---|---|
| 2012 | 1,500 | PF65 65.00 | | | | |

**KM# 442 20 ROUBLES**
33.63 g., 0.925 Silver 1.0001 oz. ASW, 38.61 mm. **Obv:** National arms and stylized DNA molecule **Rev:** Stork with baby

| Date | Mintage | VF20 | XF40 | MS60 | MS63 | MS65 |
|---|---|---|---|---|---|---|
| 2012 Proof | 10,000 | — | — | — | — | 65.00 |

**KM# 443 20 ROUBLES**
33.62 g., 0.925 Silver 0.9998 oz. ASW, 38.61 mm. **Subject:** Pottery **Obv:** National arms in stylized wreath **Rev:** Pottery filled with water

| Date | Mintage | VF20 | XF40 | MS60 | MS63 | MS65 |
|---|---|---|---|---|---|---|
| 2012 | 3,000 | PF65 65.00 | | | | |

**KM# 444 20 ROUBLES**
33.63 g., 0.925 Silver 1.0001 oz. ASW, 38.61 mm. **Subject:** Year of the Snake **Obv:** National arms and clockworks **Rev:** Coiled Viper

| Date | Mintage | VF20 | XF40 | MS60 | MS63 | MS65 |
|---|---|---|---|---|---|---|
| 2012 | 8,000 | PF65 65.00 | | | | |

**KM# 445 20 ROUBLES**
33.62 g., 0.925 Silver 0.9998 oz. ASW gilt, 38.61 mm. **Subject:** Christening of the Rus, 1025th Anniversary **Obv:** National arms and stylized cross **Rev:** Dove and angels

| Date | Mintage | VF20 | XF40 | MS60 | MS63 | MS65 |
|---|---|---|---|---|---|---|
| 2012 | 3,000 | PF65 65.00 | | | | |

**KM# 453 20 ROUBLES**
20.00 g., 0.999 Silver 0.6424 oz. ASW, 38.61 mm. **Subject:** Belarusian ballet

| Date | Mintage | VF20 | XF40 | MS60 | MS63 | MS65 |
|---|---|---|---|---|---|---|
| 2013 | Est. 10000 | PF65 75.00 | | | | |

**KM# 455 20 ROUBLES**
28.28 g., 0.925 Silver 0.841 oz. ASW, 38.61 mm. **Subject:** Zodiac - Libra

| Date | Mintage | VF20 | XF40 | MS60 | MS63 | MS65 |
|---|---|---|---|---|---|---|
| 2013 | Est. 7777 | PF65 75.00 | | | | |

**KM# 456 20 ROUBLES**
28.28 g., 0.925 Silver 0.841 oz. ASW, 38.61 mm. **Subject:** Zodiac - Scorpio

| Date | Mintage | VF20 | XF40 | MS60 | MS63 | MS65 |
|---|---|---|---|---|---|---|
| 2013 | Est. 7777 | PF65 75.00 | | | | |

**KM# 121 50 ROUBLES**
4.45 g., 0.999 Gold 0.1429 oz. AGW, 25 mm. **Subject:** Fox **Obv:** National arms **Rev:** Red fox with inset diamond eyes

| Date | Mintage | VF20 | XF40 | MS60 | MS63 | MS65 |
|---|---|---|---|---|---|---|
| 2002 | Est. 2000 | — | — | — | 1,000 | — |

**KM# 126 50 ROUBLES**
62.20 g., 0.925 Silver 1.8498 oz. ASW, 50 mm. **Subject:** 60th Anniversary of Victory **Obv:** Order of the Victory, multicolored **Rev:** Stars and arrows

| Date | Mintage | VF20 | XF40 | MS60 | MS63 | MS65 |
|---|---|---|---|---|---|---|
| 2005 | — | PF65 220 | | | | |
| 2005 | 2,000 | — | — | — | — | — |

**KM# 123 50 ROUBLES**
8.00 g., 0.900 Gold 0.2315 oz. AGW, 21 mm. **Subject:** Herring Gull **Obv:** National arms **Rev:** Herring gull in flight

| Date | Mintage | VF20 | XF40 | MS60 | MS63 | MS65 |
|---|---|---|---|---|---|---|
| 2006 | 3,000 | PF65 800 | | | | |

**KM# 125 50 ROUBLES**
8.00 g., 0.900 Gold 0.2315 oz. AGW, 21 mm. **Obv:** National arms **Rev:** Pair of common cranes

| Date | Mintage | VF20 | XF40 | MS60 | MS63 | MS65 |
|---|---|---|---|---|---|---|
| 2006 | 3,000 | PF65 800 | | | | |

**KM# 142 50 ROUBLES**
7.78 g., 0.999 Gold 0.2499 oz. AGW, 25 mm. **Subject:** Peregrine Falcon **Obv:** National arms **Rev:** Peregrine falcon with inset diamond eye

| Date | Mintage | VF20 | XF40 | MS60 | MS63 | MS65 |
|---|---|---|---|---|---|---|
| 2006 | 2,000 | — | — | 750 | 1,000 | — |

**KM# 143 50 ROUBLES**
8.00 g., 0.900 Gold 0.2315 oz. AGW, 21 mm. **Subject:** Bison **Obv:** National arms **Rev:** European bison

| Date | Mintage | VF20 | XF40 | MS60 | MS63 | MS65 |
|---|---|---|---|---|---|---|
| 2006 | 3,000 | PF65 800 | | | | |

**KM# 144 50 ROUBLES**
8.00 g., 0.900 Gold 0.2315 oz. AGW, 21 mm. **Subject:** Beaver **Obv:** National arms **Rev:** Family of Eurasian beavers

| Date | Mintage | VF20 | XF40 | MS60 | MS63 | MS65 |
|---|---|---|---|---|---|---|
| 2006 | 3,000 | PF65 800 | | | | |

**KM# 145 50 ROUBLES**
8.00 g., 0.900 Gold 0.2315 oz. AGW, 21 mm. **Subject:** Mute Swan **Obv:** National arms **Rev:** Pair of mute swans

| Date | Mintage | VF20 | XF40 | MS60 | MS63 | MS65 |
|---|---|---|---|---|---|---|
| 2006 | 3,000 | PF65 800 | | | | |

**KM# 384 50 ROUBLES**
7.78 g., 0.999 Gold 0.2499 oz. AGW, 25 mm. **Obv:** National arms **Rev:** Wolf head facing

| Date | Mintage | VF20 | XF40 | MS60 | MS63 | MS65 |
|---|---|---|---|---|---|---|
| 2007 | 2,000 | PF65 900 | | | | |

**KM# 385 50 ROUBLES**
8.00 g., 0.900 Gold 0.2315 oz. AGW, 21 mm. **Obv:** Church within frame **Rev:** Female saint icon

| Date | Mintage | VF20 | XF40 | MS60 | MS63 | MS65 |
|---|---|---|---|---|---|---|
| 2008 | 14,000 | — | — | — | — | 700 |
| 2008 | 1,000 | PF65 800 | | | | |

**KM# 386 50 ROUBLES**
8.00 g., 0.900 Gold 0.2315 oz. AGW, 21 mm. **Obv:** Church within frame **Rev:** Saint Sarowski icon

| Date | Mintage | VF20 | XF40 | MS60 | MS63 | MS65 |
|---|---|---|---|---|---|---|
| 2008 | 14,000 | — | — | — | — | 700 |
| 2008 | 1,000 | PF65 800 | | | | |

**KM# 387 50 ROUBLES**
8.00 g., 0.900 Gold 0.2315 oz. AGW, 21 mm. **Obv:** Church within frame **Rev:** Saint Sergey Radonezski icon

| Date | Mintage | VF20 | XF40 | MS60 | MS63 | MS65 |
|---|---|---|---|---|---|---|
| 2008 | 14,000 | — | — | — | — | 700 |
| 2008 | 1,000 | PF65 800 | | | | |

**KM# 388 50 ROUBLES**
8.00 g., 0.900 Gold 0.2315 oz. AGW, 21 mm. **Obv:** Church within frame **Rev:** Saint Mikplaj the miracle worker icon

| Date | Mintage | VF20 | XF40 | MS60 | MS63 | MS65 |
|---|---|---|---|---|---|---|
| 2008 | 14,000 | — | — | — | — | 700 |
| 2008 | 1,000 | PF65 800 | | | | |

**KM# 389 50 ROUBLES**
8.00 g., 0.900 Gold 0.2315 oz. AGW, 21 mm. **Obv:** Church within frame **Rev:** Saint Pantaleon icon

| Date | Mintage | VF20 | XF40 | MS60 | MS63 | MS65 |
|---|---|---|---|---|---|---|
| 2008 | 14,000 | — | — | — | — | 700 |
| 2008 | 1,000 | PF65 800 | | | | |

**KM# 390 50 ROUBLES**
7.78 g., 0.999 Silver 0.2499 oz. ASW, 25 mm. **Obv:** National arms **Rev:** Lunx head facing

| Date | Mintage | VF20 | XF40 | MS60 | MS63 | MS65 |
|---|---|---|---|---|---|---|
| 2008 | 2,000 | PF65 850 | | | | |

**KM# 391 50 ROUBLES**
7.78 g., 0.999 Gold 0.2499 oz. AGW, 25 mm. **Obv:** National arms **Rev:** Squirrel right eating nut

| Date | Mintage | VF20 | XF40 | MS60 | MS63 | MS65 |
|---|---|---|---|---|---|---|
| 2009 | 2,000 | PF65 900 | | | | |

**KM# 277 50 ROUBLES**
7.78 g., 0.999 Gold 0.2499 oz. AGW, 25 mm. **Obv:** National arms **Rev:** Owl head facing

| Date | Mintage | VF20 | XF40 | MS60 | MS63 | MS65 |
|---|---|---|---|---|---|---|
| 2010 | — | PF65 900 | | | | |

**KM# 392 50 ROUBLES**
8.64 g., 0.900 Gold 0.250 oz. AGW, 22 mm. **Subject:** Battle of Grunwald, 600th Anniversary **Obv:** Stylized figure in shape of cross **Rev:** Stylized fingerprint

| Date | Mintage | VF20 | XF40 | MS60 | MS63 | MS65 |
|---|---|---|---|---|---|---|
| 2010 | 500 | PF65 800 | | | | |

**KM# 393 50 ROUBLES**
7.78 g., 0.999 Gold 0.2499 oz. AGW, 22 mm. **Subject:** Motherhood **Obv:** Lis **Rev:** Mother and child

| Date | Mintage | VF20 | XF40 | MS60 | MS63 | MS65 |
|---|---|---|---|---|---|---|
| 2010 | 2,500 | PF65 800 | | | | |

**KM# 286 50 ROUBLES**
7.78 g., 0.999 Gold 0.2499 oz. AGW, 25 mm. **Obv:** National arms **Rev:** Hedgehog

| Date | Mintage | VF20 | XF40 | MS60 | MS63 | MS65 |
|---|---|---|---|---|---|---|
| 2011 | Est. 1000 | PF65 950 | | | | |

**KM# 421 50 ROUBLES**
7.78 g., 0.999 Gold 0.2499 oz. AGW, 25 mm. **Obv:** National arms **Rev:** Bison head facing, crystal eyes

| Date | Mintage | VF20 | XF40 | MS60 | MS63 | MS65 |
|---|---|---|---|---|---|---|
| 2012 | Est. 2000 | PF65 435 | | | | |

**KM# 450 50 ROUBLES**
7.77 g., 0.999 Gold 0.2496 oz. AGW, 22 mm. **Subject:** Belarusian Ballet

| Date | Mintage | VF20 | XF40 | MS60 | MS63 | MS65 |
|---|---|---|---|---|---|---|
| 2013 | Est. 1000 | PF65 350 | | | | |

**KM# 58 100 ROUBLES**
155.50 g., 0.925 Silver 4.6245 oz. ASW, 64 mm. **Obv:** Theater building **Rev:** Two ballet dancers **Edge:** Reeded **Note:** Illustration reduced.

| Date | Mintage | VF20 | XF40 | MS60 | MS63 | MS65 |
|---|---|---|---|---|---|---|
| 2003 | 1,000 | PF65 750 | | | | |

**KM# 216 100 ROUBLES**
17.28 g., 0.900 Gold 0.500 oz. AGW, 32 mm. **Subject:** China - Belarus relations, 15th Anniversary **Obv:** National arms **Rev:** Two archways, forest in left, Great Wall on right **Edge:** Reeded

| Date | Mintage | VF20 | XF40 | MS60 | MS63 | MS65 |
|---|---|---|---|---|---|---|
| 2007 | 1,000 | PF65 1,000 | | | | |

**KM# 192 100 ROUBLES**
155.50 g., 0.999 Silver 4.9944 oz. ASW, 65 mm. **Subject:** Figure skating **Rev:** Pair of skates and snowflakes **Note:** Illustration reduced.

| Date | Mintage | VF20 | XF40 | MS60 | MS63 | MS65 |
|---|---|---|---|---|---|---|
| 2008 | 500 | PF65 450 | | | | |

**KM# 193 100 ROUBLES**
155.50 g., 0.999 Silver 4.9944 oz. ASW, 65 mm. **Subject:** White Stork Legend **Rev:** Stylized stork

| Date | Mintage | VF20 | XF40 | MS60 | MS63 | MS65 |
|---|---|---|---|---|---|---|
| 2008 | 500 | PF65 450 | | | | |

**KM# 333 100 ROUBLES**
155.50 g., 0.999 Gold 4.9944 oz. AGW, 65 mm. **Subject:** 2012 London Olympics **Obv:** National emblem at center of star design **Rev:** Tower bridge and two stylized handball athletes above

| Date | Mintage | VF20 | XF40 | MS60 | MS63 | MS65 |
|---|---|---|---|---|---|---|
| 2009 | 800 | PF65 9,500 | | | | |

**KM# 394 100 ROUBLES**
155.50 g., 0.999 Silver 4.9944 oz. ASW, 65 mm. **Subject:** London Olympics, 2012 **Obv:** National arms and logo **Rev:** Two stylized players and Tower Bridge

| Date | Mintage | VF20 | XF40 | MS60 | MS63 | MS65 |
|---|---|---|---|---|---|---|
| 2009 Prooflike | 800 | — | — | — | — | 250 |

**KM# 395 100 ROUBLES**
15.50 g., 0.900 Gold 0.4485 oz. AGW, 30 mm. **Subject:** Zodiac - Pisces **Obv:** Sun and moon **Rev:** Two fish

| Date | Mintage | VF20 | XF40 | MS60 | MS63 | MS65 |
|---|---|---|---|---|---|---|
| 2011 | 2,000 | PF65 1,200 | | | | |

**KM# 396 100 ROUBLES**
15.50 g., 0.900 Gold 0.4485 oz. AGW, 30 mm. **Subject:** Zodiac - Ram **Obv:** Sun and moon **Rev:** Ram

| Date | Mintage | VF20 | XF40 | MS60 | MS63 | MS65 |
|---|---|---|---|---|---|---|
| 2011 | 2,000 | PF65 1,200 | | | | |

**KM# 397 100 ROUBLES**
15.50 g., 0.900 Gold 0.4485 oz. AGW, 30 mm. **Subject:** Zodiac - Taurus **Obv:** Sun and moon **Rev:** Bull

| Date | Mintage | VF20 | XF40 | MS60 | MS63 | MS65 |
|---|---|---|---|---|---|---|
| 2011 | 2,000 | PF65 1,200 | | | | |

**KM# 398 100 ROUBLES**
15.50 g., 0.900 Gold 0.4485 oz. AGW, 30 mm. **Subject:** Zodiac - Gemni **Obv:** Sun and moon **Rev:** Twins

| Date | Mintage | VF20 | XF40 | MS60 | MS63 | MS65 |
|---|---|---|---|---|---|---|
| 2011 | 2,000 | PF65 1,200 | | | | |

**KM# 399 100 ROUBLES**
15.50 g., 0.900 Gold 0.4485 oz. AGW, 30 mm. **Subject:** Zodiac - Cancer **Obv:** Sun and moon **Rev:** Crab

| Date | Mintage | VF20 | XF40 | MS60 | MS63 | MS65 |
|---|---|---|---|---|---|---|
| 2011 | 2,000 | PF65 1,200 | | | | |

**KM# 400 100 ROUBLES**
15.50 g., 0.900 Gold 0.4485 oz. AGW, 30 mm. **Subject:** Zodiac - Leo **Obv:** Sun and moon **Rev:** Lion standing left

| Date | Mintage | VF20 | XF40 | MS60 | MS63 | MS65 |
|---|---|---|---|---|---|---|
| 2011 | 2,000 | PF65 1,200 | | | | |

**KM# 401 100 ROUBLES**
15.50 g., 0.900 Gold 0.4485 oz. AGW, 30 mm. **Subject:** Zodiac - Virgo **Obv:** Sun and moon **Rev:** Girl

| Date | Mintage | VF20 | XF40 | MS60 | MS63 | MS65 |
|---|---|---|---|---|---|---|
| 2011 | 2,000 | PF65 1,200 | | | | |

**KM# 402 100 ROUBLES**
15.50 g., 0.900 Gold 0.4485 oz. AGW, 30 mm. **Subject:** Zodiac - Libra **Obv:** Sun and moon **Rev:** Balance scales

| Date | Mintage | VF20 | XF40 | MS60 | MS63 | MS65 |
|---|---|---|---|---|---|---|
| 2011 | 2,000 | PF65 1,200 | | | | |

**KM# 403 100 ROUBLES**
15.50 g., 0.900 Gold 0.4485 oz. AGW, 30 mm. **Subject:** Zodiac - Scorpion **Obv:** Sun and moon **Rev:** Scorpion

| Date | Mintage | VF20 | XF40 | MS60 | MS63 | MS65 |
|---|---|---|---|---|---|---|
| 2011 | 2,000 | PF65 1,200 | | | | |

**KM# 404 100 ROUBLES**
15.50 g., 0.900 Gold 0.4485 oz. AGW, 30 mm. **Subject:** Zodiac - Virgo **Obv:** Sun and moon **Rev:** Girl as angel with bow and arrow

| Date | Mintage | VF20 | XF40 | MS60 | MS63 | MS65 |
|---|---|---|---|---|---|---|
| 2011 | 2,000 | PF65 1,200 | | | | |

**KM# 405 100 ROUBLES**
15.50 g., 0.900 Gold 0.4485 oz. AGW, 30 mm. **Subject:** Zodiac - Capricorn **Obv:** Sun and moon **Rev:** Ram standing left

| Date | Mintage | VF20 | XF40 | MS60 | MS63 | MS65 |
|---|---|---|---|---|---|---|
| 2011 | 2,000 | PF65 1,200 | | | | |

**KM# 406 100 ROUBLES**
15.50 g., 0.900 Gold 0.4485 oz. AGW, 30 mm. **Subject:** Zodiac - Aquarius **Obv:** Sun and moon **Rev:** Child in bathtub

| Date | Mintage | VF20 | XF40 | MS60 | MS63 | MS65 |
|---|---|---|---|---|---|---|
| 2011 | 2,000 | PF65 1,200 | | | | |

**KM# 447 100 ROUBLES**
155.50 g., 0.999 Silver 4.9944 oz. ASW, 65 mm. **Subject:** 2014 FIFA World Cup Brazil

| Date | Mintage | VF20 | XF40 | MS60 | MS63 | MS65 |
|---|---|---|---|---|---|---|
| 2013 | Est. 1000 | PF65 400 | | | | |

**KM# 452 100 ROUBLES**
155.50 g., 0.999 Silver 4.9944 oz. ASW, 65 mm. **Subject:** Belarusian Ballet

| Date | Mintage | VF20 | XF40 | MS60 | MS63 | MS65 |
|---|---|---|---|---|---|---|
| 2013 | Est. 750 | PF65 400 | | | | |

**KM# 103 200 ROUBLES**
31.11 g., 0.999 Gold 0.999 oz. AGW, 40 mm. **Obv:** National arms **Rev:** Belarussian ballerina

| Date | Mintage | VF20 | XF40 | MS60 | MS63 | MS65 |
|---|---|---|---|---|---|---|
| 2005 | 1,500 | PF65 2,000 | | | | |

**KM# 408 200 ROUBLES**
34.56 g., 0.900 Gold 1.000 oz. AGW, 38.61 mm. **Subject:** Ski center in Siliczy **Obv:** Skier **Rev:** Building complex

| Date | Mintage | VF20 | XF40 | MS60 | MS63 | MS65 |
|---|---|---|---|---|---|---|
| 2006 | 2,000 | PF65 3,000 | | | | |

**KM# 409 200 ROUBLES**
31.10 g., 0.999 Gold 0.9989 oz. AGW, 40 mm. **Subject:** Ballet **Obv:** National arms **Rev:** Ballet Pair

| Date | Mintage | VF20 | XF40 | MS60 | MS63 | MS65 |
|---|---|---|---|---|---|---|
| 2006 | 1,500 | PF65 3,250 | | | | |

**KM# 407 200 ROUBLES**
31.10 g., 0.999 Gold 0.9989 oz. AGW, 40 mm. **Subject:** Ballet **Obv:** National arms **Rev:** Ballerina on point right

| Date | Mintage | VF20 | XF40 | MS60 | MS63 | MS65 |
|---|---|---|---|---|---|---|
| 2007 | 1,500 | PF65 3,000 | | | | |

## KM# 74 1000 ROUBLES

1000.00 g., 0.999 Silver 32.1186 oz. ASW, 100 mm. **Subject:** 2004 Olympics **Obv:** National arms **Rev:** Ancient charioteer **Note:** Illustration reduced.

| Date | Mintage | VF20 | XF40 | MS60 | MS63 | MS65 |
|---|---|---|---|---|---|---|
| 2004 | 650 | PF65 1,500 | | | | |

## KM# 410 1000 ROUBLES

155.50 g., 0.999 Gold 4.9944 oz. AGW, 65 mm. **Subject:** Ballet **Obv:** National arms **Rev:** Ballet pair

| Date | Mintage | VF20 | XF40 | MS60 | MS63 | MS65 |
|---|---|---|---|---|---|---|
| 2006 | 99 | PF65 10,500 | | | | |

## KM# 412 1000 ROUBLES

1000.00 g., 0.999 Silver 32.1186 oz. ASW, 100 mm. **Subject:** Beijing Olympics, 2008 **Obv:** Naitonal arms **Rev:** Classical runners around center circle

| Date | Mintage | VF20 | XF40 | MS60 | MS63 | MS65 |
|---|---|---|---|---|---|---|
| 2006 | 2,000 | PF65 2,000 | | | | |

## KM# 170 1000 ROUBLES

1000.00 g., 0.999 Silver 32.1186 oz. ASW, 100 mm. **Subject:** Belarussian Ballet **Rev:** Ballerina and mirror image **Note:** Illustration reduced.

| Date | Mintage | VF20 | XF40 | MS60 | MS63 | MS65 |
|---|---|---|---|---|---|---|
| 2007 | 300 | PF65 2,000 | | | | |

## KM# 171 1000 ROUBLES

1000.00 g., 0.999 Silver 32.1186 oz. ASW partially gilt, 100 mm. **Subject:** Cross of St. Euphrosyne of Polotsk **Obv:** Church facade **Rev:** Gold-plated pectorial cross **Note:** Illustration reduced.

| Date | Mintage | VF20 | XF40 | MS60 | MS63 | MS65 |
|---|---|---|---|---|---|---|
| 2007 Proof-like | 2,000 | PF65 2,000 | | | | |

## KM# 411 1000 ROUBLES

155.50 g., 0.999 Gold 4.9944 oz. AGW, 65 mm. **Subject:** Ballet **Obv:** National arms **Rev:** Mirror image of ballerina

| Date | Mintage | VF20 | XF40 | MS60 | MS63 | MS65 |
|---|---|---|---|---|---|---|
| 2007 | 99 | PF65 10,500 | | | | |

## KM# 449 1000 ROUBLES

155.50 g., 0.999 Gold 4.9944 oz. AGW, 65 mm. **Subject:** Belarusian Ballet

| Date | Mintage | VF20 | XF40 | MS60 | MS63 | MS65 |
|---|---|---|---|---|---|---|
| 2013 | Est. 49 | PF65 9,000 | | | | |

# BELGIUM

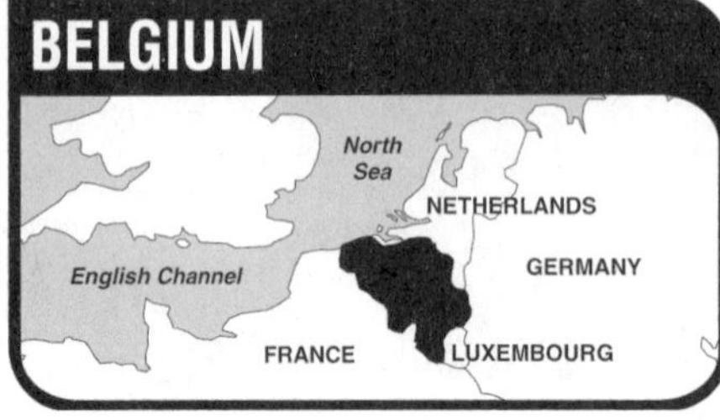


The Kingdom of Belgium, a constitutional monarchy in northwest Europe, has an area of 11,780 sq. mi. (30,519 sq. km.) and a population of 10.1 million, chiefly Dutch-speaking Flemish and French-speaking Walloons. Capital: Brussels. Agriculture, dairy farming, and the processing of raw materials for re-export are the principal industries. Beurs voor Diamant in Antwerp is the world's largest diamond trading center. Iron and steel, machinery motor vehicles, chemicals, textile yarns and fabrics comprise the principal exports.

**RULER**

Albert II, 1993-

**MINT MARK**

Angel head - Brussels

**MINTMASTERS' INITIALS & PRIVY MARKS**

Pair of scales - Roman Coenen (1987 - )
Gose feather - Serge Lesens (2010)

**NOTE**: Beginning in 1987, the letters "qp" (quality proof) appear on non-circulating coins.

**MONETARY SYSTEM**

100 Centimes = 1 Franc
1 Euro = 100 Cents

**LEGENDS**

Belgian coins are usually inscribed either in Dutch, French or both. However some modern coins are being inscribed in Latin or German. The language used is best told by noting the spelling of the name of the country.

(Fr) French: BELGIQUE or BELGES
(Du) Dutch: BELGIE or BELGEN
(La) Latin: BELGICA
(Ge) German: BELGIEN

# KINGDOM

## DECIMAL COINAGE

## KM# 149.1 50 CENTIMES

2.75 g., Bronze, 19 mm. **Ruler:** Baudouin I **Obv:** Crowned denomination divides date, legend in Dutch **Obv. Legend:** BELGIE **Rev:** Helmeted mine worker left, miner's lamp at right, large head **Edge:** Plain

| Date | Mintage | F12 | VF20 | XF40 | MS60 | MS63 |
|---|---|---|---|---|---|---|
| 2001 Sets only | 60,000 | — | — | — | 3.00 | — |
| 2001 | 5,000 | PF65 25.00 | | | | |
| Note: Medal alignment | | | | | | |
| 2007 Sets only | 60,000 | — | — | — | 2.00 | — |

## KM# 149.2 50 CENTIMES

2.75 g., Bronze, 19 mm. **Ruler:** Baudouin I **Obv:** Crowned denomination divides date, legend in French **Obv. Legend:** BELGIQUE **Rev:** Helmeted mine worker left, miner's lamp at right, large head, tip of neck 1/2 mm from rim **Edge:** Plain **Note:** Medal alignment.

| Date | Mintage | F12 | VF20 | XF40 | MS60 | MS63 |
|---|---|---|---|---|---|---|
| 2001 | — | PF65 30.00 | | | | |

## KM# 148.1 50 CENTIMES

2.70 g., Bronze, 19 mm. **Ruler:** Baudouin I **Obv:** Crowned denomination divides date, legend in French **Obv. Legend:** BELGIQUE **Rev:** Helmeted mine worker left, miner's lamp at right, large head, tip of neck 1/2 mm from rim **Edge:** Plain

| Date | Mintage | F12 | VF20 | XF40 | MS60 | MS63 |
|---|---|---|---|---|---|---|
| 2001 Sets only | 60,000 | — | — | — | 2.00 | — |
| 2001 | 5,000 | PF65 25.00 | | | | |
| Note: Medal alignment | | | | | | |

## KM# 148.2 50 CENTIMES

2.75 g., Bronze, 19 mm. **Ruler:** Baudouin I **Obv:** Crowned denomination divides date, legend in French **Obv. Legend:** BELGIQUE **Rev:** Helmeted mine worker left, miner's lamp at right, large head, tip of neck 1/2 mm from rim **Edge:** Plain **Note:** Medal alignment.

| Date | Mintage | F12 | VF20 | XF40 | MS60 | MS63 |
|---|---|---|---|---|---|---|
| 2001 | — | PF65 30.00 | | | | |

## KM# 187 FRANC

2.75 g., Nickel Plated Iron, 18 mm. **Ruler:** Albert II **Obv:** Head left, outline around back of head **Rev:** Vertical line divides date and large denomination, legend in French **Rev. Legend:** BELGIQUE **Note:** Mint mark: angel head. Unknown mintmaster's privy mark: scales.

| Date | Mintage | F12 | VF20 | XF40 | MS60 | MS63 |
|---|---|---|---|---|---|---|
| 2001 Sets only | 60,000 | — | — | — | 3.00 | — |
| 2001 | 5,000 | PF65 25.00 | | | | |
| Note: Medal alignment | | | | | | |

## KM# 188 FRANC

2.75 g., Nickel Plated Iron, 18 mm. **Ruler:** Albert II **Obv:** Head left, outline around back of head **Rev:** Vertical line divides date and large denomination, legend in Dutch **Rev. Legend:** BELGIE **Edge:** Plain

| Date | Mintage | F12 | VF20 | XF40 | MS60 | MS63 |
|---|---|---|---|---|---|---|
| 2001 Sets only | 60,000 | — | — | — | 3.00 | — |
| 2001 | 5,000 | PF65 25.00 | | | | |
| Note: Medal alignment | | | | | | |

### KM# 189 5 FRANCS (5 Frank)

5.50 g., Aluminum-Bronze, 24 mm. **Ruler:** Albert II **Obv:** Head left, outline around back of head **Rev:** Vertical line divides date and denomination, legend in French **Rev. Legend:** BELGIQUE **Note:** Mint mark: angel head. Mintmaster R. Coenen's privy mark: scale.

| Date | Mintage | F12 | VF20 | XF40 | MS60 | MS63 |
|---|---|---|---|---|---|---|
| 2001 Sets only | 60,000 | — | — | — | 4.00 | — |
| 2001 | 5,000 | PF65 25.00 | | | | |

Note: Medal alignment

### KM# 190 5 FRANCS (5 Frank)

5.50 g., Aluminum-Bronze, 24 mm. **Ruler:** Albert II **Obv:** Head left, outline around back of head **Rev:** Vertical line divides date and large denomination, legend in Dutch **Rev. Legend:** BELGIE **Note:** Mint mark: angel head. Mintmaster R. Coenen's privy mark: scale.

| Date | Mintage | F12 | VF20 | XF40 | MS60 | MS63 |
|---|---|---|---|---|---|---|
| 2001 Sets only | 60,000 | — | — | — | 4.00 | — |
| 2001 | 5,000 | PF65 25.00 | | | | |

Note: Medal alignment

### KM# 191 20 FRANCS (20 Frank)

8.50 g., Nickel-Bronze, 25.65 mm. **Ruler:** Albert II **Obv:** Head left, outline around back of head **Rev:** Vertical line divides date and large denomination, legend in French **Rev. Legend:** BELGIQUE **Note:** Mint mark: angel head. Mintmaster R. Coenen's privy mark: scale.

| Date | Mintage | F12 | VF20 | XF40 | MS60 | MS63 |
|---|---|---|---|---|---|---|
| 2001 Sets only | 60,000 | — | — | — | 4.00 | — |
| 2001 | 5,000 | PF65 25.00 | | | | |

Note: Medal alignment

### KM# 192 20 FRANCS (20 Frank)

8.50 g., Nickel-Bronze, 25.7 mm. **Ruler:** Albert II **Obv:** Head left, outline around back of head **Rev:** Vertical line divides date and large denomination, legend in Dutch **Rev. Legend:** BELGIE **Note:** Mint mark: angel head. Mintmaster R. Coenen's privy mark: scale.

| Date | Mintage | F12 | VF20 | XF40 | MS60 | MS63 |
|---|---|---|---|---|---|---|
| 2001 Sets only | 60,000 | — | — | — | 5.00 | — |
| 2001 | 5,000 | PF65 25.00 | | | | |

Note: Medal alignment

### KM# 193 50 FRANCS (50 Frank)

7.00 g., Nickel, 22.7 mm. **Ruler:** Albert II **Obv:** Head left, outline around back of head **Rev:** Vertical line divides large denomination and date, legend in French **Rev. Legend:** BELGIQUE **Note:** Mint mark: angel head. Mintmaster R. Coenen's privy mark: scale.

| Date | Mintage | F12 | VF20 | XF40 | MS60 | MS63 |
|---|---|---|---|---|---|---|
| 2001 Sets only | 60,000 | — | — | — | 8.00 | — |
| 2001 | 5,000 | PF65 25.00 | | | | |

Note: Medal alignment

### KM# 194 50 FRANCS (50 Frank)

7.00 g., Nickel, 22.75 mm. **Ruler:** Albert II **Obv:** Head left, outline around back of head **Rev:** Vertical line divides large denomination and date, legend in Dutch **Rev. Legend:** BELGIE **Note:** Mint mark: angel head. Mintmaster R. Coenen's privy mark: scale.

| Date | Mintage | F12 | VF20 | XF40 | MS60 | MS63 |
|---|---|---|---|---|---|---|
| 2001 Sets only | 60,000 | — | — | — | 8.00 | — |
| 2001 | 5,000 | PF65 25.00 | | | | |

Note: Medal alignment

### KM# 222 500 FRANCS (500 Frank)

22.85 g., 0.925 Silver 0.6795 oz. ASW, 37 mm. **Ruler:** Albert II **Subject:** Europe: Europa and the Bull **Obv:** Map and denomination **Rev:** Europa sitting on a bull **Edge:** Plain

| Date | Mintage | F12 | VF20 | XF40 | MS60 | MS63 |
|---|---|---|---|---|---|---|
| 2001 (qp) | 40,000 | PF63 45.00 | PF65 50.00 | | | |

### KM# 223 5000 FRANCS

15.55 g., 0.999 Gold 0.4994 oz. AGW, 29 mm. **Ruler:** Albert II **Subject:** Europe: Europa and the Bull **Obv:** Map and denomination **Rev:** Europa sitting on a bull **Edge:** Plain

| Date | Mintage | F12 | VF20 | XF40 | MS60 | MS63 |
|---|---|---|---|---|---|---|
| 2001 (qp) | 2,000 | PF65 875 | | | | |

## EURO COINAGE

European Union Issues

### KM# 224 EURO CENT

2.30 g., Copper Plated Steel, 16.25 mm. **Ruler:** Albert II **Obv:** Head left within inner circle, stars 3/4 surround, date below **Rev:** Denomination and globe **Edge:** Plain

| Date | Mintage | VF20 | XF40 | MS60 | MS63 | MS65 |
|---|---|---|---|---|---|---|
| 2001 | 99,840,000 | — | 0.30 | 0.75 | 1.00 | — |
| 2001 | 15,000 | PF65 12.00 | | | | |
| 2002 Sets only | 140,000 | — | — | 18.50 | 30.00 | — |
| 2002 | 15,000 | PF65 15.00 | | | | |
| 2003 | 10,135,000 | — | 0.25 | 0.60 | 0.80 | — |
| 2003 | 15,000 | PF65 12.00 | | | | |
| 2004 | 180,000,000 | — | 0.25 | 0.60 | 0.80 | — |
| 2004 | — | PF65 12.00 | | | | |
| 2005 Sets only | — | — | — | — | 18.50 | — |
| 2005 | 3,000 | PF65 12.00 | | | | |
| 2006 | 15,000,000 | — | 0.25 | 0.60 | 0.80 | — |
| 2006 | — | PF65 12.00 | | | | |
| 2007 | 60,000,000 | — | 0.25 | 0.60 | 0.80 | — |
| 2007 | — | PF65 12.00 | | | | |

### KM# 274 EURO CENT

2.30 g., Copper Plated Steel, 16.25 mm. **Ruler:** Albert II **Obv:** Head of Albert II left, crowned monogram at right, date below

| Date | Mintage | VF20 | XF40 | MS60 | MS63 | MS65 |
|---|---|---|---|---|---|---|
| 2008 | 50,000,000 | — | — | 0.35 | 0.75 | — |
| 2008 | — | PF65 12.00 | | | | |
| 2009 | 19,950,000 | — | — | 0.35 | 0.75 | — |
| 2009 | 1,500 | PF65 12.00 | | | | |
| 2010 | 30,000,000 | — | — | 0.35 | 0.75 | — |
| 2010 | 1,850 | PF65 12.00 | | | | |
| 2011 | 9,975,000 | — | — | — | 0.75 | — |
| 2011 | 1,850 | PF65 12.00 | | | | |
| 2012 | 19,950,000 | — | — | — | 0.75 | — |
| 2012 | 1,850 | PF65 12.00 | | | | |
| 2013 | 1,850 | PF65 12.00 | | | | |
| 2013 | — | — | — | — | 0.75 | — |

### KM# 225 2 EURO CENT

3.06 g., Copper Plated Steel, 18.75 mm. **Ruler:** Albert II **Obv:** Head left within circle, stars 3/4 surround, date below **Rev:** Denomination and globe **Edge:** Grooved

| Date | Mintage | VF20 | XF40 | MS60 | MS63 | MS65 |
|---|---|---|---|---|---|---|
| 2001 Sets only | 40,000 | — | — | — | 9.00 | — |
| Note: Only available in sets at present, circulation strikes not yet released | | | | | | |
| 2001 | 15,000 | PF65 15.00 | | | | |
| 2002 Sets only | 140,000 | — | — | — | 6.50 | — |
| 2002 | 15,000 | PF65 12.00 | | | | |
| 2003 | 40,135,000 | — | 0.30 | 0.75 | 1.00 | — |
| 2003 | 15,000 | PF65 12.00 | | | | |
| 2004 | 140,000,000 | — | 0.30 | 0.75 | 1.00 | — |
| 2004 | 15,000 | PF65 12.00 | | | | |
| 2005 Sets only | — | — | — | — | 1.00 | — |
| 2005 | — | PF65 12.00 | | | | |
| 2006 | 30,000,000 | — | 0.30 | 0.75 | 1.00 | — |
| 2006 | — | PF65 12.00 | | | | |
| 2007 | 70,000,000 | — | 0.30 | 0.75 | 1.00 | — |
| 2007 | — | PF65 12.00 | | | | |

### KM# 275 2 EURO CENT

3.06 g., Copper Plated Steel, 18.75 mm. **Ruler:** Albert II **Obv:** Head of Albert II left, crowned monogram at right, date below **Edge:** Grooved

| Date | Mintage | VF20 | XF40 | MS60 | MS63 | MS65 |
|---|---|---|---|---|---|---|
| 2008 | 40,000,000 | — | — | 0.75 | 1.00 | — |
| 2008 | — | PF65 12.00 | | | | |
| 2009 | 10,000,000 | — | — | 0.75 | 1.00 | — |
| 2009 | 1,500 | PF65 12.00 | | | | |
| 2010 | 20,000,000 | — | — | 0.75 | 1.00 | — |
| 2010 | 1,850 | PF65 12.00 | | | | |
| 2011 | — | — | — | — | 1.00 | — |
| 2011 | 1,850 | PF65 12.00 | | | | |
| 2012 | 15,000,000 | — | — | — | 1.00 | — |
| 2012 | 1,850 | PF65 12.00 | | | | |
| 2013 | — | — | — | — | 1.00 | — |
| 2013 | 1,850 | PF65 12.00 | | | | |

### KM# 226 5 EURO CENT

3.92 g., Copper Plated Steel, 21.25 mm. **Ruler:** Albert II **Obv:** Head left within circle, stars 3/4 surround, date below **Rev:** Denomination and globe **Edge:** Plain

| Date | Mintage | VF20 | XF40 | MS60 | MS63 | MS65 |
|---|---|---|---|---|---|---|
| 2001 Sets only | 40,000 | — | — | — | 12.50 | — |
| 2001 | 15,000 | PF65 15.00 | | | | |
| 2002 Sets only | 140,000 | — | — | — | 8.00 | — |
| 2002 | 15,000 | PF65 15.00 | | | | |
| 2003 | 30,135,000 | — | 0.30 | 0.80 | 1.20 | — |
| 2003 | 15,000 | PF65 12.00 | | | | |
| 2004 | 75,000,000 | — | 0.30 | 0.80 | 1.20 | — |
| 2004 | — | PF65 12.00 | | | | |
| 2005 | 110,000,000 | — | 0.30 | 0.80 | 1.20 | — |
| 2005 | — | PF65 12.00 | | | | |
| 2006 | 35,000,000 | — | 0.30 | 0.80 | 1.20 | — |
| 2006 | — | PF65 12.00 | | | | |
| 2007 Sets only | — | — | — | — | 8.00 | — |
| 2007 | — | PF65 12.00 | | | | |

### KM# 276 5 EURO CENT

3.92 g., Copper Plated Steel, 21.25 mm. **Ruler:** Albert II **Obv:** Redesigned head of Albert II left

| Date | Mintage | VF20 | XF40 | MS60 | MS63 | MS65 |
|---|---|---|---|---|---|---|
| 2008 | — | — | — | — | 2.00 | — |
| 2008 | — | PF65 12.00 | | | | |
| 2009 | — | — | — | — | 1.20 | — |

| Date | Mintage | VF20 | XF40 | MS60 | MS63 | MS65 |
|---|---|---|---|---|---|---|
| 2009 | 1,500 | PF65 12.00 | | | | |
| 2010 | 25,000,000 | — | — | 0.75 | 1.20 | — |
| 2010 | 1,850 | PF65 12.00 | | | | |
| 2011 | 25,000,000 | — | — | — | 1.20 | — |
| 2011 | 1,850 | PF65 12.00 | | | | |
| 2012 | 22,500,000 | — | — | — | 1.20 | — |
| 2012 | 1,850 | PF65 12.00 | | | | |
| 2013 | — | — | — | — | 1.20 | — |
| 2013 | 1,850 | PF65 12.00 | | | | |

### KM# 227 10 EURO CENT

4.10 g., Brass, 19.75 mm. **Ruler:** Albert II **Obv:** Head left within inner circle, stars 3/4 surround, date below **Rev:** Denomination and map **Edge:** Reeded

| Date | Mintage | VF20 | XF40 | MS60 | MS63 | MS65 |
|---|---|---|---|---|---|---|
| 2001 | 145,790,000 | — | — | 0.75 | 1.25 | — |
| 2001 | 15,000 | PF65 12.00 | | | | |
| 2002 Sets only | 140,000 | — | — | 6.00 | 8.00 | — |
| 2002 | 15,000 | PF65 15.00 | | | | |
| 2003 Sets only | 135,000 | — | — | 6.00 | 8.00 | — |
| 2003 | 15,000 | PF65 15.00 | | | | |
| 2004 | 20,000,000 | — | — | 1.00 | 1.50 | — |
| 2004 | — | PF65 12.00 | | | | |
| 2005 | 10,000,000 | — | — | 1.00 | 1.50 | — |
| 2005 | — | PF65 12.00 | | | | |
| 2006 Sets only | — | — | — | 1.00 | 1.50 | — |
| 2006 | — | PF65 12.00 | | | | |

### KM# 242 10 EURO CENT

4.10 g., Brass, 19.75 mm. **Ruler:** Albert II **Obv:** King's portrait **Rev:** Relief map of Western Europe, stars, lines and value **Edge:** Reeded

| Date | Mintage | VF20 | XF40 | MS60 | MS63 | MS65 |
|---|---|---|---|---|---|---|
| 2007 | — | — | — | 1.00 | 1.50 | — |
| 2007 | — | PF65 12.00 | | | | |

### KM# 277 10 EURO CENT

4.10 g., Brass, 19.75 mm. **Ruler:** Albert II **Obv:** Head of Albert II left, crowned monogram right, date below **Edge:** Reeded

| Date | Mintage | VF20 | XF40 | MS60 | MS63 | MS65 |
|---|---|---|---|---|---|---|
| 2008 | — | — | — | — | 6.00 | — |
| 2008 | — | PF65 12.00 | | | | |
| 2009 | — | — | — | — | 1.50 | — |
| 2009 | 1,500 | PF65 12.00 | | | | |
| 2010 | 20,000,000 | — | — | 1.00 | 1.50 | — |
| 2010 | 1,850 | PF65 12.00 | | | | |
| 2011 | 25,000,000 | — | — | 1.00 | 1.50 | — |
| 2011 | 1,850 | PF65 12.00 | | | | |
| 2012 | 25,000,000 | — | — | — | 1.50 | — |
| 2012 | 1,850 | PF65 12.00 | | | | |
| 2013 | — | — | — | — | 1.50 | — |
| 2013 | 1,850 | PF65 12.00 | | | | |

### KM# 228 20 EURO CENT

5.74 g., Brass, 22.25 mm. **Ruler:** Albert II **Obv:** Head left within circle, stars 3/4 surround, date below **Rev:** Denomination and map **Edge:** Notched

| Date | Mintage | VF20 | XF40 | MS60 | MS63 | MS65 |
|---|---|---|---|---|---|---|
| 2001 Sets only | 40,000 | — | — | 10.00 | 12.50 | — |
| Note: Only available in sets at present, circulation strikes not yet released | | | | | | |
| 2001 | 15,000 | PF65 15.00 | | | | |
| 2002 | 104,140,000 | — | — | 1.00 | 1.50 | — |
| 2002 | 15,000 | PF65 12.00 | | | | |
| 2003 | 30,135,000 | — | — | 1.25 | 1.75 | — |
| 2003 | 15,000 | PF65 12.00 | | | | |
| 2004 | 109,550,000 | — | — | 1.25 | 1.75 | — |
| 2004 | — | PF65 12.00 | | | | |
| 2005 | 10,000,000 | — | — | 1.25 | 1.75 | — |
| 2005 | — | PF65 12.00 | | | | |
| 2006 | 40,000,000 | — | — | 1.25 | 1.75 | — |
| 2006 | — | PF65 12.00 | | | | |

### KM# 243 20 EURO CENT

5.74 g., Brass, 22.25 mm. **Ruler:** Albert II **Obv:** King's portrait **Rev:** Relief map of Western Europe, stars, lines and value **Edge:** Notched

| Date | Mintage | VF20 | XF40 | MS60 | MS63 | MS65 |
|---|---|---|---|---|---|---|
| 2007 | — | — | — | 1.25 | 1.75 | — |
| 2007 | — | PF65 12.00 | | | | |

### KM# 278 20 EURO CENT

5.74 g., Brass, 22.25 mm. **Ruler:** Albert II **Obv:** Redesigned head of Albert II left **Edge:** Notched

| Date | Mintage | VF20 | XF40 | MS60 | MS63 | MS65 |
|---|---|---|---|---|---|---|
| 2008 | 20,000,000 | — | — | — | 2.00 | — |
| 2008 | — | PF65 12.00 | | | | |
| 2009 | 30,100,000 | — | — | 1.25 | 1.75 | — |
| 2009 | 1,500 | PF65 12.00 | | | | |
| 2010 | 15,000,000 | — | — | 1.25 | 1.75 | — |
| 2010 | 1,850 | PF65 12.00 | | | | |
| 2011 | — | — | — | 1.25 | 1.75 | — |
| 2011 | 1,850 | PF65 12.00 | | | | |
| 2012 | 42,350,000 | — | — | — | 1.75 | — |
| 2012 | 1,850 | PF65 12.00 | | | | |
| 2013 | — | — | — | — | 1.75 | — |
| 2013 | 1,850 | PF65 12.00 | | | | |

### KM# 229 50 EURO CENT

7.80 g., Brass, 24.25 mm. **Ruler:** Albert II **Obv:** Head left within circle, stars 3/4 surround, date below **Rev:** Denomination and map **Edge:** Reeded

| Date | Mintage | VF20 | XF40 | MS60 | MS63 | MS65 |
|---|---|---|---|---|---|---|
| 2001 Sets only | 40,000 | — | — | 10.00 | 12.50 | — |
| 2001 | 15,000 | PF65 15.00 | | | | |
| 2002 | 50,040,000 | — | — | 1.00 | 1.50 | — |
| 2002 | 15,000 | PF65 12.00 | | | | |
| 2003 Sets only | 135,000 | — | — | — | 12.50 | — |
| 2003 | 15,000 | PF65 12.00 | | | | |
| 2004 | 8,000,000 | — | — | 1.25 | 1.75 | — |
| 2004 | — | PF65 12.00 | | | | |
| 2005 Sets only | — | — | — | — | 12.50 | — |
| 2005 | — | PF65 12.00 | | | | |
| 2006 Sets only | — | — | — | — | 12.50 | — |
| 2006 | — | PF65 12.00 | | | | |

### KM# 244 50 EURO CENT

7.80 g., Brass, 24.25 mm. **Ruler:** Albert II **Obv:** King's portrait **Rev:** Relief map of Western Europe, stars, lines and value **Edge:** Reeded

| Date | Mintage | VF20 | XF40 | MS60 | MS63 | MS65 |
|---|---|---|---|---|---|---|
| 2007 | — | — | — | 1.25 | 1.75 | — |
| 2007 | — | PF65 12.00 | | | | |

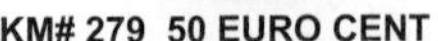

### KM# 279 50 EURO CENT

7.80 g., Brass, 24.25 mm. **Ruler:** Albert II **Obv:** Redesigned head of Albert II left **Edge:** Reeded

| Date | Mintage | VF20 | XF40 | MS60 | MS63 | MS65 |
|---|---|---|---|---|---|---|
| 2008 | 25,000,000 | — | — | — | 4.00 | — |
| 2008 | — | PF65 12.00 | | | | |
| 2009 | 30,000,000 | — | — | 2.00 | 3.00 | — |
| 2009 | 1,500 | PF65 12.00 | | | | |
| 2010 | — | — | — | — | 3.00 | — |
| 2010 | 1,850 | PF65 12.00 | | | | |
| 2011 | 15,000,000 | — | — | — | 3.00 | — |
| 2011 | 1,850 | PF65 12.00 | | | | |
| 2012 | 30,000,000 | — | — | — | 3.00 | — |
| 2012 | 1,850 | PF65 12.00 | | | | |
| 2013 | 1,850 | PF65 12.00 | | | | |
| 2013 | — | — | — | — | 3.00 | — |

### KM# 230 EURO

7.50 g., Bi-Metallic Copper-Nickel center in Nickel-Brass ring, 23.25 mm. **Ruler:** Albert II **Obv:** Head left within circle, stars 3/4 surround, date below **Rev:** Denomination and map **Edge:** Segmented reeding

| Date | Mintage | VF20 | XF40 | MS60 | MS63 | MS65 |
|---|---|---|---|---|---|---|
| 2001 Sets only | 40,000 | — | — | — | 15.00 | — |
| Note: Only available in sets at present, circulation strikes not yet released | | | | | | |
| 2001 | 15,000 | PF65 18.00 | | | | |
| 2002 | 90,640,000 | — | — | 3.00 | 5.00 | — |
| Note: Only a fraction of the mintage released at present | | | | | | |
| 2002 | 15,000 | PF65 15.00 | | | | |
| 2003 | 6,000,000 | — | — | 3.00 | 5.00 | — |
| 2003 | 15,000 | PF65 15.00 | | | | |
| 2004 | 15,000,000 | — | — | 3.00 | 5.00 | — |
| 2004 | — | PF65 15.00 | | | | |
| 2005 Sets only | — | — | — | — | 15.00 | — |
| 2005 | — | PF65 15.00 | | | | |
| 2006 Sets only | — | — | — | — | 15.00 | — |
| 2006 | — | PF65 15.00 | | | | |

### KM# 245 EURO

7.50 g., Bi-Metallic Copper-Nickel center in Nickel-Brass ring, 23.25 mm. **Ruler:** Albert II **Obv:** King's portrait **Rev:** Relief map of Western Europe, stars, lines and value **Edge:** Segmented reeding

| Date | Mintage | VF20 | XF40 | MS60 | MS63 | MS65 |
|---|---|---|---|---|---|---|
| 2007 | — | — | — | 3.00 | 5.00 | — |
| 2007 | — | PF65 15.00 | | | | |

### KM# 280 EURO

7.50 g., Bi-Metallic Copper-Nickel center in Nickel-Brass ring, 23.25 mm. **Ruler:** Albert II **Obv:** Redesigned head of Albert II left **Edge:** Segmented reeding

| Date | Mintage | VF20 | XF40 | MS60 | MS63 | MS65 |
|---|---|---|---|---|---|---|
| 2008 | 5,000,000 | — | — | — | 6.00 | — |
| 2008 | — | PF65 15.00 | | | | |
| 2009 | 10,000,000 | — | — | 3.00 | 5.00 | — |
| 2009 | 1,500 | PF65 15.00 | | | | |
| 2010 | — | — | — | — | 5.00 | — |
| 2010 | 1,850 | PF65 15.00 | | | | |
| 2011 | 15,000,000 | — | — | — | 5.00 | — |
| 2011 | 1,850 | PF65 15.00 | | | | |
| 2012 | 10,000,000 | — | — | — | 5.00 | — |
| 2012 | 1,850 | PF65 15.00 | | | | |
| 2013 | — | — | — | — | 5.00 | — |
| 2013 | 1,850 | PF65 15.00 | | | | |

**KM# 231 2 EURO**

8.50 g., Bi-Metallic Nickel-Brass center in Copper-Nickel ring, 25.75 mm. **Ruler:** Albert II **Obv:** Head left within circle, stars 3/4 surround, date below **Rev:** Denomination and map **Edge:** Reeded with 2's and stars

| Date | Mintage | VF20 | XF40 | MS60 | MS63 | MS65 |
|---|---|---|---|---|---|---|
| 2001 Sets only | 40,000 | — | — | 12.50 | 15.00 | — |
| Note: Only available in sets at present, circulation strikes not yet released | | | | | | |
| 2001 | 15,000 | PF65 20.00 | | | | |
| 2002 | 50,140,000 | — | — | 3.75 | 6.00 | — |
| 2002 | 15,000 | PF65 18.00 | | | | |
| 2003 | 30,135,000 | — | — | 3.75 | 6.00 | — |
| 2003 | 15,000 | PF65 18.00 | | | | |
| 2004 | 65,500,000 | — | — | 3.75 | 6.00 | — |
| 2004 | — | PF65 18.00 | | | | |
| 2005 | 10,500,000 | — | — | 3.75 | 6.00 | — |
| 2005 | — | PF65 18.00 | | | | |
| 2006 | 20,000,000 | — | — | 3.75 | 6.00 | — |
| 2006 | — | PF65 18.00 | | | | |

**KM# 240 2 EURO**

8.50 g., Bi-Metallic Nickel-Brass center in Copper-Nickel ring, 25.75 mm. **Ruler:** Albert II **Subject:** Schengen Agreement **Obv:** Albert II of Belgium and Henri of Luxembourg **Rev:** Value and map **Edge:** Reeded with 2's and stars

| Date | Mintage | VF20 | XF40 | MS60 | MS63 | MS65 |
|---|---|---|---|---|---|---|
| 2005 | 5,977,000 | — | — | 5.00 | 7.50 | — |
| 2005 Prooflike | 20,000 | — | — | — | 20.00 | — |
| 2005 | — | PF65 25.00 | | | | |

**KM# 241 2 EURO**

8.50 g., Bi-Metallic Nickel-Brass center in Copper-Nickel ring, 25.75 mm. **Ruler:** Albert II **Obv:** Atomic model **Rev:** Value and map **Edge:** Reeded with 2's and stars

| Date | Mintage | VF20 | XF40 | MS60 | MS63 | MS65 |
|---|---|---|---|---|---|---|
| 2006 | 4,977,000 | — | — | 4.00 | 6.00 | — |
| 2006 Prooflike | 20,000 | — | — | — | 25.00 | — |
| 2006 | 3,000 | PF63 80.00 | PF65 100 | | | |

**KM# 246 2 EURO**

8.50 g., Bi-Metallic Nickel-Brass center in Copper-Nickel ring, 25.75 mm. **Ruler:** Albert II **Obv:** King's portrait **Rev:** Relief map of Western Europe, stars, lines and value **Edge:** Reeded with 2's and stars

| Date | Mintage | VF20 | XF40 | MS60 | MS63 | MS65 |
|---|---|---|---|---|---|---|
| 2007 | — | — | — | 3.75 | 6.00 | — |
| 2007 | — | PF65 25.00 | | | | |

**KM# 247 2 EURO**

8.50 g., Bi-Metallic Nickel-Brass center in Copper-Nickel ring, 25.75 mm. **Ruler:** Albert II **Subject:** 50th Anniversary Treaty of Rome **Obv:** Open treaty book **Rev:** Large value at left, modified outline of Europe at right **Edge:** Reeded with stars and 2's

| Date | Mintage | VF20 | XF40 | MS60 | MS63 | MS65 |
|---|---|---|---|---|---|---|
| 2007 | 4,960,000 | — | — | 2.00 | 9.00 | — |
| 2007 Prooflike | 35,000 | — | — | — | 25.00 | — |
| 2007 | 10,000 | PF63 65.00 | PF65 75.00 | | | |

**KM# 248 2 EURO**

8.50 g., Bi-Metallic Nickel-Brass center in Copper-Nickel ring, 25.75 mm. **Ruler:** Albert II **Subject:** Universal Declaration of Human Rights **Obv:** Book in bow **Rev:** Large value "2" at left, modified map of Europe at right **Edge:** Reeded with 2's and stars

| Date | Mintage | VF20 | XF40 | MS60 | MS63 | MS65 |
|---|---|---|---|---|---|---|
| 2008 | — | — | — | 2.00 | 6.00 | — |

**KM# 281 2 EURO**

8.50 g., Bi-Metallic Nickel-Brass center in Copper-Nickel ring, 25.75 mm. **Ruler:** Albert II **Obv:** Head of Albert II left, crowned monogram right, date below **Edge:** Reeded with 2's and stars

| Date | Mintage | VF20 | XF40 | MS60 | MS63 | MS65 |
|---|---|---|---|---|---|---|
| 2008 | 25,000,000 | — | — | — | 7.50 | — |
| 2008 | 2,006 | PF65 18.00 | | | | |
| 2009 | 5,000,000 | — | — | 4.00 | 6.00 | — |
| 2009 | 1,506 | PF65 18.00 | | | | |
| 2010 | 15,000,000 | — | — | 4.00 | 6.00 | — |
| 2010 | 1,850 | PF65 18.00 | | | | |
| 2011 | 32,000,000 | — | — | 4.00 | 6.00 | — |
| 2011 | 1,850 | PF65 18.00 | | | | |
| 2012 Sets only | 23,000 | — | — | 4.00 | 6.00 | — |
| 2012 | 1,850 | PF65 18.00 | | | | |
| 2013 | 1,000 | PF65 18.00 | | | | |
| 2013 Sets only | 24,500 | — | — | 4.00 | 6.00 | — |

**KM# 282 2 EURO**

8.50 g., Bi-Metallic Nickel-Brass center in Copper-Nickel ring, 25.75 mm. **Ruler:** Albert II **Subject:** 10th Anniversary of EMU **Obv:** Stick figure and E symbol **Edge:** Reeded with 2's and stars

| Date | Mintage | VF20 | XF40 | MS60 | MS63 | MS65 |
|---|---|---|---|---|---|---|
| 2009 | 5,000,000 | — | — | 15.00 | — | — |
| 2009 Prooflike | — | — | — | — | 20.00 | — |
| 2009 | — | PF63 60.00 | PF65 70.00 | | | |

**KM# 288 2 EURO**

8.50 g., Bi-Metallic Nickel-Brass center in Copper-Nickel ring, 25.75 mm. **Ruler:** Albert II **Subject:** Louis Braille, 200th Anniversary of Birth **Obv:** Bust right with braile text **Edge:** Reeded with 2's and stars

| Date | Mintage | VF20 | XF40 | MS60 | MS63 | MS65 |
|---|---|---|---|---|---|---|
| 2009 | 5,000,000 | — | — | 2.00 | 5.00 | — |

**KM# 289 2 EURO**

8.50 g., Bi-Metallic Nickel-Brass center in Copper-Nickel ring, 25.75 mm. **Ruler:** Albert II **Subject:** EU Council Presidency **Rev:** eu in script **Edge:** Reeded with 2's and stars

| Date | Mintage | VF20 | XF40 | MS60 | MS63 | MS65 |
|---|---|---|---|---|---|---|
| 2010 | — | — | — | 3.00 | 7.50 | — |

**KM# 308 2 EURO**

8.50 g., Bi-Metallic Nickel-Brass center in Copper-Nickel ring, 25.75 mm. **Ruler:** Albert II **Subject:** International Women's Day, 100th Anniversary **Obv:** Portraits of I. van Diest and M. Popelin

| Date | Mintage | VF20 | XF40 | MS60 | MS63 | MS65 |
|---|---|---|---|---|---|---|
| 2011 | 5,000,000 | — | — | 9.00 | 12.50 | — |
| 2011 Special Unc. | 6,000 | — | — | — | 15.00 | — |
| 2011 | 7,500 | PF65 25.00 | | | | |

**KM# 315 2 EURO**

8.50 g., Bi-Metallic Nickel-Brass center in Copper-Nickel ring, 25.75 mm. **Ruler:** Albert II **Subject:** Euro coinage, 10th Anniversary **Obv:** Euro symbol on globe, child-like rendering around

| Date | Mintage | VF20 | XF40 | MS60 | MS63 | MS65 |
|---|---|---|---|---|---|---|
| 2012 | 6,000,000 | — | — | 6.00 | 8.00 | — |
| 2012 Special Unc. | — | — | — | — | 15.00 | — |
| 2012 | — | PF63 22.00 | PF65 25.00 | | | |

**KM# 317 2 EURO**

8.50 g., Bi-Metallic Nickel-Brass center in Copper-Nickel ring, 25.75 mm. **Ruler:** Albert II **Subject:** Queen Elizabeth Competition **Obv:** Profile of Elizabeth left, crowned monogram at center

| Date | Mintage | VF20 | XF40 | MS60 | MS63 | MS65 |
|---|---|---|---|---|---|---|
| 2012 | 5,000,000 | — | — | — | 5.00 | — |
| 2012 | — | PF63 25.00 | PF65 28.00 | | | |

**KM# 323 2 EURO**

8.50 g., Bi-Metallic Nickel-Brass center in Copper-Nickel plated Nickel ring, 25.75 mm. **Ruler:** Albert II **Subject:** Meteorological Institute, 100th Anniversary

| Date | Mintage | VF20 | XF40 | MS60 | MS63 | MS65 |
|---|---|---|---|---|---|---|
| 2013 | — | — | — | — | 5.00 | — |
| 2013 | — | PF63 25.00 | PF65 28.00 | | | |

### KM# 270 5 EURO

14.60 g., 0.925 Silver 0.4342 oz. ASW, 30 mm. **Ruler:** Albert II **Subject:** Smurfs - 50th Anniversary **Obv:** Map of Western Europe **Rev:** Smurf

| Date | Mintage | VF20 | XF40 | MS60 | MS63 | MS65 |
|---|---|---|---|---|---|---|
| 2008 | 25,000 | PF63 45.00 | PF65 50.00 | | | |

### KM# 270a 5 EURO

14.60 g., 0.925 Silver 0.4342 oz. ASW, 30 mm. **Ruler:** Albert II **Subject:** Smurf - 50th Anniversary **Obv:** Map of Western Europe **Rev:** Multicolor 50 and Smurf

| Date | Mintage | VF20 | XF40 | MS60 | MS63 | MS65 |
|---|---|---|---|---|---|---|
| 2008 | — | PF65 75.00 | | | | |

### KM# 303 5 EURO

14.60 g., 0.925 Silver 0.4342 oz. ASW, 30 mm. **Ruler:** Albert II **Subject:** Belgian Railways, 175th Anniversary

| Date | Mintage | VF20 | XF40 | MS60 | MS63 | MS65 |
|---|---|---|---|---|---|---|
| 2010 | — | PF63 45.00 | PF65 50.00 | | | |

### KM# 313 5 EURO

14.60 g., 0.925 Silver 0.4342 oz. ASW, 30 mm. **Ruler:** Albert II **Subject:** Helene Dutrieu, Belgium's first female aviator **Obv:** Euro zone map **Rev:** Female portrait at left, biplane at right

| Date | Mintage | VF20 | XF40 | MS60 | MS63 | MS65 |
|---|---|---|---|---|---|---|
| 2011 | — | PF63 45.00 | PF65 50.00 | | | |

### KM# 327 5 EURO

14.60 g., 0.925 Silver 0.4342 oz. ASW, 30 mm. **Ruler:** Albert II **Subject:** Robert Velter's Spirou, 75th Anniversary **Rev:** Bellboy Spirou from the movies

| Date | Mintage | VF20 | XF40 | MS60 | MS63 | MS65 |
|---|---|---|---|---|---|---|
| 2013 | — | PF63 55.00 | PF65 60.00 | | | |

### KM# 233 10 EURO

18.93 g., 0.925 Silver 0.563 oz. ASW, 32.9 mm. **Ruler:** Albert II **Subject:** Belgian Railway System **Obv:** Value, head at right transposed on map **Rev:** Train exiting tunnel **Edge:** Reeded

| Date | Mintage | VF20 | XF40 | MS60 | MS63 | MS65 |
|---|---|---|---|---|---|---|
| ND (2002) | 50,000 | PF63 45.00 | PF65 50.00 | | | |

### KM# 235 10 EURO

18.93 g., 0.925 Silver 0.563 oz. ASW, 32.9 mm. **Ruler:** Albert II **Subject:** Simenon **Edge:** Reeded

| Date | Mintage | VF20 | XF40 | MS60 | MS63 | MS65 |
|---|---|---|---|---|---|---|
| 2003 | 50,000 | PF63 40.00 | PF65 50.00 | | | |

### KM# 234 10 EURO

18.75 g., 0.925 Silver 0.5576 oz. ASW, 33 mm. **Ruler:** Albert II **Obv:** Value **Rev:** Western Europe map and Goddess Europa riding a bull **Edge:** Reeded

| Date | Mintage | VF20 | XF40 | MS60 | MS63 | MS65 |
|---|---|---|---|---|---|---|
| 2004 | 50,000 | PF63 35.00 | PF65 40.00 | | | |

### KM# 236 10 EURO

18.93 g., 0.925 Silver 0.563 oz. ASW, 32.9 mm. **Ruler:** Albert II **Subject:** Tintin **Edge:** Reeded

| Date | Mintage | VF20 | XF40 | MS60 | MS63 | MS65 |
|---|---|---|---|---|---|---|
| 2004 | 50,000 | PF63 75.00 | PF65 85.00 | | | |

### KM# 251 10 EURO

18.75 g., 0.925 Silver 0.5576 oz. ASW, 33 mm. **Ruler:** Albert II **Subject:** Netherland-Belgium Soccer, 75th Anniversary **Obv:** Map of Western Europe and stars **Rev:** Soccer Player

| Date | Mintage | VF20 | XF40 | MS60 | MS63 | MS65 |
|---|---|---|---|---|---|---|
| 2005 | 50,000 | PF63 40.00 | PF65 45.00 | | | |

### KM# 252 10 EURO

18.75 g., 0.925 Silver 0.5576 oz. ASW, 33 mm. **Ruler:** Albert II **Subject:** 60th Anniversary of Liberation **Obv:** Map of Western Europe and stars **Rev:** Phoenix

| Date | Mintage | VF20 | XF40 | MS60 | MS63 | MS65 |
|---|---|---|---|---|---|---|
| 2005 | 50,000 | PF63 45.00 | PF65 50.00 | | | |

### KM# 255 10 EURO

18.75 g., 0.925 Silver 0.5576 oz. ASW, 33 mm. **Ruler:** Albert II **Subject:** Justus Lipsius, 400th Anniversary of Death **Obv:** Map of Western Europe and stars **Rev:** Half-length figure of Justus Lipsius

| Date | Mintage | VF20 | XF40 | MS60 | MS63 | MS65 |
|---|---|---|---|---|---|---|
| 2006 | 50,000 | PF63 40.00 | PF65 50.00 | | | |

### KM# 257 10 EURO

18.75 g., 0.925 Silver 0.5576 oz. ASW, 33 mm. **Ruler:** Albert II **Subject:** 50th Anniversary - Mine Accident in Marcinelle **Obv:** Map of Western Europe and stars **Rev:** Male head and industrial mine scene

| Date | Mintage | VF20 | XF40 | MS60 | MS63 | MS65 |
|---|---|---|---|---|---|---|
| 2006 | 50,000 | PF63 40.00 | PF65 45.00 | | | |

### KM# 257a 10 EURO

18.75 g., 0.925 Silver 0.5576 oz. ASW, 33 mm. **Ruler:** Albert II **Subject:** 50th Anniversary, Mine Accident in Marcinelle **Obv:** Map of Western Europe and stars **Rev:** Multicolor male head and industrial mine scene

| Date | Mintage | VF20 | XF40 | MS60 | MS63 | MS65 |
|---|---|---|---|---|---|---|
| 2006 | 2,000 | PF65 75.00 | | | | |

### KM# 260 10 EURO

18.75 g., 0.925 Silver 0.5576 oz. ASW, 33 mm. **Ruler:** Albert II **Subject:** Treaty of Rome, 50th Anniversary **Obv:** Map of Western Europe **Rev:** Document and feather pen

| Date | Mintage | VF20 | XF40 | MS60 | MS63 | MS65 |
|---|---|---|---|---|---|---|
| 2007 | 40,000 | PF63 40.00 | PF65 45.00 | | | |

### KM# 263 10 EURO

18.75 g., 0.925 Silver 0.5576 oz. ASW, 33 mm. **Ruler:** Albert II **Subject:** International Polar Year **Obv:** Map of Western Europe **Rev:** Wind farm and polar station

| Date | Mintage | VF20 | XF40 | MS60 | MS63 | MS65 |
|---|---|---|---|---|---|---|
| 2007 | 40,000 | PF63 45.00 | PF65 50.00 | | | |

### KM# 266 10 EURO

18.75 g., 0.925 Silver 0.5576 oz. ASW, 33 mm. **Ruler:** Albert II **Subject:** 100th Anniversary Maurice Maeterlinck **Obv:** Map of Western Europe **Rev:** Gateway and dome in blue

| Date | Mintage | VF20 | XF40 | MS60 | MS63 | MS65 |
|---|---|---|---|---|---|---|
| 2008 | 20,000 | PF63 65.00 | PF65 75.00 | | | |

### KM# 268 10 EURO

18.75 g., 0.925 Silver 0.5576 oz. ASW, 33 mm. **Ruler:** Albert II **Subject:** Beijing Olympics **Obv:** Map of Western Europe **Rev:** Sport events, logo and torch

| Date | Mintage | VF20 | XF40 | MS60 | MS63 | MS65 |
|---|---|---|---|---|---|---|
| 2008 | 20,000 | PF63 45.00 | PF65 50.00 | | | |

### KM# 284 10 EURO

18.75 g., 0.925 Silver 0.5576 oz. ASW, 33 mm. **Ruler:** Albert II **Subject:** 75th Birthday of the King **Obv:** Head at left, laurel sprigs

| Date | Mintage | VF20 | XF40 | MS60 | MS63 | MS65 |
|---|---|---|---|---|---|---|
| 2009 | — | PF63 45.00 | PF65 50.00 | | | |

### KM# 285 10 EURO

18.75 g., 0.925 Silver 0.5576 oz. ASW **Ruler:** Albert II **Subject:** Erasmus

| Date | Mintage | VF20 | XF40 | MS60 | MS63 | MS65 |
|---|---|---|---|---|---|---|
| 2009 | — | — | — | — | 50.00 | — |

### KM# 290 10 EURO

18.75 g., 0.925 Silver 0.5576 oz. ASW, 33 mm. **Ruler:** Albert II **Subject:** Royal Museum for Central Asia 100th Anniversary

| Date | Mintage | VF20 | XF40 | MS60 | MS63 | MS65 |
|---|---|---|---|---|---|---|
| 2010 | — | — | — | — | 45.00 | — |

### KM# 291 10 EURO

18.75 g., 0.925 Silver 0.5576 oz. ASW, 33 mm. **Ruler:** Albert II **Subject:** Jean Django' Reinhart Birth Centennial

| Date | Mintage | VF20 | XF40 | MS60 | MS63 | MS65 |
|---|---|---|---|---|---|---|
| 2010 | — | PF63 40.00 | PF65 45.00 | | | |

### KM# 304 10 EURO

18.75 g., 0.925 Silver 0.5576 oz. ASW, 33 mm. **Ruler:** Albert II **Subject:** Jean "Django" Reinhardt, 100th Anniversary of Birth

| Date | Mintage | VF20 | XF40 | MS60 | MS63 | MS65 |
|---|---|---|---|---|---|---|
| 2010 | — | PF63 45.00 | PF65 50.00 | | | |

### KM# 309 10 EURO

18.75 g., 0.925 Silver 0.5576 oz. ASW, 33 mm. **Ruler:** Albert II **Subject:** Discovery of the South Pole **Obv:** Euro zone map **Rev:** Map, dog sled, Roald Amundsen

| Date | Mintage | VF20 | XF40 | MS60 | MS63 | MS65 |
|---|---|---|---|---|---|---|
| 2011 | — | PF63 45.00 | PF65 50.00 | | | |

### KM# 311 10 EURO

18.75 g., 0.925 Silver 0.5576 oz. ASW, 33 mm. **Ruler:** Albert II **Obv:** Euro zone map, partially gilt **Rev:** Belgian deep sea exploration

| Date | Mintage | VF20 | XF40 | MS60 | MS63 | MS65 |
|---|---|---|---|---|---|---|
| 2011 | — | PF63 45.00 | PF65 50.00 | | | |

**KM# 318 10 EURO**
18.75 g., 0.925 Silver 0.5576 oz. ASW, 33 mm. **Ruler:** Albert II **Subject:** Paul Delvaux, Museum at St. Idesbald, 30th Anniversary **Obv:** Value and map of Euro countries **Rev:** Bust at left, classical scene at right

| Date | Mintage | VF20 | XF40 | MS60 | MS63 | MS65 |
|---|---|---|---|---|---|---|
| 2012 | Est. 15000 | PF63 60.00 | PF65 70.00 | | | |

**KM# 319 10 EURO**
6.22 g., 0.999 Gold 0.1998 oz. AGW, 22 mm. **Ruler:** Albert II **Subject:** Paul Delvaux, Museum at St. Idesbald, 30th Anniversary **Obv:** Value and map of Euro countries **Rev:** Bust at left, classical scene at right

| Date | Mintage | VF20 | XF40 | MS60 | MS63 | MS65 |
|---|---|---|---|---|---|---|
| 2012 | Est. 1500 | PF65 550 | | | | |

**KM# 320 10 EURO**
18.75 g., 0.999 Silver 0.6022 oz. ASW, 33 mm. **Ruler:** Albert II **Subject:** 2012 Summer Olympics, London **Obv:** Value and map of Euro countries **Rev:** Half-length figure of Coubertin at right, torch at left

| Date | Mintage | VF20 | XF40 | MS60 | MS63 | MS65 |
|---|---|---|---|---|---|---|
| 2012 | Est. 10000 | PF63 60.00 | PF65 70.00 | | | |

**KM# 324 10 EURO**
18.75 g., 0.925 Silver 0.5576 oz. ASW, 33 mm. **Ruler:** Albert II **Subject:** Hugo Claus **Obv:** Value and map of Euro countries **Rev:** Profile right

| Date | Mintage | VF20 | XF40 | MS60 | MS63 | MS65 |
|---|---|---|---|---|---|---|
| 2013 | Est. 10000 | PF63 60.00 | PF65 70.00 | | | |

**KM# 326 10 EURO**
18.75 g., 0.925 Silver 0.5576 oz. ASW, 33 mm. **Ruler:** Albert II **Subject:** Flanders tour, 100th Anniversary

| Date | Mintage | VF20 | XF40 | MS60 | MS63 | MS65 |
|---|---|---|---|---|---|---|
| 2013 | Est. 10000 | PF63 60.00 | PF65 70.00 | | | |

**KM# 259 12 1/2 EURO**
1.25 g., 0.999 Gold 0.0401 oz. AGW, 13.92 mm. **Ruler:** Albert II **Subject:** Saxe-Coburg-Gotha, 175th Anniversary **Obv:** Lion and tablet with constitution **Rev:** Head of Leopold I left

| Date | Mintage | VF20 | XF40 | MS60 | MS63 | MS65 |
|---|---|---|---|---|---|---|
| 2006 | 15,000 | PF63 70.00 | PF65 80.00 | | | |

**KM# 265 12 1/2 EURO**
1.25 g., 0.999 Gold 0.0401 oz. AGW, 13.92 mm. **Subject:** 175th Anniversary Saxe-Coburg-Gotha **Obv:** Lion and tablet **Rev:** Leopold II head left

| Date | Mintage | VF20 | XF40 | MS60 | MS63 | MS65 |
|---|---|---|---|---|---|---|
| 2007 | 15,000 | PF63 70.00 | PF65 80.00 | | | |

**KM# 271 12 1/2 EURO**
1.25 g., 0.999 Gold 0.0401 oz. AGW, 13.92 mm. **Ruler:** Albert II **Subject:** 175th Anniversary - Saxe-Coburg-Gotha **Obv:** Lion and tablet **Rev:** Albert I bust right

| Date | Mintage | VF20 | XF40 | MS60 | MS63 | MS65 |
|---|---|---|---|---|---|---|
| 2008 | 15,000 | PF63 75.00 | PF65 85.00 | | | |

**KM# 292 12 1/2 EURO**
1.24 g., 0.999 Gold 0.040 oz. AGW, 14 mm. **Ruler:** Albert II **Subject:** Leopold III

| Date | Mintage | VF20 | XF40 | MS60 | MS63 | MS65 |
|---|---|---|---|---|---|---|
| 2009 | — | PF63 80.00 | PF65 90.00 | | | |

**KM# 293 12 1/2 EURO**
1.24 g., 0.999 Gold 0.040 oz. AGW, 14 mm. **Ruler:** Albert II

| Date | Mintage | VF20 | XF40 | MS60 | MS63 | MS65 |
|---|---|---|---|---|---|---|
| 2010 | — | PF63 75.00 | PF65 85.00 | | | |

**KM# 316 12 1/2 EURO**
1.25 g., 0.999 Gold 0.0401 oz. AGW, 13.92 mm. **Ruler:** Albert II **Obv:** Lion with inscribed tablet **Rev:** Crown and Albert II profile

| Date | Mintage | VF20 | XF40 | MS60 | MS63 | MS65 |
|---|---|---|---|---|---|---|
| 2011 | Est. 6000 | PF65 125 | | | | |

**KM# 321 12 1/2 EURO**
1.25 g., 0.999 Gold 0.0401 oz. AGW, 13.92 mm. **Ruler:** Albert II **Subject:** Paola Ruffo di Calabria, Queen **Obv:** Lion with inscribed tablet **Rev:** Crown and profile left

| Date | Mintage | VF20 | XF40 | MS60 | MS63 | MS65 |
|---|---|---|---|---|---|---|
| 2012 | Est. 6000 | PF65 125 | | | | |

**KM# 328 12 1/2 EURO**
1.25 g., 0.999 Gold 0.0401 oz. AGW, 13.92 mm. **Ruler:** Albert II **Subject:** Fabiola de Mora y Aragon

| Date | Mintage | VF20 | XF40 | MS60 | MS63 | MS65 |
|---|---|---|---|---|---|---|
| 2013 | Est. 6000 | PF65 225 | | | | |

**KM# 254 20 EURO**
22.85 g., 0.999 Silver 0.7339 oz. ASW, 37 mm. **Ruler:** Albert II **Subject:** FIFA World Cup in Germany **Obv:** Albert II head left **Rev:** Soccer player with ball

| Date | Mintage | VF20 | XF40 | MS60 | MS63 | MS65 |
|---|---|---|---|---|---|---|
| 2005 | 25,000 | PF63 60.00 | PF65 75.00 | | | |

**KM# 262 20 EURO**
22.85 g., 0.925 Silver 0.6795 oz. ASW, 37 mm. **Ruler:** Albert II **Subject:** Georges Remi, 100th Anniversary of Birth **Obv:** Map of Western Europe and stars **Rev:** Profile of Georges Renir and his character Tin Tin right

| Date | Mintage | VF20 | XF40 | MS60 | MS63 | MS65 |
|---|---|---|---|---|---|---|
| 2007 | 50,000 | PF63 65.00 | PF65 80.00 | | | |

**KM# 287 20 EURO**
22.85 g., 0.925 Silver 0.6795 oz. ASW, 37 mm. **Ruler:** Albert II **Obv:** Value and map of euro countries **Rev:** Fr. Damien and churches in Tremblo and Molokai, date of canionization below

| Date | Mintage | VF20 | XF40 | MS60 | MS63 | MS65 |
|---|---|---|---|---|---|---|
| 2009 | 15,000 | PF63 65.00 | PF65 80.00 | | | |

**KM# 305 20 EURO**
22.85 g., 0.925 Silver 0.6795 oz. ASW, 37 mm. **Ruler:** Albert II **Subject:** A Dog of Flanders

| Date | Mintage | VF20 | XF40 | MS60 | MS63 | MS65 |
|---|---|---|---|---|---|---|
| 2010 | — | PF63 65.00 | PF65 80.00 | | | |

**KM# 269 25 EURO**
3.11 g., 0.999 Gold 0.0999 oz. AGW, 18 mm. **Ruler:** Albert II **Subject:** Beijing Olympics **Obv:** Map of Western Europe **Rev:** Sport events, logo, torch

| Date | Mintage | VF20 | XF40 | MS60 | MS63 | MS65 |
|---|---|---|---|---|---|---|
| 2008 | 5,000 | PF65 275 | | | | |

**KM# 294 25 EURO**
3.11 g., 0.999 Gold 0.0999 oz. AGW, 18 mm. **Ruler:** Albert II **Subject:** Beijing Olympics

| Date | Mintage | VF20 | XF40 | MS60 | MS63 | MS65 |
|---|---|---|---|---|---|---|
| 2008 | 4,050 | PF65 250 | | | | |

**KM# 250 50 EURO**
6.22 g., 0.999 Gold 0.1998 oz. AGW, 21 mm. **Ruler:** Albert II **Subject:** Albert II, 70th Birthday **Obv:** Map of Western Europe and stars **Rev:** Portrait of Albert II

| Date | Mintage | VF20 | XF40 | MS60 | MS63 | MS65 |
|---|---|---|---|---|---|---|
| 2004 | 10,000 | PF65 350 | | | | |

**KM# 256 50 EURO**
6.22 g., 0.999 Gold 0.1998 oz. AGW, 21 mm. **Ruler:** Albert II **Subject:** Justus Lipsius, 400th Anniversary of Death **Obv:** Map of Western Europe and stars **Rev:** Half-length figure of Justus Lipius right

| Date | Mintage | VF20 | XF40 | MS60 | MS63 | MS65 |
|---|---|---|---|---|---|---|
| 2006 | 2,500 | PF65 365 | | | | |

**KM# 261 50 EURO**
6.22 g., 0.999 Gold 0.1998 oz. AGW, 21 mm. **Ruler:** Albert II **Subject:** Treaty of Rome, 50th Anniversary **Obv:** Map of Western Europe **Rev:** Document and feather pen

| Date | Mintage | VF20 | XF40 | MS60 | MS63 | MS65 |
|---|---|---|---|---|---|---|
| 2007 | 2,500 | PF65 365 | | | | |

**KM# 267 50 EURO**
6.22 g., 0.999 Gold 0.1998 oz. AGW, 21 mm. **Ruler:** Albert II **Subject:** 100th Anniversary Maurice Maeterlinck **Obv:** Map of Western Europe **Rev:** Gate and dove

| Date | Mintage | VF20 | XF40 | MS60 | MS63 | MS65 |
|---|---|---|---|---|---|---|
| 2008 | 2,500 | PF65 425 | | | | |

**KM# 286 50 EURO**
8.45 g., 0.999 Gold 0.2714 oz. AGW **Ruler:** Albert II **Subject:** Erasmus

| Date | Mintage | VF20 | XF40 | MS60 | MS63 | MS65 |
|---|---|---|---|---|---|---|
| 2009 | — | — | — | — | 475 | — |

**KM# 306 50 EURO**
6.22 g., 0.999 Gold 0.1998 oz. AGW, 22 mm. **Ruler:** Albert II **Subject:** Royal Museum for Central Africa

| Date | Mintage | VF20 | XF40 | MS60 | MS63 | MS65 |
|---|---|---|---|---|---|---|
| 2010 | — | PF65 400 | | | | |

**KM# 310 50 EURO**
8.45 g., 0.999 Gold 0.2714 oz. AGW, 22 mm. **Ruler:** Albert II **Obv:** Euro zone map **Rev:** Four men standing around flag, Roald Amundsen profile at right

| Date | Mintage | VF20 | XF40 | MS60 | MS63 | MS65 |
|---|---|---|---|---|---|---|
| 2011 | — | PF65 550 | | | | |

**KM# 312 50 EURO**
6.22 g., 0.999 Gold 0.1998 oz. AGW, 22 mm. **Ruler:** Albert II **Obv:** Euro zone map **Rev:** Belgian deep sea exploration

| Date | Mintage | VF20 | XF40 | MS60 | MS63 | MS65 |
|---|---|---|---|---|---|---|
| 2011 | 2,500 | PF65 550 | | | | |

**KM# 325 50 EURO**
6.22 g., 0.999 Gold 0.1998 oz. AGW, 22 mm. **Ruler:** Albert II **Subject:** Hugo Claus **Obv:** Value and map of Euro countries **Rev:** Profile facing right

| Date | Mintage | VF20 | XF40 | MS60 | MS63 | MS65 |
|---|---|---|---|---|---|---|
| 2013 | Est. 1000 | PF65 425 | | | | |

**KM# 237 100 EURO**
15.55 g., 0.999 Gold 0.4994 oz. AGW, 29 mm. **Ruler:** Albert II **Subject:** Founding Fathers

| Date | Mintage | VF20 | XF40 | MS60 | MS63 | MS65 |
|---|---|---|---|---|---|---|
| 2002 | 5,000 | PF65 875 | | | | |

**KM# 238 100 EURO**
15.55 g., 0.999 Gold 0.4994 oz. AGW, 29 mm. **Ruler:** Albert II **Subject:** 10th Anniversary of Reign

| Date | Mintage | VF20 | XF40 | MS60 | MS63 | MS65 |
|---|---|---|---|---|---|---|
| 2003 | 5,000 | PF65 875 | | | | |

**KM# 239 100 EURO**
15.55 g., 0.999 Gold 0.4994 oz. AGW, 29 mm. **Ruler:** Albert II **Subject:** Franc Germinal

| Date | Mintage | VF20 | XF40 | MS60 | MS63 | MS65 |
|---|---|---|---|---|---|---|
| 2004 | 5,000 | PF65 875 | | | | |

**KM# 253 100 EURO**
15.55 g., 0.999 Gold 0.4994 oz. AGW, 29 mm. **Ruler:** Albert II **Subject:** 175th Anniversary of Liberty **Obv:** Albert II head left **Rev:** Scene of the 1830 Revolution

| Date | Mintage | VF20 | XF40 | MS60 | MS63 | MS65 |
|---|---|---|---|---|---|---|
| 2005 | 5,000 | PF65 875 | | | | |

**KM# 258 100 EURO**
15.55 g., 0.999 Gold 0.4994 oz. AGW, 29 mm. **Ruler:** Albert II **Subject:** Saxe-Coburg-Gotha, 175th Anniversary **Obv:** Map of Western Europe and stars **Rev:** Church in Laeken, Kings monogram around

| Date | Mintage | VF20 | XF40 | MS60 | MS63 | MS65 |
|---|---|---|---|---|---|---|
| 2006 | 5,000 | PF65 875 | | | | |

**KM# 264 100 EURO**
15.55 g., 0.999 Gold 0.4994 oz. AGW, 29 mm. **Ruler:** Albert II **Subject:** Belgian Coins, 175th Anniversary **Obv:** Map of Western Europe **Rev:** Screw press, coin designs

| Date | Mintage | VF20 | XF40 | MS60 | MS63 | MS65 |
|---|---|---|---|---|---|---|
| 2007 | 5,000 | PF65 875 | | | | |

**KM# 272 100 EURO**
15.55 g., 0.999 Gold 0.4994 oz. AGW, 29 mm. **Ruler:** Albert II **Subject:** 50th Anniversary: Brussels Exposition **Obv:** Map of Western Europe

| Date | Mintage | VF20 | XF40 | MS60 | MS63 | MS65 |
|---|---|---|---|---|---|---|
| 2008 | 5,000 | PF65 875 | | | | |

### KM# 283 100 EURO

15.55 g., 0.999 Gold 0.4994 oz. AGW **Ruler:** Albert II **Subject:** Royal Wedding Anniversary **Obv:** Conjoined heads facing left

| Date | Mintage | VF20 | XF40 | MS60 | MS63 | MS65 |
|---|---|---|---|---|---|---|
| 2009 | — | PF65 875 | | | | |

### KM# 307 100 EURO

15.55 g., 0.999 Gold 0.4994 oz. AGW, 29 mm. **Ruler:** Albert II **Subject:** Prince Philippe, 50th Birthday

| Date | Mintage | VF20 | XF40 | MS60 | MS63 | MS65 |
|---|---|---|---|---|---|---|
| 2010 | 2,000 | PF65 900 | | | | |

### KM# 314 100 EURO

15.55 g., 0.999 Gold 0.4994 oz. AGW, 29 mm. **Ruler:** Albert II **Subject:** Victor Horta **Obv:** Euro zone map **Rev:** Bust at left, flora

| Date | Mintage | VF20 | XF40 | MS60 | MS63 | MS65 |
|---|---|---|---|---|---|---|
| 2011 | — | PF65 950 | | | | |

### KM# 329 100 EURO

15.55 g., 0.999 Gold 0.4994 oz. AGW, 29 mm. **Ruler:** Albert II **Subject:** Baudouin, 20th Anniversary of Death

| Date | Mintage | VF20 | XF40 | MS60 | MS63 | MS65 |
|---|---|---|---|---|---|---|
| 2013 | Est. 1500 | PF65 1,000 | | | | |

### KM# 330 20 EURO

22.85 g., 0.925 Silver 0.6795 oz. ASW, 37 mm. **Ruler:** Albert II **Subject:** Philippe as king **Rev:** Albert II and Philippe

| Date | Mintage | F12 | VF20 | XF40 | MS60 | MS63 |
|---|---|---|---|---|---|---|
| 2013 | Est. 15000 | PF63 60.00 | PF65 70.00 | | | |

### KM# 322 100 EURO

15.55 g., 0.999 Gold 0.4994 oz. AGW, 29 mm. **Ruler:** Albert II **Subject:** Gerhard Mercator, 500th Anniversary of Birth **Obv:** Value and map of Euro countries **Rev:** Bust at left, globe design background

| Date | Mintage | F12 | VF20 | XF40 | MS60 | MS63 |
|---|---|---|---|---|---|---|
| 2012 | Est. 2000 | PF65 1,000 | | | | |

## MINT SETS

| KM# | Date | Mintage | Identification | Issue Price | Mkt Val |
|---|---|---|---|---|---|
| MS14 | 2001 (10) | 60,000 | KM#148.1, 149.1, 187-194 | 15.00 | 45.00 |
| MS15 | 1999/2000/ 2001 (24) | 40,000 | Euro Intro | — | 250 |
| MS16 | 2002 (8) | 100,000 | KM#224-231, 700th Anniversary | — | 62.50 |
| MS17 | 2002 (8) | 20,000 | KM#224-231, Cycling | — | 62.50 |
| MS18 | 2002 (8) | 20,000 | KM#224-231, Euros plus waffle francs | — | 62.50 |
| MS19 | 2003 (8) | 100,000 | KM#224-231, Television 50th | — | 37.50 |
| MS20 | 2003 (8) | 15,000 | KM#224-231, Ford Production in Belgium Centennial | — | 37.50 |
| MS21 | 2003 (8) | 10,000 | KM#224-231, Rose | — | 37.50 |
| MS22 | 2003 (8) | 10,000 | KM#224-231, Baby | — | 37.50 |
| MS23.1 | 2004 (9) | 60,000 | KM#224-231, Belgian Red Cross, plain medal | — | 25.00 |
| MS23.2 | 2004 (9) | 2,000 | KM#224-231, Belgian Red Cross, enameled medal | — | 175 |
| MS24 | 2004 (9) | 5,000 | KM#224-231, Love, medal for engraving | — | 37.50 |
| MS25 | 2004 (9) | 5,000 | KM#224-231, Baby, medal for engraving | — | 37.50 |
| MS26.1 | 2005 (9) | 38,000 | KM#224-231, Grand Palace, UNESCO site, plain medal | — | 60.00 |
| MS26.2 | 2005 (9) | 2,000 | KM#224-231, Grand Palace, UNESCO site, gilt medal | — | 85.00 |
| MS27.1 | 2006 (9) | 38,000 | KM#224-231, Flemish Houses, UNESCO site, plain medal | — | 40.00 |
| MS27.2 | 2006 (9) | 2,000 | KM#224-231, Flemish Houses, UNESCO site, colored medal | — | 75.00 |
| MS28.1 | 2007 (9) | 38,000 | KM#224-226, 242-246, Canal. UNESCO site, plain medal | — | 27.50 |
| MS28.2 | 2007 (9) | 2,000 | KM#224-226, 242-246, Canal, UNESCO site, colored medal | — | 70.00 |
| MS29.1 | 2008 (9) | 25,000 | KM#274-281, Belltower, UNESCO site, plain medal | — | 75.00 |
| MS29.2 | 2008 (9) | 2,000 | KM#274-281, Belltower, UNESCO site, colored medal | — | 85.00 |
| MS30 | 2009 (8) | 25,000 | KM#274-281, plus medal | — | 45.00 |
| MS31 | 2010 (8) | 30,000 | KM#274-281, plus medal | — | 45.00 |
| MS32 | 2011 (8) | 30,000 | KM#274-281, plus medal | — | 45.00 |

## PROOF SETS

| KM# | Date | Mintage | Identification | Issue Price | Mkt Val |
|---|---|---|---|---|---|
| PS10 | 2001 (8) | 15,000 | KM#224-231 | 80.00 | 125 |
| PS11 | 2002 (8) | 3,240 | KM#224-231 | 80.00 | 115 |
| PS12 | 2003 (8) | 3,241 | KM#224-231 | 80.00 | 110 |
| PS13 | 2004 (8) | 3,006 | KM#224-231 | 80.00 | 105 |
| PS14 | 2005 (8) | 3,006 | KM#224-231 | — | 110 |
| PS15 | 2006 (8) | 3,006 | KM#224-231 | — | 115 |
| PS17 | 2007 (8) | 3,000 | KM#224-226, 242-247 | — | 175 |
| PS18 | 2008 (8) | 2,500 | KM#224-227, 276-278, 280-281 | — | 100 |
| PS19 | 2009 (8) | 1,500 | KM#274-281 | — | 110 |
| PS20 | 2010 (8) | 1,850 | KM#274-281 | — | 110 |
| PS21 | 2011 (8) | 1,850 | KM#274-281 | — | 110 |

# BELIZE

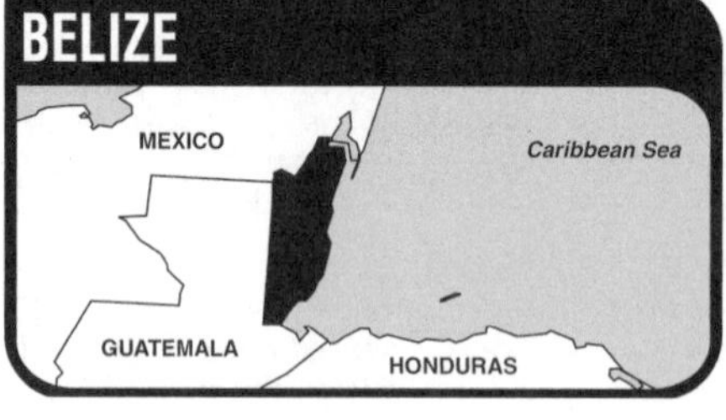


Belize, formerly British Honduras, but now a Constitutional Monarchy within the Commonwealth of Nations, is situated in Central America south of Mexico and east and north of Guatemala, with an area of 8,867 sq. mi. (22,960 sq. km.) and a population of *242,000. Capital: Belmopan. Tourism now augments Belize's economy, in addition to sugar, citrus fruits, chicle and hardwoods which are exported.

**MONETARY SYSTEM**

Commencing 1864

100 Cents = 1 Dollar

## COMMONWEALTH

## DECIMAL COINAGE

### KM# 33a CENT

0.80 g., Aluminum, 19.5 mm. **Obv:** Bust of Queen Elizabeth right **Rev:** Denomination within circle **Edge:** Smooth, scalloped

| Date | Mintage | VF20 | XF40 | MS60 | MS63 | MS65 |
|---|---|---|---|---|---|---|
| 2002 | — | — | — | 0.10 | 0.15 | 0.45 |
| 2005 | — | — | — | 0.10 | 0.15 | 0.45 |
| 2007 | — | — | — | 0.10 | 0.15 | 0.45 |
| 2010 | — | — | — | 0.10 | 0.15 | 0.45 |

### KM# 34a 5 CENTS

1.04 g., Aluminum, 20.2 mm. **Obv:** Bust of Queen Elizabeth II right **Rev:** Denomination within circle **Edge:** Plain

| Date | Mintage | VF20 | XF40 | MS60 | MS63 | MS65 |
|---|---|---|---|---|---|---|
| 2002 | — | — | — | 0.10 | 0.20 | 0.45 |
| 2003 | — | — | — | 0.10 | 0.20 | 0.45 |
| 2005 | — | — | — | 0.10 | 0.20 | 0.45 |
| 2006 | — | — | — | 0.10 | 0.20 | 0.45 |
| 2009 | — | — | — | 0.10 | 0.20 | 0.45 |

### KM# 115 5 CENTS

1.05 g., Aluminum, 20.2 mm.

| Date | Mintage | VF20 | XF40 | MS60 | MS63 | MS65 |
|---|---|---|---|---|---|---|
| 2002 | — | — | — | 0.10 | 0.20 | 0.40 |

### KM# 36 25 CENTS

5.66 g., Copper-Nickel, 23.6 mm. **Obv:** Crowned bust of Queen Elizabeth II right **Rev:** Denomination within circle, date below **Edge:** Reeded

| Date | Mintage | VF20 | XF40 | MS60 | MS63 | MS65 |
|---|---|---|---|---|---|---|
| 2003 | — | — | 0.20 | 0.35 | 0.75 | 1.50 |
| 2007 | — | — | 0.20 | 0.35 | 0.75 | 1.50 |

### KM# 37 50 CENTS

9.07 g., Copper-Nickel, 27.74 mm. **Obv:** Crowned bust of Queen Elizabeth right **Rev:** Denomination within circle, date below **Edge:** Reeded

| Date | Mintage | VF20 | XF40 | MS60 | MS63 | MS65 |
|---|---|---|---|---|---|---|
| 2010 | — | — | — | 1.00 | 2.00 | 3.00 |

### KM# 99 DOLLAR

8.90 g., Nickel-Brass, 27 mm. **Obv:** Crowned bust of Queen Elizabeth II right **Rev:** Columbus' three ships, denomination above, date below **Edge:** Alternating reeded and plain **Shape:** 10-sided

| Date | Mintage | VF20 | XF40 | MS60 | MS63 | MS65 |
|---|---|---|---|---|---|---|
| 2003 | — | — | — | 1.00 | 2.25 | 3.00 |
| 2007 | — | — | — | 1.00 | 2.25 | 3.00 |

### KM# 134 DOLLAR

30.94 g., 0.999 Silver 0.9937 oz. ASW, 39.9 mm. **Subject:** Mayan King **Obv:** National arms **Rev:** Mayan portrait in ornate headdress **Edge:** Reeded

| Date | Mintage | VF20 | XF40 | MS60 | MS63 | MS65 |
|---|---|---|---|---|---|---|
| 2002 | — | — | — | — | 40.00 | 45.00 |

### KM# 136 DOLLAR

8.90 g., Nickel-Brass, 27 mm. **Subject:** Central Bank, 30th Anniversary **Obv:** Bird in flight left **Rev:** Central Bank building **Rev. Legend:** Central Bank of Belize 30th Anniversary 1982-2012 **Edge:** alternating plain and reeded **Shape:** 10-sided

| Date | Mintage | VF20 | XF40 | MS60 | MS63 | MS65 |
|---|---|---|---|---|---|---|
| 2012 | — | — | — | — | 2.50 | 3.00 |

### KM# 137 250 DOLLARS

15.98 g., 0.916 Gold 0.4705 oz. AGW, 28.40 mm. **Subject:** Maya Heartland **Obv:** Six glyph carved stones flanked by two Maya Hero Twins **Obv. Legend:** THE MAYA HEARTLAND **Rev:** Large carved jade head of Maya Sun God Kinich Ahau **Rev. Legend:** KINICH AHAU

| Date | Mintage | VF20 | XF40 | MS60 | MS63 | MS65 |
|---|---|---|---|---|---|---|
| 2012 | Est. 500 | PF63 800 | PF65 1,000 | | | |

## BENIN

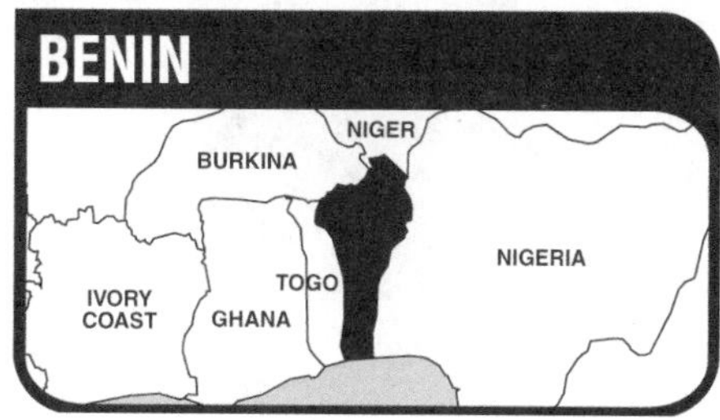


The Republic of Benin (formerly the Republic of Dahomey), located on the south side of the African bulge between Togo and Nigeria, has an area of 43,500 sq. mi. (112,620 sq. km.) and a population of 5.5 million. Capital: Porto-Novo. The principal industry of Benin, one of the poorest countries of West Africa, is the processing of palm oil products. Palm kernel oil, peanuts, cotton, and coffee are exported.

# PEOPLES REPUBLIC

## STANDARD COINAGE

### KM# 53 100 CFA FRANCS

27.00 g., Copper-Nickel Silver plated, 38.61 mm. **Rev:** Multicolor Cannabis Sativa, Aeromatic

| Date | Mintage | VF20 | XF40 | MS60 | MS63 | MS65 |
|---|---|---|---|---|---|---|
| 2010 | 2,500 | PF65 65.00 | | | | |

### KM# 53a 100 CFA FRANCS

27.00 g., Copper-Nickel gilt, 38.61 mm. **Rev:** Multicolor Cannabis Sativa, Aeromatic

| Date | Mintage | VF20 | XF40 | MS60 | MS63 | MS65 |
|---|---|---|---|---|---|---|
| 2010 | 2,500 | PF65 65.00 | | | | |

### KM# 80 1000 CFA FRANCS

31.11 g., 0.999 Silver 0.999 oz. ASW, 38.61 mm. **Obv:** National arms **Rev:** Elephant advancing left, ring of 12 elephants around rim

| Date | Mintage | VF20 | XF40 | MS60 | MS63 | MS65 |
|---|---|---|---|---|---|---|
| 2014 Prooflike | 5,000 | — | — | — | — | 40.00 |

### KM# 71 100 FRANCS

20.00 g., 0.999 Silver 0.6424 oz. ASW, 36 mm. **Obv:** State arms **Rev:** Steam train in colored forest scene

| Date | Mintage | VF20 | XF40 | MS60 | MS63 | MS65 |
|---|---|---|---|---|---|---|
| 2010 | — | PF65 55.00 | | | | |

### KM# 74 100 FRANCS

Silver Plated Base Metal, 38.61 mm. **Subject:** Man in space **Obv:** State arms **Rev:** Gagarin in color

| Date | Mintage | VF20 | XF40 | MS60 | MS63 | MS65 |
|---|---|---|---|---|---|---|
| 2011 Prooflike | 961 | — | — | — | — | 50.00 |

### KM# 75 100 FRANCS

Silver Plated Base Metal, 27 mm. **Obv:** National arms **Rev:** Rose in color and fragrant

| Date | Mintage | VF20 | XF40 | MS60 | MS63 | MS65 |
|---|---|---|---|---|---|---|
| 2011 | 2,500 | PF65 50.00 | | | | |

### KM# 76 100 FRANCS

Silver Plated Base Metal, 27 mm. **Obv:** National arms **Rev:** Convallaria majalis, French lilly in color and fragrant

| Date | Mintage | VF20 | XF40 | MS60 | MS63 | MS65 |
|---|---|---|---|---|---|---|
| 2011 | — | PF65 60.00 | | | | |

### KM# 63 500 FRANCS

Silver, 38.61 mm. **Obv:** National arms **Rev:** Euro coin motifs

| Date | Mintage | VF20 | XF40 | MS60 | MS63 | MS65 |
|---|---|---|---|---|---|---|
| 2002 | — | PF65 45.00 | | | | |

### KM# 72 500 FRANCS

Silver, 38.6 mm. **Subject:** W.A. Mozart

| Date | Mintage | VF20 | XF40 | MS60 | MS63 | MS65 |
|---|---|---|---|---|---|---|
| 2005 | — | PF65 50.00 | | | | |

### KM# 64 1000 FRANCS

Silver, 38.61 mm. **Obv:** National arms **Rev:** Zebra

| Date | Mintage | VF20 | XF40 | MS60 | MS63 | MS65 |
|---|---|---|---|---|---|---|
| 2001 | — | PF65 45.00 | | | | |

**KM# 65 1000 FRANCS**
Silver, 38.61 mm. **Obv:** National arms **Rev:** Giraffe

| Date | Mintage | VF20 | XF40 | MS60 | MS63 | MS65 |
|---|---|---|---|---|---|---|
| 2001 | — | PF65 45.00 | | | | |

**KM# 66 1000 FRANCS**
Silver, 38.61 mm. **Obv:** National arms **Rev:** Whale

| Date | Mintage | VF20 | XF40 | MS60 | MS63 | MS65 |
|---|---|---|---|---|---|---|
| 2001 | — | PF65 65.00 | | | | |

**KM# 54 1000 FRANCS**
20.00 g., 0.999 Silver 0.6424 oz. ASW, 36 mm. **Rev:** Multicolor Lockheed Orion

| Date | Mintage | VF20 | XF40 | MS60 | MS63 | MS65 |
|---|---|---|---|---|---|---|
| 2002 | — | PF63 25.00 | PF65 35.00 | | | |

**KM# 55 1000 FRANCS**
20.00 g., 0.999 Silver 0.6424 oz. ASW, 36 mm. **Rev:** Multicolor Convair 990 Coronado over mountains

| Date | Mintage | VF20 | XF40 | MS60 | MS63 | MS65 |
|---|---|---|---|---|---|---|
| 2002 | — | PF63 25.00 | PF65 35.00 | | | |

**KM# 62 1000 FRANCS**
Silver **Rev:** Klaus Stortebeker and ship

| Date | Mintage | VF20 | XF40 | MS60 | MS63 | MS65 |
|---|---|---|---|---|---|---|
| 2002 | — | PF63 32.50 | PF65 37.50 | | | |

**KM# 56 1000 FRANCS**
20.00 g., 0.999 Silver 0.6424 oz. ASW, 36 mm. **Rev:** Multicolor Douglas DC-8 at airport

| Date | Mintage | VF20 | XF40 | MS60 | MS63 | MS65 |
|---|---|---|---|---|---|---|
| 2003 | — | PF63 25.00 | PF65 35.00 | | | |

**KM# 57 1000 FRANCS**
20.00 g., 0.999 Silver 0.6424 oz. ASW, 36 mm. **Rev:** Multicolor Fokker 100 left

| Date | Mintage | VF20 | XF40 | MS60 | MS63 | MS65 |
|---|---|---|---|---|---|---|
| 2003 | — | PF63 25.00 | PF65 35.00 | | | |

**KM# 60 1000 FRANCS**
Silver **Subject:** Sir Francis Drake and the Golden Hind

| Date | Mintage | VF20 | XF40 | MS60 | MS63 | MS65 |
|---|---|---|---|---|---|---|
| 2003 | — | PF63 32.50 | PF65 37.50 | | | |

**KM# 58 1000 FRANCS**
20.00 g., 0.999 Silver 0.6424 oz. ASW, 36 mm. **Rev:** Multicolor Douglas DC-4 right

| Date | Mintage | VF20 | XF40 | MS60 | MS63 | MS65 |
|---|---|---|---|---|---|---|
| 2004 | — | PF63 25.00 | PF65 35.00 | | | |

**KM# 59 1000 FRANCS**
20.00 g., 0.999 Silver 0.6424 oz. ASW, 36 mm. **Rev:** Multicolor General Aviation GA-43 against blue sky

| Date | Mintage | VF20 | XF40 | MS60 | MS63 | MS65 |
|---|---|---|---|---|---|---|
| 2004 | — | PF63 35.00 | PF65 45.00 | | | |

**KM# 67 1000 FRANCS**
20.00 g., 0.999 Silver 0.6424 oz. ASW, 36 mm. **Obv:** National arms **Rev:** Blue plane at airport in color

| Date | Mintage | VF20 | XF40 | MS60 | MS63 | MS65 |
|---|---|---|---|---|---|---|
| 2005 | — | PF63 35.00 | PF65 45.00 | | | |

**KM# 68 1000 FRANCS**
20.00 g., 0.999 Silver 0.6424 oz. ASW, 36 mm. **Obv:** Naitonal arms **Rev:** Red plane in flight with green mountain in background

| Date | Mintage | VF20 | XF40 | MS60 | MS63 | MS65 |
|---|---|---|---|---|---|---|
| 2005 | — | PF63 35.00 | PF65 45.00 | | | |

**KM# 73 1000 FRANCS**
Silver, 38.61 mm. **Subject:** Cannabis **Rev:** Leaf in green

| Date | Mintage | VF20 | XF40 | MS60 | MS63 | MS65 |
|---|---|---|---|---|---|---|
| 2011 | — | PF65 65.00 | | | | |

**KM# 79 1000 FRANCS**
25.00 g., 0.925 Silver 0.7435 oz. ASW, 38.61 mm. **Obv:** National arms **Rev:** Lake Baikal in color

| Date | Mintage | VF20 | XF40 | MS60 | MS63 | MS65 |
|---|---|---|---|---|---|---|
| 2011 | — | PF63 40.00 | PF65 50.00 | | | |

**KM# 77 1000 FRANCS**
15.55 g., 0.999 Silver 0.4994 oz. ASW, 38.6 mm. **Obv:** National arms **Rev:** Red dragon

| Date | Mintage | VF20 | XF40 | MS60 | MS63 | MS65 |
|---|---|---|---|---|---|---|
| 2012 | — | PF63 22.00 | PF65 27.00 | | | |

**KM# 78 1000 FRANCS**
15.55 g., 0.999 Silver 0.4994 oz. ASW, 38.61 mm. **Obv:** National arms **Rev:** Blue dragon

| Date | Mintage | VF20 | XF40 | MS60 | MS63 | MS65 |
|---|---|---|---|---|---|---|
| 2012 | — | PF63 22.00 | PF65 27.00 | | | |

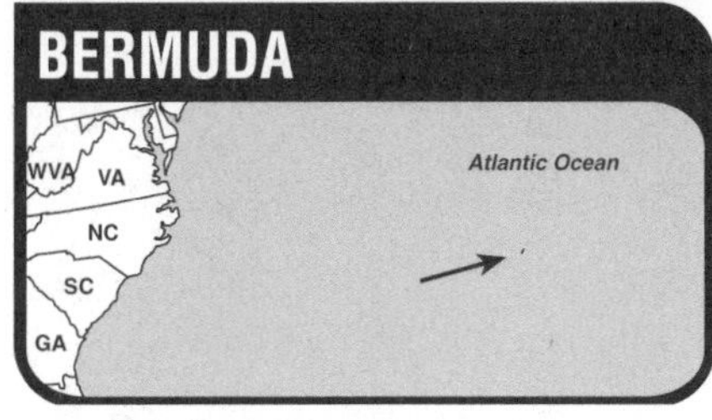


The Parliamentary British Colony of Bermuda, situated in the western Atlantic Ocean 660 miles (1,062 km.) east of North Carolina, has an area of 20.6 sq. mi. (53 sq. km.) and a population of 61,600. Capital: Hamilton. Concentrated essences, beauty preparations, and cut flowers are exported. Most Bermudians derive their livelihood from tourism. The British monarch is the head of state and is represented by a governor.

U.S. currency circulates in common with the Eastern Caribbean Dollar.

**RULER**
British

# BRITISH COLONY

## DECIMAL COINAGE

100 Cents = 1 Dollar

### KM# 107 CENT

2.50 g., Copper Plated Zinc, 19 mm. **Ruler:** Elizabeth II **Obv:** Head with tiara right **Rev:** Wild boar left **Edge:** Plain

| Date | Mintage | VF20 | XF40 | MS60 | MS63 | MS65 |
|---|---|---|---|---|---|---|
| 2001 | 1,600,000 | — | — | — | 0.50 | 0.75 |
| 2002 | 1,120,000 | — | — | — | 0.50 | 0.75 |
| 2003 | 800,000 | — | — | — | 0.50 | 0.75 |
| 2004 | 1,600,000 | — | — | — | 0.25 | 0.50 |
| 2005 | 3,200,000 | — | — | — | 0.25 | 0.50 |
| 2006 | 800,000 | — | — | — | 0.25 | 0.50 |
| 2007 | — | — | — | — | 0.25 | 0.50 |
| 2008 | 2,400,000 | — | — | — | 0.25 | 0.50 |

### KM# 107a CENT

2.50 g., Copper Plated Steel, 19 mm. **Ruler:** Elizabeth II **Obv:** Head with tiara right **Rev:** Wild boar left

| Date | Mintage | VF20 | XF40 | MS60 | MS63 | MS65 |
|---|---|---|---|---|---|---|
| 2008 | 2,400,000 | — | — | — | 0.25 | 0.50 |
| 2009 | 4,000,000 | — | — | — | 0.25 | 0.50 |

### KM# 108 5 CENTS

5.00 g., Copper-Nickel, 21.2 mm. **Ruler:** Elizabeth II **Obv:** Head with tiara right **Rev:** Queen angel fish left **Edge:** Plain

| Date | Mintage | VF20 | XF40 | MS60 | MS63 | MS65 |
|---|---|---|---|---|---|---|
| 2001 | 1,000,000 | — | — | — | 0.75 | 1.00 |
| 2002 | 700,000 | — | — | — | 0.75 | 1.00 |
| 2003 | 700,000 | — | — | — | 0.75 | 1.00 |
| 2004 | 700,000 | — | — | — | 0.75 | 1.00 |
| 2005 | 600,000 | — | — | — | 0.75 | 1.00 |
| 2008 | 500,000 | — | — | — | 0.75 | 1.00 |
| 2009 | 1,500,000 | — | — | — | 0.50 | 0.75 |

### KM# 109 10 CENTS

2.50 g., Copper-Nickel, 17.8 mm. **Ruler:** Elizabeth II **Obv:** Head with tiara right **Rev:** Bermuda lily **Edge:** Reeded

| Date | Mintage | VF20 | XF40 | MS60 | MS63 | MS65 |
|---|---|---|---|---|---|---|
| 2001 | 1,400,000 | — | — | — | 0.85 | 1.00 |
| 2002 | 800,000 | — | — | — | 0.85 | 1.00 |
| 2003 | 600,000 | — | — | — | 0.85 | 1.00 |
| 2004 | 800,000 | — | — | — | 0.85 | 1.00 |
| 2005 | 800,000 | — | — | — | 0.85 | 1.00 |
| 2008 | 2,000,000 | — | — | — | 0.50 | 0.75 |
| 2009 | 2,000,000 | — | — | — | 0.50 | 0.75 |

### KM# 110 25 CENTS

Copper-Nickel, 24 mm. **Ruler:** Elizabeth II **Obv:** Head with tiara right **Rev:** Yellow-billed tropical bird right **Edge:** Reeded

| Date | Mintage | VF20 | XF40 | MS60 | MS63 | MS65 |
|---|---|---|---|---|---|---|
| 2001 | 800,000 | — | — | — | 1.50 | 2.00 |
| 2002 | 800,000 | — | — | — | 1.50 | 2.00 |
| 2003 | 800,000 | — | — | — | 1.50 | 2.00 |
| 2004 | 800,000 | — | — | — | 1.50 | 2.00 |
| 2005 | 1,440,000 | — | — | — | 1.50 | 2.00 |
| 2006 | 320,000 | — | — | — | 1.50 | 2.00 |
| 2007 | — | — | — | — | 1.50 | 2.00 |
| 2008 | 1,200,000 | — | — | — | 1.00 | 1.50 |
| 2009 | 2,000,000 | — | — | — | 1.00 | 1.50 |

### KM# 189 25 CENTS

28.28 g., Copper-Nickel, 38.61 mm. **Ruler:** Elizabeth II **Obv:** Head with tiara right **Rev:** Bermuda bluebird with sailboats **Edge:** Reeded

| Date | Mintage | VF20 | XF40 | MS60 | MS63 | MS65 |
|---|---|---|---|---|---|---|
| 2011 | 2,000 | — | — | — | — | 25.00 |

### KM# 192 25 CENTS

28.28 g., Copper-Nickel, 38.61 mm. **Ruler:** Elizabeth II **Obv:** Head with tiara right **Rev:** Blue marlin **Edge:** Reeded

| Date | Mintage | VF20 | XF40 | MS60 | MS63 | MS65 |
|---|---|---|---|---|---|---|
| 2012 | 2,000 | — | — | — | — | 25.00 |

### KM# 195 25 CENTS

28.28 g., Copper-Nickel, 36.61 mm. **Ruler:** Elizabeth II **Obv:** Head with tiara right **Rev:** Blue angel fish **Edge:** Reeded

| Date | Mintage | VF20 | XF40 | MS60 | MS63 | MS65 |
|---|---|---|---|---|---|---|
| 2013 | 2,000 | — | — | — | — | 25.00 |

### KM# 111 DOLLAR

Nickel-Brass, 26 mm. **Ruler:** Elizabeth II **Obv:** Head with tiara right **Rev:** Sailboat

| Date | Mintage | VF20 | XF40 | MS60 | MS63 | MS65 |
|---|---|---|---|---|---|---|
| 2001 | 12,000 | — | — | — | 3.00 | 3.50 |
| 2002 | 12,000 | — | — | — | 3.00 | 3.50 |
| 2003 | 12,000 | — | — | — | 3.00 | 3.50 |
| 2004 | 12,000 | — | — | — | 3.00 | 3.50 |
| 2005 | 240,000 | — | — | — | 2.00 | 3.00 |
| 2008 | 300,000 | — | — | — | 2.00 | 3.00 |
| 2009 | 600,000 | — | — | — | 2.00 | 3.00 |

### KM# 139 DOLLAR

28.28 g., Copper-Nickel, 38.6 mm. **Ruler:** Elizabeth II **Obv:** Head with tiara right **Rev:** 4 Gombey dancers **Edge:** Reeded

| Date | Mintage | VF20 | XF40 | MS60 | MS63 | MS65 |
|---|---|---|---|---|---|---|
| 2001 | — | — | — | — | 12.00 | 14.00 |

### KM# 124 DOLLAR

28.41 g., Copper-Nickel, 38.5 mm. **Ruler:** Elizabeth II **Subject:** Queen's Golden Jubilee **Obv:** Head with tiara right **Rev:** Stylized trumpeters above monogram and date **Edge:** Reeded

| Date | Mintage | VF20 | XF40 | MS60 | MS63 | MS65 |
|---|---|---|---|---|---|---|
| 2002 | — | — | — | — | 10.00 | 12.00 |

### KM# 198 2 DOLLARS

31.60 g., 0.999 Silver 1.0151 oz. ASW, 38.61 mm. **Ruler:** Elizabeth II **Subject:** Bermuda Hawksbill Turtle **Obv:** Bust right **Rev:** Turtle **Rev. Legend:** BERMUDA HAWKSBILL TURTLE / TWO DOLLARS

| Date | Mintage | VF20 | XF40 | MS60 | MS63 | MS65 |
|---|---|---|---|---|---|---|
| 2008 | 2,500 | **PF63** 45.00 | **PF65** 50.00 | | | |

### KM# 186 2 DOLLARS

31.60 g., 0.999 Silver 1.0151 oz. ASW, 38.61 mm. **Ruler:** Elizabeth II **Subject:** Cahow **Obv:** Head of Queen Elizabeth II with tiara facing right, legend, country name, date **Obv. Legend:** ELIZABETH II **Rev:** Bird over water surrounding outline of Bermuda, denomination

| Date | Mintage | VF20 | XF40 | MS60 | MS63 | MS65 |
|---|---|---|---|---|---|---|
| 2010 | Est. 1000 | **PF65** 90.00 | | | | |

### KM# 190 2 DOLLARS

31.60 g., 0.999 Silver 1.0151 oz. ASW, 38.61 mm. **Ruler:** Elizabeth II **Obv:** Head with tiara right **Rev:** Color Bermuda bluebird with sailboats **Edge:** Reeded

| Date | Mintage | VF20 | XF40 | MS60 | MS63 | MS65 |
|---|---|---|---|---|---|---|
| 2011 | 1,000 | **PF65** 110 | | | | |

### KM# 193 2 DOLLARS

31.60 g., 0.999 Silver 1.0151 oz. ASW, 38.61 mm. **Ruler:** Elizabeth II **Obv:** Head with tiara right **Rev:** Blue marlin in color **Edge:** Reeded

| Date | Mintage | VF20 | XF40 | MS60 | MS63 | MS65 |
|---|---|---|---|---|---|---|
| 2012 | 1,000 | **PF65** 110 | | | | |

### KM# 196 2 DOLLARS

31.60 g., 0.999 Silver 1.0151 oz. ASW, 38.61 mm. **Ruler:** Elizabeth II **Obv:** Head with tiara right **Rev:** Blue angel fish in color **Edge:** Reeded

| Date | Mintage | VF20 | XF40 | MS60 | MS63 | MS65 |
|---|---|---|---|---|---|---|
| 2013 | 1,000 | **PF65** 110 | | | | |

### KM# 140 3 DOLLARS

33.63 g., 0.925 Silver 1.0001 oz. ASW, 35 mm. **Ruler:** Elizabeth II **Subject:** Shipwreck Series **Obv:** Elizabeth II **Rev:** The Mary Celestia gold-plated image **Edge:** Plain **Shape:** Triangular

| Date | Mintage | VF20 | XF40 | MS60 | MS63 | MS65 |
|---|---|---|---|---|---|---|
| 2006 | 15,000 | **PF65** 90.00 | | | | |

### KM# 141 3 DOLLARS

1.56 g., 0.999 Gold 0.0499 oz. AGW, 15 mm. **Ruler:** Elizabeth II **Subject:** Shipwreck Series **Obv:** Elizabeth II **Rev:** The Mary Celestia **Edge:** Plain **Shape:** Triangular

| Date | Mintage | VF20 | XF40 | MS60 | MS63 | MS65 |
|---|---|---|---|---|---|---|
| 2006 | 15,000 | **PF65** 100 | | | | |

### KM# 148 3 DOLLARS

33.63 g., 0.925 Silver 1.0001 oz. ASW, 35 mm. **Ruler:** Elizabeth II **Subject:** Shipwreck Series **Obv:** Elizabeth II **Rev:** The Constellation in gold-plated image **Edge:** Plain **Shape:** Triangular

| Date | Mintage | VF20 | XF40 | MS60 | MS63 | MS65 |
|---|---|---|---|---|---|---|
| 2006 | 15,000 | PF65 90.00 | | | | |

### KM# 149 3 DOLLARS

1.56 g., 0.999 Gold 0.0499 oz. AGW, 15 mm. **Ruler:** Elizabeth II **Subject:** Shipwreck Series **Obv:** Elizabeth II **Rev:** The Constellation **Edge:** Plain **Shape:** Triangular

| Date | Mintage | VF20 | XF40 | MS60 | MS63 | MS65 |
|---|---|---|---|---|---|---|
| 2006 | 15,000 | PF65 100 | | | | |

### KM# 157 3 DOLLARS

33.63 g., 0.925 Silver 1.0001 oz. ASW, 35 mm. **Ruler:** Elizabeth II **Subject:** Shipwrecks Series **Obv:** Elizabeth II **Rev:** Gold-plated image of the Hunter Galley **Edge:** Plain

| Date | Mintage | VF20 | XF40 | MS60 | MS63 | MS65 |
|---|---|---|---|---|---|---|
| 2006 | 15,000 | PF65 90.00 | | | | |

### KM# 158 3 DOLLARS

33.63 g., 0.925 Silver 1.0001 oz. ASW, 35 mm. **Ruler:** Elizabeth II **Subject:** Shipwrecks Series **Obv:** Elizabeth II **Rev:** Gold-plated image of the North Carolina **Edge:** Plain

| Date | Mintage | VF20 | XF40 | MS60 | MS63 | MS65 |
|---|---|---|---|---|---|---|
| 2006 | 15,000 | PF65 90.00 | | | | |

### KM# 159 3 DOLLARS

33.63 g., 0.925 Silver 1.0001 oz. ASW, 35 mm. **Ruler:** Elizabeth II **Subject:** Shipwrecks Series **Obv:** Elizabeth II **Rev:** Gold-plated image of the Pollockshields **Edge:** Plain

| Date | Mintage | VF20 | XF40 | MS60 | MS63 | MS65 |
|---|---|---|---|---|---|---|
| 2006 | 15,000 | PF65 90.00 | | | | |

### KM# 175 3 DOLLARS

31.49 g., 0.999 Gold 1.0114 oz. AGW, 35 mm. **Ruler:** Elizabeth II **Series:** Bermuda Shipwrecks **Subject:** The Constellation **Obv:** Head of Queen Elizabeth II with tiara facing right and legend, country name, date **Obv. Legend:** ELIZABETH II **Rev:** The Constellation, legends, denomination **Rev. Legend:** CONSTELLATION Anno Domini 1943 **Shape:** Triangular

| Date | Mintage | VF20 | XF40 | MS60 | MS63 | MS65 |
|---|---|---|---|---|---|---|
| 2006 | Est. 750 | PF63 2,000 | PF65 2,200 | | | |

### KM# 176 3 DOLLARS

31.49 g., 0.999 Gold 1.0114 oz. AGW, 35 mm. **Ruler:** Elizabeth II **Series:** Bermuda Shipwrecks **Subject:** The Hunter Galley **Obv:** Head of Queen Elizabeth II with tiara facing right, legend, country name, date **Obv. Legend:** HUNTER GALLEEY Anno Domini 1752 **Rev:** The Hunter Galley, legend, denomination **Shape:** Triangular

| Date | Mintage | VF20 | XF40 | MS60 | MS63 | MS65 |
|---|---|---|---|---|---|---|
| 2006 | — | PF63 2,000 | PF65 2,200 | | | |

### KM# 177 3 DOLLARS

31.49 g., 0.999 Gold 1.0114 oz. AGW, 35 mm. **Ruler:** Elizabeth II **Series:** Bermuda Shipwrecks **Subject:** The Mary Celestia **Obv:** Head of Queen Elizabeth II wtih tiara facing right, legend, country name, date **Obv. Legend:** ELIZABETH II **Rev:** The Mary Celestia, legends, denomination **Rev. Legend:** MARY CELESTIA Anno Domini 1864 **Shape:** Triangular

| Date | Mintage | VF20 | XF40 | MS60 | MS63 | MS65 |
|---|---|---|---|---|---|---|
| 2006 | Est. 750 | PF63 2,000 | PF65 2,200 | | | |

### KM# 178 3 DOLLARS

31.49 g., 0.999 Gold 1.0114 oz. AGW, 35 mm. **Ruler:** Elizabeth II **Series:** Bemuda Shipwrecks **Subject:** The North Carolina **Obv:** Head of Queen Elizabeth II with tiara facing right, legend, country name, date **Obv. Legend:** ELIZABETH II **Rev:** The North Carolina, legends, denomination **Rev. Legend:** NORTH CAROLINA Anno Domini 1880

| Date | Mintage | VF20 | XF40 | MS60 | MS63 | MS65 |
|---|---|---|---|---|---|---|
| 2006 | Est. 750 | PF63 2,000 | PF65 2,200 | | | |

### KM# 179 3 DOLLARS

31.49 g., 0.999 Gold 1.0114 oz. AGW, 35 mm. **Ruler:** Elizabeth II **Series:** Bermuda Shipwrecks **Subject:** The Pollockshields **Obv:** Head of Queen Elizabeth II with tiara facing right, legend, country name, date **Obv. Legend:** ELIZABETH II **Rev:** The Pollockshields, legends, denomination **Rev. Legend:** POLLOCKSHIELD Anno Domini 1915 **Shape:** Triangular

| Date | Mintage | VF20 | XF40 | MS60 | MS63 | MS65 |
|---|---|---|---|---|---|---|
| 2006 | — | PF63 2,000 | PF65 2,200 | | | |

### KM# 156 3 DOLLARS

33.63 g., 0.925 Silver 1.0001 oz. ASW, 35 mm. **Ruler:** Elizabeth II **Subject:** Shipwrecks Series **Obv:** Elizabeth II **Rev:** Gold-plated image of the Sea Venture **Edge:** Plain

| Date | Mintage | VF20 | XF40 | MS60 | MS63 | MS65 |
|---|---|---|---|---|---|---|
| 2007 | 15,000 | PF65 90.00 | | | | |

### KM# 164 3 DOLLARS

33.63 g., 0.925 Silver 1.0001 oz. ASW, 35 mm. **Ruler:** Elizabeth II **Series:** Bermuda Shipwrecks **Obv:** Head with tiara right, gilt **Rev:** Dutchman sailing ship "Manilla", gilt, 1739 **Edge:** Plain, gilt **Shape:** Triangular

| Date | Mintage | VF20 | XF40 | MS60 | MS63 | MS65 |
|---|---|---|---|---|---|---|
| 2007 | 15,000 | PF65 85.00 | | | | |

### KM# 165 3 DOLLARS

33.63 g., 0.925 Silver 1.0001 oz. ASW, 35 mm. **Ruler:** Elizabeth II **Series:** Bermuda Shipwrecks **Obv:** Head with tiara right, gilt **Rev:** 16th century Spanish sailing ship "Santa Lucia", gilt, 1584 **Edge:** Plain, gilt **Shape:** Triangular

| Date | Mintage | VF20 | XF40 | MS60 | MS63 | MS65 |
|---|---|---|---|---|---|---|
| 2007 | 15,000 | PF65 85.00 | | | | |

### KM# 166 3 DOLLARS

33.63 g., 0.925 Silver 1.0001 oz. ASW **Ruler:** Elizabeth II **Series:** Bermuda Shipwrecks **Obv:** Head with tiara right, gilt **Rev:** Spanish luxury steamship "Cristobal Colon", gilt, 1936 **Edge:** Plain

| Date | Mintage | VF20 | XF40 | MS60 | MS63 | MS65 |
|---|---|---|---|---|---|---|
| 2007 | 15,000 | PF65 85.00 | | | | |

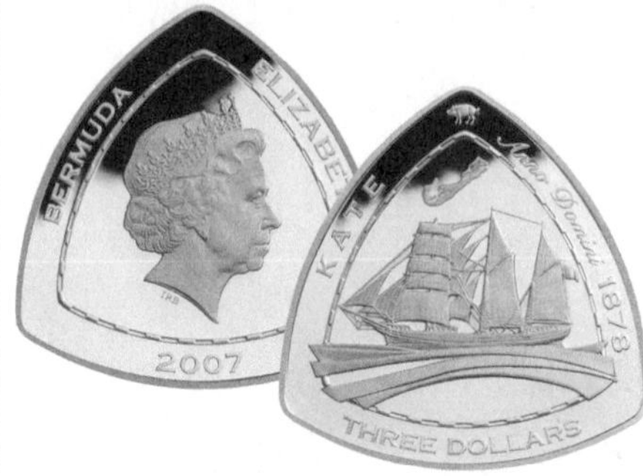


### KM# 167 3 DOLLARS

33.63 g., 0.925 Silver 1.0001 oz. ASW, 35 mm. **Ruler:** Elizabeth II **Series:** Bermuda Shipwrecks **Obv:** Head with tiara right, gilt **Rev:** English iron-hulled steamer with sails "Kate", gilt, 1878 **Edge:** Plain **Shape:** Triangular

| Date | Mintage | VF20 | XF40 | MS60 | MS63 | MS65 |
|---|---|---|---|---|---|---|
| 2007 | 15,000 | PF65 85.00 | | | | |

### KM# 168 3 DOLLARS

33.63 g., 0.925 Silver 1.0001 oz. ASW, 35 mm. **Ruler:** Elizabeth II **Series:** Bermuda Shipwrecks **Obv:** Head with tiara right, gilt **Rev:** 16th century Spanish sailing ship "San Pedro", gilt, 1596 **Edge:** Plain, gilt **Shape:** Triangular

| Date | Mintage | VF20 | XF40 | MS60 | MS63 | MS65 |
|---|---|---|---|---|---|---|
| 2007 | 15,000 | PF65 85.00 | | | | |

### KM# 169 3 DOLLARS

33.63 g., 0.925 Silver 1.0001 oz. ASW, 35 mm. **Ruler:** Elizabeth II **Series:** Bermuda Shipwrecks **Obv:** Head with tiara right, gilt **Rev:** American luxury yacht "Col. William G. Ball", gilt, 1943 **Edge:** Plain, gilt **Shape:** Triangular

| Date | Mintage | VF20 | XF40 | MS60 | MS63 | MS65 |
|---|---|---|---|---|---|---|
| 2007 | 15,000 | PF65 85.00 | | | | |

**KM# 180 3 DOLLARS**
31.49 g., 0.999 Gold 1.0114 oz. AGW, 35 mm. **Ruler:** Elizabeth II **Series:** Bermuda Shipwrecks **Subject:** The Colonel William G. Ball **Obv:** Head of Queen Elizabeth II with tiara facing right, legend, country name, date **Obv. Legend:** ELIZABETH II **Rev:** The colonel William G. Ball, legends, denomination **Rev. Legend:** WILLIAM G. BALL Anno Domini 1943 **Shape:** Triangular

| Date | Mintage | VF20 | XF40 | MS60 | MS63 | MS65 |
|---|---|---|---|---|---|---|
| 2007 | Est. 750 | PF63 2,000 | PF65 2,200 | | | |

**KM# 181 3 DOLLARS**
31.49 g., 0.999 Gold 1.0114 oz. AGW, 35 mm. **Ruler:** Elizabeth II **Series:** Bermuda Shipwrecks **Subject:** The Chistobal Colon **Obv:** Head of Queen Elizabeth II with tiara facing right, legend, country name, date **Obv. Legend:** ELIZABETH II **Rev:** The Cristobal Colon, legends, denomination **Rev. Legend:** CRISTOBAL COLON Anno Domini 1936 **Shape:** Triangular

| Date | Mintage | VF20 | XF40 | MS60 | MS63 | MS65 |
|---|---|---|---|---|---|---|
| 2007 | Est. 750 | PF63 2,000 | PF65 2,200 | | | |

**KM# 182 3 DOLLARS**
31.49 g., 0.999 Gold 1.0114 oz. AGW, 35 mm. **Ruler:** Elizabeth II **Series:** Bermuda Shipwrecks **Subject:** The Kate **Obv:** Head of Queen Elizabeth II with tiara facing right and legend, country name, date **Obv. Legend:** ELIZABETH II **Rev:** The Kate, legends, denomination **Rev. Legend:** KATE Anno Domini 1878 **Shape:** Triangular

| Date | Mintage | VF20 | XF40 | MS60 | MS63 | MS65 |
|---|---|---|---|---|---|---|
| 2007 | Est. 750 | PF63 2,000 | PF65 2,200 | | | |

**KM# 183 3 DOLLARS**
31.49 g., 0.999 Gold 1.0114 oz. AGW, 35 mm. **Ruler:** Elizabeth II **Series:** Bermuda Shipwrecks **Subject:** The San Pedro **Obv:** Head of Queen Elizabeth II with tiara facing right, legend, country name, date **Obv. Legend:** ELIZABETH II **Rev:** The San Pedro, legends, denomination **Rev. Legend:** SAN PEDRO Anno Domini 1595 **Shape:** Triangular

| Date | Mintage | VF20 | XF40 | MS60 | MS63 | MS65 |
|---|---|---|---|---|---|---|
| 2007 | Est. 750 | PF63 2,000 | PF65 2,200 | | | |

**KM# 184 3 DOLLARS**
31.49 g., 0.999 Gold 1.0114 oz. AGW, 35 mm. **Ruler:** Elizabeth II **Series:** Bermuda Shipwrecks **Subject:** The Santa Lucia **Obv:** Head of Queen Elizabeth II with tiara facing right, legend, country name, date **Obv. Legend:** ELIZABETH II **Rev:** The Santa Lucia, legends, denomination **Rev. Legend:** SANTA LUCIA Anno Domini 1584 **Shape:** Triangular

| Date | Mintage | VF20 | XF40 | MS60 | MS63 | MS65 |
|---|---|---|---|---|---|---|
| 2007 | Est. 750 | PF63 2,000 | PF65 2,200 | | | |

**KM# 185 3 DOLLARS**
31.49 g., 0.999 Gold 1.0114 oz. AGW, 35 mm. **Ruler:** Elizabeth II **Series:** Bermuda Shipwrecks **Subject:** The Manilla **Obv:** Head of Queen Elizabeth II with tiara facing right, legend, country name, date **Obv. Legend:** ELIZABETH II **Rev:** The Manilla, legends, denomination **Rev. Legend:** MANILLA Anno Domini 1739 **Shape:** Triangular

| Date | Mintage | VF20 | XF40 | MS60 | MS63 | MS65 |
|---|---|---|---|---|---|---|
| 2007 | — | PF63 2,000 | PF65 2,200 | | | |

**KM# 199 4 DOLLARS**
34.00 g., 0.925 Silver 1.0111 oz. ASW, 40 mm. **Ruler:** Elizabeth II **Obv:** Bust right **Obv. Legend:** Elizabeth II, Value, BERMUDA **Rev:** Sea venture sailing ship **Rev. Legend:** 1609-2009 400th ANNIVERSARY OF THE SETTLEMENT OF BERMUDA **Shape:** Square

| Date | Mintage | VF20 | XF40 | MS60 | MS63 | MS65 |
|---|---|---|---|---|---|---|
| ND-2009 | 2,000 | PF65 55.00 | | | | |

**KM# 120 5 DOLLARS**
28.28 g., 0.925 Silver 0.841 oz. ASW, 38.6 mm. **Ruler:** Elizabeth II **Subject:** Gombey Dancers **Obv:** Head with tiara right **Rev:** Multicolor costumed dancers **Edge:** Reeded

| Date | Mintage | VF20 | XF40 | MS60 | MS63 | MS65 |
|---|---|---|---|---|---|---|
| 2001 | 3,500 | PF63 55.00 | PF65 60.00 | | | |

**KM# 161 5 DOLLARS**
28.28 g., 0.925 Silver 0.841 oz. ASW, 38.6 mm. **Ruler:** Elizabeth II **Obv:** Bust with tiara right **Rev:** Statehouse facade, St. George's **Edge:** Reeded

| Date | Mintage | VF20 | XF40 | MS60 | MS63 | MS65 |
|---|---|---|---|---|---|---|
| 2001 | 3,500 | PF63 40.00 | PF65 45.00 | | | |

**KM# 129 5 DOLLARS**
28.28 g., 0.925 Silver 0.841 oz. ASW, 38.6 mm. **Ruler:** Elizabeth II **Subject:** Queen's Jubilee **Obv:** Gold-plated head with tiara right, denomination below **Rev:** Trumpeters, monogram and date below **Edge:** Reeded

| Date | Mintage | VF20 | XF40 | MS60 | MS63 | MS65 |
|---|---|---|---|---|---|---|
| 2002 | 20,000 | PF63 38.00 | PF65 42.00 | | | |

**KM# 162 5 DOLLARS**
28.28 g., 0.925 Silver 0.841 oz. ASW, 38.6 mm. **Ruler:** Elizabeth II **Subject:** 100th Anniversary Cup Match - Cricket **Obv:** Head with tiara right **Rev:** Two players with caps and teams shields below, multicolor **Edge:** Reeded

| Date | Mintage | VF20 | XF40 | MS60 | MS63 | MS65 |
|---|---|---|---|---|---|---|
| 2002 | 3,500 | PF63 40.00 | PF65 45.00 | | | |

**KM# 171 5 DOLLARS**
28.28 g., 0.925 Silver 0.841 oz. ASW, 38.6 mm. **Ruler:** Elizabeth II **Subject:** Queen's Golden Jubilee **Obv:** Head with tiara right **Rev:** Stylized trumpeters above monogram and date **Edge:** Reeded

| Date | Mintage | VF20 | XF40 | MS60 | MS63 | MS65 |
|---|---|---|---|---|---|---|
| 2002 | 3,500 | PF65 50.00 | | | | |

**KM# 130 5 DOLLARS**
28.28 g., 0.925 Silver 0.841 oz. ASW, 38.6 mm. **Ruler:** Elizabeth II **Subject:** Queen's Jubilee **Obv:** Gold-plated head with tiara right **Rev:** Royal visit scene **Edge:** Reeded

| Date | Mintage | VF20 | XF40 | MS60 | MS63 | MS65 |
|---|---|---|---|---|---|---|
| 2003 | 20,000 | PF63 38.00 | PF65 42.00 | | | |

**KM# 170 5 DOLLARS**
28.28 g., 0.925 Silver 0.841 oz. ASW, 38.6 mm. **Ruler:** Elizabeth II **Subject:** 100th Anniversary Fitted Dinghy Racing **Obv:** Head with tiara right **Rev:** Two dinghies, multicolor sails **Edge:** Reeded

| Date | Mintage | VF20 | XF40 | MS60 | MS63 | MS65 |
|---|---|---|---|---|---|---|
| ND-2003 | 3,500 | PF65 50.00 | | | | |

**KM# 131 5 DOLLARS**
28.28 g., 0.925 Silver 0.841 oz. ASW, 38.6 mm. **Ruler:** Elizabeth II **Obv:** Head with tiara right **Rev:** Bermudian stone quarry scene **Edge:** Reeded

| Date | Mintage | VF20 | XF40 | MS60 | MS63 | MS65 |
|---|---|---|---|---|---|---|
| 2004 | 3,500 | PF63 55.00 | PF65 60.00 | | | |

**KM# 160 5 DOLLARS**
14.50 g., 0.925 Silver 0.4312 oz. ASW partially gilt, 30.9 mm. **Ruler:** Elizabeth II **Subject:** Bermuda Quincentennial **Obv:** Head with tiara right, partially gold-plated **Rev:** Caravel sailing ship partially gold-plated compass face **Edge:** Plain **Shape:** Pentagonal

| Date | Mintage | VF20 | XF40 | MS60 | MS63 | MS65 |
|---|---|---|---|---|---|---|
| 2005 | 2,500 | PF65 45.00 | | | | |

**KM# 187 5 DOLLARS**
1.56 g., 0.999 Gold 0.0499 oz. AGW, 16 mm. **Ruler:** Elizabeth II **Subject:** Cahow **Obv:** Head of Queen Elizabeth II with tiara facing right, legend, country name, date **Obv. Legend:** ELIZABETH II **Rev:** Bird over water surrounding outline of Bermuda, denomination

| Date | Mintage | VF20 | XF40 | MS60 | MS63 | MS65 |
|---|---|---|---|---|---|---|
| 2010 | Est. 500 | PF65 150 | | | | |

**KM# 191 5 DOLLARS**
1.56 g., 0.9999 Gold 0.050 oz. AGW, 16 mm. **Ruler:** Elizabeth II **Obv:** Head with tiara right **Rev:** Bermuda bluebird with sailboats **Edge:** Reeded

| Date | Mintage | VF20 | XF40 | MS60 | MS63 | MS65 |
|---|---|---|---|---|---|---|
| 2011 | 500 | PF65 185 | | | | |

**KM# 188 5 DOLLARS**
28.28 g., 0.925 Silver 0.841 oz. ASW, 38.6 mm. **Ruler:** Elizabeth II **Rev:** Sword and decorations **Rev. Legend:** THE SYSTEM DOES DISCOVER PEOPLE WHO DO UNSUNG THINGS

| Date | Mintage | VF20 | XF40 | MS60 | MS63 | MS65 |
|---|---|---|---|---|---|---|
| 2012 | — | PF65 75.00 | | | | |

**KM# 194 5 DOLLARS**
1.56 g., 0.9999 Gold 0.050 oz. AGW, 16 mm. **Ruler:** Elizabeth II **Obv:** Head with tiara right **Rev:** Blue marlin **Edge:** Reeded

| Date | Mintage | VF20 | XF40 | MS60 | MS63 | MS65 |
|---|---|---|---|---|---|---|
| 2012 | 500 | PF65 185 | | | | |

**KM# 197 5 DOLLARS**
1.56 g., 0.9999 Gold 0.050 oz. AGW, 16 mm. **Ruler:** Elizabeth II **Obv:** Head with tiara right **Rev:** Blue angle fish **Edge:** Reeded

| Date | Mintage | VF20 | XF40 | MS60 | MS63 | MS65 |
|---|---|---|---|---|---|---|
| 2013 | 500 | PF65 185 | | | | |

**KM# 142 9 DOLLARS**
155.52 g., 0.999 Silver 4.9951 oz. ASW, 65 mm. **Ruler:** Elizabeth II **Subject:** Shipwreck Series **Obv:** Elizabeth II **Rev:** The Mary Celestia **Edge:** Plain **Shape:** Triangular

| Date | Mintage | VF20 | XF40 | MS60 | MS63 | MS65 |
|---|---|---|---|---|---|---|
| 2007 | 1,000 | PF65 200 | | | | |

**KM# 150 9 DOLLARS**
155.52 g., 0.999 Silver 4.9951 oz. ASW, 65 mm. **Ruler:** Elizabeth II **Subject:** Shipwreck Series **Obv:** Elizabeth II **Rev:** The Constellation **Edge:** Plain **Shape:** Triangular

| Date | Mintage | VF20 | XF40 | MS60 | MS63 | MS65 |
|---|---|---|---|---|---|---|
| 2007 | 1,000 | PF65 200 | | | | |

### KM# 143 30 DOLLARS

31.49 g., 0.999 Gold 1.0114 oz. AGW, 35 mm. **Ruler:** Elizabeth II **Subject:** Shipwreck Series **Obv:** Elizabeth II **Rev:** The Mary Celestia **Edge:** Plain **Shape:** Triangular

| Date | Mintage | VF20 | XF40 | MS60 | MS63 | MS65 |
|---|---|---|---|---|---|---|
| 2006 | 750 | PF65 1,750 | | | | |

### KM# 151 30 DOLLARS

31.49 g., 0.999 Gold 1.0114 oz. AGW, 35 mm. **Ruler:** Elizabeth II **Subject:** Shipwreck Series **Obv:** Elizabeth II **Rev:** The Constellation **Edge:** Plain **Shape:** Triangular

| Date | Mintage | VF20 | XF40 | MS60 | MS63 | MS65 |
|---|---|---|---|---|---|---|
| 2006 | 750 | PF65 1,750 | | | | |

### KM# 144 60 DOLLARS

1000.00 g., 0.999 Silver 32.1186 oz. ASW, 100 mm. **Ruler:** Elizabeth II **Subject:** Shipwreck Series **Obv:** Elizabeth II **Rev:** The Mary Celestia **Edge:** Plain

| Date | Mintage | VF20 | XF40 | MS60 | MS63 | MS65 |
|---|---|---|---|---|---|---|
| 2007 | 300 | PF65 1,200 | | | | |

### KM# 152 60 DOLLARS

1000.00 g., 0.999 Silver 32.1186 oz. ASW, 100 mm. **Ruler:** Elizabeth II **Subject:** Shipwreck Series **Obv:** Elizabeth II **Rev:** The Constellation **Edge:** Plain **Shape:** Triangular

| Date | Mintage | VF20 | XF40 | MS60 | MS63 | MS65 |
|---|---|---|---|---|---|---|
| 2007 | 300 | PF65 1,200 | | | | |

### KM# 145 90 DOLLARS

155.52 g., 0.999 Gold 4.9951 oz. AGW, 65 mm. **Ruler:** Elizabeth II **Subject:** Shipwreck Series **Obv:** Elizabeth II **Rev:** The Mary Celestia **Edge:** Plain **Shape:** Triangular

| Date | Mintage | VF20 | XF40 | MS60 | MS63 | MS65 |
|---|---|---|---|---|---|---|
| 2006 | 90 | PF65 8,000 | | | | |

### KM# 153 90 DOLLARS

155.52 g., 0.999 Gold 4.9951 oz. AGW, 65 mm. **Ruler:** Elizabeth II **Subject:** Shipwreck Series **Obv:** Elizabeth II **Rev:** The Constellation **Edge:** Plain **Shape:** Triangular

| Date | Mintage | VF20 | XF40 | MS60 | MS63 | MS65 |
|---|---|---|---|---|---|---|
| 2006 | 90 | PF65 8,000 | | | | |

### KM# 174 90 DOLLARS

155.52 g., 0.999 Gold 4.9951 oz. AGW, 65 mm. **Ruler:** Elizabeth II **Subject:** Sea Venture, 1609 **Obv:** Head with tiara right **Rev:** Sailing ship left **Shape:** Triangle

| Date | Mintage | VF20 | XF40 | MS60 | MS63 | MS65 |
|---|---|---|---|---|---|---|
| 2006 | — | PF65 8,000 | | | | |

### KM# 173 100 DOLLARS

1000.00 g., 0.925 Silver 29.7394 oz. ASW selective gold plating, 100 mm. **Ruler:** Elizabeth II **Subject:** 500th Anniversary of Discovery **Obv:** Head right **Rev:** Caraval within compass **Shape:** 5-sided

| Date | Mintage | VF20 | XF40 | MS60 | MS63 | MS65 |
|---|---|---|---|---|---|---|
| 2005 | 250 | PF65 1,150 | | | | |

### KM# 146 300 DOLLARS

155.52 g., 0.9995 Platinum 4.9976 oz. APW, 65 mm. **Ruler:** Elizabeth II **Subject:** Shipwrecks Series **Obv:** Elizabeth II **Rev:** The Mary Celestia **Edge:** Plain **Shape:** Triangular

| Date | Mintage | VF20 | XF40 | MS60 | MS63 | MS65 |
|---|---|---|---|---|---|---|
| 2006 | 60 | PF65 8,500 | | | | |

### KM# 154 300 DOLLARS

155.52 g., 0.9995 Platinum 4.9976 oz. APW, 65 mm. **Ruler:** Elizabeth II **Subject:** Shipwreck Series **Obv:** Elizabeth II **Rev:** The Constellation **Edge:** Plain **Shape:** Triangular

| Date | Mintage | VF20 | XF40 | MS60 | MS63 | MS65 |
|---|---|---|---|---|---|---|
| 2006 | 60 | PF65 8,500 | | | | |

### KM# 172 500 DOLLARS

31.11 g., 0.999 Gold 0.999 oz. AGW with selective silver plating, 30.89 mm. **Ruler:** Elizabeth II **Obv:** Queen Elizabeth II **Rev:** Caravel sailing ship in compass face **Edge:** Plain **Shape:** 5-sided **Note:** Bermuda Quincentennial. Prev. KM#160a.

| Date | Mintage | VF20 | XF40 | MS60 | MS63 | MS65 |
|---|---|---|---|---|---|---|
| 2005 | — | PF65 1,800 | | | | |

### KM# 147 600 DOLLARS

1096.00 g., 0.918 Gold 32.3477 oz. AGW, 100 mm. **Ruler:** Elizabeth II **Subject:** Shipwreck Series **Obv:** Elizabeth II **Rev:** The Mary Celestia **Edge:** Plain **Shape:** Triangular

| Date | Mintage | VF20 | XF40 | MS60 | MS63 | MS65 |
|---|---|---|---|---|---|---|
| 2007 | 300 | PF65 50,000 | | | | |

### KM# 155 600 DOLLARS

1096.00 g., 0.918 Gold 32.3477 oz. AGW, 100 mm. **Ruler:** Elizabeth II **Subject:** Shipwreck Series **Obv:** Elizabeth II **Rev:** The Constellation **Edge:** Plain **Shape:** Triangular

| Date | Mintage | VF20 | XF40 | MS60 | MS63 | MS65 |
|---|---|---|---|---|---|---|
| 2007 | 300 | PF65 50,000 | | | | |

## PIEDFORT

| KM# | Date | Mintage | Identification | Mkt Val |
|---|---|---|---|---|
| P3 | 2005 | 250 | 5 Dollars 0.925 Silver Gold plated bust and rim Caravel type sailing ship in partially gold plated compass face and rim | — |

## MINT SETS

| KM# | Date | Mintage | Identification | Issue Price | Mkt Val |
|---|---|---|---|---|---|
| MS8 | 2004 (5) | 2,300 | KM#107-111. | — | 10.00 |

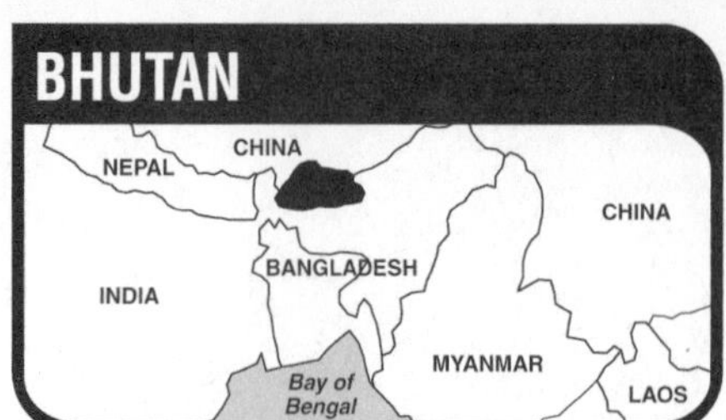


The Kingdom of Bhutan, a landlocked Himalayan country bordered by Tibet and India, has an area of 18,150 sq. mi. (38,394 sq. km.) and a population of 675,000. Capital: Thimphu. Virtually the entire population is engaged in agricultural and pastoral activities. Rice, wheat, barley, and yak butter are produced in sufficient quantity to make the country self-sufficient in food. The economy of Bhutan is primitive and many transactions are conducted on a barter basis.

**RULER**

Jigme Singye Wangchuck, 1972-2006

King Jigme Khesar Namgyel Wangchuck, 2006-

# KINGDOM

## REFORM COINAGE

1974 - 100 Chetrums (Paisa) = 1 Ngultrum (Rupee); 100 Ngultrums = 1 Sertum

### X# 105 5 CHETRUMS

3.86 g., Brass, 21.9 mm. **Obv:** Monkey right, date below **Rev:** Effigy of the old "Ma-tam", value below **Edge:** Plain **Note:** This coin is a private issue not authorized by the Royal Monetary Authority of Bhutan

| Date | Mintage | F12 | VF20 | XF40 | MS60 | MS63 |
|---|---|---|---|---|---|---|
| 2003 | — | — | — | — | 2.00 | 3.00 |

### KM# 116 NGULTRUM

8.10 g., Nickel Plated Steel **Ruler:** Jigme Khesar Namgyel Wangchuck

| Date | Mintage | VF20 | XF40 | MS60 | MS63 | MS65 |
|---|---|---|---|---|---|---|
| 2008 | — | — | — | — | 5.00 | 7.00 |

### KM# 115 100 NGULTRUMS

20.20 g., Silver, 38 mm. **Ruler:** Jigme Khesar Namgyel Wangchuck **Subject:** Coronation **Obv:** Portrait left **Rev:** Seal

| Date | Mintage | VF20 | XF40 | MS60 | MS63 | MS65 |
|---|---|---|---|---|---|---|
| 2008 | — | PF63 55.00 | PF65 60.00 | | | |

### KM# 214 100 NGULTRUMS

0.50 g., 0.999 Gold, 11 mm. **Ruler:** Jigme Khesar Namgyel Wangchuck **Subject:** Buddhist Monastery - Taktsang

| Date | Mintage | VF20 | XF40 | MS60 | MS63 | MS65 |
|---|---|---|---|---|---|---|
| 2010 | Est. 5000 | PF63 55.00 | PF65 60.00 | | | |

### KM# 224 100 NGULTRUMS

0.50 g., 0.999 Gold, 11 mm. **Ruler:** Jigme Khesar Namgyel Wangchuck **Subject:** Buddhist Monastery - Chorten Kora

| Date | Mintage | VF20 | XF40 | MS60 | MS63 | MS65 |
|---|---|---|---|---|---|---|
| 2011 | Est. 5000 | PF63 45.00 | PF65 55.00 | | | |

### KM# 229 100 NGULTRUMS

0.59 g., 0.500 Gold with 24Kt plating, 11 mm. **Ruler:** Jigme Khesar Namgyel Wangchuck **Subject:** Traditional Archery **Rev:** Archer

| Date | Mintage | VF20 | XF40 | MS60 | MS63 | MS65 |
|---|---|---|---|---|---|---|
| 2012 | 7,000 | PF63 28.00 | PF65 30.00 | | | |

### KM# 232 100 NGULTRUMS

0.50 g., 0.585 Gold AGW with 24Kt plating, 11 mm. **Subject:** Mount Everest

| Date | Mintage | VF20 | XF40 | MS60 | MS63 | MS65 |
|---|---|---|---|---|---|---|
| 2013 | Est. 5000 | PF63 45.00 | PF65 50.00 | | | |

### KM# 208 200 NGULTRUMS

1.24 g., 0.999 Gold 0.0398 oz. AGW, 13.92 mm. **Ruler:** Jigme Khesar Namgyel Wangchuck **Subject:** Buddha's of the World - Cambodia **Rev:** Head from Angkor Wat

| Date | Mintage | VF20 | XF40 | MS60 | MS63 | MS65 |
|---|---|---|---|---|---|---|
| 2010 | Est. 30000 | PF63 80.00 | PF65 90.00 | | | |

### KM# 211 200 NGULTRUMS

1.24 g., 0.999 Gold 0.0398 oz. AGW, 13.92 mm. **Ruler:** Jigme Khesar Namgyel Wangchuck **Subject:** Buddha's of the World - Korea **Rev:** Buddha seated

| Date | Mintage | VF20 | XF40 | MS60 | MS63 | MS65 |
|---|---|---|---|---|---|---|
| 2010 | — | — | — | — | — | 90.00 |

### KM# 217 200 NGULTRUMS

1.24 g., 0.999 Gold 0.0398 oz. AGW, 13.92 mm. **Ruler:** Jigme Khesar Namgyel Wangchuck **Subject:** Buddhist World Heritage - Thailand **Rev:** Wat Pho

| Date | Mintage | VF20 | XF40 | MS60 | MS63 | MS65 |
|---|---|---|---|---|---|---|
| 2011 | Est. 30000 | — | — | — | — | 100 |

### KM# 220 200 NGULTRUMS

1.24 g., 0.999 Gold 0.0398 oz. AGW, 13.92 mm. **Ruler:** Jigme Khesar Namgyel Wangchuck **Subject:** Buddhist World Heritage - China **Rev:** Great Buddha in Leshan

| Date | Mintage | VF20 | XF40 | MS60 | MS63 | MS65 |
|---|---|---|---|---|---|---|
| 2011 | Est. 30000 | — | — | — | — | 80.00 |

### KM# 181 250 NGULTRUMS

31.11 g., 0.999 Silver 0.999 oz. ASW, 38.61 mm. **Ruler:** Jigme Singye Wangchuck **Rev:** Sun Yat-Sen bust facing

| Date | Mintage | VF20 | XF40 | MS60 | MS63 | MS65 |
|---|---|---|---|---|---|---|
| 2003 | Est. 4999 | PF63 65.00 | PF65 70.00 | | | |

### KM# 185 250 NGULTRUMS

31.11 g., 0.999 Silver 0.999 oz. ASW, 38.61 mm. **Ruler:** Jigme Singye Wangchuck **Subject:** Wonders of the World - Borobudur Temple in Java

| Date | Mintage | VF20 | XF40 | MS60 | MS63 | MS65 |
|---|---|---|---|---|---|---|
| 2003 | Est. 9999 | PF63 60.00 | PF65 70.00 | | | |

### KM# 189 250 NGULTRUMS

31.11 g., 0.999 Silver 0.999 oz. ASW, 38.61 mm. **Ruler:** Jigme Singye Wangchuck **Subject:** Guanyin, Buddhist godess of mercy

| Date | Mintage | VF20 | XF40 | MS60 | MS63 | MS65 |
|---|---|---|---|---|---|---|
| 2003 | — | PF63 65.00 | PF65 70.00 | | | |

### KM# 191 250 NGULTRUMS

31.11 g., 0.999 Silver 0.999 oz. ASW, 38.61 mm. **Ruler:** Jigme Singye Wangchuck **Subject:** World Fellowship of Buddhist Youth **Rev:** Lord Buddha, the Enlightenment

| Date | Mintage | VF20 | XF40 | MS60 | MS63 | MS65 |
|---|---|---|---|---|---|---|
| 2003 | Est. 2999 | PF63 65.00 | PF65 70.00 | | | |

### KM# 170 250 NGULTRUMS

31.11 g., 0.999 Silver 0.999 oz. ASW, 38.61 mm. **Ruler:** Jigme Singye Wangchuck **Subject:** Wonders of the World - Pyramids

| Date | Mintage | VF20 | XF40 | MS60 | MS63 | MS65 |
|---|---|---|---|---|---|---|
| 2004 | Est. 4999 | PF63 65.00 | PF65 70.00 | | | |

### KM# 172 250 NGULTRUMS

31.11 g., 0.999 Silver 0.9991 oz. ASW, 38.61 mm. **Ruler:** Jigme Singye Wangchuck **Subject:** Wonders of the World - Taj Mahal

| Date | Mintage | VF20 | XF40 | MS60 | MS63 | MS65 |
|---|---|---|---|---|---|---|
| 2004 | Est. 4999 | PF63 65.00 | PF65 70.00 | | | |

### KM# 195 250 NGULTRUMS

31.11 g., 0.999 Silver 0.999 oz. ASW, 38.61 mm. **Ruler:** Jigme Singye Wangchuck **Subject:** Indonesian Games in Palembang **Rev:** Rimau, games mascot

| Date | Mintage | VF20 | XF40 | MS60 | MS63 | MS65 |
|---|---|---|---|---|---|---|
| 2004 | Est. 4999 | PF63 65.00 | PF65 75.00 | | | |

### KM# 196 250 NGULTRUMS

31.11 g., 0.999 Silver 0.999 oz. ASW, 38.61 mm. **Ruler:** Jigme Singye Wangchuck **Subject:** Indonesian Games in Palembang **Rev:** Bridge card hand

| Date | Mintage | VF20 | XF40 | MS60 | MS63 | MS65 |
|---|---|---|---|---|---|---|
| 2004 | 4,999 | PF63 65.00 | PF65 75.00 | | | |

### KM# 197 250 NGULTRUMS

31.11 g., 0.999 Silver 0.999 oz. ASW, 38.61 mm. **Ruler:** Jigme Singye Wangchuck **Subject:** Indonesian Games in Palembang **Rev:** Badminton

| Date | Mintage | VF20 | XF40 | MS60 | MS63 | MS65 |
|---|---|---|---|---|---|---|
| 2004 | Est. 4999 | PF63 65.00 | PF65 75.00 | | | |

**KM# 198 250 NGULTRUMS**
31.11 g., 0.999 Silver 0.999 oz. ASW, 38.61 mm. **Ruler:** Jigme Singye Wangchuck **Subject:** Indonesian Games in Palembang **Rev:** Sailing

| Date | Mintage | VF20 | XF40 | MS60 | MS63 | MS65 |
|---|---|---|---|---|---|---|
| 2004 | Est. 4999 | PF63 65.00 | PF65 75.00 | | | |

**KM# 199 250 NGULTRUMS**
31.11 g., 0.999 Silver 0.999 oz. ASW, 38.61 mm. **Ruler:** Jigme Singye Wangchuck **Subject:** Indonesian Games in Palembang **Rev:** Games logo

| Date | Mintage | VF20 | XF40 | MS60 | MS63 | MS65 |
|---|---|---|---|---|---|---|
| 2004 | Est. 4999 | PF63 65.00 | PF65 75.00 | | | |

**KM# 200 250 NGULTRUMS**
Bi-Metallic 25g .925 Silver and .9g .750 Gold, 38.61 mm. **Ruler:** Jigme Singye Wangchuck **Subject:** Sundial

| Date | Mintage | VF20 | XF40 | MS60 | MS63 | MS65 |
|---|---|---|---|---|---|---|
| 2004 | Est. 9999 | — | — | — | — | 125 |

**KM# 201 250 NGULTRUMS**
Bi-Metallic 25g .925 Silver with 8g Steel, 38.61 mm. **Ruler:** Jigme Singye Wangchuck **Rev:** Compass rose

| Date | Mintage | VF20 | XF40 | MS60 | MS63 | MS65 |
|---|---|---|---|---|---|---|
| 2004 | Est. 9999 | — | — | — | — | 125 |

**KM# 207 250 NGULTRUMS**
31.11 g., 0.999 Silver 0.999 oz. ASW, 40.7 mm. **Ruler:** Jigme Khesar Namgyel Wangchuck **Subject:** Buddha's of the World - Cambodia **Rev:** Head from Angkor Wat, in color

| Date | Mintage | VF20 | XF40 | MS60 | MS63 | MS65 |
|---|---|---|---|---|---|---|
| 2010 | Est. 10000 | PF63 60.00 | PF65 70.00 | | | |

**KM# 210 250 NGULTRUMS**
31.11 g., 0.999 Silver 0.999 oz. ASW, 40.7 mm. **Ruler:** Jigme Khesar Namgyel Wangchuck **Subject:** Buddha's of the World - Korea **Obv:** Dungkar design in color **Rev:** Buddha seated

| Date | Mintage | VF20 | XF40 | MS60 | MS63 | MS65 |
|---|---|---|---|---|---|---|
| 2010 | Est. 10000 | PF63 60.00 | PF65 70.00 | | | |

**KM# 216 250 NGULTRUMS**
31.11 g., 0.999 Silver 0.999 oz. ASW, 40.7 mm. **Ruler:** Jigme Khesar Namgyel Wangchuck **Subject:** Buddhist World heritage - Thailand **Obv:** Dhug in color **Rev:** Wat Pho

| Date | Mintage | VF20 | XF40 | MS60 | MS63 | MS65 |
|---|---|---|---|---|---|---|
| 2011 | Est. 10000 | PF63 60.00 | PF65 70.00 | | | |

**KM# 219 250 NGULTRUMS**
31.11 g., 0.999 Silver 0.999 oz. ASW, 40.7 mm. **Ruler:** Jigme Khesar Namgyel Wangchuck **Subject:** Buddhist World Heritage - China **Obv:** Khorto in color **Rev:** Great Buddha in Leshan

| Date | Mintage | VF20 | XF40 | MS60 | MS63 | MS65 |
|---|---|---|---|---|---|---|
| 2011 | Est. 10000 | PF63 60.00 | PF65 70.00 | | | |

**KM# 234 250 NGULTRUMS**
31.11 g., 0.999 Silver 0.999 oz. ASW, 40.7 mm. **Obv:** Knot in color **Rev:** Thousand arm Buddha

| Date | Mintage | VF20 | XF40 | MS60 | MS63 | MS65 |
|---|---|---|---|---|---|---|
| 2013 | — | PF65 70.00 | | | | |

**KM# 215 300 NGULTRUMS**
1.24 g., 0.999 Gold 0.0398 oz. AGW, 13.92 mm. **Ruler:** Jigme Khesar Namgyel Wangchuck **Subject:** Buddhist Monastery - Taktsang

| Date | Mintage | VF20 | XF40 | MS60 | MS63 | MS65 |
|---|---|---|---|---|---|---|
| 2010 | Est. 5000 | PF63 85.00 | PF65 100 | | | |

**KM# 226 300 NGULTRUMS**
28.28 g., 0.925 Silver 0.841 oz. ASW, 38.61 mm. **Ruler:** Jigme Khesar Namgyel Wangchuck **Subject:** 2014 Sochi Olympic Games -Cross Country Skiing **Rev:** Two skiers

| Date | Mintage | VF20 | XF40 | MS60 | MS63 | MS65 |
|---|---|---|---|---|---|---|
| 2012 | 5,000 | PF63 65.00 | PF65 70.00 | | | |

**KM# 227 300 NGULTRUMS**
3.11 g., 0.999 Gold 0.0999 oz. AGW, 16.5 mm. **Ruler:** Jigme Khesar Namgyel Wangchuck **Subject:** 2014 FIFA World Cup - Brazil **Rev:** Soccer Player and dragon

| Date | Mintage | VF20 | XF40 | MS60 | MS63 | MS65 |
|---|---|---|---|---|---|---|
| 2012 | 1,000 | PF65 225 | | | | |

**KM# 228 300 NGULTRUMS**
20.00 g., 0.925 Silver 0.5948 oz. ASW, 38.61 mm. **Ruler:** Jigme Khesar Namgyel Wangchuck **Subject:** Himalayan Railway **Rev:** Steam Locomotive and outline of mountains

| Date | Mintage | VF20 | XF40 | MS60 | MS63 | MS65 |
|---|---|---|---|---|---|---|
| 2012 | 3,000 | PF65 60.00 | | | | |

**KM# 230 300 NGULTRUMS**
20.00 g., 0.925 Silver 0.5948 oz. ASW, 38.61 mm. **Subject:** 2016 Olympics - Table Tennis

| Date | Mintage | VF20 | XF40 | MS60 | MS63 | MS65 |
|---|---|---|---|---|---|---|
| 2013 | Est. 10000 | PF63 70.00 | PF65 75.00 | | | |

**KM# 231 300 NGULTRUMS**
20.00 g., 0.925 Silver 0.5948 oz. ASW, 38.61 mm. **Subject:** 2014 FIFA World Cup Brazil

| Date | Mintage | VF20 | XF40 | MS60 | MS63 | MS65 |
|---|---|---|---|---|---|---|
| 2013 | Est. 10000 | PF63 70.00 | PF65 75.00 | | | |

**KM# 233 300 NGULTRUMS**
20.00 g., 0.925 Silver 0.5948 oz. ASW, 38.61 mm. **Subject:** Kalka Shimla Railway

| Date | Mintage | VF20 | XF40 | MS60 | MS63 | MS65 |
|---|---|---|---|---|---|---|
| 2013 | — | PF63 70.00 | PF65 75.00 | | | |

**KM# 203 500 NGULTRUM**
62.20 g., 0.999 Silver 1.9978 oz. ASW partially gilt **Ruler:** Jigme Singye Wangchuck **Rev:** Zodiac, partially gilt

| Date | Mintage | VF20 | XF40 | MS60 | MS63 | MS65 |
|---|---|---|---|---|---|---|
| 2006 | — | PF65 110 | | | | |

**KM# 205 500 NGULTRUM**
31.11 g., 0.999 Silver 0.999 oz. ASW, 38.7 mm. **Ruler:** Jigme Khesar Namgyel Wangchuck **Subject:** Coronation

| Date | Mintage | VF20 | XF40 | MS60 | MS63 | MS65 |
|---|---|---|---|---|---|---|
| 2008 | 5,000 | PF63 75.00 | PF65 85.00 | | | |

**KM# 222 500 NGULTRUM**
31.11 g., 0.999 Silver 0.999 oz. ASW, 40.7 mm. **Ruler:** Jigme Khesar Namgyel Wangchuck **Subject:** Royal Wedding **Rev:** Couple in color

| Date | Mintage | VF20 | XF40 | MS60 | MS63 | MS65 |
|---|---|---|---|---|---|---|
| 2011 | Est. 20000 | PF63 135 | PF65 150 | | | |

**KM# 173 1000 NGULTRUM**
10.00 g., 0.999 Gold 0.3212 oz. AGW, 26 mm. **Ruler:** Jigme Singye Wangchuck **Subject:** Wonders of the World - Taj Mahal

| Date | Mintage | VF20 | XF40 | MS60 | MS63 | MS65 |
|---|---|---|---|---|---|---|
| 2002 | Est. 3000 | PF63 650 | PF65 700 | | | |

**KM# 177 1000 NGULTRUM**
10.00 g., 0.999 Gold 0.3212 oz. AGW, 26 mm. **Ruler:** Jigme Singye Wangchuck **Subject:** World Fellowship of Buddhist Youth

| Date | Mintage | VF20 | XF40 | MS60 | MS63 | MS65 |
|---|---|---|---|---|---|---|
| 2002 | Est. 2999 | PF63 625 | PF65 650 | | | |

**KM# 182 1000 NGULTRUM**
6.22 g., 0.999 Gold 0.1998 oz. AGW, 26 mm. **Ruler:** Jigme Singye Wangchuck **Rev:** Sun Yat-Sen bust facing

| Date | Mintage | VF20 | XF40 | MS60 | MS63 | MS65 |
|---|---|---|---|---|---|---|
| 2003 | Est. 4999 | PF63 375 | PF65 425 | | | |

**KM# 183 1000 NGULTRUM**
10.00 g., 0.999 Gold 0.3212 oz. AGW, 26 mm. **Ruler:** Jigme Singye Wangchuck **Subject:** Legends of Sports - Rudy Hartono **Rev:** Bust at left, tennis serve at right

| Date | Mintage | VF20 | XF40 | MS60 | MS63 | MS65 |
|---|---|---|---|---|---|---|
| 2003 | Est. 10000 | PF63 600 | PF65 650 | | | |

**KM# 186 1000 NGULTRUM**
10.00 g., 0.999 Gold 0.3212 oz. AGW, 26 mm. **Ruler:** Jigme Singye Wangchuck **Subject:** Wonders of the World - Borobudur Temple in Java

| Date | Mintage | VF20 | XF40 | MS60 | MS63 | MS65 |
|---|---|---|---|---|---|---|
| 2003 | Est. 9999 | PF63 600 | PF65 650 | | | |

**KM# 190 1000 NGULTRUM**
10.00 g., 0.999 Gold 0.3212 oz. AGW, 26 mm. **Ruler:** Jigme Singye Wangchuck **Subject:** Guanyin, Buddhist godess of mercy

| Date | Mintage | VF20 | XF40 | MS60 | MS63 | MS65 |
|---|---|---|---|---|---|---|
| 2003 | — | PF63 625 | PF65 650 | | | |

**KM# 192 1000 NGULTRUM**
10.00 g., 0.999 Gold 0.3212 oz. AGW, 26 mm. **Ruler:** Jigme Singye Wangchuck **Subject:** World Fellowship of Buddhist Youth **Rev:** Lord Buddha, the Enlightenment

| Date | Mintage | VF20 | XF40 | MS60 | MS63 | MS65 |
|---|---|---|---|---|---|---|
| 2003 | Est. 2999 | PF63 625 | PF65 650 | | | |

**KM# 209 1000 NGULTRUM**
7.78 g., 0.999 Gold 0.2499 oz. AGW, 22 mm. **Ruler:** Jigme Khesar Namgyel Wangchuck **Subject:** Buddha's of the World - Cambodia **Rev:** Head from Angkor Wat

| Date | Mintage | VF20 | XF40 | MS60 | MS63 | MS65 |
|---|---|---|---|---|---|---|
| 2010 | Est. 6000 | PF63 500 | PF65 525 | | | |

**KM# 212 1000 NGULTRUM**
7.78 g., 0.999 Gold 0.2499 oz. AGW, 22 mm. **Ruler:** Jigme Khesar Namgyel Wangchuck **Subject:** Buddha's of the World - Korea **Rev:** Buddha seated

| Date | Mintage | VF20 | XF40 | MS60 | MS63 | MS65 |
|---|---|---|---|---|---|---|
| 2010 | Est. 6000 | PF63 500 | PF65 525 | | | |

**KM# 213 1000 NGULTRUM**
28.28 g., 0.925 Gold 0.841 oz. AGW, 38.61 mm. **Ruler:** Jigme Khesar Namgyel Wangchuck **Rev:** Charles Lindbergh and Spirit of St. Louis

| Date | Mintage | VF20 | XF40 | MS60 | MS63 | MS65 |
|---|---|---|---|---|---|---|
| 2010 | Est. 5000 | PF63 65.00 | PF65 70.00 | | | |

**KM# 218 1000 NGULTRUM**
7.78 g., 0.999 Gold 0.2499 oz. AGW, 22 mm. **Ruler:** Jigme Khesar Namgyel Wangchuck **Subject:** Buddhist World Heritage - Thailand **Rev:** Wat Pho

| Date | Mintage | VF20 | XF40 | MS60 | MS63 | MS65 |
|---|---|---|---|---|---|---|
| 2011 | — | PF63 500 | PF65 525 | | | |

**KM# 221 1000 NGULTRUM**
7.78 g., 0.999 Gold 0.2499 oz. AGW, 22 mm. **Ruler:** Jigme Khesar Namgyel Wangchuck **Subject:** Buddhist World Heritage - China **Rev:** Great Buddha in Leshan

| Date | Mintage | VF20 | XF40 | MS60 | MS63 | MS65 |
|---|---|---|---|---|---|---|
| 2011 | Est. 6000 | PF63 500 | PF65 525 | | | |

**KM# 235 1000 NGULTRUM**
7.78 g., 0.999 Gold 0.2499 oz. AGW, 22 mm. **Obv:** Knot **Rev:** Thousand arm Buddha

| Date | Mintage | VF20 | XF40 | MS60 | MS63 | MS65 |
|---|---|---|---|---|---|---|
| 2013 | — | PF65 525 | | | | |

**KM# 202 1500 NGULTRUM**
155.50 g., 0.999 Silver 4.9944 oz. ASW partially gilt, 65 mm. **Ruler:** Jigme Singye Wangchuck **Subject:** Wonders of the World - Angkor Wat **Rev:** Angkor Wat temple gilt

| Date | Mintage | VF20 | XF40 | MS60 | MS63 | MS65 |
|---|---|---|---|---|---|---|
| 2004 | — | PF65 250 | | | | |

**KM# 204 1500 NGULTRUM**
155.50 g., 0.999 Silver 4.9944 oz. ASW, 65 mm. **Ruler:** Jigme Singye Wangchuck **Subject:** Year of the Dog

| Date | Mintage | VF20 | XF40 | MS60 | MS63 | MS65 |
|---|---|---|---|---|---|---|
| 2006 | Est. 8888 | PF63 230 | PF65 250 | | | |

**KM# 167 2000 NGULTRUMS**
20.00 g., 0.999 Gold 0.6424 oz. AGW, 33 mm. **Ruler:** Jigme Singye Wangchuck **Subject:** Year of the Horse

| Date | Mintage | VF20 | XF40 | MS60 | MS63 | MS65 |
|---|---|---|---|---|---|---|
| 2002 | — | PF63 1,100 | PF65 1,250 | | | |

**KM# 171 2000 NGULTRUMS**
Bi-Metallic 31.105 g. .999 Silver and 7.78 g. .999 Gold **Ruler:** Jigme Singye Wangchuck **Subject:** Wonders of the World - Pyramids

| Date | Mintage | VF20 | XF40 | MS60 | MS63 | MS65 |
|---|---|---|---|---|---|---|
| 2002 | Est. 9999 | PF65 550 | | | | |

**KM# 193 2000 NGULTRUMS**
20.00 g., 0.999 Gold 0.6424 oz. AGW, 26 mm. **Ruler:** Jigme Singye Wangchuck **Subject:** World Fellowship of Buddhist Youth **Rev:** Lord Buddha, the Enlightenment

| Date | Mintage | VF20 | XF40 | MS60 | MS63 | MS65 |
|---|---|---|---|---|---|---|
| 2003 | — | PF63 1,100 | PF65 1,250 | | | |

**KM# 165 3000 NGULTRUM**
31.11 g., 0.999 Gold 0.999 oz. AGW, 38.61 mm. **Ruler:** Jigme Singye Wangchuck **Subject:** Year of the Snake

| Date | Mintage | VF20 | XF40 | MS60 | MS63 | MS65 |
|---|---|---|---|---|---|---|
| 2001 | Est. 18888 | PF63 1,600 | PF65 1,750 | | | |

**KM# 168 3000 NGULTRUM**
31.11 g., 0.999 Gold 0.999 oz. AGW, 38.61 mm. **Ruler:** Jigme Singye Wangchuck **Subject:** Year of the Horse

| Date | Mintage | VF20 | XF40 | MS60 | MS63 | MS65 |
|---|---|---|---|---|---|---|
| 2002 | Est. 18888 | PF63 1,600 | PF65 1,750 | | | |

**KM# 174 3000 NGULTRUM**
31.11 g., 0.999 Gold 0.999 oz. AGW, 38.61 mm. **Ruler:** Jigme Singye Wangchuck **Subject:** Wonders of the World - Taj Mahal

| Date | Mintage | VF20 | XF40 | MS60 | MS63 | MS65 |
|---|---|---|---|---|---|---|
| 2002 | Est. 18888 | PF63 1,600 | PF65 1,750 | | | |

**KM# 175 3000 NGULTRUM**
31.11 g., 0.999 Gold 0.999 oz. AGW, 38.61 mm. **Ruler:** Jigme Singye Wangchuck **Subject:** Royal Society for the Protection of Nature, 15th Anniversary **Rev:** Elephant head

| Date | Mintage | VF20 | XF40 | MS60 | MS63 | MS65 |
|---|---|---|---|---|---|---|
| 2002 | Est. 10000 | PF63 1,650 | PF65 1,800 | | | |

**KM# 176 3000 NGULTRUM**
31.11 g., 0.999 Gold 0.999 oz. AGW, 38.61 mm. **Ruler:** Jigme Singye Wangchuck **Subject:** Royal Society for the Protection of Nature, 15th Anniversary **Rev:** Two tigers

| Date | Mintage | VF20 | XF40 | MS60 | MS63 | MS65 |
|---|---|---|---|---|---|---|
| 2002 | Est. 10000 | PF63 1,650 | PF65 1,800 | | | |

**KM# 178 3000 NGULTRUM**
31.11 g., 0.999 Gold 0.999 oz. AGW, 38.61 mm. **Ruler:** Jigme Singye Wangchuck **Subject:** World Fellowship of Buddhist Youth

| Date | Mintage | VF20 | XF40 | MS60 | MS63 | MS65 |
|---|---|---|---|---|---|---|
| 2002 | Est. 10000 | PF63 1,650 | PF65 1,800 | | | |

**KM# 179 3000 NGULTRUM**
31.11 g., 0.999 Gold 0.999 oz. AGW, 38.61 mm. **Ruler:** Jigme Singye Wangchuck **Subject:** Year of the Goat **Rev:** Three rams

| Date | Mintage | VF20 | XF40 | MS60 | MS63 | MS65 |
|---|---|---|---|---|---|---|
| 2003 Proof | Est. 18888 | — | — | — | — | 1,800 |

**KM# 184 3000 NGULTRUM**
31.11 g., 0.999 Gold 0.999 oz. AGW, 38.61 mm. **Ruler:** Jigme Singye Wangchuck **Subject:** Legends of Sport - Rudy Hartono **Rev:** Bust at left, tennis serve at right

| Date | Mintage | VF20 | XF40 | MS60 | MS63 | MS65 |
|---|---|---|---|---|---|---|
| 2003 | Est. 10000 | PF63 1,650 | PF65 1,800 | | | |

**KM# 187 3000 NGULTRUM**
31.11 g., 0.999 Gold 0.999 oz. AGW, 38.61 mm. **Ruler:** Jigme Singye Wangchuck **Subject:** Wonders of the World - Borobudur Temple in Java

| Date | Mintage | VF20 | XF40 | MS60 | MS63 | MS65 |
|---|---|---|---|---|---|---|
| 2003 | Est. 30000 | PF63 1,600 | PF65 1,750 | | | |

**KM# 194 3000 NGULTRUM**
31.11 g., 0.999 Gold 0.999 oz. AGW, 38.61 mm. **Ruler:** Jigme Singye Wangchuck **Subject:** World Fellowship of Buddhist Youth **Rev:** Lord Buddha, the Enlightenment

| Date | Mintage | VF20 | XF40 | MS60 | MS63 | MS65 |
|---|---|---|---|---|---|---|
| 2003 | — | PF63 1,600 | PF65 1,750 | | | |

**KM# 166 20000 NGULTRUM**
155.52 g., 0.999 Gold 4.9951 oz. AGW, 65 mm. **Ruler:** Jigme Singye Wangchuck **Subject:** Year of the Snake

| Date | Mintage | VF20 | XF40 | MS60 | MS63 | MS65 |
|---|---|---|---|---|---|---|
| 2001 | — | PF65 9,000 | | | | |

**KM# 169 20000 NGULTRUM**
155.52 g., 0.999 Gold 4.9951 oz. AGW, 65 mm. **Ruler:** Jigme Singye Wangchuck **Subject:** Year of the Horse

| Date | Mintage | VF20 | XF40 | MS60 | MS63 | MS65 |
|---|---|---|---|---|---|---|
| 2002 | — | PF65 9,000 | | | | |

**KM# 180 20000 NGULTRUM**
155.52 g., 0.999 Gold 4.9951 oz. AGW, 65 mm. **Ruler:** Jigme Singye Wangchuck **Subject:** Year of the Goat **Rev:** Three rams

| Date | Mintage | VF20 | XF40 | MS60 | MS63 | MS65 |
|---|---|---|---|---|---|---|
| 2003 | Est. 88 | PF65 9,000 | | | | |

**KM# 188 30000 NGULTRUM**
155.52 g., 0.999 Gold 4.9951 oz. AGW, 65 mm. **Ruler:** Jigme Singye Wangchuck **Subject:** Wonders of the World - Borobudur Temple in Java

| Date | Mintage | VF20 | XF40 | MS60 | MS63 | MS65 |
|---|---|---|---|---|---|---|
| 2003 | — | PF65 9,000 | | | | |

**KM# 223 100000 NGULTRUM**
1000.00 g., 0.999 Silver 32.1186 oz. ASW, 100 mm. **Ruler:** Jigme Khesar Namgyel Wangchuck **Subject:** Royal Wedding **Rev:** Couple

| Date | Mintage | VF20 | XF40 | MS60 | MS63 | MS65 |
|---|---|---|---|---|---|---|
| 2011 | 2 | PF65 2,000 | | | | |

**KM# 225 5 SERTRUMS**
7.78 g., 0.585 Gold 0.1463 oz. AGW 24Kt plated, 25 mm. **Ruler:** Jigme Khesar Namgyel Wangchuck **Subject:** 2012 London Olympics - Archery **Rev:** Two archers and target

| Date | Mintage | VF20 | XF40 | MS60 | MS63 | MS65 |
|---|---|---|---|---|---|---|
| 2012 | 1,000 | PF65 325 | | | | |

**KM# 206 10 SERTUM**
31.11 g., 0.999 Gold 0.999 oz. AGW, 38.7 mm. **Ruler:** Jigme Khesar Namgyel Wangchuck **Subject:** Coronation

| Date | Mintage | VF20 | XF40 | MS60 | MS63 | MS65 |
|---|---|---|---|---|---|---|
| 2008 | 1,000 | PF65 1,800 | | | | |

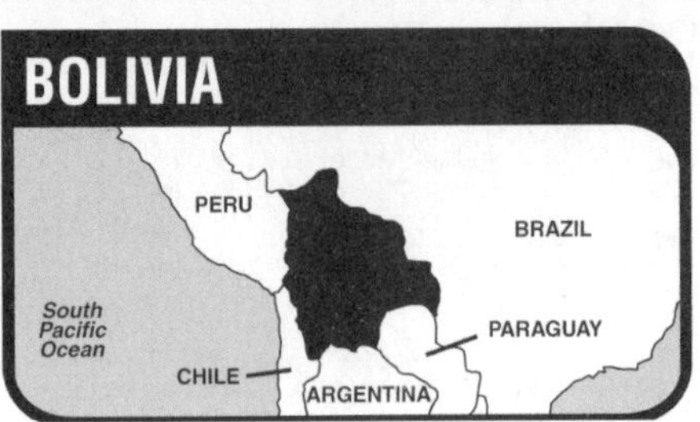


The Plurinational State of Bolivia, a landlocked country in west central South America, has an area of 424,165 sq. mi. (1,098,580 sq. km.) and a population of *8.33 million. Its capitals are: La Paz (administrative) and Sucre (constitutional). Principal exports are tin, zinc, antimony, tungsten, petroleum, natural gas, cotton and coffee.

**MINT MARK**

SA - Paris
(a) - Paris, privy marks only
CHI - Valcambia
H - Heaton
KN - Kings' Norton

# REPUBLIC

## REFORM COINAGE

1987-; 1,000,000 Peso Bolivianos = 1 Boliviano; 100 Centavos = 1 Boliviano

**KM# 202 10 CENTAVOS**
1.85 g., Stainless Steel, 19 mm. **Obv:** National arms, star below **Rev:** Denomination within circle, date below

| Date | Mintage | VF20 | XF40 | MS60 | MS63 | MS65 |
|---|---|---|---|---|---|---|
| 2006 | — | — | — | 0.20 | 0.50 | 0.70 |

**KM# 213 10 CENTAVOS**
1.85 g., Copper Clad Steel, 19 mm. **Obv:** National arms **Rev:** Value

| Date | Mintage | VF20 | XF40 | MS60 | MS63 | MS65 |
|---|---|---|---|---|---|---|
| 2001 | — | — | — | — | 0.50 | 1.00 |
| 2006 | — | — | — | — | 0.50 | 1.00 |
| 2008 | — | — | — | — | 0.50 | 1.00 |

Note: Slim and round "0" varieties in 10

**KM# 214 10 CENTAVOS**
1.85 g., Copper Plated Steel, 19 mm. **Obv:** National arms **Obv. Legend:** ESTADO PLURINACIONAL DE BOLIVIA **Rev:** Value

| Date | Mintage | VF20 | XF40 | MS60 | MS63 | MS65 |
|---|---|---|---|---|---|---|
| 2010 | — | — | — | — | 0.10 | 0.20 |

**KM# 203 20 CENTAVOS**
3.25 g., Stainless Steel, 22 mm. **Obv:** National arms, star below **Obv. Legend:** REPUBLICA DE BOLIVIA **Rev:** Denomination within circle, date below **Rev. Legend:** LA UNION ES LA FUERZA **Edge:** Plain

| Date | Mintage | VF20 | XF40 | MS60 | MS63 | MS65 |
|---|---|---|---|---|---|---|
| 2001 | — | — | — | 0.25 | 0.60 | 0.80 |
| 2006 | — | — | — | 0.25 | 0.60 | 0.80 |
| 2008 | — | — | — | 0.25 | 0.60 | 0.80 |

**KM# 215 20 CENTAVOS**
3.25 g., Stainless Steel, 22 mm. **Obv:** National arms **Obv. Legend:** ESTADO PLURINACIONAL DE BOLIVIA **Rev:** Value

| Date | Mintage | VF20 | XF40 | MS60 | MS63 | MS65 |
|---|---|---|---|---|---|---|
| 2010 | — | — | — | — | 0.15 | 0.25 |

**KM# 204 50 CENTAVOS**
3.75 g., Stainless Steel, 24 mm. **Obv:** National arms, star below **Obv. Legend:** REPUBLICA DE BOLIVIA **Rev:** Denomination within circle, date below **Rev. Legend:** LA UNION ES LA FUERZA **Edge:** Plain

| Date | Mintage | VF20 | XF40 | MS60 | MS63 | MS65 |
|---|---|---|---|---|---|---|
| 2001 | — | — | — | 0.30 | 0.75 | 1.00 |
| Note: Small and large 50 variety | | | | | | |
| 2006 | — | — | — | 0.30 | 0.75 | 1.00 |
| 2008 | — | — | — | 0.30 | 0.75 | 1.00 |

**KM# 216 50 CENTAVOS**
3.75 g., Stainless Steel, 24 mm. **Obv:** National arms **Obv. Legend:** ESTADO PLURINACIONAL DE BOLIVIA **Rev:** Value

| Date | Mintage | VF20 | XF40 | MS60 | MS63 | MS65 |
|---|---|---|---|---|---|---|
| 2010 | — | — | — | — | 0.50 | 1.00 |

**KM# 205 BOLIVIANO**
5.00 g., Stainless Steel, 27 mm. **Obv:** National arms, star below **Obv. Legend:** REPUBLICA DE BOLIVIA **Rev:** Denomination within circle, date below sprays **Rev. Legend:** LA UNION ES LA FUERZA **Edge:** Plain

| Date | Mintage | VF20 | XF40 | MS60 | MS63 | MS65 |
|---|---|---|---|---|---|---|
| 2001 | — | — | — | 0.35 | 0.90 | 1.20 |
| 2004 | — | — | — | 0.35 | 0.90 | 1.20 |
| 2008 | — | — | — | 0.35 | 0.90 | 1.20 |

**KM# 217 BOLIVIANO**
5.00 g., Stainless Steel, 27 mm. **Obv:** National arms **Obv. Legend:** ESTADO PLURINACIONAL DE BOLIVIA **Rev:** Value

| Date | Mintage | VF20 | XF40 | MS60 | MS63 | MS65 |
|---|---|---|---|---|---|---|
| 2010 | — | — | — | — | 1.50 | 2.00 |

**KM# 206.2 2 BOLIVIANOS**
6.25 g., Stainless Steel, 27 mm. **Obv:** National arms, star below **Rev:** Denomination within circle, date below **Note:** Increased size.

| Date | Mintage | VF20 | XF40 | MS60 | MS63 | MS65 |
|---|---|---|---|---|---|---|
| 2008 | — | — | — | — | 2.00 | 3.00 |

**KM# 218 2 BOLIVIANOS**
6.25 g., Stainless Steel, 27 mm. **Obv:** National arms **Obv. Legend:** ESTADO PLURINACIONAL DE BOLIVIA **Rev:** Value

| Date | Mintage | VF20 | XF40 | MS60 | MS63 | MS65 |
|---|---|---|---|---|---|---|
| 2010 | — | — | — | — | 1.50 | 2.00 |
| 2012 | — | — | — | — | 1.50 | 2.00 |

**KM# 212 5 BOLIVIANOS**
5.00 g., Bi-Metallic Bronze Plated Steel center in Stainless Steel ring, 23 mm. **Obv:** National arms **Obv. Legend:** REPUBLICA DE BOLIVIA **Rev:** Denomination **Rev. Legend:** LA UNION ES LA FUERZA **Edge:** Reeded

| Date | Mintage | VF20 | XF40 | MS60 | MS63 | MS65 |
|---|---|---|---|---|---|---|
| 2001 | — | — | — | 1.00 | 2.25 | 3.00 |
| 2004 | — | — | — | 1.00 | 2.25 | 3.00 |

**KM# 219 5 BOLIVIANOS**
5.00 g., Bi-Metallic Bronze Plated Steel center in Stainless Steel ring, 23 mm. **Obv:** National arms **Obv. Legend:** ESTADO PLURINACIONAL DE BOLIVIA **Rev:** Value **Edge:** Reeded

| Date | Mintage | VF20 | XF40 | MS60 | MS63 | MS65 |
|---|---|---|---|---|---|---|
| 2010 | — | — | — | — | 4.00 | 5.00 |

# BOSNIA - HERZEGOVINA

The Republic of Bosnia and Herzegovina borders Croatia to the north and west, Serbia to the east and Montenegro in the southeast with only 12.4 mi. of coastline. The total land area is 19,735 sq. mi. (51,129 sq. km.). They have a population of *4.34 million. Capital: Sarajevo. Electricity, mining and agriculture are leading industries.

**MONETARY SYSTEM**
1 Dinara = 100 Para, 1992-1998
1 Convertible Marka = 100 Convertible Feniga = 1 Deutschemark 1998-
**NOTE**: German Euros circulate freely.

## REPUBLIC

### REFORM COINAGE

1998-

**KM# 121 5 FENINGA**
2.66 g., Nickel Plated Steel, 18 mm. **Obv:** Denomination on map **Rev:** Triangle and stars **Edge:** Reeded

| Date | Mintage | VF20 | XF40 | MS60 | MS63 | MS65 |
|---|---|---|---|---|---|---|
| 2005 | 20,000,000 | — | — | 0.50 | 1.00 | 0.75 |
| 2008 | 10,000,000 | — | — | 0.50 | 1.00 | 0.75 |
| 2011 | 10,000,000 | — | — | 0.50 | 1.00 | 0.75 |
| 2013 | 25,000,000 | — | — | 0.50 | 1.00 | 0.75 |

**KM# 115 10 FENINGA**
3.90 g., Copper Plated Steel, 20 mm. **Obv:** Denomination on map within circle **Rev:** Triangle and stars, date at left within circle **Edge:** Plain

| Date | Mintage | VF20 | XF40 | MS60 | MS63 | MS65 |
|---|---|---|---|---|---|---|
| 2004 | 10,000,000 | — | — | 0.25 | 0.50 | 0.75 |
| 2007 | 10,000,000 | — | — | 0.25 | 0.50 | 0.75 |
| 2008 | 10,000,000 | — | — | 0.25 | 0.50 | 0.75 |
| 2011 | 10,000,000 | — | — | 0.25 | 0.50 | 0.75 |
| 2013 | 25,000,000 | — | — | 0.25 | 0.50 | 0.75 |

**KM# 116 20 FENINGA**
4.50 g., Copper Plated Steel, 22 mm. **Obv:** Denomination on map within circle **Rev:** Triangle and stars, date at left within circle **Edge:** Reeded

| Date | Mintage | VF20 | XF40 | MS60 | MS63 | MS65 |
|---|---|---|---|---|---|---|
| 2004 | 10,000,000 | — | — | 0.75 | 1.00 | 1.25 |
| 2007 | 10,000,000 | — | — | 0.75 | 1.00 | 1.25 |
| 2008 | 5,000,000 | — | — | 0.75 | 1.00 | 1.25 |
| 2009 | 5,000,000 | — | — | 0.75 | 1.00 | 1.25 |
| 2013 | 20,000,000 | — | — | 0.50 | 1.00 | 1.25 |

**KM# 117 50 FENINGA**
5.15 g., Copper Plated Steel, 24 mm. **Obv:** Denomination on map within circle **Rev:** Triangle and stars, date at left within circle

| Date | Mintage | VF20 | XF40 | MS60 | MS63 | MS65 |
|---|---|---|---|---|---|---|
| 2007 | 10,000,000 | — | — | — | — | 3.00 |
| 2013 | 3,000,000 Confirmation | | | | | |
| Note: Requires Confirmation | | | | | | |

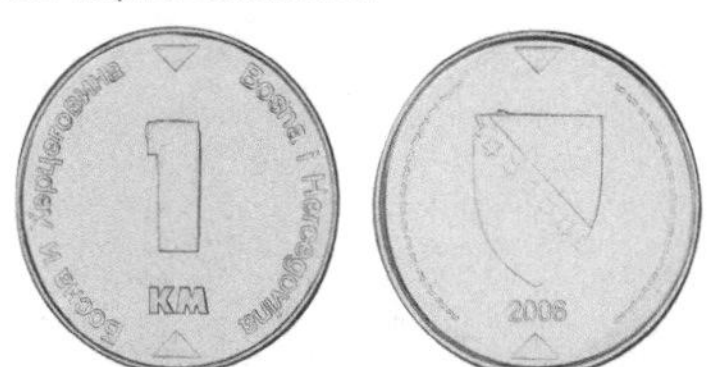

**KM# 118 KONVERTIBLE MARKA**
4.95 g., Nickel Plated Steel, 23.23 mm. **Obv:** Denomination **Rev:** Coat of arms above date **Edge:** Segmented reeding

| Date | Mintage | VF20 | XF40 | MS60 | MS63 | MS65 |
|---|---|---|---|---|---|---|
| 2002 | 7,000,000 | — | — | 2.50 | 4.00 | 6.00 |
| 2005 | 5,000,000 | — | — | 2.75 | 5.50 | 6.00 |
| Note: Requires Confirmation | | | | | | |
| 2006 | 5,000,000 | — | — | 2.00 | 4.00 | 5.00 |
| 2007 | 5,551,000 | — | — | 2.00 | 4.00 | 5.00 |
| 2008 | 5,000,000 | — | — | 2.00 | 4.00 | 5.00 |
| 2009 | 5,000,000 | — | — | 2.00 | 4.00 | 5.00 |
| 2013 | 3,000,000 | | | | | |
| Note: Requires Confirmation | | | | | | |

### KM# 119 2 KONVERTIBLE MARKA

6.90 g., Bi-Metallic Copper-Nickel center in Nickel-Brass ring, 25.75 mm. **Obv:** Denomination within circle **Rev:** Dove of Peace, date at right within circle **Edge:** Segmented reeding

| Date | Mintage | VF20 | XF40 | MS60 | MS63 | MS65 |
|---|---|---|---|---|---|---|
| 2003 | 5,060,000 | — | — | — | 3.50 | 5.00 |
| 2008 | 5,000,000 | — | — | — | 3.50 | 5.00 |

### KM# 120 5 KONVERTIBLE MARKA

10.35 g., Bi-Metallic Nickel-Brass center in Copper-Nickel ring, 30 mm. **Obv:** Denomination within circle **Rev:** Dove of Peace in flight **Edge:** Reeded

| Date | Mintage | VF20 | XF40 | MS60 | MS63 | MS65 |
|---|---|---|---|---|---|---|
| 2005 | 5,000,000 | — | — | 2.00 | 7.50 | 10.00 |
| 2009 | 10,000,000 | — | — | 2.00 | 7.50 | 10.00 |

# BOTSWANA

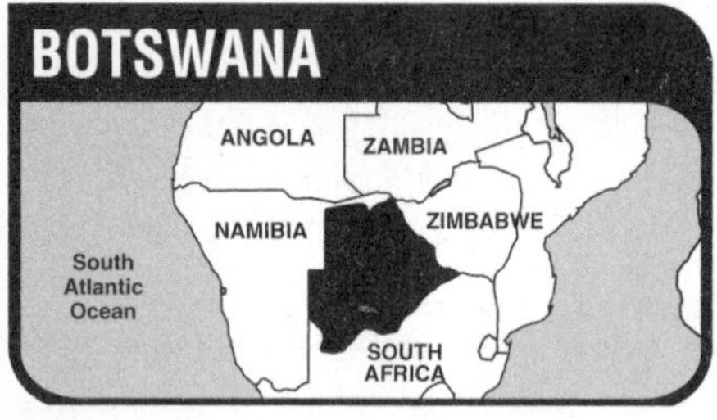


The Republic of Botswana (formerly Bechuanaland), located in south central Africa between Namibia and Zimbabwe, has an area of 224,607 sq. mi. (600,370 sq. km.) and a population of *1.62 million. Capital: Gaborone. Botswana is a member of a Customs Union with South Africa, Lesotho, and Swaziland. The economy is primarily pastoral with a rapidly developing mining industry, of which diamonds, copper and nickel are the chief elements. Meat products and diamonds comprise 85 percent of the exports.

Botswana is a member of the Commonwealth of Nations. The president is Chief of State and Head of government.

**MINT MARK**

B - Berne

**MONETARY SYSTEM**

100 Cents = 1 Thebe

## REPUBLIC

## REFORM COINAGE

100 Thebe = 1 Pula

### KM# 26 5 THEBE

2.41 g., Copper Plated Steel, 16.9 mm. **Obv:** National arms, date below **Rev:** Toko bird left, value above **Edge:** Plain **Shape:** 7-sided

| Date | Mintage | VF20 | XF40 | MS60 | MS63 | MS65 |
|---|---|---|---|---|---|---|
| 2002 | — | — | — | 0.25 | 0.50 | 1.00 |
| 2007 | — | — | — | 0.25 | 0.50 | 1.00 |
| 2009 | — | — | — | 0.25 | 0.50 | 1.00 |

### KM# 31 5 THEBE

Nickel Plated Steel, 18 mm. **Obv:** National arms **Rev:** Hornbill and value **Shape:** 7-sided

| Date | Mintage | VF20 | XF40 | MS60 | MS63 | MS65 |
|---|---|---|---|---|---|---|
| 2013 | — | — | — | 0.25 | 0.50 | 1.00 |

### KM# 27 10 THEBE

2.80 g., Nickel Plated Steel, 18 mm. **Obv:** National arms above date **Rev:** South African Oryx right, value above

| Date | Mintage | VF20 | XF40 | MS60 | MS63 | MS65 |
|---|---|---|---|---|---|---|
| 2002 | — | — | — | 0.35 | 0.75 | 1.25 |
| 2008 | — | — | — | 0.35 | 0.75 | 1.25 |

### KM# 32 10 THEBE

Nickel Plated Steel, 20 mm. **Obv:** National arms **Rev:** Gernnbok and value

| Date | Mintage | VF20 | XF40 | MS60 | MS63 | MS65 |
|---|---|---|---|---|---|---|
| 2013 | — | — | — | 0.35 | 0.75 | 1.25 |

### KM# 28 25 THEBE

3.50 g., Nickel Plated Steel, 21 mm. **Obv:** National arms, date below **Rev:** Zebu left, value above **Shape:** 7-sided

| Date | Mintage | VF20 | XF40 | MS60 | MS63 | MS65 |
|---|---|---|---|---|---|---|
| 2007 | — | — | 0.30 | 0.60 | 1.50 | 2.00 |
| 2009 | — | — | 0.30 | 0.60 | 1.50 | 2.00 |

### KM# 33 25 THEBE

Nickel Plated Steel, 22 mm. **Obv:** National arms **Rev:** Brahman bull and value **Shape:** 7-sided

| Date | Mintage | VF20 | XF40 | MS60 | MS63 | MS65 |
|---|---|---|---|---|---|---|
| 2013 | — | — | — | 1.00 | 1.50 | 2.00 |

### KM# 29 50 THEBE

4.82 g., Nickel Plated Steel, 21.5 mm. **Obv:** National arms, date below **Rev:** African Fish Eagle left, value above

| Date | Mintage | VF20 | XF40 | MS60 | MS63 | MS65 |
|---|---|---|---|---|---|---|
| 2001 | — | — | 0.50 | 1.00 | 2.00 | 2.50 |

### KM# 34 50 THEBE

Nickel Plated Steel, 24 mm. **Obv:** National arms **Rev:** Fish Eagle and value

| Date | Mintage | VF20 | XF40 | MS60 | MS63 | MS65 |
|---|---|---|---|---|---|---|
| 2013 | — | — | — | 1.50 | 2.00 | 2.50 |

### KM# 24 PULA

8.70 g., Nickel-Brass, 23.5 mm. **Obv:** National arms, date below **Rev:** Zebra left, denomination above **Shape:** 7-sided

| Date | Mintage | VF20 | XF40 | MS60 | MS63 | MS65 |
|---|---|---|---|---|---|---|
| 2007 | — | — | 1.00 | 1.75 | 3.50 | 6.00 |

### KM# 35 PULA

Brass Plated Steel, 26 mm. **Obv:** National arms **Rev:** Zebra and value

| Date | Mintage | VF20 | XF40 | MS60 | MS63 | MS65 |
|---|---|---|---|---|---|---|
| 2013 | — | — | — | 2.25 | 2.75 | 3.50 |

### KM# 25a 2 PULA

6.00 g., Brass Plated Steel, 24.5 mm. **Subject:** Wildlife **Obv:** National arms, date below **Rev:** Rhinoceros left, denomination above **Shape:** 7-sided

| Date | Mintage | VF20 | XF40 | MS60 | MS63 | MS65 |
|---|---|---|---|---|---|---|
| 2004 | — | — | — | 2.25 | 2.75 | 3.50 |

### KM# 36 2 PULA

Bi-Metallic Nickel plated steel center in Brass plated steel ring, 27 mm. **Obv:** National arms **Rev:** Square lipped rhino and value

| Date | Mintage | VF20 | XF40 | MS60 | MS63 | MS65 |
|---|---|---|---|---|---|---|
| 2013 | — | — | — | 2.75 | 3.50 | 6.00 |

### KM# 30 5 PULA

6.20 g., Bi-Metallic Copper-Nickel center in Brass ring, 23.4 mm. **Obv:** National arms, date below **Rev:** Mophane worm on a mophane leaf, denomination below within circle **Edge:** Reeded

| Date | Mintage | VF20 | XF40 | MS60 | MS63 | MS65 |
|---|---|---|---|---|---|---|
| 2007 | — | — | — | — | 6.50 | 10.00 |

### KM# 37 5 PULA

Bi-Metallic, 28 mm. **Obv:** National arms **Rev:** Phane worm on maphane tree branch and value

| Date | Mintage | VF20 | XF40 | MS60 | MS63 | MS65 |
|---|---|---|---|---|---|---|
| 2013 | — | — | — | — | 6.50 | 10.00 |

The Federative Republic of Brazil, which comprises half the continent of South America and is the only Latin American country deriving its culture and language from Portugal, has an area of 3,286,488 sq. mi. (8,511,965 sq. km.) and a population of *169.2 million. Capital: Brasilia. The economy of Brazil is as varied and complex as any in the developing world. Agriculture is a mainstay of the economy, while only 4 percent of the area is under cultivation. Known mineral resources are almost unlimited in variety and size of reserves. A large, relatively sophisticated industry ranges from basic steel and chemical production to finished consumer goods. Coffee, cotton, iron ore and cocoa are the chief exports.

**MINT MARKS**
(a) - Paris, privy marks only
B - Bahia

# REPUBLIC

## REFORM COINAGE

2750 Cruzeiros Reais = 1 Real;
100 Centavos = 1 Real
1994-present

### KM# 685 10 REIS

Gold AGW, 16 mm. **Subject:** 2016 Rio Olympics **Obv:** Rio's Christ statue **Rev:** Runner left

| Date | Mintage | VF20 | XF40 | MS60 | MS63 | MS65 |
|---|---|---|---|---|---|---|
| 2014 | — | PF65 150 | | | | |

### KM# 647 CENTAVO

2.43 g., Copper Plated Steel, 17 mm. **Obv:** Cabral bust at right **Rev:** Denomination on linear design at left, 3/4 globe with sash on right, date below **Edge:** Plain

| Date | Mintage | VF20 | XF40 | MS60 | MS63 | MS65 |
|---|---|---|---|---|---|---|
| 2001 | 242,924,000 | — | — | — | 0.10 | 0.20 |
| 2002 | 161,824,000 | — | — | — | 0.10 | 0.20 |
| 2003 | 250,000,000 | — | — | — | 0.10 | 0.20 |
| 2004 | 167,232,000 | — | — | — | 0.10 | 0.20 |

### KM# 648 5 CENTAVOS

4.10 g., Copper Plated Steel, 22 mm. **Obv:** Tiradente bust at right, dove at left **Rev:** Denomination on linear design at left, 3/4 globe with sash on right, date below **Edge:** Plain

| Date | Mintage | VF20 | XF40 | MS60 | MS63 | MS65 |
|---|---|---|---|---|---|---|
| 2001 | 175,940,000 | — | — | 0.25 | 0.45 | 0.65 |
| 2002 | 153,088,000 | — | — | 0.25 | 0.45 | 0.65 |
| 2003 | 260,000,000 | — | — | 0.25 | 0.45 | 0.65 |
| 2004 | 262,656,000 | — | — | 0.25 | 0.45 | 0.65 |
| 2005 | 230,144,000 | — | — | 0.25 | 0.45 | 0.65 |
| 2006 | 255,488,000 | — | — | 0.25 | 0.45 | 0.65 |
| 2007 | 403,968,000 | — | — | 0.25 | 0.45 | 0.65 |
| 2008 | 28,672,000 | — | — | 0.25 | 0.45 | 0.65 |
| 2009 | 400,128,000 | — | — | 0.20 | 0.30 | 0.50 |
| 2010 | 550,144,000 | — | — | 0.20 | 0.30 | 0.50 |
| 2011 | 437,504,000 | — | — | 0.20 | 0.30 | 0.50 |
| 2012 | 400,128,000 | — | — | 0.20 | 0.30 | 0.50 |
| 2013 | — | — | — | 0.20 | 0.30 | 0.50 |

### KM# 649.2 10 CENTAVOS

4.80 g., Bronze Plated Steel, 20 mm. **Obv:** Bust of Pedro at right, horseman with sword in right hand at left **Rev:** Denomination on linear design at left, 3/4 globe with sash on right, date below **Edge:** Reeded

| Date | Mintage | VF20 | XF40 | MS60 | MS63 | MS65 |
|---|---|---|---|---|---|---|
| 2001 | 134,701,000 | — | — | 0.30 | 0.60 | 0.80 |
| 2002 | 172,032,000 | — | — | 0.30 | 0.60 | 0.80 |
| 2003 | 252,666,000 | — | — | 0.30 | 0.60 | 0.80 |
| 2004 | 348,480,000 | — | — | 0.30 | 0.60 | 0.80 |
| 2005 | 362,112,000 | — | — | 0.30 | 0.60 | 0.80 |
| 2006 | 265,728,000 | — | — | 0.30 | 0.60 | 0.80 |
| 2007 | 316,800,000 | — | — | 0.30 | 0.60 | 0.80 |
| 2008 | 534,412,000 | — | — | 0.25 | 0.50 | 0.75 |
| 2009 | 205,748,000 | — | — | 0.25 | 0.50 | 0.75 |
| 2010 | 520,128,000 | — | — | 0.25 | 0.50 | 0.75 |
| 2011 | 415,104,000 | — | — | 0.25 | 0.50 | 0.75 |
| 2012 | 454,464,000 | — | — | 0.25 | 0.50 | 0.75 |
| 2013 | 380,352,000 | — | — | 0.25 | 0.50 | 0.75 |

### KM# 650 25 CENTAVOS

7.55 g., Bronze Plated Steel, 25 mm. **Obv:** Deodoro bust at right, national arms at left **Rev:** Denomination on linear design at left, 3/4 globe with sash on right, date below **Edge:** Reeded

| Date | Mintage | VF20 | XF40 | MS60 | MS63 | MS65 |
|---|---|---|---|---|---|---|
| 2001 | 92,642,000 | — | — | 0.35 | 0.75 | 1.00 |
| 2002 | 100,096,000 | — | — | 0.35 | 0.75 | 1.00 |
| 2003 | 147,200,000 | — | — | 0.35 | 0.75 | 1.00 |
| 2004 | 160,000,000 | — | — | 0.35 | 0.75 | 1.00 |
| 2005 | 100,096,000 | — | — | 0.35 | 0.75 | 1.00 |
| 2006 | 110,720,000 | — | — | 0.35 | 0.75 | 1.00 |
| 2007 | 118,784,000 | — | — | 0.35 | 0.75 | 1.00 |
| 2008 | 269,031,000 | — | — | 0.30 | 0.60 | 0.75 |
| 2009 | 200,985,000 | — | — | 0.30 | 0.60 | 0.75 |
| 2010 | 240,000,000 | — | — | 0.30 | 0.60 | 0.75 |
| 2011 | 142,592,000 | — | — | 0.30 | 0.60 | 0.75 |
| 2012 | 100,096,000 | — | — | 0.30 | 0.60 | 0.75 |
| 2013 | 190,976,000 | — | — | 0.30 | 0.60 | 0.75 |

### KM# 651 50 CENTAVOS

9.25 g., Copper-Nickel, 23 mm. **Obv:** Rio Branco bust at right, map at left **Rev:** Denomination on linear design at left, 3/4 globe with sash on right, date below **Edge Lettering:** BRASIL ORDEM E PROGRESSO

| Date | Mintage | VF20 | XF40 | MS60 | MS63 | MS65 |
|---|---|---|---|---|---|---|
| 2001 | 14,735,000 | — | — | 0.75 | 1.50 | 1.75 |

### KM# 651a 50 CENTAVOS

6.80 g., Stainless Steel, 23 mm. **Obv:** Rio Branco bust at right, map at left **Rev:** Denomination on linear design at left, 3/4 globe with sash on right, date below **Edge Lettering:** BRASIL ORDEM E PROGRESSO

| Date | Mintage | VF20 | XF40 | MS60 | MS63 | MS65 |
|---|---|---|---|---|---|---|
| 2002 | 189,952,000 | — | — | 0.65 | 1.25 | 1.50 |
| 2003 | 143,696,000 | — | — | 0.65 | 1.25 | 1.50 |
| 2005 | 122,416,000 | — | — | 0.65 | 1.25 | 1.50 |
| 2006 | 39,984,000 | — | — | 0.65 | 1.25 | 1.50 |
| 2007 | 130,032,000 | — | — | 0.65 | 1.25 | 1.50 |
| 2008 | 290,080,000 | — | — | 0.65 | 1.25 | 1.50 |
| 2009 | 300,048,000 | — | — | 0.65 | 1.25 | 1.50 |
| 2010 | 170,016,000 | — | — | 0.65 | 1.25 | 1.50 |
| 2011 | 116,928,000 | — | — | 0.65 | 1.25 | 1.50 |
| 2012 | 100,016,000 | — | — | 0.65 | 1.25 | 1.50 |
| 2013 | 259,728,000 | — | — | 0.65 | 1.25 | 1.50 |

### KM# 683 50 CENTAVOS

6.80 g., Stainless Steel, 23 mm. **Obv:** Rio Branco bust at right, map at left **Rev:** Denomination on linear design at left, 3/4 globe with sash on right, date below **Edge Lettering:** BRASIL ORDEM E PROGRESSO **Note:** Mule with the reverse for the 5 centavos coin on the 50 centavos planchet.

| Date | Mintage | VF20 | XF40 | MS60 | MS63 | MS65 |
|---|---|---|---|---|---|---|
| 2012 | — | — | — | — | 250 | — |

### KM# 652a REAL

7.00 g., Bi-Metallic Stainless Steel center in Bronze Plated Steel ring, 27 mm. **Obv:** Allegorical portrait **Rev:** Denomination on linear design at left, 3/4 globe with sash on right, date below **Edge:** Segmented reeding

| Date | Mintage | VF20 | XF40 | MS60 | MS63 | MS65 |
|---|---|---|---|---|---|---|
| 2002 | 54,192,000 | — | — | 0.75 | 1.50 | 2.00 |
| 2003 | 100,000,000 | — | — | 0.75 | 1.50 | 2.00 |
| 2004 | 150,016,000 | — | — | 0.75 | 1.50 | 2.00 |
| 2005 | 43,776,000 | — | — | 0.75 | 1.50 | 2.00 |
| 2006 | 179,968,000 | — | — | 0.50 | 1.00 | 1.25 |
| 2007 | 275,712,000 | — | — | 0.50 | 1.00 | 1.25 |
| 2008 | 664,833,000 | — | — | 0.50 | 1.00 | 1.25 |
| 2009 | 245,247,000 | — | — | 0.45 | 0.75 | 1.00 |
| 2010 | 220,032,000 | — | — | 0.45 | 0.75 | 1.00 |
| 2011 | 140,032,000 | — | — | 0.45 | 0.75 | 1.00 |
| 2012 | 150,016,000 | — | — | 0.45 | 0.75 | 1.00 |
| 2013 | 263,936,000 | — | — | 0.45 | 0.75 | 1.00 |
| 2014 | 150,016,000 | — | — | 0.45 | 0.75 | 1.00 |

### KM# 656 REAL

7.00 g., Bi-Metallic Stainless Steel center in Bronze Plated Steel ring, 27 mm. **Subject:** Centennial of Juscelino Kubitschek, president **Obv:** Head left **Rev:** Denomination on linear design at left, 3/4 globe with sash on right, date below **Edge:** Segmented reeding

| Date | Mintage | VF20 | XF40 | MS60 | MS63 | MS65 |
|---|---|---|---|---|---|---|
| 2002 | 50,000,000 | — | — | 1.00 | 1.75 | 2.25 |

### KM# 668 REAL

7.00 g., Bi-Metallic Stainless Steel center in Bronze Plated Steel ring, 27 mm. **Subject:** 40th Anniversary of Central Bank **Obv:** Monument **Rev:** Value on flag **Edge:** Segmented reeding

| Date | Mintage | VF20 | XF40 | MS60 | MS63 | MS65 |
|---|---|---|---|---|---|---|
| 2005 | 40,000,000 | — | — | 1.25 | 2.50 | 3.25 |

### KM# 679 REAL

7.00 g., Bi-Metallic Stainless Steel center in Bronze Plated Steel ring, 27 mm. **Subject:** Olympic Flag Delivery London 2012 - Rio 2016 **Obv:** Monument **Obv. Legend:** ENTREGA DA BANDEIRA OLIMPICA, LONDRES 2012 - RIO 2016 **Rev:** Value on flag **Edge:** Segmented Reeding

| Date | Mintage | VF20 | XF40 | MS60 | MS63 | MS65 |
|---|---|---|---|---|---|---|
| 2012 | 1,952,000 | — | — | 1.25 | 2.50 | 3.25 |

**KM# 657 2 REAIS**

28.00 g., 0.999 Silver 0.8993 oz. ASW, 40 mm. **Subject:** Centennial - Carlos Drummond de Andrade **Obv:** Denomination and writer **Rev:** Stylized portrait **Edge:** Reeded

| Date | Mintage | VF20 | XF40 | MS60 | MS63 | MS65 |
|---|---|---|---|---|---|---|
| ND(2002) | 4,693 | PF63 65.00 | PF65 75.00 | | | |

**KM# 658 2 REAIS**

28.00 g., 0.999 Silver 0.8993 oz. ASW, 40 mm. **Subject:** Centennial - Juscelino Kubitschek **Obv:** Bust facing in upper right, initials at left **Rev:** Denomination **Edge:** Reeded

| Date | Mintage | VF20 | XF40 | MS60 | MS63 | MS65 |
|---|---|---|---|---|---|---|
| 2002 | 8,476 | PF63 55.00 | PF65 65.00 | | | |

**KM# 663 2 REAIS**

27.00 g., 0.925 Silver 0.803 oz. ASW, 40 mm. **Obv:** Value and piano player **Rev:** Ary Barroso singing **Edge:** Reeded

| Date | Mintage | VF20 | XF40 | MS60 | MS63 | MS65 |
|---|---|---|---|---|---|---|
| 2003 | 3,663 | PF63 55.00 | PF65 65.00 | | | |

**KM# 665 2 REAIS**

27.00 g., 0.925 Silver 0.803 oz. ASW, 40 mm. **Subject:** Centennial - Cándido Con Portinari **Obv:** Starving family scene, value and country name **Rev:** Portinari's portrait, stars in squares design **Edge:** Reeded

| Date | Mintage | VF20 | XF40 | MS60 | MS63 | MS65 |
|---|---|---|---|---|---|---|
| ND(2003) | 2,000 | PF63 325 | PF65 350 | | | |

**KM# 666 2 REAIS**

27.00 g., 0.925 Silver 0.803 oz. ASW, 40 mm. **Subject:** FIFA Centennial **Obv:** Soccer ball and value **Rev:** Center part of a Brazilian flag and stars **Edge:** Reeded

| Date | Mintage | VF20 | XF40 | MS60 | MS63 | MS65 |
|---|---|---|---|---|---|---|
| 2004 | 12,166 | PF63 150 | PF65 175 | | | |

**KM# 671 2 REAIS**

27.00 g., 0.925 Silver 0.803 oz. ASW, 40 mm. **Subject:** Centennial of Flight 14 bis **Obv:** Image of 14 Bis **Obv. Legend:** Centenario Do Voo Do 14 Bis Brasil 1906-2006 **Rev:** Image and signature of Santos Dumont and value **Edge:** Reeded

| Date | Mintage | VF20 | XF40 | MS60 | MS63 | MS65 |
|---|---|---|---|---|---|---|
| 2006 | 4,000 | PF63 95.00 | PF65 110 | | | |

**KM# 672 2 REAIS**

10.17 g., Copper-Nickel, 30 mm. **Subject:** Pan-American Games XV **Obv:** Official logo of Pan-American Games XV **Rev:** Image of running athlete, XV Jogos Pan-Americanos, value, Brasil and date. **Edge:** Reeded

| Date | Mintage | VF20 | XF40 | MS60 | MS63 | MS65 |
|---|---|---|---|---|---|---|
| 2007 | 10,000 | — | — | — | — | 12.00 |

**KM# 675 2 REAIS**

10.17 g., Copper-Nickel, 30 mm. **Subject:** Japanese immigration to Brazil, 100th Anniversary **Obv:** Farmer and persimmon crop **Rev:** Ship "Kasato Maru **Edge:** Reeded

| Date | Mintage | VF20 | XF40 | MS60 | MS63 | MS65 |
|---|---|---|---|---|---|---|
| 2008 | 10,000 | — | — | — | — | 16.00 |

**KM# 661 5 REAIS**

28.00 g., 0.999 Silver 0.8993 oz. ASW, 40 mm. **Subject:** Brazil's 5th World Cup Championship **Obv:** Soccer player and Brazilian flag **Rev:** Soccer ball and value **Edge:** Reeded

| Date | Mintage | VF20 | XF40 | MS60 | MS63 | MS65 |
|---|---|---|---|---|---|---|
| 2002 | 10,149 | PF63 60.00 | PF65 65.00 | | | |

**KM# 673 5 REAIS**

27.00 g., 0.925 Silver 0.803 oz. ASW, 40 mm. **Subject:** Pan-American Games XV **Obv:** Official logo of Pan-American Games XV **Rev:** Sugar Loaf, lines of Copacabana sidewalk, "XV Jogos Pan-Americanos", value, Brasil and date. **Edge:** Reeded

| Date | Mintage | VF20 | XF40 | MS60 | MS63 | MS65 |
|---|---|---|---|---|---|---|
| 2007 | 4,000 | PF63 60.00 | PF65 70.00 | | | |

**KM# 674 5 REAIS**

27.00 g., 0.925 Silver 0.803 oz. ASW, 40 mm. **Subject:** Royal Family's arrival in Brazil, 200th Anniversary **Obv:** Ship "Martim de Freitas **Rev:** Names and dates of institutions created by Dom John **Edge:** Reeded

| Date | Mintage | VF20 | XF40 | MS60 | MS63 | MS65 |
|---|---|---|---|---|---|---|
| 2008 | 2,000 | PF63 275 | PF65 300 | | | |

**KM# 676 5 REAIS**

27.00 g., 0.925 Silver 0.803 oz. ASW, 40 mm. **Subject:** World Heritage Sites, Brasilia, 50th Anniversary **Obv:** Schematic city plan **Rev:** Brasilia's architecture montage: Congress, Cathedral, Presidential palace and Warriors sculpture **Edge:** Reeded

| Date | Mintage | VF20 | XF40 | MS60 | MS63 | MS65 |
|---|---|---|---|---|---|---|
| 2010 | 6,000 | PF63 95.00 | PF65 110 | | | |

**KM# 677 5 REAIS**

27.00 g., 0.925 Silver 0.803 oz. ASW, 40 mm. **Subject:** 2010 World Cup, South Africa **Obv:** Two players with scoccer ball, Brazil flag in background **Rev:** Map of Africa, South african savannah, soccer player at left **Edge:** Reeded

| Date | Mintage | VF20 | XF40 | MS60 | MS63 | MS65 |
|---|---|---|---|---|---|---|
| 2010 | 9,000 | PF63 85.00 | PF65 110 | | | |

**KM# 678 5 REAIS**

27.00 g., 0.925 Silver 0.803 oz. ASW, 40 mm. **Subject:** UNESCO World Heritage site. 300th Anniversary of the Foundling of the Pilar Vila Rica of Ouro Preto **Obv:** Houses and churches representing the city's architecture **Rev:** Three angels and baroque scrolls **Rev. Legend:** PATRIMONIO DA HUMANIDADE • UNESCO OURO PRETO and BRAZIL **Edge:** Reeded

| Date | Mintage | VF20 | XF40 | MS60 | MS63 | MS65 |
|---|---|---|---|---|---|---|
| 2011 | 2,000 | PF65 150 | | | | |

**KM# 680 5 REAIS**

27.00 g., 0.925 Silver 0.803 oz. ASW, 40 mm. **Subject:** Delivery of Olympic Flag London 2012 - Rio 2016 **Obv:** Olympic flag, logo of 2016 Rio de Janeiro Olympic games, legend, date **Obv. Legend:** ENTREGA DA BANDEIRA OLIMPICA **Rev:** Illustration illuding to London's Tower Bridge, Rio de Janeiro's Christ the Redeemer statue, legend, denomination, country name **Rev. Legend:** LONDRES 2012 - RIO 2016 **Edge:** Reeded

| Date | Mintage | VF20 | XF40 | MS60 | MS63 | MS65 |
|---|---|---|---|---|---|---|
| 2012 | 6,000 | PF63 95.00 | PF65 110 | | | |

**KM# 681 5 REAIS**

27.00 g., 0.925 Silver 0.803 oz. ASW, 40 mm. **Subject:** International Year of Cooperatives **Obv:** Official logo of International Year of Cooperatives, legend, date **Obv. Legend:** ANO INTERNACTIONAL DAS COOPERATIVAS **Rev:** Globe supported by three pairs of hands, legend, denomination, country name **Rev. Legend:** COOPERATIVAS CONSTROEM UM MUNDO MELHOR **Edge:** Reeded

| Date | Mintage | VF20 | XF40 | MS60 | MS63 | MS65 |
|---|---|---|---|---|---|---|
| 2012 | 5,000 | PF63 85.00 | PF65 100 | | | |

**KM# 682 5 REAIS**

27.00 g., 0.925 Silver 0.803 oz. ASW, 40 mm. **Subject:** UNESCO World Heritage site. City of Goiás **Obv:** House representing the architecture of Goiá City with Cora Coralina's house, an important poetess born in this city, on first view. **Obv. Legend:** GOIÁS 2012 **Rev:** Houses representing the architecture of Goiás City and face value on the left and part of a poem by Cora Coralina ("Eu sou estas casas encostadas cochichando umas com as outras") **Rev. Legend:** PATRIMONIO DA HUMANIDADE • UNESCO **Edge:** Reeded

| Date | Mintage | VF20 | XF40 | MS60 | MS63 | MS65 |
|---|---|---|---|---|---|---|
| 2012 | 3,000 | PF63 85.00 | PF65 100 | | | |

**KM# 684 5 REAIS**
27.00 g., 0.925 Silver 0.803 oz. ASW, 40 mm. **Subject:** UNESCO World Heritage Site - Diamantina **Obv:** Musicians on balcony of historic house **Rev:** House of Glory footbridge

| Date | Mintage | VF20 | XF40 | MS60 | MS63 | MS65 |
|---|---|---|---|---|---|---|
| 2013 | 3,000 | PF63 85.00 | PF65 100 | | | |

**KM# 686 5 REAIS**
27.00 g., 0.925 Silver 0.803 oz. ASW **Subject:** 2016 Rio Olympics **Obv:** Cycling at Floresta de aTijuca **Rev:** Dolphins

| Date | Mintage | VF20 | XF40 | MS60 | MS63 | MS65 |
|---|---|---|---|---|---|---|
| 2014 | — | PF65 75.00 | | | | |

**KM# 659 20 REAIS**
8.00 g., 0.900 Gold 0.2315 oz. AGW, 22 mm. **Obv:** Juscelino Kubitschek de Oliveira's portrait **Rev:** Value **Edge:** Reeded

| Date | Mintage | VF20 | XF40 | MS60 | MS63 | MS65 |
|---|---|---|---|---|---|---|
| 2002 | 2,499 | PF63 425 | PF65 475 | | | |

**KM# 660 20 REAIS**
8.00 g., 0.900 Gold 0.2315 oz. AGW, 22 mm. **Obv:** Carlos Drummond de Andrade portrait and value **Rev:** Andrade caricature, name and dates **Edge:** Reeded

| Date | Mintage | VF20 | XF40 | MS60 | MS63 | MS65 |
|---|---|---|---|---|---|---|
| ND(2002) | 2,499 | PF63 375 | PF65 400 | | | |

**KM# 662 20 REAIS**
8.00 g., 0.900 Gold 0.2315 oz. AGW, 22 mm. **Subject:** World Cup 2002 **Obv:** Soccer player **Rev:** Value, inscription and shooting stars **Edge:** Reeded

| Date | Mintage | VF20 | XF40 | MS60 | MS63 | MS65 |
|---|---|---|---|---|---|---|
| 2002 | 2,499 | PF63 375 | PF65 400 | | | |

**KM# 664 20 REAIS**
8.00 g., 0.900 Gold 0.2315 oz. AGW, 22 mm. **Subject:** Centennial - Ary Barroso **Obv:** Piano keyboard and musical notes above value **Rev:** Caricature of Ary Barroso **Edge:** Reeded

| Date | Mintage | VF20 | XF40 | MS60 | MS63 | MS65 |
|---|---|---|---|---|---|---|
| 2003 | 2,500 | PF63 375 | PF65 400 | | | |

**KM# 670 20 REAIS**
8.00 g., 0.900 Gold 0.2315 oz. AGW, 22 mm. **Subject:** FIFA Centennial **Obv:** Soccer ball, value, date **Obv. Legend:** BRASIL **Rev:** Christ the Redeemer, Sugar Loaf **Rev. Legend:** FUTEBUL MUNDIAL CENTENARIO DA FIFA **Edge:** Reeded

| Date | Mintage | VF20 | XF40 | MS60 | MS63 | MS65 |
|---|---|---|---|---|---|---|
| 2004 | 4,060 | PF63 600 | PF65 700 | | | |

# BRITISH ANTARCTIC TERRITORY

## BRITISH TERRITORY

### DECIMAL COINAGE

**KM# 1 2 POUNDS**
28.28 g., Copper-Nickel, 38.6 mm. **Ruler:** Elizabeth II **Subject:** 200th Anniversary of the Granting of Letters Patent **Obv:** Elizabeth II bust facing right **Rev:** Arms with denomination below **Rev. Legend:** 1908 . CENTENARY OF GRANTING OF LETTERS PATENT . 2008

| Date | Mintage | VF20 | XF40 | MS60 | MS63 | MS65 |
|---|---|---|---|---|---|---|
| 2008 | Est. 50000 | — | — | 17.50 | 20.00 | — |

**KM# 1a 2 POUNDS**
28.28 g., 0.925 Silver 0.841 oz. ASW, 38.6 mm. **Ruler:** Elizabeth II **Obv:** Bust right **Rev:** Supported arms

| Date | Mintage | VF20 | XF40 | MS60 | MS63 | MS65 |
|---|---|---|---|---|---|---|
| 2008 | Est. 10000 | PF63 55.00 | PF65 60.00 | | | |

**KM# 5 2 POUNDS**
28.28 g., Copper-Nickel, 38.6 mm. **Ruler:** Elizabeth II **Subject:** Antartic treaty **Obv:** Bust right **Rev:** Whale and other Antarctic wildlife

| Date | Mintage | VF20 | XF40 | MS60 | MS63 | MS65 |
|---|---|---|---|---|---|---|
| 2009 | 50,000 | — | — | 15.00 | 18.00 | — |

**KM# 5a 2 POUNDS**
28.28 g., 0.925 Silver 0.841 oz. ASW, 38.6 mm. **Ruler:** Elizabeth II **Obv:** Bust right **Rev:** Whale and other Antarctic wildlife

| Date | Mintage | VF20 | XF40 | MS60 | MS63 | MS65 |
|---|---|---|---|---|---|---|
| 2009 | 10,000 | PF63 40.00 | PF65 45.00 | | | |

**KM# 6 2 POUNDS**
28.28 g., Copper-Nickel, 38.61 mm. **Ruler:** Elizabeth II **Subject:** Scott's Terra Nova Expedition **Obv:** Bust in tiara right **Rev:** Captain scott, ship and men on ice flow

| Date | Mintage | VF20 | XF40 | MS60 | MS63 | MS65 |
|---|---|---|---|---|---|---|
| 2012 | — | — | — | 17.50 | 20.00 | — |

**KM# 8 2 POUNDS**
28.28 g., Copper-Nickel, 38.61 mm. **Ruler:** Elizabeth II **Subject:** Queen Elizabeth Land **Rev:** Antarctic map with boundries

| Date | Mintage | VF20 | XF40 | MS60 | MS63 | MS65 |
|---|---|---|---|---|---|---|
| 2013 | — | — | — | — | 15.00 | — |

**KM# 9 2 POUNDS**
28.28 g., Copper-Nickel, 38.61 mm. **Ruler:** Elizabeth II **Subject:** Emperor Pengiun **Rev:** Three penguin chicks

| Date | Mintage | VF20 | XF40 | MS60 | MS63 | MS65 |
|---|---|---|---|---|---|---|
| 2013 | — | — | — | — | 15.00 | — |

**KM# 2 4 POUNDS**
1.24 g., 0.9999 Gold 0.0399 oz. AGW, 13.92 mm. **Ruler:** Elizabeth II **Obv:** Bust right **Rev:** Supported arms

| Date | Mintage | VF20 | XF40 | MS60 | MS63 | MS65 |
|---|---|---|---|---|---|---|
| 2008 | Est. 10000 | PF63 80.00 | PF65 100 | | | |

**KM# 3 20 POUNDS**
6.22 g., 0.9999 Gold 0.200 oz. AGW **Ruler:** Elizabeth II **Obv:** Bust right **Rev:** Supported arms

| Date | Mintage | VF20 | XF40 | MS60 | MS63 | MS65 |
|---|---|---|---|---|---|---|
| 2008 | Est. 2000 | PF63 350 | PF65 375 | | | |

# BRITISH INDIAN OCEAN TERRITORY

## TERRITORY

### DECIMAL COINAGE

**KM# 1 2 POUNDS**
28.28 g., Copper-Nickel, 38.61 mm. **Ruler:** Elizabeth II **Obv:** Bust with tiara right **Rev:** Arms with supporters

| Date | Mintage | F12 | VF20 | XF40 | MS60 | MS63 |
|---|---|---|---|---|---|---|
| 2009 PM | — | — | — | — | — | 25.00 |

**KM# 1a 2 POUNDS**
28.28 g., 0.925 Silver 0.841 oz. ASW, 38.61 mm. **Ruler:** Elizabeth II **Subject:** First commemorative coin

| Date | Mintage | F12 | VF20 | XF40 | MS60 | MS63 |
|---|---|---|---|---|---|---|
| 2009 PM | Est. 10000 | PF63 50.00 | PF65 55.00 | | | |

**KM# 2 2 POUNDS**
22.00 g., 0.925 Silver 0.6543 oz. ASW with glass insert, 38.61 mm. **Ruler:** Elizabeth II **Obv:** Small head at top, sea turtle insert **Rev:** Circle of life of the sea turtle

| Date | Mintage | F12 | VF20 | XF40 | MS60 | MS63 |
|---|---|---|---|---|---|---|
| 2009 PM | Est. 5000 | PF63 80.00 | PF65 90.00 | | | |

**KM# 3 2 POUNDS**
28.28 g., Copper-Nickel, 38.61 mm. **Ruler:** Elizabeth II **Subject:** Engagement **Rev:** Prince William and Catherine Middleton

| Date | Mintage | F12 | VF20 | XF40 | MS60 | MS63 |
|---|---|---|---|---|---|---|
| 2010 PM | — | — | — | — | 14.00 | 17.50 |

**KM# 3a 2 POUNDS**
28.28 g., 0.925 Silver 0.841 oz. ASW, 38.61 mm. **Ruler:** Elizabeth II **Subject:** Engagement

| Date | Mintage | F12 | VF20 | XF40 | MS60 | MS63 |
|---|---|---|---|---|---|---|
| 2011 PM | Est. 10000 | PF63 50.00 | PF65 55.00 | | | |

**KM# 4 2 POUNDS**
28.28 g., Copper-Nickel, 38.61 mm. **Ruler:** Elizabeth II **Subject:** Royal Wedding **Obv:** Bust with tiara right **Rev:** Conjoined busts left of Catherine Middleton and Prince William

| Date | Mintage | F12 | VF20 | XF40 | MS60 | MS63 |
|---|---|---|---|---|---|---|
| 2011 PM | — | — | — | — | 10.00 | 12.50 |

**KM# 4a 2 POUNDS**
28.28 g., 0.925 Silver 0.841 oz. ASW, 38.61 mm. **Ruler:** Elizabeth II **Subject:** Royal Wedding

| Date | Mintage | F12 | VF20 | XF40 | MS60 | MS63 |
|---|---|---|---|---|---|---|
| 2011 PM | Est. 10000 | PF63 50.00 | PF65 55.00 | | | |

**KM# 5 2 POUNDS**
28.28 g., Copper-Nickel, 38.61 mm. **Ruler:** Elizabeth II **Subject:** Prince Philip, 90th Birthday **Obv:** Bust in tiara right **Rev:** Crowned EP cipher within circle of crosses and anchors

| Date | Mintage | F12 | VF20 | XF40 | MS60 | MS63 |
|---|---|---|---|---|---|---|
| 2011 PM | — | — | — | — | 17.50 | 20.00 |

**KM# 5a 2 POUNDS**
28.28 g., 0.925 Silver 0.841 oz. ASW **Ruler:** Elizabeth II **Subject:** Prince Philip, 90th Birthday

| Date | Mintage | F12 | VF20 | XF40 | MS60 | MS63 |
|---|---|---|---|---|---|---|
| 2011 PM | Est. 10000 | PF63 50.00 | PF65 55.00 | | | |

**KM# 6 2 POUNDS**
28.28 g., Copper-Nickel, 38.6 mm. **Ruler:** Elizabeth II **Subject:** Life of Queen Elizabeth II **Obv:** Conjoined busts left **Rev:** Elizabeth and Margaret as children riding a rocking horse

| Date | Mintage | F12 | VF20 | XF40 | MS60 | MS63 |
|---|---|---|---|---|---|---|
| 2012 PM | — | — | — | — | — | 15.00 |

**KM# 6a 2 POUNDS**
28.28 g., Silver 0.841 oz. ASW, 38.61 mm. **Ruler:** Elizabeth II **Subject:** Elizabeth II, 60th Anniversary as Queen **Rev:** Princess Elizabeth and Margaret

| Date | Mintage | F12 | VF20 | XF40 | MS60 | MS63 |
|---|---|---|---|---|---|---|
| 2012 PM | Est. 10000 | PF63 50.00 | PF65 55.00 | | | |

**KM# 7 2 POUNDS**
28.28 g., Copper-Nickel, 38.61 mm. **Ruler:** Elizabeth II **Subject:** Life of Queen Elizabeth II **Obv:** Conjoined busts right, young and current portraits **Rev:** Queen Mother waving at left, Queen Elizabeth at right

| Date | Mintage | F12 | VF20 | XF40 | MS60 | MS63 |
|---|---|---|---|---|---|---|
| 2012 PM | — | — | — | — | — | 20.00 |

**KM# 7a 2 POUNDS**
28.28 g., 0.925 Silver 0.841 oz. ASW, 38.61 mm. **Ruler:** Elizabeth II **Subject:** Elizabeth II, 60th Anniversary of reign **Rev:** Queen Mother and Elizabeth

| Date | Mintage | F12 | VF20 | XF40 | MS60 | MS63 |
|---|---|---|---|---|---|---|
| 2012 PM | Est. 10000 | PF63 50.00 | PF65 55.00 | | | |

**KM# 8 2 POUNDS**
28.28 g., Copper-Nickel, 38.61 mm. **Ruler:** Elizabeth II **Subject:** The Drive, first anniversary **Rev:** Prince William and Kate in Aston Martin DB-6 on wedding day

| Date | Mintage | F12 | VF20 | XF40 | MS60 | MS63 |
|---|---|---|---|---|---|---|
| 2012 PM | — | — | — | — | 14.00 | 17.50 |

**KM# 8a 2 POUNDS**
28.28 g., 0.925 Silver 0.841 oz. ASW, 38.61 mm. **Ruler:** Elizabeth II **Subject:** Wedding, 1st Anniversary **Rev:** Duke and Dutchess of Cambridge in Aston Martin DB-6 drive about

| Date | Mintage | F12 | VF20 | XF40 | MS60 | MS63 |
|---|---|---|---|---|---|---|
| 2012 PM | Est. 10000 | PF63 50.00 | PF65 55.00 | | | |

# BRITISH VIRGIN ISLANDS

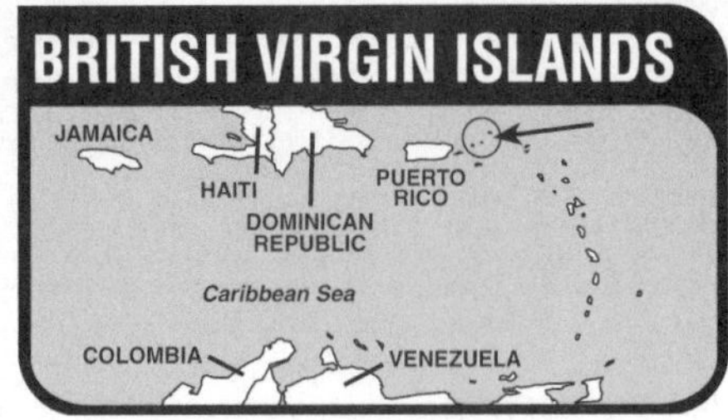


The Colony of the Virgin Islands, a British colony situated in the Caribbean Sea northeast of Puerto Rico and west of the Leeward Islands, has an area of 59 sq. mi. (155 sq. km.) and a population of 13,000. Capital: Road Town. The principal islands of the 36-island group are Tortola, Virgin Gorda, Anegada, and Jost Van Dyke. The chief industries are fishing and stock raising. Fish, livestock and bananas are exported.

## BRITISH COLONY

### STANDARD COINAGE

**KM# 180 DOLLAR**
28.28 g., Copper-Nickel, 38.6 mm. **Subject:** Sir Francis Drake **Obv:** Queen's bust right **Rev:** Ship, portrait and map **Edge:** Reeded

| Date | Mintage | VF20 | XF40 | MS60 | MS63 | MS65 |
|---|---|---|---|---|---|---|
| 2002 | — | — | — | — | 7.50 | 9.50 |

**KM# 183 DOLLAR**
28.28 g., Copper-Nickel, 38.6 mm. **Subject:** Sir Walter Raleigh **Obv:** Queen's bust right **Rev:** Ship, portrait and map **Edge:** Reeded

| Date | Mintage | VF20 | XF40 | MS60 | MS63 | MS65 |
|---|---|---|---|---|---|---|
| 2002 | — | — | — | — | 7.50 | 9.50 |

**KM# 187 DOLLAR**
28.28 g., Copper-Nickel, 38.6 mm. **Subject:** Queen's Golden Jubilee **Obv:** Queen's bust right **Rev:** Queen on horse **Edge:** Reeded

| Date | Mintage | VF20 | XF40 | MS60 | MS63 | MS65 |
|---|---|---|---|---|---|---|
| 2002 | — | — | — | — | 7.50 | 9.50 |

**KM# 190 DOLLAR**
28.28 g., Copper-Nickel, 38.6 mm. **Subject:** Queen's Golden Jubilee **Obv:** Queen's bust right **Rev:** Queen on throne **Edge:** Reeded

| Date | Mintage | VF20 | XF40 | MS60 | MS63 | MS65 |
|---|---|---|---|---|---|---|
| 2002 | — | — | — | — | 7.50 | 9.50 |

**KM# 193 DOLLAR**
28.28 g., Copper-Nickel, 38.6 mm. **Subject:** Queen's Golden Jubilee **Obv:** Queen's bust right **Rev:** Queen with President Ronald Reagan and First Lady Nancy Reagan **Edge:** Reeded

| Date | Mintage | VF20 | XF40 | MS60 | MS63 | MS65 |
|---|---|---|---|---|---|---|
| 2002 | — | — | — | — | 7.50 | 9.50 |

**KM# 196 DOLLAR**
28.28 g., Copper-Nickel, 38.6 mm. **Subject:** Queen's Golden Jubilee **Obv:** Queen's bust right **Rev:** Carnival dancers **Edge:** Reeded

| Date | Mintage | VF20 | XF40 | MS60 | MS63 | MS65 |
|---|---|---|---|---|---|---|
| 2002 | — | — | — | — | 7.50 | 9.50 |

**KM# 199 DOLLAR**
28.28 g., Copper-Nickel, 38.6 mm. **Subject:** Teddy Bear Centennial **Obv:** Queen's bust right **Rev:** Teddy bear **Edge:** Reeded

| Date | Mintage | VF20 | XF40 | MS60 | MS63 | MS65 |
|---|---|---|---|---|---|---|
| 2002 | — | — | — | — | 8.50 | 15.00 |

### KM# 204 DOLLAR

28.28 g., Copper-Nickel, 38.6 mm. **Subject:** Princess Diana **Obv:** Queen's bust right **Rev:** Diana's portrait **Edge:** Reeded

| Date | Mintage | VF20 | XF40 | MS60 | MS63 | MS65 |
|---|---|---|---|---|---|---|
| 2002 | — | — | — | — | 7.50 | 9.50 |

### KM# 207 DOLLAR

28.28 g., Copper-Nickel, 38.6 mm. **Subject:** September 11, 2001 **Obv:** Queen's bust right **Rev:** World Trade Center twin towers **Edge:** Reeded

| Date | Mintage | VF20 | XF40 | MS60 | MS63 | MS65 |
|---|---|---|---|---|---|---|
| 2002 | — | — | — | — | 12.00 | 13.50 |

### KM# 210 DOLLAR

28.28 g., Copper-Nickel, 38.6 mm. **Subject:** September 11, 2001 **Obv:** Queen's bust right **Rev:** Statue of Liberty **Edge:** Reeded

| Date | Mintage | VF20 | XF40 | MS60 | MS63 | MS65 |
|---|---|---|---|---|---|---|
| 2002 | — | — | — | — | 12.00 | 13.50 |

### KM# 213 DOLLAR

28.28 g., Copper-Nickel, 38.6 mm. **Subject:** Queen Mother **Obv:** Queen's bust right **Rev:** Queen Mother and a young Prince Charles **Edge:** Reeded

| Date | Mintage | VF20 | XF40 | MS60 | MS63 | MS65 |
|---|---|---|---|---|---|---|
| 2002 PM | — | — | — | — | 10.00 | 12.00 |

### KM# 216 DOLLAR

28.28 g., Copper-Nickel, 38.6 mm. **Subject:** Queen Mother **Obv:** Queen's bust right **Rev:** Queen Mother with four grandchildren **Edge:** Reeded

| Date | Mintage | VF20 | XF40 | MS60 | MS63 | MS65 |
|---|---|---|---|---|---|---|
| 2002 PM | — | — | — | — | 10.00 | 12.00 |

### KM# 219 DOLLAR

28.28 g., Copper-Nickel, 38.6 mm. **Subject:** Queen Mother Series **Obv:** Queen's bust right **Rev:** Queen Mother with uniformed Prince Charles **Edge:** Reeded

| Date | Mintage | VF20 | XF40 | MS60 | MS63 | MS65 |
|---|---|---|---|---|---|---|
| 2002 PM | — | — | — | — | 10.00 | 12.00 |

### KM# 222 DOLLAR

28.28 g., Copper-Nickel, 38.6 mm. **Subject:** Queen Mother Series **Obv:** Queen's bust right **Rev:** Queen Mother's coffin **Edge:** Reeded

| Date | Mintage | VF20 | XF40 | MS60 | MS63 | MS65 |
|---|---|---|---|---|---|---|
| 2002 PM | — | — | — | — | 10.00 | 12.00 |

### KM# 225 DOLLAR

28.44 g., Copper-Nickel, 38.6 mm. **Subject:** Kennedy Assassination **Obv:** Queen's bust right **Rev:** President Kennedy's portrait left **Edge:** Reeded

| Date | Mintage | VF20 | XF40 | MS60 | MS63 | MS65 |
|---|---|---|---|---|---|---|
| 2003 | — | — | — | — | 10.00 | 12.00 |

### KM# 229 DOLLAR

28.28 g., Copper-Nickel, 38.6 mm. **Subject:** Powered Flight Centennial **Obv:** Queen's bust right **Rev:** Three historic airplanes and rocket **Edge:** Reeded

| Date | Mintage | VF20 | XF40 | MS60 | MS63 | MS65 |
|---|---|---|---|---|---|---|
| 2003 | — | — | — | — | 10.00 | 12.00 |

### KM# 232 DOLLAR

28.28 g., Copper-Nickel, 38.6 mm. **Obv:** Queen's bust right **Rev:** Henry VIII and Elizabeth I **Edge:** Reeded

| Date | Mintage | VF20 | XF40 | MS60 | MS63 | MS65 |
|---|---|---|---|---|---|---|
| 2003 | — | — | — | — | 10.00 | 12.00 |

### KM# 235 DOLLAR

28.28 g., Copper-Nickel, 38.6 mm. **Obv:** Queen's bust right **Rev:** Matthew Parker, Archbishop of Canterbury **Edge:** Reeded

| Date | Mintage | VF20 | XF40 | MS60 | MS63 | MS65 |
|---|---|---|---|---|---|---|
| 2003 | — | — | — | — | 10.00 | 12.00 |

### KM# 238 DOLLAR

28.28 g., Copper-Nickel, 38.6 mm. **Obv:** Queen's bust right **Rev:** Sir Francis Drake and ships **Edge:** Reeded

| Date | Mintage | VF20 | XF40 | MS60 | MS63 | MS65 |
|---|---|---|---|---|---|---|
| 2003 | — | — | — | — | 10.00 | 12.00 |

### KM# 241 DOLLAR

28.28 g., Copper-Nickel, 38.6 mm. **Obv:** Queen's bust right **Rev:** Sir Walter Raleigh **Edge:** Reeded

| Date | Mintage | VF20 | XF40 | MS60 | MS63 | MS65 |
|---|---|---|---|---|---|---|
| 2003 | — | — | — | — | 10.00 | 12.00 |

### KM# 244 DOLLAR

28.28 g., Copper-Nickel, 38.6 mm. **Obv:** Queen's bust right **Rev:** Sir William Shakespeare **Edge:** Reeded

| Date | Mintage | VF20 | XF40 | MS60 | MS63 | MS65 |
|---|---|---|---|---|---|---|
| 2003 | — | — | — | — | 10.00 | 12.00 |

### KM# 247 DOLLAR

28.28 g., Copper-Nickel, 38.6 mm. **Obv:** Queen's bust right **Rev:** Elizabeth I above her funeral procession **Edge:** Reeded

| Date | Mintage | VF20 | XF40 | MS60 | MS63 | MS65 |
|---|---|---|---|---|---|---|
| 2003 | — | — | — | — | 10.00 | 12.00 |

### KM# 250 DOLLAR

28.28 g., Copper-Nickel, 38.6 mm. **Subject:** Olympics **Obv:** Queen's bust right **Rev:** Ancient bust, runners and coin **Edge:** Reeded

| Date | Mintage | VF20 | XF40 | MS60 | MS63 | MS65 |
|---|---|---|---|---|---|---|
| 2003 | — | — | — | — | 10.00 | 12.00 |

### KM# 253 DOLLAR

28.28 g., Copper-Nickel, 38.6 mm. **Subject:** Olympics **Obv:** Queen's bust right **Rev:** Ancient bust, charioteer and coin **Edge:** Reeded

| Date | Mintage | VF20 | XF40 | MS60 | MS63 | MS65 |
|---|---|---|---|---|---|---|
| 2003 | — | — | — | — | 10.00 | 12.00 |

### KM# 303 DOLLAR

28.28 g., Copper-Nickel, 38.6 mm. **Subject:** 2004 Athens Olympics **Obv:** Queen's bust right **Rev:** Ancient athlete's bust right, runners at lower right, ancient coin with owl at upper right **Edge:** Reeded

| Date | Mintage | VF20 | XF40 | MS60 | MS63 | MS65 |
|---|---|---|---|---|---|---|
| 2003 | — | — | — | — | 10.00 | 12.00 |

### KM# 306 DOLLAR

28.28 g., Copper-Nickel, 38.6 mm. **Subject:** 2004 Athens Olympics **Obv:** Queen's bust right **Rev:** Ancient athlete bust left, chariot race at lower left, ancient coin at upper left **Edge:** Reeded

| Date | Mintage | VF20 | XF40 | MS60 | MS63 | MS65 |
|---|---|---|---|---|---|---|
| 2003 | — | — | — | — | 10.00 | 12.00 |

### KM# 310 DOLLAR

28.28 g., Copper-Nickel, 38.6 mm. **Subject:** Queen Elizabeth's Golden Coronation Jubilee **Obv:** Elizabeth II **Rev:** Cameo portraits above the ship "Gothic **Edge:** Reeded

| Date | Mintage | VF20 | XF40 | MS60 | MS63 | MS65 |
|---|---|---|---|---|---|---|
| 2003 | — | — | — | — | 7.50 | 9.50 |

### KM# 319 DOLLAR

28.28 g., Copper-Nickel **Subject:** 50th Anniversary of Coronation **Rev:** Queen riding in automobile

| Date | Mintage | VF20 | XF40 | MS60 | MS63 | MS65 |
|---|---|---|---|---|---|---|
| 2003 | — | — | — | — | 12.00 | 15.00 |

**KM# 320 DOLLAR**
28.28 g., Copper-Nickel **Subject:** Golden Jubilee of Coronation **Rev:** Sir. Edmond Hillary on Mt. Everest, Queen II above mountain climbers

| Date | Mintage | VF20 | XF40 | MS60 | MS63 | MS65 |
|---|---|---|---|---|---|---|
| 2003 | — | — | — | — | 12.00 | 15.00 |

**KM# 321 DOLLAR**
28.28 g., Copper-Nickel **Rev:** Queen presenting Ascot Horse Racing prize

| Date | Mintage | VF20 | XF40 | MS60 | MS63 | MS65 |
|---|---|---|---|---|---|---|
| 2003 | — | — | — | — | 10.00 | 12.00 |

**KM# 265 DOLLAR**
28.28 g., Copper-Nickel, 38.6 mm. **Obv:** Queen's bust right **Rev:** Sir Francis Drake, ship and map **Edge:** Reeded

| Date | Mintage | VF20 | XF40 | MS60 | MS63 | MS65 |
|---|---|---|---|---|---|---|
| 2004 | — | — | — | — | 10.00 | 12.00 |

**KM# 267.1 DOLLAR**
28.28 g., Copper-Nickel, 38.6 mm. **Obv:** Queen's bust right **Rev:** Peter Rabbit **Edge:** Reeded

| Date | Mintage | VF20 | XF40 | MS60 | MS63 | MS65 |
|---|---|---|---|---|---|---|
| 2004 | — | — | — | — | 15.00 | 17.00 |

**KM# 267.2 DOLLAR**
28.28 g., Copper-Nickel, 38.6 mm. **Obv:** Queen's bust right **Rev:** Multicolor Peter Rabbit **Edge:** Reeded

| Date | Mintage | VF20 | XF40 | MS60 | MS63 | MS65 |
|---|---|---|---|---|---|---|
| 2004 | — | — | — | — | 20.00 | 22.00 |

**KM# 268 DOLLAR**
3.11 g., 0.999 Silver 0.0999 oz. ASW, 18 mm. **Obv:** Queen's bust right **Rev:** Peter Rabbit **Edge:** Reeded

| Date | Mintage | VF20 | XF40 | MS60 | MS63 | MS65 |
|---|---|---|---|---|---|---|
| 2004 | 10,000 | PF65 25.00 | | | | |

**KM# 281 DOLLAR**
28.28 g., Copper-Nickel, 38.6 mm. **Obv:** Queen's bust right **Rev:** Sailor above two D-Day landing craft **Edge:** Reeded

| Date | Mintage | VF20 | XF40 | MS60 | MS63 | MS65 |
|---|---|---|---|---|---|---|
| 2004 | — | — | — | — | 10.00 | 12.00 |

**KM# 286 DOLLAR**
28.28 g., Copper-Nickel, 38.6 mm. **Obv:** Queen's bust right **Rev:** Dolphin **Edge:** Reeded

| Date | Mintage | VF20 | XF40 | MS60 | MS63 | MS65 |
|---|---|---|---|---|---|---|
| 2004 | — | — | — | — | 12.00 | 14.00 |

**KM# 297 DOLLAR**
28.28 g., Copper-Nickel, 38.6 mm. **Obv:** Queen's bust right **Rev:** Soldier above tank and jeeps **Edge:** Reeded

| Date | Mintage | VF20 | XF40 | MS60 | MS63 | MS65 |
|---|---|---|---|---|---|---|
| 2004 | — | — | — | — | 10.00 | 12.00 |

**KM# 300 DOLLAR**
28.28 g., Copper-Nickel, 38.6 mm. **Obv:** Queen's bust right **Rev:** Pilot and planes above D-Day landing **Edge:** Reeded

| Date | Mintage | VF20 | XF40 | MS60 | MS63 | MS65 |
|---|---|---|---|---|---|---|
| 2004 | — | — | — | — | 10.00 | 12.00 |

**KM# 312 DOLLAR**
28.28 g., Copper-Nickel, 38.6 mm. **Obv:** Bust of Queen Elizabeth II right **Rev:** Mother and baby dolphins **Edge:** Reeded

| Date | Mintage | VF20 | XF40 | MS60 | MS63 | MS65 |
|---|---|---|---|---|---|---|
| 2005 | — | — | — | — | 12.00 | 14.00 |

**KM# 322 DOLLAR**
28.28 g., Copper-Nickel **Rev:** VJ Day, McArthur and U.S.S. Missiouri Battleship

| Date | Mintage | VF20 | XF40 | MS60 | MS63 | MS65 |
|---|---|---|---|---|---|---|
| 2005 | — | — | — | — | 10.00 | 12.00 |

**KM# 323 DOLLAR**
28.28 g., Copper-Nickel **Rev:** Warships near Atlantic coast, West Indies islands

| Date | Mintage | VF20 | XF40 | MS60 | MS63 | MS65 |
|---|---|---|---|---|---|---|
| 2005 | — | — | — | — | 10.00 | 12.00 |

**KM# 324 DOLLAR**
28.28 g., Copper-Nickel **Rev:** Death of Nelson

| Date | Mintage | VF20 | XF40 | MS60 | MS63 | MS65 |
|---|---|---|---|---|---|---|
| 2005 | — | — | — | — | 10.00 | 12.00 |

**KM# 325 DOLLAR**
28.28 g., Copper-Nickel **Rev:** Nelson and Order Star above ships

| Date | Mintage | VF20 | XF40 | MS60 | MS63 | MS65 |
|---|---|---|---|---|---|---|
| 2005 | — | — | — | — | 10.00 | 12.00 |

**KM# 326 DOLLAR**
28.28 g., Copper-Nickel **Rev:** Nelson and Napoleon

| Date | Mintage | VF20 | XF40 | MS60 | MS63 | MS65 |
|---|---|---|---|---|---|---|
| 2005 | — | — | — | — | 10.00 | 12.00 |

### KM# 327 DOLLAR

28.28 g., Copper-Nickel **Rev:** Nelson's Column, statue and ships

| Date | Mintage | VF20 | XF40 | MS60 | MS63 | MS65 |
|---|---|---|---|---|---|---|
| 2005 | — | — | — | — | 10.00 | 12.00 |

### KM# 328 DOLLAR

28.28 g., Copper-Nickel **Rev:** V.E. Day, Montgomery and Eisenhower

| Date | Mintage | VF20 | XF40 | MS60 | MS63 | MS65 |
|---|---|---|---|---|---|---|
| 2005 | — | — | — | — | 10.00 | 12.00 |

### KM# 330 DOLLAR

Copper-Nickel **Ruler:** Elizabeth II **Rev:** Battle of Britain

| Date | Mintage | VF20 | XF40 | MS60 | MS63 | MS65 |
|---|---|---|---|---|---|---|
| 2005 | — | — | — | — | 15.00 | 17.00 |

### KM# 331 DOLLAR

Copper-Nickel **Ruler:** Elizabeth II **Rev:** Battle of Berlin

| Date | Mintage | VF20 | XF40 | MS60 | MS63 | MS65 |
|---|---|---|---|---|---|---|
| 2005 | — | — | — | — | 15.00 | 17.00 |

### KM# 403 DOLLAR

28.28 g., Copper-Nickel, 38.61 mm. **Ruler:** Elizabeth II **Obv:** Bust in tiara right **Rev:** Inverted Swan postage stamp

| Date | Mintage | VF20 | XF40 | MS60 | MS63 | MS65 |
|---|---|---|---|---|---|---|
| 2005 PM | — | — | — | — | 17.50 | 20.00 |

### KM# 329 DOLLAR

Copper-Nickel **Rev:** Two dolphins

| Date | Mintage | VF20 | XF40 | MS60 | MS63 | MS65 |
|---|---|---|---|---|---|---|
| 2006 | — | — | — | — | 10.00 | 12.00 |

### KM# 349 DOLLAR

28.28 g., Copper-Nickel, 38.6 mm. **Ruler:** Elizabeth II **Subject:** 5th Anniversary Attack on Twin Towers, New York City **Obv:** Crowned bust right **Obv. Legend:** BRITISH VIRGIN ISLANDS - QUEEN ELIZABETH II **Rev:** Twin Towers in sprays, remembrance ribbon privy mark at upper right **Rev. Legend:** LEST WE FORGET **Edge:** Reeded

| Date | Mintage | VF20 | XF40 | MS60 | MS63 | MS65 |
|---|---|---|---|---|---|---|
| 2006 | — | — | — | — | 15.00 | 17.00 |

### KM# 332 DOLLAR

28.28 g., Copper-Nickel, 38.60 mm. **Ruler:** Elizabeth II **Subject:** 400th Anniversary Founding of Jamestown **Obv:** Bust with tiara right **Obv. Legend:** BRITISH VIRGIN ISLANDS - QUEEN ELIZABETH II **Rev:** British lion laying, American eagle perched on sprays **Rev. Legend:** UNITED IN FRIENDSHIP **Edge:** Reeded

| Date | Mintage | VF20 | XF40 | MS60 | MS63 | MS65 |
|---|---|---|---|---|---|---|
| 2007 | — | — | — | — | 16.50 | 18.50 |

### KM# 404 DOLLAR

28.28 g., Copper-Nickel, 38.61 mm. **Ruler:** Elizabeth II **Obv:** Bust in tiara right **Rev:** George Washington 5 cent postage stamp

| Date | Mintage | VF20 | XF40 | MS60 | MS63 | MS65 |
|---|---|---|---|---|---|---|
| 2007 PM | — | — | — | — | 17.50 | 20.00 |

### KM# 370 DOLLAR

28.28 g., Copper-Nickel, 38.6 mm. **Ruler:** Elizabeth II **Obv:** Bust right **Rev:** Two soccer players and leopard

| Date | Mintage | VF20 | XF40 | MS60 | MS63 | MS65 |
|---|---|---|---|---|---|---|
| 2009 | — | — | — | — | 12.00 | 15.00 |

### KM# 373 DOLLAR

28.28 g., Copper-Nickel, 38.6 mm. **Ruler:** Elizabeth II **Obv:** Bust right **Rev:** Queen Elizabeth I aboard ship

| Date | Mintage | VF20 | XF40 | MS60 | MS63 | MS65 |
|---|---|---|---|---|---|---|
| 2009 | — | — | — | — | 12.00 | 15.00 |

### KM# 375 DOLLAR

28.28 g., Copper-Nickel, 38.6 mm. **Ruler:** Elizabeth II **Obv:** Bust right **Rev:** Elizabeth I between two columns

| Date | Mintage | VF20 | XF40 | MS60 | MS63 | MS65 |
|---|---|---|---|---|---|---|
| 2009 | — | — | — | — | 12.00 | 15.00 |

### KM# 393 DOLLAR

28.28 g., Copper-Nickel, 38.6 mm. **Ruler:** Elizabeth II **Subject:** Peanuts 60th Anniversary **Rev:** Snoopy sleeping atop doghouse

| Date | Mintage | VF20 | XF40 | MS60 | MS63 | MS65 |
|---|---|---|---|---|---|---|
| 2010 PM | — | — | — | — | — | 25.00 |

### KM# 396 DOLLAR

28.28 g., Bronze with antique patina, 38.6 mm. **Ruler:** Elizabeth II **Subject:** Elgin Marbles **Rev:** Two horsemen

| Date | Mintage | VF20 | XF40 | MS60 | MS63 | MS65 |
|---|---|---|---|---|---|---|
| 2010 PM | — | — | — | — | 25.00 | — |

### KM# 402 DOLLAR

28.28 g., Copper-Nickel, 38.61 mm. **Ruler:** Elizabeth II **Subject:** Birth of Venus

| Date | Mintage | VF20 | XF40 | MS60 | MS63 | MS65 |
|---|---|---|---|---|---|---|
| 2010 PM | — | — | — | — | — | 15.00 |

### KM# 436 DOLLAR

28.28 g., Copper-Nickel, 38.61 mm. **Ruler:** Elizabeth II **Subject:** Orient Express

| Date | Mintage | VF20 | XF40 | MS60 | MS63 | MS65 |
|---|---|---|---|---|---|---|
| 2011 PM | — | — | — | — | — | 15.00 |

### KM# 436a DOLLAR

28.28 g., Copper-Nickel, 38.61 mm. **Ruler:** Elizabeth II **Subject:** Royal Husdon Steam Locomotive **Rev:** Locomotive in color

| Date | Mintage | VF20 | XF40 | MS60 | MS63 | MS65 |
|---|---|---|---|---|---|---|
| 2011 | — | — | — | — | — | 20.00 |

### KM# 431 DOLLAR

28.28 g., Copper-Nickel, 38.6 mm. **Ruler:** Elizabeth II **Subject:** Father of the Modern Olympics

| Date | Mintage | VF20 | XF40 | MS60 | MS63 | MS65 |
|---|---|---|---|---|---|---|
| 2012 | — | — | — | — | — | 15.00 |

### KM# 439 DOLLAR

28.28 g., Copper-Nickel, 38.61 mm. **Ruler:** Elizabeth II **Subject:** Birth of Prince George **Rev:** Prince William and blue footprints added at right

| Date | Mintage | VF20 | XF40 | MS60 | MS63 | MS65 |
|---|---|---|---|---|---|---|
| 2013 PM | — | — | — | — | — | 15.00 |

### KM# 441 DOLLAR

28.28 g., Copper-Nickel, 38.61 mm. **Ruler:** Elizabeth II **Subject:** Birth of Prince George **Rev:** Catherine and blue footprints added at right

| Date | Mintage | VF20 | XF40 | MS60 | MS63 | MS65 |
|---|---|---|---|---|---|---|
| 2013 PM | — | — | — | — | — | 15.00 |

### KM# 443 DOLLAR

28.28 g., Copper-Nickel, 38.61 mm. **Ruler:** Elizabeth II **Subject:** Last Concord Flight, 10th Anniversary **Rev:** Concord, NY and London Skyline

| Date | Mintage | VF20 | XF40 | MS60 | MS63 | MS65 |
|---|---|---|---|---|---|---|
| 2013 PM | — | — | — | — | — | 15.00 |

### KM# 443a DOLLAR

28.28 g., Copper-Nickel, 38.61 mm. **Ruler:** Elizabeth II **Subject:** Last flight of Concorde, 10th Anniversary **Rev:** Concord with tailfin in color, NY and London skyline

| Date | Mintage | VF20 | XF40 | MS60 | MS63 | MS65 |
|---|---|---|---|---|---|---|
| 2013 PM | — | — | — | — | — | 20.00 |

### KM# 446 DOLLAR

28.28 g., Copper-Nickel, 38.8 mm. **Ruler:** Elizabeth II **Obv:** Bust right **Rev:** Sea horse

| Date | Mintage | VF20 | XF40 | MS60 | MS63 | MS65 |
|---|---|---|---|---|---|---|
| 2014 | — | — | — | — | — | 15.00 |

### KM# 429 1.50 DOLLAR

47.00 g., Copper, 48 mm. **Ruler:** Elizabeth II **Subject:** Father of the Modern Olympics

| Date | Mintage | VF20 | XF40 | MS60 | MS63 | MS65 |
|---|---|---|---|---|---|---|
| 2012 | Est. 3000 | — | — | — | — | — |

### KM# 278 2 DOLLARS

58.00 g., Bronze, 50 mm. **Obv:** Queen's bust right **Rev:** 1896 Olympic medal design **Edge:** Reeded

| Date | Mintage | VF20 | XF40 | MS60 | MS63 | MS65 |
|---|---|---|---|---|---|---|
| 2004 | 3,500 | **PF65** 20.00 | | | | |

### KM# 380 2 DOLLARS

Bronze with patina, 50 mm. **Ruler:** Elizabeth II **Rev:** Turtle

| Date | Mintage | VF20 | XF40 | MS60 | MS63 | MS65 |
|---|---|---|---|---|---|---|
| 2008 PM | — | — | — | — | — | 20.00 |

### KM# 269.1 2.50 DOLLARS

7.78 g., 0.999 Silver 0.2497 oz. ASW, 26 mm. **Obv:** Queen's bust right **Rev:** Peter Rabbit **Edge:** Reeded

| Date | Mintage | VF20 | XF40 | MS60 | MS63 | MS65 |
|---|---|---|---|---|---|---|
| 2004 | — | PF65 18.00 | | | | |

### KM# 269.2 2.50 DOLLARS

7.78 g., 0.999 Silver 0.2497 oz. ASW, 26 mm. **Obv:** Queen's bust right **Rev:** Multicolor Peter Rabbit **Edge:** Reeded

| Date | Mintage | VF20 | XF40 | MS60 | MS63 | MS65 |
|---|---|---|---|---|---|---|
| 2004 | 7,500 | PF65 25.00 | | | | |

### KM# 381 4 DOLLARS

Silver **Ruler:** Elizabeth II **Subject:** 400th Anniversary of Settlement

| Date | Mintage | VF20 | XF40 | MS60 | MS63 | MS65 |
|---|---|---|---|---|---|---|
| 2009 PM | — | — | — | — | — | 35.00 |

### KM# 284 5 DOLLARS

10.00 g., 0.990 Titanium 0.3183 oz., 36.1 mm. **Obv:** Queen's bust right **Rev:** British Guiana stamp design **Edge:** Reeded

| Date | Mintage | VF20 | XF40 | MS60 | MS63 | MS65 |
|---|---|---|---|---|---|---|
| 2004 | 7,500 | PF65 95.00 | | | | |

### KM# 340 5 DOLLARS

0.9999 Bi-Metallic Silver center in Gold ring. **Ruler:** Elizabeth II **Obv:** Conjoined busts with Philip right, within gold ring **Obv. Legend:** BRITISH VIRGIN ISLANDS — QUEEN ELIZABETH II **Rev:** Conjoined busts of Princess Elizabeth and Prince Philip right within gold ring **Rev. Legend:** WITH THIS RING, I THEE WED **Edge:** Reeded

| Date | Mintage | VF20 | XF40 | MS60 | MS63 | MS65 |
|---|---|---|---|---|---|---|
| 2007 | — | PF65 500 | | | | |

### KM# 405 5 DOLLARS

28.28 g., Copper-Nickel gilt, 38.61 mm. **Ruler:** Elizabeth II **Obv:** Bust in tiara right **Rev:** Benjamin Franklin postage stamp

| Date | Mintage | VF20 | XF40 | MS60 | MS63 | MS65 |
|---|---|---|---|---|---|---|
| 2007 PM | — | — | — | — | 17.50 | 20.00 |

### KM# 414 5 DOLLARS

28.28 g., Copper-Nickel gilt, 38.61 mm. **Ruler:** Elizabeth II **Subject:** Bejing Olympics **Obv:** Bust in tiara right **Rev:** Tennis plays against Great Wall background

| Date | Mintage | VF20 | XF40 | MS60 | MS63 | MS65 |
|---|---|---|---|---|---|---|
| 2008 PM | — | PF65 25.00 | | | | |

### KM# 426 5 DOLLARS

28.28 g., Silver with gilt center, 38.61 mm. **Ruler:** Elizabeth II **Subject:** Bejing Olympics **Obv:** Bust in tiara right **Rev:** Tennis plays against Great Wall background

| Date | Mintage | VF20 | XF40 | MS60 | MS63 | MS65 |
|---|---|---|---|---|---|---|
| 2008 PM | — | PF65 50.00 | | | | |

### KM# 383 5 DOLLARS

Titanium **Ruler:** Elizabeth II **Subject:** Bejing Olympics - Tennis

| Date | Mintage | VF20 | XF40 | MS60 | MS63 | MS65 |
|---|---|---|---|---|---|---|
| 2009 PM | — | PF65 55.00 | | | | |

### KM# 384 5 DOLLARS

Titanium **Ruler:** Elizabeth II **Subject:** Bejing Olympics - Swimming

| Date | Mintage | VF20 | XF40 | MS60 | MS63 | MS65 |
|---|---|---|---|---|---|---|
| 2009 PM | — | PF65 55.00 | | | | |

### KM# 385 5 DOLLARS

Titanium **Ruler:** Elizabeth II **Subject:** Bejing Olympics

| Date | Mintage | VF20 | XF40 | MS60 | MS63 | MS65 |
|---|---|---|---|---|---|---|
| 2009 PM | — | PF65 55.00 | | | | |

### KM# 386 5 DOLLARS

Titanium **Ruler:** Elizabeth II **Subject:** Bejing Olympics

| Date | Mintage | VF20 | XF40 | MS60 | MS63 | MS65 |
|---|---|---|---|---|---|---|
| 2009 PM | — | PF65 55.00 | | | | |

### KM# 387 5 DOLLARS

Titanium **Ruler:** Elizabeth II **Subject:** Bejing Olympics

| Date | Mintage | VF20 | XF40 | MS60 | MS63 | MS65 |
|---|---|---|---|---|---|---|
| 2009 PM | — | PF65 55.00 | | | | |

### KM# 399 5 DOLLARS

7.00 g., Bi-Metallic Gold and Titanium, 38.6 mm. **Ruler:** Elizabeth II **Subject:** 175th Anniversary of Publication of Hans Christian Anderson's first book **Rev:** Scene from the Little Mermaid

| Date | Mintage | VF20 | XF40 | MS60 | MS63 | MS65 |
|---|---|---|---|---|---|---|
| 2010 PM | Est. 5000 | PF65 120 | | | | |

### KM# 400 5 DOLLARS

10.00 g., Tri-Metallic Silver, Gold and Titanium, 38.6 mm. **Ruler:** Elizabeth II **Subject:** 175th Anniversary of Publication of Hans Christian Andersen's first book **Rev:** Scene from the Little Mermaid

| Date | Mintage | VF20 | XF40 | MS60 | MS63 | MS65 |
|---|---|---|---|---|---|---|
| 2010 PM | Est. 7500 | PF65 120 | | | | |

### KM# 433 5 DOLLARS

35.50 g., Bronze, 50 mm. **Ruler:** Elizabeth II **Subject:** RMS Titanic Remembered

| Date | Mintage | VF20 | XF40 | MS60 | MS63 | MS65 |
|---|---|---|---|---|---|---|
| 2012 | Est. 7500 | — | — | — | — | — |
| Uncirculated | | | | | | |

### KM# 181 10 DOLLARS

28.28 g., 0.925 Silver 0.841 oz. ASW, 38.6 mm. **Subject:** Sir Francis Drake **Obv:** Queen's bust right **Rev:** Ship, portrait and map **Edge:** Reeded

| Date | Mintage | VF20 | XF40 | MS60 | MS63 | MS65 |
|---|---|---|---|---|---|---|
| 2002 | — | PF65 45.00 | | | | |

### KM# 184 10 DOLLARS

28.28 g., 0.925 Silver 0.841 oz. ASW, 38.6 mm. **Subject:** Sir Walter Raleigh **Obv:** Queen's bust right **Rev:** Ship, portrait and map **Edge:** Reeded

| Date | Mintage | VF20 | XF40 | MS60 | MS63 | MS65 |
|---|---|---|---|---|---|---|
| 2002 | — | PF65 45.00 | | | | |

### KM# 188 10 DOLLARS

28.28 g., 0.925 Gold Clad Silver 0.841 oz., 38.6 mm. **Subject:** Queen's Golden Jubilee **Obv:** Queen's bust right **Rev:** Queen on horse trotting left **Edge:** Reeded

| Date | Mintage | VF20 | XF40 | MS60 | MS63 | MS65 |
|---|---|---|---|---|---|---|
| 2002 | 10,000 | PF65 42.50 | | | | |

### KM# 191 10 DOLLARS

28.28 g., 0.925 Gold Clad Silver 0.841 oz., 38.6 mm. **Subject:** Queen's Golden Jubilee **Obv:** Queen's bust right **Rev:** 3/4-length Queen seated on throne **Edge:** Reeded

| Date | Mintage | VF20 | XF40 | MS60 | MS63 | MS65 |
|---|---|---|---|---|---|---|
| 2002 | 10,000 | PF65 45.00 | | | | |

**KM# 194 10 DOLLARS**
28.28 g., 0.925 Gold Clad Silver 0.841 oz., 38.6 mm. **Subject:** Queen's Golden Jubilee **Obv:** Queen's bust right **Rev:** Queen with President Ronald Reagan and First Lady Nancy Reagan **Edge:** Reeded

| Date | Mintage | VF20 | XF40 | MS60 | MS63 | MS65 |
|---|---|---|---|---|---|---|
| 2002 | — | PF65 45.00 | | | | |

**KM# 197 10 DOLLARS**
28.28 g., 0.925 Gold Clad Silver 0.841 oz., 38.6 mm. **Subject:** Queen's Golden Jubilee **Obv:** Queen's bust right **Rev:** Carnival dancers **Edge:** Reeded

| Date | Mintage | VF20 | XF40 | MS60 | MS63 | MS65 |
|---|---|---|---|---|---|---|
| 2002 | 10,000 | PF65 45.00 | | | | |

**KM# 200 10 DOLLARS**
28.28 g., 0.925 Silver 0.841 oz. ASW, 38.6 mm. **Subject:** Teddy Bear Centennial **Obv:** Queen's bust right **Rev:** Teddy bear **Edge:** Reeded

| Date | Mintage | VF20 | XF40 | MS60 | MS63 | MS65 |
|---|---|---|---|---|---|---|
| 2002 | 10,000 | PF65 40.00 | | | | |

**KM# 205 10 DOLLARS**
28.28 g., 0.925 Silver 0.841 oz. ASW, 38.6 mm. **Subject:** Princess Diana **Obv:** Queen's bust right **Rev:** Diana's portrait **Edge:** Reeded

| Date | Mintage | VF20 | XF40 | MS60 | MS63 | MS65 |
|---|---|---|---|---|---|---|
| 2002 | 10,000 | PF65 40.00 | | | | |

**KM# 208.1 10 DOLLARS**
28.28 g., 0.925 Silver 0.841 oz. ASW, 38.6 mm. **Subject:** September 11, 2001 **Obv:** Queen's bust right **Rev:** World Trade Center twin towers **Edge:** Reeded

| Date | Mintage | VF20 | XF40 | MS60 | MS63 | MS65 |
|---|---|---|---|---|---|---|
| 2002 | 10,000 | PF65 50.00 | | | | |

**KM# 208.2 10 DOLLARS**
28.28 g., 0.925 Silver 0.841 oz. ASW, 38.6 mm. **Subject:** September 11, 2001 **Obv:** Queen's bust right **Rev:** Holographic multicolor World Trade Center twin towers **Edge:** Reeded

| Date | Mintage | VF20 | XF40 | MS60 | MS63 | MS65 |
|---|---|---|---|---|---|---|
| 2002 | 10,000 | PF65 45.00 | | | | |

**KM# 211 10 DOLLARS**
28.28 g., 0.925 Silver 0.841 oz. ASW, 38.6 mm. **Subject:** September 11, 2001 **Obv:** Queen's bust right **Rev:** Statue of Liberty **Edge:** Reeded

| Date | Mintage | VF20 | XF40 | MS60 | MS63 | MS65 |
|---|---|---|---|---|---|---|
| 2002 | 10,000 | PF65 40.00 | | | | |

**KM# 214 10 DOLLARS**
28.28 g., 0.925 Silver 0.841 oz. ASW, 38.6 mm. **Subject:** Queen Mother **Obv:** Queen's bust right **Rev:** Queen Mother with young Prince Charles **Edge:** Reeded

| Date | Mintage | VF20 | XF40 | MS60 | MS63 | MS65 |
|---|---|---|---|---|---|---|
| 2002 PM | 10,000 | PF65 40.00 | | | | |

**KM# 217 10 DOLLARS**
28.28 g., 0.925 Silver 0.841 oz. ASW, 38.6 mm. **Subject:** Queen Mother Series **Obv:** Queen's bust right **Rev:** Queen Mother with four grandchildren **Edge:** Reeded

| Date | Mintage | VF20 | XF40 | MS60 | MS63 | MS65 |
|---|---|---|---|---|---|---|
| 2002 PM | 10,000 | PF65 40.00 | | | | |

**KM# 220 10 DOLLARS**
28.28 g., 0.925 Silver 0.841 oz. ASW, 38.6 mm. **Subject:** Queen Mother Series **Obv:** Queen's bust right **Rev:** Queen Mother with uniformed Prince Charles **Edge:** Reeded

| Date | Mintage | VF20 | XF40 | MS60 | MS63 | MS65 |
|---|---|---|---|---|---|---|
| 2002 PM | 10,000 | PF65 40.00 | | | | |

**KM# 223 10 DOLLARS**
28.28 g., 0.925 Silver 0.841 oz. ASW, 38.6 mm. **Subject:** Queen Mother Series **Obv:** Queen's bust right **Rev:** Queen Mother's coffin **Edge:** Reeded

| Date | Mintage | VF20 | XF40 | MS60 | MS63 | MS65 |
|---|---|---|---|---|---|---|
| 2002 PM | 10,000 | PF65 40.00 | | | | |

**KM# 226 10 DOLLARS**
28.28 g., 0.925 Silver 0.841 oz. ASW, 38.6 mm. **Subject:** Kennedy Assassination **Obv:** Queen's bust right **Rev:** President Kennedy's head left **Edge:** Reeded

| Date | Mintage | VF20 | XF40 | MS60 | MS63 | MS65 |
|---|---|---|---|---|---|---|
| 2003 | 10,000 | PF65 50.00 | | | | |

**KM# 230 10 DOLLARS**
28.28 g., 0.925 Silver 0.841 oz. ASW, 38.6 mm. **Subject:** Powered Flight Centennial **Obv:** Queen's bust right **Rev:** Three historic airplanes and rocket **Edge:** Reeded

| Date | Mintage | VF20 | XF40 | MS60 | MS63 | MS65 |
|---|---|---|---|---|---|---|
| 2003 | 10,000 | PF65 45.00 | | | | |

**KM# 233 10 DOLLARS**
28.28 g., 0.925 Silver 0.841 oz. ASW, 38.6 mm. **Obv:** Queen's bust right **Rev:** Henry VIII and Elizabeth I **Edge:** Reeded

| Date | Mintage | VF20 | XF40 | MS60 | MS63 | MS65 |
|---|---|---|---|---|---|---|
| 2003 | 10,000 | PF65 42.00 | | | | |

**KM# 236 10 DOLLARS**
28.28 g., 0.925 Silver 0.841 oz. ASW, 38.6 mm. **Obv:** Queen's bust right **Rev:** Matthew Parker, Archbishop of Canterbury **Edge:** Reeded

| Date | Mintage | VF20 | XF40 | MS60 | MS63 | MS65 |
|---|---|---|---|---|---|---|
| 2003 | 10,000 | PF65 42.00 | | | | |

**KM# 239 10 DOLLARS**
28.28 g., 0.925 Silver 0.841 oz. ASW, 38.6 mm. **Obv:** Queen's bust right **Rev:** Sir Francis Drake and ships **Edge:** Reeded

| Date | Mintage | VF20 | XF40 | MS60 | MS63 | MS65 |
|---|---|---|---|---|---|---|
| 2003 | 10,000 | PF65 42.00 | | | | |

**KM# 242 10 DOLLARS**
28.28 g., 0.925 Silver 0.841 oz. ASW, 38.6 mm. **Obv:** Queen's bust right **Rev:** Sir Walter Raleigh **Edge:** Reeded

| Date | Mintage | VF20 | XF40 | MS60 | MS63 | MS65 |
|---|---|---|---|---|---|---|
| 2003 | 10,000 | PF65 42.00 | | | | |

**KM# 245 10 DOLLARS**
28.28 g., 0.925 Silver 0.841 oz. ASW, 38.6 mm. **Obv:** Queen's bust right **Rev:** Sir William Shakespeare **Edge:** Reeded

| Date | Mintage | VF20 | XF40 | MS60 | MS63 | MS65 |
|---|---|---|---|---|---|---|
| 2003 | 10,000 | PF65 42.00 | | | | |

**KM# 248 10 DOLLARS**
28.28 g., 0.925 Silver 0.841 oz. ASW, 38.6 mm. **Obv:** Queen's bust right **Rev:** Elizabeth I above her funeral procession **Edge:** Reeded

| Date | Mintage | VF20 | XF40 | MS60 | MS63 | MS65 |
|---|---|---|---|---|---|---|
| 2003 | 10,000 | PF65 42.00 | | | | |

**KM# 251 10 DOLLARS**
28.28 g., 0.925 Silver 0.841 oz. ASW, 38.6 mm. **Subject:** Olympics **Obv:** Queen's bust right **Rev:** Ancient bust, runners and coin **Edge:** Reeded

| Date | Mintage | VF20 | XF40 | MS60 | MS63 | MS65 |
|---|---|---|---|---|---|---|
| 2003 | 10,000 | PF65 42.00 | | | | |

**KM# 254 10 DOLLARS**
28.28 g., 0.925 Silver 0.841 oz. ASW, 38.6 mm. **Subject:** Olympics **Obv:** Queen's bust right **Rev:** Ancient bust, charioteer and coin **Edge:** Reeded

| Date | Mintage | VF20 | XF40 | MS60 | MS63 | MS65 |
|---|---|---|---|---|---|---|
| 2003 | 10,000 | PF65 42.00 | | | | |

**KM# 311 10 DOLLARS**
28.30 g., 0.925 Gold Clad Silver 0.8416 oz., 38.6 mm. **Subject:** Queen Elizabeth's Golden Coronation Jubilee **Obv:** Elizabeth II **Rev:** Cameo portrait above ship "Gothic **Edge:** Reeded

| Date | Mintage | VF20 | XF40 | MS60 | MS63 | MS65 |
|---|---|---|---|---|---|---|
| 2003 | — | PF65 50.00 | | | | |

**KM# 266 10 DOLLARS**
28.28 g., 0.925 Silver 0.841 oz. ASW, 38.6 mm. **Obv:** Queen's bust right **Rev:** Sir Francis Drake, ship and map **Edge:** Reeded

| Date | Mintage | VF20 | XF40 | MS60 | MS63 | MS65 |
|---|---|---|---|---|---|---|
| 2004 | 10,000 | PF65 45.00 | | | | |

**KM# 270.1 10 DOLLARS**
28.28 g., 0.925 Silver 0.841 oz. ASW, 38.6 mm. **Obv:** Queen's bust right **Rev:** Peter Rabbit **Edge:** Reeded

| Date | Mintage | VF20 | XF40 | MS60 | MS63 | MS65 |
|---|---|---|---|---|---|---|
| 2004 | 5,000 | PF65 47.50 | | | | |

**KM# 270.2 10 DOLLARS**
28.28 g., 0.925 Silver 0.841 oz. ASW, 38.6 mm. **Obv:** Queen's bust right **Rev:** Multicolor Peter Rabbit **Edge:** Reeded

| Date | Mintage | VF20 | XF40 | MS60 | MS63 | MS65 |
|---|---|---|---|---|---|---|
| 2004 | — | PF65 65.00 | | | | |

**KM# 274 10 DOLLARS**
1.24 g., 0.9999 Gold 0.040 oz. AGW, 14 mm. **Obv:** Queen's bust right **Rev:** Hernando Pizarro **Edge:** Reeded

| Date | Mintage | VF20 | XF40 | MS60 | MS63 | MS65 |
|---|---|---|---|---|---|---|
| 2004 | 350 | PF65 85.00 | | | | |

**KM# 282 10 DOLLARS**
28.28 g., 0.925 Silver 0.841 oz. ASW, 38.6 mm. **Obv:** Queen's bust right **Rev:** Sailor above two D-Day landing craft **Edge:** Reeded

| Date | Mintage | VF20 | XF40 | MS60 | MS63 | MS65 |
|---|---|---|---|---|---|---|
| 2004 | 10,000 | PF65 50.00 | | | | |

**KM# 287 10 DOLLARS**
31.10 g., 0.999 Silver 0.999 oz. ASW, 38.6 mm. **Obv:** Queen's bust right **Rev:** Dolphin **Edge:** Reeded

| Date | Mintage | VF20 | XF40 | MS60 | MS63 | MS65 |
|---|---|---|---|---|---|---|
| 2004 | 10,000 | PF65 55.00 | | | | |

**KM# 288 10 DOLLARS**
1.24 g., 0.9999 Gold 0.040 oz. AGW, 14 mm. **Obv:** Queen's bust right **Rev:** Dolphin **Edge:** Reeded

| Date | Mintage | VF20 | XF40 | MS60 | MS63 | MS65 |
|---|---|---|---|---|---|---|
| 2004 | 10,000 | PF63 70.00 | PF65 75.00 | | | |

**KM# 298 10 DOLLARS**
28.28 g., 0.925 Silver 0.841 oz. ASW, 38.6 mm. **Obv:** Queen's bust right **Rev:** Soldier above tank and jeeps **Edge:** Reeded

| Date | Mintage | VF20 | XF40 | MS60 | MS63 | MS65 |
|---|---|---|---|---|---|---|
| 2004 | 10,000 | PF65 50.00 | | | | |

**KM# 301 10 DOLLARS**
28.28 g., 0.925 Silver 0.841 oz. ASW, 38.6 mm. **Obv:** Queen's bust right **Rev:** Pilot and planes above D-Day landing **Edge:** Reeded

| Date | Mintage | VF20 | XF40 | MS60 | MS63 | MS65 |
|---|---|---|---|---|---|---|
| 2004 | 10,000 | PF65 50.00 | | | | |

**KM# 304 10 DOLLARS**
28.28 g., 0.925 Silver 0.841 oz. ASW, 38.6 mm. **Obv:** Queen's bust right **Rev:** Ancient Olympic bust, runners and owl coin **Edge:** Reeded

| Date | Mintage | VF20 | XF40 | MS60 | MS63 | MS65 |
|---|---|---|---|---|---|---|
| 2004 | 10,000 | PF65 50.00 | | | | |

**KM# 307 10 DOLLARS**
28.28 g., 0.925 Silver 0.841 oz. ASW, 38.6 mm. **Obv:** Queen's bust right **Rev:** Ancient Olympic bust, charioteer and Zeus coin **Edge:** Reeded

| Date | Mintage | VF20 | XF40 | MS60 | MS63 | MS65 |
|---|---|---|---|---|---|---|
| 2004 | 10,000 | PF65 50.00 | | | | |

**KM# 313 10 DOLLARS**
31.10 g., 0.999 Silver 0.999 oz. ASW, 38.6 mm. **Obv:** Bust of Queen Elizabeth II right **Rev:** Mother and baby dolphin **Edge:** Reeded

| Date | Mintage | VF20 | XF40 | MS60 | MS63 | MS65 |
|---|---|---|---|---|---|---|
| 2005 | 10,000 | PF65 55.00 | | | | |

**KM# 314 10 DOLLARS**
1.24 g., 0.9999 Gold 0.040 oz. AGW, 13.92 mm. **Obv:** Bust of Queen Elizabeth II right **Rev:** Mother and baby dolphin **Edge:** Reeded

| Date | Mintage | VF20 | XF40 | MS60 | MS63 | MS65 |
|---|---|---|---|---|---|---|
| 2005 | 10,000 | PF63 70.00 | PF65 75.00 | | | |

**KM# 350 10 DOLLARS**
28.28 g., 0.925 Silver 0.841 oz. ASW, 38.60 mm. **Ruler:** Elizabeth II **Subject:** 5th Anniversary - Attack on Twin Towers, New York City **Obv:** Crowned bust right **Obv. Legend:** BRITISH VIRGIN ISLANDS — QUEEN ELIZABETH II **Rev:** Twin Towers in sprays, remembrance ribbon privy mark at upper right **Rev. Inscription:** LEST WE FORGET **Edge:** Reeded

| Date | Mintage | VF20 | XF40 | MS60 | MS63 | MS65 |
|---|---|---|---|---|---|---|
| 2006 | 10,000 | PF65 77.50 | | | | |

### KM# 333 10 DOLLARS

28.28 g., 0.9167 Silver 0.8335 oz. ASW, 38.60 mm. **Ruler:** Elizabeth II **Subject:** 400th Anniversary Founding of Jamestown **Obv:** Bust with tiara right **Obv. Legend:** BRITISH VIRGIN ISLANDS — QUEEN ELIZABETH II **Rev:** British lion laying, American eagle perched on sprays **Rev. Legend:** UNITED IN FRIENDSHIP **Edge:** Reeded

| Date | Mintage | VF20 | XF40 | MS60 | MS63 | MS65 |
|---|---|---|---|---|---|---|
| 2007 | 25,000 | PF63 65.00 | PF65 75.00 | | | |

### KM# 334 10 DOLLARS

1.24 g., 0.9999 Gold 0.040 oz. AGW, 13.92 mm. **Ruler:** Elizabeth II **Subject:** 400th Anniversary Founding of Jamestown **Obv:** Bust with tiara right **Obv. Legend:** BRITISH VIRGIN ISLANDS — QUEEN ELIZABETH II **Rev:** British lion laying, American eagle perched on sprays **Rev. Legend:** UNITED IN FRIENDSHIP **Edge:** Reeded

| Date | Mintage | VF20 | XF40 | MS60 | MS63 | MS65 |
|---|---|---|---|---|---|---|
| 2007 | 20,000 | PF63 65.00 | PF65 75.00 | | | |

### KM# 339 10 DOLLARS

28.28 g., Copper-Nickel **Ruler:** Elizabeth II **Subject:** 10th Anniversary Death of Princess Diana **Obv:** Bust with tiara right **Obv. Legend:** BRITISH VIRGIN ISLANDS — QUEEN ELIZABETH II **Rev:** Mother Teresa at left, Princess Diana at right **Rev. Legend:** MOTHER TERESA • IN LOVING MEMORY • PRINCESS DIANA **Edge:** Reeded

| Date | Mintage | VF20 | XF40 | MS60 | MS63 | MS65 |
|---|---|---|---|---|---|---|
| 2007 | — | — | — | — | 16.50 | 18.50 |

### KM# 339a 10 DOLLARS

0.9167 Silver **Ruler:** Elizabeth II **Subject:** 10th Anniversary - Death of Princess Diana **Obv:** Bust with tiara right **Obv. Legend:** BRITISH VIRGIN ISLANDS — QUEEN ELIZABETH II **Rev:** Mother Teresa at left, Princess Diana at right **Rev. Legend:** MOTHER TERESA • IN LOVING MEMORY • PRINCESS DIANA **Edge:** Reeded

| Date | Mintage | VF20 | XF40 | MS60 | MS63 | MS65 |
|---|---|---|---|---|---|---|
| 2007 | — | PF65 75.00 | | | | |

### KM# 341 10 DOLLARS

28.28 g., Copper-Nickel **Ruler:** Elizabeth II **Subject:** Diamond Wedding Anniversary **Obv:** Conjoined busts with Philip right **Obv. Legend:** BRITISH VIRGIN ISLANDS — QUEEN ELIZABETH II **Rev:** Bride to be and King George VI standing facing **Rev. Legend:** Diamond Wedding of H.M. Queen Elizabeth II & H.R.H. Prince Philip **Rev. Inscription:** THE GIVING AWAY **Edge:** Reeded

| Date | Mintage | VF20 | XF40 | MS60 | MS63 | MS65 |
|---|---|---|---|---|---|---|
| 2007 | — | — | — | — | 16.50 | 18.50 |

### KM# 341a 10 DOLLARS

28.28 g., 0.925 Silver 0.841 oz. ASW **Ruler:** Elizabeth II **Subject:** Diamond Wedding Anniversary **Obv:** Conjoined busts with Philip right **Obv. Legend:** BRITISH VIRGIN ISLANDS — QUEEN ELIZABETH II **Rev:** Bride to be and King George VI standing facing **Rev. Legend:** Diamond Wedding of H.M. Queen Elizabeth II & H.R.H. Prince Philip **Rev. Inscription:** THE GIVING AWAY **Edge:** Reeded

| Date | Mintage | VF20 | XF40 | MS60 | MS63 | MS65 |
|---|---|---|---|---|---|---|
| 2007 | — | PF65 75.00 | | | | |

### KM# 342 10 DOLLARS

28.28 g., Copper-Nickel **Ruler:** Elizabeth II **Subject:** Diamond Wedding Anniversary **Obv:** Conjoined busts with Philip right **Obv. Legend:** BRITISH VIRGIN ISLANDS — QUEEN ELIZABETH II **Rev. Legend:** Diamond Wedding of H.M. Queen Elizabeth II & H.R.H. Prince Philip **Rev. Inscription:** THE GLASS COACH **Edge:** Reeded

| Date | Mintage | VF20 | XF40 | MS60 | MS63 | MS65 |
|---|---|---|---|---|---|---|
| 2007 | — | — | — | — | 16.50 | 18.50 |

### KM# 342a 10 DOLLARS

28.28 g., 0.925 Silver 0.841 oz. ASW **Ruler:** Elizabeth II **Subject:** Diamond Wedding Anniversary **Obv:** Conjoined busts with Philip right **Obv. Legend:** BRITISH VIRGIN ISLANDS — QUEEN ELIZABETH II **Rev. Legend:** Diamond Wedding of H.M. Queen Elizabeth II & H.R.H. Prince Philip **Rev. Inscription:** THE GLASS COACH **Edge:** Reeded

| Date | Mintage | VF20 | XF40 | MS60 | MS63 | MS65 |
|---|---|---|---|---|---|---|
| 2007 | — | PF65 75.00 | | | | |

### KM# 343 10 DOLLARS

28.28 g., Copper-Nickel **Ruler:** Elizabeth II **Subject:** Diamond Wedding Anniversary **Obv:** Conjoined busts with Philip right **Obv. Legend:** BRITISH VIRGIN ISLANDS — QUEEN ELIZABETH II **Rev. Legend:** Diamond Wedding of H.M. Queen Elizabeth II & H.R.H. Prince Philip **Rev. Inscription:** THE HONEYMOON **Edge:** Reeded

| Date | Mintage | VF20 | XF40 | MS60 | MS63 | MS65 |
|---|---|---|---|---|---|---|
| 2007 | — | — | — | — | 16.50 | 18.50 |

### KM# 343a 10 DOLLARS

28.28 g., 0.925 Silver 0.841 oz. ASW **Ruler:** Elizabeth II **Subject:** Diamond Wedding Anniversary **Obv:** Conjoined busts with Philip right **Obv. Legend:** BRITISH VIRGIN ISLANDS — QUEEN ELIZABETH II **Rev. Legend:** Diamond Wedding of H.M. Queen Elizabeth II & H.R.H. Prince Philip **Rev. Inscription:** THE HONEYMOON **Edge:** Reeded

| Date | Mintage | VF20 | XF40 | MS60 | MS63 | MS65 |
|---|---|---|---|---|---|---|
| 2007 | — | PF65 75.00 | | | | |

### KM# 344 10 DOLLARS

28.28 g., Copper-Nickel **Ruler:** Elizabeth II **Subject:** Diamond Wedding Anniversary **Obv:** Conjoined busts with Philip right **Obv. Legend:** BRITISH VIRGIN ISLANDS — QUEEN ELIZABETH II **Rev. Legend:** Diamond Wedding of H.M. Queen Elizabeth II & H.R.H. Prince Philip **Rev. Inscription:** THE WEDDING PROGRAM **Edge:** Reeded

| Date | Mintage | VF20 | XF40 | MS60 | MS63 | MS65 |
|---|---|---|---|---|---|---|
| 2007 | — | — | — | — | 16.50 | 18.50 |

### KM# 344a 10 DOLLARS

28.28 g., 0.925 Silver 0.841 oz. ASW **Ruler:** Elizabeth II **Subject:** Diamond Wedding Anniversary **Obv:** Conjoined busts with Philip right **Obv. Legend:** BRITISH VIRGIN ISLANDS — QUEEN ELIZABETH II **Rev. Legend:** Diamond Wedding of H.M. Queen Elizabeth II & H.R.H. Prince Philip **Rev. Inscription:** THE WEDDING PROGRAM **Edge:** Reeded

| Date | Mintage | VF20 | XF40 | MS60 | MS63 | MS65 |
|---|---|---|---|---|---|---|
| 2007 | — | PF65 75.00 | | | | |

### KM# 411 10 DOLLARS

28.28 g., 0.925 Silver 0.841 oz. ASW, 38.61 mm. **Ruler:** Elizabeth II **Subject:** Act of Union, 300th Anniversary **Obv:** Bust in tiara right **Rev:** Flags above Queen Anne's portrait, lion and unicorn supporters flanking

| Date | Mintage | VF20 | XF40 | MS60 | MS63 | MS65 |
|---|---|---|---|---|---|---|
| 2007 PM | — | PF65 42.00 | | | | |

### KM# 371 10 DOLLARS

28.28 g., 0.925 Silver 0.841 oz. ASW, 38.6 mm. **Ruler:** Elizabeth II **Obv:** Bust right **Rev:** Two soccer players and leopard

| Date | Mintage | VF20 | XF40 | MS60 | MS63 | MS65 |
|---|---|---|---|---|---|---|
| 2009 | 10,000 | PF65 40.00 | | | | |
| 2010 | — | PF65 40.00 | | | | |

### KM# 372 10 DOLLARS

1.24 g., 0.999 Gold 0.0398 oz. AGW, 13.92 mm. **Ruler:** Elizabeth II **Obv:** Bust right **Rev:** Henry VIII facing

| Date | Mintage | VF20 | XF40 | MS60 | MS63 | MS65 |
|---|---|---|---|---|---|---|
| 2009 PM | 5,000 | PF63 75.00 | PF65 80.00 | | | |

### KM# 374 10 DOLLARS

28.28 g., 0.925 Silver 0.841 oz. ASW, 38.6 mm. **Ruler:** Elizabeth II **Obv:** Bust right **Rev:** Elizabeth I aboard ship

| Date | Mintage | VF20 | XF40 | MS60 | MS63 | MS65 |
|---|---|---|---|---|---|---|
| 2009 | 10,000 | PF65 42.00 | | | | |

### KM# 376 10 DOLLARS

28.28 g., 0.925 Silver 0.841 oz. ASW, 38.6 mm. **Ruler:** Elizabeth II **Obv:** Bust right **Rev:** Elizabeth I between two columns

| Date | Mintage | VF20 | XF40 | MS60 | MS63 | MS65 |
|---|---|---|---|---|---|---|
| 2009 | 10,000 | PF65 42.00 | | | | |

### KM# 382 10 DOLLARS

28.28 g., Copper-Nickel, 38.6 mm. **Ruler:** Elizabeth II **Subject:** Centennial of Naval Aviation **Rev:** 1936 Fairey Swordfish returning to carrier HMS Fencer

| Date | Mintage | VF20 | XF40 | MS60 | MS63 | MS65 |
|---|---|---|---|---|---|---|
| 2009 | — | — | — | — | — | 7.50 |

### KM# 382a 10 DOLLARS

28.28 g., Silver, 38.6 mm. **Ruler:** Elizabeth II **Subject:** Centennial of Naval Aviation **Rev:** 1936 Fairey Swordfish returing to carrier HMS Fencer

| Date | Mintage | VF20 | XF40 | MS60 | MS63 | MS65 |
|---|---|---|---|---|---|---|
| 2009 | 10,000 | PF65 40.00 | | | | |

### KM# 394 10 DOLLARS

28.28 g., 0.925 Silver 0.841 oz. ASW, 38.6 mm. **Ruler:** Elizabeth II **Subject:** Peanuts 60th Anniversary **Rev:** Multicolor Snoopy asleep atop doghouse

| Date | Mintage | VF20 | XF40 | MS60 | MS63 | MS65 |
|---|---|---|---|---|---|---|
| 2010 PM | 10,000 | PF65 40.00 | | | | |

### KM# 395 10 DOLLARS

1.24 g., 0.999 Gold 0.0398 oz. AGW, 13.92 mm. **Ruler:** Elizabeth II **Series:** Peanuts 60th Anniversary **Rev:** Snoopy asleep atop doghouse

| Date | Mintage | VF20 | XF40 | MS60 | MS63 | MS65 |
|---|---|---|---|---|---|---|
| 2010 PM | 10,000 | PF63 85.00 | PF65 95.00 | | | |

### KM# 397 10 DOLLARS

31.11 g., 0.999 Silver 0.9991 oz. ASW, 38.6 mm. **Ruler:** Elizabeth II **Subject:** Elgin Marbles **Rev:** Two horsemen

| Date | Mintage | VF20 | XF40 | MS60 | MS63 | MS65 |
|---|---|---|---|---|---|---|
| 2010 PM | 10,000 | PF65 50.00 | | | | |

### KM# 398 10 DOLLARS

1.22 g., 0.999 Gold 0.0392 oz. AGW, 13.92 mm. **Ruler:** Elizabeth II **Subject:** Birth of Venus

| Date | Mintage | VF20 | XF40 | MS60 | MS63 | MS65 |
|---|---|---|---|---|---|---|
| 2010 PM | Est. 10000 | PF63 85.00 | PF65 95.00 | | | |

**KM# 401 10 DOLLARS**
28.28 g., 0.925 Silver 0.841 oz. ASW, 38.6 mm. **Ruler:** Elizabeth II **Subject:** Birth of Venus

| Date | Mintage | VF20 | XF40 | MS60 | MS63 | MS65 |
|---|---|---|---|---|---|---|
| 2010 | Est. 10000 | PF65 50.00 | | | | |

**KM# 406 10 DOLLARS**
28.28 g., 0.925 Silver 0.841 oz. ASW, 38.61 mm. **Ruler:** Elizabeth II **Obv:** Bust in tiara right **Rev:** World Trade Center complex

| Date | Mintage | VF20 | XF40 | MS60 | MS63 | MS65 |
|---|---|---|---|---|---|---|
| 2011 PM | — | PF65 45.00 | | | | |

**KM# 407 10 DOLLARS**
28.28 g., 0.925 Silver 0.841 oz. ASW, 38.61 mm. **Ruler:** Elizabeth II **Subject:** Queen Elizabeth II's 85th Birthday **Obv:** Older and young busts conjoined right **Rev:** Queen on horseback left

| Date | Mintage | VF20 | XF40 | MS60 | MS63 | MS65 |
|---|---|---|---|---|---|---|
| 2011 PM | — | PF65 42.00 | | | | |

**KM# 408 10 DOLLARS**
28.28 g., 0.925 Silver 0.841 oz. ASW, 38.61 mm. **Ruler:** Elizabeth II **Subject:** Royal Wedding - Prince William and Catherine Middleton **Obv:** Bust in tiara right **Rev:** Busts of Catherine and William

| Date | Mintage | VF20 | XF40 | MS60 | MS63 | MS65 |
|---|---|---|---|---|---|---|
| 2011 PM | — | PF65 42.00 | | | | |

**KM# 409 10 DOLLARS**
1.22 g., 0.999 Gold 0.0392 oz. AGW, 13.92 mm. **Ruler:** Elizabeth II **Obv:** Bust in tiara right **Rev:** Anne Boylen bust 1/4 left

| Date | Mintage | VF20 | XF40 | MS60 | MS63 | MS65 |
|---|---|---|---|---|---|---|
| 2011 PM | — | PF63 90.00 | | PF65 100 | | |

**KM# 410 10 DOLLARS**
28.28 g., Silver with insert, 38.61 mm. **Ruler:** Elizabeth II **Subject:** Life cycle of a tree frog **Obv:** Frog at center **Rev:** Life cycle of a tree frog

| Date | Mintage | VF20 | XF40 | MS60 | MS63 | MS65 |
|---|---|---|---|---|---|---|
| 2011 PM | — | PF65 120 | | | | |

**KM# 417 10 DOLLARS**
28.28 g., 0.925 Silver 0.841 oz. ASW, 38.61 mm. **Ruler:** Elizabeth II **Subject:** Life of Queen Elizabeth II **Obv:** Current and young busts conjoined right **Rev:** Half length bust facing wearing Order sash and tiara

| Date | Mintage | VF20 | XF40 | MS60 | MS63 | MS65 |
|---|---|---|---|---|---|---|
| 2012 PM | — | PF65 50.00 | | | | |

**KM# 418 10 DOLLARS**
28.28 g., Silver, 38.6 mm. **Ruler:** Elizabeth II **Subject:** Life of Queen Elizabeth II **Obv:** Conjoined busts right **Rev:** Elizabeth II on horseback as if reviewing troops

| Date | Mintage | VF20 | XF40 | MS60 | MS63 | MS65 |
|---|---|---|---|---|---|---|
| 2012 PM Proof | — | — | — | — | — | 50.00 |

**KM# 419 10 DOLLARS**
28.28 g., Copper-Nickel, 38.6 mm. **Ruler:** Elizabeth II **Subject:** Valentine's day **Obv:** Conjoined busts right **Rev:** Crescent moon and pixi

| Date | Mintage | VF20 | XF40 | MS60 | MS63 | MS65 |
|---|---|---|---|---|---|---|
| 2012 PM | — | — | — | — | — | 15.00 |

**KM# 420 10 DOLLARS**
28.28 g., 0.925 Silver 0.841 oz. ASW, 38.6 mm. **Ruler:** Elizabeth II **Subject:** Summer Olympics, London **Obv:** Conjoined busts right **Rev:** Gymnast on pommel horse, Union Jack in color below

| Date | Mintage | VF20 | XF40 | MS60 | MS63 | MS65 |
|---|---|---|---|---|---|---|
| 2012 PM | — | PF65 50.00 | | | | |

**KM# 421 10 DOLLARS**
28.28 g., 0.925 Silver 0.841 oz. ASW, 38.6 mm. **Ruler:** Elizabeth II **Subject:** Summer Olympics, London **Obv:** Conjoined busts right **Rev:** Dressage, Union Jack in color below

| Date | Mintage | VF20 | XF40 | MS60 | MS63 | MS65 |
|---|---|---|---|---|---|---|
| 2012 PM | — | PF65 50.00 | | | | |

**KM# 422 10 DOLLARS**
28.28 g., 0.925 Silver 0.841 oz. ASW, 38.6 mm. **Ruler:** Elizabeth II **Subject:** Summer Olympics, London **Obv:** Conjoined busts right **Rev:** Fencing, Union Jack in color below

| Date | Mintage | VF20 | XF40 | MS60 | MS63 | MS65 |
|---|---|---|---|---|---|---|
| 2012 PM | — | PF65 50.00 | | | | |

**KM# 423 10 DOLLARS**
28.28 g., 0.925 Silver 0.841 oz. ASW, 38.6 mm. **Ruler:** Elizabeth II **Subject:** Summer Olympics, London **Obv:** Conjoined busts right **Rev:** Soccer players, Union Jack in color below

| Date | Mintage | VF20 | XF40 | MS60 | MS63 | MS65 |
|---|---|---|---|---|---|---|
| 2012 PM | — | **PF65** 50.00 | | | | |

**KM# 424 10 DOLLARS**
28.28 g., Copper-Nickel, 38.61 mm. **Ruler:** Elizabeth II **Rev:** Prince William

| Date | Mintage | VF20 | XF40 | MS60 | MS63 | MS65 |
|---|---|---|---|---|---|---|
| 2012 PM | — | — | — | — | — | 15.00 |

**KM# 425 10 DOLLARS**
28.28 g., Copper-Nickel, 38.61 mm. **Ruler:** Elizabeth II **Rev:** Duchess of Cambridge

| Date | Mintage | VF20 | XF40 | MS60 | MS63 | MS65 |
|---|---|---|---|---|---|---|
| 2012 PM | — | — | — | — | — | 15.00 |

**KM# 427 10 DOLLARS**
23.40 g., Silver, 38.6 mm. **Ruler:** Elizabeth II **Subject:** Year of the Dragon **Obv:** Dragon at center **Rev:** Dragon at center, Zodiac around

| Date | Mintage | VF20 | XF40 | MS60 | MS63 | MS65 |
|---|---|---|---|---|---|---|
| 2012 Proof | Est. 5000 | — | — | — | — | — |

**KM# 428 10 DOLLARS**
21.11 g., Silver, 62x61 mm. **Ruler:** Elizabeth II **Obv:** Bust with crown right **Rev:** Nefertiti Bust **Shape:** Head

| Date | Mintage | VF20 | XF40 | MS60 | MS63 | MS65 |
|---|---|---|---|---|---|---|
| 2012 | — | **PF65** 65.00 | | | | |

**KM# 430 10 DOLLARS**
28.28 g., 0.925 Silver 0.841 oz. ASW, 38.6 mm. **Ruler:** Elizabeth II **Subject:** Father of the Modern Olympics

| Date | Mintage | VF20 | XF40 | MS60 | MS63 | MS65 |
|---|---|---|---|---|---|---|
| 2012 Proof | Est. 2000 | — | — | — | — | — |

**KM# 432 10 DOLLARS**
28.28 g., Silver, 38.6 mm. **Ruler:** Elizabeth II **Subject:** Father of the Modern Olympics

| Date | Mintage | VF20 | XF40 | MS60 | MS63 | MS65 |
|---|---|---|---|---|---|---|
| 2012 Proof | Est. 10000 | — | — | — | — | — |

**KM# 437 10 DOLLARS**
31.10 g., 0.999 Silver 0.999 oz. ASW, 30 mm. **Ruler:** Elizabeth II **Rev:** Layout of pyrimids in Giza, sand encased **Note:** High relief, 4.5mm

| Date | Mintage | VF20 | XF40 | MS60 | MS63 | MS65 |
|---|---|---|---|---|---|---|
| 2013 PM | 1,999 | — | — | — | — | 35.00 |

**KM# 438 10 DOLLARS**
28.28 g., Copper-Nickel, 38.61 mm. **Ruler:** Elizabeth II **Subject:** Orient Express

| Date | Mintage | VF20 | XF40 | MS60 | MS63 | MS65 |
|---|---|---|---|---|---|---|
| 2013 PM | — | — | — | — | — | 15.00 |

**KM# 438a 10 DOLLARS**
28.28 g., 0.925 Silver 0.841 oz. ASW, 38.61 mm. **Ruler:** Elizabeth II **Subject:** Orient Express

| Date | Mintage | VF20 | XF40 | MS60 | MS63 | MS65 |
|---|---|---|---|---|---|---|
| 2013 PM | 10,000 | **PF65** 60.00 | | | | |

**KM# 440 10 DOLLARS**
28.28 g., 0.925 Silver 0.841 oz. ASW, 38.61 mm. **Ruler:** Elizabeth II **Subject:** Birth of Prince George **Rev:** Prince William with blue footprints added at right

| Date | Mintage | VF20 | XF40 | MS60 | MS63 | MS65 |
|---|---|---|---|---|---|---|
| 2013 PM | 10,000 | **PF65** 60.00 | | | | |

**KM# 442 10 DOLLARS**
28.28 g., 0.925 Silver 0.841 oz. ASW, 38.61 mm. **Ruler:** Elizabeth II **Subject:** Birth of Prince George **Rev:** Katherine and blue footprints added at right

| Date | Mintage | VF20 | XF40 | MS60 | MS63 | MS65 |
|---|---|---|---|---|---|---|
| 2013 PM | 10,000 | **PF65** 60.00 | | | | |

**KM# 444 10 DOLLARS**
28.28 g., 0.925 Silver 0.841 oz. ASW, 38.61 mm. **Ruler:** Elizabeth II **Subject:** Last flight of Concorde, 10th Anniversary **Rev:** Concorde, NY and London skyline

| Date | Mintage | VF20 | XF40 | MS60 | MS63 | MS65 |
|---|---|---|---|---|---|---|
| 2013 PM | 10,000 | **PF65** 60.00 | | | | |

### KM# 444a 10 DOLLARS

28.28 g., 0.925 Silver 0.841 oz. ASW, 38.61 mm. **Ruler:** Elizabeth II **Subject:** Last flight of Concorde, 10th Anniversary **Rev:** Concorde with tailfin in color, NY and London skyline

| Date | Mintage | VF20 | XF40 | MS60 | MS63 | MS65 |
|---|---|---|---|---|---|---|
| 2013 PM | 10,000 | PF65 60.00 | | | | |

### KM# 201 20 DOLLARS

1.24 g., 0.9999 Gold 0.040 oz. AGW, 13.92 mm. **Subject:** Teddy Bear Centennial **Obv:** Queen's bust right **Rev:** Teddy bear **Edge:** Reeded

| Date | Mintage | VF20 | XF40 | MS60 | MS63 | MS65 |
|---|---|---|---|---|---|---|
| 2002 | 10,000 | PF63 70.00 | PF65 75.00 | | | |

### KM# 227 20 DOLLARS

1.24 g., 0.9999 Gold 0.0399 oz. AGW, 13.92 mm. **Subject:** Kennedy Assassination **Obv:** Queen's bust right **Rev:** President Kennedy's portrait **Edge:** Reeded

| Date | Mintage | VF20 | XF40 | MS60 | MS63 | MS65 |
|---|---|---|---|---|---|---|
| 2003 | 10,000 | PF63 70.00 | PF65 75.00 | | | |

### KM# 271 20 DOLLARS

1.24 g., 0.9999 Gold 0.040 oz. AGW, 14 mm. **Obv:** Queen's bust right **Rev:** Peter Rabbit **Edge:** Reeded

| Date | Mintage | VF20 | XF40 | MS60 | MS63 | MS65 |
|---|---|---|---|---|---|---|
| 2004 | 5,000 | PF63 75.00 | PF65 80.00 | | | |

### KM# 279 20 DOLLARS

58.00 g., 0.999 Silver 1.8629 oz. ASW, 50 mm. **Subject:** XXVIII Olympic Games **Obv:** Bust with tiara right **Rev:** 1896 Olympic medal design **Edge:** Reeded

| Date | Mintage | VF20 | XF40 | MS60 | MS63 | MS65 |
|---|---|---|---|---|---|---|
| 2004 PM | 2,004 | PF63 75.00 | PF65 90.00 | | | |

### KM# 279a 20 DOLLARS

63.59 g., 0.999 Silver Gilt 2.0424 oz., 49.93 mm. **Ruler:** Elizabeth II **Subject:** XXVII Olympic Games **Obv:** Bust with tiara right **Rev:** 1896 Olympic medal design **Edge:** Reeded

| Date | Mintage | VF20 | XF40 | MS60 | MS63 | MS65 |
|---|---|---|---|---|---|---|
| 2004 PM | — | PF65 100 | | | | |

### KM# 345 20 DOLLARS

3.96 g., 0.750 Gold 0.0955 oz. AGW, 21.78 mm. **Ruler:** Elizabeth II **Subject:** 500th Anniversary - Death of Columbus **Obv:** Crowned bust right **Obv. Legend:** BRITISH VIRGIN ISLANDS - QUEEN ELIZABETH II **Rev:** Bust of Columbus facing 3/4 left at right, outlined map of the Americas at left **Rev. Legend:** 1451 - CHRISTOPHER COLUMBUS - 1506 **Edge:** Reeded **Note:** Struck in white gold.

| Date | Mintage | VF20 | XF40 | MS60 | MS63 | MS65 |
|---|---|---|---|---|---|---|
| 2006 | 1,506 | PF65 185 | | | | |

### KM# 346 20 DOLLARS

4.02 g., 0.750 Gold 0.0969 oz. AGW, 21.78 mm. **Ruler:** Elizabeth II **Subject:** 500th Anniversary - Death of Columbus **Obv:** Crowned bust right **Obv. Legend:** BRITISH VIRGIN ISLANDS - QUEEN ELIZABETH II **Rev:** Sailing ship "Santa Maria **Rev. Legend:** 1451 - CHRISTOPHER COLUMBUS - 1506 **Edge:** Reeded **Note:** Struck in rose gold.

| Date | Mintage | VF20 | XF40 | MS60 | MS63 | MS65 |
|---|---|---|---|---|---|---|
| 2006 | 1,506 | PF65 185 | | | | |

### KM# 347 20 DOLLARS

3.99 g., 0.750 Gold 0.0962 oz. AGW, 21.78 mm. **Ruler:** Elizabeth II **Subject:** 500th Anniversary - Death of Columbus **Obv:** Crowned bust right **Obv. Legend:** BRITISH VIRGIN ISLANDS - QUEEN ELIZABETH II **Rev:** Sailing ships "Niña" and "Pinta **Rev. Legend:** 1451 - CHRISTOPHER COLUMBUS - 1506 **Edge:** Reeded **Note:** Struck in yellow gold.

| Date | Mintage | VF20 | XF40 | MS60 | MS63 | MS65 |
|---|---|---|---|---|---|---|
| 2006 | 1,506 | PF65 200 | | | | |

### KM# 379 30 DOLLARS

155.50 g., 0.999 Silver 4.9944 oz. ASW **Ruler:** Elizabeth II **Subject:** Nelson's Victory at Trafalgar **Rev:** Two ships

| Date | Mintage | VF20 | XF40 | MS60 | MS63 | MS65 |
|---|---|---|---|---|---|---|
| 2008 | — | PF63 200 | PF65 225 | | | |

### KM# 275 25 DOLLARS

3.11 g., 0.9999 Gold 0.100 oz. AGW, 18 mm. **Obv:** Queen's bust right **Rev:** Hernando Pizarro portrait and life events pictorial **Edge:** Reeded

| Date | Mintage | VF20 | XF40 | MS60 | MS63 | MS65 |
|---|---|---|---|---|---|---|
| 2004 | 350 | PF65 185 | | | | |

### KM# 289 25 DOLLARS

3.11 g., 0.9999 Gold 0.100 oz. AGW, 18 mm. **Obv:** Queen's bust right **Rev:** Dolphin **Edge:** Reeded

| Date | Mintage | VF20 | XF40 | MS60 | MS63 | MS65 |
|---|---|---|---|---|---|---|
| 2004 | 6,000 | PF65 180 | | | | |

### KM# 315 25 DOLLARS

3.11 g., 0.9999 Gold 0.100 oz. AGW, 18 mm. **Obv:** Bust of Queen Elizabeth II right **Rev:** Mother and baby dolphins **Edge:** Reeded

| Date | Mintage | VF20 | XF40 | MS60 | MS63 | MS65 |
|---|---|---|---|---|---|---|
| 2005 | 6,000 | PF65 180 | | | | |

### KM# 335 25 DOLLARS

3.11 g., 0.9999 Gold 0.100 oz. AGW, 17.95 mm. **Ruler:** Elizabeth II **Subject:** 400th Anniversary Founding of Jamestown **Obv:** Bust with tiara right **Obv. Legend:** BRITISH VIRGIN ISLANDS - QUEEN ELIZABETH II **Rev:** British lion laying, American eagle perched on sprays **Rev. Legend:** UNITED IN FRIENDSHIP **Edge:** Reeded

| Date | Mintage | VF20 | XF40 | MS60 | MS63 | MS65 |
|---|---|---|---|---|---|---|
| 2007 | 7,500 | PF65 180 | | | | |

### KM# 412 25 DOLLARS

6.22 g., 0.999 Gold 0.1998 oz. AGW, 22 mm. **Ruler:** Elizabeth II **Subject:** Nelson's victory at Trafalgar **Obv:** Bust in tiara right **Rev:** Victory crowned Britannia standing on prow

| Date | Mintage | VF20 | XF40 | MS60 | MS63 | MS65 |
|---|---|---|---|---|---|---|
| 2008 PM | — | PF65 450 | | | | |

### KM# 202 50 DOLLARS

3.11 g., 0.9999 Gold 0.100 oz. AGW, 17.95 mm. **Subject:** Teddy Bear Centennial **Obv:** Queen's bust right **Rev:** Teddy bear **Edge:** Reeded

| Date | Mintage | VF20 | XF40 | MS60 | MS63 | MS65 |
|---|---|---|---|---|---|---|
| 2002 | — | PF65 185 | | | | |

### KM# 272 50 DOLLARS

3.11 g., 0.9999 Gold 0.100 oz. AGW, 18 mm. **Obv:** Queen's bust right **Rev:** Peter Rabbit **Edge:** Reeded

| Date | Mintage | VF20 | XF40 | MS60 | MS63 | MS65 |
|---|---|---|---|---|---|---|
| 2004 | 3,000 | PF65 190 | | | | |

### KM# 276 50 DOLLARS

6.22 g., 0.9999 Gold 0.200 oz. AGW, 22 mm. **Obv:** Queen's bust right **Rev:** Treasure ship with blue color sail **Edge:** Reeded

| Date | Mintage | VF20 | XF40 | MS60 | MS63 | MS65 |
|---|---|---|---|---|---|---|
| 2004 | 350 | PF65 400 | | | | |

### KM# 290 50 DOLLARS

6.22 g., 0.9999 Gold 0.200 oz. AGW, 22 mm. **Obv:** Queen's bust right **Rev:** Dolphin **Edge:** Reeded

| Date | Mintage | VF20 | XF40 | MS60 | MS63 | MS65 |
|---|---|---|---|---|---|---|
| 2004 | 3,500 | PF65 350 | | | | |

### KM# 316 50 DOLLARS

6.22 g., 0.9999 Gold 0.200 oz. AGW, 22 mm. **Obv:** Bust of Queen Elizabeth II right **Rev:** Large and small dolphins **Edge:** Reeded

| Date | Mintage | VF20 | XF40 | MS60 | MS63 | MS65 |
|---|---|---|---|---|---|---|
| 2005 | 3,500 | PF65 350 | | | | |

### KM# 351 50 DOLLARS

6.22 g., 0.9999 Gold 0.200 oz. AGW, 22 mm. **Ruler:** Elizabeth II **Subject:** 5th Anniversary - Attack on Twin Towers, New York City **Obv:** Crowned bust right **Obv. Legend:** BRITISH VIRGIN ISLANDS - QUEEN ELIZABETH II **Rev:** Twin Towers in sprays, remembrance ribbon privy mark at upper right **Rev. Inscription:** LEST WE FORGET **Edge:** Reeded

| Date | Mintage | VF20 | XF40 | MS60 | MS63 | MS65 |
|---|---|---|---|---|---|---|
| 2006 | 2,000 | PF65 365 | | | | |

### KM# 336 50 DOLLARS

6.22 g., 0.9999 Gold 0.2001 oz. AGW, 22 mm. **Ruler:** Elizabeth II **Subject:** 400th Anniversary Founding of Jamestown **Obv:** Bust with tiara right **Obv. Legend:** BRITISH VIRGIN ISLANDS - QUEEN ELIZABETH II **Rev:** British lion laying, American eagle perched on sprays **Rev. Legend:** UNITED IN FRIENDSHIP **Edge:** Reeded

| Date | Mintage | VF20 | XF40 | MS60 | MS63 | MS65 |
|---|---|---|---|---|---|---|
| 2007 | 5,000 | PF65 360 | | | | |

### KM# 413 50 DOLLARS

6.22 g., 0.999 Gold 0.1998 oz. AGW, 22 mm. **Ruler:** Elizabeth II **Subject:** Color photography, 100th Anniversary **Obv:** Bust in tiara right **Rev:** Conjoined portraits right in photo frame

| Date | Mintage | VF20 | XF40 | MS60 | MS63 | MS65 |
|---|---|---|---|---|---|---|
| 2007 PM | — | PF65 450 | | | | |

### KM# 377 50 DOLLARS

6.22 g., 0.999 Gold 0.1998 oz. AGW, 22 mm. **Ruler:** Elizabeth II **Obv:** Bust right **Rev:** Elizabeth II aboard ship with 1mm pearl

| Date | Mintage | VF20 | XF40 | MS60 | MS63 | MS65 |
|---|---|---|---|---|---|---|
| 2009 | 750 | PF65 375 | | | | |

### KM# 378 50 DOLLARS

6.22 g., 0.999 Gold 0.1998 oz. AGW, 22 mm. **Ruler:** Elizabeth II **Obv:** Bust right **Rev:** Elizabeth II between two columns, .01ct ruby insert

| Date | Mintage | VF20 | XF40 | MS60 | MS63 | MS65 |
|---|---|---|---|---|---|---|
| 2009 | 750 | PF65 375 | | | | |

### KM# 285 75 DOLLARS

11.00 g., Bi-Metallic .990 Titanium 2g center in .9999 Gold 9g ring, 36.5 mm. **Obv:** Queen's bust right **Rev:** British Guiana stamp design **Edge:** Reeded

| Date | Mintage | VF20 | XF40 | MS60 | MS63 | MS65 |
|---|---|---|---|---|---|---|
| 2004 | 2,500 | PF65 450 | | | | |

### KM# 389 75 DOLLARS

Bi-Metallic Titanium and gold **Ruler:** Elizabeth II **Subject:** Mozart

| Date | Mintage | VF20 | XF40 | MS60 | MS63 | MS65 |
|---|---|---|---|---|---|---|
| 2006 PM | — | PF65 450 | | | | |

### KM# 388 75 DOLLARS

Bi-Metallic Titanium and gold, 36.5 mm. **Ruler:** Elizabeth II **Subject:** Bejing Olympics **Obv:** Bust in tiara right **Rev:** Tennis plays against Great Wall background

| Date | Mintage | VF20 | XF40 | MS60 | MS63 | MS65 |
|---|---|---|---|---|---|---|
| 2009 PM | — | PF65 450 | | | | |

### KM# 182 100 DOLLARS

6.22 g., 0.999 Gold 0.1998 oz. AGW, 22 mm. **Subject:** Sir Francis Drake **Obv:** Queen's bust right **Rev:** Ship, portrait and map **Edge:** Reeded

| Date | Mintage | VF20 | XF40 | MS60 | MS63 | MS65 |
|---|---|---|---|---|---|---|
| 2002 | 5,000 | PF65 350 | | | | |

### KM# 185 100 DOLLARS

6.22 g., 0.999 Gold 0.1998 oz. AGW, 22 mm. **Subject:** Sir Walter Raleigh **Obv:** Queen's bust right **Rev:** Ship, portrait and map **Edge:** Reeded

| Date | Mintage | VF20 | XF40 | MS60 | MS63 | MS65 |
|---|---|---|---|---|---|---|
| 2002 | 5,000 | PF65 350 | | | | |

### KM# 189 100 DOLLARS

6.22 g., 0.9999 Gold 0.200 oz. AGW, 22 mm. **Subject:** Queen's Golden Jubilee **Obv:** Queen's bust right **Rev:** Queen on horse **Edge:** Reeded

| Date | Mintage | VF20 | XF40 | MS60 | MS63 | MS65 |
|---|---|---|---|---|---|---|
| 2002 | — | PF65 365 | | | | |

### KM# 192 100 DOLLARS

6.22 g., 0.9999 Gold 0.200 oz. AGW, 22 mm. **Subject:** Queen's Golden Jubilee **Obv:** Queen's bust right **Rev:** Queen on throne **Edge:** Reeded

| Date | Mintage | VF20 | XF40 | MS60 | MS63 | MS65 |
|---|---|---|---|---|---|---|
| 2002 | — | PF65 365 | | | | |

### KM# 195 100 DOLLARS

6.22 g., 0.9999 Gold 0.200 oz. AGW, 22 mm. **Subject:** Queen's Golden Jubilee **Obv:** Queen's bust right **Rev:** Queen with President Ronald Reagan and Mrs. Nancy Reagan **Edge:** Reeded

| Date | Mintage | VF20 | XF40 | MS60 | MS63 | MS65 |
|---|---|---|---|---|---|---|
| 2002 | — | PF65 365 | | | | |

### KM# 198 100 DOLLARS

6.22 g., 0.9999 Gold 0.200 oz. AGW, 22 mm. **Subject:** Queen's Golden Jubilee **Obv:** Queen's bust right **Rev:** Carnival dancers **Edge:** Reeded

| Date | Mintage | VF20 | XF40 | MS60 | MS63 | MS65 |
|---|---|---|---|---|---|---|
| 2002 | — | PF65 365 | | | | |

### KM# 203 100 DOLLARS

6.22 g., 0.9999 Gold 0.200 oz. AGW, 22 mm. **Subject:** Teddy Bear Centennial **Obv:** Queen's bust right **Rev:** Teddy bear **Edge:** Reeded

| Date | Mintage | VF20 | XF40 | MS60 | MS63 | MS65 |
|---|---|---|---|---|---|---|
| 2002 | — | PF65 350 | | | | |

### KM# 206 100 DOLLARS

6.22 g., 0.9999 Gold 0.200 oz. AGW, 22 mm. **Subject:** Princess Diana **Obv:** Queen's bust right **Rev:** Diana's portrait **Edge:** Reeded

| Date | Mintage | VF20 | XF40 | MS60 | MS63 | MS65 |
|---|---|---|---|---|---|---|
| 2002 | — | PF65 350 | | | | |

### KM# 209.1 100 DOLLARS

6.22 g., 0.9999 Gold 0.200 oz. AGW, 22 mm. **Subject:** September 11, 2001 **Obv:** Queen's bust right **Rev:** World Trade Center twin towers **Edge:** Reeded

| Date | Mintage | VF20 | XF40 | MS60 | MS63 | MS65 |
|---|---|---|---|---|---|---|
| 2002 | — | PF65 350 | | | | |

### KM# 209.2 100 DOLLARS

6.22 g., 0.9999 Gold 0.200 oz. AGW, 22 mm. **Subject:** September 11, 2001 **Obv:** Queen's bust right **Rev:** Holographic multicolor World Trade Center twin towers **Edge:** Reeded

| Date | Mintage | VF20 | XF40 | MS60 | MS63 | MS65 |
|---|---|---|---|---|---|---|
| 2002 | — | PF65 350 | | | | |

### KM# 212 100 DOLLARS

6.22 g., 0.9999 Gold 0.200 oz. AGW, 22 mm. **Subject:** September 11, 2001 **Obv:** Queen's bust right **Rev:** Statue of Liberty **Edge:** Reeded

| Date | Mintage | VF20 | XF40 | MS60 | MS63 | MS65 |
|---|---|---|---|---|---|---|
| 2002 | — | PF65 350 | | | | |

### KM# 215 100 DOLLARS

6.22 g., 0.9999 Gold 0.200 oz. AGW, 22 mm. **Subject:** Queen Mother Series **Obv:** Queen's bust right **Rev:** Queen Mother with young Prince Charles **Edge:** Reeded

| Date | Mintage | VF20 | XF40 | MS60 | MS63 | MS65 |
|---|---|---|---|---|---|---|
| 2002 PM | 5,000 | PF65 350 | | | | |

### KM# 218 100 DOLLARS

6.22 g., 0.9999 Gold 0.200 oz. AGW, 22 mm. **Subject:** Queen Mother Series **Obv:** Queen's bust right **Rev:** Queen Mother with four grandchildren **Edge:** Reeded

| Date | Mintage | VF20 | XF40 | MS60 | MS63 | MS65 |
|---|---|---|---|---|---|---|
| 2002 PM | 5,000 | PF65 350 | | | | |

### KM# 221 100 DOLLARS

6.22 g., 0.9999 Gold 0.200 oz. AGW, 22 mm. **Subject:** Queen Mother Series **Obv:** Queen's bust right **Rev:** Queen Mother with uniformed Prince Charles **Edge:** Reeded

| Date | Mintage | VF20 | XF40 | MS60 | MS63 | MS65 |
|---|---|---|---|---|---|---|
| 2002 PM | 5,000 | PF65 350 | | | | |

### KM# 224 100 DOLLARS

6.22 g., 0.9999 Gold 0.200 oz. AGW, 22 mm. **Subject:** Queen Mother Series **Obv:** Queen's bust right **Rev:** Queen Mother's coffin **Edge:** Reeded

| Date | Mintage | VF20 | XF40 | MS60 | MS63 | MS65 |
|---|---|---|---|---|---|---|
| 2002 PM | 5,000 | PF65 350 | | | | |

### KM# 228 100 DOLLARS

6.22 g., 0.9999 Gold 0.200 oz. AGW, 22 mm. **Subject:** Kennedy Assassination **Obv:** Queen's bust right **Rev:** President Kennedy's portrait **Edge:** Reeded

| Date | Mintage | VF20 | XF40 | MS60 | MS63 | MS65 |
|---|---|---|---|---|---|---|
| 2003 | 5,000 | PF65 350 | | | | |

### KM# 231 100 DOLLARS

15.55 g., 0.9999 Gold 0.4999 oz. AGW, 30 mm. **Subject:** Powered Flight Centennial **Obv:** Queen's bust right **Rev:** Three historic airplanes and rocket **Edge:** Reeded

| Date | Mintage | VF20 | XF40 | MS60 | MS63 | MS65 |
|---|---|---|---|---|---|---|
| 2003 | — | PF65 875 | | | | |

### KM# 234 100 DOLLARS

6.22 g., 0.9999 Gold 0.200 oz. AGW, 22 mm. **Obv:** Queen's bust right **Rev:** Henry VIII and Elizabeth I **Edge:** Reeded

| Date | Mintage | VF20 | XF40 | MS60 | MS63 | MS65 |
|---|---|---|---|---|---|---|
| 2003 | 5,000 | PF65 350 | | | | |

### KM# 237 100 DOLLARS

6.22 g., 0.9999 Gold 0.200 oz. AGW, 22 mm. **Obv:** Queen's bust right **Rev:** Matthew Parker, Archbishop of Canterbury **Edge:** Reeded

| Date | Mintage | VF20 | XF40 | MS60 | MS63 | MS65 |
|---|---|---|---|---|---|---|
| 2003 | 5,000 | PF65 350 | | | | |

### KM# 240 100 DOLLARS

6.22 g., 0.9999 Gold 0.200 oz. AGW, 22 mm. **Obv:** Queen's bust right **Rev:** Sir Francis Drake and ships **Edge:** Reeded

| Date | Mintage | VF20 | XF40 | MS60 | MS63 | MS65 |
|---|---|---|---|---|---|---|
| 2003 | 5,000 | PF65 350 | | | | |

### KM# 243 100 DOLLARS

6.22 g., 0.9999 Gold 0.200 oz. AGW, 22 mm. **Obv:** Queen's bust right **Rev:** Sir Walter Raleigh **Edge:** Reeded

| Date | Mintage | VF20 | XF40 | MS60 | MS63 | MS65 |
|---|---|---|---|---|---|---|
| 2003 | 5,000 | PF65 350 | | | | |

### KM# 246 100 DOLLARS

6.22 g., 0.9999 Gold 0.200 oz. AGW, 22 mm. **Obv:** Queen's bust right **Rev:** Sir William Shakespeare **Edge:** Reeded

| Date | Mintage | VF20 | XF40 | MS60 | MS63 | MS65 |
|---|---|---|---|---|---|---|
| 2003 | 5,000 | PF65 350 | | | | |

### KM# 249 100 DOLLARS

6.22 g., 0.9999 Gold 0.200 oz. AGW, 22 mm. **Obv:** Queen's bust right **Rev:** Elizabeth I above her funeral procession **Edge:** Reeded

| Date | Mintage | VF20 | XF40 | MS60 | MS63 | MS65 |
|---|---|---|---|---|---|---|
| 2003 | 5,000 | PF65 350 | | | | |

### KM# 252 100 DOLLARS

6.22 g., 0.9999 Gold 0.200 oz. AGW, 22 mm. **Subject:** Olympics **Obv:** Queen's bust right **Rev:** Ancient Olympic bust, runners in background and coin upper right **Edge:** Reeded

| Date | Mintage | VF20 | XF40 | MS60 | MS63 | MS65 |
|---|---|---|---|---|---|---|
| 2003 | 5,000 | PF65 350 | | | | |

### KM# 255 100 DOLLARS

6.22 g., 0.9999 Gold 0.200 oz. AGW, 22 mm. **Subject:** Olympics **Obv:** Queen's bust right **Rev:** Ancient bust, charioteer and coin **Edge:** Reeded

| Date | Mintage | VF20 | XF40 | MS60 | MS63 | MS65 |
|---|---|---|---|---|---|---|
| 2003 | 5,000 | PF65 350 | | | | |

### KM# 273.1 100 DOLLARS

6.22 g., 0.9999 Gold 0.200 oz. AGW, 22 mm. **Obv:** Queen's bust right **Rev:** Peter Rabbit **Edge:** Reeded

| Date | Mintage | VF20 | XF40 | MS60 | MS63 | MS65 |
|---|---|---|---|---|---|---|
| 2004 | 2,000 | PF65 365 | | | | |

### KM# 273.2 100 DOLLARS

6.22 g., 0.9999 Gold 0.200 oz. AGW, 22 mm. **Obv:** Queen's bust right **Rev:** Multicolor Peter Rabbit **Edge:** Reeded

| Date | Mintage | VF20 | XF40 | MS60 | MS63 | MS65 |
|---|---|---|---|---|---|---|
| 2004 | — | PF65 365 | | | | |

### KM# 283 100 DOLLARS

6.22 g., 0.9999 Gold 0.200 oz. AGW, 22 mm. **Obv:** Queen's bust right **Rev:** Sailor above two D-Day landing craft **Edge:** Reeded

| Date | Mintage | VF20 | XF40 | MS60 | MS63 | MS65 |
|---|---|---|---|---|---|---|
| 2004 | 5,000 | PF65 350 | | | | |

### KM# 299 100 DOLLARS

6.22 g., 0.9999 Gold 0.200 oz. AGW, 22 mm. **Obv:** Queen's bust right **Rev:** Soldier above tank and jeeps **Edge:** Reeded

| Date | Mintage | VF20 | XF40 | MS60 | MS63 | MS65 |
|---|---|---|---|---|---|---|
| 2004 | 5,000 | PF65 350 | | | | |

### KM# 302 100 DOLLARS

6.22 g., 0.9999 Gold 0.200 oz. AGW, 22 mm. **Obv:** Queen's bust right **Rev:** Pilot and planes above D-Day landing **Edge:** Reeded

| Date | Mintage | VF20 | XF40 | MS60 | MS63 | MS65 |
|---|---|---|---|---|---|---|
| 2004 | 5,000 | PF65 350 | | | | |

### KM# 305 100 DOLLARS

6.22 g., 0.9999 Gold 0.200 oz. AGW, 22 mm. **Obv:** Queen's bust right **Rev:** Ancient Olympic bust, runners and owl coin **Edge:** Reeded

| Date | Mintage | VF20 | XF40 | MS60 | MS63 | MS65 |
|---|---|---|---|---|---|---|
| 2004 | 5,000 | PF65 350 | | | | |

### KM# 308 100 DOLLARS

6.22 g., 0.9999 Gold 0.200 oz. AGW, 22 mm. **Obv:** Queen's bust right **Rev:** Ancient Olympic bust, charioteer and Zeus coin **Edge:** Reeded

| Date | Mintage | VF20 | XF40 | MS60 | MS63 | MS65 |
|---|---|---|---|---|---|---|
| 2004 | 5,000 | PF65 350 | | | | |

**KM# 434 100 DOLLARS**
1000.00 g., Silver, 120 mm. **Ruler:** Elizabeth II **Subject:** RMS Titanic Remembered

| Date | Mintage | VF20 | XF40 | MS60 | MS63 | MS65 |
|---|---|---|---|---|---|---|
| 2012 Proof | — | — | — | — | — | — |

**KM# 317 125 DOLLARS**
15.55 g., 0.9999 Gold 0.4999 oz. AGW, 30 mm. **Obv:** Bust of Queen Elizabeth II right **Rev:** Mother and baby dolphin **Edge:** Reeded

| Date | Mintage | VF20 | XF40 | MS60 | MS63 | MS65 |
|---|---|---|---|---|---|---|
| 2005 | 1,500 | **PF65** 900 | | | | |

**KM# 337 125 DOLLARS**
15.56 g., 0.9999 Gold 0.5002 oz. AGW, 30 mm. **Ruler:** Elizabeth II **Subject:** 400th Anniversary Founding of Jamestown **Obv:** Bust with tiara right **Obv. Legend:** BRITISH VIRGIN ISLANDS - QUEEN ELIZABETH II **Rev:** British lion laying, American eagle perched on sprays **Rev. Legend:** UNITED IN FRIENDSHIP **Edge:** Reeded

| Date | Mintage | VF20 | XF40 | MS60 | MS63 | MS65 |
|---|---|---|---|---|---|---|
| 2007 | 3,000 | **PF65** 875 | | | | |

**KM# 309 250 DOLLARS**
15.55 g., 0.999 Gold 0.4995 oz. AGW, 30 mm. **Obv:** Queen's bust right **Rev:** Statue of Liberty and the date "11 Sept. 2001 **Edge:** Reeded

| Date | Mintage | VF20 | XF40 | MS60 | MS63 | MS65 |
|---|---|---|---|---|---|---|
| 2002 | 250 | **PF65** 950 | | | | |

**KM# 280 250 DOLLARS**
58.00 g., 0.500 Gold 0.9324 oz. AGW, 50 mm. **Obv:** Queen's bust right **Rev:** 1896 Olympic medal design **Edge:** Reeded

| Date | Mintage | VF20 | XF40 | MS60 | MS63 | MS65 |
|---|---|---|---|---|---|---|
| 2004 | 1,000 | **PF65** 1,650 | | | | |

**KM# 318 250 DOLLARS**
31.10 g., 0.9999 Gold 0.9999 oz. AGW, 32.7 mm. **Obv:** Bust of Queen Elizabeth II right **Rev:** Mother and baby dolphin **Edge:** Reeded

| Date | Mintage | VF20 | XF40 | MS60 | MS63 | MS65 |
|---|---|---|---|---|---|---|
| 2005 | 750 | **PF65** 1,750 | | | | |

**KM# 390 250 DOLLARS**
Gold **Ruler:** Elizabeth II **Subject:** Mozart

| Date | Mintage | VF20 | XF40 | MS60 | MS63 | MS65 |
|---|---|---|---|---|---|---|
| 2006 PM | — | **PF65** 1,750 | | | | |

**KM# 338 250 DOLLARS**
31.10 g., 0.9999 Gold 0.9999 oz. AGW, 32.7 mm. **Ruler:** Elizabeth II **Subject:** 400th Anniversary Founding of Jamestown **Obv:** Bust with tiara right **Obv. Legend:** BRITISH VIRGIN ISLANDS - QUEEN ELIZABETH II **Rev:** British lion laying, American eagle perched on sprays **Rev. Legend:** UNITED IN FRIENDSHIP **Edge:** Reeded

| Date | Mintage | VF20 | XF40 | MS60 | MS63 | MS65 |
|---|---|---|---|---|---|---|
| 2007 | 1,000 | **PF65** 1,750 | | | | |

**KM# 277 500 DOLLARS**
160.76 g., 0.999 Gold 5.1633 oz. AGW, 150 mm. **Obv:** Queen's bust right **Rev:** Gold-plated portrait of Hernando Pizarro, small inset emerald above Pizarro's life events pictoral **Edge:** Reeded **Note:** Photo reduced.

| Date | Mintage | VF20 | XF40 | MS60 | MS63 | MS65 |
|---|---|---|---|---|---|---|
| 2004 | 500 | **PF65** 9,000 | | | | |

**KM# 348 500 DOLLARS**
160.76 g., 0.999 Gold 5.1633 oz. AGW, 150 mm. **Ruler:** Elizabeth II **Subject:** 500th Anniversary - Death of Columbus **Obv:** Crowned bust right **Obv. Legend:** BRITISH VIRGIN ISLANDS - QUEEN ELIZABETH II **Rev:** Ship in background at left, Columbus standing at right with right arm outstreched looking right, compass below. **Rev. Legend:** 1451 - DISCOVERER OF AMERICA - CHRISTOPHER COLUMBUS - 1506 **Edge:** Reeded

| Date | Mintage | VF20 | XF40 | MS60 | MS63 | MS65 |
|---|---|---|---|---|---|---|
| 2006 | 1,506 | **PF63** 8,700 | **PF65** 8,900 | | | |

**KM# 392 500 DOLLARS**
160.76 g., 0.999 Silver 5.1633 oz. ASW, 150 mm. **Ruler:** Elizabeth II **Subject:** Battle of Trafalgar **Rev:** Two naval ships in battle

| Date | Mintage | VF20 | XF40 | MS60 | MS63 | MS65 |
|---|---|---|---|---|---|---|
| 2008 PM | — | **PF63** 225 | **PF65** 250 | | | |

**KM# 435 500 DOLLARS**
155.51 g., Gold, 65 mm. **Ruler:** Elizabeth II **Subject:** RMS Titanic Remembered

| Date | Mintage | VF20 | XF40 | MS60 | MS63 | MS65 |
|---|---|---|---|---|---|---|
| 2012 Proof | Est. 99 | — | — | — | — | — |

## MINT SETS

| KM# | Date | Mintage | Identification | Issue Price | Mkt Val |
|---|---|---|---|---|---|
| MS12 | 2007 (4) | — | KM# 341 - 344 | 65.00 | 80.00 |

## PROOF SETS

| KM# | Date | Mintage | Identification | Issue Price | Mkt Val |
|---|---|---|---|---|---|
| PS20 | 2007 (4) | — | KM# 341a - 344a | 300 | 300 |

# BRUNEI

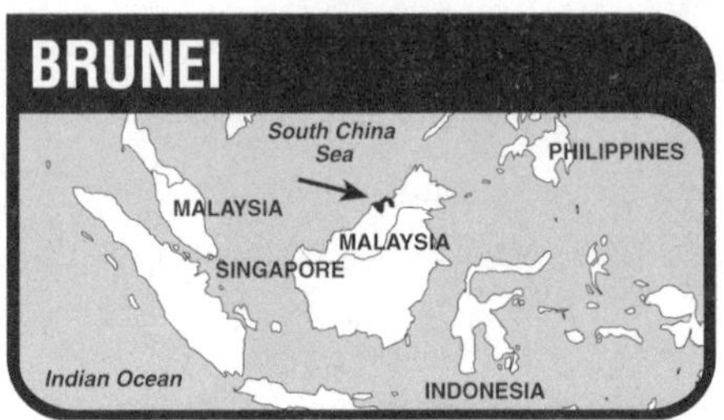


Negara Brunei Darussalam (Brunei, Adobe of Peace), an independent sultanate on the northwest coast of the island of Borneo, has an area of 2,226 sq. mi. (5,765 sq. km.) and a population of *326,000. Capital: Bandar Seri Begawan. Crude oil and rubber are exported.

**TITLES**

نكري بروني

**RULERS**
Sultan Hassanal Bolkiah, 1967-

## SULTANATE

### DECIMAL COINAGE

100 Sen = 1 Dollar (Ringgit)

**KM# 34 SEN**
1.75 g., Copper Clad Steel, 17.7 mm. **Ruler:** Sultan Hassanal Bolkiah **Obv:** Uniformed bust facing **Rev:** Native design, denomination below, date at right **Edge:** Plain

| Date | Mintage | VF20 | XF40 | MS60 | MS63 | MS65 |
|---|---|---|---|---|---|---|
| 2001 | 576,000 | — | — | 0.50 | 0.75 | 1.00 |
| 2002 | 804,900 | — | — | 0.50 | 0.75 | 1.00 |
| 2004 | — | — | — | 0.50 | 0.75 | 1.00 |
| 2005 | — | — | — | 0.50 | 0.75 | 1.00 |
| 2006 | — | — | — | 0.50 | 0.75 | 1.00 |

**KM# 34b SEN**
1.70 g., Brass, 17.7 mm. **Ruler:** Sultan Hassanal Bolkiah **Obv:** Uniformed bust facing **Rev:** Native design, denomination below, date at right

| Date | Mintage | VF20 | XF40 | MS60 | MS63 | MS65 |
|---|---|---|---|---|---|---|
| 2008 | — | — | — | 0.50 | 0.75 | 1.00 |
| 2009 | — | — | — | 0.50 | 0.75 | 1.00 |
| 2010 | — | — | — | 0.50 | 0.75 | 1.00 |
| 2011 | — | — | — | 0.50 | 0.75 | 1.00 |

### KM# 35 5 SEN

1.41 g., Copper-Nickel, 16.26 mm. **Ruler:** Sultan Hassanal Bolkiah **Obv:** Uniformed bust facing **Rev:** Native design, denomination below, date at right **Edge:** Reeded

| Date | Mintage | VF20 | XF40 | MS60 | MS63 | MS65 |
|---|---|---|---|---|---|---|
| 2001 | 808,000 | — | — | 0.75 | 1.00 | 1.50 |
| 2002 | 1,418,178 | — | — | 0.75 | 1.00 | 1.50 |
| 2004 | — | — | — | 0.75 | 1.00 | 1.50 |
| 2005 | — | — | — | 0.75 | 1.00 | 1.50 |
| 2006 | — | — | — | 0.75 | 1.00 | 1.50 |
| 2007 | — | — | — | 0.75 | 1.00 | 1.50 |
| 2008 | — | — | — | 0.75 | 1.00 | 1.50 |
| 2009 | — | — | — | 0.75 | 1.00 | 1.50 |
| 2010 | — | — | — | 0.75 | 1.00 | 1.50 |

### KM# 36 10 SEN

2.82 g., Copper-Nickel, 19.4 mm. **Ruler:** Sultan Hassanal Bolkiah **Obv:** Uniformed bust facing **Rev:** Native design, denomination below, date at right **Edge:** Reeded

| Date | Mintage | VF20 | XF40 | MS60 | MS63 | MS65 |
|---|---|---|---|---|---|---|
| 2001 | 164,000 | — | — | 0.50 | 1.00 | 1.50 |
| 2002 | 476,452 | — | — | 0.50 | 1.00 | 1.50 |
| 2004 | — | — | — | 0.50 | 1.00 | 1.50 |
| 2005 | — | — | — | 0.50 | 1.00 | 1.50 |
| 2006 | — | — | — | 0.50 | 1.00 | 1.50 |
| 2007 | — | — | — | 0.50 | 1.00 | 1.50 |
| 2008 | — | — | — | 0.50 | 1.00 | 1.50 |
| 2009 | — | — | — | 0.50 | 1.00 | 1.50 |

### KM# 37 20 SEN

5.65 g., Copper-Nickel, 23.5 mm. **Ruler:** Sultan Hassanal Bolkiah **Obv:** Uniformed bust facing **Rev:** Native design, denomination below, date at right **Edge:** Reeded

| Date | Mintage | VF20 | XF40 | MS60 | MS63 | MS65 |
|---|---|---|---|---|---|---|
| 2001 | 270,647 | — | 0.45 | 1.00 | 1.20 | 1.50 |
| 2002 | 597,272 | — | 0.45 | 1.00 | 1.20 | 1.50 |
| 2004 | — | — | 0.45 | 1.00 | 1.20 | 1.50 |
| 2005 | — | — | 0.45 | 1.00 | 1.20 | 1.50 |
| 2008 | — | — | 0.45 | 1.00 | 1.20 | 1.50 |
| 2009 | — | — | 0.45 | 1.00 | 1.20 | 1.50 |
| 2010 | — | — | 0.45 | 1.00 | 1.20 | 1.50 |

### KM# 38 50 SEN

9.33 g., Copper-Nickel, 27.7 mm. **Ruler:** Sultan Hassanal Bolkiah **Obv:** Uniformed bust facing **Rev:** National arms within circle, denomination below, date at right **Edge:** Security

| Date | Mintage | VF20 | XF40 | MS60 | MS63 | MS65 |
|---|---|---|---|---|---|---|
| 2001 | 50,000 | — | 1.00 | 1.75 | 2.50 | 3.00 |
| 2002 | 1,325 | — | 1.75 | 2.50 | 3.50 | 5.00 |
| 2004 | — | — | 0.75 | 1.50 | 2.00 | 3.00 |
| 2005 | — | — | 0.75 | 1.50 | 2.00 | 3.00 |
| 2006 | — | — | 0.75 | 1.50 | 2.00 | 3.00 |
| 2007 | — | — | 0.75 | 1.50 | 2.00 | 3.00 |
| 2008 | — | — | 0.75 | 1.50 | 2.00 | 3.00 |
| 2009 | — | — | 0.75 | 1.50 | 2.00 | 3.00 |
| 2010 | — | — | 0.75 | 1.50 | 2.00 | 3.00 |

### KM# 80 2 DOLLARS

31.10 g., Copper-Nickel, 40.7 mm. **Ruler:** Sultan Hassanal Bolkiah **Subject:** 20th Anniversary of Independence **Obv:** Bust 3/4 left, facing **Obv. Legend:** SULTAN HAJI HASSANAL BOLKIAH **Rev:** National arms **Rev. Legend:** NEGARI BRUNEI DARUSSALAM

| Date | Mintage | VF20 | XF40 | MS60 | MS63 | MS65 |
|---|---|---|---|---|---|---|
| 2004 | 4,000 | PF63 55.00 | PF65 65.00 | | | |

### KM# 86 2 DOLLARS

31.10 g., Copper-Nickel, 40.7 mm. **Ruler:** Sultan Hassanal Bolkiah **Subject:** 60th Birthday **Obv:** Bust 3/4 left, facing **Obv. Legend:** SULTAN HAJI HASSANAL BOLKIAH **Rev:** Multicolor 1/2-length figure in civilian clothes, facing

| Date | Mintage | VF20 | XF40 | MS60 | MS63 | MS65 |
|---|---|---|---|---|---|---|
| 2006 | 200 | PF65 120 | | | | |

### KM# 77 3 DOLLARS

24.00 g., Copper-Nickel, 40 mm. **Ruler:** Sultan Hassanal Bolkiah **Obv:** Uniformed bust facing **Obv. Legend:** SULTAN HAJI HASSANAL BOLKIAH **Rev:** Logo at center **Rev. Legend:** COMMONWEALTH FINANCE MINISTERS MEETING **Edge:** Reeded

| Date | Mintage | VF20 | XF40 | MS60 | MS63 | MS65 |
|---|---|---|---|---|---|---|
| 2003 | 4,000 | PF63 40.00 | PF65 45.00 | | | |

### KM# 83 3 DOLLARS

31.10 g., Copper-Nickel, 40.7 mm. **Ruler:** Sultan Hassanal Bolkiah **Subject:** Royal Wedding **Obv:** Multicolor portraits of Royal couple

| Date | Mintage | VF20 | XF40 | MS60 | MS63 | MS65 |
|---|---|---|---|---|---|---|
| 2004 | 5,000 | PF63 45.00 | PF65 50.00 | | | |

### KM# 91 10 DOLLARS

31.11 g., Copper-Nickel, 40.7 mm. **Ruler:** Sultan Hassanal Bolkiah **Subject:** ASEAN 2013 Presidency **Obv:** Bust of Suntan in color **Rev:** ASEAN logo at center in color **Shape:** 8-sided

| Date | Mintage | VF20 | XF40 | MS60 | MS63 | MS65 |
|---|---|---|---|---|---|---|
| 2013 | 800 | PF65 200 | | | | |

### KM# 81 20 DOLLARS

31.10 g., 0.999 Silver 0.9989 oz. ASW, 40.7 mm. **Ruler:** Sultan Hassanal Bolkiah **Subject:** 20th Anniversary of Independence **Obv:** Bust 3/4 left, facing **Obv. Legend:** SULTAN HAJI HASSANAL BOLKIAH **Rev:** National arms **Rev. Legend:** NEGARI BRUNEI DARUSSALAM

| Date | Mintage | VF20 | XF40 | MS60 | MS63 | MS65 |
|---|---|---|---|---|---|---|
| 2004 | 1,000 | PF65 120 | | | | |

### KM# 87 20 DOLLARS

31.10 g., 0.999 Silver 0.9989 oz. ASW, 40.7 mm. **Ruler:** Sultan Hassanal Bolkiah **Subject:** 60th Birthday **Obv:** Bust 3/4 left, facing **Obv. Legend:** SULTAN HAJI HASSANAL BOLKIAH **Rev:** Multicolor 1/2-length figure in civilian clothes, facing

| Date | Mintage | VF20 | XF40 | MS60 | MS63 | MS65 |
|---|---|---|---|---|---|---|
| 2006 | 200 | PF65 275 | | | | |

### KM# 78 30 DOLLARS

62.20 g., 0.999 Silver 1.9978 oz. ASW **Ruler:** Sultan Hassanal Bolkiah **Subject:** Commonwealth Finance Ministers' Meeting **Obv:** Logo at upper left, multicolor bust of Sultan 3/4 left, facing at right **Obv. Legend:** SULTAN HAJI HASSANAL BOLIAH **Rev:** World map at left - center, national arms at upper right **Shape:** Rectangular, 65 x 31 mm

| Date | Mintage | VF20 | XF40 | MS60 | MS63 | MS65 |
|---|---|---|---|---|---|---|
| 2003 | 1,000 | PF65 210 | | | | |

### KM# 84 30 DOLLARS

31.10 g., 0.999 Silver 0.9989 oz. ASW, 40.7 mm. **Ruler:** Sultan Hassanal Bolkiah **Subject:** Royal Wedding **Obv:** Multicolor portraits of Royal couple

| Date | Mintage | VF20 | XF40 | MS60 | MS63 | MS65 |
|---|---|---|---|---|---|---|
| 2004 | 1,000 | PF65 180 | | | | |

### KM# 90 50 DOLLARS

31.10 g., 0.999 Silver 0.9989 oz. ASW, 40.7 mm. **Ruler:** Sultan Hassanal Bolkiah **Subject:** ASEAN 2013 Presidency **Obv:** Bust facing of Sultan in color **Rev:** ASEAN logo at center in color **Shape:** 8-sided

| Date | Mintage | VF20 | XF40 | MS60 | MS63 | MS65 |
|---|---|---|---|---|---|---|
| 2013 | 400 | PF65 250 | | | | |

### KM# 89 100 DOLLARS

31.11 g., 0.999 Gold 0.999 oz. AGW **Ruler:** Sultan Hassanal Bolkiah **Subject:** ASEAN 2013 Presidency **Obv:** Bust facing of Suntan in color **Rev:** ASEAN logo at center in color **Shape:** 8-sided

| Date | Mintage | VF20 | XF40 | MS60 | MS63 | MS65 |
|---|---|---|---|---|---|---|
| 2013 | 200 | PF65 3,500 | | | | |

### KM# 82 200 DOLLARS

31.10 g., 0.9999 Gold 0.9998 oz. AGW, 32.1 mm. **Ruler:** Sultan Hassanal Bolkiah **Subject:** 20th Anniversary of Independence **Obv:** Bust 3/4 left, facing **Obv. Legend:** SULTAN HAJI HASSANAL BOLKIAH **Rev:** National arms **Rev. Legend:** NEGARI BRUNEI DARUSSALAM

| Date | Mintage | VF20 | XF40 | MS60 | MS63 | MS65 |
|---|---|---|---|---|---|---|
| 2004 | 200 | PF65 2,400 | | | | |

### KM# 85 200 DOLLARS

31.10 g., 0.9999 Gold 0.9998 oz. AGW, 32 mm. **Ruler:** Sultan Hassanal Bolkiah **Subject:** Royal Wedding **Obv:** Multicolor portraits of Royal couple

| Date | Mintage | VF20 | XF40 | MS60 | MS63 | MS65 |
|---|---|---|---|---|---|---|
| 2004 | 200 | PF65 2,400 | | | | |

### KM# 88 200 DOLLARS

31.10 g., 0.9999 Gold 0.9998 oz. AGW, 32.1 mm. **Ruler:** Sultan Hassanal Bolkiah **Subject:** 60th Birthday **Obv:** Bust 3/4 left, facing **Obv. Legend:** SULTAN HAJI HASSANAL BOLKIAH **Rev:** Multicolor 1/2-length figure in civilian clothes, facing

| Date | Mintage | VF20 | XF40 | MS60 | MS63 | MS65 |
|---|---|---|---|---|---|---|
| 2006 | 200 | PF65 2,500 | | | | |

## PROOF SETS

| KM# | Date | Mintage | Identification | Issue Price | Mkt Val |
|---|---|---|---|---|---|
| PS20 | 2003 (2) | 500 | KM#77-78 | — | 250 |
| PS21 | 2004 (3) | 200 | KM80-82 | — | 2,600 |
| PS22 | 2004 (3) | 200 | KM83-85 | — | 2,650 |
| PS23 | 2006 (3) | 200 | KM86-88 | — | 2,900 |

# BULGARIA

The Republic of Bulgaria, formerly the Peoples Republic of Bulgaria, a Balkan country on the Black Sea in southeastern Europe, has an area of 42,855 sq. mi. (110,910 sq. km.) and a population of *8.31 million. Capital: Sofia. Agriculture remains a key component of the economy but industrialization, particularly heavy industry, has been emphasized since the late 1940s. Machinery, tobacco and cigarettes, wines and spirits, clothing and metals are the chief exports. Bulgaria joined the European Union in January 2007.,

**MONETARY SYSTEM**

100 Stotinki = 1 Lev

## PEOPLES REPUBLIC

### REFORM COINAGE

## REPUBLIC

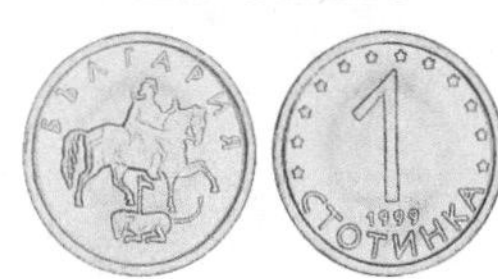

### KM# 237 STOTINKA

1.80 g., Aluminum-Bronze, 16 mm. **Obv:** Madara horseman right, animal below **Rev:** Denomination above date **Edge:** Plain

| Date | Mintage | F12 | VF20 | XF40 | MS60 | MS63 |
|---|---|---|---|---|---|---|
| 2002 | 10,000 | PF65 1.00 | | | | |

### KM# 237a STOTINKA

1.80 g., Brass Plated Steel, 16 mm. **Obv:** Madara horseman right **Rev:** Denomination above date

| Date | Mintage | F12 | VF20 | XF40 | MS60 | MS63 |
|---|---|---|---|---|---|---|
| 2002 | 10,000 | PF65 1.00 | | | | |

**KM# 238 2 STOTINKI**
2.50 g., Aluminum-Bronze, 18 mm. **Obv:** Madara horseman right, animal below **Rev:** Denomination above date **Edge:** Plain

| Date | Mintage | F12 | VF20 | XF40 | MS60 | MS63 |
|---|---|---|---|---|---|---|
| 2002 | 10,000 | PF65 1.50 | | | | |

**KM# 238a 2 STOTINKI**
2.50 g., Brass Plated Steel, 18 mm. **Obv:** Madara horseman right **Rev:** Denomination above date

| Date | Mintage | F12 | VF20 | XF40 | MS60 | MS63 |
|---|---|---|---|---|---|---|
| 2002 | 10,000 | PF65 1.50 | | | | |

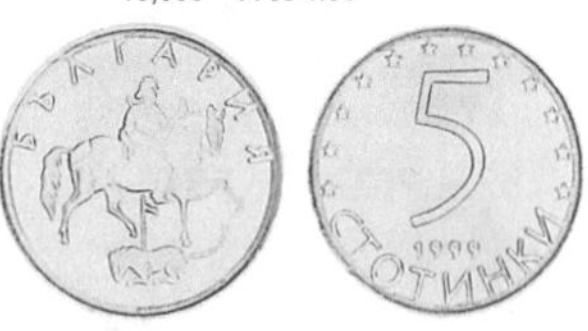

**KM# 239 5 STOTINKI**
3.50 g., Aluminum-Bronze, 20 mm. **Obv:** Madara horseman right, animal below **Rev:** Denomination above date **Edge:** Plain **Note:** Prev. KM#A239.

| Date | Mintage | F12 | VF20 | XF40 | MS60 | MS63 |
|---|---|---|---|---|---|---|
| 2002 | 10,000 | PF65 2.00 | | | | |

**KM# 239a 5 STOTINKI**
3.50 g., Brass Plated Steel, 20 mm. **Obv:** Madara horseman right **Rev:** Denomination above date

| Date | Mintage | F12 | VF20 | XF40 | MS60 | MS63 |
|---|---|---|---|---|---|---|
| 2002 | 10,000 | PF65 2.00 | | | | |

**KM# 240 10 STOTINKI**
3.00 g., Copper-Nickel-Zinc, 18.5 mm. **Obv:** Madara horseman right, animal below **Rev:** Denomination above date **Edge:** Reeded

| Date | Mintage | F12 | VF20 | XF40 | MS60 | MS63 |
|---|---|---|---|---|---|---|
| 2002 | 10,000 | PF65 2.50 | | | | |

**KM# 241 20 STOTINKI**
4.00 g., Copper-Nickel-Zinc, 20.5 mm. **Obv:** Madara horseman right, animal below **Rev:** Denomination above date **Edge:** Reeded

| Date | Mintage | F12 | VF20 | XF40 | MS60 | MS63 |
|---|---|---|---|---|---|---|
| 2002 | 10,000 | PF65 3.00 | | | | |

**KM# 242 50 STOTINKI**
5.00 g., Copper-Nickel-Zinc, 22.5 mm. **Obv:** Madara horseman right, animal below **Rev:** Denomination above date **Edge:** Reeded

| Date | Mintage | F12 | VF20 | XF40 | MS60 | MS63 |
|---|---|---|---|---|---|---|
| 2002 | 10,000 | PF65 5.00 | | | | |

**KM# 272 50 STOTINKI**
5.00 g., Copper-Nickel-Zinc, 22.5 mm. **Obv:** Stylized Bulgarian arms, lion left, NATO - 2004 under lion **Rev:** Denomination above date **Edge:** Reeded

| Date | Mintage | F12 | VF20 | XF40 | MS60 | MS63 |
|---|---|---|---|---|---|---|
| 2004 | — | — | — | — | — | 2.00 |

**KM# 282 50 STOTINKI**
5.00 g., Copper-Nickel-Zinc, 22.5 mm. **Obv:** European Union seated woman allegory **Rev:** Value above date **Edge:** Reeded **Note:** Prev. KM#274.

| Date | Mintage | F12 | VF20 | XF40 | MS60 | MS63 |
|---|---|---|---|---|---|---|
| 2005 | — | — | — | — | 0.60 | 1.25 |

**KM# 291 50 STOTINKI**
5.00 g., Copper-Nickel-Zinc, 22.5 mm. **Obv:** Value **Rev:** Pillar behind open book **Edge:** Reeded **Note:** Prev. KM#276.

| Date | Mintage | F12 | VF20 | XF40 | MS60 | MS63 |
|---|---|---|---|---|---|---|
| 2007 | 500,000 | — | — | — | 0.50 | 1.00 |

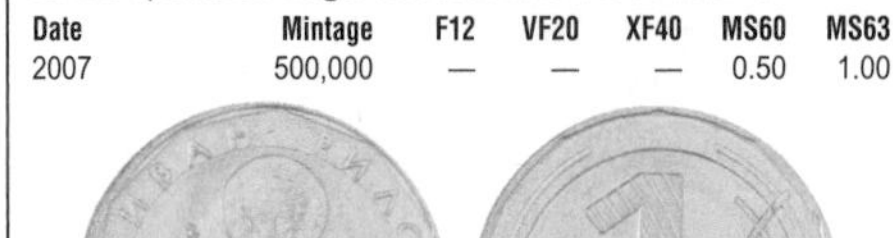

**KM# 254 LEV**
7.00 g., Bi-Metallic Copper-Nickel center in Brass ring, 24.5 mm. **Obv:** St. Ivan of Rila **Rev:** Denomination **Edge:** Segmented reeding

| Date | Mintage | F12 | VF20 | XF40 | MS60 | MS63 |
|---|---|---|---|---|---|---|
| 2002 | 24,842,000 | — | — | — | 2.00 | 3.00 |
| 2002 | 10,000 | PF63 10.00 | PF65 12.00 | | | |

**KM# 257 LEV**
15.55 g., 0.999 Gold 0.4994 oz. AGW **Obv:** St. Ivan of Rila **Rev:** Large number one **Edge:** Plain

| Date | Mintage | F12 | VF20 | XF40 | MS60 | MS63 |
|---|---|---|---|---|---|---|
| 2002 | 2,000 | PF65 875 | | | | |

**KM# 281 1.95583 LEVA**
20.00 g., 0.999 Silver 0.6424 oz. ASW, 40 mm. **Subject:** Bulgaria - EU **Obv:** National Arms, vlaue below **Rev:** Female seated within stars

| Date | Mintage | F12 | VF20 | XF40 | MS60 | MS63 |
|---|---|---|---|---|---|---|
| 2005 | 14,000 | PF65 50.00 | | | | |

**KM# 290 1.95583 LEVA**
20.00 g., 0.999 Silver 0.6424 oz. ASW Partially gold plated, 40 mm. **Subject:** Bulgaria in the EU **Obv:** National Arms **Rev:** Column and open window design

| Date | Mintage | F12 | VF20 | XF40 | MS60 | MS63 |
|---|---|---|---|---|---|---|
| 2007 | 14,000 | PF65 45.00 | | | | |

**KM# 304 2 LEVA**
16.40 g., 0.999 Copper 0.5267 oz., 34.2 mm. **Subject:** Dechko, Uzunov 110th Anniversary of Birth **Obv:** National arms **Rev:** Petar Stoikov

| Date | Mintage | F12 | VF20 | XF40 | MS60 | MS63 |
|---|---|---|---|---|---|---|
| 2009 | 8,000 | PF63 12.00 | PF65 15.00 | | | |

**KM# 310 2 LEVA**
16.40 g., Copper-Nickel, 34.2 mm. **Obv:** National arms, value below **Rev:** Zahariy Zograf's self-portriat

| Date | Mintage | F12 | VF20 | XF40 | MS60 | MS63 |
|---|---|---|---|---|---|---|
| 2010 | — | PF63 20.00 | PF65 25.00 | | | |

**KM# 317 2 LEVA**
16.40 g., Copper, 34.2 mm. **Subject:** Dimcho Debelyanov, 125th Anniversary of Birth **Obv:** National arms **Rev:** Portrait facing **Edge:** Plain

| Date | Mintage | F12 | VF20 | XF40 | MS60 | MS63 |
|---|---|---|---|---|---|---|
| 2012 | 5,000 | PF65 20.00 | | | | |

**KM# 324 2 LEVA**
16.40 g., Copper, 34.2 mm. **Subject:** Zlatyu Boyadzhiev, 110th Anniversary of Birth

| Date | Mintage | VF20 | XF40 | MS60 | MS63 | MS65 |
|---|---|---|---|---|---|---|
| 2013 | — | PF65 50.00 | | | | |

**KM# 324a 2 LEVA**
16.40 g., Copper-Nickel, 34.2 mm. **Subject:** Zlatyu Bnoyadzhiev, 110th Anniversary of Birth

| Date | Mintage | F12 | VF20 | XF40 | MS60 | MS63 |
|---|---|---|---|---|---|---|
| 2013 | — | PF65 30.00 | | | | |

**KM# 258 5 LEVA**
1.24 g., 0.999 Gold 0.0398 oz. AGW **Obv:** Denomination **Rev:** Olympic archer **Edge:** Plain

| Date | Mintage | F12 | VF20 | XF40 | MS60 | MS63 |
|---|---|---|---|---|---|---|
| 2002 | 12,000 | PF65 75.00 | | | | |

**KM# 259 5 LEVA**
1.24 g., 0.999 Gold 0.0398 oz. AGW **Obv:** Denomination **Rev:** Olympic cyclist **Edge:** Plain

| Date | Mintage | F12 | VF20 | XF40 | MS60 | MS63 |
|---|---|---|---|---|---|---|
| 2002 | 12,000 | PF65 75.00 | | | | |

**KM# 260 5 LEVA**
1.24 g., 0.999 Gold 0.0398 oz. AGW **Obv:** Denomination **Rev:** Olympic fencing **Edge:** Plain

| Date | Mintage | F12 | VF20 | XF40 | MS60 | MS63 |
|---|---|---|---|---|---|---|
| 2002 | 12,000 | PF65 75.00 | | | | |

**KM# 261 5 LEVA**
1.24 g., 0.999 Gold 0.0398 oz. AGW **Obv:** Denomination **Rev:** Olympic wrestling **Edge:** Plain

| Date | Mintage | F12 | VF20 | XF40 | MS60 | MS63 |
|---|---|---|---|---|---|---|
| 2002 | 12,000 | PF65 75.00 | | | | |

**KM# 262 5 LEVA**
1.24 g., 0.999 Gold 0.0398 oz. AGW, 14 mm. **Obv:** Denomination **Rev:** Olympic gymnastics **Edge:** Plain

| Date | Mintage | F12 | VF20 | XF40 | MS60 | MS63 |
|---|---|---|---|---|---|---|
| 2002 | 12,000 | PF65 75.00 | | | | |

**KM# 263 5 LEVA**
1.24 g., 0.999 Gold 0.0398 oz. AGW, 14 mm. **Obv:** Denomination **Rev:** Olympics founder Pierre du Coubertin **Edge:** Plain

| Date | Mintage | F12 | VF20 | XF40 | MS60 | MS63 |
|---|---|---|---|---|---|---|
| 2002 | 17,000 | PF65 75.00 | | | | |

**KM# 264 5 LEVA**
1.24 g., 0.999 Gold 0.0398 oz. AGW, 14 mm. **Obv:** Denomination **Rev:** Olympic running **Edge:** Plain

| Date | Mintage | F12 | VF20 | XF40 | MS60 | MS63 |
|---|---|---|---|---|---|---|
| 2002 | 12,000 | PF65 75.00 | | | | |

**KM# 265 5 LEVA**
1.24 g., 0.999 Gold 0.0398 oz. AGW, 14 mm. **Obv:** Denomination **Rev:** Olympic swimming **Edge:** Plain

| Date | Mintage | F12 | VF20 | XF40 | MS60 | MS63 |
|---|---|---|---|---|---|---|
| 2002 | 12,000 | PF65 75.00 | | | | |

**KM# 266 5 LEVA**
1.24 g., 0.999 Gold 0.0398 oz. AGW, 14 mm. **Obv:** Denomination **Rev:** Olympic tennis **Edge:** Plain

| Date | Mintage | F12 | VF20 | XF40 | MS60 | MS63 |
|---|---|---|---|---|---|---|
| 2002 | 12,000 | PF65 75.00 | | | | |

**KM# 267 5 LEVA**
1.24 g., 0.999 Gold 0.0398 oz. AGW, 14 mm. **Obv:** Denomination **Rev:** Olympic weight lifting **Edge:** Plain

| Date | Mintage | F12 | VF20 | XF40 | MS60 | MS63 |
|---|---|---|---|---|---|---|
| 2002 | 12,000 | PF65 75.00 | | | | |

**KM# 274 5 LEVA**
15.00 g., Copper-Nickel, 34.2 mm. **Subject:** Sourvakari **Obv:** National arms **Rev:** Multicolor children in winter clothes

| Date | Mintage | F12 | VF20 | XF40 | MS60 | MS63 |
|---|---|---|---|---|---|---|
| 2002 | 5,000 | PF63 15.00 | PF65 17.00 | | | |

**KM# 268 5 LEVA**
28.28 g., 0.925 Silver 0.841 oz. ASW, 38.5 mm. **Obv:** Denomination **Rev:** FIFA Soccer trophy cup **Edge:** reeded

| Date | Mintage | F12 | VF20 | XF40 | MS60 | MS63 |
|---|---|---|---|---|---|---|
| 2003 | 50,000 | PF63 37.00 | PF65 42.00 | | | |

**KM# 276 5 LEVA**
15.00 g., Copper-Nickel, 34.2 mm. **Obv:** National arms, date and denomination below **Rev:** Multicolor child on rocking horse **Edge:** Plain **Note:** Prev. KM#275.

| Date | Mintage | F12 | VF20 | XF40 | MS60 | MS63 |
|---|---|---|---|---|---|---|
| 2003 | 10,000 | PF63 32.00 | PF65 35.00 | | | |

**KM# 277 5 LEVA**
15.00 g., Copper-Nickel, 34.2 mm. **Subject:** Palm Sunday **Obv:** National Arms **Rev:** Bogomil Nikolov and Elena Dimitrova

| Date | Mintage | F12 | VF20 | XF40 | MS60 | MS63 |
|---|---|---|---|---|---|---|
| 2004 | 10,000 | PF63 15.00 | PF65 17.00 | | | |

**KM# 279 5 LEVA**
15.00 g., Copper-Nickel, 34.2 mm. **Subject:** Baba Marta **Obv:** National Arms **Rev:** Multicolor flora and butterfly

| Date | Mintage | F12 | VF20 | XF40 | MS60 | MS63 |
|---|---|---|---|---|---|---|
| 2005 | 10,000 | PF63 15.00 | PF65 17.00 | | | |

**KM# 284 5 LEVA**
23.30 g., 0.500 Silver 0.3746 oz. ASW, 38.6 mm. **Subject:** Bulgaria Crafts - winemaking **Obv:** National Arms **Rev:** Multicolor grapes - wine caraffe

| Date | Mintage | F12 | VF20 | XF40 | MS60 | MS63 |
|---|---|---|---|---|---|---|
| 2006 | 10,000 | PF63 25.00 | PF65 30.00 | | | |

**KM# 296 5 LEVA**
23.30 g., 0.500 Silver 0.3746 oz. ASW, 38.6 mm. **Subject:** Bulgarian Crafts - Carpet Weaving **Obv:** National Arms **Rev:** Carpet pattern in color

| Date | Mintage | F12 | VF20 | XF40 | MS60 | MS63 |
|---|---|---|---|---|---|---|
| 2007 | 7,000 | PF63 25.00 | PF65 30.00 | | | |

**KM# 305 5 LEVA**
23.30 g., 0.999 Silver 0.7484 oz. ASW, 38.6 mm. **Subject:** Bulgarian National Bank, 130th Anniversary **Obv:** Bank emblem **Rev:** Multicolor lion mozaic, fragment of stained glass

| Date | Mintage | F12 | VF20 | XF40 | MS60 | MS63 |
|---|---|---|---|---|---|---|
| 2009 | 4,000 | PF65 45.00 | | | | |

**KM# 306 5 LEVA**
0.500 Silver **Subject:** Traditional Bulgarian Crafts - Pottery **Rev:** Color pot and design

| Date | Mintage | F12 | VF20 | XF40 | MS60 | MS63 |
|---|---|---|---|---|---|---|
| 2009 | — | — | — | — | — | 30.00 |

**KM# 322 5 LEVA**
23.300 Silver ASW .5, 38.6 mm. **Subject:** Kose Bose Tale **Obv:** National arms **Rev:** Boy and Fox in color

| Date | Mintage | F12 | VF20 | XF40 | MS60 | MS63 |
|---|---|---|---|---|---|---|
| 2011 | 6,000 | — | — | — | — | — |

**KM# 321 5 LEVA**
23.30 g., 0.500 Silver 0.3746 oz. ASW, 38.6 mm. **Obv:** National arms **Rev:** Boy and the wind in color

| Date | Mintage | F12 | VF20 | XF40 | MS60 | MS63 |
|---|---|---|---|---|---|---|
| 2012 Proof | — | — | — | — | — | — |

**KM# 246 10 LEVA**
23.60 g., 0.925 Silver 0.7019 oz. ASW, 38.5 mm. **Subject:** Higher Education **Obv:** National arms, date and denomination below **Rev:** Graduate before building **Edge:** Plain

| Date | Mintage | F12 | VF20 | XF40 | MS60 | MS63 |
|---|---|---|---|---|---|---|
| 2001 | 10,000 | PF63 40.00 | PF65 45.00 | | | |

**KM# 247 10 LEVA**
23.33 g., 0.925 Silver 0.6938 oz. ASW, 38.5 mm. **Subject:** Olympics **Obv:** National arms, date and denomination below **Rev:** Ski jumper **Edge:** Plain with serial number

| Date | Mintage | F12 | VF20 | XF40 | MS60 | MS63 |
|---|---|---|---|---|---|---|
| 2001 | 25,000 | PF63 40.00 | PF65 45.00 | | | |

**KM# 275 10 LEVA**
23.30 g., 0.925 Silver 0.6929 oz. ASW, 38.6 mm. **Obv:** National arms **Rev:** Head and Star of David

| Date | Mintage | F12 | VF20 | XF40 | MS60 | MS63 |
|---|---|---|---|---|---|---|
| 2003 | 2,000 | PF65 50.00 | | | | |

**KM# 270 10 LEVA**
23.33 g., 0.999 Silver 0.7493 oz. ASW, 38.6 mm. **Subject:** National Theater Centennial **Edge:** Plain

| Date | Mintage | F12 | VF20 | XF40 | MS60 | MS63 |
|---|---|---|---|---|---|---|
| 2004 | 5,000 | PF65 50.00 | | | | |

**KM# 273 10 LEVA**
23.20 g., 0.925 Silver 0.690 oz. ASW, 38.5 mm. **Obv:** National arms, date and denomination below **Rev:** St. Nikolay Mirlikiisky Chudofvorez with gold-plated crosses and halo **Edge:** Plain

| Date | Mintage | F12 | VF20 | XF40 | MS60 | MS63 |
|---|---|---|---|---|---|---|
| 2004 | 10,000 | PF63 42.00 | PF65 45.00 | | | |

**KM# 280 10 LEVA**
23.30 g., 0.925 Silver 0.6929 oz. ASW, 38.6 mm. **Subject:** XX Olympic Games - Turino, Italy **Obv:** National arms **Rev:** Short track speed skater

| Date | Mintage | F12 | VF20 | XF40 | MS60 | MS63 |
|---|---|---|---|---|---|---|
| 2005 | 4,000 | PF65 40.00 | | | | |

**KM# 283 10 LEVA**
20.00 g., 0.999 Silver 0.6424 oz. ASW Partially gold plated, 40 mm. **Obv:** National arms **Rev:** Ancient sculpture

| Date | Mintage | F12 | VF20 | XF40 | MS60 | MS63 |
|---|---|---|---|---|---|---|
| 2005 | 10,000 | PF65 45.00 | | | | |

**KM# 285 10 LEVA**
23.30 g., 0.925 Silver 0.6929 oz. ASW, 38.6 mm. **Subject:** National Parks - Black Sea Coast **Obv:** National arms **Rev:** Map and three circular motifs

| Date | Mintage | F12 | VF20 | XF40 | MS60 | MS63 |
|---|---|---|---|---|---|---|
| 2006 | 7,000 | PF65 40.00 | | | | |

**KM# 286 10 LEVA**
20.00 g., 0.999 Silver 0.6424 oz. ASW, 40 mm. **Subject:** Treasures of Bulgaria - Letnitsa **Obv:** National arms **Rev:** Horseman statue

| Date | Mintage | F12 | VF20 | XF40 | MS60 | MS63 |
|---|---|---|---|---|---|---|
| 2006 | 10,000 | PF65 45.00 | | | | |

**KM# 292 10 LEVA**
31.10 g., 0.999 Silver 0.9989 oz. ASW, 40 mm. **Subject:** Boris Christov **Obv:** National arms **Obv. Legend:** БЪЛГАРСКА НАРОДНА БАНКА **Rev:** Early regal 1/2-length male figure facing holding orb **Rev. Legend:** ИМЕНИТИ БЪГАРСКИ ГЛАСОВЕ **Note:** Prev. KM#277.

| Date | Mintage | F12 | VF20 | XF40 | MS60 | MS63 |
|---|---|---|---|---|---|---|
| 2007 | 10,000 | PF63 45.00 | PF65 50.00 | | | |

**KM# 295 10 LEVA**
23.30 g., 0.925 Silver 0.6929 oz. ASW, 38.6 mm. **Subject:** National Parks - Pirin Mountain **Obv:** National arms **Rev:** Vanya Dimitrova

| Date | Mintage | F12 | VF20 | XF40 | MS60 | MS63 |
|---|---|---|---|---|---|---|
| 2007 | 6,000 | PF63 35.00 | PF65 40.00 | | | |

**KM# 297 10 LEVA**
20.00 g., 0.999 Silver 0.6424 oz. ASW Partially gold plated, 40 mm. **Subject:** Treasures of Bulgaria - Pegasus from Vayovo **Obv:** National arms **Rev:** Pegasus forepart

| Date | Mintage | F12 | VF20 | XF40 | MS60 | MS63 |
|---|---|---|---|---|---|---|
| 2007 | 10,000 | PF65 45.00 | | | | |

**KM# 298 10 LEVA**
23.30 g., 0.925 Silver 0.6929 oz. ASW, 38.6 mm. **Subject:** 130th Anniversary Bulgarian Liberation **Obv:** National arms **Rev:** Two figures in 19th century coats

| Date | Mintage | F12 | VF20 | XF40 | MS60 | MS63 |
|---|---|---|---|---|---|---|
| 2008 | 10,000 | PF63 35.00 | PF65 40.00 | | | |

**KM# 299 10 LEVA**
23.30 g., 0.925 Silver 0.6929 oz. ASW, 38.6 mm. **Subject:** Shooting sports **Obv:** National Arms **Rev:** Target, bowhunter, rifleman

| Date | Mintage | F12 | VF20 | XF40 | MS60 | MS63 |
|---|---|---|---|---|---|---|
| 2008 | 5,000 | PF63 35.00 | PF65 40.00 | | | |

**KM# 300 10 LEVA**
20.00 g., 0.999 Silver 0.6424 oz. ASW Partially gold plated, 40 mm. **Subject:** Treasures of Bulgaria - Sevt III **Obv:** Statue head of King Sevt III **Rev:** Elena Todorova and Todor Todorav

| Date | Mintage | F12 | VF20 | XF40 | MS60 | MS63 |
|---|---|---|---|---|---|---|
| 2008 | 8,000 | PF65 45.00 | | | | |

**KM# 301 10 LEVA**
23.30 g., 0.925 Silver 0.6929 oz. ASW, 38.6 mm. **Subject:** Bulgarian Independence - 100th Anniversary **Rev:** Crowned shield

| Date | Mintage | F12 | VF20 | XF40 | MS60 | MS63 |
|---|---|---|---|---|---|---|
| 2008 | 5,000 | PF63 35.00 | PF65 40.00 | | | |

**KM# 302 10 LEVA**
31.10 g., 0.999 Silver 0.9989 oz. ASW Partially gold plated, 40 mm. **Subject:** Great Bulgarian Voices: Nikolay Gyaurov **Obv:** National arms **Rev:** Elena Todorov and Todor Todorov

| Date | Mintage | F12 | VF20 | XF40 | MS60 | MS63 |
|---|---|---|---|---|---|---|
| 2008 | 6,000 | PF65 50.00 | | | | |

**KM# 308 10 LEVA**
23.33 g., 0.925 Silver 0.6938 oz. ASW, 38.61 mm. **Obv:** National arms **Rev:** Belogradchick rock formations

| Date | Mintage | F12 | VF20 | XF40 | MS60 | MS63 |
|---|---|---|---|---|---|---|
| 2010 | 4,000 | PF65 50.00 | | | | |

**KM# 309 10 LEVA**
23.33 g., 0.925 Silver 0.6938 oz. ASW, 38.61 mm. **Subject:** Unification, 125th Anniversary **Obv:** National arms **Rev:** Document seal gilt

| Date | Mintage | F12 | VF20 | XF40 | MS60 | MS63 |
|---|---|---|---|---|---|---|
| 2010 | 5,000 | PF65 50.00 | | | | |

**KM# 312 10 LEVA**
23.33 g., 0.925 Silver 0.6938 oz. ASW, 38.61 mm. **Obv:** St. George Zograf at right, National arms and value at left **Rev:** St. George Zograf Monastery

| Date | Mintage | F12 | VF20 | XF40 | MS60 | MS63 |
|---|---|---|---|---|---|---|
| 2011 | 6,000 | PF65 75.00 | | | | |

**KM# 313 10 LEVA**
31.10 g., 0.999 Silver 0.9989 oz. ASW, 40 mm. **Obv:** National arms **Rev:** Gena Dimitrova as Princess Turandot

| Date | Mintage | F12 | VF20 | XF40 | MS60 | MS63 |
|---|---|---|---|---|---|---|
| 2011 | 4,000 | PF65 75.00 | | | | |

**KM# 314 10 LEVA**
23.33 g., 0.925 Silver 0.6938 oz. ASW partially gilt, 38.61 mm. **Subject:** Khan Krum **Obv:** Fragment miniture from Constantine Manasses' Chronicle, Khan Krum drinks a toast **Rev:** Khan Krum pursuing the Byzantines

| Date | Mintage | F12 | VF20 | XF40 | MS60 | MS63 |
|---|---|---|---|---|---|---|
| 2011 | 5,000 | PF65 75.00 | | | | |

**KM# 318 10 LEVA**
23.33 g., 0.925 Silver 0.6938 oz. ASW, 38.6 mm. **Subject:** Slavo-Bulgraian History, 250th Anniversary **Obv:** National arms with gilt design above **Rev:** Gilt seal on documnet

| Date | Mintage | F12 | VF20 | XF40 | MS60 | MS63 |
|---|---|---|---|---|---|---|
| 2012 | 4,000 | PF65 75.00 | | | | |

**KM# 319 10 LEVA**
23.33 g., 0.925 Silver 0.6938 oz. ASW, 38.61 mm. **Subject:** Chudnite Mostove **Obv:** National arms, value below **Rev:** Natural Bridge

| Date | Mintage | F12 | VF20 | XF40 | MS60 | MS63 |
|---|---|---|---|---|---|---|
| 2012 | 4,000 | PF65 75.00 | | | | |

**KM# 320 10 LEVA**
Silver partially gilt, 38.61 mm. **Subject:** Death of Tsar Samuel **Obv:** Knights mourning Samuel **Rev:** Knights on horseback

| Date | Mintage | F12 | VF20 | XF40 | MS60 | MS63 |
|---|---|---|---|---|---|---|
| 2013 | — | PF65 100 | | | | |

**KM# 325 10 LEVA**
23.33 g., 0.925 Silver 0.6938 oz. ASW, 38.61 mm. **Subject:** Ilinden-Preobrazhenie Uprising, 110th Anniversary

| Date | Mintage | F12 | VF20 | XF40 | MS60 | MS63 |
|---|---|---|---|---|---|---|
| 2013 | — | PF65 50.00 | | | | |

**KM# 326 10 LEVA**
23.33 g., 0.925 Silver 0.6938 oz. ASW, 38.61 mm. **Subject:** Bachkovo Monastery

| Date | Mintage | VF20 | XF40 | MS60 | MS63 | MS65 |
|---|---|---|---|---|---|---|
| 2013 | — | PF65 50.00 | | | | |

**KM# 329 10 LEVA**
23.33 g., 0.925 Silver 0.6938 oz. ASW, 38.61 mm. **Subject:** Troyan Monastery

| Date | Mintage | F12 | VF20 | XF40 | MS60 | MS63 |
|---|---|---|---|---|---|---|
| 2014 | — | PF65 50.00 | | | | |

**KM# 330 10 LEVA**
23.33 g., 0.925 Silver 0.6938 oz. ASW partially gilt **Subject:** Tsar Simeon the Great

| Date | Mintage | F12 | VF20 | XF40 | MS60 | MS63 |
|---|---|---|---|---|---|---|
| 2014 | — | PF65 50.00 | | | | |

**KM# 269 20 LEVA**
1.55 g., 0.999 Gold 0.0498 oz. AGW, 16 mm. **Obv:** Denomination **Rev:** Mother of God **Edge:** Plain

| Date | Mintage | F12 | VF20 | XF40 | MS60 | MS63 |
|---|---|---|---|---|---|---|
| 2003 | 20,000 | PF63 75.00 | PF65 95.00 | | | |

**KM# 287 20 LEVA**
1.55 g., 0.999 Gold 0.0498 oz. AGW, 13.9 mm. **Subject:** Iconography St John the Baptist **Obv:** National arms **Rev:** Saint facing

| Date | Mintage | F12 | VF20 | XF40 | MS60 | MS63 |
|---|---|---|---|---|---|---|
| 2006 | 12,000 | PF63 75.00 | PF65 95.00 | | | |

**KM# 294 20 LEVA**
1.55 g., 0.999 Gold 0.0498 oz. AGW, 13.9 mm. **Subject:** Iconography - St. George the Victorious **Rev:** St. George slaying dragon

| Date | Mintage | F12 | VF20 | XF40 | MS60 | MS63 |
|---|---|---|---|---|---|---|
| 2007 | 8,000 | PF65 100 | | | | |

**KM# 303 20 LEVA**
1.55 g., 0.999 Gold 0.0498 oz. AGW, 13.9 mm. **Subject:** Tsar Boris I, the Baptist **Obv:** Half-length figure facing **Rev:** Krassimir Angelov, Borislav Kyossev, Razvigov Kolev

| Date | Mintage | F12 | VF20 | XF40 | MS60 | MS63 |
|---|---|---|---|---|---|---|
| 2008 | 8,000 | PF65 100 | | | | |

**KM# 316 20 LEVA**
1.55 g., 0.999 Gold 0.0498 oz. AGW, 13.9 mm. **Obv:** National arms **Rev:** Virgin Mary and Child

| Date | Mintage | F12 | VF20 | XF40 | MS60 | MS63 |
|---|---|---|---|---|---|---|
| 2011 | — | PF65 100 | | | | |

**KM# 293 100 LEVA**
8.64 g., 0.999 Gold 0.2775 oz. AGW **Subject:** Iconography - St. George the Victorious **Obv:** National arms **Rev:** Plamen Chernev

| Date | Mintage | F12 | VF20 | XF40 | MS60 | MS63 |
|---|---|---|---|---|---|---|
| 2007 | 1,500 | PF65 500 | | | | |

**KM# 307 100 LEVA**
7.78 g., 0.999 Gold 0.2499 oz. AGW, 22 mm. **Subject:** Bulgarian Iconography - St. Dimitar the Wonder Worker

| Date | Mintage | F12 | VF20 | XF40 | MS60 | MS63 |
|---|---|---|---|---|---|---|
| 2009 | — | PF65 475 | | | | |

**KM# 311 100 LEVA**
8.64 g., 0.999 Gold 0.2775 oz. AGW, 24 mm. **Obv:** National arms, value below **Rev:** St. Naum and Monastery of St. Naum in Ohrid

| Date | Mintage | F12 | VF20 | XF40 | MS60 | MS63 |
|---|---|---|---|---|---|---|
| 2010 | 3,000 | PF65 500 | | | | |

**KM# 323 100 LEVA**
8.64 g., 0.999 Gold 0.2775 oz. AGW, 24 mm. **Subject:** St. Petka of Bulgaria

| Date | Mintage | F12 | VF20 | XF40 | MS60 | MS63 |
|---|---|---|---|---|---|---|
| 2012 | 3,000 | PF65 450 | | | | |

**KM# 327 100 LEVA**
8.64 g., 0.999 Gold 0.2775 oz. AGW, 24 mm. **Subject:** St. Constantine and St. Helena

| Date | Mintage | F12 | VF20 | XF40 | MS60 | MS63 |
|---|---|---|---|---|---|---|
| 2013 | — | PF65 450 | | | | |

**KM# 331 100 LEVA**
8.64 g., 0.999 Gold 0.2775 oz. AGW, 24 mm. **Subject:** Holy Prophet Elias

| Date | Mintage | F12 | VF20 | XF40 | MS60 | MS63 |
|---|---|---|---|---|---|---|
| 2014 | — | PF65 450 | | | | |

**KM# 271 125 LEVA**
7.78 g., 0.999 Gold 0.2499 oz. AGW, 21 mm. **Subject:** Bulgarian National Bank 125th Anniversary

| Date | Mintage | F12 | VF20 | XF40 | MS60 | MS63 |
|---|---|---|---|---|---|---|
| 2004 | 3,000 | PF65 475 | | | | |

## PIEDFORT

| KM# | Date | Mintage | Identification | Mkt Val |
|---|---|---|---|---|
| P4 | 2004 | 5,000 | 10 Leva 0.999 Silver 100 Years - National Theatre, 38.61mm. | 75.00 |

## PROOF SETS

| KM# | Date | Mintage | Identification | Issue Price | Mkt Val |
|---|---|---|---|---|---|
| PS8 | 2002 (7) | 10,000 | KM#237-242, 254 | — | 25.00 |

# BURUNDI

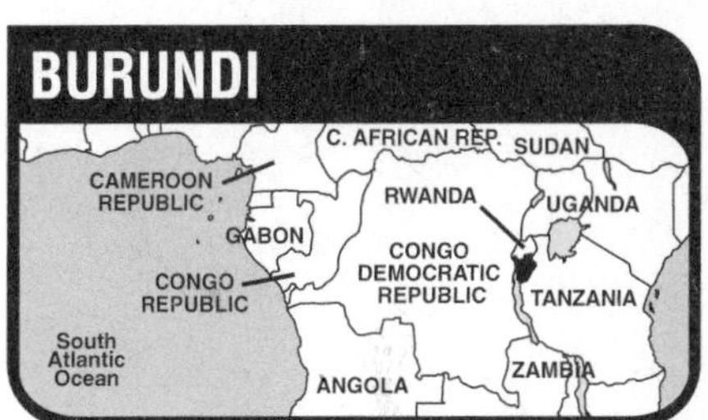


The Republic of Burundi, a landlocked country in central Africa, was a kingdom with a feudalistic society, caste system and Mwami (king) for more than 400 years before independence. It has an area of 10,740 sq. mi. (27,830 sq. km.) and a population of 6.3 million. Capital: Bujumbura. Plagued by poor soil, irregular rainfall and a single-crop economy, coffee, Burundi is barely able to feed itself. Coffee and tea are exported.

Burundi gained independence as a kingdom under Mwami Mwambutsa IV on July 1, 1962. The republic was established by military coup in 1966.

**MINT MARKS**
PM - Pobjoy Mint
(b) - Privy Marks, Brussels

**MONETARY SYSTEM**
100 Centimes = 1 Franc

## REPUBLIC

1966-

## STANDARD COINAGE

**KM# 19 FRANC**
0.87 g., Aluminum, 18.91 mm. **Obv:** Denomination **Rev:** Arms above date **Edge:** Reeded

| Date | Mintage | VF20 | XF40 | MS60 | MS63 | MS65 |
|---|---|---|---|---|---|---|
| 2003 PM | — | — | 0.50 | 1.00 | 1.50 | 2.00 |

### KM# 21 10 FRANCS

6.25 g., Nickel Plated Steel, 27 mm. **Obv:** Country name in three languages **Rev:** Value at center of wreath of bananas and wheat

| Date | Mintage | VF20 | XF40 | MS60 | MS63 | MS65 |
|---|---|---|---|---|---|---|
| 2011 | — | — | — | — | 1.00 | 2.00 |

### KM# 22 50 FRANCS

7.25 g., Nickel Plated Steel, 29 mm. **Obv:** Country name in three languages **Rev:** Drum and drummer

| Date | Mintage | VF20 | XF40 | MS60 | MS63 | MS65 |
|---|---|---|---|---|---|---|
| 2011 | — | — | — | — | 2.50 | 3.00 |

### KM# 23 5000 FRANCS

31.11 g., 0.999 Silver 0.999 oz. ASW, 38.61 mm. **Obv:** Lion head facing **Rev:** Baby leopard head faicng

| Date | Mintage | VF20 | XF40 | MS60 | MS63 | MS65 |
|---|---|---|---|---|---|---|
| 2014 Antique patina | 750 | — | — | — | — | 40.00 |

### KM# 24 5000 FRANCS

31.11 g., 0.999 Silver 0.999 oz. ASW, 38.61 mm. **Obv:** Lion head facing **Rev:** Baby Leopard in color

| Date | Mintage | VF20 | XF40 | MS60 | MS63 | MS65 |
|---|---|---|---|---|---|---|
| 2014 Antique patina | 500 | — | — | — | — | 40.00 |

# CAMBODIA

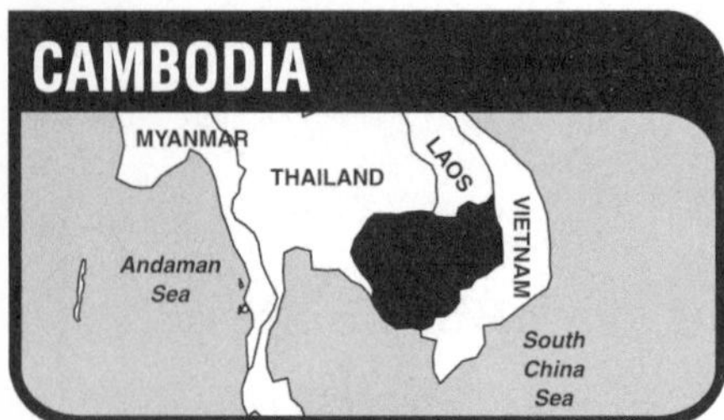


The Kingdom of Cambodia, formerly Democratic Kampuchea and the Khmer Republic, a land of paddy fields and forest-clad hills located on the Indo-Chinese peninsula, fronting on the Gulf of Thailand, has an area of 70,238 sq. mi. (181,040 sq. km.) and a population of *11.21 million. Capital: Phnom Penh. Agriculture is the basis of the economy, with rice the chief crop. Native industries include cattle breeding, weaving and rice milling. Rubber, cattle, corn, and timber are exported.

**RULERS**

Norodom Sihanouk, 1991-1993
Chairman, Supreme National Council
King, 1993-2012

## KINGDOM

1993 -

## DECIMAL COINAGE

### KM# 98 500 RIELS

19.92 g., Brass, 38.7 mm. **Subject:** Angkor Wat **Obv:** Armless statue of Jayavarman VII **Rev:** View of Angkor Wat in center **Edge:** Reeded

| Date | Mintage | VF20 | XF40 | MS60 | MS63 | MS65 |
|---|---|---|---|---|---|---|
| 2001 | 28,000 | — | — | — | 7.50 | 10.00 |

### KM# 99 3000 RIELS

1.24 g., 0.9999 Gold 0.040 oz. AGW, 13.92 mm. **Subject:** Angkor Wat **Obv:** Armless statue of Jayavarman VII **Rev:** View of Angkor Wat in center **Edge:** Reeded

| Date | Mintage | VF20 | XF40 | MS60 | MS63 | MS65 |
|---|---|---|---|---|---|---|
| 2001 | 28,000 | — | — | — | 75.00 | 85.00 |

### KM# 100 3000 RIELS

20.00 g., 0.925 Silver 0.5948 oz. ASW, 38.7 mm. **Subject:** Buddha **Obv:** Armless statue of Jayavarman VII **Rev:** Radiant Buddha next to a carved Buddha face **Edge:** Reeded

| Date | Mintage | VF20 | XF40 | MS60 | MS63 | MS65 |
|---|---|---|---|---|---|---|
| 2001 | 10,000 | PF63 45.00 | PF65 55.00 | | | |

### KM# 101 3000 RIELS

20.00 g., 0.925 Silver 0.5948 oz. ASW, 38.7 mm. **Subject:** Apsara Dance **Obv:** Armless statue of Jayavarman VII **Rev:** Dancer next to multicolor carpet pattern **Edge:** Reeded

| Date | Mintage | VF20 | XF40 | MS60 | MS63 | MS65 |
|---|---|---|---|---|---|---|
| 2001 | 10,000 | PF65 60.00 | | | | |

### KM# 103 3000 RIELS

20.00 g., 0.999 Silver 0.6424 oz. ASW, 38.7 mm. **Obv:** King Jayavarman VII (1162-1201) **Rev:** Multicolor Tutankhamen's mask **Edge:** Reeded

| Date | Mintage | VF20 | XF40 | MS60 | MS63 | MS65 |
|---|---|---|---|---|---|---|
| 2004 | 9,100 | PF65 65.00 | | | | |

### KM# 104 3000 RIELS

1.24 g., 0.999 Gold 0.040 oz. AGW, 13.92 mm. **Obv:** King Jayavarman VII (1162-1201) **Rev:** Sphinx and pyramid **Edge:** Reeded

| Date | Mintage | VF20 | XF40 | MS60 | MS63 | MS65 |
|---|---|---|---|---|---|---|
| 2004 | 27,900 | PF63 85.00 | PF65 95.00 | | | |

### KM# 124 3000 RIELS

1.24 g., 0.999 Gold 0.0398 oz. AGW, 13.92 mm. **Rev:** Pyramids

| Date | Mintage | VF20 | XF40 | MS60 | MS63 | MS65 |
|---|---|---|---|---|---|---|
| 2004 | — | — | — | — | 75.00 | 85.00 |

### KM# 139 3000 RIELS

31.11 g., 0.999 Silver 0.999 oz. ASW **Subject:** 2006 FIFA World Cup - Germany **Obv:** King Jayayarman VII **Rev:** Temple above half of a soccer ball

| Date | Mintage | VF20 | XF40 | MS60 | MS63 | MS65 |
|---|---|---|---|---|---|---|
| 2004 | — | PF63 65.00 | PF65 75.00 | | | |

### KM# 126 3000 RIELS

1.22 g., 0.999 Gold 0.0392 oz. AGW, 13.92 mm. **Rev:** Taj Mahal

| Date | Mintage | VF20 | XF40 | MS60 | MS63 | MS65 |
|---|---|---|---|---|---|---|
| 2005 | — | — | — | — | 75.00 | 85.00 |

### KM# 127 3000 RIELS

31.11 g., Silver, 38.7 mm. **Rev:** Indian Dancer, multicolor

| Date | Mintage | VF20 | XF40 | MS60 | MS63 | MS65 |
|---|---|---|---|---|---|---|
| 2005 | — | PF65 65.00 | | | | |

### KM# 110 3000 RIELS

31.11 g., 0.999 Silver 0.999 oz. ASW, 40.7 mm. **Subject:** Year of the Dog **Rev:** Multicolor St. Bernard

| Date | Mintage | VF20 | XF40 | MS60 | MS63 | MS65 |
|---|---|---|---|---|---|---|
| 2006 Prooflike | 4,000 | — | — | — | — | 80.00 |

### KM# 111 3000 RIELS

31.11 g., 0.999 Silver 0.999 oz. ASW, 40.7 mm. **Subject:** Year of the Dog **Rev:** Multicolor Bloodhound

| Date | Mintage | VF20 | XF40 | MS60 | MS63 | MS65 |
|---|---|---|---|---|---|---|
| 2006 Prooflike | 4,000 | — | — | — | — | 80.00 |

### KM# 112 3000 RIELS

31.11 g., 0.999 Silver 0.999 oz. ASW, 40.7 mm. **Subject:** Year of the Dog **Rev:** Multicolor Siberian Husky

| Date | Mintage | VF20 | XF40 | MS60 | MS63 | MS65 |
|---|---|---|---|---|---|---|
| 2006 Prooflike | 4,000 | — | — | — | — | 80.00 |

### KM# 113 3000 RIELS

31.11 g., 0.999 Silver 0.999 oz. ASW, 40.7 mm. **Subject:** Year of the Dog **Rev:** Multicolor Shar Pei

| Date | Mintage | VF20 | XF40 | MS60 | MS63 | MS65 |
|---|---|---|---|---|---|---|
| 2006 Prooflike | 4,000 | — | — | — | — | 80.00 |

### KM# 114 3000 RIELS

31.11 g., 0.999 Silver 0.999 oz. ASW, 40.7 mm. **Subject:** Year of the Dog **Rev:** Multicolor Borzaya

| Date | Mintage | VF20 | XF40 | MS60 | MS63 | MS65 |
|---|---|---|---|---|---|---|
| 2006 Prooflike | 51,000 | — | — | — | — | 80.00 |

**KM# 115 3000 RIELS**
31.11 g., 0.999 Silver 0.999 oz. ASW, 40.7 mm. **Subject:** Year of the Dog **Rev:** Multicolor Labrador

| Date | Mintage | VF20 | XF40 | MS60 | MS63 | MS65 |
|---|---|---|---|---|---|---|
| 2006 Prooflike | 51,000 | — | — | — | — | 80.00 |

**KM# 116 3000 RIELS**
31.11 g., 0.999 Silver 0.999 oz. ASW, 40.7 mm. **Subject:** Year of the Dog **Rev:** Multicolor Russian Spaniel

| Date | Mintage | VF20 | XF40 | MS60 | MS63 | MS65 |
|---|---|---|---|---|---|---|
| 2006 Prooflike | 51,000 | — | — | — | — | 80.00 |

**KM# 117 3000 RIELS**
31.11 g., 0.999 Silver 0.999 oz. ASW, 40.7 mm. **Subject:** Year of the Dog **Rev:** Multiocolor Newfoundland

| Date | Mintage | VF20 | XF40 | MS60 | MS63 | MS65 |
|---|---|---|---|---|---|---|
| 2006 Prooflike | 51,000 | — | — | — | — | 80.00 |

**KM# 129 3000 RIELS**
1.22 g., 0.999 Gold 0.0392 oz. AGW, 13.92 mm. **Rev:** Colosseum in Rome

| Date | Mintage | VF20 | XF40 | MS60 | MS63 | MS65 |
|---|---|---|---|---|---|---|
| 2006 | — | — | — | — | 75.00 | 85.00 |

**KM# 130 3000 RIELS**
Silver, 38.7 mm. **Rev:** Multicolor Roman soldier

| Date | Mintage | VF20 | XF40 | MS60 | MS63 | MS65 |
|---|---|---|---|---|---|---|
| 2006 | — | PF65 80.00 | | | | |

**KM# 118 3000 RIELS**
31.11 g., 0.999 Silver 0.999 oz. ASW, 40.7 mm. **Subject:** Year of the Pig **Rev:** Multicolor pig

| Date | Mintage | VF20 | XF40 | MS60 | MS63 | MS65 |
|---|---|---|---|---|---|---|
| 2007 Prooflike | — | — | — | — | — | 80.00 |

**KM# 132 3000 RIELS**
1.22 g., 0.999 Gold 0.0392 oz. AGW, 13.92 mm. **Rev:** Borobudur Temple, Indonesia

| Date | Mintage | VF20 | XF40 | MS60 | MS63 | MS65 |
|---|---|---|---|---|---|---|
| 2007 | 28,000 | — | — | — | 75.00 | 85.00 |

**KM# 133 3000 RIELS**
31.11 g., 0.999 Silver 0.999 oz. ASW, 38.7 mm. **Rev:** Legomo dancer, multicolor

| Date | Mintage | VF20 | XF40 | MS60 | MS63 | MS65 |
|---|---|---|---|---|---|---|
| 2007 | 10,000 | PF65 80.00 | | | | |

**KM# 135 3000 RIELS**
31.11 g., 0.999 Silver 0.999 oz. ASW, 40.7 mm. **Subject:** Year of the Pig **Rev:** Multicolor pig

| Date | Mintage | VF20 | XF40 | MS60 | MS63 | MS65 |
|---|---|---|---|---|---|---|
| 2007 Prooflike | 30,000 | — | — | — | — | 90.00 |

**KM# 136 3000 RIELS**
31.11 g., 0.999 Silver 0.999 oz. ASW, 40.7 mm. **Subject:** Year of the Pig **Rev:** Multicolor pig

| Date | Mintage | VF20 | XF40 | MS60 | MS63 | MS65 |
|---|---|---|---|---|---|---|
| 2007 Prooflike | 30,000 | — | — | — | — | 90.00 |

**KM# 137 3000 RIELS**
31.11 g., 0.999 Silver 0.999 oz. ASW, 40.7 mm. **Subject:** Year of the Pig **Rev:** Multicolor pig

| Date | Mintage | VF20 | XF40 | MS60 | MS63 | MS65 |
|---|---|---|---|---|---|---|
| 2007 Prooflike | 30,000 | — | — | — | — | 90.00 |

**KM# 138 3000 RIELS**
31.11 g., 0.999 Silver 0.999 oz. ASW, 40.7 mm. **Subject:** Year of the Pig **Rev:** Multicolor pig

| Date | Mintage | VF20 | XF40 | MS60 | MS63 | MS65 |
|---|---|---|---|---|---|---|
| 2007 Prooflike | 30,000 | — | — | — | — | 90.00 |

**KM# 121 3000 RIELS**
1.24 g., 0.999 Gold 0.0398 oz. AGW, 13.9 mm. **Subject:** Statue torso **Rev:** Shwe Dragon Pagoda, Mynamar

| Date | Mintage | VF20 | XF40 | MS60 | MS63 | MS65 |
|---|---|---|---|---|---|---|
| 2008 | — | PF63 85.00 | PF65 95.00 | | | |

**KM# 123 3000 RIELS**
31.10 g., 0.999 Silver 0.999 oz. ASW, 40.7 mm. **Obv:** Statue torso **Rev:** Multicolor Padaung

| Date | Mintage | VF20 | XF40 | MS60 | MS63 | MS65 |
|---|---|---|---|---|---|---|
| 2009 | — | PF65 75.00 | | | | |

**KM# 140 3000 RIELS**
20.00 g., 0.999 Silver 0.6424 oz. ASW, 38.7 mm. **Subject:** Japan - Cambodian friendship **Obv:** Temple **Rev:** Logo in color

| Date | Mintage | VF20 | XF40 | MS60 | MS63 | MS65 |
|---|---|---|---|---|---|---|
| 2013 | — | PF65 60.00 | | | | |

**KM# 102 10000 RIELS**
31.10 g., 0.999 Bi-Metallic 0.999 oz. Gold center in silver ring., 40.7 mm. **Subject:** Angkor Wat **Obv:** Armless statue of Jayavarman **Rev:** Multicolor holographic view of Angkor Wat in center **Edge:** Reeded

| Date | Mintage | VF20 | XF40 | MS60 | MS63 | MS65 |
|---|---|---|---|---|---|---|
| 2001 | — | PF65 350 | | | | |

**KM# 125 10000 RIELS**
31.11 g., 0.999 Silver 0.999 oz. ASW, 40.7 mm. **Rev:** Great Wall of China, holographic insert

| Date | Mintage | VF20 | XF40 | MS60 | MS63 | MS65 |
|---|---|---|---|---|---|---|
| 2003 | — | PF65 300 | | | | |

**KM# 105 10000 RIELS**
31.10 g., 0.999 Silver 0.999 oz. ASW, 40.7 mm. **Obv:** King Jayavarman VII (1162-1201) **Rev:** Sphinx and pyramid on holographic gold insert **Edge:** Reeded

| Date | Mintage | VF20 | XF40 | MS60 | MS63 | MS65 |
|---|---|---|---|---|---|---|
| 2004 | 2,100 | PF65 300 | | | | |

**KM# 119 10000 RIELS**
31.11 g., 0.999 Silver 0.999 oz. ASW, 38.7 mm. **Subject:** Zheng He 600th Anniversary **Rev:** Sailing ship with latent image

| Date | Mintage | VF20 | XF40 | MS60 | MS63 | MS65 |
|---|---|---|---|---|---|---|
| 2005 | 200 | PF65 165 | | | | |

**KM# 120 10000 RIELS**
31.11 g., 0.999 Silver 0.999 oz. ASW, 38.7 mm. **Subject:** Zheng He 600th Anniversary **Rev:** Multicolor figure standing

| Date | Mintage | VF20 | XF40 | MS60 | MS63 | MS65 |
|---|---|---|---|---|---|---|
| 2005 | 200 | PF65 150 | | | | |

**KM# 128 10000 RIELS**
31.11 g., 0.999 Silver 0.999 oz. ASW, 40.7 mm. **Rev:** Taj Mahal in multicolor hologram at center

| Date | Mintage | VF20 | XF40 | MS60 | MS63 | MS65 |
|---|---|---|---|---|---|---|
| 2005 | — | PF65 300 | | | | |

**KM# 131 10000 RIELS**
31.11 g., 0.999 Silver 0.999 oz. ASW, 40.7 mm. **Rev:** Colosseum in multicolor hologram

| Date | Mintage | VF20 | XF40 | MS60 | MS63 | MS65 |
|---|---|---|---|---|---|---|
| 2006 | — | PF65 300 | | | | |

**KM# 134 10000 RIELS**
31.11 g., 0.999 Silver 0.999 oz. ASW, 40.7 mm. **Rev:** Boraburdur temple, Indonesia

| Date | Mintage | VF20 | XF40 | MS60 | MS63 | MS65 |
|---|---|---|---|---|---|---|
| 2007 | 300 | PF65 300 | | | | |

**KM# 122 10000 RIELS**
31.10 g., 0.999 Silver 0.999 oz. ASW, 40.7 mm. **Obv:** Statue torso **Rev:** Hologram of Shwe Dragon Pagoda, Mynamar

| Date | Mintage | VF20 | XF40 | MS60 | MS63 | MS65 |
|---|---|---|---|---|---|---|
| 2009 | — | PF65 150 | | | | |

# CAMEROON

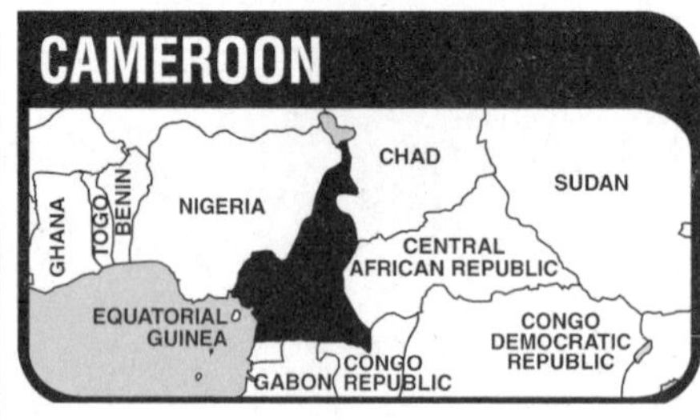


The Republic of Cameroon, located in west-central Africa on the Gulf of Guinea, has an area of 183,569 sq. mi. (475,445 sq. km.) and a population of *15.13 million. Capital: Yaounde. About 90 percent of the labor force is employed on the land; cash crops account for 80 percent of the country's export revenue. Cocoa, coffee, aluminum, cotton, rubber, and timber are exported. Cameroon is a member of the Commonwealth of Nations. The President is the Head of State; the Prime Minister is the Head of Government.

**MINT MARKS**
(a) - Paris, privy marks only
SA - Pretoria, 1943

**MONETARY SYSTEM**
100 Centimes = 1 Franc

## REPUBLIC
### STANDARD COINAGE

**KM# 56 100 FRANCS**
27.00 g., Silver Plated Copper, 40 mm. **Subject:** Soccer Championships **Obv:** National arms **Rev:** Soccer player, Brandenburg gate, map of Germany

| Date | Mintage | VF20 | XF40 | MS60 | MS63 | MS65 |
|---|---|---|---|---|---|---|
| 2012 | 10,000 | PF63 20.00 | PF65 30.00 | | | |

**KM# 57 100 FRANCS**
27.00 g., Silver Plated Copper, 40 mm. **Subject:** Soccer Championship **Obv:** National arms **Rev:** Brazilian player kneeling

| Date | Mintage | VF20 | XF40 | MS60 | MS63 | MS65 |
|---|---|---|---|---|---|---|
| 2012 | 10,000 | PF63 20.00 | PF65 30.00 | | | |

**KM# 60 100 FRANCS**
Silver Plated Copper, 38.61 mm. **Subject:** Mother Teresa beatification, 10th Anniversary **Obv:** National arms **Rev:** John Paul II and Mother Teresa in color, St. Peter's Basilica in background

| Date | Mintage | VF20 | XF40 | MS60 | MS63 | MS65 |
|---|---|---|---|---|---|---|
| 2013 Prooflike | — | — | — | — | 20.00 | — |

**KM# 25 500 FRANCS**
15.55 g., 0.925 Silver 0.4624 oz. ASW, 33 mm. **Subject:** Zodiac - Aries **Obv:** National arms

| Date | Mintage | VF20 | XF40 | MS60 | MS63 | MS65 |
|---|---|---|---|---|---|---|
| 2010 | 3,000 | — | — | — | 50.00 | 60.00 |

**KM# 26 500 FRANCS**
15.55 g., 0.925 Silver 0.4624 oz. ASW, 33 mm. **Subject:** Zodiac - Taurus **Obv:** National arms

| Date | Mintage | VF20 | XF40 | MS60 | MS63 | MS65 |
|---|---|---|---|---|---|---|
| 2010 | 3,000 | — | — | — | 50.00 | 60.00 |

**KM# 27 500 FRANCS**
15.55 g., 0.925 Silver 0.4624 oz. ASW, 33 mm. **Subject:** Zodiac - Gemini **Obv:** National arms

| Date | Mintage | VF20 | XF40 | MS60 | MS63 | MS65 |
|---|---|---|---|---|---|---|
| 2010 | 3,000 | — | — | — | 50.00 | 60.00 |

**KM# 28 500 FRANCS**
15.55 g., 0.925 Silver 0.4624 oz. ASW, 33 mm. **Subject:** Zodiac - Cancer **Obv:** National arms

| Date | Mintage | VF20 | XF40 | MS60 | MS63 | MS65 |
|---|---|---|---|---|---|---|
| 2010 | 3,000 | — | — | — | 50.00 | 60.00 |

**KM# 29 500 FRANCS**
15.55 g., 0.925 Silver 0.4624 oz. ASW **Subject:** Zodiac - Leo **Obv:** National arms

| Date | Mintage | VF20 | XF40 | MS60 | MS63 | MS65 |
|---|---|---|---|---|---|---|
| 2010 | 3,000 | — | — | — | 50.00 | 60.00 |

**KM# 30 500 FRANCS**
15.55 g., 0.925 Silver 0.4624 oz. ASW, 33 mm. **Subject:** Zodiac - Virgo **Obv:** National arms

| Date | Mintage | VF20 | XF40 | MS60 | MS63 | MS65 |
|---|---|---|---|---|---|---|
| 2010 | 3,000 | — | — | — | 50.00 | 60.00 |

**KM# 31 500 FRANCS**
15.55 g., 0.925 Silver 0.4624 oz. ASW, 33 mm. **Subject:** Zodiac - Libra **Obv:** National arms

| Date | Mintage | VF20 | XF40 | MS60 | MS63 | MS65 |
|---|---|---|---|---|---|---|
| 2010 | 3,000 | — | — | — | 50.00 | 60.00 |

**KM# 32 500 FRANCS**
15.55 g., 0.999 Silver 0.4994 oz. ASW, 33 mm. **Subject:** Zodiac - Scorpius **Obv:** National arms

| Date | Mintage | VF20 | XF40 | MS60 | MS63 | MS65 |
|---|---|---|---|---|---|---|
| 2010 | 3,000 | — | — | — | 50.00 | 60.00 |

**KM# 33 500 FRANCS**
15.55 g., 0.925 Silver 0.4624 oz. ASW, 33 mm. **Subject:** Zodiac - Sagittarius **Obv:** National arms

| Date | Mintage | VF20 | XF40 | MS60 | MS63 | MS65 |
|---|---|---|---|---|---|---|
| 2010 | 3,000 | — | — | — | 50.00 | 60.00 |

**KM# 34 500 FRANCS**
15.55 g., 0.925 Silver 0.4624 oz. ASW, 33 mm. **Subject:** Zodiac - Capricorn **Obv:** National Arms

| Date | Mintage | VF20 | XF40 | MS60 | MS63 | MS65 |
|---|---|---|---|---|---|---|
| 2010 | 3,000 | — | — | — | 50.00 | 60.00 |

**KM# 35 500 FRANCS**
15.55 g., 0.925 Silver 0.4624 oz. ASW, 33 mm. **Subject:** Zodiac - Aquarius **Obv:** National arms

| Date | Mintage | VF20 | XF40 | MS60 | MS63 | MS65 |
|---|---|---|---|---|---|---|
| 2010 | 3,000 | — | — | — | 50.00 | 60.00 |

**KM# 36 500 FRANCS**
15.55 g., 0.925 Silver 0.4624 oz. ASW, 33 mm. **Subject:** Zodiac - Pisces **Obv:** National arms

| Date | Mintage | VF20 | XF40 | MS60 | MS63 | MS65 |
|---|---|---|---|---|---|---|
| 2010 | 3,000 | — | — | — | 50.00 | 60.00 |

**KM# 61 500 FRANCS**
15.55 g., 0.999 Silver 0.4994 oz. ASW, 38.61 mm. **Subject:** Mother Teresa beatification, 10th Anniversary **Obv:** National arms **Rev:** John Paul II and Mother Teresa in color, St. Peter's Basilica in background

| Date | Mintage | VF20 | XF40 | MS60 | MS63 | MS65 |
|---|---|---|---|---|---|---|
| 2013 Prooflike | — | — | — | — | — | 25.00 |

**KM# 24 1000 FRANCS**
25.00 g., 0.925 Copper-Nickel 0.7435 oz., 38.61 mm. **Obv:** Arms **Rev:** Papillons D'Amour butterfly **Edge:** Reeded

| Date | Mintage | VF20 | XF40 | MS60 | MS63 | MS65 |
|---|---|---|---|---|---|---|
| 2010 | 2,500 | PF63 55.00 | PF65 65.00 | | | |

**KM# 37 1000 FRANCS**
25.00 g., 0.999 Silver 0.803 oz. ASW, 38.61 mm. **Subject:** Ange de l'amour **Obv:** National arms **Rev:** Cupuid

| Date | Mintage | VF20 | XF40 | MS60 | MS63 | MS65 |
|---|---|---|---|---|---|---|
| 2010 | 2,500 | PF65 80.00 | | | | |

**KM# 38 1000 FRANCS**
20.00 g., 0.925 Silver 0.5948 oz. ASW, 38.61 mm. **Obv:** National arms **Rev:** Heat sensetive image of the Shroud of Turin

| Date | Mintage | VF20 | XF40 | MS60 | MS63 | MS65 |
|---|---|---|---|---|---|---|
| 2010 | 2,010 | PF65 75.00 | | | | |

**KM# 49 1000 FRANCS**
25.00 g., Copper-Nickel, 39 mm. **Obv:** National arms **Rev:** Two swans, hologram between them

| Date | Mintage | VF20 | XF40 | MS60 | MS63 | MS65 |
|---|---|---|---|---|---|---|
| 2011 Antique Finish | — | — | — | — | 75.00 | — |
| 2011 | — | PF65 110 | | | | |

**KM# 50 1000 FRANCS**
25.00 g., Copper-Nickel, 39 mm. **Obv:** National arms **Rev:** Monarch Butterfly in 3-D and color

| Date | Mintage | VF20 | XF40 | MS60 | MS63 | MS65 |
|---|---|---|---|---|---|---|
| 2011 | — | PF65 55.00 | | | | |

**KM# 51 1000 FRANCS**
31.11 g., 0.999 Silver 0.999 oz. ASW, 38.61 mm. **Subject:** Year of the Dragon **Obv:** National arms **Rev:** Dragon in color

| Date | Mintage | VF20 | XF40 | MS60 | MS63 | MS65 |
|---|---|---|---|---|---|---|
| 2012 | — | PF65 75.00 | | | | |

**KM# 52 1000 FRANCS**
20.00 g., 0.999 Silver 0.6424 oz. ASW, 38.61 mm. **Subject:** Year of the Dragon **Obv:** National arms **Rev:** Gilt dragon and Great Wall of China

| Date | Mintage | VF20 | XF40 | MS60 | MS63 | MS65 |
|---|---|---|---|---|---|---|
| 2012 | 888 | PF65 60.00 | | | | |

**KM# 53 1000 FRANCS**
20.00 g., 0.999 Silver 0.6424 oz. ASW, 38.61 mm. **Obv:** National arms **Rev:** Unicorn and opal

| Date | Mintage | VF20 | XF40 | MS60 | MS63 | MS65 |
|---|---|---|---|---|---|---|
| 2012 | 888 | PF65 75.00 | | | | |

**KM# 58 1000 FRANCS**
20.00 g., 0.999 Silver 0.6424 oz. ASW, 38.61 mm. **Obv:** National arms **Rev:** Two Cross River Gorillas

| Date | Mintage | VF20 | XF40 | MS60 | MS63 | MS65 |
|---|---|---|---|---|---|---|
| 2012 | — | — | — | — | 50.00 | 60.00 |

**KM# 54 1000 FRANCS**
31.11 g., 0.999 Silver 0.999 oz. ASW, 40 mm. **Rev:** Cross River Gorilla

| Date | Mintage | VF20 | XF40 | MS60 | MS63 | MS65 |
|---|---|---|---|---|---|---|
| 2013 Antique patina | 1,000 | PF65 100 | | | | |

**KM# 59 1000 FRANCS**
31.11 g., 0.999 (No Composition) 0.999 oz., 38.61 mm. **Obv:** National arms **Rev:** Jesus of Nazareth in color

| Date | Mintage | VF20 | XF40 | MS60 | MS63 | MS65 |
|---|---|---|---|---|---|---|
| 2013 Antique patina | — | — | — | — | 40.00 | — |

**KM# 62 1000 FRANCS**
20.00 g., 0.999 Silver 0.6424 oz. ASW, 38.61 mm. **Obv:** National arms **Rev:** Unicorn with opal

| Date | Mintage | VF20 | XF40 | MS60 | MS63 | MS65 |
|---|---|---|---|---|---|---|
| 2013 Proof | 888 | — | — | — | 25.00 | — |

**KM# 63 1000 FRANCS**
31.11 g., 0.999 Silver 0.999 oz. ASW, 38.61 mm. **Obv:** National arms **Rev:** Cross River Gorilla head facing

| Date | Mintage | VF20 | XF40 | MS60 | MS63 | MS65 |
|---|---|---|---|---|---|---|
| 2014 Antique patina | — | — | — | — | 40.00 | — |

**KM# 64 1000 FRANCS**
31.11 g., 0.999 Silver 0.999 oz. ASW, 38.61 mm. **Obv:** National arms **Rev:** Cross River Gorilla head with crystal eyes

| Date | Mintage | VF20 | XF40 | MS60 | MS63 | MS65 |
|---|---|---|---|---|---|---|
| 2014 | — | PF65 40.00 | | | | |

**KM# 40 1500 FRANCS**
62.20 g., 0.999 Silver 1.9978 oz. ASW, 40x40 mm. **Obv:** National arms **Rev:** Black Rhinoceros head profile facing right

| Date | Mintage | VF20 | XF40 | MS60 | MS63 | MS65 |
|---|---|---|---|---|---|---|
| 2010 | — | PF63 85.00 | PF65 100 | | | |

**KM# 55 1500 FRANCS**
62.20 g., 0.999 Silver 1.9978 oz. ASW, 42 x 42 mm. **Subject:** Rare Wildlife - Black Rhino

| Date | Mintage | VF20 | XF40 | MS60 | MS63 | MS65 |
|---|---|---|---|---|---|---|
| 2010 | Est. 999 | PF65 250 | | | | |

# CANADA

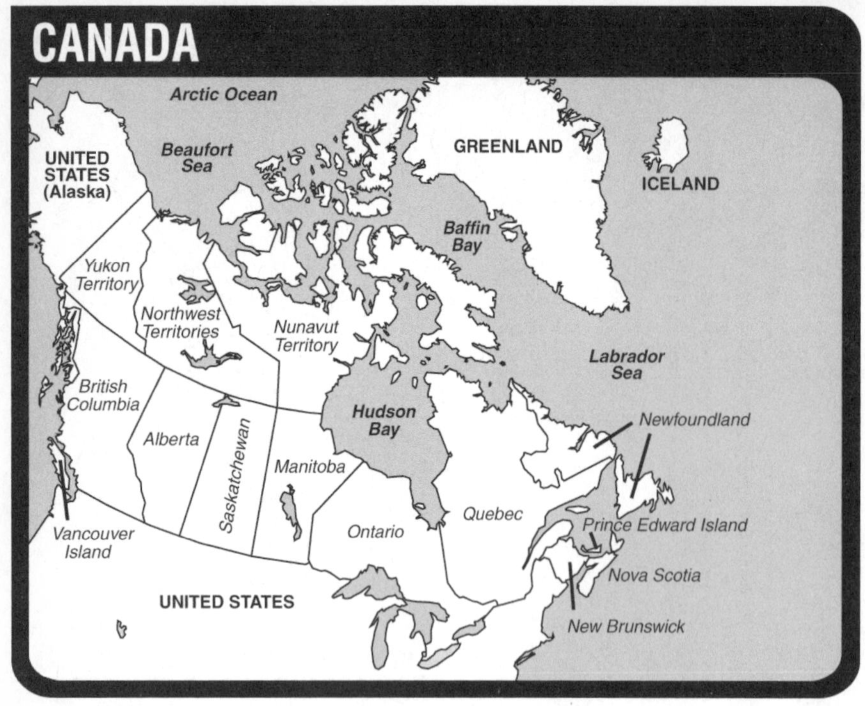


Canada is located to the north of the United States, and spans the full breadth of the northern portion of North America from Atlantic to Pacific oceans, except for the State of Alaska. It has a total area of 3,850,000 sq. mi. (9,971,550 sq. km.) and a population of 30.29 million. Capital: Ottawa.

Canada is a member of the Commonwealth of Nations. Elizabeth II is Head of State as Queen of Canada.

**RULER**
British 1763-

**MONETARY SYSTEM**
1 Dollar = 100 Cents

## CONFEDERATION

### CIRCULATION COINAGE

**KM# 289 CENT**
2.25 g., Copper Plated Steel, 19.05 mm. **Ruler:** Elizabeth II **Obv:** Crowned head right **Rev:** Maple twig design **Edge:** Round and plain

| Date | Mintage | VF20 | XF40 | MS60 | MS63 | MS65 |
|---|---|---|---|---|---|---|
| 2001 | 919,358,000 | — | — | — | 0.30 | 13.00 |
| 2001 P | — | PF65 5.00 | | | | |
| 2003 | 92,219,775 | — | — | — | 0.20 | 18.00 |
| 2003 P | — | PF65 7.50 | | | | |
| 2003 P | 235,936,799 | — | — | — | 0.20 | 13.00 |

**KM# 445 CENT**
2.25 g., Copper Plated Steel, 19.1 mm. **Ruler:** Elizabeth II **Subject:** Elizabeth II Golden Jubilee **Obv:** Crowned head right, Jubilee commemorative dates 1952-2002 **Rev:** Denomination above maple leaves **Edge:** Plain

| Date | Mintage | VF20 | XF40 | MS60 | MS63 | MS65 |
|---|---|---|---|---|---|---|
| 1952-2002 | 716,366,000 | — | — | — | 0.20 | 13.00 |
| 1952-2002 P | 114,212,000 | — | — | — | 0.45 | 13.00 |
| 1952-2002 P | 32,642 | PF65 5.00 | | | | |

**KM# 445a CENT**
0.925 Silver **Ruler:** Elizabeth II **Subject:** Elizabeth II Golden Jubilee **Obv:** Crowned head right, Jubilee commemorative dates 1952-2002 **Rev:** Denomination above maple leaves

| Date | Mintage | VF20 | XF40 | MS60 | MS63 | MS65 |
|---|---|---|---|---|---|---|
| 1952-2002 | 21,537 | PF65 3.00 | | | | |

**KM# 468 CENT**
2.50 g., Copper **Ruler:** Elizabeth II **Subject:** 50th Anniversary of the Coronation of Elizabeth II **Obv:** 1953 Effigy of the Queen, Jubilee commemorative dates 1953-2003

| Date | Mintage | VF20 | XF40 | MS60 | MS63 | MS65 |
|---|---|---|---|---|---|---|
| 1953-2003 | — | PF65 10.00 | | | | |

**KM# 490 CENT**
2.25 g., Copper Plated Zinc, 19.05 mm. **Ruler:** Elizabeth II **Obv:** New effigy of Queen Elizabeth II right **Rev:** Two maple leaves **Edge:** Plain

| Date | Mintage | VF20 | XF40 | MS60 | MS63 | MS65 |
|---|---|---|---|---|---|---|
| 2003 | 56,877,144 | — | — | — | 0.25 | — |
| 2004 | 653,317,000 | — | — | — | 0.25 | — |
| 2004 | — | PF65 7.00 | | | | |
| 2005 | 759,658,000 | — | — | — | 0.25 | — |
| 2005 | — | PF65 7.50 | | | | |
| 2006 | 886,275,000 | — | — | — | 0.25 | — |
| 2006 | — | PF65 7.00 | | | | |

**KM# 490a CENT**
2.25 g., Copper Plated Steel, 19.05 mm. **Ruler:** Elizabeth II **Obv:** Bust right **Rev:** Two maple leaves

| Date | Mintage | VF20 | XF40 | MS60 | MS63 | MS65 |
|---|---|---|---|---|---|---|
| 2003 P | 591,257,000 | — | — | — | 0.20 | 13.00 |
| 2003 WP | Inc. above | — | — | — | 0.20 | 13.00 |
| 2004 P | 134,906,000 | — | — | — | 0.20 | 13.00 |
| 2005 P | 30,525,000 | — | — | — | 0.20 | 13.00 |
| 2006 P | 137,733,000 | — | — | — | 9.00 | 27.00 |
| 2006 (ml) | Inc. above | — | — | — | 0.20 | 13.00 |
| 2007 (ml) | 938,270,000 | — | — | — | 0.20 | 13.00 |
| 2007 (ml) | — | PF65 7.00 | | | | |
| 2008 (ml) | 787,625,000 | — | — | — | 0.20 | 13.00 |
| 2008 (ml) | — | PF65 7.00 | | | | |
| 2009 (ml) | 455,680,000 | — | — | — | 0.20 | 13.00 |
| 2009 (ml) | — | PF65 7.00 | | | | |
| 2010 (ml) | — | — | — | — | 0.20 | 13.00 |
| 2010 (ml) | — | PF65 7.00 | | | | |
| 2011 (ml) | — | — | — | — | 0.20 | 13.00 |
| 2011 (ml) | — | PF65 7.00 | | | | |
| 2012 (ml) | — | — | — | — | 0.20 | 13.00 |
| 2012 (ml) | — | PF65 4.50 | | | | |

**KM# 490b CENT**
2.25 g., Copper Plated Zinc **Ruler:** Elizabeth II **Obv:** Head right **Rev:** Maple leaf, selectively gold plated **Note:** Bound into Annual Report.

| Date | Mintage | VF20 | XF40 | MS60 | MS63 | MS65 |
|---|---|---|---|---|---|---|
| 2003 | 7,746 | PF65 35.00 | | | | |

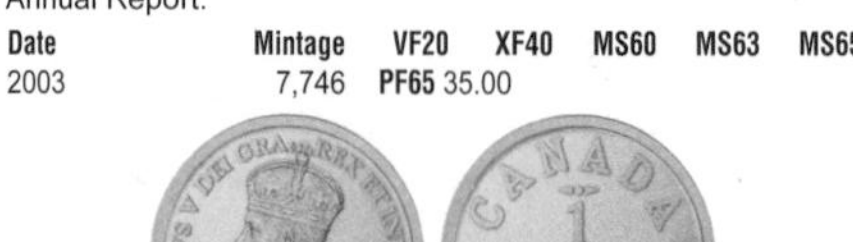

**KM# 1023 CENT**
Copper, 19.1 mm. **Ruler:** Elizabeth II **Obv:** George V bust left **Rev:** Value within wreath, dual dates below

| Date | Mintage | VF20 | XF40 | MS60 | MS63 | MS65 |
|---|---|---|---|---|---|---|
| 1935-2010 | — | PF65 10.00 | | | | |

**KM# 1153 CENT**
5.67 g., Copper, 19.1 mm. **Ruler:** Elizabeth II **Obv:** George V bust **Rev:** Value within wreath

| Date | Mintage | VF20 | XF40 | MS60 | MS63 | MS65 |
|---|---|---|---|---|---|---|
| 1911-2011 | 6,000 | PF65 10.00 | | | | |

**KM# 1342 CENT**
Silver, 25.5 mm. **Ruler:** Elizabeth II **Obv:** Edward VII crowned bust right **Rev:** Small leaves in wreath around value, country name and date

| Date | Mintage | VF20 | XF40 | MS60 | MS63 | MS65 |
|---|---|---|---|---|---|---|
| 2012 | — | PF65 20.00 | | | | |

**KM# 1343 CENT**
Silver, 25.5 mm. **Ruler:** Elizabeth II **Obv:** George V crowned bust left **Rev:** Small leaves in wreath around value and date

| Date | Mintage | VF20 | XF40 | MS60 | MS63 | MS65 |
|---|---|---|---|---|---|---|
| 2012 | — | PF65 20.00 | | | | |

**KM# 1344 CENT**
0.925 Silver, 19.1 mm. **Ruler:** Elizabeth II **Obv:** Elizabeth II bust right **Rev:** Two maple leaves

| Date | Mintage | VF20 | XF40 | MS60 | MS63 | MS65 |
|---|---|---|---|---|---|---|
| 2012 | — | PF65 20.00 | | | | |

**KM# 1345 CENT**
0.925 Silver, 19.1 mm. **Ruler:** Elizabeth II **Obv:** Elizabeth II Malouf bust right **Rev:** Dove in flight

| Date | Mintage | VF20 | XF40 | MS60 | MS63 | MS65 |
|---|---|---|---|---|---|---|
| 2012 | — | PF65 20.00 | | | | |

**KM# 1427 CENT**
157.60 g., 0.999 Silver 5.0619 oz. ASW, 65 mm. **Ruler:** Elizabeth II **Subject:** Farewell to the cent **Rev:** Two maple leaves

| Date | Mintage | VF20 | XF40 | MS60 | MS63 | MS65 |
|---|---|---|---|---|---|---|
| 2012 | Est. 1500 | PF65 500 | | | | |

**KM# 1520 CENT**
1.27 g., 0.9999 Gold 0.0408 oz. AGW, 13.92 mm. **Ruler:** Elizabeth II **Subject:** End of the Cent **Edge:** Reeded

| Date | Mintage | VF20 | XF40 | MS60 | MS63 | MS65 |
|---|---|---|---|---|---|---|
| 2012 | Est. 12000 | PF65 70.00 | | | | |

**KM# 1428 CENT**
15.87 g., 0.999 Silver 0.5097 oz. ASW, 34 mm. **Ruler:** Elizabeth II **Rev:** Two maple leaves selectively gilt

| Date | Mintage | F12 | VF20 | XF40 | MS60 | MS63 |
|---|---|---|---|---|---|---|
| 2013 | Est. 3000 | PF65 55.00 | | | | |

**KM# 410 3 CENTS**
3.11 g., 0.925 Silver 0.0925 oz. ASW Gilt, 21.3 mm. **Ruler:** Elizabeth II **Subject:** 1st Canadian Postage Stamp **Obv:** Crowned head right **Rev:** Partial stamp design **Edge:** Plain

| Date | Mintage | VF20 | XF40 | MS60 | MS63 | MS65 |
|---|---|---|---|---|---|---|
| 2001 | 59,573 | PF65 12.50 | | | | |

**KM# 182 5 CENTS**

4.60 g., Copper-Nickel, 19.55 mm. **Ruler:** Elizabeth II **Obv:** Crowned head right **Rev:** Beaver on rock divides dates and denomination **Edge:** Plain

| Date | Mintage | VF20 | XF40 | MS60 | MS63 | MS65 |
|---|---|---|---|---|---|---|
| 2001 | 30,035,000 | — | — | — | 1.25 | 65.00 |
| 2001 P | — | **PF65** 9.00 | | | | |
| 2003 | — | — | — | — | 0.60 | 22.00 |

**KM# 182a 5 CENTS**

5.35 g., 0.925 Silver 0.1591 oz. ASW, 21.2 mm. **Ruler:** Elizabeth II **Obv:** Crowned head right **Rev:** Beaver on rock divides date and denomination

| Date | Mintage | VF20 | XF40 | MS60 | MS63 | MS65 |
|---|---|---|---|---|---|---|
| 2001 | — | **PF65** 8.00 | | | | |
| 2003 | — | **PF65** 8.00 | | | | |

**KM# 182b 5 CENTS**

3.90 g., Nickel Plated Steel, 21.2 mm. **Ruler:** Elizabeth II **Obv:** Crowned head right **Rev:** Beaver on rock divides date and denomination **Edge:** Plain

| Date | Mintage | VF20 | XF40 | MS60 | MS63 | MS65 |
|---|---|---|---|---|---|---|
| 2001 P | 136,650,000 | — | — | — | 0.50 | 22.00 |
| 2003 P | 32,986,921 | — | — | — | 0.60 | 22.00 |

**KM# 413 5 CENTS**

5.35 g., 0.925 Silver 0.1591 oz. ASW, 21.2 mm. **Ruler:** Elizabeth II **Subject:** Royal Military College **Obv:** Crowned head right **Rev:** Marching cadets and arch **Edge:** Plain

| Date | Mintage | VF20 | XF40 | MS60 | MS63 | MS65 |
|---|---|---|---|---|---|---|
| 2001 | — | **PF65** 8.00 | | | | |

**KM# 446 5 CENTS**

3.95 g., Nickel Plated Steel, 21.2 mm. **Ruler:** Elizabeth II **Subject:** Elizabeth II Golden Jubilee **Obv:** Crowned head right, Jubilee commemorative dates 1952-2002 **Note:** Magnetic.

| Date | Mintage | VF20 | XF40 | MS60 | MS63 | MS65 |
|---|---|---|---|---|---|---|
| 1952-2002 P | 135,960,000 | — | — | — | 0.45 | 22.00 |
| 1952-2002 P | 32,642 | **PF65** 10.00 | | | | |

**KM# 446a 5 CENTS**

5.35 g., 0.925 Silver 0.1591 oz. ASW, 21.2 mm. **Ruler:** Elizabeth II **Subject:** Elizabeth II Golden Jubilee **Obv:** Queen, Jubilee commemorative dates 1952-2002

| Date | Mintage | VF20 | XF40 | MS60 | MS63 | MS65 |
|---|---|---|---|---|---|---|
| 1952-2002 | 21,573 | **PF65** 11.50 | | | | |

**KM# 453 5 CENTS**

5.35 g., 0.925 Silver 0.1591 oz. ASW, 21.2 mm. **Ruler:** Elizabeth II **Subject:** Vimy Ridge - WWI **Obv:** Crowned head right **Rev:** Vimy Ridge Memorial, allegorical figure and dates 1917-2002

| Date | Mintage | VF20 | XF40 | MS60 | MS63 | MS65 |
|---|---|---|---|---|---|---|
| 2002 | — | **PF65** 11.50 | | | | |

**KM# 469 5 CENTS**

5.35 g., 0.925 Silver 0.1591 oz. ASW, 21.2 mm. **Ruler:** Elizabeth II **Subject:** 50th Anniversary of the Coronation of Elizabeth II **Obv:** Crowned head right, Jubilee commemorative dates 1953-2003

| Date | Mintage | VF20 | XF40 | MS60 | MS63 | MS65 |
|---|---|---|---|---|---|---|
| 1953-2003 | 21,573 | **PF65** 11.50 | | | | |

**KM# 491 5 CENTS**

3.95 g., Nickel Plated Steel, 21.2 mm. **Ruler:** Elizabeth II **Obv:** Bare head right **Rev:** Beaver divides date and denomination **Note:** Magnetic.

| Date | Mintage | VF20 | XF40 | MS60 | MS63 | MS65 |
|---|---|---|---|---|---|---|
| 2003 P | 61,392,180 | — | — | — | 0.65 | 90.00 |
| 2004 P | 132,097,000 | — | — | — | 0.45 | 18.00 |
| 2004 P | — | **PF65** 7.00 | | | | |
| 2005 P | 89,664,000 | — | — | — | 0.45 | 18.00 |
| 2005 P | — | **PF65** 9.00 | | | | |
| 2006 P | 139,308,000 | — | — | — | 0.50 | 18.00 |
| 2006 P | — | **PF65** 7.00 | | | | |
| 2006 (ml) | 184,874,000 | — | — | — | 0.45 | 18.00 |
| 2006 (ml) | — | **PF65** 2.50 | | | | |
| 2007 (ml) | 221,472,000 | — | — | — | 0.45 | 18.00 |
| 2007 (ml) | — | **PF65** 7.00 | | | | |
| 2008 (ml) | 278,530,000 | — | — | — | 0.45 | 18.00 |
| 2008 (ml) | — | **PF65** 7.00 | | | | |
| 2009 (ml) | 266,488,000 | — | — | — | 0.45 | 18.00 |
| 2009 (ml) | — | **PF65** 7.00 | | | | |
| 2010 (ml) | — | — | — | — | 0.45 | 18.00 |
| 2010 (ml) | — | **PF65** 7.00 | | | | |
| 2011 (ml) | — | — | — | — | 0.45 | 18.00 |
| 2011 (ml) | — | **PF65** 7.00 | | | | |
| 2012 (ml) | — | — | — | — | 0.45 | 18.00 |
| 2012 (ml) | — | **PF65** 3.50 | | | | |
| 2013 (ml) | — | — | — | — | 0.45 | 18.00 |
| 2013 (ml) | — | **PF65** 2.50 | | | | |
| 2014 | — | — | — | — | 0.45 | — |
| 2014 | — | **PF63** 1.50 | **PF65** 2.50 | | | |
| 2015 | — | — | — | — | 0.45 | — |
| 2015 | — | **PF63** 1.50 | **PF65** 2.50 | | | |

**KM# 491a 5 CENTS**

5.35 g., 0.925 Silver 0.1591 oz. ASW, 21.1 mm. **Ruler:** Elizabeth II **Obv:** Crowned head right **Rev:** Beaver divides date and denomination **Edge:** Plain

| Date | Mintage | VF20 | XF40 | MS60 | MS63 | MS65 |
|---|---|---|---|---|---|---|
| 2004 | — | **PF65** 6.50 | | | | |

**KM# 506 5 CENTS**

5.35 g., 0.925 Silver 0.1591 oz. ASW, 21.3 mm. **Ruler:** Elizabeth II **Obv:** Bare head right **Rev:** Victory " design of the KM-40 reverse **Edge:** Plain **Shape:** 12-sided

| Date | Mintage | VF20 | XF40 | MS60 | MS63 | MS65 |
|---|---|---|---|---|---|---|
| 1944-2004 | 20,019 | **PF65** 15.00 | | | | |

**KM# 627 5 CENTS**

3.95 g., Nickel Plated Steel, 21.2 mm. **Ruler:** Elizabeth II **Subject:** 60th Anniversary, Victory in Europe 1945-2005 **Obv:** Head right **Rev:** Large V **Edge:** Plain

| Date | Mintage | VF20 | XF40 | MS60 | MS63 | MS65 |
|---|---|---|---|---|---|---|
| 2005 P | 59,269,192 | — | — | — | 0.65 | 18.00 |

**KM# 758 5 CENTS**

5.30 g., 0.925 Silver 0.1576 oz. ASW **Ruler:** Elizabeth II **Obv:** George VI head left **Rev:** Torch and large V

| Date | Mintage | VF20 | XF40 | MS60 | MS63 | MS65 |
|---|---|---|---|---|---|---|
| 2005 | 42,792 | **PF65** 35.00 | | | | |

**KM# 758a 5 CENTS**

5.30 g., 0.925 Silver 0.1576 oz. ASW selectively gold plated **Ruler:** Elizabeth II **Obv:** George VI head left **Rev:** Torch and large V **Note:** Bound into Annual Report.

| Date | Mintage | VF20 | XF40 | MS60 | MS63 | MS65 |
|---|---|---|---|---|---|---|
| 2005 | 6,065 | **PF65** 40.00 | | | | |

**KM# 491b 5 CENTS**

4.60 g., Copper-Nickel **Ruler:** Elizabeth II **Obv:** Bust right **Rev:** Beaver

| Date | Mintage | VF20 | XF40 | MS60 | MS63 | MS65 |
|---|---|---|---|---|---|---|
| 2006 | 43,008,000 | — | — | — | 5.00 | — |

**KM# 1024 5 CENTS**

Nickel, 21.2 mm. **Ruler:** Elizabeth II **Obv:** George V bust left **Rev:** Denomination and 1935-2010 anniversary dates, two maple leaves below

| Date | Mintage | VF20 | XF40 | MS60 | MS63 | MS65 |
|---|---|---|---|---|---|---|
| 1935-2010 | — | **PF65** 15.00 | | | | |

**KM# 1154 5 CENTS**

1.56 g., 0.925 Silver 0.0464 oz. ASW, 15.5 mm. **Ruler:** Elizabeth II **Obv:** George V bust **Rev:** Value within wreath

| Date | Mintage | VF20 | XF40 | MS60 | MS63 | MS65 |
|---|---|---|---|---|---|---|
| 1911-2011 | 6,000 | **PF65** 15.00 | | | | |

**KM# 183a 10 CENTS**

2.40 g., 0.925 Silver 0.0714 oz. ASW, 18.03 mm. **Ruler:** Elizabeth II **Obv:** Crowned head right **Rev:** Bluenose sailing left, date at right, denomination below

| Date | Mintage | VF20 | XF40 | MS60 | MS63 | MS65 |
|---|---|---|---|---|---|---|
| 2001 | — | **PF65** 5.00 | | | | |
| 2002 | — | **PF65** 7.50 | | | | |
| 2003 | — | **PF65** 7.50 | | | | |

**KM# 183b 10 CENTS**

1.77 g., Nickel Plated Steel, 18.03 mm. **Ruler:** Elizabeth II **Obv:** Crowned head right **Rev:** Bluenose sailing left, date at right, denomination below **Edge:** Reeded

| Date | Mintage | VF20 | XF40 | MS60 | MS63 | MS65 |
|---|---|---|---|---|---|---|
| 2001 P | 266,000,000 | — | — | — | 0.45 | 27.00 |
| 2003 P | 162,398,000 | — | — | — | 0.55 | 18.00 |

**KM# 412 10 CENTS**

1.77 g., Nickel Plated Steel, 18 mm. **Ruler:** Elizabeth II **Subject:** Year of the Volunteer **Obv:** Crowned head right **Rev:** Three portraits left and radiant sun **Edge:** Reeded

| Date | Mintage | VF20 | XF40 | MS60 | MS63 | MS65 |
|---|---|---|---|---|---|---|
| 2001 P | 224,714,000 | — | — | — | 0.65 | 27.00 |

**KM# 412a 10 CENTS**

2.40 g., 0.925 Silver 0.0714 oz. ASW, 18 mm. **Ruler:** Elizabeth II **Subject:** Year of the Volunteer **Obv:** Crowned head right **Rev:** Three portraits left above banner, radiant sun below **Edge:** Reeded

| Date | Mintage | VF20 | XF40 | MS60 | MS63 | MS65 |
|---|---|---|---|---|---|---|
| 2001 P | 40,634 | **PF65** 7.00 | | | | |

**KM# 447 10 CENTS**

1.77 g., Nickel Plated Steel, 18 mm. **Ruler:** Elizabeth II **Subject:** Elizabeth II Golden Jubilee **Obv:** Crowned head right, Jubilee commemorative dates 1952-2002

| Date | Mintage | VF20 | XF40 | MS60 | MS63 | MS65 |
|---|---|---|---|---|---|---|
| 1952-2002 P | 252,563,000 | — | — | — | 1.00 | — |
| 1952-2002 | 32,642 | **PF65** 2.50 | | | | |

**KM# 447a 10 CENTS**

2.32 g., 0.925 Silver 0.069 oz. ASW, 18 mm. **Ruler:** Elizabeth II **Subject:** Elizabeth II Golden Jubilee **Obv:** Crowned head right, Jubilee commemorative dates 1952-2002

| Date | Mintage | VF20 | XF40 | MS60 | MS63 | MS65 |
|---|---|---|---|---|---|---|
| 2002 | 21,537 | **PF65** 12.50 | | | | |

**KM# 470 10 CENTS**

2.32 g., 0.925 Silver 0.069 oz. ASW **Ruler:** Elizabeth II **Subject:** 50th Anniversary of the Coronation of Elizabeth II **Obv:** Head right **Rev:** Bluenose sailing left

| Date | Mintage | VF20 | XF40 | MS60 | MS63 | MS65 |
|---|---|---|---|---|---|---|
| 1953-2003 | 21,537 | **PF65** 10.00 | | | | |

**KM# 492 10 CENTS**

1.77 g., Nickel Plated Steel, 18 mm. **Ruler:** Elizabeth II **Obv:** Head right **Rev:** Bluenose sailing left

| Date | Mintage | VF20 | XF40 | MS60 | MS63 | MS65 |
|---|---|---|---|---|---|---|
| 2003 P | — | — | — | — | 0.90 | 18.00 |
| 2004 P | 211,924,000 | — | — | — | 0.60 | 18.00 |
| 2004 P | — | **PF65** 5.50 | | | | |
| 2005 P | 212,175,000 | — | — | — | 0.60 | 18.00 |
| 2005 P | — | **PF65** 5.50 | | | | |
| 2006 P | 312,122,000 | — | — | — | 0.60 | 18.00 |
| 2006 P | — | **PF65** 4.00 | | | | |
| 2007 (ml) Straight 7 | 304,110,000 | — | — | — | 0.60 | 18.00 |
| 2007 (ml) Curved 7, PL | Inc. above | — | — | — | — | 0.90 |
| 2007 (ml) | — | **PF65** 3.50 | | | | |
| 2008 (ml) | 467,495,000 | — | — | — | 0.60 | 18.00 |
| 2008 (ml) | — | **PF65** 3.50 | | | | |
| 2009 (ml) | 370,700,000 | — | — | — | 0.60 | 18.00 |

| Date | Mintage | VF20 | XF40 | MS60 | MS63 | MS65 |
|---|---|---|---|---|---|---|
| 2009 (ml) | — | PF65 3.50 | | | | |
| 2010 (ml) | — | — | — | — | 0.60 | 18.00 |
| 2010 (ml) | — | PF65 3.50 | | | | |
| 2011 (ml) | — | — | — | — | 0.60 | 18.00 |
| 2011 (ml) | — | PF65 3.50 | | | | |
| 2012 (ml) | — | — | — | — | 0.60 | 18.00 |
| 2012 (ml) | — | PF65 3.50 | | | | |
| 2013 (ml) | — | — | — | — | 0.60 | — |
| 2013 (ml) | — | PF65 2.50 | | | | |
| 2014 | — | — | — | — | 0.60 | — |
| 2014 | — | PF63 1.50 | PF65 2.50 | | | |
| 2015 | — | — | — | — | 0.60 | — |
| 2015 | — | PF63 1.50 | PF65 2.50 | | | |

### KM# 492a 10 CENTS

2.40 g., 0.925 Silver 0.0714 oz. ASW, 18 mm. **Ruler:** Elizabeth II **Obv:** Bare head right **Rev:** Sailboat **Edge:** Reeded

| Date | Mintage | VF20 | XF40 | MS60 | MS63 | MS65 |
|---|---|---|---|---|---|---|
| 2004 | — | PF65 6.00 | | | | |

### KM# 524 10 CENTS

2.40 g., 0.925 Silver 0.0714 oz. ASW, 18 mm. **Ruler:** Elizabeth II **Subject:** Golf, Championship of Canada, Centennial. **Obv:** Head right

| Date | Mintage | VF20 | XF40 | MS60 | MS63 | MS65 |
|---|---|---|---|---|---|---|
| 2004 | 39,486 | — | — | — | 10.00 | — |

### KM# 1025 10 CENTS

2.40 g., 0.925 Silver 0.0714 oz. ASW, 18.03 mm. **Ruler:** Elizabeth II **Obv:** George V bust left **Rev:** Value within wreath, dual dates below

| Date | Mintage | VF20 | XF40 | MS60 | MS63 | MS65 |
|---|---|---|---|---|---|---|
| 1935-2010 | — | PF65 20.00 | | | | |

### KM# 1155 10 CENTS

2.40 g., 0.925 Silver 0.0714 oz. ASW, 18.03 mm. **Ruler:** Elizabeth II **Obv:** George V bust **Rev:** Value within wreath

| Date | Mintage | VF20 | XF40 | MS60 | MS63 | MS65 |
|---|---|---|---|---|---|---|
| 1911-2011 | 6,000 | PF65 20.00 | | | | |

### KM# 184 25 CENTS

5.07 g., Nickel, 23.88 mm. **Ruler:** Elizabeth II **Obv:** Crowned head right **Rev:** Caribou left, denomination above, date at right

| Date | Mintage | VF20 | XF40 | MS60 | MS63 | MS65 |
|---|---|---|---|---|---|---|
| 2001 | 8,415,000 | — | — | — | 4.50 | 30.00 |
| 2001 | — | PF65 7.00 | | | | |

### KM# 184a 25 CENTS

5.90 g., 0.925 Silver 0.1755 oz. ASW, 23.88 mm. **Ruler:** Elizabeth II **Obv:** Crowned head right **Rev:** Caribou left, denomination above, date at right

| Date | Mintage | VF20 | XF40 | MS60 | MS63 | MS65 |
|---|---|---|---|---|---|---|
| 2001 | — | PF65 9.50 | | | | |
| 2003 | — | PF65 9.50 | | | | |

### KM# 184b 25 CENTS

4.40 g., Nickel Plated Steel, 23.88 mm. **Ruler:** Elizabeth II **Obv:** Crowned head right **Rev:** Caribou left, denomination above, date at right

| Date | Mintage | VF20 | XF40 | MS60 | MS63 | MS65 |
|---|---|---|---|---|---|---|
| 2001 P | 55,773,000 | — | — | — | 0.90 | 30.00 |
| 2001 P | — | PF65 5.00 | | | | |
| 2002 P | 156,105,000 | — | — | — | 0.90 | 30.00 |
| 2002 P | — | PF65 5.00 | | | | |
| 2003 P | 87,647,000 | — | — | — | 1.75 | 22.00 |
| 2003 P | — | PF65 5.00 | | | | |

### KM# 419 25 CENTS

4.40 g., Nickel Plated Steel, 23.9 mm. **Ruler:** Elizabeth II **Subject:** Canada Day **Obv:** Crowned head right **Rev:** Maple leaf at center, children holding hands below **Edge:** Reeded

| Date | Mintage | VF20 | XF40 | MS60 | MS63 | MS65 |
|---|---|---|---|---|---|---|
| 2001 PL | 96,352 | — | — | — | — | 13.00 |

### KM# 448 25 CENTS

4.40 g., Nickel Plated Steel, 23.9 mm. **Ruler:** Elizabeth II **Subject:** Elizabeth II Golden Jubilee **Obv:** Crowned head right **Rev:** Caribou left

| Date | Mintage | VF20 | XF40 | MS60 | MS63 | MS65 |
|---|---|---|---|---|---|---|
| 1952-2002 P | 152,485,000 | — | — | — | 0.90 | 30.00 |
| 1952-2002 P | 32,642 | PF65 6.00 | | | | |

### KM# 448a 25 CENTS

5.90 g., 0.925 Silver 0.1755 oz. ASW, 23.9 mm. **Ruler:** Elizabeth II **Subject:** Elizabeth II Golden Jubilee **Obv:** Crowned head right, Jubilee commemorative dates 1952-2002

| Date | Mintage | VF20 | XF40 | MS60 | MS63 | MS65 |
|---|---|---|---|---|---|---|
| 1952-2002 | 100,000 | PF65 12.50 | | | | |

### KM# 451 25 CENTS

4.40 g., Nickel Plated Steel, 23.9 mm. **Ruler:** Elizabeth II **Rev:** Small human figures supporting large maple leaf

| Date | Mintage | VF20 | XF40 | MS60 | MS63 | MS65 |
|---|---|---|---|---|---|---|
| 2002 P | 30,627,000 | — | — | — | 0.90 | 22.00 |

### KM# 451a 25 CENTS

4.40 g., Nickel Plated Steel, 23.9 mm. **Ruler:** Elizabeth II **Subject:** Canada Day **Obv:** Crowned head right **Rev:** Human figures supporting large red maple leaf **Edge:** Reeded

| Date | Mintage | VF20 | XF40 | MS60 | MS63 | MS65 |
|---|---|---|---|---|---|---|
| 2002 P | 49,901 | — | — | — | 6.00 | — |

### KM# 471 25 CENTS

5.90 g., 0.925 Silver 0.1755 oz. ASW, 23.9 mm. **Ruler:** Elizabeth II **Subject:** 50th Anniversary of the Coronation of Elizabeth II **Obv:** 1953 Effigy of the Queen, Coronation Jubilee dates 1953-2003

| Date | Mintage | VF20 | XF40 | MS60 | MS63 | MS65 |
|---|---|---|---|---|---|---|
| 1953-2003 | 21,537 | PF65 11.00 | | | | |

### KM# 474 25 CENTS

4.40 g., 0.925 Silver 0.1309 oz. ASW, 23.9 mm. **Ruler:** Elizabeth II **Subject:** Canada Day **Obv:** Queen's head right **Rev:** Polar bear and red colored maple leaves

| Date | Mintage | VF20 | XF40 | MS60 | MS63 | MS65 |
|---|---|---|---|---|---|---|
| 2003 | 63,511 | PF65 11.00 | | | | |

### KM# 493 25 CENTS

4.40 g., Nickel Plated Steel, 23.9 mm. **Ruler:** Elizabeth II **Obv:** Bare head right **Rev:** Caribou left, denomination above, date at right

| Date | Mintage | VF20 | XF40 | MS60 | MS63 | MS65 |
|---|---|---|---|---|---|---|
| 2003 P | 66,861,633 | — | — | — | 0.90 | 22.00 |
| 2003 P W PL | — | — | — | — | — | 3.50 |
| 2004 P | 177,466,000 | — | — | — | 0.65 | 22.00 |
| 2004 P | — | PF65 5.00 | | | | |
| 2005 P | 206,346,000 | — | — | — | 0.90 | 22.00 |
| 2005 P | — | PF65 5.00 | | | | |
| 2006 P | 423,189,000 | — | — | — | 0.90 | 22.00 |
| 2006 P | — | PF65 5.00 | | | | |
| 2006 (ml) | — | — | — | — | 0.90 | 22.00 |
| 2007 (ml) | 386,763,000 | — | — | — | 0.90 | 18.00 |
| 2007 (ml) | — | PF65 5.00 | | | | |
| 2008 (ml) | 387,222,000 | — | — | — | 0.90 | 18.00 |
| 2008 (ml) | — | PF65 5.00 | | | | |
| 2009 (ml) | 266,766,000 | — | — | — | 0.90 | 18.00 |
| 2009 (ml) | — | PF65 5.00 | | | | |
| 2010 (ml) | — | — | — | — | 0.90 | 18.00 |
| 2010 (ml) | — | PF65 5.00 | | | | |
| 2011 (ml) | — | — | — | — | 0.90 | 18.00 |
| 2011 (ml) | — | PF65 5.00 | | | | |
| 2012 (ml) | — | — | — | — | 0.90 | 18.00 |
| 2012 (ml) | — | PF65 5.00 | | | | |
| 2013 (ml) | — | — | — | — | 2.50 | — |
| 2013 (ml) | — | PF65 5.00 | | | | |
| 2014 | — | — | — | — | 2.50 | — |
| 2014 | — | PF63 4.00 | PF65 5.00 | | | |
| 2015 | — | — | — | — | 2.50 | — |
| 2015 | — | PF63 4.00 | PF65 5.00 | | | |

### KM# 493a 25 CENTS

5.90 g., 0.925 Silver 0.1755 oz. ASW, 23.9 mm. **Ruler:** Elizabeth II **Obv:** Bare head right **Rev:** Caribou left **Edge:** Reeded

| Date | Mintage | VF20 | XF40 | MS60 | MS63 | MS65 |
|---|---|---|---|---|---|---|
| 2004 | — | PF65 6.50 | | | | |

### KM# 510 25 CENTS

4.40 g., Nickel Plated Steel, 23.9 mm. **Ruler:** Elizabeth II **Obv:** Bare head right **Rev:** Red poppy in center of maple leaf **Edge:** Reeded

| Date | Mintage | VF20 | XF40 | MS60 | MS63 | MS65 |
|---|---|---|---|---|---|---|
| 2004 | 28,500,000 | — | — | — | 0.90 | 22.00 |

### KM# 510a 25 CENTS

5.90 g., 0.925 Silver 0.1755 oz. ASW, 23.9 mm. **Ruler:** Elizabeth II **Obv:** Bare head right **Rev:** Poppy at center of maple leaf, selectively gold plated **Edge:** Reeded **Note:** Housed in Annual Report.

| Date | Mintage | VF20 | XF40 | MS60 | MS63 | MS65 |
|---|---|---|---|---|---|---|
| 2004 | 12,677 | PF65 20.00 | | | | |

### KM# 525 25 CENTS

4.40 g., Nickel Plated Steel, 23.9 mm. **Ruler:** Elizabeth II **Obv:** Bare head right **Rev:** Maple leaf, colorized

| Date | Mintage | VF20 | XF40 | MS60 | MS63 | MS65 |
|---|---|---|---|---|---|---|
| 2004 | 16,028 | — | — | — | 8.00 | — |

### KM# 628 25 CENTS

4.40 g., Nickel Plated Steel, 23.9 mm. **Ruler:** Elizabeth II **Subject:** First Settlement, Ile Ste Croix 1604-2004 **Obv:** Bare head right **Rev:** Sailing ship Bonne-Renommee

| Date | Mintage | VF20 | XF40 | MS60 | MS63 | MS65 |
|---|---|---|---|---|---|---|
| 2004 P | 15,400,000 | — | — | — | 0.90 | 22.00 |

### KM# 698 25 CENTS

4.40 g., Nickel Plated Steel, 23.88 mm. **Ruler:** Elizabeth II **Rev:** Santa, colorized

| Date | Mintage | VF20 | XF40 | MS60 | MS63 | MS65 |
|---|---|---|---|---|---|---|
| 2004 PL | 62,777 | — | — | — | — | 30.00 |

### KM# 699 25 CENTS

4.40 g., Nickel Plated Steel, 23.9 mm. **Ruler:** Elizabeth II **Series:** Canada Day **Rev:** Moose head, humorous

| Date | Mintage | VF20 | XF40 | MS60 | MS63 | MS65 |
|---|---|---|---|---|---|---|
| 2004 PL | 44,752 | — | — | — | — | 13.00 |

### KM# 529 25 CENTS

4.40 g., Nickel Plated Steel, 23.9 mm. **Ruler:** Elizabeth II **Subject:** WWII, 60th Anniversary **Obv:** Head right **Rev:** Three soldiers and flag

| Date | Mintage | VF20 | XF40 | MS60 | MS63 | MS65 |
|---|---|---|---|---|---|---|
| 1945-2005 PL | 3,500 | — | — | — | — | 70.00 |

**KM# 530 25 CENTS**
4.40 g., Nickel Plated Steel, 23.9 mm. **Ruler:** Elizabeth II **Subject:** Alberta **Obv:** Head right **Rev:** Oil rig and sunset

| Date | Mintage | VF20 | XF40 | MS60 | MS63 | MS65 |
|---|---|---|---|---|---|---|
| 2005 P | 20,640,000 | — | — | — | 0.90 | 22.00 |

**KM# 531 25 CENTS**
4.40 g., Nickel Plated Steel, 23.9 mm. **Ruler:** Elizabeth II **Subject:** Canada Day **Obv:** Head right **Rev:** Beaver, colorized

| Date | Mintage | VF20 | XF40 | MS60 | MS63 | MS65 |
|---|---|---|---|---|---|---|
| 2005 P PL | 58,370 | — | — | — | — | 13.00 |

**KM# 532 25 CENTS**
4.40 g., Nickel Plated Steel, 23.9 mm. **Ruler:** Elizabeth II **Subject:** Saskatchewan **Obv:** Head right **Rev:** Bird on fencepost

| Date | Mintage | VF20 | XF40 | MS60 | MS63 | MS65 |
|---|---|---|---|---|---|---|
| 2005 P | 19,290,000 | — | — | — | 0.90 | 22.00 |

**KM# 533 25 CENTS**
4.40 g., Nickel Plated Steel, 23.9 mm. **Ruler:** Elizabeth II **Obv:** Head right **Rev:** Stuffed bear in Christmas stocking, colorized

| Date | Mintage | VF20 | XF40 | MS60 | MS63 | MS65 |
|---|---|---|---|---|---|---|
| 2005 P PL | 72,831 | — | — | — | — | 16.00 |

**KM# 535 25 CENTS**
4.40 g., Nickel Plated Steel, 23.9 mm. **Ruler:** Elizabeth II **Subject:** Year of the Veteran **Obv:** Head right **Rev:** Conjoined busts of young and veteran left **Edge:** Reeded

| Date | Mintage | VF20 | XF40 | MS60 | MS63 | MS65 |
|---|---|---|---|---|---|---|
| 2005 P | 29,390,000 | — | — | — | 0.90 | 22.00 |

**KM# 534 25 CENTS**
4.40 g., Nickel Plated Steel, 23.9 mm. **Ruler:** Elizabeth II **Subject:** Toronto Maple Leafs **Obv:** Head right **Rev:** Colorized team logo

| Date | Mintage | VF20 | XF40 | MS60 | MS63 | MS65 |
|---|---|---|---|---|---|---|
| 2006 P PL | 11,765 | — | — | — | — | 18.00 |

**KM# 575 25 CENTS**
4.40 g., Nickel Plated Steel, 23.9 mm. **Ruler:** Elizabeth II **Subject:** Montreal Canadiens **Obv:** Head right **Rev:** Colorized logo

| Date | Mintage | VF20 | XF40 | MS60 | MS63 | MS65 |
|---|---|---|---|---|---|---|
| 2006 P PL | 11,765 | — | — | — | — | 18.00 |

**KM# 576 25 CENTS**
4.40 g., Nickel Plated Steel, 23.9 mm. **Ruler:** Elizabeth II **Subject:** Quebec Winter Carnival **Obv:** Head right **Rev:** Snowman, colorized

| Date | Mintage | VF20 | XF40 | MS60 | MS63 | MS65 |
|---|---|---|---|---|---|---|
| 2006 PL | 8,200 | — | — | — | — | 18.00 |

**KM# 629 25 CENTS**
4.40 g., Nickel Plated Steel, 23.9 mm. **Ruler:** Elizabeth II **Obv:** Head right **Rev:** Medal of Bravery (maple leaf within wreath) **Edge:** Reeded

| Date | Mintage | VF20 | XF40 | MS60 | MS63 | MS65 |
|---|---|---|---|---|---|---|
| 2006 (ml) | 20,045,111 | — | — | — | 0.90 | 22.00 |

**KM# 632 25 CENTS**
12.61 g., Nickel Plated Steel, 35 mm. **Ruler:** Elizabeth II **Subject:** Queen Elizabeth II 80th Birthday **Rev:** Crown, colorized

| Date | Mintage | VF20 | XF40 | MS60 | MS63 | MS65 |
|---|---|---|---|---|---|---|
| 1926-2006 Specimen | 24,977 | — | — | — | — | 22.00 |

**KM# 633 25 CENTS**
4.43 g., Nickel Plated Steel, 23.9 mm. **Ruler:** Elizabeth II **Subject:** Canada Day **Obv:** Crowned head right **Rev:** Boy marching with flag, colorized

| Date | Mintage | VF20 | XF40 | MS60 | MS63 | MS65 |
|---|---|---|---|---|---|---|
| 2006 P PL | 30,328 | — | — | — | — | 13.00 |

**KM# 634 25 CENTS**
4.43 g., Nickel Plated Steel, 23.88 mm. **Ruler:** Elizabeth II **Subject:** Breast Cancer **Rev:** Four ribbons, all colorized **Note:** Sold housed in a bookmark.

| Date | Mintage | VF20 | XF40 | MS60 | MS63 | MS65 |
|---|---|---|---|---|---|---|
| 2006 P | 40,911 | — | — | — | 0.90 | 22.00 |

**KM# 635 25 CENTS**
4.43 g., Nickel Plated Steel, 23.88 mm. **Ruler:** Elizabeth II **Subject:** Breast Cancer **Rev:** Colorized pink ribbon applique in center.

| Date | Mintage | VF20 | XF40 | MS60 | MS63 | MS65 |
|---|---|---|---|---|---|---|
| 2006 P | 29,798,000 | — | — | — | 1.50 | — |

**KM# 637 25 CENTS**
4.43 g., Nickel Plated Steel, 23.88 mm. **Ruler:** Elizabeth II **Subject:** Wedding **Rev:** Colorized bouquet of flowers

| Date | Mintage | VF20 | XF40 | MS60 | MS63 | MS65 |
|---|---|---|---|---|---|---|
| 2006 (ml) | 10,318 | — | — | — | 5.00 | — |

**KM# 642 25 CENTS**
4.43 g., Nickel Plated Steel, 23.88 mm. **Ruler:** Elizabeth II **Subject:** Ottawa Senators **Obv:** Head right **Rev:** Logo

| Date | Mintage | VF20 | XF40 | MS60 | MS63 | MS65 |
|---|---|---|---|---|---|---|
| 2006 P PL | 11,765 | — | — | — | — | 18.00 |

**KM# 644 25 CENTS**
4.43 g., Nickel Plated Steel, 23.88 mm. **Ruler:** Elizabeth II **Subject:** Calgary Flames **Obv:** Head right **Rev:** Logo

| Date | Mintage | VF20 | XF40 | MS60 | MS63 | MS65 |
|---|---|---|---|---|---|---|
| 2006 (ml) | 1,082 | — | — | — | 12.50 | — |

**KM# 645 25 CENTS**
4.43 g., Nickel Plated Steel, 23.88 mm. **Ruler:** Elizabeth II **Subject:** Edmonton Oilers **Obv:** Head right **Rev:** Logo

| Date | Mintage | VF20 | XF40 | MS60 | MS63 | MS65 |
|---|---|---|---|---|---|---|
| 2006 (ml) | 2,214 | — | — | — | 12.50 | — |

**KM# 647 25 CENTS**
4.43 g., Nickel Plated Steel **Ruler:** Elizabeth II **Subject:** Santa and Rudolph **Rev:** Colorized Santa in sled lead by Rudolph

| Date | Mintage | VF20 | XF40 | MS60 | MS63 | MS65 |
|---|---|---|---|---|---|---|
| 2006 P PL | 99,258 | — | — | — | — | 16.00 |

**KM# 638 25 CENTS**
4.43 g., Nickel Plated Steel, 23.88 mm. **Ruler:** Elizabeth II **Subject:** Birthday **Rev:** Colorized balloons

| Date | Mintage | VF20 | XF40 | MS60 | MS63 | MS65 |
|---|---|---|---|---|---|---|
| 2007 (ml) PL | 24,531 | — | — | — | — | 18.00 |

**KM# 639 25 CENTS**
4.43 g., Nickel Plated Steel, 23.88 mm. **Ruler:** Elizabeth II **Subject:** Baby birth **Rev:** Colorized baby rattle **Edge:** Reeded

| Date | Mintage | VF20 | XF40 | MS60 | MS63 | MS65 |
|---|---|---|---|---|---|---|
| 2007 (ml) PL | 30,090 | — | — | — | — | 18.00 |

**KM# 640 25 CENTS**
4.43 g., Nickel Plated Steel, 23.88 mm. **Ruler:** Elizabeth II **Subject:** Oh Canada **Obv:** Head right **Rev:** Maple leaf, colorized

| Date | Mintage | VF20 | XF40 | MS60 | MS63 | MS65 |
|---|---|---|---|---|---|---|
| 2007 (ml) PL | 23,582 | — | — | — | — | 13.00 |

**KM# 641 25 CENTS**
4.43 g., Nickel Plated Steel, 23.88 mm. **Ruler:** Elizabeth II **Subject:** Congratulations **Obv:** Head right **Rev:** Fireworks, colorized

| Date | Mintage | VF20 | XF40 | MS60 | MS63 | MS65 |
|---|---|---|---|---|---|---|
| 2007 (ml) PL | 9,671 | — | — | — | — | 18.00 |

**KM# 643 25 CENTS**
4.43 g., Nickel Plated Steel, 23.88 mm. **Ruler:** Elizabeth II **Subject:** Vancouver Canucks **Obv:** Head right **Rev:** Logo

| Date | Mintage | VF20 | XF40 | MS60 | MS63 | MS65 |
|---|---|---|---|---|---|---|
| 2007 (ml) PL | 1,526 | — | — | — | — | 18.00 |

**KM# 682 25 CENTS**
4.43 g., Nickel Plated Steel **Ruler:** Elizabeth II **Subject:** Curling **Obv:** Head right

| Date | Mintage | VF20 | XF40 | MS60 | MS63 | MS65 |
|---|---|---|---|---|---|---|
| 2007 | 22,400,000 | — | — | — | 0.90 | 18.00 |
| 2008 Mule | — | — | — | — | — | — |

**KM# 683 25 CENTS**
4.43 g., Nickel Plated Steel **Ruler:** Elizabeth II **Subject:** Ice Hockey **Obv:** Head right

| Date | Mintage | VF20 | XF40 | MS60 | MS63 | MS65 |
|---|---|---|---|---|---|---|
| 2007 | 22,400,000 | — | — | — | 0.90 | 18.00 |
| 2008 Mule | — | — | — | — | — | — |

**KM# 684 25 CENTS**
4.43 g., Nickel Plated Steel, 23.8 mm. **Ruler:** Elizabeth II **Subject:** Paralympic Winter Games **Obv:** Head right **Rev:** Wheelchair curling

| Date | Mintage | VF20 | XF40 | MS60 | MS63 | MS65 |
|---|---|---|---|---|---|---|
| 2007 | 22,400,000 | — | — | — | 0.90 | 18.00 |
| 2008 Mule | — | — | — | — | — | — |

**KM# 685 25 CENTS**
4.43 g., Nickel Plated Steel **Ruler:** Elizabeth II **Subject:** Biathlon **Obv:** Head right

| Date | Mintage | VF20 | XF40 | MS60 | MS63 | MS65 |
|---|---|---|---|---|---|---|
| 2007 | 22,400,000 | — | — | — | 0.90 | 18.00 |
| 2008 Mule | — | — | — | — | — | — |

**KM# 686 25 CENTS**
4.43 g., Nickel Plated Steel, 23.8 mm. **Ruler:** Elizabeth II **Subject:** Alpine Skiing **Obv:** Head right

| Date | Mintage | VF20 | XF40 | MS60 | MS63 | MS65 |
|---|---|---|---|---|---|---|
| 2007 | 22,400,000 | — | — | — | 0.90 | 18.00 |
| 2008 Mule | — | — | — | — | 22.00 | — |

**KM# 701 25 CENTS**
4.43 g., Nickel Plated Steel, 23.88 mm. **Ruler:** Elizabeth II **Subject:** Birthday **Rev:** Party hat, multicolor

| Date | Mintage | VF20 | XF40 | MS60 | MS63 | MS65 |
|---|---|---|---|---|---|---|
| 2007 | 11,376 | — | — | — | 8.00 | — |

**KM# 702 25 CENTS**
4.43 g., Nickel Plated Steel, 23.88 mm. **Ruler:** Elizabeth II **Subject:** Congratulations **Rev:** Trophy, multicolor

| Date | Mintage | VF20 | XF40 | MS60 | MS63 | MS65 |
|---|---|---|---|---|---|---|
| 2007 PL | — | — | — | — | — | 18.00 |

**KM# 703 25 CENTS**
4.43 g., Nickel Plated Steel, 23.88 mm. **Ruler:** Elizabeth II **Subject:** Wedding **Rev:** Cake, multicolor

| Date | Mintage | VF20 | XF40 | MS60 | MS63 | MS65 |
|---|---|---|---|---|---|---|
| 2007 | — | — | — | — | 8.00 | — |

**KM# 704 25 CENTS**
4.43 g., Nickel Plated Steel, 23.88 mm. **Ruler:** Elizabeth II **Subject:** Canada Day **Rev:** Mountie, colorized

| Date | Mintage | VF20 | XF40 | MS60 | MS63 | MS65 |
|---|---|---|---|---|---|---|
| 2007 (ml) PL | 27,743 | — | — | — | — | 18.00 |

**KM# 705 25 CENTS**
4.43 g., Nickel Plated Steel, 23.88 mm. **Ruler:** Elizabeth II **Subject:** Christmas **Rev:** Multicolor tree

| Date | Mintage | VF20 | XF40 | MS60 | MS63 | MS65 |
|---|---|---|---|---|---|---|
| 2007 PL | 66,267 | — | — | — | — | 18.00 |

**KM# 706 25 CENTS**
12.61 g., Nickel Plated Steel, 35.0 mm. **Ruler:** Elizabeth II **Subject:** Red-breasted Nuthatch **Obv:** Head right **Obv. Legend:** ELIZABETH II - D • G • REGINA **Rev:** Nuthatch perched on pine branch multicolor **Rev. Legend:** CANADA **Edge:** Plain

| Date | Mintage | VF20 | XF40 | MS60 | MS63 | MS65 |
|---|---|---|---|---|---|---|
| 2007 (ml) Specimen | 11,909 | — | — | — | 300 | — |

**KM# 707 25 CENTS**
12.61 g., Nickel Plated Steel, 35 mm. **Ruler:** Elizabeth II **Obv:** Elizabeth II **Rev:** Multicolor ruby-throated hummingbird and flower **Edge:** Plain

| Date | Mintage | VF20 | XF40 | MS60 | MS63 | MS65 |
|---|---|---|---|---|---|---|
| 2007 Specimen | 17,174 | — | — | — | 125 | — |

**KM# 708 25 CENTS**
12.61 g., Nickel Plated Steel, 35 mm. **Ruler:** Elizabeth II **Subject:** Queen's 60th Wedding Anniversary **Rev:** Royal carriage in color

| Date | Mintage | VF20 | XF40 | MS60 | MS63 | MS65 |
|---|---|---|---|---|---|---|
| 1947-2007 PL, Specimen | 15,235 | — | — | — | — | 22.00 |

**KM# 713 25 CENTS**
4.40 g., Nickel Plated Steel **Ruler:** Elizabeth II **Rev:** Toronto Maple Leaf logo, colorized

| Date | Mintage | VF20 | XF40 | MS60 | MS63 | MS65 |
|---|---|---|---|---|---|---|
| 2007 (ml) PL | 5,365 | — | — | — | — | 18.00 |

**KM# 714 25 CENTS**
4.40 g., Nickel Plated Steel **Ruler:** Elizabeth II **Rev:** Ottawa Senators logo, colorized

| Date | Mintage | VF20 | XF40 | MS60 | MS63 | MS65 |
|---|---|---|---|---|---|---|
| 2007 (ml) PL | 2,474 | — | — | — | — | 18.00 |

**KM# 723 25 CENTS**
4.40 g., Nickel Plated Steel **Ruler:** Elizabeth II **Rev:** Montreal Canadiens logo, colorized

| Date | Mintage | VF20 | XF40 | MS60 | MS63 | MS65 |
|---|---|---|---|---|---|---|
| 2007 (ml) PL | 4,091 | — | — | — | — | 18.00 |

**KM# 760 25 CENTS**
4.43 g., Nickel Plated Steel, 23.88 mm. **Ruler:** Elizabeth II **Subject:** Baby **Rev:** Multicolor blue teddy bear

| Date | Mintage | VF20 | XF40 | MS60 | MS63 | MS65 |
|---|---|---|---|---|---|---|
| 2008 PL | 29,639 | — | — | — | — | 20.00 |

**KM# 761 25 CENTS**
4.43 g., Nickel Plated Steel, 23.88 mm. **Ruler:** Elizabeth II **Subject:** Birthday **Rev:** Multicolor party hat

| Date | Mintage | VF20 | XF40 | MS60 | MS63 | MS65 |
|---|---|---|---|---|---|---|
| 2008 PL | 11,376 | — | — | — | — | 18.00 |

**KM# 762 25 CENTS**
4.43 g., Nickel Plated Steel, 23.88 mm. **Ruler:** Elizabeth II **Subject:** Congratulations **Rev:** Multicolor trophy

| Date | Mintage | VF20 | XF40 | MS60 | MS63 | MS65 |
|---|---|---|---|---|---|---|
| 2008 PL | 6,821 | — | — | — | — | 18.00 |

**KM# 763 25 CENTS**
4.43 g., Nickel Plated Steel, 23.88 mm. **Ruler:** Elizabeth II **Subject:** Wedding **Rev:** Multicolor wedding cake

| Date | Mintage | VF20 | XF40 | MS60 | MS63 | MS65 |
|---|---|---|---|---|---|---|
| 2008 PL | 7,407 | — | — | — | — | 18.00 |

**KM# 764 25 CENTS**
4.43 g., Nickel Plated Steel, 23.88 mm. **Ruler:** Elizabeth II **Subject:** Santa Claus **Rev:** Multicolor Santa

| Date | Mintage | VF20 | XF40 | MS60 | MS63 | MS65 |
|---|---|---|---|---|---|---|
| 2008 PL | 42,344 | — | — | — | — | 18.00 |

**KM# 765 25 CENTS**
4.43 g., Nickel Plated Steel, 23.9 mm. **Ruler:** Elizabeth II **Subject:** Vancouver Olympics **Rev:** Freestyle skiing

| Date | Mintage | VF20 | XF40 | MS60 | MS63 | MS65 |
|---|---|---|---|---|---|---|
| 2008 | — | — | — | — | 0.90 | 18.00 |

**KM# 766 25 CENTS**
4.43 g., Nickel Plated Steel, 23.8 mm. **Ruler:** Elizabeth II **Subject:** Vancouver Olympics **Rev:** Figure skating

| Date | Mintage | VF20 | XF40 | MS60 | MS63 | MS65 |
|---|---|---|---|---|---|---|
| 2008 | — | — | — | — | 0.90 | 18.00 |

**KM# 768 25 CENTS**
4.43 g., Nickel Plated Steel, 23.88 mm. **Ruler:** Elizabeth II **Subject:** Vancouver Olympics **Rev:** Snowboarding

| Date | Mintage | VF20 | XF40 | MS60 | MS63 | MS65 |
|---|---|---|---|---|---|---|
| 2008 | — | — | — | — | 0.90 | 18.00 |

**KM# 769 25 CENTS**
4.43 g., Nickel Plated Steel, 23.88 mm. **Ruler:** Elizabeth II **Subject:** Vancouver Olympics **Rev:** Olympic mascot - Miga

| Date | Mintage | VF20 | XF40 | MS60 | MS63 | MS65 |
|---|---|---|---|---|---|---|
| 2008 PL | — | — | — | — | — | 0.90 |

**KM# 770 25 CENTS**
4.43 g., Nickel Plated Steel, 23.88 mm. **Ruler:** Elizabeth II **Subject:** Vancouver Olympics **Rev:** Olympic mascot - Quatchi

| Date | Mintage | VF20 | XF40 | MS60 | MS63 | MS65 |
|---|---|---|---|---|---|---|
| 2008 PL | — | — | — | — | — | 0.90 |

**KM# 771 25 CENTS**
4.43 g., Nickel Plated Steel, 23.88 mm. **Ruler:** Elizabeth II **Subject:** Vancouver Olympics **Rev:** Olympic mascot - Sumi

| Date | Mintage | VF20 | XF40 | MS60 | MS63 | MS65 |
|---|---|---|---|---|---|---|
| 2008 PL | — | — | — | — | — | 0.90 |

**KM# 772 25 CENTS**
4.43 g., Nickel Plated Steel, 23.88 mm. **Ruler:** Elizabeth II **Subject:** Oh Canada **Rev:** Multicolor red flag

| Date | Mintage | VF20 | XF40 | MS60 | MS63 | MS65 |
|---|---|---|---|---|---|---|
| 2008 PL | — | — | — | — | — | 18.00 |

**KM# 773 25 CENTS**
12.61 g., Nickel Plated Steel, 35 mm. **Ruler:** Elizabeth II **Obv:** Bust right **Rev:** Downy woodpecker in tree, multicolor **Edge:** Plain **Note:** Prev. KM#717.

| Date | Mintage | VF20 | XF40 | MS60 | MS63 | MS65 |
|---|---|---|---|---|---|---|
| 2008 (ml) Specimen | 14,282 | — | — | — | — | 175 |

**KM# 774 25 CENTS**
12.61 g., Nickel Plated Steel, 35 mm. **Ruler:** Elizabeth II **Obv:** Bust right **Rev:** Northern cardinal perched on branch - multicolor **Edge:** Plain **Note:** Prev. KM#718.

| Date | Mintage | VF20 | XF40 | MS60 | MS63 | MS65 |
|---|---|---|---|---|---|---|
| 2008 (ml) Specimen | 11,604 | — | — | — | — | 250 |

**KM# 775 25 CENTS**
4.43 g., Nickel Plated Steel, 23.8 mm. **Ruler:** Elizabeth II **Subject:** End of WWI, 90th Anniversary **Rev:** Multicolor poppy

| Date | Mintage | VF20 | XF40 | MS60 | MS63 | MS65 |
|---|---|---|---|---|---|---|
| 1918-2008 | 10,167 | — | — | — | — | 8.00 |

**KM# 776 25 CENTS**
12.61 g., Nickel Plated Steel, 35 mm. **Ruler:** Elizabeth II **Subject:** Anne of Green Gables **Rev:** Image of young girl, multicolor

| Date | Mintage | VF20 | XF40 | MS60 | MS63 | MS65 |
|---|---|---|---|---|---|---|
| 1908-2008 Specimen | 32,795 | — | — | — | — | 25.00 |

**KM# 841 25 CENTS**
4.43 g., Nickel Plated Steel, 23.8 mm. **Ruler:** Elizabeth II **Subject:** Vancouver Olympics **Rev:** Bobsleigh

| Date | Mintage | VF20 | XF40 | MS60 | MS63 | MS65 |
|---|---|---|---|---|---|---|
| 2008 | — | — | — | — | 0.90 | 18.00 |

**KM# 1039 25 CENTS**
4.43 g., Nickel Plated Steel, 23.9 mm. **Ruler:** Elizabeth II **Subject:** Canada Day **Rev:** Colorized moose head

| Date | Mintage | VF20 | XF40 | MS60 | MS63 | MS65 |
|---|---|---|---|---|---|---|
| 2008 PL | 11,538 | — | — | — | — | 18.00 |

**KM# 1041 25 CENTS**
4.43 g., Nickel Plated Steel **Ruler:** Elizabeth II **Subject:** WWI **Rev:** Three military men standing over tomb

| Date | Mintage | VF20 | XF40 | MS60 | MS63 | MS65 |
|---|---|---|---|---|---|---|
| 2008 (ml) | 10,167 | — | — | — | — | 12.50 |

**KM# 840 25 CENTS**
4.43 g., Nickel Plated Steel, 23.8 mm. **Ruler:** Elizabeth II **Subject:** Valcouver 2010 Olympics **Rev:** Cross-country skiing

| Date | Mintage | VF20 | XF40 | MS60 | MS63 | MS65 |
|---|---|---|---|---|---|---|
| 2009 | — | — | — | — | 0.90 | 18.00 |

**KM# 842 25 CENTS**
4.43 g., Nickel Plated Steel, 23.9 mm. **Ruler:** Elizabeth II **Subject:** Edmonton Olympics **Rev:** Speed skating

| Date | Mintage | VF20 | XF40 | MS60 | MS63 | MS65 |
|---|---|---|---|---|---|---|
| 2009 | — | — | — | — | 0.90 | 18.00 |

**KM# 885 25 CENTS**
4.40 g., Nickel Plated Steel, 23.88 mm. **Ruler:** Elizabeth II **Subject:** Canada Day **Rev:** Animals in boat with flag **Rev. Legend:** Canada 25 cents

| Date | Mintage | VF20 | XF40 | MS60 | MS63 | MS65 |
|---|---|---|---|---|---|---|
| 2009 PL | 11,091 | — | — | — | — | 16.00 |

**KM# 886 25 CENTS**
12.61 g., Nickel Plated Steel, 35 mm. **Ruler:** Elizabeth II **Subject:** Notre-Dame-Du-Saguenay **Obv:** Bust right **Obv. Legend:** Elizabeth II DG Regina **Rev:** Color photo of fjord and statue **Rev. Legend:** Canada 25 cents

| Date | Mintage | VF20 | XF40 | MS60 | MS63 | MS65 |
|---|---|---|---|---|---|---|
| 2009 Specimen | 16,653 | — | — | — | — | 18.00 |

**KM# 915 25 CENTS**
4.43 g., Nickel Plated Steel, 23.9 mm. **Ruler:** Elizabeth II **Subject:** Surprise Birthday **Obv:** Bust right **Rev:** Colorized

| Date | Mintage | VF20 | XF40 | MS60 | MS63 | MS65 |
|---|---|---|---|---|---|---|
| 2009 PL | 9,663 | — | — | — | — | 13.00 |

**KM# 916 25 CENTS**
4.43 g., Nickel Plated Steel, 23.9 mm. **Ruler:** Elizabeth II **Subject:** Share the Excitement **Obv:** Bust right **Rev:** Colorized

| Date | Mintage | VF20 | XF40 | MS60 | MS63 | MS65 |
|---|---|---|---|---|---|---|
| 2009 PL | 4,126 | — | — | — | — | 12.50 |

**KM# 917 25 CENTS**
4.43 g., Nickel Plated Steel, 23.9 mm. **Ruler:** Elizabeth II **Subject:** Share the Love **Obv:** Bust right **Rev:** Two doves, coolored

| Date | Mintage | VF20 | XF40 | MS60 | MS63 | MS65 |
|---|---|---|---|---|---|---|
| 2009 PL | 7,571 | — | — | — | — | 13.00 |

**KM# 918 25 CENTS**
4.43 g., Nickel Plated Steel, 23.9 mm. **Ruler:** Elizabeth II **Subject:** Thank You **Obv:** Bust right **Rev:** Colorized

| Date | Mintage | VF20 | XF40 | MS60 | MS63 | MS65 |
|---|---|---|---|---|---|---|
| 2009 PL | 4,415 | — | — | — | — | 13.00 |

**KM# 933 25 CENTS**
4.40 g., Nickel Plated Steel, 23.9 mm. **Ruler:** Elizabeth II **Rev:** Santa Claus, multicolor

| Date | Mintage | VF20 | XF40 | MS60 | MS63 | MS65 |
|---|---|---|---|---|---|---|
| 2009 PL | — | — | — | — | — | 16.00 |

### KM# 934 25 CENTS

4.40 g., Nickel Plated Steel, 23.9 mm. **Ruler:** Elizabeth II **Rev:** Multicolor teddy bear, crescent moon

| Date | Mintage | VF20 | XF40 | MS60 | MS63 | MS65 |
|---|---|---|---|---|---|---|
| 2009 PL | 25,182 | — | — | — | — | 16.50 |

### KM# 935 25 CENTS

4.40 g., Nickel Plated Steel, 23.9 mm. **Ruler:** Elizabeth II **Subject:** Oh Canada **Rev:** Maple leaves, yellow color

| Date | Mintage | VF20 | XF40 | MS60 | MS63 | MS65 |
|---|---|---|---|---|---|---|
| 2009 PL | 14,451 | — | — | — | — | 16.00 |

### KM# 952 25 CENTS

4.40 g., Nickel Plated Steel, 23.9 mm. **Ruler:** Elizabeth II **Rev:** Sledge hockey

| Date | Mintage | VF20 | XF40 | MS60 | MS63 | MS65 |
|---|---|---|---|---|---|---|
| 2009 | — | — | — | — | 0.90 | 18.00 |

### KM# 1063 25 CENTS

Nickel Plated Steel **Ruler:** Elizabeth II **Subject:** Men's Hockey **Rev:** Hockey player and maple leaf outline

| Date | Mintage | VF20 | XF40 | MS60 | MS63 | MS65 |
|---|---|---|---|---|---|---|
| 2009 | — | — | — | — | — | 2.50 |

### KM# 1063a 25 CENTS

Nickel Plated Steel **Ruler:** Elizabeth II **Subject:** Men's Hockey **Rev:** Hockey player and maple leaf outline in red

| Date | Mintage | VF20 | XF40 | MS60 | MS63 | MS65 |
|---|---|---|---|---|---|---|
| 2009 | — | — | — | — | 2.25 | 35.00 |

### KM# 1064 25 CENTS

Nickel Plated Steel, 23.9 mm. **Ruler:** Elizabeth II **Subject:** Women's Hockey **Rev:** Hockey player and maple leaf outline

| Date | Mintage | VF20 | XF40 | MS60 | MS63 | MS65 |
|---|---|---|---|---|---|---|
| 2009 | — | — | — | — | 0.90 | 18.00 |

### KM# 1064a 25 CENTS

Nickel Plated Steel **Ruler:** Elizabeth II **Subject:** Women's Hockey **Rev:** Hockey player and male leaf outline in red

| Date | Mintage | VF20 | XF40 | MS60 | MS63 | MS65 |
|---|---|---|---|---|---|---|
| 2009 | — | — | — | — | 2.25 | 35.00 |

### KM# 1065 25 CENTS

Nickel Plated Steel, 23.9 mm. **Ruler:** Elizabeth II **Subject:** Klassen - Female speed skater **Rev:** Skater and maple leaf outline

| Date | Mintage | VF20 | XF40 | MS60 | MS63 | MS65 |
|---|---|---|---|---|---|---|
| 2009 | — | — | — | — | 0.90 | 18.00 |

### KM# 1065a 25 CENTS

Nickel Plated Steel **Ruler:** Elizabeth II **Subject:** Klassen - female skater **Rev:** Skater and maple leaf outline in red

| Date | Mintage | VF20 | XF40 | MS60 | MS63 | MS65 |
|---|---|---|---|---|---|---|
| 2009 | — | — | — | — | 2.25 | 35.00 |

### KM# 880 25 CENTS

4.40 g., Nickel Plated Steel, 23.88 mm. **Ruler:** Elizabeth II **Subject:** Miga Mascot Vancouver Olympics **Rev:** Mica Mascot - color **Rev. Legend:** Vancouver 2010 25 cents

| Date | Mintage | VF20 | XF40 | MS60 | MS63 | MS65 |
|---|---|---|---|---|---|---|
| 2010 | 14,654 | — | — | — | — | 3.00 |

### KM# 881 25 CENTS

4.40 g., Nickel Plated Steel, 23.88 mm. **Ruler:** Elizabeth II **Subject:** Quatchi Mascot - Vancouver Olympics **Obv:** Bust right **Rev:** Quatchi Mascot color **Rev. Legend:** Vancouver 2010 25 cents

| Date | Mintage | VF20 | XF40 | MS60 | MS63 | MS65 |
|---|---|---|---|---|---|---|
| 2010 | 15,310 | — | — | — | — | 3.00 |

### KM# 882 25 CENTS

4.40 g., Nickel Plated Steel, 23.88 mm. **Ruler:** Elizabeth II **Subject:** Sumi Mascot **Rev:** Sumi Mascot color **Rev. Legend:** Vancouver 2010 25 cents

| Date | Mintage | VF20 | XF40 | MS60 | MS63 | MS65 |
|---|---|---|---|---|---|---|
| 2010 | 15,333 | — | — | — | — | 3.00 |

### KM# 953 25 CENTS

4.40 g., Nickel Plated Steel, 23.9 mm. **Ruler:** Elizabeth II **Rev:** Ice hockey

| Date | Mintage | VF20 | XF40 | MS60 | MS63 | MS65 |
|---|---|---|---|---|---|---|
| 2010 | — | — | — | — | — | 3.00 |

### KM# 953a 25 CENTS

4.40 g., Nickel Plated Steel, 23.9 mm. **Ruler:** Elizabeth II **Rev:** Ice Hockey - red enamel

| Date | Mintage | VF20 | XF40 | MS60 | MS63 | MS65 |
|---|---|---|---|---|---|---|
| 2010 | — | — | — | — | 2.25 | 35.00 |

### KM# 954 25 CENTS

4.40 g., Nickel Plated Steel, 23.9 mm. **Ruler:** Elizabeth II **Rev:** Curling

| Date | Mintage | VF20 | XF40 | MS60 | MS63 | MS65 |
|---|---|---|---|---|---|---|
| 2010 | — | — | — | — | — | 3.00 |

### KM# 954a 25 CENTS

4.40 g., Nickel Plated Steel, 23.9 mm. **Ruler:** Elizabeth II **Rev:** Curling red enamel

| Date | Mintage | VF20 | XF40 | MS60 | MS63 | MS65 |
|---|---|---|---|---|---|---|
| 2010 | — | — | — | — | — | 8.00 |

### KM# 955 25 CENTS

4.40 g., Nickel Plated Steel, 23.9 mm. **Ruler:** Elizabeth II **Rev:** Wheelchair curling

| Date | Mintage | VF20 | XF40 | MS60 | MS63 | MS65 |
|---|---|---|---|---|---|---|
| 2010 | — | — | — | — | — | 3.00 |

### KM# 955a 25 CENTS

4.40 g., Nickel Plated Steel, 23.9 mm. **Ruler:** Elizabeth II **Rev:** Wheelchair curling - red enamel

| Date | Mintage | VF20 | XF40 | MS60 | MS63 | MS65 |
|---|---|---|---|---|---|---|
| 2010 | — | — | — | — | — | 8.00 |

### KM# 956 25 CENTS

4.40 g., Nickel Plated Steel, 23.9 mm. **Ruler:** Elizabeth II **Rev:** Biathlon

| Date | Mintage | VF20 | XF40 | MS60 | MS63 | MS65 |
|---|---|---|---|---|---|---|
| 2010 | — | — | — | — | — | 3.00 |

### KM# 956a 25 CENTS

4.40 g., Nickel Plated Steel, 23.9 mm. **Ruler:** Elizabeth II **Rev:** Biathlon - red enamel

| Date | Mintage | VF20 | XF40 | MS60 | MS63 | MS65 |
|---|---|---|---|---|---|---|
| 2010 | — | — | — | — | — | 8.00 |

### KM# 957 25 CENTS

4.40 g., Nickel Plated Steel, 23.9 mm. **Ruler:** Elizabeth II **Rev:** Alpine skiing

| Date | Mintage | VF20 | XF40 | MS60 | MS63 | MS65 |
|---|---|---|---|---|---|---|
| 2010 | — | — | — | — | — | 3.00 |

### KM# 957a 25 CENTS

4.40 g., Nickel Plated Steel, 23.9 mm. **Ruler:** Elizabeth II **Rev:** Alpine skiing - red enamel

| Date | Mintage | VF20 | XF40 | MS60 | MS63 | MS65 |
|---|---|---|---|---|---|---|
| 2010 | — | — | — | — | — | 8.00 |

### KM# 958 25 CENTS

4.40 g., Nickel Plated Steel, 23.9 mm. **Ruler:** Elizabeth II **Rev:** Snowboarding

| Date | Mintage | VF20 | XF40 | MS60 | MS63 | MS65 |
|---|---|---|---|---|---|---|
| 2010 | — | — | — | — | — | 3.00 |

### KM# 958a 25 CENTS

4.40 g., Nickel Plated Steel, 23.9 mm. **Ruler:** Elizabeth II **Rev:** Snowboarding - red enamel

| Date | Mintage | VF20 | XF40 | MS60 | MS63 | MS65 |
|---|---|---|---|---|---|---|
| 2010 | — | — | — | — | — | 8.00 |

### KM# 959 25 CENTS

23.90 g., Nickel Plated Steel, 23.9 mm. **Ruler:** Elizabeth II **Rev:** Free-style skiing

| Date | Mintage | VF20 | XF40 | MS60 | MS63 | MS65 |
|---|---|---|---|---|---|---|
| 2010 | — | — | — | — | — | 3.00 |

### KM# 959a 25 CENTS

4.40 g., Nickel Plated Steel, 23.9 mm. **Ruler:** Elizabeth II **Rev:** Free-style skiing - red enamel

| Date | Mintage | VF20 | XF40 | MS60 | MS63 | MS65 |
|---|---|---|---|---|---|---|
| 2010 | — | — | — | — | — | 8.00 |

### KM# 960 25 CENTS

4.40 g., Nickel Plated Steel, 23.9 mm. **Ruler:** Elizabeth II **Rev:** Alpine skiing

| Date | Mintage | VF20 | XF40 | MS60 | MS63 | MS65 |
|---|---|---|---|---|---|---|
| 2010 | — | — | — | — | — | 3.00 |

### KM# 960a 25 CENTS

4.40 g., Nickel Plated Steel, 23.9 mm. **Ruler:** Elizabeth II **Rev:** Alpine skiing - red enamel

| Date | Mintage | VF20 | XF40 | MS60 | MS63 | MS65 |
|---|---|---|---|---|---|---|
| 2010 | — | — | — | — | — | 8.00 |

### KM# 988 25 CENTS

4.40 g., Nickel Plated Steel, 23.88 mm. **Ruler:** Elizabeth II **Rev:** Blue baby carriage

| Date | Mintage | VF20 | XF40 | MS60 | MS63 | MS65 |
|---|---|---|---|---|---|---|
| 2010 | — | — | — | — | — | 10.00 |

### KM# 989 25 CENTS

4.40 g., Nickel Plated Steel, 23.9 mm. **Ruler:** Elizabeth II **Rev:** Purple gift box

| Date | Mintage | VF20 | XF40 | MS60 | MS63 | MS65 |
|---|---|---|---|---|---|---|
| 2010 | — | — | — | — | — | 10.00 |

**KM# 990 25 CENTS**
4.40 g., Nickel Plated Steel, 23.9 mm. **Ruler:** Elizabeth II **Rev:** Four stars

| Date | Mintage | VF20 | XF40 | MS60 | MS63 | MS65 |
|---|---|---|---|---|---|---|
| 2010 | — | — | — | — | — | 10.00 |

**KM# 991 25 CENTS**
4.40 g., Nickel Plated Steel, 23.9 mm. **Ruler:** Elizabeth II **Rev:** Three maple leaves

| Date | Mintage | VF20 | XF40 | MS60 | MS63 | MS65 |
|---|---|---|---|---|---|---|
| 2010 | — | — | — | — | — | 12.50 |

**KM# 992 25 CENTS**
4.40 g., Nickel Plated Steel, 23.9 mm. **Ruler:** Elizabeth II **Rev:** Three zinnias

| Date | Mintage | VF20 | XF40 | MS60 | MS63 | MS65 |
|---|---|---|---|---|---|---|
| 2010 | — | — | — | — | — | 12.50 |

**KM# 993 25 CENTS**
4.43 g., Nickel Plated Steel, 23.9 mm. **Ruler:** Elizabeth II **Rev:** Pink hearts and roses

| Date | Mintage | VF20 | XF40 | MS60 | MS63 | MS65 |
|---|---|---|---|---|---|---|
| 2010 | — | — | — | — | — | 10.00 |

**KM# 994 25 CENTS**
12.61 g., Nickel Plated Steel, 35 mm. **Ruler:** Elizabeth II **Rev:** Goldfinch, multicolor

| Date | Mintage | VF20 | XF40 | MS60 | MS63 | MS65 |
|---|---|---|---|---|---|---|
| 2010 Specimen | Est. 14000 | — | — | — | — | 150 |

**KM# 1001 25 CENTS**
12.61 g., Nickel Plated Steel, 35 mm. **Ruler:** Elizabeth II **Subject:** Blue Jay **Rev:** Multicolor blue jay on yellow maple leaves

| Date | Mintage | VF20 | XF40 | MS60 | MS63 | MS65 |
|---|---|---|---|---|---|---|
| 2010 Specimen | Est. 14000 | — | — | — | — | 100 |

**KM# 1006 25 CENTS**
0.50 g., 0.999 Gold, 11 mm. **Ruler:** Elizabeth II **Rev:** Caribou head left

| Date | Mintage | VF20 | XF40 | MS60 | MS63 | MS65 |
|---|---|---|---|---|---|---|
| 2010 | 15,000 | **PF65** 80.00 | | | | |

**KM# 1021 25 CENTS**
Nickel Plated Steel, 23.9 mm. **Ruler:** Elizabeth II **Rev:** Santa Claus in color

| Date | Mintage | VF20 | XF40 | MS60 | MS63 | MS65 |
|---|---|---|---|---|---|---|
| 2010 | — | — | — | — | — | 15.00 |

**KM# 1026 25 CENTS**
Silver, 23.8 mm. **Ruler:** Elizabeth II **Obv:** George V bust left **Rev:** Value within wreath, dual dates below

| Date | Mintage | VF20 | XF40 | MS60 | MS63 | MS65 |
|---|---|---|---|---|---|---|
| 1935-2010 | — | **PF65** 25.00 | | | | |

**KM# 1028 25 CENTS**
4.40 g., Nickel Plated Steel, 23.9 mm. **Ruler:** Elizabeth II **Rev:** Soldier standing, two red poppies, large maple leaf behind

| Date | Mintage | VF20 | XF40 | MS60 | MS63 | MS65 |
|---|---|---|---|---|---|---|
| 2010 | — | — | — | — | — | 15.00 |

**KM# 1079 25 CENTS**
12.61 g., Nickel Plated Steel, 35 mm. **Ruler:** Elizabeth II **Rev:** Barn Swallow in color

| Date | Mintage | VF20 | XF40 | MS60 | MS63 | MS65 |
|---|---|---|---|---|---|---|
| 2011 Specimen | Est. 14000 | — | — | — | — | 50.00 |

**KM# 1080 25 CENTS**
4.43 g., Nickel Plated Steel, 23.88 mm. **Ruler:** Elizabeth II **Subject:** Oh Canada! **Rev:** Maple leaf and circular legend

| Date | Mintage | VF20 | XF40 | MS60 | MS63 | MS65 |
|---|---|---|---|---|---|---|
| 2011 | — | — | — | — | — | 2.50 |

**KM# 1081 25 CENTS**
4.43 g., Nickel Plated Steel, 23.88 mm. **Ruler:** Elizabeth II **Subject:** Wedding **Rev:** Two rings

| Date | Mintage | VF20 | XF40 | MS60 | MS63 | MS65 |
|---|---|---|---|---|---|---|
| 2011 | — | — | — | — | — | 2.50 |

**KM# 1082 25 CENTS**
4.43 g., Nickel Plated Steel, 23.88 mm. **Ruler:** Elizabeth II **Subject:** Birthday **Rev:** Year in four baloons

| Date | Mintage | VF20 | XF40 | MS60 | MS63 | MS65 |
|---|---|---|---|---|---|---|
| 2011 | — | — | — | — | — | 2.50 |

**KM# 1083 25 CENTS**
4.43 g., Nickel Plated Steel, 23.88 mm. **Ruler:** Elizabeth II **Subject:** New Baby! **Rev:** Baby's feet

| Date | Mintage | VF20 | XF40 | MS60 | MS63 | MS65 |
|---|---|---|---|---|---|---|
| 2011 | — | — | — | — | — | 2.50 |

**KM# 1084 25 CENTS**
4.43 g., Nickel Plated Steel, 23.88 mm. **Ruler:** Elizabeth II **Rev:** Tooth Fairy

| Date | Mintage | VF20 | XF40 | MS60 | MS63 | MS65 |
|---|---|---|---|---|---|---|
| 2011 | — | — | — | — | — | 2.50 |

**KM# 1110 25 CENTS**
12.61 g., Nickel Plated Steel, 35 mm. **Ruler:** Elizabeth II **Subject:** Royal Wedding **Rev:** Colored portraits left of William and Katherine

| Date | Mintage | VF20 | XF40 | MS60 | MS63 | MS65 |
|---|---|---|---|---|---|---|
| 2011 Specimen | — | — | — | — | — | 18.00 |

**KM# 1113 25 CENTS**
12.61 g., Nickel Plated Steel, 35 mm. **Ruler:** Elizabeth II **Rev:** Fantasy Furry Woods creature in color

| Date | Mintage | VF20 | XF40 | MS60 | MS63 | MS65 |
|---|---|---|---|---|---|---|
| 2011 | — | — | — | — | — | 22.00 |

**KM# 1114 25 CENTS**
12.61 g., Nickel Plated Steel, 35 mm. **Ruler:** Elizabeth II **Rev:** Fantasy sea serpent in color

| Date | Mintage | VF20 | XF40 | MS60 | MS63 | MS65 |
|---|---|---|---|---|---|---|
| 2011 | — | — | — | — | — | 22.00 |

**KM# 1115 25 CENTS**
12.61 g., Nickel Plated Steel, 35 mm. **Ruler:** Elizabeth II **Rev:** Tulip and ladybug in color

| Date | Mintage | VF20 | XF40 | MS60 | MS63 | MS65 |
|---|---|---|---|---|---|---|
| 2011 | — | — | — | — | — | 35.00 |

**KM# 1116 25 CENTS**
12.61 g., Nickel Plated Steel, 35 mm. **Ruler:** Elizabeth II **Rev:** Black capped chickadee in color

| Date | Mintage | VF20 | XF40 | MS60 | MS63 | MS65 |
|---|---|---|---|---|---|---|
| 2011 Specimen | — | — | — | — | — | 50.00 |

**KM# 1148 25 CENTS**
4.43 g., Nickel Plated Steel, 23.9 mm. **Ruler:** Elizabeth II **Obv:** Bust right **Rev:** Snowflake

| Date | Mintage | VF20 | XF40 | MS60 | MS63 | MS65 |
|---|---|---|---|---|---|---|
| 2011 | — | — | — | — | — | 7.50 |

**KM# 1156 25 CENTS**
5.90 g., 0.925 Silver 0.1755 oz. ASW, 23.8 mm. **Ruler:** Elizabeth II **Obv:** George V bust **Rev:** Value within wreath

| Date | Mintage | VF20 | XF40 | MS60 | MS63 | MS65 |
|---|---|---|---|---|---|---|
| 1911-2011 | 6,000 | PF65 25.00 | | | | |

**KM# 1168 25 CENTS**
4.40 g., Nickel Plated Steel, 23.9 mm. **Ruler:** Elizabeth II **Obv:** Bust right **Rev:** Stylized bison

| Date | Mintage | VF20 | XF40 | MS60 | MS63 | MS65 |
|---|---|---|---|---|---|---|
| 2011 | — | — | — | — | 0.90 | 18.00 |

**KM# 1168a 25 CENTS**
4.40 g., Nickel Plated Steel with color, 23.9 mm. **Ruler:** Elizabeth II **Obv:** Bust right **Rev:** Stylized bison, green circle in background

| Date | Mintage | VF20 | XF40 | MS60 | MS63 | MS65 |
|---|---|---|---|---|---|---|
| 2011 | — | — | — | — | — | 9.50 |

**KM# 1169 25 CENTS**
4.40 g., Nickel Plated Steel, 23.9 mm. **Ruler:** Elizabeth II **Obv:** Bust right **Rev:** Stylized falcon

| Date | Mintage | VF20 | XF40 | MS60 | MS63 | MS65 |
|---|---|---|---|---|---|---|
| 2011 | — | — | — | — | 0.90 | 18.00 |

**KM# 1169a 25 CENTS**
4.40 g., Nickel Plated Steel with color, 23.9 mm. **Ruler:** Elizabeth II **Obv:** Bust right **Rev:** Stylized falcon with yellow circle in background

| Date | Mintage | VF20 | XF40 | MS60 | MS63 | MS65 |
|---|---|---|---|---|---|---|
| 2011 | — | — | — | — | — | 9.50 |

**KM# 1170 25 CENTS**
4.40 g., Nickel Plated Steel, 23.9 mm. **Ruler:** Elizabeth II **Obv:** Bust right **Rev:** Stylized orca whale

| Date | Mintage | VF20 | XF40 | MS60 | MS63 | MS65 |
|---|---|---|---|---|---|---|
| 2011 | — | — | — | — | 0.90 | 18.00 |

**KM# 1170a 25 CENTS**
4.40 g., Nickel Plated Steel with color, 23.9 mm. **Ruler:** Elizabeth II **Obv:** Bust right **Rev:** Stylized orca whale with blue circle in background

| Date | Mintage | VF20 | XF40 | MS60 | MS63 | MS65 |
|---|---|---|---|---|---|---|
| 2011 | — | — | — | — | — | 9.50 |

**KM# 1171 25 CENTS**
0.50 g., 0.999 Gold, 11 mm. **Ruler:** Elizabeth II **Obv:** Bust right **Rev:** Cougar head left

| Date | Mintage | VF20 | XF40 | MS60 | MS63 | MS65 |
|---|---|---|---|---|---|---|
| 2011 | — | PF65 80.00 | | | | |

**KM# 1172 25 CENTS**
12.61 g., Copper Plated Silver gold plated, 35 mm. **Ruler:** Elizabeth II **Obv:** Bust right **Rev:** Wayne Greskey in hockey helmet left

| Date | Mintage | VF20 | XF40 | MS60 | MS63 | MS65 |
|---|---|---|---|---|---|---|
| 2011 Specimen | — | — | — | — | — | 35.00 |

**KM# 1192 25 CENTS**
4.43 g., Nickel Plated Steel, 23.9 mm. **Ruler:** Elizabeth II **Subject:** Canadian Broadcasting Company, 75th Anniversary **Obv:** Bust right **Rev:** Old-time radio microphone

| Date | Mintage | VF20 | XF40 | MS60 | MS63 | MS65 |
|---|---|---|---|---|---|---|
| 2011 | — | — | — | — | — | 2.50 |

**KM# 1193 25 CENTS**
12.61 g., Nickel Plated Steel, 35 mm. **Ruler:** Elizabeth II **Subject:** Mythical Creature - Mishepishu **Obv:** Bust right **Rev:** Horned lizard in color

| Date | Mintage | VF20 | XF40 | MS60 | MS63 | MS65 |
|---|---|---|---|---|---|---|
| 2011 | — | — | — | — | — | 22.00 |

**KM# 1227 25 CENTS**
4.43 g., Nickel Plated Steel, 23.9 mm. **Ruler:** Elizabeth II **Obv:** Bust right **Rev:** Tooth Fairy in flight

| Date | Mintage | VF20 | XF40 | MS60 | MS63 | MS65 |
|---|---|---|---|---|---|---|
| 2012 | — | — | — | — | — | 13.00 |

**KM# 1228 25 CENTS**
4.43 g., Nickel Plated Steel, 23.9 mm. **Ruler:** Elizabeth II **Subject:** Baby **Rev:** Baby's mobile

| Date | Mintage | VF20 | XF40 | MS60 | MS63 | MS65 |
|---|---|---|---|---|---|---|
| 2012 PL | — | — | — | — | — | 13.00 |

**KM# 1229 25 CENTS**
4.43 g., Nickel Plated Steel, 23.9 mm. **Ruler:** Elizabeth II **Subject:** Wedding **Rev:** Two wedding rings with small feet

| Date | Mintage | VF20 | XF40 | MS60 | MS63 | MS65 |
|---|---|---|---|---|---|---|
| 2012 PL | — | — | — | — | — | 13.00 |

**KM# 1230 25 CENTS**
4.43 g., Nickel Plated Steel, 23.9 mm. **Ruler:** Elizabeth II **Subject:** Birthday **Rev:** Cone with character face

| Date | Mintage | VF20 | XF40 | MS60 | MS63 | MS65 |
|---|---|---|---|---|---|---|
| 2012 | — | — | — | — | — | 2.50 |

**KM# 1231 25 CENTS**
4.43 g., Nickel Plated Steel, 23.9 mm. **Ruler:** Elizabeth II **Subject:** Oh, Canada ! **Rev:** Maple leaves with character faces

| Date | Mintage | VF20 | XF40 | MS60 | MS63 | MS65 |
|---|---|---|---|---|---|---|
| 2012 | — | — | — | — | — | 2.50 |

**KM# 1232 25 CENTS**
4.43 g., Nickel Plated Steel, 23.88 mm. **Ruler:** Elizabeth II **Subject:** Winnipeg Jets **Rev:** Jet superimposed on Maple leaf

| Date | Mintage | VF20 | XF40 | MS60 | MS63 | MS65 |
|---|---|---|---|---|---|---|
| 2012 | — | — | — | — | — | 2.50 |

**KM# 1233 25 CENTS**
12.51 g., Nickel Plated Steel, 35 mm. **Ruler:** Elizabeth II **Subject:** Titanic, 100th Anniversary **Obv:** Bust right **Rev:** Two views of Titanic, one at dockside, one nighttime at sea

| Date | Mintage | VF20 | XF40 | MS60 | MS63 | MS65 |
|---|---|---|---|---|---|---|
| 2012 | — | — | — | — | — | 22.00 |

**KM# 1247 25 CENTS**
12.61 g., Nickel Plated Steel, 35 mm. **Ruler:** Elizabeth II **Subject:** Coast Guard, 100th anniversary **Rev:** Rescue craft in rough seas

| Date | Mintage | VF20 | XF40 | MS60 | MS63 | MS65 |
|---|---|---|---|---|---|---|
| 2012 | — | — | — | — | — | 22.00 |

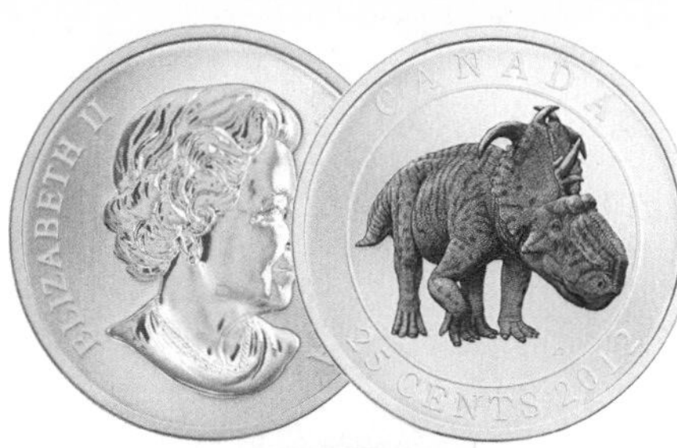

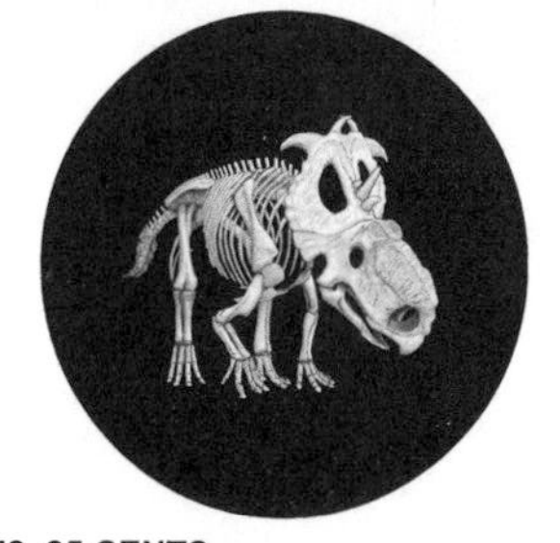

**KM# 1252 25 CENTS**
12.61 g., Nickel Plated Steel, 35 mm. **Ruler:** Elizabeth II **Subject:** Pachyrhinosaurus Lakusta **Note:** Skelton glows in the dark.

| Date | Mintage | VF20 | XF40 | MS60 | MS63 | MS65 |
|---|---|---|---|---|---|---|
| 2012 | — | — | — | — | — | 100 |

**KM# 1253 25 CENTS**
12.61 g., Nickel Plated Steel, 35 mm. **Ruler:** Elizabeth II **Subject:** Rose Breasted Grosbeak

| Date | Mintage | VF20 | XF40 | MS60 | MS63 | MS65 |
|---|---|---|---|---|---|---|
| 2012 | — | — | — | — | — | 30.00 |

**KM# 1265 25 CENTS**
12.61 g., Nickel Plated Steel, 35 mm. **Ruler:** Elizabeth II **Subject:** Aster and Bee

| Date | Mintage | VF20 | XF40 | MS60 | MS63 | MS65 |
|---|---|---|---|---|---|---|
| 2012 | — | — | — | — | — | 22.00 |

**KM# 1313 25 CENTS**
12.61 g., Copper-Nickel, 35 mm. **Ruler:** Elizabeth II **Subject:** Grey Cup, 100th Anniversary **Obv:** Bust right **Rev:** B.C. Lions logo in color

| Date | Mintage | VF20 | XF40 | MS60 | MS63 | MS65 |
|---|---|---|---|---|---|---|
| 2012 | — | PF65 25.00 | | | | |

**KM# 1314 25 CENTS**
12.61 g., Copper-Nickel, 35 mm. **Ruler:** Elizabeth II **Subject:** Grey Cup, 100th Anniversary **Obv:** Bust right **Rev:** Calgary Stampeeders logo in color

| Date | Mintage | VF20 | XF40 | MS60 | MS63 | MS65 |
|---|---|---|---|---|---|---|
| 2012 | — | PF65 22.00 | | | | |

**KM# 1315 25 CENTS**
12.61 g., Copper-Nickel, 35 mm. **Ruler:** Elizabeth II **Subject:** Grey Cup, 100th Anniversary **Obv:** Bust right **Rev:** Edmonton Eskimos logo in color

| Date | Mintage | VF20 | XF40 | MS60 | MS63 | MS65 |
|---|---|---|---|---|---|---|
| 2012 | — | PF65 25.00 | | | | |

**KM# 1316 25 CENTS**
12.61 g., Copper-Nickel, 35 mm. **Ruler:** Elizabeth II **Subject:** Grey Cup, 100th Anniversary **Obv:** Bust right **Rev:** Hamilton Tiger-Cats logo in color

| Date | Mintage | F12 | VF20 | XF40 | MS60 | MS63 |
|---|---|---|---|---|---|---|
| 2012 | — | PF65 25.00 | | | | |

**KM# 1317 25 CENTS**
12.61 g., Copper-Nickel, 35 mm. **Ruler:** Elizabeth II **Subject:** Grey Cup, 100th Anniversary **Obv:** Bust right **Rev:** Montreal Alouettes logo in color

| Date | Mintage | VF20 | XF40 | MS60 | MS63 | MS65 |
|---|---|---|---|---|---|---|
| 2012 | — | PF65 25.00 | | | | |

**KM# 1318 25 CENTS**
12.61 g., Copper-Nickel, 35 mm. **Ruler:** Elizabeth II **Subject:** Grey Cup, 100th Anniversary **Obv:** Bust right **Rev:** Saskatchewan Roughriders logo in color

| Date | Mintage | VF20 | XF40 | MS60 | MS63 | MS65 |
|---|---|---|---|---|---|---|
| 2012 | — | PF65 25.00 | | | | |

**KM# 1319 25 CENTS**
12.61 g., Copper-Nickel, 35 mm. **Ruler:** Elizabeth II **Subject:** Grey Cup, 100th Anniversary **Obv:** Bust right **Rev:** Toronto Argonauts logo in color

| Date | Mintage | VF20 | XF40 | MS60 | MS63 | MS65 |
|---|---|---|---|---|---|---|
| 2012 | — | PF65 25.00 | | | | |

**KM# 1320 25 CENTS**
12.61 g., Copper-Nickel, 35 mm. **Ruler:** Elizabeth II **Subject:** Grey Cup, 100th Anniversary **Obv:** Bust right **Rev:** Winnipeg Blue Bombers logo in color

| Date | Mintage | VF20 | XF40 | MS60 | MS63 | MS65 |
|---|---|---|---|---|---|---|
| 2012 | — | PF65 25.00 | | | | |

**KM# 1321 25 CENTS**
12.61 g., Nickel Plated Steel, 35 mm. **Ruler:** Elizabeth II **Subject:** Calgary Stampeed **Rev:** Cowboy on bucking horse in color

| Date | Mintage | VF20 | XF40 | MS60 | MS63 | MS65 |
|---|---|---|---|---|---|---|
| 2012 Specimen | — | — | — | — | — | 22.00 |

**KM# 1322 25 CENTS**
4.43 g., Nickel Plated Steel, 23.9 mm. **Ruler:** Elizabeth II **Subject:** War of 1812 - Brock **Rev:** Porrait at right

| Date | Mintage | VF20 | XF40 | MS60 | MS63 | MS65 |
|---|---|---|---|---|---|---|
| 2012 | — | — | — | — | 0.90 | 18.00 |

**KM# 1322a 25 CENTS**
4.43 g., Nickel Plated Steel, 23.9 mm. **Ruler:** Elizabeth II **Subject:** War of 1812 - Brock **Rev:** Portrait at right, red maple leaf

| Date | Mintage | VF20 | XF40 | MS60 | MS63 | MS65 |
|---|---|---|---|---|---|---|
| 2012 | — | — | — | — | — | 10.00 |

**KM# 1324 25 CENTS**
4.43 g., Nickel Plated Steel, 23.9 mm. **Ruler:** Elizabeth II **Subject:** War of 1812 - Tecumseh **Rev:** Portrait at right

| Date | Mintage | VF20 | XF40 | MS60 | MS63 | MS65 |
|---|---|---|---|---|---|---|
| 2012 | — | — | — | — | 0.90 | 18.00 |

**KM# 1324a 25 CENTS**
4.42 g., Nickel Plated Steel, 23.9 mm. **Ruler:** Elizabeth II **Subject:** War of 1812 - Tecumseh **Rev:** Portrait at right, red maple leaf

| Date | Mintage | VF20 | XF40 | MS60 | MS63 | MS65 |
|---|---|---|---|---|---|---|
| 2012 | — | — | — | — | — | 10.00 |

**KM# 1326 25 CENTS**
12.61 g., Nickel Plated Steel, 35 mm. **Ruler:** Elizabeth II **Rev:** Evening Grosbeak in color

| Date | Mintage | VF20 | XF40 | MS60 | MS63 | MS65 |
|---|---|---|---|---|---|---|
| 2012 Specimen | — | — | — | — | — | 35.00 |

**KM# 1341 25 CENTS**
12.16 g., Copper-Nickel, 35 mm. **Ruler:** Elizabeth II **Subject:** Christmas Lenticular **Rev:** Santa Claus with bag of presents

| Date | Mintage | VF20 | XF40 | MS60 | MS63 | MS65 |
|---|---|---|---|---|---|---|
| 2012 Specimen | 25,000 | — | — | — | — | 30.00 |

**KM# 1700a 25 CENTS**
4.43 g., Nickel Plated Steel, 23.9 mm. **Ruler:** Elizabeth II **Subject:** War of 1812 - Seacord **Rev:** Portrait at right, red maple leaf at left

| Date | Mintage | F12 | VF20 | XF40 | MS60 | MS63 |
|---|---|---|---|---|---|---|
| 2013 | — | — | — | — | — | 2.50 |

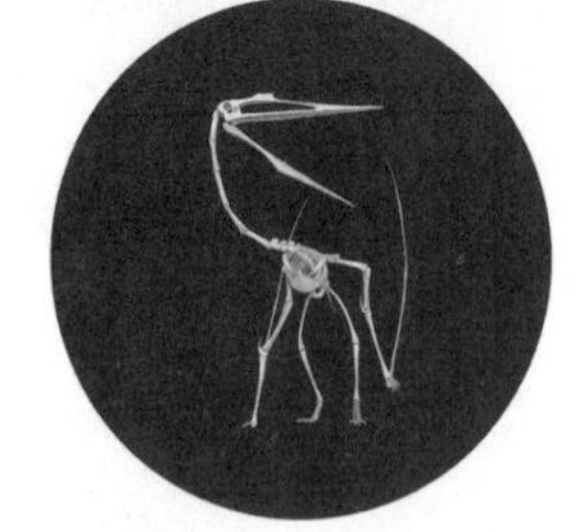

**KM# 1351 25 CENTS**
Nickel Plated Steel, 35 mm. **Ruler:** Elizabeth II **Subject:** Quetzalcoatlus **Rev:** Dinosaur in color and as glow-in-the-dark skelton

| Date | Mintage | VF20 | XF40 | MS60 | MS63 | MS65 |
|---|---|---|---|---|---|---|
| 2013 | — | — | — | — | — | 35.00 |

**KM# 1353 25 CENTS**
12.61 g., Copper-Nickel, 35 mm. **Ruler:** Elizabeth II **Rev:** Purple cone flower and butterfly in color

| Date | Mintage | VF20 | XF40 | MS60 | MS63 | MS65 |
|---|---|---|---|---|---|---|
| 2013 Specimen | 17,500 | — | — | — | — | 30.00 |

**KM# 1354 25 CENTS**
12.61 g., Copper-Nickel, 35 mm. **Ruler:** Elizabeth II **Rev:** Male and female mallards in color

| Date | Mintage | VF20 | XF40 | MS60 | MS63 | MS65 |
|---|---|---|---|---|---|---|
| 2013 Specimen | 17,500 | — | — | — | — | 27.00 |

**KM# 1368 25 CENTS**
4.43 g., Nickel Plated Steel, 23.9 mm. **Ruler:** Elizabeth II **Subject:** Oh Canada **Rev:** Maple Leaf

| Date | Mintage | VF20 | XF40 | MS60 | MS63 | MS65 |
|---|---|---|---|---|---|---|
| 2013 | — | PF65 10.00 | | | | |

**KM# 1373 25 CENTS**
12.61 g., Nickel Plated Steel, 35 mm. **Ruler:** Elizabeth II **Rev:** American Robin in color

| Date | Mintage | VF20 | XF40 | MS60 | MS63 | MS65 |
|---|---|---|---|---|---|---|
| 2013 Specimen | — | — | — | — | — | 27.00 |

**KM# 1380 25 CENTS**
0.50 g., 0.9999 Gold, 11 mm. **Ruler:** Elizabeth II **Rev:** Hummingbird in flight right

| Date | Mintage | VF20 | XF40 | MS60 | MS63 | MS65 |
|---|---|---|---|---|---|---|
| 2013 | Est. 10000 | PF65 70.00 | | | | |

**KM# 1419 25 CENTS**
4.43 g., Nickel Plated Steel, 23.9 mm. **Ruler:** Elizabeth II **Subject:** Birthday **Rev:** Birthday cake and candle

| Date | Mintage | VF20 | XF40 | MS60 | MS63 | MS65 |
|---|---|---|---|---|---|---|
| 2013 | — | PF65 20.00 | | | | |

**KM# 1420 25 CENTS**
4.43 g., Nickel Plated Steel, 23.9 mm. **Ruler:** Elizabeth II **Rev:** Two Rings

| Date | Mintage | VF20 | XF40 | MS60 | MS63 | MS65 |
|---|---|---|---|---|---|---|
| 2013 | — | PF65 20.00 | | | | |

**KM# 1432 25 CENTS**
15.50 g., Copper-Nickel, 35 mm. **Ruler:** Elizabeth II **Subject:** Coronation Anniversary **Rev:** Elizabeth standing, Victoria painting in background in color.

| Date | Mintage | VF20 | XF40 | MS60 | MS63 | MS65 |
|---|---|---|---|---|---|---|
| 2013 Specimen | Est. 15000 | — | — | — | — | 22.00 |

**KM# 1443 25 CENTS**
Copper-Nickel, 35 mm. **Ruler:** Elizabeth II **Obv:** Bust right **Rev:** Barn owl in flight left, in color

| Date | Mintage | VF20 | XF40 | MS60 | MS63 | MS65 |
|---|---|---|---|---|---|---|
| 2013 | 17,500 | PF65 27.00 | | | | |

**KM# 1460 25 CENTS**
0.50 g., Nickel Plated Steel, 23.9 mm. **Ruler:** Elizabeth II **Rev:** Baby carriage - William and Catherine names around

| Date | Mintage | VF20 | XF40 | MS60 | MS63 | MS65 |
|---|---|---|---|---|---|---|
| 2013 Specimen | — | — | — | — | — | 22.00 |

**KM# 1465 25 CENTS**
12.61 g., Nickel Plated Steel, 35 mm. **Ruler:** Elizabeth II **Rev:** Christmas wreath in color

| Date | Mintage | VF20 | XF40 | MS60 | MS63 | MS65 |
|---|---|---|---|---|---|---|
| 2013 | — | — | — | — | — | 25.00 |

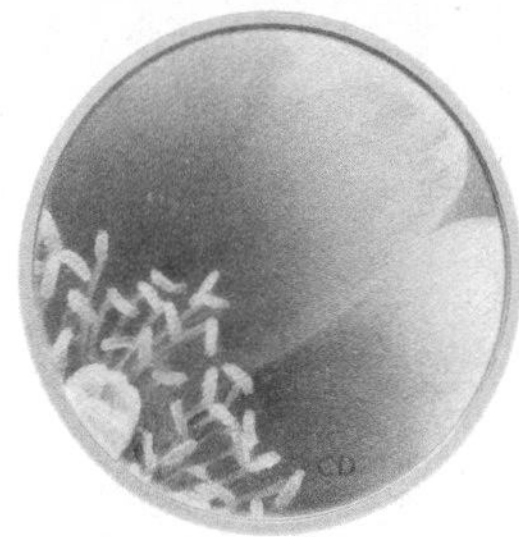

**KM# 1491 25 CENTS**
15.50 g., Copper-Nickel, 35 mm. **Ruler:** Elizabeth II **Subject:** Eastern Prickly Pear Cactus **Rev:** Partial flower in color

| Date | Mintage | VF20 | XF40 | MS60 | MS63 | MS65 |
|---|---|---|---|---|---|---|
| 2013 | 17,500 | PF65 22.00 | | | | |

**KM# 1494 25 CENTS**
0.50 g., 0.999 Gold, 11 mm. **Ruler:** Elizabeth II **Subject:** Rocky Mountain Bighorn Sheep **Rev:** Head right

| Date | Mintage | VF20 | XF40 | MS60 | MS63 | MS65 |
|---|---|---|---|---|---|---|
| 2013 | 10,000 | PF65 80.00 | | | | |

**KM# 1521 25 CENTS**
Copper-Nickel, 35 mm. **Ruler:** Elizabeth II **Rev:** Tylosaurus Pembinensis glow in the dark

| Date | Mintage | VF20 | XF40 | MS60 | MS63 | MS65 |
|---|---|---|---|---|---|---|
| 2013 | 30,000 | PF65 27.00 | | | | |

**KM# 1524 25 CENTS**
Copper-Nickel, 35 mm. **Ruler:** Elizabeth II **Rev:** Wood duck pair

| Date | Mintage | VF20 | XF40 | MS60 | MS63 | MS65 |
|---|---|---|---|---|---|---|
| 2013 | — | — | — | — | — | 30.00 |

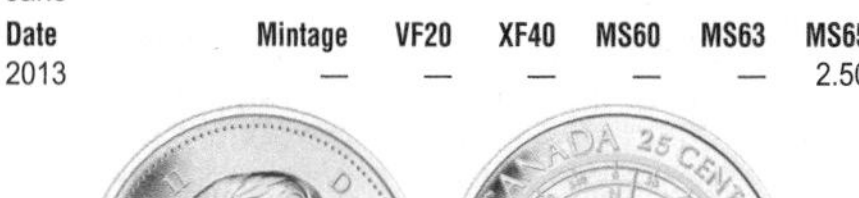

**KM# 1539 25 CENTS**
Nickel Plated Steel, 23.9 mm. **Ruler:** Elizabeth II **Obv:** Birthday cake

| Date | Mintage | VF20 | XF40 | MS60 | MS63 | MS65 |
|---|---|---|---|---|---|---|
| 2013 | — | — | — | — | — | 2.50 |

**KM# 1547 25 CENTS**
Copper-Nickel, 23.9 mm. **Ruler:** Elizabeth II **Rev:** Artic Explorers, compass rose

| Date | Mintage | VF20 | XF40 | MS60 | MS63 | MS65 |
|---|---|---|---|---|---|---|
| 2013 Frosted compass arc | — | — | — | — | — | 2.50 |
| 2013 Frosted explorers | — | — | — | — | — | 2.50 |

**KM# 1700 25 CENTS**
4.43 g., Nickel Plated Steel, 23.9 mm. **Ruler:** Elizabeth II **Subject:** War of 1812 - Secord **Rev:** Portrait at right

| Date | Mintage | F12 | VF20 | XF40 | MS60 | MS63 |
|---|---|---|---|---|---|---|
| 2013 | — | — | — | — | — | 2.50 |

**KM# 1572 25 CENTS**
12.61 g., Nickel Plated Steel, 35 mm. **Ruler:** Elizabeth II **Obv:** Bust right **Rev:** Montreal Canadians logo in color

| Date | Mintage | VF20 | XF40 | MS60 | MS63 | MS65 |
|---|---|---|---|---|---|---|
| 2014 | — | — | — | — | — | 10.00 |

**KM# 1573 25 CENTS**
12.61 g., Nickel Plated Steel, 35 mm. **Ruler:** Elizabeth II **Obv:** Bust right **Rev:** Canucks logo in color

| Date | Mintage | VF20 | XF40 | MS60 | MS63 | MS65 |
|---|---|---|---|---|---|---|
| 2014 | — | — | — | — | — | 10.00 |

**KM# 1574 25 CENTS**
12.61 g., Nickel Plated Steel, 35 mm. **Ruler:** Elizabeth II **Obv:** Bust right **Rev:** Calgary Flames logo in color

| Date | Mintage | VF20 | XF40 | MS60 | MS63 | MS65 |
|---|---|---|---|---|---|---|
| 2014 | — | — | — | — | — | 10.00 |

**KM# 1575 25 CENTS**
12.61 g., Nickel Plated Steel, 35 mm. **Ruler:** Elizabeth II **Obv:** Bust right **Rev:** Winnipeg Jets logo in color

| Date | Mintage | VF20 | XF40 | MS60 | MS63 | MS65 |
|---|---|---|---|---|---|---|
| 2014 | — | — | — | — | — | 10.00 |

**KM# 1576 25 CENTS**
12.61 g., Nickel Plated Steel, 35 mm. **Ruler:** Elizabeth II **Obv:** Bust right **Rev:** Toronto Maple Leafs logo in color

| Date | Mintage | VF20 | XF40 | MS60 | MS63 | MS65 |
|---|---|---|---|---|---|---|
| 2014 | — | — | — | — | — | 10.00 |

**KM# 1577 25 CENTS**
12.61 g., Nickel Plated Steel, 35 mm. **Ruler:** Elizabeth II **Obv:** Bust right **Rev:** Edmonton Oilers logo in color

| Date | Mintage | VF20 | XF40 | MS60 | MS63 | MS65 |
|---|---|---|---|---|---|---|
| 2014 | — | — | — | — | — | 10.00 |

**KM# 1578 25 CENTS**
12.61 g., Nickel Plated Steel, 35 mm. **Ruler:** Elizabeth II **Obv:** Bust right **Rev:** Senators logo in color

| Date | Mintage | VF20 | XF40 | MS60 | MS63 | MS65 |
|---|---|---|---|---|---|---|
| 2014 | — | — | — | — | — | 10.00 |

**KM# 1602 25 CENTS**
0.50 g., 0.999 Gold 0.0161 oz. AGW, 11 mm. **Ruler:** Elizabeth II **Obv:** Bust right **Rev:** Chipmunk

| Date | Mintage | VF20 | XF40 | MS60 | MS63 | MS65 |
|---|---|---|---|---|---|---|
| 2014 | — | PF65 80.00 | | | | |

**KM# 1618 25 CENTS**
12.61 g., Nickel Plated Steel, 35 mm. **Ruler:** Elizabeth II **Obv:** Bust right **Rev:** Eastern Meadowlark in color

| Date | Mintage | VF20 | XF40 | MS60 | MS63 | MS65 |
|---|---|---|---|---|---|---|
| 2014 | — | — | — | — | — | 35.00 |

**KM# 1619 25 CENTS**
12.61 g., Nickel Plated Steel, 35 mm. **Ruler:** Elizabeth II **Obv:** Bust right **Rev:** Tikaalik creature in glow in the dark format

| Date | Mintage | VF20 | XF40 | MS60 | MS63 | MS65 |
|---|---|---|---|---|---|---|
| 2014 | — | — | — | — | — | 25.00 |

**KM# 1630 25 CENTS**
12.61 g., Nickel Plated Steel, 35 mm. **Ruler:** Elizabeth II **Obv:** Bust right **Rev:** Pintail ducks in color

| Date | Mintage | VF20 | XF40 | MS60 | MS63 | MS65 |
|---|---|---|---|---|---|---|
| 2014 | — | — | — | — | — | 25.00 |

**KM# 1779 25 CENTS**
15.87 g., Copper-Nickel, 35 mm. **Ruler:** Elizabeth II **Obv:** Bust right **Rev:** Scarlet Tanager in color

| Date | Mintage | F12 | VF20 | XF40 | MS60 | MS63 |
|---|---|---|---|---|---|---|
| 2014 | 17,500 | — | — | — | — | 30.00 |

**KM# 1810 25 CENTS**
0.50 g., 0.999 Gold 0.0161 oz. AGW **Ruler:** Elizabeth II **Obv:** Bust right **Rev:** Grizzly Bear head left

| Date | Mintage | VF20 | XF40 | MS60 | MS63 | MS65 |
|---|---|---|---|---|---|---|
| 2015 | 10,000 | PF65 80.00 | | | | |

**KM# 290 50 CENTS**
8.10 g., Nickel, 27.1 mm. **Ruler:** Elizabeth II **Obv:** Crowned head right **Rev:** Redesigned arms **Edge:** Reeded

| Date | Mintage | VF20 | XF40 | MS60 | MS63 | MS65 |
|---|---|---|---|---|---|---|
| 2001 P | — | — | — | 0.70 | 1.50 | 30.00 |
| 2001 P | — | PF65 5.00 | | | | |
| 2002 | — | — | — | — | 15.00 | — |
| 2002 | — | PF63 15.00 | | | | |
| 2003 P PL | — | — | — | — | — | 10.00 |
| 2003 P | — | PF65 5.00 | | | | |

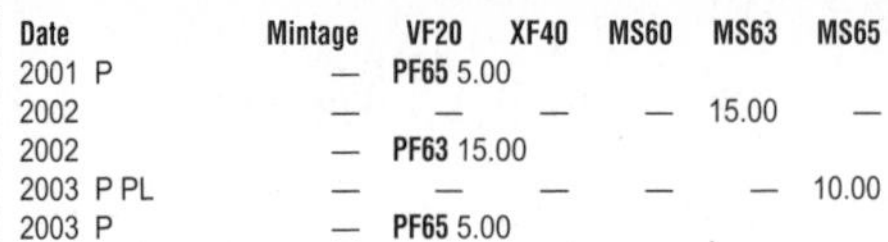

**KM# 290a 50 CENTS**
11.66 g., 0.925 Silver 0.3469 oz. ASW, 27.13 mm. **Ruler:** Elizabeth II **Obv:** Crowned head right **Rev:** Redesigned arms **Edge:** Reeded

| Date | Mintage | VF20 | XF40 | MS60 | MS63 | MS65 |
|---|---|---|---|---|---|---|
| 2001 | — | PF65 9.00 | | | | |
| 2003 | — | PF65 13.00 | | | | |

**KM# 290b 50 CENTS**
6.90 g., Nickel Plated Steel, 27.13 mm. **Ruler:** Elizabeth II **Obv:** Crowned head right **Rev:** Redesigned arms **Edge:** Reeded

| Date | Mintage | VF20 | XF40 | MS60 | MS63 | MS65 |
|---|---|---|---|---|---|---|
| 2001 P | 389,000 | — | — | 0.90 | 1.50 | 30.00 |
| 2003 P PL | — | — | — | — | — | 10.00 |

**KM# 420 50 CENTS**
9.30 g., 0.925 Silver 0.2766 oz. ASW, 27.13 mm. **Ruler:** Elizabeth II **Series:** Festivals - Quebec **Obv:** Crowned head right **Rev:** Snowman and Chateau Frontenac **Edge:** Reeded

| Date | Mintage | VF20 | XF40 | MS60 | MS63 | MS65 |
|---|---|---|---|---|---|---|
| 2001 | 58,123 | PF65 12.00 | | | | |

**KM# 421 50 CENTS**
9.30 g., 0.925 Silver 0.2766 oz. ASW, 27.13 mm. **Ruler:** Elizabeth II **Series:** Festivals - Nunavut **Obv:** Crowned head right **Rev:** Dancer, dog sled and snowmobiles **Edge:** Reeded

| Date | Mintage | VF20 | XF40 | MS60 | MS63 | MS65 |
|---|---|---|---|---|---|---|
| 2001 | — | PF65 12.00 | | | | |

**KM# 422 50 CENTS**
9.30 g., 0.925 Silver 0.2766 oz. ASW, 27.13 mm. **Ruler:** Elizabeth II **Series:** Festivals - Newfoundland **Obv:** Crowned head right **Rev:** Sailor and musical people **Edge:** Reeded

| Date | Mintage | VF20 | XF40 | MS60 | MS63 | MS65 |
|---|---|---|---|---|---|---|
| 2001 | 58,123 | PF65 12.00 | | | | |

**KM# 423 50 CENTS**
9.30 g., 0.925 Silver 0.2766 oz. ASW, 27.13 mm. **Ruler:** Elizabeth II **Series:** Festivals - Prince Edward Island **Obv:** Crowned head right **Rev:** Family, juggler and building **Edge:** Reeded

| Date | Mintage | VF20 | XF40 | MS60 | MS63 | MS65 |
|---|---|---|---|---|---|---|
| 2001 | 58,123 | PF65 12.00 | | | | |

**KM# 424 50 CENTS**
9.30 g., 0.925 Silver 0.2766 oz. ASW, 27.13 mm. **Ruler:** Elizabeth II **Series:** Folklore - The Sled **Obv:** Crowned head right **Rev:** Family scene **Edge:** Reeded

| Date | Mintage | VF20 | XF40 | MS60 | MS63 | MS65 |
|---|---|---|---|---|---|---|
| 2001 | 28,979 | PF65 12.00 | | | | |

**KM# 425 50 CENTS**
9.30 g., 0.925 Silver 0.2766 oz. ASW, 27.13 mm. **Ruler:** Elizabeth II **Series:** Folklore - The Maiden's Cave **Obv:** Crowned head right **Rev:** Woman shouting **Edge:** Reeded

| Date | Mintage | VF20 | XF40 | MS60 | MS63 | MS65 |
|---|---|---|---|---|---|---|
| 2001 | 28,979 | PF65 12.00 | | | | |

**KM# 426 50 CENTS**
9.30 g., 0.925 Silver 0.2766 oz. ASW, 27.13 mm. **Ruler:** Elizabeth II **Series:** Folklore - The Small Jumpers **Obv:** Crowned head right **Rev:** Jumping children on seashore **Edge:** Reeded

| Date | Mintage | VF20 | XF40 | MS60 | MS63 | MS65 |
|---|---|---|---|---|---|---|
| 2001 | 28,979 | PF65 12.00 | | | | |

**KM# 509 50 CENTS**
6.90 g., Nickel Plated Steel, 27.13 mm. **Ruler:** Elizabeth II **Obv:** Crowned head right **Rev:** National arms **Edge:** Reeded

| Date | Mintage | VF20 | XF40 | MS60 | MS63 | MS65 |
|---|---|---|---|---|---|---|
| 2001 P | — | — | — | — | 1.50 | — |

**KM# 444 50 CENTS**
6.90 g., Nickel Plated Steel, 27.13 mm. **Ruler:** Elizabeth II **Subject:** Queen's Golden Jubilee **Obv:** Coronation crowned head right and monogram **Rev:** Canadian arms **Edge:** Reeded

| Date | Mintage | VF20 | XF40 | MS60 | MS63 | MS65 |
|---|---|---|---|---|---|---|
| 1952-2002 P | 14,440,000 | — | — | 0.90 | 1.75 | 35.00 |

**KM# 444a 50 CENTS**
9.30 g., 0.925 Silver 0.2766 oz. ASW, 27.13 mm. **Ruler:** Elizabeth II **Subject:** Elizabeth II Golden Jubilee **Obv:** Crowned head right, Jubilee commemorative dates 1952-2002

| Date | Mintage | VF20 | XF40 | MS60 | MS63 | MS65 |
|---|---|---|---|---|---|---|
| 1952-2002 | 100,000 | PF65 17.50 | | | | |

**KM# 444b 50 CENTS**
9.30 g., 0.925 Silver 0.2766 oz. ASW 24 karat gold plated, 27.13 mm. **Ruler:** Elizabeth II **Subject:** Queen's Golden Jubilee **Obv:** Crowned head right and monogram **Rev:** Canadian arms **Edge:** Reeded

| Date | Mintage | VF20 | XF40 | MS60 | MS63 | MS65 |
|---|---|---|---|---|---|---|
| 1952-2002 | 32,642 | PF65 35.00 | | | | |

### KM# 454 50 CENTS

9.30 g., 0.925 Silver 0.2766 oz. ASW, 27.13 mm. **Ruler:** Elizabeth II **Subject:** Nova Scotia Annapolis Valley Apple Blossom Festival **Obv:** Crowned head right

| Date | Mintage | VF20 | XF40 | MS60 | MS63 | MS65 |
|---|---|---|---|---|---|---|
| 2002 | 59,998 | PF65 9.50 | | | | |

### KM# 455 50 CENTS

9.30 g., 0.925 Silver 0.2766 oz. ASW, 27.13 mm. **Ruler:** Elizabeth II **Subject:** Stratford Festival **Obv:** Crowned head right **Rev:** Couple with building in background

| Date | Mintage | VF20 | XF40 | MS60 | MS63 | MS65 |
|---|---|---|---|---|---|---|
| 2002 | 59,998 | PF65 9.50 | | | | |

### KM# 456 50 CENTS

9.30 g., 0.925 Silver 0.2766 oz. ASW, 27.13 mm. **Ruler:** Elizabeth II **Subject:** Folklorama **Obv:** Crowned head right

| Date | Mintage | VF20 | XF40 | MS60 | MS63 | MS65 |
|---|---|---|---|---|---|---|
| 2002 | 59,998 | PF65 9.50 | | | | |

### KM# 457 50 CENTS

9.30 g., 0.925 Silver 0.2766 oz. ASW, 27.13 mm. **Ruler:** Elizabeth II **Subject:** Calgary Stampede **Obv:** Crowned head right

| Date | Mintage | VF20 | XF40 | MS60 | MS63 | MS65 |
|---|---|---|---|---|---|---|
| 2002 | 59,998 | PF65 9.50 | | | | |

### KM# 458 50 CENTS

9.30 g., 0.925 Silver 0.2766 oz. ASW, 27.13 mm. **Ruler:** Elizabeth II **Subject:** Squamish Days Logger Sports **Obv:** Crowned head right

| Date | Mintage | VF20 | XF40 | MS60 | MS63 | MS65 |
|---|---|---|---|---|---|---|
| 2002 | 59,998 | PF65 9.50 | | | | |

### KM# 459 50 CENTS

9.30 g., 0.925 Silver 0.2766 oz. ASW, 27.13 mm. **Ruler:** Elizabeth II **Series:** Folklore and Legends **Obv:** Crowned head right **Rev:** The Shoemaker in Heaven

| Date | Mintage | VF20 | XF40 | MS60 | MS63 | MS65 |
|---|---|---|---|---|---|---|
| 2002 | 19,267 | PF65 11.00 | | | | |

### KM# 460 50 CENTS

9.30 g., 0.925 Silver 0.2766 oz. ASW, 27.13 mm. **Ruler:** Elizabeth II **Series:** Folklore and Legends **Subject:** The Ghost Ship **Obv:** Crowned head right

| Date | Mintage | VF20 | XF40 | MS60 | MS63 | MS65 |
|---|---|---|---|---|---|---|
| 2002 | 19,267 | PF65 11.00 | | | | |

### KM# 461 50 CENTS

9.30 g., 0.925 Silver 0.2766 oz. ASW, 27.13 mm. **Ruler:** Elizabeth II **Series:** Folklore and Legends **Subject:** The Pig That Wouldn't Get Over the Stile **Obv:** Crowned head right

| Date | Mintage | VF20 | XF40 | MS60 | MS63 | MS65 |
|---|---|---|---|---|---|---|
| 2002 | 19,267 | PF65 11.00 | | | | |

### KM# 472 50 CENTS

11.62 g., 0.925 Silver 0.3456 oz. ASW, 27.13 mm. **Ruler:** Elizabeth II **Subject:** 50th Anniversary of the Coronation of Elizabeth II **Obv:** Crowned head right, Jubilee commemorative dates 1952-2002

| Date | Mintage | VF20 | XF40 | MS60 | MS63 | MS65 |
|---|---|---|---|---|---|---|
| 2003 | 30,000 | PF65 15.00 | | | | |

### KM# 475 50 CENTS

9.30 g., 0.925 Silver 0.2766 oz. ASW, 27.13 mm. **Ruler:** Elizabeth II **Obv:** Crowned head right **Rev:** Golden daffodil

| Date | Mintage | VF20 | XF40 | MS60 | MS63 | MS65 |
|---|---|---|---|---|---|---|
| 2003 | 36,293 | PF65 25.00 | | | | |

### KM# 476 50 CENTS

9.30 g., 0.925 Silver 0.2766 oz. ASW, 27.13 mm. **Ruler:** Elizabeth II **Subject:** Yukon International Storytelling Festival **Obv:** Crowned head right

| Date | Mintage | VF20 | XF40 | MS60 | MS63 | MS65 |
|---|---|---|---|---|---|---|
| 2003 | — | PF65 11.00 | | | | |

### KM# 477 50 CENTS

9.30 g., 0.925 Silver 0.2766 oz. ASW, 27.13 mm. **Ruler:** Elizabeth II **Subject:** Festival Acadien de Caraquet **Obv:** Crowned head right **Rev:** Sailboat and couple

| Date | Mintage | VF20 | XF40 | MS60 | MS63 | MS65 |
|---|---|---|---|---|---|---|
| 2003 | — | PF65 11.00 | | | | |

### KM# 478 50 CENTS

9.30 g., 0.925 Silver 0.2766 oz. ASW, 27.13 mm. **Ruler:** Elizabeth II **Subject:** Back to Batoche **Obv:** Crowned head right

| Date | Mintage | VF20 | XF40 | MS60 | MS63 | MS65 |
|---|---|---|---|---|---|---|
| 2003 | — | PF65 11.00 | | | | |

### KM# 479 50 CENTS

9.30 g., 0.925 Silver 0.2766 oz. ASW, 27.13 mm. **Ruler:** Elizabeth II **Subject:** Great Northern Arts Festival **Obv:** Crowned head right

| Date | Mintage | VF20 | XF40 | MS60 | MS63 | MS65 |
|---|---|---|---|---|---|---|
| 2003 | — | PF65 11.00 | | | | |

### KM# 494 50 CENTS

6.90 g., Nickel Plated Steel, 27.13 mm. **Ruler:** Elizabeth II **Obv:** Crowned head right **Rev:** National arms **Edge:** Reeded

| Date | Mintage | VF20 | XF40 | MS60 | MS63 | MS65 |
|---|---|---|---|---|---|---|
| 2003 P W PL | — | — | — | — | — | 7.50 |
| 2003 P W | — | PF65 7.50 | | | | |
| 2004 P | — | — | — | — | — | 3.50 |
| 2004 P | — | PF65 7.50 | | | | |
| 2005 P | 200,000 | — | — | — | 2.00 | 22.00 |
| 2005 P | — | PF65 5.00 | | | | |
| 2006 P | 98,000 | — | — | — | 2.50 | 22.00 |
| 2006 P | — | PF65 5.00 | | | | |
| 2007 (ml) | 250,000 | — | — | — | 2.50 | 22.00 |
| 2007 (ml) | — | PF65 5.00 | | | | |
| 2008 (ml) | 211,000 | — | — | — | 2.00 | 22.00 |
| 2008 (ml) | — | PF65 5.00 | | | | |
| 2009 (ml) | 150,000 | — | — | — | 2.00 | 22.00 |
| 2009 (ml) | — | PF65 5.00 | | | | |
| 2010 (ml) | — | — | — | — | 2.00 | 22.00 |
| 2010 (ml) | — | PF65 5.00 | | | | |
| 2011 (ml) | — | — | — | — | 2.00 | 22.00 |
| 2011 (ml) | — | PF65 5.00 | | | | |
| 2012 (ml) | — | — | — | — | 2.00 | 22.00 |
| 2012 (ml) | — | PF65 5.00 | | | | |
| 2013 (ml) | — | — | — | — | 1.50 | — |
| 2013 (ml) | — | PF65 5.00 | | | | |
| 2014 | — | — | — | — | 1.50 | — |
| 2014 | — | PF63 4.00 | PF65 5.00 | | | |
| 2015 | — | — | — | — | 1.50 | — |
| 2015 | — | PF63 4.00 | PF65 5.00 | | | |

### KM# 494a 50 CENTS

9.30 g., 0.925 Silver 0.2766 oz. ASW, 27.13 mm. **Ruler:** Elizabeth II **Obv:** Crowned head right **Rev:** Canadian coat of arms **Edge:** Reeded

| Date | Mintage | VF20 | XF40 | MS60 | MS63 | MS65 |
|---|---|---|---|---|---|---|
| 2004 | — | PF65 11.00 | | | | |

### KM# 509 50 CENTS

9.30 g., 0.925 Silver 0.2766 oz. ASW, 27.13 mm. **Ruler:** Elizabeth II **Rev:** Day Lilly, gilt

| Date | Mintage | VF20 | XF40 | MS60 | MS63 | MS65 |
|---|---|---|---|---|---|---|
| 2004 | — | PF65 25.00 | | | | |

### KM# 526 50 CENTS

1.27 g., 0.9999 Gold 0.0408 oz. AGW, 14 mm. **Ruler:** Elizabeth II **Subject:** Moose **Obv:** Head right **Rev:** Moose head facing right

| Date | Mintage | VF20 | XF40 | MS60 | MS63 | MS65 |
|---|---|---|---|---|---|---|
| 2004 | — | PF65 85.00 | | | | |

### KM# 606 50 CENTS

9.30 g., 0.925 Silver 0.2766 oz. ASW, 27.13 mm. **Ruler:** Elizabeth II **Obv:** Head right **Rev:** Clouded Sulphur Butterfly, hologram

| Date | Mintage | VF20 | XF40 | MS60 | MS63 | MS65 |
|---|---|---|---|---|---|---|
| 2004 | 15,281 | PF65 35.00 | | | | |

### KM# 712 50 CENTS

9.30 g., 0.925 Silver 0.2766 oz. ASW, 27.13 mm. **Ruler:** Elizabeth II **Rev:** Hologram of Tiger Swallowtail butterfly

| Date | Mintage | VF20 | XF40 | MS60 | MS63 | MS65 |
|---|---|---|---|---|---|---|
| 2004 | 20,462 | PF65 35.00 | | | | |

### KM# 536 50 CENTS

9.30 g., 0.925 Silver 0.2766 oz. ASW with partial gold plating, 27.13 mm. **Ruler:** Elizabeth II **Subject:** Golden rose **Obv:** Head right

| Date | Mintage | VF20 | XF40 | MS60 | MS63 | MS65 |
|---|---|---|---|---|---|---|
| 2005 | 17,418 | PF65 30.00 | | | | |

### KM# 537 50 CENTS

9.30 g., 0.925 Silver 0.2766 oz. ASW, 27.13 mm. **Ruler:** Elizabeth II **Obv:** Head right **Rev:** Great Spangled Fritillary butterfly, hologram

| Date | Mintage | VF20 | XF40 | MS60 | MS63 | MS65 |
|---|---|---|---|---|---|---|
| 2005 | 20,000 | PF65 35.00 | | | | |

### KM# 538 50 CENTS

9.30 g., 0.925 Silver 0.2766 oz. ASW, 27.13 mm. **Ruler:** Elizabeth II **Subject:** Toronto Maple Leafs **Obv:** Head right **Rev:** Darryl Sittler

| Date | Mintage | VF20 | XF40 | MS60 | MS63 | MS65 |
|---|---|---|---|---|---|---|
| 2005 Specimen | 25,000 | PF65 16.00 | | | | |

### KM# 539 50 CENTS

9.30 g., 0.925 Silver 0.2766 oz. ASW, 27.13 mm. **Ruler:** Elizabeth II **Subject:** Toronto Maple Leafs **Obv:** Head right **Rev:** Dave Keon

| Date | Mintage | VF20 | XF40 | MS60 | MS63 | MS65 |
|---|---|---|---|---|---|---|
| 2005 Specimen | 25,000 | PF65 16.00 | | | | |

### KM# 540 50 CENTS

9.30 g., 0.925 Silver 0.2766 oz. ASW, 27.13 mm. **Ruler:** Elizabeth II **Subject:** Toronto Maple Leafs **Obv:** Head right **Rev:** Jonny Bover, goalie

| Date | Mintage | VF20 | XF40 | MS60 | MS63 | MS65 |
|---|---|---|---|---|---|---|
| 2005 Specimen | 25,000 | PF65 16.00 | | | | |

### KM# 541 50 CENTS

9.30 g., 0.925 Silver 0.2766 oz. ASW, 27.13 mm. **Ruler:** Elizabeth II **Subject:** Toronto Maple Leafs **Obv:** Head right **Rev:** Tim Horton

| Date | Mintage | VF20 | XF40 | MS60 | MS63 | MS65 |
|---|---|---|---|---|---|---|
| 2005 Specimen | 25,000 | PF65 16.00 | | | | |

### KM# 543 50 CENTS

9.30 g., 0.925 Silver 0.2766 oz. ASW **Ruler:** Elizabeth II **Subject:** WWII - Battle of Britain **Obv:** Head right **Rev:** Fighter plane in sky

| Date | Mintage | VF20 | XF40 | MS60 | MS63 | MS65 |
|---|---|---|---|---|---|---|
| 2005 Specimen | 20,000 | PF65 22.00 | | | | |

### KM# 544 50 CENTS

9.30 g., 0.925 Silver 0.2766 oz. ASW, 27.13 mm. **Ruler:** Elizabeth II **Subject:** WWII - Battle of Scheldt **Obv:** Head right **Rev:** Four soldiers walking down road

| Date | Mintage | VF20 | XF40 | MS60 | MS63 | MS65 |
|---|---|---|---|---|---|---|
| 2005 Specimen | 20,000 | PF65 19.00 | | | | |

### KM# 545 50 CENTS

9.30 g., 0.925 Silver 0.2766 oz. ASW, 27.13 mm. **Ruler:** Elizabeth II **Subject:** WWII - Battle of the Atlantic **Obv:** Head right **Rev:** Merchant ship sinking

| Date | Mintage | VF20 | XF40 | MS60 | MS63 | MS65 |
|---|---|---|---|---|---|---|
| 2005 Specimen | 20,000 | PF65 19.00 | | | | |

### KM# 546 50 CENTS

9.30 g., 0.925 Silver 0.2766 oz. ASW, 27.13 mm. **Ruler:** Elizabeth II **Subject:** WWII - Conquest of Sicily **Obv:** Head right **Rev:** Tank among town ruins

| Date | Mintage | VF20 | XF40 | MS60 | MS63 | MS65 |
|---|---|---|---|---|---|---|
| 2005 Specimen | 20,000 | PF65 19.00 | | | | |

### KM# 547 50 CENTS

9.30 g., 0.925 Silver 0.2766 oz. ASW, 27.13 mm. **Ruler:** Elizabeth II **Subject:** WWII - Liberation of the Netherlands **Obv:** Head right **Rev:** Soldiers in parade, one holding flag

| Date | Mintage | VF20 | XF40 | MS60 | MS63 | MS65 |
|---|---|---|---|---|---|---|
| 2005 Specimen | 20,000 | PF65 19.00 | | | | |

### KM# 548 50 CENTS

9.30 g., 0.925 Silver 0.2766 oz. ASW, 27.13 mm. **Ruler:** Elizabeth II **Subject:** WWII - Raid of Dieppe **Obv:** Head right **Rev:** Three soldiers exiting landing craft

| Date | Mintage | VF20 | XF40 | MS60 | MS63 | MS65 |
|---|---|---|---|---|---|---|
| 2005 Specimen | 20,000 | PF65 19.00 | | | | |

### KM# 577 50 CENTS

9.30 g., 0.925 Silver 0.2766 oz. ASW, 27.13 mm. **Ruler:** Elizabeth II **Subject:** Montreal Canadiens **Obv:** Head right **Rev:** Guy LaFleur

| Date | Mintage | VF20 | XF40 | MS60 | MS63 | MS65 |
|---|---|---|---|---|---|---|
| 2005 Specimen | 25,000 | PF65 17.50 | | | | |

### KM# 578 50 CENTS

9.30 g., 0.925 Silver 0.2766 oz. ASW, 27.13 mm. **Ruler:** Elizabeth II **Subject:** Montreal Canadiens **Obv:** Head right **Rev:** Jaque Plante

| Date | Mintage | VF20 | XF40 | MS60 | MS63 | MS65 |
|---|---|---|---|---|---|---|
| 2005 Specimen | 25,000 | PF65 17.50 | | | | |

### KM# 579 50 CENTS

9.30 g., 0.925 Silver 0.2766 oz. ASW, 27.13 mm. **Ruler:** Elizabeth II **Subject:** Montreal Canadiens **Obv:** Head right **Rev:** Jean Beliveau

| Date | Mintage | VF20 | XF40 | MS60 | MS63 | MS65 |
|---|---|---|---|---|---|---|
| 2005 Specimen | 25,000 | PF65 17.50 | | | | |

### KM# 580 50 CENTS

9.30 g., 0.925 Silver 0.2766 oz. ASW, 27.13 mm. **Ruler:** Elizabeth II **Subject:** Montreal Canadiens **Obv:** Head right **Rev:** Maurice Richard

| Date | Mintage | VF20 | XF40 | MS60 | MS63 | MS65 |
|---|---|---|---|---|---|---|
| 2005 Specimen | 25,000 | PF65 17.50 | | | | |

### KM# 599 50 CENTS

9.30 g., 0.925 Silver 0.2766 oz. ASW, 27.13 mm. **Ruler:** Elizabeth II **Obv:** Head right **Rev:** Monarch butterfly, colorized

| Date | Mintage | VF20 | XF40 | MS60 | MS63 | MS65 |
|---|---|---|---|---|---|---|
| 2005 | 20,000 | PF65 40.00 | | | | |

### KM# 494b 50 CENTS

6.90 g., Nickel Plated Steel partially gilt, 27.13 mm. **Ruler:** Elizabeth II **Rev:** State Arms, gilt **Note:** Housed in Mint Annual Report

| Date | Mintage | VF20 | XF40 | MS60 | MS63 | MS65 |
|---|---|---|---|---|---|---|
| 2006 | — | — | — | — | — | 15.00 |

### KM# 648 50 CENTS

9.30 g., 0.925 Silver 0.2766 oz. ASW partially gilt **Ruler:** Elizabeth II **Subject:** Golden Daisy **Obv:** Head right

| Date | Mintage | VF20 | XF40 | MS60 | MS63 | MS65 |
|---|---|---|---|---|---|---|
| 2006 | 18,190 | PF65 30.00 | | | | |

### KM# 649 50 CENTS

9.30 g., 0.925 Silver 0.2766 oz. ASW, 27.13 mm. **Ruler:** Elizabeth II **Subject:** Short-tailed swallowtail **Obv:** Head right **Rev:** Colorized butterfly

| Date | Mintage | VF20 | XF40 | MS60 | MS63 | MS65 |
|---|---|---|---|---|---|---|
| 2006 | 24,568 | PF65 45.00 | | | | |

### KM# 650 50 CENTS

9.30 g., 0.925 Silver 0.2766 oz. ASW, 27.13 mm. **Ruler:** Elizabeth II **Obv:** Head right **Rev:** Butterfly, silvery blue hologram

| Date | Mintage | VF20 | XF40 | MS60 | MS63 | MS65 |
|---|---|---|---|---|---|---|
| 2006 | 16,000 | PF65 45.00 | | | | |

### KM# 651 50 CENTS

9.30 g., 0.925 Silver 0.2766 oz. ASW **Ruler:** Elizabeth II **Subject:** Cowboy **Obv:** Head right

| Date | Mintage | VF20 | XF40 | MS60 | MS63 | MS65 |
|---|---|---|---|---|---|---|
| 2006 | — | — | — | — | 17.50 | — |

### KM# 716 50 CENTS

9.30 g., 0.925 Silver 0.2766 oz. ASW **Ruler:** Elizabeth II **Rev:** Multicolor holiday ornaments

| Date | Mintage | VF20 | XF40 | MS60 | MS63 | MS65 |
|---|---|---|---|---|---|---|
| 2006 | 16,989 | — | — | — | 17.50 | — |

### KM# 715 50 CENTS

9.30 g., 0.925 Silver 0.2766 oz. ASW with partial gold plating, 27.12 mm. **Ruler:** Elizabeth II **Rev:** Forget-me-not flower

| Date | Mintage | VF20 | XF40 | MS60 | MS63 | MS65 |
|---|---|---|---|---|---|---|
| 2007 | 22,882 | PF65 55.00 | | | | |

### KM# 778 50 CENTS

20.00 g., 0.925 Silver 0.5948 oz. ASW colorized green, 34.06 mm. **Ruler:** Elizabeth II **Subject:** Milk delivery **Obv:** Bust right **Rev:** Cow head and milk can **Shape:** Triangle

| Date | Mintage | VF20 | XF40 | MS60 | MS63 | MS65 |
|---|---|---|---|---|---|---|
| 2008 | 24,448 | PF65 35.00 | | | | |

### KM# 779 50 CENTS

9.30 g., 0.925 Silver 0.2766 oz. ASW, 35 mm. **Ruler:** Elizabeth II **Rev:** Multicolor snowman

| Date | Mintage | VF20 | XF40 | MS60 | MS63 | MS65 |
|---|---|---|---|---|---|---|
| 2008 PL | 21,679 | — | — | — | — | 17.50 |

### KM# 780 50 CENTS

9.30 g., 0.925 Silver 0.2766 oz. ASW, 29.72 mm. **Ruler:** Elizabeth II **Subject:** Ottawa Mint Centennial 1908-2008 **Obv:** Edward bust right **Rev:** Crowned value and dates within wreath

| Date | Mintage | VF20 | XF40 | MS60 | MS63 | MS65 |
|---|---|---|---|---|---|---|
| 2008 | 3,248 | PF65 20.00 | | | | |

### KM# 845 50 CENTS

9.30 g., 0.925 Silver 0.2766 oz. ASW, 27.13 mm. **Ruler:** Elizabeth II **Rev:** Calgary Flames lenticular design, old and new logos

| Date | Mintage | VF20 | XF40 | MS60 | MS63 | MS65 |
|---|---|---|---|---|---|---|
| 2009 | — | — | — | — | — | 17.00 |

### KM# 846 50 CENTS

9.30 g., 0.925 Silver 0.2766 oz. ASW, 27.13 mm. **Ruler:** Elizabeth II **Rev:** Edmonton Oiler's lenticular design, old and new logos

| Date | Mintage | VF20 | XF40 | MS60 | MS63 | MS65 |
|---|---|---|---|---|---|---|
| 2009 | — | — | — | — | — | 17.00 |

### KM# 847 50 CENTS

9.30 g., 0.925 Silver 0.2766 oz. ASW, 27.13 mm. **Ruler:** Elizabeth II **Rev:** Montreal Canadiens lenticular design, old and new logos

| Date | Mintage | VF20 | XF40 | MS60 | MS63 | MS65 |
|---|---|---|---|---|---|---|
| 2009 | — | — | — | — | — | 17.00 |

### KM# 848 50 CENTS

9.30 g., 0.925 Silver 0.2766 oz. ASW, 27.13 mm. **Ruler:** Elizabeth II **Rev:** Ottawa Senators lenticular design, old and new logos

| Date | Mintage | VF20 | XF40 | MS60 | MS63 | MS65 |
|---|---|---|---|---|---|---|
| 2009 | — | — | — | — | — | 17.00 |

### KM# 849 50 CENTS

9.30 g., 0.925 Silver 0.2766 oz. ASW, 27.13 mm. **Ruler:** Elizabeth II **Rev:** Toronto Maple Leafs lenticular design, old and new logos

| Date | Mintage | VF20 | XF40 | MS60 | MS63 | MS65 |
|---|---|---|---|---|---|---|
| 2009 | — | — | — | — | — | 17.00 |

### KM# 850 50 CENTS

9.30 g., 0.925 Silver 0.2766 oz. ASW, 27.13 mm. **Ruler:** Elizabeth II **Rev:** Vancouver Canucks lenticular design, old and new logos

| Date | Mintage | VF20 | XF40 | MS60 | MS63 | MS65 |
|---|---|---|---|---|---|---|
| 2009 | — | — | — | — | — | 17.00 |

### KM# 857 50 CENTS

6.90 g., Nickel Plated Steel, 35 mm. **Ruler:** Elizabeth II **Rev:** Calgary Flames lenticular old and new logos

| Date | Mintage | VF20 | XF40 | MS60 | MS63 | MS65 |
|---|---|---|---|---|---|---|
| 2009 | — | — | — | — | 25.00 | — |

### KM# 858 50 CENTS

6.90 g., Nickel Plated Steel, 35 mm. **Ruler:** Elizabeth II **Rev:** Edmonton Oilers lenticular old and new logos

| Date | Mintage | VF20 | XF40 | MS60 | MS63 | MS65 |
|---|---|---|---|---|---|---|
| 2009 | — | — | — | — | 25.00 | — |

### KM# 859 50 CENTS

35.00 g., Nickel Plated Steel, 35 mm. **Ruler:** Elizabeth II **Rev:** Montreal Canadians lenticular old and new logo

| Date | Mintage | VF20 | XF40 | MS60 | MS63 | MS65 |
|---|---|---|---|---|---|---|
| 2009 | — | — | — | — | 25.00 | — |

### KM# 860 50 CENTS

6.90 g., Nickel Plated Steel, 35 mm. **Ruler:** Elizabeth II **Rev:** Ottawa Senators lenticular old and new logos

| Date | Mintage | VF20 | XF40 | MS60 | MS63 | MS65 |
|---|---|---|---|---|---|---|
| 2009 | — | — | — | — | 25.00 | — |

### KM# 861 50 CENTS

6.90 g., Nickel Plated Steel, 35 mm. **Ruler:** Elizabeth II **Rev:** Toronto Maple Leafs lenticular old and new logos

| Date | Mintage | VF20 | XF40 | MS60 | MS63 | MS65 |
|---|---|---|---|---|---|---|
| 2009 | — | — | — | — | 25.00 | — |

### KM# 862 50 CENTS

6.90 g., Nickel Plated Steel, 35 mm. **Ruler:** Elizabeth II **Rev:** Vancouver Canucks lenticular old and new logos

| Date | Mintage | VF20 | XF40 | MS60 | MS63 | MS65 |
|---|---|---|---|---|---|---|
| 2009 | — | — | — | — | 25.00 | — |

### KM# 887 50 CENTS

19.10 g., Copper-Nickel, 34.06 mm. **Ruler:** Elizabeth II **Subject:** Six-string national guitar **Obv:** Bust right **Obv. Legend:** Elizabeth II DG Regina **Rev:** Hologram with 6 "strings **Rev. Legend:** 50 CENTS Canada **Shape:** Triangle

| Date | Mintage | VF20 | XF40 | MS60 | MS63 | MS65 |
|---|---|---|---|---|---|---|
| 2009 | 13,602 | **PF65** 35.00 | | | | |

### KM# 936 50 CENTS

9.30 g., Nickel **Ruler:** Elizabeth II **Rev:** Vancouver Canucks goalie jersey

| Date | Mintage | VF20 | XF40 | MS60 | MS63 | MS65 |
|---|---|---|---|---|---|---|
| 2009 | 3,563 | — | — | — | 15.00 | — |

### KM# 937 50 CENTS

6.90 g., Nickel Plated Steel, 35 mm. **Ruler:** Elizabeth II **Rev:** Calgary Flames player - colorized

| Date | Mintage | VF20 | XF40 | MS60 | MS63 | MS65 |
|---|---|---|---|---|---|---|
| 2009 | 3,518 | — | — | — | 15.00 | — |

### KM# 938 50 CENTS

6.90 g., Nickel Plated Steel, 35 mm. **Ruler:** Elizabeth II **Rev:** Edmonton Oilers player

| Date | Mintage | VF20 | XF40 | MS60 | MS63 | MS65 |
|---|---|---|---|---|---|---|
| 2009 | 3,562 | — | — | — | 15.00 | — |

### KM# 939 50 CENTS

6.90 g., Nickel Plated Steel, 35 mm. **Ruler:** Elizabeth II **Rev:** Toronto Maple Leafs player

| Date | Mintage | VF20 | XF40 | MS60 | MS63 | MS65 |
|---|---|---|---|---|---|---|
| 2009 | 5,918 | — | — | — | 15.00 | — |

### KM# 940 50 CENTS

6.90 g., Nickel Plated Steel, 35 mm. **Ruler:** Elizabeth II **Rev:** Montreal Canadiens player

| Date | Mintage | VF20 | XF40 | MS60 | MS63 | MS65 |
|---|---|---|---|---|---|---|
| 2009 | 9,865 | — | — | — | 15.00 | — |

### KM# 941 50 CENTS

6.90 g., Nickel Plated Steel, 35 mm. **Ruler:** Elizabeth II **Rev:** Ottawa Senators player

| Date | Mintage | VF20 | XF40 | MS60 | MS63 | MS65 |
|---|---|---|---|---|---|---|
| 2009 | 3,293 | — | — | — | 15.00 | — |

### KM# 1035 50 CENTS

12.61 g., Brass Plated Steel, 35 mm. **Ruler:** Elizabeth II **Subject:** Christmas toy train **Rev:** movement from far to close

| Date | Mintage | VF20 | XF40 | MS60 | MS63 | MS65 |
|---|---|---|---|---|---|---|
| 2009 | 19,103 | — | — | — | — | 26.00 |

### KM# 961 50 CENTS

6.90 g., Nickel Plated Steel, 35 mm. **Ruler:** Elizabeth II **Rev:** Bob sleigh

| Date | Mintage | VF20 | XF40 | MS60 | MS63 | MS65 |
|---|---|---|---|---|---|---|
| 2010 | — | — | — | — | 12.00 | — |

### KM# 961a 50 CENTS

6.90 g., Nickel Plated Steel, 35 mm. **Ruler:** Elizabeth II **Rev:** Bob sleigh - red enamel

| Date | Mintage | VF20 | XF40 | MS60 | MS63 | MS65 |
|---|---|---|---|---|---|---|
| 2010 | — | — | — | — | 12.00 | — |

### KM# 962 50 CENTS

6.90 g., Nickel Plated Steel, 35 mm. **Ruler:** Elizabeth II **Rev:** Speed skating

| Date | Mintage | VF20 | XF40 | MS60 | MS63 | MS65 |
|---|---|---|---|---|---|---|
| 2010 | — | — | — | — | 12.00 | — |

### KM# 962a 50 CENTS

6.90 g., Nickel Plated Steel, 35 mm. **Ruler:** Elizabeth II **Rev:** Speed skating - red enamel

| Date | Mintage | VF20 | XF40 | MS60 | MS63 | MS65 |
|---|---|---|---|---|---|---|
| 2010 | — | — | — | — | 12.00 | — |

### KM# 963 50 CENTS

6.90 g., Nickel Plated Steel, 35 mm. **Ruler:** Elizabeth II **Rev:** Migaand Quatchi in bob sleigh

| Date | Mintage | VF20 | XF40 | MS60 | MS63 | MS65 |
|---|---|---|---|---|---|---|
| 2010 | 2,119 | — | — | — | — | 9.00 |

### KM# 964 50 CENTS

6.90 g., Nickel Plated Steel, 35 mm. **Ruler:** Elizabeth II **Rev:** Miga in hockey

| Date | Mintage | VF20 | XF40 | MS60 | MS63 | MS65 |
|---|---|---|---|---|---|---|
| 2010 | 5,275 | — | — | — | — | 9.00 |

### KM# 965 50 CENTS

6.90 g., Nickel Plated Steel, 35 mm. **Ruler:** Elizabeth II **Rev:** Quatchi in ice hockey

| Date | Mintage | VF20 | XF40 | MS60 | MS63 | MS65 |
|---|---|---|---|---|---|---|
| 2010 | 5,614 | — | — | — | — | 9.00 |

### KM# 966 50 CENTS

6.90 g., Nickel Plated Steel, 35 mm. **Ruler:** Elizabeth II **Rev:** Sumi Para Sledge

| Date | Mintage | VF20 | XF40 | MS60 | MS63 | MS65 |
|---|---|---|---|---|---|---|
| 2010 | 3,707 | — | — | — | — | 9.00 |

### KM# 967 50 CENTS

6.90 g., Nickel Plated Steel, 35 mm. **Ruler:** Elizabeth II **Rev:** Miga and Quatchi Figure-skating **Edge:** Reeded

| Date | Mintage | VF20 | XF40 | MS60 | MS63 | MS65 |
|---|---|---|---|---|---|---|
| 2010 | 2,981 | — | — | — | — | 9.00 |

### KM# 968 50 CENTS

6.90 g., Nickel Plated Steel, 35 mm. **Ruler:** Elizabeth II **Rev:** Free-style mascot

| Date | Mintage | VF20 | XF40 | MS60 | MS63 | MS65 |
|---|---|---|---|---|---|---|
| 2010 | 2,114 | — | — | — | — | 9.00 |

**KM# 969 50 CENTS**
6.90 g., Nickel Plated Steel, 35 mm. **Ruler:** Elizabeth II **Rev:** Skeleton mascot

| Date | Mintage | VF20 | XF40 | MS60 | MS63 | MS65 |
|---|---|---|---|---|---|---|
| 2010 | 1,672 | — | — | — | — | 9.00 |

**KM# 970 50 CENTS**
6.90 g., Nickel Plated Steel, 35 mm. **Ruler:** Elizabeth II **Rev:** Parallel giant slalom mascot

| Date | Mintage | VF20 | XF40 | MS60 | MS63 | MS65 |
|---|---|---|---|---|---|---|
| 2010 | 1,730 | — | — | — | — | 9.00 |

**KM# 971 50 CENTS**
6.90 g., Nickel Plated Steel, 35 mm. **Ruler:** Elizabeth II **Rev:** Alpine skiing mascot

| Date | Mintage | VF20 | XF40 | MS60 | MS63 | MS65 |
|---|---|---|---|---|---|---|
| 2010 | 2,309 | — | — | — | — | 9.00 |

**KM# 972 50 CENTS**
6.90 g., Nickel Plated Steel, 35 mm. **Ruler:** Elizabeth II **Rev:** Para Olympic alpine skiing mascott

| Date | Mintage | VF20 | XF40 | MS60 | MS63 | MS65 |
|---|---|---|---|---|---|---|
| 2010 | 1,902 | — | — | — | — | 9.00 |

**KM# 973 50 CENTS**
6.90 g., Nickel Plated Steel, 35 mm. **Ruler:** Elizabeth II **Rev:** Snowboard mascot

| Date | Mintage | VF20 | XF40 | MS60 | MS63 | MS65 |
|---|---|---|---|---|---|---|
| 2010 | 2,090 | — | — | — | — | 9.00 |

**KM# 974 50 CENTS**
6.90 g., Nickel Plated Steel, 35 mm. **Ruler:** Elizabeth II **Rev:** Speed-skating mascott

| Date | Mintage | VF20 | XF40 | MS60 | MS63 | MS65 |
|---|---|---|---|---|---|---|
| 2010 | 1,825 | — | — | — | — | 9.00 |

**KM# 986 50 CENTS**
12.61 g., Brass Plated Steel, 35 mm. **Ruler:** Elizabeth II **Rev:** Dasplerosaurus Torosus - 3-D lenticular movement

| Date | Mintage | VF20 | XF40 | MS60 | MS63 | MS65 |
|---|---|---|---|---|---|---|
| 2010 | — | — | — | — | — | 18.00 |

**KM# 1015 50 CENTS**
12.61 g., Brass Plated Steel, 35 mm. **Ruler:** Elizabeth II **Rev:** Sinosauropteryx

| Date | Mintage | VF20 | XF40 | MS60 | MS63 | MS65 |
|---|---|---|---|---|---|---|
| 2010 | — | — | — | — | — | 18.00 |

**KM# 1016 50 CENTS**
12.61 g., Brass Plated Steel, 35 mm. **Ruler:** Elizabeth II **Rev:** Albertosaurus

| Date | Mintage | VF20 | XF40 | MS60 | MS63 | MS65 |
|---|---|---|---|---|---|---|
| 2010 | — | — | — | — | — | 18.00 |

**KM# 1043 50 CENTS**
Nickel Plated Steel, 34 mm. **Ruler:** Elizabeth II **Rev:** Santa Claus transforms into Rudolf the red-nosed reindeer

| Date | Mintage | VF20 | XF40 | MS60 | MS63 | MS65 |
|---|---|---|---|---|---|---|
| 2010 | — | — | — | — | — | 17.50 |

**KM# 1157 50 CENTS**
11.62 g., 0.925 Silver 0.3456 oz. ASW, 29.72 mm. **Ruler:** Elizabeth II **Obv:** George V bust **Rev:** Value within wreath

| Date | Mintage | VF20 | XF40 | MS60 | MS63 | MS65 |
|---|---|---|---|---|---|---|
| 1911-2011 | 6,000 | PF65 45.00 | | | | |

**KM# 1180 50 CENTS**
6.90 g., Nickel Plated Steel, 27.13 mm. **Ruler:** Elizabeth II **Obv:** Bust right **Rev:** Winnipeg Jets Logo, jet over maple leaf **Edge:** Reeded

| Date | Mintage | VF20 | XF40 | MS60 | MS63 | MS65 |
|---|---|---|---|---|---|---|
| 2011 | — | — | — | — | — | 13.00 |

**KM# 1191 50 CENTS**
12.61 g., Copper Plated Steel, 35 mm. **Ruler:** Elizabeth II **Obv:** Bust right **Rev:** Santa Claus checking list, and in sled over house

| Date | Mintage | VF20 | XF40 | MS60 | MS63 | MS65 |
|---|---|---|---|---|---|---|
| 2011 | — | — | — | — | — | 24.00 |

**KM# 1202 50 CENTS**
1.27 g., 0.9999 Gold 0.0408 oz. AGW, 13.92 mm. **Ruler:** Elizabeth II **Rev:** Wood Bison **Edge:** Reeded

| Date | Mintage | VF20 | XF40 | MS60 | MS63 | MS65 |
|---|---|---|---|---|---|---|
| 2011 | Est. 2500 | PF65 100 | | | | |

**KM# 1204 50 CENTS**
1.27 g., 0.9999 Gold 0.0408 oz. AGW, 13.92 mm. **Ruler:** Elizabeth II **Subject:** Boreal Forest **Rev:** Bird and tree **Edge:** Reeded

| Date | Mintage | VF20 | XF40 | MS60 | MS63 | MS65 |
|---|---|---|---|---|---|---|
| 2011 | Est. 2500 | PF65 100 | | | | |

**KM# 1206 50 CENTS**
1.27 g., 0.9999 Gold 0.0408 oz. AGW, 13.92 mm. **Ruler:** Elizabeth II **Rev:** Peregrine Falcon perched on branch

| Date | Mintage | VF20 | XF40 | MS60 | MS63 | MS65 |
|---|---|---|---|---|---|---|
| 2011 | Est. 2500 | PF65 100 | | | | |

**KM# 1208 50 CENTS**
1.27 g., 0.9999 Gold 0.0408 oz. AGW, 13.92 mm. **Ruler:** Elizabeth II **Rev:** Orca Whale **Edge:** Reeded

| Date | Mintage | VF20 | XF40 | MS60 | MS63 | MS65 |
|---|---|---|---|---|---|---|
| 2011 | Est. 2500 | PF65 100 | | | | |

**KM# 1234 50 CENTS**
12.61 g., Nickel Plated Steel, 35 mm. **Ruler:** Elizabeth II **Subject:** Titanic, 100th Anniversary **Obv:** Bust right **Rev:** Titanic sailing forward towards iceberg, colored sea

| Date | Mintage | VF20 | XF40 | MS60 | MS63 | MS65 |
|---|---|---|---|---|---|---|
| 2012 | — | PF65 65.00 | | | | |

**KM# 1264 50 CENTS**
1.27 g., 0.999 Gold 0.0408 oz. AGW, 13.92 mm. **Ruler:** Elizabeth II **Subject:** Gold Rush

| Date | Mintage | F12 | VF20 | XF40 | MS60 | MS63 |
|---|---|---|---|---|---|---|
| 2012 | — | PF65 100 | | | | |

**KM# 1293 50 CENTS**
9.30 g., 0.925 Silver 0.2766 oz. ASW, 27.13 mm. **Ruler:** Elizabeth II **Subject:** Elizabeth II Diamond Jubilee **Rev:** Crowned monogram within wreath in color

| Date | Mintage | VF20 | XF40 | MS60 | MS63 | MS65 |
|---|---|---|---|---|---|---|
| 2012 | — | — | — | — | — | 18.00 |

**KM# 1348 50 CENTS**
1.27 g., 0.9999 Gold 0.0408 oz. AGW, 13.92 mm. **Ruler:** Elizabeth II **Rev:** Bald eagle head left

| Date | Mintage | VF20 | XF40 | MS60 | MS63 | MS65 |
|---|---|---|---|---|---|---|
| 2013 | 10,000 | PF63 120 | PF65 130 | | | |

**KM# 1349 50 CENTS**
1.27 g., 0.9999 Gold 0.0408 oz. AGW, 13.92 mm. **Ruler:** Elizabeth II **Subject:** Inuit Art by Joanassie Nowkawalk

| Date | Mintage | VF20 | XF40 | MS60 | MS63 | MS65 |
|---|---|---|---|---|---|---|
| 2013 | 10,000 | PF63 120 | PF65 130 | | | |

**KM# 1435 50 CENTS**
Silver Plated Copper-Nickel, 35 mm. **Ruler:** Elizabeth II **Rev:** Canadian Tiger Swallowtail Butterfly in color

| Date | Mintage | VF20 | XF40 | MS60 | MS63 | MS65 |
|---|---|---|---|---|---|---|
| 2013 | Est. 20000 | PF65 30.00 | | | | |

**KM# 1444 50 CENTS**
12.51 g., Copper-Nickel, 35 mm. **Ruler:** Elizabeth II **Subject:** 75th Anniversary of Superman **Rev:** Superman lenticular background - then and now

| Date | Mintage | VF20 | XF40 | MS60 | MS63 | MS65 |
|---|---|---|---|---|---|---|
| 2013 | — | PF65 30.00 | | | | |

**KM# 1493 50 CENTS**
1.27 g., 0.9999 Gold 0.0408 oz. AGW, 13.92 mm. **Ruler:** Elizabeth II **Rev:** Starfish

| Date | Mintage | VF20 | XF40 | MS60 | MS63 | MS65 |
|---|---|---|---|---|---|---|
| 2013 | 10,000 | PF65 130 | | | | |

**KM# 1496 50 CENTS**
1.27 g., 0.9999 Gold 0.0408 oz. AGW, 13.92 mm. **Ruler:** Elizabeth II **Subject:** Louisbourg, 300th Anniversary **Rev:** Ship, fort gate and fish

| Date | Mintage | VF20 | XF40 | MS60 | MS63 | MS65 |
|---|---|---|---|---|---|---|
| 2013 | 1,000 | PF65 100 | | | | |

**KM# 1523 50 CENTS**
Copper-Nickel, 35 mm. **Ruler:** Elizabeth II **Rev:** Snowman, leniticular

| Date | Mintage | VF20 | XF40 | MS60 | MS63 | MS65 |
|---|---|---|---|---|---|---|
| 2013 | 20,000 | — | — | — | — | 27.00 |

**KM# 1545 50 CENTS**
Silver 31.9118 oz. ASW **Ruler:** Elizabeth II **Rev:** Superman in color **Note:** Requires confirmation.

| Date | Mintage | VF20 | XF40 | MS60 | MS63 | MS65 |
|---|---|---|---|---|---|---|
| 2013 | — | PF65 40.00 | | | | |

**KM# 1584 50 CENTS**
1.27 g., 0.999 Gold 0.0408 oz. AGW, 13.92 mm. **Ruler:** Elizabeth II **Obv:** Bust right **Rev:** Beaver left from 5 Cent coin

| Date | Mintage | VF20 | XF40 | MS60 | MS63 | MS65 |
|---|---|---|---|---|---|---|
| 2014 | — | PF65 90.00 | | | | |

**KM# 1585 50 CENTS**
Silver Plated, 35 mm. **Ruler:** Elizabeth II **Subject:** 100 Blessings of Good Fortune **Obv:** Bust right

| Date | Mintage | VF20 | XF40 | MS60 | MS63 | MS65 |
|---|---|---|---|---|---|---|
| 2014 | — | PF65 50.00 | | | | |

**KM# 1636 50 CENTS**
12.61 g., Silver Plated Copper-Nickel, 35 mm. **Ruler:** Elizabeth II **Obv:** Bust right **Rev:** Empress of Ireland

| Date | Mintage | F12 | VF20 | XF40 | MS60 | MS63 |
|---|---|---|---|---|---|---|
| 2014 | — | PF63 30.00 | PF65 35.00 | | | |

**KM# 1752 50 CENTS**
1.24 g., 0.999 Gold 0.0398 oz. AGW, 13.92 mm. **Ruler:** Elizabeth II **Subject:** Charlottetown **Obv:** Bust right **Rev:** Views within maple leaf

| Date | Mintage | VF20 | XF40 | MS60 | MS63 | MS65 |
|---|---|---|---|---|---|---|
| 2014 | — | PF65 100 | | | | |

**KM# 1775 50 CENTS**
13.70 g., Copper-Nickel, 35 mm. **Ruler:** Elizabeth II **Obv:** Bust right **Rev:** Christmas Tree lenticular

| Date | Mintage | VF20 | XF40 | MS60 | MS63 | MS65 |
|---|---|---|---|---|---|---|
| 2014 | 20,000 | PF65 30.00 | | | | |

**KM# 1842 50 CENTS**
1.27 g., 0.9999 Gold 0.0408 oz. AGW, 13.92 mm. **Ruler:** Elizabeth II **Obv:** Bust right **Rev:** Maple leaf above flag

| Date | Mintage | VF20 | XF40 | MS60 | MS63 | MS65 |
|---|---|---|---|---|---|---|
| 2015 | — | PF65 100 | | | | |

**KM# 1589 DOLLAR**
7.00 g., Aluminum-Bronze, 26.5 mm. **Ruler:** Elizabeth II **Subject:** Birthday Loon **Obv:** Bust right **Rev:** Party hats, decorations, presents

| Date | Mintage | VF20 | XF40 | MS60 | MS63 | MS65 |
|---|---|---|---|---|---|---|
| 2014 | — | — | — | — | — | — |

**KM# 186 DOLLAR**
7.00 g., Aureate-Bronze Plated Nickel, 26.5 mm. **Ruler:** Elizabeth II **Obv:** Crowned head right **Rev:** Loon right, date and denomination **Shape:** 11-sided

| Date | Mintage | VF20 | XF40 | MS60 | MS63 | MS65 |
|---|---|---|---|---|---|---|
| 2001 PL | — | — | — | — | — | 6.00 |
| 2001 | 74,194 | PF65 8.00 | | | | |
| 2002 | — | — | — | — | 3.50 | 22.00 |
| 2002 | 65,315 | PF65 10.00 | | | | |
| 2003 | — | — | — | — | 3.50 | 22.00 |

Note: Mintage of 5,101,000 includes both KM186 and KM495 examples.

| Date | Mintage | VF20 | XF40 | MS60 | MS63 | MS65 |
|---|---|---|---|---|---|---|
| 2003 | — | PF65 12.00 | | | | |

## KM# 414 DOLLAR

25.18 g., 0.925 Silver 0.7487 oz. ASW, 36 mm. **Ruler:** Elizabeth II **Subject:** National Ballet **Obv:** Crowned head right **Rev:** Ballet dancers **Edge:** Reeded

| Date | Mintage | VF20 | XF40 | MS60 | MS63 | MS65 |
|---|---|---|---|---|---|---|
| 2001 | 65,000 | — | — | — | — | 21.00 |
| 2001 | — | PF65 29.00 | | | | |

## KM# 434 DOLLAR

25.18 g., 0.925 Silver 0.7487 oz. ASW, 36 mm. **Ruler:** Elizabeth II **Obv:** Crowned head right **Rev:** Recycled 1911 pattern dollar design: denomination, country name and dates in crowned wreath **Edge:** Reeded

| Date | Mintage | VF20 | XF40 | MS60 | MS63 | MS65 |
|---|---|---|---|---|---|---|
| 1911-2001 | 24,996 | PF65 55.00 | | | | |

## KM# 186a DOLLAR

Gilt Aureate-Bronze Plated Nickel, 26.5 mm. **Ruler:** Elizabeth II **Subject:** Olympic Win

| Date | Mintage | VF20 | XF40 | MS60 | MS63 | MS65 |
|---|---|---|---|---|---|---|
| 2002 | — | PF65 40.00 | | | | |

## KM# 443 DOLLAR

25.18 g., 0.925 Silver 0.7487 oz. ASW, 36 mm. **Ruler:** Elizabeth II **Subject:** Queen's Golden Jubilee **Obv:** Crowned head right, with anniversary date at left **Rev:** Queen in her coach and a view of the coach, denomination below **Edge:** Reeded

| Date | Mintage | VF20 | XF40 | MS60 | MS63 | MS65 |
|---|---|---|---|---|---|---|
| 1952-2002 | 65,140 | — | — | — | — | 21.00 |
| 1952-2002 | 29,688 | PF65 29.00 | | | | |

## KM# 443a DOLLAR

25.18 g., 0.925 Silver Gilt 0.7488 oz., 36 mm. **Ruler:** Elizabeth II **Subject:** Queen's Golden Jubilee **Obv:** Crowned head right with anniversary date **Rev:** Queen in her coach and a view of the coach **Edge:** Reeded **Note:** Special 24 karat gold plated issue of KM#443.

| Date | Mintage | VF20 | XF40 | MS60 | MS63 | MS65 |
|---|---|---|---|---|---|---|
| 2002 | 32,642 | PF65 45.00 | | | | |

## KM# 462 DOLLAR

7.00 g., Aureate-Bronze Plated Nickel, 26 mm. **Ruler:** Elizabeth II **Obv:** Commemorative dates 1952-2002 **Rev:** Family of Loons

| Date | Mintage | VF20 | XF40 | MS60 | MS63 | MS65 |
|---|---|---|---|---|---|---|
| 2002 Specimen | 67,672 | — | — | — | — | 25.00 |

## KM# 467 DOLLAR

7.00 g., Aureate-Bronze Plated Nickel **Ruler:** Elizabeth II **Subject:** Elizabeth II Golden Jubilee **Obv:** Crowned head right, Jubilee commemorative dates 1952-2002

| Date | Mintage | VF20 | XF40 | MS60 | MS63 | MS65 |
|---|---|---|---|---|---|---|
| 2002 | 2,302,000 | — | — | — | 2.50 | — |
| 2002 | — | PF65 8.00 | | | | |

## KM# 467a DOLLAR

Gold **Ruler:** Elizabeth II **Subject:** 50th Anniversary, Accession to the Throne **Obv:** Crowned head right **Note:** Sold on the internet.

| Date | Mintage | VF20 | XF40 | MS60 | MS63 | MS65 |
|---|---|---|---|---|---|---|
| 2002 | 1 | PF65 55,500 | | | | |

## KM# 503 DOLLAR

25.18 g., 0.925 Silver 0.7487 oz. ASW, 36 mm. **Ruler:** Elizabeth II **Subject:** Queen Mother **Obv:** Crowned head right **Rev:** Queen Mother facing

| Date | Mintage | VF20 | XF40 | MS60 | MS63 | MS65 |
|---|---|---|---|---|---|---|
| 2002 | 9,994 | PF65 225 | | | | |

## KM# 450 DOLLAR

25.18 g., 0.9999 Silver 0.8093 oz. ASW, 36 mm. **Ruler:** Elizabeth II **Subject:** Cobalt Mining Centennial **Obv:** Queens portrait right **Rev:** Mine tower and fox **Edge:** Reeded

| Date | Mintage | VF20 | XF40 | MS60 | MS63 | MS65 |
|---|---|---|---|---|---|---|
| 2003 | 51,130 | — | — | — | — | 20.00 |
| 2003 | 88,536 | PF65 30.00 | | | | |

## KM# 473 DOLLAR

25.18 g., 0.9999 Silver 0.8093 oz. ASW **Ruler:** Elizabeth II **Subject:** 50th Anniversary of the Coronation of Elizabeth II **Obv:** 1953 effigy of the Queen, Jubilee dates 1953-2003 **Rev:** Voyageur, date and denomination below

| Date | Mintage | VF20 | XF40 | MS60 | MS63 | MS65 |
|---|---|---|---|---|---|---|
| 1953-2003 | 21,537 | PF65 45.00 | | | | |

## KM# 480 DOLLAR

25.18 g., 0.9999 Silver 0.8093 oz. ASW **Ruler:** Elizabeth II **Subject:** Coronation of Queen Elizabeth II **Obv:** Head right **Rev:** Voyaguers

| Date | Mintage | VF20 | XF40 | MS60 | MS63 | MS65 |
|---|---|---|---|---|---|---|
| 1953-2003 | 29,586 | PF65 50.00 | | | | |

## KM# 495 DOLLAR

7.00 g., Aureate-Bronze Plated Nickel, 26.5 mm. **Ruler:** Elizabeth II **Obv:** Bare head right **Rev:** Loon right **Shape:** 11-sided

| Date | Mintage | VF20 | XF40 | MS60 | MS63 | MS65 |
|---|---|---|---|---|---|---|
| 2003 | 5,102,000 | — | — | — | 3.50 | 22.00 |
| Note: Mintage of 5,101,000 includes both KM 186 and 495 examples. | | | | | | |
| 2003 W Prooflike | — | — | — | — | — | 7.50 |
| 2003 | 62,507 | PF65 12.00 | | | | |
| 2004 | 10,894,000 | — | — | — | 2.50 | 22.00 |
| 2004 | — | PF65 12.00 | | | | |
| 2005 | 44,375,000 | — | — | — | 3.00 | 22.00 |
| 2005 | — | PF65 10.00 | | | | |
| 2006 | 49,111,000 | — | — | — | 3.00 | — |
| 2006 | — | PF65 7.50 | | | | |
| 2006 (ml) | 49,111,000 | — | — | — | 2.25 | 13.00 |
| 2006 (ml) | — | PF65 7.50 | | | | |
| 2007 (ml) | 38,045,000 | — | — | — | 2.25 | 22.00 |
| 2007 (ml) | — | PF65 7.50 | | | | |
| 2008 (ml) | 29,561,000 | — | — | — | 2.25 | 22.00 |
| 2008 (ml) | — | PF65 7.50 | | | | |
| 2009 (ml) | 39,601,000 | — | — | — | 2.25 | 22.00 |
| 2009 (ml) | — | PF65 7.50 | | | | |
| 2010 (ml) | — | — | — | — | 2.25 | 22.00 |
| 2010 (ml) | — | PF65 7.50 | | | | |
| 2011 (ml) | — | — | — | — | 2.25 | 22.00 |
| 2011 (ml) | — | PF65 7.50 | | | | |
| 2012 (ml) | — | — | — | — | 2.25 | 22.00 |
| 2012 (ml) | — | PF65 10.00 | | | | |

## KM# 480a DOLLAR

Gold **Ruler:** Elizabeth II **Subject:** 50th Anniversary of Coronation **Rev:** Voyageur **Note:** Sold on the internet.

| Date | Mintage | VF20 | XF40 | MS60 | MS63 | MS65 |
|---|---|---|---|---|---|---|
| 1953-2003 | 1 | PF65 60,000 | | | | |

## KM# 507 DOLLAR

7.00 g., Aureate-Bronze Plated Nickel, 26.5 mm. **Ruler:** Elizabeth II **Obv:** Bare head right, date below **Rev:** Loon **Edge:** Plain **Shape:** 11-sided

| Date | Mintage | VF20 | XF40 | MS60 | MS63 | MS65 |
|---|---|---|---|---|---|---|
| 2004 | 25,105 | PF65 40.00 | | | | |

## KM# 511 DOLLAR

25.18 g., 0.9999 Silver 0.8093 oz. ASW, 36 mm. **Ruler:** Elizabeth II **Obv:** Elizabeth II **Rev:** Poppy on maple leaf **Edge:** Reeded

| Date | Mintage | VF20 | XF40 | MS60 | MS63 | MS65 |
|---|---|---|---|---|---|---|
| 2004 | 24,527 | PF65 50.00 | | | | |

## KM# 512 DOLLAR

25.18 g., 0.9999 Silver 0.8093 oz. ASW, 36 mm. **Ruler:** Elizabeth II **Subject:** First French Settlement in America **Obv:** Crowned head right **Rev:** Sailing ship **Edge:** Reeded

| Date | Mintage | VF20 | XF40 | MS60 | MS63 | MS65 |
|---|---|---|---|---|---|---|
| 2004 | 42,582 | — | — | — | — | 20.00 |
| 2004 Fleur-dis-lis privy mark | 8,315 | — | — | — | — | 60.00 |
| 2004 | 106,974 | PF65 30.00 | | | | |

## KM# 513 DOLLAR

7.00 g., Aureate-Bronze Plated Nickel, 26.5 mm. **Ruler:** Elizabeth II **Subject:** Olympics **Obv:** Bare head right **Rev:** Maple leaf, Olympic flame and rings above loon **Edge:** Plain **Shape:** 11-sided

| Date | Mintage | VF20 | XF40 | MS60 | MS63 | MS65 |
|---|---|---|---|---|---|---|
| 2004 | 6,526,000 | — | — | — | 3.50 | 22.00 |

## KM# 513a DOLLAR

9.31 g., 0.925 Silver 0.2769 oz. ASW, 26.5 mm. **Ruler:** Elizabeth II **Subject:** Olympics **Obv:** Bare head right **Rev:** Multicolor maple leaf, Olympic flame and rings above loon **Edge:** Plain **Shape:** 11-sided

| Date | Mintage | VF20 | XF40 | MS60 | MS63 | MS65 |
|---|---|---|---|---|---|---|
| 2004 | 19,994 | PF65 50.00 | | | | |

**KM# 549 DOLLAR**
25.18 g., 0.925 Silver 0.7487 oz. ASW, 36.07 mm. **Ruler:** Elizabeth II **Subject:** 40th Anniversary of National Flag **Obv:** Head right

| Date | Mintage | VF20 | XF40 | MS60 | MS63 | MS65 |
|---|---|---|---|---|---|---|
| 2005 | 50,948 | — | — | — | — | 22.00 |
| 2005 | 95,431 | PF65 35.00 | | | | |

**KM# 549a DOLLAR**
25.18 g., 0.925 Silver 0.7487 oz. ASW partially gilt, 36.07 mm. **Ruler:** Elizabeth II **Subject:** 40th Anniversary of National Flag **Obv:** Head right **Rev:** Flag partially gilt, fireworks, parliament tower

| Date | Mintage | VF20 | XF40 | MS60 | MS63 | MS65 |
|---|---|---|---|---|---|---|
| 2005 | 62,562 | — | — | — | — | 65.00 |

**KM# 549b DOLLAR**
25.18 g., 0.925 Silver 0.7488 oz. ASW, 36.07 mm. **Ruler:** Elizabeth II **Subject:** 40th Anniversary National Flag **Rev:** National flag, colorized

| Date | Mintage | VF20 | XF40 | MS60 | MS63 | MS65 |
|---|---|---|---|---|---|---|
| 2005 | 4,898 | PF65 225 | | | | |

**KM# 552 DOLLAR**
7.00 g., Aureate-Bronze Plated Nickel, 26.5 mm. **Ruler:** Elizabeth II **Obv:** Head right **Rev:** Terry Fox walking left

| Date | Mintage | VF20 | XF40 | MS60 | MS63 | MS65 |
|---|---|---|---|---|---|---|
| 2005 | 1,290,900 | — | — | — | 2.50 | 22.00 |

**KM# 553 DOLLAR**
7.00 g., Aureate-Bronze Plated Nickel **Ruler:** Elizabeth II **Subject:** Tuffed Puffin **Obv:** Head right

| Date | Mintage | VF20 | XF40 | MS60 | MS63 | MS65 |
|---|---|---|---|---|---|---|
| 2005 PL | 39,818 | — | — | — | — | 30.00 |

**KM# 581 DOLLAR**
9.31 g., 0.925 Silver 0.2769 oz. ASW **Ruler:** Elizabeth II **Subject:** Lullabies Loonie **Obv:** Head right **Rev:** Loon and moon, teddy bear in stars **Edge:** 11-sided **Shape:** 26.5

| Date | Mintage | VF20 | XF40 | MS60 | MS63 | MS65 |
|---|---|---|---|---|---|---|
| 2006 | 18,103 | — | — | — | — | 35.00 |

**KM# 582 DOLLAR**
7.00 g., Aureate-Bronze Plated Nickel, 26.5 mm. **Ruler:** Elizabeth II **Subject:** Snowy owl **Obv:** Head right **Rev:** Snowy owl with year above

| Date | Mintage | VF20 | XF40 | MS60 | MS63 | MS65 |
|---|---|---|---|---|---|---|
| 2006 Specimen | 39,935 | PF65 30.00 | | | | |

**KM# 583 DOLLAR**
25.18 g., 0.925 Silver 0.7487 oz. ASW, 36 mm. **Ruler:** Elizabeth II **Obv:** Head right **Rev:** Victoria Cross

| Date | Mintage | VF20 | XF40 | MS60 | MS63 | MS65 |
|---|---|---|---|---|---|---|
| 2006 | 27,254 | — | — | — | — | 25.00 |
| 2006 | 53,822 | PF65 40.00 | | | | |

**KM# 583a DOLLAR**
25.18 g., 0.925 Silver 0.7487 oz. ASW partially gilt, 36 mm. **Ruler:** Elizabeth II **Obv:** Head right **Rev:** Victoria Cross gilt

| Date | Mintage | VF20 | XF40 | MS60 | MS63 | MS65 |
|---|---|---|---|---|---|---|
| 2006 | 53,822 | PF65 65.00 | | | | |

**KM# 630 DOLLAR**
7.00 g., Aureate Bronze, 26.5 mm. **Ruler:** Elizabeth II **Obv:** Bust right **Rev:** Loon splashing in water

| Date | Mintage | VF20 | XF40 | MS60 | MS63 | MS65 |
|---|---|---|---|---|---|---|
| 2006 | — | — | — | — | 2.25 | 22.00 |

**KM# 630a DOLLAR**
9.31 g., 0.925 Silver 0.2769 oz. ASW, 26.5 mm. **Ruler:** Elizabeth II **Subject:** Olympic Games **Obv:** Crowned head right **Rev:** Loon in flight, color olympic logo above **Shape:** 11-sided

| Date | Mintage | VF20 | XF40 | MS60 | MS63 | MS65 |
|---|---|---|---|---|---|---|
| 2006 | 19,956 | — | — | — | 30.00 | — |

**KM# 654 DOLLAR**
7.00 g., 0.925 Silver 0.2082 oz. ASW, 26.5 mm. **Ruler:** Elizabeth II **Obv:** Head right **Rev:** Snowflake, colorized **Shape:** 11-sided
**Note:** Sold in a CD package.

| Date | Mintage | VF20 | XF40 | MS60 | MS63 | MS65 |
|---|---|---|---|---|---|---|
| 2006 (ml) | 34,014 | — | — | — | 35.00 | — |

**KM# 655 DOLLAR**
7.00 g., 0.925 Silver 0.2082 oz. ASW, 26.5 mm. **Ruler:** Elizabeth II **Subject:** Baby Rattle **Obv:** Head right **Rev:** Baby rattle **Shape:** 11-sided

| Date | Mintage | VF20 | XF40 | MS60 | MS63 | MS65 |
|---|---|---|---|---|---|---|
| 2006 | 3,207 | — | — | — | 20.00 | — |

**KM# 655a DOLLAR**
7.00 g., 0.925 Silver 0.2082 oz. ASW, 26.5 mm. **Ruler:** Elizabeth II **Obv:** Bust right **Rev:** Baby Rattle, partially gilt **Shape:** 11-sided

| Date | Mintage | VF20 | XF40 | MS60 | MS63 | MS65 |
|---|---|---|---|---|---|---|
| 2006 | 1,911 | — | — | — | 15.00 | — |

**KM# 656 DOLLAR**
28.18 g., 0.925 Silver 0.8379 oz. ASW **Ruler:** Elizabeth II **Subject:** Medal of Bravery **Obv:** Head right

| Date | Mintage | VF20 | XF40 | MS60 | MS63 | MS65 |
|---|---|---|---|---|---|---|
| 2006 | 8,343 | PF65 50.00 | | | | |

**KM# 656a DOLLAR**
28.18 g., 0.925 Silver 0.8379 oz. ASW with multicolor enamel **Ruler:** Elizabeth II **Subject:** Medal of Bravery **Obv:** Head right **Rev:** Maple leaf within wreath. Colorized.

| Date | Mintage | VF20 | XF40 | MS60 | MS63 | MS65 |
|---|---|---|---|---|---|---|
| 2006 | 4,999 | PF65 125 | | | | |

**KM# 1287 DOLLAR**
7.00 g., Aureate Bronze, 26.5 mm. **Ruler:** Elizabeth II **Rev:** Goose in flight

| Date | Mintage | VF20 | XF40 | MS60 | MS63 | MS65 |
|---|---|---|---|---|---|---|
| 2006 | — | PF65 20.00 | | | | |

**KM# 653 DOLLAR**

25.18 g., 0.925 Silver 0.7487 oz. ASW, 36.07 mm. **Ruler:** Elizabeth II **Subject:** Thayendanegea **Obv:** Head right **Rev:** Bust 3/4 facing right

| Date | Mintage | VF20 | XF40 | MS60 | MS63 | MS65 |
|---|---|---|---|---|---|---|
| 2007 | 16,378 | — | — | — | — | 23.00 |
| 2007 | — | PF65 40.00 | | | | |

**KM# 653a DOLLAR**

25.18 g., 0.925 Silver 0.7487 oz. ASW partially gilt, 36.07 mm. **Ruler:** Elizabeth II **Subject:** Thayendanega **Rev:** Bust 3/4 right, partially gold plated

| Date | Mintage | VF20 | XF40 | MS60 | MS63 | MS65 |
|---|---|---|---|---|---|---|
| 2007 | 60,000 | PF65 60.00 | | | | |

**KM# 688 DOLLAR**

7.00 g., Aureate-Bronze Plated Nickel, 26.5 mm. **Ruler:** Elizabeth II **Obv:** Head right **Rev:** Trumpeter Swan

| Date | Mintage | VF20 | XF40 | MS60 | MS63 | MS65 |
|---|---|---|---|---|---|---|
| 2007 (ml) | 40,000 | — | — | — | — | 30.00 |

**KM# 700 DOLLAR**

7.00 g., 0.925 Silver 0.2082 oz. ASW, 26.5 mm. **Ruler:** Elizabeth II **Rev:** Alphabet Letter Blocks **Shape:** 11-sided

| Date | Mintage | VF20 | XF40 | MS60 | MS63 | MS65 |
|---|---|---|---|---|---|---|
| 2007 | 3,207 | PF65 25.00 | | | | |

**KM# 719 DOLLAR**

25.18 g., 0.925 Silver 0.7488 oz. ASW, 36.07 mm. **Ruler:** Elizabeth II **Subject:** Celebration of the Arts **Rev:** Book, TV set, musical instruments, film montage **Edge:** Reeded

| Date | Mintage | VF20 | XF40 | MS60 | MS63 | MS65 |
|---|---|---|---|---|---|---|
| 2007 | 6,466 | PF65 55.00 | | | | |

**KM# 720 DOLLAR**

25.18 g., 0.925 Silver 0.7488 oz. ASW, 36.07 mm. **Ruler:** Elizabeth II **Obv:** Bust right **Rev:** Thayendanega multicolor

| Date | Mintage | VF20 | XF40 | MS60 | MS63 | MS65 |
|---|---|---|---|---|---|---|
| 2007 | 4,760 | PF65 120 | | | | |

**KM# A727 DOLLAR**

7.00 g., Aureate-Bronze Plated Nickel, 26.5 mm. **Ruler:** Elizabeth II **Subject:** Vancouver Olympic Games **Rev:** Loon splashing in water, Olympics logo at right

| Date | Mintage | VF20 | XF40 | MS60 | MS63 | MS65 |
|---|---|---|---|---|---|---|
| 2007 (ml) | 19,973 | — | — | — | 3.00 | — |

**KM# 721 DOLLAR**

7.00 g., Aureate-Bronze Plated Nickel, 26.5 mm. **Ruler:** Elizabeth II **Obv:** Bust right **Rev:** Calgary flames, multicolor in circle

| Date | Mintage | VF20 | XF40 | MS60 | MS63 | MS65 |
|---|---|---|---|---|---|---|
| 2008 | — | — | — | — | — | 18.00 |

**KM# 722 DOLLAR**

7.00 g., Aureate-Bronze Plated Nickel, 26.5 mm. **Ruler:** Elizabeth II **Obv:** Bust **Rev:** Edmonton Oilers logo, multicolor in logo

| Date | Mintage | VF20 | XF40 | MS60 | MS63 | MS65 |
|---|---|---|---|---|---|---|
| 2008 | 1,584 | — | — | — | — | 18.00 |

**KM# 723A DOLLAR**

7.00 g., Aureate-Bronze Plated Nickel, 26.5 mm. **Ruler:** Elizabeth II **Obv:** Bust right **Rev:** Montreal Canadians, multicolor logo in circle

| Date | Mintage | VF20 | XF40 | MS60 | MS63 | MS65 |
|---|---|---|---|---|---|---|
| 2008 | 2,659 | — | — | — | — | 18.00 |

**KM# 724 DOLLAR**

7.00 g., Nickel, 26.5 mm. **Ruler:** Elizabeth II **Rev:** Ottawa Senators, multicolor logo in circle

| Date | Mintage | VF20 | XF40 | MS60 | MS63 | MS65 |
|---|---|---|---|---|---|---|
| 2008 | 1,633 | — | — | — | — | 18.00 |

**KM# 725 DOLLAR**

7.00 g., Aureate-Bronze Plated Nickel, 26.5 mm. **Ruler:** Elizabeth II **Obv:** Bust right **Rev:** Toronto Maple Leafs, multicolor logo in circle

| Date | Mintage | VF20 | XF40 | MS60 | MS63 | MS65 |
|---|---|---|---|---|---|---|
| 2008 | — | — | — | — | — | 18.00 |

**KM# 726 DOLLAR**

7.00 g., Aureate-Bronze Plated Nickel, 26.5 mm. **Ruler:** Elizabeth II **Obv:** Bust left **Rev:** Vancouver Canucks, logo in center

| Date | Mintage | VF20 | XF40 | MS60 | MS63 | MS65 |
|---|---|---|---|---|---|---|
| 2008 | 1,302 | — | — | — | — | 18.00 |

**KM# 767 DOLLAR**

25.18 g., 0.925 Silver 0.7488 oz. ASW, 36.07 mm. **Ruler:** Elizabeth II **Rev:** Poppy at center of large maple leaf

| Date | Mintage | VF20 | XF40 | MS60 | MS63 | MS65 |
|---|---|---|---|---|---|---|
| 2008 | — | PF65 100 | | | | |

**KM# 781 DOLLAR**

25.18 g., 0.925 Silver 0.7488 oz. ASW partially gilt, 36.07 mm. **Ruler:** Elizabeth II **Subject:** Ottawa Mint Centennial 1908-2008 **Rev:** Maple leaf transforming into a common loon, gilt rim and 100

| Date | Mintage | VF20 | XF40 | MS60 | MS63 | MS65 |
|---|---|---|---|---|---|---|
| 2008 | 15,000 | PF65 100 | | | | |

**KM# 784 DOLLAR**

7.00 g., Aureate-Bronze Plated Nickel, 26.5 mm. **Ruler:** Elizabeth II **Rev:** Common elder

| Date | Mintage | VF20 | XF40 | MS60 | MS63 | MS65 |
|---|---|---|---|---|---|---|
| 2008 Specimen | 21,227 | — | — | — | — | 40.00 |

**KM# 785 DOLLAR**

25.18 g., 0.925 Silver 0.7488 oz. ASW, 36.07 mm. **Ruler:** Elizabeth II **Subject:** Founding of Quebec 400th Anniversary **Rev:** Samuel de Champlain, ship and town view

| Date | Mintage | VF20 | XF40 | MS60 | MS63 | MS65 |
|---|---|---|---|---|---|---|
| 2008 | 35,000 | — | — | — | — | 25.00 |
| 2008 | 65,000 | PF65 40.00 | | | | |

**KM# 785a DOLLAR**

25.18 g., 0.925 Silver 0.7488 oz. ASW partially gilt., 36.07 mm. **Ruler:** Elizabeth II **Subject:** Founding of Quebec 400th Anniversary **Rev:** Samuel de Champlain selectively gold plated, ship, town view

| Date | Mintage | VF20 | XF40 | MS60 | MS63 | MS65 |
|---|---|---|---|---|---|---|
| 2008 | 38,630 | PF65 65.00 | | | | |

**KM# 787 DOLLAR**

7.00 g., Aureate-Bronze Plated Nickel, 26.5 mm. **Ruler:** Elizabeth II **Subject:** Lucky Loonie **Rev:** Loon splashing and Olympic logo at right

| Date | Mintage | VF20 | XF40 | MS60 | MS63 | MS65 |
|---|---|---|---|---|---|---|
| 2008 | — | — | — | — | 20.00 | — |

**KM# 787a DOLLAR**
9.31 g., 0.925 Silver 0.2769 oz. ASW, 26.5 mm. **Ruler:** Elizabeth II **Rev:** Loon splashing with Olympic logo and maple leaf in color at right **Shape:** 11-sided

| Date | Mintage | VF20 | XF40 | MS60 | MS63 | MS65 |
|---|---|---|---|---|---|---|
| 2008 | 52,987 | PF65 35.00 | | | | |

**KM# 790 DOLLAR**
6.50 g., Nickel, 26.5 mm. **Ruler:** Elizabeth II **Rev:** Calgary Flames

| Date | Mintage | VF20 | XF40 | MS60 | MS63 | MS65 |
|---|---|---|---|---|---|---|
| 2008 | — | — | — | — | 25.00 | — |

**KM# 791 DOLLAR**
6.50 g., Nickel, 26.5 mm. **Ruler:** Elizabeth II **Rev:** Edmonton Oilers

| Date | Mintage | VF20 | XF40 | MS60 | MS63 | MS65 |
|---|---|---|---|---|---|---|
| 2008 | — | — | — | — | 25.00 | — |

**KM# 792 DOLLAR**
6.50 g., Nickel, 26.5 mm. **Ruler:** Elizabeth II **Rev:** Montreal Canadiens

| Date | Mintage | VF20 | XF40 | MS60 | MS63 | MS65 |
|---|---|---|---|---|---|---|
| 2008 | — | — | — | — | 25.00 | — |

**KM# 793 DOLLAR**
6.50 g., Nickel, 26.5 mm. **Ruler:** Elizabeth II **Rev:** Ottawa Senators

| Date | Mintage | VF20 | XF40 | MS60 | MS63 | MS65 |
|---|---|---|---|---|---|---|
| 2008 | — | — | — | — | 25.00 | — |

**KM# 794 DOLLAR**
6.50 g., Nickel, 26.5 mm. **Ruler:** Elizabeth II **Rev:** Toronto Maple Leafs

| Date | Mintage | VF20 | XF40 | MS60 | MS63 | MS65 |
|---|---|---|---|---|---|---|
| 2008 | — | — | — | — | 25.00 | — |

**KM# 795 DOLLAR**
6.50 g., Nickel, 26.5 mm. **Ruler:** Elizabeth II **Rev:** Vancouver Canucks

| Date | Mintage | VF20 | XF40 | MS60 | MS63 | MS65 |
|---|---|---|---|---|---|---|
| 2008 | — | — | — | — | 25.00 | — |

**KM# 851 DOLLAR**
33.65 g., Nickel, 26.5 mm. **Ruler:** Elizabeth II **Rev:** Calgary Flames Road Jersey

| Date | Mintage | VF20 | XF40 | MS60 | MS63 | MS65 |
|---|---|---|---|---|---|---|
| 2009 | 382 | — | — | — | 25.00 | — |

**KM# 852 DOLLAR**
33.65 g., Nickel, 26.5 mm. **Ruler:** Elizabeth II **Rev:** Edmonton Oilers Road Jersey

| Date | Mintage | VF20 | XF40 | MS60 | MS63 | MS65 |
|---|---|---|---|---|---|---|
| 2009 | 472 | — | — | — | 25.00 | — |

**KM# 853 DOLLAR**
33.65 g., Nickel, 26.5 mm. **Ruler:** Elizabeth II **Rev:** Montreal Canadians Road Jersey

| Date | Mintage | VF20 | XF40 | MS60 | MS63 | MS65 |
|---|---|---|---|---|---|---|
| 2009 | 4,857 | — | — | — | 25.00 | — |

**KM# 854 DOLLAR**
33.65 g., Nickel, 26.5 mm. **Ruler:** Elizabeth II **Rev:** Ottawa Senators Road Jersey

| Date | Mintage | VF20 | XF40 | MS60 | MS63 | MS65 |
|---|---|---|---|---|---|---|
| 2009 | 387 | — | — | — | 25.00 | — |

**KM# 855 DOLLAR**
33.65 g., Nickel, 26.5 mm. **Ruler:** Elizabeth II **Rev:** Toronto Maple Leafs Road Jersey

| Date | Mintage | VF20 | XF40 | MS60 | MS63 | MS65 |
|---|---|---|---|---|---|---|
| 2009 | 1,328 | — | — | — | 25.00 | — |

**KM# 856 DOLLAR**
33.65 g., Nickel, 26.5 mm. **Ruler:** Elizabeth II **Rev:** Vancouver Canucks Road Jersey

| Date | Mintage | VF20 | XF40 | MS60 | MS63 | MS65 |
|---|---|---|---|---|---|---|
| 2009 | 794 | — | — | — | 25.00 | — |

**KM# 864 DOLLAR**
7.00 g., Aureate-Bronze Plated Nickel, 26.5 mm. **Ruler:** Elizabeth II **Subject:** Montreal Canadiens, 100th Anniversary **Obv:** Bust right **Rev:** Montreal Canadiens logo and large 100 **Shape:** 11-sided

| Date | Mintage | VF20 | XF40 | MS60 | MS63 | MS65 |
|---|---|---|---|---|---|---|
| 2009 | — | — | — | — | 2.25 | 22.00 |

**KM# 865 DOLLAR**
25.17 g., 0.925 Silver 0.7485 oz. ASW, 36.07 mm. **Ruler:** Elizabeth II **Subject:** Montreal Canadiens 100th Anniversary **Obv:** Bust right **Rev:** Montreal Canadiens logo partially gilt

| Date | Mintage | VF20 | XF40 | MS60 | MS63 | MS65 |
|---|---|---|---|---|---|---|
| 2009 Proof in black case | 15,000 | PF65 75.00 | | | | |
| 2009 Proof in acrillic stand | 5,000 | PF65 150 | | | | |

**KM# 889 DOLLAR**
25.18 g., 0.925 Silver 0.7488 oz. ASW, 36.07 mm. **Ruler:** Elizabeth II **Subject:** 100th Anniversary of flight in Canada **Obv:** Bust right **Obv. Legend:** Elizabeth II DG Regina **Rev:** Silhouette with arms spread, 3 planes, plane cutout **Rev. Legend:** Canada Dollar 1909-2009

| Date | Mintage | VF20 | XF40 | MS60 | MS63 | MS65 |
|---|---|---|---|---|---|---|
| 2009 | 13,074 | — | — | — | — | 30.00 |
| 2009 | 52,549 | PF65 45.00 | | | | |

## KM# 889a DOLLAR

25.18 g., 0.925 Silver 0.7488 oz. ASW partially gilt, 36.07 mm. **Ruler:** Elizabeth II **Obv:** Bust right **Rev:** Boy silouette with arms spread, 3 planes, plane shadow partially gilt

| Date | Mintage | VF20 | XF40 | MS60 | MS63 | MS65 |
|---|---|---|---|---|---|---|
| 2009 (ml) | 27,549 | PF65 65.00 | | | | |

## KM# 914 DOLLAR

7.00 g., Aureate-Bronze Plated Nickel, 26.5 mm. **Ruler:** Elizabeth II **Obv:** Bust right **Rev:** Blue heron in flight

| Date | Mintage | VF20 | XF40 | MS60 | MS63 | MS65 |
|---|---|---|---|---|---|---|
| 2009 Specimen | 21,677 | — | — | — | — | 40.00 |

## KM# 883 DOLLAR

7.00 g., Aureate-Bronze Plated Nickel, 26.5 mm. **Ruler:** Elizabeth II **Subject:** Lucky Loonie **Obv:** Bust right **Obv. Legend:** Elizabeth II DG Regina **Rev:** Canadian Olympic logo **Rev. Legend:** Canada Dollar

| Date | Mintage | VF20 | XF40 | MS60 | MS63 | MS65 |
|---|---|---|---|---|---|---|
| 2010 | 12,000 | — | — | — | 2.50 | 22.00 |

## KM# 883a DOLLAR

9.31 g., 0.925 Silver 0.2769 oz. ASW, 26.5 mm. **Ruler:** Elizabeth II **Subject:** Lucky Loonie **Obv:** Bust right **Obv. Legend:** Elizabeth II DG Regina **Rev:** Canadian Olympic logo in color **Rev. Legend:** Vancouver 2010 Canada Dollar **Shape:** 11-sided

| Date | Mintage | VF20 | XF40 | MS60 | MS63 | MS65 |
|---|---|---|---|---|---|---|
| 2010 | 40,000 | PF65 55.00 | | | | |

## KM# 975 DOLLAR

0.925 Silver, 36 mm. **Ruler:** Elizabeth II **Rev:** Sun mask

| Date | Mintage | VF20 | XF40 | MS60 | MS63 | MS65 |
|---|---|---|---|---|---|---|
| 2010 | 1,278 | PF65 200 | | | | |

## KM# 995 DOLLAR

25.17 g., 0.925 Silver 0.7485 oz. ASW, 36.07 mm. **Ruler:** Elizabeth II **Rev:** HMCS Sackville

| Date | Mintage | VF20 | XF40 | MS60 | MS63 | MS65 |
|---|---|---|---|---|---|---|
| 2010 | — | PF65 45.00 | | | | |

## KM# 995a DOLLAR

25.17 g., 0.925 Silver 0.7485 oz. ASW partially gilt, 36.07 mm. **Ruler:** Elizabeth II **Subject:** Navy Centennial **Rev:** HMCS Sackville, sea waves in gilt

| Date | Mintage | VF20 | XF40 | MS60 | MS63 | MS65 |
|---|---|---|---|---|---|---|
| 2010 | — | PF65 70.00 | | | | |

## KM# 996 DOLLAR

7.00 g., Aureate-Bronze Plated Nickel, 26.5 mm. **Ruler:** Elizabeth II **Rev:** Northern Harrier Hawk

| Date | Mintage | VF20 | XF40 | MS60 | MS63 | MS65 |
|---|---|---|---|---|---|---|
| 2010 Prooflike | 35,000 | — | — | — | — | 30.00 |
| 2010 (ml) | — | PF65 50.00 | | | | |

## KM# 1017 DOLLAR

7.00 g., Aureate-Bronze Plated Nickel, 26.5 mm. **Ruler:** Elizabeth II **Rev:** Male and female sailors saluting, HMCS Halifax and anchor above

| Date | Mintage | VF20 | XF40 | MS60 | MS63 | MS65 |
|---|---|---|---|---|---|---|
| 2010 | — | — | — | — | 5.00 | — |

## KM# 1017a DOLLAR

7.00 g., Aureate Bronze gilt, 26.5 mm. **Ruler:** Elizabeth II **Rev:** Male and female sailors saluting, HMCS Halifax in background and anchor above

| Date | Mintage | VF20 | XF40 | MS60 | MS63 | MS65 |
|---|---|---|---|---|---|---|
| 2010 | — | PF65 50.00 | | | | |

## KM# 1027 DOLLAR

25.18 g., 0.925 Silver 0.7488 oz. ASW, 36.07 mm. **Ruler:** Elizabeth II **Obv:** George V bust left **Rev:** Voyaguers, dual dates below

| Date | Mintage | VF20 | XF40 | MS60 | MS63 | MS65 |
|---|---|---|---|---|---|---|
| 2010 | 7,500 | PF65 70.00 | | | | |

## KM# 1046 DOLLAR

Aureate-Bronze Plated Nickel, 26.5 mm. **Ruler:** Elizabeth II **Subject:** Roughriders **Rev:** S logo **Shape:** 11-sided

| Date | Mintage | VF20 | XF40 | MS60 | MS63 | MS65 |
|---|---|---|---|---|---|---|
| 2010 (ml) | — | — | — | — | 2.25 | 22.00 |

## KM# 1050 DOLLAR

25.18 g., 0.925 Silver 0.7488 oz. ASW, 36.07 mm. **Ruler:** Elizabeth II **Rev:** Red poppy in large field of poppies **Edge:** Reeded

| Date | Mintage | VF20 | XF40 | MS60 | MS63 | MS65 |
|---|---|---|---|---|---|---|
| 2010 | 5,000 | PF65 150 | | | | |

## KM# 1086 DOLLAR

7.00 g., Aureate-Bronze Plated Nickel, 26.5 mm. **Ruler:** Elizabeth II **Rev:** Great Grey Owl

| Date | Mintage | VF20 | XF40 | MS60 | MS63 | MS65 |
|---|---|---|---|---|---|---|
| 2011 Prooflike | 35,000 | — | — | — | — | 27.00 |

## KM# 1087 DOLLAR

25.18 g., 0.925 Silver 0.7488 oz. ASW, 36.07 mm. **Ruler:** Elizabeth II **Subject:** Parks Canada, 100th Anniversary **Rev:** Female head looking downward into hands holding nature scene

| Date | Mintage | VF20 | XF40 | MS60 | MS63 | MS65 |
|---|---|---|---|---|---|---|
| 2011 | — | PF65 50.00 | | | | |
| 2011 | 25,000 | — | — | — | — | 45.00 |

## KM# 1087a DOLLAR

25.18 g., 0.925 Silver 0.7488 oz. ASW partially gilt, 36.07 mm. **Ruler:** Elizabeth II **Subject:** Parks Canada, 100th Anniversary **Rev:** Female head looking downward to hands holding nature scene, partially gilt

| Date | Mintage | VF20 | XF40 | MS60 | MS63 | MS65 |
|---|---|---|---|---|---|---|
| 2011 | 45,000 | PF65 75.00 | | | | |

## KM# 1112 DOLLAR

25.17 g., 0.925 Silver 0.7485 oz. ASW, 36.07 mm. **Ruler:** Elizabeth II **Obv:** Crowned bust left of George V **Rev:** Value and date within maple wreath

| Date | Mintage | VF20 | XF40 | MS60 | MS63 | MS65 |
|---|---|---|---|---|---|---|
| 2011 | Est. 15000 | PF65 50.00 | | | | |

## KM# 1166 DOLLAR

7.00 g., Aureate-Bronze Plated Nickel, 26.5 mm. **Ruler:** Elizabeth II **Subject:** Canada Parks **Obv:** Bust right **Rev:** Stylized animals

| Date | Mintage | VF20 | XF40 | MS60 | MS63 | MS65 |
|---|---|---|---|---|---|---|
| 2011 | — | — | — | — | 2.50 | 22.00 |

## KM# 1216 DOLLAR

9.31 g., 0.925 Silver 0.2769 oz. ASW, 26.5 mm. **Ruler:** Elizabeth II **Obv:** Bust right, SP/PA below **Rev:** Loon, 1987-2012 below **Shape:** 11-sided

| Date | Mintage | VF20 | XF40 | MS60 | MS63 | MS65 |
|---|---|---|---|---|---|---|
| 2012 Specimen | — | PF65 30.00 | | | | |

## KM# 1222 DOLLAR

7.00 g., Aureate-Bronze Plated Nickel, 26.5 mm. **Ruler:** Elizabeth II **Obv:** Bust right **Rev:** Loon and two young, 1987-2012 dates

| Date | Mintage | VF20 | XF40 | MS60 | MS63 | MS65 |
|---|---|---|---|---|---|---|
| 2012 Specimen | — | PF65 40.00 | | | | |

## KM# 1225 DOLLAR

25.18 g., 0.925 Silver 0.7488 oz. ASW, 36.07 mm. **Ruler:** Elizabeth II **Subject:** War of 1812, 200th Anniversary **Obv:** Bust right **Rev:** Two soldiers and guide on patrol

| Date | Mintage | VF20 | XF40 | MS60 | MS63 | MS65 |
|---|---|---|---|---|---|---|
| 2012 | — | PF65 50.00 | | | | |
| 2012 | — | — | — | — | 50.00 | — |

## KM# 1225a DOLLAR

25.18 g., 0.925 Silver 0.7488 oz. ASW partially gilt, 36.07 mm. **Ruler:** Elizabeth II **Subject:** War of 1812, 200th Anniversary **Obv:** Bust right, gilt rim **Rev:** Two solders and guide, partially gilt

| Date | Mintage | VF20 | XF40 | MS60 | MS63 | MS65 |
|---|---|---|---|---|---|---|
| 2012 | — | PF65 65.00 | | | | |

## KM# 1244 DOLLAR

23.17 g., 0.999 Silver 0.7442 oz. ASW, 36.07 mm. **Ruler:** Elizabeth II **Subject:** Calgary Stampede

| Date | Mintage | VF20 | XF40 | MS60 | MS63 | MS65 |
|---|---|---|---|---|---|---|
| 2012 | 10,000 | PF65 55.00 | | | | |

## KM# 1254 DOLLAR

7.89 g., 0.999 Silver 0.2534 oz. ASW, 26.5 mm. **Ruler:** Elizabeth II **Subject:** Loonie, 25th Anniversary **Rev:** Two loons and large 25 **Shape:** 11-sided

| Date | Mintage | VF20 | XF40 | MS60 | MS63 | MS65 |
|---|---|---|---|---|---|---|
| 1987-2012 | 15,000 | PF65 35.00 | | | | |

## KM# 1255 DOLLAR

6.27 g., Brass Plated Steel, 26.5 mm. **Ruler:** Elizabeth II **Rev:** Loon with security feature above **Shape:** 11-sided

| Date | Mintage | VF20 | XF40 | MS60 | MS63 | MS65 |
|---|---|---|---|---|---|---|
| 2012 | — | — | — | — | 2.25 | 22.00 |
| 2012 | — | PF65 10.00 | | | | |
| 2013 | — | — | — | — | 5.00 | — |

| Date | Mintage | VF20 | XF40 | MS60 | MS63 | MS65 |
|---|---|---|---|---|---|---|
| 2013 | — | PF65 7.50 | | | | |
| 2014 | — | — | — | — | 5.00 | — |
| 2014 | — | PF65 7.50 | | | | |
| 2015 | — | — | — | — | 5.00 | — |
| 2015 | — | PF65 7.50 | | | | |

## KM# 1256 DOLLAR

6.27 g., Brass Plated Steel, 26.5 mm. **Ruler:** Elizabeth II **Subject:** Lucky Loonie **Rev:** Loon and Olympic logo **Shape:** 11-sided

| Date | Mintage | VF20 | XF40 | MS60 | MS63 | MS65 |
|---|---|---|---|---|---|---|
| 2012 | — | — | — | — | 2.50 | 22.00 |
| 2014 | — | — | — | — | 10.00 | — |

## KM# 1256a DOLLAR

12.16 g., 0.999 Silver 0.3906 oz. ASW, 26.5 mm. **Ruler:** Elizabeth II **Subject:** Lucky loonie **Rev:** Loon and olympic logo in color **Shape:** 11-sided

| Date | Mintage | VF20 | XF40 | MS60 | MS63 | MS65 |
|---|---|---|---|---|---|---|
| 2012 | 20,000 | PF65 35.00 | | | | |
| 2014 | — | PF63 30.00 | PF65 35.00 | | | |

## KM# 1274 DOLLAR

31.39 g., 0.999 Silver 1.0082 oz. ASW, 38 mm. **Ruler:** Elizabeth II **Subject:** Artistic Loonie **Rev:** Four Loons in color

| Date | Mintage | VF20 | XF40 | MS60 | MS63 | MS65 |
|---|---|---|---|---|---|---|
| 2012 | 10,000 | PF65 125 | | | | |

## KM# 1294 DOLLAR

6.27 g., Brass Plated Steel, 26.5 mm. **Ruler:** Elizabeth II **Subject:** Grey Cup, 100th Anniversary **Obv:** Bust right **Shape:** 11-sided

| Date | Mintage | VF20 | XF40 | MS60 | MS63 | MS65 |
|---|---|---|---|---|---|---|
| 2012 | — | — | — | — | 2.50 | 22.00 |

## KM# 1295 DOLLAR

25.18 g., 0.925 Silver 0.7488 oz. ASW, 36.07 mm. **Ruler:** Elizabeth II **Subject:** Grey Cup, 100th Anniversary

| Date | Mintage | VF20 | XF40 | MS60 | MS63 | MS65 |
|---|---|---|---|---|---|---|
| 2012 | — | PF65 65.00 | | | | |

### KM# 1360 DOLLAR

7.00 g., Bronze Plated Nickel, 26.5 mm. **Ruler:** Elizabeth II **Rev:** Blue wing teal standing on log

| Date | Mintage | VF20 | XF40 | MS60 | MS63 | MS65 |
|---|---|---|---|---|---|---|
| 2013 | 50,000 | PF65 40.00 | | | | |

### KM# 1387 DOLLAR

23.17 g., 0.999 Silver 0.7442 oz. ASW, 36.07 mm. **Ruler:** Elizabeth II **Subject:** Arctic Exploration - 100th Anniversary **Rev:** Three explorers and dog sled team, Company Rose in background

| Date | Mintage | VF20 | XF40 | MS60 | MS63 | MS65 |
|---|---|---|---|---|---|---|
| 2013 | Est. 40000 | PF65 50.00 | | | | |
| 2013 | 20,000 | — | — | — | — | 50.00 |

### KM# 1387a DOLLAR

23.17 g., 0.999 Silver 0.7442 oz. ASW, 36.07 mm. **Ruler:** Elizabeth II **Subject:** Arctic Exploration - 100th Anniversary **Rev:** Map of North Pole, Arctic Explorers, Selectively Gilt

| Date | Mintage | VF20 | XF40 | MS60 | MS63 | MS65 |
|---|---|---|---|---|---|---|
| 2013 | — | PF65 125 | | | | |

### KM# 1388 DOLLAR

23.17 g., 0.999 Silver 0.7442 oz. ASW, 36.07 mm. **Ruler:** Elizabeth II **Subject:** End of 7 Years War - 250th Anniversary **Rev:** Soldiers and Settlers

| Date | Mintage | VF20 | XF40 | MS60 | MS63 | MS65 |
|---|---|---|---|---|---|---|
| 2013 | Est. 10000 | PF65 60.00 | | | | |

### KM# 1394 DOLLAR

25.11 g., 0.925 Silver 0.7467 oz. ASW, 36.07 mm. **Ruler:** Elizabeth II **Obv:** Elizabeth II, Mary Glick portrait

| Date | Mintage | VF20 | XF40 | MS60 | MS63 | MS65 |
|---|---|---|---|---|---|---|
| 2013 | — | PF65 65.00 | | | | |

### KM# 1464 DOLLAR

23.17 g., 0.925 Silver 0.6891 oz. ASW, 36 mm. **Ruler:** Elizabeth II **Subject:** Korean War Armistance, 60th Anniversary **Rev:** Hercules slaying Hydra **Note:** Based on the design of the Korean Service Medal

| Date | Mintage | VF20 | XF40 | MS60 | MS63 | MS65 |
|---|---|---|---|---|---|---|
| 2013 | 10,000 | PF65 60.00 | | | | |

### KM# 1586 DOLLAR

25.18 g., 0.925 Silver 0.7488 oz. ASW, 36.07 mm. **Ruler:** Elizabeth II **Subject:** WWI **Obv:** Bust right **Rev:** Soldier and woman kissing, soldiers boarding train

| Date | Mintage | VF20 | XF40 | MS60 | MS63 | MS65 |
|---|---|---|---|---|---|---|
| 2014 | — | — | — | — | 50.00 | — |
| 2014 | — | PF65 65.00 | | | | |

### KM# 1587 DOLLAR

7.00 g., Aluminum-Bronze, 26.5 mm. **Ruler:** Elizabeth II **Subject:** Lucky Loon **Obv:** Bust right **Rev:** Loon, Olympic logo at left

| Date | Mintage | VF20 | XF40 | MS60 | MS63 | MS65 |
|---|---|---|---|---|---|---|
| 2014 | — | — | — | — | 5.00 | — |

### KM# 1586a DOLLAR

25.18 g., 0.925 Silver 0.7488 oz. ASW partially gilt, 36.07 mm. **Ruler:** Elizabeth II **Subject:** WWI, 100th Anniversary **Obv:** Bust right **Rev:** Soldier and woman kissing, soldiers boarding train, partially gilt

| Date | Mintage | F12 | VF20 | XF40 | MS60 | MS63 |
|---|---|---|---|---|---|---|
| 2014 | — | PF65 85.00 | | | | |

### KM# 1588 DOLLAR

7.00 g., Aluminum-Bronze, 26.5 mm. **Ruler:** Elizabeth II **Subject:** Baby loon **Obv:** Bust right **Rev:** Stork in flight left with baby bundle

| Date | Mintage | VF20 | XF40 | MS60 | MS63 | MS65 |
|---|---|---|---|---|---|---|
| 2014 | — | — | — | — | 5.00 | — |

### KM# 1589 DOLLAR

7.00 g., Aluminum-Bronze, 26.5 mm. **Ruler:** Elizabeth II **Subject:** Birthday Loon **Obv:** Bust right **Rev:** Party hats, decorations, presents

| Date | Mintage | VF20 | XF40 | MS60 | MS63 |
|---|---|---|---|---|---|
| 2014 | — | — | — | — | — |

### KM# 1591 DOLLAR

7.00 g., Aluminum-Bronze **Ruler:** Elizabeth II **Subject:** Oh Canada Loonie **Obv:** Bust right **Rev:** Maple leaf

| Date | Mintage | VF20 | XF40 | MS60 | MS63 | MS65 |
|---|---|---|---|---|---|---|
| 2014 | — | — | — | — | 5.00 | — |

### KM# 1627 DOLLAR

6.27 g., Brass Plated Nickel, 26.5 mm. **Ruler:** Elizabeth II **Subject:** Wedding **Obv:** Bust right **Rev:** Two birds

| Date | Mintage | VF20 | XF40 | MS60 | MS63 | MS65 |
|---|---|---|---|---|---|---|
| 2014 | — | — | — | — | 20.00 | — |

### KM# 1628 DOLLAR

6.27 g., Bronze Plated Nickel, 26.5 mm. **Ruler:** Elizabeth II **Obv:** Bust right **Rev:** Ferruginous Hawk in flight right

| Date | Mintage | VF20 | XF40 | MS60 | MS63 | MS65 |
|---|---|---|---|---|---|---|
| 2014 | 50,000 | — | — | — | 50.00 | — |
| Specimen | | | | | | |

### KM# 1702 DOLLAR

7.00 g., Brass Plated Steel **Ruler:** Elizabeth II **Obv:** Bust right **Rev:** Two reindeer and Christmas tree

| Date | Mintage | VF20 | XF40 | MS60 | MS63 | MS65 |
|---|---|---|---|---|---|---|
| 2014 | — | — | — | 20.00 | — | — |

### KM# 1724 DOLLAR

23.17 g., 0.999 Silver 0.7442 oz. ASW, 36.07 mm. **Ruler:** Elizabeth II **Subject:** World War II **Obv:** Bust right **Rev:** 3 females working on plane interior

| Date | Mintage | VF20 | XF40 | MS60 | MS63 | MS65 |
|---|---|---|---|---|---|---|
| 2014 | 7,500 | PF65 75.00 | | | | |

**KM# 1725 DOLLAR**
23.17 g., 0.999 Silver 0.7442 oz. ASW, 36.07 mm. **Ruler:** Elizabeth II **Obv:** Bust right **Rev:** WWI troops at station saying farewells

| Date | Mintage | VF20 | XF40 | MS60 | MS63 | MS65 |
|---|---|---|---|---|---|---|
| 2014 Reverse Proof | — | PF65 85.00 | | | | |

**KM# 1839 DOLLAR**
23.17 g., 0.9999 Silver 0.7449 oz. ASW, 36 mm. **Ruler:** Elizabeth II **Obv:** Bust right **Rev:** Flag above backpacker

| Date | Mintage | VF20 | XF40 | MS60 | MS63 | MS65 |
|---|---|---|---|---|---|---|
| 2015 | — | PF65 75.00 | | | | |

**KM# 1839a DOLLAR**
23.17 g., 0.9999 Silver 0.7449 oz. ASW, 36 mm. **Ruler:** Elizabeth II **Obv:** Bust right **Rev:** Color flag above backpacker

| Date | Mintage | VF20 | XF40 | MS60 | MS63 | MS65 |
|---|---|---|---|---|---|---|
| 2015 | — | PF65 75.00 | | | | |

**KM# 1840 DOLLAR**
7.00 g., Aluminum-Bronze, 26.5 mm. **Ruler:** Elizabeth II **Obv:** Bust right **Rev:** Bluejay

| Date | Mintage | VF20 | XF40 | MS60 | MS63 | MS65 |
|---|---|---|---|---|---|---|
| 2015 | — | — | — | — | — | 50.00 |

**KM# 1847 DOLLAR**
7.00 g., Aureate Bronze, 26.5 mm. **Ruler:** Elizabeth II **Obv:** Bust right **Rev:** Two swans

| Date | Mintage | VF20 | XF40 | MS60 | MS63 | MS65 |
|---|---|---|---|---|---|---|
| 2015 | — | — | — | — | — | 15.00 |

**KM# 1848 DOLLAR**
7.00 g., Aureate Bronze, 26.5 mm. **Ruler:** Elizabeth II **Obv:** Bust right **Rev:** Three baloons

| Date | Mintage | VF20 | XF40 | MS60 | MS63 | MS65 |
|---|---|---|---|---|---|---|
| 2015 | — | — | — | — | — | 15.00 |

**KM# 1849 DOLLAR**
7.00 g., Aureate Bronze, 26.5 mm. **Ruler:** Elizabeth II **Obv:** Bust right **Rev:** Fluttering Maple leaf

| Date | Mintage | VF20 | XF40 | MS60 | MS63 | MS65 |
|---|---|---|---|---|---|---|
| 2015 | — | — | — | — | — | 15.00 |

**KM# 1850 DOLLAR**
7.00 g., Aureate Bronze, 26.5 mm. **Ruler:** Elizabeth II **Obv:** Bust right **Rev:** Bear doll

| Date | Mintage | VF20 | XF40 | MS60 | MS63 | MS65 |
|---|---|---|---|---|---|---|
| 2015 | — | — | — | — | — | 15.00 |

**KM# 652 DOLLAR (Louis)**
1.50 g., 0.999 Gold 0.0482 oz. AGW, 14.1 mm. **Ruler:** Elizabeth II **Subject:** Gold Louis **Obv:** Bust right **Rev:** Crowned double L monogram within wreath

| Date | Mintage | VF20 | XF40 | MS60 | MS63 | MS65 |
|---|---|---|---|---|---|---|
| 2006 | 5,648 | PF65 90.00 | | | | |

**KM# 756 DOLLAR (Louis)**
1.56 g., 0.999 Gold 0.0499 oz. AGW, 14.1 mm. **Ruler:** Elizabeth II **Obv:** Bust right **Rev:** Crown above two oval shields

| Date | Mintage | VF20 | XF40 | MS60 | MS63 | MS65 |
|---|---|---|---|---|---|---|
| 2007 | 4,023 | PF65 110 | | | | |

**KM# 834 DOLLAR (Louis)**
1.56 g., 0.999 Gold 0.0499 oz. AGW, 14.1 mm. **Ruler:** Elizabeth II **Obv:** Bust right **Rev:** Crowned double L monogram, three lis around

| Date | Mintage | VF20 | XF40 | MS60 | MS63 | MS65 |
|---|---|---|---|---|---|---|
| 2008 | 3,793 | PF65 100 | | | | |

**KM# 270 2 DOLLARS**
7.30 g., Bi-Metallic Aluminum-Bronze center in Nickel ring, 28 mm. **Ruler:** Elizabeth II **Obv:** Crowned head right within circle, date below **Rev:** Polar bear right within circle, denomination below **Edge:** Segmented reeding

| Date | Mintage | VF20 | XF40 | MS60 | MS63 | MS65 |
|---|---|---|---|---|---|---|
| 2001 | 27,008,000 | — | — | 2.50 | 5.00 | 30.00 |
| 2001 | 74,944 | PF65 12.50 | | | | |
| 2002 | 11,910,000 | — | — | 2.50 | 5.00 | 30.00 |
| 2002 | 65,315 | PF65 12.50 | | | | |
| 2003 | 7,123,697 | — | — | 2.50 | 5.00 | 35.00 |
| 2003 | 62,007 | PF65 12.50 | | | | |

**KM# 270c 2 DOLLARS**
8.83 g., 0.925 Silver 0.2626 oz. ASW gold plated center, 28 mm. **Ruler:** Elizabeth II **Obv:** Crowned head right within circle, date below **Rev:** Polar bear right within circle, denomination below **Note:** 1.9mm thick.

| Date | Mintage | VF20 | XF40 | MS60 | MS63 | MS65 |
|---|---|---|---|---|---|---|
| 2001 | — | PF65 12.00 | | | | |

**KM# 449 2 DOLLARS**
7.30 g., Bi-Metallic Aluminum-Bronze center in Nickel ring, 28 mm. **Ruler:** Elizabeth II **Subject:** Elizabeth II Golden Jubilee **Obv:** Crowned head right, jubilee commemorative dates below **Edge:** Segmented reeding

| Date | Mintage | VF20 | XF40 | MS60 | MS63 | MS65 |
|---|---|---|---|---|---|---|
| 1952-2002 | 27,020,000 | — | — | 2.50 | 4.00 | 30.00 |

**KM# 449a 2 DOLLARS**
8.83 g., 0.925 Silver 0.2626 oz. ASW gold plated center, 28 mm. **Ruler:** Elizabeth II **Subject:** Elizabeth II Golden Jubilee **Obv:** Crowned head right, jubilee commemorative dates below

| Date | Mintage | VF20 | XF40 | MS60 | MS63 | MS65 |
|---|---|---|---|---|---|---|
| 1952-2002 | 100,000 | PF65 14.00 | | | | |

**KM# 270d 2 DOLLARS**
8.83 g., 0.925 Silver 0.2626 oz. ASW gold plated center **Ruler:** Elizabeth II **Subject:** 100th Anniversary of the Cobalt Silver Strike **Obv:** Crowned head right, within circle, date below **Rev:** Polar bear right, within circle, denomination below

| Date | Mintage | VF20 | XF40 | MS60 | MS63 | MS65 |
|---|---|---|---|---|---|---|
| 2003 | 100,000 | PF65 25.00 | | | | |

**KM# 496 2 DOLLARS**
7.30 g., Bi-Metallic Aluminum-Bronze center in Nickel ring, 28 mm. **Ruler:** Elizabeth II **Obv:** Head right **Rev:** Polar bear advancing right **Edge:** Segmented reeding

| Date | Mintage | VF20 | XF40 | MS60 | MS63 | MS65 |
|---|---|---|---|---|---|---|
| 2003 | 11,244,000 | — | — | 2.50 | 5.00 | 45.00 |
| 2003 W PL | 71,142 | — | — | — | — | 5.00 |
| 2004 | 12,908,000 | — | — | 2.50 | 5.00 | 30.00 |
| 2004 | — | PF65 12.50 | | | | |
| 2005 | 38,317,000 | — | — | 2.50 | 5.00 | 30.00 |
| 2005 | — | PF65 12.50 | | | | |
| 2006 (ml) | 35,319,000 | — | — | 2.50 | 5.00 | 30.00 |
| 2006 (ml) | — | PF65 12.50 | | | | |
| 2007 (ml) | 38,957,000 | — | — | 2.50 | 5.00 | 30.00 |
| 2007 (ml) | — | PF65 12.50 | | | | |
| 2008 (ml) | 18,400,000 | — | — | 2.50 | 5.00 | 30.00 |
| 2008 (ml) | — | PF65 12.50 | | | | |
| 2009 (ml) | 38,430,000 | — | — | 2.50 | 5.00 | 30.00 |
| 2009 (ml) | — | PF65 12.50 | | | | |
| 2010 (ml) | — | — | — | 2.50 | 5.00 | 30.00 |
| 2010 (ml) | — | PF65 12.50 | | | | |
| 2011 (ml) | — | — | — | 2.50 | 5.00 | 30.00 |
| 2011 (ml) | — | PF65 12.50 | | | | |
| 2012 (ml) | — | — | — | 4.50 | 9.00 | 45.00 |
| 2012 (ml) | — | PF65 12.50 | | | | |

**KM# 496a 2 DOLLARS**
10.84 g., 0.925 Bi-Metallic 0.3224 oz. gold plated center, 28 mm. **Ruler:** Elizabeth II **Obv:** Head right **Rev:** Polar Bear **Edge:** Segmented reeding

| Date | Mintage | VF20 | XF40 | MS60 | MS63 | MS65 |
|---|---|---|---|---|---|---|
| 2004 | — | PF65 25.00 | | | | |

**KM# 835 2 DOLLARS**
8.80 g., 0.925 Silver 0.2617 oz. ASW, 27.95 mm. **Ruler:** Elizabeth II **Rev:** Proud Polar Bear advancing right

| Date | Mintage | VF20 | XF40 | MS60 | MS63 | MS65 |
|---|---|---|---|---|---|---|
| 2004 | 12,607 | PF65 40.00 | | | | |

**KM# 631 2 DOLLARS**
7.30 g., Bi-Metallic Aluminum-Bronze center in Nickel ring, 28 mm. **Ruler:** Elizabeth II **Subject:** 10th Anniversary of $2 coin **Obv:** Crowned head right **Edge:** Segmented reeding

| Date | Mintage | VF20 | XF40 | MS60 | MS63 | MS65 |
|---|---|---|---|---|---|---|
| 2006 (ml) | 5,005,000 | — | — | 2.50 | 5.00 | 30.00 |
| 2006 (ml) | — | PF65 40.00 | | | | |

**KM# 631a 2 DOLLARS**
Bi-Metallic 24 Kt Gold center in 22 Kt Gold ring **Ruler:** Elizabeth II **Subject:** 10th Anniversary of $2 coin **Obv:** Crowned head right **Rev:** Polar bear

| Date | Mintage | VF20 | XF40 | MS60 | MS63 | MS65 |
|---|---|---|---|---|---|---|
| 2006 | 2,068 | PF65 400 | | | | |

**KM# 836 2 DOLLARS**
7.30 g., Bi-Metallic Aluminum-Bronze center in Nickel ring, 28 mm. **Ruler:** Elizabeth II **Subject:** $2 coin, 10th Anniversary **Rev:** Churchill" Polar Bear, northern lights **Edge:** Segmented reeding

| Date | Mintage | VF20 | XF40 | MS60 | MS63 | MS65 |
|---|---|---|---|---|---|---|
| 2006 (ml) | 31,636 | — | — | 2.50 | 5.00 | — |

**KM# 837 2 DOLLARS**
7.30 g., Bi-Metallic Aluminum-Bronze center in Nickel ring **Ruler:** Elizabeth II **Obv:** Bust left, date at top **Rev:** Polar Bear advancing right

| Date | Mintage | VF20 | XF40 | MS60 | MS63 | MS65 |
|---|---|---|---|---|---|---|
| 2006 (ml) | — | — | — | — | 7.50 | — |
| 2007 (ml) | 38,957,000 | — | — | — | 7.50 | — |

**KM# 796 2 DOLLARS**
8.83 g., 0.925 Silver 0.2626 oz. ASW gilt, 28.07 mm. **Ruler:** Elizabeth II **Rev:** Bear, gold plated center

| Date | Mintage | VF20 | XF40 | MS60 | MS63 | MS65 |
|---|---|---|---|---|---|---|
| 2008 | — | — | — | — | 25.00 | — |

**KM# 1040 2 DOLLARS**
7.30 g., Bi-Metallic Aluminum-Bronze center in Nickel ring, 28 mm. **Ruler:** Elizabeth II **Subject:** Quebec 400th Anniversary **Rev:** Lis and small sailing ship **Edge:** Segmented reeding

| Date | Mintage | VF20 | XF40 | MS60 | MS63 | MS65 |
|---|---|---|---|---|---|---|
| 2008 | — | — | — | 2.50 | 5.00 | 30.00 |

**KM# 1020 2 DOLLARS**
7.30 g., Bi-Metallic Aluminum-Bronze center in Nickel ring, 28 mm. **Ruler:** Elizabeth II **Rev:** Two lynx cubs **Edge:** Segmented reeding

| Date | Mintage | VF20 | XF40 | MS60 | MS63 | MS65 |
|---|---|---|---|---|---|---|
| 2010 Specimen | 15,000 | **PF65** 40.00 | | | | |

**KM# 1088 2 DOLLARS**
7.30 g., Bi-Metallic Aluminum-Bronze center in Nickel ring, 28 mm. **Ruler:** Elizabeth II **Rev:** Elk Calf **Edge:** Segmented reeding

| Date | Mintage | VF20 | XF40 | MS60 | MS63 | MS65 |
|---|---|---|---|---|---|---|
| 2011 PL | — | — | — | — | — | 40.00 |

**KM# 1167 2 DOLLARS**
7.30 g., Bi-Metallic Aluminum-Bronze center in Nickel ring, 28 mm. **Ruler:** Elizabeth II **Subject:** Canada Parks **Obv:** Bust right **Rev:** Stylized trees

| Date | Mintage | VF20 | XF40 | MS60 | MS63 | MS65 |
|---|---|---|---|---|---|---|
| 2011 | — | — | — | — | 3.50 | 30.00 |

**KM# 1257 2 DOLLARS**
6.92 g., Bi-Metallic Brass Plated Aluminum-Bronze center in Nickel Plated Steel ring, 28 mm. **Ruler:** Elizabeth II **Rev:** Polar bear with security device above **Edge:** Lettered and segmented reeding

| Date | Mintage | VF20 | XF40 | MS60 | MS63 | MS65 |
|---|---|---|---|---|---|---|
| 2012 | — | — | — | — | 3.50 | 30.00 |
| 2012 | — | **PF65** 10.00 | | | | |
| 2013 | — | — | — | 2.50 | 5.00 | 30.00 |
| 2013 | — | **PF65** 10.00 | | | | |
| 2014 | — | — | — | — | 7.50 | — |
| 2014 | — | **PF65** 10.00 | | | | |
| 2015 | — | — | — | — | 7.50 | — |
| 2015 | — | **PF65** 10.00 | | | | |

**KM# 1258 2 DOLLARS**
6.92 g., Bi-Metallic Brass Plated Aluminum-Bronze center in Nickel Plated Steel ring, 28 mm. **Ruler:** Elizabeth II **Subject:** H.M.S. Shannon **Edge:** Lettered and segmented reeding

| Date | Mintage | VF20 | XF40 | MS60 | MS63 | MS65 |
|---|---|---|---|---|---|---|
| 2012 | — | — | — | — | 3.50 | 30.00 |

**KM# 1263 2 DOLLARS**
7.30 g., Bi-Metallic Aluminum-Bronze center in Nickel Plated Steel ring, 28 mm. **Ruler:** Elizabeth II **Rev:** Wolf cubs

| Date | Mintage | VF20 | XF40 | MS60 | MS63 | MS65 |
|---|---|---|---|---|---|---|
| 2012 PL | — | — | — | — | — | 40.00 |

**KM# 1463 2 DOLLARS**
7.30 g., Bi-Metallic Aluminum-Bronze center in Nickel ring, 28 mm. **Ruler:** Elizabeth II **Rev:** Two black bear cubs playing

| Date | Mintage | VF20 | XF40 | MS60 | MS63 | MS65 |
|---|---|---|---|---|---|---|
| 2013 | 17,500 | **PF65** 50.00 | | | | |

**KM# 1638 2 DOLLARS**
6.92 g., Bi-Metallic, 28 mm. **Ruler:** Elizabeth II **Obv:** Bust right **Rev:** Two baby rabbits

| Date | Mintage | F12 | VF20 | XF40 | MS60 | MS63 |
|---|---|---|---|---|---|---|
| 2014 | — | — | — | — | — | 7.50 |

**KM# 1711 2 DOLLARS**
7.30 g., Bi-Metallic Brass Plated Aluminum-Bronze center in Nickel Plated Steel ring, 28 mm. **Ruler:** Elizabeth II **Obv:** Bust right **Rev:** WWII photo of child running after dad leaving for war

| Date | Mintage | VF20 | XF40 | MS60 | MS63 | MS65 |
|---|---|---|---|---|---|---|
| 2014 | — | — | — | — | 10.00 | — |

**KM# 657 3 DOLLARS**
11.72 g., 0.925 Silver 0.3485 oz. ASW gilt, 27x27 mm. **Ruler:** Elizabeth II **Rev:** Beaver within wreath **Shape:** Square

| Date | Mintage | VF20 | XF40 | MS60 | MS63 | MS65 |
|---|---|---|---|---|---|---|
| 2006 | 19,963 | **PF65** 225 | | | | |

**KM# 978 3 DOLLARS**
7.96 g., Silver Partially Gilt, 27 mm. **Ruler:** Elizabeth II **Rev:** Return of the Tyee (giant salmon)

| Date | Mintage | VF20 | XF40 | MS60 | MS63 | MS65 |
|---|---|---|---|---|---|---|
| 2010 | 15,000 | **PF63** 40.00 | **PF65** 50.00 | | | |

**KM# 1011 3 DOLLARS**
11.60 g., 0.925 Silver 0.345 oz. ASW gilt, 27x27 mm. **Ruler:** Elizabeth II **Rev:** Barn Owl **Shape:** Square

| Date | Mintage | VF20 | XF40 | MS60 | MS63 | MS65 |
|---|---|---|---|---|---|---|
| 2010 | 15,000 | **PF63** 55.00 | **PF65** 65.00 | | | |

**KM# 1051 3 DOLLARS**
11.60 g., 0.925 Silver 0.345 oz. ASW gilt, 27x27 mm. **Ruler:** Elizabeth II **Subject:** Wildlife conservation **Rev:** Stylized polar bear and northern lights **Shape:** square

| Date | Mintage | VF20 | XF40 | MS60 | MS63 | MS65 |
|---|---|---|---|---|---|---|
| 2010 Specimen | 15,000 | — | — | — | 55.00 | — |

**KM# 1089 3 DOLLARS**
11.60 g., 0.925 Silver 0.345 oz. ASW gilt, 27x27 mm. **Ruler:** Elizabeth II **Rev:** Orca Whale **Shape:** Square

| Date | Mintage | VF20 | XF40 | MS60 | MS63 | MS65 |
|---|---|---|---|---|---|---|
| 2011 | 15,000 | **PF63** 55.00 | **PF65** 65.00 | | | |

**KM# 1090 3 DOLLARS**
7.96 g., 0.999 Silver 0.2557 oz. ASW with red and yellow partial gilding, 27 mm. **Ruler:** Elizabeth II **Obv:** Bust right **Rev:** Eskimo mother kneeling, child on back, partially gilt

| Date | Mintage | VF20 | XF40 | MS60 | MS63 | MS65 |
|---|---|---|---|---|---|---|
| 2011 | 10,000 | **PF63** 55.00 | **PF65** 65.00 | | | |

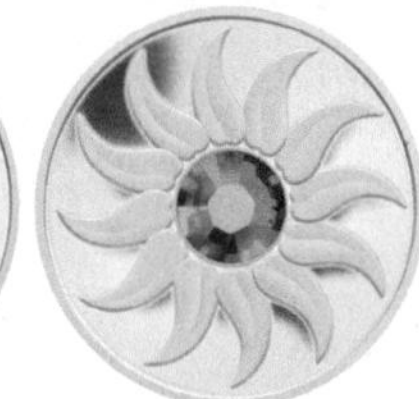

**KM# 1117 3 DOLLARS**
7.96 g., 0.9999 Silver 0.2559 oz. ASW, 27 mm. **Ruler:** Elizabeth II **Subject:** January birthstone, Garnet **Obv:** Bust left **Rev:** Birthstone at cener of artistic sunburst **Edge:** Reeded

| Date | Mintage | VF20 | XF40 | MS60 | MS63 | MS65 |
|---|---|---|---|---|---|---|
| 2011 | — | **PF63** 40.00 | **PF65** 45.00 | | | |

**KM# 1118 3 DOLLARS**

7.96 g., 0.9999 Silver 0.2559 oz. ASW, 27 mm. **Ruler:** Elizabeth II **Subject:** February birthstone, Amythest **Obv:** Bust right **Rev:** Birthstone at cener of artistic sunburst **Edge:** Reeded

| Date | Mintage | VF20 | XF40 | MS60 | MS63 | MS65 |
|---|---|---|---|---|---|---|
| 2011 | — | PF63 40.00 | PF65 45.00 | | | |

**KM# 1119 3 DOLLARS**

7.96 g., 0.9999 Silver 0.2559 oz. ASW, 27 mm. **Ruler:** Elizabeth II **Subject:** March birthstone, Aquamarine **Obv:** Bust right **Rev:** Birthstone at cener of artistic sunburst **Edge:** Reeded

| Date | Mintage | VF20 | XF40 | MS60 | MS63 | MS65 |
|---|---|---|---|---|---|---|
| 2011 | — | PF63 40.00 | PF65 45.00 | | | |

**KM# 1120 3 DOLLARS**

7.96 g., 0.9999 Silver 0.2559 oz. ASW, 27 mm. **Ruler:** Elizabeth II **Subject:** April birthstone, diamond **Obv:** Bust right **Rev:** Birthstone at cener of artistic sunburst **Edge:** Reeded

| Date | Mintage | VF20 | XF40 | MS60 | MS63 | MS65 |
|---|---|---|---|---|---|---|
| 2011 | — | PF63 40.00 | PF65 45.00 | | | |

**KM# 1121 3 DOLLARS**

7.96 g., 0.9999 Silver 0.2559 oz. ASW, 27 mm. **Ruler:** Elizabeth II **Subject:** May birthstone **Obv:** Bust right **Rev:** Birthstone at cener of artistic sunburst **Edge:** Reeded

| Date | Mintage | VF20 | XF40 | MS60 | MS63 | MS65 |
|---|---|---|---|---|---|---|
| 2011 | — | PF63 40.00 | PF65 45.00 | | | |

**KM# 1122 3 DOLLARS**

7.96 g., 0.9999 Silver 0.2559 oz. ASW, 27 mm. **Ruler:** Elizabeth II **Subject:** June birthstone, Alexandrite **Obv:** Bust right **Rev:** Birthstone at cener of artistic sunburst

| Date | Mintage | VF20 | XF40 | MS60 | MS63 | MS65 |
|---|---|---|---|---|---|---|
| 2011 | — | PF63 40.00 | PF65 45.00 | | | |

**KM# 1123 3 DOLLARS**

7.96 g., 0.9999 Silver 0.2559 oz. ASW, 27 mm. **Ruler:** Elizabeth II **Subject:** July birthstone, Ruby **Obv:** Bust right **Rev:** Birthstone at cener of artistic sunburst

| Date | Mintage | VF20 | XF40 | MS60 | MS63 | MS65 |
|---|---|---|---|---|---|---|
| 2011 | — | PF63 40.00 | PF65 45.00 | | | |

**KM# 1124 3 DOLLARS**

7.96 g., 0.9999 Silver 0.2559 oz. ASW, 27 mm. **Ruler:** Elizabeth II **Subject:** August birthstone, Priedot **Obv:** Bust right **Rev:** Birthstone at cener of artistic sunburst

| Date | Mintage | VF20 | XF40 | MS60 | MS63 | MS65 |
|---|---|---|---|---|---|---|
| 2011 | — | PF63 40.00 | PF65 45.00 | | | |

**KM# 1125 3 DOLLARS**

7.96 g., 0.9999 Silver 0.2559 oz. ASW, 27 mm. **Ruler:** Elizabeth II **Subject:** September birhtstone **Obv:** Bust right **Rev:** Birthstone at cener of artistic sunburst **Edge:** Reeded

| Date | Mintage | VF20 | XF40 | MS60 | MS63 | MS65 |
|---|---|---|---|---|---|---|
| 2011 | — | PF63 40.00 | PF65 45.00 | | | |

**KM# 1126 3 DOLLARS**

7.96 g., 0.9999 Silver 0.2559 oz. ASW, 27 mm. **Ruler:** Elizabeth II **Subject:** October birthstone **Obv:** Bust right **Rev:** Birthstone at cener of artistic sunburst

| Date | Mintage | VF20 | XF40 | MS60 | MS63 | MS65 |
|---|---|---|---|---|---|---|
| 2011 | — | PF63 40.00 | PF65 45.00 | | | |

**KM# 1127 3 DOLLARS**

7.96 g., 0.9999 Silver 0.2559 oz. ASW, 27 mm. **Ruler:** Elizabeth II **Subject:** November birthstone **Obv:** Bust right **Rev:** Birthstone at cener of artistic sunburst

| Date | Mintage | VF20 | XF40 | MS60 | MS63 | MS65 |
|---|---|---|---|---|---|---|
| 2011 | — | PF63 40.00 | PF65 45.00 | | | |

**KM# 1128 3 DOLLARS**

7.96 g., 0.9999 Silver 0.2559 oz. ASW, 27 mm. **Ruler:** Elizabeth II **Subject:** December birhtstone **Obv:** Bust right **Rev:** Birthstone at cener of artistic sunburst

| Date | Mintage | VF20 | XF40 | MS60 | MS63 | MS65 |
|---|---|---|---|---|---|---|
| 2011 | — | PF63 40.00 | PF65 45.00 | | | |

**KM# 1151 3 DOLLARS**

11.80 g., 0.925 Silver 0.3509 oz. ASW gold plated, 27x27 mm. **Ruler:** Elizabeth II **Obv:** Bust right **Rev:** Black footed ferret

| Date | Mintage | VF20 | XF40 | MS60 | MS63 | MS65 |
|---|---|---|---|---|---|---|
| 2011 | Est. 15000 | PF63 55.00 | PF65 65.00 | | | |

**KM# 1300 3 DOLLARS**

7.96 g., 0.9999 Silver 0.2559 oz. ASW, 27 mm. **Ruler:** Elizabeth II **Subject:** January birthstone, Garnet **Obv:** Bust right **Rev:** Birthstone at center of wreath

| Date | Mintage | VF20 | XF40 | MS60 | MS63 | MS65 |
|---|---|---|---|---|---|---|
| 2013 | — | PF65 50.00 | | | | |

**KM# 1301 3 DOLLARS**

7.96 g., 0.999 Silver 0.2557 oz. ASW, 27 mm. **Ruler:** Elizabeth II **Subject:** February birthstone, Amythest **Obv:** Bust right **Rev:** Birthstone at center of wreath

| Date | Mintage | VF20 | XF40 | MS60 | MS63 | MS65 |
|---|---|---|---|---|---|---|
| 2013 | — | PF65 65.00 | | | | |

**KM# 1302 3 DOLLARS**

7.96 g., 0.999 Silver 0.2557 oz. ASW, 27 mm. **Ruler:** Elizabeth II **Subject:** March birthstone, Aquamarine **Obv:** Bust right **Rev:** Birthstone at center of wreath

| Date | Mintage | VF20 | XF40 | MS60 | MS63 | MS65 |
|---|---|---|---|---|---|---|
| 2013 | — | PF65 50.00 | | | | |

**KM# 1303 3 DOLLARS**

7.96 g., 0.999 Silver 0.2557 oz. ASW, 27 mm. **Ruler:** Elizabeth II **Subject:** April birthstone, Diamond **Obv:** Bust right **Rev:** Birthstone at center of wreath

| Date | Mintage | VF20 | XF40 | MS60 | MS63 | MS65 |
|---|---|---|---|---|---|---|
| 2013 | — | PF65 50.00 | | | | |

**KM# 1304 3 DOLLARS**

7.96 g., 0.999 Silver 0.2557 oz. ASW, 27 mm. **Ruler:** Elizabeth II **Subject:** May birthstone **Obv:** Bust right **Rev:** Birthstone at center of wreath

| Date | Mintage | VF20 | XF40 | MS60 | MS63 | MS65 |
|---|---|---|---|---|---|---|
| 2013 | — | PF65 50.00 | | | | |

**KM# 1305 3 DOLLARS**

7.96 g., 0.999 Silver 0.2557 oz. ASW, 27 mm. **Ruler:** Elizabeth II **Subject:** June birthstone, Alexandrite **Obv:** Bust right **Rev:** Birthstone at center of wreath

| Date | Mintage | VF20 | XF40 | MS60 | MS63 | MS65 |
|---|---|---|---|---|---|---|
| 2013 | — | PF65 50.00 | | | | |

**KM# 1306 3 DOLLARS**

7.96 g., 0.999 Silver 0.2557 oz. ASW, 27 mm. **Ruler:** Elizabeth II **Subject:** July birthstone - Ruby **Obv:** Bust right **Rev:** Birthstone at center of wreath

| Date | Mintage | VF20 | XF40 | MS60 | MS63 | MS65 |
|---|---|---|---|---|---|---|
| 2013 | — | PF65 50.00 | | | | |

**KM# 1307 3 DOLLARS**

7.96 g., 0.999 Silver 0.2557 oz. ASW, 27 mm. **Ruler:** Elizabeth II **Subject:** August birthstone - Priedot **Obv:** Bust right **Rev:** Birthstone at center of wreath

| Date | Mintage | VF20 | XF40 | MS60 | MS63 | MS65 |
|---|---|---|---|---|---|---|
| 2013 | — | PF65 50.00 | | | | |

**KM# 1308 3 DOLLARS**

7.96 g., 0.999 Silver 0.2557 oz. ASW, 27 mm. **Ruler:** Elizabeth II **Subject:** September birthstone **Obv:** Bust right **Rev:** Birthstone at center of wreath

| Date | Mintage | VF20 | XF40 | MS60 | MS63 | MS65 |
|---|---|---|---|---|---|---|
| 2013 | — | PF65 50.00 | | | | |

**KM# 1309 3 DOLLARS**

7.96 g., 0.999 Silver 0.2557 oz. ASW, 27 mm. **Ruler:** Elizabeth II **Subject:** October birthstone **Obv:** Bust right **Rev:** Birthstone at center of wreath

| Date | Mintage | VF20 | XF40 | MS60 | MS63 | MS65 |
|---|---|---|---|---|---|---|
| 2013 | — | PF65 50.00 | | | | |

**KM# 1310 3 DOLLARS**

7.96 g., 0.999 Silver 0.2557 oz. ASW, 27 mm. **Ruler:** Elizabeth II **Subject:** November birthstone **Obv:** Bust right **Rev:** Birthstone at center of wreath

| Date | Mintage | VF20 | XF40 | MS60 | MS63 | MS65 |
|---|---|---|---|---|---|---|
| 2013 | — | PF65 50.00 | | | | |

**KM# 1311 3 DOLLARS**

7.96 g., 0.999 Silver 0.2557 oz. ASW, 27 mm. **Ruler:** Elizabeth II **Subject:** December birthstone **Obv:** Bust right **Rev:** Birthstone at center of wreath

| Date | Mintage | VF20 | XF40 | MS60 | MS63 | MS65 |
|---|---|---|---|---|---|---|
| 2013 | — | PF65 50.00 | | | | |

**KM# 1352 3 DOLLARS**

7.96 g., 0.9999 Silver 0.2559 oz. ASW, 27 mm. **Ruler:** Elizabeth II **Rev:** Hummingbirds around crystal

| Date | Mintage | VF20 | XF40 | MS60 | MS63 | MS65 |
|---|---|---|---|---|---|---|
| 2013 | 20,000 | PF63 65.00 | PF65 70.00 | | | |

**KM# 1367 3 DOLLARS**

7.96 g., 0.9999 Silver 0.2559 oz. ASW, 27 mm. **Ruler:** Elizabeth II **Subject:** Animal Architects: Bee **Rev:** Bee and Hive in color

| Date | Mintage | VF20 | XF40 | MS60 | MS63 | MS65 |
|---|---|---|---|---|---|---|
| 2013 | Est. 10000 | PF63 60.00 | PF65 70.00 | | | |

**KM# 1451 3 DOLLARS**

7.96 g., 0.9999 Silver 0.2559 oz. ASW, 27 mm. **Ruler:** Elizabeth II **Rev:** Large maple leaf and many small maple leaves

| Date | Mintage | VF20 | XF40 | MS60 | MS63 | MS65 |
|---|---|---|---|---|---|---|
| 2013 | 10,000 | PF63 50.00 | PF65 60.00 | | | |

**KM# 1481 3 DOLLARS**

19.20 g., 0.950 Copper 0.5864 oz., 35.75 mm. **Ruler:** Elizabeth II **Subject:** Banknote Allegory **Rev:** Female seated

| Date | Mintage | VF20 | XF40 | MS60 | MS63 | MS65 |
|---|---|---|---|---|---|---|
| 2013 | 15,000 | PF63 35.00 | PF65 40.00 | | | |

**KM# 1485 3 DOLLARS**

31.11 g., 0.999 Silver 0.999 oz. ASW, 38 mm. **Ruler:** Elizabeth II **Rev:** Father and son seated, fishing from lake dock, dog at their side

| Date | Mintage | VF20 | XF40 | MS60 | MS63 | MS65 |
|---|---|---|---|---|---|---|
| 2013 | — | PF63 45.00 | PF65 50.00 | | | |

**KM# 1492 3 DOLLARS**

7.96 g., 0.9999 Silver 0.2559 oz. ASW, 27 mm. **Ruler:** Elizabeth II **Rev:** Hummingbird and morning glory - crystal insert

| Date | Mintage | VF20 | XF40 | MS60 | MS63 | MS65 |
|---|---|---|---|---|---|---|
| 2013 | 20,000 | PF63 50.00 | PF65 60.00 | | | |

**KM# 1528 3 DOLLARS**

7.96 g., 0.999 Silver 0.2557 oz. ASW, 27 mm. **Ruler:** Elizabeth II **Rev:** Spider on web

| Date | Mintage | VF20 | XF40 | MS60 | MS63 | MS65 |
|---|---|---|---|---|---|---|
| 2013 | 10,000 | PF63 60.00 | PF65 70.00 | | | |

**KM# 1537 3 DOLLARS**

7.96 g., 0.999 Silver 0.2557 oz. ASW, 27 mm. **Ruler:** Elizabeth II **Rev:** Whale, realistic and Inuit designs

| Date | Mintage | VF20 | XF40 | MS60 | MS63 | MS65 |
|---|---|---|---|---|---|---|
| 2013 | 10,000 | PF63 30.00 | PF65 35.00 | | | |
| 2013 Reverse Proof | — | PF65 35.00 | | | | |

**KM# 1617 3 DOLLARS**

7.96 g., 0.999 Silver 0.2557 oz. ASW partially gilt with five crystal inserts, 27 mm. **Ruler:** Elizabeth II **Subject:** Jewel of Life **Obv:** Bust right **Rev:** Tree and crystals

| Date | Mintage | VF20 | XF40 | MS60 | MS63 | MS65 |
|---|---|---|---|---|---|---|
| 2014 | 15,000 | PF63 50.00 | PF65 60.00 | | | |

**KM# 1639 3 DOLLARS**

7.96 g., Silver, 27 mm. **Ruler:** Elizabeth II **Obv:** Bust right **Rev:** Caterpillar in color with Chrysalis in background

| Date | Mintage | F12 | VF20 | XF40 | MS60 | MS63 |
|---|---|---|---|---|---|---|
| 2014 | 10,000 | PF63 40.00 | PF65 45.00 | | | |

**KM# 1712 3 DOLLARS**

7.96 g., 0.9999 Silver 0.2559 oz. ASW, 27 mm. **Ruler:** Elizabeth II **Obv:** Bust right **Rev:** WWII photo of child running after dad leaving for war

| Date | Mintage | VF20 | XF40 | MS60 | MS63 | MS65 |
|---|---|---|---|---|---|---|
| 2014 | 15,000 | PF65 80.00 | | | | |

**KM# 728 4 DOLLARS**
15.87 g., 0.925 Silver 0.472 oz. ASW, 34 mm. **Ruler:** Elizabeth II **Subject:** Dinosaur fossil **Obv:** Bust right **Rev:** Parasaurolophus, selective enameling

| Date | Mintage | VF20 | XF40 | MS60 | MS63 | MS65 |
|---|---|---|---|---|---|---|
| 2007 | 14,946 | **PF63** 115 | **PF65** 125 | | | |

**KM# 797 4 DOLLARS**
15.87 g., 0.999 Silver 0.5097 oz. ASW, 34 mm. **Ruler:** Elizabeth II **Subject:** Dinosaur fossil **Obv:** Bust right **Rev:** Triceratops, enameled

| Date | Mintage | VF20 | XF40 | MS60 | MS63 | MS65 |
|---|---|---|---|---|---|---|
| 2008 | 13,046 | **PF63** 65.00 | **PF65** 75.00 | | | |

**KM# 890 4 DOLLARS**
15.87 g., 0.999 Silver 0.5097 oz. ASW, 34 mm. **Ruler:** Elizabeth II **Subject:** Tyrannosaurus Rex **Obv:** Bust right **Obv. Legend:** Elizabeth II DG Regina **Rev:** T-Rex skeleton in selective aging **Rev. Legend:** Canada 4 Dollars

| Date | Mintage | VF20 | XF40 | MS60 | MS63 | MS65 |
|---|---|---|---|---|---|---|
| 2009 | 13,572 | **PF63** 50.00 | **PF65** 60.00 | | | |

**KM# 942 4 DOLLARS**
15.87 g., 0.999 Silver 0.5097 oz. ASW, 34 mm. **Ruler:** Elizabeth II **Rev:** Kids hanging stocking on fireplace mantle, Christmas tree on right

| Date | Mintage | VF20 | XF40 | MS60 | MS63 | MS65 |
|---|---|---|---|---|---|---|
| 2009 | 6,011 | **PF63** 40.00 | **PF65** 45.00 | | | |

**KM# 1014 4 DOLLARS**
15.87 g., 0.999 Silver 0.5097 oz. ASW selectively plated, 34 mm. **Ruler:** Elizabeth II **Rev:** Euoplocephalus

| Date | Mintage | VF20 | XF40 | MS60 | MS63 | MS65 |
|---|---|---|---|---|---|---|
| 2010 | Est. 13000 | **PF63** 50.00 | **PF65** 60.00 | | | |

**KM# 1022 4 DOLLARS**
15.87 g., 0.999 Silver 0.5097 oz. ASW selective plating, 34 mm. **Ruler:** Elizabeth II **Rev:** Dromaeosaurus

| Date | Mintage | VF20 | XF40 | MS60 | MS63 | MS65 |
|---|---|---|---|---|---|---|
| 2010 | 8,982 | **PF63** 75.00 | **PF65** 85.00 | | | |

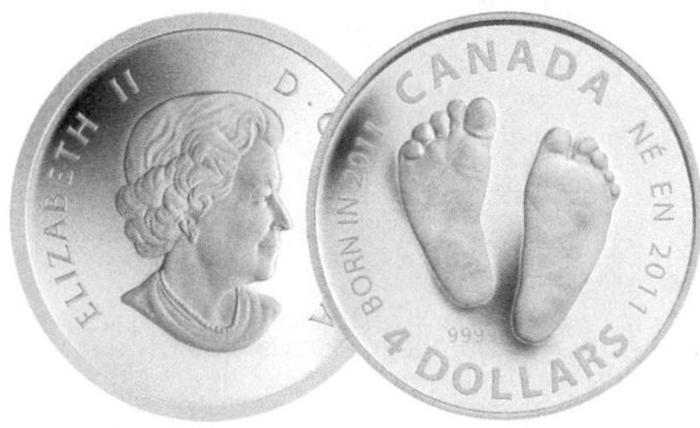

**KM# 1129 4 DOLLARS**
15.87 g., 0.9999 Silver 0.5102 oz. ASW, 34 mm. **Ruler:** Elizabeth II **Obv:** Bust right **Rev:** Baby's footprint **Edge:** Reeded

| Date | Mintage | VF20 | XF40 | MS60 | MS63 | MS65 |
|---|---|---|---|---|---|---|
| 2011 | Est. 10000 | **PF63** 50.00 | **PF65** 60.00 | | | |

**KM# 1323 4 DOLLARS**
7.96 g., 0.999 Silver 0.2557 oz. ASW, 27 mm. **Ruler:** Elizabeth II **Subject:** War of 1812 - Brock **Rev:** Portrait at right, red maple leaf

| Date | Mintage | VF20 | XF40 | MS60 | MS63 | MS65 |
|---|---|---|---|---|---|---|
| 2012 | 10,000 | **PF63** 45.00 | **PF65** 50.00 | | | |

**KM# 1325 4 DOLLARS**
7.96 g., 0.999 Silver 0.2557 oz. ASW, 27 mm. **Ruler:** Elizabeth II **Subject:** War of 1812 - Tecumseh **Rev:** Portrait at right, red maple leaf

| Date | Mintage | VF20 | XF40 | MS60 | MS63 | MS65 |
|---|---|---|---|---|---|---|
| 2012 | 10,000 | **PF63** 45.00 | **PF65** 50.00 | | | |

**KM# 1356 4 DOLLARS**
7.96 g., 0.9999 Silver 0.2559 oz. ASW, 27 mm. **Ruler:** Elizabeth II **Subject:** War of 1812 - Salaberry **Rev:** Bust at right, red maple leaf

| Date | Mintage | VF20 | XF40 | MS60 | MS63 | MS65 |
|---|---|---|---|---|---|---|
| 2013 | 10,000 | **PF63** 45.00 | **PF65** 50.00 | | | |

**KM# 1452 4 DOLLARS**
7.96 g., 0.999 Silver 0.2557 oz. ASW, 27 mm. **Ruler:** Elizabeth II **Subject:** War of 1812 - Secord **Rev:** Bust at right, maple leaf in color

| Date | Mintage | VF20 | XF40 | MS60 | MS63 | MS65 |
|---|---|---|---|---|---|---|
| 2013 | Est. 10000 | **PF63** 40.00 | **PF65** 50.00 | | | |

**KM# 435 5 DOLLARS**
16.86 g., 0.925 Silver 0.5014 oz. ASW, 28.4 mm. **Ruler:** Elizabeth II **Subject:** Guglielmo Marconi **Obv:** Crowned head right **Rev:** Gold-plated cameo portrait of Marconi **Edge:** Reeded **Note:** Only issued in two coin set with British 2 pounds KM#1014a.

| Date | Mintage | VF20 | XF40 | MS60 | MS63 | MS65 |
|---|---|---|---|---|---|---|
| 2001 | 15,011 | **PF63** 22.00 | **PF65** 30.00 | | | |

**KM# 519 5 DOLLARS**
8.36 g., 0.900 Gold 0.2419 oz. AGW, 21.6 mm. **Ruler:** Elizabeth II **Obv:** Crowned head right **Rev:** National arms **Edge:** Reeded

| Date | Mintage | VF20 | XF40 | MS60 | MS63 | MS65 |
|---|---|---|---|---|---|---|
| 1912-2002 | 2,002 | **PF65** 450 | | | | |

**KM# 603 5 DOLLARS**
31.11 g., 0.9999 Silver 0.9999 oz. ASW **Ruler:** Elizabeth II **Obv:** Head right **Rev:** Loon splashing in the water, hologram

| Date | Mintage | VF20 | XF40 | MS60 | MS63 | MS65 |
|---|---|---|---|---|---|---|
| 2002 Satin Proof | 30,000 | **PF65** 50.00 | | | | |

**KM# 518 5 DOLLARS**
31.12 g., 0.9999 Silver 1.0004 oz. ASW, 38 mm. **Ruler:** Elizabeth II **Subject:** F.I.F.A. World Cup Soccer , Germany 2006 **Obv:** Crowned head right, denomination **Rev:** Goalie on knees **Edge:** Reeded

| Date | Mintage | VF20 | XF40 | MS60 | MS63 | MS65 |
|---|---|---|---|---|---|---|
| 2003 | 21,542 | **PF63** 35.00 | **PF65** 40.00 | | | |

**KM# 514 5 DOLLARS**
31.12 g., 0.9999 Silver 1.0004 oz. ASW, 38 mm. **Ruler:** Elizabeth II **Obv:** Crowned head right **Rev:** Moose **Edge:** Reeded

| Date | Mintage | VF20 | XF40 | MS60 | MS63 | MS65 |
|---|---|---|---|---|---|---|
| 2004 | 12,822 | **PF65** 175 | | | | |

**KM# 527 5 DOLLARS**
31.12 g., 0.9999 Silver 1.0004 oz. ASW **Ruler:** Elizabeth II **Subject:** Golf, Championship of Canada, Centennial **Obv:** Head right

| Date | Mintage | VF20 | XF40 | MS60 | MS63 | MS65 |
|---|---|---|---|---|---|---|
| 2004 | 18,750 | **PF63** 25.00 | **PF65** 30.00 | | | |

**KM# 554 5 DOLLARS**
31.12 g., 0.9999 Silver 1.0004 oz. ASW **Ruler:** Elizabeth II **Subject:** Alberta

| Date | Mintage | VF20 | XF40 | MS60 | MS63 | MS65 |
|---|---|---|---|---|---|---|
| 2005 | 20,000 | **PF63** 30.00 | **PF65** 35.00 | | | |

**KM# 555 5 DOLLARS**
31.12 g., 0.9999 Silver 1.0004 oz. ASW **Ruler:** Elizabeth II **Subject:** Saskatchewan **Obv:** Head right

| Date | Mintage | VF20 | XF40 | MS60 | MS63 | MS65 |
|---|---|---|---|---|---|---|
| 2005 | 20,000 | **PF63** 30.00 | **PF65** 35.00 | | | |

**KM# 556.1 5 DOLLARS**
31.12 g., 0.999 Silver 0.9995 oz. ASW, 38.02 mm. **Ruler:** Elizabeth II **Subject:** 60th Anniversay Victory WWII - Veterans **Obv:** Bust right **Rev:** Large V and heads of sailor, soldier and aviator on large maple leaf **Edge:** Reeded

| Date | Mintage | VF20 | XF40 | MS60 | MS63 | MS65 |
|---|---|---|---|---|---|---|
| 2005 | 25,000 | — | — | — | 32.00 | — |

**KM# 556.2 5 DOLLARS**
31.12 g., 0.9999 Silver 1.0004 oz. ASW, 38.02 mm. **Ruler:** Elizabeth II **Subject:** 60th Anniversary Victory WW II - Veterans **Obv:** Bust right **Rev:** Large V and heads of sailor, soldier and aviator on maple leaf with small maple leaf added at left and right **Edge:** Reeded

| Date | Mintage | VF20 | XF40 | MS60 | MS63 | MS65 |
|---|---|---|---|---|---|---|
| 2005 | 10,000 | — | — | — | 125 | — |

**KM# 557 5 DOLLARS**
31.12 g., 0.9999 Silver 1.0004 oz. ASW, 36 mm. **Ruler:** Elizabeth II **Subject:** Walrus and calf **Obv:** Head right **Rev:** Two walrusus and calf

| Date | Mintage | VF20 | XF40 | MS60 | MS63 | MS65 |
|---|---|---|---|---|---|---|
| 2005 | 5,519 | PF63 40.00 | PF65 45.00 | | | |

**KM# 558 5 DOLLARS**
31.12 g., 0.9999 Silver 1.0004 oz. ASW, 36 mm. **Ruler:** Elizabeth II **Subject:** White tailed deer **Obv:** Head right **Rev:** Two deer standing

| Date | Mintage | VF20 | XF40 | MS60 | MS63 | MS65 |
|---|---|---|---|---|---|---|
| 2005 | 6,439 | PF63 40.00 | PF65 45.00 | | | |

**KM# 585 5 DOLLARS**
31.12 g., 0.9999 Silver 1.0004 oz. ASW, 36 mm. **Ruler:** Elizabeth II **Obv:** Head right **Rev:** Peregrine Falcon feeding young ones

| Date | Mintage | VF20 | XF40 | MS60 | MS63 | MS65 |
|---|---|---|---|---|---|---|
| 2006 | 7,226 | PF63 45.00 | PF65 50.00 | | | |

**KM# 586 5 DOLLARS**
31.12 g., 0.9999 Silver 1.0004 oz. ASW, 36 mm. **Ruler:** Elizabeth II **Subject:** Sable Island horses **Obv:** Head right **Rev:** Horse and foal standing

| Date | Mintage | VF20 | XF40 | MS60 | MS63 | MS65 |
|---|---|---|---|---|---|---|
| 2006 | 10,108 | PF63 45.00 | PF65 50.00 | | | |

**KM# 658 5 DOLLARS**
31.12 g., 0.9999 Silver 1.0004 oz. ASW, 36.07 mm. **Ruler:** Elizabeth II **Subject:** Breast Cancer Awareness **Rev:** Colorized pink ribbon

| Date | Mintage | VF20 | XF40 | MS60 | MS63 | MS65 |
|---|---|---|---|---|---|---|
| 2006 | 11,048 | PF63 45.00 | PF65 50.00 | | | |

**KM# 659 5 DOLLARS**
31.12 g., 0.9999 Silver 1.0004 oz. ASW **Ruler:** Elizabeth II **Subject:** C.A.F. Snowbirds Acrobatic Jet Flying Team **Rev:** Image of fighter jets and piolt

| Date | Mintage | VF20 | XF40 | MS60 | MS63 | MS65 |
|---|---|---|---|---|---|---|
| 2006 | 10,034 | PF63 45.00 | PF65 50.00 | | | |

**KM# 1036 5 DOLLARS**
31.12 g., 0.999 Silver 0.9995 oz. ASW **Ruler:** Elizabeth II **Subject:** 80th Anniversary **Rev:** Two deer standing, one eating branch

| Date | Mintage | VF20 | XF40 | MS60 | MS63 | MS65 |
|---|---|---|---|---|---|---|
| 2009 | 27,872 | PF63 60.00 | PF65 70.00 | | | |

**KM# 1130 5 DOLLARS**
8.50 g., 0.925 Silver 0.2528 oz. ASW with Niobium plated reverse center, 28 mm. **Ruler:** Elizabeth II **Subject:** Summer - Buck Moon **Obv:** Bust right **Rev:** Buck against summer moon

| Date | Mintage | VF20 | XF40 | MS60 | MS63 | MS65 |
|---|---|---|---|---|---|---|
| 2011 | 7,500 | PF63 115 | PF65 125 | | | |

**KM# 1131 5 DOLLARS**
8.50 g., 0.925 Silver 0.2528 oz. ASW with Niobium plated reverse center, 28 mm. **Ruler:** Elizabeth II **Subject:** Fall Moon **Obv:** Bust right **Rev:** Native American hunter seated tracking prey before Harvest Moon

| Date | Mintage | VF20 | XF40 | MS60 | MS63 | MS65 |
|---|---|---|---|---|---|---|
| 2011 | 7,500 | PF63 115 | PF65 125 | | | |

**KM# 1149 5 DOLLARS**
3.13 g., 0.9999 Gold 0.1006 oz. AGW, 16 mm. **Ruler:** Elizabeth II **Subject:** Norman Bethune **Obv:** Bust right **Rev:** Half-length figure at right, looking left

| Date | Mintage | VF20 | XF40 | MS60 | MS63 | MS65 |
|---|---|---|---|---|---|---|
| 2011 | Est. 5000 | PF65 300 | | | | |

**KM# 1132 5 DOLLARS**
8.50 g., 0.925 Silver 0.2528 oz. ASW with Niobium plated reverse center, 28 mm. **Ruler:** Elizabeth II **Subject:** Winter Moon **Obv:** Bust right **Rev:** Wolf howling before Winter Moon

| Date | Mintage | VF20 | XF40 | MS60 | MS63 | MS65 |
|---|---|---|---|---|---|---|
| 2012 | 7,500 | PF63 115 | PF65 125 | | | |

**KM# 1133 5 DOLLARS**
8.50 g., 0.925 Silver 0.2528 oz. ASW with Niobium plated reverse center., 28 mm. **Ruler:** Elizabeth II **Subject:** Spring Moon **Rev:** Phlox blossoming against a Spring Moon, field in color

| Date | Mintage | VF20 | XF40 | MS60 | MS63 | MS65 |
|---|---|---|---|---|---|---|
| 2012 | — | PF63 115 | PF65 125 | | | |

**KM# 1194 5 DOLLARS**
3.13 g., 0.999 Gold 0.1005 oz. AGW, 16 mm. **Ruler:** Elizabeth II **Obv:** Bust right **Rev:** Royal Cypher, wreath below

| Date | Mintage | VF20 | XF40 | MS60 | MS63 | MS65 |
|---|---|---|---|---|---|---|
| 2012 | — | PF65 200 | | | | |

**KM# 1220 5 DOLLARS**
3.13 g., 0.9999 Gold 0.1006 oz. AGW, 16 mm. **Ruler:** Elizabeth II **Subject:** Year of the Dragon **Obv:** Bust right **Rev:** Dragon forpart right

| Date | Mintage | VF20 | XF40 | MS60 | MS63 | MS65 |
|---|---|---|---|---|---|---|
| 2012 Specimen | — | PF65 225 | | | | |

**KM# 1236 5 DOLLARS**
8.36 g., 0.900 Gold 0.2419 oz. AGW, 21.6 mm. **Ruler:** Elizabeth II **Obv:** Bust right **Rev:** Crowned monogram in wreath

| Date | Mintage | VF20 | XF40 | MS60 | MS63 | MS65 |
|---|---|---|---|---|---|---|
| 1952-2012 | — | PF65 500 | | | | |

**KM# 1248 5 DOLLARS**
31.12 g., 0.999 Silver 0.9995 oz. ASW, 36 mm. **Ruler:** Elizabeth II **Subject:** Rick Hansen **Rev:** Wheelchair bound athlete

| Date | Mintage | VF20 | XF40 | MS60 | MS63 | MS65 |
|---|---|---|---|---|---|---|
| 2012 | — | PF63 65.00 | PF65 75.00 | | | |

**KM# 1281 5 DOLLARS**
3.13 g., 0.999 Gold 0.1005 oz. AGW, 16 mm. **Ruler:** Elizabeth II **Subject:** Year of the Dragon

| Date | Mintage | VF20 | XF40 | MS60 | MS63 | MS65 |
|---|---|---|---|---|---|---|
| 2012 | — | PF65 200 | | | | |

**KM# 1332 5 DOLLARS**
31.11 g., 0.999 Silver 0.999 oz. ASW, 36 mm. **Ruler:** Elizabeth II **Subject:** Georgia Pope **Rev:** Four female soldiers

| Date | Mintage | VF20 | XF40 | MS60 | MS63 | MS65 |
|---|---|---|---|---|---|---|
| 2012 | — | PF63 70.00 | PF65 75.00 | | | |

**KM# 1298 5 DOLLARS**
3.13 g., 0.999 Gold 0.1005 oz. AGW, 16 mm. **Ruler:** Elizabeth II **Subject:** Year of the Snake

| Date | Mintage | VF20 | XF40 | MS60 | MS63 | MS65 |
|---|---|---|---|---|---|---|
| 2013 | — | PF65 225 | | | | |

**KM# 1395 5 DOLLARS**
3.13 g., 0.9999 Gold 0.1006 oz. AGW, 16 mm. **Ruler:** Elizabeth II **Rev:** Beaver swimming with branch in mouth

| Date | Mintage | VF20 | XF40 | MS60 | MS63 | MS65 |
|---|---|---|---|---|---|---|
| 2013 | Est. 4000 | PF65 280 | | | | |

**KM# 1401 5 DOLLARS**
3.13 g., 0.9999 Gold 0.1006 oz. AGW, 16 mm. **Ruler:** Elizabeth II **Rev:** Polar Bear head

| Date | Mintage | VF20 | XF40 | MS60 | MS63 | MS65 |
|---|---|---|---|---|---|---|
| 2013 | Est. 4000 | PF65 275 | | | | |

**KM# 1426 5 DOLLARS**
23.17 g., 0.9999 Silver 0.7449 oz. ASW, 36 mm. **Ruler:** Elizabeth II **Subject:** Traditions: Hunting **Rev:** Deer and hunter teaching child

| Date | Mintage | VF20 | XF40 | MS60 | MS63 | MS65 |
|---|---|---|---|---|---|---|
| 2013 | Est. 10000 | PF63 60.00 | PF65 70.00 | | | |

**KM# 1453 5 DOLLARS**
3.13 g., 0.999 Gold 0.1005 oz. AGW, 16 mm. **Ruler:** Elizabeth II **Rev:** Caribou head

| Date | Mintage | VF20 | XF40 | MS60 | MS63 | MS65 |
|---|---|---|---|---|---|---|
| 2013 | 4,000 | PF65 275 | | | | |

**KM# 1454 5 DOLLARS**
3.13 g., 0.999 Gold 0.1005 oz. AGW, 16 mm. **Ruler:** Elizabeth II **Rev:** Wolf head

| Date | Mintage | VF20 | XF40 | MS60 | MS63 | MS65 |
|---|---|---|---|---|---|---|
| 2013 | 4,000 | PF65 275 | | | | |

**KM# 1461 5 DOLLARS**
23.17 g., 0.9999 Silver 0.7449 oz. ASW with selective gold-plating, 36 mm. **Ruler:** Elizabeth II **Subject:** Birth of Prince George **Rev:** W and C crowned in gilt center, Infant toys around

| Date | Mintage | VF20 | XF40 | MS60 | MS63 | MS65 |
|---|---|---|---|---|---|---|
| 2013 | Est. 15000 | PF63 65.00 | PF65 75.00 | | | |

**KM# 1461a 5 DOLLARS**
23.17 g., 0.9999 Silver 0.7449 oz. ASW, 36 mm. **Ruler:** Elizabeth II **Subject:** Birth of Prince George **Rev:** W and C crowned, infant toys around, gilt reverse

| Date | Mintage | VF20 | XF40 | MS60 | MS63 | MS65 |
|---|---|---|---|---|---|---|
| 2013 | Est. 15000 | PF63 65.00 | PF65 75.00 | | | |

**KM# 1475 5 DOLLARS**
8.50 g., 0.9999 Silver 0.2733 oz. ASW with Niobium plated reverse center., 28 mm. **Ruler:** Elizabeth II **Subject:** Father Ice

| Date | Mintage | VF20 | XF40 | MS60 | MS63 | MS65 |
|---|---|---|---|---|---|---|
| 2013 | 6,500 | PF63 130 | PF65 140 | | | |

**KM# 1476 5 DOLLARS**
8.50 g., 0.9999 Silver 0.2733 oz. ASW with Niobium plated reverse center, 28 mm. **Ruler:** Elizabeth II **Subject:** Mother Ice

| Date | Mintage | VF20 | XF40 | MS60 | MS63 | MS65 |
|---|---|---|---|---|---|---|
| 2013 | 6,500 | PF63 130 | PF65 140 | | | |

**KM# 1497 5 DOLLARS**
7.80 g., 0.999 Gold 0.2505 oz. AGW, 20 mm. **Ruler:** Elizabeth II **Subject:** US / Canada Devil's Brigade **Rev:** Special Forces Emblem

| Date | Mintage | VF20 | XF40 | MS60 | MS63 | MS65 |
|---|---|---|---|---|---|---|
| 2013 | 2,000 | PF65 650 | | | | |

**KM# 1498 5 DOLLARS**
23.17 g., 0.9999 Silver 0.7449 oz. ASW, 36 mm. **Ruler:** Elizabeth II **Subject:** US / Canada Devil's Brigade **Rev:** Special Forces Emblem

| Date | Mintage | VF20 | XF40 | MS60 | MS63 | MS65 |
|---|---|---|---|---|---|---|
| 2013 | 20,000 | PF63 70.00 | PF65 80.00 | | | |

**KM# 1534 5 DOLLARS**
23.00 g., 0.999 Silver 0.7387 oz. ASW, 36 mm. **Ruler:** Elizabeth II **Subject:** Traditional Hunting - Bison **Rev:** Natives advancing upon Bison herd in distance

| Date | Mintage | VF20 | XF40 | MS60 | MS63 | MS65 |
|---|---|---|---|---|---|---|
| 2013 | 10,000 | PF63 65.00 | PF65 70.00 | | | |

**KM# 1543 5 DOLLARS**
3.13 g., 0.999 Gold 0.1005 oz. AGW, 16 mm. **Ruler:** Elizabeth II **Subject:** Oh Canada **Rev:** Orca surfacing

| Date | Mintage | VF20 | XF40 | MS60 | MS63 | MS65 |
|---|---|---|---|---|---|---|
| 2013 | 4,000 | PF65 275 | | | | |

**KM# 1551 5 DOLLARS**
23.00 g., 0.9999 Silver 0.7394 oz. ASW, 36 mm. **Ruler:** Elizabeth II **Subject:** Banknote design

| Date | Mintage | VF20 | XF40 | MS60 | MS63 | MS65 |
|---|---|---|---|---|---|---|
| 2013 | — | PF65 75.00 | | | | |

**KM# 1559 5 DOLLARS**
23.00 g., 0.9999 Silver 0.7394 oz. ASW, 36 mm. **Ruler:** Elizabeth II **Obv:** Bust right **Rev:** St. George slaying dragon

| Date | Mintage | VF20 | XF40 | MS60 | MS63 | MS65 |
|---|---|---|---|---|---|---|
| 2014 | 8,500 | PF63 65.00 | PF65 75.00 | | | |

**KM# 1611 5 DOLLARS**
3.13 g., 0.999 Gold 0.1005 oz. AGW, 16 mm. **Ruler:** Elizabeth II **Obv:** Bust right **Rev:** Grizzly bear

| Date | Mintage | VF20 | XF40 | MS60 | MS63 | MS65 |
|---|---|---|---|---|---|---|
| 2014 | 4,000 | PF65 280 | | | | |

**KM# 1615 5 DOLLARS**
23.17 g., 0.999 Silver 0.7442 oz. ASW, 36.07 mm. **Ruler:** Elizabeth II **Subject:** Traditions of the Hunt - Seal Spearing **Obv:** Bust right **Rev:** Two men ready to spear seal

| Date | Mintage | VF20 | XF40 | MS60 | MS63 | MS65 |
|---|---|---|---|---|---|---|
| 2014 | 10,000 | PF63 60.00 | PF65 70.00 | | | |

**KM# 1641 5 DOLLARS**
31.12 g., 0.9999 Silver 0.9995 oz. ASW, 36 mm. **Ruler:** Elizabeth II **Obv:** Bust right **Rev:** WWI Troops and ship transports

| Date | Mintage | F12 | VF20 | XF40 | MS60 | MS63 |
|---|---|---|---|---|---|---|
| 2014 | — | PF63 170 | PF65 180 | | | |

**KM# 1642 5 DOLLARS**
3.13 g., 0.9999 Platinum 0.1006 oz. APW, 16 mm. **Ruler:** Elizabeth II **Obv:** Bust right **Rev:** Nanabzohoo

| Date | Mintage | F12 | VF20 | XF40 | MS60 | MS63 |
|---|---|---|---|---|---|---|
| 2014 | 3,000 | PF63 280 | PF65 300 | | | |

**KM# 1643 5 DOLLARS**
3.13 g., 0.9999 Gold 0.1006 oz. AGW, 16 mm. **Ruler:** Elizabeth II **Obv:** Bust right **Rev:** Nanabozhoo

| Date | Mintage | F12 | VF20 | XF40 | MS60 | MS63 |
|---|---|---|---|---|---|---|
| 2014 | 3,000 | PF63 260 | PF65 280 | | | |

**KM# 1644 5 DOLLARS**
31.39 g., 0.9999 Silver 1.0091 oz. ASW **Ruler:** Elizabeth II **Obv:** Bust right **Rev:** Arctic Fox

| Date | Mintage | F12 | VF20 | XF40 | MS60 | MS63 |
|---|---|---|---|---|---|---|
| 2014 | 750 | PF63 85.00 | PF65 90.00 | | | |

**KM# 1645 5 DOLLARS**
3.13 g., 0.9999 Gold 0.1006 oz. AGW, 16 mm. **Ruler:** Elizabeth II **Obv:** Bust right **Rev:** Canadian Goose

| Date | Mintage | F12 | VF20 | XF40 | MS60 | MS63 |
|---|---|---|---|---|---|---|
| 2014 | 4,000 | PF63 275 | PF65 290 | | | |

**KM# 1648 5 DOLLARS**
3.14 g., 0.999 Gold 0.1009 oz. AGW, 16 mm. **Ruler:** Elizabeth II **Obv:** Bust right **Rev:** Moose

| Date | Mintage | F12 | VF20 | XF40 | MS60 | MS63 |
|---|---|---|---|---|---|---|
| 2014 | 4,000 | PF63 270 | PF65 280 | | | |

**KM# 1728 5 DOLLARS**
3.11 g., 0.999 Gold 0.0999 oz. AGW, 16 mm. **Ruler:** Elizabeth II **Obv:** Bust right **Rev:** Five Blessings

| Date | Mintage | VF20 | XF40 | MS60 | MS63 | MS65 |
|---|---|---|---|---|---|---|
| 2014 | 2,000 | PF65 280 | | | | |

**KM# 1730 5 DOLLARS**
3.14 g., 0.999 Gold 0.1009 oz. AGW, 16 mm. **Ruler:** Elizabeth II **Obv:** Bust right **Rev:** Woolly Mammoth

| Date | Mintage | VF20 | XF40 | MS60 | MS63 | MS65 |
|---|---|---|---|---|---|---|
| 2014 | 3,000 | PF65 280 | | | | |

**KM# 1740 5 DOLLARS**
3.13 g., 0.999 Gold 0.1005 oz. AGW, 16 mm. **Ruler:** Elizabeth II **Obv:** Bust right **Rev:** Eagle head left

| Date | Mintage | VF20 | XF40 | MS60 | MS63 | MS65 |
|---|---|---|---|---|---|---|
| 2014 | 3,000 | PF65 100 | | | | |

**KM# 1740a 5 DOLLARS**
3.13 g., 0.999 Platinum 0.1005 oz. APW, 16 mm. **Ruler:** Elizabeth II **Obv:** Bust right **Rev:** Eagle head left

| Date | Mintage | VF20 | XF40 | MS60 | MS63 | MS65 |
|---|---|---|---|---|---|---|
| 2014 | 3,000 | PF65 100 | | | | |

**KM# 1756 5 DOLLARS**
3.14 g., 0.999 Gold 0.1009 oz. AGW, 16 mm. **Ruler:** Elizabeth II **Obv:** Bust right **Rev:** Cougar head

| Date | Mintage | VF20 | XF40 | MS60 | MS63 | MS65 |
|---|---|---|---|---|---|---|
| 2014 | — | PF65 100 | | | | |

**KM# 1756a 5 DOLLARS**
3.14 g., 0.999 Platinum 0.1009 oz. APW, 16 mm. **Ruler:** Elizabeth II **Obv:** Bust right **Rev:** Cougar head

| Date | Mintage | VF20 | XF40 | MS60 | MS63 | MS65 |
|---|---|---|---|---|---|---|
| 2014 | — | PF65 100 | | | | |

**KM# 1767 5 DOLLARS**
9.00 g., 0.9999 Silver 0.2893 oz. ASW, 28 mm. **Ruler:** Elizabeth II **Obv:** Bust right **Rev:** Pointsetta in purple niobium

| Date | Mintage | VF20 | XF40 | MS60 | MS63 | MS65 |
|---|---|---|---|---|---|---|
| 2014 | — | PF65 140 | | | | |

**KM# 1768 5 DOLLARS**
9.00 g., 0.9999 Silver 0.2893 oz. ASW, 28 mm. **Ruler:** Elizabeth II **Obv:** Bust right **Rev:** Rose in golden color niobium

| Date | Mintage | VF20 | XF40 | MS60 | MS63 | MS65 |
|---|---|---|---|---|---|---|
| 2014 | 6,000 | PF65 140 | | | | |

**KM# 1774 5 DOLLARS**
9.00 g., 0.9999 Silver 0.2891 oz. ASW, 28 mm. **Ruler:** Elizabeth II **Obv:** Bust right **Rev:** Tulip in niobium

| Date | Mintage | VF20 | XF40 | MS60 | MS63 | MS65 |
|---|---|---|---|---|---|---|
| 2014 | 6,000 | PF65 140 | | | | |

**KM# 1778 5 DOLLARS**
3.14 g., 0.999 Gold 0.1009 oz. AGW, 16 mm. **Ruler:** Elizabeth II **Obv:** Bust right **Rev:** Bison

| Date | Mintage | F12 | VF20 | XF40 | MS60 | MS63 |
|---|---|---|---|---|---|---|
| 2014 | 2,000 | PF65 280 | | | | |

**KM# 1790 5 DOLLARS**
3.14 g., 0.999 Gold 0.1009 oz. AGW, 16 mm. **Ruler:** Elizabeth II **Obv:** Bust right by Mary Gilick **Rev:** Two maple leaves

| Date | Mintage | F12 | VF20 | XF40 | MS60 | MS63 |
|---|---|---|---|---|---|---|
| 2014 | 650 | PF65 200 | | | | |

**KM# 1798 5 DOLLARS**
23.17 g., 0.999 Silver 0.7442 oz. ASW, 36.07 mm. **Ruler:** Elizabeth II **Subject:** Traditions of Hunting **Obv:** Bust right **Rev:** Bow hunting of goose in flight

| Date | Mintage | F12 | VF20 | XF40 | MS60 | MS63 |
|---|---|---|---|---|---|---|
| 2014 | 10,000 | PF65 70.00 | | | | |

**KM# 1799 5 DOLLARS**
23.17 g., 0.999 Silver 0.7442 oz. ASW, 36.07 mm. **Ruler:** Elizabeth II **Subject:** Princess to Monarch **Obv:** Bust right **Rev:** Elizabeth II reviewing troops

| Date | Mintage | F12 | VF20 | XF40 | MS60 | MS63 |
|---|---|---|---|---|---|---|
| 2014 | 10,000 | PF65 65.00 | | | | |

**KM# 1812 5 DOLLARS**
23.17 g., 0.9999 Silver 0.7449 oz. ASW, 36.07 mm. **Ruler:** Elizabeth II **Obv:** Bust right **Rev:** Ram head facing in color

| Date | Mintage | VF20 | XF40 | MS60 | MS63 | MS65 |
|---|---|---|---|---|---|---|
| 2015 | 8,888 | PF65 75.00 | | | | |

**KM# 1815 5 DOLLARS**
31.39 g., 0.999 Silver 1.0082 oz. ASW, 38 mm. **Ruler:** Elizabeth II **Obv:** Bust right **Rev:** Polar bear and cub advancing left

| Date | Mintage | VF20 | XF40 | MS60 | MS63 | MS65 |
|---|---|---|---|---|---|---|
| 2015 | 7,500 | PF65 90.00 | | | | |

**KM# 1818 5 DOLLARS**
3.15 g., 0.999 Gold 0.1012 oz. AGW, 16 mm. **Ruler:** Elizabeth II **Subject:** Year of the Ram **Obv:** Bust right **Rev:** Ram head facing

| Date | Mintage | F12 | VF20 | XF40 | MS60 | MS63 |
|---|---|---|---|---|---|---|
| 2015 | 2,888 | PF65 280 | | | | |

**KM# 1819 5 DOLLARS**
23.17 g., 0.9999 Silver 0.7449 oz. ASW, 36.07 mm. **Ruler:** Elizabeth II **Subject:** Art by Cornelius Krieghoff **Obv:** Bust right **Rev:** Moccasin Seller Crossing St. Lawrence at Quebec City

| Date | Mintage | F12 | VF20 | XF40 | MS60 | MS63 |
|---|---|---|---|---|---|---|
| 2015 | 7,000 | PF65 75.00 | | | | |

**KM# 1820 5 DOLLARS**
23.17 g., 0.9999 Silver 0.7449 oz. ASW, 36.07 mm. **Ruler:** Elizabeth II **Subject:** Art by Cornelius Krieghoff **Obv:** Bust right **Rev:** Hunter in Winter

| Date | Mintage | VF20 | XF40 | MS60 | MS63 | MS65 |
|---|---|---|---|---|---|---|
| 2015 | 7,000 | PF65 75.00 | | | | |

**KM# 1821 5 DOLLARS**
23.17 g., 0.9999 Silver 0.7449 oz. ASW, 36.07 mm. **Ruler:** Elizabeth II **Subject:** Art by Cornelius Krieghoff **Obv:** Bust right **Rev:** Wigwam in Montagnais

| Date | Mintage | F12 | VF20 | XF40 | MS60 | MS63 |
|---|---|---|---|---|---|---|
| 2015 | 7,000 | PF65 75.00 | | | | |

**KM# 515 8 DOLLARS**
28.80 g., 0.925 Silver 0.8565 oz. ASW, 39 mm. **Ruler:** Elizabeth II **Obv:** Head right **Rev:** Grizzly bear walking left **Edge:** Reeded

| Date | Mintage | VF20 | XF40 | MS60 | MS63 | MS65 |
|---|---|---|---|---|---|---|
| 2004 | 12,942 | PF65 85.00 | | | | |

**KM# 597 8 DOLLARS**
32.15 g., 0.9999 Silver 1.0335 oz. ASW partially gilt **Ruler:** Elizabeth II **Subject:** Canadian Pacific Railway, 120th Anniversary **Obv:** Head right **Rev:** Railway bridge, center is gilt

| Date | Mintage | VF20 | XF40 | MS60 | MS63 | MS65 |
|---|---|---|---|---|---|---|
| 2005 | 9,892 | PF63 60.00 | PF65 65.00 | | | |

**KM# 598 8 DOLLARS**
32.15 g., 0.9999 Silver 1.0335 oz. ASW partially gilt **Ruler:** Elizabeth II **Subject:** Canadian Pacific Railway, 120th Anniversary **Obv:** Head right **Rev:** Railway memorial to the Chinese workers, center gilt

| Date | Mintage | VF20 | XF40 | MS60 | MS63 | MS65 |
|---|---|---|---|---|---|---|
| 2005 | 9,892 | PF63 60.00 | PF65 65.00 | | | |

**KM# 730 8 DOLLARS**
25.18 g., 0.9999 Silver 0.8095 oz. ASW, 36.07 mm. **Ruler:** Elizabeth II **Obv:** Queens's head at top in circle, three Chinese characters **Rev:** Dragon and other creatures

| Date | Mintage | VF20 | XF40 | MS60 | MS63 | MS65 |
|---|---|---|---|---|---|---|
| 2007 | 19,996 | PF63 45.00 | PF65 50.00 | | | |

**KM# 731 8 DOLLARS**
25.18 g., 0.999 Silver 0.8087 oz. ASW, 36.1 mm. **Ruler:** Elizabeth II **Rev:** Maple leaf, long life hologram

| Date | Mintage | VF20 | XF40 | MS60 | MS63 | MS65 |
|---|---|---|---|---|---|---|
| 2007 | 15,000 | PF65 55.00 | | | | |

**KM# 943 8 DOLLARS**
25.18 g., 0.925 Silver 0.7488 oz. ASW, 36.1 mm. **Ruler:** Elizabeth II **Rev:** Hologram maple of wisdom at top left, crystal in center, dragons around

| Date | Mintage | VF20 | XF40 | MS60 | MS63 | MS65 |
|---|---|---|---|---|---|---|
| 2009 | 7,273 | PF63 85.00 | PF65 90.00 | | | |

**KM# 1012 8 DOLLARS**
25.30 g., 0.925 Silver 0.7524 oz. ASW, 36.07 mm. **Ruler:** Elizabeth II **Rev:** Horses around central maple leaf hologram

| Date | Mintage | VF20 | XF40 | MS60 | MS63 | MS65 |
|---|---|---|---|---|---|---|
| 2010 | 8,888 | PF63 90.00 | PF65 100 | | | |

**KM# 1535 8 DOLLARS**
46.65 g., 0.999 Silver 1.4983 oz. ASW, 38 mm. **Ruler:** Elizabeth II **Rev:** Polar bear advancing left

| Date | Mintage | VF20 | XF40 | MS60 | MS63 | MS65 |
|---|---|---|---|---|---|---|
| 2013 | — | PF65 125 | | | | |

**KM# 520 10 DOLLARS**
16.72 g., 0.900 Gold 0.4838 oz. AGW, 26.92 mm. **Ruler:** Elizabeth II **Obv:** Crowned head right **Rev:** National arms **Edge:** Reeded

| Date | Mintage | VF20 | XF40 | MS60 | MS63 | MS65 |
|---|---|---|---|---|---|---|
| 1912-2002 | 2,002 | PF65 850 | | | | |

**KM# 559 10 DOLLARS**
25.18 g., 0.9999 Silver 0.8093 oz. ASW, 36 mm. **Ruler:** Elizabeth II **Subject:** Pope John Paul II **Obv:** Head right

| Date | Mintage | VF20 | XF40 | MS60 | MS63 | MS65 |
|---|---|---|---|---|---|---|
| 2005 | 24,716 | PF63 40.00 | PF65 45.00 | | | |

**KM# 757 10 DOLLARS**
25.18 g., 0.9999 Silver 0.8093 oz. ASW **Ruler:** Elizabeth II **Subject:** Year of the Veteran **Rev:** Profile left of young and old veteran

| Date | Mintage | VF20 | XF40 | MS60 | MS63 | MS65 |
|---|---|---|---|---|---|---|
| 2005 | 6,549 | PF65 225 | | | | |

**KM# 661 10 DOLLARS**
25.18 g., 0.9999 Silver 0.8093 oz. ASW **Ruler:** Elizabeth II **Subject:** National Historic Sites **Obv:** Head right **Rev:** Fortress of Louisbourg

| Date | Mintage | VF20 | XF40 | MS60 | MS63 | MS65 |
|---|---|---|---|---|---|---|
| 2006 | 5,544 | **PF63** 35.00 | **PF65** 40.00 | | | |

**KM# 1010 10 DOLLARS**
15.87 g., 0.999 Silver 0.5097 oz. ASW **Ruler:** Elizabeth II **Subject:** 75th Anniversary Canadian Bank Notes **Rev:** Female seated

| Date | Mintage | VF20 | XF40 | MS60 | MS63 | MS65 |
|---|---|---|---|---|---|---|
| 2010 | 7,500 | **PF63** 45.00 | **PF65** 50.00 | | | |

**KM# 1096 10 DOLLARS**
27.78 g., 0.925 Silver 0.8262 oz. ASW, 40 mm. **Ruler:** Elizabeth II **Obv:** Bust right **Rev:** Blue whale diving in sea

| Date | Mintage | VF20 | XF40 | MS60 | MS63 | MS65 |
|---|---|---|---|---|---|---|
| 2010 | 10,000 | **PF63** 75.00 | **PF65** 85.00 | | | |

**KM# 1198 10 DOLLARS**
15.87 g., 0.999 Silver 0.5097 oz. ASW, 34 mm. **Ruler:** Elizabeth II **Subject:** Highway of Heroes **Obv:** Bust right **Rev:** Citizens on Highway 401 overpass with signs and flags, large maple leaf in background, Memorial Cross medal at top left. **Edge:** Reeded

| Date | Mintage | VF20 | XF40 | MS60 | MS63 | MS65 |
|---|---|---|---|---|---|---|
| 2011 | 25,000 | **PF63** 60.00 | **PF65** 70.00 | | | |

**KM# 1199 10 DOLLARS**
15.87 g., 0.9999 Silver 0.5102 oz. ASW, 34 mm. **Ruler:** Elizabeth II **Subject:** Winter Scene - Skating **Rev:** Three kids skating on pond, colored holly at left

| Date | Mintage | VF20 | XF40 | MS60 | MS63 | MS65 |
|---|---|---|---|---|---|---|
| 2011 | Est. 8000 | **PF63** 35.00 | **PF65** 40.00 | | | |

**KM# 1200 10 DOLLARS**
15.87 g., 0.9999 Silver 0.5102 oz. ASW, 34 mm. **Ruler:** Elizabeth II **Subject:** Winter scene - Two houses **Rev:** Two houses in snowy lane, colored holly flanking

| Date | Mintage | VF20 | XF40 | MS60 | MS63 | MS65 |
|---|---|---|---|---|---|---|
| 2011 | — | **PF63** 35.00 | **PF65** 40.00 | | | |

**KM# 1201 10 DOLLARS**
15.87 g., 0.9999 Silver 0.5102 oz. ASW, 34 mm. **Ruler:** Elizabeth II **Obv:** Bust right **Rev:** Wood Bison

| Date | Mintage | VF20 | XF40 | MS60 | MS63 | MS65 |
|---|---|---|---|---|---|---|
| 2011 | Est. 10000 | **PF63** 40.00 | **PF65** 50.00 | | | |

**KM# 1203 10 DOLLARS**
15.87 g., 0.9999 Silver 0.5102 oz. ASW, 34 mm. **Ruler:** Elizabeth II **Subject:** Boreal Forest **Rev:** Bird and tree

| Date | Mintage | VF20 | XF40 | MS60 | MS63 | MS65 |
|---|---|---|---|---|---|---|
| 2011 | Est. 10000 | **PF63** 40.00 | **PF65** 50.00 | | | |

**KM# 1205 10 DOLLARS**
15.87 g., 0.9999 Silver 0.5102 oz. ASW, 34 mm. **Ruler:** Elizabeth II **Obv:** Bust right **Rev:** Peregrine Falcon perched on branch

| Date | Mintage | VF20 | XF40 | MS60 | MS63 | MS65 |
|---|---|---|---|---|---|---|
| 2011 | Est. 10000 | **PF63** 40.00 | **PF65** 50.00 | | | |

**KM# 1207 10 DOLLARS**
15.87 g., 0.9999 Silver 0.5102 oz. ASW, 34 mm. **Ruler:** Elizabeth II **Obv:** Bust right **Rev:** Orca Whale

| Date | Mintage | VF20 | XF40 | MS60 | MS63 | MS65 |
|---|---|---|---|---|---|---|
| 2011 | Est. 10000 | **PF63** 40.00 | **PF65** 50.00 | | | |

**KM# 1221 10 DOLLARS**
15.87 g., 0.999 Silver 0.5097 oz. ASW, 34 mm. **Ruler:** Elizabeth II **Subject:** Year of the Dragon **Obv:** Bust right **Rev:** Dragon forepart right

| Date | Mintage | VF20 | XF40 | MS60 | MS63 | MS65 |
|---|---|---|---|---|---|---|
| 2012 Specimen | 58,888 | — | — | — | 40.00 | — |

**KM# 1235 10 DOLLARS**
25.18 g., 0.999 Silver 0.8086 oz. ASW, 36 mm. **Ruler:** Elizabeth II **Obv:** Bust right **Rev:** Titanic sailing at right, map of Eastern Canada at left

| Date | Mintage | VF20 | XF40 | MS60 | MS63 | MS65 |
|---|---|---|---|---|---|---|
| 2012 | — | **PF63** 90.00 | **PF65** 100 | | | |

**KM# 1249 10 DOLLARS**
15.87 g., 0.999 Silver 0.5097 oz. ASW, 34 mm. **Ruler:** Elizabeth II **Subject:** H.M.S. Shannon

| Date | Mintage | VF20 | XF40 | MS60 | MS63 | MS65 |
|---|---|---|---|---|---|---|
| 2012 | — | **PF63** 55.00 | **PF65** 65.00 | | | |

**KM# 1259 10 DOLLARS**
15.87 g., 0.999 Silver 0.5097 oz. ASW, 34 mm. **Ruler:** Elizabeth II **Subject:** Praying Mantis

| Date | Mintage | VF20 | XF40 | MS60 | MS63 | MS65 |
|---|---|---|---|---|---|---|
| 2012 | 7,500 | **PF63** 40.00 | **PF65** 45.00 | | | |

**KM# 1282 10 DOLLARS**
7.77 g., 0.999 Gold 0.2496 oz. AGW, 20 mm. **Ruler:** Elizabeth II **Subject:** Year of the Dragon

| Date | Mintage | VF20 | XF40 | MS60 | MS63 | MS65 |
|---|---|---|---|---|---|---|
| 2012 | — | **PF65** 450 | | | | |

**KM# 1346 10 DOLLARS**
15.55 g., 0.999 Silver 0.4994 oz. ASW, 34 mm. **Ruler:** Elizabeth II **Rev:** Baby's feet

| Date | Mintage | VF20 | XF40 | MS60 | MS63 | MS65 |
|---|---|---|---|---|---|---|
| 2012 Specimen | — | — | — | — | 27.50 | — |
| 2013 | — | — | — | — | 27.50 | — |
| 2014 | — | **PF63** 45.00 | **PF65** 50.00 | | | |

**KM# 1299 10 DOLLARS**
31.11 g., 0.999 Silver 0.999 oz. ASW, 34 mm. **Ruler:** Elizabeth II **Subject:** Year of the Snake

| Date | Mintage | VF20 | XF40 | MS60 | MS63 | MS65 |
|---|---|---|---|---|---|---|
| 2013 | — | **PF65** 50.00 | | | | |

**KM# 1355 10 DOLLARS**
30.00 g., 0.999 Silver 0.9636 oz. ASW, 36.5 mm. **Ruler:** Elizabeth II **Rev:** Male and female mallards in color

| Date | Mintage | VF20 | XF40 | MS60 | MS63 | MS65 |
|---|---|---|---|---|---|---|
| 2013 | — | **PF63** 75.00 | **PF65** 85.00 | | | |

**KM# 1357 10 DOLLARS**
15.87 g., 0.999 Silver 0.5097 oz. ASW, 34 mm. **Ruler:** Elizabeth II **Subject:** Year of the Snake **Rev:** Circular coiled snake

| Date | Mintage | VF20 | XF40 | MS60 | MS63 | MS65 |
|---|---|---|---|---|---|---|
| 2013 | 18,888 | **PF63** 40.00 | **PF65** 45.00 | | | |

**KM# 1383 10 DOLLARS**
15.87 g., 0.999 Silver 0.5097 oz. ASW, 34 mm. **Ruler:** Elizabeth II **Subject:** Ice Skating on Frozen Lake **Rev:** Winter Scene in Color

| Date | Mintage | VF20 | XF40 | MS60 | MS63 | MS65 |
|---|---|---|---|---|---|---|
| 2013 | Est. 8000 | **PF63** 55.00 | **PF65** 65.00 | | | |

**KM# 1392 10 DOLLARS**
15.87 g., 0.999 Silver 0.5097 oz. ASW, 35 mm. **Ruler:** Elizabeth II **Subject:** Oh Canada - R.C.M.P. **Rev:** Mountie on horseback

| Date | Mintage | VF20 | XF40 | MS60 | MS63 | MS65 |
|---|---|---|---|---|---|---|
| 2013 | — | **PF63** 32.00 | **PF65** 40.00 | | | |

**KM# 1392a 10 DOLLARS**
15.87 g., 0.999 Silver 0.5097 oz. ASW partially gilt, 35 mm. **Ruler:** Elizabeth II **Subject:** Oh Canada - R.C.M.P. **Rev:** Mountie on horseback within gilt border

| Date | Mintage | VF20 | XF40 | MS60 | MS63 | MS65 |
|---|---|---|---|---|---|---|
| 2013 | — | **PF63** 65.00 | **PF65** 75.00 | | | |

**KM# 1393 10 DOLLARS**
15.87 g., 0.999 Silver 0.5097 oz. ASW, 34 mm. **Ruler:** Elizabeth II **Rev:** Twelve Spotted Skimmer Dragonfly in color

| Date | Mintage | VF20 | XF40 | MS60 | MS63 | MS65 |
|---|---|---|---|---|---|---|
| 2013 | Est. 10000 | **PF63** 70.00 | **PF65** 80.00 | | | |

**KM# 1396 10 DOLLARS**
15.87 g., 0.9999 Silver 0.5102 oz. ASW, 34 mm. **Ruler:** Elizabeth II **Rev:** Bever Felling Tree

| Date | Mintage | VF20 | XF40 | MS60 | MS63 | MS65 |
|---|---|---|---|---|---|---|
| 2013 | Est. 40000 | **PF63** 35.00 | **PF65** 40.00 | | | |

**KM# 1396a 10 DOLLARS**
15.87 g., 0.999 Silver 0.5097 oz. ASW partially gilt, 34 mm. **Ruler:** Elizabeth II **Subject:** Oh Canada - Beaver **Rev:** Beaver knawing on tree

| Date | Mintage | VF20 | XF40 | MS60 | MS63 | MS65 |
|---|---|---|---|---|---|---|
| 2013 | — | **PF63** 65.00 | **PF65** 75.00 | | | |

**KM# 1400 10 DOLLARS**
15.87 g., 0.999 Silver 0.5097 oz. ASW, 34 mm. **Ruler:** Elizabeth II **Rev:** Stone formation at sea side

| Date | Mintage | VF20 | XF40 | MS60 | MS63 | MS65 |
|---|---|---|---|---|---|---|
| 2013 | 40,000 | **PF63** 35.00 | **PF65** 40.00 | | | |

**KM# 1400a 10 DOLLARS**
15.87 g., 0.999 Silver 0.5097 oz. ASW partially gilt, 34 mm. **Ruler:** Elizabeth II **Subject:** Oh Canada **Rev:** Stone formation at sea side

| Date | Mintage | VF20 | XF40 | MS60 | MS63 | MS65 |
|---|---|---|---|---|---|---|
| 2013 | — | **PF63** 65.00 | **PF65** 75.00 | | | |

**KM# 1402 10 DOLLARS**
15.57 g., 0.999 Silver 0.5001 oz. ASW, 34 mm. **Ruler:** Elizabeth II **Rev:** Polar Bear walking right

| Date | Mintage | VF20 | XF40 | MS60 | MS63 | MS65 |
|---|---|---|---|---|---|---|
| 2013 | — | **PF63** 35.00 | **PF65** 40.00 | | | |

**KM# 1402a 10 DOLLARS**
15.57 g., 0.999 Silver 0.5001 oz. ASW partially gilt **Ruler:** Elizabeth II **Subject:** Oh Canada **Rev:** Polar bear advancing right

| Date | Mintage | VF20 | XF40 | MS60 | MS63 | MS65 |
|---|---|---|---|---|---|---|
| 2013 | — | **PF63** 65.00 | **PF65** 75.00 | | | |

**KM# 1421 10 DOLLARS**
15.87 g., 0.9999 Silver 0.5102 oz. ASW, 34 mm. **Ruler:** Elizabeth II **Rev:** Caribou

| Date | Mintage | VF20 | XF40 | MS60 | MS63 | MS65 |
|---|---|---|---|---|---|---|
| 2013 | Est. 40000 | **PF63** 25.00 | **PF65** 30.00 | | | |

**KM# 1421a 10 DOLLARS**
15.87 g., 0.9999 Silver 0.5102 oz. ASW partially gilt, 34 mm. **Ruler:** Elizabeth II **Subject:** Oh Canada **Rev:** Caribou

| Date | Mintage | VF20 | XF40 | MS60 | MS63 | MS65 |
|---|---|---|---|---|---|---|
| 2013 | — | **PF63** 65.00 | **PF65** 75.00 | | | |

**KM# 1422 10 DOLLARS**
15.87 g., 0.9999 Silver 0.5102 oz. ASW, 34 mm. **Ruler:** Elizabeth II **Rev:** Niagra Falls

| Date | Mintage | VF20 | XF40 | MS60 | MS63 | MS65 |
|---|---|---|---|---|---|---|
| 2013 | Est. 40000 | **PF63** 32.00 | **PF65** 40.00 | | | |

**KM# 1422a 10 DOLLARS**
15.87 g., 0.9999 Silver 0.5102 oz. ASW partially gilt, 34 mm. **Ruler:** Elizabeth II **Subject:** Oh Canada **Rev:** Niagra Falls

| Date | Mintage | VF20 | XF40 | MS60 | MS63 | MS65 |
|---|---|---|---|---|---|---|
| 2013 | — | PF63 65.00 | PF65 75.00 | | | |

**KM# 1423 10 DOLLARS**
15.57 g., 0.9999 Silver 0.5005 oz. ASW, 34 mm. **Ruler:** Elizabeth II **Rev:** Summer lake swimming

| Date | Mintage | VF20 | XF40 | MS60 | MS63 | MS65 |
|---|---|---|---|---|---|---|
| 2013 | Est. 40000 | PF63 32.00 | PF65 40.00 | | | |

**KM# 1423a 10 DOLLARS**
15.87 g., 0.9999 Silver 0.5102 oz. ASW partially gilt, 34 mm. **Ruler:** Elizabeth II **Subject:** Oh Canada **Rev:** Summertime lake swimming

| Date | Mintage | VF20 | XF40 | MS60 | MS63 | MS65 |
|---|---|---|---|---|---|---|
| 2013 | — | PF63 65.00 | PF65 75.00 | | | |

**KM# 1424 10 DOLLARS**
15.87 g., 0.9999 Silver 0.5102 oz. ASW, 34 mm. **Ruler:** Elizabeth II **Rev:** Hand holding three Fall colored maple leaves

| Date | Mintage | VF20 | XF40 | MS60 | MS63 | MS65 |
|---|---|---|---|---|---|---|
| 2013 | Est. 40000 | PF63 32.00 | PF65 40.00 | | | |

**KM# 1424a 10 DOLLARS**
15.87 g., 0.9999 Silver 0.5102 oz. ASW, 34 mm. **Ruler:** Elizabeth II **Subject:** Oh Canada **Rev:** Hand holding three color maple leaves

| Date | Mintage | VF20 | XF40 | MS60 | MS63 | MS65 |
|---|---|---|---|---|---|---|
| 2013 | — | PF63 65.00 | PF65 75.00 | | | |

**KM# 1425 10 DOLLARS**
15.87 g., 0.9999 Silver 0.5102 oz. ASW, 34 mm. **Ruler:** Elizabeth II **Rev:** Outdoor ice hockey rink

| Date | Mintage | VF20 | XF40 | MS60 | MS63 | MS65 |
|---|---|---|---|---|---|---|
| 2013 | Est. 40000 | PF63 32.00 | PF65 40.00 | | | |

**KM# 1425a 10 DOLLARS**
15.87 g., 0.9999 Silver 0.5102 oz. ASW partially gilt, 34 mm. **Ruler:** Elizabeth II **Subject:** Oh Canada **Rev:** Winter ice rink

| Date | Mintage | VF20 | XF40 | MS60 | MS63 | MS65 |
|---|---|---|---|---|---|---|
| 2013 | — | PF63 65.00 | PF65 75.00 | | | |

**KM# 1442 10 DOLLARS**
15.87 g., 0.999 Silver 0.5097 oz. ASW, 34 mm. **Ruler:** Elizabeth II **Obv:** Bust right **Rev:** Dream catcher in color **Edge:** Reeded

| Date | Mintage | VF20 | XF40 | MS60 | MS63 | MS65 |
|---|---|---|---|---|---|---|
| 2013 | 10,000 | PF63 70.00 | PF65 80.00 | | | |

**KM# 1445 10 DOLLARS**
7.06 g., 0.999 Silver 0.2268 oz. ASW, 27 mm. **Ruler:** Elizabeth II **Subject:** 75th Anniversary of Superman **Rev:** Superman breaking chains **Rev. Legend:** Joe Shuster, DC Comics

| Date | Mintage | VF20 | XF40 | MS60 | MS63 | MS65 |
|---|---|---|---|---|---|---|
| 2013 | Est. 15000 | PF63 40.00 | PF65 45.00 | | | |

**KM# 1455 10 DOLLARS**
15.57 g., 0.999 Silver 0.5001 oz. ASW, 34 mm. **Ruler:** Elizabeth II **Rev:** Wolf standing right

| Date | Mintage | VF20 | XF40 | MS60 | MS63 | MS65 |
|---|---|---|---|---|---|---|
| 2013 | Est. 40000 | PF63 35.00 | PF65 40.00 | | | |

**KM# 1455a 10 DOLLARS**
15.57 g., 0.999 Silver 0.5001 oz. ASW partially gilt **Ruler:** Elizabeth II **Rev:** Wolf standing right

| Date | Mintage | VF20 | XF40 | MS60 | MS63 | MS65 |
|---|---|---|---|---|---|---|
| 2013 | — | PF63 65.00 | PF65 75.00 | | | |

**KM# 1529 10 DOLLARS**
15.87 g., 0.999 Silver 0.5097 oz. ASW, 34 mm. **Ruler:** Elizabeth II **Rev:** Three red candles

| Date | Mintage | VF20 | XF40 | MS60 | MS63 | MS65 |
|---|---|---|---|---|---|---|
| 2013 | 10,000 | PF63 55.00 | PF65 65.00 | | | |

**KM# 1530 10 DOLLARS**
15.87 g., 0.999 Silver 0.5097 oz. ASW, 34 mm. **Ruler:** Elizabeth II **Rev:** Partridge in a pear tree, colored greens below

| Date | Mintage | VF20 | XF40 | MS60 | MS63 | MS65 |
|---|---|---|---|---|---|---|
| 2013 | 10,000 | PF63 55.00 | PF65 65.00 | | | |

**KM# 1533 10 DOLLARS**
15.87 g., 0.999 Silver 0.5097 oz. ASW, 34 mm. **Ruler:** Elizabeth II **Subject:** World Cup, 2014 **Rev:** Soccer player, maple leaf, fans

| Date | Mintage | VF20 | XF40 | MS60 | MS63 | MS65 |
|---|---|---|---|---|---|---|
| 2013 | 10,000 | PF63 50.00 | PF65 55.00 | | | |

**KM# 1536 10 DOLLARS**
15.87 g., 0.999 Silver 0.5097 oz. ASW, 34 mm. **Ruler:** Elizabeth II **Subject:** Oh Canada - Holiday season **Rev:** Sleigh and Christmas Tree

| Date | Mintage | VF20 | XF40 | MS60 | MS63 | MS65 |
|---|---|---|---|---|---|---|
| 2013 | 40,000 | PF63 35.00 | PF65 40.00 | | | |

**KM# 1536a 10 DOLLARS**
15.87 g., 0.999 Silver 0.5097 oz. ASW partially gilt, 34 mm. **Ruler:** Elizabeth II **Subject:** Oh Canada - Holiday Season **Rev:** Sleigh and tree

| Date | Mintage | VF20 | XF40 | MS60 | MS63 | MS65 |
|---|---|---|---|---|---|---|
| 2013 | — | PF63 65.00 | PF65 75.00 | | | |

**KM# 1540 10 DOLLARS**
15.870 Silver ASW .999, 34 mm. **Ruler:** Elizabeth II **Subject:** Oh Canada **Rev:** Orca surfacing

| Date | Mintage | VF20 | XF40 | MS60 | MS63 | MS65 |
|---|---|---|---|---|---|---|
| 2013 | 40,000 | PF63 35.00 | PF65 40.00 | | | |

**KM# 1540a 10 DOLLARS**
15.87 g., 0.999 Silver 0.5097 oz. ASW partially gilt, 34 mm. **Ruler:** Elizabeth II **Subject:** Oh Canada **Rev:** Orca surfacing

| Date | Mintage | VF20 | XF40 | MS60 | MS63 | MS65 |
|---|---|---|---|---|---|---|
| 2013 | — | PF63 65.00 | PF65 75.00 | | | |

**KM# 1546 10 DOLLARS**
30.00 g., 0.999 Silver 0.9636 oz. ASW, 36.5 mm. **Ruler:** Elizabeth II **Rev:** Wood Ducks

| Date | Mintage | VF20 | XF40 | MS60 | MS63 | MS65 |
|---|---|---|---|---|---|---|
| 2013 | — | PF63 75.00 | PF65 85.00 | | | |

**KM# 1517 10 DOLLARS**
15.87 g., 0.9999 Silver 0.5102 oz. ASW, 34 mm. **Ruler:** Elizabeth II **Subject:** Year of the Horse **Obv:** Bust right **Rev:** Horse head left

| Date | Mintage | VF20 | XF40 | MS60 | MS63 | MS65 |
|---|---|---|---|---|---|---|
| 2014 | 58,888 | PF63 35.00 | PF65 40.00 | | | |

**KM# 1580 10 DOLLARS**
15.87 g., 0.999 Silver 0.5097 oz. ASW, 34 mm. **Ruler:** Elizabeth II **Obv:** Bust right **Rev:** Igloo

| Date | Mintage | VF20 | XF40 | MS60 | MS63 | MS65 |
|---|---|---|---|---|---|---|
| 2014 | — | PF63 55.00 | PF65 65.00 | | | |

**KM# 1590 10 DOLLARS**
15.87 g., 0.999 Silver 0.5097 oz. ASW, 34 mm. **Ruler:** Elizabeth II **Obv:** Bust right **Rev:** Adult teaching child how to ice skate, in color

| Date | Mintage | VF20 | XF40 | MS60 | MS63 | MS65 |
|---|---|---|---|---|---|---|
| 2014 | — | PF63 50.00 | PF65 60.00 | | | |

**KM# 1607 10 DOLLARS**
15.87 g., 0.999 Silver 0.5097 oz. ASW, 34 mm. **Ruler:** Elizabeth II **Obv:** Bust right **Rev:** Pintail ducks in color

| Date | Mintage | VF20 | XF40 | MS60 | MS63 | MS65 |
|---|---|---|---|---|---|---|
| 2014 | 10,000 | — | — | — | 35.00 | — |

**KM# 1612 10 DOLLARS**
15.87 g., 0.999 Silver 0.5097 oz. ASW, 34 mm. **Ruler:** Elizabeth II **Obv:** Bust right **Rev:** Grizzly bear left

| Date | Mintage | VF20 | XF40 | MS60 | MS63 | MS65 |
|---|---|---|---|---|---|---|
| 2014 | 40,000 | PF63 35.00 | PF65 40.00 | | | |

**KM# 1613 10 DOLLARS**
0.999 Silver ASW, 34 mm. **Ruler:** Elizabeth II **Subject:** World War I - Mobilization of a nation **Obv:** Bust right **Rev:** Soldier with gear walking up ship's gangway

| Date | Mintage | VF20 | XF40 | MS60 | MS63 | MS65 |
|---|---|---|---|---|---|---|
| 2014 | 40,000 | PF63 40.00 | PF65 45.00 | | | |

**KM# 1625 10 DOLLARS**
15.87 g., 0.999 Silver 0.5097 oz. ASW, 34 mm. **Ruler:** Elizabeth II **Obv:** Bust right **Rev:** Downhill sking

| Date | Mintage | VF20 | XF40 | MS60 | MS63 | MS65 |
|---|---|---|---|---|---|---|
| 2014 | 40,000 | PF63 35.00 | PF65 40.00 | | | |

**KM# 1649 10 DOLLARS**
15.87 g., 0.999 Silver 0.5097 oz. ASW, 34 mm. **Ruler:** Elizabeth II **Obv:** Bust right **Rev:** Moose

| Date | Mintage | F12 | VF20 | XF40 | MS60 | MS63 |
|---|---|---|---|---|---|---|
| 2014 | 40,000 | PF63 35.00 | PF65 40.00 | | | |

**KM# 1651 10 DOLLARS**
7.80 g., 0.999 Gold 0.2505 oz. AGW, 20 mm. **Ruler:** Elizabeth II **Obv:** Bust right **Rev:** Arctic Fox

| Date | Mintage | F12 | VF20 | XF40 | MS60 | MS63 |
|---|---|---|---|---|---|---|
| 2014 | 2,000 | PF63 640 | PF65 650 | | | |

**KM# 1653 10 DOLLARS**
15.87 g., 0.9999 Silver 0.5102 oz. ASW, 34 mm. **Ruler:** Elizabeth II **Obv:** Bust right **Rev:** Green Darner Dragonfly

| Date | Mintage | F12 | VF20 | XF40 | MS60 | MS63 |
|---|---|---|---|---|---|---|
| 2014 | 10,000 | PF63 75.00 | PF65 85.00 | | | |

**KM# 1713 10 DOLLARS**
15.87 g., 0.9999 Silver 0.5102 oz. ASW, 34 mm. **Ruler:** Elizabeth II **Obv:** Bust right **Rev:** WWII photo of child running after dad leaving for war, with color highlights

| Date | Mintage | VF20 | XF40 | MS60 | MS63 | MS65 |
|---|---|---|---|---|---|---|
| 2014 | 10,000 | PF65 60.00 | | | | |

**KM# 1748 10 DOLLARS**
15.87 g., 0.999 Silver 0.5097 oz. ASW, 34 mm. **Ruler:** Elizabeth II **Obv:** Bust right **Rev:** Superman lifting auto thus saving child

| Date | Mintage | VF20 | XF40 | MS60 | MS63 | MS65 |
|---|---|---|---|---|---|---|
| 2014 | 10,000 | PF65 60.00 | | | | |

**KM# 1787 10 DOLLARS**
15.87 g., Silver, 34 mm. **Ruler:** Elizabeth II **Obv:** Bust right **Rev:** Harlequin Duck in color

| Date | Mintage | F12 | VF20 | XF40 | MS60 | MS63 |
|---|---|---|---|---|---|---|
| 2014 | 10,000 | PF65 75.00 | | | | |

**KM# 1791 10 DOLLARS**
7.78 g., 0.999 Gold 0.2499 oz. AGW, 20 mm. **Ruler:** Elizabeth II **Obv:** Bust right by Mary Gilick **Rev:** Two maple leaves

| Date | Mintage | F12 | VF20 | XF40 | MS60 | MS63 |
|---|---|---|---|---|---|---|
| 2014 | 650 | PF65 475 | | | | |

**KM# 1794 10 DOLLARS**
15.87 g., 0.999 Silver 0.5097 oz. ASW, 34 mm. **Ruler:** Elizabeth II **Subject:** Frist Nations Art **Obv:** Bust right **Rev:** Salmon hologram

| Date | Mintage | F12 | VF20 | XF40 | MS60 | MS63 |
|---|---|---|---|---|---|---|
| 2014 | 10,000 | PF65 75.00 | | | | |

**KM# 1800 10 DOLLARS**
7.80 g., 0.9999 Gold 0.2508 oz. AGW, 20 mm. **Ruler:** Elizabeth II **Obv:** Gilick portrait of Elizabeth II right **Rev:** Two Maple leaves on twig

| Date | Mintage | F12 | VF20 | XF40 | MS60 | MS63 |
|---|---|---|---|---|---|---|
| 2014 Reverse Proof | 1,500 | PF65 650 | | | | |

**KM# 1811 10 DOLLARS**
7.80 g., 0.999 Gold 0.2505 oz. AGW, 20 mm. **Ruler:** Elizabeth II **Obv:** Bust right **Rev:** Polar Bear and cub

| Date | Mintage | VF20 | XF40 | MS60 | MS63 | MS65 |
|---|---|---|---|---|---|---|
| 2015 | 2,000 | PF65 650 | | | | |

**KM# 1813 10 DOLLARS**
15.87 g., 0.9999 Silver 0.5102 oz. ASW, 34 mm. **Ruler:** Elizabeth II **Obv:** Bust right **Rev:** Ram head, bamboo background

| Date | Mintage | VF20 | XF40 | MS60 | MS63 | MS65 |
|---|---|---|---|---|---|---|
| 2015 | 22,888 | PF65 40.00 | | | | |

**KM# 1826 10 DOLLARS**
15.87 g., 0.999 Silver 0.5097 oz. ASW, 34 mm. **Ruler:** Elizabeth II **Obv:** Bust right **Rev:** Calgary Flames logo

| Date | Mintage | F12 | VF20 | XF40 | MS60 | MS63 |
|---|---|---|---|---|---|---|
| 2015 | 5,000 | PF65 75.00 | | | | |

**KM# 1827 10 DOLLARS**
15.87 g., 0.999 Silver 0.5097 oz. ASW, 34 mm. **Ruler:** Elizabeth II **Obv:** Bust right **Rev:** Edmonton Oilers logo

| Date | Mintage | F12 | VF20 | XF40 | MS60 | MS63 |
|---|---|---|---|---|---|---|
| 2015 | 5,000 | PF65 75.00 | | | | |

**KM# 1828 10 DOLLARS**
15.87 g., 0.999 Silver 0.5097 oz. ASW, 34 mm. **Ruler:** Elizabeth II **Obv:** Bust right **Rev:** Montreal Canadiens logo

| Date | Mintage | F12 | VF20 | XF40 | MS60 | MS63 |
|---|---|---|---|---|---|---|
| 2015 | — | PF65 75.00 | | | | |

**KM# 1829 10 DOLLARS**
15.87 g., 0.999 Silver 0.5097 oz. ASW, 34 mm. **Ruler:** Elizabeth II **Obv:** Bust right **Rev:** Ottawa Senators logo

| Date | Mintage | VF20 | XF40 | MS60 | MS63 | MS65 |
|---|---|---|---|---|---|---|
| 2015 | 5,000 | PF65 75.00 | | | | |

**KM# 1830 10 DOLLARS**
15.87 g., 0.999 Silver 0.5097 oz. ASW, 34 mm. **Ruler:** Elizabeth II **Obv:** Bust right **Rev:** Toronto Maple Leaves logo

| Date | Mintage | VF20 | XF40 | MS60 | MS63 | MS65 |
|---|---|---|---|---|---|---|
| 2015 | 5,000 | PF65 75.00 | | | | |

**KM# 1831 10 DOLLARS**
15.87 g., 0.999 Silver 0.5097 oz. ASW, 34 mm. **Ruler:** Elizabeth II **Obv:** Bust right **Rev:** Vancouver Canucks logo

| Date | Mintage | VF20 | XF40 | MS60 | MS63 | MS65 |
|---|---|---|---|---|---|---|
| 2015 | 5,000 | PF65 75.00 | | | | |

**KM# 1832 10 DOLLARS**
15.87 g., 0.999 Silver 0.5097 oz. ASW, 34 mm. **Ruler:** Elizabeth II **Obv:** Bust right **Rev:** Winnipeg Jets logo

| Date | Mintage | VF20 | XF40 | MS60 | MS63 | MS65 |
|---|---|---|---|---|---|---|
| 2015 | — | PF65 75.00 | | | | |

**KM# 1841 10 DOLLARS**
15.87 g., 0.9999 Silver 0.5102 oz. ASW, 34 mm. **Ruler:** Elizabeth II **Obv:** Bust right **Rev:** Sir John A. McDonald standing selectively gilt

| Date | Mintage | VF20 | XF40 | MS60 | MS63 | MS65 |
|---|---|---|---|---|---|---|
| 2015 | — | PF65 85.00 | | | | |

**KM# 415 15 DOLLARS**
33.63 g., 0.925 Silver 1.0001 oz. ASW with gold insert, 40 mm. **Ruler:** Elizabeth II **Subject:** Year of the Snake **Obv:** Crowned head right **Rev:** Snake within circle of lunar calendar signs **Edge:** Reeded

| Date | Mintage | VF20 | XF40 | MS60 | MS63 | MS65 |
|---|---|---|---|---|---|---|
| 2001 | — | PF63 75.00 | PF65 85.00 | | | |

**KM# 463 15 DOLLARS**
33.63 g., 0.925 Silver 1.0001 oz. ASW with gold insert **Ruler:** Elizabeth II **Subject:** Year of the Horse **Obv:** Crowned head right **Rev:** Horse in center with Chinese Lunar calendar around

| Date | Mintage | VF20 | XF40 | MS60 | MS63 | MS65 |
|---|---|---|---|---|---|---|
| 2002 | 59,395 | PF63 75.00 | PF65 85.00 | | | |

**KM# 481 15 DOLLARS**
33.63 g., 0.925 Silver 1.0001 oz. ASW with gold insert, 40 mm. **Ruler:** Elizabeth II **Subject:** Year of the Sheep **Obv:** Crowned head right **Rev:** Sheep in center with Chinese Lunar calendar around

| Date | Mintage | VF20 | XF40 | MS60 | MS63 | MS65 |
|---|---|---|---|---|---|---|
| 2003 | 53,714 | PF63 75.00 | PF65 85.00 | | | |

**KM# 610 15 DOLLARS**
33.63 g., 0.925 Silver 1.0001 oz. ASW Gold octagon applique in center **Ruler:** Elizabeth II **Subject:** Year of the Monkey **Obv:** Crowned head right **Rev:** Monkey in center with Chinese Lunar calendar around

| Date | Mintage | VF20 | XF40 | MS60 | MS63 | MS65 |
|---|---|---|---|---|---|---|
| 2004 | 46,175 | PF65 150 | | | | |

**KM# 560 15 DOLLARS**
33.63 g., 0.925 Silver 1.0001 oz. ASW with gold insert **Ruler:** Elizabeth II **Subject:** Year of the Rooster **Obv:** Crowned head right **Rev:** Rooster in center with Chinese Lunar calendar around

| Date | Mintage | VF20 | XF40 | MS60 | MS63 | MS65 |
|---|---|---|---|---|---|---|
| 2005 | 44,690 | PF65 125 | | | | |

**KM# 587 15 DOLLARS**
33.63 g., 0.925 Silver 1.0001 oz. ASW with gold insert **Ruler:** Elizabeth II **Subject:** Year of the Dog **Obv:** Crowned head left **Rev:** Dog in center with Chinese Lunar calendar around

| Date | Mintage | VF20 | XF40 | MS60 | MS63 | MS65 |
|---|---|---|---|---|---|---|
| 2006 | 41,617 | PF63 85.00 | PF65 100 | | | |

**KM# 732 15 DOLLARS**
33.63 g., 0.925 Silver 1.0001 oz. ASW with gold insert, 40 mm. **Ruler:** Elizabeth II **Subject:** Year of the Pig **Rev:** Pig at center of lunar characters

| Date | Mintage | VF20 | XF40 | MS60 | MS63 | MS65 |
|---|---|---|---|---|---|---|
| 2007 | 48,888 | PF63 90.00 | PF65 100 | | | |

**KM# 801 15 DOLLARS**
33.63 g., 0.925 Silver 1.0001 oz. ASW with gold insert, 40 mm. **Ruler:** Elizabeth II **Subject:** Year of the Rat **Rev:** Rat, gold octagonal insert at center

| Date | Mintage | VF20 | XF40 | MS60 | MS63 | MS65 |
|---|---|---|---|---|---|---|
| 2008 | 48,888 | **PF63** 80.00 | **PF65** 90.00 | | | |

**KM# 803 15 DOLLARS**
30.00 g., 0.925 Silver 0.8922 oz. ASW, 36.15 mm. **Ruler:** Elizabeth II **Rev:** Queen Victoria's coinage portrait

| Date | Mintage | VF20 | XF40 | MS60 | MS63 | MS65 |
|---|---|---|---|---|---|---|
| 2008 | 3,442 | — | — | — | 100 | — |

**KM# 804 15 DOLLARS**
30.00 g., 0.925 Silver 0.8922 oz. ASW, 36.15 mm. **Ruler:** Elizabeth II **Rev:** Edward VII coinage portrait

| Date | Mintage | VF20 | XF40 | MS60 | MS63 | MS65 |
|---|---|---|---|---|---|---|
| 2008 | 6,261 | — | — | — | 100 | — |

**KM# 805 15 DOLLARS**
20.00 g., 0.925 Silver 0.5948 oz. ASW, 36.15 mm. **Ruler:** Elizabeth II **Rev:** George V coinage portrait

| Date | Mintage | VF20 | XF40 | MS60 | MS63 | MS65 |
|---|---|---|---|---|---|---|
| 2008 | — | — | — | — | 100 | — |

**KM# 806 15 DOLLARS**
31.56 g., 0.925 Silver 0.9386 oz. ASW, 49.8 x 28.6 mm. **Ruler:** Elizabeth II **Rev:** Queen of Spades, multicolor playing card

| Date | Mintage | VF20 | XF40 | MS60 | MS63 | MS65 |
|---|---|---|---|---|---|---|
| 2008 | 8,714 | **PF63** 80.00 | **PF65** 90.00 | | | |

**KM# 807 15 DOLLARS**
31.56 g., 0.925 Silver 0.9386 oz. ASW, 28.6x49.8 mm. **Ruler:** Elizabeth II **Rev:** Jack of Hearts, multicolor playing card

| Date | Mintage | VF20 | XF40 | MS60 | MS63 | MS65 |
|---|---|---|---|---|---|---|
| 2008 | 11,362 | **PF63** 75.00 | **PF65** 85.00 | | | |

**KM# 866 15 DOLLARS**
33.63 g., 0.925 Silver 1.0001 oz. ASW with gold insert, 40 mm. **Ruler:** Elizabeth II **Subject:** Year of the Ox **Rev:** Ox, octagon gold insert

| Date | Mintage | VF20 | XF40 | MS60 | MS63 | MS65 |
|---|---|---|---|---|---|---|
| 2009 | 48,888 | **PF63** 80.00 | **PF65** 90.00 | | | |

**KM# 919 15 DOLLARS**
31.56 g., 0.925 Silver 0.9386 oz. ASW, 49.8 x 28.6 mm. **Ruler:** Elizabeth II **Obv:** Bust right **Rev:** Ten of spades, multicolor **Shape:** rectangle

| Date | Mintage | VF20 | XF40 | MS60 | MS63 | MS65 |
|---|---|---|---|---|---|---|
| 2009 | 5,921 | **PF63** 140 | **PF65** 150 | | | |

**KM# 920 15 DOLLARS**
31.56 g., 0.925 Silver 0.9386 oz. ASW, 49.8 x 28.6 mm. **Ruler:** Elizabeth II **Obv:** Bust right **Rev:** King of hearts, multicolor **Shape:** Rectangle

| Date | Mintage | VF20 | XF40 | MS60 | MS63 | MS65 |
|---|---|---|---|---|---|---|
| 2009 | 5,798 | **PF63** 110 | **PF65** 120 | | | |

**KM# 922 15 DOLLARS**
30.00 g., 0.925 Silver 0.8922 oz. ASW, 36.15 mm. **Ruler:** Elizabeth II **Obv:** Bust right **Rev:** Paget portrait of George VI

| Date | Mintage | VF20 | XF40 | MS60 | MS63 | MS65 |
|---|---|---|---|---|---|---|
| 2009 (ml) Prooflike | — | — | — | — | 100 | — |

**KM# 923 15 DOLLARS**
30.00 g., 0.925 Silver 0.8922 oz. ASW, 36.15 mm. **Ruler:** Elizabeth II **Obv:** Bust right **Rev:** Gillick portrait of Queen Elizabeth II

| Date | Mintage | VF20 | XF40 | MS60 | MS63 | MS65 |
|---|---|---|---|---|---|---|
| 2009 (ml) Prooflike | 2,643 | — | — | — | 100 | — |

**KM# 1038 15 DOLLARS**
31.39 g., 0.999 Silver 1.0082 oz. ASW, 38 mm. **Ruler:** Elizabeth II **Subject:** Year of the tiger **Rev:** Tiger in forest **Shape:** Scalloped

| Date | Mintage | VF20 | XF40 | MS60 | MS63 | MS65 |
|---|---|---|---|---|---|---|
| 2009 | 10,268 | **PF63** 75.00 | **PF65** 85.00 | | | |

**KM# 980 15 DOLLARS**
34.00 g., 0.925 Silver 1.0111 oz. ASW, 40 mm. **Ruler:** Elizabeth II **Rev:** Tiger in gold octagon insert, zodiac animals around

| Date | Mintage | VF20 | XF40 | MS60 | MS63 | MS65 |
|---|---|---|---|---|---|---|
| 2010 | 48,888 | **PF63** 90.00 | **PF65** 100 | | | |

**KM# 1032 15 DOLLARS**
0.999 Silver **Ruler:** Elizabeth II **Subject:** Year of the tiger **Rev:** Tiger walking tiger

| Date | Mintage | VF20 | XF40 | MS60 | MS63 | MS65 |
|---|---|---|---|---|---|---|
| 2010 | 9,999 | **PF63** 75.00 | **PF65** 85.00 | | | |

**KM# 1055 15 DOLLARS**
31.11 g., 0.999 Silver 0.999 oz. ASW, 38 mm. **Ruler:** Elizabeth II **Rev:** Rabbit seated on hind legs, head turned left **Shape:** Scalloped

| Date | Mintage | VF20 | XF40 | MS60 | MS63 | MS65 |
|---|---|---|---|---|---|---|
| 2011 | 19,888 | PF63 75.00 | PF65 85.00 | | | |

**KM# 1091 15 DOLLARS**
25.11 g., 0.925 Silver 0.7468 oz. ASW, 36.15 mm. **Ruler:** Elizabeth II **Rev:** Prince Charles bust

| Date | Mintage | VF20 | XF40 | MS60 | MS63 | MS65 |
|---|---|---|---|---|---|---|
| 2011 Prooflike | 10,000 | — | — | — | 110 | — |

**KM# 1092 15 DOLLARS**
25.11 g., 0.925 Silver 0.7468 oz. ASW, 36.15 mm. **Ruler:** Elizabeth II **Rev:** Prince William

| Date | Mintage | VF20 | XF40 | MS60 | MS63 | MS65 |
|---|---|---|---|---|---|---|
| 2011 Prooflike | 10,000 | — | — | — | 110 | — |

**KM# 1093 15 DOLLARS**
25.18 g., 0.925 Silver 0.7488 oz. ASW, 36.15 mm. **Ruler:** Elizabeth II **Rev:** Prince Harry bust 1/4 right

| Date | Mintage | VF20 | XF40 | MS60 | MS63 | MS65 |
|---|---|---|---|---|---|---|
| 2011 Prooflike | 10,000 | — | — | — | 110 | — |

**KM# 1094 15 DOLLARS**
31.39 g., 0.999 Silver 1.0082 oz. ASW, 38 mm. **Ruler:** Elizabeth II **Rev:** Rabbit bounding left

| Date | Mintage | VF20 | XF40 | MS60 | MS63 | MS65 |
|---|---|---|---|---|---|---|
| 2011 | 9,999 | PF63 90.00 | PF65 100 | | | |

**KM# 1152 15 DOLLARS**
31.39 g., 0.9999 Silver 1.0091 oz. ASW, 38 mm. **Ruler:** Elizabeth II **Obv:** Bust right **Rev:** Magpie, bird of happyness in flight at top, lotus flowers at bottom, maple leaf hologram at center

| Date | Mintage | VF20 | XF40 | MS60 | MS63 | MS65 |
|---|---|---|---|---|---|---|
| 2011 | — | PF63 90.00 | PF65 100 | | | |

**KM# 1183 15 DOLLARS**
31.11 g., 0.999 Silver 0.999 oz. ASW, 36.5 mm. **Ruler:** Elizabeth II **Subject:** Year of the Dragon **Obv:** Bust right **Rev:** Dragon right

| Date | Mintage | VF20 | XF40 | MS60 | MS63 | MS65 |
|---|---|---|---|---|---|---|
| 2012 | — | PF63 65.00 | PF65 75.00 | | | |

**KM# 1186 15 DOLLARS**
31.11 g., 0.999 Silver 0.999 oz. ASW, 36.5 mm. **Ruler:** Elizabeth II **Subject:** Year of the Dragon **Obv:** Bust right **Rev:** Dragon left **Shape:** Scalloped

| Date | Mintage | VF20 | XF40 | MS60 | MS63 | MS65 |
|---|---|---|---|---|---|---|
| 2012 | — | PF63 65.00 | PF65 75.00 | | | |

**KM# 1260 15 DOLLARS**
31.39 g., 0.999 Silver 1.0082 oz. ASW, 36.5 mm. **Ruler:** Elizabeth II **Subject:** Good Fortune **Rev:** Deer and doe froclicking around central hologram

| Date | Mintage | VF20 | XF40 | MS60 | MS63 | MS65 |
|---|---|---|---|---|---|---|
| 2012 | — | PF63 65.00 | PF65 75.00 | | | |

**KM# 1358 15 DOLLARS**
31.39 g., 0.999 Silver 1.0082 oz. ASW, 36.5 mm. **Ruler:** Elizabeth II **Subject:** Year of the Snake **Rev:** Snake vertically between two Chinese characters

| Date | Mintage | VF20 | XF40 | MS60 | MS63 | MS65 |
|---|---|---|---|---|---|---|
| 2013 | 28,888 | PF65 100 | | | | |

**KM# 1359 15 DOLLARS**
26.70 g., 0.999 Silver 0.8576 oz. ASW, 38 mm. **Ruler:** Elizabeth II **Subject:** Year of the Snake **Rev:** Snake under maple leaves **Shape:** Scalloped

| Date | Mintage | VF20 | XF40 | MS60 | MS63 | MS65 |
|---|---|---|---|---|---|---|
| 2013 | 28,888 | PF63 65.00 | PF65 75.00 | | | |

**KM# 1439 15 DOLLARS**
31.39 g., 0.9999 Silver 1.0091 oz. ASW, 38 mm. **Ruler:** Elizabeth II **Subject:** Maple of Peace **Obv:** Elephant right - Maple leaf and hologram at center

| Date | Mintage | VF20 | XF40 | MS60 | MS63 | MS65 |
|---|---|---|---|---|---|---|
| 2013 | Est. 8888 | PF63 90.00 | PF65 100 | | | |

**KM# 1446 15 DOLLARS**
15.87 g., 0.999 Silver 0.5097 oz. ASW, 34 mm. **Ruler:** Elizabeth II **Subject:** 75th Anniversary of Superman **Obv:** Superman in color flying forward

| Date | Mintage | VF20 | XF40 | MS60 | MS63 | MS65 |
|---|---|---|---|---|---|---|
| 2013 | 15,000 | **PF63** 60.00 | **PF65** 70.00 | | | |

**KM# 1514 15 DOLLARS**
31.11 g., 0.9999 Silver 0.9999 oz. ASW, 38 mm. **Ruler:** Elizabeth II **Subject:** Year of the Horse **Obv:** Bust right **Rev:** Horse prancing left

| Date | Mintage | VF20 | XF40 | MS60 | MS63 | MS65 |
|---|---|---|---|---|---|---|
| 2014 | 28,888 | **PF63** 90.00 | **PF65** 100 | | | |

**KM# 1516 15 DOLLARS**
26.70 g., 0.999 (No Composition) 0.8576 oz., 38 mm. **Ruler:** Elizabeth II **Subject:** Year of the Horse **Obv:** Bust right **Rev:** Horse forepart right **Shape:** Scalloped

| Date | Mintage | VF20 | XF40 | MS60 | MS63 | MS65 |
|---|---|---|---|---|---|---|
| 2014 | 2,888 | **PF63** 90.00 | **PF65** 100 | | | |

**KM# 1657 15 DOLLARS**
23.17 g., 0.999 Silver 0.7442 oz. ASW **Ruler:** Elizabeth II **Subject:** Exploring Canada - Voyageurs **Obv:** Bust right

| Date | Mintage | F12 | VF20 | XF40 | MS60 | MS63 |
|---|---|---|---|---|---|---|
| 2014 | 15,000 | **PF65** 80.00 | | | | |

**KM# 1659 15 DOLLARS**
23.17 g., 0.999 Silver 0.7442 oz. ASW, 36.07 mm. **Ruler:** Elizabeth II **Subject:** Exploring Canada - Arctic Expedition **Obv:** Bust right

| Date | Mintage | F12 | VF20 | XF40 | MS60 | MS63 |
|---|---|---|---|---|---|---|
| 2014 | 15,000 | **PF65** 80.00 | | | | |

**KM# 1667 15 DOLLARS**
31.39 g., 0.999 Silver 1.0082 oz. ASW, 38 mm. **Ruler:** Elizabeth II **Subject:** Maple of Longevity **Obv:** Bust right **Rev:** Two cranes, chrysanthemums, tortoise, maple leaf in hologram

| Date | Mintage | F12 | VF20 | XF40 | MS60 | MS63 |
|---|---|---|---|---|---|---|
| 2014 | 8,888 | **PF63** 90.00 | **PF65** 100 | | | |

**KM# 1749 15 DOLLARS**
23.17 g., 0.999 Silver 0.7442 oz. ASW, 36.07 mm. **Ruler:** Elizabeth II **Obv:** Bust right **Rev:** Superman flying upward

| Date | Mintage | VF20 | XF40 | MS60 | MS63 | MS65 |
|---|---|---|---|---|---|---|
| 2014 | 10,000 | **PF65** 80.00 | | | | |

**KM# 1814 15 DOLLARS**
31.39 g., 0.999 Silver 1.0082 oz. ASW, 38 mm. **Ruler:** Elizabeth II **Subject:** Year of the Ram **Obv:** Bust right **Rev:** Stylized ram and sun

| Date | Mintage | F12 | VF20 | XF40 | MS60 | MS63 |
|---|---|---|---|---|---|---|
| 2015 | 18,888 | **PF65** 100 | | | | |

**KM# 1816 15 DOLLARS**
26.17 g., 0.9999 Silver 0.8413 oz. ASW, 38 mm. **Ruler:** Elizabeth II **Obv:** Bust right **Rev:** Sheep head at right **Shape:** Scalloped

| Date | Mintage | VF20 | XF40 | MS60 | MS63 | MS65 |
|---|---|---|---|---|---|---|
| 2015 | 18,888 | **PF65** 100 | | | | |

**KM# 411 20 DOLLARS**
31.10 g., 0.925 Silver 0.925 oz. ASW, 38 mm. **Ruler:** Elizabeth II **Subject:** Transportation - Steam Locomotive **Obv:** Crowned head right **Rev:** First Canadian Steel Steam Locomotive and cameo hologram **Edge:** Segmented reeding

| Date | Mintage | VF20 | XF40 | MS60 | MS63 | MS65 |
|---|---|---|---|---|---|---|
| 2001 | 15,000 | **PF63** 35.00 | **PF65** 45.00 | | | |

**KM# 427 20 DOLLARS**
31.10 g., 0.925 Silver 0.925 oz. ASW, 38 mm. **Ruler:** Elizabeth II **Series:** Transportation - The Marco Polo **Obv:** Crowned head right **Rev:** Sailship with hologram cameo **Edge:** Segmented reeding

| Date | Mintage | VF20 | XF40 | MS60 | MS63 | MS65 |
|---|---|---|---|---|---|---|
| 2001 | 15,000 | **PF63** 35.00 | **PF65** 45.00 | | | |

**KM# 428 20 DOLLARS**
31.10 g., 0.925 Silver 0.925 oz. ASW, 38 mm. **Ruler:** Elizabeth II **Series:** Transportation - Russell Touring Car **Obv:** Crowned head right **Rev:** Russell touring car with hologram cameo **Edge:** Segmented reeding

| Date | Mintage | VF20 | XF40 | MS60 | MS63 | MS65 |
|---|---|---|---|---|---|---|
| 2001 | 15,000 | **PF63** 35.00 | **PF65** 45.00 | | | |

### KM# 464 20 DOLLARS
31.10 g., 0.925 Silver 0.925 oz. ASW **Ruler:** Elizabeth II **Obv:** Crowned head right **Rev:** Gray-Dort Model 25-SM with cameo hologram

| Date | Mintage | VF20 | XF40 | MS60 | MS63 | MS65 |
|---|---|---|---|---|---|---|
| 2002 | 15,000 | PF63 35.00 | PF65 45.00 | | | |

### KM# 465 20 DOLLARS
31.10 g., 0.925 Silver 0.925 oz. ASW **Ruler:** Elizabeth II **Obv:** Crowned head right **Rev:** Sailing ship William D. Lawrence

| Date | Mintage | VF20 | XF40 | MS60 | MS63 | MS65 |
|---|---|---|---|---|---|---|
| 2002 | 15,000 | PF63 35.00 | PF65 45.00 | | | |

### KM# 482 20 DOLLARS
31.39 g., 0.9999 Silver 1.0091 oz. ASW, 38 mm. **Ruler:** Elizabeth II **Obv:** Crowned head right **Rev:** Niagara Falls hologram

| Date | Mintage | VF20 | XF40 | MS60 | MS63 | MS65 |
|---|---|---|---|---|---|---|
| 2003 | 29,967 | PF63 65.00 | PF65 75.00 | | | |

### KM# 483 20 DOLLARS
31.10 g., 0.925 Silver 0.925 oz. ASW with selective gold plating **Ruler:** Elizabeth II **Subject:** The HMCS Bras d'or (FHE-400) **Obv:** Crowned head right **Rev:** Ship in water

| Date | Mintage | VF20 | XF40 | MS60 | MS63 | MS65 |
|---|---|---|---|---|---|---|
| 2003 | 15,000 | PF63 35.00 | PF65 45.00 | | | |

### KM# 484 20 DOLLARS
31.10 g., 0.925 Silver 0.925 oz. ASW with selective gold plating **Ruler:** Elizabeth II **Subject:** Canadian National FA-1 diesel-electric locomotive **Obv:** Crowned head right

| Date | Mintage | VF20 | XF40 | MS60 | MS63 | MS65 |
|---|---|---|---|---|---|---|
| 2003 | 15,000 | PF63 35.00 | PF65 45.00 | | | |

### KM# 485 20 DOLLARS
31.10 g., 0.925 Silver 0.925 oz. ASW with selective gold plating **Ruler:** Elizabeth II **Obv:** Crowned head right **Rev:** The Bricklin SV-1

| Date | Mintage | VF20 | XF40 | MS60 | MS63 | MS65 |
|---|---|---|---|---|---|---|
| 2003 | 15,000 | PF63 35.00 | PF65 45.00 | | | |

### KM# 523 20 DOLLARS
31.39 g., 0.999 Silver 1.0082 oz. ASW, 38 mm. **Ruler:** Elizabeth II **Obv:** Crowned head right **Rev:** Canadian Rockies, multicolor

| Date | Mintage | VF20 | XF40 | MS60 | MS63 | MS65 |
|---|---|---|---|---|---|---|
| 2003 | 29,967 | PF63 45.00 | PF65 50.00 | | | |

### KM# 611 20 DOLLARS
31.39 g., 0.9999 Silver 1.0091 oz. ASW, 38 mm. **Ruler:** Elizabeth II **Obv:** Head right **Rev:** Iceberg, hologram

| Date | Mintage | VF20 | XF40 | MS60 | MS63 | MS65 |
|---|---|---|---|---|---|---|
| 2004 | 24,879 | PF63 40.00 | PF65 45.00 | | | |

### KM# 838 20 DOLLARS
31.39 g., 0.9999 Silver 1.0091 oz. ASW partially gilt, 38 mm. **Ruler:** Elizabeth II **Rev:** Hopewell Rocks, gilt

| Date | Mintage | VF20 | XF40 | MS60 | MS63 | MS65 |
|---|---|---|---|---|---|---|
| 2004 | 16,918 | PF63 35.00 | PF65 45.00 | | | |

### KM# 561 20 DOLLARS
31.39 g., 0.9999 Silver 1.0091 oz. ASW, 38 mm. **Ruler:** Elizabeth II **Obv:** Head right **Rev:** Three-masted sailing ship, hologram of the sea

| Date | Mintage | VF20 | XF40 | MS60 | MS63 | MS65 |
|---|---|---|---|---|---|---|
| 2005 | 18,276 | PF63 50.00 | PF65 55.00 | | | |

### KM# 562 20 DOLLARS
31.39 g., 0.9999 Silver 1.0091 oz. ASW, 38 mm. **Ruler:** Elizabeth II **Subject:** Northwest Territories Diamonds **Obv:** Head right **Rev:** Multicolor diamond hologram on landscape **Edge:** Reeded

| Date | Mintage | VF20 | XF40 | MS60 | MS63 | MS65 |
|---|---|---|---|---|---|---|
| 2005 | 35,000 | PF63 45.00 | PF65 50.00 | | | |

### KM# 563 20 DOLLARS
31.39 g., 0.9999 Silver 1.0091 oz. ASW **Ruler:** Elizabeth II **Subject:** Mingan Archepelago **Obv:** Head right **Rev:** Cliffs with whale tail out of water

| Date | Mintage | VF20 | XF40 | MS60 | MS63 | MS65 |
|---|---|---|---|---|---|---|
| 2005 | — | PF63 470 | PF65 45.00 | | | |

### KM# 564 20 DOLLARS
31.39 g., 0.9999 Silver 1.0091 oz. ASW **Ruler:** Elizabeth II **Subject:** Rainforests of the Pacific Northwest **Obv:** Head right **Rev:** Open winged bird

| Date | Mintage | VF20 | XF40 | MS60 | MS63 | MS65 |
|---|---|---|---|---|---|---|
| 2005 | — | PF63 40.00 | PF65 45.00 | | | |

### KM# 565 20 DOLLARS
31.39 g., 0.9999 Silver 1.0091 oz. ASW, 38 mm. **Ruler:** Elizabeth II **Subject:** Toronto Island National Park **Obv:** Head right **Rev:** Toronto Island Lighthouse, Toronto skyline in background

| Date | Mintage | VF20 | XF40 | MS60 | MS63 | MS65 |
|---|---|---|---|---|---|---|
| 2005 | — | PF63 50.00 | PF65 55.00 | | | |

### KM# 588 20 DOLLARS
31.39 g., 0.9999 Silver 1.0091 oz. ASW **Ruler:** Elizabeth II **Subject:** Georgian Bay National Park **Obv:** Head right **Rev:** Canoe and small trees on island

| Date | Mintage | VF20 | XF40 | MS60 | MS63 | MS65 |
|---|---|---|---|---|---|---|
| 2006 | — | PF63 50.00 | PF65 60.00 | | | |

### KM# 589 20 DOLLARS
31.10 g., 0.9999 Silver 0.9998 oz. ASW, 38 mm. **Ruler:** Elizabeth II **Obv:** Head right **Rev:** Notre Dame Basilica, Montreal, as a hologram

| Date | Mintage | VF20 | XF40 | MS60 | MS63 | MS65 |
|---|---|---|---|---|---|---|
| 2006 | 15,000 | PF63 45.00 | PF65 50.00 | | | |

### KM# 663 20 DOLLARS
31.39 g., 0.9999 Silver 1.0091 oz. ASW, 38 mm. **Ruler:** Elizabeth II **Subject:** Nahanni National Park **Obv:** Head right **Rev:** Bear walking along sream, cliff in background

| Date | Mintage | VF20 | XF40 | MS60 | MS63 | MS65 |
|---|---|---|---|---|---|---|
| 2006 | — | PF63 55.00 | PF65 60.00 | | | |

### KM# 664 20 DOLLARS
31.39 g., 0.9999 Silver 1.0091 oz. ASW, 38 mm. **Ruler:** Elizabeth II **Subject:** Jasper National Park **Obv:** Head right **Rev:** Cowboy on horseback in majestic scene

| Date | Mintage | VF20 | XF40 | MS60 | MS63 | MS65 |
|---|---|---|---|---|---|---|
| 2006 | — | PF63 55.00 | PF65 60.00 | | | |

### KM# 665 20 DOLLARS
31.10 g., 0.9999 Silver 0.9998 oz. ASW, 38 mm. **Ruler:** Elizabeth II **Obv:** Head right **Rev:** Holographic rendering of CN Tower

| Date | Mintage | VF20 | XF40 | MS60 | MS63 | MS65 |
|---|---|---|---|---|---|---|
| 2006 | 15,000 | PF63 55.00 | PF65 60.00 | | | |

## KM# 666 20 DOLLARS

31.10 g., 0.9999 Silver 0.9998 oz. ASW **Ruler:** Elizabeth II **Obv:** Head right **Rev:** Holographic view of Pengrowth Saddledome in Calgary

| Date | Mintage | VF20 | XF40 | MS60 | MS63 | MS65 |
|---|---|---|---|---|---|---|
| 2006 | 15,000 | PF63 50.00 | PF65 55.00 | | | |

## KM# 667 20 DOLLARS

31.39 g., 0.9999 Silver 1.0091 oz. ASW **Ruler:** Elizabeth II **Subject:** Tall Ship **Obv:** Head right **Rev:** Ketch and holographic image of thunderstorm in sky

| Date | Mintage | VF20 | XF40 | MS60 | MS63 | MS65 |
|---|---|---|---|---|---|---|
| 2006 | 10,299 | PF63 55.00 | PF65 60.00 | | | |

## KM# 734 20 DOLLARS

31.10 g., 0.999 Silver 0.9989 oz. ASW, 38 mm. **Ruler:** Elizabeth II **Rev:** Holiday sleigh ride

| Date | Mintage | VF20 | XF40 | MS60 | MS63 | MS65 |
|---|---|---|---|---|---|---|
| 2007 | 6,804 | PF63 65.00 | PF65 70.00 | | | |

## KM# 735 20 DOLLARS

31.10 g., 0.999 Silver 0.9989 oz. ASW, 38 mm. **Ruler:** Elizabeth II **Rev:** Snowflake, aquamarine crystal

| Date | Mintage | VF20 | XF40 | MS60 | MS63 | MS65 |
|---|---|---|---|---|---|---|
| 2007 | 4,989 | PF65 175 | | | | |

## KM# 737 20 DOLLARS

31.10 g., 0.999 Silver 0.9989 oz. ASW, 38 mm. **Ruler:** Elizabeth II **Subject:** International Polar Year

| Date | Mintage | VF20 | XF40 | MS60 | MS63 | MS65 |
|---|---|---|---|---|---|---|
| 2007 | 9,164 | PF63 60.00 | PF65 65.00 | | | |

## KM# 737a 20 DOLLARS

27.78 g., 0.925 Silver 0.8262 oz. ASW, 40 mm. **Ruler:** Elizabeth II **Subject:** International Polar Year **Rev:** Blue plasma coating

| Date | Mintage | VF20 | XF40 | MS60 | MS63 | MS65 |
|---|---|---|---|---|---|---|
| 2007 | 3,005 | PF65 250 | | | | |

## KM# 738 20 DOLLARS

31.39 g., 0.9999 Silver 1.0091 oz. ASW, 38 mm. **Ruler:** Elizabeth II **Subject:** Tall ships **Rev:** Brigantine in harbor, hologram

| Date | Mintage | VF20 | XF40 | MS60 | MS63 | MS65 |
|---|---|---|---|---|---|---|
| 2007 | 16,000 | PF63 55.00 | PF65 60.00 | | | |

## KM# 839 20 DOLLARS

31.39 g., 0.9999 Silver 1.0091 oz. ASW **Ruler:** Elizabeth II **Rev:** Northern lights in hologram

| Date | Mintage | VF20 | XF40 | MS60 | MS63 | MS65 |
|---|---|---|---|---|---|---|
| 2007 | — | — | — | — | 35.00 | — |

## KM# 808 20 DOLLARS

31.50 g., 0.925 Silver 0.9368 oz. ASW, 38 mm. **Ruler:** Elizabeth II **Subject:** Agriculture trade **Rev:** Team of horses plowing

| Date | Mintage | VF20 | XF40 | MS60 | MS63 | MS65 |
|---|---|---|---|---|---|---|
| 2008 | 5,802 | PF63 65.00 | PF65 70.00 | | | |

## KM# 809 20 DOLLARS

31.11 g., 0.999 Silver 0.999 oz. ASW, 38 mm. **Ruler:** Elizabeth II **Rev:** Royal Hudson Steam locomotive

| Date | Mintage | VF20 | XF40 | MS60 | MS63 | MS65 |
|---|---|---|---|---|---|---|
| 2008 | 8,345 | PF63 65.00 | PF65 70.00 | | | |

## KM# 810 20 DOLLARS

31.39 g., 0.999 Silver 1.0082 oz. ASW, 38 mm. **Ruler:** Elizabeth II **Rev:** Green leaf and crystal raindrop

| Date | Mintage | VF20 | XF40 | MS60 | MS63 | MS65 |
|---|---|---|---|---|---|---|
| 2008 | 15,000 | PF63 165 | PF65 175 | | | |

## KM# 811 20 DOLLARS

31.11 g., 0.999 Silver 0.999 oz. ASW **Ruler:** Elizabeth II **Rev:** Snowflake, amethyst crystal

| Date | Mintage | VF20 | XF40 | MS60 | MS63 | MS65 |
|---|---|---|---|---|---|---|
| 2008 | 7,172 | PF63 90.00 | PF65 95.00 | | | |

## KM# 813 20 DOLLARS

31.11 g., 0.999 Silver 0.999 oz. ASW, 38 mm. **Ruler:** Elizabeth II **Rev:** Carolers around tree

| Date | Mintage | VF20 | XF40 | MS60 | MS63 | MS65 |
|---|---|---|---|---|---|---|
| 2008 | 10,000 | PF63 60.00 | PF65 70.00 | | | |

**KM# 872 20 DOLLARS**

31.11 g., 0.999 Silver 0.999 oz. ASW, 38 mm. **Ruler:** Elizabeth II **Rev:** Snowflake, sapphire crystal

| Date | Mintage | VF20 | XF40 | MS60 | MS63 | MS65 |
|---|---|---|---|---|---|---|
| 2008 | 7,765 | PF63 90.00 | PF65 95.00 | | | |

**KM# 870 20 DOLLARS**

27.78 g., 0.925 Silver 0.8262 oz. ASW, 40 mm. **Ruler:** Elizabeth II **Rev:** Calgary Flames goalie mask multicolor on goal net

| Date | Mintage | VF20 | XF40 | MS60 | MS63 | MS65 |
|---|---|---|---|---|---|---|
| 2009 | 10,000 | PF63 60.00 | PF65 70.00 | | | |

**KM# 871 20 DOLLARS**

27.78 g., 0.925 Silver 0.8262 oz. ASW, 40 mm. **Ruler:** Elizabeth II **Rev:** Edmonton Oilers goalie mask, multicolor on goal net

| Date | Mintage | VF20 | XF40 | MS60 | MS63 | MS65 |
|---|---|---|---|---|---|---|
| 2009 | 10,000 | PF63 60.00 | PF65 70.00 | | | |

**KM# 872A 20 DOLLARS**

27.78 g., 0.925 Silver 0.8262 oz. ASW, 40 mm. **Ruler:** Elizabeth II **Rev:** Montreal Canadians goalie mask multicolor

| Date | Mintage | VF20 | XF40 | MS60 | MS63 | MS65 |
|---|---|---|---|---|---|---|
| 2009 | 10,000 | PF63 60.00 | PF65 70.00 | | | |

**KM# 873 20 DOLLARS**

27.78 g., 0.925 Silver 0.8262 oz. ASW, 40 mm. **Ruler:** Elizabeth II **Rev:** Ottawa Senators goalie mask on goal net

| Date | Mintage | VF20 | XF40 | MS60 | MS63 | MS65 |
|---|---|---|---|---|---|---|
| 2009 | 10,000 | PF63 60.00 | PF65 70.00 | | | |

**KM# 874 20 DOLLARS**

27.78 g., 0.925 Silver 0.8262 oz. ASW, 40 mm. **Ruler:** Elizabeth II **Rev:** Toronto Maple Leafs goalie mask, multicolor on goal net

| Date | Mintage | VF20 | XF40 | MS60 | MS63 | MS65 |
|---|---|---|---|---|---|---|
| 2009 | 10,000 | PF63 60.00 | PF65 70.00 | | | |

**KM# 875 20 DOLLARS**

27.78 g., 0.925 Silver 0.8262 oz. ASW, 40 mm. **Ruler:** Elizabeth II **Rev:** Vancouver Canucks goalie mask, multicolor on goal net

| Date | Mintage | VF20 | XF40 | MS60 | MS63 | MS65 |
|---|---|---|---|---|---|---|
| 2009 | 10,000 | PF63 60.00 | PF65 70.00 | | | |

**KM# 876 20 DOLLARS**

31.50 g., 0.925 Silver 0.9368 oz. ASW, 40 mm. **Ruler:** Elizabeth II **Rev:** Summer moon mask

| Date | Mintage | VF20 | XF40 | MS60 | MS63 | MS65 |
|---|---|---|---|---|---|---|
| 2009 | 2,834 | PF65 225 | | | | |

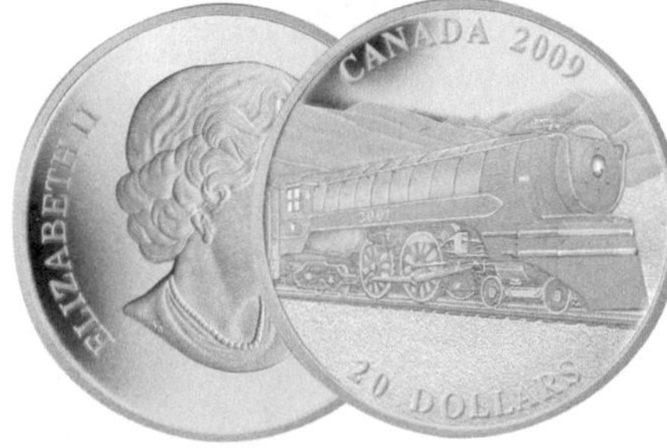


**KM# 891 20 DOLLARS**

31.39 g., 0.999 Silver 1.0082 oz. ASW, 38 mm. **Ruler:** Elizabeth II **Subject:** Great Canadian Locomotives - Jubilee **Obv:** Bust right **Obv. Legend:** Elizabeth II DG Regina **Rev:** Jubilee locomotive side view **Rev. Legend:** Canada 20 Dollars **Edge Lettering:** Jubilee

| Date | Mintage | VF20 | XF40 | MS60 | MS63 | MS65 |
|---|---|---|---|---|---|---|
| 2009 | 6,036 | PF63 65.00 | PF65 70.00 | | | |

**KM# 892 20 DOLLARS**

31.39 g., 0.999 Silver 1.0082 oz. ASW, 38 mm. **Ruler:** Elizabeth II **Subject:** Crystal raindrop **Obv:** Bust right **Rev:** Maple leaf and rain drop - fall colors

| Date | Mintage | VF20 | XF40 | MS60 | MS63 | MS65 |
|---|---|---|---|---|---|---|
| 2009 | 9,998 | PF63 75.00 | PF65 85.00 | | | |

**KM# 893 20 DOLLARS**

31.39 g., 0.999 Silver 1.0082 oz. ASW, 38 mm. **Ruler:** Elizabeth II **Subject:** Coal mining trade **Obv:** Bust right **Obv. Legend:** Elizabeth II DG Regina **Rev:** Miner pushing cart with coal **Rev. Legend:** Canada 20 Dollars

| Date | Mintage | VF20 | XF40 | MS60 | MS63 | MS65 |
|---|---|---|---|---|---|---|
| 2009 | 10,000 | PF63 65.00 | PF65 75.00 | | | |

**KM# 944 20 DOLLARS**

31.11 g., 0.999 Silver 0.999 oz. ASW, 38 mm. **Ruler:** Elizabeth II **Rev:** Snowflake - light blue crystal

| Date | Mintage | VF20 | XF40 | MS60 | MS63 | MS65 |
|---|---|---|---|---|---|---|
| 2009 | 7,477 | PF63 95.00 | PF65 100 | | | |

**KM# 945 20 DOLLARS**

31.11 g., 0.999 Silver 0.999 oz. ASW, 38 mm. **Ruler:** Elizabeth II **Rev:** Snowflake - light red crystal

| Date | Mintage | VF20 | XF40 | MS60 | MS63 | MS65 |
|---|---|---|---|---|---|---|
| 2009 | 7,004 | PF63 95.00 | PF65 100 | | | |

**KM# 987 20 DOLLARS**
31.39 g., 0.9999 Silver 1.0091 oz. ASW, 38 mm. **Ruler:** Elizabeth II **Rev:** Lotus Water Lilly in multicolor and crystal

| Date | Mintage | VF20 | XF40 | MS60 | MS63 | MS65 |
|---|---|---|---|---|---|---|
| 2010 | 10,000 | PF63 110 | PF65 120 | | | |

**KM# 1009 20 DOLLARS**
31.39 g., 0.999 Silver 1.0082 oz. ASW **Ruler:** Elizabeth II **Subject:** 75th Anniversary of Canadian Bank Notes **Rev:** Female and farmer seated

| Date | Mintage | VF20 | XF40 | MS60 | MS63 | MS65 |
|---|---|---|---|---|---|---|
| 2010 | 7,500 | PF63 65.00 | PF65 70.00 | | | |

**KM# 1013 20 DOLLARS**
31.39 g., 0.999 Silver 1.0082 oz. ASW, 38 mm. **Ruler:** Elizabeth II **Rev:** Maple leaf and crystal

| Date | Mintage | VF20 | XF40 | MS60 | MS63 | MS65 |
|---|---|---|---|---|---|---|
| 2010 | 10,000 | PF63 90.00 | PF65 100 | | | |

**KM# 1018 20 DOLLARS**
31.39 g., 0.999 Silver 1.0082 oz. ASW, 38 mm. **Ruler:** Elizabeth II **Rev:** Steam Locomotive Selkirk

| Date | Mintage | VF20 | XF40 | MS60 | MS63 | MS65 |
|---|---|---|---|---|---|---|
| 2010 | 10,000 | PF65 80.00 | | | | |

**KM# 1048 20 DOLLARS**
31.11 g., 0.9999 Silver 0.9999 oz. ASW, 38 mm. **Ruler:** Elizabeth II **Rev:** Snowflake, blue crystals

| Date | Mintage | VF20 | XF40 | MS60 | MS63 | MS65 |
|---|---|---|---|---|---|---|
| 2010 | 7,500 | PF63 85.00 | PF65 95.00 | | | |

**KM# 1049 20 DOLLARS**
31.11 g., 0.9999 Silver 0.9999 oz. ASW, 38 mm. **Ruler:** Elizabeth II **Rev:** Snowflake, tanzanite crystals

| Date | Mintage | VF20 | XF40 | MS60 | MS63 | MS65 |
|---|---|---|---|---|---|---|
| 2010 | 7,500 | PF63 85.00 | PF65 95.00 | | | |

**KM# 1066 20 DOLLARS**
31.99 g., 0.999 Silver 1.0275 oz. ASW, 38 mm. **Ruler:** Elizabeth II **Rev:** Pinecone with ruby crystals

| Date | Mintage | VF20 | XF40 | MS60 | MS63 | MS65 |
|---|---|---|---|---|---|---|
| 2010 | 5,000 | PF63 110 | PF65 120 | | | |

**KM# 1067 20 DOLLARS**
31.99 g., 0.999 Silver 1.0275 oz. ASW, 38 mm. **Ruler:** Elizabeth II **Rev:** Pinecone with moonlight blue crystals

| Date | Mintage | VF20 | XF40 | MS60 | MS63 | MS65 |
|---|---|---|---|---|---|---|
| 2010 | 5,000 | PF63 110 | PF65 120 | | | |

**KM# 1075 20 DOLLARS**
27.78 g., 0.925 Silver 0.8262 oz. ASW, 40 mm. **Ruler:** Elizabeth II **Subject:** Winter Scene **Rev:** Horse pulling cut Christmas Tree

| Date | Mintage | VF20 | XF40 | MS60 | MS63 | MS65 |
|---|---|---|---|---|---|---|
| 2011 | 8,000 | PF63 60.00 | PF65 70.00 | | | |

**KM# 1111 20 DOLLARS**
31.39 g., 0.999 Silver 1.0082 oz. ASW, 40 mm. **Ruler:** Elizabeth II **Subject:** Royal Wedding **Rev:** Portraits of Katherine and William facing each other, crystal insert

| Date | Mintage | VF20 | XF40 | MS60 | MS63 | MS65 |
|---|---|---|---|---|---|---|
| 2011 | — | PF63 70.00 | PF65 80.00 | | | |

**KM# 1134 20 DOLLARS**
31.39 g., 0.9999 Silver 1.0091 oz. ASW, 38 mm. **Ruler:** Elizabeth II **Subject:** Canadian Pacific's D-10 Steam Locomotive **Obv:** Bust right **Rev:** Steam locomotive right **Edge:** Lettered

| Date | Mintage | VF20 | XF40 | MS60 | MS63 | MS65 |
|---|---|---|---|---|---|---|
| 2011 | 10,000 | PF63 70.00 | PF65 80.00 | | | |

**KM# 1135 20 DOLLARS**
31.39 g., 0.9999 Silver 1.0091 oz. ASW, 38 mm. **Ruler:** Elizabeth II **Obv:** Bust right **Rev:** Tulip in color and Vienitian glass lady bug

| Date | Mintage | VF20 | XF40 | MS60 | MS63 | MS65 |
|---|---|---|---|---|---|---|
| 2011 | 5,000 | PF65 1,000 | | | | |

**KM# 1145 20 DOLLARS**
31.39 g., 0.9999 Silver 1.0091 oz. ASW, 38 mm. **Ruler:** Elizabeth II **Obv:** Bust right **Rev:** Wild rose in color, swarovski crystals

| Date | Mintage | VF20 | XF40 | MS60 | MS63 | MS65 |
|---|---|---|---|---|---|---|
| 2011 | Est. 10000 | PF63 125 | PF65 135 | | | |

**KM# 1147 20 DOLLARS**
31.39 g., 0.9999 Silver 1.0091 oz. ASW, 38 mm. **Ruler:** Elizabeth II **Obv:** Bust right **Rev:** Maple leaves, seeds in color, swarovski crystal drop

| Date | Mintage | VF20 | XF40 | MS60 | MS63 | MS65 |
|---|---|---|---|---|---|---|
| 2011 | — | PF63 100 | PF65 110 | | | |

**KM# 1181 20 DOLLARS**
31.39 g., 0.999 Silver 1.0082 oz. ASW, 38 mm. **Ruler:** Elizabeth II **Obv:** Bust right **Rev:** Winnipeg Jets Logo, jet over maple leaf

| Date | Mintage | VF20 | XF40 | MS60 | MS63 | MS65 |
|---|---|---|---|---|---|---|
| 2011 | 15,000 | PF63 85.00 | PF65 95.00 | | | |

**KM# 1182 20 DOLLARS**
31.99 g., 0.9999 Silver 1.0284 oz. ASW, 38 mm. **Ruler:** Elizabeth II **Obv:** Bust right **Rev:** Christmas tree with six crystals

| Date | Mintage | VF20 | XF40 | MS60 | MS63 | MS65 |
|---|---|---|---|---|---|---|
| 2011 | — | PF63 65.00 | PF65 75.00 | | | |

**KM# 1187 20 DOLLARS**
31.39 g., 0.999 Silver 1.0082 oz. ASW, 38 mm. **Ruler:** Elizabeth II **Obv:** Bust right **Rev:** Snowflake with emerald crystals

| Date | Mintage | VF20 | XF40 | MS60 | MS63 | MS65 |
|---|---|---|---|---|---|---|
| 2011 | 15,000 | PF63 75.00 | PF65 85.00 | | | |

**KM# 1188 20 DOLLARS**
31.89 g., 0.999 Silver 1.0243 oz. ASW, 38 mm. **Ruler:** Elizabeth II **Obv:** Bust right **Rev:** Snowflake with topaz crystals

| Date | Mintage | VF20 | XF40 | MS60 | MS63 | MS65 |
|---|---|---|---|---|---|---|
| 2011 | 15,000 | PF63 75.00 | PF65 85.00 | | | |

**KM# 1189 20 DOLLARS**
31.89 g., 0.999 Silver 1.0243 oz. ASW, 38 mm. **Ruler:** Elizabeth II **Obv:** Bust right **Rev:** Three snowflakes with three Hyacinth red crystals

| Date | Mintage | VF20 | XF40 | MS60 | MS63 | MS65 |
|---|---|---|---|---|---|---|
| 2011 | 15,000 | PF63 75.00 | PF65 85.00 | | | |

**KM# 1190 20 DOLLARS**
31.89 g., 0.999 Silver 1.0243 oz. ASW, 38 mm. **Ruler:** Elizabeth II **Obv:** Bust right **Rev:** Three snowflakes with three Montana blue crystals

| Date | Mintage | VF20 | XF40 | MS60 | MS63 | MS65 |
|---|---|---|---|---|---|---|
| 2011 | 15,000 | PF63 75.00 | PF65 85.00 | | | |

**KM# 1137 20 DOLLARS**
31.39 g., 0.999 Silver 1.0082 oz. ASW, 38 mm. **Ruler:** Elizabeth II **Subject:** Elizabeth II, 60th Anniversary of reign **Obv:** Bust right **Rev:** Crowned bust right with swarovski crystal insert **Edge:** Reeded

| Date | Mintage | VF20 | XF40 | MS60 | MS63 | MS65 |
|---|---|---|---|---|---|---|
| 1952-2012 | 15,000 | PF63 70.00 | PF65 80.00 | | | |

**KM# 1177 20 DOLLARS**
27.78 g., 0.925 Silver 0.8262 oz. ASW, 38 mm. **Ruler:** Elizabeth II **Obv:** Bust right **Rev:** Youthful busts right of Elizabeth II and Prince Philip

| Date | Mintage | VF20 | XF40 | MS60 | MS63 | MS65 |
|---|---|---|---|---|---|---|
| 1952-2012 | — | PF63 75.00 | PF65 85.00 | | | |

**KM# 1178 20 DOLLARS**
27.78 g., 0.925 Silver 0.8262 oz. ASW, 38 mm. **Ruler:** Elizabeth II **Obv:** Bust right **Rev:** Royal cypher, wreath below

| Date | Mintage | VF20 | XF40 | MS60 | MS63 | MS65 |
|---|---|---|---|---|---|---|
| 1952-2012 | — | PF63 75.00 | PF65 85.00 | | | |

**KM# 1238 20 DOLLARS**
30.75 g., 0.9999 Silver 0.9885 oz. ASW, 36 mm. **Ruler:** Elizabeth II **Subject:** Elizabeth II, Diamond Jubilee **Obv:** Bust right **Rev:** Elizabeth II profile left, high releif

| Date | Mintage | VF20 | XF40 | MS60 | MS63 | MS65 |
|---|---|---|---|---|---|---|
| 2012 | 7,500 | PF63 65.00 | PF65 75.00 | | | |

**KM# 1239 20 DOLLARS**

Silver 0.2557 oz. ASW **Ruler:** Elizabeth II **Subject:** Royal visit to Canada **Obv:** Young portrait right **Rev:** Elizabeth II with Mountie and horse

| Date | Mintage | VF20 | XF40 | MS60 | MS63 | MS65 |
|---|---|---|---|---|---|---|
| 1952-2012 | 25,000 | PF63 25.00 | PF65 30.00 | | | |

**KM# 1246 20 DOLLARS**

31.39 g., 0.999 Silver 1.0082 oz. ASW, 38 mm. **Ruler:** Elizabeth II **Subject:** Coast Guard, 50th Anniversary

| Date | Mintage | VF20 | XF40 | MS60 | MS63 | MS65 |
|---|---|---|---|---|---|---|
| 2012 | 7,500 | PF63 90.00 | PF65 100 | | | |

**KM# 1250 20 DOLLARS**

31.39 g., 0.999 Silver 1.0082 oz. ASW, 38 mm. **Ruler:** Elizabeth II **Subject:** F.H. Varley

| Date | Mintage | VF20 | XF40 | MS60 | MS63 | MS65 |
|---|---|---|---|---|---|---|
| 2012 | 7,000 | PF63 65.00 | PF65 75.00 | | | |

**KM# 1251 20 DOLLARS**

27.78 g., 0.925 Silver 0.8262 oz. ASW, 38 mm. **Ruler:** Elizabeth II **Subject:** Arthur Lismer

| Date | Mintage | VF20 | XF40 | MS60 | MS63 | MS65 |
|---|---|---|---|---|---|---|
| 2012 | — | PF63 65.00 | PF65 75.00 | | | |

**KM# 1266 20 DOLLARS**

31.10 g., 0.999 Silver 0.9989 oz. ASW, 38 mm. **Ruler:** Elizabeth II **Subject:** Aster and bee

| Date | Mintage | VF20 | XF40 | MS60 | MS63 | MS65 |
|---|---|---|---|---|---|---|
| 2012 | — | PF63 90.00 | PF65 100 | | | |

**KM# 1269 20 DOLLARS**

31.39 g., 0.999 Silver 1.0082 oz. ASW, 38 mm. **Ruler:** Elizabeth II **Subject:** Sugar Maple Leaf **Rev:** Leaves in color, crystal

| Date | Mintage | VF20 | XF40 | MS60 | MS63 | MS65 |
|---|---|---|---|---|---|---|
| 2012 | — | PF65 130 | | | | |

**KM# 1270 20 DOLLARS**

31.39 g., 0.999 Silver 1.0082 oz. ASW, 38 mm. **Ruler:** Elizabeth II **Rev:** Rhododendron

| Date | Mintage | VF20 | XF40 | MS60 | MS63 | MS65 |
|---|---|---|---|---|---|---|
| 2012 | — | PF65 125 | | | | |

**KM# 1280 20 DOLLARS**

31.11 g., 0.999 Silver 0.999 oz. ASW, 38 mm. **Ruler:** Elizabeth II **Subject:** Bateman Moose

| Date | Mintage | VF20 | XF40 | MS60 | MS63 | MS65 |
|---|---|---|---|---|---|---|
| 2012 | — | PF65 135 | | | | |

**KM# 1283 20 DOLLARS**

15.55 g., 0.999 Gold 0.4994 oz. AGW, 25 mm. **Ruler:** Elizabeth II **Subject:** Year of the Dragon

| Date | Mintage | VF20 | XF40 | MS60 | MS63 | MS65 |
|---|---|---|---|---|---|---|
| 2012 | — | PF65 900 | | | | |

**KM# 1333 20 DOLLARS**

31.11 g., 0.999 Silver 0.999 oz. ASW, 38 mm. **Ruler:** Elizabeth II **Rev:** Snowstorm

| Date | Mintage | VF20 | XF40 | MS60 | MS63 | MS65 |
|---|---|---|---|---|---|---|
| 2012 | — | PF63 45.00 | PF65 50.00 | | | |

**KM# 1334 20 DOLLARS**

28.02 g., 0.999 Silver 0.900 oz. ASW **Ruler:** Elizabeth II **Subject:** Christmas Play **Rev:** Three childred as the Magi, crystal

| Date | Mintage | VF20 | XF40 | MS60 | MS63 | MS65 |
|---|---|---|---|---|---|---|
| 2012 | 10,000 | PF63 110 | PF65 115 | | | |

**KM# 1335 20 DOLLARS**

27.78 g., 0.925 Silver 0.8262 oz. ASW, 38 mm. **Ruler:** Elizabeth II **Subject:** Franklin Carmichael **Rev:** Snowy Landscape

| Date | Mintage | VF20 | XF40 | MS60 | MS63 | MS65 |
|---|---|---|---|---|---|---|
| 2012 | — | PF63 70.00 | PF65 75.00 | | | |

**KM# 1347 20 DOLLARS**

31.39 g., 0.999 Silver 1.0082 oz. ASW, 38 mm. **Ruler:** Elizabeth II **Rev:** Blue flag iris in color with three crystals

| Date | Mintage | VF20 | XF40 | MS60 | MS63 | MS65 |
|---|---|---|---|---|---|---|
| 2013 | 10,000 | PF63 110 | PF65 120 | | | |

**KM# 1361 20 DOLLARS**
31.39 g., 0.999 Silver 1.0082 oz. ASW, 35 mm. **Ruler:** Elizabeth II **Rev:** Purple cone flower, butterfly in color and high relief

| Date | Mintage | VF20 | XF40 | MS60 | MS63 | MS65 |
|---|---|---|---|---|---|---|
| 2013 | — | **PF63** 50.00 | **PF65** 60.00 | | | |

**KM# 1363 20 DOLLARS**
31.39 g., 0.9999 Silver 1.0091 oz. ASW, 38 mm. **Ruler:** Elizabeth II **Subject:** Canadian Maple Canopy - Spring **Rev:** Forest Canopy in Spring, Colorized

| Date | Mintage | VF20 | XF40 | MS60 | MS63 | MS65 |
|---|---|---|---|---|---|---|
| 2013 | Est. 7500 | **PF63** 90.00 | **PF65** 100 | | | |

**KM# 1374 20 DOLLARS**
31.40 g., 0.999 Silver 1.0084 oz. ASW, 38 mm. **Ruler:** Elizabeth II **Subject:** Baseball **Rev:** Baseball Batter

| Date | Mintage | VF20 | XF40 | MS60 | MS63 | MS65 |
|---|---|---|---|---|---|---|
| 2013 | Est. 7500 | **PF63** 110 | **PF65** 115 | | | |

**KM# 1375 20 DOLLARS**
31.39 g., 0.999 Silver 1.0082 oz. ASW, 38 mm. **Ruler:** Elizabeth II **Subject:** Baseball **Rev:** Baseball Fielder

| Date | Mintage | VF20 | XF40 | MS60 | MS63 | MS65 |
|---|---|---|---|---|---|---|
| 2013 | Est. 7500 | **PF63** 110 | **PF65** 115 | | | |

**KM# 1376 20 DOLLARS**
31.39 g., 0.999 Silver 1.0082 oz. ASW, 38 mm. **Ruler:** Elizabeth II **Subject:** Baseball **Rev:** Baseball Pitcher

| Date | Mintage | VF20 | XF40 | MS60 | MS63 | MS65 |
|---|---|---|---|---|---|---|
| 2013 | — | **PF63** 110 | **PF65** 115 | | | |

**KM# 1377 20 DOLLARS**
31.39 g., 0.999 Silver 1.0082 oz. ASW, 38 mm. **Ruler:** Elizabeth II **Subject:** Baseball **Rev:** Baseball Runner

| Date | Mintage | VF20 | XF40 | MS60 | MS63 | MS65 |
|---|---|---|---|---|---|---|
| 2013 | Est. 7500 | **PF63** 110 | **PF65** 115 | | | |

**KM# 1381 20 DOLLARS**
31.11 g., 0.999 Silver 0.999 oz. ASW, 38 mm. **Ruler:** Elizabeth II **Subject:** Snow Flake With Crystal

| Date | Mintage | VF20 | XF40 | MS60 | MS63 | MS65 |
|---|---|---|---|---|---|---|
| 2013 | — | **PF63** 110 | **PF65** 120 | | | |

**KM# 1384 20 DOLLARS**
31.39 g., 0.999 Silver 1.0082 oz. ASW, 38 mm. **Ruler:** Elizabeth II **Subject:** Frank Johnston - Painter **Rev:** Painting: Guardian of the Gorge

| Date | Mintage | VF20 | XF40 | MS60 | MS63 | MS65 |
|---|---|---|---|---|---|---|
| 2013 | Est. 7000 | **PF63** 80.00 | **PF65** 90.00 | | | |

**KM# 1385 20 DOLLARS**
31.39 g., 0.999 Silver 1.0082 oz. ASW, 38 mm. **Ruler:** Elizabeth II **Subject:** Lauren S. Harris - Painter **Rev:** Painting: Toronto Street, Winter Morning

| Date | Mintage | VF20 | XF40 | MS60 | MS63 | MS65 |
|---|---|---|---|---|---|---|
| 2013 | Est. 7000 | **PF63** 80.00 | **PF65** 90.00 | | | |

**KM# 1397 20 DOLLARS**
31.39 g., 0.9999 Silver 1.0091 oz. ASW, 38 mm. **Ruler:** Elizabeth II **Rev:** Beaver gnawing on tree

| Date | Mintage | VF20 | XF40 | MS60 | MS63 | MS65 |
|---|---|---|---|---|---|---|
| 2013 | 8,500 | **PF63** 90.00 | **PF65** 100 | | | |

**KM# 1404 20 DOLLARS**
28.20 g., 0.9999 Silver 0.9066 oz. ASW, 40 mm. **Ruler:** Elizabeth II **Rev:** Arctic Fox and Northern lights in background

| Date | Mintage | VF20 | XF40 | MS60 | MS63 | MS65 |
|---|---|---|---|---|---|---|
| 2013 | — | **PF63** 75.00 | **PF65** 85.00 | | | |

**KM# 1436 20 DOLLARS**
28.02 g., 0.999 Silver 0.900 oz. ASW, 40 mm. **Ruler:** Elizabeth II **Rev:** Canadian Tiger Swallowtail Butterfly in color

| Date | Mintage | VF20 | XF40 | MS60 | MS63 | MS65 |
|---|---|---|---|---|---|---|
| 2013 | Est. 10000 | **PF63** 90.00 | **PF65** 100 | | | |

**KM# 1440 20 DOLLARS**
31.39 g., 0.9999 Silver 1.0091 oz. ASW, 38 mm. **Ruler:** Elizabeth II **Obv:** Eagle head left

| Date | Mintage | VF20 | XF40 | MS60 | MS63 | MS65 |
|---|---|---|---|---|---|---|
| 2013 | Est. 7500 | PF63 90.00 | PF65 100 | | | |

**KM# 1447 20 DOLLARS**
31.39 g., 0.999 Silver 1.0082 oz. ASW, 38 mm. **Ruler:** Elizabeth II **Rev:** Superman standing right, cape blowing

| Date | Mintage | VF20 | XF40 | MS60 | MS63 | MS65 |
|---|---|---|---|---|---|---|
| 2013 | Est. 10000 | PF63 100 | PF65 110 | | | |

**KM# 1448 20 DOLLARS**
31.39 g., 0.999 Silver 1.0082 oz. ASW, 38 mm. **Ruler:** Elizabeth II **Subject:** 75th Anniversary of Superman **Rev:** Superman flying forward, multi-color background hologram

| Date | Mintage | VF20 | XF40 | MS60 | MS63 | MS65 |
|---|---|---|---|---|---|---|
| 2013 | Est. 10000 | PF63 120 | PF65 130 | | | |

**KM# 1449 20 DOLLARS**
31.39 g., 0.999 Silver 1.0082 oz. ASW, 38 mm. **Ruler:** Elizabeth II **Subject:** 75th Anniversary of Superman **Rev:** 'S' shield logo in color

| Date | Mintage | VF20 | XF40 | MS60 | MS63 | MS65 |
|---|---|---|---|---|---|---|
| 2013 | Est. 10000 | PF63 110 | PF65 120 | | | |

**KM# 1451a 20 DOLLARS**
7.96 g., 0.9999 Silver 0.2559 oz. ASW, 38 mm. **Ruler:** Elizabeth II **Rev:** Red maple leaf in center of many small maple leaves

| Date | Mintage | VF20 | XF40 | MS60 | MS63 | MS65 |
|---|---|---|---|---|---|---|
| 2013 | Est. 10000 | PF63 100 | PF65 115 | | | |

**KM# 1459 20 DOLLARS**
31.39 g., 0.999 Silver 1.0082 oz. ASW, 38 mm. **Ruler:** Elizabeth II **Rev:** Pronghorn Antelope with northern lights in the background

| Date | Mintage | VF20 | XF40 | MS60 | MS63 | MS65 |
|---|---|---|---|---|---|---|
| 2013 | Est. 8500 | PF63 80.00 | PF65 90.00 | | | |

**KM# 1466 20 DOLLARS**
31.39 g., 0.9999 Silver 1.0091 oz. ASW, 38 mm. **Ruler:** Elizabeth II **Subject:** Birth of Prince George **Rev:** Baby sleeping in crib

| Date | Mintage | VF20 | XF40 | MS60 | MS63 | MS65 |
|---|---|---|---|---|---|---|
| 2013 | 7,500 | PF63 70.00 | PF65 80.00 | | | |

**KM# 1467 20 DOLLARS**
31.39 g., 0.9999 Silver 1.0091 oz. ASW, 38 mm. **Ruler:** Elizabeth II **Subject:** Birth of Prince George **Rev:** Parents hands holding baby's hand

| Date | Mintage | VF20 | XF40 | MS60 | MS63 | MS65 |
|---|---|---|---|---|---|---|
| 2013 | 7,500 | PF63 70.00 | PF65 80.00 | | | |

**KM# 1468 20 DOLLARS**
31.39 g., 0.9999 Silver 1.0091 oz. ASW, 38 mm. **Ruler:** Elizabeth II **Subject:** Birth of Prince George **Rev:** Mint Mascot Moose and Beaver Mountie plush dolls in crib with sleeping baby

| Date | Mintage | VF20 | XF40 | MS60 | MS63 | MS65 |
|---|---|---|---|---|---|---|
| 2013 | 7,500 | PF63 70.00 | PF65 80.00 | | | |

**KM# 1469 20 DOLLARS**
31.39 g., 0.9999 Silver 1.0091 oz. ASW, 38 mm. **Ruler:** Elizabeth II **Subject:** Autumn Bliss **Rev:** Color view of canoe, lake and trees

| Date | Mintage | VF20 | XF40 | MS60 | MS63 | MS65 |
|---|---|---|---|---|---|---|
| 2013 | 7,500 | PF63 90.00 | PF65 100 | | | |

**KM# 1470 20 DOLLARS**
31.39 g., 0.9999 Silver 1.0091 oz. ASW, 38 mm. **Ruler:** Elizabeth II **Subject:** A.Y. Jackson, painter **Rev:** Detail of painting, Sant Tile de Caps

| Date | Mintage | VF20 | XF40 | MS60 | MS63 | MS65 |
|---|---|---|---|---|---|---|
| 2013 | 7,000 | PF63 90.00 | PF65 100 | | | |

**KM# 1471 20 DOLLARS**
31.39 g., 0.9999 Silver 1.0091 oz. ASW, 38 mm. **Ruler:** Elizabeth II **Subject:** J.E.H. MacDonald, painter **Rev:** Detail of painting, Sumacs

| Date | Mintage | VF20 | XF40 | MS60 | MS63 | MS65 |
|---|---|---|---|---|---|---|
| 2013 | 7,000 | PF63 90.00 | PF65 100 | | | |

**KM# 1474 20 DOLLARS**
31.39 g., 0.999 Silver 1.0082 oz. ASW, 38 mm. **Ruler:** Elizabeth II **Subject:** Dinosaurs of Canada **Rev:** Bathygnathus advancing left

| Date | Mintage | VF20 | XF40 | MS60 | MS63 | MS65 |
|---|---|---|---|---|---|---|
| 2013 | 8,500 | PF63 80.00 | PF65 90.00 | | | |

**KM# 1479 20 DOLLARS**
31.39 g., 0.999 Silver 1.0082 oz. ASW, 38 mm. **Ruler:** Elizabeth II **Rev:** Eagle in flight left

| Date | Mintage | VF20 | XF40 | MS60 | MS63 | MS65 |
|---|---|---|---|---|---|---|
| 2013 | — | PF63 80.00 | PF65 90.00 | | | |

**KM# 1484 20 DOLLARS**
31.11 g., 0.999 Silver 0.999 oz. ASW, 38 mm. **Ruler:** Elizabeth II **Subject:** Louisbourg Settlement **Rev:** Colonial sea-side scene

| Date | Mintage | VF20 | XF40 | MS60 | MS63 | MS65 |
|---|---|---|---|---|---|---|
| 2013 | 8,500 | PF63 80.00 | PF65 90.00 | | | |

### KM# 1507 20 DOLLARS

0.999 Silver, 38 mm. **Ruler:** Elizabeth II **Subject:** Carlito Dalceggio, artist

| Date | Mintage | VF20 | XF40 | MS60 | MS63 | MS65 |
|---|---|---|---|---|---|---|
| 2013 | 7,500 | PF63 80.00 | PF65 90.00 | | | |

### KM# 1510 20 DOLLARS

31.39 g., 0.9999 Silver 1.0091 oz. ASW, 38 mm. **Ruler:** Elizabeth II **Rev:** Two eagles standing on rock

| Date | Mintage | VF20 | XF40 | MS60 | MS63 | MS65 |
|---|---|---|---|---|---|---|
| 2013 | 7,500 | PF63 75.00 | PF65 80.00 | | | |

### KM# 1513 20 DOLLARS

31.39 g., 0.9999 Silver 1.0091 oz. ASW, 38 mm. **Ruler:** Elizabeth II **Subject:** Northern Lights, the great Hare **Rev:** Hare seated watching hologram of Northern Lights

| Date | Mintage | VF20 | XF40 | MS60 | MS63 | MS65 |
|---|---|---|---|---|---|---|
| 2013 | 8,500 | PF63 100 | PF65 110 | | | |

### KM# 1522 20 DOLLARS

31.39 g., 0.999 Silver 1.0082 oz. ASW, 38 mm. **Ruler:** Elizabeth II **Rev:** Maple forest canopy, two fall leaves in color

| Date | Mintage | VF20 | XF40 | MS60 | MS63 | MS65 |
|---|---|---|---|---|---|---|
| 2013 | 7,500 | PF63 90.00 | PF65 100 | | | |

### KM# 1526 20 DOLLARS

31.39 g., 0.999 Silver 1.0082 oz. ASW, 38 mm. **Ruler:** Elizabeth II **Rev:** Pointsettia, ornament, star and candy cane in color **Note:** Venitian glass used for coloring

| Date | Mintage | VF20 | XF40 | MS60 | MS63 | MS65 |
|---|---|---|---|---|---|---|
| 2013 | 10,000 | PF63 140 | PF65 150 | | | |

### KM# 1527 20 DOLLARS

31.39 g., 0.999 Silver 1.0082 oz. ASW, 38 mm. **Ruler:** Elizabeth II **Rev:** Snowflake, crystal at center

| Date | Mintage | VF20 | XF40 | MS60 | MS63 | MS65 |
|---|---|---|---|---|---|---|
| 2013 | 10,000 | PF63 110 | PF65 115 | | | |

### KM# 1531 20 DOLLARS

31.39 g., 0.999 Silver 1.0082 oz. ASW, 38 mm. **Ruler:** Elizabeth II **Rev:** Holiday Wreath with five colored crystals

| Date | Mintage | VF20 | XF40 | MS60 | MS63 | MS65 |
|---|---|---|---|---|---|---|
| 2013 | 10,000 | PF65 175 | | | | |

### KM# 1532 20 DOLLARS

31.39 g., 0.999 Silver 1.0082 oz. ASW, 38 mm. **Ruler:** Elizabeth II **Rev:** Scutellosaurus advancing left

| Date | Mintage | VF20 | XF40 | MS60 | MS63 | MS65 |
|---|---|---|---|---|---|---|
| 2013 | 850 | PF63 80.00 | PF65 90.00 | | | |

### KM# 1548 20 DOLLARS

31.39 g., 0.999 Silver 1.0082 oz. ASW, 38 mm. **Ruler:** Elizabeth II **Rev:** Stained glass window pattern in color

| Date | Mintage | VF20 | XF40 | MS60 | MS63 | MS65 |
|---|---|---|---|---|---|---|
| 2013 | — | PF63 65.00 | PF65 75.00 | | | |

### KM# 1553 20 DOLLARS

31.39 g., 0.999 Silver 1.0082 oz. ASW, 38 mm. **Ruler:** Elizabeth II **Subject:** Pond Hockey in color **Obv:** Bust right

| Date | Mintage | VF20 | XF40 | MS60 | MS63 | MS65 |
|---|---|---|---|---|---|---|
| 2014 | 8,500 | PF63 90.00 | PF65 100 | | | |

### KM# 1556 20 DOLLARS

31.39 g., 0.9999 Silver 1.0091 oz. ASW, 38 mm. **Ruler:** Elizabeth II **Obv:** Bust right **Rev:** Polar bear walking on rocks in color

| Date | Mintage | VF20 | XF40 | MS60 | MS63 | MS65 |
|---|---|---|---|---|---|---|
| 2014 | 8,500 | PF63 90.00 | PF65 100 | | | |

### KM# 1558 20 DOLLARS

31.39 g., 0.999 Silver 1.0082 oz. ASW, 38 mm. **Ruler:** Elizabeth II **Obv:** Bust right **Rev:** Canadian UN Peacekeeper with binoculars, blue beret

| Date | Mintage | VF20 | XF40 | MS60 | MS63 | MS65 |
|---|---|---|---|---|---|---|
| 2014 | 8,500 | PF65 115 | | | | |

### KM# 1565 20 DOLLARS

31.39 g., 0.9999 Silver 1.0091 oz. ASW, 38 mm. **Ruler:** Elizabeth II **Obv:** Bust right **Rev:** Lake Superior in blue color

| Date | Mintage | VF20 | XF40 | MS60 | MS63 | MS65 |
|---|---|---|---|---|---|---|
| 2014 | 10,000 | PF63 110 | PF65 115 | | | |

### KM# 1566 20 DOLLARS

31.39 g., 0.999 Silver 1.0082 oz. ASW, 38 mm. **Obv:** Bust right **Rev:** Lake Huron in color

| Date | Mintage | VF20 | XF40 | MS60 | MS63 | MS65 |
|---|---|---|---|---|---|---|
| 2014 | 10,000 | PF63 110 | PF65 115 | | | |

**KM# 1567 20 DOLLARS**

31.39 g., 0.999 Silver 1.0082 oz. ASW, 38 mm. **Ruler:** Elizabeth II **Obv:** Bust right **Rev:** Lake Michigan in color

| Date | Mintage | VF20 | XF40 | MS60 | MS63 | MS65 |
|---|---|---|---|---|---|---|
| 2014 | 10,000 | PF63 110 | PF65 115 | | | |

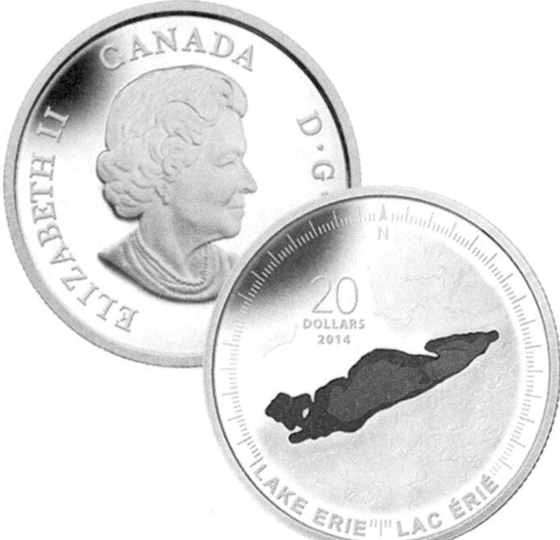


**KM# 1568 20 DOLLARS**

31.39 g., 0.999 Silver 1.0082 oz. ASW, 38 mm. **Ruler:** Elizabeth II **Obv:** Bust right **Rev:** Lake Erie in color

| Date | Mintage | VF20 | XF40 | MS60 | MS63 | MS65 |
|---|---|---|---|---|---|---|
| 2014 | 10,000 | PF63 110 | PF65 115 | | | |

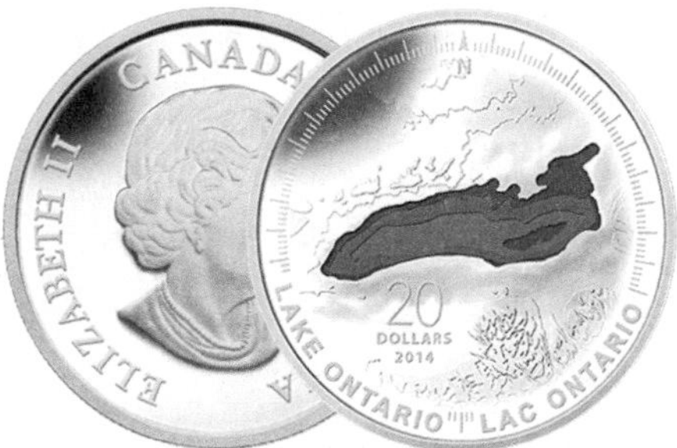


**KM# 1569 20 DOLLARS**

31.39 g., 0.999 Silver 1.0082 oz. ASW, 38 mm. **Ruler:** Elizabeth II **Obv:** Bust right **Rev:** Lake Ontario in color

| Date | Mintage | VF20 | XF40 | MS60 | MS63 | MS65 |
|---|---|---|---|---|---|---|
| 2014 | 10,000 | PF63 110 | PF65 115 | | | |

**KM# 1570 20 DOLLARS**

31.39 g., 0.9999 Silver 1.0091 oz. ASW, 38 mm. **Ruler:** Elizabeth II **Obv:** Bust right **Rev:** Caribou in color

| Date | Mintage | VF20 | XF40 | MS60 | MS63 | MS65 |
|---|---|---|---|---|---|---|
| 2014 | 8,500 | PF63 90.00 | PF65 100 | | | |

**KM# 1609 20 DOLLARS**

31.39 g., 0.999 Silver 1.0082 oz. ASW, 38 mm. **Ruler:** Elizabeth II **Obv:** Bust right **Rev:** Bison head facing

| Date | Mintage | VF20 | XF40 | MS60 | MS63 | MS65 |
|---|---|---|---|---|---|---|
| 2014 | 7,500 | PF63 90.00 | PF65 100 | | | |

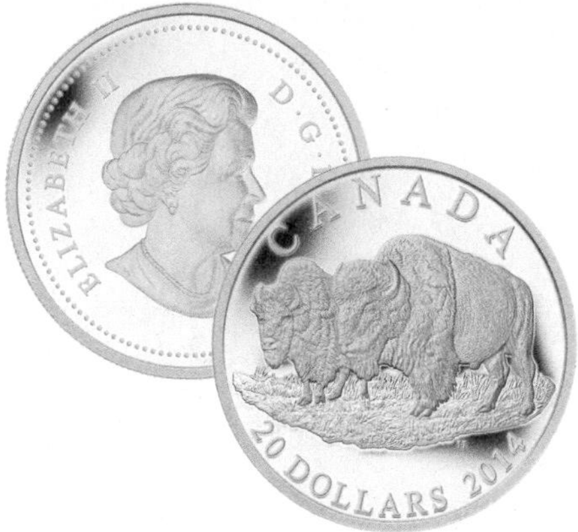


**KM# 1610 20 DOLLARS**

31.39 g., 0.999 Silver 1.0082 oz. ASW, 38 mm. **Ruler:** Elizabeth II **Obv:** Bust right **Rev:** Bison pair advancing left

| Date | Mintage | VF20 | XF40 | MS60 | MS63 | MS65 |
|---|---|---|---|---|---|---|
| 2014 | 7,500 | PF63 90.00 | PF65 100 | | | |

**KM# 1614 20 DOLLARS**

31.11 g., 0.999 Silver 0.999 oz. ASW, 40 mm. **Ruler:** Elizabeth II **Obv:** Bust right **Rev:** Wolverine with northern lights in background

| Date | Mintage | VF20 | XF40 | MS60 | MS63 | MS65 |
|---|---|---|---|---|---|---|
| 2014 | 8,500 | PF63 80.00 | PF65 90.00 | | | |

**KM# 1668 20 DOLLARS**

31.39 g., 0.999 Silver 1.0082 oz. ASW partially gilt, 38 mm. **Ruler:** Elizabeth II **Obv:** Bust right **Rev:** Nanaboozhoo and the Thunderbird

| Date | Mintage | F12 | VF20 | XF40 | MS60 | MS63 |
|---|---|---|---|---|---|---|
| 2014 | 8,500 | PF63 110 | PF65 115 | | | |

**KM# 1669 20 DOLLARS**

31.39 g., 0.9999 Silver 1.0091 oz. ASW, 38 mm. **Ruler:** Elizabeth II **Obv:** Bust right **Rev:** Nanaboozhoo and Thunderbird nest

| Date | Mintage | F12 | VF20 | XF40 | MS60 | MS63 |
|---|---|---|---|---|---|---|
| 2014 | 8,500 | PF63 85.00 | PF65 90.00 | | | |

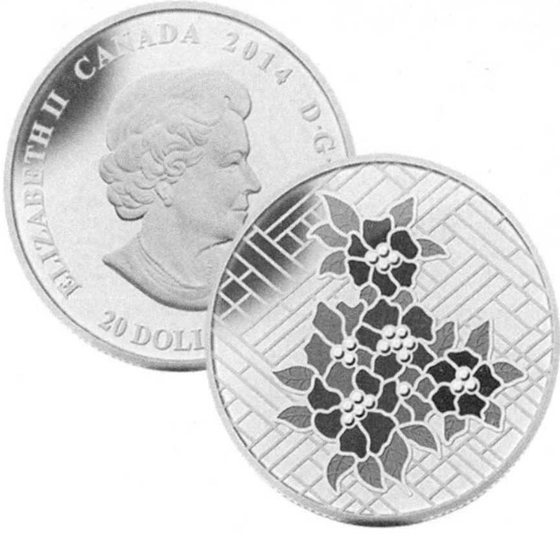


**KM# 1677 20 DOLLARS**

31.39 g., 0.9999 Silver 1.0091 oz. ASW, 38 mm. **Ruler:** Elizabeth II **Obv:** Bust right **Rev:** Floral colored glass from Craigdarroch Castle

| Date | Mintage | F12 | VF20 | XF40 | MS60 | MS63 |
|---|---|---|---|---|---|---|
| 2014 | 7,500 | PF63 125 | PF65 130 | | | |

**KM# 1678 20 DOLLARS**

31.39 g., 0.9999 Silver 1.0091 oz. ASW, 38 mm. **Ruler:** Elizabeth II **Obv:** Bust right **Rev:** River rapids in color

| Date | Mintage | F12 | VF20 | XF40 | MS60 | MS63 |
|---|---|---|---|---|---|---|
| 2014 | 7,500 | PF63 90.00 | PF65 100 | | | |

**KM# 1680 20 DOLLARS**

31.39 g., 0.9999 Silver 1.0091 oz. ASW, 38 mm. **Ruler:** Elizabeth II **Subject:** Royal Ontario Museum, 100th Anniversary **Obv:** Bust right **Rev:** Building façade, partially gilt

| Date | Mintage | F12 | VF20 | XF40 | MS60 | MS63 |
|---|---|---|---|---|---|---|
| 2014 | 8,500 | PF63 110 | PF65 115 | | | |

**KM# 1681 20 DOLLARS**

31.11 g., 0.9999 Silver 0.9999 oz. ASW, 38 mm. **Ruler:** Elizabeth II **Subject:** Royal visit, 75th Anniversary **Obv:** Bust right **Rev:** George VI and Queen Mary on back of open platform railway car

| Date | Mintage | F12 | VF20 | XF40 | MS60 | MS63 |
|---|---|---|---|---|---|---|
| 2014 Antique patina | 5,000 | — | — | — | — | 140 |

**KM# 1682 20 DOLLARS**
31.11 g., 0.9999 Silver 0.9999 oz. ASW, 38 mm. **Ruler:** Elizabeth II **Obv:** Bust right **Rev:** Howling wolf and northern lights hologram

| Date | Mintage | F12 | VF20 | XF40 | MS60 | MS63 |
|---|---|---|---|---|---|---|
| 2014 | 8,500 | PF63 105 | PF65 110 | | | |

**KM# 1684 20 DOLLARS**
31.39 g., 0.9999 Silver 1.0091 oz. ASW, 38 mm. **Ruler:** Elizabeth II **Obv:** Bust right **Rev:** Baby beaver in color

| Date | Mintage | F12 | VF20 | XF40 | MS60 | MS63 |
|---|---|---|---|---|---|---|
| 2014 | 7,500 | PF63 90.00 | PF65 100 | | | |

**KM# 1687 20 DOLLARS**
31.39 g., 0.9999 Silver 1.0091 oz. ASW, 38 mm. **Ruler:** Elizabeth II **Obv:** Bust right **Rev:** Nanaboozhoo in color

| Date | Mintage | F12 | VF20 | XF40 | MS60 | MS63 |
|---|---|---|---|---|---|---|
| 2014 | 8,500 | PF63 110 | PF65 115 | | | |

**KM# 1709 20 DOLLARS**
31.39 g., 0.999 Silver 1.0082 oz. ASW, 38 mm. **Ruler:** Elizabeth II **Obv:** Bust right **Rev:** Royal Family - Elizabeth II, Charles, William, George

| Date | Mintage | VF20 | XF40 | MS60 | MS63 | MS65 |
|---|---|---|---|---|---|---|
| 2014 | 10,000 | PF65 80.00 | | | | |

**KM# 1732 20 DOLLARS**
31.39 g., 0.999 Silver 1.0082 oz. ASW, 38 mm. **Ruler:** Elizabeth II **Subject:** Autumn Falls **Obv:** Bust right **Rev:** Waterfall and maple leaves

| Date | Mintage | VF20 | XF40 | MS60 | MS63 | MS65 |
|---|---|---|---|---|---|---|
| 2014 | 7,500 | PF65 100 | | | | |

**KM# 1734 20 DOLLARS**
31.39 g., 0.999 Silver 1.0082 oz. ASW, 38 mm. **Ruler:** Elizabeth II **Obv:** Bust right **Rev:** Chickadee on branch with red crystal berries

| Date | Mintage | VF20 | XF40 | MS60 | MS63 | MS65 |
|---|---|---|---|---|---|---|
| 2014 | 7,500 | PF65 115 | | | | |

**KM# 1735 20 DOLLARS**
31.39 g., 0.999 Silver 1.0082 oz. ASW, 38 mm. **Ruler:** Elizabeth II **Obv:** Bust right **Rev:** Bald Eagle in flight right with fish in talons

| Date | Mintage | VF20 | XF40 | MS60 | MS63 | MS65 |
|---|---|---|---|---|---|---|
| 2014 | 8,500 | PF65 100 | | | | |

**KM# 1736 20 DOLLARS**
31.39 g., 0.999 Silver 1.0082 oz. ASW partially gilt, 38 mm. **Ruler:** Elizabeth II **Obv:** Bust right **Rev:** Bald Eagle gilt, in flight left with fish in talons

| Date | Mintage | VF20 | XF40 | MS60 | MS63 | MS65 |
|---|---|---|---|---|---|---|
| 2014 | 8,500 | PF65 115 | | | | |

**KM# 1737 20 DOLLARS**
31.39 g., 0.999 Silver 1.0082 oz. ASW, 38 mm. **Ruler:** Elizabeth II **Obv:** Bust right **Rev:** Bald eagle in color, in flight right

| Date | Mintage | VF20 | XF40 | MS60 | MS63 | MS65 |
|---|---|---|---|---|---|---|
| 2014 | 8,500 | PF65 90.00 | | | | |

**KM# 1738 20 DOLLARS**
31.39 g., 0.999 Silver 1.0082 oz. ASW, 38 mm. **Ruler:** Elizabeth II **Obv:** Bust right **Rev:** Totem Forest

| Date | Mintage | VF20 | XF40 | MS60 | MS63 | MS65 |
|---|---|---|---|---|---|---|
| 2014 | 6,000 | PF65 90.00 | | | | |

**KM# 1742 20 DOLLARS**
31.39 g., 0.999 Silver 1.0082 oz. ASW, 38 mm. **Ruler:** Elizabeth II **Obv:** Bust right **Rev:** Stained glass window from Casa Loma

| Date | Mintage | F12 | VF20 | XF40 | MS60 | MS63 |
|---|---|---|---|---|---|---|
| 2014 | 7,500 | PF65 100 | | | | |

**KM# 1743 20 DOLLARS**
31.39 g., 0.999 Silver 1.0082 oz. ASW, 38 mm. **Ruler:** Elizabeth II **Obv:** Bust right **Rev:** White tail deer - Doe and two fawns

| Date | Mintage | VF20 | XF40 | MS60 | MS63 | MS65 |
|---|---|---|---|---|---|---|
| 2014 | 7,500 | PF65 80.00 | | | | |

**KM# 1744 20 DOLLARS**
31.39 g., 0.999 Silver 1.0082 oz. ASW, 38 mm. **Ruler:** Elizabeth II **Obv:** Bust right **Rev:** Two white tail deer bucks locking antlers

| Date | Mintage | VF20 | XF40 | MS60 | MS63 | MS65 |
|---|---|---|---|---|---|---|
| 2014 | 7,500 | PF65 80.00 | | | | |

**KM# 1745 20 DOLLARS**
31.39 g., 0.999 Silver 1.0082 oz. ASW, 38 mm. **Ruler:** Elizabeth II **Obv:** Bust right **Rev:** White tail deer portrait

| Date | Mintage | VF20 | XF40 | MS60 | MS63 | MS65 |
|---|---|---|---|---|---|---|
| 2014 | 7,500 | PF65 80.00 | | | | |

**KM# 1746 20 DOLLARS**
31.39 g., 0.999 Silver 1.0082 oz. ASW, 38 mm. **Ruler:** Elizabeth II **Obv:** Bust right **Rev:** Two white tail deer bounding left over fallen tree trunk

| Date | Mintage | VF20 | XF40 | MS60 | MS63 | MS65 |
|---|---|---|---|---|---|---|
| 2014 | 7,500 | PF65 100 | | | | |

**KM# 1750 20 DOLLARS**

31.39 g., 0.999 Silver 1.0082 oz. ASW, 38 mm. **Ruler:** Elizabeth II **Obv:** Bust right **Rev:** Superman breaking thru ice

| Date | Mintage | VF20 | XF40 | MS60 | MS63 | MS65 |
|---|---|---|---|---|---|---|
| 2014 | 10,000 | PF65 80.00 | | | | |

**KM# 1753 20 DOLLARS**

31.39 g., 0.999 Silver 1.0082 oz. ASW, 38 mm. **Ruler:** Elizabeth II **Obv:** Bust right **Rev:** Cougar advancing left

| Date | Mintage | VF20 | XF40 | MS60 | MS63 | MS65 |
|---|---|---|---|---|---|---|
| 2014 | — | PF65 80.00 | | | | |

**KM# 1754 20 DOLLARS**

31.39 g., 0.999 Silver 1.0082 oz. ASW, 38 mm. **Ruler:** Elizabeth II **Obv:** Bust right **Rev:** Cougar advancing, partially gilt

| Date | Mintage | VF20 | XF40 | MS60 | MS63 | MS65 |
|---|---|---|---|---|---|---|
| 2014 | — | PF65 80.00 | | | | |

**KM# 1755 20 DOLLARS**

31.39 g., 0.999 Silver 1.0082 oz. ASW, 38 mm. **Ruler:** Elizabeth II **Obv:** Bust right **Rev:** Cougar in tree, fall colors

| Date | Mintage | VF20 | XF40 | MS60 | MS63 | MS65 |
|---|---|---|---|---|---|---|
| 2014 | — | PF65 100 | | | | |

**KM# 1759 20 DOLLARS**

31.39 g., 0.999 Silver 1.0082 oz. ASW, 38 mm. **Ruler:** Elizabeth II **Obv:** Bust right **Rev:** Maple leaf canopy, autumn allure

| Date | Mintage | VF20 | XF40 | MS60 | MS63 | MS65 |
|---|---|---|---|---|---|---|
| 2014 | 7,500 | PF65 100 | | | | |

**KM# 1760 20 DOLLARS**

31.39 g., 0.999 Silver 1.0082 oz. ASW, 38 mm. **Ruler:** Elizabeth II **Obv:** Bust right **Rev:** Maple leaf impressions, large green leaf in center

| Date | Mintage | VF20 | XF40 | MS60 | MS63 | MS65 |
|---|---|---|---|---|---|---|
| 2014 | 7,500 | PF65 100 | | | | |

**KM# 1763 20 DOLLARS**

31.39 g., 0.999 Silver 1.0082 oz. ASW, 38 mm. **Ruler:** Elizabeth II **Obv:** Bust right **Rev:** Maple tree canopy, green leaves

| Date | Mintage | VF20 | XF40 | MS60 | MS63 | MS65 |
|---|---|---|---|---|---|---|
| 2014 | 7,500 | PF65 100 | | | | |

**KM# 1769 20 DOLLARS**

31.39 g., 0.999 Silver 1.0082 oz. ASW, 38 mm. **Ruler:** Elizabeth II **Obv:** Bust right **Rev:** Xenoceratopis Foremostensis dinosaur

| Date | Mintage | VF20 | XF40 | MS60 | MS63 | MS65 |
|---|---|---|---|---|---|---|
| 2014 | 8,500 | PF65 90.00 | | | | |

**KM# 1770 20 DOLLARS**

31.39 g., 0.9999 Silver 1.0091 oz. ASW, 38 mm. **Ruler:** Elizabeth II **Obv:** Bust right **Rev:** Maple leaf cluster, glow in the dark

| Date | Mintage | VF20 | XF40 | MS60 | MS63 | MS65 |
|---|---|---|---|---|---|---|
| 2014 | — | PF65 38.00 | | | | |

**KM# 1771 20 DOLLARS**

31.39 g., 0.999 Silver 1.0082 oz. ASW, 38 mm. **Ruler:** Elizabeth II **Obv:** Bust right **Rev:** Red Trillum in color and crystal dew drops

| Date | Mintage | F12 | VF20 | XF40 | MS60 | MS63 |
|---|---|---|---|---|---|---|
| 2014 | — | PF65 120 | | | | |

**KM# 1776 20 DOLLARS**

31.39 g., 0.9999 Silver 1.0091 oz. ASW, 38 mm. **Ruler:** Elizabeth II **Obv:** Bust right **Rev:** Water Lilly & Venitian glass frog **Note:** Very high relief.

| Date | Mintage | VF20 | XF40 | MS60 | MS63 | MS65 |
|---|---|---|---|---|---|---|
| 2014 | 12,500 | PF65 150 | | | | |

**KM# 1780 20 DOLLARS**

31.39 g., 0.999 Silver 1.0082 oz. ASW **Ruler:** Elizabeth II **Subject:** Canadian Space Agency **Obv:** Bust right **Rev:** Space walk and Canada arm

| Date | Mintage | F12 | VF20 | XF40 | MS60 | MS63 |
|---|---|---|---|---|---|---|
| 2014 | — | PF65 120 | | | | |

**KM# 1781 20 DOLLARS**

31.39 g., 0.999 Silver 1.0082 oz. ASW, 38 mm. **Ruler:** Elizabeth II **Subject:** Interconnections - Land **Obv:** Bust right **Rev:** Beaver hologram

| Date | Mintage | F12 | VF20 | XF40 | MS60 | MS63 |
|---|---|---|---|---|---|---|
| 2014 | 7,500 | PF65 115 | | | | |

**KM# 1782 20 DOLLARS**

31.39 g., 0.999 Silver 1.0082 oz. ASW, 38 mm. **Ruler:** Elizabeth II **Subject:** Interconnections - Air **Obv:** Bust right **Rev:** Thunderbird hologram

| Date | Mintage | F12 | VF20 | XF40 | MS60 | MS63 |
|---|---|---|---|---|---|---|
| 2014 | 7,500 | PF65 115 | | | | |

**KM# 1783 20 DOLLARS**

31.39 g., 0.999 Silver 1.0082 oz. ASW, 38 mm. **Ruler:** Elizabeth II **Subject:** Interconnections - Sea **Obv:** Bust right **Rev:** Orca hologram

| Date | Mintage | F12 | VF20 | XF40 | MS60 | MS63 |
|---|---|---|---|---|---|---|
| 2014 | 7,500 | PF65 115 | | | | |

**KM# 1788 20 DOLLARS**

31.39 g., 0.999 Silver 1.0082 oz. ASW, 38 mm. **Ruler:** Elizabeth II **Subject:** Hockey Canada, 100th Anniversary **Obv:** Bust right **Rev:** Hockey player within red and black maple leaf

| Date | Mintage | F12 | VF20 | XF40 | MS60 | MS63 |
|---|---|---|---|---|---|---|
| 2014 | — | PF65 120 | | | | |

**KM# 1795 20 DOLLARS**
31.39 g., 0.999 Silver 1.0082 oz. ASW, 38 mm. **Ruler:** Elizabeth II **Obv:** Bust right **Rev:** Snowman and house, tree in Venetian glass

| Date | Mintage | F12 | VF20 | XF40 | MS60 | MS63 |
|---|---|---|---|---|---|---|
| 2014 | 10,000 | PF65 150 | | | | |

**KM# 1796 20 DOLLARS**
31.83 g., 0.999 Silver 1.0223 oz. ASW, 40 mm. **Ruler:** Elizabeth II **Obv:** Bust right **Rev:** Red spotted purple butterfly

| Date | Mintage | F12 | VF20 | XF40 | MS60 | MS63 |
|---|---|---|---|---|---|---|
| 2014 | 10,000 | PF65 100 | | | | |

**KM# 1822 20 DOLLARS**
31.39 g., 0.999 Silver 1.0082 oz. ASW **Ruler:** Elizabeth II **Obv:** Bust right **Rev:** Family skating on ice pond

| Date | Mintage | VF20 | XF40 | MS60 | MS63 | MS65 |
|---|---|---|---|---|---|---|
| 2015 | 7,500 | PF65 75.00 | | | | |

**KM# 1823 20 DOLLARS**
31.39 g., 0.999 Silver 1.0082 oz. ASW, 38 mm. **Ruler:** Elizabeth II **Obv:** Bust right **Rev:** Albertosaurus

| Date | Mintage | F12 | VF20 | XF40 | MS60 | MS63 |
|---|---|---|---|---|---|---|
| 2015 | 8,500 | PF65 90.00 | | | | |

**KM# 1825 20 DOLLARS**
31.39 g., 0.999 Silver 1.0082 oz. ASW, 38 mm. **Ruler:** Elizabeth II **Obv:** Bust right **Rev:** Beaver at work in color

| Date | Mintage | VF20 | XF40 | MS60 | MS63 | MS65 |
|---|---|---|---|---|---|---|
| 2015 | 7,500 | PF65 100 | | | | |

**KM# 1833 20 DOLLARS**
31.39 g., 0.999 Silver 1.0082 oz. ASW, 38 mm. **Ruler:** Elizabeth II **Obv:** Bust right **Rev:** Mother and young burrowing owl in color

| Date | Mintage | VF20 | XF40 | MS60 | MS63 | MS65 |
|---|---|---|---|---|---|---|
| 2015 | 7,500 | PF65 100 | | | | |

**KM# 1844 20 DOLLARS**
31.39 g., 0.9999 Silver 1.0091 oz. ASW **Ruler:** Elizabeth II **Obv:** Bust right **Rev:** UNESCO. Mt. Fuji and Rocky Mountains

| Date | Mintage | VF20 | XF40 | MS60 | MS63 | MS65 |
|---|---|---|---|---|---|---|
| 2015 | — | PF65 75.00 | | | | |

**KM# 742 25 DOLLARS**
27.78 g., 0.925 Silver 0.8262 oz. ASW, 40 mm. **Ruler:** Elizabeth II **Subject:** Vancouver Olympics **Rev:** Alpine skiing, hologram

| Date | Mintage | VF20 | XF40 | MS60 | MS63 | MS65 |
|---|---|---|---|---|---|---|
| 2007 | 45,000 | PF63 45.00 | PF65 50.00 | | | |

**KM# 743 25 DOLLARS**
27.78 g., 0.925 Silver 0.8262 oz. ASW, 40 mm. **Ruler:** Elizabeth II **Subject:** Vancouver Olympics **Rev:** Athletics pride hologram

| Date | Mintage | VF20 | XF40 | MS60 | MS63 | MS65 |
|---|---|---|---|---|---|---|
| 2007 | 45,000 | PF63 60.00 | PF65 65.00 | | | |

**KM# 744 25 DOLLARS**
27.75 g., 0.925 Silver 0.8253 oz. ASW, 40 mm. **Ruler:** Elizabeth II **Subject:** Vancouver Olympics **Rev:** Biathleon hologram

| Date | Mintage | VF20 | XF40 | MS60 | MS63 | MS65 |
|---|---|---|---|---|---|---|
| 2007 | 54,000 | PF63 45.00 | PF65 50.00 | | | |

**KM# 745 25 DOLLARS**
27.78 g., 0.925 Silver 0.8262 oz. ASW, 40 mm. **Ruler:** Elizabeth II **Subject:** Vancouver Olympics **Rev:** Curling hologram

| Date | Mintage | VF20 | XF40 | MS60 | MS63 | MS65 |
|---|---|---|---|---|---|---|
| 2007 | — | PF63 45.00 | PF65 50.00 | | | |

**KM# 746 25 DOLLARS**
27.78 g., 0.925 Silver 0.8262 oz. ASW, 40 mm. **Ruler:** Elizabeth II **Subject:** Vancouver Olympics **Rev:** Hockey, hologram

| Date | Mintage | VF20 | XF40 | MS60 | MS63 | MS65 |
|---|---|---|---|---|---|---|
| 2007 | 45,000 | PF63 45.00 | PF65 50.00 | | | |

**KM# 814 25 DOLLARS**
27.78 g., 0.925 Silver 0.8262 oz. ASW, 40 mm. **Ruler:** Elizabeth II **Subject:** Vancouver Olympics **Rev:** Bobsleigh, hologram

| Date | Mintage | VF20 | XF40 | MS60 | MS63 | MS65 |
|---|---|---|---|---|---|---|
| 2008 | 45,000 | PF63 40.00 | PF65 50.00 | | | |

**KM# 815 25 DOLLARS**
27.78 g., 0.925 Silver 0.8262 oz. ASW, 40 mm. **Ruler:** Elizabeth II **Subject:** Vancouver Olympics **Rev:** Figure skating, hologram

| Date | Mintage | VF20 | XF40 | MS60 | MS63 | MS65 |
|---|---|---|---|---|---|---|
| 2008 | 45,000 | **PF63** 40.00 | **PF65** 50.00 | | | |

**KM# 816 25 DOLLARS**
27.78 g., 0.925 Silver 0.8262 oz. ASW, 40 mm. **Ruler:** Elizabeth II **Subject:** Vancouver Olympics **Rev:** Freestyle skating, hologram

| Date | Mintage | VF20 | XF40 | MS60 | MS63 | MS65 |
|---|---|---|---|---|---|---|
| 2008 | 45,000 | **PF63** 40.00 | **PF65** 50.00 | | | |

**KM# 817 25 DOLLARS**
27.78 g., 0.925 Silver 0.8262 oz. ASW, 40 mm. **Ruler:** Elizabeth II **Subject:** Vancouver Olympics **Rev:** Snowboarding, hologram

| Date | Mintage | VF20 | XF40 | MS60 | MS63 | MS65 |
|---|---|---|---|---|---|---|
| 2008 | 45,000 | **PF63** 40.00 | **PF65** 50.00 | | | |

**KM# 818 25 DOLLARS**
27.78 g., 0.925 Silver 0.8262 oz. ASW, 40 mm. **Ruler:** Elizabeth II **Subject:** Vancouver Olympics **Rev:** Home of the 2010 Olympics

| Date | Mintage | VF20 | XF40 | MS60 | MS63 | MS65 |
|---|---|---|---|---|---|---|
| 2008 | 45,000 | **PF63** 40.00 | **PF65** 50.00 | | | |

**KM# 903 25 DOLLARS**
27.78 g., 0.925 Silver 0.8262 oz. ASW, 40 mm. **Ruler:** Elizabeth II **Subject:** 2010 Vancouver Olympics **Obv:** Bust right **Rev:** Cross Country Skiing and hologram at left

| Date | Mintage | VF20 | XF40 | MS60 | MS63 | MS65 |
|---|---|---|---|---|---|---|
| 2009 | 45,000 | **PF63** 45.00 | **PF65** 50.00 | | | |

**KM# 904 25 DOLLARS**
27.78 g., 0.925 Silver 0.8262 oz. ASW, 40 mm. **Ruler:** Elizabeth II **Subject:** 2010 Vancouver Olympics **Obv:** Bust right **Rev:** Olympians holding torch, hologram at left

| Date | Mintage | VF20 | XF40 | MS60 | MS63 | MS65 |
|---|---|---|---|---|---|---|
| 2009 | 45,000 | **PF63** 45.00 | **PF65** 50.00 | | | |

**KM# 905 25 DOLLARS**
27.78 g., 0.925 Silver 0.8262 oz. ASW, 40 mm. **Ruler:** Elizabeth II **Subject:** 2010 Vancouver Olympics **Obv:** Bust right **Rev:** Sled, hologram at left

| Date | Mintage | VF20 | XF40 | MS60 | MS63 | MS65 |
|---|---|---|---|---|---|---|
| 2009 | 45,000 | **PF63** 45.00 | **PF65** 50.00 | | | |

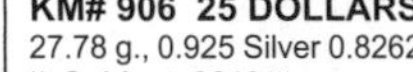

**KM# 906 25 DOLLARS**
27.78 g., 0.925 Silver 0.8262 oz. ASW, 40 mm. **Ruler:** Elizabeth II **Subject:** 2010 Vancouver Olympics **Obv:** Bust right **Rev:** Ski Jumper, hologram at left

| Date | Mintage | VF20 | XF40 | MS60 | MS63 | MS65 |
|---|---|---|---|---|---|---|
| 2009 | 45,000 | **PF63** 45.00 | **PF65** 50.00 | | | |

**KM# 907 25 DOLLARS**
27.78 g., 0.925 Silver 0.8262 oz. ASW, 40 mm. **Ruler:** Elizabeth II **Subject:** 2010 Vancouver Olympics **Obv:** Bust right **Rev:** Speed Skaters, hologram at left

| Date | Mintage | VF20 | XF40 | MS60 | MS63 | MS65 |
|---|---|---|---|---|---|---|
| 2009 | 45,000 | **PF63** 45.00 | **PF65** 50.00 | | | |

**KM# 1146 25 DOLLARS**
62.41 g., 0.9999 Silver 2.0063 oz. ASW selectively gilt, 60 mm. **Ruler:** Elizabeth II **Obv:** Bust right **Rev:** Toronto map and skyline, partilly gilt **Edge:** Reeded

| Date | Mintage | VF20 | XF40 | MS60 | MS63 | MS65 |
|---|---|---|---|---|---|---|
| 2011 | Est. 7500 | **PF63** 170 | **PF65** 180 | | | |

**KM# 1173 25 DOLLARS**
31.39 g., 0.9999 Silver 1.0091 oz. ASW, 38 mm. **Ruler:** Elizabeth II **Obv:** Bust right **Rev:** Wayne Greskey skating right, father's portrait in circle at right, 99 in hologram at lower right

| Date | Mintage | VF20 | XF40 | MS60 | MS63 | MS65 |
|---|---|---|---|---|---|---|
| 2011 | — | **PF63** 75.00 | **PF65** 85.00 | | | |

**KM# 1330 25 DOLLARS**
31.11 g., 0.999 Silver 0.999 oz. ASW, 38 mm. **Ruler:** Elizabeth II **Rev:** Grandmother Moon Mask

| Date | Mintage | VF20 | XF40 | MS60 | MS63 | MS65 |
|---|---|---|---|---|---|---|
| 2012 | — | **PF63** 70.00 | **PF65** 75.00 | | | |

**KM# 1398 25 DOLLARS**
31.39 g., 0.9999 Silver 1.0091 oz. ASW, 38 mm. **Ruler:** Elizabeth II **Rev:** Beaver with two kits

| Date | Mintage | VF20 | XF40 | MS60 | MS63 | MS65 |
|---|---|---|---|---|---|---|
| 2013 | Est. 8500 | **PF63** 80.00 | **PF65** 90.00 | | | |

### KM# 1403 25 DOLLARS

31.39 g., 0.999 Silver 1.0082 oz. ASW, 38 mm. **Ruler:** Elizabeth II **Rev:** Polar Bear and two cubs

| Date | Mintage | VF20 | XF40 | MS60 | MS63 | MS65 |
|---|---|---|---|---|---|---|
| 2013 | Est. 8500 | PF63 80.00 | PF65 90.00 | | | |

### KM# 1405 25 DOLLARS

7.77 g., 0.999 Gold 0.2496 oz. AGW, 20 mm. **Ruler:** Elizabeth II **Rev:** Arctic Fox with Northern lights in the background

| Date | Mintage | VF20 | XF40 | MS60 | MS63 | MS65 |
|---|---|---|---|---|---|---|
| 2013 | Est. 1500 | PF65 650 | | | | |

### KM# 1456 25 DOLLARS

31.39 g., 0.999 Silver 1.0082 oz. ASW, 38 mm. **Ruler:** Elizabeth II **Rev:** Caribou mother and calf

| Date | Mintage | VF20 | XF40 | MS60 | MS63 | MS65 |
|---|---|---|---|---|---|---|
| 2013 | Est. 8500 | PF63 80.00 | PF65 90.00 | | | |

### KM# 1457 25 DOLLARS

31.39 g., 0.999 Silver 1.0082 oz. ASW, 38 mm. **Ruler:** Elizabeth II **Rev:** Wolf mother and two pups

| Date | Mintage | VF20 | XF40 | MS60 | MS63 | MS65 |
|---|---|---|---|---|---|---|
| 2013 | Est. 8500 | PF63 80.00 | PF65 90.00 | | | |

### KM# 1458 25 DOLLARS

7.77 g., 0.999 Gold 0.2496 oz. AGW, 20 mm. **Ruler:** Elizabeth II **Rev:** Pronghorn Antelope with northern lights in background

| Date | Mintage | VF20 | XF40 | MS60 | MS63 | MS65 |
|---|---|---|---|---|---|---|
| 2013 | Est. 1500 | PF65 650 | | | | |

### KM# 1482 25 DOLLARS

31.11 g., 0.999 Silver 0.999 oz. ASW, 38 mm. **Ruler:** Elizabeth II **Subject:** Banknote Allegory **Rev:** Female seated

| Date | Mintage | VF20 | XF40 | MS60 | MS63 | MS65 |
|---|---|---|---|---|---|---|
| 2013 Proof | 8,500 | — | — | — | 90.00 | — |

### KM# 1483 25 DOLLARS

7.80 g., 0.9999 Gold 0.2508 oz. AGW, 20 mm. **Ruler:** Elizabeth II **Subject:** Banknote Allegory **Rev:** Seated female

| Date | Mintage | VF20 | XF40 | MS60 | MS63 | MS65 |
|---|---|---|---|---|---|---|
| 2013 | 2,000 | PF65 650 | | | | |

### KM# 1508 25 DOLLARS

30.76 g., 0.9999 Silver 0.9889 oz. ASW, 36.15 mm. **Ruler:** Elizabeth II **Subject:** Grandmother Moon Mask **Rev:** Mask carving

| Date | Mintage | VF20 | XF40 | MS60 | MS63 | MS65 |
|---|---|---|---|---|---|---|
| 2013 | 6,000 | PF63 140 | PF65 150 | | | |

### KM# 1541 25 DOLLARS

31.39 g., 0.999 Silver 1.0082 oz. ASW, 38 mm. **Ruler:** Elizabeth II **Subject:** Oh Canada **Rev:** Orca surfacing

| Date | Mintage | VF20 | XF40 | MS60 | MS63 | MS65 |
|---|---|---|---|---|---|---|
| 2013 | 8,500 | PF63 80.00 | PF65 90.00 | | | |

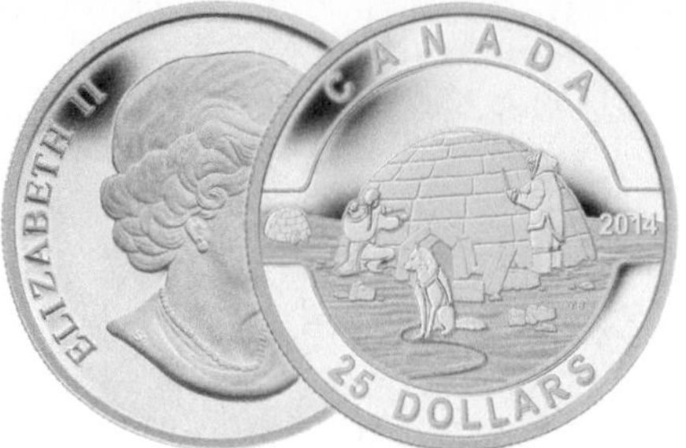


### KM# 1581 25 DOLLARS

31.39 g., 0.999 Silver 1.0082 oz. ASW, 38 mm. **Ruler:** Elizabeth II **Obv:** Bust right **Rev:** Igloo

| Date | Mintage | VF20 | XF40 | MS60 | MS63 | MS65 |
|---|---|---|---|---|---|---|
| 2014 | — | PF63 65.00 | PF65 75.00 | | | |

### KM# 1608 25 DOLLARS

7.97 g., 0.999 Gold 0.256 oz. AGW, 20 mm. **Ruler:** Elizabeth II **Obv:** Bust right **Rev:** Wolverine with northern lights in background

| Date | Mintage | VF20 | XF40 | MS60 | MS63 | MS65 |
|---|---|---|---|---|---|---|
| 2014 | 1,500 | PF65 650 | | | | |

### KM# 1626 25 DOLLARS

31.39 g., 0.999 Silver 1.0082 oz. ASW, 38 mm. **Ruler:** Elizabeth II **Obv:** Bust right **Rev:** Downhill sking

| Date | Mintage | VF20 | XF40 | MS60 | MS63 | MS65 |
|---|---|---|---|---|---|---|
| 2014 | — | PF63 80.00 | PF65 90.00 | | | |

### KM# 1689 25 DOLLARS

30.76 g., 0.9999 Silver 0.9889 oz. ASW, 36 mm. **Ruler:** Elizabeth II **Subject:** Royal visit, 75th Anniversary **Obv:** Bust right **Rev:** George VI and Queen Mary in high relief left

| Date | Mintage | F12 | VF20 | XF40 | MS60 | MS63 |
|---|---|---|---|---|---|---|
| 2014 | 6,000 | PF63 140 | PF65 150 | | | |

### KM# 1692 25 DOLLARS

31.39 g., 0.9999 Silver 1.0091 oz. ASW, 38 mm. **Ruler:** Elizabeth II **Obv:** Bust right **Rev:** Cowboy in the Rockies

| Date | Mintage | F12 | VF20 | XF40 | MS60 | MS63 |
|---|---|---|---|---|---|---|
| 2014 | — | PF65 90.00 | | | | |

### KM# 1693 25 DOLLARS

31.39 g., 0.9999 Silver 1.0091 oz. ASW, 38 mm. **Ruler:** Elizabeth II **Obv:** Bust right **Rev:** Arctic fox and northern lights

| Date | Mintage | F12 | VF20 | XF40 | MS60 | MS63 |
|---|---|---|---|---|---|---|
| 2014 | — | PF65 90.00 | | | | |

### KM# 1758 25 DOLLARS

30.76 g., 0.999 Silver 0.988 oz. ASW, 36.15 mm. **Ruler:** Elizabeth II **Obv:** Bust right **Rev:** Canadian lynx head

| Date | Mintage | VF20 | XF40 | MS60 | MS63 | MS65 |
|---|---|---|---|---|---|---|
| 2014 | 6,000 | PF65 80.00 | | | | |

### KM# 590 30 DOLLARS

31.50 g., 0.925 Silver 0.9368 oz. ASW, 38 mm. **Ruler:** Elizabeth II **Subject:** Pacific Northwest Wood Carvings **Obv:** Head right **Rev:** Welcome figure totem pole

| Date | Mintage | VF20 | XF40 | MS60 | MS63 | MS65 |
|---|---|---|---|---|---|---|
| 2006 | 9,904 | PF63 65.00 | PF65 75.00 | | | |

### KM# 668 30 DOLLARS

31.50 g., 0.925 Silver 0.9368 oz. ASW **Ruler:** Elizabeth II **Subject:** Canadarm and Col. C. Hadfield **Obv:** Head right **Rev:** Hologram of Canadarm

| Date | Mintage | VF20 | XF40 | MS60 | MS63 | MS65 |
|---|---|---|---|---|---|---|
| 2006 | 9,357 | PF63 85.00 | PF65 90.00 | | | |

**KM# 669 30 DOLLARS**
31.50 g., 0.925 Silver 0.9368 oz. ASW, 38 mm. **Ruler:** Elizabeth II **Subject:** National War Memorial **Obv:** Head right **Rev:** Statue of three soldiers

| Date | Mintage | VF20 | XF40 | MS60 | MS63 | MS65 |
|---|---|---|---|---|---|---|
| 2006 | 8,876 | PF63 80.00 | PF65 85.00 | | | |

**KM# 670 30 DOLLARS**
31.50 g., 0.925 Silver 0.9368 oz. ASW, 38 mm. **Ruler:** Elizabeth II **Subject:** Beaumont Hamel, Newfoundland **Obv:** Head right **Rev:** Caribou statue on rock outcrop

| Date | Mintage | VF20 | XF40 | MS60 | MS63 | MS65 |
|---|---|---|---|---|---|---|
| 2006 | 15,325 | PF63 90.00 | PF65 95.00 | | | |

**KM# 671 30 DOLLARS**
31.50 g., 0.925 Silver 0.9368 oz. ASW, 38 mm. **Ruler:** Elizabeth II **Obv:** Head right **Rev:** Dog Sled Team in color

| Date | Mintage | VF20 | XF40 | MS60 | MS63 | MS65 |
|---|---|---|---|---|---|---|
| 2006 | 7,384 | PF63 80.00 | PF65 85.00 | | | |

**KM# 739 30 DOLLARS**
31.50 g., 0.925 Silver 0.9368 oz. ASW, 40 mm. **Ruler:** Elizabeth II **Rev:** Niagra Falls panoramic hologram

| Date | Mintage | VF20 | XF40 | MS60 | MS63 | MS65 |
|---|---|---|---|---|---|---|
| 2007 | 7,384 | PF63 75.00 | PF65 85.00 | | | |

**KM# 741 30 DOLLARS**
31.50 g., 0.925 Silver 0.9368 oz. ASW, 40 mm. **Ruler:** Elizabeth II **Rev:** War Memorial, Vimy Ridge

| Date | Mintage | VF20 | XF40 | MS60 | MS63 | MS65 |
|---|---|---|---|---|---|---|
| 2007 | 5,335 | PF65 85.00 | | | | |

**KM# 819 30 DOLLARS**
31.50 g., 0.925 Silver 0.9368 oz. ASW, 40 mm. **Ruler:** Elizabeth II **Subject:** IMAX **Rev:** Youth reaching out to shark on large screen

| Date | Mintage | VF20 | XF40 | MS60 | MS63 | MS65 |
|---|---|---|---|---|---|---|
| 2008 | 3,861 | PF63 65.00 | PF65 75.00 | | | |

**KM# 895 30 DOLLARS**
33.75 g., 0.925 Silver 1.0037 oz. ASW, 40 mm. **Ruler:** Elizabeth II **Subject:** International year of astronomy **Obv:** Bust right **Obv. Legend:** Elizabeth II 30 Dollars DG Regina **Rev:** Observatory with planets and colored sky **Rev. Legend:** Canada

| Date | Mintage | VF20 | XF40 | MS60 | MS63 | MS65 |
|---|---|---|---|---|---|---|
| 2009 | 7,174 | PF63 80.00 | PF65 90.00 | | | |

**KM# 1623 30 DOLLARS**
62.70 g., 0.999 Silver 2.0138 oz. ASW, 54 mm. **Ruler:** Elizabeth II **Subject:** Canada thru the eyes of Tim Barnard **Obv:** Bust right **Rev:** Multitude of designs

| Date | Mintage | VF20 | XF40 | MS60 | MS63 | MS65 |
|---|---|---|---|---|---|---|
| 2014 | 5,000 | PF65 250 | | | | |

**KM# 1723 30 DOLLARS**
62.67 g., 0.999 Silver 2.0129 oz. ASW, 54 mm. **Ruler:** Elizabeth II **Subject:** Grand Trunk Railway **Obv:** Bust right **Rev:** Steam Train on Bridge

| Date | Mintage | VF20 | XF40 | MS60 | MS63 | MS65 |
|---|---|---|---|---|---|---|
| 2014 | 5,000 | PF65 200 | | | | |

**KM# 1727 30 DOLLARS**
62.67 g., 0.999 Silver 2.0129 oz. ASW, 54 mm. **Ruler:** Elizabeth II **Obv:** Bust right **Rev:** Machine gun training

| Date | Mintage | VF20 | XF40 | MS60 | MS63 | MS65 |
|---|---|---|---|---|---|---|
| 2014 | 5,000 | PF65 175 | | | | |

**KM# 1765 30 DOLLARS**
62.67 g., 0.9999 Silver 2.0147 oz. ASW, 54 mm. **Ruler:** Elizabeth II **Obv:** Bust right **Rev:** Four Aboriginies, Elk, Bear, Bison, Eagle and Wolf

| Date | Mintage | VF20 | XF40 | MS60 | MS63 | MS65 |
|---|---|---|---|---|---|---|
| 2014 | 5,000 | PF65 250 | | | | |

**KM# 566 50 DOLLARS**
12.00 g., 0.5833 Gold 0.225 oz. AGW, 27 mm. **Ruler:** Elizabeth II **Subject:** End of World War II, 60th Anniversary **Obv:** Head right **Rev:** Large V and three portraits

| Date | Mintage | VF20 | XF40 | MS60 | MS63 | MS65 |
|---|---|---|---|---|---|---|
| 2005 Specimen | 4,000 | PF65 375 | | | | |

**KM# 672 50 DOLLARS**
31.16 g., 0.9995 Palladium 1.0013 oz. APW **Ruler:** Elizabeth II **Subject:** Constellation in Spring sky position **Rev:** Large Bear at top

| Date | Mintage | VF20 | XF40 | MS60 | MS63 | MS65 |
|---|---|---|---|---|---|---|
| 2006 | 297 | PF65 1,250 | | | | |

**KM# 673 50 DOLLARS**
31.16 g., 0.9995 Palladium 1.0013 oz. APW **Ruler:** Elizabeth II **Subject:** Constellation in Summer sky position **Rev:** Large Bear at left

| Date | Mintage | VF20 | XF40 | MS60 | MS63 | MS65 |
|---|---|---|---|---|---|---|
| 2006 | 296 | PF65 1,250 | | | | |

**KM# 674 50 DOLLARS**
31.16 g., 0.9995 Palladium 1.0013 oz. APW **Ruler:** Elizabeth II **Subject:** Constellation in Autumn sky position **Rev:** Large Bear towards bottom

| Date | Mintage | VF20 | XF40 | MS60 | MS63 | MS65 |
|---|---|---|---|---|---|---|
| 2006 | 296 | PF65 1,250 | | | | |

**KM# 675 50 DOLLARS**
31.16 g., 0.9995 Palladium 1.0013 oz. APW **Ruler:** Elizabeth II **Subject:** Constellation in Winter sky position **Rev:** Large Bear towards right

| Date | Mintage | VF20 | XF40 | MS60 | MS63 | MS65 |
|---|---|---|---|---|---|---|
| 2006 | 293 | PF65 1,250 | | | | |

**KM# 709 50 DOLLARS**
155.50 g., 0.9999 Silver 4.9989 oz. ASW **Ruler:** Elizabeth II **Subject:** Queen's 60th Wedding Anniversary **Rev:** Coat of Arms and Mascots of Elizabeth and Philip

| Date | Mintage | VF20 | XF40 | MS60 | MS63 | MS65 |
|---|---|---|---|---|---|---|
| 2007 | 1,957 | PF65 350 | | | | |

**KM# 783 50 DOLLARS**
156.77 g., 0.999 Silver 5.0352 oz. ASW, 65 mm. **Ruler:** Elizabeth II **Subject:** Ottawa Mint Centennial 1908-2008 **Rev:** Mint building facade **Note:** Photo reduced.

| Date | Mintage | VF20 | XF40 | MS60 | MS63 | MS65 |
|---|---|---|---|---|---|---|
| 2008 | 2,078 | PF65 400 | | | | |

**KM# 896 50 DOLLARS**
156.77 g., 0.999 Silver 5.0352 oz. ASW, 65.25 mm. **Ruler:** Elizabeth II **Subject:** 150 Anniversary of the start of construction of the parliament buildings **Obv:** Bust right **Obv. Legend:** Elizabeth II Canada DG Regina **Rev:** Incomplete west block, original architecture **Rev. Legend:** 50 Dollars 1859-2009

| Date | Mintage | VF20 | XF40 | MS60 | MS63 | MS65 |
|---|---|---|---|---|---|---|
| 2009 | 910 | PF65 450 | | | | |

**KM# 1008 50 DOLLARS**
157.60 g., 0.999 Silver 5.0619 oz. ASW, 65.25 mm. **Ruler:** Elizabeth II **Subject:** 75th Anniverary of Canadian Bank Notes **Rev:** Female seated speaking into microphone **Note:** Photo reduced.

| Date | Mintage | VF20 | XF40 | MS60 | MS63 | MS65 |
|---|---|---|---|---|---|---|
| 2010 | 2,000 | PF65 400 | | | | |

**KM# 1243 50 DOLLARS**
157.60 g., 0.999 Silver 5.0619 oz. ASW, 65 mm. **Ruler:** Elizabeth II **Subject:** Calgary Stampede

| Date | Mintage | VF20 | XF40 | MS60 | MS63 | MS65 |
|---|---|---|---|---|---|---|
| 2012 | 1,500 | PF65 400 | | | | |

**KM# 1284 50 DOLLARS**
31.11 g., 0.999 Gold 0.999 oz. AGW, 30 mm. **Ruler:** Elizabeth II **Subject:** Year of the Dragon

| Date | Mintage | VF20 | XF40 | MS60 | MS63 | MS65 |
|---|---|---|---|---|---|---|
| 2012 | — | PF65 1,750 | | | | |

**KM# 1296 50 DOLLARS**
33.17 g., 1.000 Gold 1.0664 oz. AGW, 30 mm. **Ruler:** Elizabeth II **Subject:** Diamond Jubilee **Obv:** Bust right **Rev:** High relief bust left **Note:** Ultra high relief

| Date | Mintage | VF20 | XF40 | MS60 | MS63 | MS65 |
|---|---|---|---|---|---|---|
| 2012 | 500 | — | — | — | — | — |

**KM# 1399 50 DOLLARS**
155.55 g., 0.999 Silver 4.996 oz. ASW, 65 mm. **Ruler:** Elizabeth II **Rev:** Beaver gnawing standing tree, two others with felled tree

| Date | Mintage | VF20 | XF40 | MS60 | MS63 | MS65 |
|---|---|---|---|---|---|---|
| 2013 | — | PF65 450 | | | | |

**KM# 1417 50 DOLLARS**
155.55 g., 0.9999 Silver 5.0005 oz. ASW, 65.25 mm. **Ruler:** Elizabeth II **Obv:** Four Seasons: Spring/Fall Scene **Rev:** Winter/Summer/Large Tree

| Date | Mintage | VF20 | XF40 | MS60 | MS63 | MS65 |
|---|---|---|---|---|---|---|
| 2013 | — | PF65 250 | | | | |

**KM# 1429 50 DOLLARS**
157.60 g., 0.999 Silver 5.0619 oz. ASW, 65 mm. **Ruler:** Elizabeth II **Subject:** War of 1812 - Naval Battle **Rev:** HMS Shannon and Chesapeak

| Date | Mintage | VF20 | XF40 | MS60 | MS63 | MS65 |
|---|---|---|---|---|---|---|
| 2013 | Est. 1500 | PF65 500 | | | | |

**KM# 1433 50 DOLLARS**
157.60 g., 0.999 Silver 5.0619 oz. ASW, 62.25 mm. **Ruler:** Elizabeth II **Subject:** Coronation Anniversary **Rev:** Elizabeth II in Coronation robes - Loman image in the Victoria & Albert Museum

| Date | Mintage | VF20 | XF40 | MS60 | MS63 | MS65 |
|---|---|---|---|---|---|---|
| 2013 | Est. 1500 | PF65 525 | | | | |

**KM# 1557 50 DOLLARS**
157.60 g., 0.999 Silver 5.0619 oz. ASW, 65 mm. **Ruler:** Elizabeth II **Obv:** Bust right **Rev:** Beaver swimming with birch branch in mouth

| Date | Mintage | VF20 | XF40 | MS60 | MS63 | MS65 |
|---|---|---|---|---|---|---|
| 2014 | 1,500 | PF65 520 | | | | |

**KM# 1729 50 DOLLARS**
31.10 g., 0.999 Gold 0.9989 oz. AGW, 30 mm. **Ruler:** Elizabeth II **Obv:** Bust right **Rev:** Five Blessings with red highlights

| Date | Mintage | VF20 | XF40 | MS60 | MS63 | MS65 |
|---|---|---|---|---|---|---|
| 2014 | 350 | PF65 2,700 | | | | |

**KM# 1764 50 DOLLARS**
155.60 g., 0.999 Silver 4.9976 oz. ASW **Ruler:** Elizabeth II **Obv:** Bust right **Rev:** 3 Maple leaves

| Date | Mintage | VF20 | XF40 | MS60 | MS63 | MS65 |
|---|---|---|---|---|---|---|
| 2014 | 2,500 | PF65 520 | | | | |

**KM# 1792 50 DOLLARS**
31.39 g., 0.999 Gold 1.0082 oz. AGW, 30 mm. **Ruler:** Elizabeth II **Obv:** Bust right by Mary Gilick **Rev:** Two maple leaves

| Date | Mintage | F12 | VF20 | XF40 | MS60 | MS63 |
|---|---|---|---|---|---|---|
| 2014 | 650 | PF65 1,400 | | | | |

**KM# 1843 50 DOLLARS**
7.80 g., 0.9999 Gold 0.2508 oz. AGW **Ruler:** Elizabeth II **Obv:** Bust right **Rev:** UNESCO. Mt. Fuji and Rocky Mountains

| Date | Mintage | VF20 | XF40 | MS60 | MS63 | MS65 |
|---|---|---|---|---|---|---|
| 2015 | — | PF65 600 | | | | |

**KM# 567 75 DOLLARS**
31.44 g., 0.4166 Gold 0.4211 oz. AGW, 36.07 mm. **Ruler:** Elizabeth II **Subject:** Pope John Paul II **Obv:** Head right **Rev:** Pope giving blessing

| Date | Mintage | VF20 | XF40 | MS60 | MS63 | MS65 |
|---|---|---|---|---|---|---|
| 2005 | 1,870 | PF65 825 | | | | |

**KM# 747 75 DOLLARS**
12.00 g., 0.583 Gold 0.2249 oz. AGW, 27 mm. **Ruler:** Elizabeth II **Subject:** Vancouver Olympics - Athletics Pride **Rev:** Athletics celebrating, holding flag aloft

| Date | Mintage | VF20 | XF40 | MS60 | MS63 | MS65 |
|---|---|---|---|---|---|---|
| 2007 | 4,524 | PF65 440 | | | | |

**KM# 748 75 DOLLARS**
12.00 g., 0.583 Gold 0.2249 oz. AGW, 27 mm. **Ruler:** Elizabeth II **Obv:** Bust right **Rev:** Canada geese in flight left, multicolor

| Date | Mintage | VF20 | XF40 | MS60 | MS63 | MS65 |
|---|---|---|---|---|---|---|
| 2007 | 4,418 | PF65 440 | | | | |

**KM# 749 75 DOLLARS**
12.00 g., 0.583 Gold 0.2249 oz. AGW, 27 mm. **Ruler:** Elizabeth II **Rev:** Mountie, multicolor

| Date | Mintage | VF20 | XF40 | MS60 | MS63 | MS65 |
|---|---|---|---|---|---|---|
| 2007 | 6,687 | PF65 440 | | | | |

**KM# 820 75 DOLLARS**
12.00 g., 0.583 Gold 0.2249 oz. AGW partially silver plated, 27 mm. **Ruler:** Elizabeth II **Rev:** 2010 Olympic Inukshuk Stone man, partially silver plated

| Date | Mintage | VF20 | XF40 | MS60 | MS63 | MS65 |
|---|---|---|---|---|---|---|
| 2008 | — | PF65 420 | | | | |

**KM# 821 75 DOLLARS**
12.00 g., 0.583 Gold 0.2249 oz. AGW, 27 mm. **Ruler:** Elizabeth II **Rev:** Four Host Nations mask emblems, colored

| Date | Mintage | VF20 | XF40 | MS60 | MS63 | MS65 |
|---|---|---|---|---|---|---|
| 2008 | 8,000 | PF65 440 | | | | |

**KM# 947 75 DOLLARS**
12.00 g., 0.583 Gold 0.2249 oz. AGW, 27 mm. **Ruler:** Elizabeth II **Subject:** Vancouver Olympics **Rev:** Tent building at Olympic site, color

| Date | Mintage | VF20 | XF40 | MS60 | MS63 | MS65 |
|---|---|---|---|---|---|---|
| 2008 | 8,000 | PF63 430 | PF65 440 | | | |

### KM# 908 75 DOLLARS

12.00 g., 0.583 Gold 0.2249 oz. AGW, 27 mm. **Ruler:** Elizabeth II **Subject:** 2010 Vancouver Olympics **Obv:** Bust right **Rev:** Multicolor moose

| Date | Mintage | VF20 | XF40 | MS60 | MS63 | MS65 |
|---|---|---|---|---|---|---|
| 2009 | 4,075 | PF65 440 | | | | |

### KM# 909 75 DOLLARS

12.00 g., 0.583 Gold 0.2249 oz. AGW, 27 mm. **Ruler:** Elizabeth II **Subject:** 2010 Vancouver Olympics **Obv:** Bust right **Rev:** Multicolor athletics and torch

| Date | Mintage | VF20 | XF40 | MS60 | MS63 | MS65 |
|---|---|---|---|---|---|---|
| 2009 | 4,479 | PF65 440 | | | | |

### KM# 910 75 DOLLARS

12.00 g., 0.583 Gold 0.2249 oz. AGW, 27 mm. **Ruler:** Elizabeth II **Subject:** 2010 Vancouver Olympics **Obv:** Bust right **Rev:** Wolf, multicolor

| Date | Mintage | VF20 | XF40 | MS60 | MS63 | MS65 |
|---|---|---|---|---|---|---|
| 2009 | 4,161 | PF65 440 | | | | |

### KM# 1002 75 DOLLARS

12.00 g., 0.583 Gold 0.2249 oz. AGW, 27 mm. **Ruler:** Elizabeth II **Rev:** Spring color maple leaves

| Date | Mintage | VF20 | XF40 | MS60 | MS63 | MS65 |
|---|---|---|---|---|---|---|
| 2010 | 1,000 | PF65 500 | | | | |

### KM# 1003 75 DOLLARS

12.00 g., 0.583 Gold 0.2249 oz. AGW, 27 mm. **Ruler:** Elizabeth II **Rev:** Summer color maple leaves

| Date | Mintage | VF20 | XF40 | MS60 | MS63 | MS65 |
|---|---|---|---|---|---|---|
| 2010 | 1,000 | PF65 500 | | | | |

### KM# 1004 75 DOLLARS

12.00 g., 0.583 Gold 0.2249 oz. AGW, 27 mm. **Ruler:** Elizabeth II **Rev:** Fall color maple leaves

| Date | Mintage | VF20 | XF40 | MS60 | MS63 | MS65 |
|---|---|---|---|---|---|---|
| 2010 | 1,000 | PF65 500 | | | | |

### KM# 1005 75 DOLLARS

12.00 g., 0.583 Gold 0.2249 oz. AGW, 27 mm. **Ruler:** Elizabeth II **Rev:** Winter color maple leaves

| Date | Mintage | VF20 | XF40 | MS60 | MS63 | MS65 |
|---|---|---|---|---|---|---|
| 2010 | 1,000 | PF65 500 | | | | |

### KM# 1378 75 DOLLARS

7.77 g., 0.999 Gold 0.2496 oz. AGW, 20 mm. **Ruler:** Elizabeth II **Subject:** Baseball **Rev:** Baseball Diamond and Crossed Bats

| Date | Mintage | VF20 | XF40 | MS60 | MS63 | MS65 |
|---|---|---|---|---|---|---|
| 2013 | — | PF65 900 | | | | |

### KM# 1379 75 DOLLARS

7.77 g., 0.999 Gold 0.2496 oz. AGW, 20 mm. **Ruler:** Elizabeth II **Subject:** Baseball **Rev:** Baseball

| Date | Mintage | VF20 | XF40 | MS60 | MS63 | MS65 |
|---|---|---|---|---|---|---|
| 2013 | Est. 3500 | PF65 900 | | | | |

### KM# 1450 75 DOLLARS

12.00 g., 0.583 Gold 0.2249 oz. AGW, 27 mm. **Ruler:** Elizabeth II **Subject:** 75th Anniversary of Superman **Rev:** Superman in color, jumping on rooftop, logo name above

| Date | Mintage | VF20 | XF40 | MS60 | MS63 | MS65 |
|---|---|---|---|---|---|---|
| 2013 | Est. 2000 | PF65 750 | | | | |

### KM# 416 100 DOLLARS

13.34 g., 0.583 Gold 0.250 oz. AGW alloyed with 5.5579 g of .999 Silver, .1787 oz ASW, 27 mm. **Ruler:** Elizabeth II **Subject:** Library of Parliament **Obv:** Crowned head right **Rev:** Statue in domed building **Edge:** Reeded

| Date | Mintage | VF20 | XF40 | MS60 | MS63 | MS65 |
|---|---|---|---|---|---|---|
| 2001 | — | PF65 475 | | | | |

### KM# 452 100 DOLLARS

13.34 g., 0.583 Gold 0.250 oz. AGW, 27 mm. **Ruler:** Elizabeth II **Subject:** Discovery of Oil in Alberta **Obv:** Crowned head right **Rev:** Oil well with black oil spill on ground **Edge:** Reeded

| Date | Mintage | VF20 | XF40 | MS60 | MS63 | MS65 |
|---|---|---|---|---|---|---|
| 2002 | 9,994 | PF65 475 | | | | |

### KM# 486 100 DOLLARS

13.34 g., 0.583 Gold 0.250 oz. AGW **Ruler:** Elizabeth II **Subject:** 100th Anniversary of the Discovery of Marquis Wheat **Obv:** Head right

| Date | Mintage | VF20 | XF40 | MS60 | MS63 | MS65 |
|---|---|---|---|---|---|---|
| 2003 | 9,993 | PF65 475 | | | | |

### KM# 528 100 DOLLARS

12.00 g., 0.583 Gold 0.2249 oz. AGW **Ruler:** Elizabeth II **Subject:** St. Lawrence Seaway, 50th Anniversary **Obv:** Head right

| Date | Mintage | VF20 | XF40 | MS60 | MS63 | MS65 |
|---|---|---|---|---|---|---|
| 2004 | 7,454 | PF65 425 | | | | |

### KM# 593 100 DOLLARS

12.00 g., 0.5833 Gold 0.225 oz. AGW **Ruler:** Elizabeth II **Subject:** 130th Anniversary, Supreme Court **Obv:** Head right

| Date | Mintage | VF20 | XF40 | MS60 | MS63 | MS65 |
|---|---|---|---|---|---|---|
| 2005 | 5,092 | PF65 425 | | | | |

### KM# 591 100 DOLLARS

12.00 g., 0.5833 Gold 0.225 oz. AGW **Ruler:** Elizabeth II **Subject:** 75th Anniversary, Hockey Classic between Royal Military College and U.S. Military Academy **Obv:** Head right

| Date | Mintage | VF20 | XF40 | MS60 | MS63 | MS65 |
|---|---|---|---|---|---|---|
| 2006 | 5,439 | PF65 425 | | | | |

### KM# 689 100 DOLLARS

12.00 g., 0.5833 Gold 0.225 oz. AGW, 27 mm. **Ruler:** Elizabeth II **Subject:** 140th Anniversary Dominion **Obv:** Head right

| Date | Mintage | VF20 | XF40 | MS60 | MS63 | MS65 |
|---|---|---|---|---|---|---|
| 2007 | 4,453 | PF65 425 | | | | |

### KM# 823 100 DOLLARS

12.00 g., 0.583 Gold 0.2249 oz. AGW, 27 mm. **Ruler:** Elizabeth II **Rev:** Fraser River

| Date | Mintage | VF20 | XF40 | MS60 | MS63 | MS65 |
|---|---|---|---|---|---|---|
| 2008 | 3,089 | PF65 425 | | | | |

### KM# 898 100 DOLLARS

12.00 g., 0.583 Gold 0.2249 oz. AGW, 27 mm. **Ruler:** Elizabeth II **Subject:** 10th Anniversary of Nunavut **Obv:** Bust right **Obv. Legend:** Elizabeth II DG Regina **Rev:** Inuit dancer with 3 faces behind **Rev. Legend:** Canada 100 Dollars 1999-2009

| Date | Mintage | VF20 | XF40 | MS60 | MS63 | MS65 |
|---|---|---|---|---|---|---|
| 2009 | 2,309 | PF65 425 | | | | |

### KM# 997 100 DOLLARS

12.00 g., 0.583 Gold 0.2249 oz. AGW, 27 mm. **Ruler:** Elizabeth II **Rev:** Henry Hudson, Map of Hudson's Bay

| Date | Mintage | VF20 | XF40 | MS60 | MS63 | MS65 |
|---|---|---|---|---|---|---|
| 2010 | Est. 5000 | PF65 425 | | | | |

### KM# 1073 100 DOLLARS

12.00 g., 0.583 Gold 0.2249 oz. AGW, 27 mm. **Ruler:** Elizabeth II **Subject:** Canadian Railroads, 175th Anniversary **Rev:** Early steam locomotive

| Date | Mintage | VF20 | XF40 | MS60 | MS63 | MS65 |
|---|---|---|---|---|---|---|
| 2011 | 3,000 | PF65 425 | | | | |

### KM# 1389 100 DOLLARS

12.00 g., 0.5833 Gold 0.225 oz. AGW, 27 mm. **Ruler:** Elizabeth II **Subject:** Arctic Exploration - 100th Anniversary **Rev:** Map of the North Pole, Explorers

| Date | Mintage | VF20 | XF40 | MS60 | MS63 | MS65 |
|---|---|---|---|---|---|---|
| 2013 | — | PF65 600 | | | | |

### KM# 1441 100 DOLLARS

31.60 g., 0.999 Silver 1.0149 oz. ASW, 40 mm. **Ruler:** Elizabeth II **Rev:** Three bison advancing left

| Date | Mintage | VF20 | XF40 | MS60 | MS63 | MS65 |
|---|---|---|---|---|---|---|
| 2013 Matte Proof | Est. 50000 | PF63 100 | | | | |

### KM# 1582 100 DOLLARS

13.34 g., 0.999 Gold 0.4284 oz. AGW, 27 mm. **Ruler:** Elizabeth II **Subject:** Charlottetown Quebec, 1864 **Obv:** Bust right **Rev:** Building views

| Date | Mintage | VF20 | XF40 | MS60 | MS63 | MS65 |
|---|---|---|---|---|---|---|
| 2014 | — | PF65 475 | | | | |

### KM# 1694 100 DOLLARS

12.00 g., 0.583 Gold 0.2249 oz. AGW, 27 mm. **Ruler:** Elizabeth II **Obv:** Bust right **Rev:** Quebec & Charlottetown

| Date | Mintage | F12 | VF20 | XF40 | MS60 | MS63 |
|---|---|---|---|---|---|---|
| 2014 | 2,500 | PF65 425 | | | | |

### KM# 1751 100 DOLLARS

12.00 g., 0.583 Gold 0.2249 oz. AGW, 27 mm. **Ruler:** Elizabeth II **Obv:** Bust right **Rev:** Superman chest, black/red logo

| Date | Mintage | VF20 | XF40 | MS60 | MS63 | MS65 |
|---|---|---|---|---|---|---|
| 2014 | 2,000 | PF65 750 | | | | |

### KM# 1761 100 DOLLARS

311.50 g., 0.999 Silver 10.0049 oz. ASW, 76.25 mm. **Ruler:** Elizabeth II **Obv:** Bust right **Rev:** Majestic Maple Leaves - Large maple leaf and maple tree branch

| Date | Mintage | VF20 | XF40 | MS60 | MS63 | MS65 |
|---|---|---|---|---|---|---|
| 2014 | 2,000 | PF65 900 | | | | |

### KM# 1845 100 DOLLARS

12.00 g., 0.583 Gold 0.2249 oz. AGW **Ruler:** Elizabeth II **Obv:** Bust right **Rev:** Sir John A. McDonald and Canadian Pacific locomotive

| Date | Mintage | VF20 | XF40 | MS60 | MS63 | MS65 |
|---|---|---|---|---|---|---|
| 2015 | — | PF65 350 | | | | |

### KM# 1696 125 DOLLARS

500.00 g., 0.9999 Silver 16.0738 oz. ASW, 85 mm. **Ruler:** Elizabeth II **Obv:** Bust right **Rev:** Wolf head howling

| Date | Mintage | F12 | VF20 | XF40 | MS60 | MS63 |
|---|---|---|---|---|---|---|
| 2014 | 1,000 | PF65 1,100 | | | | |

### KM# 1824 125 DOLLARS

500.00 g., 0.999 Silver 16.0593 oz. ASW, 85.35 mm. **Ruler:** Elizabeth II **Obv:** Bust right **Rev:** Three horses galloping forwards, maple leaves

| Date | Mintage | VF20 | XF40 | MS60 | MS63 | MS65 |
|---|---|---|---|---|---|---|
| 2015 | 1,000 | PF65 1,100 | | | | |

### KM# 417 150 DOLLARS

13.61 g., 0.750 Gold 0.3282 oz. AGW, 28 mm. **Ruler:** Elizabeth II **Subject:** Year of the Snake **Obv:** Crowned head right **Rev:** Multicolor snake hologram **Edge:** Reeded

| Date | Mintage | VF20 | XF40 | MS60 | MS63 | MS65 |
|---|---|---|---|---|---|---|
| 2001 | — | PF65 625 | | | | |

### KM# 604 150 DOLLARS

13.61 g., 0.750 Gold 0.3282 oz. AGW **Ruler:** Elizabeth II **Obv:** Head right **Rev:** Stylized horse left

| Date | Mintage | VF20 | XF40 | MS60 | MS63 | MS65 |
|---|---|---|---|---|---|---|
| 2002 | 6,843 | PF65 625 | | | | |

### KM# 487 150 DOLLARS

13.61 g., 0.750 Gold 0.3282 oz. AGW, 28 mm. **Ruler:** Elizabeth II **Subject:** Year of the Ram **Obv:** Crowned head right **Rev:** Stylized ram left, hologram

| Date | Mintage | VF20 | XF40 | MS60 | MS63 | MS65 |
|---|---|---|---|---|---|---|
| 2003 | 3,927 | PF65 625 | | | | |

### KM# 614 150 DOLLARS

13.61 g., 0.750 Gold 0.3282 oz. AGW **Ruler:** Elizabeth II **Obv:** Head right **Rev:** Year of the Monkey, hologram

| Date | Mintage | VF20 | XF40 | MS60 | MS63 | MS65 |
|---|---|---|---|---|---|---|
| 2004 | 3,392 | PF65 625 | | | | |

### KM# 568 150 DOLLARS

13.61 g., 0.750 Gold 0.3282 oz. AGW **Ruler:** Elizabeth II **Subject:** Year of the Rooster **Obv:** Head right **Rev:** Rooster left, hologram

| Date | Mintage | VF20 | XF40 | MS60 | MS63 | MS65 |
|---|---|---|---|---|---|---|
| 2005 | 3,731 | PF65 625 | | | | |

### KM# 592 150 DOLLARS

13.61 g., 0.750 Gold 0.3282 oz. AGW, 28 mm. **Ruler:** Elizabeth II **Subject:** Year of the Dog, hologram **Obv:** Head right **Rev:** Stylized dog left

| Date | Mintage | VF20 | XF40 | MS60 | MS63 | MS65 |
|---|---|---|---|---|---|---|
| 2006 | 2,604 | PF65 625 | | | | |

### KM# 733 150 DOLLARS

11.84 g., 0.750 Gold 0.2855 oz. AGW, 28 mm. **Ruler:** Elizabeth II **Subject:** Year of the Pig **Obv:** Head right **Rev:** Pig in center with Chinese lunar calendar around, hologram

| Date | Mintage | VF20 | XF40 | MS60 | MS63 | MS65 |
|---|---|---|---|---|---|---|
| 2007 | 826 | PF65 675 | | | | |

### KM# 802 150 DOLLARS

11.84 g., 0.750 Gold 0.2855 oz. AGW, 28 mm. **Ruler:** Elizabeth II **Subject:** Year of the Rat **Rev:** Rat, hologram

| Date | Mintage | VF20 | XF40 | MS60 | MS63 | MS65 |
|---|---|---|---|---|---|---|
| 2008 | 582 | PF65 675 | | | | |

### KM# 867 150 DOLLARS

11.84 g., 0.750 Gold 0.2855 oz. AGW, 28 mm. **Ruler:** Elizabeth II **Subject:** Year of the Ox **Rev:** Ox, hologram

| Date | Mintage | VF20 | XF40 | MS60 | MS63 | MS65 |
|---|---|---|---|---|---|---|
| 2009 | 486 | PF65 550 | | | | |

### KM# 899 150 DOLLARS

10.40 g., 0.999 Gold 0.334 oz. AGW, 22.5 mm. **Ruler:** Elizabeth II **Subject:** Blessings of wealth **Obv:** Bust right **Obv. Legend:** Elizabeth II, DG Regina, Fine Gold 99999 or PUR **Rev:** Three goldfish surround peony, clouds **Rev. Legend:** Canada 150 Dollars (Chinese symbols of good fortune) **Edge:** Scalloped

| Date | Mintage | VF20 | XF40 | MS60 | MS63 | MS65 |
|---|---|---|---|---|---|---|
| 2009 | 1,273 | PF65 650 | | | | |

### KM# 979 150 DOLLARS

11.84 g., 0.750 Gold 0.2855 oz. AGW, 28 mm. **Ruler:** Elizabeth II **Subject:** Year of the Tiger **Rev:** Tiger in hologram

| Date | Mintage | VF20 | XF40 | MS60 | MS63 | MS65 |
|---|---|---|---|---|---|---|
| 2010 | 1,507 | PF65 550 | | | | |

### KM# 1030 150 DOLLARS

10.40 g., 0.9999 Gold 0.3343 oz. AGW **Ruler:** Elizabeth II **Subject:** Blessing of Wealth **Shape:** Scalloped

| Date | Mintage | VF20 | XF40 | MS60 | MS63 | MS65 |
|---|---|---|---|---|---|---|
| 2010 | 1,388 | PF65 650 | | | | |

### KM# 1031 150 DOLLARS

13.61 g., 0.750 Gold 0.3282 oz. AGW, 28 mm. **Ruler:** Elizabeth II **Subject:** Year of the Tiger **Rev:** Tiger walking

| Date | Mintage | VF20 | XF40 | MS60 | MS63 | MS65 |
|---|---|---|---|---|---|---|
| 2010 | 2,500 | PF65 600 | | | | |

### KM# 1053 150 DOLLARS

13.61 g., 0.750 Gold 0.3282 oz. AGW, 28 mm. **Ruler:** Elizabeth II **Subject:** Year of the rabbit **Rev:** Rabbit hologram

| Date | Mintage | VF20 | XF40 | MS60 | MS63 | MS65 |
|---|---|---|---|---|---|---|
| 2011 | — | PF65 600 | | | | |

### KM# 1054 150 DOLLARS

13.61 g., 0.750 Gold 0.3282 oz. AGW, 28 mm. **Ruler:** Elizabeth II **Subject:** Year of the rabbit **Rev:** Rabit hopping left, character at left

| Date | Mintage | VF20 | XF40 | MS60 | MS63 | MS65 |
|---|---|---|---|---|---|---|
| 2011 | 2,500 | PF65 600 | | | | |

### KM# 1184 150 DOLLARS

13.61 g., 0.750 Gold 0.3282 oz. AGW, 28 mm. **Ruler:** Elizabeth II **Subject:** Year of the Dragon **Obv:** Bust right **Rev:** Dragon left

| Date | Mintage | VF20 | XF40 | MS60 | MS63 | MS65 |
|---|---|---|---|---|---|---|
| 2012 | — | PF65 650 | | | | |

### KM# 1262 150 DOLLARS

10.40 g., 0.999 Gold 0.334 oz. AGW, 22.5 mm. **Ruler:** Elizabeth II **Subject:** Good Fortune Panda **Shape:** Scalloped

| Date | Mintage | VF20 | XF40 | MS60 | MS63 | MS65 |
|---|---|---|---|---|---|---|
| 2012 | — | PF65 650 | | | | |

### KM# 1362 150 DOLLARS

11.84 g., 0.750 Gold 0.2855 oz. AGW, 28 mm. **Ruler:** Elizabeth II **Subject:** Year of the Snake **Rev:** Snake vertical between two Chinese characters

| Date | Mintage | VF20 | XF40 | MS60 | MS63 | MS65 |
|---|---|---|---|---|---|---|
| 2013 | 2,500 | PF65 700 | | | | |

### KM# 1418 150 DOLLARS

15.59 g., Gold, 25 mm. **Ruler:** Elizabeth II **Subject:** Baseball **Rev:** Base runner with hands raised

| Date | Mintage | VF20 | XF40 | MS60 | MS63 | MS65 |
|---|---|---|---|---|---|---|
| 2013 | Est. 3500 | PF65 1,550 | | | | |

### KM# 1437 150 DOLLARS

10.40 g., 0.999 Gold 0.334 oz. AGW, 22.5 mm. **Ruler:** Elizabeth II **Subject:** Blessings of Peace **Rev:** Clouds, phoenix and feathers **Shape:** Scalloped

| Date | Mintage | VF20 | XF40 | MS60 | MS63 | MS65 |
|---|---|---|---|---|---|---|
| 2013 | Est. 888 | PF65 700 | | | | |

### KM# 1515 150 DOLLARS

11.84 g., 0.750 Gold 0.2855 oz. AGW, 28 mm. **Ruler:** Elizabeth II **Subject:** Year of the Horse **Obv:** Bust right **Rev:** Horse prancing left

| Date | Mintage | VF20 | XF40 | MS60 | MS63 | MS65 |
|---|---|---|---|---|---|---|
| 2014 | 2,500 | PF65 700 | | | | |

### KM# 1772 150 DOLLARS

10.40 g., 0.999 Gold 0.334 oz. AGW, 22.5 mm. **Ruler:** Elizabeth II **Subject:** Blessings of Longevity **Obv:** Bust right **Rev:** Two Cranes left **Shape:** Scallop

| Date | Mintage | F12 | VF20 | XF40 | MS60 | MS63 |
|---|---|---|---|---|---|---|
| 2014 | 888 | PF65 1,000 | | | | |

### KM# 418 200 DOLLARS

17.14 g., 0.9166 Gold 0.505 oz. AGW, 29 mm. **Ruler:** Elizabeth II **Subject:** Cornelius D. Krieghoff's "The Habitant farm" **Obv:** Queens head right **Edge:** Reeded

| Date | Mintage | VF20 | XF40 | MS60 | MS63 | MS65 |
|---|---|---|---|---|---|---|
| 2001 | — | PF65 975 | | | | |

### KM# 466 200 DOLLARS

17.14 g., 0.9166 Gold 0.505 oz. AGW, 29 mm. **Ruler:** Elizabeth II **Subject:** Thomas Thompson "The Jack Pine" (1916-17) **Obv:** Crowned head right

| Date | Mintage | VF20 | XF40 | MS60 | MS63 | MS65 |
|---|---|---|---|---|---|---|
| 2002 | 5,264 | PF65 975 | | | | |

**KM# 488 200 DOLLARS**
17.14 g., 0.9166 Gold 0.505 oz. AGW **Ruler:** Elizabeth II **Subject:** Fitzgerald's "Houses" (1929) **Obv:** Crowned head right **Rev:** House with trees

| Date | Mintage | VF20 | XF40 | MS60 | MS63 | MS65 |
|---|---|---|---|---|---|---|
| 2003 | 4,118 | PF65 975 | | | | |

**KM# 516 200 DOLLARS**
16.00 g., 0.9166 Gold 0.4715 oz. AGW, 29 mm. **Ruler:** Elizabeth II **Subject:** Fragments **Obv:** Crowned head right **Rev:** Fragmented face **Edge:** Reeded

| Date | Mintage | VF20 | XF40 | MS60 | MS63 | MS65 |
|---|---|---|---|---|---|---|
| 2004 | 3,917 | PF65 900 | | | | |

**KM# 569 200 DOLLARS**
16.00 g., 0.9166 Gold 0.4715 oz. AGW **Ruler:** Elizabeth II **Subject:** Fur traders **Obv:** Head right **Rev:** Men in canoe riding wave

| Date | Mintage | VF20 | XF40 | MS60 | MS63 | MS65 |
|---|---|---|---|---|---|---|
| 2005 | 3,669 | PF65 900 | | | | |

**KM# 594 200 DOLLARS**
16.00 g., 0.9166 Gold 0.4715 oz. AGW **Ruler:** Elizabeth II **Subject:** Timber trade **Obv:** Head right **Rev:** Lumberjacks felling tree

| Date | Mintage | VF20 | XF40 | MS60 | MS63 | MS65 |
|---|---|---|---|---|---|---|
| 2006 | 3,218 | PF65 900 | | | | |

**KM# 691 200 DOLLARS**
16.00 g., 0.9166 Gold 0.4715 oz. AGW, 29 mm. **Ruler:** Elizabeth II **Subject:** Fishing Trade **Obv:** Head right **Rev:** Two fishermen hauling in net

| Date | Mintage | VF20 | XF40 | MS60 | MS63 | MS65 |
|---|---|---|---|---|---|---|
| 2007 | 2,137 | PF65 900 | | | | |

**KM# 824 200 DOLLARS**
16.00 g., 0.917 Gold 0.4717 oz. AGW, 29 mm. **Ruler:** Elizabeth II **Subject:** Commerce **Rev:** Horse drawn plow

| Date | Mintage | VF20 | XF40 | MS60 | MS63 | MS65 |
|---|---|---|---|---|---|---|
| 2008 | 1,951 | PF65 900 | | | | |

**KM# 894 200 DOLLARS**
16.00 g., 0.916 Gold 0.4712 oz. AGW, 29 mm. **Ruler:** Elizabeth II **Subject:** Coal mining trade **Obv:** Bust right **Obv. Legend:** Elizabeth II DG Regina **Rev:** Miner pushing cart with black coal **Rev. Legend:** Canada 200 Dollars

| Date | Mintage | VF20 | XF40 | MS60 | MS63 | MS65 |
|---|---|---|---|---|---|---|
| 2009 | 2,241 | PF65 900 | | | | |

**KM# 1000 200 DOLLARS**
16.00 g., 0.916 Gold 0.4712 oz. AGW, 29 mm. **Ruler:** Elizabeth II **Subject:** Petroleum and Oil Trade **Rev:** Oil tank car and well head

| Date | Mintage | VF20 | XF40 | MS60 | MS63 | MS65 |
|---|---|---|---|---|---|---|
| 2010 | Est. 4000 | PF65 900 | | | | |

**KM# 1060 200 DOLLARS**
16.00 g., 0.9167 Gold 0.4716 oz. AGW, 29 mm. **Ruler:** Elizabeth II **Rev:** Olympic athletics with medal, flag and flowers

| Date | Mintage | VF20 | XF40 | MS60 | MS63 | MS65 |
|---|---|---|---|---|---|---|
| 2010 | — | PF65 900 | | | | |

**KM# 1074 200 DOLLARS**
16.00 g., 0.9167 Gold 0.4716 oz. AGW, 29 mm. **Ruler:** Elizabeth II **Rev:** SS Beaver - Seam Sail ship

| Date | Mintage | VF20 | XF40 | MS60 | MS63 | MS65 |
|---|---|---|---|---|---|---|
| 2011 | 2,800 | PF65 900 | | | | |

**KM# 1143 200 DOLLARS**
16.00 g., 0.9167 Gold 0.4716 oz. AGW, 27 mm. **Ruler:** Elizabeth II **Subject:** Wedding, Prince William and Katherine Middleton **Obv:** Bust right **Rev:** Half-length figures facing, swarovski crystal **Edge:** Reeded

| Date | Mintage | VF20 | XF40 | MS60 | MS63 | MS65 |
|---|---|---|---|---|---|---|
| 2011 | 2,000 | PF65 900 | | | | |

**KM# 1174 200 DOLLARS**
16.00 g., 0.916 Gold 0.4712 oz. AGW, 29 mm. **Ruler:** Elizabeth II **Obv:** Bust right **Rev:** Wayne Greskey skating right, father's portrait in circle at right, 99 in color at lower right

| Date | Mintage | VF20 | XF40 | MS60 | MS63 | MS65 |
|---|---|---|---|---|---|---|
| 2011 | 999 | PF65 900 | | | | |

**KM# 1219 200 DOLLARS**
16.00 g., 0.9167 Gold 0.4716 oz. AGW, 29 mm. **Ruler:** Elizabeth II **Obv:** Bust right **Rev:** Prospector panning for gold in stream

| Date | Mintage | VF20 | XF40 | MS60 | MS63 | MS65 |
|---|---|---|---|---|---|---|
| 2012 | — | PF65 900 | | | | |

**KM# 1223 200 DOLLARS**
16.00 g., 0.9167 Gold 0.4716 oz. AGW, 29 mm. **Ruler:** Elizabeth II **Obv:** Bust right **Rev:** Vikings and ship

| Date | Mintage | VF20 | XF40 | MS60 | MS63 | MS65 |
|---|---|---|---|---|---|---|
| 2012 | — | PF65 900 | | | | |

**KM# 1279 200 DOLLARS**
31.11 g., 0.999 Gold 0.999 oz. AGW, 30 mm. **Ruler:** Elizabeth II **Subject:** Bateman Moose

| Date | Mintage | VF20 | XF40 | MS60 | MS63 | MS65 |
|---|---|---|---|---|---|---|
| 2012 | — | PF65 1,850 | | | | |

**KM# 1331 200 DOLLARS**
33.33 g., 0.999 Gold 1.0705 oz. AGW, 30 mm. **Ruler:** Elizabeth II **Rev:** Grandmother Moon Mask

| Date | Mintage | VF20 | XF40 | MS60 | MS63 | MS65 |
|---|---|---|---|---|---|---|
| 2012 | 500 | PF65 3,000 | | | | |

**KM# 1390 200 DOLLARS**
15.43 g., 0.999 Gold 0.4956 oz. AGW, 29 mm. **Ruler:** Elizabeth II **Subject:** Explorer Jacques Cartier

| Date | Mintage | VF20 | XF40 | MS60 | MS63 | MS65 |
|---|---|---|---|---|---|---|
| 2013 | Est. 2000 | PF65 1,200 | | | | |

**KM# 1480 200 DOLLARS**
31.11 g., 0.999 Gold 0.999 oz. AGW, 30 mm. **Ruler:** Elizabeth II **Rev:** Eagle in nest with two chicks

| Date | Mintage | VF20 | XF40 | MS60 | MS63 | MS65 |
|---|---|---|---|---|---|---|
| 2013 Proof | 350 | — | — | — | 2,750 | — |

**KM# 1500 200 DOLLARS**
33.33 g., 0.9999 Gold 1.0715 oz. AGW, 30 mm. **Ruler:** Elizabeth II **Subject:** Grandmother Moon Mask **Rev:** Mask carving

| Date | Mintage | VF20 | XF40 | MS60 | MS63 | MS65 |
|---|---|---|---|---|---|---|
| 2013 | 500 | **PF65** 3,000 | | | | |

**KM# 1583 200 DOLLARS**
16.00 g., 0.9167 Gold 0.4716 oz. AGW, 29 mm. **Ruler:** Elizabeth II **Obv:** Bust right **Rev:** Indian and Samuel de Champlain standing next to canoes

| Date | Mintage | VF20 | XF40 | MS60 | MS63 | MS65 |
|---|---|---|---|---|---|---|
| 2014 | — | **PF65** 900 | | | | |

**KM# 1616 200 DOLLARS**
31.11 g., 0.999 Gold 0.999 oz. AGW, 30 mm. **Ruler:** Elizabeth II **Obv:** Bust right **Rev:** Howling wolf

| Date | Mintage | VF20 | XF40 | MS60 | MS63 | MS65 |
|---|---|---|---|---|---|---|
| 2014 | 2,000 | **PF65** 2,800 | | | | |

**KM# 1697 200 DOLLARS**
33.17 g., 0.999 Gold 1.0654 oz. AGW, 30 mm. **Ruler:** Elizabeth II **Obv:** Bust right **Rev:** Matriarch Moon Mask

| Date | Mintage | F12 | VF20 | XF40 | MS60 | MS63 |
|---|---|---|---|---|---|---|
| 2014 | 500 | **PF65** 3,000 | | | | |

**KM# 1698 200 DOLLARS**
33.17 g., 0.9999 Gold 1.0663 oz. AGW, 30 mm. **Ruler:** Elizabeth II **Subject:** Royal Visit, 75th Anniversary **Obv:** Bust right **Rev:** George VI and Elizabeth busts left in high relief

| Date | Mintage | F12 | VF20 | XF40 | MS60 | MS63 |
|---|---|---|---|---|---|---|
| 2014 | 500 | **PF65** 3,000 | | | | |

**KM# 1710 200 DOLLARS**
31.16 g., 0.999 Gold 1.0008 oz. AGW, 30 mm. **Ruler:** Elizabeth II **Obv:** Bust right **Rev:** Royal Family - Elizabeth II, Charles, William, George

| Date | Mintage | VF20 | XF40 | MS60 | MS63 | MS65 |
|---|---|---|---|---|---|---|
| 2014 | 350 | **PF65** 2,800 | | | | |

**KM# 1741 200 DOLLARS**
33.17 g., 1.000 Gold 1.0664 oz. AGW, 30 mm. **Ruler:** Elizabeth II **Subject:** Royal Visit, 75th Anniversary **Obv:** Conjoined busts left of George V and Elizabeth in high relief

| Date | Mintage | VF20 | XF40 | MS60 | MS63 | MS65 |
|---|---|---|---|---|---|---|
| 2014 | — | **PF65** 3,000 | | | | |

**KM# 1757 200 DOLLARS**
33.17 g., 1.000 Gold 1.0664 oz. AGW, 30 mm. **Ruler:** Elizabeth II **Obv:** Bust right **Rev:** Canadian lynx head

| Date | Mintage | VF20 | XF40 | MS60 | MS63 | MS65 |
|---|---|---|---|---|---|---|
| 2014 | 500 | **PF65** 3,000 | | | | |

**KM# 1784 200 DOLLARS**
15.43 g., 0.999 Gold 0.4956 oz. AGW, 29 mm. **Ruler:** Elizabeth II **Subject:** Interconnections - Land **Obv:** Bust right **Rev:** Beaver hologram

| Date | Mintage | F12 | VF20 | XF40 | MS60 | MS63 |
|---|---|---|---|---|---|---|
| 2014 | 1,500 | **PF65** 1,300 | | | | |

**KM# 1785 200 DOLLARS**
15.43 g., 0.999 Gold 0.4956 oz. AGW, 29 mm. **Ruler:** Elizabeth II **Subject:** Interconnections - Air **Obv:** Bust right **Rev:** Thunderbird hologram

| Date | Mintage | F12 | VF20 | XF40 | MS60 | MS63 |
|---|---|---|---|---|---|---|
| 2014 | 1,500 | **PF65** 1,300 | | | | |

**KM# 1786 200 DOLLARS**
15.43 g., 0.999 Gold 0.4956 oz. AGW, 29 mm. **Ruler:** Elizabeth II **Subject:** Interconnections - Sea **Obv:** Bust right **Rev:** Orca hologram

| Date | Mintage | F12 | VF20 | XF40 | MS60 | MS63 |
|---|---|---|---|---|---|---|
| 2014 | 1,500 | **PF65** 1,300 | | | | |

**KM# 1846 200 DOLLARS**
15.43 g., 0.9999 Gold 0.496 oz. AGW **Ruler:** Elizabeth II **Obv:** Bust right **Rev:** Henry Hudson

| Date | Mintage | VF20 | XF40 | MS60 | MS63 | MS65 |
|---|---|---|---|---|---|---|
| 2015 | — | **PF65** 500 | | | | |

**KM# 677 250 DOLLARS**
45.00 g., 0.5833 Gold 0.8439 oz. AGW, 40 mm. **Ruler:** Elizabeth II **Rev:** Dog Sled Team

| Date | Mintage | VF20 | XF40 | MS60 | MS63 | MS65 |
|---|---|---|---|---|---|---|
| 2006 | 953 | **PF65** 1,625 | | | | |

**KM# 751 250 DOLLARS**
1000.00 g., 0.9999 Silver 32.1475 oz. ASW, 101.6 mm. **Ruler:** Elizabeth II **Subject:** Vancouver Olympics, 2010 **Rev:** Early Canada motif **Note:** Illustration reduced.

| Date | Mintage | VF20 | XF40 | MS60 | MS63 | MS65 |
|---|---|---|---|---|---|---|
| 2007 | 2,500 | **PF65** 1,250 | | | | |

**KM# 833 250 DOLLARS**
1000.00 g., 0.999 Silver 32.1186 oz. ASW, 101.6 mm. **Ruler:** Elizabeth II **Subject:** Vancouver Olympics 2010 **Rev:** Towards confederation **Note:** Illustration reduced.

| Date | Mintage | VF20 | XF40 | MS60 | MS63 | MS65 |
|---|---|---|---|---|---|---|
| 2008 | 2,500 | **PF65** 1,350 | | | | |

**KM# 913 250 DOLLARS**
1000.00 g., 0.9999 Silver 32.1475 oz. ASW, 101.5 mm. **Ruler:** Elizabeth II **Obv:** Bust right **Rev:** Mask with fish - Surviving the flood **Note:** Illustration reduced.

| Date | Mintage | VF20 | XF40 | MS60 | MS63 | MS65 |
|---|---|---|---|---|---|---|
| 2009 | 815 | PF65 1,350 | | | | |

**KM# 949 250 DOLLARS**
1000.00 g., 0.999 Silver 32.1186 oz. ASW, 101.6 mm. **Ruler:** Elizabeth II **Rev:** Modern Canada

| Date | Mintage | VF20 | XF40 | MS60 | MS63 | MS65 |
|---|---|---|---|---|---|---|
| 2009 | 905 | PF65 1,350 | | | | |

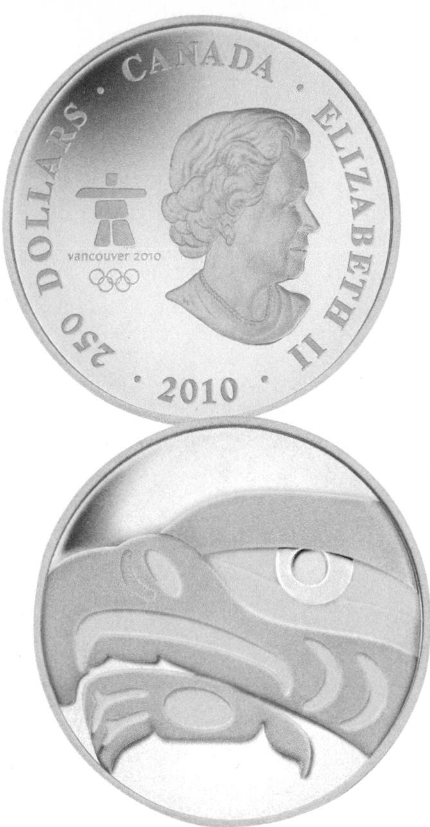


**KM# 981 250 DOLLARSW**
1000.00 g., 0.999 Silver 32.1186 oz. ASW, 101.6 mm. **Ruler:** Elizabeth II **Rev:** Eagle head

| Date | Mintage | VF20 | XF40 | MS60 | MS63 | MS65 |
|---|---|---|---|---|---|---|
| 2010 Antique Patina | 500 | — | — | — | 1,350 | — |
| 2010 | 500 | PF65 1,400 | | | | |

**KM# 981a 250 DOLLARS**
1000.00 g., 0.999 Silver 32.1186 oz. ASW, 101.6 mm. **Ruler:** Elizabeth II **Rev:** Eagle head, blue enamel

| Date | Mintage | VF20 | XF40 | MS60 | MS63 | MS65 |
|---|---|---|---|---|---|---|
| 2010 | 500 | PF65 1,400 | | | | |

**KM# 1044 250 DOLLARS**
1000.00 g., 0.999 Silver 32.1186 oz. ASW, 101.6 mm. **Ruler:** Elizabeth II **Subject:** Baniff, 125th Anniversary of resort founding **Rev:** Features of Baniff

| Date | Mintage | VF20 | XF40 | MS60 | MS63 | MS65 |
|---|---|---|---|---|---|---|
| 2010 | 750 | PF65 1,650 | | | | |

**KM# 1285 250 DOLLARS**
1000.00 g., 0.999 Silver 32.1186 oz. ASW, 101 mm. **Ruler:** Elizabeth II **Subject:** Olympic views

| Date | Mintage | VF20 | XF40 | MS60 | MS63 | MS65 |
|---|---|---|---|---|---|---|
| 2010 | — | PF65 1,350 | | | | |

**KM# 1150 250 DOLLARS**
1000.00 g., 0.9999 Silver 32.1475 oz. ASW, 100 mm. **Ruler:** Elizabeth II **Rev:** Lacrosse

| Date | Mintage | VF20 | XF40 | MS60 | MS63 | MS65 |
|---|---|---|---|---|---|---|
| 2011 | — | PF65 1,350 | | | | |

## KM# 1185 250 DOLLARS

1000.00 g., 0.999 Silver 32.1186 oz. ASW, 101.6 mm. **Ruler:** Elizabeth II **Subject:** Year of the Dragon **Obv:** Bust left **Rev:** Dragon left

| Date | Mintage | VF20 | XF40 | MS60 | MS63 | MS65 |
|---|---|---|---|---|---|---|
| 2012 | — | PF65 1,550 | | | | |

## KM# 1277 250 DOLLARS

1000.00 g., 0.999 Silver 32.1186 oz. ASW, 101 mm. **Ruler:** Elizabeth II **Subject:** Bateman Moose

| Date | Mintage | VF20 | XF40 | MS60 | MS63 | MS65 |
|---|---|---|---|---|---|---|
| 2012 | — | PF65 1,650 | | | | |

## KM# 1340 250 DOLLARS

1000.00 g., 0.9999 Silver 32.1475 oz. ASW, 102 mm. **Ruler:** Elizabeth II **Subject:** War of 1812, Battle of Queenstown Heights **Rev:** Battle scene

| Date | Mintage | VF20 | XF40 | MS60 | MS63 | MS65 |
|---|---|---|---|---|---|---|
| 2012 | 7,000 | PF65 2,250 | | | | |

## KM# 1366 250 DOLLARS

1000.00 g., 0.9999 Silver 32.1475 oz. ASW **Ruler:** Elizabeth II **Subject:** Year of the Snake **Rev:** Snake under maple leaves

| Date | Mintage | VF20 | XF40 | MS60 | MS63 | MS65 |
|---|---|---|---|---|---|---|
| 2013 | Est. 888 | PF65 2,250 | | | | |

## KM# 1369 250 DOLLARS

1000.00 g., 0.999 Silver 32.1186 oz. ASW **Ruler:** Elizabeth II **Subject:** End of 7 Years War **Rev:** Map of North America with Arms of France and Great Britain

| Date | Mintage | VF20 | XF40 | MS60 | MS63 | MS65 |
|---|---|---|---|---|---|---|
| 2013 | Est. 500 | PF65 2,250 | | | | |

## KM# 1371 250 DOLLARS

1000.00 g., 0.999 Silver 32.1186 oz. ASW, 101 mm. **Ruler:** Elizabeth II **Subject:** Arctic Coastline

| Date | Mintage | VF20 | XF40 | MS60 | MS63 | MS65 |
|---|---|---|---|---|---|---|
| 2013 | Est. 750 | PF65 2,250 | | | | |

**KM# 1438 250 DOLLARS**
1000.00 g., 0.9999 Silver 32.1475 oz. ASW, 102.1 mm. **Ruler:** Elizabeth II **Rev:** Two maple leaves - gilt

| Date | Mintage | VF20 | XF40 | MS60 | MS63 | MS65 |
|---|---|---|---|---|---|---|
| 2013 | Est. 600 | PF65 2,300 | | | | |

**KM# 1477 250 DOLLARS**
1000.00 g., 0.9999 Silver 32.1475 oz. ASW, 102.1 mm. **Ruler:** Elizabeth II **Subject:** Battle of Chateauguay **Rev:** Henri Julien's painting of the battle

| Date | Mintage | VF20 | XF40 | MS60 | MS63 | MS65 |
|---|---|---|---|---|---|---|
| 2013 | 500 | PF65 2,250 | | | | |

**KM# 1502 250 DOLLARS**
1000.00 g., 0.9999 Silver 32.1475 oz. ASW, 102.1 mm. **Ruler:** Elizabeth II **Rev:** Two caribou advancing left

| Date | Mintage | VF20 | XF40 | MS60 | MS63 | MS65 |
|---|---|---|---|---|---|---|
| 2013 | 500 | PF65 2,500 | | | | |

**KM# 1518 250 DOLLARS**
1000.00 g., 0.9999 Silver 32.1475 oz. ASW, 102.1 mm. **Ruler:** Elizabeth II **Subject:** Year of the Horse **Obv:** Bust right **Rev:** Horse rearing up left

| Date | Mintage | VF20 | XF40 | MS60 | MS63 | MS65 |
|---|---|---|---|---|---|---|
| 2014 | 388 | PF65 2,250 | | | | |

**KM# 1579 250 DOLLARS**
1000.00 g., 0.9999 Silver 32.1475 oz. ASW, 101 mm. **Ruler:** Elizabeth II **Subject:** Year of the Horse **Obv:** Bust right

| Date | Mintage | VF20 | XF40 | MS60 | MS63 | MS65 |
|---|---|---|---|---|---|---|
| 2014 | — | PF65 1,350 | | | | |

**KM# 1605 250 DOLLARS**
1000.00 g., 0.9999 Silver 32.1475 oz. ASW, 101 mm. **Ruler:** Elizabeth II **Obv:** Bust right **Rev:** Snowy owl, yellow eyes

| Date | Mintage | VF20 | XF40 | MS60 | MS63 | MS65 |
|---|---|---|---|---|---|---|
| 2014 | — | PF65 1,650 | | | | |

**KM# 1622 250 DOLLARS**
62.34 g., 0.999 Gold 2.0023 oz. AGW, 42 mm. **Ruler:** Elizabeth II **Subject:** Canada thru the eyes of Tim Barnard **Obv:** Bust right **Rev:** Multitude of designs

| Date | Mintage | VF20 | XF40 | MS60 | MS63 | MS65 |
|---|---|---|---|---|---|---|
| 2014 | 300 | PF65 5,200 | | | | |

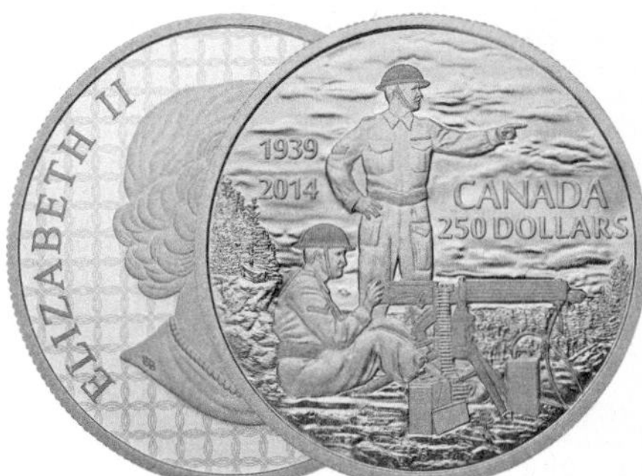

**KM# 1701 250 DOLLARS**
62.34 g., 0.9999 Gold 2.0041 oz. AGW, 42 mm. **Ruler:** Elizabeth II **Obv:** Bust right **Rev:** Machine Gunner Training

| Date | Mintage | VF20 | XF40 | MS60 | MS63 | MS65 |
|---|---|---|---|---|---|---|
| 2014 | 200 | PF65 5,200 | | | | |

**KM# 1722 250 DOLLARS**
62.34 g., 0.999 Gold 2.0023 oz. AGW, 42 mm. **Ruler:** Elizabeth II **Subject:** Grand Trunk Railway **Obv:** Bust right **Rev:** Steam Train on Bridge

| Date | Mintage | VF20 | XF40 | MS60 | MS63 | MS65 |
|---|---|---|---|---|---|---|
| 2014 | 300 | PF65 5,200 | | | | |

**KM# 1747 250 DOLLARS**
31.16 g., 0.999 Silver 1.0008 oz. ASW, 30 mm. **Ruler:** Elizabeth II **Obv:** Bust right **Rev:** White tail deer doe and two fawns

| Date | Mintage | VF20 | XF40 | MS60 | MS63 | MS65 |
|---|---|---|---|---|---|---|
| 2014 | 350 | PF65 30.00 | | | | |

**KM# 1762 250 DOLLARS**
1000.00 g., 0.999 Silver 32.1186 oz. ASW, 102.1 mm. **Ruler:** Elizabeth II **Obv:** Bust right **Rev:** 2 Maple leaves - one red and one green, rays in background

| Date | Mintage | VF20 | XF40 | MS60 | MS63 | MS65 |
|---|---|---|---|---|---|---|
| 2014 | 600 | PF65 2,300 | | | | |

**KM# 1817 250 DOLLARS**
1000.00 g., 0.999 Silver 32.1186 oz. ASW, 102 mm. **Ruler:** Elizabeth II **Subject:** Year of the Ram **Obv:** Bust right **Rev:** Sheep head at right, red tree, gilt chinese character

| Date | Mintage | F12 | VF20 | XF40 | MS60 | MS63 |
|---|---|---|---|---|---|---|
| 2015 | 388 | PF65 2,300 | | | | |

**KM# 1834 250 DOLLARS**
60.08 g., 0.9999 Gold 1.9314 oz. AGW, 38 mm. **Ruler:** Elizabeth II **Obv:** Bust right **Rev:** Tulup in glass

| Date | Mintage | VF20 | XF40 | MS60 | MS63 | MS65 |
|---|---|---|---|---|---|---|
| 2015 | 100 | PF65 4,700 | | | | |

**KM# 1835 250 DOLLARS**
60.08 g., 0.9999 Gold 1.9314 oz. AGW, 38 mm. **Ruler:** Elizabeth II **Obv:** Bust right **Rev:** Water Lilly in glass

| Date | Mintage | VF20 | XF40 | MS60 | MS63 | MS65 |
|---|---|---|---|---|---|---|
| 2015 | 100 | PF65 4,700 | | | | |

**KM# 1836 250 DOLLARS**
60.08 g., 0.9999 Gold 1.9314 oz. AGW, 38 mm. **Ruler:** Elizabeth II **Obv:** Bust right **Rev:** Aster in glass

| Date | Mintage | VF20 | XF40 | MS60 | MS63 | MS65 |
|---|---|---|---|---|---|---|
| 2015 | 100 | PF65 4,700 | | | | |

**KM# 501 300 DOLLARS**
60.00 g., 0.5833 Gold 1.1252 oz. AGW, 50 mm. **Ruler:** Elizabeth II **Obv:** Triple cameo portraits of Queen Elizabeth II by Gillick, Machin and de Pedery-Hunt, each in 14K gold, rose in center **Rev:** Dates "1952-2002" and denomination in legend, rose in center **Note:** Housed in anodized gold-colored aluminum box with cherrywood stained siding

| Date | Mintage | VF20 | XF40 | MS60 | MS63 | MS65 |
|---|---|---|---|---|---|---|
| 1952-2002 | 999 | PF65 2,150 | | | | |

**KM# 517 300 DOLLARS**
60.00 g., 0.5833 Gold 1.1252 oz. AGW, 50 mm. **Ruler:** Elizabeth II **Obv:** Four coinage portraits of Elizabeth II **Rev:** Canadian arms above value **Edge:** Plain

| Date | Mintage | VF20 | XF40 | MS60 | MS63 | MS65 |
|---|---|---|---|---|---|---|
| 2004 | 998 | PF65 2,150 | | | | |

**KM# 570.1 300 DOLLARS**
45.00 g., 0.5833 Gold 0.8439 oz. AGW, 40 mm. **Ruler:** Elizabeth II **Subject:** Standard Time - 4 AM Pacific **Obv:** Head right **Rev:** Roman numeral clock with world inside

| Date | Mintage | VF20 | XF40 | MS60 | MS63 | MS65 |
|---|---|---|---|---|---|---|
| 2005 | 200 | PF65 1,650 | | | | |

**KM# 570.2 300 DOLLARS**
45.00 g., 0.583 Gold 0.8435 oz. AGW, 40 mm. **Ruler:** Elizabeth II **Subject:** Standard Time - Mountian 5 AM **Obv:** Head right **Rev:** Roman numeral clock with world inside.

| Date | Mintage | VF20 | XF40 | MS60 | MS63 | MS65 |
|---|---|---|---|---|---|---|
| 2005 | 200 | PF65 1,650 | | | | |

**KM# 570.3 300 DOLLARS**
45.00 g., 0.583 Gold 0.8435 oz. AGW, 40 mm. **Ruler:** Elizabeth II **Subject:** Standard Time - Central 6 PM **Obv:** Head right **Rev:** Roman numeral clock with world inside

| Date | Mintage | VF20 | XF40 | MS60 | MS63 | MS65 |
|---|---|---|---|---|---|---|
| 2005 | 200 | PF65 1,650 | | | | |

**KM# 570.4 300 DOLLARS**
45.00 g., 0.583 Gold 0.8435 oz. AGW, 40 mm. **Ruler:** Elizabeth II **Subject:** Standard Time - Eastern 7 AM **Obv:** Head right **Rev:** Roman numeral clock with world inside

| Date | Mintage | VF20 | XF40 | MS60 | MS63 | MS65 |
|---|---|---|---|---|---|---|
| 2005 | 200 | PF65 1,650 | | | | |

**KM# 570.5 300 DOLLARS**
45.00 g., 0.583 Gold 0.8435 oz. AGW, 40 mm. **Ruler:** Elizabeth II **Subject:** Standard Time - Atlantic 8 AM **Obv:** Head right **Rev:** Roman numeral clock with world inside

| Date | Mintage | VF20 | XF40 | MS60 | MS63 | MS65 |
|---|---|---|---|---|---|---|
| 2005 | 200 | PF65 1,650 | | | | |

**KM# 570.6 300 DOLLARS**
45.00 g., 0.583 Gold 0.8435 oz. AGW, 40 mm. **Ruler:** Elizabeth II **Subject:** Standard Time - Newfoundland 8:30 **Obv:** Head right **Rev:** Roman numeral clock with world inside

| Date | Mintage | VF20 | XF40 | MS60 | MS63 | MS65 |
|---|---|---|---|---|---|---|
| 2005 | 200 | PF65 1,650 | | | | |

**KM# 596 300 DOLLARS**
60.00 g., 0.5833 Gold 1.1252 oz. AGW, 50 mm. **Ruler:** Elizabeth II **Subject:** Shinplaster **Obv:** Head right **Rev:** Britannia bust, spear over shoulder

| Date | Mintage | VF20 | XF40 | MS60 | MS63 | MS65 |
|---|---|---|---|---|---|---|
| 2005 | 994 | PF65 2,150 | | | | |

**KM# 600 300 DOLLARS**
60.00 g., 0.5833 Gold 1.1252 oz. AGW, 40 mm. **Ruler:** Elizabeth II **Subject:** Welcome Figure Totem Pole **Obv:** Head right **Rev:** Men with totem pole

| Date | Mintage | VF20 | XF40 | MS60 | MS63 | MS65 |
|---|---|---|---|---|---|---|
| 2005 | 948 | PF65 2,150 | | | | |

**KM# 595 300 DOLLARS**
60.00 g., 0.5833 Gold 1.1252 oz. AGW, 50 mm. **Ruler:** Elizabeth II **Subject:** Shinplaster **Obv:** Head right **Rev:** Seated Britannia with shield

| Date | Mintage | VF20 | XF40 | MS60 | MS63 | MS65 |
|---|---|---|---|---|---|---|
| 2006 | 940 | PF65 2,150 | | | | |

**KM# 678 300 DOLLARS**
45.00 g., 0.5833 Gold 0.8439 oz. AGW, 40 mm. **Ruler:** Elizabeth II **Rev:** Hologram of Canadarm, Col. C. Hadfield in spacewalk

| Date | Mintage | VF20 | XF40 | MS60 | MS63 | MS65 |
|---|---|---|---|---|---|---|
| 2006 | 581 | PF65 1,650 | | | | |

**KM# 679 300 DOLLARS**
60.00 g., 0.5833 Gold 1.1252 oz. AGW, 50 mm. **Ruler:** Elizabeth II **Subject:** Queen Elizabeth's 80th Birthday **Rev:** State Crown, colorized

| Date | Mintage | VF20 | XF40 | MS60 | MS63 | MS65 |
|---|---|---|---|---|---|---|
| 2006 | 996 | PF65 2,150 | | | | |

**KM# 680 300 DOLLARS**
60.00 g., 0.5833 Gold 1.1252 oz. AGW, 50 mm. **Ruler:** Elizabeth II **Subject:** Crystal Snowflake

| Date | Mintage | VF20 | XF40 | MS60 | MS63 | MS65 |
|---|---|---|---|---|---|---|
| 2006 | 998 | PF65 2,150 | | | | |

**KM# 692 300 DOLLARS**
60.00 g., 0.5833 Gold 1.1252 oz. AGW, 50 mm. **Ruler:** Elizabeth II **Subject:** Shinplaster **Rev:** 1923 25 cent bank note

| Date | Mintage | VF20 | XF40 | MS60 | MS63 | MS65 |
|---|---|---|---|---|---|---|
| 2007 | 778 | PF65 2,150 | | | | |

**KM# 740 300 DOLLARS**
45.00 g., 0.583 Gold 0.8435 oz. AGW, 40 mm. **Ruler:** Elizabeth II **Rev:** Canadian Rockies panoramic hologram

| Date | Mintage | VF20 | XF40 | MS60 | MS63 | MS65 |
|---|---|---|---|---|---|---|
| 2007 | 511 | PF65 1,750 | | | | |

**KM# 752 300 DOLLARS**
60.00 g., 0.583 Gold 1.1246 oz. AGW, 50 mm. **Ruler:** Elizabeth II **Subject:** Vancouver Olympics **Rev:** Olympic ideals, classic figures and torch

| Date | Mintage | VF20 | XF40 | MS60 | MS63 | MS65 |
|---|---|---|---|---|---|---|
| 2007 | 953 | PF65 2,150 | | | | |

**KM# 825 300 DOLLARS**
45.00 g., 0.583 Gold 0.8435 oz. AGW, 50 mm. **Ruler:** Elizabeth II **Rev:** Alberta Coat of Arms

| Date | Mintage | VF20 | XF40 | MS60 | MS63 | MS65 |
|---|---|---|---|---|---|---|
| 2008 | 344 | PF65 1,750 | | | | |

**KM# 826 300 DOLLARS**
60.00 g., 0.583 Gold 1.1246 oz. AGW, 50 mm. **Ruler:** Elizabeth II **Rev:** Newfoundland and Labrador Coat of Arms

| Date | Mintage | VF20 | XF40 | MS60 | MS63 | MS65 |
|---|---|---|---|---|---|---|
| 2008 | 472 | PF65 2,150 | | | | |

**KM# 827 300 DOLLARS**
45.00 g., 0.583 Gold 0.8435 oz. AGW, 40 mm. **Ruler:** Elizabeth II **Subject:** Canadian achievements IMAX **Rev:** Kid in audience reaching out to shark on big screen

| Date | Mintage | VF20 | XF40 | MS60 | MS63 | MS65 |
|---|---|---|---|---|---|---|
| 2008 | — | PF65 1,650 | | | | |

**KM# 828 300 DOLLARS**
60.00 g., 0.583 Gold 1.1246 oz. AGW, 50 mm. **Ruler:** Elizabeth II **Rev:** Four seasons moon mask in color, blue design in border

| Date | Mintage | VF20 | XF40 | MS60 | MS63 | MS65 |
|---|---|---|---|---|---|---|
| 2008 | 544 | PF65 3,800 | | | | |

**KM# 830 300 DOLLARS**
60.00 g., 0.583 Gold 1.1246 oz. AGW, 50 mm. **Ruler:** Elizabeth II **Subject:** Vancouver Olympics **Rev:** Olympic competition, athletics and torch

| Date | Mintage | VF20 | XF40 | MS60 | MS63 | MS65 |
|---|---|---|---|---|---|---|
| 2008 | 334 | PF65 2,250 | | | | |

**KM# 877 300 DOLLARS**
60.00 g., 0.583 Gold 1.1246 oz. AGW, 50 mm. **Ruler:** Elizabeth II **Rev:** Summer moon mask, enameled

| Date | Mintage | VF20 | XF40 | MS60 | MS63 | MS65 |
|---|---|---|---|---|---|---|
| 2009 | — | PF65 2,250 | | | | |

**KM# 900 300 DOLLARS**
60.00 g., 0.583 Gold 1.1246 oz. AGW, 50 mm. **Ruler:** Elizabeth II **Subject:** Yukon Coat of Arms **Obv:** Bust right **Obv. Legend:** Elizabeth II DG Regina **Rev:** Yukon Coat of Arms **Rev. Legend:** Canada 300 Dollars

| Date | Mintage | VF20 | XF40 | MS60 | MS63 | MS65 |
|---|---|---|---|---|---|---|
| 2009 | 325 | PF65 2,150 | | | | |

**KM# 911 300 DOLLARS**
60.00 g., 0.583 Gold 1.1246 oz. AGW, 50 mm. **Ruler:** Elizabeth II **Subject:** 2010 Vancouver Olympics **Obv:** Bust right **Rev:** Athletics with torch - Olympic firendship

| Date | Mintage | VF20 | XF40 | MS60 | MS63 | MS65 |
|---|---|---|---|---|---|---|
| 2009 | 880 | PF65 2,150 | | | | |

**KM# 999 300 DOLLARS**
54.00 g., 0.583 Gold 1.0122 oz. AGW, 50 mm. **Ruler:** Elizabeth II **Rev:** British Columbia Arms

| Date | Mintage | VF20 | XF40 | MS60 | MS63 | MS65 |
|---|---|---|---|---|---|---|
| 2010 | 500 | PF65 1,900 | | | | |

**KM# 1047 300 DOLLARS**
60.00 g., 0.583 Gold 1.1246 oz. AGW, 50 mm. **Ruler:** Elizabeth II **Rev:** Snowflake, white crystals

| Date | Mintage | VF20 | XF40 | MS60 | MS63 | MS65 |
|---|---|---|---|---|---|---|
| 2010 | 750 | PF65 2,150 | | | | |

**KM# 1078 300 DOLLARS**
60.00 g., 0.583 Gold 1.1246 oz. AGW, 50 mm. **Ruler:** Elizabeth II **Rev:** New Brunswick Coat of arms

| Date | Mintage | VF20 | XF40 | MS60 | MS63 | MS65 |
|---|---|---|---|---|---|---|
| 2010 | 500 | PF65 2,150 | | | | |

**KM# 1095 300 DOLLARS**
60.00 g., 0.9167 Gold 1.7684 oz. AGW, 50 mm. **Ruler:** Elizabeth II **Rev:** Manitoba Coat of arms

| Date | Mintage | VF20 | XF40 | MS60 | MS63 | MS65 |
|---|---|---|---|---|---|---|
| 2011 | 500 | PF65 3,300 | | | | |

**KM# 1215 300 DOLLARS**
60.00 g., 0.917 Gold 1.7689 oz. AGW, 50 mm. **Ruler:** Elizabeth II **Obv:** Bust right **Rev:** Arms of Nova Scotia

| Date | Mintage | VF20 | XF40 | MS60 | MS63 | MS65 |
|---|---|---|---|---|---|---|
| 2011 | — | PF65 3,300 | | | | |

**KM# 1195 300 DOLLARS**
45.00 g., 0.583 Gold 0.8435 oz. AGW, 40 mm. **Ruler:** Elizabeth II **Subject:** Elizabeth II, Diamond Jubilee **Obv:** Bust right **Rev:** Youthful bust with crown right, insert crystal at right

| Date | Mintage | VF20 | XF40 | MS60 | MS63 | MS65 |
|---|---|---|---|---|---|---|
| 1952-2012 | — | PF65 1,600 | | | | |

**KM# 1224 300 DOLLARS**
60.00 g., 0.9167 Gold 1.7684 oz. AGW, 50 mm. **Ruler:** Elizabeth II **Obv:** Bust right **Rev:** Shield of Quebec

| Date | Mintage | VF20 | XF40 | MS60 | MS63 | MS65 |
|---|---|---|---|---|---|---|
| 2012 | — | PF65 3,300 | | | | |

**KM# 1242 300 DOLLARS**
16.00 g., 0.916 Gold 0.4712 oz. AGW, 29 mm. **Ruler:** Elizabeth II **Subject:** Calgary Stampede

| Date | Mintage | VF20 | XF40 | MS60 | MS63 | MS65 |
|---|---|---|---|---|---|---|
| 2012 | — | PF65 900 | | | | |

**KM# 1278 300 DOLLARS**
31.11 g., 0.999 Platinum 0.9992 oz. APW, 30 mm. **Ruler:** Elizabeth II **Subject:** Bateman Moose

| Date | Mintage | VF20 | XF40 | MS60 | MS63 | MS65 |
|---|---|---|---|---|---|---|
| 2012 | — | PF65 1,750 | | | | |

**KM# 1338 300 DOLLARS**
60.00 g., 0.917 Gold 1.7689 oz. AGW, 50 mm. **Ruler:** Elizabeth II **Subject:** Nunavut Province **Rev:** Provincial Arms

| Date | Mintage | VF20 | XF40 | MS60 | MS63 | MS65 |
|---|---|---|---|---|---|---|
| 2012 | — | PF65 4,000 | | | | |

**KM# 1430 300 DOLLARS**
31.16 g., 0.9995 Platinum 1.0013 oz. APW, 30 mm. **Ruler:** Elizabeth II **Subject:** War of 1812 - Naval Battle **Rev:** HMS Shannon and Chesapeake

| Date | Mintage | VF20 | XF40 | MS60 | MS63 | MS65 |
|---|---|---|---|---|---|---|
| 2013 | Est. 250 | PF65 3,000 | | | | |

**KM# 1549 300 DOLLARS**
60.00 g., 0.9176 Gold 1.7701 oz. AGW, 50 mm. **Ruler:** Elizabeth II **Subject:** Northwest Territories **Rev:** Provincial Arms

| Date | Mintage | VF20 | XF40 | MS60 | MS63 | MS65 |
|---|---|---|---|---|---|---|
| 2013 | — | PF65 4,000 | | | | |

**KM# 1571 300 DOLLARS**
60.00 g., 0.917 Gold 1.7689 oz. AGW, 50 mm. **Ruler:** Elizabeth II **Obv:** Bust right **Rev:** Arms of Ontario

| Date | Mintage | VF20 | XF40 | MS60 | MS63 | MS65 |
|---|---|---|---|---|---|---|
| 2013 | 3,300 | PF65 4,000 | | | | |

**KM# 1592 300 DOLLARS**
60.00 g., 0.999 Gold 1.9271 oz. AGW, 50 mm. **Ruler:** Elizabeth II **Obv:** Bust right **Rev:** Saskashawan coat of arms

| Date | Mintage | VF20 | XF40 | MS60 | MS63 | MS65 |
|---|---|---|---|---|---|---|
| 2014 | — | PF65 3,300 | | | | |

**KM# 1699 300 DOLLARS**
60.00 g., 0.583 Gold 1.1246 oz. AGW, 50 mm. **Ruler:** Elizabeth II **Obv:** Bust right **Rev:** National Arms of Canada

| Date | Mintage | F12 | VF20 | XF40 | MS60 | MS63 |
|---|---|---|---|---|---|---|
| 2014 | 500 | PF65 2,700 | | | | |

**KM# 433 350 DOLLARS**
38.05 g., 0.9999 Gold 1.2232 oz. AGW, 34 mm. **Ruler:** Elizabeth II **Subject:** The Mayflower Flower **Obv:** Crowned head right **Rev:** Two flowers **Edge:** Reeded

| Date | Mintage | VF20 | XF40 | MS60 | MS63 | MS65 |
|---|---|---|---|---|---|---|
| 2001 | 1,988 | PF65 2,350 | | | | |

**KM# 502 350 DOLLARS**
38.05 g., 0.9999 Gold 1.2232 oz. AGW, 34 mm. **Ruler:** Elizabeth II **Subject:** The Wild Rose **Obv:** Crowned head right **Rev:** Wild rose plant

| Date | Mintage | VF20 | XF40 | MS60 | MS63 | MS65 |
|---|---|---|---|---|---|---|
| 2002 | 2,001 | PF65 2,350 | | | | |

**KM# 504 350 DOLLARS**
38.05 g., 0.9999 Gold 1.2232 oz. AGW, 34 mm. **Ruler:** Elizabeth II **Subject:** The White Trillium **Obv:** Crowned head right **Rev:** White Trillium

| Date | Mintage | VF20 | XF40 | MS60 | MS63 | MS65 |
|---|---|---|---|---|---|---|
| 2003 | 1,865 | PF65 2,350 | | | | |

**KM# 601 350 DOLLARS**
38.05 g., 0.9999 Gold 1.2232 oz. AGW **Ruler:** Elizabeth II **Subject:** Western Red Lilly **Obv:** Head right **Rev:** Western Red Lilies

| Date | Mintage | VF20 | XF40 | MS60 | MS63 | MS65 |
|---|---|---|---|---|---|---|
| 2005 | 1,634 | PF65 2,350 | | | | |

**KM# 626 350 DOLLARS**
38.05 g., 0.9999 Gold 1.2232 oz. AGW, 34 mm. **Ruler:** Elizabeth II **Subject:** Iris Vericolor **Obv:** Crowned head right **Rev:** Iris

| Date | Mintage | VF20 | XF40 | MS60 | MS63 | MS65 |
|---|---|---|---|---|---|---|
| 2006 | 1,995 | PF65 2,350 | | | | |

**KM# 754 350 DOLLARS**
35.00 g., 0.9999 Gold 1.1252 oz. AGW, 34 mm. **Ruler:** Elizabeth II **Rev:** Purple violet

| Date | Mintage | VF20 | XF40 | MS60 | MS63 | MS65 |
|---|---|---|---|---|---|---|
| 2007 | 1,392 | PF65 2,200 | | | | |

**KM# 832 350 DOLLARS**
35.00 g., 0.9999 Gold 1.1252 oz. AGW, 34 mm. **Ruler:** Elizabeth II **Rev:** Purple saxifrage

| Date | Mintage | VF20 | XF40 | MS60 | MS63 | MS65 |
|---|---|---|---|---|---|---|
| 2008 | 1,313 | PF65 2,200 | | | | |

**KM# 901 350 DOLLARS**
35.00 g., 1.000 Gold 1.1253 oz. AGW, 34 mm. **Ruler:** Elizabeth II **Subject:** Pitcher plant **Obv:** Bust right **Obv. Legend:** Elizabeth II Canada DG Regina Fine Gold 350 Dollars or PUR 99999 **Rev:** Cluster of pitcher flowers **Rev. Legend:** Julie Wilson

| Date | Mintage | VF20 | XF40 | MS60 | MS63 | MS65 |
|---|---|---|---|---|---|---|
| 2009 | 1,003 | PF65 2,200 | | | | |

**KM# 1019 350 DOLLARS**
35.00 g., 0.999 Gold 1.1242 oz. AGW, 34 mm. **Ruler:** Elizabeth II **Rev:** Praire Crocus

| Date | Mintage | VF20 | XF40 | MS60 | MS63 | MS65 |
|---|---|---|---|---|---|---|
| 2010 | Est. 1400 | PF65 2,200 | | | | |

**KM# 1136 350 DOLLARS**
35.00 g., 0.9999 Gold 1.1252 oz. AGW, 34 mm. **Ruler:** Elizabeth II **Obv:** Bust right **Rev:** Mountain Avens in bloom **Edge:** Reeded

| Date | Mintage | VF20 | XF40 | MS60 | MS63 | MS65 |
|---|---|---|---|---|---|---|
| 2011 | 1,300 | PF65 2,200 | | | | |

**KM# 1327 350 DOLLARS**
35.00 g., 0.999 Gold 1.1242 oz. AGW, 34 mm. **Ruler:** Elizabeth II **Subject:** War of 1812 - Sir Issac Brock **Rev:** Putti crowning funeral urn, design of 1816 Half-penny token

| Date | Mintage | VF20 | XF40 | MS60 | MS63 | MS65 |
|---|---|---|---|---|---|---|
| 2012 | 1,000 | PF65 2,800 | | | | |

**KM# 1499 350 DOLLARS**
35.00 g., 0.9999 Gold 1.1252 oz. AGW, 34 mm. **Ruler:** Elizabeth II **Rev:** Polar Bear

| Date | Mintage | VF20 | XF40 | MS60 | MS63 | MS65 |
|---|---|---|---|---|---|---|
| 2013 | 600 | PF65 2,800 | | | | |

**KM# 1793 350 DOLLARS**
35.00 g., 0.999 Gold 1.1242 oz. AGW, 34 mm. **Ruler:** Elizabeth II **Obv:** Bust right **Rev:** Moose advancing left

| Date | Mintage | F12 | VF20 | XF40 | MS60 | MS63 |
|---|---|---|---|---|---|---|
| 2014 | 600 | PF65 2,800 | | | | |

**KM# 710 500 DOLLARS**
156.50 g., 0.9999 Gold 5.0311 oz. AGW, 60 mm. **Ruler:** Elizabeth II **Subject:** Queen's 60th Wedding **Rev:** Coat of Arms and Mascots of Elizabeth and Philip

| Date | Mintage | VF20 | XF40 | MS60 | MS63 | MS65 |
|---|---|---|---|---|---|---|
| 2007 | 198 | — | — | — | 9,150 | — |

**KM# 782 500 DOLLARS**
155.76 g., 0.999 Gold 5.0028 oz. AGW, 60 mm. **Ruler:** Elizabeth II **Subject:** Ottawa Mint Centennial 1908-2008 **Rev:** Mint building facade **Note:** Illustration reduced.

| Date | Mintage | VF20 | XF40 | MS60 | MS63 | MS65 |
|---|---|---|---|---|---|---|
| 2008 | 248 | — | — | — | 9,150 | — |

**KM# 897 500 DOLLARS**
156.05 g., 0.999 Gold 5.0121 oz. AGW, 60 mm. **Ruler:** Elizabeth II **Subject:** 150th Anniversary of the start of construction of the Parliament Buildings **Obv:** Bust right **Rev:** Incomplete west block, original architecture **Rev. Legend:** 500 Dollars 1859-2009

| Date | Mintage | VF20 | XF40 | MS60 | MS63 | MS65 |
|---|---|---|---|---|---|---|
| 2009 | 77 | PF65 9,150 | | | | |

**KM# 1007 500 DOLLARS**
156.50 g., 0.999 Gold 5.0266 oz. AGW, 60 mm. **Ruler:** Elizabeth II **Subject:** 75th Anniversary of Canadian Bank Notes **Rev:** Abundance seated under tree

| Date | Mintage | VF20 | XF40 | MS60 | MS63 | MS65 |
|---|---|---|---|---|---|---|
| 2010 | 200 | PF65 9,150 | | | | |

**KM# 1179 500 DOLLARS**
156.50 g., 0.9999 Gold 5.0311 oz. AGW, 60 mm. **Ruler:** Elizabeth II **Obv:** Crowned bust of George V **Rev:** Arms of Canada, dual dates and denomination below **Edge:** Serially numbered

| Date | Mintage | VF20 | XF40 | MS60 | MS63 | MS65 |
|---|---|---|---|---|---|---|
| 1912-2012 | 200 | PF65 9,150 | | | | |

**KM# 1431 500 DOLLARS**
156.05 g., 0.999 Gold 5.0121 oz. AGW, 60 mm. **Ruler:** Elizabeth II **Subject:** War of 1812 - Naval Battle **Rev:** HMS Shannon and Chesapeake

| Date | Mintage | VF20 | XF40 | MS60 | MS63 | MS65 |
|---|---|---|---|---|---|---|
| 2013 | Est. 200 | PF65 12,000 | | | | |

**KM# 1495 500 DOLLARS**
156.00 g., 0.9999 Gold 5.015 oz. AGW, 60.15 mm. **Ruler:** Elizabeth II **Subject:** Aboriginal art **Rev:** Artic animals, aboriginal in canoe

| Date | Mintage | VF20 | XF40 | MS60 | MS63 | MS65 |
|---|---|---|---|---|---|---|
| 2013 | 1,000 | **PF65** 12,000 | | | | |

**KM# 1538 500 DOLLARS**
5000.00 g., 0.999 Silver 160.5929 oz. ASW, 180 mm. **Ruler:** Elizabeth II **Rev:** Tsatsisnukomi

| Date | Mintage | VF20 | XF40 | MS60 | MS63 | MS65 |
|---|---|---|---|---|---|---|
| 2013 | 100 | **PF65** 10,500 | | | | |

**KM# 1707 500 DOLLARS**
500.00 g., 0.999 Gold 16.0593 oz. AGW, 85.35 mm. **Ruler:** Elizabeth II **Obv:** Bust right **Rev:** Howling Wolf

| Date | Mintage | VF20 | XF40 | MS60 | MS63 | MS65 |
|---|---|---|---|---|---|---|
| 2014 | 25 | **PF65** 32,000 | | | | |

**KM# 1733 500 DOLLARS**
156.05 g., 0.999 Gold 5.0121 oz. AGW, 60 mm. **Ruler:** Elizabeth II **Obv:** Bust right **Rev:** Legend of the Spirit Bear

| Date | Mintage | VF20 | XF40 | MS60 | MS63 | MS65 |
|---|---|---|---|---|---|---|
| 2014 | 50 | **PF65** 12,000 | | | | |

**KM# 1766 500 DOLLARS**
5000.00 g., 0.999 Silver 160.5929 oz. ASW, 180 mm. **Ruler:** Elizabeth II **Obv:** Bust right **Rev:** Four Aboriginies, Elk, Bear, Bison, Eagle and Wolf

| Date | Mintage | VF20 | XF40 | MS60 | MS63 | MS65 |
|---|---|---|---|---|---|---|
| 2014 | 150 | **PF65** 10,500 | | | | |

**KM# 1721 1000 DOLLARS**
311.50 g., 0.9999 Gold 10.0139 oz. AGW, 76.1 mm. **Ruler:** Elizabeth II **Obv:** Bust right **Rev:** WWI troops on ship's stern with last sight of land in distance

| Date | Mintage | VF20 | XF40 | MS60 | MS63 | MS65 |
|---|---|---|---|---|---|---|
| 2014 | 40 | **PF65** 21,000 | | | | |

**KM# 681 2500 DOLLARS**
1000.00 g., 0.9999 Gold 32.1475 oz. AGW, 101.6 mm. **Ruler:** Elizabeth II **Subject:** Kilo **Rev:** Common Characters, Early Canada

| Date | Mintage | VF20 | XF40 | MS60 | MS63 | MS65 |
|---|---|---|---|---|---|---|
| 2007 | 20 | — | — | — | 57,000 | — |

**KM# 1288 2500 DOLLARS**
1000.00 g., 0.999 Gold 32.1186 oz. AGW, 101 mm. **Ruler:** Elizabeth II **Subject:** Old town view

| Date | Mintage | VF20 | XF40 | MS60 | MS63 | MS65 |
|---|---|---|---|---|---|---|
| 2008 | — | **PF65** 57,000 | | | | |

**KM# 902 2500 DOLLARS**
1000.00 g., 0.999 Silver 32.1186 oz. ASW, 101.6 mm. **Ruler:** Elizabeth II **Series:** History and Culture Collection **Subject:** Modern Canada **Obv:** Bust right **Obv. Legend:** Vancouver 2010, 2500 Dollars, Elizabeth II **Rev:** Canadian landscape with modern elements

| Date | Mintage | VF20 | XF40 | MS60 | MS63 | MS65 |
|---|---|---|---|---|---|---|
| 2009 | 2,500 | **PF65** 1,250 | | | | |

### KM# 902a 2500 DOLLARS

1000.00 g., 0.999 Gold 32.1186 oz. AGW, 101.6 mm. **Ruler:** Elizabeth II **Series:** History and Culture Collection **Subject:** Modern Canada **Obv:** Bust right **Obv. Legend:** Vancouver 2010, 2500 Dollars, Elizabeth II **Rev:** Canadian landscape with modern elements

| Date | Mintage | VF20 | XF40 | MS60 | MS63 | MS65 |
|---|---|---|---|---|---|---|
| 2009 | 50 | PF65 57,000 | | | | |

### KM# 912 2500 DOLLARS

1000.00 g., 0.9999 Gold 32.1475 oz. AGW, 101 mm. **Ruler:** Elizabeth II **Obv:** Bust right **Rev:** Mask with fish - Surviving the flood

| Date | Mintage | VF20 | XF40 | MS60 | MS63 | MS65 |
|---|---|---|---|---|---|---|
| 2009 | 40 | PF65 58,000 | | | | |

### KM# 984 2500 DOLLARS

1000.00 g., 0.999 Gold 32.1186 oz. AGW, 101 mm. **Ruler:** Elizabeth II

| Date | Mintage | VF20 | XF40 | MS60 | MS63 | MS65 |
|---|---|---|---|---|---|---|
| 2010 | 20 | PF65 60,000 | | | | |

### KM# 1045 2500 DOLLARS

1000.00 g., 0.9999 Gold 32.1475 oz. AGW, 101 mm. **Ruler:** Elizabeth II **Subject:** Baniff, 125th Anniversary **Rev:** Highlights of Baniff

| Date | Mintage | VF20 | XF40 | MS60 | MS63 | MS65 |
|---|---|---|---|---|---|---|
| 2010 | — | PF65 60,000 | | | | |

### KM# 1286 2500 DOLLARS

1000.00 g., 0.999 Gold 32.1186 oz. AGW, 101 mm. **Ruler:** Elizabeth II **Subject:** Olympic views

| Date | Mintage | VF20 | XF40 | MS60 | MS63 | MS65 |
|---|---|---|---|---|---|---|
| 2010 | — | PF65 60,000 | | | | |

### KM# 1197 2500 DOLLARS

1000.00 g., 0.9999 Gold 32.1475 oz. AGW, 101 mm. **Ruler:** Elizabeth II **Obv:** Bust right **Rev:** Early lacrosse game

| Date | Mintage | VF20 | XF40 | MS60 | MS63 | MS65 |
|---|---|---|---|---|---|---|
| 2011 | 35 | PF65 60,000 | | | | |

### KM# 1276 2500 DOLLARS

1000.00 g., 0.999 Gold 32.1186 oz. AGW, 101 mm. **Ruler:** Elizabeth II **Subject:** Bateman Moose

| Date | Mintage | VF20 | XF40 | MS60 | MS63 | MS65 |
|---|---|---|---|---|---|---|
| 2012 | — | PF65 58,000 | | | | |

### KM# 1339 2500 DOLLARS

1000.00 g., 0.9999 Gold 32.1475 oz. AGW, 101 mm. **Ruler:** Elizabeth II **Subject:** War of 1812, Battle of Queenston Heights **Rev:** Battle scene

| Date | Mintage | VF20 | XF40 | MS60 | MS63 | MS65 |
|---|---|---|---|---|---|---|
| 2012 | 20 | PF65 69,000 | | | | |

**KM# 1364 2500 DOLLARS**
1000.00 g., 0.9999 Gold 32.1475 oz. AGW, 101.6 mm. **Ruler:** Elizabeth II **Subject:** Year of the Snake **Rev:** Snake under maple leaves

| Date | Mintage | VF20 | XF40 | MS60 | MS63 | MS65 |
|---|---|---|---|---|---|---|
| 2013 | Est. 25 | PF65 69,000 | | | | |

**KM# 1372 2500 DOLLARS**
1000.00 g., 0.999 Gold 32.1186 oz. AGW, 101.6 mm. **Ruler:** Elizabeth II **Subject:** Arctic Coastline

| Date | Mintage | VF20 | XF40 | MS60 | MS63 | MS65 |
|---|---|---|---|---|---|---|
| 2013 | Est. 20 | PF65 69,000 | | | | |

**KM# 1501 2500 DOLLARS**
1000.00 g., 0.9999 Gold 32.1475 oz. AGW, 101.6 mm. **Ruler:** Elizabeth II **Rev:** Two caribou advancing left

| Date | Mintage | VF20 | XF40 | MS60 | MS63 | MS65 |
|---|---|---|---|---|---|---|
| 2013 | 20 | PF65 69,000 | | | | |

**KM# 1370 2500 DOLLARS**
1000.00 g., 0.999 Gold 32.1186 oz. AGW, 102 mm. **Ruler:** Elizabeth II **Series:** End of 7 Years War - 250th Anniversary **Rev:** Map of North America and Arms of France and Great Britain.

| Date | Mintage | VF20 | XF40 | MS60 | MS63 | MS65 |
|---|---|---|---|---|---|---|
| 2013 | Est. 20 | PF65 69,000 | | | | |

**KM# 1478 2500 DOLLARS**
1000.00 g., 0.9999 Gold 32.1475 oz. AGW, 101 mm. **Ruler:** Elizabeth II **Subject:** Battle of Chateauguay and Crysler's Farm

| Date | Mintage | VF20 | XF40 | MS60 | MS63 | MS65 |
|---|---|---|---|---|---|---|
| 2013 | 20 | PF65 69,000 | | | | |

**KM# 1519 2500 DOLLARS**
1000.00 g., 0.9999 Gold 32.1475 oz. AGW, 101.6 mm. **Ruler:** Elizabeth II **Subject:** Year of the Horse **Obv:** Bust right **Rev:** Horse rearing up left

| Date | Mintage | VF20 | XF40 | MS60 | MS63 | MS65 |
|---|---|---|---|---|---|---|
| 2014 | 18 | PF65 69,000 | | | | |

**KM# 1606 2500 DOLLARS**
1000.00 g., 0.9999 Gold 32.1475 oz. AGW, 101 mm. **Ruler:** Elizabeth II **Obv:** Bust right **Rev:** Snowy owl, colored eyes

| Date | Mintage | VF20 | XF40 | MS60 | MS63 | MS65 |
|---|---|---|---|---|---|---|
| 2014 | — | PF65 60,000 | | | | |

**KM# 1708 2500 DOLLARS**
1000.00 g., 0.999 Gold 32.1186 oz. AGW, 101.6 mm. **Ruler:** Elizabeth II **Obv:** Bust right **Rev:** War of 1812 - Battle of Lundy's Lane

| Date | Mintage | VF20 | XF40 | MS60 | MS63 | MS65 |
|---|---|---|---|---|---|---|
| 2014 | 10 | PF65 69,000 | | | | |

## SILVER BULLION COINAGE

**KM# 617 DOLLAR**
1.56 g., 0.9999 Silver 0.050 oz. ASW, 16 mm. **Ruler:** Elizabeth II **Obv:** Crowned head right **Rev:** Holographic Maple leaf **Edge:** Reeded

| Date | Mintage | VF20 | XF40 | MS60 | MS63 | MS65 |
|---|---|---|---|---|---|---|
| 2003 | — | PF65 4.50 | | | | |

**KM# 621 DOLLAR**
1.56 g., 0.9999 Silver 0.050 oz. ASW, 17 mm. **Ruler:** Elizabeth II **Obv:** Crowned head right **Rev:** Maple leaf **Edge:** Reeded

| Date | Mintage | VF20 | XF40 | MS60 | MS63 | MS65 |
|---|---|---|---|---|---|---|
| 2004 Mint logo privy mark | 13,859 | PF63 3.50 | PF65 4.50 | | | |

**KM# 718 DOLLAR**
15.55 g., 0.999 Silver 0.4994 oz. ASW, 32 mm. **Ruler:** Elizabeth II **Obv:** Bust right **Rev:** Grey Wolf standing with moon in background **Edge:** Reeded

| Date | Mintage | VF20 | XF40 | MS60 | MS63 | MS65 |
|---|---|---|---|---|---|---|
| 2005 | 106,800 | — | — | — | 40.00 | — |
| 2006 | — | — | — | — | 40.00 | — |
| 2007 | — | — | — | — | 40.00 | — |

**KM# 1489 DOLLAR**
1.000 Silver **Ruler:** Elizabeth II **Rev:** Maple leaf tilted left **Note:** Thick planchet.

| Date | Mintage | VF20 | XF40 | MS60 | MS63 | MS65 |
|---|---|---|---|---|---|---|
| 2010 | — | PF63 65.00 | PF65 75.00 | | | |

**KM# 1406 DOLLAR**
1.55 g., 0.9999 Silver 0.0498 oz. ASW, 17 mm. **Ruler:** Elizabeth II **Rev:** Three Maple Leaves

| Date | Mintage | VF20 | XF40 | MS60 | MS63 | MS65 |
|---|---|---|---|---|---|---|
| 2013 | — | PF63 18.00 | PF65 20.00 | | | |

**KM# 1593 DOLLAR**
1.56 g., 0.9999 Silver 0.050 oz. ASW Partially gilt, 16 mm. **Ruler:** Elizabeth II **Obv:** Bust right **Rev:** Two maple leaves, one gilt

| Date | Mintage | VF20 | XF40 | MS60 | MS63 | MS65 |
|---|---|---|---|---|---|---|
| 2014 | — | — | — | — | 5.00 | — |

**KM# 1805 DOLLAR**
1.63 g., 0.9999 Silver 0.0524 oz. ASW, 16 mm. **Ruler:** Elizabeth II **Obv:** Bust right **Rev:** Maple Leaf

| Date | Mintage | VF20 | XF40 | MS60 | MS63 | MS65 |
|---|---|---|---|---|---|---|
| 2015 | 9,999 | PF65 15.00 | | | | |

**KM# 618 2 DOLLARS**
3.11 g., 0.9999 Silver 0.100 oz. ASW, 20.1 mm. **Ruler:** Elizabeth II **Obv:** Crowned head right **Rev:** Holographic Maple leaf **Edge:** Reeded

| Date | Mintage | VF20 | XF40 | MS60 | MS63 | MS65 |
|---|---|---|---|---|---|---|
| 2003 | — | PF65 7.50 | | | | |

**KM# 622 2 DOLLARS**
3.11 g., 0.9999 Silver 0.100 oz. ASW, 21 mm. **Ruler:** Elizabeth II **Obv:** Crowned head right **Rev:** Maple leaf **Edge:** Reeded

| Date | Mintage | VF20 | XF40 | MS60 | MS63 | MS65 |
|---|---|---|---|---|---|---|
| 2004 Mint logo privy mark | 13,859 | PF63 6.50 | PF65 7.50 | | | |

**KM# 571 2 DOLLARS**
3.11 g., 0.9999 Silver 0.100 oz. ASW, 21 mm. **Ruler:** Elizabeth II **Obv:** Head right **Rev:** Lynx

| Date | Mintage | VF20 | XF40 | MS60 | MS63 | MS65 |
|---|---|---|---|---|---|---|
| 2005 | — | PF63 6.50 | PF65 7.50 | | | |

**KM# 1407 2 DOLLARS**
3.11 g., 0.999 Silver 0.0999 oz. ASW **Ruler:** Elizabeth II **Rev:** Three Maple Leaves

| Date | Mintage | VF20 | XF40 | MS60 | MS63 | MS65 |
|---|---|---|---|---|---|---|
| 2013 | — | PF63 25.00 | PF65 30.00 | | | |

**KM# 1594 2 DOLLARS**
3.11 g., 0.9999 Silver 0.100 oz. ASW partially gilt, 20.1 mm. **Ruler:** Elizabeth II **Obv:** Bust right **Rev:** Two maple leaves, one gilt

| Date | Mintage | VF20 | XF40 | MS60 | MS63 | MS65 |
|---|---|---|---|---|---|---|
| 2014 | — | — | — | — | 10.00 | — |

**KM# 1806 2 DOLLARS**
3.23 g., 0.9999 Silver 0.1038 oz. ASW, 20 mm. **Ruler:** Elizabeth II **Obv:** Bust right **Rev:** Maple Leaf

| Date | Mintage | VF20 | XF40 | MS60 | MS63 | MS65 |
|---|---|---|---|---|---|---|
| 2015 | 9,999 | PF65 30.00 | | | | |

**KM# 619 3 DOLLARS**
7.78 g., 0.9999 Silver 0.250 oz. ASW, 26.9 mm. **Ruler:** Elizabeth II **Obv:** Crowned head right **Rev:** Holographic Maple leaf **Edge:** Reeded

| Date | Mintage | VF20 | XF40 | MS60 | MS63 | MS65 |
|---|---|---|---|---|---|---|
| 2003 | — | PF65 15.00 | | | | |

**KM# 623 3 DOLLARS**
7.78 g., 0.9999 Silver 0.250 oz. ASW, 27 mm. **Ruler:** Elizabeth II **Obv:** Crowned head right **Rev:** Maple leaf **Edge:** Reeded

| Date | Mintage | VF20 | XF40 | MS60 | MS63 | MS65 |
|---|---|---|---|---|---|---|
| 2004 Mint logo privy mark | 13,859 | PF63 11.00 | PF65 12.50 | | | |

**KM# 1415 3 DOLLARS**
7.77 g., 0.999 Silver 0.2496 oz. ASW, 27 mm. **Ruler:** Elizabeth II **Rev:** Fox

| Date | Mintage | VF20 | XF40 | MS60 | MS63 | MS65 |
|---|---|---|---|---|---|---|
| 2004 | — | PF63 30.00 | PF65 35.00 | | | |

**KM# 572 3 DOLLARS**
7.78 g., 0.9999 Silver 0.250 oz. ASW, 27 mm. **Ruler:** Elizabeth II **Obv:** Head right **Rev:** Lynx

| Date | Mintage | VF20 | XF40 | MS60 | MS63 | MS65 |
|---|---|---|---|---|---|---|
| 2005 | — | PF63 11.00 | PF65 12.50 | | | |

**KM# 1408 3 DOLLARS**
7.78 g., 0.9999 Silver 0.250 oz. ASW, 27 mm. **Ruler:** Elizabeth II **Rev:** Three Maple Leaves

| Date | Mintage | VF20 | XF40 | MS60 | MS63 | MS65 |
|---|---|---|---|---|---|---|
| 2012 | — | PF63 35.00 | PF65 40.00 | | | |

**KM# 1595 3 DOLLARS**
7.77 g., 0.9999 Silver 0.2498 oz. ASW partially gilt, 27 mm. **Ruler:** Elizabeth II **Obv:** Bust right **Rev:** Two maple leaves, one gilt

| Date | Mintage | VF20 | XF40 | MS60 | MS63 | MS65 |
|---|---|---|---|---|---|---|
| 2014 | — | — | — | — | 15.00 | — |

**KM# 1807 3 DOLLARS**
7.96 g., 0.9999 Silver 0.2559 oz. ASW **Ruler:** Elizabeth II **Obv:** Bust right **Rev:** Maple Leaf

| Date | Mintage | VF20 | XF40 | MS60 | MS63 | MS65 |
|---|---|---|---|---|---|---|
| 2015 | 9,999 | PF65 75.00 | | | | |

**KM# 620 4 DOLLARS**
15.55 g., 0.9999 Silver 0.4999 oz. ASW, 33.9 mm. **Ruler:** Elizabeth II **Obv:** Crowned head right **Rev:** Holographic Maple leaf **Edge:** Reeded

| Date | Mintage | VF20 | XF40 | MS60 | MS63 | MS65 |
|---|---|---|---|---|---|---|
| 2003 | — | PF63 22.00 | PF65 25.00 | | | |

**KM# 624 4 DOLLARS**
15.55 g., 0.9999 Silver 0.4999 oz. ASW, 34 mm. **Ruler:** Elizabeth II **Obv:** Crowned head right **Rev:** Maple leaf **Edge:** Reeded

| Date | Mintage | VF20 | XF40 | MS60 | MS63 | MS65 |
|---|---|---|---|---|---|---|
| 2004 Mint logo privy mark Reverse Proof | 13,859 | PF65 22.50 | | | | |

**KM# 573 4 DOLLARS**
15.55 g., 0.9999 Silver 0.4999 oz. ASW, 34 mm. **Ruler:** Elizabeth II **Obv:** Head right **Rev:** Lynx

| Date | Mintage | VF20 | XF40 | MS60 | MS63 | MS65 |
|---|---|---|---|---|---|---|
| 2005 | — | PF63 20.00 | PF65 22.50 | | | |

**KM# 1409 4 DOLLARS**
15.55 g., 0.9999 Silver 0.4999 oz. ASW, 33.9 mm. **Ruler:** Elizabeth II **Rev:** Three maple leaves

| Date | Mintage | VF20 | XF40 | MS60 | MS63 | MS65 |
|---|---|---|---|---|---|---|
| 2013 | — | PF63 35.00 | PF65 40.00 | | | |

**KM# 1596 4 DOLLARS**
15.55 g., 0.9999 Silver 0.4999 oz. ASW partially gilt, 34 mm. **Ruler:** Elizabeth II **Obv:** Bust right **Rev:** Two maple leaves, one gilt

| Date | Mintage | VF20 | XF40 | MS60 | MS63 | MS65 |
|---|---|---|---|---|---|---|
| 2014 | — | — | — | — | 22.50 | — |

**KM# 1808 4 DOLLARS**
15.87 g., 0.9999 Silver 0.5102 oz. ASW, 34 mm. **Ruler:** Elizabeth II **Obv:** Bust right **Rev:** Maple Leaf

| Date | Mintage | VF20 | XF40 | MS60 | MS63 | MS65 |
|---|---|---|---|---|---|---|
| 2015 | 9,999 | PF65 100 | | | | |

**KM# 187 5 DOLLARS**
31.10 g., 0.9999 Silver 0.9998 oz. ASW **Ruler:** Elizabeth II **Obv:** Crowned head right, date and denomination below **Rev:** Maple leaf flanked by 9999

| Date | Mintage | VF20 | XF40 | MS60 | MS63 | MS65 |
|---|---|---|---|---|---|---|
| 2001 | 398,563 | — | — | — | 35.00 | — |
| 2001 Reverse proof, Snake privy mark | 25,000 | PF63 35.00 | PF65 45.00 | | | |
| 2002 | 576,196 | — | — | — | 35.00 | — |
| 2002 Reverse proof, Horse privy mark | 25,000 | PF63 35.00 | PF65 45.00 | | | |
| 2003 | — | — | — | — | 35.00 | — |
| 2003 Reverse proof, sheep privy mark | 25,000 | PF63 35.00 | PF65 45.00 | | | |

**KM# 436 5 DOLLARS**
31.10 g., 0.9999 Silver 0.9999 oz. ASW, 38 mm. **Ruler:** Elizabeth II **Obv:** Crowned head right, date and denomination below **Rev:** Three maple leaves in autumn colors, 9999 flanks **Edge:** Reeded

| Date | Mintage | VF20 | XF40 | MS60 | MS63 | MS65 |
|---|---|---|---|---|---|---|
| 2001 | 49,709 | PF63 30.00 | PF65 40.00 | | | |

**KM# 437 5 DOLLARS**
31.10 g., 0.9999 Silver 0.9999 oz. ASW, 38 mm. **Ruler:** Elizabeth II **Obv:** Crowned head right, date and denomination below **Rev:** Radiant maple leaf hologram **Edge:** Reeded

| Date | Mintage | VF20 | XF40 | MS60 | MS63 | MS65 |
|---|---|---|---|---|---|---|
| 2001 Good fortune privy mark | 29,906 | — | — | — | 75.00 | — |

### KM# 505 5 DOLLARS

31.10 g., 0.9999 Silver 0.9999 oz. ASW, 38 mm. **Ruler:** Elizabeth II **Obv:** Crowned head right, date and denomination below **Rev:** Two maple leaves in spring color (green) **Edge:** Reeded

| Date | Mintage | VF20 | XF40 | MS60 | MS63 | MS65 |
|---|---|---|---|---|---|---|
| 2002 | 29,509 | — | — | — | 37.50 | — |

### KM# 521 5 DOLLARS

31.10 g., 0.9999 Silver 0.9999 oz. ASW **Ruler:** Elizabeth II **Obv:** Head right **Rev:** Maple leaf, summer colors

| Date | Mintage | VF20 | XF40 | MS60 | MS63 | MS65 |
|---|---|---|---|---|---|---|
| 2003 | 29,416 | — | — | — | 37.50 | — |

### KM# 508 5 DOLLARS

31.10 g., 0.9999 Silver 0.9999 oz. ASW, 38 mm. **Ruler:** Elizabeth II **Obv:** Crowned head right, date and denomination below **Rev:** Holographic Maple leaf flanked by 9999 **Edge:** Reeded

| Date | Mintage | VF20 | XF40 | MS60 | MS63 | MS65 |
|---|---|---|---|---|---|---|
| 2003 | — | PF63 35.00 | PF65 37.50 | | | |

### KM# 522 5 DOLLARS

31.11 g., 0.9999 Silver 0.9999 oz. ASW **Ruler:** Elizabeth II **Obv:** Head right **Rev:** Maple leaf, winter color

| Date | Mintage | VF20 | XF40 | MS60 | MS63 | MS65 |
|---|---|---|---|---|---|---|
| 2004 | 26,763 | — | — | — | 35.00 | — |

### KM# 607 5 DOLLARS

31.12 g., 0.9999 Silver 1.0004 oz. ASW **Ruler:** Elizabeth II **Obv:** Head right **Rev:** Maple leaf, winter colors

| Date | Mintage | VF20 | XF40 | MS60 | MS63 | MS65 |
|---|---|---|---|---|---|---|
| 2004 | — | — | — | — | 37.50 | — |

### KM# 625 5 DOLLARS

31.10 g., 0.9999 Silver 0.9999 oz. ASW, 38 mm. **Ruler:** Elizabeth II **Obv:** Bust right **Rev:** Maple leaf **Edge:** Reeded

| Date | Mintage | VF20 | XF40 | MS60 | MS63 | MS65 |
|---|---|---|---|---|---|---|
| 2004 Mint logo privy mark Specimen | 13,859 | PF65 37.50 | | | | |
| 2004 Monkey privy mark Specimen | 25,000 | PF65 37.50 | | | | |
| 2004 D-Day privy mark Specimen | 11,698 | PF65 37.50 | | | | |
| 2004 Desjardins privy mark | 15,000 | — | — | — | 37.50 | — |
| 2004 Capricorn privy Mark Reverse proof | 5,000 | PF65 37.50 | | | | |
| 2004 Aquarius privy mark Reverse proof | 5,000 | PF65 37.50 | | | | |
| 2004 Pisces privy mark Reverse proof | 5,000 | PF65 37.50 | | | | |
| 2004 Aries privy mark Reverse proof | 5,000 | PF65 37.50 | | | | |
| 2004 Taurus privy mark Reverse proof | 5,000 | PF65 37.50 | | | | |
| 2004 Gemini privy mark Reverse proof | 5,000 | PF65 37.50 | | | | |
| 2004 Cancer privy mark Reverse proof | 5,000 | PF65 37.50 | | | | |
| 2004 Leo privy mark Reverse proof | 5,000 | PF65 37.50 | | | | |
| 2004 Virgo privy mark Reverse proof | 5,000 | PF65 37.50 | | | | |
| 2004 Libra privy mark Reverse proof | 5,000 | PF65 37.50 | | | | |
| 2004 Scorpio privy mark Reverse proof | 5,000 | PF65 37.50 | | | | |
| 2004 Sagittarius privy mark Reverse proof | 5,000 | PF65 50.00 | | | | |
| 2005 | — | — | — | — | 35.00 | — |
| 2005 Tulip privy mark Reverse proof | 3,500 | PF65 50.00 | | | | |
| 2005 Tank privy mark Reverse proof | 7,000 | PF65 60.00 | | | | |
| 2005 USS Missouri privy mark Reverse proof | 7,000 | PF65 60.00 | | | | |
| 2005 Rooster privy mark Reverse proof | 15,000 | PF65 50.00 | | | | |
| 2006 | — | — | — | — | 35.00 | — |
| 2006 Dog privy mark Reverse proof | — | PF65 50.00 | | | | |
| 2007 | — | — | — | — | 35.00 | — |
| 2007 F12 privy mark Reverse proof | — | PF65 130 | | | | |
| 2007 Pig privy mark Reverse proof | — | PF65 50.00 | | | | |
| 2008 | — | — | — | — | 35.00 | — |
| 2008 F12 privy mark Reverse proof | — | PF65 130 | | | | |
| 2008 Rat privy mark Reverse proof | — | PF65 50.00 | | | | |
| 2009 | — | — | — | — | 35.00 | — |
| 2009 Brandenberg Gate privy mark Reverse proof | — | PF65 50.00 | | | | |
| 2009 Tower Bridge privy mark Reverse proof | — | PF65 50.00 | | | | |
| 2009 Ox Privy mark Reverse proof | — | PF65 50.00 | | | | |
| 2010 | — | — | — | — | 35.00 | — |
| 2010 Fabulous 15 privy mark Reverse proof | — | PF65 50.00 | | | | |
| 2011 | — | — | — | — | 35.00 | — |
| 2012 | — | — | — | — | 35.00 | — |
| 2012 Dragon privy mark Reverse proof | — | PF65 50.00 | | | | |
| 2012 Titanic privy mark Reverse proof | — | PF65 50.00 | | | | |
| 2012 Pisa privy mark | — | — | — | — | 35.00 | — |
| 2012 Fabulous 15 privy mark Reverse proof | — | PF65 75.00 | | | | |
| 2013 | — | — | — | — | 35.00 | — |
| 2014 | — | — | — | — | 35.00 | — |
| 2014 World Money Fair Berlin privy mark Reverse proof | — | PF65 50.00 | | | | |

### KM# 550 5 DOLLARS

31.10 g., 0.9999 Silver 0.9999 oz. ASW, 38 mm. **Ruler:** Elizabeth II **Obv:** Head right **Rev:** Big Leaf Maple and seed pod, color

| Date | Mintage | VF20 | XF40 | MS60 | MS63 | MS65 |
|---|---|---|---|---|---|---|
| 2005 | 21,233 | — | — | — | 35.00 | — |

### KM# 574 5 DOLLARS

31.10 g., 0.9999 Silver 0.9999 oz. ASW, 38 mm. **Ruler:** Elizabeth II **Obv:** Head right **Rev:** Lynx

| Date | Mintage | VF20 | XF40 | MS60 | MS63 | MS65 |
|---|---|---|---|---|---|---|
| 2005 | — | PF63 35.00 | PF65 37.50 | | | |

### KM# 924 5 DOLLARS

31.11 g., 0.9999 Silver 0.9999 oz. ASW **Ruler:** Elizabeth II **Rev:** Maple Leaf, laser engraved

| Date | Mintage | VF20 | XF40 | MS60 | MS63 | MS65 |
|---|---|---|---|---|---|---|
| 2005 | 25,000 | PF63 50.00 | PF65 60.00 | | | |

### KM# 660 5 DOLLARS

31.10 g., 0.999 Silver 0.999 oz. ASW **Ruler:** Elizabeth II **Obv:** Bust right **Rev:** Silver maple, colorized

| Date | Mintage | VF20 | XF40 | MS60 | MS63 | MS65 |
|---|---|---|---|---|---|---|
| 2006 | 14,157 | — | — | — | 37.50 | — |

**KM# 625a 5 DOLLARS**

31.11 g., 0.9999 Silver 0.9999 oz. ASW, 38 mm. **Ruler:** Elizabeth II **Rev:** Maple leaf, gilt

| Date | Mintage | VF20 | XF40 | MS60 | MS63 | MS65 |
|---|---|---|---|---|---|---|
| 2007 | — | — | — | — | 75.00 | — |
| 2008 | — | — | — | — | 75.00 | — |
| 2009 | — | — | — | — | 75.00 | — |
| 2009 Tower Bridge Privy Mark | — | — | — | — | 75.00 | — |
| 2010 | — | — | — | — | 75.00 | — |

**KM# 729 5 DOLLARS**

31.11 g., 0.999 Silver 0.999 oz. ASW, 38 mm. **Ruler:** Elizabeth II **Obv:** Bust right **Rev:** Maple leaf orange multicolor

| Date | Mintage | VF20 | XF40 | MS60 | MS63 | MS65 |
|---|---|---|---|---|---|---|
| 2007 | — | **PF63** 40.00 | **PF65** 45.00 | | | |

**KM# 925 5 DOLLARS**

31.11 g., 0.999 Silver 0.999 oz. ASW **Ruler:** Elizabeth II **Obv:** Bust right **Rev:** Sugar maple, colorized

| Date | Mintage | VF20 | XF40 | MS60 | MS63 | MS65 |
|---|---|---|---|---|---|---|
| 2007 | 11,495 | — | — | — | 37.50 | — |

**KM# 928 5 DOLLARS**

31.39 g., 0.999 Silver 1.0082 oz. ASW, 38 mm. **Ruler:** Elizabeth II **Rev:** Orange sugar maple leaf

| Date | Mintage | VF20 | XF40 | MS60 | MS63 | MS65 |
|---|---|---|---|---|---|---|
| 2007 Specimen | 20,000 | — | — | — | 100 | — |

**KM# 798 5 DOLLARS**

31.11 g., 0.999 Silver 0.999 oz. ASW, 38 mm. **Ruler:** Elizabeth II **Subject:** Maple Leaf 20th Anniversary **Rev:** Maple Leaf, selective gold plating

| Date | Mintage | VF20 | XF40 | MS60 | MS63 | MS65 |
|---|---|---|---|---|---|---|
| 2008 | 10,000 | **PF63** 65.00 | **PF65** 75.00 | | | |

**KM# 799 5 DOLLARS**

31.11 g., 0.999 Silver 0.999 oz. ASW, 38 mm. **Ruler:** Elizabeth II **Subject:** Breast Cancer Awareness **Rev:** Multicolor, green maple leaf and pink ribbon

| Date | Mintage | VF20 | XF40 | MS60 | MS63 | MS65 |
|---|---|---|---|---|---|---|
| 2008 | 11,048 | — | — | — | 85.00 | — |

**KM# 800 5 DOLLARS**

31.11 g., 0.999 Silver 0.999 oz. ASW, 38 mm. **Ruler:** Elizabeth II **Subject:** Vancouver Olympics **Obv:** Bust right **Rev:** Maple leaf, Olympic logo at left, turtle

| Date | Mintage | VF20 | XF40 | MS60 | MS63 | MS65 |
|---|---|---|---|---|---|---|
| 2008 | — | — | — | — | 37.50 | — |
| 2009 | — | — | — | — | 37.50 | — |
| 2010 | — | — | — | — | 37.50 | — |

**KM# 800a 5 DOLLARS**

31.11 g., 0.9999 Silver 0.9999 oz. ASW partially gilt, 38 mm. **Ruler:** Elizabeth II **Rev:** Maple leaf gilt, olympic logo at left

| Date | Mintage | VF20 | XF40 | MS60 | MS63 | MS65 |
|---|---|---|---|---|---|---|
| 2008 | — | — | — | — | 50.00 | — |

**KM# 1056 5 DOLLARS**

31.11 g., 0.9999 Silver 0.9999 oz. ASW, 38 mm. **Ruler:** Elizabeth II **Rev:** Maple leaf in brown color, card diamond

| Date | Mintage | VF20 | XF40 | MS60 | MS63 | MS65 |
|---|---|---|---|---|---|---|
| 2008 | — | — | — | — | 50.00 | — |

**KM# 1057 5 DOLLARS**

31.11 g., 0.9999 Silver 0.9999 oz. ASW, 38 mm. **Ruler:** Elizabeth II **Rev:** Maple Leaf in green color, card heart

| Date | Mintage | VF20 | XF40 | MS60 | MS63 | MS65 |
|---|---|---|---|---|---|---|
| 2008 | — | — | — | — | 50.00 | — |

**KM# 1058 5 DOLLARS**

31.11 g., 0.9999 Silver 0.9999 oz. ASW, 38 mm. **Ruler:** Elizabeth II **Rev:** Maple leaf in green color, card club

| Date | Mintage | VF20 | XF40 | MS60 | MS63 | MS65 |
|---|---|---|---|---|---|---|
| 2008 | — | — | — | — | 50.00 | — |

**KM# 1059 5 DOLLARS**

31.11 g., 0.9999 Silver 0.9999 oz. ASW, 38 mm. **Ruler:** Elizabeth II **Rev:** Maple Leaf in red color, card spade

| Date | Mintage | VF20 | XF40 | MS60 | MS63 | MS65 |
|---|---|---|---|---|---|---|
| 2008 | — | — | — | — | 50.00 | — |

**KM# 863 5 DOLLARS**

31.11 g., 0.9999 Silver 0.9999 oz. ASW, 38 mm. **Ruler:** Elizabeth II **Subject:** Vancouver Olympics **Rev:** Thunderbird Totem

| Date | Mintage | VF20 | XF40 | MS60 | MS63 | MS65 |
|---|---|---|---|---|---|---|
| 2009 | — | — | — | — | 50.00 | — |

**KM# 863a 5 DOLLARS**

31.11 g., 0.9999 Silver 0.9999 oz. ASW partially gilt, 38 mm. **Ruler:** Elizabeth II **Rev:** Thunderbird, gilt

| Date | Mintage | VF20 | XF40 | MS60 | MS63 | MS65 |
|---|---|---|---|---|---|---|
| 2009 | — | — | — | — | 60.00 | — |

**KM# 1061 5 DOLLARS**
31.11 g., 0.9999 Silver 0.9999 oz. ASW, 38 mm. **Ruler:** Elizabeth II **Rev:** Maple leaf in red color, support our troops yellow ribbon

| Date | Mintage | VF20 | XF40 | MS60 | MS63 | MS65 |
|---|---|---|---|---|---|---|
| 2009 | — | — | — | — | 70.00 | — |

**KM# 998 5 DOLLARS**
31.12 g., 0.999 Silver 0.9995 oz. ASW, 38 mm. **Ruler:** Elizabeth II **Rev:** Olympic Hockey

| Date | Mintage | VF20 | XF40 | MS60 | MS63 | MS65 |
|---|---|---|---|---|---|---|
| 2010 | — | PF63 38.00 | | PF65 42.00 | | |

**KM# 998a 5 DOLLARS**
31.11 g., 0.9999 Silver 0.9999 oz. ASW partially gilt, 38 mm. **Ruler:** Elizabeth II **Rev:** Hockey player, gilt maple leaves flanking

| Date | Mintage | VF20 | XF40 | MS60 | MS63 | MS65 |
|---|---|---|---|---|---|---|
| 2010 | — | — | — | — | 50.00 | — |

**KM# 1077 5 DOLLARS**
31.39 g., 0.999 Silver 1.0082 oz. ASW, 34 mm. **Ruler:** Elizabeth II **Rev:** Maple leaf on 45 degree angle left **Note:** Piedfort.

| Date | Mintage | VF20 | XF40 | MS60 | MS63 | MS65 |
|---|---|---|---|---|---|---|
| 2010 Reverse Proof | 9,000 | PF65 80.00 | | | | |

**KM# 1289 5 DOLLARS**
31.11 g., 0.9999 Silver 0.9999 oz. ASW, 38 mm. **Ruler:** Elizabeth II **Rev:** Maple leaf in green with crystal

| Date | Mintage | VF20 | XF40 | MS60 | MS63 | MS65 |
|---|---|---|---|---|---|---|
| 2010 | — | — | — | — | 65.00 | — |

**KM# 1290 5 DOLLARS**
31.11 g., 0.999 Silver 0.999 oz. ASW, 38 mm. **Ruler:** Elizabeth II **Rev:** Maple leaf in red with crystal

| Date | Mintage | VF20 | XF40 | MS60 | MS63 | MS65 |
|---|---|---|---|---|---|---|
| 2010 | — | — | — | — | 65.00 | — |

**KM# 1291 5 DOLLARS**
31.11 g., 0.9999 Silver 0.9999 oz. ASW, 38 mm. **Ruler:** Elizabeth II **Rev:** Maple leaf in dark green with crystal

| Date | Mintage | VF20 | XF40 | MS60 | MS63 | MS65 |
|---|---|---|---|---|---|---|
| 2010 | — | — | — | — | 65.00 | — |

**KM# 1292 5 DOLLARS**
31.11 g., 0.9999 Silver 0.9999 oz. ASW, 38 mm. **Ruler:** Elizabeth II **Rev:** Maple leaf in color with crystal

| Date | Mintage | VF20 | XF40 | MS60 | MS63 | MS65 |
|---|---|---|---|---|---|---|
| 2010 | — | — | — | — | 65.00 | — |

**KM# 1052 5 DOLLARS**
31.11 g., 0.9999 Silver 0.9999 oz. ASW, 38 mm. **Ruler:** Elizabeth II **Rev:** Wolf standing with moonlight in background

| Date | Mintage | VF20 | XF40 | MS60 | MS63 | MS65 |
|---|---|---|---|---|---|---|
| 2011 | 1,000,000 | — | — | — | 42.00 | — |

**KM# 1109 5 DOLLARS**
31.11 g., 0.999 Silver 0.999 oz. ASW, 38 mm. **Ruler:** Elizabeth II **Rev:** Grizzly Bear walking right

| Date | Mintage | VF20 | XF40 | MS60 | MS63 | MS65 |
|---|---|---|---|---|---|---|
| 2011 | 1,000,000 | — | — | — | 40.00 | — |

**KM# 1164 5 DOLLARS**
31.11 g., 0.999 Silver 0.999 oz. ASW, 38 mm. **Ruler:** Elizabeth II **Rev:** Cougar

| Date | Mintage | VF20 | XF40 | MS60 | MS63 | MS65 |
|---|---|---|---|---|---|---|
| 2012 | 1,000,000 | — | — | — | 40.00 | — |

**KM# 1241 5 DOLLARS**
31.14 g., 0.9999 Silver 1.0009 oz. ASW, 38 mm. **Ruler:** Elizabeth II **Obv:** Bust right **Rev:** Moose left **Edge:** Reeded

| Date | Mintage | VF20 | XF40 | MS60 | MS63 | MS65 |
|---|---|---|---|---|---|---|
| 2012 | 1,000,000 | — | — | — | 42.00 | — |

**KM# 1297 5 DOLLARS**
31.11 g., 0.999 Silver 0.999 oz. ASW, 38 mm. **Ruler:** Elizabeth II **Obv:** Bust right **Rev:** Antelope

| Date | Mintage | VF20 | XF40 | MS60 | MS63 | MS65 |
|---|---|---|---|---|---|---|
| 2013 | — | — | — | — | 42.00 | — |

**KM# 1382 5 DOLLARS**
31.11 g., 0.999 Silver 0.999 oz. ASW, 38 mm. **Ruler:** Elizabeth II **Subject:** Silver Maple Leaf - 25th Anniversary **Rev:** Maple leaf and gilt shadow of maple leaf

| Date | Mintage | VF20 | XF40 | MS60 | MS63 | MS65 |
|---|---|---|---|---|---|---|
| 2013 | Est. 10000 | **PF63** 100 | **PF65** 110 | | | |

**KM# 1410 5 DOLLARS**
31.11 g., 0.9999 Silver 0.9999 oz. ASW, 38 mm. **Ruler:** Elizabeth II **Rev:** Three maple leaves

| Date | Mintage | VF20 | XF40 | MS60 | MS63 | MS65 |
|---|---|---|---|---|---|---|
| 2013 | — | — | — | — | 45.00 | — |

**KM# 1434 5 DOLLARS**
31.11 g., 0.9999 Silver 0.9999 oz. ASW, 38 mm. **Ruler:** Elizabeth II **Rev:** Wood bison advancing left

| Date | Mintage | VF20 | XF40 | MS60 | MS63 | MS65 |
|---|---|---|---|---|---|---|
| 2013 | — | — | — | — | 40.00 | — |

**KM# 1525 5 DOLLARS**
31.39 g., 0.999 Silver 1.0082 oz. ASW, 34 mm. **Ruler:** Elizabeth II **Rev:** Maple leaves **Note:** Thick planchet piedfort

| Date | Mintage | VF20 | XF40 | MS60 | MS63 | MS65 |
|---|---|---|---|---|---|---|
| 2013 | 10,000 | **PF63** 45.00 | **PF65** 50.00 | | | |

**KM# 1542 5 DOLLARS**
31.39 g., 0.9999 Silver 1.0091 oz. ASW, 38 mm. **Ruler:** Elizabeth II **Rev:** Large 25 on maple leaf

| Date | Mintage | VF20 | XF40 | MS60 | MS63 | MS65 |
|---|---|---|---|---|---|---|
| 2013 | — | — | — | — | 75.00 | — |

**KM# 1597 5 DOLLARS**
31.10 g., 0.9999 Silver 0.9999 oz. ASW partially gilt, 38 mm. **Ruler:** Elizabeth II **Obv:** Bust right **Rev:** Two maple leaves, one gilt

| Date | Mintage | VF20 | XF40 | MS60 | MS63 | MS65 |
|---|---|---|---|---|---|---|
| 2014 | — | — | — | — | 40.00 | — |

**KM# 1601 5 DOLLARS**
31.11 g., 0.9999 Silver 0.9999 oz. ASW, 38 mm. **Ruler:** Elizabeth II **Obv:** Bust right, rays in field **Rev:** Maple leaf, rays in field

| Date | Mintage | VF20 | XF40 | MS60 | MS63 | MS65 |
|---|---|---|---|---|---|---|
| 2014 | — | — | — | — | 50.00 | — |

**KM# 1719 5 DOLLARS**
31.39 g., 0.999 Silver 1.0082 oz. ASW, 38 mm. **Ruler:** Elizabeth II **Obv:** Bust right **Rev:** Eagle in flight left with fish

| Date | Mintage | F12 | VF20 | XF40 | MS60 | MS63 |
|---|---|---|---|---|---|---|
| 2014 | 7,500 | — | — | — | — | 65.00 |

**KM# 1809 5 DOLLARS**
31.39 g., 0.9999 Silver 1.0091 oz. ASW, 38 mm. **Ruler:** Elizabeth II **Obv:** Bust right **Rev:** Maple leaf in red color

| Date | Mintage | VF20 | XF40 | MS60 | MS63 | MS65 |
|---|---|---|---|---|---|---|
| 2015 | 9,999 | **PF65** 125 | | | | |

**KM# 1158 10 DOLLARS**
31.11 g., 0.9999 Silver 0.9999 oz. ASW, 38 mm. **Ruler:** Elizabeth II **Obv:** Bust right **Rev:** Branch with three maple leaves

| Date | Mintage | VF20 | XF40 | MS60 | MS63 | MS65 |
|---|---|---|---|---|---|---|
| 2011 | — | **PF63** 45.00 | **PF65** 50.00 | | | |

**KM# 1268 10 DOLLARS**
31.11 g., 0.999 Silver 0.999 oz. ASW, 38 mm. **Ruler:** Elizabeth II **Subject:** Maple Leaf Forever

| Date | Mintage | VF20 | XF40 | MS60 | MS63 | MS65 |
|---|---|---|---|---|---|---|
| 2012 | — | **PF63** 40.00 | **PF65** 50.00 | | | |

**KM# 1473 10 DOLLARS**
15.87 g., 0.9999 Silver 0.5102 oz. ASW, 34 mm. **Ruler:** Elizabeth II **Rev:** Two maple leaves

| Date | Mintage | VF20 | XF40 | MS60 | MS63 | MS65 |
|---|---|---|---|---|---|---|
| 2013 | 5,000 | **PF63** 35.00 | **PF65** 40.00 | | | |

**KM# 1062 20 DOLLARS**
7.96 g., 0.9999 Silver 0.2559 oz. ASW, 27 mm. **Ruler:** Elizabeth II **Rev:** Five Maple leaves at left

| Date | Mintage | VF20 | XF40 | MS60 | MS63 | MS65 |
|---|---|---|---|---|---|---|
| 2011 | 200,000 | — | — | — | 25.00 | — |

### KM# 1176 20 DOLLARS

7.96 g., 0.9999 Silver 0.2559 oz. ASW, 27 mm. **Ruler:** Elizabeth II **Obv:** Bust right **Rev:** Canoe and reflection **Edge:** Reeded

| Date | Mintage | VF20 | XF40 | MS60 | MS63 | MS65 |
|---|---|---|---|---|---|---|
| 2011 | 200,000 | — | — | — | 30.00 | — |

### KM# 1226 20 DOLLARS

7.96 g., 0.9999 Silver 0.2559 oz. ASW, 27 mm. **Ruler:** Elizabeth II **Obv:** Bust right **Rev:** Waterline view of polar bear swimming **Edge:** Reeded

| Date | Mintage | VF20 | XF40 | MS60 | MS63 | MS65 |
|---|---|---|---|---|---|---|
| 2012 | 250,000 | — | — | — | 25.00 | — |

### KM# 1237 20 DOLLARS

7.96 g., 0.9999 Silver 0.2559 oz. ASW, 27 mm. **Ruler:** Elizabeth II **Subject:** Commemorating the end of the Canadian Cent **Obv:** Bust right **Rev:** Maple leaves floating on water

| Date | Mintage | VF20 | XF40 | MS60 | MS63 | MS65 |
|---|---|---|---|---|---|---|
| 2012 | — | — | — | — | 20.00 | — |

### KM# 1337 20 DOLLARS

7.96 g., 0.999 Silver 0.2557 oz. ASW, 27 mm. **Ruler:** Elizabeth II **Rev:** Reindeer

| Date | Mintage | VF20 | XF40 | MS60 | MS63 | MS65 |
|---|---|---|---|---|---|---|
| 2012 | — | — | — | — | 27.50 | — |

### KM# 1350 20 DOLLARS

15.50 g., 0.9999 Silver 0.4983 oz. ASW, 34 mm. **Ruler:** Elizabeth II **Obv:** Bust right **Rev:** Elizabeth II bust at left wearing hat

| Date | Mintage | F12 | VF20 | XF40 | MS60 | MS63 |
|---|---|---|---|---|---|---|
| 2012 | — | — | — | — | — | 25.00 |

### KM# 1365 20 DOLLARS

7.96 g., 0.999 Silver 0.2557 oz. ASW, 27 mm. **Ruler:** Elizabeth II **Subject:** Year of the Snake **Rev:** Snake in Tree

| Date | Mintage | VF20 | XF40 | MS60 | MS63 | MS65 |
|---|---|---|---|---|---|---|
| 2013 | Est. 128888 | PF63 25.00 | PF65 30.00 | | | |

### KM# 1511 20 DOLLARS

7.96 g., 0.999 Silver 0.2557 oz. ASW, 27 mm. **Ruler:** Elizabeth II **Rev:** Wolf

| Date | Mintage | VF20 | XF40 | MS60 | MS63 | MS65 |
|---|---|---|---|---|---|---|
| 2013 | 250,000 | — | — | — | 25.00 | — |

### KM# 1512 20 DOLLARS

7.70 g., 0.9999 Silver 0.2475 oz. ASW, 27 mm. **Ruler:** Elizabeth II **Rev:** Iceberg and whale

| Date | Mintage | VF20 | XF40 | MS60 | MS63 | MS65 |
|---|---|---|---|---|---|---|
| 2013 | 225,000 | — | — | — | 25.00 | — |

### KM# 1554 20 DOLLARS

7.96 g., 0.999 Silver 0.2557 oz. ASW, 27 mm. **Ruler:** Elizabeth II **Rev:** Santa

| Date | Mintage | VF20 | XF40 | MS60 | MS63 | MS65 |
|---|---|---|---|---|---|---|
| 2013 | 225,000 | — | — | — | 20.00 | — |

### KM# 1777 20 DOLLARS

31.11 g., 0.999 Silver 0.999 oz. ASW, 27 mm. **Ruler:** Elizabeth II **Rev:** Snowman throwing snowball

| Date | Mintage | F12 | VF20 | XF40 | MS60 | MS63 |
|---|---|---|---|---|---|---|
| 2014 | — | — | — | — | — | 25.00 |

### KM# 1561 20 DOLLARS

7.96 g., 0.999 Silver 0.2557 oz. ASW **Ruler:** Elizabeth II **Obv:** Bust right **Rev:** Goose in flight right

| Date | Mintage | VF20 | XF40 | MS60 | MS63 | MS65 |
|---|---|---|---|---|---|---|
| 2014 | 225,000 | — | — | — | 20.00 | — |

### KM# 1562 20 DOLLARS

7.96 g., 0.999 Silver 0.2557 oz. ASW, 27 mm. **Ruler:** Elizabeth II **Obv:** Bust right **Rev:** Bobcat

| Date | Mintage | VF20 | XF40 | MS60 | MS63 | MS65 |
|---|---|---|---|---|---|---|
| 2014 | 225,000 | — | — | — | 20.00 | — |

### KM# 1563 20 DOLLARS

7.96 g., 0.999 Silver 0.2557 oz. ASW, 27 mm. **Ruler:** Elizabeth II **Obv:** Bust right **Rev:** Summertime

| Date | Mintage | VF20 | XF40 | MS60 | MS63 | MS65 |
|---|---|---|---|---|---|---|
| 2014 | 225,000 | — | — | — | 20.00 | — |

### KM# 1564 20 DOLLARS

7.96 g., 0.999 Silver 0.2557 oz. ASW, 27 mm. **Ruler:** Elizabeth II **Obv:** Bust right **Rev:** Holiday Candles

| Date | Mintage | VF20 | XF40 | MS60 | MS63 | MS65 |
|---|---|---|---|---|---|---|
| 2014 | 225,000 | — | — | — | 20.00 | — |

### KM# 1714 20 DOLLARS

7.96 g., 0.9999 Silver 0.2559 oz. ASW, 27 mm. **Ruler:** Elizabeth II **Obv:** Bust right **Rev:** Bobcat jumping forward

| Date | Mintage | VF20 | XF40 | MS60 | MS63 | MS65 |
|---|---|---|---|---|---|---|
| 2014 | — | — | — | — | 25.00 | — |

### KM# 1715 20 DOLLARS

7.96 g., 0.9999 Silver 0.2559 oz. ASW, 27 mm. **Ruler:** Elizabeth II **Obv:** Bust right **Rev:** Summertime - Boy jumping into lake

| Date | Mintage | VF20 | XF40 | MS60 | MS63 | MS65 |
|---|---|---|---|---|---|---|
| 2014 | — | — | — | — | 25.00 | — |

### KM# 1716 20 DOLLARS

7.96 g., 0.9999 Silver 0.2559 oz. ASW, 27 mm. **Ruler:** Elizabeth II **Obv:** Bust right **Rev:** Goose in flight

| Date | Mintage | VF20 | XF40 | MS60 | MS63 | MS65 |
|---|---|---|---|---|---|---|
| 2014 | — | — | — | — | 25.00 | — |

### KM# 1509 50 DOLLARS

157.60 g., 0.9999 Silver 5.0664 oz. ASW, 65 mm. **Ruler:** Elizabeth II **Subject:** Maple Leaf Bullion, 25th Anniversary **Rev:** Three maple leaves

| Date | Mintage | VF20 | XF40 | MS60 | MS63 | MS65 |
|---|---|---|---|---|---|---|
| 2013 | 2,500 | PF65 500 | | | | |

### KM# 1550 50 DOLLARS

155.56 g., 0.999 Silver 4.9964 oz. ASW partially gilt, 60 mm. **Ruler:** Elizabeth II **Subject:** Silver Maple Leaf, 25th Anniversary

| Date | Mintage | VF20 | XF40 | MS60 | MS63 | MS65 |
|---|---|---|---|---|---|---|
| 2013 | — | — | — | — | — | — |

### KM# 1624 50 DOLLARS

157.60 g., 0.999 Silver 5.0619 oz. ASW, 65.25 mm. **Ruler:** Elizabeth II **Obv:** Bust right **Rev:** Three maple leaves

| Date | Mintage | VF20 | XF40 | MS60 | MS63 | MS65 |
|---|---|---|---|---|---|---|
| 2014 | 2,500 | PF65 520 | | | | |

### KM# 1717 50 DOLLARS

15.87 g., 0.9999 Silver 0.5102 oz. ASW, 34 mm. **Ruler:** Elizabeth II **Obv:** Bust right **Rev:** Snowy Owl in flight forward

| Date | Mintage | VF20 | XF40 | MS60 | MS63 | MS65 |
|---|---|---|---|---|---|---|
| 2014 | — | — | — | — | 60.00 | — |

### KM# 1718 50 DOLLARS

15.87 g., 0.9999 Silver 0.5102 oz. ASW, 34 mm. **Ruler:** Elizabeth II **Obv:** Bust right **Rev:** Polar Bear at stream

| Date | Mintage | VF20 | XF40 | MS60 | MS63 | MS65 |
|---|---|---|---|---|---|---|
| 2014 | — | — | — | — | 60.00 | — |

### KM# 1555 100 DOLLARS

31.60 g., 0.9999 Silver 1.0159 oz. ASW, 40 mm. **Ruler:** Elizabeth II **Obv:** Bust right **Rev:** Bear eating salmon in river

| Date | Mintage | VF20 | XF40 | MS60 | MS63 | MS65 |
|---|---|---|---|---|---|---|
| 2014 | 50,000 | — | — | — | 100 | — |

### KM# 1620 100 DOLLARS

31.60 g., 0.999 Silver 1.0149 oz. ASW, 40 mm. **Ruler:** Elizabeth II **Obv:** Bust right **Rev:** Eagle in flight

| Date | Mintage | VF20 | XF40 | MS60 | MS63 | MS65 |
|---|---|---|---|---|---|---|
| 2014 Matte Proof | 50,000 | PF63 115 | | | | |

### KM# 1621 100 DOLLARS

31.60 g., 0.999 Silver 1.0149 oz. ASW, 40 mm. **Ruler:** Elizabeth II **Obv:** Bust right **Rev:** Two big horn sheep butting heads

| Date | Mintage | VF20 | XF40 | MS60 | MS63 | MS65 |
|---|---|---|---|---|---|---|
| 2014 Matte Proof | 45,000 | PF63 115 | | | | |

### KM# 676 250 DOLLARS

1000.00 g., 0.9999 Silver 32.1475 oz. ASW **Ruler:** Elizabeth II **Subject:** Kilo

| Date | Mintage | VF20 | XF40 | MS60 | MS63 | MS65 |
|---|---|---|---|---|---|---|
| 2006 | — | — | — | — | 1,350 | — |

### KM# 1160 250 DOLLARS

1000.00 g., 0.9999 Silver 32.1475 oz. ASW, 101 mm. **Ruler:** Elizabeth II **Obv:** Bust right **Rev:** Three maple leaves on branch

| Date | Mintage | VF20 | XF40 | MS60 | MS63 | MS65 |
|---|---|---|---|---|---|---|
| 2011 | 999 | PF65 2,000 | | | | |

### KM# 1272 250 DOLLARS

1000.00 g., 0.999 Silver 32.1186 oz. ASW, 101 mm. **Ruler:** Elizabeth II **Subject:** Maple Leaf Forever

| Date | Mintage | VF20 | XF40 | MS60 | MS63 | MS65 |
|---|---|---|---|---|---|---|
| 2012 | — | PF65 1,450 | | | | |

### KM# 1472 250 DOLLARS

1000.00 g., 0.999 Silver 32.1186 oz. ASW Partially gilt, 102.1 mm. **Ruler:** Elizabeth II **Rev:** Two maple leaves, gilt

| Date | Mintage | VF20 | XF40 | MS60 | MS63 | MS65 |
|---|---|---|---|---|---|---|
| 2013 | 600 | PF65 2,300 | | | | |

### KM# 1245 500 DOLLARS

5000.00 g., 0.9999 Silver 160.7375 oz. ASW, 180 mm. **Ruler:** Elizabeth II **Subject:** Haida sculpture

| Date | Mintage | VF20 | XF40 | MS60 | MS63 | MS65 |
|---|---|---|---|---|---|---|
| 2012 | 100 | PF65 7,500 | | | | |

## GOLD BULLION COINAGE

### KM# 542 50 CENTS

1.27 g., 0.999 Gold 0.0408 oz. AGW, 13.92 mm. **Ruler:** Elizabeth II **Rev:** Voyagers with northern lights above

| Date | Mintage | VF20 | XF40 | MS60 | MS63 | MS65 |
|---|---|---|---|---|---|---|
| 2005 | — | PF65 100 | | | | |

### KM# 717 50 CENTS

1.24 g., 0.999 Gold 0.0398 oz. AGW, 13.9 mm. **Ruler:** Elizabeth II **Rev:** Wolf

| Date | Mintage | VF20 | XF40 | MS60 | MS63 | MS65 |
|---|---|---|---|---|---|---|
| 2006 | — | PF63 90.00 | PF65 100 | | | |

### KM# 926 50 CENTS

1.24 g., 0.999 Gold 0.0398 oz. AGW, 13.9 mm. **Ruler:** Elizabeth II **Rev:** Cowboy and bronco rider

| Date | Mintage | VF20 | XF40 | MS60 | MS63 | MS65 |
|---|---|---|---|---|---|---|
| 2006 | — | PF63 90.00 | PF65 100 | | | |

### KM# 927 50 CENTS

1.24 g., 0.999 Gold 0.0398 oz. AGW, 13.9 mm. **Ruler:** Elizabeth II **Subject:** Gold Louis

| Date | Mintage | VF20 | XF40 | MS60 | MS63 | MS65 |
|---|---|---|---|---|---|---|
| 2007 | — | PF63 90.00 | PF65 100 | | | |

### KM# 777 50 CENTS

1.24 g., 0.999 Gold 0.0398 oz. AGW, 13.9 mm. **Ruler:** Elizabeth II **Subject:** DeHavilland beaver

| Date | Mintage | VF20 | XF40 | MS60 | MS63 | MS65 |
|---|---|---|---|---|---|---|
| 2008 | 20,000 | PF63 90.00 | PF65 100 | | | |

### KM# 888 50 CENTS

1.27 g., 0.999 Gold 0.0408 oz. AGW, 13.92 mm. **Ruler:** Elizabeth II **Subject:** Red maple **Obv:** Bust right **Obv. Legend:** Elizabeth II 50 cents **Rev:** Two maple leaves **Rev. Legend:** Canada, Fine gold 1/25 oz or PUR 9999

| Date | Mintage | VF20 | XF40 | MS60 | MS63 | MS65 |
|---|---|---|---|---|---|---|
| 2009 | 150,000 | PF63 75.00 | PF65 90.00 | | | |

### KM# 985 50 CENTS

1.24 g., 0.999 Gold 0.0398 oz. AGW, 13.92 mm. **Ruler:** Elizabeth II **Subject:** RCMP **Obv:** Bust right **Rev:** Mountie on horseback

| Date | Mintage | VF20 | XF40 | MS60 | MS63 | MS65 |
|---|---|---|---|---|---|---|
| 2010 | Est. 14000 | PF63 90.00 | PF65 100 | | | |

### KM# 1085 50 CENTS

1.27 g., 0.999 Gold 0.0408 oz. AGW, 13.92 mm. **Ruler:** Elizabeth II **Rev:** Geese in flight left

| Date | Mintage | VF20 | XF40 | MS60 | MS63 | MS65 |
|---|---|---|---|---|---|---|
| 2011 | 10,000 | PF63 80.00 | PF65 90.00 | | | |

### KM# 1214 50 CENTS

1.27 g., 1.000 Gold 0.0408 oz. AGW, 13.92 mm. **Ruler:** Elizabeth II **Obv:** Bust right **Rev:** Three maple leaves, 2007-2012 above

| Date | Mintage | VF20 | XF40 | MS60 | MS63 | MS65 |
|---|---|---|---|---|---|---|
| 2012 | — | PF63 80.00 | PF65 90.00 | | | |

### KM# 1218 50 CENTS

1.27 g., 0.9999 Gold 0.0408 oz. AGW, 13.92 mm. **Ruler:** Elizabeth II **Obv:** Bust right **Rev:** Schooner sailing left

| Date | Mintage | VF20 | XF40 | MS60 | MS63 | MS65 |
|---|---|---|---|---|---|---|
| 2012 | — | PF65 90.00 | | | | |

### KM# 1348 50 CENTS

1.27 g., 0.9999 Gold 0.0408 oz. AGW, 13.92 mm. **Ruler:** Elizabeth II **Rev:** Bald eagle head left

| Date | Mintage | VF20 | XF40 | MS60 | MS63 | MS65 |
|---|---|---|---|---|---|---|
| 2013 | 10,000 | PF63 120 | PF65 130 | | | |

### KM# 1349 50 CENTS

1.27 g., 0.9999 Gold 0.0408 oz. AGW, 13.92 mm. **Ruler:** Elizabeth II **Subject:** Inuit Art by Joanassie Nowkawalk

| Date | Mintage | VF20 | XF40 | MS60 | MS63 | MS65 |
|---|---|---|---|---|---|---|
| 2013 | 10,000 | PF63 120 | PF65 130 | | | |

### KM# 238 DOLLAR

1.56 g., 0.9999 Gold 0.050 oz. AGW **Ruler:** Elizabeth II **Obv:** Crowned head right, denomination and date below **Rev:** Maple leaf flanked by 9999

| Date | Mintage | VF20 | XF40 | MS60 | MS63 | MS65 |
|---|---|---|---|---|---|---|
| 2001 | — | — | — | — | 79.00 | — |

### KM# 438 DOLLAR

1.58 g., 0.999 Gold 0.0508 oz. AGW, 14.1 mm. **Ruler:** Elizabeth II **Subject:** Holographic Maple Leaves **Obv:** Crowned head right **Rev:** Three maple leaves multicolor hologram **Edge:** Reeded

| Date | Mintage | VF20 | XF40 | MS60 | MS63 | MS65 |
|---|---|---|---|---|---|---|
| 2001 | 600 | — | — | — | 85.00 | — |

### KM# 1416 DOLLAR

1.55 g., 0.9999 Gold 0.0498 oz. AGW, 14 mm. **Ruler:** Elizabeth II **Obv:** Bust right **Rev:** Maple Leaf

| Date | Mintage | VF20 | XF40 | MS60 | MS63 | MS65 |
|---|---|---|---|---|---|---|
| 2009 | — | PF63 115 | PF65 125 | | | |

### KM# 1490 DOLLAR

1.000 Gold **Ruler:** Elizabeth II **Rev:** Maple leaf tilted left **Note:** Thick planchet.

| Date | Mintage | VF20 | XF40 | MS60 | MS63 | MS65 |
|---|---|---|---|---|---|---|
| 2010 Proof | — | — | — | — | — | — |

### KM# 1138 DOLLAR

1.56 g., 0.9999 Gold 0.0502 oz. AGW, 14 mm. **Ruler:** Elizabeth II **Obv:** Bust right **Rev:** Maple leaf

| Date | Mintage | VF20 | XF40 | MS60 | MS63 | MS65 |
|---|---|---|---|---|---|---|
| 1911-2011 | — | — | — | — | 100 | — |

### KM# 1213 DOLLAR

1.58 g., 1.000 Gold 0.0508 oz. AGW, 14.1 mm. **Ruler:** Elizabeth II **Obv:** Bust right **Rev:** Three maple leaves, 2007-2012 above

| Date | Mintage | VF20 | XF40 | MS60 | MS63 | MS65 |
|---|---|---|---|---|---|---|
| 2012 | — | PF63 100 | PF65 110 | | | |

### KM# 1411 DOLLAR

1.55 g., 0.999 Gold 0.0498 oz. AGW **Ruler:** Elizabeth II **Rev:** Two maple leaves

| Date | Mintage | VF20 | XF40 | MS60 | MS63 | MS65 |
|---|---|---|---|---|---|---|
| 2013 | — | PF63 115 | PF65 125 | | | |

### KM# 1506 DOLLAR

1.58 g., 0.9999 Gold 0.0508 oz. AGW, 14.1 mm. **Ruler:** Elizabeth II **Rev:** Two maple leaves

| Date | Mintage | VF20 | XF40 | MS60 | MS63 | MS65 |
|---|---|---|---|---|---|---|
| 2013 Reverse proof | — | PF65 150 | | | | |

### KM# 1703 DOLLAR

1.58 g., 0.9999 Gold 0.0508 oz. AGW, 14.1 mm. **Ruler:** Elizabeth II **Obv:** Bust right **Rev:** 3 Sugar Maple Leaves

| Date | Mintage | VF20 | XF40 | MS60 | MS63 | MS65 |
|---|---|---|---|---|---|---|
| 2014 | 600 | PF65 175 | | | | |

### KM# 1789 DOLLAR

1.24 g., 0.999 Gold 0.0398 oz. AGW, 14.1 mm. **Ruler:** Elizabeth II **Obv:** Bust right by Mary Glick **Rev:** Two maple leaves

| Date | Mintage | F12 | VF20 | XF40 | MS60 | MS63 |
|---|---|---|---|---|---|---|
| 2014 | 650 | PF65 100 | | | | |

### KM# 1801 DOLLAR

1.58 g., 0.9999 Gold 0.0508 oz. AGW, 14.1 mm. **Ruler:** Elizabeth II **Obv:** Bust right **Rev:** Silver maple leaf drifting downward **Note:** Edge numbered.

| Date | Mintage | VF20 | XF40 | MS60 | MS63 | MS65 |
|---|---|---|---|---|---|---|
| 2015 | 600 | PF65 125 | | | | |

### KM# 188 5 DOLLARS

3.12 g., 0.9999 Gold 0.1003 oz. AGW **Ruler:** Elizabeth II **Obv:** Elizabeth II effigy **Rev:** Maple leaf

| Date | Mintage | VF20 | XF40 | MS60 | MS63 | MS65 |
|---|---|---|---|---|---|---|
| 2001 | — | — | — | — | 139 | — |

### KM# 439 5 DOLLARS

3.13 g., 0.9999 Gold 0.1007 oz. AGW, 16 mm. **Ruler:** Elizabeth II **Subject:** Holographic Maple Leaves **Obv:** Crowned head right **Rev:** Three maple leaves multicolor hologram **Edge:** Reeded

| Date | Mintage | VF20 | XF40 | MS60 | MS63 | MS65 |
|---|---|---|---|---|---|---|
| 2001 | 600 | — | — | — | 200 | — |

### KM# 929 5 DOLLARS

3.13 g., 0.999 Gold 0.1005 oz. AGW, 16 mm. **Ruler:** Elizabeth II **Rev:** Maple leaf

| Date | Mintage | VF20 | XF40 | MS60 | MS63 | MS65 |
|---|---|---|---|---|---|---|
| 2007 | — | PF65 200 | | | | |
| 2008 | — | PF65 200 | | | | |
| 2009 | — | PF65 200 | | | | |
| 2010 | — | PF65 200 | | | | |
| 2011 | — | PF65 200 | | | | |

### KM# 1139 5 DOLLARS

3.13 g., 0.999 Gold 0.1005 oz. AGW, 16 mm. **Ruler:** Elizabeth II **Obv:** Bust right **Rev:** Maple leaf

| Date | Mintage | VF20 | XF40 | MS60 | MS63 | MS65 |
|---|---|---|---|---|---|---|
| 1911-2011 | — | — | — | — | 225 | — |

### KM# 1212 5 DOLLARS

3.13 g., 1.000 Gold 0.1006 oz. AGW, 16 mm. **Ruler:** Elizabeth II **Obv:** Bust right **Rev:** Three maple leaves, 2007-2012 above

| Date | Mintage | VF20 | XF40 | MS60 | MS63 | MS65 |
|---|---|---|---|---|---|---|
| 2012 | — | PF65 200 | | | | |

### KM# 1267 5 DOLLARS

3.13 g., 0.999 Gold 0.1005 oz. AGW, 16 mm. **Ruler:** Elizabeth II **Subject:** Maple Leaf Forever

| Date | Mintage | VF20 | XF40 | MS60 | MS63 | MS65 |
|---|---|---|---|---|---|---|
| 2012 | — | PF65 200 | | | | |

### KM# 1412 5 DOLLARS

3.11 g., 0.9999 Gold 0.100 oz. AGW, 16 mm. **Ruler:** Elizabeth II **Rev:** Two maple leaves

| Date | Mintage | VF20 | XF40 | MS60 | MS63 | MS65 |
|---|---|---|---|---|---|---|
| 2013 | — | PF65 250 | | | | |

### KM# 1505 5 DOLLARS

3.13 g., 0.9999 Gold 0.1006 oz. AGW, 16 mm. **Ruler:** Elizabeth II **Rev:** Two maple leaves

| Date | Mintage | VF20 | XF40 | MS60 | MS63 | MS65 |
|---|---|---|---|---|---|---|
| 2013 Reverse Proof | — | PF65 225 | | | | |

### KM# 1598 5 DOLLARS

3.11 g., 0.9999 Gold 0.100 oz. AGW, 16 mm. **Ruler:** Elizabeth II **Obv:** Bust right **Rev:** Three maple leaves

| Date | Mintage | VF20 | XF40 | MS60 | MS63 | MS65 |
|---|---|---|---|---|---|---|
| 2014 | — | PF65 200 | | | | |

### KM# 1704 5 DOLLARS

3.13 g., 0.9999 Gold 0.1006 oz. AGW, 16 mm. **Ruler:** Elizabeth II **Obv:** Bust right **Rev:** 3 Sugar Maple Leaves

| Date | Mintage | VF20 | XF40 | MS60 | MS63 | MS65 |
|---|---|---|---|---|---|---|
| 2014 | 600 | PF65 400 | | | | |

### KM# 1802 5 DOLLARS

3.14 g., 0.9999 Gold 0.1009 oz. AGW, 16 mm. **Ruler:** Elizabeth II **Obv:** Bust right **Rev:** Silver maple leaf drifting downward **Note:** Edge numbered.

| Date | Mintage | VF20 | XF40 | MS60 | MS63 | MS65 |
|---|---|---|---|---|---|---|
| 2015 | 600 | PF65 250 | | | | |

### KM# 189 10 DOLLARS

7.79 g., 0.9999 Gold 0.2503 oz. AGW **Ruler:** Elizabeth II **Obv:** Crowned head right, date and denomination below **Rev:** Maple leaf flanked by 9999

| Date | Mintage | VF20 | XF40 | MS60 | MS63 | MS65 |
|---|---|---|---|---|---|---|
| 2001 | — | — | — | — | 349 | — |

### KM# 440 10 DOLLARS

7.80 g., 0.9999 Gold 0.2507 oz. AGW, 20 mm. **Ruler:** Elizabeth II **Subject:** Holographic Maples Leaves **Obv:** Crowned head right **Rev:** Three maple leaves multicolor hologram **Edge:** Reeded

| Date | Mintage | VF20 | XF40 | MS60 | MS63 | MS65 |
|---|---|---|---|---|---|---|
| 2001 | 15,000 | — | — | — | 475 | — |

### KM# 1140 10 DOLLARS

7.80 g., 0.9999 Gold 0.2507 oz. AGW, 20 mm. **Ruler:** Elizabeth II **Obv:** Bust right **Rev:** Maple leaf

| Date | Mintage | VF20 | XF40 | MS60 | MS63 | MS65 |
|---|---|---|---|---|---|---|
| 1911-2011 | — | — | — | — | 485 | — |

### KM# 1312 10 DOLLARS

6.22 g., 0.999 Gold 0.1998 oz. AGW **Ruler:** Elizabeth II **Obv:** Bust right **Rev:** Maple leaf **Note:** Piedfort

| Date | Mintage | VF20 | XF40 | MS60 | MS63 | MS65 |
|---|---|---|---|---|---|---|
| 2011 | — | — | — | — | 400 | — |

### KM# 1211 10 DOLLARS

7.80 g., 1.000 Gold 0.2507 oz. AGW, 20 mm. **Ruler:** Elizabeth II **Obv:** Bust right **Rev:** Three maple leaves, 2007-2012 above

| Date | Mintage | VF20 | XF40 | MS60 | MS63 | MS65 |
|---|---|---|---|---|---|---|
| 2012 | — | PF65 475 | | | | |

### KM# 1275 10 DOLLARS

7.77 g., 0.9999 Gold 0.2498 oz. AGW, 20 mm. **Ruler:** Elizabeth II **Subject:** War of 1812

| Date | Mintage | VF20 | XF40 | MS60 | MS63 | MS65 |
|---|---|---|---|---|---|---|
| 2012 | — | PF65 500 | | | | |

### KM# 1413 10 DOLLARS

7.77 g., 0.9999 Gold 0.2498 oz. AGW, 20 mm. **Ruler:** Elizabeth II **Rev:** Two maple leaves

| Date | Mintage | VF20 | XF40 | MS60 | MS63 | MS65 |
|---|---|---|---|---|---|---|
| 2013 | — | PF65 500 | | | | |

### KM# 1504 10 DOLLARS

7.77 g., 0.999 Gold 0.2496 oz. AGW, 20 mm. **Ruler:** Elizabeth II **Rev:** Two maple leaves

| Date | Mintage | VF20 | XF40 | MS60 | MS63 | MS65 |
|---|---|---|---|---|---|---|
| 2013 Reverse proof | 600 | PF65 400 | | | | |

### KM# 1599 10 DOLLARS

7.77 g., 0.9999 Gold 0.2498 oz. AGW, 20 mm. **Ruler:** Elizabeth II **Obv:** Bust right **Rev:** Three maple leaves

| Date | Mintage | VF20 | XF40 | MS60 | MS63 | MS65 |
|---|---|---|---|---|---|---|
| 2014 | — | PF65 475 | | | | |

### KM# 1705 10 DOLLARS

7.80 g., 0.9999 Gold 0.2508 oz. AGW, 20 mm. **Ruler:** Elizabeth II **Obv:** Bust right **Rev:** 3 Sugar Maple Leaves

| Date | Mintage | VF20 | XF40 | MS60 | MS63 | MS65 |
|---|---|---|---|---|---|---|
| 2014 | 600 | PF65 800 | | | | |

### KM# 1803 10 DOLLARS

7.80 g., 0.9999 Gold 0.2508 oz. AGW, 20 mm. **Ruler:** Elizabeth II **Obv:** Bust right **Rev:** Silver maple leaf drifting downward **Note:** Edge numbered.

| Date | Mintage | VF20 | XF40 | MS60 | MS63 | MS65 |
|---|---|---|---|---|---|---|
| 2015 | 600 | PF65 750 | | | | |

### KM# 190 20 DOLLARS

15.55 g., 0.9999 Gold 0.4999 oz. AGW **Ruler:** Elizabeth II **Obv:** Crowned head right, date and denomination below **Rev:** Maple leaf flanked by 9999

| Date | Mintage | VF20 | XF40 | MS60 | MS63 | MS65 |
|---|---|---|---|---|---|---|
| 2001 | — | — | — | — | 680 | — |

### KM# 441 20 DOLLARS

15.58 g., 0.9999 Gold 0.501 oz. AGW, 25 mm. **Ruler:** Elizabeth II **Subject:** Holographic Maples Leaves **Obv:** Crowned head right **Rev:** Three maple leaves multicolor hologram **Edge:** Reeded

| Date | Mintage | VF20 | XF40 | MS60 | MS63 | MS65 |
|---|---|---|---|---|---|---|
| 2001 | 600 | — | — | — | 925 | — |

### KM# 191 50 DOLLARS

31.10 g., 0.9999 Gold 0.9999 oz. AGW **Ruler:** Elizabeth II **Obv:** Crowned head right, date and denomination below **Rev:** Maple leaf flanked by .9999

| Date | Mintage | VF20 | XF40 | MS60 | MS63 | MS65 |
|---|---|---|---|---|---|---|
| 2001 | — | — | — | — | 1,299 | — |

### KM# 442 50 DOLLARS

31.15 g., 0.9999 Gold 1.0014 oz. AGW, 30 mm. **Ruler:** Elizabeth II **Subject:** Holographic Maples Leaves **Obv:** Crowned head right **Rev:** Three maple leaves multicolor hologram **Edge:** Reeded

| Date | Mintage | VF20 | XF40 | MS60 | MS63 | MS65 |
|---|---|---|---|---|---|---|
| 2001 | 600 | — | — | — | 1,850 | — |

### KM# 1042 50 DOLLARS

31.11 g., 0.999 Gold 0.999 oz. AGW, 30 mm. **Ruler:** Elizabeth II **Rev:** Vancouver logo and maple leaf **Edge:** Reeded

| Date | Mintage | VF20 | XF40 | MS60 | MS63 | MS65 |
|---|---|---|---|---|---|---|
| 2008 P | — | — | — | — | 1,850 | — |

### KM# 1042a 50 DOLLARS

31.11 g., 0.9999 Gold 0.9999 oz. AGW, 30 mm. **Ruler:** Elizabeth II **Rev:** Maple leaf in red enamel, olympic logo at left

| Date | Mintage | VF20 | XF40 | MS60 | MS63 | MS65 |
|---|---|---|---|---|---|---|
| 2008 | — | — | — | — | 1,850 | — |

### KM# 1037 50 DOLLARS

31.11 g., 0.9999 Gold 0.9999 oz. AGW, 30 mm. **Ruler:** Elizabeth II **Rev:** Thunderbird **Edge:** Reeded

| Date | Mintage | VF20 | XF40 | MS60 | MS63 | MS65 |
|---|---|---|---|---|---|---|
| 2009 | — | — | — | — | 1,850 | — |

### KM# 1037a 50 DOLLARS

31.11 g., 0.9999 Gold 0.9999 oz. AGW, 30 mm. **Ruler:** Elizabeth II **Rev:** Thunderbird, stars in red enamel highlights

| Date | Mintage | VF20 | XF40 | MS60 | MS63 | MS65 |
|---|---|---|---|---|---|---|
| 2009 | — | — | — | — | 1,850 | — |

### KM# 1029 50 DOLLARS

31.11 g., 0.9999 Gold 0.9999 oz. AGW, 30 mm. **Ruler:** Elizabeth II **Rev:** Hockey player flanked by maple leaves

| Date | Mintage | VF20 | XF40 | MS60 | MS63 | MS65 |
|---|---|---|---|---|---|---|
| 2010 | — | — | — | — | 1,850 | — |

### KM# 1029a 50 DOLLARS

31.11 g., 0.9999 Gold 0.9999 oz. AGW, 30 mm. **Ruler:** Elizabeth II **Rev:** Hockey player, red enameled maple leaves flanking

| Date | Mintage | VF20 | XF40 | MS60 | MS63 | MS65 |
|---|---|---|---|---|---|---|
| 2010 | — | — | — | — | 1,850 | — |

### KM# 1141 50 DOLLARS

31.11 g., 0.9999 Gold 0.9999 oz. AGW, 30 mm. **Ruler:** Elizabeth II **Obv:** Bust right **Rev:** Maple leaf

| Date | Mintage | VF20 | XF40 | MS60 | MS63 | MS65 |
|---|---|---|---|---|---|---|
| 1911-2011 | — | — | — | — | 1,850 | — |

### KM# 1210 50 DOLLARS

31.11 g., 1.000 Gold 1.000 oz. AGW, 30 mm. **Ruler:** Elizabeth II **Obv:** Bust right **Rev:** Three maple leaves, 2007-2012 above

| Date | Mintage | VF20 | XF40 | MS60 | MS63 | MS65 |
|---|---|---|---|---|---|---|
| 2012 | — | **PF65** 1,850 | | | | |

### KM# 1414 50 DOLLARS

31.10 g., 0.9999 Gold 0.9999 oz. AGW, 30 mm. **Ruler:** Elizabeth II **Rev:** Two Maple Leaves

| Date | Mintage | VF20 | XF40 | MS60 | MS63 | MS65 |
|---|---|---|---|---|---|---|
| 2013 | — | — | — | — | 1,800 | — |

### KM# 1488 50 DOLLARS

31.11 g., 0.9999 Gold 0.9999 oz. AGW, 30 mm. **Ruler:** Elizabeth II **Rev:** Maple Leaf, security feature added

| Date | Mintage | VF20 | XF40 | MS60 | MS63 | MS65 |
|---|---|---|---|---|---|---|
| 2013 | — | — | — | — | 1,250 | — |
| 2014 | — | — | — | — | 1,250 | — |

### KM# 1503 50 DOLLARS

31.11 g., 0.9999 Gold 0.9999 oz. AGW, 30 mm. **Ruler:** Elizabeth II **Rev:** Two maple leaves

| Date | Mintage | VF20 | XF40 | MS60 | MS63 | MS65 |
|---|---|---|---|---|---|---|
| 2013 Reverse Proof | 600 | **PF65** 1,800 | | | | |

### KM# 1600 50 DOLLARS

31.11 g., 0.9999 Gold 0.9999 oz. AGW, 30 mm. **Ruler:** Elizabeth II **Obv:** Bust right **Rev:** Three maple leaves

| Date | Mintage | VF20 | XF40 | MS60 | MS63 | MS65 |
|---|---|---|---|---|---|---|
| 2014 | — | **PF65** 1,500 | | | | |

### KM# 1706 50 DOLLARS

31.10 g., 0.9999 Gold 0.9998 oz. AGW, 30 mm. **Ruler:** Elizabeth II **Obv:** Bust right **Rev:** 3 Sugar Maple Leaves

| Date | Mintage | VF20 | XF40 | MS60 | MS63 | MS65 |
|---|---|---|---|---|---|---|
| 2014 | 600 | **PF65** 1,600 | | | | |

### KM# 1804 50 DOLLARS

31.16 g., 0.9999 Gold 1.0017 oz. AGW, 30 mm. **Ruler:** Elizabeth II **Obv:** Bust right **Rev:** Silver maple leaf drifting downward **Note:** Edge numbered.

| Date | Mintage | VF20 | XF40 | MS60 | MS63 | MS65 |
|---|---|---|---|---|---|---|
| 2015 | 600 | **PF65** 1,400 | | | | |

**KM# 750 200 DOLLARS**
31.11 g., 1.000 Gold 1.000 oz. AGW, 30 mm. **Ruler:** Elizabeth II **Rev:** Three maple leaves

| Date | Mintage | VF20 | XF40 | MS60 | MS63 | MS65 |
|---|---|---|---|---|---|---|
| 2007 Proof, T/E privy mark | 500 | PF65 1,850 | | | | |

**KM# 786 200 DOLLARS**
31.11 g., 1.000 Gold 1.000 oz. AGW, 30 mm. **Ruler:** Elizabeth II **Obv:** Bust right on lathe-work background **Rev:** Two maple leaves on lathe-work background

| Date | Mintage | VF20 | XF40 | MS60 | MS63 | MS65 |
|---|---|---|---|---|---|---|
| 2008 | — | PF65 1,850 | | | | |

**KM# 1162 200 DOLLARS**
31.11 g., 1.000 Gold 1.000 oz. AGW, 30 mm. **Ruler:** Elizabeth II **Rev:** Maple leaf with lathe background

| Date | Mintage | VF20 | XF40 | MS60 | MS63 | MS65 |
|---|---|---|---|---|---|---|
| 2009 | — | PF65 1,850 | | | | |

**KM# 1163 200 DOLLARS**
31.11 g., 0.999 Gold 0.999 oz. AGW, 30 mm. **Ruler:** Elizabeth II **Subject:** Celebrating win **Rev:** Three athletics with hands raised

| Date | Mintage | VF20 | XF40 | MS60 | MS63 | MS65 |
|---|---|---|---|---|---|---|
| 2010 | — | PF65 1,850 | | | | |

**KM# 1165 200 DOLLARS**
31.11 g., 1.000 Gold 1.000 oz. AGW, 30 mm. **Ruler:** Elizabeth II **Rev:** Mountie on horseback, lathe backgound

| Date | Mintage | VF20 | XF40 | MS60 | MS63 | MS65 |
|---|---|---|---|---|---|---|
| 2011 | — | — | — | — | 1,850 | — |

**KM# 1487 200 DOLLARS**
31.11 g., 0.9999 Gold 0.9999 oz. AGW, 30 mm. **Ruler:** Elizabeth II **Rev:** Three maple leaves, engine turned background

| Date | Mintage | VF20 | XF40 | MS60 | MS63 | MS65 |
|---|---|---|---|---|---|---|
| 2012 | — | PF65 1,800 | | | | |

**KM# 1328 500 DOLLARS**
155.55 g., 0.9999 Gold 5.0005 oz. AGW, 55 mm. **Ruler:** Elizabeth II **Rev:** Three Maple Leaves

| Date | Mintage | VF20 | XF40 | MS60 | MS63 | MS65 |
|---|---|---|---|---|---|---|
| 2012 | — | PF65 10,000 | | | | |

**KM# 1161 2500 DOLLARS**
1000.00 g., 0.9999 Gold 32.1475 oz. AGW, 101 mm. **Ruler:** Elizabeth II **Rev:** Three maple leaves on branch

| Date | Mintage | VF20 | XF40 | MS60 | MS63 | MS65 |
|---|---|---|---|---|---|---|
| 2011 | — | PF65 56,000 | | | | |

**KM# 1271 2500 DOLLARS**
1000.00 g., 0.999 Gold 32.1186 oz. AGW, 101 mm. **Ruler:** Elizabeth II **Subject:** Maple Leaf Forever

| Date | Mintage | VF20 | XF40 | MS60 | MS63 | MS65 |
|---|---|---|---|---|---|---|
| 2012 | — | PF65 56,000 | | | | |

**KM# 1486 2500 DOLLARS**
1000.00 g., 0.9999 Gold 32.1475 oz. AGW, 101 mm. **Ruler:** Elizabeth II **Rev:** Three maple leaves

| Date | Mintage | VF20 | XF40 | MS60 | MS63 | MS65 |
|---|---|---|---|---|---|---|
| 2012 | — | PF65 69,000 | | | | |

**KM# 1209 100000 DOLLARS**
10000.00 g., 1.000 Gold 321.504 oz. AGW **Ruler:** Elizabeth II **Obv:** Bust right **Rev:** Bill Reid's sculpture: Spirit of Haida Gwaii **Note:** The sculpture is at the Canadian Embassy in Washington, D.C.

| Date | Mintage | VF20 | XF40 | MS60 | MS63 | MS65 |
|---|---|---|---|---|---|---|
| 2011 | — | PF65 565,000 | | | | |

**KM# 755 1000000 DOLLARS**
100000.00 g., 0.9999 Gold 3214.7508 oz. AGW **Ruler:** Elizabeth II **Obv:** Bust right **Rev:** Three maple leaves **Note:** Cast

| Date | Mintage | VF20 | XF40 | MS60 | MS63 | MS65 |
|---|---|---|---|---|---|---|
| 2007 | 10 | — | — | — | 5,630,000 | — |

## PLATINUM BULLION COINAGE

**KM# 429 30 DOLLARS**
3.11 g., 0.9995 Platinum 0.0999 oz. APW, 16 mm. **Ruler:** Elizabeth II **Obv:** Crowned head right **Rev:** Harlequin duck's head **Edge:** Reeded

| Date | Mintage | VF20 | XF40 | MS60 | MS63 | MS65 |
|---|---|---|---|---|---|---|
| 2001 | 448 | PF65 200 | | | | |

**KM# 1097 30 DOLLARS**
3.11 g., 0.9995 Platinum 0.0999 oz. APW, 16 mm. **Ruler:** Elizabeth II **Rev:** Great Blue Heron

| Date | Mintage | VF20 | XF40 | MS60 | MS63 | MS65 |
|---|---|---|---|---|---|---|
| 2002 | 344 | PF65 200 | | | | |

**KM# 1101 30 DOLLARS**
3.11 g., 0.9995 Platinum 0.0999 oz. APW, 16 mm. **Ruler:** Elizabeth II **Rev:** Atlantic Walrus

| Date | Mintage | VF20 | XF40 | MS60 | MS63 | MS65 |
|---|---|---|---|---|---|---|
| 2003 | 365 | PF65 250 | | | | |

**KM# 1105 30 DOLLARS**
3.11 g., 0.9995 Platinum 0.0999 oz. APW, 16 mm. **Ruler:** Elizabeth II **Rev:** Grizzly Bear

| Date | Mintage | VF20 | XF40 | MS60 | MS63 | MS65 |
|---|---|---|---|---|---|---|
| 2004 | 380 | PF65 250 | | | | |

**KM# 430 75 DOLLARS**
7.78 g., 0.9995 Platinum 0.2499 oz. APW, 20 mm. **Ruler:** Elizabeth II **Obv:** Crowned head right **Rev:** Harlequin duck in flight **Edge:** Reeded

| Date | Mintage | VF20 | XF40 | MS60 | MS63 | MS65 |
|---|---|---|---|---|---|---|
| 2001 | 448 | PF65 500 | | | | |

**KM# 1098 75 DOLLARS**
7.77 g., 0.9995 Platinum 0.2497 oz. APW, 20 mm. **Ruler:** Elizabeth II **Rev:** Great Blue Heron

| Date | Mintage | VF20 | XF40 | MS60 | MS63 | MS65 |
|---|---|---|---|---|---|---|
| 2002 | 344 | PF65 525 | | | | |

**KM# 1102 75 DOLLARS**
7.77 g., 0.9995 Platinum 0.2497 oz. APW, 20 mm. **Ruler:** Elizabeth II **Rev:** Atlantic Walrus

| Date | Mintage | VF20 | XF40 | MS60 | MS63 | MS65 |
|---|---|---|---|---|---|---|
| 2003 | 365 | PF65 550 | | | | |

**KM# 1106 75 DOLLARS**
7.77 g., 0.9995 Platinum 0.2497 oz. APW, 20 mm. **Ruler:** Elizabeth II **Rev:** Grizzly Bear

| Date | Mintage | VF20 | XF40 | MS60 | MS63 | MS65 |
|---|---|---|---|---|---|---|
| 2004 | 380 | PF65 550 | | | | |

**KM# 431 150 DOLLARS**
15.55 g., 0.9995 Platinum 0.4997 oz. APW, 25 mm. **Ruler:** Elizabeth II **Obv:** Crowned head right **Rev:** Two harlequin ducks **Edge:** Reeded

| Date | Mintage | VF20 | XF40 | MS60 | MS63 | MS65 |
|---|---|---|---|---|---|---|
| 2001 | 448 | **PF65** 1,000 | | | | |

**KM# 1099 150 DOLLARS**
15.55 g., 0.9995 Platinum 0.4997 oz. APW, 25 mm. **Ruler:** Elizabeth II **Rev:** Great Blue Heron

| Date | Mintage | VF20 | XF40 | MS60 | MS63 | MS65 |
|---|---|---|---|---|---|---|
| 2002 | 344 | **PF65** 1,000 | | | | |

**KM# 1103 150 DOLLARS**
15.55 g., 0.9995 Platinum 0.4997 oz. APW, 25 mm. **Ruler:** Elizabeth II **Rev:** Atlantic Walrus

| Date | Mintage | VF20 | XF40 | MS60 | MS63 | MS65 |
|---|---|---|---|---|---|---|
| 2003 | 365 | **PF65** 1,000 | | | | |

**KM# 1107 150 DOLLARS**
15.55 g., 0.9995 Platinum 0.4997 oz. APW, 25 mm. **Ruler:** Elizabeth II **Rev:** Grizzly Bear

| Date | Mintage | VF20 | XF40 | MS60 | MS63 | MS65 |
|---|---|---|---|---|---|---|
| 2004 | 380 | **PF65** 1,000 | | | | |

**KM# 432 300 DOLLARS**
31.10 g., 0.9995 Platinum 0.9995 oz. APW, 30 mm. **Ruler:** Elizabeth II **Obv:** Crowned head right **Rev:** Two standing harlequin ducks **Edge:** Reeded

| Date | Mintage | VF20 | XF40 | MS60 | MS63 | MS65 |
|---|---|---|---|---|---|---|
| 2001 | 448 | **PF65** 1,900 | | | | |

**KM# 1100 300 DOLLARS**
31.11 g., 0.9995 Platinum 0.9995 oz. APW, 30 mm. **Ruler:** Elizabeth II **Rev:** Great Blue Heron

| Date | Mintage | VF20 | XF40 | MS60 | MS63 | MS65 |
|---|---|---|---|---|---|---|
| 2002 | 344 | **PF65** 1,950 | | | | |

**KM# 1104 300 DOLLARS**
31.11 g., 0.9995 Platinum 0.9995 oz. APW, 30 mm. **Ruler:** Elizabeth II **Rev:** Atlantic Walrus

| Date | Mintage | VF20 | XF40 | MS60 | MS63 | MS65 |
|---|---|---|---|---|---|---|
| 2003 | 365 | **PF65** 1,950 | | | | |

**KM# 1108 300 DOLLARS**
31.11 g., 0.9995 Platinum 0.9995 oz. APW, 30 mm. **Ruler:** Elizabeth II **Rev:** Grizzly Bear

| Date | Mintage | VF20 | XF40 | MS60 | MS63 | MS65 |
|---|---|---|---|---|---|---|
| 2004 | 380 | **PF65** 1,950 | | | | |

**KM# 753 300 DOLLARS**
31.11 g., 0.9999 Platinum 0.9999 oz. APW **Ruler:** Elizabeth II **Rev:** Wooly mammoth

| Date | Mintage | VF20 | XF40 | MS60 | MS63 | MS65 |
|---|---|---|---|---|---|---|
| 2007 | 400 | **PF65** 3,200 | | | | |

**KM# 831 300 DOLLARS**
31.11 g., 0.999 Platinum 0.999 oz. APW, 30 mm. **Ruler:** Elizabeth II **Rev:** Saber Tooth Scimitar cat

| Date | Mintage | VF20 | XF40 | MS60 | MS63 | MS65 |
|---|---|---|---|---|---|---|
| 2008 | 200 | **PF65** 3,500 | | | | |

**KM# 951 300 DOLLARS**
31.16 g., 0.999 Platinum 1.0008 oz. APW, 30 mm. **Ruler:** Elizabeth II **Rev:** Steppe Bison

| Date | Mintage | VF20 | XF40 | MS60 | MS63 | MS65 |
|---|---|---|---|---|---|---|
| 2009 | 200 | **PF65** 3,500 | | | | |

**KM# 1159 300 DOLLARS**
31.11 g., 0.999 Platinum 0.999 oz. APW, 30 mm. **Ruler:** Elizabeth II **Rev:** Ground Sloth

| Date | Mintage | VF20 | XF40 | MS60 | MS63 | MS65 |
|---|---|---|---|---|---|---|
| 2010 | 200 | **PF65** 1,900 | | | | |

**KM# 1175 300 DOLLARS**
31.11 g., 0.9995 Platinum 0.9995 oz. APW, 30 mm. **Ruler:** Elizabeth II **Obv:** Bust right **Rev:** Cougar head left

| Date | Mintage | VF20 | XF40 | MS60 | MS63 | MS65 |
|---|---|---|---|---|---|---|
| 2011 | 200 | **PF65** 1,950 | | | | |

**KM# 1273 300 DOLLARS**
31.11 g., 0.999 Platinum 0.999 oz. APW, 30 mm. **Ruler:** Elizabeth II **Subject:** Maple Leaf Forever

| Date | Mintage | VF20 | XF40 | MS60 | MS63 | MS65 |
|---|---|---|---|---|---|---|
| 2012 | — | **PF65** 1,950 | | | | |

**KM# 1386 300 DOLLARS**
31.11 g., 0.999 Platinum 0.999 oz. APW, 30 mm. **Ruler:** Elizabeth II **Subject:** Maple Leaf - 25th Anniversary **Rev:** Maple Leaf - Gilt Shadow

| Date | Mintage | VF20 | XF40 | MS60 | MS63 | MS65 |
|---|---|---|---|---|---|---|
| 2013 | Est. 250 | **PF65** 3,000 | | | | |

**KM# 1391 300 DOLLARS**
31.11 g., 0.999 Platinum 0.9992 oz. APW, 30 mm. **Ruler:** Elizabeth II **Rev:** Two Bald Eagles at Nest

| Date | Mintage | VF20 | XF40 | MS60 | MS63 | MS65 |
|---|---|---|---|---|---|---|
| 2013 | — | **PF65** 2,250 | | | | |

**KM# 1544 300 DOLLARS**
31.11 g., 0.999 Platinum 0.9992 oz. APW, 30 mm. **Ruler:** Elizabeth II **Rev:** Two bison

| Date | Mintage | VF20 | XF40 | MS60 | MS63 | MS65 |
|---|---|---|---|---|---|---|
| 2013 | — | **PF65** 2,250 | | | | |

**KM# 1552 300 DOLLARS**
31.16 g., 0.9995 Platinum 1.0013 oz. APW, 30 mm. **Ruler:** Elizabeth II **Obv:** Bust right **Rev:** Two bison with heads butting

| Date | Mintage | VF20 | XF40 | MS60 | MS63 | MS65 |
|---|---|---|---|---|---|---|
| 2014 | 200 | **PF65** 3,000 | | | | |

**KM# 1560 300 DOLLARS**
31.16 g., 0.9995 Platinum 1.0013 oz. APW, 30 mm. **Ruler:** Elizabeth II **Obv:** Bust right **Rev:** Bighorn Sheep

| Date | Mintage | VF20 | XF40 | MS60 | MS63 | MS65 |
|---|---|---|---|---|---|---|
| 2014 | 250 | **PF65** 3,000 | | | | |

## MINT SETS

| KM# | Date | Mintage | Identification | Issue Price | Mkt Val |
|---|---|---|---|---|---|
| MS8 | 2001 (5) | 600 | KM438-442 | 1,996 | 2,950 |
| MS9 | 2002 (7) | 135,000 | Double-dated 1952-2002, KM#444-449, 467 Elizabeth II Golden Jubilee | 11.75 | 16.00 |
| MS10 | 2002 (7) | — | KM#444-449, 467, Oh! Canada! 135th Birthday Gift set. | 17.00 | 16.00 |
| MS11 | 2002 (7) | — | KM#444-449, 467, Tiny Treasures Uncirculated Gift Set | 17.00 | 16.00 |
| MS12 | 2003 (7) | 135,000 | KM#289, 182b, 183b, 184b, 290, 186, 270 | 12.00 | 16.00 |
| MS13 | 2003 (7) | 75,000 | KM490-496 | 13.25 | 20.00 |
| MS14 | 2003 (7) | — | KM289, 182-184, 290, 186, 270, Oh! Canada! | 17.75 | 16.00 |
| MS15 | 2003 (7) | — | KM289, 182-184, 290, 186, 270, Tiny Treasures Uncirculated Gift Set | 17.75 | 16.00 |

## PROOF SETS

| KM# | Date | Mintage | Identification | Issue Price | Mkt Val |
|---|---|---|---|---|---|
| PS51 | 2001 (4) | — | KM429, 430, 431, 432 | — | 3,600 |
| PS52 | 2002 (8) | 100,000 | KM#443, 444a, 445, 446a-449a, 467 Elizabeth II Golden Jubilee | 60.00 | 125 |
| PS53 | 2002 (3) | — | KM#459-461 Canadian Folklore and Legends Collection | 57.50 | 35.00 |
| PS54 | 2002 (2) | — | KM#519, 520 | 750 | 1,125 |
| PS55 | 2003 (8) | 100,000 | KM#182a, 183a, 184a, 186, 270d, 289, 290a, 450 100th Anniversary of the Cobalt Silver Strike | 62.50 | 125 |
| PS56 | 2003 (6) | 30,000 | KM#468-473 50th Anniversary of the Coronation of Elizabeth II | 75.00 | 100 |
| PS57 | 2004 (8) | — | KM#490, 491a-494a, 495, 496a, 512 | — | 115 |
| PS58 | 2004 (5) | 25,000 | KM#621-625 | — | 100 |

## SPECIMEN SETS (SS)

| KM# | Date | Mintage | Identification | Issue Price | Mkt Val |
|---|---|---|---|---|---|
| SS90 | 2002 (7) | 75,000 | KM#444-449,462 Elizabeth II Golden Jubilee | 30.00 | 65.00 |
| SS91 | 2003 (3) | 75,000 | KM#(uncertain), 270, 289, 290 | 30.00 | 50.00 |

# CAPE VERDE

The Republic of Cape Verde, Africa's smallest republic, is located in the Atlantic Ocean, about 370 miles (595 km.) west of Dakar, Senegal, off the coast of Africa. The 14-island republic has an area of 1,557 sq. mi. (4,033 sq. km.) and a population of 435,983. Capital: Praia. The refueling of ships and aircraft is the chief economic function of the country. Fishing is important and agriculture is widely practiced, but the Cape Verdes are not self-sufficient in food. Fish products, salt, bananas, and shellfish are exported.

After 500 years of Portuguese rule, the Cape Verdes became independent on July 5, 1975. At the first general election, all seats of the new national assembly were won by the Party for the Independence of Guinea-Bissau and Cape Verde (PAIGC). The PAIGC linked the two former colonies into one state. Antonio Mascarenhas Monteiro won the first free presidential election in 1991.

**MONETARY SYSTEM**
100 Centavos = 1 Escudo

## REPUBLIC

### DECIMAL COINAGE

**KM# 46 25 ESCUDOS**
15.55 g., 0.999 Silver 0.4995 oz. ASW, 30.4 mm. **Obv:** Value above national arms **Rev:** Jesus **Edge:** Plain

| Date | Mintage | VF20 | XF40 | MS60 | MS63 | MS65 |
|---|---|---|---|---|---|---|
| 2006 | — | PF63 35.00 | PF65 40.00 | | | |

**KM# 47 50 ESCUDOS**
1.56 g., 0.999 Gold 0.0499 oz. AGW, 16 mm. **Obv:** Value above national arms **Rev:** Jesus **Edge:** Plain

| Date | Mintage | VF20 | XF40 | MS60 | MS63 | MS65 |
|---|---|---|---|---|---|---|
| 2006 | — | PF63 90.00 | PF65 100 | | | |

**KM# 48 50 ESCUDOS**
25.00 g., 0.925 Silver 0.7435 oz. ASW, 38.8 mm. **Subject:** 500th Anniversary Death of Christopher Columbus **Obv:** National arms **Obv. Legend:** CABO VERDE **Rev:** Sailing ship "Santa Maria **Rev. Legend:** A SANTA MARIA DE CHRIST?V?O COLOMBO **Edge:** Reeded

| Date | Mintage | VF20 | XF40 | MS60 | MS63 | MS65 |
|---|---|---|---|---|---|---|
| 2006 | — | PF63 50.00 | PF65 55.00 | | | |

**KM# 49 50 ESCUDOS**
25.00 g., 0.925 Silver 0.7435 oz. ASW, 38.6 mm. **Subject:** Appearance in Grotto **Obv:** National arms **Obv. Legend:** CABO VERDE **Rev:** Maria standing facing 3/4 left at right **Rev. Legend:** AVE MARIA - LOURDES **Edge:** Reeded

| Date | Mintage | VF20 | XF40 | MS60 | MS63 | MS65 |
|---|---|---|---|---|---|---|
| 2006 | — | PF63 60.00 | PF65 65.00 | | | |

**KM# 50 50 ESCUDOS**
25.00 g., 0.925 Silver 0.7435 oz. ASW **Obv:** National arms **Rev:** Red Kite bird

| Date | Mintage | VF20 | XF40 | MS60 | MS63 | MS65 |
|---|---|---|---|---|---|---|
| 2006 | — | PF63 60.00 | PF65 65.00 | | | |

**KM# 52 50 ESCUDOS**
25.00 g., 0.925 Silver 0.7435 oz. ASW, 38.6 mm. **Rev:** East India Company's Princess Louisa and 1/2 real from shipwreck

| Date | Mintage | VF20 | XF40 | MS60 | MS63 | MS65 |
|---|---|---|---|---|---|---|
| 2006 | Est. 1500 | PF63 75.00 | PF65 80.00 | | | |

**KM# 53 50 ESCUDOS**
25.00 g., 0.925 Silver 0.7435 oz. ASW, 38.6 mm. **Rev:** Princess Louisa hitting the reef, 1/2 real from shipwreck

| Date | Mintage | VF20 | XF40 | MS60 | MS63 | MS65 |
|---|---|---|---|---|---|---|
| 2006 | Est. 1500 | PF63 75.00 | PF65 80.00 | | | |

**KM# 45 200 ESCUDOS**
7.80 g., Copper-Nickel, 29.5 mm. **Subject:** 30th Anniversary of Independence **Obv:** National arms in number 2 of 200 **Rev:** Symbolic education design **Edge:** Reeded **Shape:** Round

| Date | Mintage | VF20 | XF40 | MS60 | MS63 | MS65 |
|---|---|---|---|---|---|---|
| 2005 | — | — | — | — | 8.00 | 10.00 |

**KM# 45a 200 ESCUDOS**
18.28 g., 0.925 Silver 0.5436 oz. ASW **Subject:** 30th Anniversary of Independence **Obv:** National arms in number 2 of 200 **Rev:** Symbolic education design **Edge:** Reeded **Shape:** Round

| Date | Mintage | VF20 | XF40 | MS60 | MS63 | MS65 |
|---|---|---|---|---|---|---|
| 2005 | — | PF63 60.00 | PF65 70.00 | | | |

**KM# 51 250 ESCUDOS**
Copper-Nickel **Subject:** Independence, 35th Anniversary **Obv:** Ship sailing forward **Rev:** Arms

| Date | Mintage | VF20 | XF40 | MS60 | MS63 | MS65 |
|---|---|---|---|---|---|---|
| 2010 | — | — | — | — | 12.00 | 15.00 |

# CAYMAN ISLANDS

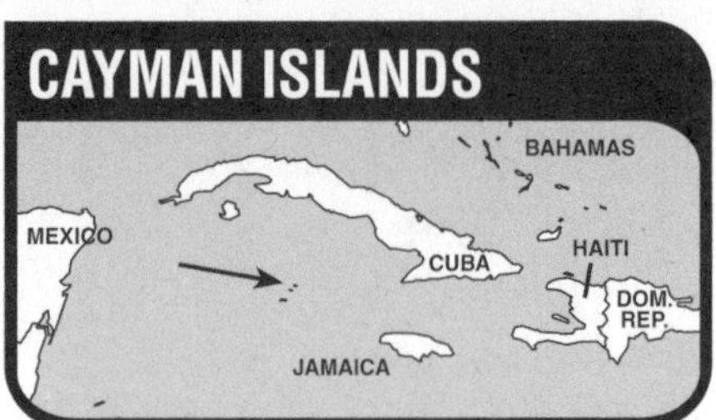


The Cayman Islands is a British Crown Colony situated about 180 miles (280 km) northwest of Jamaica. It consists of three islands: Grand Cayman, Little Cayman, and Cayman Brac. The islands have an area of 102 sq. mi. (259 sq. km.) and a population of 33,200. Capital: George Town. Seafaring, commerce, banking, and tourism are the principal industries. Rope, turtle shells, and sharkskins are exported.

**RULER**
British

**MINT MARKS**
CHI - Valcambi

**MONETARY SYSTEM**
100 Cents = 1 Dollar

## BRITISH COLONY

### DECIMAL COINAGE

**KM# 131 CENT**
2.55 g., Copper Plated Steel, 17 mm. **Ruler:** Elizabeth II **Obv:** Crowned head right **Rev:** Grand Caiman thrush **Edge:** Plain

| Date | Mintage | VF20 | XF40 | MS60 | MS63 | MS65 |
|---|---|---|---|---|---|---|
| 2002 | 10,000,000 | — | 0.15 | 0.35 | 0.75 | 1.00 |
| 2005 | 16,220,000 | — | 0.15 | 0.35 | 0.75 | 1.00 |
| 2008 | 12,000,000 | — | 0.15 | 0.35 | 0.75 | 1.00 |

**KM# 132 5 CENTS**
2.00 g., Nickel Plated Steel, 18 mm. **Ruler:** Elizabeth II **Obv:** Crowned head right **Rev:** Pink-spotted shrimp **Edge:** Plain

| Date | Mintage | VF20 | XF40 | MS60 | MS63 | MS65 |
|---|---|---|---|---|---|---|
| 2002 | 2,500,000 | — | 0.15 | 0.35 | 0.50 | 0.85 |
| 2005 | 2,500,000 | — | 0.15 | 0.35 | 0.50 | 0.85 |
| 2008 | 3,000,000 | — | 0.15 | 0.35 | 0.50 | 0.85 |

**KM# 133 10 CENTS**
3.45 g., Nickel Plated Steel, 21 mm. **Ruler:** Elizabeth II **Obv:** Head with tiara right **Rev:** Green turtle surfacing **Edge:** Reeded

| Date | Mintage | VF20 | XF40 | MS60 | MS63 | MS65 |
|---|---|---|---|---|---|---|
| 2002 | 3,000,000 | 0.25 | 0.40 | 0.60 | 0.75 | 1.00 |
| 2005 | 3,000,000 | 0.25 | 0.40 | 0.60 | 0.75 | 1.00 |
| 2008 | 3,500,000 | 0.25 | 0.40 | 0.60 | 0.75 | 1.00 |

**KM# 134 25 CENTS**
5.10 g., Nickel Plated Steel, 24.26 mm. **Ruler:** Elizabeth II **Obv:** Head with tiara right **Rev:** Schooner sailing right **Edge:** Reeded

| Date | Mintage | VF20 | XF40 | MS60 | MS63 | MS65 |
|---|---|---|---|---|---|---|
| 2002 | 2,500,000 | — | 0.60 | 1.00 | 1.25 | 1.50 |
| 2005 | 2,500,000 | — | 0.60 | 1.00 | 1.25 | 1.50 |
| 2008 | 3,000,000 | — | 0.60 | 1.00 | 1.25 | 1.50 |

### KM# 136 2 DOLLARS

28.34 g., 0.925 Silver 0.8428 oz. ASW, 38.6 mm. **Ruler:** Elizabeth II **Obv:** Gold plated Queen Elizabeth II **Rev:** British crown and value **Edge:** Reeded

| Date | Mintage | VF20 | XF40 | MS60 | MS63 | MS65 |
|---|---|---|---|---|---|---|
| 2002 | — | PF63 50.00 | PF65 55.00 | | | |

### KM# 135 2 DOLLARS

28.28 g., 0.925 Silver 0.841 oz. ASW, 38.6 mm. **Ruler:** Elizabeth II **Subject:** 500th Anniversary - Christopher Columbus First Recorded Sighting of the Cayman Islands **Obv:** Crowned head right **Rev:** Quincentennial Celebrations Logo in color

| Date | Mintage | VF20 | XF40 | MS60 | MS63 | MS65 |
|---|---|---|---|---|---|---|
| 2003 | 1,500 | PF63 50.00 | PF65 55.00 | | | |

### KM# 138 2 DOLLARS

28.28 g., 0.925 Silver 0.841 oz. ASW, 38.61 mm. **Ruler:** Elizabeth II **Subject:** Royal Horticulture Society **Obv:** Head right, gilt portrait **Rev:** RHS Tent and flowers

| Date | Mintage | VF20 | XF40 | MS60 | MS63 | MS65 |
|---|---|---|---|---|---|---|
| 2003 | — | PF63 50.00 | PF65 55.00 | | | |

### KM# 137 5 DOLLARS

28.28 g., 0.925 Silver 0.841 oz. ASW, 38.6 mm. **Ruler:** Elizabeth II **Subject:** Elizabeth II's 80th Birthday **Obv:** Crowned head right - gilt **Obv. Legend:** CAYMAN ISLANDS - ELIZABETH II **Rev:** Queen crowning Charles as Prince of Wales

| Date | Mintage | VF20 | XF40 | MS60 | MS63 | MS65 |
|---|---|---|---|---|---|---|
| 2006 | 25,000 | PF63 45.00 | PF65 50.00 | | | |

### KM# 145 5 DOLLARS

28.28 g., 0.925 Silver 0.841 oz. ASW, 38.61 mm. **Ruler:** Elizabeth II **Subject:** Queen Elizabeth, 80th Birthday **Rev:** Elizabeth and Philip in the state coach

| Date | Mintage | VF20 | XF40 | MS60 | MS63 | MS65 |
|---|---|---|---|---|---|---|
| 2006 | Est. 25000 | PF63 45.00 | PF65 50.00 | | | |

### KM# 149 5 DOLLARS

28.28 g., 0.925 Silver 0.841 oz. ASW, 38.6 mm. **Ruler:** Elizabeth II **Obv:** Head in tiara right, gilt face and rim **Rev:** Queen and Prince Philip in carriage, gilt 80 above

| Date | Mintage | VF20 | XF40 | MS60 | MS63 | MS65 |
|---|---|---|---|---|---|---|
| 2006 | — | PF63 50.00 | PF65 55.00 | | | |

### KM# 139 5 DOLLARS

28.28 g., 0.925 Silver 0.841 oz. ASW, 38.61 mm. **Ruler:** Elizabeth II **Subject:** Cayman Islands Monetary Authority, 10th Anniversary **Obv:** Bust right **Rev:** Island's coat of arms

| Date | Mintage | VF20 | XF40 | MS60 | MS63 | MS65 |
|---|---|---|---|---|---|---|
| 2007 | 200 | PF63 100 | PF65 110 | | | |

### KM# 146 5 DOLLARS

28.28 g., 0.925 Silver 0.841 oz. ASW, 38.61 mm. **Ruler:** Elizabeth II **Subject:** End of World War I, 90th Anniversary

| Date | Mintage | VF20 | XF40 | MS60 | MS63 | MS65 |
|---|---|---|---|---|---|---|
| 2008 | — | PF63 50.00 | PF65 55.00 | | | |

### KM# 147 5 DOLLARS

28.28 g., 0.925 Silver 0.841 oz. ASW, 38.61 mm. **Ruler:** Elizabeth II **Subject:** End of World War I, 90th Anniversary

| Date | Mintage | VF20 | XF40 | MS60 | MS63 | MS65 |
|---|---|---|---|---|---|---|
| 2008 | — | PF63 50.00 | PF65 55.00 | | | |

### KM# 141 5 DOLLARS

28.28 g., 0.925 Silver 0.841 oz. ASW, 38.6 mm. **Ruler:** Elizabeth II **Subject:** Constitutional Government, 50th Anniversary **Obv:** Bust right **Rev:** Coat of arms

| Date | Mintage | VF20 | XF40 | MS60 | MS63 | MS65 |
|---|---|---|---|---|---|---|
| 2009 | 300 | PF63 75.00 | PF65 85.00 | | | |

### KM# 150 5 DOLLARS

28.28 g., 0.925 Silver 0.841 oz. ASW, 38.61 mm. **Ruler:** Elizabeth II **Subject:** Royal Yacht Britannia, 60th Anniversary **Rev:** HMY Britannia, flags **Rev. Legend:** I NAME THIS SHIP BRITANNIA

| Date | Mintage | VF20 | XF40 | MS60 | MS63 | MS65 |
|---|---|---|---|---|---|---|
| 2012 | — | PF65 110 | | | | |

### KM# 151 5 DOLLARS

28.28 g., 0.925 Silver 0.841 oz. ASW partially gilt, 38.61 mm. **Ruler:** Elizabeth II **Subject:** Heroes Day, 10th Anniversary **Obv:** Coat of arms, gilt **Rev:** Statues of father and son sitting on ship's deck, woman holding the earth in her hands, three small catboats in the water

| Date | Mintage | VF20 | XF40 | MS60 | MS63 | MS65 |
|---|---|---|---|---|---|---|
| 2013 | 200 | PF65 115 | | | | |

### KM# 140 10 DOLLARS

7.99 g., 0.9167 Gold 0.2354 oz. AGW, 22.1 mm. **Ruler:** Elizabeth II **Subject:** Cayman Islands Monetary Authority, 10th Anniversary **Obv:** Bust right **Rev:** Island's coat of arms

| Date | Mintage | VF20 | XF40 | MS60 | MS63 | MS65 |
|---|---|---|---|---|---|---|
| 2007 | 75 | PF63 450 | PF65 500 | | | |

### KM# 152 10 DOLLARS

28.28 g., 0.925 Silver 0.841 oz. ASW, 38.61 mm. **Ruler:** Elizabeth II **Subject:** Royal Family **Shape:** 7-Sided

| Date | Mintage | VF20 | XF40 | MS60 | MS63 | MS65 |
|---|---|---|---|---|---|---|
| 2007 | Est. 30000 | PF63 35.00 | PF65 40.00 | | | |

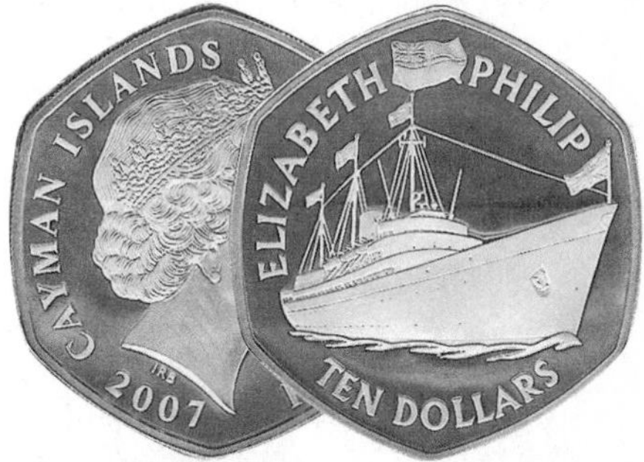


### KM# 153 10 DOLLARS

28.28 g., 0.925 Silver 0.841 oz. ASW, 38.61 mm. **Ruler:** Elizabeth II **Subject:** Royal Yacht Britannia **Shape:** 7-Sided

| Date | Mintage | VF20 | XF40 | MS60 | MS63 | MS65 |
|---|---|---|---|---|---|---|
| 2007 | Est. 30000 | PF63 35.00 | PF65 40.00 | | | |

### KM# 154 10 DOLLARS

28.28 g., 0.925 Silver 0.841 oz. ASW, 38.61 mm. **Ruler:** Elizabeth II **Shape:** 7-Sided

| Date | Mintage | VF20 | XF40 | MS60 | MS63 | MS65 |
|---|---|---|---|---|---|---|
| 2007 | Est. 30000 | PF63 35.00 | PF65 40.00 | | | |

### KM# 142 10 DOLLARS

7.99 g., 0.9167 Gold 0.2354 oz. AGW, 22.1 mm. **Ruler:** Elizabeth II **Subject:** Constitutional Government, 50th Anniversary **Obv:** Bust right **Rev:** Coat of Arms

| Date | Mintage | VF20 | XF40 | MS60 | MS63 | MS65 |
|---|---|---|---|---|---|---|
| 2009 | 125 | PF63 425 | PF65 475 | | | |

### KM# 148 50 DOLLARS

155.50 g., 0.925 Silver 4.6245 oz. ASW, 65 mm. **Ruler:** Elizabeth II **Subject:** End of World War I, 90th Anniversary **Rev:** Soldier in the field with barbed wire

| Date | Mintage | VF20 | XF40 | MS60 | MS63 | MS65 |
|---|---|---|---|---|---|---|
| 2008 | Est. 150 | PF63 250 | PF65 300 | | | |

# CENTRAL AFRICAN STATES

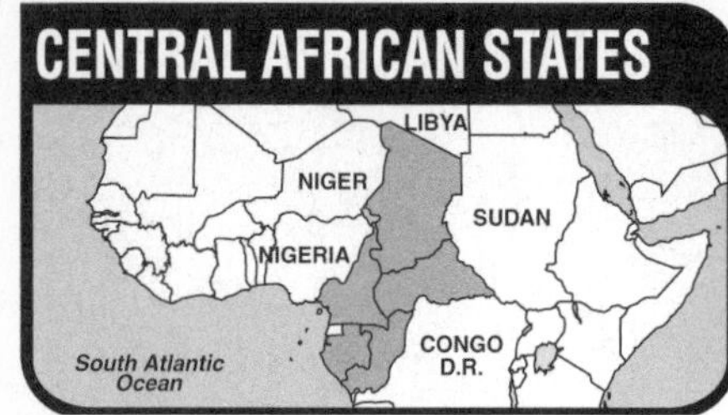


The Central African States, a monetary union comprised of Equatorial Guinea (a former Spanish possession), the former French possessions and now independent states of the Republic of Congo (Brazzaville), Gabon, Central African Republic, Chad and Cameroon, issues a common currency for the member states from a common central bank. The monetary unit, the African Financial Community franc, is tied to and supported by the French franc.

In 1960, an attempt was made to form a union of the newly independent republics of Chad, Congo, Central Africa and Gabon. The proposal was discarded when Chad refused to become a constituent member. The four countries then linked into an Equatorial Customs Unit, to which Cameroon became an associate member in 1961. A more extensive cooperation of the five republics, identified as the Central African Customs and Economic Union, was entered into force at the beginning of 1966.

In 1974 the Central Bank of the Equatorial African States, which had issued coins and paper currency in its own name and with the names of the constituent member nations, changed its name to the Bank of the Central African States. Equatorial Guinea converted to the CFA currency system issuing its first 100 Franc in 1985.

## MONETARY UNION

### STANDARD COINAGE

**KM# 8 FRANC**
1.30 g., Aluminum, 23 mm. **Obv:** Three giant eland left, date below **Rev:** Denomination within wreath

| Date | Mintage | VF20 | XF40 | MS60 | MS63 | MS65 |
|---|---|---|---|---|---|---|
| 2003 | — | 0.40 | 0.80 | 1.00 | 2.00 | — |

**KM# 16 FRANC**
1.61 g., Stainless Steel, 14.9 mm. **Obv:** Value **Rev:** Value above produce **Edge:** Plain

| Date | Mintage | VF20 | XF40 | MS60 | MS63 | MS65 |
|---|---|---|---|---|---|---|
| 2006 (a) | — | — | — | — | 0.15 | 0.25 |

**KM# 17 2 FRANCS**
2.43 g., Stainless Steel, 17.9 mm. **Obv:** Value **Rev:** Value above produce **Edge:** Plain

| Date | Mintage | VF20 | XF40 | MS60 | MS63 | MS65 |
|---|---|---|---|---|---|---|
| 2006 (a) | — | — | — | — | 0.25 | 0.35 |

**KM# 7 5 FRANCS**
3.00 g., Aluminum-Bronze, 20 mm. **Obv:** Three giant eland left, date below **Rev:** Denomination within wreath

| Date | Mintage | VF20 | XF40 | MS60 | MS63 | MS65 |
|---|---|---|---|---|---|---|
| 2003 | — | 0.30 | 0.60 | 0.75 | 1.25 | 2.50 |

**KM# 18 5 FRANCS**
2.41 g., Brass, 15.9 mm. **Obv:** Value **Rev:** Value above produce **Edge:** Reeded

| Date | Mintage | VF20 | XF40 | MS60 | MS63 | MS65 |
|---|---|---|---|---|---|---|
| 2006 (a) | — | — | — | — | 0.50 | 0.65 |

**KM# 9 10 FRANCS**
4.00 g., Aluminum-Bronze, 23 mm. **Obv:** Three giant eland left, date below **Rev:** Denomination within wreath

| Date | Mintage | VF20 | XF40 | MS60 | MS63 | MS65 |
|---|---|---|---|---|---|---|
| 2003 (a) | — | 0.35 | 0.75 | 1.00 | 1.50 | 3.00 |

**KM# 19 10 FRANCS**
3.00 g., Brass, 17.9 mm. **Obv:** Value **Rev:** Value above produce **Edge:** Reeded

| Date | Mintage | VF20 | XF40 | MS60 | MS63 | MS65 |
|---|---|---|---|---|---|---|
| 2006 (a) | — | — | — | — | 0.75 | 1.00 |

**KM# 10 25 FRANCS**
8.00 g., Aluminum-Bronze, 27.2 mm. **Obv:** Three giant eland left, date below **Rev:** Denomination within wreath

| Date | Mintage | VF20 | XF40 | MS60 | MS63 | MS65 |
|---|---|---|---|---|---|---|
| 2003 (a) | — | 0.50 | 1.00 | 1.50 | 2.00 | 5.00 |

**KM# 20 25 FRANCS**
4.20 g., Brass, 22.7 mm. **Obv:** Value **Rev:** Value above produce **Edge:** Reeded

| Date | Mintage | VF20 | XF40 | MS60 | MS63 | MS65 |
|---|---|---|---|---|---|---|
| 2006 (a) | — | — | — | — | 1.00 | 1.25 |

**KM# 11 50 FRANCS**
4.70 g., Nickel, 21.5 mm. **Obv:** Three giant eland left, date below **Rev:** Denomination within flower design **Edge:** Reeded **Note:** Starting in 1996 an extra flora item was added where the mintmark was formerly located.

| Date | Mintage | VF20 | XF40 | MS60 | MS63 | MS65 |
|---|---|---|---|---|---|---|
| 2003 (a) | — | 1.25 | 2.00 | 3.00 | 5.00 | 9.00 |

**KM# 21 50 FRANCS**
4.90 g., Stainless Steel, 22 mm. **Obv:** Value **Rev:** Value above produce **Edge:** Reeded

| Date | Mintage | VF20 | XF40 | MS60 | MS63 | MS65 |
|---|---|---|---|---|---|---|
| 2006 (a) | — | — | — | — | 1.25 | 1.50 |

**KM# 13 100 FRANCS**
7.05 g., Nickel, 25.5 mm. **Obv:** Three giant eland **Rev:** Denomination

| Date | Mintage | VF20 | XF40 | MS60 | MS63 | MS65 |
|---|---|---|---|---|---|---|
| 2003 | — | — | — | 2.00 | 4.50 | 6.00 |

**KM# 15 100 FRANCS**
6.00 g., Bi-Metallic Stainless Steel center in Brass ring, 23.9 mm. **Obv:** Denomination above initials within beaded circle **Rev:** Value above produce **Edge:** Reeded

| Date | Mintage | VF20 | XF40 | MS60 | MS63 | MS65 |
|---|---|---|---|---|---|---|
| 2006 (a) | — | — | — | — | 5.00 | 6.50 |

**KM# 22 500 FRANCS**
8.10 g., Copper-Nickel, 26 mm. **Obv:** Value above produce **Rev:** Value **Edge:** Segmented reeding and lettering

| Date | Mintage | VF20 | XF40 | MS60 | MS63 | MS65 |
|---|---|---|---|---|---|---|
| 2006 (a) | — | — | — | 8.00 | 10.00 | |

**KM# 23 1000 FRANCS**
22.20 g., 0.900 Silver 0.6424 oz. ASW, 37 mm. **Subject:** FIFA World Cup, England, 2004 **Edge:** Plain

| Date | Mintage | VF20 | XF40 | MS60 | MS63 | MS65 |
|---|---|---|---|---|---|---|
| 2004 (a) | — | — | — | — | 35.00 | 40.00 |
| 2004 (a) | — | PF63 40.00 | PF65 45.00 | | | |

# CHAD

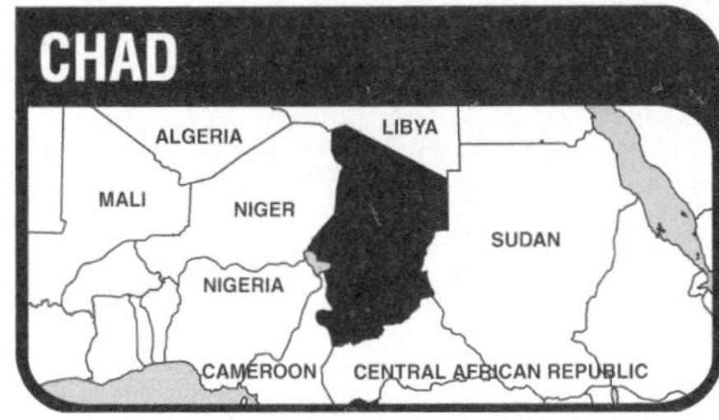


The Republic of Chad, a landlocked country of central Africa, is the largest country of former French Equatorial Africa. It has an area of 495,755 sq. mi. (1,284,000 sq. km.) and a population of *7.27 million. Capital: N'Djamena. An expanding livestock industry produces camels, cattle and sheep. Cotton (the chief product), ivory and palm oil are important exports.

**NOTE**: For earlier and related coinage see French Equatorial Africa and the Equatorial African States. For later coinage see Central African States.

**MINT MARKS**

(a) - Paris, privy marks only
(b) = Brussels
NI - Numismatic Italiana, Arezzo, Italy

## REPUBLIC

### DECIMAL COINAGE

**KM# 30 500 FRANCS**
Silver, 31 mm. **Obv:** Native portrait within circle **Rev:** Rhino mom and baby

| Date | Mintage | VF20 | XF40 | MS60 | MS63 | MS65 |
|---|---|---|---|---|---|---|
| 2001 Proof | — | — | — | — | — | — |

**KM# 20 1000 FRANCS**
15.00 g., 0.999 Silver 0.4818 oz. ASW, 35 mm. **Obv:** Native portrait within circle, denomination below **Rev:** Ancient Arabic war ship **Edge:** Plain

| Date | Mintage | VF20 | XF40 | MS60 | MS63 | MS65 |
|---|---|---|---|---|---|---|
| 2001 | — | PF65 40.00 | | | | |

**KM# 21 1000 FRANCS**
25.10 g., 0.999 Silver 0.8062 oz. ASW, 40 mm. **Obv:** Native portrait within circle, denomination below **Rev:** Soccer player and stadium **Edge:** Reeded

| Date | Mintage | VF20 | XF40 | MS60 | MS63 | MS65 |
|---|---|---|---|---|---|---|
| 2001 | — | PF63 45.00 | PF65 50.00 | | | |

**KM# 29 1000 FRANCS**
15.00 g., 0.999 Silver 0.4818 oz. ASW, 36 mm. **Obv:** Native portrait within circle **Rev:** Multicolor orang-outan

| Date | Mintage | VF20 | XF40 | MS60 | MS63 | MS65 |
|---|---|---|---|---|---|---|
| 2001 | — | PF65 35.00 | | | | |

**KM# 35 1000 FRANCS**
20.00 g., Silver, 40 mm. **Subject:** African Fauna **Obv:** Native portrait within circle **Rev:** Balearica Pavonina (two birds)

| Date | Mintage | VF20 | XF40 | MS60 | MS63 | MS65 |
|---|---|---|---|---|---|---|
| 2001 | — | PF63 40.00 | PF65 45.00 | | | |

**KM# 22 1000 FRANCS**
20.00 g., 0.999 Silver 0.6424 oz. ASW, 40 mm. **Obv:** Native portrait within circle, denomination below **Rev:** Horizontal soccer player above stadium **Edge:** Reeded

| Date | Mintage | VF20 | XF40 | MS60 | MS63 | MS65 |
|---|---|---|---|---|---|---|
| 2002 | 5,000 | PF63 40.00 | PF65 45.00 | | | |

**KM# 23 1000 FRANCS**
20.15 g., 0.999 Silver 0.6472 oz. ASW, 40 mm. **Obv:** Native portrait within circle, denomination below **Rev:** Soccer player and Arch of Triumph **Edge:** Reeded

| Date | Mintage | VF20 | XF40 | MS60 | MS63 | MS65 |
|---|---|---|---|---|---|---|
| 2002 | — | PF63 37.00 | PF65 42.00 | | | |

**KM# 31 1000 FRANCS**
15.00 g., 0.985 Silver 0.475 oz. ASW, 34 mm. **Rev:** Multicolor McDonnell-Douglass DC-10 landing left

| Date | Mintage | VF20 | XF40 | MS60 | MS63 | MS65 |
|---|---|---|---|---|---|---|
| 2002 | — | PF65 35.00 | | | | |

**KM# 32 1000 FRANCS**
15.00 g., 0.985 Silver 0.475 oz. ASW, 34 mm. **Rev:** Multicolor Boeing 747 taking-off right

| Date | Mintage | VF20 | XF40 | MS60 | MS63 | MS65 |
|---|---|---|---|---|---|---|
| 2002 | — | PF65 35.00 | | | | |

**KM# 33 1000 FRANCS**
15.00 g., 0.985 Silver 0.475 oz. ASW, 34 mm. **Rev:** Multicolor McDonnell-Douglass DC-9 over mountains

| Date | Mintage | VF20 | XF40 | MS60 | MS63 | MS65 |
|---|---|---|---|---|---|---|
| 2003 | — | PF65 35.00 | | | | |

**KM# 34 1000 FRANCS**
15.00 g., 0.985 Silver 0.475 oz. ASW, 34 mm. **Rev:** Multicolor Fokker F-7a top wing

| Date | Mintage | VF20 | XF40 | MS60 | MS63 | MS65 |
|---|---|---|---|---|---|---|
| 2003 | — | PF65 35.00 | | | | |

**KM# 36 1000 FRANCS**
20.00 g., Silver, 40 mm. **Subject:** Animals in Peril **Obv:** Native portrait within circle **Rev:** Leopard

| Date | Mintage | VF20 | XF40 | MS60 | MS63 | MS65 |
|---|---|---|---|---|---|---|
| 2003 | — | PF63 35.00 | PF65 40.00 | | | |

The Republic of Chile, a ribbon-like country on the Pacific coast of southern South America, has an area of 292,135 sq. mi. (756,950 sq. km.) and a population of *15.21 million. Capital: Santiago. Historically, the economic base of Chile has been the rich mineral deposits of its northern provinces. Copper has accounted for more than 75 percent of Chile's export earnings in recent years. Other important mineral exports are iron ore, iodine and nitrate of soda. Fresh fruits and vegetables, as well as wine are increasingly significant in inter-hemispheric trade.

**MINT MARK**

So - Santiago
(ml) - Maple leaf - Royal Canadian Mint (RCM)

# REPUBLIC

## REFORM COINAGE

100 Centavos = 1 Peso; 1000 Old Escudos = 1 Peso

### KM# 231 PESO

0.70 g., Aluminum, 15.5 mm. **Obv:** Gen. Bernardo O'Higgins bust right **Obv. Legend:** REPUBLICA - DE CHILE **Rev:** Denomination above date within wreath **Edge:** Plain **Shape:** 8-sided **Note:** Varieties exist.

| Date | Mintage | VF20 | XF40 | MS60 | MS63 | MS65 |
|---|---|---|---|---|---|---|
| 2001 So Narrow date | — | — | — | — | 0.10 | 0.20 |
| 2002 So Narrow date | — | — | — | — | 0.10 | 0.20 |
| 2003 So Narrow date | — | — | — | — | 0.10 | 0.20 |
| 2004 So Wide date | — | — | — | — | 0.10 | 0.20 |
| 2005 So Wide date | — | — | — | — | 0.10 | 0.20 |
| 2006 So Wide date | — | — | — | — | 0.10 | 0.20 |
| 2008 So Wide date | — | — | — | — | 0.10 | 0.20 |
| 2009 So Wide date | — | — | — | — | 0.10 | 0.20 |
| 2011 So Wide date | — | — | — | — | 0.10 | 0.20 |
| 2012 So Wide date | — | — | — | — | 0.10 | 0.20 |
| 2013 So Wide date | — | — | — | — | 0.10 | 0.20 |

### KM# 232 5 PESOS

2.20 g., Aluminum-Bronze, 15.5 mm. **Obv:** Gen. Bernardo O'Higgins bust right **Obv. Legend:** REPUBLICA - DE CHILE **Rev:** Denomination above date within wreath **Edge:** Plain **Shape:** 8-sided **Note:** Varieties exist.

| Date | Mintage | VF20 | XF40 | MS60 | MS63 | MS65 |
|---|---|---|---|---|---|---|
| 2001 So Narrow date | — | — | 0.10 | 0.20 | 0.35 | 0.60 |
| 2001 (sa) Wide date | — | — | 0.15 | 0.25 | 0.50 | 0.75 |
| Note: Without name of sculptor | | | | | | |
| 2002 So Narrow date | — | — | 0.15 | 0.25 | 0.50 | 0.75 |
| 2002 (a) Wide date | — | — | 0.10 | 0.20 | 0.35 | 0.60 |
| 2003 So | — | — | 0.10 | 0.20 | 0.35 | 0.60 |
| 2004 So | — | — | 0.10 | 0.20 | 0.35 | 0.60 |
| 2005 So | — | — | 0.10 | 0.20 | 0.35 | 0.60 |
| 2006 So | — | — | 0.10 | 0.20 | 0.35 | 0.60 |
| 2007 So | — | — | 0.10 | 0.20 | 0.35 | 0.60 |
| 2008 So | — | — | 0.10 | 0.20 | 0.35 | 0.60 |
| 2009 So | — | — | 0.10 | 0.20 | 0.35 | 0.60 |
| 2010 So | — | — | 0.10 | 0.20 | 0.35 | 0.60 |
| 2011 So | — | — | 0.10 | 0.20 | 0.35 | 0.60 |
| 2012 So (Minted in Madrid) | — | — | 0.10 | 0.20 | 0.35 | 0.60 |
| 2013 So | — | — | 0.10 | 0.20 | 0.35 | 0.60 |

### KM# 228.2 10 PESOS

3.50 g., Aluminum-Bronze, 21 mm. **Obv:** Bust of Gen. Bernardo O'Higgins right **Obv. Legend:** REPUBLICA - DE CHILE **Rev:** Denomination above date within sprays **Edge:** Reeded **Note:** All 9's are curl tail 9's except for the 1999 date, these are straight tail 9's. Normal rim.

| Date | Mintage | VF20 | XF40 | MS60 | MS63 | MS65 |
|---|---|---|---|---|---|---|
| 2002 So | — | — | 0.20 | 0.30 | 0.50 | 0.65 |
| 2003 So | — | — | 0.20 | 0.30 | 0.50 | 0.65 |
| 2004 So | — | — | 0.20 | 0.30 | 0.50 | 0.65 |
| 2005 So | — | — | 0.20 | 0.30 | 0.50 | 0.65 |
| 2006 So | — | — | 0.20 | 0.30 | 0.50 | 0.65 |
| 2007 | — | — | 0.20 | 0.30 | 0.50 | 0.65 |
| Note: Struck in Canada | | | | | | |
| 2008 So | — | — | 0.20 | 0.30 | 0.50 | 0.65 |
| 2009 So | — | — | 0.20 | 0.30 | 0.50 | 0.65 |
| 2010 So | — | — | 0.20 | 0.30 | 0.50 | 0.65 |
| 2011 So | — | — | 0.20 | 0.30 | 0.50 | 0.65 |
| 2012 So | — | — | 0.20 | 0.30 | 0.50 | 0.65 |
| 2013 So | — | — | 0.20 | 0.30 | 0.50 | 0.65 |

### KM# 219.2 50 PESOS

7.00 g., Aluminum-Bronze, 25 mm. **Obv:** Bust of Gen. Bernardo O'Higgins right **Obv. Legend:** REPUBLICA - DE CHILE **Rev:** Denomination above date within sprays **Edge:** Ornamented **Shape:** 10-sided **Note:** Narrow date.

| Date | Mintage | VF20 | XF40 | MS60 | MS63 | MS65 |
|---|---|---|---|---|---|---|
| 2001 So | — | — | 0.50 | 0.75 | 1.25 | 1.50 |
| 2002 So | — | — | 0.50 | 0.75 | 1.25 | 1.50 |
| 2005 So | — | — | — | 0.50 | 1.00 | 1.25 |
| 2006 So | — | — | — | 0.50 | 1.00 | 1.25 |
| 2007 | — | — | — | 0.50 | 1.00 | 1.25 |
| Note: Struck in Canada | | | | | | |
| 2009 So | — | — | — | 0.50 | 1.00 | 1.25 |
| 2010 So | — | — | — | 0.50 | 1.00 | 1.25 |
| 2011 So | — | — | — | 0.50 | 1.00 | 1.25 |
| 2012 So | — | — | — | 0.50 | 1.00 | 1.25 |
| 2013 So | — | — | — | 0.50 | 1.00 | 1.25 |

### KM# 219.3 50 PESOS

7.00 g., Aluminum-Bronze, 25 mm. **Obv:** Bust of Gen. Bernardo O'Higgins right **Obv. Legend:** REPUBLICA DE CHIIE **Rev:** Denomination above date within sprays **Note:** Error spelling in legend of CHILE.

| Date | Mintage | VF20 | XF40 | MS60 | MS63 | MS65 |
|---|---|---|---|---|---|---|
| 2008 | — | — | — | 2.00 | 3.00 | 4.50 |

### KM# 236 100 PESOS

7.58 g., Bi-Metallic Copper-Nickel-Zinc center in Aluminum-Bronze ring, 23.5 mm. **Subject:** Native people **Obv:** Bust of native Mapuche girl facing **Obv. Legend:** REPUBLICA DE CHILE - PUEBLOS ORIGINARIOS **Rev:** National arms above denomination **Edge:** Segmented reeding

| Date | Mintage | VF20 | XF40 | MS60 | MS63 | MS65 |
|---|---|---|---|---|---|---|
| 2001 So | — | 0.35 | 0.65 | 0.85 | 1.25 | 2.25 |
| 2003 So | — | 0.35 | 0.65 | 0.85 | 1.25 | 2.25 |
| 2004 So | — | 0.35 | 0.65 | 0.85 | 1.25 | 2.25 |
| 2005 So | — | 0.35 | 0.65 | 0.85 | 1.25 | 2.25 |
| 2006 So | — | 0.35 | 0.65 | 0.85 | 1.25 | 2.25 |
| 2008 So | — | 0.35 | 0.65 | 0.85 | 1.25 | 2.25 |
| 2009 So | — | 0.35 | 0.65 | 0.85 | 1.25 | 2.25 |
| 2010 So | — | 0.35 | 0.65 | 0.85 | 1.25 | 2.25 |
| 2011 So | — | 0.35 | 0.65 | 0.85 | 1.25 | 2.25 |
| 2012 So | — | 0.35 | 0.65 | 0.85 | 1.25 | 2.25 |
| 2013 So | — | 0.35 | 0.65 | 0.85 | 1.25 | 2.25 |

### KM# 235 500 PESOS

6.50 g., Bi-Metallic Aluminum-Bronze center in Copper-Nickel-Zinc ring, 26 mm. **Subject:** Cardinal Raul Silva Henriquez **Obv:** Bust of cardinal within inner ring facing left **Rev:** Denomination above date within wreath **Edge:** Reeded

| Date | Mintage | VF20 | XF40 | MS60 | MS63 | MS65 |
|---|---|---|---|---|---|---|
| 2001 So | — | — | — | 2.50 | 5.00 | 6.50 |
| 2002 So 4.1mm date | — | — | — | 2.50 | 5.00 | 6.50 |
| 2002 So 5.2mm date | — | — | — | 2.50 | 5.00 | 6.50 |
| 2003 So | — | — | — | 2.50 | 5.00 | 6.50 |
| 2008 So | — | — | — | 2.50 | 5.00 | 6.50 |
| 2009 So | — | — | — | 2.50 | 5.00 | 6.50 |
| 2010 So | — | — | — | 2.50 | 5.00 | 6.50 |
| 2011 So | — | — | — | 2.50 | 5.00 | 6.50 |
| 2012 So | — | — | — | 2.50 | 5.00 | 6.50 |
| 2013 So | — | — | — | 2.50 | 5.00 | 6.50 |

The Peoples Republic of China, located in eastern Asia, has an area of 3,696,100 sq. mi. (9,596,960 sq. km.) (including Manchuria and Tibet) and a population of *1.20 billion. Capital: Peking (Beijing). The economy is based on agriculture, mining, and manufacturing. Textiles, clothing, metal ores, tea and rice are exported.

**MONETARY SYSTEM**

10 Fen (Cents) = 1 Jiao
10 Jiao = 1 Renminbi Yuan

**MINT MARKS**

(b) - Beijing (Peking)
(s) - Shanghai
(y) - Shenyang (Mukden)

**OBVERSE LEGENDS**

中华人民共和国

ZHONGHUA RENMIN GONGHEGUO
(Peoples Republic of China)

中国人民银行

ZHONGGUO RENMIN YINHANG
(Peoples Bank of China)

# PEOPLES REPUBLIC

## STANDARD COINAGE

### KM# 1 FEN

0.70 g., Aluminum, 18 mm. **Obv:** National emblem **Rev:** Value in wreath, date below **Edge:** Reeded **Note:** Prev. Y#1.

| Date | Mintage | VF20 | XF40 | MS60 | MS63 | MS65 |
|---|---|---|---|---|---|---|
| 2005 | — | — | — | 0.15 | 0.25 | — |
| 2006 | — | — | — | 0.15 | 0.25 | — |
| 2007 | — | — | — | 0.15 | 0.25 | — |
| 2008 | — | — | — | 0.15 | 0.25 | — |
| 2009 | — | — | — | 0.15 | 0.25 | — |
| 2010 | — | — | — | 0.15 | 0.25 | — |
| 2011 | — | — | — | 0.15 | 0.25 | — |

### KM# 1210 JIAO

1.12 g., Aluminum, 19 mm. **Obv:** Denomination, date below **Rev:** Orchid **Rev. Legend:** ZHONGGUA RENMIN YINHANG **Edge:** Plain **Note:** Prev. Y#1068.

| Date | Mintage | VF20 | XF40 | MS60 | MS63 | MS65 |
|---|---|---|---|---|---|---|
| 2001 | — | — | — | 0.50 | 0.75 | — |
| 2002 | — | — | — | 0.50 | 0.75 | — |
| 2003 | — | — | — | 0.50 | 0.75 | — |

### KM# 1210a JIAO

Copper-Nickel, 19 mm. **Obv:** Denomination, date below **Note:** Prev. Y#1068a.

| Date | Mintage | VF20 | XF40 | MS60 | MS63 | MS65 |
|---|---|---|---|---|---|---|
| 2005 | — | — | — | 0.50 | 0.75 | — |

### KM# 1210b JIAO

3.20 g., Stainless Steel, 19 mm. **Obv:** Value, date below **Rev:** Orchid **Rev. Legend:** ZHONGGUA RENMIN YINHANG **Edge:** Plain **Note:** Prev. Y#1068b.

| Date | Mintage | VF20 | XF40 | MS60 | MS63 | MS65 |
|---|---|---|---|---|---|---|
| 2005 | — | — | — | — | 2.00 | — |
| 2006 | — | — | — | — | 0.25 | — |
| 2007 | — | — | — | — | 0.25 | — |
| 2008 | — | — | — | — | 0.25 | — |
| 2009 | — | — | — | — | 0.25 | — |
| 2010 | — | — | — | — | 0.25 | — |
| 2011 | — | — | — | — | 0.25 | — |
| 2012 | — | — | — | — | 0.25 | — |
| 2013 | — | — | — | — | 0.25 | — |

### KM# 336 5 JIAO

3.80 g., Brass, 20.5 mm. **Obv:** National emblem, date below **Rev:** Denomination above flowers **Edge:** Segmented reeding **Note:** Prev. Y#329.

| Date | Mintage | VF20 | XF40 | MS60 | MS63 | MS65 |
|---|---|---|---|---|---|---|
| 2001 | — | — | — | 1.00 | 1.25 | — |

### KM# 1411 5 JIAO

3.80 g., Brass Plated Steel, 20.5 mm. **Obv:** Denomination **Rev:** Flower **Rev. Legend:** ZHONGGUA RENMIN YINHANG **Edge:** Segmented reeding **Note:** Prev. Y#1106.

| Date | Mintage | VF20 | XF40 | MS60 | MS63 | MS65 |
|---|---|---|---|---|---|---|
| 2002 | — | — | — | 1.50 | 1.75 | — |
| 2003 | — | — | — | 1.50 | 1.75 | — |
| 2004 | — | — | — | 1.50 | 1.75 | — |
| 2005 | — | — | — | 1.50 | 1.75 | — |
| 2006 | — | — | — | 1.50 | 1.75 | — |
| 2007 | — | — | — | 1.50 | 1.75 | — |
| 2008 | — | — | — | 1.50 | 1.75 | — |
| 2009 | — | — | — | 1.50 | 1.75 | — |
| 2010 | — | — | — | 1.50 | 1.75 | — |
| 2011 | — | — | — | 1.50 | 1.75 | — |
| 2012 | — | — | — | 1.50 | 1.75 | — |
| 2013 | — | — | — | 1.50 | 1.75 | — |

### KM# 1212 YUAN

6.10 g., Nickel Plated Steel, 24.9 mm. **Obv:** Denomination, date below **Rev:** Chrysanthemum **Rev. Legend:** ZHONGGUA RENMIN YINHANG **Edge:** RMB" three times **Note:** Prev. Y#1069.

| Date | Mintage | VF20 | XF40 | MS60 | MS63 | MS65 |
|---|---|---|---|---|---|---|
| 2001 | — | — | — | 2.00 | 2.50 | — |
| 2002 | — | — | — | 2.00 | 2.50 | — |
| 2003 | — | — | — | 2.00 | 2.50 | — |
| 2004 | — | — | — | 2.00 | 2.50 | — |
| 2005 | — | — | — | 2.00 | 2.50 | — |
| 2006 | — | — | — | 2.00 | 2.50 | — |
| 2007 | — | — | — | 2.00 | 2.50 | — |
| 2008 | — | — | — | 2.00 | 2.50 | — |
| 2009 | — | — | — | 2.00 | 2.50 | — |
| 2010 | — | — | — | 2.00 | 2.50 | — |
| 2011 | — | — | — | 2.00 | 2.50 | — |
| 2012 | — | — | — | 2.00 | 2.50 | — |
| 2013 | — | — | — | 2.00 | 2.50 | — |

### KM# 1465 YUAN

6.85 g., Brass, 25 mm. **Obv:** Value **Rev:** Celebrating child and ram **Edge:** Lettered **Edge Lettering:** RMB" three times **Note:** Prev. Y#1125.

| Date | Mintage | VF20 | XF40 | MS60 | MS63 | MS65 |
|---|---|---|---|---|---|---|
| 2003 | — | — | — | 5.00 | 6.00 | — |

### KM# 1521 YUAN

6.750 Brass, 25 mm. **Obv:** Denomination **Rev:** Celebrating Child **Note:** Prev. Y#1247.

| Date | Mintage | VF20 | XF40 | MS60 | MS63 | MS65 |
|---|---|---|---|---|---|---|
| 2004 | — | — | — | 2.50 | 3.00 | — |

### KM# 1522 YUAN

6.00 g., Nickel Plated Steel, 25 mm. **Obv:** Palace **Rev:** Deng Xiao Ping 1904-2004 **Note:** Prev. Y#1248.

| Date | Mintage | VF20 | XF40 | MS60 | MS63 | MS65 |
|---|---|---|---|---|---|---|
| 2004 | — | — | — | 3.50 | 4.00 | — |

### KM# 1523 YUAN

6.00 g., Nickel Plated Steel, 25 mm. **Subject:** 50th Year of Peoples Congress **Obv:** Congress building **Note:** Prev. Y#1249.

| Date | Mintage | VF20 | XF40 | MS60 | MS63 | MS65 |
|---|---|---|---|---|---|---|
| 2004 | — | — | — | 3.50 | 4.00 | — |

### KM# 1574 YUAN

5.96 g., Nickel Clad Steel, 25 mm. **Obv:** Building **Rev:** Bust of Chenyun **Edge:** Lettered **Note:** Prev. Y#1208.

| Date | Mintage | VF20 | XF40 | MS60 | MS63 | MS65 |
|---|---|---|---|---|---|---|
| 2005 | — | — | — | 3.50 | 4.00 | — |

### KM# 1575 YUAN

6.75 g., Brass, 25 mm. **Subject:** Year of the Rooster **Obv:** Denomination **Rev:** Celebrating Child **Note:** Prev. Y#1250.

| Date | Mintage | VF20 | XF40 | MS60 | MS63 | MS65 |
|---|---|---|---|---|---|---|
| 2005 | — | — | — | 3.00 | 3.50 | — |

### KM# 1650 YUAN

6.75 g., Brass, 25 mm. **Subject:** Year of the Dog **Obv:** Denomination **Rev:** Celebrating Child **Note:** Prev. Y#1251.

| Date | Mintage | VF20 | XF40 | MS60 | MS63 | MS65 |
|---|---|---|---|---|---|---|
| 2006 | — | — | — | 7.00 | 8.00 | — |

### KM# 1775 YUAN

6.75 g., Brass, 25 mm. **Subject:** 29th Olympics **Obv:** Stylized Olympics logo **Rev:** Cartoon swimmer **Edge:** Reeded **Note:** Issued in 2006. Prev. Y#1256.

| Date | Mintage | VF20 | XF40 | MS60 | MS63 | MS65 |
|---|---|---|---|---|---|---|
| 2008 (y) | — | — | — | 5.00 | 6.00 | — |

### KM# 1776 YUAN

6.75 g., Brass, 25 mm. **Subject:** 29th Olympics **Obv:** Stylized Olympics logo **Rev:** Cartoon Weight Lifter **Edge:** Reeded **Note:** Issued in 2006. Prev. Y#1257.

| Date | Mintage | VF20 | XF40 | MS60 | MS63 | MS65 |
|---|---|---|---|---|---|---|
| 2008 | — | — | — | 5.00 | 6.00 | — |

### KM# 1652 YUAN

6.75 g., Brass, 25 mm. **Subject:** Year of the Pig

| Date | Mintage | VF20 | XF40 | MS60 | MS63 | MS65 |
|---|---|---|---|---|---|---|
| 2007 | 10,000,000 | — | — | — | 8.00 | — |

### KM# 1671 YUAN

6.75 g., Brass, 25 mm. **Subject:** 29th Summer Olympics, Bejing **Obv:** Olympic Logo **Rev:** Yingying mascot on pomel horse, latent image

| Date | Mintage | VF20 | XF40 | MS60 | MS63 | MS65 |
|---|---|---|---|---|---|---|
| 2008 | — | — | — | — | 5.00 | — |

### KM# 1672 YUAN

6.75 g., Brass, 25 mm. **Subject:** 29th Summer Olympics, Bejing **Obv:** Olympic games logo **Rev:** Jingjing mascot with bow and arrow, latent images

| Date | Mintage | VF20 | XF40 | MS60 | MS63 | MS65 |
|---|---|---|---|---|---|---|
| 2008 | — | — | — | — | 5.00 | — |

### KM# 1673 YUAN

6.75 g., Brass, 25 mm. **Subject:** 29th Summer Olympics, Bejing **Obv:** Olympics logo **Rev:** Huanhuan mascot playing soccer, latent image

| Date | Mintage | VF20 | XF40 | MS60 | MS63 | MS65 |
|---|---|---|---|---|---|---|
| 2008 | — | — | — | — | 5.00 | — |

### KM# 1810 YUAN

6.75 g., Brass, 25 mm. **Obv:** Beijing Olympic logo **Rev:** Character playing ping-pong

| Date | Mintage | VF20 | XF40 | MS60 | MS63 | MS65 |
|---|---|---|---|---|---|---|
| 2008 | — | — | — | 2.50 | 3.00 | — |

### KM# 1811 YUAN

6.750 Brass, 25 mm. **Obv:** Beijing Olympic logo **Rev:** Character fencing with bow and arrow

| Date | Mintage | VF20 | XF40 | MS60 | MS63 | MS65 |
|---|---|---|---|---|---|---|
| 2008 | — | — | — | 2.50 | 3.00 | — |

### KM# 1812 YUAN

6.75 g., Brass, 25 mm. **Obv:** Beijing Olympic logo **Rev:** Character on horseback

| Date | Mintage | VF20 | XF40 | MS60 | MS63 | MS65 |
|---|---|---|---|---|---|---|
| 2008 | — | — | — | 2.50 | 3.00 | — |

### KM# 1813 YUAN

6.75 g., Brass, 25 mm. **Obv:** Large value **Rev:** Boy with rat pattern chinese knot & cluster of fireworks

| Date | Mintage | VF20 | XF40 | MS60 | MS63 | MS65 |
|---|---|---|---|---|---|---|
| 2008 | 10,000,000 | — | — | 2.50 | 3.00 | — |

### KM# 1790 YUAN

6.75 g., Brass, 25 mm. **Subject:** Year of the Bull

| Date | Mintage | VF20 | XF40 | MS60 | MS63 | MS65 |
|---|---|---|---|---|---|---|
| 2009 | 30,000,000 | — | — | — | 5.00 | — |

### KM# 1791 YUAN

6.75 g., Brass, 25 mm. **Subject:** Conservation **Rev:** Eye and leaf on globe

| Date | Mintage | VF20 | XF40 | MS60 | MS63 | MS65 |
|---|---|---|---|---|---|---|
| 2009 | 10,000,000 | — | — | — | 5.00 | — |

### KM# 1792 YUAN

6.75 g., Brass, 25 mm. **Subject:** Harmony **Rev:** Haromony in seal script

| Date | Mintage | VF20 | XF40 | MS60 | MS63 | MS65 |
|---|---|---|---|---|---|---|
| 2009 | 10,000,000 | — | — | — | 5.00 | — |

### KM# 1988 YUAN

Nickel Plated Brass, 25 mm. **Subject:** Shanghai Expo **Obv:** Expo logo **Rev:** Skyline and expo mascot

| Date | Mintage | VF20 | XF40 | MS60 | MS63 | MS65 |
|---|---|---|---|---|---|---|
| 2010 | 60,000,000 | — | — | 6.00 | 8.00 | — |

### KM# 1989 YUAN

6.75 g., Brass, 25 mm. **Subject:** Year of the Tiger **Obv:** Large value **Rev:** Child dancing

| Date | Mintage | VF20 | XF40 | MS60 | MS63 | MS65 |
|---|---|---|---|---|---|---|
| 2010 | 60,000,000 | — | — | 5.00 | 7.50 | — |

### KM# 1990 YUAN

6.75 g., Brass, 25 mm. **Subject:** Enviornmental protection **Obv:** State emblem **Rev:** Caligraphy - Peace-Harmony

| Date | Mintage | VF20 | XF40 | MS60 | MS63 | MS65 |
|---|---|---|---|---|---|---|
| 2010 | 10,000,000 | — | — | 6.00 | 8.00 | — |

### KM# 1991 YUAN

6.75 g., Brass, 25 mm. **Subject:** Environmental protection **Obv:** National emblem **Rev:** Family dancing, globe

| Date | Mintage | VF20 | XF40 | MS60 | MS63 | MS65 |
|---|---|---|---|---|---|---|
| 2010 | 10,000,000 | — | — | 6.00 | 8.00 | — |

### KM# 1993 YUAN

6.75 g., Brass, 25 mm. **Subject:** Year of the Rabbit **Obv:** Large value **Rev:** Child playing

| Date | Mintage | VF20 | XF40 | MS60 | MS63 | MS65 |
|---|---|---|---|---|---|---|
| 2011 | 60,000,000 | — | — | 6.00 | 8.00 | — |

### KM# 2041 YUAN

6.75 g., Brass, 25 mm. **Subject:** Year of the Dragon **Obv:** Large numeral value **Rev:** Child dancing with lantern, dragon in background

| Date | Mintage | VF20 | XF40 | MS60 | MS63 | MS65 |
|---|---|---|---|---|---|---|
| 2012 | 80,000,000 | — | — | — | 3.00 | — |

### KM# 2080 YUAN

6.75 g., Brass, 25 mm. **Obv:** Large 1 **Rev:** Two children with kite

| Date | Mintage | VF20 | XF40 | MS60 | MS63 | MS65 |
|---|---|---|---|---|---|---|
| 2013 | 80,000,000 | — | — | 2.00 | 3.50 | — |

### KM# 2058 3 YUAN

7.78 g., 0.999 Silver 0.2499 oz. ASW, 25 mm. **Subject:** Panda, 30th Anniversary **Obv:** Temple of Heaven **Rev:** Panda

| Date | Mintage | VF20 | XF40 | MS60 | MS63 | MS65 |
|---|---|---|---|---|---|---|
| 2012 | 300,000 | PF63 25.00 | PF65 30.00 | | | |

### KM# 1068 5 YUAN

22.00 g., 0.900 Silver 0.6366 oz. ASW, 36 mm. **Obv:** Great Wall **Rev:** Gymnast, denomination at right **Edge:** Reeded **Note:** Prev. Y#1189.

| Date | Mintage | VF20 | XF40 | MS60 | MS63 | MS65 |
|---|---|---|---|---|---|---|
| 2005 (y) | — | — | — | 75.00 | 85.00 | — |

### KM# 1363 5 YUAN

12.80 g., Brass, 30 mm. **Subject:** 50th Anniversary - Chinese Occupation of Tibet **Obv:** National emblem **Rev:** Potala Palace, value and two dancers **Edge:** Reeded **Note:** Prev. Y#1126.

| Date | Mintage | VF20 | XF40 | MS60 | MS63 | MS65 |
|---|---|---|---|---|---|---|
| 2001 (y) | 10,000,000 | — | — | 8.00 | — | — |

### KM# 1364 5 YUAN

12.80 g., Brass, 30 mm. **Subject:** Revolution: 90th Anniversary **Obv:** National emblem **Rev:** Battle scene **Edge:** Reeded **Note:** Prev. Y#1109.

| Date | Mintage | VF20 | XF40 | MS60 | MS63 | MS65 |
|---|---|---|---|---|---|---|
| 2001 | — | — | — | 7.50 | 8.50 | — |

### KM# 1412 5 YUAN

12.80 g., Brass, 30 mm. **Subject:** The Great Wall **Obv:** State arms, icroscopic inscription repeated four times on the inner raised rim **Obv. Inscription:** SHI JIE WEN HUA YI CHAN **Rev:** Two views of the Great Wall **Edge:** Reeded **Note:** Prev. Y#1107.

| Date | Mintage | VF20 | XF40 | MS60 | MS63 | MS65 |
|---|---|---|---|---|---|---|
| 2002 | — | — | — | 7.00 | 8.00 | — |

### KM# 1413 5 YUAN

12.80 g., Brass, 30 mm. **Subject:** Terra Cotta Army **Obv:** State arms and the microscopic inscription repeated four times on the raised inner rim. **Obv. Inscription:** SHI JIE WEN HUA YI CHAN **Rev:** Terra Cotta Soldier close-up with many more in background **Edge:** Reeded **Note:** Prev. Y#1108.

| Date | Mintage | VF20 | XF40 | MS60 | MS63 | MS65 |
|---|---|---|---|---|---|---|
| 2002 | — | — | — | 7.00 | 8.00 | — |

### KM# 1461 5 YUAN

12.80 g., Brass, 30 mm. **Obv:** National emblem **Rev:** Chaotian Temple in Beigang Taiwan **Edge:** Reeded **Note:** Prev. Y#1127.

| Date | Mintage | VF20 | XF40 | MS60 | MS63 | MS65 |
|---|---|---|---|---|---|---|
| 2003 | 10,000,000 | — | — | 7.00 | 8.00 | — |

### KM# 1462 5 YUAN

12.80 g., Brass, 30 mm. **Obv:** National emblem **Rev:** Chikan Tower on Treasure Island Taiwan **Edge:** Reeded **Note:** Prev. Y#1128.

| Date | Mintage | VF20 | XF40 | MS60 | MS63 | MS65 |
|---|---|---|---|---|---|---|
| 2003 (y) | 10,000,000 | — | — | 7.00 | 8.00 | — |

### KM# 1463 5 YUAN

12.80 g., Brass, 30 mm. **Subject:** Chaotian Temple in Beijing **Obv:** State emblem **Rev:** Buildings **Edge:** Reeded **Note:** Prev. Y#1230.

| Date | Mintage | VF20 | XF40 | MS60 | MS63 | MS65 |
|---|---|---|---|---|---|---|
| 2003 | 10,000,000 | — | — | 7.00 | 8.00 | — |

### KM# 1464 5 YUAN

12.80 g., Brass, 30 mm. **Obv:** National emblem **Rev:** Imperial Palace **Note:** Prev. Y#1252.

| Date | Mintage | VF20 | XF40 | MS60 | MS63 | MS65 |
|---|---|---|---|---|---|---|
| 2003 | — | — | — | 7.00 | 8.00 | — |

### KM# 1524 5 YUAN

12.80 g., Brass, 30 mm. **Obv:** National emblem **Rev:** Island scene **Note:** Prev. Y#1253.

| Date | Mintage | VF20 | XF40 | MS60 | MS63 | MS65 |
|---|---|---|---|---|---|---|
| 2004 | — | — | — | 6.00 | 7.00 | — |

### KM# 1525 5 YUAN

12.800 Brass, 30 mm. **Obv:** National emblem **Rev:** Lighthouse **Note:** Prev. Y#1254.

| Date | Mintage | VF20 | XF40 | MS60 | MS63 | MS65 |
|---|---|---|---|---|---|---|
| 2004 | — | — | — | 6.00 | 7.00 | — |

### KM# 1526 5 YUAN

12.70 g., Brass, 30 mm. **Obv:** National emblem **Rev:** Peking Man bust and discovery site view **Edge:** Reeded **Note:** Prev. Y#1201.

| Date | Mintage | VF20 | XF40 | MS60 | MS63 | MS65 |
|---|---|---|---|---|---|---|
| 2004 | 6,000,000 | — | — | 6.00 | 7.00 | — |

### KM# 1527 5 YUAN

12.80 g., Brass, 30 mm. **Obv:** National emblem **Rev:** Pavillion and bridge **Edge:** Reeded **Note:** Prev. Y#1202.

| Date | Mintage | VF20 | XF40 | MS60 | MS63 | MS65 |
|---|---|---|---|---|---|---|
| 2004 | 6,000,000 | — | — | 6.00 | 7.00 | — |

### KM# 1576 5 YUAN

12.80 g., Brass, 30 mm. **Obv:** National emblem **Rev:** Lijiang building **Edge:** Reeded **Note:** Prev. Y#1209.

| Date | Mintage | VF20 | XF40 | MS60 | MS63 | MS65 |
|---|---|---|---|---|---|---|
| 2005 | — | — | — | 6.00 | 7.00 | — |

**KM# 1577 5 YUAN**
12.80 g., Brass, 30 mm. **Subject:** Taiwan **Obv:** State emblem **Rev:** Tower and terrace **Edge:** Reeded **Note:** Prev. Y#1231.

| Date | Mintage | VF20 | XF40 | MS60 | MS63 | MS65 |
|---|---|---|---|---|---|---|
| 2005 | — | — | — | 6.00 | 7.00 | — |

**KM# 1578 5 YUAN**
12.80 g., Brass, 30 mm. **Obv:** National emblem **Rev:** Green City Hall **Edge:** Reeded **Note:** Prev. Y#1210.

| Date | Mintage | VF20 | XF40 | MS60 | MS63 | MS65 |
|---|---|---|---|---|---|---|
| 2005 | — | — | — | 6.00 | 7.00 | — |

**KM# 1651 5 YUAN**
12.80 g., Brass, 30 mm. **Subject:** UNESCO World Heritage site - Summer Palace Pagoda

| Date | Mintage | VF20 | XF40 | MS60 | MS63 | MS65 |
|---|---|---|---|---|---|---|
| 2006 | — | — | — | 6.00 | 7.00 | — |

**KM# 1731 5 YUAN**
12.80 g., Brass, 30 mm. **Obv:** State emblem **Rev:** Large statue head

| Date | Mintage | VF20 | XF40 | MS60 | MS63 | MS65 |
|---|---|---|---|---|---|---|
| 2006 | 10,000,000 | PF65 3.00 | | | | |

**KM# 1826 5 YUAN**
15.57 g., 0.999 Silver 0.5001 oz. ASW, 33 mm. **Subject:** 12th Special Olympics in Shanghai **Obv:** Logo in color

| Date | Mintage | VF20 | XF40 | MS60 | MS63 | MS65 |
|---|---|---|---|---|---|---|
| 2007 | 40,000 | PF65 60.00 | | | | |

**KM# 1992 5 YUAN**
12.80 g., Brass, 30 mm. **Subject:** Chinese Communist Party, 90th Anniversary **Obv:** National emblem **Rev:** Banner, hammer and sythe, stars, birds in flight

| Date | Mintage | VF20 | XF40 | MS60 | MS63 | MS65 |
|---|---|---|---|---|---|---|
| 2011 | 60,000,000 | — | — | 7.50 | 9.00 | — |

**KM# 2081 5 YUAN**
12.80 g., Brass, 30 mm. **Obv:** National arms **Rev:** Character "He" - harmony

| Date | Mintage | VF20 | XF40 | MS60 | MS63 | MS65 |
|---|---|---|---|---|---|---|
| 2013 | 50,000,000 | — | — | 3.00 | 5.00 | — |

**KM# 1384 10 YUAN**
31.10 g., 0.999 Silver 0.999 oz. ASW **Series:** Folk Fairy Tales **Rev:** Heroic figure putting ax to mountains

| Date | Mintage | VF20 | XF40 | MS60 | MS63 | MS65 |
|---|---|---|---|---|---|---|
| 2001 | 30,000 | PF65 120 | | | | |

**KM# 1385 10 YUAN**
31.10 g., 0.999 Silver 0.999 oz. ASW, 40 mm. **Series:** Folk Fairy Tales **Rev:** Multicolor angelic figure

| Date | Mintage | VF20 | XF40 | MS60 | MS63 | MS65 |
|---|---|---|---|---|---|---|
| 2001 | 30,000 | PF65 120 | | | | |

**KM# 1395 10 YUAN**
31.10 g., 0.999 Silver 0.999 oz. ASW, 40 mm. **Subject:** 2008 Olympics Beijing bid **Obv:** Gold-plated "V" design **Rev:** Radiant Temple of Heaven **Edge:** Reeded **Note:** Prev. Y#1103.

| Date | Mintage | VF20 | XF40 | MS60 | MS63 | MS65 |
|---|---|---|---|---|---|---|
| 2001 | 60,000 | PF63 45.00 | PF65 50.00 | | | |

**KM# 1396 10 YUAN**
31.10 g., 0.999 Silver 0.999 oz. ASW, 40 mm. **Series:** Folk customs - Mid Autumn Festival **Rev:** Flora and sun

| Date | Mintage | VF20 | XF40 | MS60 | MS63 | MS65 |
|---|---|---|---|---|---|---|
| 2001 | 40,000 | PF65 180 | | | | |

**KM# 1397 10 YUAN**
31.10 g., 0.999 Silver 0.999 oz. ASW, 32 mm. **Subject:** Bejing International Coin Expo **Obv:** Globe hemisphere view **Rev:** Bejing city view

| Date | Mintage | VF20 | XF40 | MS60 | MS63 | MS65 |
|---|---|---|---|---|---|---|
| 2001 | 40,000 | PF65 125 | | | | |

**KM# 1398 10 YUAN**
31.10 g., 0.999 Silver 0.999 oz. ASW, 40 mm. **Subject:** Bejing opera **Rev:** Two multicolor actors, one with hankie

| Date | Mintage | VF20 | XF40 | MS60 | MS63 | MS65 |
|---|---|---|---|---|---|---|
| 2001 | 38,000 | PF65 100 | | | | |

**KM# 1399 10 YUAN**
31.10 g., 0.999 Silver 0.999 oz. ASW, 40 mm. **Subject:** Bejing opera **Rev:** Two actors, one with blue ribbon

| Date | Mintage | VF20 | XF40 | MS60 | MS63 | MS65 |
|---|---|---|---|---|---|---|
| 2001 | 38,000 | PF65 120 | | | | |

**KM# 1400 10 YUAN**
31.10 g., 0.999 Silver 0.999 oz. ASW, 40 mm. **Subject:** Bejing opera **Rev:** Two multicolor actors, one with tassles

| Date | Mintage | VF20 | XF40 | MS60 | MS63 | MS65 |
|---|---|---|---|---|---|---|
| 2001 | 38,000 | PF65 60.00 | | | | |

**KM# 1401 10 YUAN**
31.10 g., 0.999 Silver 0.999 oz. ASW, 40 mm. **Subject:** Bejing opera **Rev:** Two multicolor actors, white or black beard

| Date | Mintage | VF20 | XF40 | MS60 | MS63 | MS65 |
|---|---|---|---|---|---|---|
| 2001 | 38,000 | PF65 120 | | | | |

**KM# 1428 10 YUAN**
31.10 g., 0.999 Silver 0.999 oz. ASW, 40 mm. **Series:** Folk Fairy Tales **Rev:** Multicolor male figure seated

| Date | Mintage | VF20 | XF40 | MS60 | MS63 | MS65 |
|---|---|---|---|---|---|---|
| 2002 | 30,000 | PF65 120 | | | | |

**KM# 1429 10 YUAN**
31.10 g., 0.999 Silver 0.999 oz. ASW Colorized, 40 mm. **Series:** Folk fairy tails **Rev:** Male figure brandishing sword

| Date | Mintage | VF20 | XF40 | MS60 | MS63 | MS65 |
|---|---|---|---|---|---|---|
| 2002 | 30,000 | PF65 120 | | | | |

**KM# 1438 10 YUAN**
31.10 g., 0.999 Silver 0.999 oz. ASW, 40 mm. **Series:** Folk customs **Rev:** Dragon boat

| Date | Mintage | VF20 | XF40 | MS60 | MS63 | MS65 |
|---|---|---|---|---|---|---|
| 2002 | 40,000 | PF65 120 | | | | |

**KM# 1441 10 YUAN**
31.10 g., 0.999 Silver 0.999 oz. ASW Colorized, 40 mm. **Series:** Classic literature **Rev:** Black and red dressed women seated **Shape:** Octagon

| Date | Mintage | VF20 | XF40 | MS60 | MS63 | MS65 |
|---|---|---|---|---|---|---|
| 2002 | 38,000 | PF65 100 | | | | |

**KM# 1442 10 YUAN**
31.10 g., 0.999 Silver 0.999 oz. ASW, 40 mm. **Series:** Classic literature **Rev:** Multicolor white dressed woman standing **Shape:** Octagon

| Date | Mintage | VF20 | XF40 | MS60 | MS63 | MS65 |
|---|---|---|---|---|---|---|
| 2002 | 38,000 | PF65 100 | | | | |

**KM# 1443 10 YUAN**
31.10 g., 0.999 Silver 0.999 oz. ASW, 40 mm. **Series:** Classic literature **Rev:** Multicolor yellow dressed woman walking left **Shape:** Octagon

| Date | Mintage | VF20 | XF40 | MS60 | MS63 | MS65 |
|---|---|---|---|---|---|---|
| 2002 | 38,000 | PF65 100 | | | | |

**KM# 1444 10 YUAN**
31.10 g., 0.999 Silver 0.999 oz. ASW, 40 mm. **Series:** Classic literature **Obv:** Multicolor purple dressed woman **Shape:** Octagon

| Date | Mintage | VF20 | XF40 | MS60 | MS63 | MS65 |
|---|---|---|---|---|---|---|
| 2002 | 38,000 | PF65 100 | | | | |

**KM# 1447 10 YUAN**
31.10 g., 0.999 Silver 0.999 oz. ASW, 40 mm. **Subject:** Bejing Coin and Stamp Fair **Obv:** Hemisphere map **Rev:** Highway design

| Date | Mintage | VF20 | XF40 | MS60 | MS63 | MS65 |
|---|---|---|---|---|---|---|
| 2002 | 40,000 | PF65 95.00 | | | | |

**KM# 1448 10 YUAN**
31.10 g., 0.999 Silver 0.999 oz. ASW, 40 mm. **Subject:** Table tennis, 50th anniversary **Rev:** Trophies, flag

| Date | Mintage | VF20 | XF40 | MS60 | MS63 | MS65 |
|---|---|---|---|---|---|---|
| 2002 | 50,000 | PF65 100 | | | | |

**KM# 1449 10 YUAN**
31.10 g., 0.999 Silver 0.999 oz. ASW, 40 mm. **Series:** Bejing opera **Rev:** Two multicolor characters, one seated

| Date | Mintage | VF20 | XF40 | MS60 | MS63 | MS65 |
|---|---|---|---|---|---|---|
| 2002 | 38,000 | PF65 65.00 | | | | |

**KM# 1450 10 YUAN**
31.10 g., 0.999 Silver 0.999 oz. ASW, 40 mm. **Series:** Bejing opera **Rev:** Two multicolor characters, white and green

| Date | Mintage | VF20 | XF40 | MS60 | MS63 | MS65 |
|---|---|---|---|---|---|---|
| 2002 | 38,000 | PF65 125 | | | | |

**KM# 1451 10 YUAN**
31.10 g., 0.999 Silver 0.999 oz. ASW, 40 mm. **Series:** Bejing opera **Rev:** Bearded character, black

| Date | Mintage | VF20 | XF40 | MS60 | MS63 | MS65 |
|---|---|---|---|---|---|---|
| 2002 | 38,000 | PF65 125 | | | | |

**KM# 1452 10 YUAN**
31.10 g., 0.999 Silver 0.999 oz. ASW, 40 mm. **Series:** Bejing opera **Rev:** Multicolor bearded character, red

| Date | Mintage | VF20 | XF40 | MS60 | MS63 | MS65 |
|---|---|---|---|---|---|---|
| 2002 | 38,000 | PF65 125 | | | | |

**KM# 1455 10 YUAN**
31.10 g., 0.999 Silver 0.999 oz. ASW, 40 mm. **Subject:** Shanghai World Expo of 2010 **Obv:** Flower design with inset pearl **Rev:** 2010 Logo incorporating a tower **Edge:** Reeded **Note:** Prev. Y#1233.

| Date | Mintage | VF20 | XF40 | MS60 | MS63 | MS65 |
|---|---|---|---|---|---|---|
| 2002 | 50,000 | PF63 115 | PF65 125 | | | |

**KM# A1455 10 YUAN**
31.10 g., 0.999 Silver 0.999 oz. ASW, 40 mm. **Subject:** World Expo 2010 **Rev:** Tower

| Date | Mintage | VF20 | XF40 | MS60 | MS63 | MS65 |
|---|---|---|---|---|---|---|
| 2002 | 50,000 | PF63 90.00 | PF65 100 | | | |

**KM# 1487 10 YUAN**
31.10 g., 0.999 Silver 0.999 oz. ASW, 40 mm. **Rev:** Two Koi

| Date | Mintage | VF20 | XF40 | MS60 | MS63 | MS65 |
|---|---|---|---|---|---|---|
| 2003 | 100,000 | PF63 75.00 | PF65 90.00 | | | |

**KM# 1489 10 YUAN**
31.10 g., 0.999 Silver 0.999 oz. ASW, 40 mm. **Subject:** Arbor Day **Rev:** Trees with bike riders

| Date | Mintage | VF20 | XF40 | MS60 | MS63 | MS65 |
|---|---|---|---|---|---|---|
| 2003 | 30,000 | PF63 80.00 | PF65 90.00 | | | |

**KM# 1490 10 YUAN**
31.10 g., 0.999 Silver 0.999 oz. ASW, 40 mm. **Subject:** Arbor Day **Rev:** Close-up of leaves, birds in flight

| Date | Mintage | VF20 | XF40 | MS60 | MS63 | MS65 |
|---|---|---|---|---|---|---|
| 2003 | 30,000 | PF63 110 | PF65 120 | | | |

**KM# 1491 10 YUAN**
31.10 g., 0.999 Silver 0.999 oz. ASW, 40 mm. **Series:** Fairy tails **Rev:** Multicolor blue female

| Date | Mintage | VF20 | XF40 | MS60 | MS63 | MS65 |
|---|---|---|---|---|---|---|
| 2003 | 30,000 | PF65 120 | | | | |

**KM# 1492 10 YUAN**
31.10 g., 0.999 Silver 0.999 oz. ASW, 40 mm. **Subject:** Fairy tails **Rev:** Multicolor red bloused girl

| Date | Mintage | VF20 | XF40 | MS60 | MS63 | MS65 |
|---|---|---|---|---|---|---|
| 2003 | 30,000 | PF65 120 | | | | |

**KM# 1496 10 YUAN**
31.10 g., 0.999 Silver 0.999 oz. ASW, 40 mm. **Series:** Class literature **Rev:** Multicolor purple cloaked man and monkey

| Date | Mintage | VF20 | XF40 | MS60 | MS63 | MS65 |
|---|---|---|---|---|---|---|
| 2003 | 38,000 | PF65 120 | | | | |

**KM# 1497 10 YUAN**
31.10 g., 0.999 Silver 0.999 oz. ASW, 40 mm. **Series:** Classic literature **Rev:** Two multicolor men fighting in clouds

| Date | Mintage | VF20 | XF40 | MS60 | MS63 | MS65 |
|---|---|---|---|---|---|---|
| 2003 | 38,000 | PF65 120 | | | | |

**KM# 1498 10 YUAN**
31.10 g., 0.999 Silver 0.999 oz. ASW, 40 mm. **Rev:** Multicolor female standing, black dress **Shape:** Octagon

| Date | Mintage | VF20 | XF40 | MS60 | MS63 | MS65 |
|---|---|---|---|---|---|---|
| 2003 | 38,000 | PF65 120 | | | | |

**KM# 1499 10 YUAN**
31.10 g., 0.999 Silver 0.999 oz. ASW, 40 mm. **Series:** Classic Literature **Rev:** Multicolor female kneeling **Shape:** Octagon

| Date | Mintage | VF20 | XF40 | MS60 | MS63 | MS65 |
|---|---|---|---|---|---|---|
| 2003 | 38,000 | PF65 120 | | | | |

**KM# 1500 10 YUAN**
31.10 g., 0.999 Silver 0.999 oz. ASW, 40 mm. **Series:** Classic literature **Rev:** Multicolor female walking, rose dress **Shape:** Octagon

| Date | Mintage | VF20 | XF40 | MS60 | MS63 | MS65 |
|---|---|---|---|---|---|---|
| 2003 | — | PF65 120 | | | | |

**KM# 1501 10 YUAN**
31.10 g., 0.999 Silver 0.999 oz. ASW, 40 mm. **Series:** Classic literature **Rev:** Multicolor female kneeling, red dress **Shape:** Octagon

| Date | Mintage | VF20 | XF40 | MS60 | MS63 | MS65 |
|---|---|---|---|---|---|---|
| 2003 | — | PF65 120 | | | | |

**KM# 1507 10 YUAN**
31.10 g., 0.999 Silver 0.999 oz. ASW, 40 mm. **Obv:** Stylized forest **Rev:** Cyclists in forest **Edge:** Reeded **Note:** Prev. Y#1132.

| Date | Mintage | VF20 | XF40 | MS60 | MS63 | MS65 |
|---|---|---|---|---|---|---|
| 2003 | 30,000 | PF63 115 | PF65 125 | | | |

**KM# 1508 10 YUAN**
31.10 g., 0.999 Silver 0.999 oz. ASW, 40 mm. **Obv:** Stylized forest **Rev:** Birds flying over forest **Edge:** Reeded **Note:** Prev. Y#1133.

| Date | Mintage | VF20 | XF40 | MS60 | MS63 | MS65 |
|---|---|---|---|---|---|---|
| 2003 (y) | 30,000 | PF63 115 | PF65 125 | | | |

**KM# 1510 10 YUAN**
31.10 g., 0.999 Silver 0.999 oz. ASW, 40 mm. **Obv:** Solar system design **Rev:** Multicolor Chinese Astronaut **Edge:** Reeded **Note:** Prev. Y#1134.

| Date | Mintage | VF20 | XF40 | MS60 | MS63 | MS65 |
|---|---|---|---|---|---|---|
| 2003 (y) | 60,000 | PF65 90.00 | | | | |

**KM# 1539 10 YUAN**
31.10 g., 0.999 Silver 0.999 oz. ASW, 40 mm. **Subject:** 20th Anniversary / Bank of China Industrial and Commercial **Rev:** Panda walking with cub

| Date | Mintage | VF20 | XF40 | MS60 | MS63 | MS65 |
|---|---|---|---|---|---|---|
| 2004 | 120,000 | PF63 75.00 | PF65 90.00 | | | |

**KM# 1541 10 YUAN**
31.10 g., 0.999 Silver 0.999 oz. ASW, 40 mm. **Subject:** 50th Anniversary China Construction Bank **Rev:** Panda walking with cub

| Date | Mintage | VF20 | XF40 | MS60 | MS63 | MS65 |
|---|---|---|---|---|---|---|
| 2004 | 170,000 | PF63 75.00 | PF65 90.00 | | | |

**KM# 1543 10 YUAN**
31.10 g., 0.999 Silver 0.999 oz. ASW, 40 mm. **Subject:** Bejing International Coin Expo **Rev:** Panda walking with cub, gold plated center

| Date | Mintage | VF20 | XF40 | MS60 | MS63 | MS65 |
|---|---|---|---|---|---|---|
| 2004 | 30,000 | PF63 110 | PF65 120 | | | |

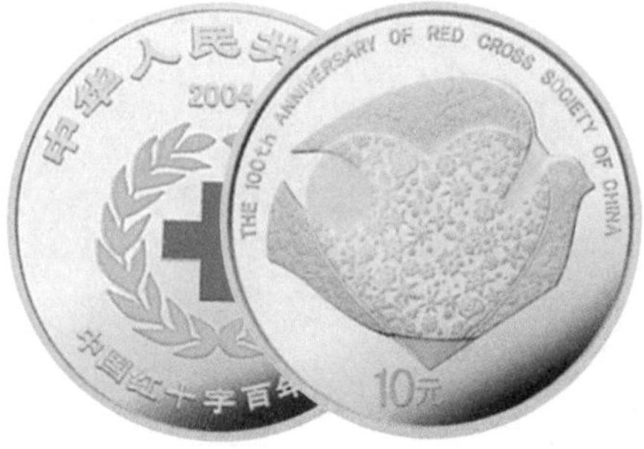

**KM# 1555 10 YUAN**
31.10 g., 0.999 Silver 0.999 oz. ASW, 40 mm. **Subject:** 100th Anniversary Red Cross **Obv:** Red Cross within wreath **Rev:** Dove **Note:** Colorized

| Date | Mintage | VF20 | XF40 | MS60 | MS63 | MS65 |
|---|---|---|---|---|---|---|
| 2004 | 60,000 | PF65 85.00 | | | | |

**KM# 1557 10 YUAN**
31.10 g., 0.999 Silver 0.999 oz. ASW, 40 mm. **Series:** Folk customs **Subject:** Lantern Festival **Rev:** Boy holding lantern **Note:** Colorized

| Date | Mintage | VF20 | XF40 | MS60 | MS63 | MS65 |
|---|---|---|---|---|---|---|
| 2004 | 60,000 | PF65 100 | | | | |

**KM# 1558 10 YUAN**
31.10 g., 0.999 Silver 0.999 oz. ASW, 40 mm. **Obv:** Monkey King leading the Master over bridge **Rev:** Multicolor Pig carrying Monkey King piggy-back style **Edge:** Reeded **Note:** Prev. Y#1215.

| Date | Mintage | VF20 | XF40 | MS60 | MS63 | MS65 |
|---|---|---|---|---|---|---|
| 2004 | 38,000 | PF65 110 | | | | |

**KM# 1559 10 YUAN**
31.10 g., 0.999 Silver 0.999 oz. ASW, 40 mm. **Obv:** Monkey King leading the Master over bridge **Rev:** Multicolor Monkey King fighting the "Ox Fiend **Edge:** Reeded **Note:** Prev. Y#1214.

| Date | Mintage | VF20 | XF40 | MS60 | MS63 | MS65 |
|---|---|---|---|---|---|---|
| 2004 | 38,000 | PF65 110 | | | | |

**KM# 1566 10 YUAN**
31.10 g., 0.999 Silver 0.999 oz. ASW, 40 mm. **Obv:** Guangan Exposition Hall **Rev:** Deng Xiaoping and value **Edge:** Reeded **Note:** Prev. Y#1240. Photo reduced.

| Date | Mintage | VF20 | XF40 | MS60 | MS63 | MS65 |
|---|---|---|---|---|---|---|
| 2004 | 80,000 | PF63 75.00 | PF65 90.00 | | | |

**KM# 1570 10 YUAN**
31.10 g., 0.999 Silver 0.999 oz. ASW, 40 mm. **Obv:** National arms above People's Congress Hall and ornamental column **Rev:** Multicolor hologram depicting the hall's overhead lighting **Edge:** Reeded **Note:** Prev. KM#1212.

| Date | Mintage | VF20 | XF40 | MS60 | MS63 | MS65 |
|---|---|---|---|---|---|---|
| 2004 | 50,000 | PF65 100 | | | | |

**KM# 1580 10 YUAN**
31.10 g., 0.999 Silver 0.999 oz. ASW, 40 mm. **Subject:** 600th Anniversary of Zheng He's voyage **Obv:** Multicolor stylized sailboat on water **Rev:** Ancient Chinese navigational instruments **Edge:** Reeded **Note:** Prev. Y#1239.

| Date | Mintage | VF20 | XF40 | MS60 | MS63 | MS65 |
|---|---|---|---|---|---|---|
| 2005 (y) | — | PF65 100 | | | | |

**KM# 1592 10 YUAN**
31.11 g., 0.999 Silver 0.999 oz. ASW gilt rim, 40 mm. **Obv:** Temple of Heaven **Rev:** Panda cub and mom seated in bamboo **Note:** Gilt rim

| Date | Mintage | VF20 | XF40 | MS60 | MS63 | MS65 |
|---|---|---|---|---|---|---|
| 2005 | 30,000 | PF63 75.00 | PF65 85.00 | | | |

**KM# 1601 10 YUAN**
31.11 g., 0.999 Silver 0.999 oz. ASW, 40 mm. **Subject:** Foundation of Industrial & Commercial Bank **Obv:** Temple of Heaven, gilt rim **Rev:** Panda cub and mom seated in bamboo

| Date | Mintage | VF20 | XF40 | MS60 | MS63 | MS65 |
|---|---|---|---|---|---|---|
| 2005 | 100,000 | PF63 65.00 | PF65 75.00 | | | |

**KM# 1603 10 YUAN**
31.11 g., 0.999 Silver 0.999 oz. ASW, 40 mm. **Subject:** 100th Anniversary of Bank of Shanghai **Obv:** Temple of Heaven **Rev:** Panda cub and mom seated in bamboo

| Date | Mintage | VF20 | XF40 | MS60 | MS63 | MS65 |
|---|---|---|---|---|---|---|
| 2005 | 50,000 | PF63 70.00 | PF65 80.00 | | | |

**KM# 1618 10 YUAN**
31.11 g., 0.999 Silver 0.999 oz. ASW, 40 mm. **Subject:** 2006 World Cup - Germany **Obv:** Multicolor logo **Rev:** Classical soccer player and goal net **Note:** Prev - Y1255, KM1670

| Date | Mintage | VF20 | XF40 | MS60 | MS63 | MS65 |
|---|---|---|---|---|---|---|
| 2005 | 50,000 | PF63 75.00 | PF65 85.00 | | | |

**KM# 1626 10 YUAN**
31.11 g., 0.999 Silver 0.999 oz. ASW, 40 mm. **Subject:** 600th Anniversary - Zheng He's Voyages **Obv:** Multicolor logo **Rev:** Nautical invention

| Date | Mintage | VF20 | XF40 | MS60 | MS63 | MS65 |
|---|---|---|---|---|---|---|
| 2005 | 60,000 | PF63 65.00 | PF65 75.00 | | | |

**KM# 1628 10 YUAN**
31.11 g., 0.999 Silver 0.999 oz. ASW, 40 mm. **Subject:** Chen Yun Birth Centennial **Obv:** House **Rev:** Half-length figure facing

| Date | Mintage | VF20 | XF40 | MS60 | MS63 | MS65 |
|---|---|---|---|---|---|---|
| 2005 | 15,000 | PF65 150 | | | | |

**KM# 1629 10 YUAN**
31.11 g., 0.999 Silver 0.999 oz. ASW, 40 mm. **Subject:** Chen Yun Birth Centennial **Obv:** House **Rev:** Figure seated in chair, arm outstretched

| Date | Mintage | VF20 | XF40 | MS60 | MS63 | MS65 |
|---|---|---|---|---|---|---|
| 2005 | 15,000 | PF65 150 | | | | |

**KM# 1631 10 YUAN**
31.11 g., 0.999 Silver 0.999 oz. ASW, 40 mm. **Subject:** 60th Anniversary of Victory - War of Resistance **Obv:** Monument **Rev:** People celebrating

| Date | Mintage | VF20 | XF40 | MS60 | MS63 | MS65 |
|---|---|---|---|---|---|---|
| 2005 | 30,000 | PF63 130 | PF65 140 | | | |

**KM# 1636 10 YUAN**
31.11 g., 0.999 Silver 0.999 oz. ASW, 40 mm. **Series:** Classical Literature **Obv:** Horseman on arch bridge **Rev:** Multicolor monkey and female

| Date | Mintage | VF20 | XF40 | MS60 | MS63 | MS65 |
|---|---|---|---|---|---|---|
| 2005 | 38,000 | PF65 130 | | | | |

**KM# 1637 10 YUAN**
31.11 g., 0.999 Silver 0.999 oz. ASW, 40 mm. **Series:** Classical Literature **Obv:** Horseman on arch bridge **Rev:** Multicolor man slaying spider on web

| Date | Mintage | VF20 | XF40 | MS60 | MS63 | MS65 |
|---|---|---|---|---|---|---|
| 2005 | 38,000 | PF65 130 | | | | |

**KM# 1639 10 YUAN**
31.11 g., 0.999 Silver 0.999 oz. ASW, 40 mm. **Subject:** Chinese Movie Centennial **Obv:** Winged column **Rev:** Old time movie camera

| Date | Mintage | VF20 | XF40 | MS60 | MS63 | MS65 |
|---|---|---|---|---|---|---|
| 2005 | 60,000 | PF63 75.00 | PF65 85.00 | | | |

**KM# 1666 10 YUAN**
31.11 g., 0.999 Silver 0.999 oz. ASW, 40 mm. **Obv:** Temple of Heaven **Rev:** Two pandas seated with bamboo

| Date | Mintage | VF20 | XF40 | MS60 | MS63 | MS65 |
|---|---|---|---|---|---|---|
| 2006 | 50,000 | PF63 65.00 | PF65 75.00 | | | |

**KM# 1668 10 YUAN**
31.11 g., 0.999 Silver 0.999 oz. ASW, 40 mm. **Subject:** 10th Anniversary of China Minsheng Banking Corp **Obv:** Temple of Heaven **Rev:** Two pandas seated with bamboo

| Date | Mintage | VF20 | XF40 | MS60 | MS63 | MS65 |
|---|---|---|---|---|---|---|
| 2006 | 70,000 | PF63 75.00 | PF65 85.00 | | | |

**KM# 1670 10 YUAN**
31.10 g., 0.999 Silver 0.999 oz. ASW **Subject:** World Cup Soccer **Obv:** Colorized logo **Rev:** Classically dressed athlete scoring goal **Note:** Prev. Y#1255.

| Date | Mintage | VF20 | XF40 | MS60 | MS63 | MS65 |
|---|---|---|---|---|---|---|
| 2006 | — | PF65 100 | | | | |

**KM# A1670 10 YUAN**
31.11 g., 0.999 Silver 0.999 oz. ASW, 40 mm. **Subject:** Shengang Horticultural Expo **Obv:** Temple of Heaven **Rev:** Two pandas seated with bamboo

| Date | Mintage | VF20 | XF40 | MS60 | MS63 | MS65 |
|---|---|---|---|---|---|---|
| 2006 | 30,000 | PF63 75.00 | PF65 85.00 | | | |

**KM# 1675 10 YUAN**
31.11 g., 0.999 Silver 0.999 oz. ASW, 40 mm. **Subject:** 10th Anniversary Jinan City Commercial Bank **Obv:** Temple of Heaven **Rev:** Two pandas seated with bamboo

| Date | Mintage | VF20 | XF40 | MS60 | MS63 | MS65 |
|---|---|---|---|---|---|---|
| 2006 | 20,000 | PF63 75.00 | PF65 85.00 | | | |

**KM# 1676 10 YUAN**
31.11 g., 0.999 Silver 0.999 oz. ASW Gold plated outer ring, 40 mm. **Subject:** Beijing International Stamp and Coin Expo **Obv:** Temple of Heaven **Rev:** Two pandas seated with bamboo

| Date | Mintage | VF20 | XF40 | MS60 | MS63 | MS65 |
|---|---|---|---|---|---|---|
| 2006 | 20,000 | PF63 90.00 | PF65 100 | | | |

**KM# 1690 10 YUAN**
31.11 g., 0.999 Silver 0.999 oz. ASW, 40 mm. **Subject:** Yvelv Academy **Obv:** Front door of Academy **Rev:** Exterior view

| Date | Mintage | VF20 | XF40 | MS60 | MS63 | MS65 |
|---|---|---|---|---|---|---|
| 2006 | 40,000 | PF63 75.00 | PF65 85.00 | | | |

**KM# 1691 10 YUAN**
31.11 g., 0.999 Silver 0.999 oz. ASW, 40 mm. **Subject:** Qinghai - Tibet Railway Opening **Obv:** Lhasa Railway Station with mountains in background **Rev:** Yvante Bridge over the Yangtze River and tibetan antelope and yak

| Date | Mintage | VF20 | XF40 | MS60 | MS63 | MS65 |
|---|---|---|---|---|---|---|
| 2006 | 36,000 | PF65 150 | | | | |

**KM# 1693 10 YUAN**
31.11 g., 0.999 Silver 0.999 oz. ASW, 40 mm. **Obv:** Map of marches and hammer and sickle **Rev:** Group of marchers in snow

| Date | Mintage | VF20 | XF40 | MS60 | MS63 | MS65 |
|---|---|---|---|---|---|---|
| 2006 | 25,000 | PF65 110 | | | | |

**KM# 1653 10 YUAN**
31.10 g., 0.999 Silver 0.999 oz. ASW, 40 mm. **Subject:** Chengdu multi-purpose warplanes, 10th Anniversary

| Date | Mintage | VF20 | XF40 | MS60 | MS63 | MS65 |
|---|---|---|---|---|---|---|
| 2007 | 20,000 | PF63 65.00 | PF65 75.00 | | | |

**KM# 1729 10 YUAN**
31.11 g., 0.999 Silver 0.999 oz. ASW, 40 mm. **Subject:** 60th Anniversary - Foundry of Mongolia Autonomous Region **Obv:** Wheel of Mongolian Lele Cart **Rev:** Grassland view of Mongolia, huts and horsemen

| Date | Mintage | VF20 | XF40 | MS60 | MS63 | MS65 |
|---|---|---|---|---|---|---|
| 2007 | 20,000 | PF65 110 | | | | |

**KM# 1828 10 YUAN**

31.10 g., 0.999 Silver 0.999 oz. ASW, 40 mm. **Subject:** Chinese aerospace **Obv:** Solar System **Rev:** Chang'e 1 in lunar orbit

| Date | Mintage | VF20 | XF40 | MS60 | MS63 | MS65 |
|---|---|---|---|---|---|---|
| 2007 | 40,000 | PF63 65.00 | PF65 75.00 | | | |

**KM# 1861 10 YUAN**

31.10 g., 0.999 Silver 0.999 oz. ASW, 40 mm. **Subject:** Chinese Peoples Liberation Army, 80th Anniversary **Obv:** Military personel saluting, flag in background **Rev:** Ship, tank, plane

| Date | Mintage | VF20 | XF40 | MS60 | MS63 | MS65 |
|---|---|---|---|---|---|---|
| 2007 | — | PF63 65.00 | PF65 75.00 | | | |

**KM# 1863 10 YUAN**

31.10 g., 0.999 Silver 0.999 oz. ASW, 40 mm. **Subject:** Xi'an City Commercial Bank **Obv:** Temple of Heaven **Rev:** Panda

| Date | Mintage | VF20 | XF40 | MS60 | MS63 | MS65 |
|---|---|---|---|---|---|---|
| 2007 | 20,000 | — | — | — | 300 | — |

**KM# 1864 10 YUAN**

31.10 g., 0.999 Silver 0.999 oz. ASW, 40 mm. **Subject:** China International Trust and Investment Co., 20th Anniversary **Obv:** Temple of Heaven **Rev:** Panda

| Date | Mintage | VF20 | XF40 | MS60 | MS63 | MS65 |
|---|---|---|---|---|---|---|
| 2007 | 20,000 | — | — | — | 300 | — |

**KM# 1674 10 YUAN**

31.11 g., 0.999 Silver 0.999 oz. ASW, 40 mm. **Subject:** 29th Summer Olympics, Bejing **Rev:** Great Wall, ornament at left in color

| Date | Mintage | VF20 | XF40 | MS60 | MS63 | MS65 |
|---|---|---|---|---|---|---|
| 2008 S | 160,000 | PF65 75.00 | | | | |
| 2008 Y | Inc. above | PF65 75.00 | | | | |
| 2008 Z | Inc. above | PF65 75.00 | | | | |

**KM# 1688 10 YUAN**

31.11 g., 0.999 Silver 0.999 oz. ASW, 40 mm. **Subject:** 29th Summer Olympics, Bejing **Rev:** Summer Palace, Bejing; flower at left in color

| Date | Mintage | VF20 | XF40 | MS60 | MS63 | MS65 |
|---|---|---|---|---|---|---|
| 2008 S | 160,000 | PF65 75.00 | | | | |
| 2008 Y | Inc. above | PF65 75.00 | | | | |
| 2008 Z | Inc. above | PF65 75.00 | | | | |

**KM# 1702 10 YUAN**

31.11 g., 0.999 Silver 0.999 oz. ASW, 40 mm. **Subject:** 2007 Summer Olympics **Obv:** Beijing Olympic logo **Rev:** Child with kite, multicolor design **Note:** Issued in 2006

| Date | Mintage | VF20 | XF40 | MS60 | MS63 | MS65 |
|---|---|---|---|---|---|---|
| 2008 S | 160,000 | PF65 75.00 | | | | |
| 2008 Y | Inc. above | PF65 75.00 | | | | |
| 2008 Z | Inc. above | PF65 75.00 | | | | |

**KM# 1703 10 YUAN**

31.11 g., 0.999 Silver 0.999 oz. ASW, 40 mm. **Subject:** 2007 Summer Olympics **Obv:** Beijing Olympics logo **Rev:** Two children playing leapfrog, multicolor **Note:** Issued in 2006

| Date | Mintage | VF20 | XF40 | MS60 | MS63 | MS65 |
|---|---|---|---|---|---|---|
| 2008 S | 160,000 | PF65 75.00 | | | | |
| 2008 Y | Inc. above | PF65 75.00 | | | | |
| 2008 Z | Inc. above | PF65 75.00 | | | | |

**KM# 1704 10 YUAN**

31.11 g., 0.999 Silver 0.999 oz. ASW, 40 mm. **Subject:** 2007 Summer Olympics **Obv:** Beijing Olympics logo **Rev:** Child rolling ring with stick, multicolor **Note:** Issued in 2006

| Date | Mintage | VF20 | XF40 | MS60 | MS63 | MS65 |
|---|---|---|---|---|---|---|
| 2008 S | 160,000 | PF65 75.00 | | | | |
| 2008 Y | Inc. above | PF65 75.00 | | | | |
| 2008 Z | Inc. above | PF65 75.00 | | | | |

**KM# 1705 10 YUAN**

31.11 g., 0.999 Silver 0.999 oz. ASW, 40 mm. **Subject:** 2007 Summer Olympics **Obv:** Beijing Olympic's logo **Rev:** Young girl dancing, multicolor **Note:** Issued in 2006

| Date | Mintage | VF20 | XF40 | MS60 | MS63 | MS65 |
|---|---|---|---|---|---|---|
| 2008 S | 160,000 | PF65 75.00 | | | | |
| 2008 Y | Inc. above | PF65 75.00 | | | | |
| 2008 Z | Inc. above | PF65 75.00 | | | | |

**KM# 1732 10 YUAN**

31.11 g., 0.999 Silver 0.999 oz. ASW, 40 mm. **Subject:** 29th Summer Games, Beijing **Rev:** White Pagoda, North Sea Park

| Date | Mintage | VF20 | XF40 | MS60 | MS63 | MS65 |
|---|---|---|---|---|---|---|
| 2008 | 160,000 | PF65 75.00 | | | | |
| 2008 | Inc. above | PF65 75.00 | | | | |
| 2008 | Inc. above | PF65 75.00 | | | | |

**KM# 1733 10 YUAN**

31.11 g., 0.999 Silver 0.999 oz. ASW, 40 mm. **Subject:** 29th Summer Olympics, Beijing **Obv:** Olympics logo **Rev:** Traditonal residence, flower at left in color

| Date | Mintage | VF20 | XF40 | MS60 | MS63 | MS65 |
|---|---|---|---|---|---|---|
| 2008 S | 160,000 | PF65 75.00 | | | | |
| 2008 Y | Inc. above | PF65 75.00 | | | | |
| 2008 Z | Inc. above | PF65 75.00 | | | | |

**KM# 1734 10 YUAN**

31.10 g., 0.999 Silver 0.999 oz. ASW, 40 mm. **Obv:** Solar system **Rev:** Man walkking in space in color

| Date | Mintage | VF20 | XF40 | MS60 | MS63 | MS65 |
|---|---|---|---|---|---|---|
| 2008 | 60,000 | PF65 75.00 | | | | |

**KM# 1736 10 YUAN**

31.11 g., 0.999 Silver 0.999 oz. ASW, 40 mm. **Subject:** Economic Reform in China, 30th Anniversary **Rev:** Economic Growth

| Date | Mintage | VF20 | XF40 | MS60 | MS63 | MS65 |
|---|---|---|---|---|---|---|
| 2008 | 80,000 | PF63 55.00 | PF65 65.00 | | | |

**KM# 1739 10 YUAN**

31.10 g., 0.999 Silver 0.999 oz. ASW, 40 mm. **Subject:** Banknote Printing Works, Beijing, 100th Anniversary **Obv:** Temple of Heaven **Rev:** Two pandas

| Date | Mintage | VF20 | XF40 | MS60 | MS63 | MS65 |
|---|---|---|---|---|---|---|
| 2008 | 20,000 | — | — | — | 275 | — |

**KM# 1825 10 YUAN**

31.11 g., 0.999 Silver 0.999 oz. ASW, 40 mm. **Subject:** Bank of Communications, Centennial

| Date | Mintage | VF20 | XF40 | MS60 | MS63 | MS65 |
|---|---|---|---|---|---|---|
| 2008 | — | PF63 75.00 | PF65 85.00 | | | |

**KM# 1843 10 YUAN**

31.11 g., 0.999 Silver 0.999 oz. ASW, 40 mm. **Subject:** Beijing Olympics **Rev:** Multicolor mask, stall tea scene

| Date | Mintage | VF20 | XF40 | MS60 | MS63 | MS65 |
|---|---|---|---|---|---|---|
| 2008 | 160,000 | PF65 55.00 | | | | |

**KM# 1844 10 YUAN**

31.11 g., 0.999 Silver 0.999 oz. ASW, 40 mm. **Subject:** Beijing Olympics **Rev:** Multicolor mask, lion dancer

| Date | Mintage | VF20 | XF40 | MS60 | MS63 | MS65 |
|---|---|---|---|---|---|---|
| 2008 | 160,000 | PF65 55.00 | | | | |

**KM# 1845 10 YUAN**

31.11 g., 0.999 Silver 0.999 oz. ASW, 40 mm. **Subject:** Beijing Olympics **Rev:** Multicolor mask, Yangtze dancer

| Date | Mintage | VF20 | XF40 | MS60 | MS63 | MS65 |
|---|---|---|---|---|---|---|
| 2008 | 160,000 | PF65 55.00 | | | | |

**KM# 1846 10 YUAN**

31.11 g., 0.999 Silver 0.999 oz. ASW, 40 mm. **Subject:** Beijing Olympics **Rev:** Multicolor mask, Beijing Opera

| Date | Mintage | VF20 | XF40 | MS60 | MS63 | MS65 |
|---|---|---|---|---|---|---|
| 2008 | 160,000 | PF65 55.00 | | | | |

**KM# 1852 10 YUAN**

31.11 g., 0.999 Silver 0.999 oz. ASW, 40 mm. **Subject:** Hainan Special Economic Zone

| Date | Mintage | VF20 | XF40 | MS60 | MS63 | MS65 |
|---|---|---|---|---|---|---|
| 2008 | 20,000 | PF63 80.00 | PF65 90.00 | | | |

### KM# 1854 10 YUAN
31.11 g., 0.999 Silver 0.999 oz. ASW, 40 mm. **Subject:** Para Olympics

| Date | Mintage | VF20 | XF40 | MS60 | MS63 | MS65 |
|---|---|---|---|---|---|---|
| 2008 | 30,000 | PF63 90.00 | PF65 100 | | | |

### KM# 1856 10 YUAN
31.11 g., 0.999 Silver 0.999 oz. ASW, 40 mm. **Subject:** Ningxia Hui Autonomous Region

| Date | Mintage | VF20 | XF40 | MS60 | MS63 | MS65 |
|---|---|---|---|---|---|---|
| 2008 | 20,000 | PF63 110 | PF65 120 | | | |

### KM# 1858 10 YUAN
31.11 g., 0.999 Silver 0.999 oz. ASW, 40 mm. **Subject:** Beijing Coin and Stamp Expo

| Date | Mintage | VF20 | XF40 | MS60 | MS63 | MS65 |
|---|---|---|---|---|---|---|
| 2008 | 30,000 | PF63 65.00 | PF65 75.00 | | | |

### KM# 1859 10 YUAN
31.11 g., 0.999 Silver 0.999 oz. ASW, 40 mm. **Subject:** Guangxi Zhuang Autonomous Region

| Date | Mintage | VF20 | XF40 | MS60 | MS63 | MS65 |
|---|---|---|---|---|---|---|
| 2008 | 20,000 | PF63 100 | PF65 110 | | | |

### KM# 1891 10 YUAN
31.11 g., 0.999 Silver 0.999 oz. ASW, 40 mm. **Subject:** Precious Metal Commemoratives, 30th Anniversary

| Date | Mintage | VF20 | XF40 | MS60 | MS63 | MS65 |
|---|---|---|---|---|---|---|
| 2009 | 300,000 | — | — | — | 40.00 | — |

### KM# 1892 10 YUAN
31.11 g., 0.999 Silver 0.999 oz. ASW, 40 mm. **Subject:** Beijing International Coin & Stamp Show

| Date | Mintage | VF20 | XF40 | MS60 | MS63 | MS65 |
|---|---|---|---|---|---|---|
| 2009 | 30,000 | — | — | — | 60.00 | — |

### KM# 1896 10 YUAN
31.10 g., 0.999 Silver 0.999 oz. ASW, 40 mm. **Subject:** Stock Exchange trading in Shenzhen **Obv:** Temple of Heaven **Rev:** Two pandas

| Date | Mintage | VF20 | XF40 | MS60 | MS63 | MS65 |
|---|---|---|---|---|---|---|
| 2009 | 30,000 | PF65 150 | | | | |

### KM# 1898 10 YUAN
31.11 g., 0.999 Silver 0.999 oz. ASW, 40 mm. **Subject:** P.R.C. 60th Anniversary **Rev:** Multicolor

| Date | Mintage | VF20 | XF40 | MS60 | MS63 | MS65 |
|---|---|---|---|---|---|---|
| 2009 | 100,000 | PF65 65.00 | | | | |

### KM# 1902 10 YUAN
31.11 g., 0.999 Silver 0.999 oz. ASW, 40 mm. **Subject:** Outlaws of the Marsh, series 1 **Rev:** Multicolor

| Date | Mintage | VF20 | XF40 | MS60 | MS63 | MS65 |
|---|---|---|---|---|---|---|
| 2009 | 60,000 | PF65 95.00 | | | | |

### KM# 1903 10 YUAN
31.11 g., 0.999 Silver 0.999 oz. ASW, 40 mm. **Subject:** Outlaws of the Marsh, series 1 **Rev:** Multicolor

| Date | Mintage | VF20 | XF40 | MS60 | MS63 | MS65 |
|---|---|---|---|---|---|---|
| 2009 | 60,000 | PF65 95.00 | | | | |

### KM# 1905 10 YUAN
31.11 g., 0.999 Silver 0.999 oz. ASW, 40 mm. **Subject:** 16th Asian Games

| Date | Mintage | VF20 | XF40 | MS60 | MS63 | MS65 |
|---|---|---|---|---|---|---|
| 2009 | 60,000 | PF63 45.00 | PF65 50.00 | | | |

### KM# 1907 10 YUAN
31.11 g., 0.999 Silver 0.999 oz. ASW, 40 mm. **Subject:** Shanghai Expo

| Date | Mintage | VF20 | XF40 | MS60 | MS63 | MS65 |
|---|---|---|---|---|---|---|
| 2009 | — | PF65 60.00 | | | | |

### KM# 1908 10 YUAN
31.11 g., 0.999 Silver 0.999 oz. ASW, 40 mm. **Subject:** Shanghai Expo

| Date | Mintage | VF20 | XF40 | MS60 | MS63 | MS65 |
|---|---|---|---|---|---|---|
| 2009 | — | PF63 45.00 | PF65 50.00 | | | |

### KM# 1910 10 YUAN
31.11 g., 0.999 Silver 0.999 oz. ASW, 40 mm. **Subject:** China Agricultural Bank

| Date | Mintage | VF20 | XF40 | MS60 | MS63 | MS65 |
|---|---|---|---|---|---|---|
| 2009 | 100,000 | — | — | — | 45.00 | 55.00 |

### KM# 1793 10 YUAN
31.11 g., 0.999 Silver 0.999 oz. ASW **Subject:** Agricultural Bank, IPO **Obv:** Temple of Heaven **Rev:** Panda

| Date | Mintage | VF20 | XF40 | MS60 | MS63 | MS65 |
|---|---|---|---|---|---|---|
| 2010 | 70,000 | — | — | — | 275 | — |

### KM# 1795 10 YUAN
31.10 g., 0.999 Silver 0.999 oz. ASW, 40 mm. **Subject:** Capital Market in the Peoples Republic of China, 20th Anniversary **Obv:** Temple of Heaven **Rev:** Panda

| Date | Mintage | VF20 | XF40 | MS60 | MS63 | MS65 |
|---|---|---|---|---|---|---|
| 2010 Proof | 40,000 | — | — | — | 120 | — |

### KM# 1796 10 YUAN
31.10 g., 0.999 Silver 0.999 oz. ASW, 40 mm. **Subject:** Shanghai Mint, 90th Anniversary **Obv:** Temple of Heaven **Rev:** Panda

| Date | Mintage | VF20 | XF40 | MS60 | MS63 | MS65 |
|---|---|---|---|---|---|---|
| 2010 | 20,000 | — | — | — | 275 | — |

### KM# 1939 10 YUAN
31.11 g., 0.999 Silver 0.999 oz. ASW, 40 mm. **Series:** Outlaws of the Marsh, series 2 **Rev:** Multicolor

| Date | Mintage | VF20 | XF40 | MS60 | MS63 | MS65 |
|---|---|---|---|---|---|---|
| 2010 | 70,000 | PF65 90.00 | | | | |

### KM# 1940 10 YUAN
31.11 g., 0.999 Silver 0.999 oz. ASW, 40 mm. **Series:** Outlaws of the Marsh, series 2 **Rev:** Multicolor

| Date | Mintage | VF20 | XF40 | MS60 | MS63 | MS65 |
|---|---|---|---|---|---|---|
| 2010 | 70,000 | PF65 90.00 | | | | |

### KM# 1942 10 YUAN
10.36 g., 0.999 Gold 0.3327 oz. AGW **Subject:** Shanghai World Expo, 2010

| Date | Mintage | VF20 | XF40 | MS60 | MS63 | MS65 |
|---|---|---|---|---|---|---|
| 2010 | 60,000 | PF65 600 | | | | |

### KM# 1943 10 YUAN
31.11 g., 0.999 Silver 0.999 oz. ASW, 40 mm. **Subject:** Shanghai World Expo, 2010

| Date | Mintage | VF20 | XF40 | MS60 | MS63 | MS65 |
|---|---|---|---|---|---|---|
| 2010 | 80,000 | PF63 60.00 | PF65 70.00 | | | |

### KM# 1944 10 YUAN
31.11 g., 0.999 Silver 0.999 oz. ASW, 40 mm. **Subject:** Shanghai World Expo, 2010

| Date | Mintage | VF20 | XF40 | MS60 | MS63 | MS65 |
|---|---|---|---|---|---|---|
| 2010 | 80,000 | PF63 60.00 | PF65 70.00 | | | |

### KM# 1946 10 YUAN
31.11 g., 0.999 Silver 0.999 oz. ASW, 40 mm. **Subject:** Wudang Mountain

| Date | Mintage | VF20 | XF40 | MS60 | MS63 | MS65 |
|---|---|---|---|---|---|---|
| 2010 | 60,000 | PF63 65.00 | PF65 75.00 | | | |

### KM# 1953 10 YUAN
31.11 g., 0.999 Silver 0.999 oz. ASW **Subject:** Shenzhen Economic Zone

| Date | Mintage | VF20 | XF40 | MS60 | MS63 | MS65 |
|---|---|---|---|---|---|---|
| 2010 | 30,000 | PF63 60.00 | PF65 70.00 | | | |

### KM# 1955 10 YUAN
31.11 g., 0.999 Silver 0.999 oz. ASW, 40 mm. **Subject:** 16th Asian Games

| Date | Mintage | VF20 | XF40 | MS60 | MS63 | MS65 |
|---|---|---|---|---|---|---|
| 2010 | 60,000 | PF63 55.00 | PF65 65.00 | | | |

### KM# 1957 10 YUAN
31.11 g., 0.999 Silver 0.999 oz. ASW, 40 mm. **Subject:** Bejing Opera, series 1 **Rev:** Multicolor face mask

| Date | Mintage | VF20 | XF40 | MS60 | MS63 | MS65 |
|---|---|---|---|---|---|---|
| 2010 | 50,000 | PF65 65.00 | | | | |

### KM# 1958 10 YUAN
31.11 g., 0.999 Silver 0.999 oz. ASW, 40 mm. **Subject:** Bejing Opera, series 1 **Rev:** Multicolor face mask

| Date | Mintage | VF20 | XF40 | MS60 | MS63 | MS65 |
|---|---|---|---|---|---|---|
| 2010 | 50,000 | PF65 65.00 | | | | |

### KM# 1959 10 YUAN
31.11 g., 0.999 Silver 0.999 oz. ASW, 40 mm. **Subject:** Bejing Stamp & Coin Expo

| Date | Mintage | VF20 | XF40 | MS60 | MS63 | MS65 |
|---|---|---|---|---|---|---|
| 2010 | 30,000 | PF63 50.00 | PF65 60.00 | | | |

### KM# 1798 10 YUAN
31.10 g., 0.999 Silver 0.999 oz. ASW, 40 mm. **Subject:** World Wildlife Fund, 50th Anniversary **Rev:** Tibetian antelope

| Date | Mintage | VF20 | XF40 | MS60 | MS63 | MS65 |
|---|---|---|---|---|---|---|
| 2011 | 30,000 | PF63 60.00 | PF65 70.00 | | | |

### KM# 1800 10 YUAN
31.10 g., 0.999 Silver 0.999 oz. ASW, 40 mm. **Subject:** Tsinghua University, 100th Anniversary **Rev:** Old University entrance

| Date | Mintage | VF20 | XF40 | MS60 | MS63 | MS65 |
|---|---|---|---|---|---|---|
| 2011 | Est. 50000 | PF63 65.00 | PF65 75.00 | | | |

### KM# 1804 10 YUAN
31.11 g., 0.999 Silver 0.999 oz. ASW, 40 mm. **Subject:** 23rd Beijing International Stamp and Coin Exposition **Rev:** Byzantine coin and Song Dynasty coin

| Date | Mintage | VF20 | XF40 | MS60 | MS63 | MS65 |
|---|---|---|---|---|---|---|
| 2011 | Est. 30000 | PF65 125 | | | | |

### KM# 1805 10 YUAN
31.10 g., 0.999 Silver 0.999 oz. ASW, 40 mm. **Subject:** Chinese Literature **Rev:** Archer and geese in color

| Date | Mintage | VF20 | XF40 | MS60 | MS63 | MS65 |
|---|---|---|---|---|---|---|
| 2011 | 70,000 | PF65 75.00 | | | | |

### KM# 1806 10 YUAN
31.11 g., 0.999 Silver 0.999 oz. ASW, 40 mm. **Subject:** Chinese Literature **Rev:** Li Kui as black wind in color

| Date | Mintage | VF20 | XF40 | MS60 | MS63 | MS65 |
|---|---|---|---|---|---|---|
| 2011 | 70,000 | PF65 75.00 | | | | |

### KM# 1985 10 YUAN
31.11 g., 0.999 Silver 0.999 oz. ASW, 40 mm. **Subject:** Peking Opera art **Rev:** Lu Zhishen, the "Flowery Monk" character from Water Margin

| Date | Mintage | VF20 | XF40 | MS60 | MS63 | MS65 |
|---|---|---|---|---|---|---|
| 2011 | 50,000 | PF63 75.00 | PF65 85.00 | | | |

### KM# 1986 10 YUAN
31.11 g., 0.999 Silver 0.999 oz. ASW, 40 mm. **Subject:** Peking Opera art **Rev:** Shan Ziongxin

| Date | Mintage | VF20 | XF40 | MS60 | MS63 | MS65 |
|---|---|---|---|---|---|---|
| 2011 | 50,000 | PF63 75.00 | PF65 85.00 | | | |

### KM# 1994 10 YUAN
31.11 g., 0.999 Silver 0.999 oz. ASW, 40 mm. **Subject:** Bejing-Shanghai High Speed Rail **Obv:** Temple of Heaven **Rev:** Two pandas

| Date | Mintage | VF20 | XF40 | MS60 | MS63 | MS65 |
|---|---|---|---|---|---|---|
| 2011 | 30,000 | PF65 200 | | | | |

### KM# 1996 10 YUAN
31.11 g., 0.999 Silver 0.999 oz. ASW, 40 mm. **Subject:** Xi-an Hortaculture Exposition **Obv:** Temple of Heaven **Rev:** Two pandas

| Date | Mintage | VF20 | XF40 | MS60 | MS63 | MS65 |
|---|---|---|---|---|---|---|
| 2011 | 20,000 | PF65 235 | | | | |

### KM# 1998 10 YUAN
31.11 g., 0.999 Silver 0.999 oz. ASW, 40 mm. **Subject:** 26th Summer Universade, Shezhuan **Obv:** Colored wreath logo **Rev:** Cubic building

| Date | Mintage | VF20 | XF40 | MS60 | MS63 | MS65 |
|---|---|---|---|---|---|---|
| 2011 | 30,000 | PF65 200 | | | | |

### KM# 2000 10 YUAN
31.11 g., 0.999 Silver 0.999 oz. ASW, 40 mm. **Subject:** Peaceful liberation, 60th Anniversary **Obv:** National emblem **Rev:** Ornate design

| Date | Mintage | VF20 | XF40 | MS60 | MS63 | MS65 |
|---|---|---|---|---|---|---|
| 2011 Proof | 30,000 | — | — | — | 200 | — |

### KM# 2002 10 YUAN
31.11 g., 0.999 Silver 0.999 oz. ASW, 40 mm. **Subject:** 100th Anniversary of the Revolution **Obv:** National emblem **Rev:** Revolutionary army advancing right - Wuchang Uprising

| Date | Mintage | VF20 | XF40 | MS60 | MS63 | MS65 |
|---|---|---|---|---|---|---|
| 2011 | 160,000 | PF65 100 | | | | |

### KM# 2004 10 YUAN
31.11 g., 0.999 Silver 0.999 oz. ASW, 40 mm. **Subject:** Avation Industry in the P.R.C., 60th Anniversary **Obv:** Temple of Heaven **Rev:** Two pandas

| Date | Mintage | VF20 | XF40 | MS60 | MS63 | MS65 |
|---|---|---|---|---|---|---|
| 2011 | 20,000 | PF65 200 | | | | |

### KM# 2007 10 YUAN
31.11 g., 0.999 Silver 0.999 oz. ASW, 40 mm. **Subject:** World Heritage Site **Obv:** National emblem **Rev:** Songyue Temple Pagoda

| Date | Mintage | VF20 | XF40 | MS60 | MS63 | MS65 |
|---|---|---|---|---|---|---|
| 2011 | 60,000 | PF65 150 | | | | |

### KM# 2034 10 YUAN

31.10 g., 0.999 Silver 0.999 oz. ASW **Subject:** National Committee of the Chinese Financial Workers Union, 60th Anniversary **Rev:** Mother and cub panda

| Date | Mintage | VF20 | XF40 | MS60 | MS63 | MS65 |
|---|---|---|---|---|---|---|
| 2011 | 30,000 | — | — | — | 200 | — |

### KM# 2035 10 YUAN

31.10 g., 0.999 Silver 0.999 oz. ASW, 40 mm. **Subject:** Shanghai Gold Exchange, 10th Anniversary **Rev:** Mother and cub panda

| Date | Mintage | VF20 | XF40 | MS60 | MS63 | MS65 |
|---|---|---|---|---|---|---|
| 2011 | 30,000 | — | — | — | 140 | — |

### KM# 2037 10 YUAN

31.10 g., 0.999 Silver 0.999 oz. ASW, 40 mm. **Subject:** Xiamen Special Economic Zone, 30th Anniversary **Rev:** Mother and cub panda

| Date | Mintage | VF20 | XF40 | MS60 | MS63 | MS65 |
|---|---|---|---|---|---|---|
| 2011 | 20,000 | — | — | — | 200 | — |

### KM# 2039 10 YUAN

31.10 g., 0.999 Silver 0.999 oz. ASW, 40 mm. **Subject:** Rual Credit Cooperatives, 60th Anniversary **Rev:** Mother and cub panda

| Date | Mintage | VF20 | XF40 | MS60 | MS63 | MS65 |
|---|---|---|---|---|---|---|
| 2011 | 60,000 | — | — | — | 100 | — |

### KM# 2047 10 YUAN

31.10 g., 0.999 Silver 0.999 oz. ASW, 40 mm. **Subject:** Bejing Opera Masks **Rev:** Zhang Fei mask in color

| Date | Mintage | VF20 | XF40 | MS60 | MS63 | MS65 |
|---|---|---|---|---|---|---|
| 2012 | 50,000 | **PF65** 85.00 | | | | |

### KM# 2048 10 YUAN

31.10 g., 0.999 Silver 0.999 oz. ASW, 40 mm. **Subject:** Bejing Opera Mask **Rev:** Tao Hong mask in color

| Date | Mintage | VF20 | XF40 | MS60 | MS63 | MS65 |
|---|---|---|---|---|---|---|
| 2012 | 50,000 | **PF65** 80.00 | | | | |

### KM# 2052 10 YUAN

31.10 g., 0.999 Silver 0.999 oz. ASW, 40 mm. **Subject:** Bronze Age vessels **Rev:** Three water vessels from the Shang Dynasty, Zianwen find

| Date | Mintage | VF20 | XF40 | MS60 | MS63 | MS65 |
|---|---|---|---|---|---|---|
| 2012 | 80,000 | **PF63** 70.00 | **PF65** 80.00 | | | |

### KM# 2057 10 YUAN

31.10 g., Silver, 40 mm. **Subject:** Beijing International Stamp and Coin Exposition

| Date | Mintage | VF20 | XF40 | MS60 | MS63 | MS65 |
|---|---|---|---|---|---|---|
| 2012 | 30,000 | **PF63** 115 | **PF65** 125 | | | |

### KM# 2063 10 YUAN

31.10 g., 0.999 Silver 0.999 oz. ASW, 40 mm. **Subject:** Bank of China, 100th Anniversary **Obv:** Temple of Heaven **Rev:** Mother and cub panda seated

| Date | Mintage | VF20 | XF40 | MS60 | MS63 | MS65 |
|---|---|---|---|---|---|---|
| 2012 | 260,000 | — | — | — | 85.00 | — |

### KM# 2076 10 YUAN

31.11 g., 0.999 Silver 0.999 oz. ASW, 40 mm. **Subject:** Hua Xia Bank, 20th Anniversary

| Date | Mintage | VF20 | XF40 | MS60 | MS63 | MS65 |
|---|---|---|---|---|---|---|
| 2013 | 50,000 | — | — | — | 75.00 | — |

### KM# 2078 10 YUAN

31.13 g., 0.999 Silver 0.9999 oz. ASW, 40 mm. **Subject:** China Merchants Bank, 25th Anniversary

| Date | Mintage | VF20 | XF40 | MS60 | MS63 | MS65 |
|---|---|---|---|---|---|---|
| 2012 | 30,000 | — | — | — | 75.00 | — |

### KM# 2065 10 YUAN

31.13 g., 0.999 Silver 0.9999 oz. ASW, 40 mm. **Subject:** Year of the Snake **Obv:** National arms **Rev:** Snake **Shape:** Scalloped

| Date | Mintage | VF20 | XF40 | MS60 | MS63 | MS65 |
|---|---|---|---|---|---|---|
| 2013 | Est. 60000 | **PF65** 75.00 | | | | |

### KM# 2066 10 YUAN

31.13 g., 0.999 Silver 0.9999 oz. ASW **Subject:** Year of the Snake **Obv:** National arms **Rev:** Snake **Shape:** Arc

| Date | Mintage | VF20 | XF40 | MS60 | MS63 | MS65 |
|---|---|---|---|---|---|---|
| 2013 | Est. 80000 | **PF65** 75.00 | | | | |

### KM# 2067 10 YUAN

31.13 g., 0.999 Silver 0.9999 oz. ASW, 40 mm. **Subject:** Year of the Snake **Obv:** National arms **Rev:** Snake

| Date | Mintage | VF20 | XF40 | MS60 | MS63 | MS65 |
|---|---|---|---|---|---|---|
| 2013 | Est. 200000 | **PF65** 75.00 | | | | |

### KM# 2082 10 YUAN

31.13 g., 0.999 Silver 0.9999 oz. ASW, 40 mm. **Subject:** Year of the Snake **Obv:** National emblem **Rev:** Snake in color

| Date | Mintage | VF20 | XF40 | MS60 | MS63 | MS65 |
|---|---|---|---|---|---|---|
| 2013 | Est. 220000 | **PF65** 60.00 | | | | |

### KM# 1388 20 YUAN

62.21 g., 0.999 Silver 1.998 oz. ASW, 40 mm. **Subject:** Mogao Grottos **Obv:** 8-story building **Rev:** Buddha-like statue **Edge:** Reeded **Note:** Prev. Y#1082.

| Date | Mintage | VF20 | XF40 | MS60 | MS63 | MS65 |
|---|---|---|---|---|---|---|
| 2001 | — | **PF65** 150 | | | | |

### KM# 1432 20 YUAN

62.21 g., 0.999 Silver 1.998 oz. ASW, 40 mm. **Rev:** Buddha-like statue

| Date | Mintage | VF20 | XF40 | MS60 | MS63 | MS65 |
|---|---|---|---|---|---|---|
| 2002 | 30,000 | **PF65** 150 | | | | |

### KM# 1563 20 YUAN

31.10 g., 0.999 Silver 0.999 oz. ASW, 40 mm. **Series:** Maijishan grotto art **Rev:** Two figures standing

| Date | Mintage | VF20 | XF40 | MS60 | MS63 | MS65 |
|---|---|---|---|---|---|---|
| 2004 | 20,000 | **PF65** 90.00 | | | | |

### KM# 2042 20 YUAN

62.27 g., 0.999 Silver 2.000 oz. ASW, 40 mm. **Subject:** UNESCO **Rev:** Budda statue in Riwo Tsenga

| Date | Mintage | VF20 | XF40 | MS60 | MS63 | MS65 |
|---|---|---|---|---|---|---|
| 2012 | Est. 100000 | **PF63** 135 | **PF65** 150 | | | |

### KM# 1386 50 YUAN

155.52 g., 0.999 Silver 4.995 oz. ASW, 90 x 40 mm. **Series:** Folk fairy tails **Rev:** Seven multicolor figures on beach **Shape:** Rectangle

| Date | Mintage | VF20 | XF40 | MS60 | MS63 | MS65 |
|---|---|---|---|---|---|---|
| 2001 | 10,000 | **PF65** 300 | | | | |

### KM# 1389 50 YUAN

3.11 g., 0.999 Gold 0.0999 oz. AGW **Subject:** Mogao Grottoes **Obv:** Eight story building **Rev:** Buddha-like statue **Edge:** Reeded. **Note:** Prev. Y#1084.

| Date | Mintage | VF20 | XF40 | MS60 | MS63 | MS65 |
|---|---|---|---|---|---|---|
| 2001 | — | **PF65** 250 | | | | |

### KM# 1390 50 YUAN

155.52 g., 0.999 Silver 4.995 oz. ASW, 70 mm. **Subject:** Mogao Grottoes **Obv:** Eight story building **Rev:** Four musicians **Edge:** Reeded. **Note:** Prev. Y#1083.

| Date | Mintage | VF20 | XF40 | MS60 | MS63 | MS65 |
|---|---|---|---|---|---|---|
| 2001 | — | **PF65** 300 | | | | |

### KM# 1394 50 YUAN

155.52 g., 0.999 Silver 4.995 oz. ASW, 90 x 40 mm. **Subject:** Han Xizai's Dinner Party **Obv:** Tang Dynasty buildings **Rev:** Multicolor "Five Dynasties" painting **Edge:** Plain **Shape:** Rectangular **Note:** Prev. Y#1104.

| Date | Mintage | VF20 | XF40 | MS60 | MS63 | MS65 |
|---|---|---|---|---|---|---|
| 2001 | 18,800 | **PF65** 275 | | | | |

### KM# 1402 50 YUAN

155.52 g., 0.999 Silver 4.995 oz. ASW, 90 x 50 mm. **Subject:** Bejing opera **Rev:** Four multicolor actors **Shape:** Rectangle

| Date | Mintage | VF20 | XF40 | MS60 | MS63 | MS65 |
|---|---|---|---|---|---|---|
| 2001 | 11,800 | **PF65** 300 | | | | |

### KM# 1430 50 YUAN

155.79 g., 0.999 Silver 5.0038 oz. ASW, 90 x 40 mm. **Series:** Folk fairy tails **Rev:** Multicolor female with red ribbon **Shape:** Rectangle

| Date | Mintage | VF20 | XF40 | MS60 | MS63 | MS65 |
|---|---|---|---|---|---|---|
| 2002 | — | **PF65** 375 | | | | |

### KM# 1433 50 YUAN

155.52 g., 0.999 Silver 4.995 oz. ASW, 70 mm. **Series:** Long men grottoes **Rev:** Two figures

| Date | Mintage | VF20 | XF40 | MS60 | MS63 | MS65 |
|---|---|---|---|---|---|---|
| 2002 | 8,000 | **PF65** 300 | | | | |

### KM# 1437 50 YUAN

3.11 g., 0.999 Gold 0.0999 oz. AGW, 18 mm. **Subject:** Kuan yin

| Date | Mintage | VF20 | XF40 | MS60 | MS63 | MS65 |
|---|---|---|---|---|---|---|
| 2002 | 33,000 | **PF65** 225 | | | | |

### KM# 1445 50 YUAN

155.52 g., 0.999 Silver 4.995 oz. ASW, 65 x 26 mm. **Series:** Classic literature **Rev:** Multicolor crowd of women **Shape:** Fan-like

| Date | Mintage | VF20 | XF40 | MS60 | MS63 | MS65 |
|---|---|---|---|---|---|---|
| 2002 | 11,800 | **PF65** 250 | | | | |

### KM# 1453 50 YUAN

155.52 g., 0.999 Silver 4.995 oz. ASW, 90 x 40 mm. **Series:** Bejing opera **Rev:** Three multicolor characters one with spikes in costume **Shape:** Rectangle

| Date | Mintage | VF20 | XF40 | MS60 | MS63 | MS65 |
|---|---|---|---|---|---|---|
| 2002 | 11,800 | **PF65** 300 | | | | |

### KM# 1493 50 YUAN

155.35 g., 0.999 Silver 4.9896 oz. ASW, 90 x 40 mm. **Series:** Fairy tails **Rev:** Multicolor man with two boys in buckets, jenole in flight at left **Shape:** Rectangle

| Date | Mintage | VF20 | XF40 | MS60 | MS63 | MS65 |
|---|---|---|---|---|---|---|
| 2003 | 10,000 | **PF65** 350 | | | | |

### KM# 1502 50 YUAN

155.50 g., 0.999 Silver 4.9944 oz. ASW, 80 x 50 mm. **Series:** Class literature **Rev:** Multicolor man lying on couch **Shape:** Rectangle

| Date | Mintage | VF20 | XF40 | MS60 | MS63 | MS65 |
|---|---|---|---|---|---|---|
| 2003 | 10,000 | **PF65** 350 | | | | |

### KM# 1503 50 YUAN

155.15 g., 0.999 Silver 4.9832 oz. ASW, 65 x 125 mm. **Series:** Class literature **Rev:** Six people **Shape:** Arc **Note:** Colorized

| Date | Mintage | VF20 | XF40 | MS60 | MS63 | MS65 |
|---|---|---|---|---|---|---|
| 2003 | 11,800 | **PF65** 350 | | | | |

### KM# 1512 50 YUAN

3.11 g., 0.999 Gold 0.0999 oz. AGW, 18 mm. **Obv:** Putuo Mountain Pilgrimage Gate **Rev:** Seated Kuanyin with holographic background **Edge:** Reeded **Note:** Prev. Y#1234.

| Date | Mintage | VF20 | XF40 | MS60 | MS63 | MS65 |
|---|---|---|---|---|---|---|
| 2003 | 33,000 | **PF65** 225 | | | | |

### KM# 1560 50 YUAN

155.52 g., 0.999 Silver 4.995 oz. ASW, 80x50 mm. **Obv:** Monkey King leading the Master over bridge **Rev:** Multicolor Monkey King fighting the Pig Demon of Bones **Edge:** Plain **Shape:** Rectangle **Note:** Prev. Y#1216.

| Date | Mintage | VF20 | XF40 | MS60 | MS63 | MS65 |
|---|---|---|---|---|---|---|
| 2004 | 10,000 | **PF65** 375 | | | | |

**KM# 1572 50 YUAN**
3.11 g., 0.999 Gold 0.0999 oz. AGW, 18 mm. **Obv:** Putuo Mountain Pilgrimage Gate **Rev:** Kuanyin and value **Edge:** Reeded **Note:** Prev. Y#1237.

| Date | Mintage | VF20 | XF40 | MS60 | MS63 | MS65 |
|---|---|---|---|---|---|---|
| 2004 | 33,000 | **PF65** 225 | | | | |

**KM# 1635 50 YUAN**
155.00 g., 0.999 Silver 4.9784 oz. ASW, 80 x 50 mm. **Series:** Classical Literature **Obv:** Horseman on arch bridge **Rev:** Multicolor female and lion **Shape:** Rectangle **Note:** Illustration reduced.

| Date | Mintage | VF20 | XF40 | MS60 | MS63 | MS65 |
|---|---|---|---|---|---|---|
| 2005 | 10,000 | **PF65** 350 | | | | |

**KM# 1901 50 YUAN**
155.50 g., 0.999 Silver 4.9944 oz. ASW, 80x50 mm. **Subject:** Outlaws of the Marsh, series 1 **Rev:** Multicolor **Shape:** Rectangle

| Date | Mintage | VF20 | XF40 | MS60 | MS63 | MS65 |
|---|---|---|---|---|---|---|
| 2009 | 10,000 | **PF65** 250 | | | | |

**KM# 1938 50 YUAN**
155.50 g., 0.999 Silver 4.9944 oz. ASW, 80x50 mm. **Subject:** Outlaws of the Marsh, series 2 **Rev:** Multicolor **Shape:** Regtangle

| Date | Mintage | VF20 | XF40 | MS60 | MS63 | MS65 |
|---|---|---|---|---|---|---|
| 2010 | 12,000 | **PF65** 225 | | | | |

**KM# 1951 50 YUAN**
62.10 g., 0.999 Silver 1.9946 oz. ASW **Subject:** Yungang Grotto Art

| Date | Mintage | VF20 | XF40 | MS60 | MS63 | MS65 |
|---|---|---|---|---|---|---|
| 2010 | 20,000 | **PF65** 120 | | | | |

**KM# 1807 50 YUAN**
155.67 g., 0.999 Silver 4.9999 oz. ASW, 80x50 mm. **Subject:** Chinese Literature **Rev:** Yan Qing and Ren Yuan in color

| Date | Mintage | VF20 | XF40 | MS60 | MS63 | MS65 |
|---|---|---|---|---|---|---|
| 2011 | 12,000 | **PF65** 325 | | | | |

**KM# 2049 50 YUAN**
155.67 g., 0.999 Silver 4.9999 oz. ASW, 70 mm. **Subject:** Beijing Opera Masks **Rev:** Zhong Kui mask in color

| Date | Mintage | VF20 | XF40 | MS60 | MS63 | MS65 |
|---|---|---|---|---|---|---|
| 2012 | 10,000 | **PF65** 350 | | | | |

**KM# 2053 50 YUAN**
155.67 g., 0.999 Silver 4.9999 oz. ASW, 70 mm. **Subject:** Vessels of the Bronze Age **Rev:** Shang Dynasty kettle

| Date | Mintage | VF20 | XF40 | MS60 | MS63 | MS65 |
|---|---|---|---|---|---|---|
| 2012 | 10,000 | **PF65** 350 | | | | |

**KM# 2059 50 YUAN**
155.67 g., 0.999 Silver 4.9999 oz. ASW, 70 mm. **Subject:** Panda, 30th Anniversary **Obv:** Temple of Heaven **Rev:** Panda

| Date | Mintage | VF20 | XF40 | MS60 | MS63 | MS65 |
|---|---|---|---|---|---|---|
| 2012 | 30,000 | **PF65** 350 | | | | |

**KM# 2060 50 YUAN**
3.11 g., 0.999 Gold 0.0999 oz. AGW, 18 mm. **Subject:** Panda, 30th Anniversary **Obv:** Temple of Heaven **Rev:** Panda

| Date | Mintage | VF20 | XF40 | MS60 | MS63 | MS65 |
|---|---|---|---|---|---|---|
| 2012 | 100,000 | **PF65** 300 | | | | |

**KM# 2068 50 YUAN**
155.67 g., 0.999 Silver 4.9999 oz. ASW, 80x50 mm. **Subject:** Year of the Snake **Obv:** National emblem **Rev:** Snake **Shape:** Rectangle

| Date | Mintage | VF20 | XF40 | MS60 | MS63 | MS65 |
|---|---|---|---|---|---|---|
| 2013 | Est. 20000 | **PF65** 375 | | | | |

**KM# 2070 50 YUAN**
3.11 g., 0.999 Gold 0.0999 oz. AGW, 18 mm. **Subject:** Year of the Snake **Obv:** National emblem **Rev:** Snake

| Date | Mintage | VF20 | XF40 | MS60 | MS63 | MS65 |
|---|---|---|---|---|---|---|
| 2013 | Est. 120000 | **PF65** 275 | | | | |

**KM# 2084 50 YUAN**
155.67 g., 0.999 Silver 4.9999 oz. ASW, 70 mm. **Subject:** Year of the Snake **Obv:** National emblem **Rev:** Snake in color

| Date | Mintage | VF20 | XF40 | MS60 | MS63 | MS65 |
|---|---|---|---|---|---|---|
| 2013 | Est. 30000 | **PF65** 375 | | | | |

**KM# 2084 50 YUAN**
3.11 g., 0.999 Gold 0.0999 oz. AGW, 18 mm. **Subject:** Year of the Snake **Obv:** National arms **Rev:** Snake in color

| Date | Mintage | VF20 | XF40 | MS60 | MS63 | MS65 |
|---|---|---|---|---|---|---|
| 2013 | Est. 120000 | **PF65** 250 | | | | |

**KM# 1514 100 YUAN**
3.10 g., 0.999 Platinum 0.0996 oz. APW, 18 mm. **Series:** Guan Yi

| Date | Mintage | VF20 | XF40 | MS60 | MS63 | MS65 |
|---|---|---|---|---|---|---|
| 2003 | 33,000 | **PF65** 225 | | | | |

**KM# 1534 100 YUAN**
15.55 g., 0.999 Palladium 0.4994 oz. APW, 27 mm. **Obv:** Temple of Heaven **Rev:** Panda mother and cub, "kissing pandas **Edge:** Reeded **Note:** Prev. Y#1211.

| Date | Mintage | VF20 | XF40 | MS60 | MS63 | MS65 |
|---|---|---|---|---|---|---|
| 2004 | 8,000 | **PF65** 550 | | | | |

**KM# 1540 100 YUAN**
7.85 g., 0.999 Gold 0.2521 oz. AGW, 22 mm. **Subject:** 20th Anniversary / Bank of China Industrial and Commercial **Rev:** Panda walking with cub

| Date | Mintage | VF20 | XF40 | MS60 | MS63 | MS65 |
|---|---|---|---|---|---|---|
| 2004 | 50,000 | **PF65** 500 | | | | |

**KM# 1542 100 YUAN**
7.84 g., 0.999 Gold 0.2518 oz. AGW, 22 mm. **Subject:** 50th Anniversary China Construction Bank **Rev:** Panda walking with cub

| Date | Mintage | VF20 | XF40 | MS60 | MS63 | MS65 |
|---|---|---|---|---|---|---|
| 2004 | 60,000 | **PF65** 500 | | | | |

**KM# 1573 100 YUAN**
3.11 g., 0.9995 Platinum 0.0999 oz. APW, 18 mm. **Obv:** Putuo Mountain Pilgrimage Gate **Rev:** Kuanyin and value **Edge:** Reeded **Note:** Prev. Y#1238.

| Date | Mintage | VF20 | XF40 | MS60 | MS63 | MS65 |
|---|---|---|---|---|---|---|
| 2004 | 33,000 | **PF65** 225 | | | | |

**KM# 1600 100 YUAN**
7.77 g., 0.999 Gold 0.2496 oz. AGW, 22 mm. **Subject:** Foundation of Industrial & Commercial Bank **Obv:** Temple of Heaven **Rev:** Panda cub and mom seated in bamboo

| Date | Mintage | VF20 | XF40 | MS60 | MS63 | MS65 |
|---|---|---|---|---|---|---|
| 2005 | 40,000 | PF65 500 | | | | |

**KM# 1602 100 YUAN**
7.77 g., 0.999 Gold 0.2496 oz. AGW, 22 mm. **Subject:** 100th Anniversary of Bank of Shanghai **Obv:** Temple of Heaven **Rev:** Panda cub and mom seated in bamboo

| Date | Mintage | VF20 | XF40 | MS60 | MS63 | MS65 |
|---|---|---|---|---|---|---|
| 2005 | 40,000 | PF65 500 | | | | |

**KM# 1616 100 YUAN**
7.70 g., 0.999 Gold 0.2473 oz. AGW, 22 mm. **Subject:** 2006 World Cup - Germany **Obv:** Multicolor logo **Rev:** Temple of Heaven and soccer ball

| Date | Mintage | VF20 | XF40 | MS60 | MS63 | MS65 |
|---|---|---|---|---|---|---|
| 2005 | 10,000 | PF65 550 | | | | |

**KM# A979 100 YUAN**
8.50 g., 0.999 Gold 0.273 oz. AGW, 22 mm. **Subject:** 10th Anniversary Bank of Beijing **Obv:** Temple of Heaven **Rev:** Two pandas

| Date | Mintage | VF20 | XF40 | MS60 | MS63 | MS65 |
|---|---|---|---|---|---|---|
| 2006 | 100 | — | — | — | 800 | — |

**KM# A980 100 YUAN**
8.50 g., 0.999 Gold 0.273 oz. AGW, 22 mm. **Subject:** 10th Anniversary China Minsheng Banking Corp. **Obv:** Temple of Heaven **Rev:** Two Pandas munching on bamboo

| Date | Mintage | VF20 | XF40 | MS60 | MS63 | MS65 |
|---|---|---|---|---|---|---|
| 2006 | 100 | — | — | — | 800 | — |

**KM# 1665 100 YUAN**
7.77 g., 0.999 Gold 0.2496 oz. AGW, 22 mm. **Subject:** 10th Anniversary Bank of Beijing **Obv:** Temple of Heaven **Rev:** Two pandas seated with bamboo

| Date | Mintage | VF20 | XF40 | MS60 | MS63 | MS65 |
|---|---|---|---|---|---|---|
| 2006 | 150,000 | PF65 500 | | | | |

**KM# 1667 100 YUAN**
7.77 g., 0.999 Silver 0.2496 oz. ASW, 22 mm. **Subject:** 10th Anniversary - China Minsheng Banking Corp **Obv:** Temple of Heaven **Rev:** Two pandas seated with bamboo

| Date | Mintage | VF20 | XF40 | MS60 | MS63 | MS65 |
|---|---|---|---|---|---|---|
| 2006 | 20,000 | PF65 550 | | | | |

**KM# 1669 100 YUAN**
7.77 g., 0.999 Gold 0.2496 oz. AGW, 22 mm. **Subject:** Shenyang Horticultural Expo **Obv:** Temple of Heaven **Rev:** Two pandas seated with bamboo

| Date | Mintage | VF20 | XF40 | MS60 | MS63 | MS65 |
|---|---|---|---|---|---|---|
| 2006 | 10,000 | PF65 550 | | | | |

**KM# 1694 100 YUAN**
7.77 g., 0.999 Gold 0.2496 oz. AGW, 22 mm. **Subject:** Qinghai - Tibet Railway Opening **Obv:** Map of railway route and track layer **Rev:** Kun Lun Tunnel Portal

| Date | Mintage | VF20 | XF40 | MS60 | MS63 | MS65 |
|---|---|---|---|---|---|---|
| 2006 | 16,000 | PF65 550 | | | | |

**KM# 1730 100 YUAN**
7.77 g., 0.999 Gold 0.2496 oz. AGW, 22 mm. **Subject:** 60th Anniversary - Foundry of Mongolia Autonomous Region **Obv:** Wheel of Mongolian Lele Cart **Rev:** Female Mongolian in posture of welcome

| Date | Mintage | VF20 | XF40 | MS60 | MS63 | MS65 |
|---|---|---|---|---|---|---|
| 2007 | 10,000 | PF65 550 | | | | |

**KM# 1827 100 YUAN**
7.78 g., 0.999 Gold 0.2499 oz. AGW, 22 mm. **Subject:** 12th Special Olympics in Shanghai **Obv:** Logo in color **Rev:** Runner

| Date | Mintage | VF20 | XF40 | MS60 | MS63 | MS65 |
|---|---|---|---|---|---|---|
| 2007 | 20,000 | PF65 650 | | | | |

**KM# 1737 100 YUAN**
7.78 g., 0.999 Gold 0.2499 oz. AGW, 22 mm. **Subject:** Economic Reform in China, 30th Anniversary **Rev:** Flowers and fireworks

| Date | Mintage | VF20 | XF40 | MS60 | MS63 | MS65 |
|---|---|---|---|---|---|---|
| 2008 | 30,000 | PF65 600 | | | | |

**KM# 1824 100 YUAN**
7.77 g., 0.999 Gold 0.2496 oz. AGW, 23 mm. **Subject:** Bank of Communications, Centennial **Rev:** Panda

| Date | Mintage | VF20 | XF40 | MS60 | MS63 | MS65 |
|---|---|---|---|---|---|---|
| 2008 | 10,000 | PF65 550 | | | | |

**KM# 1853 100 YUAN**
7.77 g., 0.999 Gold 0.2496 oz. AGW **Subject:** Hainan Special Economic Zone

| Date | Mintage | VF20 | XF40 | MS60 | MS63 | MS65 |
|---|---|---|---|---|---|---|
| 2008 | 10,000 | PF65 550 | | | | |

**KM# 1857 100 YUAN**
7.77 g., 0.999 Gold 0.2496 oz. AGW **Subject:** Ningxia Hui Autonomous Region

| Date | Mintage | VF20 | XF40 | MS60 | MS63 | MS65 |
|---|---|---|---|---|---|---|
| 2008 | 10,000 | PF65 550 | | | | |

**KM# 1860 100 YUAN**
7.77 g., 0.999 Gold 0.2496 oz. AGW **Subject:** Guangzi Zhuang Autonomous Region

| Date | Mintage | VF20 | XF40 | MS60 | MS63 | MS65 |
|---|---|---|---|---|---|---|
| 2008 | 10,000 | PF65 550 | | | | |

**KM# 1890 100 YUAN**
7.77 g., 0.999 Gold 0.2496 oz. AGW, 23 mm. **Subject:** Precious Metal Commemoratives, 30th Anniversary **Obv:** Temple of Heaven **Rev:** Two pandas seated

| Date | Mintage | VF20 | XF40 | MS60 | MS63 | MS65 |
|---|---|---|---|---|---|---|
| 2009 | 10,000 | — | — | — | 550 | — |

**KM# 1895 100 YUAN**
7.77 g., 0.999 Gold 0.2496 oz. AGW, 22 mm. **Subject:** P.R.C. 60th Anniversary

| Date | Mintage | VF20 | XF40 | MS60 | MS63 | MS65 |
|---|---|---|---|---|---|---|
| 2009 | 100,000 | PF65 500 | | | | |

**KM# 1904 100 YUAN**
7.77 g., 0.999 Gold 0.2496 oz. AGW, 22 mm. **Subject:** 16th Asian Games

| Date | Mintage | VF20 | XF40 | MS60 | MS63 | MS65 |
|---|---|---|---|---|---|---|
| 2009 | 30,000 | PF65 525 | | | | |

**KM# 1909 100 YUAN**
7.77 g., 0.999 Gold 0.2496 oz. AGW, 22 mm. **Subject:** China Agricultural Bank

| Date | Mintage | VF20 | XF40 | MS60 | MS63 | MS65 |
|---|---|---|---|---|---|---|
| 2009 | 100,000 | — | — | — | 500 | — |

**KM# 1794 100 YUAN**
7.78 g., 0.999 Gold 0.2499 oz. AGW, 22 mm. **Subject:** Agricultural Bank, IPO **Obv:** Temple of Heaven **Rev:** Panda

| Date | Mintage | VF20 | XF40 | MS60 | MS63 | MS65 |
|---|---|---|---|---|---|---|
| 2010 | 60,000 | — | — | — | 500 | — |

**KM# 1797 100 YUAN**
7.78 g., 0.999 Gold 0.2499 oz. AGW, 22 mm. **Subject:** Shanghai Mint, 90th Anniversary **Obv:** Temple of Heaven **Rev:** Panda

| Date | Mintage | VF20 | XF40 | MS60 | MS63 | MS65 |
|---|---|---|---|---|---|---|
| 2010 | 5,000 | — | — | — | 500 | — |

**KM# 1945 100 YUAN**
7.77 g., 0.999 Gold 0.2496 oz. AGW **Subject:** Wudang Mountain

| Date | Mintage | VF20 | XF40 | MS60 | MS63 | MS65 |
|---|---|---|---|---|---|---|
| 2010 | 30,000 | PF65 525 | | | | |

**KM# 1952 100 YUAN**
7.77 g., 0.999 Gold 0.2496 oz. AGW **Subject:** Shenzhen Economic Zone

| Date | Mintage | VF20 | XF40 | MS60 | MS63 | MS65 |
|---|---|---|---|---|---|---|
| 2010 | 20,000 | PF65 525 | | | | |

**KM# 1954 100 YUAN**
7.77 g., 0.999 Gold 0.2496 oz. AGW **Subject:** 16th Asian Games

| Date | Mintage | VF20 | XF40 | MS60 | MS63 | MS65 |
|---|---|---|---|---|---|---|
| 2010 | 30,000 | PF65 525 | | | | |

**KM# 1956 100 YUAN**
7.77 g., 0.999 Gold 0.2496 oz. AGW **Subject:** Bejing Opera, series 1 **Rev:** Multicolor

| Date | Mintage | VF20 | XF40 | MS60 | MS63 | MS65 |
|---|---|---|---|---|---|---|
| 2010 | 30,000 | PF65 525 | | | | |

**KM# 1799 100 YUAN**
7.78 g., 0.999 Gold 0.2499 oz. AGW, 22 mm. **Subject:** World Wildlife Fund, 50th Anniversary **Rev:** Large 50 and WWF logo

| Date | Mintage | VF20 | XF40 | MS60 | MS63 | MS65 |
|---|---|---|---|---|---|---|
| 2011 | 10,000 | PF65 600 | | | | |

**KM# 1801 100 YUAN**
7.78 g., 0.999 Gold 0.2499 oz. AGW, 22 mm. **Subject:** Tsinghua University **Rev:** Original main building

| Date | Mintage | VF20 | XF40 | MS60 | MS63 | MS65 |
|---|---|---|---|---|---|---|
| 2011 | Est. 20000 | PF65 550 | | | | |

**KM# 1987 100 YUAN**
7.77 g., 0.999 Gold 0.2496 oz. AGW, 22 mm. **Subject:** Peking Opera art **Rev:** Mask of Guan Yu

| Date | Mintage | VF20 | XF40 | MS60 | MS63 | MS65 |
|---|---|---|---|---|---|---|
| 2011 | 30,000 | PF65 525 | | | | |

**KM# 1995 100 YUAN**
7.77 g., 0.999 Gold 0.2496 oz. AGW, 22 mm. **Subject:** Bejing-Shanghai High Speed Rail **Obv:** Temple of Heaven **Rev:** Two pandas

| Date | Mintage | VF20 | XF40 | MS60 | MS63 | MS65 |
|---|---|---|---|---|---|---|
| 2011 | 10,000 | PF65 600 | | | | |

**KM# 1997 100 YUAN**
7.77 g., 0.999 Gold 0.2496 oz. AGW, 22 mm. **Subject:** Xi-an Horticulture Exposition **Obv:** Temple of Heaven **Rev:** Two pandas

| Date | Mintage | VF20 | XF40 | MS60 | MS63 | MS65 |
|---|---|---|---|---|---|---|
| 2011 | 3,000 | PF65 750 | | | | |

**KM# 1999 100 YUAN**
7.77 g., 0.999 Gold 0.2496 oz. AGW, 22 mm. **Subject:** 26th Summer Universade, Shezhuan **Obv:** Colored wreath logo **Rev:** Rays and smile face design

| Date | Mintage | VF20 | XF40 | MS60 | MS63 | MS65 |
|---|---|---|---|---|---|---|
| 2011 | 20,000 | PF65 750 | | | | |

**KM# 2001 100 YUAN**
7.77 g., 0.999 Gold 0.2496 oz. AGW, 22 mm. **Subject:** Peaceful Liberation, 60th Anniversary **Obv:** National emblem **Rev:** Ornate design

| Date | Mintage | VF20 | XF40 | MS60 | MS63 | MS65 |
|---|---|---|---|---|---|---|
| 2011 | 20,000 | PF65 750 | | | | |

**KM# 2003 100 YUAN**
7.77 g., 0.999 Gold 0.2496 oz. AGW, 22 mm. **Subject:** 100th Anniversary of the Revolution **Obv:** National emblem **Rev:** Sun Yat-sen bust facing

| Date | Mintage | VF20 | XF40 | MS60 | MS63 | MS65 |
|---|---|---|---|---|---|---|
| 2011 | 100,000 | PF65 650 | | | | |

### KM# 2005 100 YUAN
7.77 g., 0.999 Gold 0.2496 oz. AGW, 22 mm. **Subject:** Avation Industry in the P.R.C., 60th Anniversary **Obv:** Temple of Heaven **Rev:** Two pandas

| Date | Mintage | VF20 | XF40 | MS60 | MS63 | MS65 |
|---|---|---|---|---|---|---|
| 2011 | 5,000 | PF65 750 | | | | |

### KM# 2008 100 YUAN
7.77 g., 0.999 Gold 0.2496 oz. AGW, 22 mm. **Subject:** World Heritage Site **Obv:** National emblem **Rev:** Gate of the Shaolin Temple

| Date | Mintage | VF20 | XF40 | MS60 | MS63 | MS65 |
|---|---|---|---|---|---|---|
| 2011 | 30,000 | PF65 650 | | | | |

### KM# 2036 100 YUAN
7.78 g., 0.999 Gold 0.2499 oz. AGW, 22 mm. **Subject:** Shanghai Gold Exchange **Rev:** Mother and cub panda

| Date | Mintage | VF20 | XF40 | MS60 | MS63 | MS65 |
|---|---|---|---|---|---|---|
| 2011 | 6,000 | — | — | — | 550 | — |

### KM# 2038 100 YUAN
7.78 g., 0.999 Gold 0.2499 oz. AGW, 22 mm. **Subject:** Xiamen Special Economic Zone, 30th Anniversary **Rev:** Mother and cub panda

| Date | Mintage | VF20 | XF40 | MS60 | MS63 | MS65 |
|---|---|---|---|---|---|---|
| 2011 | 5,000 | — | — | — | 550 | — |

### KM# 2040 100 YUAN
7.78 g., 0.999 Gold 0.2499 oz. AGW, 22 mm. **Subject:** Rural Credit Cooperatives, 60th Anniversary **Rev:** Mother and cub panda

| Date | Mintage | VF20 | XF40 | MS60 | MS63 | MS65 |
|---|---|---|---|---|---|---|
| 2011 | 25,000 | — | — | — | 550 | — |

### KM# 2044 100 YUAN
7.78 g., 0.999 Gold 0.2499 oz. AGW, 22 mm. **Subject:** UNESCO **Rev:** Pusading Temple

| Date | Mintage | VF20 | XF40 | MS60 | MS63 | MS65 |
|---|---|---|---|---|---|---|
| 2012 | 60,000 | PF65 550 | | | | |

### KM# 2050 100 YUAN
7.78 g., 0.999 Gold 0.2499 oz. AGW, 22 mm. **Subject:** Beijing Opera Mask **Rev:** Monkey King in color

| Date | Mintage | VF20 | XF40 | MS60 | MS63 | MS65 |
|---|---|---|---|---|---|---|
| 2012 | 30,000 | PF65 550 | | | | |

### KM# 2055 100 YUAN
7.78 g., 0.999 Gold 0.2499 oz. AGW, 22 mm. **Subject:** Bronze Age vessels **Rev:** Tripod drinking glass, Xia Dynasty, Yanshi find

| Date | Mintage | VF20 | XF40 | MS60 | MS63 | MS65 |
|---|---|---|---|---|---|---|
| 2012 | 50,000 | PF65 550 | | | | |

### KM# 2064 100 YUAN
7.78 g., 0.999 Gold 0.2499 oz. AGW, 22 mm. **Subject:** Bank of China, 100th Anniversary **Obv:** Temple of Heaven **Rev:** Mother and cub panda

| Date | Mintage | VF20 | XF40 | MS60 | MS63 | MS65 |
|---|---|---|---|---|---|---|
| 2012 | 55,000 | — | — | — | 550 | — |

### KM# 2079 100 YUAN
7.78 g., 0.999 Silver 0.2499 oz. ASW, 20 mm. **Subject:** China Merchants Bank, 25th Anniversary

| Date | Mintage | VF20 | XF40 | MS60 | MS63 | MS65 |
|---|---|---|---|---|---|---|
| 2012 | 20,000 | — | — | — | 375 | — |

### KM# 1488 150 YUAN
10.05 g., 0.999 Gold 0.3228 oz. AGW, 23 mm. **Subject:** Spring festival **Obv:** Tree with berries **Rev:** Two Koi in ribbon sea

| Date | Mintage | VF20 | XF40 | MS60 | MS63 | MS65 |
|---|---|---|---|---|---|---|
| 2003 | 50,000 | PF65 600 | | | | |

### KM# 1511 150 YUAN
10.13 g., 0.999 Gold 0.3254 oz. AGW, 23 mm. **Subject:** Space flight **Rev:** Multicolor astronaut and ship

| Date | Mintage | VF20 | XF40 | MS60 | MS63 | MS65 |
|---|---|---|---|---|---|---|
| 2003 | 30,000 | PF65 625 | | | | |

### KM# 1556 150 YUAN
10.50 g., 0.999 Gold 0.3372 oz. AGW, 23 mm. **Series:** Folk customs **Subject:** Lantern Festival **Rev:** Boy holding lantern **Note:** Colorized

| Date | Mintage | VF20 | XF40 | MS60 | MS63 | MS65 |
|---|---|---|---|---|---|---|
| 2004 | 20,000 | PF65 650 | | | | |

### KM# 1638 150 YUAN
10.05 g., 0.999 Gold 0.3228 oz. AGW, 23 mm. **Subject:** Chinese Movie Centennial **Obv:** Winged column **Rev:** Movie clipboard

| Date | Mintage | VF20 | XF40 | MS60 | MS63 | MS65 |
|---|---|---|---|---|---|---|
| 2005 | 20,000 | PF65 650 | | | | |

### KM# 1654 150 YUAN
10.36 g., 0.999 Gold 0.3327 oz. AGW, 23 mm. **Subject:** Chengdu multi-purpose war planes, 10th Anniversary

| Date | Mintage | VF20 | XF40 | MS60 | MS63 | MS65 |
|---|---|---|---|---|---|---|
| 2007 | 10,000 | PF65 850 | | | | |

### KM# 1829 150 YUAN
10.36 g., 0.999 Gold 0.3327 oz. AGW, 23 mm. **Subject:** Chinese aerospace **Obv:** Solar system **Rev:** Chang'e 1 in lunar orbit

| Date | Mintage | VF20 | XF40 | MS60 | MS63 | MS65 |
|---|---|---|---|---|---|---|
| 2007 | 20,000 | PF65 850 | | | | |

### KM# 1696 150 YUAN
10.36 g., 0.999 Gold 0.3327 oz. AGW, 23 mm. **Subject:** 29th Summer Olympics, Beijing **Rev:** Swimmer entering water at race start

| Date | Mintage | VF20 | XF40 | MS60 | MS63 | MS65 |
|---|---|---|---|---|---|---|
| 2008 S | 60,000 | PF65 600 | | | | |
| 2008 Y | Inc. above | PF65 600 | | | | |
| 2008 Z | Inc. above | PF65 600 | | | | |

### KM# 1697 150 YUAN
10.36 g., 0.999 Gold 0.3327 oz. AGW, 23 mm. **Subject:** 29th Summer Olympics, Beijing **Obv:** Olympics Logo **Rev:** Ancient Chinese weightlifter

| Date | Mintage | VF20 | XF40 | MS60 | MS63 | MS65 |
|---|---|---|---|---|---|---|
| 2008 S | 60,000 | PF65 600 | | | | |
| 2008 Y | Inc. above | PF65 600 | | | | |
| 2008 Z | Inc. above | PF65 600 | | | | |

### KM# 1700 150 YUAN
10.05 g., 0.999 Gold 0.3228 oz. AGW, 23 mm. **Subject:** 29th Summer Olympics **Obv:** Beijing Olympic logo **Rev:** Ancient horsemaid and new logo **Note:** Issued in 2006

| Date | Mintage | VF20 | XF40 | MS60 | MS63 | MS65 |
|---|---|---|---|---|---|---|
| 2008 S | 60,000 | PF65 600 | | | | |
| 2008 Y | Inc. above | PF65 600 | | | | |
| 2008 Z | Inc. above | PF65 600 | | | | |

### KM# 1701 150 YUAN
10.05 g., 0.999 Gold 0.3228 oz. AGW, 23 mm. **Subject:** 29th Summer Olympics **Obv:** Beijing Olympic logo **Rev:** Ancient archer and new logo **Note:** Issued in 2006

| Date | Mintage | VF20 | XF40 | MS60 | MS63 | MS65 |
|---|---|---|---|---|---|---|
| 2008 S | 60,000 | PF65 600 | | | | |
| 2008 Y | Inc. above | PF65 600 | | | | |
| 2008 Z | Inc. above | PF65 600 | | | | |

### KM# 1735 150 YUAN
10.36 g., 0.999 Gold 0.3327 oz. AGW, 23 mm. **Obv:** Solar system **Rev:** Man walking in space

| Date | Mintage | VF20 | XF40 | MS60 | MS63 | MS65 |
|---|---|---|---|---|---|---|
| 2008 | 30,000 | PF65 900 | | | | |

### KM# 1847 150 YUAN
10.10 g., 0.999 Gold 0.3244 oz. AGW, 23 mm. **Subject:** Beijing Olympics **Rev:** Classical wrestlers

| Date | Mintage | VF20 | XF40 | MS60 | MS63 | MS65 |
|---|---|---|---|---|---|---|
| 2008 | 60,000 | PF65 600 | | | | |

### KM# 1848 150 YUAN
10.10 g., 0.999 Gold 0.3244 oz. AGW, 23 mm. **Subject:** Beijing Olympics **Obv:** Beijing Olympics **Rev:** Classical soccer player

| Date | Mintage | VF20 | XF40 | MS60 | MS63 | MS65 |
|---|---|---|---|---|---|---|
| 2008 | 60,000 | PF65 600 | | | | |

### KM# 1855 150 YUAN
10.10 g., 0.999 Gold 0.3244 oz. AGW **Subject:** Para Olympics

| Date | Mintage | VF20 | XF40 | MS60 | MS63 | MS65 |
|---|---|---|---|---|---|---|
| 2008 | 15,000 | PF65 700 | | | | |

### KM# 1900 150 YUAN
10.36 g., 0.999 Gold 0.3327 oz. AGW, 23 mm. **Subject:** Outlaws of the Marsh, series 1 **Rev:** Multicolor

| Date | Mintage | VF20 | XF40 | MS60 | MS63 | MS65 |
|---|---|---|---|---|---|---|
| 2009 | 30,000 | PF65 650 | | | | |

### KM# 1906 150 YUAN
10.35 g., 0.999 Gold 0.3324 oz. AGW **Subject:** Shanghai Expo

| Date | Mintage | VF20 | XF40 | MS60 | MS63 | MS65 |
|---|---|---|---|---|---|---|
| 2009 | — | PF65 650 | | | | |

### KM# 1937 150 YUAN
10.35 g., 0.999 Gold 0.3324 oz. AGW **Subject:** Outlaws of the Marsh, series 2 **Rev:** Multicolor

| Date | Mintage | VF20 | XF40 | MS60 | MS63 | MS65 |
|---|---|---|---|---|---|---|
| 2010 | 35,000 | PF65 650 | | | | |

### KM# 1941 150 YUAN
155.55 g., 0.999 Gold 4.996 oz. AGW **Subject:** Shanghai World Expo, 2010

| Date | Mintage | VF20 | XF40 | MS60 | MS63 | MS65 |
|---|---|---|---|---|---|---|
| 2010 | 1,000 | PF65 9,500 | | | | |

### KM# 1809 150 YUAN
1036.00 g., 0.999 Gold 33.2748 oz. AGW, 23 mm. **Subject:** Chinese Literature **Rev:** Wu Yong reviewing the plan in color

| Date | Mintage | VF20 | XF40 | MS60 | MS63 | MS65 |
|---|---|---|---|---|---|---|
| 2011 | 35,000 | PF65 60,000 | | | | |

### KM# 2071 150 YUAN
10.36 g., 0.999 Gold 0.3327 oz. AGW **Subject:** Year of the Snake **Obv:** National emblem **Rev:** Snake **Shape:** Arc

| Date | Mintage | VF20 | XF40 | MS60 | MS63 | MS65 |
|---|---|---|---|---|---|---|
| 2013 | Est. 30000 | PF65 650 | | | | |

### KM# 1387 200 YUAN
15.55 g., 0.999 Gold 0.4995 oz. AGW, 27 mm. **Series:** Folk fairy tails **Rev:** Multicolor heroic figure putting ax to clouds

| Date | Mintage | VF20 | XF40 | MS60 | MS63 | MS65 |
|---|---|---|---|---|---|---|
| 2001 | 8,800 | PF65 1,050 | | | | |

### KM# 1391 200 YUAN
15.55 g., 0.999 Gold 0.4995 oz. AGW, 27 mm. **Subject:** Mogao Grottoes **Obv:** Eight story building **Rev:** Dancing drummer **Edge:** Reeded. **Note:** Prev. Y#1085.

| Date | Mintage | VF20 | XF40 | MS60 | MS63 | MS65 |
|---|---|---|---|---|---|---|
| 2001 | — | PF65 1,050 | | | | |

### KM# 1393 200 YUAN
15.55 g., 0.999 Gold 0.4995 oz. AGW, 27 mm. **Subject:** 50th Anniversary Chinese Occupation of Tibet **Obv:** Five stars **Rev:** Denomination in flower **Edge:** Reeded **Note:** Prev. Y#1087.

| Date | Mintage | VF20 | XF40 | MS60 | MS63 | MS65 |
|---|---|---|---|---|---|---|
| 2001 | 15,000 | PF65 950 | | | | |

### KM# 1403 200 YUAN
15.55 g., 0.999 Gold 0.4995 oz. AGW, 27 mm. **Subject:** Bejing opera **Rev:** Multicolor ribbon dancer

| Date | Mintage | VF20 | XF40 | MS60 | MS63 | MS65 |
|---|---|---|---|---|---|---|
| 2001 | 8,000 | PF65 1,100 | | | | |

### KM# 1431 200 YUAN
15.50 g., 0.999 Gold 0.4978 oz. AGW **Subject:** Art **Rev:** Multicolor male with snake and staff **Note:** Prev. Y#1148.

| Date | Mintage | VF20 | XF40 | MS60 | MS63 | MS65 |
|---|---|---|---|---|---|---|
| 2002 | 8,800 | PF65 1,050 | | | | |

### KM# 1434 200 YUAN
15.55 g., 0.999 Gold 0.4994 oz. AGW, 27 mm. **Subject:** Buddha **Note:** Prev. Y#1145.

| Date | Mintage | VF20 | XF40 | MS60 | MS63 | MS65 |
|---|---|---|---|---|---|---|
| 2002 | 8,800 | PF65 1,050 | | | | |

### KM# 1439 200 YUAN
15.52 g., 0.999 Gold 0.4984 oz. AGW, 27 mm. **Subject:** Sichuan Sanxingdui relics **Obv:** Museum building **Rev:** Face mask

| Date | Mintage | VF20 | XF40 | MS60 | MS63 | MS65 |
|---|---|---|---|---|---|---|
| 2002 | 8,800 | PF65 1,050 | | | | |

### KM# 1440 200 YUAN
15.50 g., 0.999 Gold 0.4978 oz. AGW **Subject:** Ceremonial Mask **Note:** Prev. Y#1149.

| Date | Mintage | VF20 | XF40 | MS60 | MS63 | MS65 |
|---|---|---|---|---|---|---|
| 2002 | 5,000 | PF65 1,100 | | | | |

### KM# 1446 200 YUAN
15.50 g., 0.999 Gold 0.4978 oz. AGW **Subject:** Dream of the Red Mansion **Shape:** Octagon **Note:** Prev. Y#1147.

| Date | Mintage | VF20 | XF40 | MS60 | MS63 | MS65 |
|---|---|---|---|---|---|---|
| 2002 | 8,000 | PF65 1,100 | | | | |

### KM# 1454 200 YUAN
15.50 g., 0.999 Gold 0.4978 oz. AGW **Subject:** Peking Opera **Note:** Prev. Y#1146.

| Date | Mintage | VF20 | XF40 | MS60 | MS63 | MS65 |
|---|---|---|---|---|---|---|
| 2002 | 8,000 | PF65 1,050 | | | | |

**KM# 1456 200 YUAN**
15.52 g., 0.999 Gold 0.4984 oz. AGW, 27 mm. **Subject:** World Expo 2010 **Rev:** Skyline

| Date | Mintage | VF20 | XF40 | MS60 | MS63 | MS65 |
|---|---|---|---|---|---|---|
| 2002 | 5,000 | PF65 1,100 | | | | |

**KM# 1494 200 YUAN**
15.55 g., 0.9999 Gold 0.500 oz. AGW **Subject:** Chinese Mythical Folk Tales **Note:** Prev. Y#1160.

| Date | Mintage | VF20 | XF40 | MS60 | MS63 | MS65 |
|---|---|---|---|---|---|---|
| 2003 | 8,800 | PF65 1,050 | | | | |

**KM# 1495 200 YUAN**
15.52 g., 0.999 Gold 0.4983 oz. AGW, 27 mm. **Subject:** Finger Sarira of Sakyanmunt **Obv:** Tall tower **Rev:** Flora design

| Date | Mintage | VF20 | XF40 | MS60 | MS63 | MS65 |
|---|---|---|---|---|---|---|
| 2003 | 12,000 | PF65 950 | | | | |

**KM# 1504 200 YUAN**
15.55 g., 0.9999 Gold 0.500 oz. AGW **Subject:** Pilgrimage to the West **Note:** Prev. Y#1159.

| Date | Mintage | VF20 | XF40 | MS60 | MS63 | MS65 |
|---|---|---|---|---|---|---|
| 2003 | 11,800 | PF65 950 | | | | |

**KM# 1506 200 YUAN**
15.51 g., 0.999 Gold 0.4983 oz. AGW, 40 mm. **Series:** Classical literature **Rev:** Multicolor blue seated female **Shape:** Hexagon

| Date | Mintage | VF20 | XF40 | MS60 | MS63 | MS65 |
|---|---|---|---|---|---|---|
| 2003 | 8,000 | PF65 1,050 | | | | |

**KM# 1509 200 YUAN**
15.52 g., 0.999 Gold 0.4983 oz. AGW, 27 mm. **Series:** Wulingyan Scenic Resort

| Date | Mintage | VF20 | XF40 | MS60 | MS63 | MS65 |
|---|---|---|---|---|---|---|
| 2003 | 8,000 | PF65 950 | | | | |

**KM# 1561 200 YUAN**
15.55 g., 0.999 Gold 0.4994 oz. AGW, 27 mm. **Obv:** Monkey King leading the Master over bridge **Rev:** Multicolor Monkey King on one knee meeting the Master **Edge:** Reeded **Note:** Prev. Y#1217.

| Date | Mintage | VF20 | XF40 | MS60 | MS63 | MS65 |
|---|---|---|---|---|---|---|
| 2004 | 11,800 | PF65 950 | | | | |

**KM# 1564 200 YUAN**
15.56 g., 0.999 Gold 0.4998 oz. AGW, 27 mm. **Series:** Maijishan grotto art **Rev:** Buddha statue

| Date | Mintage | VF20 | XF40 | MS60 | MS63 | MS65 |
|---|---|---|---|---|---|---|
| 2004 | 8,800 | PF65 1,050 | | | | |

**KM# 1567 200 YUAN**
15.55 g., 0.999 Gold 0.4995 oz. AGW, 27 mm. **Obv:** Guangan Exposition Hall **Rev:** Deng Xiaoping and value **Edge:** Reeded **Note:** Prev. Y#1241.

| Date | Mintage | VF20 | XF40 | MS60 | MS63 | MS65 |
|---|---|---|---|---|---|---|
| 2004 | 10,000 | PF65 950 | | | | |

**KM# 1571 200 YUAN**
15.55 g., 0.999 Gold 0.4994 oz. AGW, 27 mm. **Obv:** National arms above People's Congress Hall and ornamental column **Rev:** Multicolor hologram depicting the hall's overhead lighting **Edge:** Reeded **Note:** Prev. Y#1213.

| Date | Mintage | VF20 | XF40 | MS60 | MS63 | MS65 |
|---|---|---|---|---|---|---|
| 2004 | 5,000 | PF65 1,050 | | | | |

**KM# 1625 200 YUAN**
15.55 g., 0.999 Gold 0.4994 oz. AGW, 27 mm. **Subject:** 600th Anniversary of Zheng He's Voyages **Obv:** Multicolor logo **Rev:** Zheng He portrait in linear form

| Date | Mintage | VF20 | XF40 | MS60 | MS63 | MS65 |
|---|---|---|---|---|---|---|
| 2005 | 6,000 | PF65 950 | | | | |

**KM# 1627 200 YUAN**
15.55 g., 0.999 Gold 0.4994 oz. AGW, 27 mm. **Subject:** Chen Yun Birth Centennial **Obv:** House **Rev:** Head 3/4 right

| Date | Mintage | VF20 | XF40 | MS60 | MS63 | MS65 |
|---|---|---|---|---|---|---|
| 2005 | 5,000 | PF65 1,100 | | | | |

**KM# 1630 200 YUAN**
15.55 g., 0.999 Gold 0.4994 oz. AGW, 27 mm. **Subject:** 60th Anniverasary of Victory - War of Resistance **Obv:** Monument **Rev:** Mob of Peoples Army

| Date | Mintage | VF20 | XF40 | MS60 | MS63 | MS65 |
|---|---|---|---|---|---|---|
| 2005 | 5,000 | PF65 1,100 | | | | |

**KM# 1633 200 YUAN**
15.55 g., 0.999 Gold 0.4994 oz. AGW, 27 mm. **Series:** Classical Literature **Obv:** Horseman on arch bridge **Rev:** Two multicolor women, one with monkey, other with rabbit

| Date | Mintage | VF20 | XF40 | MS60 | MS63 | MS65 |
|---|---|---|---|---|---|---|
| 2005 | 11,800 | PF65 950 | | | | |

**KM# 1689 200 YUAN**
15.55 g., 0.999 Gold 0.4994 oz. AGW, 27 mm. **Subject:** Yvelv Academy **Obv:** Front door of Academy **Rev:** Interior room

| Date | Mintage | VF20 | XF40 | MS60 | MS63 | MS65 |
|---|---|---|---|---|---|---|
| 2006 | 7,000 | PF65 950 | | | | |

**KM# 1692 200 YUAN**
15.55 g., 0.999 Gold 0.4994 oz. AGW, 27 mm. **Subject:** 70th Anniversary of Long March **Obv:** Route of the marches, hammer and sickle symbol **Rev:** Group of marchers advancing with rifles

| Date | Mintage | VF20 | XF40 | MS60 | MS63 | MS65 |
|---|---|---|---|---|---|---|
| 2006 | 10,000 | PF65 950 | | | | |

**KM# 1862 200 YUAN**
15.57 g., 0.999 Gold 0.5001 oz. AGW, 27 mm. **Subject:** Chinese Peoples Liberation Army, 80th Anniversary **Obv:** Three military men saluting, flag in background **Rev:** Ship, tank, plane

| Date | Mintage | VF20 | XF40 | MS60 | MS63 | MS65 |
|---|---|---|---|---|---|---|
| 2007 | 10,000 | PF65 1,100 | | | | |

**KM# 1949 200 YUAN**
15.55 g., 0.999 Gold 0.4994 oz. AGW **Subject:** Yungang Grotto Art

| Date | Mintage | VF20 | XF40 | MS60 | MS63 | MS65 |
|---|---|---|---|---|---|---|
| 2010 | 10,000 | PF65 975 | | | | |

**KM# 2072 200 YUAN**
15.57 g., 0.999 Gold 0.5001 oz. AGW, 27 mm. **Subject:** Year of the Snake **Obv:** National emblem **Rev:** Snake

| Date | Mintage | VF20 | XF40 | MS60 | MS63 | MS65 |
|---|---|---|---|---|---|---|
| 2013 | Est. 8000 | PF65 1,000 | | | | |

**KM# 1435 300 YUAN**
1000.00 g., 0.999 Silver 32.1186 oz. ASW, 100 mm. **Series:** Long men grottoes **Rev:** Large female statue

| Date | Mintage | VF20 | XF40 | MS60 | MS63 | MS65 |
|---|---|---|---|---|---|---|
| 2002 | 8,000 | PF65 1,750 | | | | |

**KM# 1513 300 YUAN**
1000.00 g., 0.999 Silver 32.1186 oz. ASW, 100 mm. **Series:** Guan Yi

| Date | Mintage | VF20 | XF40 | MS60 | MS63 | MS65 |
|---|---|---|---|---|---|---|
| 2003 | 3,800 | PF65 3,500 | | | | |

**KM# 1568 300 YUAN**
1000.00 g., 0.999 Silver 32.1186 oz. ASW, 100 mm. **Obv:** Guangan Exposition Hall **Rev:** Deng Xiaoping and value **Edge:** Reeded **Note:** Prev. Y#1242.

| Date | Mintage | VF20 | XF40 | MS60 | MS63 | MS65 |
|---|---|---|---|---|---|---|
| 2004 | 5,000 | PF65 1,850 | | | | |

**KM# 1579 300 YUAN**
1000.00 g., 0.999 Silver 32.1186 oz. ASW, 100 mm. **Series:** Kuan Yin **Rev:** Female seated holding flower

| Date | Mintage | VF20 | XF40 | MS60 | MS63 | MS65 |
|---|---|---|---|---|---|---|
| 2004 | 3,800 | PF65 2,000 | | | | |

**KM# 1617 300 YUAN**
1000.00 g., 0.999 Silver 32.1186 oz. ASW, 100 mm. **Subject:** 2006 World Cup - Germany **Obv:** Multicolor logo **Rev:** World Cup Trophy

| Date | Mintage | VF20 | XF40 | MS60 | MS63 | MS65 |
|---|---|---|---|---|---|---|
| 2005 | 3,000 | PF65 2,250 | | | | |

**KM# 1634 300 YUAN**
1000.00 g., 0.999 Silver 32.1186 oz. ASW, 100 mm. **Series:** Classical Literature **Obv:** Horseman on arch bridge **Rev:** Multicolor heavenly buddha

| Date | Mintage | VF20 | XF40 | MS60 | MS63 | MS65 |
|---|---|---|---|---|---|---|
| 2005 | 5,000 | PF65 2,250 | | | | |

**KM# 1695 300 YUAN**
1000.00 g., 0.999 Silver 32.1186 oz. ASW, 100 mm. **Subject:** 29th Summer Olympics, Beijing **Obv:** Olympics Logo **Rev:** Riding and rowing

| Date | Mintage | VF20 | XF40 | MS60 | MS63 | MS65 |
|---|---|---|---|---|---|---|
| 2008 | 20,008 | PF65 2,000 | | | | |

**KM# 1849 300 YUAN**
1000.00 g., 0.999 Silver 32.1186 oz. ASW, 100 mm. **Subject:** Beijing Olympics **Obv:** Multicolor logo **Rev:** Classical tug of war **Note:** Photo reduced.

| Date | Mintage | VF20 | XF40 | MS60 | MS63 | MS65 |
|---|---|---|---|---|---|---|
| 2008 | 20,008 | PF65 2,250 | | | | |

**KM# 1897 300 YUAN**
1000.00 g., 0.999 Silver 32.1186 oz. ASW, 100 mm. **Subject:** P.R.C. 60th Anniversary

| Date | Mintage | VF20 | XF40 | MS60 | MS63 | MS65 |
|---|---|---|---|---|---|---|
| 2009 | 6,000 | PF65 2,100 | | | | |

**KM# 1950 300 YUAN**
1000.00 g., 0.999 Silver 32.1186 oz. ASW **Subject:** Yungang Grotto Art

| Date | Mintage | VF20 | XF40 | MS60 | MS63 | MS65 |
|---|---|---|---|---|---|---|
| 2010 | 3,800 | PF65 2,100 | | | | |

**KM# 1808 300 YUAN**
1000.00 g., 0.999 Silver 32.1186 oz. ASW, 100 mm. **Subject:** Chinese Literature **Rev:** Meeting of the Heroes in the great hall in color

| Date | Mintage | VF20 | XF40 | MS60 | MS63 | MS65 |
|---|---|---|---|---|---|---|
| 2011 | 10,000 | PF65 1,650 | | | | |

**KM# 2006 300 YUAN**
1000.00 g., 0.999 Silver 32.1186 oz. ASW, 100 mm. **Subject:** World Heritage Site **Obv:** National emblem **Rev:** Tianzhong Pavillon at the Zhongyue Temple

| Date | Mintage | VF20 | XF40 | MS60 | MS63 | MS65 |
|---|---|---|---|---|---|---|
| 2011 | 5,000 | PF65 1,750 | | | | |

**KM# 2043 300 YUAN**
1000.00 g., 0.999 Silver 32.1186 oz. ASW, 100 mm. **Subject:** UNESCO **Rev:** Tayuan Temple

| Date | Mintage | VF20 | XF40 | MS60 | MS63 | MS65 |
|---|---|---|---|---|---|---|
| 2012 | — | PF65 1,600 | | | | |

**KM# 2069 300 YUAN**
1000.00 g., 0.999 Silver 32.1186 oz. ASW, 100 mm. **Subject:** Year of the Snake **Obv:** National emblem **Rev:** Snake

| Date | Mintage | VF20 | XF40 | MS60 | MS63 | MS65 |
|---|---|---|---|---|---|---|
| 2013 | Est. 3800 | PF65 1,350 | | | | |

**KM# 2061 500 YUAN**
31.10 g., 0.999 Gold 0.999 oz. AGW, 32 mm. **Subject:** Panda, 30th Anniversary **Obv:** Temple of Heaven **Rev:** Panda

| Date | Mintage | VF20 | XF40 | MS60 | MS63 | MS65 |
|---|---|---|---|---|---|---|
| 2012 | 30,000 | PF65 2,250 | | | | |

**KM# 1392 2000 YUAN**
155.52 g., 0.999 Gold 4.995 oz. AGW, 60 mm. **Subject:** Mogao Grottoes **Obv:** Eight story building **Rev:** Two dancers **Edge:** Reeded **Note:** Prev. #Y1086.

| Date | Mintage | VF20 | XF40 | MS60 | MS63 | MS65 |
|---|---|---|---|---|---|---|
| 2001 | — | PF65 25,000 | | | | |

**KM# 1436 2000 YUAN**
155.52 g., 0.999 Gold 4.995 oz. AGW, 60 mm. **Subject:** Chinese grottos art - Longmen **Note:** Prev. #Y1151.

| Date | Mintage | VF20 | XF40 | MS60 | MS63 | MS65 |
|---|---|---|---|---|---|---|
| 2002 | 288 | PF65 13,500 | | | | |

**KM# 1505 2000 YUAN**
155.50 g., 0.999 Gold 4.9944 oz. AGW, 64 x 40 mm. **Series:** Class literature **Rev:** Two multicolor monkey kings **Shape:** Rectangle **Note:** Illustration reduced.

| Date | Mintage | VF20 | XF40 | MS60 | MS63 | MS65 |
|---|---|---|---|---|---|---|
| 2003 | 500 | PF65 11,500 | | | | |

**KM# 1562 2000 YUAN**
155.52 g., 0.999 Gold 4.995 oz. AGW, 64x40 mm. **Obv:** Monkey King leading Master over bridge **Rev:** Multicolor Monkey King fighting the Pig "Demon of Bones **Edge:** Plain **Shape:** Ingot **Note:** Prev. #Y1218. Illustration reduced.

| Date | Mintage | VF20 | XF40 | MS60 | MS63 | MS65 |
|---|---|---|---|---|---|---|
| 2004 | 500 | PF65 11,500 | | | | |

**KM# 1565 2000 YUAN**
155.52 g., 0.999 Gold 4.995 oz. AGW, 60 mm. **Subject:** Maijishan Grottos **Obv:** Grotto view **Rev:** Buddha portrait within halo of flying devatas **Edge:** Reeded **Note:** Prev. #Y1206.

| Date | Mintage | VF20 | XF40 | MS60 | MS63 | MS65 |
|---|---|---|---|---|---|---|
| 2004 (y) | 288 | PF65 14,500 | | | | |

**KM# 1569 2000 YUAN**
155.52 g., 0.999 Gold 4.995 oz. AGW, 60 mm. **Obv:** Guangan Exposition Hall **Rev:** Deng Xiaoping and value **Edge:** Reeded **Note:** Prev. #Y1243.

| Date | Mintage | VF20 | XF40 | MS60 | MS63 | MS65 |
|---|---|---|---|---|---|---|
| 2004 | 600 | PF65 13,500 | | | | |

**KM# 1632 2000 YUAN**
155.00 g., 0.999 Gold 4.9784 oz. AGW, 64 x 40 mm. **Series:** Classic Literature Pilgrimage To The West **Obv:** Horseback rider on arch bridge **Rev:** Multicolor court scene **Shape:** Rectangle

| Date | Mintage | VF20 | XF40 | MS60 | MS63 | MS65 |
|---|---|---|---|---|---|---|
| 2005 | 500 | PF65 13,500 | | | | |

**KM# 1698 2000 YUAN**
155.52 g., 0.999 Gold 4.9951 oz. AGW, 60 mm. **Subject:** 29th Summer Olympics, Beijing **Obv:** Olympics Logo **Rev:** Athletics and team sports

| Date | Mintage | VF20 | XF40 | MS60 | MS63 | MS65 |
|---|---|---|---|---|---|---|
| 2008 | 2,008 | PF65 9,000 | | | | |

**KM# 1738 2000 YUAN**
155.67 g., 0.999 Gold 4.9999 oz. AGW, 60 mm. **Subject:** Economic Reform in China, 30th Anniversary **Rev:** Flowers and Fireworks

| Date | Mintage | VF20 | XF40 | MS60 | MS63 | MS65 |
|---|---|---|---|---|---|---|
| 2008 | 800 | PF65 9,500 | | | | |

**KM# 1850 2000 YUAN**
155.55 g., 0.999 Gold 4.996 oz. AGW, 60 mm. **Subject:** Beijing Olympics **Obv:** Multicolor logo **Rev:** Four sports

| Date | Mintage | VF20 | XF40 | MS60 | MS63 | MS65 |
|---|---|---|---|---|---|---|
| 2008 | — | PF65 16,500 | | | | |

**KM# 1894 2000 YUAN**
155.50 g., 0.999 Gold 4.9944 oz. AGW, 60 mm. **Subject:** P.R.C. 60th Anniversary

| Date | Mintage | VF20 | XF40 | MS60 | MS63 | MS65 |
|---|---|---|---|---|---|---|
| 2009 | 600 | PF65 12,000 | | | | |

**KM# 1899 2000 YUAN**
155.50 g., 0.999 Gold 4.9944 oz. AGW, 64c40 mm. **Subject:** Outlaws of the Marsh, series 1 **Rev:** Multicolor **Shape:** Rectangle

| Date | Mintage | VF20 | XF40 | MS60 | MS63 | MS65 |
|---|---|---|---|---|---|---|
| 2009 | 800 | PF65 12,000 | | | | |

**KM# 1936 2000 YUAN**
155.55 g., 0.999 Gold 4.996 oz. AGW, 64x40 mm. **Series:** Outlaws of the Marsh, series 2 **Rev:** Multicolor **Shape:** Rectangle

| Date | Mintage | VF20 | XF40 | MS60 | MS63 | MS65 |
|---|---|---|---|---|---|---|
| 2010 | 900 | PF65 12,000 | | | | |

**KM# 1948 2000 YUAN**
155.50 g., 0.999 Gold 4.9944 oz. AGW **Subject:** Yungang Grotto Art

| Date | Mintage | VF20 | XF40 | MS60 | MS63 | MS65 |
|---|---|---|---|---|---|---|
| 2010 | 800 | PF65 12,000 | | | | |

**KM# 1802 2000 YUAN**
155.67 g., 0.999 Gold 4.9999 oz. AGW, 90 mm. **Subject:** UNESCO **Rev:** Taishi Que

| Date | Mintage | VF20 | XF40 | MS60 | MS63 | MS65 |
|---|---|---|---|---|---|---|
| 2011 | Est. 1000 | PF65 10,000 | | | | |

**KM# 1819 2000 YUAN**
155.67 g., 0.999 Gold 4.9999 oz. AGW, 64x40 mm. **Subject:** Chinese Literature **Rev:** Huyan Zhuo and Guan Sheng in color

| Date | Mintage | VF20 | XF40 | MS60 | MS63 | MS65 |
|---|---|---|---|---|---|---|
| 2011 | 900 | PF65 11,000 | | | | |

**KM# 2045 2000 YUAN**
155.67 g., 0.999 Gold 4.9999 oz. AGW, 60 mm. **Subject:** UNESCO **Rev:** Xiantong Temple

| Date | Mintage | VF20 | XF40 | MS60 | MS63 | MS65 |
|---|---|---|---|---|---|---|
| 2012 | 3,000 | PF65 11,000 | | | | |

**KM# 2051 2000 YUAN**
155.67 g., 0.999 Gold 4.9999 oz. AGW, 60 mm. **Subject:** Beijing Opera Masks **Rev:** Guan Yu mask in color

| Date | Mintage | VF20 | XF40 | MS60 | MS63 | MS65 |
|---|---|---|---|---|---|---|
| 2012 | 2,000 | PF65 11,000 | | | | |

**KM# 2056 2000 YUAN**
155.67 g., 0.999 Gold 4.9999 oz. AGW, 40 mm. **Subject:** Bronze Age Containers **Rev:** Storrage vessel from the Shang Dynastie, Zhengzhou find

| Date | Mintage | VF20 | XF40 | MS60 | MS63 | MS65 |
|---|---|---|---|---|---|---|
| 2012 | 30,000 | PF65 8,500 | | | | |

**KM# 2062 2000 YUAN**
155.67 g., 0.999 Gold 4.9999 oz. AGW, 60 mm. **Subject:** Panda, 30th Anniversary **Obv:** Temple of Heaven **Rev:** Panda

| Date | Mintage | VF20 | XF40 | MS60 | MS63 | MS65 |
|---|---|---|---|---|---|---|
| 2012 | 3,000 | PF65 11,500 | | | | |

**KM# 2073 2000 YUAN**
155.67 g., 0.999 Gold 4.9999 oz. AGW **Subject:** Year of the Snake **Obv:** National arms **Rev:** Snake **Shape:** Arc

| Date | Mintage | VF20 | XF40 | MS60 | MS63 | MS65 |
|---|---|---|---|---|---|---|
| 2013 | Est. 2000 | PF65 9,000 | | | | |

**KM# 2085 2000 YUAN**
155.67 g., 0.999 Gold 4.9999 oz. AGW, 60 mm. **Subject:** Year of the Snake **Obv:** National emblem **Rev:** Snake in color

| Date | Mintage | VF20 | XF40 | MS60 | MS63 | MS65 |
|---|---|---|---|---|---|---|
| 2013 | Est. 3000 | PF65 7,000 | | | | |

**KM# 2054 3000 YUAN**
1000.00 g., 0.999 Silver 32.1186 oz. ASW, 100 mm. **Subject:** Bronze Age Vessels **Rev:** Shang Dynasty wine container

| Date | Mintage | VF20 | XF40 | MS60 | MS63 | MS65 |
|---|---|---|---|---|---|---|
| 2012 | 6,000 | PF65 1,750 | | | | |

**KM# 1893 10000 YUAN**
1000.00 g., 0.999 Gold 32.1186 oz. AGW, 90 mm. **Subject:** P.R.C. 60th Anniversary

| Date | Mintage | VF20 | XF40 | MS60 | MS63 | MS65 |
|---|---|---|---|---|---|---|
| 2009 | 100 | PF65 60,000 | | | | |

**KM# 1947 10000 YUAN**
1000.00 g., 0.999 Gold 32.1186 oz. AGW **Subject:** Yungang Grotto Art

| Date | Mintage | VF20 | XF40 | MS60 | MS63 | MS65 |
|---|---|---|---|---|---|---|
| 2010 | 100 | PF65 60,000 | | | | |

**KM# 1803 10000 YUAN**
1000.00 g., 0.999 Gold 32.1186 oz. AGW, 90 mm. **Subject:** UNESCO **Rev:** Observatory

| Date | Mintage | VF20 | XF40 | MS60 | MS63 | MS65 |
|---|---|---|---|---|---|---|
| 2011 | 200 | PF65 60,000 | | | | |

**KM# 1869 10000 YUAN**
1000.00 g., 0.999 Gold 32.1186 oz. AGW, 90 mm. **Subject:** Chinese Literature **Rev:** Meeting in the great hall in color

| Date | Mintage | VF20 | XF40 | MS60 | MS63 | MS65 |
|---|---|---|---|---|---|---|
| 2011 | 200 | PF65 60,000 | | | | |

**KM# 2046 10000 YUAN**
1000.00 g., 0.999 Gold 32.1186 oz. AGW, 90 mm. **Subject:** UNESCO **Rev:** Foguang Temple

| Date | Mintage | VF20 | XF40 | MS60 | MS63 | MS65 |
|---|---|---|---|---|---|---|
| 2012 | 300 | PF65 60,000 | | | | |

**KM# 2074 10000 YUAN**
1000.00 g., 0.999 Gold 32.1186 oz. AGW, 100 mm. **Subject:** Year of the Snake **Obv:** National emblem **Rev:** Snake **Shape:** Scalloped

| Date | Mintage | VF20 | XF40 | MS60 | MS63 | MS65 |
|---|---|---|---|---|---|---|
| 2013 | Est. 118 | PF65 45,000 | | | | |

**KM# 1851 100000 YUAN**
10000.00 g., 0.999 Gold 321.1857 oz. AGW, 180 mm. **Subject:** Beijing Olympics **Obv:** Multicolor logo **Rev:** Sports montage, Temple of Heaven

| Date | Mintage | VF20 | XF40 | MS60 | MS63 | MS65 |
|---|---|---|---|---|---|---|
| 2008 | 29 | PF65 650,000 | | | | |

**KM# 2075 100000 YUAN**
10000.00 g., 0.999 Gold 321.1857 oz. AGW, 180 mm. **Subject:** Year of the Snake **Obv:** National emblem **Rev:** Snake

| Date | Mintage | VF20 | XF40 | MS60 | MS63 | MS65 |
|---|---|---|---|---|---|---|
| 2013 | Est. 18 | PF65 425,000 | | | | |

## SILVER BULLION COINAGE

Lunar Series

**KM# 1375 10 YUAN**
31.10 g., 0.999 Silver 0.999 oz. ASW, 40 mm. **Subject:** Year of the Snake **Rev:** Multicolor

| Date | Mintage | VF20 | XF40 | MS60 | MS63 | MS65 |
|---|---|---|---|---|---|---|
| 2001 | 6,800 | PF65 150 | | | | |

**KM# 1379 10 YUAN**
30.84 g., 0.999 Silver 0.9905 oz. ASW, 39.9 mm. **Subject:** Year of the Snake **Obv:** Traditional style building **Rev:** Snake **Shape:** Scalloped **Note:** Prev. Y#1041.

| Date | Mintage | VF20 | XF40 | MS60 | MS63 | MS65 |
|---|---|---|---|---|---|---|
| 2001 | 6,800 | PF65 165 | | | | |

**KM# 1382 10 YUAN**
31.10 g., 0.999 Silver 0.999 oz. ASW **Subject:** Year of the Snake **Shape:** Fan-like **Note:** Prev. Y#1042.

| Date | Mintage | VF20 | XF40 | MS60 | MS63 | MS65 |
|---|---|---|---|---|---|---|
| 2001 | 66,000 | — | — | 100 | 115 | — |

**KM# 1414 10 YUAN**
31.10 g., 0.999 Silver 0.999 oz. ASW, 40 mm. **Subject:** Year of the Horse **Rev:** Multicolor horse prancing right

| Date | Mintage | VF20 | XF40 | MS60 | MS63 | MS65 |
|---|---|---|---|---|---|---|
| 2002 | 10,000 | PF65 150 | | | | |

**KM# 1418 10 YUAN**
31.10 g., 0.999 Silver 0.999 oz. ASW, 40 mm. **Subject:** Year of the Horse **Obv:** Da Zheng Hall **Rev:** Stylized horse head **Edge:** Reeded **Note:** Prev. Y#1232.

| Date | Mintage | VF20 | XF40 | MS60 | MS63 | MS65 |
|---|---|---|---|---|---|---|
| 2002 | 50,000 | — | — | — | 140 | — |

**KM# 1423 10 YUAN**
31.10 g., 0.999 Silver 0.999 oz. ASW, 40 mm. **Subject:** Year of the Horse **Shape:** Fan-like

| Date | Mintage | VF20 | XF40 | MS60 | MS63 | MS65 |
|---|---|---|---|---|---|---|
| 2002 | 50,000 | PF65 175 | | | | |

**KM# 1425 10 YUAN**
31.10 g., 0.999 Silver 0.999 oz. ASW, 40 mm. **Subject:** Year of the Horse **Shape:** Scalloped

| Date | Mintage | VF20 | XF40 | MS60 | MS63 | MS65 |
|---|---|---|---|---|---|---|
| 2002 | 6,800 | PF65 400 | | | | |

**KM# 1477 10 YUAN**
31.10 g., 0.999 Silver 0.999 oz. ASW, 40 mm. **Subject:** Year of the Sheep **Rev:** Multicolor

| Date | Mintage | VF20 | XF40 | MS60 | MS63 | MS65 |
|---|---|---|---|---|---|---|
| 2003 | 6,800 | PF65 150 | | | | |

**KM# A1477 10 YUAN**
31.10 g., 0.999 Silver 0.999 oz. ASW, 40 mm. **Subject:** Year of the Sheep

| Date | Mintage | VF20 | XF40 | MS60 | MS63 | MS65 |
|---|---|---|---|---|---|---|
| 2003 | 66,000 | PF65 150 | | | | |

**KM# 1480 10 YUAN**
31.10 g., 0.999 Silver 0.999 oz. ASW, 40 mm. **Subject:** Year of the sheep **Shape:** Scalloped

| Date | Mintage | VF20 | XF40 | MS60 | MS63 | MS65 |
|---|---|---|---|---|---|---|
| 2003 | 50,000 | PF65 70.00 | | | | |

**KM# 1485 10 YUAN**
31.10 g., 0.999 Silver 0.999 oz. ASW, 30 x 85 mm. **Subject:** Year of the Sheep **Shape:** Fan-like

| Date | Mintage | VF20 | XF40 | MS60 | MS63 | MS65 |
|---|---|---|---|---|---|---|
| 2003 | 66,000 | PF65 175 | | | | |

**KM# 1545 10 YUAN**
31.10 g., 0.999 Silver 0.999 oz. ASW, 40 mm. **Series:** Lunar New Year **Subject:** Year of the Monkey

| Date | Mintage | VF20 | XF40 | MS60 | MS63 | MS65 |
|---|---|---|---|---|---|---|
| 2004 | 80,000 | PF65 150 | | | | |

**KM# A1545 10 YUAN**
31.10 g., 0.999 Silver 0.999 oz. ASW, 40 mm. **Series:** Lunar New Year **Subject:** Year of the Monkey **Rev:** Multicolor monkey

| Date | Mintage | VF20 | XF40 | MS60 | MS63 | MS65 |
|---|---|---|---|---|---|---|
| 2004 | — | PF65 150 | | | | |

**KM# 1548 10 YUAN**
31.10 g., 0.999 Silver 0.999 oz. ASW, 40 mm. **Subject:** Lunar New Year **Rev:** Monkey **Shape:** Scalloped

| Date | Mintage | VF20 | XF40 | MS60 | MS63 | MS65 |
|---|---|---|---|---|---|---|
| 2004 | 6,800 | PF65 190 | | | | |

**KM# 1553 10 YUAN**
31.10 g., 0.999 Silver 0.999 oz. ASW, 30 x 85 mm. **Series:** Lunar New Year **Subject:** Year of the Monkey **Rev:** Monkey **Shape:** Fan-like

| Date | Mintage | VF20 | XF40 | MS60 | MS63 | MS65 |
|---|---|---|---|---|---|---|
| 2004 | 66,000 | PF65 175 | | | | |

**KM# 1612 10 YUAN**
31.11 g., 0.999 Silver 0.999 oz. ASW, 40 mm. **Subject:** Year of the rooster **Obv:** Classical rooster **Rev:** Multicolor rooster

| Date | Mintage | VF20 | XF40 | MS60 | MS63 | MS65 |
|---|---|---|---|---|---|---|
| 2005 | 100,000 | PF65 190 | | | | |

**KM# 1613 10 YUAN**
31.11 g., 0.999 Silver 0.999 oz. ASW, 40 mm. **Subject:** Year of the rooster **Obv:** Classical rooster **Rev:** Rooster, hen and chicks **Shape:** Scallop

| Date | Mintage | VF20 | XF40 | MS60 | MS63 | MS65 |
|---|---|---|---|---|---|---|
| 2005 | 60,000 | **PF65** 125 | | | | |

**KM# 1614 10 YUAN**
31.11 g., 0.999 Silver 0.999 oz. ASW, 40 mm. **Subject:** Year of the rooster **Obv:** Classical rooster **Rev:** Rooster, hen and chicks

| Date | Mintage | VF20 | XF40 | MS60 | MS63 | MS65 |
|---|---|---|---|---|---|---|
| 2005 | 8,000 | **PF65** 150 | | | | |

**KM# 1615 10 YUAN**
31.11 g., 0.999 Silver 0.999 oz. ASW, 30 x 85 mm. **Subject:** Year of the rooster **Obv:** Temple **Rev:** Rooster, hen and chicks **Shape:** Fan-like **Note:** Photo reduced.

| Date | Mintage | VF20 | XF40 | MS60 | MS63 | MS65 |
|---|---|---|---|---|---|---|
| 2005 | 66,000 | **PF65** 190 | | | | |

**KM# 1684 10 YUAN**
31.10 g., 0.999 Silver 0.999 oz. ASW, 40 mm. **Obv:** Dog-shaped belt-hook from ancient Chinese bronze ware, decorative design of dog tail-shaped plant leaves **Rev:** 2 smart dogs **Note:** Prev. Y#1225; 1657.

| Date | Mintage | VF20 | XF40 | MS60 | MS63 | MS65 |
|---|---|---|---|---|---|---|
| 2006 | 80,000 | — | — | — | 125 | — |

**KM# 1685 10 YUAN**
31.10 g., 0.999 Silver 0.999 oz. ASW, 40 mm. **Obv:** Dog-shaped belt-hook depicted from ancient Chinese bronze ware and a decorative design of dog tail-shaped plant leaves **Rev:** 2 smart dogs **Shape:** Scalloped **Note:** Prev. Y#1223; KM#1655.

| Date | Mintage | VF20 | XF40 | MS60 | MS63 | MS65 |
|---|---|---|---|---|---|---|
| 2006 | 60,000 | **PF65** 140 | | | | |

**KM# 1686 10 YUAN**
31.10 g., 0.999 Silver 0.999 oz. ASW **Obv:** Qing Yuan Gate of the China Great Wall **Rev:** 2 dogs at play **Shape:** Fan-like **Note:** Prev. Y#1219; KM#1651. Photo reduced.

| Date | Mintage | VF20 | XF40 | MS60 | MS63 | MS65 |
|---|---|---|---|---|---|---|
| 2006 | 66,000 | **PF65** 165 | | | | |

**KM# 1687 10 YUAN**
31.10 g., 0.999 Silver 0.999 oz. ASW, 40 mm. **Obv:** Belt-hook in dog shape from Chinese ancient bronze ware and a decorative design of dog tail-shaped plant leaves **Rev:** 2 dogs at play **Note:** Prev. Y#1221; KM#1653.

| Date | Mintage | VF20 | XF40 | MS60 | MS63 | MS65 |
|---|---|---|---|---|---|---|
| 2006 | 100,000 | **PF65** 125 | | | | |

**KM# 1716 10 YUAN**
31.11 g., 0.999 Silver 0.999 oz. ASW, 40 mm. **Subject:** Year of the Pig **Obv:** Classical pig **Rev:** Pig walking right

| Date | Mintage | VF20 | XF40 | MS60 | MS63 | MS65 |
|---|---|---|---|---|---|---|
| 2007 | 80,000 | **PF65** 140 | | | | |

**KM# 1717 10 YUAN**
31.11 g., 0.999 Silver 0.999 oz. ASW, 40 mm. **Subject:** Year of the Pig **Obv:** Classical pig **Rev:** Multicolor sow and four piglets sucking

| Date | Mintage | VF20 | XF40 | MS60 | MS63 | MS65 |
|---|---|---|---|---|---|---|
| 2007 | 100,000 | **PF65** 125 | | | | |

**KM# 1718 10 YUAN**
31.11 g., 0.999 Silver 0.999 oz. ASW, 85 x 60 mm. **Subject:** Year of the Pig **Obv:** Temple **Rev:** Sow and four pigletts **Shape:** Fan-like

| Date | Mintage | VF20 | XF40 | MS60 | MS63 | MS65 |
|---|---|---|---|---|---|---|
| 2007 | 66,000 | **PF65** 190 | | | | |

**KM# 1719 10 YUAN**
31.11 g., 0.999 Silver 0.999 oz. ASW, 40 mm. **Subject:** Year of the Pig **Obv:** Classical pig **Rev:** Pig walking right **Shape:** Scalloped

| Date | Mintage | VF20 | XF40 | MS60 | MS63 | MS65 |
|---|---|---|---|---|---|---|
| 2007 | 60,000 | **PF65** 140 | | | | |

**KM# 1830 10 YUAN**
31.11 g., 0.999 Silver 0.999 oz. ASW, 40 mm. **Rev:** Multicolor

| Date | Mintage | VF20 | XF40 | MS60 | MS63 | MS65 |
|---|---|---|---|---|---|---|
| 2008 | — | **PF65** 60.00 | | | | |

**KM# 1831 10 YUAN**
31.11 g., 0.999 Silver 0.999 oz. ASW, 40 mm. **Subject:** Year of the Rat

| Date | Mintage | VF20 | XF40 | MS60 | MS63 | MS65 |
|---|---|---|---|---|---|---|
| 2008 | — | **PF65** 140 | | | | |

**KM# 1832 10 YUAN**
31.11 g., 0.999 Silver 0.999 oz. ASW, 40 mm. **Subject:** Year of the Rat **Shape:** Scallop

| Date | Mintage | VF20 | XF40 | MS60 | MS63 | MS65 |
|---|---|---|---|---|---|---|
| 2008 | — | **PF65** 140 | | | | |

**KM# 1833 10 YUAN**
31.11 g., 0.999 Silver 0.999 oz. ASW, 85 x 60 mm. **Subject:** Year of the Rat **Shape:** Fan-like

| Date | Mintage | VF20 | XF40 | MS60 | MS63 | MS65 |
|---|---|---|---|---|---|---|
| 2008 | — | **PF65** 190 | | | | |

**KM# 1875 10 YUAN**
31.11 g., 0.999 Silver 0.999 oz. ASW, 40 mm. **Rev:** Multicolor

| Date | Mintage | VF20 | XF40 | MS60 | MS63 | MS65 |
|---|---|---|---|---|---|---|
| 2009 | — | **PF65** 125 | | | | |

**KM# 1876 10 YUAN**
31.11 g., 0.999 Silver 0.999 oz. ASW, 40 mm. **Subject:** Year of the Ox

| Date | Mintage | VF20 | XF40 | MS60 | MS63 | MS65 |
|---|---|---|---|---|---|---|
| 2009 | 100,000 | **PF63** 115 **PF65** 125 | | | | |

**KM# 1877 10 YUAN**
31.11 g., 0.999 Silver 0.999 oz. ASW **Subject:** Year of the Ox

| Date | Mintage | VF20 | XF40 | MS60 | MS63 | MS65 |
|---|---|---|---|---|---|---|
| 2009 | 66,000 | **PF63** 135 **PF65** 145 | | | | |

**KM# 1878 10 YUAN**
31.11 g., 0.999 Silver 0.999 oz. ASW **Shape:** Fan-like

| Date | Mintage | VF20 | XF40 | MS60 | MS63 | MS65 |
|---|---|---|---|---|---|---|
| 2009 | 66,000 | **PF65** 190 | | | | |

**KM# 1922 10 YUAN**
31.11 g., 0.999 Silver 0.999 oz. ASW **Subject:** Year of the Tiger **Shape:** Arc

| Date | Mintage | VF20 | XF40 | MS60 | MS63 | MS65 |
|---|---|---|---|---|---|---|
| 2010 | 66,000 | — | — | — | 100 | — |

**KM# 1923 10 YUAN**
31.11 g., 0.999 Silver 0.999 oz. ASW **Subject:** Year of the Tiger **Shape:** Scalloped

| Date | Mintage | VF20 | XF40 | MS60 | MS63 | MS65 |
|---|---|---|---|---|---|---|
| 2010 | 60,000 | **PF65** 145 | | | | |

**KM# 1924 10 YUAN**
31.11 g., 0.999 Silver 0.999 oz. ASW **Subject:** Year of the Tiger

| Date | Mintage | VF20 | XF40 | MS60 | MS63 | MS65 |
|---|---|---|---|---|---|---|
| 2010 | 100,000 | PF65 115 | | | | |

**KM# 1925 10 YUAN**
31.11 g., 0.999 Silver 0.999 oz. ASW **Subject:** Year of the Tiger **Rev:** Multicolor

| Date | Mintage | VF20 | XF40 | MS60 | MS63 | MS65 |
|---|---|---|---|---|---|---|
| 2010 | 100,000 | PF65 135 | | | | |

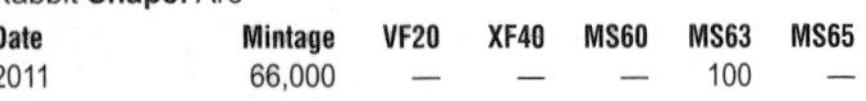

**KM# 1971 10 YUAN**
31.11 g., 0.999 Silver 0.999 oz. ASW **Subject:** Year of the Rabbit **Shape:** Arc

| Date | Mintage | VF20 | XF40 | MS60 | MS63 | MS65 |
|---|---|---|---|---|---|---|
| 2011 | 66,000 | — | — | — | 100 | — |

**KM# 1972 10 YUAN**
31.11 g., 0.999 Silver 0.999 oz. ASW **Subject:** Year of the Rabbit **Shape:** Scalloped

| Date | Mintage | VF20 | XF40 | MS60 | MS63 | MS65 |
|---|---|---|---|---|---|---|
| 2011 | 60,000 | PF65 120 | | | | |

**KM# 1973 10 YUAN**
31.11 g., 0.999 Silver 0.999 oz. ASW, 40 mm. **Subject:** Year of the Rabbit

| Date | Mintage | VF20 | XF40 | MS60 | MS63 | MS65 |
|---|---|---|---|---|---|---|
| 2011 | 100,000 | PF65 100 | | | | |

**KM# 1974 10 YUAN**
31.11 g., 0.999 Silver 0.999 oz. ASW **Subject:** Year of the Rabbit **Rev:** Multicolor

| Date | Mintage | VF20 | XF40 | MS60 | MS63 | MS65 |
|---|---|---|---|---|---|---|
| 2011 | 100,000 | PF65 100 | | | | |

**KM# 2020 10 YUAN**
31.11 g., 0.999 Silver 0.999 oz. ASW **Subject:** Year of the Dragon **Shape:** Fan

| Date | Mintage | VF20 | XF40 | MS60 | MS63 | MS65 |
|---|---|---|---|---|---|---|
| 2012 | — | PF65 145 | | | | |

**KM# 2021 10 YUAN**
31.11 g., 0.999 Silver 0.999 oz. ASW, 40 mm. **Subject:** Year of the Dragon **Shape:** Scalloped

| Date | Mintage | VF20 | XF40 | MS60 | MS63 | MS65 |
|---|---|---|---|---|---|---|
| 2012 proof | — | PF65 125 | | | | |

**KM# 2022 10 YUAN**
31.11 g., 0.999 Silver 0.999 oz. ASW, 40 mm. **Subject:** Year of the Dragon

| Date | Mintage | VF20 | XF40 | MS60 | MS63 | MS65 |
|---|---|---|---|---|---|---|
| 2012 | — | PF65 75.00 | | | | |

**KM# 2023 10 YUAN**
31.11 g., 0.999 Silver 0.999 oz. ASW **Subject:** Year of the Dragon **Rev:** Colored dragon

| Date | Mintage | VF20 | XF40 | MS60 | MS63 | MS65 |
|---|---|---|---|---|---|---|
| 2012 | — | PF65 110 | | | | |

**KM# 1377 50 YUAN**
155.44 g., 0.999 Silver 4.9925 oz. ASW, 80.6 x 50.5 mm. **Subject:** Year of the Snake **Obv:** Traditional style building **Rev:** Snake **Edge:** Plain **Shape:** Rectangle **Note:** Illustration reduced. Prev. Y#1040.

| Date | Mintage | VF20 | XF40 | MS60 | MS63 | MS65 |
|---|---|---|---|---|---|---|
| 2001 | 1,888 | PF65 1,250 | | | | |

**KM# 1421 50 YUAN**
155.52 g., 0.999 Silver 4.995 oz. ASW, 80 x 50 mm. **Subject:** Year of the Horse **Rev:** Three horses running left **Shape:** Rectangle

| Date | Mintage | VF20 | XF40 | MS60 | MS63 | MS65 |
|---|---|---|---|---|---|---|
| 2002 | 1,888 | PF65 2,000 | | | | |

**KM# 1484 50 YUAN**
155.50 g., 0.999 Silver 4.9944 oz. ASW, 80 x 50 mm. **Subject:** Year of the Sheep **Shape:** Rectangle

| Date | Mintage | VF20 | XF40 | MS60 | MS63 | MS65 |
|---|---|---|---|---|---|---|
| 2003 | 1,888 | PF65 1,250 | | | | |

**KM# 1551 50 YUAN**
155.50 g., 0.999 Silver 4.9944 oz. ASW, 80 x 50 mm. **Series:** Lunar New Year **Subject:** Year of the Monkey **Rev:** Monkey **Shape:** Rectangle **Note:** Photo reduced.

| Date | Mintage | VF20 | XF40 | MS60 | MS63 | MS65 |
|---|---|---|---|---|---|---|
| 2004 | 1,888 | PF65 1,250 | | | | |

**KM# 1611 50 YUAN**
155.00 g., 0.999 Silver 4.9784 oz. ASW, 80 x 50 mm. **Subject:** Year of the Rooster **Obv:** Classical rooster **Rev:** Rooster, hen and chicks **Shape:** Rectangle **Note:** Photo reduced.

| Date | Mintage | VF20 | XF40 | MS60 | MS63 | MS65 |
|---|---|---|---|---|---|---|
| 2005 | 1,888 | PF65 1,250 | | | | |

**KM# 1683 50 YUAN**
155.44 g., 0.999 Silver 4.9925 oz. ASW, 60 x 50 mm. **Subject:** Year of the Dog **Obv:** Classical dog **Rev:** Two dogs **Shape:** Rectangle **Note:** Photo reduced.

| Date | Mintage | VF20 | XF40 | MS60 | MS63 | MS65 |
|---|---|---|---|---|---|---|
| 2006 | 1,888 | PF65 1,250 | | | | |

### KM# 1720 50 YUAN

155.55 g., 0.999 Silver 4.996 oz. ASW, 80 x 50 mm. **Subject:** Year of the Pig **Obv:** Classical pig **Rev:** Sow and four piglets **Shape:** Rectangle

| Date | Mintage | VF20 | XF40 | MS60 | MS63 | MS65 |
|---|---|---|---|---|---|---|
| 2007 | 1,888 | **PF65** 1,250 | | | | |

### KM# 1834 50 YUAN

155.50 g., 0.999 Silver 4.9944 oz. ASW, 80 x 50 mm. **Subject:** Year of the Rat **Shape:** Rectangle

| Date | Mintage | VF20 | XF40 | MS60 | MS63 | MS65 |
|---|---|---|---|---|---|---|
| 2008 | — | **PF65** 1,250 | | | | |

### KM# 1879 50 YUAN

Silver **Subject:** Year of the Ox

| Date | Mintage | VF20 | XF40 | MS60 | MS63 | MS65 |
|---|---|---|---|---|---|---|
| 2009 | 1,888 | **PF65** 1,250 | | | | |

### KM# 1920 50 YUAN

155.50 g., 0.999 Silver 4.9944 oz. ASW **Subject:** Year of the Tiger **Shape:** Rectangle

| Date | Mintage | VF20 | XF40 | MS60 | MS63 | MS65 |
|---|---|---|---|---|---|---|
| 2010 | 1,888 | **PF65** 1,250 | | | | |

### KM# 1921 50 YUAN

155.50 g., 0.999 Silver 4.9944 oz. ASW **Subject:** Year of the Tiger

| Date | Mintage | VF20 | XF40 | MS60 | MS63 | MS65 |
|---|---|---|---|---|---|---|
| 2010 | 8,800 | **PF65** 850 | | | | |

### KM# 1969 50 YUAN

155.50 g., 0.999 Silver 4.9944 oz. ASW, 80x50 mm. **Subject:** Year of the Rabbit **Shape:** Rectangle **Note:** Photo reduced.

| Date | Mintage | VF20 | XF40 | MS60 | MS63 | MS65 |
|---|---|---|---|---|---|---|
| 2011 | 1,888 | **PF65** 1,250 | | | | |

### KM# 1970 50 YUAN

155.50 g., 0.999 Silver 4.9944 oz. ASW **Subject:** Year of the Rabbit **Rev:** Multicolor

| Date | Mintage | VF20 | XF40 | MS60 | MS63 | MS65 |
|---|---|---|---|---|---|---|
| 2011 | 8,800 | **PF65** 750 | | | | |

### KM# 2018 50 YUAN

155.55 g., 0.999 Silver 4.996 oz. ASW, 80x50 mm. **Subject:** Year of the Dragon **Shape:** Rectangle

| Date | Mintage | VF20 | XF40 | MS60 | MS63 | MS65 |
|---|---|---|---|---|---|---|
| 2012 | — | **PF65** 850 | | | | |

### KM# 2019 50 YUAN

155.55 g., 0.999 Silver 4.996 oz. ASW **Subject:** Year of the Dragon **Rev:** Colored dragon

| Date | Mintage | VF20 | XF40 | MS60 | MS63 | MS65 |
|---|---|---|---|---|---|---|
| 2012 proof | — | **PF65** 750 | | | | |

### KM# 1420 300 YUAN

1000.00 g., 0.999 Silver 32.1186 oz. ASW, 100 mm. **Series:** Lunar **Subject:** Year of the Horse

| Date | Mintage | VF20 | XF40 | MS60 | MS63 | MS65 |
|---|---|---|---|---|---|---|
| 2002 | 3,800 | **PF65** 6,500 | | | | |

### KM# 1479 300 YUAN

1000.00 g., 0.999 Silver 32.1186 oz. ASW, 100 mm. **Subject:** Year of the Sheep

| Date | Mintage | VF20 | XF40 | MS60 | MS63 | MS65 |
|---|---|---|---|---|---|---|
| 2003 | 3,800 | **PF65** 7,500 | | | | |

### KM# 1547 300 YUAN

1000.00 g., 0.999 Silver 32.1186 oz. ASW, 100 mm. **Series:** Lunar New Year **Subject:** Year of the Monkey **Rev:** Monkey

| Date | Mintage | VF20 | XF40 | MS60 | MS63 | MS65 |
|---|---|---|---|---|---|---|
| 2004 | 3,800 | **PF65** 9,000 | | | | |

### KM# 1610 300 YUAN

1000.00 g., 0.999 Silver 32.1186 oz. ASW, 100 mm. **Subject:** Year of the Rooster **Obv:** Classical rooster **Rev:** Rooster strutting **Note:** Photo reduced.

| Date | Mintage | VF20 | XF40 | MS60 | MS63 | MS65 |
|---|---|---|---|---|---|---|
| 2005 | 3,800 | **PF65** 5,000 | | | | |

### KM# 1682 300 YUAN

1000.00 g., 0.999 Silver 32.1186 oz. ASW, 100 mm. **Obv:** Dog-shaped belt-hook from ancient Chinese bronze ware, decorative design of dog tail-shaped plant leaves **Rev:** 2 dogs **Note:** Prev. Y#1227; KM#1659. Photo reduced.

| Date | Mintage | VF20 | XF40 | MS60 | MS63 | MS65 |
|---|---|---|---|---|---|---|
| 2006 | 3,800 | **PF65** 4,500 | | | | |

### KM# 1725 300 YUAN

1000.00 g., 0.999 Silver 32.1186 oz. ASW, 100 mm. **Subject:** Year of the Pig **Obv:** Classical pig **Rev:** Three pigs

| Date | Mintage | VF20 | XF40 | MS60 | MS63 | MS65 |
|---|---|---|---|---|---|---|
| 2007 | 3,800 | **PF65** 5,000 | | | | |

### KM# 1839 300 YUAN

1000.00 g., 0.999 Silver 32.1186 oz. ASW, 100 mm. **Subject:** Year of the Rat

| Date | Mintage | VF20 | XF40 | MS60 | MS63 | MS65 |
|---|---|---|---|---|---|---|
| 2008 | — | **PF65** 5,000 | | | | |

### KM# 1884 300 YUAN

1000.00 g., 0.999 Silver 32.1186 oz. ASW **Subject:** Year of the Ox

| Date | Mintage | VF20 | XF40 | MS60 | MS63 | MS65 |
|---|---|---|---|---|---|---|
| 2009 | 3,800 | **PF65** 5,000 | | | | |

### KM# 1919 300 YUAN

1000.00 g., 0.999 Silver 32.1186 oz. ASW **Subject:** Year of the Tiger

| Date | Mintage | VF20 | XF40 | MS60 | MS63 | MS65 |
|---|---|---|---|---|---|---|
| 2010 | 3,800 | **PF65** 4,500 | | | | |

### KM# 1968 300 YUAN

1000.00 g., 0.999 Silver 32.1186 oz. ASW, 100 mm. **Subject:** Year of the Rabbit **Note:** Photo reduced.

| Date | Mintage | VF20 | XF40 | MS60 | MS63 | MS65 |
|---|---|---|---|---|---|---|
| 2011 | 1,888 | **PF65** 4,500 | | | | |

**KM# 2017 300 YUAN**
1000.00 g., 0.999 Silver 32.1186 oz. ASW, 100 mm. **Subject:** Year of the Dragon

| Date | Mintage | VF20 | XF40 | MS60 | MS63 | MS65 |
|---|---|---|---|---|---|---|
| 2012 | — | PF65 1,250 | | | | |

## SILVER BULLION COINAGE
Panda Series

**KM# 1740 3 YUAN**
7.77 g., 0.999 Silver 0.2496 oz. ASW, 25 mm. **Obv:** Temple of Heaven **Rev:** Panda seated with branch

| Date | Mintage | VF20 | XF40 | MS60 | MS63 | MS65 |
|---|---|---|---|---|---|---|
| 2007 | 30,000 | PF63 25.00 | PF65 30.00 | | | |

**KM# 1742 3 YUAN**
7.77 g., 0.999 Silver 0.2496 oz. ASW, 25 mm. **Obv:** Temple of Heaven **Rev:** Panda walking right

| Date | Mintage | VF20 | XF40 | MS60 | MS63 | MS65 |
|---|---|---|---|---|---|---|
| 2007 | 30,000 | PF63 25.00 | PF65 30.00 | | | |

**KM# 1744 3 YUAN**
7.77 g., 0.999 Silver 0.2496 oz. ASW, 25 mm. **Obv:** Temple of Heaven **Rev:** Panda seated with bamboo branch

| Date | Mintage | VF20 | XF40 | MS60 | MS63 | MS65 |
|---|---|---|---|---|---|---|
| 2007 | 30,000 | PF63 25.00 | PF65 30.00 | | | |

**KM# 1746 3 YUAN**
7.77 g., 0.999 Silver 0.2496 oz. ASW **Obv:** Temple of Heaven **Rev:** Panda hanging from branch

| Date | Mintage | VF20 | XF40 | MS60 | MS63 | MS65 |
|---|---|---|---|---|---|---|
| 2007 | 30,000 | PF63 25.00 | PF65 30.00 | | | |

**KM# 1748 3 YUAN**
7.77 g., 0.999 Silver 0.2496 oz. ASW, 25 mm. **Obv:** Temple of Heaven **Rev:** Panda walking forward

| Date | Mintage | VF20 | XF40 | MS60 | MS63 | MS65 |
|---|---|---|---|---|---|---|
| 2007 | 30,000 | PF63 25.00 | PF65 30.00 | | | |

**KM# 1750 3 YUAN**
7.77 g., 0.999 Silver 0.2496 oz. ASW, 25 mm. **Obv:** Temple of Heaven **Rev:** Panda drinking water

| Date | Mintage | VF20 | XF40 | MS60 | MS63 | MS65 |
|---|---|---|---|---|---|---|
| 2007 | 30,000 | PF63 25.00 | PF65 30.00 | | | |

**KM# 1752 3 YUAN**
7.77 g., 0.999 Silver 0.2496 oz. ASW, 25 mm. **Obv:** Tample of Heaven **Rev:** Panda seated in oval with branch

| Date | Mintage | VF20 | XF40 | MS60 | MS63 | MS65 |
|---|---|---|---|---|---|---|
| 2007 | 30,000 | PF63 25.00 | PF65 30.00 | | | |

**KM# 1754 3 YUAN**
7.77 g., 0.999 Silver 0.2496 oz. ASW, 25 mm. **Obv:** Temple of Heaven **Rev:** Panda seated on geometric background

| Date | Mintage | VF20 | XF40 | MS60 | MS63 | MS65 |
|---|---|---|---|---|---|---|
| 2007 | 30,000 | PF63 25.00 | PF65 30.00 | | | |

**KM# 1756 3 YUAN**
7.77 g., 0.999 Silver 0.2496 oz. ASW, 10 mm. **Obv:** Temple of Heaven **Rev:** Panda on rock

| Date | Mintage | VF20 | XF40 | MS60 | MS63 | MS65 |
|---|---|---|---|---|---|---|
| 2007 | 30,000 | PF63 25.00 | PF65 30.00 | | | |

**KM# 1758 3 YUAN**
7.77 g., 0.999 Silver 0.2496 oz. ASW, 25 mm. **Obv:** Temple of Heaven **Rev:** Panda seated on river bank

| Date | Mintage | VF20 | XF40 | MS60 | MS63 | MS65 |
|---|---|---|---|---|---|---|
| 2007 | 30,000 | PF63 25.00 | PF65 30.00 | | | |

**KM# 1760 3 YUAN**
7.77 g., 0.999 Silver 0.2496 oz. ASW, 25 mm. **Obv:** Temple of Heaven **Rev:** Panda on tree branch

| Date | Mintage | VF20 | XF40 | MS60 | MS63 | MS65 |
|---|---|---|---|---|---|---|
| 2007 | 30,000 | PF63 25.00 | PF65 30.00 | | | |

**KM# 1762 3 YUAN**
7.77 g., 0.999 Silver 0.2496 oz. ASW, 25 mm. **Obv:** Temple of Heaven **Rev:** Panda on rock ledge

| Date | Mintage | VF20 | XF40 | MS60 | MS63 | MS65 |
|---|---|---|---|---|---|---|
| 2007 | 30,000 | PF63 25.00 | PF65 30.00 | | | |

**KM# 1764 3 YUAN**
7.77 g., 0.999 Silver 0.2496 oz. ASW, 25 mm. **Obv:** Temple of Heaven **Rev:** Panda seated munching bamboo

| Date | Mintage | VF20 | XF40 | MS60 | MS63 | MS65 |
|---|---|---|---|---|---|---|
| 2007 | 30,000 | PF63 25.00 | PF65 30.00 | | | |

**KM# 1766 3 YUAN**
7.77 g., 0.999 Silver 0.2496 oz. ASW, 25 mm. **Obv:** Temple of Heaven **Rev:** Panda pulling bamboo

| Date | Mintage | VF20 | XF40 | MS60 | MS63 | MS65 |
|---|---|---|---|---|---|---|
| 2007 | 30,000 | PF63 25.00 | PF65 30.00 | | | |

**KM# 1768 3 YUAN**
7.77 g., 0.999 Silver 0.2496 oz. ASW, 25 mm. **Obv:** Temple of Heaven **Rev:** Panda in tree

| Date | Mintage | VF20 | XF40 | MS60 | MS63 | MS65 |
|---|---|---|---|---|---|---|
| 2007 | 30,000 | PF63 25.00 | PF65 30.00 | | | |

**KM# 1770 3 YUAN**
7.77 g., 0.999 Silver 0.2496 oz. ASW, 25 mm. **Obv:** Temple of Heaven **Rev:** Panda looking over branch

| Date | Mintage | VF20 | XF40 | MS60 | MS63 | MS65 |
|---|---|---|---|---|---|---|
| 2007 | 30,000 | PF63 25.00 | PF65 30.00 | | | |

**KM# 1772 3 YUAN**
7.77 g., 0.999 Silver 0.2496 oz. ASW, 25 mm. **Obv:** Temple of Heaven **Rev:** Panda seated on rock

| Date | Mintage | VF20 | XF40 | MS60 | MS63 | MS65 |
|---|---|---|---|---|---|---|
| 2007 | 30,000 | PF63 25.00 | PF65 30.00 | | | |

**KM# 1774 3 YUAN**
7.77 g., 0.999 Silver 0.2496 oz. ASW, 25 mm. **Obv:** Temple of Heaven **Rev:** Panda looking out over rock

| Date | Mintage | VF20 | XF40 | MS60 | MS63 | MS65 |
|---|---|---|---|---|---|---|
| 2007 | 30,000 | PF63 25.00 | PF65 30.00 | | | |

**KM# A1776 3 YUAN**
7.77 g., 0.999 Silver 0.2496 oz. ASW, 25 mm. **Obv:** Temple of Heaven **Rev:** Panda seated on frosted background

| Date | Mintage | VF20 | XF40 | MS60 | MS63 | MS65 |
|---|---|---|---|---|---|---|
| 2007 | 30,000 | PF63 25.00 | PF65 30.00 | | | |

**KM# 1778 3 YUAN**
7.77 g., 0.999 Silver 0.2496 oz. ASW, 25 mm. **Obv:** Temple of Heaven **Rev:** Panda walking amongst bamboo

| Date | Mintage | VF20 | XF40 | MS60 | MS63 | MS65 |
|---|---|---|---|---|---|---|
| 2007 | 30,000 | PF63 25.00 | PF65 30.00 | | | |

**KM# 1780 3 YUAN**
7.77 g., 0.999 Silver 0.2496 oz. ASW, 25 mm. **Obv:** Temple of Heaven **Rev:** Panda looking forward

| Date | Mintage | VF20 | XF40 | MS60 | MS63 | MS65 |
|---|---|---|---|---|---|---|
| 2007 | 30,000 | PF63 25.00 | PF65 30.00 | | | |

**KM# 1782 3 YUAN**
7.77 g., 0.999 Silver 0.2496 oz. ASW, 25 mm. **Obv:** Temple of Heaven **Rev:** Panda and cub walking right

| Date | Mintage | VF20 | XF40 | MS60 | MS63 | MS65 |
|---|---|---|---|---|---|---|
| 2007 | 30,000 | PF63 25.00 | PF65 30.00 | | | |

**KM# 1784 3 YUAN**
7.77 g., 0.999 Silver 0.2496 oz. ASW, 25 mm. **Obv:** Temple of Heaven **Rev:** Panda seated with cub on left

| Date | Mintage | VF20 | XF40 | MS60 | MS63 | MS65 |
|---|---|---|---|---|---|---|
| 2007 | 30,000 | PF63 25.00 | PF65 30.00 | | | |

**KM# 1786 3 YUAN**
7.77 g., 0.999 Silver 0.2496 oz. ASW, 25 mm. **Obv:** Temple of Heaven **Rev:** Panda seated with cub on right

| Date | Mintage | VF20 | XF40 | MS60 | MS63 | MS65 |
|---|---|---|---|---|---|---|
| 2007 | 30,000 | PF63 25.00 | PF65 30.00 | | | |

**KM# 1788 3 YUAN**
7.77 g., 0.999 Silver 0.2496 oz. ASW, 25 mm. **Obv:** Temple of Heaven **Rev:** Panda seated with cub, both munching bamboo

| Date | Mintage | VF20 | XF40 | MS60 | MS63 | MS65 |
|---|---|---|---|---|---|---|
| 2007 | 30,000 | PF63 25.00 | PF65 30.00 | | | |

**KM# 1365 10 YUAN**
31.10 g., 0.999 Silver 0.999 oz. ASW, 40.1 mm. **Obv:** Temple of Heaven with incuse legend **Rev:** Panda walking left through bamboo **Edge:** Oblique reeding **Note:** Large and small date varieties exist. Prev. Y#1111.

| Date | Mintage | VF20 | XF40 | MS60 | MS63 | MS65 |
|---|---|---|---|---|---|---|
| 2001 | 250,000 | — | — | 50.00 | 45.00 | — |
| 2001 D | — | PF63 65.00 | PF65 75.00 | | | |
| 2002 | — | PF63 65.00 | PF65 75.00 | | | |

**KM# A1365 10 YUAN**
31.23 g., 0.999 Silver 1.0031 oz. ASW, 40 mm. **Obv:** Temple of Heaven, incuse legend **Rev:** Multicolor panda walking in bamboo **Edge:** Slanted reeding **Note:** Large and small date varieties exist.

| Date | Mintage | VF20 | XF40 | MS60 | MS63 | MS65 |
|---|---|---|---|---|---|---|
| 2002 | — | PF63 80.00 | PF65 90.00 | | | |

Note: Privately colored

**KM# 1466 10 YUAN**
31.10 g., 0.999 Silver 0.999 oz. ASW, 40 mm. **Obv:** Temple of Heaven **Rev:** Panda eating bamboo in a frosted circle **Edge:** Slant reeded **Note:** Prev. Y#1244.

| Date | Mintage | VF20 | XF40 | MS60 | MS63 | MS65 |
|---|---|---|---|---|---|---|
| 2003 | — | PF63 80.00 | PF65 90.00 | | | |

**KM# 1528 10 YUAN**
31.10 g., 0.999 Silver 0.999 oz. ASW, 40 mm. **Obv:** Temple of Heaven **Rev:** Panda nuzzling her cub **Edge:** Slant reeded **Note:** Prev. Y#1245.

| Date | Mintage | VF20 | XF40 | MS60 | MS63 | MS65 |
|---|---|---|---|---|---|---|
| 2004 | — | PF63 80.00 | PF65 90.00 | | | |

**KM# 1589 10 YUAN**
31.11 g., 0.999 Silver 0.999 oz. ASW, 40 mm. **Obv:** Temple of Heaven **Rev:** Panda cub and mom seated in bamboo

| Date | Mintage | VF20 | XF40 | MS60 | MS63 | MS65 |
|---|---|---|---|---|---|---|
| 2005 | 60,000 | PF63 80.00 | PF65 90.00 | | | |

**KM# 1664 10 YUAN**
31.11 g., 0.999 Silver 0.999 oz. ASW, 40 mm. **Obv:** Temple of Heaven **Rev:** Two pandas seated with bamboo

| Date | Mintage | VF20 | XF40 | MS60 | MS63 | MS65 |
|---|---|---|---|---|---|---|
| 2006 | 600,000 | PF63 65.00 | PF65 75.00 | | | |

**KM# 1706 10 YUAN**
31.11 g., 0.999 Silver 0.999 oz. ASW, 40 mm. **Obv:** Temple of Heaven **Rev:** Two pandas, one walking, one seated

| Date | Mintage | VF20 | XF40 | MS60 | MS63 | MS65 |
|---|---|---|---|---|---|---|
| 2007 | 600,000 | PF63 65.00 | PF65 75.00 | | | |

**KM# 1814 10 YUAN**
31.11 g., 0.999 Silver 0.999 oz. ASW, 40 mm. **Rev:** Panda cub pawing mom

| Date | Mintage | VF20 | XF40 | MS60 | MS63 | MS65 |
|---|---|---|---|---|---|---|
| 2008 | — | PF63 60.00 | PF65 70.00 | | | |

### KM# 1865 10 YUAN

31.11 g., 0.999 Silver 0.999 oz. ASW, 40 mm. **Obv:** Temple of Heaven **Rev:** Adult panda at left, facing left, cub on right facing left, cub seated

| Date | Mintage | VF20 | XF40 | MS60 | MS63 | MS65 |
|---|---|---|---|---|---|---|
| 2008 | — | PF63 60.00 | PF65 70.00 | | | |

### KM# 1931 10 YUAN

31.11 g., 0.999 Silver 0.999 oz. ASW, 40 mm. **Obv:** Temple of Heaven **Rev:** Two pandas, one lying on back

| Date | Mintage | VF20 | XF40 | MS60 | MS63 | MS65 |
|---|---|---|---|---|---|---|
| 2010 | 800,000 | — | — | — | 60.00 | — |

### KM# 1980 10 YUAN

31.11 g., 0.999 Silver 0.999 oz. ASW, 40 mm.

| Date | Mintage | VF20 | XF40 | MS60 | MS63 | MS65 |
|---|---|---|---|---|---|---|
| 2011 | — | — | — | — | 45.00 | 55.00 |

### KM# 2029 10 YUAN

31.11 g., 0.999 Silver 0.999 oz. ASW, 40 mm.

| Date | Mintage | VF20 | XF40 | MS60 | MS63 | MS65 |
|---|---|---|---|---|---|---|
| 2012 | — | — | — | — | 50.00 | — |

### KM# 1468 50 YUAN

151.50 g., 0.999 Silver 4.866 oz. ASW, 80 x 50 mm. **Shape:** Rectangle

| Date | Mintage | VF20 | XF40 | MS60 | MS63 | MS65 |
|---|---|---|---|---|---|---|
| 2003 | 1,888 | PF65 1,150 | | | | |

### KM# 1530 50 YUAN

155.50 g., 0.999 Silver 4.9944 oz. ASW, 70 mm. **Rev:** Panda walking with cub **Note:** Illustration reduced.

| Date | Mintage | VF20 | XF40 | MS60 | MS63 | MS65 |
|---|---|---|---|---|---|---|
| 2004 | 10,000 | PF65 600 | | | | |

### KM# 1588 50 YUAN

155.00 g., 0.999 Silver 4.9784 oz. ASW, 70 mm. **Obv:** Temple of Heaven **Rev:** Panda cub and mom seated in bamboo

| Date | Mintage | VF20 | XF40 | MS60 | MS63 | MS65 |
|---|---|---|---|---|---|---|
| 2005 | 10,000 | PF65 550 | | | | |

### KM# 1663 50 YUAN

155.55 g., 0.999 Silver 4.996 oz. ASW, 70 mm. **Obv:** Temple of Heaven **Rev:** Two pandas seated with bamboo

| Date | Mintage | VF20 | XF40 | MS60 | MS63 | MS65 |
|---|---|---|---|---|---|---|
| 2006 | 10,000 | PF65 550 | | | | |

### KM# 1708 50 YUAN

155.55 g., 0.999 Silver 4.996 oz. ASW, 70 mm. **Obv:** Temple of Heaven **Rev:** Two pandas, one walking, one seated

| Date | Mintage | VF20 | XF40 | MS60 | MS63 | MS65 |
|---|---|---|---|---|---|---|
| 2007 | 10,000 | PF65 550 | | | | |

### KM# 1816 50 YUAN

155.50 g., Silver, 70 mm. **Rev:** Panda cub pawing mom

| Date | Mintage | VF20 | XF40 | MS60 | MS63 | MS65 |
|---|---|---|---|---|---|---|
| 2008 | — | PF65 550 | | | | |

### KM# 1867 50 YUAN

155.50 g., 0.999 Silver 4.9944 oz. ASW

| Date | Mintage | VF20 | XF40 | MS60 | MS63 | MS65 |
|---|---|---|---|---|---|---|
| 2008 | — | PF65 550 | | | | |

### KM# 1935 50 YUAN

155.55 g., 0.999 Silver 4.996 oz. ASW **Obv:** Temple of Heaven **Rev:** Two pandas, one lying on back

| Date | Mintage | VF20 | XF40 | MS60 | MS63 | MS65 |
|---|---|---|---|---|---|---|
| 2010 | 10,000 | PF65 650 | | | | |

### KM# 1984 50 YUAN

155.55 g., 0.999 Silver 4.996 oz. ASW

| Date | Mintage | VF20 | XF40 | MS60 | MS63 | MS65 |
|---|---|---|---|---|---|---|
| 2011 | — | PF65 500 | | | | |

### KM# 2033 50 YUAN

155.55 g., 0.999 Silver 4.996 oz. ASW, 70 mm.

| Date | Mintage | VF20 | XF40 | MS60 | MS63 | MS65 |
|---|---|---|---|---|---|---|
| 2012 | — | PF65 650 | | | | |

### KM# 1370 300 YUAN

1000.00 g., 0.999 Silver 32.1186 oz. ASW, 100 mm. **Rev:** Panda walking thru bamboo

| Date | Mintage | VF20 | XF40 | MS60 | MS63 | MS65 |
|---|---|---|---|---|---|---|
| 2001 D | 2,000 | PF65 2,500 | | | | |

### KM# 1416 300 YUAN

1000.00 g., 0.999 Silver 32.1186 oz. ASW, 100 mm. **Subject:** Panda Coinage 20th Anniversary **Obv:** Temple of Heaven **Rev:** Two gold inserts with the 1982 and 2002 panda designs on bamboo leaves **Edge:** Plain **Note:** Large and small date varieties exist. Prev. Y#1116.

| Date | Mintage | VF20 | XF40 | MS60 | MS63 | MS65 |
|---|---|---|---|---|---|---|
| 2002 | 6,000 | PF65 3,000 | | | | |

### KM# 1473 300 YUAN

1000.00 g., 0.999 Silver 32.1186 oz. ASW **Rev:** Panda and bamboo **Shape:** 100

| Date | Mintage | VF20 | XF40 | MS60 | MS63 | MS65 |
|---|---|---|---|---|---|---|
| 2003 | 7,500 | PF65 2,000 | | | | |

### KM# 1536 300 YUAN

1000.00 g., 0.999 Silver 32.1186 oz. ASW, 100 mm. **Rev:** Panda walking with cub

| Date | Mintage | VF20 | XF40 | MS60 | MS63 | MS65 |
|---|---|---|---|---|---|---|
| 2004 | 4,000 | PF65 2,000 | | | | |

### KM# 1587 300 YUAN

1000.00 g., 0.999 Silver 32.1186 oz. ASW, 100 mm. **Obv:** Temple of Heaven **Rev:** Panda cub and mom seated in bamboo **Note:** Photo reduced.

| Date | Mintage | VF20 | XF40 | MS60 | MS63 | MS65 |
|---|---|---|---|---|---|---|
| 2005 | 4,000 | PF65 2,250 | | | | |

### KM# 1662 300 YUAN

1000.00 g., 0.999 Silver 32.1186 oz. ASW, 100 mm. **Obv:** Temple of Heaven **Rev:** Two pandas seated with bamboo **Note:** Photo reduced.

| Date | Mintage | VF20 | XF40 | MS60 | MS63 | MS65 |
|---|---|---|---|---|---|---|
| 2006 | 4,000 | PF65 2,250 | | | | |

**KM# 1712 300 YUAN**
1000.00 g., 0.999 Silver 32.1186 oz. ASW, 100 mm. **Obv:** Temple of Heaven **Rev:** Two pandas, one walking, one seated

| Date | Mintage | VF20 | XF40 | MS60 | MS63 | MS65 |
|---|---|---|---|---|---|---|
| 2007 | 4,000 | PF65 2,250 | | | | |

**KM# 1820 300 YUAN**
1000.00 g., 0.999 Silver 32.1186 oz. ASW, 100 mm. **Rev:** Panda cub pawing mom

| Date | Mintage | VF20 | XF40 | MS60 | MS63 | MS65 |
|---|---|---|---|---|---|---|
| 2008 | — | PF65 2,000 | | | | |

**KM# 1871 300 YUAN**
1000.00 g., 0.999 Silver 32.1186 oz. ASW

| Date | Mintage | VF20 | XF40 | MS60 | MS63 | MS65 |
|---|---|---|---|---|---|---|
| 2008 | — | PF65 2,000 | | | | |

**KM# 1934 300 YUAN**
1000.00 g., 0.999 Silver 32.1186 oz. ASW **Obv:** Temple of Heaven **Rev:** Two pandas, one lying on back

| Date | Mintage | VF20 | XF40 | MS60 | MS63 | MS65 |
|---|---|---|---|---|---|---|
| 2010 | 4,000 | PF65 1,500 | | | | |

**KM# 1983 300 YUAN**
1000.00 g., 0.999 Silver 32.1186 oz. ASW, 100 mm.

| Date | Mintage | VF20 | XF40 | MS60 | MS63 | MS65 |
|---|---|---|---|---|---|---|
| 2011 | — | PF65 1,250 | | | | |

**KM# 2032 300 YUAN**
1000.00 g., 0.999 Silver 32.1186 oz. ASW, 100 mm.

| Date | Mintage | VF20 | XF40 | MS60 | MS63 | MS65 |
|---|---|---|---|---|---|---|
| 2012 | — | PF65 1,500 | | | | |

## GOLD BULLION COINAGE

Panda Series

**KM# 1741 15 YUAN**
1.24 g., 0.999 Gold 0.0398 oz. AGW, 12 mm. **Obv:** Temple of Heaven **Rev:** Panda seated with branch

| Date | Mintage | VF20 | XF40 | MS60 | MS63 | MS65 |
|---|---|---|---|---|---|---|
| 2007 | 18,000 | PF65 95.00 | | | | |

**KM# 1743 15 YUAN**
1.24 g., 0.999 Gold 0.0398 oz. AGW, 12 mm. **Obv:** Temple of heaven **Rev:** Panda walking right

| Date | Mintage | VF20 | XF40 | MS60 | MS63 | MS65 |
|---|---|---|---|---|---|---|
| 2007 | 18,000 | PF65 95.00 | | | | |

**KM# 1745 15 YUAN**
1.24 g., 0.999 Gold 0.0398 oz. AGW, 12 mm. **Obv:** Temple of heaven **Rev:** Panda seated with bamboo branch

| Date | Mintage | VF20 | XF40 | MS60 | MS63 | MS65 |
|---|---|---|---|---|---|---|
| 2007 | 18,000 | PF65 95.00 | | | | |

**KM# 1747 15 YUAN**
1.24 g., 0.999 Gold 0.0398 oz. AGW, 12 mm. **Obv:** Temple of Heaven **Rev:** Panda hanging from branch

| Date | Mintage | VF20 | XF40 | MS60 | MS63 | MS65 |
|---|---|---|---|---|---|---|
| 2007 | 18,000 | PF65 95.00 | | | | |

**KM# 1749 15 YUAN**
1.24 g., 0.999 Gold 0.0398 oz. AGW, 12 mm. **Obv:** Temple of Heaven **Rev:** Panda walking forward

| Date | Mintage | VF20 | XF40 | MS60 | MS63 | MS65 |
|---|---|---|---|---|---|---|
| 2007 | 18,000 | PF65 95.00 | | | | |

**KM# 1751 15 YUAN**
1.24 g., 0.999 Gold 0.0398 oz. AGW, 12 mm. **Obv:** Temple of Heaven **Rev:** Panda drinking water

| Date | Mintage | VF20 | XF40 | MS60 | MS63 | MS65 |
|---|---|---|---|---|---|---|
| 2007 | 18,000 | PF65 95.00 | | | | |

**KM# 1753 15 YUAN**
1.24 g., 0.999 Gold 0.0398 oz. AGW, 12 mm. **Obv:** Temple of Heaven **Rev:** Panda seated in oval with branch

| Date | Mintage | VF20 | XF40 | MS60 | MS63 | MS65 |
|---|---|---|---|---|---|---|
| 2007 | 18,000 | PF65 95.00 | | | | |

**KM# 1755 15 YUAN**
1.24 g., 0.999 Gold 0.0398 oz. AGW, 12 mm. **Rev:** Panda seated on geometric background

| Date | Mintage | VF20 | XF40 | MS60 | MS63 | MS65 |
|---|---|---|---|---|---|---|
| 2007 | 18,000 | PF65 95.00 | | | | |

**KM# 1757 15 YUAN**
1.24 g., 0.999 Gold 0.0398 oz. AGW, 12 mm. **Obv:** Temple of Heaven **Rev:** Panda on rock

| Date | Mintage | VF20 | XF40 | MS60 | MS63 | MS65 |
|---|---|---|---|---|---|---|
| 2007 | 18,000 | PF65 95.00 | | | | |

**KM# 1759 15 YUAN**
1.24 g., 0.999 Gold 0.0398 oz. AGW, 12 mm. **Obv:** Temple of Heaven **Rev:** Panda seated on river bank

| Date | Mintage | VF20 | XF40 | MS60 | MS63 | MS65 |
|---|---|---|---|---|---|---|
| 2007 | 18,000 | PF65 95.00 | | | | |

**KM# 1761 15 YUAN**
1.24 g., 0.999 Gold 0.0398 oz. AGW, 12 mm. **Obv:** Temple of Heaven **Rev:** Panda on tree branch

| Date | Mintage | VF20 | XF40 | MS60 | MS63 | MS65 |
|---|---|---|---|---|---|---|
| 2007 | 18,000 | PF65 95.00 | | | | |

**KM# 1763 15 YUAN**
1.24 g., 0.999 Gold 0.0398 oz. AGW, 12 mm. **Obv:** Temple of Heaven **Rev:** Panda on rock ledge

| Date | Mintage | VF20 | XF40 | MS60 | MS63 | MS65 |
|---|---|---|---|---|---|---|
| 2007 | 18,000 | PF65 95.00 | | | | |

**KM# 1765 15 YUAN**
1.24 g., 0.999 Gold 0.0398 oz. AGW, 12 mm. **Obv:** Temple of Heaven **Rev:** Panda seated munching bamboo

| Date | Mintage | VF20 | XF40 | MS60 | MS63 | MS65 |
|---|---|---|---|---|---|---|
| 2007 | 18,000 | PF65 95.00 | | | | |

**KM# 1767 15 YUAN**
1.24 g., 0.999 Gold 0.0398 oz. AGW **Obv:** Temple of Heaven **Rev:** Panda pulling bamboo **Shape:** 12

| Date | Mintage | VF20 | XF40 | MS60 | MS63 | MS65 |
|---|---|---|---|---|---|---|
| 2007 | 1,800 | PF65 95.00 | | | | |

**KM# 1769 15 YUAN**
1.24 g., 0.999 Gold 0.0398 oz. AGW, 12 mm. **Obv:** Temple of Heaven **Rev:** Panda in tree

| Date | Mintage | VF20 | XF40 | MS60 | MS63 | MS65 |
|---|---|---|---|---|---|---|
| 2007 | 18,000 | PF65 95.00 | | | | |

**KM# 1771 15 YUAN**
1.24 g., 0.999 Gold 0.0398 oz. AGW **Obv:** Temple of Heaven **Rev:** Panda looking over branch

| Date | Mintage | VF20 | XF40 | MS60 | MS63 | MS65 |
|---|---|---|---|---|---|---|
| 2007 | 18,000 | PF65 95.00 | | | | |

**KM# 1773 15 YUAN**
1.24 g., 0.999 Gold 0.0398 oz. AGW, 12 mm. **Obv:** Temple of Heaven **Rev:** Panda seated on rock

| Date | Mintage | VF20 | XF40 | MS60 | MS63 | MS65 |
|---|---|---|---|---|---|---|
| 2007 | 18,000 | PF65 95.00 | | | | |

**KM# A1775 15 YUAN**
1.24 g., 0.999 Gold 0.0398 oz. AGW, 12 mm. **Obv:** Temple of Heaven **Rev:** Panda looking out from rock

| Date | Mintage | VF20 | XF40 | MS60 | MS63 | MS65 |
|---|---|---|---|---|---|---|
| 2007 | 18,000 | PF65 95.00 | | | | |

**KM# 1777 15 YUAN**
1.24 g., 0.999 Gold 0.0398 oz. AGW, 12 mm. **Obv:** Temple of Heaven **Rev:** Panda seated on frosted background

| Date | Mintage | VF20 | XF40 | MS60 | MS63 | MS65 |
|---|---|---|---|---|---|---|
| 2007 | 18,000 | PF65 95.00 | | | | |

**KM# 1779 15 YUAN**
1.24 g., 0.999 Gold 0.0398 oz. AGW, 12 mm. **Obv:** Temple of Heaven **Rev:** Panda walking amongst bamboo

| Date | Mintage | VF20 | XF40 | MS60 | MS63 | MS65 |
|---|---|---|---|---|---|---|
| 2007 | 18,000 | PF65 95.00 | | | | |

**KM# 1781 15 YUAN**
1.24 g., 0.999 Gold 0.0398 oz. AGW, 12 mm. **Obv:** Temple of Heaven **Rev:** Panda looking forward

| Date | Mintage | VF20 | XF40 | MS60 | MS63 | MS65 |
|---|---|---|---|---|---|---|
| 2007 | 18,000 | PF65 95.00 | | | | |

**KM# 1783 15 YUAN**
1.24 g., 0.999 Gold 0.0398 oz. AGW, 12 mm. **Obv:** Temple of Heaven **Rev:** Panda and cub walking right

| Date | Mintage | VF20 | XF40 | MS60 | MS63 | MS65 |
|---|---|---|---|---|---|---|
| 2007 | 18,000 | PF65 95.00 | | | | |

**KM# 1785 15 YUAN**
1.24 g., 0.999 Gold 0.0398 oz. AGW, 12 mm. **Obv:** Temple of Heaven **Rev:** Panda seated with cub on left

| Date | Mintage | VF20 | XF40 | MS60 | MS63 | MS65 |
|---|---|---|---|---|---|---|
| 2007 | 18,000 | PF65 95.00 | | | | |

**KM# 1787 15 YUAN**
1.24 g., 0.999 Gold 0.0398 oz. AGW, 12 mm. **Obv:** Temple of Heaven **Rev:** Panda seated with cub on right

| Date | Mintage | VF20 | XF40 | MS60 | MS63 | MS65 |
|---|---|---|---|---|---|---|
| 2007 | 18,000 | PF65 95.00 | | | | |

**KM# 1789 15 YUAN**
1.24 g., 0.999 Gold 0.0398 oz. AGW, 12 mm. **Obv:** Temple of Heaven **Rev:** Panda seated with cub, both munching bamboo

| Date | Mintage | VF20 | XF40 | MS60 | MS63 | MS65 |
|---|---|---|---|---|---|---|
| 2007 | 18,000 | PF65 95.00 | | | | |

**KM# 1366 20 YUAN**
1.56 g., 0.999 Gold 0.0501 oz. AGW, 14 mm. **Obv:** Temple of Heaven **Rev:** Panda walking left through bamboo **Edge:** Reeded **Note:** Large and small date varieties exist. Prev. Y#1112.

| Date | Mintage | VF20 | XF40 | MS60 | MS63 | MS65 |
|---|---|---|---|---|---|---|
| 2001 | 200,000 | — | — | 100 | 115 | — |
| 2001 D | Inc. above | — | — | 100 | 115 | — |
| 2002 | 74,601 | — | — | 100 | 115 | — |

**KM# 1467 20 YUAN**
1.56 g., 0.9999 Gold 0.050 oz. AGW, 14.5 mm. **Subject:** Panda **Obv:** Temple of Heaven **Rev:** Panda facing, walking through bamboo **Edge:** Reeded **Note:** Large and small date varieties exist. Prev. Y#1154.

| Date | Mintage | VF20 | XF40 | MS60 | MS63 | MS65 |
|---|---|---|---|---|---|---|
| 2003 | 117,000 | — | — | — | 110 | — |

**KM# 1529 20 YUAN**
1.56 g., 0.9999 Gold 0.050 oz. AGW, 14 mm. **Rev:** Panda walking with cub **Note:** Large and small date varieties exist. Prev. Y#1172.

| Date | Mintage | VF20 | XF40 | MS60 | MS63 | MS65 |
|---|---|---|---|---|---|---|
| 2004 | 101,000 | — | — | — | 120 | — |

**KM# 1586 20 YUAN**
1.55 g., 0.999 Gold 0.0498 oz. AGW, 14 mm. **Obv:** Temple of Heaven **Rev:** Panda cub and mom seated in bamboo

| Date | Mintage | VF20 | XF40 | MS60 | MS63 | MS65 |
|---|---|---|---|---|---|---|
| 2005 | 89,500 | PF65 125 | | | | |

**KM# 1661 20 YUAN**
1.56 g., 0.999 Gold 0.050 oz. AGW, 14 mm. **Obv:** Temple of Heaven **Rev:** Two pandas seated with bamboo

| Date | Mintage | VF20 | XF40 | MS60 | MS63 | MS65 |
|---|---|---|---|---|---|---|
| 2006 | 62,000 | PF65 145 | | | | |

**KM# 1707 20 YUAN**
1.56 g., 0.999 Gold 0.050 oz. AGW, 14 mm. **Obv:** Temple of Heaven **Rev:** Two pandas, one walking, one seated

| Date | Mintage | VF20 | XF40 | MS60 | MS63 | MS65 |
|---|---|---|---|---|---|---|
| 2007 | 200,000 | PF65 100 | | | | |

**KM# 1815 20 YUAN**
1.56 g., 0.999 Gold 0.050 oz. AGW, 14 mm. **Rev:** Panda cut pawing mom

| Date | Mintage | VF20 | XF40 | MS60 | MS63 | MS65 |
|---|---|---|---|---|---|---|
| 2008 | — | PF65 100 | | | | |

**KM# 1866 20 YUAN**
1.56 g., 0.999 Gold 0.050 oz. AGW

| Date | Mintage | VF20 | XF40 | MS60 | MS63 | MS65 |
|---|---|---|---|---|---|---|
| 2008 | — | PF65 100 | | | | |

**KM# 1930 20 YUAN**
1.55 g., 0.999 Gold 0.0498 oz. AGW **Obv:** Temple of Heaven **Rev:** Two pandas, one lying on back

| Date | Mintage | VF20 | XF40 | MS60 | MS63 | MS65 |
|---|---|---|---|---|---|---|
| 2010 | 120,000 | — | — | — | 110 | — |

**KM# 1979 20 YUAN**
1.55 g., 0.999 Gold 0.0498 oz. AGW, 14 mm.

| Date | Mintage | VF20 | XF40 | MS60 | MS63 | MS65 |
|---|---|---|---|---|---|---|
| 2011 | — | — | — | — | 110 | — |

**KM# 2028 20 YUAN**
1.55 g., 0.999 Gold 0.0498 oz. AGW, 14 mm.

| Date | Mintage | VF20 | XF40 | MS60 | MS63 | MS65 |
|---|---|---|---|---|---|---|
| 2012 | — | — | — | — | 110 | — |

**KM# 1817 30 YUAN**
3.11 g., 0.999 Gold 0.0999 oz. AGW, 18 mm. **Rev:** Panda cub pawing mom

| Date | Mintage | VF20 | XF40 | MS60 | MS63 | MS65 |
|---|---|---|---|---|---|---|
| 2008 | — | PF65 215 | | | | |

**KM# 1367 50 YUAN**
3.11 g., 0.999 Gold 0.0999 oz. AGW, 18 mm. **Obv:** Temple of Heaven **Rev:** Panda walking left through bamboo **Edge:** Reeded **Note:** Large and small date varieties exist. Prev. Y#1113.

| Date | Mintage | VF20 | XF40 | MS60 | MS63 | MS65 |
|---|---|---|---|---|---|---|
| 2001 D | 150,000 | — | — | — | 250 | — |
| 2001 | 50,000 | — | — | — | 200 | — |

**KM# 1457 50 YUAN**
3.11 g., 0.9999 Gold 0.100 oz. AGW **Subject:** Temple of Heaven **Rev:** Panda walking

| Date | Mintage | VF20 | XF40 | MS60 | MS63 | MS65 |
|---|---|---|---|---|---|---|
| 2002 | 36,092 | — | — | — | 225 | — |

**KM# 1469 50 YUAN**
3.11 g., 0.9999 Gold 0.100 oz. AGW **Subject:** Panda **Note:** Large and small date varieties exist. Prev. Y#1157.

| Date | Mintage | VF20 | XF40 | MS60 | MS63 | MS65 |
|---|---|---|---|---|---|---|
| 2003 | 47,500 | — | — | — | 215 | — |

**KM# 1531 50 YUAN**
3.11 g., 0.9999 Gold 0.100 oz. AGW **Subject:** Panda **Note:** Large and small date varieties exist. Prev. Y#1173.

| Date | Mintage | VF20 | XF40 | MS60 | MS63 | MS65 |
|---|---|---|---|---|---|---|
| 2004 | — | — | — | — | 200 | — |

**KM# 1585 50 YUAN**
3.11 g., 0.999 Gold 0.0999 oz. AGW, 18 mm. **Obv:** Temple of Heaven **Rev:** Panda cub and mom seated in bamboo

| Date | Mintage | VF20 | XF40 | MS60 | MS63 | MS65 |
|---|---|---|---|---|---|---|
| 2005 | 150,000 | — | — | — | 200 | — |

**KM# 1660 50 YUAN**
3.11 g., 0.999 Gold 0.0999 oz. AGW, 18 mm. **Obv:** Temple of Heaven **Rev:** Two pandas seated with bamboo

| Date | Mintage | VF20 | XF40 | MS60 | MS63 | MS65 |
|---|---|---|---|---|---|---|
| 2006 | 150,000 | — | — | — | 200 | — |

**KM# 1709 50 YUAN**
3.11 g., 0.999 Gold 0.0999 oz. AGW, 18 mm. **Obv:** Temple of Heaven **Rev:** Two pandas, one walking, one seated

| Date | Mintage | VF20 | XF40 | MS60 | MS63 | MS65 |
|---|---|---|---|---|---|---|
| 2007 | 150,000 | — | — | — | 200 | — |

**KM# 1868 50 YUAN**
3.10 g., 0.999 Gold 0.0996 oz. AGW, 18 mm. **Rev:** Panda cub pawing mom

| Date | Mintage | VF20 | XF40 | MS60 | MS63 | MS65 |
|---|---|---|---|---|---|---|
| 2008 | — | — | — | — | 200 | — |

**KM# 1929 50 YUAN**
3.11 g., 0.999 Gold 0.0999 oz. AGW **Obv:** Temple of Heaven **Rev:** Two pandas, one lying on back

| Date | Mintage | VF20 | XF40 | MS60 | MS63 | MS65 |
|---|---|---|---|---|---|---|
| 2010 | 120,000 | — | — | — | 200 | — |

**KM# 1978 50 YUAN**
3.11 g., 0.999 Gold 0.0999 oz. AGW, 18 mm.

| Date | Mintage | VF20 | XF40 | MS60 | MS63 | MS65 |
|---|---|---|---|---|---|---|
| 2011 | — | — | — | — | 200 | — |

**KM# 2027 50 YUAN**
3.11 g., 0.999 Gold 0.0999 oz. AGW, 18 mm.

| Date | Mintage | VF20 | XF40 | MS60 | MS63 | MS65 |
|---|---|---|---|---|---|---|
| 2012 | — | — | — | — | 200 | — |

**KM# 1368 100 YUAN**
7.78 g., 0.999 Gold 0.2498 oz. AGW, 22 mm. **Obv:** Temple of Heaven **Rev:** Panda walking left through bamboo **Edge:** Reeded **Note:** Large and small date varieties exist. Prev. Y#1114.

| Date | Mintage | VF20 | XF40 | MS60 | MS63 | MS65 |
|---|---|---|---|---|---|---|
| 2001 | 85,010 | — | — | — | 475 | — |
| 2001 D | Inc. above | — | — | — | 525 | — |

**KM# 1458 100 YUAN**
7.78 g., 0.9999 Gold 0.250 oz. AGW **Obv:** Temple of Heaven **Rev:** Panda walking

| Date | Mintage | VF20 | XF40 | MS60 | MS63 | MS65 |
|---|---|---|---|---|---|---|
| 2002 | 19,205 | — | — | — | 500 | — |

**KM# 1471 100 YUAN**
7.78 g., 0.9999 Gold 0.250 oz. AGW **Subject:** Panda **Note:** Large and small date varieties exist. Prev. Y#1158.

| Date | Mintage | VF20 | XF40 | MS60 | MS63 | MS65 |
|---|---|---|---|---|---|---|
| 2003 | 28,000 | — | — | — | 475 | — |

**KM# 1533 100 YUAN**
7.78 g., 0.9999 Gold 0.250 oz. AGW **Subject:** Panda **Note:** Large and small date varieties exist. Prev. Y#1174. Photo reduced.

| Date | Mintage | VF20 | XF40 | MS60 | MS63 | MS65 |
|---|---|---|---|---|---|---|
| 2004 | 41,000 | — | — | — | 475 | — |

**KM# 1584 100 YUAN**
7.77 g., 0.999 Gold 0.2496 oz. AGW, 22 mm. **Obv:** Temple of Heaven **Rev:** Panda cub and mom seated in bamboo

| Date | Mintage | VF20 | XF40 | MS60 | MS63 | MS65 |
|---|---|---|---|---|---|---|
| 2005 | 40,000 | — | — | — | 475 | — |

**KM# 1659 100 YUAN**
7.77 g., 0.999 Gold 0.2496 oz. AGW, 22 mm. **Obv:** Temple of Heaven **Rev:** Two pandas seated with bamboo

| Date | Mintage | VF20 | XF40 | MS60 | MS63 | MS65 |
|---|---|---|---|---|---|---|
| 2006 | 28,500 | — | — | — | 500 | — |

**KM# 1710 100 YUAN**
7.77 g., 0.999 Gold 0.2496 oz. AGW, 22 mm. **Obv:** Temple of Heaven **Rev:** Two pandas, one walking, one seated

| Date | Mintage | VF20 | XF40 | MS60 | MS63 | MS65 |
|---|---|---|---|---|---|---|
| 2007 | 60,000 | — | — | — | 475 | — |

**KM# 1818 100 YUAN**
7.77 g., 0.999 Gold 0.2496 oz. AGW, 22 mm. **Rev:** Panda cub pawing mom

| Date | Mintage | VF20 | XF40 | MS60 | MS63 | MS65 |
|---|---|---|---|---|---|---|
| 2008 | — | — | — | — | 475 | — |

**KM# 1928 100 YUAN**
7.77 g., 0.999 Gold 0.2496 oz. AGW **Obv:** Temple of Heaven **Rev:** Two panda, one lying on back

| Date | Mintage | VF20 | XF40 | MS60 | MS63 | MS65 |
|---|---|---|---|---|---|---|
| 2010 | 120,000 | — | — | — | 500 | — |

**KM# 1977 100 YUAN**
7.77 g., 0.999 Gold 0.2496 oz. AGW, 22 mm.

| Date | Mintage | VF20 | XF40 | MS60 | MS63 | MS65 |
|---|---|---|---|---|---|---|
| 2011 | — | — | — | — | 500 | — |

**KM# 2026 100 YUAN**
7.77 g., 0.999 Gold 0.2496 oz. AGW, 22 mm.

| Date | Mintage | VF20 | XF40 | MS60 | MS63 | MS65 |
|---|---|---|---|---|---|---|
| 2012 | — | — | — | — | 450 | — |

**KM# 1369 200 YUAN**
15.55 g., 0.999 Gold 0.4995 oz. AGW, 27 mm. **Obv:** Temple of Heaven **Rev:** Panda in bamboo forest **Edge:** Slanted reeding **Note:** Illustration reduced. Large and small date varieties exist. Prev. Y#1105.

| Date | Mintage | VF20 | XF40 | MS60 | MS63 | MS65 |
|---|---|---|---|---|---|---|
| 2001 D | 100,000 | — | — | — | 875 | — |
| 2001 | 33,215 | — | — | — | 900 | — |

**KM# 1459 200 YUAN**
15.55 g., 0.9999 Gold 0.500 oz. AGW **Rev:** Panda

| Date | Mintage | VF20 | XF40 | MS60 | MS63 | MS65 |
|---|---|---|---|---|---|---|
| 2002 | 28,514 | — | — | — | 900 | — |

**KM# 1472 200 YUAN**
15.55 g., 0.9999 Gold 0.500 oz. AGW **Subject:** Panda **Note:** Large and small date varieties exist. Prev. Y#1162.

| Date | Mintage | VF20 | XF40 | MS60 | MS63 | MS65 |
|---|---|---|---|---|---|---|
| 2003 | 25,000 | — | — | — | 900 | — |

**KM# 1535 200 YUAN**
15.55 g., 0.999 Gold 0.4995 oz. AGW **Subject:** Panda **Note:** Large and small date varieties exist. Prev. Y#1175.

| Date | Mintage | VF20 | XF40 | MS60 | MS63 | MS65 |
|---|---|---|---|---|---|---|
| 2004 | 42,000 | — | — | — | 875 | — |

**KM# 1583 200 YUAN**
15.55 g., 0.999 Gold 0.4995 oz. AGW, 27 mm. **Obv:** Temple of Heaven **Rev:** Panda cub and mom seated in bamboo

| Date | Mintage | VF20 | XF40 | MS60 | MS63 | MS65 |
|---|---|---|---|---|---|---|
| 2005 | 36,410 | — | — | — | 875 | — |

**KM# 1658 200 YUAN**
15.55 g., 0.999 Gold 0.4994 oz. AGW, 27 mm. **Obv:** Temple of Heaven **Rev:** Two pandas seated with bamboo

| Date | Mintage | VF20 | XF40 | MS60 | MS63 | MS65 |
|---|---|---|---|---|---|---|
| 2006 | 25,600 | — | — | — | 900 | — |

**KM# 1711 200 YUAN**
15.55 g., 0.999 Gold 0.4994 oz. AGW **Obv:** Temple of Heaven **Rev:** Two pandas, one walking, one seated

| Date | Mintage | VF20 | XF40 | MS60 | MS63 | MS65 |
|---|---|---|---|---|---|---|
| 2007 | 60,000 | — | — | — | 875 | — |

**KM# 1870 200 YUAN**
15.50 g., 0.999 Gold 0.4978 oz. AGW

| Date | Mintage | VF20 | XF40 | MS60 | MS63 | MS65 |
|---|---|---|---|---|---|---|
| 2009 | — | — | — | — | 875 | — |

**KM# 1927 200 YUAN**
15.55 g., 0.999 Gold 0.4994 oz. AGW **Obv:** Temple of Heaven **Rev:** Two pandas, one lying on back

| Date | Mintage | VF20 | XF40 | MS60 | MS63 | MS65 |
|---|---|---|---|---|---|---|
| 2010 | 120,000 | — | — | — | 900 | — |

**KM# 1976 200 YUAN**
15.55 g., 0.999 Gold 0.4994 oz. AGW

| Date | Mintage | VF20 | XF40 | MS60 | MS63 | MS65 |
|---|---|---|---|---|---|---|
| 2011 | — | — | — | — | 900 | — |

**KM# 2025 200 YUAN**
15.55 g., 0.999 Gold 0.4994 oz. AGW, 27 mm.

| Date | Mintage | VF20 | XF40 | MS60 | MS63 | MS65 |
|---|---|---|---|---|---|---|
| 2012 | — | — | — | — | 900 | — |

**KM# 1371 500 YUAN**
31.10 g., 0.999 Gold 0.999 oz. AGW, 32 mm. **Obv:** Temple of Heaven **Rev:** Panda walking through bamboo **Edge:** Reeded **Note:** Prev. Y#1088.

| Date | Mintage | VF20 | XF40 | MS60 | MS63 | MS65 |
|---|---|---|---|---|---|---|
| 2001 D | 150,000 | — | — | — | — | 1,396 |
| 2001 | — | — | — | — | — | 1,396 |

**KM# 1405 500 YUAN**
31.11 g., 0.9999 Gold 0.9999 oz. AGW **Rev:** Panda

| Date | Mintage | VF20 | XF40 | MS60 | MS63 | MS65 |
|---|---|---|---|---|---|---|
| 2001 | 41,411 | — | — | — | — | 1,397 |

**KM# 1460 500 YUAN**
31.11 g., 0.9999 Gold 0.9999 oz. AGW **Rev:** Panda

| Date | Mintage | VF20 | XF40 | MS60 | MS63 | MS65 |
|---|---|---|---|---|---|---|
| 2002 | 28,345 | — | — | — | — | 1,460 |

**KM# 1474 500 YUAN**
31.13 g., 0.9999 Gold 1.0008 oz. AGW **Subject:** Panda **Note:** Large and small date varieties exist. Prev. Y#1164.

| Date | Mintage | VF20 | XF40 | MS60 | MS63 | MS65 |
|---|---|---|---|---|---|---|
| 2003 | 36,300 | — | — | — | — | 1,424 |

**KM# 1537 500 YUAN**
31.10 g., 0.9999 Gold 0.9999 oz. AGW **Subject:** Panda **Note:** Large and small date varieties exist. Prev. Y#1176.

| Date | Mintage | VF20 | XF40 | MS60 | MS63 | MS65 |
|---|---|---|---|---|---|---|
| 2004 | 55,000 | — | — | — | — | 1,397 |

**KM# 1582 500 YUAN**
31.11 g., 0.999 Gold 0.999 oz. AGW, 32 mm. **Obv:** Temple of Heaven **Rev:** Panda cub and mom seated in bamboo

| Date | Mintage | VF20 | XF40 | MS60 | MS63 | MS65 |
|---|---|---|---|---|---|---|
| 2005 | 50,300 | **PF65** 1,396 | | | | |

**KM# 1657 500 YUAN**
31.11 g., 0.999 Gold 0.999 oz. AGW, 32 mm. **Obv:** Temple of Heaven **Rev:** Two panda's seated with bamboo

| Date | Mintage | VF20 | XF40 | MS60 | MS63 | MS65 |
|---|---|---|---|---|---|---|
| 2006 | 115,600 | **PF65** 1,396 | | | | |

**KM# 1713 500 YUAN**
31.11 g., 0.999 Gold 0.999 oz. AGW, 32 mm. **Obv:** Temple of Heaven **Rev:** Two pandas, one walking, one seated

| Date | Mintage | VF20 | XF40 | MS60 | MS63 | MS65 |
|---|---|---|---|---|---|---|
| 2007 | 150,000 | **PF65** 1,396 | | | | |

**KM# 1821 500 YUAN**
31.11 g., 0.999 Gold 0.999 oz. AGW, 32 mm. **Rev:** Panda cub pawing mom

| Date | Mintage | VF20 | XF40 | MS60 | MS63 | MS65 |
|---|---|---|---|---|---|---|
| 2008 | — | **PF65** 1,396 | | | | |

**KM# 1872 500 YUAN**
31.11 g., 0.999 Gold 0.999 oz. AGW

| Date | Mintage | VF20 | XF40 | MS60 | MS63 | MS65 |
|---|---|---|---|---|---|---|
| 2009 | — | **PF65** 1,396 | | | | |

**KM# 1926 500 YUAN**
31.11 g., 0.999 Gold 0.999 oz. AGW **Obv:** Temple of Heaven **Rev:** Two pandas, one lying on back

| Date | Mintage | VF20 | XF40 | MS60 | MS63 | MS65 |
|---|---|---|---|---|---|---|
| 2010 | 300,000 | — | — | — | — | 1,396 |

**KM# 1975 500 YUAN**
31.11 g., 0.999 Gold 0.999 oz. AGW

| Date | Mintage | VF20 | XF40 | MS60 | MS63 | MS65 |
|---|---|---|---|---|---|---|
| 2011 | — | — | — | — | — | 1,396 |

**KM# 2024 500 YUAN**
31.11 g., 0.999 Gold 0.999 oz. AGW, 32 mm.

| Date | Mintage | VF20 | XF40 | MS60 | MS63 | MS65 |
|---|---|---|---|---|---|---|
| 2012 | — | — | — | — | — | 1,396 |

**KM# 1581 2000 YUAN**
155.00 g., 0.999 Gold 4.9784 oz. AGW, 60 mm. **Obv:** Temple of Heaven **Rev:** Panda cub and mom seated in bamboo **Note:** Photo reduced.

| Date | Mintage | VF20 | XF40 | MS60 | MS63 | MS65 |
|---|---|---|---|---|---|---|
| 2005 | 1,000 | **PF65** 7,271 | | | | |

**KM# 1656 2000 YUAN**
155.55 g., 0.999 Gold 4.996 oz. AGW, 60 mm. **Obv:** Temple of Heaven **Rev:** Two pandas seated with bamboo **Note:** Photo reduced.

| Date | Mintage | VF20 | XF40 | MS60 | MS63 | MS65 |
|---|---|---|---|---|---|---|
| 2006 | 1,000 | **PF65** 7,297 | | | | |

**KM# 1714 2000 YUAN**
155.55 g., 0.999 Gold 4.996 oz. AGW, 60 mm. **Obv:** Temple of Heaven **Rev:** Two pandas, one walking, one seated

| Date | Mintage | VF20 | XF40 | MS60 | MS63 | MS65 |
|---|---|---|---|---|---|---|
| 2007 | 1,000 | **PF65** 7,297 | | | | |

**KM# 1822 2000 YUAN**
155.50 g., 0.999 Gold 4.9944 oz. AGW, 60 mm. **Rev:** Panda cub pawing mom

| Date | Mintage | VF20 | XF40 | MS60 | MS63 | MS65 |
|---|---|---|---|---|---|---|
| 2008 | 1,000 | **PF65** 7,294 | | | | |

**KM# 1873 2000 YUAN**
155.50 g., 0.999 Gold 4.9944 oz. AGW

| Date | Mintage | VF20 | XF40 | MS60 | MS63 | MS65 |
|---|---|---|---|---|---|---|
| 2009 | 1,000 | **PF65** 7,294 | | | | |

**KM# 1914 2000 YUAN**
155.50 g., 0.999 Gold 4.9944 oz. AGW **Subject:** Year of the Tiger **Rev:** Multicolor

| Date | Mintage | VF20 | XF40 | MS60 | MS63 | MS65 |
|---|---|---|---|---|---|---|
| 2010 | 1,800 | **PF65** 6,977 | | | | |

**KM# 1933 2000 YUAN**
155.50 g., 0.999 Gold 4.9944 oz. AGW **Obv:** Temple of Heaven **Rev:** Two pandas, one lying on back

| Date | Mintage | VF20 | XF40 | MS60 | MS63 | MS65 |
|---|---|---|---|---|---|---|
| 2010 | 1,000 | **PF65** 7,294 | | | | |

**KM# 1982 2000 YUAN**
155.55 g., 0.999 Gold 4.996 oz. AGW, 60 mm.

| Date | Mintage | VF20 | XF40 | MS60 | MS63 | MS65 |
|---|---|---|---|---|---|---|
| 2011 | — | **PF65** 6,979 | | | | |

**KM# 1372 10000 YUAN**
1000.00 g., 0.999 Gold 32.1186 oz. AGW **Subject:** Panda **Note:** Large and small date varieties exist. Prev. #Y1138.

| Date | Mintage | VF20 | XF40 | MS60 | MS63 | MS65 |
|---|---|---|---|---|---|---|
| 2001 | 68 | — | — | — | — | 50,988 |

**KM# A1475 10000 YUAN**
1000.00 g., 0.9999 Gold 32.1475 oz. AGW **Subject:** Panda **Note:** Large and small date varieties exist. Prev. #Y1165.

| Date | Mintage | VF20 | XF40 | MS60 | MS63 | MS65 |
|---|---|---|---|---|---|---|
| 2002 | 68 | — | — | — | — | 51,034 |

**KM# 1475 10000 YUAN**
1000.00 g., 0.999 Gold 32.1186 oz. AGW, 100 mm. **Rev:** Panda and bamboo

| Date | Mintage | VF20 | XF40 | MS60 | MS63 | MS65 |
|---|---|---|---|---|---|---|
| 2003 | 68 | **PF65** 50,988 | | | | |

**KM# 1538 10000 YUAN**
1000.00 g., 0.9999 Gold 32.1475 oz. AGW **Subject:** Panda **Note:** Large and small date varieties exist. Prev. #Y1177.

| Date | Mintage | VF20 | XF40 | MS60 | MS63 | MS65 |
|---|---|---|---|---|---|---|
| 2004 | 68 | — | — | — | — | 51,034 |

**KM# A1580 10000 YUAN**
1000.00 g., 0.999 Gold 32.1186 oz. AGW, 90 mm. **Obv:** Temple of Heaven **Rev:** Panda cub and mom seated in bamboo **Note:** Photo reduced.

| Date | Mintage | VF20 | XF40 | MS60 | MS63 | MS65 |
|---|---|---|---|---|---|---|
| 2005 | 100 | **PF65** 50,988 | | | | |

**KM# 1655 10000 YUAN**
1000.00 g., 0.999 Gold 32.1186 oz. AGW, 90 mm. **Obv:** Temple of Heaven **Rev:** Two pandas seated with bamboo **Note:** Photo reduced.

| Date | Mintage | VF20 | XF40 | MS60 | MS63 | MS65 |
|---|---|---|---|---|---|---|
| 2006 | 200 | **PF65** 48,949 | | | | |

### KM# 1715 10000 YUAN
1000.00 g., 0.999 Gold 32.1186 oz. AGW **Obv:** Temple of Heaven **Rev:** Two pandas, one walking, one seated

| Date | Mintage | VF20 | XF40 | MS60 | MS63 | MS65 |
|---|---|---|---|---|---|---|
| 2007 | 200 | PF65 48,949 | | | | |

### KM# 1823 10000 YUAN
1000.00 g., 0.999 Gold 32.1186 oz. AGW, 90 mm. **Rev:** Panda cub pawing mom

| Date | Mintage | VF20 | XF40 | MS60 | MS63 | MS65 |
|---|---|---|---|---|---|---|
| 2008 | 200 | PF65 48,949 | | | | |

### KM# 1874 10000 YUAN
1000.00 g., 0.999 Gold 32.1186 oz. AGW

| Date | Mintage | VF20 | XF40 | MS60 | MS63 | MS65 |
|---|---|---|---|---|---|---|
| 2009 | 200 | PF65 48,949 | | | | |

### KM# 1932 10000 YUAN
1000.00 g., 0.999 Gold 32.1186 oz. AGW **Obv:** Temple of Heaven **Rev:** Two pandas, one lying on back

| Date | Mintage | VF20 | XF40 | MS60 | MS63 | MS65 |
|---|---|---|---|---|---|---|
| 2010 | 200 | PF65 48,949 | | | | |

### KM# 1981 10000 YUAN
1000.00 g., 0.999 Gold 32.1186 oz. AGW, 90 mm.

| Date | Mintage | VF20 | XF40 | MS60 | MS63 | MS65 |
|---|---|---|---|---|---|---|
| 2011 | — | PF65 48,949 | | | | |

### KM# 2030 10000 YUAN
1000.00 g., 0.999 Gold 32.1186 oz. AGW, 90 mm.

| Date | Mintage | VF20 | XF40 | MS60 | MS63 | MS65 |
|---|---|---|---|---|---|---|
| 2012 | — | PF65 48,949 | | | | |

## GOLD BULLION COINAGE

Lunar Series

### KM# 1967 20 YUAN
3.11 g., 0.999 Gold 0.0999 oz. AGW, 18 mm. **Subject:** Year of the Rabbit **Rev:** Multicolor

| Date | Mintage | VF20 | XF40 | MS60 | MS63 | MS65 |
|---|---|---|---|---|---|---|
| 2011 | 80,000 | PF65 225 | | | | |

### KM# 1374 50 YUAN
3.11 g., 0.999 Gold 0.0999 oz. AGW, 18 mm. **Subject:** Year of the Snake **Note:** Prev. Y#1141.1; 1043.

| Date | Mintage | VF20 | XF40 | MS60 | MS63 | MS65 |
|---|---|---|---|---|---|---|
| 2001 | 48,000 | — | — | — | — | 265 |

### KM# 1376 50 YUAN
3.11 g., 0.9999 Gold 0.100 oz. AGW **Subject:** Year of the Snake **Rev:** Multicolor. **Note:** Prev. Y#1141.2.

| Date | Mintage | VF20 | XF40 | MS60 | MS63 | MS65 |
|---|---|---|---|---|---|---|
| 2001 | 30,000 | — | — | — | — | 350 |

### KM# 1417 50 YUAN
3.11 g., 0.9999 Gold 0.0998 oz. AGW **Subject:** Year of the Horse **Rev:** Multicolor horse prancing forward **Note:** Prev. Y#1143.2.

| Date | Mintage | VF20 | XF40 | MS60 | MS63 | MS65 |
|---|---|---|---|---|---|---|
| 2002 | 30,000 | — | — | — | — | 425 |

### KM# 1419 50 YUAN
3.11 g., 0.9999 Gold 0.0998 oz. AGW **Subject:** Year of the Horse **Rev:** Dramatic horse profile right **Note:** Prev. Y#1143.1.

| Date | Mintage | VF20 | XF40 | MS60 | MS63 | MS65 |
|---|---|---|---|---|---|---|
| 2002 | 48,000 | — | — | — | — | 240 |

### KM# 1478 50 YUAN
3.11 g., 0.9999 Gold 0.100 oz. AGW **Subject:** Year of the Goat **Note:** Prev. Y#1155.1.

| Date | Mintage | VF20 | XF40 | MS60 | MS63 | MS65 |
|---|---|---|---|---|---|---|
| 2003 | 48,000 | — | — | — | — | 275 |

### KM# A1478 50 YUAN
3.11 g., 0.9999 Gold 0.100 oz. AGW **Subject:** Year of the Goat **Rev:** Multicolor. **Note:** Prev. Y#1155.2

| Date | Mintage | VF20 | XF40 | MS60 | MS63 | MS65 |
|---|---|---|---|---|---|---|
| 2003 | 30,000 | — | — | — | — | 400 |

### KM# 1544 50 YUAN
3.11 g., 0.9999 Gold 0.100 oz. AGW, 18 mm. **Subject:** Year of the Monkey **Note:** Prev. Y#1167.1.

| Date | Mintage | VF20 | XF40 | MS60 | MS63 | MS65 |
|---|---|---|---|---|---|---|
| 2004 | 48,000 | — | — | — | — | 275 |

### KM# 1546 50 YUAN
3.11 g., 0.9999 Gold 0.100 oz. AGW **Subject:** Year of the Monkey **Rev:** Multicolor monkey and baby **Note:** Prev. Y#1167.2

| Date | Mintage | VF20 | XF40 | MS60 | MS63 | MS65 |
|---|---|---|---|---|---|---|
| 2004 | 30,000 | — | — | — | — | 425 |

### KM# 1608 50 YUAN
3.11 g., 0.999 Gold 0.0999 oz. AGW, 18 mm. **Subject:** Year of the Rooster **Obv:** Classical rooster **Rev:** Multicolor rooster

| Date | Mintage | VF20 | XF40 | MS60 | MS63 | MS65 |
|---|---|---|---|---|---|---|
| 2005 | 30,000 | PF65 375 | | | | |

### KM# 1609 50 YUAN
3.11 g., 0.999 Gold 0.0999 oz. AGW, 18 mm. **Subject:** Year of the Rooster **Obv:** Classical rooster **Rev:** Rooster, hen and chicks

| Date | Mintage | VF20 | XF40 | MS60 | MS63 | MS65 |
|---|---|---|---|---|---|---|
| 2005 | 60,000 | PF65 300 | | | | |

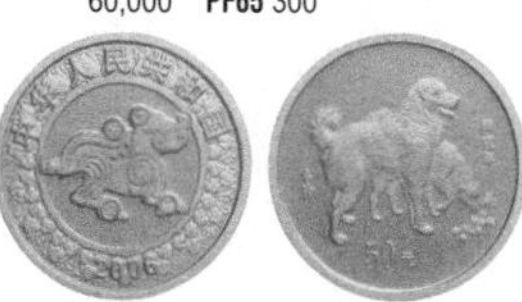

### KM# 1680 50 YUAN
3.11 g., 0.999 Gold 0.0999 oz. AGW, 18 mm. **Obv:** Dog-shaped belt-hook from ancient Chinese bronze ware, decorative design of dog tail-shaped plant leaves **Rev:** 2 smart dogs **Note:** Prev. Y#1226; KM#1658.

| Date | Mintage | VF20 | XF40 | MS60 | MS63 | MS65 |
|---|---|---|---|---|---|---|
| 2006 | 60,000 | — | — | — | — | 225 |

### KM# 1681 50 YUAN
3.11 g., 0.999 Gold 0.0999 oz. AGW, 18 mm. **Obv:** Dog-shaped belt-hook , an ancient Chinese bronze ware, decorative disign of dog tail-shaped plant leaves **Rev:** 2 dogs at play **Note:** Prev. Y#1222; KM#1654.

| Date | Mintage | VF20 | XF40 | MS60 | MS63 | MS65 |
|---|---|---|---|---|---|---|
| 2006 | 30,000 | PF65 220 | | | | |

### KM# 1721 50 YUAN
3.10 g., 0.999 Gold 0.0996 oz. AGW, 18 mm. **Subject:** Year of the Pig **Obv:** Classical pig **Rev:** Pig walking right

| Date | Mintage | VF20 | XF40 | MS60 | MS63 | MS65 |
|---|---|---|---|---|---|---|
| 2007 | — | PF65 225 | | | | |

### KM# 1722 50 YUAN
3.10 g., 0.999 Gold 0.0996 oz. AGW, 18 mm. **Subject:** Year of the Pig **Obv:** Classical pig **Rev:** Multicolor sow and piglets sucking

| Date | Mintage | VF20 | XF40 | MS60 | MS63 | MS65 |
|---|---|---|---|---|---|---|
| 2007 | 30,000 | PF65 550 | | | | |

### KM# 1835 50 YUAN
3.11 g., 0.999 Gold 0.0999 oz. AGW **Subject:** Year of the Rat **Rev:** Multicolor **Shape:** 18

| Date | Mintage | VF20 | XF40 | MS60 | MS63 | MS65 |
|---|---|---|---|---|---|---|
| 2008 | 30,000 | PF65 350 | | | | |

### KM# 1836 50 YUAN
3.11 g., 0.999 Gold 0.0999 oz. AGW, 18 mm. **Subject:** Year of the Rat

| Date | Mintage | VF20 | XF40 | MS60 | MS63 | MS65 |
|---|---|---|---|---|---|---|
| 2008 | 60,000 | PF65 225 | | | | |

### KM# 1880 50 YUAN
3.11 g., 0.999 Gold 0.0999 oz. AGW **Subject:** Year of the Ox colorized

| Date | Mintage | VF20 | XF40 | MS60 | MS63 | MS65 |
|---|---|---|---|---|---|---|
| 2009 | 30,000 | PF65 400 | | | | |

### KM# 1881 50 YUAN
3.11 g., 0.999 Gold 0.0999 oz. AGW **Subject:** Year of the Ox

| Date | Mintage | VF20 | XF40 | MS60 | MS63 | MS65 |
|---|---|---|---|---|---|---|
| 2009 | 80,000 | PF65 200 | | | | |

### KM# 1917 50 YUAN
3.11 g., 0.999 Gold 0.0999 oz. AGW **Subject:** Year of the Tiger

| Date | Mintage | VF20 | XF40 | MS60 | MS63 | MS65 |
|---|---|---|---|---|---|---|
| 2010 | 80,000 | PF65 225 | | | | |

### KM# 1918 50 YUAN
3.11 g., 0.999 Gold 0.0999 oz. AGW **Subject:** Year of the Tiger **Rev:** Multicolor

| Date | Mintage | VF20 | XF40 | MS60 | MS63 | MS65 |
|---|---|---|---|---|---|---|
| 2010 | 80,000 | PF65 225 | | | | |

### KM# 1966 50 YUAN
3.11 g., 0.999 Gold 0.0999 oz. AGW, 18 mm. **Subject:** Year of the Rabbit

| Date | Mintage | VF20 | XF40 | MS60 | MS63 | MS65 |
|---|---|---|---|---|---|---|
| 2011 | 80,000 | PF65 225 | | | | |

### KM# 2015 50 YUAN
3.11 g., 0.999 Gold 0.0997 oz. AGW, 18 mm. **Subject:** Year of the Dragon

| Date | Mintage | VF20 | XF40 | MS60 | MS63 | MS65 |
|---|---|---|---|---|---|---|
| 2012 | — | PF65 225 | | | | |

### KM# 2016 50 YUAN
3.11 g., 0.999 Gold 0.0997 oz. AGW, 18 mm. **Subject:** Year of the Dragon **Rev:** Colored

| Date | Mintage | VF20 | XF40 | MS60 | MS63 | MS65 |
|---|---|---|---|---|---|---|
| 2012 | — | PF65 225 | | | | |

### KM# 1380 200 YUAN
15.55 g., 0.999 Gold 0.4995 oz. AGW **Subject:** Year of the Snake **Shape:** Flower **Note:** Prev. Y#1045.

| Date | Mintage | VF20 | XF40 | MS60 | MS63 | MS65 |
|---|---|---|---|---|---|---|
| 2001 | 2,300 | PF65 1,250 | | | | |

### KM# 1383 200 YUAN
15.55 g., 0.999 Gold 0.4995 oz. AGW **Subject:** Year of the Snake **Rev:** Fan **Note:** Prev. Y#1044.

| Date | Mintage | VF20 | XF40 | MS60 | MS63 | MS65 |
|---|---|---|---|---|---|---|
| 2001 | 6,600 | — | — | — | — | 950 |

### KM# 1424 200 YUAN
15.55 g., 0.999 Gold 0.4994 oz. AGW **Subject:** Year of the Horse **Shape:** Fan

| Date | Mintage | VF20 | XF40 | MS60 | MS63 | MS65 |
|---|---|---|---|---|---|---|
| 2002 | 6,600 | — | — | — | — | 1,000 |

### KM# 1426 200 YUAN
15.50 g., 0.999 Gold 0.4978 oz. AGW **Subject:** Year of the Horse **Shape:** Flower **Note:** Prev. Y#1150.

| Date | Mintage | VF20 | XF40 | MS60 | MS63 | MS65 |
|---|---|---|---|---|---|---|
| 2002 | 2,300 | — | — | — | — | 1,350 |

### KM# 1475.1 200 YUAN
15.55 g., 0.9999 Gold 0.4999 oz. AGW **Subject:** Year of the Goat **Shape:** Fan

| Date | Mintage | VF20 | XF40 | MS60 | MS63 | MS65 |
|---|---|---|---|---|---|---|
| 2003 | 6,600 | — | — | — | — | 950 |

### KM# 1481 200 YUAN
15.55 g., 0.9999 Gold 0.500 oz. AGW **Subject:** Year of the Goat **Shape:** Flower **Note:** Prev. Y#1161.

| Date | Mintage | VF20 | XF40 | MS60 | MS63 | MS65 |
|---|---|---|---|---|---|---|
| 2003 | 2,300 | — | — | — | — | 1,350 |

### KM# 1486 200 YUAN
15.51 g., 0.999 Gold 0.4983 oz. AGW, 58 x 30 mm. **Subject:** Year of the Sheep **Shape:** Fan

| Date | Mintage | VF20 | XF40 | MS60 | MS63 | MS65 |
|---|---|---|---|---|---|---|
| 2003 | 6,600 | PF65 1,100 | | | | |

### KM# 1549 200 YUAN
15.55 g., 0.9999 Gold 0.500 oz. AGW **Subject:** Year of the Monkey **Shape:** Flower **Note:** Prev. Y#1169.

| Date | Mintage | VF20 | XF40 | MS60 | MS63 | MS65 |
|---|---|---|---|---|---|---|
| 2004 | 2,300 | — | — | — | — | 1,350 |

**KM# 1554 200 YUAN**
15.55 g., 0.9999 Gold 0.500 oz. AGW **Subject:** Year of the Monkey **Shape:** Fan **Note:** Illustration reduced. Prev. Y#1168.

| Date | Mintage | VF20 | XF40 | MS60 | MS63 | MS65 |
|---|---|---|---|---|---|---|
| 2004 | 6,600 | — | — | — | — | 1,100 |

**KM# 1606 200 YUAN**
15.55 g., 0.999 Gold 0.4994 oz. AGW, 27 mm. **Series:** Classical rooster **Subject:** Year of the Rooster **Obv:** Rooster, hen and chicks **Shape:** Scallops

| Date | Mintage | VF20 | XF40 | MS60 | MS63 | MS65 |
|---|---|---|---|---|---|---|
| 2005 | 8,000 | **PF65** 925 | | | | |

**KM# 1607 200 YUAN**
15.55 g., 0.999 Gold 0.4994 oz. AGW, 58 x 30 mm. **Subject:** Year of the Rooster **Obv:** Temple **Rev:** Rooster, hen and chicks **Shape:** Fan **Note:** Illustration reduced.

| Date | Mintage | VF20 | XF40 | MS60 | MS63 | MS65 |
|---|---|---|---|---|---|---|
| 2005 | 6,600 | **PF65** 950 | | | | |

**KM# 1677 200 YUAN**
15.63 g., 0.999 Gold 0.502 oz. AGW, 27 mm. **Subject:** Year of the Dog **Obv:** Dog-shaped belt-hook from ancient Chinese bronze ware, decorative design of dog tail-shaped plant leaves **Rev:** 2 smart dogs **Shape:** Scalloped **Note:** Prev. Y#1224; KM#1656.

| Date | Mintage | VF20 | XF40 | MS60 | MS63 | MS65 |
|---|---|---|---|---|---|---|
| 2006 | 8,000 | **PF65** 1,350 | | | | |

**KM# 1679 200 YUAN**
15.63 g., 0.999 Gold 0.502 oz. AGW **Subject:** Year of the Dog **Obv:** Qing Yuan Gate of the China Great Wall **Rev:** 2 dogs at play **Shape:** 30× Fan **Note:** Prev. Y#1220; KM#1652. Illustration reduced.

| Date | Mintage | VF20 | XF40 | MS60 | MS63 | MS65 |
|---|---|---|---|---|---|---|
| 2006 | 6,600 | **PF65** 1,100 | | | | |

**KM# 1723 200 YUAN**
15.50 g., 0.999 Gold 0.4978 oz. AGW, 58 x 39 mm. **Subject:** Year of the Pig **Obv:** Temple **Rev:** Sow and four pigletts **Shape:** Fan

| Date | Mintage | VF20 | XF40 | MS60 | MS63 | MS65 |
|---|---|---|---|---|---|---|
| 2007 | 6,600 | **PF65** 1,150 | | | | |

**KM# 1724 200 YUAN**
15.55 g., 0.999 Gold 0.4994 oz. AGW, 27 mm. **Subject:** Year of the Pig **Obv:** Classical pig **Rev:** Pig walking right **Shape:** Flower

| Date | Mintage | VF20 | XF40 | MS60 | MS63 | MS65 |
|---|---|---|---|---|---|---|
| 2007 | 8,000 | **PF65** 950 | | | | |

**KM# 1837 200 YUAN**
15.50 g., 0.999 Gold 0.4978 oz. AGW, 27 mm. **Subject:** Year of the Rat **Shape:** Flower

| Date | Mintage | VF20 | XF40 | MS60 | MS63 | MS65 |
|---|---|---|---|---|---|---|
| 2008 | 8,000 | **PF65** 950 | | | | |

**KM# 1838 200 YUAN**
15.50 g., 0.999 Gold 0.4978 oz. AGW, 58 x 39 mm. **Subject:** Year of the Rat **Shape:** Fan

| Date | Mintage | VF20 | XF40 | MS60 | MS63 | MS65 |
|---|---|---|---|---|---|---|
| 2008 | 6,600 | **PF65** 1,000 | | | | |

**KM# 1882 200 YUAN**
15.50 g., 0.999 Gold 0.4978 oz. AGW **Subject:** Year of the Ox **Shape:** Flower

| Date | Mintage | VF20 | XF40 | MS60 | MS63 | MS65 |
|---|---|---|---|---|---|---|
| 2009 | 8,000 | **PF65** 950 | | | | |

**KM# 1883 200 YUAN**
15.50 g., 0.999 Gold 0.4978 oz. AGW **Subject:** Year of the Ox **Shape:** Fan

| Date | Mintage | VF20 | XF40 | MS60 | MS63 | MS65 |
|---|---|---|---|---|---|---|
| 2009 | 6,600 | **PF65** 1,000 | | | | |

**KM# 1915 200 YUAN**
15.55 g., 0.999 Gold 0.4994 oz. AGW **Subject:** Year of the Tiger **Shape:** Arc

| Date | Mintage | VF20 | XF40 | MS60 | MS63 | MS65 |
|---|---|---|---|---|---|---|
| 2010 | 6,600 | — | — | — | — | 975 |

**KM# 1916 200 YUAN**
15.55 g., 0.999 Gold 0.4994 oz. AGW **Subject:** Year of the Tiger **Shape:** Scalloped

| Date | Mintage | VF20 | XF40 | MS60 | MS63 | MS65 |
|---|---|---|---|---|---|---|
| 2010 | 8,000 | **PF65** 925 | | | | |

**KM# 1964 200 YUAN**
15.50 g., 0.999 Gold 0.4978 oz. AGW **Subject:** Year of the Rabbit **Shape:** Arc **Note:** Photo reduced.

| Date | Mintage | VF20 | XF40 | MS60 | MS63 | MS65 |
|---|---|---|---|---|---|---|
| 2011 | 6,600 | — | — | — | — | 975 |

**KM# 1965 200 YUAN**
15.55 g., 0.999 Gold 0.4994 oz. AGW, 27 mm. **Subject:** Year of the Rabbit **Shape:** Scallop

| Date | Mintage | VF20 | XF40 | MS60 | MS63 | MS65 |
|---|---|---|---|---|---|---|
| 2011 | 8,000 | **PF65** 925 | | | | |

**KM# 2013 200 YUAN**
15.55 g., 0.999 Gold 0.4994 oz. AGW **Subject:** Year of the Dragon **Shape:** Fan

| Date | Mintage | VF20 | XF40 | MS60 | MS63 | MS65 |
|---|---|---|---|---|---|---|
| 2012 | — | **PF65** 1,000 | | | | |

**KM# 2014 200 YUAN**
15.55 g., 0.999 Gold 0.4994 oz. AGW, 27 mm. **Subject:** Year of the Dragon **Shape:** Scalloped

| Date | Mintage | VF20 | XF40 | MS60 | MS63 | MS65 |
|---|---|---|---|---|---|---|
| 2012 | — | **PF65** 950 | | | | |

**KM# 1378 2000 YUAN**
155.52 g., 0.999 Gold 4.995 oz. AGW, 80 x 50 mm. **Subject:** Year of the Snake **Shape:** Rectangle **Note:** Prev. #Y1046.

| Date | Mintage | VF20 | XF40 | MS60 | MS63 | MS65 |
|---|---|---|---|---|---|---|
| 2001 | 118 | **PF65** 22,500 | | | | |

**KM# 1422 2000 YUAN**
155.52 g., 0.9999 Gold 4.9995 oz. AGW **Subject:** Year of the Horse **Shape:** Rectangle **Note:** Prev. #Y1152.

| Date | Mintage | VF20 | XF40 | MS60 | MS63 | MS65 |
|---|---|---|---|---|---|---|
| 2002 | 118 | **PF65** 22,500 | | | | |

**KM# 1483 2000 YUAN**
155.52 g., 0.9999 Gold 4.9995 oz. AGW **Subject:** Year of the Goat **Note:** Prev. #Y1163.

| Date | Mintage | VF20 | XF40 | MS60 | MS63 | MS65 |
|---|---|---|---|---|---|---|
| 2003 | 118 | **PF65** 22,500 | | | | |

### KM# 1552 2000 YUAN

155.18 g., 0.9999 Gold 4.9885 oz. AGW **Subject:** Year of the Monkey **Note:** Prev. #Y1170. Illustration reduced.

| Date | Mintage | VF20 | XF40 | MS60 | MS63 | MS65 |
|---|---|---|---|---|---|---|
| 2004 | 118 | **PF65** 22,500 | | | | |

### KM# 1605 2000 YUAN

155.55 g., 0.999 Gold 4.996 oz. AGW, 64 x 40 mm. **Subject:** Year of the Rooster **Obv:** Classical rooster **Rev:** Rooster, hen and chicks **Shape:** Rectangle **Note:** Photo reduced.

| Date | Mintage | VF20 | XF40 | MS60 | MS63 | MS65 |
|---|---|---|---|---|---|---|
| 2005 | 118 | **PF65** 22,500 | | | | |

### KM# 1678 2000 YUAN

155.55 g., 0.999 Gold 4.996 oz. AGW, 64 x 40 mm. **Subject:** Year of the Dog **Obv:** Classical dog **Rev:** Two dogs **Note:** Photo reduced.

| Date | Mintage | VF20 | XF40 | MS60 | MS63 | MS65 |
|---|---|---|---|---|---|---|
| 2006 | 118 | **PF65** 22,500 | | | | |

### KM# 1726 2000 YUAN

155.55 g., 0.999 Gold 4.996 oz. AGW, 64 x 40 mm. **Subject:** Year of the Pig **Obv:** Classical pig **Rev:** Sow and four piglets **Shape:** Rectangle

| Date | Mintage | VF20 | XF40 | MS60 | MS63 | MS65 |
|---|---|---|---|---|---|---|
| 2007 | 118 | **PF65** 22,500 | | | | |

### KM# 1840 2000 YUAN

155.00 g., 0.999 Gold 4.9784 oz. AGW, 64 x 40 mm. **Subject:** Year of the Rat **Shape:** Rectangle

| Date | Mintage | VF20 | XF40 | MS60 | MS63 | MS65 |
|---|---|---|---|---|---|---|
| 2008 | 118 | **PF65** 22,500 | | | | |

### KM# 1885 2000 YUAN

155.50 g., 0.999 Gold 4.9944 oz. AGW, 64x40 mm. **Subject:** Year of the Ox **Shape:** Rectangle

| Date | Mintage | VF20 | XF40 | MS60 | MS63 | MS65 |
|---|---|---|---|---|---|---|
| 2009 | 118 | **PF65** 22,500 | | | | |

### KM# 1913 2000 YUAN

155.20 g., 0.999 Gold 4.9848 oz. AGW, 64x40 mm. **Subject:** Year of the Tiger **Shape:** Rectangle

| Date | Mintage | VF20 | XF40 | MS60 | MS63 | MS65 |
|---|---|---|---|---|---|---|
| 2010 | 118 | **PF65** 20,000 | | | | |

### KM# 1962 2000 YUAN

155.50 g., 0.999 Gold 4.9944 oz. AGW, 64x40 mm. **Subject:** Year of the Rabbit **Shape:** Rectangle **Note:** Photo reduced.

| Date | Mintage | VF20 | XF40 | MS60 | MS63 | MS65 |
|---|---|---|---|---|---|---|
| 2011 | 118 | **PF65** 20,000 | | | | |

### KM# 1963 2000 YUAN

155.50 g., 0.999 Gold 4.9944 oz. AGW **Subject:** Year of the Rabbit **Rev:** Multicolor **Note:** Photo reduced.

| Date | Mintage | VF20 | XF40 | MS60 | MS63 | MS65 |
|---|---|---|---|---|---|---|
| 2011 | 1,800 | **PF65** 9,500 | | | | |

### KM# 2011 2000 YUAN

155.55 g., 0.999 Gold 4.996 oz. AGW, 64x40 mm. **Subject:** Year of the Dragon **Shape:** Rectangle

| Date | Mintage | VF20 | XF40 | MS60 | MS63 | MS65 |
|---|---|---|---|---|---|---|
| 2012 | — | **PF65** 20,000 | | | | |

### KM# 2012 2000 YUAN

155.55 g., 0.999 Gold 4.996 oz. AGW **Subject:** Year of the Dragon **Rev:** Colored Dragon

| Date | Mintage | VF20 | XF40 | MS60 | MS63 | MS65 |
|---|---|---|---|---|---|---|
| 2012 | — | **PF65** 9,500 | | | | |

### KM# 2031 2000 YUAN

155.55 g., 0.999 Gold 4.996 oz. AGW, 60 mm.

| Date | Mintage | VF20 | XF40 | MS60 | MS63 | MS65 |
|---|---|---|---|---|---|---|
| 2012 | — | **PF65** 11,000 | | | | |

### KM# 1381 10000 YUAN

1000.00 g., 0.999 Gold 32.1186 oz. AGW **Subject:** Year of the Snake **Shape:** Scalloped **Note:** Prev. #Y1047.

| Date | Mintage | VF20 | XF40 | MS60 | MS63 | MS65 |
|---|---|---|---|---|---|---|
| 2001 | 15 | **PF65** 125,000 | | | | |

### KM# 1427 10000 YUAN

1000.00 g., 0.9999 Gold 32.1475 oz. AGW **Subject:** Year of the Horse **Shape:** Scalloped **Note:** Prev. #Y1153.

| Date | Mintage | VF20 | XF40 | MS60 | MS63 | MS65 |
|---|---|---|---|---|---|---|
| 2002 | 15 | **PF65** 90,000 | | | | |

### KM# 1482 10000 YUAN

1000.00 g., 0.9999 Gold 32.1475 oz. AGW, 100 mm. **Subject:** Year of the Goat **Shape:** Scalloped **Note:** Prev. #Y1166.

| Date | Mintage | VF20 | XF40 | MS60 | MS63 | MS65 |
|---|---|---|---|---|---|---|
| 2003 | 15 | **PF65** 75,000 | | | | |

### KM# 1550 10000 YUAN

1000.00 g., 0.9999 Gold 32.1475 oz. AGW, 100 mm. **Subject:** Year of the Monkey **Shape:** Scalloped **Note:** Prev. #Y1171.

| Date | Mintage | VF20 | XF40 | MS60 | MS63 | MS65 |
|---|---|---|---|---|---|---|
| 2004 | 15 | **PF65** 90,000 | | | | |

### KM# 1604 10000 YUAN

1000.00 g., 0.999 Gold 32.1186 oz. AGW, 100 mm. **Obv:** Classical rooster **Rev:** Rooster strutting **Edge:** Scalloped **Note:** Photo reduced.

| Date | Mintage | VF20 | XF40 | MS60 | MS63 | MS65 |
|---|---|---|---|---|---|---|
| 2005 | 15 | **PF65** 75,000 | | | | |

**KM# 1727 10000 YUAN**
1000.00 g., 0.999 Gold 32.1186 oz. AGW, 100 mm. **Subject:** Year of the Pig **Obv:** Classical pig **Rev:** Three pigs **Shape:** Scalloped

| Date | Mintage | VF20 | XF40 | MS60 | MS63 | MS65 |
|---|---|---|---|---|---|---|
| 2007 | 118 | PF65 70,000 | | | | |

**KM# 1841 10000 YUAN**
1000.00 g., 0.999 Gold 32.1186 oz. AGW, 100 mm. **Subject:** Year of the Rat **Shape:** Scalloped

| Date | Mintage | VF20 | XF40 | MS60 | MS63 | MS65 |
|---|---|---|---|---|---|---|
| 2008 | 118 | PF65 70,000 | | | | |

**KM# 1912 10000 YUAN**
1000.00 g., 0.999 Gold 32.1186 oz. AGW, 100 mm. **Subject:** Year of the Tiger **Shape:** Scalloped

| Date | Mintage | VF20 | XF40 | MS60 | MS63 | MS65 |
|---|---|---|---|---|---|---|
| 2010 | 118 | PF65 68,000 | | | | |

**KM# 1961 10000 YUAN**
1000.00 g., 0.999 Gold 32.1186 oz. AGW, 100 mm. **Subject:** Year of the Rabbit **Shape:** Scalloped **Note:** Photo reduced.

| Date | Mintage | VF20 | XF40 | MS60 | MS63 | MS65 |
|---|---|---|---|---|---|---|
| 2011 | 118 | PF65 68,000 | | | | |

**KM# 2010 10000 YUAN**
1000.00 g., 0.999 Gold 32.1186 oz. AGW, 100 mm. **Subject:** Year of the Dragon

| Date | Mintage | VF20 | XF40 | MS60 | MS63 | MS65 |
|---|---|---|---|---|---|---|
| 2012 | — | PF65 75,000 | | | | |

**KM# 1728 100000 YUAN**
10000.00 g., 0.999 Gold 321.1857 oz. AGW, 180 mm. **Subject:** Year of the Pig **Obv:** Classical pig **Rev:** Sow with four pigletts sucking

| Date | Mintage | VF20 | XF40 | MS60 | MS63 | MS65 |
|---|---|---|---|---|---|---|
| 2007 | 18 | PF65 600,000 | | | | |

**KM# 1842 100000 YUAN**
10000.00 g., 0.999 Gold 321.1857 oz. AGW, 180 mm.

| Date | Mintage | VF20 | XF40 | MS60 | MS63 | MS65 |
|---|---|---|---|---|---|---|
| 2008 | 18 | PF65 600,000 | | | | |

**KM# 1886 100000 YUAN**
1000.00 g., 0.999 Gold 32.1186 oz. AGW, 180 mm. **Subject:** Year of the Ox

| Date | Mintage | VF20 | XF40 | MS60 | MS63 | MS65 |
|---|---|---|---|---|---|---|
| 2009 | 118 | PF65 70,000 | | | | |

**KM# 1887 100000 YUAN**
10000.00 g., 0.999 Gold 321.1857 oz. AGW, 180 mm. **Subject:** Year of the Ox

| Date | Mintage | VF20 | XF40 | MS60 | MS63 | MS65 |
|---|---|---|---|---|---|---|
| 2009 | — | PF65 700,000 | | | | |

**KM# 1911 100000 YUAN**
10000.00 g., 0.999 Gold 321.1857 oz. AGW, 180 mm. **Subject:** Year of the Tiger

| Date | Mintage | VF20 | XF40 | MS60 | MS63 | MS65 |
|---|---|---|---|---|---|---|
| 2010 | 18 | PF65 700,000 | | | | |

**KM# 1960 100000 YUAN**
10000.00 g., 0.999 Gold 321.1857 oz. AGW, 180 mm. **Subject:** Year of the Rabbit **Note:** Photo reduced.

| Date | Mintage | VF20 | XF40 | MS60 | MS63 | MS65 |
|---|---|---|---|---|---|---|
| 2011 | 18 | PF65 700,000 | | | | |

**KM# 2009 100000 YUAN**
10000.00 g., 0.999 Gold 321.1857 oz. AGW, 180 mm. **Subject:** Year of the Dragon

| Date | Mintage | VF20 | XF40 | MS60 | MS63 | MS65 |
|---|---|---|---|---|---|---|
| 2012 | — | PF65 700,000 | | | | |

## PALLADIUM BULLION COINAGE

Panda Series

**KM# A1531 100 YUAN**
15.56 g., 0.999 Palladium 0.4997 oz. APW, 14 mm. **Rev:** Panda walking with cub

| Date | Mintage | VF20 | XF40 | MS60 | MS63 | MS65 |
|---|---|---|---|---|---|---|
| 2004 | 8,000 | PF65 500 | | | | |

**KM# 1590 100 YUAN**
15.55 g., 0.999 Palladium 0.4994 oz. APW, 30 mm. **Obv:** Temple of Heaven **Rev:** Panda cub and mom seated in bamboo

| Date | Mintage | VF20 | XF40 | MS60 | MS63 | MS65 |
|---|---|---|---|---|---|---|
| 2005 | 8,000 | PF65 530 | | | | |

## PLATINUM BULLION COINAGE

Panda Series

**KM# 1470 50 YUAN**
1.55 g., 0.9995 Platinum 0.0498 oz. APW, 14.03 mm. **Obv:** Temple of Heaven, incuse legend **Rev:** Panda standing facing eating bamboo **Edge:** Reeded

| Date | Mintage | VF20 | XF40 | MS60 | MS63 | MS65 |
|---|---|---|---|---|---|---|
| 2003 | 50,000 | PF65 135 | | | | |

**KM# 1532 50 YUAN**
1.45 g., 0.9995 Platinum 0.0466 oz. APW, 14 mm. **Obv:** Temple of Heaven, incuse legend **Rev:** Panda standing facing with cub **Edge:** Reeded

| Date | Mintage | VF20 | XF40 | MS60 | MS63 | MS65 |
|---|---|---|---|---|---|---|
| 2004 | 50,000 | PF65 135 | | | | |

**KM# 1415 100 YUAN**
3.11 g., 0.9995 Platinum 0.0999 oz. APW, 18 mm. **Subject:** Panda Coinage 20th Anniversary **Obv:** Seated panda design of 1982 **Rev:** Walking panda design of 2002 **Edge:** Reeded **Note:** Prev. Y#1115.

| Date | Mintage | VF20 | XF40 | MS60 | MS63 | MS65 |
|---|---|---|---|---|---|---|
| 2002 | 20,000 | PF65 250 | | | | |

**KM# 1591 100 YUAN**
3.11 g., 0.999 Platinum 0.0999 oz. APW, 18 mm. **Obv:** Temple of Heaven **Rev:** Panda cub and mom seated in bamboo

| Date | Mintage | VF20 | XF40 | MS60 | MS63 | MS65 |
|---|---|---|---|---|---|---|
| 2005 | 30,000 | PF65 200 | | | | |

# TAIWAN

The Republic of China, comprising Taiwan (an island located 90 miles (145 km.) off the southeastern coast of mainland China), the offshore islands of Quemoy and Matsu and nearby islets of the Pescadores chain, has an area of 14,000 sq. mi. (35,980 sq. km.) and a population of 20.2 million. Capital: Taipei. During the past decade, manufacturing has replaced agriculture in importance. Fruits, vegetables, plywood, textile yarns and fabrics and clothing are exported.

The coins of Nationalist China do not carry A.D. dating, but are dated according to the year of the republic, which was established in 1911. However, republican years are added to 1911 to find the western year. Thus republican year 90 plus 1911 equals Gregorian calendar year 2001AD.

## REPUBLIC

## STANDARD COINAGE

**Y# 550 1/2 YUAN**
3.00 g., Bronze, 18 mm. **Obv:** Orchid **Rev:** Value and Chinese symbols **Edge:** Plain

| Date | Mintage | F12 | VF20 | XF40 | MS60 | MS63 |
|---|---|---|---|---|---|---|
| 90(2001) | — | PF60 10.00 | | | | |
| 92(2003) | — | PF60 10.00 | | | | |
| 92(2003) | — | — | — | 0.30 | 1.00 | 1.25 |
| 93(2004) | — | — | — | 0.30 | 1.00 | 1.25 |

**Y# 551 YUAN**

3.80 g., Aluminum-Bronze, 20 mm. **Obv:** Bust of Chiang Kai-shek left **Rev:** Chinese value in center, 1 below **Edge:** Reeded

| Date | Mintage | F12 | VF20 | XF40 | MS60 | MS63 |
|---|---|---|---|---|---|---|
| 90(2001) | — | PF60 12.50 | | | | |
| 92(2003) | — | — | — | 0.15 | 0.30 | 0.45 |
| 92(2003) | — | PF60 12.50 | | | | |
| 94 (2005) | — | — | — | 0.15 | 0.30 | 0.45 |
| 95(2006) | — | — | — | 0.15 | 0.30 | 0.45 |
| 96(2007) | — | — | — | 0.15 | 0.30 | 0.45 |
| 97(2008) | — | — | — | 0.15 | 0.30 | 0.45 |
| 98(2009) | — | — | — | 0.15 | 0.30 | 0.45 |
| 99(2010) | — | — | — | 0.15 | 0.30 | 0.45 |
| 100(2011) | — | — | — | 0.15 | 0.30 | 0.45 |
| 101(2012) | — | — | — | 0.15 | 0.30 | 0.45 |
| 102(2013) | — | — | — | 0.15 | — | 0.30 |

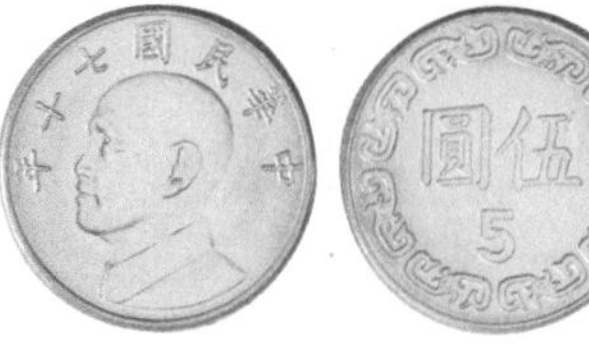

**Y# 552 5 YUAN**

4.40 g., Copper-Nickel, 22 mm. **Obv:** Bust of Chiang Kai-shek left **Rev:** Chinese value in center, 5 below **Edge:** Reeded

| Date | Mintage | F12 | VF20 | XF40 | MS60 | MS63 |
|---|---|---|---|---|---|---|
| 90(2001) | — | PF60 12.50 | | | | |
| 92(2003) | — | — | — | 0.25 | 0.50 | 0.75 |
| 92(2003) | — | PF60 12.50 | | | | |
| 97(2008) | — | — | — | 0.25 | 0.50 | 0.75 |
| 100(2011) | — | — | — | 0.25 | 0.50 | 0.75 |
| 101 (2012) | — | — | — | 0.25 | 0.50 | 0.75 |
| 102(2013) | — | — | — | 0.25 | 0.50 | 0.75 |

**Y# 553 10 YUAN**

7.50 g., Copper-Nickel, 26 mm. **Obv:** Bust of Chiang Kai-shek left **Rev:** Chinese value in center, 10 below **Edge:** Reeded

| Date | Mintage | F12 | VF20 | XF40 | MS60 | MS63 |
|---|---|---|---|---|---|---|
| 90(2001) | — | PF60 15.00 | | | | |
| 92(2003) | — | — | 0.25 | 0.45 | 0.75 | 1.00 |
| 92(2003) | — | PF60 15.00 | | | | |
| 93(2004) | — | — | — | 0.45 | 0.75 | 1.00 |
| 94(2005) | — | — | — | 0.45 | 0.75 | 1.00 |
| 95(2006) | — | — | — | 0.45 | 0.75 | 1.00 |
| 96(2007) | — | — | — | 0.45 | 0.75 | 1.00 |
| 96(2007) | — | PF60 15.00 | | | | |
| 97(2008) | — | — | — | 0.45 | 0.75 | 1.00 |
| 98(2009) | — | — | — | 0.45 | 0.75 | 1.00 |
| 99(2010) | — | — | — | 0.45 | 0.75 | 1.00 |

**Y# 567 10 YUAN**

7.43 g., Copper-Nickel, 26 mm. **Subject:** 90th Anniversary of the Republic **Obv:** Bust of Sun Yat-sen facing **Rev:** Holographic design and denomination **Edge:** Reeded

| Date | Mintage | F12 | VF20 | XF40 | MS60 | MS63 |
|---|---|---|---|---|---|---|
| 90 (2001) | 30,000,000 | — | — | — | 2.50 | 3.00 |

**Y# 572 10 YUAN**

7.50 g., Copper-Nickel, 26 mm. **Subject:** Chiang Ching-kuo, president **Obv:** Portriat facing **Rev:** Two legends in latent format, large value below

| Date | Mintage | F12 | VF20 | XF40 | MS60 | MS63 |
|---|---|---|---|---|---|---|
| 100 (2010) | — | — | — | — | 2.00 | 3.00 |

**Y# 573 10 YUAN**

7.50 g., Copper-Nickel, 26 mm. **Subject:** Chiang Wei-shui **Obv:** Portrait facing **Rev:** Two legends as latent images, large value below

| Date | Mintage | F12 | VF20 | XF40 | MS60 | MS63 |
|---|---|---|---|---|---|---|
| 100 (2010) | — | — | — | — | 2.00 | 3.00 |

**Y# 574 10 YUAN**

7.50 g., Copper-Nickel, 26 mm. **Obv:** Sun Yat-sen bust facing **Rev:** Two legends as latent images, large value below

| Date | Mintage | F12 | VF20 | XF40 | MS60 | MS63 |
|---|---|---|---|---|---|---|
| 100 (2011) | — | — | — | — | 2.00 | 3.00 |
| 101 (2012) | — | — | — | — | 2.00 | 3.00 |
| 102 (2013) | — | — | — | — | 2.00 | 3.00 |

**Y# 565 20 YUAN**

8.50 g., Bi-Metallic Copper-Nickel center in Aluminum-Bronze ring., 26.85 mm. **Subject:** Mona Rudao, Sediq chieftain **Obv:** Male portrait **Rev:** Three boats **Edge:** Reeded

| Date | Mintage | F12 | VF20 | XF40 | MS60 | MS63 |
|---|---|---|---|---|---|---|
| 90(2001) | — | — | — | — | 3.50 | 4.50 |
| 90(2001) | — | PF60 18.00 | | | | |
| 92(2003) | — | — | — | — | 3.50 | 4.50 |
| 92(2003) | — | PF60 18.00 | | | | |
| 101(2012) | — | — | — | — | 3.50 | 4.50 |
| 101(2012) | — | PF65 18.00 | | | | |
| 102(2013) | — | — | — | — | 3.50 | 4.50 |
| 102(2013) | — | PF65 18.00 | | | | |

**Y# 568 50 YUAN**

10.00 g., Aluminum-Bronze, 28 mm. **Obv:** Bust **Rev:** Denomination above latent image denomination **Edge:** Reeding and denomination

| Date | Mintage | F12 | VF20 | XF40 | MS60 | MS63 |
|---|---|---|---|---|---|---|
| 90-2001 | — | PF60 20.00 | | | | |
| 91-2002 | — | — | — | — | 7.50 | 10.00 |
| 92-2003 | — | — | — | — | 7.50 | 10.00 |
| 92-2003 | — | PF60 20.00 | | | | |
| 93-2004 | — | — | — | — | 7.50 | 10.00 |
| 94-2005 | — | — | — | — | 7.50 | 10.00 |
| 95-2006 | — | — | — | — | 7.50 | 10.00 |
| 95-2006 | — | PF60 20.00 | | | | |
| 96-2007 | — | — | — | — | 7.50 | 10.00 |
| 97-2008 | — | — | — | — | 7.50 | 10.00 |
| 101-2012 | — | — | — | — | 7.50 | 10.00 |
| 101-2012 | — | PF65 20.00 | | | | |
| 102-2013 | — | — | — | — | 7.50 | 10.00 |
| 102-2013 | — | PF65 20.00 | | | | |

**Y# 570 50 YUAN**

15.57 g., 0.999 Silver 0.500 oz. ASW, 33 mm. **Subject:** World Cup Baseball **Obv:** Player at bat with ball background **Rev:** Mount Jade above denomination **Edge:** Reeded

| Date | Mintage | F12 | VF20 | XF40 | MS60 | MS63 |
|---|---|---|---|---|---|---|
| 90(2001) | 130,000 | — | — | — | 25.00 | 27.50 |

**Y# 569 50 YUAN**

15.57 g., 0.999 Silver 0.500 oz. ASW, 33 mm. **Subject:** 90th Anniversary of the Republic **Obv:** Portrait of Sun Yat-sen **Rev:** Latent image above denomination **Edge:** Reeded

| Date | Mintage | F12 | VF20 | XF40 | MS60 | MS63 |
|---|---|---|---|---|---|---|
| 90(2001) | 230,000 | — | — | — | 25.00 | 27.50 |

**Y# 571 50 YUAN**

31.10 g., 0.999 Silver 0.999 oz. ASW, 38 mm. **Subject:** Third National Expressway **Obv:** Multicolor island map **Rev:** Kao Ping Hsi bridge **Edge:** Reeded

| Date | Mintage | F12 | VF20 | XF40 | MS60 | MS63 |
|---|---|---|---|---|---|---|
| 93-2004 | 20,000 | — | — | — | 45.00 | 50.00 |

**Y# 578 100 YUAN**

31.14 g., 0.999 Silver 1.000 oz. ASW, 38 mm. **Subject:** Year of the Rooster

| Date | Mintage | F12 | VF20 | XF40 | MS60 | MS63 |
|---|---|---|---|---|---|---|
| 2005 | 150,000 | PF63 130 | PF65 150 | | | |

**Y# 579 100 YUAN**

31.14 g., 0.999 Silver 1.000 oz. ASW, 38 mm. **Subject:** Asian International Stamp Exhibition 2005, Taipei

| Date | Mintage | F12 | VF20 | XF40 | MS60 | MS63 |
|---|---|---|---|---|---|---|
| 2005 | 25,000 | PF63 100 | PF65 115 | | | |

**Y# 580 100 YUAN**

31.14 g., 0.999 Silver 1.000 oz. ASW **Subject:** Lunar Year of the Dog

| Date | Mintage | F12 | VF20 | XF40 | MS60 | MS63 |
|---|---|---|---|---|---|---|
| 2006 | 150,000 | PF63 125 | PF65 140 | | | |

### Y# 581 100 YUAN

31.14 g., 0.999 Silver 1.000 oz. ASW, 38 mm. **Subject:** Taiwan High Speed Rail

| Date | Mintage | F12 | VF20 | XF40 | MS60 | MS63 |
|---|---|---|---|---|---|---|
| 2006 | 30,000 | PF63 100 | PF65 115 | | | |

### Y# 582 100 YUAN

31.14 g., 0.999 Silver 1.000 oz. ASW **Subject:** Lunar Year of the Pig

| Date | Mintage | F12 | VF20 | XF40 | MS60 | MS63 |
|---|---|---|---|---|---|---|
| 2007 | 150,000 | PF63 125 | PF65 140 | | | |

### Y# 583 100 YUAN

31.14 g., 0.999 Silver 1.000 oz. ASW **Subject:** Lunar Year of the Rat

| Date | Mintage | F12 | VF20 | XF40 | MS60 | MS63 |
|---|---|---|---|---|---|---|
| 2008 | 150,000 | PF63 125 | PF65 140 | | | |

### Y# 584 100 YUAN

31.14 g., 0.999 Silver 1.000 oz. ASW, 38 mm. **Subject:** 2008 Asian International Stamp Exposition, Taipai

| Date | Mintage | F12 | VF20 | XF40 | MS60 | MS63 |
|---|---|---|---|---|---|---|
| 2008 | 20,000 | PF63 100 | PF65 115 | | | |

### Y# 587 100 YUAN

31.14 g., 0.999 Silver 1.000 oz. ASW, 38 mm. **Subject:** Lunar Year of the Buffalo

| Date | Mintage | F12 | VF20 | XF40 | MS60 | MS63 |
|---|---|---|---|---|---|---|
| 2009 | 150,000 | PF63 125 | PF65 140 | | | |

### Y# 588 100 YUAN

31.14 g., 0.999 Silver 1.000 oz. ASW, 38 mm. **Subject:** Lunar Year of the Tiger

| Date | Mintage | F12 | VF20 | XF40 | MS60 | MS63 |
|---|---|---|---|---|---|---|
| 2010 | 150,000 | PF63 130 | PF65 150 | | | |

### Y# 589 100 YUAN

31.14 g., 0.999 Silver 1.000 oz. ASW, 38 mm. **Subject:** Lunar Year of the Rabbit

| Date | Mintage | F12 | VF20 | XF40 | MS60 | MS63 |
|---|---|---|---|---|---|---|
| 2011 | 150,000 | PF63 125 | PF65 140 | | | |

### Y# 590 100 YUAN

31.14 g., 0.999 Silver 1.000 oz. ASW, 38 mm. **Subject:** 100th Anniversary of the Republic of China

| Date | Mintage | F12 | VF20 | XF40 | MS60 | MS63 |
|---|---|---|---|---|---|---|
| 2011 | 120,000 | PF63 90.00 | PF65 110 | | | |

### Y# 591 100 YUAN

31.14 g., 0.999 Silver 1.000 oz. ASW, 38 mm. **Subject:** Lunar Year of the Water Dragon

| Date | Mintage | F12 | VF20 | XF40 | MS60 | MS63 |
|---|---|---|---|---|---|---|
| 2012 | 150,000 | PF63 125 | PF65 140 | | | |

### Y# 576 200 YUAN

31.14 g., 0.999 Silver 1.000 oz. ASW, 38 mm. **Subject:** Inauguration of the President of the People's Republic of China

| Date | Mintage | F12 | VF20 | XF40 | MS60 | MS63 |
|---|---|---|---|---|---|---|
| 2004 | 65,000 | PF63 100 | PF65 115 | | | |

### Y# 585 200 YUAN

31.14 g., 0.999 Silver 1.000 oz. ASW, 38 mm. **Subject:** Inauguration of the President and Vice President of the People's Republic of China

| Date | Mintage | F12 | VF20 | XF40 | MS60 | MS63 |
|---|---|---|---|---|---|---|
| 2008 | 120,000 | PF63 100 | PF65 115 | | | |

### Y# 592 200 YUAN

31.14 g., 0.925 Silver 0.9259 oz. ASW, 38 mm. **Subject:** Election of the President of the People's Republic of China

| Date | Mintage | F12 | VF20 | XF40 | MS60 | MS63 |
|---|---|---|---|---|---|---|
| 2012 | — | PF63 100 | PF65 115 | | | |

### Y# 577 2000 YUAN

31.11 g., 0.9999 Gold 1.000 oz. AGW, 33 mm. **Subject:** Inauguration of the President of the People's Republic of China

| Date | Mintage | F12 | VF20 | XF40 | MS60 | MS63 |
|---|---|---|---|---|---|---|
| 2004 | — | PF63 1,500 | PF65 1,900 | | | |

### Y# 586 2000 YUAN

31.11 g., 0.9999 Gold 1.000 oz. AGW, 33 mm. **Subject:** Inauguration of the President and Vice President of The People's Republic of China

| Date | Mintage | F12 | VF20 | XF40 | MS60 | MS63 |
|---|---|---|---|---|---|---|
| 2008 | 60,000 | PF63 1,750 | PF65 2,000 | | | |

### Y# 593 2000 YUAN

31.11 g., 0.9999 Gold 1.000 oz. AGW, 33 mm. **Subject:** Election of the President of the People's Republic of China

| Date | Mintage | F12 | VF20 | XF40 | MS60 | MS63 |
|---|---|---|---|---|---|---|
| 2012 | — | PF63 1,750 | PF65 2,000 | | | |

## MINT SETS

| KM# | Date | Mintage | Identification | Issue Price | Mkt Val |
|---|---|---|---|---|---|
| MS9 | 92(2003) (6) | — | Y550-553, 565, 568 plus C-N Year of the Goat medal | — | 20.00 |

## PROOF SETS

| KM# | Date | Mintage | Identification | Issue Price | Mkt Val |
|---|---|---|---|---|---|
| PS10 | 90(2001) (6) | 210,000 | Y#550-553, 565, 568 plus medal | 29.40 | 90.00 |
| PS12 | 92(2003) (6) | — | Y550-553, 565, 568 plus silver Year of the Goat Medal | — | 100 |

# COLOMBIA

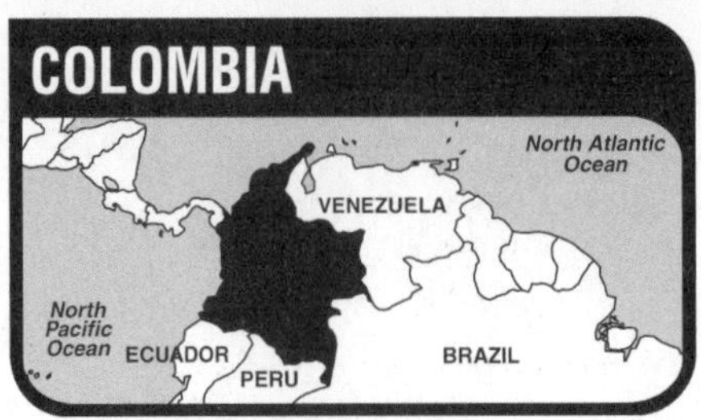


The Republic of Colombia, in the northwestern corner of South America, has an area of 440,831 sq. mi. (1,138,910 sq. km.) and a population of*42.3 million. Capital: Bogota. The economy is primarily agricultural with a mild, rich coffee being the chief crop. Colombia has the world's largest platinum deposits and important reserves of coal, iron ore, petroleum and limestone; other precious metals and emeralds are also mined. Coffee, crude oil, bananas, sugar and emeralds are exported.

## REPUBLIC

## DECIMAL COINAGE

100 Centavos = 1 Peso

### KM# 282.2 20 PESOS

3.60 g., Aluminum-Bronze, 20.25 mm. **Obv:** Flagged arms, 68 beads circle around the rim **Rev:** Denomination within wreath

| Date | Mintage | VF20 | XF40 | MS60 | MS63 | MS65 |
|---|---|---|---|---|---|---|
| 2003 | 15,900,000 | — | — | 0.25 | 0.50 | 0.75 |

### KM# 294 20 PESOS

2.00 g., Brass, 17.2 mm. **Obv:** Head of Simon Bolivar left **Rev:** Value **Edge:** Reeded

| Date | Mintage | VF20 | XF40 | MS60 | MS63 | MS65 |
|---|---|---|---|---|---|---|
| 2004 | 22,700,000 | — | — | 0.15 | 0.25 | 0.50 |
| 2005 | 56,100,000 | — | — | 0.15 | 0.25 | 0.50 |
| 2006 | 63,012,500 | — | — | 0.15 | 0.25 | 0.50 |
| 2007 | 87,300,000 | — | — | 0.15 | 0.25 | 0.50 |
| 2008 | 5,850,000 | — | — | 0.20 | 0.30 | 0.60 |

### KM# 283.2 50 PESOS

4.60 g., Copper-Nickel-Zinc, 21.8 mm. **Obv:** National arms, date below **Rev:** Denomination within wreath, 72 beads circle around rim **Edge:** Reeded

| Date | Mintage | VF20 | XF40 | MS60 | MS63 | MS65 |
|---|---|---|---|---|---|---|
| 2003 | 59,842,620 | — | 0.30 | 0.50 | 0.75 | 1.00 |
| 2004 | 51,700,000 | — | 0.30 | 0.50 | 0.75 | 1.00 |
| 2005 | 47,200,000 | — | 0.30 | 0.50 | 0.75 | 1.00 |
| 2006 | 22,000,000 | — | 0.30 | 0.50 | 0.75 | 1.00 |
| 2007 | 14,500,000 | — | 0.30 | 0.50 | 0.75 | 1.00 |
| 2008 | 67,500,000 | — | 0.30 | 0.50 | 0.75 | 1.00 |

### KM# 283.2a 50 PESOS

Stainless Steel, 21.8 mm. **Obv:** National Arms, date below **Rev:** Denomination within wreath, 72 beads circle around rim **Edge:** Reeded

| Date | Mintage | VF20 | XF40 | MS60 | MS63 | MS65 |
|---|---|---|---|---|---|---|
| 2007 | 14,824,000 | — | 0.30 | 0.50 | 0.75 | 1.00 |
| 2008 | 67,500,000 | — | 0.30 | 0.50 | 0.75 | 1.00 |
| 2009 | 3,000,000 | — | 0.30 | 0.50 | 0.85 | 1.20 |
| 2010 | 55,100,000 | — | 0.30 | 0.50 | 0.75 | 1.00 |
| 2011 | 19,100,000 | — | 0.30 | 0.50 | 0.75 | 1.00 |
| 2012 | 22,300,000 | — | 0.30 | 0.50 | 0.75 | 1.00 |

### KM# 295 50 PESOS

2.00 g., Nickel Plated Steel, 17 mm. **Obv:** Value at center **Rev:** Spectacled bear (Tremarctos ornatus)

| Date | Mintage | VF20 | XF40 | MS60 | MS63 | MS65 |
|---|---|---|---|---|---|---|
| 2012 | 30,816,000 | — | 0.30 | 0.50 | 0.75 | 1.00 |
| 2013 | — | — | 0.30 | 0.50 | 0.75 | 1.00 |

### KM# 285.2 100 PESOS

5.31 g., Aluminum-Bronze, 23 mm. **Obv:** Flagged arms above date **Rev:** Denomination within wreath, numerals 6mm tall **Edge:** Segmented reeding and lettered **Edge Lettering:** CIEN PESOS (twice) **Note:** Edge varieties exist.

| Date | Mintage | VF20 | XF40 | MS60 | MS63 | MS65 |
|---|---|---|---|---|---|---|
| 2006 | 59,000,000 | — | 0.50 | 0.75 | 1.00 | 1.50 |
| 2007 | 55,000,000 | — | 0.50 | 0.75 | 1.00 | 1.50 |
| 2008 | 120,200,000 | — | 0.50 | 0.75 | 1.00 | 1.50 |
| 2009 | 41,800,000 | — | 0.50 | 0.75 | 1.00 | 1.50 |
| 2010 | 85,400,000 | — | 0.50 | 0.75 | 1.00 | 1.50 |
| 2011 | 108,500,000 | — | 0.50 | 0.75 | 1.00 | 1.50 |
| 2012 | 20,000,000 | — | 0.50 | 0.75 | 1.00 | 1.50 |

### KM# 296 100 PESOS

3.24 g., Brass Plated Steel, 20.3 mm. **Obv:** Value at center **Rev:** Colombian fruit frailejon

| Date | Mintage | VF20 | XF40 | MS60 | MS63 | MS65 |
|---|---|---|---|---|---|---|
| 2012 | — | — | — | — | 1.00 | 1.50 |
| 2013 | — | — | — | — | 1.00 | 1.25 |

### KM# 287 200 PESOS

7.08 g., Copper-Nickel-Zinc, 24.4 mm. **Obv:** Denomination within lined circle, date below **Rev:** Quimbaya artwork **Edge Lettering:** MOTIVO QUIMBAYA - 200 PESOS

| Date | Mintage | VF20 | XF40 | MS60 | MS63 | MS65 |
|---|---|---|---|---|---|---|
| 2003 | 26,600,000 | — | 0.50 | 0.75 | 1.00 | 1.50 |
| 2004 | 31,200,000 | — | 0.50 | 0.75 | 1.00 | 1.50 |
| 2005 | 49,700,000 | — | 0.50 | 0.75 | 1.00 | 1.50 |
| 2006 | 75,462,500 | — | 0.50 | 0.75 | 1.00 | 1.50 |
| 2007 | 85,000,000 | — | 0.50 | 0.75 | 1.00 | 1.50 |
| 2008 | 110,400,000 | — | 0.50 | 0.75 | 1.00 | 1.50 |
| 2009 | 42,200,000 | — | 0.50 | 0.75 | 1.00 | 1.50 |
| 2010 | 85,600,000 | — | 0.50 | 0.75 | 1.00 | 1.50 |
| 2011 | 104,000,000 | — | 0.50 | 0.75 | 1.00 | 1.50 |
| 2012 | 45,000,000 | — | 0.50 | 0.75 | 1.00 | 1.50 |

### KM# 297 200 PESOS

4.61 g., Copper-Nickel-Zinc, 22.4 mm. **Obv:** Value at center **Rev:** Scarlet macaw (Ara macao)

| Date | Mintage | VF20 | XF40 | MS60 | MS63 | MS65 |
|---|---|---|---|---|---|---|
| 2012 | 55,000,000 | — | 0.50 | 0.75 | 1.00 | 1.50 |
| 2013 | — | — | 0.50 | 0.75 | 1.00 | 1.50 |

### KM# 286 500 PESOS

7.14 g., Bi-Metallic Aluminum-Bronze center in Copper-Zinc-Nickel ring, 23.7 mm. **Obv:** Guacari tree within circle **Rev:** Denomination within circle, date below **Edge:** Segmented reeding

| Date | Mintage | VF20 | XF40 | MS60 | MS63 | MS65 |
|---|---|---|---|---|---|---|
| 2002 | 38,800,000 | — | 0.75 | 1.25 | 2.00 | 3.00 |
| 2003 | 26,410,000 | — | 0.75 | 1.25 | 2.00 | 3.00 |
| 2004 | 90,454,000 | — | 0.75 | 1.25 | 2.00 | 3.00 |
| 2005 | 97,664,000 | — | 0.75 | 1.25 | 2.00 | 3.00 |
| 2006 | 70,700,000 | — | 0.75 | 1.25 | 2.00 | 3.00 |
| 2007 | 109,624,000 | — | 0.75 | 1.25 | 2.00 | 3.00 |
| 2008 | 132,400,000 | — | 0.75 | 1.25 | 2.00 | 3.00 |
| 2009 | 39,700,000 | — | 0.75 | 1.25 | 2.00 | 3.00 |
| 2010 | 35,800,000 | — | 0.75 | 1.25 | 2.00 | 3.00 |
| 2011 | 76,200,000 | — | 0.75 | 1.25 | 2.00 | 3.00 |
| 2012 | 40,000,000 | — | 0.75 | 1.25 | 2.00 | 3.00 |

### KM# 298 500 PESOS

7.14 g., Bi-Metallic Aluminum-Bronze center in Copper-Nickel-Zinc ring, 23.7 mm. **Obv:** Value at center **Rev:** Glass frog (Hyalinobatrachium pellucidum) **Edge:** Segmented reeding

| Date | Mintage | VF20 | XF40 | MS60 | MS63 | MS65 |
|---|---|---|---|---|---|---|
| 2012 | 22,738,000 | — | 0.75 | 1.25 | 2.00 | 3.00 |

### KM# 299 1000 PESOS

9.95 g., Bi-Metallic Copper-Nickel-Zinc center in Aluminum-Bronze ring, 26.7 mm. **Obv:** Value at center with waves below **Rev:** Loggerhead sea turtle (Caretta caretta) and sea waves design **Edge:** Reeded & Security

| Date | Mintage | VF20 | XF40 | MS60 | MS63 | MS65 |
|---|---|---|---|---|---|---|
| 2012 | — | — | — | 1.50 | 3.00 | 5.00 |
| 2013 | — | — | — | 1.00 | 2.00 | 3.00 |

# COMOROS

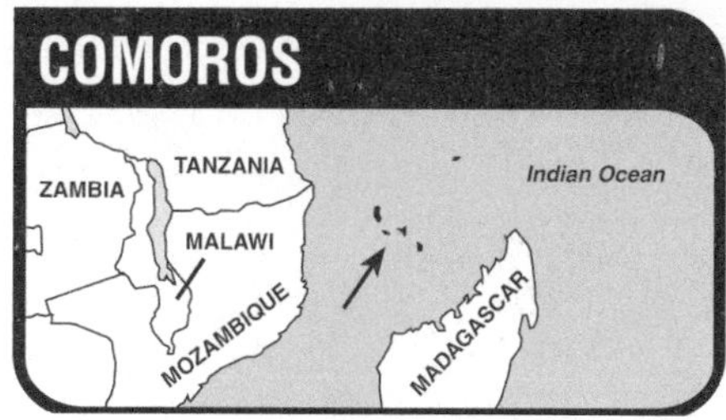


The Federal Islamic Republic of the Comoros, a volcanic archipelago located in the Mozambique Channel of the Indian Ocean 300 miles (483 km.) northwest of Madagascar, has an area of 719 sq. mi. (2,171 sq. km.) and a population of *714,000. Capital: Moroni. The economy of the islands is based on agriculture. There are practically no mineral resources. Vanilla, essence for perfumes, copra, and sisal are exported.

Ancient Phoenician traders were probably the first visitors to the Comoro Islands, but the first detailed knowledge of the area was gathered by Arab sailors. Arab dominion and culture were firmly established when the Portuguese, Dutch, and French arrived in the 16th century. In 1843 a Malagasy ruler ceded the island of Mayotte to France; the other three principal islands of the archipelago-Anjouan, Moheli, and Grand Comore came under French protection in 1886. The islands were joined administratively with Madagascar in 1912. The Comoros became partially autonomous, with the status of a French overseas territory, in 1946, and achieved complete internal autonomy in 1961. On Dec. 31, 1975, after 133 years of French association, the Comoro Islands became the independent Republic of the Comoros.

Mayotte retained the option of determining its future ties and in 1976 voted to remain French. Its present status is that of a French Territorial Collectivity. French currency now circulates there.

**MINT MARKS**

(a) - Paris, privy marks only
A - Paris

**MONETARY SYSTEM**

100 Centimes = 1 Franc

## FEDERAL ISLAMIC REPUBLIC

### BANQUE CENTRAL COINAGE

**KM# 19 10 FRANCS**
2.40 g., Steel, 17 mm. **Obv:** Crescent and four stars **Rev:** Value

| Date | Mintage | VF20 | XF40 | MS60 | MS63 | MS65 |
|---|---|---|---|---|---|---|
| 2001 (a) | — | — | — | — | 7.00 | 12.00 |

**KM# 14a 25 FRANCS**
3.97 g., Nickel Plated Steel, 20 mm. **Series:** F.A.O. **Obv:** Eggs and chicks **Rev:** Denomination above date

| Date | Mintage | VF20 | XF40 | MS60 | MS63 | MS65 |
|---|---|---|---|---|---|---|
| 2001 (a) Horseshoe | — | — | 0.20 | 0.40 | 0.80 | 2.00 |
| 2013 | — | — | — | — | 0.80 | 2.00 |

**KM# 16 50 FRANCS**
5.60 g., Nickel, 23.93 mm. **Obv:** Crescent and stars above denomination, date below **Rev:** Building with tall tower **Edge:** Reeded

| Date | Mintage | VF20 | XF40 | MS60 | MS63 | MS65 |
|---|---|---|---|---|---|---|
| 2001 (a) horseshoe | — | — | — | — | 2.50 | 3.50 |

**KM# 16a 50 FRANCS**
Nickel Plated Steel, 23.9 mm. **Obv:** Crescent and stars above denomination, date below **Rev:** Building with tall tower **Edge:** Reeded

| Date | Mintage | VF20 | XF40 | MS60 | MS63 | MS65 |
|---|---|---|---|---|---|---|
| 2001 (a) | — | 0.25 | 0.50 | 1.00 | 2.50 | 3.50 |
| 2013 | — | — | — | 1.00 | 2.50 | 3.50 |

**KM# 18a 100 FRANCS**
10.20 g., Copper-Nickel, 28 mm. **Obv:** Crescent and stars above denomination, date below **Rev:** Boat and fish

| Date | Mintage | VF20 | XF40 | MS60 | MS63 | MS65 |
|---|---|---|---|---|---|---|
| 2003 (a) | — | — | — | — | 3.50 | 5.00 |
| 2013 | — | — | — | — | 3.50 | 5.00 |

**KM# 20 1000 FRANCS**
22.20 g., 0.900 Silver 0.6424 oz. ASW, 37 mm. **Obv:** Crescent and four stars **Rev:** Mosque of the Sultans

| Date | Mintage | VF20 | XF40 | MS60 | MS63 | MS65 |
|---|---|---|---|---|---|---|
| 2002 | 500 | **PF63** 100 | **PF65** 120 | | | |

**KM# 21 250 FRANCS**
Bi-Metallic **Subject:** Central Bank, 30th Anniversary **Obv:** Large value at center **Rev:** Crescent and vertical stars

| Date | Mintage | VF20 | XF40 | MS60 | MS63 | MS65 |
|---|---|---|---|---|---|---|
| 2013 | — | — | — | — | 10.00 | 15.00 |

# CONGO DEMOCRATIC REPUBLIC

The Democratic Republic of the Congo (formerly the Republic of Zaire, and earlier the Belgian Congo), located in the south-central part of Africa, has an area of 905,568 sq. mi. (2,345,410 sq. km.) and a population of *47.4 million. Capital: Kinshasa. The mineral-rich country produces copper, tin, diamonds, gold, zinc, cobalt and uranium.

## DEMOCRATIC REPUBLIC

1998 -

### REFORM COINAGE

Congo Francs; July 1998

**KM# 76 25 CENTIMES**
0.88 g., Aluminum, 19.90 mm. **Obv:** Lion left **Rev:** Mongoose **Edge:** Plain

| Date | Mintage | VF20 | XF40 | MS60 | MS63 | MS65 |
|---|---|---|---|---|---|---|
| 2002 | — | — | — | 0.75 | 1.00 | 1.25 |

**KM# 77 25 CENTIMES**
0.85 g., Aluminum, 20 mm. **Obv:** Lion left **Rev:** Ram right, looking left **Edge:** Plain

| Date | Mintage | VF20 | XF40 | MS60 | MS63 | MS65 |
|---|---|---|---|---|---|---|
| 2002 | — | — | — | 0.75 | 1.00 | 1.25 |

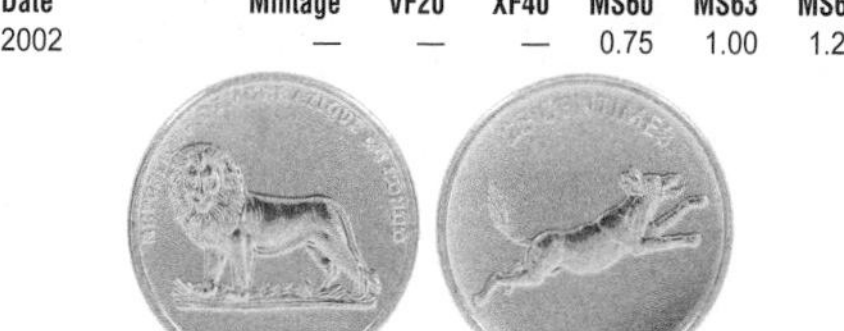

**KM# 83 25 CENTIMES**
1.30 g., Aluminum, 20 mm. **Obv:** Lion left **Rev:** Wild leaping dog right **Edge:** Plain

| Date | Mintage | VF20 | XF40 | MS60 | MS63 | MS65 |
|---|---|---|---|---|---|---|
| 2002 | — | — | — | 0.75 | 1.00 | 1.25 |

**KM# 75 50 CENTIMES**
2.20 g., Aluminum, 26.97 mm. **Obv:** Lion left **Rev:** Soccer player right, bumping ball with head **Edge:** Plain

| Date | Mintage | VF20 | XF40 | MS60 | MS63 | MS65 |
|---|---|---|---|---|---|---|
| 2002 | — | — | — | 1.25 | 1.50 | 1.75 |

**KM# 78 50 CENTIMES**
2.16 g., Aluminum, 27 mm. **Obv:** Lion left **Rev:** Giraffe right, looking left **Edge:** Plain

| Date | Mintage | VF20 | XF40 | MS60 | MS63 | MS65 |
|---|---|---|---|---|---|---|
| 2002 | — | — | — | 1.25 | 1.50 | 1.75 |

**KM# 79 50 CENTIMES**
2.20 g., Aluminum, 26.92 mm. **Obv:** Lion left **Rev:** Gorilla facing, looking left **Edge:** Plain

| Date | Mintage | VF20 | XF40 | MS60 | MS63 | MS65 |
|---|---|---|---|---|---|---|
| 2002 | — | — | — | 1.00 | 1.25 | 1.50 |

**KM# 80 50 CENTIMES**
2.16 g., Aluminum, 27 mm. **Obv:** Lion left **Rev:** Butterfly **Edge:** Plain

| Date | Mintage | VF20 | XF40 | MS60 | MS63 | MS65 |
|---|---|---|---|---|---|---|
| 2002 | — | — | — | 1.50 | 1.75 | 2.00 |

### KM# 123 50 CENTIMES

3.92 g., Stainless Steel, 22.3 mm. **Obv:** Lion left above denomination **Rev:** Verney L. Cameroon **Edge:** Plain

| Date | Mintage | VF20 | XF40 | MS60 | MS63 | MS65 |
|---|---|---|---|---|---|---|
| 2002 | — | — | — | 1.00 | 1.25 | 1.50 |

### KM# 81 FRANC

4.57 g., Brass, 20.31 mm. **Obv:** Lion left **Rev:** Turtle **Edge:** Plain

| Date | Mintage | VF20 | XF40 | MS60 | MS63 | MS65 |
|---|---|---|---|---|---|---|
| 2002 | — | — | — | 1.25 | 1.50 | 1.75 |

### KM# 82 FRANC

4.52 g., Brass, 20.32 mm. **Obv:** Lion left **Rev:** Chicken **Edge:** Plain

| Date | Mintage | VF20 | XF40 | MS60 | MS63 | MS65 |
|---|---|---|---|---|---|---|
| 2002 | — | — | — | 1.50 | 1.75 | 2.00 |

### KM# 156 FRANC

5.00 g., Nickel Clad Steel, 24.8 mm. **Subject:** 25th Anniversary - Pope John Paul II's Visit **Obv:** Lion left **Rev:** Pope John Paul II as a priest in 1946 **Edge:** Plain

| Date | Mintage | VF20 | XF40 | MS60 | MS63 | MS65 |
|---|---|---|---|---|---|---|
| 2004 | — | — | — | 2.00 | 2.50 | 3.00 |

### KM# 157 FRANC

5.00 g., Nickel Clad Steel, 24.8 mm. **Subject:** 25th Anniversary - Pope John Paul II's Visit **Obv:** Lion left **Rev:** Pope John Paul II as a Cardinal in 1967 **Edge:** Plain

| Date | Mintage | VF20 | XF40 | MS60 | MS63 | MS65 |
|---|---|---|---|---|---|---|
| 2004 | — | — | — | 2.00 | 2.50 | 3.00 |

### KM# 158 FRANC

5.00 g., Nickel Clad Steel, 24.8 mm. **Subject:** 25th Anniversary - Pope John Paul II's Visit **Obv:** Lion left **Rev:** Pope John Paul II as newly elected pope in 1978 **Edge:** Plain

| Date | Mintage | VF20 | XF40 | MS60 | MS63 | MS65 |
|---|---|---|---|---|---|---|
| 2004 | — | — | — | 2.00 | 2.50 | 3.00 |

### KM# 159 FRANC

5.00 g., Nickel Clad Steel, 24.8 mm. **Subject:** 25th Anniversary - Pope John Paul II's Visit **Obv:** Lion left **Rev:** Pope John Paul II wearing a mitre **Edge:** Plain

| Date | Mintage | VF20 | XF40 | MS60 | MS63 | MS65 |
|---|---|---|---|---|---|---|
| 2004 | — | — | — | 2.00 | 2.50 | 3.00 |

### KM# 174 FRANC

6.00 g., Copper-Nickel, 21 mm. **Obv:** Lion left **Rev:** African Golden Cat right **Edge:** Plain

| Date | Mintage | VF20 | XF40 | MS60 | MS63 | MS65 |
|---|---|---|---|---|---|---|
| 2004 | 5,000 | — | — | 5.00 | 7.00 | 9.00 |

### KM# 174a FRANC

8.00 g., 0.999 Silver 0.2569 oz. ASW, 21 mm. **Obv:** Lion left **Rev:** African Golden Cat right **Edge:** Plain

| Date | Mintage | VF20 | XF40 | MS60 | MS63 | MS65 |
|---|---|---|---|---|---|---|
| 2004 | 25 | — | — | — | 270 | 300 |

### KM# 56 5 FRANCS

22.40 g., Copper-Nickel, 39.8 mm. **Series:** Wild Life Protection **Obv:** Lion left **Rev:** Multicolor swallowtail butterfly hologram **Edge:** Reeded **Note:** Prev. KM#79.

| Date | Mintage | VF20 | XF40 | MS60 | MS63 | MS65 |
|---|---|---|---|---|---|---|
| 2002 | 20,000 | — | — | — | 35.00 | 40.00 |

### KM# 57 5 FRANCS

22.40 g., Copper-Nickel, 39.8 mm. **Series:** Wild Life Protection **Obv:** Lion left **Rev:** Multicolor dark greenish butterfly hologram **Edge:** Reeded **Note:** Prev. KM#80.

| Date | Mintage | VF20 | XF40 | MS60 | MS63 | MS65 |
|---|---|---|---|---|---|---|
| 2002 | 20,000 | — | — | — | 35.00 | 40.00 |

### KM# 58 5 FRANCS

22.40 g., Copper-Nickel, 39.8 mm. **Series:** Wild Life Protection **Obv:** Lion left **Rev:** Multicolor red and black butterfly hologram **Edge:** Reeded **Note:** Prev. KM#81.

| Date | Mintage | VF20 | XF40 | MS60 | MS63 | MS65 |
|---|---|---|---|---|---|---|
| 2002 | 20,000 | — | — | — | 35.00 | 40.00 |

### KM# 170 5 FRANCS

24.30 g., Copper-Nickel, 38.5 mm. **Obv:** Lion left **Rev:** Multicolor German 1 mark coin dated 2001 **Edge:** Reeded

| Date | Mintage | VF20 | XF40 | MS60 | MS63 | MS65 |
|---|---|---|---|---|---|---|
| 2002 | — | — | — | — | 15.00 | 20.00 |

### KM# 198 5 FRANCS

Copper-Nickel, 38.6 mm. **Obv:** Lion left **Rev:** Cameleon on branch in color

| Date | Mintage | VF20 | XF40 | MS60 | MS63 | MS65 |
|---|---|---|---|---|---|---|
| 2003 | — | — | — | — | — | 25.00 |

**KM# 214 5 FRANCS**
22.40 g., Copper-Nickel, 38.6 mm. **Subject:** Wild Life protection **Obv:** Lion left **Rev:** Loggerhead sea turtle

| Date | Mintage | VF20 | XF40 | MS60 | MS63 | MS65 |
|---|---|---|---|---|---|---|
| 2003 | — | — | — | — | — | 45.00 |

**KM# 215 5 FRANCS**
22.40 g., Copper-Nickel, 38.6 mm. **Subject:** Wild Life Protection **Obv:** Lion left **Rev:** Dolphin as prism

| Date | Mintage | VF20 | XF40 | MS60 | MS63 | MS65 |
|---|---|---|---|---|---|---|
| 2003 | — | — | — | — | — | 40.00 |

**KM# 216 5 FRANCS**
22.40 g., Copper-Nickel, 38.6 mm. **Subject:** Wild Life Protection **Obv:** Lion left **Rev:** Orca whale as prism

| Date | Mintage | VF20 | XF40 | MS60 | MS63 | MS65 |
|---|---|---|---|---|---|---|
| 2003 | — | — | — | — | — | 40.00 |

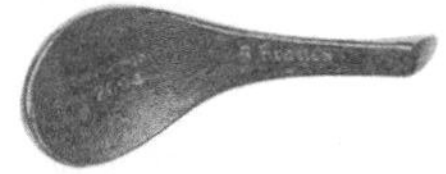

**KM# 128 5 FRANCS**
8.00 g., Iron, 27.26x14.13 mm. **Obv:** Country name, lion and date in the bowl part of the spoon; value on the handle part **Edge:** Reeded **Note:** This is the Spoon part of the Compass and Spoon set. See also 10 Francs, KM#127 (The spoon is the compass needle.)

| Date | Mintage | VF20 | XF40 | MS60 | MS63 | MS65 |
|---|---|---|---|---|---|---|
| 2004 | 5,000 | — | — | — | 15.00 | — |

**KM# 146 5 FRANCS**
27.00 g., Copper-Nickel, 38.6 mm. **Obv:** Lion left **Rev:** Multicolor Quetzal bird **Edge:** Reeded

| Date | Mintage | VF20 | XF40 | MS60 | MS63 | MS65 |
|---|---|---|---|---|---|---|
| 2004 | 5,000 | PF65 35.00 | | | | |

**KM# 147 5 FRANCS**
27.00 g., Copper-Nickel, 38.6 mm. **Obv:** Lion left **Rev:** Multicolor Bird of Paradise **Edge:** Reeded

| Date | Mintage | VF20 | XF40 | MS60 | MS63 | MS65 |
|---|---|---|---|---|---|---|
| 2004 | 5,000 | PF65 35.00 | | | | |

**KM# 148 5 FRANCS**
27.00 g., Copper-Nickel, 38.6 mm. **Obv:** Lion left **Rev:** Multicolor Kingfisher bird **Edge:** Reeded

| Date | Mintage | VF20 | XF40 | MS60 | MS63 | MS65 |
|---|---|---|---|---|---|---|
| 2004 | 5,000 | PF65 35.00 | | | | |

**KM# 164 5 FRANCS**
25.40 g., Copper-Nickel, 38.8 mm. **Subject:** Papal Visit **Obv:** Lion left **Rev:** Pope John Paul II with staff and mitre **Edge:** Reeded

| Date | Mintage | VF20 | XF40 | MS60 | MS63 | MS65 |
|---|---|---|---|---|---|---|
| 2004 | — | PF65 25.00 | | | | |

**KM# 165 5 FRANCS**
49.50 g., Copper-Nickel, 45.1 mm. **Obv:** Lion left **Rev:** Rotating 50 year calender **Edge:** Reeded

| Date | Mintage | VF20 | XF40 | MS60 | MS63 | MS65 |
|---|---|---|---|---|---|---|
| ND-2004 Matte | — | — | — | — | 75.00 | — |

**KM# 166 5 FRANCS**
2.16 g., Wood Maple, 39.4 mm. **Obv:** Lion, brown ink **Rev:** Gorilla, brown ink **Edge:** Plain

| Date | Mintage | VF20 | XF40 | MS60 | MS63 | MS65 |
|---|---|---|---|---|---|---|
| 2005 | 2,000 | — | — | — | 22.00 | — |

**KM# 179 5 FRANCS**
25.92 g., Copper-Nickel, 38.6 mm. **Series:** Wildlife Protection **Obv:** Lion standing left **Obv. Legend:** REPUBLIQUE DEMOCRATIQUE DU CONGO **Rev:** Butterfly Fish, multicolor **Edge:** Reeded

| Date | Mintage | VF20 | XF40 | MS60 | MS63 | MS65 |
|---|---|---|---|---|---|---|
| 2005 | 5,000 | — | — | — | — | 25.00 |

**KM# 180 5 FRANCS**
25.92 g., Copper-Nickel, 38.6 mm. **Series:** Wildlife Protection **Obv:** Lion standing left **Obv. Legend:** REPUBLIQUE DEMOCRATIQYE DU CONGO **Rev:** African Moony Fish, multicolor **Edge:** Reeded

| Date | Mintage | VF20 | XF40 | MS60 | MS63 | MS65 |
|---|---|---|---|---|---|---|
| 2005 | 5,000 | — | — | — | — | 25.00 |

**KM# 181 5 FRANCS**
25.92 g., Copper-Nickel, 38.6 mm. **Series:** Wildlife Protection **Obv:** Lion standing laft **Obv. Legend:** REPUBLIQUE DENOCRATIQUE DU CONGO **Rev:** Red Perch, multicolor **Edge:** Reeded

| Date | Mintage | VF20 | XF40 | MS60 | MS63 | MS65 |
|---|---|---|---|---|---|---|
| 2005 | 5,000 | — | — | — | — | 20.00 |

**KM# 182 5 FRANCS**
Copper-Nickel, 38.6 mm. **Obv:** Lion standing left **Rev:** Two cupids embracing, roses - multicolor **Rev. Legend:** Endless Love **Edge:** Reeded **Shape:** Heart

| Date | Mintage | VF20 | XF40 | MS60 | MS63 | MS65 |
|---|---|---|---|---|---|---|
| 2005 | 5,000 | PF65 30.00 | | | | |

**KM# 220 5 FRANCS**
Silver, 38.6 mm. **Obv:** Lion standing left **Rev:** Swiss Guard standing at right in hallway

| Date | Mintage | VF20 | XF40 | MS60 | MS63 | MS65 |
|---|---|---|---|---|---|---|
| 2006 | — | PF65 45.00 | | | | |

**KM# 178 5 FRANCS**
26.30 g., Silver Plated Bronze, 38.6 mm. **Obv:** Lion **Rev:** Multicolor Pope John Paul II wearing a mitre **Edge:** Reeded

| Date | Mintage | VF20 | XF40 | MS60 | MS63 | MS65 |
|---|---|---|---|---|---|---|
| 2007 | — | PF65 35.00 | | | | |

**KM# 38 10 FRANCS**
31.30 g., 0.925 Silver 0.9308 oz. ASW, 27 x 47.1 mm. **Subject:** Illusion **Obv:** Lion left **Rev:** Multicolor couple in flower picture **Edge:** Plain **Shape:** Rectangular **Note:** Prev. KM#61.

| Date | Mintage | VF20 | XF40 | MS60 | MS63 | MS65 |
|---|---|---|---|---|---|---|
| 2001 | — | PF65 50.00 | | | | |

**KM# 59 10 FRANCS**
25.95 g., 0.925 Silver 0.7717 oz. ASW, 39.9 mm. **Series:** Wild Life Protection **Obv:** Lion left **Rev:** Multicolor swallowtail butterfly hologram **Edge:** Reeded **Note:** Prev. KM#82.

| Date | Mintage | VF20 | XF40 | MS60 | MS63 | MS65 |
|---|---|---|---|---|---|---|
| 2002 | 15,000 | PF65 65.00 | | | | |

**KM# 60 10 FRANCS**
25.95 g., 0.925 Silver 0.7717 oz. ASW, 39.9 mm. **Series:** Wild Life Protection **Obv:** Lion left **Rev:** Multicolor dark greenish butterfly hologram **Edge:** Reeded **Note:** Prev. KM#83.

| Date | Mintage | VF20 | XF40 | MS60 | MS63 | MS65 |
|---|---|---|---|---|---|---|
| 2002 | 15,000 | PF65 65.00 | | | | |

**KM# 61 10 FRANCS**
25.95 g., 0.925 Silver 0.7717 oz. ASW, 39.9 mm. **Series:** Wild Life Protection **Obv:** Lion left **Rev:** Multicolor red and black butterfly hologram **Edge:** Reeded **Note:** Prev. KM#84.

| Date | Mintage | VF20 | XF40 | MS60 | MS63 | MS65 |
|---|---|---|---|---|---|---|
| 2002 | 15,000 | PF65 65.00 | | | | |

**KM# 65 10 FRANCS**
20.00 g., 0.925 Silver 0.5948 oz. ASW, 40.1 mm. **Series:** Airplanes **Obv:** Lion left **Rev:** Vickers Vimy twin engine biplane flying left **Edge:** Reeded **Note:** Prev. KM#88.

| Date | Mintage | VF20 | XF40 | MS60 | MS63 | MS65 |
|---|---|---|---|---|---|---|
| 2001 | — | PF63 42.00 | PF65 45.00 | | | |

**KM# 66 10 FRANCS**
20.00 g., 0.925 Silver 0.5948 oz. ASW, 40.1 mm. **Series:** Airplanes **Obv:** Lion left **Rev:** Fokker DR1 triplane flying left **Edge:** Reeded **Note:** Prev. KM#89.

| Date | Mintage | VF20 | XF40 | MS60 | MS63 | MS65 |
|---|---|---|---|---|---|---|
| 2001 | — | **PF63** 42.00 | **PF65** 45.00 | | | |

**KM# 67 10 FRANCS**
20.00 g., 0.925 Silver 0.5948 oz. ASW, 40.1 mm. **Series:** Airplanes **Obv:** Lion left **Rev:** Lockheed Vega flying left **Edge:** Reeded **Note:** Prev. KM#90.

| Date | Mintage | VF20 | XF40 | MS60 | MS63 | MS65 |
|---|---|---|---|---|---|---|
| 2001 | — | **PF63** 42.00 | **PF65** 45.00 | | | |

**KM# 68 10 FRANCS**
20.00 g., 0.925 Silver 0.5948 oz. ASW, 40.1 mm. **Series:** Airplanes **Obv:** Lion left **Rev:** Boeing 314 Clipper flying left **Edge:** Reeded **Note:** Prev. KM#91.

| Date | Mintage | VF20 | XF40 | MS60 | MS63 | MS65 |
|---|---|---|---|---|---|---|
| 2001 | — | **PF63** 42.00 | **PF65** 45.00 | | | |

**KM# 69 10 FRANCS**
20.00 g., 0.925 Silver 0.5948 oz. ASW, 40.1 mm. **Series:** Airplanes **Obv:** Lion left **Rev:** Junkers JU-87 Stuka in a dive **Edge:** Reeded **Note:** Prev. KM#92.

| Date | Mintage | VF20 | XF40 | MS60 | MS63 | MS65 |
|---|---|---|---|---|---|---|
| 2001 | — | **PF63** 42.00 | **PF65** 45.00 | | | |

**KM# 70 10 FRANCS**
20.00 g., 0.925 Silver 0.5948 oz. ASW, 40.1 mm. **Series:** Airplanes **Obv:** Lion left **Rev:** B-29 Enola Gay flying left **Edge:** Reeded **Note:** Prev. KM#93.

| Date | Mintage | VF20 | XF40 | MS60 | MS63 | MS65 |
|---|---|---|---|---|---|---|
| 2001 | — | **PF63** 42.00 | **PF65** 45.00 | | | |

**KM# 71 10 FRANCS**
20.00 g., 0.925 Silver 0.5948 oz. ASW, 40.1 mm. **Series:** Airplanes **Obv:** Lion left **Rev:** Bell X-1 rocket plane flying left **Edge:** Reeded **Note:** Prev. KM#94.

| Date | Mintage | VF20 | XF40 | MS60 | MS63 | MS65 |
|---|---|---|---|---|---|---|
| 2001 | — | **PF63** 42.00 | **PF65** 45.00 | | | |

**KM# 72 10 FRANCS**
20.00 g., 0.925 Silver 0.5948 oz. ASW, 40.1 mm. **Series:** Airplanes **Obv:** Lion left **Rev:** Mikoyan-Gurevich Mig 21 fighter flying left **Edge:** Reeded

| Date | Mintage | VF20 | XF40 | MS60 | MS63 | MS65 |
|---|---|---|---|---|---|---|
| 2001 | — | **PF63** 42.00 | **PF65** 45.00 | | | |

**KM# 74 10 FRANCS**
31.10 g., 0.999 Silver 0.999 oz. ASW, 40 mm. **Subject:** 2004 Olympics **Obv:** Lion left **Rev:** Convex chariot **Edge:** Reeded

| Date | Mintage | VF20 | XF40 | MS60 | MS63 | MS65 |
|---|---|---|---|---|---|---|
| 2001 Antique Finish | 15,000 | — | — | 45.00 | — | — |

**KM# 167 10 FRANCS**
20.00 g., 0.925 Silver 0.5948 oz. ASW, 40.1 mm. **Obv:** Lion left **Rev:** SS Bremen ship at sea **Edge:** Reeded

| Date | Mintage | VF20 | XF40 | MS60 | MS63 | MS65 |
|---|---|---|---|---|---|---|
| 2001 | — | **PF65** 35.00 | | | | |

**KM# 168 10 FRANCS**
20.00 g., 0.925 Silver 0.5948 oz. ASW, 40.1 mm. **Obv:** Lion left **Rev:** RMS Queen Elizabeth 2 at sea **Edge:** Reeded

| Date | Mintage | VF20 | XF40 | MS60 | MS63 | MS65 |
|---|---|---|---|---|---|---|
| 2001 | — | **PF65** 35.00 | | | | |

**KM# 169 10 FRANCS**
20.00 g., 0.925 Silver 0.5948 oz. ASW, 30 mm. **Obv:** Lion left **Rev:** Sail Ship America **Edge:** Reeded

| Date | Mintage | VF20 | XF40 | MS60 | MS63 | MS65 |
|---|---|---|---|---|---|---|
| 2001 | — | **PF65** 35.00 | | | | |

**KM# 175 10 FRANCS**
25.83 g., Silver, 40 mm. **Obv:** Lion left **Rev:** 3 players **Edge:** Reeded

| Date | Mintage | VF20 | XF40 | MS60 | MS63 | MS65 |
|---|---|---|---|---|---|---|
| 2001 | — | — | — | — | — | 50.00 |

**KM# 197 10 FRANCS**
20.00 g., 0.5948 Silver 0.3825 oz. ASW, 40.1 mm. **Obv:** LIon left **Rev:** SS Andrea Doria sailing left

| Date | Mintage | VF20 | XF40 | MS60 | MS63 | MS65 |
|---|---|---|---|---|---|---|
| 2001 | — | PF65 45.00 | | | | |

**KM# 199 10 FRANCS**
Silver, 40.1 mm. **Obv:** Lion left **Rev:** M.S. Voyager of the Seas sailing left

| Date | Mintage | VF20 | XF40 | MS60 | MS63 | MS65 |
|---|---|---|---|---|---|---|
| 2001 | — | PF65 45.00 | | | | |

**KM# 91 10 FRANCS**
31.10 g., 0.999 Silver 0.9989 oz. ASW, 40 mm. **Subject:** Olympics **Obv:** Lion left **Rev:** Ancient athlete incuse design **Edge:** Plain **Note:** Design hubs with the design of the 500 sika coin KM-42 of Ghana

| Date | Mintage | VF20 | XF40 | MS60 | MS63 | MS65 |
|---|---|---|---|---|---|---|
| 2002 Antiqued finish | — | — | — | 40.00 | — | — |

**KM# 93 10 FRANCS**
31.23 g., 0.999 Silver 1.0031 oz. ASW, 38.7 mm. **Obv:** Lion left **Rev:** Bearded portrait of Verney L. Camereon **Edge:** Reeded

| Date | Mintage | VF20 | XF40 | MS60 | MS63 | MS65 |
|---|---|---|---|---|---|---|
| 2002 | — | — | — | — | 40.00 | 45.00 |

**KM# 94 10 FRANCS**
26.15 g., Copper-Nickel, 40.3 mm. **Subject:** Historic Automobiles **Obv:** Lion left **Rev:** 1908 Berliet car **Edge:** Reeded

| Date | Mintage | VF20 | XF40 | MS60 | MS63 | MS65 |
|---|---|---|---|---|---|---|
| 2002 | — | PF63 13.50 | PF65 15.00 | | | |

**KM# 95 10 FRANCS**
26.15 g., Copper-Nickel, 40.3 mm. **Subject:** Historic Automobiles **Obv:** Lion left **Rev:** 1919 Hispano Suiza H6 car right **Edge:** Reeded

| Date | Mintage | VF20 | XF40 | MS60 | MS63 | MS65 |
|---|---|---|---|---|---|---|
| 2002 | — | PF63 13.50 | PF65 15.00 | | | |

**KM# 96 10 FRANCS**
32.00 g., Silver Plated Copper, 40 mm. **Subject:** World Cup Soccer **Obv:** Lion left **Rev:** Soccer player and multicolor American flag **Edge:** Reeded

| Date | Mintage | VF20 | XF40 | MS60 | MS63 | MS65 |
|---|---|---|---|---|---|---|
| 2002 | 20,000 | PF65 50.00 | | | | |

**KM# 97 10 FRANCS**
32.00 g., Silver Plated Copper, 40 mm. **Subject:** World Cup Soccer **Obv:** Lion left **Rev:** Two soccer players and multicolor flag of Ecuador **Edge:** Reeded

| Date | Mintage | VF20 | XF40 | MS60 | MS63 | MS65 |
|---|---|---|---|---|---|---|
| 2002 | 20,000 | PF65 50.00 | | | | |

**KM# 103 10 FRANCS**
19.00 g., 0.999 Silver 0.6103 oz. ASW, 40 mm. **Series:** Airplanes **Obv:** Lion left **Rev:** WWI German Gotha Ursinus G bomber flying left at 8 o'clock **Edge:** Reeded

| Date | Mintage | VF20 | XF40 | MS60 | MS63 | MS65 |
|---|---|---|---|---|---|---|
| 2002 | — | PF63 42.00 | PF65 45.00 | | | |

**KM# 104 10 FRANCS**
19.00 g., 0.999 Silver 0.6103 oz. ASW, 40 mm. **Series:** Airplanes **Obv:** Lion left **Rev:** WWII ME 109 German fighter plane flying left **Edge:** Reeded

| Date | Mintage | VF20 | XF40 | MS60 | MS63 | MS65 |
|---|---|---|---|---|---|---|
| 2002 | — | PF63 42.00 | PF65 45.00 | | | |

**KM# 105 10 FRANCS**
19.00 g., 0.999 Silver 0.6103 oz. ASW, 40 mm. **Series:** Airplanes **Obv:** Lion left **Rev:** Savoia-Marchetti S 55 seaplane flying left **Edge:** Reeded

| Date | Mintage | VF20 | XF40 | MS60 | MS63 | MS65 |
|---|---|---|---|---|---|---|
| 2002 | — | **PF63** 42.00 | **PF65** 45.00 | | | |

**KM# 106 10 FRANCS**
19.00 g., 0.999 Silver 0.6103 oz. ASW, 40 mm. **Series:** Airplanes **Obv:** Lion left **Rev:** B-58 Hustler Delta wing bomber flying left at 8 o'clock **Edge:** Reeded

| Date | Mintage | VF20 | XF40 | MS60 | MS63 | MS65 |
|---|---|---|---|---|---|---|
| 2002 | — | **PF63** 42.00 | **PF65** 45.00 | | | |

**KM# 107 10 FRANCS**
19.00 g., 0.999 Silver 0.6103 oz. ASW, 40 mm. **Series:** Airplanes **Obv:** Lion left **Rev:** CF-105 Arrow jet fighter plane flying right, nose up **Edge:** Reeded

| Date | Mintage | VF20 | XF40 | MS60 | MS63 | MS65 |
|---|---|---|---|---|---|---|
| 2002 | — | **PF63** 42.00 | **PF65** 45.00 | | | |

**KM# 108 10 FRANCS**
19.00 g., 0.999 Silver 0.6103 oz. ASW, 40 mm. **Series:** Airplanes **Obv:** Lion left **Rev:** XB-70 Valkyrie experimental jet bomber flying right **Edge:** Reeded

| Date | Mintage | VF20 | XF40 | MS60 | MS63 | MS65 |
|---|---|---|---|---|---|---|
| 2002 | — | **PF63** 42.00 | **PF65** 45.00 | | | |

**KM# 124 10 FRANCS**
26.00 g., 0.925 Silver 0.7732 oz. ASW, 40 mm. **Subject:** Field Marshal Erwin Rommel **Obv:** Lion left above value **Rev:** Rommel, tank and map **Edge:** Reeded

| Date | Mintage | VF20 | XF40 | MS60 | MS63 | MS65 |
|---|---|---|---|---|---|---|
| 2002 | 15,000 | **PF65** 42.50 | | | | |

**KM# 125 10 FRANCS**
26.00 g., 0.925 Silver 0.7732 oz. ASW, 40 mm. **Subject:** George S. Patton **Obv:** Lion left above value **Rev:** Patton, tank and map **Edge:** Reeded

| Date | Mintage | VF20 | XF40 | MS60 | MS63 | MS65 |
|---|---|---|---|---|---|---|
| 2002 | 15,000 | **PF65** 42.50 | | | | |

**KM# 162 10 FRANCS**
20.20 g., 0.999 Silver 0.6488 oz. ASW, 40 mm. **Obv:** Lion left **Rev:** Space shuttle and five astronauts **Edge:** Reeded

| Date | Mintage | VF20 | XF40 | MS60 | MS63 | MS65 |
|---|---|---|---|---|---|---|
| 2002 | — | **PF65** 40.00 | | | | |

**KM# 187 10 FRANCS**
26.15 g., Copper-Nickel, 40.3 mm. **Series:** Automobiles **Obv:** Lion standing left **Rev:** Buick **Edge:** Reeded

| Date | Mintage | VF20 | XF40 | MS60 | MS63 | MS65 |
|---|---|---|---|---|---|---|
| 2002 | — | **PF63** 13.50 | **PF65** 15.00 | | | |

**KM# 188 10 FRANCS**
26.15 g., Copper-Nickel, 40.3 mm. **Series:** Automobiles **Obv:** Lion standing left **Rev:** Land Rover **Edge:** Reeded

| Date | Mintage | VF20 | XF40 | MS60 | MS63 | MS65 |
|---|---|---|---|---|---|---|
| 2002 | — | **PF63** 13.50 | **PF65** 15.00 | | | |

**KM# 189 10 FRANCS**
26.15 g., Copper-Nickel, 40.3 mm. **Series:** Automobiles **Obv:** Lion standing left **Rev:** Rolls Royce **Edge:** Reeded

| Date | Mintage | VF20 | XF40 | MS60 | MS63 | MS65 |
|---|---|---|---|---|---|---|
| 2002 | — | **PF63** 13.50 | **PF65** 15.00 | | | |

**KM# 190 10 FRANCS**
26.15 g., Copper-Nickel, 40.3 mm. **Series:** Automobiles **Obv:** Lion standing left **Rev:** Peujeot

| Date | Mintage | VF20 | XF40 | MS60 | MS63 | MS65 |
|---|---|---|---|---|---|---|
| 2002 | — | **PF63** 13.50 | **PF65** 15.00 | | | |

**KM# 191 10 FRANCS**
26.15 g., Copper-Nickel, 40.3 mm. **Series:** Automobiles **Obv:** Lion standing left **Rev:** Opel **Edge:** Reeded

| Date | Mintage | VF20 | XF40 | MS60 | MS63 | MS65 |
|---|---|---|---|---|---|---|
| 2002 | — | **PF63** 13.50 | **PF65** 15.00 | | | |

**KM# 192 10 FRANCS**
26.15 g., Copper-Nickel, 40.3 mm. **Series:** Automobiles **Obv:** Lion standing left **Rev:** Cadillac

| Date | Mintage | VF20 | XF40 | MS60 | MS63 | MS65 |
|---|---|---|---|---|---|---|
| 2002 | — | **PF63** 13.50 | **PF65** 15.00 | | | |

**KM# 193 10 FRANCS**
26.15 g., Copper-Nickel, 40.3 mm. **Series:** Automobiles **Obv:** Lion standing left **Rev:** Benz **Shape:** Reeded

| Date | Mintage | VF20 | XF40 | MS60 | MS63 | MS65 |
|---|---|---|---|---|---|---|
| 2002 | — | **PF63** 13.50 | **PF65** 15.00 | | | |

**KM# 194 10 FRANCS**
26.15 g., Copper-Nickel, 40.3 mm. **Series:** Automobiles **Obv:** Lion standing left **Rev:** Audi **Edge:** Reeded

| Date | Mintage | VF20 | XF40 | MS60 | MS63 | MS65 |
|---|---|---|---|---|---|---|
| 2002 | — | **PF63** 13.50 | **PF65** 15.00 | | | |

**KM# 195 10 FRANCS**
26.15 g., Copper-Nickel, 40.3 mm. **Series:** Automobiles **Obv:** Lion standing left **Rev:** Alfa Romero

| Date | Mintage | VF20 | XF40 | MS60 | MS63 | MS65 |
|---|---|---|---|---|---|---|
| 2002 | — | **PF63** 13.50 | **PF65** 15.00 | | | |

**KM# 196 10 FRANCS**
26.15 g., Copper-Nickel, 40.3 mm. **Series:** Automobiles **Obv:** Lion standing left **Rev:** Ford Model 'T' **Edge:** Reeded

| Date | Mintage | VF20 | XF40 | MS60 | MS63 | MS65 |
|---|---|---|---|---|---|---|
| 2002 | — | **PF63** 13.50 | **PF65** 15.00 | | | |

**KM# 99.1 10 FRANCS**
24.91 g., 0.925 Silver 0.7408 oz. ASW, 38.6 mm. **Obv:** Lion left **Rev:** Chameleon **Edge:** Reeded

| Date | Mintage | VF20 | XF40 | MS60 | MS63 | MS65 |
|---|---|---|---|---|---|---|
| 2003 | — | **PF65** 45.00 | | | | |

**KM# 99.2 10 FRANCS**
24.91 g., 0.925 Silver 0.7408 oz. ASW, 38.6 mm. **Obv:** Lion left **Rev:** Multicolor chameleon **Edge:** Reeded

| Date | Mintage | VF20 | XF40 | MS60 | MS63 | MS65 |
|---|---|---|---|---|---|---|
| 2003 | — | **PF65** 50.00 | | | | |

**KM# 100 10 FRANCS**
24.91 g., 0.925 Silver 0.7408 oz. ASW, 38.6 mm. **Obv:** Lion left **Rev:** Striped skunk **Edge:** Reeded

| Date | Mintage | VF20 | XF40 | MS60 | MS63 | MS65 |
|---|---|---|---|---|---|---|
| 2003 | — | **PF65** 475 | | | | |

**KM# 101 10 FRANCS**
24.91 g., 0.925 Silver 0.7408 oz. ASW, 38.6 mm. **Obv:** Lion left **Rev:** Porcupine on rock, right **Edge:** Reeded

| Date | Mintage | VF20 | XF40 | MS60 | MS63 | MS65 |
|---|---|---|---|---|---|---|
| 2003 | — | **PF65** 50.00 | | | | |

**KM# 102 10 FRANCS**
24.91 g., 0.925 Silver 0.7408 oz. ASW, 38.6 mm. **Obv:** Lion left **Rev:** Giant Pangolin on rock right **Edge:** Reeded

| Date | Mintage | VF20 | XF40 | MS60 | MS63 | MS65 |
|---|---|---|---|---|---|---|
| 2003 | — | PF65 50.00 | | | | |

**KM# 109 10 FRANCS**
19.00 g., 0.999 Silver 0.6103 oz. ASW, 40 mm. **Obv:** Lion left **Rev:** 14 BIS early aircraft in flight **Edge:** Reeded

| Date | Mintage | VF20 | XF40 | MS60 | MS63 | MS65 |
|---|---|---|---|---|---|---|
| 2003 | — | PF63 42.00 | PF65 45.00 | | | |

**KM# 110 10 FRANCS**
19.00 g., 0.999 Silver 0.6103 oz. ASW, 40 mm. **Obv:** Lion left **Rev:** WWI Sopwith Camel fighter plane flying right **Edge:** Reeded

| Date | Mintage | VF20 | XF40 | MS60 | MS63 | MS65 |
|---|---|---|---|---|---|---|
| 2003 | — | PF63 42.00 | PF65 45.00 | | | |

**KM# 111 10 FRANCS**
19.00 g., 0.999 Silver 0.6103 oz. ASW, 40 mm. **Obv:** Lion left **Rev:** Curtiss NC-4 early seaplane flying left **Edge:** Reeded

| Date | Mintage | VF20 | XF40 | MS60 | MS63 | MS65 |
|---|---|---|---|---|---|---|
| 2003 | — | PF63 42.00 | PF65 45.00 | | | |

**KM# 112 10 FRANCS**
19.00 g., 0.999 Silver 0.6103 oz. ASW, 40 mm. **Obv:** Lion left **Rev:** Macchi-Castoldi MC-72 seaplane flying left at 8 o'clock **Edge:** Reeded

| Date | Mintage | VF20 | XF40 | MS60 | MS63 | MS65 |
|---|---|---|---|---|---|---|
| 2003 | — | PF63 42.00 | PF65 45.00 | | | |

**KM# 113 10 FRANCS**
19.00 g., 0.999 Silver 0.6103 oz. ASW, 40 mm. **Obv:** Lion left **Rev:** WWII CA-12 Boomerang fighter plane flying above map at 10 o'clock **Edge:** Reeded

| Date | Mintage | VF20 | XF40 | MS60 | MS63 | MS65 |
|---|---|---|---|---|---|---|
| 2003 | — | PF63 42.00 | PF65 45.00 | | | |

**KM# 114 10 FRANCS**
19.00 g., 0.999 Silver 0.6103 oz. ASW, 40 mm. **Obv:** Lion left **Rev:** B-50A Superfortress bomber flying left **Edge:** Reeded

| Date | Mintage | VF20 | XF40 | MS60 | MS63 | MS65 |
|---|---|---|---|---|---|---|
| 2003 | — | PF63 42.00 | PF65 45.00 | | | |

**KM# 115 10 FRANCS**
19.00 g., 0.999 Silver 0.6103 oz. ASW, 40 mm. **Obv:** Lion left **Rev:** WWII Heinkel-178 German jet plane flying left **Edge:** Reeded

| Date | Mintage | VF20 | XF40 | MS60 | MS63 | MS65 |
|---|---|---|---|---|---|---|
| 2003 | — | PF63 42.00 | PF65 45.00 | | | |

**KM# 116 10 FRANCS**
19.00 g., 0.999 Silver 0.6103 oz. ASW, 40 mm. **Obv:** Lion left **Rev:** Early De Havilland Comet jet liner flying left **Edge:** Reeded

| Date | Mintage | VF20 | XF40 | MS60 | MS63 | MS65 |
|---|---|---|---|---|---|---|
| 2003 | — | PF63 42.00 | PF65 45.00 | | | |

**KM# 117 10 FRANCS**
19.00 g., 0.999 Silver 0.6103 oz. ASW, 40 mm. **Obv:** Lion left **Rev:** Panavia Tornado jet fighter-bomber flying left **Edge:** Reeded

| Date | Mintage | VF20 | XF40 | MS60 | MS63 | MS65 |
|---|---|---|---|---|---|---|
| 2003 | — | PF63 42.00 | PF65 45.00 | | | |

**KM# 118 10 FRANCS**
19.00 g., 0.999 Silver 0.6103 oz. ASW, 40 mm. **Obv:** Lion left **Rev:** Hindustan HF24 jet fighter flying left **Edge:** Reeded

| Date | Mintage | VF20 | XF40 | MS60 | MS63 | MS65 |
|---|---|---|---|---|---|---|
| 2003 | — | PF63 42.00 | PF65 45.00 | | | |

**KM# 119 10 FRANCS**
19.00 g., 0.999 Silver 0.6103 oz. ASW, 40 mm. **Obv:** Lion left **Rev:** Lockheed F-117 Stealth fighter flying left **Edge:** Reeded

| Date | Mintage | VF20 | XF40 | MS60 | MS63 | MS65 |
|---|---|---|---|---|---|---|
| 2003 | — | PF63 42.00 | PF65 45.00 | | | |

**KM# 120 10 FRANCS**
19.00 g., 0.999 Silver 0.6103 oz. ASW, 40 mm. **Obv:** Lion left **Rev:** North American X-15 experimental rocket plane flying right at 1 o'clock **Edge:** Reeded

| Date | Mintage | VF20 | XF40 | MS60 | MS63 | MS65 |
|---|---|---|---|---|---|---|
| 2003 | — | **PF63** 42.00 | | **PF65** 45.00 | | |

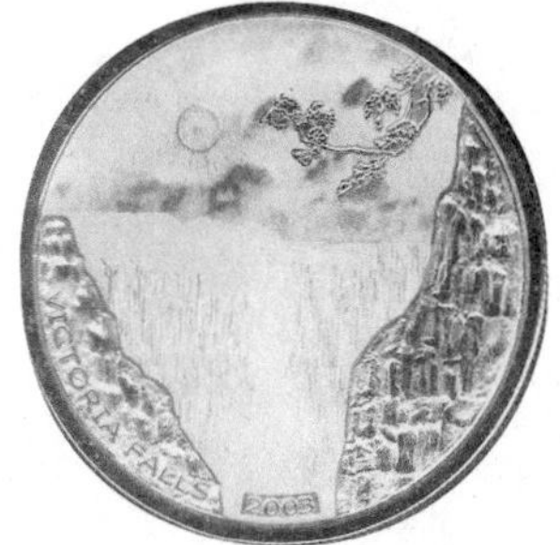

**KM# 122 10 FRANCS**
25.00 g., 0.925 Silver 0.7435 oz. ASW, 38.6 mm. **Obv:** Lion left **Rev:** Multicolor 3D hologram view of Victoria Falls **Edge:** Reeded

| Date | Mintage | VF20 | XF40 | MS60 | MS63 | MS65 |
|---|---|---|---|---|---|---|
| 2003 | 5,000 | **PF63** 50.00 | | **PF65** 70.00 | | |

**KM# 132 10 FRANCS**
25.00 g., 0.900 Silver 0.7234 oz. ASW, 40 mm. **Obv:** Lion left **Rev:** Multicolor dolphin leaping left **Edge:** Reeded

| Date | Mintage | VF20 | XF40 | MS60 | MS63 | MS65 |
|---|---|---|---|---|---|---|
| 2003 | 5,000 | **PF65** 30.00 | | | | |

**KM# 133 10 FRANCS**
25.00 g., 0.900 Silver 0.7234 oz. ASW, 40 mm. **Obv:** Lion left **Rev:** Multicolor sea turtle left **Edge:** Reeded

| Date | Mintage | VF20 | XF40 | MS60 | MS63 | MS65 |
|---|---|---|---|---|---|---|
| 2003 | 5,000 | **PF65** 30.00 | | | | |

**KM# 134 10 FRANCS**
25.00 g., 0.900 Silver 0.7234 oz. ASW, 40 mm. **Obv:** Lion left **Rev:** Multicolor killer whale jumping right **Edge:** Reeded

| Date | Mintage | VF20 | XF40 | MS60 | MS63 | MS65 |
|---|---|---|---|---|---|---|
| 2003 | 5,000 | **PF65** 30.00 | | | | |

**KM# 135 10 FRANCS**
26.00 g., 0.999 Silver 0.8351 oz. ASW, 40 mm. **Obv:** Lion left **Rev:** Pope John Paul II with staff and mitre, waving **Edge:** Reeded

| Date | Mintage | VF20 | XF40 | MS60 | MS63 | MS65 |
|---|---|---|---|---|---|---|
| 2003 | — | **PF65** 55.00 | | | | |

**KM# 163 10 FRANCS**
39.10 g., Acrylic, 49.9 mm. **Obv:** Old World Swallowtail butterfly above lion and value **Rev:** Rear view of the obverse **Edge:** Plain

| Date | Mintage | VF20 | XF40 | MS60 | MS63 | MS65 |
|---|---|---|---|---|---|---|
| 2003 | — | — | — | 75.00 | — | — |

**KM# 171 10 FRANCS**
39.10 g., Acrylic, 49.9 mm. **Obv:** Gorch Fock sail ship above lion and value **Rev:** Rear view of the obverse design **Edge:** Plain

| Date | Mintage | VF20 | XF40 | MS60 | MS63 | MS65 |
|---|---|---|---|---|---|---|
| 2003 | 1,000 | — | — | 75.00 | — | — |

**KM# 126 10 FRANCS**
25.00 g., 0.925 Silver 0.7435 oz. ASW, 38.6 mm. **Obv:** Lion left above value **Rev:** Sundial face with collapsible gnomon **Edge:** Reeded

| Date | Mintage | VF20 | XF40 | MS60 | MS63 | MS65 |
|---|---|---|---|---|---|---|
| 2004 | 5,000 | **PF65** 50.00 | | | | |

**KM# 127 10 FRANCS**
25.00 g., 0.925 Silver 0.7435 oz. ASW, 38.6 mm. **Obv:** Lion left above value **Rev:** Compass face **Edge:** Reeded **Note:** Compass part of the compass and spoon set. See also 5 Francs, (KM#128)

| Date | Mintage | VF20 | XF40 | MS60 | MS63 | MS65 |
|---|---|---|---|---|---|---|
| 2004 | 5,000 | **PF65** 50.00 | | | | |

**KM# 141 10 FRANCS**
25.00 g., 0.925 Silver 0.7435 oz. ASW, 38.6 mm. **Obv:** Lion left **Rev:** Multicolor Emperor fish swimming left **Edge:** Reeded

| Date | Mintage | VF20 | XF40 | MS60 | MS63 | MS65 |
|---|---|---|---|---|---|---|
| 2004 | 5,000 | **PF65** 55.00 | | | | |

**KM# 142 10 FRANCS**
25.00 g., 0.925 Silver 0.7435 oz. ASW, 38.6 mm. **Obv:** Lion left **Rev:** Multicolor octopus facing **Edge:** Reeded

| Date | Mintage | VF20 | XF40 | MS60 | MS63 | MS65 |
|---|---|---|---|---|---|---|
| 2004 | 5,000 | **PF65** 75.00 | | | | |

**KM# 143 10 FRANCS**
25.00 g., 0.925 Silver 0.7435 oz. ASW, 38.6 mm. **Obv:** Lion left **Rev:** Formula 1 and GT race cars **Edge:** Reeded

| Date | Mintage | VF20 | XF40 | MS60 | MS63 | MS65 |
|---|---|---|---|---|---|---|
| 2004 | 5,000 | **PF65** 45.00 | | | | |

**KM# 145 10 FRANCS**
25.00 g., 0.925 Silver 0.7435 oz. ASW, 27x47 mm. **Obv:** Lion left **Rev:** Pope with crucifix **Edge:** Plain **Shape:** Rectangular

| Date | Mintage | VF20 | XF40 | MS60 | MS63 | MS65 |
|---|---|---|---|---|---|---|
| 2004 | 5,000 | PF65 50.00 | | | | |

**KM# 149 10 FRANCS**
25.00 g., 0.925 Silver 0.7435 oz. ASW, 38.6 mm. **Obv:** Lion left **Rev:** Multicolor Quetzal bird **Edge:** Reeded

| Date | Mintage | VF20 | XF40 | MS60 | MS63 | MS65 |
|---|---|---|---|---|---|---|
| 2004 | 5,000 | PF65 35.00 | | | | |

**KM# 150 10 FRANCS**
25.00 g., 0.925 Silver 0.7435 oz. ASW, 38.6 mm. **Obv:** Lion left **Rev:** Multicolor Bird of Paradise on branch left **Edge:** Reeded

| Date | Mintage | VF20 | XF40 | MS60 | MS63 | MS65 |
|---|---|---|---|---|---|---|
| 2004 | 5,000 | PF65 35.00 | | | | |

**KM# 151 10 FRANCS**
25.00 g., 0.925 Silver 0.7435 oz. ASW, 38.6 mm. **Obv:** Lion left **Rev:** Multicolor Kingfisher bird left **Edge:** Reeded

| Date | Mintage | VF20 | XF40 | MS60 | MS63 | MS65 |
|---|---|---|---|---|---|---|
| 2004 | 5,000 | PF65 35.00 | | | | |

**KM# 155 10 FRANCS**
Acrylic Clear, 50 mm. **Obv:** Etched nine-masted sailing junk above lion, value and country name **Edge:** Plain

| Date | Mintage | VF20 | XF40 | MS60 | MS63 | MS65 |
|---|---|---|---|---|---|---|
| 2004 | 2,000 | — | — | — | — | 55.00 |

**KM# 172 10 FRANCS**
25.00 g., Silver, 38.6 mm. **Obv:** Lion left **Rev:** Pope waving half facing at left, cross at upper right, Vatican at lower right

| Date | Mintage | VF20 | XF40 | MS60 | MS63 | MS65 |
|---|---|---|---|---|---|---|
| 2005 | 3,000 | PF65 50.00 | | | | |

**KM# 179a 10 FRANCS**
25.00 g., 0.925 Silver 0.7435 oz. ASW, 38.58 mm. **Series:** Wildlife Protection **Obv:** Lion standing left **Obv. Legend:** REPUBLIQUE DEMOCRATIQUE DU CONGO **Rev:** Butterfly Fish, multicolor **Edge:** Reeded

| Date | Mintage | VF20 | XF40 | MS60 | MS63 | MS65 |
|---|---|---|---|---|---|---|
| 2005 | 5,000 | PF65 45.00 | | | | |

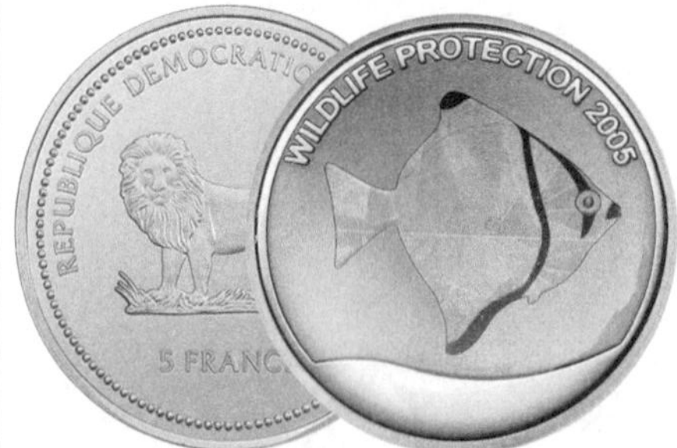


**KM# 180a 10 FRANCS**
25.00 g., 0.925 Silver 0.7435 oz. ASW, 38.58 mm. **Series:** Wildlife Protection **Obv:** Lion standing left **Obv. Legend:** REPUBLIQUE DEMOCRATIQUE DU CONGO **Rev:** African Moony Fish, multicolor **Edge:** Reeded

| Date | Mintage | VF20 | XF40 | MS60 | MS63 | MS65 |
|---|---|---|---|---|---|---|
| 2005 | 5,000 | PF65 45.00 | | | | |

**KM# 181a 10 FRANCS**
25.00 g., 0.925 Silver 0.7435 oz. ASW, 38.58 mm. **Series:** Wildlife Protection **Obv:** Lion standing left **Obv. Legend:** REPUBLIQUE DEMOCRATIQUE DU CONGO **Rev:** Red Perch, multicolor **Edge:** Reeded

| Date | Mintage | VF20 | XF40 | MS60 | MS63 | MS65 |
|---|---|---|---|---|---|---|
| 2005 | 5,000 | PF65 45.00 | | | | |

**KM# 217 10 FRANCS**
39.00 g., Acrylic, 50 mm. **Obv:** John Paul II, lion and cross

| Date | Mintage | VF20 | XF40 | MS60 | MS63 | MS65 |
|---|---|---|---|---|---|---|
| 2005 | — | — | — | — | — | 50.00 |

**KM# 218 10 FRANCS**
39.10 g., Acrylic, 50 mm. **Obv:** Sailing training vessel Amergo Vespucci

| Date | Mintage | VF20 | XF40 | MS60 | MS63 | MS65 |
|---|---|---|---|---|---|---|
| 2005 | — | — | — | — | — | 50.00 |

**KM# 176 10 FRANCS**
32.00 g., 0.999 Silver 1.0278 oz. ASW, 40 mm. **Obv:** Lion standing left **Obv. Legend:** REPUBLIQUE DEMOCRATIQUE DU CONGO **Rev:** World Trade Center Twin Towers as they were before 9-11 **Edge:** Reeded

| Date | Mintage | VF20 | XF40 | MS60 | MS63 | MS65 |
|---|---|---|---|---|---|---|
| 2006 | — | PF65 50.00 | | | | |

**KM# 219 10 FRANCS**
39.00 g., Acrylic, 50 mm. **Obv:** Sailing ship Shtandart

| Date | Mintage | VF20 | XF40 | MS60 | MS63 | MS65 |
|---|---|---|---|---|---|---|
| 2006 | — | — | — | — | — | 50.00 |

**KM# 221 10 FRANCS**
Silver, 38.6 mm. **Obv:** Lion standing left **Rev:** Swiss Guard standing taking oath on flag

| Date | Mintage | VF20 | XF40 | MS60 | MS63 | MS65 |
|---|---|---|---|---|---|---|
| 2006 | — | PF65 70.00 | | | | |

**KM# 222 10 FRANCS**
39.10 g., Acrylic, 50 mm. **Obv:** Admiral Michiel de Ruyter and sailing ship

| Date | Mintage | VF20 | XF40 | MS60 | MS63 | MS65 |
|---|---|---|---|---|---|---|
| 2007 | — | — | — | — | — | 50.00 |

**KM# 200 10 FRANCS**
Silver Plated Copper, 40 mm. **Subject:** Aviation Centennial 1903-2003 **Obv:** National arms **Rev:** Early aircraft and bust

| Date | Mintage | VF20 | XF40 | MS60 | MS63 | MS65 |
|---|---|---|---|---|---|---|
| 2008 | — | PF65 15.00 | | | | |

**KM# 201 10 FRANCS**
Silver Plated Copper, 40 mm. **Subject:** Warriors of the World **Obv:** National arms **Rev:** Spartan standing

| Date | Mintage | VF20 | XF40 | MS60 | MS63 | MS65 |
|---|---|---|---|---|---|---|
| 2010 | — | PF63 25.00 | PF65 30.00 | | | |

**KM# 202 10 FRANCS**
Silver Plated Copper, 40 mm. **Subject:** Warriors of the World **Obv:** National arms **Rev:** Centurian

| Date | Mintage | VF20 | XF40 | MS60 | MS63 | MS65 |
|---|---|---|---|---|---|---|
| 2010 | — | PF63 25.00 | PF65 30.00 | | | |

**KM# 203 10 FRANCS**
Silver Plated Copper, 40 mm. **Subject:** Warriors of the World **Obv:** National arms **Rev:** Gladiator standing

| Date | Mintage | VF20 | XF40 | MS60 | MS63 | MS65 |
|---|---|---|---|---|---|---|
| 2010 | — | PF63 25.00 | PF65 30.00 | | | |

**KM# 204 10 FRANCS**
Silver Plated Copper, 40 mm. **Subject:** Warriors of the World **Obv:** Naitonal arms **Rev:** Chinese warrior

| Date | Mintage | VF20 | XF40 | MS60 | MS63 | MS65 |
|---|---|---|---|---|---|---|
| 2010 | — | PF63 25.00 | PF65 30.00 | | | |

**KM# 205 10 FRANCS**
Silver Plated Copper, 40 mm. **Subject:** Warriors of the World **Obv:** Naitonal Arms **Rev:** Celtic Warrior

| Date | Mintage | VF20 | XF40 | MS60 | MS63 | MS65 |
|---|---|---|---|---|---|---|
| 2010 | — | PF63 25.00 | PF65 30.00 | | | |

**KM# 206 10 FRANCS**
Silver Plated Copper, 40 mm. **Subject:** Warriors of the World **Obv:** National arms **Rev:** Mongolian warrior on horseback

| Date | Mintage | VF20 | XF40 | MS60 | MS63 | MS65 |
|---|---|---|---|---|---|---|
| 2010 | — | PF63 25.00 | PF65 30.00 | | | |

**KM# 207 10 FRANCS**
Silver Plated Copper, 40 mm. **Subject:** Warriors of the World **Obv:** National arms **Rev:** Viking standing

| Date | Mintage | VF20 | XF40 | MS60 | MS63 | MS65 |
|---|---|---|---|---|---|---|
| 2010 | — | PF63 25.00 | PF65 30.00 | | | |

**KM# 208 10 FRANCS**
Silver Plated Copper, 40 mm. **Subject:** Warriors of the World **Obv:** National arms **Rev:** English Archer

| Date | Mintage | VF20 | XF40 | MS60 | MS63 | MS65 |
|---|---|---|---|---|---|---|
| 2010 | — | PF63 25.00 | PF65 30.00 | | | |

**KM# 209 10 FRANCS**
Silver Plated Copper, 40 mm. **Subject:** Warriors of the World **Obv:** National arms **Rev:** Templar Knight on horseback

| Date | Mintage | VF20 | XF40 | MS60 | MS63 | MS65 |
|---|---|---|---|---|---|---|
| 2010 | — | PF63 25.00 | PF65 30.00 | | | |

**KM# 210 10 FRANCS**
Silver Plated Copper, 40 mm. **Subject:** Warriors of the World **Obv:** National arms **Rev:** Ninja standing

| Date | Mintage | VF20 | XF40 | MS60 | MS63 | MS65 |
|---|---|---|---|---|---|---|
| 2010 | — | PF63 25.00 | PF65 30.00 | | | |

**KM# 211 10 FRANCS**
Silver Plated Copper, 40 mm. **Subject:** Warriors of the World **Obv:** National arms **Rev:** Samurai warrior standing

| Date | Mintage | VF20 | XF40 | MS60 | MS63 | MS65 |
|---|---|---|---|---|---|---|
| 2010 | — | PF63 25.00 | PF65 30.00 | | | |

**KM# 212 10 FRANCS**
Silver Plated Copper, 40 mm. **Subject:** Warriors of the World **Obv:** National arms **Rev:** Zulu warrior standing

| Date | Mintage | VF20 | XF40 | MS60 | MS63 | MS65 |
|---|---|---|---|---|---|---|
| 2010 | — | PF63 25.00 | PF65 30.00 | | | |

**KM# 136 20 FRANCS**
1.24 g., 0.9999 Gold 0.040 oz. AGW, 13.92 mm. **Obv:** Lion left **Rev:** Pope John Paul II with staff and mitre, waving **Edge:** Plain

| Date | Mintage | VF20 | XF40 | MS60 | MS63 | MS65 |
|---|---|---|---|---|---|---|
| 2003 | — | PF65 75.00 | | | | |

**KM# 137 20 FRANCS**
1.24 g., 0.9999 Gold 0.040 oz. AGW, 13.92 mm. **Obv:** Lion left **Rev:** Skunk **Edge:** Plain

| Date | Mintage | VF20 | XF40 | MS60 | MS63 | MS65 |
|---|---|---|---|---|---|---|
| 2003 | 25,000 | PF65 75.00 | | | | |

**KM# 138 20 FRANCS**
1.24 g., 0.9999 Gold 0.040 oz. AGW, 13.92 mm. **Obv:** Lion left **Rev:** Giant anteater right **Edge:** Plain

| Date | Mintage | VF20 | XF40 | MS60 | MS63 | MS65 |
|---|---|---|---|---|---|---|
| 2003 | 25,000 | PF65 75.00 | | | | |

**KM# 139 20 FRANCS**
1.24 g., 0.9999 Gold 0.040 oz. AGW, 13.92 mm. **Obv:** Lion left **Rev:** Porcupine right **Edge:** Plain

| Date | Mintage | VF20 | XF40 | MS60 | MS63 | MS65 |
|---|---|---|---|---|---|---|
| 2003 | 25,000 | PF65 75.00 | | | | |

**KM# 140 20 FRANCS**
1.24 g., 0.9999 Gold 0.040 oz. AGW, 13.92 mm. **Obv:** Lion left **Rev:** Chameleon **Edge:** Plain

| Date | Mintage | VF20 | XF40 | MS60 | MS63 | MS65 |
|---|---|---|---|---|---|---|
| 2003 | 25,000 | PF65 75.00 | | | | |

**KM# 184 20 FRANCS**
1.22 g., 0.9999 Gold 0.0392 oz. AGW, 13.74 mm. **Subject:** XXVIII Summer Olympics - Athens **Obv:** Lion standing right **Rev:** Athenian tetradrachm featuring owl perched **Edge:** Reeded

| Date | Mintage | VF20 | XF40 | MS60 | MS63 | MS65 |
|---|---|---|---|---|---|---|
| 2003 | 25,000 | PF65 75.00 | | | | |

**KM# 144 20 FRANCS**
1.24 g., 0.9999 Gold 0.040 oz. AGW, 13.92 mm. **Obv:** Lion left **Rev:** Ferrari coat of arms **Edge:** Plain

| Date | Mintage | VF20 | XF40 | MS60 | MS63 | MS65 |
|---|---|---|---|---|---|---|
| 2004 | 5,000 | PF65 75.00 | | | | |

**KM# 186 20 FRANCS**
1.24 g., 0.9999 Gold 0.040 oz. AGW, 13.92 mm. **Subject:** Christmas **Obv:** Lion standing left **Rev:** Jesus lying in manger

| Date | Mintage | VF20 | XF40 | MS60 | MS63 | MS65 |
|---|---|---|---|---|---|---|
| ND-2004 | 25,000 | PF65 75.00 | | | | |

**KM# 173 20 FRANCS**
1.53 g., 0.999 Gold 0.0491 oz. AGW, 13.9 mm. **Obv:** Lion left **Rev:** Pope waving at left, cross at upper right, Vatican at lower right

| Date | Mintage | VF20 | XF40 | MS60 | MS63 | MS65 |
|---|---|---|---|---|---|---|
| 2005 | 25,000 | PF65 95.00 | | | | |

**KM# 213 25 FRANCS**
Acrylic, 50mm mm. **Rev:** H.M. Bark Endeavour at center; Captian James Cook bust at top left, National arms at bottom center

| Date | Mintage | VF20 | XF40 | MS60 | MS63 | MS65 |
|---|---|---|---|---|---|---|
| 2009 | — | — | — | — | — | 55.00 |

**KM# 223 30 FRANCS**
20.00 g., 0.999 Silver 0.6424 oz. ASW, 38.61 mm. **Subject:** Big Cats - Lion

| Date | Mintage | VF20 | XF40 | MS60 | MS63 | MS65 |
|---|---|---|---|---|---|---|
| 2011 | 3,000 | PF65 50.00 | | | | |

**KM# 224 30 FRANCS**
20.00 g., 0.999 Silver 0.6424 oz. ASW, 38.61 mm. **Subject:** Big cats - Leopard

| Date | Mintage | VF20 | XF40 | MS60 | MS63 | MS65 |
|---|---|---|---|---|---|---|
| 2011 | 3,000 | PF65 50.00 | | | | |

**KM# 225 30 FRANCS**
20.00 g., 0.999 Silver 0.6424 oz. ASW, 38.61 mm. **Subject:** Big cats - Chetah

| Date | Mintage | VF20 | XF40 | MS60 | MS63 | MS65 |
|---|---|---|---|---|---|---|
| 2011 | 3,000 | PF65 50.00 | | | | |

**KM# 226 30 FRANCS**
20.00 g., 0.999 Silver 0.6424 oz. ASW, 38.61 mm. **Subject:** Big cats - Tiger

| Date | Mintage | VF20 | XF40 | MS60 | MS63 | MS65 |
|---|---|---|---|---|---|---|
| 2011 | 3,000 | PF65 50.00 | | | | |

**KM# 185 75 FRANCS**
15.55 g., 0.9999 Gold 0.4999 oz. AGW **Subject:** XXVIII Summer Olympics - Athens **Obv:** Lion standing right **Rev:** Athenian tetradrachm featuring owl perched **Edge:** Reeded

| Date | Mintage | VF20 | XF40 | MS60 | MS63 | MS65 |
|---|---|---|---|---|---|---|
| 2003 | 500 | PF65 900 | | | | |

**KM# 129 100 FRANCS**
31.10 g., 0.9999 Gold 0.9998 oz. AGW, 40 mm. **Series:** Wild Life Protection **Obv:** Lion left **Rev:** Reflective multicolor swallowtail butterfly **Edge:** Reeded

| Date | Mintage | VF20 | XF40 | MS60 | MS63 | MS65 |
|---|---|---|---|---|---|---|
| 2002 | 50 | PF65 1,800 | | | | |

**KM# 130 100 FRANCS**
31.10 g., 0.9999 Gold 0.9998 oz. AGW, 40 mm. **Series:** Wild Life Protection **Obv:** Lion left **Rev:** Reflective multicolor dark greenish butterfly **Edge:** Reeded

| Date | Mintage | VF20 | XF40 | MS60 | MS63 | MS65 |
|---|---|---|---|---|---|---|
| 2002 | 50 | PF65 1,800 | | | | |

**KM# 131 100 FRANCS**
31.10 g., 0.9999 Gold 0.9998 oz. AGW, 40 mm. **Series:** Wild Life Protection **Obv:** Lion left **Rev:** Reflective multicolor red and black butterfly **Edge:** Reeded

| Date | Mintage | VF20 | XF40 | MS60 | MS63 | MS65 |
|---|---|---|---|---|---|---|
| 2002 | 50 | PF65 1,800 | | | | |

**KM# 152 100 FRANCS**
31.10 g., 0.9999 Gold 0.9999 oz. AGW, 38.6 mm. **Obv:** Lion left **Rev:** Multicolor Quetzal bird **Edge:** Reeded

| Date | Mintage | VF20 | XF40 | MS60 | MS63 | MS65 |
|---|---|---|---|---|---|---|
| 2004 | 25 | PF65 1,800 | | | | |

**KM# 153 100 FRANCS**
31.10 g., 0.9999 Gold 0.9999 oz. AGW, 38.6 mm. **Obv:** Lion left **Rev:** Multicolor Bird of Paradise left **Edge:** Reeded

| Date | Mintage | VF20 | XF40 | MS60 | MS63 | MS65 |
|---|---|---|---|---|---|---|
| 2004 | 25 | PF65 1,800 | | | | |

**KM# 154 100 FRANCS**
31.10 g., 0.9999 Gold 0.9999 oz. AGW, 38.6 mm. **Obv:** Lion left **Rev:** Multicolor Kingfisher bird **Edge:** Reeded

| Date | Mintage | VF20 | XF40 | MS60 | MS63 | MS65 |
|---|---|---|---|---|---|---|
| 2004 | 25 | PF65 1,800 | | | | |

**KM# 179b 100 FRANCS**
31.10 g., 0.999 Gold 0.9989 oz. AGW, 38.58 mm. **Series:** Wildlife Protection **Obv:** Lion standing left **Obv. Legend:** REPUBLIQUE DEMOCRATIQUE DU CONGO **Rev:** Butterfly Fish, multicolor **Edge:** Reeded

| Date | Mintage | VF20 | XF40 | MS60 | MS63 | MS65 |
|---|---|---|---|---|---|---|
| 2005 | 25 | PF65 1,800 | | | | |

**KM# 180b 100 FRANCS**
31.10 g., 0.999 Gold 0.9989 oz. AGW, 38.58 mm. **Series:** Wildlife Protection **Obv:** Lion standing left **Obv. Legend:** REPUBLIQUE DEMOCRATIQUE DU CONGO **Rev:** African Mooney Fish, muticolor **Edge:** Reeded

| Date | Mintage | VF20 | XF40 | MS60 | MS63 | MS65 |
|---|---|---|---|---|---|---|
| 2005 | 25 | PF65 1,800 | | | | |

**KM# 181b 100 FRANCS**
31.10 g., 0.999 Gold 0.9989 oz. AGW, 38.58 mm. **Series:** Wildlife Protection **Obv:** Lion standing left **Obv. Legend:** REPUBLIQUE DEMOCRATIQUE DU CONGO **Rev:** Red Perch, multicolor **Edge:** Reeded

| Date | Mintage | VF20 | XF40 | MS60 | MS63 | MS65 |
|---|---|---|---|---|---|---|
| 2005 | 25 | PF65 1,800 | | | | |

## MINT SETS

| KM# | Date | Mintage | Identification | Issue Price | Mkt Val |
|---|---|---|---|---|---|
| MS2 | 2004 (4) | — | KM#156-159 | — | 12.50 |

# CONGO REPUBLIC

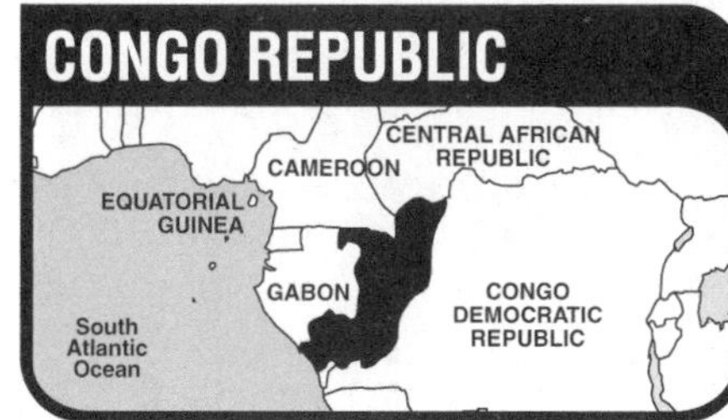


The Republic of the Congo (formerly the Peoples Republic of the Congo), located on the equator in west-central Africa, has an area of 132,047 sq. mi. (342,000 sq. km.) and a population of *2.98 million. Capital: Brazzaville. Agriculture forestry, mining, and food processing are the principal industries. Timber, industrial diamonds, potash, peanuts, and cocoa beans are exported.

**NOTE**: For earlier and related coinage see French Equatorial Africa and the Equatorial African States. For later coinage see Central African States.

**MINT MARK**
(a) - Paris, privy marks only

**MONETARY SYSTEM**
100 Centimes = 1 Franc

# REPUBLIC

Republique du Congo

## DECIMAL COINAGE

**KM# 110 500 FRANCS**
Silver **Subject:** History of aviation **Rev:** Swiss Air jet over mountains, 1931-2001, in color

| Date | Mintage | VF20 | XF40 | MS60 | MS63 | MS65 |
|---|---|---|---|---|---|---|
| 2002 | — | PF65 50.00 | | | | |

**KM# 47 1000 FRANCS**
15.00 g., 0.999 Silver 0.4818 oz. ASW, 35 mm. **Obv:** Seated woman with tablet **Rev:** Two soccer players and colosseum **Edge:** Plain

| Date | Mintage | VF20 | XF40 | MS60 | MS63 | MS65 |
|---|---|---|---|---|---|---|
| 2001 | — | PF65 42.00 | | | | |

**KM# 48 1000 FRANCS**
20.00 g., 0.999 Silver 0.6424 oz. ASW, 38 mm. **Obv:** Seated woman with tablet **Rev:** Two soccer players and Mexican pyramid **Edge:** Reeded

| Date | Mintage | VF20 | XF40 | MS60 | MS63 | MS65 |
|---|---|---|---|---|---|---|
| 2001 | — | PF65 45.00 | | | | |

**KM# 112 1000 FRANCS**
Silver, 38 mm. **Subject:** Thomas W. Lawson **Obv:** Female holding tablets **Rev:** Seven-masted Great Lakes Sconner sailing right

| Date | Mintage | VF20 | XF40 | MS60 | MS63 | MS65 |
|---|---|---|---|---|---|---|
| 2001 | — | PF63 35.00 | PF65 40.00 | | | |

**KM# 67 1000 FRANCS**
31.11 g., 0.999 Silver 0.999 oz. ASW, 40 mm. **Rev:** Eifle tower and franc coin in color

| Date | Mintage | VF20 | XF40 | MS60 | MS63 | MS65 |
|---|---|---|---|---|---|---|
| 2002 | Est. 2001 | PF65 90.00 | | | | |

**KM# 68 1000 FRANCS**
Silver **Subject:** African Wildlife **Shape:** Rectangle

| Date | Mintage | VF20 | XF40 | MS60 | MS63 | MS65 |
|---|---|---|---|---|---|---|
| 2002 Proof | — | — | — | — | — | — |

**KM# 109 1000 FRANCS**
20.00 g., 0.999 Silver 0.6424 oz. ASW, 38.6 mm. **Obv:** Seated woman with tablets **Rev:** Portuguese merchant ship

| Date | Mintage | VF20 | XF40 | MS60 | MS63 | MS65 |
|---|---|---|---|---|---|---|
| 2002 | — | PF63 40.00 | PF65 45.00 | | | |

**KM# 113 1000 FRANCS**
Silver, 38 mm. **Obv:** Female with tablets **Rev:** Hohenzollern castle

| Date | Mintage | VF20 | XF40 | MS60 | MS63 | MS65 |
|---|---|---|---|---|---|---|
| 2002 | — | PF63 35.00 | PF65 40.00 | | | |

**KM# 114 1000 FRANCS**
Silver, 38 mm. **Obv:** Female seated with tablets **Rev:** Nymphenburg palace

| Date | Mintage | VF20 | XF40 | MS60 | MS63 | MS65 |
|---|---|---|---|---|---|---|
| 2002 | — | PF63 35.00 | PF65 40.00 | | | |

**KM# 115 1000 FRANCS**
20.00 g., 0.999 Silver 0.6424 oz. ASW, 38.6 mm. **Obv:** Seated female with two tablets **Rev:** DC-3 aircraft in clouds

| Date | Mintage | VF20 | XF40 | MS60 | MS63 | MS65 |
|---|---|---|---|---|---|---|
| 2002 | — | PF65 50.00 | | | | |

**KM# 116 1000 FRANCS**
20.00 g., 0.999 Silver 0.6424 oz. ASW, 38.6 mm. **Obv:** Seated female with two tablets **Rev:** Swiss A-3000 flying over mountains

| Date | Mintage | VF20 | XF40 | MS60 | MS63 | MS65 |
|---|---|---|---|---|---|---|
| 2002 | — | PF65 50.00 | | | | |

**KM# 50 1000 FRANCS**
20.20 g., Silver, 40 mm. **Series:** Endangered Wildlife **Obv:** Seated woman with tablet **Obv. Legend:** REPUBLIQUE DU CONGO **Rev:** Gorilla seated with infant **Rev. Legend:** - LE MONDE ANIMAL EN PERIL **Edge:** Reeded

| Date | Mintage | VF20 | XF40 | MS60 | MS63 | MS65 |
|---|---|---|---|---|---|---|
| 2003 | — | PF65 50.00 | | | | |

**KM# 108 1000 FRANCS**
20.00 g., 0.999 Silver 0.6424 oz. ASW, 38.6 mm. **Obv:** Seated woman with two tablets **Rev:** James Cook and the Endeavour

| Date | Mintage | VF20 | XF40 | MS60 | MS63 | MS65 |
|---|---|---|---|---|---|---|
| 2003 | — | PF63 40.00 | PF65 45.00 | | | |

**KM# 117 1000 FRANCS**
20.00 g., 0.999 Silver 0.6424 oz. ASW, 38.6 mm. **Obv:** Seated female with two tablets **Rev:** MD-11 aircraft on runway

| Date | Mintage | VF20 | XF40 | MS60 | MS63 | MS65 |
|---|---|---|---|---|---|---|
| 2003 | — | PF65 50.00 | | | | |

**KM# 111 1000 FRANCS**
Silver, 38 mm. **Subject:** Konrad Duden **Obv:** Female holding tablets **Rev:** Bust facing, writing

| Date | Mintage | VF20 | XF40 | MS60 | MS63 | MS65 |
|---|---|---|---|---|---|---|
| 2004 | — | PF63 35.00 | PF65 40.00 | | | |

**KM# 118 1000 FRANCS**
20.00 g., 0.999 Silver 0.6424 oz. ASW, 38.6 mm. **Obv:** Seated female with two tablets **Rev:** BAC-111 on grasy runway

| Date | Mintage | VF20 | XF40 | MS60 | MS63 | MS65 |
|---|---|---|---|---|---|---|
| 2004 | — | PF65 50.00 | | | | |

**KM# 119 1000 FRANCS**
20.00 g., 0.999 Silver 0.6424 oz. ASW, 38.6 mm. **Obv:** Seated female with two tablets **Rev:** DC-2 in clouds

| Date | Mintage | VF20 | XF40 | MS60 | MS63 | MS65 |
|---|---|---|---|---|---|---|
| 2004 | — | PF65 50.00 | | | | |

**KM# 120 1000 FRANCS**
20.00 g., 0.999 Silver 0.6424 oz. ASW, 38.6 mm. **Obv:** Seated female with two tablets **Rev:** DC-7 at airport

| Date | Mintage | VF20 | XF40 | MS60 | MS63 | MS65 |
|---|---|---|---|---|---|---|
| 2004 | — | PF65 50.00 | | | | |

**KM# 51 1000 FRANCS**
15.50 g., Silver, 35.02 mm. **Obv:** Seated woman with tablet **Obv. Legend:** REPUBLIQUE DU CONGO **Rev:** Head of Michelangelo 3/4 right **Edge:** Plain

| Date | Mintage | VF20 | XF40 | MS60 | MS63 | MS65 |
|---|---|---|---|---|---|---|
| 2005 | — | PF63 35.00 | PF65 40.00 | | | |

**KM# 72 1000 FRANCS**
0.999 Silver **Obv:** National Arms **Rev:** Steam locomotive Limmat and Spanish Bon trasport (1847) from Baden to Zurich

| Date | Mintage | VF20 | XF40 | MS60 | MS63 | MS65 |
|---|---|---|---|---|---|---|
| 2007 | — | PF65 75.00 | | | | |

**KM# 75 1000 FRANCS**
31.11 g., 0.999 Silver 0.999 oz. ASW, 40 mm. **Obv:** National arms **Rev:** Colored Easter eggs and candle in cake, set on table; Orthodox church in background

| Date | Mintage | VF20 | XF40 | MS60 | MS63 | MS65 |
|---|---|---|---|---|---|---|
| 2011 | 2,000 | PF63 100 | | | | |

**KM# 73 1000 FRANCS**
31.11 g., 0.999 Silver 0.999 oz. ASW, 40 mm. **Obv:** National arms **Rev:** Rhino facing, map of Africa at right

| Date | Mintage | VF20 | XF40 | MS60 | MS63 | MS65 |
|---|---|---|---|---|---|---|
| 2012 Antique patina | 2,000 | — | — | — | 100 | — |

**KM# 74 1000 FRANCS**
31.11 g., 0.999 Silver 0.999 oz. ASW, 40 mm. **Obv:** National arms **Rev:** Two lion cubs, map of Africa at right

| Date | Mintage | VF20 | XF40 | MS60 | MS63 | MS65 |
|---|---|---|---|---|---|---|
| 2012 Antique patina | 2,000 | — | — | — | 100 | — |

**KM# 69 1500 FRANCS**
1.24 g., 0.999 Gold 0.0398 oz. AGW, 13.92 mm. **Rev:** Ferdinand Graf von Zeppelin

| Date | Mintage | VF20 | XF40 | MS60 | MS63 | MS65 |
|---|---|---|---|---|---|---|
| 2005 | — | PF63 90.00 | PF65 100 | | | |

**KM# 70 1500 FRANCS**
1.24 g., 0.999 Gold 0.0398 oz. AGW, 13.92 mm. **Rev:** Spinx and Pyramids

| Date | Mintage | VF20 | XF40 | MS60 | MS63 | MS65 |
|---|---|---|---|---|---|---|
| 2005 | — | PF63 90.00 | PF65 100 | | | |

**KM# 71 1500 FRANCS**
1.24 g., 0.999 Gold 0.0398 oz. AGW, 13.94 mm. **Rev:** Neuschwanstein castle

| Date | Mintage | VF20 | XF40 | MS60 | MS63 | MS65 |
|---|---|---|---|---|---|---|
| 2005 | — | PF63 90.00 | PF65 100 | | | |

# COOK ISLANDS

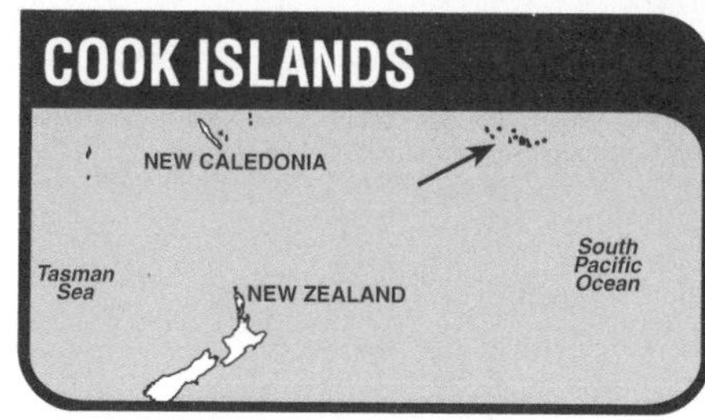


Cook Islands, a self-governing dependency of New Zealand consisting of 15 islands, is located in the South Pacific Ocean about 2,000 miles (3,218 km.) northeast of New Zealand. It has an area of 93 sq. mi. (234 sq. km.) and a population of 17,185. Capital: Avarua. The United States claims the islands of Danger, Manahiki, Penrhyn, and Rakahanga atolls. Citrus and canned fruits and juices, copra, clothing, jewelry, and mother-of-pearl shell are exported.

**RULER**
British

**MINT MARKS**
PM - Pobjoy Mint

**MONETARY SYSTEM**
100 Cents = 1 Dollar

## DEPENDENCY OF NEW ZEALAND

### DECIMAL COINAGE

**KM# 419 CENT**
1.44 g., Aluminum, 21.9 mm. **Ruler:** Elizabeth II **Obv:** Crowned head right, date below **Rev:** Bust of Capt. James Cook right, denomination below **Edge:** Plain

| Date | Mintage | VF20 | XF40 | MS60 | MS63 | MS65 |
|---|---|---|---|---|---|---|
| 2003 | — | — | — | 1.25 | 1.50 | — |

**KM# 420 CENT**
1.44 g., Aluminum, 21.9 mm. **Ruler:** Elizabeth II **Obv:** Crowned head right, date below **Rev:** Collie dog right, denomination below **Edge:** Plain

| Date | Mintage | VF20 | XF40 | MS60 | MS63 | MS65 |
|---|---|---|---|---|---|---|
| 2003 | — | — | — | 0.75 | 1.00 | — |

**KM# 421 CENT**
1.44 g., Aluminum, 21.9 mm. **Ruler:** Elizabeth II **Obv:** Crowned head right, date below **Rev:** Pointer dog right, denomination above **Edge:** Plain

| Date | Mintage | VF20 | XF40 | MS60 | MS63 | MS65 |
|---|---|---|---|---|---|---|
| 2003 | — | — | — | 0.75 | 1.00 | — |

**KM# 422 CENT**
1.44 g., Aluminum, 21.9 mm. **Ruler:** Elizabeth II **Obv:** Crowned head right, date below **Rev:** Rooster right, denomination above **Edge:** Plain

| Date | Mintage | VF20 | XF40 | MS60 | MS63 | MS65 |
|---|---|---|---|---|---|---|
| 2003 | — | — | — | 0.75 | 1.00 | — |

**KM# 423 CENT**
1.44 g., Aluminum, 22 mm. **Ruler:** Elizabeth II **Obv:** Crowned head right, date below **Rev:** Monkey on branch, denomination at left **Edge:** Plain

| Date | Mintage | VF20 | XF40 | MS60 | MS63 | MS65 |
|---|---|---|---|---|---|---|
| 2003 | — | — | — | 0.75 | 1.00 | — |

**KM# 756 CENT**
3.64 g., Brass Plated Steel, 11.8 mm. **Ruler:** Elizabeth II **Obv:** Bust right **Rev:** Female Hula dancer

| Date | Mintage | VF20 | XF40 | MS60 | MS63 | MS65 |
|---|---|---|---|---|---|---|
| 2010 | — | — | — | 0.75 | 1.00 | — |

**KM# 757 2 CENTS**
5.10 g., Brass Plated Steel, 19.8 mm. **Ruler:** Elizabeth II **Obv:** Bust right **Rev:** The Endeavor

| Date | Mintage | VF20 | XF40 | MS60 | MS63 | MS65 |
|---|---|---|---|---|---|---|
| 2010 | — | — | — | 0.75 | 1.00 | — |

**KM# 758 5 CENTS**
6.15 g., Brass Plated Steel, 21.7 mm. **Ruler:** Elizabeth II **Obv:** Bust right **Rev:** Tiare Maori flower

| Date | Mintage | VF20 | XF40 | MS60 | MS63 | MS65 |
|---|---|---|---|---|---|---|
| 2010 | — | — | — | 1.00 | 1.50 | — |

**KM# 759 10 CENTS**
11.50 g., Nickel Plated Steel, 20.5 mm. **Ruler:** Elizabeth II **Obv:** Bust right **Rev:** Yellowfin tuna

| Date | Mintage | VF20 | XF40 | MS60 | MS63 | MS65 |
|---|---|---|---|---|---|---|
| 2010 | — | — | — | 1.00 | 1.50 | — |

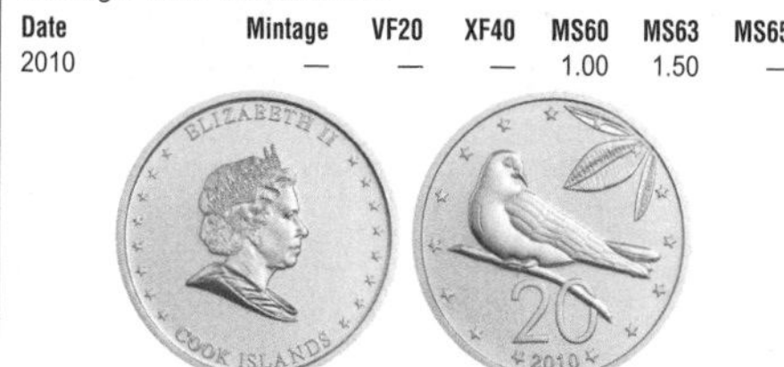


**KM# 760 20 CENTS**
14.13 g., Nickel Plated Steel, 21.75 mm. **Ruler:** Elizabeth II **Obv:** Bust right **Rev:** Bird

| Date | Mintage | VF20 | XF40 | MS60 | MS63 | MS65 |
|---|---|---|---|---|---|---|
| 2010 | — | — | — | 1.50 | 2.00 | — |

**KM# 1116 50 CENTS**
28.28 g., Copper-Nickel, 38.61 mm. **Ruler:** Elizabeth II **Subject:** Elizabeth II Corronation, 50th Anniversary

| Date | Mintage | VF20 | XF40 | MS60 | MS63 | MS65 |
|---|---|---|---|---|---|---|
| 2002 | — | — | — | — | 20.00 | — |

**KM# 1144 50 CENTS**
Copper-Nickel **Ruler:** Elizabeth II **Rev:** Edward "Ned" Kelley in color

| Date | Mintage | VF20 | XF40 | MS60 | MS63 | MS65 |
|---|---|---|---|---|---|---|
| 2004 | Est. 10000 | PF65 15.00 | | | | |

**KM# 761 50 CENTS**
Nickel Plated Steel, 34 mm. **Ruler:** Elizabeth II **Obv:** Bust right **Rev:** The Endeavor **Edge Lettering:** Reeded

| Date | Mintage | VF20 | XF40 | MS60 | MS63 | MS65 |
|---|---|---|---|---|---|---|
| 2010 | — | — | — | 2.00 | 2.50 | — |

**KM# 1114 DOLLAR**
32.00 g., Copper-Nickel, 40 mm. **Ruler:** Elizabeth II **Subject:** 2002 Winter Olympics, Salt Lake City

| Date | Mintage | VF20 | XF40 | MS60 | MS63 | MS65 |
|---|---|---|---|---|---|---|
| 2001 | — | — | — | — | — | 15.00 |

**KM# 1115 DOLLAR**
9.50 g., 0.999 Silver 0.3051 oz. ASW, 22.5 mm. **Ruler:** Elizabeth II **Series:** 2002 Commonwealth Games, Manchester **Rev:** Track field and medals on ribbons

| Date | Mintage | VF20 | XF40 | MS60 | MS63 | MS65 |
|---|---|---|---|---|---|---|
| 2001 | Est. 5000 | PF65 20.00 | | | | |

**KM# 396 DOLLAR**
24.88 g., 0.999 Silver 0.7992 oz. ASW with Acrylic capsule center containing tiny rubies, sapphires and cubic zirconias, 40.6 mm. **Ruler:** Elizabeth II **Subject:** Crown Jewels **Obv:** Crowned head right, legend **Rev:** Crowns and royal regalia **Edge:** Reeded

| Date | Mintage | VF20 | XF40 | MS60 | MS63 | MS65 |
|---|---|---|---|---|---|---|
| 2002 | 50,000 | PF65 32.50 | | | | |

**KM# 1117 DOLLAR**
0.999 Silver **Ruler:** Elizabeth II **Subject:** 2002 Winter Olumpics, Salt Lake City **Rev:** Figure skating

| Date | Mintage | VF20 | XF40 | MS60 | MS63 | MS65 |
|---|---|---|---|---|---|---|
| 2002 | — | PF65 37.50 | | | | |

**KM# 1118 DOLLAR**
Copper-Nickel **Ruler:** Elizabeth II **Subject:** XVII World Cup, Korea and Japan **Rev:** Soccer player and ball

| Date | Mintage | VF20 | XF40 | MS60 | MS63 | MS65 |
|---|---|---|---|---|---|---|
| 2002 | — | PF65 15.00 | | | | |

**KM# 416 DOLLAR**
10.75 g., Copper-Nickel, 28.5 mm. **Ruler:** Elizabeth II **Obv:** Queen's new portrait **Rev:** Tangaroa statue and value **Shape:** Scalloped

| Date | Mintage | VF20 | XF40 | MS60 | MS63 | MS65 |
|---|---|---|---|---|---|---|
| 2003 | — | — | — | — | 2.50 | 3.00 |
| 2010 | — | — | — | — | 2.50 | 3.00 |

**KM# 424 DOLLAR**
8.50 g., 0.999 Silver 0.273 oz. ASW, 25.1 mm. **Ruler:** Elizabeth II **Subject:** Zodiac Gemstones - Cancer **Obv:** Crowned head above ornamental center **Rev:** Encapsulated emeralds above Crab (Cancer) **Edge:** Reeded

| Date | Mintage | VF20 | XF40 | MS60 | MS63 | MS65 |
|---|---|---|---|---|---|---|
| ND(2003) | 10,000 | PF65 25.00 | | | | |

**KM# 424a DOLLAR**
8.50 g., 0.999 Silver Gilt 0.273 oz., 25.1 mm. **Ruler:** Elizabeth II **Obv:** Crowned head above ornamental center **Rev:** Encapsulated emeralds above Crab (cancer)

| Date | Mintage | VF20 | XF40 | MS60 | MS63 | MS65 |
|---|---|---|---|---|---|---|
| ND(2003) | 10,000 | PF65 60.00 | | | | |

**KM# 425 DOLLAR**
8.50 g., 0.999 Silver 0.273 oz. ASW, 25.1 mm. **Ruler:** Elizabeth II **Subject:** Zodiac Gemstones - Aquarius **Obv:** Crowned head above ornamental center **Rev:** Encapsulated garnets with Aquarius in background **Edge:** Reeded

| Date | Mintage | VF20 | XF40 | MS60 | MS63 | MS65 |
|---|---|---|---|---|---|---|
| ND(2004) | 10,000 | PF65 25.00 | | | | |

**KM# 425a DOLLAR**
8.50 g., 0.999 Silver Gilt 0.273 oz., 25.1 mm. **Ruler:** Elizabeth II **Obv:** Crowned head above ornamental center **Rev:** Encapsulated garnets with Aquarius in background

| Date | Mintage | VF20 | XF40 | MS60 | MS63 | MS65 |
|---|---|---|---|---|---|---|
| ND(2003) | 10,000 | PF65 60.00 | | | | |

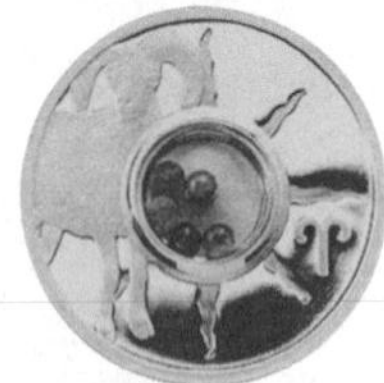

**KM# 426 DOLLAR**
8.50 g., 0.999 Silver 0.273 oz. ASW, 25.1 mm. **Ruler:** Elizabeth II **Subject:** Zodiac Gemstones - Aries **Obv:** Crowned head above ornamental center **Rev:** Encapsulated Bloodstones in center with ram at left **Edge:** Reeded

| Date | Mintage | VF20 | XF40 | MS60 | MS63 | MS65 |
|---|---|---|---|---|---|---|
| ND(2003) | 10,000 | PF65 25.00 | | | | |

**KM# 426a DOLLAR**
8.50 g., 0.999 Silver Gilt 0.273 oz., 25.1 mm. **Ruler:** Elizabeth II **Obv:** Crowned head above ornamental center **Rev:** Encapsulated Bloodstones in center with ram at left

| Date | Mintage | VF20 | XF40 | MS60 | MS63 | MS65 |
|---|---|---|---|---|---|---|
| ND(2003) | 10,000 | PF65 60.00 | | | | |

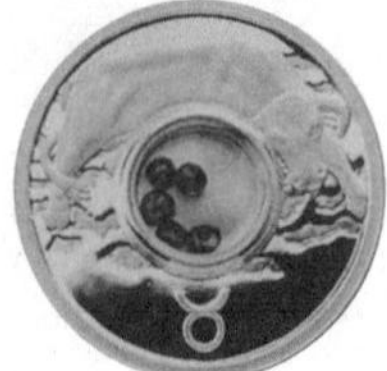

**KM# 427 DOLLAR**
8.50 g., 0.999 Silver 0.273 oz. ASW, 25.1 mm. **Ruler:** Elizabeth II **Subject:** Zodiac Gemstones - Taurus **Obv:** Crowned head above ornamental center **Rev:** Encapsulated Sapphires with bull in background **Edge:** Reeded

| Date | Mintage | VF20 | XF40 | MS60 | MS63 | MS65 |
|---|---|---|---|---|---|---|
| ND(2003) | 10,000 | PF65 25.00 | | | | |

**KM# 427a DOLLAR**
8.50 g., 0.999 Silver Gilt 0.273 oz., 25.1 mm. **Ruler:** Elizabeth II **Subject:** Zodiac Gemstones - Taurus **Obv:** Crowned head above ornamental center **Rev:** Encapsulated Sapphires with bull in background **Edge:** Reeded

| Date | Mintage | VF20 | XF40 | MS60 | MS63 | MS65 |
|---|---|---|---|---|---|---|
| ND(2003) | 10,000 | PF65 60.00 | | | | |

**KM# 428 DOLLAR**
8.50 g., 0.999 Silver 0.273 oz. ASW, 25.1 mm. **Ruler:** Elizabeth II **Obv:** Crowned head above ornamental center **Rev:** Encapsulated Agates between twins **Edge:** Reeded

| Date | Mintage | VF20 | XF40 | MS60 | MS63 | MS65 |
|---|---|---|---|---|---|---|
| ND(2003) | 10,000 | PF65 25.00 | | | | |

**KM# 428a DOLLAR**
8.50 g., 0.999 Silver Gilt 0.273 oz., 25.1 mm. **Ruler:** Elizabeth II **Obv:** Crowned head above ornamental center **Rev:** Encapsulated Agates between twins **Edge:** Reeded

| Date | Mintage | VF20 | XF40 | MS60 | MS63 | MS65 |
|---|---|---|---|---|---|---|
| ND(2003) | 10,000 | PF65 60.00 | | | | |

**KM# 429 DOLLAR**
8.50 g., 0.999 Silver 0.273 oz. ASW, 25.1 mm. **Ruler:** Elizabeth II **Obv:** Crowned head above ornamental center **Rev:** Encapsulated Onyx stones with lion at right **Edge:** Reeded

| Date | Mintage | VF20 | XF40 | MS60 | MS63 | MS65 |
|---|---|---|---|---|---|---|
| ND(2003) | 10,000 | PF65 25.00 | | | | |

**KM# 429a DOLLAR**
8.50 g., 0.999 Silver Gilt 0.273 oz., 25.1 mm. **Ruler:** Elizabeth II **Obv:** Crowned head above ornamental center **Rev:** Encapsulated Onyx stones with lion at right **Edge:** Reeded

| Date | Mintage | VF20 | XF40 | MS60 | MS63 | MS65 |
|---|---|---|---|---|---|---|
| ND(2003) | 10,000 | PF65 60.00 | | | | |

**KM# 430 DOLLAR**
8.50 g., 0.999 Silver 0.273 oz. ASW, 25.1 mm. **Ruler:** Elizabeth II **Subject:** Zodiac Gemstones - Virgo **Obv:** Crowned head above ornamented center **Rev:** Encapsulated Carnelian stones with woman at right **Edge:** Reeded

| Date | Mintage | VF20 | XF40 | MS60 | MS63 | MS65 |
|---|---|---|---|---|---|---|
| ND(2003) | 10,000 | PF65 25.00 | | | | |

**KM# 430a DOLLAR**
8.50 g., 0.999 Silver Gilt 0.273 oz., 25.1 mm. **Ruler:** Elizabeth II **Subject:** Zodiac Gemstones - Virgo **Obv:** Crowned head above ornamented center **Rev:** Encapsulated Carnelian stones with Virgo at right **Edge:** Reeded

| Date | Mintage | VF20 | XF40 | MS60 | MS63 | MS65 |
|---|---|---|---|---|---|---|
| ND(2003) | 10,000 | PF65 60.00 | | | | |

**KM# 431 DOLLAR**
8.50 g., 0.999 Silver 0.273 oz. ASW, 25.1 mm. **Ruler:** Elizabeth II **Subject:** Zodiac Gemstones - Libra **Obv:** Crowned head above ornamented center **Rev:** Encapsulated Peridot stones with balance scale **Edge:** Reeded

| Date | Mintage | VF20 | XF40 | MS60 | MS63 | MS65 |
|---|---|---|---|---|---|---|
| ND(2003) | 10,000 | PF65 25.00 | | | | |

**KM# 431a DOLLAR**
8.50 g., 0.999 Silver Gilt 0.273 oz., 25.1 mm. **Ruler:** Elizabeth II **Subject:** Zodiac Gemstones - Libra **Obv:** Crowned head above ornamented center **Rev:** Encapsulated Peridot stones with balance scale **Edge:** Reeded

| Date | Mintage | VF20 | XF40 | MS60 | MS63 | MS65 |
|---|---|---|---|---|---|---|
| ND(2003) | 10,000 | PF65 60.00 | | | | |

**KM# 432 DOLLAR**
8.50 g., 0.999 Silver 0.273 oz. ASW, 25.1 mm. **Ruler:** Elizabeth II **Subject:** Zodiac Gemstones - Scorpio **Obv:** Crowned head above ornamented center **Rev:** Encapsulated Aquamarine stones with scorpion at lower right **Edge:** Reeded

| Date | Mintage | VF20 | XF40 | MS60 | MS63 | MS65 |
|---|---|---|---|---|---|---|
| ND(2003) | 10,000 | PF65 25.00 | | | | |

**KM# 432a DOLLAR**
8.50 g., 0.999 Silver Gilt 0.273 oz., 25.1 mm. **Ruler:** Elizabeth II **Subject:** Zodiac Gemstones - Scorpio **Obv:** Crowned head above ornamented center **Rev:** Encapsulated Aquamarine stones with scorpion at lower right **Edge:** Reeded

| Date | Mintage | VF20 | XF40 | MS60 | MS63 | MS65 |
|---|---|---|---|---|---|---|
| ND(2003) | 10,000 | PF65 60.00 | | | | |

**KM# 433 DOLLAR**
8.50 g., 0.999 Silver 0.273 oz. ASW, 25.1 mm. **Ruler:** Elizabeth II **Subject:** Zodiac Gemstones - Sagittarius **Obv:** Crowned head above ornamented center **Rev:** Encapsulated Topaz stones with centaur at right **Edge:** Reeded

| Date | Mintage | VF20 | XF40 | MS60 | MS63 | MS65 |
|---|---|---|---|---|---|---|
| ND(2003) | 10,000 | PF65 25.00 | | | | |

**KM# 433a DOLLAR**
8.50 g., 0.999 Silver Gilt 0.273 oz., 25.1 mm. **Ruler:** Elizabeth II **Subject:** Zodiac Gemstones - Sagittarius **Obv:** Crowned head above ornamented center **Rev:** Encapsulated Topaz stones with centaur at right **Edge:** Reeded

| Date | Mintage | VF20 | XF40 | MS60 | MS63 | MS65 |
|---|---|---|---|---|---|---|
| ND(2003) | 10,000 | PF65 60.00 | | | | |

**KM# 434 DOLLAR**
8.50 g., 0.999 Silver 0.273 oz. ASW, 25.1 mm. **Ruler:** Elizabeth II **Subject:** Zodiac Gemstones - Capricorn **Obv:** Crowned head above ornamented center **Rev:** Encapsulated rubies with goat at right **Edge:** Reeded

| Date | Mintage | VF20 | XF40 | MS60 | MS63 | MS65 |
|---|---|---|---|---|---|---|
| ND(2003) | 10,000 | PF65 25.00 | | | | |

**KM# 434a DOLLAR**
8.50 g., 0.999 Silver Gilt 0.273 oz., 25.1 mm. **Ruler:** Elizabeth II **Subject:** Zodiac Gemstones - Capricorn **Obv:** Crowned head above ornamented center **Rev:** Encapsulated Rubies with goat at right **Edge:** Reeded

| Date | Mintage | VF20 | XF40 | MS60 | MS63 | MS65 |
|---|---|---|---|---|---|---|
| ND(2003) | 10,000 | PF65 60.00 | | | | |

**KM# 435 DOLLAR**
8.50 g., 0.999 Silver 0.273 oz. ASW, 25.1 mm. **Ruler:** Elizabeth II **Subject:** Zodiac Gemstones - Pices **Obv:** Crowned head above ornamented center **Rev:** Encapsulated Amethyst stones and two fish **Edge:** Reeded

| Date | Mintage | VF20 | XF40 | MS60 | MS63 | MS65 |
|---|---|---|---|---|---|---|
| ND(2003) | 10,000 | PF65 25.00 | | | | |

**KM# 435a DOLLAR**
8.50 g., 0.999 Silver Gilt 0.273 oz., 25.1 mm. **Ruler:** Elizabeth II **Subject:** Zodiac Gemstones - Pices **Obv:** Crowned head above ornamented center **Rev:** Encapsulated Amethyst stones and 2 fish **Edge:** Reeded

| Date | Mintage | VF20 | XF40 | MS60 | MS63 | MS65 |
|---|---|---|---|---|---|---|
| ND(2003) | 10,000 | PF65 60.00 | | | | |

**KM# 455 DOLLAR**
23.90 g., Copper-Nickel, 38.5 mm. **Ruler:** Elizabeth II **Obv:** Queen Elizabeth II **Rev:** 50th Anniversary - Playboy magazine logo **Edge:** Reeded

| Date | Mintage | VF20 | XF40 | MS60 | MS63 | MS65 |
|---|---|---|---|---|---|---|
| 2003 | — | — | — | — | 7.00 | 9.00 |

**KM# 455a DOLLAR**
25.27 g., Copper-Nickel partiall gilt, 38.3 mm. **Ruler:** Elizabeth II **Obv:** Elizabeth II **Rev:** Playboy magazine's 50th Anniversary logo **Edge:** Reeded

| Date | Mintage | VF20 | XF40 | MS60 | MS63 | MS65 |
|---|---|---|---|---|---|---|
| 2003 | 50,000 | PF63 18.00 | PF65 20.00 | | | |

**KM# 455b DOLLAR**
25.27 g., 0.999 Silver 0.8116 oz. ASW, 38.3 mm. **Ruler:** Elizabeth II **Obv:** Elizabeth II **Rev:** Playboy magazine's 50th Anniversary logo **Edge:** Reeded

| Date | Mintage | VF20 | XF40 | MS60 | MS63 | MS65 |
|---|---|---|---|---|---|---|
| 2003 | — | PF63 37.00 | PF65 40.00 | | | |

**KM# 455c DOLLAR**
25.27 g., 0.999 Silver Gilt 0.8116 oz., 38.3 mm. **Ruler:** Elizabeth II **Obv:** Elizabeth II **Rev:** Playboy magazine's 50th Anniversary logo **Edge:** Reeded

| Date | Mintage | VF20 | XF40 | MS60 | MS63 | MS65 |
|---|---|---|---|---|---|---|
| 2003 | — | PF63 45.00 | PF65 50.00 | | | |

**KM# 462 DOLLAR**
Copper-Nickel, 41 mm. **Ruler:** Elizabeth II **Rev:** Face of 5 Euro Banknote

| Date | Mintage | VF20 | XF40 | MS60 | MS63 | MS65 |
|---|---|---|---|---|---|---|
| 2003 | — | — | — | — | 7.00 | 9.00 |

**KM# 463 DOLLAR**
Copper-Nickel, 41 mm. **Ruler:** Elizabeth II **Rev:** Face of 10 Euro Banknote

| Date | Mintage | VF20 | XF40 | MS60 | MS63 | MS65 |
|---|---|---|---|---|---|---|
| 2003 | — | — | — | — | 7.00 | 9.00 |

**KM# 464 DOLLAR**
Copper-Nickel, 41 mm. **Ruler:** Elizabeth II **Rev:** Face of 20 Euro Banknote

| Date | Mintage | VF20 | XF40 | MS60 | MS63 | MS65 |
|---|---|---|---|---|---|---|
| 2003 | — | — | — | — | 7.00 | 9.00 |

**KM# 465 DOLLAR**
Copper-Nickel, 41 mm. **Ruler:** Elizabeth II **Rev:** Face of 50 Euro Banknote

| Date | Mintage | VF20 | XF40 | MS60 | MS63 | MS65 |
|---|---|---|---|---|---|---|
| 2003 | — | — | — | — | 7.00 | 9.00 |

**KM# 466 DOLLAR**
Copper-Nickel, 41 mm. **Ruler:** Elizabeth II **Rev:** Face of 100 Euro Banknote

| Date | Mintage | VF20 | XF40 | MS60 | MS63 | MS65 |
|---|---|---|---|---|---|---|
| 2003 | — | — | — | — | 7.00 | 9.00 |

**KM# 467 DOLLAR**
Copper-Nickel, 41 mm. **Ruler:** Elizabeth II **Rev:** Face of 500 Euro Banknote

| Date | Mintage | VF20 | XF40 | MS60 | MS63 | MS65 |
|---|---|---|---|---|---|---|
| 2003 | — | — | — | — | 7.00 | 9.00 |

**KM# 746 DOLLAR**
24.90 g., Copper-Nickel, 38 mm. **Ruler:** Elizabeth II **Subject:** Historic ships - Espusi

| Date | Mintage | VF20 | XF40 | MS60 | MS63 | MS65 |
|---|---|---|---|---|---|---|
| 2003 | — | — | — | — | 15.00 | 20.00 |

**KM# 747 DOLLAR**
24.90 g., Copper-Nickel, 38 mm. **Ruler:** Elizabeth II **Subject:** Historic ships - Gorch Foch

| Date | Mintage | VF20 | XF40 | MS60 | MS63 | MS65 |
|---|---|---|---|---|---|---|
| 2003 | — | — | — | — | 15.00 | 20.00 |

**KM# 748 DOLLAR**
24.90 g., Copper-Nickel, 38 mm. **Ruler:** Elizabeth II **Subject:** Historic ships - Constitution

| Date | Mintage | VF20 | XF40 | MS60 | MS63 | MS65 |
|---|---|---|---|---|---|---|
| 2003 | — | — | — | — | 15.00 | 20.00 |

**KM# 749 DOLLAR**
24.90 g., Copper-Nickel, 38 mm. **Ruler:** Elizabeth II **Subject:** Historic ships - Beagle

| Date | Mintage | VF20 | XF40 | MS60 | MS63 | MS65 |
|---|---|---|---|---|---|---|
| 2003 | — | — | — | — | 15.00 | 20.00 |

**KM# 750 DOLLAR**
24.90 g., Copper-Nickel, 38 mm. **Ruler:** Elizabeth II **Subject:** Historic ship - Endeavour

| Date | Mintage | VF20 | XF40 | MS60 | MS63 | MS65 |
|---|---|---|---|---|---|---|
| 2003 | — | — | — | — | 15.00 | 20.00 |

**KM# 751 DOLLAR**
24.90 g., Copper-Nickel, 38 mm. **Ruler:** Elizabeth II **Subject:** Historic Ship - Vasa

| Date | Mintage | VF20 | XF40 | MS60 | MS63 | MS65 |
|---|---|---|---|---|---|---|
| 2003 | — | — | — | — | 15.00 | 20.00 |

**KM# 1127 DOLLAR**
31.64 g., 0.999 Silver 1.0161 oz. ASW, 40.5 mm. **Ruler:** Elizabeth II **Rev:** James Cook and sailing ship

| Date | Mintage | VF20 | XF40 | MS60 | MS63 | MS65 |
|---|---|---|---|---|---|---|
| 2003 | Est. 4999 | PF65 50.00 | | | | |

**KM# 1130 DOLLAR**
31.11 g., 0.999 Silver 0.999 oz. ASW, 38.6 mm. **Ruler:** Elizabeth II **Subject:** Full Gospel Business Men's Fellowship, 50th Anniversary

| Date | Mintage | VF20 | XF40 | MS60 | MS63 | MS65 |
|---|---|---|---|---|---|---|
| 2003 | Est. 4999 | PF65 55.00 | | | | |

**KM# 1143 DOLLAR**
28.28 g., 0.925 Silver 0.841 oz. ASW partially gilt, 38.61 mm. **Ruler:** Elizabeth II **Series:** Elizabeth II, 50th Anniversary of Corronation

| Date | Mintage | VF20 | XF40 | MS60 | MS63 | MS65 |
|---|---|---|---|---|---|---|
| 2003 Proof | Est. 20000 | — | — | — | — | 45.00 |

**KM# 438 DOLLAR**
31.10 g., 0.999 Silver 0.999 oz. ASW, 40.5 mm. **Ruler:** Elizabeth II **Obv:** Crowned head right **Rev:** Multicolor Deng Xiaoping on Chinese map **Edge:** Plain **Shape:** As a map

| Date | Mintage | VF20 | XF40 | MS60 | MS63 | MS65 |
|---|---|---|---|---|---|---|
| 2004 | 20,000 | — | — | — | 70.00 | 75.00 |

### KM# 454 DOLLAR

27.53 g., 0.999 Silver Clad Copper-Nickel 0.8842 oz., 38.6 mm. **Ruler:** Elizabeth II **Subject:** 60th Anniversary - D-Day Invasion **Obv:** Crowned bust right, new portrait **Rev:** Invasion scene of soldiers storming the beaches (Sword, Gold, Juno, Omaha, and Utah) of Normandy

| Date | Mintage | VF20 | XF40 | MS60 | MS63 | MS65 |
|---|---|---|---|---|---|---|
| 2004 | — | — | — | — | 18.00 | 20.00 |

### KM# 1146 DOLLAR

31.64 g., 0.999 Silver 1.0161 oz. ASW **Ruler:** Elizabeth II **Subject:** Cobb & Co. 150th Anniversary **Rev:** Hackney Cab in color

| Date | Mintage | VF20 | XF40 | MS60 | MS63 | MS65 |
|---|---|---|---|---|---|---|
| 2004 | — | **PF65** 60.00 | | | | |

### KM# 1147 DOLLAR

31.64 g., 0.999 Silver 1.0161 oz. ASW **Ruler:** Elizabeth II **Subject:** 90th Anniversary, Battle of the Emden and Sydney I

| Date | Mintage | VF20 | XF40 | MS60 | MS63 | MS65 |
|---|---|---|---|---|---|---|
| 2004 | Est. 5000 | **PF65** 60.00 | | | | |

### KM# 1148 DOLLAR

10.75 g., Copper-Nickel, 28.28 mm. **Ruler:** Elizabeth II **Rev:** Elvis Presley

| Date | Mintage | VF20 | XF40 | MS60 | MS63 | MS65 |
|---|---|---|---|---|---|---|
| 2004 | — | — | — | — | — | 15.00 |

### KM# 1150 DOLLAR

31.11 g., 0.999 Silver 0.999 oz. ASW, 45 mm. **Ruler:** Elizabeth II **Subject:** XXVIII Summer Olympics, Athens **Rev:** Cyclist in color

| Date | Mintage | VF20 | XF40 | MS60 | MS63 | MS65 |
|---|---|---|---|---|---|---|
| 2004 | Est. 5000 | — | — | — | — | 45.00 |

### KM# 1151 DOLLAR

31.11 g., 0.999 Silver 0.999 oz. ASW, 45 mm. **Ruler:** Elizabeth II **Rev:** Gymnast

| Date | Mintage | VF20 | XF40 | MS60 | MS63 | MS65 |
|---|---|---|---|---|---|---|
| 2004 | Est. 5000 | — | — | — | — | 45.00 |

### KM# 1152 DOLLAR

31.11 g., 0.999 Silver 0.999 oz. ASW, 45 mm. **Ruler:** Elizabeth II **Subject:** XXVIII Summer Olympics, Athens **Rev:** Two basketball players in color

| Date | Mintage | VF20 | XF40 | MS60 | MS63 | MS65 |
|---|---|---|---|---|---|---|
| 2004 | Est. 5000 | — | — | — | — | 45.00 |

### KM# 1153 DOLLAR

31.11 g., 0.999 Silver 0.999 oz. ASW, 45 mm. **Ruler:** Elizabeth II **Subject:** XVIII Summer Olympics, Athens **Rev:** Sprinter in color

| Date | Mintage | VF20 | XF40 | MS60 | MS63 | MS65 |
|---|---|---|---|---|---|---|
| 2004 | — | — | — | — | — | 45.00 |

### KM# 1154 DOLLAR

31.11 g., 0.999 Silver 0.999 oz. ASW, 45 mm. **Ruler:** Elizabeth II **Subject:** XXVIII Summer Olympics, Athens **Rev:** Archer in color

| Date | Mintage | VF20 | XF40 | MS60 | MS63 | MS65 |
|---|---|---|---|---|---|---|
| 2004 | Est. 5000 | — | — | — | — | 45.00 |

### KM# 1155 DOLLAR

31.11 g., 0.999 Silver 0.999 oz. ASW, 45 mm. **Ruler:** Elizabeth II **Subject:** XXVIII Summer Olympics, Athens **Rev:** Weightlifter in color

| Date | Mintage | VF20 | XF40 | MS60 | MS63 | MS65 |
|---|---|---|---|---|---|---|
| 2004 Proof | Est. 5000 | — | — | — | — | 45.00 |

### KM# 1156 DOLLAR

24.00 g., Copper-Nickel, 38 mm. **Ruler:** Elizabeth II **Rev:** Mohandas Ghandhi

| Date | Mintage | VF20 | XF40 | MS60 | MS63 | MS65 |
|---|---|---|---|---|---|---|
| 2004 | — | — | — | — | 15.00 | 18.00 |

### KM# 443 DOLLAR

23.90 g., Copper-Nickel, 38.5 mm. **Ruler:** Elizabeth II **Subject:** Battle of Trafalgar **Obv:** Crowned bust right, new portrait **Rev:** HMS Victory and color portrait of Nelson **Edge:** Reeded

| Date | Mintage | VF20 | XF40 | MS60 | MS63 | MS65 |
|---|---|---|---|---|---|---|
| 2005 | — | — | — | — | 15.00 | 18.00 |

### KM# 470 DOLLAR

26.00 g., Bronze silver plated, 39 mm. **Ruler:** Elizabeth II **Obv:** Statue of Liberty and Twin Towers **Rev:** Statue of Liberty and Freedom Tower **Edge:** Plain

| Date | Mintage | VF20 | XF40 | MS60 | MS63 | MS65 |
|---|---|---|---|---|---|---|
| 2005 | — | **PF65** 15.00 | | | | |
| 2007 | — | **PF65** 15.00 | | | | |
| 2008 | — | **PF65** 15.00 | | | | |

### KM# 470a DOLLAR

31.16 g., 0.999 Silver 1.0008 oz. ASW, 39.02 mm. **Ruler:** Elizabeth II **Obv:** Twin Towers and Statue of Liberty, Queens Head below **Obv. Legend:** COOK ISLANDS / WE WILL NEVER FORGET **Rev:** Freedoom Tower and Statue of Liberty **Rev. Inscription:** LET / FREEDOM / RING - FREEDOM TOWER **Edge:** Reeded and plain with lettering **Edge Lettering:** 1 TROY OZ. .999 FINE SILVER

| Date | Mintage | VF20 | XF40 | MS60 | MS63 | MS65 |
|---|---|---|---|---|---|---|
| 2006 | — | **PF65** 30.00 | | | | |

### KM# 1107 DOLLAR

31.11 g., 0.999 Silver 0.999 oz. ASW partially gilt, 40 mm. **Ruler:** Elizabeth II **Rev:** Pope Benedict XVI partially gilt

| Date | Mintage | VF20 | XF40 | MS60 | MS63 | MS65 |
|---|---|---|---|---|---|---|
| 2005 | — | **PF65** 45.00 | | | | |

### KM# 1133 DOLLAR

Copper-Nickel, 38.6 mm. **Ruler:** Elizabeth II **Subject:** Star Wars, 30th Anniversary

| Date | Mintage | VF20 | XF40 | MS60 | MS63 | MS65 |
|---|---|---|---|---|---|---|
| 2005 | Est. 9999 | **PF65** 20.00 | | | | |

### KM# 1157 DOLLAR

31.64 g., 0.999 Silver 1.0161 oz. ASW **Ruler:** Elizabeth II **Subject:** Australian Automobiles

| Date | Mintage | VF20 | XF40 | MS60 | MS63 | MS65 |
|---|---|---|---|---|---|---|
| 2005 | Est. 1500 | **PF65** 60.00 | | | | |

### KM# 1158 DOLLAR

31.64 g., 0.999 Silver 1.0161 oz. ASW **Ruler:** Elizabeth II **Subject:** Australian Automobiles

| Date | Mintage | VF20 | XF40 | MS60 | MS63 | MS65 |
|---|---|---|---|---|---|---|
| 2005 | Est. 1500 | **PF65** 60.00 | | | | |

### KM# 1159 DOLLAR

31.64 g., 0.999 Silver 1.0161 oz. ASW **Ruler:** Elizabeth II **Subject:** Australian Automobiles

| Date | Mintage | VF20 | XF40 | MS60 | MS63 | MS65 |
|---|---|---|---|---|---|---|
| 2005 | Est. 1500 | **PF65** 60.00 | | | | |

### KM# 1160 DOLLAR

31.64 g., 0.999 Silver 1.0161 oz. ASW **Ruler:** Elizabeth II **Subject:** Australian Automobiles

| Date | Mintage | VF20 | XF40 | MS60 | MS63 | MS65 |
|---|---|---|---|---|---|---|
| 2005 | Est. 1500 | **PF65** 60.00 | | | | |

### KM# 1161 DOLLAR

31.64 g., 0.999 Silver 1.0161 oz. ASW **Ruler:** Elizabeth II **Subject:** Australian Automobiles

| Date | Mintage | VF20 | XF40 | MS60 | MS63 | MS65 |
|---|---|---|---|---|---|---|
| 2005 | Est. 1500 | **PF65** 60.00 | | | | |

### KM# 1162 DOLLAR

31.64 g., 0.999 Silver 1.0161 oz. ASW **Ruler:** Elizabeth II **Subject:** Australian Automobiles

| Date | Mintage | VF20 | XF40 | MS60 | MS63 | MS65 |
|---|---|---|---|---|---|---|
| 2005 | Est. 1500 | **PF65** 60.00 | | | | |

### KM# 1163 DOLLAR

31.64 g., 0.999 Silver 1.0161 oz. ASW **Ruler:** Elizabeth II **Subject:** Australian Automobiles

| Date | Mintage | VF20 | XF40 | MS60 | MS63 | MS65 |
|---|---|---|---|---|---|---|
| 2005 | Est. 1500 | **PF65** 60.00 | | | | |

### KM# 1164 DOLLAR

31.64 g., 0.999 Silver 1.0161 oz. ASW **Ruler:** Elizabeth II **Subject:** Australian Automobiles

| Date | Mintage | VF20 | XF40 | MS60 | MS63 | MS65 |
|---|---|---|---|---|---|---|
| 2005 | Est. 1500 | **PF65** 60.00 | | | | |

### KM# 1165 DOLLAR

31.64 g., 0.999 Silver 1.0161 oz. ASW **Ruler:** Elizabeth II **Subject:** Australian Automobiles

| Date | Mintage | VF20 | XF40 | MS60 | MS63 | MS65 |
|---|---|---|---|---|---|---|
| 2005 | Est. 1500 | **PF65** 60.00 | | | | |

### KM# 1166 DOLLAR

31.64 g., 0.999 Silver 1.0161 oz. ASW **Ruler:** Elizabeth II **Subject:** Australian Automobiles

| Date | Mintage | VF20 | XF40 | MS60 | MS63 | MS65 |
|---|---|---|---|---|---|---|
| 2005 | 1,500 | **PF65** 60.00 | | | | |

### KM# 1167 DOLLAR

31.64 g., 0.999 Silver 1.0161 oz. ASW **Ruler:** Elizabeth II **Subject:** Australian Automobiles

| Date | Mintage | VF20 | XF40 | MS60 | MS63 | MS65 |
|---|---|---|---|---|---|---|
| 2005 | Est. 1500 | **PF65** 60.00 | | | | |

### KM# 1168 DOLLAR

31.64 g., 0.999 Silver 1.0161 oz. ASW **Ruler:** Elizabeth II **Subject:** Australian Automobiles

| Date | Mintage | VF20 | XF40 | MS60 | MS63 | MS65 |
|---|---|---|---|---|---|---|
| 2005 | Est. 1500 | **PF65** 60.00 | | | | |

### KM# 1173 DOLLAR

32.00 g., Copper-Nickel, 40 mm. **Ruler:** Elizabeth II **Rev:** Snowflake, building tower hockey play and figure skater

| Date | Mintage | VF20 | XF40 | MS60 | MS63 | MS65 |
|---|---|---|---|---|---|---|
| 2005 | 20,000 | — | — | — | 10.00 | 12.00 |

### KM# 1174 DOLLAR

Copper-Nickel **Ruler:** Elizabeth II **Subject:** Marriage of Prince Charles and Camilla Parker-Bowles

| Date | Mintage | VF20 | XF40 | MS60 | MS63 | MS65 |
|---|---|---|---|---|---|---|
| 2005 | Est. 5000 | — | — | — | — | 15.00 |

### KM# 1177 DOLLAR

31.64 g., 0.999 Silver 1.0161 oz. ASW **Ruler:** Elizabeth II **Rev:** Pope John Paul II in color

| Date | Mintage | VF20 | XF40 | MS60 | MS63 | MS65 |
|---|---|---|---|---|---|---|
| 2005 | 5,000 | **PF65** 125 | | | | |

### KM# 1621 DOLLAR

20.00 g., 0.500 Silver 0.3215 oz. ASW **Ruler:** Elizabeth II **Subject:** Battle of Hastings

| Date | Mintage | VF20 | XF40 | MS60 | MS63 | MS65 |
|---|---|---|---|---|---|---|
| 2005 | — | **PF65** 20.00 | | | | |

### KM# 479 DOLLAR

Copper-Nickel, 38.6 mm. **Ruler:** Elizabeth II **Subject:** Gun ships of the world **Rev:** HMS Redoutable

| Date | Mintage | VF20 | XF40 | MS60 | MS63 | MS65 |
|---|---|---|---|---|---|---|
| 2006 | — | — | — | — | — | 25.00 |

**KM# 480 DOLLAR**
24.90 g., Copper-Nickel, 38 mm. **Ruler:** Elizabeth II **Subject:** Gunships of the world **Obv:** Crowned bust right **Rev:** Ark Royal in color **Edge:** Reeded

| Date | Mintage | VF20 | XF40 | MS60 | MS63 | MS65 |
|---|---|---|---|---|---|---|
| 2006 | — | — | — | — | — | 25.00 |

**KM# 752 DOLLAR**
24.90 g., Copper-Nickel, 38 mm. **Ruler:** Elizabeth II **Subject:** Gun ships - Chesapeak **Rev:** Multicolor naval ship

| Date | Mintage | VF20 | XF40 | MS60 | MS63 | MS65 |
|---|---|---|---|---|---|---|
| 2006 | — | — | — | — | 15.00 | 20.00 |

**KM# 753 DOLLAR**
24.90 g., Copper-Nickel, 38 mm. **Ruler:** Elizabeth II **Subject:** Gun ships - Syvende **Rev:** Multicolor naval ship

| Date | Mintage | VF20 | XF40 | MS60 | MS63 | MS65 |
|---|---|---|---|---|---|---|
| 2006 | — | — | — | — | 15.00 | 20.00 |

**KM# 754 DOLLAR**
24.90 g., Copper-Nickel, 38 mm. **Ruler:** Elizabeth II **Rev:** Multicolor Naval ship

| Date | Mintage | VF20 | XF40 | MS60 | MS63 | MS65 |
|---|---|---|---|---|---|---|
| 2006 | — | — | — | — | 15.00 | 20.00 |

**KM# 755 DOLLAR**
24.90 g., Copper-Nickel, 38 mm. **Ruler:** Elizabeth II **Subject:** Gun Ships - Mary Rose **Rev:** Multicolor Naval ship

| Date | Mintage | VF20 | XF40 | MS60 | MS63 | MS65 |
|---|---|---|---|---|---|---|
| 2006 | — | — | — | — | 15.00 | 20.00 |

**KM# 1137 DOLLAR**
31.64 g., 0.999 Silver 1.0161 oz. ASW **Ruler:** Elizabeth II **Subject:** 1923 New South Wales Garford Fire

| Date | Mintage | VF20 | XF40 | MS60 | MS63 | MS65 |
|---|---|---|---|---|---|---|
| 2006 | Est. 5000 | PF65 55.00 | | | | |

**KM# 1169 DOLLAR**
0.50 g., 0.999 Gold **Ruler:** Elizabeth II **Rev:** Pope Benedict XVI

| Date | Mintage | VF20 | XF40 | MS60 | MS63 | MS65 |
|---|---|---|---|---|---|---|
| 2006 | — | PF65 45.00 | | | | |

**KM# 1179 DOLLAR**
Silver **Ruler:** Elizabeth II **Subject:** David Livingstone

| Date | Mintage | VF20 | XF40 | MS60 | MS63 | MS65 |
|---|---|---|---|---|---|---|
| 2006 | — | PF65 45.00 | | | | |

**KM# 1180 DOLLAR**
Silver **Ruler:** Elizabeth II **Subject:** Ferdinanad Magellan

| Date | Mintage | VF20 | XF40 | MS60 | MS63 | MS65 |
|---|---|---|---|---|---|---|
| 2006 | — | PF65 45.00 | | | | |

**KM# 1181 DOLLAR**
Silver **Ruler:** Elizabeth II **Subject:** Roald Amundsen

| Date | Mintage | VF20 | XF40 | MS60 | MS63 | MS65 |
|---|---|---|---|---|---|---|
| 2006 | — | PF65 45.00 | | | | |

**KM# 1182 DOLLAR**
Silver **Ruler:** Elizabeth II **Subject:** Christopher Columbus

| Date | Mintage | VF20 | XF40 | MS60 | MS63 | MS65 |
|---|---|---|---|---|---|---|
| 2006 | — | PF65 45.00 | | | | |

**KM# 1183 DOLLAR**
Silver **Ruler:** Elizabeth II **Subject:** Juan Sebastian de Elcano

| Date | Mintage | VF20 | XF40 | MS60 | MS63 | MS65 |
|---|---|---|---|---|---|---|
| 2006 | — | PF65 45.00 | | | | |

**KM# 1428 DOLLAR**
Copper-Nickel, 38.61 mm. **Ruler:** Elizabeth II **Subject:** Television, 80th anniversary

| Date | Mintage | VF20 | XF40 | MS60 | MS63 | MS65 |
|---|---|---|---|---|---|---|
| 2006 | — | — | — | — | 10.00 | 12.00 |

**KM# 1623 DOLLAR**
Silver Plated **Ruler:** Elizabeth II **Subject:** Television, 80th Anniversary

| Date | Mintage | VF20 | XF40 | MS60 | MS63 | MS65 |
|---|---|---|---|---|---|---|
| 2006 | — | PF65 15.00 | | | | |

**KM# 471 DOLLAR**
35.80 g., 0.999 Silver 1.1498 oz. ASW **Ruler:** Elizabeth II **Subject:** Sputnik 50th Anniversary - 1957-2007 **Obv:** Small bust divides legend above, center globe with color applique **Rev:** Satellite orbiting Earth with color applique **Rev. Legend:** SPUTNIK 50th ANNIVERSARY 1957 - 2007 **Edge:** Plain **Note:** Center piece rotates freely

| Date | Mintage | VF20 | XF40 | MS60 | MS63 | MS65 |
|---|---|---|---|---|---|---|
| 2007 | — | PF65 95.00 | | | | |

**KM# 490 DOLLAR**
31.10 g., 0.999 Silver 0.999 oz. ASW, 40.6 mm. **Ruler:** Elizabeth II **Subject:** Historical Australian Coins **Obv:** Head with tiara right **Rev:** 1757 New South Wales Holey Dollar **Edge:** Reeded

| Date | Mintage | VF20 | XF40 | MS60 | MS63 | MS65 |
|---|---|---|---|---|---|---|
| 2007 | 1,500 | PF65 125 | | | | |

**KM# 491 DOLLAR**
31.10 g., 0.999 Silver 0.999 oz. ASW, 40.6 mm. **Ruler:** Elizabeth II **Subject:** Historical Australian Coins **Obv:** Head with tiara right **Rev:** Gilt 1857 Sydney Mint Sovereign **Edge:** Reeded

| Date | Mintage | VF20 | XF40 | MS60 | MS63 | MS65 |
|---|---|---|---|---|---|---|
| 2007 | 1,500 | PF65 125 | | | | |

**KM# 492 DOLLAR**
31.10 g., 0.999 Silver 0.999 oz. ASW Selective copper plating, 40.6 mm. **Ruler:** Elizabeth II **Subject:** Historical Australian Coins **Obv:** Head with tiarra right **Rev:** Copper 1937 pattern penny **Edge:** Reeded

| Date | Mintage | VF20 | XF40 | MS60 | MS63 | MS65 |
|---|---|---|---|---|---|---|
| 2007 | 1,500 | PF65 125 | | | | |

**KM# 733 DOLLAR**
25.09 g., Copper-Nickel, 38.8 mm. **Ruler:** Elizabeth II **Rev:** HMS Victory **Rev. Legend:** England expects that every man will do his duty

| Date | Mintage | VF20 | XF40 | MS60 | MS63 | MS65 |
|---|---|---|---|---|---|---|
| 2007 | — | — | — | — | — | 15.00 |

**KM# 734 DOLLAR**
25.09 g., Copper-Nickel, 38.8 mm. **Ruler:** Elizabeth II **Rev:** Admiral Nelson and two naval vessels **Rev. Legend:** England expects that every man will do his duty

| Date | Mintage | VF20 | XF40 | MS60 | MS63 | MS65 |
|---|---|---|---|---|---|---|
| 2007 | — | — | — | — | — | 15.00 |

**KM# 735 DOLLAR**
0.50 g., 0.999 Gold, 11 mm. **Ruler:** Elizabeth II **Rev:** Treaty of Rome - Slovenia

| Date | Mintage | VF20 | XF40 | MS60 | MS63 | MS65 |
|---|---|---|---|---|---|---|
| 2007 | — | PF65 40.00 | | | | |

**KM# 736 DOLLAR**
0.50 g., 0.999 Gold **Ruler:** Elizabeth II **Rev:** Benedict XVI's 2 Euro Coin

| Date | Mintage | VF20 | XF40 | MS60 | MS63 | MS65 |
|---|---|---|---|---|---|---|
| 2007 | — | PF65 40.00 | | | | |

**KM# 1138 DOLLAR**
0.50 g., 0.999 Gold, 11 mm. **Ruler:** Elizabeth II **Subject:** Treaty of Rome, 50th Anniversary **Rev:** San Marino

| Date | Mintage | VF20 | XF40 | MS60 | MS63 | MS65 |
|---|---|---|---|---|---|---|
| 2007 | — | PF65 50.00 | | | | |

**KM# 1196 DOLLAR**
25.00 g., Copper-Nickel gilt, 38.6 mm. **Ruler:** Elizabeth II **Rev:** Photo of Elizabeth II and Prince Philip in State Crown and uniform

| Date | Mintage | VF20 | XF40 | MS60 | MS63 | MS65 |
|---|---|---|---|---|---|---|
| 2007 | Est. 50000 | PF65 17.50 | | | | |

**KM# 1197 DOLLAR**
25.00 g., Copper-Nickel gilt, 38.6 mm. **Ruler:** Elizabeth II **Rev:** Photo of Elizabeth II and Prince Philip riding in state coach

| Date | Mintage | VF20 | XF40 | MS60 | MS63 | MS65 |
|---|---|---|---|---|---|---|
| 2007 | — | PF65 17.50 | | | | |

**KM# 1198 DOLLAR**
25.00 g., Copper-Nickel gilt, 38.6 mm. **Ruler:** Elizabeth II **Rev:** Photo Elizabeth II in wedding dress and Prince Philip in uniform

| Date | Mintage | VF20 | XF40 | MS60 | MS63 | MS65 |
|---|---|---|---|---|---|---|
| 2007 | — | PF65 17.50 | | | | |

**KM# 1199 DOLLAR**
25.00 g., Copper-Nickel, 38.6 mm. **Ruler:** Elizabeth II **Rev:** Photo of Elizabeth II in wedding dress and Prince Philip in uniform, both waving

| Date | Mintage | VF20 | XF40 | MS60 | MS63 | MS65 |
|---|---|---|---|---|---|---|
| 2007 | Est. 50000 | PF65 17.50 | | | | |

**KM# 1200 DOLLAR**
25.00 g., Copper-Nickel gilt, 38.6 mm. **Ruler:** Elizabeth II **Rev:** Recent photo of Elizabeth in blue hat and Prince Philip in uniform

| Date | Mintage | VF20 | XF40 | MS60 | MS63 | MS65 |
|---|---|---|---|---|---|---|
| 2007 | Est. 50000 | PF65 17.50 | | | | |

**KM# 1445 DOLLAR**
25.00 g., Copper-Nickel gilt, 38.6 mm. **Ruler:** Elizabeth II **Rev:** Modern photo of Elizabeth II in red dress and Prince Philip in suit

| Date | Mintage | VF20 | XF40 | MS60 | MS63 | MS65 |
|---|---|---|---|---|---|---|
| 2007 | Est. 50000 | PF65 17.50 | | | | |

**KM# 1466 DOLLAR**
28.28 g., 0.925 Silver 0.841 oz. ASW, 38.61 mm. **Ruler:** Elizabeth II **Rev:** Horatio Nelson and the Battle of Trafalgar

| Date | Mintage | VF20 | XF40 | MS60 | MS63 | MS65 |
|---|---|---|---|---|---|---|
| 2007 | Est. 5000 | PF65 55.00 | | | | |

**KM# 1468 DOLLAR**
0.50 g., 0.999 Gold, 11 mm. **Ruler:** Elizabeth II **Rev:** Sugar Maple leaf

| Date | Mintage | VF20 | XF40 | MS60 | MS63 | MS65 |
|---|---|---|---|---|---|---|
| 2007 | Est. 5000 | PF65 50.00 | | | | |

**KM# 1520 DOLLAR**
0.50 g., 1.000 Gold **Ruler:** Elizabeth II **Subject:** 2007 Walking Liberty

| Date | Mintage | VF20 | XF40 | MS60 | MS63 | MS65 |
|---|---|---|---|---|---|---|
| 2007 | Est. 15000 | PF65 70.00 | | | | |

**KM# 1521 DOLLAR**
0.50 g., 1.000 Gold, 11 mm. **Ruler:** Elizabeth II **Subject:** 2007 Eagle

| Date | Mintage | VF20 | XF40 | MS60 | MS63 | MS65 |
|---|---|---|---|---|---|---|
| 2007 | Est. 15000 | PF65 50.00 | | | | |

**KM# 493 DOLLAR**
31.10 g., 0.999 Silver 0.999 oz. ASW, 40.6 mm. **Ruler:** Elizabeth II **Subject:** Historical Australian Coins **Obv:** Head with tiara right **Rev:** 1823 MacIntosh and Degraves Shilling **Edge:** Reeded

| Date | Mintage | VF20 | XF40 | MS60 | MS63 | MS65 |
|---|---|---|---|---|---|---|
| 2008 | 1,500 | PF65 125 | | | | |

**KM# 494 DOLLAR**
31.10 g., 0.999 Silver 0.999 oz. ASW Selective gold plating, 40.6 mm. **Ruler:** Elizabeth II **Subject:** Historic Australian Coins **Obv:** Head with tiara right **Rev:** Gilt 1788 George III Spade Guinea **Edge:** Reeded

| Date | Mintage | VF20 | XF40 | MS60 | MS63 | MS65 |
|---|---|---|---|---|---|---|
| 2008 | 1,500 | PF65 125 | | | | |

**KM# 495 DOLLAR**
31.10 g., 0.999 Silver 0.999 oz. ASW, 40.6 mm. **Ruler:** Elizabeth II **Subject:** Historic Australian Coins **Obv:** Head with tiara right **Rev:** Australian 1910 Florin **Edge:** Reeded

| Date | Mintage | VF20 | XF40 | MS60 | MS63 | MS65 |
|---|---|---|---|---|---|---|
| 2008 | 1,500 | PF65 125 | | | | |

**KM# 496 DOLLAR**
31.10 g., 0.999 Silver 0.999 oz. ASW Selective gold plating, 40.6 mm. **Ruler:** Elizabeth II **Subject:** Historic Australian Coins **Obv:** Head with tiara right **Rev:** Gilt 1808-1815 Gold Pagoda **Edge:** Reeded

| Date | Mintage | VF20 | XF40 | MS60 | MS63 | MS65 |
|---|---|---|---|---|---|---|
| 2008 | 1,500 | PF65 125 | | | | |

**KM# 497 DOLLAR**
31.10 g., 0.999 Silver 0.999 oz. ASW, 40.6 mm. **Ruler:** Elizabeth II **Subject:** Historic Australian Coins **Obv:** Head with tiara right **Rev:** 1850's Taylor's sixpence pattern **Edge:** Reeded

| Date | Mintage | VF20 | XF40 | MS60 | MS63 | MS65 |
|---|---|---|---|---|---|---|
| 2008 | 1,500 | PF65 125 | | | | |

**KM# 498 DOLLAR**
31.11 g., 0.999 Silver 0.999 oz. ASW Selective copper plating, 40.6 mm. **Ruler:** Elizabeth II **Subject:** Historic Australian Coins **Obv:** Head with tiara right **Rev:** Copper Australian WWII Interment Camp Token **Edge:** Reeded

| Date | Mintage | VF20 | XF40 | MS60 | MS63 | MS65 |
|---|---|---|---|---|---|---|
| 2008 | 1,500 | PF65 125 | | | | |

**KM# 499 DOLLAR**
31.10 g., 0.999 Silver 0.999 oz. ASW, 40.6 mm. **Ruler:** Elizabeth II **Subject:** Historic Australian Coins **Obv:** Head with tiara right **Rev:** Australian 1946 Perth Mint Shilling **Edge:** Reeded

| Date | Mintage | VF20 | XF40 | MS60 | MS63 | MS65 |
|---|---|---|---|---|---|---|
| 2008 | 1,500 | PF65 125 | | | | |

**KM# 500 DOLLAR**
31.10 g., 0.999 Silver 0.999 oz. ASW, 40.6 mm. **Ruler:** Elizabeth II **Subject:** Historic Australian Coins **Obv:** Head with tiara right **Rev:** Australian 1938 Crown **Edge:** Reeded

| Date | Mintage | VF20 | XF40 | MS60 | MS63 | MS65 |
|---|---|---|---|---|---|---|
| 2008 | 1,500 | PF65 125 | | | | |

**KM# 501 DOLLAR**
31.10 g., 0.999 Silver 0.999 oz. ASW, 40.6 mm. **Ruler:** Elizabeth II **Subject:** Historic Australian Coins **Obv:** Head with tiara right **Rev:** Copper Australian 1930 Penny **Edge:** Reeded

| Date | Mintage | VF20 | XF40 | MS60 | MS63 | MS65 |
|---|---|---|---|---|---|---|
| 2008 | 1,500 | PF65 125 | | | | |

**KM# 502 DOLLAR**
31.10 g., 0.999 Silver 0.999 oz. ASW, 40.6 mm. **Ruler:** Elizabeth II **Subject:** World War I **Obv:** Head with tiara right **Rev:** Multicolor image of Australian WWI soldier in Europe **Edge:** Reeded

| Date | Mintage | VF20 | XF40 | MS60 | MS63 | MS65 |
|---|---|---|---|---|---|---|
| 2008 | 1,918 | PF65 85.00 | | | | |

**KM# 504 DOLLAR**
31.10 g., 0.999 Silver 0.999 oz. ASW, 40.6 mm. **Ruler:** Elizabeth II **Subject:** WWI **Obv:** Head with tiara right **Rev:** Multicolor image of Australian WWI soldier in Mid-East scene **Edge:** Reeded

| Date | Mintage | VF20 | XF40 | MS60 | MS63 | MS65 |
|---|---|---|---|---|---|---|
| 2008 | 1,918 | PF65 85.00 | | | | |

**KM# 506 DOLLAR**
31.10 g., 0.999 Silver 0.999 oz. ASW, 40.6 mm. **Ruler:** Elizabeth II **Subject:** Captain Cook **Obv:** Head with tiara right **Rev:** Multicolor image of James Cook within letter C **Edge:** Reeded

| Date | Mintage | VF20 | XF40 | MS60 | MS63 | MS65 |
|---|---|---|---|---|---|---|
| 2008 | 1,779 | PF65 100 | | | | |

**KM# 507 DOLLAR**
31.10 g., 0.999 Silver 0.999 oz. ASW, 40.6 mm. **Ruler:** Elizabeth II **Subject:** Captain Cook **Obv:** Head with tiara right **Rev:** Multicolor image of James Cook, Bottany Bay all within letter O **Edge:** Reeded

| Date | Mintage | VF20 | XF40 | MS60 | MS63 | MS65 |
|---|---|---|---|---|---|---|
| 2008 | 1,779 | PF65 100 | | | | |

**KM# 508 DOLLAR**
31.10 g., 0.999 Silver 0.999 oz. ASW, 40.6 mm. **Ruler:** Elizabeth II **Subject:** Captain Cook **Obv:** Head with tiara right **Rev:** Multicolor image of James Cook, a new world all within letter O **Edge:** Reeded

| Date | Mintage | VF20 | XF40 | MS60 | MS63 | MS65 |
|---|---|---|---|---|---|---|
| 2008 | 1,779 | PF65 100 | | | | |

**KM# 509 DOLLAR**
31.10 g., 0.999 Silver 0.999 oz. ASW, 40.6 mm. **Ruler:** Elizabeth II **Subject:** Captain Cook **Obv:** Head with tiara right **Rev:** Multicolor image of James Cook, striking the reef, large letter K in background **Edge:** Reeded

| Date | Mintage | VF20 | XF40 | MS60 | MS63 | MS65 |
|---|---|---|---|---|---|---|
| 2008 | 1,779 | PF65 100 | | | | |

**KM# 765 DOLLAR**
35.80 g., 0.999 Silver 1.1498 oz. ASW, 40 mm. **Ruler:** Elizabeth II **Subject:** 1961 First man in Space

| Date | Mintage | VF20 | XF40 | MS60 | MS63 | MS65 |
|---|---|---|---|---|---|---|
| 2008 | — | PF65 115 | | | | |

**KM# 801 DOLLAR**
31.11 g., 0.999 Silver 0.999 oz. ASW, 40 mm. **Ruler:** Elizabeth II **Rev:** An-2, partially gilt

| Date | Mintage | VF20 | XF40 | MS60 | MS63 | MS65 |
|---|---|---|---|---|---|---|
| 2008 | — | PF65 50.00 | | | | |

**KM# 802 DOLLAR**
31.11 g., 0.999 Silver 0.999 oz. ASW, 40 mm. **Ruler:** Elizabeth II **Rev:** An-74, partially gilt

| Date | Mintage | VF20 | XF40 | MS60 | MS63 | MS65 |
|---|---|---|---|---|---|---|
| 2008 | — | PF65 50.00 | | | | |

**KM# 803 DOLLAR**
31.11 g., 0.999 Silver 0.999 oz. ASW, 40 mm. **Ruler:** Elizabeth II **Rev:** An-124, partially gilt

| Date | Mintage | VF20 | XF40 | MS60 | MS63 | MS65 |
|---|---|---|---|---|---|---|
| 2008 | — | PF65 50.00 | | | | |

**KM# 804 DOLLAR**
31.11 g., 0.999 Silver 0.999 oz. ASW, 40 mm. **Ruler:** Elizabeth II **Rev:** An-148, partially gilt

| Date | Mintage | VF20 | XF40 | MS60 | MS63 | MS65 |
|---|---|---|---|---|---|---|
| 2008 | — | PF65 50.00 | | | | |

**KM# 805 DOLLAR**
31.11 g., 0.999 Silver 0.999 oz. ASW, 40 mm. **Ruler:** Elizabeth II **Rev:** An-225, partially gilt

| Date | Mintage | VF20 | XF40 | MS60 | MS63 | MS65 |
|---|---|---|---|---|---|---|
| 2008 | — | PF65 50.00 | | | | |

**KM# 1208 DOLLAR**
0.50 g., 0.999 Gold, 11 mm. **Ruler:** Elizabeth II **Subject:** British Monarchs - Henry V

| Date | Mintage | VF20 | XF40 | MS60 | MS63 | MS65 |
|---|---|---|---|---|---|---|
| 2008 | Est. 14500 | PF65 45.00 | | | | |

**KM# 1209 DOLLAR**
0.50 g., 0.999 Gold, 11 mm. **Ruler:** Elizabeth II **Subject:** British Monarchs - Henry VIII

| Date | Mintage | VF20 | XF40 | MS60 | MS63 | MS65 |
|---|---|---|---|---|---|---|
| 2008 | Est. 50000 | PF65 45.00 | | | | |

**KM# 1209a DOLLAR**
0.50 g., 0.999 Platinum APW, 11 mm. **Ruler:** Elizabeth II **Subject:** British Monarchs - Henry VIII

| Date | Mintage | VF20 | XF40 | MS60 | MS63 | MS65 |
|---|---|---|---|---|---|---|
| 2008 | Est. 50000 | PF65 50.00 | | | | |

**KM# 1210 DOLLAR**
0.50 g., 0.999 Gold, 11 mm. **Ruler:** Elizabeth II **Subject:** British Monarchs - Elizabeth I

| Date | Mintage | VF20 | XF40 | MS60 | MS63 | MS65 |
|---|---|---|---|---|---|---|
| 2008 | Est. 50000 | PF65 45.00 | | | | |

**KM# 1522 DOLLAR**
0.50 g., 1.000 Gold, 11 mm. **Ruler:** Elizabeth II **Subject:** 2008 Indian Head

| Date | Mintage | VF20 | XF40 | MS60 | MS63 | MS65 |
|---|---|---|---|---|---|---|
| 2008 | Est. 15000 | PF65 70.00 | | | | |

**KM# 1632 DOLLAR**
0.50 g., 0.999 Gold AGW, 11 mm. **Ruler:** Elizabeth II **Rev:** British monarchs - James I

| Date | Mintage | VF20 | XF40 | MS60 | MS63 | MS65 |
|---|---|---|---|---|---|---|
| 2008 | — | PF65 45.00 | | | | |

**KM# 1633 DOLLAR**
0.50 g., 0.999 Gold AGW, 11 mm. **Ruler:** Elizabeth II **Rev:** British monarchs - William I

| Date | Mintage | VF20 | XF40 | MS60 | MS63 | MS65 |
|---|---|---|---|---|---|---|
| 2008 | — | PF65 45.00 | | | | |

**KM# 701 DOLLAR**
31.11 g., 0.999 Silver 0.999 oz. ASW, 39 mm. **Ruler:** Elizabeth II **Subject:** First Man on the Moon, 40th Anniversary **Obv:** Head right at top, multicolor moon in center **Rev:** Rocket, orbiter, moon walk. moon in multicolor at center

| Date | Mintage | VF20 | XF40 | MS60 | MS63 | MS65 |
|---|---|---|---|---|---|---|
| 2009 | 25,000 | PF65 110 | | | | |

**KM# 702 DOLLAR**
31.11 g., 0.999 Silver 0.999 oz. ASW, 33x33 mm. **Ruler:** Elizabeth II **Subject:** Cook's Cottage, 75th Anniversary of relocation **Obv:** Head right **Rev:** Cottage and multicolor Captain Cook image **Shape:** Square

| Date | Mintage | VF20 | XF40 | MS60 | MS63 | MS65 |
|---|---|---|---|---|---|---|
| 2009 | 5,000 | PF65 95.00 | | | | |

**KM# 706 DOLLAR**
0.50 g., 0.999 Gold, 11 mm. **Ruler:** Elizabeth II **Subject:** Pope Benedict XVI visits the Holy Land **Rev:** Dome of the Rock

| Date | Mintage | VF20 | XF40 | MS60 | MS63 | MS65 |
|---|---|---|---|---|---|---|
| 2009 | 25,000 | PF65 35.00 | | | | |

**KM# 772 DOLLAR**
27.00 g., Copper silver plated, 40 mm. **Ruler:** Elizabeth II **Subject:** Year of Astronomy **Rev:** Sun, multicolor

| Date | Mintage | VF20 | XF40 | MS60 | MS63 | MS65 |
|---|---|---|---|---|---|---|
| 2009 | — | — | — | — | — | 20.00 |

**KM# 773 DOLLAR**
27.00 g., Copper silver plated, 40 mm. **Ruler:** Elizabeth II **Subject:** Year of Astronomy **Rev:** Mercury, multicolor

| Date | Mintage | VF20 | XF40 | MS60 | MS63 | MS65 |
|---|---|---|---|---|---|---|
| 2009 | — | — | — | — | — | 20.00 |

**KM# 774 DOLLAR**
27.00 g., Copper silver plated, 40 mm. **Ruler:** Elizabeth II **Subject:** Year of Astronomy **Rev:** Venus, multicolor

| Date | Mintage | VF20 | XF40 | MS60 | MS63 | MS65 |
|---|---|---|---|---|---|---|
| 2009 | — | — | — | — | — | 25.00 |

**KM# 775 DOLLAR**
27.00 g., Copper silver plated, 40 mm. **Ruler:** Elizabeth II **Subject:** Year of Astronomy **Rev:** Earth, multicolor

| Date | Mintage | VF20 | XF40 | MS60 | MS63 | MS65 |
|---|---|---|---|---|---|---|
| 2009 | — | — | — | — | — | 22.00 |

**KM# 776 DOLLAR**
27.00 g., Copper silver plated, 40 mm. **Ruler:** Elizabeth II **Subject:** Year of Astronomy **Rev:** Mars, multicolor

| Date | Mintage | VF20 | XF40 | MS60 | MS63 | MS65 |
|---|---|---|---|---|---|---|
| 2009 | — | — | — | — | — | 22.00 |

### KM# 777 DOLLAR

27.00 g., Copper silver plated, 40 mm. **Ruler:** Elizabeth II **Subject:** Year of Astronomy **Rev:** Jupiter, multicolor

| Date | Mintage | VF20 | XF40 | MS60 | MS63 | MS65 |
|---|---|---|---|---|---|---|
| 2009 | — | — | — | — | — | 22.00 |

### KM# 778 DOLLAR

27.00 g., Copper silver plated, 40 mm. **Ruler:** Elizabeth II **Subject:** Year of Astronomy **Rev:** Saturn, multicolor

| Date | Mintage | VF20 | XF40 | MS60 | MS63 | MS65 |
|---|---|---|---|---|---|---|
| 2009 | — | — | — | — | — | 22.00 |

### KM# 779 DOLLAR

27.00 g., Copper silver plated, 40 mm. **Ruler:** Elizabeth II **Subject:** Year of Astronomy **Rev:** Uranus, multicolor

| Date | Mintage | VF20 | XF40 | MS60 | MS63 | MS65 |
|---|---|---|---|---|---|---|
| 2009 | — | — | — | — | — | 22.00 |

### KM# 780 DOLLAR

27.00 g., Copper silver plated, 40 mm. **Ruler:** Elizabeth II **Subject:** Year of Astronomy **Rev:** Neptune, multicolor

| Date | Mintage | VF20 | XF40 | MS60 | MS63 | MS65 |
|---|---|---|---|---|---|---|
| 2009 | — | — | — | — | — | 22.00 |

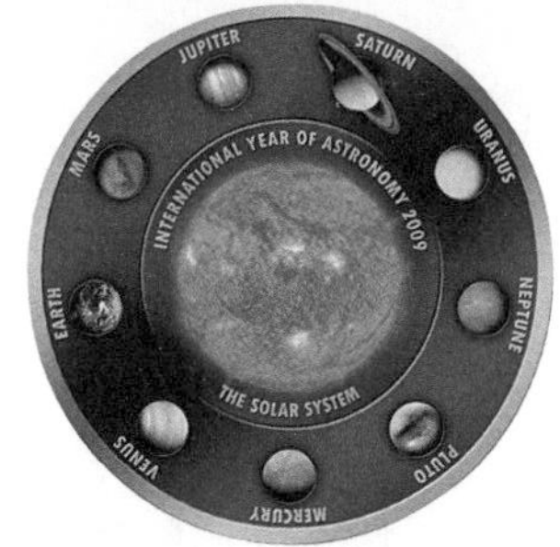


### KM# 781 DOLLAR

27.00 g., Copper silver plated, 40 mm. **Ruler:** Elizabeth II **Subject:** Year of Astronomy **Rev:** Solar System, multicolor

| Date | Mintage | VF20 | XF40 | MS60 | MS63 | MS65 |
|---|---|---|---|---|---|---|
| 2009 | — | — | — | — | — | 22.00 |

### KM# 794 DOLLAR

Copper-Nickel silver plated, 40 mm. **Ruler:** Elizabeth II **Rev:** Nessie, multicolor

| Date | Mintage | VF20 | XF40 | MS60 | MS63 | MS65 |
|---|---|---|---|---|---|---|
| 2009 | — | — | — | — | — | 22.00 |

### KM# 795 DOLLAR

Copper-Nickel silver plated, 40 mm. **Ruler:** Elizabeth II **Rev:** Bigfoot, multicolor

| Date | Mintage | VF20 | XF40 | MS60 | MS63 | MS65 |
|---|---|---|---|---|---|---|
| 2009 | — | — | — | — | — | 22.00 |

### KM# 796 DOLLAR

Copper-Nickel, 40 mm. **Ruler:** Elizabeth II **Rev:** Medussa, multicolor

| Date | Mintage | VF20 | XF40 | MS60 | MS63 | MS65 |
|---|---|---|---|---|---|---|
| 2009 | — | — | — | — | — | 22.00 |

### KM# 797 DOLLAR

Copper-Nickel, 40 mm. **Ruler:** Elizabeth II **Rev:** Pegasus, multicolor

| Date | Mintage | VF20 | XF40 | MS60 | MS63 | MS65 |
|---|---|---|---|---|---|---|
| 2009 | — | — | — | — | — | 22.00 |

### KM# 798 DOLLAR

Silver, 40 mm. **Ruler:** Elizabeth II **Rev:** Baba Yaga, multicolor

| Date | Mintage | VF20 | XF40 | MS60 | MS63 | MS65 |
|---|---|---|---|---|---|---|
| 2009 | — | — | — | — | — | 22.00 |

### KM# 799 DOLLAR

Copper-Nickel, 40 mm. **Ruler:** Elizabeth II **Rev:** Phoenix, multicolor

| Date | Mintage | VF20 | XF40 | MS60 | MS63 | MS65 |
|---|---|---|---|---|---|---|
| 2009 | — | — | — | — | — | 22.00 |

### KM# 1172 DOLLAR

27.00 g., Copper-Nickel, 38.6 mm. **Ruler:** Elizabeth II **Subject:** Moon Landing, 40th Anniversary **Rev:** Landing module Eagle and moon in color

| Date | Mintage | VF20 | XF40 | MS60 | MS63 | MS65 |
|---|---|---|---|---|---|---|
| 2009 | — | — | — | — | — | 17.50 |

### KM# 1231 DOLLAR

25.00 g., Copper-Nickel partially gilt, 38.6 mm. **Ruler:** Elizabeth II **Subject:** British Monarchs - Henry VIII

| Date | Mintage | VF20 | XF40 | MS60 | MS63 | MS65 |
|---|---|---|---|---|---|---|
| 2009 | Est. 50000 | — | — | — | — | 17.50 |

### KM# 1241 DOLLAR

31.14 g., 0.999 Silver 1.000 oz. ASW, 38.61 mm. **Ruler:** Elizabeth II **Subject:** Battle of Gettysburg and General Meade **Rev:** Battle scene at left, Meade in color at right

| Date | Mintage | VF20 | XF40 | MS60 | MS63 | MS65 |
|---|---|---|---|---|---|---|
| 2009 | — | PF65 65.00 | | | | |

**KM# 1327 DOLLAR**
Silver **Ruler:** Elizabeth II **Subject:** Mystical creatures - Drago **Rev:** Dragon in color

| Date | Mintage | VF20 | XF40 | MS60 | MS63 | MS65 |
|---|---|---|---|---|---|---|
| 2009 | — | PF65 75.00 | | | | |

**KM# 1328 DOLLAR**
Copper-Nickel **Ruler:** Elizabeth II **Subject:** Wonders of the World **Rev:** Ayers Rock in color

| Date | Mintage | VF20 | XF40 | MS60 | MS63 | MS65 |
|---|---|---|---|---|---|---|
| 2009 | — | — | — | — | — | 20.00 |

**KM# 1478 DOLLAR**
27.00 g., Silver Plated Copper, 40 mm. **Ruler:** Elizabeth II **Rev:** Mount Everest in color

| Date | Mintage | VF20 | XF40 | MS60 | MS63 | MS65 |
|---|---|---|---|---|---|---|
| 2009 | Est. 5000 | — | — | — | — | 25.00 |

**KM# 1479 DOLLAR**
27.00 g., Silver Plated Copper, 40 mm. **Ruler:** Elizabeth II **Rev:** Niagara Falls in color

| Date | Mintage | VF20 | XF40 | MS60 | MS63 | MS65 |
|---|---|---|---|---|---|---|
| 2009 | Est. 5000 | — | — | — | — | 25.00 |

**KM# 1480 DOLLAR**
27.00 g., Silver Plated Copper, 40 mm. **Ruler:** Elizabeth II **Rev:** Grand Canyon in color

| Date | Mintage | VF20 | XF40 | MS60 | MS63 | MS65 |
|---|---|---|---|---|---|---|
| 2009 | Est. 5000 | — | — | — | — | 25.00 |

**KM# 1481 DOLLAR**
27.00 g., Silver Plated Copper, 40 mm. **Ruler:** Elizabeth II **Rev:** Mt. Aetna volcano in color

| Date | Mintage | VF20 | XF40 | MS60 | MS63 | MS65 |
|---|---|---|---|---|---|---|
| 2009 | Est. 5000 | — | — | — | — | 25.00 |

**KM# 1482 DOLLAR**
27.00 g., Silver Plated Copper, 40 mm. **Ruler:** Elizabeth II **Rev:** Northern lights in color

| Date | Mintage | VF20 | XF40 | MS60 | MS63 | MS65 |
|---|---|---|---|---|---|---|
| 2009 | Est. 5000 | — | — | — | — | 25.00 |

**KM# 1483 DOLLAR**
27.00 g., Silver Plated Copper, 40 mm. **Ruler:** Elizabeth II **Rev:** Strokkur geyser in Iceland

| Date | Mintage | VF20 | XF40 | MS60 | MS63 | MS65 |
|---|---|---|---|---|---|---|
| 2009 | 5,000 | — | — | — | — | 25.00 |

**KM# 1493 DOLLAR**
0.50 g., 0.999 Gold, 11 mm. **Ruler:** Elizabeth II **Subject:** James Cook, 200th Anniversary of Death **Rev:** H.M.S. Endeavour

| Date | Mintage | VF20 | XF40 | MS60 | MS63 | MS65 |
|---|---|---|---|---|---|---|
| 2009 | Est. 10000 | PF65 35.00 | | | | |

**KM# 1517 DOLLAR**
26.03 g., Silver Plated Copper, 38.61 mm. **Ruler:** Elizabeth II **Subject:** 2012 London Olympic Games - Sailing

| Date | Mintage | VF20 | XF40 | MS60 | MS63 | MS65 |
|---|---|---|---|---|---|---|
| 2009 | Est. 30000 | PF65 12.00 | | | | |

**KM# 1534 DOLLAR**
5.67 g., 0.999 Silver 0.1821 oz. ASW, 35 mm. **Ruler:** Elizabeth II **Subject:** Ships and Explorers - Amundsen and Fram

| Date | Mintage | VF20 | XF40 | MS60 | MS63 | MS65 |
|---|---|---|---|---|---|---|
| 2009 | Est. 5000 | PF65 15.00 | | | | |

**KM# 1535 DOLLAR**
5.67 g., 0.999 Silver 0.1821 oz. ASW, 35 mm. **Ruler:** Elizabeth II **Series:** Sips and Explorers - Gorch Fock

| Date | Mintage | VF20 | XF40 | MS60 | MS63 | MS65 |
|---|---|---|---|---|---|---|
| 2009 | — | PF65 15.00 | | | | |

**KM# 1536 DOLLAR**
5.67 g., 0.999 Silver 0.1821 oz. ASW, 35 mm. **Ruler:** Elizabeth II **Subject:** Ships and Explorers - Henry the Seafarer

| Date | Mintage | VF20 | XF40 | MS60 | MS63 | MS65 |
|---|---|---|---|---|---|---|
| 2009 | Est. 5000 | PF65 15.00 | | | | |

**KM# 1568 DOLLAR**
34.00 g., Gold Plated Copper plus silver plated pop-up insert, 38.6 mm. **Ruler:** Elizabeth II **Subject:** World Monuments - Brandenburg Gate Berlin

| Date | Mintage | VF20 | XF40 | MS60 | MS63 | MS65 |
|---|---|---|---|---|---|---|
| 2009 | Est. 20000 | — | — | — | — | 65.00 |

**KM# 1569 DOLLAR**
34.00 g., Gold Plated Copper plus silver plated pop-up insert, 38.6 mm. **Ruler:** Elizabeth II **Subject:** World Monuments - Holsten Gate in Lubeck

| Date | Mintage | VF20 | XF40 | MS60 | MS63 | MS65 |
|---|---|---|---|---|---|---|
| 2009 | Est. 7500 | — | — | — | — | 80.00 |

**KM# 1570 DOLLAR**
34.00 g., Gold Plated Copper plus silver plated pop up insert, 38.6 mm. **Ruler:** Elizabeth II **Subject:** World Monuments - Semper Opera in Dresden

| Date | Mintage | VF20 | XF40 | MS60 | MS63 | MS65 |
|---|---|---|---|---|---|---|
| 2009 | — | — | — | — | — | 80.00 |

**KM# 1571 DOLLAR**
34.00 g., Gold Plated Copper plus silver plated pop-up insert, 38.6 mm. **Ruler:** Elizabeth II **Subject:** World MOnuments - Memorial Church in Berlin

| Date | Mintage | VF20 | XF40 | MS60 | MS63 | MS65 |
|---|---|---|---|---|---|---|
| 2009 | Est. 7500 | — | — | — | — | 80.00 |

**KM# 1572 DOLLAR**
34.00 g., Gold Plated Copper plus silver plated pop-up insert, 38.6 mm. **Ruler:** Elizabeth II **Subject:** World Monuments - CHurch of Our Lady in Dresden

| Date | Mintage | VF20 | XF40 | MS60 | MS63 | MS65 |
|---|---|---|---|---|---|---|
| 2009 | — | — | — | — | — | 80.00 |

**KM# 1576 DOLLAR**
34.00 g., Gold Plated Copper plus silver plated pop-up insert, 38.6 mm. **Ruler:** Elizabeth II **Subject:** World Monuments - Porta Nigra in Trier

| Date | Mintage | VF20 | XF40 | MS60 | MS63 | MS65 |
|---|---|---|---|---|---|---|
| 2009 | Est. 7500 | — | — | — | — | 80.00 |

**KM# 1634 DOLLAR**
0.50 g., 0.999 Gold AGW, 11 mm. **Ruler:** Elizabeth II **Rev:** British monarch - Charles I

| Date | Mintage | VF20 | XF40 | MS60 | MS63 | MS65 |
|---|---|---|---|---|---|---|
| 2009 | — | PF65 45.00 | | | | |

**KM# 1635 DOLLAR**
0.50 g., 0.999 Gold AGW, 11 mm. **Ruler:** Elizabeth II **Rev:** British monarchs - George I

| Date | Mintage | VF20 | XF40 | MS60 | MS63 | MS65 |
|---|---|---|---|---|---|---|
| 2009 | — | PF65 45.00 | | | | |

**KM# 720 DOLLAR**
0.12 g., 0.999 Silver, 4 mm. **Ruler:** Elizabeth II **Rev:** Fisherman's God statue **Note:** Illustration enlarged.

| Date | Mintage | VF20 | XF40 | MS60 | MS63 | MS65 |
|---|---|---|---|---|---|---|
| 2010 Prooflike | 5,000 | — | — | — | — | 10.00 |

**KM# 739 DOLLAR**
31.11 g., 0.999 Silver 0.999 oz. ASW, 37.65 mm. **Ruler:** Elizabeth II **Subject:** Niko & the way to the stars **Obv:** Head crowned left **Rev:** Multicolor deer **Shape:** 7-sided

| Date | Mintage | VF20 | XF40 | MS60 | MS63 | MS65 |
|---|---|---|---|---|---|---|
| 2010 | 3,500 | PF65 60.00 | | | | |

**KM# 740 DOLLAR**
31.11 g., 0.999 Silver 0.999 oz. ASW, 37.65 mm. **Ruler:** Elizabeth II **Subject:** Niko & the way to the stars **Obv:** Head crowned left **Rev:** Multicolor wolf **Shape:** 7-sided

| Date | Mintage | VF20 | XF40 | MS60 | MS63 | MS65 |
|---|---|---|---|---|---|---|
| 2010 | 3,500 | PF65 60.00 | | | | |

**KM# 741 DOLLAR**
31.11 g., 0.999 Silver 0.999 oz. ASW, 37.65 mm. **Ruler:** Elizabeth II **Subject:** Niko & the way to the stars **Obv:** Head crowned left **Rev:** Multicolor flying squirrel **Shape:** 7-sided

| Date | Mintage | VF20 | XF40 | MS60 | MS63 | MS65 |
|---|---|---|---|---|---|---|
| 2010 | 3,500 | PF65 60.00 | | | | |

**KM# 742 DOLLAR**
31.11 g., 0.999 Silver 0.999 oz. ASW, 37.65 mm. **Ruler:** Elizabeth II **Subject:** Niko and the way to the stars **Obv:** Head crowned right **Rev:** Multicolor Ermine **Shape:** 7-sided

| Date | Mintage | VF20 | XF40 | MS60 | MS63 | MS65 |
|---|---|---|---|---|---|---|
| 2010 | 3,500 | PF65 60.00 | | | | |

**KM# 743 DOLLAR**
31.11 g., 0.999 Silver 0.999 oz. ASW, 37.65 mm. **Ruler:** Elizabeth II **Subject:** Niko and the way to the stars **Obv:** Head crowned right **Rev:** Multicolor deer, flying squirrel and ermine **Shape:** 7-sided

| Date | Mintage | VF20 | XF40 | MS60 | MS63 | MS65 |
|---|---|---|---|---|---|---|
| 2010 | 3,500 | PF65 60.00 | | | | |

**KM# 744 DOLLAR**
31.14 g., 0.999 Silver 1.000 oz. ASW, 40.6 mm. **Ruler:** Elizabeth II **Subject:** Battle of Trafalgar, 1805 **Rev:** Multicolor battle scene, HMS Victory

| Date | Mintage | VF20 | XF40 | MS60 | MS63 | MS65 |
|---|---|---|---|---|---|---|
| 2010 | 5,000 | PF65 80.00 | | | | |

**KM# 762 DOLLAR**
10.93 g., Bi-Metallic Copper Nickel center in Aluminum-Bronze ring. **Ruler:** Elizabeth II **Obv:** Bust right **Rev:** Carved Maori figure (Tangaroa)

| Date | Mintage | VF20 | XF40 | MS60 | MS63 | MS65 |
|---|---|---|---|---|---|---|
| 2010 | — | — | — | — | 5.00 | 6.00 |

**KM# 770 DOLLAR**
31.11 g., 0.999 Silver 0.999 oz. ASW, 40 mm. **Ruler:** Elizabeth II **Subject:** Battle of Hampton Roads, Va. **Rev:** Monitor, multicolor background

| Date | Mintage | VF20 | XF40 | MS60 | MS63 | MS65 |
|---|---|---|---|---|---|---|
| 2010 | 5,000 | PF65 80.00 | | | | |

### KM# 771 DOLLAR

31.11 g., 0.999 Silver 0.999 oz. ASW, 40 mm. **Ruler:** Elizabeth II **Subject:** Battle of Salams **Rev:** Trireame, multicolor insert

| Date | Mintage | VF20 | XF40 | MS60 | MS63 | MS65 |
|---|---|---|---|---|---|---|
| 2010 | 5,000 | PF65 100 | | | | |

### KM# 1243 DOLLAR

31.14 g., 0.999 Silver 1.000 oz. ASW, 40.6 mm. **Ruler:** Elizabeth II **Subject:** Battle of Midway **Rev:** Aircraft carrier

| Date | Mintage | VF20 | XF40 | MS60 | MS63 | MS65 |
|---|---|---|---|---|---|---|
| 2010 | 5,000 | PF65 100 | | | | |

### KM# 1256 DOLLAR

31.14 g., 0.999 Silver 1.000 oz. ASW, 40.6 mm. **Ruler:** Elizabeth II **Subject:** Battle of Grunwald

| Date | Mintage | VF20 | XF40 | MS60 | MS63 | MS65 |
|---|---|---|---|---|---|---|
| 2010 | — | PF65 50.00 | | | | |

### KM# 1295 DOLLAR

0.50 g., 0.999 Gold, 11 mm. **Ruler:** Elizabeth II **Rev:** Martin Luther King

| Date | Mintage | VF20 | XF40 | MS60 | MS63 | MS65 |
|---|---|---|---|---|---|---|
| 2010 | — | PF65 50.00 | | | | |

### KM# 1296 DOLLAR

0.50 g., 0.999 Gold, 11 mm. **Ruler:** Elizabeth II **Rev:** Barack Obama

| Date | Mintage | VF20 | XF40 | MS60 | MS63 | MS65 |
|---|---|---|---|---|---|---|
| 2010 | — | PF65 50.00 | | | | |

### KM# 1458 DOLLAR

25.00 g., Copper-Nickel gilt, 38.61 mm. **Ruler:** Elizabeth II **Rev:** Photo of William and Kate

| Date | Mintage | VF20 | XF40 | MS60 | MS63 | MS65 |
|---|---|---|---|---|---|---|
| 2010 | — | PF65 20.00 | | | | |

### KM# 1573 DOLLAR

34.00 g., Gold Plated Copper plus silver plated pop-up insert, 38.6 mm. **Ruler:** Elizabeth II **Subject:** World Monuments - Cathedral of Cologne

| Date | Mintage | VF20 | XF40 | MS60 | MS63 | MS65 |
|---|---|---|---|---|---|---|
| 2010 | Est. 7500 | — | — | — | — | 80.00 |

### KM# 1574 DOLLAR

34.00 g., Gold Plated Copper plus silver plated pop-up insert, 38.6 mm. **Ruler:** Elizabeth II **Subject:** World Monuments - Memorial of the Battle of the Peoples

| Date | Mintage | VF20 | XF40 | MS60 | MS63 | MS65 |
|---|---|---|---|---|---|---|
| 2010 | Est. 7500 | — | — | — | — | 80.00 |

### KM# 1575 DOLLAR

34.00 g., Gold Plated Copper plus silver plated pop-up insert, 38.6 mm. **Ruler:** Elizabeth II **Subject:** World Monuments - Castle Neuschwanstein

| Date | Mintage | VF20 | XF40 | MS60 | MS63 | MS65 |
|---|---|---|---|---|---|---|
| 2010 | Est. 7500 | — | — | — | — | 80.00 |

### KM# 1577 DOLLAR

34.00 g., Gold Plated Copper plus silver plated pop-up insert, 38.6 mm. **Ruler:** Elizabeth II **Subject:** World Monuments - German Reichstag in Berlin

| Date | Mintage | VF20 | XF40 | MS60 | MS63 | MS65 |
|---|---|---|---|---|---|---|
| 2010 | — | — | — | — | — | 80.00 |

### KM# 1578 DOLLAR

34.00 g., Gold Plated Copper plus silver plated pop-up insert, 38.6 mm. **Ruler:** Elizabeth II **Subject:** World Monuments - Wartburg

| Date | Mintage | VF20 | XF40 | MS60 | MS63 | MS65 |
|---|---|---|---|---|---|---|
| 2010 | — | — | — | — | — | 80.00 |

### KM# 1579 DOLLAR

34.00 g., Gold Plated Copper plus silver plated pop-up insert, 38.6 mm. **Ruler:** Elizabeth II **Series:** World Monuments - Castle Sanssouci

| Date | Mintage | VF20 | XF40 | MS60 | MS63 | MS65 |
|---|---|---|---|---|---|---|
| 2010 | Est. 7500 | — | — | — | — | 80.00 |

### KM# 1580 DOLLAR

34.00 g., Gold Plated Copper plus silver plated pop-up insert, 38.6 mm. **Ruler:** Elizabeth II **Subject:** World Monuments - Elbphilharmonie in Hamburg

| Date | Mintage | VF20 | XF40 | MS60 | MS63 | MS65 |
|---|---|---|---|---|---|---|
| 2010 | — | — | — | — | — | 80.00 |

### KM# 1581 DOLLAR

34.00 g., Gold Plated Copper plus silver plated pop-up insert, 38.6 mm. **Ruler:** Elizabeth II **Subject:** World Monuments - Bellevue Palace in Berlin

| Date | Mintage | VF20 | XF40 | MS60 | MS63 | MS65 |
|---|---|---|---|---|---|---|
| 2010 | Est. 7500 | — | — | — | — | 80.00 |

### KM# 1582 DOLLAR

34.00 g., Gold Plated Copper plus silver plated pop-up insert, 38.6 mm. **Ruler:** Elizabeth II **Subject:** World Monuments - Ulmer Munster

| Date | Mintage | VF20 | XF40 | MS60 | MS63 | MS65 |
|---|---|---|---|---|---|---|
| 2010 | — | — | — | — | — | 80.00 |

### KM# 1235 DOLLAR

31.14 g., 0.999 Silver 1.000 oz. ASW, 40.6 mm. **Ruler:** Elizabeth II **Subject:** Battle of Jutland, 1916 **Rev:** Multicolor battleship

| Date | Mintage | VF20 | XF40 | MS60 | MS63 | MS65 |
|---|---|---|---|---|---|---|
| 2011 | 5,000 | PF65 85.00 | | | | |

**KM# 1269 DOLLAR**
31.14 g., 0.999 Silver 1.000 oz. ASW, 47.6x27.6 mm. **Ruler:** Elizabeth II **Subject:** Year of the Rabbit **Rev:** Two brown rabbits **Shape:** Rectangle

| Date | Mintage | VF20 | XF40 | MS60 | MS63 | MS65 |
|---|---|---|---|---|---|---|
| 2011 | 3,000 | **PF65** 100 | | | | |

**KM# 1270 DOLLAR**
31.14 g., 0.999 Silver 1.000 oz. ASW, 47.6x27.6 mm. **Ruler:** Elizabeth II **Subject:** Year of the Rabbit **Rev:** Two white rabbits **Shape:** Rectangle

| Date | Mintage | VF20 | XF40 | MS60 | MS63 | MS65 |
|---|---|---|---|---|---|---|
| 2011 | 3,000 | **PF65** 100 | | | | |

**KM# 1271 DOLLAR**
31.14 g., 0.999 Silver 1.000 oz. ASW, 47.6x27.6 mm. **Ruler:** Elizabeth II **Subject:** Year of the Rabbit **Rev:** One black rabbit **Shape:** Rectangle

| Date | Mintage | VF20 | XF40 | MS60 | MS63 | MS65 |
|---|---|---|---|---|---|---|
| 2011 | 3,000 | **PF65** 100 | | | | |

**KM# 1272 DOLLAR**
31.14 g., 0.999 Silver 1.000 oz. ASW, 47.6x27.6 mm. **Ruler:** Elizabeth II **Subject:** Year of the Rabbit **Rev:** One black rabbit **Shape:** Rectangle

| Date | Mintage | VF20 | XF40 | MS60 | MS63 | MS65 |
|---|---|---|---|---|---|---|
| 2011 | 3,000 | **PF65** 100 | | | | |

**KM# 1283 DOLLAR**
31.10 g., 0.999 Silver 0.9989 oz. ASW, 40.6 mm. **Ruler:** Elizabeth II **Subject:** Florin - 1927 design

| Date | Mintage | VF20 | XF40 | MS60 | MS63 | MS65 |
|---|---|---|---|---|---|---|
| 2011 | 1,500 | **PF65** 75.00 | | | | |

**KM# 1284 DOLLAR**
31.10 g., 0.999 Silver 0.9989 oz. ASW, 40.6 mm. **Ruler:** Elizabeth II **Subject:** Florin - 1934-35 Centenary

| Date | Mintage | VF20 | XF40 | MS60 | MS63 | MS65 |
|---|---|---|---|---|---|---|
| 2011 | 1,500 | **PF65** 75.00 | | | | |

**KM# 1285 DOLLAR**
31.10 g., 0.999 Silver 0.9989 oz. ASW, 40.6 mm. **Ruler:** Elizabeth II **Subject:** Florin - 1901-51 Jubilee

| Date | Mintage | VF20 | XF40 | MS60 | MS63 | MS65 |
|---|---|---|---|---|---|---|
| 2011 | 1,500 | **PF65** 75.00 | | | | |

**KM# 1286 DOLLAR**
31.10 g., 0.999 Silver 0.9989 oz. ASW, 40.6 mm. **Ruler:** Elizabeth II **Subject:** Florin - 1954 Royal Visit

| Date | Mintage | VF20 | XF40 | MS60 | MS63 | MS65 |
|---|---|---|---|---|---|---|
| 2011 | 1,500 | **PF65** 75.00 | | | | |

**KM# 1313 DOLLAR**
27.00 g., Silver Plated Copper, 38.61 mm. **Ruler:** Elizabeth II **Subject:** Marilyn Monroe, 85th Birthday

| Date | Mintage | VF20 | XF40 | MS60 | MS63 | MS65 |
|---|---|---|---|---|---|---|
| 2011 | 2,500 | **PF65** 25.00 | | | | |

**KM# 1313a DOLLAR**
31.11 g., 0.999 Silver 0.999 oz. ASW, 38.61 mm. **Ruler:** Elizabeth II **Subject:** Marylin Monroe, 80th Birthday **Rev:** Marylin Monroe in color pose

| Date | Mintage | VF20 | XF40 | MS60 | MS63 | MS65 |
|---|---|---|---|---|---|---|
| 2011 | — | **PF65** 125 | | | | |

### KM# 1342 DOLLAR

31.11 g., 0.999 Silver 0.999 oz. ASW, 38.61 mm. **Ruler:** Elizabeth II **Subject:** Planets - Mercury **Rev:** with color

| Date | Mintage | VF20 | XF40 | MS60 | MS63 | MS65 |
|---|---|---|---|---|---|---|
| 2011 | — | PF65 75.00 | | | | |

### KM# 1343 DOLLAR

31.11 g., 0.999 Silver 0.999 oz. ASW, 38.61 mm. **Ruler:** Elizabeth II **Subject:** Plants - Venus **Rev:** with color

| Date | Mintage | VF20 | XF40 | MS60 | MS63 | MS65 |
|---|---|---|---|---|---|---|
| 2011 | — | PF65 75.00 | | | | |

### KM# 1344 DOLLAR

31.11 g., 0.999 Silver 0.999 oz. ASW, 38.61 mm. **Ruler:** Elizabeth II **Subject:** Planets - Earth **Rev:** with color

| Date | Mintage | VF20 | XF40 | MS60 | MS63 | MS65 |
|---|---|---|---|---|---|---|
| 2011 | — | PF65 75.00 | | | | |

### KM# 1345 DOLLAR

31.11 g., 0.999 Silver 0.999 oz. ASW, 38.61 mm. **Ruler:** Elizabeth II **Subject:** Plants - Mars **Rev:** with color

| Date | Mintage | VF20 | XF40 | MS60 | MS63 | MS65 |
|---|---|---|---|---|---|---|
| 2011 | — | PF65 75.00 | | | | |

### KM# 1346 DOLLAR

31.11 g., 0.999 Silver 0.999 oz. ASW, 38.61 mm. **Ruler:** Elizabeth II **Subject:** Planets - Jupiter **Rev:** Jupiter and Sagittarius with color

| Date | Mintage | VF20 | XF40 | MS60 | MS63 | MS65 |
|---|---|---|---|---|---|---|
| 2011 | — | PF65 75.00 | | | | |

### KM# 1347 DOLLAR

31.11 g., 0.999 Silver 0.999 oz. ASW, 38.61 mm. **Ruler:** Elizabeth II **Subject:** Planets - Saturn **Rev:** Saturn and Capricorn with color

| Date | Mintage | VF20 | XF40 | MS60 | MS63 | MS65 |
|---|---|---|---|---|---|---|
| 2011 | — | PF65 75.00 | | | | |

### KM# 1348 DOLLAR

31.11 g., 0.999 Silver 0.999 oz. ASW, 38.61 mm. **Ruler:** Elizabeth II **Subject:** Planets - Uranis **Rev:** Uranis and Aquarius with color

| Date | Mintage | VF20 | XF40 | MS60 | MS63 | MS65 |
|---|---|---|---|---|---|---|
| 2011 | — | PF65 75.00 | | | | |

### KM# 1396 DOLLAR

31.11 g., 0.999 Silver 0.999 oz. ASW, 38.61 mm. **Ruler:** Elizabeth II **Subject:** Hollywood Legends - Elizabeth Taylor **Rev:** Elizabeth Taylor facing photo

| Date | Mintage | VF20 | XF40 | MS60 | MS63 | MS65 |
|---|---|---|---|---|---|---|
| 2011 | — | PF65 125 | | | | |

### KM# 1459 DOLLAR

25.00 g., Copper-Nickel gilt, 38.61 mm. **Ruler:** Elizabeth II **Rev:** Photo of William and Kate

| Date | Mintage | VF20 | XF40 | MS60 | MS63 | MS65 |
|---|---|---|---|---|---|---|
| 2011 | — | PF65 25.00 | | | | |

### KM# 1638 DOLLAR

25.00 g., Silver Plated Copper **Ruler:** Elizabeth II **Subject:** Space Shuttle Program, 30th Anniversary **Rev:** Space shuttle and earth in color

| Date | Mintage | VF20 | XF40 | MS60 | MS63 | MS65 |
|---|---|---|---|---|---|---|
| 2012 | 981 | PF65 50.00 | | | | |

### KM# 1375 DOLLAR

0.50 g., 0.999 Gold, 11 mm. **Ruler:** Elizabeth II **Obv:** Head with tiara right **Rev:** Titanic sailing left

| Date | Mintage | VF20 | XF40 | MS60 | MS63 | MS65 |
|---|---|---|---|---|---|---|
| 2012 | — | PF65 50.00 | | | | |

### KM# 1391 DOLLAR

31.11 g., 0.999 Silver 0.999 oz. ASW, 47.6x27.6 mm. **Ruler:** Elizabeth II **Obv:** Head with crown right **Rev:** Orange dragon at right

| Date | Mintage | VF20 | XF40 | MS60 | MS63 | MS65 |
|---|---|---|---|---|---|---|
| 2012 | 3,000 | PF65 125 | | | | |

### KM# 1392 DOLLAR

31.11 g., 0.999 Silver 0.999 oz. ASW, 47.6x27.6 mm. **Ruler:** Elizabeth II **Obv:** Head with crown right **Rev:** Blue dragon at left center

| Date | Mintage | VF20 | XF40 | MS60 | MS63 | MS65 |
|---|---|---|---|---|---|---|
| 2012 | 3,000 | PF65 125 | | | | |

### KM# 1393 DOLLAR

31.11 g., 0.999 Silver 0.999 oz. ASW, 47.6x27.6 mm. **Ruler:** Elizabeth II **Obv:** Head with crown right **Rev:** Brown dragon at center

| Date | Mintage | VF20 | XF40 | MS60 | MS63 | MS65 |
|---|---|---|---|---|---|---|
| 2012 | 3,000 | PF65 125 | | | | |

**KM# 1394 DOLLAR**
31.11 g., 0.999 Silver 0.999 oz. ASW, 47.6x27.6 mm. **Ruler:** Elizabeth II **Obv:** Head with crown right **Rev:** Orange dragon at left

| Date | Mintage | VF20 | XF40 | MS60 | MS63 | MS65 |
|---|---|---|---|---|---|---|
| 2012 | 3,000 | PF65 125 | | | | |

**KM# 1424 DOLLAR**
Silver Plated Copper-Nickel, 38.61 mm. **Ruler:** Elizabeth II **Subject:** Ctyrlistek Cartoons **Rev:** Characters in color

| Date | Mintage | VF20 | XF40 | MS60 | MS63 | MS65 |
|---|---|---|---|---|---|---|
| 2012 | 100 | PF65 35.00 | | | | |

**KM# 1441 DOLLAR**
15.50 g., 0.999 Silver 0.4978 oz. ASW partially gilt **Ruler:** Elizabeth II **Subject:** Year of the Dragon **Rev:** Blue dragon **Shape:** Arc **Note:** One of four which form circle.

| Date | Mintage | VF20 | XF40 | MS60 | MS63 | MS65 |
|---|---|---|---|---|---|---|
| 2012 | — | PF65 50.00 | | | | |

**KM# 1442 DOLLAR**
15.50 g., 0.999 Silver 0.4978 oz. ASW partially gilt **Ruler:** Elizabeth II **Subject:** Year of the Dragon **Rev:** Orange dragon **Shape:** Arc **Note:** One of four which form circle.

| Date | Mintage | VF20 | XF40 | MS60 | MS63 | MS65 |
|---|---|---|---|---|---|---|
| 2012 | — | PF65 50.00 | | | | |

**KM# 1443 DOLLAR**
15.50 g., 0.999 Silver 0.4978 oz. ASW partially gilt **Ruler:** Elizabeth II **Subject:** Year of the Dragon **Rev:** Red dragon **Shape:** Arc **Note:** One of four which form circle.

| Date | Mintage | VF20 | XF40 | MS60 | MS63 | MS65 |
|---|---|---|---|---|---|---|
| 2012 | — | PF65 50.00 | | | | |

**KM# 1444 DOLLAR**
15.50 g., 0.999 Silver 0.4978 oz. ASW partially gilt **Ruler:** Elizabeth II **Subject:** Year of the Dragon **Rev:** Green dragon **Shape:** Arc **Note:** One of four which form circle.

| Date | Mintage | VF20 | XF40 | MS60 | MS63 | MS65 |
|---|---|---|---|---|---|---|
| 2012 | — | PF65 50.00 | | | | |

**KM# 1449 DOLLAR**
Silver Plated Copper, 38.61 mm. **Ruler:** Elizabeth II **Subject:** Abu Simbel **Rev:** Statues in color

| Date | Mintage | VF20 | XF40 | MS60 | MS63 | MS65 |
|---|---|---|---|---|---|---|
| 2012 | — | PF65 40.00 | | | | |

**KM# 1456 DOLLAR**
25.00 g., Copper-Nickel gilt, 38.61 mm. **Ruler:** Elizabeth II **Subject:** Space Walk **Rev:** Photo of Space Walk

| Date | Mintage | VF20 | XF40 | MS60 | MS63 | MS65 |
|---|---|---|---|---|---|---|
| 2012 | — | PF65 60.00 | | | | |

**KM# 1457 DOLLAR**
Silver **Ruler:** Elizabeth II **Subject:** Everlasting love **Rev:** Flowers in color **Shape:** Heart

| Date | Mintage | VF20 | XF40 | MS60 | MS63 | MS65 |
|---|---|---|---|---|---|---|
| 2012 | — | PF65 100 | | | | |

**KM# 1599 DOLLAR**
20.12 g., 0.925 Silver 0.5984 oz. ASW, 38.6 mm. **Ruler:** Elizabeth II **Subject:** Gold Cup, Royal Ascot **Rev:** Gold Cup trophy, horse forepart at right

| Date | Mintage | VF20 | XF40 | MS60 | MS63 | MS65 |
|---|---|---|---|---|---|---|
| 2012 | — | PF65 75.00 | | | | |

**KM# 1460 DOLLAR**
31.11 g., 0.999 Silver 0.999 oz. ASW, 27x47 mm. **Ruler:** Elizabeth II **Subject:** Year of the Snake **Rev:** Blue lipped sea snake **Shape:** Rectangle

| Date | Mintage | VF20 | XF40 | MS60 | MS63 | MS65 |
|---|---|---|---|---|---|---|
| 2013 | 3,000 | PF65 100 | | | | |

**KM# 1461 DOLLAR**
31.11 g., 0.999 Silver 0.999 oz. ASW, 27x47 mm. **Ruler:** Elizabeth II **Subject:** Year of the Snake **Rev:** Yellow banded wolf snake **Shape:** Rectangle

| Date | Mintage | VF20 | XF40 | MS60 | MS63 | MS65 |
|---|---|---|---|---|---|---|
| 2013 | 3,000 | PF65 100 | | | | |

**KM# 1462 DOLLAR**
31.11 g., 0.999 Silver 0.999 oz. ASW, 38.61 mm. **Ruler:** Elizabeth II **Subject:** Year of the Snake **Rev:** Red bamboo rat snake

| Date | Mintage | VF20 | XF40 | MS60 | MS63 | MS65 |
|---|---|---|---|---|---|---|
| 2013 | 3,000 | PF65 100 | | | | |

**KM# 1463 DOLLAR**
31.11 g., 0.999 Silver 0.999 oz. ASW, 38.61 mm. **Ruler:** Elizabeth II **Subject:** Year of the Snake **Rev:** Chinese green tree viper

| Date | Mintage | VF20 | XF40 | MS60 | MS63 | MS65 |
|---|---|---|---|---|---|---|
| 2013 | 3,000 | PF65 100 | | | | |

**KM# 1464 DOLLAR**
15.50 g., 0.999 Silver 0.4978 oz. ASW, 49x24 mm. **Ruler:** Elizabeth II **Subject:** Year of the Snake **Shape:** Fan

| Date | Mintage | VF20 | XF40 | MS60 | MS63 | MS65 |
|---|---|---|---|---|---|---|
| 2013 | 7,500 | PF65 75.00 | | | | |

**KM# 1595 DOLLAR**
27.00 g., Copper-Nickel, 38.61 mm. **Ruler:** Elizabeth II **Subject:** Cyrlistek Cartoons - Pinda

| Date | Mintage | VF20 | XF40 | MS60 | MS63 | MS65 |
|---|---|---|---|---|---|---|
| 2013 | Est. 1000 | PF65 80.00 | | | | |

**KM# 1596 DOLLAR**
27.00 g., Silver, 38.61 mm. **Ruler:** Elizabeth II **Subject:** Ctyrlistek Cartoon - Myspulin

| Date | Mintage | VF20 | XF40 | MS60 | MS63 | MS65 |
|---|---|---|---|---|---|---|
| 2013 | Est. 1000 | PF65 80.00 | | | | |

**KM# 1597 DOLLAR**
27.00 g., Copper-Nickel, 38.61 mm. **Ruler:** Elizabeth II **Subject:** Ctyrlistek Cartoons - Fifinka

| Date | Mintage | VF20 | XF40 | MS60 | MS63 | MS65 |
|---|---|---|---|---|---|---|
| 2013 | Est. 1000 | PF65 80.00 | | | | |

**KM# 1598 DOLLAR**
27.00 g., Copper-Nickel, 38.61 mm. **Ruler:** Elizabeth II **Subject:** Ctyrlistek Cartoons - Bobik

| Date | Mintage | VF20 | XF40 | MS60 | MS63 | MS65 |
|---|---|---|---|---|---|---|
| 2013 | Est. 1000 | PF65 80.00 | | | | |

**KM# 1603 DOLLAR**
0.925 Silver ASW partially gilt **Ruler:** Elizabeth II **Subject:** 2016 Olympics Transfer from London to Rio

| Date | Mintage | VF20 | XF40 | MS60 | MS63 | MS65 |
|---|---|---|---|---|---|---|
| 2013 | Est. 10000 | PF65 50.00 | | | | |

**KM# 1604 DOLLAR**
0.50 g., 0.999 Gold AGW with selective .585 gold plating, 11 mm. **Ruler:** Elizabeth II **Subject:** 2016 Olympics - Transfer from London to Rio

| Date | Mintage | VF20 | XF40 | MS60 | MS63 | MS65 |
|---|---|---|---|---|---|---|
| 2013 | Est. 1000 | PF65 50.00 | | | | |

**KM# 1607 DOLLAR**
0.50 g., 0.585 Gold AGW with 24Kt plating, 11 mm. **Ruler:** Elizabeth II **Subject:** Vincent van Gogh

| Date | Mintage | VF20 | XF40 | MS60 | MS63 | MS65 |
|---|---|---|---|---|---|---|
| 2013 | Est. 5000 | PF65 50.00 | | | | |

**KM# 1612 DOLLAR**
7.30 g., 0.333 Silver 0.0782 oz. ASW, 30 mm. **Ruler:** Elizabeth II **Subject:** 2014 FIFA World Cup - Brazil Trophy

| Date | Mintage | VF20 | XF40 | MS60 | MS63 | MS65 |
|---|---|---|---|---|---|---|
| 2013 | Est. 25000 | PF65 40.00 | | | | |

**KM# 1613 DOLLAR**
7.30 g., 0.333 Silver 0.0782 oz. ASW, 30 mm. **Ruler:** Elizabeth II **Subject:** 2014 FIFA World Cup Brazil - Mascot

| Date | Mintage | VF20 | XF40 | MS60 | MS63 | MS65 |
|---|---|---|---|---|---|---|
| 2013 | Est. 25000 | PF65 50.00 | | | | |

**KM# 1651 DOLLAR**
0.50 g., 0.999 Gold AGW, 13.92 mm. **Ruler:** Elizabeth II **Rev:** Marilyn Monroe color image

| Date | Mintage | VF20 | XF40 | MS60 | MS63 | MS65 |
|---|---|---|---|---|---|---|
| 2013 | — | PF65 75.00 | | | | |

**KM# 1652 DOLLAR**
0.50 g., 0.999 Gold AGW, 13.92 mm. **Ruler:** Elizabeth II **Rev:** S.S. Republic

| Date | Mintage | VF20 | XF40 | MS60 | MS63 | MS65 |
|---|---|---|---|---|---|---|
| 2013 | — | PF65 75.00 | | | | |

**KM# 551 2 DOLLARS**
31.11 g., 0.999 Silver 0.999 oz. ASW, 40.5 mm. **Ruler:** Elizabeth II **Subject:** Asian wildlife **Rev:** Multicolor Mikado Pheasant

| Date | Mintage | VF20 | XF40 | MS60 | MS63 | MS65 |
|---|---|---|---|---|---|---|
| 2001 | 5,000 | PF65 85.00 | | | | |

**KM# 552 2 DOLLARS**
31.11 g., 0.999 Silver 0.999 oz. ASW, 40.5 mm. **Ruler:** Elizabeth II **Subject:** Asian wildlife **Rev:** Multicolor black-faced spoonbill

| Date | Mintage | VF20 | XF40 | MS60 | MS63 | MS65 |
|---|---|---|---|---|---|---|
| 2001 | 5,000 | PF65 85.00 | | | | |

**KM# 553 2 DOLLARS**
31.11 g., 0.999 Silver 0.999 oz. ASW, 40.5 mm. **Ruler:** Elizabeth II **Subject:** Asian wildlife **Rev:** Multicolor Indian Pitta

| Date | Mintage | VF20 | XF40 | MS60 | MS63 | MS65 |
|---|---|---|---|---|---|---|
| 2001 | 3,000 | PF65 85.00 | | | | |

**KM# 554 2 DOLLARS**
31.11 g., 0.999 Silver 0.999 oz. ASW, 40.5 mm. **Ruler:** Elizabeth II **Subject:** Asian wildlife **Rev:** Multicolored pheasant-tailed Jacana

| Date | Mintage | VF20 | XF40 | MS60 | MS63 | MS65 |
|---|---|---|---|---|---|---|
| 2001 | 3,000 | PF65 85.00 | | | | |

**KM# 468 2 DOLLARS**
Copper-Nickel **Ruler:** Elizabeth II **Rev:** Football championship

| Date | Mintage | VF20 | XF40 | MS60 | MS63 | MS65 |
|---|---|---|---|---|---|---|
| 2002 | — | — | — | 5.00 | 7.00 | 9.00 |

**KM# 1119 2 DOLLARS**
Copper-Nickel, 30 mm. **Ruler:** Elizabeth II **Subject:** XXVIII Summer Olympics, Athens **Rev:** Discus thrower

| Date | Mintage | VF20 | XF40 | MS60 | MS63 | MS65 |
|---|---|---|---|---|---|---|
| 2002 | — | PF65 15.00 | | | | |

**KM# 1120 2 DOLLARS**
Silver **Ruler:** Elizabeth II **Subject:** Endangered Wildlife **Rev:** Lion family

| Date | Mintage | VF20 | XF40 | MS60 | MS63 | MS65 |
|---|---|---|---|---|---|---|
| 2002 | — | PF65 25.00 | | | | |

**KM# 1282 2 DOLLARS**
31.14 g., 0.999 Silver 1.000 oz. ASW, 40.6 mm. **Ruler:** Elizabeth II **Subject:** Taiwan New Koala Family **Obv:** Head crowned right **Rev:** Multicolor Koala seated with leaves

| Date | Mintage | VF20 | XF40 | MS60 | MS63 | MS65 |
|---|---|---|---|---|---|---|
| 2002 | — | PF65 135 | | | | |

**KM# 417 2 DOLLARS**
7.55 g., Copper-Nickel, 26 mm. **Ruler:** Elizabeth II **Obv:** Crowned bust right, new portrait **Rev:** Mortar and pestle from Atiu Island **Shape:** Triangle

| Date | Mintage | VF20 | XF40 | MS60 | MS63 | MS65 |
|---|---|---|---|---|---|---|
| 2003 | — | — | — | 3.00 | 3.50 | 5.00 |
| 2010 | — | — | — | 3.00 | 3.50 | 5.00 |

**KM# 1123 2 DOLLARS**
62.77 g., 0.999 Silver 2.0161 oz. ASW, 50 mm. **Ruler:** Elizabeth II **Rev:** Edward "Ned" Kelly in color

| Date | Mintage | VF20 | XF40 | MS60 | MS63 | MS65 |
|---|---|---|---|---|---|---|
| 2003 | Est. 2500 | PF65 125 | | | | |

**KM# 1124 2 DOLLARS**
62.77 g., 0.999 Silver 2.0161 oz. ASW, 50 mm. **Ruler:** Elizabeth II **Rev:** Daniel Morgan in color

| Date | Mintage | VF20 | XF40 | MS60 | MS63 | MS65 |
|---|---|---|---|---|---|---|
| 2003 | — | PF65 125 | | | | |

**KM# 1125 2 DOLLARS**
62.77 g., 0.999 Silver 2.0161 oz. ASW **Ruler:** Elizabeth II **Rev:** Ben Hall in color

| Date | Mintage | VF20 | XF40 | MS60 | MS63 | MS65 |
|---|---|---|---|---|---|---|
| 2003 | Est. 2500 | PF65 125 | | | | |

**KM# 1126 2 DOLLARS**
62.77 g., 0.999 Silver 2.0161 oz. ASW, 50 mm. **Ruler:** Elizabeth II **Rev:** Fred Ward "Captain Thunderbolt" in color

| Date | Mintage | VF20 | XF40 | MS60 | MS63 | MS65 |
|---|---|---|---|---|---|---|
| 2003 | Est. 2500 | PF65 125 | | | | |

**KM# 1139 2 DOLLARS**
0.999 Silver, 30 mm. **Ruler:** Elizabeth II **Subject:** John F. Kennedy, 40th Anniversary of Death

| Date | Mintage | VF20 | XF40 | MS60 | MS63 | MS65 |
|---|---|---|---|---|---|---|
| 2003 | — | PF65 45.00 | | | | |

**KM# 1141 2 DOLLARS**
Gold **Ruler:** Elizabeth II **Rev:** Red cardinal in color

| Date | Mintage | VF20 | XF40 | MS60 | MS63 | MS65 |
|---|---|---|---|---|---|---|
| 2003 | Est. 5000 | PF65 85.00 | | | | |

**KM# 1142 2 DOLLARS**
Gold **Ruler:** Elizabeth II **Subject:** Love swing **Rev:** Bird in color

| Date | Mintage | VF20 | XF40 | MS60 | MS63 | MS65 |
|---|---|---|---|---|---|---|
| 2003 | Est. 5000 | PF65 85.00 | | | | |

**KM# 536 2 DOLLARS**
31.11 g., 0.999 Silver 0.999 oz. ASW, 40.7 mm. **Ruler:** Elizabeth II **Subject:** Birds of New Zealand **Rev:** Multicolor tui

| Date | Mintage | VF20 | XF40 | MS60 | MS63 | MS65 |
|---|---|---|---|---|---|---|
| 2005 Prooflike | 8,000 | — | — | — | — | 85.00 |

**KM# 537 2 DOLLARS**
31.11 g., 0.999 Silver 0.999 oz. ASW, 40.7 mm. **Ruler:** Elizabeth II **Subject:** Birds of New Zealand **Rev:** Multicolor bell bird

| Date | Mintage | VF20 | XF40 | MS60 | MS63 | MS65 |
|---|---|---|---|---|---|---|
| 2005 Prooflike | 8,000 | — | — | — | — | 85.00 |

**KM# 538 2 DOLLARS**
31.11 g., 0.999 Silver 0.999 oz. ASW, 40.7 mm. **Ruler:** Elizabeth II **Subject:** Birds of New Zealand **Rev:** Multicolor New Zealand Pigeon

| Date | Mintage | VF20 | XF40 | MS60 | MS63 | MS65 |
|---|---|---|---|---|---|---|
| 2005 Prooflike | 8,000 | — | — | — | — | 85.00 |

**KM# 539 2 DOLLARS**
31.11 g., 0.999 Silver 0.999 oz. ASW, 40.7 mm. **Ruler:** Elizabeth II **Subject:** Birds of New Zealand **Rev:** Multicolor yellow crowned parakeet

| Date | Mintage | VF20 | XF40 | MS60 | MS63 | MS65 |
|---|---|---|---|---|---|---|
| 2005 Prooflike | 8,000 | — | — | — | — | 85.00 |

**KM# 1619 2 DOLLARS**
31.11 g., 0.999 Silver 0.999 oz. ASW selectively gilt, 40 mm. **Ruler:** Elizabeth II **Subject:** Year of the Rooster **Obv:** Head with tiara right **Rev:** Formosan Golden Hen

| Date | Mintage | VF20 | XF40 | MS60 | MS63 | MS65 |
|---|---|---|---|---|---|---|
| 2005 | — | PF65 125 | | | | |

**KM# 524 2 DOLLARS**
31.11 g., 0.999 Silver 0.999 oz. ASW, 40.7 mm. **Ruler:** Elizabeth II **Subject:** Classic Speedsters from the 1930's **Rev:** Multicolor 1935 Auburn 851 Speedster

| Date | Mintage | VF20 | XF40 | MS60 | MS63 | MS65 |
|---|---|---|---|---|---|---|
| 2006 Prooflike | 6,000 | — | — | — | — | 75.00 |

**KM# 525 2 DOLLARS**
31.11 g., 0.999 Silver 0.999 oz. ASW, 40.7 mm. **Ruler:** Elizabeth II **Subject:** Classic Speedsters from the 1930's **Rev:** Multicolor 1935 Bugatti Type 57SC Atlantic Speedster

| Date | Mintage | VF20 | XF40 | MS60 | MS63 | MS65 |
|---|---|---|---|---|---|---|
| 2006 Prooflike | 6,000 | — | — | — | — | 75.00 |

**KM# 526 2 DOLLARS**
31.11 g., 0.999 Silver 0.999 oz. ASW, 40.7 mm. **Ruler:** Elizabeth II **Subject:** Speedsters from the 1930's **Rev:** Multicolor 1936 Duesenberg SSJ Speedster

| Date | Mintage | VF20 | XF40 | MS60 | MS63 | MS65 |
|---|---|---|---|---|---|---|
| 2006 Prooflike | — | — | — | — | — | 75.00 |

**KM# 527 2 DOLLARS**
31.11 g., 0.999 Silver 0.999 oz. ASW, 40.7 mm. **Ruler:** Elizabeth II **Subject:** Speedsters from the 1930's **Rev:** Multicolor 1930 Packard 734 Boattail Speedster

| Date | Mintage | VF20 | XF40 | MS60 | MS63 | MS65 |
|---|---|---|---|---|---|---|
| 2006 Prooflike | 6,000 | — | — | — | — | 75.00 |

**KM# 1170 2 DOLLARS**
10.00 g., 0.925 Silver 0.2974 oz. ASW, 30 mm. **Ruler:** Elizabeth II **Rev:** Motion Pictures, 100th Anniversary

| Date | Mintage | VF20 | XF40 | MS60 | MS63 | MS65 |
|---|---|---|---|---|---|---|
| 2006 | Est. 2500 | — | — | — | — | 35.00 |

**KM# 1288 2 DOLLARS**
31.11 g., 0.999 Silver 0.999 oz. ASW, 40.7 mm. **Ruler:** Elizabeth II **Rev:** Supermarine S-6B race plane in color

| Date | Mintage | VF20 | XF40 | MS60 | MS63 | MS65 |
|---|---|---|---|---|---|---|
| 2006 Prooflike | 6,000 | — | — | — | — | 65.00 |

**KM# 1289 2 DOLLARS**
31.11 g., 0.999 Silver 0.999 oz. ASW, 40.7 mm. **Ruler:** Elizabeth II **Rev:** GeeBee race plane in color

| Date | Mintage | VF20 | XF40 | MS60 | MS63 | MS65 |
|---|---|---|---|---|---|---|
| 2006 Prooflike | 6,000 | — | — | — | — | 65.00 |

**KM# 1290 2 DOLLARS**
31.11 g., 0.999 Silver 0.999 oz. ASW, 40.7 mm. **Ruler:** Elizabeth II **Rev:** Hughes H-1 race plane in color

| Date | Mintage | VF20 | XF40 | MS60 | MS63 | MS65 |
|---|---|---|---|---|---|---|
| 2006 Prooflike | 6,000 | — | — | — | — | 65.00 |

**KM# 1291 2 DOLLARS**
31.11 g., 0.999 Silver 0.999 oz. ASW, 40.7 mm. **Ruler:** Elizabeth II **Rev:** Polikarpov I-16 race plane in color

| Date | Mintage | VF20 | XF40 | MS60 | MS63 | MS65 |
|---|---|---|---|---|---|---|
| 2006 Prooflike | 6,000 | — | — | — | — | 65.00 |

**KM# 1626 2 DOLLARS**
31.11 g., 0.999 Silver 0.999 oz. ASW, 40 mm. **Ruler:** Elizabeth II **Rev:** Boris Pasternak in color

| Date | Mintage | VF20 | XF40 | MS60 | MS63 | MS65 |
|---|---|---|---|---|---|---|
| 2006 | 6,000 | PF65 100 | | | | |

**KM# 1627 2 DOLLARS**
31.11 g., 0.999 Silver 0.999 oz. ASW, 40 mm. **Ruler:** Elizabeth II **Rev:** Anna Akhmatova in color

| Date | Mintage | VF20 | XF40 | MS60 | MS63 | MS65 |
|---|---|---|---|---|---|---|
| 2006 | 6,000 | PF65 100 | | | | |

**KM# 514 2 DOLLARS**
31.11 g., 0.999 Silver 0.999 oz. ASW, 40.7 mm. **Ruler:** Elizabeth II **Subject:** Great Motorcycles from the 1930's **Rev:** Multicolor 1930 BSA Sloper

| Date | Mintage | VF20 | XF40 | MS60 | MS63 | MS65 |
|---|---|---|---|---|---|---|
| 2007 Prooflike | 6,000 | — | — | — | — | 70.00 |

**KM# 515 2 DOLLARS**
31.11 g., 0.999 Silver 0.999 oz. ASW, 40.7 mm. **Ruler:** Elizabeth II **Subject:** Great motorcycles from the 1930's **Rev:** Multicolor 1937 Ariel 1000 Squarefour

| Date | Mintage | VF20 | XF40 | MS60 | MS63 | MS65 |
|---|---|---|---|---|---|---|
| 2007 Prooflike | 6,000 | — | — | — | — | 70.00 |

**KM# 516 2 DOLLARS**
31.11 g., 0.999 Silver 0.999 oz. ASW, 40.7 mm. **Ruler:** Elizabeth II **Subject:** Great motorcycles from the 1930's **Rev:** Multicolor 1938 12H 8

| Date | Mintage | VF20 | XF40 | MS60 | MS63 | MS65 |
|---|---|---|---|---|---|---|
| 2007 Prooflike | 6,000 | — | — | — | — | 70.00 |

**KM# 517 2 DOLLARS**
31.11 g., 0.999 Silver 0.999 oz. ASW, 40.7 mm. **Ruler:** Elizabeth II **Subject:** Great motorcycles from the 1930's **Rev:** Multicolor 1931 Matchless Silver Hawk

| Date | Mintage | VF20 | XF40 | MS60 | MS63 | MS65 |
|---|---|---|---|---|---|---|
| 2007 Prooflike | 6,000 | — | — | — | — | 70.00 |

**KM# 518 2 DOLLARS**
31.11 g., 0.999 Silver 0.999 oz. ASW, 40.7 mm. **Ruler:** Elizabeth II **Subject:** Great motocycles from the 1930's **Rev:** Multicolor 1932 Brough Superior SS100

| Date | Mintage | VF20 | XF40 | MS60 | MS63 | MS65 |
|---|---|---|---|---|---|---|
| 2007 Prooflike | 6,000 | — | — | — | — | 70.00 |

**KM# 529 2 DOLLARS**
31.11 g., 0.999 Silver 0.999 oz. ASW, 40.7 mm. **Ruler:** Elizabeth II **Subject:** International Women's Day **Rev:** Multicolor tulips, large 8

| Date | Mintage | VF20 | XF40 | MS60 | MS63 | MS65 |
|---|---|---|---|---|---|---|
| 2007 Prooflike | 4,000 | — | — | — | — | 65.00 |

**KM# 532 2 DOLLARS**
31.11 g., 0.999 Silver 0.999 oz. ASW, 40.7 mm. **Ruler:** Elizabeth II **Subject:** Sherlock Holmes **Rev:** Multicolor portrait

| Date | Mintage | VF20 | XF40 | MS60 | MS63 | MS65 |
|---|---|---|---|---|---|---|
| 2007 Prooflike | 8,000 | — | — | — | — | 100 |

**KM# 1184 2 DOLLARS**
31.11 g., 0.999 Silver 0.999 oz. ASW, 40.7 mm. **Ruler:** Elizabeth II **Subject:** Birds of Fiji **Rev:** Island Thrush in color

| Date | Mintage | VF20 | XF40 | MS60 | MS63 | MS65 |
|---|---|---|---|---|---|---|
| 2007 | — | — | — | — | — | 45.00 |

**KM# 1185 2 DOLLARS**
31.11 g., 0.999 Silver 0.999 oz. ASW, 40.7 mm. **Ruler:** Elizabeth II **Subject:** Birds of Fiji **Rev:** Vampire Bat in color

| Date | Mintage | VF20 | XF40 | MS60 | MS63 | MS65 |
|---|---|---|---|---|---|---|
| 2007 | Est. 4000 | — | — | — | — | 45.00 |

**KM# 1186 2 DOLLARS**
31.11 g., 0.999 Silver 0.999 oz. ASW, 40.7 mm. **Ruler:** Elizabeth II **Subject:** Birds of Fiji **Rev:** Kingfisher in color

| Date | Mintage | VF20 | XF40 | MS60 | MS63 | MS65 |
|---|---|---|---|---|---|---|
| 2007 | 4,000 | — | — | — | — | 45.00 |

**KM# 1187 2 DOLLARS**
31.11 g., 0.999 Silver 0.999 oz. ASW, 40.7 mm. **Ruler:** Elizabeth II **Subject:** Birds of Fiji **Rev:** Lori in color

| Date | Mintage | VF20 | XF40 | MS60 | MS63 | MS65 |
|---|---|---|---|---|---|---|
| 2007 | 4,000 | — | — | — | — | 45.00 |

**KM# 1316 2 DOLLARS**
Silver **Ruler:** Elizabeth II **Rev:** Motorcycle - Brough in color

| Date | Mintage | VF20 | XF40 | MS60 | MS63 | MS65 |
|---|---|---|---|---|---|---|
| 2007 | — | PF65 45.00 | | | | |

**KM# 1317 2 DOLLARS**
Silver **Ruler:** Elizabeth II **Rev:** Motorcycle - BSA Sloper in color

| Date | Mintage | VF20 | XF40 | MS60 | MS63 | MS65 |
|---|---|---|---|---|---|---|
| 2007 | — | PF65 45.00 | | | | |

**KM# 1318 2 DOLLARS**
Silver **Ruler:** Elizabeth II **Rev:** Motorcycle - IZH 8

| Date | Mintage | VF20 | XF40 | MS60 | MS63 | MS65 |
|---|---|---|---|---|---|---|
| 2007 | — | PF65 45.00 | | | | |

**KM# 510 2 DOLLARS**
31.11 g., 0.999 Silver 0.999 oz. ASW, 40.7 mm. **Ruler:** Elizabeth II **Subject:** Year of the Rat **Rev:** Multicolor scene of little girl from Russian animated cartoon

| Date | Mintage | VF20 | XF40 | MS60 | MS63 | MS65 |
|---|---|---|---|---|---|---|
| 2008 Prooflike | 10,000 | — | — | — | — | 80.00 |

**KM# 511 2 DOLLARS**
31.11 g., 0.999 Silver 0.999 oz. ASW, 40.7 mm. **Ruler:** Elizabeth II **Subject:** Year of the Rat **Rev:** Multicolor scene of nutcracker from Russian animated cartoon

| Date | Mintage | VF20 | XF40 | MS60 | MS63 | MS65 |
|---|---|---|---|---|---|---|
| 2008 Prooflike | 10,000 | — | — | — | — | 80.00 |

**KM# 512 2 DOLLARS**
39.11 g., 0.999 Silver 1.256 oz. ASW, 40.7 mm. **Ruler:** Elizabeth II **Rev:** Multicolor scene of Adventure of Cat Leopold Russian animated cartoon

| Date | Mintage | VF20 | XF40 | MS60 | MS63 | MS65 |
|---|---|---|---|---|---|---|
| 2008 Prooflike | 10,000 | — | — | — | — | 100 |

**KM# 513 2 DOLLARS**
31.11 g., 0.999 Silver 0.999 oz. ASW, 40.7 mm. **Ruler:** Elizabeth II **Subject:** Year of the Rat **Rev:** Multicolor scene of tough toy soldier from Russian animated cartoon

| Date | Mintage | VF20 | XF40 | MS60 | MS63 | MS65 |
|---|---|---|---|---|---|---|
| 2008 Prooflike | 10,000 | — | — | — | — | 80.00 |

**KM# 519 2 DOLLARS**
31.11 g., 0.999 Silver 0.999 oz. ASW, 40.7 mm. **Ruler:** Elizabeth II **Subject:** Racers from the 1930's **Rev:** Multicolor Gee Bee

| Date | Mintage | VF20 | XF40 | MS60 | MS63 | MS65 |
|---|---|---|---|---|---|---|
| 2008 Prooflike | 6,000 | — | — | — | — | 70.00 |

**KM# 520 2 DOLLARS**
31.11 g., 0.999 Silver 0.999 oz. ASW, 40.7 mm. **Ruler:** Elizabeth II **Subject:** Racers from the 1930's **Rev:** Multicolor, Hughes H-1 Racer

| Date | Mintage | VF20 | XF40 | MS60 | MS63 | MS65 |
|---|---|---|---|---|---|---|
| 2008 Prooflike | 6,000 | — | — | — | — | 70.00 |

**KM# 521 2 DOLLARS**
31.11 g., 0.999 Silver 0.999 oz. ASW, 40.7 mm. **Ruler:** Elizabeth II **Subject:** Racers from the 1930's **Rev:** Multicolor Laird Turner LTR-14 Meteor

| Date | Mintage | VF20 | XF40 | MS60 | MS63 | MS65 |
|---|---|---|---|---|---|---|
| 2008 Prooflike | 6,000 | — | — | — | — | 70.00 |

**KM# 522 2 DOLLARS**
31.11 g., 0.999 Silver 0.999 oz. ASW, 40.7 mm. **Ruler:** Elizabeth II **Subject:** Racers from the 1930's **Rev:** Multicolor Spuermarine S.6B Floatplane

| Date | Mintage | VF20 | XF40 | MS60 | MS63 | MS65 |
|---|---|---|---|---|---|---|
| 2008 Prooflike | 6,000 | — | — | — | — | 70.00 |

**KM# 523 2 DOLLARS**
31.11 g., 0.999 Silver 0.999 oz. ASW, 40.7 mm. **Ruler:** Elizabeth II **Subject:** Racers from the 1930's **Rev:** Multicolor Polikarpov I-16

| Date | Mintage | VF20 | XF40 | MS60 | MS63 | MS65 |
|---|---|---|---|---|---|---|
| 2008 Prooflike | 6,000 | — | — | — | — | 70.00 |

**KM# 528 2 DOLLARS**
31.11 g., 0.999 Silver 0.999 oz. ASW, 40.7 mm. **Ruler:** Elizabeth II **Subject:** Valentines (Love) **Rev:** Multicolor pair of swans **Rev. Legend:** Love is precious

| Date | Mintage | VF20 | XF40 | MS60 | MS63 | MS65 |
|---|---|---|---|---|---|---|
| 2008 Prooflike | 16,000 | — | — | — | — | 90.00 |

**KM# 530 2 DOLLARS**
31.11 g., 0.999 Silver 0.999 oz. ASW, 40.7 mm. **Ruler:** Elizabeth II **Subject:** Mikhail Kalasknikov **Rev:** Multicolor portrait in uniform with siver gun

| Date | Mintage | VF20 | XF40 | MS60 | MS63 | MS65 |
|---|---|---|---|---|---|---|
| 2008 Prooflike | 20,000 | — | — | — | — | 100 |

**KM# 531 2 DOLLARS**
31.11 g., 0.999 Silver 0.999 oz. ASW, 40.7 mm. **Ruler:** Elizabeth II **Subject:** Mikhail Kalashnikov **Rev:** Multicolor red star, soldier and gun

| Date | Mintage | VF20 | XF40 | MS60 | MS63 | MS65 |
|---|---|---|---|---|---|---|
| 2008 Prooflike | 20,000 | — | — | — | — | 100 |

**KM# 533 2 DOLLARS**
31.11 g., 0.999 Silver 0.999 oz. ASW, 40.7 mm. **Ruler:** Elizabeth II **Subject:** Sherlock Holmes **Rev:** Multicolor scene from Hound of the Baskervilles

| Date | Mintage | VF20 | XF40 | MS60 | MS63 | MS65 |
|---|---|---|---|---|---|---|
| 2008 Prooflike | 8,000 | — | — | — | — | 100 |

**KM# 534 2 DOLLARS**
31.11 g., 0.999 Silver 0.999 oz. ASW, 40.7 mm. **Ruler:** Elizabeth II **Subject:** Sherlock Holmes **Rev:** Multicolor scehe from the Final Problem

| Date | Mintage | VF20 | XF40 | MS60 | MS63 | MS65 |
|---|---|---|---|---|---|---|
| 2008 Prooflike | 8,000 | — | — | — | — | 100 |

**KM# 535 2 DOLLARS**
31.11 g., 0.999 Silver 0.999 oz. ASW, 40.7 mm. **Ruler:** Elizabeth II **Subject:** Sherlock Holmes **Rev:** Multicolor scene from the Sign of the Four

| Date | Mintage | VF20 | XF40 | MS60 | MS63 | MS65 |
|---|---|---|---|---|---|---|
| 2008 Prooflike | 8,000 | — | — | — | — | 100 |

**KM# 540 2 DOLLARS**
31.11 g., 0.999 Silver 0.999 oz. ASW, 40.7 mm. **Ruler:** Elizabeth II **Subject:** Ballet dancers **Rev:** Multicolor Vasley Nijinnsky

| Date | Mintage | VF20 | XF40 | MS60 | MS63 | MS65 |
|---|---|---|---|---|---|---|
| 2008 Prooflike | 8,000 | — | — | — | — | 85.00 |

**KM# 541 2 DOLLARS**
31.11 g., 0.999 Silver 0.999 oz. ASW, 40.7 mm. **Ruler:** Elizabeth II **Subject:** Ballet Dancers **Rev:** Multicolor Matuilda Kshesinskaya

| Date | Mintage | VF20 | XF40 | MS60 | MS63 | MS65 |
|---|---|---|---|---|---|---|
| 2008 Prooflike | 8,000 | — | — | — | — | 85.00 |

**KM# 542 2 DOLLARS**
31.11 g., 0.999 Silver 0.999 oz. ASW, 40.7 mm. **Ruler:** Elizabeth II **Subject:** Ballet dancers **Rev:** Multicolor Sergey Lifar

| Date | Mintage | VF20 | XF40 | MS60 | MS63 | MS65 |
|---|---|---|---|---|---|---|
| 2008 Prooflike | 8,000 | — | — | — | — | 85.00 |

**KM# 543 2 DOLLARS**
31.11 g., 0.999 Silver 0.999 oz. ASW, 40.7 mm. **Ruler:** Elizabeth II **Subject:** Ballet dancers **Rev:** Multicolor Anna Pavlova

| Date | Mintage | VF20 | XF40 | MS60 | MS63 | MS65 |
|---|---|---|---|---|---|---|
| 2008 Prooflike | — | — | — | — | — | 85.00 |

**KM# 544 2 DOLLARS**
31.11 g., 0.999 Silver 0.999 oz. ASW, 40.7 mm. **Ruler:** Elizabeth II **Subject:** White Army **Rev:** Multicolor Anton Denkin

| Date | Mintage | VF20 | XF40 | MS60 | MS63 | MS65 |
|---|---|---|---|---|---|---|
| 2008 Prooflike | 6,000 | — | — | — | — | 85.00 |

**KM# 545 2 DOLLARS**
31.11 g., 0.999 Silver 0.999 oz. ASW, 40.7 mm. **Ruler:** Elizabeth II **Subject:** White Army **Rev:** Multicolor Pytor Vrangel

| Date | Mintage | VF20 | XF40 | MS60 | MS63 | MS65 |
|---|---|---|---|---|---|---|
| 2008 Prooflike | 6,000 | — | — | — | — | 85.00 |

**KM# 546 2 DOLLARS**
31.11 g., 0.999 Silver 0.999 oz. ASW, 40.7 mm. **Ruler:** Elizabeth II **Subject:** White Army **Rev:** Multicolor Alexander Kutepov

| Date | Mintage | VF20 | XF40 | MS60 | MS63 | MS65 |
|---|---|---|---|---|---|---|
| 2008 Prooflike | 6,000 | — | — | — | — | 85.00 |

**KM# 547 2 DOLLARS**
31.11 g., 0.999 Silver 0.999 oz. ASW, 40.7 mm. **Ruler:** Elizabeth II **Subject:** White Army **Rev:** Multicolor Alexander Kolchak

| Date | Mintage | VF20 | XF40 | MS60 | MS63 | MS65 |
|---|---|---|---|---|---|---|
| 2008 Prooflike | 6,000 | — | — | — | — | 85.00 |

**KM# 721 2 DOLLARS**
0.12 g., 0.999 Gold, 4 mm. **Ruler:** Elizabeth II **Rev:** Lady Penrhyn sailing ship **Note:** Illustration enlarged.

| Date | Mintage | VF20 | XF40 | MS60 | MS63 | MS65 |
|---|---|---|---|---|---|---|
| 2010 Prooflike | 5,000 | — | — | — | — | 12.00 |

**KM# 722 2 DOLLARS**
0.12 g., 0.995 Platinum APW, 4 mm. **Ruler:** Elizabeth II **Rev:** Humpback whale **Note:** Illustration enlarged.

| Date | Mintage | VF20 | XF40 | MS60 | MS63 | MS65 |
|---|---|---|---|---|---|---|
| 2010 Prooflike | 5,000 | — | — | — | — | 15.00 |

**KM# 1294 2 DOLLARS**
31.11 g., 0.999 Silver 0.999 oz. ASW, 33 mm. **Ruler:** Elizabeth II **Rev:** Fish with crown partially gilt

| Date | Mintage | VF20 | XF40 | MS60 | MS63 | MS65 |
|---|---|---|---|---|---|---|
| 2010 | — | PF65 55.00 | | | | |

**KM# 1312 2 DOLLARS**
15.55 g., 0.925 Silver 0.4624 oz. ASW partially gilt, 33 mm. **Ruler:** Elizabeth II **Subject:** Good Luck

| Date | Mintage | VF20 | XF40 | MS60 | MS63 | MS65 |
|---|---|---|---|---|---|---|
| 2010 | 1,000 | — | — | — | — | 45.00 |

**KM# 1384 2 DOLLARS**
31.11 g., 0.999 Silver 0.999 oz. ASW, 40.7 mm. **Ruler:** Elizabeth II **Subject:** Polish President's death, 1st Anniversary **Rev:** Portrait at right, plane crash site in color at left

| Date | Mintage | VF20 | XF40 | MS60 | MS63 | MS65 |
|---|---|---|---|---|---|---|
| 2011 | — | — | — | — | — | 75.00 |

**KM# 1405 2 DOLLARS**
15.50 g., 0.925 Silver 0.461 oz. ASW, 15.5x35 mm. **Ruler:** Elizabeth II **Subject:** Hieronymus Bosch, pater **Rev:** Paradise in color **Shape:** Vertical rectangle

| Date | Mintage | VF20 | XF40 | MS60 | MS63 | MS65 |
|---|---|---|---|---|---|---|
| 2011 | 500 | **PF65** 150 | | | | |

**KM# 1407 2 DOLLARS**
15.50 g., 0.925 Silver 0.461 oz. ASW, 15.5x35 mm. **Ruler:** Elizabeth II **Subject:** Hieronymus Bosch, pater **Rev:** Hell in color **Shape:** Vertical rectangle

| Date | Mintage | VF20 | XF40 | MS60 | MS63 | MS65 |
|---|---|---|---|---|---|---|
| 2011 | 500 | **PF65** 150 | | | | |

**KM# 1411 2 DOLLARS**
31.11 g., 0.999 Silver 0.999 oz. ASW, 38.61 mm. **Ruler:** Elizabeth II **Subject:** Soyuzmultfilm - Old dog and wolf **Rev:** Wolf in color

| Date | Mintage | VF20 | XF40 | MS60 | MS63 | MS65 |
|---|---|---|---|---|---|---|
| 2011 | 2,000 | **PF65** 100 | | | | |

**KM# 1412 2 DOLLARS**
31.11 g., 0.999 Silver 0.9991 oz. ASW, 38.61 mm. **Ruler:** Elizabeth II **Subject:** Kipling's Jungle Book **Rev:** Mowgli and Aklea in color

| Date | Mintage | VF20 | XF40 | MS60 | MS63 | MS65 |
|---|---|---|---|---|---|---|
| 2011 | 2,000 | **PF65** 100 | | | | |

**KM# 1413 2 DOLLARS**
31.11 g., 0.999 Silver 0.999 oz. ASW, 38.61 mm. **Ruler:** Elizabeth II **Subject:** Kipling's Jungle Book characters **Rev:** Kaa, snake

| Date | Mintage | VF20 | XF40 | MS60 | MS63 | MS65 |
|---|---|---|---|---|---|---|
| 2011 | 2,000 | **PF65** 100 | | | | |

**KM# 1414 2 DOLLARS**
31.11 g., 0.999 Silver 0.999 oz. ASW, 38.61 mm. **Ruler:** Elizabeth II **Subject:** Kipling's Jungle Book characters **Rev:** Baloo (bear) in color

| Date | Mintage | VF20 | XF40 | MS60 | MS63 | MS65 |
|---|---|---|---|---|---|---|
| 2011 | 2,000 | **PF65** 100 | | | | |

**KM# 1415 2 DOLLARS**
31.11 g., 0.999 Silver 0.999 oz. ASW, 38.61 mm. **Ruler:** Elizabeth II **Subject:** Kipling's Jungle Book characters **Rev:** Bagheera and Kaa, panther and crow

| Date | Mintage | VF20 | XF40 | MS60 | MS63 | MS65 |
|---|---|---|---|---|---|---|
| 2011 | 2,000 | **PF65** 100 | | | | |

**KM# 1416 2 DOLLARS**
31.11 g., 0.999 Silver 0.999 oz. ASW, 38.61 mm. **Ruler:** Elizabeth II **Subject:** Kipling's Jungle Book characters **Rev:** Shere Khan (tiger) in color

| Date | Mintage | VF20 | XF40 | MS60 | MS63 | MS65 |
|---|---|---|---|---|---|---|
| 2011 | 2,000 | **PF65** 100 | | | | |

**KM# 1645 2 DOLLARS**
31.11 g., 0.999 Silver 0.999 oz. ASW partially gilt **Ruler:** Elizabeth II **Subject:** Year of the Monkey **Rev:** Monkey, gilt

| Date | Mintage | VF20 | XF40 | MS60 | MS63 | MS65 |
|---|---|---|---|---|---|---|
| 2011 | — | **PF65** 145 | | | | |

**KM# 1593 2 DOLLARS**
15.55 g., 0.925 Silver 0.4624 oz. ASW, 35 mm. **Ruler:** Elizabeth II **Subject:** Venomous Spiders - Brazilian Wandering Spider

| Date | Mintage | VF20 | XF40 | MS60 | MS63 | MS65 |
|---|---|---|---|---|---|---|
| 2013 | Est. 1000 | **PF65** 60.00 | | | | |

**KM# 1121 5 DOLLARS**
Silver **Ruler:** Elizabeth II **Rev:** Sir Francis Drake

| Date | Mintage | VF20 | XF40 | MS60 | MS63 | MS65 |
|---|---|---|---|---|---|---|
| 2002 | — | **PF65** 35.00 | | | | |

**KM# 1122 5 DOLLARS**
Silver **Ruler:** Elizabeth II **Rev:** Kon Tiki and Thor Heyerdahl

| Date | Mintage | VF20 | XF40 | MS60 | MS63 | MS65 |
|---|---|---|---|---|---|---|
| 2002 | — | **PF65** 45.00 | | | | |

**KM# 418 5 DOLLARS**
14.00 g., Aluminum-Bronze, 31.5 mm. **Ruler:** Elizabeth II **Obv:** Crowned bust right, new portrait **Rev:** Conch shell and value **Shape:** 12-sided

| Date | Mintage | VF20 | XF40 | MS60 | MS63 | MS65 |
|---|---|---|---|---|---|---|
| 2003 | — | — | — | — | 6.00 | 8.00 |

**KM# 1140 5 DOLLARS**
20.00 g., 0.999 Silver 0.6424 oz. ASW **Ruler:** Elizabeth II **Subject:** Vincent van Gogh, 150th Anniversary of Birth

| Date | Mintage | VF20 | XF40 | MS60 | MS63 | MS65 |
|---|---|---|---|---|---|---|
| 2003 | — | **PF65** 35.00 | | | | |

**KM# 469 5 DOLLARS**
Copper-Nickel, 40 mm. **Ruler:** Elizabeth II **Obv:** USPS logo, Queens head above **Rev:** 5 cent 1847 Benjamin Franklin stamp

| Date | Mintage | VF20 | XF40 | MS60 | MS63 | MS65 |
|---|---|---|---|---|---|---|
| 2004 | — | — | — | — | 10.00 | 12.00 |

**KM# 469a 5 DOLLARS**
Silver, 40 mm. **Ruler:** Elizabeth II **Obv:** USPS logo, Queens head above **Rev:** 5 cent 1847 Benjamin Franklin stamp **Edge:** Reeded

| Date | Mintage | VF20 | XF40 | MS60 | MS63 | MS65 |
|---|---|---|---|---|---|---|
| 2004 | — | **PF65** 30.00 | | | | |

**KM# 1149 5 DOLLARS**
31.64 g., 0.999 Silver 1.0161 oz. ASW **Ruler:** Elizabeth II **Subject:** Apollo Moon Landing, 35th Anniversary **Rev:** Astronaut in Solar System

| Date | Mintage | VF20 | XF40 | MS60 | MS63 | MS65 |
|---|---|---|---|---|---|---|
| 2004 | Est. 10000 | **PF65** 55.00 | | | | |

**KM# 1108 5 DOLLARS**
25.00 g., 0.925 Silver 0.7435 oz. ASW **Ruler:** Elizabeth II **Subject:** Ferrari F2

| Date | Mintage | VF20 | XF40 | MS60 | MS63 | MS65 |
|---|---|---|---|---|---|---|
| 2005 | Est. 8000 | **PF63** 25.00 | **PF65** 30.00 | | | |

**KM# 1109 5 DOLLARS**
25.00 g., 0.925 Silver 0.7435 oz. ASW **Ruler:** Elizabeth II **Rev:** Ferrari F 2004 in color

| Date | Mintage | VF20 | XF40 | MS60 | MS63 | MS65 |
|---|---|---|---|---|---|---|
| 2005 | Est. 8000 | **PF63** 25.00 | **PF65** 30.00 | | | |

**KM# 1134 5 DOLLARS**
31.11 g., 0.999 Silver 0.999 oz. ASW, 38.6 mm. **Ruler:** Elizabeth II **Subject:** Star Wars, 30th Anniversary

| Date | Mintage | VF20 | XF40 | MS60 | MS63 | MS65 |
|---|---|---|---|---|---|---|
| 2005 | — | **PF65** 50.00 | | | | |

**KM# 1135 5 DOLLARS**
31.11 g., 0.999 Silver 0.999 oz. ASW, 38.6 mm. **Ruler:** Elizabeth II **Subject:** Star Wars, 30th Anniversary

| Date | Mintage | VF20 | XF40 | MS60 | MS63 | MS65 |
|---|---|---|---|---|---|---|
| 2005 | Est. 9999 | **PF65** 50.00 | | | | |

**KM# 1175 5 DOLLARS**
25.00 g., 0.925 Silver 0.7435 oz. ASW **Ruler:** Elizabeth II **Subject:** Marriage of Prince Charles and Camilla Parker-Bowles

| Date | Mintage | VF20 | XF40 | MS60 | MS63 | MS65 |
|---|---|---|---|---|---|---|
| 2005 | — | **PF65** 45.00 | | | | |

**KM# 478 5 DOLLARS**
Silver Gilt **Ruler:** Elizabeth II **Subject:** Pope Benedict XVI's visit to Valencia, Spain **Obv:** Bust right **Rev:** Valencia Cathedral **Shape:** Cathedral outline **Note:** Jeweled cathedral.

| Date | Mintage | VF20 | XF40 | MS60 | MS63 | MS65 |
|---|---|---|---|---|---|---|
| 2006 | 2,500 | **PF65** 100 | | | | |

**KM# 560 5 DOLLARS**
25.00 g., 0.925 Silver 0.7435 oz. ASW partially gilt, 35x31 mm. **Ruler:** Elizabeth II **Subject:** Benedict XVI Annus Secundus **Rev:** Cross in crystals and gilt Papal Arms **Shape:** 6-sided

| Date | Mintage | VF20 | XF40 | MS60 | MS63 | MS65 |
|---|---|---|---|---|---|---|
| 2006 | 5,000 | **PF63** 65.00 | **PF65** 75.00 | | | |

**KM# 561 5 DOLLARS**
25.00 g., 0.999 Silver 0.803 oz. ASW partially gilt, 42x49 mm. **Ruler:** Elizabeth II **Subject:** Benedict XVI visits Germany **Rev:** Cathedral gilt, crystal inserts **Shape:** oval

| Date | Mintage | VF20 | XF40 | MS60 | MS63 | MS65 |
|---|---|---|---|---|---|---|
| 2006 | 5,000 | **PF63** 65.00 | **PF65** 75.00 | | | |

**KM# 562 5 DOLLARS**
25.00 g., 0.999 Silver 0.803 oz. ASW, 35x35 mm. **Ruler:** Elizabeth II **Subject:** Benedict XVI **Rev:** Profile at left, cross in crystal inserts **Shape:** Square

| Date | Mintage | VF20 | XF40 | MS60 | MS63 | MS65 |
|---|---|---|---|---|---|---|
| 2006 | 5,000 | **PF63** 65.00 | **PF65** 75.00 | | | |

**KM# 563 5 DOLLARS**
25.00 g., 0.999 Silver 0.803 oz. ASW partially gilt, 35x38 mm. **Ruler:** Elizabeth II **Subject:** Christmas in St. Peter's Square **Rev:** St. Peter's partially gilt, star crystal insert **Shape:** Triange

| Date | Mintage | VF20 | XF40 | MS60 | MS63 | MS65 |
|---|---|---|---|---|---|---|
| 2006 | 5,000 | **PF63** 65.00 | **PF65** 75.00 | | | |

**KM# 564 5 DOLLARS**
25.00 g., 0.999 Silver 0.803 oz. ASW, 20x44 mm. **Ruler:** Elizabeth II **Subject:** benedict XVI visits Poland **Rev:** Polish icon, partially gilt, crystal insert **Shape:** Candle

| Date | Mintage | VF20 | XF40 | MS60 | MS63 | MS65 |
|---|---|---|---|---|---|---|
| 2006 | 564 | **PF63** 65.00 | **PF65** 75.00 | | | |

**KM# 565 5 DOLLARS**
25.00 g., 0.999 Silver 0.803 oz. ASW partially gilt, 38.6 mm. **Ruler:** Elizabeth II **Rev:** St. Peter's Basilica, partially gilt, crystals as stars

| Date | Mintage | VF20 | XF40 | MS60 | MS63 | MS65 |
|---|---|---|---|---|---|---|
| 2006 | 5,000 | **PF63** 65.00 | **PF65** 75.00 | | | |

**KM# 566 5 DOLLARS**
25.00 g., 0.999 Silver 0.803 oz. ASW partially gilt, 35x35 mm. **Ruler:** Elizabeth II **Subject:** Swiss Guards, 500th Anniversary **Rev:** Four Swiss guards, partially gilt, crystal insert **Shape:** Diamond

| Date | Mintage | VF20 | XF40 | MS60 | MS63 | MS65 |
|---|---|---|---|---|---|---|
| 2006 | 5,000 | **PF63** 65.00 | **PF65** 75.00 | | | |

**KM# 567 5 DOLLARS**
25.00 g., 0.999 Silver 0.803 oz. ASW, 40x25 mm. **Ruler:** Elizabeth II **Subject:** Benedict XVI visits Turkey **Rev:** Pope and Patrarch, partially gilt, crystal insert **Shape:** Rectangle

| Date | Mintage | VF20 | XF40 | MS60 | MS63 | MS65 |
|---|---|---|---|---|---|---|
| 2006 | 5,000 | **PF63** 65.00 | **PF65** 75.00 | | | |

**KM# 568 5 DOLLARS**
25.00 g., 0.999 Silver 0.803 oz. ASW, 40x25 mm. **Ruler:** Elizabeth II **Subject:** Urbi et Orbi message **Rev:** Benedict XVI giving blessing, partially gilt, crystal insert **Shape:** Rectangle

| Date | Mintage | VF20 | XF40 | MS60 | MS63 | MS65 |
|---|---|---|---|---|---|---|
| 2006 | 5,000 | **PF63** 65.00 | **PF65** 75.00 | | | |

**KM# 569 5 DOLLARS**
0.25 g., 0.999 Silver partially gilt, 29x42 mm. **Ruler:** Elizabeth II **Subject:** Benedict XVI visits Vallencia **Rev:** Valencia cathedral façade, partially gilt, crystal inserts **Shape:** Irregular

| Date | Mintage | VF20 | XF40 | MS60 | MS63 | MS65 |
|---|---|---|---|---|---|---|
| 2006 | 5,000 | **PF65** 75.00 | | | | |

**KM# 570 5 DOLLARS**
31.10 g., 0.999 Silver 0.9989 oz. ASW, 38.6 mm. **Ruler:** Elizabeth II **Rev:** Statue of Liberty gilt pop-up

| Date | Mintage | VF20 | XF40 | MS60 | MS63 | MS65 |
|---|---|---|---|---|---|---|
| 2006 | 5,000 | **PF65** 90.00 | | | | |

**KM# 571 5 DOLLARS**
31.10 g., 0.999 Silver 0.9989 oz. ASW, 38.6 mm. **Ruler:** Elizabeth II **Rev:** Ludwig's castle gilt pop-up

| Date | Mintage | VF20 | XF40 | MS60 | MS63 | MS65 |
|---|---|---|---|---|---|---|
| 2006 | 5,000 | **PF65** 90.00 | | | | |

**KM# 572 5 DOLLARS**
25.00 g., 0.999 Silver 0.803 oz. ASW partially gilt, 35x35 mm. **Ruler:** Elizabeth II **Subject:** Benedict XVI visits Marianzell **Rev:** Our Lady or Marianzell, partially gilt, crystal inserts **Shape:** Tablet

| Date | Mintage | VF20 | XF40 | MS60 | MS63 | MS65 |
|---|---|---|---|---|---|---|
| 2007 | 5,000 | **PF63** 75.00 | **PF65** 85.00 | | | |

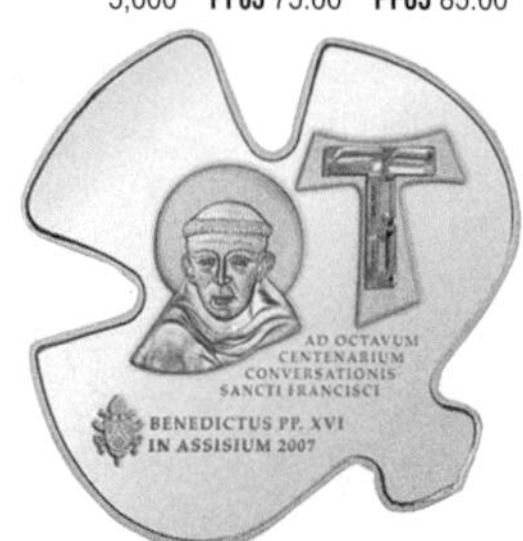

**KM# 573 5 DOLLARS**
25.00 g., 0.999 Silver 0.803 oz. ASW, 35x35 mm. **Ruler:** Elizabeth II **Rev:** St. Francis, tau cross, partially gilt, crystal insert **Shape:** Dove

| Date | Mintage | VF20 | XF40 | MS60 | MS63 | MS65 |
|---|---|---|---|---|---|---|
| 2007 | 5,000 | **PF63** 65.00 | **PF65** 75.00 | | | |

**KM# 574 5 DOLLARS**
25.00 g., 0.999 Silver 0.803 oz. ASW, 31x40 mm. **Ruler:** Elizabeth II **Rev:** Benedict XVI bust left, partially gilt, crystal insert **Shape:** Irregular

| Date | Mintage | VF20 | XF40 | MS60 | MS63 | MS65 |
|---|---|---|---|---|---|---|
| 2007 | 5,000 | **PF63** 65.00 | **PF65** 75.00 | | | |

**KM# 575 5 DOLLARS**
25.00 g., 0.999 Silver 0.803 oz. ASW, 35x45 mm. **Ruler:** Elizabeth II **Subject:** Benedict XVI visits Brazil **Rev:** Christ statue in Rio, partially gilt, crystal insert **Shape:** Diamond

| Date | Mintage | VF20 | XF40 | MS60 | MS63 | MS65 |
|---|---|---|---|---|---|---|
| 2007 | 5,000 | **PF63** 65.00 | **PF65** 75.00 | | | |

**KM# 576 5 DOLLARS**
25.00 g., 0.999 Silver 0.803 oz. ASW, 37 mm. **Ruler:** Elizabeth II **Subject:** Princess Diana, 10th Anniversary of death **Rev:** Bust at left, multicolored rose **Shape:** Heart

| Date | Mintage | VF20 | XF40 | MS60 | MS63 | MS65 |
|---|---|---|---|---|---|---|
| 2007 | 1,997 | **PF65** 75.00 | | | | |

**KM# 577 5 DOLLARS**
25.00 g., 0.999 Silver 0.803 oz. ASW partially gilt, 39x24 mm. **Ruler:** Elizabeth II **Subject:** Docrine of the Immaculate Conception **Rev:** Virgin Mary and cathedral, partially gilt, crystal insert **Shape:** Rectangle

| Date | Mintage | VF20 | XF40 | MS60 | MS63 | MS65 |
|---|---|---|---|---|---|---|
| 2007 | 5,000 | **PF63** 65.00 | **PF65** 75.00 | | | |

**KM# 578 5 DOLLARS**
25.00 g., 0.999 Silver 0.803 oz. ASW, 31x35 mm. **Ruler:** Elizabeth II **Subject:** Benedict XVI visits Loredo **Rev:** Pope blessing crowd, cathedral, partially gilt, crystal insert **Shape:** 6-sided

| Date | Mintage | VF20 | XF40 | MS60 | MS63 | MS65 |
|---|---|---|---|---|---|---|
| 2007 | 5,000 | **PF63** 65.00 | **PF65** 75.00 | | | |

**KM# 579 5 DOLLARS**
25.00 g., 0.999 Silver 0.803 oz. ASW, 35x35 mm. **Ruler:** Elizabeth II **Subject:** Santo Subito **Rev:** Pope John Paul II, partially gilt, crystal insert **Shape:** Cross

| Date | Mintage | VF20 | XF40 | MS60 | MS63 | MS65 |
|---|---|---|---|---|---|---|
| 2007 | 5,000 | **PF65** 100 | | | | |

**KM# 580 5 DOLLARS**
25.00 g., 0.999 Silver 0.803 oz. ASW, 30x45 mm. **Ruler:** Elizabeth II **Subject:** Way of the Cross **Rev:** Benedict XVI holdign cross, collesum in background, partially gilt, crystal insert **Shape:** Vertical oval

| Date | Mintage | VF20 | XF40 | MS60 | MS63 | MS65 |
|---|---|---|---|---|---|---|
| 2007 | 5,000 | **PF63** 65.00 | **PF65** 75.00 | | | |

### KM# 581 5 DOLLARS

31.10 g., 0.999 Silver 0.9989 oz. ASW, 38.6 mm. **Ruler:** Elizabeth II **Rev:** Parthenon gilt pop-up

| Date | Mintage | VF20 | XF40 | MS60 | MS63 | MS65 |
|---|---|---|---|---|---|---|
| 2007 | 5,000 | PF65 90.00 | | | | |

### KM# 583 5 DOLLARS

31.10 g., 0.999 Silver 0.9989 oz. ASW, 38.6 mm. **Ruler:** Elizabeth II **Rev:** Rio's Christ statue gilt pop-up

| Date | Mintage | VF20 | XF40 | MS60 | MS63 | MS65 |
|---|---|---|---|---|---|---|
| 2007 | 5,000 | PF65 100 | | | | |

### KM# 584 5 DOLLARS

31.10 g., 0.999 Silver 0.9989 oz. ASW, 38.6 mm. **Ruler:** Elizabeth II **Rev:** Collesum gilt pop-up

| Date | Mintage | VF20 | XF40 | MS60 | MS63 | MS65 |
|---|---|---|---|---|---|---|
| 2007 | 5,000 | PF65 90.00 | | | | |

### KM# 586 5 DOLLARS

31.10 g., 0.999 Silver 0.9989 oz. ASW, 38.6 mm. **Ruler:** Elizabeth II **Rev:** Eifle Tower gilt pop-up

| Date | Mintage | VF20 | XF40 | MS60 | MS63 | MS65 |
|---|---|---|---|---|---|---|
| 2007 | 5,000 | PF65 90.00 | | | | |

### KM# 763 5 DOLLARS

20.00 g., Silver, 38.61 mm. **Ruler:** Elizabeth II **Subject:** Brenham Meteor **Obv:** Bust right **Rev:** Meteorite and fragment inset

| Date | Mintage | VF20 | XF40 | MS60 | MS63 | MS65 |
|---|---|---|---|---|---|---|
| 2007 | 2,500 | PF65 100 | | | | |

### KM# 1188 5 DOLLARS

20.00 g., 0.925 Silver 0.5948 oz. ASW, 38.61 mm. **Ruler:** Elizabeth II **Subject:** Elvis Presley, 30th Anniversary of death

| Date | Mintage | VF20 | XF40 | MS60 | MS63 | MS65 |
|---|---|---|---|---|---|---|
| 2007 | Est. 50000 | PF65 70.00 | | | | |

### KM# 1189 5 DOLLARS

20.00 g., 0.925 Silver 0.5948 oz. ASW, 38.61 mm. **Ruler:** Elizabeth II **Subject:** Elvis Presely, 30th Anniversary of Death **Rev:** Love me Tender, 1956

| Date | Mintage | VF20 | XF40 | MS60 | MS63 | MS65 |
|---|---|---|---|---|---|---|
| 2007 | Est. 50000 | PF65 70.00 | | | | |

### KM# 1201 5 DOLLARS

25.00 g., Copper-Nickel partially gilt, 38.6 mm. **Ruler:** Elizabeth II **Subject:** Lady Diana, 10th Anniversary of Death **Rev:** Diana partially gilt

| Date | Mintage | VF20 | XF40 | MS60 | MS63 | MS65 |
|---|---|---|---|---|---|---|
| 2007 | Est. 50000 | PF65 22.50 | | | | |

### KM# 1202 5 DOLLARS

25.00 g., Copper-Nickel partially gilt, 38.6 mm. **Ruler:** Elizabeth II **Subject:** Princess Diana, 10th Anniversary of Death **Rev:** Diana in wedding dress, partially gilt

| Date | Mintage | VF20 | XF40 | MS60 | MS63 | MS65 |
|---|---|---|---|---|---|---|
| 2007 | Est. 14500 | PF65 22.50 | | | | |

### KM# 1203 5 DOLLARS

155.50 g., Copper-Nickel partially gilt, 65 mm. **Ruler:** Elizabeth II **Subject:** Princess Diana, 10th Anniversary of Death **Rev:** Lady Diana, partially gilt

| Date | Mintage | VF20 | XF40 | MS60 | MS63 | MS65 |
|---|---|---|---|---|---|---|
| 2007 | Est. 1961 | PF65 85.00 | | | | |

### KM# 594 5 DOLLARS

25.00 g., 0.999 Silver 0.803 oz. ASW, 35x35 mm. **Ruler:** Elizabeth II **Subject:** Pope John Paul II Election 30th Anniversary **Rev:** John Paul II coat-of-arms, aprtially gilt, crystal insert **Shape:** Diamond

| Date | Mintage | VF20 | XF40 | MS60 | MS63 | MS65 |
|---|---|---|---|---|---|---|
| 2008 | 5,000 | PF65 120 | | | | |

### KM# 595 5 DOLLARS

25.00 g., 0.999 Silver 0.803 oz. ASW, 30x45 mm. **Ruler:** Elizabeth II **Subject:** Lourdes, 150th Anniversary **Rev:** Statue of Our Lady of Lourdes, partially gilt, crystal insert **Shape:** Vertical oval

| Date | Mintage | VF20 | XF40 | MS60 | MS63 | MS65 |
|---|---|---|---|---|---|---|
| 2008 | 5,000 | PF65 110 | | | | |

### KM# 596 5 DOLLARS

25.00 g., 0.999 Silver 0.803 oz. ASW, 30x45 mm. **Ruler:** Elizabeth II **Subject:** Lourdes, 150th Anniversary **Rev:** Our Lady of Lourdes, holigram, partially gilt, crystal insert **Shape:** Vertical oval

| Date | Mintage | VF20 | XF40 | MS60 | MS63 | MS65 |
|---|---|---|---|---|---|---|
| 2008 | 5,000 | PF65 120 | | | | |

### KM# 597 5 DOLLARS

25.00 g., 0.999 Silver 0.803 oz. ASW, 40x25 mm. **Ruler:** Elizabeth II **Subject:** Benedict XVI Annus Novas **Rev:** Benedict XVI and dove **Shape:** Oval

| Date | Mintage | VF20 | XF40 | MS60 | MS63 | MS65 |
|---|---|---|---|---|---|---|
| 2008 | 5,000 | PF65 100 | | | | |

### KM# 598 5 DOLLARS

25.00 g., 0.999 Silver 0.803 oz. ASW, 32x41 mm. **Ruler:** Elizabeth II **Rev:** St. Peter's Square, cresch and christmas tree, partially gilt, crystal insert **Shape:** Triangle

| Date | Mintage | VF20 | XF40 | MS60 | MS63 | MS65 |
|---|---|---|---|---|---|---|
| 2008 | 5,000 | PF65 100 | | | | |

### KM# 599 5 DOLLARS

25.00 g., 0.999 Silver 0.803 oz. ASW, 35x35 mm. **Ruler:** Elizabeth II **Subject:** Crufifixio Domini **Rev:** Benedict XVI before cross, partially gilt, crystal inserts **Shape:** Cross

| Date | Mintage | VF20 | XF40 | MS60 | MS63 | MS65 |
|---|---|---|---|---|---|---|
| 2008 | 5,000 | PF65 100 | | | | |

### KM# 600 5 DOLLARS

25.00 g., 0.999 Silver 0.803 oz. ASW, 29x42 mm. **Ruler:** Elizabeth II **Subject:** Paulus year **Rev:** Benedict XVI in Basicilica, partially gilt, crystal insert **Shape:** Vertical rectangle

| Date | Mintage | VF20 | XF40 | MS60 | MS63 | MS65 |
|---|---|---|---|---|---|---|
| 2008 | 5,000 | PF65 100 | | | | |

### KM# 601 5 DOLLARS

25.00 g., 0.999 Silver 0.803 oz. ASW, 40x25 mm. **Ruler:** Elizabeth II **Subject:** Sistine Chapel, 500th Anniversary **Rev:** Adam and god, Sistine Chapel ceiling, partially gilt, crystal insert **Shape:** Rectangle

| Date | Mintage | VF20 | XF40 | MS60 | MS63 | MS65 |
|---|---|---|---|---|---|---|
| 2008 | 5,000 | PF65 120 | | | | |

### KM# 602 5 DOLLARS

25.00 g., 0.999 Silver 0.803 oz. ASW, 40x42 mm. **Ruler:** Elizabeth II **Rev:** St Martin on horseback, partially gilt, crystal insert **Shape:** 8-sided

| Date | Mintage | VF20 | XF40 | MS60 | MS63 | MS65 |
|---|---|---|---|---|---|---|
| 2008 | 5,000 | PF65 100 | | | | |

### KM# 603 5 DOLLARS

25.00 g., 0.999 Silver 0.803 oz. ASW, 45x34 mm. **Ruler:** Elizabeth II **Subject:** Benedict XVI visits Sydney **Rev:** Sydney Harbor Bridge and Sydney Opera House, partially gilt, crystal insert **Shape:** Irregular oval

| Date | Mintage | VF20 | XF40 | MS60 | MS63 | MS65 |
|---|---|---|---|---|---|---|
| 2008 | 5,000 | PF65 100 | | | | |

### KM# 604 5 DOLLARS

25.00 g., 0.999 Silver 0.803 oz. ASW, 35x35 mm. **Ruler:** Elizabeth II **Subject:** Tu Es Peterus **Rev:** Cross Keys, Christ handing keys to kneeling St. Peter. Partially gilt, crystal insert. **Shape:** Square

| Date | Mintage | VF20 | XF40 | MS60 | MS63 | MS65 |
|---|---|---|---|---|---|---|
| 2008 | 5,000 | PF65 120 | | | | |

### KM# 605 5 DOLLARS

25.00 g., 0.999 Silver 0.803 oz. ASW, 38.6 mm. **Ruler:** Elizabeth II **Rev:** Pope blessing crowd, partially gilt, crystal inserts

| Date | Mintage | VF20 | XF40 | MS60 | MS63 | MS65 |
|---|---|---|---|---|---|---|
| 2008 | 5,000 | PF65 110 | | | | |

### KM# 606 5 DOLLARS

25.00 g., 0.999 Silver 0.803 oz. ASW, 42x29 mm. **Ruler:** Elizabeth II **Subject:** Benedict XVI visits the United States **Rev:** Benedict XVI, the White House, Statue of Liberty, UN Building, partially gilt, crystal inserts **Shape:** Irregular US Map shape

| Date | Mintage | VF20 | XF40 | MS60 | MS63 | MS65 |
|---|---|---|---|---|---|---|
| 2008 | 5,000 | PF65 110 | | | | |

### KM# 607 5 DOLLARS

25.00 g., 0.999 Silver 0.803 oz. ASW, 40x42 mm. **Ruler:** Elizabeth II **Rev:** St. George slaying dragon, partially gilt, crystal insert **Shape:** 8-sided

| Date | Mintage | VF20 | XF40 | MS60 | MS63 | MS65 |
|---|---|---|---|---|---|---|
| 2008 | 5,000 | PF65 100 | | | | |

### KM# 608 5 DOLLARS

31.11 g., 0.999 Silver 0.999 oz. ASW, 38.6 mm. **Ruler:** Elizabeth II **Subject:** Conversion of Russia, 1000th Anniversary **Rev:** Baptism scene **Note:** Exclusive to the Russian Market.

| Date | Mintage | VF20 | XF40 | MS60 | MS63 | MS65 |
|---|---|---|---|---|---|---|
| 2008 | 500 | PF65 120 | | | | |

**KM# 609 5 DOLLARS**
31.11 g., 0.999 Silver 0.999 oz. ASW, 47x27 mm. **Ruler:** Elizabeth II **Subject:** Orthodox Communication **Rev:** Patriarch's meeting **Shape:** Rectangle **Note:** Exclusive to the Russian Market.

| Date | Mintage | VF20 | XF40 | MS60 | MS63 | MS65 |
|---|---|---|---|---|---|---|
| 2008 | 500 | PF65 120 | | | | |

**KM# 610 5 DOLLARS**
25.00 g., 0.999 Silver 0.803 oz. ASW, 30x38 mm. **Ruler:** Elizabeth II **Rev:** Icon - Theotokos of Vladimir, wood insert **Shape:** Rectangle **Note:** Exclusive to the Russian Market.

| Date | Mintage | VF20 | XF40 | MS60 | MS63 | MS65 |
|---|---|---|---|---|---|---|
| 2008 | 2,500 | PF65 120 | | | | |

**KM# 611 5 DOLLARS**
31.11 g., 0.999 Silver 0.999 oz. ASW, 38.6 mm. **Ruler:** Elizabeth II **Subject:** Kiev Churches **Rev:** Church of All Saints **Note:** Exclusive to the Russian Market.

| Date | Mintage | VF20 | XF40 | MS60 | MS63 | MS65 |
|---|---|---|---|---|---|---|
| 2008 | 500 | PF65 120 | | | | |

**KM# 612 5 DOLLARS**
31.11 g., 0.999 Silver 0.999 oz. ASW, 38.6 mm. **Ruler:** Elizabeth II **Subject:** Kiev Churches **Rev:** Dormotion of Theotokos **Note:** Exclusive to the Russian Market.

| Date | Mintage | VF20 | XF40 | MS60 | MS63 | MS65 |
|---|---|---|---|---|---|---|
| 2008 | 500 | PF65 120 | | | | |

**KM# 613 5 DOLLARS**
31.11 g., 0.999 Silver 0.999 oz. ASW **Ruler:** Elizabeth II **Subject:** Kiev Churches **Rev:** Refractory of Pechersky **Shape:** 38.6 **Note:** Exclusive to the Russian Market.

| Date | Mintage | VF20 | XF40 | MS60 | MS63 | MS65 |
|---|---|---|---|---|---|---|
| 2008 | 500 | PF65 120 | | | | |

**KM# 614 5 DOLLARS**
31.11 g., 0.999 Silver 0.999 oz. ASW, 38.6 mm. **Ruler:** Elizabeth II **Subject:** Kiev Churches **Rev:** Troitskaya Barbican **Note:** Exclusive to the Russian Market.

| Date | Mintage | VF20 | XF40 | MS60 | MS63 | MS65 |
|---|---|---|---|---|---|---|
| 2008 | 500 | PF65 120 | | | | |

**KM# 615 5 DOLLARS**
25.00 g., 0.925 Silver 0.7435 oz. ASW, 37 mm. **Ruler:** Elizabeth II **Rev:** Cupid and roses **Rev. Legend:** My Everlasting Love **Shape:** Heart

| Date | Mintage | VF20 | XF40 | MS60 | MS63 | MS65 |
|---|---|---|---|---|---|---|
| 2008 | 2,500 | PF65 70.00 | | | | |

**KM# 616 5 DOLLARS**
25.00 g., 0.925 Silver 0.7435 oz. ASW, 38.6 mm. **Ruler:** Elizabeth II **Subject:** Endangered Wildlife - Arctic **Rev:** Polar bear and cubs, crystal inserts

| Date | Mintage | VF20 | XF40 | MS60 | MS63 | MS65 |
|---|---|---|---|---|---|---|
| 2008 | 2,500 | PF65 70.00 | | | | |

**KM# 617 5 DOLLARS**
25.00 g., 0.925 Silver 0.7435 oz. ASW, 38.6 mm. **Ruler:** Elizabeth II **Subject:** Engangered wildlife - Antarctic **Rev:** Penguin, crystal insert

| Date | Mintage | VF20 | XF40 | MS60 | MS63 | MS65 |
|---|---|---|---|---|---|---|
| 2008 | 2,500 | PF65 70.00 | | | | |

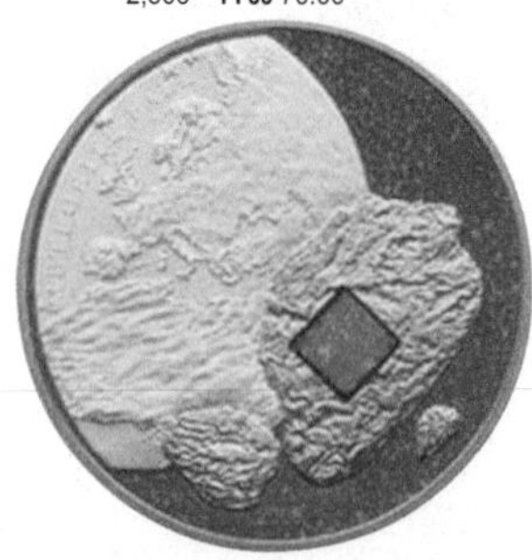

**KM# 618 5 DOLLARS**
25.00 g., 0.925 Silver 0.7435 oz. ASW, 38.6 mm. **Ruler:** Elizabeth II **Subject:** Pultusk Meteorite **Rev:** Earth and Meteorite fragment insert

| Date | Mintage | VF20 | XF40 | MS60 | MS63 | MS65 |
|---|---|---|---|---|---|---|
| 2008 | 2,500 | PF65 85.00 | | | | |

**KM# 666 5 DOLLARS**
141.40 g., 0.999 Silver 4.5416 oz. ASW, 65 mm. **Ruler:** Elizabeth II **Subject:** Tall ships **Obv:** Bust right **Rev:** Germany's Preussen, 5-masted square rigger

| Date | Mintage | VF20 | XF40 | MS60 | MS63 | MS65 |
|---|---|---|---|---|---|---|
| 2008 | — | PF65 285 | | | | |

**KM# 667 5 DOLLARS**
141.40 g., 0.999 Silver 4.5416 oz. ASW, 65 mm. **Ruler:** Elizabeth II **Subject:** Tall ships **Rev:** France's France II

| Date | Mintage | VF20 | XF40 | MS60 | MS63 | MS65 |
|---|---|---|---|---|---|---|
| 2008 | — | PF65 285 | | | | |

**KM# 668 5 DOLLARS**
141.40 g., 0.999 Silver 4.5416 oz. ASW, 65 mm. **Ruler:** Elizabeth II **Subject:** Tall Ships **Rev:** America's Thomas W. Lawson, 7-masted schooner

| Date | Mintage | VF20 | XF40 | MS60 | MS63 | MS65 |
|---|---|---|---|---|---|---|
| 2008 | — | PF65 285 | | | | |

**KM# 669 5 DOLLARS**
141.40 g., 0.999 Silver 4.5416 oz. ASW, 65 mm. **Ruler:** Elizabeth II **Subject:** Tall Ships **Rev:** Russia's Sedov, 4-masted barque

| Date | Mintage | VF20 | XF40 | MS60 | MS63 | MS65 |
|---|---|---|---|---|---|---|
| 2008 | — | PF65 285 | | | | |

**KM# 670 5 DOLLARS**
141.40 g., 0.999 Silver 4.5416 oz. ASW, 65 mm. **Ruler:** Elizabeth II **Subject:** Tall Ships **Rev:** Norway's Christian Radich

| Date | Mintage | VF20 | XF40 | MS60 | MS63 | MS65 |
|---|---|---|---|---|---|---|
| 2008 | — | PF65 285 | | | | |

**KM# 671 5 DOLLARS**
141.40 g., 0.999 Silver 4.5416 oz. ASW, 65 mm. **Ruler:** Elizabeth II **Subject:** Tall Ships **Rev:** Russian 4-masted barque Kruzenshtern

| Date | Mintage | VF20 | XF40 | MS60 | MS63 | MS65 |
|---|---|---|---|---|---|---|
| 2008 | — | PF65 285 | | | | |

**KM# 766 5 DOLLARS**
31.11 g., 0.999 Silver 0.999 oz. ASW, 40 mm. **Ruler:** Elizabeth II **Subject:** First man on the Moon **Rev:** Moon and rock fragment

| Date | Mintage | VF20 | XF40 | MS60 | MS63 | MS65 |
|---|---|---|---|---|---|---|
| 2008 | — | PF65 120 | | | | |

**KM# 1207 5 DOLLARS**
0.50 g., 0.999 Gold, 11 mm. **Ruler:** Elizabeth II **Rev:** American Bison

| Date | Mintage | VF20 | XF40 | MS60 | MS63 | MS65 |
|---|---|---|---|---|---|---|
| 2008 | Est. 10000 | PF65 70.00 | | | | |

**KM# 1211 5 DOLLARS**
155.50 g., Copper-Nickel partially gilt, 65 mm. **Ruler:** Elizabeth II **Subject:** British Monarchs - Elizabeth I

| Date | Mintage | VF20 | XF40 | MS60 | MS63 | MS65 |
|---|---|---|---|---|---|---|
| 2008 | Est. 450 | PF65 85.00 | | | | |

**KM# 1320 5 DOLLARS**
Silver **Ruler:** Elizabeth II **Rev:** Copernicus with solar system, partially gilt

| Date | Mintage | VF20 | XF40 | MS60 | MS63 | MS65 |
|---|---|---|---|---|---|---|
| 2008 | — | PF65 50.00 | | | | |

**KM# 1526 5 DOLLARS**
0.50 g., 1.000 Gold, 11 mm. **Ruler:** Elizabeth II **Subject:** Aristotle

| Date | Mintage | VF20 | XF40 | MS60 | MS63 | MS65 |
|---|---|---|---|---|---|---|
| 2008 | Est. 10000 | PF65 50.00 | | | | |

**KM# 640 5 DOLLARS**
25.00 g., 0.999 Silver 0.803 oz. ASW, 38.6 mm. **Ruler:** Elizabeth II **Rev:** Papal Tiara above crossed keys, partially gilt, crystal inserts

| Date | Mintage | VF20 | XF40 | MS60 | MS63 | MS65 |
|---|---|---|---|---|---|---|
| 2009 | 5,000 | PF65 120 | | | | |

**KM# 641 5 DOLLARS**
25.00 g., 0.999 Silver 0.803 oz. ASW **Ruler:** Elizabeth II **Subject:** Benedict XVI visits Israel **Rev:** Benedict XVI and "Dome of the Rock", partially gilt, crystal inserts **Shape:** Diamond

| Date | Mintage | VF20 | XF40 | MS60 | MS63 | MS65 |
|---|---|---|---|---|---|---|
| 2009 | 5,000 | PF65 115 | | | | |

**KM# 642 5 DOLLARS**
25.00 g., 0.999 Silver 0.803 oz. ASW **Ruler:** Elizabeth II **Subject:** Benedict XVI visits Africa **Rev:** Bust at left, partially gilt, crystal inserts **Shape:** Irregular, Africa shape

| Date | Mintage | VF20 | XF40 | MS60 | MS63 | MS65 |
|---|---|---|---|---|---|---|
| 2009 | 5,000 | PF65 115 | | | | |

**KM# 643 5 DOLLARS**
25.00 g., 0.999 Silver 0.803 oz. ASW **Ruler:** Elizabeth II **Subject:** Easter 2009 **Rev:** Statue of the risen Christ, partially gilt, crystal inserts **Shape:** Fish

| Date | Mintage | VF20 | XF40 | MS60 | MS63 | MS65 |
|---|---|---|---|---|---|---|
| 2009 | 5,000 | PF65 115 | | | | |

**KM# 644 5 DOLLARS**
25.00 g., 0.999 Silver 0.803 oz. ASW, 35 mm. **Ruler:** Elizabeth II **Rev:** Star of the Magi, partially gilt, crystal inserts **Shape:** Star

| Date | Mintage | VF20 | XF40 | MS60 | MS63 | MS65 |
|---|---|---|---|---|---|---|
| 2009 | 5,000 | PF65 115 | | | | |

**KM# 645 5 DOLLARS**
25.00 g., 0.999 Silver 0.803 oz. ASW, 35x35 mm. **Ruler:** Elizabeth II **Rev:** Cathedral of Santiago de Compostela, partially gilt, crystal inserts

| Date | Mintage | VF20 | XF40 | MS60 | MS63 | MS65 |
|---|---|---|---|---|---|---|
| 2009 | 5,000 | PF65 120 | | | | |

**KM# 646 5 DOLLARS**
25.00 g., 0.999 Silver 0.803 oz. ASW, 25x35 mm. **Ruler:** Elizabeth II **Rev:** Michangelo's Pieta, partially gilt, crystal inserts **Shape:** Rectangle

| Date | Mintage | VF20 | XF40 | MS60 | MS63 | MS65 |
|---|---|---|---|---|---|---|
| 2009 | 5,000 | PF65 115 | | | | |

**KM# 647 5 DOLLARS**
25.00 g., 0.999 Silver 0.803 oz. ASW, 30x34 mm. **Ruler:** Elizabeth II **Rev:** St. Christopher, partially gilt, crystal inserts **Shape:** Oval

| Date | Mintage | VF20 | XF40 | MS60 | MS63 | MS65 |
|---|---|---|---|---|---|---|
| 2009 | 5,000 | PF65 115 | | | | |

**KM# 648 5 DOLLARS**
25.00 g., 0.999 Silver 0.803 oz. ASW, 40x25 mm. **Ruler:** Elizabeth II **Subject:** Benedict XVI visits the Czech Republic **Rev:** Benedict XVI in Wenceleses square, partially gilt, crystal inserts **Shape:** Rectangle

| Date | Mintage | VF20 | XF40 | MS60 | MS63 | MS65 |
|---|---|---|---|---|---|---|
| 2009 | 5,000 | PF65 115 | | | | |

**KM# 649 5 DOLLARS**
25.00 g., 0.999 Silver 0.803 oz. ASW **Ruler:** Elizabeth II **Rev:** Christmas, village scene, partially gilt, crystal inserts **Shape:** Diamond

| Date | Mintage | VF20 | XF40 | MS60 | MS63 | MS65 |
|---|---|---|---|---|---|---|
| 2009 | 5,000 | PF65 115 | | | | |

**KM# 650 5 DOLLARS**
31.11 g., 0.999 Silver 0.999 oz. ASW, 38.6 mm. **Ruler:** Elizabeth II **Subject:** Kiev Churches **Rev:** Andreevskaya Church **Note:** Exclusive to the Russian Market.

| Date | Mintage | VF20 | XF40 | MS60 | MS63 | MS65 |
|---|---|---|---|---|---|---|
| 2009 | 500 | PF65 125 | | | | |

**KM# 651 5 DOLLARS**
31.11 g., 0.999 Silver 0.999 oz. ASW, 38.6 mm. **Ruler:** Elizabeth II **Subject:** Kiev Churches **Rev:** Kirillovskaya Church **Note:** Exclusive to the Russian Market.

| Date | Mintage | VF20 | XF40 | MS60 | MS63 | MS65 |
|---|---|---|---|---|---|---|
| 2009 | 500 | PF65 125 | | | | |

**KM# 652 5 DOLLARS**
31.11 g., 0.999 Silver 0.999 oz. ASW, 38.6 mm. **Ruler:** Elizabeth II **Subject:** Kiev Chruches **Rev:** Mikailovsky Monastery **Note:** Exclusive to the Russian Market.

| Date | Mintage | VF20 | XF40 | MS60 | MS63 | MS65 |
|---|---|---|---|---|---|---|
| 2009 | 500 | PF65 125 | | | | |

**KM# 653 5 DOLLARS**
31.11 g., 0.999 Silver 0.999 oz. ASW, 38.6 mm. **Ruler:** Elizabeth II **Subject:** Kiev Churches **Rev:** Cathedral of St. Sophia **Note:** Exclusive to the Russian Market.

| Date | Mintage | VF20 | XF40 | MS60 | MS63 | MS65 |
|---|---|---|---|---|---|---|
| 2009 | 500 | PF65 125 | | | | |

**KM# 654 5 DOLLARS**
31.11 g., 0.999 Silver 0.999 oz. ASW, 38.61 mm. **Ruler:** Elizabeth II **Subject:** Ukraine Landmarks - Bendrological park, Sofiyivka **Rev:** Statue and gardens **Note:** Exclusive to the Russian Market.

| Date | Mintage | VF20 | XF40 | MS60 | MS63 | MS65 |
|---|---|---|---|---|---|---|
| 2009 | 500 | PF65 120 | | | | |

**KM# 655 5 DOLLARS**
31.11 g., 0.999 Silver 0.999 oz. ASW, 38.61 mm. **Ruler:** Elizabeth II **Subject:** Ukraine Landmarks - Holy Dormition Kiev Pechersk Lavra **Rev:** Churches **Note:** Exclusive to the Russian Market.

| Date | Mintage | VF20 | XF40 | MS60 | MS63 | MS65 |
|---|---|---|---|---|---|---|
| 2009 | 500 | PF65 120 | | | | |

**KM# 656 5 DOLLARS**
31.11 g., 0.999 Silver 0.999 oz. ASW, 38.61 mm. **Ruler:** Elizabeth II **Subject:** Ukraine Landmarks - Holy Dormition Pochayiv Lavra **Rev:** Buildings **Note:** Exclusive to the Russian Market.

| Date | Mintage | VF20 | XF40 | MS60 | MS63 | MS65 |
|---|---|---|---|---|---|---|
| 2009 | 500 | PF65 120 | | | | |

**KM# 657 5 DOLLARS**
31.11 g., 0.999 Silver 0.999 oz. ASW, 38.61 mm. **Ruler:** Elizabeth II **Subject:** Ukraine Landmarks - Holy Dormition Sviatohirsk Lavra **Rev:** Virgin Mary and Church **Note:** Exclusive to the Russian Market.

| Date | Mintage | VF20 | XF40 | MS60 | MS63 | MS65 |
|---|---|---|---|---|---|---|
| 2009 | 500 | **PF65** 120 | | | | |

**KM# 658 5 DOLLARS**
31.11 g., 0.999 Silver 0.999 oz. ASW, 38.61 mm. **Ruler:** Elizabeth II **Subject:** Ukraine Landmarks - Kamyanets National Reserve **Rev:** Fortress **Note:** Exclusive to the Russian Market.

| Date | Mintage | VF20 | XF40 | MS60 | MS63 | MS65 |
|---|---|---|---|---|---|---|
| 2009 | 500 | **PF65** 120 | | | | |

**KM# 659 5 DOLLARS**
31.11 g., 0.999 Silver 0.999 oz. ASW, 38.6 mm. **Ruler:** Elizabeth II **Subject:** Ukraine Landmarks - Khersones Tavrijsky National Reserve **Rev:** Roman ruins **Note:** Exclusive to the Russian Market.

| Date | Mintage | VF20 | XF40 | MS60 | MS63 | MS65 |
|---|---|---|---|---|---|---|
| 2009 | 500 | **PF65** 120 | | | | |

**KM# 660 5 DOLLARS**
31.11 g., 0.999 Silver 0.999 oz. ASW, 38.6 mm. **Ruler:** Elizabeth II **Subject:** Ukraine Landmarks - Khortytsia National Reserve **Rev:** Stone carvings and bridge **Note:** Exclusive to the Russian Market.

| Date | Mintage | VF20 | XF40 | MS60 | MS63 | MS65 |
|---|---|---|---|---|---|---|
| 2009 | 500 | **PF65** 120 | | | | |

**KM# 661 5 DOLLARS**
31.11 g., 0.999 Silver 0.999 oz. ASW, 38.6 mm. **Ruler:** Elizabeth II **Subject:** Ukraine Landmarks - National Theatre of Odessa **Rev:** Opera House **Note:** Exclusive to the Russian Market.

| Date | Mintage | VF20 | XF40 | MS60 | MS63 | MS65 |
|---|---|---|---|---|---|---|
| 2009 | 500 | **PF65** 120 | | | | |

**KM# 662 5 DOLLARS**
31.11 g., 0.999 Silver 0.999 oz. ASW, 38.6 mm. **Ruler:** Elizabeth II **Subject:** Ukraine Landmarks - Olesko Castle **Rev:** Hillside dwelling **Note:** Exclusive to the Russian Market.

| Date | Mintage | VF20 | XF40 | MS60 | MS63 | MS65 |
|---|---|---|---|---|---|---|
| 2009 | 500 | **PF65** 120 | | | | |

**KM# 663 5 DOLLARS**
31.11 g., 0.999 Silver 0.999 oz. ASW, 38.6 mm. **Ruler:** Elizabeth II **Subject:** Ukraine Landmarks - Palanok Castle in Mukachevo **Rev:** Hilltop fortress **Note:** Exclusive to the Russian Market.

| Date | Mintage | VF20 | XF40 | MS60 | MS63 | MS65 |
|---|---|---|---|---|---|---|
| 2009 | 500 | **PF65** 120 | | | | |

**KM# 664 5 DOLLARS**
31.11 g., 0.999 Silver 0.999 oz. ASW, 38.6 mm. **Ruler:** Elizabeth II **Subject:** Ukraine Landmarks - Khotyn Fortress Reserve **Rev:** Road to castle **Note:** Exclusive to the Russian Market.

| Date | Mintage | VF20 | XF40 | MS60 | MS63 | MS65 |
|---|---|---|---|---|---|---|
| 2009 | 500 | **PF65** 120 | | | | |

**KM# 665 5 DOLLARS**
31.11 g., 0.999 Silver 0.999 oz. ASW, 38.6 mm. **Ruler:** Elizabeth II **Subject:** Ukraine Landmarks - Upper Castle of Lutsk **Rev:** Tower **Note:** Exclusive to the Russian Market.

| Date | Mintage | VF20 | XF40 | MS60 | MS63 | MS65 |
|---|---|---|---|---|---|---|
| 2009 | 500 | **PF65** 120 | | | | |

**KM# 672 5 DOLLARS**
25.00 g., 0.925 Silver 0.7435 oz. ASW, 38.6 mm. **Ruler:** Elizabeth II **Rev:** HMS Endeavour and James Cook portrait

| Date | Mintage | VF20 | XF40 | MS60 | MS63 | MS65 |
|---|---|---|---|---|---|---|
| 2009 | 2,500 | **PF65** 45.00 | | | | |

**KM# 673 5 DOLLARS**
25.00 g., 0.500 Silver 0.4019 oz. ASW, 38.6 mm. **Ruler:** Elizabeth II **Rev:** Ferrari F-2008 Carbon

| Date | Mintage | VF20 | XF40 | MS60 | MS63 | MS65 |
|---|---|---|---|---|---|---|
| ND2009 | 2,008 | **PF65** 50.00 | | | | |

**KM# 674 5 DOLLARS**
20.00 g., 0.925 Silver 0.5948 oz. ASW, 38.61 mm. **Ruler:** Elizabeth II **Subject:** Endangered Wildlife **Rev:** Giant Anteater

| Date | Mintage | VF20 | XF40 | MS60 | MS63 | MS65 |
|---|---|---|---|---|---|---|
| 2009 | 5,000 | **PF65** 50.00 | | | | |

**KM# 675 5 DOLLARS**
31.11 g., 0.925 Silver 0.925 oz. ASW, 38.6 mm. **Ruler:** Elizabeth II **Series:** International Womens Day **Rev:** Roses and butterfly **Note:** Exclusive to the Russian Market

| Date | Mintage | VF20 | XF40 | MS60 | MS63 | MS65 |
|---|---|---|---|---|---|---|
| 2009 | 500 | PF65 120 | | | | |

**KM# 676 5 DOLLARS**
25.00 g., 0.925 Silver 0.7435 oz. ASW, 38.6 mm. **Ruler:** Elizabeth II **Rev:** Sir Lancelot with color

| Date | Mintage | VF20 | XF40 | MS60 | MS63 | MS65 |
|---|---|---|---|---|---|---|
| 2009 | 300 | PF65 75.00 | | | | |

**KM# 677 5 DOLLARS**
0.925 Silver **Ruler:** Elizabeth II **Subject:** Masters of Europe - Vermeer **Rev:** Girl with a pearl earing, multicolor **Shape:** Vertical rectangle

| Date | Mintage | VF20 | XF40 | MS60 | MS63 | MS65 |
|---|---|---|---|---|---|---|
| 2009 | — | PF65 65.00 | | | | |

**KM# 678 5 DOLLARS**
0.925 Silver **Ruler:** Elizabeth II **Subject:** Masters of Europe - DaVinci **Rev:** Lady with an ermine, multicolor **Shape:** Vertical rectangle

| Date | Mintage | VF20 | XF40 | MS60 | MS63 | MS65 |
|---|---|---|---|---|---|---|
| 2009 | — | PF65 75.00 | | | | |

**KM# 679 5 DOLLARS**
0.925 Silver **Ruler:** Elizabeth II **Subject:** Masters of Europe - Jan Matejko **Rev:** Wernyhora, multicolor **Shape:** Vertical rectangle

| Date | Mintage | VF20 | XF40 | MS60 | MS63 | MS65 |
|---|---|---|---|---|---|---|
| 2009 | — | PF65 65.00 | | | | |

**KM# 680 5 DOLLARS**
Silver **Ruler:** Elizabeth II **Subject:** 50th Anniversary of Space exploration, 40th Anniversary of Apollo 11 **Obv:** Moon **Rev:** Moonscape and moon rock implant

| Date | Mintage | VF20 | XF40 | MS60 | MS63 | MS65 |
|---|---|---|---|---|---|---|
| 2009 Matte | 1,969 | — | — | — | — | 300 |

**KM# 681 5 DOLLARS**
25.00 g., 0.925 Silver 0.7435 oz. ASW copper plated **Ruler:** Elizabeth II **Subject:** 400th Anniversary of Mars observations **Obv:** Bust with tiara right **Rev:** Mars landscape

| Date | Mintage | VF20 | XF40 | MS60 | MS63 | MS65 |
|---|---|---|---|---|---|---|
| 2009 Matte | 2,500 | — | — | — | — | 250 |

**KM# 682 5 DOLLARS**
25.00 g., 0.925 Silver 0.7435 oz. ASW, 38.61 mm. **Ruler:** Elizabeth II **Subject:** Year of the Ox **Rev:** Child riding oxen, partially gilt **Note:** Exclusive to the Russian market

| Date | Mintage | VF20 | XF40 | MS60 | MS63 | MS65 |
|---|---|---|---|---|---|---|
| 2009 | 1,000 | PF65 200 | | | | |

**KM# 683 5 DOLLARS**
25.00 g., 0.999 Silver 0.803 oz. ASW **Ruler:** Elizabeth II **Subject:** World of Flowers - Pansey **Rev:** Pansey, multicolor cloisonne

| Date | Mintage | VF20 | XF40 | MS60 | MS63 | MS65 |
|---|---|---|---|---|---|---|
| 2009 | 2,500 | PF65 75.00 | | | | |

**KM# 684 5 DOLLARS**
25.00 g., 0.999 Silver 0.803 oz. ASW, 38.6 mm. **Ruler:** Elizabeth II **Subject:** World of flowers - Poppy **Rev:** Poppy, multicolor closinne

| Date | Mintage | VF20 | XF40 | MS60 | MS63 | MS65 |
|---|---|---|---|---|---|---|
| 2009 | 2,500 | PF65 75.00 | | | | |

**KM# 685 5 DOLLARS**
25.00 g., 0.925 Silver 0.7435 oz. ASW, 30x43 mm. **Ruler:** Elizabeth II **Obv:** Bust right **Rev:** Easter chick, thermal image changing **Shape:** Egg

| Date | Mintage | VF20 | XF40 | MS60 | MS63 | MS65 |
|---|---|---|---|---|---|---|
| 2009 | 2,500 | PF65 70.00 | | | | |

**KM# 686 5 DOLLARS**
25.00 g., 0.925 Silver 0.7435 oz. ASW, 35x35 mm. **Ruler:** Elizabeth II **Rev:** Season's greetings, rocking horse **Shape:** Square

| Date | Mintage | VF20 | XF40 | MS60 | MS63 | MS65 |
|---|---|---|---|---|---|---|
| 2009 | 2,500 | PF65 60.00 | | | | |

**KM# 687 5 DOLLARS**
25.00 g., 0.999 Silver 0.803 oz. ASW, 30x38 mm. **Ruler:** Elizabeth II **Rev:** Kazan Virgin icon **Shape:** Vertical rectangle **Note:** Exclusive to the Russian market

| Date | Mintage | VF20 | XF40 | MS60 | MS63 | MS65 |
|---|---|---|---|---|---|---|
| 2009 | 2,500 | PF65 125 | | | | |

**KM# 764 5 DOLLARS**
Silver, 25x40 mm. **Ruler:** Elizabeth II **Subject:** Ferrari, the Legend **Rev:** Car and enameled shield **Shape:** Vertical rectangle

| Date | Mintage | VF20 | XF40 | MS60 | MS63 | MS65 |
|---|---|---|---|---|---|---|
| 2009 | — | PF65 125 | | | | |

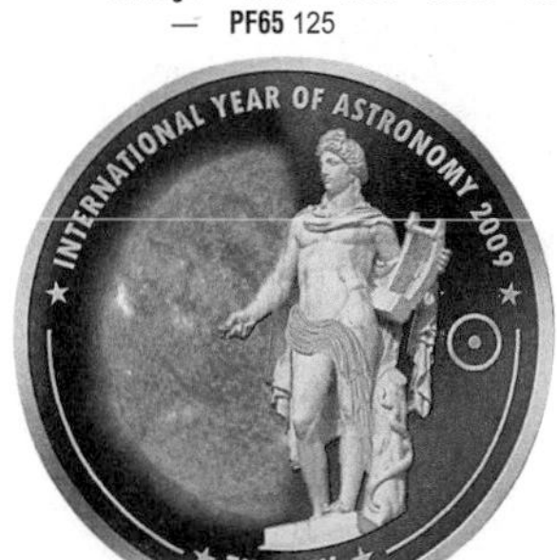

**KM# 782 5 DOLLARS**
20.00 g., 0.999 Silver 0.6424 oz. ASW, 40 mm. **Ruler:** Elizabeth II **Subject:** Year of Astronomy **Rev:** Sun, multicolor

| Date | Mintage | VF20 | XF40 | MS60 | MS63 | MS65 |
|---|---|---|---|---|---|---|
| 2009 | — | — | — | — | — | 50.00 |

**KM# 783 5 DOLLARS**
20.00 g., 0.999 Silver 0.6424 oz. ASW, 40 mm. **Ruler:** Elizabeth II **Subject:** Year of Astronomy **Rev:** Mercury, multicolor

| Date | Mintage | VF20 | XF40 | MS60 | MS63 | MS65 |
|---|---|---|---|---|---|---|
| 2009 | — | — | — | — | — | 50.00 |

**KM# 784 5 DOLLARS**
20.00 g., 0.999 Silver 0.6424 oz. ASW, 40 mm. **Ruler:** Elizabeth II **Subject:** Year of Astronomy **Rev:** Venus, multicolor

| Date | Mintage | VF20 | XF40 | MS60 | MS63 | MS65 |
|---|---|---|---|---|---|---|
| 2009 | — | — | — | — | — | 55.00 |

**KM# 785 5 DOLLARS**
20.00 g., 0.999 Silver 0.6424 oz. ASW, 40 mm. **Ruler:** Elizabeth II **Subject:** Year of Astronomy **Rev:** Earth, multicolor

| Date | Mintage | VF20 | XF40 | MS60 | MS63 | MS65 |
|---|---|---|---|---|---|---|
| 2009 | — | — | — | — | — | 50.00 |

**KM# 786 5 DOLLARS**
20.00 g., 0.999 Silver 0.6424 oz. ASW, 40 mm. **Ruler:** Elizabeth II **Subject:** Year of Astronomy **Rev:** Mars, multicolor

| Date | Mintage | VF20 | XF40 | MS60 | MS63 | MS65 |
|---|---|---|---|---|---|---|
| 2009 | — | — | — | — | — | 50.00 |

**KM# 787 5 DOLLARS**
20.00 g., 0.999 Silver 0.6424 oz. ASW, 40 mm. **Ruler:** Elizabeth II **Subject:** Year of Astronomy **Rev:** Jupiter, multicolor

| Date | Mintage | VF20 | XF40 | MS60 | MS63 | MS65 |
|---|---|---|---|---|---|---|
| 2009 | — | — | — | — | — | 50.00 |

**KM# 788 5 DOLLARS**
20.00 g., 0.999 Silver 0.6424 oz. ASW, 40 mm. **Ruler:** Elizabeth II **Subject:** Year of Astronomy **Rev:** Saturn, multicolor

| Date | Mintage | VF20 | XF40 | MS60 | MS63 | MS65 |
|---|---|---|---|---|---|---|
| 2009 | — | — | — | — | — | 50.00 |

**KM# 789 5 DOLLARS**
20.00 g., 0.999 Silver 0.6424 oz. ASW, 40 mm. **Ruler:** Elizabeth II **Subject:** Year of Astronomy **Rev:** Uranus, multicolor

| Date | Mintage | VF20 | XF40 | MS60 | MS63 | MS65 |
|---|---|---|---|---|---|---|
| 2009 | — | — | — | — | — | 50.00 |

**KM# 790 5 DOLLARS**
20.00 g., 0.999 Silver 0.6424 oz. ASW, 40 mm. **Ruler:** Elizabeth II **Subject:** Year of Astronomy **Rev:** Neptune, multicolor

| Date | Mintage | VF20 | XF40 | MS60 | MS63 | MS65 |
|---|---|---|---|---|---|---|
| 2009 | — | — | — | — | — | 50.00 |

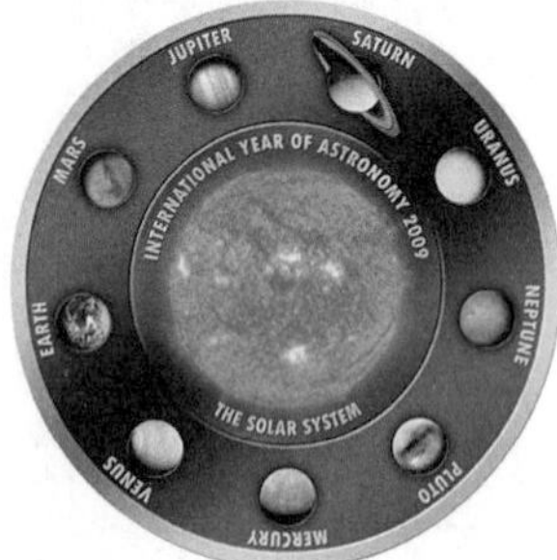


**KM# 791 5 DOLLARS**
20.00 g., 0.999 Silver 0.6424 oz. ASW, 40 mm. **Ruler:** Elizabeth II **Subject:** Year of Astronomy **Rev:** Solar System, multicolor

| Date | Mintage | VF20 | XF40 | MS60 | MS63 | MS65 |
|---|---|---|---|---|---|---|
| 2009 | — | — | — | — | — | 50.00 |

**KM# 1225 5 DOLLARS**
28.28 g., 0.925 Silver 0.841 oz. ASW, 38.6 mm. **Ruler:** Elizabeth II **Subject:** Ikuko Shimizu's Hello Kitty **Rev:** Kitty and London Bus in color

| Date | Mintage | VF20 | XF40 | MS60 | MS63 | MS65 |
|---|---|---|---|---|---|---|
| 2009 | Est. 3000 | **PF65** 110 | | | | |

**KM# 1226 5 DOLLARS**
28.28 g., 0.925 Silver 0.841 oz. ASW, 38.6 mm. **Ruler:** Elizabeth II **Subject:** Ikuko Shimizu's Hello Kitty **Rev:** Kitty playing polo in multicolor

| Date | Mintage | VF20 | XF40 | MS60 | MS63 | MS65 |
|---|---|---|---|---|---|---|
| 2009 | Est. 3000 | **PF65** 110 | | | | |

**KM# 1227 5 DOLLARS**
28.28 g., 0.925 Silver 0.841 oz. ASW, 38.6 mm. **Ruler:** Elizabeth II **Subject:** Ikuko Shimizu's Hello Kitty **Rev:** Kitty and Daniel with Tower Bridge in multicolor

| Date | Mintage | VF20 | XF40 | MS60 | MS63 | MS65 |
|---|---|---|---|---|---|---|
| 2009 | — | **PF65** 110 | | | | |

**KM# 1236 5 DOLLARS**
25.00 g., 0.925 Silver 0.7435 oz. ASW, 38.61 mm. **Ruler:** Elizabeth II **Subject:** Lady of the Lake

| Date | Mintage | VF20 | XF40 | MS60 | MS63 | MS65 |
|---|---|---|---|---|---|---|
| 2009 | 300 | **PF65** 75.00 | | | | |

**KM# 1237 5 DOLLARS**
25.00 g., 0.925 Silver 0.7435 oz. ASW, 38.61 mm. **Ruler:** Elizabeth II **Rev:** Excalibur set into rock in color

| Date | Mintage | VF20 | XF40 | MS60 | MS63 | MS65 |
|---|---|---|---|---|---|---|
| 2009 | 300 | **PF65** 75.00 | | | | |

**KM# 1238 5 DOLLARS**
25.00 g., 0.925 Silver 0.7435 oz. ASW, 38.61 mm. **Ruler:** Elizabeth II **Subject:** King Arthur with color

| Date | Mintage | VF20 | XF40 | MS60 | MS63 | MS65 |
|---|---|---|---|---|---|---|
| 2009 | 300 | **PF65** 75.00 | | | | |

**KM# 1239 5 DOLLARS**
25.00 g., 0.925 Silver 0.7435 oz. ASW, 38.61 mm. **Ruler:** Elizabeth II **Rev:** Sir Galahad with color

| Date | Mintage | VF20 | XF40 | MS60 | MS63 | MS65 |
|---|---|---|---|---|---|---|
| 2009 | 300 | **PF65** 75.00 | | | | |

**KM# 1240 5 DOLLARS**
25.00 g., 0.925 Silver 0.7435 oz. ASW, 38.61 mm. **Ruler:** Elizabeth II **Rev:** The Holy Grail gilt, knights of the roundtable in background

| Date | Mintage | VF20 | XF40 | MS60 | MS63 | MS65 |
|---|---|---|---|---|---|---|
| 2009 | 300 | **PF65** 75.00 | | | | |

**KM# 1329 5 DOLLARS**
Silver **Ruler:** Elizabeth II **Subject:** Banker's Day **Rev:** Map of Ukraine, locations pinpointed

| Date | Mintage | VF20 | XF40 | MS60 | MS63 | MS65 |
|---|---|---|---|---|---|---|
| 2009 Antique patina | — | — | — | — | 85.00 | — |

**KM# 1330 5 DOLLARS**
Silver **Ruler:** Elizabeth II **Rev:** European Bison, partially gilt

| Date | Mintage | VF20 | XF40 | MS60 | MS63 | MS65 |
|---|---|---|---|---|---|---|
| 2009 | — | **PF65** 50.00 | | | | |

**KM# 1331 5 DOLLARS**
Silver **Ruler:** Elizabeth II **Rev:** Napoleon on horseback in battle in color

| Date | Mintage | VF20 | XF40 | MS60 | MS63 | MS65 |
|---|---|---|---|---|---|---|
| 2009 | — | **PF65** 65.00 | | | | |

**KM# 1430 5 DOLLARS**
Copper-Nickel, 38.61 mm. **Ruler:** Elizabeth II **Subject:** First Crusade

| Date | Mintage | VF20 | XF40 | MS60 | MS63 | MS65 |
|---|---|---|---|---|---|---|
| 2009 | — | — | — | — | — | 25.00 |

**KM# 1490 5 DOLLARS**
0.50 g., 0.999 Gold, 11 mm. **Ruler:** Elizabeth II **Rev:** Man with golden helmet by Rembrant

| Date | Mintage | VF20 | XF40 | MS60 | MS63 | MS65 |
|---|---|---|---|---|---|---|
| 2009 | Est. 10000 | **PF65** 60.00 | | | | |

**KM# 1523 5 DOLLARS**
0.50 g., 1.000 Gold, 11 mm. **Ruler:** Elizabeth II **Subject:** Greek Mythology Artemis

| Date | Mintage | VF20 | XF40 | MS60 | MS63 | MS65 |
|---|---|---|---|---|---|---|
| 2009 | Est. 10000 | **PF65** 50.00 | | | | |

**KM# 1524 5 DOLLARS**
0.50 g., 1.000 Gold, 11 mm. **Ruler:** Elizabeth II **Subject:** Greek Mythology Ares

| Date | Mintage | VF20 | XF40 | MS60 | MS63 | MS65 |
|---|---|---|---|---|---|---|
| 2009 | Est. 10000 | **PF65** 50.00 | | | | |

**KM# 1525 5 DOLLARS**
0.50 g., 1.000 Gold, 11 mm. **Ruler:** Elizabeth II **Subject:** Greek Mythology Helios

| Date | Mintage | VF20 | XF40 | MS60 | MS63 | MS65 |
|---|---|---|---|---|---|---|
| 2009 | Est. 10000 | **PF65** 50.00 | | | | |

**KM# 1527 5 DOLLARS**
0.50 g., 1.000 Gold, 11 mm. **Ruler:** Elizabeth II **Subject:** 10 Years of Euro Introduction

| Date | Mintage | VF20 | XF40 | MS60 | MS63 | MS65 |
|---|---|---|---|---|---|---|
| 2009 | Est. 10000 | **PF65** 50.00 | | | | |

**KM# 1528 5 DOLLARS**
0.50 g., 0.999 Gold, 11 mm. **Ruler:** Elizabeth II **Subject:** Orpheus

| Date | Mintage | VF20 | XF40 | MS60 | MS63 | MS65 |
|---|---|---|---|---|---|---|
| 2009 | Est. 10000 | PF65 50.00 | | | | |

**KM# 1529 5 DOLLARS**
0.50 g., 0.999 Gold, 11 mm. **Ruler:** Elizabeth II **Subject:** Eurydice

| Date | Mintage | VF20 | XF40 | MS60 | MS63 | MS65 |
|---|---|---|---|---|---|---|
| 2009 | Est. 10000 | PF65 60.00 | | | | |

**KM# 1630 5 DOLLARS**
25.00 g., 0.999 Silver 0.803 oz. ASW partially gilt, 30x35 mm. **Ruler:** Elizabeth II **Rev:** Apollo Belvidere statue and crystals **Shape:** Vertical rectangle

| Date | Mintage | VF20 | XF40 | MS60 | MS63 | MS65 |
|---|---|---|---|---|---|---|
| 2009 | 5,000 | PF65 120 | | | | |

**KM# 1631 5 DOLLARS**
28.28 g., 0.925 Silver 0.841 oz. ASW, 38.61 mm. **Ruler:** Elizabeth II **Rev:** Hello Kitty playing polo

| Date | Mintage | VF20 | XF40 | MS60 | MS63 | MS65 |
|---|---|---|---|---|---|---|
| 2009 | 3,000 | PF65 170 | | | | |

**KM# 1636 5 DOLLARS**
25.00 g., 0.999 Silver 0.803 oz. ASW partially gilt, 30x35 mm. **Ruler:** Elizabeth II **Subject:** Vatican Art **Rev:** Pieta **Shape:** Vertical rectangle

| Date | Mintage | VF20 | XF40 | MS60 | MS63 | MS65 |
|---|---|---|---|---|---|---|
| 2009 | 5,000 | PF65 120 | | | | |

**KM# 723 5 DOLLARS**
31.11 g., 0.999 Silver 0.999 oz. ASW, 24x47 mm. **Ruler:** Elizabeth II **Subject:** War of 1812 **Rev:** Peter Bagraton

| Date | Mintage | VF20 | XF40 | MS60 | MS63 | MS65 |
|---|---|---|---|---|---|---|
| 2010 Antique patina | 2,000 | — | — | — | 55.00 | — |

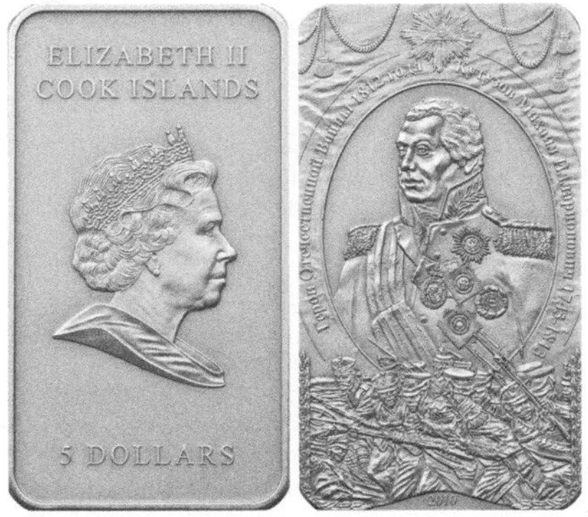


**KM# 724 5 DOLLARS**
31.11 g., 0.999 Silver 0.999 oz. ASW **Ruler:** Elizabeth II **Subject:** War of 1812 **Rev:** Mikhail Kutuzov **Shape:** 24x47

| Date | Mintage | VF20 | XF40 | MS60 | MS63 | MS65 |
|---|---|---|---|---|---|---|
| 2010 Antique patina | 2,000 | — | — | — | 55.00 | — |

**KM# 725 5 DOLLARS**
31.11 g., 0.999 Silver 0.999 oz. ASW, 27x47 mm. **Ruler:** Elizabeth II **Subject:** War of 1812 **Rev:** Bikoly Raevsky

| Date | Mintage | VF20 | XF40 | MS60 | MS63 | MS65 |
|---|---|---|---|---|---|---|
| 2010 Antique finish | 2,000 | — | — | — | 55.00 | — |

**KM# 726 5 DOLLARS**
20.00 g., 0.999 Silver 0.6424 oz. ASW, 30x43 mm. **Ruler:** Elizabeth II **Subject:** Imperial Eggs **Rev:** Blue egg

| Date | Mintage | VF20 | XF40 | MS60 | MS63 | MS65 |
|---|---|---|---|---|---|---|
| 2010 | 2,500 | PF65 65.00 | | | | |

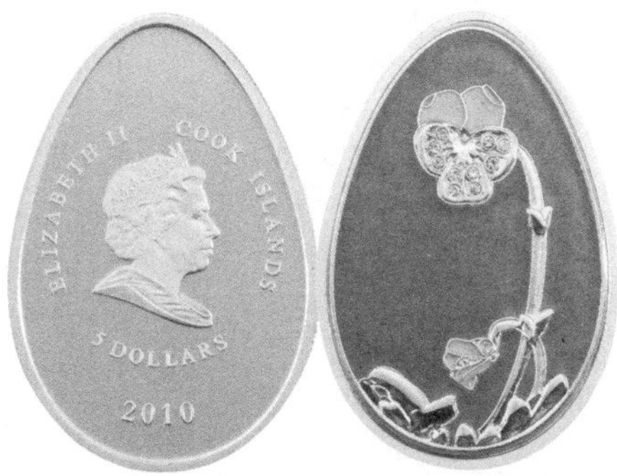


**KM# 727 5 DOLLARS**
20.00 g., 0.999 Silver 0.6424 oz. ASW, 30x43 mm. **Ruler:** Elizabeth II **Subject:** Imperial Egg **Rev:** Green cloisonne

| Date | Mintage | VF20 | XF40 | MS60 | MS63 | MS65 |
|---|---|---|---|---|---|---|
| 2010 | 2,500 | PF65 65.00 | | | | |

**KM# 728 5 DOLLARS**
20.00 g., 0.999 Silver 0.6424 oz. ASW, 30x43 mm. **Ruler:** Elizabeth II **Subject:** Imperial Egg **Rev:** Yellow cloisonne and Bohemian crystals

| Date | Mintage | VF20 | XF40 | MS60 | MS63 | MS65 |
|---|---|---|---|---|---|---|
| 2010 | 2,500 | PF65 65.00 | | | | |

**KM# 729 5 DOLLARS**
25.00 g., 0.999 Silver 0.803 oz. ASW, 38.6 mm. **Ruler:** Elizabeth II **Rev:** Martin Luther King, pointing **Note:** Fits together with KM#730.

| Date | Mintage | VF20 | XF40 | MS60 | MS63 | MS65 |
|---|---|---|---|---|---|---|
| 2010 Antique finish | 2,500 | — | — | — | 45.00 | — |

**KM# 730 5 DOLLARS**
25.00 g., 0.999 Silver 0.803 oz. ASW, 38.6 mm. **Ruler:** Elizabeth II **Rev:** Barack Obama, pointing **Note:** Fits together with KM#729.

| Date | Mintage | VF20 | XF40 | MS60 | MS63 | MS65 |
|---|---|---|---|---|---|---|
| 2010 Antique finish | 2,500 | — | — | — | 45.00 | — |

**KM# 731 5 DOLLARS**
25.00 g., 0.925 Silver 0.7435 oz. ASW, 38.6 mm. **Ruler:** Elizabeth II **Subject:** Tender Love **Rev:** Rose in relief hologram

| Date | Mintage | VF20 | XF40 | MS60 | MS63 | MS65 |
|---|---|---|---|---|---|---|
| 2010 | 2,500 | PF65 50.00 | | | | |

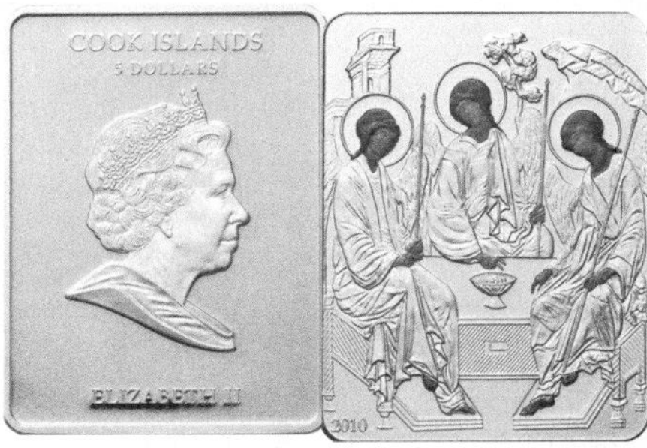


**KM# 732 5 DOLLARS**
25.00 g., 0.925 Silver 0.7435 oz. ASW, 30x38 mm. **Ruler:** Elizabeth II **Rev:** Holy Trinity icon

| Date | Mintage | VF20 | XF40 | MS60 | MS63 | MS65 |
|---|---|---|---|---|---|---|
| 2010 | 2,500 | PF65 65.00 | | | | |

### KM# 1244 5 DOLLARS

25.00 g., 0.925 Silver 0.7435 oz. ASW, 30x38 mm. **Ruler:** Elizabeth II **Subject:** Vasily Tropinin, 1776-1857 **Rev:** The Lacemaker, multicolor **Shape:** Vertical rectangle

| Date | Mintage | VF20 | XF40 | MS60 | MS63 | MS65 |
|---|---|---|---|---|---|---|
| 2010 | 2,500 | PF65 65.00 | | | | |

### KM# 1245 5 DOLLARS

25.00 g., 0.925 Silver 0.7435 oz. ASW, 40.6 mm. **Ruler:** Elizabeth II **Subject:** Don Juan, Battle of Lepanto

| Date | Mintage | VF20 | XF40 | MS60 | MS63 | MS65 |
|---|---|---|---|---|---|---|
| 2010 | 1,000 | PF65 75.00 | | | | |

### KM# 1250 5 DOLLARS

26.00 g., 0.925 Silver 0.7732 oz. ASW, 30x38 mm. **Ruler:** Elizabeth II **Subject:** Peter Brandl **Shape:** Vertical rectangle

| Date | Mintage | VF20 | XF40 | MS60 | MS63 | MS65 |
|---|---|---|---|---|---|---|
| 2010 | 2,500 | PF65 60.00 | | | | |

### KM# 1251 5 DOLLARS

25.00 g., 0.925 Silver 0.7435 oz. ASW, 30x38 mm. **Ruler:** Elizabeth II **Subject:** Michangelo's David **Shape:** Vertical rectangle

| Date | Mintage | VF20 | XF40 | MS60 | MS63 | MS65 |
|---|---|---|---|---|---|---|
| 2010 | 2,500 | PF65 45.00 | | | | |

### KM# 1252 5 DOLLARS

25.00 g., 0.925 Silver 0.7435 oz. ASW, 38.61 mm. **Ruler:** Elizabeth II **Subject:** Hollywood Stars - Ginger Rogers

| Date | Mintage | VF20 | XF40 | MS60 | MS63 | MS65 |
|---|---|---|---|---|---|---|
| 2010 | 2,500 | PF65 55.00 | | | | |

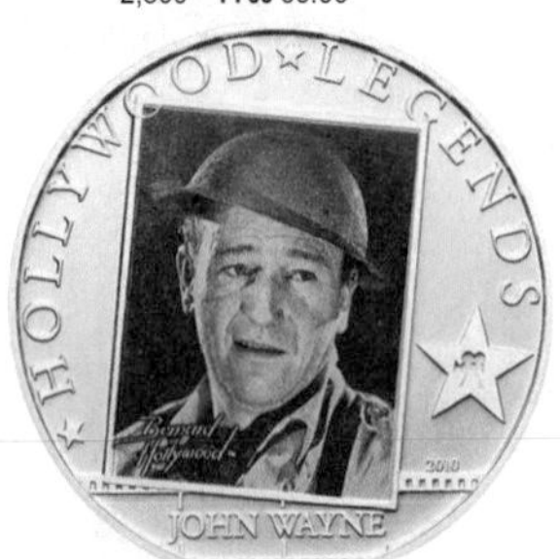

### KM# 1253 5 DOLLARS

25.00 g., 0.925 Silver 0.7435 oz. ASW, 38.61 mm. **Ruler:** Elizabeth II **Subject:** Hollywood Stars - John Wayne

| Date | Mintage | VF20 | XF40 | MS60 | MS63 | MS65 |
|---|---|---|---|---|---|---|
| 2010 | 2,500 | PF65 55.00 | | | | |

### KM# 1254 5 DOLLARS

25.00 g., 0.925 Silver 0.7435 oz. ASW, 38.61 mm. **Ruler:** Elizabeth II **Subject:** Hollywood Stars - Clark Gable

| Date | Mintage | VF20 | XF40 | MS60 | MS63 | MS65 |
|---|---|---|---|---|---|---|
| 2010 | 2,500 | PF65 55.00 | | | | |

### KM# 1255 5 DOLLARS

25.00 g., 0.925 Silver 0.7435 oz. ASW, 38.61 mm. **Ruler:** Elizabeth II **Subject:** Gdansk **Rev:** Town view, statue in copper **Note:** Antique patina.

| Date | Mintage | VF20 | XF40 | MS60 | MS63 | MS65 |
|---|---|---|---|---|---|---|
| 2010 | 1,000 | PF65 60.00 | | | | |

### KM# 1281 5 DOLLARS

Silver, 27x47 mm. **Ruler:** Elizabeth II **Subject:** Ferrari 250 GTO and 599 GTO **Rev:** Car at top and bottom, yellow logo at center **Shape:** Vertical rectangle

| Date | Mintage | VF20 | XF40 | MS60 | MS63 | MS65 |
|---|---|---|---|---|---|---|
| 2010 | 1,010 | PF65 135 | | | | |

### KM# 1292 5 DOLLARS

25.00 g., 0.999 Silver 0.803 oz. ASW, 30x38 mm. **Ruler:** Elizabeth II **Subject:** Russian Icons **Rev:** Icon of St. Nicolas **Shape:** Vertical rectangle

| Date | Mintage | VF20 | XF40 | MS60 | MS63 | MS65 |
|---|---|---|---|---|---|---|
| 2010 | — | PF65 120 | | | | |

### KM# 1299 5 DOLLARS

25.00 g., 0.925 Silver 0.7435 oz. ASW, 38.61 mm. **Ruler:** Elizabeth II **Rev:** HAH 280 Meteorite in color

| Date | Mintage | VF20 | XF40 | MS60 | MS63 | MS65 |
|---|---|---|---|---|---|---|
| 2010 Antique Patina | 2,500 | — | — | — | 250 | — |

### KM# 1300 5 DOLLARS

31.11 g., 0.925 Silver 0.925 oz. ASW, 38.61 mm. **Ruler:** Elizabeth II **Subject:** Yugra district **Rev:** Bear

| Date | Mintage | VF20 | XF40 | MS60 | MS63 | MS65 |
|---|---|---|---|---|---|---|
| 2010 | 2,000 | PF65 75.00 | | | | |

### KM# 1301 5 DOLLARS

31.11 g., 0.925 Silver 0.925 oz. ASW, 38.61 mm. **Ruler:** Elizabeth II **Subject:** Yugra District **Rev:** Crude Oil

| Date | Mintage | VF20 | XF40 | MS60 | MS63 | MS65 |
|---|---|---|---|---|---|---|
| 2010 | 2,000 | PF65 75.00 | | | | |

### KM# 1302 5 DOLLARS

31.11 g., 0.925 Silver 0.925 oz. ASW, 38.61 mm. **Ruler:** Elizabeth II **Subject:** Yugra District **Rev:** Sledge Jump

| Date | Mintage | VF20 | XF40 | MS60 | MS63 | MS65 |
|---|---|---|---|---|---|---|
| 2010 | 2,000 | PF65 75.00 | | | | |

### KM# 1303 5 DOLLARS

31.11 g., 0.999 Silver 0.999 oz. ASW, 38.61 mm. **Ruler:** Elizabeth II **Subject:** Day of Prudence

| Date | Mintage | VF20 | XF40 | MS60 | MS63 | MS65 |
|---|---|---|---|---|---|---|
| 2010 Antique patina | 500 | — | — | — | 75.00 | — |

**KM# 1304 5 DOLLARS**
25.00 g., 0.999 Silver 0.803 oz. ASW, 30x38 mm. **Ruler:** Elizabeth II **Subject:** Russian Icons **Rev:** The Holy Face of Christ **Shape:** Vertical rectangle

| Date | Mintage | VF20 | XF40 | MS60 | MS63 | MS65 |
|---|---|---|---|---|---|---|
| 2010 | 2,500 | PF65 75.00 | | | | |

**KM# 1305 5 DOLLARS**
25.00 g., 0.999 Silver 0.803 oz. ASW, 30x38 mm. **Ruler:** Elizabeth II **Subject:** Russian Icons **Rev:** St. Sergius of Radonezh **Shape:** Vertical rectangle

| Date | Mintage | VF20 | XF40 | MS60 | MS63 | MS65 |
|---|---|---|---|---|---|---|
| 2010 | 2,500 | PF65 75.00 | | | | |

**KM# 1307 5 DOLLARS**
25.00 g., 0.925 Silver 0.7435 oz. ASW, 38.61 mm. **Ruler:** Elizabeth II **Rev:** Wedding day, color and partially gilt

| Date | Mintage | VF20 | XF40 | MS60 | MS63 | MS65 |
|---|---|---|---|---|---|---|
| 2010 | 2,000 | PF65 75.00 | | | | |

**KM# 1308 5 DOLLARS**
31.11 g., 0.999 Silver 0.999 oz. ASW, 38.61 mm. **Ruler:** Elizabeth II **Subject:** Dear Grandmother

| Date | Mintage | VF20 | XF40 | MS60 | MS63 | MS65 |
|---|---|---|---|---|---|---|
| 2010 | 500 | PF65 75.00 | | | | |

**KM# 1309 5 DOLLARS**
25.00 g., 0.925 Silver 0.7435 oz. ASW, 38.61 mm. **Ruler:** Elizabeth II **Rev:** Cats at night

| Date | Mintage | VF20 | XF40 | MS60 | MS63 | MS65 |
|---|---|---|---|---|---|---|
| 2010 | 2,000 | PF65 75.00 | | | | |

**KM# 1310 5 DOLLARS**
25.00 g., 0.999 Silver 0.803 oz. ASW, 30x38 mm. **Ruler:** Elizabeth II **Subject:** Patron saints **Rev:** St. Helena **Shape:** Vertical rectangle

| Date | Mintage | VF20 | XF40 | MS60 | MS63 | MS65 |
|---|---|---|---|---|---|---|
| 2010 | 2,500 | PF65 75.00 | | | | |

**KM# 1311 5 DOLLARS**
25.00 g., 0.999 Silver 0.803 oz. ASW, 30x38 mm. **Ruler:** Elizabeth II **Subject:** Patron Saints **Rev:** St. Constantine **Shape:** Vertical rectangle

| Date | Mintage | VF20 | XF40 | MS60 | MS63 | MS65 |
|---|---|---|---|---|---|---|
| 2010 | 2,500 | PF65 75.00 | | | | |

**KM# 1334 5 DOLLARS**
Silver, 40 mm. **Ruler:** Elizabeth II **Subject:** 2nd Crusade

| Date | Mintage | VF20 | XF40 | MS60 | MS63 | MS65 |
|---|---|---|---|---|---|---|
| 2010 Antique patina | — | — | — | — | 100 | — |

**KM# 1335 5 DOLLARS**
Silver, 40 mm. **Ruler:** Elizabeth II **Subject:** 3rd Crusade

| Date | Mintage | VF20 | XF40 | MS60 | MS63 | MS65 |
|---|---|---|---|---|---|---|
| 2010 Antique patina | — | — | — | — | 100 | — |

**KM# 1336 5 DOLLARS**
Silver **Ruler:** Elizabeth II **Subject:** 4th Crusade

| Date | Mintage | VF20 | XF40 | MS60 | MS63 | MS65 |
|---|---|---|---|---|---|---|
| 2010 Antique patina | — | — | — | — | 100 | — |

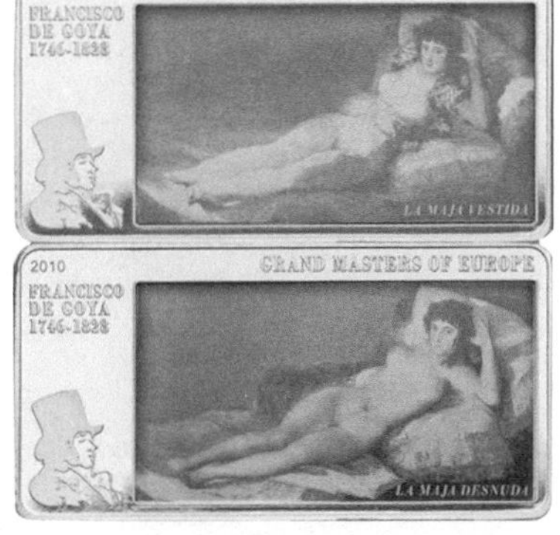


**KM# 1337 5 DOLLARS**
Silver **Ruler:** Elizabeth II **Subject:** Clothed and nude Maya **Shape:** Rectangle **Note:** Detachable clothing over image.

| Date | Mintage | VF20 | XF40 | MS60 | MS63 | MS65 |
|---|---|---|---|---|---|---|
| 2010 | — | PF65 80.00 | | | | |

**KM# 1338 5 DOLLARS**
Silver **Ruler:** Elizabeth II **Subject:** Lubek

| Date | Mintage | VF20 | XF40 | MS60 | MS63 | MS65 |
|---|---|---|---|---|---|---|
| 2010 Antique patina | — | — | — | — | 100 | — |

**KM# 1339 5 DOLLARS**
Silver **Ruler:** Elizabeth II **Subject:** Zutphen

| Date | Mintage | VF20 | XF40 | MS60 | MS63 | MS65 |
|---|---|---|---|---|---|---|
| 2010 Antque patina | — | — | — | — | 100 | — |

**KM# 1340 5 DOLLARS**
Silver **Ruler:** Elizabeth II **Subject:** Trafalgar **Rev:** HMS Victory in color

| Date | Mintage | VF20 | XF40 | MS60 | MS63 | MS65 |
|---|---|---|---|---|---|---|
| 2010 | — | PF65 80.00 | | | | |

**KM# 1429 5 DOLLARS**
Silver, 38.61 mm. **Ruler:** Elizabeth II **Rev:** Boticelli's Natalis Domini, partially gilt, crystal inserts above **Shape:** Half-circle

| Date | Mintage | VF20 | XF40 | MS60 | MS63 | MS65 |
|---|---|---|---|---|---|---|
| 2010 | — | PF65 75.00 | | | | |

**KM# 1530 5 DOLLARS**
0.50 g., 1.000 Gold, 11 mm. **Ruler:** Elizabeth II **Subject:** Rose of Dubai

| Date | Mintage | VF20 | XF40 | MS60 | MS63 | MS65 |
|---|---|---|---|---|---|---|
| 2010 | — | PF65 70.00 | | | | |

**KM# 1531 5 DOLLARS**
0.50 g., 0.9999 Gold, 11 mm. **Ruler:** Elizabeth II **Subject:** Mexican Gold

| Date | Mintage | VF20 | XF40 | MS60 | MS63 | MS65 |
|---|---|---|---|---|---|---|
| 2010 | Est. 5000 | PF65 50.00 | | | | |

**KM# 1532 5 DOLLARS**
0.50 g., 0.999 Gold, 11 mm. **Ruler:** Elizabeth II **Subject:** St. George and the Dragon

| Date | Mintage | VF20 | XF40 | MS60 | MS63 | MS65 |
|---|---|---|---|---|---|---|
| 2010 | Est. 10000 | PF65 50.00 | | | | |

**KM# 1617 5 DOLLARS**
25.00 g., 0.925 Silver 0.7435 oz. ASW, 40 mm. **Ruler:** Elizabeth II **Subject:** Kaliningrad (Koingsberg) **Rev:** Copper-plated knight standing at left, town view at right

| Date | Mintage | VF20 | XF40 | MS60 | MS63 | MS65 |
|---|---|---|---|---|---|---|
| 2010 Antique patina | — | — | — | — | 60.00 | — |

**KM# 1637 5 DOLLARS**
25.00 g., 0.999 Silver 0.803 oz. ASW partially gilt, 30x35 mm. **Ruler:** Elizabeth II **Subject:** Vatican Art **Rev:** St. Peter sculpture **Shape:** Vertical rectangle

| Date | Mintage | VF20 | XF40 | MS60 | MS63 | MS65 |
|---|---|---|---|---|---|---|
| 2010 | 5,000 | PF65 120 | | | | |

**KM# 1261 5 DOLLARS**
25.00 g., 0.925 Silver 0.7435 oz. ASW, 38.61 mm. **Ruler:** Elizabeth II **Subject:** Flowers - Daisy

| Date | Mintage | VF20 | XF40 | MS60 | MS63 | MS65 |
|---|---|---|---|---|---|---|
| 2011 | 2,500 | PF65 75.00 | | | | |

**KM# 1262 5 DOLLARS**
25.00 g., 0.925 Silver 0.7435 oz. ASW, 38.61 mm. **Ruler:** Elizabeth II **Subject:** Hollywood Stars - Sophia Loren

| Date | Mintage | VF20 | XF40 | MS60 | MS63 | MS65 |
|---|---|---|---|---|---|---|
| 2011 | 2,500 | PF65 55.00 | | | | |

**KM# 1263 5 DOLLARS**
25.00 g., 0.925 Silver 0.7435 oz. ASW, 38.61 mm. **Ruler:** Elizabeth II **Subject:** Hollywood Stars - Elizabeth Taylor

| Date | Mintage | VF20 | XF40 | MS60 | MS63 | MS65 |
|---|---|---|---|---|---|---|
| 2011 | 2,500 | PF65 55.00 | | | | |

**KM# 1264 5 DOLLARS**
25.00 g., 0.925 Silver 0.7435 oz. ASW, 38.61 mm. **Ruler:** Elizabeth II **Subject:** Hollywood Stars - Marylin Monroe

| Date | Mintage | VF20 | XF40 | MS60 | MS63 | MS65 |
|---|---|---|---|---|---|---|
| 2011 | 2,500 | PF65 85.00 | | | | |

**KM# 1265 5 DOLLARS**
25.00 g., 0.925 Silver 0.7435 oz. ASW, 38.61 mm. **Ruler:** Elizabeth II **Subject:** Terminator-2, 20th Anniversary **Rev:** Walking through flames

| Date | Mintage | VF20 | XF40 | MS60 | MS63 | MS65 |
|---|---|---|---|---|---|---|
| 2011 | — | PF65 60.00 | | | | |

**KM# 1266 5 DOLLARS**
25.00 g., 0.925 Silver 0.7435 oz. ASW, 38.61 mm. **Ruler:** Elizabeth II **Subject:** Terminator-2, 20th Anniversary **Rev:** Riding motorcycle

| Date | Mintage | VF20 | XF40 | MS60 | MS63 | MS65 |
|---|---|---|---|---|---|---|
| 2011 | — | PF65 60.00 | | | | |

**KM# 1267 5 DOLLARS**
25.00 g., 0.925 Silver 0.7435 oz. ASW **Ruler:** Elizabeth II **Subject:** Terminator-2, 20th Anniversary **Rev:** Head shot **Shape:** 38.61

| Date | Mintage | VF20 | XF40 | MS60 | MS63 | MS65 |
|---|---|---|---|---|---|---|
| 2011 | — | PF65 60.00 | | | | |

**KM# 1287 5 DOLLARS**
31.10 g., 0.925 Silver 0.9249 oz. ASW, 38.6 mm. **Ruler:** Elizabeth II **Subject:** Scent of Austalia - Eucalyptus **Rev:** Koala, eucalyptus leaves and gum berries

| Date | Mintage | VF20 | XF40 | MS60 | MS63 | MS65 |
|---|---|---|---|---|---|---|
| 2011 | 2,500 | — | — | — | — | 100 |

**KM# 1314 5 DOLLARS**
25.00 g., 0.925 Silver 0.7435 oz. ASW, 38.61 mm. **Ruler:** Elizabeth II **Subject:** Marilyn Monroe, 85th Birthday

| Date | Mintage | VF20 | XF40 | MS60 | MS63 | MS65 |
|---|---|---|---|---|---|---|
| 2011 | 1,926 | PF65 95.00 | | | | |

**KM# 1353 5 DOLLARS**
25.00 g., 0.925 Silver 0.7435 oz. ASW, 30x38 mm. **Ruler:** Elizabeth II **Subject:** Patron Saints **Rev:** St. Mary Magalene **Shape:** Vertical rectangle

| Date | Mintage | VF20 | XF40 | MS60 | MS63 | MS65 |
|---|---|---|---|---|---|---|
| 2011 | — | PF65 75.00 | | | | |

**KM# 1355 5 DOLLARS**
25.00 g., 0.925 Silver 0.7435 oz. ASW, 30x38 mm. **Ruler:** Elizabeth II **Subject:** Patron Saints **Rev:** St. Catherine Icon **Shape:** Vertical rectangle

| Date | Mintage | VF20 | XF40 | MS60 | MS63 | MS65 |
|---|---|---|---|---|---|---|
| 2011 | — | PF65 75.00 | | | | |

**KM# 1357 5 DOLLARS**
25.00 g., Silver, 30x38 mm. **Ruler:** Elizabeth II **Subject:** Patrol Saints **Rev:** St. Oleg Icon **Shape:** Vertical rectangle

| Date | Mintage | VF20 | XF40 | MS60 | MS63 | MS65 |
|---|---|---|---|---|---|---|
| 2011 | — | PF65 75.00 | | | | |

**KM# 1358 5 DOLLARS**
25.00 g., 0.925 Silver 0.7435 oz. ASW, 30x38 mm. **Ruler:** Elizabeth II **Subject:** Patron Saints **Rev:** St. Vladimir Icon **Shape:** Vertical rectangle

| Date | Mintage | VF20 | XF40 | MS60 | MS63 | MS65 |
|---|---|---|---|---|---|---|
| 2011 | — | PF65 75.00 | | | | |

**KM# 1361 5 DOLLARS**
31.11 g., 0.999 Silver 0.999 oz. ASW, 38.61 mm. **Ruler:** Elizabeth II **Subject:** Soyuzmultfilm 75th Anniversary - Winnie the Pooh **Rev:** Winnie the Pooh in color **Edge:** Reeded

| Date | Mintage | VF20 | XF40 | MS60 | MS63 | MS65 |
|---|---|---|---|---|---|---|
| 2011 | 2,000 | PF65 90.00 | | | | |

**KM# 1362 5 DOLLARS**
31.11 g., 0.999 Silver 0.999 oz. ASW, 38.61 mm. **Ruler:** Elizabeth II **Subject:** Soyuzmultfilm 75th Anniversary - Winnie the Pooh **Rev:** Piglet in color **Edge:** Reeded

| Date | Mintage | VF20 | XF40 | MS60 | MS63 | MS65 |
|---|---|---|---|---|---|---|
| 2011 | 2,000 | PF65 85.00 | | | | |

**KM# 1363 5 DOLLARS**
31.11 g., 0.999 Silver 0.999 oz. ASW, 38.61 mm. **Ruler:** Elizabeth II **Subject:** Soyuzmultfilm 75th Anniversary - Winnie the Pooh **Rev:** Owl in color **Edge:** Reeded

| Date | Mintage | VF20 | XF40 | MS60 | MS63 | MS65 |
|---|---|---|---|---|---|---|
| 2011 | 2,000 | PF65 85.00 | | | | |

**KM# 1364 5 DOLLARS**
31.11 g., 0.999 Silver 0.999 oz. ASW, 38.61 mm. **Ruler:** Elizabeth II **Subject:** Soyuzmultfilm 75th Anniversary - Winnie the Pooh **Rev:** Eyore in color **Edge:** Reeded

| Date | Mintage | VF20 | XF40 | MS60 | MS63 | MS65 |
|---|---|---|---|---|---|---|
| 2011 | 2,000 | PF65 85.00 | | | | |

**KM# 1365 5 DOLLARS**
31.11 g., 0.999 Silver 0.999 oz. ASW, 38.61 mm. **Ruler:** Elizabeth II **Subject:** Soyuzmultfilm 75th Anniversary - Winnie the Pooh **Rev:** Rabbit in color **Edge:** Reeded

| Date | Mintage | VF20 | XF40 | MS60 | MS63 | MS65 |
|---|---|---|---|---|---|---|
| 2011 | 2,000 | PF65 85.00 | | | | |

**KM# 1367 5 DOLLARS**
31.11 g., 0.999 Silver 0.999 oz. ASW, 38.61 mm. **Ruler:** Elizabeth II **Subject:** Soyuzmultfilm 75th Anniversary - Little Boy and Karlsson-on-the-Roof **Rev:** Little Boy and dog in color **Edge:** Reeded

| Date | Mintage | VF20 | XF40 | MS60 | MS63 | MS65 |
|---|---|---|---|---|---|---|
| 2011 | 2,000 | PF65 85.00 | | | | |

**KM# 1368 5 DOLLARS**
31.11 g., 0.999 Silver 0.999 oz. ASW, 38.61 mm. **Ruler:** Elizabeth II **Subject:** Soyuzmultfilm 75th Anniversary - Little Boy and Karlsson-on-the-Roof **Rev:** Karlsson in color **Edge:** Reeded

| Date | Mintage | VF20 | XF40 | MS60 | MS63 | MS65 |
|---|---|---|---|---|---|---|
| 2011 | 2,000 | PF65 90.00 | | | | |

**KM# 1369 5 DOLLARS**
31.11 g., 0.999 Silver 0.999 oz. ASW, 38.61 mm. **Ruler:** Elizabeth II **Subject:** Soyuzmultfilm 75th Anniversary - Little Boy and Karlsson-on-the-Roof **Rev:** Freken Bok in color **Edge:** Reeded

| Date | Mintage | VF20 | XF40 | MS60 | MS63 | MS65 |
|---|---|---|---|---|---|---|
| 2011 | 2,000 | PF65 90.00 | | | | |

**KM# 1371 5 DOLLARS**
31.11 g., 0.999 Silver 0.999 oz. ASW, 38.61 mm. **Ruler:** Elizabeth II **Subject:** Soyuzmultfilm 75th Anniversary - Cheburashka and Crocodile Gena **Rev:** Cheburashka with orange in color **Edge:** Reeded

| Date | Mintage | VF20 | XF40 | MS60 | MS63 | MS65 |
|---|---|---|---|---|---|---|
| 2011 | 2,000 | PF65 85.00 | | | | |

**KM# 1372 5 DOLLARS**
31.11 g., 0.999 Silver 0.999 oz. ASW, 38.61 mm. **Ruler:** Elizabeth II **Subject:** Soyuzmultfilm 75th Anniversary - Cheburashka and Crocodile Gena **Rev:** Madame Shapoklyak and dog in color **Edge:** Reeded

| Date | Mintage | VF20 | XF40 | MS60 | MS63 | MS65 |
|---|---|---|---|---|---|---|
| 2011 | 2,000 | PF65 90.00 | | | | |

**KM# 1373 5 DOLLARS**
31.11 g., 0.999 Silver 0.999 oz. ASW, 38.61 mm. **Ruler:** Elizabeth II **Subject:** Soyuzmultfilm 75th Anniversary - Cheburashka and Crocodile Gena **Rev:** Crocodile Gena in color **Edge:** Reeded

| Date | Mintage | VF20 | XF40 | MS60 | MS63 | MS65 |
|---|---|---|---|---|---|---|
| 2011 | 2,000 | PF65 85.00 | | | | |

**KM# 1374 5 DOLLARS**
31.11 g., 0.999 Silver 0.999 oz. ASW, 38.61 mm. **Ruler:** Elizabeth II **Subject:** Soyuzmultfilm 75th Anniversary - Hedgehog in a fog **Rev:** Hedgehog in a fog in color **Edge:** Reeded

| Date | Mintage | VF20 | XF40 | MS60 | MS63 | MS65 |
|---|---|---|---|---|---|---|
| 2011 | 2,000 | PF65 90.00 | | | | |

**KM# 1380 5 DOLLARS**
Silver, 30x28.5 mm. **Ruler:** Elizabeth II **Subject:** Seeds of Love **Rev:** Vine and half of a heart shaped red crystal

| Date | Mintage | VF20 | XF40 | MS60 | MS63 | MS65 |
|---|---|---|---|---|---|---|
| 2011 Antique patina | — | PF65 75.00 | | | | |

**KM# 1381 5 DOLLARS**
20.00 g., 0.925 Silver 0.5948 oz. ASW, 40 mm. **Ruler:** Elizabeth II **Subject:** Muonionalusta Meteor **Obv:** Head with tiara right **Rev:** View of meteor falling and fragment insert

| Date | Mintage | VF20 | XF40 | MS60 | MS63 | MS65 |
|---|---|---|---|---|---|---|
| 2011 | 2,500 | PF65 125 | | | | |

**KM# 1398 5 DOLLARS**
31.14 g., 0.999 Silver 1.000 oz. ASW, 38.61 mm. **Ruler:** Elizabeth II **Subject:** Soyuzmultfilm animation - Cat named Woof **Obv:** Head with crown right **Rev:** Dog and kitten in color **Edge:** Reeded

| Date | Mintage | VF20 | XF40 | MS60 | MS63 | MS65 |
|---|---|---|---|---|---|---|
| 2011 | 2,000 | PF65 90.00 | | | | |

**KM# 1399 5 DOLLARS**
31.14 g., 0.999 Silver 1.000 oz. ASW, 38.61 mm. **Ruler:** Elizabeth II **Subject:** Soyuzmultfilm animation - Umka **Obv:** Head with crown right **Rev:** Polar bear and cub in color **Edge:** Reeded

| Date | Mintage | VF20 | XF40 | MS60 | MS63 | MS65 |
|---|---|---|---|---|---|---|
| 2011 | 2,000 | PF65 90.00 | | | | |

**KM# 1400 5 DOLLARS**
31.14 g., 0.999 Silver 1.000 oz. ASW, 38.61 mm. **Ruler:** Elizabeth II **Subject:** Soyuzmultfilm animation - Cat named Woof **Obv:** Head with crown right **Rev:** Cat and dog in color **Edge:** Reeded

| Date | Mintage | VF20 | XF40 | MS60 | MS63 | MS65 |
|---|---|---|---|---|---|---|
| 2011 | 2,000 | PF65 90.00 | | | | |

**KM# 1401 5 DOLLARS**
31.14 g., 0.999 Silver 1.000 oz. ASW, 38.61 mm. **Ruler:** Elizabeth II **Subject:** Soyuzmultfilm animation - Lion and turtle **Obv:** Head with crown right **Rev:** Turtle and lion **Edge:** Reeded

| Date | Mintage | VF20 | XF40 | MS60 | MS63 | MS65 |
|---|---|---|---|---|---|---|
| 2011 | 2,000 | PF65 90.00 | | | | |

**KM# 1406 5 DOLLARS**
31.10 g., 0.925 Silver 0.9249 oz. ASW, 35x35 mm. **Ruler:** Elizabeth II **Subject:** Hieronymus Bosch, pater **Rev:** The Garden (of Eden), in color **Shape:** Square

| Date | Mintage | VF20 | XF40 | MS60 | MS63 | MS65 |
|---|---|---|---|---|---|---|
| 2011 | 500 | PF65 300 | | | | |

**KM# 1409 5 DOLLARS**
31.11 g., 0.999 Silver 0.999 oz. ASW, 38.61 mm. **Ruler:** Elizabeth II **Subject:** Holidays of Bonifaciya **Rev:** Lion in color

| Date | Mintage | VF20 | XF40 | MS60 | MS63 | MS65 |
|---|---|---|---|---|---|---|
| 2011 | 2,000 | PF65 100 | | | | |

**KM# 1410 5 DOLLARS**
31.11 g., 0.999 Silver 0.999 oz. ASW, 38.61 mm. **Ruler:** Elizabeth II **Subject:** Soyuzmultfilm Anniversary - Old dog and wolf **Rev:** Wolf dog in color

| Date | Mintage | VF20 | XF40 | MS60 | MS63 | MS65 |
|---|---|---|---|---|---|---|
| 2011 | 2,000 | PF65 100 | | | | |

**KM# 1417 5 DOLLARS**
155.50 g., 0.999 Silver 4.9944 oz. ASW, 65 mm. **Ruler:** Elizabeth II **Subject:** Brothers Grimm - Bremen Town Musicians **Rev:** Troubador and animals on cart

| Date | Mintage | VF20 | XF40 | MS60 | MS63 | MS65 |
|---|---|---|---|---|---|---|
| 2011 | 500 | PF65 250 | | | | |

**KM# 1418 5 DOLLARS**
31.11 g., 0.999 Silver 0.999 oz. ASW, 38.61 mm. **Ruler:** Elizabeth II **Subject:** Brothers Grimm - Bremen Town Musicians **Rev:** Troubador in color

| Date | Mintage | VF20 | XF40 | MS60 | MS63 | MS65 |
|---|---|---|---|---|---|---|
| 2011 | 2,000 | PF65 100 | | | | |

**KM# 1419 5 DOLLARS**
31.11 g., 0.999 Silver 0.999 oz. ASW, 38.61 mm. **Ruler:** Elizabeth II **Subject:** Brothers Grimm - Bremen Town Musicians **Rev:** Musical coach in color

| Date | Mintage | VF20 | XF40 | MS60 | MS63 | MS65 |
|---|---|---|---|---|---|---|
| 2011 | 2,000 | PF65 100 | | | | |

**KM# 1420 5 DOLLARS**
31.11 g., 0.999 Silver 0.999 oz. ASW, 38.61 mm. **Ruler:** Elizabeth II **Subject:** Brothers Grimm - Bremen Town Musicians **Rev:** Queen and cannoner in color

| Date | Mintage | VF20 | XF40 | MS60 | MS63 | MS65 |
|---|---|---|---|---|---|---|
| 2011 | 2,000 | PF65 100 | | | | |

**KM# 1421 5 DOLLARS**
31.11 g., 0.999 Silver 0.999 oz. ASW, 38.61 mm. **Ruler:** Elizabeth II **Subject:** Brothers Grimm - Bremen Town Musicians **Rev:** Polynesian dancers in color

| Date | Mintage | VF20 | XF40 | MS60 | MS63 | MS65 |
|---|---|---|---|---|---|---|
| 2011 | 2,000 | PF65 100 | | | | |

**KM# 1422 5 DOLLARS**
31.11 g., 0.999 Silver 0.999 oz. ASW, 38.61 mm. **Ruler:** Elizabeth II **Subject:** Brothers Grimm - Bremen Town Musicians **Rev:** Rock and Roll group in color

| Date | Mintage | VF20 | XF40 | MS60 | MS63 | MS65 |
|---|---|---|---|---|---|---|
| 2011 | 2,000 | PF65 100 | | | | |

**KM# 1427 5 DOLLARS**
25.00 g., 0.925 Silver 0.7435 oz. ASW, 38.61 mm. **Ruler:** Elizabeth II **Subject:** 5th Crusade **Rev:** John of Brienne

| Date | Mintage | VF20 | XF40 | MS60 | MS63 | MS65 |
|---|---|---|---|---|---|---|
| 2011 Antique patina | 1,000 | PF65 75.00 | | | | |

**KM# 1431 5 DOLLARS**
Silver, 38.61 mm. **Ruler:** Elizabeth II **Subject:** Muonionalusta meteorite **Rev:** Meteorite fragment flying over forest lake

| Date | Mintage | VF20 | XF40 | MS60 | MS63 | MS65 |
|---|---|---|---|---|---|---|
| 2011 | — | PF65 125 | | | | |

**KM# 1503 5 DOLLARS**
145.00 g., Copper Plated Tombac, 65 mm. **Ruler:** Elizabeth II **Subject:** Elizabeth II, 60th anniversary of reign **Rev:** Elizabeth II photo in color by Julian Calder

| Date | Mintage | VF20 | XF40 | MS60 | MS63 | MS65 |
|---|---|---|---|---|---|---|
| 2011 | Est. 2012 | PF65 45.00 | | | | |

**KM# 1504 5 DOLLARS**
0.50 g., 0.999 Gold, 11 mm. **Ruler:** Elizabeth II **Rev:** Tiki Art Tangaroa

| Date | Mintage | VF20 | XF40 | MS60 | MS63 | MS65 |
|---|---|---|---|---|---|---|
| 2011 | Est. 10000 | PF65 55.00 | | | | |

**KM# 1533 5 DOLLARS**
0.50 g., 1.000 Gold, 11 mm. **Ruler:** Elizabeth II **Subject:** 20 Years of Ballerina

| Date | Mintage | VF20 | XF40 | MS60 | MS63 | MS65 |
|---|---|---|---|---|---|---|
| 2011 | Est. 5000 | PF65 50.00 | | | | |

**KM# 1376 5 DOLLARS**
25.00 g., 0.925 Silver 0.7435 oz. ASW, 45x30 mm. **Ruler:** Elizabeth II **Obv:** Head with tiara right **Rev:** Titanic sailing left in color, coal fragment insert **Shape:** Horizontal oval

| Date | Mintage | VF20 | XF40 | MS60 | MS63 | MS65 |
|---|---|---|---|---|---|---|
| 2012 | 2,012 | PF65 70.00 | | | | |

**KM# 1377 5 DOLLARS**
20.00 g., 0.999 Silver 0.6424 oz. ASW, 30x43 mm. **Ruler:** Elizabeth II **Subject:** Imperial Egg - Swan **Obv:** Head with tiara right **Rev:** Pink coloring

| Date | Mintage | VF20 | XF40 | MS60 | MS63 | MS65 |
|---|---|---|---|---|---|---|
| 2012 | — | PF65 65.00 | | | | |

**KM# 1378 5 DOLLARS**
20.00 g., 0.999 Silver 0.6424 oz. ASW, 30x43 mm. **Ruler:** Elizabeth II **Subject:** Imperial egg - Elephant **Obv:** Head with tiara right **Rev:** Blue coloring

| Date | Mintage | VF20 | XF40 | MS60 | MS63 | MS65 |
|---|---|---|---|---|---|---|
| 2012 | — | PF65 65.00 | | | | |

**KM# 1379 5 DOLLARS**
20.00 g., 0.999 Silver 0.6424 oz. ASW, 30x43 mm. **Ruler:** Elizabeth II **Subject:** Imperial egg **Obv:** Head in tiara right **Rev:** Multicolor closonne

| Date | Mintage | VF20 | XF40 | MS60 | MS63 | MS65 |
|---|---|---|---|---|---|---|
| 2012 | — | PF65 65.00 | | | | |

**KM# 1382 5 DOLLARS**
31.11 g., 0.999 Silver 0.999 oz. ASW, 38.61 mm. **Ruler:** Elizabeth II **Subject:** History of Egypt **Rev:** Tutankhamun's gold mask in color

| Date | Mintage | VF20 | XF40 | MS60 | MS63 | MS65 |
|---|---|---|---|---|---|---|
| 2012 | — | PF65 85.00 | | | | |

**KM# 1390 5 DOLLARS**
31.11 g., 0.999 Silver 0.999 oz. ASW, 38.61 mm. **Ruler:** Elizabeth II **Subject:** Titanic, 100th Anniversary **Rev:** Titanic side view sailing left, recovered coal fragment insert

| Date | Mintage | VF20 | XF40 | MS60 | MS63 | MS65 |
|---|---|---|---|---|---|---|
| 2012 | — | PF65 125 | | | | |

**KM# 1395 5 DOLLARS**
31.11 g., 0.999 Silver 0.999 oz. ASW, 38.61 mm. **Ruler:** Elizabeth II **Obv:** Head with tiara right **Rev:** Cherry Blossom in color

| Date | Mintage | VF20 | XF40 | MS60 | MS63 | MS65 |
|---|---|---|---|---|---|---|
| 2012 | — | PF65 60.00 | | | | |

**KM# 1425 5 DOLLARS**
20.00 g., 0.925 Silver 0.5948 oz. ASW, 30x35 mm. **Ruler:** Elizabeth II **Subject:** Love conquers all **Rev:** Roman Cupids by Caravaggio **Shape:** Vertical oval

| Date | Mintage | VF20 | XF40 | MS60 | MS63 | MS65 |
|---|---|---|---|---|---|---|
| 2012 | 1,000 | PF65 80.00 | | | | |

**KM# 1437 5 DOLLARS**
25.00 g., 0.925 Silver 0.7435 oz. ASW, 38.61 mm. **Ruler:** Elizabeth II **Subject:** Hollywood Stars - Marlene Dietrich

| Date | Mintage | VF20 | XF40 | MS60 | MS63 | MS65 |
|---|---|---|---|---|---|---|
| 2012 | 2,500 | PF65 65.00 | | | | |

**KM# 1438 5 DOLLARS**
25.00 g., 0.925 Silver 0.7435 oz. ASW, 38.61 mm. **Ruler:** Elizabeth II **Subject:** Hollywood Stars - Anita Ekberg

| Date | Mintage | VF20 | XF40 | MS60 | MS63 | MS65 |
|---|---|---|---|---|---|---|
| 2012 | 2,500 | PF65 65.00 | | | | |

**KM# 1439 5 DOLLARS**
25.00 g., 0.925 Silver 0.7435 oz. ASW, 38.61 mm. **Ruler:** Elizabeth II **Subject:** Hollywood Stars - Robert Mitchum

| Date | Mintage | VF20 | XF40 | MS60 | MS63 | MS65 |
|---|---|---|---|---|---|---|
| 2012 | 2,500 | PF65 65.00 | | | | |

**KM# 1440 5 DOLLARS**
20.00 g., 0.925 Silver 0.5948 oz. ASW, 38.6 mm. **Ruler:** Elizabeth II **Subject:** Seymchan Meteorite **Rev:** Meteorite fragment in color scene

| Date | Mintage | VF20 | XF40 | MS60 | MS63 | MS65 |
|---|---|---|---|---|---|---|
| 2012 | 2,500 | PF65 125 | | | | |

**KM# 1446 5 DOLLARS**
31.11 g., 0.999 Silver 0.999 oz. ASW, 38.61 mm. **Ruler:** Elizabeth II **Subject:** Yes of the Dragon **Rev:** Golden dragon

| Date | Mintage | VF20 | XF40 | MS60 | MS63 | MS65 |
|---|---|---|---|---|---|---|
| 2012 | — | PF65 165 | | | | |

**KM# 1447 5 DOLLARS**
31.11 g., 0.999 Silver 0.999 oz. ASW, 38.61 mm. **Ruler:** Elizabeth II **Subject:** Year of the Dragon **Rev:** Blue dragon

| Date | Mintage | VF20 | XF40 | MS60 | MS63 | MS65 |
|---|---|---|---|---|---|---|
| 2012 | — | PF65 165 | | | | |

**KM# 1450 5 DOLLARS**
20.00 g., 0.925 Silver 0.5948 oz. ASW, 38.61 mm. **Ruler:** Elizabeth II **Subject:** PGA Tour - Golf ball insert

| Date | Mintage | VF20 | XF40 | MS60 | MS63 | MS65 |
|---|---|---|---|---|---|---|
| 2012 | 2,500 | PF65 55.00 | | | | |

**KM# 1451 5 DOLLARS**
20.00 g., 0.925 Silver 0.5948 oz. ASW, 38.61 mm. **Ruler:** Elizabeth II **Subject:** Amerigo Vespucci, 500th Anniversary of voyage of discovery **Rev:** Sailing ship

| Date | Mintage | VF20 | XF40 | MS60 | MS63 | MS65 |
|---|---|---|---|---|---|---|
| 2012 | 2,500 | PF65 75.00 | | | | |

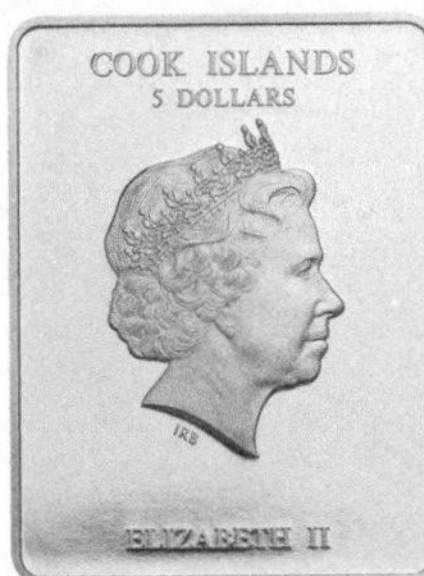

**KM# 1452 5 DOLLARS**

25.00 g., 0.925 Silver 0.7435 oz. ASW, 30x38 mm. **Ruler:** Elizabeth II **Rev:** Nativity of the Blessed Virgin Mary **Shape:** Vertical rectangle

| Date | Mintage | VF20 | XF40 | MS60 | MS63 | MS65 |
|---|---|---|---|---|---|---|
| 2012 | 2,500 | PF65 100 | | | | |

**KM# 1453 5 DOLLARS**

31.11 g., 0.999 Silver 0.999 oz. ASW, 38.61 mm. **Ruler:** Elizabeth II **Subject:** Year of the Dragon **Rev:** Color dragon

| Date | Mintage | VF20 | XF40 | MS60 | MS63 | MS65 |
|---|---|---|---|---|---|---|
| 2012 | — | PF65 100 | | | | |

**KM# 1587 5 DOLLARS**

0.50 g., 0.585 Gold With 24K Gold-Plating, 11 mm. **Ruler:** Elizabeth II **Subject:** Smallest Gold Coins - James Cook

| Date | Mintage | VF20 | XF40 | MS60 | MS63 | MS65 |
|---|---|---|---|---|---|---|
| 2012 | Est. 10000 | PF65 32.00 | | | | |

**KM# 1594 5 DOLLARS**

20.00 g., 0.925 Silver 0.5948 oz. ASW, 38.61 mm. **Ruler:** Elizabeth II **Subject:** Black Squirrel

| Date | Mintage | VF20 | XF40 | MS60 | MS63 | MS65 |
|---|---|---|---|---|---|---|
| 2013 | Est. 999 | PF65 75.00 | | | | |

**KM# 1605 5 DOLLARS**

0.50 g., 0.585 Gold AGW with 24Kt plating, 11 mm. **Ruler:** Elizabeth II **Subject:** Zeppelin

| Date | Mintage | VF20 | XF40 | MS60 | MS63 | MS65 |
|---|---|---|---|---|---|---|
| 2013 | Est. 5000 | PF65 50.00 | | | | |

**KM# 1606 5 DOLLARS**

0.50 g., 0.585 Gold AGW with 24kt plating, 11 mm. **Ruler:** Elizabeth II **Subject:** Ned Kelly

| Date | Mintage | VF20 | XF40 | MS60 | MS63 | MS65 |
|---|---|---|---|---|---|---|
| 2013 | Est. 5000 | PF65 50.00 | | | | |

**KM# 1608 5 DOLLARS**

0.50 g., 0.999 Gold AGW, 11 mm. **Ruler:** Elizabeth II **Subject:** Vincent van Gogh

| Date | Mintage | VF20 | XF40 | MS60 | MS63 | MS65 |
|---|---|---|---|---|---|---|
| 2013 | Est. 5000 | PF65 50.00 | | | | |

**KM# 1609 5 DOLLARS**

0.50 g., 0.999 Gold AGW, 11 mm. **Ruler:** Elizabeth II **Subject:** Buffalo, 100th Anniversary

| Date | Mintage | VF20 | XF40 | MS60 | MS63 | MS65 |
|---|---|---|---|---|---|---|
| 2013 | Est. 5000 | PF65 50.00 | | | | |

**KM# 1610 5 DOLLARS**

0.50 g., 0.999 Gold AGW, 11 mm. **Ruler:** Elizabeth II **Subject:** Troy

| Date | Mintage | VF20 | XF40 | MS60 | MS63 | MS65 |
|---|---|---|---|---|---|---|
| 2013 | Est. 7500 | PF65 50.00 | | | | |

**KM# 1650 5 DOLLARS**

25.00 g., 0.925 Silver 0.7435 oz. ASW, 38.61 mm. **Ruler:** Elizabeth II **Subject:** Chelyabinsk Meteorite

| Date | Mintage | VF20 | XF40 | MS60 | MS63 | MS65 |
|---|---|---|---|---|---|---|
| 2013 | 2,500 | PF65 75.00 | | | | |

**KM# 1653 5 DOLLARS**

25.00 g., 0.925 Silver 0.7435 oz. ASW, 45x30 mm. **Ruler:** Elizabeth II **Rev:** S.S. Republic in color, coal insert **Shape:** Horizontal oval

| Date | Mintage | VF20 | XF40 | MS60 | MS63 | MS65 |
|---|---|---|---|---|---|---|
| 2013 | 5,000 | PF65 45.00 | | | | |

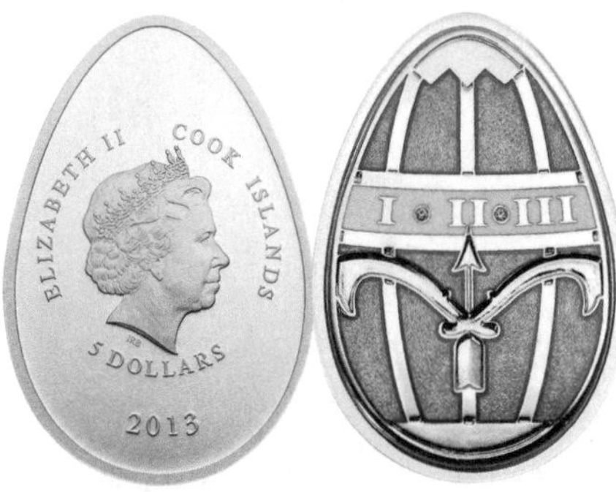

**KM# 1659 5 DOLLARS**

20.00 g., 0.999 Silver 0.6424 oz. ASW **Ruler:** Elizabeth II **Subject:** Easter Egg cloisonné - Time **Edge:** 30x43 **Shape:** Egg

| Date | Mintage | VF20 | XF40 | MS60 | MS63 | MS65 |
|---|---|---|---|---|---|---|
| 2013 | 2,500 | PF65 75.00 | | | | |

**KM# 1660 5 DOLLARS**

20.00 g., 0.999 Silver 0.6424 oz. ASW, 30x43 mm. **Ruler:** Elizabeth II **Subject:** Easter Egg cloisonné - Red **Shape:** Egg

| Date | Mintage | VF20 | XF40 | MS60 | MS63 | MS65 |
|---|---|---|---|---|---|---|
| 2013 | 2,500 | PF65 75.00 | | | | |

**KM# 1661 5 DOLLARS**

20.00 g., 0.999 Silver 0.6424 oz. ASW, 30x43 mm. **Ruler:** Elizabeth II **Rev:** Easter Egg cloisonné - Green **Shape:** Egg

| Date | Mintage | VF20 | XF40 | MS60 | MS63 | MS65 |
|---|---|---|---|---|---|---|
| 2013 | 2,500 | PF65 75.00 | | | | |

**KM# 1662 5 DOLLARS**

20.00 g., 0.999 Silver 0.6424 oz. ASW, 30x43 mm. **Ruler:** Elizabeth II **Rev:** Easter Egg cloisonné - White **Shape:** Egg

| Date | Mintage | VF20 | XF40 | MS60 | MS63 | MS65 |
|---|---|---|---|---|---|---|
| 2013 | 2,500 | PF65 75.00 | | | | |

**KM# 473 10 DOLLARS**

20.12 g., Silver, 38.62 mm. **Ruler:** Elizabeth II **Subject:** 2004 Summer Olympics - Athens **Obv:** Crowned bust right **Rev:** Male discus thrower **Edge:** Reeded

| Date | Mintage | VF20 | XF40 | MS60 | MS63 | MS65 |
|---|---|---|---|---|---|---|
| 2001 | — | PF65 37.50 | | | | |

**KM# 549 10 DOLLARS**
10.00 g., 0.9999 Gold 0.3215 oz. AGW, 25 mm. **Ruler:** Elizabeth II **Rev:** Multicolored Mikado Pheasant

| Date | Mintage | VF20 | XF40 | MS60 | MS63 | MS65 |
|---|---|---|---|---|---|---|
| 2001 | 1,000 | **PF65** 600 | | | | |

**KM# 550 10 DOLLARS**
10.00 g., 0.9999 Gold 0.3215 oz. AGW, 25 mm. **Ruler:** Elizabeth II **Rev:** Multicolor black-faced spoonbill

| Date | Mintage | VF20 | XF40 | MS60 | MS63 | MS65 |
|---|---|---|---|---|---|---|
| 2001 | 1,000 | **PF65** 600 | | | | |

**KM# 453 10 DOLLARS**
186.83 g., 0.999 Silver Gilt 6.0007 oz., 89 mm. **Ruler:** Elizabeth II **Obv:** Crowned bust right, unique portrait for Cook Is. **Rev:** Queen Victoria standing with lion **Edge:** Reeded

| Date | Mintage | VF20 | XF40 | MS60 | MS63 | MS65 |
|---|---|---|---|---|---|---|
| 2003 | 198 | **PF65** 375 | | | | |

**KM# 1110 10 DOLLARS**
1.24 g., 0.999 Gold 0.0398 oz. AGW **Ruler:** Elizabeth II **Rev:** Emblem

| Date | Mintage | VF20 | XF40 | MS60 | MS63 | MS65 |
|---|---|---|---|---|---|---|
| 2005 | Est. 8000 | **PF65** 85.00 | | | | |

**KM# 1136 10 DOLLARS**
1.24 g., 0.999 Gold 0.0398 oz. AGW, 13.92 mm. **Ruler:** Elizabeth II **Subject:** Star Wars, 30th Anniversary

| Date | Mintage | VF20 | XF40 | MS60 | MS63 | MS65 |
|---|---|---|---|---|---|---|
| 2005 | 9,999 | **PF63** 85.00 | **PF65** 95.00 | | | |

**KM# 1176 10 DOLLARS**
1.24 g., 0.999 Gold 0.0398 oz. AGW **Ruler:** Elizabeth II **Subject:** Marriage of Prince Charles and Camilla Parker-Bowles

| Date | Mintage | VF20 | XF40 | MS60 | MS63 | MS65 |
|---|---|---|---|---|---|---|
| 2005 | — | **PF63** 85.00 | **PF65** 95.00 | | | |

**KM# 1178 10 DOLLARS**
1.24 g., 0.999 Gold 0.0398 oz. AGW, 13.92 mm. **Ruler:** Elizabeth II **Rev:** Pope John Paul II

| Date | Mintage | VF20 | XF40 | MS60 | MS63 | MS65 |
|---|---|---|---|---|---|---|
| 2005 | — | **PF63** 85.00 | **PF65** 95.00 | | | |

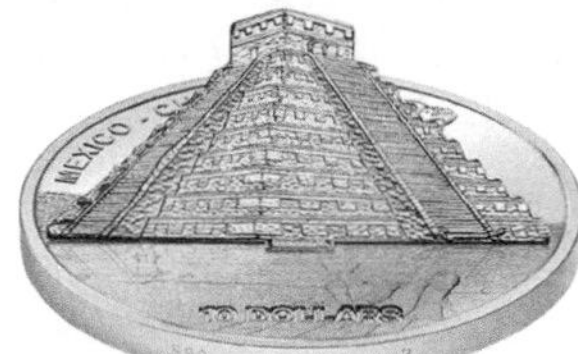

**KM# 582 10 DOLLARS**
31.10 g., 0.999 Silver 0.9989 oz. ASW, 38.6 mm. **Ruler:** Elizabeth II **Rev:** Chichen Itza gilt pop-up

| Date | Mintage | VF20 | XF40 | MS60 | MS63 | MS65 |
|---|---|---|---|---|---|---|
| 2007 | 5,000 | **PF65** 65.00 | | | | |

**KM# 585 10 DOLLARS**
31.10 g., 0.999 Silver 0.9989 oz. ASW, 38.6 mm. **Ruler:** Elizabeth II **Rev:** Easter Island status gilt pop-up

| Date | Mintage | VF20 | XF40 | MS60 | MS63 | MS65 |
|---|---|---|---|---|---|---|
| 2007 | 5,000 | **PF65** 100 | | | | |

**KM# 587 10 DOLLARS**
31.10 g., 0.999 Silver 0.9989 oz. ASW, 38.6 mm. **Ruler:** Elizabeth II **Rev:** Pyrmids gilt pop-up

| Date | Mintage | VF20 | XF40 | MS60 | MS63 | MS65 |
|---|---|---|---|---|---|---|
| 2007 | 5,000 | **PF65** 65.00 | | | | |

**KM# 588 10 DOLLARS**
31.10 g., 0.999 Silver 0.9989 oz. ASW, 38.6 mm. **Ruler:** Elizabeth II **Rev:** Golden Gate Bridge gilt pop-up

| Date | Mintage | VF20 | XF40 | MS60 | MS63 | MS65 |
|---|---|---|---|---|---|---|
| 2007 | 5,000 | **PF65** 65.00 | | | | |

**KM# 589 10 DOLLARS**
31.10 g., 0.999 Silver 0.9989 oz. ASW, 38.6 mm. **Ruler:** Elizabeth II **Rev:** Great Wall of China gilt pop-up

| Date | Mintage | VF20 | XF40 | MS60 | MS63 | MS65 |
|---|---|---|---|---|---|---|
| 2007 | 5,000 | **PF65** 65.00 | | | | |

**KM# 590 10 DOLLARS**
31.10 g., 0.999 Silver 0.9989 oz. ASW, 38.6 mm. **Ruler:** Elizabeth II **Rev:** Sydney Harbor Bridge gilt pop-up

| Date | Mintage | VF20 | XF40 | MS60 | MS63 | MS65 |
|---|---|---|---|---|---|---|
| 2007 | 5,000 | **PF65** 65.00 | | | | |

**KM# 591 10 DOLLARS**
31.10 g., 0.999 Silver 0.9989 oz. ASW, 38.6 mm. **Ruler:** Elizabeth II **Rev:** Machu Pichu gilt pop-up

| Date | Mintage | VF20 | XF40 | MS60 | MS63 | MS65 |
|---|---|---|---|---|---|---|
| 2007 | 5,000 | **PF65** 65.00 | | | | |

**KM# 592 10 DOLLARS**
31.10 g., 0.999 Silver 0.9989 oz. ASW, 38.6 mm. **Ruler:** Elizabeth II **Rev:** Petra Treasury gilt pop-up

| Date | Mintage | VF20 | XF40 | MS60 | MS63 | MS65 |
|---|---|---|---|---|---|---|
| 2007 | 5,000 | **PF65** 65.00 | | | | |

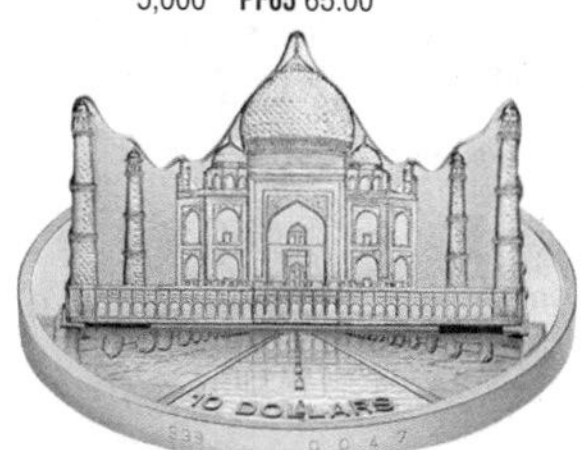

**KM# 593 10 DOLLARS**
31.10 g., 0.999 Silver 0.9989 oz. ASW, 38.6 mm. **Ruler:** Elizabeth II **Rev:** Taj mahal gilt pop-up

| Date | Mintage | VF20 | XF40 | MS60 | MS63 | MS65 |
|---|---|---|---|---|---|---|
| 2007 | 5,000 | **PF65** 65.00 | | | | |

**KM# 1113 10 DOLLARS**
0.50 g., 0.999 Gold, 11 mm. **Ruler:** Elizabeth II **Subject:** Treaty of rome, 50th Anniversary **Rev:** Monaco

| Date | Mintage | VF20 | XF40 | MS60 | MS63 | MS65 |
|---|---|---|---|---|---|---|
| 2007 | Est. 5000 | **PF65** 50.00 | | | | |

**KM# 1171 10 DOLLARS**
0.50 g., 0.999 Gold, 11 mm. **Ruler:** Elizabeth II **Subject:** Treaty of Rome, 50th Anniversary **Rev:** Vatican City

| Date | Mintage | VF20 | XF40 | MS60 | MS63 | MS65 |
|---|---|---|---|---|---|---|
| 2007 | Est. 5000 | **PF65** 50.00 | | | | |

**KM# 1192 10 DOLLARS**
1.24 g., 0.999 Gold 0.0398 oz. AGW, 13.92 mm. **Ruler:** Elizabeth II **Subject:** European Monarchs **Rev:** Elizabeth II

| Date | Mintage | VF20 | XF40 | MS60 | MS63 | MS65 |
|---|---|---|---|---|---|---|
| 2007 | Est. 10000 | **PF65** 85.00 | | | | |

**KM# 1193 10 DOLLARS**
1.24 g., 0.999 Gold 0.0398 oz. AGW **Ruler:** Elizabeth II **Subject:** European Monarchs **Rev:** Juan Carlos I

| Date | Mintage | VF20 | XF40 | MS60 | MS63 | MS65 |
|---|---|---|---|---|---|---|
| 2007 | Est. 10000 | **PF65** 85.00 | | | | |

**KM# 1194 10 DOLLARS**
1.24 g., 0.999 Gold 0.0398 oz. AGW **Ruler:** Elizabeth II **Subject:** European Monarchs **Rev:** Carl XVI Gustaf

| Date | Mintage | VF20 | XF40 | MS60 | MS63 | MS65 |
|---|---|---|---|---|---|---|
| 2007 | Est. 10000 | **PF65** 85.00 | | | | |

**KM# 1195 10 DOLLARS**
1.24 g., Gold, 13.92 mm. **Ruler:** Elizabeth II **Subject:** European Monarchs **Rev:** Beatrix

| Date | Mintage | VF20 | XF40 | MS60 | MS63 | MS65 |
|---|---|---|---|---|---|---|
| 2007 | Est. 10000 | **PF65** 85.00 | | | | |

**KM# 1204 10 DOLLARS**
1.24 g., 0.999 Gold 0.0398 oz. AGW, 13.92 mm. **Ruler:** Elizabeth II **Subject:** Christmas **Rev:** Cherib seated on rock

| Date | Mintage | VF20 | XF40 | MS60 | MS63 | MS65 |
|---|---|---|---|---|---|---|
| 2007 proof | Est. 15000 | **PF65** 85.00 | | | | |

**KM# 619 10 DOLLARS**
31.10 g., 0.999 Silver 0.9989 oz. ASW, 38.6 mm. **Ruler:** Elizabeth II **Rev:** Angor Wat temple gilt pop-up

| Date | Mintage | VF20 | XF40 | MS60 | MS63 | MS65 |
|---|---|---|---|---|---|---|
| 2008 | 5,000 | **PF65** 65.00 | | | | |

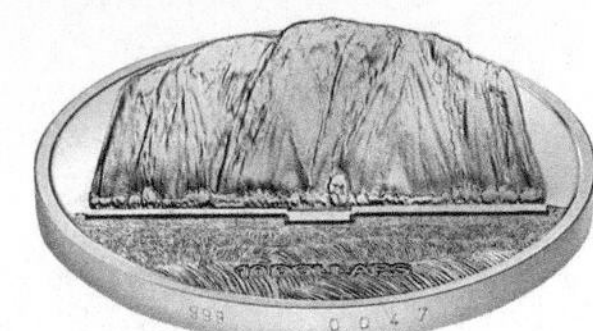

**KM# 620 10 DOLLARS**
31.10 g., 0.999 Silver 0.9989 oz. ASW, 38.6 mm. **Ruler:** Elizabeth II **Rev:** Ayer's Rock gilt pop-up

| Date | Mintage | VF20 | XF40 | MS60 | MS63 | MS65 |
|---|---|---|---|---|---|---|
| 2008 | 5,000 | **PF65** 65.00 | | | | |

**KM# 621 10 DOLLARS**
31.10 g., 0.999 Silver 0.9989 oz. ASW, 38.6 mm. **Ruler:** Elizabeth II **Rev:** Parliament Buildings and Big Ben pop-up

| Date | Mintage | VF20 | XF40 | MS60 | MS63 | MS65 |
|---|---|---|---|---|---|---|
| 2008 | 5,000 | **PF65** 65.00 | | | | |

**KM# 622 10 DOLLARS**
31.10 g., 0.999 Silver 0.9989 oz. ASW, 38.6 mm. **Ruler:** Elizabeth II **Rev:** Mt. Rushmore figures gilt pop-up

| Date | Mintage | VF20 | XF40 | MS60 | MS63 | MS65 |
|---|---|---|---|---|---|---|
| 2008 | 5,000 | **PF65** 65.00 | | | | |

**KM# 623 10 DOLLARS**
31.10 g., 0.999 Silver 0.9989 oz. ASW, 38.6 mm. **Ruler:** Elizabeth II **Rev:** Sydney Opera House gilt pop-up

| Date | Mintage | VF20 | XF40 | MS60 | MS63 | MS65 |
|---|---|---|---|---|---|---|
| 2008 | 5,000 | **PF65** 65.00 | | | | |

**KM# 624 10 DOLLARS**
31.10 g., 0.999 Silver 0.9989 oz. ASW, 38.6 mm. **Ruler:** Elizabeth II **Rev:** Malaysian Twin Towers gilt pop-up

| Date | Mintage | VF20 | XF40 | MS60 | MS63 | MS65 |
|---|---|---|---|---|---|---|
| 2008 | 5,000 | **PF65** 65.00 | | | | |

**KM# 625 10 DOLLARS**
31.10 g., 0.999 Silver 0.9989 oz. ASW, 38.6 mm. **Ruler:** Elizabeth II **Rev:** Sphinx gilt pop-up

| Date | Mintage | VF20 | XF40 | MS60 | MS63 | MS65 |
|---|---|---|---|---|---|---|
| 2008 | 5,000 | **PF65** 65.00 | | | | |

**KM# 626 10 DOLLARS**
31.10 g., 0.999 Silver 0.9989 oz. ASW, 38.6 mm. **Ruler:** Elizabeth II **Rev:** Stonehedge gilt pop-up

| Date | Mintage | VF20 | XF40 | MS60 | MS63 | MS65 |
|---|---|---|---|---|---|---|
| 2008 | 5,000 | **PF65** 65.00 | | | | |

**KM# 627 10 DOLLARS**
62.21 g., 0.999 Silver 1.9979 oz. ASW, 50 mm. **Ruler:** Elizabeth II **Rev:** Tsar Alexander II, multicolor **Note:** Exclusive to the Russian Market.

| Date | Mintage | VF20 | XF40 | MS60 | MS63 | MS65 |
|---|---|---|---|---|---|---|
| 2008 | 500 | **PF65** 350 | | | | |

**KM# 628 10 DOLLARS**
62.21 g., 0.999 Silver 1.9979 oz. ASW **Ruler:** Elizabeth II **Rev:** Tsar Alexi, multicolor **Note:** Exclusive to the Russian Market.

| Date | Mintage | VF20 | XF40 | MS60 | MS63 | MS65 |
|---|---|---|---|---|---|---|
| 2008 | 500 | **PF65** 350 | | | | |

**KM# 629 10 DOLLARS**
62.21 g., 0.999 Silver 1.9979 oz. ASW, 50 mm. **Ruler:** Elizabeth II **Rev:** Tsarina Anna, multicolor

| Date | Mintage | VF20 | XF40 | MS60 | MS63 | MS65 |
|---|---|---|---|---|---|---|
| 2008 | 500 | **PF65** 350 | | | | |

**KM# 630 10 DOLLARS**
62.21 g., 0.999 Silver 1.9979 oz. ASW, 50 mm. **Ruler:** Elizabeth II **Rev:** Tsarina Elizabeth, multicolor

| Date | Mintage | VF20 | XF40 | MS60 | MS63 | MS65 |
|---|---|---|---|---|---|---|
| 2008 | 500 | **PF65** 350 | | | | |

**KM# 631 10 DOLLARS**
62.21 g., 0.999 Silver 1.9979 oz. ASW, 50 mm. **Ruler:** Elizabeth II **Rev:** Tsar Mikhail, multicolor

| Date | Mintage | VF20 | XF40 | MS60 | MS63 | MS65 |
|---|---|---|---|---|---|---|
| 2008 | 500 | **PF65** 350 | | | | |

**KM# 632 10 DOLLARS**
62.21 g., 0.999 Silver 1.9979 oz. ASW, 50 mm. **Ruler:** Elizabeth II **Rev:** Tsar Paul I, multicolor

| Date | Mintage | VF20 | XF40 | MS60 | MS63 | MS65 |
|---|---|---|---|---|---|---|
| 2008 | 500 | **PF65** 350 | | | | |

**KM# 633 10 DOLLARS**
31.10 g., 0.999 Silver 0.9989 oz. ASW, 40 mm. **Ruler:** Elizabeth II **Rev:** Nathan Rothschild bust at right, partially gilt

| Date | Mintage | VF20 | XF40 | MS60 | MS63 | MS65 |
|---|---|---|---|---|---|---|
| 2008 | 10,000 | **PF65** 55.00 | | | | |

**KM# 634 10 DOLLARS**
31.11 g., 0.999 Silver 0.999 oz. ASW, 40 mm. **Ruler:** Elizabeth II **Rev:** Henry Ford at left and Model-A car at right, partially gilt

| Date | Mintage | VF20 | XF40 | MS60 | MS63 | MS65 |
|---|---|---|---|---|---|---|
| 2008 | 10,000 | PF65 55.00 | | | | |

**KM# 635 10 DOLLARS**
31.10 g., 0.999 Silver 0.9989 oz. ASW, 40 mm. **Ruler:** Elizabeth II **Rev:** John D. Rockefeller Sr., bust right, oil derrick, partially gilt.

| Date | Mintage | VF20 | XF40 | MS60 | MS63 | MS65 |
|---|---|---|---|---|---|---|
| 2008 | 10,000 | PF65 60.00 | | | | |

**KM# 704 10 DOLLARS**
1.00 g., 0.999 Gold 0.0321 oz. AGW, 13.9 mm. **Ruler:** Elizabeth II **Subject:** Gorch Fock **Rev:** Sailing vessel right

| Date | Mintage | VF20 | XF40 | MS60 | MS63 | MS65 |
|---|---|---|---|---|---|---|
| 2008 | 15,000 | PF65 70.00 | | | | |

**KM# 705 10 DOLLARS**
62.21 g., 0.999 Silver 1.9981 oz. ASW, 50 mm. **Ruler:** Elizabeth II **Subject:** Kiev Churches **Rev:** Lavra bell tower

| Date | Mintage | VF20 | XF40 | MS60 | MS63 | MS65 |
|---|---|---|---|---|---|---|
| 2008 Proof | 500 | — | — | — | — | 200 |

**KM# 1205 10 DOLLARS**
1.00 g., 0.999 Gold 0.0321 oz. AGW, 13.92 mm. **Ruler:** Elizabeth II **Rev:** Gorch Fock I, 1933

| Date | Mintage | VF20 | XF40 | MS60 | MS63 | MS65 |
|---|---|---|---|---|---|---|
| 2008 | — | PF65 70.00 | | | | |

**KM# 1206 10 DOLLARS**
1.00 g., 0.999 Gold 0.0321 oz. AGW, 13.92 mm. **Ruler:** Elizabeth II **Subject:** Endangered Wildlife **Rev:** Polar Bear

| Date | Mintage | VF20 | XF40 | MS60 | MS63 | MS65 |
|---|---|---|---|---|---|---|
| 2008 | Est. 25000 | PF65 60.00 | | | | |

**KM# 1469 10 DOLLARS**
31.11 g., 0.999 Silver 0.999 oz. ASW with gold pop-up, 38.61 mm. **Ruler:** Elizabeth II **Rev:** Koln Cathedral 4 gr. gold pop-up

| Date | Mintage | VF20 | XF40 | MS60 | MS63 | MS65 |
|---|---|---|---|---|---|---|
| 2008 | Est. 5000 | — | — | — | — | 80.00 |

**KM# 1515 10 DOLLARS**
7.78 g., 0.585 Gold 0.1463 oz. AGW 24K Gold Plating, 25 mm. **Ruler:** Elizabeth II **Subject:** 2008 Vancouver Olympic Games - Transfer Coin

| Date | Mintage | VF20 | XF40 | MS60 | MS63 | MS65 |
|---|---|---|---|---|---|---|
| 2008 | Est. 1000 | PF65 320 | | | | |

**KM# 1543 10 DOLLARS**
28.28 g., 0.925 Silver 0.841 oz. ASW, 38.61 mm. **Ruler:** Elizabeth II **Subject:** Railways - Big Boy

| Date | Mintage | VF20 | XF40 | MS60 | MS63 | MS65 |
|---|---|---|---|---|---|---|
| 2008 | Est. 5000 | PF65 45.00 | | | | |

**KM# 688 10 DOLLARS**
31.11 g., 0.999 Silver 0.999 oz. ASW, 38.6 mm. **Ruler:** Elizabeth II **Subject:** World Monuments - Egypt, Abu Simbel **Rev:** Statues of Ramesses II at Abu Simbel gilt pop-up

| Date | Mintage | VF20 | XF40 | MS60 | MS63 | MS65 |
|---|---|---|---|---|---|---|
| 2009 | Est. 3000 | PF65 75.00 | | | | |

**KM# 689 10 DOLLARS**
31.11 g., 0.999 Silver 0.999 oz. ASW, 38.6 mm. **Ruler:** Elizabeth II **Subject:** World Monuments- France, Arc de Triomphe **Rev:** Arc de Triumph gilt pop-up

| Date | Mintage | VF20 | XF40 | MS60 | MS63 | MS65 |
|---|---|---|---|---|---|---|
| 2009 | Est. 3000 | PF65 75.00 | | | | |

**KM# 690 10 DOLLARS**
31.11 g., 0.999 Silver 0.999 oz. ASW, 38.6 mm. **Ruler:** Elizabeth II **Subject:** Wold Monuments - Turkey, Hagia Sophia **Rev:** Hagia Sofia gilt pop-up

| Date | Mintage | VF20 | XF40 | MS60 | MS63 | MS65 |
|---|---|---|---|---|---|---|
| 2009 | Est. 3000 | PF65 75.00 | | | | |

**KM# 691 10 DOLLARS**
31.11 g., 0.999 Silver 0.999 oz. ASW, 38.6 mm. **Ruler:** Elizabeth II **Subject:** World Monuments - China, Temple of Heaven **Rev:** Temple of Heaven gilt pop-up

| Date | Mintage | VF20 | XF40 | MS60 | MS63 | MS65 |
|---|---|---|---|---|---|---|
| 2009 | — | PF65 75.00 | | | | |

**KM# 692 10 DOLLARS**
31.11 g., 0.999 Silver 0.999 oz. ASW, 38.6 mm. **Ruler:** Elizabeth II **Subject:** World Monuments - Germany Holsten Gate Lubeck **Rev:** Holstein Gate gilt pop-up

| Date | Mintage | VF20 | XF40 | MS60 | MS63 | MS65 |
|---|---|---|---|---|---|---|
| 2009 | Est. 3000 | PF65 75.00 | | | | |

**KM# 693 10 DOLLARS**
31.11 g., 0.999 Silver 0.999 oz. ASW, 38.6 mm. **Ruler:** Elizabeth II **Subject:** World Monuments - Germany, Kaiser Wilhelm Memorial Church **Rev:** Ruins of Kaiser Church in Berlin, gilt pop-up

| Date | Mintage | VF20 | XF40 | MS60 | MS63 | MS65 |
|---|---|---|---|---|---|---|
| 2009 | Est. 3000 | PF65 75.00 | | | | |

**KM# 694 10 DOLLARS**
31.11 g., 0.999 Silver 0.999 oz. ASW, 38.6 mm. **Ruler:** Elizabeth II **Rev:** Statue of Peter I gilt pop-up

| Date | Mintage | VF20 | XF40 | MS60 | MS63 | MS65 |
|---|---|---|---|---|---|---|
| 2009 | 5,000 | PF65 65.00 | | | | |

**KM# 695 10 DOLLARS**
31.11 g., 0.999 Silver 0.999 oz. ASW, 38.6 mm. **Ruler:** Elizabeth II **Subject:** World Monuments - Italy, Venice Rialto Bridge **Rev:** Bridge in Venice, gilt pop-up

| Date | Mintage | VF20 | XF40 | MS60 | MS63 | MS65 |
|---|---|---|---|---|---|---|
| 2009 | Est. 3000 | PF65 75.00 | | | | |

**KM# 696 10 DOLLARS**
31.11 g., 0.999 Silver 0.999 oz. ASW, 38.6 mm. **Ruler:** Elizabeth II **Subject:** World Monuments - Germany Semper Opera **Rev:** Opera house, gilt pop-up

| Date | Mintage | VF20 | XF40 | MS60 | MS63 | MS65 |
|---|---|---|---|---|---|---|
| 2009 | Est. 3000 | PF65 75.00 | | | | |

**KM# 703 10 DOLLARS**
25.00 g., 0.999 Silver 0.803 oz. ASW, 38.6 mm. **Ruler:** Elizabeth II **Subject:** Nicolaus Copernicus **Rev:** Bust facing and orbit of the planets, crystal insert, partially gold plated

| Date | Mintage | VF20 | XF40 | MS60 | MS63 | MS65 |
|---|---|---|---|---|---|---|
| 2009 | 7,500 | PF65 75.00 | | | | |

**KM# 708 10 DOLLARS**
1.00 g., 0.999 Gold 0.0321 oz. AGW, 13.9 mm. **Ruler:** Elizabeth II **Rev:** Bridge

| Date | Mintage | VF20 | XF40 | MS60 | MS63 | MS65 |
|---|---|---|---|---|---|---|
| 2009 | 250 | PF65 70.00 | | | | |

**KM# 709 10 DOLLARS**
1.00 g., 0.999 Gold 0.0321 oz. AGW, 13.9 mm. **Ruler:** Elizabeth II **Rev:** Statue and gardens

| Date | Mintage | VF20 | XF40 | MS60 | MS63 | MS65 |
|---|---|---|---|---|---|---|
| 2009 | 250 | PF65 70.00 | | | | |

**KM# 710 10 DOLLARS**
1.00 g., 0.999 Gold 0.0321 oz. AGW, 13.9 mm. **Ruler:** Elizabeth II **Rev:** City Gate tower

| Date | Mintage | VF20 | XF40 | MS60 | MS63 | MS65 |
|---|---|---|---|---|---|---|
| 2009 | 250 | PF65 70.00 | | | | |

**KM# 711 10 DOLLARS**
1.00 g., 0.999 Gold 0.0321 oz. AGW, 13.9 mm. **Ruler:** Elizabeth II **Rev:** Virgin Mary statue and church in background

| Date | Mintage | VF20 | XF40 | MS60 | MS63 | MS65 |
|---|---|---|---|---|---|---|
| 2009 | 250 | PF65 70.00 | | | | |

**KM# 712 10 DOLLARS**
1.00 g., 0.999 Gold 0.0321 oz. AGW, 13.9 mm. **Ruler:** Elizabeth II **Rev:** Multiple church spires

| Date | Mintage | VF20 | XF40 | MS60 | MS63 | MS65 |
|---|---|---|---|---|---|---|
| 2009 | 250 | PF65 70.00 | | | | |

**KM# 713 10 DOLLARS**
1.00 g., 0.999 Gold 0.0321 oz. AGW, 13.9 mm. **Ruler:** Elizabeth II **Rev:** National Theater

| Date | Mintage | VF20 | XF40 | MS60 | MS63 | MS65 |
|---|---|---|---|---|---|---|
| 2009 | 250 | PF65 70.00 | | | | |

**KM# 714 10 DOLLARS**
1.00 g., 0.999 Gold 0.0321 oz. AGW, 13.9 mm. **Ruler:** Elizabeth II **Rev:** Castle

| Date | Mintage | VF20 | XF40 | MS60 | MS63 | MS65 |
|---|---|---|---|---|---|---|
| 2009 | 250 | PF65 70.00 | | | | |

**KM# 715 10 DOLLARS**
1.00 g., 0.999 Gold 0.0321 oz. AGW, 13.9 mm. **Ruler:** Elizabeth II **Rev:** Castle on a hill

| Date | Mintage | VF20 | XF40 | MS60 | MS63 | MS65 |
|---|---|---|---|---|---|---|
| 2009 | 250 | PF65 70.00 | | | | |

**KM# 716 10 DOLLARS**
1.00 g., 0.999 Gold 0.0321 oz. AGW, 13.9 mm. **Ruler:** Elizabeth II **Rev:** Castle

| Date | Mintage | VF20 | XF40 | MS60 | MS63 | MS65 |
|---|---|---|---|---|---|---|
| 2009 | 250 | PF65 70.00 | | | | |

**KM# 717 10 DOLLARS**
1.00 g., 0.999 Gold 0.0321 oz. AGW, 13.9 mm. **Ruler:** Elizabeth II **Rev:** Castle

| Date | Mintage | VF20 | XF40 | MS60 | MS63 | MS65 |
|---|---|---|---|---|---|---|
| 2009 | 250 | PF65 70.00 | | | | |

**KM# 718 10 DOLLARS**
1.00 g., 0.999 Gold 0.0321 oz. AGW, 13.9 mm. **Ruler:** Elizabeth II **Rev:** Church

| Date | Mintage | VF20 | XF40 | MS60 | MS63 | MS65 |
|---|---|---|---|---|---|---|
| 2009 | 250 | PF65 70.00 | | | | |

**KM# 719 10 DOLLARS**
1.00 g., 0.999 Gold 0.0321 oz. AGW, 13.9 mm. **Ruler:** Elizabeth II **Rev:** Ancient ruins

| Date | Mintage | VF20 | XF40 | MS60 | MS63 | MS65 |
|---|---|---|---|---|---|---|
| 2009 | 250 | PF65 70.00 | | | | |

**KM# 792 10 DOLLARS**
31.11 g., 0.999 Silver 0.999 oz. ASW, 40 mm. **Ruler:** Elizabeth II **Subject:** Tycoons - Alfred Nobel **Rev:** Nobel bust at right, Prize Medal partially gilt at right

| Date | Mintage | VF20 | XF40 | MS60 | MS63 | MS65 |
|---|---|---|---|---|---|---|
| 2009 | 10,000 | PF65 55.00 | | | | |

**KM# 793 10 DOLLARS**
31.11 g., 0.999 Silver 0.999 oz. ASW, 40 mm. **Ruler:** Elizabeth II **Subject:** Tycoons **Rev:** Cecil Rhodes, partially gilt

| Date | Mintage | VF20 | XF40 | MS60 | MS63 | MS65 |
|---|---|---|---|---|---|---|
| 2009 | 10,000 | PF65 55.00 | | | | |

**KM# 1228 10 DOLLARS**
155.50 g., 0.925 Silver 4.6245 oz. ASW, 65 mm. **Ruler:** Elizabeth II **Subject:** Ikuko Shimizu's Hello Kitty **Rev:** Kitty and Buckingham Palace in multicolor

| Date | Mintage | VF20 | XF40 | MS60 | MS63 | MS65 |
|---|---|---|---|---|---|---|
| 2009 | Est. 1500 | PF65 350 | | | | |

**KM# 1232 10 DOLLARS**
1.24 g., 0.999 Gold 0.0398 oz. AGW, 13.92 mm. **Ruler:** Elizabeth II **Subject:** Knut Hamsun, 150th Anniversary of Birth

| Date | Mintage | VF20 | XF40 | MS60 | MS63 | MS65 |
|---|---|---|---|---|---|---|
| 2009 | Est. 1000 | PF65 85.00 | | | | |

**KM# 1233 10 DOLLARS**
1.24 g., 0.999 Gold 0.0398 oz. AGW, 13.92 mm. **Ruler:** Elizabeth II **Subject:** Sweedish King Oscar II

| Date | Mintage | VF20 | XF40 | MS60 | MS63 | MS65 |
|---|---|---|---|---|---|---|
| 2009 | Est. 10000 | PF65 85.00 | | | | |

**KM# 1332 10 DOLLARS**
1.24 g., 0.999 Gold 0.0398 oz. AGW, 13.92 mm. **Ruler:** Elizabeth II **Subject:** 40th Anniversary of Moon landing

| Date | Mintage | VF20 | XF40 | MS60 | MS63 | MS65 |
|---|---|---|---|---|---|---|
| 2009 | — | PF65 100 | | | | |

**KM# 1333 10 DOLLARS**
1.24 g., 0.999 Gold 0.0398 oz. AGW, 13.92 mm. **Ruler:** Elizabeth II **Subject:** James Cook and the H.M.S Endeavor

| Date | Mintage | VF20 | XF40 | MS60 | MS63 | MS65 |
|---|---|---|---|---|---|---|
| 2009 | — | PF65 100 | | | | |

**KM# 1484 10 DOLLARS**
31.11 g., 0.999 Silver 0.999 oz. ASW with 4 gr. gold insert, 38.61 mm. **Ruler:** Elizabeth II **Subject:** World Monuments - Germany, Porta Nigra **Rev:** Porta Nigra in Trier

| Date | Mintage | VF20 | XF40 | MS60 | MS63 | MS65 |
|---|---|---|---|---|---|---|
| 2009 | Est. 3000 | — | — | — | — | 80.00 |

**KM# 1485 10 DOLLARS**
31.11 g., 0.999 Silver 0.999 oz. ASW with 4gr gold insert, 38.61 mm. **Ruler:** Elizabeth II **Rev:** Semper Opera House in Dresden

| Date | Mintage | VF20 | XF40 | MS60 | MS63 | MS65 |
|---|---|---|---|---|---|---|
| 2009 | Est. 3000 | — | — | — | — | 80.00 |

**KM# 1486 10 DOLLARS**
31.11 g., 0.999 Silver 0.999 oz. ASW with 4 gr. gold insert, 38.61 mm. **Ruler:** Elizabeth II **Subject:** World Monuments - Germany, Memorial for the Battle of the Peoples in Leipzig **Rev:** Battle monument in Leipzig

| Date | Mintage | VF20 | XF40 | MS60 | MS63 | MS65 |
|---|---|---|---|---|---|---|
| 2009 | — | — | — | — | — | 80.00 |

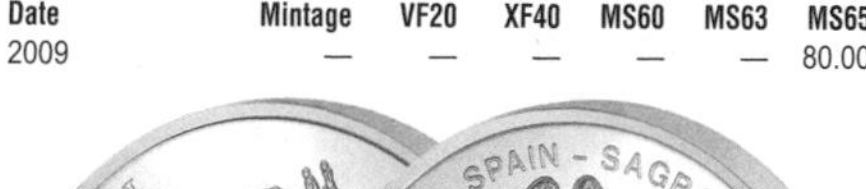

**KM# 1487 10 DOLLARS**
31.11 g., 0.999 Silver 0.999 oz. ASW plus 4 gr. gold insert, 38.61 mm. **Ruler:** Elizabeth II **Subject:** World Monuments - Spain, Sagrada Familia **Rev:** Holy Family Cathedral in Barcelona

| Date | Mintage | VF20 | XF40 | MS60 | MS63 | MS65 |
|---|---|---|---|---|---|---|
| 2009 | Est. 3000 | — | — | — | — | 80.00 |

**KM# 1488 10 DOLLARS**
31.11 g., 0.999 Silver 0.999 oz. ASW with 4 gr. gold insert, 38.61 mm. **Ruler:** Elizabeth II **Subject:** World Monuments - United Arab Emirates, Burj Al Arab **Rev:** Burj al Arab ni Dubai

| Date | Mintage | VF20 | XF40 | MS60 | MS63 | MS65 |
|---|---|---|---|---|---|---|
| 2009 Proof | Est. 3000 | — | — | — | — | 80.00 |

**KM# 1489 10 DOLLARS**
28.28 g., 0.925 Silver 0.841 oz. ASW, 38.61 mm. **Ruler:** Elizabeth II **Subject:** Railways - Steam Locomotive GS4 The Daylight **Rev:** Southern Pacific's GS-4 Daylight Limited

| Date | Mintage | VF20 | XF40 | MS60 | MS63 | MS65 |
|---|---|---|---|---|---|---|
| 2009 | Est. 5000 | PF65 55.00 | | | | |

**KM# 1491 10 DOLLARS**
Silver **Ruler:** Elizabeth II **Subject:** Wold Cup Soccer, South Africa

| Date | Mintage | VF20 | XF40 | MS60 | MS63 | MS65 |
|---|---|---|---|---|---|---|
| 2009 | Est. 10000 | PF65 55.00 | | | | |

**KM# 1492 10 DOLLARS**
1.00 g., 0.999 Gold 0.0321 oz. AGW, 13.92 mm. **Ruler:** Elizabeth II **Subject:** World Cup Soccer in South Africa

| Date | Mintage | VF20 | XF40 | MS60 | MS63 | MS65 |
|---|---|---|---|---|---|---|
| 2009 | Est. 5000 | PF65 70.00 | | | | |

**KM# 1516 10 DOLLARS**
28.28 g., 0.925 Silver 0.841 oz. ASW, 38.61 mm. **Ruler:** Elizabeth II **Subject:** 2012 London Olympic Games - Sailing

| Date | Mintage | VF20 | XF40 | MS60 | MS63 | MS65 |
|---|---|---|---|---|---|---|
| 2009 | Est. 10000 | PF65 55.00 | | | | |

**KM# 1249 10 DOLLARS**
31.14 g., 0.999 Silver 1.000 oz. ASW, 45 mm. **Ruler:** Elizabeth II **Subject:** Albert Durer **Rev:** Rabbit illustration with crystals

| Date | Mintage | VF20 | XF40 | MS60 | MS63 | MS65 |
|---|---|---|---|---|---|---|
| 2010 | 3,000 | PF65 75.00 | | | | |

**KM# 1258 10 DOLLARS**
50.00 g., 0.925 Silver 1.487 oz. ASW, 50 mm. **Ruler:** Elizabeth II **Subject:** Windows of Heaven **Rev:** Cologne Cathedral, stained glass windows, facade and ceiling arch plan

| Date | Mintage | VF20 | XF40 | MS60 | MS63 | MS65 |
|---|---|---|---|---|---|---|
| 2010 | 2,000 | PF65 500 | | | | |

**KM# 1293 10 DOLLARS**
31.11 g., 0.999 Silver 0.999 oz. ASW, 45 mm. **Ruler:** Elizabeth II **Subject:** Oberg **Rev:** Rural Russian folk scene

| Date | Mintage | VF20 | XF40 | MS60 | MS63 | MS65 |
|---|---|---|---|---|---|---|
| 2010 | — | PF65 75.00 | | | | |

**KM# 1296 10 DOLLARS**
0.50 g., 0.999 Gold AGW, 11 mm. **Ruler:** Elizabeth II **Rev:** Barack Obama

| Date | Mintage | F12 | VF20 | XF40 | MS60 | MS63 |
|---|---|---|---|---|---|---|
| 2010 | — | PF65 50.00 | | | | |

**KM# 1297 10 DOLLARS**
1.00 g., 0.999 Gold 0.0321 oz. AGW, 13.92 mm. **Ruler:** Elizabeth II **Rev:** Martin Luther King

| Date | Mintage | VF20 | XF40 | MS60 | MS63 | MS65 |
|---|---|---|---|---|---|---|
| 2010 | — | PF65 75.00 | | | | |

**KM# 1298 10 DOLLARS**
1.00 g., 0.999 Gold 0.0321 oz. AGW, 13.92 mm. **Ruler:** Elizabeth II **Rev:** Barack Obama

| Date | Mintage | VF20 | XF40 | MS60 | MS63 | MS65 |
|---|---|---|---|---|---|---|
| 2010 | — | PF65 75.00 | | | | |

**KM# 1495 10 DOLLARS**
31.11 g., 0.999 Silver 0.999 oz. ASW plus 4 gr. gold insert, 38.61 mm. **Ruler:** Elizabeth II **Rev:** Sanssouci Palace in Potsdam

| Date | Mintage | VF20 | XF40 | MS60 | MS63 | MS65 |
|---|---|---|---|---|---|---|
| 2010 | Est. 3000 | — | — | — | — | 80.00 |

**KM# 1496 10 DOLLARS**
31.11 g., 0.999 Silver 0.999 oz. ASW plus 4 gr. gold insert, 38.61 mm. **Ruler:** Elizabeth II **Subject:** World Monuments - Bellevue Palace Berlin **Rev:** Castle in Eisenach

| Date | Mintage | VF20 | XF40 | MS60 | MS63 | MS65 |
|---|---|---|---|---|---|---|
| 2010 | Est. 3000 | — | — | — | — | 80.00 |

**KM# 1497 10 DOLLARS**
31.11 g., 0.999 Silver 0.999 oz. ASW plus 4 gr. gold insert, 38.61 mm. **Ruler:** Elizabeth II **Subject:** World Monuments - Belgium Atomium **Rev:** The Atomium in Brussels

| Date | Mintage | VF20 | XF40 | MS60 | MS63 | MS65 |
|---|---|---|---|---|---|---|
| 2010 Proof | — | — | — | — | — | 80.00 |

**KM# 1498 10 DOLLARS**
31.11 g., 0.999 Silver 0.999 oz. ASW plus 4 gr. gold insert, 38.61 mm. **Ruler:** Elizabeth II **Subject:** World Monuments - Denmark, Little Mermaid **Rev:** Little Mermaid statue in Copenhagen

| Date | Mintage | VF20 | XF40 | MS60 | MS63 | MS65 |
|---|---|---|---|---|---|---|
| 2010 | Est. 3000 | — | — | — | — | 80.00 |

**KM# 1499 10 DOLLARS**
31.11 g., 0.999 Silver 0.999 oz. ASW plus 4 gr. gold insert, 38.61 mm. **Ruler:** Elizabeth II **Subject:** World Monuments - France, Fort Carcassonne **Rev:** Comtal castle in Carcassonne

| Date | Mintage | VF20 | XF40 | MS60 | MS63 | MS65 |
|---|---|---|---|---|---|---|
| 2010 | Est. 3000 | — | — | — | — | 80.00 |

**KM# 1500 10 DOLLARS**
31.11 g., 0.999 Silver 0.999 oz. ASW plus 4 gr. gold insert, 38.61 mm. **Ruler:** Elizabeth II **Rev:** Belem tower in Lisbon

| Date | Mintage | VF20 | XF40 | MS60 | MS63 | MS65 |
|---|---|---|---|---|---|---|
| 2010 | Est. 3000 | — | — | — | — | 80.00 |

**KM# 1501 10 DOLLARS**
31.11 g., 0.999 Silver 0.999 oz. ASW, 38.61 mm. **Ruler:** Elizabeth II **Subject:** World Monuments - Laos, That Luang **Rev:** That Luang in Viet Nam

| Date | Mintage | VF20 | XF40 | MS60 | MS63 | MS65 |
|---|---|---|---|---|---|---|
| 2010 Proof | Est. 3000 | — | — | — | — | 80.00 |

**KM# 1502 10 DOLLARS**
31.11 g., 0.999 Silver 0.999 oz. ASW plus 4 gr. gold insert, 38.61 mm. **Ruler:** Elizabeth II **Subject:** World Monuments - Tibet, Portala Palace **Rev:** Dala Lama's palace in Tibet

| Date | Mintage | VF20 | XF40 | MS60 | MS63 | MS65 |
|---|---|---|---|---|---|---|
| 2010 | Est. 3000 | — | — | — | — | 80.00 |

**KM# 1518 10 DOLLARS**
28.28 g., 0.925 Silver 0.841 oz. ASW, 38.61 mm. **Ruler:** Elizabeth II **Subject:** 2014 Sochi Olympic Games - Transfer Coin "From Vancouver to Sochi", Colorized

| Date | Mintage | VF20 | XF40 | MS60 | MS63 | MS65 |
|---|---|---|---|---|---|---|
| 2010 | Est. 5000 | PF65 55.00 | | | | |
| 2011 | Est. 5000 | PF65 55.00 | | | | |

**KM# 1519 10 DOLLARS**
7.78 g., 0.585 Gold 0.1463 oz. AGW 24K Gold Plated and Partially Colored, 25 mm. **Ruler:** Elizabeth II **Subject:** 2014 Sotchi Olympic Games - Transfer Coin "From Vancouver to Sotchi", Colorized

| Date | Mintage | VF20 | XF40 | MS60 | MS63 | MS65 |
|---|---|---|---|---|---|---|
| 2010 | Est. 500 | PF65 350 | | | | |
| 2011 | — | PF65 350 | | | | |

**KM# 1544 10 DOLLARS**
28.28 g., 0.925 Silver 0.841 oz. ASW, 38.61 mm. **Ruler:** Elizabeth II **Subject:** Railways - California Zephyr

| Date | Mintage | VF20 | XF40 | MS60 | MS63 | MS65 |
|---|---|---|---|---|---|---|
| 2010 | Est. 5000 | PF65 45.00 | | | | |

**KM# 1545 10 DOLLARS**
31.11 g., 0.999 Silver 0.999 oz. ASW plus 4 gr. gold insert, 38.61 mm. **Ruler:** Elizabeth II **Subject:** World Monuments - Germany, Wartburg

| Date | Mintage | VF20 | XF40 | MS60 | MS63 | MS65 |
|---|---|---|---|---|---|---|
| 2010 | Est. 3000 | — | — | — | — | 80.00 |

**KM# 1546 10 DOLLARS**
31.11 g., 0.999 Silver 0.999 oz. ASW plus 4 gr. gold insert, 38.61 mm. **Ruler:** Elizabeth II **Subject:** World Monuments - Ukraine - St. Sophia Cathedral

| Date | Mintage | VF20 | XF40 | MS60 | MS63 | MS65 |
|---|---|---|---|---|---|---|
| 2010 | Est. 3000 | — | — | — | — | 80.00 |

**KM# 1547 10 DOLLARS**
31.11 g., 0.999 Silver 0.999 oz. ASW plus 4 gr. gold insert, 38.61 mm. **Ruler:** Elizabeth II **Subject:** World Monuments - United Arab Emirates, Burj Dubai

| Date | Mintage | VF20 | XF40 | MS60 | MS63 | MS65 |
|---|---|---|---|---|---|---|
| 2010 | Est. 3000 | — | — | — | — | 80.00 |

**KM# 1548 10 DOLLARS**
31.11 g., 0.999 Silver 0.999 oz. ASW plus 4 gr. gold insert, 38.61 mm. **Ruler:** Elizabeth II **Subject:** World Monuments - USA, Empire State Building

| Date | Mintage | VF20 | XF40 | MS60 | MS63 | MS65 |
|---|---|---|---|---|---|---|
| 2010 | Est. 3000 | **PF65** 80.00 | | | | |

**KM# 1549 10 DOLLARS**
31.11 g., 0.999 Silver 0.999 oz. ASW plus 4 gr. gold insert, 38.61 mm. **Ruler:** Elizabeth II **Subject:** World Monuments - England, Buckingham Palace

| Date | Mintage | VF20 | XF40 | MS60 | MS63 | MS65 |
|---|---|---|---|---|---|---|
| 2010 | — | — | — | — | — | 80.00 |

**KM# 1550 10 DOLLARS**
31.11 g., 0.999 Silver 0.999 oz. ASW plus 4 gr. gold insert, 38.61 mm. **Ruler:** Elizabeth II **Subject:** World Monuments - Liechtenstein, Vaduz Castle

| Date | Mintage | VF20 | XF40 | MS60 | MS63 | MS65 |
|---|---|---|---|---|---|---|
| 2010 | Est. 3000 | — | — | — | — | 80.00 |

**KM# 1551 10 DOLLARS**
31.11 g., 0.999 Silver 0.999 oz. ASW plus 4 gr. gold insert, 38.61 mm. **Ruler:** Elizabeth II **Subject:** World Monuments - German Reunification

| Date | Mintage | VF20 | XF40 | MS60 | MS63 | MS65 |
|---|---|---|---|---|---|---|
| 2010 | — | — | — | — | — | 80.00 |

**KM# 1552 10 DOLLARS**
31.11 g., 0.999 Silver 0.999 oz. ASW plus 4 gr. gold insert, 38.61 mm. **Ruler:** Elizabeth II **Subject:** World Monuments - Portugal, Sintra

| Date | Mintage | VF20 | XF40 | MS60 | MS63 | MS65 |
|---|---|---|---|---|---|---|
| 2010 | — | — | — | — | — | 80.00 |

**KM# 1553 10 DOLLARS**
31.11 g., 0.999 Silver 0.999 oz. ASW plus 4 gr. gold insert, 38.61 mm. **Ruler:** Elizabeth II **Subject:** World Monuments - German Reunification

| Date | Mintage | VF20 | XF40 | MS60 | MS63 | MS65 |
|---|---|---|---|---|---|---|
| 2010 3000 | — | — | — | — | — | 80.00 |

**KM# 1259 10 DOLLARS**
50.00 g., 0.999 Silver 1.6059 oz. ASW, 50 mm. **Ruler:** Elizabeth II **Subject:** Windows of Heaven **Rev:** Westminister Abbey, stained glass windows, floor plan and facade

| Date | Mintage | VF20 | XF40 | MS60 | MS63 | MS65 |
|---|---|---|---|---|---|---|
| 2011 | 2,000 | **PF65** 350 | | | | |

**KM# 1388 10 DOLLARS**
50.00 g., 0.999 Silver 1.6059 oz. ASW, 50 mm. **Ruler:** Elizabeth II **Subject:** St. Issac's Cathedral, St. Petersburg **Rev:** Stained glass window and floor plan

| Date | Mintage | VF20 | XF40 | MS60 | MS63 | MS65 |
|---|---|---|---|---|---|---|
| 2011 | 2,000 | **PF65** 300 | | | | |

**KM# 1389 10 DOLLARS**
50.00 g., 0.999 Silver 1.6059 oz. ASW, 50 mm. **Ruler:** Elizabeth II **Subject:** Seville Cathedral **Rev:** Stained glass window, floor plan and façade

| Date | Mintage | VF20 | XF40 | MS60 | MS63 | MS65 |
|---|---|---|---|---|---|---|
| 2011 | 2,000 | **PF65** 250 | | | | |

**KM# 1505 10 DOLLARS**
31.11 g., 0.999 Silver 0.999 oz. ASW, 65 mm. **Ruler:** Elizabeth II **Series:** Biggest Silver Ounces of the World **Subject:** The Five Continents: Europe **Rev:** Moose before Bandenburg Gate and European Tuscany

| Date | Mintage | VF20 | XF40 | MS60 | MS63 | MS65 |
|---|---|---|---|---|---|---|
| 2011 | Est. 3000 | PF65 85.00 | | | | |

**KM# 1506 10 DOLLARS**
31.11 g., 0.999 Silver 0.999 oz. ASW, 65 mm. **Ruler:** Elizabeth II **Series:** Biggest Silver Ounces of the World **Subject:** The Five Continents: America **Rev:** Grizley bear before Statue of Liberty and cattle ranchers in America

| Date | Mintage | VF20 | XF40 | MS60 | MS63 | MS65 |
|---|---|---|---|---|---|---|
| 2011 | Est. 3000 | PF65 85.00 | | | | |

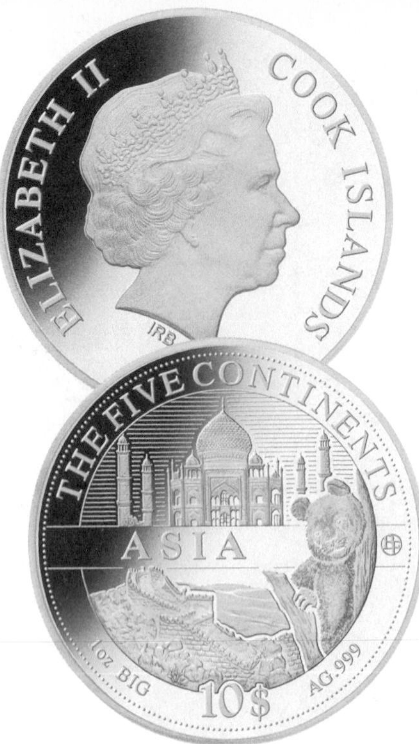


**KM# 1507 10 DOLLARS**
31.11 g., 0.999 Silver 0.999 oz. ASW, 65 mm. **Ruler:** Elizabeth II **Series:** Biggest Silver Ounces of the World **Subject:** The Five Continents: Asia **Rev:** Panda before Taj Mahal and Great Wall of China

| Date | Mintage | VF20 | XF40 | MS60 | MS63 | MS65 |
|---|---|---|---|---|---|---|
| 2011 | — | PF65 85.00 | | | | |

**KM# 1508 10 DOLLARS**
31.11 g., 0.999 Silver 0.999 oz. ASW, 65 mm. **Ruler:** Elizabeth II **Series:** Biggest Silver Ounces of the World **Subject:** The Five Continents: Australia **Rev:** Kangaroo before Harbor Bridge and Ayers Rock in Australia

| Date | Mintage | VF20 | XF40 | MS60 | MS63 | MS65 |
|---|---|---|---|---|---|---|
| 2011 | Est. 3000 | PF65 85.00 | | | | |

**KM# 1509 10 DOLLARS**
31.11 g., 0.999 Silver 0.999 oz. ASW, 65 mm. **Ruler:** Elizabeth II **Series:** Biggest Silver Ounces of the World **Subject:** The Five Continents: Africa **Rev:** Elephant before Great Sphinx and Mt. Kilimanjaro in Africa

| Date | Mintage | VF20 | XF40 | MS60 | MS63 | MS65 |
|---|---|---|---|---|---|---|
| 2011 | Est. 3000 | PF65 85.00 | | | | |

**KM# 1537 10 DOLLARS**
15.55 g., 0.999 Silver 0.4994 oz. ASW, 33 mm. **Ruler:** Elizabeth II **Series:** History of Silver - Black Swan Treasure

| Date | Mintage | VF20 | XF40 | MS60 | MS63 | MS65 |
|---|---|---|---|---|---|---|
| 2011 | Est. 8000 | PF65 30.00 | | | | |

**KM# 1538 10 DOLLARS**
15.55 g., 0.999 Silver 0.4994 oz. ASW, 33 mm. **Ruler:** Elizabeth II **Subject:** History of Silver - ANcient Coins of Lydia

| Date | Mintage | VF20 | XF40 | MS60 | MS63 | MS65 |
|---|---|---|---|---|---|---|
| 2011 | Est. 8000 | PF65 30.00 | | | | |

**KM# 1539 10 DOLLARS**
15.55 g., 0.999 Silver 0.4994 oz. ASW, 33 mm. **Ruler:** Elizabeth II **Subject:** History of Silver - Chinese Acupuntcture

| Date | Mintage | VF20 | XF40 | MS60 | MS63 | MS65 |
|---|---|---|---|---|---|---|
| 2011 | Est. 8000 | PF65 30.00 | | | | |

### KM# 1540 10 DOLLARS

15.55 g., 0.999 Silver 0.4994 oz. ASW, 33 mm. **Ruler:** Elizabeth II **Subject:** History of Silver - Rio de la Plata

| Date | Mintage | VF20 | XF40 | MS60 | MS63 | MS65 |
|---|---|---|---|---|---|---|
| 2011 | Est. 8000 | PF65 30.00 | | | | |

### KM# 1541 10 DOLLARS

15.55 g., 0.999 Silver 0.4994 oz. ASW, 33 mm. **Ruler:** Elizabeth II **Subject:** History of Silver - Navajo

| Date | Mintage | VF20 | XF40 | MS60 | MS63 | MS65 |
|---|---|---|---|---|---|---|
| 2011 | Est. 8000 | PF65 30.00 | | | | |

### KM# 1542 10 DOLLARS

15.55 g., 0.999 Silver 0.4994 oz. ASW, 33 mm. **Ruler:** Elizabeth II **Subject:** History of Silver - Cerro Rico - Potosi

| Date | Mintage | VF20 | XF40 | MS60 | MS63 | MS65 |
|---|---|---|---|---|---|---|
| 2011 | Est. 8000 | PF65 30.00 | | | | |

### KM# 1554 10 DOLLARS

31.11 g., 0.999 Silver 0.999 oz. ASW plus 4 gr. gold insert, 38.61 mm. **Ruler:** Elizabeth II **Subject:** World Monuments - Japan, Giant Kamakura Buddha

| Date | Mintage | VF20 | XF40 | MS60 | MS63 | MS65 |
|---|---|---|---|---|---|---|
| 2011 | Est. 3000 | — | — | — | — | 80.00 |

### KM# 1555 10 DOLLARS

31.11 g., 0.999 Silver 0.999 oz. ASW plus 4 gr. gold insert, 38.61 mm. **Ruler:** Elizabeth II **Subject:** World Monuments - USA Space Needle

| Date | Mintage | VF20 | XF40 | MS60 | MS63 | MS65 |
|---|---|---|---|---|---|---|
| 2011 | Est. 3000 | PF65 80.00 | | | | |

### KM# 1556 10 DOLLARS

31.11 g., 0.999 Silver 0.999 oz. ASW plus 4 gr. gold insert, 38.61 mm. **Ruler:** Elizabeth II **Subject:** World Monuments - France, Notre Dame

| Date | Mintage | VF20 | XF40 | MS60 | MS63 | MS65 |
|---|---|---|---|---|---|---|
| 2011 | Est. 3000 | — | — | — | — | 80.00 |

### KM# 1557 10 DOLLARS

31.11 g., 0.999 Silver 0.999 oz. ASW plus 4 gr. gold insert, 38.61 mm. **Ruler:** Elizabeth II **Subject:** World Monuments - Germany, Eltz Castle

| Date | Mintage | VF20 | XF40 | MS60 | MS63 | MS65 |
|---|---|---|---|---|---|---|
| 2011 | Est. 3000 | — | — | — | — | 80.00 |

### KM# 1558 10 DOLLARS

31.11 g., 0.999 Silver 0.9926 oz. ASW, 38.61 mm. **Ruler:** Elizabeth II **Subject:** World Monuments - USA, World Trade Center

| Date | Mintage | F12 | VF20 | XF40 | MS60 | MS63 |
|---|---|---|---|---|---|---|
| 2011 | Est. 3000 | PF65 80.00 | | | | |

### KM# 1559 10 DOLLARS

31.11 g., 0.999 Silver 0.999 oz. ASW plus 4 gr. gold insert, 38.61 mm. **Ruler:** Elizabeth II **Subject:** World Monuments - USA, White House

| Date | Mintage | VF20 | XF40 | MS60 | MS63 | MS65 |
|---|---|---|---|---|---|---|
| 2011 | Est. 3000 | — | — | — | — | 80.00 |

### KM# 1560 10 DOLLARS

31.11 g., 0.999 Silver 0.999 oz. ASW, 38.61 mm. **Ruler:** Elizabeth II **Subject:** World Monuments - Holland Kinderdijk Windmills

| Date | Mintage | VF20 | XF40 | MS60 | MS63 | MS65 |
|---|---|---|---|---|---|---|
| 2011 | Est. 3000 | — | — | — | — | 80.00 |

### KM# 1561 10 DOLLARS

31.11 g., 0.999 Silver 0.999 oz. ASW plus 4 gr. gold insert **Ruler:** Elizabeth II **Subject:** World Monuments - Italy, Famous Landmarks **Edge:** 38.61

| Date | Mintage | VF20 | XF40 | MS60 | MS63 | MS65 |
|---|---|---|---|---|---|---|
| 2011 | Est. 3000 | — | — | — | — | 80.00 |

**KM# 1562 10 DOLLARS**
31.11 g., 0.999 Silver 0.999 oz. ASW plus 4 gr. gold insert, 38.61 mm. **Ruler:** Elizabeth II **Subject:** World Monuments - Temple Mount

| Date | Mintage | VF20 | XF40 | MS60 | MS63 | MS65 |
|---|---|---|---|---|---|---|
| 2011 | Est. 3000 | — | — | — | — | 80.00 |

**KM# 1563 10 DOLLARS**
31.11 g., 0.999 Silver 0.999 oz. ASW plus 4 gr. gold insert, 38.61 mm. **Ruler:** Elizabeth II **Subject:** World Monuments - Germany, Speyer Cathedral

| Date | Mintage | VF20 | XF40 | MS60 | MS63 | MS65 |
|---|---|---|---|---|---|---|
| 2011 | Est. 3000 | — | — | — | — | 80.00 |

**KM# 1564 10 DOLLARS**
31.11 g., 0.999 Silver 0.999 oz. ASW plus 4 gr. gold insert, 38.61 mm. **Ruler:** Elizabeth II **Subject:** World Monuments - UK, Windsor Castle

| Date | Mintage | VF20 | XF40 | MS60 | MS63 | MS65 |
|---|---|---|---|---|---|---|
| 2011 | Est. 3000 | — | — | — | — | 80.00 |

**KM# 1565 10 DOLLARS**
31.11 g., 0.999 Silver 0.999 oz. ASW plus 4 gr. gold insert, 38.61 mm. **Ruler:** Elizabeth II **Subject:** World Monuments - Castle Schwerin

| Date | Mintage | VF20 | XF40 | MS60 | MS63 | MS65 |
|---|---|---|---|---|---|---|
| 2011 | Est. 3000 | — | — | — | — | 80.00 |

**KM# 1566 10 DOLLARS**
31.11 g., 0.999 Silver 0.999 oz. ASW, 38.61 mm. **Ruler:** Elizabeth II **Subject:** World Monuments - England, Westminister Abby

| Date | Mintage | VF20 | XF40 | MS60 | MS63 | MS65 |
|---|---|---|---|---|---|---|
| 2011 | Est. 3000 | — | — | — | — | 85.00 |

**KM# 1567 10 DOLLARS**
31.11 g., 0.999 Silver 0.999 oz. ASW plus 4 gr. gold insert **Ruler:** Elizabeth II **Subject:** World Monuments - Austria, Famous Landmarks **Shape:** 38.61

| Date | Mintage | VF20 | XF40 | MS60 | MS63 | MS65 |
|---|---|---|---|---|---|---|
| 2011 | Est. 3000 | — | — | — | — | 85.00 |

**KM# 1583 10 DOLLARS**
31.10 g., 0.999 Silver 0.9989 oz. ASW, 40.6 mm. **Ruler:** Elizabeth II **Subject:** Diamond Jubilee of Queen Elizabeth II - Trooping the Color, Colorized

| Date | Mintage | VF20 | XF40 | MS60 | MS63 | MS65 |
|---|---|---|---|---|---|---|
| 2011 | Est. 10000 | PF65 60.00 | | | | |

**KM# 1642 10 DOLLARS**
50.00 g., 0.925 Silver 1.487 oz. ASW, 50 mm. **Ruler:** Elizabeth II **Rev:** Titanic and staircase skylight window

| Date | Mintage | VF20 | XF40 | MS60 | MS63 | MS65 |
|---|---|---|---|---|---|---|
| 2011 Prooflike | — | — | — | — | — | 250 |

**KM# 1643 10 DOLLARS**
50.00 g., 0.925 Silver 1.487 oz. ASW, 50 mm. **Ruler:** Elizabeth II **Rev:** Notre Dame and window

| Date | Mintage | VF20 | XF40 | MS60 | MS63 | MS65 |
|---|---|---|---|---|---|---|
| 2011 Prooflike | 2,000 | — | — | — | — | 350 |

**KM# 1644 10 DOLLARS**
31.11 g., 0.999 Silver 0.999 oz. ASW, 38.61 mm. **Ruler:** Elizabeth II **Rev:** Queen on horseback, Queen in royal coach

| Date | Mintage | VF20 | XF40 | MS60 | MS63 | MS65 |
|---|---|---|---|---|---|---|
| 2011 | — | PF65 65.00 | | | | |

**KM# 1433 10 DOLLARS**
50.00 g., 0.925 Silver 1.487 oz. ASW, 50 mm. **Ruler:** Elizabeth II **Subject:** Window's of Heaven, Church of St. Francis, Krakow, Poland **Rev:** Stained glass window

| Date | Mintage | VF20 | XF40 | MS60 | MS63 | MS65 |
|---|---|---|---|---|---|---|
| 2012 | 2,000 | PF65 250 | | | | |

**KM# 1434 10 DOLLARS**
50.00 g., 0.925 Silver 1.487 oz. ASW, 50 mm. **Ruler:** Elizabeth II **Subject:** Window's of Heaven - St. Isaac's Cethedral, St. Petersburg, Russia **Rev:** Stained glass window

| Date | Mintage | VF20 | XF40 | MS60 | MS63 | MS65 |
|---|---|---|---|---|---|---|
| 2012 | 2,000 | PF65 285 | | | | |

**KM# 1510 10 DOLLARS**
31.11 g., 0.999 Silver 0.999 oz. ASW, 65 mm. **Ruler:** Elizabeth II **Subject:** Ancient Cultures - Babylon

| Date | Mintage | VF20 | XF40 | MS60 | MS63 | MS65 |
|---|---|---|---|---|---|---|
| 2012 | — | PF65 75.00 | | | | |

**KM# 1511 10 DOLLARS**
31.11 g., 0.999 Silver 0.9991 oz. ASW, 65 mm. **Ruler:** Elizabeth II **Subject:** Ancient Cultures - Chinese

| Date | Mintage | VF20 | XF40 | MS60 | MS63 | MS65 |
|---|---|---|---|---|---|---|
| 2012 | — | PF65 75.00 | | | | |

**KM# 1512 10 DOLLARS**
31.11 g., 0.999 Silver 0.999 oz. ASW, 65 mm. **Ruler:** Elizabeth II **Subject:** Ancient Cultures - Egyptian

| Date | Mintage | VF20 | XF40 | MS60 | MS63 | MS65 |
|---|---|---|---|---|---|---|
| 2012 | — | PF65 75.00 | | | | |

**KM# 1513 10 DOLLARS**
31.11 g., 0.999 Silver 0.999 oz. ASW, 65 mm. **Ruler:** Elizabeth II **Subject:** Ancient Cultures - Greek

| Date | Mintage | VF20 | XF40 | MS60 | MS63 | MS65 |
|---|---|---|---|---|---|---|
| 2012 | — | PF65 75.00 | | | | |

**KM# 1514 10 DOLLARS**
31.11 g., 0.999 Silver 0.999 oz. ASW, 65 mm. **Ruler:** Elizabeth II **Subject:** Ancient Cultures - Aztec

| Date | Mintage | VF20 | XF40 | MS60 | MS63 | MS65 |
|---|---|---|---|---|---|---|
| 2012 | — | PF65 75.00 | | | | |

**KM# 1585 10 DOLLARS**
20.00 g., 0.925 Gold 0.5948 oz. AGW With Partial Gold-Plating, 38.61 mm. **Ruler:** Elizabeth II **Subject:** 2016 Rio Olympic Games - Transfer Coin "From London to Rio

| Date | Mintage | VF20 | XF40 | MS60 | MS63 | MS65 |
|---|---|---|---|---|---|---|
| 2012 | Est. 10000 | PF65 1,380 | | | | |

**KM# 1586 10 DOLLARS**
28.28 g., 0.925 Silver 0.841 oz. ASW, 38.61 mm. **Ruler:** Elizabeth II **Subject:** 2014 Sochi Olympic Games - Halfpipe Skiing

| Date | Mintage | VF20 | XF40 | MS60 | MS63 | MS65 |
|---|---|---|---|---|---|---|
| 2012 | Est. 5000 | PF65 40.00 | | | | |

**KM# 1588 10 DOLLARS**
20.00 g., 0.925 Silver 0.5948 oz. ASW, 38.61 mm. **Ruler:** Elizabeth II **Subject:** 2014 FIFA World Cup Brazil - Indian and Soccer Player

| Date | Mintage | VF20 | XF40 | MS60 | MS63 | MS65 |
|---|---|---|---|---|---|---|
| 2012 | Est. 10000 | PF65 35.00 | | | | |

**KM# 1589 10 DOLLARS**
20.00 g., 0.925 Silver 0.5948 oz. ASW, 38.61 mm. **Ruler:** Elizabeth II **Subject:** Raliways - Empire State Express No. 999

| Date | Mintage | VF20 | XF40 | MS60 | MS63 | MS65 |
|---|---|---|---|---|---|---|
| 2012 | — | PF65 35.00 | | | | |

**KM# 1590 10 DOLLARS**
31.10 g., 0.999 Silver 0.9989 oz. ASW, 38.61 mm. **Ruler:** Elizabeth II **Subject:** Tiki Silver Ounce

| Date | Mintage | VF20 | XF40 | MS60 | MS63 | MS65 |
|---|---|---|---|---|---|---|
| 2012 | Est. 5000 | PF65 40.00 | | | | |

**KM# 1600 10 DOLLARS**
Silver **Ruler:** Elizabeth II **Subject:** Sistine Chapel

| Date | Mintage | VF20 | XF40 | MS60 | MS63 | MS65 |
|---|---|---|---|---|---|---|
| 2012 | — | PF65 75.00 | | | | |

**KM# 1616 10 DOLLARS**
1.00 g., 0.999 Gold 0.0321 oz. AGW, 11 mm. **Ruler:** Elizabeth II **Rev:** Trans-Atlantic Liner "Deutschland"

| Date | Mintage | VF20 | XF40 | MS60 | MS63 | MS65 |
|---|---|---|---|---|---|---|
| 2012 | — | PF65 75.00 | | | | |

**KM# 1647 10 DOLLARS**
50.00 g., 0.925 Silver 1.487 oz. ASW, 50 mm. **Ruler:** Elizabeth II **Rev:** Church of St. Catherine in Bethlehem, window

| Date | Mintage | VF20 | XF40 | MS60 | MS63 | MS65 |
|---|---|---|---|---|---|---|
| 2012 Prooflike | 2,000 | — | — | — | — | 275 |

**KM# 1648 10 DOLLARS**
50.00 g., 0.925 Silver 1.487 oz. ASW **Ruler:** Elizabeth II **Subject:** Nano Technology **Rev:** Globe held on hand

| Date | Mintage | VF20 | XF40 | MS60 | MS63 | MS65 |
|---|---|---|---|---|---|---|
| 2012 | 1,000 | PF65 275 | | | | |

**KM# 1611 10 DOLLARS**
20.00 g., 0.925 Silver 0.5948 oz. ASW, 38.61 mm. **Ruler:** Elizabeth II **Subject:** 2014 FIFA World Cup - Brazil Mascot

| Date | Mintage | VF20 | XF40 | MS60 | MS63 | MS65 |
|---|---|---|---|---|---|---|
| 2013 | Est. 10000 | PF65 75.00 | | | | |

**KM# 1615 10 DOLLARS**
31.11 g., 0.999 Silver 0.999 oz. ASW, 65 mm. **Ruler:** Elizabeth II **Subject:** Christopher Columbus

| Date | Mintage | VF20 | XF40 | MS60 | MS63 | MS65 |
|---|---|---|---|---|---|---|
| 2013 | Est. 3000 | PF65 50.00 | | | | |

**KM# 1655 10 DOLLARS**
50.00 g., 0.925 Silver 1.487 oz. ASW, 50 mm. **Ruler:** Elizabeth II **Rev:** Chatre Cathedral and window

| Date | Mintage | VF20 | XF40 | MS60 | MS63 | MS65 |
|---|---|---|---|---|---|---|
| 2013 | 2,000 | PF65 250 | | | | |

**KM# 1656 10 DOLLARS**
50.00 g., 0.925 Silver 1.487 oz. ASW, 50 mm. **Ruler:** Elizabeth II **Subject:** Grand Central Terminal, New York City, 100th Anniversary **Obv:** Clock and waiting room Chandelier **Rev:** Exterior clock sculpture

| Date | Mintage | VF20 | XF40 | MS60 | MS63 | MS65 |
|---|---|---|---|---|---|---|
| 2013 | 2,000 | PF65 225 | | | | |

**KM# 1657 10 DOLLARS**
50.00 g., 0.925 Silver 1.487 oz. ASW, 50 mm. **Ruler:** Elizabeth II **Obv:** Head with tiara, window of Mary **Rev:** Lourdes Basilica and window of Mary

| Date | Mintage | VF20 | XF40 | MS60 | MS63 | MS65 |
|---|---|---|---|---|---|---|
| 2013 | 2,000 | PF65 200 | | | | |

**KM# 1658 10 DOLLARS**
50.00 g., 0.925 Silver 1.487 oz. ASW, 50 mm. **Ruler:** Elizabeth II **Obv:** Head in tiara, window of St. Michael **Rev:** Milan Cathedral floor plan, window

| Date | Mintage | VF20 | XF40 | MS60 | MS63 | MS65 |
|---|---|---|---|---|---|---|
| 2013 | 2,000 | PF65 225 | | | | |

**KM# 1131 12 DOLLARS**
10.00 g., 0.9999 Gold 0.3215 oz. AGW, 26 mm. **Ruler:** Elizabeth II **Subject:** Full Gospel Business Men's Fellowship, 50th Anniversary **Rev:** Jesus Christ

| Date | Mintage | VF20 | XF40 | MS60 | MS63 | MS65 |
|---|---|---|---|---|---|---|
| 2003 | Est. 4999 | PF65 600 | | | | |

**KM# 894 20 DOLLARS**
31.11 g., 0.925 Silver 0.925 oz. ASW **Ruler:** Elizabeth II **Rev:** Marco Polo visits the Khubla Khan in China

| Date | Mintage | VF20 | XF40 | MS60 | MS63 | MS65 |
|---|---|---|---|---|---|---|
| 2007 | — | PF65 60.00 | | | | |

**KM# 636 20 DOLLARS**
93.30 g., 0.999 Silver 2.9967 oz. ASW, 55 mm. **Ruler:** Elizabeth II **Rev:** Michangelo, Creation of Adam, multicolor with crystal inserts

| Date | Mintage | VF20 | XF40 | MS60 | MS63 | MS65 |
|---|---|---|---|---|---|---|
| 2008 | 1,000 | PF65 650 | | | | |

**KM# 637 20 DOLLARS**
93.30 g., 0.999 Silver 2.9967 oz. ASW, 55 mm. **Ruler:** Elizabeth II **Rev:** DaVinci, Last Supper, multicolor with crystal inserts

| Date | Mintage | VF20 | XF40 | MS60 | MS63 | MS65 |
|---|---|---|---|---|---|---|
| 2008 | 1,000 | PF65 750 | | | | |

**KM# 638 20 DOLLARS**
93.30 g., 0.999 Silver 2.9967 oz. ASW, 55 mm. **Ruler:** Elizabeth II **Rev:** Raffaello, School of Athens, multicolor with crystal inserts

| Date | Mintage | VF20 | XF40 | MS60 | MS63 | MS65 |
|---|---|---|---|---|---|---|
| 2008 | 1,000 | PF65 600 | | | | |

**KM# 639 20 DOLLARS**
93.30 g., 0.999 Silver 2.9967 oz. ASW, 55 mm. **Ruler:** Elizabeth II **Rev:** Botticelli, Birth of Venus, multicolor with crystal inserts

| Date | Mintage | VF20 | XF40 | MS60 | MS63 | MS65 |
|---|---|---|---|---|---|---|
| 2008 | 1,458 | PF65 425 | | | | |

**KM# 1477 20 DOLLARS**
93.30 g., 0.999 Silver 2.9967 oz. ASW, 55 mm. **Ruler:** Elizabeth II **Rev:** Vatican City 100 Euro design

| Date | Mintage | VF20 | XF40 | MS60 | MS63 | MS65 |
|---|---|---|---|---|---|---|
| 2008 | Est. 960 | PF65 225 | | | | |

**KM# 697 20 DOLLARS**
93.32 g., 0.999 Silver 2.9971 oz. ASW, 55 mm. **Ruler:** Elizabeth II **Subject:** European Masters - DaVinci **Rev:** Mona Lisa, 12 crystals imbedded

| Date | Mintage | VF20 | XF40 | MS60 | MS63 | MS65 |
|---|---|---|---|---|---|---|
| 2009 | 999 | PF65 1,450 | | | | |

**KM# 698 20 DOLLARS**
93.32 g., 0.999 Silver 2.9971 oz. ASW, 55 mm. **Ruler:** Elizabeth II **Subject:** European Masters - Rembrandt **Rev:** The Night watch, crystals embedded

| Date | Mintage | VF20 | XF40 | MS60 | MS63 | MS65 |
|---|---|---|---|---|---|---|
| 2009 | 1,642 | PF65 475 | | | | |

**KM# 699 20 DOLLARS**
93.32 g., 0.999 Silver 2.9971 oz. ASW, 55 mm. **Ruler:** Elizabeth II **Subject:** European Masters - Raffaelo **Rev:** Sistine Chapel Madonna, crystals embedded

| Date | Mintage | VF20 | XF40 | MS60 | MS63 | MS65 |
|---|---|---|---|---|---|---|
| 2009 | 1,512 | PF65 475 | | | | |

**KM# 700 20 DOLLARS**
93.32 g., 0.999 Silver 2.9971 oz. ASW, 55 mm. **Ruler:** Elizabeth II **Subject:** European Masters - Spitzwig **Rev:** The Poor Poet, crystals embedded

| Date | Mintage | VF20 | XF40 | MS60 | MS63 | MS65 |
|---|---|---|---|---|---|---|
| 2009 | — | PF65 425 | | | | |

**KM# 769 20 DOLLARS**
93.32 g., 0.999 Silver 2.9971 oz. ASW partially gilt, 55 mm. **Ruler:** Elizabeth II **Rev:** Vetruvian man

| Date | Mintage | VF20 | XF40 | MS60 | MS63 | MS65 |
|---|---|---|---|---|---|---|
| 2010 | — | PF65 550 | | | | |

**KM# 1246 20 DOLLARS**
93.30 g., 0.999 Silver 2.9967 oz. ASW, 55 mm. **Ruler:** Elizabeth II **Subject:** Carlo Maratta **Rev:** Holy Night, color image of Mary and child, crystals

| Date | Mintage | VF20 | XF40 | MS60 | MS63 | MS65 |
|---|---|---|---|---|---|---|
| 2010 | 1,655 | — | — | — | — | 450 |

**KM# 1248 20 DOLLARS**
93.30 g., 0.999 Silver 2.9967 oz. ASW, 55 mm. **Ruler:** Elizabeth II **Subject:** Rembrandt **Rev:** Man in a Golden Helmet, plus crystals

| Date | Mintage | VF20 | XF40 | MS60 | MS63 | MS65 |
|---|---|---|---|---|---|---|
| 2010 | 1,655 | PF65 450 | | | | |

**KM# 1341 20 DOLLARS**
93.14 g., 0.999 Silver 2.9914 oz. ASW, 55 mm. **Ruler:** Elizabeth II **Subject:** Van Gogh, Sunflowers

| Date | Mintage | VF20 | XF40 | MS60 | MS63 | MS65 |
|---|---|---|---|---|---|---|
| 2010 | — | PF65 435 | | | | |

**KM# 1494 20 DOLLARS**
93.30 g., 0.999 Silver 2.9967 oz. ASW plus 7.78 gr. .999 gold inlay, 55 mm. **Ruler:** Elizabeth II **Rev:** Man drawing by DaVinci

| Date | Mintage | VF20 | XF40 | MS60 | MS63 | MS65 |
|---|---|---|---|---|---|---|
| 2010 | Est. 999 | PF65 525 | | | | |

**KM# 1387 20 DOLLARS**
93.14 g., 0.999 Silver 2.9914 oz. ASW, 55 mm. **Ruler:** Elizabeth II **Subject:** Charles LeBrun, painter **Obv:** Head with tiara right **Rev:** Adoration of the Shepards painting **Edge:** Reeded

| Date | Mintage | VF20 | XF40 | MS60 | MS63 | MS65 |
|---|---|---|---|---|---|---|
| 2011 | 1,689 | **PF65** 450 | | | | |

**KM# 1402 20 DOLLARS**
93.30 g., 0.999 Silver 2.9967 oz. ASW, 55 mm. **Ruler:** Elizabeth II **Subject:** Vincent van Gogh **Rev:** Sunflowers

| Date | Mintage | VF20 | XF40 | MS60 | MS63 | MS65 |
|---|---|---|---|---|---|---|
| 2011 | 1,655 | **PF65** 400 | | | | |

**KM# 1403 20 DOLLARS**
93.30 g., 0.999 Silver 2.9967 oz. ASW, 55 mm. **Ruler:** Elizabeth II **Subject:** Franz Marc, painter **Rev:** Blue Horse

| Date | Mintage | VF20 | XF40 | MS60 | MS63 | MS65 |
|---|---|---|---|---|---|---|
| 2011 proof | 1,911 | **PF65** 415 | | | | |

**KM# 1404 20 DOLLARS**
93.30 g., 0.999 Silver 2.9967 oz. ASW, 55 mm. **Ruler:** Elizabeth II **Subject:** Giovanni Canalello Bucentoro **Rev:** St. Mark's and Doge's Palace, Venice

| Date | Mintage | VF20 | XF40 | MS60 | MS63 | MS65 |
|---|---|---|---|---|---|---|
| 2011 | 1,732 | **PF65** 450 | | | | |

**KM# 1448 20 DOLLARS**
93.30 g., 0.999 Silver 2.9967 oz. ASW, 65 mm. **Ruler:** Elizabeth II **Subject:** Vatican Art **Rev:** Giovanni Canaletto's St. Mark's Square and the Doge's palace

| Date | Mintage | VF20 | XF40 | MS60 | MS63 | MS65 |
|---|---|---|---|---|---|---|
| 2011 | — | **PF65** 450 | | | | |

**KM# 1454 20 DOLLARS**
100.00 g., 0.999 Silver 3.2119 oz. ASW, 25x36 mm. **Ruler:** Elizabeth II **Subject:** The Luxury lifestyle **Rev:** Large blue crystal insert **Shape:** Vertical rectangle

| Date | Mintage | VF20 | XF40 | MS60 | MS63 | MS65 |
|---|---|---|---|---|---|---|
| 2011 | 2,000 | **PF65** 550 | | | | |

**KM# 1639 20 DOLLARS**
100.00 g., 0.999 Silver 3.2119 oz. ASW, 50x85 mm. **Ruler:** Elizabeth II **Subject:** Luxury Line - Blue Crystal insert **Shape:** Vertical rectangle

| Date | Mintage | VF20 | XF40 | MS60 | MS63 | MS65 |
|---|---|---|---|---|---|---|
| 2011 | 2,000 | **PF65** 300 | | | | |

**KM# 1640 20 DOLLARS**
93.30 g., 0.999 Silver 2.9967 oz. ASW, 55 mm. **Ruler:** Elizabeth II **Subject:** Franz Marc **Rev:** Horse painting and crystals

| Date | Mintage | VF20 | XF40 | MS60 | MS63 | MS65 |
|---|---|---|---|---|---|---|
| 2011 | 1,111 | **PF65** 250 | | | | |

**KM# 1641 20 DOLLARS**
Silver ASW 93.3g .999 Silver and 7.78g .999 Gold, 55 mm. **Ruler:** Elizabeth II **Rev:** Tutankhamen Mask as gold insert. 26 crystals in frame

| Date | Mintage | VF20 | XF40 | MS60 | MS63 | MS65 |
|---|---|---|---|---|---|---|
| 2011 | 999 | PF65 2,750 | | | | |

**KM# 1397 20 DOLLARS**
93.30 g., 0.999 Silver 2.9967 oz. ASW, 55 mm. **Ruler:** Elizabeth II **Obv:** Bust with tiara right **Rev:** Nefertiti head in color at center, crystal frame around

| Date | Mintage | VF20 | XF40 | MS60 | MS63 | MS65 |
|---|---|---|---|---|---|---|
| 2012 | — | PF65 350 | | | | |

**KM# 1432 20 DOLLARS**
93.30 g., 0.999 Silver 2.9967 oz. ASW, 55 mm. **Ruler:** Elizabeth II **Subject:** Portrait of Adele **Rev:** Painting image

| Date | Mintage | VF20 | XF40 | MS60 | MS63 | MS65 |
|---|---|---|---|---|---|---|
| 2012 | 1,897 | PF65 250 | | | | |

**KM# 1435 20 DOLLARS**
93.30 g., 0.999 Silver 2.9967 oz. ASW, 55 mm. **Ruler:** Elizabeth II **Subject:** Vatican Art **Rev:** Renoir's Sleeping Bather

| Date | Mintage | VF20 | XF40 | MS60 | MS63 | MS65 |
|---|---|---|---|---|---|---|
| 2012 | — | PF65 325 | | | | |

**KM# 1436 20 DOLLARS**
93.30 g., 0.999 Silver 2.9967 oz. ASW, 55 mm. **Ruler:** Elizabeth II **Subject:** Vatican Art **Rev:** Neferititi

| Date | Mintage | VF20 | XF40 | MS60 | MS63 | MS65 |
|---|---|---|---|---|---|---|
| 2012 | — | PF65 450 | | | | |

**KM# 1455 20 DOLLARS**
93.30 g., 0.999 Silver 2.9967 oz. ASW, 65 mm. **Ruler:** Elizabeth II **Subject:** Art - Gustav Klemt **Rev:** Adele 3 in color

| Date | Mintage | VF20 | XF40 | MS60 | MS63 | MS65 |
|---|---|---|---|---|---|---|
| 2012 | — | PF65 400 | | | | |

**KM# 1646 20 DOLLARS**
93.30 g., 0.999 Silver 2.9967 oz. ASW, 55 mm. **Ruler:** Elizabeth II **Rev:** The Sleeping Bather and crystals

| Date | Mintage | VF20 | XF40 | MS60 | MS63 | MS65 |
|---|---|---|---|---|---|---|
| 2012 | 1,897 | PF65 425 | | | | |

**KM# 1649 20 DOLLARS**
93.30 g., 0.999 Silver 2.9967 oz. ASW, 55 mm. **Ruler:** Elizabeth II **Rev:** Niccolo Bambini's Adoration of the Kings

| Date | Mintage | VF20 | XF40 | MS60 | MS63 | MS65 |
|---|---|---|---|---|---|---|
| 2013 | 1,897 | PF65 200 | | | | |

**KM# 1654 20 DOLLARS**
93.30 g., 0.999 Silver 2.9967 oz. ASW, 55 mm. **Ruler:** Elizabeth II **Rev:** de la Croix's "Liberte" painting, crystal frame

| Date | Mintage | VF20 | XF40 | MS60 | MS63 | MS65 |
|---|---|---|---|---|---|---|
| 2013 | 1,830 | PF65 475 | | | | |

**KM# 1145 25 DOLLARS**
7.87 g., 0.9999 Gold 0.253 oz. AGW **Ruler:** Elizabeth II **Rev:** Edward "Ned"Kelley in color

| Date | Mintage | VF20 | XF40 | MS60 | MS63 | MS65 |
|---|---|---|---|---|---|---|
| 2004 proof | Est. 1000 | PF63 350 | PF65 425 | | | |

**KM# 1622 25 DOLLARS**
155.50 g., 0.999 Silver 4.9944 oz. ASW **Ruler:** Elizabeth II **Subject:** Japan's imperial Birth Celebration **Obv:** Head with crown right **Rev:** Mythical Crane

| Date | Mintage | VF20 | XF40 | MS60 | MS63 | MS65 |
|---|---|---|---|---|---|---|
| 2006 | — | PF65 800 | | | | |

**KM# 1190 25 DOLLARS**
155.50 g., 0.925 Silver 4.6245 oz. ASW, 65 mm. **Ruler:** Elizabeth II **Subject:** Elvis Presely, 30th Anniversary of death **Rev:** That's All right, Mama

| Date | Mintage | VF20 | XF40 | MS60 | MS63 | MS65 |
|---|---|---|---|---|---|---|
| 2007 | Est. 1977 | PF65 350 | | | | |

**KM# 1321 25 DOLLARS**
Silver **Ruler:** Elizabeth II **Rev:** Christian Radish

| Date | Mintage | VF20 | XF40 | MS60 | MS63 | MS65 |
|---|---|---|---|---|---|---|
| 2008 | — | PF65 125 | | | | |

### KM# 1322 25 DOLLARS

Silver **Ruler:** Elizabeth II **Rev:** France II

| Date | Mintage | VF20 | XF40 | MS60 | MS63 | MS65 |
|---|---|---|---|---|---|---|
| 2008 | — | PF65 125 | | | | |

### KM# 1325 25 DOLLARS

Silver **Ruler:** Elizabeth II **Rev:** Sedov

| Date | Mintage | VF20 | XF40 | MS60 | MS63 | MS65 |
|---|---|---|---|---|---|---|
| 2008 | — | PF65 85.00 | | | | |

### KM# 1326 25 DOLLARS

Silver **Ruler:** Elizabeth II **Rev:** Thomas Lawson

| Date | Mintage | VF20 | XF40 | MS60 | MS63 | MS65 |
|---|---|---|---|---|---|---|
| 2008 | — | PF65 85.00 | | | | |

### KM# 1423 25 DOLLARS

7.77 g., 0.999 Gold 0.2496 oz. AGW **Ruler:** Elizabeth II **Subject:** Pultusk Meteroite

| Date | Mintage | VF20 | XF40 | MS60 | MS63 | MS65 |
|---|---|---|---|---|---|---|
| 2008 | — | PF65 500 | | | | |

### KM# 1628 25 DOLLARS

155.50 g., 0.999 Silver 4.9944 oz. ASW, 65 mm. **Ruler:** Elizabeth II **Obv:** Head with tiara right **Rev:** Queen Elizabeth I

| Date | Mintage | VF20 | XF40 | MS60 | MS63 | MS65 |
|---|---|---|---|---|---|---|
| 2008 | 450 | PF65 350 | | | | |

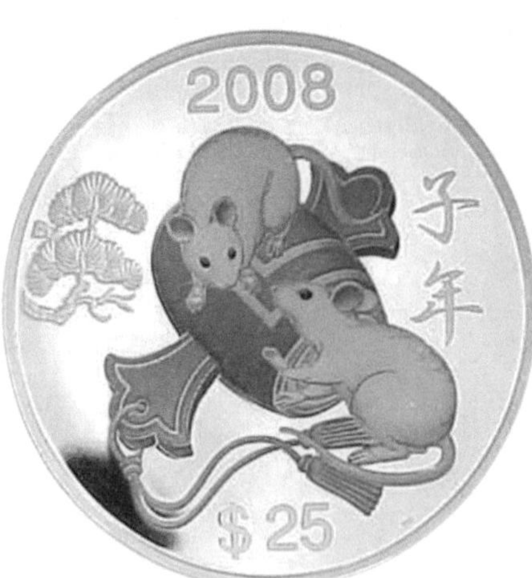

### KM# 1629 25 DOLLARS

155.50 g., 0.999 Silver 4.9944 oz. ASW, 65 mm. **Ruler:** Elizabeth II **Subject:** Year of the Rat **Obv:** Bust right **Rev:** Two mice in color

| Date | Mintage | VF20 | XF40 | MS60 | MS63 | MS65 |
|---|---|---|---|---|---|---|
| 2008 | — | PF65 400 | | | | |

### KM# 767 25 DOLLARS

155.50 g., 0.999 Silver 4.9944 oz. ASW, 65 mm. **Ruler:** Elizabeth II **Subject:** Year of the Ox **Rev:** Child riding back of ox, partially gilt **Note:** Photo reduced.

| Date | Mintage | VF20 | XF40 | MS60 | MS63 | MS65 |
|---|---|---|---|---|---|---|
| 2009 | — | PF65 675 | | | | |

### KM# 1229 25 DOLLARS

7.98 g., 0.916 Gold 0.235 oz. AGW, 22.05 mm. **Ruler:** Elizabeth II **Subject:** Ikuko Shimizu's Hello Kitty **Rev:** Kitty and Union Jack flag in multicolor

| Date | Mintage | VF20 | XF40 | MS60 | MS63 | MS65 |
|---|---|---|---|---|---|---|
| 2009 | Est. 1000 | PF65 650 | | | | |

### KM# 1584 25 DOLLARS

92.05 g., 0.999 Silver 2.9565 oz. ASW Two sculptures, one gold-plated plus one colored, 55 mm. **Ruler:** Elizabeth II **Subject:** World Monuments - Sculpture Coin, Fall of the Berlin Wall

| Date | Mintage | VF20 | XF40 | MS60 | MS63 | MS65 |
|---|---|---|---|---|---|---|
| 2009 | 1,989 | — | — | — | — | 130 |

### KM# 1242 25 DOLLARS

4.00 g., 0.999 Gold 0.1285 oz. AGW, 14x23.3 mm. **Ruler:** Elizabeth II **Subject:** Shroud of Turin **Rev:** Image of the face of Jesus, 3 red crystals

| Date | Mintage | VF20 | XF40 | MS60 | MS63 | MS65 |
|---|---|---|---|---|---|---|
| 2010 | 2,000 | PF65 500 | | | | |

**KM# 1323 25 DOLLARS**
Silver **Ruler:** Elizabeth II **Rev:** Krulzernen

| Date | Mintage | VF20 | XF40 | MS60 | MS63 | MS65 |
|---|---|---|---|---|---|---|
| 2011 | — | **PF65** 125 | | | | |

**KM# 1324 25 DOLLARS**
Silver **Ruler:** Elizabeth II **Rev:** Preussen

| Date | Mintage | VF20 | XF40 | MS60 | MS63 | MS65 |
|---|---|---|---|---|---|---|
| 2011 | — | **PF65** 125 | | | | |

**KM# 1360 25 DOLLARS**
155.50 g., 0.999 Silver 4.9944 oz. ASW, 65 mm. **Ruler:** Elizabeth II **Subject:** Soyuzmultfilm 75th Anniversary - Winnie the Pooh **Rev:** Winnie the Pooh characters in color **Edge:** Reeded **Note:** Photo reduced.

| Date | Mintage | VF20 | XF40 | MS60 | MS63 | MS65 |
|---|---|---|---|---|---|---|
| 2011 | 500 | **PF65** 420 | | | | |

**KM# 1366 25 DOLLARS**
155.50 g., 0.999 Silver 4.9944 oz. ASW, 65 mm. **Ruler:** Elizabeth II **Subject:** Soyuzmultfilm 75th Anniversary - Little Boy and Karlsson-on-the-Roof **Rev:** Little Boy, Karlsson and Freken Bok in color **Edge:** Reeded **Note:** Photo reduced.

| Date | Mintage | VF20 | XF40 | MS60 | MS63 | MS65 |
|---|---|---|---|---|---|---|
| 2011 | 500 | **PF65** 425 | | | | |

**KM# 1370 25 DOLLARS**
155.50 g., 0.999 Silver 4.9944 oz. ASW, 65 mm. **Ruler:** Elizabeth II **Subject:** Soyuzmultfilm 75th Anniversary - Cheburashka and Crocodile Gena **Rev:** Cheburashka, Crocodile Gena and Madame Shapoklyak in color **Edge:** Reeded **Note:** Photo reduced.

| Date | Mintage | VF20 | XF40 | MS60 | MS63 | MS65 |
|---|---|---|---|---|---|---|
| 2011 | 500 | **PF65** 420 | | | | |

**KM# 1408 25 DOLLARS**
155.50 g., 0.999 Silver 4.9944 oz. ASW, 65 mm. **Ruler:** Elizabeth II **Subject:** Kipling's Mowgli story characters **Rev:** Characters in color

| Date | Mintage | VF20 | XF40 | MS60 | MS63 | MS65 |
|---|---|---|---|---|---|---|
| 2011 | Est. 500 | **PF65** 250 | | | | |

**KM# 1426 25 DOLLARS**
25.00 g., 0.925 Silver 0.7435 oz. ASW, 38.61 mm. **Ruler:** Elizabeth II **Rev:** King Cobra (Ophiophagus hannah)

| Date | Mintage | VF20 | XF40 | MS60 | MS63 | MS65 |
|---|---|---|---|---|---|---|
| 2011 | 1,000 | **PF65** 75.00 | | | | |

**KM# 439 30 DOLLARS**
10.00 g., 0.9999 Gold 0.3215 oz. AGW, 16.1 mm. **Ruler:** Elizabeth II **Obv:** Crowned head right, date below **Rev:** Multicolor Peony flower and denomination **Edge:** Reeded

| Date | Mintage | VF20 | XF40 | MS60 | MS63 | MS65 |
|---|---|---|---|---|---|---|
| 2004 | 10,000 | — | — | — | — | 600 |

### KM# 1620 30 DOLLARS

1000.00 g., 0.999 Silver 32.1186 oz. ASW partially gilt, 101 mm. **Ruler:** Elizabeth II **Subject:** Gods of the North, East, South and West **Obv:** Crowned head right **Rev:** Turtle and serpent / Phoenix / Dragon / Tiger

| Date | Mintage | VF20 | XF40 | MS60 | MS63 | MS65 |
|---|---|---|---|---|---|---|
| 2005 | — | PF65 1,100 | | | | |

### KM# 1128 35 DOLLARS

10.02 g., 0.999 Gold 0.3219 oz. AGW, 25 mm. **Ruler:** Elizabeth II **Rev:** James Cook and sailing ship

| Date | Mintage | VF20 | XF40 | MS60 | MS63 | MS65 |
|---|---|---|---|---|---|---|
| 2003 | Est. 4999 | PF65 625 | | | | |

### KM# 440 35 DOLLARS

10.00 g., 0.9999 Gold 0.3215 oz. AGW, 16.1 mm. **Ruler:** Elizabeth II **Obv:** Crowned head right, date below **Rev:** Multicolor Chinese man beating a tiger and denomination **Edge:** Reeded

| Date | Mintage | VF20 | XF40 | MS60 | MS63 | MS65 |
|---|---|---|---|---|---|---|
| 2004 | 6,000 | — | — | — | — | 600 |

### KM# 441 35 DOLLARS

10.00 g., 0.9999 Gold 0.3215 oz. AGW, 16.1 mm. **Ruler:** Elizabeth II **Obv:** Crowned head right, date below **Rev:** Multicolor Chinese man riding a horse and denomination **Edge:** Reeded

| Date | Mintage | VF20 | XF40 | MS60 | MS63 | MS65 |
|---|---|---|---|---|---|---|
| 2004 | 10,000 | — | — | — | — | 600 |

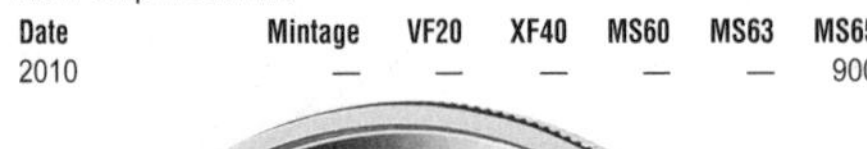


### KM# 442 35 DOLLARS

10.00 g., 0.9999 Gold 0.3215 oz. AGW, 25 x 15 mm. **Ruler:** Elizabeth II **Obv:** Crowned head right, date below **Rev:** Multicolor "Eight immortals crossing the sea" and denomination **Edge:** Plain **Shape:** Ingot

| Date | Mintage | VF20 | XF40 | MS60 | MS63 | MS65 |
|---|---|---|---|---|---|---|
| 2004 | 3,000 | — | — | — | — | 650 |

### KM# 1132 50 DOLLARS

31.11 g., 0.9999 Gold 0.9999 oz. AGW, 38.6 mm. **Ruler:** Elizabeth II **Subject:** Full Gospel Business Men's Fellowship, 50th Anniversary **Rev:** Jesus Christ

| Date | Mintage | VF20 | XF40 | MS60 | MS63 | MS65 |
|---|---|---|---|---|---|---|
| 2003 | Est. 2999 | PF65 1,800 | | | | |

### KM# 1624 50 DOLLARS

31.11 g., 0.999 Gold 0.999 oz. AGW **Ruler:** Elizabeth II **Subject:** Henry VIII **Note:** Sold as a set with colored gilt bonze medals of the six wives.

| Date | Mintage | VF20 | XF40 | MS60 | MS63 | MS65 |
|---|---|---|---|---|---|---|
| 2006 | 250 | PF65 1,500 | | | | |

### KM# 1191 50 DOLLARS

7.78 g., 0.750 Gold 0.1876 oz. AGW, 26 mm. **Ruler:** Elizabeth II **Subject:** Elvis Presley, 30th Anniversary of death

| Date | Mintage | VF20 | XF40 | MS60 | MS63 | MS65 |
|---|---|---|---|---|---|---|
| 2007 | 500 | PF65 420 | | | | |

### KM# 1319 50 DOLLARS

Silver **Ruler:** Elizabeth II **Subject:** Worlf Wildlife Fund **Rev:** Two deer

| Date | Mintage | VF20 | XF40 | MS60 | MS63 | MS65 |
|---|---|---|---|---|---|---|
| 2007 | — | PF65 100 | | | | |

### KM# 800 50 DOLLARS

155.50 g., 0.999 Silver 4.9944 oz. ASW, 65 mm. **Ruler:** Elizabeth II **Subject:** Tales of the Carribean **Rev:** Sea monster atacking Pirate ship

| Date | Mintage | VF20 | XF40 | MS60 | MS63 | MS65 |
|---|---|---|---|---|---|---|
| 2008 | 500 | — | — | — | — | 1,000 |

### KM# 1230 50 DOLLARS

15.61 g., 0.999 Gold 0.5014 oz. AGW, 26.5 mm. **Ruler:** Elizabeth II **Subject:** Ikuko Shimizu's Hello Kitty **Rev:** Kitty and Daniel in automobile near Westminster and Big Ben in multicolor

| Date | Mintage | VF20 | XF40 | MS60 | MS63 | MS65 |
|---|---|---|---|---|---|---|
| 2009 | Est. 1000 | PF65 1,000 | | | | |

### KM# 738 50 DOLLARS

31.11 g., 0.9999 Palladium 0.9999 oz. APW **Ruler:** Elizabeth II **Rev:** Ship model left

| Date | Mintage | VF20 | XF40 | MS60 | MS63 | MS65 |
|---|---|---|---|---|---|---|
| 2010 | — | — | — | — | — | 900 |

### KM# 1465 50 DOLLARS

155.50 g., 0.999 Silver 4.9944 oz. ASW, 65 mm. **Ruler:** Elizabeth II **Rev:** Airship Hindenburg in flight over New York skyline engraved on mother-of-pearl insert

| Date | Mintage | VF20 | XF40 | MS60 | MS63 | MS65 |
|---|---|---|---|---|---|---|
| 2013 | 750 | PF65 350 | | | | |

### KM# 1591 50 DOLLARS

155.50 g., Silver, 65 mm. **Ruler:** Elizabeth II **Subject:** Year of the Snake **Obv:** Head and Tiara right **Rev:** Snake on hand in green mother of pearl

| Date | Mintage | VF20 | XF40 | MS60 | MS63 | MS65 |
|---|---|---|---|---|---|---|
| 2013 | — | PF65 350 | | | | |

### KM# 1592 50 DOLLARS

155.55 g., 0.999 Silver 4.996 oz. ASW, 65 mm. **Ruler:** Elizabeth II **Subject:** Jules Verne's 20,000 Leagues Under the Sea **Obv:** Nautalus and sea creature in mother of pearl

| Date | Mintage | VF20 | XF40 | MS60 | MS63 | MS65 |
|---|---|---|---|---|---|---|
| 2014 | 750 | PF65 350 | | | | |

### KM# 1601 50 DOLLARS

155.50 g., 0.999 Silver 4.9944 oz. ASW, 65 mm. **Ruler:** Elizabeth II **Subject:** Year of the Horse **Rev:** Horse engraved in mother of pearl

| Date | Mintage | VF20 | XF40 | MS60 | MS63 | MS65 |
|---|---|---|---|---|---|---|
| 2014 | 888 | PF65 500 | | | | |

### KM# 397 100 DOLLARS

23.33 g., 0.9999 Gold 0.7499 oz. AGW Acrylic capsule center containing tiny diamonds, rubies and sapphires, 32.1 mm. **Ruler:** Elizabeth II **Subject:** Crown Jewels **Obv:** Crowned bust right, legend **Rev:** Crowns and royal regalia **Edge:** Reeded

| Date | Mintage | VF20 | XF40 | MS60 | MS63 | MS65 |
|---|---|---|---|---|---|---|
| 2002 | 5,000 | PF65 1,350 | | | | |

### KM# 1129 100 DOLLARS

31.16 g., 0.999 Gold 1.0009 oz. AGW, 32 mm. **Ruler:** Elizabeth II **Rev:** James Cook and sailing ship

| Date | Mintage | VF20 | XF40 | MS60 | MS63 | MS65 |
|---|---|---|---|---|---|---|
| 2003 | Est. 2999 | PF65 1,700 | | | | |

### KM# 503 100 DOLLARS

31.10 g., 0.9999 Gold 0.9999 oz. AGW, 40.6 mm. **Ruler:** Elizabeth II **Subject:** WWI **Obv:** Head with tiara right **Rev:** Multicolor image of Australian WWI soldier in Europe **Edge:** Reeded

| Date | Mintage | VF20 | XF40 | MS60 | MS63 | MS65 |
|---|---|---|---|---|---|---|
| 2008 | 90 | PF65 2,000 | | | | |

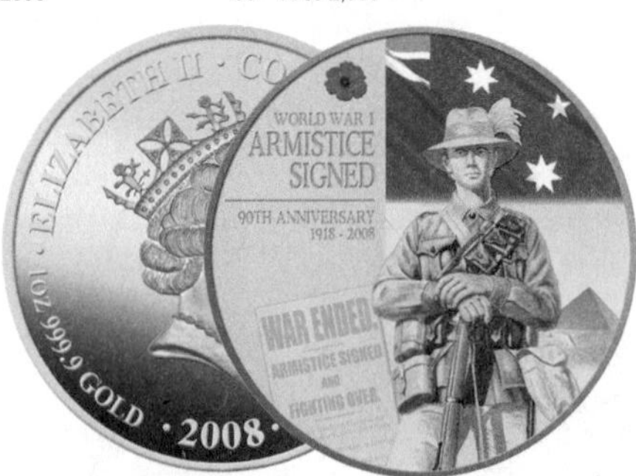


### KM# 505 100 DOLLARS

31.10 g., 0.9999 Gold 0.9999 oz. AGW, 40.6 mm. **Ruler:** Elizabeth II **Subject:** WWI **Obv:** Head with tiara right **Rev:** Multicolor image of Australian WWI soldier in Mid-East scene **Edge:** Reeded

| Date | Mintage | VF20 | XF40 | MS60 | MS63 | MS65 |
|---|---|---|---|---|---|---|
| 2008 | 90 | PF65 2,000 | | | | |

### KM# 737 100 DOLLARS

31.11 g., 0.9999 Platinum 0.9999 oz. APW **Ruler:** Elizabeth II **Rev:** Ship model left

| Date | Mintage | VF20 | XF40 | MS60 | MS63 | MS65 |
|---|---|---|---|---|---|---|
| 2010 | — | — | — | — | — | 2,250 |

### KM# 1614 100 DOLLARS

3.11 g., 0.999 Gold 0.0999 oz. AGW, 16.5 mm. **Ruler:** Elizabeth II **Subject:** 2014 FIFA World Cup - Brazil Mascot

| Date | Mintage | VF20 | XF40 | MS60 | MS63 | MS65 |
|---|---|---|---|---|---|---|
| 2013 | Est. 1000 | PF65 175 | | | | |

### KM# 1618 150 DOLLARS

62.20 g., Bi-Metallic 1.5 oz. Gold and .5 oz. Silver **Ruler:** Elizabeth II **Subject:** Great White Shark

| Date | Mintage | VF20 | XF40 | MS60 | MS63 | MS65 |
|---|---|---|---|---|---|---|
| 2005 | — | PF65 2,200 | | | | |

### KM# 1212 200 DOLLARS

31.16 g., 0.9999 Gold 1.0018 oz. AGW, 32 mm. **Ruler:** Elizabeth II **Subject:** John Marshall's Cow Parade **Rev:** Cow in multicolor

| Date | Mintage | VF20 | XF40 | MS60 | MS63 | MS65 |
|---|---|---|---|---|---|---|
| 2008 | Est. 100 | — | — | — | — | 1,850 |

### KM# 1213 200 DOLLARS

31.16 g., 0.999 Gold 1.0009 oz. AGW, 32 mm. **Ruler:** Elizabeth II **Subject:** John Marshall's Cow Parade **Rev:** African Moonlight Cow in multicolor

| Date | Mintage | VF20 | XF40 | MS60 | MS63 | MS65 |
|---|---|---|---|---|---|---|
| 2008 | Est. 100 | — | — | — | — | 1,850 |

**KM# 1214 200 DOLLARS**
31.17 g., 0.999 Gold 1.001 oz. AGW, 32 mm. **Ruler:** Elizabeth II **Subject:** John Marshall's Cow Parade **Rev:** Discount Motivated in multicolor

| Date | Mintage | VF20 | XF40 | MS60 | MS63 | MS65 |
|---|---|---|---|---|---|---|
| 2008 | Est. 100 | — | — | — | — | 1,850 |

**KM# 1215 200 DOLLARS**
31.17 g., 0.9999 Gold 1.0019 oz. AGW **Ruler:** Elizabeth II **Subject:** John Marshall's Cow Parade **Rev:** Moodonna in multicolor

| Date | Mintage | VF20 | XF40 | MS60 | MS63 | MS65 |
|---|---|---|---|---|---|---|
| 2008 | Est. 100 | — | — | — | — | 1,850 |

**KM# 1216 200 DOLLARS**
31.17 g., 0.999 Gold 1.001 oz. AGW, 32 mm. **Ruler:** Elizabeth II **Subject:** John Marshall's Cow Parade **Rev:** Moodiba in multicolor

| Date | Mintage | VF20 | XF40 | MS60 | MS63 | MS65 |
|---|---|---|---|---|---|---|
| 2008 | Est. 100 | — | — | — | — | 1,850 |

**KM# 1217 200 DOLLARS**
31.17 g., 0.9999 Gold 1.0019 oz. AGW, 32 mm. **Ruler:** Elizabeth II **Subject:** John Marshall's Cow Parade **Rev:** Railbow Cowwow in multicolor

| Date | Mintage | VF20 | XF40 | MS60 | MS63 | MS65 |
|---|---|---|---|---|---|---|
| 2008 | Est. 100 | — | — | — | — | 1,850 |

**KM# 1218 200 DOLLARS**
31.17 g., 0.9999 Gold 1.0019 oz. AGW, 32 mm. **Ruler:** Elizabeth II **Subject:** John Marshall's Cow Parade **Rev:** Picowso in multicolor

| Date | Mintage | VF20 | XF40 | MS60 | MS63 | MS65 |
|---|---|---|---|---|---|---|
| 2008 | Est. 100 | — | — | — | — | 1,850 |

**KM# 1219 200 DOLLARS**
31.17 g., 0.999 Gold 1.001 oz. AGW, 32 mm. **Ruler:** Elizabeth II **Subject:** John Marshall's Cow Parade **Rev:** Location Cow in multicolor

| Date | Mintage | VF20 | XF40 | MS60 | MS63 | MS65 |
|---|---|---|---|---|---|---|
| 2008 | Est. 100 | — | — | — | — | 1,850 |

**KM# 1220 200 DOLLARS**
31.17 g., 0.9999 Gold 1.0019 oz. AGW, 32 mm. **Ruler:** Elizabeth II **Subject:** John Marshall's Cow Parade **Rev:** Milking in the Farmhouse in multicolor

| Date | Mintage | VF20 | XF40 | MS60 | MS63 | MS65 |
|---|---|---|---|---|---|---|
| 2008 | Est. 100 | — | — | — | — | 1,850 |

**KM# 1221 200 DOLLARS**
31.17 g., 0.9999 Gold 1.0019 oz. AGW, 32 mm. **Ruler:** Elizabeth II **Subject:** John Marshall's Cow Parade **Rev:** Evening Cows in multicolor

| Date | Mintage | VF20 | XF40 | MS60 | MS63 | MS65 |
|---|---|---|---|---|---|---|
| 2008 | Est. 100 | — | — | — | — | 1,850 |

**KM# 1222 200 DOLLARS**
31.17 g., 0.9999 Gold 1.0019 oz. AGW, 32 mm. **Ruler:** Elizabeth II **Subject:** John Marshall's Cow Parade **Rev:** Cultural Moosic Cow in multicolor

| Date | Mintage | VF20 | XF40 | MS60 | MS63 | MS65 |
|---|---|---|---|---|---|---|
| 2008 | Est. 100 | — | — | — | — | 1,850 |

**KM# 1223 200 DOLLARS**
31.17 g., 0.9999 Gold 1.0019 oz. AGW, 32 mm. **Ruler:** Elizabeth II **Subject:** John Marshall's Cow Parade **Rev:** Freedomoo Cow in multicolor

| Date | Mintage | VF20 | XF40 | MS60 | MS63 | MS65 |
|---|---|---|---|---|---|---|
| 2008 | Est. 100 | — | — | — | — | 1,850 |

**KM# 1224 200 DOLLARS**
31.17 g., 0.9999 Gold 1.0019 oz. AGW, 32 mm. **Ruler:** Elizabeth II **Subject:** John Marshall's Cow Parade **Rev:** Bovingham Palace Cow in multicolor

| Date | Mintage | VF20 | XF40 | MS60 | MS63 | MS65 |
|---|---|---|---|---|---|---|
| 2008 | Est. 100 | — | — | — | — | 1,850 |

**KM# 768 200 DOLLARS**
31.11 g., 0.999 Gold 0.999 oz. AGW, 40.6 mm. **Ruler:** Elizabeth II **Subject:** Year of the Ox **Rev:** Child riding back of ox

| Date | Mintage | VF20 | XF40 | MS60 | MS63 | MS65 |
|---|---|---|---|---|---|---|
| 2009 | — | PF65 1,850 | | | | |

**KM# 389 500 DOLLARS**
2000.00 g., 0.999 Silver 64.2371 oz. ASW, 105 mm. **Ruler:** Elizabeth II **Subject:** Moby Dick **Obv:** Crowned head right **Rev:** Whale jumping over a six-man rowboat **Edge:** Plain **Note:** Illustration reduced.

| Date | Mintage | VF20 | XF40 | MS60 | MS63 | MS65 |
|---|---|---|---|---|---|---|
| 2001 | — | PF65 2,300 | | | | |

**KM# 548 500 DOLLARS**
113.00 g., 1.000 Gold 3.633 oz. AGW, 50 mm. **Ruler:** Elizabeth II **Subject:** Jack Nicklaus **Rev:** Portrait facing - two golf poses flanking

| Date | Mintage | VF20 | XF40 | MS60 | MS63 | MS65 |
|---|---|---|---|---|---|---|
| 2006 | 113 | PF65 6,250 | | | | |

**KM# 1602**
155.50 g., 0.999 Gold 4.9944 oz. AGW **Ruler:** Elizabeth II **Subject:** Year of the Horse **Rev:** Horse in mother of pearl

| Date | Mintage | VF20 | XF40 | MS60 | MS63 | MS65 |
|---|---|---|---|---|---|---|
| 2014 Proof | 25 | — | — | — | — | — |

## BULLION COINAGE

**KM# 1473 DOLLAR**
31.11 g., 0.999 Silver 0.999 oz. ASW, 39 mm. **Ruler:** Elizabeth II **Rev:** H.M.A.V. Bounty

| Date | Mintage | VF20 | XF40 | MS60 | MS63 | MS65 |
|---|---|---|---|---|---|---|
| 2009 | — | — | — | — | — | 40.00 |

**KM# 1470 5 DOLLARS**
100.00 g., 0.999 Silver 3.2119 oz. ASW **Ruler:** Elizabeth II **Rev:** H.M.A.V. Bounty

| Date | Mintage | VF20 | XF40 | MS60 | MS63 | MS65 |
|---|---|---|---|---|---|---|
| 2009 | — | — | — | — | — | 135 |

**KM# 1474 10 DOLLARS**
3.11 g., 0.999 Gold 0.0999 oz. AGW **Ruler:** Elizabeth II **Rev:** H.M.A.V. Bounty

| Date | Mintage | VF20 | XF40 | MS60 | MS63 | MS65 |
|---|---|---|---|---|---|---|
| 2009 | — | — | — | — | — | 185 |

**KM# 1475 25 DOLLARS**
7.78 g., 0.999 Gold 0.2499 oz. AGW **Ruler:** Elizabeth II **Rev:** H.M.A.V. Bounty

| Date | Mintage | VF20 | XF40 | MS60 | MS63 | MS65 |
|---|---|---|---|---|---|---|
| 2009 | — | — | — | — | — | 475 |

**KM# 1467 30 DOLLARS**
1000.00 g., 0.999 Silver 32.1186 oz. ASW, 50x105 mm. **Ruler:** Elizabeth II **Shape:** Rectangle

| Date | Mintage | VF20 | XF40 | MS60 | MS63 | MS65 |
|---|---|---|---|---|---|---|
| 2007 | — | — | — | — | — | 1,200 |

**KM# 1234 50 DOLLARS**
31.11 g., 0.999 Palladium 0.999 oz. APW, 38.6 mm. **Ruler:** Elizabeth II **Rev:** H.M.A.V. Bounty, as full hull model

| Date | Mintage | VF20 | XF40 | MS60 | MS63 | MS65 |
|---|---|---|---|---|---|---|
| 2009 | — | — | — | — | — | 1,000 |

**KM# 1471 100 DOLLARS**
3110.00 g., 0.999 Silver 99.8888 oz. ASW, 89x182 mm. **Ruler:** Elizabeth II **Rev:** H.M.A.V. Bounty

| Date | Mintage | VF20 | XF40 | MS60 | MS63 | MS65 |
|---|---|---|---|---|---|---|
| 2008 | — | — | — | — | — | 3,500 |

**KM# 1476 100 DOLLARS**
31.11 g., 0.999 Gold 0.999 oz. AGW **Ruler:** Elizabeth II **Rev:** H.M.A.V. Bounty

| Date | Mintage | VF20 | XF40 | MS60 | MS63 | MS65 |
|---|---|---|---|---|---|---|
| 2009 | — | — | — | — | — | 1,900 |

**KM# 1472 150 DOLLARS**
5000.00 g., 0.999 Silver 160.5929 oz. ASW, 89x182 mm. **Ruler:** Elizabeth II **Rev:** H.M.A.V. Bounty

| Date | Mintage | VF20 | XF40 | MS60 | MS63 | MS65 |
|---|---|---|---|---|---|---|
| 2008 | — | — | — | — | — | 5,500 |

## MAUNDY MONEY

Ceremonial Sterling Pence

**KM# 449 PENNY**
0.48 g., 0.999 Silver, 11.1 mm. **Ruler:** Elizabeth II **Subject:** Maundy **Obv:** Crowned bust right **Rev:** Crowned denomination divides date within wreath **Edge:** Plain

| Date | Mintage | VF20 | XF40 | MS60 | MS63 | MS65 |
|---|---|---|---|---|---|---|
| 2002 | 5,000 | PF65 8.00 | | | | |

**KM# 450 2 PENCE**
0.94 g., 0.999 Silver, 13.4 mm. **Ruler:** Elizabeth II **Subject:** Maundy **Obv:** Crowned bust right **Rev:** Crowned denomination divides date within wreath **Edge:** Plain

| Date | Mintage | VF20 | XF40 | MS60 | MS63 | MS65 |
|---|---|---|---|---|---|---|
| 2002 | 5,000 | PF65 10.00 | | | | |

**KM# 451 3 PENCE**
1.44 g., 0.999 Silver 0.0463 oz. ASW, 16.1 mm. **Ruler:** Elizabeth II **Subject:** Maundy **Obv:** Crowned bust right **Rev:** Crowned denomination divides date within wreath **Edge:** Plain

| Date | Mintage | VF20 | XF40 | MS60 | MS63 | MS65 |
|---|---|---|---|---|---|---|
| 2002 | 5,000 | PF65 12.00 | | | | |

**KM# 452 4 PENCE**
1.93 g., 0.999 Silver 0.062 oz. ASW, 17.5 mm. **Ruler:** Elizabeth II **Subject:** Maundy **Obv:** Crowned bust right **Rev:** Crowned denomination divides date within wreath **Edge:** Plain

| Date | Mintage | VF20 | XF40 | MS60 | MS63 | MS65 |
|---|---|---|---|---|---|---|
| 2002 | 5,000 | PF65 15.00 | | | | |

## PROOF SETS

| KM# | Date | Mintage | Identification | Issue Price | Mkt Val |
|---|---|---|---|---|---|
| PS25 | 2002 (4) | 5,000 | KM#449-452 Maundy Set | — | 45.00 |

# COSTA RICA

The Republic of Costa Rica, located in southern Central America between Nicaragua and Panama, has an area of 19,730 sq. mi. (51,100 sq. km.) and a population of 3.4 million. Capital: San Jose. Agriculture predominates; tourism and coffee, bananas, beef and sugar contribute heavily to the country's export earnings.

**KEY TO MINT IDENTIFICATION**

| Key Letter | Mint |
|---|---|
| (a) | Armant Metalurgica, Santiago, Chile |
| (c) | Casa de Moneda, Mexico City Mint |
| (cc) | Casa de Moneda, Brazil |
| (co) | Colombia Republican Banko |
| (g) | Guatemala Mint |
| (i) | Italcambio Mint |
| (p) or (P) | Philadelphia Mint, USA |
| (r) RCM | Royal Canadian Mint |
| (rm) | Royal Mint, London |
| (s) | San Francisco |
| (sj) | San Jose |
| (sm) | Sherrit Mint, Toronto |
| (v) | Vereingte Deutsche Metallwerke, Karlsruhe |
| (w) | Westain, Toronto |

## REPUBLIC

### REFORM COINAGE

1920, 100 Centimos = 1 Colon

**KM# 227a.2 5 COLONES**
4.00 g., Brass, 21.6 mm. **Obv:** National arms, date below, large letters in legend, large date, shield is not outlined **Rev:** Denomination above spray, B.C.C.R. below, thin '5' **Edge:** Segmented reeding

| Date | Mintage | VF20 | XF40 | MS60 | MS63 | MS65 |
|---|---|---|---|---|---|---|
| 2001 (a) | 35,000,000 | — | — | 0.50 | 1.00 | 1.00 |

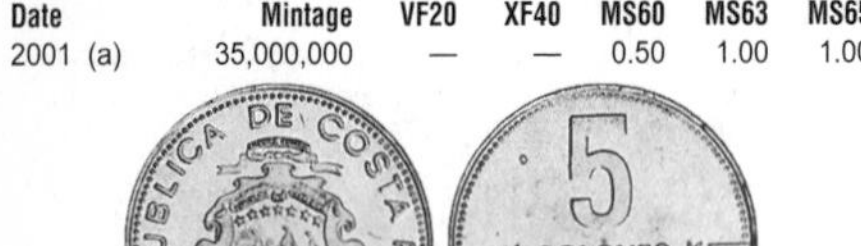

**KM# 227b 5 COLONES**
0.90 g., Aluminum, 21.4 mm. **Obv:** National arms **Obv. Legend:** REPUBLICA DE COSTA RICA **Rev:** Denomination above sprays, B.C.C.R. **Edge:** Plain

| Date | Mintage | VF20 | XF40 | MS60 | MS63 | MS65 |
|---|---|---|---|---|---|---|
| 2005 | 55,000,000 | — | — | 0.35 | 0.50 | 0.75 |
| 2008 | 300,000,000 | — | — | 0.35 | 0.50 | 0.75 |

**KM# 228.2 10 COLONES**
5.00 g., Copper-Aluminum-Nickel, 23.5 mm. **Obv:** National arms, date below, large legend and date, shield not outlined **Rev:** Denomination above spray, B.C.C.R. below, thick '1' **Edge:** Segmented reeding

| Date | Mintage | VF20 | XF40 | MS60 | MS63 | MS65 |
|---|---|---|---|---|---|---|
| 2002 (a) | 15,000,000 | — | — | 0.75 | 1.00 | 1.25 |

**KM# 228b 10 COLONES**
1.13 g., Aluminum, 22.97 mm. **Obv:** National arms **Obv. Legend:** REPUBLICA DE COSTA RICA **Rev:** Denomination above sprays, B.C.C.R. **Edge:** Reeded

| Date | Mintage | VF20 | XF40 | MS60 | MS63 | MS65 |
|---|---|---|---|---|---|---|
| 2005 | 50,000,000 | — | — | 0.50 | 0.75 | 1.00 |
| Note: Fine letters | | | | | | |
| 2008 | 200,000,000 | — | — | 0.50 | 0.75 | 1.00 |
| Note: Bold letters | | | | | | |
| 2012 | 230,000,000 | — | — | 0.50 | 0.75 | 1.00 |

**KM# 229a 25 COLONES**
7.00 g., Copper-Aluminum-Nickel, 25.5 mm. **Obv:** National arms **Obv. Legend:** REPUBLICA DE COSTA RICA **Rev:** Value above sprays, B.C.C.R. below **Edge:** Segmented reeding

| Date | Mintage | VF20 | XF40 | MS60 | MS63 | MS65 |
|---|---|---|---|---|---|---|
| 2001 (a) | 10,000,000 | — | — | 0.75 | 1.00 | 1.50 |
| 2003 | 15,000,000 | — | — | 0.75 | 1.00 | 1.50 |

**KM# 229b 25 COLONES**
7.00 g., Brass, 25.5 mm. **Obv:** National arms, date below **Rev:** Value above sprays, B.C.C.R. below **Edge:** Plain **Note:** Prev.#229a.1

| Date | Mintage | VF20 | XF40 | MS60 | MS63 | MS65 |
|---|---|---|---|---|---|---|
| 2005 | 30,000,000 | — | — | 0.75 | 1.00 | 1.50 |

**KM# 229c 25 COLONES**
Brass Plated Steel, 25.5 mm. **Obv:** National arms, country name and date **Rev:** Sprays, legend B.C.C.R. and denomination

| Date | Mintage | VF20 | XF40 | MS60 | MS63 | MS65 |
|---|---|---|---|---|---|---|
| 2007 | 90,000,000 | — | — | 0.75 | 1.00 | 1.50 |

**KM# 231.1a 50 COLONES**
7.92 g., Copper-Aluminum-Nickel, 27.5 mm. **Obv:** National arms, date below **Rev:** Value with spray below **Rev. Legend:** B. C. C. R. **Edge:** Segmented reeding

| Date | Mintage | VF20 | XF40 | MS60 | MS63 | MS65 |
|---|---|---|---|---|---|---|
| 2002 | 15,000,000 | — | — | 1.00 | 1.50 | 2.00 |

**KM# 231.1b 50 COLONES**
7.84 g., Brass Plated Steel, 27.5 mm. **Obv:** National arms above date **Rev:** Value above sprays, B.C.C.R. below **Edge:** Segmented reeding

| Date | Mintage | VF20 | XF40 | MS60 | MS63 | MS65 |
|---|---|---|---|---|---|---|
| 2006 | 5,000,000 | — | — | 1.00 | 1.50 | 2.00 |
| 2007 | 36,000,000 | — | — | 1.00 | 1.50 | 2.00 |

**KM# 240a 100 COLONES**
9.00 g., Brass Plated Steel, 29.5 mm. **Obv:** National arms above date **Rev:** Value above sprays **Edge:** Reeded

| Date | Mintage | VF20 | XF40 | MS60 | MS63 | MS65 |
|---|---|---|---|---|---|---|
| 2006 | 14,000,000 | — | — | 1.00 | 1.50 | 2.50 |
| 2007 | 108,000,000 | — | — | 1.00 | 1.50 | 2.50 |

**KM# 239.1 500 COLONES**
11.00 g., Copper-Aluminum-Nickel, 33 mm. **Obv:** National arms **Obv. Legend:** REPUBLICA DE COSTA RICA **Rev:** Value above sprays, B.C.C.R. below, thick numerals **Edge:** Segmented reeding

| Date | Mintage | VF20 | XF40 | MS60 | MS63 | MS65 |
|---|---|---|---|---|---|---|
| 2003 (a) | 15,000,000 | — | 0.85 | 1.25 | 1.75 | — |
| 2005 | 10,000,000 | — | 0.85 | 1.25 | 1.75 | — |

**KM# 239.2 500 COLONES**
Brass, 32.9 mm. **Obv:** National arms, date below **Obv. Legend:** REPUBLICA DE COSTA RICA **Rev:** Denomination above sprays, B.C.C.R. below, thin numerals **Edge:** Segmented reeding

| Date | Mintage | VF20 | XF40 | MS60 | MS63 | MS65 |
|---|---|---|---|---|---|---|
| 2003 | 100 | — | — | — | 250 | — |

**KM# 239.1a 500 COLONES**
11.00 g., Brass Plated Steel, 33 mm. **Obv:** National arms, date below **Rev:** Value above sprays, B.C.C.R. below **Edge:** Segmented reeding

| Date | Mintage | VF20 | XF40 | MS60 | MS63 | MS65 |
|---|---|---|---|---|---|---|
| 2006 | 6,000,000 | — | 0.85 | 1.25 | 1.75 | — |
| 2007 | 38,200,000 | — | 0.85 | 1.25 | 1.75 | — |

# CREEK NATION

## POARCH CREEK INDIANS

## SOVEREIGN NATION

### MILLED COINAGE

**KM# 1 DOLLAR**
31.13 g., 0.999 Silver 1.000 oz. ASW, 39 mm. **Subject:** Peace **Obv:** Tribal seal **Obv. Legend:** CREEK NATION OF INDIANS **Rev:** Indian on horseback left **Rev. Legend:** PEACE **Edge:** Reeded

| Date | Mintage | VF20 | XF40 | MS60 | MS63 | MS65 |
|---|---|---|---|---|---|---|
| 2004 | 10,000 | PF63 45.00 | PF65 50.00 | | | |
| 2004 | 20,000 | — | — | — | 35.00 | 40.00 |

**KM# 2 DOLLAR**
31.11 g., 0.999 Silver 0.999 oz. ASW, 39 mm. **Subject:** 20th Anniversary of Recognition **Obv:** Young sky dancer right, symbol **Obv. Legend:** CREEK NATION OF INDIANS **Rev:** Busts of 5 tribal chiefs, symbol below **Rev. Legend:** SOVEREIGN NATION **Edge:** Reeded

| Date | Mintage | VF20 | XF40 | MS60 | MS63 | MS65 |
|---|---|---|---|---|---|---|
| 2004 | 10,000 | PF63 45.00 | PF65 50.00 | | | |
| 2004 | 20,000 | — | — | — | 35.00 | 40.00 |

**KM# 7 DOLLAR**
31.11 g., 0.999 Silver 0.999 oz. ASW, 40.52 mm. **Obv:** Tribal seal **Obv. Legend:** CREEK NATION OF INDIANS **Rev:** Bust of Chief Menawa 3/4 left **Rev. Legend:** CHIEF MENAWA "THE GREAT WARRIOR **Edge:** Reeded

| Date | Mintage | VF20 | XF40 | MS60 | MS63 | MS65 |
|---|---|---|---|---|---|---|
| 2005 | 20,000 | — | — | — | 35.00 | 40.00 |
| 2005 | 10,000 | PF63 45.00 | PF65 50.00 | | | |

**KM# 8 DOLLAR**
31.11 g., 0.999 Silver 0.999 oz. ASW, 40.55 mm. **Obv:** Tribal seal **Obv. Legend:** CREEK NATION OF INDIANS **Rev:** Tchow-ee-put-o-kaw 3/4 right **Rev. Legend:** TCOW-EE-PUT-O-KAW **Edge:** Reeded

| Date | Mintage | VF20 | XF40 | MS60 | MS63 | MS65 |
|---|---|---|---|---|---|---|
| 2005 | 10,000 | PF63 45.00 | PF65 50.00 | | | |
| 2005 | 20,000 | — | — | — | 35.00 | 40.00 |

**KM# 10 DOLLAR**
31.12 g., 0.999 Silver 0.9995 oz. ASW, 41.61 mm. **Obv:** Dancer left at center right, a tribal seal at lower left **Obv. Legend:** CREEK NATION - OF INDIANS **Rev:** Warrior horseback 3/4 right **Rev. Legend:** SOVEREIGN NATION **Edge:** Reeded

| Date | Mintage | VF20 | XF40 | MS60 | MS63 | MS65 |
|---|---|---|---|---|---|---|
| 2006 | 20,000 | — | — | — | 35.00 | 40.00 |
| 2006 | 10,000 | PF63 45.00 | PF65 50.00 | | | |

**KM# 11 DOLLAR**
31.17 g., 0.999 Silver 1.0011 oz. ASW, 40.58 mm. **Obv:** Tribal seal **Obv. Legend:** CREEK NATION OF INDIANS **Rev:** Facing busts of Chief Tomochichi and his son with eagle **Rev. Legend:** CHIEF TOMOCHICHI **Edge:** Reeded

| Date | Mintage | VF20 | XF40 | MS60 | MS63 | MS65 |
|---|---|---|---|---|---|---|
| 2006 | 20,000 | — | — | — | 35.00 | 40.00 |
| 2006 | 10,000 | PF63 45.00 | PF65 50.00 | | | |

**KM# 13 DOLLAR**
31.11 g., 0.999 Silver 0.999 oz. ASW, 40.58 mm. **Obv:** Sky Dancer **Obv. Legend:** CREEK NATION OF INDIANS **Rev:** Warrior on horseback **Rev. Legend:** CHIEF OPOTHLE YOHOLO **Edge:** Reeded

| Date | Mintage | VF20 | XF40 | MS60 | MS63 | MS65 |
|---|---|---|---|---|---|---|
| 2007 | 10,000 | PF63 45.00 | PF65 50.00 | | | |
| 2007 | — | — | — | — | 35.00 | 40.00 |

**KM# 4 5 DOLLARS**
6.17 g., 0.999 Gold 0.1982 oz. AGW, 22 mm. **Subject:** Peace **Issuer:** Panda America **Obv:** Symbol **Obv. Legend:** CREEK NATION OF INDIANS **Rev:** Indian horseback left **Edge:** Reeded

| Date | Mintage | VF20 | XF40 | MS60 | MS63 | MS65 |
|---|---|---|---|---|---|---|
| 2004 | — | PF63 350 | PF65 375 | | | |

**KM# 9 5 DOLLARS**
6.17 g., 0.999 Gold 0.1982 oz. AGW, 22.18 mm. **Obv:** Tribal seal **Obv. Legend:** CREEK NATION OF INDIANS **Rev:** Busts of Chief Hopothle Mico and George Washington 3/4 left **Rev. Legend:** CHIEF HOPOTHLE MICO • GEORGE WASHINGTON **Edge:** Reeded

| Date | Mintage | VF20 | XF40 | MS60 | MS63 | MS65 |
|---|---|---|---|---|---|---|
| 2005 | 2,500 | PF63 350 | PF65 375 | | | |

**KM# 12 5 DOLLARS**
6.17 g., 0.999 Gold 0.1982 oz. AGW, 22.2 mm. **Obv:** Tribal seal **Obv. Legend:** CREEK NATION OF INDIANS **Rev:** Bust of Chief Stee•Chaco•Me•Co **Rev. Legend:** CHIEF STEE • CHACO • ME • CO **Edge:** Reeded

| Date | Mintage | VF20 | XF40 | MS60 | MS63 | MS65 |
|---|---|---|---|---|---|---|
| 2006 | 2,500 | PF63 350 | PF65 375 | | | |

**KM# 14 5 DOLLARS**
6.17 g., 0.999 Gold 0.1982 oz. AGW, 22.2 mm. **Obv:** Tribal seal **Obv. Legend:** CREEK NATION OF INDIANS **Rev. Legend:** CHIEF CALVIN MCGHEE **Edge:** Reeded

| Date | Mintage | VF20 | XF40 | MS60 | MS63 | MS65 |
|---|---|---|---|---|---|---|
| 2007 | 2,500 | PF63 350 | PF65 375 | | | |

**KM# 5 10 DOLLARS**
15.55 g., 0.9995 Palladium 0.4997 oz. APW, 30 mm. **Subject:** 20th Anniversary of Recognition **Obv:** Young sky dancer right, symbol **Obv. Legend:** CREEK NATION OF INDIANS **Rev:** Busts of 5 tribal chiefs, symbol below **Rev. Legend:** SOVEREIGN NATION **Edge:** Reeded

| Date | Mintage | VF20 | XF40 | MS60 | MS63 | MS65 |
|---|---|---|---|---|---|---|
| 2004 | 250 | PF65 650 | | | | |

**KM# 6 100 DOLLARS**
31.11 g., 0.999 Gold 0.999 oz. AGW, 31.94 mm. **Subject:** Treaty for Autonomy, 20th Anniversary **Obv:** Native dancer right at left center, tribal seal at right **Obv. Legend:** CREEK NATION - OF INDIANS **Rev:** Five portraits left to right, tribal seal below **Rev. Legend:** • SOVEREIGN NATION • **Edge:** Reeded

| Date | Mintage | VF20 | XF40 | MS60 | MS63 | MS65 |
|---|---|---|---|---|---|---|
| 2004 | 250 | PF65 1,850 | | | | |

The Republic of Croatia, (Hrvatska) bordered on the west by the Adriatic Sea and the northeast by Hungary, has an area of 21,829 sq. mi. (56,538 sq. km.) and a population of 4.7 million. Capital: Zagreb.

**NOTE:** Coin dates starting with 1994 are followed by a period. Example: 1994.

# REPUBLIC

## REFORM COINAGE

For the circulating minor coins, the reverse legend (name of item) is in Croatian for odd dated years and Latin for even dated years. May 30, 1994 - 1000 Dinara = 1 Kuna; 100 Lipa = 1 Kuna

### KM# 3 LIPA

0.70 g., Aluminum, 17 mm. **Obv:** Denomination above crowned arms **Obv. Legend:** REPUBLIKA HRVATSKA **Rev:** Ears of corn, date below **Rev. Legend:** KUKURUZ **Edge:** Plain

| Date | Mintage | VF20 | XF40 | MS60 | MS63 | MS65 |
|---|---|---|---|---|---|---|
| 2001 | 2,000,000 | — | 0.20 | 0.35 | 0.50 | — |
| 2001 | 1,000 | PF65 2.50 | | | | |
| 2003 | 1,500,000 | — | 0.20 | 0.35 | 0.50 | — |
| 2003 | 1,000 | PF65 2.50 | | | | |
| 2005 | — | — | 0.20 | 0.35 | 0.50 | — |
| 2005 | 2,000 | PF65 2.00 | | | | |
| 2007 | — | — | 0.20 | 0.35 | 0.50 | — |
| 2007 | 1,000 | PF65 2.00 | | | | |
| 2009 Sets only | — | — | — | — | 1.00 | — |
| 2009 | — | PF65 2.00 | | | | |
| 2011 | — | PF65 2.00 | | | | |

### KM# 12 LIPA

0.70 g., Aluminum, 17 mm. **Obv:** Denomination above crowned arms **Obv. Legend:** REPUBLIKA HRVATSKA **Rev:** Ears of corn, date below **Rev. Legend:** ZEA MAYS **Edge:** Plain

| Date | Mintage | VF20 | XF40 | MS60 | MS63 | MS65 |
|---|---|---|---|---|---|---|
| 2002 | 3,000,000 | — | 0.40 | 0.75 | 1.00 | — |
| 2002 | 1,000 | PF65 2.50 | | | | |
| 2004 | 2,000,000 | — | 0.40 | 0.75 | 1.00 | — |
| 2004 | 2,000 | PF65 1.50 | | | | |
| 2006 | — | — | 0.40 | 0.75 | 1.00 | — |
| 2006 | 1,000 | PF65 1.50 | | | | |
| 2008 | — | — | 0.40 | 0.75 | 1.00 | — |
| 2008 | 1,000 | PF65 1.50 | | | | |
| 2010 | — | PF65 1.50 | | | | |
| 2012 | — | — | 0.40 | 0.75 | 1.00 | — |
| 2012 | — | PF65 1.50 | | | | |

### KM# 4 2 LIPE

0.92 g., Aluminum, 19 mm. **Obv:** Denomination above crowned arms on half braid **Obv. Legend:** REPUBLIKA HRVATSKA **Rev:** Grapevine, date below **Rev. Legend:** VINOVA LOZA **Edge:** Plain

| Date | Mintage | VF20 | XF40 | MS60 | MS63 | MS65 |
|---|---|---|---|---|---|---|
| 2001 | 2,986,000 | — | 0.40 | 0.75 | 1.00 | — |
| 2001 | 1,000 | PF65 3.00 | | | | |
| 2003 | 2,000,000 | — | 0.40 | 0.75 | 1.00 | — |
| 2003 | 1,000 | PF65 3.00 | | | | |
| 2005 | — | — | 0.40 | 0.75 | 1.00 | — |
| 2005 | 2,000 | PF65 3.00 | | | | |
| 2007 | — | — | 0.40 | 0.75 | 1.00 | — |
| 2007 | 1,000 | PF65 3.00 | | | | |
| 2009 Sets only | — | — | — | — | 2.00 | — |
| 2009 | — | PF65 3.00 | | | | |
| 2011 | — | PF65 3.00 | | | | |

### KM# 14 2 LIPE

0.92 g., Aluminum, 19 mm. **Obv:** Denomination above crowned arms on half braid **Obv. Legend:** REPUBLIKA HRVATSKA **Rev:** Grapevine, date below **Rev. Legend:** VITIS VINIFERA **Edge:** Plain

| Date | Mintage | VF20 | XF40 | MS60 | MS63 | MS65 |
|---|---|---|---|---|---|---|
| 2002 | 2,000,000 | — | 0.80 | 1.25 | 2.00 | — |
| 2002 | 1,000 | PF65 3.00 | | | | |
| 2004 | 2,000,000 | — | 0.80 | 1.25 | 2.00 | — |
| 2004 | 2,000 | PF65 2.50 | | | | |
| 2006 | — | — | 0.80 | 1.25 | 2.00 | — |
| 2006 | 1,000 | PF65 2.50 | | | | |
| 2008 | — | — | 0.80 | 1.25 | 2.00 | — |
| 2008 | 1,000 | PF65 2.50 | | | | |
| 2010 | — | PF65 2.50 | | | | |
| 2012 | — | — | 0.80 | 1.25 | 2.00 | — |
| 2012 | — | PF65 2.50 | | | | |

### KM# 5 5 LIPA

2.50 g., Brass Plated Steel, 18 mm. **Obv:** Denomination above crowned arms **Obv. Legend:** REPUBLIKA HRVATSKA **Rev:** Oak leaves, date below **Rev. Legend:** HRAST LUZNJAK **Edge:** Plain

| Date | Mintage | VF20 | XF40 | MS60 | MS63 | MS65 |
|---|---|---|---|---|---|---|
| 2001 | 6,598,000 | — | 0.40 | 0.60 | 1.00 | — |
| 2001 | 1,000 | PF65 4.00 | | | | |
| 2003 | 13,000,000 | — | 0.40 | 0.60 | 1.00 | — |
| 2003 | 2,000 | PF65 3.50 | | | | |
| 2005 | — | — | 0.40 | 0.60 | 1.00 | — |
| 2005 | 2,000 | PF65 3.50 | | | | |
| 2007 | — | — | 0.40 | 0.60 | 1.00 | — |
| 2007 | 1,000 | PF65 3.50 | | | | |
| 2009 | — | — | 0.40 | 0.60 | 1.00 | — |
| 2009 | — | PF65 3.50 | | | | |
| 2011 | — | — | 0.40 | 0.60 | 1.00 | — |
| 2011 | — | PF65 3.50 | | | | |
| 2013 | — | — | — | — | — | — |
| 2013 | — | PF65 3.50 | | | | |

### KM# 15 5 LIPA

2.50 g., Brass Plated Steel, 18 mm. **Obv:** Denomination above crowned arms **Obv. Legend:** REPUBLIKA HRVATSKA **Rev:** Oak leaves, date below **Rev. Legend:** QUERCUS ROBUR **Edge:** Plain

| Date | Mintage | VF20 | XF40 | MS60 | MS63 | MS65 |
|---|---|---|---|---|---|---|
| 2002 | 3,500,000 | — | 0.80 | 1.25 | 2.00 | — |
| 2002 | 1,000 | PF65 4.00 | | | | |
| 2004 | 2,000,000 | — | 0.80 | 1.25 | 2.00 | — |
| 2004 | 2,000 | PF65 3.00 | | | | |
| 2006 | — | — | 0.80 | 1.25 | 2.00 | — |
| 2006 | 1,000 | PF65 3.00 | | | | |
| 2008 | — | — | 0.80 | 1.25 | 2.00 | — |
| 2008 | 1,000 | PF65 3.00 | | | | |
| 2010 | — | — | 0.80 | 1.25 | 2.00 | — |
| 2010 | — | PF65 3.00 | | | | |
| 2012 | — | — | 0.80 | 1.25 | 2.00 | — |
| 2012 | — | PF65 3.00 | | | | |
| 2014 | — | — | — | — | 2.00 | — |
| 2014 | — | PF65 3.00 | | | | |

### KM# 6 10 LIPA

3.25 g., Brass Plated Steel, 20 mm. **Obv:** Denomination above crowned arms **Obv. Legend:** REPUBLIKA HRVATSKA **Rev:** Tobacco plant, date below **Rev. Legend:** DUHAN **Edge:** Plain

| Date | Mintage | VF20 | XF40 | MS60 | MS63 | MS65 |
|---|---|---|---|---|---|---|
| 2001 | 31,500,000 | — | 0.40 | 0.75 | 1.50 | — |
| 2001 | 1,000 | PF65 5.00 | | | | |
| 2003 | 12,000,000 | — | 0.40 | 0.75 | 1.50 | — |
| 2003 | 1,000 | PF65 5.00 | | | | |
| 2005 | — | — | 0.40 | 0.75 | 1.50 | — |
| 2005 | 2,000 | PF65 5.00 | | | | |
| 2007 | — | — | 0.40 | 0.75 | 1.50 | — |
| 2007 | 1,000 | PF65 5.00 | | | | |
| 2009 | — | — | 0.40 | 0.75 | 1.50 | — |
| 2009 | 1,000 | PF65 5.00 | | | | |
| 2011 | — | — | 0.40 | 0.75 | 1.50 | — |
| 2011 | — | PF65 5.00 | | | | |
| 2013 | — | — | — | 0.75 | 1.50 | — |
| 2013 | — | PF65 5.00 | | | | |

### KM# 16 10 LIPA

3.25 g., Brass Plated Steel, 20 mm. **Obv:** Denomination above crowned arms on half braid **Obv. Legend:** REPUBLIKA HRVATSKA **Rev:** Tobacco plant, date below **Rev. Legend:** NICOTIANA TABACUM **Edge:** Plain

| Date | Mintage | VF20 | XF40 | MS60 | MS63 | MS65 |
|---|---|---|---|---|---|---|
| 2002 | 2,000,000 | — | 0.80 | 1.25 | 2.50 | — |
| 2002 | 1,000 | PF65 5.00 | | | | |
| 2004 | 2,000,000 | — | 0.80 | 1.25 | 2.50 | — |
| 2004 | 2,000 | PF65 4.50 | | | | |
| 2006 | — | — | 0.80 | 1.25 | 2.50 | — |
| 2006 | 1,000 | PF65 4.50 | | | | |
| 2008 | — | — | 0.80 | 1.25 | 2.50 | — |
| 2008 | 1,000 | PF65 4.50 | | | | |
| 2010 | — | — | 0.80 | 1.25 | 2.50 | — |
| 2010 | 1,000 | PF65 4.50 | | | | |
| 2012 | — | — | 0.80 | 1.25 | 2.50 | — |
| 2012 | — | PF65 4.50 | | | | |
| 2014 | — | — | — | 1.25 | 2.50 | — |
| 2014 | — | PF65 4.50 | | | | |

### KM# 7 20 LIPA

2.90 g., Nickel Plated Steel, 18.5 mm. **Obv:** Denomination above crowned arms on half braid **Obv. Legend:** REPUBLIKA HRVATSKA **Rev:** Olive branch, date below **Rev. Legend:** MASLINA **Edge:** Plain

| Date | Mintage | VF20 | XF40 | MS60 | MS63 | MS65 |
|---|---|---|---|---|---|---|
| 2001 | 23,000,000 | — | 0.45 | 0.75 | 1.50 | — |
| 2001 | 1,000 | PF65 5.00 | | | | |
| 2003 | 12,500,000 | — | 0.45 | 0.75 | 1.50 | — |
| 2003 | 1,000 | PF65 5.00 | | | | |
| 2005 | — | — | 0.45 | 0.75 | 1.50 | — |
| 2005 | 2,000 | PF65 5.00 | | | | |
| 2007 | — | — | 0.45 | 0.75 | 1.50 | — |
| 2007 | 1,000 | PF65 5.00 | | | | |
| 2009 | — | — | 0.45 | 0.75 | 1.50 | — |
| 2009 | — | PF65 5.00 | | | | |
| 2011 | — | — | 0.45 | 0.75 | 1.50 | — |
| 2011 | — | PF65 5.00 | | | | |
| 2013 | — | — | — | 0.75 | 1.50 | — |
| 2013 | — | PF65 5.00 | | | | |

### KM# 17 20 LIPA

2.90 g., Nickel Plated Steel, 18.5 mm. **Obv:** Denomination above crowned arms on half braid **Obv. Legend:** REPUBLIKA HRVATSKA **Rev:** Olive branch, date below **Rev. Legend:** OLEA EUROPAEA **Edge:** Plain

| Date | Mintage | VF20 | XF40 | MS60 | MS63 | MS65 |
|---|---|---|---|---|---|---|
| 2002 | 2,000,000 | — | 0.80 | 1.25 | 2.50 | — |
| 2002 | 1,000 | PF65 5.00 | | | | |
| 2004 | 2,000,000 | — | 0.80 | 1.25 | 2.50 | — |
| 2004 | 2,000 | PF65 4.50 | | | | |
| 2006 | — | — | 0.80 | 1.25 | 2.50 | — |
| 2006 | 1,000 | PF65 4.50 | | | | |
| 2008 | — | — | 0.80 | 1.25 | 2.50 | — |
| 2008 | 1,000 | PF65 4.50 | | | | |
| 2010 | — | — | 0.80 | 1.25 | 2.50 | — |
| 2010 | 1,000 | PF65 4.50 | | | | |
| 2012 | — | — | 0.80 | 1.25 | 2.50 | — |
| 2012 | — | PF65 4.50 | | | | |
| 2014 | — | — | — | 1.25 | 2.50 | — |
| 2014 | — | PF65 4.50 | | | | |

### KM# 8 50 LIPA

3.65 g., Nickel Plated Steel, 20.5 mm. **Obv:** Denomination above crowned arms on half braid **Obv. Legend:** REPUBLIKA HRVATSKA **Rev:** Flowers, date below **Rev. Legend:** VELEBITSKA DEGENIJA **Edge:** Plain

| Date | Mintage | VF20 | XF40 | MS60 | MS63 | MS65 |
|---|---|---|---|---|---|---|
| 2001 | 5,500,000 | — | 0.60 | 0.80 | 1.50 | — |
| 2001 | 1,000 | PF65 5.50 | | | | |
| 2003 | 8,000,000 | — | 0.60 | 0.80 | 1.50 | — |
| 2003 | 1,000 | PF65 5.50 | | | | |
| 2005 | — | — | 0.60 | 0.80 | 1.50 | — |
| 2005 | 2,000 | PF65 5.00 | | | | |
| 2007 | — | — | 0.60 | 0.80 | 1.50 | — |
| 2007 | 1,000 | PF65 5.00 | | | | |
| 2009 | — | — | 0.60 | 0.80 | 1.50 | — |
| 2009 | — | PF65 5.00 | | | | |
| 2011 | — | — | 0.60 | 0.80 | 1.50 | — |
| 2011 | — | PF65 5.00 | | | | |
| 2013 | — | — | — | 0.80 | 1.50 | — |
| 2013 | — | PF65 5.00 | | | | |

### KM# 19 50 LIPA

3.65 g., Nickel Plated Steel, 20.5 mm. **Obv:** Denomination above crowned arms on half braid **Obv. Legend:** REPUBLIKA HRVATSKA **Rev:** Flowers, date below **Rev. Legend:** DEGENIA VELEBITICA **Edge:** Plain

| Date | Mintage | VF20 | XF40 | MS60 | MS63 | MS65 |
|---|---|---|---|---|---|---|
| 2002 | 2,000,000 | — | 0.80 | 1.25 | 2.50 | — |
| 2002 | 1,000 | PF65 5.00 | | | | |
| 2004 | 2,000,000 | — | 0.80 | 1.25 | 2.50 | — |
| 2004 | 2,000 | PF65 4.50 | | | | |
| 2006 | — | — | 0.80 | 1.25 | 2.50 | — |
| 2006 | 1,000 | PF65 4.50 | | | | |
| 2008 | — | — | 0.80 | 1.25 | 2.50 | — |
| 2008 | 1,000 | PF65 4.50 | | | | |
| 2010 | — | — | 0.80 | 1.25 | 2.50 | — |
| 2010 | 1,000 | PF65 4.50 | | | | |
| 2012 | — | — | 0.80 | 1.25 | 2.50 | — |
| 2012 | — | PF65 4.50 | | | | |
| 2014 | — | — | — | 1.25 | 2.50 | — |
| 2014 | — | PF65 4.50 | | | | |

### KM# 9.1 KUNA

5.00 g., Copper-Nickel-Zinc, 22.5 mm. **Obv:** Marten back of numeral, arms divide branches below **Obv. Legend:** REPUBLIKA HRVATSKA **Rev:** Nightingale left, two dates **Rev. Legend:** SLAVUJ **Edge:** Reeded

| Date | Mintage | VF20 | XF40 | MS60 | MS63 | MS65 |
|---|---|---|---|---|---|---|
| 2001 | 1,000,000 | — | 0.75 | 1.65 | 2.00 | — |
| 2001 | 1,000 | PF65 4.50 | | | | |
| 2003 | 2,000,000 | — | 0.75 | 1.65 | 2.00 | — |
| 2003 | 1,000 | PF65 4.50 | | | | |
| 2005 | — | — | 0.75 | 1.65 | 2.00 | — |
| 2005 | 2,000 | PF65 4.50 | | | | |
| 2007 | — | — | 0.75 | 1.65 | 2.00 | — |
| 2007 | 1,000 | PF65 4.50 | | | | |
| 2009 | — | — | 0.75 | 1.65 | 2.00 | — |
| 2009 | — | PF65 4.50 | | | | |
| 2011 | — | — | 0.75 | 1.65 | 2.00 | — |
| 2011 | — | PF65 4.50 | | | | |
| 2013 | — | — | — | 1.65 | 2.00 | — |
| 2013 | — | PF65 4.50 | | | | |

### KM# 9.2 KUNA

5.00 g., Copper-Nickel-Zinc, 22.5 mm. **Obv:** Crowned arms flanked by sprays, denomination above on marten **Rev:** Nightingale, left, '1994' above, date below **Edge:** Reeded

| Date | Mintage | VF20 | XF40 | MS60 | MS63 | MS65 |
|---|---|---|---|---|---|---|
| 2001 | — | PF65 4.00 | | | | |

### KM# 20.1 KUNA

5.00 g., Copper-Nickel-Zinc, 22.5 mm. **Obv:** Marten back of numeral, arms divide branches below **Rev:** Nightingale left, date below **Rev. Legend:** Error spelling "LUSCINNIA" MEGARHYNCHOS **Edge:** Reeded **Note:** Formerly KM-20

| Date | Mintage | VF20 | XF40 | MS60 | MS63 | MS65 |
|---|---|---|---|---|---|---|
| 2002 | — | — | — | — | 2.00 | — |

### KM# 20.2 KUNA

5.00 g., Copper-Nickel-Zinc, 22.5 mm. **Obv:** Marten back of numeral, arms divide branches below **Obv. Legend:** REPUBLIKA HRVATSKA **Rev:** Nightingale left, date below **Rev. Legend:** Correct spelling "LUSCINIA" MEGARHYNCHOS **Edge:** Reeded

| Date | Mintage | VF20 | XF40 | MS60 | MS63 | MS65 |
|---|---|---|---|---|---|---|
| 2002 | 1,000,000 | — | 1.00 | 3.00 | 4.00 | — |
| 2002 | 1,000 | PF65 5.00 | | | | |
| 2006 | — | — | 1.00 | 3.00 | 4.00 | — |
| 2006 | 1,000 | PF65 5.00 | | | | |
| 2008 | — | — | 1.00 | 3.00 | 4.00 | — |
| 2008 | 1,000 | PF65 5.00 | | | | |
| 2010 | — | — | 1.00 | 3.00 | 4.00 | — |
| 2010 | — | PF65 5.00 | | | | |
| 2012 | — | — | 1.00 | 3.00 | 4.00 | — |
| 2012 | — | PF65 5.00 | | | | |
| 2014 | — | — | 1.00 | 3.00 | 4.00 | — |
| 2014 | — | PF65 5.00 | | | | |

### KM# 79 KUNA

5.00 g., Copper-Nickel-Zinc, 22.5 mm. **Subject:** 10th Anniversary of National Currency **Obv:** Crowned arms flanked by sprays, denomination above on marten **Obv. Legend:** REPUBLIKA HRVATSKA **Rev:** Nightingale left, date below **Rev. Legend:** MEGARHYNCHOS **Edge:** Reeded

| Date | Mintage | VF20 | XF40 | MS60 | MS63 | MS65 |
|---|---|---|---|---|---|---|
| ND(2004) | 30,000 | — | 1.00 | 3.00 | 4.00 | — |
| ND(2004) | 2,000 | PF65 5.00 | | | | |

### KM# 10 2 KUNE

6.20 g., Copper-Nickel-Zinc, 24.5 mm. **Obv:** Marten back of numeral, arms divide branches below **Obv. Legend:** REPUBLIKA HRVATSKA **Rev:** Bluefin tuna right, date below **Rev. Legend:** TUNJ **Edge:** Reeded

| Date | Mintage | VF20 | XF40 | MS60 | MS63 | MS65 |
|---|---|---|---|---|---|---|
| 2001 | 1,250,000 | — | 1.00 | 2.00 | 3.00 | — |
| 2001 | 1,000 | PF65 6.50 | | | | |
| 2003 | 7,250,000 | — | 1.00 | 2.00 | 3.00 | — |
| 2003 | 1,000 | PF65 6.50 | | | | |
| 2005 | — | — | 1.00 | 2.00 | 3.00 | — |
| 2005 | 2,000 | PF65 6.50 | | | | |
| 2007 | — | — | 1.00 | 2.00 | 3.00 | — |
| 2007 | 1,000 | PF65 6.50 | | | | |
| 2009 | — | — | 1.00 | 2.00 | 3.00 | — |
| 2009 | — | PF65 6.50 | | | | |
| 2011 | — | — | 1.00 | 2.00 | 3.00 | — |
| 2011 | — | PF65 6.50 | | | | |
| 2013 | — | — | — | 2.00 | 3.00 | — |
| 2013 | — | PF65 6.50 | | | | |

### KM# 21 2 KUNE

6.20 g., Copper-Nickel-Zinc, 24.5 mm. **Obv:** Marten back of numeral, arms divide branches below **Obv. Legend:** REPUBLIKA HRVATSKA **Rev:** Bluefin tuna right, date below **Rev. Legend:** THUNNUS - THYNNUS **Edge:** Reeded

| Date | Mintage | VF20 | XF40 | MS60 | MS63 | MS65 |
|---|---|---|---|---|---|---|
| 2002 | 1,000,000 | — | 1.50 | 3.00 | 4.00 | — |
| 2002 | 1,000 | PF65 6.00 | | | | |
| 2004 | 2,000,000 | — | 1.50 | 3.00 | 4.00 | — |
| 2004 | 2,000 | PF65 5.50 | | | | |
| 2006 | — | — | 1.50 | 3.00 | 4.00 | — |
| 2006 | 1,000 | PF65 5.50 | | | | |
| 2008 | — | — | 1.50 | 3.00 | 4.00 | — |
| 2008 | 1,000 | PF65 5.50 | | | | |
| 2010 | — | — | 1.50 | 3.00 | 4.00 | — |
| 2010 | — | PF65 5.50 | | | | |
| 2012 | — | — | 1.50 | 3.00 | 4.00 | — |
| 2012 | — | PF65 5.50 | | | | |
| 2014 | — | — | 1.50 | 3.00 | 4.00 | — |
| 2014 | — | PF65 5.50 | | | | |

### KM# 11 5 KUNA

7.45 g., Copper-Nickel-Zinc, 26.7 mm. **Obv:** Marten back of numeral, arms divide branches below **Obv. Legend:** REPUBLIKA HRVATSKA **Rev:** Brown bear left, date below **Rev. Legend:** MRKI MEDVJED **Edge:** Reeded

| Date | Mintage | VF20 | XF40 | MS60 | MS63 | MS65 |
|---|---|---|---|---|---|---|
| 2001 | 17,300,000 | — | 1.50 | 5.00 | 10.00 | — |
| 2001 | 1,000 | PF65 9.00 | | | | |
| 2003 | 1,000,000 | — | 1.50 | 5.00 | 10.00 | — |
| 2003 | 1,000 | PF65 9.00 | | | | |
| 2005 | — | — | 1.50 | 5.00 | 10.00 | — |
| 2005 | 2,000 | PF65 9.00 | | | | |
| 2007 | — | — | 1.50 | 5.00 | 10.00 | — |
| 2007 | 1,000 | PF65 9.00 | | | | |
| 2009 | — | — | 1.50 | 5.00 | 10.00 | — |
| 2009 | — | PF65 9.00 | | | | |
| 2011 | — | — | 1.50 | 5.00 | 10.00 | — |
| 2011 | — | PF65 9.00 | | | | |
| 2013 | — | — | — | 5.00 | 10.00 | — |
| 2013 | — | PF65 9.00 | | | | |

### KM# 23 5 KUNA

7.45 g., Copper-Nickel-Zinc, 26.5 mm. **Obv:** Marten back of numeral, arms divide branches below **Obv. Legend:** REPUBLIKA HRVATSKA **Rev:** Brown bear left, date below **Rev. Legend:** URSUS ARCTOS **Edge:** Reeded

| Date | Mintage | VF20 | XF40 | MS60 | MS63 | MS65 |
|---|---|---|---|---|---|---|
| 2002 | 2,000,000 | — | 2.00 | 5.00 | 9.00 | — |
| 2002 | 1,000 | PF65 9.00 | | | | |
| 2004 | 2,000,000 | — | 2.00 | 5.00 | 9.00 | — |
| 2004 | 2,000 | PF65 8.00 | | | | |
| 2006 | — | — | 2.00 | 5.00 | 9.00 | — |
| 2006 | 1,000 | PF65 8.00 | | | | |
| 2008 | — | — | 2.00 | 5.00 | 9.00 | — |

| Date | Mintage | VF20 | XF40 | MS60 | MS63 | MS65 |
|---|---|---|---|---|---|---|
| 2008 | 1,000 | PF65 8.00 | | | | |
| 2010 | — | — | 2.00 | 5.00 | 9.00 | — |
| 2010 | — | PF65 8.00 | | | | |
| 2012 | — | — | 2.00 | 5.00 | 9.00 | — |
| 2012 | — | PF65 8.00 | | | | |
| 2014 | — | — | — | 5.00 | 9.00 | — |
| 2014 | — | PF65 8.00 | | | | |

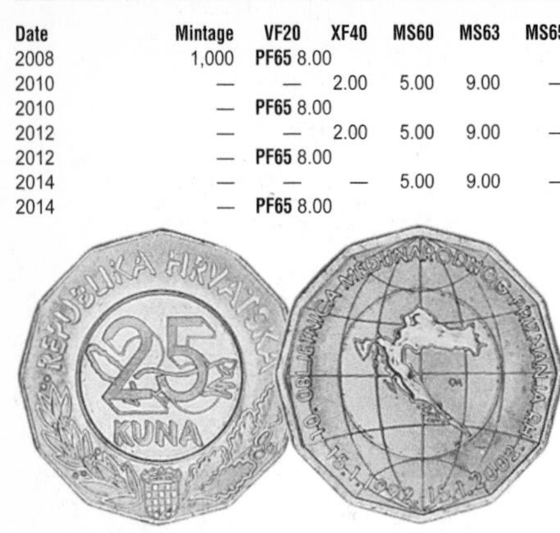

### KM# 66 25 KUNA

12.75 g., Bi-Metallic Brass center in Copper-Nickel ring, 32 mm. **Subject:** 10th Anniversary of International Recognition **Obv:** Denomination in 3-D on outlined marten within circle, arms divide sprays below **Rev:** National map **Edge:** Plain **Shape:** 12-sided

| Date | Mintage | VF20 | XF40 | MS60 | MS63 | MS65 |
|---|---|---|---|---|---|---|
| ND-2002 | 200,000 | — | — | — | 8.50 | — |

### KM# 78 25 KUNA

12.75 g., Bi-Metallic Brass center in Copper-Nickel ring, 32 mm. **Subject:** Croatian European Union Candidacy **Obv:** Denomination in 3-D on outlined marten within circle, arms divide sprays below **Rev:** Joined squares within circle of stars **Edge:** Plain **Shape:** 12-sided

| Date | Mintage | VF20 | XF40 | MS60 | MS63 | MS65 |
|---|---|---|---|---|---|---|
| ND (2004) | 30,000 | — | — | — | 10.00 | 12.00 |
| ND (2004) | — | PF63 22.00 | PF65 25.00 | | | |

### KM# 93 25 KUNA

12.75 g., Bi-Metallic Brass center in Copper-Nickel ring, 32 mm. **Subject:** EBRD Annual Meeting, Zagreb **Obv:** Large value at center **Rev:** Stylized old and new skyline

| Date | Mintage | VF20 | XF40 | MS60 | MS63 | MS65 |
|---|---|---|---|---|---|---|
| 2010 | — | — | — | — | 10.00 | 12.00 |

### KM# 94 25 KUNA

12.75 g., Bi-Metallic Brass center in Copper-Nickel ring, 32 mm. **Subject:** Croatian entry into European Union **Obv:** Shield and country names **Rev:** Group of 28 stars **Shape:** 12-sided

| Date | Mintage | VF20 | XF40 | MS60 | MS63 | MS65 |
|---|---|---|---|---|---|---|
| 2013 | — | — | — | — | 15.00 | — |
| 2013 | — | PF63 25.00 | PF65 30.00 | | | |

### KM# 83 150 KUNA

24.00 g., 0.925 Silver 0.7137 oz. ASW, 37 mm. **Subject:** 2006 Winter Olympics - Italy **Obv:** National arms below denomination **Rev:** Slalom skiing

| Date | Mintage | VF20 | XF40 | MS60 | MS63 | MS65 |
|---|---|---|---|---|---|---|
| ND-2006 | 15,000 | PF63 35.00 | PF65 40.00 | | | |

### KM# 84 150 KUNA

24.00 g., 0.925 Silver 0.7137 oz. ASW, 37 mm. **Subject:** 2006 World Soccer Championship - Germany **Obv:** National arms below denomination **Rev:** Soccer player

| Date | Mintage | VF20 | XF40 | MS60 | MS63 | MS65 |
|---|---|---|---|---|---|---|
| ND-2006 | 50,000 | PF63 30.00 | PF65 35.00 | | | |

### KM# 85 150 KUNA

24.00 g., 0.925 Silver 0.7137 oz. ASW, 37 mm. **Subject:** 2006 World Soccer Championship - Germany **Obv:** National arms above denomination **Rev:** Vignette

| Date | Mintage | VF20 | XF40 | MS60 | MS63 | MS65 |
|---|---|---|---|---|---|---|
| ND-2006 | 10,000 | PF63 40.00 | PF65 45.00 | | | |

### KM# 86 150 KUNA

24.00 g., 0.925 Silver 0.7137 oz. ASW, 37 mm. **Subject:** 150th Anniversary - Birth of Nikola Tesla **Obv:** National arms above induction motor and denomination **Rev:** Bust of Tesla

| Date | Mintage | VF20 | XF40 | MS60 | MS63 | MS65 |
|---|---|---|---|---|---|---|
| ND-2006 | 5,000 | PF63 47.00 | PF65 50.00 | | | |

### KM# 87 150 KUNA

24.00 g., 0.925 Silver 0.7137 oz. ASW, 37 mm. **Subject:** 2008 Olympic Games - Peoples Republic of China **Issuer:** Croatian National Bank **Obv:** National arms, value in laurel wreath **Rev:** T'ai-ho Tien gate in Beijing, athlete **Edge:** Plain **Edge Lettering:** Ag 925/1000 24 g 37 mm PP HNZ

| Date | Mintage | VF20 | XF40 | MS60 | MS63 | MS65 |
|---|---|---|---|---|---|---|
| ND-2006 | 20,000 | PF63 35.00 | PF65 40.00 | | | |

### KM# 88 150 KUNA

24.00 g., 0.925 Silver 0.7137 oz. ASW, 37 mm. **Subject:** Ican Mestrovic **Obv:** Squares and shamrocks **Rev:** Female kneeling with Irish harp

| Date | Mintage | VF20 | XF40 | MS60 | MS63 | MS65 |
|---|---|---|---|---|---|---|
| 2007 | 4,000 | — | — | — | 45.00 | 55.00 |

### KM# 89 150 KUNA

24.00 g., 0.925 Silver 0.7137 oz. ASW, 37 mm. **Subject:** Benedikt Kotruljevic **Obv:** Pile of coins **Rev:** Bust right

| Date | Mintage | VF20 | XF40 | MS60 | MS63 | MS65 |
|---|---|---|---|---|---|---|
| 2007 | 10,000 | — | — | — | 40.00 | 45.00 |

### KM# 90 150 KUNA

24.00 g., 0.925 Silver 0.7137 oz. ASW, 37 mm. **Subject:** Historic Ships - Dubrovnik Karaka **Obv:** Sail within compass **Rev:** Ship

| Date | Mintage | VF20 | XF40 | MS60 | MS63 | MS65 |
|---|---|---|---|---|---|---|
| 2007 | 10,000 | — | — | — | 40.00 | 45.00 |

### KM# 91 1000 KUNA

7.00 g., 0.986 Gold 0.2219 oz. AGW, 22 mm. **Subject:** Andrija Monorovicic, 150th Anniversary of Birth **Obv:** Globe bisected showing layers **Rev:** Bust facing

| Date | Mintage | VF20 | XF40 | MS60 | MS63 | MS65 |
|---|---|---|---|---|---|---|
| 2007 | 2,000 | — | — | — | 425 | 450 |

### KM# 92 1000 KUNA

7.00 g., 0.986 Gold 0.2219 oz. AGW, 22 mm. **Subject:** Marin Drzic **Obv:** Shield flanked by comedy and tragedy masks **Rev:** Half-length figure right

| Date | Mintage | VF20 | XF40 | MS60 | MS63 | MS65 |
|---|---|---|---|---|---|---|
| 2008 | 2,000 | — | — | — | 425 | 450 |

### KM# 95 1000 KUNA

7.00 g., 0.986 Gold 0.2219 oz. AGW, 22 mm. **Subject:** Croatian entry into European Union **Obv:** Three stars and shield **Rev:** Group of 28 stars

| Date | Mintage | VF20 | XF40 | MS60 | MS63 | MS65 |
|---|---|---|---|---|---|---|
| 2013 | — | PF63 425 | PF65 450 | | | |

## MINT SETS

| KM# | Date | Mintage | Identification | Issue Price | Mkt Val |
|---|---|---|---|---|---|
| MS2 | 2002 (9) | — | KM#12, 14-17, 19, 20.1, 21, 23 | — | 25.00 |

## PROOF SETS

| KM# | Date | Mintage | Identification | Issue Price | Mkt Val |
|---|---|---|---|---|---|
| PS36 | 2001 (9) | — | KM#3-8, 9.2, 10, 11 | — | 45.00 |
| PS37 | 2002 (9) | — | KM#12, 14-17, 19, 20.2, 21, 23 | — | 45.00 |
| PS38 | 2003 (9) | — | KM#3-8, 9.1, 10, 11 | — | 45.00 |
| PS39 | 2004 (9) | — | KM#12, 14-17, 19, 21, 23, 79 | — | 40.00 |
| PS40 | 2005 (9) | — | KM#3-8, 9.1, 10-11 | — | 45.00 |
| PS41 | 2006 (9) | — | KM#12, 14-17, 19, 20.2, 21, 23 | — | 40.00 |
| PS42 | 2007 (9) | — | KM#3-8, 9.1, 10-11 | — | 45.00 |
| PS43 | 2008 (9) | — | KM#12, 14-17, 19, 20.2, 21, 23 | — | 40.00 |
| PS44 | 2009 (9) | — | KM#3-8, 9.1, 10-11. | — | 45.00 |
| PS45 | 2010 (9) | — | KM#12, 14-17, 19, 20.2, 21, 23 | — | 45.00 |
| PS46 | 2011 (9) | — | KM#3-8, 9.1, 10-11. | — | 45.00 |
| PS47 | 2012 (9) | — | KM#12, 14-17, 19, 20.2, 21, 23. | — | 45.00 |

# CUBA

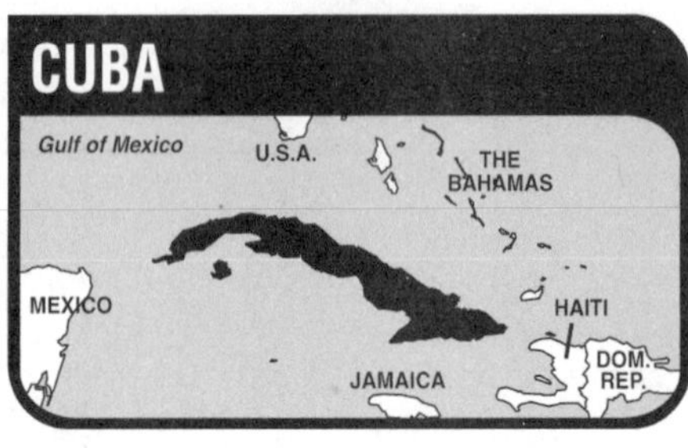


The Republic of Cuba, situated at the northern edge of the Caribbean Sea about 90 miles (145 km.) south of Florida, has an area of 42,804 sq. mi. (110,860 sq. km.) and a population of *11.2 million. Capital: Havana. The Cuban economy is based on the cultivation and refining of sugar, which provides 80 percent of export earnings.

**MINT MARK**

Key - Havana, 1977-

**MONETARY SYSTEM**

100 Centavos = 1 Peso

## SECOND REPUBLIC

1962 - Present

## DECIMAL COINAGE

### KM# 33.3 CENTAVO

0.75 g., Aluminum, 16.76 mm. **Obv:** Cuban arms within wreath, denomination below **Rev:** Roman denomination within circle of star, date below **Edge:** Plain **Note:** Shield varieties exist.

| Date | Mintage | VF20 | XF40 | MS60 | MS63 | MS65 |
|---|---|---|---|---|---|---|
| 2001 | — | — | 0.40 | 0.80 | 1.75 | 2.00 |
| 2002 | — | — | 0.40 | 0.80 | 1.75 | 2.00 |
| 2003 | — | — | 0.40 | 0.80 | 1.75 | 2.00 |
| 2004 | — | — | 0.40 | 0.80 | 1.75 | 2.00 |
| 2005 | — | — | 0.40 | 0.80 | 1.75 | 2.00 |
| 2006 | — | — | 0.40 | 0.80 | 1.75 | 2.00 |
| 2007 | — | — | 0.40 | 0.80 | 1.75 | 2.00 |
| 2008 | — | — | — | 0.80 | 1.75 | 2.00 |
| 2010 | — | — | — | 0.80 | 1.75 | 2.00 |
| 2012 | — | — | — | 0.80 | 1.75 | 2.00 |

### KM# 34 5 CENTAVOS

1.50 g., Aluminum, 21.21 mm. **Obv:** National arms within wreath, denomination below **Rev:** Roman denomination within circle of star, date below **Note:** Shield varieties exist.

| Date | Mintage | VF20 | XF40 | MS60 | MS63 | MS65 |
|---|---|---|---|---|---|---|
| 2001 | 6,703,331 | 0.10 | 0.25 | 0.75 | 1.50 | 1.75 |
| 2002 | 14,830,000 | — | 0.25 | 0.75 | 1.50 | 1.75 |
| Note: High or low dates exist. | | | | | | |
| 2003 | 62,520,000 | — | 0.25 | 0.75 | 1.50 | 1.75 |

| Date | Mintage | VF20 | XF40 | MS60 | MS63 | MS65 |
|---|---|---|---|---|---|---|
| 2004 | 62,520,000 | — | 0.25 | 0.75 | 1.50 | 1.75 |
| 2006 | 62,520,000 | — | 0.25 | 0.75 | 1.50 | 1.75 |
| 2007 | 62,520,000 | — | 0.25 | 0.75 | 1.50 | 1.75 |
| 2008 | — | — | 0.25 | 0.75 | 1.50 | 1.75 |
| 2009 | — | — | 0.25 | 0.75 | 1.50 | 1.75 |
| 2010 | — | — | 0.25 | 0.75 | 1.50 | 1.75 |

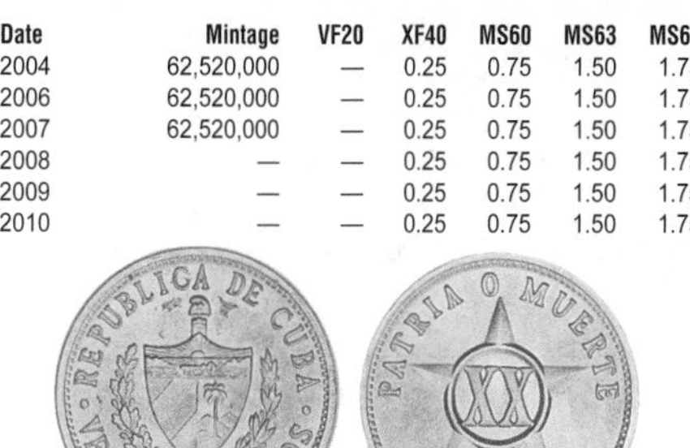


## KM# 35.1 20 CENTAVOS

2.00 g., Aluminum, 24 mm. **Obv:** Cuban arms within wreath, denomination below **Rev:** Roman denomination within circle of star, date below **Note:** Shield varieties exist.

| Date | Mintage | VF20 | XF40 | MS60 | MS63 | MS65 |
|---|---|---|---|---|---|---|
| 2002 | 25,000,000 | 0.50 | 1.00 | 2.00 | 3.50 | 5.00 |
| 2003 | 11,911,000 | 0.50 | 1.00 | 2.00 | 3.50 | 5.00 |
| 2005 | — | 0.50 | 1.00 | 2.00 | 3.50 | 5.00 |
| 2006 | — | 0.50 | 1.00 | 2.00 | 3.50 | 5.00 |
| 2007 | — | 0.50 | 1.00 | 2.00 | 3.50 | 5.00 |

## KM# 35.2 20 CENTAVOS

2.00 g., Aluminum, 24 mm. **Obv:** National arms, revised shield **Rev:** Roman denomination within circle of star

| Date | Mintage | VF20 | XF40 | MS60 | MS63 | MS65 |
|---|---|---|---|---|---|---|
| 2002 | — | 7.00 | 10.00 | 15.00 | — | — |
| Note: Large and small dates exist. | | | | | | |
| 2003 | — | 7.00 | 10.00 | 15.00 | — | — |
| 2005 | — | 7.00 | 10.00 | 15.00 | — | — |
| 2006 | — | 7.00 | 10.00 | 15.00 | — | — |

## KM# 347 PESO

5.52 g., Brass Plated Steel, 24.5 mm. **Subject:** Jose Marti **Obv:** National arms within wreath, denomination below **Rev:** Smaller Bust facing, denomination at left **Rev. Legend:** PATRIA O MUERTE **Note:** Rim varieties exist.

| Date | Mintage | VF20 | XF40 | MS60 | MS63 | MS65 |
|---|---|---|---|---|---|---|
| 2001 | — | — | 1.00 | 2.00 | 3.00 | 4.00 |
| 2002 | — | — | 1.00 | 2.00 | 3.00 | 4.00 |
| 2012 | — | — | 1.00 | 2.00 | 3.00 | 4.00 |

## KM# 829 PESO

12.70 g., Nickel Plated Steel, 32.5 mm. **Obv:** National arms **Rev:** Carpenter bird perched - multicolor **Rev. Legend:** FAUNA CUBANA - PAJERO CARPINTERO **Edge:** Plain

| Date | Mintage | VF20 | XF40 | MS60 | MS63 | MS65 |
|---|---|---|---|---|---|---|
| 2001 | — | — | — | — | 15.00 | — |

## KM# 830 PESO

12.70 g., Nickel Plated Steel, 32.5 mm. **Obv:** National arms **Rev:** Parrot perched - multicolor **Rev. Legend:** FAUNA CUBANA - COTORRA **Edge:** Plain

| Date | Mintage | VF20 | XF40 | MS60 | MS63 | MS65 |
|---|---|---|---|---|---|---|
| 2001 | — | — | — | — | 15.00 | — |

## KM# 831 PESO

12.70 g., Nickel Plated Steel, 32.5 mm. **Obv:** National arms **Rev:** Pink orchid - multicolor **Rev. Legend:** FLORA CUBANA - ORQUIDEAS **Edge:** Plain

| Date | Mintage | VF20 | XF40 | MS60 | MS63 | MS65 |
|---|---|---|---|---|---|---|
| 2001 | — | — | — | — | 20.00 | — |

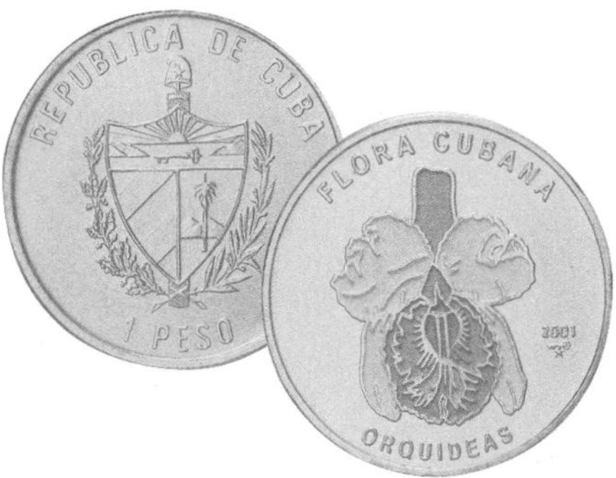


## KM# 832 PESO

12.70 g., Nickel Plated Steel, 32.5 mm. **Obv:** National arms **Rev:** Yellow orchid - multicolor **Rev. Legend:** FLORA CUBANA - ORQUIDEAS **Edge:** Plain

| Date | Mintage | VF20 | XF40 | MS60 | MS63 | MS65 |
|---|---|---|---|---|---|---|
| 2001 | — | — | — | — | 20.00 | — |

## KM# 833 PESO

12.70 g., Nickel Plated Steel, 32.5 mm. **Obv:** National arms **Rev:** White orchid - multicolor **Rev. Legend:** FLORA CUBANA - ORQUIDEAS **Edge:** Plain

| Date | Mintage | VF20 | XF40 | MS60 | MS63 | MS65 |
|---|---|---|---|---|---|---|
| 2001 | — | — | — | — | 20.00 | — |

## KM# 844 PESO

26.00 g., Copper-Nickel, 38 mm. **Subject:** Bolivar, 175th Anniversary of Liberation **Rev:** Bust

| Date | Mintage | VF20 | XF40 | MS60 | MS63 | MS65 |
|---|---|---|---|---|---|---|
| 2001 | — | — | — | — | — | 15.00 |

## KM# 845 PESO

26.00 g., Copper-Nickel, 38 mm. **Subject:** Bolivar - 175th Anniversary of Liberation **Rev:** Birthplace

| Date | Mintage | VF20 | XF40 | MS60 | MS63 | MS65 |
|---|---|---|---|---|---|---|
| 2001 | — | — | — | — | — | 15.00 |

## KM# 846 PESO

Copper-Nickel, 38 mm. **Subject:** Boliver, 175th Anniversary of Liberation **Rev:** Battle scene

| Date | Mintage | VF20 | XF40 | MS60 | MS63 | MS65 |
|---|---|---|---|---|---|---|
| 2001 | — | — | — | — | — | 15.00 |

## KM# 847 PESO

12.70 g., Nickel Plated Steel, 32.5 mm. **Subject:** Cuban Fauna - Avellaneda Butterfly **Rev:** Butterfly

| Date | Mintage | VF20 | XF40 | MS60 | MS63 | MS65 |
|---|---|---|---|---|---|---|
| 2001 | — | — | — | — | — | 15.00 |

## KM# 848 PESO

26.00 g., Copper-Nickel, 38 mm. **Subject:** Global Conference Three

| Date | Mintage | VF20 | XF40 | MS60 | MS63 | MS65 |
|---|---|---|---|---|---|---|
| 2001 | 200 | — | — | — | — | 50.00 |

## KM# 849 PESO

26.00 g., Copper-Nickel, 38 mm. **Subject:** Monuments of Cuba **Rev:** Havana Cathedral

| Date | Mintage | VF20 | XF40 | MS60 | MS63 | MS65 |
|---|---|---|---|---|---|---|
| 2001 | — | — | — | — | — | 15.00 |

## KM# 850 PESO

26.00 g., Copper-Nickel, 38 mm. **Subject:** Monuments of Cuba **Rev:** Trinidad Cathedral

| Date | Mintage | VF20 | XF40 | MS60 | MS63 | MS65 |
|---|---|---|---|---|---|---|
| 2001 | — | — | — | — | — | 15.00 |

### KM# 851 PESO

Copper-Nickel, 38 mm. **Subject:** Monuments of Cuba **Rev:** Templete

| Date | Mintage | VF20 | XF40 | MS60 | MS63 | MS65 |
|---|---|---|---|---|---|---|
| 2001 | — | — | — | — | — | 15.00 |

### KM# 852 PESO

26.00 g., Copper-Nickel, 38 mm. **Subject:** Playa Giron

| Date | Mintage | VF20 | XF40 | MS60 | MS63 | MS65 |
|---|---|---|---|---|---|---|
| 2001 | — | — | — | — | — | 15.00 |

### KM# 853 PESO

26.00 g., Copper-Nickel, 38 mm. **Subject:** Federico Engels

| Date | Mintage | VF20 | XF40 | MS60 | MS63 | MS65 |
|---|---|---|---|---|---|---|
| 2002 | — | — | — | — | — | 15.00 |

### KM# 854 PESO

26.00 g., Copper-Nickel, 38 mm. **Subject:** Lenin

| Date | Mintage | VF20 | XF40 | MS60 | MS63 | MS65 |
|---|---|---|---|---|---|---|
| 2002 | — | — | — | — | — | 15.00 |

### KM# 855 PESO

26.00 g., Copper-Nickel, 38 mm. **Subject:** Mao Tse Tung

| Date | Mintage | VF20 | XF40 | MS60 | MS63 | MS65 |
|---|---|---|---|---|---|---|
| 2002 | — | — | — | — | — | 15.00 |

### KM# 856 PESO

26.00 g., Copper-Nickel, 38 mm. **Subject:** Karl Marx

| Date | Mintage | VF20 | XF40 | MS60 | MS63 | MS65 |
|---|---|---|---|---|---|---|
| 2002 | — | — | — | — | — | 15.00 |

### KM# 951 PESO

Copper-Nickel **Rev:** Birds in color

| Date | Mintage | VF20 | XF40 | MS60 | MS63 | MS65 |
|---|---|---|---|---|---|---|
| 2002 | — | PF65 60.00 | | | | |

### KM# 728 PESO

Silver **Subject:** Endangered Wildlife **Rev:** Crocodile

| Date | Mintage | VF20 | XF40 | MS60 | MS63 | MS65 |
|---|---|---|---|---|---|---|
| 2003 | — | PF65 45.00 | | | | |

### KM# 857 PESO

26.00 g., Copper-Nickel, 38 mm. **Subject:** Che Guevara, 75th Anniversary of Birth

| Date | Mintage | VF20 | XF40 | MS60 | MS63 | MS65 |
|---|---|---|---|---|---|---|
| 2003 | — | — | — | — | — | 15.00 |

### KM# 858 PESO

26.00 g., Copper-Nickel, 38 mm. **Subject:** Che Guevara, 75th Anniversary of Birth

| Date | Mintage | VF20 | XF40 | MS60 | MS63 | MS65 |
|---|---|---|---|---|---|---|
| 2003 | — | — | — | — | — | 15.00 |

### KM# 953 PESO

20.00 g., Copper, 38 mm. **Subject:** Ernesto "Che" Guevara, 75th Birthday **Rev:** Bust

| Date | Mintage | VF20 | XF40 | MS60 | MS63 | MS65 |
|---|---|---|---|---|---|---|
| 2003 | — | — | — | — | — | 50.00 |

### KM# 859 PESO

26.00 g., Copper-Nickel, 38 mm. **Subject:** Fauna - Hawk Pilgrin

| Date | Mintage | VF20 | XF40 | MS60 | MS63 | MS65 |
|---|---|---|---|---|---|---|
| 2004 | — | — | — | — | — | 17.00 |

### KM# 860 PESO

26.00 g., Copper-Nickel, 38 mm. **Subject:** Fauna Iberian Lynx

| Date | Mintage | VF20 | XF40 | MS60 | MS63 | MS65 |
|---|---|---|---|---|---|---|
| 2004 | — | — | — | — | — | 17.00 |

### KM# 861 PESO

26.00 g., Copper-Nickel, 38 mm. **Subject:** Fauna - Imperial Eagle

| Date | Mintage | VF20 | XF40 | MS60 | MS63 | MS65 |
|---|---|---|---|---|---|---|
| 2004 | — | — | — | — | — | 17.00 |

### KM# 862 PESO

26.00 g., Copper-Nickel, 38 mm. **Subject:** Fauna Lobo Gris

| Date | Mintage | VF20 | XF40 | MS60 | MS63 | MS65 |
|---|---|---|---|---|---|---|
| 2004 | — | — | — | — | — | 17.00 |

### KM# 863 PESO

26.00 g., Copper-Nickel, 38 mm. **Subject:** Fauna - Oso Pards

| Date | Mintage | VF20 | XF40 | MS60 | MS63 | MS65 |
|---|---|---|---|---|---|---|
| 2004 | — | — | — | — | — | 17.00 |

### KM# 864 PESO

26.00 g., Copper-Nickel, 38 mm. **Subject:** Fauna - Osprey

| Date | Mintage | VF20 | XF40 | MS60 | MS63 | MS65 |
|---|---|---|---|---|---|---|
| 2004 | — | — | — | — | — | 17.00 |

### KM# 865 PESO

Copper-Nickel, 38 mm. **Subject:** Cuban Tobacco

| Date | Mintage | VF20 | XF40 | MS60 | MS63 | MS65 |
|---|---|---|---|---|---|---|
| 2005 | — | — | — | — | — | 17.00 |

### KM# 866 PESO

26.00 g., Nickel Plated Steel, 32.8 mm. **Subject:** Tropical Fish - Pygoplites **Obv:** National arms within wreath **Rev:** Pyglopites dicanthus

| Date | Mintage | VF20 | XF40 | MS60 | MS63 | MS65 |
|---|---|---|---|---|---|---|
| 2005 | — | — | — | — | — | 15.00 |

### KM# 867 PESO

26.00 g., Nickel Plated Steel, 32.8 mm. **Subject:** Tropical Fish - Zanclus **Obv:** National arms within wreath **Rev:** Zanclus canescens

| Date | Mintage | VF20 | XF40 | MS60 | MS63 | MS65 |
|---|---|---|---|---|---|---|
| 2005 | — | — | — | — | — | 15.00 |

### KM# 868 PESO

26.00 g., Nickel Plated Steel, 32.8 mm. **Subject:** Tropical Fish - Rhinecanthus **Obv:** National arms

| Date | Mintage | VF20 | XF40 | MS60 | MS63 | MS65 |
|---|---|---|---|---|---|---|
| 2005 | — | — | — | — | — | 15.00 |

### KM# 924 PESO

Nickel Plated Steel **Subject:** Cuban Tobacco, 500th Anniversary **Rev:** Tobacco traders before caraval sailing ship

| Date | Mintage | VF20 | XF40 | MS60 | MS63 | MS65 |
|---|---|---|---|---|---|---|
| 2005 Proof | — | — | — | — | — | 10.00 |

### KM# 869 PESO

26.00 g., Nickel Plated Steel, 38 mm. **Obv:** National arms within wreath **Rev:** Toucan

| Date | Mintage | VF20 | XF40 | MS60 | MS63 | MS65 |
|---|---|---|---|---|---|---|
| 2006 | — | — | — | — | — | 15.00 |

**KM# 870 PESO**
26.00 g., Copper-Nickel, 38 mm. **Subject:** 29th Summer Olympics

| Date | Mintage | VF20 | XF40 | MS60 | MS63 | MS65 |
|---|---|---|---|---|---|---|
| 2006 | — | — | — | — | — | 15.00 |

**KM# 871 PESO**
26.00 g., Copper-Nickel, 38 mm. **Subject:** Che Guevara, 40th Anniversary of his Death **Obv:** National arms within wreath **Rev:** Bust facing

| Date | Mintage | VF20 | XF40 | MS60 | MS63 | MS65 |
|---|---|---|---|---|---|---|
| 2007 | — | — | — | — | — | 15.00 |

**KM# 871a PESO**
26.00 g., Copper, 38 mm. **Obv:** Che Guevara, 40th Anniversary of his Death

| Date | Mintage | VF20 | XF40 | MS60 | MS63 | MS65 |
|---|---|---|---|---|---|---|
| 2007 | — | — | — | — | — | 15.00 |

**KM# 873 PESO**
26.00 g., Copper-Nickel **Subject:** Fauna - Buitre (Condor)

| Date | Mintage | VF20 | XF40 | MS60 | MS63 | MS65 |
|---|---|---|---|---|---|---|
| 2007 | — | — | — | — | — | 17.00 |

**KM# 874 PESO**
26.00 g., Copper-Nickel, 38 mm. **Subject:** Fauna - Burro

| Date | Mintage | VF20 | XF40 | MS60 | MS63 | MS65 |
|---|---|---|---|---|---|---|
| 2007 | — | — | — | — | — | 17.00 |

**KM# 875 PESO**
26.00 g., Copper-Nickel, 38 mm. **Subject:** Fauna - Cobra Montesa

| Date | Mintage | VF20 | XF40 | MS60 | MS63 | MS65 |
|---|---|---|---|---|---|---|
| 2007 | — | — | — | — | — | 17.00 |

**KM# 876 PESO**
26.00 g., Copper-Nickel **Subject:** Fauna - Gato Montes

| Date | Mintage | VF20 | XF40 | MS60 | MS63 | MS65 |
|---|---|---|---|---|---|---|
| 2007 | — | — | — | — | — | 17.00 |

**KM# 877 PESO**
26.00 g., Copper-Nickel, 38 mm. **Subject:** Fauma - Mastin Espanol

| Date | Mintage | VF20 | XF40 | MS60 | MS63 | MS65 |
|---|---|---|---|---|---|---|
| 2007 | — | — | — | — | — | 17.00 |

**KM# 878 PESO**
26.00 g., Copper-Nickel, 26 mm. **Subject:** Fauna - Urogallo

| Date | Mintage | VF20 | XF40 | MS60 | MS63 | MS65 |
|---|---|---|---|---|---|---|
| 2007 | — | — | — | — | — | 17.00 |

**KM# 879 PESO**
26.00 g., Copper-Nickel, 38 mm. **Subject:** Fortress - El Morro

| Date | Mintage | VF20 | XF40 | MS60 | MS63 | MS65 |
|---|---|---|---|---|---|---|
| 2007 | — | — | — | — | — | 17.00 |

**KM# 880 PESO**
26.00 g., Copper-Nickel, 38 mm. **Subject:** Fortress - La Fuerza

| Date | Mintage | VF20 | XF40 | MS60 | MS63 | MS65 |
|---|---|---|---|---|---|---|
| 2007 | — | — | — | — | — | 15.00 |

**KM# 881 PESO**
26.00 g., Copper-Nickel, 38 mm. **Subject:** Fortress - La Punta

| Date | Mintage | VF20 | XF40 | MS60 | MS63 | MS65 |
|---|---|---|---|---|---|---|
| 2007 | — | — | — | — | — | 15.00 |

**KM# 882 PESO**
26.00 g., Copper-Nickel, 38 mm. **Subject:** Garibaldi

| Date | Mintage | VF20 | XF40 | MS60 | MS63 | MS65 |
|---|---|---|---|---|---|---|
| 2007 | — | — | — | — | — | 15.00 |

**KM# 883 PESO**
26.00 g., Copper-Nickel, 38 mm. **Subject:** Santa Ana Ship

| Date | Mintage | VF20 | XF40 | MS60 | MS63 | MS65 |
|---|---|---|---|---|---|---|
| 2007 | — | — | — | — | — | 15.00 |

**KM# 884 PESO**
26.00 g., Copper-Nickel, 38 mm. **Subject:** Sputnik

| Date | Mintage | VF20 | XF40 | MS60 | MS63 | MS65 |
|---|---|---|---|---|---|---|
| 2007 | — | — | — | — | — | 15.00 |

**KM# 901 PESO**
38.00 g., Copper-Nickel, 38 mm. **Subject:** Ship - Principe Asturias

| Date | Mintage | VF20 | XF40 | MS60 | MS63 | MS65 |
|---|---|---|---|---|---|---|
| 2008 | — | — | — | — | — | 15.00 |

**KM# 902 PESO**
26.00 g., Copper-Nickel, 38 mm. **Subject:** Ship San Carlos

| Date | Mintage | VF20 | XF40 | MS60 | MS63 | MS65 |
|---|---|---|---|---|---|---|
| 2008 | — | — | — | — | — | 15.00 |

**KM# 903 PESO**
38.00 g., Copper-Nickel, 38 mm. **Subject:** Ship- San Hermene

| Date | Mintage | VF20 | XF40 | MS60 | MS63 | MS65 |
|---|---|---|---|---|---|---|
| 2008 | — | — | — | — | — | 15.00 |

**KM# 907 PESO**
41.00 g., Copper, 45 mm. **Subject:** Revolution, 50th Anniversary **Obv:** National arms within wreath **Rev:** Five scenes in medallions

| Date | Mintage | VF20 | XF40 | MS60 | MS63 | MS65 |
|---|---|---|---|---|---|---|
| 2009 Antique patina | 2,009 | — | — | — | — | 15.00 |

**KM# 908 PESO**
26.00 g., Copper-Nickel, 38 mm. **Subject:** Fidel & Raul Castro **Obv:** National arms within wreath

| Date | Mintage | VF20 | XF40 | MS60 | MS63 | MS65 |
|---|---|---|---|---|---|---|
| 2009 | 5,000 | — | — | — | — | 15.00 |

**KM# 908a PESO**
26.00 g., Copper, 38 mm. **Subject:** Fidel and Raul Castro

| Date | Mintage | VF20 | XF40 | MS60 | MS63 | MS65 |
|---|---|---|---|---|---|---|
| 2009 | 5,000 | — | — | — | — | 15.00 |

**KM# 910 PESO**
26.00 g., Copper-Nickel, 38 mm. **Subject:** Manatee

| Date | Mintage | VF20 | XF40 | MS60 | MS63 | MS65 |
|---|---|---|---|---|---|---|
| 2009 | — | — | — | — | — | 15.00 |

**KM# 956 PESO**
Gold, 45 mm. **Subject:** Revolution, 50th Anniversary

| Date | Mintage | VF20 | XF40 | MS60 | MS63 | MS65 |
|---|---|---|---|---|---|---|
| 2009 | 50 | PF65 2,000 | | | | |

**KM# 954 PESO**
26.00 g., Copper-Nickel, 38 mm. **Obv:** National arms within wreath **Rev:** Castro and Hemingway

| Date | Mintage | VF20 | XF40 | MS60 | MS63 | MS65 |
|---|---|---|---|---|---|---|
| 2010 | 5,000 | — | — | — | — | 15.00 |

**KM# 954a PESO**
26.00 g., Copper, 38 mm. **Obv:** National arms within wreath **Rev:** Castro and Hemingway

| Date | Mintage | VF20 | XF40 | MS60 | MS63 | MS65 |
|---|---|---|---|---|---|---|
| 2010 | 5,000 | — | — | — | — | 15.00 |

**KM# 954b PESO**
20.00 g., 0.999 Silver 0.6424 oz. ASW, 38 mm. **Obv:** National arms within wreath **Rev:** Castro and Hemingway

| Date | Mintage | VF20 | XF40 | MS60 | MS63 | MS65 |
|---|---|---|---|---|---|---|
| 2010 | 5,000 | PF65 45.00 | | | | |

**KM# 955 PESO**
26.00 g., Copper-Nickel, 38 mm. **Subject:** Independence of the Americas, 200th Anniversary **Obv:** National arms at left and legend at right **Rev:** Sunburst and map of the Americas

| Date | Mintage | VF20 | XF40 | MS60 | MS63 | MS65 |
|---|---|---|---|---|---|---|
| 2011 | — | — | — | — | — | 15.00 |

**KM# 955a PESO**
26.00 g., Copper, 38 mm. **Subject:** Independence of the Americas, 200th Anniversary **Obv:** National arms within wreath at left, legend at right **Rev:** Sunburst and map of the Americas

| Date | Mintage | VF20 | XF40 | MS60 | MS63 | MS65 |
|---|---|---|---|---|---|---|
| 2011 | — | — | — | — | — | 15.00 |

**KM# 955b PESO**
20.00 g., 0.999 Silver 0.6424 oz. ASW, 38 mm. **Subject:** Independence of the Americas, 200th Anniversary **Obv:** National arms at left, legend at right **Rev:** Sunburst and map of the Americas

| Date | Mintage | VF20 | XF40 | MS60 | MS63 | MS65 |
|---|---|---|---|---|---|---|
| 2011 | 1,810 | PF65 45.00 | | | | |

**KM# 346a 3 PESOS**
8.00 g., Nickel Plated Steel, 26.5 mm. **Obv:** National arms within wreath, denomination below **Rev:** Head facing, date below **Note:** Shield varieties exist.

| Date | Mintage | VF20 | XF40 | MS60 | MS63 | MS65 |
|---|---|---|---|---|---|---|
| 2002 | — | — | 2.50 | 5.00 | 7.00 | — |

**KM# 739 5 PESOS**
1.24 g., Gold, 14 mm. **Subject:** Wonders of the Ancient World **Obv:** Cuban arms **Rev:** Ancient lighthouse of Alexandria

| Date | Mintage | VF20 | XF40 | MS60 | MS63 | MS65 |
|---|---|---|---|---|---|---|
| 2005 | 5,000 | PF65 85.00 | | | | |

**KM# 740 5 PESOS**
1.24 g., Gold, 14 mm. **Subject:** Wonders of the Ancient World **Obv:** Cuban arms **Rev:** Colossus of Rhodes

| Date | Mintage | VF20 | XF40 | MS60 | MS63 | MS65 |
|---|---|---|---|---|---|---|
| 2005 | 5,000 | PF65 75.00 | | | | |

**KM# 741 5 PESOS**
1.24 g., Gold, 14 mm. **Subject:** Wonders of the Ancient World **Obv:** Cuban arms **Rev:** Hanging Gardens of Babylon

| Date | Mintage | VF20 | XF40 | MS60 | MS63 | MS65 |
|---|---|---|---|---|---|---|
| 2005 | 5,000 | PF65 75.00 | | | | |

**KM# 742 5 PESOS**
1.24 g., Gold, 14 mm. **Subject:** Wonders of the Ancient World **Obv:** Cuban arms **Rev:** Egyptian Pyramids

| Date | Mintage | VF20 | XF40 | MS60 | MS63 | MS65 |
|---|---|---|---|---|---|---|
| 2005 | 5,000 | PF65 75.00 | | | | |

**KM# 743 5 PESOS**
1.24 g., Gold, 14 mm. **Subject:** Wonders of the Ancient World **Obv:** Cuban arms **Rev:** Temple of Artemis

| Date | Mintage | VF20 | XF40 | MS60 | MS63 | MS65 |
|---|---|---|---|---|---|---|
| 2005 | 5,000 | PF65 75.00 | | | | |

**KM# 744 5 PESOS**
1.24 g., Gold, 14 mm. **Subject:** Wonders of the Ancient World **Obv:** Cuban arms **Rev:** Statue of Jupiter

| Date | Mintage | VF20 | XF40 | MS60 | MS63 | MS65 |
|---|---|---|---|---|---|---|
| 2005 | 5,000 | PF65 75.00 | | | | |

**KM# 745 5 PESOS**
1.24 g., Gold, 14 mm. **Subject:** Wonders of the Ancient World **Obv:** Cuban arms **Rev:** Mausoleum of Halicarnas

| Date | Mintage | VF20 | XF40 | MS60 | MS63 | MS65 |
|---|---|---|---|---|---|---|
| 2005 | 5,000 | PF65 75.00 | | | | |

**KM# 746 5 PESOS**
1.24 g., Gold, 14 mm. **Obv:** Cuban arms **Rev:** Cortes, Montezuma and Aztec Pyramid

| Date | Mintage | VF20 | XF40 | MS60 | MS63 | MS65 |
|---|---|---|---|---|---|---|
| 2005 | 15,000 | PF65 75.00 | | | | |

**KM# 885 5 PESOS**
12.00 g., Silver, 30 mm. **Subject:** Che Guevara, 40th Anniversary of his Death

| Date | Mintage | VF20 | XF40 | MS60 | MS63 | MS65 |
|---|---|---|---|---|---|---|
| 2007 | — | PF63 40.00 | PF65 45.00 | | | |

**KM# 762 10 PESOS**
31.10 g., 0.999 Silver 0.999 oz. ASW, 38 mm. **Obv:** Cuban arms **Rev:** Two Bee hummingbirds

| Date | Mintage | VF20 | XF40 | MS60 | MS63 | MS65 |
|---|---|---|---|---|---|---|
| 2001 | 20,000 | PF63 35.00 | PF65 40.00 | | | |

**KM# 763 10 PESOS**
20.00 g., 0.999 Silver 0.6424 oz. ASW, 38 mm. **Subject:** Third Globalization Conference **Obv:** Cuban arms **Rev:** World map

| Date | Mintage | VF20 | XF40 | MS60 | MS63 | MS65 |
|---|---|---|---|---|---|---|
| 2001 | 100 | PF65 200 | | | | |

**KM# 764 10 PESOS**
20.00 g., 0.999 Silver 0.6424 oz. ASW, 38 mm. **Subject:** 40th Anniversary - Battle of Giron **Obv:** Cuban arms **Rev:** Soldiers on tank

| Date | Mintage | VF20 | XF40 | MS60 | MS63 | MS65 |
|---|---|---|---|---|---|---|
| 2001 | — | — | — | — | — | 30.00 |
| 2001 | 3,000 | PF63 40.00 | PF65 45.00 | | | |

**KM# 765 10 PESOS**
31.10 g., 0.999 Silver 0.999 oz. ASW, 38 mm. **Subject:** 106th Anniversary - Jose Marti's **Obv:** Cuban arms **Rev:** Monument

| Date | Mintage | VF20 | XF40 | MS60 | MS63 | MS65 |
|---|---|---|---|---|---|---|
| 2001 | — | PF63 40.00 | PF65 45.00 | | | |

**KM# 766 10 PESOS**
15.00 g., 0.999 Silver 0.4818 oz. ASW, 35 mm. **Subject:** Cuban Fauna **Obv:** Cuban arms **Rev:** Red-splashed Sulphur butterfly

| Date | Mintage | VF20 | XF40 | MS60 | MS63 | MS65 |
|---|---|---|---|---|---|---|
| 2001 | — | PF65 35.00 | | | | |

**KM# 767 10 PESOS**
15.00 g., 0.999 Silver 0.4818 oz. ASW, 35 mm. **Subject:** Cuban Fauna **Obv:** Cuban arms **Rev:** Cuban Parrot

| Date | Mintage | VF20 | XF40 | MS60 | MS63 | MS65 |
|---|---|---|---|---|---|---|
| 2001 | — | PF65 35.00 | | | | |

**KM# 768 10 PESOS**
15.00 g., 0.999 Silver 0.4818 oz. ASW, 35 mm. **Obv:** National arms **Rev:** Cuban (Green) woodpecker

| Date | Mintage | VF20 | XF40 | MS60 | MS63 | MS65 |
|---|---|---|---|---|---|---|
| 2001 | — | PF65 35.00 | | | | |

**KM# 769 10 PESOS**
15.00 g., 0.999 Silver 0.4818 oz. ASW, 35 mm. **Obv:** Cuban arms **Rev:** Multicolor white orchid

| Date | Mintage | VF20 | XF40 | MS60 | MS63 | MS65 |
|---|---|---|---|---|---|---|
| 2001 | — | PF65 30.00 | | | | |

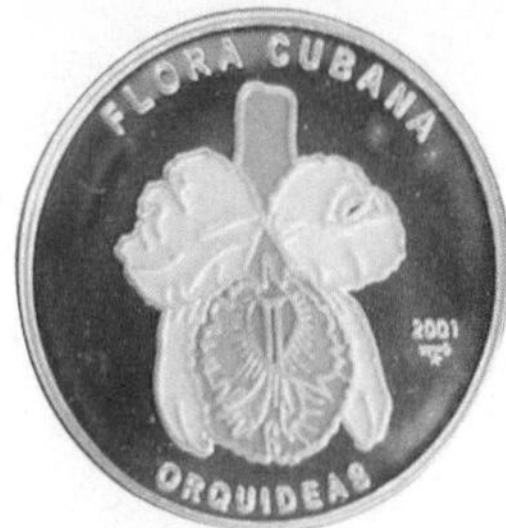


**KM# 770 10 PESOS**
15.00 g., 0.999 Silver 0.4818 oz. ASW, 35 mm. **Subject:** Cuban Flora **Obv:** Cuban arms **Rev:** Multicolor yellow orchid

| Date | Mintage | VF20 | XF40 | MS60 | MS63 | MS65 |
|---|---|---|---|---|---|---|
| 2001 | — | PF65 30.00 | | | | |

**KM# 771 10 PESOS**
15.00 g., 0.999 Silver 0.4818 oz. ASW, 35 mm. **Subject:** Cuban Flora **Obv:** Cuban arms **Rev:** Multicolor pink orchid

| Date | Mintage | VF20 | XF40 | MS60 | MS63 | MS65 |
|---|---|---|---|---|---|---|
| 2001 | — | PF65 30.00 | | | | |

**KM# 772 10 PESOS**
31.10 g., 0.999 Silver 0.999 oz. ASW, 42 mm. **Obv:** Cuban arms **Rev:** Multicolor Santa Maria

| Date | Mintage | VF20 | XF40 | MS60 | MS63 | MS65 |
|---|---|---|---|---|---|---|
| 2001 | — | PF65 50.00 | | | | |

**KM# 773 10 PESOS**
15.00 g., 0.999 Silver 0.4818 oz. ASW, 35 mm. **Subject:** World Cup Soccer Champions **Obv:** Cuban arms **Rev:** Soccer player and stadium

| Date | Mintage | VF20 | XF40 | MS60 | MS63 | MS65 |
|---|---|---|---|---|---|---|
| 2001 | — | PF63 25.00 | PF65 30.00 | | | |

**KM# 774 10 PESOS**
20.00 g., 0.999 Silver 0.6424 oz. ASW, 38 mm. **Subject:** Cuban Monuments **Obv:** Cuban arms **Rev:** Trinidad street view

| Date | Mintage | VF20 | XF40 | MS60 | MS63 | MS65 |
|---|---|---|---|---|---|---|
| 2001 | — | PF63 35.00 | PF65 40.00 | | | |

**KM# 775 10 PESOS**
20.00 g., 0.999 Silver 0.6424 oz. ASW, 38 mm. **Subject:** Cuban Monuments **Obv:** Cuban arms **Rev:** Havana Cathedral

| Date | Mintage | VF20 | XF40 | MS60 | MS63 | MS65 |
|---|---|---|---|---|---|---|
| 2001 | — | PF63 35.00 | PF65 40.00 | | | |

**KM# 776 10 PESOS**
20.00 g., 0.999 Silver 0.6424 oz. ASW, 38 mm. **Subject:** Cuban Monuments **Obv:** Cuban arms **Rev:** Template building

| Date | Mintage | VF20 | XF40 | MS60 | MS63 | MS65 |
|---|---|---|---|---|---|---|
| 2001 | — | PF63 35.00 | PF65 40.00 | | | |

**KM# 777 10 PESOS**
31.10 g., 0.999 Silver 0.999 oz. ASW, 38 mm. **Obv:** Cuban arms **Rev:** Bolivar standing at his birthplace

| Date | Mintage | VF20 | XF40 | MS60 | MS63 | MS65 |
|---|---|---|---|---|---|---|
| 2001 | — | PF63 45.00 | PF65 50.00 | | | |

**KM# 778 10 PESOS**
31.10 g., 0.999 Silver 0.999 oz. ASW, 38 mm. **Obv:** Cuban arms **Rev:** Bolivar and map of South America

| Date | Mintage | VF20 | XF40 | MS60 | MS63 | MS65 |
|---|---|---|---|---|---|---|
| 2001 | — | PF63 45.00 | PF65 50.00 | | | |

**KM# 779 10 PESOS**
31.10 g., 0.999 Silver 0.999 oz. ASW, 38 mm. **Subject:** 180th Anniversary of the Battle of Carabobo **Obv:** Cuban arms **Rev:** Bolivar leading troops

| Date | Mintage | VF20 | XF40 | MS60 | MS63 | MS65 |
|---|---|---|---|---|---|---|
| 2001 | — | PF63 45.00 | PF65 50.00 | | | |

**KM# 828 10 PESOS**
20.00 g., 0.999 Silver 0.6424 oz. ASW **Subject:** XVII World Soccer Championship - Korea and Japan 2002 **Obv:** National arms

| Date | Mintage | VF20 | XF40 | MS60 | MS63 | MS65 |
|---|---|---|---|---|---|---|
| 2001 proof | — | PF65 45.00 | | | | |

**KM# 734 10 PESOS**
20.00 g., 0.999 Silver 0.6424 oz. ASW, 37.9 mm. **Subject:** Olympics **Obv:** Cuban arms **Rev:** Runner and ancient ruins **Edge:** Reeded

| Date | Mintage | VF20 | XF40 | MS60 | MS63 | MS65 |
|---|---|---|---|---|---|---|
| 2002 | — | PF65 38.00 | | | | |

**KM# 780 10 PESOS**
20.00 g., 0.999 Silver 0.6424 oz. ASW, 38 mm. **Subject:** World Cup Soccer Champions **Obv:** Cuban arms **Rev:** Soccer player and map above "CHILE 1962

| Date | Mintage | VF20 | XF40 | MS60 | MS63 | MS65 |
|---|---|---|---|---|---|---|
| 2002 | — | PF63 32.00 | PF65 38.00 | | | |

**KM# 781 10 PESOS**
20.00 g., 0.999 Silver 0.6424 oz. ASW, 38 mm. **Subject:** World Cup Soccer Champions **Obv:** Cuban arms **Rev:** Soccer player and Cuauhtemoc head below MEXICO 1970

| Date | Mintage | VF20 | XF40 | MS60 | MS63 | MS65 |
|---|---|---|---|---|---|---|
| 2002 | — | PF63 32.00 | PF65 38.00 | | | |

**KM# 782 10 PESOS**
20.00 g., 0.999 Silver 0.6424 oz. ASW, 38 mm. **Obv:** Cuban arms **Rev:** Vasco De Gama and ship

| Date | Mintage | VF20 | XF40 | MS60 | MS63 | MS65 |
|---|---|---|---|---|---|---|
| 2002 | — | PF63 35.00 | PF65 40.00 | | | |

**KM# 783 10 PESOS**
20.00 g., 0.999 Silver 0.6424 oz. ASW, 38 mm. **Obv:** Cuban arms **Rev:** Americo Vespucio and ship

| Date | Mintage | VF20 | XF40 | MS60 | MS63 | MS65 |
|---|---|---|---|---|---|---|
| 2002 | — | PF63 35.00 | PF65 40.00 | | | |

**KM# 784 10 PESOS**
31.10 g., 0.999 Silver 0.999 oz. ASW, 38 mm. **Subject:** Leaders of Communism **Obv:** Cuban arms **Rev:** Head of Mao Tse Tung left

| Date | Mintage | VF20 | XF40 | MS60 | MS63 | MS65 |
|---|---|---|---|---|---|---|
| 2002 | — | PF65 50.00 | | | | |

**KM# 785 10 PESOS**
31.10 g., 0.999 Silver 0.999 oz. ASW, 38 mm. **Subject:** Leaders of Communism **Obv:** Cuban arms **Rev:** Head of Karl Marx 3/4 left

| Date | Mintage | VF20 | XF40 | MS60 | MS63 | MS65 |
|---|---|---|---|---|---|---|
| 2002 | — | PF65 50.00 | | | | |

**KM# 786 10 PESOS**
31.10 g., 0.999 Silver 0.999 oz. ASW, 38 mm. **Subject:** Leaders of Communism **Obv:** Cuban arms **Rev:** Head of Vladimir Lenin right

| Date | Mintage | VF20 | XF40 | MS60 | MS63 | MS65 |
|---|---|---|---|---|---|---|
| 2002 | — | PF65 60.00 | | | | |

**KM# 787 10 PESOS**
31.10 g., 0.999 Silver 0.999 oz. ASW, 38 mm. **Subject:** Leaders of Communism **Obv:** Cuban arms **Rev:** Head of Federico Engels 3/4 right

| Date | Mintage | VF20 | XF40 | MS60 | MS63 | MS65 |
|---|---|---|---|---|---|---|
| 2002 | — | PF65 50.00 | | | | |

**KM# 788 10 PESOS**
27.00 g., 0.999 Silver 0.8672 oz. ASW, 40 mm. **Subject:** IBERO-AMERICA Series **Obv:** Circle of arms around Cuban arms **Rev:** Santisima Trinidad ship

| Date | Mintage | VF20 | XF40 | MS60 | MS63 | MS65 |
|---|---|---|---|---|---|---|
| 2002 | 14,000 | PF63 40.00 | PF65 45.00 | | | |

**KM# 952 10 PESOS**
27.00 g., 0.925 Silver 0.803 oz. ASW **Obv:** National Arms surrounded by 10 older arms **Rev:** Santisima Trinidad, sailing ship

| Date | Mintage | VF20 | XF40 | MS60 | MS63 | MS65 |
|---|---|---|---|---|---|---|
| 2002 | — | PF63 50.00 | PF65 55.00 | | | |

**KM# 727 10 PESOS**
Silver **Subject:** Endangered wildlife **Rev:** Iguana

| Date | Mintage | VF20 | XF40 | MS60 | MS63 | MS65 |
|---|---|---|---|---|---|---|
| 2003 | — | PF65 40.00 | | | | |

**KM# 789 10 PESOS**
31.10 g., 0.999 Silver 0.999 oz. ASW, 38 mm. **Subject:** Jose Marti's 150th Birthday **Obv:** Cuban arms **Rev:** Numbered infield behind head right

| Date | Mintage | VF20 | XF40 | MS60 | MS63 | MS65 |
|---|---|---|---|---|---|---|
| 2003 | 150 | PF65 150 | | | | |

**KM# 790 10 PESOS**
20.00 g., 0.999 Silver 0.6424 oz. ASW, 38 mm. **Obv:** Cuban arms **Rev:** Ferdinand Magellan, ship, and astrolab

| Date | Mintage | VF20 | XF40 | MS60 | MS63 | MS65 |
|---|---|---|---|---|---|---|
| 2003 | 5,000 | PF63 35.00 | PF65 40.00 | | | |

**KM# 791 10 PESOS**
20.00 g., 0.999 Silver 0.6424 oz. ASW, 38 mm. **Obv:** Cuban arms **Rev:** Sailing ship, Sovereign of the Seas

| Date | Mintage | VF20 | XF40 | MS60 | MS63 | MS65 |
|---|---|---|---|---|---|---|
| 2003 | 5,000 | PF63 35.00 | PF65 40.00 | | | |

**KM# 792 10 PESOS**
20.00 g., 0.999 Silver 0.6424 oz. ASW, 38 mm. **Obv:** Cuban arms **Rev:** Che Guevara, 75th Anniversary of Birth

| Date | Mintage | VF20 | XF40 | MS60 | MS63 | MS65 |
|---|---|---|---|---|---|---|
| 2003 | 5,000 | PF63 35.00 | PF65 40.00 | | | |

**KM# 793 10 PESOS**
31.10 g., 0.999 Silver 0.9989 oz. ASW, 38 mm. **Subject:** World Cup Soccer - Germany 2006 **Obv:** Cuban arms **Rev:** 5 soccer players

| Date | Mintage | VF20 | XF40 | MS60 | MS63 | MS65 |
|---|---|---|---|---|---|---|
| 2003 | 50,000 | PF63 40.00 | PF65 45.00 | | | |

**KM# 794 10 PESOS**
20.00 g., 0.999 Silver 0.6424 oz. ASW, 38 mm. **Subject:** Endangered Wildlife **Obv:** Cuban arms **Rev:** Cuban Crocodile

| Date | Mintage | VF20 | XF40 | MS60 | MS63 | MS65 |
|---|---|---|---|---|---|---|
| 2003 | 5,000 | PF65 45.00 | | | | |

**KM# 795 10 PESOS**
20.00 g., 0.999 Silver 0.6424 oz. ASW, 38 mm. **Subject:** Endangered Wildlife **Obv:** Cuban arms **Rev:** Ocelot

| Date | Mintage | VF20 | XF40 | MS60 | MS63 | MS65 |
|---|---|---|---|---|---|---|
| 2003 | 5,000 | PF65 45.00 | | | | |

**KM# 921 10 PESOS**
Silver **Subject:** World Cup, Germany **Rev:** Five soccer players

| Date | Mintage | VF20 | XF40 | MS60 | MS63 | MS65 |
|---|---|---|---|---|---|---|
| 2003 | 50,000 | PF65 55.00 | | | | |

**KM# 796 10 PESOS**
20.00 g., 0.999 Silver 0.6424 oz. ASW, 38 mm. **Obv:** Cuban arms **Rev:** John Cabot's portrait in cameo above ship

| Date | Mintage | VF20 | XF40 | MS60 | MS63 | MS65 |
|---|---|---|---|---|---|---|
| 2004 | 5,000 | PF63 35.00 | PF65 40.00 | | | |

**KM# 797 10 PESOS**
15.00 g., 0.999 Silver 0.4818 oz. ASW, 35 mm. **Subject:** Hippocampus Kuda **Obv:** Cuban arms **Rev:** Spotted seahorse

| Date | Mintage | VF20 | XF40 | MS60 | MS63 | MS65 |
|---|---|---|---|---|---|---|
| 2004 | 5,000 | PF65 45.00 | | | | |

**KM# 798 10 PESOS**
20.00 g., 0.999 Silver 0.6424 oz. ASW, 38 mm. **Obv:** Cuban arms **Rev:** Murphy's Petrel bird on rock

| Date | Mintage | VF20 | XF40 | MS60 | MS63 | MS65 |
|---|---|---|---|---|---|---|
| 2004 | 5,000 | PF65 45.00 | | | | |

**KM# 799 10 PESOS**
20.00 g., 0.999 Silver 0.6424 oz. ASW, 38 mm. **Obv:** Cuban arms **Rev:** Cuban Rock Iguana on branch

| Date | Mintage | VF20 | XF40 | MS60 | MS63 | MS65 |
|---|---|---|---|---|---|---|
| 2004 | 5,000 | PF65 45.00 | | | | |

**KM# 800 10 PESOS**
31.10 g., 0.999 Silver 0.9989 oz. ASW, 38 mm. **Obv:** Cuban arms **Rev:** Imperial eagle perched on branch

| Date | Mintage | VF20 | XF40 | MS60 | MS63 | MS65 |
|---|---|---|---|---|---|---|
| 2004 | 1,000 | PF65 58.00 | | | | |

**KM# 801 10 PESOS**
31.10 g., 0.999 Silver 0.9989 oz. ASW, 38 mm. **Obv:** Cuban arms **Rev:** Bearded vulture in flight

| Date | Mintage | VF20 | XF40 | MS60 | MS63 | MS65 |
|---|---|---|---|---|---|---|
| 2004 | 1,000 | PF65 58.00 | | | | |

**KM# 802 10 PESOS**
31.10 g., 0.999 Silver 0.9989 oz. ASW, 38 mm. **Obv:** Cuban arms **Rev:** Iberian Lynx

| Date | Mintage | VF20 | XF40 | MS60 | MS63 | MS65 |
|---|---|---|---|---|---|---|
| 2004 | 1,000 | PF65 58.00 | | | | |

**KM# 803 10 PESOS**
31.10 g., 0.999 Silver 0.9989 oz. ASW, 38 mm. **Obv:** Cuban arms **Rev:** 2 grey wolves

| Date | Mintage | VF20 | XF40 | MS60 | MS63 | MS65 |
|---|---|---|---|---|---|---|
| 2004 | 1,000 | PF65 60.00 | | | | |

**KM# 804 10 PESOS**
31.10 g., 0.999 Silver 0.9989 oz. ASW, 38 mm. **Obv:** Cuban arms **Rev:** Brown bear

| Date | Mintage | VF20 | XF40 | MS60 | MS63 | MS65 |
|---|---|---|---|---|---|---|
| 2004 | — | — | — | — | — | 40.00 |
| 2004 | 1,000 | PF65 60.00 | | | | |

**KM# 805 10 PESOS**
31.10 g., 0.999 Silver 0.9989 oz. ASW, 38 mm. **Obv:** Cuban arms **Rev:** Peregrine Falcon perches on branch

| Date | Mintage | VF20 | XF40 | MS60 | MS63 | MS65 |
|---|---|---|---|---|---|---|
| 2004 | 1,000 | PF65 60.00 | | | | |

**KM# 806 10 PESOS**
20.00 g., 0.999 Silver 0.6424 oz. ASW, 38 mm. **Subject:** Monuments of Cuba **Obv:** Cuban arms **Rev:** University of Havana building

| Date | Mintage | VF20 | XF40 | MS60 | MS63 | MS65 |
|---|---|---|---|---|---|---|
| 2004 | 1,500 | PF63 47.00 | PF65 50.00 | | | |

**KM# 807 10 PESOS**
20.00 g., 0.999 Silver 0.6424 oz. ASW, 38 mm. **Subject:** Monuments of Cuba **Obv:** Cuban arms **Rev:** Fountain of India

| Date | Mintage | VF20 | XF40 | MS60 | MS63 | MS65 |
|---|---|---|---|---|---|---|
| 2004 | 1,500 | PF63 47.00 | PF65 50.00 | | | |

**KM# 808 10 PESOS**
20.00 g., 0.999 Silver 0.6424 oz. ASW, 38 mm. **Subject:** Monuments of Cuba **Obv:** Cuban arms **Rev:** Plaza building

| Date | Mintage | VF20 | XF40 | MS60 | MS63 | MS65 |
|---|---|---|---|---|---|---|
| 2004 | 1,500 | PF63 47.00 | PF65 50.00 | | | |

**KM# 923 10 PESOS**
15.00 g., 0.999 Silver 0.4818 oz. ASW **Rev:** Sea Horse and coral reef in color

| Date | Mintage | VF20 | XF40 | MS60 | MS63 | MS65 |
|---|---|---|---|---|---|---|
| 2004 | — | PF65 35.00 | | | | |

**KM# 809 10 PESOS**
27.00 g., 0.925 Silver 0.803 oz. ASW, 40 mm. **Obv:** Cuban arms within circle of arms **Rev:** Portions of the old Havana Wall

| Date | Mintage | VF20 | XF40 | MS60 | MS63 | MS65 |
|---|---|---|---|---|---|---|
| 2005 | 12,000 | PF63 60.00 | PF65 70.00 | | | |

**KM# 810 10 PESOS**
20.00 g., 0.999 Silver 0.6424 oz. ASW, 38 mm. **Subject:** Tobacco **Obv:** Cuban arms **Rev:** Indian showing tobacco to Columbus, ship in background

| Date | Mintage | VF20 | XF40 | MS60 | MS63 | MS65 |
|---|---|---|---|---|---|---|
| 2005 | 2,000 | PF65 50.00 | | | | |

**KM# 811 10 PESOS**
20.00 g., 0.925 Silver 0.5948 oz. ASW, 38 mm. **Subject:** Columbus' Ships **Obv:** Cuban arms **Rev:** The Santa Maria under sail

| Date | Mintage | VF20 | XF40 | MS60 | MS63 | MS65 |
|---|---|---|---|---|---|---|
| 2005 | 5,000 | PF63 40.00 | PF65 42.00 | | | |

**KM# 812 10 PESOS**
20.00 g., 0.925 Silver 0.5948 oz. ASW, 38 mm. **Subject:** Columbus' Ships **Obv:** Cuban arms **Rev:** The Nina under sail

| Date | Mintage | VF20 | XF40 | MS60 | MS63 | MS65 |
|---|---|---|---|---|---|---|
| 2005 | 5,000 | PF63 40.00 | PF65 42.00 | | | |

**KM# 813 10 PESOS**
20.00 g., 0.925 Silver 0.5948 oz. ASW, 38 mm. **Subject:** Columbus' Ships **Obv:** Cuban arms **Rev:** The Pinta under sail

| Date | Mintage | VF20 | XF40 | MS60 | MS63 | MS65 |
|---|---|---|---|---|---|---|
| 2005 | 5,000 | PF63 40.00 | PF65 42.00 | | | |

**KM# 814 10 PESOS**
20.00 g., 0.925 Silver 0.5948 oz. ASW, 38 mm. **Obv:** Cuban arms **Rev:** Cuban Solenodon on branch

| Date | Mintage | VF20 | XF40 | MS60 | MS63 | MS65 |
|---|---|---|---|---|---|---|
| 2005 | 5,000 | PF65 42.00 | | | | |

**KM# 815 10 PESOS**
15.00 g., 0.999 Silver 0.4818 oz. ASW, 35 mm. **Obv:** Cuban arms **Rev:** Multicolor Solenodon on branch

| Date | Mintage | VF20 | XF40 | MS60 | MS63 | MS65 |
|---|---|---|---|---|---|---|
| 2005 | 5,000 | PF65 40.00 | | | | |

**KM# 816 10 PESOS**
15.00 g., 0.925 Silver 0.4461 oz. ASW, 35 mm. **Subject:** Tropical Fish **Obv:** Cuban arms **Rev:** Picassofish (triggerfish)

| Date | Mintage | VF20 | XF40 | MS60 | MS63 | MS65 |
|---|---|---|---|---|---|---|
| 2005 | 2,000 | PF65 40.00 | | | | |

**KM# 817 10 PESOS**
15.00 g., 0.925 Silver 0.4461 oz. ASW, 35 mm. **Subject:** Tropical Fish **Obv:** Cuban arms **Rev:** Moorish Idol fish

| Date | Mintage | VF20 | XF40 | MS60 | MS63 | MS65 |
|---|---|---|---|---|---|---|
| 2005 | 2,000 | PF65 40.00 | | | | |

**KM# 818 10 PESOS**
15.00 g., 0.925 Silver 0.4461 oz. ASW, 35 mm. **Subject:** Tropical Fish **Obv:** Cuban arms **Rev:** Regal Angel fish

| Date | Mintage | VF20 | XF40 | MS60 | MS63 | MS65 |
|---|---|---|---|---|---|---|
| 2005 | 2,000 | PF65 40.00 | | | | |

**KM# 819 10 PESOS**
20.00 g., 0.999 Silver 0.6424 oz. ASW, 38 mm. **Subject:** Don Quijote, 400th Anniversary **Obv:** Cuban arms **Rev:** Don Quijote and Sancho looking at two windmills

| Date | Mintage | VF20 | XF40 | MS60 | MS63 | MS65 |
|---|---|---|---|---|---|---|
| 2005 | 5,000 | PF63 45.00 | PF65 50.00 | | | |

**KM# 820 10 PESOS**
31.10 g., 0.999 Silver 0.9989 oz. ASW, 38 mm. **Subject:** Maximo Gomez Centennial of Death **Obv:** Cuban arms **Rev:** Bust 3/4 left, numbered behind neck

| Date | Mintage | VF20 | XF40 | MS60 | MS63 | MS65 |
|---|---|---|---|---|---|---|
| 2005 | 100 | PF65 220 | | | | |

**KM# 925 10 PESOS**
27.00 g., 0.925 Silver 0.803 oz. ASW, 40 mm. **Subject:** Ibero American sites **Rev:** Old City Wall

| Date | Mintage | VF20 | XF40 | MS60 | MS63 | MS65 |
|---|---|---|---|---|---|---|
| 2005 | — | PF63 50.00 | PF65 55.00 | | | |

**KM# 821 10 PESOS**
20.00 g., 0.925 Silver 0.5948 oz. ASW, 38 mm. **Subject:** XXIX Olympics **Obv:** Cuban arms **Rev:** Baseball player with bat, baseball background

| Date | Mintage | VF20 | XF40 | MS60 | MS63 | MS65 |
|---|---|---|---|---|---|---|
| 2006 | 15,000 | PF63 35.00 | PF65 40.00 | | | |

**KM# 886 10 PESOS**
20.00 g., Silver, 38 mm. **Subject:** Che Guevara, 40th Anniversary of his Death

| Date | Mintage | VF20 | XF40 | MS60 | MS63 | MS65 |
|---|---|---|---|---|---|---|
| 2007 | — | PF65 40.00 | | | | |

**KM# 887 10 PESOS**
20.00 g., Silver, 38 mm. **Subject:** Fauna - Buitre (Condor)

| Date | Mintage | VF20 | XF40 | MS60 | MS63 | MS65 |
|---|---|---|---|---|---|---|
| 2007 | — | PF65 40.00 | | | | |

**KM# 888 10 PESOS**
20.00 g., Silver **Subject:** Fauna Burro

| Date | Mintage | VF20 | XF40 | MS60 | MS63 | MS65 |
|---|---|---|---|---|---|---|
| 2007 | — | PF65 40.00 | | | | |

**KM# 889 10 PESOS**
20.00 g., Silver, 38 mm. **Subject:** Fauna - Cobra Montesa

| Date | Mintage | VF20 | XF40 | MS60 | MS63 | MS65 |
|---|---|---|---|---|---|---|
| 2007 | — | PF65 45.00 | | | | |

**KM# 890 10 PESOS**
20.00 g., Silver, 38 mm. **Subject:** Fauna - Gato Montes

| Date | Mintage | VF20 | XF40 | MS60 | MS63 | MS65 |
|---|---|---|---|---|---|---|
| 2007 | — | PF65 40.00 | | | | |

**KM# 891 10 PESOS**
20.00 g., Silver, 38 mm. **Subject:** Fauna - Mastin Espanol

| Date | Mintage | VF20 | XF40 | MS60 | MS63 | MS65 |
|---|---|---|---|---|---|---|
| 2007 | — | PF65 40.00 | | | | |

**KM# 892 10 PESOS**
20.00 g., Silver, 38 mm. **Subject:** Fauna - Urogallo

| Date | Mintage | VF20 | XF40 | MS60 | MS63 | MS65 |
|---|---|---|---|---|---|---|
| 2007 | — | PF65 40.00 | | | | |

**KM# 893 10 PESOS**
20.00 g., Silver, 38 mm. **Subject:** Fortress - El Morro

| Date | Mintage | VF20 | XF40 | MS60 | MS63 | MS65 |
|---|---|---|---|---|---|---|
| 2007 | — | PF65 40.00 | | | | |

**KM# 894 10 PESOS**
20.00 g., Silver, 38 mm. **Subject:** Fortress - La Fuerza

| Date | Mintage | VF20 | XF40 | MS60 | MS63 | MS65 |
|---|---|---|---|---|---|---|
| 2007 | — | PF65 40.00 | | | | |

**KM# 895 10 PESOS**
20.00 g., Silver, 38 mm. **Subject:** La Punta

| Date | Mintage | VF20 | XF40 | MS60 | MS63 | MS65 |
|---|---|---|---|---|---|---|
| 2007 | — | PF65 40.00 | | | | |

**KM# 896 10 PESOS**
20.00 g., Silver, 38 mm. **Subject:** Garabaldi

| Date | Mintage | VF20 | XF40 | MS60 | MS63 | MS65 |
|---|---|---|---|---|---|---|
| 2007 | — | PF65 40.00 | | | | |

**KM# 897 10 PESOS**
27.00 g., 0.925 Silver 0.803 oz. ASW, 40 mm. **Subject:** Ibero - American Series - Javelin

| Date | Mintage | VF20 | XF40 | MS60 | MS63 | MS65 |
|---|---|---|---|---|---|---|
| 2007 | — | PF63 40.00 | PF65 45.00 | | | |

**KM# 898 10 PESOS**
20.00 g., Silver, 38 mm. **Subject:** Sputnik

| Date | Mintage | VF20 | XF40 | MS60 | MS63 | MS65 |
|---|---|---|---|---|---|---|
| 2007 | — | **PF63** 35.00 | **PF65** 40.00 | | | |

**KM# 899 10 PESOS**
20.00 g., Silver, 38 mm. **Subject:** World Championship Soccer England

| Date | Mintage | VF20 | XF40 | MS60 | MS63 | MS65 |
|---|---|---|---|---|---|---|
| 2007 | — | **PF63** 35.00 | **PF65** 40.00 | | | |

**KM# 904 10 PESOS**
20.00 g., 0.999 Silver 0.6424 oz. ASW, 38 mm. **Subject:** Ship Principe Asturias

| Date | Mintage | VF20 | XF40 | MS60 | MS63 | MS65 |
|---|---|---|---|---|---|---|
| 2008 | — | **PF65** 40.00 | | | | |

**KM# 905 10 PESOS**
20.00 g., 0.999 Silver 0.6424 oz. ASW, 40 mm. **Subject:** Ship - San Carlos **Obv:** National arms within wreath

| Date | Mintage | VF20 | XF40 | MS60 | MS63 | MS65 |
|---|---|---|---|---|---|---|
| 2008 | — | **PF65** 40.00 | | | | |

**KM# 906 10 PESOS**
20.00 g., 0.999 Silver 0.6424 oz. ASW, 40 mm. **Subject:** Ship - San Hermene

| Date | Mintage | VF20 | XF40 | MS60 | MS63 | MS65 |
|---|---|---|---|---|---|---|
| 2008 | — | **PF65** 40.00 | | | | |

**KM# 911 10 PESOS**
20.00 g., 0.999 Silver 0.6424 oz. ASW, 38 mm. **Subject:** Fidel and Raul Castro

| Date | Mintage | VF20 | XF40 | MS60 | MS63 | MS65 |
|---|---|---|---|---|---|---|
| 2009 | 5,000 | **PF65** 40.00 | | | | |

**KM# 912 10 PESOS**
20.00 g., 0.999 Silver 0.6424 oz. ASW, 38 mm. **Subject:** Manatee **Obv:** National arms in wreath

| Date | Mintage | VF20 | XF40 | MS60 | MS63 | MS65 |
|---|---|---|---|---|---|---|
| 2009 | — | **PF65** 40.00 | | | | |

**KM# 926 10 PESOS**
27.00 g., 0.925 Silver 0.803 oz. ASW, 40 mm. **Subject:** Ibero-American series - Historic coins **Obv:** Cuban arms at center of circle of other national arms **Rev:** Historic coin

| Date | Mintage | VF20 | XF40 | MS60 | MS63 | MS65 |
|---|---|---|---|---|---|---|
| 2010 | 12,000 | **PF63** 50.00 | **PF65** 55.00 | | | |

**KM# 900 20 PESOS**
62.20 g., 0.999 Silver 1.9978 oz. ASW, 45 mm. **Subject:** Che Guevara - 40th Anniversary of Death

| Date | Mintage | VF20 | XF40 | MS60 | MS63 | MS65 |
|---|---|---|---|---|---|---|
| 2007 | — | **PF63** 85.00 | **PF65** 95.00 | | | |

**KM# 913 20 PESOS**
62.21 g., 0.999 Silver 1.9981 oz. ASW, 45 mm. **Subject:** Revolution 50th Anniversary

| Date | Mintage | VF20 | XF40 | MS60 | MS63 | MS65 |
|---|---|---|---|---|---|---|
| 2009 | 1,959 | **PF63** 130 | **PF65** 150 | | | |

**KM# 922 25 PESOS**
7.78 g., 0.999 Gold 0.2499 oz. AGW **Subject:** Wold Cup, Germany **Rev:** Socer player and globe

| Date | Mintage | VF20 | XF40 | MS60 | MS63 | MS65 |
|---|---|---|---|---|---|---|
| 2004 | 25,000 | **PF63** 425 | **PF65** 475 | | | |

**KM# 822 100 PESOS**
31.10 g., 0.999 Gold 0.9989 oz. AGW, 38 mm. **Subject:** 100th Anniversary - Death of Marti **Obv:** Cuban arms **Rev:** Monument

| Date | Mintage | VF20 | XF40 | MS60 | MS63 | MS65 |
|---|---|---|---|---|---|---|
| 2001 | 100 | **PF65** 1,850 | | | | |

## PESO CONVERTIBLE SERIES

**KM# 729 CENTAVO**
1.70 g., Copper Plated Steel, 15 mm. **Obv:** National arms within wreath, denomination below **Rev:** Tower and denomination **Edge:** Reeded

| Date | Mintage | VF20 | XF40 | MS60 | MS63 | MS65 |
|---|---|---|---|---|---|---|
| 2002 | — | — | — | 3.00 | — | — |
| 2006 | — | — | — | 3.00 | — | — |
| 2007 | — | — | — | 3.00 | — | — |
| 2013 | — | — | — | 3.00 | — | — |

**KM# 733 CENTAVO**
0.75 g., Aluminum, 16.75 mm. **Obv:** Cuban arms **Rev:** Tower and denomination **Edge:** Plain

| Date | Mintage | VF20 | XF40 | MS60 | MS63 | MS65 |
|---|---|---|---|---|---|---|
| 2001 | — | — | — | 2.00 | — | — |
| 2002 | — | — | — | 2.00 | — | — |
| 2003 | — | — | — | 2.00 | — | — |
| 2005 | — | — | — | 2.00 | — | — |
| 2007 | — | — | — | 2.00 | — | — |

**KM# 575.2 5 CENTAVOS**
2.65 g., Nickel Plated Steel, 18 mm. **Obv:** National arms **Rev:** Casa Colonial **Note:** Coin alignment, recut designs.

| Date | Mintage | VF20 | XF40 | MS60 | MS63 | MS65 |
|---|---|---|---|---|---|---|
| 2001 | — | — | — | 1.00 | — | — |
| 2002 | — | — | — | 1.00 | — | — |
| 2003 | — | — | — | 1.00 | — | — |
| 2004 | — | — | — | 1.00 | — | — |
| 2006 | — | — | — | 1.00 | — | — |
| 2007 | — | — | — | 1.00 | — | — |
| 2008 | — | — | — | 1.00 | — | — |
| 2009 | — | — | — | 1.00 | — | — |

**KM# 576.2 10 CENTAVOS**
4.00 g., Nickel Plated Steel, 20 mm. **Obv:** National arms **Rev:** Castillo de la Fuerza **Note:** Coin alignment, recut designs.

| Date | Mintage | VF20 | XF40 | MS60 | MS63 | MS65 |
|---|---|---|---|---|---|---|
| 2002 | — | — | — | 2.00 | — | — |
| 2003 | — | — | — | 2.00 | — | — |
| 2008 | — | — | — | 2.00 | — | — |
| 2009 | — | — | — | 2.00 | — | — |

**KM# 577.2 25 CENTAVOS**
5.65 g., Nickel Plated Steel, 23 mm. **Obv:** National arms **Rev:** Trinidad **Note:** Coin alignment.

| Date | Mintage | VF20 | XF40 | MS60 | MS63 | MS65 |
|---|---|---|---|---|---|---|
| 2001 | — | — | — | 3.00 | — | — |
| 2002 | — | — | — | 3.00 | — | — |
| 2003 | — | — | — | 3.00 | — | — |
| 2006 | — | — | — | 3.00 | — | — |
| 2007 | — | — | — | 3.00 | — | — |
| 2008 | — | — | — | 3.00 | — | — |

**KM# 578.2 50 CENTAVOS**
7.53 g., Nickel Plated Steel, 25 mm. **Obv:** Cuban arms **Rev:** Havana Cathedral **Note:** Coin alignment.

| Date | Mintage | VF20 | XF40 | MS60 | MS63 | MS65 |
|---|---|---|---|---|---|---|
| 2002 | — | — | — | 5.00 | — | — |
| 2007 | — | — | — | 5.00 | — | — |

**KM# 579.2 PESO**
8.50 g., Nickel Plated Steel, 27 mm. **Obv:** National arms **Rev:** Guama **Edge:** Reeded **Note:** Coin alignment.

| Date | Mintage | VF20 | XF40 | MS60 | MS63 | MS65 |
|---|---|---|---|---|---|---|
| 2001 | — | — | — | — | 5.00 | — |
| 2007 | — | — | — | — | 5.00 | — |
| 2012 | — | — | — | — | 5.00 | — |

## MINT SETS

| KM# | Date | Mintage | Identification | Issue Price | Mkt Val |
|---|---|---|---|---|---|
| MS3 | 2001 (3) | — | KM#831-833 | — | 62.50 |

# CYPRUS

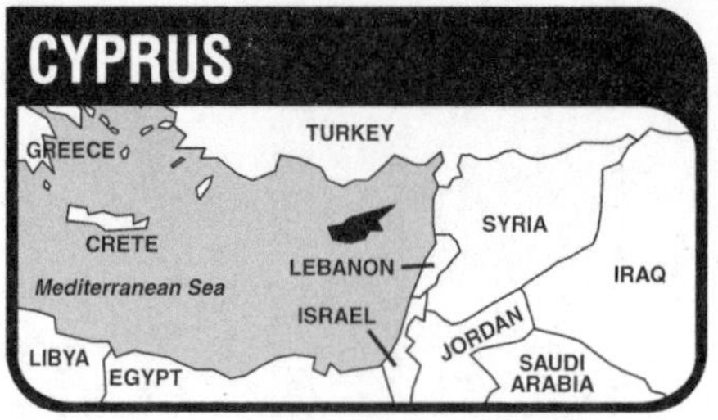


The island of Cyprus lies in the eastern Mediterranean Sea 44 miles (71 km.) south of Turkey and 60 miles (97 km.) off the Syrian coast. It is the third largest island in the Mediterranean Sea, having an area of 3,572 sq. mi. (9,251 sq. km.) and a population of 736,636. Capital: Nicosia. Agriculture, light manufacturing and tourism are the chief industries. Citrus fruit, potatoes, footwear and clothing are exported

Cyprus is a member of the Commonwealth of Nations. The president is Chief of State and Head of Government. Cyprus is also a member of the European Union.

**MINT MARKS**
no mint mark - Royal Mint, London, England
H - Birmingham, England

## REPUBLIC

### REFORM COINAGE

100 Cents = 1 Pound

**KM# 53.3 CENT**
2.00 g., Nickel-Brass, 16.5 mm. **Obv:** Shielded arms within altered wreath, date below **Rev:** Stylized bird on a branch, denomination at left **Edge:** Plain

| Date | Mintage | VF20 | XF40 | MS60 | MS63 | MS65 |
|---|---|---|---|---|---|---|
| 2003 | 5,000,000 | — | 0.10 | 0.20 | 0.30 | 0.45 |
| 2004 Narrow figures | 12,000,000 | — | 0.10 | 0.20 | 0.30 | 0.45 |

**KM# 54.3 2 CENTS**
2.50 g., Nickel-Brass, 19 mm. **Obv:** Shielded arms within altered wreath, date below **Rev:** Stylized goats, denomination upper right **Edge:** Plain

| Date | Mintage | VF20 | XF40 | MS60 | MS63 | MS65 |
|---|---|---|---|---|---|---|
| 2003 | 5,000,000 | — | 0.15 | 0.25 | 0.35 | 0.50 |
| 2004 | 7,000,000 | — | 0.15 | 0.25 | 0.35 | 0.50 |

**KM# 55.3 5 CENTS**
3.75 g., Nickel-Brass, 22 mm. **Obv:** Altered wreath around arms **Rev:** Stylized bull's head above denomination **Edge:** Plain

| Date | Mintage | VF20 | XF40 | MS60 | MS63 | MS65 |
|---|---|---|---|---|---|---|
| 2001 | 15,000,000 | — | 0.20 | 0.50 | 0.75 | 1.00 |
| 2004 | 15,000,000 | — | 0.20 | 0.50 | 0.75 | 1.00 |

**KM# 56.3 10 CENTS**
5.50 g., Nickel-Brass, 24.5 mm. **Obv:** Altered wreath around arms **Rev:** Decorative vase, denomination above **Edge:** Reeded

| Date | Mintage | VF20 | XF40 | MS60 | MS63 | MS65 |
|---|---|---|---|---|---|---|
| 2002 | 10,000,000 | — | 0.35 | 0.75 | 1.00 | 1.25 |
| 2004 Narrow figures | 7,000,000 | — | 0.35 | 0.75 | 1.00 | 1.25 |

**KM# 62.2 20 CENTS**
7.75 g., Nickel-Brass, 27.25 mm. **Obv:** Altered wreath around arms **Rev:** Head left, denomination at right **Edge:** Reeded

| Date | Mintage | VF20 | XF40 | MS60 | MS63 | MS65 |
|---|---|---|---|---|---|---|
| 2001 | 15,000,000 | — | — | 1.00 | 1.25 | 1.50 |
| 2004 | 4,000,000 | — | — | 1.00 | 1.25 | 1.50 |

**KM# 66 50 CENTS**
7.00 g., Copper-Nickel, 26 mm. **Subject:** Abduction of Europa **Obv:** National arms, date below **Rev:** Female figure riding bull right within square, denomination below **Edge:** Plain **Shape:** 7-sided

| Date | Mintage | VF20 | XF40 | MS60 | MS63 | MS65 |
|---|---|---|---|---|---|---|
| 2002 | 7,000,000 | — | — | 1.75 | 2.50 | 3.25 |
| 2004 | 5,000,000 | — | — | 1.75 | 2.50 | 3.25 |

**KM# 96 POUND**
28.28 g., Copper-Nickel, 38.6 mm. **Obv:** National arms **Rev:** Butterfly on branch

| Date | Mintage | VF20 | XF40 | MS60 | MS63 | MS65 |
|---|---|---|---|---|---|---|
| 2002 | — | **PF63** 45.00 | **PF65** 50.00 | | | |

**KM# 75 POUND**
28.28 g., Copper-Nickel, 38.6 mm. **Subject:** Cyprus Joins the European Union **Obv:** National arms **Rev:** Map in center with Triton trumpeting through a seashell **Edge:** Plain

| Date | Mintage | VF20 | XF40 | MS60 | MS63 | MS65 |
|---|---|---|---|---|---|---|
| 2004 | 3,000 | — | — | 25.00 | 50.00 | — |

**KM# 75a POUND**
28.28 g., 0.925 Silver 0.841 oz. ASW, 38.6 mm. **Subject:** Cyprus Joins the European Union **Obv:** National arms **Rev:** Map and Triton trumpeting through a sea shell **Edge:** Plain

| Date | Mintage | VF20 | XF40 | MS60 | MS63 | MS65 |
|---|---|---|---|---|---|---|
| 2004 | 3,000 | **PF63** 75.00 | **PF65** 80.00 | | | |

**KM# 76 POUND**
28.27 g., Copper-Nickel, 38.5 mm. **Obv:** National arms **Rev:** Mediterranean Monk Seal **Edge:** Plain

| Date | Mintage | VF20 | XF40 | MS60 | MS63 | MS65 |
|---|---|---|---|---|---|---|
| 2005 | 4,000 | PF63 45.00 | PF65 50.00 | | | |

**KM# 76a POUND**
28.28 g., 0.925 Silver 0.841 oz. ASW, 38.61 mm. **Obv:** National arms **Rev:** Mediterranean Monk Seal **Edge:** Plain

| Date | Mintage | VF20 | XF40 | MS60 | MS63 | MS65 |
|---|---|---|---|---|---|---|
| 2005 | 4,000 | PF63 60.00 | PF65 65.00 | | | |

**KM# 77 POUND**
28.28 g., Copper-Nickel, 38.6 mm. **Obv:** National arms **Rev:** Akamas Centaurea flowers **Edge:** Plain

| Date | Mintage | VF20 | XF40 | MS60 | MS63 | MS65 |
|---|---|---|---|---|---|---|
| 2006 | 6,000 | PF63 25.00 | PF65 30.00 | | | |

**KM# 77a POUND**
28.28 g., 0.925 Silver 0.841 oz. ASW, 38.61 mm. **Obv:** National arms **Rev:** Akamas Centaurea flowers **Edge:** Plain

| Date | Mintage | VF20 | XF40 | MS60 | MS63 | MS65 |
|---|---|---|---|---|---|---|
| 2006 | 3,000 | PF63 70.00 | PF65 75.00 | | | |

**KM# 86 POUND**
28.28 g., Copper-Nickel, 38.6 mm. **Subject:** 50th Anniversary Treaty of Rome **Obv:** National arms **Rev:** Open Treaty Book **Edge:** Plain

| Date | Mintage | VF20 | XF40 | MS60 | MS63 | MS65 |
|---|---|---|---|---|---|---|
| 2007 Prooflike | 10,000 | PF63 28.00 | PF65 32.00 | | | |

**KM# 87 20 POUNDS**
7.99 g., Gold, 22.05 mm. **Obv:** National arms **Rev:** Greek god Triton, trumpeter (messenger) of the deep sea below outlined map of Cyprus

| Date | Mintage | VF20 | XF40 | MS60 | MS63 | MS65 |
|---|---|---|---|---|---|---|
| 2004 | 1,500 | PF65 1,000 | | | | |

## EURO COINAGE

European Union Issues

**KM# 78 EURO CENT**
2.30 g., Copper Plated Steel, 16.25 mm. **Obv:** Two Mouflons **Rev:** Large value at left, globe at lower right **Edge:** Plain

| Date | Mintage | VF20 | XF40 | MS60 | MS63 | MS65 |
|---|---|---|---|---|---|---|
| 2008 | 40,000,000 | — | — | 0.35 | 0.50 | 0.75 |
| 2009 | 20,000,000 | — | — | 0.35 | 0.50 | 0.75 |
| 2010 | 200,000 | — | — | 0.35 | 0.50 | 0.75 |
| 2011 | 15,200,000 | — | — | 0.35 | 0.50 | 0.75 |
| 2012 | 988,000 | — | — | 0.35 | 0.50 | 0.75 |
| 2013 | — | — | — | 0.35 | 0.50 | 0.75 |
| 2014 | — | — | — | 0.35 | 0.50 | 0.75 |

**KM# 79 2 EURO CENT**
3.06 g., Copper Plated Steel, 18.75 mm. **Obv:** Two Mouflons **Rev:** Large value at left, globe at lower right **Edge:** Grooved

| Date | Mintage | VF20 | XF40 | MS60 | MS63 | MS65 |
|---|---|---|---|---|---|---|
| 2008 | 100,000,000 | — | — | 0.50 | 0.75 | 1.00 |
| 2009 | 1,000,000 | — | — | 0.50 | 0.75 | 1.00 |
| 2010 | 200,000 | — | — | 0.50 | 0.75 | 1.00 |
| 2011 | 200,000 | — | — | 0.50 | 0.75 | 1.00 |
| 2012 | 988,000 | — | — | 0.50 | 0.75 | 1.00 |
| 2013 | — | — | — | 0.50 | 0.75 | 1.00 |
| 2014 | — | — | — | 0.50 | 0.75 | 1.00 |

**KM# 80 5 EURO CENT**
3.92 g., Copper Plated Steel, 21.25 mm. **Obv:** Two Mouflons **Rev:** Large value at left, globe at lower right **Edge:** Plain

| Date | Mintage | VF20 | XF40 | MS60 | MS63 | MS65 |
|---|---|---|---|---|---|---|
| 2008 | 60,000,000 | — | — | 1.00 | 1.25 | 1.50 |
| 2009 | 6,000,000 | — | — | 1.00 | 1.25 | 1.50 |
| 2010 | 200,000 | — | — | 1.00 | 1.25 | 1.50 |
| 2011 | 30,200,000 | — | — | 1.00 | 1.25 | 1.50 |
| 2012 | 988,000 | — | — | 1.00 | 1.25 | 1.50 |
| 2013 | — | — | — | 1.00 | 1.25 | 1.50 |
| 2014 | — | — | — | 1.00 | 1.25 | 1.50 |

**KM# 81 10 EURO CENT**
4.10 g., Brass, 19.75 mm. **Obv:** Early sailing boat **Rev:** Modified outline of Europe at left, large value at right **Edge:** Reeded

| Date | Mintage | VF20 | XF40 | MS60 | MS63 | MS65 |
|---|---|---|---|---|---|---|
| 2008 | 70,000,000 | — | — | 1.25 | 1.50 | 1.75 |
| 2009 | 1,000,000 | — | — | 1.25 | 1.50 | 1.75 |
| 2010 | 200,000 | — | — | 1.25 | 1.50 | 1.75 |
| 2011 | 200,000 | — | — | 1.25 | 1.50 | 1.75 |
| 2012 | 988,000 | — | — | 1.25 | 1.50 | 1.75 |
| 2013 | — | — | — | 1.25 | 1.50 | 1.75 |
| 2014 | — | — | — | 1.25 | 1.50 | 1.75 |

**KM# 82 20 EURO CENT**
5.74 g., Brass, 22.25 mm. **Obv:** Early sailing boat **Rev:** Modified outline of Europe at left, large value at right **Edge:** Notched

| Date | Mintage | VF20 | XF40 | MS60 | MS63 | MS65 |
|---|---|---|---|---|---|---|
| 2008 | 65,000,000 | — | — | 1.50 | 2.00 | 2.25 |
| 2009 | 1,000,000 | — | — | 1.50 | 2.00 | 2.25 |
| 2010 | 200,000 | — | — | 1.50 | 2.00 | 2.25 |
| 2011 | 200,000 | — | — | 1.50 | 2.00 | 2.25 |
| 2012 | 988,000 | — | — | 1.50 | 2.00 | 2.25 |
| 2013 | — | — | — | 1.50 | 2.00 | 2.25 |
| 2014 | — | — | — | 1.50 | 2.00 | 2.25 |

**KM# 83 50 EURO CENT**
7.80 g., Brass, 24.25 mm. **Obv:** Early sailing boat **Rev:** Modified outline of Europe at left, large value at right **Edge:** Reeded

| Date | Mintage | VF20 | XF40 | MS60 | MS63 | MS65 |
|---|---|---|---|---|---|---|
| 2008 | 30,000,000 | — | — | 2.00 | 2.50 | 2.75 |
| 2009 | 1,000,000 | — | — | 2.00 | 2.50 | 2.75 |
| 2010 | 200,000 | — | — | 2.00 | 2.50 | 2.75 |
| 2011 | 200,000 | — | — | 2.00 | 2.50 | 2.75 |
| 2012 | 988,000 | — | — | 2.00 | 2.50 | 2.75 |
| 2013 | — | — | — | 2.00 | 2.50 | 2.75 |
| 2014 | — | — | — | 2.00 | 2.50 | 2.75 |

**KM# 84 EURO**
7.50 g., Bi-Metallic Copper-Nickel center in Nickel-Brass ring, 23.25 mm. **Obv:** Ancient cross shaped idol discovered in the village of Pomos in the distrct of Paphos. **Rev:** Large value at left, modified outline of Europe at right **Edge:** Segmented reeding

| Date | Mintage | VF20 | XF40 | MS60 | MS63 | MS65 |
|---|---|---|---|---|---|---|
| 2008 | 28,000,000 | — | — | 3.50 | 4.50 | 5.50 |
| 2009 | 4,000,000 | — | — | 3.50 | 4.50 | 5.50 |
| 2010 | 200,000 | — | — | 3.50 | 4.50 | 5.50 |
| 2011 | 200,000 | — | — | 3.50 | 4.50 | 5.50 |
| 2012 | 988,000 | — | — | 3.50 | 4.50 | 5.50 |
| 2013 | — | — | — | 3.50 | 4.50 | 5.50 |
| 2014 | — | — | — | 3.50 | 4.50 | 5.50 |

**KM# 85 2 EURO**
8.50 g., Bi-Metallic Nickel-Brass center in Copper-Nickel ring, 25.75 mm. **Obv:** Ancient cross shaped idol discovered in the village of Pomos in the distrct of Paphos. **Rev:** Large value at left, modified outline of Europe at right

| Date | Mintage | VF20 | XF40 | MS60 | MS63 | MS65 |
|---|---|---|---|---|---|---|
| 2008 | 25,000,000 | — | — | 5.00 | 6.00 | 7.00 |
| 2009 | 5,000,000 | — | — | 5.00 | 6.00 | 7.00 |
| 2010 | 200,000 | — | — | 5.00 | 6.00 | 7.00 |
| 2011 | 200,000 | — | — | 5.00 | 6.00 | 7.00 |
| 2012 | 988,000 | — | — | 5.00 | 6.00 | 7.00 |
| 2013 | — | — | — | 5.00 | 6.00 | 7.00 |
| 2014 | — | — | — | 5.00 | 6.00 | 7.00 |

**KM# 89 2 EURO**
8.50 g., Bi-Metallic Nickel-Brass center in Copper-Nickel ring, 25.75 mm. **Subject:** 10th Anniversary of Euro **Obv:** Ancient statue wearing a cross found in Solol **Rev:** Childs drawing of a stick figure and 2E

| Date | Mintage | VF20 | XF40 | MS60 | MS63 | MS65 |
|---|---|---|---|---|---|---|
| 2009 | 980,000 | — | — | 5.00 | 6.00 | 7.00 |
| 2009 Special Unc. | 20,000 | — | — | — | 15.00 | 17.00 |
| 2009 | — | PF65 25.00 | | | | |

**KM# 97 2 EURO**
8.50 g., Bi-Metallic Nickel-Brass center in Copper-Nickel ring, 25.75 mm. **Subject:** Euro Coinage, 10th Anniversary **Obv:** Euro symbol on globe, child-like rendering around

| Date | Mintage | VF20 | XF40 | MS60 | MS63 | MS65 |
|---|---|---|---|---|---|---|
| 2012 | 1,000,000 | — | — | 6.00 | 8.00 | 10.00 |
| 2012 Special Unc. | 5,000 | — | — | — | 15.00 | 17.00 |
| 2012 | 8,000 | PF65 25.00 | | | | |

### KM# 88 5 EURO

28.28 g., 0.925 Silver 0.841 oz. ASW, 38.61 mm. **Subject:** Entry into Euro Zone **Obv:** National arms **Rev:** Euro band around outlined Europe and Cyprus **Edge:** Reeded

| Date | Mintage | VF20 | XF40 | MS60 | MS63 | MS65 |
|---|---|---|---|---|---|---|
| 2008 | 15,000 | PF63 70.00 | PF65 75.00 | | | |

### KM# 94 5 EURO

28.28 g., 0.925 Silver 0.841 oz. ASW, 38.61 mm. **Subject:** Republic of Cyprus, 50th Anniversary **Obv:** National arms **Rev:** Bird in stylized tree

| Date | Mintage | VF20 | XF40 | MS60 | MS63 | MS65 |
|---|---|---|---|---|---|---|
| 2010 | 5,000 | PF63 60.00 | PF65 65.00 | | | |

### KM# 98 5 EURO

28.28 g., 0.925 Silver 0.841 oz. ASW, 38.61 mm. **Subject:** Cyprian presidency of European Council

| Date | Mintage | VF20 | XF40 | MS60 | MS63 | MS65 |
|---|---|---|---|---|---|---|
| 2012 | 8,000 | PF65 85.00 | | | | |

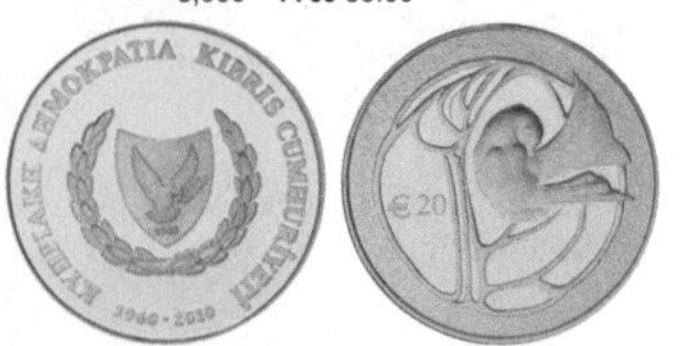

### KM# 95 20 EURO

7.99 g., 0.900 Gold 0.2312 oz. AGW, 22 mm. **Subject:** Republic of Cyprus, 50th Anniversary **Obv:** National arms **Rev:** Bird in stylized tree **Edge:** Reeded

| Date | Mintage | VF20 | XF40 | MS60 | MS63 | MS65 |
|---|---|---|---|---|---|---|
| 2010 | 750 | PF65 450 | | | | |

## MINT SETS

| KM# | Date | Mintage | Identification | Issue Price | Mkt Val |
|---|---|---|---|---|---|
| MS20 | 2008 (8) | 70,000 | KM#78-85 | — | 50.00 |
| MS21 | 2009 (9) | 15,000 | KM#78-85, 89 | — | 60.00 |
| MS22 | 2011 (8) | 10,000 | KM#78-85 | — | 50.00 |
| MS23 | 2012 (8) | — | KM#78-85 | — | 50.00 |

# CZECH REPUBLIC

The Czech Republic was formerly united with Slovakia as Czechoslovakia. It is bordered in the west by Germany, to the north by Poland, to the east by Slovakia and to the south by Austria. It consists of 3 major regions: Bohemia, Moravia and Silesia and has an area of 30,450 sq. mi. (78,864 sq. km.) and a population of 10.4 million. Capital: Prague (Praha). Agriculture and livestock are chief occupations while coal deposits are the main mineral resources.

**MINT MARKS**

(c) - castle = Hamburg
(cr) - cross = British Royal Mint
(l) - leaf = Royal Canadian
(m) - crowned *b* or *CM* = Jablonec nad Nisou
(mk) - *MK* in circle = Kremnica
(o) - broken circle = Vienna (Wien)

**MONETARY SYSTEM**

1 Czechoslovak Koruna (Kcs) = 1 Czech Koruna (Kc)
1 Koruna = 100 Haleru

## REPUBLIC

## STANDARD COINAGE

### KM# 6 10 HALERU

0.60 g., Aluminum, 15.5 mm. **Obv:** Crowned Czech lion left, date below **Rev:** Denomination and stylized river **Edge:** Plain **Note:** Two varieties of mint marks exist for 1994.

| Date | Mintage | VF20 | XF40 | MS60 | MS63 | MS65 |
|---|---|---|---|---|---|---|
| 2001 (m) | 40,525,000 | — | — | — | 0.20 | 0.25 |
| 2001 (m) | — | PF65 10.00 | | | | |
| 2002 (m) | 81,496,000 | — | — | — | 0.20 | 0.25 |
| 2002 (m) | — | PF65 10.00 | | | | |
| 2003 (m) | 3,022,350 | — | — | — | 0.20 | 0.25 |
| 2003 (m) | — | PF65 7.00 | | | | |
| 2004 (m) | — | — | — | — | 0.20 | 0.25 |
| 2004 (m) | — | PF65 7.00 | | | | |
| 2005 (m) | — | — | — | — | 0.20 | 0.25 |

### KM# 2.3 20 HALERU

0.74 g., Aluminum, 17 mm. **Obv:** Crowned Czech lion left, date above **Rev:** Open 2 in denomination, "h" above angle line **Edge:** Reeded **Note:** Medal alignment.

| Date | Mintage | VF20 | XF40 | MS60 | MS63 | MS65 |
|---|---|---|---|---|---|---|
| 2001 (m) | 44,425,000 | — | — | — | 0.30 | 0.40 |
| 2001 (m) | — | PF65 12.50 | | | | |
| 2002 (m) | 20,000 | — | — | — | 0.30 | 0.40 |
| 2002 (m) | — | PF65 12.50 | | | | |
| 2003 (m) | 22,200 | — | — | — | 0.30 | 0.40 |
| 2003 (m) | 3,000 | PF65 7.50 | | | | |
| 2004 (m) | — | — | — | — | 0.30 | 0.40 |
| 2004 (m) | — | PF65 7.50 | | | | |

### KM# 3.1 50 HALERU

0.90 g., Aluminum, 19 mm. **Obv:** Crowned Czech lion left, date below **Rev:** Large denomination **Edge:** Segmented reeding **Note:** Prev. KM#3.

| Date | Mintage | VF20 | XF40 | MS60 | MS63 | MS65 |
|---|---|---|---|---|---|---|
| 2001 (m) | 21,425,000 | — | — | — | 0.50 | 0.60 |
| 2001 (m) | 2,500 | PF65 12.50 | | | | |

### KM# 3.2 50 HALERU

0.90 g., Aluminum, 19 mm. **Obv:** Crowned Czech lion left, date below **Rev:** Large denomination **Edge:** Segmented reeding **Note:** Outlined lettering and larger mint mark

| Date | Mintage | VF20 | XF40 | MS60 | MS63 | MS65 |
|---|---|---|---|---|---|---|
| 2001 (m) | 21,425,000 | — | — | — | 0.50 | 0.60 |
| 2001 (m) | — | PF65 12.50 | | | | |
| 2002 (m) | 26,246,298 | — | — | — | 0.50 | 0.60 |
| 2002 (m) | 3,490 | PF65 12.50 | | | | |
| 2003 (m) | 41,548,000 | — | — | — | 0.50 | 0.60 |
| 2003 (m) | 3,000 | PF65 7.50 | | | | |
| 2004 (m) | 931,145 | — | — | — | 0.50 | 0.60 |
| 2004 (m) | 4,000 | PF65 7.50 | | | | |
| 2005 (m) | 36,814,000 | — | — | — | 0.50 | 0.60 |
| 2005 (m) | 3,000 | PF65 7.50 | | | | |
| 2006 (m) | 40,030,500 | — | — | — | 0.50 | 0.60 |
| 2006 (m) | 2,500 | PF65 7.50 | | | | |
| 2007 (m) | 35,020,500 | — | — | — | 0.50 | 0.60 |
| 2007 (m) | 2,500 | PF65 7.50 | | | | |
| 2008 (m) | 17,000 | — | — | — | 0.50 | 0.60 |
| 2008 (m) | 2,500 | PF65 3.00 | | | | |
| 2009 (m) | — | — | — | — | 0.50 | 0.60 |
| 2009 (m) | 2,500 | PF65 3.00 | | | | |

### KM# 7 KORUNA

3.60 g., Nickel Plated Steel, 20 mm. **Obv:** Crowned Czech lion left, date below **Rev:** Denomination above crown **Edge:** Reeded **Note:** Two varieties of mint marks exist for 1996. 2000-03 have two varieties in the artist monogram.

| Date | Mintage | VF20 | XF40 | MS60 | MS63 | MS65 |
|---|---|---|---|---|---|---|
| 2001 (m) | 15,938,353 | — | — | — | 0.60 | 0.75 |
| 2001 (m) | — | PF65 20.00 | | | | |
| 2002 (m) | 26,244,666 | — | — | — | 0.60 | 0.75 |
| 2002 (m) | — | PF65 20.00 | | | | |
| 2003 (m) | 36,877,440 | — | — | — | 0.60 | 0.75 |
| 2003 (m) | 3,000 | PF65 10.00 | | | | |
| 2004 (m) | 30,500 | — | — | — | 0.60 | 0.75 |
| 2004 (m) | — | PF65 10.00 | | | | |
| 2005 (m) | 14,000 | — | — | — | 0.60 | 0.75 |
| 2005 (m) | 3,000 | PF65 10.00 | | | | |
| 2006 (m) | 27,097,500 | — | — | — | 0.60 | 0.75 |
| 2006 (m) | 2,500 | PF65 10.00 | | | | |
| 2007 (m) | 14,170,500 | — | — | — | 0.60 | 0.75 |
| 2007 (m) | 2,500 | PF65 10.00 | | | | |
| 2008 (m) | 29,617,000 | — | — | — | 0.60 | 0.75 |
| 2008 (m) | 2,500 | PF65 6.00 | | | | |
| 2009 (m) | 38,367,400 | — | — | — | 0.60 | 0.75 |
| 2009 (m) | 3,200 | PF65 6.00 | | | | |
| 2010 (m) | 15,004,602 | — | — | — | 0.60 | 0.75 |
| 2010 (m) | 3,200 | PF65 6.00 | | | | |
| 2011 (m) | 4,000,600 | — | — | — | 0.60 | 0.75 |
| 2011 (m) | 2,500 | PF65 6.00 | | | | |
| 2012 (m) | 19,000,000 | — | — | — | 0.60 | 0.75 |
| 2012 (m) | — | PF63 6.00 | | | | |
| 2013 (m) | — | — | — | — | 0.60 | 0.75 |

### KM# 9 2 KORUNY

3.70 g., Nickel Plated Steel, 21.5 mm. **Obv:** Crowned Czech lion left, date below **Rev:** Large denomination, pendant design at left **Edge:** Plain **Shape:** 11-sided **Note:** Two varieties of designer monograms exist for 2001-04.

| Date | Mintage | VF20 | XF40 | MS60 | MS63 | MS65 |
|---|---|---|---|---|---|---|
| 2001 (m) | 26,117,000 | — | — | — | 0.65 | 0.80 |
| 2001 (m) | — | PF65 20.00 | | | | |
| 2002 (m) | 20,941,084 | — | — | — | 0.65 | 0.80 |
| 2002 (m) | — | PF65 20.00 | | | | |
| 2003 (m) | 20,955,000 | — | — | — | 0.65 | 0.80 |
| 2003 (m) | — | PF65 12.50 | | | | |
| 2004 (m) | 15,658,556 | — | — | — | 0.65 | 0.80 |
| 2004 (m) | — | PF65 10.00 | | | | |
| 2005 (m) | 14,000 | — | — | — | 0.65 | 0.80 |
| 2005 (m) | 3,000 | PF65 7.50 | | | | |
| 2006 (m) | 30,500 | — | — | — | 0.65 | 0.80 |
| 2006 (m) | 2,500 | PF65 7.50 | | | | |

| Date | Mintage | VF20 | XF40 | MS60 | MS63 | MS65 |
|---|---|---|---|---|---|---|
| 2007 (m) | 30,020,500 | — | — | — | 0.65 | 0.80 |
| 2007 (m) | 2,500 | PF65 7.50 | | | | |
| 2008 (m) | 26,267,000 | — | — | — | 0.65 | 0.80 |
| 2008 (m) | 2,500 | PF65 5.00 | | | | |
| 2009 (m) | 25,418,000 | — | — | — | 0.65 | 0.80 |
| 2009 (m) | 3,200 | PF65 5.00 | | | | |
| 2010 (m) | 26,054,000 | — | — | — | 0.65 | 0.80 |
| 2010 (m) | 3,200 | PF65 5.00 | | | | |
| 2011 (m) | 12,000,000 | — | — | — | 0.65 | 0.80 |
| 2011 (m) | 2,500 | PF65 5.00 | | | | |
| 2012 (m) | 13,000,000 | — | — | — | 0.65 | 0.80 |
| 2012 (m) | — | PF65 5.00 | | | | |
| 2013 (m) | — | — | — | — | 0.65 | 0.80 |
| 2013 | — | PF65 5.00 | | | | |

### KM# 8 5 KORUN

4.80 g., Nickel Plated Steel, 23 mm. **Obv:** Crowned Czech lion left, date below **Rev:** Large denomination, Charles bridge and linden leaf **Edge:** Plain

| Date | Mintage | VF20 | XF40 | MS60 | MS63 | MS65 |
|---|---|---|---|---|---|---|
| 2001 (m) | 25,000 | — | — | — | 1.00 | 1.25 |
| 2001 (m) | — | PF65 27.50 | | | | |
| 2002 (m) | 21,344,995 | — | — | — | 1.00 | 1.25 |
| 2002 (m) | — | PF65 27.50 | | | | |
| 2003 (m) | 22,000 | — | — | — | 1.00 | 1.25 |
| 2003 (m) | — | PF65 15.00 | | | | |
| 2004 (m) | 34,940 | — | — | — | 1.00 | 1.25 |
| 2004 (m) | — | PF65 12.00 | | | | |
| 2005 (m) | 14,000 | — | — | — | 1.00 | 1.25 |
| 2005 (m) | 3,000 | PF65 10.00 | | | | |
| 2006 (m) | 25,030,500 | — | — | — | 1.00 | 1.25 |
| 2006 (m) | 2,500 | PF65 10.00 | | | | |
| 2007 (m) | 20,500 | — | — | — | 1.00 | 1.25 |
| 2007 (m) | 2,500 | PF65 10.00 | | | | |
| 2008 (m) | 11,617,000 | — | — | — | 1.00 | 1.25 |
| 2008 (m) | 2,500 | PF65 6.00 | | | | |
| 2009 (m) | 19,911,000 | — | — | — | 1.00 | 1.25 |
| 2009 (m) | 3,200 | PF65 6.00 | | | | |
| 2010 (m) | 14,711,000 | — | — | — | 1.00 | 1.25 |
| 2010 (m) | 3,200 | PF65 6.00 | | | | |
| 2011 (m) | — | — | — | — | 1.00 | 1.25 |
| 2011 (m) | 5,500 | PF65 6.00 | | | | |
| 2012 (m) | — | — | — | — | 1.00 | 1.25 |
| 2012 (m) | — | PF65 6.00 | | | | |
| 2013 (m) | — | — | — | — | 1.00 | 1.25 |

### KM# 4 10 KORUN

7.62 g., Copper Plated Steel, 24.5 mm. **Obv:** Crowned Czech lion left, date below **Rev:** Brno Cathedral, denomination below **Edge:** Reeded **Note:** Position of designer's initials on reverse change during the 1995 strike.

| Date | Mintage | VF20 | XF40 | MS60 | MS63 | MS65 |
|---|---|---|---|---|---|---|
| 2001 (m) | 25,000 | — | — | — | 1.50 | 1.75 |
| 2001 (m) | 2,500 | PF65 28.00 | | | | |
| 2002 (m) | 20,156 | — | — | — | 1.50 | 1.75 |
| 2002 (m) | — | PF65 28.00 | | | | |
| 2003 (m) | 18,747,000 | — | — | — | 1.50 | 1.75 |
| 2003 (m) | — | PF65 17.50 | | | | |
| 2004 (m) | 2,255,740 | — | — | — | 1.50 | 1.75 |
| 2004 (m) | — | PF65 14.00 | | | | |
| 2005 (m) | 14,000 | — | — | — | 1.50 | 1.75 |
| 2005 (m) | 3,000 | PF65 10.00 | | | | |
| 2006 (m) | 30,500 | — | — | — | 1.50 | 1.75 |
| 2006 (m) | 2,500 | PF65 10.00 | | | | |
| 2007 (m) | 20,500 | — | — | — | 1.50 | 1.75 |
| 2007 (m) | 2,500 | PF65 10.00 | | | | |
| 2008 (m) | 10,092,000 | — | — | — | 1.50 | 1.75 |
| 2008 (m) | 2,500 | PF65 7.00 | | | | |
| 2009 (m) | 10,511,000 | — | — | — | 1.50 | 1.75 |
| 2009 (m) | 3,200 | PF65 7.00 | | | | |
| 2010 (m) | 16,811,000 | — | — | — | 1.50 | 1.75 |
| 2010 (m) | 3,200 | PF65 7.00 | | | | |
| 2011 (m) | — | — | — | — | 1.50 | 1.75 |
| 2011 (m) | 5,500 | PF65 7.00 | | | | |
| 2012 (m) | — | — | — | — | 1.50 | 1.75 |
| 2012 (m) | — | PF65 7.00 | | | | |
| 2013 (m) | — | — | — | — | 1.50 | 1.75 |

### KM# 5 20 KORUN

8.43 g., Brass Plated Steel, 26 mm. **Obv:** Crowned Czech lion left, date below **Rev:** St. Wenceslas (Duke Vaclav) on horse **Edge:** Plain **Shape:** 13-sided **Note:** Two varieties of mint marks and style of 9's exist for 1997.

| Date | Mintage | VF20 | XF40 | MS60 | MS63 | MS65 |
|---|---|---|---|---|---|---|
| 2001 (m) | 25,000 | — | — | — | 2.50 | 2.75 |
| 2001 (m) | — | PF65 40.00 | | | | |
| 2002 (m) | 20,996,500 | — | — | — | 2.50 | 2.75 |
| 2002 (m) | — | PF65 40.00 | | | | |
| 2003 (m) | 22,000 | — | — | — | 2.50 | 2.75 |
| 2003 (m) | — | PF65 25.00 | | | | |
| 2004 (m) | 8,249,507 | — | — | — | 2.50 | 2.75 |
| 2004 (m) | — | PF65 22.50 | | | | |
| 2005 (m) | 9,866,778 | — | — | — | 2.50 | 2.75 |
| 2005 (m) | 3,000 | PF65 22.50 | | | | |
| 2006 (m) | 2,096,500 | — | — | — | 2.50 | 2.75 |
| 2006 (m) | 2,500 | PF65 22.50 | | | | |
| 2007 (m) | 20,500 | — | — | — | 2.50 | 2.75 |
| 2007 (m) | 2,500 | PF65 22.50 | | | | |
| 2008 (m) | 17,000 | — | — | — | 2.50 | 2.75 |
| 2008 (m) | 2,500 | PF65 10.00 | | | | |
| 2009 (m) | 11,000 | — | — | — | 2.50 | 2.75 |
| 2009 (m) | 3,200 | PF65 10.00 | | | | |
| 2010 (m) | 11,000 | — | — | — | 2.50 | 2.75 |
| 2010 (m) | 3,200 | PF65 10.00 | | | | |
| 2011 (m) | 8,000,000 | — | — | — | 2.50 | 2.75 |
| 2011 (m) | 5,500 | PF65 10.00 | | | | |
| 2012 (m) | 8,000,000 | — | — | — | 2.50 | 2.75 |
| 2012 (m) | — | PF65 10.00 | | | | |
| 2013 | — | — | — | — | 2.50 | 2.75 |

### KM# 1 50 KORUN

9.70 g., Bi-Metallic Brass Plated Steel center in Copper Plated Steel ring, 27.5 mm. **Obv:** Crowned Czech lion left **Rev:** Prague city view **Edge:** Plain

| Date | Mintage | VF20 | XF40 | MS60 | MS63 | MS65 |
|---|---|---|---|---|---|---|
| 2001 (m) | 16,000 | — | — | — | 9.00 | 9.50 |
| 2001 (m) | — | PF65 80.00 | | | | |
| 2002 (m) | 16,771 | — | — | — | 9.00 | 9.50 |
| 2002 (m) | — | PF65 80.00 | | | | |
| 2003 (m) | 22,000 | — | — | — | 9.00 | 9.50 |
| 2003 (m) | — | PF65 50.00 | | | | |
| 2004 (m) | 34,555 | — | — | — | 9.00 | 9.50 |
| 2004 (m) | — | PF65 40.00 | | | | |
| 2005 (m) | 14,000 | — | — | — | 9.00 | 9.50 |
| 2005 (m) | 3,000 | PF65 25.00 | | | | |
| 2006 (m) | 30,500 | — | — | — | 9.00 | 9.50 |
| 2006 (m) | 2,500 | PF65 25.00 | | | | |
| 2007 (m) | 20,500 | — | — | — | 9.00 | 9.50 |
| 2007 (m) | 2,500 | PF65 25.00 | | | | |
| 2008 (m) | 9,528,300 | — | — | — | 9.00 | 9.50 |
| 2008 (m) | 2,500 | PF65 20.00 | | | | |
| 2009 (m) | 36,719,050 | — | — | — | 9.00 | 9.50 |
| 2009 (m) | 3,200 | PF65 20.00 | | | | |
| 2010 (m) | 17,210,000 | — | — | — | 9.00 | 9.50 |
| 2010 (m) | 32,000 | PF65 20.00 | | | | |
| 2011 (m) | 10,000,000 | — | — | — | 9.00 | 9.50 |
| 2011 (m) | 5,500 | PF65 20.00 | | | | |
| 2012 (m) | 10,000,000 | — | — | — | 9.00 | 9.50 |
| 2012 (m) | — | PF65 20.00 | | | | |
| 2013 (m) | — | — | — | — | 9.00 | 9.50 |

### KM# 51 200 KORUN

13.00 g., 0.900 Silver 0.3762 oz. ASW, 31 mm. **Subject:** Jaroslav Seifert **Obv:** Quartered arms above denomination **Rev:** Head right, dates at left **Note:** 1,680 pieces uncirculated and 2 proof remelted.

| Date | Mintage | VF20 | XF40 | MS60 | MS63 | MS65 |
|---|---|---|---|---|---|---|
| ND-2001 | 11,746 | — | — | — | 18.00 | 20.00 |
| Note: Milled edge | | | | | | |
| ND-2001 | 3,186 | PF65 165 | | | | |
| Note: Plain edge with CESKA NARODNI BANKA *0.900* 13g | | | | | | |

### KM# 52 200 KORUN

13.00 g., 0.900 Silver 0.3762 oz. ASW, 31 mm. **Subject:** Soccer **Obv:** Quartered arms on square, denomination below **Rev:** Rampant lion on soccer ball **Note:** 2,350 pieces uncirculated and 1 proof remelted.

| Date | Mintage | VF20 | XF40 | MS60 | MS63 | MS65 |
|---|---|---|---|---|---|---|
| ND-2001 | 12,050 | — | — | — | 18.00 | 20.00 |
| Note: Milled edge | | | | | | |
| ND-2001 | 3,896 | PF65 165 | | | | |
| Note: Plain edge with CESKA NARODNI BANKA *0.900* 13g | | | | | | |

### KM# 53 200 KORUN

13.00 g., 0.900 Silver 0.3762 oz. ASW, 31 mm. **Subject:** 250th Anniversary - Death of Kilian Ignac Dientzenhofer **Obv:** Quartered arms, denomination at right **Rev:** Doorway and caliper **Note:** 1,840 pieces uncirculated and 104 proof remelted.

| Date | Mintage | VF20 | XF40 | MS60 | MS63 | MS65 |
|---|---|---|---|---|---|---|
| ND(2001) | 11,565 | — | — | — | 18.00 | 20.00 |
| Note: Milled edge | | | | | | |
| ND(2001) | 3,282 | PF65 150 | | | | |
| Note: Plain edge with CESKA NARODNI BANKA *0.900* 13g | | | | | | |

### KM# 54 200 KORUN

13.00 g., 0.900 Silver 0.3762 oz. ASW, 31 mm. **Subject:** Euro Currency System **Obv:** National arms **Rev:** Prague gros coin design **Note:** 134 pieces uncirculated and 1 proof remelted.

| Date | Mintage | VF20 | XF40 | MS60 | MS63 | MS65 |
|---|---|---|---|---|---|---|
| ND-2001 | 3,995 | PF65 200 | | | | |
| Note: Plain edge with CESKA NARODNI BANKA *0.900* 13g | | | | | | |
| ND-2001 | 13,730 | — | — | — | 18.00 | 20.00 |
| Note: Milled edge | | | | | | |

**KM# 58 200 KORUN**

13.00 g., 0.900 Silver 0.3762 oz. ASW, 31 mm. **Subject:** Frantisek Skroup **Obv:** Quartered, elongated arms above date **Rev:** Portrait and name **Note:** 1,480 pieces uncirculated and 13 proof remelted.

| Date | Mintage | VF20 | XF40 | MS60 | MS63 | MS65 |
|---|---|---|---|---|---|---|
| ND-2001 | 11,944 | — | — | — | 18.00 | 20.00 |
| Note: Milled edge | | | | | | |
| ND-2001 | 3,179 | PF65 175 | | | | |
| Note: Plain edge with CESKA NARODNI BANKA *0.900* 13g | | | | | | |

**KM# 55 200 KORUN**

13.00 g., 0.900 Silver 0.3762 oz. ASW, 31 mm. **Subject:** St. Zdislava **Obv:** Old and new arms form diamond above denomination **Rev:** Saint feeding sick person **Note:** 865 pieces uncirculated remelted.

| Date | Mintage | VF20 | XF40 | MS60 | MS63 | MS65 |
|---|---|---|---|---|---|---|
| ND-2002 | 12,083 | — | — | — | 18.00 | 20.00 |
| Note: Milled edge | | | | | | |
| ND-2002 | 3,596 | PF65 300 | | | | |
| Note: Plain edge with CESKA NARODNI BANKA *0.900* 13g | | | | | | |

**KM# 56 200 KORUN**

13.00 g., 0.900 Silver 0.3762 oz. ASW, 30.9 mm. **Subject:** Emil Holub **Obv:** National arms, eagles and lions, denomination below **Rev:** Traveler and African dancers **Note:** 1,350 pieces uncirculated and 7 proof remelted.

| Date | Mintage | VF20 | XF40 | MS60 | MS63 | MS65 |
|---|---|---|---|---|---|---|
| ND-2002 | 3,588 | PF65 165 | | | | |
| Note: Plain edge with CESKA NARODNI BANKA *0.900* 13g | | | | | | |
| ND-2002 | 11,602 | — | — | — | 18.00 | 20.00 |
| Note: Milled edge | | | | | | |

**KM# 57 200 KORUN**

13.00 g., 0.900 Silver 0.3762 oz. ASW, 30.9 mm. **Subject:** Jiri of Podebrady **Obv:** Overlapped arms **Rev:** Head right **Note:** 1,200 pieces uncirculated and 5 proof remelted.

| Date | Mintage | VF20 | XF40 | MS60 | MS63 | MS65 |
|---|---|---|---|---|---|---|
| ND-2002 | 11,729 | — | — | — | 18.00 | 20.00 |
| Note: Milled edge | | | | | | |
| ND-2002 | 3,591 | PF65 200 | | | | |
| Note: Plain edge with CESKA NARODNI BANKA *0.900* 13g | | | | | | |

**KM# 59 200 KORUN**

13.00 g., 0.900 Silver 0.3762 oz. ASW, 31 mm. **Subject:** Mikolas Ales **Obv:** Four coats of arms above denomination **Rev:** Horse and rider **Note:** 573 pieces uncirculated and 139 proof remelted.

| Date | Mintage | VF20 | XF40 | MS60 | MS63 | MS65 |
|---|---|---|---|---|---|---|
| ND(2002) | 11,879 | — | — | — | 18.00 | 20.00 |
| Note: Milled edge | | | | | | |
| ND-2002 (m) | 4,258 | PF65 165 | | | | |
| Note: Plain edge with CESKA NARODNI BANKA *0.900* 13g | | | | | | |

**KM# 60 200 KORUN**

13.00 g., 0.900 Silver 0.3762 oz. ASW, 31 mm. **Subject:** Jaroslav Vrchlicky **Obv:** Denomination and quill **Rev:** Bust with hat facing **Note:** 889 pieces uncirculated and 5 proof remelted.

| Date | Mintage | VF20 | XF40 | MS60 | MS63 | MS65 |
|---|---|---|---|---|---|---|
| ND-2003 | 10,583 | — | — | — | 18.00 | 20.00 |
| Note: Milled edge | | | | | | |
| ND-2003 | 3,692 | PF65 135 | | | | |
| Note: Plain edge with CESKA NARODNI BANKA *0.900* 13g | | | | | | |

**KM# 62 200 KORUN**

13.00 g., 0.900 Silver 0.3762 oz. ASW, 30.9 mm. **Subject:** Josef Thomayer **Obv:** National arms **Rev:** Portrait **Note:** 783 uncirculated and 12 proof were remelted.

| Date | Mintage | VF20 | XF40 | MS60 | MS63 | MS65 |
|---|---|---|---|---|---|---|
| ND(2003) | 10,525 | — | — | — | 18.00 | 20.00 |
| Note: Milled edge | | | | | | |
| ND-2003 | 3,981 | PF65 135 | | | | |
| Note: Plain edge with CESKA NARODNI BANKA *0.900* 13g | | | | | | |

**KM# 63 200 KORUN**

13.00 g., 0.900 Silver 0.3762 oz. ASW, 31 mm. **Subject:** Tabor-Bechyne Electric Railway **Obv:** Head left **Rev:** Railroad station scene **Note:** 808 Uncirculated were remelted.

| Date | Mintage | VF20 | XF40 | MS60 | MS63 | MS65 |
|---|---|---|---|---|---|---|
| ND(2003) | 10,986 | — | — | — | 18.00 | 20.00 |
| Note: Milled edge | | | | | | |
| ND-2003 | 4,097 | PF65 125 | | | | |
| Note: Plain edge with CESKA NARODNI BANKA *0.900* 13g | | | | | | |

**KM# 64 200 KORUN**

13.00 g., 0.900 Silver 0.3762 oz. ASW, 31 mm. **Subject:** Bohemian Skiers' Union **Obv:** Head 3/4 left **Rev:** Skier **Note:** 680 Uncirculated and 13 proof were remelted.

| Date | Mintage | VF20 | XF40 | MS60 | MS63 | MS65 |
|---|---|---|---|---|---|---|
| ND(2003) | 10,801 | — | — | — | 18.00 | 20.00 |
| Note: Milled edge | | | | | | |
| ND-2003 | 4,284 | PF65 120 | | | | |
| Note: Plain edge with CESKA NARODNI BANKA *0.900* 13g | | | | | | |

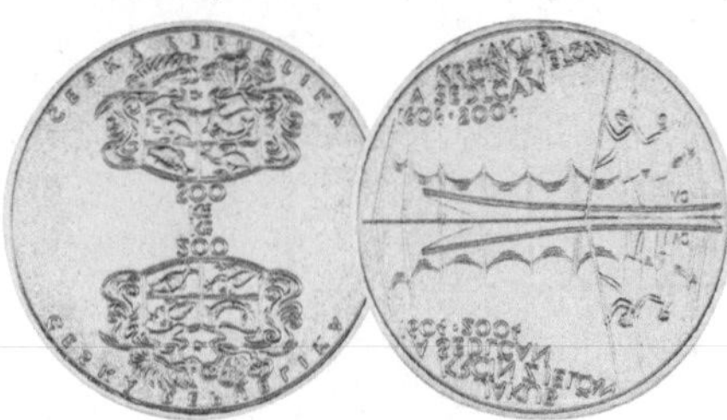

**KM# 70 200 KORUN**

13.00 g., 0.900 Silver 0.3762 oz. ASW, 31 mm. **Subject:** 300th Anniversary - Death of pond builder Jakub Krcin **Obv:** Coat of arms above value with reflected design below **Rev:** Two fishermen in boat with reflection on water below **Note:** 656 uncirculated remelted.

| Date | Mintage | VF20 | XF40 | MS60 | MS63 | MS65 |
|---|---|---|---|---|---|---|
| ND(2004) (m) | 10,685 | — | — | — | 18.00 | 20.00 |
| Note: Milled edge | | | | | | |
| ND-2004 | 3,995 | PF65 120 | | | | |
| Note: Plain edge with CESKA NARODNI BANKA *0.900* 13g | | | | | | |

**KM# 71 200 KORUN**

13.00 g., 0.900 Silver 0.3762 oz. ASW **Subject:** Entry into the European Union **Rev:** State emblems of 15 members of the European Union

| Date | Mintage | VF20 | XF40 | MS60 | MS63 | MS65 |
|---|---|---|---|---|---|---|
| 2004 | 13,918 | — | — | — | 18.00 | 20.00 |
| Note: Plain edge with codes for EU countries | | | | | | |
| 2004 | 9,994 | PF65 65.00 | | | | |
| Note: Plain edge with CESKA NARODNI BANKA *0.900* 13g | | | | | | |

**KM# 72 200 KORUN**

13.00 g., 0.900 Silver 0.3762 oz. ASW, 31 mm. **Subject:** Prokop Diviš **Obv:** Lighting conductor modulator **Rev:** Head of Diviš

| Date | Mintage | VF20 | XF40 | MS60 | MS63 | MS65 |
|---|---|---|---|---|---|---|
| 2004 | 10,145 | — | — | — | 18.00 | 20.00 |
| Note: Milled edge | | | | | | |
| 2004 | 3,897 | PF65 85.00 | | | | |
| Note: Plain edge with CESKA NARODNI BANKA *0.900* 13g | | | | | | |

**KM# 73 200 KORUN**

13.00 g., 0.900 Silver 0.3762 oz. ASW **Subject:** Leos Janacek **Rev:** Head of Janacek

| Date | Mintage | VF20 | XF40 | MS60 | MS63 | MS65 |
|---|---|---|---|---|---|---|
| 2004 | 10,143 | — | — | — | 18.00 | 20.00 |
| Note: Milled edge | | | | | | |
| 2004 | — | PF65 75.00 | | | | |
| Note: Plain edge with CESKA NARODNI BANKA *0.900* 13g | | | | | | |

**KM# 74 200 KORUN**
13.00 g., 0.900 Silver 0.3762 oz. ASW **Subject:** Kralice Bible **Obv:** Enlargement of bible page **Rev:** Bible page

| Date | Mintage | VF20 | XF40 | MS60 | MS63 | MS65 |
|---|---|---|---|---|---|---|
| 2004 | 10,975 | — | — | — | 18.00 | 20.00 |
| Note: Reeded | | | | | | |
| 2004 | — | PF65 95.00 | | | | |

**KM# 77 200 KORUN**
13.00 g., 0.900 Silver 0.3762 oz. ASW, 31 mm. **Obv:** Prokop Divis **Rev:** Lightning conductor

| Date | Mintage | VF20 | XF40 | MS60 | MS63 | MS65 |
|---|---|---|---|---|---|---|
| 2004 | 4,600 | PF65 85.00 | | | | |
| Note: Plain edge with CESKA NARODNI BANKA * Ag 0.900 * 13g * | | | | | | |
| 2004 | 14,000 | — | — | — | 18.00 | 20.00 |
| Note: Reeded | | | | | | |

**KM# 78 200 KORUN**
13.00 g., 0.900 Silver 0.3762 oz. ASW, 31 mm. **Subject:** 100th Anniversary of Jan Werich and Jiri Voskovec

| Date | Mintage | VF20 | XF40 | MS60 | MS63 | MS65 |
|---|---|---|---|---|---|---|
| 2005 | 4,997 | PF65 135 | | | | |
| Note: Plain edge with CESKA NARODNI BANKA *0.900* 13g | | | | | | |
| 2005 | 10,884 | — | — | — | 18.00 | 20.00 |
| Note: Milled edge | | | | | | |

**KM# 79 200 KORUN**
13.00 g., 0.900 Silver 0.3762 oz. ASW, 31 mm. **Subject:** 100th Anniversary of Production of 1st Car in Mlada Boleslav **Rev:** 1st car of LK factory

| Date | Mintage | VF20 | XF40 | MS60 | MS63 | MS65 |
|---|---|---|---|---|---|---|
| 2005 | 10,797 | PF65 65.00 | | | | |
| Note: Plain edge with CESKA NARODNI BANKA *0.900* 13g | | | | | | |
| 2005 | 13,225 | — | — | — | 18.00 | 20.00 |

**KM# 80 200 KORUN**
13.00 g., 0.900 Silver 0.3762 oz. ASW, 31 mm. **Subject:** 450th Anniversary - Birth of Mikulas Dacicky **Obv:** Arms of Dacicky **Rev:** Head of Mikulas Dacicky z Heslova

| Date | Mintage | VF20 | XF40 | MS60 | MS63 | MS65 |
|---|---|---|---|---|---|---|
| 2005 | 5,597 | PF65 70.00 | | | | |
| Note: Plain edge with CESKA NARODNI BANKA *0.900* 13g | | | | | | |
| 2005 | 10,076 | — | — | — | 18.00 | 20.00 |
| Note: Milled edge | | | | | | |

**KM# 81 200 KORUN**
13.00 g., 0.900 Silver 0.3762 oz. ASW, 31 mm. **Subject:** 250th Anniversary - Birth of F.J. Gerstner

| Date | Mintage | VF20 | XF40 | MS60 | MS63 | MS65 |
|---|---|---|---|---|---|---|
| 2006 | 6,194 | PF65 50.00 | | | | |
| Note: Plain edge with CESKA NARODNI BANKA *0.900* 13g | | | | | | |
| 2006 | 11,101 | — | — | — | 18.00 | 20.00 |
| Note: Milled edge | | | | | | |

**KM# 82 200 KORUN**
13.00 g., 0.900 Silver 0.3762 oz. ASW, 31 mm. **Subject:** 150th Anniversary - School of Glass Making in Kamenicky Senov **Obv:** Image of National Arms within glass cube **Rev:** Artistic image within glass cube

| Date | Mintage | VF20 | XF40 | MS60 | MS63 | MS65 |
|---|---|---|---|---|---|---|
| 2006 | 6,494 | PF65 50.00 | | | | |
| Note: Plain edge with CESKA NARODNI BANKA *0.900* 13g | | | | | | |
| 2006 | 9,546 | — | — | — | 20.00 | 22.00 |
| Note: Milled edge | | | | | | |

**KM# 83 200 KORUN**
13.00 g., 0.900 Silver 0.3762 oz. ASW, 31 mm. **Subject:** 500th Anniversary - Death of Matej Rejsek **Obv:** Pulpit in the church of St. Laurer in Kank **Rev:** Portrait of Rejsek on the Prasna gate in Prague

| Date | Mintage | VF20 | XF40 | MS60 | MS63 | MS65 |
|---|---|---|---|---|---|---|
| 2006 | 6,494 | PF65 50.00 | | | | |
| Note: Plain edge with CESKA NARODNI BANKA *0.900* 13g | | | | | | |
| 2006 | 9,594 | — | — | — | 20.00 | 22.00 |
| Note: Milled edge | | | | | | |

**KM# 84 200 KORUN**
13.00 g., 0.900 Silver 0.3762 oz. ASW, 31 mm. **Subject:** 700th Anniversary - Death of Vaclav III **Obv:** Sword between two shields positioned top-to-top **Rev:** King Vaclav III between shields of Bohemia and Moravia

| Date | Mintage | VF20 | XF40 | MS60 | MS63 | MS65 |
|---|---|---|---|---|---|---|
| 2006 | 10,471 | — | — | — | 18.00 | 20.00 |
| Note: Milled edge | | | | | | |
| 2006 | 7,497 | PF65 50.00 | | | | |
| Note: Plain edge with CESKA NARODNI BANKA *0.900* 13g | | | | | | |

**KM# 85 200 KORUN**
13.00 g., 0.900 Silver 0.3762 oz. ASW, 31 mm. **Subject:** 100th Anniversary - Birth of Jaroslav Jezek **Obv:** Musical score **Rev:** Caricature looking at score

| Date | Mintage | VF20 | XF40 | MS60 | MS63 | MS65 |
|---|---|---|---|---|---|---|
| 2006 (m) | 15,442 | PF65 30.00 | | | | |
| Note: Plain edge with CESKA NARODNI BANKA *0.900* 13g | | | | | | |
| 2006 (m) | 10,192 | — | — | — | 18.00 | 20.00 |
| Note: Milled edge | | | | | | |

**KM# 91 200 KORUN**
13.00 g., 0.900 Silver 0.3762 oz. ASW, 31 mm. **Subject:** Founding of Jednota Bratrska, 550th Anniversary **Obv:** Emblem of Jednota Bratrska, tree, ram with flag. **Rev:** Chalice with ram with flag

| Date | Mintage | VF20 | XF40 | MS60 | MS63 | MS65 |
|---|---|---|---|---|---|---|
| 2007 | 8,297 | PF65 65.00 | | | | |
| Note: Plain edge with CESKA NARODNI BANKA *0.900* 13g | | | | | | |
| 2007 | 10,471 | — | — | — | 20.00 | 22.00 |
| Note: Milled edge | | | | | | |

**KM# 92 200 KORUN**
13.00 g., 0.900 Silver 0.3762 oz. ASW, 31 mm. **Subject:** Charles Bridge cornerstone, 650th anniversary

| Date | Mintage | VF20 | XF40 | MS60 | MS63 | MS65 |
|---|---|---|---|---|---|---|
| 2007 | 18,746 | PF65 32.00 | | | | |
| Note: Plain edge with CESKA NARODNI BANKA *0.900* 13g | | | | | | |
| 2007 | 10,772 | — | — | — | 20.00 | 22.00 |
| Note: Milled edge | | | | | | |

**KM# 93 200 KORUN**
13.00 g., 0.900 Silver 0.3762 oz. ASW, 31 mm. **Subject:** Jarmila Novotná, 100th Anniversary of Birth **Obv:** Names of the operas in which Novotna sang **Rev:** Head of Novotna

| Date | Mintage | VF20 | XF40 | MS60 | MS63 | MS65 |
|---|---|---|---|---|---|---|
| 2007 Proof | 12,788 | PF65 32.00 | | | | |
| Note: Plain edge with CESKA NARODNI BANKA *0.900* 13g | | | | | | |
| 2007 | 9,584 | — | — | — | 20.00 | 22.00 |
| Note: Milled edge | | | | | | |

**KM# 94 200 KORUN**
13.00 g., 0.900 Silver 0.3737 oz. ASW, 31 mm. **Subject:** Earth Satelite Launch, 50th Anniversary **Obv:** Satelite and sound signal of satelite **Rev:** Plentary system with satelite

| Date | Mintage | VF20 | XF40 | MS60 | MS63 | MS65 |
|---|---|---|---|---|---|---|
| 2007 | 10,148 | — | — | — | 30.00 | 50.00 |
| Note: Milled edge | | | | | | |
| 2007 | 14,797 | PF65 42.50 | | | | |
| Note: Plain edge with CESKA NARODNI BANKA *0.900* 13g | | | | | | |

**KM# 97 200 KORUN**
13.00 g., 0.900 Silver 0.3762 oz. ASW, 31 mm. **Subject:** Charles IV Vineyard Planting decree

| Date | Mintage | VF20 | XF40 | MS60 | MS63 | MS65 |
|---|---|---|---|---|---|---|
| 2008 | 9,768 | — | — | — | 20.00 | 22.00 |
| Note: Milled edge | | | | | | |
| 2008 | 16,997 | PF65 32.00 | | | | |
| Note: Plain edge with CESKA NARODNI BANKA *0.900* 13g | | | | | | |

**KM# 98 200 KORUN**
13.00 g., 0.900 Silver 0.3762 oz. ASW **Subject:** Josef Hlavka, 100th Anniversary of Death **Obv:** Wing over architectural element **Rev:** Facing portrait of Hlavka

| Date | Mintage | VF20 | XF40 | MS60 | MS63 | MS65 |
|---|---|---|---|---|---|---|
| 2008 | 9,559 | — | — | — | 20.00 | 22.00 |
| Note: Milled edge | | | | | | |
| 2008 | 15,976 | PF65 32.00 | | | | |
| Note: Plain edge with CESKA NARODNI BANKA *0.900* 13g | | | | | | |

**KM# 99 200 KORUN**
13.00 g., 0.900 Silver 0.3762 oz. ASW, 31 mm. **Subject:** Schengen Convention **Obv:** Arms **Rev:** Opening of the frontiers

| Date | Mintage | VF20 | XF40 | MS60 | MS63 | MS65 |
|---|---|---|---|---|---|---|
| 2008 | 15,743 | PF65 32.00 | | | | |
| Note: Plain edge with CESKA NARODNI BANKA *0.900* 13g | | | | | | |
| 2008 | 9,739 | — | — | — | 20.00 | 22.00 |
| Note: Milled edge | | | | | | |

**KM# 100 200 KORUN**
13.00 g., 0.900 Silver 0.3762 oz. ASW, 31 mm. **Subject:** Viktor Ponrepo,150th Anniversary **Obv:** Tripod camera **Rev:** Mustache and top hat

| Date | Mintage | VF20 | XF40 | MS60 | MS63 | MS65 |
|---|---|---|---|---|---|---|
| 2008 | 14,997 | PF65 32.00 | | | | |
| Note: Plain edge with CESKA NARODNI BANKA *0.900* 13g | | | | | | |
| 2008 | 9,572 | — | — | — | 20.00 | 22.00 |
| Note: Milled edge | | | | | | |

**KM# 101 200 KORUN**
13.00 g., 0.900 Silver 0.3737 oz. ASW, 31 mm. **Subject:** National Technical Museum **Obv:** Steam Locomotive and driving wheel **Rev:** Museum façade and clock face

| Date | Mintage | VF20 | XF40 | MS60 | MS63 | MS65 |
|---|---|---|---|---|---|---|
| 2008 | 14,997 | PF65 35.00 | | | | |
| Note: Plain edge with CESKA NARODNI BANKA *0.900* 13g | | | | | | |
| 2008 | 9,972 | — | — | — | 22.00 | 25.00 |
| Note: Milled edge | | | | | | |

**KM# 102 200 KORUN**
13.00 g., 0.900 Silver 0.3762 oz. ASW, 31 mm. **Subject:** Czech Ice Hockey Association - 100th Anniversary **Obv:** Hockey Player **Rev:** Logo

| Date | Mintage | VF20 | XF40 | MS60 | MS63 | MS65 |
|---|---|---|---|---|---|---|
| 2008 | 10,272 | — | — | — | 20.00 | 22.00 |
| Note: Milled edge | | | | | | |
| 2008 | 15,097 | PF65 55.00 | | | | |
| Note: Plain edge with CESKA NARODNI BANKA *0.900* 13g | | | | | | |

**KM# 105 200 KORUN**
13.00 g., 0.900 Silver 0.3737 oz. ASW, 31 mm. **Subject:** Czech Presidency to Council of the European Union **Obv:** Arms in circle **Rev:** Czech flag and circle of stars

| Date | Mintage | VF20 | XF40 | MS60 | MS63 | MS65 |
|---|---|---|---|---|---|---|
| 2009 | 13,172 | — | — | — | 20.00 | 22.00 |
| Note: Milled edge | | | | | | |
| 2009 | 19,697 | PF65 32.00 | | | | |
| Note: Plain edge with CESKA NARODNI BANKA *0.900* 13g | | | | | | |

**KM# 106 200 KORUN**
13.00 g., 0.900 Silver 0.3762 oz. ASW, 31 mm. **Subject:** Nordic World Ski Championships in Liberec **Obv:** Logo with skis **Rev:** Cross country skiers and ski jumpers

| Date | Mintage | VF20 | XF40 | MS60 | MS63 | MS65 |
|---|---|---|---|---|---|---|
| 2009 | 15,197 | PF65 32.00 | | | | |
| Note: Plain edge with CESKA NARODNI BANKA *0.900* 13g | | | | | | |
| 2009 | 10,772 | — | — | — | 20.00 | 22.00 |
| Note: Milled edge | | | | | | |

**KM# 107 200 KORUN**
13.00 g., 0.900 Silver 0.3762 oz. ASW, 31 mm. **Subject:** North Pole Exploration **Obv:** Facing Explorer **Rev:** Sled and Northern Lights

| Date | Mintage | VF20 | XF40 | MS60 | MS63 | MS65 |
|---|---|---|---|---|---|---|
| 2009 | 10,172 | — | — | — | 20.00 | 22.00 |
| Note: Milled edge | | | | | | |
| 2009 | 16,767 | PF65 37.50 | | | | |
| Note: Plain edge with CESKA NARODNI BANKA *0.900* 13g | | | | | | |

**KM# 108 200 KORUN**
13.00 g., 0.900 Silver 0.3762 oz. ASW, 31 mm. **Subject:** Rabbi Jehuda Löw **Obv:** Star of David and dates **Rev:** Symbols of Rabbi Low

| Date | Mintage | VF20 | XF40 | MS60 | MS63 | MS65 |
|---|---|---|---|---|---|---|
| 2009 | 18,100 | PF65 32.00 | | | | |
| Note: Plain edge with CESKA NARODNI BANKA *0.900* 13g | | | | | | |
| 2009 | 11,275 | — | — | — | 20.00 | 22.00 |
| Note: Milled edge | | | | | | |

**KM# 109 200 KORUN**
13.00 g., 0.900 Silver 0.3762 oz. ASW, 31 mm. **Subject:** Kepler's Planetary Motion Laws **Obv:** Kepler's plan of Mars **Rev:** Portrait of Kepler

| Date | Mintage | VF20 | XF40 | MS60 | MS63 | MS65 |
|---|---|---|---|---|---|---|
| 2009 | 10,472 | — | — | — | 20.00 | 22.00 |
| Note: Milled edge | | | | | | |
| 2009 | 19,687 | **PF65** 95.00 | | | | |
| Note: Plain edge with CESKA NARODNI BANKA *0.900* 13g | | | | | | |

**KM# 112 200 KORUN**
13.00 g., 0.900 Silver 0.3762 oz. ASW, 31 mm. **Subject:** Astronomical Clock, Prague **Obv:** Figures of four apostles and rooster **Rev:** Clock works

| Date | Mintage | VF20 | XF40 | MS60 | MS63 | MS65 |
|---|---|---|---|---|---|---|
| 2010 | 10,372 | — | — | — | 18.00 | 20.00 |
| Note: Milled edge | | | | | | |
| 2010 | 16,097 | **PF65** 32.50 | | | | |
| Note: Plain edge with CESKA NARODNI BANKA *0.900* 13g | | | | | | |

**KM# 113 200 KORUN**
13.00 g., 0.900 Silver 0.3762 oz. ASW, 31 mm. **Subject:** Gustav Mahler **Obv:** Part of Mahler's 5th symphony **Rev:** Portrait of Mahler

| Date | Mintage | VF20 | XF40 | MS60 | MS63 | MS65 |
|---|---|---|---|---|---|---|
| 2010 | 9,672 | — | — | — | 18.00 | 20.00 |
| Note: Milled edge | | | | | | |
| 2010 | 15,047 | **PF65** 32.50 | | | | |
| Note: Plain edge with CESKA NARODNI BANKA *0.900* 13g | | | | | | |

**KM# 114 200 KORUN**
13.00 g., 0.900 Silver 0.3762 oz. ASW, 31 mm. **Subject:** Alfons Mucha **Obv:** Print of Music by Mucha **Rev:** Facing portrait of Mucha

| Date | Mintage | VF20 | XF40 | MS60 | MS63 | MS65 |
|---|---|---|---|---|---|---|
| 2010 | 10,072 | — | — | — | 18.00 | 20.00 |
| Note: Milled edge | | | | | | |
| 2010 | 15,897 | **PF65** 75.00 | | | | |
| Note: Plain edge with CESKA NARODNI BANKA *0.900* 13g | | | | | | |

**KM# 115 200 KORUN**
13.00 g., 0.900 Silver 0.3762 oz. ASW, 31 mm. **Subject:** John of Luxembourg, 700th Wedding Anniversary **Obv:** Czech lion on tapestry background **Rev:** John and wife standing

| Date | Mintage | VF20 | XF40 | MS60 | MS63 | MS65 |
|---|---|---|---|---|---|---|
| 2010 | 9,572 | — | — | — | 18.00 | 20.00 |
| Note: Milled edge | | | | | | |
| 2010 | 13,897 | **PF65** 32.00 | | | | |
| Note: Plain edge with CESKA NARODNI BANKA *0.900* 13g | | | | | | |

**KM# 116 200 KORUN**
13.00 g., 0.900 Silver 0.3762 oz. ASW, 31 mm. **Subject:** Karel Zeman, 100th Anniversary of Birth **Obv:** Marionettes of Zeman's cinemas **Rev:** Submarine, airship, octopus of Zeman's cinemas

| Date | Mintage | VF20 | XF40 | MS60 | MS63 | MS65 |
|---|---|---|---|---|---|---|
| 2010 | 9,275 | — | — | — | 18.00 | 20.00 |
| Note: Milled edge | | | | | | |
| 2010 | 13,000 | **PF65** 32.00 | | | | |
| Note: Plain edge with CESKA NARODNI BANKA *0.900* 13g | | | | | | |

**KM# 119 200 KORUN**
13.00 g., 0.925 Silver 0.3866 oz. ASW, 31 mm. **Subject:** Prague Conservatory, 200th Anniversary

| Date | Mintage | VF20 | XF40 | MS60 | MS63 | MS65 |
|---|---|---|---|---|---|---|
| 2011 | 11,500 | **PF65** 32.00 | | | | |
| Note: Plain edge with CESKA NARODNI BANKA *0.900* 13g | | | | | | |
| 2011 | 7,777 | — | — | — | 18.00 | 20.00 |
| Note: Milled edge | | | | | | |

**KM# 120 200 KORUN**
13.00 g., 0.925 Silver 0.3866 oz. ASW, 31 mm. **Subject:** Jan Kaspar, 100th Anniversary of First Flight

| Date | Mintage | VF20 | XF40 | MS60 | MS63 | MS65 |
|---|---|---|---|---|---|---|
| 2011 | 7,777 | — | — | — | 18.00 | 20.00 |
| Note: Milled edge | | | | | | |
| 2011 | 11,600 | **PF65** 32.00 | | | | |
| Note: Plain edge with CESKA NARODNI BANKA *0.900* 13g | | | | | | |

**KM# 121 200 KORUN**
13.00 g., 0.925 Silver 0.3866 oz. ASW, 31 mm. **Subject:** Jiri Melantrich, 500th Anniversary of Birth

| Date | Mintage | VF20 | XF40 | MS60 | MS63 | MS65 |
|---|---|---|---|---|---|---|
| 2011 | 7,877 | — | — | — | 18.00 | 20.00 |
| Note: Milled edge | | | | | | |
| 2011 | 11,600 | **PF65** 32.00 | | | | |
| Note: Plain edge with CESKA NARODNI BANKA *0.900* 13g | | | | | | |

**KM# 122 200 KORUN**
13.00 g., 0.925 Silver 0.3866 oz. ASW, 31 mm. **Subject:** Petr Vok, 400th Anniversary of Death

| Date | Mintage | VF20 | XF40 | MS60 | MS63 | MS65 |
|---|---|---|---|---|---|---|
| 2011 | 8,200 | — | — | — | 18.00 | 20.00 |
| Note: Milled edge | | | | | | |
| 2011 | 12,200 | **PF65** 32.00 | | | | |
| Note: Plain edge with CESKA NARODNI BANKA *0.900* 13g | | | | | | |

**KM# 126 200 KORUN**
13.00 g., 0.925 Silver 0.3841 oz. ASW, 31 mm. **Subject:** Emperor Rudolf II, 400th Anniversary of Death **Obv:** Emperor on horseback, Prague city view in backgorund **Rev:** Portrait, signature and arms

| Date | Mintage | VF20 | XF40 | MS60 | MS63 | MS65 |
|---|---|---|---|---|---|---|
| 2012 | 12,600 | **PF65** 32.00 | | | | |
| 2012 | 8,100 | — | — | — | — | 25.00 |
| Note: Milled edge | | | | | | |

**KM# 127 200 KORUN**
13.00 g., 0.925 Silver 0.3866 oz. ASW, 31 mm. **Subject:** Sokol, 150th Anniversary **Obv:** SOKOL logo and stylized gymnasts in background **Rev:** Falcon, stylized gymnasts in background

| Date | Mintage | VF20 | XF40 | MS60 | MS63 | MS65 |
|---|---|---|---|---|---|---|
| 2012 | 12,200 | **PF65** 32.00 | | | | |
| 2012 | 8,000 | — | — | — | — | 25.00 |
| Note: Milled edge | | | | | | |

**KM# 128 200 KORUN**

13.00 g., 0.925 Silver 0.3866 oz. ASW, 31 mm. **Subject:** Czech Scouts - Junak, 100th Anniversary **Obv:** Scouting emblems **Rev:** A. B. Svojsik, founder of Czeck scouting

| Date | Mintage | VF20 | XF40 | MS60 | MS63 | MS65 |
|---|---|---|---|---|---|---|
| 2012 | 12,200 | PF65 32.00 | | | | |
| 2012 | 8,000 | — | — | — | — | 50.00 |

Note: Milled edge

**KM# 129 200 KORUN**

13.00 g., 0.925 Silver 0.3866 oz. ASW, 31 mm. **Subject:** Kamil Lhoták, 100th Anniversary of Birth

| Date | Mintage | VF20 | XF40 | MS60 | MS63 | MS65 |
|---|---|---|---|---|---|---|
| 2012 | 13,200 | PF65 32.00 | | | | |
| 2012 | 7,700 | — | — | — | — | 25.00 |

**KM# 130 200 KORUN**

13.00 g., 0.925 Silver 0.3866 oz. ASW, 31 mm. **Subject:** Prague Municipal House, 100th Anniversary

| Date | Mintage | VF20 | XF40 | MS60 | MS63 | MS65 |
|---|---|---|---|---|---|---|
| 2012 | 7,700 | — | — | — | — | 25.00 |
| 2012 | 13,600 | PF65 32.00 | | | | |

**KM# 138 200 KORUN**

13.00 g., 0.925 Silver 0.3866 oz. ASW, 31 mm. **Subject:** Josef Bican, 100th Anniversary of Birth

| Date | Mintage | VF20 | XF40 | MS60 | MS63 | MS65 |
|---|---|---|---|---|---|---|
| 2013 | — | — | — | — | — | 25.00 |
| 2013 | — | PF65 32.00 | | | | |

**KM# 135 200 KORUN**

13.00 g., 0.925 Silver 0.3866 oz. ASW, 31 mm. **Subject:** Czech National Bank, 20th Anniversary

| Date | Mintage | VF20 | XF40 | MS60 | MS63 | MS65 |
|---|---|---|---|---|---|---|
| 2013 | — | — | — | — | — | 25.00 |
| 2013 | — | PF65 32.00 | | | | |

**KM# 136 200 KORUN**

13.00 g., 0.925 Silver 0.3866 oz. ASW, 31 mm. **Subject:** Aloys Klar, 250th Anniversary of Birth

| Date | Mintage | VF20 | XF40 | MS60 | MS63 | MS65 |
|---|---|---|---|---|---|---|
| 2013 | — | — | — | — | — | 25.00 |
| 2013 | — | PF65 32.00 | | | | |

**KM# 137 200 KORUN**

13.00 g., 0.925 Silver 0.3866 oz. ASW, 31 mm. **Subject:** Zlatá Koruna monastery, 750th Anniversary

| Date | Mintage | VF20 | XF40 | MS60 | MS63 | MS65 |
|---|---|---|---|---|---|---|
| 2013 | — | — | — | — | — | 25.00 |
| 2013 | — | PF65 32.00 | | | | |

**KM# 139 200 KORUN**

13.00 g., 0.925 Silver 0.3866 oz. ASW, 31 mm. **Subject:** Otto Wichterle, 100th Anniversary of Birth

| Date | Mintage | VF20 | XF40 | MS60 | MS63 | MS65 |
|---|---|---|---|---|---|---|
| 2013 | — | — | — | — | — | 25.00 |
| 2013 | — | PF65 32.00 | | | | |

**KM# 123 500 KORUN**

25.00 g., 0.925 Silver 0.7435 oz. ASW, 40 mm. **Subject:** Karel Jaromir Erben, 200th Anniversary of Birth **Obv:** Floral bouquet **Rev:** Portrait 1/4 left

| Date | Mintage | VF20 | XF40 | MS60 | MS63 | MS65 |
|---|---|---|---|---|---|---|
| 2011 | 7,300 | — | — | — | — | 35.00 |
| Note: Milled edge | | | | | | |
| 2011 | 10,800 | PF65 45.00 | | | | |

Note: Plain edge with CESKA NARODNI BANKA *0.900* 13g

**KM# 131 500 KORUN**

25.00 g., 0.925 Silver 0.7387 oz. ASW, 40 mm. **Subject:** Jiri Trnka, 100th Anniversary of Birth **Rev:** Profile left

| Date | Mintage | VF20 | XF40 | MS60 | MS63 | MS65 |
|---|---|---|---|---|---|---|
| 2012 | 12,100 | PF65 40.00 | | | | |
| 2012 | 6,800 | — | — | — | — | 35.00 |

Note: Milled edge.

**KM# 140 500 KORUN**

25.00 g., 0.925 Silver 0.7435 oz. ASW, 40 mm. **Subject:** Beno Blachut, 100th Anniversary of Birth

| Date | Mintage | VF20 | XF40 | MS60 | MS63 | MS65 |
|---|---|---|---|---|---|---|
| 2013 | — | — | — | — | — | 35.00 |
| 2013 | — | PF65 40.00 | | | | |

**KM# 65 2000 KORUN**

6.22 g., 0.9999 Gold 0.200 oz. AGW, 20 mm. **Subject:** Romanesque - Znojmo Rotunda **Obv:** Three heraldic animals **Rev:** Farmer and round building

| Date | Mintage | VF20 | XF40 | MS60 | MS63 | MS65 |
|---|---|---|---|---|---|---|
| ND-2001 | 2,197 | — | — | — | — | 375 |
| Note: Milled edge | | | | | | |
| ND-2001 | — | PF65 400 | | | | |

Note: Plain edge

**KM# 61 2000 KORUN**

6.22 g., 0.9999 Gold 0.200 oz. AGW, 20 mm. **Subject:** Renaissance - Litomysl Castle **Obv:** Three heraldic animals above mermaid **Rev:** Aerial castle view and mythical creature

| Date | Mintage | VF20 | XF40 | MS60 | MS63 | MS65 |
|---|---|---|---|---|---|---|
| 2002 | 2,094 | — | — | — | — | 375 |
| Note: Milled edge | | | | | | |
| 2002 | — | PF65 400 | | | | |

Note: Plain edge

**KM# 67 2000 KORUN**

6.22 g., 0.9999 Gold 0.200 oz. AGW, 20 mm. **Subject:** Gothic - Fountain in Kutna Hora **Obv:** Three heraldic animals **Rev:** Fountain enclosure

| Date | Mintage | VF20 | XF40 | MS60 | MS63 | MS65 |
|---|---|---|---|---|---|---|
| 2002 | 2,195 | — | — | — | — | 375 |
| Note: Milled edge | | | | | | |
| 2002 | — | PF65 400 | | | | |

Note: Plain edge

**KM# 68 2000 KORUN**
6.22 g., 0.9999 Gold 0.200 oz. AGW, 20 mm. **Subject:** Renaissance - Slavonice House Gables **Obv:** Three heraldic animals above city view **Rev:** City arms

| Date | Mintage | VF20 | XF40 | MS60 | MS63 | MS65 |
|---|---|---|---|---|---|---|
| 2003 | 1,994 | — | — | — | — | 375 |
| Note: Milled edge | | | | | | |
| 2003 | 2,996 | PF65 400 | | | | |
| Note: Plain edge | | | | | | |

**KM# 69 2000 KORUN**
6.22 g., 0.9999 Gold 0.200 oz. AGW, 20 mm. **Subject:** Baroque - Buchlovice Palace **Obv:** Three heraldic animals above palace **Rev:** Palace view

| Date | Mintage | VF20 | XF40 | MS60 | MS63 | MS65 |
|---|---|---|---|---|---|---|
| 2003 | 1,994 | — | — | — | — | 375 |
| Note: Milled edge | | | | | | |
| 2003 | — | PF65 400 | | | | |
| Note: Plain edge | | | | | | |

**KM# 75 2000 KORUN**
6.22 g., 0.9999 Gold 0.200 oz. AGW, 20 mm. **Obv:** Ornamental porch below three heraldic animals **Rev:** Hluboka Castle with coat of arms in foreground

| Date | Mintage | VF20 | XF40 | MS60 | MS63 | MS65 |
|---|---|---|---|---|---|---|
| 2004 | 1,994 | — | — | — | — | 375 |
| Note: Milled edge | | | | | | |
| 2004 | 2,997 | PF65 400 | | | | |
| Note: Plain edge | | | | | | |

**KM# 86 2000 KORUN**
6.22 g., 0.999 Gold 0.1998 oz. AGW, 20 mm. **Subject:** Kacina Castle

| Date | Mintage | VF20 | XF40 | MS60 | MS63 | MS65 |
|---|---|---|---|---|---|---|
| 2004 | 2,996 | PF65 400 | | | | |
| Note: Plain edge | | | | | | |
| 2004 | 1,994 | — | — | — | — | 375 |
| Note: Milled edge | | | | | | |

**KM# 87 2000 KORUN**
6.22 g., 0.999 Gold 0.1998 oz. AGW, 20 mm. **Subject:** Lazne Bohdanec Spa **Obv:** Gocar Spa Pavillion, full facade **Rev:** Gocar Spa Pavillion central area

| Date | Mintage | VF20 | XF40 | MS60 | MS63 | MS65 |
|---|---|---|---|---|---|---|
| 2005 | 2,996 | PF65 400 | | | | |
| Note: Plain edge | | | | | | |
| 2005 | 1,997 | — | — | — | — | 375 |
| Note: Milled edge | | | | | | |

**KM# 88 2000 KORUN**
6.22 g., 0.999 Gold 0.1998 oz. AGW, 20 mm. **Subject:** Dancing House in Prague **Rev:** Exterior view of Dancing House

| Date | Mintage | VF20 | XF40 | MS60 | MS63 | MS65 |
|---|---|---|---|---|---|---|
| 2005 | 3,297 | PF65 400 | | | | |
| Note: Plain edge | | | | | | |
| 2005 | 1,996 | — | — | — | — | 375 |
| Note: Milled edge | | | | | | |

**KM# 76 2500 KORUN**
31.10 g., Bi-Metallic .9999 Gold 7.776g center in .999 Silver 23.328g ring, 40 mm. **Subject:** Czech entry into the European Union **Obv:** Value within circle of shields **Rev:** "1.5.2004" within circle of dates and text **Edge:** Lettered **Edge Lettering:** CNB * Ag 0.999 * 23,328 g CNB Au 999.9 * 7,776g *

| Date | Mintage | VF20 | XF40 | MS60 | MS63 | MS65 |
|---|---|---|---|---|---|---|
| ND (2004) | 8,117 | PF65 500 | | | | |

**KM# 89 2500 KORUN**
7.78 g., 0.999 Gold 0.2498 oz. AGW, 22 mm. **Subject:** Hand Paper Mill at Velke Losiny

| Date | Mintage | VF20 | XF40 | MS60 | MS63 | MS65 |
|---|---|---|---|---|---|---|
| 2006 | 3,000 | PF65 3,000 | | | | |
| Note: Plain edge | | | | | | |
| 2006 | 1,800 | — | — | — | 1,500 | — |
| Note: Milled edge | | | | | | |

**KM# 90 2500 KORUN**
7.79 g., 0.999 Gold 0.250 oz. AGW, 22 mm. **Subject:** Observatory at Prague Klementinum **Obv:** Sun's rays thru clouds **Rev:** Building tower, rays and moon **Note:** Prev. KM #86.

| Date | Mintage | VF20 | XF40 | MS60 | MS63 | MS65 |
|---|---|---|---|---|---|---|
| 2006 | 3,797 | PF65 1,000 | | | | |
| Note: Plain edge | | | | | | |
| 2006 | 1,897 | — | — | — | — | 700 |
| Note: Milled edge | | | | | | |

**KM# 95 2500 KORUN**
7.78 g., 0.999 Gold 0.2498 oz. AGW, 22 mm. **Subject:** Sevcinsky Mine at Pribram-Brezove Hory **Rev:** Head-gear tower at mine

| Date | Mintage | VF20 | XF40 | MS60 | MS63 | MS65 |
|---|---|---|---|---|---|---|
| 2007 | 5,097 | PF65 500 | | | | |
| Note: Plain edge | | | | | | |
| 2007 | 2,097 | — | — | — | — | 475 |
| Note: Milled edge | | | | | | |

**KM# 96 2500 KORUN**
7.78 g., 0.999 Gold 0.2498 oz. AGW, 22 mm. **Subject:** Water Mill at Slup **Obv:** Water Mill **Rev:** Water Mill

| Date | Mintage | VF20 | XF40 | MS60 | MS63 | MS65 |
|---|---|---|---|---|---|---|
| 2007 | 6,297 | PF65 500 | | | | |
| 2007 | 2,297 | — | — | — | — | 475 |

**KM# 103 2500 KORUN**
7.78 g., 0.999 Gold 0.2499 oz. AGW, 22 mm. **Subject:** Stadlec Suspension Bridge **Obv:** Side view of bridge **Rev:** View of bridge thru arch

| Date | Mintage | VF20 | XF40 | MS60 | MS63 | MS65 |
|---|---|---|---|---|---|---|
| 2008 | 10,897 | PF65 500 | | | | |
| Note: Plain edge | | | | | | |
| 2008 | 3,097 | — | — | — | — | 475 |
| Note: Milled edge | | | | | | |

**KM# 104 2500 KORUN**
7.78 g., 0.999 Gold 0.2499 oz. AGW, 22 mm. **Subject:** Plzen Brewery **Obv:** Copper vats **Rev:** Plzen Brewery façade and wooden barrels

| Date | Mintage | VF20 | XF40 | MS60 | MS63 | MS65 |
|---|---|---|---|---|---|---|
| 2008 | 10,797 | PF65 500 | | | | |
| Note: Plain edge | | | | | | |
| 2008 | 3,197 | — | — | — | — | 475 |
| Note: Milled edge | | | | | | |

**KM# 110 2500 KORUN**
7.78 g., 0.999 Gold 0.2498 oz. AGW, 22 mm. **Subject:** Elbe Sluice under Strekov Castle **Obv:** Turbine in sluice in the Labe (Elbe) river **Rev:** Sluice under Strekov castle

| Date | Mintage | VF20 | XF40 | MS60 | MS63 | MS65 |
|---|---|---|---|---|---|---|
| 2009 | 10,497 | PF65 500 | | | | |
| Note: Plain edge | | | | | | |
| 2009 | 3,497 | — | — | — | — | 475 |
| Note: Milled edge | | | | | | |

**KM# 111 2500 KORUN**
7.78 g., 0.999 Gold 0.2498 oz. AGW, 22 mm. **Subject:** Windmill at Ruprechtov

| Date | Mintage | VF20 | XF40 | MS60 | MS63 | MS65 |
|---|---|---|---|---|---|---|
| 2009 | 10,497 | PF65 500 | | | | |
| 2009 | 3,497 | — | — | — | — | 475 |

### KM# 117 2500 KORUN

7.77 g., 0.999 Gold 0.2496 oz. AGW, 22 mm. **Subject:** Hammer Mill in Dobriv

| Date | Mintage | VF20 | XF40 | MS60 | MS63 | MS65 |
|---|---|---|---|---|---|---|
| 2010 | 3,797 | — | — | — | — | 475 |
| Note: Milled edge | | | | | | |
| 2010 | 9,997 | PF65 500 | | | | |
| Note: Plain edge | | | | | | |

### KM# 118 2500 KORUN

7.77 g., 0.999 Gold 0.2496 oz. AGW, 22 mm. **Subject:** Michael Mine in Ostrana **Obv:** Turbine **Rev:** Mine shaft

| Date | Mintage | VF20 | XF40 | MS60 | MS63 | MS65 |
|---|---|---|---|---|---|---|
| 2010 | 3,697 | — | — | — | — | 475 |
| Note: Milled edge | | | | | | |
| 2010 | 9,097 | PF65 500 | | | | |
| Note: Plain edge | | | | | | |

### KM# 124 5000 KORUN

15.55 g., 0.9999 Gold 0.500 oz. AGW, 28 mm. **Subject:** Gothic Bridge in Pisek

| Date | Mintage | VF20 | XF40 | MS60 | MS63 | MS65 |
|---|---|---|---|---|---|---|
| 2011 | 2,600 | — | — | — | — | 900 |
| 2011 | 6,900 | PF65 950 | | | | |

### KM# 125 5000 KORUN

15.55 g., 0.9999 Gold 0.500 oz. AGW, 28 mm. **Subject:** Renaissance Bridge in Stribro

| Date | Mintage | VF20 | XF40 | MS60 | MS63 | MS65 |
|---|---|---|---|---|---|---|
| 2011 | 2,700 | — | — | — | — | 900 |
| Note: Milled edge | | | | | | |
| 2011 | 7,300 | PF65 950 | | | | |
| Note: Plain edge | | | | | | |

### KM# 132 5000 KORUN

15.55 g., 0.9999 Gold 0.500 oz. AGW, 28 mm. **Subject:** Banocco Bridge in Namest nad Oslavou

| Date | Mintage | VF20 | XF40 | MS60 | MS63 | MS65 |
|---|---|---|---|---|---|---|
| 2012 | 3,200 | — | — | — | — | 950 |
| 2012 | 9,000 | PF65 950 | | | | |

### KM# 133 5000 KORUN

15.55 g., 0.9999 Gold 0.500 oz. AGW, 28 mm. **Subject:** Negrelli viaduct in Prague

| Date | Mintage | VF20 | XF40 | MS60 | MS63 | MS65 |
|---|---|---|---|---|---|---|
| 2012 | 3,900 | — | — | — | — | 900 |
| 2012 | 12,200 | PF65 950 | | | | |

### KM# 141 5000 KORUN

15.55 g., 0.9999 Gold 0.4999 oz. AGW, 28 mm. **Subject:** Covered Wooden Bridge at Lenora

| Date | Mintage | VF20 | XF40 | MS60 | MS63 | MS65 |
|---|---|---|---|---|---|---|
| 2013 | — | — | — | — | — | 800 |
| 2013 | — | PF65 850 | | | | |

### KM# 142 5000 KORUN

15.55 g., 0.9999 Gold 0.4999 oz. AGW, 28 mm. **Subject:** Railway bridge in Zampach

| Date | Mintage | VF20 | XF40 | MS60 | MS63 | MS65 |
|---|---|---|---|---|---|---|
| 2013 | — | — | — | — | — | 800 |
| 2013 | — | PF65 850 | | | | |

### KM# 134 10000 KORUN

31.11 g., 0.9999 Gold 1.000 oz. AGW, 34 mm. **Subject:** Gold Bulla of Sicily, 800th Anniversary

| Date | Mintage | VF20 | XF40 | MS60 | MS63 | MS65 |
|---|---|---|---|---|---|---|
| 2012 | 3,100 | — | — | — | — | 1,900 |
| 2012 | 10,900 | PF65 2,000 | | | | |

### KM# 143 10000 KORUN

31.11 g., 0.9999 Gold 1.000 oz. AGW, 34 mm. **Subject:** St. Cyril and Methodius, 1150th Anniversary of arrival in Czech lands

| Date | Mintage | VF20 | XF40 | MS60 | MS63 | MS65 |
|---|---|---|---|---|---|---|
| 2013 | — | — | — | — | — | 1,500 |
| 2013 | — | PF65 1,600 | | | | |

## MINT SETS

| KM# | Date | Mintage | Identification | Issue Price | Mkt Val |
|---|---|---|---|---|---|
| MS14 | 2001 (9) | 11,500 | KM#1, 2.3, 3.2, 4-9, Tyn Church folder | — | 17.50 |
| MS15 | 2002 (9) | 11,885 | KM#1, 2.3, 3.2, 4-9, Castles | — | 60.00 |
| MS16 | 2002 (9) | 5,115 | KM#1, 2.3, 3.2, 4-9, NATO Summit folder | — | 17.50 |
| MS17 | 2003 (9) | 22,000 | KM#1, 2.3, 3.2, 4-9, CNB 10th Anniversary | — | 30.00 |
| MS18 | 2004 (7) | 7,500 | KM#1, 3.2, 4-5, 7-9, Football | — | 30.00 |
| MS19 | 2004 (7) | 13,000 | KM#1, 3.2, 4-5, 7-9, EU Entry | — | 40.00 |
| MS20 | 2004 (7) | 10,000 | KM#1, 3.2, 4-5, 7-9 IIHF Hockey Year | — | 16.00 |
| MS21 | 2005 (8) | 13,015 | KM#1, 3.2, 4-5, 7-9, plus Smetna/Dvorak Medal and CD | — | 17.50 |
| MS22 | 2006 (7) | 9,000 | KM#1, 3.2, 4-5, 7-9. UNESCO Folder | — | 16.00 |
| MS23 | 2006 (7) | 5,139 | KM#1, 3.2, 4-5, 7-9, Football Championship | — | 40.00 |
| MS24 | 2006 (7) | 9,784 | KM#1, 3.2, 4-5, 7-9, plus Euro Medal | — | 45.00 |
| MS25 | 2007 (7) | 8,500 | KM#1, 3.2, 4-5, 7-9, UNESCO Kunta Hora folder | — | 25.00 |
| MS26 | 2007 (14) | 10,000 | KM#1, 3.2, 4-5, 7-9. Natural beauties with Slovakia coins | — | 35.00 |
| MS27 | 2008 (7) | 9,000 | KM#1, 3.2, 4-5, 7-9, plus UNESCO Medal | — | 30.00 |
| MS28 | 2008 (8) | 6,000 | KM#1, 3.2, 4-5, 7-9. Soccer medal and package | — | 17.50 |
| MS29 | 2009 (8) | 10,000 | KM#1, 3.2, 4-5, 7-9 plus brass Southern Bohemia Medal | — | 17.50 |
| MS30 | 2010 (6) | 10,000 | KM#1, 3.2, 4-5, 7-9, Zlin Region folder | — | 17.50 |
| MS31 | 2011 (6) | 10,000 | KM#1, 4-5, 7-9, Plzen Region folder | — | 17.50 |
| MS32 | 2011 (6) | 5,000 | KM#1, 4-5, 7-9. Baby set. | — | 17.50 |
| MS33 | 2011 (6) | 450 | KM# 1, 4-5, 7-9. ENA and CNB official distribution | 12.00 | 15.00 |

## PROOF SETS

| KM# | Date | Mintage | Identification | Issue Price | Mkt Val |
|---|---|---|---|---|---|
| PS6 | 2001 (9) | 2,500 | KM#1, 2.3, 3.1, 4-9 | 35.00 | 250 |
| PS7 | 2002 (9) | 3,490 | KM#1, 2.3, 3.2, 4-9 | 35.00 | 250 |
| PS8 | 2003 (9) | 3,000 | KM#1, 2.3, 3.2, 4-9 | 35.00 | 150 |
| PS9 | 2004 (7) | 4,000 | KM#1, 3.2, 4-5, 7-9 | 35.00 | 100 |
| PS10 | 2005 (8) | 3,000 | KM#1, 3.2, 4-5, 7-9, and silver strike of Czechoslovakia KM#4 | — | 100 |
| PS11 | 2006 (8) | 2,500 | KM#1, 3.2, 4-5, 7-9, and silver strike of Czechoslovakia KM#2 | — | 120 |
| PS12 | 2007 (8) | 2,500 | KM#1, 3.2, 4-5, 7-9, and silver Unesco medal | — | 120 |
| PS13 | 2008 (8) | 2,500 | KM#1, 3.2, 4-5, 7-9, and silver medal for 15th Anniversary of Republic | — | 150 |
| PS14 | 2009 (8) | 3,200 | KM#1, 3.2, 4-5, 7-9, and silver medal for the Czech Presidency of the EU | — | 85.00 |
| PS15 | 2010 (7) | 3,200 | KM#1, 4-5, 7-9, plus silver T. G. Masaryk medal | — | 85.00 |
| PS16 | 2011 (7) | 3,500 | KM#1, 4-5, 7-9, plus silver Ema Destinnova medal in a velvet case | — | 85.00 |
| PS17 | 2011 (7) | 2,000 | KM#1, 4-5, 7-9, plus silver Ema Destinnova medal in a leather case | — | 120 |

# DENMARK

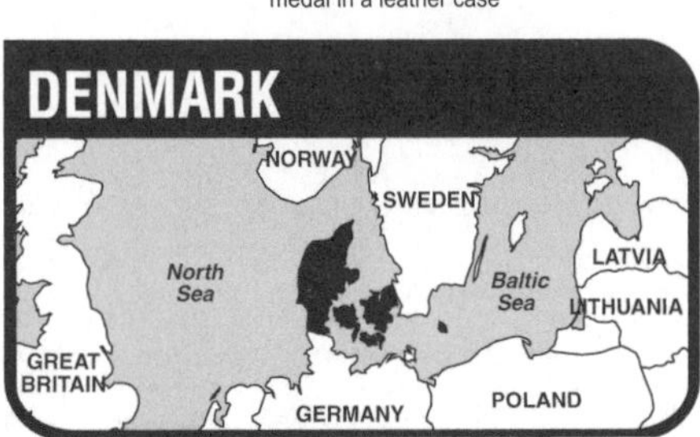


The Kingdom of Denmark (Danmark), a constitutional monarchy located at the mouth of the Baltic Sea, has an area of 16,639 sq. mi. (43,070 sq. km.) and a population of 5.2 million. Capital: Copenhagen. Most of the country is arable. Agriculture is conducted by large farms served by cooperatives. The largest industries are food processing, iron and metal, and shipping. Machinery, meats (chiefly bacon), dairy products and chemicals are exported.

The present decimal system of currency was introduced in 1874. As a result of a referendum held September 28, 2000, the currency of the European Monetary Union, the Euro, will not be introduced in Denmark in the foreseeable future.

**RULERS**

Christian IX, 1863-1906
Frederik VIII, 1906-1912
Christian X, 1912-1947
Frederik IX, 1947-1972
Margrethe II, 1972—

**MINT MARKS**

(h) - Copenhagen, heart

**MINT OFFICIALS' INITIALS**

**Copenhagen Mint**

| Letter | Date | Name |
|---|---|---|
| *P, VBP | 1893-1918 | Vilhelm Buchard Poulsen |
| HCN | 1919-1927 | Hans Christian Nielsen |
| N | 1927-1955 | Niels Peter Nielsen |
| C | 1956-1971 | Alfred Frederik Christiansen |
| S | 1971-1978 | Vagn Sorensen |
| B | 1978-1981 | Peter M Biarno |
| R, NR | 1982-1989 | N. Norregaard Rasmussen |
| LG - JP | 1990-2001 | Laust Grove / J Petersen |

**NOTE:** The letter P was only used on Danish West Indies coins and on Denmark, KM#802.

**MONEYERS' INITIALS**

**Copenhagen Mint**

| Letter | Date | Name |
|---|---|---|
| GI, GJ | 1901-1933 | Knud Gunnar Jensen |
| GI, GJ | 1901-1933 | Knud Gunnar Jensen |
| AH | 1908-1924 | Andreas Frederik Vilhelm Hansen |
| HS, S | 1933-1968 | Harald Salomon |
| B | 1968-1983 | Frode Bahnsen |
| A | 1986- | Johan Alkjaer (designer) |
| HV | 1986- | Hanne Varming (sculptor) |
| JP | 1989- | Jan Petersen |

**MONETARY SYSTEM**

100 Øre = 1 Krone

# KINGDOM

## DECIMAL COINAGE

100 Øre = 1 Krone; 1874-present

### KM# 868.1 25 ØRE

2.80 g., Bronze, 17.5 mm. **Ruler:** Margrethe II **Obv:** Large crown divides date above, initial to right of country **Rev:** Denomination, small heart above, mint mark and initials LG-JP below **Note:** Beginning in 1996 and ending with 1998, the words "DANMARK" and "ØRE" have raised edges. Heart mint mark under "ØRE"; Prev. KM#868.

| Date | Mintage | VF20 | XF40 | MS60 | MS63 | MS65 |
|---|---|---|---|---|---|---|
| 2001 LG; JP; A | 10,530,000 | — | — | — | — | 0.15 |

### KM# 868.2 25 ØRE

2.80 g., Bronze, 17.5 mm. **Ruler:** Margrethe II **Obv:** Large crown divides date above **Rev:** Denomination, small heart above **Edge:** Plain **Note:** Without initials

| Date | Mintage | VF20 | XF40 | MS60 | MS63 | MS65 |
|---|---|---|---|---|---|---|
| 2002 | 12,000,000 | — | — | — | — | 0.15 |
| 2003 | 17,590,000 | — | — | — | — | 0.15 |
| 2004 | 7,040,304 | — | — | — | — | 0.15 |
| 2004 | 3,000 | PF63 15.00 | | PF65 18.00 | | |
| 2005 | 19,039,000 | — | — | — | — | 0.15 |
| 2005 | 2,650 | PF63 15.00 | | PF65 18.00 | | |
| 2006 | 16,796,000 | — | — | — | — | 0.15 |
| 2006 | 1,800 | PF63 15.00 | | PF65 18.00 | | |
| 2007 | 20,592,000 | — | — | — | — | 0.15 |
| 2007 | 1,400 | PF63 15.00 | | PF65 18.00 | | |
| 2008 | 2,049,000 | — | — | — | — | 0.15 |
| 2008 | 1,000 | PF63 15.00 | | PF65 18.00 | | |

### KM# 866.2 50 ØRE

4.30 g., Bronze, 21.5 mm. **Ruler:** Margrethe II **Obv:** Large crown divides date above, initial to right of country name **Rev:** Large heart above value, mint mark and initials LG-JP below **Note:** Beginning in 1996 and ending with 1998, the words "DANMARK" and "ØRE" have raised edges. Heart mint mark under the word "ØRE".

| Date | Mintage | VF20 | XF40 | MS60 | MS63 | MS65 |
|---|---|---|---|---|---|---|
| 2001 LG; JP; A | 12,270,000 | — | — | — | — | 0.30 |

### KM# 866.3 50 ØRE

4.30 g., Bronze, 21.5 mm. **Ruler:** Margrethe II **Obv:** Large crown divides date above **Rev:** Small heart above denomination **Edge:** Plain **Note:** No initials

| Date | Mintage | VF20 | XF40 | MS60 | MS63 | MS65 |
|---|---|---|---|---|---|---|
| 2002 | 3,900,000 | — | — | — | — | 0.50 |
| 2003 | 8,817,000 | — | — | — | — | 0.30 |
| 2004 | 10,040,706 | — | — | — | — | 0.25 |
| 2004 | 3,000 | PF63 15.00 | | PF65 18.00 | | |
| 2005 | 12,037,000 | — | — | — | — | 0.25 |
| 2005 | 2,650 | PF63 15.00 | | PF65 18.00 | | |
| 2006 | 14,843,000 | — | — | — | — | 0.25 |
| 2006 | 1,800 | PF63 15.00 | | PF65 18.00 | | |
| 2007 | 10,198,000 | — | — | — | — | 0.25 |
| 2007 | 1,400 | PF63 15.00 | | PF65 18.00 | | |
| 2008 | 2,573,000 | — | — | — | — | 0.25 |
| 2008 | 1,000 | PF63 15.00 | | PF65 18.00 | | |
| 2009 | 1,050 | PF63 15.00 | | PF65 18.00 | | |
| 2010 | 1,010 | PF63 15.00 | | PF65 18.00 | | |
| 2011 | 1,000 | PF63 15.00 | | PF65 18.00 | | |
| 2012 | 1,090 | PF63 15.00 | | PF65 18.00 | | |
| 2013 | — | — | — | — | — | 1.00 |
| 2013 | — | PF63 15.00 | | PF65 18.00 | | |
| 2014 | — | — | — | — | — | 1.00 |
| 2014 | — | PF65 18.00 | | | | |

### KM# 873.1 KRONE

3.60 g., Copper-Nickel, 20.25 mm. **Ruler:** Margrethe II **Obv:** 3 crowned MII monograms around center hole, date, mint mark, and initials LG-JP-A below **Rev:** Wave design surrounds center hole, value above, hearts flank **Edge:** Reeded **Note:** Prev. KM#873.

| Date | Mintage | VF20 | XF40 | MS60 | MS63 | MS65 |
|---|---|---|---|---|---|---|
| 2001 LG; JP; A | 14,640,000 | — | — | — | — | 0.40 |

### KM# 873.2 KRONE

3.60 g., Copper-Nickel, 20.25 mm. **Ruler:** Margrethe II **Obv:** 3 crowned MII monograms around center hole, date below **Rev:** Design surounds center hole, value above, hearts flank **Edge:** Reeded **Note:** Without initials

| Date | Mintage | VF20 | XF40 | MS60 | MS63 | MS65 |
|---|---|---|---|---|---|---|
| 2002 | 9,000,000 | — | — | — | — | 0.40 |
| 2003 | 5,231,000 | — | — | — | — | 0.40 |
| 2004 | 16,139,596 | — | — | — | — | 0.40 |
| 2004 | 3,000 | PF63 18.00 | | PF65 22.00 | | |
| 2005 | 16,757,000 | — | — | — | — | 0.40 |
| 2005 | 2,650 | PF63 18.00 | | PF65 22.00 | | |
| 2006 | 21,026,000 | — | — | — | — | 0.40 |
| 2006 | 1,800 | PF63 18.00 | | PF65 22.00 | | |
| 2007 | 11,729,000 | — | — | — | — | 0.40 |
| 2007 | 1,400 | PF63 18.00 | | PF65 22.00 | | |
| 2008 | 13,339,000 | — | — | — | — | 0.40 |
| 2008 | 1,000 | PF63 18.00 | | PF65 22.00 | | |
| 2009 | 624,000 | — | — | — | — | 2.00 |
| 2009 | 1,050 | PF63 18.00 | | PF65 22.00 | | |
| 2010 Sets only | 26,000 | — | — | — | — | 2.00 |
| 2010 | 1,010 | PF63 18.00 | | PF65 22.00 | | |
| 2011 Sets only | 21,000 | — | — | — | — | 2.00 |
| 2011 | 1,000 | PF63 18.00 | | PF65 22.00 | | |
| 2012 | 17,170 | — | — | — | — | 2.00 |
| 2012 | 1,090 | PF63 18.00 | | PF65 22.00 | | |
| 2013 | — | — | — | — | — | 0.40 |
| 2013 | — | PF63 18.00 | | PF65 22.00 | | |
| 2014 | — | — | — | — | — | 0.40 |
| 2014 | — | PF65 22.00 | | | | |

### KM# 874.1 2 KRONER

5.90 g., Copper-Nickel, 24.5 mm. **Ruler:** Margrethe II **Obv:** 3 crowned MII monograms around center hole, date and initials LG-JP-A below **Rev:** Design surrounds center hole, denomination above, hearts flank **Edge:** Segmented reeding **Note:** Prev. KM#874.

| Date | Mintage | VF20 | XF40 | MS60 | MS63 | MS65 |
|---|---|---|---|---|---|---|
| 2001 LG; JP; A | 11,180,000 | — | — | — | — | 0.80 |

### KM# 874.2 2 KRONER

5.90 g., Copper-Nickel, 24.5 mm. **Ruler:** Margrethe II **Obv:** 3 crowned MII monograms around center hole, date and initials LGpJP-A below **Rev:** Wave design surrounds center hole, denomination above, hearts flank **Edge:** Segmented reeding **Note:** Without initials

| Date | Mintage | VF20 | XF40 | MS60 | MS63 | MS65 |
|---|---|---|---|---|---|---|
| 2002 | 6,159,000 | — | — | — | — | 0.80 |
| 2004 | 7,381,531 | — | — | — | — | 0.80 |
| 2004 | 3,000 | PF63 22.00 | | PF65 25.00 | | |
| 2005 | 16,684,000 | — | — | — | — | 0.80 |
| 2005 | 2,650 | PF63 22.00 | | PF65 25.00 | | |
| 2006 | 7,331,000 | — | — | — | — | 0.80 |
| 2006 | 1,800 | PF63 22.00 | | PF65 25.00 | | |
| 2007 | 22,060,000 | — | — | — | — | 0.80 |
| 2007 | 1,400 | PF63 22.00 | | PF65 25.00 | | |
| 2008 | 2,623,000 | — | — | — | — | 0.80 |
| 2008 | 1,000 | PF63 22.00 | | PF65 25.00 | | |
| 2009 Sets only | 27,000 | — | — | — | — | 2.50 |
| 2009 | 1,050 | PF63 22.00 | | PF65 25.00 | | |
| 2010 Sets only | 25,000 | — | — | — | — | 2.50 |
| 2010 | 1,010 | PF63 22.00 | | PF65 25.00 | | |
| 2011 | 920,000 | — | — | — | — | 1.00 |
| 2011 | 1,000 | PF63 22.00 | | PF65 25.00 | | |
| 2012 Sets only | 18,000 | — | — | — | — | 1.00 |
| 2012 | 1,090 | PF63 22.00 | | PF65 25.00 | | |
| 2013 | — | — | — | — | — | 0.80 |
| 2013 | — | PF63 22.00 | | PF65 25.00 | | |
| 2014 | — | — | — | — | — | 0.80 |
| 2014 | — | PF65 25.00 | | | | |

### KM# 869.1 5 KRONER

9.20 g., Copper-Nickel, 28.5 mm. **Ruler:** Margrethe II **Obv:** 3 crowned MII monograms around center hole, date and initials LG-JP-A below **Rev:** Wave design surrounds center hole, denomination above, hearts flank **Edge:** Reeded **Note:** Large and small date varieties exist.

| Date | Mintage | VF20 | XF40 | MS60 | MS63 | MS65 |
|---|---|---|---|---|---|---|
| 2001 LG; JP; A | 5,700,000 | — | — | — | — | 1.75 |

### KM# 869.2 5 KRONER

9.20 g., Copper-Nickel, 28.5 mm. **Ruler:** Margrethe II **Obv:** 3 crowned MII monograms around center hole, date below **Rev:** Wave design surrounds center hole, denomination above, hearts flank **Edge:** Reeded **Note:** Without initials

| Date | Mintage | VF20 | XF40 | MS60 | MS63 | MS65 |
|---|---|---|---|---|---|---|
| 2002 | 5,980,000 | — | — | — | — | 1.75 |
| 2004 | 1,415,925 | — | — | — | — | 1.50 |
| 2004 | 3,000 | PF63 30.00 | | PF65 35.00 | | |
| 2005 | 7,073,000 | — | — | — | — | 1.50 |
| 2005 | 2,650 | PF63 30.00 | | PF65 35.00 | | |
| 2006 | 3,431,000 | — | — | — | — | 1.50 |
| 2006 | 1,800 | PF63 30.00 | | PF65 35.00 | | |
| 2007 | 4,983,000 | — | — | — | — | 1.50 |
| 2007 | 1,400 | PF63 30.00 | | PF65 35.00 | | |
| 2008 | 7,506,000 | — | — | — | — | 1.50 |
| 2008 | 1,000 | PF63 30.00 | | PF65 35.00 | | |
| 2009 Sets only | 25,700 | — | — | — | — | 3.00 |
| 2009 | 1,050 | PF63 30.00 | | PF65 35.00 | | |
| 2010 Sets only | 24,300 | — | — | — | — | 3.00 |
| 2010 | 1,010 | PF63 30.00 | | PF65 35.00 | | |
| 2011 Sets only | 19,900 | — | — | — | — | 3.00 |
| 2011 | 1,000 | PF63 30.00 | | PF65 35.00 | | |
| 2012 Sets only | 17,170 | — | — | — | — | 3.00 |
| 2012 | 1,090 | PF63 30.00 | | PF65 35.00 | | |
| 2013 | — | — | — | — | — | 1.50 |
| 2013 | — | PF63 30.00 | | PF65 35.00 | | |
| 2014 | — | — | — | — | — | 1.50 |
| 2014 | — | PF65 35.00 | | | | |

### KM# 887.1 10 KRONER

7.00 g., Aluminum-Bronze, 23.35 mm. **Ruler:** Margrethe II **Obv:** Crowned head right within inner circle, date, initials LG-JP-A below, mint mark after II in title **Obv. Legend:** MARGRETHE II - DANMARKS DRONNING **Rev:** Crowned arms within inner circle above denomination **Edge:** Plain

| Date | Mintage | VF20 | XF40 | MS60 | MS63 | MS65 |
|---|---|---|---|---|---|---|
| 2001 (h) LG; JP; A | 4,800,000 | — | — | — | — | 4.00 |

## KM# 887.2 10 KRONER

7.00 g., Aluminum-Bronze, 23.35 mm. **Ruler:** Margrethe II **Obv:** Crowned bust right, mint mark after II in title **Obv. Legend:** MARGRETHE II - DANMARKS DRONNING **Rev:** Crowned arms and denomination **Edge:** Plain **Note:** Without initials

| Date | Mintage | VF20 | XF40 | MS60 | MS63 | MS65 |
|---|---|---|---|---|---|---|
| 2002 (h) | 7,299,900 | — | — | — | — | 3.00 |

## KM# 896 10 KRONER

7.00 g., Aluminum-Bronze, 23.35 mm. **Ruler:** Margrethe II **Obv:** Crowned bust right within circle, date below **Obv. Legend:** MARGRETHE II - DANMARKS DRONNING **Rev:** Crowned arms above denomination **Edge:** Plain

| Date | Mintage | VF20 | XF40 | MS60 | MS63 | MS65 |
|---|---|---|---|---|---|---|
| 2004 (h) | 5,835,426 | — | — | — | — | 3.00 |
| 2004 (h) | 3,000 | PF63 35.00 | PF65 40.00 | | | |
| 2005 (h) | 2,614,000 | — | — | — | — | 3.00 |
| 2005 (h) | 2,650 | PF63 35.00 | PF65 40.00 | | | |
| 2006 (h) | 3,530,000 | — | — | — | — | 3.00 |
| 2006 (h) | 1,800 | PF63 35.00 | PF65 40.00 | | | |
| 2007 (h) | 3,294,000 | — | — | — | — | 3.00 |
| 2007 (h) | 1,400 | PF63 35.00 | PF65 40.00 | | | |
| 2008 (h) | 2,258,000 | — | — | — | — | 3.00 |
| 2008 (h) | 1,000 | PF63 35.00 | PF65 40.00 | | | |
| 2009 (h) | 1,701,000 | — | — | — | — | 4.00 |
| 2009 (h) | 1,050 | PF63 35.00 | PF65 40.00 | | | |
| 2010 (h) Sets only | 24,300 | — | — | — | — | 7.00 |
| 2010 (h) | 1,010 | PF63 35.00 | PF65 40.00 | | | |

## KM# 898 10 KRONER

7.00 g., Aluminum-Bronze, 23.35 mm. **Ruler:** Margrethe II **Series:** Fairy Tales **Subject:** Hans Christian Andersen's Ugly duckling story **Obv:** Crowned bust right within circle, date below **Obv. Legend:** MARGRETHE II - DANMARKS DRONNING **Rev:** Swan and reflection on water within circle, value below **Edge:** Plain

| Date | Mintage | VF20 | XF40 | MS60 | MS63 | MS65 |
|---|---|---|---|---|---|---|
| 2005 (h) | 1,206,675 | — | — | — | 2.75 | 4.00 |

## KM# 900 10 KRONER

7.00 g., Aluminum-Bronze, 23.35 mm. **Ruler:** Margrethe II **Series:** Fairy Tales **Subject:** Hans Christian Andersen's Little Mermaid **Obv:** Crowned bust right within circle, date below **Obv. Legend:** MARGRETHE II - DANMARKS DRONNING **Rev:** Little Mermaid **Edge:** Plain

| Date | Mintage | VF20 | XF40 | MS60 | MS63 | MS65 |
|---|---|---|---|---|---|---|
| 2005 (h) | 1,206,675 | — | — | — | 2.75 | 4.00 |

## KM# 906 10 KRONER

31.10 g., 0.999 Silver 0.9989 oz. ASW, 38 mm. **Ruler:** Margrethe II **Series:** Fairy Tales **Subject:** Hans Christian Andersen's The Ugly Duckling **Obv:** Crowned bust right **Obv. Legend:** MARGRETHE II - DANMARKS DRONNING **Rev:** Swan and reflection on water

| Date | Mintage | VF20 | XF40 | MS60 | MS63 | MS65 |
|---|---|---|---|---|---|---|
| 2005 (h) | 75,000 | — | — | — | — | 35.00 |

## KM# 907 10 KRONER

8.65 g., 0.900 Gold 0.2503 oz. AGW, 22 mm. **Ruler:** Margrethe II **Series:** Fairy Tales **Subject:** Hans Christian Andersen's The Ugly Duckling **Obv:** Crowned bust right **Obv. Legend:** MARGRETHE II - DANMARKS DRONNING **Rev:** Swan and reflection on water

| Date | Mintage | VF20 | XF40 | MS60 | MS63 | MS65 |
|---|---|---|---|---|---|---|
| 2005 (h) | 7,000 | — | — | — | 425 | — |

## KM# 908 10 KRONER

31.10 g., 0.999 Silver 0.9989 oz. ASW, 38 mm. **Ruler:** Margrethe II **Series:** Fairy Tales **Subject:** Hans Christian Andersen's Little Mermaid **Obv:** Crowned bust right, date below **Obv. Legend:** MARGRETHE II - DANMARKS DRONNING **Rev:** Little Mermaid

| Date | Mintage | VF20 | XF40 | MS60 | MS63 | MS65 |
|---|---|---|---|---|---|---|
| 2005 (h) | 40,220 | PF63 35.00 | PF65 40.00 | | | |

## KM# 911 10 KRONER

8.65 g., 0.900 Gold 0.2503 oz. AGW, 22 mm. **Ruler:** Margrethe II **Series:** Fairy Tales **Subject:** Hans Christian Andersen's Little Mermaid **Obv:** Crowned bust right **Obv. Legend:** MARGRETHE II - DANMARKS DRONNING **Rev:** Little Mermaid

| Date | Mintage | VF20 | XF40 | MS60 | MS63 | MS65 |
|---|---|---|---|---|---|---|
| 2005 (h) | 4,220 | — | — | — | 425 | — |

## KM# 903 10 KRONER

7.00 g., Aluminum-Bronze, 23.35 mm. **Ruler:** Margrethe II **Series:** Fairy Tales **Subject:** H.C. Andersen's "The Shadow **Obv:** Crowned bust right within circle, date below **Obv. Legend:** MARGRETHE II - DANMARKS DRONNING **Rev:** Stylized figures **Edge:** Plain

| Date | Mintage | VF20 | XF40 | MS60 | MS63 | MS65 |
|---|---|---|---|---|---|---|
| 2006 (h) | 1,206,675 | — | — | — | 2.75 | 4.00 |

## KM# 909 10 KRONER

31.10 g., 0.999 Silver 0.9989 oz. ASW, 38 mm. **Ruler:** Margrethe II **Series:** Fairy Tales **Subject:** H.C. Andersen's "Skyggen" (The Shadow) **Obv:** Crowned bust right **Obv. Legend:** MARGRETHE II - DANMARKS DRONNING **Rev:** Stylized figures

| Date | Mintage | VF20 | XF40 | MS60 | MS63 | MS65 |
|---|---|---|---|---|---|---|
| 2006 (h) | 22,317 | PF63 45.00 | PF65 50.00 | | | |

## KM# 910 10 KRONER

8.65 g., 0.900 Gold 0.2503 oz. AGW, 22 mm. **Ruler:** Margrethe II **Series:** Fairy Tales **Subject:** H.C. Andersen's "Skyggen" (The Shadow) **Obv:** Crowned bust right **Obv. Legend:** MARGRETHE II - DANMARKS DRONNING **Rev:** Stylized figures

| Date | Mintage | VF20 | XF40 | MS60 | MS63 | MS65 |
|---|---|---|---|---|---|---|
| 2006 (h) | 3,070 | — | — | — | 425 | — |

## KM# 914 10 KRONER

7.00 g., Aluminum-Bronze, 23.35 mm. **Ruler:** Margrethe II **Series:** Fairy Tales **Subject:** Hans Christian Andersen's Snow Queen **Obv:** Crowned bust right **Obv. Legend:** MARGRETHE II - DANMARKS DRONNING **Rev:** Ice pieces

| Date | Mintage | VF20 | XF40 | MS60 | MS63 | MS65 |
|---|---|---|---|---|---|---|
| 2006 (h) | 1,206,675 | — | — | — | 2.75 | 4.00 |

## KM# 951 10 KRONER

31.10 g., 0.999 Silver 0.9989 oz. ASW, 38 mm. **Ruler:** Margrethe II **Series:** Fairy Tales **Subject:** Hans Christian Andersen's Snow Queen **Obv:** Crowned bust right **Obv. Legend:** MARGRETHE II - DANMARKS DRONNING **Rev:** Ice pieces

| Date | Mintage | VF20 | XF40 | MS60 | MS63 | MS65 |
|---|---|---|---|---|---|---|
| 2006 (h) | 25,758 | — | — | — | 40.00 | — |

## KM# 952 10 KRONER

8.65 g., 0.900 Gold 0.2503 oz. AGW, 22 mm. **Ruler:** Margrethe II **Series:** Fairy Tales **Subject:** The Snow Queen **Obv:** Crowned bust right **Obv. Legend:** MARGRETHE II - DANMARKS DRONNING **Rev:** Ice pieces

| Date | Mintage | VF20 | XF40 | MS60 | MS63 | MS65 |
|---|---|---|---|---|---|---|
| 2006 (h) | 3,075 | — | — | — | 475 | — |

## KM# 916 10 KRONER

7.00 g., Aluminum-Bronze, 23.35 mm. **Ruler:** Margrethe II **Subject:** International Polar Year 2007-2009 **Obv:** Head with tiara right **Obv. Legend:** MARGRETHE II - DANMARKS DRONNING **Rev:** Polar bear facing, walking on ice flow **Rev. Legend:** POLARÅR 2007-2009 **Edge:** Plain

| Date | Mintage | VF20 | XF40 | MS60 | MS63 | MS65 |
|---|---|---|---|---|---|---|
| 2007 (h) | 1,200,000 | — | — | — | 2.75 | 4.00 |

## KM# 923 10 KRONER

7.00 g., Aluminum-Bronze, 23.35 mm. **Ruler:** Margrethe II **Series:** Fairy Tales **Subject:** H.C. Anderson's 'The Nightingale' **Rev:** Bird

| Date | Mintage | VF20 | XF40 | MS60 | MS63 | MS65 |
|---|---|---|---|---|---|---|
| 2007 | 1,206,675 | — | — | — | 2.75 | 4.00 |

## KM# 949 10 KRONER

31.10 g., 0.999 Silver 0.9989 oz. ASW, 38 mm. **Ruler:** Margrethe II **Series:** Fairy Tales **Subject:** H.C. Anderson's 'The Nightengale' **Rev:** Bird

| Date | Mintage | VF20 | XF40 | MS60 | MS63 | MS65 |
|---|---|---|---|---|---|---|
| 2007 | 18,117 | PF63 40.00 | PF65 45.00 | | | |

## KM# 950 10 KRONER

8.65 g., 0.900 Gold 0.2503 oz. AGW, 22 mm. **Ruler:** Margrethe II **Series:** Fairy Tales **Subject:** H.C. Anderson's 'The Nightengale' **Rev:** Bird

| Date | Mintage | VF20 | XF40 | MS60 | MS63 | MS65 |
|---|---|---|---|---|---|---|
| 2007 | 2,964 | — | — | — | 475 | — |

## KM# 925 10 KRONER

7.00 g., Aluminum-Bronze, 23.35 mm. **Ruler:** Margrethe II **Series:** International Polar Year 2007-2009 **Obv:** Head with tiara right **Rev:** Outlined globe **Rev. Legend:** POLARÅR 2007-2009 **Edge:** Plain

| Date | Mintage | VF20 | XF40 | MS60 | MS63 | MS65 |
|---|---|---|---|---|---|---|
| 2008 (h) | 1,200,000 | — | — | — | 2.75 | 4.00 |

## KM# 932 10 KRONER

7.00 g., Aluminum-Bronze, 23.35 mm. **Ruler:** Margrethe II **Rev:** Ice scape, Northern Lights

| Date | Mintage | VF20 | XF40 | MS60 | MS63 | MS65 |
|---|---|---|---|---|---|---|
| 2009 | 1,200,000 | — | — | — | 2.75 | 4.00 |

## KM# 943 10 KRONER

7.00 g., Aluminum-Bronze, 23.35 mm. **Ruler:** Margrethe II **Obv:** Head right **Obv. Legend:** MARGRETHE II DANMARKS DRONNING **Rev:** Crowned shield and value **Edge:** Plain

| Date | Mintage | VF20 | XF40 | MS60 | MS63 | MS65 |
|---|---|---|---|---|---|---|
| 2011 (h) | 2,339,000 | — | — | — | 2.75 | 4.00 |
| 2011 Special Unc | 3,010 | — | — | — | 25.00 | — |
| 2011 (h) | 1,000 | PF63 25.00 | PF65 28.00 | | | |
| 2012 Sets only | 24,000 | — | — | — | — | 6.00 |
| 2012 | 1,090 | PF63 25.00 | PF65 28.00 | | | |

## KM# 954 10 KRONER

7.00 g., Aluminum-Bronze, 23.35 mm. **Ruler:** Margrethe II **Obv:** Bust right **Rev:** Crown, three lions and denomination **Edge:** Plain

| Date | Mintage | VF20 | XF40 | MS60 | MS63 | MS65 |
|---|---|---|---|---|---|---|
| 2013 | — | — | — | — | 5.00 | — |
| 2013 | — | PF63 28.00 | PF65 32.00 | | | |
| 2014 | — | — | — | — | 5.00 | — |
| 2014 | — | PF65 32.00 | | | | |

**KM# 888.1 20 KRONER**

9.30 g., Aluminum-Bronze, 27 mm. **Ruler:** Margrethe II **Obv:** Crowned bust right within circle, date and initials LG-JP-A below, mint mark after II in legend **Obv. Legend:** MARGRETHE II - DANMARKS DRONNING **Rev:** Crowned arms within ornaments and value **Edge:** Alternating reeded and plain sections

| Date | Mintage | VF20 | XF40 | MS60 | MS63 | MS65 |
|---|---|---|---|---|---|---|
| 2001 (h) LG; JP; A | 2,900,000 | — | — | — | — | 5.00 |

**KM# 888.2 20 KRONER**

9.30 g., Aluminum-Bronze, 27 mm. **Ruler:** Margrethe II **Obv:** Crowned bust right within circle, mint mark after II in legend **Obv. Legend:** MARGRETHE II - DANMARKS DRONNING **Rev:** Crowned arms within ornaments and value **Edge:** Alternate reeded and plain sections **Note:** Without initials.

| Date | Mintage | VF20 | XF40 | MS60 | MS63 | MS65 |
|---|---|---|---|---|---|---|
| 2002 (h) | 5,500,000 | — | — | — | — | 5.00 |

**KM# 889 20 KRONER**

9.30 g., Aluminum-Bronze, 27 mm. **Ruler:** Margrethe II **Series:** Danish Towers **Obv:** Crowned bust right within circle date below, mint mark after II in legend **Obv. Legend:** MARGRETHE II - DANMARKS DRONNING **Rev:** Aarhus City Hall **Edge:** Reeded and plain sections

| Date | Mintage | VF20 | XF40 | MS60 | MS63 | MS65 |
|---|---|---|---|---|---|---|
| 2002 (h) | 1,208,600 | — | — | — | — | 5.00 |

**KM# 890 20 KRONER**

9.30 g., Aluminum-Bronze, 27 mm. **Ruler:** Margrethe II **Series:** Danish Towers **Obv:** Crowned bust right within circle, mint mark and date **Obv. Legend:** MARGRETHE II - DANMARKS DRONNING **Rev:** Copenhagen Old Stock Exchange spire with four intertwined dragon tails **Edge:** Alternate reeded and plain sections

| Date | Mintage | VF20 | XF40 | MS60 | MS63 | MS65 |
|---|---|---|---|---|---|---|
| 2003 (h) | 1,208,600 | — | — | — | — | 5.00 |

**KM# 891 20 KRONER**

9.30 g., Aluminum-Bronze, 27 mm. **Ruler:** Margrethe II **Obv:** Crowned bust right within circle, mint mark and date **Obv. Legend:** MARGRETHE II - DANMARKS DRONNING **Rev:** Crowned arms above denomination **Edge:** Alternate reeded and plain sections

| Date | Mintage | VF20 | XF40 | MS60 | MS63 | MS65 |
|---|---|---|---|---|---|---|
| 2003 (h) | 5,720,000 | — | — | — | — | 5.00 |
| 2004 (h) | 6,922,182 | — | — | — | — | 5.00 |
| 2004 (h) | 3,000 | PF63 | 50.00 | PF65 | 55.00 | |
| 2005 (h) | 4,194,000 | — | — | — | — | 5.00 |
| 2005 (h) | 2,650 | PF63 | 50.00 | PF65 | 55.00 | |
| 2006 (h) | 3,051,000 | — | — | — | — | 5.00 |
| 2006 (h) | 1,800 | PF63 | 50.00 | PF65 | 55.00 | |
| 2007 (h) | 2,409,000 | — | — | — | — | 5.00 |
| 2007 (h) | 1,400 | PF63 | 50.00 | PF65 | 55.00 | |
| 2008 (h) | 1,982,000 | — | — | — | — | 5.00 |
| 2008 (h) | 1,000 | PF63 | 50.00 | PF65 | 55.00 | |
| 2009 (h) | 2,021,000 | — | — | — | — | 5.00 |
| 2009 (h) | 1,050 | PF63 | 50.00 | PF65 | 55.00 | |
| 2010 (h) Sets only | 24,300 | — | — | — | — | 7.00 |
| 2010 (h) | 1,010 | PF63 | 50.00 | PF65 | 55.00 | |

**KM# 892 20 KRONER**

9.30 g., Aluminum-Bronze, 27 mm. **Ruler:** Margrethe II **Series:** Danish towers **Obv:** Crowned bust right within circle, mint mark and date **Obv. Legend:** MARGRETHE II - DANMARKS DRONNING **Rev:** Christiansborg Castle (parliament) tower and Danish flag **Edge:** Alternate reeded and plain sections

| Date | Mintage | VF20 | XF40 | MS60 | MS63 | MS65 |
|---|---|---|---|---|---|---|
| 2003 (h) | 1,208,600 | — | — | — | — | 5.00 |

**KM# 893 20 KRONER**

9.30 g., Aluminum-Bronze, 27 mm. **Ruler:** Margrethe II **Series:** Danish Towers **Obv:** Crowned bust right within circle, date below **Obv. Legend:** MARGRETHE II - DANMARKS DRONNING **Rev:** Gåsetårnet tower **Edge:** Alternate reeded and plain sections

| Date | Mintage | VF20 | XF40 | MS60 | MS63 | MS65 |
|---|---|---|---|---|---|---|
| 2004 (h) | 1,208,600 | — | — | — | — | 5.00 |

**KM# 894 20 KRONER**

9.30 g., Aluminum-Bronze, 27 mm. **Ruler:** Margrethe II **Subject:** Crown Prince's Wedding **Obv:** Crowned bust right within circle, date below **Obv. Legend:** MARGRETHE II - DANMARKS DRONNING **Rev:** Crown Prince Frederik and Crown Princess Mary **Edge:** Alternate reeded and plain sections

| Date | Mintage | VF20 | XF40 | MS60 | MS63 | MS65 |
|---|---|---|---|---|---|---|
| 2004 (h) | 1,200,000 | — | — | — | — | 5.00 |

**KM# 897 20 KRONER**

9.30 g., Aluminum-Bronze, 27 mm. **Ruler:** Margrethe II **Series:** Danish Towers **Obv:** Crowned bust right within circle, date below **Obv. Legend:** MARGRETHE II - DANMARKS DRONNING **Rev:** Svaneke water tower, Bornholm **Edge:** Alternate reeded and plain sections

| Date | Mintage | VF20 | XF40 | MS60 | MS63 | MS65 |
|---|---|---|---|---|---|---|
| 2004 (h) | 1,208,600 | — | — | — | — | 5.00 |

**KM# 899 20 KRONER**

9.30 g., Aluminum-Bronze, 27 mm. **Ruler:** Margrethe II **Series:** Danish Towers **Obv:** Crowned bust right within circle, date below **Obv. Legend:** MARGRETHE II - DANMARKS DRONNING **Rev:** Landet Kirke, with elements from the story of Elvira Madigan and Sixten Sparre, including a revolver among leaves of chestnut-trees **Edge:** Segmented reeding

| Date | Mintage | VF20 | XF40 | MS60 | MS63 | MS65 |
|---|---|---|---|---|---|---|
| 2005 (h) | 1,208,600 | — | — | — | — | 5.00 |

**KM# 901 20 KRONER**

9.30 g., Aluminum-Bronze, 27 mm. **Ruler:** Margrethe II **Series:** Danish Towers **Obv:** Crowned bust right within circle, date below **Obv. Legend:** MARGRETHE II - DANMARKS DRONNING **Rev:** Lighthouse of Nolsoy (Faeroe Islands) **Edge:** Alternate plain and reeded segments

| Date | Mintage | VF20 | XF40 | MS60 | MS63 | MS65 |
|---|---|---|---|---|---|---|
| 2005 (h) | 1,208,600 | — | — | — | — | 5.00 |

**KM# 902 20 KRONER**

9.30 g., Aluminum-Bronze, 27 mm. **Ruler:** Margrethe II **Series:** Danish Towers **Obv:** Crowned bust right within circle, date below **Obv. Legend:** MARGRETHE II - DANMARKS DRONNING **Rev:** Gråsten Castle Bell Tower **Edge:** Segmented reeding

| Date | Mintage | VF20 | XF40 | MS60 | MS63 | MS65 |
|---|---|---|---|---|---|---|
| 2006 (h) | 1,208,600 | — | — | — | — | 5.00 |

**KM# 913 20 KRONER**

9.30 g., Aluminum-Bronze, 27 mm. **Ruler:** Margrethe II **Series:** Danish Towers **Obv:** Crowned bust right within circle, date below **Obv. Legend:** MARGRETHE II - DANMARKS DRONNING **Rev:** The Greenland Cairns: Nukaritt/Three Brothers **Rev. Legend:** TRE BRØDRE **Edge:** Alternate plain and reeded segments

| Date | Mintage | VF20 | XF40 | MS60 | MS63 | MS65 |
|---|---|---|---|---|---|---|
| 2006 (h) | 1,208,600 | — | — | — | — | 5.00 |

**KM# 919 20 KRONER**

9.30 g., Aluminum-Bronze, 27 mm. **Ruler:** Margrethe II **Series:** Danish Towers **Obv:** Bust with tiarra right **Obv. Legend:** MARGRETHE II - DANMARKS DRONNING **Rev:** City Hall in Copenhagen **Rev. Legend:** KØBENHAVNS RÅDHUS **Edge:** Alternate plain and reeded segments

| Date | Mintage | VF20 | XF40 | MS60 | MS63 | MS65 |
|---|---|---|---|---|---|---|
| 2007 (h) | 1,208,600 | — | — | — | — | 5.00 |

**KM# 920 20 KRONER**

9.30 g., Aluminum-Bronze, 27 mm. **Ruler:** Margrethe II **Series:** Danish Ships **Obv:** Crowned bust right **Obv. Legend:** MARGRETHE II - DANMARKS DRONNING **Rev:** Sailing ship Jylland **Rev. Legend:** FREGATTEN - JYLLAND **Edge:** Segmented reeding

| Date | Mintage | VF20 | XF40 | MS60 | MS63 | MS65 |
|---|---|---|---|---|---|---|
| 2007 (h) | 1,200,000 | — | — | — | — | 5.00 |

**KM# 921 20 KRONER**

9.30 g., Aluminum-Bronze, 27 mm. **Ruler:** Margrethe II **Series:** Danish ships **Subject:** The Galathea 3 expedition **Obv:** Crowned bust right **Obv. Legend:** MARGRETHE II - DANMARKS DRONNING **Rev:** Ship Vaedderen, route map in background **Rev. Legend:** VAEDDEREN **Edge:** Segmented reeding

| Date | Mintage | VF20 | XF40 | MS60 | MS63 | MS65 |
|---|---|---|---|---|---|---|
| 2007 (h) | 1,200,000 | — | — | — | — | 5.00 |

**KM# 926 20 KRONER**

9.30 g., Aluminum-Bronze, 27 mm. **Ruler:** Margrethe II **Series:** Danish Ships **Obv:** Head with tiara right **Rev:** World's first ocean-going diesel-engine merchant ship, built 1912 **Rev. Legend:** SELANDIA **Edge:** Segmented reeding

| Date | Mintage | VF20 | XF40 | MS60 | MS63 | MS65 |
|---|---|---|---|---|---|---|
| 2008 (h) | 1,200,000 | — | — | — | — | 5.00 |
| 2008 (h) | 1,500 | PF63 60.00 | PF65 65.00 | | | |

**KM# 927 20 KRONER**

9.30 g., Aluminum-Bronze, 27 mm. **Ruler:** Margrethe II **Series:** Danish Ships **Subject:** Voyage to Dublin, Irelend, with full size replica Viking ship, HAVHINGSTEN **Obv:** Crowned bust right **Obv. Legend:** MARGRETHE II - DANMARKS DRONNING **Rev:** Sailing vessel at sea **Rev. Legend:** HAVHINGSTEN / 20 KRONER **Edge:** Segmented reeding

| Date | Mintage | VF20 | XF40 | MS60 | MS63 | MS65 |
|---|---|---|---|---|---|---|
| 2008 | 1,200,000 | — | — | — | — | 5.00 |
| 2008 | 1,500 | PF63 60.00 | PF65 65.00 | | | |

**KM# 928 20 KRONER**

9.30 g., Aluminum-Bronze, 27 mm. **Ruler:** Margrethe II **Series:** Danish Ships **Rev:** Royal Yacht Dannebrog **Edge:** Segmented reeding

| Date | Mintage | VF20 | XF40 | MS60 | MS63 | MS65 |
|---|---|---|---|---|---|---|
| 2008 | 1,200,000 | — | — | — | 5.00 | — |
| 2008 | 1,500 | PF63 60.00 | PF65 65.00 | | | |

**KM# 935 20 KRONER**

9.30 g., Aluminum-Bronze, 27 mm. **Ruler:** Margrethe II **Series:** Danish Ships **Obv:** Crowned bust right **Obv. Legend:** MARGRETHE II - DANMARKS DRONNING **Rev:** Lightship XVII (built 1895) on duty **Edge:** Segmented reeding

| Date | Mintage | VF20 | XF40 | MS60 | MS63 | MS65 |
|---|---|---|---|---|---|---|
| 2009 | 1,100,000 | — | — | — | 9.00 | 5.00 |
| 2009 | 1,500 | PF63 60.00 | PF65 65.00 | | | |

**KM# 936 20 KRONER**

9.30 g., Aluminum-Bronze, 27 mm. **Ruler:** Margrethe II **Series:** Danish Ships **Obv:** Crowned bust facing right **Rev:** FAERØBÅD (Boat of Faeroe Islands) **Edge:** Segmented reeding

| Date | Mintage | VF20 | XF40 | MS60 | MS63 | MS65 |
|---|---|---|---|---|---|---|
| 2009 | 900,000 | — | — | — | — | 5.00 |
| 2009 | 2,825 | PF63 60.00 | PF65 65.00 | | | |

**KM# 937 20 KRONER**

9.30 g., Aluminum-Bronze, 27 mm. **Ruler:** Margrethe II **Subject:** Queen's 70th Birthday **Obv:** Head right **Rev:** Crowned shield against background of daisies

| Date | Mintage | VF20 | XF40 | MS60 | MS63 | MS65 |
|---|---|---|---|---|---|---|
| 2010 | 1,440,000 | — | — | — | — | 5.00 |
| 2010 | 4,100 | PF63 60.00 | PF65 65.00 | | | |

**KM# 940 20 KRONER**

9.30 g., Aluminum-Bronze, 27 mm. **Ruler:** Margrethe II **Series:** Danish Ships **Subject:** Greenland kayak - women's ship **Obv:** Bust facing right **Rev:** Kayak-Umak **Rev. Legend:** KAJAK • KONEBÅD **Edge:** Segmented reeding

| Date | Mintage | VF20 | XF40 | MS60 | MS63 | MS65 |
|---|---|---|---|---|---|---|
| 2010 | 972,000 | — | — | — | — | 5.00 |
| 2010 | 1,877 | PF63 60.00 | PF65 65.00 | | | |

**KM# 942 20 KRONER**

9.30 g., Aluminum-Bronze, 27 mm. **Ruler:** Margrethe II **Subject:** The Emma Maersk, a container ship **Obv:** Head right **Obv. Legend:** MARGRETHE II DANMARKS DRONNING **Rev:** Emma Maersk, container ship, right **Edge:** Segmented reeding

| Date | Mintage | VF20 | XF40 | MS60 | MS63 | MS65 |
|---|---|---|---|---|---|---|
| 2011 | 800,000 | — | — | — | — | 5.00 |
| 2011 | 3,810 | PF63 60.00 | PF65 65.00 | | | |

**KM# 941 20 KRONER**

9.30 g., Aluminum-Bronze, 27 mm. **Ruler:** Margrethe II **Series:** Danish Ships **Subject:** The Hjejlen, a paddle steamer **Obv:** Head right **Obv. Legend:** MARGRETHE II DANMARKS DRONNING **Rev:** The Hjejlen and value **Edge:** Segmented reeding

| Date | Mintage | VF20 | XF40 | MS60 | MS63 | MS65 |
|---|---|---|---|---|---|---|
| 2011 | 700,000 | — | — | — | — | 5.00 |
| 2011 | 2,662 | PF63 60.00 | PF65 65.00 | | | |

**KM# 944 20 KRONER**

9.30 g., Aluminum-Bronze, 27 mm. **Ruler:** Margrethe II **Obv:** Head right **Obv. Legend:** MARGRETHE II DANMARKS DRONNING **Rev:** Crowned shield and value **Edge:** Segmented reeding

| Date | Mintage | VF20 | XF40 | MS60 | MS63 | MS65 |
|---|---|---|---|---|---|---|
| 2011 (h) | 1,035,000 | — | — | 6.25 | — | — |
| 2011 Special Unc | 3,019 | — | — | — | 6.00 | — |
| 2011 (h) | 1,000 | PF63 50.00 | PF65 55.00 | | | |
| 2012 Sets only | 276,000 | — | — | 6.25 | — | — |
| 2012 | 1,090 | PF63 50.00 | PF65 55.00 | | | |

**KM# 945 20 KRONER**

9.30 g., Aluminum-Bronze, 27 mm. **Ruler:** Margrethe II **Subject:** 40th Jubilee of Queen Margrethe II **Obv:** Bust of Queen Margrethe II facing right **Obv. Legend:** MARGRETHE II DANMARKS DRONNING **Rev:** Design, legend 1972 14 JANUAR 2012 and denomination **Edge:** Segmented reeding

| Date | Mintage | VF20 | XF40 | MS60 | MS63 | MS65 |
|---|---|---|---|---|---|---|
| 2012 | 750,000 | — | — | — | — | 5.00 |
| 2012 | 3,180 | PF63 60.00 | PF65 65.00 | | | |

**KM# 948 20 KRONER**

9.30 g., Aluminum-Bronze, 27 mm. **Ruler:** Margrethe II **Series:** Danish Ships **Subject:** The Kong Frederik IX, a ferry **Obv:** Bust of Queen Margrethe II facing right **Obv. Legend:** MARGRETHE II DANMARKS DRONNING **Rev:** The Kong Frederik IX, legend KONG FREDERIK IX and denomination **Edge:** Segmented reeding

| Date | Mintage | VF20 | XF40 | MS60 | MS63 | MS65 |
|---|---|---|---|---|---|---|
| 2012 | 349,000 | — | — | — | — | 5.00 |
| 2012 | 2,331 | PF63 60.00 | PF65 65.00 | | | |

**KM# 953 20 KRONER**

9.30 g., Aluminum-Bronze, 27 mm. **Ruler:** Margrethe II **Obv:** Bust right **Rev:** Fishing vessel and denomination **Rev. Inscription:** FISKEKUTTER **Edge:** Segmented reeding

| Date | Mintage | VF20 | XF40 | MS60 | MS63 | MS65 |
|---|---|---|---|---|---|---|
| 2012 | 257,000 | — | — | — | 5.00 | — |
| 2012 | 1,732 | PF63 28.00 | PF65 32.00 | | | |

**KM# 955 20 KRONER**
9.30 g., Aluminum-Bronze, 27 mm. **Ruler:** Margrethe II **Obv:** Bust right **Rev:** Crown, three lions and denomination **Edge:** Segmented reeding

| Date | Mintage | VF20 | XF40 | MS60 | MS63 | MS65 |
|---|---|---|---|---|---|---|
| 2013 | — | — | — | — | 5.00 | — |
| 2013 | — | PF63 35.00 | PF65 38.00 | | | |
| 2014 | — | — | — | — | — | 5.00 |
| 2014 | — | PF65 38.00 | | | | |

**KM# 956 20 KRONER**
9.30 g., Aluminum-Bronze, 27 mm. **Ruler:** Margrethe II **Subject:** Niels Bohr **Obv:** Bust right **Rev:** Atom design **Edge:** Segmented reeding

| Date | Mintage | VF20 | XF40 | MS60 | MS63 | MS65 |
|---|---|---|---|---|---|---|
| 2013 | 250,000 | — | — | — | 5.50 | — |
| 2013 | — | PF63 35.00 | PF65 38.00 | | | |

**KM# 958 20 KRONER**
9.30 g., Aluminum-Bronze, 27 mm. **Ruler:** Margrethe II **Subject:** H.C. Ørsted **Obv:** Bust right **Rev:** Electromagnet with poles connected **Edge:** Segmented reeding

| Date | Mintage | VF20 | XF40 | MS60 | MS63 | MS65 |
|---|---|---|---|---|---|---|
| 2013 | 250,000 | — | — | — | 5.50 | — |
| 2013 | — | PF63 35.00 | PF65 38.00 | | | |

**KM# 960 20 KRONER**
9.30 g., Aluminum-Bronze, 27 mm. **Ruler:** Margrethe II **Subject:** Ole Rømer **Obv:** Bust right **Rev:** Sun and orbiting planets and moons

| Date | Mintage | VF20 | XF40 | MS60 | MS63 | MS65 |
|---|---|---|---|---|---|---|
| 2013 | 250,000 | — | — | — | 5.50 | — |
| 2013 | — | PF63 35.00 | PF65 38.00 | | | |

**KM# 962 20 KRONER**
9.30 g., Aluminum-Bronze, 27 mm. **Ruler:** Margrethe II **Subject:** Tycho Brahe **Obv:** Bust right **Rev:** Sun and constellations **Edge:** Segmented reeding

| Date | Mintage | VF20 | XF40 | MS60 | MS63 | MS65 |
|---|---|---|---|---|---|---|
| 2013 | 250,000 | — | — | — | 5.50 | — |
| 2013 | — | PF63 35.00 | PF65 38.00 | | | |

**KM# 917 100 KRONER**
31.00 g., 0.999 Silver 0.9957 oz. ASW, 38 mm. **Ruler:** Margrethe II **Subject:** International Polar Year 2007-2009 **Obv:** Crowned bust right **Obv. Legend:** MARGRETHE II - DANMARKS DRONNING **Rev:** Polar bear facing, walking on ice flow **Rev. Legend:** POLARÅR 2007-2009

| Date | Mintage | VF20 | XF40 | MS60 | MS63 | MS65 |
|---|---|---|---|---|---|---|
| 2007 (h) | 43,048 | — | — | — | — | 45.00 |

**KM# 930 100 KRONER**
31.10 g., 0.999 Silver 0.9989 oz. ASW, 38 mm. **Ruler:** Margrethe II **Subject:** International Polar Year 2007-2009 **Rev:** Globe and dog sled

| Date | Mintage | VF20 | XF40 | MS60 | MS63 | MS65 |
|---|---|---|---|---|---|---|
| 2008 | 15,631 | — | — | — | — | 50.00 |

**KM# 933 100 KRONER**
31.10 g., 0.999 Silver 0.9989 oz. ASW, 38 mm. **Ruler:** Margrethe II **Subject:** International Polar Year 2007-2009 **Rev:** Ice scape, Northern Lights

| Date | Mintage | VF20 | XF40 | MS60 | MS63 | MS65 |
|---|---|---|---|---|---|---|
| 2009 | 10,600 | — | — | — | — | 55.00 |

**KM# 895 200 KRONER**
31.10 g., 0.999 Silver 0.9989 oz. ASW, 38.3 mm. **Ruler:** Margrethe II **Subject:** Wedding of Crown Prince **Obv:** Crowned bust right within circle, date below **Obv. Legend:** MARGRETHE II - DANMARKS DRONNING **Rev:** Crown Prince Frederik and Crown Princess Mary **Edge:** Plain **Note:** No initials.

| Date | Mintage | VF20 | XF40 | MS60 | MS63 | MS65 |
|---|---|---|---|---|---|---|
| 2004 (h) | 125,000 | — | — | — | 45.00 | — |

**KM# 929 500 KRONER**
31.10 g., 0.999 Silver 0.9989 oz. ASW, 38 mm. **Ruler:** Margrethe II **Rev:** Royal Yacht Dannebrog

| Date | Mintage | VF20 | XF40 | MS60 | MS63 | MS65 |
|---|---|---|---|---|---|---|
| 2008 | 31,700 | — | — | — | — | 100 |

**KM# 938 500 KRONER**
31.10 g., 0.999 Silver 0.9989 oz. ASW, 38 mm. **Ruler:** Margrethe II **Subject:** Queen's 70th Birthday **Obv:** Head right **Rev:** Crowned shield against a background of daisies

| Date | Mintage | VF20 | XF40 | MS60 | MS63 | MS65 |
|---|---|---|---|---|---|---|
| 2010 | 28,236 | — | — | — | — | 100 |

**KM# 946 500 KRONER**
31.10 g., 0.999 Silver 0.9989 oz. ASW, 38 mm. **Ruler:** Margrethe II **Subject:** 40th Jubilee of Queen Margrethe II **Obv:** Bust of the Queen Margrethe II facing right **Obv. Legend:** MARGRETHE II DANMARKS DRONNING **Rev:** Design, legend 1972, 14 JANUAR 2012 and denomination

| Date | Mintage | VF20 | XF40 | MS60 | MS63 | MS65 |
|---|---|---|---|---|---|---|
| 2012 | 16,881 | — | — | — | — | 100 |

**KM# 957 500 KRONER**
31.11 g., 0.999 Silver 0.999 oz. ASW, 38 mm. **Ruler:** Margrethe II **Subject:** Niels Bohr, Atomic Theory **Obv:** Bust right **Rev:** Design of atom

| Date | Mintage | VF20 | XF40 | MS60 | MS63 | MS65 |
|---|---|---|---|---|---|---|
| 2013 | — | — | — | — | 95.00 | — |

**KM# 959 500 KRONER**
31.11 g., 0.999 Silver 0.999 oz. ASW, 38 mm. **Ruler:** Margrethe II **Subject:** H.C. Ørsted **Obv:** Bust right **Rev:** Electromagnet with wire connecting poles

| Date | Mintage | VF20 | XF40 | MS60 | MS63 | MS65 |
|---|---|---|---|---|---|---|
| 2013 | — | — | — | — | 95.00 | — |

**KM# 961 500 KRONER**
31.11 g., 0.999 Silver 0.999 oz. ASW, 38 mm. **Ruler:** Margrethe II **Subject:** Ole Rømer **Obv:** Bust right **Rev:** Sun and orbiting planets and moon

| Date | Mintage | VF20 | XF40 | MS60 | MS63 | MS65 |
|---|---|---|---|---|---|---|
| 2013 | — | — | — | — | 95.00 | — |

**KM# 963 500 KRONER**
31.11 g., 0.999 Silver 0.999 oz. ASW, 38 mm. **Ruler:** Margrethe II **Subject:** Tycho Brahe **Obv:** Bust right **Rev:** Sun and constellation of stars

| Date | Mintage | VF20 | XF40 | MS60 | MS63 | MS65 |
|---|---|---|---|---|---|---|
| 2013 | — | — | — | — | 95.00 | — |

**KM# 918 1000 KRONER**
8.65 g., 0.900 Gold 0.2503 oz. AGW, 22 mm. **Ruler:** Margrethe II **Subject:** International Polar Year 2007-2009 **Obv:** Crowned bust right **Obv. Legend:** MARGRETHE II - DANMARKS DRONNING **Rev:** Polar bear facing, walking on ice flow **Rev. Legend:** POLARÅR 2007-2009 **Note:** Struck from gold from Greenland having a small polar bear to right of denomination.

| Date | Mintage | VF20 | XF40 | MS60 | MS63 | MS65 |
|---|---|---|---|---|---|---|
| 2007 (h) | 6,000 | **PF63** 425 | **PF65** 450 | | | |

**KM# 931 1000 KRONER**
8.65 g., 0.900 Gold 0.2503 oz. AGW, 22 mm. **Ruler:** Margrethe II **Subject:** International Polar Year 2007-2009 **Rev:** Globe and dog sled

| Date | Mintage | VF20 | XF40 | MS60 | MS63 | MS65 |
|---|---|---|---|---|---|---|
| 2008 | 3,604 | **PF63** 425 | **PF65** 450 | | | |

**KM# 934 1000 KRONER**
8.65 g., 0.900 Gold 0.2503 oz. AGW, 22 mm. **Ruler:** Margrethe II **Subject:** International Polar Year 2007-2009 **Rev:** Ice scape, Northern Lights

| Date | Mintage | VF20 | XF40 | MS60 | MS63 | MS65 |
|---|---|---|---|---|---|---|
| 2009 | 2,400 | **PF63** 425 | **PF65** 450 | | | |

**KM# 939 1000 KRONER**
8.65 g., 0.900 Gold 0.2503 oz. AGW, 22 mm. **Ruler:** Margrethe II **Subject:** Queen's 70th Birthday **Obv:** Bust right **Rev:** Crowned shield against background of daisies

| Date | Mintage | VF20 | XF40 | MS60 | MS63 | MS65 |
|---|---|---|---|---|---|---|
| 2010 | 2,639 | **PF63** 475 | **PF65** 500 | | | |

**KM# 947 3000 KRONER**
8.65 g., 0.900 Gold 0.2503 oz. AGW, 22 mm. **Ruler:** Margrethe II **Subject:** 40th Jubilee of Queen Margrethe II **Obv:** Bust of Queen Margrethe II facing right **Obv. Legend:** MARGRETHE II DANMARKS DRONNING **Rev:** Design, legend 1972 14 JANUAR 2012 and denomination **Edge:** Segmented reeding

| Date | Mintage | VF20 | XF40 | MS60 | MS63 | MS65 |
|---|---|---|---|---|---|---|
| 2012 | 2,325 | — | — | — | — | 600 |

## MINT SETS

| KM# | Date | Mintage | Identification | Issue Price | Mkt Val |
|---|---|---|---|---|---|
| MS46 | 2001 (5) | 28,000 | KM866.2, 868, 869, 873, 874, 887, 888 | 15.00 | 37.50 |
| MS47 | 2002 (7) | 28,000 | KM866.3, 868.2, 869.2, 873.2, 874.2, 887.2, 888.2 | 17.50 | 35.00 |
| MS48 | 2003 (6) | 30,000 | KM866.3, 868.2, 873.2, 889, 890, 891 | 17.50 | 35.00 |
| MS49 | 2004 (8) | 33,000 | KM#866.3, 868.2, 869.2, 873.2, 874.2, 891, 894, 896, plus Battle of Kōge Bay medal in Nordic gold | 34.50 | 75.00 |
| MS50 | 2005 (8) | 26,700 | KM#866.3, 868.2, 869.2, 873.2, 874.2, 891, 896, 898, plus Battle of Copenhagen medal in Nordic gold | 34.50 | 50.00 |
| MS51 | 2006 (8) | 25,000 | KM#866.3, 868.2, 869.2, 873.2, 874.2, 891, 896, plus Floating Dock medal in Copenhagen sound medal in Nordic gold | 40.00 | 42.00 |
| MS52 | 2006 (8) | 5,000 | KM#866.3, 868.2, 869.2, 873.2, 874.2, 891, 896 plus children's medal in Nordic gold. (Children's coin set). | — | 48.00 |
| MS55 | 2007 (8) | 23,000 | KM#866.3, 868.2, 869.2, 873.2, 874.2, 891, 896 plus Galathea medal in Nordic gold. | — | 42.00 |
| MS56 | 2007 (7) | 2,700 | KM#866.3, 868.2, 869.2, 873.2, 874.2, 891, 896 plus Children's medal in Nordic gold (Children's coin set) | 46.00 | 50.00 |
| MS57 | 2008 (7) | 1,000 | KM#866.3, 868.2, 869.2, 873.2, 874.2, 891, 896 plus Children's medal in Nordic gold (Children's coin set). | — | 50.00 |
| MS58 | 2008 (8) | 20,350 | KM#866.3, 868.2, 869.2, 873.2, 874.2, 891, 896 plus Battle of Kronberg Castle Coast (Elsinore) medal in Nordic gold. | — | 45.00 |
| MS59 | 2009 (6) | 1,450 | KM#866.3, 869.2, 873.2, 874.2, 891, 896 plus Children's medal in Nordic gold (Children's coin set) | — | 65.00 |
| MS60 | 2009 (7) | 24,250 | KM#866.3, 869.2, 873.2, 874.2, 891, 896 plus Neptune admiring Naval fleet medal in Nordic gold. | — | 60.00 |
| MS61 | 2010 (7) | 1,300 | KM#866.3, 869.2, 873.2, 874.2, 891, 896 plus children's medal in Nordic gold (Children's coin set). | — | 45.00 |
| MS62 | 2010 (7) | 23,000 | KM#866.3, 869.2, 873.2, 874.2, 891, 896 plus Danish Navy's first dry dock medal in Nordic gold | — | 45.00 |
| MS63 | 2011 (6) | 1,750 | KM#866.3, 869.2, 873.2, 874.2, 943-944 plus children's medal in Nordic gold. | — | 45.00 |
| MS64 | 2011 (6) | 17,150 | KM#866.3, 869.2, 873.2, 874.2, 943-944 | — | 40.00 |
| MS65 | 2012 (6) | — | KM#866.3, 869.2, 873.2, 874.2, 943, 944 | — | 40.00 |
| MS66 | 2012 (6) | — | KM#866.3, 869.2, 873.2, 874.2, 943, 944, plus Children's medal in Nordic gold (Children's coin set) | — | 45.00 |

## PROOF SETS

| KM# | Date | Mintage | Identification | Issue Price | Mkt Val |
|---|---|---|---|---|---|
| PS1 | 2004 (8) | 3,000 | KM#866.3, 868.2, 869.2, 873.2, 874.2, 891, 896, plus Royal Wedding medal in .925 Silver | 150 | 250 |
| PS2 | 2005 (8) | 2,650 | KM866.3, 868.2, 869.2, 873.2, 874.2, 896, 891 plus 1801 Battle of Copenhagen medal in .925 Silver | 150 | 185 |
| PS3 | 2006 (8) | 1,800 | KM#866.3, 868.2, 869.2, 873.2, 874.2, 896, 891 plus 1691 Floating Dock medal in .925 Silver | 160 | 185 |
| PS4 | 2007 (8) | 1,400 | KM#866.3, 868.2, 869.2, 873.2, 874.2, 896, 891, plus Galathea medal in .925 silver | 160 | 185 |
| PS5 | 2008 (8) | 1,000 | KM#866.3, 868.2, 869.2, 873.2, 874.2, 896, 891, plus medal in .925 Silver | — | 200 |
| PS6 | 2009 (7) | 1,050 | KM#866.3, 869.2, 873.2, 874.2, 891, 896 plus Neptune admiring Naval fleet medal in .925 Silver. | — | 250 |
| PS7 | 2010 (7) | 1,010 | KM#866.3, 869.2, 873.2, 874.2, 891, 896 plus Danish Navy's first dry dock medal in .925 Silver. | — | 185 |
| PS8 | 2011 (2) | 3,010 | KM#943-944 | — | 75.00 |
| PS9 | 2011 (6) | 1,000 | KM#866.3, 869.2, 873.2, 874.2, 943-944 | — | 185 |

# DJIBOUTI

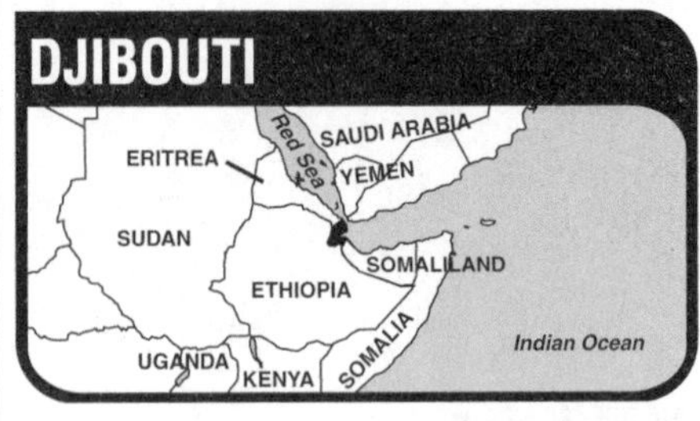


The Republic of Djibouti (formerly French Somaliland and the French Overseas Territory of Afars and Issas), located in northeast Africa at the Bab el Mandeb Strait connecting the Suez Canal and the Red Sea with the Gulf of Aden and the Indian Ocean, has an area of 8,950 sq. mi. (22,000 sq. km.) and a population of 421,320. Capital: Djibouti. The tiny nation has less than one sq. mi. of arable land, and no natural resources except salt, sand, and camels. The commercial activities of the transshipment port of Djibouti and the Addis Abada-Djibouti railroad are the basis of the economy. Salt, fish and hides are exported.

## REPUBLIC

### STANDARD COINAGE

**KM# 23 10 FRANCS**
3.00 g., Aluminum-Bronze, 20 mm. **Obv:** National arms within wreath, date below **Rev:** Boats on water, denomination above **Note:** Varieties exist.

| Date | Mintage | F12 | VF20 | XF40 | MS60 | MS63 |
|---|---|---|---|---|---|---|
| 2004 (a) | — | — | — | — | 2.50 | 4.50 |
| 2007 (a) | — | — | — | — | 2.50 | 4.50 |
| 2010 (a) | — | — | — | — | 2.50 | 4.50 |

**KM# 34 10 FRANCS**
3.40 g., Copper-Nickel, 20.9 mm. **Obv:** National arms **Rev:** Chimpanzee **Edge:** Plain

| Date | Mintage | F12 | VF20 | XF40 | MS60 | MS63 |
|---|---|---|---|---|---|---|
| 2003 | — | — | — | — | 2.00 | 4.00 |

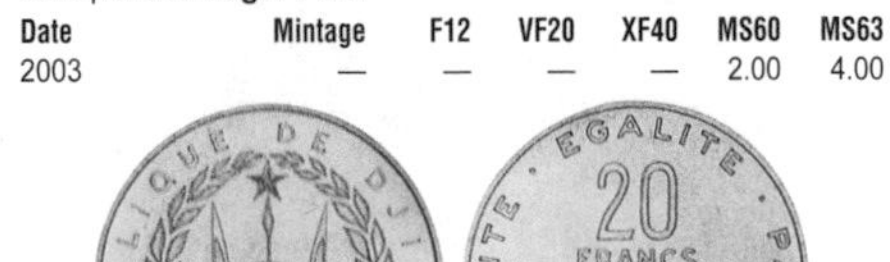

**KM# 24 20 FRANCS**
4.00 g., Aluminum-Bronze, 23.5 mm. **Obv:** National arms within wreath, date below **Rev:** Boats on water, denomination above **Note:** Varieties exist.

| Date | Mintage | F12 | VF20 | XF40 | MS60 | MS63 |
|---|---|---|---|---|---|---|
| 2007 (a) | — | — | — | — | 2.50 | 4.50 |
| 2010 (a) | — | — | — | — | 2.50 | 4.50 |

**KM# 25 50 FRANCS**
7.05 g., Copper-Nickel, 25.7 mm. **Obv:** National arms within wreath, date below **Rev:** Pair of dromedary camels right, denomination above

| Date | Mintage | F12 | VF20 | XF40 | MS60 | MS63 |
|---|---|---|---|---|---|---|
| 2007 (a) | — | — | — | — | 6.00 | 9.00 |
| 2010 (a) | — | — | — | — | 6.00 | 9.00 |

**KM# 26 100 FRANCS**
12.00 g., Copper-Nickel, 30 mm. **Obv:** National arms within wreath, date below **Rev:** Pair of dromedary camels right, denomination above

| Date | Mintage | F12 | VF20 | XF40 | MS60 | MS63 |
|---|---|---|---|---|---|---|
| 2004 (a) | — | — | — | 2.50 | 8.00 | 12.00 |
| 2007 (a) | — | — | — | 2.50 | 8.00 | 11.00 |
| 2010 (a) | — | — | — | 2.50 | 8.00 | 10.00 |

**KM# 38 100 FRANCS**
Nickel Possibly Copper-Nickel-Zinc, confirmation of magnetic quality requested, 35 mm. **Subject:** 25th Anniversary of Independence **Obv:** Small national arms on state flag **Obv. Legend:** REPUBLIQUE DE DJIBOUTI **Rev:** UNITÉ in color **Rev. Legend:** UNITÉ ... ÉGALITÉ ... PAIX

| Date | Mintage | F12 | VF20 | XF40 | MS60 | MS63 |
|---|---|---|---|---|---|---|
| ND-2002 | — | — | — | — | — | 180 |

**KM# 39 100 FRANCS**
Nickel Possibly Copper-Nickel-Zinc, confirmation of magnetic quality requested, 35 mm. **Subject:** 25th Anniversary of Independence **Obv:** Small national arms on state flag **Obv. Legend:** REPUBLIQUE DE DJIBOUTI **Rev:** É/GAL/ITÉ in color **Rev. Legend:** UNITÉ ... ÉGALITÉ ... PAIX

| Date | Mintage | F12 | VF20 | XF40 | MS60 | MS63 |
|---|---|---|---|---|---|---|
| AH-2002 | — | — | — | — | — | 180 |

**KM# 40 100 FRANCS**
Nickel Possibly Copper-Nickel-Zinc, confirmation of magnetic quality requested, 35 mm. **Subject:** 25th Anniversary of Independence **Obv:** Small national arms on state flag **Obv. Legend:** REPUBLIQUE DE DJIBOUTI **Rev:** PAI/X in color **Rev. Legend:** UNITÉ ... ÉGALITÉ ... PAIX

| Date | Mintage | F12 | VF20 | XF40 | MS60 | MS63 |
|---|---|---|---|---|---|---|
| ND-2002 | — | — | — | — | — | 180 |

**KM# 41 250 FRANCS**
22.20 g., 0.900 Silver 0.6424 oz. ASW **Obv:** National arms **Obv. Legend:** REPUBLIQUE DE DJIBOUTI **Rev:** Two dromedary camels right **Rev. Legend:** UNITÉ - ÉGALITÉ - PAIX

| Date | Mintage | F12 | VF20 | XF40 | MS60 | MS63 |
|---|---|---|---|---|---|---|
| 2002 (a) Proof | — | — | — | — | — | — |

Note: Confirmation requested

**KM# 42 250 FRANCS**
10.00 g., Bi-Metallic Copper-Nickel center in Aluminum-Bronze ring **Obv:** National arms **Rev:** Djibouti bird **Rev. Legend:** UNITE EGALITE PAIX

| Date | Mintage | F12 | VF20 | XF40 | MS60 | MS63 |
|---|---|---|---|---|---|---|
| 2012 | — | — | — | 5.00 | 9.00 | 12.00 |

**KM# 27 500 FRANCS**
Aluminum-Bronze **Obv:** National arms within wreath, date below **Rev:** Denomination within sprays

| Date | Mintage | VF20 | XF40 | MS60 | MS63 | MS65 |
|---|---|---|---|---|---|---|
| 2010 (a) | — | — | 5.00 | 8.00 | 12.00 | 15.00 |

# DOMINICAN REPUBLIC

The Dominican Republic, which occupies the eastern two-thirds of the island of Hispaniola, has an area of 18,704 sq. mi. (48,734 sq. km.) and a population of 7.9 million. Capital: Santo Domingo. The largely agricultural economy produces sugar, coffee, tobacco and cocoa. Tourism and casino gaming are also a rising source of revenue.

## REPUBLIC

### REFORM COINAGE

1937: 100 Centavos = 1 Peso Oro

**KM# 80.2 PESO**
6.49 g., Brass, 25 mm. **Subject:** Juan Pablo Duarte **Obv:** National arms and denomination **Rev:** DUARTE below bust, date below **Note:** Coin die alignment.

| Date | Mintage | VF20 | XF40 | MS60 | MS63 | MS65 |
|---|---|---|---|---|---|---|
| 2002 | — | — | — | 2.00 | 2.50 | 3.50 |
| 2005 | — | — | — | 2.00 | 2.50 | 3.50 |
| 2008 | — | — | — | 2.00 | 2.50 | 3.50 |

**KM# 90 PESO**
12.50 g., Copper-Nickel, 30.6 mm. **Obv:** Pan American Games logo **Rev:** National arms and denomination **Edge:** Reeded

| Date | Mintage | VF20 | XF40 | MS60 | MS63 | MS65 |
|---|---|---|---|---|---|---|
| 2003 | — | PF63 12.00 | PF65 15.00 | | | |

**KM# 89 5 PESOS**
6.06 g., Bi-Metallic Stainless Steel center in Brass ring, 23 mm. **Subject:** Sanchez **Obv:** National arms and denomination **Rev:** Portrait facing within circle, date below **Edge:** Segmented reeding

| Date | Mintage | VF20 | XF40 | MS60 | MS63 | MS65 |
|---|---|---|---|---|---|---|
| 2002 | — | — | — | 2.50 | 3.00 | 4.50 |
| 2005 | — | — | — | 2.50 | 3.00 | 4.50 |
| 2007 | — | — | — | 2.50 | 3.00 | 4.50 |
| 2008 | — | — | — | 2.50 | 3.00 | 4.50 |

**KM# 106 10 PESOS**
8.20 g., Bi-Metallic Brass center in Copper-Nickel ring, 27 mm. **Obv:** Value at left of national arms **Obv. Legend:** • REPUBLICA DOMINICANA • **Rev:** Bust of General Mella facing **Rev. Legend:** BANCO CENTRAL DE LA REPUBLICA DOMINICANA **Edge:** Segmented reeding

| Date | Mintage | VF20 | XF40 | MS60 | MS63 | MS65 |
|---|---|---|---|---|---|---|
| 2005 | — | — | — | 4.00 | 6.00 | 8.00 |
| 2007 | — | — | — | 4.00 | 6.00 | 8.00 |
| 2008 | — | — | — | 4.00 | 6.00 | 8.00 |
| 2010 | — | — | — | 4.00 | 6.00 | 8.00 |

**KM# 107 25 PESOS**
8.56 g., Copper-Nickel, 28.82 mm. **Obv:** Value at left of national arms **Obv. Legend:** REPUBLICA DOMINICANA **Rev:** Bust of General Luperon facing **Rev. Legend:** BANCO CENTRAL DE LA REPUBLICA DOMINICANA **Rev. Inscription:** HEROE DE LA RESTAURACION **Edge:** Reeded

| Date | Mintage | VF20 | XF40 | MS60 | MS63 | MS65 |
|---|---|---|---|---|---|---|
| 2005 | — | — | — | 3.00 | 5.00 | 7.00 |
| 2008 | — | — | — | 3.00 | 5.00 | 7.00 |
| 2010 | — | — | — | 3.00 | 5.00 | 7.00 |

# EAST CARIBBEAN STATES

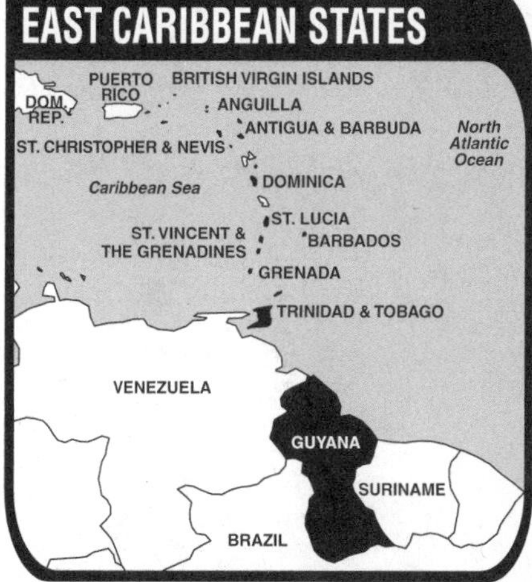


The East Caribbean States, formerly the British Caribbean Territories (Eastern Group), formed a currency board in 1950 to provide the constituent territories of Trinidad & Tobago, Barbados, British Guiana (now Guyana), British Virgin Islands, Anguilla, St. Kitts, Nevis, Antigua, Dominica, St. Lucia, St. Vincent and Grenada with a common currency, thereby permitting withdrawal of the regular British Pound currency. This was dissolved in 1965 and after the breakup, the East Caribbean Territories, a grouping including Barbados, the Leeward and Windward Islands, came into being. Coinage of the dissolved 'Eastern Group' continues to circulate. Paper currency of the East Caribbean Authority was first issued in 1965 and although Barbados withdrew from the group they continued using them prior to 1973 when Barbados issued a decimal coinage.

A series of 4-dollar coins tied to the FAO coinage program were released in 1970 under the name of the Caribbean Development Bank by eight loosely federated island groupings in the eastern Caribbean. These issues are listed individually in this volume under Antigua, Barbados, Dominica, Grenada, Montserrat, St. Kitts, St. Lucia and St. Vincent.

## STANDARD COINAGE

100 Cents = 1 Dollar

### KM# 10 CENT

0.90 g., Aluminum, 18.4 mm. **Ruler:** Elizabeth II **Obv:** Young bust right **Rev:** Wreath divides denomination, date upper right **Shape:** Scalloped **Note:** Prev. KM#1.

| Date | Mintage | VF20 | XF40 | MS60 | MS63 | MS65 |
|---|---|---|---|---|---|---|
| 2001 | — | — | — | 0.20 | 0.30 | 0.40 |

### KM# 34 CENT

1.03 g., Aluminum, 18.42 mm. **Ruler:** Elizabeth II **Obv:** Crowned head right **Rev:** Denomination **Edge:** Plain

| Date | Mintage | VF20 | XF40 | MS60 | MS63 | MS65 |
|---|---|---|---|---|---|---|
| 2002 | — | — | — | 0.20 | 0.30 | 0.40 |
| 2004 | — | — | — | 0.20 | 0.30 | 0.40 |
| 2008 | — | — | — | 0.20 | 0.30 | 0.40 |
| 2011 | — | — | — | 0.20 | 0.30 | 0.40 |

### KM# 35 2 CENTS

1.42 g., Aluminum, 21.46 mm. **Ruler:** Elizabeth II **Obv:** Crowned head right **Rev:** Denomination **Edge:** Plain

| Date | Mintage | VF20 | XF40 | MS60 | MS63 | MS65 |
|---|---|---|---|---|---|---|
| 2002 | — | — | — | 0.25 | 0.35 | 0.50 |
| 2004 | — | — | — | 0.25 | 0.35 | 0.50 |
| 2008 | — | — | — | 0.25 | 0.35 | 0.50 |

### KM# 36 5 CENTS

1.74 g., Aluminum, 23.11 mm. **Ruler:** Elizabeth II **Obv:** Crowned head right **Rev:** Denomination **Edge:** Plain

| Date | Mintage | VF20 | XF40 | MS60 | MS63 | MS65 |
|---|---|---|---|---|---|---|
| 2002 | — | — | — | 0.30 | 0.45 | 0.65 |
| 2004 | — | — | — | 0.30 | 0.45 | 0.65 |
| 2008 | — | — | — | 0.30 | 0.45 | 0.65 |
| 2010 | — | — | — | 0.30 | 0.45 | 0.65 |

### KM# 37 10 CENTS

2.59 g., Copper-Nickel, 18.06 mm. **Ruler:** Elizabeth II **Obv:** Crowned head right **Rev:** Sir Francis Drake's Golden Hind and denomination **Edge:** Reeded

| Date | Mintage | VF20 | XF40 | MS60 | MS63 | MS65 |
|---|---|---|---|---|---|---|
| 2002 | — | — | — | 0.40 | 0.60 | 0.75 |
| 2004 | — | — | — | 0.40 | 0.60 | 0.75 |
| 2007 | — | — | — | 0.40 | 0.60 | 0.75 |

### KM# 37a 10 CENTS

Nickel Plated Steel, 18 mm. **Ruler:** Elizabeth II **Obv:** Crowned head right **Rev:** Sir Francis Drake's Golden Hind and denomination **Edge:** Reeded

| Date | Mintage | VF20 | XF40 | MS60 | MS63 | MS65 |
|---|---|---|---|---|---|---|
| 2009 | — | — | — | 0.40 | 0.60 | 0.75 |

### KM# 38 25 CENTS

6.48 g., Copper-Nickel, 23.98 mm. **Ruler:** Elizabeth II **Obv:** Crowned head right **Rev:** Sir Francis Drake's Golden Hind and denomination **Edge:** Reeded

| Date | Mintage | VF20 | XF40 | MS60 | MS63 | MS65 |
|---|---|---|---|---|---|---|
| 2002 | — | — | — | 0.50 | 0.75 | 1.00 |
| 2004 | — | — | — | 0.50 | 0.75 | 1.00 |
| 2007 | — | — | — | 0.50 | 0.75 | 1.00 |

### KM# 38a 25 CENTS

Nickel Plated Steel, 24 mm. **Ruler:** Elizabeth II **Obv:** Crowned head right **Rev:** Sir Francis Drake's Golden Hind and denomination **Edge:** Reeded

| Date | Mintage | VF20 | XF40 | MS60 | MS63 | MS65 |
|---|---|---|---|---|---|---|
| 2010 | — | — | — | 0.50 | 0.75 | 1.00 |

### KM# 39 DOLLAR

7.98 g., Copper-Nickel, 26.5 mm. **Ruler:** Elizabeth II **Obv:** Crowned head right **Rev:** Sir Francis Drake's Golden Hind and denomination **Edge:** Segmented reeding

| Date | Mintage | VF20 | XF40 | MS60 | MS63 | MS65 |
|---|---|---|---|---|---|---|
| 2002 | — | — | — | 2.00 | 2.50 | 3.00 |
| 2004 | — | — | — | 2.00 | 2.50 | 3.00 |
| 2007 | — | — | — | 2.00 | 2.50 | 3.00 |

### KM# 40 DOLLAR

28.28 g., Copper-Nickel Gilt, 38.6 mm. **Ruler:** Elizabeth II **Subject:** Golden Jubilee Monarchs **Obv:** Crowned head right **Rev:** Henry III (1216-1277) **Edge:** Reeded

| Date | Mintage | VF20 | XF40 | MS60 | MS63 | MS65 |
|---|---|---|---|---|---|---|
| 2002 | 5,000 | — | — | 20.00 | 22.50 | 25.00 |

### KM# 42 DOLLAR

28.28 g., Copper-Nickel Gilt, 38.6 mm. **Ruler:** Elizabeth II **Subject:** Golden Jubilee Monarchs **Obv:** Crowned head right **Rev:** Edward III (1327-1377) **Edge:** Reeded

| Date | Mintage | VF20 | XF40 | MS60 | MS63 | MS65 |
|---|---|---|---|---|---|---|
| 2002 | 5,000 | — | — | 20.00 | 22.50 | 25.00 |

### KM# 44 DOLLAR

28.28 g., Copper-Nickel Gilt, 38.6 mm. **Ruler:** Elizabeth II **Subject:** Golden Jubilee Monarchs **Obv:** Crowned head right **Rev:** George III (1760-1820) **Edge:** Reeded

| Date | Mintage | VF20 | XF40 | MS60 | MS63 | MS65 |
|---|---|---|---|---|---|---|
| 2002 | 5,000 | — | — | 20.00 | 22.50 | 25.00 |

### KM# 46 DOLLAR

28.28 g., Copper-Nickel Gilt, 38.6 mm. **Ruler:** Elizabeth II **Subject:** Golden Jubilee Monarchs **Obv:** Crowned head right **Rev:** Queen Victoria (1837-1901) **Edge:** Reeded

| Date | Mintage | VF20 | XF40 | MS60 | MS63 | MS65 |
|---|---|---|---|---|---|---|
| 2002 | 5,000 | — | — | 20.00 | 22.50 | 25.00 |

### KM# 48 DOLLAR

28.28 g., Copper-Nickel Gilt, 38.6 mm. **Ruler:** Elizabeth II **Subject:** Golden Jubilee Monarchs **Obv:** Crowned head right **Rev:** Queen Elizabeth II (1952- ) **Edge:** Reeded

| Date | Mintage | VF20 | XF40 | MS60 | MS63 | MS65 |
|---|---|---|---|---|---|---|
| 2002 | 5,000 | — | — | 20.00 | 22.50 | 25.00 |

### KM# 86 DOLLAR

27.73 g., Copper-Nickel, 38.5 mm. **Ruler:** Elizabeth II **Subject:** Coronation Jubilee **Obv:** Crowned head right **Rev:** Fireworks display above building **Edge:** Reeded

| Date | Mintage | VF20 | XF40 | MS60 | MS63 | MS65 |
|---|---|---|---|---|---|---|
| 2002 | — | — | — | 7.00 | 10.00 | 12.00 |

### KM# 58 DOLLAR

7.98 g., Copper-Nickel, 26.5 mm. **Ruler:** Elizabeth II **Subject:** 25th Anniversary **Obv:** Head right **Rev:** Motto within wreath

| Date | Mintage | VF20 | XF40 | MS60 | MS63 | MS65 |
|---|---|---|---|---|---|---|
| 2008 | 500,000 | — | — | — | 5.00 | 7.00 |

### KM# 51 2 DOLLARS

56.56 g., Copper-Nickel Gilt, 38.6 mm. **Ruler:** Elizabeth II **Subject:** British Military Leaders **Obv:** Crowned head right **Rev:** Wellington's portrait and battle scene **Edge:** Reeded

| Date | Mintage | VF20 | XF40 | MS60 | MS63 | MS65 |
|---|---|---|---|---|---|---|
| 2002 | 10,000 | PF63 35.00 | PF65 45.00 | | | |

### KM# 54 2 DOLLARS

56.56 g., Copper-Nickel Gilt, 38.6 mm. **Ruler:** Elizabeth II **Subject:** British Military Leaders **Obv:** Crowned head right **Rev:** Admiral Nelson's portrait and naval battle scene **Edge:** Reeded

| Date | Mintage | VF20 | XF40 | MS60 | MS63 | MS65 |
|---|---|---|---|---|---|---|
| 2003 | 10,000 | PF63 35.00 | PF65 45.00 | | | |

### KM# 57 2 DOLLARS

56.56 g., Copper-Nickel Gilt, 38.6 mm. **Ruler:** Elizabeth II **Subject:** British Military Leaders **Obv:** Crowned head right **Rev:** Churchill's portrait and air battle scene **Edge:** Reeded

| Date | Mintage | VF20 | XF40 | MS60 | MS63 | MS65 |
|---|---|---|---|---|---|---|
| 2003 | 10,000 | PF63 35.00 | PF65 45.00 | | | |

### KM# 60 2 DOLLARS

Copper-Nickel, 38.6 mm. **Ruler:** Elizabeth II **Subject:** Financial Information Month **Obv:** Head in tiara right **Rev:** Tree seedling growing in palm of hand

| Date | Mintage | VF20 | XF40 | MS60 | MS63 | MS65 |
|---|---|---|---|---|---|---|
| 2011 | — | PF63 35.00 | PF65 45.00 | | | |

### KM# 87 2 DOLLARS

11.35 g., Copper-Nickel, 30 mm. **Ruler:** Elizabeth II **Subject:** Financial Information Month, 10th Anniversary **Rev:** Hands holding tree **Edge:** Reeded

| Date | Mintage | VF20 | XF40 | MS60 | MS63 | MS65 |
|---|---|---|---|---|---|---|
| 2011 | — | — | — | 4.00 | 5.00 | 6.00 |

### KM# 61 8 DOLLARS

Copper-Nickel, 38.61 mm. **Ruler:** Elizabeth II **Subject:** OECS Economic Union **Obv:** Head in tiara right **Rev:** Flags in color

| Date | Mintage | VF20 | XF40 | MS60 | MS63 | MS65 |
|---|---|---|---|---|---|---|
| 2011 | — | PF65 100 | | | | |

### KM# 41 10 DOLLARS

28.28 g., 0.925 Silver 0.841 oz. ASW with gold cameo, 38.6 mm. **Ruler:** Elizabeth II **Subject:** Golden Jubilee Monarchs **Obv:** Crowned head right **Rev:** Henry III (1216-1272) **Edge:** Reeded

| Date | Mintage | VF20 | XF40 | MS60 | MS63 | MS65 |
|---|---|---|---|---|---|---|
| 2002 | 10,000 | PF65 65.00 | | | | |

### KM# 41a 10 DOLLARS

39.94 g., 0.9166 Gold 1.177 oz. AGW, 38.6 mm. **Ruler:** Elizabeth II **Subject:** Golden Jubilee Monarchs **Obv:** Crowned head right **Rev:** Henry III (1216-1272) **Edge:** Reeded

| Date | Mintage | VF20 | XF40 | MS60 | MS63 | MS65 |
|---|---|---|---|---|---|---|
| 2002 | 100 | PF65 2,150 | | | | |

### KM# 43 10 DOLLARS

28.28 g., 0.925 Silver 0.841 oz. ASW, 38.6 mm. **Ruler:** Elizabeth II **Subject:** Golden Jubile Monarchs **Obv:** Crowned head right **Rev:** Edward III (1327-1377) **Edge:** Reeded

| Date | Mintage | VF20 | XF40 | MS60 | MS63 | MS65 |
|---|---|---|---|---|---|---|
| 2002 | 10,000 | PF65 65.00 | | | | |

### KM# 43a 10 DOLLARS

39.94 g., 0.9166 Gold 1.177 oz. AGW, 38.6 mm. **Ruler:** Elizabeth II **Subject:** Golden Jubilee Monarchs **Obv:** Crowned head right **Rev:** Edward III (1327-1377) **Edge:** Reeded

| Date | Mintage | VF20 | XF40 | MS60 | MS63 | MS65 |
|---|---|---|---|---|---|---|
| 2002 | 100 | PF65 2,150 | | | | |

### KM# 45 10 DOLLARS

28.28 g., 0.925 Silver 0.841 oz. ASW with gold cameo, 38.6 mm. **Subject:** Golden Jubilee Monarchs **Obv:** Crowned head right **Rev:** George III (1760-1820) **Edge:** Reeded

| Date | Mintage | VF20 | XF40 | MS60 | MS63 | MS65 |
|---|---|---|---|---|---|---|
| 2002 | 10,000 | PF65 65.00 | | | | |

### KM# 45a 10 DOLLARS

39.94 g., 0.9166 Gold 1.177 oz. AGW, 38.6 mm. **Ruler:** Elizabeth II **Subject:** Golden Jubilee Monarchs **Obv:** Crowned head right **Rev:** George III (1760-1820) **Edge:** Reeded

| Date | Mintage | VF20 | XF40 | MS60 | MS63 | MS65 |
|---|---|---|---|---|---|---|
| 2002 | 100 | PF65 2,150 | | | | |

**KM# 47 10 DOLLARS**
28.28 g., 0.925 Silver 0.841 oz. ASW with partial gold plating, 38.6 mm. **Ruler:** Elizabeth II **Subject:** Golden Jubilee Monarchs **Obv:** Crowned head right **Rev:** Queen Victoria (1837-1901) **Edge:** Reeded

| Date | Mintage | VF20 | XF40 | MS60 | MS63 | MS65 |
|---|---|---|---|---|---|---|
| 2002 | 10,000 | PF65 65.00 | | | | |

**KM# 47a 10 DOLLARS**
39.94 g., 0.9166 Gold 1.177 oz. AGW, 38.6 mm. **Ruler:** Elizabeth II **Subject:** Golden Jubilee Monarchs **Obv:** Crowned head right **Rev:** Queen Victoria (1837-1901) **Edge:** Reeded

| Date | Mintage | VF20 | XF40 | MS60 | MS63 | MS65 |
|---|---|---|---|---|---|---|
| 2002 | 100 | PF65 2,150 | | | | |

**KM# 49 10 DOLLARS**
28.28 g., 0.925 Silver 0.841 oz. ASW with gold cameo, 38.6 mm. **Ruler:** Elizabeth II **Subject:** Golden Jubilee Monarchs **Obv:** Crowned head right **Rev:** Queen Elizabeth II (1952- ) **Edge:** Reeded

| Date | Mintage | VF20 | XF40 | MS60 | MS63 | MS65 |
|---|---|---|---|---|---|---|
| 2002 | 10,000 | PF65 65.00 | | | | |

**KM# 49a 10 DOLLARS**
39.94 g., 0.9166 Gold 1.177 oz. AGW, 38.6 mm. **Ruler:** Elizabeth II **Subject:** Golden Jubilee Monarchs **Obv:** Crowned head right **Rev:** Queen Elizabeth II (1952- ) **Edge:** Reeded

| Date | Mintage | VF20 | XF40 | MS60 | MS63 | MS65 |
|---|---|---|---|---|---|---|
| 2002 | 100 | PF65 2,150 | | | | |

**KM# 59 10 DOLLARS**
Silver partially gilt, 39 mm. **Ruler:** Elizabeth II **Obv:** Head right, partially gilt **Rev:** Fireworks display above Buckingham Palace

| Date | Mintage | VF20 | XF40 | MS60 | MS63 | MS65 |
|---|---|---|---|---|---|---|
| 2002 | — | PF63 45.00 | PF65 50.00 | | | |

**KM# 88 10 DOLLARS**
28.28 g., 0.925 Silver 0.841 oz. ASW, 38.61 mm. **Ruler:** Elizabeth II **Subject:** Queen Elizabeth II Celebration **Shape:** 7-Sided

| Date | Mintage | VF20 | XF40 | MS60 | MS63 | MS65 |
|---|---|---|---|---|---|---|
| 2007 | Est. 30000 | PF63 32.00 | PF65 40.00 | | | |

**KM# 89 10 DOLLARS**
28.28 g., 0.925 Silver 0.841 oz. ASW, 38.61 mm. **Ruler:** Elizabeth II **Subject:** Queen Elizabeth II - Country Life **Shape:** 7-Sided

| Date | Mintage | VF20 | XF40 | MS60 | MS63 | MS65 |
|---|---|---|---|---|---|---|
| 2007 | Est. 30000 | PF63 32.00 | PF65 40.00 | | | |

**KM# 90 10 DOLLARS**
28.28 g., 0.925 Silver 0.841 oz. ASW, 38.61 mm. **Ruler:** Elizabeth II **Subject:** Queen Elizabeth II 60th Wedding Anniversary **Shape:** 7-Sided

| Date | Mintage | VF20 | XF40 | MS60 | MS63 | MS65 |
|---|---|---|---|---|---|---|
| 2007 | Est. 30000 | PF63 32.00 | PF65 40.00 | | | |

**KM# 91 10 DOLLARS**
28.28 g., 0.925 Silver 0.841 oz. ASW, 38.6 mm. **Ruler:** Elizabeth II **Rev:** Military colors and trumpants **Rev. Legend:** THE COLOURS THAT I AM PRESENTING TO YOU

| Date | Mintage | VF20 | XF40 | MS60 | MS63 | MS65 |
|---|---|---|---|---|---|---|
| 2012 | — | PF65 75.00 | | | | |

# EAST TIMOR

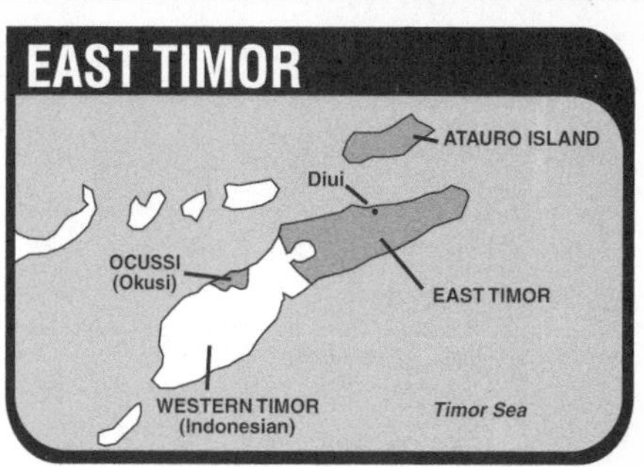


East Timor, population: 522,433, area: 7332 sq. miles, capital: Dili, is primarily located on the eastern half of the island of Timor, just northwest of Australia at the eastern end of the Indonesian archipelago. Formerly a Portuguese colony, Timor declared its independence from Portugal on November 28, 1975. After nine short days of fledgling autonomy, a guerilla faction sympathetic to the Indonesian territorial claim to East Timor seized the government. On July 17, 1976 the Provisional government enacted a law, which dissolved the free republic and made East Timor the 24th province of Indonesia. Violent rule and civil unrest plagued the province, with great loss of life and extreme damage to property and natural resources until independence was again achieved with United Nations assistance during a period from 1999 to 2002. Emerging as the Democratic Republic of Timor-Leste and commonly known as East Timor the country has worked, with international assistance to rebuild its decimated infrastructure. Natural resources waiting to be tapped include rich oil reserves, though current exports are most dependent on coffee, sandalwood and marble. The first coins of the new republic were issued in 2003.

## DEMOCRATIC REPUBLIC OF TIMOR-LESTE

### DECIMAL COINAGE

**KM# 1 CENTAVO**
3.10 g., Nickel Clad Steel, 17 mm. **Obv:** Nautilus above date **Rev:** Denomination within circle **Edge:** Plain

| Date | Mintage | VF20 | XF40 | MS60 | MS63 | MS65 |
|---|---|---|---|---|---|---|
| 2003 | 1,500,000 | — | — | 1.50 | 2.00 | 2.50 |
| 2003 | 12,500 | PF65 8.00 | | | | |
| 2004 | 1,500,000 | — | — | 1.50 | 2.00 | 2.50 |
| 2005 | — | — | — | 1.50 | 2.00 | 2.50 |
| 2005 | 12,500 | PF65 8.00 | | | | |
| 2012 | — | — | — | 1.50 | 2.00 | 2.50 |
| 2012 | 2,000 | PF65 8.00 | | | | |

**KM# 2 5 CENTAVOS**
4.10 g., Nickel Clad Steel, 18.75 mm. **Obv:** Rice plant above date **Rev:** Denomination within circle **Edge:** Plain

| Date | Mintage | VF20 | XF40 | MS60 | MS63 | MS65 |
|---|---|---|---|---|---|---|
| 2003 | 1,500,000 | — | — | 2.00 | 2.50 | 3.00 |
| 2003 | 12,500 | PF65 10.00 | | | | |
| 2004 | 1,500,000 | — | — | 2.00 | 2.50 | 3.00 |
| 2005 | — | — | — | 2.00 | 2.50 | 3.00 |
| 2005 | 12,500 | PF65 10.00 | | | | |
| 2006 | — | — | — | 2.00 | 2.50 | 3.00 |
| 2010 | — | — | — | 2.00 | 2.50 | 3.00 |
| 2012 | — | — | — | 2.00 | 2.50 | 3.00 |
| 2012 | 2,000 | PF65 10.00 | | | | |

**KM# 3 10 CENTAVOS**
5.20 g., Nickel Clad Steel, 20.75 mm. **Obv:** Rooster left above date **Rev:** Denomination within circle **Edge:** Plain

| Date | Mintage | VF20 | XF40 | MS60 | MS63 | MS65 |
|---|---|---|---|---|---|---|
| 2003 | 2,500,000 | — | — | 2.50 | 3.25 | 4.00 |
| 2003 | 12,500 | PF65 12.00 | | | | |
| 2004 | 2,500,000 | — | — | 2.50 | 3.25 | 4.00 |
| 2005 | — | — | — | 2.50 | 3.25 | 4.00 |
| 2005 | 12,500 | PF65 12.00 | | | | |
| 2006 | — | — | — | 2.50 | 3.25 | 4.00 |
| 2010 | — | — | — | 2.50 | 3.25 | 4.00 |
| 2011 | — | — | — | 2.50 | 3.25 | 4.00 |
| 2012 | — | — | — | 2.50 | 3.25 | 4.00 |
| 2012 | — | PF65 12.00 | | | | |

**KM# 4 25 CENTAVOS**
5.85 g., Nickel-Brass, 21.25 mm. **Obv:** Sail boat above date **Rev:** Denomination within circle **Edge:** Reeded

| Date | Mintage | VF20 | XF40 | MS60 | MS63 | MS65 |
|---|---|---|---|---|---|---|
| 2003 | 1,500,000 | — | — | 2.50 | 3.50 | 5.00 |
| 2003 | 12,500 | PF65 16.00 | | | | |
| 2004 | 1,500,000 | — | — | 3.00 | 4.00 | 5.00 |
| 2005 | — | — | — | 3.00 | 4.00 | 5.00 |
| 2005 | 12,500 | PF65 16.00 | | | | |
| 2006 | — | — | — | 3.00 | 4.00 | 5.00 |
| 2011 | — | — | — | 3.00 | 4.00 | 5.00 |
| 2012 | — | — | — | 3.00 | 4.00 | 5.00 |
| 2012 | 2,000 | PF65 16.00 | | | | |

**KM# 5 50 CENTAVOS**
6.50 g., Nickel-Brass, 25 mm. **Obv:** Coffee plant with beans above date **Rev:** Denomination within circle **Edge:** Reeded

| Date | Mintage | VF20 | XF40 | MS60 | MS63 | MS65 |
|---|---|---|---|---|---|---|
| 2003 | 1,000,000 | — | — | 5.00 | 6.00 | 7.00 |
| 2003 | 12,500 | PF65 22.00 | | | | |
| 2004 | 1,000,000 | — | — | 5.00 | 6.00 | 7.00 |
| 2005 | — | — | — | 5.00 | 6.00 | 7.00 |
| 2005 | 12,500 | PF65 22.00 | | | | |
| 2006 | — | — | — | 5.00 | 6.00 | 7.00 |
| 2011 | — | — | — | 5.00 | 6.00 | 7.00 |
| 2012 | — | — | — | 5.00 | 6.00 | 7.00 |
| 2012 | 2,000 | PF65 22.00 | | | | |

**KM# 6 50 CENTAVOS**
Nickel-Brass

| Date | Mintage | VF20 | XF40 | MS60 | MS63 | MS65 |
|---|---|---|---|---|---|---|
| 2012 | — | — | — | 10.00 | 12.00 | 15.00 |
| 2012 | 2,000 | PF65 25.00 | | | | |

## MINT SETS

| KM# | Date | Mintage | Identification | Issue Price | Mkt Val |
|---|---|---|---|---|---|
| MS1 | 2003 (5) | 25,000 | KM#1-5 | 27.84 | 35.00 |
| MS2 | 2004 (5) | 25,000 | KM#1-5 | — | 35.00 |
| MS3 | 2012 (6) | 2,000 | KM#1-6 | — | 45.00 |

## PROOF SETS

| KM# | Date | Mintage | Identification | Issue Price | Mkt Val |
|---|---|---|---|---|---|
| PS1 | 2003 (5) | 12,500 | KM#1-5 | 57.25 | 70.00 |
| PS2 | 2005 (5) | 12,500 | KM#1-5 | — | 82.00 |
| PS3 | 2012 (6) | 2,000 | KM#1-6 | — | 95.00 |

# ECUADOR

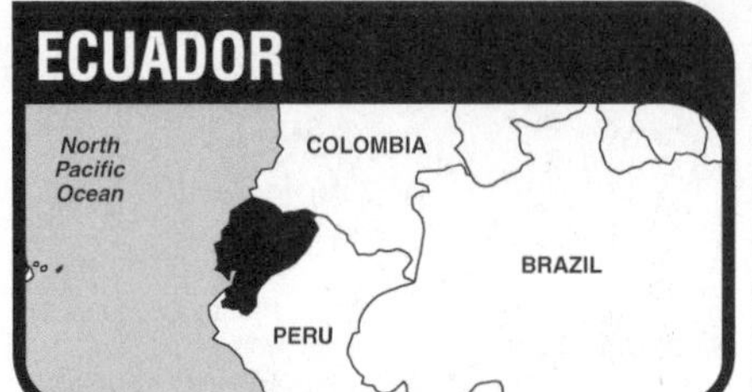


The Republic of Ecuador, located astride the equator on the Pacific Coast of South America, has an area of 105,037 sq. mi. (283,560 sq. km.) and a population of 10.9 million. Capital: Quito. Agriculture is the mainstay of the economy but there are appreciable deposits of minerals and petroleum. It is one of the world's largest exporters of bananas and balsa wood. Coffee, cacao, sugar and petroleum are also valuable exports.

## REPUBLIC

### REFORM COINAGE

100 Centavos = 1 Dollar

**KM# 104 CENTAVO (UN)**
2.52 g., Brass, 19 mm. **Obv:** Map of the Americas within circle **Rev:** Denomination **Edge:** Plain

| Date | Mintage | VF20 | XF40 | MS60 | MS63 | MS65 |
|---|---|---|---|---|---|---|
| 2003 | — | — | — | 0.20 | 0.40 | 0.50 |
| 2004 | — | — | — | 0.20 | 0.40 | 0.50 |

**KM# 104a CENTAVO (UN)**
2.42 g., Copper Plated Steel, 19 mm. **Obv:** Map of the Americas **Rev:** Denomination **Edge:** Plain

| Date | Mintage | VF20 | XF40 | MS60 | MS63 | MS65 |
|---|---|---|---|---|---|---|
| 2003 | — | — | — | 0.30 | 0.50 | 0.70 |

**KM# 105 5 CENTAVOS (CINCO)**
5.00 g., Steel, 21.2 mm. **Subject:** Juan Montalvo **Obv:** Bust 3/4 facing and arms **Rev:** Denomination **Edge:** Plain

| Date | Mintage | VF20 | XF40 | MS60 | MS63 | MS65 |
|---|---|---|---|---|---|---|
| 2003 | — | — | — | 0.50 | 0.75 | 1.00 |

**KM# 115 SUCRE (UN)**
8.36 g., 0.900 Gold 0.2419 oz. AGW, 22 mm. **Subject:** Homage to Jefferson Pérez Quezada **Obv:** National arms **Obv. Legend:** BANCO CENTRAL DEL ECUADOR **Rev:** 3/4 length figure of Perez running **Rev. Legend:** BICAMPEON MUNDIAL - CAMPEON OLIMPICO ATLANTA 1996

| Date | Mintage | VF20 | XF40 | MS60 | MS63 | MS65 |
|---|---|---|---|---|---|---|
| 2006 | — | PF65 450 | | | | |

**KM# 118 SUCRE (UN)**
8.36 g., 0.900 Gold 0.2419 oz. AGW, 13.9 mm. **Subject:** World Cup Soccer **Obv:** National arms **Rev:** Ecuadorian Soccer player holding a soccer ball

| Date | Mintage | VF20 | XF40 | MS60 | MS63 | MS65 |
|---|---|---|---|---|---|---|
| 2006 | — | PF65 150 | | | | |

**KM# 119 SUCRE (UN)**
27.10 g., 0.925 Silver 0.8059 oz. ASW, 40 mm. **Obv:** National arms within circle of other state arms **Rev:** Runner on track

| Date | Mintage | VF20 | XF40 | MS60 | MS63 | MS65 |
|---|---|---|---|---|---|---|
| 2007 | — | PF65 60.00 | | | | |

**KM# 116 SUCRE (UN)**
31.10 g., 0.999 Silver 0.9989 oz. ASW, 39 mm. **Subject:** Independence 200th Anniversary

| Date | Mintage | VF20 | XF40 | MS60 | MS63 | MS65 |
|---|---|---|---|---|---|---|
| 2009 | 200 | PF65 75.00 | | | | |

**KM# 117 SUCRE (UN)**
31.10 g., 0.999 Silver 0.9989 oz. ASW, 39 mm. **Subject:** Massacre, 200th Anniversary

| Date | Mintage | VF20 | XF40 | MS60 | MS63 | MS65 |
|---|---|---|---|---|---|---|
| 2010 | — | PF65 100 | | | | |

**KM# 112 25000 SUCRES**
27.10 g., 0.925 Silver 0.8059 oz. ASW, 40 mm. **Subject:** IBERO-AMERICA Series **Obv:** Coats of arms **Rev:** Balsawood sailing raft **Edge:** Reeded

| Date | Mintage | VF20 | XF40 | MS60 | MS63 | MS65 |
|---|---|---|---|---|---|---|
| 2002 | — | PF60 30.00 | PF63 45.00 | PF65 60.00 | | |

**KM# 113 25000 SUCRES**
27.00 g., 0.925 Silver 0.803 oz. ASW, 40 mm. **Obv:** National arms **Rev:** Capital building in Quito **Edge:** Reeded

| Date | Mintage | VF20 | XF40 | MS60 | MS63 | MS65 |
|---|---|---|---|---|---|---|
| 2004 | 1,000 | PF60 45.00 | PF63 60.00 | PF65 75.00 | | |

**KM# 114 25000 SUCRES**
27.20 g., 0.925 Silver 0.8089 oz. ASW, 40 mm. **Subject:** 2006 World Cup Soccer **Obv:** National arms **Rev:** Ecuadorian Soccer player torso holding a soccer ball **Edge:** Reeded

| Date | Mintage | VF20 | XF40 | MS60 | MS63 | MS65 |
|---|---|---|---|---|---|---|
| ND(2006) | — | PF60 35.00 | PF63 45.00 | PF65 55.00 | | |

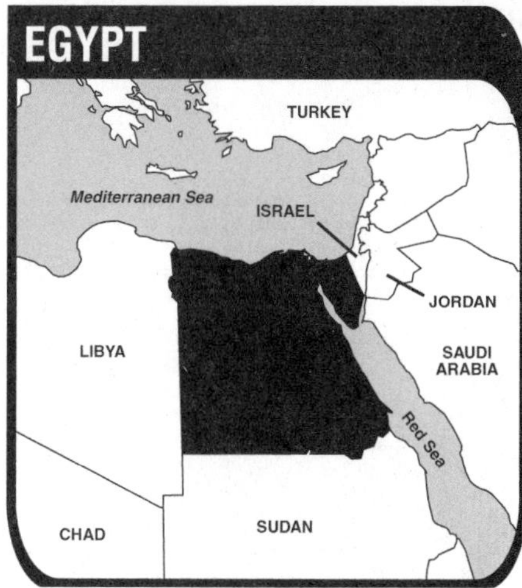


The Arab Republic of Egypt, located on the northeastern corner of Africa, has an area of 385,229 sq. mi. (1,1001,450 sq. km.) and a population of 62.4 million. Capital: Cairo. Although Egypt is an almost rainless expanse of desert, its economy is predominantly agricultural. Cotton, rice and petroleum are exported. Other main sources of income are revenues from the Suez Canal, remittances of Egyptian workers abroad and tourism.

# ARAB REPUBLIC

AH1391- / 1971- AD

## DECIMAL COINAGE

### KM# 941 5 PIASTRES

1.95 g., Brass, 18 mm. **Obv:** Denomination divides dates below, legend above **Rev:** Antique pottery vase **Edge:** Plain

| Date | Mintage | VF20 | XF40 | MS60 | MS63 | MS65 |
|---|---|---|---|---|---|---|
| AH1425-2004 | — | — | — | — | 1.50 | 2.00 |

### KM# 941a 5 PIASTRES

1.50 g., Copper Plated Steel, 18 mm. **Obv:** Denomination divides dates below, legend above **Rev:** Antique pottery vase

| Date | Mintage | VF20 | XF40 | MS60 | MS63 | MS65 |
|---|---|---|---|---|---|---|
| AH1429/2008 | — | — | — | — | 1.50 | 2.00 |

### KM# 922 10 PIASTRES

4.52 g., Copper-Nickel, 24.8 mm. **Subject:** National Women's Council **Obv:** Value **Rev:** Woman standing next to Sphinx **Edge:** Reeded **Mint:** Cairo

| Date | Mintage | VF20 | XF40 | MS60 | MS63 | MS65 |
|---|---|---|---|---|---|---|
| AH1425-2004 | — | — | — | — | 1.50 | 2.00 |

### KM# 990 10 PIASTRES

3.41 g., Nickel Plated Steel, 19.03 mm. **Obv:** Text, date and value **Rev:** Mosque

| Date | Mintage | VF20 | XF40 | MS60 | MS63 | MS65 |
|---|---|---|---|---|---|---|
| AH1429 (2008) | — | — | — | — | 1.00 | 1.50 |

### KM# 923 20 PIASTRES

6.00 g., Copper-Nickel, 26.8 mm. **Subject:** National Women's Council **Obv:** Value **Rev:** Woman standing next to Sphinx **Edge:** Reeded **Mint:** Cairo

| Date | Mintage | VF20 | XF40 | MS60 | MS63 | MS65 |
|---|---|---|---|---|---|---|
| AH1425-2004 | — | — | — | — | 2.50 | 3.50 |

### KM# 991 25 PIASTRES

4.50 g., Nickel Plated Steel, 21 mm. **Obv:** Value at center, Arabic legend at top, dates below **Rev:** Value at center, Arabic at top, English value below **Edge:** Reeded

| Date | Mintage | VF20 | XF40 | MS60 | MS63 | MS65 |
|---|---|---|---|---|---|---|
| AH1429-2008 | — | — | — | — | 2.50 | 3.50 |
| AH1430-2009 | — | — | — | — | 2.50 | 3.50 |
| AH1431-2010 | — | — | — | — | 2.50 | 3.50 |

### KM# 942.1 50 PIASTRES

6.50 g., Brass, 25 mm. **Obv:** Value **Rev:** Bust of Cleopatra left **Edge:** Reeded **Mint:** Cairo **Note:** Non-magnetic.

| Date | Mintage | VF20 | XF40 | MS60 | MS63 | MS65 |
|---|---|---|---|---|---|---|
| AH1426-2005 | — | — | — | 1.20 | 3.00 | 4.00 |
| AH1427-2006 | — | — | — | 1.20 | 3.00 | 4.00 |

### KM# 942.2 50 PIASTRES

6.50 g., Brass Plated Steel, 23 mm. **Obv:** Value **Rev:** Bust of Cleopatra left **Edge:** Reeded **Note:** Magnetic

| Date | Mintage | VF20 | XF40 | MS60 | MS63 | MS65 |
|---|---|---|---|---|---|---|
| AH1428-2007 | — | — | — | — | 1.00 | 1.50 |
| AH1429-2008 | — | — | — | — | 1.00 | 1.50 |
| AH1430-2009 | — | — | — | — | 1.00 | 1.50 |
| AH1431-2010 | — | — | — | — | 1.00 | 1.50 |
| AH1433-2012 | — | — | — | — | 1.00 | 1.50 |

### KM# 903 1/2 POUND

4.00 g., 0.875 Gold 0.1125 oz. AGW, 18 mm. **Subject:** Egyptian Museum Centennial **Obv:** Value **Rev:** Building **Edge:** Reeded **Mint:** Cairo

| Date | Mintage | VF20 | XF40 | MS60 | MS63 | MS65 |
|---|---|---|---|---|---|---|
| AH1423-2002 | — | — | — | 250 | 275 | 300 |

### KM# 930 POUND

15.00 g., 0.720 Silver 0.3472 oz. ASW, 35 mm. **Subject:** National Women's Council **Obv:** Value **Rev:** Woman standing next to Sphinx **Edge:** Reeded **Mint:** Cairo

| Date | Mintage | VF20 | XF40 | MS60 | MS63 | MS65 |
|---|---|---|---|---|---|---|
| AH1421-2001 | 600 | — | — | 45.00 | 50.00 | 60.00 |

### KM# 904 POUND

15.00 g., 0.720 Silver 0.3472 oz. ASW, 35 mm. **Subject:** Egyptian Museum Centennial **Obv:** Value **Rev:** Building, centennial numerals in background **Edge:** Reeded **Mint:** Cairo

| Date | Mintage | VF20 | XF40 | MS60 | MS63 | MS65 |
|---|---|---|---|---|---|---|
| AH1423-2002 | 1,500 | — | — | 35.00 | 40.00 | 45.00 |

### KM# 905 POUND

8.00 g., 0.875 Gold 0.2251 oz. AGW, 24 mm. **Subject:** Egyptian Museum Centennial **Obv:** Value **Rev:** Building, centennial numerals in background **Edge:** Reeded **Mint:** Cairo

| Date | Mintage | VF20 | XF40 | MS60 | MS63 | MS65 |
|---|---|---|---|---|---|---|
| AH1423-2002 | 300 | — | — | 400 | 425 | 450 |

### KM# 909 POUND

15.00 g., 0.720 Silver 0.3472 oz. ASW, 35 mm. **Subject:** International Ear, Nose and Throat Conference **Obv:** King Tut's Gold Mask **Rev:** IFOS" on world map **Edge:** Reeded **Mint:** Cairo

| Date | Mintage | VF20 | XF40 | MS60 | MS63 | MS65 |
|---|---|---|---|---|---|---|
| AH1423-2002 | 2,500 | — | — | 30.00 | 35.00 | 40.00 |

### KM# 910 POUND

15.00 g., 0.720 Silver 0.3472 oz. ASW, 35 mm. **Subject:** 50th Anniversary of Egyptian Revolution **Obv:** Value **Rev:** Soldier with flag **Edge:** Reeded **Mint:** Cairo

| Date | Mintage | VF20 | XF40 | MS60 | MS63 | MS65 |
|---|---|---|---|---|---|---|
| AH1423-2002 | 1,500 | — | — | 35.00 | 40.00 | 45.00 |

### KM# 912 POUND

15.00 g., 0.720 Silver 0.3472 oz. ASW, 35 mm. **Subject:** Alexandria Library **Obv:** Legend and inscription **Rev:** Inscribed arches above library roof **Edge:** Reeded **Mint:** Cairo

| Date | Mintage | VF20 | XF40 | MS60 | MS63 | MS65 |
|---|---|---|---|---|---|---|
| AH1423-2002 | 8,000 | — | — | 30.00 | 35.00 | 40.00 |

### KM# 913 POUND

15.00 g., 0.720 Silver 0.3472 oz. ASW, 35 mm. **Subject:** Body Building Championships **Obv:** Arabic and English legends **Rev:** Mr. Universe cartoon **Edge:** Reeded **Mint:** Cairo

| Date | Mintage | VF20 | XF40 | MS60 | MS63 | MS65 |
|---|---|---|---|---|---|---|
| AH1423-2002 | 1,000 | — | — | 30.00 | 35.00 | 40.00 |

### KM# 936 POUND

8.00 g., 0.875 Gold 0.2251 oz. AGW, 24 mm. **Subject:** 50th Anniversary of Egyptian Revolution **Obv:** Value **Rev:** Soldier with flag, pyramids and radiant sun **Edge:** Reeded **Mint:** Cairo

| Date | Mintage | VF20 | XF40 | MS60 | MS63 | MS65 |
|---|---|---|---|---|---|---|
| AH1423-2002 | 400 | — | — | 400 | 425 | 450 |

**KM# 938 POUND**
8.00 g., 0.875 Gold 0.2251 oz. AGW, 24 mm. **Subject:** Alexandria Library **Obv:** Cufic text in center **Rev:** Arched inscription above slanted library roof **Edge:** Reeded **Mint:** Cairo

| Date | Mintage | VF20 | XF40 | MS60 | MS63 | MS65 |
|---|---|---|---|---|---|---|
| AH1423-2002 | 750 | — | — | 400 | 425 | 450 |

**KM# 955 POUND**
8.00 g., 0.875 Gold 0.2251 oz. AGW, 24 mm. **Subject:** Golden Jubilee Ein Shams University **Obv:** Value **Rev:** Obelisk with bird standing at left and right **Edge:** Reeded **Mint:** Cairo

| Date | Mintage | VF20 | XF40 | MS60 | MS63 | MS65 |
|---|---|---|---|---|---|---|
| AH1422-2002 | 400 | — | — | 400 | 425 | 450 |

**KM# 956 POUND**
8.00 g., 0.875 Gold 0.2251 oz. AGW, 24 mm. **Subject:** Police Day **Obv:** Police eagle with wings spread, value **Rev:** Police badge **Edge:** Reeded **Mint:** Cairo

| Date | Mintage | VF20 | XF40 | MS60 | MS63 | MS65 |
|---|---|---|---|---|---|---|
| AH1422-2002 | 400 | — | — | 400 | 425 | 450 |

**KM# 915 POUND**
15.00 g., 0.720 Silver 0.3472 oz. ASW, 35 mm. **Subject:** 30th Anniversary of the October War **Obv:** Value, dates and legend **Rev:** Soldier with flag above pyramids **Edge:** Reeded **Mint:** Cairo

| Date | Mintage | VF20 | XF40 | MS60 | MS63 | MS65 |
|---|---|---|---|---|---|---|
| AH1424-2003 | 1,000 | — | — | 30.00 | 35.00 | 40.00 |

**KM# 917 POUND**
15.00 g., 0.720 Silver 0.3472 oz. ASW, 35 mm. **Subject:** 25th Anniversary of the Commerce Society **Obv:** Value, dates and legend **Rev:** Radiant sun above lattice work **Edge:** Reeded **Mint:** Cairo

| Date | Mintage | VF20 | XF40 | MS60 | MS63 | MS65 |
|---|---|---|---|---|---|---|
| AH1424-2003 | 1,200 | — | — | 30.00 | 35.00 | 40.00 |

**KM# 957 POUND**
8.00 g., 0.875 Gold 0.2251 oz. AGW, 24 mm. **Subject:** 30th Anniversary October War Victory **Obv:** Value **Rev:** Soldier holding flag on top of pyramid **Edge:** Reeded **Mint:** Cairo

| Date | Mintage | VF20 | XF40 | MS60 | MS63 | MS65 |
|---|---|---|---|---|---|---|
| AH1424-2003 | 200 | — | — | 425 | 445 | 475 |

**KM# 958 POUND**
8.00 g., 0.875 Gold 0.2251 oz. AGW, 24 mm. **Series:** Value **Subject:** Radio and Television Festival **Obv:** Modern abstract design **Edge:** Reeded **Mint:** Cairo

| Date | Mintage | VF20 | XF40 | MS60 | MS63 | MS65 |
|---|---|---|---|---|---|---|
| AH1424-2003 | 1,000 | — | — | 375 | 400 | 425 |

**KM# 959 POUND**
8.00 g., 0.875 Gold 0.2251 oz. AGW, 24 mm. **Subject:** 50th Anniversary El Gomhoreya Newspaper - Hosni Mubarak **Obv:** Value **Rev:** Bust facing at left, building in background **Edge:** Reeded **Mint:** Cairo

| Date | Mintage | VF20 | XF40 | MS60 | MS63 | MS65 |
|---|---|---|---|---|---|---|
| AH1424-2003 | 400 | — | — | 400 | 425 | 450 |

**KM# 924 POUND**
15.00 g., 0.720 Silver 0.3472 oz. ASW, 35 mm. **Subject:** 90th Anniversary Scouts **Obv:** Value **Rev:** Combined scouting badge **Edge:** Reeded **Mint:** Cairo

| Date | Mintage | VF20 | XF40 | MS60 | MS63 | MS65 |
|---|---|---|---|---|---|---|
| AH1425-2004 | 2,000 | — | — | 30.00 | 35.00 | 40.00 |

**KM# 934 POUND**
15.00 g., 0.725 Silver 0.3496 oz. ASW, 35 mm. **Subject:** Golden Jubilee - Military Production **Obv:** Value **Rev:** Ancient chariot, horse and rider **Edge:** Reeded **Mint:** Cairo

| Date | Mintage | VF20 | XF40 | MS60 | MS63 | MS65 |
|---|---|---|---|---|---|---|
| AH1425-2004 | 1,000 | — | — | 30.00 | 35.00 | 40.00 |

**KM# 960 POUND**
8.00 g., 0.875 Gold 0.2251 oz. AGW, 24 mm. **Subject:** Golden Jubilee Military Production **Obv:** Value **Rev:** Ancient chariot, horse and rider left **Edge:** Reeded **Mint:** Cairo

| Date | Mintage | VF20 | XF40 | MS60 | MS63 | MS65 |
|---|---|---|---|---|---|---|
| AH1425-2004 | 750 | — | — | 375 | 400 | 425 |

**KM# 940 POUND**
8.50 g., Bi-Metallic Brass center in Copper-Nickel ring, 25.1 mm. **Obv:** Value **Rev:** King Tutankhaman's gold mask **Edge:** Reeded **Mint:** Cairo

| Date | Mintage | VF20 | XF40 | MS60 | MS63 | MS65 |
|---|---|---|---|---|---|---|
| AH1426-2005 | — | — | — | — | 3.00 | 5.00 |
| AH1427-2006 | — | — | — | — | 3.00 | 5.00 |

**KM# 961 POUND**
8.00 g., 0.875 Gold 0.2251 oz. AGW, 24 mm. **Subject:** World Environment Day **Obv:** Value **Rev:** Stylized tree, emblem at left, bird standing at right **Edge:** Reeded **Mint:** Cairo

| Date | Mintage | VF20 | XF40 | MS60 | MS63 | MS65 |
|---|---|---|---|---|---|---|
| AH1427-2006 | 200 | — | — | 425 | 445 | 475 |

**KM# 962 POUND**
8.00 g., 0.875 Gold 0.2251 oz. AGW, 24 mm. **Subject:** Golden Jubilee Suez Canal Nationalization **Obv:** Value **Rev:** Large "50" above government buildings **Edge:** Reeded **Mint:** Cairo

| Date | Mintage | VF20 | XF40 | MS60 | MS63 | MS65 |
|---|---|---|---|---|---|---|
| AH1427-2006 | 1,000 | — | — | 375 | 400 | 425 |

**KM# 965 POUND**
15.00 g., 0.720 Silver 0.3472 oz. ASW, 35 mm. **Subject:** Golden Jubilee Suez Canal Nationalization **Obv:** Value **Rev:** Large "50" above government buildings **Edge:** Reeded **Mint:** Cairo

| Date | Mintage | VF20 | XF40 | MS60 | MS63 | MS65 |
|---|---|---|---|---|---|---|
| AH1427-2006 | 1,750 | — | — | 35.00 | 40.00 | 45.00 |

**KM# 966 POUND**
15.00 g., 0.720 Silver 0.3472 oz. ASW, 35 mm. **Subject:** 60th Anniversary UNESCO **Obv:** Value **Rev:** Logo **Edge:** Reeded **Mint:** Cairo

| Date | Mintage | VF20 | XF40 | MS60 | MS63 | MS65 |
|---|---|---|---|---|---|---|
| AH1427-2006 | 800 | — | — | 100 | 125 | 145 |

**KM# 967 POUND**
15.00 g., 0.720 Silver 0.3472 oz. ASW, 35 mm. **Subject:** 13th General Population Census **Obv:** Value **Rev:** Stylized couple leaning left at left **Edge:** Reeded **Mint:** Cairo

| Date | Mintage | VF20 | XF40 | MS60 | MS63 | MS65 |
|---|---|---|---|---|---|---|
| AH1427-2006 | 2,000 | — | — | 45.00 | 50.00 | 55.00 |

**KM# 940a POUND**
8.50 g., Bi-Metallic Brass Plated Steel center in Nickel Plated Steel ring, 25.1 mm. **Obv:** Value at center **Rev:** King Tutankhaman's gold mask **Edge:** Reeded **Mint:** Cairo **Note:** Magnetic

| Date | Mintage | VF20 | XF40 | MS60 | MS63 | MS65 |
|---|---|---|---|---|---|---|
| AH1428-2007 | — | — | — | — | 3.00 | 5.00 |
| AH1429-2008 | — | — | — | — | 3.00 | 4.00 |
| AH1430-2009 | — | — | — | — | 3.00 | 4.00 |
| AH1431-2010 | — | — | — | — | 3.00 | 4.00 |

**KM# 944 POUND**
15.00 g., 0.720 Silver 0.3472 oz. ASW, 35.00 mm. **Subject:** Air Force Diamond Jubilee **Obv:** Value **Rev:** Air Force insignia **Edge:** Reeded **Mint:** Cairo

| Date | Mintage | VF20 | XF40 | MS60 | MS63 | MS65 |
|---|---|---|---|---|---|---|
| AH1428-2007 | — | — | — | 45.00 | 50.00 | 55.00 |

**KM# 963 POUND**
8.00 g., 0.875 Gold 0.2251 oz. AGW, 24 mm. **Subject:** Silver Jubilee Egyptian Enviromental Protection **Obv:** Value **Rev:** World globe **Edge:** Reeded **Mint:** Cairo

| Date | Mintage | VF20 | XF40 | MS60 | MS63 | MS65 |
|---|---|---|---|---|---|---|
| AH1428-2007 | 300 | — | — | 420 | 440 | 465 |

**KM# 964 POUND**
8.00 g., 0.875 Gold 0.2251 oz. AGW, 24 mm. **Subject:** Diamond Jubilee Air Force **Obv:** Value **Rev:** Air Force emblem **Edge:** Reeded **Mint:** Cairo

| Date | Mintage | VF20 | XF40 | MS60 | MS63 | MS65 |
|---|---|---|---|---|---|---|
| AH1428-2007 | 130 | — | — | 500 | 550 | 600 |

**KM# 968 POUND**
15.00 g., 0.720 Silver 0.3472 oz. ASW, 35 mm. **Subject:** 100th Anniversary Ahly Club **Obv:** Value **Rev:** Large "100" with linked zeroes **Edge:** Reeded **Mint:** Cairo

| Date | Mintage | VF20 | XF40 | MS60 | MS63 | MS65 |
|---|---|---|---|---|---|---|
| AH1428-2007 | 5,000 | — | — | 45.00 | 50.00 | 55.00 |

**KM# 996 POUND**
15.00 g., 0.720 Silver 0.3472 oz. ASW, 35 mm. **Subject:** Susan Mubarak

| Date | Mintage | VF20 | XF40 | MS60 | MS63 | MS65 |
|---|---|---|---|---|---|---|
| AH1431-2010 | — | — | — | 45.00 | 50.00 | 55.00 |

**KM# 998 POUND**
15.00 g., 0.720 Silver 0.3472 oz. ASW, 35 mm. **Subject:** 50th Anniversary

| Date | Mintage | VF20 | XF40 | MS60 | MS63 | MS65 |
|---|---|---|---|---|---|---|
| AH1431-2010 | — | — | — | 45.00 | 50.00 | 55.00 |

**KM# 931 5 POUNDS**
17.50 g., 0.720 Silver 0.4051 oz. ASW, 37 mm. **Subject:** National Women's Council **Obv:** Value **Rev:** Woman standing next to Sphinx **Edge:** Reeded **Mint:** Cairo

| Date | Mintage | VF20 | XF40 | MS60 | MS63 | MS65 |
|---|---|---|---|---|---|---|
| AH1421-2001 | 600 | — | — | 55.00 | 60.00 | 70.00 |

**KM# 906 5 POUNDS**
17.50 g., 0.720 Silver 0.4051 oz. ASW, 37 mm. **Subject:** Egyptian Museum Centennial **Obv:** Value **Rev:** Building, centennial numerals in background **Edge:** Reeded **Mint:** Cairo

| Date | Mintage | VF20 | XF40 | MS60 | MS63 | MS65 |
|---|---|---|---|---|---|---|
| AH1423-2002 | 1,500 | — | — | 45.00 | 48.00 | 52.00 |

**KM# 907 5 POUNDS**
26.00 g., 0.875 Gold 0.7314 oz. AGW, 33 mm. **Subject:** Egyptian Museum Centennial **Obv:** Value **Rev:** Building, centennial numerals in background **Edge:** Reeded **Mint:** Cairo

| Date | Mintage | VF20 | XF40 | MS60 | MS63 | MS65 |
|---|---|---|---|---|---|---|
| AH1423-2002 | 250 | — | — | 1,250 | 1,350 | 1,500 |

**KM# 911 5 POUNDS**
17.55 g., 0.925 Silver 0.5219 oz. ASW, 37 mm. **Subject:** 50th Anniversary of the Egyptian Revolution **Obv:** Value **Rev:** Soldier with flag **Edge:** Reeded **Mint:** Cairo

| Date | Mintage | VF20 | XF40 | MS60 | MS63 | MS65 |
|---|---|---|---|---|---|---|
| AH1423-2002 | 1,500 | — | — | 45.00 | 48.00 | 52.00 |

**KM# 914 5 POUNDS**
17.50 g., 0.720 Silver 0.4051 oz. ASW, 37 mm. **Subject:** Body Building Championships **Obv:** Arabic and English legends **Rev:** Mr. Universe cartoon **Edge:** Reeded **Mint:** Cairo

| Date | Mintage | VF20 | XF40 | MS60 | MS63 | MS65 |
|---|---|---|---|---|---|---|
| AH1423-2002 | 800 | — | — | 40.00 | 45.00 | 55.00 |

**KM# 932 5 POUNDS**
17.50 g., 0.720 Silver 0.4051 oz. ASW, 37 mm. **Subject:** 50th Anniversary of the National Police **Obv:** Value and police logo **Rev:** Ceremonial design **Edge:** Reeded **Mint:** Cairo

| Date | Mintage | VF20 | XF40 | MS60 | MS63 | MS65 |
|---|---|---|---|---|---|---|
| AH1422-2002 | 750 | — | — | 45.00 | 50.00 | 60.00 |

**KM# 916 5 POUNDS**
17.50 g., 0.720 Silver 0.4051 oz. ASW, 37 mm. **Subject:** 30th Anniversary of the October War **Obv:** Value and legend **Rev:** Soldier with flag above pyramids **Edge:** Reeded **Mint:** Cairo

| Date | Mintage | VF20 | XF40 | MS60 | MS63 | MS65 |
|---|---|---|---|---|---|---|
| AH1424-2003 | 800 | — | — | 40.00 | 45.00 | 55.00 |

**KM# 918 5 POUNDS**
17.50 g., 0.720 Silver 0.4051 oz. ASW, 37 mm. **Obv:** Value and legend **Rev:** Geo-Physical Institute **Edge:** Reeded **Mint:** Cairo

| Date | Mintage | VF20 | XF40 | MS60 | MS63 | MS65 |
|---|---|---|---|---|---|---|
| AH1424-2003 | 800 | — | — | 40.00 | 45.00 | 55.00 |

**KM# 919 5 POUNDS**
17.50 g., 0.720 Silver 0.4051 oz. ASW, 37 mm. **Subject:** 50th Anniversary of the Republic **Obv:** Value and legend **Rev:** Portrait and building **Edge:** Reeded **Mint:** Cairo

| Date | Mintage | VF20 | XF40 | MS60 | MS63 | MS65 |
|---|---|---|---|---|---|---|
| AH1424-2003 | 3,000 | — | — | 37.00 | 42.00 | 48.00 |

**KM# 920 5 POUNDS**
17.50 g., 0.720 Silver 0.4051 oz. ASW, 37 mm. **Subject:** 25th Anniversary of the Delta Bank **Obv:** Value and legend **Rev:** Delta on world globe **Edge:** Reeded **Mint:** Cairo

| Date | Mintage | VF20 | XF40 | MS60 | MS63 | MS65 |
|---|---|---|---|---|---|---|
| AH1424-2004 | 1,500 | — | — | 37.00 | 42.00 | 48.00 |

**KM# 925 5 POUNDS**
17.50 g., 0.720 Silver 0.4051 oz. ASW, 37 mm. **Obv:** Value **Rev:** Balance scale **Edge:** Reeded **Mint:** Cairo

| Date | Mintage | VF20 | XF40 | MS60 | MS63 | MS65 |
|---|---|---|---|---|---|---|
| AH1425-2004 | 3,300 | — | — | 37.00 | 42.00 | 48.00 |

**KM# 933 5 POUNDS**
17.50 g., 0.720 Silver 0.4051 oz. ASW, 37 mm. **Subject:** 90th Anniversary - Egyptian Scouts Organization - 1914-2004 **Obv:** Value **Rev:** Combined scouting emblem **Edge:** Reeded **Mint:** Cairo

| Date | Mintage | VF20 | XF40 | MS60 | MS63 | MS65 |
|---|---|---|---|---|---|---|
| AH1425-2004 | — | — | — | 37.00 | 42.00 | 48.00 |

**KM# 935 5 POUNDS**
17.50 g., 0.720 Silver 0.4051 oz. ASW, 37 mm. **Subject:** Golden Jubilee - Military Production **Obv:** Value **Rev:** Ancient chariot, horse and rider left **Edge:** Reeded **Mint:** Cairo

| Date | Mintage | VF20 | XF40 | MS60 | MS63 | MS65 |
|---|---|---|---|---|---|---|
| AH1425-2004 | 800 | — | — | 40.00 | 45.00 | 55.00 |

**KM# 974 5 POUNDS**
17.50 g., 0.720 Silver 0.4051 oz. ASW, 37 mm. **Subject:** Golden Jubilee Cairo Mint **Obv:** Value **Rev:** National arms above mint building **Edge:** Reeded **Mint:** Cairo

| Date | Mintage | VF20 | XF40 | MS60 | MS63 | MS65 |
|---|---|---|---|---|---|---|
| AH1425-2004 | 1,750 | — | — | 45.00 | 50.00 | 55.00 |

**KM# 975 5 POUNDS**
17.50 g., 0.720 Silver 0.4051 oz. ASW, 37 mm. **Subject:** 60th Anniversary Arab League **Obv:** Value **Rev:** Logo in center of ornate background **Edge:** Reeded **Mint:** Cairo

| Date | Mintage | VF20 | XF40 | MS60 | MS63 | MS65 |
|---|---|---|---|---|---|---|
| AH1426-2005 | 2,000 | — | — | 55.00 | 60.00 | 65.00 |

**KM# 976 5 POUNDS**
17.50 g., 0.720 Silver 0.4051 oz. ASW, 37 mm. **Subject:** World Environment Day **Obv:** Value **Rev:** Stylized tree with logo at left, bird at right **Edge:** Reeded **Mint:** Cairo

| Date | Mintage | VF20 | XF40 | MS60 | MS63 | MS65 |
|---|---|---|---|---|---|---|
| AH1427-2006 | 1,000 | — | — | 70.00 | 80.00 | 90.00 |

**KM# 977 5 POUNDS**
17.50 g., 0.720 Silver 0.4051 oz. ASW, 35 mm. **Subject:** Golden jubilee Suez Canal Nationalization **Obv:** Value **Rev:** Large "50" above government buildings **Edge:** Reeded **Mint:** Cairo

| Date | Mintage | VF20 | XF40 | MS60 | MS63 | MS65 |
|---|---|---|---|---|---|---|
| AH1427-2006 | 1,750 | — | — | 45.00 | 50.00 | 55.00 |

**KM# 978 5 POUNDS**
17.50 g., 0.720 Silver 0.4051 oz. ASW, 37 mm. **Subject:** 60th Anniversary UNESCO **Obv:** Value **Rev:** Logo **Edge:** Reeded **Mint:** Cairo

| Date | Mintage | VF20 | XF40 | MS60 | MS63 | MS65 |
|---|---|---|---|---|---|---|
| AH1427-2006 | 800 | — | — | 100 | 125 | 145 |

**KM# 979 5 POUNDS**
17.50 g., 0.720 Silver 0.4051 oz. ASW, 37 mm. **Subject:** Diamond Jubilee Academy of Arab Language **Obv:** Value **Rev:** Globe on open book **Edge:** Reeded **Mint:** Cairo

| Date | Mintage | VF20 | XF40 | MS60 | MS63 | MS65 |
|---|---|---|---|---|---|---|
| AH1427-2006 | 1,000 | — | — | 70.00 | 80.00 | 90.00 |

**KM# 980 5 POUNDS**
17.50 g., 0.720 Silver 0.4051 oz. ASW, 37 mm. **Subject:** 13th General Population Census **Obv:** Circle with inscription in center **Rev:** Stylized couple leaning left at left **Edge:** Reeded **Mint:** Cairo

| Date | Mintage | VF20 | XF40 | MS60 | MS63 | MS65 |
|---|---|---|---|---|---|---|
| AH1427-2006 | 1,500 | — | — | 65.00 | 75.00 | 85.00 |

**KM# 943 5 POUNDS**
17.50 g., 0.720 Silver 0.4051 oz. ASW, 37 mm. **Subject:** 11th Pan-Arab Games **Obv:** Value **Rev:** Logo with outlined map of Arab nations in background **Edge:** Reeded **Mint:** Cairo

| Date | Mintage | VF20 | XF40 | MS60 | MS63 | MS65 |
|---|---|---|---|---|---|---|
| AH1428-2007 | 6,300 | — | — | 30.00 | 35.00 | 40.00 |

**KM# 945 5 POUNDS**
17.50 g., 0.720 Silver 0.4051 oz. ASW, 37 mm. **Subject:** Air Force Diamond Jubilee **Obv:** Value **Rev:** Air Force insignia **Edge:** Reeded **Mint:** Cairo

| Date | Mintage | VF20 | XF40 | MS60 | MS63 | MS65 |
|---|---|---|---|---|---|---|
| AH1428-2007 | 600 | — | — | 55.00 | 60.00 | 70.00 |

**KM# 981 5 POUNDS**
17.50 g., 0.720 Silver 0.4051 oz. ASW, 37 mm. **Subject:** 100th Anniversary Ahly Club **Obv:** Value **Rev:** Large "100" With linked zeroes **Edge:** Reeded **Mint:** Cairo

| Date | Mintage | VF20 | XF40 | MS60 | MS63 | MS65 |
|---|---|---|---|---|---|---|
| AH1428-2007 | 3,000 | — | — | 45.00 | 50.00 | 55.00 |

**KM# 982 5 POUNDS**
17.50 g., 0.720 Silver 0.4051 oz. ASW, 37 mm. **Subject:** Diamond Jubilee Court of Cassation **Obv:** Balance scale above inscriptions **Rev:** Court building **Edge:** Reeded **Mint:** Cairo

| Date | Mintage | VF20 | XF40 | MS60 | MS63 | MS65 |
|---|---|---|---|---|---|---|
| AH1428-2007 | 450 | — | — | 125 | 150 | 175 |

**KM# 983 5 POUNDS**
17.50 g., 0.720 Silver 0.4051 oz. ASW, 37 mm. **Subject:** Silver Jubilee Enviromental Protection Agency **Obv:** Value **Rev:** World globe **Edge:** Reeded **Mint:** Cairo

| Date | Mintage | VF20 | XF40 | MS60 | MS63 | MS65 |
|---|---|---|---|---|---|---|
| AH1428-2007 | 1,300 | — | — | 55.00 | 60.00 | 70.00 |

**KM# 984 5 POUNDS**
17.50 g., 0.720 Silver 0.4051 oz. ASW, 37 mm. **Subject:** 11th Arab Sports Championship - Egypt **Obv:** Value **Rev:** Stylized player on map of Arab countries **Edge:** Reeded **Mint:** Cairo

| Date | Mintage | VF20 | XF40 | MS60 | MS63 | MS65 |
|---|---|---|---|---|---|---|
| AH1428-2007 | 6,300 | — | — | 45.00 | 50.00 | 55.00 |

**KM# 994 5 POUNDS**
17.50 g., 0.720 Silver 0.4051 oz. ASW, 37 mm. **Subject:** Ras Muhammad Reserve protection

| Date | Mintage | VF20 | XF40 | MS60 | MS63 | MS65 |
|---|---|---|---|---|---|---|
| AH1431-2010 | — | — | — | 37.00 | 42.00 | 48.00 |

**KM# 995 5 POUNDS**
17.50 g., 0.720 Silver 0.4051 oz. ASW, 37 mm. **Subject:** Egypt Olympic Committee

| Date | Mintage | VF20 | XF40 | MS60 | MS63 | MS65 |
|---|---|---|---|---|---|---|
| AH1431-2010 | — | — | — | 37.00 | 42.00 | 48.00 |

**KM# 997 5 POUNDS**
17.50 g., 0.720 Silver 0.4051 oz. ASW, 37 mm. **Subject:** Susan Mubarak

| Date | Mintage | VF20 | XF40 | MS60 | MS63 | MS65 |
|---|---|---|---|---|---|---|
| AH1431-2010 | — | — | — | 45.00 | 50.00 | 55.00 |

**KM# 999 5 POUNDS**
17.50 g., 0.720 Silver 0.4051 oz. ASW, 37 mm. **Subject:** 50th Anniversary

| Date | Mintage | VF20 | XF40 | MS60 | MS63 | MS65 |
|---|---|---|---|---|---|---|
| AH1431-2010 | — | — | — | 45.00 | 50.00 | 55.00 |

**KM# 908 10 POUNDS**
40.00 g., 0.875 Gold 1.1253 oz. AGW, 37 mm. **Subject:** Egyptian Museum Centennial **Obv:** Denomination **Rev:** Building, centennial numerals in background **Edge:** Reeded **Mint:** Cairo

| Date | Mintage | VF20 | XF40 | MS60 | MS63 | MS65 |
|---|---|---|---|---|---|---|
| AH1423-2002 | 150 | — | — | — | 2,000 | 2,200 |

**KM# 989 10 POUNDS**
40.00 g., 0.875 Gold 1.1253 oz. AGW, 37 mm. **Subject:** Golden Jubilee Police Day **Obv:** Eagle left with wings spread **Rev:** Police emblem **Edge:** Reeded **Mint:** Cairo

| Date | Mintage | VF20 | XF40 | MS60 | MS63 | MS65 |
|---|---|---|---|---|---|---|
| AH1422-2002 | 150 | — | — | — | 2,000 | 2,200 |

**KM# 985 10 POUNDS**
40.00 g., 0.875 Gold 1.1253 oz. AGW, 37 mm. **Subject:** 50th Anniversary El Gomhoreya News **Obv:** Value **Rev:** Bust of Hosni Mubarak facing at left, building in background **Edge:** Reeded **Mint:** Cairo

| Date | Mintage | VF20 | XF40 | MS60 | MS63 | MS65 |
|---|---|---|---|---|---|---|
| AH1424-2003 | 50 | — | — | — | 2,150 | 2,350 |

**KM# 986 10 POUNDS**
40.00 g., 0.875 Gold 1.1253 oz. AGW, 37 mm. **Subject:** Golden Jubilee Military Production **Obv:** Value **Rev:** Ancient chariot, horse and rider left **Edge:** Reeded **Mint:** Cairo

| Date | Mintage | VF20 | XF40 | MS60 | MS63 | MS65 |
|---|---|---|---|---|---|---|
| AH1425-2004 | 85 | — | — | — | 2,100 | 2,300 |

**KM# 987 10 POUNDS**
40.00 g., 0.875 Gold 1.1253 oz. AGW, 37 mm. **Subject:** 60th Anniversary Arab League **Obv:** Value **Rev:** Emblem at center, ornate background **Edge:** Reeded **Mint:** Cairo

| Date | Mintage | VF20 | XF40 | MS60 | MS63 | MS65 |
|---|---|---|---|---|---|---|
| AH1426-2005 | 50 | — | — | — | 2,150 | 2,350 |

**KM# 988 10 POUNDS**
40.00 g., 0.875 Gold 1.1253 oz. AGW, 37 mm. **Subject:** Diamond Jubilee Air Force **Obv:** Value **Rev:** Air Force emblem **Edge:** Reeded **Mint:** Cairo

| Date | Mintage | VF20 | XF40 | MS60 | MS63 | MS65 |
|---|---|---|---|---|---|---|
| AH1428-2007 | 25 | — | — | — | 2,250 | 2,500 |

# ESTONIA

The Republic of Estonia (formerly the Estonian Soviet Socialist Republic of the U.S.S.R.) is the northernmost of the three Baltic States in Eastern Europe. It has an area of 17,462 sq. mi. (45,100 sq. km.) and a population of 1.6 million. Capital: Tallinn. Agriculture and dairy farming are the principal industries. Butter, eggs, bacon, timber and petroleum are exported.

## MODERN REPUBLIC

1991 - present

### STANDARD COINAGE

**KM# 22 10 SENTI**
1.85 g., Aluminum-Bronze, 17.1 mm. **Obv:** Three lions left divide date **Rev:** Denomination **Rev. Legend:** EESTI VABARIIK **Edge:** Plain

| Date | Mintage | VF20 | XF40 | MS60 | MS63 | MS65 |
|---|---|---|---|---|---|---|
| 2002 | 30,000,000 | — | 0.20 | 0.50 | 1.00 | 1.50 |
| 2006 | 31,000,000 | — | 0.20 | 0.50 | 1.00 | 1.50 |
| 2008 | 15,000,000 | — | 0.20 | 0.50 | 1.00 | 1.50 |

**KM# 23a 20 SENTI**
2.00 g., Nickel Plated Steel, 18.9 mm. **Obv:** National arms divide date **Rev:** Denomination **Rev. Legend:** EESTI VABARIIK **Edge:** Plain

| Date | Mintage | VF20 | XF40 | MS60 | MS63 | MS65 |
|---|---|---|---|---|---|---|
| 2003 | 11,100,000 | — | — | 0.60 | 1.25 | 1.75 |
| 2004 | 20,000,000 | — | — | 0.60 | 1.25 | 1.75 |
| 2006 | 2,000,000 | — | — | 0.60 | 1.25 | 1.75 |
| 2008 | 12,000,000 | — | — | 0.60 | 1.25 | 1.75 |

**KM# 24 50 SENTI**
2.90 g., Aluminum-Bronze, 19.5 mm. **Obv:** National arms divide date **Rev:** Denomination **Rev. Legend:** EESTI VABARIIK **Edge:** Plain

| Date | Mintage | VF20 | XF40 | MS60 | MS63 | MS65 |
|---|---|---|---|---|---|---|
| 2004 | 10,000,000 | — | — | 1.00 | 1.50 | 2.00 |
| 2006 | 7,000,000 | — | — | 1.00 | 1.50 | 2.00 |
| 2007 | 17,000,000 | — | — | 1.00 | 1.50 | 2.00 |

**KM# 35 KROON**
5.00 g., Aluminum-Bronze, 23.5 mm. **Obv:** National arms **Rev:** Large, thick denomination **Rev. Legend:** EESTI VABARIIK **Edge:** Segmented reeding

| Date | Mintage | VF20 | XF40 | MS60 | MS63 | MS65 |
|---|---|---|---|---|---|---|
| 2001 | 15,000,000 | — | 0.50 | 1.50 | 2.00 | 2.50 |
| 2003 | 15,000,000 | — | 0.50 | 1.50 | 2.00 | 2.50 |
| 2006 | 15,170,000 | — | 0.50 | 1.50 | 2.00 | 2.50 |

**KM# 44 KROON**
4.80 g., Aluminum-Bronze, 23.21 mm. **Obv:** National arms **Rev:** Stylized plant in circle **Rev. Legend:** EESTI VABARIIK **Edge:** Segmented reeding

| Date | Mintage | VF20 | XF40 | MS60 | MS63 | MS65 |
|---|---|---|---|---|---|---|
| 2008 | 20,000,000 | — | 1.00 | 2.00 | 3.00 | 4.00 |

**KM# 38 10 KROONI**
28.28 g., 0.999 Silver 0.9083 oz. ASW, 38.6 mm. **Subject:** Tartu University **Obv:** National arms **Rev:** Building in oval, value at left **Edge:** Reeded

| Date | Mintage | VF20 | XF40 | MS60 | MS63 | MS65 |
|---|---|---|---|---|---|---|
| 2002 | 10,000 | **PF63** 70.00 | **PF65** 80.00 | | | |

**KM# 40 10 KROONI**
28.28 g., 0.999 Silver 0.9083 oz. ASW, 38.6 mm. **Subject:** Estonian Flag **Obv:** National arms **Rev:** Round multicolor flag design **Edge:** Reeded

| Date | Mintage | VF20 | XF40 | MS60 | MS63 | MS65 |
|---|---|---|---|---|---|---|
| 2004 | 10,000 | **PF63** 65.00 | **PF65** 75.00 | | | |

**KM# 42 10 KROONI**
28.28 g., 0.999 Silver 0.9083 oz. ASW, 38.6 mm. **Subject:** Torino Winter Olympics **Obv:** National arms **Rev:** Gold inset cross country skier in semi-circle above Olympic flame **Edge:** Reeded

| Date | Mintage | VF20 | XF40 | MS60 | MS63 | MS65 |
|---|---|---|---|---|---|---|
| 2006 | 10,000 | **PF65** 150 | | | | |

**KM# 46 10 KROONI**
28.28 g., 0.999 Silver 0.9083 oz. ASW, 38.61 mm. **Subject:** 90th Anniversary of Independence **Obv:** National arms **Obv. Legend:** EESTI VARBARIIK **Rev:** Wiiralt oak tree **Edge:** Plain

| Date | Mintage | VF20 | XF40 | MS60 | MS63 | MS65 |
|---|---|---|---|---|---|---|
| 2008 | 10,000 | PF65 85.00 | | | | |

**KM# 48 10 KROONI**
28.28 g., 0.999 Silver 0.9083 oz. ASW, 38.61 mm. **Subject:** Olympics **Obv:** Arms **Rev:** Torch and geometric patterns

| Date | Mintage | VF20 | XF40 | MS60 | MS63 | MS65 |
|---|---|---|---|---|---|---|
| 2008 | — | PF65 50.00 | | | | |

**KM# 49 10 KROONI**
24.10 g., 0.999 Silver 0.7741 oz. ASW, 38.61 mm. **Subject:** National Museum **Obv:** National arms within starburst **Rev:** Design in star

| Date | Mintage | VF20 | XF40 | MS60 | MS63 | MS65 |
|---|---|---|---|---|---|---|
| 2008 | — | PF65 85.00 | | | | |

**KM# 51 10 KROONI**
31.11 g., 0.999 Silver 0.999 oz. ASW, 40.6 mm. **Subject:** Song and Dance Festival **Obv:** National Arms **Rev:** Circle of dancers

| Date | Mintage | VF20 | XF40 | MS60 | MS63 | MS65 |
|---|---|---|---|---|---|---|
| 2009 | — | PF65 75.00 | | | | |

**KM# 53 10 KROONI**
28.28 g., 0.999 Silver 0.9083 oz. ASW, 38.61 mm. **Subject:** Vancouver Winter Olympics **Obv:** National arms within wreath, date below **Rev:** Two stylized cross county skiers right

| Date | Mintage | VF20 | XF40 | MS60 | MS63 | MS65 |
|---|---|---|---|---|---|---|
| 2010 | — | PF65 60.00 | | | | |

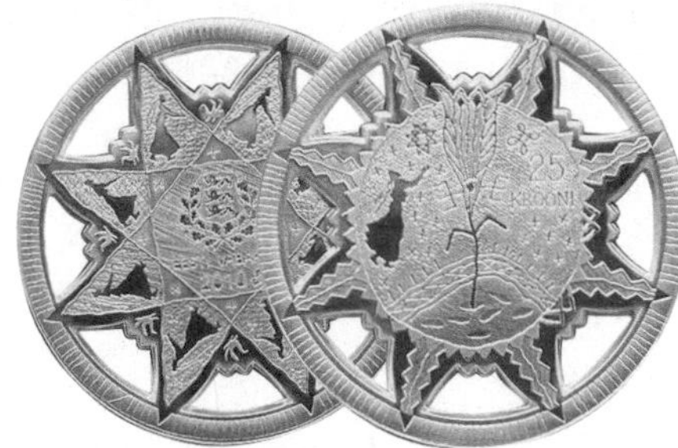

**KM# 55 25 KROONI**
24.10 g., 0.9999 Silver 0.7748 oz. ASW, 38.61 mm.

| Date | Mintage | VF20 | XF40 | MS60 | MS63 | MS65 |
|---|---|---|---|---|---|---|
| 2010 | — | PF65 75.00 | | | | |

**KM# 50 50 KROONI**
8.64 g., 0.999 Gold 0.2775 oz. AGW, 22 mm. **Obv:** National Arms and laurel branch **Rev:** Windmill

| Date | Mintage | VF20 | XF40 | MS60 | MS63 | MS65 |
|---|---|---|---|---|---|---|
| 2008 | — | PF65 650 | | | | |

**KM# 54 50 KROONI**
24.50 g., 0.999 Silver 0.7869 oz. ASW with Wood insert, 38.61 mm. **Subject:** Estonian Nature **Obv:** Arms and legned

| Date | Mintage | VF20 | XF40 | MS60 | MS63 | MS65 |
|---|---|---|---|---|---|---|
| 2010 | — | PF65 60.00 | | | | |

**KM# 39 100 KROONI**
7.78 g., 0.9999 Gold 0.250 oz. AGW **Subject:** Monetary Reform **Obv:** National arms **Rev:** Cross design **Edge:** Reeded

| Date | Mintage | VF20 | XF40 | MS60 | MS63 | MS65 |
|---|---|---|---|---|---|---|
| 2002 | 2,000 | — | — | — | — | 625 |

**KM# 41 100 KROONI**
7.78 g., 0.9999 Gold 0.250 oz. AGW, 22 mm. **Subject:** Olympic Games **Obv:** National arms within wreath **Rev:** Olympic flame above rings in center **Edge:** Reeded

| Date | Mintage | VF20 | XF40 | MS60 | MS63 | MS65 |
|---|---|---|---|---|---|---|
| 2004 Prooflike | 5,000 | — | — | — | — | 550 |

**KM# 43 100 KROONI**
28.28 g., 0.999 Silver 0.9083 oz. ASW, 38.6 mm. **Subject:** National Opera **Obv:** National arms **Rev:** Building front **Edge:** Plain

| Date | Mintage | VF20 | XF40 | MS60 | MS63 | MS65 |
|---|---|---|---|---|---|---|
| 2006 | 10,000 | PF63 75.00 | PF65 85.00 | | | |

**KM# 45 100 KROONI**
7.78 g., 0.9999 Gold 0.2501 oz. AGW **Subject:** 15th Anniversary Reintroduction of the Estonian Kroon **Obv:** National arms **Obv. Legend:** EESTI VARBARIIK **Rev:** Cornflower **Rev. Legend:** KROONI TAAS- / KEHTESTAMISE / 15. AASTAPAEV **Edge:** Plain **Shape:** Triangular

| Date | Mintage | VF20 | XF40 | MS60 | MS63 | MS65 |
|---|---|---|---|---|---|---|
| 2007 Prooflike | 6,000 | PF63 600 | | | | |

**KM# 47 100 KROONI**
7.78 g., 0.999 Platinum 0.2497 oz. APW, 18 mm. **Subject:** 90th Anniversary of Republic **Rev:** Three birds on wire

| Date | Mintage | VF20 | XF40 | MS60 | MS63 | MS65 |
|---|---|---|---|---|---|---|
| 2008 | 3,000 | PF65 675 | | | | |

**KM# 52 100 KROONI**
7.78 g., 0.999 Gold 0.2499 oz. AGW, 22 mm. **Subject:** Song and dance festival **Obv:** Arms **Rev:** Stylized chorus on stage

| Date | Mintage | VF20 | XF40 | MS60 | MS63 | MS65 |
|---|---|---|---|---|---|---|
| 2009 | — | PF65 600 | | | | |

**KM# 56 100 KROONI**
7.78 g., 0.999 Gold 0.2499 oz. AGW, 22 mm.

| Date | Mintage | VF20 | XF40 | MS60 | MS63 | MS65 |
|---|---|---|---|---|---|---|
| 2010 | — | PF65 650 | | | | |

## EURO COINAGE

### KM# 61 EURO CENT

2.30 g., Copper Plated Steel, 16.25 mm. **Obv:** Map of Estonia **Rev:** Denomination and globe

| Date | Mintage | VF20 | XF40 | MS60 | MS63 | MS65 |
|---|---|---|---|---|---|---|
| 2011 | 32,000,000 | — | — | 0.35 | 0.50 | 0.75 |
| 2011 Special Unc | 50,000 | — | — | — | 2.00 | 3.00 |
| 2011 | 3,500 | **PF65** 6.00 | | | | |
| 2012 | 25,000,000 | — | — | 0.35 | 0.50 | 0.75 |

### KM# 62 2 EURO CENT

3.06 g., Copper Plated Steel, 18.75 mm. **Obv:** Map of Estonia **Rev:** Denomination and globe **Edge:** Grooved

| Date | Mintage | VF20 | XF40 | MS60 | MS63 | MS65 |
|---|---|---|---|---|---|---|
| 2011 | 30,000,000 | — | — | 0.50 | 1.00 | 1.50 |
| 2011 Special Unc | 50,000 | — | — | — | 3.00 | 5.00 |
| 2011 | 3,500 | **PF65** 7.00 | | | | |
| 2012 | 25,000,000 | — | — | 0.50 | 1.00 | 1.50 |

### KM# 63 5 EURO CENT

3.92 g., Copper Plated Steel, 21.25 mm. **Obv:** Map of Estonia **Rev:** Denomination and globe

| Date | Mintage | VF20 | XF40 | MS60 | MS63 | MS65 |
|---|---|---|---|---|---|---|
| 2011 | 30,000,000 | — | — | 0.75 | 1.50 | 2.00 |
| 2011 Special Unc | 50,000 | — | — | — | 4.00 | 6.00 |
| 2011 | 3,500 | **PF65** 8.00 | | | | |

### KM# 64 10 EURO CENT

4.10 g., Brass, 19.75 mm. **Obv:** Map of Estonia **Rev:** Relief map of Western Europe, stars, line and value **Edge:** Reeded

| Date | Mintage | VF20 | XF40 | MS60 | MS63 | MS65 |
|---|---|---|---|---|---|---|
| 2011 | 30,000,000 | — | — | 1.50 | 2.00 | 3.00 |
| 2011 Special Unc | 50,000 | — | — | — | 5.00 | 7.00 |
| 2011 | 3,500 | **PF65** 9.00 | | | | |

### KM# 65 20 EURO CENT

5.74 g., Brass, 22.25 mm. **Obv:** Map of Estonia **Rev:** Relief map of Western Europe, stars, line and value **Edge:** Notched

| Date | Mintage | VF20 | XF40 | MS60 | MS63 | MS65 |
|---|---|---|---|---|---|---|
| 2011 | 25,000,000 | — | — | 1.00 | 1.50 | 2.00 |
| 2011 Special Unc | 50,000 | — | — | — | 5.00 | 7.00 |
| 2011 | 3,500 | **PF65** 9.00 | | | | |

### KM# 66 50 EURO CENT

7.80 g., Brass, 24.25 mm. **Obv:** Map of Estonia **Rev:** Relief map of Western Europe, stars, line and value **Edge:** Reeded

| Date | Mintage | VF20 | XF40 | MS60 | MS63 | MS65 |
|---|---|---|---|---|---|---|
| 2011 | 20,000,000 | — | — | 1.50 | 2.00 | 3.00 |
| 2011 Special Unc | 50,000 | — | — | — | 5.00 | 7.00 |
| 2011 | 3,500 | **PF65** 15.00 | | | | |

### KM# 67 EURO

7.50 g., Bi-Metallic Copper-Nickel center in Nickel-Brass ring, 23.35 mm. **Obv:** Map of Estonia **Rev:** Relief map of Western Europe, stars, lines and value **Edge:** Segmented reeding

| Date | Mintage | VF20 | XF40 | MS60 | MS63 | MS65 |
|---|---|---|---|---|---|---|
| 2011 | 16,000,000 | — | — | 2.50 | 4.00 | 6.00 |
| 2011 Special Unc | 50,000 | — | — | — | 7.50 | 10.00 |
| 2011 | 3,500 | **PF65** 15.00 | | | | |

### KM# 68 2 EURO

8.50 g., Bi-Metallic Nickel-Brass center in Copper-Nickel ring, 25.75 mm. **Obv:** Map of Estonia **Rev:** Relief map of Western Europe, stars, lines and value **Edge:** Reeded and lettered

| Date | Mintage | VF20 | XF40 | MS60 | MS63 | MS65 |
|---|---|---|---|---|---|---|
| 2011 | 11,000,000 | — | — | 4.00 | 6.00 | — |
| 2011 Special Unc | 50,000 | — | — | — | 8.00 | 12.00 |
| 2011 | 3,500 | **PF65** 30.00 | | | | |

### KM# 70 2 EURO

8.50 g., Bi-Metallic Nickel-Brass center in Copper-Nickel ring, 25.75 mm. **Subject:** Euro Coinage, 10th Anniversary **Obv:** Euro symbol on globe at center, child-like rendering around

| Date | Mintage | VF20 | XF40 | MS60 | MS63 | MS65 |
|---|---|---|---|---|---|---|
| 2012 | 2,000,000 | — | — | 4.00 | 6.00 | — |

### KM# 73 7 EURO

28.28 g., 0.925 Silver 0.841 oz. ASW, 38.61 mm. **Subject:** Raymond Valgre **Obv:** National arms **Rev:** Musical notes and Valgre signature

| Date | Mintage | VF20 | XF40 | MS60 | MS63 | MS65 |
|---|---|---|---|---|---|---|
| 2013 | 7,500 | **PF65** 70.00 | | | | |

### KM# 71 10 EURO

28.80 g., 0.9999 Silver 0.9258 oz. ASW, 38.61 mm. **Subject:** Estonia's Future **Obv:** National arms **Rev:** Two dancing figures, value at top **Edge Lettering:** Ag 999.9

| Date | Mintage | VF20 | XF40 | MS60 | MS63 | MS65 |
|---|---|---|---|---|---|---|
| 2011 | 30,000 | **PF65** 65.00 | | | | |

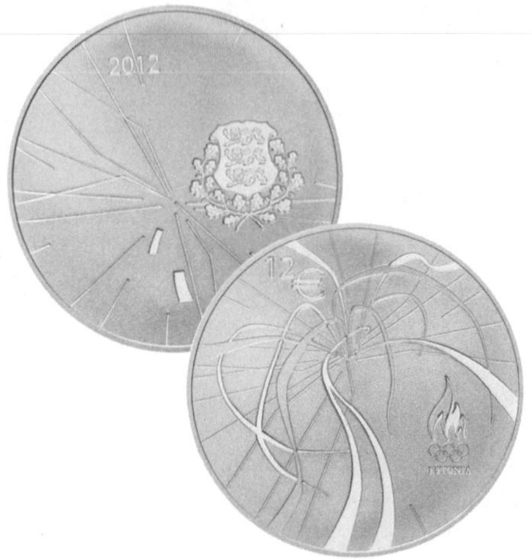

### KM# 72 12 EURO

28.28 g., 0.999 Silver 0.9083 oz. ASW, 38.61 mm. **Subject:** London Olympics **Obv:** National arms **Rev:** Ribbons, Olympic rings and flame

| Date | Mintage | VF20 | XF40 | MS60 | MS63 | MS65 |
|---|---|---|---|---|---|---|
| 2012 | 7,500 | **PF65** 100 | | | | |

### KM# 69 20 EURO

14.60 g., Bi-Metallic .9999 Gold center in .9999 Silver ring, 27.25 mm. **Subject:** Estonia's entry into Eurozone **Obv:** National arms **Rev:** Lace

| Date | Mintage | VF20 | XF40 | MS60 | MS63 | MS65 |
|---|---|---|---|---|---|---|
| 2011 | 10,000 | **PF65** 650 | | | | |

## MINT SETS

| KM# | Date | Mintage | Identification | Issue Price | Mkt Val |
|---|---|---|---|---|---|
| MS2 | 2011 (8) | 50,000 | KM#61-68 | — | 25.00 |

## PROOF SETS

| KM# | Date | Mintage | Identification | Issue Price | Mkt Val |
|---|---|---|---|---|---|
| PS1 | 2011 (8) | 3,500 | KM#61-68 | — | 95.00 |

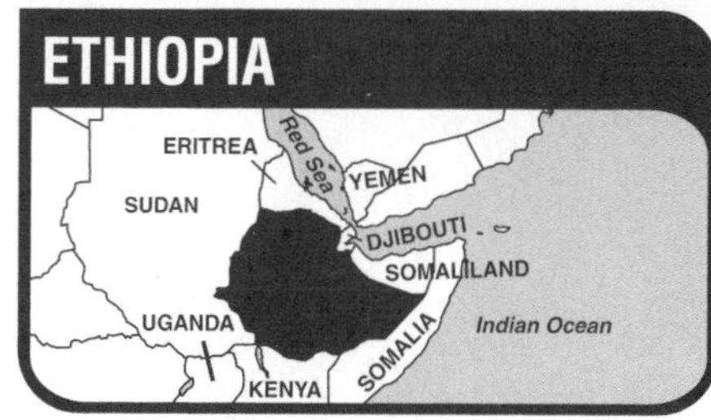


The People's Federal Republic of Ethiopia (formerly the Peoples Democratic Republic and the Empire of Ethiopia), Africa's oldest independent nation, faces the Red Sea in East-Central Africa. The country has an area of 424,214 sq. mi. (1,004,390 sq. km.) and a population of 56 million people who are divided among 40 tribes that speak some 270 languages and dialects. Capital: Addis Ababa. The economy is predominantly agricultural and pastoral. Gold and platinum are mined and petroleum fields are being developed. Coffee, oilseeds, hides and cereals are exported.

DATING

Ethiopian coinage is dated by the Ethiopian Era calendar (E.E.), which commenced 7 years and 8 months after the advent of A.D. dating.

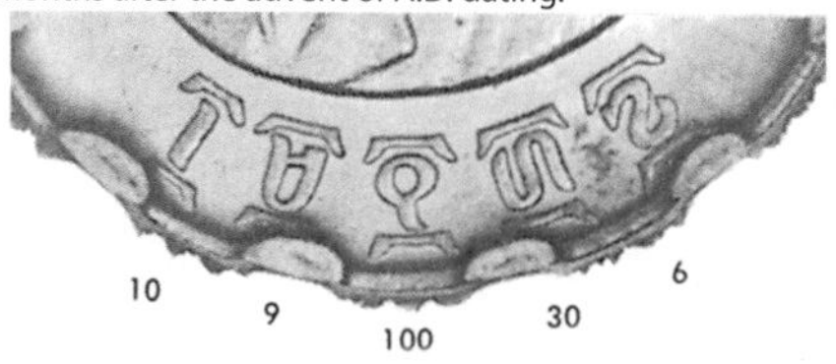


EXAMPLE
1900 (10 and 9 = 19 x 100)
36 (Add 30 and 6)
1936 E.E.
8 (Add)
1943/4 AD

## PEOPLES DEMOCRATIC REPUBLIC

### DECIMAL COINAGE

100 Santeems (Cents) = 1 Birr (Dollar)
100 Matonas = 100 Santeems

**KM# 44.3 5 CENTS**
3.00 g., Brass Plated Steel, 20 mm. **Obv:** Large lion head, right **Rev:** Denomination left of figure

| Date | Mintage | VF20 | XF40 | MS60 | MS63 | MS65 |
|---|---|---|---|---|---|---|
| EE1996 (2004) | — | — | — | — | 1.00 | 1.25 |
| EE1998 (2006) | — | — | — | — | 1.00 | 1.25 |
| EE1999 (2007) | — | — | — | — | 1.00 | 1.25 |
| EE2000 (2008) | — | — | — | — | 1.00 | 1.25 |
| EE2004 (2012) | — | — | — | — | 1.00 | 1.25 |

**KM# 45.3 10 CENTS**
4.50 g., Brass Plated Steel, 23 mm. **Obv:** Large lion head right **Rev:** Mountain Nyala, denomination at right

| Date | Mintage | VF20 | XF40 | MS60 | MS63 | MS65 |
|---|---|---|---|---|---|---|
| EE1996 (2004) | — | — | — | — | 1.25 | 1.50 |
| EE1997 (2005) | — | — | — | — | 1.25 | 1.50 |
| EE1998 (2006) | — | — | — | — | 1.25 | 1.50 |
| EE2000 (2008) | — | — | — | — | 1.25 | 1.50 |
| EE2004 (2012) | — | — | — | — | 1.25 | 1.50 |

**KM# 46.3 25 CENTS**
3.70 g., Copper-Nickel Plated Steel, 21.45 mm. **Obv:** Large lion head right **Rev:** Man and woman with arms raised divide denomination

| Date | Mintage | VF20 | XF40 | MS60 | MS63 | MS65 |
|---|---|---|---|---|---|---|
| EE1996 (2004) | — | — | — | — | 1.25 | 1.50 |
| EE1997 (2005) | — | — | — | — | 1.25 | 1.50 |
| EE2000 (2008) | — | — | — | — | 1.25 | 1.50 |
| EE2004 (2012) | — | — | — | — | 1.25 | 1.50 |

**KM# 47.2 50 CENTS**
6.00 g., Copper-Nickel Plated Steel, 25 mm. **Obv:** Small lion head, two long chin whiskers at left nearly touch date **Rev:** People of the republic, denomination above

| Date | Mintage | VF20 | XF40 | MS60 | MS63 | MS65 |
|---|---|---|---|---|---|---|
| EE1996 (2004) | — | — | — | 1.75 | 2.75 | 3.25 |
| EE1997 (2005) | — | — | — | 1.75 | 2.75 | 3.25 |
| EE2000 (2008) | — | — | — | 1.75 | 2.75 | 3.25 |
| EE2004 (2012) | — | — | — | 1.75 | 2.75 | 3.25 |

## FEDERAL DEMOCRATIC REPUBLIC

**KM# 78 BIRR**
6.82 g., Bi-Metallic Brass Plated Steel center in Nickel Plated Steel ring, 27 mm. **Obv:** Large lion right in center **Rev:** Balance scale

| Date | Mintage | VF20 | XF40 | MS60 | MS63 | MS65 |
|---|---|---|---|---|---|---|
| EE2002 (2010) | 416,000,000 | — | — | 2.25 | 4.50 | 5.50 |

**KM# 76 20 BIRR**
30.00 g., 0.900 Silver 0.8681 oz. ASW, 40 mm. **Obv:** Vertical symbol with ribbon **Rev:** Reconstructed skeleton

| Date | Mintage | VF20 | XF40 | MS60 | MS63 | MS65 |
|---|---|---|---|---|---|---|
| EE2000 (2007) | Est. 50000 | **PF63** 65.00 | **PF65** 75.00 | | | |

**KM# 77 600 BIRR**
20.00 g., Gold, 34 mm. **Rev:** Selam Skull

| Date | Mintage | VF20 | XF40 | MS60 | MS63 | MS65 |
|---|---|---|---|---|---|---|
| EE2000 (2007) | Est. 1000 | **PF63** 1,100 | **PF65** 1,250 | | | |

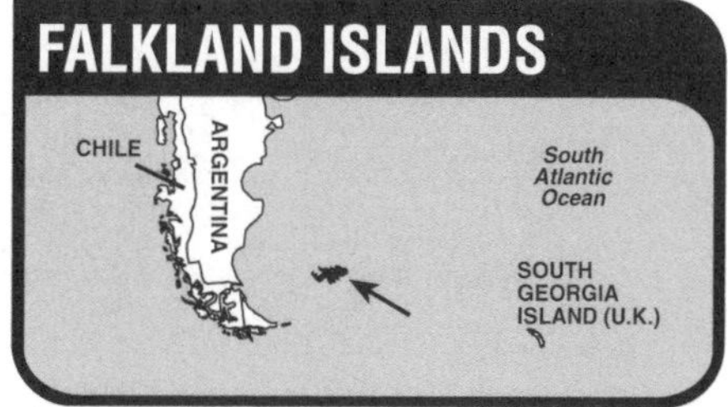


The Colony of the Falkland Islands and Dependencies, a British colony located in the South Atlantic about 500 miles northeast of Cape Horn, has an area of 4,700 sq. mi. (12,170 sq. km.) and a population of 2,121. East Falkland, West Falkland, South Georgia, and South Sandwich are the largest of the 200 islands. Capital: Stanley. Sheep grazing is the main industry. Wool, whale oil, and seal oil are exported.

**RULER**
British

**MONETARY SYSTEM**
100 Pence = 1 Pound

## BRITISH COLONY

### DECIMAL COINAGE

**KM# 130 PENNY**
3.56 g., Copper Plated Steel, 20.3 mm. **Ruler:** Elizabeth II **Obv:** Head with tiara right **Obv. Legend:** QUEEN ELIZABETH THE SECOND **Rev:** Two Gentoo penguins flank value **Rev. Legend:** FALKLAND ISLANDS **Edge:** Plain

| Date | Mintage | VF20 | XF40 | MS60 | MS63 | MS65 |
|---|---|---|---|---|---|---|
| 2004 | — | — | — | 0.25 | 0.50 | 0.75 |

**KM# 131 2 PENCE**
7.12 g., Copper Plated Steel, 25.9 mm. **Ruler:** Elizabeth II **Obv:** Head with tiara right **Obv. Legend:** QUEEN ELIZABETH THE SECOND **Rev:** Upland goose alighting, value above **Rev. Legend:** FALKLAND ISLANDS **Edge:** Plain

| Date | Mintage | VF20 | XF40 | MS60 | MS63 | MS65 |
|---|---|---|---|---|---|---|
| 2004 | — | — | — | 0.25 | 0.50 | 1.00 |

**KM# 132 5 PENCE**
3.25 g., Copper-Nickel, 18 mm. **Ruler:** Elizabeth II **Obv:** Head with tiara right **Obv. Legend:** QUEEN ELIZABETH THE SECOND **Rev:** Black-browed Albatross in flight, value below **Rev. Legend:** FALKLAND - ISLANDS **Edge:** Reeded

| Date | Mintage | VF20 | XF40 | MS60 | MS63 | MS65 |
|---|---|---|---|---|---|---|
| 2004 | — | — | — | 0.35 | 0.75 | 1.00 |

**KM# 133 10 PENCE**
6.50 g., Copper-Nickel, 24.5 mm. **Ruler:** Elizabeth II **Obv:** Head with tiara right **Obv. Legend:** QUEEN ELIZABETH THE SECOND **Rev:** Ursine seal with cub, value below **Rev. Legend:** FALKLAND ISLANDS **Edge:** Reeded

| Date | Mintage | VF20 | XF40 | MS60 | MS63 | MS65 |
|---|---|---|---|---|---|---|
| 2004 | — | — | — | 0.75 | 1.50 | 3.00 |

**KM# 134 20 PENCE**
5.00 g., Copper-Nickel, 21.4 mm. **Ruler:** Elizabeth II **Obv:** Head with tiara right **Obv. Legend:** QUEEN ELIZABETH THE SECOND **Rev:** Romney marsh sheep standing left, value above **Rev. Legend:** FALKLAND ISLANDS **Edge:** Plain **Shape:** 7-sided

| Date | Mintage | VF20 | XF40 | MS60 | MS63 | MS65 |
|---|---|---|---|---|---|---|
| 2004 | — | — | — | 1.00 | 2.00 | 4.00 |

**KM# 70 50 PENCE**
29.10 g., Copper-Nickel, 38.6 mm. **Ruler:** Elizabeth II **Subject:** Centennial of Queen Victoria's Death **Obv:** Crowned bust right, denomination below **Rev:** Crowned head left, three dates **Edge:** Reeded

| Date | Mintage | VF20 | XF40 | MS60 | MS63 | MS65 |
|---|---|---|---|---|---|---|
| 2001 | — | — | — | 4.00 | 6.00 | 7.00 |

**KM# 70a 50 PENCE**
28.28 g., 0.925 Silver 0.841 oz. ASW, 38.6 mm. **Ruler:** Elizabeth II **Obv:** Crowned bust right, denomination below **Rev:** Crowned head left, three dates **Edge:** Reeded

| Date | Mintage | VF20 | XF40 | MS60 | MS63 | MS65 |
|---|---|---|---|---|---|---|
| 2001 | 10,000 | PF65 50.00 | | | | |

**KM# 70b 50 PENCE**
47.54 g., 0.917 Gold 1.4016 oz. AGW, 38.61 mm. **Ruler:** Elizabeth II **Subject:** Centennial of Queen Victoria's Death **Obv:** Crowned bust right, denomination below **Rev:** Victoria's crowned bust left, three dates **Edge:** Reeded

| Date | Mintage | VF20 | XF40 | MS60 | MS63 | MS65 |
|---|---|---|---|---|---|---|
| 2001 | 100 | PF65 2,500 | | | | |

**KM# 71 50 PENCE**
29.10 g., Copper-Nickel, 38.6 mm. **Ruler:** Elizabeth II **Subject:** Queen Elizabeth's 75th Birthday **Obv:** Crowned bust right, denomination below **Rev:** Bust of Queen Elizabeth II left **Edge:** Reeded

| Date | Mintage | VF20 | XF40 | MS60 | MS63 | MS65 |
|---|---|---|---|---|---|---|
| 2001 | — | — | — | 4.00 | 6.00 | 7.00 |

**KM# 71b 50 PENCE**
47.54 g., 0.917 Gold 1.4016 oz. AGW, 38.61 mm. **Ruler:** Elizabeth II **Subject:** Queen Elizabeth's 75th Birthday **Obv:** Crowned bust right, denomination below **Rev:** Bust of Queen Elizabeth II left

| Date | Mintage | VF20 | XF40 | MS60 | MS63 | MS65 |
|---|---|---|---|---|---|---|
| 2001 | Est. 100 | PF65 2,500 | | | | |

**KM# 86 50 PENCE**
28.28 g., Copper-Nickel, 38.6 mm. **Ruler:** Elizabeth II **Obv:** Crowned bust right, denomination below **Rev:** Edward IV (1461-83) with Rose Ryal gold coin design **Edge:** Reeded

| Date | Mintage | VF20 | XF40 | MS60 | MS63 | MS65 |
|---|---|---|---|---|---|---|
| 2001 | — | — | — | 7.00 | 9.00 | 10.00 |

**KM# 86a 50 PENCE**
28.28 g., 0.925 Silver 0.841 oz. ASW, 38.6 mm. **Ruler:** Elizabeth II **Obv:** Crowned bust right, denomination below **Rev:** Edward IV (1461-83) with gold-plated Rose Ryal gold coin design **Edge:** Reeded

| Date | Mintage | VF20 | XF40 | MS60 | MS63 | MS65 |
|---|---|---|---|---|---|---|
| 2001 | 5,000 | PF65 50.00 | | | | |

**KM# 87 50 PENCE**
28.28 g., Copper-Nickel, 38.6 mm. **Ruler:** Elizabeth II **Obv:** Crowned bust right, denomination below **Rev:** Henry VII (1485-1509) with 1489 Gold Sovereign coin design **Edge:** Reeded

| Date | Mintage | VF20 | XF40 | MS60 | MS63 | MS65 |
|---|---|---|---|---|---|---|
| 2001 | — | — | — | 7.00 | 9.00 | 10.00 |

**KM# 87a 50 PENCE**
28.28 g., 0.925 Silver 0.841 oz. ASW, 38.6 mm. **Ruler:** Elizabeth II **Obv:** Crowned bust right, denomination below **Rev:** Henry VII (1485-1509) with gold-plated 1489 gold Sovereign coin design **Edge:** Reeded

| Date | Mintage | VF20 | XF40 | MS60 | MS63 | MS65 |
|---|---|---|---|---|---|---|
| 2001 | 5,000 | PF65 50.00 | | | | |

**KM# 88 50 PENCE**
28.28 g., Copper-Nickel, 38.6 mm. **Ruler:** Elizabeth II **Obv:** Crowned bust right, denomination below **Rev:** Charles II (1660-85) with 1663 gold Guinea coin design **Edge:** Reeded

| Date | Mintage | VF20 | XF40 | MS60 | MS63 | MS65 |
|---|---|---|---|---|---|---|
| 2001 | — | — | — | 7.00 | 9.00 | 10.00 |

**KM# 88a 50 PENCE**
28.28 g., 0.925 Silver 0.841 oz. ASW, 38.6 mm. **Ruler:** Elizabeth II **Obv:** Crowned bust right, denomination below **Rev:** Charles II (1660-85) with gold-plated Gold Guinea coin design **Edge:** Reeded

| Date | Mintage | VF20 | XF40 | MS60 | MS63 | MS65 |
|---|---|---|---|---|---|---|
| 2001 | 5,000 | PF65 50.00 | | | | |

**KM# 89 50 PENCE**
28.28 g., Copper-Nickel, 38.6 mm. **Ruler:** Elizabeth II **Obv:** Crowned bust right, denomination below **Rev:** Queen Victoria with Gold Sovereign coin design **Edge:** Reeded

| Date | Mintage | VF20 | XF40 | MS60 | MS63 | MS65 |
|---|---|---|---|---|---|---|
| 2001 | — | — | — | 7.00 | 9.00 | 10.00 |

**KM# 89a 50 PENCE**
28.28 g., 0.925 Silver 0.841 oz. ASW, 38.6 mm. **Ruler:** Elizabeth II **Obv:** Crowned bust right, denomination below **Rev:** Queen Victoria with gold-plated Gold Sovereign coin design **Edge:** Reeded

| Date | Mintage | VF20 | XF40 | MS60 | MS63 | MS65 |
|---|---|---|---|---|---|---|
| 2001 | 5,000 | PF65 50.00 | | | | |

**KM# 73.1 50 PENCE**
28.13 g., Copper-Nickel, 38.6 mm. **Ruler:** Elizabeth II **Subject:** Queen's Golden Jubilee **Obv:** Crowned head right, denomination below **Rev:** Queen Elizabeth II on throne in inner circle below multicolor bunting **Edge:** Reeded

| Date | Mintage | VF20 | XF40 | MS60 | MS63 | MS65 |
|---|---|---|---|---|---|---|
| 2002(2001) | — | PF65 8.00 | | | | |

**KM# 73.2 50 PENCE**
Copper-Nickel **Ruler:** Elizabeth II **Subject:** Queen's Golden Jubilee **Obv:** Crowned bust right, denomination below **Rev:** With plain bunting

| Date | Mintage | VF20 | XF40 | MS60 | MS63 | MS65 |
|---|---|---|---|---|---|---|
| 2002 | — | — | — | 4.00 | 6.00 | 7.00 |

**KM# 73a.1 50 PENCE**
28.28 g., 0.925 Silver 0.841 oz. ASW, 38.6 mm. **Ruler:** Elizabeth II **Subject:** Queen's Golden Jubilee **Obv:** Crowned bust right, denomination below **Rev:** Queen on throne below multicolor bunting **Edge:** Reeded

| Date | Mintage | VF20 | XF40 | MS60 | MS63 | MS65 |
|---|---|---|---|---|---|---|
| 2002 | 25,000 | PF65 45.00 | | | | |

**KM# 73a.2 50 PENCE**
28.28 g., 0.925 Silver 0.841 oz. ASW, 38.61 mm. **Ruler:** Elizabeth II **Obv:** Crowned bust right, denomination below **Rev:** With plain bunting

| Date | Mintage | VF20 | XF40 | MS60 | MS63 | MS65 |
|---|---|---|---|---|---|---|
| 2002 | — | PF65 45.00 | | | | |

**KM# 73b.1 50 PENCE**
39.94 g., 0.917 Gold 1.1775 oz. AGW, 38.61 mm. **Ruler:** Elizabeth II **Obv:** Crowned bust right, denomination below **Rev:** Crowned queen with scepter and orb below multicolor bunting **Edge:** Reeded

| Date | Mintage | VF20 | XF40 | MS60 | MS63 | MS65 |
|---|---|---|---|---|---|---|
| 2002 | 150 | PF65 2,100 | | | | |

**KM# 74.1 50 PENCE**
28.13 g., Copper-Nickel, 38.6 mm. **Ruler:** Elizabeth II **Subject:** Queen's Golden Jubilee **Obv:** Crowned bust right, denomination below **Rev:** Queen on horse half left in inner circle below multicolor bunting **Edge:** Reeded

| Date | Mintage | VF20 | XF40 | MS60 | MS63 | MS65 |
|---|---|---|---|---|---|---|
| 2002(2001) | — | PF65 8.00 | | | | |

**KM# 74.2 50 PENCE**
Copper-Nickel **Ruler:** Elizabeth II **Subject:** Queen's Golden Jubilee **Obv:** Crowned bust right, denomination below **Rev:** With plain bunting

| Date | Mintage | VF20 | XF40 | MS60 | MS63 | MS65 |
|---|---|---|---|---|---|---|
| 2002 | — | — | — | 5.00 | 7.00 | 8.00 |

**KM# 74a.1 50 PENCE**
28.28 g., 0.925 Silver 0.841 oz. ASW, 38.6 mm. **Ruler:** Elizabeth II **Subject:** Queen's Golden Jubilee **Obv:** Crowned bust right, denomination below **Edge:** Reeded

| Date | Mintage | VF20 | XF40 | MS60 | MS63 | MS65 |
|---|---|---|---|---|---|---|
| 2002 | 25,000 | PF65 45.00 | | | | |

**KM# 74a.2 50 PENCE**
28.28 g., 0.925 Silver 0.841 oz. ASW, 38.61 mm. **Ruler:** Elizabeth II **Subject:** Queen's Golden Jubilee **Obv:** Crowned bust right, denomination below **Rev:** With plain bunting

| Date | Mintage | VF20 | XF40 | MS60 | MS63 | MS65 |
|---|---|---|---|---|---|---|
| 2002 | — | PF65 45.00 | | | | |

**KM# 74b.1 50 PENCE**
39.94 g., 0.917 Gold 1.1775 oz. AGW, 38.61 mm. **Ruler:** Elizabeth II **Subject:** Queen's Golden Jubilee **Obv:** Crowned bust right, denomination below **Rev:** Queen on horseback below multicolored bunting **Edge:** Reeded

| Date | Mintage | VF20 | XF40 | MS60 | MS63 | MS65 |
|---|---|---|---|---|---|---|
| 2002 | 150 | PF65 2,050 | | | | |

**KM# 74b.2 50 PENCE**
39.94 g., 0.917 Gold 1.1775 oz. AGW, 38.61 mm. **Ruler:** Elizabeth II **Subject:** Queen's Golden Jubilee **Obv:** Crowned bust right, denomination below **Rev:** With plain bunting

| Date | Mintage | VF20 | XF40 | MS60 | MS63 | MS65 |
|---|---|---|---|---|---|---|
| 2002 | — | PF65 2,100 | | | | |

**KM# 75.1 50 PENCE**
28.13 g., Copper-Nickel, 38.6 mm. **Ruler:** Elizabeth II **Subject:** Queen's Golden Jubilee **Obv:** Crowned bust right, denomination below **Rev:** Queen Elizabeth II talking into microphone below multicolor bunting **Edge:** Reeded

| Date | Mintage | VF20 | XF40 | MS60 | MS63 | MS65 |
|---|---|---|---|---|---|---|
| 2002(2001) | — | PF65 8.00 | | | | |

**KM# 75.2 50 PENCE**
Copper-Nickel **Ruler:** Elizabeth II **Subject:** Queen's Golden Jubilee **Obv:** Crowned bust right, denomination below **Rev:** With plain bunting

| Date | Mintage | VF20 | XF40 | MS60 | MS63 | MS65 |
|---|---|---|---|---|---|---|
| 2002 | — | — | — | 4.00 | 6.00 | 7.00 |

**KM# 75a.1 50 PENCE**
28.28 g., 0.925 Silver 0.841 oz. ASW, 38.6 mm. **Ruler:** Elizabeth II **Subject:** Queen's Golden Jubilee **Obv:** Crowned bust right, denomination below **Rev:** Queen speaking into a radio microphone below multicolored bunting **Edge:** Reeded

| Date | Mintage | VF20 | XF40 | MS60 | MS63 | MS65 |
|---|---|---|---|---|---|---|
| 2002 | 25,000 | PF65 45.00 | | | | |

**KM# 75a.2 50 PENCE**
28.28 g., 0.925 Silver 0.841 oz. ASW, 38.61 mm. **Ruler:** Elizabeth II **Subject:** Queen's Golden Jubilee **Obv:** Crowned bust right, denomination below **Rev:** With plain bunting

| Date | Mintage | VF20 | XF40 | MS60 | MS63 | MS65 |
|---|---|---|---|---|---|---|
| 2002 | — | PF65 45.00 | | | | |

**KM# 75b.1 50 PENCE**
39.94 g., 0.917 Gold 1.1775 oz. AGW, 38.61 mm. **Ruler:** Elizabeth II **Subject:** Queen's Golden Jubilee **Obv:** Crowned bust right, denomination below **Rev:** Elizabeth speaking into a radio microphone below multicolored bunting **Edge:** Reeded

| Date | Mintage | VF20 | XF40 | MS60 | MS63 | MS65 |
|---|---|---|---|---|---|---|
| 2002 | 50 | PF65 2,150 | | | | |

**KM# 75b.2 50 PENCE**
39.94 g., 0.917 Gold 1.1775 oz. AGW, 38.61 mm. **Ruler:** Elizabeth II **Subject:** Queen's Golden Jubilee **Obv:** Crowned bust right, denomination below **Rev:** With plain bunting

| Date | Mintage | VF20 | XF40 | MS60 | MS63 | MS65 |
|---|---|---|---|---|---|---|
| 2002 | — | PF65 2,100 | | | | |

**KM# 76.1 50 PENCE**
28.13 g., Copper-Nickel, 38.6 mm. **Ruler:** Elizabeth II **Subject:** Queen's Golden Jubilee **Obv:** Crowned bust right, denomination below **Rev:** Queen walking to left in front of a crowd below multicolored bunting **Edge:** Reeded

| Date | Mintage | VF20 | XF40 | MS60 | MS63 | MS65 |
|---|---|---|---|---|---|---|
| 2002(2001) | — | PF65 8.00 | | | | |

**KM# 76.2 50 PENCE**
Copper-Nickel **Ruler:** Elizabeth II **Subject:** Queen's Golden Jubilee **Obv:** Crowned bust right, denomination below **Rev:** With plain bunting

| Date | Mintage | VF20 | XF40 | MS60 | MS63 | MS65 |
|---|---|---|---|---|---|---|
| 2002 | — | — | — | 4.00 | 6.00 | 7.00 |

**KM# 76a.1 50 PENCE**
28.28 g., 0.925 Silver 0.841 oz. ASW, 38.6 mm. **Ruler:** Elizabeth II **Subject:** Queen's Golden Jubilee **Obv:** Crowned bust right, denomination below **Rev:** Queen standing before crowd below multicolored bunting **Edge:** Reeded

| Date | Mintage | VF20 | XF40 | MS60 | MS63 | MS65 |
|---|---|---|---|---|---|---|
| 2002 | 15,000 | PF65 45.00 | | | | |

**KM# 76a.2 50 PENCE**
28.28 g., 0.925 Silver 0.841 oz. ASW, 38.61 mm. **Ruler:** Elizabeth II **Subject:** Queen's Golden Jubilee **Obv:** Crowned bust right, denomination below **Rev:** With plain bunting

| Date | Mintage | VF20 | XF40 | MS60 | MS63 | MS65 |
|---|---|---|---|---|---|---|
| 2002 | — | PF65 45.00 | | | | |

**KM# 76b.1 50 PENCE**
39.94 g., 0.917 Gold 1.1775 oz. AGW, 38.61 mm. **Ruler:** Elizabeth II **Subject:** Queen's Golden Jubilee **Obv:** Crowned bust right, denomination below **Rev:** Queen standing before a crowd below multicolored bunting **Edge:** Reeded

| Date | Mintage | VF20 | XF40 | MS60 | MS63 | MS65 |
|---|---|---|---|---|---|---|
| 2002 | 50 | PF65 2,150 | | | | |

**KM# 76b.2 50 PENCE**
39.94 g., 0.917 Gold 1.1775 oz. AGW, 38.61 mm. **Ruler:** Elizabeth II **Subject:** Queen's Golden Jubilee **Obv:** Crowned bust right, denomination below **Rev:** With plain bunting

| Date | Mintage | VF20 | XF40 | MS60 | MS63 | MS65 |
|---|---|---|---|---|---|---|
| 2002 | — | PF65 2,100 | | | | |

### KM# 77.1 50 PENCE

28.13 g., Copper-Nickel, 38.6 mm. **Ruler:** Elizabeth II **Subject:** Queen's Golden Jubilee **Obv:** Crowned bust right, denomination below **Rev:** Conjoined busts of Queen Elizabeth, Prince Charles, Prince William facing left in inner circle below multicolor bunting **Edge:** Reeded

| Date | Mintage | VF20 | XF40 | MS60 | MS63 | MS65 |
|---|---|---|---|---|---|---|
| 2002(2001) | — | PF65 8.00 | | | | |

### KM# 77.2 50 PENCE

Copper-Nickel **Ruler:** Elizabeth II **Subject:** Queen's Golden Jubilee **Obv:** Crowned bust right, denomination below **Rev:** With plain bunting

| Date | Mintage | VF20 | XF40 | MS60 | MS63 | MS65 |
|---|---|---|---|---|---|---|
| 2002 | — | — | — | 4.00 | 6.00 | 7.00 |

### KM# 77a.1 50 PENCE

28.28 g., 0.925 Silver 0.841 oz. ASW, 38.6 mm. **Ruler:** Elizabeth II **Subject:** Queen's Golden Jubilee **Obv:** Crowned bust right, denomination below **Rev:** Queen, Prince Charles and Prince William below multicolor bunting **Edge:** Reeded

| Date | Mintage | VF20 | XF40 | MS60 | MS63 | MS65 |
|---|---|---|---|---|---|---|
| 2002 | 15,000 | PF65 45.00 | | | | |

### KM# 77a.2 50 PENCE

28.28 g., 0.925 Silver 0.841 oz. ASW, 38.61 mm. **Ruler:** Elizabeth II **Subject:** Queen's Golden Jubilee **Obv:** Crowned bust right, denomination below **Rev:** With plain bunting

| Date | Mintage | VF20 | XF40 | MS60 | MS63 | MS65 |
|---|---|---|---|---|---|---|
| 2002 | — | PF65 45.00 | | | | |

### KM# 77b.1 50 PENCE

39.94 g., 0.917 Gold 1.1775 oz. AGW, 38.61 mm. **Ruler:** Elizabeth II **Subject:** Queen's Golden Jubilee **Obv:** Crowned bust right, denomination below **Rev:** Elizabeth II, Prince Charles and his son William below multicolored bunting **Edge:** Reeded

| Date | Mintage | VF20 | XF40 | MS60 | MS63 | MS65 |
|---|---|---|---|---|---|---|
| 2002 | 50 | PF65 2,150 | | | | |

### KM# 77b.2 50 PENCE

39.94 g., 0.917 Gold 1.1775 oz. AGW, 38.61 mm. **Ruler:** Elizabeth II **Subject:** Queen's Golden Jubilee **Obv:** Crowned bust right, denomination below **Rev:** With plain bunting

| Date | Mintage | VF20 | XF40 | MS60 | MS63 | MS65 |
|---|---|---|---|---|---|---|
| 2002 | — | PF65 2,100 | | | | |

### KM# 78.1 50 PENCE

28.13 g., Copper-Nickel, 38.6 mm. **Ruler:** Elizabeth II **Subject:** Queen's Golden Jubilee **Obv:** Crowned bust right, denomination below **Rev:** Royal coach below multicolor bunting **Edge:** Reeded

| Date | Mintage | VF20 | XF40 | MS60 | MS63 | MS65 |
|---|---|---|---|---|---|---|
| 2002 | — | PF65 8.00 | | | | |

### KM# 78.2 50 PENCE

Copper-Nickel **Ruler:** Elizabeth II **Subject:** Queen's Golden Jubilee **Obv:** Crowned bust right, denomination below **Rev:** With plain bunting

| Date | Mintage | VF20 | XF40 | MS60 | MS63 | MS65 |
|---|---|---|---|---|---|---|
| 2002 | — | — | — | 4.00 | 6.00 | 7.00 |

### KM# 78a.1 50 PENCE

28.28 g., 0.925 Silver 0.841 oz. ASW, 38.6 mm. **Ruler:** Elizabeth II **Subject:** Queen's Golden Jubilee **Obv:** Crowned bust right, denomination below **Rev:** Coronation coach below multicolor bunting **Edge:** Reeded

| Date | Mintage | VF20 | XF40 | MS60 | MS63 | MS65 |
|---|---|---|---|---|---|---|
| 2002 | 15,000 | PF65 45.00 | | | | |

### KM# 78b.1 50 PENCE

39.94 g., 0.917 Gold 1.1775 oz. AGW, 38.61 mm. **Ruler:** Elizabeth II **Subject:** Queen's Golden Jubilee **Obv:** Crowned bust right, denomination below **Rev:** Coronation coach below multicolor bunting **Edge:** Reeded

| Date | Mintage | VF20 | XF40 | MS60 | MS63 | MS65 |
|---|---|---|---|---|---|---|
| 2002 | 150 | PF65 2,150 | | | | |

### KM# 78b.2 50 PENCE

39.94 g., 0.917 Gold 1.1775 oz. AGW, 38.61 mm. **Ruler:** Elizabeth II **Subject:** Queen's Golden Jubilee **Obv:** Crowned bust right, denomination below **Rev:** With plain bunting

| Date | Mintage | VF20 | XF40 | MS60 | MS63 | MS65 |
|---|---|---|---|---|---|---|
| 2002 | — | PF65 2,100 | | | | |

### KM# 79.1 50 PENCE

28.13 g., Copper-Nickel, 38.6 mm. **Ruler:** Elizabeth II **Subject:** Queen's Golden Jubilee **Obv:** Crowned bust right, denomination below **Rev:** Scepter and orb below multicolor bunting **Edge:** Reeded

| Date | Mintage | VF20 | XF40 | MS60 | MS63 | MS65 |
|---|---|---|---|---|---|---|
| 2002 | — | PF65 8.00 | | | | |

### KM# 79.2 50 PENCE

Copper-Nickel **Ruler:** Elizabeth II **Subject:** Queen's Golden Jubilee **Obv:** Crowned bust right, denomination below **Rev:** With plain bunting

| Date | Mintage | VF20 | XF40 | MS60 | MS63 | MS65 |
|---|---|---|---|---|---|---|
| 2002 | — | — | — | 4.00 | 6.00 | 7.00 |

### KM# 79a.1 50 PENCE

28.28 g., 0.925 Silver 0.841 oz. ASW, 38.6 mm. **Ruler:** Elizabeth II **Subject:** Queen's Golden Jubilee **Obv:** Crowned bust right, denomination below **Rev:** Orb and scepter below multicolor bunting **Edge:** Reeded

| Date | Mintage | VF20 | XF40 | MS60 | MS63 | MS65 |
|---|---|---|---|---|---|---|
| 2002 | 15,000 | PF65 45.00 | | | | |

### KM# 79a.2 50 PENCE

28.28 g., 0.925 Silver 0.841 oz. ASW, 38.61 mm. **Ruler:** Elizabeth II **Subject:** Queen's Golden Jubilee **Obv:** Crowned bust right, denomination below **Rev:** With plain bunting

| Date | Mintage | VF20 | XF40 | MS60 | MS63 | MS65 |
|---|---|---|---|---|---|---|
| 2002 | — | PF65 45.00 | | | | |

### KM# 79b.1 50 PENCE

39.94 g., 0.917 Gold 1.1775 oz. AGW, 38.61 mm. **Ruler:** Elizabeth II **Subject:** Queen's Golden Jubilee **Obv:** Crowned bust right, denomination below **Rev:** Orb and scepter below multicolor bunting **Edge:** Reeded

| Date | Mintage | VF20 | XF40 | MS60 | MS63 | MS65 |
|---|---|---|---|---|---|---|
| 2002 | 150 | PF65 2,150 | | | | |

### KM# 79b.2 50 PENCE

39.94 g., 0.917 Gold 1.1775 oz. AGW, 38.61 mm. **Ruler:** Elizabeth II **Subject:** Queen's Golden Jubilee **Obv:** Crowned bust right, denomination below **Rev:** With plain bunting

| Date | Mintage | VF20 | XF40 | MS60 | MS63 | MS65 |
|---|---|---|---|---|---|---|
| 2002 | — | PF65 2,100 | | | | |

### KM# 80.1 50 PENCE

28.13 g., Copper-Nickel, 38.6 mm. **Ruler:** Elizabeth II **Subject:** Queen's Golden Jubilee **Obv:** Crowned bust right, denomination below **Rev:** Crown below multicolor bunting **Edge:** Reeded

| Date | Mintage | VF20 | XF40 | MS60 | MS63 | MS65 |
|---|---|---|---|---|---|---|
| 2002 | — | PF65 8.00 | | | | |

### KM# 80.2 50 PENCE

Copper-Nickel **Ruler:** Elizabeth II **Subject:** Queen's Golden Jubilee **Obv:** Crowned bust right, denomination below **Rev:** With plain bunting

| Date | Mintage | VF20 | XF40 | MS60 | MS63 | MS65 |
|---|---|---|---|---|---|---|
| 2002 | — | — | — | 4.00 | 6.00 | 7.00 |

### KM# 80a.1 50 PENCE

28.28 g., 0.925 Silver 0.841 oz. ASW, 38.6 mm. **Ruler:** Elizabeth II **Subject:** Queen's Golden Jubilee **Obv:** Crowned bust right, denomination below **Rev:** Crown below multicolor bunting **Edge:** Reeded

| Date | Mintage | VF20 | XF40 | MS60 | MS63 | MS65 |
|---|---|---|---|---|---|---|
| 2002 | 15,000 | PF65 45.00 | | | | |

### KM# 80a.2 50 PENCE

28.28 g., 0.925 Silver 0.841 oz. ASW, 38.61 mm. **Ruler:** Elizabeth II **Subject:** Queen's Golden Jubilee **Obv:** Crowned bust right, denomination below **Rev:** With plain bunting

| Date | Mintage | VF20 | XF40 | MS60 | MS63 | MS65 |
|---|---|---|---|---|---|---|
| 2002 | — | PF65 45.00 | | | | |

**KM# 80b.1 50 PENCE**
39.94 g., 0.917 Gold 1.1775 oz. AGW, 38.61 mm. **Ruler:** Elizabeth II **Subject:** Queen's Golden Jubilee **Obv:** Crowned bust right, denomination below **Rev:** Crown below multicolor bunting **Edge:** Reeded

| Date | Mintage | VF20 | XF40 | MS60 | MS63 | MS65 |
|---|---|---|---|---|---|---|
| 2002 | 150 | PF65 2,150 | | | | |

**KM# 80b.2 50 PENCE**
39.94 g., 0.917 Gold 1.1775 oz. AGW, 38.61 mm. **Ruler:** Elizabeth II **Subject:** Queen's Golden Jubilee **Obv:** Crowned bust right, denomination below **Rev:** With plain bunting

| Date | Mintage | VF20 | XF40 | MS60 | MS63 | MS65 |
|---|---|---|---|---|---|---|
| 2002 | — | PF65 2,100 | | | | |

**KM# 81.1 50 PENCE**
28.13 g., Copper-Nickel, 38.6 mm. **Ruler:** Elizabeth II **Subject:** Queen's Golden Jubilee **Obv:** Crowned bust right, denomination below **Rev:** Throne below multicolor bunting **Edge:** Reeded

| Date | Mintage | VF20 | XF40 | MS60 | MS63 | MS65 |
|---|---|---|---|---|---|---|
| 2002 | — | PF65 8.00 | | | | |

**KM# 81.2 50 PENCE**
Copper-Nickel **Ruler:** Elizabeth II **Subject:** Queen's Golden Jubilee **Obv:** Crowned bust right, denomination below **Rev:** With plain bunting

| Date | Mintage | VF20 | XF40 | MS60 | MS63 | MS65 |
|---|---|---|---|---|---|---|
| 2002 | — | — | — | 4.00 | 6.00 | 7.00 |

**KM# 81a.1 50 PENCE**
28.28 g., 0.925 Silver 0.841 oz. ASW, 38.6 mm. **Ruler:** Elizabeth II **Subject:** Queen's Golden Jubilee **Obv:** Crowned bust right, denomination below **Rev:** Coronation throne below multicolor bunting **Edge:** Reeded

| Date | Mintage | VF20 | XF40 | MS60 | MS63 | MS65 |
|---|---|---|---|---|---|---|
| 2002 | 15,000 | PF65 45.00 | | | | |

**KM# 81a.2 50 PENCE**
28.28 g., 0.925 Silver 0.841 oz. ASW, 38.61 mm. **Ruler:** Elizabeth II **Subject:** Queen's Golden Jubilee **Obv:** Crowned bust right, denomination below **Rev:** With plain bunting

| Date | Mintage | VF20 | XF40 | MS60 | MS63 | MS65 |
|---|---|---|---|---|---|---|
| 2002 | — | PF65 45.00 | | | | |

**KM# 81b.1 50 PENCE**
39.94 g., 0.917 Gold 1.1775 oz. AGW, 38.61 mm. **Ruler:** Elizabeth II **Subject:** Queen's Golden Jubilee **Obv:** Crowned bust right, denomination below **Rev:** Coronation Throne below multicolored bunting **Edge:** Reeded

| Date | Mintage | VF20 | XF40 | MS60 | MS63 | MS65 |
|---|---|---|---|---|---|---|
| 2002 | 150 | PF65 2,150 | | | | |

**KM# 81b.2 50 PENCE**
39.94 g., 0.917 Gold 1.1775 oz. AGW, 38.61 mm. **Ruler:** Elizabeth II **Subject:** Queen's Golden Jubilee **Obv:** Crowned bust right, denomination below **Rev:** With plain bunting

| Date | Mintage | VF20 | XF40 | MS60 | MS63 | MS65 |
|---|---|---|---|---|---|---|
| 2002 | — | PF65 2,100 | | | | |

**KM# 82.1 50 PENCE**
28.13 g., Copper-Nickel, 38.6 mm. **Ruler:** Elizabeth II **Subject:** Queen's Golden Jubilee **Obv:** Crowned bust right, denomination below **Rev:** Queen on throne below multicolor bunting **Edge:** Reeded

| Date | Mintage | VF20 | XF40 | MS60 | MS63 | MS65 |
|---|---|---|---|---|---|---|
| 2002 Proof | — | — | — | 4.00 | 6.00 | 7.00 |

**KM# 82.2 50 PENCE**
Copper-Nickel **Ruler:** Elizabeth II **Subject:** Queen's Golden Jubilee **Obv:** Crowned bust right, denomination below **Rev:** With plain bunting

| Date | Mintage | VF20 | XF40 | MS60 | MS63 | MS65 |
|---|---|---|---|---|---|---|
| 2002 | — | — | — | 4.00 | 6.00 | 7.00 |

**KM# 82a.1 50 PENCE**
28.28 g., 0.925 Silver 0.841 oz. ASW, 38.6 mm. **Ruler:** Elizabeth II **Subject:** Queen's Golden Jubilee **Obv:** Crowned bust right, denomination below **Rev:** Queen on throne below multicolor bunting **Edge:** Reeded

| Date | Mintage | VF20 | XF40 | MS60 | MS63 | MS65 |
|---|---|---|---|---|---|---|
| 2002 | 15,000 | PF65 45.00 | | | | |

**KM# 82a.2 50 PENCE**
28.28 g., 0.925 Silver 0.841 oz. ASW, 38.61 mm. **Ruler:** Elizabeth II **Subject:** Queen's Golden Jubilee **Obv:** Crowned bust right, denomination below **Rev:** With plain bunting

| Date | Mintage | VF20 | XF40 | MS60 | MS63 | MS65 |
|---|---|---|---|---|---|---|
| 2002 | — | PF65 45.00 | | | | |

**KM# 82b.1 50 PENCE**
39.94 g., 0.917 Gold 1.1775 oz. AGW, 38.61 mm. **Ruler:** Elizabeth II **Subject:** Queen's Golden Jubilee **Obv:** Crowned bust right, denomination below **Rev:** Queen seated on throne below multicolor bunting **Edge:** Reeded

| Date | Mintage | VF20 | XF40 | MS60 | MS63 | MS65 |
|---|---|---|---|---|---|---|
| 2002 | 50 | PF65 2,150 | | | | |

**KM# 82b.2 50 PENCE**
39.94 g., 0.917 Gold 1.1775 oz. AGW, 38.61 mm. **Ruler:** Elizabeth II **Subject:** Queen's Golden Jubilee **Obv:** Crowned bust right, denomination below **Rev:** With plain bunting

| Date | Mintage | VF20 | XF40 | MS60 | MS63 | MS65 |
|---|---|---|---|---|---|---|
| 2002 | — | PF65 2,100 | | | | |

**KM# 83.1 50 PENCE**
28.13 g., Copper-Nickel, 38.6 mm. **Ruler:** Elizabeth II **Subject:** Queen's Golden Jubilee **Obv:** Crowned bust right, denomination below **Rev:** Queen and young family below multicolor bunting **Edge:** Reeded

| Date | Mintage | VF20 | XF40 | MS60 | MS63 | MS65 |
|---|---|---|---|---|---|---|
| 2002 Proof | — | — | — | 4.00 | 6.00 | 7.00 |

**KM# 83a.1 50 PENCE**
28.28 g., 0.925 Silver 0.841 oz. ASW, 38.6 mm. **Ruler:** Elizabeth II **Subject:** Queen's Golden Jubilee **Obv:** Crowned bust right, denomination below **Rev:** Royal family below multicolor bunting **Edge:** Reeded

| Date | Mintage | VF20 | XF40 | MS60 | MS63 | MS65 |
|---|---|---|---|---|---|---|
| 2002 | 15,000 | PF65 45.00 | | | | |

**KM# 83a.2 50 PENCE**
28.28 g., 0.925 Silver 0.841 oz. ASW, 38.61 mm. **Ruler:** Elizabeth II **Subject:** Queen's Golden Jubilee **Obv:** Crowned bust right, denomination below **Rev:** With plain bunting

| Date | Mintage | VF20 | XF40 | MS60 | MS63 | MS65 |
|---|---|---|---|---|---|---|
| 2002 | — | PF65 45.00 | | | | |

**KM# 83b.1 50 PENCE**
39.94 g., 0.917 Gold 1.1775 oz. AGW, 38.61 mm. **Ruler:** Elizabeth II **Subject:** Queen's Golden Jubilee **Obv:** Crowned bust right, denomination below **Rev:** Royal Family below multicolor bunting **Edge:** Reeded

| Date | Mintage | VF20 | XF40 | MS60 | MS63 | MS65 |
|---|---|---|---|---|---|---|
| 2002 | 50 | PF65 2,150 | | | | |

**KM# 83b.2 50 PENCE**
39.94 g., 0.917 Gold 1.1775 oz. AGW, 38.61 mm. **Ruler:** Elizabeth II **Subject:** Queen's Golden Jubilee **Obv:** Crowned bust right, denomination below **Rev:** With plain bunting

| Date | Mintage | VF20 | XF40 | MS60 | MS63 | MS65 |
|---|---|---|---|---|---|---|
| 2002 | — | PF65 2,100 | | | | |

**KM# 84.1 50 PENCE**
28.13 g., Copper-Nickel, 38.6 mm. **Ruler:** Elizabeth II **Subject:** Queen's Golden Jubilee **Obv:** Crowned bust right, denomination below **Rev:** Queens head and tree house below multicolor bunting **Edge:** Reeded

| Date | Mintage | VF20 | XF40 | MS60 | MS63 | MS65 |
|---|---|---|---|---|---|---|
| 2002 | — | PF65 8.00 | | | | |

### KM# 84.2 50 PENCE

Copper-Nickel **Ruler:** Elizabeth II **Subject:** Queen's Golden Jubilee **Obv:** Crowned bust right, denomination below **Rev:** With plain bunting

| Date | Mintage | VF20 | XF40 | MS60 | MS63 | MS65 |
|---|---|---|---|---|---|---|
| 2002 | — | — | — | 4.00 | 6.00 | 7.00 |

### KM# 84a.1 50 PENCE

28.28 g., 0.925 Silver 0.841 oz. ASW, 38.6 mm. **Ruler:** Elizabeth II **Subject:** Queen's Golden Jubilee **Obv:** Crowned bust right, denomination below **Rev:** Queen and tree house below multicolor bunting **Edge:** Reeded

| Date | Mintage | VF20 | XF40 | MS60 | MS63 | MS65 |
|---|---|---|---|---|---|---|
| 2002 | 25,000 | PF65 45.00 | | | | |

### KM# 84a.2 50 PENCE

28.28 g., 0.925 Silver 0.841 oz. ASW, 38.61 mm. **Ruler:** Elizabeth II **Subject:** Queen's Golden Jubilee **Obv:** Crowned bust right, denomination below **Rev:** With plain bunting

| Date | Mintage | VF20 | XF40 | MS60 | MS63 | MS65 |
|---|---|---|---|---|---|---|
| 2002 | — | PF65 45.00 | | | | |

### KM# 84b.1 50 PENCE

39.94 g., 0.917 Gold 1.1775 oz. AGW, 38.61 mm. **Ruler:** Elizabeth II **Subject:** Queen's Golden Jubilee **Obv:** Crowned bust right, denomination below **Rev:** Queen and tree house below multicolor bunting **Edge:** Reeded

| Date | Mintage | VF20 | XF40 | MS60 | MS63 | MS65 |
|---|---|---|---|---|---|---|
| 2002 | 50 | PF65 2,150 | | | | |

### KM# 84b.2 50 PENCE

39.94 g., 0.917 Gold 1.1775 oz. AGW, 38.61 mm. **Ruler:** Elizabeth II **Subject:** Queen's Golden Jubilee **Obv:** Crowned bust right, denomination below **Rev:** With plain bunting

| Date | Mintage | VF20 | XF40 | MS60 | MS63 | MS65 |
|---|---|---|---|---|---|---|
| 2002 | — | PF65 2,100 | | | | |

### KM# 90 50 PENCE

28.28 g., Copper-Nickel, 38.6 mm. **Ruler:** Elizabeth II **Obv:** Crowned bust right, denomination below **Rev:** Conjoined busts of Elizabeth and Philip below multicolor bunting **Edge:** Reeded

| Date | Mintage | VF20 | XF40 | MS60 | MS63 | MS65 |
|---|---|---|---|---|---|---|
| 2002 | — | — | — | 4.00 | 6.00 | 7.00 |

### KM# 90a.1 50 PENCE

28.28 g., 0.925 Silver 0.841 oz. ASW, 38.6 mm. **Ruler:** Elizabeth II **Obv:** Crowned bust right, denomination below **Rev:** Elizabeth and Philip below multicolor bunting **Edge:** Reeded

| Date | Mintage | VF20 | XF40 | MS60 | MS63 | MS65 |
|---|---|---|---|---|---|---|
| 2002 | 15,000 | PF65 45.00 | | | | |

### KM# 90a.2 50 PENCE

28.28 g., 0.925 Silver 0.841 oz. ASW, 38.6 mm. **Ruler:** Elizabeth II **Obv:** Crowned bust right, denomination below **Rev:** With plain bunting

| Date | Mintage | VF20 | XF40 | MS60 | MS63 | MS65 |
|---|---|---|---|---|---|---|
| 2002 | — | PF65 45.00 | | | | |

### KM# 90b.1 50 PENCE

39.94 g., 0.917 Gold 1.1775 oz. AGW, 38.61 mm. **Ruler:** Elizabeth II **Obv:** Crowned bust right, denomination below **Rev:** Elizabeth and Philip below multicolor bunting **Edge:** Reeded

| Date | Mintage | VF20 | XF40 | MS60 | MS63 | MS65 |
|---|---|---|---|---|---|---|
| 2002 | 50 | PF65 2,150 | | | | |

### KM# 90b.2 50 PENCE

39.94 g., 0.917 Gold 1.1775 oz. AGW, 38.61 mm. **Ruler:** Elizabeth II **Obv:** Crowned bust right, denomination below **Rev:** With plain bunting **Edge:** Reeded

| Date | Mintage | VF20 | XF40 | MS60 | MS63 | MS65 |
|---|---|---|---|---|---|---|
| 2002 | — | PF65 2,100 | | | | |

### KM# 91 50 PENCE

28.28 g., Copper-Nickel, 38.6 mm. **Ruler:** Elizabeth II **Obv:** Crowned bust right, denomination below **Rev:** Queen and Aborigine dancers below multicolor bunting **Edge:** Reeded

| Date | Mintage | VF20 | XF40 | MS60 | MS63 | MS65 |
|---|---|---|---|---|---|---|
| 2002 | — | — | — | 4.00 | 6.00 | 7.00 |

### KM# 91a.1 50 PENCE

28.28 g., 0.925 Silver 0.841 oz. ASW, 38.6 mm. **Ruler:** Elizabeth II **Obv:** Crowned bust right, denomination below **Rev:** Queen and Aborigine dancers below multicolor bunting **Edge:** Reeded

| Date | Mintage | VF20 | XF40 | MS60 | MS63 | MS65 |
|---|---|---|---|---|---|---|
| 2002 | 15,000 | PF65 45.00 | | | | |

### KM# 91a.2 50 PENCE

28.28 g., 0.925 Silver 0.841 oz. ASW, 38.6 mm. **Ruler:** Elizabeth II **Obv:** Crowned bust right, denomination below **Rev:** With plain bunting **Edge:** Reeded

| Date | Mintage | VF20 | XF40 | MS60 | MS63 | MS65 |
|---|---|---|---|---|---|---|
| 2002 | — | PF65 45.00 | | | | |

### KM# 91b.1 50 PENCE

39.94 g., 0.917 Gold 1.1775 oz. AGW, 38.61 mm. **Ruler:** Elizabeth II **Obv:** Crowned bust right, denomination below **Rev:** Queen and Aborigine dancers below multicolor bunting **Edge:** Reeded

| Date | Mintage | VF20 | XF40 | MS60 | MS63 | MS65 |
|---|---|---|---|---|---|---|
| 2002 | 50 | PF65 2,150 | | | | |

### KM# 91b.2 50 PENCE

39.94 g., 0.917 Gold 1.1775 oz. AGW, 38.61 mm. **Ruler:** Elizabeth II **Obv:** Crowned bust right, denomination below **Rev:** With plain bunting **Edge:** Reeded

| Date | Mintage | VF20 | XF40 | MS60 | MS63 | MS65 |
|---|---|---|---|---|---|---|
| 2002 | — | PF65 2,100 | | | | |

### KM# 92 50 PENCE

28.28 g., Copper-Nickel, 38.6 mm. **Ruler:** Elizabeth II **Obv:** Crowned bust right, denomination below **Rev:** Queen and St. Paul's Cathedral dome below multicolor bunting **Edge:** Reeded

| Date | Mintage | VF20 | XF40 | MS60 | MS63 | MS65 |
|---|---|---|---|---|---|---|
| 2002 | — | — | — | 4.00 | 6.00 | 7.00 |

### KM# 92a.1 50 PENCE

28.28 g., 0.925 Silver 0.841 oz. ASW, 38.6 mm. **Ruler:** Elizabeth II **Obv:** Crowned bust right, denomination below **Rev:** Queen and St. Paul's Cathedral dome below multicolor bunting **Edge:** Reeded

| Date | Mintage | VF20 | XF40 | MS60 | MS63 | MS65 |
|---|---|---|---|---|---|---|
| 2002 | 15,000 | PF65 45.00 | | | | |

### KM# 92a.2 50 PENCE

28.28 g., 0.925 Silver 0.841 oz. ASW, 38.6 mm. **Ruler:** Elizabeth II **Obv:** Crowned bust right, denomination below **Rev:** With plain bunting **Edge:** Reeded

| Date | Mintage | VF20 | XF40 | MS60 | MS63 | MS65 |
|---|---|---|---|---|---|---|
| 2002 | — | PF65 45.00 | | | | |

### KM# 92b.1 50 PENCE

39.94 g., 0.917 Gold 1.1775 oz. AGW, 38.61 mm. **Ruler:** Elizabeth II **Obv:** Crowned bust right, denomination below **Rev:** Queen and St. Paul's Cathedral dome below multicolor bunting **Edge:** Reeded

| Date | Mintage | VF20 | XF40 | MS60 | MS63 | MS65 |
|---|---|---|---|---|---|---|
| 2002 | 50 | PF65 2,150 | | | | |

### KM# 92b.2 50 PENCE

39.94 g., 0.917 Gold 1.1775 oz. AGW, 38.61 mm. **Ruler:** Elizabeth II **Obv:** Crowned bust right, denomination below **Rev:** With plain bunting **Edge:** Reeded

| Date | Mintage | VF20 | XF40 | MS60 | MS63 | MS65 |
|---|---|---|---|---|---|---|
| 2002 | — | PF65 2,100 | | | | |

### KM# 93 50 PENCE

28.28 g., Copper-Nickel, 38.6 mm. **Ruler:** Elizabeth II **Obv:** Crowned bust right, denomination below **Rev:** Elizabeth and Philip in coronation coach below multicolor bunting **Edge:** Reeded

| Date | Mintage | VF20 | XF40 | MS60 | MS63 | MS65 |
|---|---|---|---|---|---|---|
| 2002 | — | — | — | 4.00 | 6.00 | 7.00 |

### KM# 93a.1 50 PENCE

28.28 g., 0.925 Silver 0.841 oz. ASW, 38.6 mm. **Ruler:** Elizabeth II **Obv:** Crowned bust right, denomination below **Rev:** Elizabeth and Philip in coronation coach below multicolor bunting **Edge:** Reeded

| Date | Mintage | VF20 | XF40 | MS60 | MS63 | MS65 |
|---|---|---|---|---|---|---|
| 2002 | 15,000 | PF65 45.00 | | | | |

### KM# 93a.2 50 PENCE

28.28 g., 0.925 Silver 0.841 oz. ASW, 38.6 mm. **Ruler:** Elizabeth II **Obv:** Crowned bust right, denomination below **Rev:** With plain bunting **Edge:** Reeded

| Date | Mintage | VF20 | XF40 | MS60 | MS63 | MS65 |
|---|---|---|---|---|---|---|
| 2002 | — | PF65 45.00 | | | | |

### KM# 93b.1 50 PENCE

39.94 g., 0.917 Gold 1.1775 oz. AGW, 38.61 mm. **Ruler:** Elizabeth II **Obv:** Crowned bust right, denomination below **Rev:** Elizabeth and Philip in coronation coach below multicolor bunting **Edge:** Reeded

| Date | Mintage | VF20 | XF40 | MS60 | MS63 | MS65 |
|---|---|---|---|---|---|---|
| 2002 | 50 | PF65 2,150 | | | | |

### KM# 93b.2 50 PENCE

39.94 g., 0.917 Gold 1.1775 oz. AGW, 38.61 mm. **Ruler:** Elizabeth II **Obv:** Crowned bust right, denomination below **Rev:** With plain bunting **Edge:** Reeded

| Date | Mintage | VF20 | XF40 | MS60 | MS63 | MS65 |
|---|---|---|---|---|---|---|
| 2002 | — | PF65 2,100 | | | | |

### KM# 94 50 PENCE

28.28 g., Copper-Nickel, 38.6 mm. **Ruler:** Elizabeth II **Obv:** Crowned bust right, denomination below **Rev:** Elizabeth and Prince Charles at flower show below multicolor bunting **Edge:** Reeded

| Date | Mintage | VF20 | XF40 | MS60 | MS63 | MS65 |
|---|---|---|---|---|---|---|
| 2002 | — | — | — | 4.00 | 6.00 | 7.00 |

**KM# 94a.1 50 PENCE**
28.28 g., 0.925 Silver 0.841 oz. ASW, 38.6 mm. **Ruler:** Elizabeth II **Obv:** Crowned bust right, denomination below **Rev:** Queen and Prince Charles at flower show below multicolor bunting **Edge:** Reeded

| Date | Mintage | VF20 | XF40 | MS60 | MS63 | MS65 |
|---|---|---|---|---|---|---|
| 2002 | 15,000 | PF65 45.00 | | | | |

**KM# 94a.2 50 PENCE**
28.28 g., 0.925 Silver 0.841 oz. ASW, 38.6 mm. **Ruler:** Elizabeth II **Obv:** Crowned bust right, denomination below **Rev:** With plain bunting **Edge:** Reeded

| Date | Mintage | VF20 | XF40 | MS60 | MS63 | MS65 |
|---|---|---|---|---|---|---|
| 2002 | — | PF65 45.00 | | | | |

**KM# 94b.1 50 PENCE**
39.94 g., 0.917 Gold 1.1775 oz. AGW, 38.61 mm. **Ruler:** Elizabeth II **Obv:** Crowned bust right, denomination below **Rev:** Queen and Prince Charles at flower show below multicolor bunting **Edge:** Reeded

| Date | Mintage | VF20 | XF40 | MS60 | MS63 | MS65 |
|---|---|---|---|---|---|---|
| 2002 | 50 | PF65 2,150 | | | | |

**KM# 94b.2 50 PENCE**
39.94 g., 0.917 Gold 1.1775 oz. AGW, 38.61 mm. **Ruler:** Elizabeth II **Obv:** Crowned bust right, denomination below **Rev:** With plain bunting **Edge:** Reeded

| Date | Mintage | VF20 | XF40 | MS60 | MS63 | MS65 |
|---|---|---|---|---|---|---|
| 2002 | — | PF65 2,100 | | | | |

**KM# 95 50 PENCE**
28.28 g., Copper-Nickel, 38.6 mm. **Ruler:** Elizabeth II **Obv:** Crowned bust right, denomination below **Rev:** Elizabeth and Philip on balcony below multicolor bunting **Edge:** Reeded

| Date | Mintage | VF20 | XF40 | MS60 | MS63 | MS65 |
|---|---|---|---|---|---|---|
| 2002 | — | — | — | 4.00 | 6.00 | 7.00 |

**KM# 95a.1 50 PENCE**
28.28 g., 0.925 Silver 0.841 oz. ASW, 38.6 mm. **Ruler:** Elizabeth II **Obv:** Crowned bust right, denomination below **Rev:** Elizabeth and Philip on balcony below colored bunting **Edge:** Reeded

| Date | Mintage | VF20 | XF40 | MS60 | MS63 | MS65 |
|---|---|---|---|---|---|---|
| 2002 | 15,000 | PF65 45.00 | | | | |

**KM# 95a.2 50 PENCE**
28.28 g., 0.925 Silver 0.841 oz. ASW, 38.6 mm. **Ruler:** Elizabeth II **Obv:** Crowned bust right, denomination below **Rev:** With plain bunting **Edge:** Reeded

| Date | Mintage | VF20 | XF40 | MS60 | MS63 | MS65 |
|---|---|---|---|---|---|---|
| 2002 | — | PF65 45.00 | | | | |

**KM# 95b.1 50 PENCE**
39.94 g., 0.917 Gold 1.1775 oz. AGW, 38.61 mm. **Ruler:** Elizabeth II **Obv:** Crowned bust right, denomination below **Rev:** Elizabeth and Philip on balcony below multicolor bunting **Edge:** Reeded

| Date | Mintage | VF20 | XF40 | MS60 | MS63 | MS65 |
|---|---|---|---|---|---|---|
| 2002 | 50 | PF65 2,150 | | | | |

**KM# 95b.2 50 PENCE**
39.94 g., 0.917 Gold 1.1775 oz. AGW, 38.61 mm. **Ruler:** Elizabeth II **Obv:** Crowned bust right, denomination below **Rev:** With plain bunting **Edge:** Reeded

| Date | Mintage | VF20 | XF40 | MS60 | MS63 | MS65 |
|---|---|---|---|---|---|---|
| 2002 | — | PF65 2,100 | | | | |

**KM# 96 50 PENCE**
28.28 g., Copper-Nickel, 38.6 mm. **Ruler:** Elizabeth II **Obv:** Crowned bust right, denomination below **Rev:** Multicolor jets below multicolor bunting **Edge:** Reeded

| Date | Mintage | VF20 | XF40 | MS60 | MS63 | MS65 |
|---|---|---|---|---|---|---|
| 2002 | — | — | — | 4.00 | 6.00 | 7.00 |

**KM# 96a.1 50 PENCE**
28.28 g., 0.925 Silver 0.841 oz. ASW, 38.6 mm. **Ruler:** Elizabeth II **Obv:** Crowned bust right, denomination below **Rev:** Multicolor jets below multicolor bunting **Edge:** Reeded

| Date | Mintage | VF20 | XF40 | MS60 | MS63 | MS65 |
|---|---|---|---|---|---|---|
| 2002 | 15,000 | PF65 45.00 | | | | |

**KM# 96a.2 50 PENCE**
28.28 g., 0.925 Silver 0.841 oz. ASW, 38.6 mm. **Ruler:** Elizabeth II **Obv:** Crowned bust right, denomination below **Rev:** With plain bunting **Edge:** Reeded

| Date | Mintage | VF20 | XF40 | MS60 | MS63 | MS65 |
|---|---|---|---|---|---|---|
| 2002 | — | PF65 45.00 | | | | |

**KM# 96b.1 50 PENCE**
39.94 g., 0.917 Gold 1.1775 oz. AGW, 38.61 mm. **Ruler:** Elizabeth II **Obv:** Crowned bust right, denomination below **Rev:** Multicolor jets below multicolor bunting **Edge:** Reeded

| Date | Mintage | VF20 | XF40 | MS60 | MS63 | MS65 |
|---|---|---|---|---|---|---|
| 2002 | 50 | PF65 2,150 | | | | |

**KM# 96b.2 50 PENCE**
39.94 g., 0.917 Gold 1.1775 oz. AGW, 38.61 mm. **Ruler:** Elizabeth II **Obv:** Crowned bust right, denomination below **Rev:** With plain bunting **Edge:** Reeded

| Date | Mintage | VF20 | XF40 | MS60 | MS63 | MS65 |
|---|---|---|---|---|---|---|
| 2002 | — | PF65 2,100 | | | | |

**KM# 97 50 PENCE**
28.28 g., Copper-Nickel, 38.6 mm. **Ruler:** Elizabeth II **Obv:** Crowned bust right, denomination below **Rev:** Queen and fireworks below multicolor bunting **Edge:** Reeded

| Date | Mintage | VF20 | XF40 | MS60 | MS63 | MS65 |
|---|---|---|---|---|---|---|
| 2002 | — | — | — | 4.00 | 6.00 | 7.00 |

**KM# 97a.1 50 PENCE**
28.28 g., 0.925 Silver 0.841 oz. ASW, 38.61 mm. **Ruler:** Elizabeth II **Obv:** Crowned bust right, denomination below **Rev:** Queen and fireworks below multicolor bunting **Edge:** Reeded

| Date | Mintage | VF20 | XF40 | MS60 | MS63 | MS65 |
|---|---|---|---|---|---|---|
| 2002 | 15,000 | PF65 45.00 | | | | |

**KM# 97a.2 50 PENCE**
28.28 g., 0.925 Silver 0.841 oz. ASW, 38.6 mm. **Ruler:** Elizabeth II **Obv:** Crowned bust right, denomination below **Rev:** With plain bunting **Edge:** Reeded

| Date | Mintage | VF20 | XF40 | MS60 | MS63 | MS65 |
|---|---|---|---|---|---|---|
| 2002 | — | PF65 45.00 | | | | |

**KM# 97b.1 50 PENCE**
39.94 g., 0.917 Gold 1.1775 oz. AGW, 38.61 mm. **Ruler:** Elizabeth II **Obv:** Crowned bust right, denomination below **Rev:** Queen and fireworks below multicolor bunting **Edge:** Reeded

| Date | Mintage | VF20 | XF40 | MS60 | MS63 | MS65 |
|---|---|---|---|---|---|---|
| 2002 | 50 | PF65 2,150 | | | | |

**KM# 97b.2 50 PENCE**
39.94 g., 0.917 Gold 1.1775 oz. AGW, 38.61 mm. **Ruler:** Elizabeth II **Obv:** Crowned bust right, denomination below **Rev:** With plain bunting **Edge:** Reeded

| Date | Mintage | VF20 | XF40 | MS60 | MS63 | MS65 |
|---|---|---|---|---|---|---|
| 2002 | — | PF65 2,100 | | | | |

**KM# 98 50 PENCE**
28.28 g., Copper-Nickel, 38.6 mm. **Ruler:** Elizabeth II **Obv:** Crowned bust right, denomination below **Rev:** UK map and flags below multicolor bunting **Edge:** Reeded

| Date | Mintage | VF20 | XF40 | MS60 | MS63 | MS65 |
|---|---|---|---|---|---|---|
| 2002 | — | — | — | 4.00 | 6.00 | 7.00 |

**KM# 98a.1 50 PENCE**
28.28 g., 0.925 Silver 0.841 oz. ASW, 38.6 mm. **Ruler:** Elizabeth II **Obv:** Crowned bust right, denomination below **Rev:** UK and four flags below multicolor bunting **Edge:** Reeded

| Date | Mintage | VF20 | XF40 | MS60 | MS63 | MS65 |
|---|---|---|---|---|---|---|
| 2002 | 15,000 | PF65 45.00 | | | | |

**KM# 98a.2 50 PENCE**
28.28 g., 0.925 Silver 0.841 oz. ASW, 38.6 mm. **Ruler:** Elizabeth II **Obv:** Crowned bust right, denomination below **Rev:** With plain bunting **Edge:** Reeded

| Date | Mintage | VF20 | XF40 | MS60 | MS63 | MS65 |
|---|---|---|---|---|---|---|
| 2002 | — | PF65 45.00 | | | | |

**KM# 98b.1 50 PENCE**
39.94 g., 0.917 Gold 1.1775 oz. AGW, 38.61 mm. **Ruler:** Elizabeth II **Obv:** Crowned bust right, denomination below **Rev:** UK map and four flags below multicolor bunting **Edge:** Reeded

| Date | Mintage | VF20 | XF40 | MS60 | MS63 | MS65 |
|---|---|---|---|---|---|---|
| 2002 | 50 | PF65 2,150 | | | | |

**KM# 98b.2 50 PENCE**
39.94 g., 0.917 Gold 1.1775 oz. AGW, 38.61 mm. **Ruler:** Elizabeth II **Obv:** Crowned bust right, denomination below **Rev:** With plain bunting **Edge:** Reeded

| Date | Mintage | VF20 | XF40 | MS60 | MS63 | MS65 |
|---|---|---|---|---|---|---|
| 2002 | — | PF65 2,100 | | | | |

**KM# 99 50 PENCE**
28.28 g., Copper-Nickel, 38.6 mm. **Ruler:** Elizabeth II **Obv:** Crowned bust right, denomination below **Rev:** Queen and two Commonwealth Games athletes below multicolor bunting **Edge:** Reeded

| Date | Mintage | VF20 | XF40 | MS60 | MS63 | MS65 |
|---|---|---|---|---|---|---|
| 2002 | — | — | — | 4.00 | 6.00 | 7.00 |

**KM# 99a.1 50 PENCE**
28.28 g., 0.925 Silver 0.841 oz. ASW, 38.6 mm. **Ruler:** Elizabeth II **Obv:** Crowned bust right, denomination below **Rev:** Queen and two Commonwealth Games athletes below multicolor bunting **Edge:** Reeded

| Date | Mintage | VF20 | XF40 | MS60 | MS63 | MS65 |
|---|---|---|---|---|---|---|
| 2002 | 15,000 | PF65 45.00 | | | | |

**KM# 99a.2 50 PENCE**
28.28 g., 0.925 Silver 0.841 oz. ASW, 38.6 mm. **Ruler:** Elizabeth II **Obv:** Crowned bust right, denomination below **Rev:** With plain bunting **Edge:** Reeded

| Date | Mintage | VF20 | XF40 | MS60 | MS63 | MS65 |
|---|---|---|---|---|---|---|
| 2002 | — | PF65 45.00 | | | | |

**KM# 99b.1 50 PENCE**
39.94 g., 0.917 Gold 1.1775 oz. AGW, 38.61 mm. **Ruler:** Elizabeth II **Obv:** Crowned bust right, denomination below **Rev:** Queen and two Commonwealth Games athletes below multicolor bunting **Edge:** Reeded

| Date | Mintage | VF20 | XF40 | MS60 | MS63 | MS65 |
|---|---|---|---|---|---|---|
| 2002 | 50 | PF65 2,150 | | | | |

**KM# 99b.2 50 PENCE**
39.94 g., 0.917 Gold 1.1775 oz. AGW, 38.61 mm. **Ruler:** Elizabeth II **Obv:** Crowned bust right, denomination below **Rev:** With plain bunting **Edge:** Reeded

| Date | Mintage | VF20 | XF40 | MS60 | MS63 | MS65 |
|---|---|---|---|---|---|---|
| 2002 | — | PF65 2,100 | | | | |

**KM# 100 50 PENCE**
28.28 g., Copper-Nickel, 38.6 mm. **Ruler:** Elizabeth II **Obv:** Crowned bust right, denomination below **Rev:** Royal Ascot Carriage scene below multicolor bunting **Edge:** Reeded

| Date | Mintage | VF20 | XF40 | MS60 | MS63 | MS65 |
|---|---|---|---|---|---|---|
| 2002 | — | — | — | 4.00 | 6.00 | 7.00 |

### KM# 100a.1 50 PENCE

28.28 g., 0.925 Silver 0.841 oz. ASW, 38.6 mm. **Ruler:** Elizabeth II **Obv:** Crowned bust right, denomination below **Rev:** Royal Ascot Carriage scene below multicolor bunting **Edge:** Reeded

| Date | Mintage | VF20 | XF40 | MS60 | MS63 | MS65 |
|---|---|---|---|---|---|---|
| 2002 | 15,000 | PF65 45.00 | | | | |

### KM# 100a.2 50 PENCE

28.28 g., 0.925 Silver 0.841 oz. ASW, 38.6 mm. **Ruler:** Elizabeth II **Obv:** Crowned bust right, denomination below **Rev:** With plain bunting **Edge:** Reeded

| Date | Mintage | VF20 | XF40 | MS60 | MS63 | MS65 |
|---|---|---|---|---|---|---|
| 2002 | — | PF65 45.00 | | | | |

### KM# 100b.1 50 PENCE

39.94 g., 0.917 Gold 1.1775 oz. AGW, 38.61 mm. **Ruler:** Elizabeth II **Obv:** Crowned bust right, denomination below **Rev:** Royal Ascot Carriage scene below multicolor bunting **Edge:** Reeded

| Date | Mintage | VF20 | XF40 | MS60 | MS63 | MS65 |
|---|---|---|---|---|---|---|
| 2002 | 50 | PF65 2,150 | | | | |

### KM# 100b.2 50 PENCE

39.94 g., 0.917 Gold 1.1775 oz. AGW, 38.61 mm. **Ruler:** Elizabeth II **Obv:** Crowned bust right, denomination below **Rev:** With plain bunting **Edge:** Reeded

| Date | Mintage | VF20 | XF40 | MS60 | MS63 | MS65 |
|---|---|---|---|---|---|---|
| 2002 | — | PF65 2,100 | | | | |

### KM# 101 50 PENCE

28.28 g., Copper-Nickel, 38.6 mm. **Ruler:** Elizabeth II **Obv:** Crowned bust right, denomination below **Rev:** Queen and two hockey players below multicolor bunting **Edge:** Reeded

| Date | Mintage | VF20 | XF40 | MS60 | MS63 | MS65 |
|---|---|---|---|---|---|---|
| 2002 | — | — | — | 4.00 | 6.00 | 7.00 |

### KM# 101a.1 50 PENCE

28.28 g., 0.925 Silver 0.841 oz. ASW, 38.6 mm. **Ruler:** Elizabeth II **Obv:** Crowned bust right, denomination below **Rev:** Queen and two hockey players below multicolor bunting **Edge:** Reeded

| Date | Mintage | VF20 | XF40 | MS60 | MS63 | MS65 |
|---|---|---|---|---|---|---|
| 2002 | 15,000 | PF65 45.00 | | | | |

### KM# 101a.2 50 PENCE

28.28 g., 0.925 Silver 0.841 oz. ASW, 38.6 mm. **Ruler:** Elizabeth II **Obv:** Crowned bust right, denomination below **Rev:** With plain bunting **Edge:** Reeded

| Date | Mintage | VF20 | XF40 | MS60 | MS63 | MS65 |
|---|---|---|---|---|---|---|
| 2002 | — | PF65 45.00 | | | | |

### KM# 101b.1 50 PENCE

39.94 g., 0.917 Gold 1.1775 oz. AGW, 38.61 mm. **Ruler:** Elizabeth II **Obv:** Crowned bust right, denomination below **Rev:** Queen and two hockey players below multicolor bunting **Edge:** Reeded

| Date | Mintage | VF20 | XF40 | MS60 | MS63 | MS65 |
|---|---|---|---|---|---|---|
| 2002 | 50 | PF65 2,150 | | | | |

### KM# 101b.2 50 PENCE

39.94 g., 0.917 Gold 1.1775 oz. AGW, 38.61 mm. **Ruler:** Elizabeth II **Obv:** Crowned bust right, denomination below **Rev:** With plain bunting **Edge:** Reeded

| Date | Mintage | VF20 | XF40 | MS60 | MS63 | MS65 |
|---|---|---|---|---|---|---|
| 2002 | — | PF65 2,100 | | | | |

### KM# 102 50 PENCE

28.28 g., Copper-Nickel, 38.6 mm. **Ruler:** Elizabeth II **Obv:** Crowned bust right, denomination below **Rev:** Queen Mother as a young lady and as an elderly lady **Edge:** Reeded

| Date | Mintage | VF20 | XF40 | MS60 | MS63 | MS65 |
|---|---|---|---|---|---|---|
| ND(2002) | — | — | — | 7.00 | 9.00 | 10.00 |

### KM# 102a 50 PENCE

28.28 g., 0.925 Silver 0.841 oz. ASW, 38.6 mm. **Ruler:** Elizabeth II **Obv:** Crowned bust right, denomination below **Rev:** Queen Mother as a young lady and as an elderly lady **Edge:** Reeded

| Date | Mintage | VF20 | XF40 | MS60 | MS63 | MS65 |
|---|---|---|---|---|---|---|
| ND(2002) | 10,000 | PF65 45.00 | | | | |

### KM# 135 50 PENCE

8.00 g., Copper-Nickel, 27.3 mm. **Ruler:** Elizabeth II **Obv:** Crowned bust right **Rev:** Fox standing right **Shape:** 7-sided

| Date | Mintage | VF20 | XF40 | MS60 | MS63 | MS65 |
|---|---|---|---|---|---|---|
| 2003 | — | — | — | 3.50 | 5.00 | 7.50 |
| 2004 | — | — | — | 3.50 | 5.00 | 7.50 |

### KM# 149 50 PENCE

28.28 g., 0.925 Silver 0.841 oz. ASW, 38.6 mm. **Ruler:** Elizabeth II **Subject:** Queen's 80th Birthday **Obv:** Head with tiara right - gilt **Obv. Legend:** QUEEN ELIZABETH II - FALKLAND ISLANDS **Rev:** Elizabeth seated at left, Queen Mother at right holding baby

| Date | Mintage | VF20 | XF40 | MS60 | MS63 | MS65 |
|---|---|---|---|---|---|---|
| 2006 | — | PF65 45.00 | | | | |

### KM# 163 50 PENCE

8.00 g., Copper-Nickel, 27.3 mm. **Ruler:** Elizabeth II **Subject:** 25th Annivery of Liberation **Obv:** Head in tiara right **Rev:** Soldier in full gear standing before map of Falklands **Shape:** 7-sided

| Date | Mintage | VF20 | XF40 | MS60 | MS63 | MS65 |
|---|---|---|---|---|---|---|
| 2007 PM | — | — | — | 3.50 | 5.00 | 7.50 |

### KM# 136 POUND

9.50 g., Nickel-Brass, 22.5 mm. **Ruler:** Elizabeth II **Obv:** Crowned bust right **Rev:** Shield

| Date | Mintage | VF20 | XF40 | MS60 | MS63 | MS65 |
|---|---|---|---|---|---|---|
| 2004 | — | — | — | — | 2.00 | 3.50 |

### KM# 137 2 POUNDS

12.00 g., Bi-Metallic Copper-Nickel center in Nickel-Brass ring, 28.4 mm. **Ruler:** Elizabeth II **Obv:** Head with tiara right **Obv. Legend:** QUEEN ELIZABETH THE SECOND **Rev:** Sun and map surrounded by wildlife **Edge:** Reeded and lettered **Edge Lettering:** 30 YEARS OF FALKLAND ISLANDS COINAGE

| Date | Mintage | VF20 | XF40 | MS60 | MS63 | MS65 |
|---|---|---|---|---|---|---|
| 2004 | — | — | — | — | 10.00 | 12.00 |

### KM# 103 25 POUNDS

7.81 g., 0.9999 Gold 0.2511 oz. AGW, 22 mm. **Ruler:** Elizabeth II **Obv:** Crowned bust right, denomination below **Rev:** Queen Mother as a young lady and as an elderly lady **Edge:** Reeded

| Date | Mintage | VF20 | XF40 | MS60 | MS63 | MS65 |
|---|---|---|---|---|---|---|
| ND(2002) | 1,000 | PF65 475 | | | | |

## CROWN COINAGE

### KM# 161 1/25 CROWN

0.50 g., 0.9999 Gold, 11 mm. **Ruler:** Elizabeth II **Subject:** Henry Dunant, Founder, International Red Cross and 1901 Nobel Peace Prize winner **Obv:** Bust with tiara right **Rev:** Dunant bust facing

| Date | Mintage | VF20 | XF40 | MS60 | MS63 | MS65 |
|---|---|---|---|---|---|---|
| 2010 PM | — | PF65 80.00 | | | | |

### KM# 141 1/5 CROWN

6.22 g., 0.9999 Gold 0.200 oz. AGW **Ruler:** Elizabeth II **Subject:** Diamond Wedding Anniversary **Obv:** Conjoined busts with Prince Philip right **Obv. Legend:** QUEEN ELIZABETH II - FALKLAND ISLANDS **Rev:** Bride and groom standing facing at wedding cake; .01 carat x 1.3mm diamond embedded at top **Rev. Legend:** Diamond Wedding of H.M. Queen Elizabeth II & H.R.H. Prince Philip **Edge:** Reeded

| Date | Mintage | VF20 | XF40 | MS60 | MS63 | MS65 |
|---|---|---|---|---|---|---|
| 2007 PM | — | PF65 450 | | | | |

### KM# 129 CROWN

Copper-Nickel **Ruler:** Elizabeth II **Rev:** Nelson and the H.M.S. Victory

| Date | Mintage | VF20 | XF40 | MS60 | MS63 | MS65 |
|---|---|---|---|---|---|---|
| 2005 | — | — | — | — | 10.00 | 12.00 |

### KM# 151 CROWN

Copper-Nickel, 38.61 mm. **Ruler:** Elizabeth II **Subject:** I. K. Burnel **Rev:** S. S. Great Britain sailing right

| Date | Mintage | VF20 | XF40 | MS60 | MS63 | MS65 |
|---|---|---|---|---|---|---|
| 2006 PM | — | — | — | — | 12.00 | 15.00 |

### KM# 152 CROWN

Copper-Nickel, 38.61 mm. **Ruler:** Elizabeth II **Subject:** Artic and Antarctic - John Ross and James Clark Ross **Rev:** Ships Victory and Erebus

| Date | Mintage | VF20 | XF40 | MS60 | MS63 | MS65 |
|---|---|---|---|---|---|---|
| 2006 PM | — | — | — | — | 12.00 | 15.00 |

### KM# 138 CROWN

Copper-Nickel **Ruler:** Elizabeth II **Rev:** Winston Churchill

| Date | Mintage | VF20 | XF40 | MS60 | MS63 | MS65 |
|---|---|---|---|---|---|---|
| 2007 | — | — | — | — | 15.00 | 17.00 |

### KM# 139 CROWN

Copper-Nickel **Ruler:** Elizabeth II **Rev:** Queen Elizabeth I

| Date | Mintage | VF20 | XF40 | MS60 | MS63 | MS65 |
|---|---|---|---|---|---|---|
| 2007 | — | — | — | — | 15.00 | 17.00 |

### KM# 140 CROWN

Copper-Nickel **Ruler:** Elizabeth II **Rev:** Charles Darwin

| Date | Mintage | VF20 | XF40 | MS60 | MS63 | MS65 |
|---|---|---|---|---|---|---|
| 2007 | — | — | — | — | 15.00 | 17.00 |

### KM# 142 CROWN

Copper-Nickel **Ruler:** Elizabeth II **Subject:** Diamond Wedding Anniversary **Obv:** Conjoined busts with Prince Philip right **Obv. Legend:** QUEEN ELIZABETH II - FALKLAND ISLANDS **Rev:** King George VI standing at left giving Philip standing at right his consent to a contract of matrimony **Rev. Legend:** Diamond Wedding of H.M. Queen Elizabeth II & H.R.H. Prince Philip **Edge:** Reeded

| Date | Mintage | VF20 | XF40 | MS60 | MS63 | MS65 |
|---|---|---|---|---|---|---|
| 2007 PM | — | — | — | — | 17.00 | 20.00 |

### KM# 142a CROWN

0.9167 Silver **Ruler:** Elizabeth II **Subject:** Diamond Wedding Anniversary **Obv:** Conjoined busts with Prince Philip right **Obv. Legend:** QUEEN ELIZABETH II - FALKLAND ISLANDS **Rev:** King George VI, standing at left, giving Philip, standing at right, his consent to a contract of matrimony **Rev. Legend:** Diamond Wedding of H.M. Queen Elizabeth II & H.R.H. Prince Philip **Edge:** Reeded

| Date | Mintage | VF20 | XF40 | MS60 | MS63 | MS65 |
|---|---|---|---|---|---|---|
| 2007 PM | — | PF65 40.00 | | | | |

### KM# 143 CROWN

Copper-Nickel **Ruler:** Elizabeth II **Subject:** Diamond Wedding Anniversary **Obv:** Conjoined busts with Prince Philip right **Obv. Legend:** QUEEN ELIZABETH II - FALKLAND ISLANDS **Rev:** Bride and groom standing facing at wedding cake **Rev. Legend:** Diamond Wedding of H.M. Queen Elizabeth II & H.R.H. Prince Philip **Edge:** Reeded

| Date | Mintage | VF20 | XF40 | MS60 | MS63 | MS65 |
|---|---|---|---|---|---|---|
| 2007 PM | — | — | — | — | 17.00 | 20.00 |

### KM# 143a CROWN

0.9167 Silver **Ruler:** Elizabeth II **Subject:** Diamond Wedding Anniversary **Obv:** Conjoined busts with Prince Philip right **Obv. Legend:** QUEEN ELIZABETH II - FALKLAND ISLANDS **Rev:** Bride and groom standing facing at wedding cake **Rev. Legend:** Diamond Wedding of H.M. Queen Elizabeth II & H.R.H. Prince Philip **Edge:** Reeded

| Date | Mintage | VF20 | XF40 | MS60 | MS63 | MS65 |
|---|---|---|---|---|---|---|
| 2007 PM | — | PF65 40.00 | | | | |

### KM# 144 CROWN

Copper-Nickel **Ruler:** Elizabeth II **Subject:** Diamond Wedding Anniversary **Obv:** Conjoined busts with Prince Philip right **Obv. Legend:** QUEEN ELIZABETH II - FALKLAND ISLANDS **Rev:** Bridesmaids and Page Boys **Rev. Legend:** Diamond Wedding of H.M. Queen Elizabeth II & H.R.H. Prince Philip **Edge:** Reeded

| Date | Mintage | VF20 | XF40 | MS60 | MS63 | MS65 |
|---|---|---|---|---|---|---|
| 2007 PM | — | — | — | — | 17.00 | 20.00 |

### KM# 144a CROWN

0.9167 Silver **Ruler:** Elizabeth II **Subject:** Diamond Wedding Anniversary **Obv:** Conjoined busts with Prince Philip right **Obv. Legend:** QUEEN ELIZABETH II - FALKLAND ISLANDS **Rev:** Bridesmaids and Page Boys **Rev. Legend:** Diamond Wedding of H.M. Queen Elizabeth II & H.R.H. Prince Philip **Edge:** Reeded

| Date | Mintage | VF20 | XF40 | MS60 | MS63 | MS65 |
|---|---|---|---|---|---|---|
| 2007 PM | — | PF65 40.00 | | | | |

### KM# 145 CROWN

Copper-Nickel **Ruler:** Elizabeth II **Subject:** Diamond Wedding Anniversary **Obv:** Conjoined busts with Prince Philip right **Obv. Legend:** QUEEN ELIZABETH II - FALKLAND ISLANDS **Rev:** Buckingham Palace facade **Rev. Legend:** Diamond Wedding of H.M. Queen Elizabeth II & H.R.H. Prince Philip **Edge:** Reeded

| Date | Mintage | VF20 | XF40 | MS60 | MS63 | MS65 |
|---|---|---|---|---|---|---|
| 2007 PM | — | — | — | — | 17.00 | 20.00 |

### KM# 145a CROWN

0.9167 Silver **Ruler:** Elizabeth II **Subject:** Diamond Wedding Anniversary **Obv:** Conjoined busts with Prince Philip right **Obv. Legend:** QUEEN ELIZABETH II - FALKLAND ISLANDS **Rev:** Buckingham Palace facade **Rev. Legend:** Diamond Wedding of H.M. Queen Elizabeth II & H.R.H. Prince Philip **Edge:** Reeded

| Date | Mintage | VF20 | XF40 | MS60 | MS63 | MS65 |
|---|---|---|---|---|---|---|
| 2007 PM | — | PF65 40.00 | | | | |

### KM# 146 CROWN

Copper-Nickel **Ruler:** Elizabeth II **Subject:** 10th Anniversary - Death of Princess Diana **Obv:** Bust with tiara right **Obv. Legend:** QUEEN ELIZABETH II - FALKLAND ISLANDS **Rev:** Bust of Princess Diana facing 3/4 right **Rev. Legend:** 1961 - 1997 • DIANA — PRINCESS OF WALES **Edge:** Reeded

| Date | Mintage | VF20 | XF40 | MS60 | MS63 | MS65 |
|---|---|---|---|---|---|---|
| 2007 PM | — | — | — | — | 17.00 | 20.00 |

### KM# 146a CROWN

0.9167 Silver **Ruler:** Elizabeth II **Subject:** 10th Anniversary Death of Princess Diana **Obv:** Bust with tiara right **Obv. Legend:** QUEEN ELIZABETH II - FALKLAND ISLANDS **Rev:** Bust of Princess Diana facing 3/4 right **Rev. Legend:** 1961 - 1997 ? DIANA ? PRINCESS OF WALES **Edge:** Reeded

| Date | Mintage | VF20 | XF40 | MS60 | MS63 | MS65 |
|---|---|---|---|---|---|---|
| 2007 PM | — | PF65 75.00 | | | | |

### KM# 147 CROWN

Copper-Nickel, 38 mm. **Ruler:** Elizabeth II **Subject:** 20th Anniversary - Falkland Islands Fishery **Obv:** Bust right of Queen Elizabeth II **Rev:** Shortfin Squid (Illex Argentinca) **Edge:** Reeded

| Date | Mintage | VF20 | XF40 | MS60 | MS63 | MS65 |
|---|---|---|---|---|---|---|
| 2007 PM | — | — | — | — | 17.00 | 20.00 |

### KM# 148 CROWN

Copper-Nickel, 39 mm. **Ruler:** Elizabeth II **Subject:** Scouting Centennial **Obv:** Crowned bust right **Obv. Legend:** QUEEN ELIZABETH II FALKLAND ISLANDS 2007 **Rev:** Baden-Powell bust 3/4 left, scout saluting, tent flanking within circle on animal tracks **Rev. Legend:** 1857 ROBERT BADEN-POWELL 1941 ONE CROWN **Edge:** Reeded

| Date | Mintage | VF20 | XF40 | MS60 | MS63 | MS65 |
|---|---|---|---|---|---|---|
| 2007 PM | — | — | — | — | 12.00 | 15.00 |

### KM# 148a CROWN

28.28 g., 0.925 Silver 0.841 oz. ASW, 38.5 mm. **Ruler:** Elizabeth II **Subject:** Scouting Centennial **Obv:** Crowned bust right **Obv. Legend:** QUEEN ELIZABETH II FALKLAND ISLANDS 2007 **Rev:** Baden-Powell bust 3/4 facing left, scout saluting and tent flanking, within circle of animal tracks and rope **Rev. Legend:** 1857 ROBERT BADEN-POWELL 1941 ONE CROWN **Edge:** Reeded

| Date | Mintage | VF20 | XF40 | MS60 | MS63 | MS65 |
|---|---|---|---|---|---|---|
| 2007 PM | 10,000 | PF65 65.00 | | | | |

### KM# 156 CROWN

28.28 g., Copper-Nickel, 38.61 mm. **Ruler:** Elizabeth II **Subject:** International Polar Year - Discovery **Obv:** Bust in tiara right **Rev:** Icebound ship

| Date | Mintage | VF20 | XF40 | MS60 | MS63 | MS65 |
|---|---|---|---|---|---|---|
| 2007 PM | — | — | — | — | 17.50 | 20.00 |

### KM# 157 CROWN

Copper-Nickel, 38.61 mm. **Ruler:** Elizabeth II **Subject:** 25th Anniversary of Liberation **Obv:** Bust in tiara right **Rev:** Britannia standing before map of the Falkland Islands

| Date | Mintage | VF20 | XF40 | MS60 | MS63 | MS65 |
|---|---|---|---|---|---|---|
| 2007 PM | — | — | — | — | 17.50 | 20.00 |

### KM# 158 CROWN

28.28 g., Copper-Nickel, 38.61 mm. **Ruler:** Elizabeth II **Subject:** Race for the South Pole **Obv:** Bust in tiara right **Rev:** Portrats of Scott and Amundsen, dog-sleds, and man-pulled sleds.

| Date | Mintage | VF20 | XF40 | MS60 | MS63 | MS65 |
|---|---|---|---|---|---|---|
| 2007 PM | — | — | — | — | 17.50 | 20.00 |

**KM# 150 CROWN**
28.28 g., Copper-Nickel, 38.6 mm. **Ruler:** Elizabeth II **Subject:** Royal Air Force, 90th anniversary

| Date | Mintage | VF20 | XF40 | MS60 | MS63 | MS65 |
|---|---|---|---|---|---|---|
| 2008 | — | — | — | — | 12.00 | 15.00 |

**KM# 153 CROWN**
Copper-Nickel, 38.61 mm. **Ruler:** Elizabeth II **Subject:** Spitfire **Obv:** Bust in tiara right **Rev:** Two planes in flight

| Date | Mintage | VF20 | XF40 | MS60 | MS63 | MS65 |
|---|---|---|---|---|---|---|
| 2008 | — | — | — | — | 12.00 | 15.00 |

**KM# 154 CROWN**
Copper-Nickel, 38.61 mm. **Ruler:** Elizabeth II **Subject:** Port Louis **Obv:** Bust in tiara right **Rev:** Flag raising over fort

| Date | Mintage | VF20 | XF40 | MS60 | MS63 | MS65 |
|---|---|---|---|---|---|---|
| 2008 | — | — | — | — | 12.00 | 15.00 |

**KM# 162 CROWN**
28.28 g., Copper-Nickel, 38.61 mm. **Ruler:** Elizabeth II **Obv:** Bust in tiara right **Rev:** Charles Darwin bust left

| Date | Mintage | VF20 | XF40 | MS60 | MS63 | MS65 |
|---|---|---|---|---|---|---|
| 2009 PM | — | — | — | — | 18.50 | 22.00 |

**KM# 159 CROWN**
Copper-Nickel, 38.61 mm. **Ruler:** Elizabeth II **Subject:** RAF Search and Rescue 70th anniversary **Obv:** Bust in tiara right **Rev:** RAF Search and Rescue Helicopter

| Date | Mintage | VF20 | XF40 | MS60 | MS63 | MS65 |
|---|---|---|---|---|---|---|
| 2011 PM | — | — | — | — | 17.50 | 20.00 |

**KM# 160 CROWN**
Copper-Nickel, 38.61 mm. **Ruler:** Elizabeth II **Subject:** Royal Wedding - Prince William and Catherine Middleton **Obv:** Bust in tiara right **Rev:** Busts left

| Date | Mintage | VF20 | XF40 | MS60 | MS63 | MS65 |
|---|---|---|---|---|---|---|
| 2011 PM | — | — | — | — | 17.50 | 20.00 |

**KM# 164 CROWN**
Copper-Nickel, 38.61 mm. **Ruler:** Elizabeth II **Subject:** Elizabeth and Philip 60th Wedding anniversary **Obv:** Bust in tiara right **Rev:** Lion on crown and Plumes

| Date | Mintage | VF20 | XF40 | MS60 | MS63 | MS65 |
|---|---|---|---|---|---|---|
| 2011 PM | — | — | — | — | 17.50 | 20.00 |

**KM# 165 CROWN**
28.28 g., Copper-Nickel, 38.6 mm. **Ruler:** Elizabeth II **Subject:** Life of Queen Elizabeth II **Obv:** Conjoined busts right **Rev:** Elizabeth, the Queen mother in robes of the Order of the Garter

| Date | Mintage | VF20 | XF40 | MS60 | MS63 | MS65 |
|---|---|---|---|---|---|---|
| 2012 PM | — | — | — | — | 12.00 | 15.00 |

**KM# 166 CROWN**
28.28 g., Copper-Nickel, 38.6 mm. **Ruler:** Elizabeth II **Subject:** Life of Queen Elizabeth II **Obv:** Conjoined busts right **Rev:** Elizabeth as WWII nurse

| Date | Mintage | VF20 | XF40 | MS60 | MS63 | MS65 |
|---|---|---|---|---|---|---|
| 2012 PM | — | — | — | — | 12.00 | 15.00 |

**KM# 167 CROWN**
Silver with glass insert, 38.6 mm. **Ruler:** Elizabeth II **Obv:** Head at top, butterfly in glass **Rev:** Life of the butterfly around central image

| Date | Mintage | VF20 | XF40 | MS60 | MS63 | MS65 |
|---|---|---|---|---|---|---|
| 2012 PM | — | PF65 85.00 | | | | |

**KM# 168 CROWN**
Copper-Nickel **Ruler:** Elizabeth II **Subject:** Stanley Sports Association, 100th Anniversary **Obv:** Double busts right **Rev:** Horse facing left

| Date | Mintage | VF20 | XF40 | MS60 | MS63 | MS65 |
|---|---|---|---|---|---|---|
| 2012 | — | PF65 85.00 | | | | |

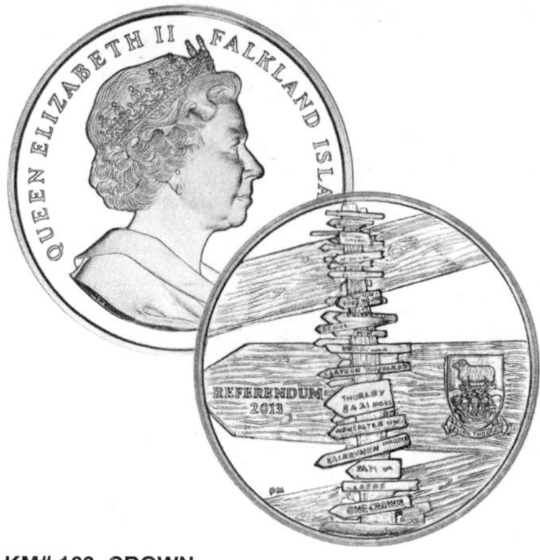

**KM# 169 CROWN**

28.28 g., Copper-Nickel, 38.6 mm. **Ruler:** Elizabeth II **Subject:** Falkland Islands Referendum

| Date | Mintage | VF20 | XF40 | MS60 | MS63 | MS65 |
|---|---|---|---|---|---|---|
| 2013 | — | — | — | — | 12.00 | 15.00 |

**KM# 169a CROWN**

28.28 g., 0.925 Silver 0.841 oz. ASW, 38.6 mm. **Ruler:** Elizabeth II **Subject:** Falkland Islands Referendum

| Date | Mintage | VF20 | XF40 | MS60 | MS63 | MS65 |
|---|---|---|---|---|---|---|
| 2012 PM | Est. 10,000 | **PF65** 85.00 | | | | |

**KM# 170 CROWN**

28.28 g., Copper-Nickel, 38.6 mm. **Obv:** Bust right **Rev:** Margaret Thatcher bust facing

| Date | Mintage | VF20 | XF40 | MS60 | MS63 | MS65 |
|---|---|---|---|---|---|---|
| 2013 | — | — | — | — | 12.00 | 15.00 |

## PIEDFORT

| KM# | Date | Mintage | Identification | Mkt Val |
|---|---|---|---|---|
| P4 | 2001 | 500 | 50 Pence 0.925 Silver Proof KM#86a. | 95.00 |
| P5 | 2001 | 500 | 50 Pence 0.925 Silver Proof KM#70a. | 110 |
| P6 | 2001 | — | 50 Pence 0.925 Silver Queen's portrait Edward's portrait with two gold plated coin designs | — |
| P7 | 2001 | — | 50 Pence 0.925 Silver Queen's portrait Henry's portrait with two gold plated coin designs | — |
| P8 | 2001 | — | 50 Pence 0.925 Silver Queen's portrait Charles' portrait with two gold plated coin designs | — |
| P9 | 2001 | — | 50 Pence 0.925 Silver Queen's portrait Victoria's portrait with two gold plated coin designs | — |
| P10 | 2001 | 500 | 50 Pence 0.925 Silver | 90.00 |
| P11 | 2001 | 500 | 50 Pence 0.925 Silver | 95.00 |
| P12 | 2001 | 500 | 50 Pence 0.925 Silver | 95.00 |
| P13 | 2001 | 500 | 50 Pence 0.925 Silver | 110 |
| P14 | 2002 | 500 | 50 Pence 0.925 Silver Proof KM#73a. | 95.00 |
| P15 | 2002 | 500 | 50 Pence 0.925 Silver Proof KM#74a. | 110 |
| P16 | 2002 | 500 | 50 Pence 0.925 Silver Proof KM#75a. | 95.00 |
| P17 | 2002 | 500 | 50 Pence 0.925 Silver Proof KM#76a. | 95.00 |
| P18 | 2002 | 500 | 50 Pence 0.925 Silver Proof KM#77a. | 95.00 |
| P19 | 2002 | 500 | 50 Pence 0.925 Silver Proof KM#78a. | 95.00 |
| P20 | 2002 | 500 | 50 Pence 0.925 Silver Proof KM#79a. | 95.00 |
| P21 | 2002 | 500 | 50 Pence 0.925 Silver Proof KM#80a. | 95.00 |
| P23 | 2002 | 500 | 50 Pence 0.925 Silver Proof KM#82a. | 95.00 |
| P24 | 2002 | 500 | 50 Pence 0.925 Silver Proof KM#83a. | 95.00 |
| P25 | 2002 | 500 | 50 Pence 0.925 Silver Proof KM#84a. | 95.00 |
| P26 | ND(2002) | 500 | 50 Pence 0.925 Silver Proof KM#102a. | 95.00 |

# FIJI

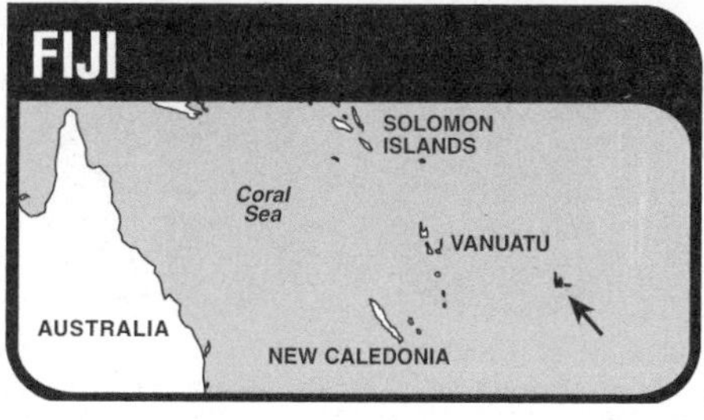


The Republic of Fiji consists of about 320 islands located in the southwestern Pacific 1,100 miles (1,770 km.) north of New Zealand. The islands have a combined area of 7,056 sq. mi. (18,274 sq. km.) and a population of 772,891. Capital: Suva. Fiji's economy is based on agriculture and mining. Sugar, coconut products, manganese, and gold are exported. Fiji is a member of the Commonwealth of Nations, but has been subject to periodic short suspensions.

**MINT MARK**

(o) - Royal Canadian Mint, Ottawa

## REPUBLIC

British Administration until 1970

### DECIMAL COINAGE

100 Cents = 1 Dollar

**KM# 49a CENT**

1.58 g., Copper Plated Zinc, 17.53 mm. **Ruler:** Elizabeth II **Obv:** Crowned head right, date at right **Rev:** Tanoa kava bowl divides denomination

| Date | Mintage | VF20 | XF40 | MS60 | MS63 | MS65 |
|---|---|---|---|---|---|---|
| 2001 (o) | — | — | — | 0.20 | 0.40 | 0.65 |
| 2002 (o) | 5,880,000 | — | — | 0.20 | 0.40 | 0.65 |
| 2003 (o) | 8,030,000 | — | — | 0.20 | 0.40 | 0.65 |
| 2004 (o) | 8,840,000 | — | — | 0.20 | 0.40 | 0.65 |
| 2005 (o) | 9,720,000 | — | — | 0.20 | 0.40 | 0.65 |

**KM# 49b CENT**

1.76 g., Copper Plated Steel, 17.5 mm. **Ruler:** Elizabeth II **Obv:** Crowned head right, date at right **Rev:** Tanoa kava bowl

| Date | Mintage | VF20 | XF40 | MS60 | MS63 | MS65 |
|---|---|---|---|---|---|---|
| 2006 (o) | — | — | — | 0.25 | 0.35 | 0.50 |

**KM# 50a 2 CENTS**

3.16 g., Copper Plated Zinc, 21.08 mm. **Ruler:** Elizabeth II **Obv:** Crowned head right, date at right **Rev:** Palm fan and denomination

| Date | Mintage | VF20 | XF40 | MS60 | MS63 | MS65 |
|---|---|---|---|---|---|---|
| 2001 (o) | 2,830,000 | — | — | 0.30 | 0.50 | 0.85 |
| 2002 (o) | 5,000,000 | — | — | 0.30 | 0.50 | 0.85 |
| 2003 (o) | 6,410,000 | — | — | 0.30 | 0.50 | 0.85 |
| 2004 (o) | 7,050,000 | — | — | 0.30 | 0.50 | 0.85 |
| 2005 (o) | 7,760,000 | — | — | 0.30 | 0.50 | 0.85 |

**KM# 51a 5 CENTS**

2.34 g., Nickel Plated Steel, 19.41 mm. **Ruler:** Elizabeth II **Obv:** Crowned head right **Rev:** Fijian drum - lali divides denomination **Edge:** Reeded

| Date | Mintage | VF20 | XF40 | MS60 | MS63 | MS65 |
|---|---|---|---|---|---|---|
| 2006 (l) | — | — | — | 0.50 | 0.75 | 1.00 |

**KM# 119 5 CENTS**

2.34 g., Nickel Plated Steel, 19.5 mm. **Ruler:** Elizabeth II **Obv:** Crowned head right **Rev:** Fijian drum - Lali divides denomination **Edge:** Plain

| Date | Mintage | VF20 | XF40 | MS60 | MS63 | MS65 |
|---|---|---|---|---|---|---|
| 2009 | — | — | — | 0.50 | 0.75 | 1.00 |
| 2010 | — | — | — | 0.50 | 0.75 | 1.00 |

**KM# 332 5 CENTS**

2.34 g., Nickel Plated Steel, 19.5 mm. **Ruler:** Elizabeth II **Obv:** Luga roro (Foxfaced Rabbit Fish) **Rev:** Lalt (Wooden drum)

| Date | Mintage | VF20 | XF40 | MS60 | MS63 | MS65 |
|---|---|---|---|---|---|---|
| 2012 | — | — | — | — | 0.25 | 0.50 |

**KM# 52a 10 CENTS**

4.75 g., Nickel Plated Steel, 23.6 mm. **Ruler:** Elizabeth II **Obv:** Crowned head right **Rev:** Throwing club - ula tava tava divides value **Edge:** Reeded

| Date | Mintage | VF20 | XF40 | MS60 | MS63 | MS65 |
|---|---|---|---|---|---|---|
| 2006 | — | — | — | 0.50 | 1.00 | 1.25 |

**KM# 120 10 CENTS**

3.55 g., Nickel Plated Steel, 21.5 mm. **Ruler:** Elizabeth II **Obv:** Crowned head right **Rev:** Throwing club - ula tava tava divides value **Edge:** Reeded

| Date | Mintage | VF20 | XF40 | MS60 | MS63 | MS65 |
|---|---|---|---|---|---|---|
| 2009 | — | — | — | 0.50 | 1.00 | 1.25 |

**KM# 333 10 CENTS**

3.55 g., Nickel Plated Steel, 21.5 mm. **Ruler:** Elizabeth II **Obv:** Beka Mirimiri (Fiji Flying Fox) handing upside down **Rev:** Lula Tavatava (War club)

| Date | Mintage | VF20 | XF40 | MS60 | MS63 | MS65 |
|---|---|---|---|---|---|---|
| 2012 | — | — | — | — | 0.50 | 0.75 |
| 2013 | — | — | — | — | 0.50 | 0.75 |

**KM# 53a 20 CENTS**

10.50 g., Nickel Plated Steel, 28.5 mm. **Ruler:** Elizabeth II **Obv:** Crowned head right **Rev:** Tabua on braided sennit cord divides denomination **Edge:** Reeded

| Date | Mintage | VF20 | XF40 | MS60 | MS63 | MS65 |
|---|---|---|---|---|---|---|
| 2006 (l) | — | 0.20 | 0.35 | 0.75 | 1.25 | 1.50 |

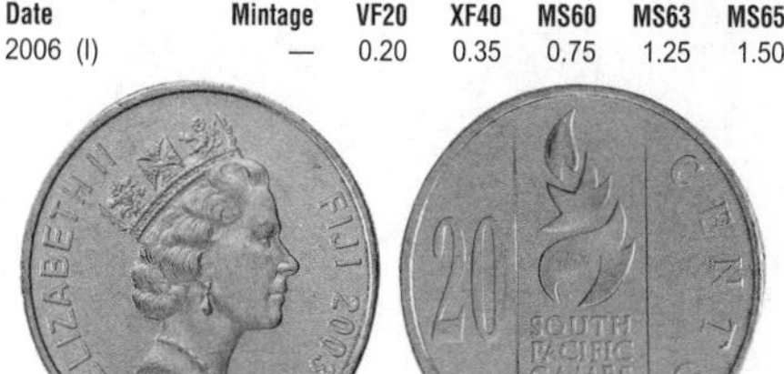

**KM# 95 20 CENTS**

11.24 g., Copper-Nickel, 28.5 mm. **Ruler:** Elizabeth II **Obv:** Crowned head right, date at right **Rev:** South Pacific Games flame logo **Edge:** Reeded **Note:** Prooflike examples issued in special cards.

| Date | Mintage | VF20 | XF40 | MS60 | MS63 | MS65 |
|---|---|---|---|---|---|---|
| 2003 | 1,540,000 | — | — | 0.75 | 1.50 | 2.50 |
| 2003 Prooflike | — | — | — | — | — | 6.00 |

### KM# 121 20 CENTS

4.68 g., Nickel Plated Steel, 24 mm. **Ruler:** Elizabeth II **Obv:** Crowned head right **Rev:** Tabua, a ceremonial whale's tooth divides denomination **Edge:** Segmented reeding

| Date | Mintage | VF20 | XF40 | MS60 | MS63 | MS65 |
|---|---|---|---|---|---|---|
| 2009 | — | — | 0.35 | 0.75 | 1.25 | 1.50 |
| 2010 | — | — | 0.35 | 0.75 | 1.25 | 1.50 |

### KM# 334 20 CENTS

4.68 g., Nickel Plated Steel, 24 mm. **Ruler:** Elizabeth II **Obv:** Kaka (Kadavu Shining Parrot) **Rev:** Tabua (Whale's tooth)

| Date | Mintage | VF20 | XF40 | MS60 | MS63 | MS65 |
|---|---|---|---|---|---|---|
| 2012 | — | — | — | 0.50 | 1.00 | 1.50 |
| 2013 | — | — | — | 0.50 | 1.00 | 1.50 |

### KM# 259 50 CENTS

Copper-Nickel **Ruler:** Elizabeth II **Subject:** Taiwan Wildlife, a Blackfaced Loffler

| Date | Mintage | VF20 | XF40 | MS60 | MS63 | MS65 |
|---|---|---|---|---|---|---|
| 2003 | — | — | — | — | — | 15.00 |

### KM# 260 50 CENTS

Copper-Nickel **Ruler:** Elizabeth II **Subject:** Taiwan Wildlife - Neon pitta

| Date | Mintage | VF20 | XF40 | MS60 | MS63 | MS65 |
|---|---|---|---|---|---|---|
| 2003 | — | — | — | — | — | 15.00 |

### KM# 122 50 CENTS

6.50 g., Nickel Plated Steel, 26.5 mm. **Ruler:** Elizabeth II **Obv:** Crowned head right **Rev:** Sailing canoe - Takia, denomination below **Edge:** Reeded

| Date | Mintage | VF20 | XF40 | MS60 | MS63 | MS65 |
|---|---|---|---|---|---|---|
| 2009 | — | — | — | 1.00 | 2.00 | 3.00 |

### KM# 164 50 CENTS

27.22 g., Copper-Nickel, 38.74 mm. **Ruler:** Elizabeth II **Subject:** Year of the Tiger **Obv:** Female goddess facing **Rev:** Multicolor Formosan Tiger

| Date | Mintage | VF20 | XF40 | MS60 | MS63 | MS65 |
|---|---|---|---|---|---|---|
| 2010 (c) | 6,000 | — | — | — | — | 50.00 |

### KM# 335 50 CENTS

6.50 g., Nickel Plated Steel, 26.5 mm. **Ruler:** Elizabeth II **Obv:** Varivoce (Humphead Urasse Fish) **Rev:** Camakau (Sail Catamaran)

| Date | Mintage | VF20 | XF40 | MS60 | MS63 | MS65 |
|---|---|---|---|---|---|---|
| 2012 | — | — | — | — | 1.50 | 2.50 |
| 2013 | — | — | — | — | 1.50 | 2.50 |

### KM# 515 50 CENTS

8.00 g., Copper-Nickel, 27.3 mm. **Subject:** Iliesa Delana, paralympian High Jump Medallist **Obv:** National arms **Rev:** High jumper

| Date | Mintage | VF20 | XF40 | MS60 | MS63 | MS65 |
|---|---|---|---|---|---|---|
| 2013 | — | — | — | — | 3.00 | 5.00 |

### KM# 254 DOLLAR

28.28 g., Copper-Nickel, 38.61 mm. **Ruler:** Elizabeth II **Subject:** Elizabeth II, 50th Anniversary of Reign **Rev:** Draped sword

| Date | Mintage | VF20 | XF40 | MS60 | MS63 | MS65 |
|---|---|---|---|---|---|---|
| 2002 | — | — | — | — | — | 20.00 |

### KM# 255 DOLLAR

28.28 g., Copper-Nickel, 38.61 mm. **Ruler:** Elizabeth II **Subject:** Elizabeth II, 50th Anniversary of Reign **Rev:** Boys Choir in Westminster Abbey

| Date | Mintage | VF20 | XF40 | MS60 | MS63 | MS65 |
|---|---|---|---|---|---|---|
| 2002 | — | — | — | — | — | 20.00 |

### KM# 261 DOLLAR

31.11 g., 0.999 Silver 0.999 oz. ASW, 38.7 mm. **Ruler:** Elizabeth II **Subject:** Song Meiling, 1st Anniversary of Death **Obv:** National arms **Rev:** Song Meiling and Jiang Jieshi

| Date | Mintage | VF20 | XF40 | MS60 | MS63 | MS65 |
|---|---|---|---|---|---|---|
| 2004 | — | PF65 55.00 | | | | |

### KM# 262 DOLLAR

31.11 g., 0.999 Silver 0.999 oz. ASW, 38.7 mm. **Ruler:** Elizabeth II **Subject:** Song Meiling, 1st Anniversary of Death **Rev:** Song Meiling and Chrysanthemen

| Date | Mintage | VF20 | XF40 | MS60 | MS63 | MS65 |
|---|---|---|---|---|---|---|
| 2004 | — | PF65 55.00 | | | | |

### KM# 114 DOLLAR

31.11 g., 0.999 Silver 0.999 oz. ASW, 40.7 mm. **Ruler:** Elizabeth II **Subject:** Sputnik I, 50th Anniversary **Rev:** Multicolor earth, satellite rocket

| Date | Mintage | VF20 | XF40 | MS60 | MS63 | MS65 |
|---|---|---|---|---|---|---|
| 2007 Prooflike | 6,000 | — | — | — | — | 110 |

### KM# 233 DOLLAR

0.50 g., 0.9999 Gold 0.0161 oz. AGW, 11 mm. **Ruler:** Elizabeth II **Obv:** Head in tiara right **Rev:** Britannia seated left

| Date | Mintage | VF20 | XF40 | MS60 | MS63 | MS65 |
|---|---|---|---|---|---|---|
| 2007 | 15,000 | PF65 50.00 | | | | |

### KM# 234 DOLLAR

0.50 g., 0.9999 Gold 0.0161 oz. AGW, 11 mm. **Ruler:** Elizabeth II **Obv:** Head in tiara right **Rev:** Victory from Mexico's Libertad bullion coinage

| Date | Mintage | VF20 | XF40 | MS60 | MS63 | MS65 |
|---|---|---|---|---|---|---|
| 2007 | 15,000 | PF65 50.00 | | | | |

### KM# 115 DOLLAR

31.11 g., 0.999 Silver 0.999 oz. ASW **Ruler:** Elizabeth II **Subject:** Birds of Fiji **Rev:** Multicolor - blue crested broadbill

| Date | Mintage | VF20 | XF40 | MS60 | MS63 | MS65 |
|---|---|---|---|---|---|---|
| 2008 Prooflike | 4,000 | — | — | — | — | 95.00 |

### KM# 116 DOLLAR

31.11 g., 0.999 Silver 0.999 oz. ASW **Ruler:** Elizabeth II **Subject:** Birds of Fiji **Rev:** Multicolor collared lory

| Date | Mintage | VF20 | XF40 | MS60 | MS63 | MS65 |
|---|---|---|---|---|---|---|
| 2008 Prooflike | 4,000 | — | — | — | — | 95.00 |

### KM# 117 DOLLAR

31.11 g., 0.999 Silver 0.999 oz. ASW **Ruler:** Elizabeth II **Subject:** Birds of Fiji **Rev:** Multicolor - Island Thrush

| Date | Mintage | VF20 | XF40 | MS60 | MS63 | MS65 |
|---|---|---|---|---|---|---|
| 2008 Prooflike | 4,000 | — | — | — | — | 95.00 |

### KM# 118 DOLLAR

31.11 g., 0.999 Silver 0.999 oz. ASW **Ruler:** Elizabeth II **Subject:** Birds of Fiji **Rev:** Multicolor white collared kingfisher

| Date | Mintage | VF20 | XF40 | MS60 | MS63 | MS65 |
|---|---|---|---|---|---|---|
| 2008 Prooflike | 4,000 | — | — | — | — | 95.00 |

### KM# 237 DOLLAR

28.28 g., 0.925 Silver 0.841 oz. ASW, 38.61 mm. **Ruler:** Elizabeth II **Subject:** History fo Seafaring **Obv:** Head with tiara right **Rev:** Pamir sailing right

| Date | Mintage | VF20 | XF40 | MS60 | MS63 | MS65 |
|---|---|---|---|---|---|---|
| 2008 | 1,500 | PF63 32.00 | PF65 35.00 | | | |

### KM# 124 DOLLAR

Copper-Nickel **Ruler:** Elizabeth II **Subject:** Barack Obama elected U.S. President

| Date | Mintage | VF20 | XF40 | MS60 | MS63 | MS65 |
|---|---|---|---|---|---|---|
| 2009 | — | — | — | — | — | 15.00 |

### KM# 130 DOLLAR

Copper-Nickel partially gilt, 40 mm. **Ruler:** Elizabeth II **Subject:** Pacific Explorers - Sir Francis Drake **Rev:** Ship, portrait in oval

| Date | Mintage | VF20 | XF40 | MS60 | MS63 | MS65 |
|---|---|---|---|---|---|---|
| 2009 | — | PF65 15.00 | | | | |

### KM# 131 DOLLAR

Copper-Nickel partially gilt, 40 mm. **Ruler:** Elizabeth II **Subject:** Pacific Explorers - Ferdinand Magellan **Rev:** Ship, portrait in oval

| Date | Mintage | VF20 | XF40 | MS60 | MS63 | MS65 |
|---|---|---|---|---|---|---|
| 2009 | — | PF65 15.00 | | | | |

### KM# 132 DOLLAR

Copper-Nickel partially gilt, 40 mm. **Ruler:** Elizabeth II **Subject:** Pacific Explorers - James Cook **Rev:** Ship, portrait in oval

| Date | Mintage | VF20 | XF40 | MS60 | MS63 | MS65 |
|---|---|---|---|---|---|---|
| 2009 | — | PF65 15.00 | | | | |

### KM# 133 DOLLAR

Copper-Nickel partially gilt, 40 mm. **Ruler:** Elizabeth II **Subject:** Pacific Explorers - Abel Tasman **Rev:** Ship, portrait in oval

| Date | Mintage | VF20 | XF40 | MS60 | MS63 | MS65 |
|---|---|---|---|---|---|---|
| 2009 | — | PF65 15.00 | | | | |

### KM# 134 DOLLAR

Copper-Nickel partially gilt **Ruler:** Elizabeth II **Subject:** Pacific Explorers - Jacob DeMare & William Schouten **Rev:** Ship, portraits in oval

| Date | Mintage | VF20 | XF40 | MS60 | MS63 | MS65 |
|---|---|---|---|---|---|---|
| 2009 | — | PF65 15.00 | | | | |

### KM# 135 DOLLAR

Copper-Nickel partially gilt **Ruler:** Elizabeth II **Subject:** Pacific Explorers - William Bligh **Rev:** Ship, portrait in oval

| Date | Mintage | VF20 | XF40 | MS60 | MS63 | MS65 |
|---|---|---|---|---|---|---|
| 2009 | — | — | — | — | — | 15.00 |

### KM# 137 DOLLAR

Copper-Nickel, 38.61 mm. **Ruler:** Elizabeth II **Subject:** Great animals of the World - Panda **Rev:** Panda seated, fur pattern as background

| Date | Mintage | VF20 | XF40 | MS60 | MS63 | MS65 |
|---|---|---|---|---|---|---|
| 2009 | — | — | — | — | — | 15.00 |

### KM# 137a DOLLAR

Copper-Nickel gilt **Ruler:** Elizabeth II **Subject:** Great animals of the World - Panda

| Date | Mintage | VF20 | XF40 | MS60 | MS63 | MS65 |
|---|---|---|---|---|---|---|
| 2009 | — | — | — | — | — | 15.00 |

### KM# 138 DOLLAR

Copper-Nickel, 38.61 mm. **Ruler:** Elizabeth II **Subject:** Great animals of the World - Koi **Rev:** Koi fish swimming right, scale pattern as background

| Date | Mintage | VF20 | XF40 | MS60 | MS63 | MS65 |
|---|---|---|---|---|---|---|
| 2009 | — | — | — | — | — | 15.00 |

### KM# 138a DOLLAR

Copper-Nickel gilt **Ruler:** Elizabeth II **Subject:** Great animals of the World - Koi

| Date | Mintage | VF20 | XF40 | MS60 | MS63 | MS65 |
|---|---|---|---|---|---|---|
| 2009 | — | — | — | — | — | 15.00 |

### KM# 139 DOLLAR

Copper-Nickel **Ruler:** Elizabeth II **Subject:** Great animals of the World - Zebra

| Date | Mintage | VF20 | XF40 | MS60 | MS63 | MS65 |
|---|---|---|---|---|---|---|
| 2009 | — | — | — | — | — | 15.00 |

### KM# 139a DOLLAR

Copper-Nickel gilt, 38.61 mm. **Ruler:** Elizabeth II **Subject:** Great animals of the World - Zebra

| Date | Mintage | VF20 | XF40 | MS60 | MS63 | MS65 |
|---|---|---|---|---|---|---|
| 2009 | — | — | — | — | — | 15.00 |

### KM# 140 DOLLAR

Copper-Nickel **Ruler:** Elizabeth II **Subject:** Great animals of the World - Elephant

| Date | Mintage | VF20 | XF40 | MS60 | MS63 | MS65 |
|---|---|---|---|---|---|---|
| 2009 | — | — | — | — | — | 15.00 |

### KM# 140a DOLLAR

Copper-Nickel gilt **Ruler:** Elizabeth II **Subject:** Great animals of the World - Elephant

| Date | Mintage | VF20 | XF40 | MS60 | MS63 | MS65 |
|---|---|---|---|---|---|---|
| 2009 | — | — | — | — | — | 15.00 |

### KM# 141 DOLLAR

Copper-Nickel, 38.61 mm. **Ruler:** Elizabeth II **Subject:** Great animals of the world - Cheeta **Rev:** Cheets standing left, fur pattern background

| Date | Mintage | VF20 | XF40 | MS60 | MS63 | MS65 |
|---|---|---|---|---|---|---|
| 2009 | — | — | — | — | — | 15.00 |

### KM# 141a DOLLAR

Copper-Nickel gilt **Ruler:** Elizabeth II **Subject:** Great animals of the World - Cheeta

| Date | Mintage | VF20 | XF40 | MS60 | MS63 | MS65 |
|---|---|---|---|---|---|---|
| 2009 | — | — | — | — | — | 15.00 |

### KM# 142 DOLLAR

Copper-Nickel, 38.61 mm. **Ruler:** Elizabeth II **Subject:** Great animals of teh World - Leopard **Rev:** Leopard walking left, leopard skin background

| Date | Mintage | VF20 | XF40 | MS60 | MS63 | MS65 |
|---|---|---|---|---|---|---|
| 2009 | — | — | — | — | — | 15.00 |

### KM# 142a DOLLAR

Copper-Nickel gilt **Ruler:** Elizabeth II **Subject:** Great animals of the World - Leopard

| Date | Mintage | VF20 | XF40 | MS60 | MS63 | MS65 |
|---|---|---|---|---|---|---|
| 2009 | — | — | — | — | — | 15.00 |

### KM# 143 DOLLAR

Copper-Nickel **Ruler:** Elizabeth II **Subject:** Great animals of the World - Giraffe

| Date | Mintage | VF20 | XF40 | MS60 | MS63 | MS65 |
|---|---|---|---|---|---|---|
| 2009 | — | — | — | — | — | 15.00 |

### KM# 143a DOLLAR

Copper-Nickel gilt **Ruler:** Elizabeth II **Subject:** Great animals of the World - Giraffe

| Date | Mintage | VF20 | XF40 | MS60 | MS63 | MS65 |
|---|---|---|---|---|---|---|
| 2009 | — | — | — | — | — | 15.00 |

### KM# 144 DOLLAR

Copper-Nickel, 38.61 mm. **Ruler:** Elizabeth II **Subject:** Great animals of the World - Tiger **Rev:** Tiger advancing right, fur pattern as background

| Date | Mintage | VF20 | XF40 | MS60 | MS63 | MS65 |
|---|---|---|---|---|---|---|
| 2009 | — | — | — | — | — | 15.00 |

### KM# 144a DOLLAR

Copper-Nickel gilt **Ruler:** Elizabeth II **Subject:** Great animals of the World - Tiger

| Date | Mintage | VF20 | XF40 | MS60 | MS63 | MS65 |
|---|---|---|---|---|---|---|
| 2009 | — | — | — | — | — | 15.00 |

### KM# 145 DOLLAR

Copper-Nickel silver plated **Ruler:** Elizabeth II **Subject:** Tropical fish - Yellow pointed nose

| Date | Mintage | VF20 | XF40 | MS60 | MS63 | MS65 |
|---|---|---|---|---|---|---|
| 2009 | — | — | — | — | — | 15.00 |

### KM# 146 DOLLAR

Copper-Nickel silver plated **Ruler:** Elizabeth II **Subject:** Tropical fish - Albino yellow fish

| Date | Mintage | VF20 | XF40 | MS60 | MS63 | MS65 |
|---|---|---|---|---|---|---|
| 2009 | — | — | — | — | — | 15.00 |

### KM# 147 DOLLAR

Copper-Nickel silver plated **Ruler:** Elizabeth II **Subject:** Tropical fish - Striped Butterfly fish

| Date | Mintage | VF20 | XF40 | MS60 | MS63 | MS65 |
|---|---|---|---|---|---|---|
| 2009 | — | — | — | — | — | 15.00 |

### KM# 148 DOLLAR

Copper-Nickel silver plated **Ruler:** Elizabeth II **Subject:** Tropical fish - Damsel fish

| Date | Mintage | VF20 | XF40 | MS60 | MS63 | MS65 |
|---|---|---|---|---|---|---|
| 2009 | — | — | — | — | — | 15.00 |

### KM# 149 DOLLAR

Copper-Nickel silver plated, 38.6 mm. **Ruler:** Elizabeth II **Subject:** Tropical fish - Surgern fish **Rev:** Colored fish below ship

| Date | Mintage | VF20 | XF40 | MS60 | MS63 | MS65 |
|---|---|---|---|---|---|---|
| 2009 | — | — | — | — | — | 15.00 |

### KM# 150 DOLLAR

Copper-Nickel silver plated **Ruler:** Elizabeth II **Subject:** Tropical fish - Clown fish

| Date | Mintage | VF20 | XF40 | MS60 | MS63 | MS65 |
|---|---|---|---|---|---|---|
| 2009 | — | — | — | — | — | 15.00 |

### KM# 293 DOLLAR

25.00 g., Aluminum-Bronze, 38.61 mm. **Ruler:** Elizabeth II **Rev:** Mary and Christ child

| Date | Mintage | VF20 | XF40 | MS60 | MS63 | MS65 |
|---|---|---|---|---|---|---|
| 2009 | — | — | — | — | — | 10.00 |

### KM# 126 DOLLAR

Silver **Ruler:** Elizabeth II **Subject:** H.C. Andersen - Steadfast Tin Soldier **Rev:** Multicolor toy soldier in flames

| Date | Mintage | VF20 | XF40 | MS60 | MS63 | MS65 |
|---|---|---|---|---|---|---|
| 2010 | — | PF65 50.00 | | | | |

### KM# 127 DOLLAR

Silver **Ruler:** Elizabeth II **Subject:** H.C. Andersen - The Nightengale **Rev:** Multicolor bird

| Date | Mintage | VF20 | XF40 | MS60 | MS63 | MS65 |
|---|---|---|---|---|---|---|
| 2010 | — | PF65 65.00 | | | | |

### KM# 128 DOLLAR

Silver **Ruler:** Elizabeth II **Subject:** H.C. Andersen - Thumbelina **Rev:** Multicolor Pixi

| Date | Mintage | VF20 | XF40 | MS60 | MS63 | MS65 |
|---|---|---|---|---|---|---|
| 2010 | — | PF65 50.00 | | | | |

### KM# 129 DOLLAR

Silver **Ruler:** Elizabeth II **Subject:** H.C. Andersen - The little match girl **Rev:** Multicolor girl with match

| Date | Mintage | VF20 | XF40 | MS60 | MS63 | MS65 |
|---|---|---|---|---|---|---|
| 2010 | — | PF65 50.00 | | | | |

**KM# 152 DOLLAR**
31.11 g., 0.999 Silver 0.999 oz. ASW, 46x29 mm. **Ruler:** Elizabeth II **Subject:** Siberian Tiger **Shape:** Irregular

| Date | Mintage | VF20 | XF40 | MS60 | MS63 | MS65 |
|---|---|---|---|---|---|---|
| 2010 | 10,000 | PF65 60.00 | | | | |

**KM# 153 DOLLAR**
31.11 g., 0.999 Silver 0.999 oz. ASW, 46x29 mm. **Ruler:** Elizabeth II **Subject:** Bengal Tiger **Shape:** Irregular

| Date | Mintage | VF20 | XF40 | MS60 | MS63 | MS65 |
|---|---|---|---|---|---|---|
| 2010 | 10,000 | PF65 60.00 | | | | |

**KM# 154 DOLLAR**
Tri-Metallic Copper center, Brass inner ring, Copper-Nickel outer ring., 40 mm. **Ruler:** Elizabeth II **Subject:** FIAA World Cup - South Africa **Rev:** Pretoria stadium and antelopes

| Date | Mintage | VF20 | XF40 | MS60 | MS63 | MS65 |
|---|---|---|---|---|---|---|
| 2010 | — | — | — | — | 20.00 | 25.00 |

**KM# 155 DOLLAR**
Tri-Metallic Copper center, Brass inner ring, Copper-Nickel outer ring., 40 mm. **Ruler:** Elizabeth II **Subject:** FIAA World Cup - South Africa **Rev:** Kapstadt stadium and Zebra

| Date | Mintage | VF20 | XF40 | MS60 | MS63 | MS65 |
|---|---|---|---|---|---|---|
| 2010 | — | — | — | — | 20.00 | 25.00 |

**KM# 156 DOLLAR**
Tri-Metallic Copper center, Brass inner ring, Copper-Nickel outer ring., 40 mm. **Ruler:** Elizabeth II **Subject:** FIAA World Cup - South Africa **Rev:** Johannesburg Stadium and Rhinos

| Date | Mintage | VF20 | XF40 | MS60 | MS63 | MS65 |
|---|---|---|---|---|---|---|
| 2010 | — | — | — | — | 20.00 | 25.00 |

**KM# 157 DOLLAR**
Tri-Metallic Copper center, Brass inner ring, Copper-Nickel outer ring., 40 mm. **Ruler:** Elizabeth II **Subject:** FIAA World Cup - South Africa **Rev:** Johannesburg Stadium and Leopard

| Date | Mintage | VF20 | XF40 | MS60 | MS63 | MS65 |
|---|---|---|---|---|---|---|
| 2010 | — | — | — | — | 20.00 | 25.00 |

**KM# 158 DOLLAR**
Tri-Metallic Copper center, Brass inner ring, Copper-Nickel outer ring., 40 mm. **Ruler:** Elizabeth II **Subject:** FIAA World Cup - South Africa **Rev:** Rustenburg Stadium and Lion

| Date | Mintage | VF20 | XF40 | MS60 | MS63 | MS65 |
|---|---|---|---|---|---|---|
| 2010 | — | — | — | — | 20.00 | 25.00 |

**KM# 159 DOLLAR**
Tri-Metallic Copper center, Brass inner ring, Copper-Nickel outer ring., 40 mm. **Ruler:** Elizabeth II **Subject:** FIAA World Cup - South Africa **Rev:** Durban Stadium and Giraffes

| Date | Mintage | VF20 | XF40 | MS60 | MS63 | MS65 |
|---|---|---|---|---|---|---|
| 2010 | — | — | — | — | 20.00 | 25.00 |

**KM# 160 DOLLAR**
Tri-Metallic Copper center, Brass inner ring, Copper-Nickel outer ring., 40 mm. **Ruler:** Elizabeth II **Subject:** FIAA World Cup - South Africa **Rev:** Polokwane Stadium and Elephant

| Date | Mintage | VF20 | XF40 | MS60 | MS63 | MS65 |
|---|---|---|---|---|---|---|
| 2010 | — | — | — | — | 20.00 | 25.00 |

**KM# 161 DOLLAR**
Tri-Metallic Copper center, Brass inner ring, Copper-Nickel outer ring., 40 mm. **Ruler:** Elizabeth II **Subject:** FIAA World Cup - South Africa **Rev:** Nelspruit stadium and Water buffalo

| Date | Mintage | VF20 | XF40 | MS60 | MS63 | MS65 |
|---|---|---|---|---|---|---|
| 2010 | — | — | — | — | 20.00 | 25.00 |

**KM# 162 DOLLAR**
Tri-Metallic Copper center, Brass inner ring, Copper-Nickel outer ring., 40 mm. **Ruler:** Elizabeth II **Subject:** FIAA World Cup - South Africa **Rev:** Bloemfontein stadium and Lemurs

| Date | Mintage | VF20 | XF40 | MS60 | MS63 | MS65 |
|---|---|---|---|---|---|---|
| 2010 | — | — | — | — | 20.00 | 25.00 |

**KM# 163 DOLLAR**
Tri-Metallic Copper center, Brass inner ring, Copper-Nickel outer ring., 40 mm. **Ruler:** Elizabeth II **Subject:** FIAA World Cup - South Africa **Rev:** Port Elizabeth stadium and Animal

| Date | Mintage | VF20 | XF40 | MS60 | MS63 | MS65 |
|---|---|---|---|---|---|---|
| 2010 | — | — | — | — | 20.00 | 25.00 |

**KM# 181 DOLLAR**
31.11 g., 0.999 Silver 0.999 oz. ASW, 38.61 mm. **Ruler:** Elizabeth II **Subject:** Year of the Tiger **Obv:** Head with crown right **Rev:** Bengal Tiger in color **Shape:** Yin-Yang

| Date | Mintage | VF20 | XF40 | MS60 | MS63 | MS65 |
|---|---|---|---|---|---|---|
| 2010 | — | PF65 50.00 | | | | |

**KM# 182 DOLLAR**
31.11 g., 0.999 Silver 0.999 oz. ASW, 38.61 mm. **Ruler:** Elizabeth II **Obv:** Head with crown right **Rev:** Siberian tiger in color **Shape:** Yin-Yang

| Date | Mintage | VF20 | XF40 | MS60 | MS63 | MS65 |
|---|---|---|---|---|---|---|
| 2010 | — | PF65 50.00 | | | | |

**KM# 238 DOLLAR**
0.50 g., 0.999 Gold 0.0161 oz. AGW, 11 mm. **Ruler:** Elizabeth II **Subject:** Johann Philipp Reis **Obv:** Head in tiara right **Rev:** Reis portrait

| Date | Mintage | VF20 | XF40 | MS60 | MS63 | MS65 |
|---|---|---|---|---|---|---|
| 2010 | 5,000 | PF65 50.00 | | | | |

**KM# 240 DOLLAR**
26.03 g., Copper Plated Silver, 38.61 mm. **Ruler:** Elizabeth II **Subject:** London Olympics, 2012 **Obv:** Head with tiara right **Rev:** Triathlon sports

| Date | Mintage | VF20 | XF40 | MS60 | MS63 | MS65 |
|---|---|---|---|---|---|---|
| 2010 | 10,000 | PF63 20.00 | PF65 22.00 | | | |

**KM# 242 DOLLAR**
6.22 g., 0.999 Silver 0.1998 oz. ASW, 35 mm. **Ruler:** Elizabeth II **Subject:** Vitus Bering **Obv:** Head with tiara right **Rev:** Vitus J. Bering and ship Saint Peter

| Date | Mintage | VF20 | XF40 | MS60 | MS63 | MS65 |
|---|---|---|---|---|---|---|
| 2010 | 5,000 | PF63 32.00 | PF65 35.00 | | | |

**KM# 170 DOLLAR**
31.11 g., 0.999 Silver 0.999 oz. ASW, 38.6 mm. **Ruler:** Elizabeth II **Subject:** Year of the Dragon **Obv:** Characters, Filigree center **Rev:** Characters, Filigree center

| Date | Mintage | VF20 | XF40 | MS60 | MS63 | MS65 |
|---|---|---|---|---|---|---|
| 2011 | 10,000 | PF65 120 | | | | |

**KM# 176 DOLLAR**
31.11 g., 0.999 Silver 0.999 oz. ASW, 38.61 mm. **Ruler:** Elizabeth II **Subject:** Year of the Rabbit **Obv:** Head with crown right **Rev:** Rabbit eating carrot, carrots in color

| Date | Mintage | VF20 | XF40 | MS60 | MS63 | MS65 |
|---|---|---|---|---|---|---|
| 2011 | — | PF65 60.00 | | | | |

**KM# 177 DOLLAR**
31.11 g., 0.999 Silver 0.999 oz. ASW, 38.61 mm. **Ruler:** Elizabeth II **Subject:** Year of the Rabbit **Obv:** Head at left, rabbit in center cut-out **Rev:** Rabbit in center, leatuce leaves around

| Date | Mintage | VF20 | XF40 | MS60 | MS63 | MS65 |
|---|---|---|---|---|---|---|
| 2011 | — | PF65 145 | | | | |

**KM# 179 DOLLAR**
31.11 g., 0.999 Silver 0.999 oz. ASW, 38.61 mm. **Ruler:** Elizabeth II **Subject:** Year of the Rabbit **Obv:** Head in crown right **Rev:** Snow rabbit in color **Shape:** Yin-Yang

| Date | Mintage | VF20 | XF40 | MS60 | MS63 | MS65 |
|---|---|---|---|---|---|---|
| 2011 | — | PF65 90.00 | | | | |

**KM# 180 DOLLAR**
31.11 g., 0.999 Silver 0.999 oz. ASW, 38.61 mm. **Ruler:** Elizabeth II **Subject:** Year of the Rabbit **Obv:** Head with crown right **Rev:** Summer rabbit **Shape:** Yin-Yang

| Date | Mintage | VF20 | XF40 | MS60 | MS63 | MS65 |
|---|---|---|---|---|---|---|
| 2011 | — | PF65 90.00 | | | | |

**KM# 183 DOLLAR**
Copper-Nickel Silver plated, partially gilt, 38.61 mm. **Ruler:** Elizabeth II **Obv:** Bust right **Rev:** Sun, gilt figure

| Date | Mintage | VF20 | XF40 | MS60 | MS63 | MS65 |
|---|---|---|---|---|---|---|
| 2011 | — | — | — | — | — | 30.00 |

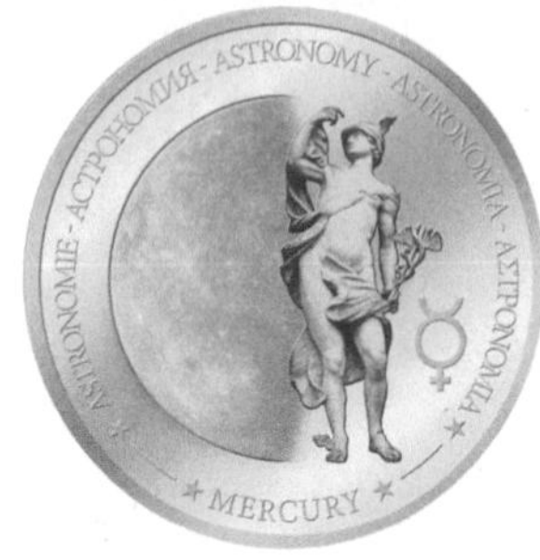


**KM# 184 DOLLAR**
Copper-Nickel Silver plated, partially gilt, 38.61 mm. **Ruler:** Elizabeth II **Obv:** Bust right **Rev:** Mercury, gilt figure

| Date | Mintage | VF20 | XF40 | MS60 | MS63 | MS65 |
|---|---|---|---|---|---|---|
| 2011 | — | — | — | — | — | 30.00 |

**KM# 185 DOLLAR**
Copper-Nickel Silver plated, partially gilt, 38.6 mm. **Ruler:** Elizabeth II **Obv:** Bust right **Rev:** Venus, gilt statue

| Date | Mintage | VF20 | XF40 | MS60 | MS63 | MS65 |
|---|---|---|---|---|---|---|
| 2011 | — | — | — | — | — | 30.00 |

**KM# 186 DOLLAR**
Copper-Nickel Silver plated, partially gilt, 38.61 mm. **Ruler:** Elizabeth II **Obv:** Bust right **Rev:** Earth, gilt statue

| Date | Mintage | VF20 | XF40 | MS60 | MS63 | MS65 |
|---|---|---|---|---|---|---|
| 2011 | — | — | — | — | — | 30.00 |

**KM# 187 DOLLAR**
Copper-Nickel Silver plated, partially gilt, 38.61 mm. **Ruler:** Elizabeth II **Obv:** Bust right **Rev:** Mars, gilt statue

| Date | Mintage | VF20 | XF40 | MS60 | MS63 | MS65 |
|---|---|---|---|---|---|---|
| 2011 | — | — | — | — | — | 30.00 |

**KM# 188 DOLLAR**
Copper-Nickel Silver plated, partially gilt, 38.61 mm. **Ruler:** Elizabeth II **Obv:** Bust right **Rev:** Jupiter, gilt statue

| Date | Mintage | VF20 | XF40 | MS60 | MS63 | MS65 |
|---|---|---|---|---|---|---|
| 2011 | — | — | — | — | — | 30.00 |

**KM# 189 DOLLAR**
Copper-Nickel Silver plated, partially gilt, 38.61 mm. **Ruler:** Elizabeth II **Obv:** Bust right **Rev:** Saturn, gilt statue

| Date | Mintage | VF20 | XF40 | MS60 | MS63 | MS65 |
|---|---|---|---|---|---|---|
| 2011 | — | — | — | — | — | 30.00 |

**KM# 190 DOLLAR**
Copper-Nickel Silver plated, partially gilt, 38.6 mm. **Ruler:** Elizabeth II **Obv:** Bust right **Rev:** Uranus, gilt statue

| Date | Mintage | VF20 | XF40 | MS60 | MS63 | MS65 |
|---|---|---|---|---|---|---|
| 2011 | — | — | — | — | — | 30.00 |

**KM# 191 DOLLAR**
Copper-Nickel Silver plated, partially gilt, 38.61 mm. **Ruler:** Elizabeth II **Obv:** Bust right **Rev:** Nepture, gilt statue

| Date | Mintage | VF20 | XF40 | MS60 | MS63 | MS65 |
|---|---|---|---|---|---|---|
| 2011 | — | — | — | — | — | 30.00 |

**KM# 192 DOLLAR**
Copper-Nickel Silver plated, partially gilt, 38.61 mm. **Ruler:** Elizabeth II **Obv:** Bust right **Rev:** Pluto, gilt statue

| Date | Mintage | VF20 | XF40 | MS60 | MS63 | MS65 |
|---|---|---|---|---|---|---|
| 2011 | — | — | — | — | — | 30.00 |

**KM# 246 DOLLAR**
0.50 g., 0.999 Gold 0.0161 oz. AGW, 11 mm. **Ruler:** Elizabeth II **Obv:** Head with tiara right **Rev:** Nero head right

| Date | Mintage | VF20 | XF40 | MS60 | MS63 | MS65 |
|---|---|---|---|---|---|---|
| 2011 | 5,000 | PF65 50.00 | | | | |

**KM# 171 DOLLAR**
15.55 g., 0.999 Silver 0.4994 oz. ASW with color., 38.6 mm. **Ruler:** Elizabeth II **Subject:** Year of the Dragon **Rev:** Red dragon **Shape:** Yin

| Date | Mintage | VF20 | XF40 | MS60 | MS63 | MS65 |
|---|---|---|---|---|---|---|
| 2012 | 10,000 | PF65 85.00 | | | | |

**KM# 172 DOLLAR**
15.55 g., 0.999 Silver 0.4994 oz. ASW with color, 38.6 mm. **Ruler:** Elizabeth II **Subject:** Year of the Dragon **Rev:** Blue dragon **Shape:** Yang

| Date | Mintage | VF20 | XF40 | MS60 | MS63 | MS65 |
|---|---|---|---|---|---|---|
| 2012 | — | PF65 85.00 | | | | |

**KM# 200 DOLLAR**
20.00 g., Copper-Nickel Silver plated, 38.61 mm. **Ruler:** Elizabeth II **Subject:** Carnival - Rio

| Date | Mintage | VF20 | XF40 | MS60 | MS63 | MS65 |
|---|---|---|---|---|---|---|
| 2012 | 2,500 | — | — | — | — | 40.00 |

**KM# 201 DOLLAR**
20.00 g., Copper-Nickel Silver plated, 38.6 mm. **Ruler:** Elizabeth II **Subject:** Carnival - Venice **Obv:** Head with tiara right

| Date | Mintage | VF20 | XF40 | MS60 | MS63 | MS65 |
|---|---|---|---|---|---|---|
| 2012 | 2,500 | — | — | — | — | 50.00 |

**KM# 202 DOLLAR**
20.00 g., Copper-Nickel Silver plated, 38.6 mm. **Ruler:** Elizabeth II **Subject:** Carnival - Nice **Obv:** Head with tiara right

| Date | Mintage | VF20 | XF40 | MS60 | MS63 | MS65 |
|---|---|---|---|---|---|---|
| 2012 | 2,500 | — | — | — | — | 50.00 |

**KM# 203 DOLLAR**
20.00 g., Copper-Nickel Silver plated, 38.6 mm. **Ruler:** Elizabeth II **Subject:** Carnival - New Orleans **Obv:** Head with tiara right

| Date | Mintage | VF20 | XF40 | MS60 | MS63 | MS65 |
|---|---|---|---|---|---|---|
| 2012 | 2,500 | — | — | — | — | 50.00 |

**KM# 204 DOLLAR**
20.00 g., Copper-Nickel Silver plated, 38.6 mm. **Ruler:** Elizabeth II **Subject:** Carnival - Cologne **Obv:** Head with tiara right

| Date | Mintage | VF20 | XF40 | MS60 | MS63 | MS65 |
|---|---|---|---|---|---|---|
| 2012 | 2,500 | — | — | — | — | 50.00 |

**KM# 205 DOLLAR**
20.00 g., Copper-Nickel Silver plated, 38.6 mm. **Ruler:** Elizabeth II **Subject:** Carnival - Basel **Obv:** Head with tiara right

| Date | Mintage | VF20 | XF40 | MS60 | MS63 | MS65 |
|---|---|---|---|---|---|---|
| 2012 | 2,500 | — | — | — | — | 50.00 |

**KM# 212 DOLLAR**
20.00 g., Silver Plated Copper, 38.6 mm. **Ruler:** Elizabeth II **Subject:** Music - Chanson

| Date | Mintage | VF20 | XF40 | MS60 | MS63 | MS65 |
|---|---|---|---|---|---|---|
| 2012 | 2,500 | PF65 20.00 | | | | |

**KM# 213 DOLLAR**
20.00 g., Silver Plated Copper, 38.6 mm. **Ruler:** Elizabeth II **Subject:** Music - Bob Marley

| Date | Mintage | VF20 | XF40 | MS60 | MS63 | MS65 |
|---|---|---|---|---|---|---|
| 2012 | 2,500 | PF65 20.00 | | | | |

**KM# 214 DOLLAR**
20.00 g., Silver Plated Copper, 38.6 mm. **Ruler:** Elizabeth II **Subject:** Music - Elvis Presley

| Date | Mintage | VF20 | XF40 | MS60 | MS63 | MS65 |
|---|---|---|---|---|---|---|
| 2012 | 2,500 | PF65 20.00 | | | | |

**KM# 319 DOLLAR**
0.50 g., 0.585 Gold 0.0094 oz. AGW 24K Gold Plating, 11 mm. **Ruler:** Elizabeth II **Subject:** Smallest Gold Coins - Pirogue of the Fiji Islands

| Date | Mintage | VF20 | XF40 | MS60 | MS63 | MS65 |
|---|---|---|---|---|---|---|
| 2012 | — | PF65 35.00 | | | | |

**KM# 320 DOLLAR**
0.50 g., 0.9999 Gold 0.0161 oz. AGW, 11 mm. **Ruler:** Elizabeth II **Subject:** Smallest Gold Coins - Diamond Jubilee

| Date | Mintage | VF20 | XF40 | MS60 | MS63 | MS65 |
|---|---|---|---|---|---|---|
| 2012 | Est. 5000 | PF65 50.00 | | | | |

**KM# 336 DOLLAR**
5.05 g., Brass Plated Steel, 23 mm. **Ruler:** Elizabeth II **Obv:** Vokai (Banded Iguana) **Rev:** Saqamoli (Drinking vessel)

| Date | Mintage | VF20 | XF40 | MS60 | MS63 | MS65 |
|---|---|---|---|---|---|---|
| 2012 | — | — | — | — | — | 2.00 |
| 2013 | — | — | — | — | — | 2.00 |

**KM# 352 DOLLAR**
20.00 g., 0.999 Silver 0.6424 oz. ASW, 40 mm. **Ruler:** Elizabeth II **Obv:** Bust with tiara right **Rev:** Horus eye in color

| Date | Mintage | VF20 | XF40 | MS60 | MS63 | MS65 |
|---|---|---|---|---|---|---|
| 2012 | 999 | PF65 65.00 | | | | |

**KM# 353 DOLLAR**
20.00 g., 0.999 Silver 0.6424 oz. ASW, 40 mm. **Ruler:** Elizabeth II **Obv:** Bust with tiara right **Rev:** Horus statue left, gilt and in color **Note:** Edge numbered

| Date | Mintage | VF20 | XF40 | MS60 | MS63 | MS65 |
|---|---|---|---|---|---|---|
| 2012 | 999 | PF65 65.00 | | | | |

**KM# 354 DOLLAR**
20.00 g., 0.999 Silver 0.6424 oz. ASW, 40 mm. **Ruler:** Elizabeth II **Obv:** Bust with tiara right **Rev:** Winged Isis in color **Note:** Edge numbered

| Date | Mintage | VF20 | XF40 | MS60 | MS63 | MS65 |
|---|---|---|---|---|---|---|
| 2012 | 999 | PF65 65.00 | | | | |

**KM# 355 DOLLAR**
20.00 g., 0.999 Silver 0.6424 oz. ASW, 40 mm. **Ruler:** Elizabeth II **Obv:** Bust with tiara right **Rev:** Nefertiti in color **Edge:** Plain **Note:** Edge numbered

| Date | Mintage | VF20 | XF40 | MS60 | MS63 | MS65 |
|---|---|---|---|---|---|---|
| 2012 | 999 | PF65 65.00 | | | | |

**KM# 356 DOLLAR**
20.00 g., 0.999 Silver 0.6424 oz. ASW, 40 mm. **Ruler:** Elizabeth II **Obv:** Bust with tiara right **Rev:** Tutankhamen mask in gold and color **Note:** Edge numbered

| Date | Mintage | VF20 | XF40 | MS60 | MS63 | MS65 |
|---|---|---|---|---|---|---|
| 2012 | 999 | PF65 65.00 | | | | |

**KM# 393 DOLLAR**
20.00 g., Gold Plated Copper, 40 mm. **Ruler:** Elizabeth II **Obv:** Head with tiara right **Rev:** Simon in color

| Date | Mintage | VF20 | XF40 | MS60 | MS63 | MS65 |
|---|---|---|---|---|---|---|
| 2012 Prooflike | 2,500 | — | — | — | — | 15.00 |

**KM# 395 DOLLAR**
20.00 g., Gold Plated Copper, 40 mm. **Ruler:** Elizabeth II **Obv:** Head with tiara right **Rev:** Thaddeus in color

| Date | Mintage | VF20 | XF40 | MS60 | MS63 | MS65 |
|---|---|---|---|---|---|---|
| 2012 Prooflike | 2,500 | — | — | — | — | 15.00 |

**KM# 396 DOLLAR**
20.00 g., Gold Plated Copper, 40 mm. **Ruler:** Elizabeth II **Obv:** Head with tiara right **Rev:** Philip in color

| Date | Mintage | VF20 | XF40 | MS60 | MS63 | MS65 |
|---|---|---|---|---|---|---|
| 2012 Prooflike | 2,500 | — | — | — | — | 15.00 |

**KM# 397 DOLLAR**
20.00 g., Gold Plated Copper, 40 mm. **Ruler:** Elizabeth II **Obv:** Head with tiara right **Rev:** James the Greater in color

| Date | Mintage | VF20 | XF40 | MS60 | MS63 | MS65 |
|---|---|---|---|---|---|---|
| 2012 Prooflike | 2,500 | — | — | — | — | 15.00 |

**KM# 398 DOLLAR**
20.00 g., Gold Plated Copper, 40 mm. **Ruler:** Elizabeth II **Obv:** Head with tiara right **Rev:** James the Lesser in color

| Date | Mintage | VF20 | XF40 | MS60 | MS63 | MS65 |
|---|---|---|---|---|---|---|
| 2012 Prooflike | 2,500 | — | — | — | — | 15.00 |

**KM# 399 DOLLAR**
20.00 g., Gold Plated Copper, 40 mm. **Ruler:** Elizabeth II **Obv:** Head with tiara right **Rev:** Bartholomew in color

| Date | Mintage | VF20 | XF40 | MS60 | MS63 | MS65 |
|---|---|---|---|---|---|---|
| 2012 Prooflike | 2,500 | — | — | — | — | 15.00 |

**KM# 400 DOLLAR**
20.00 g., Gold Plated Copper, 40 mm. **Ruler:** Elizabeth II **Obv:** Head with tiara right **Rev:** Andrew in color

| Date | Mintage | VF20 | XF40 | MS60 | MS63 | MS65 |
|---|---|---|---|---|---|---|
| 2012 Prooflike | 2,500 | — | — | — | — | 15.00 |

**KM# 401 DOLLAR**
20.00 g., Gold Plated Copper, 40 mm. **Ruler:** Elizabeth II **Obv:** head with tiara right **Rev:** John in color

| Date | Mintage | VF20 | XF40 | MS60 | MS63 | MS65 |
|---|---|---|---|---|---|---|
| 2012 Prooflike | 2,500 | — | — | — | — | 15.00 |

**KM# 402 DOLLAR**
20.00 g., Gold Plated Copper, 40 mm. **Ruler:** Elizabeth II **Obv:** Head with tiara right **Rev:** Matthew in color

| Date | Mintage | VF20 | XF40 | MS60 | MS63 | MS65 |
|---|---|---|---|---|---|---|
| 2012 Prooflike | 2,500 | — | — | — | — | 15.00 |

**KM# 403 DOLLAR**
20.00 g., Gold Plated Copper, 40 mm. **Ruler:** Elizabeth II **Obv:** Head with tiara right **Rev:** Peter in color

| Date | Mintage | VF20 | XF40 | MS60 | MS63 | MS65 |
|---|---|---|---|---|---|---|
| 2012 Prooflike | 2,500 | — | — | — | — | 15.00 |

**KM# 404 DOLLAR**
20.00 g., Gold Plated Copper, 40 mm. **Ruler:** Elizabeth II **Obv:** Head with tiara right **Rev:** Judas Iscariot in color

| Date | Mintage | VF20 | XF40 | MS60 | MS63 | MS65 |
|---|---|---|---|---|---|---|
| 2012 Prooflike | 2,500 | — | — | — | — | 15.00 |

**KM# 406 DOLLAR**
20.00 g., Silver Plated Copper, 38.61 mm. **Ruler:** Elizabeth II **Subject:** Music - Gospel **Obv:** Head with tiara right

| Date | Mintage | VF20 | XF40 | MS60 | MS63 | MS65 |
|---|---|---|---|---|---|---|
| 2012 | 2,500 | **PF65** 20.00 | | | | |

**KM# 407 DOLLAR**
20.00 g., Silver Plated Copper, 38.61 mm. **Ruler:** Elizabeth II **Subject:** Music - Jazz **Obv:** Head with tiara right

| Date | Mintage | VF20 | XF40 | MS60 | MS63 | MS65 |
|---|---|---|---|---|---|---|
| 2012 | 2,500 | **PF65** 20.00 | | | | |

**KM# 408 DOLLAR**
20.00 g., Silver Plated Copper, 40 mm. **Ruler:** Elizabeth II **Subject:** Music - Blues **Obv:** Head with tiara right

| Date | Mintage | VF20 | XF40 | MS60 | MS63 | MS65 |
|---|---|---|---|---|---|---|
| 2012 | 2,500 | **PF65** 20.00 | | | | |

**KM# 447 DOLLAR**
20.00 g., 0.999 Silver 0.6424 oz. ASW, 40 mm. **Ruler:** Elizabeth II **Obv:** Bust with tiara right **Rev:** Great Wall and koi fish, white pearls encased **Edge:** Plain **Note:** Edge numbered

| Date | Mintage | VF20 | XF40 | MS60 | MS63 | MS65 |
|---|---|---|---|---|---|---|
| 2012 | 999 | **PF65** 100 | | | | |

**KM# 448 DOLLAR**
20.00 g., 0.999 Silver 0.6424 oz. ASW, 40 mm. **Ruler:** Elizabeth II **Obv:** Bust with tiara right **Rev:** Sea Horse and hill-top pagoda; pink pearls encased **Edge:** Plain **Note:** Edge numbered

| Date | Mintage | VF20 | XF40 | MS60 | MS63 | MS65 |
|---|---|---|---|---|---|---|
| 2012 | 999 | **PF65** 100 | | | | |

**KM# 449 DOLLAR**
20.00 g., 0.999 Silver 0.6424 oz. ASW, 40 mm. **Ruler:** Elizabeth II **Obv:** Bust with tiara right **Rev:** Snake, mountain, grey pearls encased **Note:** Edge numbered

| Date | Mintage | VF20 | XF40 | MS60 | MS63 | MS65 |
|---|---|---|---|---|---|---|
| 2012 | 999 | **PF65** 100 | | | | |

**KM# 450 DOLLAR**
20.00 g., 0.999 Silver 0.6424 oz. ASW, 40 mm. **Ruler:** Elizabeth II **Obv:** Bust with tiara right **Rev:** Turtle, coral; violet pearls encased **Note:** Edge numbered

| Date | Mintage | VF20 | XF40 | MS60 | MS63 | MS65 |
|---|---|---|---|---|---|---|
| 2012 | 999 | **PF65** 100 | | | | |

**KM# 451 DOLLAR**
20.00 g., 0.999 Silver 0.6424 oz. ASW, 40 mm. **Ruler:** Elizabeth II **Obv:** Bust with tiara right **Rev:** Eagle and Bridge, Peridot encased **Edge:** Plain **Note:** Edge numbered

| Date | Mintage | VF20 | XF40 | MS60 | MS63 | MS65 |
|---|---|---|---|---|---|---|
| 2012 | — | **PF65** 100 | | | | |

**KM# 452 DOLLAR**
20.00 g., 0.999 Silver 0.6424 oz. ASW, 40 mm. **Ruler:** Elizabeth II **Obv:** Bust with tiara right **Rev:** Puma and building, Amethyst encased **Note:** Edge numbered

| Date | Mintage | VF20 | XF40 | MS60 | MS63 | MS65 |
|---|---|---|---|---|---|---|
| 2012 | 999 | **PF65** 100 | | | | |

**KM# 453 DOLLAR**
20.00 g., 0.999 Silver 0.6424 oz. ASW, 40 mm. **Ruler:** Elizabeth II **Obv:** Bust with tiara right **Rev:** Antelope and mountains, Smoky Quartz encased **Note:** Edge numbered

| Date | Mintage | VF20 | XF40 | MS60 | MS63 | MS65 |
|---|---|---|---|---|---|---|
| 2012 | 999 | **PF65** 100 | | | | |

**KM# 454 DOLLAR**
20.00 g., 0.999 Silver 0.6424 oz. ASW, 40 mm. **Ruler:** Elizabeth II **Obv:** Bust with tiara right **Rev:** Wolf and mountains, White topaz encased **Note:** Edge numbered

| Date | Mintage | VF20 | XF40 | MS60 | MS63 | MS65 |
|---|---|---|---|---|---|---|
| 2012 | 999 | **PF65** 100 | | | | |

**KM# 455 DOLLAR**
22.00 g., 0.999 Silver 0.7066 oz. ASW, 40 mm. **Ruler:** Elizabeth II **Obv:** Bust with tiara right **Rev:** Camel and mountains; silver encased **Note:** Edge numbered

| Date | Mintage | VF20 | XF40 | MS60 | MS63 | MS65 |
|---|---|---|---|---|---|---|
| 2012 | 999 | **PF65** 100 | | | | |

**KM# 456 DOLLAR**
20.00 g., 0.999 Silver 0.6424 oz. ASW, 40 mm. **Ruler:** Elizabeth II **Obv:** Bust with tiara right **Rev:** Tiger and tree; gold encased **Note:** Edge numbered

| Date | Mintage | VF20 | XF40 | MS60 | MS63 | MS65 |
|---|---|---|---|---|---|---|
| 2012 | 999 | **PF65** 100 | | | | |

**KM# 457 DOLLAR**
20.00 g., 0.999 Silver 0.6424 oz. ASW, 40 mm. **Ruler:** Elizabeth II **Obv:** Bust with tiara right **Rev:** Kangaroo and Sydney Opera House, Palladium encased **Note:** Edge numbered

| Date | Mintage | VF20 | XF40 | MS60 | MS63 | MS65 |
|---|---|---|---|---|---|---|
| 2012 | 999 | **PF65** 100 | | | | |

**KM# 458 DOLLAR**
20.00 g., 0.999 Silver 0.6424 oz. ASW, 40 mm. **Ruler:** Elizabeth II **Obv:** Bust with tiara right **Rev:** Eagle and cactus; Rhodium encased **Note:** Edge numbered

| Date | Mintage | VF20 | XF40 | MS60 | MS63 | MS65 |
|---|---|---|---|---|---|---|
| 2012 | 999 | **PF65** 100 | | | | |

**KM# 459 DOLLAR**
20.00 g., 0.999 Silver 0.6424 oz. ASW, 40 mm. **Ruler:** Elizabeth II **Obv:** Bust with tiara right **Rev:** Bear and mountains; Platinum encased **Note:** Edge numbered

| Date | Mintage | VF20 | XF40 | MS60 | MS63 | MS65 |
|---|---|---|---|---|---|---|
| 2012 | 999 | **PF65** 100 | | | | |

**KM# 466 DOLLAR**
20.00 g., 0.999 Silver 0.6424 oz. ASW, 40 mm. **Ruler:** Elizabeth II **Obv:** Bust with tiara right **Rev:** Osiris statues gilt and in color **Edge:** Plain **Note:** Edge numbered

| Date | Mintage | VF20 | XF40 | MS60 | MS63 | MS65 |
|---|---|---|---|---|---|---|
| 2012 | 999 | **PF65** 65.00 | | | | |

**KM# 467 DOLLAR**
20.00 g., 0.999 Silver 0.6424 oz. ASW, 40 mm. **Ruler:** Elizabeth II **Obv:** Bust with tiara right **Rev:** Anubis bust right in color **Edge:** Plain **Note:** Edge numbered

| Date | Mintage | VF20 | XF40 | MS60 | MS63 | MS65 |
|---|---|---|---|---|---|---|
| 2012 | 999 | **PF65** 65.00 | | | | |

**KM# 349 DOLLAR**
0.50 g., 0.585 Gold 0.0094 oz. AGW with 24Kt plating, 11 mm. **Ruler:** Elizabeth II **Subject:** H.M.S. Bounty

| Date | Mintage | VF20 | XF40 | MS60 | MS63 | MS65 |
|---|---|---|---|---|---|---|
| 2013 | Est. 5000 | **PF65** 40.00 | | | | |

**KM# 351 DOLLAR**
0.50 g., 0.585 Gold 0.0094 oz. AGW with 24Kt plating, 11 mm. **Ruler:** Elizabeth II **Subject:** Gutenberg

| Date | Mintage | VF20 | XF40 | MS60 | MS63 | MS65 |
|---|---|---|---|---|---|---|
| 2013 | Est. 5000 | PF65 40.00 | | | | |

**KM# 108 2 DOLLARS**
10.00 g., 0.925 Silver 0.2974 oz. ASW, 30 mm. **Ruler:** Elizabeth II **Subject:** XVIII FIFA World Rootball Championship - Germany 2006 **Obv:** Crowned head right **Obv. Legend:** ELIZABETH II - FIJI **Rev:** World cup

| Date | Mintage | VF20 | XF40 | MS60 | MS63 | MS65 |
|---|---|---|---|---|---|---|
| 2004 | 50,000 | PF60 17.00 | PF63 20.00 | PF65 22.00 | | |

**KM# 193 2 DOLLARS**
Silver, 38.61 mm. **Ruler:** Elizabeth II **Obv:** Head crowned right **Rev:** Orthodox church in color

| Date | Mintage | VF20 | XF40 | MS60 | MS63 | MS65 |
|---|---|---|---|---|---|---|
| 2009 | — | PF65 50.00 | | | | |

**KM# 194 2 DOLLARS**
Silver, 38.61 mm. **Ruler:** Elizabeth II **Obv:** Head crowned right **Rev:** Nicholas II Romanoff wedding portrait in color

| Date | Mintage | VF20 | XF40 | MS60 | MS63 | MS65 |
|---|---|---|---|---|---|---|
| 2009 | — | PF65 50.00 | | | | |

**KM# 195 2 DOLLARS**
Silver, 38.61 mm. **Ruler:** Elizabeth II **Obv:** Head crowned right **Rev:** Romanoff family portrait in color

| Date | Mintage | VF20 | XF40 | MS60 | MS63 | MS65 |
|---|---|---|---|---|---|---|
| 2009 | — | PF65 50.00 | | | | |

**KM# 273 2 DOLLARS**
0.999 Silver, 45x31 mm. **Ruler:** Elizabeth II **Rev:** British airship R34 in color **Shape:** Oval

| Date | Mintage | VF20 | XF40 | MS60 | MS63 | MS65 |
|---|---|---|---|---|---|---|
| 2009 | 20,000 | PF63 90.00 | PF65 100 | | | |

**KM# 274 2 DOLLARS**
0.999 Silver, 45x31 mm. **Ruler:** Elizabeth II **Rev:** Soviet airship B6 in color **Shape:** Oval

| Date | Mintage | VF20 | XF40 | MS60 | MS63 | MS65 |
|---|---|---|---|---|---|---|
| 2009 | 20,000 | PF63 90.00 | PF65 100 | | | |

**KM# 275 2 DOLLARS**
0.999 Silver, 45x31 mm. **Ruler:** Elizabeth II **Rev:** U.S. Airship Akron in color **Shape:** Oval

| Date | Mintage | VF20 | XF40 | MS60 | MS63 | MS65 |
|---|---|---|---|---|---|---|
| 2009 | 20,000 | PF63 90.00 | PF65 100 | | | |

**KM# 276 2 DOLLARS**
0.999 Silver, 45x31 mm. **Ruler:** Elizabeth II **Rev:** German airship Hindenburg in color **Shape:** Oval

| Date | Mintage | VF20 | XF40 | MS60 | MS63 | MS65 |
|---|---|---|---|---|---|---|
| 2009 | 20,000 | PF63 90.00 | PF65 100 | | | |

**KM# 166 2 DOLLARS**
31.11 g., 0.999 Silver 0.999 oz. ASW, 45x31 mm. **Ruler:** Elizabeth II **Rev:** Submarine Ohio in color **Shape:** Oval

| Date | Mintage | VF20 | XF40 | MS60 | MS63 | MS65 |
|---|---|---|---|---|---|---|
| 2010 Prooflike | 15,000 | — | — | — | — | 90.00 |

**KM# 167 2 DOLLARS**
31.11 g., 0.999 Silver 0.999 oz. ASW, 45x31 mm. **Ruler:** Elizabeth II **Rev:** Submarine Triomphant in color **Shape:** Oval

| Date | Mintage | VF20 | XF40 | MS60 | MS63 | MS65 |
|---|---|---|---|---|---|---|
| 2010 Prooflike | 15,000 | — | — | — | — | 90.00 |

**KM# 168 2 DOLLARS**
31.11 g., 0.999 Silver 0.999 oz. ASW, 45x31 mm. **Ruler:** Elizabeth II **Rev:** Submarine Typhoon in color **Shape:** Oval

| Date | Mintage | VF20 | XF40 | MS60 | MS63 | MS65 |
|---|---|---|---|---|---|---|
| 2010 Prooflike | 15,000 | — | — | — | — | 90.00 |

**KM# 169 2 DOLLARS**
31.11 g., 0.999 Silver 0.999 oz. ASW, 45x31 mm. **Ruler:** Elizabeth II **Rev:** Submarine Vanguard in color **Shape:** Oval

| Date | Mintage | VF20 | XF40 | MS60 | MS63 | MS65 |
|---|---|---|---|---|---|---|
| 2010 Prooflike | 15,000 | — | — | — | — | 90.00 |

**KM# 369 2 DOLLARS**
25.00 g., 0.999 Silver 0.803 oz. ASW, 38.61 mm. **Ruler:** Elizabeth II **Obv:** Head crowned right **Rev:** Mnemosyne

| Date | Mintage | VF20 | XF40 | MS60 | MS63 | MS65 |
|---|---|---|---|---|---|---|
| 2011 | 4,000 | PF65 50.00 | | | | |

**KM# 370 2 DOLLARS**
25.00 g., 0.999 Silver 0.803 oz. ASW, 38.61 mm. **Ruler:** Elizabeth II **Obv:** Head crowned right **Rev:** Calliope

| Date | Mintage | VF20 | XF40 | MS60 | MS63 | MS65 |
|---|---|---|---|---|---|---|
| 2011 | 4,000 | PF65 50.00 | | | | |

**KM# 371 2 DOLLARS**
25.00 g., 0.999 Silver 0.803 oz. ASW, 38.61 mm. **Ruler:** Elizabeth II **Obv:** Head crowned right **Rev:** Orpheus

| Date | Mintage | VF20 | XF40 | MS60 | MS63 | MS65 |
|---|---|---|---|---|---|---|
| 2011 | 4,000 | PF65 50.00 | | | | |

**KM# 372 2 DOLLARS**
25.00 g., 0.999 Silver 0.803 oz. ASW, 38.61 mm. **Ruler:** Elizabeth II **Obv:** Head crowned right **Rev:** Clio

| Date | Mintage | VF20 | XF40 | MS60 | MS63 | MS65 |
|---|---|---|---|---|---|---|
| 2011 | 4,000 | PF65 50.00 | | | | |

**KM# 373 2 DOLLARS**
25.00 g., 0.999 Silver 0.803 oz. ASW, 38.61 mm. **Ruler:** Elizabeth II **Obv:** Head crowned right **Rev:** Erato

| Date | Mintage | VF20 | XF40 | MS60 | MS63 | MS65 |
|---|---|---|---|---|---|---|
| 2011 | 4,000 | PF65 50.00 | | | | |

**KM# 374 2 DOLLARS**
25.00 g., 0.999 Silver 0.803 oz. ASW, 38.61 mm. **Ruler:** Elizabeth II **Obv:** Head crowned right **Rev:** Euterpe

| Date | Mintage | VF20 | XF40 | MS60 | MS63 | MS65 |
|---|---|---|---|---|---|---|
| 2011 | 4,000 | PF65 50.00 | | | | |

**KM# 375 2 DOLLARS**
25.00 g., 0.999 Silver 0.803 oz. ASW, 38.61 mm. **Ruler:** Elizabeth II **Obv:** Head crowned right **Rev:** Melpomene

| Date | Mintage | VF20 | XF40 | MS60 | MS63 | MS65 |
|---|---|---|---|---|---|---|
| 2011 | 4,000 | PF65 50.00 | | | | |

**KM# 376 2 DOLLARS**
25.00 g., 0.999 Silver 0.803 oz. ASW, 38.61 mm. **Ruler:** Elizabeth II **Obv:** Head crowned right **Rev:** Polyhymnia

| Date | Mintage | VF20 | XF40 | MS60 | MS63 | MS65 |
|---|---|---|---|---|---|---|
| 2011 | 4,000 | PF65 50.00 | | | | |

**KM# 377 2 DOLLARS**
25.00 g., 0.999 Silver 0.803 oz. ASW, 38.61 mm. **Ruler:** Elizabeth II **Obv:** Head crowned right **Rev:** Therpsichore

| Date | Mintage | VF20 | XF40 | MS60 | MS63 | MS65 |
|---|---|---|---|---|---|---|
| 2011 | 4,000 | PF65 50.00 | | | | |

**KM# 378 2 DOLLARS**
25.00 g., 0.999 Silver 0.803 oz. ASW, 38.61 mm. **Ruler:** Elizabeth II **Obv:** Head crowned right **Rev:** Thalia

| Date | Mintage | VF20 | XF40 | MS60 | MS63 | MS65 |
|---|---|---|---|---|---|---|
| 2011 | 4,000 | PF65 50.00 | | | | |

**KM# 379 2 DOLLARS**
25.00 g., 0.999 Silver 0.803 oz. ASW, 38.61 mm. **Ruler:** Elizabeth II **Obv:** Head crowned right **Rev:** Urania

| Date | Mintage | VF20 | XF40 | MS60 | MS63 | MS65 |
|---|---|---|---|---|---|---|
| 2011 | 4,000 | PF65 50.00 | | | | |

**KM# 380 2 DOLLARS**
25.00 g., 0.999 Silver 0.803 oz. ASW, 38.61 mm. **Ruler:** Elizabeth II **Obv:** Head crowned right **Rev:** Apollo

| Date | Mintage | VF20 | XF40 | MS60 | MS63 | MS65 |
|---|---|---|---|---|---|---|
| 2011 | 4,000 | PF65 50.00 | | | | |

**KM# 252 2 DOLLARS**
31.11 g., 0.999 Silver 0.999 oz. ASW **Ruler:** Elizabeth II **Rev:** Muhammad Ali, color portrait

| Date | Mintage | VF20 | XF40 | MS60 | MS63 | MS65 |
|---|---|---|---|---|---|---|
| 2012 | 7,500 | PF65 100 | | | | |

**KM# 337 2 DOLLARS**
(No Composition), 27.5 mm. **Ruler:** Elizabeth II **Obv:** Gani Yatu (Peregrine Falcon) **Rev:** Tanoa (Drinking vessel)

| Date | Mintage | VF20 | XF40 | MS60 | MS63 | MS65 |
|---|---|---|---|---|---|---|
| 2012 | — | — | — | — | — | 4.00 |
| 2013 | — | — | — | — | — | 4.00 |

**KM# 338 2 DOLLARS**
31.11 g., 0.999 Silver 0.999 oz. ASW with red zirconia stone insert **Ruler:** Elizabeth II **Obv:** National Arms **Rev:** Yorkshire Terrier (My Little Puppy)

| Date | Mintage | VF20 | XF40 | MS60 | MS63 | MS65 |
|---|---|---|---|---|---|---|
| 2013 | Est. 5000 | PF65 50.00 | | | | |

### KM# 339 2 DOLLARS

31.11 g., 0.999 Silver 0.999 oz. ASW with yellow zirconia insert, 40 mm. **Ruler:** Elizabeth II **Obv:** National arms **Rev:** Basset Hound (My Best Friend)

| Date | Mintage | VF20 | XF40 | MS60 | MS63 | MS65 |
|---|---|---|---|---|---|---|
| 2013 | Est. 5000 | **PF65** 50.00 | | | | |

### KM# 340 2 DOLLARS

31.11 g., 0.999 Silver 0.999 oz. ASW with blue zirconia stone insert, 40 mm. **Ruler:** Elizabeth II **Obv:** National arms **Rev:** Boxer (My Great Protector)

| Date | Mintage | VF20 | XF40 | MS60 | MS63 | MS65 |
|---|---|---|---|---|---|---|
| 2013 | Est. 5000 | **PF65** 50.00 | | | | |

### KM# 341 2 DOLLARS

31.11 g., 0.999 Silver 0.999 oz. ASW with blue zirconia stone insert, 40 mm. **Ruler:** Elizabeth II **Obv:** National arms **Rev:** American Curl (Fluffy Cat)

| Date | Mintage | VF20 | XF40 | MS60 | MS63 | MS65 |
|---|---|---|---|---|---|---|
| 2013 | Est. 5000 | **PF65** 50.00 | | | | |

### KM# 342 2 DOLLARS

31.11 g., 0.999 Silver 0.999 oz. ASW with pink zirconia stone insert, 40 mm. **Ruler:** Elizabeth II **Obv:** National arms **Rev:** Sphynx (Super Cat)

| Date | Mintage | VF20 | XF40 | MS60 | MS63 | MS65 |
|---|---|---|---|---|---|---|
| 2013 | Est. 5000 | **PF65** 50.00 | | | | |

### KM# 343 2 DOLLARS

31.10 g., 0.999 Silver 0.999 oz. ASW With yellow zirconia insert, 40 mm. **Ruler:** Elizabeth II **Obv:** National arms **Rev:** Felis Margarita (Wild Cat)

| Date | Mintage | VF20 | XF40 | MS60 | MS63 | MS65 |
|---|---|---|---|---|---|---|
| 2013 | Est. 5000 | **PF65** 50.00 | | | | |

### KM# 367 2 DOLLARS

31.10 g., 0.999 Silver 0.9989 oz. ASW, 30x51 mm. **Ruler:** Elizabeth II **Subject:** Collared Lory **Obv:** National arms and bird in color **Shape:** Vertical rectangle

| Date | Mintage | VF20 | XF40 | MS60 | MS63 | MS65 |
|---|---|---|---|---|---|---|
| 2013 | 3,000 | **PF65** 50.00 | | | | |

### KM# 93 5 DOLLARS

1.56 g., 0.9999 Gold 0.050 oz. AGW **Ruler:** Elizabeth II **Obv:** Crowned head right, date at right **Rev:** Arms

| Date | Mintage | VF20 | XF40 | MS60 | MS63 | MS65 |
|---|---|---|---|---|---|---|
| 2002 | 3,000 | **PF63** 90.00 | **PF65** 100 | | | |

### KM# 115A 5 DOLLARS

1.56 g., 0.9999 Gold 0.0498 oz. AGW, 13.9 mm. **Ruler:** Elizabeth II **Rev:** Coat of Arms

| Date | Mintage | VF20 | XF40 | MS60 | MS63 | MS65 |
|---|---|---|---|---|---|---|
| 2002 | 3,000 | **PF63** 200 | **PF65** 220 | | | |

### KM# 173 5 DOLLARS

Silver partially gilt, 39 mm. **Ruler:** Elizabeth II **Subject:** Queen Elizabeth II, 80th Birthday

| Date | Mintage | VF20 | XF40 | MS60 | MS63 | MS65 |
|---|---|---|---|---|---|---|
| 2006 | — | **PF65** 50.00 | | | | |

### KM# 265 5 DOLLARS

Silver partially gilt **Ruler:** Elizabeth II **Subject:** Christopher Columbus, 500th Anniversary of Death **Rev:** Santa Maria and Columbus portrait

| Date | Mintage | VF20 | XF40 | MS60 | MS63 | MS65 |
|---|---|---|---|---|---|---|
| 2006 | 3,000 | **PF65** 35.00 | | | | |

### KM# 266 5 DOLLARS

1.24 g., 0.585 Gold 0.0233 oz. AGW, 13.92 mm. **Ruler:** Elizabeth II **Rev:** Stonehedge

| Date | Mintage | VF20 | XF40 | MS60 | MS63 | MS65 |
|---|---|---|---|---|---|---|
| 2006 | 7,500 | **PF63** 45.00 | **PF65** 50.00 | | | |

### KM# 267 5 DOLLARS

1.24 g., 0.585 Gold 0.0233 oz. AGW, 13.92 mm. **Ruler:** Elizabeth II **Rev:** Easter Island rock sculptures

| Date | Mintage | VF20 | XF40 | MS60 | MS63 | MS65 |
|---|---|---|---|---|---|---|
| 2006 | 7,500 | **PF63** 45.00 | **PF65** 50.00 | | | |

### KM# 268 5 DOLLARS

1.24 g., 0.585 Gold 0.0233 oz. AGW, 13.92 mm. **Ruler:** Elizabeth II **Rev:** Bird glyph on Nazca Plateau

| Date | Mintage | VF20 | XF40 | MS60 | MS63 | MS65 |
|---|---|---|---|---|---|---|
| 2006 | 7,500 | **PF63** 45.00 | **PF65** 50.00 | | | |

### KM# 269 5 DOLLARS

1.24 g., 0.585 Gold 0.0233 oz. AGW, 13.92 mm. **Ruler:** Elizabeth II **Rev:** Seven castles

| Date | Mintage | VF20 | XF40 | MS60 | MS63 | MS65 |
|---|---|---|---|---|---|---|
| 2006 | 7,500 | **PF63** 45.00 | **PF65** 50.00 | | | |

### KM# 270 5 DOLLARS

1.24 g., 0.585 Gold 0.0233 oz. AGW, 13.92 mm. **Ruler:** Elizabeth II **Rev:** Atlantis

| Date | Mintage | VF20 | XF40 | MS60 | MS63 | MS65 |
|---|---|---|---|---|---|---|
| 2006 | 7,500 | **PF63** 45.00 | **PF65** 50.00 | | | |

### KM# 271 5 DOLLARS

1.24 g., 0.585 Gold 0.0233 oz. AGW, 13.92 mm. **Ruler:** Elizabeth II **Rev:** Ayers Rock

| Date | Mintage | VF20 | XF40 | MS60 | MS63 | MS65 |
|---|---|---|---|---|---|---|
| 2006 | 7,500 | **PF63** 45.00 | **PF65** 50.00 | | | |

### KM# 272 5 DOLLARS

1.24 g., 0.585 Gold 0.0233 oz. AGW, 13.92 mm. **Ruler:** Elizabeth II **Rev:** Sailing ship in Bermuda triangle

| Date | Mintage | VF20 | XF40 | MS60 | MS63 | MS65 |
|---|---|---|---|---|---|---|
| 2006 | 7,500 | **PF63** 45.00 | **PF65** 50.00 | | | |

### KM# 206 5 DOLLARS

62.20 g., 0.999 Silver 1.9978 oz. ASW partially gilt, 60 mm. **Ruler:** Elizabeth II **Subject:** Map - New York City, Manhattan Island

| Date | Mintage | VF20 | XF40 | MS60 | MS63 | MS65 |
|---|---|---|---|---|---|---|
| 2011 | 5,000 | **PF65** 125 | | | | |

**KM# 207 5 DOLLARS**
62.20 g., 0.999 Silver 1.9978 oz. ASW partially gilt, 60 mm. **Ruler:** Elizabeth II **Subject:** Map - Paris

| Date | Mintage | VF20 | XF40 | MS60 | MS63 | MS65 |
|---|---|---|---|---|---|---|
| 2011 | 5,000 | PF65 125 | | | | |

**KM# 208 5 DOLLARS**
62.20 g., 0.999 Silver 1.9978 oz. ASW partially gilt, 60 mm. **Ruler:** Elizabeth II **Subject:** Map - Tokyo

| Date | Mintage | VF20 | XF40 | MS60 | MS63 | MS65 |
|---|---|---|---|---|---|---|
| 2011 | 5,000 | PF65 125 | | | | |

**KM# 209 5 DOLLARS**
62.20 g., 0.999 Silver 1.9978 oz. ASW partially gilt, 60 mm. **Ruler:** Elizabeth II **Subject:** Map - Sidney

| Date | Mintage | VF20 | XF40 | MS60 | MS63 | MS65 |
|---|---|---|---|---|---|---|
| 2011 | 5,000 | PF65 125 | | | | |

**KM# 210 5 DOLLARS**
62.20 g., 0.999 Silver 1.9978 oz. ASW partially gilt, 60 mm. **Ruler:** Elizabeth II **Subject:** Map - Berlin

| Date | Mintage | VF20 | XF40 | MS60 | MS63 | MS65 |
|---|---|---|---|---|---|---|
| 2011 | 5,000 | PF65 125 | | | | |

**KM# 318 5 DOLLARS**
28.28 g., 0.925 Silver 0.841 oz. ASW, 38.61 mm. **Ruler:** Elizabeth II **Subject:** Diamond Jubilee of Queen Elizabeth II - Imperial State Crown

| Date | Mintage | VF20 | XF40 | MS60 | MS63 | MS65 |
|---|---|---|---|---|---|---|
| 2012 | Est. 10000 | PF65 50.00 | | | | |

**KM# 82 10 DOLLARS**
31.62 g., 0.925 Silver 0.9404 oz. ASW, 38.6 mm. **Ruler:** Elizabeth II **Obv:** Crowned head right, date at right **Rev:** William Bligh's - HMS Providence **Edge:** Reeded

| Date | Mintage | VF20 | XF40 | MS60 | MS63 | MS65 |
|---|---|---|---|---|---|---|
| 2001 | — | PF63 35.00 | PF65 40.00 | | | |

**KM# 83 10 DOLLARS**
28.28 g., 0.925 Silver 0.841 oz. ASW, 38.6 mm. **Ruler:** Elizabeth II **Subject:** Queen Elizabeth II - 50 Years of Reign **Obv:** Queen's head right, gilded **Rev:** Cloth draped sword hilt, legend and denomination **Rev. Legend:** Defender of the Faith... **Edge:** Reeded

| Date | Mintage | VF20 | XF40 | MS60 | MS63 | MS65 |
|---|---|---|---|---|---|---|
| 2002 | 15,000 | PF63 37.00 | PF65 42.00 | | | |

**KM# 84 10 DOLLARS**
28.28 g., 0.925 Silver 0.841 oz. ASW, 38.6 mm. **Ruler:** Elizabeth II **Subject:** Queen Elizabeth II - 50th Year of Reign **Obv:** Head right, gilded **Rev:** Four man chorus, legend, and denomination **Rev. Legend:** Westminster Abbey June 1953. **Edge:** Reeded

| Date | Mintage | VF20 | XF40 | MS60 | MS63 | MS65 |
|---|---|---|---|---|---|---|
| 2002 | 15,000 | PF63 37.00 | PF65 42.00 | | | |

**KM# 94 10 DOLLARS**
3.11 g., 0.9999 Gold 0.100 oz. AGW **Ruler:** Elizabeth II **Obv:** Crowned head right, date at right **Rev:** Arms **Edge:** Reeded

| Date | Mintage | VF20 | XF40 | MS60 | MS63 | MS65 |
|---|---|---|---|---|---|---|
| 2002 | 2,000 | PF63 175 | PF65 200 | | | |

**KM# 101 10 DOLLARS**
31.10 g., 0.999 Silver 0.9989 oz. ASW, 40 mm. **Ruler:** Elizabeth II **Series:** Save the Whales **Obv:** Crowned head right, date at right **Obv. Legend:** ELIZABETH II - FIJI **Rev:** Sperm Whale on mother-of-pearl inset **Edge:** Plain

| Date | Mintage | VF20 | XF40 | MS60 | MS63 | MS65 |
|---|---|---|---|---|---|---|
| 2002 | 2,000 | PF65 85.00 | | | | |

**KM# 104 10 DOLLARS**
28.28 g., 0.925 Silver 0.841 oz. ASW, 38.6 mm. **Ruler:** Elizabeth II **Series:** Endangered Wildlife **Obv:** Crowned head right **Obv. Legend:** ELIZABETH II - FIJI **Rev:** Head of Peregrine Falcon right

| Date | Mintage | VF20 | XF40 | MS60 | MS63 | MS65 |
|---|---|---|---|---|---|---|
| 2002 | — | PF63 42.00 | PF65 45.00 | | | |

**KM# 105 10 DOLLARS**
28.28 g., 0.925 Silver 0.841 oz. ASW, 38.6 mm. **Ruler:** Elizabeth II **Obv:** Crowned head right **Obv. Legend:** ELIZABETH II - FIJI **Rev:** Sailing ship "Vostok

| Date | Mintage | VF20 | XF40 | MS60 | MS63 | MS65 |
|---|---|---|---|---|---|---|
| 2002 | — | PF63 35.00 | PF65 40.00 | | | |

**KM# 106 10 DOLLARS**
1.24 g., 0.9999 Gold 0.0399 oz. AGW, 13.88 mm. **Ruler:** Elizabeth II **Obv:** Crowned head right **Obv. Legend:** ELIZABETH II - FIJI **Rev:** Sailing ship at left, naval bust 3/4 left at right **Rev. Legend:** HMS INVESTIGATOR * MATTHEW FLINDERS **Edge:** Reeded

| Date | Mintage | VF20 | XF40 | MS60 | MS63 | MS65 |
|---|---|---|---|---|---|---|
| 2002 | — | PF63 75.00 | PF65 85.00 | | | |

**KM# 258 10 DOLLARS**
31.11 g., 0.999 Silver 0.999 oz. ASW, 40 mm. **Ruler:** Elizabeth II **Subject:** Fairwell to the Irish Pfund **Rev:** Coin motif in color

| Date | Mintage | VF20 | XF40 | MS60 | MS63 | MS65 |
|---|---|---|---|---|---|---|
| 2002 | Est. 2001 | PF65 80.00 | | | | |

### KM# 114A 10 DOLLARS

3.11 g., 0.9999 Gold 0.0993 oz. AGW, 16 mm. **Ruler:** Elizabeth II **Rev:** Coat of Arms

| Date | Mintage | VF20 | XF40 | MS60 | MS63 | MS65 |
|---|---|---|---|---|---|---|
| 2002 | 2,000 | PF63 325 | PF65 350 | | | |

### KM# 107 10 DOLLARS

28.26 g., 0.925 Silver 0.8404 oz. ASW, 38.61 mm. **Ruler:** Elizabeth II **Obv:** Crowned head right **Obv. Legend:** ELIZABETH II - FIJI **Rev:** Sailing ship at left, naval bust 3/4 left at right **Rev. Legend:** HMS INVESTIGATOR * MATTHEW FLINDERS **Edge:** Reeded

| Date | Mintage | VF20 | XF40 | MS60 | MS63 | MS65 |
|---|---|---|---|---|---|---|
| 2003 | — | PF63 42.00 | PF65 45.00 | | | |

### KM# 109 10 DOLLARS

28.28 g., 0.925 Silver 0.841 oz. ASW, 38.61 mm. **Ruler:** Elizabeth II **Subject:** XXVIII Summer Olympics - Athens 2004 **Obv:** Crowned head right **Obv. Legend:** ELIZABETH II - FIJI **Rev:** Regatta **Edge:** Reeded

| Date | Mintage | VF20 | XF40 | MS60 | MS63 | MS65 |
|---|---|---|---|---|---|---|
| 2003 | — | PF63 38.00 | PF65 42.00 | | | |

### KM# 113 10 DOLLARS

1.24 g., Gold, 13.91 mm. **Ruler:** Elizabeth II **Subject:** Lost Treasure of King Richard **Obv:** Crowned head right **Rev:** Bust of King Richard facing **Edge:** Reeded

| Date | Mintage | VF20 | XF40 | MS60 | MS63 | MS65 |
|---|---|---|---|---|---|---|
| 2003 | — | PF63 70.00 | PF65 80.00 | | | |

### KM# 110 10 DOLLARS

Copper-Nickel-Zinc, 38.6 mm. **Ruler:** Elizabeth II **Subject:** XVIII FIFA World Football Championship - Germany 2006 **Obv:** Crowned head right **Obv. Legend:** ELIZABETH II - FIJI **Rev:** Digital countdown clock

| Date | Mintage | VF20 | XF40 | MS60 | MS63 | MS65 |
|---|---|---|---|---|---|---|
| 2005 | 50,000 | — | — | — | — | 45.00 |

### KM# 263 10 DOLLARS

31.11 g., 0.999 Silver 0.999 oz. ASW with gold inlay, 38.61 mm. **Ruler:** Elizabeth II **Subject:** FIFA World Cup **Rev:** Trophy

| Date | Mintage | VF20 | XF40 | MS60 | MS63 | MS65 |
|---|---|---|---|---|---|---|
| 2005 | — | — | — | — | — | 80.00 |

### KM# 111 10 DOLLARS

1.24 g., 0.9999 Gold 0.0399 oz. AGW **Ruler:** Elizabeth II **Subject:** 500th Anniversary Death of Christopher Columbus **Obv:** Crowned head right **Obv. Legend:** ELIZABETH II - FIJI **Rev:** Sailing ship "Santa Maria

| Date | Mintage | VF20 | XF40 | MS60 | MS63 | MS65 |
|---|---|---|---|---|---|---|
| 2006 | 15,000 | PF63 70.00 | PF65 80.00 | | | |

### KM# 330 10 DOLLARS

28.28 g., 0.925 Silver 0.841 oz. ASW, 38.61 mm. **Ruler:** Elizabeth II **Subject:** Queen Elizabeth II 60th Wedding Anniversary **Shape:** 7-Sided

| Date | Mintage | VF20 | XF40 | MS60 | MS63 | MS65 |
|---|---|---|---|---|---|---|
| 2007 | — | PF65 40.00 | | | | |

### KM# 331 10 DOLLARS

28.28 g., 0.925 Silver 0.841 oz. ASW, 38.61 mm. **Ruler:** Elizabeth II **Subject:** Balmoral Castle **Shape:** 7-Sided

| Date | Mintage | VF20 | XF40 | MS60 | MS63 | MS65 |
|---|---|---|---|---|---|---|
| 2007 | Est. 30000 | PF65 40.00 | | | | |

### KM# 235 10 DOLLARS

28.28 g., 0.925 Silver 0.841 oz. ASW, 38.61 mm. **Ruler:** Elizabeth II **Subject:** James Watt **Obv:** Head in tiara right **Rev:** James Watt and steam engine

| Date | Mintage | VF20 | XF40 | MS60 | MS63 | MS65 |
|---|---|---|---|---|---|---|
| 2008 | 5,000 | PF65 35.00 | | | | |

### KM# 236 10 DOLLARS

1.00 g., 0.9999 Gold 0.0321 oz. AGW, 13.92 mm. **Ruler:** Elizabeth II **Subject:** Lapita art **Obv:** Head with Tiara right **Rev:** Artistic design

| Date | Mintage | VF20 | XF40 | MS60 | MS63 | MS65 |
|---|---|---|---|---|---|---|
| 2008 | 15,000 | PF65 75.00 | | | | |

### KM# 125 10 DOLLARS

31.11 g., 0.999 Silver 0.999 oz. ASW **Ruler:** Elizabeth II **Obv:** Crowned head right **Rev:** Yes we can!

| Date | Mintage | VF20 | XF40 | MS60 | MS63 | MS65 |
|---|---|---|---|---|---|---|
| 2009 | — | PF65 50.00 | | | | |

### KM# 178 10 DOLLARS

28.28 g., 0.925 Silver 0.841 oz. ASW, 38.61 mm. **Ruler:** Elizabeth II **Obv:** Head with tiara right **Rev:** Barak Obama at left

| Date | Mintage | VF20 | XF40 | MS60 | MS63 | MS65 |
|---|---|---|---|---|---|---|
| 2009 | — | PF65 50.00 | | | | |

### KM# 277 10 DOLLARS

28.28 g., 0.925 Silver 0.841 oz. ASW, 38.61 mm. **Ruler:** Elizabeth II **Rev:** Butterfly fish in color

| Date | Mintage | VF20 | XF40 | MS60 | MS63 | MS65 |
|---|---|---|---|---|---|---|
| 2009 | — | PF65 45.00 | | | | |

### KM# 277a 10 DOLLARS

39.00 g., 0.916 Gold 1.1486 oz. AGW, 38.61 mm. **Ruler:** Elizabeth II **Rev:** Butterfly fish

| Date | Mintage | VF20 | XF40 | MS60 | MS63 | MS65 |
|---|---|---|---|---|---|---|
| 2009 | — | PF63 1,950 | PF65 2,100 | | | |

### KM# 278 10 DOLLARS

28.28 g., 0.925 Silver 0.841 oz. ASW, 38.61 mm. **Ruler:** Elizabeth II **Rev:** Imperial Angler fish in color

| Date | Mintage | VF20 | XF40 | MS60 | MS63 | MS65 |
|---|---|---|---|---|---|---|
| 2009 | — | PF65 45.00 | | | | |

### KM# 278a 10 DOLLARS

39.00 g., 0.916 Gold 1.1486 oz. AGW, 38.61 mm. **Ruler:** Elizabeth II **Rev:** Imperial Angler

| Date | Mintage | VF20 | XF40 | MS60 | MS63 | MS65 |
|---|---|---|---|---|---|---|
| 2009 | — | PF63 1,950 | PF65 2,100 | | | |

### KM# 279 10 DOLLARS

28.28 g., 0.925 Silver 0.841 oz. ASW, 38.61 mm. **Ruler:** Elizabeth II **Rev:** Clown fish in color

| Date | Mintage | VF20 | XF40 | MS60 | MS63 | MS65 |
|---|---|---|---|---|---|---|
| 2009 | — | PF65 45.00 | | | | |

### KM# 279a 10 DOLLARS

39.00 g., 0.916 Gold 1.1486 oz. AGW, 38.61 mm. **Ruler:** Elizabeth II **Rev:** Clown fish

| Date | Mintage | VF20 | XF40 | MS60 | MS63 | MS65 |
|---|---|---|---|---|---|---|
| 2009 | — | PF63 1,950 | PF65 2,100 | | | |

### KM# 280 10 DOLLARS

28.28 g., 0.925 Silver 0.841 oz. ASW, 38.61 mm. **Ruler:** Elizabeth II **Rev:** Flame dwarf angel fish in color

| Date | Mintage | VF20 | XF40 | MS60 | MS63 | MS65 |
|---|---|---|---|---|---|---|
| 2009 | — | PF65 45.00 | | | | |

### KM# 280a 10 DOLLARS

39.00 g., 0.916 Gold 1.1486 oz. AGW, 38.61 mm. **Ruler:** Elizabeth II **Rev:** Flame dwarf angel fish

| Date | Mintage | VF20 | XF40 | MS60 | MS63 | MS65 |
|---|---|---|---|---|---|---|
| 2009 | — | PF63 1,950 | PF65 2,100 | | | |

### KM# 281 10 DOLLARS

28.28 g., 0.925 Silver 0.841 oz. ASW, 38.61 mm. **Ruler:** Elizabeth II **Rev:** Pallet surgeon fish in color

| Date | Mintage | VF20 | XF40 | MS60 | MS63 | MS65 |
|---|---|---|---|---|---|---|
| 2009 | — | PF65 45.00 | | | | |

### KM# 281a 10 DOLLARS

39.00 g., 0.916 Gold 1.1486 oz. AGW, 38.61 mm. **Ruler:** Elizabeth II **Rev:** Pallet surgeon fish

| Date | Mintage | VF20 | XF40 | MS60 | MS63 | MS65 |
|---|---|---|---|---|---|---|
| 2009 | — | PF63 1,950 | PF65 2,100 | | | |

### KM# 282 10 DOLLARS

28.28 g., 0.925 Silver 0.841 oz. ASW, 38.61 mm. **Ruler:** Elizabeth II **Rev:** Yellow nose surgeon fish in color

| Date | Mintage | VF20 | XF40 | MS60 | MS63 | MS65 |
|---|---|---|---|---|---|---|
| 2009 Proof | — | — | — | — | — | 45.00 |

### KM# 282a 10 DOLLARS

39.00 g., 0.916 Gold 1.1486 oz. AGW, 38.61 mm. **Ruler:** Elizabeth II **Rev:** Yellow nose surgeon fish

| Date | Mintage | VF20 | XF40 | MS60 | MS63 | MS65 |
|---|---|---|---|---|---|---|
| 2009 | — | PF63 1,950 | PF65 2,100 | | | |

### KM# 283 10 DOLLARS

28.28 g., 0.925 Silver 0.841 oz. ASW, 38.61 mm. **Ruler:** Elizabeth II **Rev:** Cheetah

| Date | Mintage | VF20 | XF40 | MS60 | MS63 | MS65 |
|---|---|---|---|---|---|---|
| 2009 | — | PF65 45.00 | | | | |

### KM# 283a 10 DOLLARS

39.00 g., 0.916 Gold 1.1486 oz. AGW, 38.61 mm. **Ruler:** Elizabeth II **Rev:** Cheetah

| Date | Mintage | VF20 | XF40 | MS60 | MS63 | MS65 |
|---|---|---|---|---|---|---|
| 2009 | — | PF63 1,950 | PF65 2,100 | | | |

### KM# 284 10 DOLLARS

28.28 g., 0.925 Silver 0.841 oz. ASW, 38.61 mm. **Ruler:** Elizabeth II **Rev:** Elephant

| Date | Mintage | VF20 | XF40 | MS60 | MS63 | MS65 |
|---|---|---|---|---|---|---|
| 2009 | — | PF65 45.00 | | | | |

### KM# 284a 10 DOLLARS

39.00 g., 0.916 Gold 1.1486 oz. AGW, 38.61 mm. **Ruler:** Elizabeth II **Rev:** Elephant

| Date | Mintage | VF20 | XF40 | MS60 | MS63 | MS65 |
|---|---|---|---|---|---|---|
| 2009 | — | PF63 1,950 | PF65 2,100 | | | |

### KM# 285 10 DOLLARS

28.28 g., 0.925 Silver 0.841 oz. ASW, 38.61 mm. **Ruler:** Elizabeth II **Rev:** Giraffe

| Date | Mintage | VF20 | XF40 | MS60 | MS63 | MS65 |
|---|---|---|---|---|---|---|
| 2009 | — | PF65 45.00 | | | | |

### KM# 285a 10 DOLLARS

39.00 g., 0.916 Gold 1.1486 oz. AGW, 38.61 mm. **Ruler:** Elizabeth II **Rev:** Giraffe

| Date | Mintage | VF20 | XF40 | MS60 | MS63 | MS65 |
|---|---|---|---|---|---|---|
| 2009 | — | PF63 1,950 | PF65 2,100 | | | |

### KM# 286 10 DOLLARS

28.28 g., 0.925 Silver 0.841 oz. ASW, 38.61 mm. **Ruler:** Elizabeth II **Rev:** Koi

| Date | Mintage | VF20 | XF40 | MS60 | MS63 | MS65 |
|---|---|---|---|---|---|---|
| 2009 | — | PF65 45.00 | | | | |

### KM# 286a 10 DOLLARS

39.00 g., 0.916 Gold 1.1486 oz. AGW, 38.61 mm. **Ruler:** Elizabeth II **Rev:** Koi

| Date | Mintage | VF20 | XF40 | MS60 | MS63 | MS65 |
|---|---|---|---|---|---|---|
| 2009 | — | PF63 1,950 | PF65 2,100 | | | |

### KM# 287 10 DOLLARS

28.28 g., 0.925 Silver 0.841 oz. ASW, 38.61 mm. **Ruler:** Elizabeth II **Rev:** Leopard

| Date | Mintage | VF20 | XF40 | MS60 | MS63 | MS65 |
|---|---|---|---|---|---|---|
| 2009 | — | PF65 45.00 | | | | |

### KM# 287a 10 DOLLARS

39.00 g., 0.916 Gold 1.1486 oz. AGW, 38.61 mm. **Ruler:** Elizabeth II **Rev:** Leopard

| Date | Mintage | VF20 | XF40 | MS60 | MS63 | MS65 |
|---|---|---|---|---|---|---|
| 2009 | — | PF63 1,950 | PF65 2,100 | | | |

**KM# 288 10 DOLLARS**
28.28 g., 0.925 Silver 0.841 oz. ASW, 38.61 mm. **Ruler:** Elizabeth II **Rev:** Panda

| Date | Mintage | VF20 | XF40 | MS60 | MS63 | MS65 |
|---|---|---|---|---|---|---|
| 2009 | — | PF65 45.00 | | | | |

**KM# 288a 10 DOLLARS**
39.00 g., 0.916 Gold 1.1486 oz. AGW, 38.61 mm. **Ruler:** Elizabeth II **Rev:** Panda

| Date | Mintage | VF20 | XF40 | MS60 | MS63 | MS65 |
|---|---|---|---|---|---|---|
| 2009 | — | PF63 1,950 | PF65 2,100 | | | |

**KM# 289 10 DOLLARS**
28.28 g., 0.925 Silver 0.841 oz. ASW, 38.61 mm. **Ruler:** Elizabeth II **Rev:** Tiger

| Date | Mintage | VF20 | XF40 | MS60 | MS63 | MS65 |
|---|---|---|---|---|---|---|
| 2009 | — | PF65 45.00 | | | | |

**KM# 289a 10 DOLLARS**
39.00 g., 0.916 Gold 1.1486 oz. AGW, 38.61 mm. **Ruler:** Elizabeth II **Rev:** Tiger

| Date | Mintage | VF20 | XF40 | MS60 | MS63 | MS65 |
|---|---|---|---|---|---|---|
| 2009 | — | PF63 1,950 | PF65 2,100 | | | |

**KM# 290 10 DOLLARS**
28.28 g., 0.925 Silver 0.841 oz. ASW, 38.61 mm. **Ruler:** Elizabeth II **Rev:** Zebra

| Date | Mintage | VF20 | XF40 | MS60 | MS63 | MS65 |
|---|---|---|---|---|---|---|
| 2009 | — | PF65 45.00 | | | | |

**KM# 290a 10 DOLLARS**
39.00 g., 0.916 Gold 1.1486 oz. AGW, 38.61 mm. **Ruler:** Elizabeth II **Rev:** Zebra

| Date | Mintage | VF20 | XF40 | MS60 | MS63 | MS65 |
|---|---|---|---|---|---|---|
| 2009 | — | PF63 1,950 | PF65 2,100 | | | |

**KM# 291 10 DOLLARS**
Silver **Ruler:** Elizabeth II **Subject:** Wold Cup Soccer, South Africa

| Date | Mintage | VF20 | XF40 | MS60 | MS63 | MS65 |
|---|---|---|---|---|---|---|
| 2009 | Est. 10000 | PF65 55.00 | | | | |

**KM# 292 10 DOLLARS**
1.00 g., 0.999 Gold 0.0321 oz. AGW, 13.92 mm. **Ruler:** Elizabeth II **Subject:** World Cup Soccer, South Africa

| Date | Mintage | VF20 | XF40 | MS60 | MS63 | MS65 |
|---|---|---|---|---|---|---|
| 2009 | Est. 5000 | PF65 70.00 | | | | |

**KM# 294 10 DOLLARS**
28.28 g., 0.925 Silver 0.841 oz. ASW, 38.61 mm. **Ruler:** Elizabeth II **Rev:** Mary and Christ child

| Date | Mintage | VF20 | XF40 | MS60 | MS63 | MS65 |
|---|---|---|---|---|---|---|
| 2009 | — | PF65 45.00 | | | | |

**KM# 294a 10 DOLLARS**
39.00 g., 0.916 Gold 1.1486 oz. AGW, 38.61 mm. **Ruler:** Elizabeth II **Rev:** Mary and Christ child

| Date | Mintage | VF20 | XF40 | MS60 | MS63 | MS65 |
|---|---|---|---|---|---|---|
| 2009 | — | PF63 1,950 | PF65 2,100 | | | |

**KM# 216 10 DOLLARS**
0.50 g., 0.999 Gold 0.0161 oz. AGW, 11 mm. **Ruler:** Elizabeth II **Obv:** Head in tiara right **Rev:** Sun, statue and symbol

| Date | Mintage | VF20 | XF40 | MS60 | MS63 | MS65 |
|---|---|---|---|---|---|---|
| 2010 | 2,000 | PF65 40.00 | | | | |

**KM# 217 10 DOLLARS**
0.50 g., 0.999 Gold 0.0161 oz. AGW, 11 mm. **Ruler:** Elizabeth II **Obv:** Head with tiara right **Rev:** Mercury, statue and symbol

| Date | Mintage | VF20 | XF40 | MS60 | MS63 | MS65 |
|---|---|---|---|---|---|---|
| 2010 | 2,000 | PF65 40.00 | | | | |

**KM# 218 10 DOLLARS**
0.50 g., 0.999 Gold 0.0161 oz. AGW, 11 mm. **Ruler:** Elizabeth II **Obv:** Head with tiara right **Rev:** Venus, statue and symbol

| Date | Mintage | VF20 | XF40 | MS60 | MS63 | MS65 |
|---|---|---|---|---|---|---|
| 2010 | 2,000 | PF65 40.00 | | | | |

**KM# 219 10 DOLLARS**
0.50 g., 0.999 Gold 0.0161 oz. AGW, 11 mm. **Ruler:** Elizabeth II **Obv:** Head with tiara right **Rev:** Earth, statue and symbol

| Date | Mintage | VF20 | XF40 | MS60 | MS63 | MS65 |
|---|---|---|---|---|---|---|
| 2010 | 2,000 | PF65 40.00 | | | | |

**KM# 220 10 DOLLARS**
0.50 g., 0.999 Gold 0.0161 oz. AGW, 11 mm. **Ruler:** Elizabeth II **Obv:** Head with tiara right **Rev:** Mars, statue and symbol

| Date | Mintage | VF20 | XF40 | MS60 | MS63 | MS65 |
|---|---|---|---|---|---|---|
| 2010 | 2,000 | PF65 40.00 | | | | |

**KM# 221 10 DOLLARS**
0.50 g., 0.999 Gold 0.0161 oz. AGW, 11 mm. **Ruler:** Elizabeth II **Obv:** Head with tiara right **Rev:** Jupiter, statue and symbol

| Date | Mintage | VF20 | XF40 | MS60 | MS63 | MS65 |
|---|---|---|---|---|---|---|
| 2010 | 2,000 | PF65 40.00 | | | | |

**KM# 222 10 DOLLARS**
0.50 g., 0.999 Gold 0.0161 oz. AGW, 11 mm. **Ruler:** Elizabeth II **Obv:** Head with tiara right **Rev:** Saturn, statue and symbol

| Date | Mintage | VF20 | XF40 | MS60 | MS63 | MS65 |
|---|---|---|---|---|---|---|
| 2010 | 2,000 | PF65 40.00 | | | | |

**KM# 223 10 DOLLARS**
0.50 g., 0.999 Gold 0.0161 oz. AGW, 11 mm. **Ruler:** Elizabeth II **Obv:** Head with tiara right **Rev:** Uranus, statue and symbol

| Date | Mintage | VF20 | XF40 | MS60 | MS63 | MS65 |
|---|---|---|---|---|---|---|
| 2010 | 2,000 | PF65 40.00 | | | | |

**KM# 224 10 DOLLARS**
0.50 g., 0.999 Gold 0.0161 oz. AGW, 11 mm. **Ruler:** Elizabeth II **Obv:** Head with tiara right **Rev:** Neptune, statue and symbol

| Date | Mintage | VF20 | XF40 | MS60 | MS63 | MS65 |
|---|---|---|---|---|---|---|
| 2010 | 2,000 | PF65 40.00 | | | | |

**KM# 225 10 DOLLARS**
0.50 g., 0.999 Gold 0.0161 oz. AGW, 11 mm. **Ruler:** Elizabeth II **Obv:** Head with tiara right **Rev:** Pluto, statue and symbol

| Date | Mintage | VF20 | XF40 | MS60 | MS63 | MS65 |
|---|---|---|---|---|---|---|
| 2010 | 2,000 | PF65 40.00 | | | | |

**KM# 239 10 DOLLARS**
28.28 g., 0.925 Silver 0.841 oz. ASW, 38.61 mm. **Ruler:** Elizabeth II **Subject:** John Bull, steam locomotive **Obv:** Head with tiara right **Rev:** Steam locomotive left

| Date | Mintage | VF20 | XF40 | MS60 | MS63 | MS65 |
|---|---|---|---|---|---|---|
| 2010 | 5,000 | PF65 35.00 | | | | |

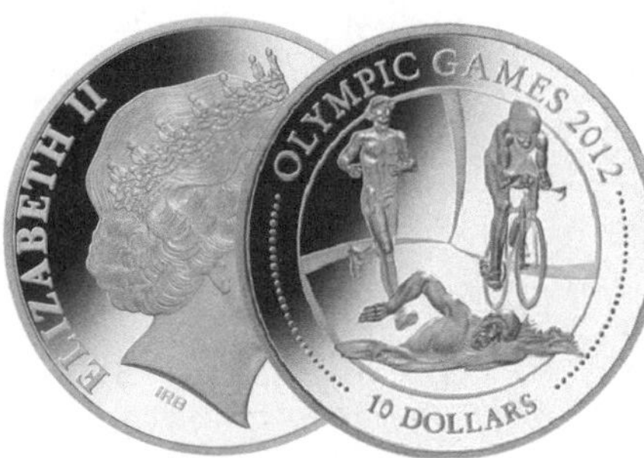


**KM# 241 10 DOLLARS**
28.28 g., 0.925 Silver 0.841 oz. ASW, 38.61 mm. **Ruler:** Elizabeth II **Subject:** London Olympics, 2012 **Obv:** Head with tiara right **Rev:** Triathlon sports

| Date | Mintage | VF20 | XF40 | MS60 | MS63 | MS65 |
|---|---|---|---|---|---|---|
| 2010 | 5,000 | PF65 35.00 | | | | |

**KM# 295 10 DOLLARS**
0.50 g., 0.999 Gold 0.0161 oz. AGW, 11 mm. **Ruler:** Elizabeth II **Rev:** Eye of Horus

| Date | Mintage | VF20 | XF40 | MS60 | MS63 | MS65 |
|---|---|---|---|---|---|---|
| 2010 | — | PF63 32.00 | PF65 35.00 | | | |

**KM# 296 10 DOLLARS**
0.50 g., 0.999 Gold 0.0161 oz. AGW, 11 mm. **Ruler:** Elizabeth II **Rev:** Gold mask of Tutanchamun

| Date | Mintage | VF20 | XF40 | MS60 | MS63 | MS65 |
|---|---|---|---|---|---|---|
| 2010 | — | PF63 32.00 | PF65 35.00 | | | |

**KM# 297 10 DOLLARS**
0.50 g., 0.999 Gold 0.0161 oz. AGW, 11 mm. **Ruler:** Elizabeth II **Rev:** Egyptian dog-headed god

| Date | Mintage | VF20 | XF40 | MS60 | MS63 | MS65 |
|---|---|---|---|---|---|---|
| 2010 | — | PF63 32.00 | PF65 35.00 | | | |

**KM# 409 10 DOLLARS**
0.50 g., 0.9999 Gold 0.0161 oz. AGW, 11 mm. **Ruler:** Elizabeth II **Obv:** Head with tiara right **Rev:** Nefertiti statue left

| Date | Mintage | VF20 | XF40 | MS60 | MS63 | MS65 |
|---|---|---|---|---|---|---|
| 2010 | 2,000 | PF65 50.00 | | | | |

**KM# 410 10 DOLLARS**
0.50 g., 0.9999 Gold 0.0161 oz. AGW, 11 mm. **Ruler:** Elizabeth II **Obv:** Head with tiara right **Rev:** Winged Isis statue

| Date | Mintage | VF20 | XF40 | MS60 | MS63 | MS65 |
|---|---|---|---|---|---|---|
| 2010 | 2,000 | PF65 50.00 | | | | |

**KM# 411 10 DOLLARS**
0.50 g., 0.9999 Gold 0.0161 oz. AGW, 11 mm. **Ruler:** Elizabeth II **Obv:** Head with tiara right **Rev:** Tutankhamen throne

| Date | Mintage | VF20 | XF40 | MS60 | MS63 | MS65 |
|---|---|---|---|---|---|---|
| 2010 | 2,000 | PF65 50.00 | | | | |

**KM# 413 10 DOLLARS**
0.50 g., 0.9999 Gold 0.0161 oz. AGW, 11 mm. **Ruler:** Elizabeth II **Obv:** Head with tiara right **Rev:** Female beer brewer

| Date | Mintage | VF20 | XF40 | MS60 | MS63 | MS65 |
|---|---|---|---|---|---|---|
| 2010 | 2,000 | PF65 50.00 | | | | |

**KM# 414 10 DOLLARS**
0.50 g., 0.9999 Gold 0.0161 oz. AGW, 11 mm. **Ruler:** Elizabeth II **Obv:** Head with tiara right **Rev:** Scarab of Tutankhamen

| Date | Mintage | VF20 | XF40 | MS60 | MS63 | MS65 |
|---|---|---|---|---|---|---|
| 2010 | 2,000 | PF65 50.00 | | | | |

**KM# 415 10 DOLLARS**
0.50 g., 0.9999 Gold 0.0161 oz. AGW, 11 mm. **Ruler:** Elizabeth II **Obv:** Head with tiara right **Rev:** Scribe seated

| Date | Mintage | VF20 | XF40 | MS60 | MS63 | MS65 |
|---|---|---|---|---|---|---|
| 2010 | 2,000 | PF65 50.00 | | | | |

**KM# 416 10 DOLLARS**
0.50 g., 0.9999 Gold 0.0161 oz. AGW, 11 mm. **Ruler:** Elizabeth II **Obv:** Head with tiara right **Rev:** Falcon breastplate

| Date | Mintage | VF20 | XF40 | MS60 | MS63 | MS65 |
|---|---|---|---|---|---|---|
| 2010 | 2,000 | PF65 50.00 | | | | |

**KM# 417 10 DOLLARS**
0.50 g., 0.9999 Gold 0.0161 oz. AGW, 11 mm. **Ruler:** Elizabeth II **Obv:** Head with tiara right **Rev:** Sennefer (male and female statues)

| Date | Mintage | VF20 | XF40 | MS60 | MS63 | MS65 |
|---|---|---|---|---|---|---|
| 2010 | 2,000 | PF65 50.00 | | | | |

**KM# 418 10 DOLLARS**
0.50 g., 0.9999 Gold 0.0161 oz. AGW, 11 mm. **Ruler:** Elizabeth II **Obv:** Head with tiara right **Rev:** Scarab

| Date | Mintage | VF20 | XF40 | MS60 | MS63 | MS65 |
|---|---|---|---|---|---|---|
| 2010 | 2,000 | PF65 50.00 | | | | |

**KM# 419 10 DOLLARS**
0.50 g., 0.9999 Gold 0.0161 oz. AGW, 11 mm. **Ruler:** Elizabeth II **Obv:** Head with tiara right **Rev:** Horus head left

| Date | Mintage | VF20 | XF40 | MS60 | MS63 | MS65 |
|---|---|---|---|---|---|---|
| 2010 | 2,000 | PF65 50.00 | | | | |

**KM# 420 10 DOLLARS**
0.50 g., 0.9999 Gold 0.0161 oz. AGW, 11 mm. **Ruler:** Elizabeth II **Obv:** Head with tiara right **Rev:** Gold mummy mask

| Date | Mintage | VF20 | XF40 | MS60 | MS63 | MS65 |
|---|---|---|---|---|---|---|
| 2010 | 2,000 | PF65 50.00 | | | | |

**KM# 421 10 DOLLARS**
0.50 g., 0.9999 Gold 0.0161 oz. AGW, 11 mm. **Ruler:** Elizabeth II **Obv:** Head with tiara right **Rev:** Mask of Psusennes

| Date | Mintage | VF20 | XF40 | MS60 | MS63 | MS65 |
|---|---|---|---|---|---|---|
| 2010 | 2,000 | PF65 50.00 | | | | |

**KM# 422 10 DOLLARS**
0.50 g., 0.9999 Gold 0.0161 oz. AGW, 11 mm. **Ruler:** Elizabeth II **Obv:** Head with tiara right **Rev:** God Amun-Re

| Date | Mintage | VF20 | XF40 | MS60 | MS63 | MS65 |
|---|---|---|---|---|---|---|
| 2010 | 2,000 | PF65 50.00 | | | | |

**KM# 423 10 DOLLARS**
0.50 g., 0.999 Gold 0.0161 oz. AGW, 11 mm. **Ruler:** Elizabeth II **Obv:** Head with tiara right **Rev:** Younger Memnon

| Date | Mintage | VF20 | XF40 | MS60 | MS63 | MS65 |
|---|---|---|---|---|---|---|
| 2010 | 2,000 | PF65 50.00 | | | | |

**KM# 424 10 DOLLARS**
0.50 g., 0.999 Gold 0.0161 oz. AGW, 11 mm. **Ruler:** Elizabeth II **Obv:** Head with tiara right **Rev:** Nubian Servant

| Date | Mintage | VF20 | XF40 | MS60 | MS63 | MS65 |
|---|---|---|---|---|---|---|
| 2010 | 2,000 | PF65 50.00 | | | | |

**KM# 425 10 DOLLARS**
0.50 g., 0.9999 Gold 0.0161 oz. AGW, 11 mm. **Ruler:** Elizabeth II **Obv:** Head with tiara right **Rev:** Duamutef

| Date | Mintage | VF20 | XF40 | MS60 | MS63 | MS65 |
|---|---|---|---|---|---|---|
| 2010 | 2,000 | PF65 50.00 | | | | |

**KM# 243 10 DOLLARS**
28.28 g., 0.925 Silver 0.841 oz. ASW, 38.61 mm. **Ruler:** Elizabeth II **Subject:** Etrich II Taube **Obv:** Head with tiara right **Rev:** Early experimental aircraft

| Date | Mintage | VF20 | XF40 | MS60 | MS63 | MS65 |
|---|---|---|---|---|---|---|
| 2011 | 5,000 | PF63 32.00 | PF65 35.00 | | | |

**KM# 245 10 DOLLARS**

28.28 g., 0.925 Silver 0.841 oz. ASW partially gilt, 38.6 mm. **Ruler:** Elizabeth II **Subject:** Lady Diana Spencer **Obv:** Head with tiara right **Rev:** Bust at right, gilt rose at left

| Date | Mintage | VF20 | XF40 | MS60 | MS63 | MS65 |
|---|---|---|---|---|---|---|
| 2011 | 7,500 | **PF65** 35.00 | | | | |

**KM# 247 10 DOLLARS**

28.28 g., 0.925 Silver 0.841 oz. ASW, 38.61 mm. **Ruler:** Elizabeth II **Subject:** London Olympics, 2012 **Obv:** Head with tiara right **Rev:** Rowing

| Date | Mintage | VF20 | XF40 | MS60 | MS63 | MS65 |
|---|---|---|---|---|---|---|
| 2011 | 5,000 | **PF63** 32.00 | **PF65** 35.00 | | | |

**KM# 249 10 DOLLARS**

28.28 g., 0.925 Silver 0.841 oz. ASW selectively gilt, 38.6 mm. **Ruler:** Elizabeth II **Subject:** Lady Diana **Obv:** Head with tiara right **Rev:** Diana with Prince William and Prince Harry

| Date | Mintage | VF20 | XF40 | MS60 | MS63 | MS65 |
|---|---|---|---|---|---|---|
| 2011 | 7,500 | **PF65** 35.00 | | | | |

**KM# 250 10 DOLLARS**

28.28 g., 0.925 Silver 0.841 oz. ASW partially gilt, 38.6 mm. **Ruler:** Elizabeth II **Subject:** Princess Diana **Obv:** Head with tiara right **Rev:** Diana and AIDS baby, gilt rose at left

| Date | Mintage | VF20 | XF40 | MS60 | MS63 | MS65 |
|---|---|---|---|---|---|---|
| 2011 | 7,500 | **PF65** 35.00 | | | | |

**KM# 251 10 DOLLARS**

28.28 g., 0.925 Silver 0.841 oz. ASW partially gilt, 38.6 mm. **Ruler:** Elizabeth II **Subject:** Lady Diana **Obv:** Head with tiara right **Rev:** Bust left, gilt rose to left

| Date | Mintage | VF20 | XF40 | MS60 | MS63 | MS65 |
|---|---|---|---|---|---|---|
| 2011 | 7,500 | **PF65** 35.00 | | | | |

**KM# 298 10 DOLLARS**

0.50 g., 0.585 Gold 0.0094 oz. AGW, 11 mm. **Ruler:** Elizabeth II **Rev:** Matterhorn

| Date | Mintage | VF20 | XF40 | MS60 | MS63 | MS65 |
|---|---|---|---|---|---|---|
| 2011 | Est. 5000 | **PF63** 32.00 | **PF65** 35.00 | | | |

**KM# 299 10 DOLLARS**

0.50 g., 0.585 Gold 0.0094 oz. AGW, 11 mm. **Ruler:** Elizabeth II **Rev:** Bay of Halong, Viet Nam

| Date | Mintage | VF20 | XF40 | MS60 | MS63 | MS65 |
|---|---|---|---|---|---|---|
| 2011 | Est. 5000 | **PF63** 32.00 | **PF65** 35.00 | | | |

**KM# 300 10 DOLLARS**

0.50 g., 0.585 Gold 0.0094 oz. AGW, 11 mm. **Ruler:** Elizabeth II **Rev:** Amazon in Brazil

| Date | Mintage | VF20 | XF40 | MS60 | MS63 | MS65 |
|---|---|---|---|---|---|---|
| 2011 | — | **PF63** 32.00 | **PF65** 35.00 | | | |

**KM# 301 10 DOLLARS**

0.50 g., 0.585 Gold 0.0094 oz. AGW, 11 mm. **Ruler:** Elizabeth II **Rev:** Monument Valley in the USA

| Date | Mintage | VF20 | XF40 | MS60 | MS63 | MS65 |
|---|---|---|---|---|---|---|
| 2011 | Est. 5000 | **PF63** 32.00 | **PF65** 35.00 | | | |

**KM# 302 10 DOLLARS**

0.50 g., 0.585 Gold 0.0094 oz. AGW, 11 mm. **Ruler:** Elizabeth II **Rev:** Pamukkale in Turkey

| Date | Mintage | VF20 | XF40 | MS60 | MS63 | MS65 |
|---|---|---|---|---|---|---|
| 2011 | — | **PF63** 32.00 | **PF65** 35.00 | | | |

**KM# 303 10 DOLLARS**

0.50 g., 0.585 Gold 0.0094 oz. AGW, 11 mm. **Ruler:** Elizabeth II **Rev:** Mesa in South Africa

| Date | Mintage | VF20 | XF40 | MS60 | MS63 | MS65 |
|---|---|---|---|---|---|---|
| 2011 | Est. 5000 | **PF63** 32.00 | **PF65** 35.00 | | | |

**KM# 304 10 DOLLARS**

0.50 g., 0.585 Gold 0.0094 oz. AGW, 11 mm. **Ruler:** Elizabeth II **Rev:** Sossusvlei, Namibia feature

| Date | Mintage | VF20 | XF40 | MS60 | MS63 | MS65 |
|---|---|---|---|---|---|---|
| 2011 | — | **PF63** 32.00 | **PF65** 35.00 | | | |

**KM# 305 10 DOLLARS**

0.50 g., 0.999 Gold 0.0161 oz. AGW, 11 mm. **Ruler:** Elizabeth II **Subject:** Euro motif **Rev:** Map of Estonia

| Date | Mintage | VF20 | XF40 | MS60 | MS63 | MS65 |
|---|---|---|---|---|---|---|
| 2011 | — | **PF63** 32.00 | **PF65** 35.00 | | | |

**KM# 426 10 DOLLARS**

0.50 g., 0.585 Gold 0.0094 oz. AGW, 11 mm. **Ruler:** Elizabeth II **Subject:** Niagara Falls **Rev:** Bust with tiara right

| Date | Mintage | VF20 | XF40 | MS60 | MS63 | MS65 |
|---|---|---|---|---|---|---|
| 2011 | 5,000 | **PF65** 40.00 | | | | |

**KM# 427 10 DOLLARS**

0.50 g., 0.585 Gold 0.0094 oz. AGW, 11 mm. **Ruler:** Elizabeth II **Obv:** Bust with tiara right **Rev:** Grand Canyon

| Date | Mintage | VF20 | XF40 | MS60 | MS63 | MS65 |
|---|---|---|---|---|---|---|
| 2011 | 5,000 | **PF65** 40.00 | | | | |

**KM# 428 10 DOLLARS**

0.50 g., 0.585 Gold 0.0094 oz. AGW, 11 mm. **Ruler:** Elizabeth II **Obv:** Bust with tiara right **Rev:** Strokker Geyser, Iceland

| Date | Mintage | VF20 | XF40 | MS60 | MS63 | MS65 |
|---|---|---|---|---|---|---|
| 2011 | 5,000 | **PF65** 40.00 | | | | |

**KM# 429 10 DOLLARS**

0.50 g., 0.585 Gold 0.0094 oz. AGW, 11 mm. **Ruler:** Elizabeth II **Obv:** Bust with tiara right **Rev:** Mount Everest

| Date | Mintage | VF20 | XF40 | MS60 | MS63 | MS65 |
|---|---|---|---|---|---|---|
| 2011 | 5,000 | **PF65** 40.00 | | | | |

**KM# 430 10 DOLLARS**

0.50 g., 0.585 Gold 0.0094 oz. AGW, 11 mm. **Ruler:** Elizabeth II **Obv:** Bust with tiara right **Rev:** Mt. Etna

| Date | Mintage | VF20 | XF40 | MS60 | MS63 | MS65 |
|---|---|---|---|---|---|---|
| 2011 | 5,000 | **PF65** 40.00 | | | | |

**KM# 431 10 DOLLARS**

0.50 g., 0.585 Gold 0.0094 oz. AGW, 11 mm. **Ruler:** Elizabeth II **Obv:** Bust with tiara right **Rev:** Ayers Rock

| Date | Mintage | VF20 | XF40 | MS60 | MS63 | MS65 |
|---|---|---|---|---|---|---|
| 2011 | 5,000 | **PF65** 40.00 | | | | |

**KM# 432 10 DOLLARS**

0.50 g., 0.585 Gold 0.0094 oz. AGW, 11 mm. **Ruler:** Elizabeth II **Obv:** Bust with tiara right **Rev:** Aurora Borealis

| Date | Mintage | VF20 | XF40 | MS60 | MS63 | MS65 |
|---|---|---|---|---|---|---|
| 2011 | 5,000 | **PF65** 40.00 | | | | |

**KM# 198 10 DOLLARS**

Silver, 38.61 mm. **Ruler:** Elizabeth II **Obv:** Jewels at center **Rev:** Sunset

| Date | Mintage | VF20 | XF40 | MS60 | MS63 | MS65 |
|---|---|---|---|---|---|---|
| 2012 | — | **PF65** 60.00 | | | | |

**KM# 199 10 DOLLARS**

Silver, 38.6 mm. **Ruler:** Elizabeth II **Obv:** Foral with blue jewel insert as cut out **Rev:** Flowers around blue jewel insert

| Date | Mintage | VF20 | XF40 | MS60 | MS63 | MS65 |
|---|---|---|---|---|---|---|
| 2012 | — | **PF65** 60.00 | | | | |

**KM# 226 10 DOLLARS**
20.00 g., 0.925 Silver 0.5948 oz. ASW, 54x32 mm. **Ruler:** Elizabeth II **Subject:** Aztec Calender **Obv:** Head with tiara right, insert at left **Rev:** Aztec design, insert at left **Shape:** Horizontal oval

| Date | Mintage | VF20 | XF40 | MS60 | MS63 | MS65 |
|---|---|---|---|---|---|---|
| 2012 | 1,000 | — | — | — | — | 125 |

**KM# 227 10 DOLLARS**
20.00 g., 0.925 Silver 0.5948 oz. ASW, 32x54 mm. **Ruler:** Elizabeth II **Obv:** Head in tiara right, insert **Rev:** Atlas holding up world on shoulders, insert **Shape:** Vertical oval

| Date | Mintage | VF20 | XF40 | MS60 | MS63 | MS65 |
|---|---|---|---|---|---|---|
| 2012 | 1,000 | — | — | — | — | 75.00 |

**KM# 230 10 DOLLARS**
31.11 g., 0.999 Silver 0.999 oz. ASW, 40 mm. **Ruler:** Elizabeth II **Subject:** Year of the Dragon **Obv:** Head with tiara right **Rev:** Gilt dragon and pearl

| Date | Mintage | VF20 | XF40 | MS60 | MS63 | MS65 |
|---|---|---|---|---|---|---|
| 2012 | 8,888 | PF65 100 | | | | |

**KM# 253 10 DOLLARS**
20.00 g., 0.999 Silver 0.6424 oz. ASW **Ruler:** Elizabeth II **Subject:** End of World War I **Rev:** Fireworks in color over Kremlin skyline

| Date | Mintage | VF20 | XF40 | MS60 | MS63 | MS65 |
|---|---|---|---|---|---|---|
| 2012 | — | PF65 100 | | | | |

**KM# 308 10 DOLLARS**
28.28 g., 0.925 Silver 0.841 oz. ASW, 38.61 mm. **Ruler:** Elizabeth II **Subject:** 2014 Sochi Olympic Games - Men's Giant Slalom

| Date | Mintage | VF20 | XF40 | MS60 | MS63 | MS65 |
|---|---|---|---|---|---|---|
| 2012 | Est. 5000 | PF65 32.00 | | | | |

**KM# 309 10 DOLLARS**
20.00 g., 0.925 Silver 0.5948 oz. ASW, 38.61 mm. **Ruler:** Elizabeth II **Subject:** 2014 FIFA World Cup Brazil - Colorized Soccer Players

| Date | Mintage | VF20 | XF40 | MS60 | MS63 | MS65 |
|---|---|---|---|---|---|---|
| 2012 | Est. 10000 | PF65 28.00 | | | | |

**KM# 310 10 DOLLARS**
2.84 g., 0.999 Gold 0.0911 oz. AGW, 16.5 mm. **Ruler:** Elizabeth II **Subject:** 2014 FIFA World Cup Brazil

| Date | Mintage | VF20 | XF40 | MS60 | MS63 | MS65 |
|---|---|---|---|---|---|---|
| 2012 | Est. 1000 | PF65 180 | | | | |

**KM# 317 10 DOLLARS**
20.00 g., 0.925 Silver 0.5948 oz. ASW, 38.61 mm. **Ruler:** Elizabeth II **Subject:** Ruler Series - Constantine the Great

| Date | Mintage | VF20 | XF40 | MS60 | MS63 | MS65 |
|---|---|---|---|---|---|---|
| 2012 | Est. 30000 | PF65 28.00 | | | | |

**KM# 321 10 DOLLARS**
20.00 g., 0.925 Silver 0.5948 oz. ASW, 38.61 mm. **Ruler:** Elizabeth II **Subject:** Intercity Railways in Europe

| Date | Mintage | VF20 | XF40 | MS60 | MS63 | MS65 |
|---|---|---|---|---|---|---|
| 2012 | Est. 5000 | PF65 40.00 | | | | |

**KM# 322 10 DOLLARS**
28.35 g., 0.999 Silver 0.9106 oz. ASW, 53x36 mm. **Ruler:** Elizabeth II **Subject:** Cities at Night - New York

| Date | Mintage | VF20 | XF40 | MS60 | MS63 | MS65 |
|---|---|---|---|---|---|---|
| 2012 | Est. 3500 | PF65 80.00 | | | | |

**KM# 323 10 DOLLARS**
28.35 g., 0.999 Silver 0.9106 oz. ASW, 53x36 mm. **Ruler:** Elizabeth II **Subject:** Cities at Night - London

| Date | Mintage | VF20 | XF40 | MS60 | MS63 | MS65 |
|---|---|---|---|---|---|---|
| 2012 | Est. 3500 | PF65 80.00 | | | | |

**KM# 324 10 DOLLARS**
28.35 g., 0.999 Silver 0.9106 oz. ASW, 53x36 mm. **Ruler:** Elizabeth II **Subject:** Cities at Night - Paris

| Date | Mintage | VF20 | XF40 | MS60 | MS63 | MS65 |
|---|---|---|---|---|---|---|
| 2012 | Est. 3500 | PF65 80.00 | | | | |

**KM# 325 10 DOLLARS**
20.00 g., 0.999 Silver 0.6424 oz. ASW, 40 mm. **Ruler:** Elizabeth II **Subject:** Kainsaz Russia 1937 Meteorite **Obv:** Bust right above fragments **Rev:** Color application of Kainsaz Meteorite

| Date | Mintage | VF20 | XF40 | MS60 | MS63 | MS65 |
|---|---|---|---|---|---|---|
| 2012 | Est. 999 | PF65 65.00 | | | | |

**KM# 326 10 DOLLARS**
31.11 g., 0.999 Silver 0.999 oz. ASW, 38.61 mm. **Ruler:** Elizabeth II **Obv:** Michaelangelo's head gilt

| Date | Mintage | VF20 | XF40 | MS60 | MS63 | MS65 |
|---|---|---|---|---|---|---|
| 2012 | — | PF65 50.00 | | | | |

**KM# 327 10 DOLLARS**
31.11 g., 0.999 Silver 0.999 oz. ASW, 38.61 mm. **Ruler:** Elizabeth II **Subject:** Raphael - gilt bust

| Date | Mintage | VF20 | XF40 | MS60 | MS63 | MS65 |
|---|---|---|---|---|---|---|
| 2012 | — | PF65 50.00 | | | | |

**KM# 328 10 DOLLARS**
20.00 g., 0.999 Silver 0.6424 oz. ASW, 40 mm. **Ruler:** Elizabeth II **Subject:** Jillin Meteorite 1976 **Rev:** Color application of meteorite

| Date | Mintage | VF20 | XF40 | MS60 | MS63 | MS65 |
|---|---|---|---|---|---|---|
| 2012 | Est. 999 | PF65 65.00 | | | | |

**KM# 329 10 DOLLARS**
20.00 g., 0.999 Silver 0.6424 oz. ASW, 40 mm. **Ruler:** Elizabeth II **Subject:** Abee 1952 Meteorite **Rev:** Color application of meteorite

| Date | Mintage | VF20 | XF40 | MS60 | MS63 | MS65 |
|---|---|---|---|---|---|---|
| 2012 | Est. 999 | PF65 65.00 | | | | |

**KM# 381 10 DOLLARS**
20.00 g., 0.925 Silver 0.5948 oz. ASW, 32x54 mm. **Ruler:** Elizabeth II **Subject:** Galileo explaining the planets **Shape:** Vertical oval

| Date | Mintage | VF20 | XF40 | MS60 | MS63 | MS65 |
|---|---|---|---|---|---|---|
| 2012 Antique patina | 1,000 | — | — | — | — | 75.00 |

### KM# 382 10 DOLLARS

20.00 g., 0.925 Silver 0.5948 oz. ASW, 32x54 mm. **Ruler:** Elizabeth II **Subject:** Ptolemy's planetary model **Shape:** Vertical oval

| Date | Mintage | VF20 | XF40 | MS60 | MS63 | MS65 |
|---|---|---|---|---|---|---|
| 2012 Antique patina | 1,000 | — | — | — | — | 75.00 |

### KM# 383 10 DOLLARS

0.50 g., 0.999 Gold 0.0161 oz. AGW, 11 mm. **Ruler:** Elizabeth II **Obv:** Head with tiara right **Rev:** Belem tower - Portugal

| Date | Mintage | VF20 | XF40 | MS60 | MS63 | MS65 |
|---|---|---|---|---|---|---|
| 2012 | 1,000 | PF65 50.00 | | | | |

### KM# 384 10 DOLLARS

0.50 g., 0.999 Gold 0.0161 oz. AGW, 11 mm. **Ruler:** Elizabeth II **Obv:** Head with tiara right **Rev:** Coliseum - Rome, Italy

| Date | Mintage | VF20 | XF40 | MS60 | MS63 | MS65 |
|---|---|---|---|---|---|---|
| 2012 | 1,000 | PF65 50.00 | | | | |

### KM# 385 10 DOLLARS

0.50 g., 0.999 Gold 0.0161 oz. AGW, 11 mm. **Ruler:** Elizabeth II **Obv:** Head with tiara right **Rev:** Christ the Redeemer statue - Rio, Brazil

| Date | Mintage | VF20 | XF40 | MS60 | MS63 | MS65 |
|---|---|---|---|---|---|---|
| 2012 | 1,000 | PF65 50.00 | | | | |

### KM# 386 10 DOLLARS

0.50 g., 0.999 Gold 0.0161 oz. AGW, 11 mm. **Ruler:** Elizabeth II **Obv:** Head with tiara right **Rev:** Hagia Sophia, Istanbul, Turkey

| Date | Mintage | VF20 | XF40 | MS60 | MS63 | MS65 |
|---|---|---|---|---|---|---|
| 2012 | 1,000 | PF65 50.00 | | | | |

### KM# 387 10 DOLLARS

0.50 g., 0.999 Gold 0.0161 oz. AGW, 11 mm. **Ruler:** Elizabeth II **Obv:** Head with tiara right **Rev:** Kizhi, Russia

| Date | Mintage | VF20 | XF40 | MS60 | MS63 | MS65 |
|---|---|---|---|---|---|---|
| 2012 | 1,000 | PF65 50.00 | | | | |

### KM# 388 10 DOLLARS

0.50 g., 0.999 Gold 0.0161 oz. AGW, 11 mm. **Ruler:** Elizabeth II **Obv:** Head with tiara right **Rev:** Statue of Liberty, New York, USA

| Date | Mintage | VF20 | XF40 | MS60 | MS63 | MS65 |
|---|---|---|---|---|---|---|
| 2012 | 1,000 | PF65 50.00 | | | | |

### KM# 389 10 DOLLARS

0.50 g., 0.999 Gold 0.0161 oz. AGW, 11 mm. **Ruler:** Elizabeth II **Obv:** Head with tiara right **Rev:** Meteora, Greece

| Date | Mintage | VF20 | XF40 | MS60 | MS63 | MS65 |
|---|---|---|---|---|---|---|
| 2012 | 1,000 | PF65 50.00 | | | | |

### KM# 390 10 DOLLARS

0.50 g., 0.999 Gold 0.0161 oz. AGW, 11 mm. **Ruler:** Elizabeth II **Obv:** Head with tiara right **Rev:** Bode Museum, Museum Island, Berlin, Germany

| Date | Mintage | VF20 | XF40 | MS60 | MS63 | MS65 |
|---|---|---|---|---|---|---|
| 2012 | 1,000 | PF65 50.00 | | | | |

### KM# 391 10 DOLLARS

0.50 g., 0.999 Gold 0.0161 oz. AGW, 11 mm. **Ruler:** Elizabeth II **Obv:** Head with tiara right **Rev:** Stonehenge, United Kingdom

| Date | Mintage | VF20 | XF40 | MS60 | MS63 | MS65 |
|---|---|---|---|---|---|---|
| 2012 | 1,000 | PF65 50.00 | | | | |

### KM# 392 10 DOLLARS

0.50 g., 0.999 Gold 0.0161 oz. AGW, 11 mm. **Ruler:** Elizabeth II **Obv:** Head with tiara right **Rev:** City of Valletta, Malta

| Date | Mintage | VF20 | XF40 | MS60 | MS63 | MS65 |
|---|---|---|---|---|---|---|
| 2012 | 1,000 | PF65 50.00 | | | | |

### KM# 433 10 DOLLARS

0.50 g., 0.585 Gold 0.0094 oz. AGW, 11 mm. **Ruler:** Elizabeth II **Obv:** Bust with tiara right **Rev:** Chichen Itza

| Date | Mintage | VF20 | XF40 | MS60 | MS63 | MS65 |
|---|---|---|---|---|---|---|
| 2012 | 5,000 | PF65 40.00 | | | | |

### KM# 434 10 DOLLARS

0.50 g., 0.585 Gold 0.0094 oz. AGW, 11 mm. **Ruler:** Elizabeth II **Obv:** Bust with tiara right **Rev:** Christ the Redeemer statue, Rio

| Date | Mintage | VF20 | XF40 | MS60 | MS63 | MS65 |
|---|---|---|---|---|---|---|
| 2012 | 5,000 | PF65 40.00 | | | | |

### KM# 435 10 DOLLARS

0.50 g., 0.585 Gold 0.0094 oz. AGW, 11 mm. **Ruler:** Elizabeth II **Obv:** Bust with tiara right **Rev:** Coliseum

| Date | Mintage | VF20 | XF40 | MS60 | MS63 | MS65 |
|---|---|---|---|---|---|---|
| 2012 | 5,000 | PF65 40.00 | | | | |

### KM# 436 10 DOLLARS

0.50 g., 0.585 Gold 0.0094 oz. AGW, 11 mm. **Ruler:** Elizabeth II **Obv:** Bust with tiara right **Rev:** Giza Necropolis

| Date | Mintage | VF20 | XF40 | MS60 | MS63 | MS65 |
|---|---|---|---|---|---|---|
| 2012 | 5,000 | PF65 40.00 | | | | |

### KM# 437 10 DOLLARS

0.50 g., 0.585 Gold 0.0094 oz. AGW, 11 mm. **Ruler:** Elizabeth II **Obv:** Bust with tiara right **Rev:** Hagia Sophia

| Date | Mintage | VF20 | XF40 | MS60 | MS63 | MS65 |
|---|---|---|---|---|---|---|
| 2012 | 5,000 | PF65 40.00 | | | | |

### KM# 438 10 DOLLARS

0.50 g., 0.585 Gold 0.0094 oz. AGW, 11 mm. **Ruler:** Elizabeth II **Obv:** Bust with tiara right **Rev:** Machu Picchu

| Date | Mintage | VF20 | XF40 | MS60 | MS63 | MS65 |
|---|---|---|---|---|---|---|
| 2012 | 5,000 | PF65 40.00 | | | | |

### KM# 439 10 DOLLARS

0.50 g., 0.585 Gold 0.0094 oz. AGW, 11 mm. **Ruler:** Elizabeth II **Obv:** Bust with tiara right **Rev:** Taj Mahal

| Date | Mintage | VF20 | XF40 | MS60 | MS63 | MS65 |
|---|---|---|---|---|---|---|
| 2012 | 5,000 | PF65 40.00 | | | | |

### KM# 440 10 DOLLARS

0.50 g., 0.585 Gold 0.0094 oz. AGW, 11 mm. **Ruler:** Elizabeth II **Obv:** Bust with tiara right **Rev:** Kilimanjaro

| Date | Mintage | VF20 | XF40 | MS60 | MS63 | MS65 |
|---|---|---|---|---|---|---|
| 2012 | 5,000 | PF65 40.00 | | | | |

### KM# 441 10 DOLLARS

0.50 g., 0.585 Gold 0.0094 oz. AGW, 11 mm. **Ruler:** Elizabeth II **Obv:** Bust with tiara right **Rev:** Geiranger fjord

| Date | Mintage | VF20 | XF40 | MS60 | MS63 | MS65 |
|---|---|---|---|---|---|---|
| 2012 | 5,000 | PF65 40.00 | | | | |

### KM# 442 10 DOLLARS

0.50 g., 0.585 Gold 0.0094 oz. AGW, 11 mm. **Ruler:** Elizabeth II **Obv:** Bust with tiara right **Rev:** Colorado Provencal

| Date | Mintage | VF20 | XF40 | MS60 | MS63 | MS65 |
|---|---|---|---|---|---|---|
| 2012 | 5,000 | PF65 40.00 | | | | |

### KM# 443 10 DOLLARS

0.50 g., 0.585 Gold 0.0094 oz. AGW, 11 mm. **Ruler:** Elizabeth II **Obv:** Bust with tiara right **Rev:** Great Barrier Reef

| Date | Mintage | VF20 | XF40 | MS60 | MS63 | MS65 |
|---|---|---|---|---|---|---|
| 2012 | 5,000 | PF65 40.00 | | | | |

### KM# 444 10 DOLLARS

0.50 g., 0.585 Gold 0.0094 oz. AGW, 11 mm. **Ruler:** Elizabeth II **Obv:** Bust with tiara right **Rev:** White Desert, Egypt

| Date | Mintage | VF20 | XF40 | MS60 | MS63 | MS65 |
|---|---|---|---|---|---|---|
| 2012 | 5,000 | PF65 40.00 | | | | |

### KM# 445 10 DOLLARS

0.50 g., 0.585 Gold 0.0094 oz. AGW, 11 mm. **Ruler:** Elizabeth II **Obv:** Bust with tiara right **Rev:** Tierra del Fuego

| Date | Mintage | VF20 | XF40 | MS60 | MS63 | MS65 |
|---|---|---|---|---|---|---|
| 2012 | 5,000 | PF65 40.00 | | | | |

### KM# 446 10 DOLLARS

0.50 g., 0.585 Gold 0.0094 oz. AGW, 11 mm. **Ruler:** Elizabeth II **Obv:** Bust with tiara right **Rev:** Lake Baikal, Russia

| Date | Mintage | VF20 | XF40 | MS60 | MS63 | MS65 |
|---|---|---|---|---|---|---|
| 2012 | 5,000 | PF65 40.00 | | | | |

### KM# 460 10 DOLLARS

Silver Plated Copper-Nickel, 40 mm. **Ruler:** Elizabeth II **Obv:** Bust with tiara right **Rev:** Tiger and tree; Gold encased

| Date | Mintage | VF20 | XF40 | MS60 | MS63 | MS65 |
|---|---|---|---|---|---|---|
| 2012 | 10,000 | PF65 60.00 | | | | |

### KM# 461 10 DOLLARS

Silver Plated Copper-Nickel, 40 mm. **Ruler:** Elizabeth II **Obv:** Head with tiara right **Rev:** Cactus and Eagle on branch; Rhodium encased

| Date | Mintage | VF20 | XF40 | MS60 | MS63 | MS65 |
|---|---|---|---|---|---|---|
| 2012 | 10,000 | PF65 60.00 | | | | |

### KM# 462 10 DOLLARS

Silver Plated Copper-Nickel, 40 mm. **Ruler:** Elizabeth II **Obv:** Bust with tiara right **Rev:** Kangaroo and Sydney Opera House; Palladium encased

| Date | Mintage | VF20 | XF40 | MS60 | MS63 | MS65 |
|---|---|---|---|---|---|---|
| 2012 | 10,000 | PF65 60.00 | | | | |

### KM# 463 10 DOLLARS

Silver Plated Copper-Nickel, 40 mm. **Ruler:** Elizabeth II **Obv:** Bust with tiara right **Rev:** Bear and mountains; Platinum encased

| Date | Mintage | VF20 | XF40 | MS60 | MS63 | MS65 |
|---|---|---|---|---|---|---|
| 2012 | 10,000 | PF65 60.00 | | | | |

### KM# 464 10 DOLLARS

Silver Plated Copper-Nickel, 40 mm. **Ruler:** Elizabeth II **Obv:** Bust with tiara right **Rev:** Great wall and koi fish; White Pearl encased

| Date | Mintage | VF20 | XF40 | MS60 | MS63 | MS65 |
|---|---|---|---|---|---|---|
| 2012 | 10,000 | PF65 60.00 | | | | |

### KM# 465 10 DOLLARS

Silver Plated Copper-Nickel, 40 mm. **Ruler:** Elizabeth II **Obv:** Bust with tiara right **Rev:** Neuschwanstein Meteorite, Germany 2002 fragment encased

| Date | Mintage | VF20 | XF40 | MS60 | MS63 | MS65 |
|---|---|---|---|---|---|---|
| 2012 | 20,000 | PF65 70.00 | | | | |

### KM# 488 10 DOLLARS

0.50 g., 0.585 Gold 0.0094 oz. AGW, 11 mm. **Ruler:** Elizabeth II **Obv:** Bust with tiara right **Rev:** Puma and building, Amethyst insert

| Date | Mintage | VF20 | XF40 | MS60 | MS63 | MS65 |
|---|---|---|---|---|---|---|
| 2012 | 5,000 | PF65 45.00 | | | | |

### KM# 489 10 DOLLARS

0.50 g., 0.585 Gold 0.0094 oz. AGW, 11 mm. **Obv:** Bust with tiara right **Rev:** Great wall and koi fish; White pearl insert

| Date | Mintage | VF20 | XF40 | MS60 | MS63 | MS65 |
|---|---|---|---|---|---|---|
| 2012 | 5,000 | PF65 45.00 | | | | |

### KM# 491 10 DOLLARS

0.50 g., 0.585 Gold 0.0094 oz. AGW, 11 mm. **Ruler:** Elizabeth II **Obv:** Bust with tiara ight **Rev:** Wolf and mountains; White Topaz insert

| Date | Mintage | VF20 | XF40 | MS60 | MS63 | MS65 |
|---|---|---|---|---|---|---|
| 2012 | 5,000 | PF65 45.00 | | | | |

### KM# 492 10 DOLLARS

20.00 g., 0.999 Silver 0.6424 oz. ASW, 40 mm. **Ruler:** Elizabeth II **Obv:** Bust with tiara right **Rev:** Neuschwanstein Meteorite fragments and color

| Date | Mintage | VF20 | XF40 | MS60 | MS63 | MS65 |
|---|---|---|---|---|---|---|
| 2012 | 999 | PF65 100 | | | | |

### KM# 493 10 DOLLARS

20.00 g., 0.999 Silver 0.6424 oz. ASW, 40 mm. **Ruler:** Elizabeth II **Obv:** Bust with tiara right **Rev:** Abee meteorite and color

| Date | Mintage | VF20 | XF40 | MS60 | MS63 | MS65 |
|---|---|---|---|---|---|---|
| 2012 | 999 | PF65 100 | | | | |

### KM# 494 10 DOLLARS

20.00 g., 0.999 Silver 0.6424 oz. ASW, 40 mm. **Ruler:** Elizabeth II **Obv:** Bust with tiara right **Rev:** Brenham meteorite fragments and color

| Date | Mintage | VF20 | XF40 | MS60 | MS63 | MS65 |
|---|---|---|---|---|---|---|
| 2012 | 999 | PF65 100 | | | | |

### KM# 495 10 DOLLARS

20.00 g., 0.999 Silver 0.6424 oz. ASW, 40 mm. **Ruler:** Elizabeth II **Obv:** Bust with tiara right **Rev:** Jilin meteorite and color

| Date | Mintage | VF20 | XF40 | MS60 | MS63 | MS65 |
|---|---|---|---|---|---|---|
| 2012 | 999 | PF65 100 | | | | |

### KM# 496 10 DOLLARS

20.00 g., 0.999 Silver 0.6424 oz. ASW, 40 mm. **Ruler:** Elizabeth II **Obv:** Bust with tiara right **Rev:** Kainsaz meteorite and color

| Date | Mintage | VF20 | XF40 | MS60 | MS63 | MS65 |
|---|---|---|---|---|---|---|
| 2012 | 999 | PF65 100 | | | | |

### KM# 497 10 DOLLARS

20.00 g., 0.999 Silver 0.6424 oz. ASW, 40 mm. **Ruler:** Elizabeth II **Obv:** Bust with tiara right **Rev:** Chassigny meteorite and color

| Date | Mintage | VF20 | XF40 | MS60 | MS63 | MS65 |
|---|---|---|---|---|---|---|
| 2012 | 999 | PF65 100 | | | | |

### KM# 500 10 DOLLARS

20.00 g., 0.999 Silver 0.6424 oz. ASW, 40 mm. **Ruler:** Elizabeth II **Obv:** Bust with tiara right **Rev:** Bjurbole meteorite fragments with color

| Date | Mintage | VF20 | XF40 | MS60 | MS63 | MS65 |
|---|---|---|---|---|---|---|
| 2012 | 999 | PF65 100 | | | | |

### KM# 501 10 DOLLARS

20.00 g., 0.999 Silver 0.6424 oz. ASW, 40 mm. **Ruler:** Elizabeth II **Obv:** Bust with tiara right **Rev:** Murchuison meteorite fragments with color

| Date | Mintage | VF20 | XF40 | MS60 | MS63 | MS65 |
|---|---|---|---|---|---|---|
| 2012 | 999 | PF65 100 | | | | |

### KM# 504 10 DOLLARS

20.00 g., 0.999 Silver 0.6424 oz. ASW, 40 mm. **Obv:** National arms **Rev:** Pisces zodiac sign in color, Amethyst encased **Shape:** Plain **Note:** Edge numbered

| Date | Mintage | VF20 | XF40 | MS60 | MS63 | MS65 |
|---|---|---|---|---|---|---|
| 2012 | 999 | PF65 100 | | | | |

### KM# 346 10 DOLLARS

20.00 g., 0.925 Silver 0.5948 oz. ASW, 38.61 mm. **Ruler:** Elizabeth II **Subject:** 2016 Olympics - Rugby

| Date | Mintage | VF20 | XF40 | MS60 | MS63 | MS65 |
|---|---|---|---|---|---|---|
| 2013 | Est. 5000 | PF63 65.00 | PF65 75.00 | | | |

### KM# 366 10 DOLLARS

93.30 g., 0.999 Silver 2.9967 oz. ASW, 55 mm. **Ruler:** Elizabeth II **Subject:** Malachite Room - Hermitage

| Date | Mintage | VF20 | XF40 | MS60 | MS63 | MS65 |
|---|---|---|---|---|---|---|
| 2013 Antique patina | 999 | — | — | — | 350 | — |

### KM# 368 10 DOLLARS

20.00 g., 0.999 Silver 0.6424 oz. ASW **Ruler:** Elizabeth II **Subject:** Diamonds of Nature - Clouded Leopard

| Date | Mintage | VF20 | XF40 | MS60 | MS63 | MS65 |
|---|---|---|---|---|---|---|
| 2013 | 1,000 | PF65 125 | | | | |

### KM# 470 10 DOLLARS

62.20 g., 0.999 Silver 1.9978 oz. ASW **Ruler:** Elizabeth II **Subject:** Tiffany Art - Gothic **Obv:** Venice's Doge's Palace

| Date | Mintage | VF20 | XF40 | MS60 | MS63 | MS65 |
|---|---|---|---|---|---|---|
| 2013 Antique patina | 999 | — | — | — | 425 | — |

### KM# 471 10 DOLLARS

31.11 g., 0.999 Silver 0.999 oz. ASW, 52x38 mm. **Obv:** National arms **Rev:** Bald eagle with crystal eye inserts **Edge:** Plain **Shape:** Oval **Note:** Edge numbered

| Date | Mintage | VF20 | XF40 | MS60 | MS63 | MS65 |
|---|---|---|---|---|---|---|
| 2013 Antique patina | 999 | — | — | — | 125 | — |

### KM# 472 10 DOLLARS

31.11 g., 0.999 Silver 0.999 oz. ASW, 52x38 mm. **Obv:** National arms **Rev:** Panda, crystal eye inserts **Edge:** Plain **Shape:** Oval **Note:** Edge numbered

| Date | Mintage | VF20 | XF40 | MS60 | MS63 | MS65 |
|---|---|---|---|---|---|---|
| 2013 Antique patina | 999 | — | — | — | 125 | — |

### KM# 473 10 DOLLARS

31.11 g., 0.999 Silver 0.999 oz. ASW, 52x38 mm. **Obv:** National arms **Rev:** Maki with crystal eye inserts **Shape:** Oval **Note:** Edge numbered

| Date | Mintage | VF20 | XF40 | MS60 | MS63 | MS65 |
|---|---|---|---|---|---|---|
| 2013 Antique Patina | 999 | — | — | — | 125 | — |

### KM# 474 10 DOLLARS

31.11 g., 0.999 Silver 0.999 oz. ASW, 52x38 mm. **Obv:** National arms **Rev:** Koala pair with crystal eye inserts **Shape:** Oval **Note:** Edge numbered

| Date | Mintage | VF20 | XF40 | MS60 | MS63 | MS65 |
|---|---|---|---|---|---|---|
| 2013 Antique patina | 999 | — | — | — | 125 | — |

### KM# 475 10 DOLLARS

31.11 g., 0.999 Silver 0.999 oz. ASW, 52x38 mm. **Obv:** National arms **Rev:** Listaffe - cotton top tamarin with crystal eye inserts **Shape:** Oval **Note:** Edge numbered

| Date | Mintage | VF20 | XF40 | MS60 | MS63 | MS65 |
|---|---|---|---|---|---|---|
| 2013 Antique patina | 999 | — | — | — | 125 | — |

### KM# 477 10 DOLLARS

20.00 g., 0.999 Silver 0.6424 oz. ASW, 32x54 mm. **Obv:** National arms **Rev:** Locomotive Merddin Emrys in color, printed glass insert below **Shape:** Vertical oval

| Date | Mintage | VF20 | XF40 | MS60 | MS63 | MS65 |
|---|---|---|---|---|---|---|
| 2013 | 1,999 | PF65 100 | | | | |

### KM# 478 10 DOLLARS

20.00 g., 0.999 Silver 0.6424 oz. ASW, 32x54 mm. **Obv:** National arms **Rev:** Locomotive LDE Saxonia in color, printed glass insert below **Shape:** Vertical oval

| Date | Mintage | VF20 | XF40 | MS60 | MS63 | MS65 |
|---|---|---|---|---|---|---|
| 2013 | 1,999 | PF65 100 | | | | |

## KM# 479 10 DOLLARS

20.00 g., 0.999 Silver 0.6424 oz. ASW, 32x54 mm. **Obv:** National arms **Rev:** Union Pacific No.119 in color, printed glass insert below **Shape:** Vertical oval

| Date | Mintage | VF20 | XF40 | MS60 | MS63 | MS65 |
|---|---|---|---|---|---|---|
| 2013 | 1,999 | PF65 100 | | | | |

## KM# 480 10 DOLLARS

31.11 g., 0.999 Silver 0.999 oz. ASW, 38x52 mm. **Obv:** National arms **Rev:** Gladiatrix shooting arrow from chariot, color background **Shape:** Vertical oval

| Date | Mintage | VF20 | XF40 | MS60 | MS63 | MS65 |
|---|---|---|---|---|---|---|
| 2013 Antique patina | 999 | — | — | — | 100 | — |

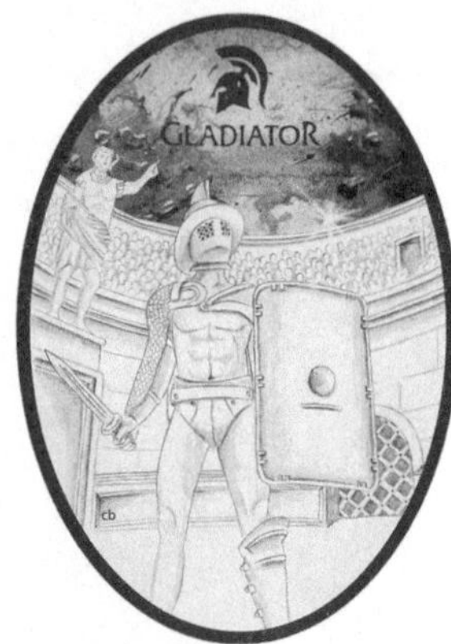


## KM# 481 10 DOLLARS

31.11 g., 0.999 Silver 0.999 oz. ASW, 38x52 mm. **Obv:** National arms **Rev:** Murmillo holding short sword and rectangle shield, color background **Shape:** Vertical oval

| Date | Mintage | VF20 | XF40 | MS60 | MS63 | MS65 |
|---|---|---|---|---|---|---|
| 2013 Antique patina | 999 | — | — | — | 100 | — |

## KM# 482 10 DOLLARS

31.11 g., 0.999 Silver 0.999 oz. ASW, 38x52 mm. **Obv:** National arms **Rev:** Provocator gladiator with helmet and gorgon shield, color background

| Date | Mintage | VF20 | XF40 | MS60 | MS63 | MS65 |
|---|---|---|---|---|---|---|
| 2013 Antique patina | 999 | — | — | — | 100 | — |

## KM# 483 10 DOLLARS

20.00 g., 0.999 Silver 0.6424 oz. ASW, 40 mm. **Obv:** National arms **Rev:** Mount St. Helens, gold obsidian insert

| Date | Mintage | VF20 | XF40 | MS60 | MS63 | MS65 |
|---|---|---|---|---|---|---|
| 2013 | 999 | PF65 100 | | | | |

## KM# 484 10 DOLLARS

31.11 g., 0.999 Silver 0.999 oz. ASW, 40 mm. **Obv:** National arms **Rev:** Kronotsky volcano; Rhylite encased

| Date | Mintage | VF20 | XF40 | MS60 | MS63 | MS65 |
|---|---|---|---|---|---|---|
| 2013 | 999 | PF65 100 | | | | |

## KM# 485 10 DOLLARS

20.00 g., 0.999 Silver 0.6424 oz. ASW, 40 mm. **Obv:** National arms **Rev:** Awatscha volcano; Silver obsidian insert

| Date | Mintage | VF20 | XF40 | MS60 | MS63 | MS65 |
|---|---|---|---|---|---|---|
| 2013 | 999 | PF65 100 | | | | |

## KM# 486 10 DOLLARS

20.00 g., 0.999 Silver 0.6424 oz. ASW, 40 mm. **Subject:** Mt. Vesuvs, Beige Obsidian insert **Rev:** National arms

| Date | Mintage | VF20 | XF40 | MS60 | MS63 | MS65 |
|---|---|---|---|---|---|---|
| 2013 | 999 | PF65 100 | | | | |

## KM# 487 10 DOLLARS

20.00 g., 0.999 Silver 0.6424 oz. ASW, 40 mm. **Obv:** National arms **Rev:** Stromboli volcano, Nodule Obsidian insert

| Date | Mintage | VF20 | XF40 | MS60 | MS63 | MS65 |
|---|---|---|---|---|---|---|
| 2013 | 999 | PF65 100 | | | | |

## KM# 490 10 DOLLARS

0.50 g., 0.585 Gold 0.0094 oz. AGW, 11 mm. **Obv:** Bust with tiara right **Rev:** Sea horse and pagoda; Pink pearl insert

| Date | Mintage | VF20 | XF40 | MS60 | MS63 | MS65 |
|---|---|---|---|---|---|---|
| 2013 | 5,000 | PF65 45.00 | | | | |

## KM# 503 10 DOLLARS

20.00 g., 0.999 Silver-Bronze 0.6424 oz., 40 mm. **Obv:** National arms **Rev:** Aquarius zodiac signs in color, Onyx encased **Edge:** Plain **Note:** Edge numbered

| Date | Mintage | VF20 | XF40 | MS60 | MS63 | MS65 |
|---|---|---|---|---|---|---|
| 2013 | 999 | PF65 100 | | | | |

## KM# 505 10 DOLLARS

20.00 g., 0.999 Silver 0.6424 oz. ASW, 40 mm. **Obv:** National arms **Rev:** Aries zodiac sign in color, red carnelian encased **Edge:** Plain **Note:** Edge numbered

| Date | Mintage | VF20 | XF40 | MS60 | MS63 | MS65 |
|---|---|---|---|---|---|---|
| 2013 | 999 | PF65 100 | | | | |

## KM# 506 10 DOLLARS

20.00 g., 0.999 Silver 0.6424 oz. ASW, 40 mm. **Obv:** National arms **Rev:** Taurus zodiac sign in color, aventurin encased **Edge:** Plain **Note:** Edge numbered

| Date | Mintage | VF20 | XF40 | MS60 | MS63 | MS65 |
|---|---|---|---|---|---|---|
| 2013 | 999 | PF65 100 | | | | |

## KM# 507 10 DOLLARS

20.00 g., 0.999 Silver 0.6424 oz. ASW, 40 mm. **Obv:** National arms **Rev:** Gemini zodiac in color, tigerauge encased **Edge:** Plain **Note:** Edge numbered

| Date | Mintage | VF20 | XF40 | MS60 | MS63 | MS65 |
|---|---|---|---|---|---|---|
| 2013 | 999 | PF65 100 | | | | |

## KM# 508 10 DOLLARS

20.00 g., 0.999 Silver 0.6424 oz. ASW, 40 mm. **Obv:** National arms **Rev:** Cancer zodiac sign in color, aventurin encased **Edge:** Plain **Note:** Edge numbered

| Date | Mintage | VF20 | XF40 | MS60 | MS63 | MS65 |
|---|---|---|---|---|---|---|
| 2013 | 999 | PF65 100 | | | | |

## KM# 509 10 DOLLARS

20.00 g., 0.999 Silver 0.6424 oz. ASW, 40 mm. **Obv:** National arms **Rev:** Leo zodiac sign in color, tigerauge encased **Edge:** Plain **Note:** Edge numbered

| Date | Mintage | VF20 | XF40 | MS60 | MS63 | MS65 |
|---|---|---|---|---|---|---|
| 2013 | 999 | PF65 100 | | | | |

## KM# 510 10 DOLLARS

20.00 g., 0.999 Silver 0.6424 oz. ASW, 40 mm. **Obv:** National arms **Rev:** Virgo zodiac signs in color, red carnelian encased **Edge:** Plain **Note:** Edge numbered

| Date | Mintage | VF20 | XF40 | MS60 | MS63 | MS65 |
|---|---|---|---|---|---|---|
| 2013 | 999 | PF65 100 | | | | |

## KM# 511 10 DOLLARS

20.00 g., 0.999 Silver 0.6424 oz. ASW, 40 mm. **Obv:** National arms **Rev:** Libra zodiac sign in color; red jasper encased **Edge:** Plain **Note:** Edge numbered

| Date | Mintage | VF20 | XF40 | MS60 | MS63 | MS65 |
|---|---|---|---|---|---|---|
| 2013 | 999 | PF65 100 | | | | |

## KM# 512 10 DOLLARS

20.00 g., 0.999 Silver 0.6424 oz. ASW, 40 mm. **Obv:** National arms **Rev:** Scorpio zodiac sign in color, green agate encased **Edge:** Plain **Note:** Edge numbered

| Date | Mintage | VF20 | XF40 | MS60 | MS63 | MS65 |
|---|---|---|---|---|---|---|
| 2013 | 999 | PF65 100 | | | | |

## KM# 513 10 DOLLARS

20.00 g., 0.999 Silver 0.6424 oz. ASW, 40 mm. **Obv:** National arms **Rev:** Sagittarius zodiac sign in color, Sodalith encased **Edge:** Plain **Note:** Edge numbered

| Date | Mintage | VF20 | XF40 | MS60 | MS63 | MS65 |
|---|---|---|---|---|---|---|
| 2013 | 999 | PF65 100 | | | | |

**KM# 514 10 DOLLARS**
20.00 g., 0.999 Silver 0.6424 oz. ASW, 40 mm. **Obv:** National arms **Rev:** Capricorn zodiac sign in color, onyx encased **Edge:** Plain **Note:** Edge numbered

| Date | Mintage | VF20 | XF40 | MS60 | MS63 | MS65 |
|---|---|---|---|---|---|---|
| 2013 | 999 | **PF65** 100 | | | | |

**KM# 344 10 DOLLARS**
31.11 g., 0.999 Silver 0.999 oz. ASW, 40 mm. **Ruler:** Elizabeth II **Subject:** Year of the Horse **Rev:** Horse head left in color

| Date | Mintage | VF20 | XF40 | MS60 | MS63 | MS65 |
|---|---|---|---|---|---|---|
| 2014 | 3,888 | **PF63** 75.00 | **PF65** 85.00 | | | |

**KM# 345 10 DOLLARS**
31.11 g., 0.999 Silver 0.999 oz. ASW partially gilt, 40 mm. **Ruler:** Elizabeth II **Subject:** Year of the Horse **Obv:** National arms in center **Rev:** Three gilt horses around center red stone

| Date | Mintage | VF20 | XF40 | MS60 | MS63 | MS65 |
|---|---|---|---|---|---|---|
| 2014 | 8,800 | **PF63** 90.00 | **PF65** 100 | | | |

**KM# 256 20 DOLLARS**
Platinum APW **Ruler:** Elizabeth II **Subject:** Elizabeth II, 50th Anniversary of Reign **Rev:** Draped sword

| Date | Mintage | VF20 | XF40 | MS60 | MS63 | MS65 |
|---|---|---|---|---|---|---|
| 2002 Proof | — | — | — | — | — | — |

**KM# 257 20 DOLLARS**
Platinum APW **Ruler:** Elizabeth II **Subject:** Elizabeth II, 50th Anniversary of Reign **Rev:** Boys Choir in Westminister Abbey

| Date | Mintage | VF20 | XF40 | MS60 | MS63 | MS65 |
|---|---|---|---|---|---|---|
| 2002 Proof | — | — | — | — | — | — |

**KM# 231 20 DOLLARS**
62.20 g., 0.999 Silver 1.9978 oz. ASW, 50.2 mm. **Ruler:** Elizabeth II **Subject:** Year of the Dragon **Obv:** Head with tiara right **Rev:** Fire Red Dragon with ruby insert

| Date | Mintage | VF20 | XF40 | MS60 | MS63 | MS65 |
|---|---|---|---|---|---|---|
| 2012 | 888 | **PF63** 225 | **PF65** 250 | | | |

**KM# 313 20 DOLLARS**
56.70 g., 0.999 Silver 1.8211 oz. ASW, 32x66 mm. **Ruler:** Elizabeth II **Subject:** Painter Series - Colorized Sixtine Madonna (Complete Painting)

| Date | Mintage | VF20 | XF40 | MS60 | MS63 | MS65 |
|---|---|---|---|---|---|---|
| 2012 | — | **PF65** 100 | | | | |

**KM# 314 20 DOLLARS**
56.70 g., 0.999 Silver 1.8211 oz. ASW, 66x32 mm. **Ruler:** Elizabeth II **Subject:** Painter Series - Colorized, Sixtine Madonna (Angels)

| Date | Mintage | VF20 | XF40 | MS60 | MS63 | MS65 |
|---|---|---|---|---|---|---|
| 2012 | Est. 500 | **PF65** 100 | | | | |

**KM# 315 20 DOLLARS**
56.70 g., 0.999 Silver 1.8211 oz. ASW, 66x32 mm. **Ruler:** Elizabeth II **Subject:** Painter Series - Colorized, The Creation of Adam

| Date | Mintage | VF20 | XF40 | MS60 | MS63 | MS65 |
|---|---|---|---|---|---|---|
| 2012 | Est. 500 | **PF65** 100 | | | | |

**KM# 316 20 DOLLARS**
56.70 g., 0.999 Silver 1.8211 oz. ASW, 66 x 32 mm. **Ruler:** Elizabeth II **Subject:** Painter Series - The Creation of Adam (Hands)

| Date | Mintage | VF20 | XF40 | MS60 | MS63 | MS65 |
|---|---|---|---|---|---|---|
| 2012 | Est. 500 | **PF65** 100 | | | | |

**KM# 394 20 DOLLARS**
20.00 g., Gold Plated Copper, 40 mm. **Ruler:** Elizabeth II **Obv:** Head with tiara right **Rev:** Thomas in color

| Date | Mintage | VF20 | XF40 | MS60 | MS63 | MS65 |
|---|---|---|---|---|---|---|
| 2012 Prooflike | 2,500 | — | — | — | — | 15.00 |

**KM# 348 20 DOLLARS**
62.20 g., 0.999 Silver 1.9978 oz. ASW with precious stones, 50 mm. **Ruler:** Elizabeth II **Subject:** Year of the Snake

| Date | Mintage | VF20 | XF40 | MS60 | MS63 | MS65 |
|---|---|---|---|---|---|---|
| 2013 | Est. 888 | **PF63** 200 | **PF65** 210 | | | |

**KM# 405 20 DOLLARS**
62.20 g., 0.999 Silver 1.9978 oz. ASW, 50 mm. **Ruler:** Elizabeth II **Obv:** National arms **Rev:** Two fish in color

| Date | Mintage | VF20 | XF40 | MS60 | MS63 | MS65 |
|---|---|---|---|---|---|---|
| 2013 | — | — | — | — | — | 85.00 |

**KM# 112 25 DOLLARS**
155.50 g., 0.999 Silver 4.9944 oz. ASW **Ruler:** Elizabeth II **Obv:** Crowned head right **Obv. Legend:** ELIZABETH II - FIJI **Rev:** Sailing ship "Vostok

| Date | Mintage | VF20 | XF40 | MS60 | MS63 | MS65 |
|---|---|---|---|---|---|---|
| 2002 | — | **PF63** 185 | **PF65** 220 | | | |

**KM# 350 25 DOLLARS**
93.30 g., 0.999 Silver 2.9967 oz. ASW with malachite stone inserts, 55 mm. **Ruler:** Elizabeth II **Subject:** 2014 FIFA World Cup - Brazil

| Date | Mintage | VF20 | XF40 | MS60 | MS63 | MS65 |
|---|---|---|---|---|---|---|
| 2013 | Est. 500 | **PF65** 400 | | | | |

**KM# 468 25 DOLLARS**
96.90 g., 0.999 Silver 3.1123 oz. ASW, 55 mm. **Obv:** National arms **Rev:** Soccer player and six malachite inserts

| Date | Mintage | VF20 | XF40 | MS60 | MS63 | MS65 |
|---|---|---|---|---|---|---|
| 2013 | 500 | **PF65** 175 | | | | |

**KM# 264 50 DOLLARS**
155.00 g., 0.999 Silver 4.9784 oz. ASW, 65 mm. **Ruler:** Elizabeth II **Rev:** Marine life - coral reef

| Date | Mintage | VF20 | XF40 | MS60 | MS63 | MS65 |
|---|---|---|---|---|---|---|
| 2005 | 500 | **PF65** 275 | | | | |

**KM# 244 50 DOLLARS**
7.78 g., 0.9999 Gold 0.2501 oz. AGW, 22 mm. **Ruler:** Elizabeth II **Subject:** Diana Princess of Wales **Obv:** Head with tiara right **Rev:** Bust right, while colored rose at right

| Date | Mintage | VF20 | XF40 | MS60 | MS63 | MS65 |
|---|---|---|---|---|---|---|
| 2011 | Est. 3000 | **PF63** 450 | **PF65** 475 | | | |

**KM# 248 50 DOLLARS**
7.77 g., 0.5833 Gold 0.1457 oz. AGW with a 24 kt. gold plating, 25 mm. **Ruler:** Elizabeth II **Subject:** London Olympics, 2012 **Obv:** Head with tiara right **Rev:** Rowing

| Date | Mintage | VF20 | XF40 | MS60 | MS63 | MS65 |
|---|---|---|---|---|---|---|
| 2011 | 1,000 | **PF65** 325 | | | | |

**KM# 196 50 DOLLARS**
155.50 g., 0.999 Silver 4.9944 oz. ASW, 65 mm. **Ruler:** Elizabeth II **Subject:** Year of the Dragon **Obv:** Head crowned right **Rev:** Dragon etched in mother of pearl

| Date | Mintage | VF20 | XF40 | MS60 | MS63 | MS65 |
|---|---|---|---|---|---|---|
| 2012 | 750 | **PF65** 400 | | | | |

**KM# 197 50 DOLLARS**
155.50 g., 0.999 Silver 4.9944 oz. ASW, 65 mm. **Ruler:** Elizabeth II **Obv:** Head crowned right **Rev:** Titanic etched mother of pearl

| Date | Mintage | VF20 | XF40 | MS60 | MS63 | MS65 |
|---|---|---|---|---|---|---|
| 2012 | 750 | PF65 450 | | | | |

**KM# 228 50 DOLLARS**
62.20 g., 0.999 Silver 1.9978 oz. ASW, 65 mm. **Ruler:** Elizabeth II **Obv:** Head in tiara right **Rev:** Tutankhamun in color

| Date | Mintage | VF20 | XF40 | MS60 | MS63 | MS65 |
|---|---|---|---|---|---|---|
| 2012 | 999 | PF63 175 | PF65 200 | | | |

**KM# 229 50 DOLLARS**
62.20 g., 0.999 Silver 1.9978 oz. ASW, 65 mm. **Ruler:** Elizabeth II **Obv:** Head in tiara right **Rev:** Neferititi head in color

| Date | Mintage | VF20 | XF40 | MS60 | MS63 | MS65 |
|---|---|---|---|---|---|---|
| 2012 | 999 | PF63 175 | PF65 200 | | | |

**KM# 306 50 DOLLARS**
155.50 g., 0.999 Silver 4.9944 oz. ASW, 65 mm. **Ruler:** Elizabeth II **Rev:** Dragon with the pearl of wisdom in gold

| Date | Mintage | VF20 | XF40 | MS60 | MS63 | MS65 |
|---|---|---|---|---|---|---|
| 2012 | 888 | PF63 225 | PF65 250 | | | |

**KM# 312 50 DOLLARS**
155.50 g., 0.999 Silver 4.9944 oz. ASW, 65 mm. **Ruler:** Elizabeth II **Subject:** Lunar Year of the Dragon with Mother of Pearl Inlay

| Date | Mintage | VF20 | XF40 | MS60 | MS63 | MS65 |
|---|---|---|---|---|---|---|
| 2012 | — | PF65 250 | | | | |

**KM# 360 50 DOLLARS**
62.21 g., 0.999 Silver 1.998 oz. ASW, 65 mm. **Ruler:** Elizabeth II **Obv:** Bust with tiara right **Rev:** Hatshepsut bust at left, gilt and in color

| Date | Mintage | VF20 | XF40 | MS60 | MS63 | MS65 |
|---|---|---|---|---|---|---|
| 2012 | 2,000 | PF65 200 | | | | |

**KM# 361 50 DOLLARS**
62.21 g., 0.999 Silver 1.998 oz. ASW, 65 mm. **Ruler:** Elizabeth II **Obv:** Bust with tiara right **Rev:** Tutankhamen mask gilt and in color

| Date | Mintage | VF20 | XF40 | MS60 | MS63 | MS65 |
|---|---|---|---|---|---|---|
| 2012 | 2,000 | PF65 200 | | | | |

**KM# 362 50 DOLLARS**
62.21 g., 0.999 Silver 1.998 oz. ASW, 65 mm. **Ruler:** Elizabeth II **Obv:** Bust with tiara right **Rev:** Cleopatra at left, obelisk and cartouche at right, gilt and in color

| Date | Mintage | VF20 | XF40 | MS60 | MS63 | MS65 |
|---|---|---|---|---|---|---|
| 2012 | 2,000 | PF65 200 | | | | |

**KM# 363 50 DOLLARS**
62.21 g., Silver, 65 mm. **Ruler:** Elizabeth II **Obv:** Bust with tiara right **Rev:** Nefertiti bust right gilt and in color **Edge:** Plain

| Date | Mintage | VF20 | XF40 | MS60 | MS63 | MS65 |
|---|---|---|---|---|---|---|
| 2012 | 2,000 | PF65 200 | | | | |

**KM# 364 50 DOLLARS**
62.21 g., 0.999 Silver 1.998 oz. ASW, 65 mm. **Ruler:** Elizabeth II **Obv:** Bust with tiara right **Rev:** Horus statue gilt and in color

| Date | Mintage | VF20 | XF40 | MS60 | MS63 | MS65 |
|---|---|---|---|---|---|---|
| 2012 | 2,000 | PF65 200 | | | | |

**KM# 476 50 DOLLARS**
155.55 g., 0.999 Silver 4.996 oz. ASW **Obv:** National arms **Rev:** Bald Eagle head with crystal eye inserts **Edge:** Plain **Shape:** Oval **Note:** Edge numbered

| Date | Mintage | VF20 | XF40 | MS60 | MS63 | MS65 |
|---|---|---|---|---|---|---|
| 2013 Antique patina | 499 | — | — | — | 450 | — |

**KM# 502 50 DOLLARS**
10.00 g., 0.999 Gold 0.3212 oz. AGW, 40 mm. **Obv:** National arms **Rev:** Neuschwanstein meteorite fragment and color

| Date | Mintage | VF20 | XF40 | MS60 | MS63 | MS65 |
|---|---|---|---|---|---|---|
| 2013 | 999 | PF65 700 | | | | |

**KM# 99 100 DOLLARS**
7.78 g., 0.585 Gold 0.1463 oz. AGW **Ruler:** Elizabeth II **Subject:** 2006 FIFA World Cup - Germany **Obv:** Crowned head right, date at right **Rev:** World Cup **Edge:** Reeded

| Date | Mintage | VF20 | XF40 | MS60 | MS63 | MS65 |
|---|---|---|---|---|---|---|
| 2003 | 25,000 | PF63 250 | PF65 275 | | | |

**KM# 347 200 DOLLARS**
31.11 g., 0.999 Gold 0.999 oz. AGW with malachite stone inserts, 38.61 mm. **Ruler:** Elizabeth II **Subject:** 2014 FIFA World Cup - Brazil

| Date | Mintage | VF20 | XF40 | MS60 | MS63 | MS65 |
|---|---|---|---|---|---|---|
| 2013 | Est. 150 | PF63 1,500 | PF65 1,500 | | | |

**KM# 469 200 DOLLARS**
31.11 g., 0.999 Gold 0.999 oz. AGW, 38.61 mm. **Obv:** National arms **Rev:** Football player and 6 malachite inserts

| Date | Mintage | VF20 | XF40 | MS60 | MS63 | MS65 |
|---|---|---|---|---|---|---|
| 2014 | 150 | PF65 2,000 | | | | |

**KM# 311 1000 DOLLARS**
141.75 g., 0.999 Gold 4.5528 oz. AGW, 65 mm. **Ruler:** Elizabeth II **Subject:** R.M.S. Titanic with Blue Mother of Pearl

| Date | Mintage | VF20 | XF40 | MS60 | MS63 | MS65 |
|---|---|---|---|---|---|---|
| 2012 | Est. 25 | PF65 9,600 | | | | |

## SILVER BULLION COINAGE

**KM# 211 DOLLAR**
15.50 g., 0.999 Silver 0.4978 oz. ASW, 32.5 mm. **Ruler:** Elizabeth II **Obv:** Head with crown right **Rev:** Hawksbill turtle

| Date | Mintage | VF20 | XF40 | MS60 | MS63 | MS65 |
|---|---|---|---|---|---|---|
| 2012 Prooflike | — | — | — | — | — | 22.50 |

**KM# 151 2 DOLLARS**
31.11 g., 0.999 Silver 0.999 oz. ASW, 40.5 mm. **Ruler:** Elizabeth II **Rev:** Hawksbill Taku Turtle

| Date | Mintage | VF20 | XF40 | MS60 | MS63 | MS65 |
|---|---|---|---|---|---|---|
| 2010 Prooflike | — | — | — | — | — | 50.00 |
| 2011 Prooflike | — | — | — | — | — | 50.00 |
| 2012 Prooflike | — | — | — | — | — | 50.00 |

**KM# 151a 2 DOLLARS**
31.11 g., 0.999 Silver 0.999 oz. ASW partially gilt, 40 mm. **Ruler:** Elizabeth II **Rev:** Hawksbill Taku Turtle, gilt

| Date | Mintage | VF20 | XF40 | MS60 | MS63 | MS65 |
|---|---|---|---|---|---|---|
| 2010 | Est. 5000 | PF65 65.00 | | | | |
| 2012 | — | PF65 65.00 | | | | |

**KM# 165 2 DOLLARS**
31.11 g., 0.999 Silver 0.999 oz. ASW partially gilt, 40.7 mm. **Ruler:** Elizabeth II **Rev:** Pacific Swordfish gilt

| Date | Mintage | VF20 | XF40 | MS60 | MS63 | MS65 |
|---|---|---|---|---|---|---|
| 2011 Prooflike | 5,000 | — | — | — | — | 80.00 |

**KM# 232 10 DOLLARS**
155.50 g., 0.999 Silver 4.9944 oz. ASW **Ruler:** Elizabeth II **Obv:** Head with tiara right **Rev:** Hawkbill turtle

| Date | Mintage | VF20 | XF40 | MS60 | MS63 | MS65 |
|---|---|---|---|---|---|---|
| 2012 Prooflike | — | — | — | — | — | 185 |

## GOLD BULLION COINAGE

### KM# 136 PACIFIC SOVEREIGN

31.11 g., 0.999 Gold 0.999 oz. AGW, 32 mm. **Ruler:** Elizabeth II **Rev:** Beach scene, two palm trees at right

| Date | Mintage | VF20 | XF40 | MS60 | MS63 | MS65 |
|---|---|---|---|---|---|---|
| 2009 Proof-like | — | — | — | — | 1,650 | 1,750 |

### KM# 215 PACIFIC SOVEREIGN

31.14 g., 0.999 Gold 1.000 oz. AGW, 32.1 mm. **Ruler:** Elizabeth II **Obv:** Head crowned right **Rev:** Beach scene, one palm tree at left

| Date | Mintage | VF20 | XF40 | MS60 | MS63 | MS65 |
|---|---|---|---|---|---|---|
| 2011 | — | PF63 1,700 | PF65 1,800 | | | |

### KM# 520

20.00 g., 0.999 Silver 0.6424 oz. ASW, 54x32 mm. **Subject:** Year of the Snake **Obv:** National arms **Rev:** Coiled snake at left, greenish hologram of Roman coin at right **Shape:** Oval

| Date | Mintage | VF20 | XF40 | MS60 | MS63 | MS65 |
|---|---|---|---|---|---|---|
| 2013 Antique patina | — | — | — | — | 100 | — |

# FINLAND

The Republic of Finland, the third most northerly state of the European continent, has an area of 130,559 sq. mi. (338,127 sq. km.) and a population of 5.1 million. Capital: Helsinki. Lumbering, shipbuilding, metal and woodworking are the leading industries. Paper, timber, wood pulp, plywood and metal products are exported.

**MONETARY SYSTEM**

100 Pennia = 1 Markka until 2001
100 Euro Cent = 1 Euro 2001 -

**MINT MARKS**

H - Birmingham 1921
Heart (h) - Copenhagen 1922
No mm – Helsinki
M – 1987-2006
FI – FINLAND – 2007-
Rampant lion in a circle – 2010-

**MINT OFFICIALS' INITIALS**

| Letter | Date | Name |
|---|---|---|
| J-M | 2002 | Toivo Jaatinen & Raimo Makkonen |
| L-M | 2000-03 | Maija Lavonen & Raimo Makkonen |
| K-M | 2004 | Heli Kauhanen & Raimo Makkonen |
| K-M | 2005-06 | Tapio Kettunen & Raimo Makkonen |
| M-M | 2002-06 | Pertti Mäkinen & Raimo Makkonen |
| N-M | 2001 | Antti Neuvonen & Raimo Makkonen |
| P-M | 2003 | Matti Peltokangas & Raimo Makkonen |
| P-M | 2001, 2005-07 | Reijo Paavilainen & Raimo Makkonen |
| S-M | 2003 | Anneli Sigriläinen & Raimo Makkonen |
| VV-M | 2002 | Erkki Vainio & Hannu Veijalainen & Raimo Makkonen |

# REPUBLIC

## REFORM COINAGE

100 Old Markkaa = 1 New Markkaa 1963

### KM# 65 10 PENNI'A'

1.80 g., Copper-Nickel, 16.3 mm. **Obv:** Flower pods and stems, date at right **Rev:** Denomination to right of honeycombs

| Date | Mintage | VF20 | XF40 | MS60 | MS63 | MS65 |
|---|---|---|---|---|---|---|
| 2001 M | 25,000,000 | — | — | — | 1.00 | 1.50 |
| 2001 M | — | PF65 7.00 | | | | |

### KM# 66 50 PENNI'A'

3.30 g., Copper-Nickel, 19.7 mm. **Obv:** Polar bear, date below **Rev:** Denomination above flower heads **Edge:** Reeded

| Date | Mintage | VF20 | XF40 | MS60 | MS63 | MS65 |
|---|---|---|---|---|---|---|
| 2001 M | 200,000 | — | — | 0.20 | 1.00 | 1.50 |
| 2001 M | — | PF65 8.00 | | | | |

### KM# 76 MARKKA

5.00 g., Aluminum-Bronze, 22.2 mm. **Obv:** Rampant lion left within circle, date below **Rev:** Ornaments flank denomination within circle

| Date | Mintage | VF20 | XF40 | MS60 | MS63 | MS65 |
|---|---|---|---|---|---|---|
| 2001 M | 200,000 | — | 0.25 | 0.50 | 1.00 | 1.50 |
| 2001 M | — | PF65 10.00 | | | | |

### KM# 95 MARKKA

8.64 g., 0.750 Gold 0.2083 oz. AGW, 22 mm. **Subject:** Last Markka Coin **Obv:** Rampant lion with sword left **Rev:** Stylized tree with roots **Edge:** Reeded

| Date | Mintage | VF20 | XF40 | MS60 | MS63 | MS65 |
|---|---|---|---|---|---|---|
| 2001 M P-M | 55,000 | PF63 350 | PF65 375 | | | |

### KM# 106 MARKKA

6.10 g., Copper-Nickel, 24 mm. **Subject:** Remembrance Markka **Obv:** Rampant lion with sword left **Rev:** Denomination and pine tree **Edge:** Plain **Note:** This coin is encased in acrylic resin and sealed in a display card.

| Date | Mintage | VF20 | XF40 | MS60 | MS63 | MS65 |
|---|---|---|---|---|---|---|
| 2001 M N-M | 500,000 | — | — | — | 5.00 | 6.50 |

### KM# 73 5 MARKKAA

5.50 g., Copper-Aluminum-Nickel, 24.5 mm. **Obv:** Lake Saimaa ringed seal, date below **Rev:** Denomination, dragonfly and lily pad leaves

| Date | Mintage | VF20 | XF40 | MS60 | MS63 | MS65 |
|---|---|---|---|---|---|---|
| 2001 M | 200,000 | — | — | 2.00 | 3.00 | 3.50 |
| 2001 M | — | PF65 12.00 | | | | |

### KM# 77 10 MARKKAA

8.80 g., Bi-Metallic Brass center in Copper-Nickel ring, 27.25 mm. **Obv:** Capercaillie bird within circle, date above **Rev:** Denomination and branches

| Date | Mintage | VF20 | XF40 | MS60 | MS63 | MS65 |
|---|---|---|---|---|---|---|
| 2001 M | 200,000 | — | 2.00 | 3.00 | 4.00 | 5.00 |
| 2001 M | — | PF65 18.00 | | | | |

### KM# 96 25 MARKKAA

20.20 g., Bi-Metallic Brass center in Copper-Nickel ring, 35 mm. **Subject:** First Nordic Ski Championship, "Lahti 2001 **Obv:** Stylized woman's face **Rev:** Female torso, landscape **Edge:** Plain

| Date | Mintage | VF20 | XF40 | MS60 | MS63 | MS65 |
|---|---|---|---|---|---|---|
| 2001 M Prooflike | 100,000 | — | — | 25.00 | 30.00 | 35.00 |

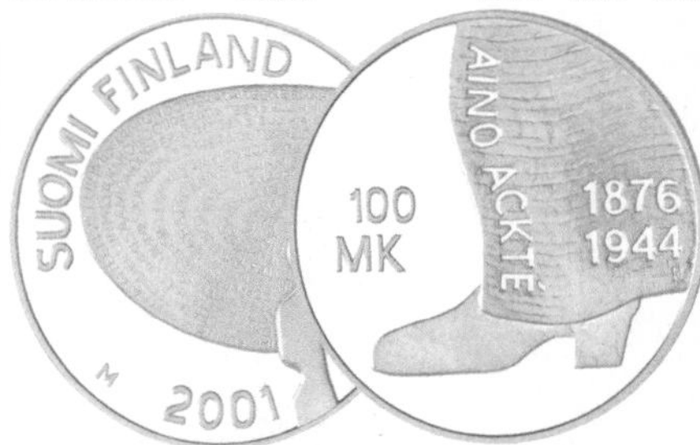

### KM# 97 100 MARKKAA

31.00 g., 0.925 Silver 0.9219 oz. ASW, 35 mm. **Subject:** Aino Ackte **Obv:** Partial portrait **Rev:** High heel boot and trouser bottom **Edge:** Plain

| Date | Mintage | VF20 | XF40 | MS60 | MS63 | MS65 |
|---|---|---|---|---|---|---|
| 2001 M | 33,000 | — | — | — | 32.00 | 45.00 |
| 2001 M | 12,000 | PF63 60.00 | PF65 70.00 | | | |

## EURO COINAGE

European Union Issues

### KM# 98 EURO CENT

2.30 g., Copper Plated Steel, 16.25 mm. **Obv:** Rampant lion left surrounded by stars, date at left **Rev:** Denomination and globe **Edge:** Plain

| Date | Mintage | VF20 | XF40 | MS60 | MS63 | MS65 |
|---|---|---|---|---|---|---|
| 2001 M | 500,000 | — | — | — | — | 10.00 |
| 2001 M Proof | 15,000 | — | — | — | — | — |
| 2002 M | 659,000 | — | — | — | — | 5.00 |
| 2002 M | 13,000 | PF65 15.00 | | | | |
| 2003 M | 6,790,000 | — | — | — | — | 1.00 |
| 2003 M | 14,500 | PF65 15.00 | | | | |
| 2004 M | 9,690,000 | — | — | — | — | 1.00 |
| 2004 M | 5,000 | PF65 15.00 | | | | |
| 2005 M | 5,800,000 | — | — | — | — | 1.00 |
| 2005 M | 3,000 | PF65 15.00 | | | | |
| 2006 M | 4,000,000 | — | — | — | — | 1.00 |
| 2006 M | 3,300 | PF65 15.00 | | | | |
| 2007 FI | 3,000,000 | — | — | — | — | 1.00 |
| 2007 FI | — | PF65 15.00 | | | | |
| 2008 FI | 1,500,000 | — | — | — | — | 1.00 |
| 2008 FI | 2,500 | PF65 15.00 | | | | |
| 2009 FI | 936,500 | — | — | — | — | 1.00 |
| 2009 FI | 2,500 | PF65 15.00 | | | | |
| 2010 FI | 738,000 | — | — | — | — | 1.00 |
| 2010 FI | 2,000 | PF65 15.00 | | | | |
| 2011 FI | 755,000 | — | — | — | — | 1.00 |
| 2011 FI | 755,000 | PF65 15.00 | | | | |
| 2012 FI | 724,000 | — | — | — | — | 1.00 |
| 2012 FI | 724,000 | PF65 15.00 | | | | |

| Date | Mintage | VF20 | XF40 | MS60 | MS63 | MS65 |
|---|---|---|---|---|---|---|
| 2013 FI | — | — | — | — | — | 1.00 |
| 2013 FI | — | PF65 15.00 | | | | |
| 2014 | 200,000 | — | — | — | — | 2.00 |
| 2014 | 1,200 | PF65 15.00 | | | | |

### KM# 99 2 EURO CENT

3.06 g., Copper Plated Steel, 18.75 mm. **Obv:** Rampant lion surrounded by stars, date at left **Rev:** Denomination and globe **Edge:** Grooved

| Date | Mintage | VF20 | XF40 | MS60 | MS63 | MS65 |
|---|---|---|---|---|---|---|
| 2001 M | 500,000 | — | — | — | — | 10.00 |
| 2001 M | 15,000 | PF65 15.00 | | | | |
| 2002 M | 659,000 | — | — | — | — | 5.00 |
| 2002 M | 13,000 | PF65 15.00 | | | | |
| 2003 M | 6,790,000 | — | — | — | — | 2.00 |
| 2003 M | 14,500 | PF65 15.00 | | | | |
| 2004 M | 8,024,000 | — | — | — | — | 2.00 |
| 2004 M | 5,000 | PF65 15.00 | | | | |
| 2005 M | 5,800,000 | — | — | — | — | 2.50 |
| 2005 M | 3,000 | PF65 15.00 | | | | |
| 2006 M | 4,000,000 | — | — | — | — | 2.00 |
| 2006 M | 3,300 | PF65 15.00 | | | | |
| 2007 FI | 3,000,000 | — | — | — | — | 2.00 |
| 2007 FI | — | PF65 15.00 | | | | |
| 2008 FI | 1,500,000 | — | — | — | — | 2.00 |
| 2008 FI | 2,500 | PF65 15.00 | | | | |
| 2009 FI | 936,500 | — | — | — | — | 2.00 |
| 2009 FI | 2,500 | PF65 15.00 | | | | |
| 2010 FI | 738,000 | — | — | — | — | 2.00 |
| 2010 FI | 2,000 | PF65 15.00 | | | | |
| 2011 FI | 755,000 | — | — | — | — | 3.00 |
| 2011 FI | — | PF65 15.00 | | | | |
| 2012 FI | — | — | — | — | — | 3.00 |
| 2012 FI | 724,000 | PF65 15.00 | | | | |
| 2013 FI | — | — | — | — | — | 3.00 |
| 2013 FI | — | PF65 15.00 | | | | |
| 2014 | 200,000 | — | — | — | — | 4.00 |
| 2014 | 1,200 | PF65 15.00 | | | | |

### KM# 100 5 EURO CENT

3.92 g., Copper Plated Steel, 21.25 mm. **Obv:** Rampant lion left surrounded by stars, date at left **Rev:** Denomination and globe **Edge:** Plain

| Date | Mintage | VF20 | XF40 | MS60 | MS63 | MS65 |
|---|---|---|---|---|---|---|
| 2001 M | 213,756,000 | — | — | — | — | 0.50 |
| 2001 M | 15,000 | PF65 15.00 | | | | |
| 2002 M | 101,824,000 | — | — | — | — | 0.50 |
| 2002 M | 13,000 | PF65 15.00 | | | | |
| 2003 M | 790,000 | — | — | — | — | 2.00 |
| 2003 M | 14,500 | PF65 15.00 | | | | |
| 2004 M | 629,000 | — | — | — | — | 2.00 |
| 2004 M | 5,000 | PF65 15.00 | | | | |
| 2005 M | 800,000 | — | — | — | — | 2.00 |
| 2005 M | 3,000 | PF65 15.00 | | | | |
| 2006 M | 1,000,000 | — | — | — | — | 1.00 |
| 2006 M | 3,000 | PF65 15.00 | | | | |
| 2007 FI | 1,000,000 | — | — | — | — | 1.00 |
| 2007 FI | — | PF65 15.00 | | | | |
| 2008 FI | 1,000,000 | — | — | — | — | 1.00 |
| 2008 FI | 2,500 | PF65 15.00 | | | | |
| 2009 FI | 936,500 | — | — | — | — | 1.00 |
| 2009 FI | 2,500 | PF65 15.00 | | | | |
| 2010 FI | 738,000 | — | — | — | — | 1.00 |
| 2010 FI | 2,000 | PF65 15.00 | | | | |
| 2011 FI | 755,000 | — | — | — | — | 1.00 |
| 2011 FI | — | PF65 15.00 | | | | |
| 2012 FI | — | — | — | — | — | 1.00 |
| 2012 FI | 724,000 | PF65 15.00 | | | | |
| 2013 FI | — | — | — | — | — | 1.00 |
| 2013 FI | — | PF65 15.00 | | | | |
| 2014 | — | — | — | — | — | 1.00 |
| 2014 | 1,200 | PF65 15.00 | | | | |

### KM# 101 10 EURO CENT

4.10 g., Brass, 19.75 mm. **Obv:** Rampant lion left surrounded by stars, date at left **Rev:** Denomination and map **Edge:** Reeded

| Date | Mintage | VF20 | XF40 | MS60 | MS63 | MS65 |
|---|---|---|---|---|---|---|
| 2001 M | 14,730,000 | — | — | — | — | 10.00 |
| 2001 M | 15,000 | PF65 18.00 | | | | |
| 2002 M | 1,499,000 | — | — | — | — | 10.00 |
| 2002 M | 13,000 | PF65 18.00 | | | | |
| 2003 M | 790,000 | — | — | — | — | 5.00 |
| 2003 M | 14,500 | PF65 18.00 | | | | |
| 2004 M | 629,000 | — | — | — | — | 5.00 |
| 2004 M | 5,000 | PF65 18.00 | | | | |
| 2005 M | 800,000 | — | — | — | — | 3.00 |
| 2005 M | 3,000 | PF65 18.00 | | | | |
| 2006 M | 1,000,000 | — | — | — | — | 3.00 |
| 2006 M | 3,300 | PF65 18.00 | | | | |

### KM# 126 10 EURO CENT

4.10 g., Brass, 19.75 mm. **Obv:** Rampant lion surrounded by stars **Rev:** Relief map of Western Europe, stars, lines and value **Edge:** Reeded **Note:** In different years, varieties exist in the position of the mint mark and mintmaster symbols.

| Date | Mintage | VF20 | XF40 | MS60 | MS63 | MS65 |
|---|---|---|---|---|---|---|
| 2007 FI | 1,000,000 | — | — | — | — | 2.50 |
| 2007 FI | — | PF65 18.00 | | | | |
| 2008 FI | 1,000,000 | — | — | — | — | 2.50 |
| 2008 FI | 2,500 | PF65 18.00 | | | | |
| 2009 FI | 936,500 | — | — | — | — | 2.50 |
| 2009 FI | 2,500 | PF65 18.00 | | | | |
| 2010 FI | 738,000 | — | — | — | — | 2.50 |
| 2010 FI | 2,000 | PF65 18.00 | | | | |
| 2011 FI | — | — | — | — | — | 2.50 |
| 2011 FI | 755,000 | PF65 18.00 | | | | |
| 2012 FI | 10,724,000 | — | — | — | — | 2.50 |
| 2012 FI | — | PF65 18.00 | | | | |
| 2013 FI | — | — | — | — | — | 2.50 |
| 2013 FI | — | PF65 18.00 | | | | |
| 2014 | 200,000 | — | — | — | — | 5.00 |
| 2014 | 1,200 | PF65 18.00 | | | | |

### KM# 102 20 EURO CENT

5.74 g., Brass, 22.25 mm. **Obv:** Rampant lion left surrounded by stars, date at left **Rev:** Denomination and map **Edge:** Notched

| Date | Mintage | VF20 | XF40 | MS60 | MS63 | MS65 |
|---|---|---|---|---|---|---|
| 2001 M | 121,763,000 | — | — | — | — | 2.00 |
| 2001 M | 15,000 | PF65 20.00 | | | | |
| 2002 M | 100,759,000 | — | — | — | — | 2.00 |
| 2002 M | 13,000 | PF65 20.00 | | | | |
| 2003 M | 790,000 | — | — | — | — | 3.00 |
| 2003 M | 14,500 | PF65 20.00 | | | | |
| 2004 M | 629,000 | — | — | — | — | 3.00 |
| 2004 M | 5,000 | PF65 20.00 | | | | |
| 2005 M | 800,000 | — | — | — | — | 3.00 |
| 2005 M | 3,000 | PF65 20.00 | | | | |
| 2006 M | 1,000,000 | — | — | — | — | 2.00 |
| 2006 M | 3,300 | PF65 20.00 | | | | |

### KM# 127 20 EURO CENT

5.74 g., Brass, 22.25 mm. **Obv:** Rampant lion surrounded by stars **Rev:** Relief map of Western Europe, stars, lines and value **Edge:** Notched

| Date | Mintage | VF20 | XF40 | MS60 | MS63 | MS65 |
|---|---|---|---|---|---|---|
| 2007 FI | 1,000,000 | — | — | — | — | 2.00 |
| 2007 FI | — | PF65 20.00 | | | | |
| 2008 FI | 1,000,000 | — | — | — | — | 2.00 |
| 2008 FI | 2,500 | PF65 20.00 | | | | |
| 2009 FI | 936,500 | — | — | — | — | 2.00 |
| 2009 FI | 2,500 | PF65 20.00 | | | | |
| 2010 FI | 738,000 | — | — | — | — | 1.75 |
| 2010 FI | 2,000 | PF65 20.00 | | | | |
| 2011 FI | 8,755,000 | — | — | — | — | 1.75 |
| 2011 FI | — | PF65 20.00 | | | | |
| 2012 FI | 10,724,000 | — | — | — | — | 1.75 |
| 2012 FI | — | PF65 20.00 | | | | |
| 2013 FI | — | — | — | — | — | 1.75 |
| 2013 FI | — | PF65 20.00 | | | | |
| 2014 | 200,000 | — | — | — | — | 3.50 |
| 2014 | 1,200 | PF65 20.00 | | | | |

### KM# 103 50 EURO CENT

7.80 g., Brass, 24.25 mm. **Obv:** Rampant lion left surrounded by stars, date at left **Rev:** Denomination and map **Edge:** Reeded

| Date | Mintage | VF20 | XF40 | MS60 | MS63 | MS65 |
|---|---|---|---|---|---|---|
| 2001 M | 4,432,000 | — | — | — | — | 5.00 |
| 2001 M | 15,000 | PF65 22.00 | | | | |
| 2002 M | 1,147,000 | — | — | — | — | 10.00 |
| 2002 M | 13,000 | PF65 22.00 | | | | |
| 2003 M | 790,000 | — | — | — | — | 5.00 |
| 2003 M | 14,500 | PF65 22.00 | | | | |
| 2004 M | 629,000 | — | — | — | — | 5.00 |
| 2004 M | 5,000 | PF65 22.00 | | | | |
| 2005 M | 4,800,000 | — | — | — | — | 5.00 |
| 2005 M | 3,000 | PF65 22.00 | | | | |
| 2006 M | 6,850,000 | — | — | — | — | 3.00 |
| 2006 M | 3,300 | PF65 22.00 | | | | |

### KM# 128 50 EURO CENT

7.80 g., Brass, 24.25 mm. **Obv:** Rampant lion surrounded by stars **Rev:** Relief map of Western Europe, stars, lines and value **Edge:** Reeded

| Date | Mintage | VF20 | XF40 | MS60 | MS63 | MS65 |
|---|---|---|---|---|---|---|
| 2007 FI | 1,000,000 | — | — | — | — | 3.00 |
| 2007 FI | — | PF65 22.00 | | | | |
| 2008 FI | 8,000,000 | — | — | — | — | 3.00 |
| 2008 FI | 2,500 | PF65 22.00 | | | | |
| 2009 FI | 6,936,500 | — | — | — | — | 3.00 |
| 2009 FI | 2,500 | PF65 22.00 | | | | |
| 2010 FI | 738,000 | — | — | — | — | 3.00 |
| 2010 FI | 2,000 | PF65 22.00 | | | | |
| 2011 FI | — | — | — | — | — | 5.00 |
| 2011 FI | 3,755,000 | PF65 22.00 | | | | |
| 2012 FI | 4,724,000 | — | — | — | — | 3.00 |
| 2012 FI | — | PF65 22.00 | | | | |
| 2013 FI | — | — | — | — | — | 5.00 |
| 2013 FI | — | PF65 22.00 | | | | |
| 2014 | 200,000 | — | — | — | — | 10.00 |
| 2014 | 1,200 | PF65 22.00 | | | | |

### KM# 104 EURO

7.50 g., Bi-Metallic Copper-Nickel center in Nickel-Brass ring, 23.25 mm. **Obv:** 2 flying swans, date below, surrounded by stars on outer ring **Rev:** Denomination and map **Edge:** Segmented reeding

| Date | Mintage | VF20 | XF40 | MS60 | MS63 | MS65 |
|---|---|---|---|---|---|---|
| 2001 M | 13,862,000 | — | — | — | — | 5.00 |
| 2001 M | 15,000 | PF65 25.00 | | | | |
| 2002 M | 14,114,000 | — | — | — | — | 5.00 |
| 2002 M | 13,000 | PF65 25.00 | | | | |
| 2003 M | 790,000 | — | — | — | — | 10.00 |
| 2003 M | 14,500 | PF65 25.00 | | | | |
| 2004 M | 5,529,000 | — | — | — | — | 6.50 |
| 2004 M | 5,000 | PF65 25.00 | | | | |
| 2005 M | 7,935,000 | — | — | — | — | 6.50 |
| 2005 M | 3,000 | PF65 25.00 | | | | |
| 2006 M | 1,705,000 | — | — | — | — | 5.00 |
| 2006 M | 3,300 | PF65 25.00 | | | | |

**KM# 129 EURO**

7.50 g., Bi-Metallic Copper-Nickel center in Nickel-Brass ring, 23.25 mm. **Obv:** 2 flying swans surrounded by stars on outer ring **Rev:** Relief map of western Europe, stars, lines and value **Edge:** Segmented reeding **Note:** In different years, varieties exist in the position of the mint mark and mintmaster symbols.

| Date | Mintage | VF20 | XF40 | MS60 | MS63 | MS65 |
|---|---|---|---|---|---|---|
| 2007 FI | 1,000,000 | — | — | — | — | 5.00 |
| 2007 FI | — | PF65 25.00 | | | | |
| 2008 FI | 1,000,000 | — | — | — | — | 5.00 |
| 2008 FI | 2,500 | PF65 25.00 | | | | |
| 2009 FI | 936,500 | — | — | — | — | 5.00 |
| 2009 FI | 2,500 | PF65 25.00 | | | | |
| 2010 FI | 738,000 | — | — | — | — | 5.00 |
| 2010 FI | 2,000 | PF65 25.00 | | | | |
| 2011 FI | 755,000 | — | — | — | — | 6.50 |
| 2011 FI | — | PF65 25.00 | | | | |
| 2012 FI | 724,000 | — | — | — | — | 6.50 |
| 2012 FI | — | PF65 25.00 | | | | |
| 2013 FI | — | — | — | — | — | 6.50 |
| 2013 FI | — | PF65 25.00 | | | | |
| 2014 | 200,000 | — | — | — | 13.00 | 15.00 |

**KM# 105 2 EURO**

8.50 g., Bi-Metallic Nickel-Brass center in Copper-Nickel ring, 25.75 mm. **Obv:** 2 cloudberry flowers surrounded by stars on outer ring **Rev:** Denomination and map **Edge:** Reeded and lettered **Edge Lettering:** SUOMI FINLAND

| Date | Mintage | VF20 | XF40 | MS60 | MS63 | MS65 |
|---|---|---|---|---|---|---|
| 2001 M | 29,132,000 | — | — | — | — | 5.00 |
| 2001 M | 15,000 | PF65 30.00 | | | | |
| 2002 M | 1,386,000 | — | — | — | — | 15.00 |
| 2002 M | 13,000 | PF65 30.00 | | | | |
| 2003 M | 9,080,000 | — | — | — | — | 7.50 |
| 2003 M | 14,500 | PF65 30.00 | | | | |
| 2004 M | 10,029,000 | — | — | — | — | 7.00 |
| 2004 M | 5,000 | PF65 30.00 | | | | |
| 2005 M | 10,800,000 | — | — | — | — | 7.00 |
| 2005 M | 3,000 | PF65 30.00 | | | | |
| 2006 M | 11,000,000 | — | — | — | — | 5.00 |
| 2006 M | 3,300 | PF65 30.00 | | | | |

**KM# 114 2 EURO**

8.50 g., Bi-Metallic Nickel-Brass center in Copper-Nickel ring, 25.75 mm. **Subject:** EU Expansion **Obv:** Stylized flower **Rev:** Denomination and map **Edge:** Reeded and lettered

| Date | Mintage | VF20 | XF40 | MS60 | MS63 | MS65 |
|---|---|---|---|---|---|---|
| 2004 M M | 1,000,000 | — | — | — | — | 11.50 |
| 2004 M M | — | PF65 30.00 | | | | |

**KM# 119 2 EURO**

8.50 g., Bi-Metallic Nickel-Brass center in Copper-Nickel ring, 25.75 mm. **Subject:** 60th Anniversary - Finland - UN **Obv:** Dove on a puzzle **Rev:** Denomination over map **Edge Lettering:** YK 1945-2005 FN

| Date | Mintage | VF20 | XF40 | MS60 | MS63 | MS65 |
|---|---|---|---|---|---|---|
| 2005 M K | 2,000,000 | — | — | — | 6.00 | 7.50 |

**KM# 125 2 EURO**

8.50 g., Bi-Metallic Nickel-Brass center in Copper-Nickel ring, 25.75 mm. **Subject:** Centennial of Universal Suffrage **Obv:** Two faces **Rev:** Value and map **Edge Lettering:** SUOMI FINLAND

| Date | Mintage | VF20 | XF40 | MS60 | MS63 | MS65 |
|---|---|---|---|---|---|---|
| 2006 M M | 2,500,000 | — | — | — | 6.00 | 7.50 |

**KM# 130 2 EURO**

8.50 g., Bi-Metallic Nickel-Brass center in Copper-Nickel ring, 25.75 mm. **Obv:** 2 cloudberry flowers surrounded by stars on outer ring **Rev:** Relief map of Western Europe, stars, lines and value **Edge:** Reeded and lettered **Edge Lettering:** SUOMI FINLAND

| Date | Mintage | VF20 | XF40 | MS60 | MS63 | MS65 |
|---|---|---|---|---|---|---|
| 2006 M Error die pairing | — | — | 40.00 | 50.00 | 75.00 | 100 |
| 2007 FI | 8,600,000 | — | — | — | 6.00 | 7.50 |
| 2007 FI | — | PF65 30.00 | | | | |
| 2008 FI | 9,800,000 | — | — | — | 6.00 | 7.50 |
| 2008 FI | 2,500 | PF65 30.00 | | | | |
| 2009 FI | 6,256,500 | — | — | — | 6.00 | 7.50 |
| 2009 FI | 2,500 | PF65 30.00 | | | | |
| 2010 FI | 3,938,000 | — | — | — | 6.00 | 7.50 |
| 2010 FI | 2,000 | PF65 30.00 | | | | |
| 2011 FI | 5,155,000 | — | — | — | 6.00 | 7.50 |
| 2011 FI | — | PF65 30.00 | | | | |
| 2012 FI | — | — | — | — | 6.00 | 7.50 |
| 2012 FI | 3,234,000 | PF65 30.00 | | | | |
| 2013 FI | — | — | — | — | 6.00 | 7.50 |
| 2013 FI | — | PF65 30.00 | | | | |
| 2014 | 200,000 | — | — | — | — | 15.00 |
| 2014 | 1,200 | PF65 30.00 | | | | |

**KM# 138 2 EURO**

8.50 g., Bi-Metallic Nickel-Brass center in Copper-Nickel ring, 25.75 mm. **Subject:** 50th Anniversary Treaty of Rome **Obv:** Open treaty book **Rev:** Large value at left, modified outline of Europe at right **Edge:** Reeded and lettered

| Date | Mintage | VF20 | XF40 | MS60 | MS63 | MS65 |
|---|---|---|---|---|---|---|
| 2007 | — | — | — | — | 7.00 | 9.00 |
| 2007 | — | PF65 75.00 | | | | |

**KM# 139 2 EURO**

8.50 g., Bi-Metallic Nickel-Brass center in Copper-Nickel ring, 25.75 mm. **Subject:** 90th Anniversary of Independence **Obv:** Longboat rowing together **Edge:** Reeded and lettered

| Date | Mintage | VF20 | XF40 | MS60 | MS63 | MS65 |
|---|---|---|---|---|---|---|
| 2007 M | 2,000,000 | — | — | — | — | 6.00 |
| 2007 M | 20,000 | PF65 20.00 | | | | |

**KM# 143 2 EURO**

8.50 g., Bi-Metallic Nickel-Brass center in Copper-Nickel ring, 25.75 mm. **Subject:** Universal Declaration of Human Rights **Obv:** Human figure within heart in landscape **Rev:** Segmented reeding

| Date | Mintage | VF20 | XF40 | MS60 | MS63 | MS65 |
|---|---|---|---|---|---|---|
| 2008 | 2,500,000 | — | — | — | 6.00 | 7.50 |
| 2008 | 2,500 | PF63 22.00 | PF65 25.00 | | | |

**KM# 144 2 EURO**

8.50 g., Bi-Metallic Nickel-Brass center in Copper-Nickel ring, 25.75 mm. **Subject:** EMU 10th Anniversary **Obv:** Stick figure and E symbol **Edge:** Reeded and lettered

| Date | Mintage | VF20 | XF40 | MS60 | MS63 | MS65 |
|---|---|---|---|---|---|---|
| 2009 | 25,000 | PF63 28.00 | PF65 30.00 | | | |
| 2009 | 1,400,000 | — | — | — | 6.00 | 7.50 |

**KM# 149 2 EURO**

8.50 g., Bi-Metallic Nickel-Brass center in Copper-Nickel ring, 25.75 mm. **Subject:** Finnish Autonomy, 200th Anniversary **Obv:** Classical Pyramid **Edge:** Lettered

| Date | Mintage | VF20 | XF40 | MS60 | MS63 | MS65 |
|---|---|---|---|---|---|---|
| 2009 | 2,500 | PF63 25.00 | PF65 30.00 | | | |
| 2009 | 1,600,000 | — | — | — | 6.00 | 7.50 |

**KM# 154 2 EURO**

8.50 g., Bi-Metallic Nickel-Brass center in Copper-Nickel ring, 25.75 mm. **Subject:** Finnish Currency, 150th Anniversary

| Date | Mintage | VF20 | XF40 | MS60 | MS63 | MS65 |
|---|---|---|---|---|---|---|
| 2010 | 25,000 | PF63 25.00 | PF65 30.00 | | | |
| 2010 | 1,600,000 | — | — | — | 6.00 | 7.50 |

**KM# 163 2 EURO**

8.50 g., Bi-Metallic Nickel-Brass center in Copper-Nickel ring, 25.75 mm. **Subject:** Bank of Finland, 200th Anniversary **Obv:** Swan in Flight

| Date | Mintage | VF20 | XF40 | MS60 | MS63 | MS65 |
|---|---|---|---|---|---|---|
| 2011 | 25,000 | PF63 25.00 | PF65 30.00 | | | |
| 2011 | — | — | — | — | 6.00 | 7.50 |

**KM# 178 2 EURO**
8.50 g., Bi-Metallic Nickel-Brass center in Copper-Nickel ring, 25.75 mm. **Subject:** Euro coinage, 10th Anniversary **Obv:** Euro symbol on globe at center, child-like rendering around

| Date | Mintage | VF20 | XF40 | MS60 | MS63 | MS65 |
|---|---|---|---|---|---|---|
| 2012 M | — | — | — | — | — | 15.00 |
| Special Unc. | | | | | | |
| 2012 M | 1,500,000 | — | — | — | 6.00 | 8.00 |
| 2012 | 25,000 | PF63 20.00 | PF65 25.00 | | | |

**KM# 182 2 EURO**
8.50 g., Bi-Metallic Nickel-Brass center in Copper-Nickel ring, 25.75 mm. **Subject:** Helene Schjerfbeck, 150th Anniversary of Birth **Obv:** Helene Schjerfbeck

| Date | Mintage | VF20 | XF40 | MS60 | MS63 | MS65 |
|---|---|---|---|---|---|---|
| 2012 | 13,000 | PF63 25.00 | PF65 30.00 | | | |
| 2012 | 1,987,000 | — | — | — | 6.00 | 7.50 |

**KM# 193 2 EURO**
8.50 g., Bi-Metallic Nickel-Brass center in Copper-Nickel ring, 25.75 mm. **Subject:** Frans Eemil Sillanpää, 125th Anniversary of Birth

| Date | Mintage | VF20 | XF40 | MS60 | MS63 | MS65 |
|---|---|---|---|---|---|---|
| 2013 | 1,000,000 | — | — | — | 6.00 | 8.00 |
| 2013 | 11,000 | PF63 30.00 | PF65 35.00 | | | |

**KM# 194 2 EURO**
8.50 g., Bi-Metallic Nickel-Brass center in Copper-Nickel ring, 25.75 mm. **Subject:** Tove Jansson, 100th Anniversary of Birth **Obv:** Head facing

| Date | Mintage | VF20 | XF40 | MS60 | MS63 | MS65 |
|---|---|---|---|---|---|---|
| 2014 | — | — | — | — | 6.00 | 8.00 |
| 2014 Proof | — | PF65 30.00 | | | | |

**KM# 190 2 EURO**
8.50 g., Bi-Metallic Nickel-Brass center in Copper-Nickel ring, 25.75 mm. **Subject:** Parliament, 150th Anniversary **Obv:** Stylized 1863 date

| Date | Mintage | VF20 | XF40 | MS60 | MS63 | MS65 |
|---|---|---|---|---|---|---|
| 2013 | 989,000 | — | — | — | 6.00 | 8.00 |
| 2013 | 11,000 | PF63 30.00 | PF65 35.00 | | | |

**KM# 194 2 EURO**
8.50 g., Bi-Metallic Nickel-Brass center in Copper-Nickel ring, 25.75 mm. **Subject:** Tove Jansson, 100th Anniversary of Birth **Obv:** Head facing

| Date | Mintage | F12 | VF20 | XF40 | MS60 | MS63 |
|---|---|---|---|---|---|---|
| 2014 | — | — | — | — | 6.00 | 7.50 |
| 2014 | — | PF65 30.00 | | | | |

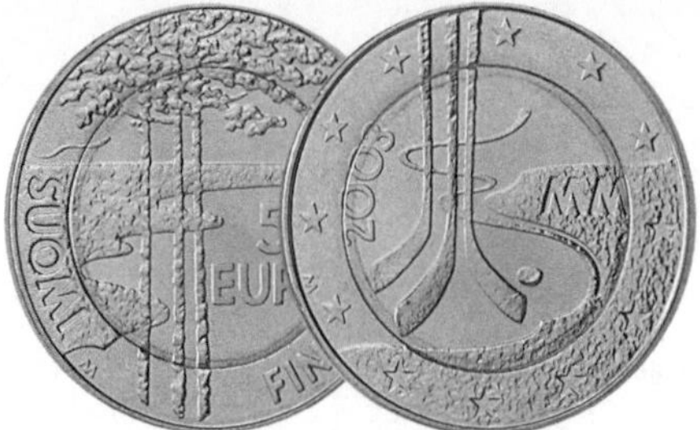

**KM# 111 5 EURO**
20.10 g., Bi-Metallic Copper-Nickel center in Brass ring, 34.9 mm. **Subject:** Ice Hockey World Championships **Obv:** Summer landscape and denomination **Rev:** Three hockey sticks and a puck **Edge:** Plain

| Date | Mintage | VF20 | XF40 | MS60 | MS63 | MS65 |
|---|---|---|---|---|---|---|
| 2003 M M-M | 150,000 | — | — | — | 25.00 | 30.00 |

**KM# 118 5 EURO**
19.80 g., Bi-Metallic Brass center in Copper-Nickel ring, 35 mm. **Subject:** 10th Anniversary - IAAF World Championships in Athletics **Obv:** Female javelin thrower, denomination **Rev:** Running feet **Edge:** Plain

| Date | Mintage | VF20 | XF40 | MS60 | MS63 | MS65 |
|---|---|---|---|---|---|---|
| 2005 M K-M | 170,000 | — | — | — | 15.00 | 20.00 |
| 2005 M K-M | 5,000 | PF63 25.00 | PF65 30.00 | | | |

**KM# 123 5 EURO**
18.70 g., Brass, 35 mm. **Subject:** 150th Anniversary - Demilitarization of Aland **Obv:** Boat, Dove of Peace on the helm **Rev:** Tree **Edge Lettering:** AHVENANMAAN DEMILITARISOINTI 150 VUOTTA*

| Date | Mintage | VF20 | XF40 | MS60 | MS63 | MS65 |
|---|---|---|---|---|---|---|
| 2006 M-M | 55,000 | — | — | — | 20.00 | 25.00 |

**KM# 131 5 EURO**
9.81 g., Bi-Metallic Copper-Nickel center in Aluminum-Bronze ring, 27.25 mm. **Subject:** Finland Presidency of European Union **Obv:** Letter decorations with 2006 and SUOMI-FINLAND **Rev:** 5 EURO below letter decoration

| Date | Mintage | VF20 | XF40 | MS60 | MS63 | MS65 |
|---|---|---|---|---|---|---|
| 2006 M P-M | 100,000 | — | — | — | 15.00 | 20.00 |

**KM# 135 5 EURO**
19.81 g., Bi-Metallic Aluminum-Bronze center in Copper-Nickel ring, 35 mm. **Subject:** 90th Anniversary of Finland's Independence

| Date | Mintage | VF20 | XF40 | MS60 | MS63 | MS65 |
|---|---|---|---|---|---|---|
| 2007 P | 130,000 | — | — | — | 15.00 | 20.00 |
| 2007 P | 20,000 | PF63 25.00 | PF65 30.00 | | | |

**KM# 146 5 EURO**
19.81 g., Bi-Metallic Aluminum-Bronze center in Copper-Nickel ring., 35 mm. **Subject:** Independence, 90th Anniversary **Obv:** Petroglif of a longboat

| Date | Mintage | VF20 | XF40 | MS60 | MS63 | MS65 |
|---|---|---|---|---|---|---|
| 2007 P | 130,000 | — | — | — | — | 15.00 |
| 2007 P | 20,000 | PF63 30.00 | PF65 35.00 | | | |

**KM# 141 5 EURO**
19.81 g., Bi-Metallic Copper-Nickel center in Aluminum-Bronze ring, 35 mm. **Subject:** Science and Research

| Date | Mintage | VF20 | XF40 | MS60 | MS63 | MS65 |
|---|---|---|---|---|---|---|
| 2008 K | 20,000 | PF63 25.00 | PF65 30.00 | | | |
| 2008 K | 25,000 | — | — | — | 15.00 | 20.00 |

**KM# 156 5 EURO**
9.80 g., Bi-Metallic Copper-Nickel center in Aluminum-Bronze ring, 27.25 mm. **Subject:** Provinces - Satakunta

| Date | Mintage | VF20 | XF40 | MS60 | MS63 | MS65 |
|---|---|---|---|---|---|---|
| 2010 T | — | — | — | — | — | 12.00 |
| 2010 T | — | PF63 25.00 | PF65 30.00 | | | |

**KM# 158 5 EURO**
9.80 g., Bi-Metallic Copper-Nickel center in Aluminum-Bronze ring, 27.5 mm. **Subject:** Provinces - Varsinais - Suomi

| Date | Mintage | VF20 | XF40 | MS60 | MS63 | MS65 |
|---|---|---|---|---|---|---|
| 2010 T | 90,000 | — | — | — | — | 12.00 |
| 2010 T | 30,000 | PF63 25.00 | PF65 30.00 | | | |

**KM# 159 5 EURO**
9.80 g., Bi-Metallic Copper-Nickel center in Aluminum-Bronze ring, 27.25 mm. **Subject:** Provinces - Karjala **Rev:** Shield

| Date | Mintage | VF20 | XF40 | MS60 | MS63 | MS65 |
|---|---|---|---|---|---|---|
| 2011 T | 20,000 | PF63 25.00 | PF65 30.00 | | | |
| 2011 T | 100,000 | — | — | — | 13.00 | 15.00 |

**KM# 160 5 EURO**
9.80 g., Bi-Metallic Copper-Nickel center in Aluminum-Bronze ring, 27.5 mm. **Subject:** Provinces - Uusimaa

| Date | Mintage | VF20 | XF40 | MS60 | MS63 | MS65 |
|---|---|---|---|---|---|---|
| 2011 T | 100,000 | — | — | — | 15.00 | 20.00 |
| 2011 T | 20,000 | PF63 25.00 | PF65 30.00 | | | |

**KM# 161 5 EURO**
9.80 g., Bi-Metallic Copper-Nickel center in Aluminum-Bronze ring, 27.5 mm. **Subject:** Provinces - Häme

| Date | Mintage | VF20 | XF40 | MS60 | MS63 | MS65 |
|---|---|---|---|---|---|---|
| 2011 T | 100,000 | — | — | — | — | 12.00 |
| 2011 T | 20,000 | PF63 20.00 PF65 25.00 | | | | |

**KM# 162 5 EURO**
9.80 g., Bi-Metallic Copper-Nickel center in Aluminum-Bronze ring, 27.5 mm. **Subject:** Provinces - Savo

| Date | Mintage | VF20 | XF40 | MS60 | MS63 | MS65 |
|---|---|---|---|---|---|---|
| 2011 T | 100,000 | — | — | — | 15.00 | 20.00 |
| 2011 T | 20,000 | PF63 25.00 PF65 30.00 | | | | |

**KM# 170 5 EURO**
9.80 g., Bi-Metallic Copper-Nickel center in Aluminum-Bronze ring, 27.25 mm. **Subject:** Provinces - Lappi **Obv:** Shield **Rev:** Antler

| Date | Mintage | VF20 | XF40 | MS60 | MS63 | MS65 |
|---|---|---|---|---|---|---|
| 2011 T | 100,000 | — | — | — | 13.00 | 15.00 |
| 2011 T | 20,000 | PF63 25.00 PF65 30.00 | | | | |

**KM# 171 5 EURO**
9.80 g., Bi-Metallic Copper-Nickel center in Aluminum-Bronze ring, 27.25 mm. **Subject:** Provinces - Pohjanmea **Obv:** Shield **Rev:** Wood

| Date | Mintage | VF20 | XF40 | MS60 | MS63 | MS65 |
|---|---|---|---|---|---|---|
| 2011 T | — | — | — | — | — | 12.00 |
| 2011 T | — | PF63 25.00 PF65 30.00 | | | | |

**KM# 177 5 EURO**
9.80 g., Bi-Metallic Copper-Nickel center in Aluminum-Bronze ring., 27.25 mm. **Series:** Provinces - Ahvenamnas **Obv:** Needle sewing fishing net **Rev:** Shield

| Date | Mintage | VF20 | XF40 | MS60 | MS63 | MS65 |
|---|---|---|---|---|---|---|
| 2011 T | 20,000 | PF63 25.00 PF65 30.00 | | | | |
| 2011 T | 100,000 | — | — | — | — | 18.00 |

**KM# 181 5 EURO**
9.00 g., Aluminum-Bronze, 27.25 mm. **Subject:** World Design Capital Helsinki 2012 **Obv:** Angular **Rev:** Angular

| Date | Mintage | VF20 | XF40 | MS60 | MS63 | MS65 |
|---|---|---|---|---|---|---|
| 2012 | 100,000 | — | — | — | — | 110 |

**KM# 183 5 EURO**
9.80 g., Bi-Metallic Copper-Nickel center in Aluminum-Bronze ring, 27.25 mm. **Subject:** IIHF Ice Hockey World Championship **Obv:** Puck flying into the goal **Rev:** Hockey player

| Date | Mintage | VF20 | XF40 | MS60 | MS63 | MS65 |
|---|---|---|---|---|---|---|
| 2012 N | 180,000 | — | — | — | — | 5.00 |
| 2012 N | 20,000 | PF65 18.00 | | | | |

**KM# 184 5 EURO**
9.80 g., Bi-Metallic Copper-Nickel center in Aluminum-Bronze ring, 27.25 mm. **Subject:** Northern Nature - Flora **Obv:** Crowfoot framed by moss and lichen

| Date | Mintage | VF20 | XF40 | MS60 | MS63 | MS65 |
|---|---|---|---|---|---|---|
| 2012 P | 7,000 | PF65 45.00 | | | | |
| 2012 P | 50,000 | — | — | — | 7.00 | 8.00 |

**KM# 185 5 EURO**
9.80 g., Bi-Metallic Copper-Nickel center in Aluminum-Bronze ring, 27.25 mm. **Subject:** Northern Nature - Fauna **Obv:** Paw trail of the arctic fox **Rev:** 5 EURO SUOMI FINLAND

| Date | Mintage | VF20 | XF40 | MS60 | MS63 | MS65 |
|---|---|---|---|---|---|---|
| 2012 P | 50,000 | — | — | — | 7.00 | 8.00 |
| 2012 P | 7,000 | PF65 45.00 | | | | |

**KM# 186 5 EURO**
9.80 g., Bi-Metallic Copper-Nickel center in Aluminum-Bronze ring, 27.25 mm. **Subject:** Northern Nature - Winter **Obv:** Northern lights **Rev:** Animal tracks in the snow

| Date | Mintage | VF20 | XF40 | MS60 | MS63 | MS65 |
|---|---|---|---|---|---|---|
| 2012 P | 50,000 | — | — | — | 7.00 | 8.00 |
| 2012 P | 7,000 | PF65 45.00 | | | | |

**KM# 191 5 EURO**
9.80 g., Bi-Metallic, 27.25 mm. **Subject:** Buildings of the Provinces **Obv:** Helsinki and Uspenski Cathedral **Rev:** Shield and Denomination

| Date | Mintage | VF20 | XF40 | MS60 | MS63 | MS65 |
|---|---|---|---|---|---|---|
| 2012 T | Est. 55000 | — | — | — | 7.00 | 8.00 |
| 2012 T | Est. 10000 | PF65 40.00 | | | | |

**KM# 192 5 EURO**
9.80 g., Bi-Metallic, 27.25 mm. **Subject:** Buildings of the Provinces-Lappi **Obv:** Jätkänkynttilä Bridge in Rovaniemi **Rev:** Shield and denomination

| Date | Mintage | VF20 | XF40 | MS60 | MS63 | MS65 |
|---|---|---|---|---|---|---|
| 2012 T | 10,000 | PF65 40.00 | | | | |
| 2012 T | 55,000 | — | — | — | 7.00 | 8.00 |

**KM# 195 5 EURO**
9.00 g., Bi-Metallic Copper-Nickel center in Aluminum-Bronze ring, 27.25 mm. **Obv:** Imatra Dam **Rev:** Shield and denomination

| Date | Mintage | VF20 | XF40 | MS60 | MS63 | MS65 |
|---|---|---|---|---|---|---|
| 2013 | 55,000 | — | — | 17.00 | 20.00 | 22.00 |
| 2013 | 10,000 | PF63 30.00 PF65 35.00 | | | | |

**KM# 196 5 EURO**
9.80 g., Bi-Metallic Copper-Nickel center in Aluminum-Bronze ring, 27.25 mm. **Subject:** Northern Nature - Summer **Obv:** Water lilies **Rev:** Lakeside landscape

| Date | Mintage | VF20 | XF40 | MS60 | MS63 | MS65 |
|---|---|---|---|---|---|---|
| 2013 | 50,000 | — | — | 17.00 | 20.00 | 22.00 |
| 2013 | 7,000 | PF63 32.00 PF65 40.00 | | | | |

**KM# 197 5 EURO**
9.80 g., Bi-Metallic Copper-Nickel center in Aluminum-Bronze ring, 27.25 mm. **Obv:** Church of St. Lawrence in Janakkala **Rev:** Shield and denomination

| Date | Mintage | VF20 | XF40 | MS60 | MS63 | MS65 |
|---|---|---|---|---|---|---|
| 2013 | 55,000 | — | — | 17.00 | 20.00 | 22.00 |
| 2013 | 10,000 | PF63 30.00 PF65 35.00 | | | | |

**KM# 198 5 EURO**
9.80 g., Bi-Metallic Copper-Nickel center in Aluminum-Bronze ring, 27.25 mm. **Obv:** Sammallahdenmäki - bronze age burial mounds in Lappi **Rev:** Shield and denomination

| Date | Mintage | VF20 | XF40 | MS60 | MS63 | MS65 |
|---|---|---|---|---|---|---|
| 2013 | 55,000 | — | — | 17.00 | 20.00 | 22.00 |
| 2013 | 10,000 | PF63 30.00 PF65 35.00 | | | | |

**KM# 199 5 EURO**

9.80 g., Bi-Metallic Copper-Nickel center in Aluminum-Bronze ring, 27.25 mm. **Obv:** St. Olaf's Castle **Rev:** Shield and denomination

| Date | Mintage | VF20 | XF40 | MS60 | MS63 | MS65 |
|---|---|---|---|---|---|---|
| 2013 | 55,000 | — | — | 17.00 | 20.00 | 22.00 |
| 2013 | 10,000 | PF63 30.00 | PF65 35.00 | | | |

**KM# 200 5 EURO**

9.80 g., Bi-Metallic Copper-Nickel center in Aluminum-Bronze ring, 27.25 mm. **Obv:** Salskar Lighthouse, Aland **Rev:** Shield and denomination

| Date | Mintage | VF20 | XF40 | MS60 | MS63 | MS65 |
|---|---|---|---|---|---|---|
| 2013 | 55,000 | — | — | 17.00 | 20.00 | 22.00 |
| 2013 | 10,000 | PF63 30.00 | PF65 35.00 | | | |

**KM# 205 5 EURO**

9.80 g., Bi-Metallic Copper-Nickel center in Aluminum-Bronze ring, 27.25 mm. **Obv:** House **Rev:** Shield

| Date | Mintage | VF20 | XF40 | MS60 | MS63 | MS65 |
|---|---|---|---|---|---|---|
| 2013 | — | — | — | — | 17.00 | 20.00 |
| 2013 | — | PF65 35.00 | | | | |

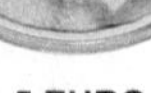

**KM# 213 5 EURO**

9.80 g., Bi-Metallic Copper-Nickel center in Aluminum-Bronze ring, 27.25 mm. **Obv:** Turku Cathedral **Rev:** Shield

| Date | Mintage | VF20 | XF40 | MS60 | MS63 | MS65 |
|---|---|---|---|---|---|---|
| 2013 | — | — | — | — | 17.00 | 20.00 |
| 2013 | — | PF65 35.00 | | | | |

**KM# 107 10 EURO**

27.40 g., 0.925 Silver 0.8149 oz. ASW, 38.6 mm. **Subject:** 50th Anniversary - Helsinki Olympics **Obv:** Flames and denomination above globe with map of Finland **Rev:** Tower and partial coin design **Edge:** Plain

| Date | Mintage | VF20 | XF40 | MS60 | MS63 | MS65 |
|---|---|---|---|---|---|---|
| 2002 M VV-M | 10,000 | — | — | — | 25.00 | 30.00 |
| 2002 M VV-M | 34,800 | PF63 35.00 | PF65 40.00 | | | |

**KM# 108 10 EURO**

27.40 g., 0.925 Silver 0.8149 oz. ASW, 38.6 mm. **Subject:** Elias Lönnrot **Obv:** Ribbon with stars **Rev:** Quill and signature **Edge:** Plain

| Date | Mintage | VF20 | XF40 | MS60 | MS63 | MS65 |
|---|---|---|---|---|---|---|
| 2002 M M-M | 40,000 | — | — | — | 25.00 | 30.00 |
| 2002 M M-M | 40,000 | PF63 35.00 | PF65 40.00 | | | |

**KM# 110 10 EURO**

27.40 g., 0.925 Silver 0.8149 oz. ASW, 38.6 mm. **Subject:** Anders Chydenius **Obv:** Stylized design **Rev:** Name and book **Edge:** Plain

| Date | Mintage | VF20 | XF40 | MS60 | MS63 | MS65 |
|---|---|---|---|---|---|---|
| 2003 M | 30,000 | PF63 40.00 | PF65 45.00 | | | |
| 2003 M L-M | 30,000 | — | — | — | 25.00 | 30.00 |

**KM# 112 10 EURO**

27.40 g., 0.925 Silver 0.8149 oz. ASW, 38.6 mm. **Subject:** Mannerheim and St. Petersburg **Obv:** Head 3/4 facing **Rev:** Fortress, denomination at right

| Date | Mintage | VF20 | XF40 | MS60 | MS63 | MS65 |
|---|---|---|---|---|---|---|
| 2003 S-M | 29,000 | PF63 35.00 | PF65 40.00 | | | |
| 2003 S-M | 6,000 | — | — | — | 30.00 | 35.00 |

**KM# 115 10 EURO**

27.40 g., 0.925 Silver 0.8149 oz. ASW, 38.6 mm. **Subject:** 200th Birthday of Johan Ludwig Runeberg **Obv:** Head of Runeberg **Rev:** Text of 1831 Helsingfors Tidningar newspaper

| Date | Mintage | VF20 | XF40 | MS60 | MS63 | MS65 |
|---|---|---|---|---|---|---|
| 2004 K-M | 5,600 | — | — | — | 30.00 | 35.00 |
| 2004 K-M | 22,750 | PF65 40.00 | | | | |

**KM# 116 10 EURO**

27.40 g., 0.925 Silver 0.8149 oz. ASW, 38.6 mm. **Subject:** Tove Jansson **Obv:** Three inhabitants of Moominland - Moomintroll, Little My and Snork maiden **Rev:** Jansson head at left, artist pallet at right

| Date | Mintage | VF20 | XF40 | MS60 | MS63 | MS65 |
|---|---|---|---|---|---|---|
| 2004 M-M | 20,000 | PF65 50.00 | | | | |
| 2004 M-M | 50,000 | — | — | — | 30.00 | 40.00 |

**KM# 120 10 EURO**

25.50 g., 0.925 Silver 0.7584 oz. ASW, 38.6 mm. **Subject:** 60 years of Peace **Obv:** Dove of peace **Rev:** Flowering plant

| Date | Mintage | VF20 | XF40 | MS60 | MS63 | MS65 |
|---|---|---|---|---|---|---|
| 2005 M-M | 55,000 | — | — | — | 28.00 | 35.00 |
| 2005 | 5,000 | PF63 40.00 | PF65 45.00 | | | |

**KM# 122 10 EURO**

25.50 g., 0.925 Silver 0.7584 oz. ASW, 38.6 mm. **Subject:** Unknown Soldier and Finnish Film Art **Obv:** Trench **Rev:** Soldier with helmet on top of a film

| Date | Mintage | VF20 | XF40 | MS60 | MS63 | MS65 |
|---|---|---|---|---|---|---|
| 2005 P-M | 25,000 | — | — | — | 30.00 | 32.00 |
| 2005 P-M | 15,000 | PF63 37.00 | PF65 40.00 | | | |

**KM# 124 10 EURO**

25.50 g., 0.925 Silver 0.7584 oz. ASW, 38.6 mm. **Subject:** 200th Birthday - Johan Vilhelm Snellman **Obv:** Sun rising over the lake **Rev:** Snellman

| Date | Mintage | VF20 | XF40 | MS60 | MS63 | MS65 |
|---|---|---|---|---|---|---|
| 2006 K-M | — | — | — | — | 30.00 | 35.00 |
| 2006 K-M | — | PF63 30.00 | PF65 35.00 | | | |

**KM# 132 10 EURO**

25.50 g., 0.925 Silver 0.7584 oz. ASW, 38.6 mm. **Subject:** 100th Anniversary of Parliamentary Reform **Obv:** Two stylist heads female and male with text SUOMI FINLAND 10 EURO **Rev:** Male and female fingers inserting ballot paper into ballot box with text 100V EDUSKUNTAUUDISTUS 2006 **Edge Lettering:** LANTDAGSREFORMEN 1906

| Date | Mintage | VF20 | XF40 | MS60 | MS63 | MS65 |
|---|---|---|---|---|---|---|
| 2006 M M-M | 40,000 | — | — | — | 30.00 | 40.00 |
| 2006 M M-M | 20,000 | **PF63** 40.00 | **PF65** 45.00 | | | |

**KM# 134 10 EURO**

25.50 g., 0.925 Silver 0.7584 oz. ASW, 38.6 mm. **Subject:** A.E. Nordenskiöld and the Northeast Passage **Rev:** Sailor at ship's wheel during foul weather

| Date | Mintage | VF20 | XF40 | MS60 | MS63 | MS65 |
|---|---|---|---|---|---|---|
| 2007 M P | 7,000 | — | — | — | 30.00 | 35.00 |
| 2007 M P | 33,000 | **PF63** 37.00 | **PF65** 40.00 | | | |

**KM# 136 10 EURO**

25.50 g., 0.925 Silver 0.7584 oz. ASW, 38.6 mm. **Subject:** Mikael Agricola - Finnish Language **Obv:** Quill pen and lettering **Rev:** Alphabet Letters

| Date | Mintage | VF20 | XF40 | MS60 | MS63 | MS65 |
|---|---|---|---|---|---|---|
| 2007 P | 6,000 | — | — | — | 30.00 | 35.00 |
| 2007 P | 24,000 | **PF63** 40.00 | **PF65** 50.00 | | | |

**KM# 140 10 EURO**

25.50 g., 0.925 Silver 0.7584 oz. ASW, 38.6 mm. **Subject:** Finnish Flag **Obv:** SUOMI FINLAND 2008 and flag **Rev:** SUOMEN LIPPU 1918-2008-FINLANDS FLAGGA and value

| Date | Mintage | VF20 | XF40 | MS60 | MS63 | MS65 |
|---|---|---|---|---|---|---|
| 2008 K | 9,000 | — | — | — | 30.00 | 32.00 |
| 2008 K | 26,000 | **PF63** 35.00 | **PF65** 40.00 | | | |

**KM# 142 10 EURO**

25.50 g., 0.925 Silver 0.7584 oz. ASW, 38.6 mm. **Subject:** Mika Waltari **Obv:** Signature and 1908-1879 **Rev:** Egyptian pharaoh hound and value

| Date | Mintage | VF20 | XF40 | MS60 | MS63 | MS65 |
|---|---|---|---|---|---|---|
| 2008 P | 5,000 | — | — | — | 30.00 | 32.00 |
| 2008 P | 15,000 | **PF63** 35.00 | **PF65** 40.00 | | | |

**KM# 148 10 EURO**

25.50 g., 0.925 Silver 0.7584 oz. ASW, 38.6 mm. **Subject:** Fredrik Pacius **Obv:** Opening notes to Kung Karls Jakt, first opera of Pacius **Rev:** Stage curtian opening

| Date | Mintage | VF20 | XF40 | MS60 | MS63 | MS65 |
|---|---|---|---|---|---|---|
| 2009 M | 7,000 | — | — | — | 35.00 | 58.00 |
| 2009 M | 28,000 | **PF63** 75.00 | **PF65** 80.00 | | | |

**KM# 173 10 EURO**

25.50 g., 0.925 Silver 0.7584 oz. ASW **Subject:** Council of State, 200th Anniversary

| Date | Mintage | VF20 | XF40 | MS60 | MS63 | MS65 |
|---|---|---|---|---|---|---|
| 2009 P | 15,000 | **PF63** 70.00 | **PF65** 80.00 | | | |
| 2009 P | 5,000 | — | — | — | — | 50.00 |

**KM# 151 10 EURO**

25.50 g., 0.925 Silver 0.7584 oz. ASW, 38.6 mm. **Subject:** Eero Saarinen, 100th Anniversary of Birth **Obv:** Tulip chair **Rev:** St. Louis Arch

| Date | Mintage | VF20 | XF40 | MS60 | MS63 | MS65 |
|---|---|---|---|---|---|---|
| 2010 K | 20,000 | **PF63** 75.00 | **PF65** 80.00 | | | |
| 2010 K | 6,000 | — | — | — | — | 50.00 |

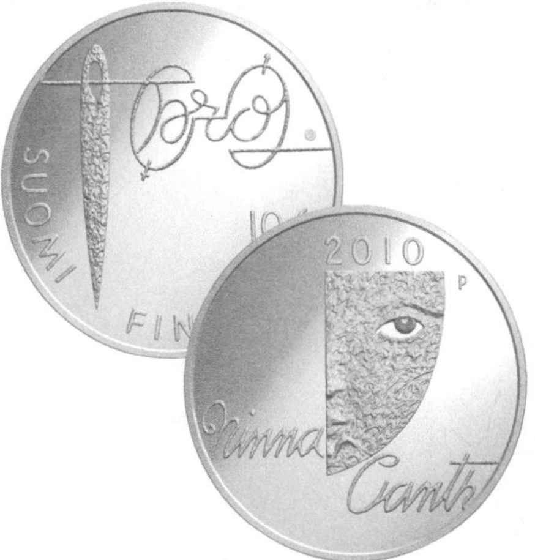


**KM# 152 10 EURO**

25.50 g., 0.925 Silver 0.7584 oz. ASW, 38.6 mm. **Subject:** Minna Cauth, author

| Date | Mintage | VF20 | XF40 | MS60 | MS63 | MS65 |
|---|---|---|---|---|---|---|
| 2010 P | 16,000 | **PF63** 75.00 | **PF65** 80.00 | | | |
| 2010 P | 4,000 | — | — | — | — | 50.00 |

**KM# 157 10 EURO**
25.50 g., 0.925 Silver 0.7584 oz. ASW, 38.6 mm. **Subject:** Konsta Jylhä, 100th Anniversary of Birth

| Date | Mintage | VF20 | XF40 | MS60 | MS63 | MS65 |
|---|---|---|---|---|---|---|
| 2010 P | — | PF63 | 75.00 | PF65 | 80.00 | |
| 2010 P | — | — | — | — | 32.00 | 50.00 |

**KM# 165 10 EURO**
25.50 g., 0.925 Silver 0.7584 oz. ASW, 38.6 mm. **Subject:** Hella Wuolijoki and Equality

| Date | Mintage | VF20 | XF40 | MS60 | MS63 | MS65 |
|---|---|---|---|---|---|---|
| 2011 P | 7,000 | PF63 | 75.00 | PF65 | 80.00 | |
| 2011 P | 5,000 | — | — | — | 30.00 | 70.00 |

**KM# 166 10 EURO**
25.50 g., 0.925 Silver 0.7584 oz. ASW, 38.6 mm. **Subject:** Kaj Franck and industrial art **Obv:** Franck's signature

| Date | Mintage | VF20 | XF40 | MS60 | MS63 | MS65 |
|---|---|---|---|---|---|---|
| 2011 P | 5,000 | — | — | — | 30.00 | 70.00 |
| 2011 P | 10,000 | PF63 | 75.00 | PF65 | 80.00 | |

**KM# 167 10 EURO**
25.50 g., 0.925 Silver 0.7584 oz. ASW, 38.6 mm. **Subject:** Pehr Kalm and European Explorers **Obv:** Mountain laurel - kalmia latifolia **Rev:** Surveyor before Niagara Falls

| Date | Mintage | VF20 | XF40 | MS60 | MS63 | MS65 |
|---|---|---|---|---|---|---|
| 2011 V | 14,000 | PF63 | 65.00 | PF65 | 70.00 | |
| 2011 V | 6,000 | — | — | — | 30.00 | 35.00 |

**KM# 168 10 EURO**
25.50 g., 0.500 Silver 0.4099 oz. ASW, 38.6 mm. **Subject:** Juhani Aho and Finnish Literature **Rev:** Pen point and manuscript

| Date | Mintage | VF20 | XF40 | MS60 | MS63 | MS65 |
|---|---|---|---|---|---|---|
| 2011 P | 8,000 | — | — | — | — | 50.00 |

**KM# 168a 10 EURO**
25.50 g., 0.925 Silver 0.7584 oz. ASW, 38.6 mm. **Subject:** Juhani Aho and Finnish Literature

| Date | Mintage | VF20 | XF40 | MS60 | MS63 | MS65 |
|---|---|---|---|---|---|---|
| 2011 P | 7,000 | PF63 | 80.00 | | | |

**KM# 179 10 EURO**
25.50 g., 0.925 Silver 0.7584 oz. ASW, 38.6 mm. **Subject:** Henrik Wigström, 150th Anniversary of Birth **Obv:** Swan swimming left, Lilly pads nearby **Rev:** Floral Easter egg ball

| Date | Mintage | VF20 | XF40 | MS60 | MS63 | MS65 |
|---|---|---|---|---|---|---|
| 2012 M | 15,000 | PF65 | 75.00 | | | |
| 2012 M | 15,000 | — | — | — | 30.00 | 70.00 |

**KM# 187 10 EURO**
25.50 g., 0.925 Silver 0.7584 oz. ASW, 38.6 mm. **Subject:** Arvo Ylppö and Medicin **Obv:** Colored alphabet letters **Rev:** Baby nestled in stethoscope

| Date | Mintage | VF20 | XF40 | MS60 | MS63 | MS65 |
|---|---|---|---|---|---|---|
| 2012 M | 20,000 | — | — | — | — | 70.00 |
| 2012 M | 20,000 | PF65 | 80.00 | | | |

**KM# 188 10 EURO**
25.50 g., 0.925 Silver 0.7584 oz. ASW, 38.6 mm. **Subject:** Armi Ratia and Industrial Art **Obv:** Armi Ratia 1912-1973 **Rev:** Unikko flower

| Date | Mintage | VF20 | XF40 | MS60 | MS63 | MS65 |
|---|---|---|---|---|---|---|
| 2012 | 20,000 | — | — | — | — | 70.00 |
| 2012 | 20,000 | PF65 | 80.00 | | | |

**KM# 201 10 EURO**
25.50 g., 0.925 Silver 0.7584 oz. ASW, 38.6 mm. **Obv:** Frans Eemil Sillanpää **Rev:** Art of Sillanpää

| Date | Mintage | VF20 | XF40 | MS60 | MS63 | MS65 |
|---|---|---|---|---|---|---|
| 2013 | 20,000 | — | — | — | — | 70.00 |
| 2013 | 20,000 | PF65 | 80.00 | | | |

**KM# 202 10 EURO**
25.50 g., 0.925 Silver 0.7584 oz. ASW, 38.6 mm. **Subject:** Sophie Mannerheim, 150th Anniversary of Birth **Obv:** Sophie Mannerheim **Rev:** Woman and children

| Date | Mintage | VF20 | XF40 | MS60 | MS63 | MS65 |
|---|---|---|---|---|---|---|
| 2013 | 20,000 | — | — | — | — | 70.00 |
| 2013 | 20,000 | PF65 | 80.00 | | | |

### KM# 214 10 EURO

25.50 g., 0.925 Silver 0.7584 oz. ASW, 38.6 mm. **Subject:** Eero Järnefelt, 150th Anniversary of Birth **Obv:** Rugged landscape painting **Rev:** Artist painting at easel

| Date | Mintage | VF20 | XF40 | MS60 | MS63 | MS65 |
|---|---|---|---|---|---|---|
| 2013 | 17,000 | **PF65** 55.00 | | | | |

### KM# 121 20 EURO

1.73 g., 0.900 Gold 0.0501 oz. AGW, 13.9 mm. **Subject:** 10th Anniversary - IAAF World Championships in Athletics **Obv:** Helsinki Stadium **Rev:** Two faces

| Date | Mintage | VF20 | XF40 | MS60 | MS63 | MS65 |
|---|---|---|---|---|---|---|
| 2005 M-M | 30,000 | **PF63** 90.00 | **PF65** 100 | | | |

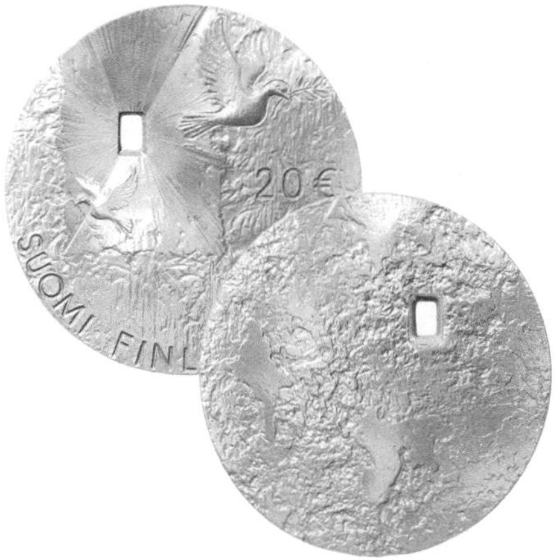


### KM# 172 20 EURO

25.50 g., 0.925 Silver 0.7584 oz. ASW, 38.6 mm. **Subject:** Peace and security **Obv:** Two peace doves with a twig

| Date | Mintage | VF20 | XF40 | MS60 | MS63 | MS65 |
|---|---|---|---|---|---|---|
| 2009 K | 11,500 | **PF65** 120 | | | | |
| 2009 K | 3,500 | — | — | — | 32.00 | 40.00 |

### KM# 153 20 EURO

33.62 g., 0.925 Silver 0.9998 oz. ASW, 38.61 mm. **Subject:** Children's creativity

| Date | Mintage | VF20 | XF40 | MS60 | MS63 | MS65 |
|---|---|---|---|---|---|---|
| 2010 M | 10,000 | **PF65** 120 | | | | |
| 2010 M | 3,500 | — | — | — | — | 100 |

### KM# 169 20 EURO

33.62 g., 0.500 Silver 0.5405 oz. ASW, 38.6 mm. **Subject:** Protecting Baltic Sea **Obv:** Fishing boat and map of the Baltic Sea **Rev:** Seal and fish

| Date | Mintage | VF20 | XF40 | MS60 | MS63 | MS65 |
|---|---|---|---|---|---|---|
| 2011 K | 7,000 | — | — | — | — | 80.00 |

### KM# 169a 20 EURO

33.62 g., 0.925 Silver 0.9998 oz. ASW, 38.6 mm. **Subject:** Protecting the Baltic **Obv:** Fishing boat and map of the Baltic Sea **Rev:** Seal and fish

| Date | Mintage | VF20 | XF40 | MS60 | MS63 | MS65 |
|---|---|---|---|---|---|---|
| 2011 K | 8,000 | **PF63** 110 | | | | |

### KM# 189 20 EURO

33.62 g., 0.925 Silver 0.9998 oz. ASW, 38.6 mm. **Subject:** Equity and Tolerance **Obv:** World map **Rev:** Human faces and value

| Date | Mintage | VF20 | XF40 | MS60 | MS63 | MS65 |
|---|---|---|---|---|---|---|
| 2012 P | 20,000 | — | — | — | — | 110 |
| 2012 P | 20,000 | **PF65** 120 | | | | |

### KM# 204 20 EURO

25.50 g., 0.925 Silver 0.7584 oz. ASW, 38.6 mm. **Subject:** Multicultural

| Date | Mintage | VF20 | XF40 | MS60 | MS63 | MS65 |
|---|---|---|---|---|---|---|
| 2013 | — | **PF65** 75.00 | | | | |

### KM# 113 50 EURO

13.20 g., Bi-Metallic .75 Gold center in .925 Silver ring, 27.25 mm. **Subject:** Finnish art and design **Obv:** Snowflake design within box, beaded circle surrounds **Rev:** Snowflake design within beaded circle

| Date | Mintage | VF20 | XF40 | MS60 | MS63 | MS65 |
|---|---|---|---|---|---|---|
| 2003 P-M | 10,600 | **PF65** 375 | | | | |

### KM# 133 50 EURO

12.80 g., Bi-Metallic .75 Gold center in .925 Silver ring, 27.25 mm. **Subject:** Finland Presidency of European Union **Obv:** Letter decorations with 2006 and SUOMI-FINLAND **Rev:** 50 EURO below letter decoration

| Date | Mintage | VF20 | XF40 | MS60 | MS63 | MS65 |
|---|---|---|---|---|---|---|
| 2006 M P-M | 8,000 | **PF65** 400 | | | | |

### KM# 180 50 EURO

10.80 g., Bi-Metallic 5.75 g gold center in 5.8 g .925 Silver ring, 27.25 mm. **Subject:** World Design Capital Helsinki 2012 **Obv:** WORLD DESIGN CAPITAL HELSINKI around angular patterns **Rev:** 50 above angular patterns

| Date | Mintage | VF20 | XF40 | MS60 | MS63 | MS65 |
|---|---|---|---|---|---|---|
| 2012 L | 5,000 | **PF65** 600 | | | | |

### KM# 109 100 EURO

8.64 g., 0.900 Gold 0.250 oz. AGW, 22 mm. **Subject:** Lapland **Obv:** Small tree and mountain stream **Rev:** Lake landscape beneath the midnight sun **Edge:** Plain with serial number

| Date | Mintage | VF20 | XF40 | MS60 | MS63 | MS65 |
|---|---|---|---|---|---|---|
| 2002 M J-M | 25,000 | **PF65** 450 | | | | |

### KM# 176 100 EURO

5.65 g., Gold, 22 mm. **Obv:** Tree branch **Rev:** Eternal sunlight

| Date | Mintage | VF20 | XF40 | MS60 | MS63 | MS65 |
|---|---|---|---|---|---|---|
| 2002 T | — | **PF65** 525 | | | | |

### KM# 117 100 EURO

8.64 g., 0.900 Gold 0.250 oz. AGW, 22 mm. **Subject:** 150th Birthday of Albert Edelfelt **Obv:** Flower **Rev:** Head of Edelfelt

| Date | Mintage | VF20 | XF40 | MS60 | MS63 | MS65 |
|---|---|---|---|---|---|---|
| 2004 M-M | 8,500 | **PF65** 475 | | | | |

### KM# 175 100 EURO

5.65 g., 0.917 Gold 0.1666 oz. AGW, 22 mm. **Subject:** Albert Edelfelt **Obv:** Floser **Rev:** Head facing

| Date | Mintage | VF20 | XF40 | MS60 | MS63 | MS65 |
|---|---|---|---|---|---|---|
| 2004 T | — | **PF65** 525 | | | | |

**KM# 137 100 EURO**

8.48 g., 0.917 Gold 0.250 oz. AGW **Subject:** 90th Anniversary of Finland's Independence **Obv:** Finland and the years of independence **Rev:** Abstract composition

| Date | Mintage | VF20 | XF40 | MS60 | MS63 | MS65 |
|---|---|---|---|---|---|---|
| 2007 P | — | — | — | — | 450 | 465 |
| 2007 P | — | PF65 475 | | | | |

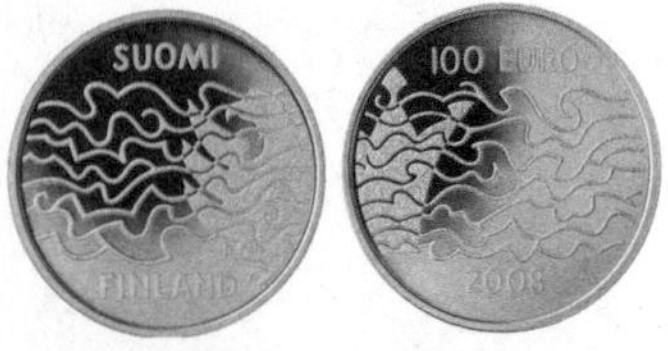

**KM# 174 100 EURO**

8.48 g., 0.917 Gold 0.250 oz. AGW, 22 mm. **Subject:** Finnish War and the Birth of Autonomy **Obv:** Half of an Eagle at left **Rev:** Half of a Crown at right

| Date | Mintage | VF20 | XF40 | MS60 | MS63 | MS65 |
|---|---|---|---|---|---|---|
| 2008 P | 9,000 | PF65 625 | | | | |

**KM# 145 100 EURO**

6.78 g., 0.917 Gold 0.1999 oz. AGW, 22 mm. **Subject:** Diet of Porvoo **Rev:** Porvoo

| Date | Mintage | VF20 | XF40 | MS60 | MS63 | MS65 |
|---|---|---|---|---|---|---|
| 2009 P | 7,500 | PF65 375 | | | | |

**KM# 150 100 EURO**

5.65 g., 0.917 Gold 0.1666 oz. AGW, 22 mm. **Subject:** Finnish Currency, 150th Anniversary **Obv:** Finnish Lion **Rev:** Composition of figures

| Date | Mintage | VF20 | XF40 | MS60 | MS63 | MS65 |
|---|---|---|---|---|---|---|
| 2010 P | — | PF65 550 | | | | |

**KM# 164 100 EURO**

5.65 g., 0.917 Gold 0.1666 oz. AGW, 22 mm. **Subject:** Bank of Finland, 200th Anniversary **Obv:** Swan in flight **Rev:** Left wing of swan SUOMI FINLAND value and date

| Date | Mintage | VF20 | XF40 | MS60 | MS63 | MS65 |
|---|---|---|---|---|---|---|
| 2011 V | 8,000 | PF65 525 | | | | |

**KM# 203 100 EURO**

5.65 g., 0.917 Gold 0.1666 oz. AGW, 22 mm. **Subject:** Parliament, 150th Anniversary

| Date | Mintage | VF20 | XF40 | MS60 | MS63 | MS65 |
|---|---|---|---|---|---|---|
| 2013 | — | PF65 525 | | | | |

## MINT SETS

| KM# | Date | Mintage | Identification | Issue Price | Mkt Val |
|---|---|---|---|---|---|
| MS58 | 2001 (5) | 20,000 | KM#65, 66, 73, 76, 77 plus 1865 coin design medal | 18.00 | 22.50 |
| MS59 | 2001 (5) | — | KM#65, 66, 73, 76, 77, medal (Johan Vilhelm Snellman) | — | 22.50 |
| MS60 | 2002 (8) | 130,000 | KM#98-105, Church medal | — | 40.00 |
| MS61 | 2003 (8) | 170,000 | KM#98-105, Golden Medal, goldpanning in Lappland | — | 37.50 |
| MS62 | 2002 (8) | 2,000 | KM#98-105, Baby | — | 100 |
| MS63 | 2003 (9) | 8,000 | KM#98-105, Silver medal, goldpanning in Lappland | — | 125 |
| MS64 | 2003 (8) | 15,000 | KM#98-105, Ice Hockey | — | 60.00 |
| MS65 | 2003 (9) | 3,000 | KM#98-105, medal and teddy bear | — | — |
| MS66 | 2003 (9) | 5,000 | KM#98-105, Baby, medal | — | 37.50 |
| MS67 | 2003 (9) | 4,000 | KM#98-105, Rose, medal | — | 60.00 |
| MS68 | 2003 (9) | 30,000 | KM#98-105, Christmas, golden medal | — | 37.50 |
| MS69 | 2004 (8) | 55,000 | KM#98-105, Euro zone, medal | — | 40.00 |
| MS70 | 2004 (8) | 5,000 | KM#98-105, 114, baby, medal | — | 35.00 |
| MS71 | 2004 (8) | 18,000 | KM#98-105, Tove Jansson, 90th Birthday | — | 42.50 |
| MS72 | 2004 (9) | 4,000 | KM#98-105, Music, medal | — | 60.00 |
| MS73 | 2005 (8) | 40,000 | KM#98-105, Wildlife, medal | — | 42.50 |
| MS74 | 2005 (9) | 30,000 | KM#98-105, 118, Paraolympics | — | 55.00 |
| MS75 | 2005 (9) | 4,000 | KM#98-105, Baby, medal | — | 45.00 |
| MS76 | 2005 (9) | 3,000 | KM#98-105, Music, medal | — | 55.00 |
| MS77 | 2006 (9) | 40,000 | KM#98-105, 119, Lighthouse | — | 45.00 |
| MS78 | 2006 (9) | 20,000 | KM#98-105, 125, Centennial of Parlament reform, suffrage | — | 55.00 |
| MS79 | 2006 (9) | 3,200 | KM#98-105, Music, medal | — | 55.00 |
| MS80 | 2006 (9) | 4,000 | KM#98-105, Wedding, medal | — | 55.00 |
| MS81 | 2006 (9) | 4,600 | KM#98-105, Baby, medal | — | 55.00 |
| MS82 | 2006 (9) | 4,000 | KM#98-105, Aland | — | 45.00 |
| MS83 | 2007 (9) | 30,000 | KM#98-100, 126-130, Lighthouse, medal | — | 30.00 |
| MS84 | 2007 (9) | 3,000 | KM#98-100, 126-130, Rose, medal | — | 70.00 |
| MS85 | 2007 (9) | 3,000 | KM#98-100, 126-130, Marriage, medal | — | 55.00 |
| MS86 | 2007 (9) | 4,000 | KM#98-100, 126-130, Baby, medal | — | 65.00 |
| MS87 | 2007 (10) | 20,000 | KM#98-100, 126-130, 138, European Song Festival, medal | — | 45.00 |
| MS88 | 2007 (8) | 4,000 | KM#98-100, 126-130, Aland | — | 40.00 |
| MS89 | 2007 (9) | 20,000 | KM#98-100, 126-130, 139, Swans | — | 50.00 |
| MS90 | 2007 (3) | — | KM98-100 | — | 10.00 |
| MS91 | 2008 (9) | 30,000 | KM#98-100, 126-130, Lighthouse, medal | — | 35.00 |
| MS92 | 2008 (9) | 3,000 | KM#98-100, 126-130, Rose, medal | — | 55.00 |
| MS93 | 2008 (9) | 3,000 | KM#98-100, 126-130, Wedding, medal | — | 45.00 |
| MS94 | 2008 (9) | 4,000 | KM#98-100, 126-130, Baby, medal | — | 50.00 |
| MS95 | 2008 (9) | 4,000 | KM#98-100, 126-130, Aland medal | — | 25.00 |
| MS96 | 2008 (9) | 30,000 | KM#98-100, 126-130, 143 | — | 25.00 |
| MS97 | 2009 (10) | 20,000 | KM#98-100, 126-130, 149 plus medal | — | 40.00 |
| MS98 | 2009 (10) | 30,000 | KM#98-100, 126-130, 149 plus lighthouse medal | — | 45.00 |
| MS99 | 2009 (10) | 2,200 | KM#98-100, 126-130, 149 Aland | — | 40.00 |
| MS100 | 2009 (10) | 1,500 | KM#98-100, 126-130, 149, Wedding, plus medal | — | 45.00 |
| MS101 | 2009 (10) | 3,000 | KM#98-100, 126-130, 149, Music plus medal | — | 45.00 |
| MS102 | 2009 (10) | 4,000 | KM#98-100, 126-130, 149, Baby, plus medal | — | 45.00 |
| MS103 | 2010 (10) | 30,000 | KM#98-100, 126-130, 154 and Lighthouse medal | — | 45.00 |
| MS104 | 2010 (10) | 15,000 | KM#98-100, 126-130, 154 plus Biology medal | — | 45.00 |
| MS105 | 2010 (10) | 2,500 | KM#98-100, 126-130, 154 plus Music medal | — | 45.00 |
| MS106 | 2010 (10) | 2 | KM#98-100, 126-130, 154 plus Wedding medal | — | 45.00 |
| MS107 | 2010 (10) | 3,000 | KM#98-100, 126-130, 154 plus Kids medal | — | 45.00 |
| MS108 | 2010 (3) | 7,000 | KM#98-100 | — | 12.50 |
| MS109 | 2011 (10) | 20,000 | KM#98-100, 126-130, 163 plus Lighthouse medal | — | 45.00 |
| MS110 | 2011 (10) | 15,000 | KM#98-100, 126-130, 163 plus Nature medal | — | 45.00 |
| MS111 | 2011 (10) | 3,000 | KM#98-100, 126-130, 163 plus Kids medal | — | 45.00 |
| MS112 | 2011 (10) | 2,500 | KM#98-100, 126-130, 163 plus Music medal | — | 45.00 |
| MS113 | 2011 (10) | 2,500 | KM#98-100, 126-130, 163 plus Wedding medal | — | 45.00 |
| MS114 | 2011 (3) | 10,000 | KM#98-100 | — | 15.00 |

## PROOF SETS

| KM# | Date | Mintage | Identification | Issue Price | Mkt Val |
|---|---|---|---|---|---|
| PS9 | 2001 (6) | — | KM#65-66, 73, 76-77, medal (Suomen Markka 1864-2001) | — | 60.00 |
| PS10 | 2002 (9) | 5,000 | KM#98-105, European Union gold medal | — | 550 |
| PS11 | 2002 (9) | 8,000 | KM#98-105, National Theater silver medal | — | 185 |
| PS12 | 2003 (9) | 500 | KM#98-105, Gold medal | — | 350 |
| PS13 | 2003 (9) | 5,000 | KM#98-105, Gold medal with diamond chip | — | 500 |
| PS14 | 2003 (9) | 1,000 | KM#98-105, Silver medal | — | 400 |
| PS15 | 2003 (9) | 8,000 | KM#98-105, Silver medal with diamond chip | — | 150 |
| PS16 | 2004 (10) | 5,000 | KM#98-105, 114, Silver medal | — | 225 |
| PS17 | 2005 (10) | 3,000 | KM#98-105, 118, Silver medal | — | 200 |
| PS18 | 2005 (4) | 2,005 | KM#118, 121 plus 2 older coins. | — | 225 |
| PS19 | 2006 (10) | 3,300 | KM#98-105, 125, Salmon medal | — | 200 |
| PS20 | 2007 (10) | 2,500 | KM#98-100, 126-130, 138, Silver medal. | — | 150 |
| PS21 | 2008 (10) | 2,500 | KM#98-100, 126-130, 143 plus medal | — | 185 |
| PS22 | 2009 (11) | 2,500 | KM#98-100, 126-130, 144, 149, plus medal | — | 225 |
| PS23 | 2010 (10) | 2,000 | KM#98-100, 126-130, 154 plus medal | — | 200 |
| PS24 | 2011 (10) | — | KM#98-100, 126-130, 163 plus medal | — | 200 |
| PS25 | 2010 (3) | 7,000 | KM#150 plus Russian 1863 Kopek and Finnish 1864 Pennia | — | 475 |

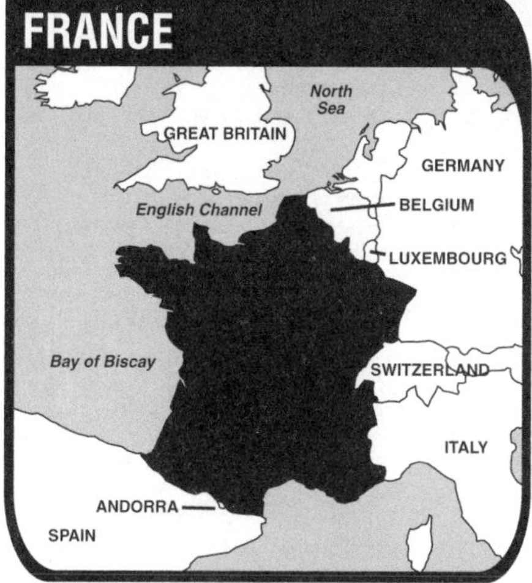


The French Republic, largest of the West European nations, has an area of 210,026 sq. mi. (547,030 sq. km.) and a population of 58.1 million. Capital: Paris. Agriculture, manufacturing, tourist industry and financial services are the most important elements of France's diversified economy. Textiles and clothing, steel products, machinery and transportation equipment, chemicals, pharmaceuticals, nuclear electricity, agricultural products and wine are exported.

**ENGRAVER GENERALS' PRIVY MARKS**

| Mark | Desc. | Date | Name |
|---|---|---|---|
| | Horseshoe | 2000-2002 | Gérard Buquoi |
| | SL Heart-shaped monogram | 2002-2003 | Serge Levet |
| | French horn w/fish in water | 2003-2010 | Hubert Larivière |

**MINT DIRECTORS' PRIVY MARKS**

Some modern coins struck from dies produced at the Paris Mint have the 'A' mint mark. In the absence of a mint mark, the cornucopia privy mark serves to attribute a coin to Paris design.

**A - Paris, Central Mint**

# MODERN REPUBLICS

1870-present

## REFORM COINAGE

1 Old Franc = 1 New Centime;
100 New Centimes = 1 New Franc

### KM# 928 CENTIME

1.65 g., Stainless Steel, 15 mm. **Obv:** Cursive legend surrounds grain sprig **Rev:** Cursive denomination, date at top **Edge:** Plain **Mint:** Paris **Note:** 1991-1993 dated coins, non-Proof, exist in both coin and medal alignment. Values given here are for medal alignment examples. Pieces struck in coin alignment have been traded for as much as $50.00.

| Date | Mintage | VF20 | XF40 | MS60 | MS63 | MS65 |
|---|---|---|---|---|---|---|
| 2001 In sets only | — | — | — | — | — | 1.50 |
| 2001 | — | PF65 2.00 | | | | |

### KM# 928a CENTIME

2.50 g., 0.750 Gold 0.0603 oz. AGW **Obv:** Cursive legend surrounds grain sprig, medallic alignment **Rev:** Cursive denomination, date above, medallic alignment **Edge:** Plain **Mint:** Paris **Note:** Last Centime.

| Date | Mintage | VF20 | XF40 | MS60 | MS63 | MS65 |
|---|---|---|---|---|---|---|
| 2001 | — | — | — | — | — | 250 |

### KM# 933 5 CENTIMES

2.00 g., Aluminum-Bronze, 17 mm. **Obv:** Liberty bust left **Rev:** Denomination above date, grain sprig below, laurel branch at left **Edge:** Plain **Mint:** Paris **Note:** 1991-1993 dated coins, non-Proof exist in both coin and medal alignment.

| Date | Mintage | VF20 | XF40 | MS60 | MS63 | MS65 |
|---|---|---|---|---|---|---|
| 2001 In sets only | — | — | — | — | — | 2.50 |
| 2001 | — | PF65 1.00 | | | | |

### KM# 929 10 CENTIMES

3.00 g., Aluminum-Bronze, 20 mm. **Obv:** Liberty bust left **Rev:** Denomination above date, grain sprig below, laurel branch at left **Edge:** Plain **Mint:** Paris **Note:** Without mint mark. 1991-1993 dated coins, non-Proof, exist in both coin and medal alignment.

| Date | Mintage | VF20 | XF40 | MS60 | MS63 | MS65 |
|---|---|---|---|---|---|---|
| 2001 In sets only | — | — | — | — | — | 3.00 |
| 2001 | — | PF65 1.00 | | | | |

### KM# 930 20 CENTIMES

4.00 g., Aluminum-Bronze, 23.5 mm. **Obv:** Liberty bust left **Rev:** Denomination above date, grain sprig below, laurel branch at left **Edge:** Plain **Mint:** Paris **Note:** Without mint mark. 1991-1993 dated coins, non-Proof, exist in both coin and medal alignment.

| Date | Mintage | VF20 | XF40 | MS60 | MS63 | MS65 |
|---|---|---|---|---|---|---|
| 2001 In sets only | — | — | — | — | — | 3.00 |
| 2001 | — | PF65 1.00 | | | | |

### KM# 931.1 1/2 FRANC

4.50 g., Nickel, 19.5 mm. **Obv:** The Seed Sower **Rev:** Laurel divides denomination and date **Edge:** Reeded **Mint:** Paris **Note:** Without mint mark.

| Date | Mintage | VF20 | XF40 | MS60 | MS63 | MS65 |
|---|---|---|---|---|---|---|
| 2001 In sets only | — | — | — | 1.00 | 2.00 | 3.00 |

### KM# 931.2 1/2 FRANC

4.50 g., Nickel, 19.5 mm. **Obv:** Modified sower, engraver's signature: "O. ROTY" preceded by "D'AP **Rev:** Laurel divides date and denomination **Edge:** Plain

| Date | Mintage | VF20 | XF40 | MS60 | MS63 | MS65 |
|---|---|---|---|---|---|---|
| 2001 | — | — | — | 0.25 | 0.40 | 0.60 |
| 2001 | — | PF65 1.50 | | | | |

### KM# 925.1 FRANC

6.00 g., Nickel, 24 mm. **Obv:** The Seed Sower **Rev:** Laurel branch divides denomination and date **Edge:** Reeded **Mint:** Paris **Note:** Without mint mark.

| Date | Mintage | VF20 | XF40 | MS60 | MS63 | MS65 |
|---|---|---|---|---|---|---|
| 2001 | 20,000,000 | — | — | 0.25 | 0.40 | 0.60 |

### KM# 925.2 FRANC

6.00 g., Nickel, 24 mm. **Obv:** Modified sower, engraver's signature: O. ROTY, preceded by D'AP **Rev:** Laurel divides date and denomination **Edge:** Plain

| Date | Mintage | VF20 | XF40 | MS60 | MS63 | MS65 |
|---|---|---|---|---|---|---|
| 2001 | — | — | — | 0.25 | 0.40 | 0.60 |
| 2001 | — | PF65 2.50 | | | | |

### KM# 925.1a FRANC

8.00 g., 0.750 Gold 0.1929 oz. AGW, 24 mm. **Obv:** The Seed Sower **Rev:** Laurel divides date and denomination **Edge:** Reeded **Mint:** Paris **Note:** Medallic alignment.

| Date | Mintage | VF20 | XF40 | MS60 | MS63 | MS65 |
|---|---|---|---|---|---|---|
| 2001 | Est. 9941 | — | — | 234 | 285 | 365 |

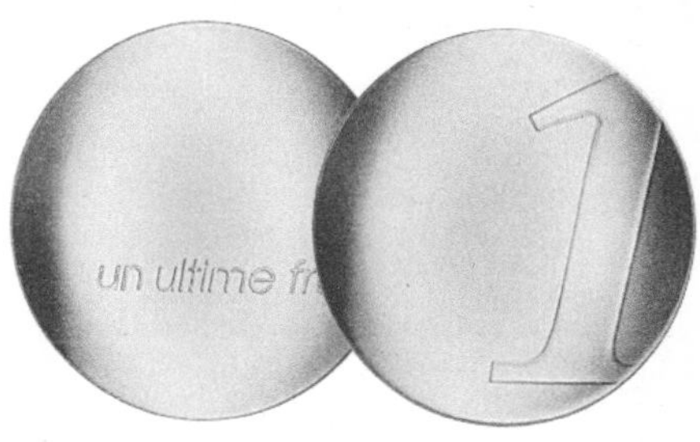

### KM# 1290 FRANC

17.77 g., 0.980 Silver 0.5599 oz. ASW **Subject:** The Last Franc **Obv:** Legend on polished field **Obv. Legend:** UN ULTIME FRANC **Rev:** Number "1" on polished field **Edge Lettering:** REPUBLIQUE FRANCAISE STARCK LIBERTE EGALITE FRATERNITE (2001). **Mint:** Paris **Note:** The coin is intentionally warped and the edge inscription is very faint. Struck at Paris Mint.

| Date | Mintage | VF20 | XF40 | MS60 | MS63 | MS65 |
|---|---|---|---|---|---|---|
| 2001 Matte | 49,838 | PF63 150 | | | | |

### KM# 1290a FRANC

26.10 g., 0.750 Gold 0.6294 oz. AGW **Subject:** The Last Franc **Obv:** Legend on polished field **Obv. Legend:** UN ULTIME FRANC **Rev:** Number "1" on polished field **Edge Lettering:** REPUBLIQUE FRANCAISE. STARCK. LIBERTE. EGALITE. FRATERNITE (cornucopia) 2001 **Mint:** Paris **Note:** This coin has an intentionally warped surface and the edge inscription is very weak.

| Date | Mintage | VF20 | XF40 | MS60 | MS63 | MS65 |
|---|---|---|---|---|---|---|
| 2001 Matte | 4,963 | — | — | 1,250 | 1,700 | — |

### KM# 942.1 2 FRANCS

7.50 g., Nickel, 26.5 mm. **Obv:** The Seed Sower **Rev:** Denomination on branches, date below **Edge:** Wide reeded

| Date | Mintage | VF20 | XF40 | MS60 | MS63 | MS65 |
|---|---|---|---|---|---|---|
| 2001 Bee | — | — | — | 0.50 | 0.75 | 1.25 |

### KM# 942.2 2 FRANCS

7.50 g., Nickel, 26.5 mm. **Obv:** The Seed Sower **Rev:** Denomination on branches, date below **Edge:** Plain

| Date | Mintage | VF20 | XF40 | MS60 | MS63 | MS65 |
|---|---|---|---|---|---|---|
| 2001 | — | — | — | 0.50 | 0.75 | 1.25 |
| 2001 | — | PF65 3.50 | | | | |

### KM# 926a.1 5 FRANCS

10.00 g., Nickel Clad Copper-Nickel, 29 mm. **Obv:** The Seed Sower **Rev:** Branches divide denomination and date **Edge:** Reeded **Mint:** Paris

| Date | Mintage | VF20 | XF40 | MS60 | MS63 | MS65 |
|---|---|---|---|---|---|---|
| 2001 In sets only | — | — | — | 3.50 | 5.00 | 7.50 |

### KM# 926a.2 5 FRANCS

10.00 g., Nickel Clad Copper-Nickel, 29 mm. **Obv:** Modified sower, engraver's signature: "O. ROTY" preceded by "D'AP **Rev:** Branches divide date and denomination **Edge:** Plain **Mint:** Paris

| Date | Mintage | VF20 | XF40 | MS60 | MS63 | MS65 |
|---|---|---|---|---|---|---|
| 2001 | — | PF65 6.50 | | | | |
| 2001 | — | — | — | 1.25 | 1.65 | 2.50 |

**KM# 1309 5 FRANCS**
12.00 g., 0.900 Silver 0.3472 oz. ASW, 29 mm. **Subject:** Last Year of the Franc **Obv:** The Seed Sower **Rev:** Denomination and date **Edge:** Lettered **Edge Lettering:** * LIBERTY * EGALITE * FRATERNITE * **Mint:** Paris

| Date | Mintage | VF20 | XF40 | MS60 | MS63 | MS65 |
|---|---|---|---|---|---|---|
| 2001 | 25,000 | — | — | — | 22.50 | 25.00 |

**KM# 1265.1 6.55957 FRANCS**
13.00 g., 0.900 Silver 0.3762 oz. ASW **Subject:** Last Year of the French Franc **Obv:** French and other European euro currency equivalents **Rev:** Europa allegorical portrait, date below, "last year of the franc" logo after the date **Edge:** Reeded **Mint:** Paris

| Date | Mintage | VF20 | XF40 | MS60 | MS63 | MS65 |
|---|---|---|---|---|---|---|
| 2001 | — | — | — | — | 25.00 | 50.00 |

**KM# 1265.2 6.55957 FRANCS**
22.20 g., 0.900 Silver 0.6424 oz. ASW **Obv:** French and other European euro currency equivalents **Rev:** Europa allegorical portrait, date below, "last year of the franc" logo after the date **Edge:** Plain

| Date | Mintage | VF20 | XF40 | MS60 | MS63 | MS65 |
|---|---|---|---|---|---|---|
| 2001 | Est. 10000 | **PF63** 60.00 | **PF65** 65.00 | | | |

**KM# 1276 6.55957 FRANCS**
22.20 g., 0.900 Silver 0.6424 oz. ASW, 36 mm. **Subject:** Mottos **Obv:** Denomination **Rev:** FRATERNITE in red letters **Edge:** Reeded **Mint:** Paris

| Date | Mintage | VF20 | XF40 | MS60 | MS63 | MS65 |
|---|---|---|---|---|---|---|
| 2001 | 2,171 | **PF63** 50.00 | **PF65** 55.00 | | | |

**KM# 1277 6.55957 FRANCS**
22.20 g., 0.900 Silver 0.6424 oz. ASW, 36 mm. **Subject:** Mottos **Obv:** Denomination **Rev:** EGALITE in white letters

| Date | Mintage | VF20 | XF40 | MS60 | MS63 | MS65 |
|---|---|---|---|---|---|---|
| 2001 | 2,190 | **PF63** 50.00 | **PF65** 55.00 | | | |

**KM# 1278 6.55957 FRANCS**
22.20 g., 0.900 Silver 0.6424 oz. ASW, 36 mm. **Subject:** Mottos **Obv:** Denomination **Rev:** LIBERTE in red letters

| Date | Mintage | VF20 | XF40 | MS60 | MS63 | MS65 |
|---|---|---|---|---|---|---|
| 2001 | 2,259 | **PF63** 50.00 | **PF65** 55.00 | | | |

**KM# 964.2 10 FRANCS**
Aluminum-Bronze, 23 mm. **Obv:** Winged figure divides RF **Rev:** Patterned denomination above date **Edge:** Plain

| Date | Mintage | VF20 | XF40 | MS60 | MS63 | MS65 |
|---|---|---|---|---|---|---|
| 2001 | — | **PF65** 15.00 | | | | |
| 2001 | — | — | — | 4.00 | 6.00 | 7.50 |

**KM# 1268 10 FRANCS**
22.20 g., 0.900 Silver 0.6424 oz. ASW, 36 mm. **Subject:** Monuments of France - Palace of Versailles **Obv:** Stylized French map **Rev:** 1/2 bust of Louis XIV at right, internal and external palace views at left **Edge:** Plain **Mint:** Paris

| Date | Mintage | VF20 | XF40 | MS60 | MS63 | MS65 |
|---|---|---|---|---|---|---|
| 2001 | Est. 2561 | **PF63** 50.00 | **PF65** 55.00 | | | |

**KM# 1270 10 FRANCS**
22.20 g., 0.900 Silver 0.6424 oz. ASW, 36 mm. **Subject:** Monuments of France - Arch of Triumph **Obv:** Stylized French map **Rev:** Arch of Triumph on the Champs Elysees partial close up and aerial views

| Date | Mintage | VF20 | XF40 | MS60 | MS63 | MS65 |
|---|---|---|---|---|---|---|
| 2001 | Est. 2882 | **PF63** 50.00 | **PF65** 55.00 | | | |

**KM# 1272 10 FRANCS**
22.20 g., 0.900 Silver 0.6424 oz. ASW, 1272 mm. **Subject:** Monuments of France - Notre Dame Cathedral **Obv:** Stylized French map **Rev:** Gargoyle at left, cathedral views at right

| Date | Mintage | VF20 | XF40 | MS60 | MS63 | MS65 |
|---|---|---|---|---|---|---|
| 2001 | Est. 2877 | **PF63** 50.00 | **PF65** 55.00 | | | |

**KM# 1274 10 FRANCS**
22.20 g., 0.900 Silver 0.6424 oz. ASW, 36 mm. **Subject:** Monuments of France - Eiffel Tower **Obv:** Stylized French map **Rev:** Two tower views

| Date | Mintage | VF20 | XF40 | MS60 | MS63 | MS65 |
|---|---|---|---|---|---|---|
| 2001 | Est. 3888 | **PF63** 45.00 | **PF65** 50.00 | | | |

**KM# 1008.2 20 FRANCS**
9.00 g., Tri-Metallic Copper-Aluminum-Nickel center, Nickel inner ring, Copper-Aluminum-Nickel outer ring, 27 mm. **Obv:** Mont St. Michel **Rev:** Patterned denomination above date **Edge:** 5 milled bands, reeded or plain

| Date | Mintage | VF20 | XF40 | MS60 | MS63 | MS65 |
|---|---|---|---|---|---|---|
| 2001 | — | **PF65** 25.00 | | | | |
| 2001 | — | — | — | 6.00 | 8.00 | 10.00 |

**KM# 1266 65.5997 FRANCS**
8.45 g., 0.920 Gold 0.2499 oz. AGW **Subject:** Last Year of the French Franc **Obv:** French and other European euro currency equivalents **Rev:** Europa allegorical portrait, date below, "last year of the franc" logo after the date **Edge:** Reeded **Mint:** Paris

| Date | Mintage | VF20 | XF40 | MS60 | MS63 | MS65 |
|---|---|---|---|---|---|---|
| 2001 | 3,000 | **PF65** 600 | | | | |

**KM# 1269 100 FRANCS**
17.00 g., 0.920 Gold 0.5028 oz. AGW **Subject:** Palace of Versailles **Obv:** Stylized French map **Rev:** Louis XIV with internal and external palace views **Edge:** Plain **Mint:** Paris

| Date | Mintage | VF20 | XF40 | MS60 | MS63 | MS65 |
|---|---|---|---|---|---|---|
| 2001 | 105 | **PF63** 875 | **PF65** 900 | | | |

**KM# 1271 100 FRANCS**
17.00 g., 0.920 Gold 0.5028 oz. AGW **Obv:** Champs-Elysees **Rev:** Arch of Triumph partial close up and aerial views

| Date | Mintage | VF20 | XF40 | MS60 | MS63 | MS65 |
|---|---|---|---|---|---|---|
| 2001 | 115 | **PF63** 875 | **PF65** 900 | | | |

**KM# 1273 100 FRANCS**
17.00 g., 0.920 Gold 0.5028 oz. AGW **Obv:** Notre-Dame Cathedral **Rev:** Gargoyle and cathedral views

| Date | Mintage | VF20 | XF40 | MS60 | MS63 | MS65 |
|---|---|---|---|---|---|---|
| 2001 | 116 | **PF63** 875 | **PF65** 900 | | | |

**KM# 1275 100 FRANCS**
17.00 g., 0.920 Gold 0.5028 oz. AGW **Obv:** Eiffel Tower **Rev:** Two tower views

| Date | Mintage | VF20 | XF40 | MS60 | MS63 | MS65 |
|---|---|---|---|---|---|---|
| 2001 | 170 | **PF63** 875 | **PF65** 900 | | | |

**KM# 1994 100 FRANCS**
155.55 g., 0.999 Gold 4.996 oz. AGW **Obv:** Cruved cross with coins **Rev:** Europa facing at right, flags at left **Mint:** Paris

| Date | Mintage | VF20 | XF40 | MS60 | MS63 | MS65 |
|---|---|---|---|---|---|---|
| 2003 | 99 | **PF65** 9,500 | | | | |

**KM# 2001 100 FRANCS**
155.55 g., 0.999 Gold 4.996 oz. AGW **Subject:** Athletic World Championships **Obv:** Winner Podium before buildings **Rev:** Runner **Mint:** Paris

| Date | Mintage | VF20 | XF40 | MS60 | MS63 | MS65 |
|---|---|---|---|---|---|---|
| 2003 | 369 | **PF65** 10,000 | | | | |

**KM# 2002 100 FRANCS**
155.55 g., 0.999 Gold 4.996 oz. AGW **Subject:** Louisana Purchase, 200th Anniversary **Obv:** Thomas Jefferson and Napoleon Bonaparte with map of purchase **Rev:** Celebration of Lousiana: plantation mansion, jazz, riverboat **Mint:** Paris

| Date | Mintage | VF20 | XF40 | MS60 | MS63 | MS65 |
|---|---|---|---|---|---|---|
| 2003 | 99 | **PF65** 10,000 | | | | |

**KM# 1267 655.957 FRANCS**
31.10 g., 0.999 Gold 0.999 oz. AGW **Subject:** Last Year of the French Franc **Obv:** French and other European euro currency equivalents **Rev:** Europa allegorical portrait, date below, "last year of the franc" logo after the date **Edge:** Plain **Mint:** Paris

| Date | Mintage | VF20 | XF40 | MS60 | MS63 | MS65 |
|---|---|---|---|---|---|---|
| 2001 | 2,000 | **PF65** 2,100 | | | | |

**KM# 1267.1 655.957 FRANCS**
155.52 g., 0.999 Gold 4.995 oz. AGW **Obv:** French and other European euro currency equivalents **Rev:** Europa allegorical portrait, date below, "last year of the franc" after the date **Edge:** Plain

| Date | Mintage | VF20 | XF40 | MS60 | MS63 | MS65 |
|---|---|---|---|---|---|---|
| 2001 | 99 | **PF65** 9,500 | | | | |

**KM# 1279 655.957 FRANCS**
17.00 g., 0.920 Gold 0.5028 oz. AGW, 29 mm. **Subject:** Motto Series **Obv:** Denomination **Rev:** FRATERNITE **Edge:** Reeded **Mint:** Paris

| Date | Mintage | VF20 | XF40 | MS60 | MS63 | MS65 |
|---|---|---|---|---|---|---|
| 2001 | 62 | **PF63** 1,000 | **PF65** 1,100 | | | |

**KM# 1280 655.957 FRANCS**
17.00 g., 0.920 Gold 0.5028 oz. AGW, 29 mm. **Subject:** Motto Series **Obv:** Denomination **Rev:** EGALITE

| Date | Mintage | VF20 | XF40 | MS60 | MS63 | MS65 |
|---|---|---|---|---|---|---|
| 2001 | 64 | PF63 1,000 | PF65 1,100 | | | |

**KM# 1281 655.957 FRANCS**
17.00 g., 0.920 Gold 0.5028 oz. AGW, 29 mm. **Subject:** Motto Series **Obv:** Denomination **Rev:** LIBERTE

| Date | Mintage | VF20 | XF40 | MS60 | MS63 | MS65 |
|---|---|---|---|---|---|---|
| 2001 | 63 | PF63 1,000 | PF65 1,100 | | | |

## EURO COINAGE

European Union Issues

**KM# 1282 EURO CENT**
2.27 g., Copper Plated Steel, 16.3 mm. **Obv:** Human face **Rev:** Denomination and globe **Edge:** Plain **Mint:** Paris

| Date | Mintage | VF20 | XF40 | MS60 | MS63 | MS65 |
|---|---|---|---|---|---|---|
| 2001 | 300,681,580 | — | — | 0.35 | 0.50 | 0.75 |
| 2001 | 15,000 | PF65 10.00 | | | | |
| 2002 | 200,000 | — | — | — | — | 10.00 |
| 2002 | 21,453 | PF65 8.00 | | | | |
| 2003 | 160,017,000 | — | — | 1.00 | 1.50 | 2.00 |
| 2003 | 40,000 | PF65 8.00 | | | | |
| 2004 | 400,032,000 | — | — | 0.35 | 0.50 | 0.75 |
| 2004 | 20,000 | PF65 10.00 | | | | |
| 2005 | 240,320,000 | — | — | 0.35 | 0.50 | 0.75 |
| 2005 | 10,000 | PF65 12.00 | | | | |
| 2006 | 343,078,000 | — | — | 0.35 | 0.50 | 0.75 |
| 2006 | 10,000 | PF65 12.00 | | | | |
| 2007 | 300,058,000 | — | — | 0.35 | 0.50 | 0.75 |
| 2007 | 7,500 | PF65 14.00 | | | | |
| 2008 | 462,757,000 | — | — | 0.35 | 0.50 | 0.75 |
| 2008 | 7,500 | PF65 14.00 | | | | |
| 2009 | 404,050,500 | — | — | 0.35 | 0.50 | 0.75 |
| 2009 | 7,500 | PF65 14.00 | | | | |
| 2010 | 336,000,000 | — | — | 0.35 | 0.50 | 0.75 |
| 2010 | — | PF65 15.00 | | | | |
| 2011 | 320,118,000 | — | — | 0.35 | 0.50 | 0.75 |
| 2011 | — | PF65 15.00 | | | | |
| 2012 | 358,566,000 | — | — | 0.35 | 0.50 | 0.75 |
| 2012 | — | PF65 15.00 | | | | |
| 2013 | — | — | — | 0.35 | 0.50 | 0.75 |
| 2013 | — | PF65 15.00 | | | | |
| 2014 | — | — | — | 0.35 | 0.50 | 0.75 |
| 2014 | — | PF65 14.00 | | | | |

**KM# 1283 2 EURO CENT**
3.03 g., Copper Plated Steel, 18.7 mm. **Obv:** Human face **Rev:** Denomination and globe **Edge:** Grooved **Mint:** Paris

| Date | Mintage | VF20 | XF40 | MS60 | MS63 | MS65 |
|---|---|---|---|---|---|---|
| 2001 | 249,101,580 | — | — | 0.50 | 0.75 | 1.00 |
| 2001 | 15,000 | PF65 10.00 | | | | |
| 2002 In sets only | 100,000 | — | — | — | — | 12.50 |
| 2002 | 21,453 | PF65 8.00 | | | | |
| 2003 | 160,175,000 | — | — | 1.25 | 2.00 | 2.50 |
| 2003 | 40,000 | PF65 8.00 | | | | |
| 2004 | 300,024,000 | — | — | — | 1.00 | 1.25 |
| 2004 | 20,000 | PF65 10.00 | | | | |
| 2005 | 2,603,202,000 | — | — | — | 1.00 | 1.25 |
| 2005 | 10,000 | PF65 12.00 | | | | |
| 2006 | 283,278,000 | — | — | — | 1.00 | 1.25 |
| 2006 | 10,000 | PF65 12.00 | | | | |
| 2007 | 213,258,000 | — | — | — | 1.00 | 1.25 |
| 2007 | 7,500 | PF65 14.00 | | | | |
| 2008 | 386,557,000 | — | — | — | 1.00 | 1.25 |
| 2008 | 7,500 | PF65 14.00 | | | | |
| 2009 | 317,050,500 | — | — | — | 1.00 | 1.25 |
| 2009 | 7,500 | PF65 14.00 | | | | |
| 2010 | 277,000,000 | — | — | — | 1.00 | 1.25 |
| 2010 | — | PF65 14.00 | | | | |
| 2011 | 250,128,000 | — | — | — | 1.00 | 1.25 |
| 2011 | — | PF65 14.00 | | | | |
| 2012 | 277,668,000 | — | — | — | 1.00 | 1.25 |
| 2012 | — | PF65 14.00 | | | | |
| 2013 | — | — | — | — | 1.00 | 1.25 |
| 2013 | — | PF65 14.00 | | | | |
| 2014 | — | — | — | — | 1.00 | 1.25 |
| 2014 | — | PF65 14.00 | | | | |

**KM# 1284 5 EURO CENT**
3.86 g., Copper Plated Steel, 21.2 mm. **Obv:** Human face **Rev:** Denomination and globe **Edge:** Plain **Mint:** Paris

| Date | Mintage | VF20 | XF40 | MS60 | MS63 | MS65 |
|---|---|---|---|---|---|---|
| 2001 | 217,324,477 | — | — | 0.75 | 1.25 | 1.50 |
| 2001 | 15,000 | PF65 12.00 | | | | |
| 2002 | 186,400,000 | — | — | 0.75 | 1.25 | 1.50 |
| 2002 | 21,453 | PF65 10.00 | | | | |
| 2003 | 101,175,000 | — | — | 1.00 | 1.50 | 2.00 |
| 2003 | 40,000 | PF65 10.00 | | | | |
| 2004 | 60,162,000 | — | — | — | 1.25 | 1.50 |
| 2004 | 20,000 | PF65 12.00 | | | | |
| 2005 | 20,320,000 | — | — | — | 1.25 | 1.50 |
| 2005 | 10,000 | PF65 14.00 | | | | |
| 2006 | 132,078,000 | — | — | — | 1.25 | 1.50 |
| 2006 | 10,000 | PF65 14.00 | | | | |
| 2007 | 130,058,000 | — | — | — | 1.25 | 1.50 |
| 2007 | 7,500 | PF65 16.00 | | | | |
| 2008 | 218,257,000 | — | — | — | 1.25 | 1.50 |
| 2008 | 7,500 | PF65 16.00 | | | | |
| 2009 | 184,550,500 | — | — | — | 1.25 | 1.50 |
| 2009 | 7,500 | PF65 16.00 | | | | |
| 2010 | 184,000,000 | — | — | — | 1.25 | 1.50 |
| 2010 | — | PF65 16.00 | | | | |
| 2011 | 144,900,000 | — | — | — | 1.25 | 1.50 |
| 2011 | — | PF65 16.00 | | | | |
| 2012 | 139,104,000 | — | — | — | 1.25 | 1.50 |
| 2012 | — | PF65 16.00 | | | | |
| 2013 | — | — | — | — | 1.25 | 1.50 |
| 2013 | — | PF65 16.00 | | | | |
| 2014 | — | — | — | — | 1.25 | 1.50 |
| 2014 | — | PF65 16.00 | | | | |

**KM# 1285 10 EURO CENT**
4.07 g., Brass, 19.7 mm. **Obv:** The seed sower divides date and RF **Rev:** Denomination and map **Edge:** Reeded **Mint:** Paris

| Date | Mintage | VF20 | XF40 | MS60 | MS63 | MS65 |
|---|---|---|---|---|---|---|
| 2001 | 144,513,261 | — | — | 1.25 | 2.00 | 2.50 |
| 2001 | 15,000 | PF65 12.00 | | | | |
| 2002 | 206,700,000 | — | — | 0.75 | 1.25 | 1.50 |
| 2002 | 21,453 | PF65 10.00 | | | | |
| 2003 | 180,875,000 | — | — | 1.25 | 2.00 | 2.50 |
| 2003 | 40,000 | PF65 10.00 | | | | |
| 2004 | 5,000,000 | — | — | — | 1.50 | 2.00 |
| 2004 In sets only | 140,000 | — | — | — | — | 6.00 |
| 2004 | 20,000 | PF65 12.00 | | | | |
| 2005 | 45,120,000 | — | — | — | 1.50 | 2.00 |
| 2005 | 10,000 | PF65 14.00 | | | | |
| 2006 | 60,278,000 | — | — | — | 1.50 | 2.00 |
| 2006 | 10,000 | PF65 14.00 | | | | |
| 2007 | 90,158,000 | — | — | — | 1.50 | 2.00 |
| 2007 | 7,500 | PF65 14.00 | | | | |
| 2008 | 178,757,000 | — | — | — | 1.50 | 2.00 |
| 2008 | 7,500 | PF65 14.00 | | | | |
| 2009 | 142,550,500 | — | — | — | 1.50 | 2.00 |
| 2009 | 7,500 | PF65 14.00 | | | | |
| 2010 | — | — | — | — | 1.50 | 2.00 |
| 2010 | — | PF65 14.00 | | | | |
| 2011 | — | — | — | — | 1.50 | 2.00 |
| 2011 | — | PF65 14.00 | | | | |
| 2012 | — | — | — | — | 1.50 | 2.00 |
| 2012 | — | PF65 14.00 | | | | |
| 2013 | — | — | — | — | 1.50 | 2.00 |
| 2013 | — | PF65 14.00 | | | | |
| 2014 | — | — | — | — | 1.50 | 2.00 |
| 2014 | — | PF65 14.00 | | | | |

**KM# 1410 10 EURO CENT**
4.07 g., Brass, 19.7 mm. **Obv:** Sower **Rev:** Relief map of Western Europe, stars, lines and value **Edge:** Reeded **Mint:** Paris

**KM# 1286 20 EURO CENT**
5.73 g., Brass, 22.2 mm. **Obv:** The seed sower divides date and RF **Rev:** Denomination and map **Edge:** Notched **Mint:** Paris

| Date | Mintage | VF20 | XF40 | MS60 | MS63 | MS65 |
|---|---|---|---|---|---|---|
| 2001 | 256,342,108 | — | — | 1.00 | 1.50 | 2.00 |
| 2001 | 15,000 | PF65 14.00 | | | | |
| 2002 | 192,100,000 | — | — | 1.00 | 1.50 | 2.00 |
| 2002 | 21,453 | PF65 12.00 | | | | |
| 2003 In sets only | 180,000 | — | — | — | — | 9.50 |
| 2003 | 40,000 | PF65 12.00 | | | | |
| 2004 In sets only | 160,000 | — | — | — | — | 9.50 |
| 2004 | 20,000 | PF65 14.00 | | | | |
| 2005 In sets only | 120,000 | — | — | — | — | 9.50 |
| 2005 | 10,000 | PF65 16.00 | | | | |
| 2006 In sets only | 67,600 | — | — | — | — | 9.50 |
| 2006 | 10,000 | PF65 16.00 | | | | |

**KM# 1411 20 EURO CENT**
5.73 g., Brass, 22.2 mm. **Obv:** Sower **Rev:** Relief map of Western Europe, stars, lines and value **Edge:** Notched **Mint:** Paris

| Date | Mintage | VF20 | XF40 | MS60 | MS63 | MS65 |
|---|---|---|---|---|---|---|
| 2007 | 40,258,000 | — | — | — | 1.50 | 2.00 |
| 2007 | 7,500 | PF65 14.00 | | | | |
| 2008 | 25,557,000 | — | — | — | 1.50 | 2.00 |
| 2008 | 7,500 | PF65 14.00 | | | | |
| 2009 | 82,550,500 | — | — | — | 1.50 | 2.00 |
| 2009 | 7,500 | PF65 14.00 | | | | |
| 2010 | — | — | — | — | 1.50 | 2.00 |
| 2010 | — | PF65 14.00 | | | | |
| 2011 | — | — | — | — | 1.50 | 2.00 |
| 2011 | — | PF65 14.00 | | | | |
| 2012 | — | — | — | — | 1.50 | 2.00 |
| 2012 | — | PF65 14.00 | | | | |
| 2013 | — | — | — | — | 1.50 | 2.00 |
| 2013 | — | PF65 14.00 | | | | |
| 2014 | — | — | — | — | 1.50 | 2.00 |
| 2014 | — | PF65 14.00 | | | | |

**KM# 1293 1/4 EURO**
12.50 g., Aluminum-Bronze, 30 mm. **Subject:** Childrens Design **Obv:** Euro globe with children **Rev:** Denomination and stars **Edge:** Plain **Mint:** Paris

| Date | Mintage | VF20 | XF40 | MS60 | MS63 | MS65 |
|---|---|---|---|---|---|---|
| 2002 | 61,431 | — | — | — | 6.50 | 8.50 |

**KM# 1293a 1/4 EURO**
13.00 g., 0.900 Silver 0.3762 oz. ASW, 30 mm. **Subject:** Childrens Design **Obv:** Euro globe with children **Rev:** Denomination **Edge:** Plain **Mint:** Paris

| Date | Mintage | VF20 | XF40 | MS60 | MS63 | MS65 |
|---|---|---|---|---|---|---|
| 2002 | 10,000 | PF63 45.00 | PF65 50.00 | | | |

**KM# 1300 1/4 EURO**
13.00 g., 0.900 Silver 0.3762 oz. ASW, 30 mm. **Subject:** Europa **Obv:** Eight French euro coin designs **Rev:** Portrait and flags design of 6.55957 francs coin KM-1265 **Edge:** Reeded **Mint:** Paris

| Date | Mintage | VF20 | XF40 | MS60 | MS63 | MS65 |
|---|---|---|---|---|---|---|
| 2002 | 20,000 | — | — | — | 20.00 | 22.00 |

**KM# 1331 1/4 EURO**
3.11 g., 0.999 Gold 0.0999 oz. AGW, 15 mm. **Subject:** Children's Design **Obv:** Euro globe with children **Rev:** Denomination **Edge:** Plain **Mint:** Paris

| Date | Mintage | VF20 | XF40 | MS60 | MS63 | MS65 |
|---|---|---|---|---|---|---|
| 2002 | 5,000 | PF63 185 | PF65 200 | | | |

**KM# 1293a 1/4 EURO**
13.00 g., 0.900 Silver 0.3762 oz. ASW, 30 mm. **Obv:** Euro globe with children **Rev:** Denomination **Edge:** Plain **Mint:** Paris

| Date | Mintage | VF20 | XF40 | MS60 | MS63 | MS65 |
|---|---|---|---|---|---|---|
| 2002 Proof | 10,000 | — | — | — | — | 35.00 |

**KM# 1983 1/4 EURO**
13.00 g., 0.900 Silver 0.3762 oz. ASW, 30 mm. **Obv:** Soccer ball and syylized map of France **Rev:** Two soccer players and stadium plan **Mint:** Paris

| Date | Mintage | VF20 | XF40 | MS60 | MS63 | MS65 |
|---|---|---|---|---|---|---|
| 2002 | 9,033 | — | — | — | — | 35.00 |

**KM# 1350 1/4 EURO**
3.11 g., 0.9999 Gold 0.100 oz. AGW, 15 mm. **Obv:** Obverse design of first one franc coin **Rev:** Reverse design of first one franc coin **Edge:** Plain **Mint:** Paris

| Date | Mintage | VF20 | XF40 | MS60 | MS63 | MS65 |
|---|---|---|---|---|---|---|
| 2003 | 1,143 | PF63 185 | PF65 200 | | | |

**KM# 1991 1/4 EURO**
13.00 g., 0.900 Silver 0.3762 oz. ASW, 30 mm. **Obv:** Curved cross pattern with coins **Rev:** Europa head at right, flags at left **Mint:** Paris

| Date | Mintage | VF20 | XF40 | MS60 | MS63 | MS65 |
|---|---|---|---|---|---|---|
| 2003 | 16,035 | — | — | — | — | 25.00 |

**KM# 1995 1/4 EURO**
13.00 g., 0.900 Silver 0.3762 oz. ASW, 30 mm. **Subject:** Tour de France, 100th Anniversary **Mint:** Paris

| Date | Mintage | VF20 | XF40 | MS60 | MS63 | MS65 |
|---|---|---|---|---|---|---|
| 2003 | 71,257 | — | — | — | — | 20.00 |

**KM# 1372 1/4 EURO**
22.20 g., 0.900 Silver 0.6424 oz. ASW, 37 mm. **Obv:** Samuel de Champlain **Rev:** Sail ship **Edge:** Plain **Mint:** Paris

| Date | Mintage | VF20 | XF40 | MS60 | MS63 | MS65 |
|---|---|---|---|---|---|---|
| 2004 | 15,105 | — | — | — | 27.50 | 32.50 |

**KM# 1390 1/4 EURO**
13.00 g., 0.900 Silver 0.3762 oz. ASW, 30 mm. **Subject:** European Union Expansion **Obv:** Partial face and flags **Rev:** Puzzle map **Edge:** Plain **Mint:** Paris

| Date | Mintage | VF20 | XF40 | MS60 | MS63 | MS65 |
|---|---|---|---|---|---|---|
| 2004 | 10,066 | — | — | — | 22.00 | 25.00 |

**KM# 2017 1/4 EURO**
22.20 g., 0.900 Silver 0.6424 oz. ASW, 37 mm. **Subject:** Chinese - French culture **Obv:** Rooster and dragon **Rev:** Temple of Heaven and Eiffel tower **Mint:** Paris

| Date | Mintage | VF20 | XF40 | MS60 | MS63 | MS65 |
|---|---|---|---|---|---|---|
| 2004 | 10,000 | — | — | — | — | 100 |

**KM# 1402 1/4 EURO**
11.00 g., Aluminum-Bronze, 30 mm. **Subject:** Jules Verne **Obv:** Various scenes from Jules Verne's novels **Rev:** Jules Verne's portrait left of value and date **Mint:** Paris

| Date | Mintage | VF20 | XF40 | MS60 | MS63 | MS65 |
|---|---|---|---|---|---|---|
| 2005 | 22,256 | — | — | — | — | 10.00 |

**KM# 1415 1/4 EURO**
22.20 g., 0.900 Silver 0.6424 oz. ASW, 37 mm. **Obv:** Jean de la Fontaine, value, Chinese astrological animals, date, Paris mint privy marks but without national identification **Rev:** Dog in wreath **Edge:** Reeded **Mint:** Paris **Note:** Anonymous coinage

| Date | Mintage | VF20 | XF40 | MS60 | MS63 | MS65 |
|---|---|---|---|---|---|---|
| 2006 | 10,000 | — | — | — | 32.00 | 35.00 |

**KM# 1442 1/4 EURO**
22.20 g., 0.900 Silver 0.6424 oz. ASW, 37 mm. **Obv:** Bust of Franklin facing slightly right at left, his diplomatic and technical successes at right **Obv. Legend:** BENJAMIN FRANKLIN 1706-2006 **Obv. Inscription:** AMI DE LA FRANCE **Rev:** French flag at left, American flag at right **Rev. Inscription:** PHILOSOPHE / DIPLOMATE / ÉCRIVAIN / SAVANT **Mint:** Paris

| Date | Mintage | VF20 | XF40 | MS60 | MS63 | MS65 |
|---|---|---|---|---|---|---|
| 2006 | 15,000 | — | — | — | 32.00 | 35.00 |

**KM# 1445 1/4 EURO**
22.20 g., 0.900 Silver 0.6424 oz. ASW, 37 mm. **Subject:** Marshall Bernadotte under Napoleon **Rev:** Military bust facing 3/4 right at left, building in backgound at right **Rev. Legend:** LIBERTÉ / ÉGALITÉ / FRATERNITÉ - KARL XIV JOHAN ROI DE SUÈDE **Mint:** Paris

| Date | Mintage | VF20 | XF40 | MS60 | MS63 | MS65 |
|---|---|---|---|---|---|---|
| 2006 Proof | 10,000 | — | — | — | 32.00 | 35.00 |

**KM# 1457 1/4 EURO**
22.20 g., 0.900 Silver 0.6424 oz. ASW, 37 mm. **Subject:** Hèpitaux de France Foundation **Obv:** Foundation logo **Rev:** TGV train, money box on outlined map of France **Mint:** Paris

| Date | Mintage | VF20 | XF40 | MS60 | MS63 | MS65 |
|---|---|---|---|---|---|---|
| 2006 | 50,000 | — | — | — | 28.00 | 30.00 |

**KM# 2061 1/4 EURO**
22.20 g., 0.900 Silver 0.6424 oz. ASW, 37 mm. **Subject:** Wolfgang Amadeus Mozart, 250th Anniversary of Birth **Obv:** Youthful bust **Rev:** Hand on piano keys, music above **Mint:** Paris

| Date | Mintage | VF20 | XF40 | MS60 | MS63 | MS65 |
|---|---|---|---|---|---|---|
| 2006 | 5,000 | — | — | — | — | 55.00 |

**KM# 1417 1/4 EURO**
22.20 g., 0.900 Silver 0.6424 oz. ASW, 37 mm. **Obv:** Jean de la Fontaine, value, Chinese astrological animals, date, Paris mint privy marks but without national identification **Rev:** Pig in wreath **Edge:** Reeded **Mint:** Paris **Note:** Anonymous issue.

| Date | Mintage | VF20 | XF40 | MS60 | MS63 | MS65 |
|---|---|---|---|---|---|---|
| 2007 | 10,000 | — | — | — | 32.00 | 35.00 |

**KM# 1419 1/4 EURO**
13.00 g., 0.900 Silver 0.3762 oz. ASW, 30 mm. **Obv:** Military bust of Lafayette facing 3/4 left **Obv. Legend:** LA FAYETTE. HÉROS DE LA RÉVOLUTION AMÉRICAINE **Obv. Inscription:** 1757/1854 at left, RF monogram at right **Rev:** Sailing ship L' Hermione **Rev. Legend:** LA FAYETTE, HERO OF THE AMERICAN REVOLUTION **Edge:** Plain **Mint:** Paris

| Date | Mintage | VF20 | XF40 | MS60 | MS63 | MS65 |
|---|---|---|---|---|---|---|
| 2007 (a) Proof-like | 4,740 | — | — | — | 32.00 | 35.00 |

**KM# 1421 1/4 EURO**
15.00 g., 0.900 Silver 0.434 oz. ASW, 30x21 mm. **Subject:** 90th Anniversary Death of Degas **Obv:** Ballerina "The Star" at left **Obv. Inscription:** Degas **Rev:** Paint brushes and oils multicolor at left, self portrait at right **Rev. Inscription:** LIBERTÉ / ÉGALITÉ / FRATERNITÉ **Shape:** Rectangle **Mint:** Paris

| Date | Mintage | VF20 | XF40 | MS60 | MS63 | MS65 |
|---|---|---|---|---|---|---|
| 2007 | 5,000 | — | — | — | 42.00 | 45.00 |

**KM# 1461 1/4 EURO**
13.00 g., 0.900 Silver 0.3762 oz. ASW, 30 mm. **Subject:** Sebastien Le Prestre de Vauban, 300th Anniversary of Death **Obv:** Arms above funeral coach, book at left **Rev:** Vauban standing; plans of fortress

| Date | Mintage | VF20 | XF40 | MS60 | MS63 | MS65 |
|---|---|---|---|---|---|---|
| 2007 | 4,051 | PF63 22.00 | PF65 25.00 | | | |

**KM# 1483 1/4 EURO**
13.00 g., 0.900 Silver 0.3762 oz. ASW, 30 mm. **Subject:** 2007 Rugby World Cup **Obv:** Two Rugby players **Rev:** Logo and goal

| Date | Mintage | VF20 | XF40 | MS60 | MS63 | MS65 |
|---|---|---|---|---|---|---|
| 2007 | Est. 4944 | — | — | — | 32.00 | 35.00 |

**KM# 1570 1/4 EURO**
15.00 g., 0.900 Silver 0.434 oz. ASW, 30 x 21 mm. **Subject:** Edward Manet **Obv:** Manet's "Olympia" painting **Rev:** Multicolor paint brushes and Manet's portrait **Shape:** Rectangle

| Date | Mintage | VF20 | XF40 | MS60 | MS63 | MS65 |
|---|---|---|---|---|---|---|
| 2008 | 7,695 | — | — | — | — | 65.00 |

**KM# 1572 1/4 EURO**
22.20 g., 0.900 Silver 0.6424 oz. ASW, 37 mm. **Subject:** Lunar New Year - Year of the Rat **Obv:** Bust of Jean de la Fontaine and twelve awards **Rev:** Rat within border

| Date | Mintage | VF20 | XF40 | MS60 | MS63 | MS65 |
|---|---|---|---|---|---|---|
| 2008 | 5,267 | — | — | — | 32.00 | 35.00 |

**KM# 1287 50 EURO CENT**
7.81 g., Brass, 24.2 mm. **Obv:** The Seed Sower divides date and RF **Rev:** Denomination and map **Edge:** Reeded **Mint:** Paris

| Date | Mintage | VF20 | XF40 | MS60 | MS63 | MS65 |
|---|---|---|---|---|---|---|
| 2001 | 276,287,274 | — | — | — | 1.25 | 2.00 |
| 2001 | 15,000 | PF65 15.00 | | | | |
| 2002 | 226,500,000 | — | — | — | 1.25 | 2.00 |
| 2002 | 21,453 | PF65 14.00 | | | | |
| 2003 In sets only | 180,000 | — | — | — | — | 11.50 |
| 2003 | 40,000 | PF65 14.00 | | | | |
| 2004 In sets only | 160,000 | — | — | — | — | 11.50 |
| 2004 | 20,000 | PF65 15.00 | | | | |
| 2005 In sets only | 120,000 | — | — | — | — | 11.50 |
| 2005 | 10,000 | PF65 17.00 | | | | |
| 2006 In sets only | 67,600 | — | — | — | — | 11.50 |
| 2006 | 10,000 | PF65 17.00 | | | | |

**KM# 1412 50 EURO CENT**
7.81 g., Brass, 24.2 mm. **Obv:** Sower **Rev:** Relief map of Western Europe, stars, lines and value **Edge:** Reeded **Mint:** Paris

| Date | Mintage | VF20 | XF40 | MS60 | MS63 | MS65 |
|---|---|---|---|---|---|---|
| 2007 In sets only | 58,000 | — | — | — | — | 11.50 |
| 2007 | 7,500 | PF65 16.00 | | | | |
| 2008 In sets only | 57,000 | — | — | — | — | 3.00 |
| 2008 | 7,500 | PF65 16.00 | | | | |
| 2009 In sets only | 50,500 | — | — | — | — | 3.00 |
| 2009 | 7,500 | PF65 16.00 | | | | |
| 2010 | — | — | — | — | 2.00 | 3.00 |
| 2010 | — | PF65 16.00 | | | | |
| 2011 | — | — | — | — | 2.00 | 3.00 |
| 2011 | — | PF65 16.00 | | | | |
| 2012 | — | — | — | — | 2.00 | 3.00 |
| 2012 | — | PF65 16.00 | | | | |
| 2013 | — | — | — | — | 2.00 | 3.00 |
| 2013 | — | PF65 16.00 | | | | |
| 2014 | — | — | — | — | 2.00 | 3.00 |
| 2014 | — | PF65 16.00 | | | | |

**KM# 1288 EURO**
7.50 g., Bi-Metallic Copper-Nickel center in Nickel-Brass ring, 23.25 mm. **Obv:** Stylized tree divides RF within circle, date below **Rev:** Denomination and map **Edge:** Segmented reeding **Mint:** Paris

| Date | Mintage | VF20 | XF40 | MS60 | MS63 | MS65 |
|---|---|---|---|---|---|---|
| 2001 | 150,251,624 | — | — | — | 2.75 | 4.00 |
| 2001 | 15,000 | PF65 18.00 | | | | |
| 2002 | 129,400,000 | — | — | — | 2.50 | 3.75 |
| 2002 | 21,453 | PF65 16.00 | | | | |
| 2003 In sets only | 100,000 | — | — | — | — | 12.00 |
| 2003 | 20,000 | PF65 18.00 | | | | |
| 2004 In sets only | 160,000 | — | — | — | — | 3.00 |
| 2004 | 20,000 | PF65 18.00 | | | | |
| 2005 In sets only | 120,000 | — | — | — | — | 3.00 |
| 2005 | 10,000 | PF65 20.00 | | | | |
| 2006 In sets only | 78,000 | — | — | — | — | 3.00 |
| 2006 | 10,000 | PF65 20.00 | | | | |

**KM# 1413 EURO**
7.50 g., Bi-Metallic Copper-Nickel center in Nickel-Brass ring, 23.25 mm. **Obv:** Stylized tree **Rev:** Relief map of Western Europe, stars, lines and value **Edge:** Segmented reeding **Mint:** Paris

| Date | Mintage | VF20 | XF40 | MS60 | MS63 | MS65 |
|---|---|---|---|---|---|---|
| 2007 In sets only | 58,000 | — | — | — | — | 12.00 |
| 2007 | 7,500 | PF65 20.00 | | | | |
| 2008 In sets only | 57,000 | — | — | — | — | 3.00 |
| 2008 | 7,500 | PF65 20.00 | | | | |
| 2009 In sets only | 50,500 | — | — | — | — | 3.00 |
| 2009 | 7,500 | PF65 20.00 | | | | |
| 2010 | — | — | — | — | 2.50 | 3.00 |
| 2010 | — | PF65 20.00 | | | | |
| 2011 | — | — | — | — | 2.50 | 3.00 |
| 2011 | — | PF65 20.00 | | | | |
| 2012 | — | — | — | — | 2.50 | 3.00 |
| 2012 | — | PF65 20.00 | | | | |
| 2013 | — | — | — | — | 2.50 | 3.00 |
| 2013 | — | PF65 20.00 | | | | |
| 2014 | — | — | — | — | 2.50 | 3.00 |
| 2014 | — | PF65 20.00 | | | | |

**KM# 1464 EURO**
155.55 g., 0.950 Silver 4.751 oz. ASW, 50 mm. **Subject:** Sebastien Le Prestre de Vauban, 300th Anniversary of Death

| Date | Mintage | VF20 | XF40 | MS60 | MS63 | MS65 |
|---|---|---|---|---|---|---|
| 2007 | 500 | PF63 350 | PF65 375 | | | |

**KM# 1470 EURO**
17.00 g., 0.920 Gold 0.5028 oz. AGW, 31 mm. **Subject:** Le Petit Prince, 60th Anniversary **Obv:** Prince standing with rabbit

| Date | Mintage | VF20 | XF40 | MS60 | MS63 | MS65 |
|---|---|---|---|---|---|---|
| 2007 | 2,000 | PF63 875 | PF65 900 | | | |

**KM# 1486 EURO**
17.00 g., 0.920 Gold 0.5028 oz. AGW, 31 mm. **Subject:** 2007 Rugby World Cup **Obv:** Two players and goal **Rev:** Logo and goal

| Date | Mintage | VF20 | XF40 | MS60 | MS63 | MS65 |
|---|---|---|---|---|---|---|
| 2007 | 500 | PF63 875 | PF65 900 | | | |

**KM# 1490 EURO**
22.00 g., 0.900 Silver 0.6366 oz. ASW, 37 mm. **Subject:** UNESCO **Obv:** Great Wall of China

| Date | Mintage | VF20 | XF40 | MS60 | MS63 | MS65 |
|---|---|---|---|---|---|---|
| 2007 | 5,000 | PF63 60.00 | PF65 70.00 | | | |

**KM# 1491 EURO**
8.45 g., 0.920 Gold 0.2499 oz. AGW, 22 mm. **Subject:** Unesco **Obv:** Great Wall of China **Rev:** Unesco Building and emblem

| Date | Mintage | VF20 | XF40 | MS60 | MS63 | MS65 |
|---|---|---|---|---|---|---|
| 2007 | 500 | PF63 450 | PF65 475 | | | |

**KM# 1492 EURO**
22.20 g., 0.900 Silver 0.6424 oz. ASW, 37 mm. **Subject:** Point Neuf 400th Anniversary **Obv:** Monuments of France logo **Rev:** Point Neuf Bridge, Paris Mint Museum

| Date | Mintage | VF20 | XF40 | MS60 | MS63 | MS65 |
|---|---|---|---|---|---|---|
| 2007 | 3,000 | PF63 80.00 | PF65 90.00 | | | |

**KM# 1493 EURO**
8.45 g., 0.920 Gold 0.2499 oz. AGW, 22 mm. **Subject:** Point Neuf, 400th Anniversary **Obv:** Monuments of France logo **Rev:** Point Neuf Brudge, Paris Mint Building

| Date | Mintage | VF20 | XF40 | MS60 | MS63 | MS65 |
|---|---|---|---|---|---|---|
| 2007 | 500 | PF63 450 | PF65 475 | | | |

**KM# 1495 EURO**
8.45 g., 0.920 Gold 0.2499 oz. AGW, 22 mm. **Subject:** Cannes Film Festival **Obv:** Cinema screen and stage, Golden Palm Award

| Date | Mintage | VF20 | XF40 | MS60 | MS63 | MS65 |
|---|---|---|---|---|---|---|
| 2007 | 500 | PF63 450 | PF65 475 | | | |

**KM# 1514 EURO**
17.00 g., 0.920 Gold 0.5028 oz. AGW, 31 mm. **Subject:** Stanislas Lesczynski **Obv:** Bust, shield **Rev:** Palac Stanislas - Nancy

| Date | Mintage | VF20 | XF40 | MS60 | MS63 | MS65 |
|---|---|---|---|---|---|---|
| 2007 | 500 | PF63 875 | PF65 900 | | | |

**KM# 1587 EURO**
8.45 g., 0.920 Gold 0.2499 oz. AGW, 22 mm. **Subject:** Court of Human Rights, 50th Anniversary **Obv:** Sower left **Rev:** Text

| Date | Mintage | VF20 | XF40 | MS60 | MS63 | MS65 |
|---|---|---|---|---|---|---|
| 2009 P | 500 | PF63 450 | PF65 475 | | | |

**KM# 1301 1-1/2 EURO**
22.20 g., 0.900 Silver 0.6424 oz. ASW, 37 mm. **Subject:** Europa **Obv:** Eight French euro coins design **Rev:** Portrait and flags design of 6.55957 francs KM-1265 **Edge:** Plain **Mint:** Paris

| Date | Mintage | VF20 | XF40 | MS60 | MS63 | MS65 |
|---|---|---|---|---|---|---|
| 2002 | 50,000 | PF63 45.00 | PF65 50.00 | | | |

**KM# 1305 1-1/2 EURO**
22.20 g., 0.900 Silver 0.6424 oz. ASW, 37 mm. **Subject:** French Landmarks **Obv:** French map **Rev:** Le Mont St. Michel **Edge:** Plain **Mint:** Paris

| Date | Mintage | VF20 | XF40 | MS60 | MS63 | MS65 |
|---|---|---|---|---|---|---|
| 2002 | 9,520 | PF63 50.00 | PF65 55.00 | | | |

**KM# 1307 1-1/2 EURO**
22.20 g., 0.900 Silver 0.6424 oz. ASW, 37 mm. **Subject:** French Landmarks **Obv:** French map **Rev:** La Butte Montmartre **Edge:** Plain **Mint:** Paris

| Date | Mintage | VF20 | XF40 | MS60 | MS63 | MS65 |
|---|---|---|---|---|---|---|
| 2002 | 6,095 | PF63 47.50 | PF65 50.00 | | | |

**KM# 1310 1-1/2 EURO**
22.20 g., 0.900 Silver 0.6424 oz. ASW, 37 mm. **Subject:** First West to East Transatlantic Flight **Obv:** Denomination, map and Lindbergh portrait **Rev:** Spirit of St. Louis (airplane) and map **Edge:** Plain **Mint:** Paris

| Date | Mintage | VF20 | XF40 | MS60 | MS63 | MS65 |
|---|---|---|---|---|---|---|
| 2002 | 10,000 | PF63 50.00 | PF65 55.00 | | | |

**KM# 1332 1-1/2 EURO**
22.20 g., 0.900 Silver 0.6424 oz. ASW, 37 mm. **Obv:** Victor Hugo, denomination and map **Rev:** Multicolor "Gavroche **Edge:** Plain **Mint:** Paris

| Date | Mintage | VF20 | XF40 | MS60 | MS63 | MS65 |
|---|---|---|---|---|---|---|
| 2002 | 10,000 | PF63 55.00 | PF65 60.00 | | | |

**KM# 1840 1-1/2 EURO**
22.20 g., 0.900 Silver 0.6424 oz. ASW, 37 mm. **Subject:** Snow White **Rev:** Scenes from the book, color

| Date | Mintage | VF20 | XF40 | MS60 | MS63 | MS65 |
|---|---|---|---|---|---|---|
| 2002 | 9,751 | PF63 55.00 | PF65 60.00 | | | |

**KM# 1841 1-1/2 EURO**
22.20 g., 0.900 Silver 0.6424 oz. ASW, 37 mm. **Subject:** Cinderella **Rev:** Scenes from the book, color

| Date | Mintage | VF20 | XF40 | MS60 | MS63 | MS65 |
|---|---|---|---|---|---|---|
| 2002 | 9,907 | PF63 55.00 | PF65 60.00 | | | |

**KM# 1842 1-1/2 EURO**
22.20 g., 0.900 Silver 0.6424 oz. ASW, 37 mm. **Subject:** Pinocchio **Rev:** Scenes form the book, color

| Date | Mintage | VF20 | XF40 | MS60 | MS63 | MS65 |
|---|---|---|---|---|---|---|
| 2002 | — | PF63 55.00 | PF65 60.00 | | | |

**KM# 1321 1-1/2 EURO**
22.20 g., 0.900 Silver 0.6424 oz. ASW, 37 mm. **Obv:** Tour de France logo **Rev:** Cyclist going left **Edge:** Plain **Mint:** Paris

| Date | Mintage | VF20 | XF40 | MS60 | MS63 | MS65 |
|---|---|---|---|---|---|---|
| 2003 | 22,905 | PF63 50.00 | PF65 55.00 | | | |

**KM# 1322 1-1/2 EURO**
22.20 g., 0.900 Silver 0.6424 oz. ASW, 37 mm. **Obv:** Tour de France logo **Rev:** Group of cyclists and Arch de Triumph **Edge:** Plain **Mint:** Paris

| Date | Mintage | VF20 | XF40 | MS60 | MS63 | MS65 |
|---|---|---|---|---|---|---|
| 2003 (Ht) | 16,532 | **PF63** 50.00 | **PF65** 55.00 | | | |

**KM# 1323 1-1/2 EURO**
22.20 g., 0.900 Silver 0.6424 oz. ASW, 37 mm. **Obv:** Tour de France logo **Rev:** Two cyclists and spectators **Edge:** Plain **Mint:** Paris

| Date | Mintage | VF20 | XF40 | MS60 | MS63 | MS65 |
|---|---|---|---|---|---|---|
| 2003 (Ht) | 15,934 | **PF63** 50.00 | **PF65** 55.00 | | | |

**KM# 1324 1-1/2 EURO**
22.20 g., 0.900 Silver 0.6424 oz. ASW, 37 mm. **Obv:** Tour de France logo **Rev:** Two groups of cyclists **Edge:** Plain **Mint:** Paris

| Date | Mintage | VF20 | XF40 | MS60 | MS63 | MS65 |
|---|---|---|---|---|---|---|
| 2003 (Ht) | 16,317 | **PF63** 50.00 | **PF65** 55.00 | | | |

**KM# 1325 1-1/2 EURO**
22.20 g., 0.900 Silver 0.6424 oz. ASW, 37 mm. **Obv:** Tour de France logo **Rev:** Cyclists, stopwatch and gears **Edge:** Plain **Mint:** Paris

| Date | Mintage | VF20 | XF40 | MS60 | MS63 | MS65 |
|---|---|---|---|---|---|---|
| 2003 (Ht) | 5,589 | **PF63** 50.00 | **PF65** 55.00 | | | |

**KM# 1336 1-1/2 EURO**
22.20 g., 0.900 Silver 0.6424 oz. ASW, 37 mm. **Obv:** Jefferson and Napoleon with Louisiana Purchase map **Rev:** Jazz musician, mansion and river boat **Edge:** Plain **Mint:** Paris

| Date | Mintage | VF20 | XF40 | MS60 | MS63 | MS65 |
|---|---|---|---|---|---|---|
| 2003 | 10,000 | **PF63** 55.00 | **PF65** 60.00 | | | |

**KM# 1338 1-1/2 EURO**
22.20 g., 0.900 Silver 0.6424 oz. ASW, 37 mm. **Obv:** Curved cross design with multiple values **Rev:** Goddess Europa and flags **Edge:** Plain **Mint:** Paris

| Date | Mintage | VF20 | XF40 | MS60 | MS63 | MS65 |
|---|---|---|---|---|---|---|
| 2003 | 24,501 | **PF63** 50.00 | **PF65** 55.00 | | | |

**KM# 1341 1-1/2 EURO**
22.20 g., 0.900 Silver 0.6424 oz. ASW, 37 mm. **Obv:** Denomination and compass face **Rev:** SS Normandie and New York City **Edge:** Plain **Mint:** Paris

| Date | Mintage | VF20 | XF40 | MS60 | MS63 | MS65 |
|---|---|---|---|---|---|---|
| 2003 | 2,422 | **PF63** 55.00 | **PF65** 60.00 | | | |

**KM# 1343 1-1/2 EURO**
22.20 g., 0.900 Silver 0.6424 oz. ASW, 37 mm. **Obv:** Denomination and compass face **Rev:** Airplane and Tokyo Geisha **Edge:** Plain **Mint:** Paris

| Date | Mintage | VF20 | XF40 | MS60 | MS63 | MS65 |
|---|---|---|---|---|---|---|
| 2003 | 2,285 | **PF63** 55.00 | **PF65** 60.00 | | | |

**KM# 1345 1-1/2 EURO**
22.20 g., 0.900 Silver 0.6424 oz. ASW, 37 mm. **Obv:** Paul Gauguin **Rev:** Native woman **Edge:** Plain **Mint:** Paris

| Date | Mintage | VF20 | XF40 | MS60 | MS63 | MS65 |
|---|---|---|---|---|---|---|
| 2003 | 3,198 | **PF63** 70.00 | **PF65** 80.00 | | | |

**KM# 1351 1-1/2 EURO**
22.20 g., 0.900 Silver 0.6424 oz. ASW, 37 mm. **Obv:** Obverse design of first one franc coin **Rev:** Reverse design of first one franc coin **Edge:** Plain **Mint:** Paris

| Date | Mintage | VF20 | XF40 | MS60 | MS63 | MS65 |
|---|---|---|---|---|---|---|
| 2003 | 15,000 | **PF63** 55.00 | **PF65** 60.00 | | | |

**KM# 1353 1-1/2 EURO**
22.20 g., 0.900 Silver 0.6424 oz. ASW, 37 mm. **Obv:** Mona Lisa **Rev:** Leonardo da Vinci **Edge:** Plain **Mint:** Paris

| Date | Mintage | VF20 | XF40 | MS60 | MS63 | MS65 |
|---|---|---|---|---|---|---|
| 2003 | 8,139 | **PF63** 55.00 | **PF65** 60.00 | | | |

**KM# 1355 1-1/2 EURO**
22.20 g., 0.900 Silver 0.6424 oz. ASW, 37 mm. **Obv:** Map and denomination **Rev:** Chateau Chambord **Edge:** Plain **Mint:** Paris

| Date | Mintage | VF20 | XF40 | MS60 | MS63 | MS65 |
|---|---|---|---|---|---|---|
| 2003 | 3,094 | **PF63** 50.00 | **PF65** 55.00 | | | |

**KM# 1357 1-1/2 EURO**
22.20 g., 0.900 Silver 0.6424 oz. ASW, 37 mm. **Obv:** Denomination in swirling design **Rev:** Multicolor Hansel and Gretel, witch and house **Edge:** Plain **Mint:** Paris

| Date | Mintage | VF20 | XF40 | MS60 | MS63 | MS65 |
|---|---|---|---|---|---|---|
| 2003 | 3,124 | **PF63** 55.00 | **PF65** 60.00 | | | |

**KM# 1359 1-1/2 EURO**
22.20 g., 0.900 Silver 0.6424 oz. ASW, 37 mm. **Obv:** Denomination in swirling design **Rev:** Multicolor Alice in Wonderland **Edge:** Plain **Mint:** Paris

| Date | Mintage | VF20 | XF40 | MS60 | MS63 | MS65 |
|---|---|---|---|---|---|---|
| 2003 | 3,096 | **PF63** 55.00 | **PF65** 60.00 | | | |

**KM# 1361 1-1/2 EURO**
22.20 g., 0.900 Silver 0.6424 oz. ASW, 37 mm. **Obv:** Pierre de Coubertin **Rev:** Olympic runners **Edge:** Plain **Mint:** Paris

| Date | Mintage | VF20 | XF40 | MS60 | MS63 | MS65 |
|---|---|---|---|---|---|---|
| 2003 | 50,000 | **PF63** 50.00 | **PF65** 55.00 | | | |

**KM# 1843 1-1/2 EURO**
22.20 g., 0.900 Silver 0.6424 oz. ASW, 37 mm. **Subject:** Athletic Games **Rev:** Shot Put athlete and stadium

| Date | Mintage | VF20 | XF40 | MS60 | MS63 | MS65 |
|---|---|---|---|---|---|---|
| 2003 | 4,195 | **PF63** 55.00 | **PF65** 60.00 | | | |

**KM# 1996 1-1/2 EURO**
22.20 g., 0.900 Silver 0.6424 oz. ASW, 37 mm. **Subject:** Athletic World Championships **Obv:** Winner podium before buildigns **Rev:** Runners by Pont des Arts **Mint:** Paris

| Date | Mintage | VF20 | XF40 | MS60 | MS63 | MS65 |
|---|---|---|---|---|---|---|
| 2003 | 4,425 | **PF63** 45.00 | **PF65** 50.00 | | | |

**KM# 1997 1-1/2 EURO**
22.20 g., 0.900 Silver 0.6424 oz. ASW, 37 mm. **Subject:** Athletic Wordl Championships **Obv:** Winner podium before buildings **Rev:** High jumper before Pont au Double **Mint:** Paris

| Date | Mintage | VF20 | XF40 | MS60 | MS63 | MS65 |
|---|---|---|---|---|---|---|
| 2003 | 4,169 | **PF63** 45.00 | **PF65** 50.00 | | | |

**KM# 2003 1-1/2 EURO**
22.20 g., 0.900 Silver 0.6424 oz. ASW, 37 mm. **Obv:** Sower advancing left **Rev:** Stars and map of European Union **Mint:** Paris

| Date | Mintage | VF20 | XF40 | MS60 | MS63 | MS65 |
|---|---|---|---|---|---|---|
| 2003 | 6,100 | **PF63** 55.00 | **PF65** 65.00 | | | |

**KM# 2006 1-1/2 EURO**
22.20 g., 0.900 Silver 0.6424 oz. ASW, 37 mm. **Subject:** Orient Express, Hagia Sophia in Istanbul **Mint:** Paris

| Date | Mintage | VF20 | XF40 | MS60 | MS63 | MS65 |
|---|---|---|---|---|---|---|
| 2003 | Est. 3821 | **PF63** 45.00 | **PF65** 50.00 | | | |

**KM# 2008 1-1/2 EURO**
22.20 g., 0.900 Silver 0.6424 oz. ASW, 37 mm. **Subject:** Childhood Fairy Tales **Rev:** Sleeping Beauty **Mint:** Paris

| Date | Mintage | VF20 | XF40 | MS60 | MS63 | MS65 |
|---|---|---|---|---|---|---|
| 2003 | 3,246 | **PF63** 55.00 | **PF65** 65.00 | | | |

**KM# 1364 1-1/2 EURO**
22.20 g., 0.900 Silver 0.6424 oz. ASW, 37 mm. **Obv:** Map with denomination **Rev:** Avignon Popes Palace **Edge:** Plain **Mint:** Paris

| Date | Mintage | VF20 | XF40 | MS60 | MS63 | MS65 |
|---|---|---|---|---|---|---|
| 2004 | 3,504 | **PF63** 50.00 | **PF65** 55.00 | | | |

**KM# 1366 1-1/2 EURO**
22.20 g., 0.900 Silver 0.6424 oz. ASW, 37 mm. **Obv:** Book, eagle and denomination **Rev:** Napoleon and coronation scene in background **Edge:** Plain **Mint:** Paris

| Date | Mintage | VF20 | XF40 | MS60 | MS63 | MS65 |
|---|---|---|---|---|---|---|
| 2004 | 9,705 | **PF63** 45.00 | **PF65** 50.00 | | | |

**KM# 1369 1-1/2 EURO**
22.20 g., 0.900 Silver 0.6424 oz. ASW, 37 mm. **Obv:** Soldiers and Normandy invasion scene **Rev:** D-DAY" above denomination **Edge:** Plain **Mint:** Paris

| Date | Mintage | VF20 | XF40 | MS60 | MS63 | MS65 |
|---|---|---|---|---|---|---|
| 2004 | 3,343 | **PF63** 50.00 | **PF65** 55.00 | | | |

**KM# 1373 1-1/2 EURO**
22.20 g., 0.900 Silver 0.6424 oz. ASW, 37 mm. **Obv:** Emile Loubet and King Edward VII **Rev:** Marianne and Britannia **Edge:** Plain **Mint:** Paris

| Date | Mintage | VF20 | XF40 | MS60 | MS63 | MS65 |
|---|---|---|---|---|---|---|
| 2004 | 4,022 | **PF63** 50.00 | **PF65** 55.00 | | | |

**KM# 1374 1-1/2 EURO**
22.20 g., 0.900 Silver 0.6424 oz. ASW, 37 mm. **Obv:** Soccer ball and denomination **Rev:** Rooster and quill **Edge:** Plain **Mint:** Paris

| Date | Mintage | VF20 | XF40 | MS60 | MS63 | MS65 |
|---|---|---|---|---|---|---|
| 2004 | 25,000 | **PF63** 55.00 | **PF65** 60.00 | | | |

**KM# 1378 1-1/2 EURO**
22.20 g., 0.900 Silver 0.6424 oz. ASW, 37 mm. **Obv:** Compass rose **Rev:** Ocean liner **Edge:** Plain **Mint:** Paris

| Date | Mintage | VF20 | XF40 | MS60 | MS63 | MS65 |
|---|---|---|---|---|---|---|
| 2004 | 1,708 | **PF63** 50.00 | **PF65** 55.00 | | | |

**KM# 1380 1-1/2 EURO**
22.20 g., 0.900 Silver 0.6424 oz. ASW, 37 mm. **Obv:** Compass rose **Rev:** Trans-Siberian Railroad **Edge:** Plain **Mint:** Paris

| Date | Mintage | VF20 | XF40 | MS60 | MS63 | MS65 |
|---|---|---|---|---|---|---|
| 2004 | 2,958 | **PF63** 50.00 | **PF65** 55.00 | | | |

**KM# 1382 1-1/2 EURO**
22.20 g., 0.900 Silver 0.6424 oz. ASW, 37 mm. **Obv:** Compass rose **Rev:** Half-track vehicle **Edge:** Plain **Mint:** Paris

| Date | Mintage | VF20 | XF40 | MS60 | MS63 | MS65 |
|---|---|---|---|---|---|---|
| 2004 | 1,743 | **PF63** 47.50 | **PF65** 50.00 | | | |

**KM# 1384 1-1/2 EURO**
22.20 g., 0.900 Silver 0.6424 oz. ASW, 37 mm. **Obv:** Compass rose **Rev:** Biplane airliner **Edge:** Plain **Mint:** Paris

| Date | Mintage | VF20 | XF40 | MS60 | MS63 | MS65 |
|---|---|---|---|---|---|---|
| 2004 | 1,548 | **PF63** 47.50 | **PF65** 50.00 | | | |

**KM# 1386 1-1/2 EURO**
22.20 g., 0.900 Silver 0.6424 oz. ASW, 37 mm. **Obv:** F.A. Bartholdi **Rev:** Statue of Liberty **Edge:** Plain **Mint:** Paris

| Date | Mintage | VF20 | XF40 | MS60 | MS63 | MS65 |
|---|---|---|---|---|---|---|
| 2004 | 3,303 | **PF63** 47.50 | **PF65** 50.00 | | | |

**KM# 1391 1-1/2 EURO**
22.20 g., 0.900 Silver 0.6424 oz. ASW, 37 mm. **Subject:** European Union Expansion **Obv:** Puzzle map of Europe **Rev:** Partial face and flags **Edge:** Plain **Mint:** Paris

| Date | Mintage | VF20 | XF40 | MS60 | MS63 | MS65 |
|---|---|---|---|---|---|---|
| 2004 | 40,000 | **PF63** 42.50 | **PF65** 50.00 | | | |

**KM# 1844 1-1/2 EURO**
22.20 g., 0.900 Silver 0.6424 oz. ASW, 37 mm. **Obv:** Sower advancing left within stars **Rev:** Head at left, stars at right

| Date | Mintage | VF20 | XF40 | MS60 | MS63 | MS65 |
|---|---|---|---|---|---|---|
| 2004 | Est. 5000 | **PF63** 55.00 | **PF65** 60.00 | | | |

**KM# 2013 1-1/2 EURO**
22.20 g., 0.900 Silver 0.6424 oz. ASW, 37 mm. **Subject:** Childhood stories **Rev:** Aladdin and lamp in color **Mint:** Paris

| Date | Mintage | VF20 | XF40 | MS60 | MS63 | MS65 |
|---|---|---|---|---|---|---|
| 2004 | 2,222 | **PF63** 70.00 | **PF65** 80.00 | | | |

**KM# 2014 1-1/2 EURO**
22.20 g., 0.900 Silver 0.6424 oz. ASW, 37 mm. **Subject:** Childhood stories **Rev:** Peter Pan in color **Mint:** Paris

| Date | Mintage | VF20 | XF40 | MS60 | MS63 | MS65 |
|---|---|---|---|---|---|---|
| 2004 | 2,469 | **PF63** 70.00 | **PF65** 80.00 | | | |

**KM# 1423 1-1/2 EURO**
22.20 g., 0.900 Silver 0.6424 oz. ASW, 37 mm. **Subject:** Biathlon **Rev:** Skier at right facing 3/4 left, mountain peaks in background **Rev. Inscription:** JEUX D'HIVER **Mint:** Paris

| Date | Mintage | VF20 | XF40 | MS60 | MS63 | MS65 |
|---|---|---|---|---|---|---|
| 2005 | 4,903 | **PF63** 45.00 | **PF65** 50.00 | | | |

**KM# 1425 1-1/2 EURO**
22.20 g., 0.900 Silver 0.6424 oz. ASW, 37 mm. **Series:** Jules Verne **Subject:** From the Earth to the Moon **Rev:** Crowd observing at lower left, volcano erupting above, moon at upper right, Verne in spaceship at lower right, factory chimneys belching smoke in bachground **Rev. Legend:** DE LA TERRE... LA LUNE **Mint:** Paris

| Date | Mintage | VF20 | XF40 | MS60 | MS63 | MS65 |
|---|---|---|---|---|---|---|
| 2005 | 1,336 | **PF63** 65.00 | **PF65** 75.00 | | | |

**KM# 1427 1-1/2 EURO**
22.20 g., 0.900 Silver 0.6424 oz. ASW, 37 mm. **Rev:** Kitty and poodle at table at cafe, multicolor **Rev. Legend:** Hello Kitty **Mint:** Paris

| Date | Mintage | VF20 | XF40 | MS60 | MS63 | MS65 |
|---|---|---|---|---|---|---|
| 2005 | 4,000 | **PF63** 65.00 | **PF65** 75.00 | | | |

**KM# 1428 1-1/2 EURO**
22.20 g., 0.900 Silver 0.6424 oz. ASW, 37 mm. **Rev:** Kitty on the Champs-Elysees, multicolor **Rev. Legend:** Hello Kitty **Mint:** Paris

| Date | Mintage | VF20 | XF40 | MS60 | MS63 | MS65 |
|---|---|---|---|---|---|---|
| 2005 | 4,000 | **PF63** 65.00 | **PF65** 75.00 | | | |

**KM# 1431 1-1/2 EURO**
22.20 g., 0.900 Silver 0.6424 oz. ASW, 37 mm. **Subject:** Bicentennial Victory at Austerlitz **Rev:** Battle scene **Rev. Legend:** LIBERTÉ ÉGALITÉ FRATERNITÉ **Mint:** Paris

| Date | Mintage | VF20 | XF40 | MS60 | MS63 | MS65 |
|---|---|---|---|---|---|---|
| 2005 | 7,203 | **PF63** 50.00 | **PF65** 55.00 | | | |

**KM# 1434 1-1/2 EURO**
22.20 g., 0.900 Silver 0.6424 oz. ASW, 37 mm. **Subject:** 50th Anniversary of the Europe flag **Rev:** Stars at left, partial flag at center right **Mint:** Paris

| Date | Mintage | VF20 | XF40 | MS60 | MS63 | MS65 |
|---|---|---|---|---|---|---|
| 2005 | 7,861 | **PF63** 50.00 | **PF65** 55.00 | | | |

**KM# 1436 1-1/2 EURO**
22.20 g., 0.900 Silver 0.6424 oz. ASW, 37 mm. **Subject:** Centenary Law of Dec. 9, 1905 **Obv:** Sower" left in ring of stars **Mint:** Paris

| Date | Mintage | VF20 | XF40 | MS60 | MS63 | MS65 |
|---|---|---|---|---|---|---|
| 2005 | 3,110 | **PF63** 50.00 | **PF65** 55.00 | | | |
| 2006 | 10,000 | **PF63** 50.00 | **PF65** 55.00 | | | |

**KM# 1438 1-1/2 EURO**
22.20 g., 0.900 Silver 0.6424 oz. ASW, 37 mm. **Series:** Jules Verne **Subject:** 20,000 Leagues Under the Sea **Rev:** Submarine above plants and divers **Rev. Legend:** VINGT MILLE LIEUES SOUS LES MERS **Mint:** Paris

| Date | Mintage | VF20 | XF40 | MS60 | MS63 | MS65 |
|---|---|---|---|---|---|---|
| 2005 | 4,463 | **PF63** 65.00 | **PF65** 75.00 | | | |

**KM# 1440 1-1/2 EURO**
22.20 g., 0.900 Silver 0.6424 oz. ASW, 37 mm. **Subject:** 150th Anniversary of Classification of Bordeaux Wines **Rev:** Stylized female with grapes between various names of wines at her feet **Mint:** Paris

| Date | Mintage | VF20 | XF40 | MS60 | MS63 | MS65 |
|---|---|---|---|---|---|---|
| 2005 | 2,832 | **PF63** 65.00 | **PF65** 75.00 | | | |

**KM# 1441 1-1/2 EURO**
22.20 g., 0.900 Silver 0.6424 oz. ASW, 37 mm. **Subject:** 60th Anniversary - End of World War II **Rev:** Doves in flight **Rev. Inscription:** L'EUROPE FAIT LA PAIX **Mint:** Paris

| Date | Mintage | VF20 | XF40 | MS60 | MS63 | MS65 |
|---|---|---|---|---|---|---|
| 2005 | 44,532 | **PF63** 45.00 | **PF65** 50.00 | | | |

**KM# 2020 1-1/2 EURO**
22.20 g., 0.900 Silver 0.6424 oz. ASW, 37 mm. **Subject:** World Cup Soccer **Obv:** Trophy and soccer ball motif **Rev:** Value within map of France **Mint:** Paris

| Date | Mintage | VF20 | XF40 | MS60 | MS63 | MS65 |
|---|---|---|---|---|---|---|
| 2005 | 1,883 | **PF63** 45.00 | **PF65** 50.00 | | | |

**KM# 2027 1-1/2 EURO**

22.20 g., 0.900 Silver 0.6424 oz. ASW **Subject:** Frederic Chopin, 195th Anniversary of Birth **Obv:** Profile at left, piano keys at right vertically **Rev:** Monument in Wausau park at left, piano keys at right vertically **Mint:** Paris

| Date | Mintage | VF20 | XF40 | MS60 | MS63 | MS65 |
|---|---|---|---|---|---|---|
| 2005 | 3,000 | PF63 300 | PF65 325 | | | |

**KM# 2029 1-1/2 EURO**

22.20 g., 0.900 Silver 0.6424 oz. ASW, 37 mm. **Subject:** Jules Verne, 100th Anniversary of Death **Obv:** Around the World in 80 days **Mint:** Paris

| Date | Mintage | VF20 | XF40 | MS60 | MS63 | MS65 |
|---|---|---|---|---|---|---|
| 2005 | 4,998 | PF63 100 | PF65 120 | | | |

**KM# 2036 1-1/2 EURO**

22.20 g., 0.900 Silver 0.6424 oz. ASW, 37 mm. **Subject:** Hello Kitty **Rev:** Kitty with umbrella in color flying above Paris skyline **Mint:** Paris

| Date | Mintage | VF20 | XF40 | MS60 | MS63 | MS65 |
|---|---|---|---|---|---|---|
| 2005 | Est. 4000 | PF63 55.00 | PF65 65.00 | | | |

**KM# 1444 1-1/2 EURO**

22.20 g., 0.900 Silver 0.6424 oz. ASW, 37 mm. **Subject:** 100th Anniversary - French Grand Prix **Obv:** Steering wheel with early race car in upper segment, two gauges at lower left, R / F at lower right **Obv. Legend:** LE MANS 1906 - CENTENAIRE du 1er GRAND PRIX de l'AUTOMOBILE CLUB de FRANCE **Rev:** Modern racing car's steering wheel **Rev. Legend:** MAGNY-COURS **Mint:** Paris

| Date | Mintage | VF20 | XF40 | MS60 | MS63 | MS65 |
|---|---|---|---|---|---|---|
| 2006 | 4,235 | PF63 65.00 | PF65 75.00 | | | |

**KM# 1447 1-1/2 EURO**

22.20 g., 0.900 Silver 0.6424 oz. ASW, 37 mm. **Obv:** Strogoff on horseback wielding sword, city at left, soldiers at lower left, calvalry at right **Obv. Legend:** MICHEL STROGOFF **Rev:** Head of Verne facing 3/4 right at left center, instruments and anchor in curved band **Rev. Legend:** 1828 JULES VERNE 1905 - LIBERTÉ . ÉGALITÉ . FRATERNITÉ **Mint:** Paris

| Date | Mintage | VF20 | XF40 | MS60 | MS63 | MS65 |
|---|---|---|---|---|---|---|
| 2006 | 2,468 | PF63 100 | PF65 125 | | | |

**KM# 1450 1-1/2 EURO**

22.20 g., 0.900 Silver 0.6424 oz. ASW, 37 mm. **Subject:** Jules Verne **Obv:** Hot air balloon, parrots at left, native masks at lower left, foliage at right, native huts below, map of Africa in background **Obv. Legend:** CINQ SEMAINES EN BAILON **Rev:** Head of Verne facing 3/4 right at left center, instruments and anchor in curved band **Rev. Legend:** 1828 JULES VERNE 1905 **Mint:** Paris

| Date | Mintage | VF20 | XF40 | MS60 | MS63 | MS65 |
|---|---|---|---|---|---|---|
| 2006 | 2,287 | PF63 65.00 | PF65 75.00 | | | |

**KM# 1452 1-1/2 EURO**

22.20 g., 0.900 Silver 0.6424 oz. ASW, 37 mm. **Subject:** Formula 1 World Championship **Obv:** Race car outline on checker board background **Obv. Legend:** LIBERTÉ ÉGALITÉ FRATERNITÉ **Rev:** Race car outline in victory sprays with star **Rev. Legend:** RENAULT - CHAMPION DU MONDE FIA 2005 DES CONSTRUCTEURS DE FORMULE 1 **Mint:** Paris

| Date | Mintage | VF20 | XF40 | MS60 | MS63 | MS65 |
|---|---|---|---|---|---|---|
| 2006 | 10,000 | PF63 50.00 | PF65 55.00 | | | |

**KM# 1453 1-1/2 EURO**

22.20 g., 0.900 Silver 0.6424 oz. ASW, 37 mm. **Subject:** 100th Anniversary - Death of Paul Cézanne **Obv:** Self portrait **Obv. Inscription:** PAUL / CÉZANNE **Rev:** The Card Players **Rev. Legend:** LIBERTÉ ÉGALITÉ FRATERNITÉ **Mint:** Paris

| Date | Mintage | VF20 | XF40 | MS60 | MS63 | MS65 |
|---|---|---|---|---|---|---|
| 2006 | 5,000 | PF63 65.00 | PF65 75.00 | | | |

**KM# 1455 1-1/2 EURO**

22.20 g., 0.900 Silver 0.6424 oz. ASW, 37 mm. **Obv:** Map of the Basilica **Rev:** Bust of Pope Benedict XVI with arms outstretched facing 3/4 right at lower left, Basilica in background **Rev. Legend:** 500 ANS de la BASILIQUE SAINT-PIERRE **Mint:** Paris

| Date | Mintage | VF20 | XF40 | MS60 | MS63 | MS65 |
|---|---|---|---|---|---|---|
| 2006 | 5,000 | PF63 65.00 | PF65 75.00 | | | |

**KM# 1456 1-1/2 EURO**

22.20 g., 0.900 Silver 0.6424 oz. ASW, 37 mm. **Rev:** Half of Arc at left, eternal flame above WW I plaque at right **Rev. Legend:** ARC DE TRIOMPHE **Mint:** Paris

| Date | Mintage | VF20 | XF40 | MS60 | MS63 | MS65 |
|---|---|---|---|---|---|---|
| 2006 | 3,620 | PF63 50.00 | PF65 55.00 | | | |

**KM# 1458 1-1/2 EURO**

22.20 g., 0.900 Silver 0.6424 oz. ASW, 37 mm. **Subject:** 300th Anniversary - Completion of the Dome of Les Invalides **Rev:** Dome between Jules-Hardouin Mansart at left, Louis XIV at right **Rev. Legend:** SAINT-LOUIS - DES INVALIDES **Rev. Inscription:** 28/AOÛT - 1706 **Mint:** Paris

| Date | Mintage | VF20 | XF40 | MS60 | MS63 | MS65 |
|---|---|---|---|---|---|---|
| 2006 | 2,891 | PF63 50.00 | PF65 55.00 | | | |

**KM# 2037 1-1/2 EURO**

22.20 g., 0.900 Silver 0.6424 oz. ASW, 37 mm. **Subject:** Robert Schuman, 120th Anniversary of Birth **Mint:** Paris

| Date | Mintage | VF20 | XF40 | MS60 | MS63 | MS65 |
|---|---|---|---|---|---|---|
| 2006 | 21,517 | PF63 35.00 | PF65 40.00 | | | |

**KM# 2041 1-1/2 EURO**

22.20 g., 0.900 Silver 0.6424 oz. ASW, 37 mm. **Subject:** Bejing Olympics **Obv:** Three fencing foils on globe map pointing at Bejing **Rev:** Two fencers **Mint:** Paris

| Date | Mintage | VF20 | XF40 | MS60 | MS63 | MS65 |
|---|---|---|---|---|---|---|
| 2006 | 10,000 | PF63 45.00 | PF65 50.00 | | | |

**KM# 2048 1-1/2 EURO**

22.20 g., 0.900 Silver 0.6424 oz. ASW, 37 mm. **Subject:** Marie Amélie of Orleans and Carlos I of Portugal, 120th Anniversary of Marriage **Obv:** Bust in tiara left **Rev:** Two shields crowned **Mint:** Paris

| Date | Mintage | VF20 | XF40 | MS60 | MS63 | MS65 |
|---|---|---|---|---|---|---|
| 2006 | 3,000 | PF63 150 | PF65 175 | | | |

**KM# 2055 1-1/2 EURO**

22.20 g., 0.900 Silver 0.6424 oz. ASW, 37 mm. **Subject:** Abolition of the Death Penalty, 25th Anniversary **Obv:** Sower advancing left **Rev:** Guillotine **Mint:** Paris

| Date | Mintage | VF20 | XF40 | MS60 | MS63 | MS65 |
|---|---|---|---|---|---|---|
| 2006 | 3,110 | PF63 45.00 | PF65 50.00 | | | |

**KM# 2064 1-1/2 EURO**

22.20 g., 0.900 Silver 0.6424 oz. ASW, 37 mm. **Subject:** Jules Verne, 100th Anniversary of Death **Obv:** Voyage to the center of the Earth **Mint:** Paris

| Date | Mintage | VF20 | XF40 | MS60 | MS63 | MS65 |
|---|---|---|---|---|---|---|
| 2006 | 2,411 | PF63 100 | PF65 120 | | | |

**KM# 1462 1-1/2 EURO**

22.00 g., 0.900 Silver 0.6366 oz. ASW, 37 mm. **Subject:** Sebastien Le Prestre de Vauban, 300th Anniversary of Death

| Date | Mintage | VF20 | XF40 | MS60 | MS63 | MS65 |
|---|---|---|---|---|---|---|
| 2007 | 14,364 | PF63 40.00 | PF65 45.00 | | | |

**KM# 1465 1-1/2 EURO**

22.20 g., 0.900 Silver 0.6424 oz. ASW, 37 mm. **Subject:** Le Petit Prince, 60th Anniversary **Obv:** Prince standing, multicolor

| Date | Mintage | VF20 | XF40 | MS60 | MS63 | MS65 |
|---|---|---|---|---|---|---|
| 2007 | 3,000 | PF63 55.00 | PF65 60.00 | | | |

**KM# 1467 1-1/2 EURO**

22.20 g., 0.900 Silver 0.6424 oz. ASW, 37 mm. **Subject:** Le Petit Prince, 60th Anniversary **Obv:** Prince lying in field, multicolor

| Date | Mintage | VF20 | XF40 | MS60 | MS63 | MS65 |
|---|---|---|---|---|---|---|
| 2007 | 3,000 | PF63 55.00 | PF65 60.00 | | | |

**KM# 1469 1-1/2 EURO**

22.20 g., 0.900 Silver 0.6424 oz. ASW, 37 mm. **Subject:** Le Petite Prince, 60th Anniversary **Obv:** Prince standing with fox, multicolor

| Date | Mintage | VF20 | XF40 | MS60 | MS63 | MS65 |
|---|---|---|---|---|---|---|
| 2007 | 3,000 | PF63 55.00 | PF65 60.00 | | | |

**KM# 1473 1-1/2 EURO**

22.20 g., 0.900 Silver 0.6424 oz. ASW, 37 mm. **Subject:** Paul E. Victor, 100th Birthday **Obv:** International Polar Year Logo **Rev:** Bust at left, Islands

| Date | Mintage | VF20 | XF40 | MS60 | MS63 | MS65 |
|---|---|---|---|---|---|---|
| 2007 | 5,000 | PF63 55.00 | PF65 60.00 | | | |

**KM# 1475 1-1/2 EURO**

22.20 g., 0.900 Silver 0.6424 oz. ASW, 37 mm. **Obv:** Formula 1 race car on checkered background **Rev:** Legend in wreath on checkered background

| Date | Mintage | VF20 | XF40 | MS60 | MS63 | MS65 |
|---|---|---|---|---|---|---|
| 2007//2006 | 4,554 | PF63 55.00 | PF65 60.00 | | | |

**KM# 1477 1-1/2 EURO**

22.20 g., 0.900 Silver 0.6424 oz. ASW, 37 mm. **Subject:** 29th Summer Olympic Games Beijing **Obv:** Rider on horseback, globe map of China **Rev:** Equestrian jump over orienteal fence

| Date | Mintage | VF20 | XF40 | MS60 | MS63 | MS65 |
|---|---|---|---|---|---|---|
| 2007 | 10,000 | PF63 50.00 | PF65 55.00 | | | |

**KM# 1479 1-1/2 EURO**

22.20 g., 0.900 Silver 0.6424 oz. ASW, 37 mm. **Subject:** Airbus A380 **Obv:** Airplane **Rev:** Europa head and flags

| Date | Mintage | VF20 | XF40 | MS60 | MS63 | MS65 |
|---|---|---|---|---|---|---|
| 2007 | 5,000 | PF63 50.00 | PF65 55.00 | | | |

**KM# 1484 1-1/2 EURO**

22.20 g., 0.900 Silver 0.6424 oz. ASW, 37 mm. **Subject:** 2007 Rugby World Cup **Obv:** Two players and goal **Rev:** Logo and goal

| Date | Mintage | VF20 | XF40 | MS60 | MS63 | MS65 |
|---|---|---|---|---|---|---|
| 2007 | 4,915 | PF63 50.00 | PF65 55.00 | | | |

**KM# 1488 1-1/2 EURO**

22.20 g., 0.900 Silver 0.6424 oz. ASW, 37 mm. **Obv:** Christian Dior bust **Rev:** Dior Museum building

| Date | Mintage | VF20 | XF40 | MS60 | MS63 | MS65 |
|---|---|---|---|---|---|---|
| 2007 | 4,799 | PF63 75.00 | PF65 85.00 | | | |

**KM# 1501 1-1/2 EURO**

22.20 g., 0.900 Silver 0.6424 oz. ASW, 37 mm. **Subject:** Georges Pompendev Center, 30th Anniversary

| Date | Mintage | VF20 | XF40 | MS60 | MS63 | MS65 |
|---|---|---|---|---|---|---|
| 2007 | — | PF63 50.00 | PF65 55.00 | | | |

**KM# 1505 1-1/2 EURO**

22.20 g., 0.900 Silver 0.6424 oz. ASW, 37 mm. **Subject:** George Remir Centennial **Obv:** Wand and sparkles **Rev:** Tin Tin and the Professor calculus in multicolor

| Date | Mintage | VF20 | XF40 | MS60 | MS63 | MS65 |
|---|---|---|---|---|---|---|
| 2007 | 10,000 | PF63 60.00 | PF65 70.00 | | | |

**KM# 1506 1-1/2 EURO**

22.20 g., 0.900 Silver 0.6424 oz. ASW, 37 mm. **Subject:** Georges Remi Centennial **Obv:** Wand and sparkles **Rev:** Tin Tin and Captain Haddock in multicolor

| Date | Mintage | VF20 | XF40 | MS60 | MS63 | MS65 |
|---|---|---|---|---|---|---|
| 2007 | 5,043 | PF63 65.00 | PF65 75.00 | | | |

**KM# 1507 1-1/2 EURO**

22.20 g., 0.900 Silver 0.6424 oz. ASW, 37 mm. **Subject:** Georges Remi Centennial **Obv:** Wand and sparkles **Rev:** Tin Tin and Chang in multicolor

| Date | Mintage | VF20 | XF40 | MS60 | MS63 | MS65 |
|---|---|---|---|---|---|---|
| 2007 | 4,648 | PF63 65.00 | PF65 75.00 | | | |

**KM# 1511 1-1/2 EURO**
22.20 g., 0.900 Silver 0.6424 oz. ASW, 37 mm. **Subject:** Aristides de Sousa Mendes, Portuguese diplomat **Obv:** Bust right **Rev:** Plaque

| Date | Mintage | VF20 | XF40 | MS60 | MS63 | MS65 |
|---|---|---|---|---|---|---|
| 2007 | 3,000 | PF63 55.00 | PF65 60.00 | | | |

**KM# 1516 1-1/2 EURO**
22.20 g., 0.900 Silver 0.6424 oz. ASW, 37 mm. **Subject:** Asterix **Rev:** The Banquet

| Date | Mintage | VF20 | XF40 | MS60 | MS63 | MS65 |
|---|---|---|---|---|---|---|
| 2007 | 2,994 | PF63 60.00 | PF65 70.00 | | | |

**KM# 1517 1-1/2 EURO**
22.20 g., 0.900 Silver 0.6424 oz. ASW, 37 mm. **Subject:** Asterix **Rev:** The posion

| Date | Mintage | VF20 | XF40 | MS60 | MS63 | MS65 |
|---|---|---|---|---|---|---|
| 2007 | 2,996 | PF63 60.00 | PF65 70.00 | | | |

**KM# 1518 1-1/2 EURO**
22.20 g., 0.900 Silver 0.6424 oz. ASW, 37 mm. **Subject:** Asterix **Rev:** The Chase

| Date | Mintage | VF20 | XF40 | MS60 | MS63 | MS65 |
|---|---|---|---|---|---|---|
| 2007 | 2,996 | PF63 60.00 | PF65 70.00 | | | |

**KM# 1527 1-1/2 EURO**
22.20 g., 0.900 Silver 0.6424 oz. ASW, 37 mm. **Subject:** French Presidency of European Union **Obv:** Text written stars **Rev:** Europa head and flags

| Date | Mintage | VF20 | XF40 | MS60 | MS63 | MS65 |
|---|---|---|---|---|---|---|
| 2008 | 4,412 | PF63 50.00 | PF65 55.00 | | | |

**KM# 1532 1-1/2 EURO**
22.20 g., 0.900 Silver 0.6424 oz. ASW, 37 mm. **Subject:** Eurpean Parliament, 50th Anniversary **Obv:** Map of EU within stars **Rev:** European Parliament Building in Strasboury

| Date | Mintage | VF20 | XF40 | MS60 | MS63 | MS65 |
|---|---|---|---|---|---|---|
| 2008 | 13,802 | PF63 50.00 | PF65 55.00 | | | |

**KM# 1537 1-1/2 EURO**
22.20 g., 0.900 Silver 0.6424 oz. ASW, 37 mm. **Subject:** 5th Republic, 50th Anniversasry **Obv:** Sower **Rev:** deGaulle head right

| Date | Mintage | VF20 | XF40 | MS60 | MS63 | MS65 |
|---|---|---|---|---|---|---|
| 2008 | 6,631 | PF63 50.00 | PF65 55.00 | | | |

**KM# 1543 1-1/2 EURO**
22.20 g., 0.900 Silver 0.6424 oz. ASW, 37 mm. **Subject:** 29th Summer Olympic Games - Beijing **Obv:** Swimmer and globe **Rev:** Diver and oriental screen

| Date | Mintage | VF20 | XF40 | MS60 | MS63 | MS65 |
|---|---|---|---|---|---|---|
| 2008 | 3,824 | PF63 65.00 | PF65 75.00 | | | |

**KM# 1546 1-1/2 EURO**
22.20 g., 0.900 Silver 0.6382 oz. ASW, 37 mm. **Subject:** UEFA **Obv:** French soccer team **Rev:** UEFA logo

| Date | Mintage | F12 | VF20 | XF40 | MS60 | MS63 |
|---|---|---|---|---|---|---|
| 2008 | 5,000 | PF63 55.00 | PF65 60.00 | | | |

**KM# 1548 1-1/2 EURO**
22.20 g., 0.900 Silver 0.6424 oz. ASW, 37 mm. **Subject:** Franco - Japanese Relators, 150th Anniversary **Obv:** Eiffel Tower and Kimono forming logo **Rev:** Delacroix's "La Liberte"

| Date | Mintage | VF20 | XF40 | MS60 | MS63 | MS65 |
|---|---|---|---|---|---|---|
| 2008 | 4,866 | PF63 65.00 | PF65 75.00 | | | |

**KM# 1549 1-1/2 EURO**
22.20 g., 0.900 Silver 0.6424 oz. ASW, 37 mm. **Subject:** Franco - Japanese Relators - 150th Anniversary **Obv:** Eillfel Tower and Kimono forming logo **Rev:** Ichikawa Ebizo IV portrait painting

| Date | Mintage | VF20 | XF40 | MS60 | MS63 | MS65 |
|---|---|---|---|---|---|---|
| 2008 | 4,735 | PF63 65.00 | PF65 75.00 | | | |

**KM# 1550 1-1/2 EURO**
22.20 g., 0.900 Silver 0.6424 oz. ASW, 37 mm. **Subject:** Franco - Japanese Relators - 150th Anniversary **Obv:** Eillfel Tower and Kimono forming logo **Rev:** Scenes of Paris and Tokyo - Eillfel Tower and Pagoda Sensoji

| Date | Mintage | VF20 | XF40 | MS60 | MS63 | MS65 |
|---|---|---|---|---|---|---|
| 2008 | 48,914 | PF63 65.00 | PF65 75.00 | | | |

**KM# 1551 1-1/2 EURO**
22.20 g., 0.900 Silver 0.6424 oz. ASW, 37 mm. **Subject:** Franco - Japanese Relators - 150th Anniversary **Obv:** Eiflfel Tower and Kimono forming logo **Rev:** Japanese cash coin of "Kanei Tsuho

| Date | Mintage | VF20 | XF40 | MS60 | MS63 | MS65 |
|---|---|---|---|---|---|---|
| 2008 | 4,873 | PF63 65.00 | PF65 75.00 | | | |

**KM# 1555 1-1/2 EURO**
22.20 g., 0.900 Silver 0.6424 oz. ASW, 37 mm. **Subject:** André Citronën **Obv:** First front wheel drive auto **Rev:** Bust 1/4 left

| Date | Mintage | VF20 | XF40 | MS60 | MS63 | MS65 |
|---|---|---|---|---|---|---|
| 2008 | 3,814 | PF63 65.00 | PF65 75.00 | | | |

**KM# 1558 1-1/2 EURO**
22.20 g., 0.900 Silver 0.6424 oz. ASW, 37 mm. **Subject:** Rouen Armada **Obv:** Cape Horn, sextant, hour glass **Rev:** Sailing ship

| Date | Mintage | VF20 | XF40 | MS60 | MS63 | MS65 |
|---|---|---|---|---|---|---|
| 2008 | 2,790 | PF63 65.00 | PF65 75.00 | | | |

**KM# 1561 1-1/2 EURO**
22.20 g., 0.900 Silver 0.6424 oz. ASW, 37 mm. **Subject:** Lourdes, 150th Anniversary **Obv:** Church of Notre Dame at Lourdes **Rev:** Cross with Pope John Paul II, Pope Benedict XVI and Bernadette Soubirous in quadrants

| Date | Mintage | VF20 | XF40 | MS60 | MS63 | MS65 |
|---|---|---|---|---|---|---|
| 2008 | 8,001 | PF63 60.00 | PF65 70.00 | | | |

**KM# 1566 1-1/2 EURO**
22.20 g., 0.900 Silver 0.6424 oz. ASW, 37 mm. **Subject:** Gabrielle Chanel **Obv:** Bust right in hat **Rev:** Value on "Matelassé" pattern

| Date | Mintage | VF20 | XF40 | MS60 | MS63 | MS65 |
|---|---|---|---|---|---|---|
| 2008 | 9,987 | PF63 65.00 | PF65 75.00 | | | |

**KM# 1574 1-1/2 EURO**
22.20 g., 0.900 Silver 0.6424 oz. ASW, 37 mm. **Subject:** UNESCO - Grand Canyon **Obv:** Grand Canyon **Rev:** UNESCO logos

| Date | Mintage | VF20 | XF40 | MS60 | MS63 | MS65 |
|---|---|---|---|---|---|---|
| 2008 | 3,647 | PF63 65.00 | PF65 75.00 | | | |

**KM# 1576 1-1/2 EURO**
22.20 g., 0.900 Silver 0.6424 oz. ASW, 37 mm. **Subject:** International Polar Year **Obv:** IPY logo **Rev:** Emperor Penguin and map of Antartica

| Date | Mintage | VF20 | XF40 | MS60 | MS63 | MS65 |
|---|---|---|---|---|---|---|
| 2008 | 3,553 | PF63 65.00 | PF65 75.00 | | | |

**KM# 1578 1-1/2 EURO**
22.20 g., 0.900 Silver 0.6424 oz. ASW, 37 mm. **Subject:** Spirou, 70th Anniversary **Obv:** Character Spirou in thought **Rev:** 70th Anniversary logo

| Date | Mintage | VF20 | XF40 | MS60 | MS63 | MS65 |
|---|---|---|---|---|---|---|
| 2008 | 3,672 | PF63 60.00 | PF65 70.00 | | | |

**KM# 1633 1-1/2 EURO**
11.00 g., Aluminum-Bronze, 30 mm. **Obv:** Stadium view, soccer player **Rev:** Shield of Olympique Lyonnais

| Date | Mintage | VF20 | XF40 | MS60 | MS63 | MS65 |
|---|---|---|---|---|---|---|
| 2009 | 8,455 | — | — | 12.00 | 15.00 | 20.00 |

**KM# 1723 1-1/2 EURO**
11.00 g., Aluminum-Bronze, 30 mm. **Obv:** Soccer player **Rev:** Girondins de Bordeaux logo **Mint:** Paris

| Date | Mintage | VF20 | XF40 | MS60 | MS63 | MS65 |
|---|---|---|---|---|---|---|
| 2010 | 25,000 | — | — | 12.00 | 15.00 | 20.00 |

**KM# 1754 1-1/2 EURO**
11.00 g., Aluminum-Bronze, 30 mm. **Subject:** Olympique de Marseille **Obv:** Soccer player **Rev:** OM logo **Mint:** Paris

| Date | Mintage | VF20 | XF40 | MS60 | MS63 | MS65 |
|---|---|---|---|---|---|---|
| 2011 | 25,000 | — | — | — | — | 15.00 |

**KM# 1918 1-1/2 EURO**
11.00 g., Aluminum-Bronze, 30 mm. **Subject:** Paris Saint Germain **Obv:** Stadium and player **Rev:** Team logo **Mint:** Paris

| Date | Mintage | VF20 | XF40 | MS60 | MS63 | MS65 |
|---|---|---|---|---|---|---|
| 2012 (a) | 25,000 | — | — | — | — | 15.00 |

**KM# 1289 2 EURO**
8.50 g., Bi-Metallic Nickel-Brass center in Copper-Nickel ring, 25.75 mm. **Obv:** Stylized tree divides RF within circle, date below **Rev:** Denomination and map **Edge:** Reeded with 2's and stars **Mint:** Paris

| Date | Mintage | VF20 | XF40 | MS60 | MS63 | MS65 |
|---|---|---|---|---|---|---|
| 2001 | 237,950,793 | — | — | — | 3.75 | 6.00 |
| 2001 | 15,000 | PF65 20.00 | | | | |
| 2002 | 153,700,000 | — | — | — | 3.75 | 6.00 |
| 2002 | 21,453 | PF65 18.00 | | | | |
| 2003 In sets only | 180,000 | — | — | — | — | 13.50 |
| 2003 | 40,000 | PF65 20.00 | | | | |
| 2004 In sets only | 160,000 | — | — | — | — | 13.50 |
| 2004 | 20,000 | PF65 20.00 | | | | |
| 2005 In sets only | 120,000 | — | — | — | — | 13.50 |
| 2005 | 10,000 | PF65 20.00 | | | | |
| 2006 In sets only | 67,600 | — | — | — | — | 13.50 |
| 2006 | 10,000 | PF65 20.00 | | | | |

### KM# 1414 2 EURO

8.50 g., Bi-Metallic Nickel-Brass center in Copper-Nickel ring, 25.75 mm. **Obv:** Stylized tree divides RF within circle, date below **Rev:** Relief map of Western Europe, stars, lines and value **Edge:** Reeded with 2's and stars **Mint:** Paris

| Date | Mintage | VF20 | XF40 | MS60 | MS63 | MS65 |
|---|---|---|---|---|---|---|
| 2007 In sets only | 58,000 | — | — | — | — | 15.00 |
| 2007 | 7,500 | **PF65** 25.00 | | | | |
| 2008 In sets only | 57,000 | — | — | — | — | 6.00 |
| 2008 | 7,500 | **PF65** 25.00 | | | | |
| 2009 In sets only | 50,500 | — | — | — | — | 6.00 |
| 2009 | 7,500 | **PF65** 25.00 | | | | |
| 2010 | — | — | — | — | — | 6.00 |
| 2010 | — | **PF65** 25.00 | | | | |
| 2011 | — | — | — | — | — | 6.00 |
| 2011 | — | **PF65** 25.00 | | | | |
| 2012 | — | — | — | — | — | 6.00 |
| 2012 | — | **PF65** 25.00 | | | | |
| 2013 | — | — | — | — | — | 6.00 |
| 2013 | — | **PF65** 25.00 | | | | |
| 2014 | — | — | — | — | — | 6.00 |
| 2014 | — | **PF65** 25.00 | | | | |

### KM# 1460 2 EURO

8.50 g., Bi-Metallic Nickel-Brass center in Copper-Nickel ring, 25.75 mm. **Subject:** Treaty of Rome 50th Anniversary **Edge:** Reeded with 2's and stars **Mint:** Paris

| Date | Mintage | VF20 | XF40 | MS60 | MS63 | MS65 |
|---|---|---|---|---|---|---|
| 2007 | 9,600,000 | — | — | — | 5.50 | 6.50 |

### KM# 1459 2 EURO

8.50 g., Bi-Metallic Nickel-Brass center in Copper-Nickel ring, 25.75 mm. **Subject:** European Union Presidency **Obv:** Inscription **Obv. Inscription:** PRÉSIDENCE / FRANÇAISE / UNION / EUROPÉENNE / RF **Rev:** Large value "2" at left, modified map of Europe at right **Edge:** Reeded with 2's and stars **Mint:** Paris

| Date | Mintage | VF20 | XF40 | MS60 | MS63 | MS65 |
|---|---|---|---|---|---|---|
| 2008 (a) | 20,100,000 | — | — | — | 5.50 | 6.50 |

### KM# 1542 2 EURO

8.50 g., Bi-Metallic Nickel-Brass center in Copper-Nickel ring, 25.75 mm. **Subject:** 5th Republic, 50th Anniversary **Obv:** Text within stars **Rev:** Value at left, relief map of the EU at right **Edge:** Reeded with 2's and stars **Mint:** Paris

| Date | Mintage | VF20 | XF40 | MS60 | MS63 | MS65 |
|---|---|---|---|---|---|---|
| 2008 (a) Sets only | 20,000 | — | — | — | — | 20.00 |
| 2008 (a) | 10,000,000 | — | — | — | 6.50 | 7.50 |
| 2008 (a) | 10,000 | **PF63** 40.00 | **PF65** 45.00 | | | |

### KM# 1590 2 EURO

8.50 g., Bi-Metallic Nickel-Brass center in Copper-Nickel ring, 25.75 mm. **Subject:** EMU 10th Anniversary **Obv:** Stick figure and E design **Edge:** Reeded with 2's and stars **Mint:** Paris

| Date | Mintage | VF20 | XF40 | MS60 | MS63 | MS65 |
|---|---|---|---|---|---|---|
| 2009 | 6,801 | **PF63** 15.00 | **PF65** 18.00 | | | |
| 2009 | 7,284 | — | — | — | 8.00 | 10.00 |

### KM# 1676 2 EURO

8.50 g., Bi-Metallic Nickel-Brass center in Copper-Nickel ring, 25.75 mm. **Subject:** 70th Anniversary, June 18th Appeal **Obv:** General Charles DeGaulle giving BBC speech **Rev:** Value and map **Edge:** Reeded with 2's and stars **Mint:** Paris

| Date | Mintage | VF20 | XF40 | MS60 | MS63 | MS65 |
|---|---|---|---|---|---|---|
| 2010 | 20,000 | — | — | — | 8.00 | 10.00 |
| 2010 | 10,000 | **PF63** 15.00 | **PF65** 18.00 | | | |

### KM# 1789 2 EURO

8.50 g., Bi-Metallic Nickel-Brass center in Copper-Nickel ring, 25.75 mm. **Subject:** International Music Day, 30th Anniversary **Obv:** Youth jamming **Rev:** Value and map of Western Europe **Edge:** Reeded with 2's and stars **Mint:** Paris

| Date | Mintage | VF20 | XF40 | MS60 | MS63 | MS65 |
|---|---|---|---|---|---|---|
| 2011 | 10,000,000 | — | — | — | — | 5.00 |
| 2011 Special Unc. | 20,000 | — | — | — | — | 8.00 |
| 2011 | 10,000 | **PF63** 15.00 | **PF65** 18.00 | | | |

### KM# 1846 2 EURO

8.50 g., Bi-Metallic Nickel-Brass center in Copper-Nickel ring, 25.75 mm. **Subject:** Euro coinage, 10th Anniversary **Obv:** Euro symbol on globe, child-like drawing around **Mint:** Paris

| Date | Mintage | VF20 | XF40 | MS60 | MS63 | MS65 |
|---|---|---|---|---|---|---|
| 2012 (a) | 10,000,000 | — | — | — | 6.50 | 7.50 |
| 2012 (a) Special Unc. | | — | — | — | 8.00 | 10.00 |
| 2012 (a) | — | **PF63** 15.00 | **PF65** 18.00 | | | |

### KM# 1847 2 EURO

22.20 g., 0.900 Silver 0.6424 oz. ASW, 37 mm. **Obv:** Sailing ship L'Hermione **Rev:** Ship figurehead at right, ship's wheel at bottom **Mint:** Paris

| Date | Mintage | VF20 | XF40 | MS60 | MS63 | MS65 |
|---|---|---|---|---|---|---|
| 2012 (a) | 10,000 | **PF63** 35.00 | **PF65** 40.00 | | | |

### KM# 1894 2 EURO

8.50 g., Bi-Metallic Nickel-Brass center in Copper-Nickel ring, 25.75 mm. **Subject:** abbé Pierre, 100th anniversary of Birth **Obv:** Portrait facing of abbé Pierre, wearing beret **Mint:** Paris

| Date | Mintage | VF20 | XF40 | MS60 | MS63 | MS65 |
|---|---|---|---|---|---|---|
| 2012 (a) | 1,000,000 | — | — | — | 6.00 | 7.00 |
| 2012 (a) Special Unc. | 10,000 | — | — | — | 8.00 | 10.00 |
| 2012 (a) | 10,000 | **PF63** 25.00 | **PF65** 30.00 | | | |

### KM# 2094 2 EURO

8.50 g., Bi-Metallic Nickel-Brass center in Copper-Nickel ring, 25.75 mm. **Subject:** French-German Friendship, 50th Anniversary **Mint:** Paris

| Date | Mintage | VF20 | XF40 | MS60 | MS63 | MS65 |
|---|---|---|---|---|---|---|
| 2013 | — | — | — | — | 8.00 | 10.00 |
| 2013 | — | **PF63** 15.00 | **PF65** 18.00 | | | |

### KM# 2102 2 EURO

8.50 g., Bi-Metallic Nickel-Brass center in Copper-Nickel ring, 25.75 mm. **Subject:** Pierre de Coubertin 150th Anniversary of Birth **Rev:** Rings at left, facing bust at right

| Date | Mintage | VF20 | XF40 | MS60 | MS63 | MS65 |
|---|---|---|---|---|---|---|
| 2013 | — | — | — | — | 8.00 | 10.00 |
| 2013 Special Unc | — | — | — | — | 8.00 | 10.00 |
| 2013 | — | **PF63** 15.00 | **PF65** 18.00 | | | |

### KM# 1347 5 EURO

24.90 g., 0.900 Bi-Metallic 0.7205 oz. .900 Silver 22.2g planchet with .750 Gold 2.7g insert, 37 mm. **Obv:** The Seed Sower on gold insert **Rev:** Denomination and map **Edge:** Plain **Mint:** Paris

| Date | Mintage | VF20 | XF40 | MS60 | MS63 | MS65 |
|---|---|---|---|---|---|---|
| 2002 | 8,408 | **PF63** 550 | **PF65** 575 | | | |

### KM# 1371 5 EURO

24.90 g., Bi-Metallic .750 Gold 2.7 g insert on .900 Silver 22.2g planchet, 37 mm. **Obv:** The Seed Sower on gold insert **Rev:** French face map and denomination **Edge:** Plain **Mint:** Paris

| Date | Mintage | VF20 | XF40 | MS60 | MS63 | MS65 |
|---|---|---|---|---|---|---|
| 2004 | 3,000 | **PF63** 550 | **PF65** 575 | | | |

### KM# 2010 5 EURO

12.00 g., 0.900 Silver 0.3472 oz. ASW, 29 mm. **Obv:** Tree within hexagon **Rev:** Pantheon and large value **Mint:** Paris

| Date | Mintage | VF20 | XF40 | MS60 | MS63 | MS65 |
|---|---|---|---|---|---|---|
| 2004 | — | **PF63** 25.00 | **PF65** 30.00 | | | |
| 2005 | — | **PF63** 25.00 | **PF65** 30.00 | | | |
| 2006 | — | **PF63** 25.00 | **PF65** 30.00 | | | |

### KM# 1523 5 EURO

22.20 g., 0.900 Silver 0.6424 oz. ASW, 37 mm. **Subject:** Euro - 5th Anniversary **Obv:** The Seed Sower

| Date | Mintage | VF20 | XF40 | MS60 | MS63 | MS65 |
|---|---|---|---|---|---|---|
| 2007 | 5,000 | **PF63** 55.00 | **PF65** 60.00 | | | |

### KM# 1524 5 EURO

163.80 g., 0.950 Silver 5.003 oz. ASW, 50 mm. **Subject:** Euro 5th Anniversary **Obv:** Sower

| Date | Mintage | VF20 | XF40 | MS60 | MS63 | MS65 |
|---|---|---|---|---|---|---|
| 2007 | 493 | **PF63** 325 | **PF65** 350 | | | |

### KM# 1525 5 EURO

1.24 g., 0.999 Gold 0.0398 oz. AGW, 13.9 mm. **Subject:** Euro 5th Anniversary **Obv:** The Seed Sower

| Date | Mintage | VF20 | XF40 | MS60 | MS63 | MS65 |
|---|---|---|---|---|---|---|
| 2007 | 9,951 | **PF63** 75.00 | **PF65** 85.00 | | | |

### KM# 1526 5 EURO

31.11 g., 0.920 Gold 0.920 oz. AGW, 31 mm. **Subject:** Euro 5th Anniversary **Obv:** The Seed Sower

| Date | Mintage | VF20 | XF40 | MS60 | MS63 | MS65 |
|---|---|---|---|---|---|---|
| 2007 | 472 | **PF65** 1,600 | | | | |

### KM# 1534 5 EURO

10.00 g., 0.500 Silver 0.1608 oz. ASW, 27 mm. **Obv:** Sower, full length **Rev:** Value within hexagon design

| Date | Mintage | VF20 | XF40 | MS60 | MS63 | MS65 |
|---|---|---|---|---|---|---|
| 2008 | 2,000,000 | **PF63** 15.00 | **PF65** 18.00 | | | |

### KM# 1538 5 EURO

1.24 g., 0.999 Gold 0.0398 oz. AGW, 13.9 mm. **Subject:** 5th Republic, 50th Anniversary **Obv:** Sower **Rev:** de Gaulle head right

| Date | Mintage | VF20 | XF40 | MS60 | MS63 | MS65 |
|---|---|---|---|---|---|---|
| 2008 | 9,757 | **PF63** 75.00 | **PF65** 85.00 | | | |

**KM# 1586 5 EURO**
1.24 g., 0.999 Gold 0.0398 oz. AGW, 13.9 mm. **Subject:** Court of Human Rights, 50th Anniversary **Obv:** The Seed Sower left **Rev:** Text

| Date | Mintage | VF20 | XF40 | MS60 | MS63 | MS65 |
|---|---|---|---|---|---|---|
| 2009 P | 8,118 | PF63 75.00 | PF65 85.00 | | | |

**KM# 1625 5 EURO**
15.00 g., 0.900 Silver 0.434 oz. ASW, 30 x 21 mm. **Subject:** Monet **Obv:** Le Bassin Aux Nympheas, 1900 painting **Rev:** Multicolor pallet and brushes, portrait **Shape:** Rectangle

| Date | Mintage | VF20 | XF40 | MS60 | MS63 | MS65 |
|---|---|---|---|---|---|---|
| 2009 P | 3,865 | — | — | — | 45.00 | 50.00 |

**KM# 1627 5 EURO**
22.20 g., 0.900 Silver 0.6424 oz. ASW, 37 mm. **Subject:** Year of the Ox **Obv:** Oxen within Asia screen garden **Rev:** Portrait of La Fontaine

| Date | Mintage | VF20 | XF40 | MS60 | MS63 | MS65 |
|---|---|---|---|---|---|---|
| 2009 P | 4,738 | PF63 35.00 | PF65 40.00 | | | |

**KM# 1643 5 EURO**
15.00 g., 0.900 Silver 0.434 oz. ASW, 30x21 mm. **Subject:** Pierre Auguste Renoir **Obv:** Boaters Lunch in color **Rev:** Portrait and paint brushes **Shape:** Rectangle **Mint:** Paris

| Date | Mintage | VF20 | XF40 | MS60 | MS63 | MS65 |
|---|---|---|---|---|---|---|
| 2009 | 2,799 | — | — | — | 45.00 | 50.00 |

**KM# 1674 5 EURO**
1.24 g., 0.999 Gold 0.0398 oz. AGW, 13.9 mm. **Obv:** The Seed Sower left **Rev:** Wheat and olive branch **Mint:** Paris

| Date | Mintage | VF20 | XF40 | MS60 | MS63 | MS65 |
|---|---|---|---|---|---|---|
| 2010 | 10,000 | PF63 75.00 | PF65 85.00 | | | |

**KM# 1680 5 EURO**
0.50 g., 0.999 Gold, 11 mm. **Subject:** Cluny Abbey, 1100th Anniversary **Obv:** Europa head facing **Rev:** Cluny Abbey **Mint:** Paris

| Date | Mintage | VF20 | XF40 | MS60 | MS63 | MS65 |
|---|---|---|---|---|---|---|
| 2010 | 20,000 | PF63 45.00 | PF65 50.00 | | | |

**KM# 1715 5 EURO**
22.20 g., 0.900 Silver 0.6424 oz. ASW, 37 mm. **Obv:** Tiger within border **Rev:** La Fontaine bust at left, animals at right **Mint:** Paris

| Date | Mintage | VF20 | XF40 | MS60 | MS63 | MS65 |
|---|---|---|---|---|---|---|
| 2010 | 10,000 | PF63 65.00 | PF65 75.00 | | | |

**KM# 1785 5 EURO**
1.24 g., 0.999 Gold 0.040 oz. AGW, 13.9 mm. **Subject:** Euro Starter Kit, 10th Anniversary **Obv:** Sower **Rev:** Euro starter kit **Mint:** Paris

| Date | Mintage | VF20 | XF40 | MS60 | MS63 | MS65 |
|---|---|---|---|---|---|---|
| 2011 | 10,000 | PF63 100 | PF65 120 | | | |

**KM# 1791 5 EURO**
0.50 g., 0.999 Gold, 11 mm. **Subject:** International Music Day, 30th Anniversary **Obv:** Europa **Rev:** Youth jamming **Mint:** Paris

| Date | Mintage | VF20 | XF40 | MS60 | MS63 | MS65 |
|---|---|---|---|---|---|---|
| 2011 | 20,000 | PF63 100 | PF65 120 | | | |

**KM# 1810 5 EURO**
0.50 g., 0.999 Gold, 11 mm. **Subject:** UNESCO World Heritage Site - Palace of Versailles **Mint:** Paris

| Date | Mintage | VF20 | XF40 | MS60 | MS63 | MS65 |
|---|---|---|---|---|---|---|
| 2011 | 20,000 | PF63 100 | PF65 120 | | | |

**KM# 1833 5 EURO**
22.20 g., 0.900 Silver 0.6424 oz. ASW, 37 mm. **Subject:** Year of the Rabbit **Obv:** Rabbit seated facing right **Rev:** Fontaine and animals **Mint:** Paris

| Date | Mintage | VF20 | XF40 | MS60 | MS63 | MS65 |
|---|---|---|---|---|---|---|
| 2011 | 10,000 | PF63 50.00 | PF65 55.00 | | | |

**KM# 1851 5 EURO**
0.50 g., 0.999 Gold, 11 mm. **Subject:** Eurocorps, 20th Anniversary **Obv:** Mitterrand and Kohl standing clasping hands **Rev:** Europa facing **Mint:** Paris

| Date | Mintage | VF20 | XF40 | MS60 | MS63 | MS65 |
|---|---|---|---|---|---|---|
| 2012 (a) | 10,000 | PF63 65.00 | PF65 75.00 | | | |

**KM# 1890 5 EURO**
0.50 g., 0.999 Gold, 11 mm. **Subject:** Euro, 10th Anniversary **Obv:** The Sower advancing left **Rev:** Value on globe with child-like renderings around **Mint:** Paris

| Date | Mintage | VF20 | XF40 | MS60 | MS63 | MS65 |
|---|---|---|---|---|---|---|
| 2012 (a) | 10,000 | PF63 75.00 | PF65 85.00 | | | |

**KM# 1896 5 EURO**
1.24 g., 0.999 Gold 0.040 oz. AGW, 13.9 mm. **Subject:** abbé Pierre, 100th anniversary of Birth **Obv:** Pierre's bust at left, shaddow figure at right **Rev:** Emmaus International logo and quote **Mint:** Paris

| Date | Mintage | VF20 | XF40 | MS60 | MS63 | MS65 |
|---|---|---|---|---|---|---|
| 2012 (a) | 10,000 | PF63 100 | PF65 120 | | | |

**KM# 1907 5 EURO**
0.50 g., 0.999 Gold, 11 mm. **Subject:** UNESCO - World Heritage Site **Obv:** Abu Simbel temple **Rev:** Sphinx and Pyramids **Mint:** Paris

| Date | Mintage | VF20 | XF40 | MS60 | MS63 | MS65 |
|---|---|---|---|---|---|---|
| 2012 (a) | 10,000 | PF63 75.00 | PF65 85.00 | | | |

**KM# 1758 5 EURO**
7.30 g., 0.333 Silver 0.0782 oz. ASW, 26 mm. **Obv:** Value within horizontal wreath **Rev:** LIBERTE **Mint:** Paris

| Date | Mintage | VF20 | XF40 | MS60 | MS63 | MS65 |
|---|---|---|---|---|---|---|
| 2013 | 2,000,000 | — | — | — | 12.50 | 15.00 |

**KM# 1759 5 EURO**
7.30 g., 0.333 Silver 0.0782 oz. ASW, 26 mm. **Obv:** Value within horizontal wreath **Rev:** EGALITE **Mint:** Paris

| Date | Mintage | VF20 | XF40 | MS60 | MS63 | MS65 |
|---|---|---|---|---|---|---|
| 2013 | 2,000,000 | — | — | — | 12.50 | 15.00 |

**KM# 1760 5 EURO**
7.30 g., 0.333 Silver 0.0782 oz. ASW, 26 mm. **Rev:** FRATERNTE **Mint:** Paris

| Date | Mintage | VF20 | XF40 | MS60 | MS63 | MS65 |
|---|---|---|---|---|---|---|
| 2013 | 2,000,000 | — | — | — | 12.50 | 15.00 |

**KM# 2092 5 EURO**
0.50 g., 0.999 Gold, 11 mm. **Subject:** French - German Friendship **Rev:** Europa head facing at right, banners at left **Mint:** Paris

| Date | Mintage | VF20 | XF40 | MS60 | MS63 | MS65 |
|---|---|---|---|---|---|---|
| 2013 | — | PF63 75.00 | PF65 85.00 | | | |

**KM# 2099 5 EURO**
0.50 g., 0.999 Gold, 11 mm. **Subject:** Notre Dame, 850th Anniversary **Obv:** Seal at right, cathedral details **Rev:** Seal at left, cathedral details **Mint:** Paris

| Date | Mintage | VF20 | XF40 | MS60 | MS63 | MS65 |
|---|---|---|---|---|---|---|
| 2013 | 15,000 | PF63 100 | PF65 120 | | | |

**KM# 2114 5 EURO**
0.50 g., 0.999 Gold AGW, 11 mm. **Subject:** Tour de France, 100th Anniversary **Mint:** Paris

| Date | Mintage | VF20 | XF40 | MS60 | MS63 | MS65 |
|---|---|---|---|---|---|---|
| 2013 | 15,000 | PF63 65.00 | PF65 75.00 | | | |

**KM# 1302 10 EURO**
8.45 g., 0.999 Gold 0.2714 oz. AGW, 22 mm. **Subject:** Europa **Obv:** Eight French euro coin designs **Rev:** Portrait and flags design of 6.55957 francs KM-1265 **Edge:** Reeded **Mint:** Paris

| Date | Mintage | VF20 | XF40 | MS60 | MS63 | MS65 |
|---|---|---|---|---|---|---|
| 2002 | 3,000 | PF65 525 | | | | |

**KM# 1326 10 EURO**
8.45 g., 0.920 Gold 0.2499 oz. AGW, 22 mm. **Obv:** Tour de France logo **Rev:** Cyclist going left **Edge:** Reeded **Mint:** Paris

| Date | Mintage | VF20 | XF40 | MS60 | MS63 | MS65 |
|---|---|---|---|---|---|---|
| 2003 (Ht) | 5,000 | PF63 500 | PF65 525 | | | |

**KM# 1348 10 EURO**
8.45 g., 0.920 Gold 0.2499 oz. AGW, 22 mm. **Obv:** The seed sower **Rev:** Denomination and map **Edge:** Plain **Mint:** Paris

| Date | Mintage | VF20 | XF40 | MS60 | MS63 | MS65 |
|---|---|---|---|---|---|---|
| 2003 | 5,779 | PF63 475 | PF65 500 | | | |

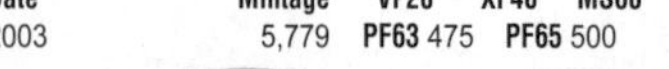

**KM# 1352 10 EURO**
8.45 g., 0.920 Gold 0.2499 oz. AGW, 22 mm. **Obv:** Obverse design of first one franc coin **Rev:** Reverse design of first one franc coin **Edge:** Plain **Mint:** Paris

| Date | Mintage | VF20 | XF40 | MS60 | MS63 | MS65 |
|---|---|---|---|---|---|---|
| 2003 | 1,761 | PF63 475 | PF65 500 | | | |

**KM# 1362 10 EURO**
8.45 g., 0.920 Gold 0.2499 oz. AGW, 22 mm. **Obv:** Pierre de Coubertin **Rev:** Olympic runners **Edge:** Plain **Mint:** Paris

| Date | Mintage | VF20 | XF40 | MS60 | MS63 | MS65 |
|---|---|---|---|---|---|---|
| 2003 | 1,635 | PF63 475 | PF65 500 | | | |

**KM# 1992 10 EURO**
8.45 g., 0.920 Gold 0.2499 oz. AGW, 22 mm. **Obv:** Curved cross with coins **Rev:** Europa head at right, flags at left **Mint:** Paris

| Date | Mintage | VF20 | XF40 | MS60 | MS63 | MS65 |
|---|---|---|---|---|---|---|
| 2003 | Est. 7000 | PF63 550 | PF65 575 | | | |

**KM# 1367 10 EURO**
6.41 g., 0.900 Gold 0.1855 oz. AGW, 22 mm. **Obv:** Book, denomination and eagle **Rev:** Napoleon and coronation scene **Edge:** Plain **Mint:** Paris

| Date | Mintage | VF20 | XF40 | MS60 | MS63 | MS65 |
|---|---|---|---|---|---|---|
| 2004 | 5,000 | PF63 400 | PF65 425 | | | |

**KM# 1375 10 EURO**
8.45 g., 0.920 Gold 0.2499 oz. AGW, 22 mm. **Obv:** Half soccer ball and denomination **Rev:** Eiffel tower and soccer balls **Edge:** Plain **Mint:** Paris

| Date | Mintage | VF20 | XF40 | MS60 | MS63 | MS65 |
|---|---|---|---|---|---|---|
| 2004 | 10,000 | PF63 475 | PF65 500 | | | |

**KM# 1392 10 EURO**
8.45 g., 0.920 Gold 0.2499 oz. AGW, 22 mm. **Subject:** European Union Expansion **Obv:** Partial face and flags **Rev:** Puzzle map **Edge:** Reeded **Mint:** Paris

| Date | Mintage | VF20 | XF40 | MS60 | MS63 | MS65 |
|---|---|---|---|---|---|---|
| 2004 | 5,000 | PF63 500 | PF65 525 | | | |

**KM# 1403 10 EURO**
8.45 g., 0.920 Gold 0.2499 oz. AGW, 22 mm. **Subject:** Jules Verne **Obv:** Various scenes from Verne's novel "Around The World in 80 Days **Rev:** Jules Verne's portrait left of value and date **Mint:** Paris

| Date | Mintage | VF20 | XF40 | MS60 | MS63 | MS65 |
|---|---|---|---|---|---|---|
| 2005 | 811 | PF63 575 | PF65 600 | | | |

**KM# 1424 10 EURO**
8.45 g., 0.920 Gold 0.2499 oz. AGW, 22 mm. **Subject:** Biathlon **Rev:** Skier at right facing 3/4 left, mountain peaks in background **Rev. Inscription:** JEUX D'HIVER **Mint:** Paris

| Date | Mintage | VF20 | XF40 | MS60 | MS63 | MS65 |
|---|---|---|---|---|---|---|
| 2005 | 700 | PF63 475 | PF65 500 | | | |

**KM# 1426 10 EURO**
8.45 g., 0.920 Gold 0.2499 oz. AGW, 22 mm. **Series:** Jules Verne **Subject:** From the earth to the moon **Rev:** Crowd observing at lower left, volcano erupting above, moon at upper right, Verne in spaceship at lower right, chimneys belching smoke in backgroud **Rev. Legend:** DE LA TERRE À LA LUNE **Mint:** Paris

| Date | Mintage | VF20 | XF40 | MS60 | MS63 | MS65 |
|---|---|---|---|---|---|---|
| 2005 | 414 | PF63 500 | PF65 525 | | | |

**KM# 1429 10 EURO**
8.45 g., 0.920 Gold 0.2499 oz. AGW, 22 mm. **Rev:** Kitty at the Spectacle, multicolor **Rev. Legend:** Hello Kitty **Mint:** Paris

| Date | Mintage | VF20 | XF40 | MS60 | MS63 | MS65 |
|---|---|---|---|---|---|---|
| 2005 | 1,000 | PF63 550 | PF65 575 | | | |

**KM# 1432 10 EURO**
6.41 g., 0.900 Gold 0.1855 oz. AGW, 21 mm. **Subject:** Bicentennial - Victory at Austerlitz **Rev:** Battle scene **Rev. Legend:** LIBERTÉ ÉGALITÉ FRATERNITÉ **Mint:** Paris

| Date | Mintage | VF20 | XF40 | MS60 | MS63 | MS65 |
|---|---|---|---|---|---|---|
| 2005 | 451 | PF63 400 | PF65 425 | | | |

**KM# 1435 10 EURO**
8.45 g., 0.920 Gold 0.2499 oz. AGW, 22 mm. **Subject:** 50th Anniversary - Flag of Europe **Rev:** Stars at left, partial flag at center right **Mint:** Paris

| Date | Mintage | VF20 | XF40 | MS60 | MS63 | MS65 |
|---|---|---|---|---|---|---|
| 2005 | 1,798 | PF63 475 | PF65 500 | | | |

**KM# 1439 10 EURO**
8.45 g., 0.920 Gold 0.2499 oz. AGW, 22 mm. **Series:** Jules Verne **Subject:** 20,000 Leagues Under the Sea **Rev:** Submarine above plants and divers **Rev. Legend:** VINGT MILLE LIEUES SOUS LES MERS **Mint:** Paris

| Date | Mintage | VF20 | XF40 | MS60 | MS63 | MS65 |
|---|---|---|---|---|---|---|
| 2005 | 490 | PF63 500 | PF65 525 | | | |

**KM# 2021 10 EURO**
8.45 g., 0.920 Gold 0.2499 oz. AGW, 22 mm. **Subject:** World Cup Soccer **Obv:** World Cup Trophy and soccer ball **Rev:** Large value and map of France **Mint:** Paris

| Date | Mintage | VF20 | XF40 | MS60 | MS63 | MS65 |
|---|---|---|---|---|---|---|
| 2005 | 1,518 | PF63 550 | PF65 575 | | | |

**KM# 2023 10 EURO**
8.45 g., 0.920 Gold 0.2499 oz. AGW, 22 mm. **Obv:** Globe and map of Europe **Rev:** Doves in flight above globe **Mint:** Paris

| Date | Mintage | VF20 | XF40 | MS60 | MS63 | MS65 |
|---|---|---|---|---|---|---|
| 2005 | 3,000 | PF63 550 | PF65 575 | | | |

**KM# 2026 10 EURO**
8.45 g., 0.920 Gold 0.2499 oz. AGW, 22 mm. **Subject:** Bordeaux, 150th Anniversary **Obv:** Female holding bounty **Rev:** Stylized fingers and a grape **Mint:** Paris

| Date | Mintage | VF20 | XF40 | MS60 | MS63 | MS65 |
|---|---|---|---|---|---|---|
| 2005 | 500 | PF63 550 | PF65 575 | | | |

**KM# 1416 10 EURO**
8.45 g., 0.920 Gold 0.2499 oz. AGW, 22 mm. **Obv:** Jean de la Fontaine, value, Chinese astrological animals, date, Paris mint privy marks but without national identification **Rev:** Dog in wreath **Edge:** Reeded **Mint:** Paris

| Date | Mintage | VF20 | XF40 | MS60 | MS63 | MS65 |
|---|---|---|---|---|---|---|
| 2006 | 500 | PF63 525 | PF65 550 | | | |

**KM# 1446 10 EURO**
8.45 g., 0.920 Gold 0.2499 oz. AGW, 22 mm. **Subject:** Marshal Bernadotte under Napoleon **Rev:** Military bust facing 3/4 right at left, building in backgound at right **Rev. Legend:** LIBERTÉ GALITÉ FRATERNITÉ - KARL XIV JOHAN ROI DE SUÉDE **Mint:** Paris

| Date | Mintage | VF20 | XF40 | MS60 | MS63 | MS65 |
|---|---|---|---|---|---|---|
| 2006 | 1,000 | PF63 500 | PF65 525 | | | |

**KM# 1448 10 EURO**
8.45 g., 0.920 Gold 0.2499 oz. AGW, 22 mm. **Subject:** 20,000 Leagues Under the Sea **Obv:** Strogoff horseback wielding a sword, city at left, soldiers at lower left, calvary at right - the Tartars, Siberia and the Tsar's Army **Obv. Legend:** MICHEL STROGOFF **Rev:** Head of Verne facing 3/4 right at left center, instruments and anchor in curved band **Rev. Legend:** 1828 JULES VERNE 1905 **Mint:** Paris

| Date | Mintage | VF20 | XF40 | MS60 | MS63 | MS65 |
|---|---|---|---|---|---|---|
| 2006 | 500 | PF63 525 | PF65 550 | | | |

**KM# 1449 10 EURO**
8.45 g., 0.920 Gold 0.2499 oz. AGW, 22 mm. **Subject:** 20,000 Leagues Under the Sea **Obv:** Hot air balloon, parrots at left, native masks below left, foliage at right, huts below, map of Africa in background. **Obv. Legend:** CINQ SEMAINES EN BALLON **Rev:** Head of Verne facing 3/4 right at left center, instruments and anchor in curved band **Rev. Legend:** 1828 JULES VERNE 1905 - LIBERTÉ . ÉGALITÉ . FRATERNITÉ **Mint:** Paris

| Date | Mintage | VF20 | XF40 | MS60 | MS63 | MS65 |
|---|---|---|---|---|---|---|
| 2006 | 500 | PF63 525 | PF65 550 | | | |

**KM# 1451 10 EURO**
8.45 g., 0.920 Gold 0.2499 oz. AGW, 22 mm. **Subject:** 100th Anniversary - French Grand Prix **Obv:** Steering wheel with early race car in upper segment, two gauges at lower left, R / F at lower right **Obv. Legend:** LE MANS 1906 - CENTENAIRE du 1er GRAND PRIX de l'AUTOMOBILE CLUB de FRANCE **Rev. Legend:** MAGNY-COURS **Mint:** Paris

| Date | Mintage | VF20 | XF40 | MS60 | MS63 | MS65 |
|---|---|---|---|---|---|---|
| 2006 | 500 | PF63 525 | PF65 550 | | | |

**KM# 2038 10 EURO**
8.45 g., 0.920 Gold 0.2499 oz. AGW, 22 mm. **Subject:** Robert Schuman, 120th Anniversary of Birth **Mint:** Paris

| Date | Mintage | VF20 | XF40 | MS60 | MS63 | MS65 |
|---|---|---|---|---|---|---|
| 2006 | — | PF63 550 | PF65 575 | | | |

**KM# 2042 10 EURO**
8.45 g., 0.920 Gold 0.2499 oz. AGW, 22 mm. **Subject:** Bejing Olympics **Obv:** Three fencing foils on globe map pointing toward Bejing **Rev:** Two fencers **Mint:** Paris

| Date | Mintage | VF20 | XF40 | MS60 | MS63 | MS65 |
|---|---|---|---|---|---|---|
| 2006 | 1,000 | PF63 550 | PF65 575 | | | |

**KM# 2043 10 EURO**
8.45 g., 0.920 Gold 0.2499 oz. AGW, 22 mm. **Subject:** Benjamin Franklin, 300th anniversary of Birth **Obv:** Bust at left, kite in thunderclouds at right **Rev:** French and American flags **Mint:** Paris

| Date | Mintage | VF20 | XF40 | MS60 | MS63 | MS65 |
|---|---|---|---|---|---|---|
| 2006 | 1,000 | PF63 525 | PF65 550 | | | |

**KM# 2045 10 EURO**
8.45 g., 0.920 Gold 0.2499 oz. AGW **Subject:** St. Peter's Basilica, 500th Anniversary **Obv:** Floorplan of St. Peter's **Rev:** Façade and Pope Benedict XVI **Mint:** Paris

| Date | Mintage | VF20 | XF40 | MS60 | MS63 | MS65 |
|---|---|---|---|---|---|---|
| 2006 | 1,000 | PF63 525 | PF65 550 | | | |

**KM# 2049 10 EURO**
8.45 g., 0.920 Gold 0.2499 oz. AGW, 22 mm. **Subject:** Marie Amélie of Orleans and Carlos I of Portugal, 120th Anniversary of Marriage **Obv:** Bust with tiara left **Rev:** Two shields crowned **Mint:** Paris

| Date | Mintage | VF20 | XF40 | MS60 | MS63 | MS65 |
|---|---|---|---|---|---|---|
| 2006 | 500 | PF63 600 | PF65 625 | | | |

**KM# 2053 10 EURO**
8.45 g., 0.920 Gold 0.2499 oz. AGW, 22 mm. **Obv:** Partial monuments forming map of France **Rev:** Arc de Triomphe and Tomb of Unknown Soldier **Mint:** Paris

| Date | Mintage | VF20 | XF40 | MS60 | MS63 | MS65 |
|---|---|---|---|---|---|---|
| 2006 | 500 | PF63 525 | PF65 550 | | | |

**KM# 2054 10 EURO**
8.45 g., 0.920 Gold 0.2499 oz. AGW, 22 mm. **Subject:** Church of St. Louis des Invalides **Obv:** Monument fragments forming map of France **Rev:** Church façade flanked by two men **Mint:** Paris

| Date | Mintage | VF20 | XF40 | MS60 | MS63 | MS65 |
|---|---|---|---|---|---|---|
| 2006 | 500 | PF63 525 | PF65 550 | | | |

**KM# 2063 10 EURO**
8.45 g., 0.920 Gold 0.2499 oz. AGW, 22 mm. **Subject:** Wolfgang Amadeus Mozart, 250th Anniversary of Birth **Obv:** Youthful bust **Rev:** Hands at piano keys, music above **Mint:** Paris

| Date | Mintage | VF20 | XF40 | MS60 | MS63 | MS65 |
|---|---|---|---|---|---|---|
| 2006 | 1,000 | PF63 525 | PF65 550 | | | |

**KM# 2068 10 EURO**
8.45 g., 0.920 Gold 0.2499 oz. AGW, 22 mm. **Subject:** Jules Verne, 100th Anniversary of Death **Obv:** Voyage to the center of the Earth **Mint:** Paris

| Date | Mintage | VF20 | XF40 | MS60 | MS63 | MS65 |
|---|---|---|---|---|---|---|
| 2006 | 500 | PF63 525 | PF65 550 | | | |

**KM# 1418 10 EURO**
8.45 g., 0.920 Gold 0.2499 oz. AGW, 22 mm. **Obv:** Jean de la Fontaine, value, Chinese astrological animals, date, Paris mint privy marks but without national identification **Rev:** Pig in wreath **Edge:** Reeded **Mint:** Paris **Note:** anonymous issue

| Date | Mintage | VF20 | XF40 | MS60 | MS63 | MS65 |
|---|---|---|---|---|---|---|
| 2007 | 500 | PF63 525 | PF65 550 | | | |

**KM# 1420 10 EURO**
8.45 g., 0.920 Gold 0.2499 oz. AGW, 22 mm. **Obv:** Military bust of Lafayette facing 3/4 left **Obv. Legend:** LA FAYETTE. HÉROS DELA RÉVOLUTION AMÉRICAINE **Obv. Inscription:** 1757/1854 at left, RF monogram at right **Rev:** Sailing ship L' Hermione **Rev. Legend:** LA FAYETTE, HERO OF THE AMERICAN REVOLUTION **Edge:** Plain **Mint:** Paris

| Date | Mintage | VF20 | XF40 | MS60 | MS63 | MS65 |
|---|---|---|---|---|---|---|
| 2007 (a) | 499 | PF63 525 | PF65 550 | | | |

**KM# 1463 10 EURO**
8.45 g., 0.920 Gold 0.2499 oz. AGW, 22 mm. **Subject:** Sebastien Le Prestre de Vauban, 300th Anniversary of Death

| Date | Mintage | VF20 | XF40 | MS60 | MS63 | MS65 |
|---|---|---|---|---|---|---|
| 2007 | 1,838 | PF63 475 | PF65 500 | | | |

**KM# 1474 10 EURO**
8.45 g., 0.920 Gold 0.2499 oz. AGW, 22 mm. **Subject:** Paul E. Victor, 100th birthday **Obv:** International polar year logo **Rev:** Bust at left, Islands

| Date | Mintage | VF20 | XF40 | MS60 | MS63 | MS65 |
|---|---|---|---|---|---|---|
| 2007 | 500 | — | — | — | — | 500 |

### KM# 1476 10 EURO

8.45 g., 0.920 Gold 0.2499 oz. AGW, 22 mm. **Obv:** Formula 1 race car on checkered background **Rev:** Legend in wreath on checkered background

| Date | Mintage | VF20 | XF40 | MS60 | MS63 | MS65 |
|---|---|---|---|---|---|---|
| 2007//2006 | 500 | PF63 525 | PF65 550 | | | |

### KM# 1478 10 EURO

8.45 g., 0.920 Gold 0.2499 oz. AGW, 22 mm. **Subject:** 29th Summer Olympic Games Beijing **Obv:** Rider on horseback, globe map of China **Rev:** Equestrian jump over oriental fence

| Date | Mintage | VF20 | XF40 | MS60 | MS63 | MS65 |
|---|---|---|---|---|---|---|
| 2007 | 1,000 | PF63 525 | PF65 550 | | | |

### KM# 1480 10 EURO

8.45 g., 0.920 Gold 0.2499 oz. AGW, 22 mm. **Subject:** Airbus A380 **Obv:** Airplane **Rev:** Europa head and flags

| Date | Mintage | VF20 | XF40 | MS60 | MS63 | MS65 |
|---|---|---|---|---|---|---|
| 2007 | 1,000 | PF63 500 | PF65 525 | | | |

### KM# 1485 10 EURO

8.45 g., 0.920 Gold 0.2499 oz. AGW, 22 mm. **Subject:** 2007 Rugby World Cup **Obv:** Two players and goal **Rev:** Logo and goal

| Date | Mintage | VF20 | XF40 | MS60 | MS63 | MS65 |
|---|---|---|---|---|---|---|
| 2007 | 500 | PF63 525 | PF65 550 | | | |

### KM# 1489 10 EURO

8.45 g., 0.920 Gold 0.2499 oz. AGW, 22 mm. **Obv:** Christian Dior **Rev:** Dior Museum building

| Date | Mintage | VF20 | XF40 | MS60 | MS63 | MS65 |
|---|---|---|---|---|---|---|
| 2007 | 500 | PF63 525 | PF65 550 | | | |

### KM# 1502 10 EURO

8.45 g., 0.920 Gold 0.2499 oz. AGW, 22 mm. **Subject:** Georges Pompidou Center, 30th Anniversary

| Date | Mintage | VF20 | XF40 | MS60 | MS63 | MS65 |
|---|---|---|---|---|---|---|
| 2007 | — | PF63 525 | PF65 550 | | | |

### KM# 1508 10 EURO

8.45 g., 0.920 Gold 0.2499 oz. AGW, 22 mm. **Subject:** Georges Remi Centennial **Obv:** Wand and sparkles **Rev:** Tin Tin raising cap

| Date | Mintage | VF20 | XF40 | MS60 | MS63 | MS65 |
|---|---|---|---|---|---|---|
| 2007 | 1,000 | PF63 500 | PF65 525 | | | |

### KM# 1512 10 EURO

8.45 g., 0.920 Gold 0.2499 oz. AGW, 22 mm. **Subject:** Aristides de Sousa Mendes, Portuguese diplomat **Obv:** Bust right **Rev:** Plaque

| Date | Mintage | VF20 | XF40 | MS60 | MS63 | MS65 |
|---|---|---|---|---|---|---|
| 2007 | 500 | PF63 525 | PF65 550 | | | |

### KM# 1519 10 EURO

8.45 g., 0.920 Gold 0.2499 oz. AGW, 22 mm. **Subject:** Asterix **Rev:** Character with torch

| Date | Mintage | VF20 | XF40 | MS60 | MS63 | MS65 |
|---|---|---|---|---|---|---|
| 2007 | 480 | PF63 525 | PF65 550 | | | |

### KM# 1528 10 EURO

8.45 g., 0.920 Gold 0.2499 oz. AGW, 22 mm. **Subject:** French Presidency of European Union **Obv:** Text within stars **Rev:** Europa head and flags

| Date | Mintage | VF20 | XF40 | MS60 | MS63 | MS65 |
|---|---|---|---|---|---|---|
| 2008 | 999 | PF63 500 | PF65 525 | | | |

### KM# 1533 10 EURO

8.45 g., 0.920 Gold 0.2499 oz. AGW, 22 mm. **Subject:** European Parliament, 50th Anniversary **Obv:** Map of EU within stars **Rev:** European Parliament Building in Strasbourg

| Date | Mintage | VF20 | XF40 | MS60 | MS63 | MS65 |
|---|---|---|---|---|---|---|
| 2008 | 1,845 | PF63 475 | PF65 500 | | | |

### KM# 1539 10 EURO

8.45 g., 0.999 Gold 0.2714 oz. AGW, 22 mm. **Subject:** 5th Republic, 50th Anniversary **Obv:** The Seed Sower **Rev:** de Gaulle head right

| Date | Mintage | VF20 | XF40 | MS60 | MS63 | MS65 |
|---|---|---|---|---|---|---|
| 2008 | 620 | PF63 500 | PF65 525 | | | |

### KM# 1544 10 EURO

8.45 g., 0.920 Gold 0.2499 oz. AGW, 22 mm. **Subject:** 29th Summer Olympic Games - Beijing **Obv:** Swimmer and globe **Rev:** Diver and oriental screen

| Date | Mintage | VF20 | XF40 | MS60 | MS63 | MS65 |
|---|---|---|---|---|---|---|
| 2008 | 988 | PF63 500 | PF65 525 | | | |

### KM# 1547 10 EURO

8.45 g., 0.920 Gold 0.2483 oz. AGW, 22 mm. **Subject:** UEFA **Obv:** French soccer team **Rev:** UEFA logo

| Date | Mintage | F12 | VF20 | XF40 | MS60 | MS63 |
|---|---|---|---|---|---|---|
| 2008 | 500 | PF63 525 | PF65 550 | | | |

### KM# 1552 10 EURO

8.45 g., 0.920 Gold 0.2499 oz. AGW, 22 mm. **Subject:** Franco - Japanese Relators - 150th Anniversary **Obv:** Eiffel Tower and Kimono forming logo **Rev:** Delacroix's "La Liberte

| Date | Mintage | VF20 | XF40 | MS60 | MS63 | MS65 |
|---|---|---|---|---|---|---|
| 2008 | 1,726 | PF63 475 | PF65 500 | | | |

### KM# 1553 10 EURO

8.45 g., 0.920 Gold 0.2499 oz. AGW, 22 mm. **Subject:** Franco - Japanese Relators - 150th Anniversary **Obv:** Eiffel Tower and Kimono forming logo **Rev:** Ichikawa Ebizo IV" portrait painting

| Date | Mintage | VF20 | XF40 | MS60 | MS63 | MS65 |
|---|---|---|---|---|---|---|
| 2008 | 1,657 | PF63 475 | PF65 500 | | | |

### KM# 1554 10 EURO

8.45 g., 0.920 Gold 0.2499 oz. AGW, 22 mm. **Subject:** Franco - Japanese Relators - 150th Anniversary **Obv:** Eiffel Tower and Kimono forming logo **Rev:** Japanese cash coin from "Kanci Tsuho

| Date | Mintage | VF20 | XF40 | MS60 | MS63 | MS65 |
|---|---|---|---|---|---|---|
| 2008 | 1,848 | PF63 475 | PF65 500 | | | |

### KM# 1556 10 EURO

8.45 g., 0.920 Gold 0.2499 oz. AGW, 22 mm. **Subject:** André Citronë **Obv:** First front wheel drive auto **Rev:** Bust 1/4 left

| Date | Mintage | VF20 | XF40 | MS60 | MS63 | MS65 |
|---|---|---|---|---|---|---|
| 2008 | 500 | PF63 525 | PF65 550 | | | |

### KM# 1559 10 EURO

8.45 g., 0.920 Gold 0.2499 oz. AGW, 22 mm. **Subject:** Rouen Armada **Obv:** Cape Hown, sextant, hour glass **Edge:** Sailing ship

| Date | Mintage | VF20 | XF40 | MS60 | MS63 | MS65 |
|---|---|---|---|---|---|---|
| 2008 | 500 | PF63 525 | PF65 550 | | | |

### KM# 1562 10 EURO

8.45 g., 0.920 Gold 0.2499 oz. AGW, 22 mm. **Subject:** Lourdes, 150th Anniversary **Obv:** Church of Notre Dame at Lourdes **Rev:** Cross with Pope John Paul II, Pope Benedict XVI and Bernadette Soubirous in quadrants

| Date | Mintage | VF20 | XF40 | MS60 | MS63 | MS65 |
|---|---|---|---|---|---|---|
| 2008 | 999 | PF63 500 | PF65 525 | | | |

### KM# 1567 10 EURO

8.45 g., 0.920 Gold 0.2499 oz. AGW, 22 mm. **Subject:** Gabrielle Chanel **Obv:** Portrait in hat, right **Rev:** Value on "Matelassé" pattern

| Date | Mintage | VF20 | XF40 | MS60 | MS63 | MS65 |
|---|---|---|---|---|---|---|
| 2008 | 500 | PF63 475 | PF65 500 | | | |

### KM# 1573 10 EURO

8.45 g., 0.920 Gold 0.2499 oz. AGW, 22 mm. **Subject:** Lunar New Year - Year of the Rat **Obv:** Bust of Jean de la Fontaine and twelve awards **Rev:** Rat within border

| Date | Mintage | VF20 | XF40 | MS60 | MS63 | MS65 |
|---|---|---|---|---|---|---|
| 2008 | 500 | PF63 525 | PF65 550 | | | |

### KM# 1575 10 EURO

8.45 g., 0.920 Gold 0.2499 oz. AGW, 22 mm. **Subject:** UNESCO - Grand Canyon **Obv:** Grand Canyon **Rev:** UNESCO logos

| Date | Mintage | VF20 | XF40 | MS60 | MS63 | MS65 |
|---|---|---|---|---|---|---|
| 2008 | 500 | PF63 525 | PF65 550 | | | |

### KM# 1577 10 EURO

8.45 g., 0.920 Gold 0.2499 oz. AGW, 22 mm. **Subject:** International Polar Year **Obv:** IPY logo **Rev:** Emperor Penguin and map of Antartica

| Date | Mintage | VF20 | XF40 | MS60 | MS63 | MS65 |
|---|---|---|---|---|---|---|
| 2008 | 500 | PF63 525 | PF65 550 | | | |

### KM# 1579 10 EURO

8.45 g., 0.920 Gold 0.2499 oz. AGW, 22 mm. **Subject:** Spirou, 70th Anniversary **Obv:** Character Spirou in thought **Rev:** 70th Aniversary logo

| Date | Mintage | VF20 | XF40 | MS60 | MS63 | MS65 |
|---|---|---|---|---|---|---|
| 2008 | 387 | PF63 525 | PF65 550 | | | |

### KM# 1580 10 EURO

12.00 g., 0.900 Silver 0.3472 oz. ASW, 29 mm. **Obv:** Modernistic sower advancing right **Rev:** Wreath and value

| Date | Mintage | VF20 | XF40 | MS60 | MS63 | MS65 |
|---|---|---|---|---|---|---|
| 2009 P | 2,000,000 | — | — | — | 17.50 | 22.50 |

### KM# 1584 10 EURO

22.20 g., 0.900 Silver 0.6424 oz. ASW, 37 mm. **Subject:** Court of Human Rights, 50th Anniversary **Obv:** Sower left **Rev:** Text

| Date | Mintage | VF20 | XF40 | MS60 | MS63 | MS65 |
|---|---|---|---|---|---|---|
| 2009 P | 8,284 | PF63 35.00 | PF65 40.00 | | | |

### KM# 1591 10 EURO

27.20 g., 0.900 Silver 0.787 oz. ASW, 37 mm. **Subject:** Europa - Fall of Berlin Wall **Obv:** Brandenburg gate and doves in flight **Rev:** Head facing and flags

| Date | Mintage | VF20 | XF40 | MS60 | MS63 | MS65 |
|---|---|---|---|---|---|---|
| 2009 P | 10,000 | PF63 37.50 | PF65 40.00 | | | |

### KM# 1596 10 EURO

22.20 g., 0.900 Silver 0.6424 oz. ASW, 37 mm. **Subject:** Concorde 40th Anniversary **Obv:** Concorde in flight **Rev:** Tail emblems

| Date | Mintage | VF20 | XF40 | MS60 | MS63 | MS65 |
|---|---|---|---|---|---|---|
| 2009 P | 15,077 | PF63 40.00 | PF65 45.00 | | | |

### KM# 1601 10 EURO

20.89 g., 0.900 Silver 0.6045 oz. ASW, 37 mm. **Obv:** Eiffel Tower Structure **Rev:** Gustave Eiffel at left

| Date | Mintage | VF20 | XF40 | MS60 | MS63 | MS65 |
|---|---|---|---|---|---|---|
| 2009 P | 7,989 | PF63 35.00 | PF65 40.00 | | | |

### KM# 1606 10 EURO

27.20 g., 0.900 Silver 0.787 oz. ASW, 37 mm. **Subject:** Bugatti 100th Anniversary **Obv:** Ettore Bugatti at left **Rev:** Race car and quilt motif

| Date | Mintage | VF20 | XF40 | MS60 | MS63 | MS65 |
|---|---|---|---|---|---|---|
| 2009 P | 3,547 | PF63 40.00 | PF65 45.00 | | | |

**KM# 1611 10 EURO**
22.20 g., 0.900 Silver 0.6424 oz. ASW, 37 mm. **Subject:** Curie Institute, 100th Anniversary

| Date | Mintage | VF20 | XF40 | MS60 | MS63 | MS65 |
|---|---|---|---|---|---|---|
| 2009 P | 10,000 | PF63 35.00 | PF65 40.00 | | | |

**KM# 1616 10 EURO**
27.20 g., 0.900 Silver 0.787 oz. ASW, 37 mm. **Subject:** Unesco site - The Kremlin in Moscow **Obv:** Wall Tower and cathedral

| Date | Mintage | VF20 | XF40 | MS60 | MS63 | MS65 |
|---|---|---|---|---|---|---|
| 2009 P | 5,205 | PF63 37.00 | PF65 42.00 | | | |

**KM# 1621 10 EURO**
22.20 g., 0.900 Silver 0.6424 oz. ASW, 37 mm. **Subject:** First Moon Landing, 40th Anniversary **Obv:** Footprint on the moon

| Date | Mintage | VF20 | XF40 | MS60 | MS63 | MS65 |
|---|---|---|---|---|---|---|
| 2009 P | 9,996 | PF63 35.00 | PF65 40.00 | | | |

**KM# 1629 10 EURO**
22.20 g., 0.900 Silver 0.6424 oz. ASW, 37 mm. **Subject:** Comic strip heroes **Obv:** Wanted posted **Rev:** Lucky Luke on horseback

| Date | Mintage | VF20 | XF40 | MS60 | MS63 | MS65 |
|---|---|---|---|---|---|---|
| 2009 P | 5,000 | PF63 45.00 | PF65 50.00 | | | |

**KM# 1631 10 EURO**
22.20 g., 0.900 Silver 0.6424 oz. ASW, 37 mm. **Obv:** Soccer player **Rev:** Shield of Stade Francais in color

| Date | Mintage | VF20 | XF40 | MS60 | MS63 | MS65 |
|---|---|---|---|---|---|---|
| 2009 P | 2,206 | PF63 40.00 | PF65 45.00 | | | |

**KM# 1634 10 EURO**
27.20 g., 0.900 Silver 0.787 oz. ASW, 37 mm. **Subject:** Alpine skiing **Obv:** Globe and downhill skier **Rev:** Downhill skier on mountainside

| Date | Mintage | VF20 | XF40 | MS60 | MS63 | MS65 |
|---|---|---|---|---|---|---|
| 2009 P | 10,000 | PF63 37.00 | PF65 42.00 | | | |

**KM# 1636 10 EURO**
22.20 g., 0.900 Silver 0.6424 oz. ASW, 37 mm. **Subject:** FIFA World Cup, South Africa **Obv:** Soccer player on field **Rev:** Soccerball, map of Africa, Prorea flower

| Date | Mintage | VF20 | XF40 | MS60 | MS63 | MS65 |
|---|---|---|---|---|---|---|
| 2009 P | 6,404 | PF63 35.00 | PF65 40.00 | | | |

**KM# 1675 10 EURO**
22.20 g., 0.900 Silver 0.6424 oz. ASW, 37 mm. **Obv:** Sower left **Rev:** Wheat and olive branch **Mint:** Paris

| Date | Mintage | VF20 | XF40 | MS60 | MS63 | MS65 |
|---|---|---|---|---|---|---|
| 2009 | — | — | — | — | 27.00 | 30.00 |
| 2010 | 10,000 | PF63 35.00 | PF65 40.00 | | | |

**KM# 1645 10 EURO**
12.00 g., 0.900 Silver 0.3472 oz. ASW, 29 mm. **Subject:** Aquitaine **Rev:** Value at center, wreath horizontal **Mint:** Paris

| Date | Mintage | VF20 | XF40 | MS60 | MS63 | MS65 |
|---|---|---|---|---|---|---|
| 2010 | 7,690 | — | — | — | 22.50 | 27.00 |

**KM# 1646 10 EURO**
12.00 g., 0.900 Silver 0.3472 oz. ASW, 29 mm. **Subject:** Auvergne **Rev:** Value at center, wreath horizontal **Mint:** Paris

| Date | Mintage | VF20 | XF40 | MS60 | MS63 | MS65 |
|---|---|---|---|---|---|---|
| 2010 | 7,690 | — | — | — | 22.50 | 27.00 |

**KM# 1647 10 EURO**
12.00 g., 0.900 Silver 0.3472 oz. ASW, 29 mm. **Subject:** Basse - Normandie **Rev:** Value at center, wreath horizontal **Mint:** Paris

| Date | Mintage | VF20 | XF40 | MS60 | MS63 | MS65 |
|---|---|---|---|---|---|---|
| 2010 | 7,690 | — | — | — | 22.50 | 27.00 |

**KM# 1648 10 EURO**
12.00 g., 0.900 Silver 0.3472 oz. ASW, 29 mm. **Subject:** Bretagne **Rev:** Value at center, wreath horizontal **Mint:** Paris

| Date | Mintage | VF20 | XF40 | MS60 | MS63 | MS65 |
|---|---|---|---|---|---|---|
| 2010 | 7,690 | — | — | — | 22.50 | 27.00 |

**KM# 1649 10 EURO**
12.00 g., 0.900 Silver 0.3472 oz. ASW, 29 mm. **Subject:** Burgundy **Rev:** Value at center, wreath horizontal **Mint:** Paris

| Date | Mintage | VF20 | XF40 | MS60 | MS63 | MS65 |
|---|---|---|---|---|---|---|
| 2010 | 7,690 | — | — | — | 22.50 | 27.00 |

**KM# 1650 10 EURO**
12.00 g., 0.900 Silver 0.3472 oz. ASW, 29 mm. **Subject:** Centre **Rev:** Value at center, wreath horizontal **Mint:** Paris

| Date | Mintage | VF20 | XF40 | MS60 | MS63 | MS65 |
|---|---|---|---|---|---|---|
| 2010 | 7,690 | — | — | — | 22.50 | 27.00 |

**KM# 1651 10 EURO**
12.00 g., 0.900 Silver 0.3472 oz. ASW, 29 mm. **Subject:** Champagne - Ardenne **Rev:** Value at center, wreath horizontal **Mint:** Paris

| Date | Mintage | VF20 | XF40 | MS60 | MS63 | MS65 |
|---|---|---|---|---|---|---|
| 2010 | 7,690 | — | — | — | 22.50 | 27.00 |

**KM# 1652 10 EURO**
12.00 g., 0.900 Silver 0.3472 oz. ASW, 29 mm. **Subject:** Alsace **Rev:** Value at center, wreath horizontal **Mint:** Paris

| Date | Mintage | VF20 | XF40 | MS60 | MS63 | MS65 |
|---|---|---|---|---|---|---|
| 2010 | 7,690 | — | — | — | 22.50 | 27.00 |

**KM# 1653 10 EURO**
12.00 g., 0.900 Silver 0.3472 oz. ASW, 29 mm. **Subject:** French - Comte **Rev:** Value at center, wreath horizontal **Mint:** Paris

| Date | Mintage | VF20 | XF40 | MS60 | MS63 | MS65 |
|---|---|---|---|---|---|---|
| 2010 | 7,690 | — | — | — | 22.50 | 27.00 |

**KM# 1654 10 EURO**
12.00 g., 0.900 Silver 0.3472 oz. ASW, 29 mm. **Subject:** French Guiana **Rev:** Value at center, wreath horizontal **Mint:** Paris

| Date | Mintage | VF20 | XF40 | MS60 | MS63 | MS65 |
|---|---|---|---|---|---|---|
| 2010 | 7,690 | — | — | — | 25.00 | 28.00 |

**KM# 1655 10 EURO**
12.00 g., 0.900 Silver 0.3472 oz. ASW, 29 mm. **Subject:** Guadeloupe **Rev:** Value at center, wreath horizontal **Mint:** Paris

| Date | Mintage | VF20 | XF40 | MS60 | MS63 | MS65 |
|---|---|---|---|---|---|---|
| 2010 | 7,690 | — | — | — | 25.00 | 28.00 |

**KM# 1656 10 EURO**
12.00 g., 0.900 Silver 0.3472 oz. ASW, 29 mm. **Subject:** Haute - Normandie **Rev:** Value at center, wreath horizontal **Mint:** Paris

| Date | Mintage | VF20 | XF40 | MS60 | MS63 | MS65 |
|---|---|---|---|---|---|---|
| 2010 | 7,690 | — | — | — | 22.50 | 27.00 |

**KM# 1657 10 EURO**
12.00 g., 0.900 Silver 0.3472 oz. ASW, 29 mm. **Subject:** Ile-de-France **Rev:** Value at center, wreath horizontal **Mint:** Paris

| Date | Mintage | VF20 | XF40 | MS60 | MS63 | MS65 |
|---|---|---|---|---|---|---|
| 2010 | 7,690 | — | — | — | 22.50 | 27.00 |

**KM# 1658 10 EURO**
12.00 g., 0.900 Silver 0.3472 oz. ASW, 29 mm. **Subject:** Corsica **Rev:** Value at center, wreath horizontal **Mint:** Paris

| Date | Mintage | VF20 | XF40 | MS60 | MS63 | MS65 |
|---|---|---|---|---|---|---|
| 2010 | 7,690 | — | — | — | 25.00 | 28.00 |

**KM# 1659 10 EURO**
12.00 g., 0.900 Silver 0.3472 oz. ASW, 29 mm. **Subject:** Languedoc - Roussillon **Rev:** Value at center, wreath horizontal **Mint:** Paris

| Date | Mintage | VF20 | XF40 | MS60 | MS63 | MS65 |
|---|---|---|---|---|---|---|
| 2010 | 7,690 | — | — | — | 22.50 | 27.00 |

**KM# 1660 10 EURO**
12.00 g., 0.900 Silver 0.3472 oz. ASW, 29 mm. **Subject:** Limousin **Rev:** Value at center, wreath horizontal **Mint:** Paris

| Date | Mintage | VF20 | XF40 | MS60 | MS63 | MS65 |
|---|---|---|---|---|---|---|
| 2010 | 7,690 | — | — | — | 22.50 | 27.00 |

**KM# 1661 10 EURO**
12.00 g., 0.900 Silver 0.3472 oz. ASW, 29 mm. **Subject:** Lorroaine **Rev:** Value at center, wreath horizontal **Mint:** Paris

| Date | Mintage | VF20 | XF40 | MS60 | MS63 | MS65 |
|---|---|---|---|---|---|---|
| 2010 | 7,690 | — | — | — | 22.50 | 27.00 |

**KM# 1662 10 EURO**
12.00 g., 0.900 Silver 0.3472 oz. ASW, 29 mm. **Subject:** Martinique **Rev:** Value at center, wreath horizontal **Mint:** Paris

| Date | Mintage | VF20 | XF40 | MS60 | MS63 | MS65 |
|---|---|---|---|---|---|---|
| 2010 | 7,690 | — | — | — | 25.00 | 28.00 |

**KM# 1663 10 EURO**
12.00 g., 0.900 Silver 0.3472 oz. ASW, 29 mm. **Subject:** Midi - Pyrenees **Rev:** Value at center, wreath horizontal **Mint:** Paris

| Date | Mintage | VF20 | XF40 | MS60 | MS63 | MS65 |
|---|---|---|---|---|---|---|
| 2010 | 7,690 | — | — | — | 22.50 | 27.00 |

**KM# 1664 10 EURO**
12.00 g., 0.900 Silver 0.3472 oz. ASW, 29 mm. **Subject:** Nord - Pas de - Calais **Rev:** Value at center, wreath horizontal **Mint:** Paris

| Date | Mintage | VF20 | XF40 | MS60 | MS63 | MS65 |
|---|---|---|---|---|---|---|
| 2010 | 7,690 | — | — | — | 22.50 | 27.00 |

**KM# 1665 10 EURO**
12.00 g., 0.900 Silver 0.3472 oz. ASW, 29 mm. **Subject:** Pays de la Loire **Rev:** Value at center, wreath horizontal **Mint:** Paris

| Date | Mintage | VF20 | XF40 | MS60 | MS63 | MS65 |
|---|---|---|---|---|---|---|
| 2010 | 7,690 | — | — | — | 22.50 | 27.00 |

**KM# 1666 10 EURO**
12.00 g., 0.900 Silver 0.3472 oz. ASW, 29 mm. **Subject:** Picardie **Rev:** Value at center, wreath horizontal **Mint:** Paris

| Date | Mintage | VF20 | XF40 | MS60 | MS63 | MS65 |
|---|---|---|---|---|---|---|
| 2010 | 7,690 | — | — | — | 22.50 | 27.00 |

**KM# 1667 10 EURO**
12.00 g., 0.900 Silver 0.3472 oz. ASW, 29 mm. **Subject:** Poitou - Charentes **Rev:** Value at center, wreath horizontal **Mint:** Paris

| Date | Mintage | VF20 | XF40 | MS60 | MS63 | MS65 |
|---|---|---|---|---|---|---|
| 2010 | 7,690 | — | — | — | 22.50 | 27.00 |

**KM# 1668 10 EURO**
12.00 g., 0.900 Silver 0.3472 oz. ASW, 29 mm. **Subject:** Provence - Alpes - Cote d'Azur **Rev:** Value at center, wreath horizontal **Mint:** Paris

| Date | Mintage | VF20 | XF40 | MS60 | MS63 | MS65 |
|---|---|---|---|---|---|---|
| 2010 | 7,690 | — | — | — | 22.50 | 27.00 |

**KM# 1669 10 EURO**
12.00 g., 0.900 Silver 0.3472 oz. ASW, 29 mm. **Subject:** Reunion **Rev:** Value at center, wreath horizontal **Mint:** Paris

| Date | Mintage | VF20 | XF40 | MS60 | MS63 | MS65 |
|---|---|---|---|---|---|---|
| 2010 | 7,690 | — | — | — | 25.00 | 28.00 |

**KM# 1670 10 EURO**
12.00 g., 0.900 Silver 0.3472 oz. ASW, 29 mm. **Subject:** Rhone - Alpes **Rev:** Value at center, wreath horizontal **Mint:** Paris

| Date | Mintage | VF20 | XF40 | MS60 | MS63 | MS65 |
|---|---|---|---|---|---|---|
| 2010 | 7,690 | — | — | — | 22.50 | 27.00 |

**KM# 1681 10 EURO**
22.20 g., 0.999 Silver 0.713 oz. ASW, 37 mm. **Subject:** Cluny Abbey, 1100th Anniversary **Obv:** Europa head facing **Rev:** Cluny Abbey **Mint:** Paris

| Date | Mintage | VF20 | XF40 | MS60 | MS63 | MS65 |
|---|---|---|---|---|---|---|
| 2010 | 10,000 | PF63 50.00 | PF65 55.00 | | | |

**KM# 1686 10 EURO**
22.20 g., 0.900 Silver 0.6424 oz. ASW, 37 mm. **Obv:** Georges Pompidou Center design **Rev:** Design detail **Mint:** Paris

| Date | Mintage | VF20 | XF40 | MS60 | MS63 | MS65 |
|---|---|---|---|---|---|---|
| 2010 | 30,000 | PF63 40.00 | PF65 45.00 | | | |

**KM# 1691 10 EURO**
22.20 g., Nickel-Copper Aeronotical alloy, 37 mm. **Obv:** Marcel Dassault **Rev:** Mirage III plane **Mint:** Paris

| Date | Mintage | VF20 | XF40 | MS60 | MS63 | MS65 |
|---|---|---|---|---|---|---|
| 2010 | 20,000 | PF63 45.00 | PF65 50.00 | | | |

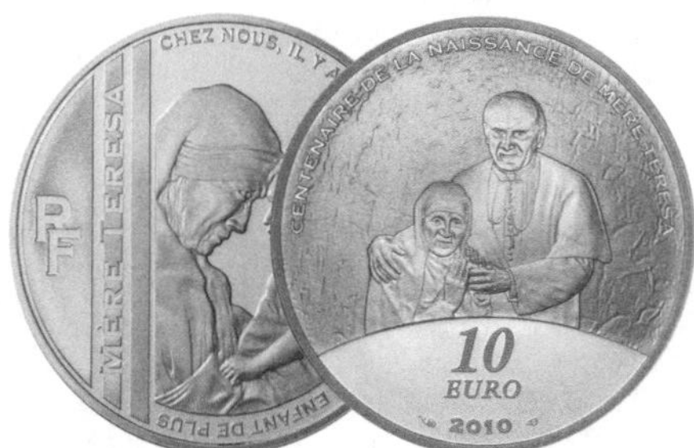


**KM# 1695 10 EURO**
22.20 g., 0.900 Silver 0.6424 oz. ASW, 37 mm. **Obv:** Mother Teresa and child **Rev:** Mother Teresa and Pope John Paul II **Mint:** Paris

| Date | Mintage | VF20 | XF40 | MS60 | MS63 | MS65 |
|---|---|---|---|---|---|---|
| 2010 | 20,000 | PF63 40.00 | PF65 45.00 | | | |

**KM# 1700 10 EURO**
22.20 g., 0.900 Silver 0.6424 oz. ASW, 37 mm. **Obv:** Taj Mahal **Rev:** UNESCO offices **Mint:** Paris

| Date | Mintage | VF20 | XF40 | MS60 | MS63 | MS65 |
|---|---|---|---|---|---|---|
| 2010 | 10,000 | PF63 55.00 | PF65 65.00 | | | |

**KM# 1705 10 EURO**
22.20 g., 0.900 Silver 0.6424 oz. ASW, 37 mm. **Obv:** Lille station and route map **Rev:** Three TGV trains **Mint:** Paris

| Date | Mintage | VF20 | XF40 | MS60 | MS63 | MS65 |
|---|---|---|---|---|---|---|
| 2010 | 30,000 | PF63 35.00 | PF65 40.00 | | | |

**KM# 1708 10 EURO**
15.00 g., 0.900 Silver 0.434 oz. ASW, 30x21 mm. **Rev:** Georges Braque **Shape:** Rectangle **Mint:** Paris

| Date | Mintage | VF20 | XF40 | MS60 | MS63 | MS65 |
|---|---|---|---|---|---|---|
| 2010 | 20,000 | PF63 60.00 | PF65 70.00 | | | |

**KM# 1713 10 EURO**
15.00 g., 0.900 Silver 0.434 oz. ASW, 30x21 mm. **Rev:** Picasso **Shape:** Rectangle **Mint:** Paris

| Date | Mintage | VF20 | XF40 | MS60 | MS63 | MS65 |
|---|---|---|---|---|---|---|
| 2010 | 20,000 | PF63 70.00 | PF65 80.00 | | | |

**KM# 1717 10 EURO**
22.20 g., 0.900 Silver 0.6424 oz. ASW, 37 mm. **Obv:** Blake and Mortimer **Rev:** Secret of the Swordfish" scene, arrest of Col. Olrik. **Mint:** Paris

| Date | Mintage | VF20 | XF40 | MS60 | MS63 | MS65 |
|---|---|---|---|---|---|---|
| 2010 | 10,000 | PF63 50.00 | PF65 60.00 | | | |

**KM# 1720 10 EURO**
22.20 g., 0.900 Silver 0.6424 oz. ASW, 37 mm. **Obv:** Handball player and globe **Rev:** Handball player, net and Big Ben **Mint:** Paris

| Date | Mintage | VF20 | XF40 | MS60 | MS63 | MS65 |
|---|---|---|---|---|---|---|
| 2010 | 10,000 | PF63 40.00 | PF65 45.00 | | | |

**KM# 1722 10 EURO**
22.20 g., 0.900 Silver 0.6424 oz. ASW, 37 mm. **Obv:** Soccer player **Rev:** Stade Toulousain logo, multicolor **Mint:** Paris

| Date | Mintage | VF20 | XF40 | MS60 | MS63 | MS65 |
|---|---|---|---|---|---|---|
| 2010 | 5,000 | PF63 50.00 | PF65 55.00 | | | |

**KM# 1726 10 EURO**
10.00 g., 0.500 Silver 0.1608 oz. ASW, 29 mm. **Subject:** Mayotte **Obv:** Value at center, wreath horizontal **Mint:** Paris

| Date | Mintage | VF20 | XF40 | MS60 | MS63 | MS65 |
|---|---|---|---|---|---|---|
| 2011 | 50,000 | — | — | — | 20.00 | 25.00 |

**KM# 1727 10 EURO**
10.00 g., 0.500 Silver 0.1608 oz. ASW, 29 mm. **Subject:** Aquitaine **Mint:** Paris

| Date | Mintage | VF20 | XF40 | MS60 | MS63 | MS65 |
|---|---|---|---|---|---|---|
| 2011 | 150,000 | — | — | — | 20.00 | 25.00 |

**KM# 1728 10 EURO**
10.00 g., 0.500 Silver 0.1608 oz. ASW, 29 mm. **Subject:** Auvergne **Mint:** Paris

| Date | Mintage | VF20 | XF40 | MS60 | MS63 | MS65 |
|---|---|---|---|---|---|---|
| 2011 | 80,000 | — | — | — | 20.00 | 25.00 |

**KM# 1729 10 EURO**
10.00 g., 0.500 Silver 0.1608 oz. ASW, 29 mm. **Subject:** Basse - Normindie **Mint:** Paris

| Date | Mintage | VF20 | XF40 | MS60 | MS63 | MS65 |
|---|---|---|---|---|---|---|
| 2011 | 100,000 | — | — | — | 20.00 | 25.00 |

**KM# 1730 10 EURO**
10.00 g., 0.500 Silver 0.1608 oz. ASW, 29 mm. **Subject:** Bretagne **Mint:** Paris

| Date | Mintage | VF20 | XF40 | MS60 | MS63 | MS65 |
|---|---|---|---|---|---|---|
| 2011 | 150,000 | — | — | — | 20.00 | 25.00 |

**KM# 1731 10 EURO**
10.00 g., 0.500 Silver 0.1608 oz. ASW, 29 mm. **Subject:** Burgundy **Mint:** Paris

| Date | Mintage | VF20 | XF40 | MS60 | MS63 | MS65 |
|---|---|---|---|---|---|---|
| 2011 | — | — | — | — | 20.00 | 25.00 |

**KM# 1732 10 EURO**
10.00 g., 0.500 Silver 0.1608 oz. ASW, 29 mm. **Subject:** Centre **Mint:** Paris

| Date | Mintage | VF20 | XF40 | MS60 | MS63 | MS65 |
|---|---|---|---|---|---|---|
| 2011 | 80,000 | — | — | — | 20.00 | 25.00 |

**KM# 1733 10 EURO**
10.00 g., 0.500 Silver 0.1608 oz. ASW, 29 mm. **Subject:** Campagne - Ardenne **Mint:** Paris

| Date | Mintage | VF20 | XF40 | MS60 | MS63 | MS65 |
|---|---|---|---|---|---|---|
| 2011 | 50,000 | — | — | — | 20.00 | 25.00 |

**KM# 1734 10 EURO**
10.00 g., 0.500 Silver 0.1608 oz. ASW, 29 mm. **Subject:** Alsace **Mint:** Paris

| Date | Mintage | VF20 | XF40 | MS60 | MS63 | MS65 |
|---|---|---|---|---|---|---|
| 2011 | 100,000 | — | — | — | 20.00 | 25.00 |

**KM# 1735 10 EURO**
10.00 g., 0.500 Silver 0.1608 oz. ASW, 29 mm. **Subject:** France - Comte **Mint:** Paris

| Date | Mintage | VF20 | XF40 | MS60 | MS63 | MS65 |
|---|---|---|---|---|---|---|
| 2011 | 80,000 | — | — | — | 20.00 | 25.00 |

**KM# 1736 10 EURO**
10.00 g., 0.500 Silver 0.1608 oz. ASW, 29 mm. **Subject:** Guyane **Mint:** Paris

| Date | Mintage | VF20 | XF40 | MS60 | MS63 | MS65 |
|---|---|---|---|---|---|---|
| 2011 | 50,000 | — | — | — | 25.00 | 28.00 |

**KM# 1737 10 EURO**
10.00 g., 0.500 Silver 0.1608 oz. ASW, 29 mm. **Subject:** Guadeloupe **Mint:** Paris

| Date | Mintage | VF20 | XF40 | MS60 | MS63 | MS65 |
|---|---|---|---|---|---|---|
| 2011 | 50,000 | — | — | — | 25.00 | 28.00 |

**KM# 1738 10 EURO**
10.00 g., 0.500 Silver 0.1608 oz. ASW, 29 mm. **Subject:** Haute - Normandie **Mint:** Paris

| Date | Mintage | VF20 | XF40 | MS60 | MS63 | MS65 |
|---|---|---|---|---|---|---|
| 2011 | 80,000 | — | — | — | 20.00 | 25.00 |

**KM# 1739 10 EURO**
10.00 g., 0.500 Silver 0.1608 oz. ASW, 29 mm. **Subject:** Ile de France **Mint:** Paris

| Date | Mintage | VF20 | XF40 | MS60 | MS63 | MS65 |
|---|---|---|---|---|---|---|
| 2011 | 310,000 | — | — | — | 20.00 | 25.00 |

**KM# 1740 10 EURO**
10.00 g., 0.500 Silver 0.1608 oz. ASW, 29 mm. **Subject:** Corsica **Mint:** Paris

| Date | Mintage | VF20 | XF40 | MS60 | MS63 | MS65 |
|---|---|---|---|---|---|---|
| 2011 | 80,000 | — | — | — | 25.00 | 28.00 |

**KM# 1741 10 EURO**
10.00 g., 0.500 Silver 0.1608 oz. ASW, 29 mm. **Subject:** Languedoc - Rossillon **Mint:** Paris

| Date | Mintage | VF20 | XF40 | MS60 | MS63 | MS65 |
|---|---|---|---|---|---|---|
| 2011 | 120,000 | — | — | — | 20.00 | 25.00 |

**KM# 1742 10 EURO**
10.00 g., 0.500 Silver 0.1608 oz. ASW, 29 mm. **Subject:** Limousin **Mint:** Paris

| Date | Mintage | VF20 | XF40 | MS60 | MS63 | MS65 |
|---|---|---|---|---|---|---|
| 2011 | 80,000 | — | — | — | 20.00 | 25.00 |

**KM# 1743 10 EURO**
10.00 g., 0.500 Silver 0.1608 oz. ASW, 29 mm. **Subject:** Lorraine **Mint:** Paris

| Date | Mintage | VF20 | XF40 | MS60 | MS63 | MS65 |
|---|---|---|---|---|---|---|
| 2011 | 100,000 | — | — | — | 20.00 | 25.00 |

**KM# 1744 10 EURO**
10.00 g., 0.500 Silver 0.1608 oz. ASW, 29 mm. **Subject:** Martinique **Mint:** Paris

| Date | Mintage | VF20 | XF40 | MS60 | MS63 | MS65 |
|---|---|---|---|---|---|---|
| 2011 | 50,000 | — | — | — | 25.00 | 28.00 |

**KM# 1745 10 EURO**
10.00 g., 0.500 Silver 0.1608 oz. ASW, 29 mm. **Subject:** Nord Pas de Calais **Mint:** Paris

| Date | Mintage | VF20 | XF40 | MS60 | MS63 | MS65 |
|---|---|---|---|---|---|---|
| 2011 | 180,000 | — | — | — | 20.00 | 25.00 |

**KM# 1746 10 EURO**
10.00 g., 0.500 Silver 0.1608 oz. ASW, 29 mm. **Subject:** Pays de la Loire **Mint:** Paris

| Date | Mintage | VF20 | XF40 | MS60 | MS63 | MS65 |
|---|---|---|---|---|---|---|
| 2011 | — | — | — | — | 20.00 | 25.00 |

**KM# 1747 10 EURO**
10.00 g., 0.500 Silver 0.1608 oz. ASW, 29 mm. **Subject:** Picardie **Mint:** Paris

| Date | Mintage | VF20 | XF40 | MS60 | MS63 | MS65 |
|---|---|---|---|---|---|---|
| 2011 | 100,000 | — | — | — | 20.00 | 25.00 |

**KM# 1748 10 EURO**
10.00 g., 0.500 Silver 0.1608 oz. ASW, 29 mm. **Subject:** Poitou - Charentes **Mint:** Paris

| Date | Mintage | VF20 | XF40 | MS60 | MS63 | MS65 |
|---|---|---|---|---|---|---|
| 2011 | 100,000 | — | — | — | 20.00 | 25.00 |

**KM# 1749 10 EURO**
10.00 g., 0.500 Silver 0.1608 oz. ASW, 29 mm. **Subject:** Province - Alpes - Cote d'Azur **Mint:** Paris

| Date | Mintage | VF20 | XF40 | MS60 | MS63 | MS65 |
|---|---|---|---|---|---|---|
| 2011 | 220,000 | — | — | — | 20.00 | 25.00 |

**KM# 1750 10 EURO**
10.00 g., 0.500 Silver 0.1608 oz. ASW, 29 mm. **Subject:** Reunion **Mint:** Paris

| Date | Mintage | VF20 | XF40 | MS60 | MS63 | MS65 |
|---|---|---|---|---|---|---|
| 2011 | 70,000 | — | — | — | 25.00 | 28.00 |

**KM# 1751 10 EURO**
10.00 g., 0.500 Silver 0.1608 oz. ASW, 29 mm. **Subject:** Rhone - Alpes **Mint:** Paris

| Date | Mintage | VF20 | XF40 | MS60 | MS63 | MS65 |
|---|---|---|---|---|---|---|
| 2011 | 220,000 | — | — | — | 20.00 | 25.00 |

**KM# 1752 10 EURO**
10.00 g., 0.500 Silver 0.1608 oz. ASW, 29 mm. **Subject:** Midi - Pyreneis **Mint:** Paris

| Date | Mintage | VF20 | XF40 | MS60 | MS63 | MS65 |
|---|---|---|---|---|---|---|
| 2011 | 120,000 | — | — | — | 20.00 | 25.00 |

**KM# 1755 10 EURO**
22.20 g., 0.900 Silver 0.6424 oz. ASW, 37 mm. **Obv:** Bicycle racer **Rev:** Metro 92 logo **Mint:** Paris

| Date | Mintage | VF20 | XF40 | MS60 | MS63 | MS65 |
|---|---|---|---|---|---|---|
| 2011 | 5,000 | PF63 50.00 | PF65 55.00 | | | |

**KM# 1784 10 EURO**
22.20 g., 0.900 Silver 0.6424 oz. ASW, 37 mm. **Subject:** Euro Starter Kit, 10th Anniversary **Obv:** Sower left **Rev:** Euro starter kit **Mint:** Paris

| Date | Mintage | VF20 | XF40 | MS60 | MS63 | MS65 |
|---|---|---|---|---|---|---|
| 2011 | 10,000 | PF63 40.00 | PF65 45.00 | | | |

**KM# 1790 10 EURO**
22.20 g., 0.900 Silver 0.6424 oz. ASW, 37 mm. **Subject:** International Music Day, 30th Anniversary **Obv:** Europa **Rev:** Youth jamming **Mint:** Paris

| Date | Mintage | VF20 | XF40 | MS60 | MS63 | MS65 |
|---|---|---|---|---|---|---|
| 2011 | 10,000 | PF63 40.00 | PF65 45.00 | | | |

**KM# 1795 10 EURO**
22.20 g., 0.900 Silver 0.6424 oz. ASW, 37 mm. **Subject:** Great Explorers - Jacques Cartier **Obv:** The Grand Hermine sailing away **Rev:** Cartier, globe and compass rose **Mint:** Paris

| Date | Mintage | VF20 | XF40 | MS60 | MS63 | MS65 |
|---|---|---|---|---|---|---|
| 2011 | 30,000 | PF63 50.00 | PF65 55.00 | | | |

**KM# 1800 10 EURO**
22.20 g., 0.900 Silver 0.6424 oz. ASW, 37 mm. **Subject:** Colvis, 481-511 **Obv:** Hands over chalice, reign dates at left, value at right **Rev:** Crowned head left **Mint:** Paris

| Date | Mintage | VF20 | XF40 | MS60 | MS63 | MS65 |
|---|---|---|---|---|---|---|
| 2011 | 20,000 | PF63 50.00 | PF65 55.00 | | | |

**KM# 1802 10 EURO**
22.20 g., 0.900 Silver 0.6424 oz. ASW, 37 mm. **Subject:** Charlemagne, 768-814 **Obv:** Cross on orb, reight dates at left, value at right **Rev:** Crowned head left **Mint:** Paris

| Date | Mintage | VF20 | XF40 | MS60 | MS63 | MS65 |
|---|---|---|---|---|---|---|
| 2011 | 20,000 | PF63 50.00 | PF65 55.00 | | | |

**KM# 1804 10 EURO**
22.20 g., 0.900 Silver 0.6424 oz. ASW, 37 mm. **Subject:** Charles II, 840-877 **Obv:** KARLOS monogram **Rev:** Crowned head left **Mint:** Paris

| Date | Mintage | VF20 | XF40 | MS60 | MS63 | MS65 |
|---|---|---|---|---|---|---|
| 2011 | 20,000 | PF63 50.00 | PF65 55.00 | | | |

**KM# 1806 10 EURO**
22.20 g., 0.900 Silver 0.6424 oz. ASW, 37 mm. **Subject:** WWF - Audouin's Gull **Obv:** Gull in flight right **Rev:** Gull standing right, WWF panda logo **Mint:** Paris

| Date | Mintage | VF20 | XF40 | MS60 | MS63 | MS65 |
|---|---|---|---|---|---|---|
| 2011 | 20,000 | PF63 55.00 | PF65 60.00 | | | |

**KM# 1809 10 EURO**
22.20 g., 0.900 Silver 0.6424 oz. ASW, 37 mm. **Subject:** UNESCO World Heritage Site - Palace of Versailles **Obv:** Building and garden plan **Rev:** Top view of UNESCO's Paris headquarters **Mint:** Paris

| Date | Mintage | VF20 | XF40 | MS60 | MS63 | MS65 |
|---|---|---|---|---|---|---|
| 2011 | 20,000 | PF63 50.00 | PF65 55.00 | | | |

**KM# 1814 10 EURO**
22.20 g., 0.900 Silver 0.6424 oz. ASW, 37 mm. **Obv:** Metz railroad station **Rev:** TGV and ICE trains **Mint:** Paris

| Date | Mintage | VF20 | XF40 | MS60 | MS63 | MS65 |
|---|---|---|---|---|---|---|
| 2011 | 10,000 | PF63 50.00 | PF65 55.00 | | | |

**KM# 1819 10 EURO**
15.00 g., 0.900 Silver 0.434 oz. ASW, 30x21 mm. **Subject:** Vassily Kandinsky **Shape:** Rectangle **Mint:** Paris

| Date | Mintage | VF20 | XF40 | MS60 | MS63 | MS65 |
|---|---|---|---|---|---|---|
| 2011 | 10,000 | PF63 70.00 | PF65 80.00 | | | |

**KM# 1823 10 EURO**
15.00 g., 0.900 Silver 0.434 oz. ASW, 31 mm. **Subject:** Andy Warhol **Obv:** Portrait facing **Rev:** Dollar sign in color **Mint:** Paris

| Date | Mintage | VF20 | XF40 | MS60 | MS63 | MS65 |
|---|---|---|---|---|---|---|
| 2011 | 10,000 | PF63 65.00 | PF65 75.00 | | | |

**KM# 1827 10 EURO**
22.20 g., 0.900 Silver 0.6424 oz. ASW, 37 mm. **Obv:** Cosette - Les Miserables **Rev:** Victor Hugo **Mint:** Paris

| Date | Mintage | VF20 | XF40 | MS60 | MS63 | MS65 |
|---|---|---|---|---|---|---|
| 2011 | 10,000 | PF63 50.00 | PF65 55.00 | | | |

**KM# 1829 10 EURO**
22.20 g., 0.900 Silver 0.6424 oz. ASW, 37 mm. **Obv:** Nana **Rev:** Emile Zola **Mint:** Paris

| Date | Mintage | VF20 | XF40 | MS60 | MS63 | MS65 |
|---|---|---|---|---|---|---|
| 2011 | 5,000 | PF63 50.00 | PF65 55.00 | | | |

**KM# 1831 10 EURO**
22.20 g., 0.900 Silver 0.6424 oz. ASW, 37 mm. **Obv:** The Stranger **Rev:** Albert Camus **Mint:** Paris

| Date | Mintage | VF20 | XF40 | MS60 | MS63 | MS65 |
|---|---|---|---|---|---|---|
| 2011 | — | PF63 50.00 | PF65 55.00 | | | |

**KM# 1835 10 EURO**
22.20 g., 0.900 Silver 0.6424 oz. ASW, 37 mm. **Subject:** Comic Strip XIII **Obv:** Montage of characters **Rev:** Profile left and large XIII **Mint:** Paris

| Date | Mintage | VF20 | XF40 | MS60 | MS63 | MS65 |
|---|---|---|---|---|---|---|
| 2011 | 10,000 | PF63 50.00 | PF65 55.00 | | | |

**KM# 1838 10 EURO**
22.20 g., 0.900 Silver 0.6424 oz. ASW, 37 mm. **Obv:** Female figure skater and globe **Rev:** Figure skating pair **Mint:** Paris

| Date | Mintage | VF20 | XF40 | MS60 | MS63 | MS65 |
|---|---|---|---|---|---|---|
| 2011 | 10,000 | PF63 50.00 | PF65 55.00 | | | |

**KM# 1850 10 EURO**
22.20 g., 0.900 Silver 0.6424 oz. ASW, 37 mm. **Subject:** Eurocorps, 20th Anniversary **Obv:** Mitterrand and Kohl standing clasping hands **Rev:** Europa facing **Mint:** Paris

| Date | Mintage | VF20 | XF40 | MS60 | MS63 | MS65 |
|---|---|---|---|---|---|---|
| 2012 (a) | 10,000 | PF63 35.00 | PF65 40.00 | | | |

**KM# 1856 10 EURO**
22.20 g., 0.900 Silver 0.6424 oz. ASW, 37 mm. **Subject:** Hugues Capet **Obv:** Crowned head faicing **Rev:** Right hand raised in benidiction **Mint:** Paris

| Date | Mintage | VF20 | XF40 | MS60 | MS63 | MS65 |
|---|---|---|---|---|---|---|
| 2012 (a) | 20,000 | PF63 35.00 | PF65 40.00 | | | |

**KM# 1857 10 EURO**
22.20 g., 0.900 Silver 0.6424 oz. ASW, 37 mm. **Subject:** Saint Louis **Obv:** Crowned head facing **Rev:** Oak tree **Mint:** Paris

| Date | Mintage | VF20 | XF40 | MS60 | MS63 | MS65 |
|---|---|---|---|---|---|---|
| 2012 (a) | 20,000 | PF63 35.00 | PF65 40.00 | | | |

**KM# 1859 10 EURO**
22.20 g., 0.900 Silver 0.6424 oz. ASW, 37 mm. **Subject:** The Three Musketeers **Obv:** D'Artagnan, cross emblem and three musketeers standing with swords raised **Rev:** Musketeers motto: "Un pour tours..." at left, Alexandre Dumas portrait at right **Mint:** Paris

| Date | Mintage | VF20 | XF40 | MS60 | MS63 | MS65 |
|---|---|---|---|---|---|---|
| 2012 (a) | 5,000 | PF63 35.00 | PF65 40.00 | | | |

**KM# 1862 10 EURO**
10.00 g., 0.500 Silver 0.1608 oz. ASW, 29 mm. **Subject:** Mayotte **Obv:** Value at center, wreath horizontal **Mint:** Paris

| Date | Mintage | VF20 | XF40 | MS60 | MS63 | MS65 |
|---|---|---|---|---|---|---|
| 2012 (a) | — | — | — | — | 20.00 | 25.00 |

**KM# 1863 10 EURO**
10.00 g., 0.500 Silver 0.1608 oz. ASW, 29 mm. **Subject:** Aquitaine **Obv:** Value at center, wreath horizontal **Mint:** Paris

| Date | Mintage | VF20 | XF40 | MS60 | MS63 | MS65 |
|---|---|---|---|---|---|---|
| 2012 (a) | — | — | — | — | 20.00 | 25.00 |

**KM# 1864 10 EURO**
10.00 g., 0.500 Silver 0.1608 oz. ASW, 29 mm. **Subject:** Auvergne **Obv:** Value at center, wreath horizontal **Mint:** Paris

| Date | Mintage | VF20 | XF40 | MS60 | MS63 | MS65 |
|---|---|---|---|---|---|---|
| 2012 (a) | — | — | — | — | 20.00 | 25.00 |

**KM# 1865 10 EURO**
10.00 g., 0.500 Silver 0.1608 oz. ASW, 29 mm. **Subject:** Basse - Normandie **Obv:** Value at center, wreath horizontal **Mint:** Paris

| Date | Mintage | VF20 | XF40 | MS60 | MS63 | MS65 |
|---|---|---|---|---|---|---|
| 2012 (a) | — | — | — | — | 20.00 | 25.00 |

**KM# 1866 10 EURO**
10.00 g., 0.500 Silver 0.1608 oz. ASW, 29 mm. **Subject:** Bretagne **Obv:** Value at center, wreath horizontal **Mint:** Paris

| Date | Mintage | VF20 | XF40 | MS60 | MS63 | MS65 |
|---|---|---|---|---|---|---|
| 2012 (a) | — | — | — | — | 20.00 | 25.00 |

**KM# 1867 10 EURO**
10.00 g., 0.500 Silver 0.1608 oz. ASW, 29 mm. **Subject:** Burgundy **Obv:** Value at center, wreath horizontal **Mint:** Paris

| Date | Mintage | VF20 | XF40 | MS60 | MS63 | MS65 |
|---|---|---|---|---|---|---|
| 2012 (a) | — | — | — | — | 20.00 | 25.00 |

**KM# 1868 10 EURO**
10.00 g., 0.500 Silver 0.1608 oz. ASW, 29 mm. **Subject:** Centre **Obv:** Value at center, wreath horizontal **Mint:** Paris

| Date | Mintage | VF20 | XF40 | MS60 | MS63 | MS65 |
|---|---|---|---|---|---|---|
| 2012 (a) | — | — | — | — | 20.00 | 25.00 |

**KM# 1869 10 EURO**
10.00 g., 0.500 Silver 0.1608 oz. ASW, 29 mm. **Subject:** Champagne - Ardenne **Obv:** Value at center, wreath horizontal **Mint:** Paris

| Date | Mintage | VF20 | XF40 | MS60 | MS63 | MS65 |
|---|---|---|---|---|---|---|
| 2012 (a) | — | — | — | — | 20.00 | 25.00 |

**KM# 1870 10 EURO**
10.00 g., 0.500 Silver 0.1608 oz. ASW, 29 mm. **Subject:** Alsace **Obv:** Value at center, wreath horizontal **Mint:** Paris

| Date | Mintage | VF20 | XF40 | MS60 | MS63 | MS65 |
|---|---|---|---|---|---|---|
| 2012 (a) | — | — | — | — | 20.00 | 25.00 |

**KM# 1871 10 EURO**
10.00 g., 0.500 Silver 0.1608 oz. ASW, 29 mm. **Subject:** France - Comte **Mint:** Paris

| Date | Mintage | VF20 | XF40 | MS60 | MS63 | MS65 |
|---|---|---|---|---|---|---|
| 2012 (a) | — | — | — | — | 20.00 | 25.00 |

**KM# 1872 10 EURO**
10.00 g., 0.500 Silver 0.1608 oz. ASW, 29 mm. **Subject:** French Guiana **Obv:** Value at center, wreath horizontal **Mint:** Paris

| Date | Mintage | VF20 | XF40 | MS60 | MS63 | MS65 |
|---|---|---|---|---|---|---|
| 2012 (a) | — | — | — | — | 25.00 | 28.00 |

**KM# 1873 10 EURO**
10.00 g., 0.500 Silver 0.1608 oz. ASW, 29 mm. **Subject:** Guadeloupe **Obv:** Value at center, wreath horizontal **Mint:** Paris

| Date | Mintage | VF20 | XF40 | MS60 | MS63 | MS65 |
|---|---|---|---|---|---|---|
| 2012 (a) | — | — | — | — | 25.00 | 28.00 |

**KM# 1874 10 EURO**
10.00 g., 0.500 Silver 0.1608 oz. ASW, 29 mm. **Subject:** Haute - Normandie **Obv:** Value at center, wreath horizontal **Mint:** Paris

| Date | Mintage | VF20 | XF40 | MS60 | MS63 | MS65 |
|---|---|---|---|---|---|---|
| 2012 (a) | — | — | — | — | 20.00 | 25.00 |

**KM# 1875 10 EURO**
10.00 g., 0.500 Silver 0.1608 oz. ASW, 29 mm. **Subject:** Ile de France **Obv:** Value at center, wreath horizontal **Mint:** Paris

| Date | Mintage | VF20 | XF40 | MS60 | MS63 | MS65 |
|---|---|---|---|---|---|---|
| 2012 (a) | — | — | — | — | 20.00 | 25.00 |

**KM# 1876 10 EURO**
10.00 g., 0.500 Silver 0.1608 oz. ASW, 29 mm. **Subject:** Corsica **Obv:** Value at center, wreath horizontal **Mint:** Paris

| Date | Mintage | VF20 | XF40 | MS60 | MS63 | MS65 |
|---|---|---|---|---|---|---|
| 2012 (a) | — | — | — | — | 25.00 | 28.00 |

**KM# 1877 10 EURO**
10.00 g., 0.500 Silver 0.1608 oz. ASW, 29 mm. **Subject:** Languedoc - Rossillon **Obv:** Value at center, wreath horizontal **Mint:** Paris

| Date | Mintage | VF20 | XF40 | MS60 | MS63 | MS65 |
|---|---|---|---|---|---|---|
| 2012 (a) | — | — | — | — | 20.00 | 25.00 |

**KM# 1878 10 EURO**
10.00 g., 0.500 Silver 0.1608 oz. ASW, 29 mm. **Subject:** Limousin **Obv:** Value at center, wreath horizontal **Mint:** Paris

| Date | Mintage | VF20 | XF40 | MS60 | MS63 | MS65 |
|---|---|---|---|---|---|---|
| 2012 (a) | — | — | — | — | 20.00 | 25.00 |

**KM# 1879 10 EURO**
10.00 g., 0.500 Silver 0.1608 oz. ASW, 29 mm. **Subject:** Martinique **Obv:** Value at center, wreath horizontal **Mint:** Paris

| Date | Mintage | VF20 | XF40 | MS60 | MS63 | MS65 |
|---|---|---|---|---|---|---|
| 2012 (a) | — | — | — | — | 25.00 | 28.00 |

**KM# 1880 10 EURO**
10.00 g., 0.500 Silver 0.1608 oz. ASW, 29 mm. **Subject:** Nord Pas de Calais **Obv:** Value at center, wreath horizontal **Mint:** Paris

| Date | Mintage | VF20 | XF40 | MS60 | MS63 | MS65 |
|---|---|---|---|---|---|---|
| 2012 (a) | — | — | — | — | 20.00 | 25.00 |

**KM# 1881 10 EURO**
10.00 g., 0.500 Silver 0.1608 oz. ASW, 29 mm. **Subject:** Pays de la Loire **Obv:** Value at center, wreath horizontal **Mint:** Paris

| Date | Mintage | VF20 | XF40 | MS60 | MS63 | MS65 |
|---|---|---|---|---|---|---|
| 2012 (a) | — | — | — | — | 20.00 | 25.00 |

**KM# 1882 10 EURO**
10.00 g., 0.500 Silver 0.1608 oz. ASW, 29 mm. **Subject:** Picardie **Obv:** Value at center, wreath horizontal **Mint:** Paris

| Date | Mintage | VF20 | XF40 | MS60 | MS63 | MS65 |
|---|---|---|---|---|---|---|
| 2012 (a) | — | — | — | — | 20.00 | 25.00 |

**KM# 1883 10 EURO**
10.00 g., 0.500 Silver 0.1608 oz. ASW, 29 mm. **Subject:** Poitou - Charentes **Obv:** Value at center, wreath horizontal **Mint:** Paris

| Date | Mintage | VF20 | XF40 | MS60 | MS63 | MS65 |
|---|---|---|---|---|---|---|
| 2012 (a) | — | — | — | — | 20.00 | 25.00 |

**KM# 1884 10 EURO**
10.00 g., 0.500 Silver 0.1608 oz. ASW, 29 mm. **Subject:** Province - Alpes - Cote d'Azur **Obv:** Value at center, wreath horizontal **Mint:** Paris

| Date | Mintage | VF20 | XF40 | MS60 | MS63 | MS65 |
|---|---|---|---|---|---|---|
| 2012 (a) | — | — | — | — | 20.00 | 25.00 |

**KM# 1885 10 EURO**
10.00 g., 0.500 Silver 0.1608 oz. ASW, 29 mm. **Subject:** Reunion **Obv:** Value at center, wreath horizontal **Mint:** Paris

| Date | Mintage | VF20 | XF40 | MS60 | MS63 | MS65 |
|---|---|---|---|---|---|---|
| 2012 (a) | — | — | — | — | 25.00 | 28.00 |

**KM# 1886 10 EURO**
10.00 g., 0.500 Silver 0.1608 oz. ASW, 29 mm. **Subject:** Rhone - Alpes **Obv:** Value at center, wreath horizontal **Mint:** Paris

| Date | Mintage | VF20 | XF40 | MS60 | MS63 | MS65 |
|---|---|---|---|---|---|---|
| 2012 (a) | — | — | — | — | 20.00 | 25.00 |

**KM# 1887 10 EURO**
10.00 g., 0.500 Silver 0.1608 oz. ASW, 29 mm. **Subject:** Midi - Pyrenees **Obv:** Value at center, wreath horizontal **Mint:** Paris

| Date | Mintage | VF20 | XF40 | MS60 | MS63 | MS65 |
|---|---|---|---|---|---|---|
| 2012 (a) | — | — | — | — | 20.00 | 25.00 |

**KM# 1888 10 EURO**
10.00 g., 0.500 Silver 0.1608 oz. ASW, 29 mm. **Subject:** Lorraine **Obv:** Value at center, wreath horizontal **Mint:** Paris

| Date | Mintage | VF20 | XF40 | MS60 | MS63 | MS65 |
|---|---|---|---|---|---|---|
| 2012 (a) | — | — | — | — | 20.00 | 25.00 |

**KM# 1889 10 EURO**
22.20 g., 0.900 Silver 0.6424 oz. ASW, 37 mm. **Subject:** Euro, 10th Anniversary **Obv:** The Sower advancing left **Rev:** Value at center on globe, child-like drawings around **Mint:** Paris

| Date | Mintage | VF20 | XF40 | MS60 | MS63 | MS65 |
|---|---|---|---|---|---|---|
| 2012 (a) | 15,000 | PF63 35.00 | PF65 40.00 | | | |

**KM# 1895 10 EURO**
22.20 g., 0.900 Silver 0.6424 oz. ASW, 37 mm. **Subject:** abbé Pierre, 100th anniversary of Birth **Obv:** Pierre at left, shadow at right **Rev:** Emmaus International logo and quote **Mint:** Paris

| Date | Mintage | VF20 | XF40 | MS60 | MS63 | MS65 |
|---|---|---|---|---|---|---|
| 2012 (a) | 10,000 | PF63 35.00 | PF65 40.00 | | | |

**KM# 1905 10 EURO**
22.20 g., 0.900 Silver 0.6424 oz. ASW, 37 mm. **Subject:** UNESCO - World Heritage Site **Obv:** Abu Simbel temple **Mint:** Paris

| Date | Mintage | VF20 | XF40 | MS60 | MS63 | MS65 |
|---|---|---|---|---|---|---|
| 2012 (a) | 10,000 | PF63 35.00 | PF65 40.00 | | | |

**KM# 1911 10 EURO**
22.20 g., 0.900 Silver 0.6424 oz. ASW, 37 mm. **Subject:** TGV South-East **Obv:** Lyon Saint-Exupery station **Rev:** Two modern locomotives **Mint:** Paris

| Date | Mintage | VF20 | XF40 | MS60 | MS63 | MS65 |
|---|---|---|---|---|---|---|
| 2012 (a) | 5,000 | PF63 35.00 | PF65 40.00 | | | |

**KM# 1916 10 EURO**
22.20 g., 0.900 Silver 0.6424 oz. ASW, 37 mm. **Subject:** Comic strip hero **Obv:** Largo Winch and building **Rev:** Winch riding motorcycle being chased by two cars **Mint:** Paris

| Date | Mintage | VF20 | XF40 | MS60 | MS63 | MS65 |
|---|---|---|---|---|---|---|
| 2012 (a) | 5,000 | PF63 35.00 | PF65 40.00 | | | |

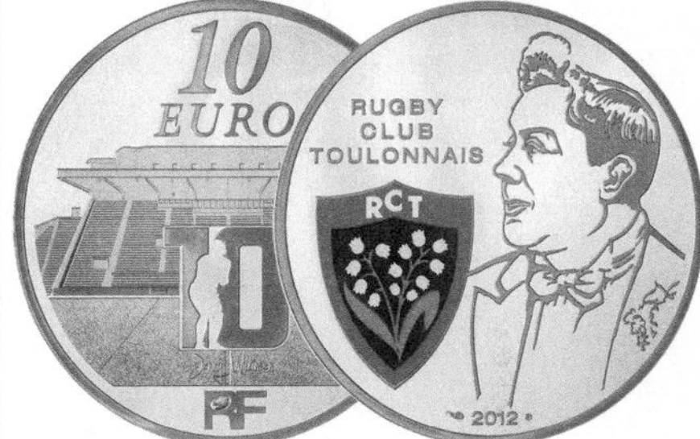

**KM# 1919 10 EURO**
22.20 g., 0.900 Silver 0.6424 oz. ASW, 37 mm. **Subject:** Toulonnais Rugby Club **Obv:** Value and Stadium field view **Rev:** Colored shield and portrait Felix Mayol **Mint:** Paris

| Date | Mintage | VF20 | XF40 | MS60 | MS63 | MS65 |
|---|---|---|---|---|---|---|
| 2012 (a) | 5,000 | PF63 45.00 | PF65 50.00 | | | |

**KM# 1921 10 EURO**
22.20 g., 0.900 Silver 0.6424 oz. ASW, 37 mm. **Subject:** 2012 Summer Olympics, London **Obv:** Two judo athletes and map of Europe **Rev:** Two judo athletes **Mint:** Paris

| Date | Mintage | VF20 | XF40 | MS60 | MS63 | MS65 |
|---|---|---|---|---|---|---|
| 2012 (a) | 10,000 | PF63 35.00 | PF65 40.00 | | | |

**KM# 1924 10 EURO**
22.20 g., 0.900 Silver 0.6424 oz. ASW, 37 mm. **Subject:** Year of the Dragon **Obv:** Dragon **Rev:** La Fontaine and zodiac animals **Mint:** Paris

| Date | Mintage | VF20 | XF40 | MS60 | MS63 | MS65 |
|---|---|---|---|---|---|---|
| 2012 (a) | 10,000 | PF63 55.00 | PF65 65.00 | | | |

**KM# 2073 10 EURO**
10.00 g., 0.500 Silver 0.1608 oz. ASW, 29 mm. **Obv:** Horizontal wreath, value within **Rev:** Hercules group standing **Mint:** Paris

| Date | Mintage | VF20 | XF40 | MS60 | MS63 | MS65 |
|---|---|---|---|---|---|---|
| 2012 | 491,000 | — | — | — | 15.00 | 20.00 |
| 2012 | 19,000 | PF63 35.00 | PF65 40.00 | | | |
| 2013 | — | — | — | — | 15.00 | 20.00 |
| 2013 | — | PF63 35.00 | PF65 40.00 | | | |

**KM# 2075 10 EURO**
22.20 g., 0.900 Silver 0.6424 oz. ASW, 37 mm. **Obv:** Palice de Louvre **Rev:** Philipp II August, head facing **Mint:** Paris

| Date | Mintage | VF20 | XF40 | MS60 | MS63 | MS65 |
|---|---|---|---|---|---|---|
| 2012 | Est. 20000 | — | — | — | — | 65.00 |

**KM# 2078 10 EURO**
22.20 g., 0.900 Silver 0.6424 oz. ASW, 37 mm. **Obv:** Aircraft Carrier Jean de Arc **Rev:** Anchor chain below convoy of ships **Mint:** Paris

| Date | Mintage | VF20 | XF40 | MS60 | MS63 | MS65 |
|---|---|---|---|---|---|---|
| 2012 | Est. 10000 | PF63 45.00 | PF65 50.00 | | | |

**KM# 2079 10 EURO**
22.20 g., 0.900 Silver 0.6424 oz. ASW, 37 mm. **Obv:** Trans-atlantic liner France **Rev:** Two winged smoke-stacks, partial porthole **Mint:** Paris

| Date | Mintage | VF20 | XF40 | MS60 | MS63 | MS65 |
|---|---|---|---|---|---|---|
| 2012 | Est. 10000 | PF63 45.00 | PF65 50.00 | | | |

**KM# 2084 10 EURO**
22.20 g., 0.900 Silver 0.6424 oz. ASW, 37 mm. **Obv:** Roxane on the Balcony **Rev:** Edmond Rostand and quote **Mint:** Paris

| Date | Mintage | VF20 | XF40 | MS60 | MS63 | MS65 |
|---|---|---|---|---|---|---|
| 2012 | Est. 5000 | PF63 35.00 | PF65 40.00 | | | |

**KM# 2085 10 EURO**
22.20 g., 0.900 Silver 0.6424 oz. ASW, 37 mm. **Obv:** Puss in boots **Rev:** Charles Perrault and quote **Mint:** Paris

| Date | Mintage | VF20 | XF40 | MS60 | MS63 | MS65 |
|---|---|---|---|---|---|---|
| 2012 | Est. 5000 | PF63 35.00 | PF65 40.00 | | | |

**KM# 2087 10 EURO**
22.20 g., 0.900 Silver 0.6424 oz. ASW, 37 mm. **Obv:** Yves Klein, blue hand **Rev:** Klein artwork **Mint:** Paris

| Date | Mintage | VF20 | XF40 | MS60 | MS63 | MS65 |
|---|---|---|---|---|---|---|
| 2012 | — | PF63 40.00 | PF65 45.00 | | | |

**KM# 1766 10 EURO**
22.20 g., 0.900 Silver 0.6424 oz. ASW, 37 mm. **Subject:** Year of the Snake **Obv:** Snake **Rev:** La Fontaine and lunar year animals **Mint:** Paris

| Date | Mintage | VF20 | XF40 | MS60 | MS63 | MS65 |
|---|---|---|---|---|---|---|
| 2013 | 10,000 | PF65 75.00 | | | | |

**KM# 1770 10 EURO**
22.20 g., 0.900 Silver 0.6424 oz. ASW, 37 mm. **Obv:** Steam ship l'Amazone **Rev:** Two ship funnels from SS France **Mint:** Paris

| Date | Mintage | VF20 | XF40 | MS60 | MS63 | MS65 |
|---|---|---|---|---|---|---|
| 2013 | — | PF63 45.00 | PF65 50.00 | | | |

**KM# 1772 10 EURO**
22.20 g., 0.900 Silver 0.6424 oz. ASW, 37 mm. **Subject:** Asterix **Mint:** Paris

| Date | Mintage | VF20 | XF40 | MS60 | MS63 | MS65 |
|---|---|---|---|---|---|---|
| 2013 | 10,000 | PF63 45.00 | PF65 50.00 | | | |

**KM# 1775 10 EURO**
22.20 g., 0.900 Silver 0.6424 oz. ASW, 37 mm. **Subject:** Francois I **Mint:** Paris

| Date | Mintage | VF20 | XF40 | MS60 | MS63 | MS65 |
|---|---|---|---|---|---|---|
| 2013 | 10,000 | — | — | — | — | 65.00 |

**KM# 1778 10 EURO**
22.20 g., 0.900 Silver 0.6424 oz. ASW, 37 mm. **Obv:** Sailing ship La Gloire **Mint:** Paris

| Date | Mintage | VF20 | XF40 | MS60 | MS63 | MS65 |
|---|---|---|---|---|---|---|
| 2013 | 10,000 | PF63 35.00 | PF65 40.00 | | | |

**KM# 1779 10 EURO**
22.20 g., 0.900 Silver 0.6424 oz. ASW, 37 mm. **Subject:** Henri IV **Mint:** Paris

| Date | Mintage | VF20 | XF40 | MS60 | MS63 | MS65 |
|---|---|---|---|---|---|---|
| 2013 | 10,000 | — | — | — | — | 65.00 |

**KM# 1781 10 EURO**
22.20 g., 0.900 Silver 0.6424 oz. ASW, 37 mm. **Subject:** Julien Sorel **Mint:** Paris

| Date | Mintage | VF20 | XF40 | MS60 | MS63 | MS65 |
|---|---|---|---|---|---|---|
| 2013 | — | PF63 35.00 | PF65 40.00 | | | |

**KM# 1783 10 EURO**
22.20 g., 0.900 Silver 0.6424 oz. ASW, 37 mm. **Subject:** Louis XI **Mint:** Paris

| Date | Mintage | VF20 | XF40 | MS60 | MS63 | MS65 |
|---|---|---|---|---|---|---|
| 2013 | — | — | — | — | — | 65.00 |

**KM# 1900 10 EURO**
22.20 g., 0.900 Silver 0.6424 oz. ASW, 37 mm. **Subject:** Louis XI **Mint:** Paris

| Date | Mintage | VF20 | XF40 | MS60 | MS63 | MS65 |
|---|---|---|---|---|---|---|
| 2013 | — | — | — | — | — | 65.00 |

**KM# 1902 10 EURO**
22.20 g., 0.900 Silver-Bronze 0.6424 oz., 37 mm. **Subject:** Madame Bovary **Mint:** Paris

| Date | Mintage | VF20 | XF40 | MS60 | MS63 | MS65 |
|---|---|---|---|---|---|---|
| 2013 | — | PF63 45.00 | PF65 50.00 | | | |

**KM# 2091 10 EURO**
22.20 g., 0.900 Silver 0.6424 oz. ASW, 37 mm. **Subject:** French-German Friendship, 50th Anniversary **Rev:** Europa head facing at right, banners at left **Mint:** Paris

| Date | Mintage | VF20 | XF40 | MS60 | MS63 | MS65 |
|---|---|---|---|---|---|---|
| 2013 | — | PF63 35.00 | PF65 40.00 | | | |

**KM# 2095 10 EURO**
22.20 g., 0.900 Silver 0.6424 oz. ASW, 37 mm. **Subject:** Rudolf Nureyev **Obv:** Portrait at right **Rev:** Dancer and National Theater **Mint:** Paris

| Date | Mintage | VF20 | XF40 | MS60 | MS63 | MS65 |
|---|---|---|---|---|---|---|
| 2013 | — | PF63 35.00 | PF65 40.00 | | | |

**KM# 2097 10 EURO**
22.20 g., 0.900 Silver 0.6424 oz. ASW, 37 mm. **Subject:** Notre Dame, 850th Anniversary **Obv:** Seal at right, cathedral details, blue highlights **Rev:** Seal at left, cathedral details, blue highlights **Mint:** Paris

| Date | Mintage | VF20 | XF40 | MS60 | MS63 | MS65 |
|---|---|---|---|---|---|---|
| 2013 | — | PF63 50.00 | PF65 55.00 | | | |

**KM# 2103 10 EURO**
22.20 g., 0.900 Silver 0.6424 oz. ASW, 37 mm. **Subject:** Odette de Crecy **Mint:** Paris

| Date | Mintage | VF20 | XF40 | MS60 | MS63 | MS65 |
|---|---|---|---|---|---|---|
| 2013 | — | PF63 45.00 | PF65 50.00 | | | |

**KM# 2111 10 EURO**
22.20 g., 0.900 Silver 0.6424 oz. ASW, 37 mm. **Subject:** Pessac Industrial Site, 40th Anniversary **Obv:** Sower **Mint:** Paris

| Date | Mintage | VF20 | XF40 | MS60 | MS63 | MS65 |
|---|---|---|---|---|---|---|
| 2013 | — | PF63 45.00 | PF65 50.00 | | | |

**KM# 2117 10 EURO**
22.20 g., 0.900 Silver 0.6424 oz. ASW, 37 mm. **Subject:** Tour de France, 100th Anniversary **Rev:** Bike rider with green jacket **Mint:** Paris

| Date | Mintage | VF20 | XF40 | MS60 | MS63 | MS65 |
|---|---|---|---|---|---|---|
| 2013 | — | PF63 45.00 | PF65 55.00 | | | |

**KM# 2118 10 EURO**
22.20 g., 0.900 Silver 0.6424 oz. ASW, 37 mm. **Subject:** Tour de France, 100th Anniversary **Rev:** Bike rider with white shirt **Mint:** Paris

| Date | Mintage | VF20 | XF40 | MS60 | MS63 | MS65 |
|---|---|---|---|---|---|---|
| 2013 | — | PF63 45.00 | PF65 55.00 | | | |

**KM# 2119 10 EURO**
22.20 g., 0.900 Silver 0.6424 oz. ASW, 37 mm. **Subject:** Tour de France, 100th Anniversary **Rev:** Bike rider with yellow shirt **Mint:** Paris

| Date | Mintage | VF20 | XF40 | MS60 | MS63 | MS65 |
|---|---|---|---|---|---|---|
| 2013 | — | PF63 45.00 | PF65 55.00 | | | |

**KM# 2120 10 EURO**
22.20 g., 0.900 Silver 0.6424 oz. ASW, 37 mm. **Subject:** Tour de France, 100th Anniversary **Rev:** Bike rider with red spotted shirt **Mint:** Paris

| Date | Mintage | VF20 | XF40 | MS60 | MS63 | MS65 |
|---|---|---|---|---|---|---|
| 2013 | — | PF63 45.00 | PF65 55.00 | | | |

**KM# 2122 15 EURO**
0.500 Silver ASW, 27 mm. **Obv:** Value within horizontal wreath **Rev:** Hercules **Mint:** Paris

| Date | Mintage | VF20 | XF40 | MS60 | MS63 | MS65 |
|---|---|---|---|---|---|---|
| 2013 | — | — | — | — | 15.00 | 20.00 |

**KM# 2123 10 EURO**
22.20 g., 0.900 Silver 0.6424 oz. ASW, 37 mm. **Subject:** Sochi Snowboard **Mint:** Paris

| Date | Mintage | VF20 | XF40 | MS60 | MS63 | MS65 |
|---|---|---|---|---|---|---|
| 2013 | — | PF63 45.00 | PF65 55.00 | | | |

**KM# 2125 10 EURO**
22.20 g., 0.900 Silver 0.6424 oz. ASW, 37 mm. **Subject:** TVG - Gare Nord **Mint:** Paris

| Date | Mintage | VF20 | XF40 | MS60 | MS63 | MS65 |
|---|---|---|---|---|---|---|
| 2013 | — | PF63 45.00 | PF65 55.00 | | | |

**KM# A1450 15 EURO**
31.00 g., 0.900 Silver 0.897 oz. ASW, 31 mm. **Rev:** Pantheon

| Date | Mintage | VF20 | XF40 | MS60 | MS63 | MS65 |
|---|---|---|---|---|---|---|
| 2007 | 7,500 | PF63 75.00 | PF65 85.00 | | | |

**KM# 1535 15 EURO**
15.00 g., 0.900 Silver 0.434 oz. ASW, 31 mm. **Obv:** Sower, half length advancing right **Rev:** Value within hexagon

| Date | Mintage | VF20 | XF40 | MS60 | MS63 | MS65 |
|---|---|---|---|---|---|---|
| 2008 | 7,500 | PF63 55.00 | PF65 60.00 | | | |
| 2008 | 500,000 | — | — | — | — | 45.00 |
| 2009 | 7,500 | PF63 55.00 | PF65 60.00 | | | |
| 2010 | 9,000 | PF63 55.00 | PF65 60.00 | | | |

**KM# 1306 20 EURO**
17.00 g., 0.920 Gold 0.5028 oz. AGW, 31 mm. **Subject:** French Landmarks **Obv:** French map **Rev:** Le Mont St. Michel **Edge:** Plain **Mint:** Paris

| Date | Mintage | VF20 | XF40 | MS60 | MS63 | MS65 |
|---|---|---|---|---|---|---|
| 2002 | 1,000 | PF63 950 | PF65 1,000 | | | |

**KM# 1308 20 EURO**
17.00 g., 0.920 Gold 0.5028 oz. AGW, 31 mm. **Subject:** French Landmarks **Obv:** French map **Rev:** La Butte Montmartre **Edge:** Plain **Mint:** Paris

| Date | Mintage | VF20 | XF40 | MS60 | MS63 | MS65 |
|---|---|---|---|---|---|---|
| 2002 | 1,000 | PF63 875 | PF65 900 | | | |

**KM# 1333 20 EURO**
17.00 g., 0.920 Gold 0.5028 oz. AGW, 31 mm. **Obv:** Victor Hugo, denomination and map **Rev:** Gavroche **Edge:** Plain **Mint:** Paris

| Date | Mintage | VF20 | XF40 | MS60 | MS63 | MS65 |
|---|---|---|---|---|---|---|
| 2002 | 2,000 | PF63 900 | PF65 925 | | | |

**KM# 1982 20 EURO**
17.00 g., 0.920 Gold 0.5028 oz. AGW, 31 mm. **Obv:** French euro coin designs **Rev:** Europa head facing, flags at left **Mint:** Paris

| Date | Mintage | VF20 | XF40 | MS60 | MS63 | MS65 |
|---|---|---|---|---|---|---|
| 2002 | 3,000 | PF63 1,000 | PF65 1,100 | | | |

**KM# 1984 20 EURO**
17.00 g., 0.920 Gold 0.5028 oz. AGW, 31 mm. **Subject:** Charles Lindburg's Flight, 75th Anniversary **Obv:** Map of Northern France, portrait of Lindburg **Rev:** Spirit of St. Louis plane and U.S. Coastline **Mint:** Paris

| Date | Mintage | VF20 | XF40 | MS60 | MS63 | MS65 |
|---|---|---|---|---|---|---|
| 2002 | 1,000 | PF63 1,000 | PF65 1,100 | | | |

**KM# 1986 20 EURO**
163.80 g., 0.950 Silver 5.003 oz. ASW, 50 mm. **Obv:** Victor Hugo bust facing at left **Rev:** Street scene from Les Miserables **Rev. Legend:** GAVROCHE **Mint:** Paris

| Date | Mintage | VF20 | XF40 | MS60 | MS63 | MS65 |
|---|---|---|---|---|---|---|
| 2002 | 500 | PF63 1,400 | PF65 1,500 | | | |

**KM# 1987 20 EURO**
17.00 g., 0.920 Gold 0.5028 oz. AGW, 31 mm. **Subject:** Children's stories **Rev:** Cinderilla **Mint:** Paris

| Date | Mintage | VF20 | XF40 | MS60 | MS63 | MS65 |
|---|---|---|---|---|---|---|
| 2002 | 926 | PF63 1,000 | PF65 1,100 | | | |

**KM# 1988 20 EURO**
17.00 g., 0.920 Gold 0.5028 oz. AGW, 31 mm. **Subject:** Children's Stories **Rev:** Snow White **Mint:** Paris

| Date | Mintage | VF20 | XF40 | MS60 | MS63 | MS65 |
|---|---|---|---|---|---|---|
| 2002 | 950 | PF63 1,000 | PF65 1,100 | | | |

**KM# 1989 20 EURO**
17.00 g., 0.920 Gold 0.5028 oz. AGW, 31 mm. **Subject:** Children's Stories **Rev:** Pinocchio **Mint:** Paris

| Date | Mintage | VF20 | XF40 | MS60 | MS63 | MS65 |
|---|---|---|---|---|---|---|
| 2002 | 1,000 | PF63 1,000 | PF65 1,100 | | | |

**KM# 1990 20 EURO**
17.00 g., 0.920 Gold 0.5028 oz. AGW, 31 mm. **Obv:** Sower advancing left **Rev:** Large value and map of Europe **Mint:** Paris

| Date | Mintage | VF20 | XF40 | MS60 | MS63 | MS65 |
|---|---|---|---|---|---|---|
| 2002 | 4,182 | PF63 1,000 | PF65 1,100 | | | |

**KM# 1327 20 EURO**
8.45 g., 0.920 Gold 0.2499 oz. AGW, 31 mm. **Obv:** Tour de France logo **Rev:** Group of cyclists and Arch de Triumph **Edge:** Reeded **Mint:** Paris

| Date | Mintage | VF20 | XF40 | MS60 | MS63 | MS65 |
|---|---|---|---|---|---|---|
| 2003 A | 2,127 | PF63 475 | PF65 500 | | | |

**KM# 1328 20 EURO**
8.45 g., 0.920 Gold 0.2499 oz. AGW, 31 mm. **Obv:** Tour de France logo **Rev:** Two cyclists and spectators **Edge:** Reeded **Mint:** Paris

| Date | Mintage | VF20 | XF40 | MS60 | MS63 | MS65 |
|---|---|---|---|---|---|---|
| 2003 A | 2,100 | PF63 475 | PF65 500 | | | |

**KM# 1329 20 EURO**
8.45 g., 0.920 Gold 0.2499 oz. AGW, 31 mm. **Obv:** Tour de France logo **Rev:** Two groups of cyclists **Edge:** Reeded **Mint:** Paris

| Date | Mintage | VF20 | XF40 | MS60 | MS63 | MS65 |
|---|---|---|---|---|---|---|
| 2003 A | 2,103 | PF63 475 | PF65 500 | | | |

**KM# 1330 20 EURO**
8.45 g., 0.920 Gold 0.2499 oz. AGW, 31 mm. **Obv:** Tour de France logo **Rev:** Cyclist, stop watch and gears **Edge:** Reeded **Mint:** Paris

| Date | Mintage | VF20 | XF40 | MS60 | MS63 | MS65 |
|---|---|---|---|---|---|---|
| 2003 A | 2,107 | PF63 475 | PF65 500 | | | |

**KM# 1334 20 EURO**
17.00 g., 0.920 Gold 0.5028 oz. AGW, 31 mm. **Obv:** Tour de France logo **Rev:** Cyclist going left **Edge:** Plain **Mint:** Paris

| Date | Mintage | VF20 | XF40 | MS60 | MS63 | MS65 |
|---|---|---|---|---|---|---|
| 2003 | 5,000 | PF63 875 | PF65 900 | | | |

**KM# 1337 20 EURO**
17.00 g., 0.920 Gold 0.5028 oz. AGW, 31 mm. **Obv:** Jefferson and Napoleon with Louisiana Purchase map **Rev:** Jazz musician, mansion and river boat **Edge:** Plain **Mint:** Paris

| Date | Mintage | VF20 | XF40 | MS60 | MS63 | MS65 |
|---|---|---|---|---|---|---|
| 2003 | 761 | PF63 900 | PF65 925 | | | |

**KM# 1339 20 EURO**
17.00 g., 0.920 Gold 0.5028 oz. AGW, 31 mm. **Obv:** Curved cross design with multiple values **Rev:** Goddess Europa and flags **Edge:** Plain **Mint:** Paris

| Date | Mintage | VF20 | XF40 | MS60 | MS63 | MS65 |
|---|---|---|---|---|---|---|
| 2003 | 2,322 | PF63 875 | PF65 900 | | | |

**KM# 1342 20 EURO**
17.00 g., 0.920 Gold 0.5028 oz. AGW, 31 mm. **Obv:** Denomination and compass face **Rev:** SS Normandie and New York City skyline **Edge:** Plain **Mint:** Paris

| Date | Mintage | VF20 | XF40 | MS60 | MS63 | MS65 |
|---|---|---|---|---|---|---|
| 2003 | 389 | PF63 900 | PF65 925 | | | |

**KM# 1344 20 EURO**
17.00 g., 0.920 Gold 0.5028 oz. AGW, 31 mm. **Obv:** Denomination and compass face **Rev:** Airplane and Tokyo Geisha **Edge:** Plain **Mint:** Paris

| Date | Mintage | VF20 | XF40 | MS60 | MS63 | MS65 |
|---|---|---|---|---|---|---|
| 2003 | 580 | PF63 900 | PF65 925 | | | |

**KM# 1346 20 EURO**
17.00 g., 0.920 Gold 0.5028 oz. AGW, 31 mm. **Obv:** Paul Gauguin **Rev:** Native woman **Edge:** Plain **Mint:** Paris

| Date | Mintage | VF20 | XF40 | MS60 | MS63 | MS65 |
|---|---|---|---|---|---|---|
| 2003 | 628 | PF63 875 | | | | |

**KM# 1349 20 EURO**
17.00 g., 0.920 Gold 0.5028 oz. AGW, 31 mm. **Obv:** The Seed Sower **Rev:** Denomination and map **Edge:** Plain **Mint:** Paris

| Date | Mintage | VF20 | XF40 | MS60 | MS63 | MS65 |
|---|---|---|---|---|---|---|
| 2003 | 1,166 | PF63 875 | PF65 900 | | | |

**KM# 1354 20 EURO**
17.00 g., 0.920 Gold 0.5028 oz. AGW, 31 mm. **Obv:** Mona Lisa **Rev:** Leonardo da Vinci and denomination **Edge:** Plain **Mint:** Paris

| Date | Mintage | VF20 | XF40 | MS60 | MS63 | MS65 |
|---|---|---|---|---|---|---|
| 2003 | 808 | PF63 900 | PF65 925 | | | |

**KM# 1356 20 EURO**
17.00 g., 0.920 Gold 0.5028 oz. AGW, 31 mm. **Obv:** Map and denomination **Rev:** Chateau Chambord **Edge:** Plain **Mint:** Paris

| Date | Mintage | VF20 | XF40 | MS60 | MS63 | MS65 |
|---|---|---|---|---|---|---|
| 2003 | 561 | PF63 900 | PF65 925 | | | |

**KM# 1358 20 EURO**
17.00 g., 0.920 Gold 0.5028 oz. AGW, 31 mm. **Obv:** Denomination in swirling design **Rev:** Hansel and Gretel, witch and house **Edge:** Plain **Mint:** Paris

| Date | Mintage | VF20 | XF40 | MS60 | MS63 | MS65 |
|---|---|---|---|---|---|---|
| 2003 | 310 | PF63 900 | PF65 925 | | | |

**KM# 1360 20 EURO**
17.00 g., 0.920 Gold 0.5028 oz. AGW, 31 mm. **Obv:** Denomination in swirling design **Rev:** Alice in Wonderland **Edge:** Plain **Mint:** Paris

| Date | Mintage | VF20 | XF40 | MS60 | MS63 | MS65 |
|---|---|---|---|---|---|---|
| 2003 | 314 | PF63 900 | PF65 925 | | | |

**KM# 1363 20 EURO**
17.00 g., 0.920 Gold 0.5028 oz. AGW, 31 mm. **Obv:** Pierre de Coubertin **Rev:** Olympic runners **Edge:** Plain **Mint:** Paris

| Date | Mintage | VF20 | XF40 | MS60 | MS63 | MS65 |
|---|---|---|---|---|---|---|
| 2003 | 334 | PF63 875 | PF65 900 | | | |

**KM# 1998 20 EURO**
17.00 g., 0.920 Gold 0.5028 oz. AGW, 31 mm. **Subject:** Athletic World Championships **Obv:** Winner podium before buildings **Rev:** Runner **Mint:** Paris

| Date | Mintage | VF20 | XF40 | MS60 | MS63 | MS65 |
|---|---|---|---|---|---|---|
| 2003 | 1,165 | PF63 1,000 | PF65 1,100 | | | |

**KM# 1999 20 EURO**
17.00 g., 0.920 Gold 0.5028 oz. AGW, 31 mm. **Subject:** Athletic World Championships **Obv:** Winner podium before buildings **Rev:** High jumper **Mint:** Paris

| Date | Mintage | VF20 | XF40 | MS60 | MS63 | MS65 |
|---|---|---|---|---|---|---|
| 2003 | 863 | PF63 1,000 | PF65 1,100 | | | |

**KM# 2000 20 EURO**
17.00 g., 0.920 Gold 0.5028 oz. AGW, 31 mm. **Subject:** Athletic World Championships **Obv:** Winner podium before buildings **Mint:** Paris

| Date | Mintage | VF20 | XF40 | MS60 | MS63 | MS65 |
|---|---|---|---|---|---|---|
| 2003 | 867 | PF63 1,000 PF65 1,100 | | | | |

**KM# 2004 20 EURO**
163.80 g., 0.950 Silver 5.003 oz. ASW, 50 mm. **Obv:** Mona Lisa **Rev:** Leonardo DaVinci bust at left, large value at right **Mint:** Paris

| Date | Mintage | VF20 | XF40 | MS60 | MS63 | MS65 |
|---|---|---|---|---|---|---|
| 2003 | 999 | PF63 400 PF65 425 | | | | |

**KM# 2007 20 EURO**
17.00 g., 0.920 Gold 0.5028 oz. AGW, 31 mm. **Subject:** Orient Express, Hagia Sophia in Istanbul **Obv:** Compass Rose **Rev:** Steam locomotive **Mint:** Paris

| Date | Mintage | VF20 | XF40 | MS60 | MS63 | MS65 |
|---|---|---|---|---|---|---|
| 2003 | 402 | PF63 1,000 PF65 1,100 | | | | |

**KM# 2009 20 EURO**
17.00 g., 0.920 Gold 0.5028 oz. AGW, 31 mm. **Subject:** Childhood Fairy Tales **Rev:** Sleeping Beauty **Mint:** Paris

| Date | Mintage | VF20 | XF40 | MS60 | MS63 | MS65 |
|---|---|---|---|---|---|---|
| 2003 | 309 | PF63 1,250 PF65 1,350 | | | | |

**KM# 1365 20 EURO**
17.00 g., 0.920 Gold 0.5028 oz. AGW, 31 mm. **Obv:** Map with denomination **Rev:** Avignon Popes Palace **Edge:** Plain **Mint:** Paris

| Date | Mintage | VF20 | XF40 | MS60 | MS63 | MS65 |
|---|---|---|---|---|---|---|
| 2004 | 595 | PF63 900 PF65 925 | | | | |

**KM# 1370 20 EURO**
17.00 g., 0.920 Gold 0.5028 oz. AGW, 31 mm. **Obv:** Soldiers and Normandy invasion scene **Rev:** D-DAY" above denomination **Edge:** Plain **Mint:** Paris

| Date | Mintage | VF20 | XF40 | MS60 | MS63 | MS65 |
|---|---|---|---|---|---|---|
| 2004 | 531 | PF63 875 PF65 900 | | | | |

**KM# 1376 20 EURO**
17.00 g., 0.920 Gold 0.5028 oz. AGW, 31 mm. **Subject:** Centenary Law of Dec. 9, 1905 **Obv:** Sower" left in ring of stars **Rev:** Denomination and French map face design **Edge:** Plain **Mint:** Paris

| Date | Mintage | VF20 | XF40 | MS60 | MS63 | MS65 |
|---|---|---|---|---|---|---|
| 2004 | 874 | PF63 875 PF65 900 | | | | |
| 2006 | 1,000 | PF63 900 PF65 925 | | | | |

**KM# 1379 20 EURO**
17.00 g., 0.920 Gold 0.5028 oz. AGW, 31 mm. **Obv:** Compass rose **Rev:** Ocean liner **Edge:** Plain **Mint:** Paris

| Date | Mintage | VF20 | XF40 | MS60 | MS63 | MS65 |
|---|---|---|---|---|---|---|
| 2004 | 281 | PF63 900 PF65 925 | | | | |

**KM# 1381 20 EURO**
17.00 g., 0.920 Gold 0.5028 oz. AGW, 31 mm. **Obv:** Compass rose **Rev:** Trans-Siberian Railroad **Edge:** Plain **Mint:** Paris

| Date | Mintage | VF20 | XF40 | MS60 | MS63 | MS65 |
|---|---|---|---|---|---|---|
| 2004 | 299 | PF63 900 PF65 925 | | | | |

**KM# 1383 20 EURO**
17.00 g., 0.920 Gold 0.5028 oz. AGW, 31 mm. **Obv:** Compass rose **Rev:** Half-track vehicle **Edge:** Plain **Mint:** Paris

| Date | Mintage | VF20 | XF40 | MS60 | MS63 | MS65 |
|---|---|---|---|---|---|---|
| 2004 | 273 | PF63 900 PF65 925 | | | | |

**KM# 1385 20 EURO**
17.00 g., 0.920 Gold 0.5028 oz. AGW, 31 mm. **Obv:** Compass rose **Rev:** Biplane airliner **Edge:** Plain **Mint:** Paris

| Date | Mintage | VF20 | XF40 | MS60 | MS63 | MS65 |
|---|---|---|---|---|---|---|
| 2004 | 273 | PF63 900 PF65 925 | | | | |

**KM# 1388 20 EURO**
17.00 g., 0.920 Gold 0.5028 oz. AGW, 31 mm. **Obv:** Statue of Liberty **Rev:** F. A. Bartholdi **Edge:** Plain **Mint:** Paris

| Date | Mintage | VF20 | XF40 | MS60 | MS63 | MS65 |
|---|---|---|---|---|---|---|
| 2004 | 320 | PF63 875 PF65 900 | | | | |

**KM# 1393 20 EURO**
17.00 g., 0.920 Gold 0.5028 oz. AGW, 31 mm. **Subject:** European Union Expansion **Obv:** Partial face and flags **Rev:** Puzzle map **Edge:** Plain **Mint:** Paris

| Date | Mintage | VF20 | XF40 | MS60 | MS63 | MS65 |
|---|---|---|---|---|---|---|
| 2004 | 1,280 | PF63 875 PF65 900 | | | | |

**KM# 2011 20 EURO**
17.00 g., 0.920 Gold 0.5028 oz. AGW, 31 mm. **Subject:** French-English Treaty, 100th Anniversary **Obv:** Two busts and treaty document **Rev:** Marianne and Britannia **Mint:** Paris

| Date | Mintage | VF20 | XF40 | MS60 | MS63 | MS65 |
|---|---|---|---|---|---|---|
| 2004 | 339 | PF63 1,500 PF65 1,600 | | | | |

**KM# 2015 20 EURO**
17.00 g., 0.920 Gold 0.5028 oz. AGW, 31 mm. **Subject:** Childhood stories **Rev:** Aladdin **Mint:** Paris

| Date | Mintage | VF20 | XF40 | MS60 | MS63 | MS65 |
|---|---|---|---|---|---|---|
| 2004 | 316 | PF63 1,200 PF65 1,300 | | | | |

**KM# 2016 20 EURO**
17.00 g., 0.920 Gold 0.5028 oz. AGW, 31 mm. **Subject:** Childhood stories **Rev:** Peter Pan **Mint:** Paris

| Date | Mintage | VF20 | XF40 | MS60 | MS63 | MS65 |
|---|---|---|---|---|---|---|
| 2004 | 362 | PF63 1,000 PF65 1,100 | | | | |

**KM# 1433 20 EURO**
17.00 g., 0.920 Gold 0.5028 oz. AGW, 31 mm. **Subject:** Bicentennial Victory at Austerlitz **Rev:** Battle scene **Rev. Legend:** LIBERTÉ ÉGALITÉ FRATERNITÉ **Mint:** Paris

| Date | Mintage | VF20 | XF40 | MS60 | MS63 | MS65 |
|---|---|---|---|---|---|---|
| 2005 | 1,431 | PF63 875 PF65 900 | | | | |

**KM# 1437 20 EURO**
17.00 g., 0.920 Gold 0.5028 oz. AGW, 31 mm. **Subject:** Centenary - Law of Dec. 9, 1905 **Obv:** Sower" at left in ring of stars **Mint:** Paris

| Date | Mintage | VF20 | XF40 | MS60 | MS63 | MS65 |
|---|---|---|---|---|---|---|
| 2005 | 436 | PF63 875 PF65 900 | | | | |

**KM# 2022 20 EURO**
17.00 g., 0.920 Gold 0.5028 oz. AGW, 31 mm. **Subject:** World Cup Soccer **Obv:** World Cup trophy and soccer ball **Rev:** Large value and map of France **Mint:** Paris

| Date | Mintage | VF20 | XF40 | MS60 | MS63 | MS65 |
|---|---|---|---|---|---|---|
| 2005 | Est. 102 | PF63 1,000 PF65 1,100 | | | | |

**KM# 2028 20 EURO**
17.00 g., 0.920 Gold 0.5028 oz. AGW, 31 mm. **Subject:** Frederic Chopin, 195th Anniversary of Birth **Obv:** Profile at left, piano keys at right vertically **Rev:** Statue in Wausau park at left, piano keys at right vertically **Mint:** Paris

| Date | Mintage | VF20 | XF40 | MS60 | MS63 | MS65 |
|---|---|---|---|---|---|---|
| 2005 | 500 | PF65 3,000 | | | | |

**KM# 2030 20 EURO**
163.80 g., 0.950 Silver 5.003 oz. ASW, 50 mm. **Subject:** Jules Verne, 100th Anniversary of Death **Obv:** Around the World in 80 days **Mint:** Paris

| Date | Mintage | VF20 | XF40 | MS60 | MS63 | MS65 |
|---|---|---|---|---|---|---|
| 2005 | 500 | PF63 350 PF65 375 | | | | |

**KM# 2031 20 EURO**
163.50 g., 0.950 Silver 4.9938 oz. ASW, 50 mm. **Subject:** Jules Verne, 100th Anniversary of Death **Obv:** 20,000 leagues under the sea **Mint:** Paris

| Date | Mintage | VF20 | XF40 | MS60 | MS63 | MS65 |
|---|---|---|---|---|---|---|
| 2005 | 500 | PF63 350 PF65 375 | | | | |

**KM# 2032 20 EURO**
163.50 g., 0.950 Silver 4.9938 oz. ASW, 50 mm. **Subject:** Jules Verne, 100th Anniversary of Death **Rev:** From the earth to the moon **Mint:** Paris

| Date | Mintage | VF20 | XF40 | MS60 | MS63 | MS65 |
|---|---|---|---|---|---|---|
| 2005 | 500 | PF63 350 PF65 375 | | | | |

**KM# 1443 20 EURO**
155.52 g., 0.950 Silver 4.7501 oz. ASW, 50 mm. **Obv:** Bust of Franklin facing slightly right at left, his diplomatic and technical successes at right **Obv. Legend:** BENJAMIN FRANKLIN 1706-2006 **Obv. Inscription:** AMI DE LA FRANCE **Mint:** Paris

| Date | Mintage | VF20 | XF40 | MS60 | MS63 | MS65 |
|---|---|---|---|---|---|---|
| 2006 | 500 | PF63 300 PF65 325 | | | | |

**KM# 1454 20 EURO**
155.50 g., 0.950 Silver 4.7495 oz. ASW, 50 mm. **Subject:** 100th Anniversary - Paul Cézanne's death **Obv:** Self portrait **Rev:** The Card Players **Rev. Legend:** LIBERTÉ ÉGALITÉ FRATERNITÉ **Mint:** Paris

| Date | Mintage | VF20 | XF40 | MS60 | MS63 | MS65 |
|---|---|---|---|---|---|---|
| 2006 | 500 | PF63 300 PF65 325 | | | | |

**KM# 2050 20 EURO**
163.80 g., 0.950 Silver 5.003 oz. ASW, 50 mm. **Subject:** Marie Curie, 100th Anniversary of Sorbonne Professorship **Obv:** Bust and atom **Rev:** Building tower and students **Mint:** Paris

| Date | Mintage | VF20 | XF40 | MS60 | MS63 | MS65 |
|---|---|---|---|---|---|---|
| 2006 | 500 | PF63 500 PF65 525 | | | | |

**KM# 2051 20 EURO**
17.00 g., 0.920 Gold 0.5028 oz. AGW, 31 mm. **Subject:** Marie Curie, 100th Anniversary of Sorbonne Professorship **Obv:** Bust and atom **Rev:** Building tower and students **Mint:** Paris

| Date | Mintage | VF20 | XF40 | MS60 | MS63 | MS65 |
|---|---|---|---|---|---|---|
| 2006 | 500 | PF63 1,400 PF65 1,500 | | | | |

**KM# 2052 20 EURO**
163.80 g., 0.950 Silver 5.003 oz. ASW, 50 mm. **Obv:** Monument parts as map of France **Rev:** Arc de Triomphe and tomb of Unknown soldier **Mint:** Paris

| Date | Mintage | VF20 | XF40 | MS60 | MS63 | MS65 |
|---|---|---|---|---|---|---|
| 2006 | 500 | PF63 300 PF65 325 | | | | |

Note: Individually numbered

**KM# 2056 20 EURO**
17.00 g., 0.920 Gold 0.5028 oz. AGW, 31 mm. **Subject:** Abolition of the Death Penalty, 25th Anniversary **Obv:** Sower advancing left **Rev:** Guillotine **Mint:** Paris

| Date | Mintage | VF20 | XF40 | MS60 | MS63 | MS65 |
|---|---|---|---|---|---|---|
| 2006 | 652 | PF63 1,000 PF65 1,100 | | | | |

**KM# 2059 20 EURO**
17.00 g., 0.920 Gold 0.5028 oz. AGW, 31 mm. **Subject:** Paul Cézanne, 100th Anniversary of Death **Obv:** Bust **Rev:** Two men seated at table, wine bottle between them **Mint:** Paris

| Date | Mintage | VF20 | XF40 | MS60 | MS63 | MS65 |
|---|---|---|---|---|---|---|
| 2006 | 500 | PF63 1,100 PF65 1,200 | | | | |

**KM# 2062 20 EURO**
163.80 g., 0.950 Silver 5.003 oz. ASW, 50 mm. **Subject:** Wolfgang Amadeus Mozart, 250th Anniversary of Birth **Obv:** Youthful bust **Rev:** Hands at piano keys, music above **Mint:** Paris

| Date | Mintage | VF20 | XF40 | MS60 | MS63 | MS65 |
|---|---|---|---|---|---|---|
| 2006 | 500 | PF63 400 PF65 425 | | | | |

Note: Individually numbered

**KM# 2065 20 EURO**
163.80 g., 0.950 Silver 5.003 oz. ASW, 50 mm. **Subject:** Jules Verne, 100th Anniversary of Death **Obv:** Voyage to the center of the earth **Mint:** Paris

| Date | Mintage | VF20 | XF40 | MS60 | MS63 | MS65 |
|---|---|---|---|---|---|---|
| 2006 | 500 | PF63 400 PF65 425 | | | | |

**KM# 2066 20 EURO**
165.30 g., 0.999 Silver 5.3092 oz. ASW, 50 mm. **Subject:** Jules Verne, 100th Anniversary of Death **Obv:** Michel Strogoff, the curier of the Tsar **Mint:** Paris

| Date | Mintage | VF20 | XF40 | MS60 | MS63 | MS65 |
|---|---|---|---|---|---|---|
| 2006 | 500 | PF63 400 PF65 425 | | | | |

**KM# 2067 20 EURO**
163.80 g., 0.999 Silver 5.261 oz. ASW, 50 mm. **Subject:** Jules Verne, 100th Anniversary of Death **Obv:** Five weeks in a balloon **Mint:** Paris

| Date | Mintage | VF20 | XF40 | MS60 | MS63 | MS65 |
|---|---|---|---|---|---|---|
| 2006 | 500 | PF63 400 PF65 425 | | | | |

**KM# 1422 20 EURO**
17.00 g., 0.920 Gold 0.5028 oz. AGW, 30 x 21 mm. **Subject:** Edgar Degas, 90th Anniversary of Seuth **Obv:** Degas painting of dancer **Rev:** Brushes and Degas portrait **Shape:** Rectangle

| Date | Mintage | VF20 | XF40 | MS60 | MS63 | MS65 |
|---|---|---|---|---|---|---|
| 2007 | 500 | PF63 1,000 PF65 1,100 | | | | |

**KM# 1468 20 EURO**
17.00 g., 0.920 Gold 0.5028 oz. AGW, 31 mm. **Subject:** Le Petit Prince, 60th Anniversary **Obv:** Prince lying in field

| Date | Mintage | VF20 | XF40 | MS60 | MS63 | MS65 |
|---|---|---|---|---|---|---|
| 2007 | 1,475 | PF63 875 PF65 900 | | | | |

**KM# 1471 20 EURO**
155.55 g., 0.950 Silver 4.751 oz. ASW, 50 mm. **Obv:** Two dragons in flight **Rev:** Merlin and Excalibur

| Date | Mintage | VF20 | XF40 | MS60 | MS63 | MS65 |
|---|---|---|---|---|---|---|
| 2007 | 498 | PF63 400 PF65 425 | | | | |

**KM# 1472 20 EURO**
17.00 g., 0.920 Gold 0.5028 oz. AGW, 31 mm. **Obv:** Two dragons in flight **Rev:** Merlin & Excalibur

| Date | Mintage | VF20 | XF40 | MS60 | MS63 | MS65 |
|---|---|---|---|---|---|---|
| 2007 | 500 | PF63 900 PF65 925 | | | | |

**KM# 1494 20 EURO**
155.55 g., 0.950 Silver 4.751 oz. ASW, 50 mm. **Subject:** Point Neuf - 400th Anniversary **Obv:** Moments of France logo **Rev:** Point Neuf Bridge and Paris Mint Building

| Date | Mintage | VF20 | XF40 | MS60 | MS63 | MS65 |
|---|---|---|---|---|---|---|
| 2007 | 434 | PF63 300 PF65 325 | | | | |

**KM# 1496 20 EURO**
155.55 g., 0.950 Silver 4.751 oz. ASW, 50 mm. **Subject:** Cannes Film Festival, 60th Anniversary **Obv:** Cinema screen and stage, Golden Palm Award

| Date | Mintage | VF20 | XF40 | MS60 | MS63 | MS65 |
|---|---|---|---|---|---|---|
| 2007 | 369 | PF63 300 PF65 325 | | | | |

**KM# 1509 20 EURO**
100.00 g., 0.950 Silver 3.0543 oz. ASW, 49 mm. **Subject:** Georges Remi Centennial **Rev:** Tin Tin and Snowy

| Date | Mintage | VF20 | XF40 | MS60 | MS63 | MS65 |
|---|---|---|---|---|---|---|
| 2007 | 488 | PF63 325 PF65 350 | | | | |

**KM# 1513 20 EURO**
155.50 g., 0.950 Silver 4.7495 oz. ASW, 50 mm. **Subject:** Stanislas Leszczynski **Obv:** Bust and shield **Rev:** Palace Stanislas - Nancy

| Date | Mintage | VF20 | XF40 | MS60 | MS63 | MS65 |
|---|---|---|---|---|---|---|
| 2007 | 500 | PF63 325 PF65 350 | | | | |

**KM# 1520 20 EURO**
155.50 g., 0.950 Silver 4.7495 oz. ASW, 50 mm. **Subject:** Asterix **Rev:** Character running downhill

| Date | Mintage | VF20 | XF40 | MS60 | MS63 | MS65 |
|---|---|---|---|---|---|---|
| 2007 | 500 | PF63 425 PF65 450 | | | | |

**KM# 1521 20 EURO**
17.00 g., 0.920 Gold 0.5028 oz. AGW, 31 mm. **Subject:** Asterix **Rev:** Asterix and Cleopatria

| Date | Mintage | VF20 | XF40 | MS60 | MS63 | MS65 |
|---|---|---|---|---|---|---|
| 2007 | 490 | **PF63** 900 | **PF65** 925 | | | |

**KM# 1529 20 EURO**
163.80 g., 0.950 Silver 5.003 oz. ASW, 50 mm. **Subject:** French Presidency of European Union **Obv:** Text within stars **Rev:** Europa head and flags

| Date | Mintage | VF20 | XF40 | MS60 | MS63 | MS65 |
|---|---|---|---|---|---|---|
| 2008 | 500 | **PF63** 300 | **PF65** 325 | | | |

**KM# 1540 20 EURO**
163.80 g., 0.950 Silver 5.003 oz. ASW, 50 mm. **Subject:** 5th Republic, 50th Anniversary **Obv:** Sower **Rev:** de Gaulle head right

| Date | Mintage | VF20 | XF40 | MS60 | MS63 | MS65 |
|---|---|---|---|---|---|---|
| 2008 | 500 | **PF63** 300 | **PF65** 325 | | | |

**KM# 1541 20 EURO**
17.00 g., 0.9205 Gold 0.5031 oz. AGW, 31 mm. **Subject:** 5th Republic, 50th Anniversary **Obv:** Sower **Rev:** de Gaulle head right

| Date | Mintage | VF20 | XF40 | MS60 | MS63 | MS65 |
|---|---|---|---|---|---|---|
| 2008 | 500 | **PF63** 900 | **PF65** 925 | | | |

**KM# 1557 20 EURO**
163.80 g., 0.950 Silver 5.003 oz. ASW, 50 mm. **Subject:** André Citronë **Obv:** First front wheel drive auto **Rev:** Bust 1/4 left

| Date | Mintage | VF20 | XF40 | MS60 | MS63 | MS65 |
|---|---|---|---|---|---|---|
| 2008 | 500 | **PF63** 425 | **PF65** 450 | | | |

**KM# 1560 20 EURO**
163.80 g., 0.950 Silver 5.003 oz. ASW, 50 mm. **Subject:** Rouen Armada **Obv:** Cape Horn, sextant, hour glass **Rev:** Sailing ship

| Date | Mintage | VF20 | XF40 | MS60 | MS63 | MS65 |
|---|---|---|---|---|---|---|
| 2008 | — | **PF63** 450 | **PF65** 475 | | | |

**KM# 1563 20 EURO**
163.80 g., 0.950 Silver 5.003 oz. ASW, 50 mm. **Subject:** Lourdes, 150th Anniversary **Obv:** Church of Notre Dame at Lourdes **Rev:** Cross with Pope John Paul II, Pope Benedict XVI and Bernadette Soubirous in quadrants

| Date | Mintage | VF20 | XF40 | MS60 | MS63 | MS65 |
|---|---|---|---|---|---|---|
| 2008 | 500 | **PF63** 400 | **PF65** 425 | | | |

**KM# 1568 20 EURO**
163.80 g., 0.950 Silver 5.003 oz. ASW, 50 mm. **Subject:** Gabrielle Chanel **Obv:** Portrait in hat, right **Rev:** Value on "Matelassé" pattern

| Date | Mintage | VF20 | XF40 | MS60 | MS63 | MS65 |
|---|---|---|---|---|---|---|
| 2008 | 499 | **PF63** 400 | **PF65** 425 | | | |

**KM# 1571 20 EURO**
17.00 g., 0.920 Gold 0.5028 oz. AGW, 30 x 21 mm. **Subject:** Edward Manet **Obv:** Manet's "Olympia" painting **Rev:** Paint brushes and Manet's portrait **Shape:** Rectangle

| Date | Mintage | VF20 | XF40 | MS60 | MS63 | MS65 |
|---|---|---|---|---|---|---|
| 2008 | 500 | **PF63** 950 | **PF65** 975 | | | |

**KM# 1602 20 EURO**
44.40 g., 0.900 Silver 1.2847 oz. ASW, 37 mm. **Obv:** Eiffel Tower Structure **Rev:** Gustave Eiffel at left

| Date | Mintage | VF20 | XF40 | MS60 | MS63 | MS65 |
|---|---|---|---|---|---|---|
| 2009 P | 2,522 | **PF63** 100 | **PF65** 120 | | | |

**KM# 1607 20 EURO**
44.40 g., 0.900 Silver 1.2847 oz. ASW, 37 mm. **Subject:** Bugatti 100th Anniversary **Obv:** Ettore Bugatti at left **Rev:** Race car and grill motif

| Date | Mintage | VF20 | XF40 | MS60 | MS63 | MS65 |
|---|---|---|---|---|---|---|
| 2009 P | 789 | **PF63** 100 | **PF65** 120 | | | |

**KM# 1612 20 EURO**
44.40 g., 0.900 Silver 1.2847 oz. ASW, 37 mm. **Subject:** Curie Institute, 100th Anniversary

| Date | Mintage | VF20 | XF40 | MS60 | MS63 | MS65 |
|---|---|---|---|---|---|---|
| 2009 P | 5,000 | **PF63** 70.00 | **PF65** 80.00 | | | |

**KM# 1617 20 EURO**
163.80 g., 0.950 Silver 5.003 oz. ASW, 50 mm. **Subject:** Unesco site - The Kremlin in Moscow **Obv:** Wall Tower and cathedral

| Date | Mintage | VF20 | XF40 | MS60 | MS63 | MS65 |
|---|---|---|---|---|---|---|
| 2009 P | 500 | **PF63** 300 | **PF65** 325 | | | |

**KM# 1690 20 EURO**
44.40 g., 0.900 Silver 1.2847 oz. ASW, 37 mm. **Obv:** Marcel Dassault **Rev:** Mirage III plane **Mint:** Paris

| Date | Mintage | VF20 | XF40 | MS60 | MS63 | MS65 |
|---|---|---|---|---|---|---|
| 2010 | 2,000 | **PF63** 75.00 | **PF65** 85.00 | | | |

**KM# 1704 20 EURO**
44.40 g., 0.900 Silver 1.2847 oz. ASW, 37 mm. **Obv:** Lille station and route map **Rev:** Three TGV trains **Mint:** Paris

| Date | Mintage | VF20 | XF40 | MS60 | MS63 | MS65 |
|---|---|---|---|---|---|---|
| 2010 | 2,000 | **PF63** 75.00 | **PF65** 85.00 | | | |

**KM# 1815 20 EURO**
44.40 g., 0.900 Silver 1.2847 oz. ASW, 37 mm. **Obv:** Metz railroad station **Rev:** TGV and ICE trains **Mint:** Paris

| Date | Mintage | VF20 | XF40 | MS60 | MS63 | MS65 |
|---|---|---|---|---|---|---|
| 2011 | 1,000 | **PF63** 100 | **PF65** 120 | | | |

**KM# 2070 20 EURO**
15.00 g., 0.900 Silver 0.434 oz. ASW, 31 mm. **Subject:** G-20 Meeting in Cannes **Obv:** Sower advancing right **Rev:** Laurel tree and oak tree in the shape of a Euro symbol with value specification in the hexagon as stylization national borders **Mint:** Paris

| Date | Mintage | VF20 | XF40 | MS60 | MS63 | MS65 |
|---|---|---|---|---|---|---|
| 2011 | 2,000 | — | — | — | — | 100 |

**KM# 1912 20 EURO**
44.40 g., 0.900 Silver 1.2847 oz. ASW, 37 mm. **Subject:** TGV South East **Obv:** Lyon Saint-Exupery station **Rev:** Two modern locomotives **Mint:** Paris

| Date | Mintage | VF20 | XF40 | MS60 | MS63 | MS65 |
|---|---|---|---|---|---|---|
| 2012 (a) | 1,000 | **PF63** 75.00 | **PF65** 85.00 | | | |

**KM# 1581 25 EURO**
18.00 g., 0.900 Silver 0.5208 oz. ASW, 33 mm. **Obv:** Modernistic sower advancing right **Rev:** Value and wreath

| Date | Mintage | VF20 | XF40 | MS60 | MS63 | MS65 |
|---|---|---|---|---|---|---|
| 2009 P | 250,000 | — | — | — | — | 35.00 |

**KM# 1761 25 EURO**
18.00 g., 0.500 Silver 0.2894 oz. ASW, 33 mm. **Obv:** Value within horizontal wreath **Rev:** JUSTICE **Mint:** Paris

| Date | Mintage | VF20 | XF40 | MS60 | MS63 | MS65 |
|---|---|---|---|---|---|---|
| 2013 | 100,000 | — | — | — | — | 45.00 |

**KM# 1762 25 EURO**
18.00 g., 0.500 Silver 0.2894 oz. ASW, 33 mm. **Obv:** Value within horizontal wreath **Rev:** RESPECT **Mint:** Paris

| Date | Mintage | VF20 | XF40 | MS60 | MS63 | MS65 |
|---|---|---|---|---|---|---|
| 2013 | 100,000 | — | — | — | — | 45.00 |

**KM# 1763 25 EURO**
18.00 g., 0.500 Silver 0.2894 oz. ASW, 33 mm. **Obv:** Value within horizontal wreath **Rev:** LAICITE **Mint:** Paris

| Date | Mintage | VF20 | XF40 | MS60 | MS63 | MS65 |
|---|---|---|---|---|---|---|
| 2013 | 100,000 | — | — | — | — | 45.00 |

**KM# 1303 50 EURO**
31.00 g., 0.999 Gold 0.9957 oz. AGW, 37 mm. **Subject:** Europa **Obv:** Eight French euro coin designs **Rev:** Portrait and flags design of 6.55957 francs KM-1265 **Edge:** Plain **Mint:** Paris

| Date | Mintage | VF20 | XF40 | MS60 | MS63 | MS65 |
|---|---|---|---|---|---|---|
| 2002 | 2,000 | **PF65** 1,800 | | | | |

**KM# 1335 50 EURO**
31.10 g., 0.999 Gold 0.9989 oz. AGW, 37 mm. **Obv:** Tour de France logo **Rev:** Cyclist going left **Edge:** Plain **Mint:** Paris

| Date | Mintage | VF20 | XF40 | MS60 | MS63 | MS65 |
|---|---|---|---|---|---|---|
| 2002 | 5,000 | **PF65** 1,750 | | | | |

**KM# 1340 50 EURO**
1000.00 g., 0.950 Silver 30.5432 oz. ASW, 100 mm. **Obv:** Curved cross design with multiple values **Rev:** Goddess Europa and flags **Edge:** Plain with three line inscription at six o'clock **Mint:** Paris

| Date | Mintage | VF20 | XF40 | MS60 | MS63 | MS65 |
|---|---|---|---|---|---|---|
| 2003 | 5,528 | **PF63** 1,150 | **PF65** 1,200 | | | |

**KM# 1993 50 EURO**
31.11 g., 0.999 Gold 0.999 oz. AGW **Obv:** Curved cross with coins **Rev:** Europa head at right, flags at left **Mint:** Paris

| Date | Mintage | VF20 | XF40 | MS60 | MS63 | MS65 |
|---|---|---|---|---|---|---|
| 2003 | 2,000 | **PF65** 1,850 | | | | |

**KM# 1368 50 EURO**
31.10 g., 0.999 Gold 0.9989 oz. AGW, 37 mm. **Obv:** Book, denomination and eagle **Rev:** Napoleon and coronation scene **Edge:** Plain **Mint:** Paris

| Date | Mintage | VF20 | XF40 | MS60 | MS63 | MS65 |
|---|---|---|---|---|---|---|
| 2004 | 2,000 | **PF65** 1,800 | | | | |

**KM# 1394 50 EURO**
31.10 g., 0.999 Gold 0.999 oz. AGW, 37 mm. **Subject:** European Union Expansion **Obv:** Partial face and flags **Rev:** Puzzle map **Edge:** Plain **Mint:** Paris

| Date | Mintage | VF20 | XF40 | MS60 | MS63 | MS65 |
|---|---|---|---|---|---|---|
| 2004 | 618 | **PF65** 1,800 | | | | |

**KM# 1430 50 EURO**
31.10 g., 0.999 Gold 0.999 oz. AGW, 37 mm. **Rev:** Kitty and Daniel in Versailles **Rev. Legend:** Hello Kitty **Mint:** Paris

| Date | Mintage | VF20 | XF40 | MS60 | MS63 | MS65 |
|---|---|---|---|---|---|---|
| 2005 | 1,260 | **PF65** 1,850 | | | | |

**KM# 2018 50 EURO**
31.10 g., 0.999 Gold 0.9989 oz. AGW **Subject:** European Union, 50th Anniversary **Obv:** Flag of the European Union **Rev:** Europa head facing at right, banners at left **Mint:** Paris

| Date | Mintage | VF20 | XF40 | MS60 | MS63 | MS65 |
|---|---|---|---|---|---|---|
| 2005 | 500 | **PF65** 1,800 | | | | |

**KM# 2039 50 EURO**
31.10 g., 0.999 Gold 0.9989 oz. AGW **Subject:** Robert Schuman, 120th Anniversary of Birth **Rev:** Europa head facing at right, with color highlights **Mint:** Paris

| Date | Mintage | VF20 | XF40 | MS60 | MS63 | MS65 |
|---|---|---|---|---|---|---|
| 2006 | 500 | **PF65** 1,900 | | | | |

**KM# 2046 50 EURO**
31.11 g., 0.999 Gold 0.999 oz. AGW, 22 mm. **Subject:** St. Peter's Bascilica, 500th Anniversary **Obv:** St. Peter's floor plan **Rev:** Façade of St. Peter's, Pope Benedict XVI **Mint:** Paris

| Date | Mintage | VF20 | XF40 | MS60 | MS63 | MS65 |
|---|---|---|---|---|---|---|
| 2006 | 500 | **PF65** 1,900 | | | | |

**KM# 2057 50 EURO**
31.11 g., 0.999 Gold 0.999 oz. AGW **Subject:** Abolishment of the Death Penalty, 25th Anniversary **Obv:** Sower advancing left **Rev:** Guillotine **Mint:** Paris

| Date | Mintage | VF20 | XF40 | MS60 | MS63 | MS65 |
|---|---|---|---|---|---|---|
| 2006 | Est. 500 | **PF65** 1,800 | | | | |

**KM# 1466 50 EURO**
31.11 g., 0.999 Gold 0.999 oz. AGW, 37 mm. **Subject:** Le Petit Prince, 60th Anniversary **Obv:** Prince standing

| Date | Mintage | VF20 | XF40 | MS60 | MS63 | MS65 |
|---|---|---|---|---|---|---|
| 2007 | 1,491 | **PF65** 1,800 | | | | |

**KM# 1481 50 EURO**
31.10 g., 0.999 Gold 0.9989 oz. AGW, 37 mm. **Subject:** Airbus A380 **Obv:** Airplane **Rev:** Europa and flags

| Date | Mintage | VF20 | XF40 | MS60 | MS63 | MS65 |
|---|---|---|---|---|---|---|
| 2007 | 500 | **PF65** 1,900 | | | | |

**KM# 1487 50 EURO**
1000.00 g., 0.950 Silver 30.5432 oz. ASW **Subject:** 2007 Rugby World Cup **Obv:** Two players and goal **Rev:** Logo and goal **Shape:** Oval

| Date | Mintage | VF20 | XF40 | MS60 | MS63 | MS65 |
|---|---|---|---|---|---|---|
| 2007 | 298 | **PF65** 1,500 | | | | |

**KM# 1510 50 EURO**
31.11 g., 0.999 Gold 0.999 oz. AGW, 37 mm. **Subject:** Georges Remi Centennial **Obv:** Wand and sparkles **Rev:** Tin Tin and dog Snowy

| Date | Mintage | VF20 | XF40 | MS60 | MS63 | MS65 |
|---|---|---|---|---|---|---|
| 2007 | 500 | **PF65** 1,900 | | | | |

**KM# 1522 50 EURO**
31.05 g., 0.999 Gold 0.9973 oz. AGW, 37 mm. **Subject:** Asterix **Rev:** Asterix and the Butcher of Arverne

| Date | Mintage | VF20 | XF40 | MS60 | MS63 | MS65 |
|---|---|---|---|---|---|---|
| 2007 | 500 | **PF65** 1,900 | | | | |

**KM# 1530 50 EURO**
31.10 g., 0.999 Gold 0.999 oz. AGW, 37 mm. **Subject:** French Presidency of the Euopean Union **Obv:** Text within stars **Rev:** Europa head within flags

| Date | Mintage | VF20 | XF40 | MS60 | MS63 | MS65 |
|---|---|---|---|---|---|---|
| 2008 | 497 | **PF65** 1,900 | | | | |

**KM# 1564 50 EURO**
31.10 g., 0.999 Gold 0.999 oz. AGW, 37 mm. **Subject:** Lourdes, 150th Anniversary **Obv:** Church of Notre Dame at Lourdes **Rev:** Cross with Pope John Paul II, Pope Benedict XVI and Bernadette Soubirous in quadrants

| Date | Mintage | VF20 | XF40 | MS60 | MS63 | MS65 |
|---|---|---|---|---|---|---|
| 2008 | 500 | **PF65** 1,900 | | | | |

**KM# 1585 50 EURO**
163.80 g., 0.950 Silver 5.003 oz. ASW, 50 mm. **Subject:** Court of Human Rights, 50th Anniversary **Obv:** Sower left **Rev:** Text

| Date | Mintage | VF20 | XF40 | MS60 | MS63 | MS65 |
|---|---|---|---|---|---|---|
| 2009 P | 251 | **PF63** 325 | **PF65** 350 | | | |

**KM# 1592 50 EURO**
8.45 g., 0.920 Gold 0.2499 oz. AGW, 22 mm. **Subject:** Europa - Fall of Berlin Wall **Obv:** Brandenburg gate and doves in flight **Rev:** Head facing and flags

| Date | Mintage | VF20 | XF40 | MS60 | MS63 | MS65 |
|---|---|---|---|---|---|---|
| 2009 P | 1,000 | **PF63** 500 | **PF65** 525 | | | |

**KM# 1597 50 EURO**
163.80 g., 0.950 Silver 5.003 oz. ASW, 50 mm. **Subject:** Concorde 40th Anniversary **Obv:** Concorde in flight **Rev:** Tail emblems

| Date | Mintage | VF20 | XF40 | MS60 | MS63 | MS65 |
|---|---|---|---|---|---|---|
| 2009 P | 1,000 | **PF63** 300 | **PF65** 325 | | | |

**KM# 1598 50 EURO**
8.45 g., 0.920 Gold 0.2499 oz. AGW, 22 mm. **Subject:** Concorde 40th Anniversary **Obv:** Concorde in flight **Rev:** Tail emblems

| Date | Mintage | VF20 | XF40 | MS60 | MS63 | MS65 |
|---|---|---|---|---|---|---|
| 2009 P | 2,135 | **PF63** 475 | **PF65** 500 | | | |

**KM# 1603 50 EURO**
163.80 g., 0.950 Silver 5.003 oz. ASW, 50 mm. **Obv:** Eiffel Tower Structure **Rev:** Gustave Eiffel at left

| Date | Mintage | VF20 | XF40 | MS60 | MS63 | MS65 |
|---|---|---|---|---|---|---|
| 2009 P | 554 | **PF63** 400 | **PF65** 425 | | | |

**KM# 1604 50 EURO**
8.45 g., 0.920 Gold 0.2499 oz. AGW, 22 mm. **Obv:** Eiffel Tower Structure **Rev:** Gustave Eiffel at left

| Date | Mintage | VF20 | XF40 | MS60 | MS63 | MS65 |
|---|---|---|---|---|---|---|
| 2009 P | 793 | **PF63** 500 | **PF65** 525 | | | |

**KM# 1608 50 EURO**
163.80 g., 0.950 Silver 5.003 oz. ASW, 50 mm. **Subject:** Bugatti 100th Anniverary **Obv:** Ettore Bugatti at left **Rev:** Race car and grill motif

| Date | Mintage | VF20 | XF40 | MS60 | MS63 | MS65 |
|---|---|---|---|---|---|---|
| 2009 P | 269 | **PF63** 475 | **PF65** 500 | | | |

**KM# 1609 50 EURO**
8.45 g., 0.920 Gold 0.2499 oz. AGW, 22 mm. **Subject:** Bugatti 100th Anniversary **Obv:** Ettore Bugatti at left **Rev:** Race car and grill motif

| Date | Mintage | VF20 | XF40 | MS60 | MS63 | MS65 |
|---|---|---|---|---|---|---|
| 2009 P | 854 | **PF63** 500 | **PF65** 525 | | | |

**KM# 1613 50 EURO**
163.80 g., 0.950 Silver 5.003 oz. ASW, 50 mm. **Subject:** Curie Institute, 100th Anniversary

| Date | Mintage | VF20 | XF40 | MS60 | MS63 | MS65 |
|---|---|---|---|---|---|---|
| 2009 P | 500 | **PF63** 350 | **PF65** 375 | | | |

KM# 1614 50 EURO
8.45 g., 0.920 Gold 0.2499 oz. AGW, 22 mm. **Subject:** Curie Institute, 100th Anniversary

| Date | Mintage | VF20 | XF40 | MS60 | MS63 | MS65 |
|---|---|---|---|---|---|---|
| 2009 P | 1,000 | PF63 500 | PF65 525 | | | |

KM# 1618 50 EURO
163.80 g., 0.950 Silver 5.003 oz. ASW, 50 mm. **Subject:** UNESCO Site - The Kremlin in Moscow

| Date | Mintage | VF20 | XF40 | MS60 | MS63 | MS65 |
|---|---|---|---|---|---|---|
| 2009 | 497 | PF63 300 | PF65 325 | | | |

KM# 1622 50 EURO
163.80 g., 0.950 Silver 5.003 oz. ASW, 50 mm. **Subject:** First Moon Landing, 40th Anniversary **Obv:** Footprint on the moon

| Date | Mintage | VF20 | XF40 | MS60 | MS63 | MS65 |
|---|---|---|---|---|---|---|
| 2009 P | 371 | PF63 350 | PF65 375 | | | |

KM# 1623 50 EURO
8.45 g., 0.920 Gold 0.2499 oz. AGW, 22 mm. **Subject:** First Moon Landing, 40th Anniversary **Obv:** Footprint on the moon

| Date | Mintage | VF20 | XF40 | MS60 | MS63 | MS65 |
|---|---|---|---|---|---|---|
| 2009 P | 986 | PF63 475 | PF65 500 | | | |

KM# 1628 50 EURO
8.45 g., 0.920 Gold 0.2499 oz. AGW, 22 mm. **Subject:** Year of the Ox **Obv:** Oxen within Asian screen **Rev:** Portrait of LaFontaine

| Date | Mintage | VF20 | XF40 | MS60 | MS63 | MS65 |
|---|---|---|---|---|---|---|
| 2009 P | 497 | PF63 525 | PF65 550 | | | |

KM# 1630 50 EURO
8.45 g., 0.920 Gold 0.2499 oz. AGW, 22 mm. **Subject:** Comic strip heroes **Obv:** Wanted Poster **Rev:** Lucky Luke on horseback

| Date | Mintage | VF20 | XF40 | MS60 | MS63 | MS65 |
|---|---|---|---|---|---|---|
| 2009 P | 967 | PF63 500 | PF65 525 | | | |

KM# 1632 50 EURO
8.45 g., 0.920 Gold 0.2499 oz. AGW, 22 mm. **Obv:** Rugby player **Rev:** State Francais

| Date | Mintage | VF20 | XF40 | MS60 | MS63 | MS65 |
|---|---|---|---|---|---|---|
| 2009 P | 325 | PF63 525 | PF65 550 | | | |

KM# 1635 50 EURO
8.45 g., 0.920 Gold 0.2499 oz. AGW, 22 mm. **Subject:** Alpine skiing **Obv:** Globe and downhill skier **Rev:** Downhill skier on mountainside

| Date | Mintage | VF20 | XF40 | MS60 | MS63 | MS65 |
|---|---|---|---|---|---|---|
| 2009 P | 974 | PF63 500 | PF65 525 | | | |

KM# 1637 50 EURO
163.80 g., 0.950 Silver 5.003 oz. ASW, 50 mm. **Subject:** FIFA World Cup, South Africa 2010 **Obv:** Soccer player on field **Rev:** Soccerball, Map of Africa, Protrea flower

| Date | Mintage | VF20 | XF40 | MS60 | MS63 | MS65 |
|---|---|---|---|---|---|---|
| 2009 P | 500 | PF63 400 | PF65 425 | | | |

KM# 1638 50 EURO
8.45 g., 0.920 Gold 0.2499 oz. AGW, 22 mm. **Subject:** FIFA World Cup, South Africa 2010 **Obv:** Soccer Player on field **Rev:** Soccerball, Map of Africa, Protea flower

| Date | Mintage | VF20 | XF40 | MS60 | MS63 | MS65 |
|---|---|---|---|---|---|---|
| 2009 P | 6,287 | PF63 475 | PF65 500 | | | |

KM# 1644 50 EURO
36.00 g., 0.900 Silver 1.0417 oz. ASW, 36 mm. **Obv:** The Seed Sower advancing right, sun rays from above **Rev:** Value at center, wreath horizontal **Mint:** Paris

| Date | Mintage | VF20 | XF40 | MS60 | MS63 | MS65 |
|---|---|---|---|---|---|---|
| 2010 | 100,000 | — | — | — | — | 45.00 |

KM# 1673 50 EURO
8.45 g., 0.920 Gold 0.2499 oz. AGW, 22 mm. **Obv:** The Seed Sower left **Rev:** Wheat and olive branch **Mint:** Paris

| Date | Mintage | VF20 | XF40 | MS60 | MS63 | MS65 |
|---|---|---|---|---|---|---|
| 2010 | 500 | PF63 525 | PF65 550 | | | |

KM# 1679 50 EURO
8.45 g., 0.925 Gold 0.2513 oz. AGW, 22 mm. **Subject:** Cluny Abbey, 1100th Anniversary **Obv:** Europa head facing **Rev:** Cluney Abbey **Mint:** Paris

| Date | Mintage | VF20 | XF40 | MS60 | MS63 | MS65 |
|---|---|---|---|---|---|---|
| 2010 | 1,000 | PF63 500 | PF65 525 | | | |

KM# 1684 50 EURO
8.45 g., 0.920 Gold 0.2499 oz. AGW, 22 mm. **Obv:** Georges Pompidou Center design **Rev:** Design detail **Mint:** Paris

| Date | Mintage | VF20 | XF40 | MS60 | MS63 | MS65 |
|---|---|---|---|---|---|---|
| 2010 | 3,000 | PF63 475 | PF65 500 | | | |

KM# 1685 50 EURO
163.80 g., 0.950 Silver 5.003 oz. ASW, 50 mm. **Obv:** Georges Pompidou Center design **Rev:** Design detail **Mint:** Paris

| Date | Mintage | VF20 | XF40 | MS60 | MS63 | MS65 |
|---|---|---|---|---|---|---|
| 2010 | 1,000 | PF63 300 | PF65 325 | | | |

**KM# 1688 50 EURO**
8.45 g., 0.920 Gold 0.2499 oz. AGW, 22 mm. **Obv:** Marcel Dassault **Rev:** Mirage III plane **Mint:** Paris

| Date | Mintage | VF20 | XF40 | MS60 | MS63 | MS65 |
|---|---|---|---|---|---|---|
| 2010 | 1,000 | PF63 500 | PF65 525 | | | |

**KM# 1694 50 EURO**
8.45 g., 0.920 Gold 0.2499 oz. AGW, 22 mm. **Obv:** Mother Teresa and child **Rev:** Mother Teresa and Pope John Paul II **Mint:** Paris

| Date | Mintage | VF20 | XF40 | MS60 | MS63 | MS65 |
|---|---|---|---|---|---|---|
| 2010 | 1,000 | PF63 500 | PF65 525 | | | |

**KM# 1699 50 EURO**
8.45 g., 0.920 Gold 0.2499 oz. AGW, 22 mm. **Obv:** Taj Mahal **Rev:** UNESCO offices **Mint:** Paris

| Date | Mintage | VF20 | XF40 | MS60 | MS63 | MS65 |
|---|---|---|---|---|---|---|
| 2010 | 1,000 | PF63 500 | PF65 525 | | | |

**KM# 1702 50 EURO**
8.45 g., 0.920 Gold 0.2499 oz. AGW, 22 mm. **Obv:** Lille station and route map **Rev:** Three TGV trains **Mint:** Paris

| Date | Mintage | VF20 | XF40 | MS60 | MS63 | MS65 |
|---|---|---|---|---|---|---|
| 2010 | 1,000 | PF63 500 | PF65 525 | | | |

**KM# 1703 50 EURO**
163.80 g., 0.950 Silver 5.003 oz. ASW, 50 mm. **Obv:** Lille station and route map **Rev:** Three TGV trains **Mint:** Paris

| Date | Mintage | VF20 | XF40 | MS60 | MS63 | MS65 |
|---|---|---|---|---|---|---|
| 2010 | 500 | PF63 350 | PF65 375 | | | |

**KM# 1714 50 EURO**
8.45 g., 0.920 Gold 0.2499 oz. AGW, 22 mm. **Obv:** Tiger within border **Rev:** La Fontaine bust at left, animals at right **Mint:** Paris

| Date | Mintage | VF20 | XF40 | MS60 | MS63 | MS65 |
|---|---|---|---|---|---|---|
| 2010 | 500 | PF63 525 | PF65 550 | | | |

**KM# 1716 50 EURO**
8.45 g., 0.920 Gold 0.2499 oz. AGW, 22 mm. **Obv:** Blake and Mortimer **Rev:** Secret of the Swordfish" scene, the arrest of Col. Olrik **Mint:** Paris

| Date | Mintage | VF20 | XF40 | MS60 | MS63 | MS65 |
|---|---|---|---|---|---|---|
| 2010 | 500 | PF63 525 | PF65 550 | | | |

**KM# 1719 50 EURO**
8.45 g., 0.920 Gold 0.2499 oz. AGW, 22 mm. **Obv:** Handball player on globe **Rev:** Handball player, net, Big Ben **Mint:** Paris

| Date | Mintage | VF20 | XF40 | MS60 | MS63 | MS65 |
|---|---|---|---|---|---|---|
| 2010 | 1,000 | PF63 500 | PF65 525 | | | |

**KM# 1721 50 EURO**
8.45 g., 0.920 Gold 0.2499 oz. AGW, 22 mm. **Obv:** Soccer player **Rev:** Stade Toulousain logo, multicolor **Mint:** Paris

| Date | Mintage | VF20 | XF40 | MS60 | MS63 | MS65 |
|---|---|---|---|---|---|---|
| 2010 | 500 | PF63 525 | PF65 550 | | | |

**KM# 1756 50 EURO**
8.45 g., 0.920 Gold 0.2499 oz. AGW, 22 mm. **Obv:** Bicycle racer **Rev:** Metro 92 logo **Mint:** Paris

| Date | Mintage | VF20 | XF40 | MS60 | MS63 | MS65 |
|---|---|---|---|---|---|---|
| 2011 | 500 | PF63 500 | PF65 525 | | | |

**KM# 1786 50 EURO**
8.45 g., 0.920 Gold 0.2499 oz. AGW, 22 mm. **Subject:** Euro Starter Kit, 10th Anniversary **Obv:** Sower **Rev:** Euro starter kit **Mint:** Paris

| Date | Mintage | VF20 | XF40 | MS60 | MS63 | MS65 |
|---|---|---|---|---|---|---|
| 2011 | 3,000 | PF63 475 | PF65 500 | | | |

**KM# 1792 50 EURO**
8.45 g., 0.920 Gold 0.2499 oz. AGW, 22 mm. **Subject:** International Music Day, 30th Anniversary **Obv:** Europa **Rev:** Youth jamming **Mint:** Paris

| Date | Mintage | VF20 | XF40 | MS60 | MS63 | MS65 |
|---|---|---|---|---|---|---|
| 2011 | 3,000 | PF63 475 | PF65 500 | | | |

**KM# 1796 50 EURO**
8.45 g., 0.920 Gold 0.2499 oz. AGW, 22 mm. **Subject:** Great Explorers - Jacques Cartier **Obv:** The Grande Hermine sailing away **Rev:** Carter, globe and compass rose **Mint:** Paris

| Date | Mintage | VF20 | XF40 | MS60 | MS63 | MS65 |
|---|---|---|---|---|---|---|
| 2011 | 3,000 | PF63 475 | PF65 500 | | | |

**KM# 1801 50 EURO**
8.45 g., 0.920 Gold 0.2499 oz. AGW, 22 mm. **Subject:** Clovis, 481-511 **Obv:** Hands over chalice, reign dates at left, value at right **Rev:** Crowned head left **Mint:** Paris

| Date | Mintage | VF20 | XF40 | MS60 | MS63 | MS65 |
|---|---|---|---|---|---|---|
| 2011 | 1,500 | PF63 485 | PF65 500 | | | |

**KM# 1803 50 EURO**
8.45 g., 0.920 Gold 0.2499 oz. AGW, 22 mm. **Subject:** Charlemagne, 768-814 **Obv:** Cross on orb, reight dates at left, value at right **Rev:** Crowned head left **Mint:** Paris

| Date | Mintage | VF20 | XF40 | MS60 | MS63 | MS65 |
|---|---|---|---|---|---|---|
| 2011 | 1,500 | PF63 485 | PF65 500 | | | |

**KM# 1805 50 EURO**
8.45 g., 0.920 Gold 0.2499 oz. AGW, 22 mm. **Subject:** Charles II, 840-877 **Obv:** KARLOS monogram **Rev:** Crowned head left **Mint:** Paris

| Date | Mintage | VF20 | XF40 | MS60 | MS63 | MS65 |
|---|---|---|---|---|---|---|
| 2011 | 1,500 | PF63 485 | PF65 500 | | | |

**KM# 1807 50 EURO**
8.45 g., 0.920 Gold 0.2499 oz. AGW, 22 mm. **Subject:** WWF - Audouin's Gull **Obv:** Gull in flight right **Rev:** Gull standing right, WWF logo at right **Mint:** Paris

| Date | Mintage | VF20 | XF40 | MS60 | MS63 | MS65 |
|---|---|---|---|---|---|---|
| 2011 | 1,000 | PF63 500 | PF65 525 | | | |

**KM# 1811 50 EURO**
8.45 g., 0.920 Gold 0.2499 oz. AGW, 22 mm. **Subject:** UNESCO World Heritage Site - Palace of Versailles **Mint:** Paris

| Date | Mintage | VF20 | XF40 | MS60 | MS63 | MS65 |
|---|---|---|---|---|---|---|
| 2011 | 1,000 | PF63 500 | PF65 525 | | | |

**KM# 1816 50 EURO**
163.80 g., 0.950 Silver 5.003 oz. ASW, 50 mm. **Obv:** Metz railroad station **Rev:** TGV and ICE trains **Mint:** Paris

| Date | Mintage | VF20 | XF40 | MS60 | MS63 | MS65 |
|---|---|---|---|---|---|---|
| 2011 | 500 | PF63 300 | PF65 325 | | | |

**KM# 1817 50 EURO**
8.45 g., 0.920 Gold 0.2499 oz. AGW, 22 mm. **Obv:** Metz railroad station **Rev:** TGV and ICE trains **Mint:** Paris

| Date | Mintage | VF20 | XF40 | MS60 | MS63 | MS65 |
|---|---|---|---|---|---|---|
| 2011 | 1,000 | PF63 500 | PF65 525 | | | |

**KM# 1828 50 EURO**
8.45 g., 0.920 Gold 0.2499 oz. AGW, 22 mm. **Obv:** Cosette - Les Miserables **Rev:** Victor Hugo **Mint:** Paris

| Date | Mintage | VF20 | XF40 | MS60 | MS63 | MS65 |
|---|---|---|---|---|---|---|
| 2011 | 3,000 | PF63 475 | PF65 500 | | | |

**KM# 1830 50 EURO**
8.45 g., 0.920 Gold 0.2499 oz. AGW, 22 mm. **Obv:** Nana **Rev:** Emile Zola **Mint:** Paris

| Date | Mintage | VF20 | XF40 | MS60 | MS63 | MS65 |
|---|---|---|---|---|---|---|
| 2011 | 1,000 | PF63 500 | PF65 525 | | | |

**KM# 1832 50 EURO**
8.45 g., 0.920 Gold 0.2499 oz. AGW, 22 mm. **Obv:** The Stranger **Rev:** Albert Camus **Mint:** Paris

| Date | Mintage | VF20 | XF40 | MS60 | MS63 | MS65 |
|---|---|---|---|---|---|---|
| 2011 | — | PF63 500 | PF65 525 | | | |

**KM# 1834 50 EURO**
8.45 g., 0.920 Gold 0.2499 oz. AGW, 22 mm. **Subject:** Year of the Rabbit **Obv:** Rabbit seated facing right **Rev:** Fontaine and animals **Mint:** Paris

| Date | Mintage | VF20 | XF40 | MS60 | MS63 | MS65 |
|---|---|---|---|---|---|---|
| 2011 | 500 | PF63 525 | PF65 550 | | | |

**KM# 1837 50 EURO**
8.45 g., 0.920 Gold 0.2499 oz. AGW, 22 mm. **Obv:** Comic Characters **Rev:** Profile left and large XIII **Mint:** Paris

| Date | Mintage | VF20 | XF40 | MS60 | MS63 | MS65 |
|---|---|---|---|---|---|---|
| 2011 | 1,000 | PF63 500 | PF65 525 | | | |

**KM# 1839 50 EURO**
8.45 g., 0.920 Gold 0.2499 oz. AGW, 22 mm. **Obv:** Female figure skater on globe **Rev:** Figure skating pair **Mint:** Paris

| Date | Mintage | VF20 | XF40 | MS60 | MS63 | MS65 |
|---|---|---|---|---|---|---|
| 2011 | 1,000 | PF63 500 | PF65 525 | | | |

**KM# 2071 50 EURO**
36.00 g., 0.900 Silver 1.0417 oz. ASW, 41 mm. **Subject:** G-20 Meeting in Cannes **Obv:** Sower advancing right **Rev:** Laurel tree and oak tree in the shape of a Euro symbol with value specification in the hexagon as stylization national borders **Mint:** Paris

| Date | Mintage | VF20 | XF40 | MS60 | MS63 | MS65 |
|---|---|---|---|---|---|---|
| 2011 | 200 | — | — | — | — | 200 |

**KM# 1848 50 EURO**
163.80 g., 0.925 Silver 4.8713 oz. ASW, 50 mm. **Obv:** Battleship Jeanne de Arc **Rev:** WWII convoy image, anchor chain below **Mint:** Paris

| Date | Mintage | VF20 | XF40 | MS60 | MS63 | MS65 |
|---|---|---|---|---|---|---|
| 2012 (a) | 500 | PF63 350 | PF65 375 | | | |

**KM# 1849 50 EURO**
8.45 g., 0.920 Gold 0.2499 oz. AGW, 22 mm. **Obv:** SS France waterline view **Rev:** Winged funnels, porthole detail below **Mint:** Paris

| Date | Mintage | VF20 | XF40 | MS60 | MS63 | MS65 |
|---|---|---|---|---|---|---|
| 2012 (a) | 1,500 | PF63 485 | PF65 500 | | | |

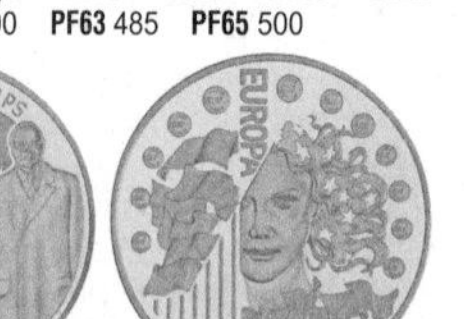


**KM# 1852 50 EURO**
8.45 g., 0.920 Gold 0.2499 oz. AGW, 22 mm. **Subject:** Eurocorps, 20th Anniversary **Obv:** Mitterrand and Kohl standing clasping hands **Rev:** Europa facing **Mint:** Paris

| Date | Mintage | VF20 | XF40 | MS60 | MS63 | MS65 |
|---|---|---|---|---|---|---|
| 2012 (a) | 1,500 | PF63 475 | PF65 500 | | | |

**KM# 1858 50 EURO**
8.45 g., 0.920 Gold 0.2499 oz. AGW, 22 mm. **Subject:** Philippe II Auguste **Obv:** Crowned head facing **Rev:** The Louvre's original design **Mint:** Paris

| Date | Mintage | VF20 | XF40 | MS60 | MS63 | MS65 |
|---|---|---|---|---|---|---|
| 2012 (a) | 1,500 | PF63 485 | PF65 500 | | | |

**KM# 1860 50 EURO**
8.45 g., 0.920 Gold 0.2499 oz. AGW, 22 mm. **Subject:** Savinien Cyrano de Bergerac **Obv:** Half-length figure of Cyrano at left, Roxane on balcony at top right **Rev:** Quote at left, Edmond Rostand portrait at right **Mint:** Paris

| Date | Mintage | VF20 | XF40 | MS60 | MS63 | MS65 |
|---|---|---|---|---|---|---|
| 2012 (a) | 1,000 | PF63 500 | PF65 525 | | | |

**KM# 1861 50 EURO**
8.45 g., 0.920 Gold 0.2499 oz. AGW, 22 mm. **Subject:** Puss in boots **Obv:** Puss in boots standing, castle in background **Rev:** Quote at left, Charles Perrault portrait at right **Mint:** Paris

| Date | Mintage | VF20 | XF40 | MS60 | MS63 | MS65 |
|---|---|---|---|---|---|---|
| 2012 (a) | 1,000 | PF63 500 | PF65 525 | | | |

**KM# 1891 50 EURO**
8.45 g., 0.920 Gold 0.2499 oz. AGW, 22 mm. **Subject:** Euro, 10th Anniversary **Obv:** The Sower advancing left **Rev:** Value on globe, child-like renderings around **Mint:** Paris

| Date | Mintage | VF20 | XF40 | MS60 | MS63 | MS65 |
|---|---|---|---|---|---|---|
| 2012 (a) | 1,000 | PF63 500 | PF65 525 | | | |

**KM# 1897 50 EURO**
8.45 g., 0.920 Gold 0.2499 oz. AGW, 22 mm. **Subject:** abbé Pierre, 100th anniversary of Birth **Obv:** Pierre's bust at left, shaddow figure at right **Rev:** Emmaus International logo and quote **Mint:** Paris

| Date | Mintage | VF20 | XF40 | MS60 | MS63 | MS65 |
|---|---|---|---|---|---|---|
| 2012 (a) | 1,000 | PF63 500 | PF65 525 | | | |

**KM# 1906 50 EURO**
163.80 g., 0.950 Silver 5.003 oz. ASW, 50 mm. **Subject:** UNESCO - World Heritage Site **Obv:** Abu Simbel temple **Mint:** Paris

| Date | Mintage | VF20 | XF40 | MS60 | MS63 | MS65 |
|---|---|---|---|---|---|---|
| 2012 (a) | 500 | PF63 375 | PF65 400 | | | |

**KM# 1908 50 EURO**
8.45 g., 0.920 Gold 0.2499 oz. AGW, 22 mm. **Subject:** UNESCO - World Heritage Site **Obv:** Abu Simbel temple **Mint:** Paris

| Date | Mintage | VF20 | XF40 | MS60 | MS63 | MS65 |
|---|---|---|---|---|---|---|
| 2012 (a) | 1,500 | PF63 485 | PF65 500 | | | |

**KM# 1913 50 EURO**
163.80 g., 0.950 Silver 5.003 oz. ASW, 50 mm. **Subject:** TGV South-East **Obv:** Lyon Saint-Exupery station **Rev:** Two modern locomotives **Mint:** Paris

| Date | Mintage | VF20 | XF40 | MS60 | MS63 | MS65 |
|---|---|---|---|---|---|---|
| 2012 (a) | 500 | PF63 300 | PF65 325 | | | |

**KM# 1914 50 EURO**
8.45 g., 0.920 Gold 0.2499 oz. AGW, 22 mm. **Subject:** TGV Sud-East **Obv:** Lyon Saint-Exupery station **Rev:** Two modern locomotives **Mint:** Paris

| Date | Mintage | VF20 | XF40 | MS60 | MS63 | MS65 |
|---|---|---|---|---|---|---|
| 2012 (a) | 1,000 | PF63 500 | PF65 525 | | | |

**KM# 1917 50 EURO**
8.45 g., 0.920 Gold 0.2499 oz. AGW, 22 mm. **Subject:** Comic strip hero **Obv:** Largo Winch and building **Rev:** Winch riding motocycle being chased by two cars **Mint:** Paris

| Date | Mintage | VF20 | XF40 | MS60 | MS63 | MS65 |
|---|---|---|---|---|---|---|
| 2012 (a) | 500 | PF63 525 | PF65 550 | | | |

**KM# 1920 50 EURO**
8.45 g., 0.920 Gold 0.2499 oz. AGW, 22 mm. **Subject:** Toulonnais Rugby Club **Obv:** Value and stadium field view **Rev:** Shield and portrait of Felix Mayol **Mint:** Paris

| Date | Mintage | VF20 | XF40 | MS60 | MS63 | MS65 |
|---|---|---|---|---|---|---|
| 2012 (a) | 500 | PF63 525 | PF65 550 | | | |

**KM# 1922 50 EURO**
8.45 g., 0.920 Gold 0.2499 oz. AGW, 22 mm. **Subject:** 2012 Summer Olympics, London **Obv:** Two judo athletes and map of Europe **Rev:** Two judo athletes **Mint:** Paris

| Date | Mintage | VF20 | XF40 | MS60 | MS63 | MS65 |
|---|---|---|---|---|---|---|
| 2012 (a) | 1,000 | PF63 500 | PF65 525 | | | |

**KM# 1925 50 EURO**
8.45 g., 0.920 Gold 0.2499 oz. AGW, 22 mm. **Subject:** Year of the Dragon **Obv:** Dragon **Rev:** La Fontaine and zodiac animals **Mint:** Paris

| Date | Mintage | VF20 | XF40 | MS60 | MS63 | MS65 |
|---|---|---|---|---|---|---|
| 2012 (a) | 1,000 | PF63 500 | PF65 525 | | | |

**KM# 2076 50 EURO**
8.45 g., 0.920 Gold 0.2499 oz. AGW, 22 mm. **Obv:** Hand raised in benediction **Rev:** Hugues Capet head facing **Mint:** Paris

| Date | Mintage | VF20 | XF40 | MS60 | MS63 | MS65 |
|---|---|---|---|---|---|---|
| 2012 | Est. 1500 | — | — | — | — | 500 |

**KM# 2077 50 EURO**
8.45 g., 0.920 Gold 0.2499 oz. AGW **Obv:** Oak tree **Rev:** Saint Louis head facing **Mint:** Paris

| Date | Mintage | VF20 | XF40 | MS60 | MS63 | MS65 |
|---|---|---|---|---|---|---|
| 2012 | Est. 1500 | — | — | — | — | 500 |

**KM# 2080 50 EURO**
163.80 g., 0.950 Silver 5.003 oz. ASW, 50 mm. **Obv:** Sailing ship Hermione **Rev:** Ship wheel, sails, figurehead **Mint:** Paris

| Date | Mintage | VF20 | XF40 | MS60 | MS63 | MS65 |
|---|---|---|---|---|---|---|
| 2012 | Est. 500 | PF63 300 | PF65 325 | | | |

**KM# 2081 50 EURO**
163.80 g., 0.950 Silver 5.003 oz. ASW, 50 mm. **Obv:** Trans-atlantic liner France **Rev:** Winged smoke stacks, partial porthole **Mint:** Paris

| Date | Mintage | VF20 | XF40 | MS60 | MS63 | MS65 |
|---|---|---|---|---|---|---|
| 2012 | Est. 500 | PF63 300 | PF65 325 | | | |

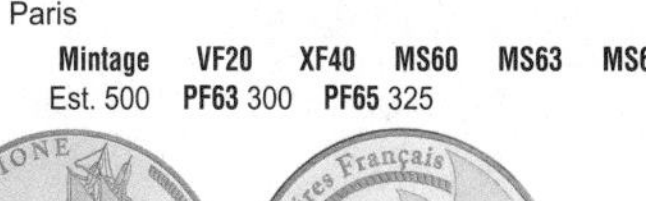

**KM# 2082 50 EURO**
8.45 g., 0.920 Gold 0.2499 oz. AGW, 22 mm. **Obv:** Sailing ship Hermione **Rev:** Ship wheel, sails, figurehead **Mint:** Paris

| Date | Mintage | VF20 | XF40 | MS60 | MS63 | MS65 |
|---|---|---|---|---|---|---|
| 2012 | Est. 1500 | PF63 500 | PF65 525 | | | |

**KM# 2083 50 EURO**
8.45 g., 0.920 Gold 0.2499 oz. AGW, 22 mm. **Obv:** Cruiser Jean d'Arc **Rev:** Anchor chain below convoy of ships **Mint:** Paris

| Date | Mintage | VF20 | XF40 | MS60 | MS63 | MS65 |
|---|---|---|---|---|---|---|
| 2012 | Est. 1500 | PF63 500 | PF65 525 | | | |

**KM# 2086 50 EURO**
8.45 g., 0.920 Gold 0.2499 oz. AGW, 22 mm. **Obv:** d'Artagnan **Rev:** Alexander Dumas and quote **Mint:** Paris

| Date | Mintage | VF20 | XF40 | MS60 | MS63 | MS65 |
|---|---|---|---|---|---|---|
| 2012 | Est. 1000 | PF63 500 | PF65 525 | | | |

**KM# 2088 50 EURO**
163.80 g., 0.950 Silver 5.003 oz. ASW, 50 mm. **Obv:** Yves Klein, blue hand **Rev:** Klein artwork **Mint:** Paris

| Date | Mintage | VF20 | XF40 | MS60 | MS63 | MS65 |
|---|---|---|---|---|---|---|
| 2012 | — | PF63 300 | PF65 325 | | | |

**KM# 2090 50 EURO**
8.45 g., 0.920 Gold 0.2499 oz. AGW, 22 mm. **Obv:** Yves Klein and hand **Rev:** Klein artwork **Mint:** Paris

| Date | Mintage | VF20 | XF40 | MS60 | MS63 | MS65 |
|---|---|---|---|---|---|---|
| 2012 | — | PF63 525 | PF65 550 | | | |

**KM# 1767 50 EURO**
8.45 g., 0.920 Gold 0.2499 oz. AGW, 22 mm. **Subject:** Year of the Snake **Obv:** Snake **Rev:** La Fontaine and lunar year animals **Mint:** Paris

| Date | Mintage | VF20 | XF40 | MS60 | MS63 | MS65 |
|---|---|---|---|---|---|---|
| 2013 | 1,000 | PF63 525 | PF65 550 | | | |

**KM# 1768 50 EURO**
8.45 g., 0.920 Gold 0.2499 oz. AGW, 22 mm. **Obv:** Steam ship l'Amazone **Rev:** Two ship funnels from SS France **Mint:** Paris

| Date | Mintage | VF20 | XF40 | MS60 | MS63 | MS65 |
|---|---|---|---|---|---|---|
| 2013 | — | PF63 485 | PF65 500 | | | |

**KM# 1769 50 EURO**
163.80 g., 0.925 Silver 4.8713 oz. ASW, 50 mm. **Obv:** Steam ship l'Amazone **Rev:** Two ship funnels from SS France **Mint:** Paris

| Date | Mintage | VF20 | XF40 | MS60 | MS63 | MS65 |
|---|---|---|---|---|---|---|
| 2013 | — | PF63 350 | PF65 375 | | | |

**KM# 1773 50 EURO**
8.45 g., 0.920 Gold 0.2499 oz. AGW, 22 mm. **Subject:** Asterix **Mint:** Paris

| Date | Mintage | VF20 | XF40 | MS60 | MS63 | MS65 |
|---|---|---|---|---|---|---|
| 2013 | 1,000 | PF63 600 | PF65 625 | | | |

**KM# 1774 50 EURO**
8.45 g., 0.920 Gold 0.2499 oz. AGW, 22 mm. **Subject:** Francios I **Mint:** Paris

| Date | Mintage | VF20 | XF40 | MS60 | MS63 | MS65 |
|---|---|---|---|---|---|---|
| 2013 | 1,500 | — | — | — | — | 500 |

**KM# 1776 50 EURO**
8.45 g., 0.920 Gold 0.2499 oz. AGW, 22 mm. **Obv:** Sailing ship La Gloire **Mint:** Paris

| Date | Mintage | VF20 | XF40 | MS60 | MS63 | MS65 |
|---|---|---|---|---|---|---|
| 2013 | 1,000 | PF63 500 | PF65 525 | | | |

**KM# 1777 50 EURO**
163.80 g., 0.950 Silver 5.003 oz. ASW, 50 mm. **Obv:** Sailing ship La Gloire **Mint:** Paris

| Date | Mintage | VF20 | XF40 | MS60 | MS63 | MS65 |
|---|---|---|---|---|---|---|
| 2013 | 500 | PF63 350 | PF65 375 | | | |

**KM# 1780 50 EURO**
8.45 g., 0.920 Gold 0.2499 oz. AGW, 22 mm. **Subject:** Henri IV **Mint:** Paris

| Date | Mintage | VF20 | XF40 | MS60 | MS63 | MS65 |
|---|---|---|---|---|---|---|
| 2013 | 1,500 | — | — | — | — | 500 |

**KM# 1782 50 EURO**
8.45 g., 0.920 Gold 0.2499 oz. AGW, 22 mm. **Subject:** Julien Sorel **Mint:** Paris

| Date | Mintage | VF20 | XF40 | MS60 | MS63 | MS65 |
|---|---|---|---|---|---|---|
| 2013 | — | PF63 500 | PF65 525 | | | |

**KM# 1901 50 EURO**
8.45 g., 0.920 Gold 0.2499 oz. AGW, 22 mm. **Subject:** Louis XI **Mint:** Paris

| Date | Mintage | VF20 | XF40 | MS60 | MS63 | MS65 |
|---|---|---|---|---|---|---|
| 2013 | — | — | — | — | — | 500 |

**KM# 1903 50 EURO**
8.45 g., 0.920 Gold 0.2499 oz. AGW, 22 mm. **Subject:** Madame Bovary **Mint:** Paris

| Date | Mintage | VF20 | XF40 | MS60 | MS63 | MS65 |
|---|---|---|---|---|---|---|
| 2013 | — | — | — | — | — | 500 |

**KM# 2093 50 EURO**
8.45 g., 0.920 Gold 0.2499 oz. AGW, 22 mm. **Subject:** French-German Friendship, 50th Anniversary **Rev:** Europa head facing at right, banners at left **Mint:** Paris

| Date | Mintage | VF20 | XF40 | MS60 | MS63 | MS65 |
|---|---|---|---|---|---|---|
| 2013 | — | PF63 525 | PF65 550 | | | |

**KM# 2096 50 EURO**
8.45 g., 0.920 Gold 0.2499 oz. AGW, 22 mm. **Subject:** Rudolf Nureyev **Obv:** Portrait at right **Rev:** Dancer and National Theater **Mint:** Paris

| Date | Mintage | VF20 | XF40 | MS60 | MS63 | MS65 |
|---|---|---|---|---|---|---|
| 2013 | — | PF63 525 | PF65 550 | | | |

**KM# 2098 50 EURO**
163.80 g., 0.950 Silver 5.003 oz. ASW, 50 mm. **Subject:** Notre Dame, 850th Anniversary **Obv:** Seal at right, cathedral details, blue highlights **Rev:** Seal at left, cathedral details, blue highlights **Mint:** Paris

| Date | Mintage | VF20 | XF40 | MS60 | MS63 | MS65 |
|---|---|---|---|---|---|---|
| 2013 | 850 | PF63 300 | PF65 325 | | | |

**KM# 2100 50 EURO**
8.45 g., 0.920 Gold 0.2499 oz. AGW, 22 mm. **Subject:** Notre Dame, 850th Anniversary **Obv:** Seal at right, cathedral details **Rev:** Seal at left, cathedral details **Mint:** Paris

| Date | Mintage | VF20 | XF40 | MS60 | MS63 | MS65 |
|---|---|---|---|---|---|---|
| 2013 | 1,000 | PF63 600 | PF65 625 | | | |

**KM# 2104 50 EURO**
8.45 g., 0.920 Gold 0.2499 oz. AGW, 22 mm. **Subject:** Odette de Crecy **Mint:** Paris

| Date | Mintage | VF20 | XF40 | MS60 | MS63 | MS65 |
|---|---|---|---|---|---|---|
| 2013 | — | PF63 500 | PF65 525 | | | |

**KM# 2105 50 EURO**
163.80 g., 0.950 Silver 5.003 oz. ASW, 50 mm. **Subject:** Pen Duick **Mint:** Paris

| Date | Mintage | VF20 | XF40 | MS60 | MS63 | MS65 |
|---|---|---|---|---|---|---|
| 2013 | — | PF63 300 | PF65 325 | | | |

**KM# 2106 50 EURO**
8.45 g., 0.920 Gold 0.2499 oz. AGW, 22 mm. **Subject:** Pen Duick **Mint:** Paris

| Date | Mintage | VF20 | XF40 | MS60 | MS63 | MS65 |
|---|---|---|---|---|---|---|
| 2013 | — | PF63 500 | PF65 525 | | | |

**KM# 2112 50 EURO**
8.45 g., 0.920 Gold 0.2499 oz. AGW, 22 mm. **Subject:** Pessac Industrial Site, 40th Anniversary **Obv:** Sower **Mint:** Paris

| Date | Mintage | VF20 | XF40 | MS60 | MS63 | MS65 |
|---|---|---|---|---|---|---|
| 2013 | — | PF63 500 | PF65 525 | | | |

**KM# 2115 50 EURO**
8.45 g., 0.920 Gold 0.2499 oz. AGW, 22 mm. **Subject:** Tour de France, 100th Anniversary **Mint:** Paris

| Date | Mintage | VF20 | XF40 | MS60 | MS63 | MS65 |
|---|---|---|---|---|---|---|
| 2013 | 1,500 | PF63 500 | PF65 525 | | | |

**KM# 2124 50 EURO**
8.45 g., 0.920 Gold 0.2499 oz. AGW, 22 mm. **Subject:** Sochi Snowboard **Mint:** Paris

| Date | Mintage | VF20 | XF40 | MS60 | MS63 | MS65 |
|---|---|---|---|---|---|---|
| 2013 | — | PF63 500 | PF65 525 | | | |

**KM# 2126 50 EURO**
8.45 g., 0.920 Gold 0.2499 oz. AGW, 22 mm. **Subject:** TGV - Gare Nord **Mint:** Paris

| Date | Mintage | VF20 | XF40 | MS60 | MS63 | MS65 |
|---|---|---|---|---|---|---|
| 2013 | — | PF63 500 | PF65 525 | | | |

**KM# 1304 100 EURO**
155.52 g., 0.999 Gold 4.995 oz. AGW, 50 mm. **Subject:** Europa **Obv:** Eight French euro coin designs **Rev:** Portrait and flags design of 6.55957 francs KM-1265 **Edge:** Plain **Mint:** Paris

| Date | Mintage | VF20 | XF40 | MS60 | MS63 | MS65 |
|---|---|---|---|---|---|---|
| 2002 | 99 | PF65 10,000 | | | | |

**KM# 1985 100 EURO**
155.55 g., 0.999 Gold 4.996 oz. AGW, 50 mm. **Subject:** Charles Lindbergh, 75th Anniververary of Flight **Obv:** Map of Northern France **Rev:** Spirit of St. Louis, U.S. Coastline **Mint:** Paris

| Date | Mintage | VF20 | XF40 | MS60 | MS63 | MS65 |
|---|---|---|---|---|---|---|
| 2002 | 99 | PF65 12,500 | | | | |

**KM# 2005 100 EURO**
155.55 g., 0.999 Gold 4.996 oz. AGW, 50 mm. **Obv:** Mona Lisa **Rev:** Leonardo DaVinci head left, large value right **Mint:** Paris

| Date | Mintage | VF20 | XF40 | MS60 | MS63 | MS65 |
|---|---|---|---|---|---|---|
| 2003 | 99 | PF65 10,000 | | | | |

**KM# 1377 100 EURO**
155.52 g., 0.999 Gold 4.995 oz. AGW, 50 mm. **Subject:** D-Day 60th Anniversary **Obv:** Soldiers and Normandy invasion scene **Rev:** D-Day" inscription above denomination **Edge:** Plain **Mint:** Paris

| Date | Mintage | VF20 | XF40 | MS60 | MS63 | MS65 |
|---|---|---|---|---|---|---|
| 2004 | 68 | PF65 9,500 | | | | |

**KM# 1387 100 EURO**
155.50 g., 0.950 Gold 4.7495 oz. AGW, 50 mm. **Obv:** Statue of Liberty **Rev:** F. A. Bartholdi **Edge:** Plain **Mint:** Paris

| Date | Mintage | VF20 | XF40 | MS60 | MS63 | MS65 |
|---|---|---|---|---|---|---|
| 2004 | 99 | PF65 10,000 | | | | |

**KM# 1389 100 EURO**
155.50 g., 0.999 Gold 4.9944 oz. AGW, 50 mm. **Obv:** Statue of Liberty **Rev:** F. A. Bartholdi **Edge:** Plain **Mint:** Paris

| Date | Mintage | VF20 | XF40 | MS60 | MS63 | MS65 |
|---|---|---|---|---|---|---|
| 2004 | 99 | PF65 10,000 | | | | |

**KM# 1395 100 EURO**
155.55 g., 0.999 Gold 4.996 oz. AGW, 50 mm. **Subject:** European Union Expansion **Obv:** Partial face and flags **Rev:** Puzzle map **Edge:** Plain **Mint:** Paris

| Date | Mintage | VF20 | XF40 | MS60 | MS63 | MS65 |
|---|---|---|---|---|---|---|
| 2004 | 99 | PF65 10,000 | | | | |

**KM# 2012 100 EURO**
155.55 g., 0.999 Gold 4.996 oz. AGW, 50 mm. **Subject:** Napoleon's coronation, 200th Anniversary **Obv:** Napoleon, laureate **Rev:** Notre Dame cathedral façade **Mint:** Paris

| Date | Mintage | VF20 | XF40 | MS60 | MS63 | MS65 |
|---|---|---|---|---|---|---|
| 2004 | 99 | PF65 10,000 | | | | |

**KM# 2019 100 EURO**
155.55 g., 0.999 Gold 4.996 oz. AGW, 50 mm. **Subject:** European Union, 50th Anniversary **Obv:** European Union Flag **Rev:** Europa head facing at right, banners at left **Mint:** Paris

| Date | Mintage | VF20 | XF40 | MS60 | MS63 | MS65 |
|---|---|---|---|---|---|---|
| 2005 | 99 | PF65 10,000 | | | | |

**KM# 2024 100 EURO**
155.55 g., 0.999 Gold 4.996 oz. AGW, 50 mm. **Obv:** Stars and map of Europe **Rev:** Doves in flight above globe **Mint:** Paris

| Date | Mintage | VF20 | XF40 | MS60 | MS63 | MS65 |
|---|---|---|---|---|---|---|
| 2005 | Est. 99 | PF65 10,000 | | | | |

**KM# 2025 100 EURO**
155.55 g., 0.999 Gold 4.996 oz. AGW, 50 mm. **Obv:** Napoleon looking out over land towards sunrise **Rev:** Napoleon and troops in the field **Mint:** Paris

| Date | Mintage | VF20 | XF40 | MS60 | MS63 | MS65 |
|---|---|---|---|---|---|---|
| 2005 | Est. 99 | PF65 10,000 | | | | |

**KM# 2033 100 EURO**
155.55 g., 0.999 Gold 4.996 oz. AGW, 50 mm. **Subject:** Jules Verne, 100th Anniversary of Death **Obv:** Around the world in 80 days **Mint:** Paris

| Date | Mintage | VF20 | XF40 | MS60 | MS63 | MS65 |
|---|---|---|---|---|---|---|
| 2005 | 80 | PF65 11,000 | | | | |

**KM# 2034 100 EURO**
155.55 g., 0.999 Gold 4.996 oz. AGW, 50 mm. **Subject:** Jules Verne, 100th Anniversary of Death **Obv:** 20,000 leagues under the sea **Mint:** Paris

| Date | Mintage | VF20 | XF40 | MS60 | MS63 | MS65 |
|---|---|---|---|---|---|---|
| 2005 | 71 | PF65 11,000 | | | | |

**KM# 2035 100 EURO**
155.55 g., 0.999 Gold 4.996 oz. AGW, 50 mm. **Subject:** Jules Verne, 100th Anniversary of Death **Obv:** From the earth to the moon **Mint:** Paris

| Date | Mintage | VF20 | XF40 | MS60 | MS63 | MS65 |
|---|---|---|---|---|---|---|
| 2005 | 71 | PF65 11,000 | | | | |

**KM# 2040 100 EURO**
155.55 g., 0.999 Gold 4.996 oz. AGW, 50 mm. **Subject:** Robert Schuman, 120th Anniversary of Birth **Rev:** Europa head facing at right, color highlights **Mint:** Paris

| Date | Mintage | VF20 | XF40 | MS60 | MS63 | MS65 |
|---|---|---|---|---|---|---|
| 2006 | 99 | PF65 10,000 | | | | |

Note: Individually numbered

**KM# 2044 100 EURO**
155.55 g., 0.999 Gold 4.996 oz. AGW, 50 mm. **Subject:** Benjamin Franklin, 300th Anniversary of Birth **Obv:** Bust at left, kite in thunderclouds at right **Rev:** French and American flags **Mint:** Paris

| Date | Mintage | VF20 | XF40 | MS60 | MS63 | MS65 |
|---|---|---|---|---|---|---|
| 2006 | 99 | PF65 10,000 | | | | |

Note: Individually numbered

**KM# 2047 100 EURO**
155.55 g., 0.999 Gold 4.996 oz. AGW, 50 mm. **Subject:** St. Peter's Basilica, 500th Anniversary **Obv:** St. Peter's floor plan **Rev:** Façade of St. Peter's, Pope Benedict XVI **Mint:** Paris

| Date | Mintage | VF20 | XF40 | MS60 | MS63 | MS65 |
|---|---|---|---|---|---|---|
| 2006 | 99 | PF65 10,000 | | | | |

Note: Individually numbered

**KM# 2058 100 EURO**
155.55 g., 0.999 Gold 4.996 oz. AGW, 50 mm. **Subject:** Abolishment of the Death Penalty, 25th Anniversary **Obv:** Sower advancing left **Rev:** Guillotine **Mint:** Paris

| Date | Mintage | VF20 | XF40 | MS60 | MS63 | MS65 |
|---|---|---|---|---|---|---|
| 2006 | — | PF65 10,000 | | | | |

Note: Individually numbered

**KM# 2060 100 EURO**
155.55 g., 0.999 Gold 4.996 oz. AGW, 50 mm. **Subject:** Paul Cézanne, 100th Anniversary of Death **Obv:** Bust **Rev:** Two men seated at table, wine bottle between them **Mint:** Paris

| Date | Mintage | VF20 | XF40 | MS60 | MS63 | MS65 |
|---|---|---|---|---|---|---|
| 2006 | — | PF65 10,000 | | | | |

Note: Individually numbered

**KM# 2069 100 EURO**
155.50 g., 0.999 Gold 4.9944 oz. AGW **Subject:** Jules Verne, 100th Anniversary of Death **Obv:** Voyage to the center of the Earth **Mint:** Paris

| Date | Mintage | VF20 | XF40 | MS60 | MS63 | MS65 |
|---|---|---|---|---|---|---|
| 2006 | 92 | PF65 10,000 | | | | |

**KM# 1482 100 EURO**
155.55 g., 0.999 Gold 4.996 oz. AGW, 50 mm. **Subject:** Airbus A380 **Rev:** Europa head and flags

| Date | Mintage | VF20 | XF40 | MS60 | MS63 | MS65 |
|---|---|---|---|---|---|---|
| 2007 | 99 | PF65 10,000 | | | | |

**KM# 1497 100 EURO**
155.50 g., 0.999 Gold 4.9944 oz. AGW, 50 mm. **Subject:** Cannes Film Festival, 60th Anniversary **Obv:** Cinema screen and stage, Golden Palm Award

| Date | Mintage | VF20 | XF40 | MS60 | MS63 | MS65 |
|---|---|---|---|---|---|---|
| 2007 | 99 | PF65 10,000 | | | | |

**KM# 1531 100 EURO**
155.50 g., 0.999 Gold 4.9944 oz. AGW, 50 mm. **Subject:** French Presidency of the European Union **Obv:** Text within stars **Rev:** Europa head and flags

| Date | Mintage | VF20 | XF40 | MS60 | MS63 | MS65 |
|---|---|---|---|---|---|---|
| 2008 | 99 | PF65 10,000 | | | | |

**KM# 1536 100 EURO**
3.10 g., 0.999 Gold 0.0996 oz. AGW, 15 mm. **Obv:** Modernistic sower advancing right **Rev:** Value and wreath **Mint:** Paris

| Date | Mintage | VF20 | XF40 | MS60 | MS63 | MS65 |
|---|---|---|---|---|---|---|
| 2008 | 50,000 | — | — | — | — | 180 |
| 2009 | 50,000 | — | — | — | — | 180 |
| 2010 | 50,000 | — | — | — | — | 180 |

**KM# 1545 100 EURO**
155.50 g., 0.999 Gold 4.9944 oz. AGW, 50 mm. **Subject:** 29th Summer Olympic Games - Beijing **Obv:** Swimmer and globe **Rev:** Diver and oriental screen

| Date | Mintage | VF20 | XF40 | MS60 | MS63 | MS65 |
|---|---|---|---|---|---|---|
| 2008 | 98 | PF65 10,000 | | | | |

**KM# 1565 100 EURO**
155.50 g., 0.999 Gold 4.9944 oz. AGW, 50 mm. **Subject:** Lourdes, 150th Anniversary **Obv:** Church of Notre Dame at Lourdes **Rev:** Cross with Pope John Paul II, Pope Benedict XVI and Bernadette Soubirous in quadrants

| Date | Mintage | VF20 | XF40 | MS60 | MS63 | MS65 |
|---|---|---|---|---|---|---|
| 2008 | 99 | PF65 10,000 | | | | |

**KM# 1582 100 EURO**
155.50 g., 0.999 Gold 4.9944 oz. AGW, 50 mm. **Subject:** CoCo Chanel, 125th Anniversary of Birth **Obv:** Profile at left **Rev:** Diamond handbag pattern **Mint:** Paris

| Date | Mintage | VF20 | XF40 | MS60 | MS63 | MS65 |
|---|---|---|---|---|---|---|
| 2008 | Est. 99 | PF65 9,500 | | | | |

**KM# 1588 100 EURO**
31.11 g., 0.920 Gold 0.920 oz. AGW, 47 mm. **Subject:** Court of Human Rights, 50th Anniversary **Obv:** The Seed Sower left **Rev:** Text

| Date | Mintage | VF20 | XF40 | MS60 | MS63 | MS65 |
|---|---|---|---|---|---|---|
| 2009 P | 500 | PF65 1,750 | | | | |

**KM# 1626 100 EURO**
17.00 g., 0.920 Gold 0.5028 oz. AGW, 30 x 21 mm. **Subject:** Renoir **Obv:** Le dejuner des canotiers, 1881 painting **Rev:** Brushes and portrait **Shape:** Rectangle

| Date | Mintage | VF20 | XF40 | MS60 | MS63 | MS65 |
|---|---|---|---|---|---|---|
| 2009 P | 317 | PF65 1,000 | | | | |

**KM# 1641 100 EURO**
17.00 g., 0.920 Gold 0.5028 oz. AGW, 30x21 mm. **Subject:** Claude Monet **Obv:** Bassin of the Nymphs in color **Rev:** Portrait and paint brushes **Shape:** Rectangle **Mint:** Paris

| Date | Mintage | VF20 | XF40 | MS60 | MS63 | MS65 |
|---|---|---|---|---|---|---|
| 2009 | 361 | PF63 950 | PF65 975 | | | |

**KM# 1672 100 EURO**
17.00 g., 0.920 Gold 0.5028 oz. AGW, 18 mm. **Obv:** The Seed Sower left **Rev:** Wheat and olive branch **Mint:** Paris

| Date | Mintage | VF20 | XF40 | MS60 | MS63 | MS65 |
|---|---|---|---|---|---|---|
| 2010 | 500 | PF63 925 | PF65 950 | | | |

**KM# 1689 100 EURO**
327.60 g., 0.950 Silver 10.0059 oz. ASW, 65 mm. **Obv:** Marcel Dassault **Rev:** Mirage III plane **Mint:** Paris

| Date | Mintage | VF20 | XF40 | MS60 | MS63 | MS65 |
|---|---|---|---|---|---|---|
| 2010 | 500 | PF63 400 | PF65 425 | | | |

**KM# 1707 100 EURO**
17.00 g., 0.920 Gold 0.5028 oz. AGW, 30x21 mm. **Rev:** Georges Braque **Shape:** Rectangle **Mint:** Paris

| Date | Mintage | VF20 | XF40 | MS60 | MS63 | MS65 |
|---|---|---|---|---|---|---|
| 2010 | 500 | PF63 975 | PF65 1,000 | | | |

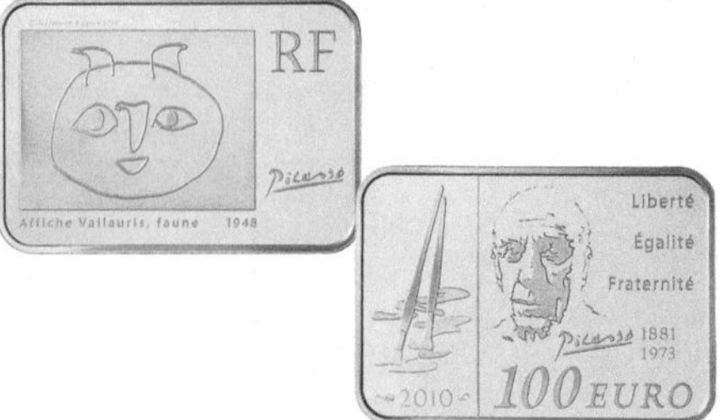

**KM# 1711 100 EURO**
17.00 g., 0.920 Gold 0.5028 oz. AGW, 30x21 mm. **Rev:** Picasso **Shape:** Rectangle **Mint:** Paris

| Date | Mintage | VF20 | XF40 | MS60 | MS63 | MS65 |
|---|---|---|---|---|---|---|
| 2010 | 500 | PF63 1,000 | PF65 1,100 | | | |

**KM# 1724 100 EURO**
50.00 g., 0.900 Silver 1.4468 oz. ASW, 47 mm. **Obv:** Value at center, wreath horizontal **Rev:** Hercules goup **Mint:** Paris

| Date | Mintage | VF20 | XF40 | MS60 | MS63 | MS65 |
|---|---|---|---|---|---|---|
| 2011 | 50,000 | — | — | — | — | 150 |
| 2012 | 50,000 | — | — | — | — | 150 |
| 2013 | — | — | — | — | — | 150 |

**KM# 1787 100 EURO**
17.00 g., 0.920 Gold 0.5028 oz. AGW, 31 mm. **Subject:** Euro Starter Kit, 10th Anniversary **Obv:** Sower **Rev:** Euro starter kit **Mint:** Paris

| Date | Mintage | VF20 | XF40 | MS60 | MS63 | MS65 |
|---|---|---|---|---|---|---|
| 2011 | 500 | **PF63** 925 **PF65** 950 | | | | |

**KM# 1820 100 EURO**
17.00 g., 0.920 Gold 0.5028 oz. AGW, 30x21 mm. **Subject:** Vassily Kandinsky **Shape:** Rectangle **Mint:** Paris

| Date | Mintage | VF20 | XF40 | MS60 | MS63 | MS65 |
|---|---|---|---|---|---|---|
| 2011 | 500 | **PF63** 975 **PF65** 1,000 | | | | |

**KM# 1824 100 EURO**
17.00 g., 0.920 Gold 0.5028 oz. AGW, 31 mm. **Subject:** Andy Warhol **Obv:** Portrait facing **Rev:** Dollar sign **Mint:** Paris

| Date | Mintage | VF20 | XF40 | MS60 | MS63 | MS65 |
|---|---|---|---|---|---|---|
| 2011 | 500 | **PF63** 975 **PF65** 1,000 | | | | |

**KM# 1836 100 EURO**
327.60 g., 0.950 Silver 10.0059 oz. ASW, 75 mm. **Obv:** Commic characters **Rev:** Profile left and large XIII **Mint:** Paris

| Date | Mintage | VF20 | XF40 | MS60 | MS63 | MS65 |
|---|---|---|---|---|---|---|
| 2011 | 500 | **PF63** 400 **PF65** 425 | | | | |

**KM# 1892 100 EURO**
17.00 g., 0.920 Gold 0.5028 oz. AGW, 31 mm. **Subject:** Euro, 10th Anniversary **Obv:** The Sower advancing left **Rev:** Value on globe at center, child-like renderings around **Mint:** Paris

| Date | Mintage | VF20 | XF40 | MS60 | MS63 | MS65 |
|---|---|---|---|---|---|---|
| 2012 (a) | 500 | **PF63** 950 **PF65** 975 | | | | |

**KM# 2089 100 EURO**
327.60 g., 0.950 Silver 10.0059 oz. ASW, 75 mm. **Obv:** Yves Klein and blue hand **Rev:** Klein artwork **Mint:** Paris

| Date | Mintage | VF20 | XF40 | MS60 | MS63 | MS65 |
|---|---|---|---|---|---|---|
| 2012 | 500 | **PF63** 1,250 **PF65** 1,350 | | | | |

**KM# 1771 100 EURO**
17.00 g., 0.920 Gold 0.5028 oz. AGW, 31 mm. **Subject:** Asterix **Mint:** Paris

| Date | Mintage | VF20 | XF40 | MS60 | MS63 | MS65 |
|---|---|---|---|---|---|---|
| 2013 | 500 | **PF63** 950 **PF65** 975 | | | | |

**KM# 2113 100 EURO**
17.00 g., 0.920 Gold 0.5028 oz. AGW, 37 mm. **Subject:** Pessac Industrial Site, 40th Anniversary **Obv:** Sower **Mint:** Paris

| Date | Mintage | VF20 | XF40 | MS60 | MS63 | MS65 |
|---|---|---|---|---|---|---|
| 2013 | — | **PF63** 925 **PF65** 950 | | | | |

**KM# 2135 100 EURO**
17.00 g., 0.920 Gold 0.5028 oz. AGW, 31 mm. **Obv:** Sower **Rev:** Deniers of Charles the Bald **Mint:** Paris

| Date | Mintage | VF20 | XF40 | MS60 | MS63 | MS65 |
|---|---|---|---|---|---|---|
| 2014 | 500 | **PF65** 900 | | | | |

**KM# 1589 200 EURO**
31.10 g., 0.999 Gold 0.999 oz. AGW, 37 mm. **Subject:** Court of Human Rights - 50th Anniversary **Obv:** The Seed Sower left **Rev:** Text

| Date | Mintage | VF20 | XF40 | MS60 | MS63 | MS65 |
|---|---|---|---|---|---|---|
| 2009 P | 500 | **PF65** 1,850 | | | | |

**KM# 1593 200 EURO**
31.10 g., 0.999 Gold 0.999 oz. AGW, 37 mm. **Subject:** Europa - Fall of Berlin Wall **Obv:** Brandenburg gate and doves in flight **Rev:** Head facing and flags

| Date | Mintage | VF20 | XF40 | MS60 | MS63 | MS65 |
|---|---|---|---|---|---|---|
| 2009 P | 500 | **PF65** 1,850 | | | | |

**KM# 1624 200 EURO**
31.10 g., 0.999 Gold 0.999 oz. AGW, 37 mm. **Subject:** First Moon Landing, 40th Anniversary **Obv:** Footprint on the moon

| Date | Mintage | VF20 | XF40 | MS60 | MS63 | MS65 |
|---|---|---|---|---|---|---|
| 2009 P | 1,000 | **PF65** 1,850 | | | | |

**KM# 1639 200 EURO**
31.10 g., 0.999 Gold 0.999 oz. AGW, 37 mm. **Subject:** FIFA World Cup, South Africa 2010 **Obv:** Soccer player on field **Rev:** Soccerball, Map of Africa, Protea flower

| Date | Mintage | VF20 | XF40 | MS60 | MS63 | MS65 |
|---|---|---|---|---|---|---|
| 2009 P | 125 | **PF65** 1,850 | | | | |

**KM# 1678 200 EURO**
31.10 g., 0.999 Gold 0.999 oz. AGW, 37 mm. **Subject:** Cluny Abbey, 1100th Anniversary **Obv:** Europa head facing **Rev:** Cluny Abbey **Mint:** Paris

| Date | Mintage | VF20 | XF40 | MS60 | MS63 | MS65 |
|---|---|---|---|---|---|---|
| 2010 | 500 | PF65 1,850 | | | | |

**KM# 1683 200 EURO**
31.10 g., 0.999 Gold 0.999 oz. AGW, 37 mm. **Obv:** Georges Pompidou Center design **Rev:** Design detail **Mint:** Paris

| Date | Mintage | VF20 | XF40 | MS60 | MS63 | MS65 |
|---|---|---|---|---|---|---|
| 2010 | 500 | PF65 1,850 | | | | |

**KM# 1693 200 EURO**
31.10 g., 0.999 Gold 0.999 oz. AGW, 37 mm. **Obv:** Mother Teresa and child **Rev:** Mother Teresa and Pope John Paul II **Mint:** Paris

| Date | Mintage | VF20 | XF40 | MS60 | MS63 | MS65 |
|---|---|---|---|---|---|---|
| 2010 | 500 | PF65 1,850 | | | | |

**KM# 1698 200 EURO**
31.10 g., 0.999 Gold 0.999 oz. AGW, 37 mm. **Obv:** Taj Mahal **Rev:** UNESCO offices **Mint:** Paris

| Date | Mintage | VF20 | XF40 | MS60 | MS63 | MS65 |
|---|---|---|---|---|---|---|
| 2010 | 1,000 | PF65 1,800 | | | | |

**KM# 1701 200 EURO**
31.10 g., 0.999 Gold 0.999 oz. AGW, 37 mm. **Obv:** Lille station and route map **Rev:** Three TGV trains **Mint:** Paris

| Date | Mintage | VF20 | XF40 | MS60 | MS63 | MS65 |
|---|---|---|---|---|---|---|
| 2010 | 500 | PF65 1,850 | | | | |

**KM# 1757 200 EURO**
4.00 g., 0.999 Gold 0.1285 oz. AGW, 21 mm. **Obv:** French region names around RF within stylized map of France **Rev:** Value within wreath **Mint:** Paris

| Date | Mintage | VF20 | XF40 | MS60 | MS63 | MS65 |
|---|---|---|---|---|---|---|
| 2011 (a) Proof | 50,000 | — | — | — | — | 265 |

**KM# 1793 200 EURO**
31.10 g., 0.999 Gold 0.999 oz. AGW, 37 mm. **Subject:** International Music Day, 30th Anniversary **Obv:** Europa **Rev:** Youth jamming **Mint:** Paris

| Date | Mintage | VF20 | XF40 | MS60 | MS63 | MS65 |
|---|---|---|---|---|---|---|
| 2011 | 500 | PF65 1,900 | | | | |

**KM# 1797 200 EURO**
31.10 g., 0.999 Gold 0.999 oz. AGW, 37 mm. **Subject:** Great Explorers - Jacques Cartier **Obv:** The Grande Hermine sailing away **Rev:** Cartier, globe and compass rose **Mint:** Paris

| Date | Mintage | VF20 | XF40 | MS60 | MS63 | MS65 |
|---|---|---|---|---|---|---|
| 2011 | 500 | PF65 1,850 | | | | |

**KM# 1808 200 EURO**
31.10 g., 0.999 Gold 0.999 oz. AGW, 37 mm. **Subject:** WWF - Audouin's Gull **Obv:** Gull in flight right **Rev:** Gull standing right, WWF logo right **Mint:** Paris

| Date | Mintage | VF20 | XF40 | MS60 | MS63 | MS65 |
|---|---|---|---|---|---|---|
| 2011 | 500 | PF65 1,850 | | | | |

**KM# 1818 200 EURO**
31.10 g., 0.999 Gold 0.999 oz. AGW, 37 mm. **Obv:** Metz railroad station **Rev:** TGV and ICE trains **Mint:** Paris

| Date | Mintage | VF20 | XF40 | MS60 | MS63 | MS65 |
|---|---|---|---|---|---|---|
| 2011 | — | PF65 1,850 | | | | |

**KM# 2072 200 EURO**
4.00 g., 0.999 Gold 0.1285 oz. AGW, 21 mm. **Subject:** G-20 Meeting in Cannes **Obv:** Sower advancing right **Rev:** Laurel tree and oak tree in the shape of a Euro symbol with value specification in the hexagon as stylization national borders **Mint:** Paris

| Date | Mintage | VF20 | XF40 | MS60 | MS63 | MS65 |
|---|---|---|---|---|---|---|
| 2011 | 100 | — | — | — | — | 400 |

**KM# 1853 200 EURO**
31.10 g., 0.999 Gold 0.999 oz. AGW, 37 mm. **Subject:** Eurocorps, 20th Anniversary **Obv:** Mitterrand and Kohl standing clasping hands **Rev:** Europa facing **Mint:** Paris

| Date | Mintage | VF20 | XF40 | MS60 | MS63 | MS65 |
|---|---|---|---|---|---|---|
| 2012 (a) | 500 | PF65 1,850 | | | | |

**KM# 1898 200 EURO**
31.10 g., 0.999 Gold 0.999 oz. AGW, 37 mm. **Subject:** abbé Pierre, 100th anniversary of Birth **Obv:** Pierre's bust at left, shaddow figure at right **Rev:** Emmaus International logo, quote below **Mint:** Paris

| Date | Mintage | VF20 | XF40 | MS60 | MS63 | MS65 |
|---|---|---|---|---|---|---|
| 2012 (a) | 500 | PF65 1,850 | | | | |

**KM# 1915 200 EURO**

31.10 g., 0.999 Gold 0.999 oz. AGW, 37 mm. **Subject:** TGV South-East **Obv:** Lyon Saint-Exupery station **Rev:** Two modern locomotives **Mint:** Paris

| Date | Mintage | VF20 | XF40 | MS60 | MS63 | MS65 |
|---|---|---|---|---|---|---|
| 2012 (a) | 500 | PF65 1,850 | | | | |

**KM# 1923 200 EURO**

31.10 g., 0.999 Gold 0.999 oz. AGW, 37 mm. **Subject:** 2012 Summer Olympics, London **Obv:** Two judo athletes and map of Europe **Rev:** Two judo athletes **Mint:** Paris

| Date | Mintage | VF20 | XF40 | MS60 | MS63 | MS65 |
|---|---|---|---|---|---|---|
| 2012 (a) | 500 | PF65 1,850 | | | | |

**KM# 1926 200 EURO**

31.10 g., 0.999 Gold 0.999 oz. AGW, 37 mm. **Subject:** Year of the Dragon **Obv:** Dragon **Rev:** La Fontaine and zodiac animals **Mint:** Paris

| Date | Mintage | VF20 | XF40 | MS60 | MS63 | MS65 |
|---|---|---|---|---|---|---|
| 2012 (a) | 500 | PF65 1,850 | | | | |

**KM# 2074 200 EURO**

4.00 g., 0.999 Gold 0.1285 oz. AGW, 21 mm. **Obv:** French province names in horizontal lines, RF in center in stylized map of France **Rev:** Laural and oak wreath, value within **Mint:** Paris

| Date | Mintage | VF20 | XF40 | MS60 | MS63 | MS65 |
|---|---|---|---|---|---|---|
| 2012 | 50,000 | — | — | — | — | 325 |

**KM# 2101 200 EURO**

31.11 g., 0.999 Gold 0.999 oz. AGW, 37 mm. **Subject:** Notre Dame, 850th Anniversary **Obv:** Seal at right, cathedral details **Rev:** Seal at left, cathedral details **Mint:** Paris

| Date | Mintage | VF20 | XF40 | MS60 | MS63 | MS65 |
|---|---|---|---|---|---|---|
| 2013 | 500 | PF65 2,750 | | | | |

**KM# 2116 200 EURO**

31.10 g., 0.999 Gold 0.999 oz. AGW, 37 mm. **Subject:** Tour de France, 100th Anniversary **Mint:** Paris

| Date | Mintage | VF20 | XF40 | MS60 | MS63 | MS65 |
|---|---|---|---|---|---|---|
| 2013 | 500 | PF65 1,850 | | | | |

**KM# 2121 200 EURO**

31.10 g., 0.999 Gold 0.999 oz. AGW, 37 mm. **Subject:** Elysee Treaty, 50th Anniversary **Mint:** Paris

| Date | Mintage | VF20 | XF40 | MS60 | MS63 | MS65 |
|---|---|---|---|---|---|---|
| 2013 | — | PF65 1,850 | | | | |

**KM# 1583 250 EURO**

8.45 g., 0.920 Gold 0.2499 oz. AGW, 22 mm. **Obv:** Modernistic sower advancing right **Rev:** Value and wreath

| Date | Mintage | VF20 | XF40 | MS60 | MS63 | MS65 |
|---|---|---|---|---|---|---|
| 2009 P | 25,000 | — | — | — | — | 500 |

**KM# 1671 250 EURO**

62.21 g., 0.999 Gold 1.998 oz. AGW, 37 mm. **Obv:** The Seed Sower left **Rev:** Wheat and olive branch **Mint:** Paris

| Date | Mintage | VF20 | XF40 | MS60 | MS63 | MS65 |
|---|---|---|---|---|---|---|
| 2010 | 500 | PF65 3,550 | | | | |

**KM# 1788 250 EURO**

62.21 g., 0.999 Gold 1.998 oz. AGW, 37 mm. **Subject:** Euro Starter Kit, 10th Anniversary **Obv:** Sower **Rev:** Euro starter kit **Mint:** Paris **Note:** Thick planchet.

| Date | Mintage | VF20 | XF40 | MS60 | MS63 | MS65 |
|---|---|---|---|---|---|---|
| 2011 | 500 | PF65 3,550 | | | | |

**KM# 1893 250 EURO**

62.21 g., 0.999 Gold 1.998 oz. AGW, 37 mm. **Subject:** Euro, 10th Anniversary **Obv:** The Sower advancing left **Rev:** Value on globe at center, child-like renderings around **Mint:** Paris

| Date | Mintage | VF20 | XF40 | MS60 | MS63 | MS65 |
|---|---|---|---|---|---|---|
| 2012 (a) | 500 | PF65 3,600 | | | | |

**KM# 1764 250 EURO**

3.89 g., 0.9999 Gold 0.1251 oz. AGW, 23 mm. **Obv:** Value within horizontal wreath **Rev:** Dove and PEACE in various languages **Mint:** Paris

| Date | Mintage | VF20 | XF40 | MS60 | MS63 | MS65 |
|---|---|---|---|---|---|---|
| 2013 | 50,000 | — | — | — | — | 400 |

**KM# 1396 500 EURO**

1000.00 g., 0.999 Gold 32.1186 oz. AGW, 85 mm. **Subject:** European Union Expansion **Obv:** Partial face and flags **Rev:** Puzzle map **Edge:** Plain **Mint:** Paris **Note:** Illustration reduced.

| Date | Mintage | VF20 | XF40 | MS60 | MS63 | MS65 |
|---|---|---|---|---|---|---|
| 2004 | 20 | PF65 60,000 | | | | |

**KM# 1594 500 EURO**

155.50 g., 0.999 Gold 4.9944 oz. AGW, 50 mm. **Subject:** Europa - Fall of Berlin Wall **Obv:** Brandenburg gate and doves in flight **Rev:** Head facing and flags

| Date | Mintage | VF20 | XF40 | MS60 | MS63 | MS65 |
|---|---|---|---|---|---|---|
| 2009 P | 99 | PF65 9,250 | | | | |

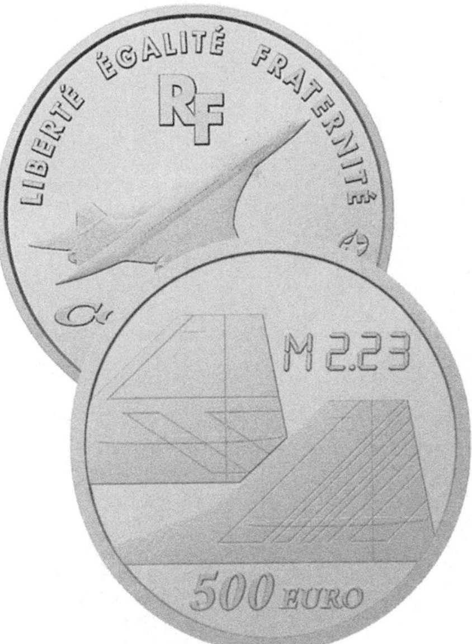


**KM# 1599 500 EURO**

155.50 g., 0.999 Gold 4.9944 oz. AGW, 50 mm. **Subject:** Concorde 40th Anniversary **Obv:** Concorde in flight **Rev:** Tail emblems

| Date | Mintage | VF20 | XF40 | MS60 | MS63 | MS65 |
|---|---|---|---|---|---|---|
| 2009 P | 90 | PF65 9,250 | | | | |

**KM# 1605 500 EURO**

155.50 g., 0.999 Gold 4.9944 oz. AGW, 50 mm. **Obv:** Eiffel Tower Structure **Rev:** Gustave Eiffel at left

| Date | Mintage | VF20 | XF40 | MS60 | MS63 | MS65 |
|---|---|---|---|---|---|---|
| 2009 P | 65 | PF65 9,250 | | | | |

**KM# 1610 500 EURO**

155.50 g., 0.999 Gold 4.9944 oz. AGW, 50 mm. **Subject:** Bugatti 100th Anniversary **Obv:** Ettore Bugatti at left **Rev:** Race car and grill motif

| Date | Mintage | VF20 | XF40 | MS60 | MS63 | MS65 |
|---|---|---|---|---|---|---|
| 2009 P | 85 | PF65 9,975 | | | | |

**KM# 1615 500 EURO**
155.50 g., 0.999 Gold 4.9944 oz. AGW, 50 mm. **Subject:** Curie Institute, 100th Anniversary

| Date | Mintage | VF20 | XF40 | MS60 | MS63 | MS65 |
|---|---|---|---|---|---|---|
| 2009 P | 99 | PF65 9,250 | | | | |

**KM# 1619 500 EURO**
155.50 g., 0.999 Gold 4.9944 oz. AGW, 50 mm. **Subject:** Unesco site - The Kremlin in Moscow **Obv:** Wall Tower and cathedral

| Date | Mintage | VF20 | XF40 | MS60 | MS63 | MS65 |
|---|---|---|---|---|---|---|
| 2009 P | 99 | PF65 9,250 | | | | |

**KM# 1640 500 EURO**
155.50 g., 0.999 Gold 4.9944 oz. AGW, 50 mm. **Subject:** FIFA World Cup, South Africa 2010 **Obv:** Soccer player on field **Rev:** Soccerball, Map of Africa, Protea flower

| Date | Mintage | VF20 | XF40 | MS60 | MS63 | MS65 |
|---|---|---|---|---|---|---|
| 2009 P | 22 | PF65 9,250 | | | | |

**KM# 1642 500 EURO**
12.00 g., 0.999 Gold 0.3854 oz. AGW, 31 mm. **Obv:** The Seed Sower advancing right, sun rays from below **Rev:** Value in center, wreath horizontal

| Date | Mintage | VF20 | XF40 | MS60 | MS63 | MS65 |
|---|---|---|---|---|---|---|
| 2010 | 25,000 | — | — | — | — | 700 |

**KM# 1687 500 EURO**
155.50 g., 0.999 Gold 4.9944 oz. AGW, 50 mm. **Obv:** Marcel Dassault **Rev:** Mirage III plane **Mint:** Paris

| Date | Mintage | VF20 | XF40 | MS60 | MS63 | MS65 |
|---|---|---|---|---|---|---|
| 2010 | 99 | PF65 9,250 | | | | |

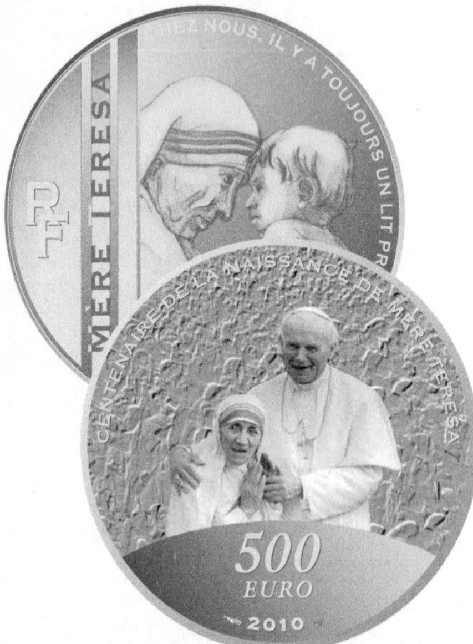


**KM# 1692 500 EURO**
155.50 g., 0.999 Gold 4.9944 oz. AGW, 50 mm. **Obv:** Mother Teresa and child **Rev:** Mother Teresa and Pope John Paul II **Mint:** Paris

| Date | Mintage | VF20 | XF40 | MS60 | MS63 | MS65 |
|---|---|---|---|---|---|---|
| 2010 | 99 | PF65 9,250 | | | | |

**KM# 1697 500 EURO**
155.50 g., 0.999 Gold 4.9944 oz. AGW, 50 mm. **Obv:** Taj Mahal **Rev:** UNESCO offices **Mint:** Paris

| Date | Mintage | VF20 | XF40 | MS60 | MS63 | MS65 |
|---|---|---|---|---|---|---|
| 2010 | 99 | PF65 9,250 | | | | |

**KM# 1706 500 EURO**
155.50 g., 0.999 Gold 4.9944 oz. AGW, 50 mm. **Obv:** Doves **Rev:** Georges Baraque **Mint:** Paris

| Date | Mintage | VF20 | XF40 | MS60 | MS63 | MS65 |
|---|---|---|---|---|---|---|
| 2010 | 99 | PF65 9,250 | | | | |

**KM# 1710 500 EURO**
155.50 g., 0.999 Gold 4.9944 oz. AGW, 50 mm. **Rev:** Picasso **Mint:** Paris

| Date | Mintage | VF20 | XF40 | MS60 | MS63 | MS65 |
|---|---|---|---|---|---|---|
| 2010 | 99 | PF65 9,250 | | | | |

**KM# 1712 500 EURO**
1000.00 g., 0.950 Silver 30.5432 oz. ASW, 100 mm. **Rev:** Picasso **Mint:** Paris

| Date | Mintage | VF20 | XF40 | MS60 | MS63 | MS65 |
|---|---|---|---|---|---|---|
| 2010 | 500 | PF63 1,200 | PF65 1,300 | | | |

**KM# 1718 500 EURO**
155.50 g., 0.999 Gold 4.9944 oz. AGW, 50 mm. **Obv:** Handball player on globe **Rev:** Handball player, net, Big Ben **Mint:** Paris

| Date | Mintage | VF20 | XF40 | MS60 | MS63 | MS65 |
|---|---|---|---|---|---|---|
| 2010 | 99 | PF65 9,250 | | | | |

**KM# 1798 500 EURO**
155.50 g., 0.999 Gold 4.9944 oz. AGW, 50 mm. **Subject:** Great Explorers - Jacques Cartier **Obv:** The Grande Hermine sailing away **Rev:** Cartier, globe and compass rose **Mint:** Paris

| Date | Mintage | VF20 | XF40 | MS60 | MS63 | MS65 |
|---|---|---|---|---|---|---|
| 2011 | 99 | PF65 9,500 | | | | |

**KM# 1812 500 EURO**
155.50 g., 0.999 Gold 4.9944 oz. AGW, 50 mm. **Subject:** UNESCO World Heritage Site - Palace of Versailles **Mint:** Paris

| Date | Mintage | VF20 | XF40 | MS60 | MS63 | MS65 |
|---|---|---|---|---|---|---|
| 2011 | 99 | PF65 9,250 | | | | |

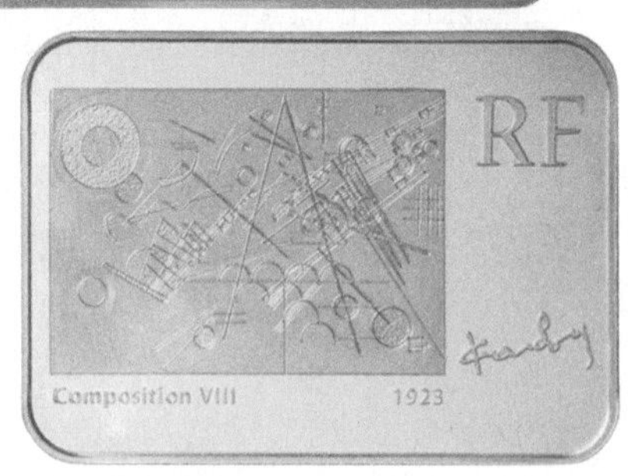


**KM# 1821 500 EURO**
155.50 g., 0.999 Gold 4.9944 oz. AGW, 53x37 mm. **Subject:** Vassily Kandinsky **Shape:** Rectangle **Mint:** Paris

| Date | Mintage | VF20 | XF40 | MS60 | MS63 | MS65 |
|---|---|---|---|---|---|---|
| 2011 | 99 | PF65 9,975 | | | | |

**KM# 1825 500 EURO**
155.50 g., 0.999 Gold 4.9944 oz. AGW, 53x37 mm. **Subject:** Andy Warhol **Shape:** Rectangle **Mint:** Paris

| Date | Mintage | VF20 | XF40 | MS60 | MS63 | MS65 |
|---|---|---|---|---|---|---|
| 2011 | 99 | PF65 9,500 | | | | |

**KM# 1854 500 EURO**
155.59 g., 0.999 Gold 4.9973 oz. AGW, 50 mm. **Subject:** Eurocorps, 20th Anniversary **Obv:** Mitterrand and Kohl standing clasping hands **Rev:** Europa facing **Mint:** Paris

| Date | Mintage | VF20 | XF40 | MS60 | MS63 | MS65 |
|---|---|---|---|---|---|---|
| 2012 (a) | 99 | PF65 9,250 | | | | |

**KM# 1899 500 EURO**
155.50 g., 0.999 Gold 4.9944 oz. AGW, 50 mm. **Subject:** abbé Pierre, 100th anniversary of Birth **Obv:** Pierre's bust at left, shadow at right **Rev:** Emmaus International logo, quote below **Mint:** Paris

| Date | Mintage | VF20 | XF40 | MS60 | MS63 | MS65 |
|---|---|---|---|---|---|---|
| 2012 (a) | 99 | PF65 9,250 | | | | |

**KM# 1909 500 EURO**
155.50 g., 0.999 Gold 4.9944 oz. AGW, 50 mm. **Subject:** UNESCO - World Heritage Site **Obv:** Abu Simbel temple **Rev:** Sphinx and Pyramids **Mint:** Paris

| Date | Mintage | VF20 | XF40 | MS60 | MS63 | MS65 |
|---|---|---|---|---|---|---|
| 2012 (a) | 99 | PF65 9,250 | | | | |

**KM# 1927 500 EURO**
155.50 g., 0.999 Gold 4.9944 oz. AGW, 50 mm. **Subject:** Year of the Dragon **Obv:** Dragon **Rev:** La Fontaine and zodiac animals **Mint:** Paris

| Date | Mintage | VF20 | XF40 | MS60 | MS63 | MS65 |
|---|---|---|---|---|---|---|
| 2012 (a) | 99 | PF65 9,250 | | | | |

**KM# 1765 500 EURO**
7.78 g., 0.9999 Gold 0.2501 oz. AGW, 29 mm. **Obv:** Value within horizontal wreath **Rev:** Words around La REPUBLIQUE **Mint:** Paris

| Date | Mintage | VF20 | XF40 | MS60 | MS63 | MS65 |
|---|---|---|---|---|---|---|
| 2013 | 25,000 | — | — | — | — | 750 |

**KM# 1595 1000 EURO**
311.00 g., 0.999 Gold 9.9889 oz. AGW, 65 mm. **Subject:** Europa - Fall of Berlin Wall **Obv:** Brandenburg gate and doves in flight **Rev:** Head facing and flags

| Date | Mintage | VF20 | XF40 | MS60 | MS63 | MS65 |
|---|---|---|---|---|---|---|
| 2009 P | 20 | PF65 18,500 | | | | |

**KM# 1600 1000 EURO**
311.00 g., 0.999 Gold 9.9889 oz. AGW, 65 mm. **Subject:** Concorde 40 Anniversary **Obv:** Concorde in flight **Rev:** Tail emblems

| Date | Mintage | VF20 | XF40 | MS60 | MS63 | MS65 |
|---|---|---|---|---|---|---|
| 2009 P | 20 | PF65 18,500 | | | | |

**KM# 1677 1000 EURO**
31.10 g., 0.999 Gold 0.9989 oz. AGW, 65 mm. **Subject:** Cluny Abbey, 1100th Anniversary **Obv:** Europa head facing **Rev:** Cluny Abby view **Mint:** Paris

| Date | Mintage | VF20 | XF40 | MS60 | MS63 | MS65 |
|---|---|---|---|---|---|---|
| 2010 | 39 | PF65 18,500 | | | | |

**KM# 1682 1000 EURO**
311.00 g., 0.999 Gold 9.9889 oz. AGW, 65 mm. **Obv:** Georges Pompidou Center design **Rev:** Design detail **Mint:** Paris

| Date | Mintage | VF20 | XF40 | MS60 | MS63 | MS65 |
|---|---|---|---|---|---|---|
| 2010 | 39 | PF65 18,500 | | | | |

**KM# 1725 1000 EURO**
20.00 g., 0.999 Gold 0.6424 oz. AGW, 39 mm. **Obv:** Value at center, wreath horizontal **Rev:** Hercules group **Mint:** Paris

| Date | Mintage | VF20 | XF40 | MS60 | MS63 | MS65 |
|---|---|---|---|---|---|---|
| 2011 | 10,000 | — | — | — | — | 1,250 |
| 2012 | 10,000 | — | — | — | — | 1,250 |
| 2013 | — | — | — | — | — | 1,250 |

**KM# 1794 1000 EURO**
311.00 g., 0.999 Gold 9.9889 oz. AGW, 65 mm. **Subject:** International Music Day, 30th Anniversary **Obv:** Europa **Rev:** Youth jamming **Mint:** Paris

| Date | Mintage | VF20 | XF40 | MS60 | MS63 | MS65 |
|---|---|---|---|---|---|---|
| 2011 | 39 | PF65 18,500 | | | | |

**KM# 1799 1000 EURO**
311.00 g., 0.999 Gold 9.9889 oz. AGW, 65 mm. **Subject:** Great Explorers - Jacques Cartier **Obv:** The Grande Hermine sailing away **Rev:** Cartier, globe and compass rose **Mint:** Paris

| Date | Mintage | VF20 | XF40 | MS60 | MS63 | MS65 |
|---|---|---|---|---|---|---|
| 2011 | 39 | PF65 18,500 | | | | |

**KM# 1855 1000 EURO**
311.00 g., 0.999 Gold 9.9889 oz. AGW, 65 mm. **Subject:** Eurocorps, 20th Anniversary **Obv:** Mitterrand and Kohl standing clasping hands **Rev:** Europa facing **Mint:** Paris

| Date | Mintage | VF20 | XF40 | MS60 | MS63 | MS65 |
|---|---|---|---|---|---|---|
| 2012 (a) | 39 | PF65 18,500 | | | | |

**KM# 1620 5000 EURO**
1000.00 g., 0.999 Gold 32.1186 oz. AGW, 85 mm. **Subject:** Unesco site - The Kremlin in Moscow **Obv:** Wall Tower and cathedral

| Date | Mintage | VF20 | XF40 | MS60 | MS63 | MS65 |
|---|---|---|---|---|---|---|
| 2009 P | 23 | PF65 60,000 | | | | |

**KM# 1696 5000 EURO**
1000.00 g., 0.999 Gold 32.1186 oz. AGW, 85 mm. **Obv:** Taj Mahal and diamond inserts **Rev:** UNESCO offices **Mint:** Paris

| Date | Mintage | VF20 | XF40 | MS60 | MS63 | MS65 |
|---|---|---|---|---|---|---|
| 2010 | 29 | PF65 60,000 | | | | |

**KM# 1709 5000 EURO**
1000.00 g., 0.999 Gold 32.1186 oz. AGW, 85 mm. **Rev:** Picasso **Mint:** Paris

| Date | Mintage | VF20 | XF40 | MS60 | MS63 | MS65 |
|---|---|---|---|---|---|---|
| 2010 | 29 | PF65 60,000 | | | | |

**KM# 1813 5000 EURO**
1000.00 g., 0.999 Gold 32.1186 oz. AGW, 85 mm. **Subject:** UNESCO World Heritage Site - Palace of Versailles **Mint:** Paris

| Date | Mintage | VF20 | XF40 | MS60 | MS63 | MS65 |
|---|---|---|---|---|---|---|
| 2011 | 29 | **PF65** 60,000 | | | | |

**KM# 1822 5000 EURO**
1000.00 g., 0.999 Gold 32.1186 oz. AGW, 90x63 mm. **Subject:** Andy Warhol **Shape:** Rectangle **Mint:** Paris

| Date | Mintage | VF20 | XF40 | MS60 | MS63 | MS65 |
|---|---|---|---|---|---|---|
| 2011 | 29 | **PF65** 60,000 | | | | |

**KM# 1910 5000 EURO**
1000.00 g., 0.999 Gold 32.1186 oz. AGW, 85 mm. **Subject:** UNESCO - World Heritage Site **Obv:** Abu Simbel temple **Rev:** Sphinx and Pyramids **Mint:** Paris

| Date | Mintage | VF20 | XF40 | MS60 | MS63 | MS65 |
|---|---|---|---|---|---|---|
| 2012 (a) | 29 | **PF65** 60,000 | | | | |

**KM# 1928 5000 EURO**
75.00 g., 0.999 Gold 2.4089 oz. AGW, 45 mm. **Obv:** Value at center, wreath horizontal **Rev:** Hercules group **Mint:** Paris

| Date | Mintage | VF20 | XF40 | MS60 | MS63 | MS65 |
|---|---|---|---|---|---|---|
| 2012 (a) | 2,000 | — | — | — | — | 4,500 |
| 2013 | 2,000 | — | — | — | — | 4,500 |

**KM# 2127 5000 EURO**
1000.00 g., 0.999 Gold 32.1186 oz. AGW, 85 mm. **Subject:** Notre Dame, 850th Anniversary **Mint:** Paris

| Date | Mintage | VF20 | XF40 | MS60 | MS63 | MS65 |
|---|---|---|---|---|---|---|
| 2013 | 29 | **PF65** 45,000 | | | | |

**KM# 2128 5000 EURO**
100.00 g., 0.999 Gold 3.2119 oz. AGW, 45 mm. **Obv:** Value within horizontal wreath **Rev:** Rooster crowing right **Mint:** Paris

| Date | Mintage | VF20 | XF40 | MS60 | MS63 | MS65 |
|---|---|---|---|---|---|---|
| 2014 | 2,000 | — | — | — | — | 4,850 |

## MINT SETS

| KM# | Date | Mintage | Identification | Issue Price | Mkt Val |
|---|---|---|---|---|---|
| MS20 | 2001 (2) | 10,000 | KM#925.1a, 928a | — | 590 |
| MS21 | 2001 (8) | 35,000 | KM#1282-1289 | 20.25 | 20.00 |
| MS22 | 2002 (8) | 35,000 | KM#1282-1289 | 20.25 | 40.00 |
| MS23 | 2003 (8) | — | KM#1282-89 | — | 55.00 |
| MS24 | 2004 (8) | — | KM#1282-1289 | — | 45.00 |
| MS25 | 2005 (8) | — | KM#1282-1289 | — | 45.00 |
| MS26 | 2005 (8) | 40,000 | KM#1282-1289 Moebius set plus token | 45.00 | 55.00 |
| MS27 | 2005 (8) | 10,000 | KM1282-1289, French Memories - Bordeaux | 45.00 | 45.00 |
| MS28 | 2006 (8) | 70,000 | KM#1282-1289 | 36.50 | 42.50 |
| MS29 | 2006 (8) | 500 | KM#1282-1289, Denver, Colorado special ANA Coin Convention Set | 45.00 | 70.00 |
| MS30 | 2006 (8) | 500 | KM#1282-1289, Berlin Coin Fair set | 45.00 | 55.00 |
| MS31 | 2006 (8) | 500 | KM1282-1289, Pierre Curie set | 45.00 | 50.00 |
| MS32 | 2006 (8) | 500 | KM#1282-1289, Musee de la Monnaie set | 45.00 | 50.00 |
| MS33 | 2006 (8) | 500 | KM#1282-1289, Journees du Patrimoine set | 45.00 | 50.00 |
| MS34 | 2006 (8) | 500 | KM#1282-1289, Bourgogne set | 45.00 | 50.00 |
| MS35 | 2006 (8) | 500 | KM#1282-1289, "Coree set" (Korea) | 45.00 | 50.00 |
| MS36 | 2006 (8) | 500 | KM#1282-1289, Nord Pas-de-Calais set | 45.00 | 50.00 |
| MS37 | 2006 (8) | 500 | KM#1282-1289, Jacques Chirac set | 45.00 | 50.00 |
| MS38 | 2006 (8) | 500 | KM#1282-1289, Mitterand & Khol | 45.00 | 50.00 |
| MS39 | 2006 (8) | 500 | KM#1282-1289, Birthday 1 set | 45.00 | 45.00 |
| MS40 | 2006 (8) | 500 | KM#1282-1289, Birthday 2 set | 45.00 | 45.00 |
| MS41 | 2006 (8) | 500 | KM#1282-1289, Tokyo set | 45.00 | 50.00 |
| MS42 | 2006 (8) | 500 | KM#1282-1289, Viaduc de Millau set | 45.00 | 50.00 |
| MS43 | 2006 (8) | 500 | KM#1282-1289, Ile-de-France set | 45.00 | 50.00 |

## PROOF SETS

| KM# | Date | Mintage | Identification | Issue Price | Mkt Val |
|---|---|---|---|---|---|
| PS21 | 2001 (8) | 15,000 | KM#1282-1289 | 59.00 | 125 |
| PS22 | 2002 (8) | 40,000 | KM#1282-1289 | 59.00 | 110 |
| PS23 | 2003 (5) | 150,000 | KM#1321, 1322, 1323, 1324, 1325 | — | 260 |
| PS24 | 2003 (5) | 5,000 | KM#1326, 1327, 1328, 1329, 1330 | — | 1,900 |
| PS25 | 2003 (8) | — | KM#1282-1289 | — | 110 |
| PS26 | 2004 (9) | 20,000 | KM#1282-1289 plus Pantheon 5 Euro | — | 150 |
| PS27 | 2005 (9) | 10,000 | KM#1282-1289 plus Pantheon 5 Euro | — | 150 |
| PS28 | 2006 (9) | 10,000 | KM#1282-1289 plus Pantheon 5 Euro | — | 150 |
| PS29 | 2007 (9) | 7,500 | KM#1282-84, 1410-1414 plus 15 Euro | — | 150 |
| PS30 | 2008 (10) | 7,500 | KM#1282-84, 1410-1414, 1535 | — | 200 |
| PS31 | 2009 (10) | 7,500 | KM#1282-84, 1410-1414, 1535 | — | 200 |
| PS32 | 2010 (9) | 9,000 | KM#1282-84, 1410-1414 plus 15 Euro | — | 150 |
| PS33 | 2011 (9) | 9,000 | KM#1282-84, 1410-1414, 1795 | — | 200 |
| PS34 | 2012 (9) | 10,000 | KM#1282-84, 1410-1414 plus Hercules 10 Euro | — | 150 |

# FRENCH POLYNESIA

The Territory of French Polynesia (formerly French Oceania) has an area of 1,544 sq. mi. (3,941 sq. km.) and a population of 220,000. It is comprised of the same five archipelagoes that were grouped administratively to form French Oceania.

The colony of French Oceania became the Territory of French Polynesia by act of the French National Assembly in March, 1957. In Sept. of 1958 it voted in favor of the new constitution of the Fifth Republic, thereby electing to remain within the new French Community.

Picturesque, mountainous Tahiti, the setting of many tales of adventure and romance, is one of the most inspiringly beautiful islands in the world. Robert Louis Stevenson called it 'God's sweetest works'. It was there that Paul Gaugin, one of the pioneers of the Impressionist movement, painted the brilliant, exotic pictures that later made him famous. The arid coral atolls of Tuamotu comprise the most economically valuable area of French Polynesia. Pearl oysters thrive in the warm, limpid lagoons, and extensive portions of the atolls are valuable phosphate rock.

**RULER**
French

**MINT MARKS**
(a) - Paris, privy marks only
(b)

**MONETARY SYSTEM**
100 Centimes = 1 Franc

## FRENCH OVERSEAS TERRITORY

## DECIMAL COINAGE

### KM# 11 FRANC

1.30 g., Aluminum, 23 mm. **Obv:** Seated Liberty with torch and cornucopia right, date below, legend added flanking figure's feet **Obv. Legend:** I. E. O. M. **Rev:** Legend and island scene divide denomination

| Date | Mintage | VF20 | XF40 | MS60 | MS63 | MS65 |
|---|---|---|---|---|---|---|
| 2001 (a) | 2,900,000 | — | — | 0.50 | 0.75 | 1.00 |
| 2002 (a) | 1,600,000 | — | — | 0.50 | 0.75 | 1.00 |
| 2003 (a) | 4,200,000 | — | — | 0.50 | 0.75 | 1.00 |
| 2004 (a) | 2,400,000 | — | — | 0.50 | 0.75 | 1.00 |
| 2005 (a) | — | — | — | 0.50 | 0.75 | 1.00 |
| 2006 (a) | 2,100,000 | — | — | 0.50 | 0.75 | 1.00 |
| 2007 (a) Coin rotation | 3,400,000 | — | — | 0.50 | 0.75 | 1.00 |
| 2007 (a) Medal rotation | Inc. above | — | — | — | — | 30.00 |
| 2008 (a) | 4,800,000 | — | — | 0.50 | 0.75 | 1.00 |
| 2009 (a) | 3,200,000 | — | — | 0.50 | 0.75 | 1.00 |
| 2010 (a) | 2,100,000 | — | — | 0.50 | 0.75 | 1.00 |
| 2011 (a) | — | — | — | 0.50 | 0.75 | 1.00 |

### KM# 10 2 FRANCS

2.30 g., Aluminum, 27 mm. **Obv:** Seated Liberty with torch and cornucopia right, date below, legend added flanking figure's feet **Obv. Legend:** I. E. O. M. **Rev:** Legend and island scene divide denomination

| Date | Mintage | VF20 | XF40 | MS60 | MS63 | MS65 |
|---|---|---|---|---|---|---|
| 2001 (a) | 2,400,000 | — | — | 0.75 | 1.25 | 1.50 |
| 2002 (a) | 2,500,000 | — | — | 0.75 | 1.25 | 1.50 |
| 2003 (a) | 3,200,000 | — | — | 0.75 | 1.25 | 1.50 |
| 2004 (a) | 3,000,000 | — | — | 0.75 | 1.25 | 1.50 |
| 2005 (a) | 900,000 | — | — | 0.75 | 1.25 | 1.50 |
| 2006 (a) | 1,600,000 | — | — | 0.75 | 1.25 | 1.50 |
| 2007 (a) | 640,000 | — | — | 0.75 | 1.25 | 1.50 |
| 2008 (a) | 1,900,000 | — | — | 0.75 | 1.25 | 1.50 |
| 2009 (a) | 1,600,000 | — | — | 0.75 | 1.25 | 1.50 |
| 2010 (a) | 2,400,000 | — | — | 0.75 | 1.25 | 1.50 |
| 2011 (a) | 1,600,000 | — | — | 0.75 | 1.25 | 1.50 |

### KM# 12 5 FRANCS

3.75 g., Aluminum, 31 mm. **Obv:** Seated Liberty with torch and cornucopia right, date below, legend added flanking figure's feet **Obv. Legend:** I. E. O. M. **Rev:** Legend and island divide denomination

| Date | Mintage | VF20 | XF40 | MS60 | MS63 | MS65 |
|---|---|---|---|---|---|---|
| 2001 (a) | 1,600,000 | — | — | 1.00 | 1.50 | 2.00 |
| 2002 (a) | 400,000 | — | — | 1.00 | 1.50 | 2.00 |
| 2003 (a) | 1,000,000 | — | — | 1.00 | 1.50 | 2.00 |
| 2004 (a) | 600,000 | — | — | 1.00 | 1.50 | 2.00 |
| 2005 (a) | 600,000 | — | — | 1.00 | 1.50 | 2.00 |
| 2006 (a) | 720,000 | — | — | 1.00 | 1.50 | 2.00 |
| 2007 (a) | 1,000,000 | — | — | 1.00 | 1.50 | 2.00 |
| 2008 (a) | 1,060,000 | — | — | 1.00 | 1.50 | 2.00 |
| 2009 (a) | 900,000 | — | — | 1.00 | 1.50 | 2.00 |
| 2010 (a) | 700,000 | — | — | 1.00 | 1.50 | 2.00 |
| 2011 (a) | 900,000 | — | — | 1.00 | 1.50 | 2.00 |

### KM# 8 10 FRANCS

6.00 g., Nickel, 24 mm. **Obv:** Capped head left, date and legend below **Obv. Legend:** I. E. O. M. **Rev:** Native art, denomination below **Edge:** Reeded

| Date | Mintage | VF20 | XF40 | MS60 | MS63 | MS65 |
|---|---|---|---|---|---|---|
| 2001 (a) | 500,000 | — | — | 1.25 | 2.00 | 2.75 |
| 2002 (a) | 600,000 | — | — | 1.25 | 2.00 | 2.75 |
| 2003 (a) | 1,000,000 | — | — | 1.25 | 2.00 | 2.75 |
| 2004 (a) | 600,000 | — | — | 1.25 | 2.00 | 2.75 |
| 2005 (a) | 200,000 | — | — | 1.25 | 2.00 | 2.75 |

### KM# 8a 10 FRANCS

6.00 g., Copper-Nickel, 24 mm. **Obv:** Capped head left, date and legend below **Obv. Legend:** I. E. O. M. **Rev:** Native art, denomination below **Edge:** Reeded

| Date | Mintage | VF20 | XF40 | MS60 | MS63 | MS65 |
|---|---|---|---|---|---|---|
| 2006 (a) | 620,000 | — | — | 1.25 | 2.00 | 2.75 |
| 2007 (a) | 800,000 | — | — | 1.25 | 2.00 | 2.75 |
| 2008 (a) | 820,000 | — | — | 1.25 | 2.00 | 2.75 |
| 2009 (a) | 1,000,000 | — | — | 1.25 | 2.00 | 2.75 |
| 2010 (a) | 500,000 | — | — | 1.25 | 2.00 | 2.75 |
| 2011 (a) | 200,000 | — | — | 1.25 | 2.00 | 2.75 |

### KM# 9 20 FRANCS

10.00 g., Nickel, 28.3 mm. **Obv:** Capped head left, date and legend below **Obv. Legend:** I. E. O. M. **Rev:** Flowers, vanilla shoots, bread fruit **Edge:** Reeded

| Date | Mintage | VF20 | XF40 | MS60 | MS63 | MS65 |
|---|---|---|---|---|---|---|
| 2001 (a) | 500,000 | — | — | 1.75 | 2.75 | 3.25 |
| 2002 (a) | 300,000 | — | — | 1.75 | 2.75 | 3.25 |
| 2003 (a) | 700,000 | — | — | 1.75 | 2.25 | 3.00 |
| 2004 (a) | 600,000 | — | — | 1.75 | 2.25 | 3.00 |
| 2005 (a) | 30,000 | — | — | 20.00 | 25.00 | 35.00 |

### KM# 9a 20 FRANCS

10.00 g., Copper-Nickel, 28.3 mm. **Obv:** Capped head left, date and legend below **Obv. Legend:** I. E. O. M. **Rev:** Flowers, vanilla shoots, bread fruit **Edge:** Reeded

| Date | Mintage | VF20 | XF40 | MS60 | MS63 | MS65 |
|---|---|---|---|---|---|---|
| 2006 (a) | 300,000 | — | — | 1.75 | 2.50 | 3.00 |
| 2007 (a) | 450,000 | — | — | 1.75 | 2.50 | 3.00 |
| 2008 (a) | 610,000 | — | — | 1.75 | 2.50 | 3.00 |
| 2009 (a) | 750,000 | — | — | 1.75 | 2.50 | 3.00 |
| 2010 (a) | 200,000 | — | — | 1.75 | 2.50 | 3.00 |
| 2011 (a) | 400,000 | — | — | 1.75 | 2.50 | 3.00 |

### KM# 13 50 FRANCS

15.00 g., Nickel, 33 mm. **Obv:** Capped head left, date and legend below **Obv. Legend:** I. E. O. M. **Rev:** Denomination above Moorea Harbor **Edge:** Reeded

| Date | Mintage | VF20 | XF40 | MS60 | MS63 | MS65 |
|---|---|---|---|---|---|---|
| 2001 (a) | 300,000 | — | — | 2.00 | 3.00 | 4.00 |
| 2002 (a) | — | — | — | 2.00 | 3.00 | 4.00 |
| 2003 (a) | 240,000 | — | — | 2.00 | 3.00 | 4.00 |
| 2004 (a) | 100,000 | — | — | 2.00 | 3.00 | 4.00 |
| 2005 (a) | 100,000 | — | — | 2.00 | 3.00 | 4.00 |

### KM# 13a 50 FRANCS

15.00 g., Copper-Nickel, 33 mm. **Obv:** Capped head left, date and legend below **Obv. Legend:** I. E. O. M. **Rev:** Denomination above Moorea Harbor **Edge:** Reeded

| Date | Mintage | VF20 | XF40 | MS60 | MS63 | MS65 |
|---|---|---|---|---|---|---|
| 2006 (a) | 15,000 | — | — | 3.00 | 4.00 | 5.00 |
| 2007 (a) | 310,000 | — | — | 2.00 | 3.00 | 4.00 |
| 2008 (a) | 200,000 | — | — | 2.00 | 3.00 | 4.00 |
| 2009 (a) | 300,000 | — | — | 2.00 | 3.00 | 4.00 |
| 2010 (a) | 120,000 | — | — | 2.00 | 3.00 | 4.00 |
| 2011 (a) | 130,000 | — | — | 2.00 | 3.00 | 4.00 |

### KM# 14 100 FRANCS

10.00 g., Nickel-Bronze, 30 mm. **Obv:** Capped head left, date below **Rev:** Denomination above Moorea Harbor **Edge:** Reeded

| Date | Mintage | VF20 | XF40 | MS60 | MS63 | MS65 |
|---|---|---|---|---|---|---|
| 2001 (a) | 200,000 | — | — | 3.00 | 4.00 | 5.00 |
| 2002 (a) | — | — | — | 3.00 | 4.00 | 5.00 |
| 2003 (a) | 600,000 | — | — | 2.75 | 3.50 | 5.00 |
| 2004 (a) | 450,000 | — | — | 2.75 | 3.50 | 5.00 |
| 2005 (a) | 300,000 | — | — | 2.75 | 3.50 | 5.00 |

### KM# 14a 100 FRANCS

10.00 g., Aluminum-Bronze, 30 mm. **Obv:** Capped head left, date below **Obv. Legend:** I. E. O. M. **Rev:** Denomination above Moorea Harbor **Edge:** Reeded

| Date | Mintage | VF20 | XF40 | MS60 | MS63 | MS65 |
|---|---|---|---|---|---|---|
| 2006 (a) | 200,000 | — | — | 2.75 | 3.50 | 5.00 |
| 2007 (a) | 650,000 | — | — | 2.75 | 3.50 | 5.00 |
| 2008 (a) | 690,000 | — | — | 2.75 | 3.50 | 5.00 |
| 2009 (a) | — | — | — | 2.75 | 3.50 | 5.00 |
| 2010 (a) | — | — | — | 2.75 | 3.50 | 5.00 |
| 2011 (a) | — | — | — | 2.75 | 3.50 | 5.00 |

## MINT SETS

| KM# | Date | Mintage | Identification | Issue Price | Mkt Val |
|---|---|---|---|---|---|
| MS1 | 2001 (7) | 3,000 | KM#8-14 | — | 22.50 |
| MS2 | 2002 (7) | 5,000 | KM#8-14 | — | 22.50 |
| MS3 | 2003 (7) | 3,000 | KM#8-14 | — | 22.50 |

# GABON

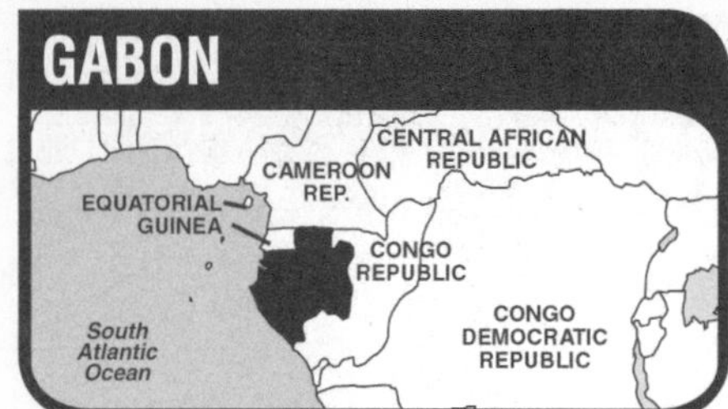


The Gabonese Republic, a member of the French Community, straddles the equator on the west coast of Africa. The hot and humid rain forest country has an area of 103,347 sq. mi. (267,670 sq. km.) and a population of 1.2 million, almost all of Bantu origin. Capital: Libreville. Extravagantly rich in resources, Gabon exports crude oil, manganese ore, gold and timbers.

For earlier coinage see French Equatorial Africa, Central African States and the Equatorial African States.

**MINT MARKS**

(a) - Paris, privy marks only

(t) - Poissy, privy marks only, thunderbolt

## REPUBLIC

### DECIMAL COINAGE

**KM# 18 1000 FRANCS**

31.14 g., 0.999 Silver 1.000 oz. ASW, 40 mm. **Obv:** National arms **Rev:** Male lion

| Date | Mintage | VF20 | XF40 | MS60 | MS63 | MS65 |
|---|---|---|---|---|---|---|
| 2012 | 2,000 | PF63 55.00 | PF65 60.00 | | | |

**KM# 19 1000 FRANCS**

31.14 g., 0.999 Silver 1.000 oz. ASW, 40 mm. **Obv:** National arms **Rev:** Elephant

| Date | Mintage | VF20 | XF40 | MS60 | MS63 | MS65 |
|---|---|---|---|---|---|---|
| 2012 | 2,000 | PF63 55.00 | PF65 60.00 | | | |

**KM# 20 1000 FRANCS**

31.14 g., 0.999 Silver 1.000 oz. ASW, 40 mm. **Obv:** National arms **Rev:** Gazelle

| Date | Mintage | VF20 | XF40 | MS60 | MS63 | MS65 |
|---|---|---|---|---|---|---|
| 2012 | 2,000 | PF63 55.00 | PF65 60.00 | | | |

**KM# 21 1000 FRANCS**

31.14 g., 0.999 Silver 1.000 oz. ASW, 40 mm. **Obv:** National arms **Rev:** Baby elephants

| Date | Mintage | VF20 | XF40 | MS60 | MS63 | MS65 |
|---|---|---|---|---|---|---|
| 2012 | 2,000 | PF63 55.00 | PF65 60.00 | | | |

**KM# 22 1000 FRANCS**

31.11 g., 0.999 Silver 0.999 oz. ASW, 38.61 mm. **Rev:** Elephant facing

| Date | Mintage | VF20 | XF40 | MS60 | MS63 | MS65 |
|---|---|---|---|---|---|---|
| 2012 | — | PF63 70.00 | PF65 75.00 | | | |

# GAMBIA

The Republic of The Gambia, occupies a strip of land 7 miles (11km.) to 20 miles (32 km.) wide and 200 miles (322 km.) long encompassing both sides of West Africa's Gambia River, and completely surrounded by Senegal. The republic, one of Africa's smallest countries, has an area of 4,127 sq. mi. (11,300 sq. km.) and a population of 989,273. Capital: Banjul. Agriculture and tourism are the principal industries. Peanuts constitute 95 per cent of export earnings.

The Gambia was once part of the great empires of Ghana and Songhay. When Portuguese gold seekers and slave traders visited The Gambia in the 15th century, it was part of the Kingdom of Mali. In 1588 the territory became, through purchase, the first British colony in Africa. English slavers established Fort James, the first settlement, on a small island a dozen miles up the Gambia River in 1664. After alternate periods of union with Sierra Leone and existence as a separate colony The Gambia became a British colony in 1888. On Feb. 18, 1965, The Gambia achieved independence as a constitutional monarchy within the Commonwealth of Nations, with Elizabeth II as Head of State as Queen of The Gambia. It became a republic on April 24, 1970, remaining a member of the Commonwealth, but with the president as Chief of State and Head of Government.

Together with Senegal, The Gambia formed a confederation on February 1, 1982. This confederation was officially dissolved on September 21, 1989. In July, 1994 a military junta took control of The Gambia and disbanded its elected government.

For earlier coinage see British West Africa.

**RULER**

British until 1970

## REPUBLIC

### DECIMAL COINAGE

100 Bututs = 1 Dalasi

**KM# 58 50 BUTUTS**

9.84 g., Nickel Plated Steel, 28.8 mm. **Obv:** National arms, date below **Rev:** African domestic ox divides denomination

| Date | Mintage | VF20 | XF40 | MS60 | MS63 | MS65 |
|---|---|---|---|---|---|---|
| 2008 | — | — | — | 1.00 | 1.50 | 2.00 |
| 2011 | — | — | — | 1.00 | 1.50 | 2.00 |

**KM# 72 DALASI**

Gold **Subject:** 7th Conference of the African Union in Banjul

| Date | Mintage | VF20 | XF40 | MS60 | MS63 | MS65 |
|---|---|---|---|---|---|---|
| 2006 Proof | — | — | — | — | — | — |

**KM# 59a DALASI**

8.67 g., Nickel Plated Steel, 28 mm. **Obv:** National arms, date below **Rev:** Slender-snouted crocodile, denomination at right **Shape:** 7-sided

| Date | Mintage | VF20 | XF40 | MS60 | MS63 | MS65 |
|---|---|---|---|---|---|---|
| 2008 | — | — | 2.75 | 4.00 | 6.00 | 7.50 |
| 2011 | — | — | 2.75 | 4.00 | 6.00 | 7.50 |

# GEORGIA

Georgia (formerly the Georgian Social Democratic Republic under the U.S.S.R.), is bounded by the Black Sea to the west and by Turkey, Armenia and Azerbaijan. It occupies the western part of Transcaucasia covering an area of 26,900 sq. mi. (69,700 sq. km.) and a population of 5.7 million. Capitol: Tbilisi. Hydro-electricity, minerals, forestry and agriculture are the chief industries.

Germano - Georgian treaty was signed on May 28, 1918, followed by a Turko-Georgian peace treaty on June 4. The end of WW I and the collapse of the central powers allowed free The collapse of the U.S.S.R. allowed full transition to independence and on April 9, 1991 a unanimous vote declared the republic an independent state based on its original treaty of independence of May 1918.

**MONETARY SYSTEM**

100 Thetri = 1 Lari

## INDEPENDENT STATE (C.I.S.)

### STANDARD COINAGE

100 Thetri = 1 Lari

**KM# 89 50 THETRI**

6.50 g., Copper-Nickel, 24 mm. **Obv:** National arms **Rev:** Value **Edge:** Reeded and lettered

| Date | Mintage | VF20 | XF40 | MS60 | MS63 | MS65 |
|---|---|---|---|---|---|---|
| 2006 | — | — | — | 3.00 | 4.00 | 5.00 |

**KM# 95 LARI**

28.28 g., 0.999 Silver 0.9083 oz. ASW, 38.61 mm. **Subject:** World Cup Soccer, 2006 Germany **Obv:** Map of Georgia, flag **Rev:** World Cup trophy, two soccer players

| Date | Mintage | VF20 | XF40 | MS60 | MS63 | MS65 |
|---|---|---|---|---|---|---|
| 2004 | 50,000 | PF63 40.00 | PF65 45.00 | | | |

**KM# 90 LARI**

7.80 g., Copper-Nickel, 26.2 mm. **Obv:** National arms **Rev:** Value **Edge:** Reeded and lettered

| Date | Mintage | VF20 | XF40 | MS60 | MS63 | MS65 |
|---|---|---|---|---|---|---|
| 2006 | — | — | — | 5.00 | 6.00 | 7.00 |

**KM# 92 2 LARI**

12.92 g., Copper-Nickel, 31 mm. **Obv:** Trophy cup, value and date **Rev:** UEFA Winners Cup and soccer player **Edge:** Plain

| Date | Mintage | VF20 | XF40 | MS60 | MS63 | MS65 |
|---|---|---|---|---|---|---|
| 2006 | 10,000 | — | — | 14.00 | 18.00 | 20.00 |

**KM# 94 2 LARI**

8.00 g., Bi-Metallic Aluminum-Bronze center in Copper-Nickel ring, 27 mm. **Obv:** National arms **Rev:** Large value **Edge:** Reeded and lettered

| Date | Mintage | VF20 | XF40 | MS60 | MS63 | MS65 |
|---|---|---|---|---|---|---|
| 2006 | — | — | — | 7.00 | 9.00 | 11.00 |

**KM# 103 2 LARI**
28.28 g., 0.925 Silver 0.841 oz. ASW, 38.61 mm. **Obv:** Trophy cup, value and date **Rev:** UEFA Winners Cup and soccer player

| Date | Mintage | VF20 | XF40 | MS60 | MS63 | MS65 |
|---|---|---|---|---|---|---|
| 2006 | 6,000 | PF63 60.00 | PF65 65.00 | | | |

**KM# 93 3 LARI**
12.80 g., Copper-Nickel, 31 mm. **Obv:** Three oil wells **Rev:** Map with "Baku-Tbilisi-Ceyhan" route **Edge:** Lettered

| Date | Mintage | VF20 | XF40 | MS60 | MS63 | MS65 |
|---|---|---|---|---|---|---|
| 2006 | 3,000 | — | — | — | 25.00 | 28.00 |

**KM# 102 3 LARI**
28.28 g., Silver, 38.61 mm. **Obv:** Three oil wells **Rev:** Map with "Baku-Tbilisi-Ceyhan" route

| Date | Mintage | VF20 | XF40 | MS60 | MS63 | MS65 |
|---|---|---|---|---|---|---|
| 2006 | 5,000 | PF63 60.00 | PF65 65.00 | | | |

**KM# 106 10 LARI**
28.28 g., 0.925 Silver 0.841 oz. ASW, 38.61 mm. **Subject:** St. George's Day **Obv:** Drawing of church by Don Christoforo de Castelli **Rev:** Church of St. george in Ilora

| Date | Mintage | VF20 | XF40 | MS60 | MS63 | MS65 |
|---|---|---|---|---|---|---|
| 2009 | 1,500 | PF63 75.00 | PF65 85.00 | | | |

**KM# 104 20 LARI**
28.28 g., 0.925 Silver 0.841 oz. ASW, 38.61 mm. **Obv:** Two classical runners **Rev:** Exterior of Bird's Nest Stadium, torch

| Date | Mintage | VF20 | XF40 | MS60 | MS63 | MS65 |
|---|---|---|---|---|---|---|
| 2008 | 1,500 | PF63 75.00 | PF65 85.00 | | | |

**KM# 105 20 LARI**
8.50 g., 0.900 Gold 0.246 oz. AGW, 25 mm. **Obv:** Two classical runners **Rev:** Exterior of Bird's Nest Stadium, torch

| Date | Mintage | VF20 | XF40 | MS60 | MS63 | MS65 |
|---|---|---|---|---|---|---|
| 2008 | — | PF63 450 | PF65 500 | | | |

## BULLION COINAGE

**KM# 96 10 LARI**
3.11 g., 0.999 Gold 0.0999 oz. AGW, 16 mm. **Obv:** Ancient sailing vessel, trade route **Rev:** Golden Fleece

| Date | Mintage | VF20 | XF40 | MS60 | MS63 | MS65 |
|---|---|---|---|---|---|---|
| 2006 | 4,000 | — | — | — | — | 175 |

**KM# 97 25 LARI**
7.78 g., 0.999 Gold 0.2499 oz. AGW, 22 mm. **Obv:** Ancient sailing ship trade route map **Rev:** Golden Feece

| Date | Mintage | VF20 | XF40 | MS60 | MS63 | MS65 |
|---|---|---|---|---|---|---|
| 2006 | — | — | — | — | — | 450 |

**KM# 98 50 LARI**
28.00 g., 0.999 Gold 0.8993 oz. AGW, 28 mm. **Obv:** Ancient sailing ship, trade route map **Rev:** Golden Fleece

| Date | Mintage | VF20 | XF40 | MS60 | MS63 | MS65 |
|---|---|---|---|---|---|---|
| 2006 | — | — | — | — | — | 1,600 |

**KM# 99 100 LARI**
31.11 g., 0.999 Gold 0.999 oz. AGW, 37 mm. **Obv:** Ancient sailing ship, trade route map **Rev:** Golden Fleece

| Date | Mintage | VF20 | XF40 | MS60 | MS63 | MS65 |
|---|---|---|---|---|---|---|
| 2006 | — | — | — | — | — | 1,750 |

**KM# 100 300 LARI**
155.50 g., 0.999 Gold 4.9944 oz. AGW, 50 mm. **Obv:** Ancient sailing ship, trade route map **Rev:** Golden Fleece

| Date | Mintage | VF20 | XF40 | MS60 | MS63 | MS65 |
|---|---|---|---|---|---|---|
| 2006 | — | — | — | — | — | 9,000 |

**KM# 101 1000 LARI**
311.00 g., 0.999 Gold 9.9889 oz. AGW, 60 mm. **Obv:** Ancient sailing ship, trade route map **Rev:** Golden Fleece

| Date | Mintage | VF20 | XF40 | MS60 | MS63 | MS65 |
|---|---|---|---|---|---|---|
| 2006 | — | — | — | — | — | 17,500 |

The Federal Republic of Germany, located in north-central Europe, has an area of 137,744 sq. mi. (356,910sq. km.) and a population of 81.1 million. Capital: Berlin. The economy centers about one of the world's foremost industrial establishments. Machinery, motor vehicles, iron, steel, yarns and fabrics are exported.

**MINT MARKS**
A - Berlin
D - Munich
F - Stuttgart
G - Karlsruhe
J - Hamburg

**MONETARY SYSTEM**
100 Pfennig = 1 Deutsche Mark (DM)

# FEDERAL REPUBLIC

## STANDARD COINAGE

**KM# 105 PFENNIG**
2.00 g., Copper Plated Steel, 16.5 mm. **Obv:** Five oak leaves, date below **Obv. Legend:** BUNDESREPUBLIK DEUTSCHLAND **Rev:** Denomination

| Date | Mintage | F12 | VF20 | XF40 | MS60 | MS63 |
|---|---|---|---|---|---|---|
| 2001 A Sets only | 130,000 | — | — | — | — | 5.00 |
| 2001 A | 78,000 | PF63 5.00 | | | | |
| 2001 D Sets only | 130,000 | — | — | — | — | 5.00 |
| 2001 D | 78,000 | PF63 5.00 | | | | |
| 2001 F Sets only | 130,000 | — | — | — | — | 5.00 |
| 2001 F | 78,000 | PF63 5.00 | | | | |
| 2001 G Sets only | 130,000 | — | — | — | — | 5.00 |
| 2001 G | 78,000 | PF63 5.00 | | | | |
| 2001 J Sets only | 130,000 | — | — | — | — | 5.00 |
| 2001 J | 78,000 | PF63 5.00 | | | | |

**KM# 106a 2 PFENNIG**
2.90 g., Copper Plated Steel, 19.25 mm. **Obv:** Five oak leaves, date below **Rev:** Denomination

| Date | Mintage | F12 | VF20 | XF40 | MS60 | MS63 |
|---|---|---|---|---|---|---|
| 2001 A Sets only | 130,000 | — | — | — | — | 5.00 |
| 2001 A | 78,000 | PF65 5.00 | | | | |
| 2001 D Sets only | 130,000 | — | — | — | — | 5.00 |
| 2001 D | 78,000 | PF65 5.00 | | | | |
| 2001 F Sets only | 130,000 | — | — | — | — | 5.00 |
| 2001 F | 78,000 | PF65 5.00 | | | | |
| 2001 G Sets only | 130,000 | — | — | — | — | 5.00 |
| 2001 G | 78,000 | PF65 5.00 | | | | |
| 2001 J Sets only | 130,000 | — | — | — | — | 5.00 |
| 2001 J | 78,000 | PF65 5.00 | | | | |

**KM# 107 5 PFENNIG**
3.00 g., Brass Clad Steel, 18.5 mm. **Obv:** Five oak leaves, date below **Obv. Legend:** BUNDESREPUBLIK DEUTSCHLAND **Rev:** Denomination

| Date | Mintage | F12 | VF20 | XF40 | MS60 | MS63 |
|---|---|---|---|---|---|---|
| 2001 A Sets only | 130,000 | — | — | — | — | 5.00 |
| 2001 A | 78,000 | PF63 5.00 | | | | |
| 2001 D Sets only | 130,000 | — | — | — | — | 5.00 |
| 2001 D | 78,000 | PF63 5.00 | | | | |
| 2001 F Sets only | 130,000 | — | — | — | — | 5.00 |
| 2001 F | 78,000 | PF63 5.00 | | | | |
| 2001 G Sets only | 130,000 | — | — | — | — | 5.00 |
| 2001 G | 78,000 | PF63 5.00 | | | | |
| 2001 J Sets only | 130,000 | — | — | — | — | 5.00 |
| 2001 J | 78,000 | PF63 5.00 | | | | |

**KM# 108 10 PFENNIG**
4.00 g., Brass Clad Steel, 21.5 mm. **Obv:** Five oak leaves, date below **Obv. Legend:** BUNDESREPUBLIK DEUTSCHLAND **Rev:** Denomination **Edge:** Plain

| Date | Mintage | F12 | VF20 | XF40 | MS60 | MS63 |
|---|---|---|---|---|---|---|
| 2001 A Sets only | 135,808 | — | — | — | — | 5.00 |
| 2001 A | 78,000 | PF63 5.00 | | | | |
| 2001 D Sets only | 135,808 | — | — | — | — | 5.00 |
| 2001 D | 78,000 | PF63 5.00 | | | | |
| 2001 F Sets only | 135,808 | — | — | — | — | 5.00 |

| Date | Mintage | F12 | VF20 | XF40 | MS60 | MS63 |
|---|---|---|---|---|---|---|
| 2001 F | 78,000 | PF63 5.00 | | | | |
| 2001 G Sets only | 153,018 | — | — | — | — | 5.00 |
| 2001 G | 78,000 | PF63 5.00 | | | | |
| 2001 J Sets only | 135,808 | — | — | — | — | 5.00 |
| 2001 J | 78,000 | PF63 5.00 | | | | |

### KM# 109.2 50 PFENNIG

3.50 g., Copper-Nickel, 20 mm. **Obv:** Denomination **Obv. Legend:** BUNDESREPUBLIK DEUTSCHLAND **Rev:** Woman planting an oak seedling **Edge:** Plain

| Date | Mintage | F12 | VF20 | XF40 | MS60 | MS63 |
|---|---|---|---|---|---|---|
| 2001 A Sets only | 130,000 | — | — | — | — | 10.00 |
| 2001 A | 78,000 | PF63 10.00 | | | | |
| 2001 D Sets only | 130,000 | — | — | — | — | 10.00 |
| 2001 D | 78,000 | PF63 10.00 | | | | |
| 2001 F Sets only | 130,000 | — | — | — | — | 10.00 |
| 2001 F | 78,000 | PF63 10.00 | | | | |
| 2001 G Sets only | 130,000 | — | — | — | — | 10.00 |
| 2001 G | 78,000 | PF63 10.00 | | | | |
| 2001 J Sets only | 130,000 | — | — | — | — | 10.00 |
| 2001 J | 78,000 | PF63 10.00 | | | | |

### KM# 110 MARK

5.50 g., Copper-Nickel, 23.5 mm. **Obv:** Eagle **Rev:** Denomination flanked by oak leaves, date below

| Date | Mintage | F12 | VF20 | XF40 | MS60 | MS63 |
|---|---|---|---|---|---|---|
| 2001 A Sets only | 130,000 | — | — | — | — | 15.00 |
| 2001 A | 78,000 | PF63 15.00 | | | | |
| 2001 D Sets only | 130,000 | — | — | — | — | 15.00 |
| 2001 D | 78,000 | PF63 15.00 | | | | |
| 2001 F Sets only | 130,000 | — | — | — | — | 15.00 |
| 2001 F | 78,000 | PF63 15.00 | | | | |
| 2001 G Sets only | 130,000 | — | — | — | — | 15.00 |
| 2001 G | 78,000 | PF63 15.00 | | | | |
| 2001 J Sets only | 130,000 | — | — | — | — | 15.00 |
| 2001 J | 78,000 | PF63 15.00 | | | | |

### KM# 203 MARK

12.00 g., 0.9999 Gold 0.3858 oz. AGW, 23.5 mm. **Subject:** Retirement of the Mark Currency **Obv:** Eagle **Rev:** Denomination flanked by oak leaves, date below **Edge:** Arabeskes

| Date | Mintage | F12 | VF20 | XF40 | MS60 | MS63 |
|---|---|---|---|---|---|---|
| 2001 A | 200,000 | PF63 750 | | | | |
| 2001 D | 200,000 | PF63 750 | | | | |
| 2001 G | 200,000 | PF63 750 | | | | |
| 2001 J | 200,000 | PF63 750 | | | | |
| 2001 F | 200,000 | PF63 750 | | | | |

### KM# 170 2 MARK

7.00 g., Copper-Nickel Clad Nickel, 26.75 mm. **Subject:** Ludwig Erhard **Obv:** Eagle above denomination **Rev:** Head facing divides dates **Edge Lettering:** EINIGKEIT UND RECHT UND FREIHEIT

| Date | Mintage | F12 | VF20 | XF40 | MS60 | MS63 |
|---|---|---|---|---|---|---|
| 2001 A Sets only | 130,000 | — | — | — | — | 10.00 |
| 2001 A | 78,000 | PF63 10.00 | | | | |
| 2001 D Sets only | 130,000 | — | — | — | — | 10.00 |
| 2001 D | 78,000 | PF63 10.00 | | | | |
| 2001 F Sets only | 130,000 | — | — | — | — | 10.00 |
| 2001 F | 78,000 | PF63 10.00 | | | | |
| 2001 G Sets only | 130,000 | — | — | — | — | 10.00 |

| Date | Mintage | F12 | VF20 | XF40 | MS60 | MS63 |
|---|---|---|---|---|---|---|
| 2001 G | 78,000 | PF63 10.00 | | | | |
| 2001 J Sets only | 130,000 | — | — | — | — | 10.00 |
| 2001 J | 78,000 | PF63 10.00 | | | | |

### KM# 175 2 MARK

7.04 g., Copper-Nickel Clad Nickel, 26.8 mm. **Subject:** Franz Joseph Strauss **Obv:** Eagle above denomination **Rev:** Head left divides dates **Edge Lettering:** EINIGKEIT UND RECHT UND FREIHEIT

| Date | Mintage | F12 | VF20 | XF40 | MS60 | MS63 |
|---|---|---|---|---|---|---|
| 2001 A Sets only | 130,000 | — | — | — | — | 10.00 |
| 2001 A | 78,000 | PF63 10.00 | | | | |
| 2001 D Sets only | 130,000 | — | — | — | — | 10.00 |
| 2001 D | 78,000 | PF63 10.00 | | | | |
| 2001 F Sets only | 130,000 | — | — | — | — | 10.00 |
| 2001 F | 78,000 | PF63 10.00 | | | | |
| 2001 G Sets only | 130,000 | — | — | — | — | 10.00 |
| 2001 G | 78,000 | PF63 10.00 | | | | |
| 2001 J Sets only | 130,000 | — | — | — | — | 10.00 |
| 2001 J | 78,000 | PF63 10.00 | | | | |

### KM# 183 2 MARK

7.00 g., Copper-Nickel Clad Nickel, 26.75 mm. **Subject:** Willy Brandt **Obv:** Eagle above denomination **Rev:** Head facing divides dates **Edge Lettering:** EINIGKEIT UND RECHT UND FREIHEIT

| Date | Mintage | F12 | VF20 | XF40 | MS60 | MS63 |
|---|---|---|---|---|---|---|
| 2001 A Sets only | 130,000 | — | — | — | — | 10.00 |
| 2001 A | 78,000 | PF63 10.00 | | | | |
| 2001 D Sets only | 130,000 | — | — | — | — | 10.00 |
| 2001 D | 78,000 | PF63 10.00 | | | | |
| 2001 F Sets only | 130,000 | — | — | — | — | 10.00 |
| 2001 F | 78,000 | PF63 10.00 | | | | |
| 2001 G Sets only | 130,000 | — | — | — | — | 10.00 |
| 2001 G | 78,000 | PF63 10.00 | | | | |
| 2001 J Sets only | 130,000 | — | — | — | — | 10.00 |
| 2001 J | 78,000 | PF63 10.00 | | | | |

### KM# 140.1 5 MARK

10.00 g., Copper-Nickel Clad Nickel, 29 mm. **Obv:** Denomination within rounded square therefore nicknamed "TV-Fives **Rev:** Eagle above date **Edge Lettering:** EINIGKEIT UND RECHT UND FREIHEIT

| Date | Mintage | F12 | VF20 | XF40 | MS60 | MS63 |
|---|---|---|---|---|---|---|
| 2001 A Sets only | 130,000 | — | — | — | — | 30.00 |
| 2001 A | 78,000 | PF63 30.00 | | | | |
| 2001 D Sets only | 130,000 | — | — | — | — | 30.00 |
| 2001 D | 78,000 | PF63 30.00 | | | | |
| 2001 F Sets only | 130,000 | — | — | — | — | 30.00 |
| 2001 F | 78,000 | PF63 30.00 | | | | |
| 2001 G Sets only | 130,000 | — | — | — | — | 30.00 |
| 2001 G | 78,000 | PF63 30.00 | | | | |
| 2001 J Sets only | 130,000 | — | — | — | — | 30.00 |
| 2001 J | 78,000 | PF63 30.00 | | | | |

## COMMEMORATIVE COINAGE

### KM# 204 10 MARK

15.50 g., 0.925 Silver 0.461 oz. ASW, 32.5 mm. **Obv:** Imperial eagle above denomination **Rev:** Naval Museum, Stralsund **Edge Lettering:** OHNE WASSER KEIN LEBEN

| Date | Mintage | F12 | VF20 | XF40 | MS60 | MS63 |
|---|---|---|---|---|---|---|
| 2001 A | 2,500,000 | — | — | — | 16.00 | 18.00 |
| 2001 A | 163,000 | PF65 22.00 | | | | |
| 2001 D | 163,000 | PF65 22.00 | | | | |
| 2001 F | 163,000 | PF65 22.00 | | | | |
| 2001 G | 163,000 | PF65 22.00 | | | | |
| 2001 J | 163,000 | PF65 22.00 | | | | |

### KM# 205 10 MARK

15.50 g., 0.925 Silver 0.461 oz. ASW, 32.5 mm. **Subject:** 200th Anniversary - Birth of Albert Gustav Lortzing **Obv:** Stylized eagle above denomination **Rev:** Portrait and music **Edge Lettering:** * WILDSCHUETZ * UNDINE * ZAR UND ZIMMERMANN *

| Date | Mintage | F12 | VF20 | XF40 | MS60 | MS63 |
|---|---|---|---|---|---|---|
| 2001 J | 2,500,000 | — | — | — | 16.00 | 18.00 |
| 2001 J | 163,000 | PF65 22.00 | | | | |
| 2001 | 163,000 | PF65 22.00 | | | | |
| 2001 | 163,000 | PF65 22.00 | | | | |
| 2001 | 163,000 | PF65 22.00 | | | | |
| 2001 | 163,000 | PF65 22.00 | | | | |

### KM# 206 10 MARK

15.50 g., 0.925 Silver 0.461 oz. ASW, 32.5 mm. **Subject:** Federal Court of Constitution: 50th Anniversary **Obv:** Stylized eagle above denomination **Rev:** Justice holding books and scale **Edge:** Lettered **Edge Lettering:** FÜR DAS GESAMTE DEUTSCHE VOLK

| Date | Mintage | F12 | VF20 | XF40 | MS60 | MS63 |
|---|---|---|---|---|---|---|
| 2001 G | 2,000,000 | — | — | — | 16.00 | 18.00 |
| 2001 G | 151,000 | PF65 22.00 | | | | |
| 2001 A | 151,000 | PF65 22.00 | | | | |
| 2001 D | 151,000 | PF65 22.00 | | | | |
| 2001 F | 151,000 | PF65 22.00 | | | | |
| 2001 J | 151,000 | PF65 22.00 | | | | |

## EURO COINAGE

European Union Issues

### KM# 207 EURO CENT

2.30 g., Copper Plated Steel, 16.25 mm. **Obv:** Oak leaves **Rev:** Denomination and globe **Edge:** Plain

| Date | Mintage | F12 | VF20 | XF40 | MS60 | MS63 |
|---|---|---|---|---|---|---|
| 2002 A | 800,090,000 | — | — | — | 0.35 | 0.50 |
| 2002 A | 75,000 | PF65 1.00 | | | | |
| 2002 D | 840,090,000 | — | — | — | 0.35 | 0.50 |
| 2002 D | 75,000 | PF65 1.00 | | | | |

| Date | Mintage | F12 | VF20 | XF40 | MS60 | MS63 |
|---|---|---|---|---|---|---|
| 2002 F | 960,090,000 | — | — | — | 0.35 | 0.50 |
| 2002 F | 75,000 | PF65 1.00 | | | | |
| 2002 G | 560,090,000 | — | — | — | 0.35 | 0.50 |
| 2002 G | 75,000 | PF65 1.00 | | | | |
| 2002 J | 840,090,000 | — | — | — | 0.35 | 0.50 |
| 2002 J | 75,000 | PF65 1.00 | | | | |
| 2003 A Sets only | 90,000 | — | — | — | — | 4.50 |
| 2003 A | 75,000 | PF65 1.00 | | | | |
| 2003 D Sets only | 90,000 | — | — | — | — | 4.50 |
| 2003 D | 75,000 | PF65 1.00 | | | | |
| 2003 F Sets only | 90,000 | — | — | — | — | 4.50 |
| 2003 F | 75,000 | PF65 1.00 | | | | |
| 2003 G Sets only | 90,000 | — | — | — | — | 4.50 |
| 2003 G | 75,000 | PF65 1.00 | | | | |
| 2003 J Sets only | 90,000 | — | — | — | — | 4.50 |
| 2003 J | 75,000 | PF65 1.00 | | | | |
| 2004 A | 280,090,000 | — | — | — | 0.35 | 0.50 |
| 2004 A | 75,000 | PF65 1.00 | | | | |
| 2004 D | 294,090,000 | — | — | — | 0.35 | 0.50 |
| 2004 D | 75,000 | PF65 1.00 | | | | |
| 2004 F | 336,090,000 | — | — | — | 0.35 | 0.50 |
| 2004 F | 75,000 | PF65 1.00 | | | | |
| 2004 G | 196,090,000 | — | — | — | 0.35 | 0.50 |
| 2004 G | 75,000 | PF65 1.00 | | | | |
| 2004 J | 294,090,000 | — | — | — | 0.35 | 0.50 |
| 2004 J | 75,000 | PF65 1.00 | | | | |
| 2005 A | 120,090,000 | — | — | — | 0.35 | 0.50 |
| 2005 A | 75,000 | PF65 1.00 | | | | |
| 2005 D | 126,090,000 | — | — | — | 0.35 | 0.50 |
| 2005 D | 75,000 | PF65 1.00 | | | | |
| 2005 F | 144,090,000 | — | — | — | 0.35 | 0.50 |
| 2005 F | 75,000 | PF65 1.00 | | | | |
| 2005 G | 84,090,000 | — | — | — | 0.35 | 0.50 |
| 2005 G | 75,000 | PF65 1.00 | | | | |
| 2005 J | 126,090,000 | — | — | — | 0.35 | 0.50 |
| 2005 J | 75,000 | PF65 1.00 | | | | |
| 2006 A Sets only | 90,000 | — | — | — | — | 4.50 |
| 2006 A | 75,000 | PF65 1.00 | | | | |
| 2006 D Sets only | 90,000 | — | — | — | — | 4.50 |
| 2006 D | 75,000 | PF65 1.00 | | | | |
| 2006 F Sets only | 90,000 | — | — | — | — | 4.50 |
| 2006 F | 75,000 | PF65 1.00 | | | | |
| 2006 G Sets only | 90,000 | — | — | — | — | 4.50 |
| 2006 G | 75,000 | PF65 1.00 | | | | |
| 2006 J Sets only | 90,000 | — | — | — | — | 4.50 |
| 2006 J | 75,000 | PF65 1.00 | | | | |
| 2007 A | 119,490,000 | — | — | — | 0.35 | 0.50 |
| 2007 A | 75,000 | PF65 1.00 | | | | |
| 2007 D | 125,460,000 | — | — | — | 0.35 | 0.50 |
| 2007 D | 75,000 | PF65 1.00 | | | | |
| 2007 F | 143,370,000 | — | — | — | 0.35 | 0.50 |
| 2007 F | 75,000 | PF65 1.00 | | | | |
| 2007 G | 83,670,000 | — | — | — | 0.35 | 0.50 |
| 2007 G | 75,000 | PF65 1.00 | | | | |
| 2007 J | 125,460,000 | — | — | — | 0.35 | 0.50 |
| 2007 J | 75,000 | PF65 1.00 | | | | |
| 2008 A | 101,280,000 | — | — | — | 0.35 | 0.50 |
| 2008 A | 70,000 | PF65 1.00 | | | | |
| 2008 D | 106,340,000 | — | — | — | 0.35 | 0.50 |
| 2008 D | 70,000 | PF65 1.00 | | | | |
| 2008 F | 121,520,000 | — | — | — | 0.35 | 0.50 |
| 2008 F | 70,000 | PF65 1.00 | | | | |
| 2008 G | 70,920,000 | — | — | — | 0.35 | 0.50 |
| 2008 G | 70,000 | PF65 1.00 | | | | |
| 2008 J | 106,340,000 | — | — | — | 0.35 | 0.50 |
| 2008 J | 70,000 | PF65 1.00 | | | | |
| 2009 A | 100,060,000 | — | — | — | 0.35 | 0.50 |
| 2009 A | 50,000 | PF65 1.00 | | | | |
| 2009 D | 105,060,000 | — | — | — | 0.35 | 0.50 |
| 2009 D | 50,000 | PF65 1.00 | | | | |
| 2009 F | 120,060,000 | — | — | — | 0.35 | 0.50 |
| 2009 F | 50,000 | PF65 1.00 | | | | |
| 2009 G | 70,060,000 | — | — | — | 0.35 | 0.50 |
| 2009 G | 50,000 | PF65 1.00 | | | | |
| 2009 J | 105,060,000 | — | — | — | 0.35 | 0.50 |
| 2009 J | 50,000 | PF65 1.00 | | | | |
| 2010 A | 94,454,000 | — | — | — | 0.35 | 0.50 |
| 2010 A | 45,150 | PF65 1.00 | | | | |
| 2010 D | 99,167,000 | — | — | — | 0.35 | 0.50 |
| 2010 D | 40,120 | PF65 1.00 | | | | |
| 2010 F | 113,327,000 | — | — | — | 0.35 | 0.50 |
| 2010 F | 40,120 | PF65 1.00 | | | | |
| 2010 G | 66,127,000 | — | — | — | 0.35 | 0.50 |
| 2010 G | 40,120 | PF65 1.00 | | | | |
| 2010 J | 99,167,000 | — | — | — | 0.35 | 0.50 |
| 2010 J | 40,120 | PF65 1.00 | | | | |
| 2011 A | 118,448,000 | — | — | — | 0.35 | 0.50 |
| 2011 A | 43,000 | PF65 1.25 | | | | |
| 2011 D | 124,364,000 | — | — | — | 0.35 | 0.50 |
| 2011 D | 37,000 | PF65 1.25 | | | | |
| 2011 F | 142,124,000 | — | — | — | 0.35 | 0.50 |
| 2011 F | 37,000 | PF65 1.25 | | | | |
| 2011 G | 82,924,000 | — | — | — | 0.35 | 0.50 |
| 2011 G | 37,000 | PF65 1.25 | | | | |
| 2011 J | 124,364,000 | — | — | — | 0.35 | 0.50 |
| 2011 J | 37,000 | PF65 1.25 | | | | |
| 2012 A | 104,245,000 | — | — | — | 0.35 | 0.50 |
| 2012 A | 40,000 | PF65 1.25 | | | | |
| 2012 D | 109,450,000 | — | — | — | 0.35 | 0.50 |
| 2012 D | Est. 40000 | PF65 1.25 | | | | |
| 2012 F | 125,080,000 | — | — | — | 0.35 | 0.50 |
| 2012 F | Est. 40000 | PF65 1.25 | | | | |
| 2012 G | Est. 72990 | — | — | — | 0.35 | 0.50 |
| 2012 G | Est. 40000 | PF65 1.25 | | | | |
| 2012 J | 109,450,000 | — | — | — | 0.35 | 0.50 |
| 2012 J | 32,000 | PF65 1.25 | | | | |
| 2013 A | Est. 60045000 | — | — | — | 0.20 | 0.35 |
| 2013 A | 35,000 | PF65 1.25 | | | | |
| 2013 D | — | — | — | — | 0.20 | 0.35 |
| 2013 D | Est. 40000 | PF65 1.25 | | | | |
| 2013 F | Est. 72040000 | — | — | — | 0.20 | 0.35 |
| 2013 F | Est. 40000 | PF65 1.25 | | | | |
| 2013 G | — | — | — | — | 0.20 | 0.35 |
| 2013 G | Est. 40000 | PF65 1.25 | | | | |
| 2013 J | Est. 63040000 | — | — | — | 0.20 | 0.35 |
| 2013 J | Est. 40000 | PF65 1.25 | | | | |
| 2014 A | — | — | — | — | 0.20 | 0.35 |
| 2014 A | — | PF65 1.25 | | | | |
| 2014 D | — | — | — | — | 0.20 | 0.35 |
| 2014 D | — | PF65 1.25 | | | | |
| 2014 F | — | — | — | — | 0.20 | 0.35 |
| 2014 F | — | PF65 1.25 | | | | |
| 2014 G | — | — | — | — | 0.20 | 0.35 |
| 2014 G | — | PF65 1.25 | | | | |
| 2014 J | — | — | — | — | 0.20 | 0.35 |
| 2014 J | — | PF65 1.25 | | | | |

## KM# 208 2 EURO CENT

3.06 g., Copper Plated Steel, 18.75 mm. **Obv:** Oak leaves **Rev:** Denomination and globe **Edge:** Grooved

| Date | Mintage | F12 | VF20 | XF40 | MS60 | MS63 |
|---|---|---|---|---|---|---|
| 2002 A | 360,090,000 | — | — | — | 0.50 | 0.65 |
| 2002 A | 75,000 | PF65 1.50 | | | | |
| 2002 D | 483,090,000 | — | — | — | 0.50 | 0.65 |
| 2002 D | 75,000 | PF65 1.50 | | | | |
| 2002 F | 507,890,000 | — | — | — | 0.50 | 0.65 |
| 2002 F | 75,000 | PF65 1.50 | | | | |
| 2002 G | 311,890,000 | — | — | — | 0.50 | 0.65 |
| 2002 G | 75,000 | PF65 1.50 | | | | |
| 2002 J | 419,490,000 | — | — | — | 0.50 | 0.65 |
| 2002 J | 75,000 | PF65 1.50 | | | | |
| 2003 A | 200,090,000 | — | — | — | 0.50 | 0.65 |
| 2003 A | 75,000 | PF65 1.50 | | | | |
| 2003 D | 105,090,000 | — | — | — | 0.50 | 0.65 |
| 2003 D | 75,000 | PF65 1.50 | | | | |
| 2003 F | 164,290,000 | — | — | — | 0.50 | 0.65 |
| 2003 F | 75,000 | PF65 1.50 | | | | |
| 2003 G | 80,290,000 | — | — | — | 0.50 | 0.65 |
| 2003 G | 75,000 | PF65 1.50 | | | | |
| 2003 J | 168,690,000 | — | — | — | 0.50 | 0.65 |
| 2003 J | 75,000 | PF65 1.50 | | | | |
| 2004 A | 127,090,000 | — | — | — | 0.50 | 0.65 |
| 2004 A | 75,000 | PF65 1.50 | | | | |
| 2004 D | 133,440,000 | — | — | — | 0.50 | 0.65 |
| 2004 D | 75,000 | PF65 1.50 | | | | |
| 2004 F | 152,490,000 | — | — | — | 0.50 | 0.65 |
| 2004 F | 75,000 | PF65 1.50 | | | | |
| 2004 G | 88,990,000 | — | — | — | 0.50 | 0.65 |
| 2004 G | 75,000 | PF65 1.50 | | | | |
| 2004 J | 133,440,000 | — | — | — | 0.50 | 0.65 |
| 2004 J | 75,000 | PF65 1.50 | | | | |
| 2005 A | 73,090,000 | — | — | — | 0.50 | 0.65 |
| 2005 A | 75,000 | PF65 1.50 | | | | |
| 2005 D | 76,740,000 | — | — | — | 0.50 | 0.65 |
| 2005 D | 75,000 | PF65 1.50 | | | | |
| 2005 F | 87,690,000 | — | — | — | 0.50 | 0.65 |
| 2005 F | 75,000 | PF65 1.50 | | | | |
| 2005 G | 51,590,000 | — | — | — | 0.50 | 0.65 |
| 2005 G | 75,000 | PF65 1.50 | | | | |
| 2005 J | 76,740,000 | — | — | — | 0.50 | 0.65 |
| 2005 J | 75,000 | PF65 1.50 | | | | |
| 2006 A | 108,090,000 | — | — | — | 0.50 | 0.65 |
| 2006 A | 75,000 | PF65 1.50 | | | | |
| 2006 D | 113,490,000 | — | — | — | 0.50 | 0.65 |
| 2006 D | 75,000 | PF65 1.50 | | | | |
| 2006 F | 129,690,000 | — | — | — | 0.50 | 0.65 |
| 2006 F | 75,000 | PF65 1.50 | | | | |
| 2006 G | 75,690,000 | — | — | — | 0.50 | 0.65 |
| 2006 G | 75,000 | PF65 1.50 | | | | |
| 2006 J | 148,490,000 | — | — | — | 0.50 | 0.65 |
| 2006 J | 75,000 | PF65 1.50 | | | | |
| 2007 A | 100,090,000 | — | — | — | 0.50 | 0.65 |
| 2007 A | 75,000 | PF65 1.50 | | | | |
| 2007 D | 105,090,000 | — | — | — | 0.50 | 0.65 |
| 2007 D | 75,000 | PF65 1.50 | | | | |
| 2007 F | 120,090,000 | — | — | — | 0.50 | 0.65 |
| 2007 F | 75,000 | PF65 1.50 | | | | |
| 2007 G | 70,090,000 | — | — | — | 0.50 | 0.65 |
| 2007 G | 75,000 | PF65 1.50 | | | | |
| 2007 J | 105,090,000 | — | — | — | 0.50 | 0.65 |
| 2007 J | 75,000 | PF65 1.50 | | | | |
| 2008 A | 80,080,000 | — | — | — | 0.50 | 0.65 |
| 2008 A | 70,000 | PF65 1.50 | | | | |
| 2008 D | 84,080,000 | — | — | — | 0.50 | 0.65 |
| 2008 D | 70,000 | PF65 1.50 | | | | |
| 2008 F | 96,080,000 | — | — | — | 0.50 | 0.65 |
| 2008 F | 70,000 | PF65 1.50 | | | | |
| 2008 G | 56,080,000 | — | — | — | 0.50 | 0.65 |
| 2008 G | 70,000 | PF65 1.50 | | | | |
| 2008 J | 84,080,000 | — | — | — | 0.50 | 0.65 |
| 2008 J | 70,000 | PF65 1.50 | | | | |
| 2009 A | 59,060,000 | — | — | — | 0.50 | 0.65 |
| 2009 A | 50,000 | PF65 1.50 | | | | |
| 2009 D | 62,010,000 | — | — | — | 0.50 | 0.65 |
| 2009 D | 50,000 | PF65 1.50 | | | | |
| 2009 F | 70,860,000 | — | — | — | 0.50 | 0.65 |
| 2009 F | 50,000 | PF65 1.50 | | | | |
| 2009 G | 41,360,000 | — | — | — | 0.50 | 0.65 |
| 2009 G | 50,000 | PF65 1.50 | | | | |
| 2009 J | 62,010,000 | — | — | — | 0.50 | 0.65 |
| 2009 J | 50,000 | PF65 1.50 | | | | |
| 2010 A | 72,854,000 | — | — | — | 0.50 | 0.65 |
| 2010 A | 45,150 | PF65 1.50 | | | | |
| 2010 D | 76,487,000 | — | — | — | 0.50 | 0.65 |
| 2010 D | 40,120 | PF65 1.50 | | | | |
| 2010 F | 87,407,000 | — | — | — | 0.50 | 0.65 |
| 2010 F | 40,120 | PF65 1.50 | | | | |
| 2010 G | 51,007,000 | — | — | — | 0.50 | 0.65 |
| 2010 G | 40,120 | PF65 1.50 | | | | |
| 2010 J | 76,487,000 | — | — | — | 0.50 | 0.65 |
| 2010 J | 40,120 | PF65 1.50 | | | | |
| 2011 A | 100,448,000 | — | — | — | 0.50 | 0.65 |
| 2011 A | Est. 43000 | PF65 1.50 | | | | |
| 2011 D | 105,464,000 | — | — | — | 0.50 | 0.65 |
| 2011 D | 37,000 | PF65 1.50 | | | | |
| 2011 F | 120,524,000 | — | — | — | 0.50 | 0.65 |
| 2011 F | Est. 37000 | PF65 1.50 | | | | |
| 2011 G | 70,324,000 | — | — | — | 0.50 | 0.65 |
| 2011 G | 37,000 | PF65 1.50 | | | | |
| 2011 G | 105,464,000 | — | — | — | 0.50 | 0.65 |
| 2011 J | Est. 37000 | PF65 1.50 | | | | |
| 2012 A | Est. 77490000 | — | — | — | 0.50 | 0.65 |
| 2012 A | Est. 40000 | PF65 1.75 | | | | |
| 2012 D | Est. 81320000 | — | — | — | 0.50 | 0.65 |
| 2012 D | Est. 40000 | PF65 1.75 | | | | |
| 2012 F | Est. 92930000 | — | — | — | 0.50 | 0.65 |
| 2012 F | 32,000 | PF65 1.75 | | | | |
| 2012 G | Est. 54230000 | — | — | — | 0.50 | 0.65 |
| 2012 G | Est. 40000 | PF65 1.75 | | | | |
| 2012 J | Est. 81320000 | — | — | — | 0.50 | 0.65 |
| 2012 J | Est. 40000 | PF65 1.75 | | | | |
| 2013 A | Est. 60045000 | — | — | — | 0.50 | 0.65 |
| 2013 A | Est. 35000 | PF65 1.75 | | | | |
| 2013 D | Est. 63040000 | — | — | — | 0.50 | 0.65 |
| 2013 D | Est. 30000 | PF65 1.75 | | | | |
| 2013 F | Est. 72040000 | — | — | — | 0.50 | 0.65 |
| 2013 F | Est. 30000 | PF65 1.75 | | | | |
| 2013 G | Est. 42040000 | — | — | — | 0.50 | 0.65 |
| 2013 G | Est. 30000 | PF65 1.75 | | | | |
| 2013 J | Est. 63040000 | — | — | — | 0.50 | 0.65 |
| 2013 J | Est. 30000 | PF65 1.75 | | | | |
| 2014 A | — | — | — | — | 0.50 | 0.65 |
| 2014 A | — | PF65 1.75 | | | | |
| 2014 D | — | — | — | — | 0.50 | 0.65 |
| 2014 D | — | PF65 1.75 | | | | |
| 2014 F | — | — | — | — | 0.50 | 0.65 |
| 2014 F | — | PF65 1.75 | | | | |
| 2014 G | — | — | — | — | 0.50 | 0.65 |
| 2014 G | — | PF65 1.75 | | | | |
| 2014 J | — | — | — | — | 0.50 | 0.65 |
| 2014 J | — | PF65 1.75 | | | | |

## KM# 209 5 EURO CENT

3.92 g., Copper Plated Steel, 21.25 mm. **Obv:** Oak leaves **Rev:** Denomination and globe **Edge:** Plain

| Date | Mintage | F12 | VF20 | XF40 | MS60 | MS63 |
|---|---|---|---|---|---|---|
| 2002 A | 480,090,000 | — | — | — | 0.75 | 1.00 |
| 2002 A | 75,000 | PF65 2.00 | | | | |
| 2002 D | 504,090,000 | — | — | — | 0.75 | 1.00 |
| 2002 D | 75,000 | PF65 2.00 | | | | |
| 2002 F | 576,090,000 | — | — | — | 0.75 | 1.00 |
| 2002 F | 75,000 | PF65 2.00 | | | | |
| 2002 G | 336,090,000 | — | — | — | 0.75 | 1.00 |
| 2002 G | 75,000 | PF65 2.00 | | | | |
| 2002 J | 504,090,000 | — | — | — | 0.75 | 1.00 |
| 2002 J | 90,000 | PF65 2.00 | | | | |
| 2003 A Sets only | 75,000 | — | — | — | — | 4.50 |
| 2003 A | 90,000 | PF65 2.00 | | | | |
| 2003 D Sets only | 75,000 | — | — | — | — | 4.50 |

| Date | Mintage | F12 | VF20 | XF40 | MS60 | MS63 |
|---|---|---|---|---|---|---|
| 2003 D | 90,000 | PF65 2.00 | | | | |
| 2003 F Sets only | 75,000 | — | — | — | — | 4.50 |
| 2003 F | 90,000 | PF65 2.00 | | | | |
| 2003 G Sets only | 75,000 | — | — | — | — | 4.50 |
| 2003 G | 90,000 | PF65 2.00 | | | | |
| 2003 J Sets only | 90,000 | — | — | — | — | 4.50 |
| 2003 J | 75,000 | PF65 2.00 | | | | |
| 2004 A | 112,090,000 | — | — | — | 0.75 | 1.00 |
| 2004 A | 75,000 | PF65 2.00 | | | | |
| 2004 D | 117,690,000 | — | — | — | 0.75 | 1.00 |
| 2004 D | 75,000 | PF65 2.00 | | | | |
| 2004 F | 134,490,000 | — | — | — | 0.75 | 1.00 |
| 2004 F | 75,000 | PF65 2.00 | | | | |
| 2004 G | 78,490,000 | — | — | — | 0.75 | 1.00 |
| 2004 G | 75,000 | PF65 2.00 | | | | |
| 2004 J | 117,690,000 | — | — | — | 0.75 | 1.00 |
| 2004 J | 75,000 | PF65 2.00 | | | | |
| 2005 A | 44,090,000 | — | — | — | 0.75 | 1.00 |
| 2005 A | 75,000 | PF65 2.00 | | | | |
| 2005 D | 46,290,000 | — | — | — | 0.75 | 1.00 |
| 2005 D | 75,000 | PF65 2.00 | | | | |
| 2005 F | 52,890,000 | — | — | — | 0.75 | 1.00 |
| 2005 F | 75,000 | PF65 2.00 | | | | |
| 2005 G | 30,890,000 | — | — | — | 0.75 | 1.00 |
| 2005 G | 75,000 | PF65 2.00 | | | | |
| 2005 J | 46,290,000 | — | — | — | 0.75 | 1.00 |
| 2005 J | 75,000 | PF65 2.00 | | | | |
| 2006 A | 27,090,000 | — | — | — | 0.75 | 1.00 |
| 2006 A | 75,000 | PF65 2.00 | | | | |
| 2006 D | 28,440,000 | — | — | — | 0.75 | 1.00 |
| 2006 D | 75,000 | PF65 2.00 | | | | |
| 2006 F | 32,490,000 | — | — | — | 0.75 | 1.00 |
| 2006 F | 75,000 | PF65 2.00 | | | | |
| 2006 G | 18,990,000 | — | — | — | 0.75 | 1.00 |
| 2006 G | 75,000 | PF65 2.00 | | | | |
| 2006 J | 28,440,000 | — | — | — | 0.75 | 1.00 |
| 2006 J | 75,000 | PF65 2.00 | | | | |
| 2007 A | 52,490,000 | — | — | — | 0.75 | 1.00 |
| 2007 A | 75,000 | PF65 2.00 | | | | |
| 2007 D | 55,110,000 | — | — | — | 0.75 | 1.00 |
| 2007 D | 75,000 | PF65 2.00 | | | | |
| 2007 F | 62,970,000 | — | — | — | 0.75 | 1.00 |
| 2007 F | 75,000 | PF65 2.00 | | | | |
| 2007 G | 36,770,000 | — | — | — | 0.75 | 1.00 |
| 2007 G | 75,000 | PF65 2.00 | | | | |
| 2007 J | 55,110,000 | — | — | — | 0.75 | 1.00 |
| 2007 J | 75,000 | PF65 2.00 | | | | |
| 2008 A | 29,280,000 | — | — | — | 0.75 | 1.00 |
| 2008 A | 70,000 | PF65 2.00 | | | | |
| 2008 D | 30,740,000 | — | — | — | 0.75 | 1.00 |
| 2008 D | 70,000 | PF65 2.00 | | | | |
| 2008 F | 35,120,000 | — | — | — | 0.75 | 1.00 |
| 2008 F | 70,000 | PF65 2.00 | | | | |
| 2008 G | 24,520,000 | — | — | — | 0.75 | 1.00 |
| 2008 G | 70,000 | PF65 2.00 | | | | |
| 2008 J | 30,740,000 | — | — | — | 0.75 | 1.00 |
| 2008 J | 70,000 | PF65 2.00 | | | | |
| 2009 A | 39,660,000 | — | — | — | 0.75 | 1.00 |
| 2009 A | 50,000 | PF65 2.00 | | | | |
| 2009 D | 41,640,000 | — | — | — | 0.75 | 1.00 |
| 2009 D | 50,000 | PF65 2.00 | | | | |
| 2009 F | 47,580,000 | — | — | — | 0.75 | 1.00 |
| 2009 F | 50,000 | PF65 2.00 | | | | |
| 2009 G | 27,780,000 | — | — | — | 0.75 | 1.00 |
| 2009 G | 50,000 | PF65 2.00 | | | | |
| 2009 J | 41,640,000 | — | — | — | 0.75 | 1.00 |
| 2009 J | 50,000 | PF65 2.00 | | | | |
| 2010 A | 39,854,000 | — | — | — | 0.75 | 1.00 |
| 2010 A | 45,150 | PF65 2.00 | | | | |
| 2010 D | 41,837,000 | — | — | — | 0.75 | 1.00 |
| 2010 D | 40,120 | PF65 2.00 | | | | |
| 2010 F | 47,807,000 | — | — | — | 0.75 | 1.00 |
| 2010 F | 40,120 | PF65 2.00 | | | | |
| 2010 G | 20,903,000 | — | — | — | 0.75 | 1.00 |
| 2010 G | 40,120 | PF65 2.00 | | | | |
| 2010 J | 41,837,000 | — | — | — | 0.75 | 1.00 |
| 2010 J | 40,120 | PF65 2.00 | | | | |
| 2011 A | 59,248,000 | — | — | — | 0.75 | 1.00 |
| 2011 A | Est. 43000 | PF65 2.25 | | | | |
| 2011 D | 62,204,000 | — | — | — | 0.75 | 1.00 |
| 2011 D | Est. 37000 | PF65 2.25 | | | | |
| 2011 F | 71,084,000 | — | — | — | 0.75 | 1.00 |
| 2011 F | Est. 37000 | PF65 2.25 | | | | |
| 2011 G | 41,484,000 | — | — | — | 0.75 | 1.00 |
| 2011 G | 37,000 | PF65 2.25 | | | | |
| 2011 J | 62,204,000 | — | — | — | 0.75 | 1.00 |
| 2011 J | Est. 37000 | PF65 2.25 | | | | |
| 2012 A | 41,845,000 | — | — | — | 0.75 | 1.00 |
| 2012 A | 40,000 | PF65 2.25 | | | | |
| 2012 D | 43,930,000 | — | — | — | 0.75 | 1.00 |
| 2012 D | Est. 40000 | PF65 2.25 | | | | |
| 2012 F | 50,200,000 | — | — | — | 0.75 | 1.00 |
| 2012 F | Est. 40000 | PF65 2.25 | | | | |
| 2012 G | 29,300,000 | — | — | — | 0.75 | 1.00 |
| 2012 G | Est. 40000 | PF65 2.25 | | | | |
| 2012 J | 43,930,000 | — | — | — | 0.75 | 1.00 |
| 2012 J | Est. 40000 | PF65 2.25 | | | | |
| 2013 A | Est. 32040000 | — | — | — | 0.40 | 0.75 |
| 2013 A | Est. 40000 | PF65 2.25 | | | | |
| 2013 D | Est. 33640000 | — | — | — | 0.40 | 0.75 |
| 2013 D | Est. 40000 | PF65 2.25 | | | | |
| 2013 F | Est. 38440000 | — | — | — | 0.40 | 0.75 |
| 2013 F | Est. 40000 | PF65 2.25 | | | | |
| 2013 G | Est. 22040000 | — | — | — | 0.40 | 0.75 |
| 2013 G | Est. 40000 | PF65 2.25 | | | | |
| 2013 J | Est. 33640000 | — | — | — | 0.40 | 0.75 |
| 2013 J | Est. 40000 | PF65 2.50 | | | | |
| 2014 A | — | — | — | — | 0.75 | 1.00 |
| 2014 D | — | — | — | — | 0.75 | 1.00 |
| 2014 F | — | — | — | — | 0.75 | 1.00 |
| 2014 G | — | — | — | — | 0.75 | 1.00 |
| 2014 J | — | — | — | — | 0.75 | 1.00 |

### KM# 210 10 EURO CENT

4.10 g., Brass, 19.75 mm. **Obv:** Brandenburg Gate **Rev:** Denomination and map **Edge:** Reeded

| Date | Mintage | F12 | VF20 | XF40 | MS60 | MS63 |
|---|---|---|---|---|---|---|
| 2002 A | 696,240,000 | — | — | — | 0.75 | 1.00 |
| 2002 A | 75,000 | PF65 2.00 | | | | |
| 2002 D | 722,040,000 | — | — | — | 0.75 | 1.00 |
| 2002 D | 75,000 | PF65 2.00 | | | | |
| 2002 F | 838,890,000 | — | — | — | 0.75 | 1.00 |
| 2002 F | 75,000 | PF65 2.00 | | | | |
| 2002 G | 494,390,000 | — | — | — | 0.75 | 1.00 |
| 2002 G | 75,000 | PF65 2.00 | | | | |
| 2002 J | 758,730,000 | — | — | — | 0.75 | 1.00 |
| 2002 J | 75,000 | PF65 2.00 | | | | |
| 2003 A | 50,750,000 | — | — | — | 1.25 | 1.50 |
| 2003 A | 75,000 | PF65 2.00 | | | | |
| 2003 D | 50,940,000 | — | — | — | 1.25 | 1.50 |
| 2003 D | 75,000 | PF65 2.00 | | | | |
| 2003 F | 6,090,000 | — | — | — | 2.00 | 2.50 |
| 2003 F | 75,000 | PF65 2.00 | | | | |
| 2003 G | 13,090,000 | — | — | — | 1.25 | 1.50 |
| 2003 G | 75,000 | PF65 2.00 | | | | |
| 2003 J | 25,590,000 | — | — | — | 1.25 | 1.50 |
| 2003 J | 75,000 | PF65 2.00 | | | | |
| 2004 A Sets only | 99,000 | — | — | — | — | 4.50 |
| 2004 A | 75,000 | PF65 2.00 | | | | |
| 2004 D | 11,290,000 | — | — | — | 1.25 | 1.50 |
| 2004 D | 75,000 | PF65 2.00 | | | | |
| 2004 F | 51,450,000 | — | — | — | 1.25 | 1.50 |
| 2004 F | 75,000 | PF65 2.00 | | | | |
| 2004 G | 15,550,000 | — | — | — | 1.25 | 1.50 |
| 2004 G | 75,000 | PF65 2.00 | | | | |
| 2004 J Sets only | 90,000 | — | — | — | — | 4.50 |
| 2004 J | 75,000 | PF65 2.00 | | | | |
| 2005 A Sets only | 90,000 | — | — | — | — | 4.50 |
| 2005 A | 75,000 | PF65 2.00 | | | | |
| 2005 D Sets only | 90,000 | — | — | — | — | 4.50 |
| 2005 D | 75,000 | PF65 2.00 | | | | |
| 2005 F Sets only | 90,000 | — | — | — | — | 4.50 |
| 2005 F | 75,000 | PF65 2.00 | | | | |
| 2005 G Sets only | 90,000 | — | — | — | — | 4.50 |
| 2005 G | 75,000 | PF65 2.00 | | | | |
| 2005 J Sets only | 90,000 | — | — | — | — | 4.50 |
| 2005 J | 75,000 | PF65 2.00 | | | | |
| 2006 A Sets only | 90,000 | — | — | — | — | 4.50 |
| 2006 A | 75,000 | PF65 2.00 | | | | |
| 2006 D Sets only | 90,000 | — | — | — | — | 4.50 |
| 2006 D | 75,000 | PF65 2.00 | | | | |
| 2006 F Sets only | 90,000 | — | — | — | — | 4.50 |
| 2006 F | 75,000 | PF65 2.00 | | | | |
| 2006 G Sets only | 90,000 | — | — | — | — | 4.50 |
| 2006 G | 75,000 | PF65 2.00 | | | | |
| 2006 J Sets only | 90,000 | — | — | — | — | 4.50 |
| 2006 J | 75,000 | PF65 2.00 | | | | |

### KM# 254 10 EURO CENT

4.10 g., Brass, 19.75 mm. **Obv:** Brandenburg Gate **Rev:** Relief map of Western Europe, stars, lines and value **Edge:** Reeded

| Date | Mintage | F12 | VF20 | XF40 | MS60 | MS63 |
|---|---|---|---|---|---|---|
| 2007 A Sets only | 90,000 | — | — | — | — | 4.50 |
| 2007 A | 75,000 | PF65 2.00 | | | | |
| 2007 D Sets only | 90,000 | — | — | — | — | 4.50 |
| 2007 D | 75,000 | PF65 2.00 | | | | |
| 2007 F Sets only | 90,000 | — | — | — | — | 4.50 |
| 2007 F | 75,000 | PF65 2.00 | | | | |
| 2007 G Sets only | 90,000 | — | — | — | — | 4.50 |
| 2007 G | 75,000 | PF65 2.00 | | | | |
| 2007 J Sets only | 90,000 | — | — | — | — | 4.50 |
| 2007 J | 75,000 | PF65 2.00 | | | | |
| 2008 A Sets only | 80,000 | — | — | — | — | 4.50 |
| 2008 A | 70,000 | PF65 2.00 | | | | |
| 2008 D Sets only | 80,000 | — | — | — | — | 4.50 |
| 2008 D | 70,000 | PF65 2.00 | | | | |
| 2008 F Sets only | 80,000 | — | — | — | — | 4.50 |
| 2008 F | 70,000 | PF65 2.00 | | | | |
| 2008 G Sets only | 80,000 | — | — | — | — | 4.50 |
| 2008 G | 70,000 | PF65 2.00 | | | | |
| 2008 J Sets only | 80,000 | — | — | — | — | 4.50 |
| 2008 J | 70,000 | PF65 2.00 | | | | |
| 2009 A Sets only | 60,000 | — | — | — | — | 4.50 |
| 2009 A | 50,000 | PF65 2.00 | | | | |
| 2009 D Sets only | 60,000 | — | — | — | — | 4.50 |
| 2009 D | 50,000 | PF65 2.00 | | | | |
| 2009 F Sets only | 60,000 | — | — | — | — | 4.50 |
| 2009 F | 50,000 | PF65 2.00 | | | | |
| 2009 G Sets only | 60,000 | — | — | — | — | 4.50 |
| 2009 G | 50,000 | PF65 2.00 | | | | |
| 2009 J Sets only | 60,000 | — | — | — | — | 4.50 |
| 2009 J | 50,000 | PF65 2.00 | | | | |
| 2010 A Sets only | 53,800 | — | — | — | — | 4.00 |
| 2010 A | 45,150 | PF65 2.00 | | | | |
| 2010 D Sets only | 46,800 | — | — | — | — | 4.00 |
| 2010 D | 40,120 | PF65 2.00 | | | | |
| 2010 F Sets only | 46,800 | — | — | — | — | 4.00 |
| 2010 F | 40,120 | PF65 2.00 | | | | |
| 2010 G Sets only | 46,800 | — | — | — | — | 4.00 |
| 2010 G | 40,120 | PF65 2.00 | | | | |
| 2010 J Sets only | 46,800 | — | — | — | — | 4.00 |
| 2010 J | 40,120 | PF65 2.00 | | | | |
| 2011 A Sets only | Est. 55000 | — | — | — | — | 4.00 |
| 2011 A | 48,000 | PF65 2.75 | | | | |
| 2011 D Sets only | 44,000 | — | — | — | — | 4.00 |
| 2011 D | 37,000 | PF65 2.75 | | | | |
| 2011 F Sets only | 44,000 | — | — | — | — | 4.00 |
| 2011 F | 37,000 | PF65 2.75 | | | | |
| 2011 G Sets only | 44,000 | — | — | — | — | 4.00 |
| 2011 G | 37,000 | PF65 2.75 | | | | |
| 2011 J Sets only | 44,000 | — | — | — | — | 4.00 |
| 2011 J | 37,000 | PF65 2.75 | | | | |
| 2012 A Sets only | 40,000 | — | — | — | — | 3.00 |
| 2012 A | — | PF65 2.75 | | | | |
| 2012 D Sets only | Est. 50000 | — | — | — | — | 3.00 |
| 2012 D | Est. 40000 | PF65 2.75 | | | | |
| 2012 F Sets only | Est. 50000 | — | — | — | — | 3.00 |
| 2012 F | Est. 40000 | PF65 2.75 | | | | |
| 2012 G Sets only | Est. 50000 | — | — | — | — | 3.00 |
| 2012 G | Est. 40000 | PF65 2.75 | | | | |
| 2012 J Sets only | Est. 50000 | — | — | — | — | 3.00 |
| 2012 J | Est. 40000 | PF65 2.75 | | | | |
| 2013 A Sets only | Est. 40000 | — | — | — | — | 3.00 |
| 2013 A | 35,000 | PF65 2.75 | | | | |
| 2013 D Sets only | Est. 35000 | — | — | — | — | 3.00 |
| 2013 D | 30,000 | PF65 2.75 | | | | |
| 2013 F Sets only | Est. 35000 | — | — | — | — | 3.00 |
| 2013 F | Est. 40000 | PF65 2.75 | | | | |
| 2013 F Sets only | Est. 30000 | — | — | — | — | 3.00 |
| 2013 G | — | PF65 2.75 | | | | |
| 2013 J Sets only | Est. 35000 | — | — | — | — | 3.00 |
| 2013 J | Est. 40000 | PF65 2.75 | | | | |
| 2014 A | — | — | — | — | — | 3.00 |
| 2014 A | — | PF65 2.75 | | | | |
| 2014 D | — | — | — | — | — | 3.00 |
| 2014 F | — | — | — | — | — | 3.00 |
| 2014 F | — | PF65 2.75 | | | | |
| 2014 G | — | — | — | — | — | 3.00 |
| 2014 G | — | PF65 2.75 | | | | |
| 2014 J | — | — | — | — | — | 3.00 |
| 2014 J | — | PF65 2.75 | | | | |
| 2014 D | — | PF65 2.75 | | | | |

### KM# 211 20 EURO CENT

5.74 g., Brass, 22.25 mm. **Obv:** Brandenburg Gate **Rev:** Denomination and map **Edge:** Notched

| Date | Mintage | F12 | VF20 | XF40 | MS60 | MS63 |
|---|---|---|---|---|---|---|
| 2002 A | 378,240,000 | — | — | — | 1.00 | 1.50 |
| 2002 A | 75,000 | PF65 3.00 | | | | |
| 2002 D | 367,090,000 | — | — | — | 1.00 | 1.50 |
| 2002 D | 75,000 | PF65 3.00 | | | | |
| 2002 F | 421,690,000 | — | — | — | 1.00 | 1.50 |
| 2002 F | 75,000 | PF65 3.00 | | | | |
| 2002 G | 251,990,000 | — | — | — | 1.00 | 1.50 |
| 2002 G | 75,000 | PF65 3.00 | | | | |
| 2002 J | 441,090,000 | — | — | — | 1.00 | 1.50 |
| 2002 J | 75,000 | PF65 3.00 | | | | |
| 2003 A | 41,950,000 | — | — | — | 1.00 | 1.50 |
| 2003 A | 75,000 | PF65 3.00 | | | | |
| 2003 D | 24,190,000 | — | — | — | 1.00 | 1.50 |
| 2003 D | 75,000 | PF65 3.00 | | | | |
| 2003 F | 82,490,000 | — | — | — | 1.00 | 1.50 |
| 2003 F | 75,000 | PF65 3.00 | | | | |
| 2003 G | 42,190,000 | — | — | — | 1.00 | 1.50 |
| 2003 G | 75,000 | PF65 3.00 | | | | |
| 2003 J Sets only | 90,000 | — | — | — | — | 4.50 |
| 2003 J | 75,000 | PF65 3.00 | | | | |
| 2004 A Sets only | 90,000 | — | — | — | — | 4.50 |
| 2004 A | 75,000 | PF65 3.00 | | | | |
| 2004 D | 49,850,000 | — | — | — | — | 2.50 |

| Date | Mintage | F12 | VF20 | XF40 | MS60 | MS63 |
|---|---|---|---|---|---|---|
| 2004 D | 75,000 | PF65 3.00 | | | | |
| 2004 F Sets only | 90,000 | — | — | — | — | 4.50 |
| 2004 F | 75,000 | PF65 3.00 | | | | |
| 2004 G Sets only | 90,000 | — | — | — | — | 4.50 |
| 2004 G | 75,000 | PF65 3.00 | | | | |
| 2004 J Sets only | 90,000 | — | — | — | — | 4.50 |
| 2004 J | 75,000 | PF65 3.00 | | | | |
| 2005 A | 8,090,000 | — | — | — | 1.00 | 1.50 |
| 2005 A | 75,000 | PF65 3.00 | | | | |
| 2005 D | 8,490,000 | — | — | — | 1.00 | 1.50 |
| 2005 D | 75,000 | PF65 3.00 | | | | |
| 2005 F | 9,690,000 | — | — | — | 1.00 | 1.50 |
| 2005 F | 75,000 | PF65 3.00 | | | | |
| 2005 G | 5,690,000 | — | — | — | 1.00 | 1.50 |
| 2005 G | 75,000 | PF65 3.00 | | | | |
| 2005 J | 8,490,000 | — | — | — | 1.00 | 1.50 |
| 2005 J | 75,000 | PF65 3.00 | | | | |
| 2006 A | 39,090,000 | — | — | — | 1.00 | 1.50 |
| 2006 A | 75,000 | PF65 3.00 | | | | |
| 2006 D | 41,040,000 | — | — | — | 1.00 | 1.50 |
| 2006 D | 75,000 | PF65 3.00 | | | | |
| 2006 F | 46,890,000 | — | — | — | 1.00 | 1.50 |
| 2006 F | 75,000 | PF65 3.00 | | | | |
| 2006 G | 27,390,000 | — | — | — | 1.00 | 1.50 |
| 2006 G | 75,000 | PF65 3.00 | | | | |
| 2006 J | 41,040,000 | — | — | — | 1.00 | 1.50 |
| 2006 J | 75,000 | PF65 3.00 | | | | |
| 2007 F Error die paring | — | — | — | 50.00 | 65.00 | 85.00 |

## KM# 255 20 EURO CENT

5.74 g., Brass, 22.25 mm. **Obv:** Brandenburg Gate **Rev:** Relief map of Western Europe, stars, lines and value **Edge:** Notched

| Date | Mintage | F12 | VF20 | XF40 | MS60 | MS63 |
|---|---|---|---|---|---|---|
| 2007 A | 21,690,000 | — | — | — | 1.00 | 1.50 |
| 2007 A | 75,000 | PF65 3.00 | | | | |
| 2007 D | 22,770,000 | — | — | — | 1.00 | 1.50 |
| 2007 D | 75,000 | PF65 3.00 | | | | |
| 2007 F | 26,010,000 | — | — | — | 1.00 | 1.50 |
| 2007 F | 75,000 | PF65 3.00 | | | | |
| 2007 G | 15,210,000 | — | — | — | 1.00 | 1.50 |
| 2007 G | 75,000 | PF65 3.00 | | | | |
| 2007 J | 23,020,000 | — | — | — | 1.00 | 1.50 |
| 2007 J | 75,000 | PF65 3.00 | | | | |
| 2008 A | 15,880,000 | — | — | — | 1.00 | 1.50 |
| 2008 A | 70,000 | PF65 3.00 | | | | |
| 2008 D | 16,670,000 | — | — | — | 1.00 | 1.50 |
| 2008 D | 70,000 | PF65 3.00 | | | | |
| 2008 F | 19,040,000 | — | — | — | 1.00 | 1.50 |
| 2008 F | 70,000 | PF65 3.00 | | | | |
| 2008 G | 11,140,000 | — | — | — | 1.00 | 1.50 |
| 2008 G | 70,000 | PF65 3.00 | | | | |
| 2008 J | 16,420,000 | — | — | — | 1.00 | 1.50 |
| 2008 J | 70,000 | PF65 3.00 | | | | |
| 2009 A | 21,660,000 | — | — | — | 1.00 | 1.50 |
| 2009 A | 50,000 | PF65 3.00 | | | | |
| 2009 D | 22,740,000 | — | — | — | 1.00 | 1.50 |
| 2009 D | 50,000 | PF65 3.00 | | | | |
| 2009 F | 25,980,000 | — | — | — | 1.00 | 1.50 |
| 2009 F | 50,000 | PF65 3.00 | | | | |
| 2009 G | 15,180,000 | — | — | — | 1.00 | 1.50 |
| 2009 G | 50,000 | PF65 3.00 | | | | |
| 2009 J | 22,740,000 | — | — | — | 1.00 | 1.50 |
| 2009 J | 50,000 | PF65 3.00 | | | | |
| 2010 A | 24,454,000 | — | — | — | 1.00 | 1.50 |
| 2010 A | 45,150 | PF65 3.00 | | | | |
| 2010 D | 25,667,000 | — | — | — | 1.00 | 1.50 |
| 2010 D | 40,120 | PF65 3.00 | | | | |
| 2010 F | 29,327,000 | — | — | — | 1.00 | 1.50 |
| 2010 F | 40,120 | PF65 3.00 | | | | |
| 2010 G | 17,127,000 | — | — | — | 1.00 | 1.50 |
| 2010 G | 40,120 | PF65 3.00 | | | | |
| 2010 J | 25,667,000 | — | — | — | 1.00 | 1.50 |
| 2010 J | 40,120 | PF65 3.00 | | | | |
| 2011 A | 33,048,000 | — | — | — | 1.00 | 1.50 |
| 2011 A | 43,000 | PF65 3.00 | | | | |
| 2011 D | 34,694,000 | — | — | — | 1.00 | 1.50 |
| 2011 D | 37,000 | PF65 3.00 | | | | |
| 2011 F | 39,644,000 | — | — | — | 1.00 | 1.50 |
| 2011 F | 37,000 | PF65 3.00 | | | | |
| 2011 G | 23,144,000 | — | — | — | 1.00 | 1.50 |
| 2011 F | 37,000 | PF65 3.00 | | | | |
| 2011 J | 34,694,000 | — | — | — | 1.00 | 1.50 |
| 2011 J | 37,000 | PF65 3.00 | | | | |
| 2012 A | 21,245,000 | — | — | — | 1.00 | 1.50 |
| 2012 A | Est. 40000 | PF65 3.00 | | | | |
| 2012 D | Est. 23810000 | — | — | — | 1.00 | 1.50 |
| 2012 D | 32,000 | PF65 3.00 | | | | |
| 2012 F | Est. 25490000 | — | — | — | 1.00 | 1.50 |
| 2012 F | Est. 40000 | PF65 3.00 | | | | |
| 2012 G | Est. 11240000 | — | — | — | 1.00 | 1.50 |
| 2012 G | Est. 40000 | PF65 3.00 | | | | |
| 2012 J | Est. 22310000 | — | — | — | 1.00 | 1.50 |
| 2012 J | Est. 40000 | PF65 3.00 | | | | |
| 2013 A | Est. 16045000 | — | — | — | 0.75 | 1.25 |
| 2013 A | 35,000 | PF65 3.00 | | | | |
| 2013 D | Est. 16840000 | — | — | — | 0.75 | 1.25 |
| 2013 D | Est. 40000 | PF65 3.00 | | | | |
| 2013 F | Est. 19240000 | — | — | — | 0.75 | 1.25 |
| 2013 F | 30,000 | PF65 3.00 | | | | |
| 2013 G | — | — | — | — | 0.75 | 1.25 |
| 2013 G | Est. 40000 | PF65 3.00 | | | | |
| 2013 J | Est. 16840000 | — | — | — | 0.75 | 1.25 |
| 2013 J | Est. 40000 | PF65 3.00 | | | | |
| 2014 A | — | — | — | — | 1.00 | 1.50 |
| 2014 A | — | PF65 3.00 | | | | |
| 2014 D | — | — | — | — | 1.00 | 1.50 |
| 2014 D | — | PF65 3.00 | | | | |
| 2014 F | — | — | — | — | 1.00 | 1.50 |
| 2014 F | — | PF65 3.00 | | | | |
| 2014 G | — | — | — | — | 1.00 | 1.50 |
| 2014 G | — | PF65 3.00 | | | | |
| 2014 J | — | — | — | — | — | 40.00 |
| 2014 J | — | PF65 3.00 | | | | |

## KM# 212 50 EURO CENT

7.80 g., Brass, 24.25 mm. **Obv:** Brandenburg Gate **Rev:** Denomination and map **Edge:** Reeded

| Date | Mintage | F12 | VF20 | XF40 | MS60 | MS63 |
|---|---|---|---|---|---|---|
| 2002 A | 337,840,000 | — | — | — | 1.75 | 2.00 |
| 2002 A | 75,000 | PF65 4.00 | | | | |
| 2002 D | 370,330,000 | — | — | — | 1.75 | 2.00 |
| 2002 D | 75,000 | PF65 4.00 | | | | |
| 2002 F | 430,570,000 | — | — | — | 1.75 | 2.00 |
| 2002 F | 75,000 | PF65 4.00 | | | | |
| 2002 G | 256,650,000 | — | — | — | 1.75 | 2.00 |
| 2002 G | 75,000 | PF65 4.00 | | | | |
| 2002 J | 401,490,000 | — | — | — | 1.75 | 2.00 |
| 2002 J | 75,000 | PF65 4.00 | | | | |
| 2003 A Sets only | 90,000 | — | — | — | — | 4.50 |
| 2003 A | 75,000 | PF65 4.00 | | | | |
| 2003 D | 70,710,000 | — | — | — | 2.00 | 3.00 |
| 2003 D | 75,000 | PF65 4.00 | | | | |
| 2003 F Sets only | 90,000 | — | — | — | — | 4.50 |
| 2003 F | 75,000 | PF65 4.00 | | | | |
| 2003 G Sets only | 90,000 | — | — | — | — | 4.50 |
| 2003 G | 75,000 | PF65 4.00 | | | | |
| 2003 J | 39,690,000 | — | — | — | 1.75 | 2.00 |
| 2003 J | 75,000 | PF65 4.00 | | | | |
| 2004 A | 82,350,000 | — | — | — | 1.75 | 2.00 |
| 2004 A | 75,000 | PF65 4.00 | | | | |
| 2004 D Sets only | 90,000 | — | — | — | — | 4.50 |
| 2004 D | 75,000 | PF65 4.00 | | | | |
| 2004 F | 73,610,000 | — | — | — | 1.75 | 2.00 |
| 2004 F | 75,000 | PF65 4.00 | | | | |
| 2004 G | 37,530,000 | — | — | — | 1.75 | 2.00 |
| 2004 G | 75,000 | PF65 4.00 | | | | |
| 2004 J Sets only | 90,000 | — | — | — | — | 4.50 |
| 2004 J | 75,000 | PF65 4.00 | | | | |
| 2005 A Sets only | 90,000 | — | — | — | — | 4.50 |
| 2005 A | 75,000 | PF65 4.00 | | | | |
| 2005 D Sets only | 90,000 | — | — | — | — | 4.50 |
| 2005 D | 75,000 | PF65 4.00 | | | | |
| 2005 F Sets only | 90,000 | — | — | — | — | 4.50 |
| 2005 F | 75,000 | PF65 4.00 | | | | |
| 2005 G Sets only | 90,000 | — | — | — | — | 4.50 |
| 2005 G | 75,000 | PF65 4.00 | | | | |
| 2005 J Sets only | 90,000 | — | — | — | — | 4.50 |
| 2005 J | 75,000 | PF65 4.00 | | | | |
| 2006 A Sets only | 90,000 | — | — | — | — | 4.50 |
| 2006 A | 75,000 | PF65 4.00 | | | | |
| 2006 D Sets only | 90,000 | — | — | — | — | 4.50 |
| 2006 D | 75,000 | PF65 4.00 | | | | |
| 2006 F Sets only | 90,000 | — | — | — | — | 4.50 |
| 2006 F | 75,000 | PF65 4.00 | | | | |
| 2006 G Sets only | 90,000 | — | — | — | — | 4.50 |
| 2006 G | 75,000 | PF65 4.00 | | | | |
| 2006 J Sets only | 90,000 | — | — | — | — | 4.50 |
| 2006 J | 75,000 | PF65 4.00 | | | | |

## KM# 256 50 EURO CENT

7.80 g., Brass, 24.25 mm. **Obv:** Brandenburg Gate **Rev:** Relief map of Western Europe, stars, lines and value **Edge:** Reeded

| Date | Mintage | F12 | VF20 | XF40 | MS60 | MS63 |
|---|---|---|---|---|---|---|
| 2007 A Sets only | 90,000 | — | — | — | — | 4.50 |
| 2007 A | 75,000 | PF65 4.00 | | | | |
| 2007 D Sets only | 90,000 | — | — | — | — | 4.50 |
| 2007 D | 75,000 | PF65 4.00 | | | | |
| 2007 F Sets only | 90,000 | — | — | — | — | 4.50 |
| 2007 F | 75,000 | PF65 4.00 | | | | |
| 2007 G Sets only | 90,000 | — | — | — | — | 4.50 |
| 2007 G | 75,000 | PF65 4.00 | | | | |
| 2007 J Sets only | 90,000 | — | — | — | — | 4.50 |
| 2007 J | 75,000 | PF65 4.00 | | | | |
| 2008 A Sets only | 80,000 | — | — | — | — | 4.50 |
| 2008 A | 70,000 | PF65 4.00 | | | | |
| 2008 D Sets only | 80,000 | — | — | — | — | 4.50 |
| 2008 D | 70,000 | PF65 4.00 | | | | |
| 2008 F Sets only | 80,000 | — | — | — | — | 4.50 |
| 2008 F | 70,000 | PF65 4.00 | | | | |
| 2008 G Sets only | 80,000 | — | — | — | — | 4.50 |
| 2008 G | 70,000 | PF65 4.00 | | | | |
| 2008 J Sets only | 80,000 | — | — | — | — | 4.50 |
| 2008 J | 70,000 | PF65 4.00 | | | | |
| 2009 A Sets only | 60,000 | — | — | — | — | 4.50 |
| 2009 A | 50,000 | PF65 4.00 | | | | |
| 2009 D Sets only | 60,000 | — | — | — | — | 4.50 |
| 2009 D | 50,000 | PF65 4.00 | | | | |
| 2009 F Sets only | 60,000 | — | — | — | — | 4.50 |
| 2009 F | 50,000 | PF65 4.00 | | | | |
| 2009 G Sets only | 60,000 | — | — | — | — | 4.50 |
| 2009 G | 50,000 | PF65 4.00 | | | | |
| 2009 J Sets only | 60,000 | — | — | — | — | 4.50 |
| 2009 J | 50,000 | PF65 4.00 | | | | |
| 2010 A Sets only | 53,800 | — | — | — | — | 4.00 |
| 2010 A | 45,150 | PF65 4.00 | | | | |
| 2010 D Sets only | 46,800 | — | — | — | — | 4.00 |
| 2010 D | 40,120 | PF65 4.00 | | | | |
| 2010 F Sets only | 46,800 | — | — | — | — | 4.00 |
| 2010 F | 40,120 | PF65 4.00 | | | | |
| 2010 G Sets only | 46,800 | — | — | — | — | 4.00 |
| 2010 G | 40,120 | PF65 4.00 | | | | |
| 2010 J Sets only | 46,800 | — | — | — | — | 4.00 |
| 2010 J | 40,120 | PF65 4.00 | | | | |
| 2011 A Sets only | 48,000 | — | — | — | — | 4.00 |
| 2011 A | Est. 43000 | PF65 4.00 | | | | |
| 2011 D Sets only | Est. 44000 | — | — | — | — | 4.00 |
| 2011 D | 37,000 | PF65 4.00 | | | | |
| 2011 F Sets only | Est. 44000 | — | — | — | — | 4.00 |
| 2011 F | 37,000 | PF65 4.00 | | | | |
| 2011 G Sets only | Est. 44000 | — | — | — | — | 4.00 |
| 2011 G | Est. 37000 | PF65 4.00 | | | | |
| 2011 J Sets only | Est. 44000 | — | — | — | — | 4.00 |
| 2011 J | Est. 37000 | PF65 4.00 | | | | |
| 2012 A Sets only | 40,000 | — | — | — | — | 4.00 |
| 2012 A | Est. 40000 | PF65 4.00 | | | | |
| 2012 D Sets only | 40,000 | — | — | — | — | 4.00 |
| 2012 D | Est. 40000 | PF65 4.00 | | | | |
| 2012 F Sets only | Est. 50000 | — | — | — | — | 4.00 |
| 2012 F | Est. 40000 | PF65 4.00 | | | | |
| 2012 G Sets only | Est. 50000 | — | — | — | — | 4.00 |
| 2012 G | Est. 40000 | PF65 4.00 | | | | |
| 2012 J Sets only | Est. 50000 | — | — | — | — | 4.00 |
| 2012 J | Est. 40000 | PF65 4.00 | | | | |
| 2013 A Sets only | — | — | — | — | — | 4.00 |
| 2013 A | Est. 40000 | PF65 4.00 | | | | |
| 2013 D Sets only | Est. 35000 | — | — | — | — | 4.00 |
| 2013 D | Est. 40000 | PF65 4.00 | | | | |
| 2013 F Sets only | Est. 35000 | — | — | — | — | 4.00 |
| 2013 F | Est. 40000 | PF65 4.00 | | | | |
| 2013 G Sets only | Est. 35000 | — | — | — | — | 4.00 |
| 2013 G | Est. 40000 | PF65 4.00 | | | | |
| 2013 J Sets only | Est. 35000 | — | — | — | — | 4.00 |
| 2013 J | Est. 40000 | PF65 4.00 | | | | |
| 2014 A | — | — | — | — | — | 4.00 |
| 2014 A | — | PF65 4.00 | | | | |
| 2014 D | — | — | — | — | — | 4.00 |
| 2014 D | — | — | — | — | — | 4.00 |
| 2014 D | — | PF65 4.00 | | | | |
| 2014 F | — | — | — | — | — | 4.00 |
| 2014 F | — | PF65 4.00 | | | | |
| 2014 G | — | — | — | — | — | 4.00 |
| 2014 G | — | PF65 4.00 | | | | |
| 2014 J | — | — | — | — | — | 4.00 |
| 2014 J | — | PF65 4.00 | | | | |

## KM# 213 EURO

7.50 g., Bi-Metallic Copper-Nickel center in Nickel-Brass ring, 23.25 mm. **Obv:** Stylized eagle **Rev:** Denomination over map **Edge:** Segmented reeding

| Date | Mintage | F12 | VF20 | XF40 | MS60 | MS63 |
|---|---|---|---|---|---|---|
| 2002 A | 367,990,000 | — | — | — | 2.50 | 3.00 |
| 2002 A | 75,000 | PF65 6.50 | | | | |
| 2002 D | 372,690,000 | — | — | — | 2.50 | 3.00 |
| 2002 D | 75,000 | PF65 6.50 | | | | |
| 2002 F | 439,890,000 | — | — | — | 2.50 | 3.00 |
| 2002 F | 75,000 | PF65 6.50 | | | | |
| 2002 G | 266,440,000 | — | — | — | 2.50 | 3.00 |

| Date | Mintage | F12 | VF20 | XF40 | MS60 | MS63 |
|---|---|---|---|---|---|---|
| 2002 G | 75,000 | PF65 6.50 | | | | |
| 2002 J | 372,400,000 | — | — | — | 2.50 | 3.00 |
| 2002 J | 75,000 | PF65 6.50 | | | | |
| 2003 A | 50,340,000 | — | — | — | 2.50 | 3.00 |
| 2003 A | 75,000 | PF65 6.50 | | | | |
| 2003 D Sets only | 90,000 | — | — | — | — | 5.50 |
| 2003 D | 75,000 | PF65 6.50 | | | | |
| 2003 F Sets only | 90,000 | — | — | — | — | 5.50 |
| 2003 F | 75,000 | PF65 6.50 | | | | |
| 2003 G Sets only | 90,000 | — | — | — | — | 5.50 |
| 2003 G | 75,000 | PF65 6.50 | | | | |
| 2003 J | 29,940,000 | — | — | — | 2.50 | 3.00 |
| 2003 J | 75,000 | PF65 6.50 | | | | |
| 2004 A | 21,950,000 | — | — | — | 2.50 | 3.00 |
| 2004 A | 75,000 | PF65 6.50 | | | | |
| 2004 D | 89,350,000 | — | — | — | 2.50 | 3.00 |
| 2004 D | 75,000 | PF65 6.50 | | | | |
| 2004 F | 88,290,000 | — | — | — | 2.50 | 3.00 |
| 2004 F | 75,000 | PF65 6.50 | | | | |
| 2004 G | 41,740,000 | — | — | — | 2.50 | 3.00 |
| 2004 G | 75,000 | PF65 6.50 | | | | |
| 2004 J Sets only | 90,000 | — | — | — | — | 5.50 |
| 2004 J | 75,000 | PF65 6.50 | | | | |
| 2005 A Sets only | 90,000 | — | — | — | — | 5.50 |
| 2005 A | 75,000 | PF65 5.00 | | | | |
| 2005 D Sets only | 90,000 | — | — | — | — | 5.50 |
| 2005 D | 75,000 | PF65 5.00 | | | | |
| 2005 F Sets only | 90,000 | — | — | — | — | 5.50 |
| 2005 F | 75,000 | PF65 5.00 | | | | |
| 2005 G Sets only | 90,000 | — | — | — | — | 5.50 |
| 2005 G | 75,000 | PF65 5.00 | | | | |
| 2005 J | 59,930,000 | — | — | — | 2.50 | 3.00 |
| 2005 J | 75,000 | PF65 5.00 | | | | |
| 2006 A Sets only | 90,000 | — | — | — | — | 5.50 |
| 2006 A | 75,000 | PF65 5.00 | | | | |
| 2006 D Sets only | 90,000 | — | — | — | — | 5.50 |
| 2006 D | 75,000 | PF65 5.00 | | | | |
| 2006 F Sets only | 90,000 | — | — | — | — | 5.50 |
| 2006 F | 75,000 | PF65 5.00 | | | | |
| 2006 G Sets only | 90,000 | — | — | — | — | 5.50 |
| 2006 G | 75,000 | PF65 5.00 | | | | |
| 2006 J Sets only | 90,000 | — | — | — | — | 5.50 |
| 2006 J | 75,000 | PF65 5.00 | | | | |

### KM# 257 EURO

7.50 g., Bi-Metallic Copper-Nickel center in Nickel-Brass ring, 23.25 mm. **Obv:** Stylized eagle **Rev:** Relief map of Western Europe, stars, lines and value **Edge:** Segmented reeding

| Date | Mintage | F12 | VF20 | XF40 | MS60 | MS63 |
|---|---|---|---|---|---|---|
| 2007 A Sets only | 90,000 | — | — | — | — | 5.50 |
| 2007 A | 75,000 | PF65 5.00 | | | | |
| 2007 D Sets only | 90,000 | — | — | — | — | 5.50 |
| 2007 D | 75,000 | PF65 5.00 | | | | |
| 2007 F Sets only | 90,000 | — | — | — | — | 5.50 |
| 2007 F | 75,000 | PF65 5.00 | | | | |
| 2007 G Sets only | 90,000 | — | — | — | — | 5.50 |
| 2007 G | 75,000 | PF65 5.00 | | | | |
| 2007 J Sets only | 90,000 | — | — | — | — | 5.50 |
| 2007 J | 75,000 | PF65 5.00 | | | | |
| 2008 A Sets only | 80,000 | — | — | — | — | 5.50 |
| 2008 A | 70,000 | PF65 5.00 | | | | |
| 2008 D Sets only | 80,000 | — | — | — | — | 5.50 |
| 2008 D | 70,000 | PF65 5.00 | | | | |
| 2008 F Sets only | 80,000 | — | — | — | — | 5.50 |
| 2008 F | 70,000 | PF65 5.00 | | | | |
| 2008 G Sets only | 80,000 | — | — | — | — | 5.50 |
| 2008 G | 70,000 | PF65 5.00 | | | | |
| 2008 J Sets only | 80,000 | — | — | — | — | 5.50 |
| 2008 J | 70,000 | PF65 5.00 | | | | |
| 2009 A Sets only | 60,000 | — | — | — | — | 5.50 |
| 2009 A | 50,000 | PF65 5.00 | | | | |
| 2009 D Sets only | 60,000 | — | — | — | — | 5.50 |
| 2009 D | 50,000 | PF65 5.00 | | | | |
| 2009 F Sets only | 60,000 | — | — | — | — | 5.50 |
| 2009 F | 50,000 | PF65 5.00 | | | | |
| 2009 G Sets only | 60,000 | — | — | — | — | 5.50 |
| 2009 G | 50,000 | PF65 5.00 | | | | |
| 2009 J Sets only | 60,000 | — | — | — | — | 5.50 |
| 2009 J | 50,000 | PF65 5.00 | | | | |
| 2010 A Sets only | 53,800 | — | — | — | — | 4.00 |
| 2010 A | 45,150 | PF65 5.00 | | | | |
| 2010 D Sets only | 46,800 | — | — | — | — | 4.00 |
| 2010 D | 40,120 | PF65 5.00 | | | | |
| 2010 F Sets only | 46,800 | — | — | — | — | 4.00 |
| 2010 F | 40,120 | PF65 5.00 | | | | |
| 2010 G Sets only | 46,800 | — | — | — | — | 4.00 |
| 2010 G | 40,120 | PF65 5.00 | | | | |
| 2010 J Sets only | 46,800 | — | — | — | — | 4.00 |
| 2010 J | 40,120 | PF65 5.00 | | | | |
| 2011 A Sets only | 48,000 | — | — | — | — | 4.00 |
| 2011 A | 43,000 | PF65 5.00 | | | | |
| 2011 D Sets only | 44,000 | — | — | — | — | 4.00 |
| 2011 D | 37,000 | PF65 5.00 | | | | |
| 2011 F Sets only | 44,000 | — | — | — | — | 4.00 |
| 2011 F | 37,000 | PF65 5.00 | | | | |
| 2011 G Sets only | 44,000 | — | — | — | — | 4.00 |
| 2011 G | 37,000 | PF65 5.00 | | | | |
| 2011 J Sets only | 44,000 | — | — | — | — | 4.00 |
| 2011 J | 37,000 | PF65 5.00 | | | | |

| Date | Mintage | F12 | VF20 | XF40 | MS60 | MS63 |
|---|---|---|---|---|---|---|
| 2012 A Sets only | 45,000 | — | — | — | — | 4.00 |
| 2012 A | 40,000 | PF65 5.00 | | | | |
| 2012 D Sets only | Est. 50000 | — | — | — | — | 4.00 |
| 2012 D | Est. 40000 | PF65 5.00 | | | | |
| 2012 F Sets only | Est. 50000 | — | — | — | — | 4.00 |
| 2012 F | 32,000 | PF65 5.00 | | | | |
| 2012 G Sets only | Est. 50000 | — | — | — | — | 4.00 |
| 2012 G | Est. 40000 | PF65 5.00 | | | | |
| 2012 J Sets only | Est. 50000 | — | — | — | — | 4.00 |
| 2012 J | 30,000 | PF65 5.00 | | | | |
| 2013 A Sets only | Est. 50000 | — | — | — | — | 4.00 |
| 2013 A | Est. 40000 | PF65 5.00 | | | | |
| 2013 D Sets only | Est. 50000 | — | — | — | — | 4.00 |
| 2013 D | Est. 40000 | PF65 5.00 | | | | |
| 2013 F Sets only | Est. 50000 | — | — | — | — | 4.00 |
| 2013 F | Est. 40000 | PF65 5.00 | | | | |
| 2013 G Sets only | Est. 50000 | — | — | — | — | 4.00 |
| 2013 G | Est. 40000 | PF65 5.00 | | | | |
| 2013 J Sets only | Est. 50000 | — | — | — | — | 4.00 |
| 2013 J | Est. 40000 | PF65 5.00 | | | | |
| 2014 A | — | — | — | — | — | 4.00 |
| 2014 A | — | PF65 5.00 | | | | |
| 2014 D | — | — | — | — | — | 4.00 |
| 2014 D | — | PF65 5.00 | | | | |
| 2014 F | — | — | — | — | — | 4.00 |
| 2014 F | — | PF65 5.00 | | | | |
| 2014 G | — | — | — | — | — | 4.00 |
| 2014 G | — | PF65 5.00 | | | | |
| 2014 J | — | — | — | — | — | 4.00 |
| 2014 J | — | PF65 5.00 | | | | |

### KM# 214 2 EURO

8.50 g., Bi-Metallic Nickel-Brass center in Copper-Nickel ring, 25.75 mm. **Obv:** Stylized eagle **Rev:** Denomination and map **Edge:** Reeded and "EINIGKEIT UND RECHT UND FREIHEIT

| Date | Mintage | F12 | VF20 | XF40 | MS60 | MS63 |
|---|---|---|---|---|---|---|
| 2002 A | 239,010,000 | — | — | — | 4.50 | 6.00 |
| 2002 A | 75,000 | PF65 12.50 | | | | |
| 2002 D | 231,390,000 | — | — | — | 4.50 | 6.00 |
| 2002 D | 75,000 | PF65 12.50 | | | | |
| 2002 F | 281,180,000 | — | — | — | 4.50 | 6.00 |
| 2002 F | 75,000 | PF65 12.50 | | | | |
| 2002 G | 181,040,000 | — | — | — | 4.50 | 6.00 |
| 2002 G | 75,000 | PF65 12.50 | | | | |
| 2002 J | 257,910,000 | — | — | — | 4.50 | 6.00 |
| 2002 J | 75,000 | PF65 12.50 | | | | |
| 2003 A | 20,560,000 | — | — | — | 4.50 | 6.00 |
| 2003 A | 75,000 | PF65 12.50 | | | | |
| 2003 D | 22,260,000 | — | — | — | 4.50 | 6.00 |
| 2003 D | 75,000 | PF65 12.50 | | | | |
| 2003 F | 24,550,000 | — | — | — | 4.50 | 6.00 |
| 2003 F | 75,000 | PF65 12.50 | | | | |
| 2003 G | 29,230,000 | — | — | — | 4.50 | 6.00 |
| 2003 G | 75,000 | PF65 12.50 | | | | |
| 2003 J | 19,590,000 | — | — | — | 4.50 | 6.00 |
| 2003 J | 75,000 | PF65 12.50 | | | | |
| 2004 A | 31,660,000 | — | — | — | 4.50 | 6.00 |
| 2004 A | 75,000 | PF65 12.50 | | | | |
| 2004 D | 19,930,000 | — | — | — | 4.50 | 6.00 |
| 2004 D | 75,000 | PF65 12.50 | | | | |
| 2004 F Sets only | 90,000 | — | — | — | — | 6.50 |
| 2004 F | 75,000 | PF65 12.50 | | | | |
| 2004 G Sets only | 90,000 | — | — | — | — | 6.50 |
| 2004 G | 75,000 | PF65 12.50 | | | | |
| 2004 J | 22,600,000 | — | — | — | 4.50 | 6.00 |
| 2004 J | 75,000 | PF65 12.50 | | | | |
| 2005 A Sets only | 90,000 | — | — | — | — | 6.50 |
| 2005 A | 75,000 | PF65 10.00 | | | | |
| 2005 D Sets only | 90,000 | — | — | — | — | 6.50 |
| 2005 D | 75,000 | PF65 10.00 | | | | |
| 2005 F Sets only | 90,000 | — | — | — | — | 6.50 |
| 2005 F | 75,000 | PF65 10.00 | | | | |
| 2005 G Sets only | 90,000 | — | — | — | — | 6.50 |
| 2005 G | 75,000 | PF65 10.00 | | | | |
| 2005 J Sets only | 90,000 | — | — | — | — | 6.50 |
| 2005 J | 75,000 | PF65 10.00 | | | | |
| 2006 A Sets only | 90,000 | — | — | — | — | 6.50 |
| 2006 A | 75,000 | PF65 10.00 | | | | |
| 2006 D Sets only | 90,000 | — | — | — | — | 6.50 |
| 2006 D | 75,000 | PF65 10.00 | | | | |
| 2006 F Sets only | 90,000 | — | — | — | — | 6.50 |
| 2006 F | 75,000 | PF65 10.00 | | | | |
| 2006 G Sets only | 90,000 | — | — | — | — | 6.50 |
| 2006 G | 75,000 | PF65 10.00 | | | | |
| 2006 J Sets only | 90,000 | — | — | — | — | 6.50 |
| 2006 J | 75,000 | PF65 10.00 | | | | |

### KM# 253 2 EURO

8.50 g., Bi-Metallic Nickel-Brass center in Copper-Nickel ring, 25.75 mm. **Obv:** Schleswig Holstein castle **Obv. Legend:** BUNDESREPUBLIK DEUTSCHLAND **Obv. Inscription:** SCHLESWIG- / HOLSTEIN **Rev:** Denomination over map

| Date | Mintage | F12 | VF20 | XF40 | MS60 | MS63 |
|---|---|---|---|---|---|---|
| 2006 A | 6,170,000 | — | — | — | 5.00 | 6.00 |
| 2006 A | 145,000 | PF63 8.00 | PF65 10.00 | | | |
| 2006 D | 6,470,000 | — | — | — | 5.00 | 6.00 |
| 2006 D | 145,000 | PF63 8.00 | PF65 10.00 | | | |
| 2006 F | 7,370,000 | — | — | — | 5.00 | 6.00 |
| 2006 F | 145,000 | PF63 8.00 | PF65 10.00 | | | |
| 2006 G | 4,370,000 | — | — | — | 5.00 | 6.00 |
| 2006 G | 145,000 | PF63 8.00 | PF65 10.00 | | | |
| 2006 J | 6,470,000 | — | — | — | 5.00 | 6.00 |
| 2006 J | 145,000 | PF63 8.00 | PF65 10.00 | | | |

### KM# 259 2 EURO

8.50 g., Bi-Metallic Nickel-Brass center in Copper-Nickel ring, 25.75 mm. **Subject:** 50th Anniversary Treaty of Rome **Obv:** Open treaty book **Obv. Legend:** BUNDESREPUBLIK DEUTSCHLAND **Rev:** Large value at left, modified outline of Europe at right **Edge Lettering:** EINIGKEIT UND RECHT UND FREIHEIT

| Date | Mintage | F12 | VF20 | XF40 | MS60 | MS63 |
|---|---|---|---|---|---|---|
| 2007 A | 1,090,000 | — | — | — | 4.00 | 5.00 |
| 2007 A | 125,000 | PF63 8.00 | PF65 10.00 | | | |
| 2007 D | 14,590,000 | — | — | — | 4.00 | 5.50 |
| 2007 D | 125,000 | PF63 8.00 | PF65 10.00 | | | |
| 2007 F | 8,090,000 | — | — | — | 4.00 | 5.50 |
| 2007 F | 125,000 | PF63 8.00 | PF65 10.00 | | | |
| 2007 G | 5,090,000 | — | — | — | 4.00 | 5.50 |
| 2007 G | 125,000 | PF63 8.00 | PF65 10.00 | | | |
| 2007 J | 1,590,000 | — | — | — | 4.00 | 5.50 |
| 2007 J | 125,000 | PF63 8.00 | PF65 10.00 | | | |

### KM# 260 2 EURO

8.50 g., Bi-Metallic Nickel-Brass center in Copper-Nickel ring, 25.75 mm. **Obv:** City buildings, Mecklenburg's Schwerin Castle **Obv. Legend:** BUNDESREPUBLIK DEUTSCHLAND **Obv. Inscription:** MECKLENBURG- / VORPOMMERN **Rev:** Large value at left, modified map of Europe at right **Edge Lettering:** EINIGKEIT UND RECHT UND FREIHEIT

| Date | Mintage | F12 | VF20 | XF40 | MS60 | MS63 |
|---|---|---|---|---|---|---|
| 2007 A | 1,210,000 | — | — | — | 4.00 | 5.50 |
| 2007 A | 145,000 | PF63 8.00 | PF65 10.00 | | | |
| 2007 D | 12,010,000 | — | — | — | 4.00 | 5.50 |
| 2007 D | 145,000 | PF63 8.00 | PF65 10.00 | | | |
| 2007 F | 12,110,000 | — | — | — | 4.00 | 5.50 |
| 2007 F | 145,000 | PF63 8.00 | PF65 10.00 | | | |
| 2007 G | 4,370,000 | — | — | — | 4.00 | 5.50 |
| 2007 G | 145,000 | PF63 8.00 | PF65 10.00 | | | |
| 2007 J | 1,240,000 | — | — | — | 4.00 | 5.50 |
| 2007 J | 145,000 | PF63 8.00 | PF65 10.00 | | | |

### KM# 258 2 EURO

8.50 g., Bi-Metallic Nickel-Brass center in Copper-Nickel ring, 25.75 mm. **Obv:** Stylized eagle **Rev:** Relief map of Western Europe, stars, lines and value **Edge Lettering:** EINIGKEIT UND RECHT UND FREIHEIT

| Date | Mintage | F12 | VF20 | XF40 | MS60 | MS63 |
|---|---|---|---|---|---|---|
| 2008 A | 11,480,000 | — | — | — | 4.50 | 6.00 |
| 2008 A | 70,000 | PF63 8.00 | PF65 10.00 | | | |
| 2008 D | 12,050,000 | — | — | — | 4.50 | 6.00 |
| 2008 D | 70,000 | PF63 8.00 | PF65 10.00 | | | |
| 2008 F | 13,760,000 | — | — | — | 4.50 | 6.00 |
| 2008 F | 70,000 | PF63 8.00 | PF65 10.00 | | | |
| 2008 G | 8,060,000 | — | — | — | 4.50 | 6.00 |
| 2008 G | 70,000 | PF63 8.00 | PF65 10.00 | | | |
| 2008 J | 12,050,000 | — | — | — | 4.50 | 6.00 |
| 2008 J | 70,000 | PF63 8.00 | PF65 10.00 | | | |
| 2010 A | 19,654,000 | — | — | — | 4.50 | 6.00 |
| 2010 A | 45,150 | PF63 8.00 | PF65 10.00 | | | |
| 2010 D | 20,627,000 | — | — | — | 4.50 | 6.00 |
| 2010 D | 40,120 | PF63 8.00 | PF65 10.00 | | | |
| 2010 F | 23,567,000 | — | — | — | 4.50 | 6.00 |
| 2010 F | 40,120 | PF63 8.00 | PF65 10.00 | | | |
| 2010 G | 13,767,000 | — | — | — | 4.50 | 6.00 |
| 2010 G | 40,120 | PF63 8.00 | PF65 10.00 | | | |
| 2010 J | 20,627,000 | — | — | — | 4.50 | 6.00 |
| 2010 J | 40,120 | PF63 8.00 | PF65 10.00 | | | |
| 2011 A | 23,848,000 | — | — | — | 4.50 | 6.00 |
| 2011 A | 43,000 | PF63 8.00 | PF65 10.00 | | | |
| 2011 D | 25,034,000 | — | — | — | 4.50 | 6.00 |
| 2011 D | 37,000 | PF63 8.00 | PF65 10.00 | | | |
| 2011 F | 28,604,000 | — | — | — | 4.50 | 6.00 |
| 2011 F | 37,000 | PF63 8.00 | PF65 10.00 | | | |
| 2011 G | 16,704,000 | — | — | — | 4.50 | 6.00 |
| 2011 G | 37,000 | PF63 8.00 | PF65 10.00 | | | |
| 2011 J | 25,034,000 | — | — | — | 4.50 | 6.00 |
| 2011 J | 37,000 | PF63 8.00 | PF65 10.00 | | | |

### KM# 261 2 EURO

8.50 g., Bi-Metallic Nickel-Brass center in Copper-Nickel ring, 25.75 mm. **Obv:** Hamburg Cathedral **Obv. Legend:** BUNDESREPUBLIK DEUTSCHLAND **Obv. Inscription:** HAMBURG **Rev:** Large value at left, modified outline of Europe at right **Edge Lettering:** EINIGKEIT UND RECHT UND FREIHEIT

| Date | Mintage | F12 | VF20 | XF40 | MS60 | MS63 |
|---|---|---|---|---|---|---|
| 2008 A | 1,160,000 | — | — | — | 4.00 | 5.50 |
| 2008 A | 140,000 | PF63 8.00 | PF65 10.00 | | | |
| 2008 D | 9,060,000 | — | — | — | 4.00 | 5.50 |
| 2008 D | 140,000 | PF63 8.00 | PF65 10.00 | | | |
| 2008 F | 9,760,000 | — | — | — | 4.00 | 5.50 |
| 2008 F | 140,000 | PF63 8.00 | PF65 10.00 | | | |
| 2008 G | 4,360,000 | — | — | — | 4.00 | 5.50 |
| 2008 G | 140,000 | PF63 8.00 | PF65 10.00 | | | |
| 2008 J | 6,460,000 | — | — | — | 4.00 | 5.50 |
| 2008 J | 140,000 | PF63 8.00 | PF65 10.00 | | | |

### KM# A261 2 EURO

8.50 g., Bi-Metallic Nickel-Brass center in Copper-Nickel ring, 25.75 mm. **Obv:** Hamburg Cathedral **Rev:** Denomination over map **Edge Lettering:** EINIGKEIT UND RECHT UND FREIHEIT **Note:** Mule with old reverse Euro Zone map.

| Date | Mintage | F12 | VF20 | XF40 | MS60 | MS63 |
|---|---|---|---|---|---|---|
| 2008 F | Inc. above | — | — | — | — | 30.00 |

### KM# 276 2 EURO

8.50 g., Bi-Metallic Nickel-Brass center in Copper-Nickel ring, 25.75 mm. **Obv:** Building in Saarland **Rev:** Value and map

| Date | Mintage | F12 | VF20 | XF40 | MS60 | MS63 |
|---|---|---|---|---|---|---|
| 2009 A | 6,110,000 | — | — | — | 4.50 | 5.00 |
| 2009 A | 100,000 | PF63 8.00 | PF65 10.00 | | | |
| 2009 D | 6,410,000 | — | — | — | 4.50 | 5.00 |
| 2009 D | 100,000 | PF63 8.00 | PF65 10.00 | | | |
| 2009 F | 7,310,000 | — | — | — | 4.50 | 5.00 |
| 2009 F | 100,000 | PF63 8.00 | PF65 10.00 | | | |
| 2009 G | 4,310,000 | — | — | — | 4.50 | 5.00 |
| 2009 G | 100,000 | PF63 8.00 | PF65 10.00 | | | |
| 2009 J | 6,410,000 | — | — | — | 4.50 | 5.00 |
| 2009 J | 100,000 | PF63 8.00 | PF65 10.00 | | | |

### KM# 277 2 EURO

8.50 g., Bi-Metallic Nickel-Brass center in Copper-Nickel ring, 25.75 mm. **Subject:** EMU, 10th Anniversary **Obv:** Stick figure and E symbol

| Date | Mintage | F12 | VF20 | XF40 | MS60 | MS63 |
|---|---|---|---|---|---|---|
| 2009 A | 6,060,000 | — | — | — | 4.50 | 5.00 |
| 2009 A | 80,000 | PF63 8.00 | PF65 10.00 | | | |
| 2009 D | 6,360,000 | — | — | — | 4.50 | 5.00 |
| 2009 D | 80,000 | PF63 8.00 | PF65 10.00 | | | |
| 2009 F | 7,260,000 | — | — | — | 4.50 | 5.00 |
| 2009 F | 80,000 | PF63 8.00 | PF65 10.00 | | | |
| 2009 G | 4,260,000 | — | — | — | 4.50 | 5.00 |
| 2009 G | 80,000 | PF63 8.00 | PF65 10.00 | | | |
| 2009 J | 6,360,000 | — | — | — | 4.50 | 5.00 |
| 2009 J | 80,000 | PF63 8.00 | PF65 10.00 | | | |

### KM# 285 2 EURO

8.50 g., Bi-Metallic Nickel-Brass center in Copper-Nickel ring, 25.75 mm. **Obv:** Bremen town hall and statue and knight statue **Rev:** Value and map

| Date | Mintage | F12 | VF20 | XF40 | MS60 | MS63 |
|---|---|---|---|---|---|---|
| 2010 A | 6,104,000 | — | — | — | 4.50 | 5.00 |
| 2010 A | 100,000 | PF63 8.00 | PF65 10.00 | | | |
| 2010 D | 6,397,000 | — | — | — | 4.50 | 5.00 |
| 2010 D | 100,000 | PF63 8.00 | PF65 10.00 | | | |
| 2010 F | 7,297,000 | — | — | — | 4.50 | 5.00 |
| 2010 F | 100,000 | PF63 8.00 | PF65 10.00 | | | |
| 2010 G | 4,297,000 | — | — | — | 4.50 | 5.00 |
| 2010 G | 100,000 | PF63 8.00 | PF65 10.00 | | | |
| 2010 J | 6,397,000 | — | — | — | 4.50 | 5.00 |
| 2010 J | 100,000 | PF63 8.00 | PF65 10.00 | | | |

### KM# 293 2 EURO

8.50 g., Bi-Metallic Nickel-Brass center in Copper-Nickel ring, 25.75 mm. **Obv:** Cologne Cathedral **Obv. Legend:** NORDRHEIN - WESTFALEN

| Date | Mintage | F12 | VF20 | XF40 | MS60 | MS63 |
|---|---|---|---|---|---|---|
| 2011 A | 6,102,000 | — | — | — | 5.00 | 7.50 |
| 2011 A | 102,000 | PF63 8.00 | PF65 10.00 | | | |
| 2011 D | 6,402,000 | — | — | — | 5.00 | 7.50 |
| 2011 D | 102,000 | PF63 8.00 | PF65 10.00 | | | |
| 2011 F | 7,302,000 | — | — | — | 5.00 | 7.50 |
| 2011 F | 102,000 | PF63 8.00 | PF65 10.00 | | | |
| 2011 G | 4,302,000 | — | — | — | 5.00 | 7.50 |
| 2011 G | 102,000 | PF63 8.00 | PF65 10.00 | | | |
| 2011 J | 6,402,000 | — | — | — | 5.00 | 7.50 |
| 2011 J | 102,000 | PF63 8.00 | PF65 10.00 | | | |

### KM# 305 2 EURO

8.50 g., Bi-Metallic Nickel-Brass center in Copper-Nickel ring, 25.75 mm. **Series:** German States **Subject:** Bavaria, Neuschwanstein Castle **Rev:** Relief map of Europe, stars, lines and value **Edge Lettering:** EINIGKEIT UND RECHT UND FREIHEIT

| Date | Mintage | F12 | VF20 | XF40 | MS60 | MS63 |
|---|---|---|---|---|---|---|
| 2012 A | Est. 6100000 | — | — | — | 4.00 | 5.00 |
| 2012 A | 95,000 | PF63 8.00 | PF65 10.00 | | | |
| 2012 D | Est. 6400000 | — | — | — | 4.00 | 5.00 |
| 2012 D | 87,000 | PF63 8.00 | PF65 10.00 | | | |
| 2012 F | Est. 7300000 | — | — | — | 4.00 | 5.00 |
| 2012 F | 87,000 | PF63 8.00 | PF65 10.00 | | | |
| 2012 G | Est. 4300000 | — | — | — | 4.00 | 5.00 |
| 2012 G | 87,000 | PF63 8.00 | PF65 10.00 | | | |
| 2012 J | Est. 6400000 | — | — | — | 4.00 | 5.00 |
| 2012 J | 87,000 | PF63 8.00 | PF65 10.00 | | | |

### KM# 306 2 EURO

8.50 g., Bi-Metallic Nickel-Brass center in Copper-Nickel ring, 25.75 mm. **Subject:** Euro coinage, 10th Anniversary **Obv:** Euro symbol on globe at center, child-like rendering around **Rev:** Reliev map of Europe, stars, lines and value **Edge Lettering:** EINIGKEIT UND RECHT UND FREIHEIT

| Date | Mintage | F12 | VF20 | XF40 | MS60 | MS63 |
|---|---|---|---|---|---|---|
| 2012 A | Est. 6100000 | — | — | — | 4.00 | 5.00 |
| 2012 A | 95,000 | PF63 8.00 | PF65 10.00 | | | |
| 2012 D | Est. 6400000 | — | — | — | 4.00 | 5.00 |
| 2012 D | 87,000 | PF63 8.00 | PF65 10.00 | | | |
| 2012 F | Est. 7300000 | — | — | — | 4.00 | 5.00 |
| 2012 F | 87,000 | PF63 8.00 | PF65 10.00 | | | |
| 2012 G | 4,240,000 | — | — | — | 4.00 | 5.00 |
| 2012 G | 87,000 | PF63 8.00 | PF65 10.00 | | | |
| 2012 J | Est. 6400000 | — | — | — | 4.00 | 5.00 |
| 2012 J | 87,000 | PF63 8.00 | PF65 10.00 | | | |

### KM# 314 2 EURO

8.50 g., Bi-Metallic Nickel-Brass center in Copper-Nickel ring, 25.75 mm. **Series:** German States **Subject:** Baden-Württemberg, Maulbronn Cloister **Obv:** Maulbronn Cloiser **Obv. Legend:** BADEN-WÜRTTEMBERG **Rev:** Relief map of Europe, stars, lines and value **Edge Lettering:** EINIGKEIT UND RECHT UND FREIHEIT

| Date | Mintage | F12 | VF20 | XF40 | MS60 | MS63 |
|---|---|---|---|---|---|---|
| 2013 A | Est. 6087000 | — | — | — | 4.00 | 5.00 |
| 2013 A | Est. 89000 | PF63 7.00 | PF65 9.00 | | | |
| 2013 D | Est. 6400000 | — | — | — | 4.00 | 5.00 |
| 2013 D | Est. 82000 | PF63 7.00 | PF65 9.00 | | | |
| 2013 F | Est. 7282000 | — | — | — | 4.00 | 5.00 |
| 2013 F | Est. 82000 | PF63 7.00 | PF65 9.00 | | | |
| 2013 G | Est. 4300000 | — | — | — | 4.00 | 5.00 |
| 2013 G | Est. 82000 | PF63 7.00 | PF65 9.00 | | | |
| 2013 J | Est. 6400000 | — | — | — | 4.00 | 5.00 |
| 2013 J | Est. 82000 | PF63 7.00 | PF65 9.00 | | | |

### KM# 315 2 EURO

8.50 g., Bi-Metallic Nickel-Brass center in Copper-Nickel ring, 25.75 mm. **Subject:** Fiftieth Anniversary of the Elysée (Paris) Treaty **Obv:** Heads of Konrad Adenauer and Charles de Gaulle **Rev:** Relief map of Europe, stars, lines and value **Rev. Legend:** TRAITÉ DE L' ÉLYSÉE, ÉLYSÉE-VERTAG and 50 ANS JAHRE **Edge Lettering:** EINIGKEIT UND RECHT UND FREIHEIT

| Date | Mintage | F12 | VF20 | XF40 | MS60 | MS63 |
|---|---|---|---|---|---|---|
| 2013 A | Est. 2300000 | — | — | — | 4.00 | 5.00 |
| 2013 A | Est. 84000 | PF63 7.00 | PF65 9.00 | | | |
| 2013 D | Est. 2410000 | — | — | — | 4.00 | 5.00 |
| 2013 D | Est. 77000 | PF63 7.00 | PF65 9.00 | | | |
| 2013 F | Est. 2740000 | — | — | — | 4.00 | 5.00 |
| 2013 F | Est. 77000 | PF63 7.00 | PF65 9.00 | | | |
| 2013 G | Est. 1575000 | — | — | — | 4.00 | 5.00 |
| 2013 G | Est. 77000 | PF63 7.00 | PF65 9.00 | | | |
| 2013 J | Est. 2410000 | — | — | — | 4.00 | 5.00 |
| 2013 J | Est. 77000 | PF63 7.00 | PF65 9.00 | | | |

**KM# 215 10 EURO**
18.00 g., 0.925 Silver 0.5353 oz. ASW, 32.5 mm. **Subject:** Introduction of the Euro Currency **Obv:** Stylized round eagle **Rev:** Euro symbol and map **Edge Lettering:** IM ZEICHEN DER EINIGUNG EUROPAS

| Date | Mintage | F12 | VF20 | XF40 | MS60 | MS63 |
|---|---|---|---|---|---|---|
| 2002 F | 2,000,000 | — | — | — | 22.00 | 25.00 |
| 2002 F | 400,000 | PF63 28.00 | PF65 30.00 | | | |

**KM# 216 10 EURO**
18.00 g., 0.925 Silver 0.5353 oz. ASW, 32.5 mm. **Subject:** Berlin Subway Centennial **Obv:** Stylized squarish eagle **Rev:** Elevated and subterranean train views **Edge Lettering:** HISTORISCH UND ZUKUNFTS WEISEND

| Date | Mintage | F12 | VF20 | XF40 | MS60 | MS63 |
|---|---|---|---|---|---|---|
| 2002 D | 2,000,000 | — | — | — | 22.00 | 25.00 |
| 2002 D | 400,000 | PF63 28.00 | PF65 30.00 | | | |

**KM# 217 10 EURO**
18.00 g., 0.925 Silver 0.5353 oz. ASW, 32.5 mm. **Subject:** Documenta Kassel Art Exposition **Obv:** Stylized eagle above inscription **Rev:** Exposition logo **Edge Lettering:** ART (in nine languages)

| Date | Mintage | F12 | VF20 | XF40 | MS60 | MS63 |
|---|---|---|---|---|---|---|
| 2002 J | 2,000,000 | — | — | — | 22.00 | 25.00 |
| 2002 J | 300,000 | PF63 28.00 | PF65 30.00 | | | |

**KM# 218 10 EURO**
18.00 g., 0.925 Silver 0.5353 oz. ASW, 32.5 mm. **Subject:** Museum Island, Berlin **Obv:** Stylized eagle **Rev:** Aerial view of museum complex **Edge Lettering:** FREISTÄTTE FÜR KUNST UND WISSENSCHAFT

| Date | Mintage | F12 | VF20 | XF40 | MS60 | MS63 |
|---|---|---|---|---|---|---|
| 2002 A | 2,000,000 | — | — | — | 22.00 | 25.00 |
| 2002 A | 280,000 | PF63 28.00 | PF65 30.00 | | | |

**KM# 219 10 EURO**
18.00 g., 0.925 Silver 0.5353 oz. ASW, 32.5 mm. **Subject:** 50 Years - German Television **Obv:** Stylized eagle silhouette **Rev:** Television screen silhouette **Edge Lettering:** BILDUNG UNTERHALTUNG INFORMATION

| Date | Mintage | F12 | VF20 | XF40 | MS60 | MS63 |
|---|---|---|---|---|---|---|
| 2002 G | 2,000,000 | — | — | — | 22.00 | 25.00 |
| 2002 G | 290,000 | PF63 30.00 | PF65 32.00 | | | |

**KM# 222 10 EURO**
18.00 g., 0.925 Silver 0.5353 oz. ASW, 32.5 mm. **Subject:** Justus von Liebig **Obv:** Eagle above denomination **Rev:** Liebig's portrait **Edge Lettering:** FORSCHEN • LEHREN • ANWENDEN •

| Date | Mintage | F12 | VF20 | XF40 | MS60 | MS63 |
|---|---|---|---|---|---|---|
| 2003 J | 2,050,000 | — | — | — | 22.00 | 25.00 |
| 2003 J | 350,000 | PF63 28.00 | PF65 30.00 | | | |

**KM# 223 10 EURO**
18.00 g., 0.925 Silver 0.5353 oz. ASW, 32.5 mm. **Subject:** World Cup Soccer **Obv:** Stylized round eagle above denomination **Rev:** German map on soccer ball **Edge Lettering:** DIE WELT ZU GAST BEI FREUNDEN A • D • F • G • J • **Note:** Mint is determined by which letter "E" in the edge inscription has a short center bar. If the first letter "E" has the short center bar the coin is from the Berlin mint. Second "E"= Munich, third "E"=Stuttgart, fourth "E"=Karlsruhe, fifth "E"=Hamburg

| Date | Mintage | F12 | VF20 | XF40 | MS60 | MS63 |
|---|---|---|---|---|---|---|
| 2003 A | 710,000 | — | — | — | 22.00 | 25.00 |
| 2003 A | 80,000 | PF63 30.00 | PF65 32.00 | | | |
| 2003 D | 710,000 | — | — | — | 22.00 | 25.00 |
| 2003 D | 80,000 | PF63 30.00 | PF65 32.00 | | | |
| 2003 F | 710,000 | — | — | — | 22.00 | 25.00 |
| 2003 F | 80,000 | PF63 30.00 | PF65 32.00 | | | |
| 2003 G | 710,000 | — | — | — | 22.00 | 25.00 |
| 2003 G | 80,000 | PF63 30.00 | PF65 32.00 | | | |
| 2003 J | 710,000 | — | — | — | 22.00 | 25.00 |
| 2003 J | 80,000 | PF63 30.00 | PF65 32.00 | | | |

**KM# 224 10 EURO**
18.00 g., 0.925 Silver 0.5353 oz. ASW, 32.5 mm. **Subject:** Ruhr Industrial District **Obv:** Stylized eagle, denomination below **Rev:** Various city views **Edge Lettering:** RUHRPOTT KULTURLANDSCHAFT

| Date | Mintage | F12 | VF20 | XF40 | MS60 | MS63 |
|---|---|---|---|---|---|---|
| 2003 F | 2,050,000 | — | — | — | 22.00 | 25.00 |
| 2003 F | 350,000 | PF63 28.00 | PF65 30.00 | | | |

**KM# 225 10 EURO**
18.00 g., 0.925 Silver 0.5353 oz. ASW, 32.5 mm. **Subject:** German Museum München Centennial **Obv:** Stylized eagle, denomination at left **Rev:** Abstract design **Edge Lettering:** SAMMELN • AUSSTELLEN • FORSCHEN • BILDEN •

| Date | Mintage | F12 | VF20 | XF40 | MS60 | MS63 |
|---|---|---|---|---|---|---|
| 2003 D | 350,000 | PF63 28.00 | PF65 30.00 | | | |
| 2003 D | 2,050,000 | — | — | — | 22.00 | 25.00 |

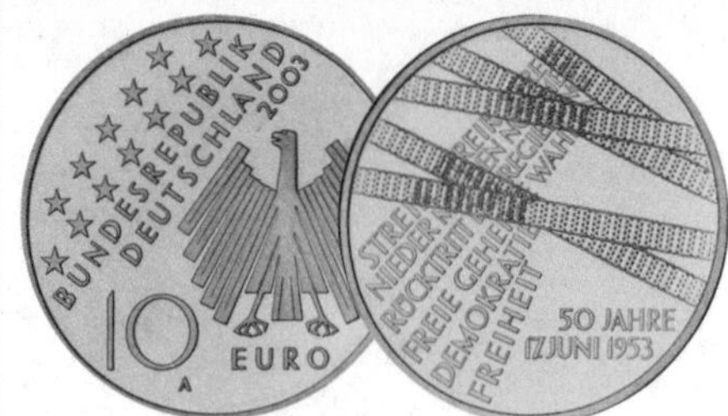


**KM# 226 10 EURO**
18.00 g., 0.925 Silver 0.5353 oz. ASW, 32.5 mm. **Subject:** 50th Anniversary of the Ill-fated East German Revolution **Obv:** Stylized eagle, denomination at left **Rev:** Tank tracks over slogans **Edge Lettering:** ERINNERUNG AN DEN VOLKSAUFSTAND IN DER DDR

| Date | Mintage | F12 | VF20 | XF40 | MS60 | MS63 |
|---|---|---|---|---|---|---|
| 2003 A | 2,050,000 | — | — | — | 22.00 | 25.00 |
| 2003 A | 350,000 | PF63 28.00 | PF65 30.00 | | | |

**KM# 227 10 EURO**
18.00 g., 0.925 Silver 0.5353 oz. ASW, 32.5 mm. **Obv:** Stylized eagle above denomination **Rev:** Gottfried Semper and floor plan **Edge Lettering:** ARCHITEKT • FORSCHER • KOSMOPOLIT • DEMOKRAT•

| Date | Mintage | F12 | VF20 | XF40 | MS60 | MS63 |
|---|---|---|---|---|---|---|
| 2003 G | 350,000 | PF63 28.00 | PF65 30.00 | | | |
| 2003 G | 2,050,000 | — | — | — | 22.00 | 25.00 |

**KM# 229 10 EURO**
18.00 g., 0.925 Silver 0.5353 oz. ASW, 32.5 mm. **Obv:** Stylized eagle, denomination below **Rev:** Soccer ball orbiting the earth **Edge Lettering:** DIE WELT ZU GAST BEI FREUNDEN A D F G J **Note:** Soccer Series: Mint determination same as KM-223

| Date | Mintage | F12 | VF20 | XF40 | MS60 | MS63 |
|---|---|---|---|---|---|---|
| 2004 A | 800,000 | — | — | — | 22.00 | 25.00 |
| 2004 A | 80,000 | PF63 28.00 | PF65 30.00 | | | |
| 2004 D | 800,000 | — | — | — | 22.00 | 25.00 |
| 2004 D | 80,000 | PF63 28.00 | PF65 30.00 | | | |
| 2004 F | 800,000 | — | — | — | 22.00 | 25.00 |
| 2004 F | 80,000 | PF63 28.00 | PF65 30.00 | | | |
| 2004 G | 800,000 | — | — | — | 22.00 | 25.00 |
| 2004 G | 80,000 | PF63 28.00 | PF65 30.00 | | | |
| 2004 J | 800,000 | — | — | — | 22.00 | 25.00 |
| 2004 J | 80,000 | PF63 28.00 | PF65 30.00 | | | |

**KM# 230 10 EURO**
18.00 g., 0.925 Silver 0.5353 oz. ASW, 32.5 mm. **Obv:** Stylized eagle, stars and denomination **Rev:** Bauhaus Dessau geometric shapes design **Edge Lettering:** KUNST TECHNIK LEHRE

| Date | Mintage | F12 | VF20 | XF40 | MS60 | MS63 |
|---|---|---|---|---|---|---|
| 2004 A | 1,800,000 | — | — | — | 22.00 | 25.00 |
| 2004 A | 300,000 | PF63 28.00 | PF65 30.00 | | | |

**KM# 231 10 EURO**

18.00 g., 0.925 Silver 0.5353 oz. ASW, 32.5 mm. **Obv:** Stylized eagle above denomination **Rev:** European Union country names and dates **Edge Lettering:** FREUDE SCHÖNER GÖTTERFUNKEN

| Date | Mintage | F12 | VF20 | XF40 | MS60 | MS63 |
|---|---|---|---|---|---|---|
| 2004 G | 1,800,000 | — | — | — | 22.00 | 25.00 |
| 2004 G | 300,000 | PF63 28.00 | PF65 30.00 | | | |

**KM# 232 10 EURO**

18.00 g., 0.925 Silver 0.5353 oz. ASW, 32.5 mm. **Obv:** Stylized eagle and denomination **Rev:** Geese flying over Wattenmeer National Park **Edge Lettering:** MEERESGRUND TRIFFT HORIZONT

| Date | Mintage | F12 | VF20 | XF40 | MS60 | MS63 |
|---|---|---|---|---|---|---|
| 2004 J | 300,000 | PF63 28.00 | PF65 30.00 | | | |
| 2004 J | 1,800,000 | — | — | — | 22.00 | 25.00 |

**KM# 233 10 EURO**

18.00 g., 0.925 Silver 0.5353 oz. ASW, 32.5 mm. **Obv:** Stylized eagle **Rev:** Eduard Moerike **Edge Lettering:** OHNE DAS SCHÖNE WAS SOLL DER GEWINN

| Date | Mintage | F12 | VF20 | XF40 | MS60 | MS63 |
|---|---|---|---|---|---|---|
| 2004 F | 300,000 | PF63 28.00 | PF65 30.00 | | | |
| 2004 F | 1,800,000 | — | — | — | 22.00 | 25.00 |

**KM# 234 10 EURO**

18.00 g., 0.925 Silver 0.5353 oz. ASW, 32.5 mm. **Obv:** Stylized eagle, denomination below **Rev:** Space station above the earth **Edge Lettering:** RAUMFAHRT VERBINDET DIE WELT

| Date | Mintage | F12 | VF20 | XF40 | MS60 | MS63 |
|---|---|---|---|---|---|---|
| 2004 D | 300,000 | PF63 28.00 | PF65 30.00 | | | |
| 2004 D | 1,800,000 | — | — | — | 22.00 | 25.00 |

**KM# 238 10 EURO**

18.00 g., 0.925 Silver 0.5353 oz. ASW, 32.5 mm. **Subject:** Albert Einstein **Obv:** Stylized eagle within circle, denomination below **Rev:** E=mc2 on a sphere resting on a net **Edge Lettering:** NICHT AUFHOREN ZU FRAGEN

| Date | Mintage | F12 | VF20 | XF40 | MS60 | MS63 |
|---|---|---|---|---|---|---|
| 2005 J | 1,800,000 | — | — | — | 22.00 | 25.00 |
| 2005 J | 300,000 | PF63 28.00 | PF65 30.00 | | | |

**KM# 239 10 EURO**

18.00 g., 0.925 Silver 0.5353 oz. ASW, 32.5 mm. **Subject:** Friedrich von Schiller **Obv:** Stylized eagle **Rev:** Schiller portrait **Edge Lettering:** ERNST IST DAS LEBEN. HEITER IST DIE KUNST

| Date | Mintage | F12 | VF20 | XF40 | MS60 | MS63 |
|---|---|---|---|---|---|---|
| 2005 G | 1,800,000 | — | — | — | 22.00 | 25.00 |
| 2005 G | 300,000 | PF63 28.00 | PF65 30.00 | | | |

**KM# 240 10 EURO**

18.00 g., 0.925 Silver 0.5353 oz. ASW, 32.5 mm. **Subject:** Magdeburg **Obv:** Stylized eagle, denomination below **Rev:** Church flanked by landmarks and objects **Edge Lettering:** MAGADOBURG 805 • MAGDEBURG 2005 •

| Date | Mintage | F12 | VF20 | XF40 | MS60 | MS63 |
|---|---|---|---|---|---|---|
| 2005 A | 300,000 | PF63 28.00 | PF65 30.00 | | | |
| 2005 A | 1,800,000 | — | — | — | 22.00 | 25.00 |

**KM# 241 10 EURO**

18.00 g., 0.925 Silver 0.5353 oz. ASW, 32.5 mm. **Subject:** Bavarian Forest National Park **Obv:** Stylized eagle **Rev:** Various park scenes **Edge:** Lettered

| Date | Mintage | F12 | VF20 | XF40 | MS60 | MS63 |
|---|---|---|---|---|---|---|
| 2005 D | 1,800,000 | — | — | — | 22.00 | 25.00 |
| 2005 D | 300,000 | PF63 28.00 | PF65 30.00 | | | |

**KM# 242 10 EURO**

18.00 g., 0.925 Silver 0.5353 oz. ASW, 32.5 mm. **Subject:** Bertha von Suttner **Obv:** Stylized eagle above stars **Rev:** Suttner's portrait **Edge Lettering:** EIPHNH PAX FRIEDEN twice

| Date | Mintage | F12 | VF20 | XF40 | MS60 | MS63 |
|---|---|---|---|---|---|---|
| 2005 F | 300,000 | PF63 28.00 | PF65 30.00 | | | |
| 2005 F | 1,800,000 | — | — | — | 22.00 | 25.00 |

**KM# 243 10 EURO**

18.00 g., 0.925 Silver 0.5353 oz. ASW, 32.5 mm. **Subject:** World Cup Soccer **Obv:** Round stylized eagle **Rev:** Ball and legs seen through a net **Edge Lettering:** DIE WELT ZU GAST BEI FREUNDEN

| Date | Mintage | F12 | VF20 | XF40 | MS60 | MS63 |
|---|---|---|---|---|---|---|
| 2005 A | 800,000 | — | — | — | 22.00 | 25.00 |
| 2005 A | 80,000 | PF63 30.00 | PF65 32.00 | | | |
| 2005 D | 800,000 | — | — | — | 22.00 | 25.00 |
| 2005 D | 80,000 | PF63 30.00 | PF65 32.00 | | | |
| 2005 F | 800,000 | — | — | — | 22.00 | 25.00 |
| 2005 F | 80,000 | PF63 30.00 | PF65 32.00 | | | |
| 2005 G | 800,000 | — | — | — | 22.00 | 25.00 |
| 2005 G | 80,000 | PF63 30.00 | PF65 32.00 | | | |
| 2005 J | 800,000 | — | — | — | 22.00 | 25.00 |
| 2005 J | 80,000 | PF63 30.00 | PF65 32.00 | | | |

**KM# 245 10 EURO**

18.00 g., 0.925 Silver 0.5353 oz. ASW, 32.5 mm. **Subject:** Karl Friedrich Schinkel **Obv:** Stylized eagle **Rev:** Kneeling brick layer **Edge Lettering:** DER MENSCH BILDE SICH IN ALLEM SCHÖN

| Date | Mintage | F12 | VF20 | XF40 | MS60 | MS63 |
|---|---|---|---|---|---|---|
| 2006 F | 300,000 | PF63 28.00 | PF65 30.00 | | | |
| 2006 F | 1,600,000 | — | — | — | 22.00 | 25.00 |

**KM# 246 10 EURO**

18.00 g., 0.925 Silver 0.5353 oz. ASW, 32.5 mm. **Subject:** Dresden **Obv:** Stylized eagle **Rev:** City view and reflection **Edge Lettering:** 1206 1485 1547 1697 1832 1945 1989 2006

| Date | Mintage | F12 | VF20 | XF40 | MS60 | MS63 |
|---|---|---|---|---|---|---|
| 2006 A | 1,600,000 | — | — | — | 22.00 | 25.00 |
| 2006 A | 300,000 | PF63 28.00 | PF65 30.00 | | | |

**KM# 247 10 EURO**
18.00 g., 0.925 Silver 0.5353 oz. ASW, 32.5 mm. **Subject:** Hanseatic League **Obv:** Stylized eagle **Rev:** Old sail boat **Edge Lettering:** Wandel durch Handel - von der Hanse nach Europa

| Date | Mintage | F12 | VF20 | XF40 | MS60 | MS63 |
|---|---|---|---|---|---|---|
| 2006 J | 300,000 | **PF63** 28.00 | **PF65** 30.00 | | | |
| 2006 J | 1,600,000 | — | — | — | 22.00 | 25.00 |

**KM# 248 10 EURO**
18.00 g., 0.925 Silver 0.5353 oz. ASW, 32.5 mm. **Subject:** Mozart **Obv:** Stylized eagle, music and denomination above **Rev:** Bust left, dates above **Edge Lettering:** -- MOZART -- DIE WELT HAT EINEN SINN

| Date | Mintage | F12 | VF20 | XF40 | MS60 | MS63 |
|---|---|---|---|---|---|---|
| 2006 D | 1,600,000 | — | — | — | 22.00 | 25.00 |
| 2006 D | 300,000 | **PF63** 28.00 | **PF65** 30.00 | | | |

**KM# 249 10 EURO**
18.00 g., 0.925 Silver 0.5353 oz. ASW, 32.5 mm. **Subject:** World Cup Soccer **Obv:** Stylized eagle **Rev:** Brandenburg Gate on ball on globe **Edge Lettering:** DIE WELT ZU GAST BEI FREUNDEN - ADFGJ **Note:** Mint is determined by which letter "E" in the edge inscription has a short center bar. If the first letter "E" has the short center bar the coin is from the Berlin mint. Second "E"= Munich, third "E"=Stuttgart, fourth "E"=Karlsruhe, fifth "E"=Hamburg

| Date | Mintage | F12 | VF20 | XF40 | MS60 | MS63 |
|---|---|---|---|---|---|---|
| 2006 A | 800,000 | — | — | — | 20.00 | 22.00 |
| 2006 A | 80,000 | **PF63** 23.00 | **PF65** 25.00 | | | |
| 2006 D | 800,000 | — | — | — | 20.00 | 22.00 |
| 2006 D | 80,000 | **PF63** 23.00 | **PF65** 25.00 | | | |
| 2006 F | 800,000 | — | — | — | 20.00 | 22.00 |
| 2006 F | 80,000 | **PF63** 23.00 | **PF65** 25.00 | | | |
| 2006 G | 800,000 | — | — | — | 20.00 | 22.00 |
| 2006 G | 80,000 | **PF63** 23.00 | **PF65** 25.00 | | | |
| 2006 J | 800,000 | — | — | — | 20.00 | 22.00 |
| 2006 J | 80,000 | **PF63** 23.00 | **PF65** 25.00 | | | |

**KM# 263 10 EURO**
18.00 g., 0.925 Silver 0.5353 oz. ASW, 32.5 mm. **Subject:** Saarland, 50th Anniversary of German control **Obv:** Eagle **Rev:** Modern town view, four stylized heads

| Date | Mintage | F12 | VF20 | XF40 | MS60 | MS63 |
|---|---|---|---|---|---|---|
| 2007 G | 1,600,000 | — | — | — | 22.00 | 25.00 |
| 2007 G | 300,000 | **PF63** 28.00 | **PF65** 30.00 | | | |

**KM# 264 10 EURO**
18.00 g., 0.925 Silver 0.5353 oz. ASW, 32.5 mm. **Subject:** Treaty of Rome, 50th Anniversary **Obv:** Eagle **Rev:** Map of Central Europe and stars

| Date | Mintage | F12 | VF20 | XF40 | MS60 | MS63 |
|---|---|---|---|---|---|---|
| 2007 F | 1,600,000 | — | — | — | 22.00 | 25.00 |
| 2007 F | 300,000 | **PF63** 28.00 | **PF65** 30.00 | | | |

**KM# 265 10 EURO**
18.00 g., 0.925 Silver 0.5353 oz. ASW, 32.5 mm. **Subject:** Wilhelm Busch, 175th Anniversary of Birth **Obv:** Eagle within square **Rev:** Portrait of Busch, characters Helene, Max and Moritz flanking

| Date | Mintage | F12 | VF20 | XF40 | MS60 | MS63 |
|---|---|---|---|---|---|---|
| 2007 D | 1,600,000 | — | — | — | 22.00 | 25.00 |
| 2007 D | 300,000 | **PF63** 28.00 | **PF65** 30.00 | | | |

**KM# 266 10 EURO**
18.00 g., 0.925 Silver 0.5353 oz. ASW, 32.5 mm. **Subject:** Deutsche Bundesbank, 50th Aniversary **Obv:** Eagle on rectangle design **Rev:** Buildings on graph

| Date | Mintage | F12 | VF20 | XF40 | MS60 | MS63 |
|---|---|---|---|---|---|---|
| 2007 J | 1,600,000 | — | — | — | 22.00 | 25.00 |
| 2007 J | 300,000 | **PF63** 28.00 | **PF65** 30.00 | | | |

**KM# 268 10 EURO**
18.00 g., 0.925 Silver 0.5353 oz. ASW, 32.5 mm. **Subject:** Eagle **Rev:** St. Elisabeth von Thuringen

| Date | Mintage | F12 | VF20 | XF40 | MS60 | MS63 |
|---|---|---|---|---|---|---|
| 2007 A | 1,600,000 | — | — | — | 22.00 | 25.00 |
| 2007 A | 300,000 | **PF63** 28.00 | **PF65** 30.00 | | | |

**KM# 271 10 EURO**
18.00 g., 0.925 Silver 0.5353 oz. ASW, 32.5 mm. **Subject:** Franz Kafka, 125th Anniversary of Birth **Obv:** Eagle **Rev:** Prague Cathedral, writings & portrait **Edge Lettering:** EIN KÄFIG GING EINEN VOGEL SUCHEN

| Date | Mintage | F12 | VF20 | XF40 | MS60 | MS63 |
|---|---|---|---|---|---|---|
| 2008 G | 1,500,000 | — | — | — | 22.00 | 25.00 |
| 2008 G | 260,000 | **PF63** 28.00 | **PF65** 30.00 | | | |

**KM# 272 10 EURO**
18.00 g., 0.925 Silver 0.5353 oz. ASW, 32.5 mm. **Subject:** Max Planck, 150th Anniversary of Birth **Obv:** Eagle **Rev:** Graph and portrait **Edge Lettering:** DEM ANWENDEN MUSS DAS + ERKENNEN VORAUSGEHEN

| Date | Mintage | F12 | VF20 | XF40 | MS60 | MS63 |
|---|---|---|---|---|---|---|
| 2008 F | 1,500,000 | — | — | — | 22.00 | 25.00 |
| 2008 F | 260,000 | **PF63** 28.00 | **PF65** 30.00 | | | |

**KM# 273 10 EURO**
18.00 g., 0.925 Silver 0.5353 oz. ASW **Subject:** Carl Spitzweg - 200th Anniversary of Birth **Obv:** Eagle **Rev:** Spitzweg reclining in bed with books, umbrella above **Edge Lettering:** ACH, DIE VERGANGENHEIT ÌST SCHÖN **Shape:** 32.5

| Date | Mintage | F12 | VF20 | XF40 | MS60 | MS63 |
|---|---|---|---|---|---|---|
| 2008 D | 1,500,000 | — | — | — | 22.00 | 25.00 |
| 2008 D | 260,000 | **PF63** 28.00 | **PF65** 30.00 | | | |

**KM# 274 10 EURO**
18.00 g., 0.925 Silver 0.5353 oz. ASW, 32.5 mm. **Subject:** Gorch Fock II, 50th Anniversary **Obv:** Eagle **Rev:** Naval training sailing ship Gorch Fock II **Edge Lettering:** SEEFAHRT ÌST NOT

| Date | Mintage | F12 | VF20 | XF40 | MS60 | MS63 |
|---|---|---|---|---|---|---|
| 2008 J | 1,500,000 | — | — | — | 22.00 | 25.00 |
| 2008 J | 260,000 | **PF63** 28.00 | **PF65** 30.00 | | | |

**KM# 294 10 EURO**
18.00 g., 0.925 Silver 0.5353 oz. ASW, 32.5 mm. **Subject:** Archaology in Germany **Obv:** Eagle, stars flanking **Rev:** Sun, moon and star shield

| Date | Mintage | F12 | VF20 | XF40 | MS60 | MS63 |
|---|---|---|---|---|---|---|
| 2008 A | 1,500,000 | — | — | — | 22.00 | 25.00 |
| 2008 A | 260,000 | **PF63** 28.00 | **PF65** 30.00 | | | |

**KM# 279 10 EURO**
18.00 g., 0.925 Silver 0.5353 oz. ASW, 32.5 mm. **Subject:** IAAF World Championships - Berlin **Obv:** Eagle and value **Rev:** Female javelin thrower in stadium **Note:** Mint Marks letters are in Morse Code.

| Date | Mintage | F12 | VF20 | XF40 | MS60 | MS63 |
|---|---|---|---|---|---|---|
| 2009 A | 362,000 | — | — | — | 22.00 | 25.00 |
| 2009 A | 40,000 | **PF63** 28.00 | **PF65** 30.00 | | | |
| 2009 D | 362,000 | — | — | — | 22.00 | 25.00 |
| 2009 D | 40,000 | **PF63** 28.00 | **PF65** 30.00 | | | |
| 2009 F | 362,000 | — | — | — | 22.00 | 25.00 |
| 2009 F | 40,000 | **PF63** 28.00 | **PF65** 30.00 | | | |
| 2009 G | 362,000 | — | — | — | 22.00 | 25.00 |
| 2009 G | 40,000 | **PF63** 28.00 | **PF65** 30.00 | | | |
| 2009 J | 362,000 | — | — | — | 22.00 | 25.00 |
| 2009 J | 40,000 | **PF63** 28.00 | **PF65** 30.00 | | | |

**KM# 280 10 EURO**
18.00 g., 0.925 Silver 0.5353 oz. ASW, 32.5 mm. **Subject:** Kepler's Laws - 400th Anniversary **Obv:** Eagle above value **Rev:** Portrait and geometric diagram demonstrating planetary orbits

| Date | Mintage | F12 | VF20 | XF40 | MS60 | MS63 |
|---|---|---|---|---|---|---|
| 2009 F | 1,643,000 | — | — | — | 22.00 | 25.00 |
| 2009 F | 200,000 | **PF63** 28.00 | **PF65** 30.00 | | | |

**KM# 281 10 EURO**
18.00 g., 0.925 Silver 0.5353 oz. ASW, 32.5 mm. **Subject:** International Aerospace Expo, 100th Anniversary **Obv:** Eagle above value **Rev:** Plane landing, montage of plane development

| Date | Mintage | F12 | VF20 | XF40 | MS60 | MS63 |
|---|---|---|---|---|---|---|
| 2009 D | 1,650,000 | — | — | — | 22.00 | 25.00 |
| 2009 D | 200,000 | **PF63** 28.00 | **PF65** 30.00 | | | |

**KM# 281a 10 EURO**
18.00 g., 0.925 Silver 0.5353 oz. ASW partially gilt, 32.5 mm. **Subject:** International Air Travel, 100th Anniversary **Obv:** Stylized eagle **Rev:** Airplanes, partially gilt

| Date | Mintage | F12 | VF20 | XF40 | MS60 | MS63 |
|---|---|---|---|---|---|---|
| 2009 D | 1,650,000 | — | — | — | 22.00 | 25.00 |
| 2009 D | 200,000 | **PF63** 28.00 | **PF65** 30.00 | | | |

**KM# 282 10 EURO**
18.00 g., 0.925 Silver 0.5353 oz. ASW, 32.5 mm. **Subject:** Leipzig University - 600th Anniversary **Obv:** Eagle above value **Rev:** University seal, portrait of Gottfried Wilhelm Leibniz

| Date | Mintage | F12 | VF20 | XF40 | MS60 | MS63 |
|---|---|---|---|---|---|---|
| 2009 A | 1,613,000 | — | — | — | 22.00 | 25.00 |
| 2009 G | 200,000 | **PF63** 28.00 | **PF65** 30.00 | | | |

**KM# 283 10 EURO**
18.00 g., 0.925 Silver 0.5353 oz. ASW, 32.5 mm. **Subject:** Youth hostels - 100th Anniversary **Obv:** Eagle and value **Rev:** Stylized mountain, Alternal hostel in Westphalia

| Date | Mintage | F12 | VF20 | XF40 | MS60 | MS63 |
|---|---|---|---|---|---|---|
| 2009 G | 1,610,000 | — | — | — | 22.00 | 25.00 |
| 2009 G | 200,000 | **PF63** 28.00 | **PF65** 30.00 | | | |

**KM# 284 10 EURO**
18.00 g., 0.925 Silver 0.5353 oz. ASW, 32.5 mm. **Subject:** Marion Countess Donhoff - 100th Anniversary of Birth **Obv:** Eagle and value **Rev:** Profile right

| Date | Mintage | F12 | VF20 | XF40 | MS60 | MS63 |
|---|---|---|---|---|---|---|
| 2009 J | 1,600,000 | — | — | — | 22.00 | 25.00 |
| 2009 J | 200,000 | **PF63** 28.00 | **PF65** 30.00 | | | |

**KM# 287 10 EURO**
18.00 g., 0.925 Silver 0.5353 oz. ASW, 32.5 mm. **Subject:** Porcelain Production in Germany, 300th Anniversary

| Date | Mintage | F12 | VF20 | XF40 | MS60 | MS63 |
|---|---|---|---|---|---|---|
| 2010 F | 1,749,000 | — | — | — | 20.00 | 22.00 |
| 2010 F | 182,900 | **PF63** 23.00 | **PF65** 25.00 | | | |

**KM# 288 10 EURO**
18.00 g., 0.925 Silver 0.5353 oz. ASW, 32.5 mm. **Subject:** Robert Schumann - 200th Birth Anniversary

| Date | Mintage | F12 | VF20 | XF40 | MS60 | MS63 |
|---|---|---|---|---|---|---|
| 2010 J | 1,700,000 | — | — | — | 20.00 | 22.00 |
| 2010 J | 182,900 | **PF63** 23.00 | **PF65** 25.00 | | | |

**KM# 289 10 EURO**
14.00 g., 0.925 Silver 0.4164 oz. ASW, 32.5 mm. **Subject:** Konrad Zuse, 100th Birth Anniversary

| Date | Mintage | F12 | VF20 | XF40 | MS60 | MS63 |
|---|---|---|---|---|---|---|
| 2010 G | 1,706,000 | — | — | — | 20.00 | 22.00 |
| 2010 G | 182,900 | **PF63** 23.00 | **PF65** 25.00 | | | |

**KM# 290 10 EURO**
18.00 g., 0.925 Silver 0.5353 oz. ASW, 32.5 mm. **Subject:** German Unification, 20th Anniversary **Edge Lettering:** EINIGKEIT UND RECHT UND FREIHEIT

| Date | Mintage | F12 | VF20 | XF40 | MS60 | MS63 |
|---|---|---|---|---|---|---|
| 2010 A | 2,100,000 | — | — | — | 20.00 | 22.00 |
| 2010 A | 184,200 | **PF63** 23.00 | **PF65** 25.00 | | | |

**KM# 291 10 EURO**
18.00 g., 0.925 Silver 0.5353 oz. ASW **Subject:** 175th Anniversary of German Railroads **Edge Lettering:** AUF VEREINTEN GLEISEN 1835-2010

| Date | Mintage | F12 | VF20 | XF40 | MS60 | MS63 |
|---|---|---|---|---|---|---|
| 2010 D | 2,041,000 | — | — | — | 21.00 | 23.00 |
| 2010 D | 186,000 | **PF63** 28.00 | **PF65** 30.00 | | | |

**KM# 295 10 EURO**
16.00 g., 0.625 Silver 0.3215 oz. ASW, 32.5 mm. **Subject:** Franz Liszt, 200th Anniversary of Birth **Edge Lettering:** CGME OBLICE - GENIE VEPPUCHIT

| Date | Mintage | F12 | VF20 | XF40 | MS60 | MS63 |
|---|---|---|---|---|---|---|
| 2011 G | 2,187,000 | — | — | — | 15.00 | 16.00 |
| 2011 G | 178,000 | **PF63** 28.00 | **PF65** 30.00 | | | |

**KM# 296a 10 EURO**
14.00 g., 0.625 Silver 0.2813 oz. ASW, 32.5 mm. **Subject:** 125th Anniversary of the Automobile **Obv:** Stylized eagle, stars, country name, denomination and date **Obv. Legend:** 125 JAHRE AUTOMOBIL **Rev:** Hand on steering wheel, zig-sag roadway **Edge Lettering:** WAS UNS BEWEGT

| Date | Mintage | F12 | VF20 | XF40 | MS60 | MS63 |
|---|---|---|---|---|---|---|
| 2011 F | 223,000 | **PF63** 28.00 | **PF65** 30.00 | | | |

**KM# 298 10 EURO**
18.00 g., 0.925 Silver 0.5353 oz. ASW, 32.5 mm. **Subject:** FIS World Alpine Ski Championships **Edge Lettering:** FESTSPIELE IM SHNEE (Issued in 2010)

| Date | Mintage | F12 | VF20 | XF40 | MS60 | MS63 |
|---|---|---|---|---|---|---|
| 2011 A | 400,000 | — | — | — | 21.00 | 23.00 |
| 2011 A | 41,400 | PF63 28.00 | PF65 30.00 | | | |
| 2011 D | 400,000 | — | — | — | 21.00 | 23.00 |
| 2011 D | 41,400 | PF63 28.00 | PF65 30.00 | | | |
| 2011 F | 400,000 | — | — | — | 21.00 | 23.00 |
| 2011 F | 41,400 | PF63 28.00 | PF65 30.00 | | | |
| 2011 G | 400,000 | — | — | — | 21.00 | 23.00 |
| 2011 G | 41,400 | PF63 28.00 | PF65 30.00 | | | |
| 2011 J | 400,000 | — | — | — | 21.00 | 23.00 |
| 2011 J | 41,400 | PF63 28.00 | PF65 30.00 | | | |

**KM# 299 10 EURO**
14.00 g., Copper-Nickel, 32.5 mm. **Subject:** Soccer (Football) Women's World Cup in Germany **Edge Lettering:** DIE ZUKUNFT DES FUSSBALLS IST WEIBLICH

| Date | Mintage | F12 | VF20 | XF40 | MS60 | MS63 |
|---|---|---|---|---|---|---|
| 2011 A | 444,800 | — | — | — | 15.00 | 16.00 |
| 2011 D | 444,800 | — | — | — | 15.00 | 16.00 |
| 2011 F | 444,800 | — | — | — | 15.00 | 16.00 |
| 2011 G | 444,800 | — | — | — | 15.00 | 16.00 |
| 2011 J | 444,800 | — | — | — | 15.00 | 16.00 |

**KM# 299a 10 EURO**
16.00 g., 0.625 Silver 0.3215 oz. ASW, 32.5 mm. **Subject:** Soccer (Football) Women's World Cup in Germany **Edge Lettering:** DIE ZUKUNFT DES FUSSBALLS IST WEIBLICH

| Date | Mintage | F12 | VF20 | XF40 | MS60 | MS63 |
|---|---|---|---|---|---|---|
| 2011 A | 47,000 | PF63 28.00 | PF65 30.00 | | | |
| 2011 D | 47,000 | PF63 28.00 | PF65 30.00 | | | |
| 2011 F | 47,000 | PF63 28.00 | PF65 30.00 | | | |
| 2011 G | 47,000 | PF63 28.00 | PF65 30.00 | | | |
| 2011 J | 47,000 | PF63 28.00 | PF65 30.00 | | | |

**KM# 300 10 EURO**
14.00 g., Copper-Nickel, 32.5 mm. **Subject:** Till Eulenspiegel, 500th Anniversary **Edge Lettering:** SO BIN ICH DOCH HIE GEWESEN

| Date | Mintage | F12 | VF20 | XF40 | MS60 | MS63 |
|---|---|---|---|---|---|---|
| 2011 D | Est. 1800000 | — | — | — | 15.00 | 16.00 |

**KM# 300a 10 EURO**
16.00 g., 0.625 Silver 0.3215 oz. ASW, 32.5 mm. **Subject:** Til Eulenspiegel, 500th Anniversary **Edge Lettering:** SO BIN ICH DOCH HIE GEWESEN

| Date | Mintage | F12 | VF20 | XF40 | MS60 | MS63 |
|---|---|---|---|---|---|---|
| 2011 D | 223,000 | PF63 28.00 | PF65 30.00 | | | |

**KM# 301 10 EURO**
14.00 g., Copper-Nickel, 32.5 mm. **Subject:** Discovery of the Archaeopteryx, 150th Anniversary **Edge Lettering:** ARCHAEOPTERYX - ZEUGE DER EVOLUTION

| Date | Mintage | F12 | VF20 | XF40 | MS60 | MS63 |
|---|---|---|---|---|---|---|
| 2011 A | Est. 2093000 | — | — | — | 15.00 | 16.00 |

**KM# 301a 10 EURO**
16.00 g., 0.625 Silver 0.3215 oz. ASW, 32.5 mm. **Subject:** Discovery of the Archaeopteryx, 150th Anniversary **Edge Lettering:** ARCHAEOPTERYX - ZEUGE DER EVOLUTION

| Date | Mintage | F12 | VF20 | XF40 | MS60 | MS63 |
|---|---|---|---|---|---|---|
| 2011 A | 223,000 | PF63 28.00 | PF65 30.00 | | | |

**KM# 302 10 EURO**
14.00 g., Copper-Nickel, 32.5 mm. **Subject:** Elbe Tunnel, Hamburg, 100th Anniversary **Edge Lettering:** VERBINDUNG VON STADT UND HAFEN

| Date | Mintage | F12 | VF20 | XF40 | MS60 | MS63 |
|---|---|---|---|---|---|---|
| 2011 J | Est. 1900000 | — | — | — | 15.00 | 16.00 |

**KM# 302a 10 EURO**
16.00 g., 0.625 Silver 0.3215 oz. ASW, 32.5 mm. **Subject:** Elbe Tunnel, Hamburg, 100th Anniversary **Edge Lettering:** VERBINDUNG VON STADT UND HAFEN

| Date | Mintage | F12 | VF20 | XF40 | MS60 | MS63 |
|---|---|---|---|---|---|---|
| 2011 J | 223,000 | PF63 28.00 | PF65 30.00 | | | |

**KM# 308 10 EURO**
16.00 g., 0.625 Silver 0.3215 oz. ASW, 32.5 mm. **Subject:** Friedrich der Grosse, 300th Anniversary of Birth **Obv:** Head of Friedrich the Great facing left **Obv. Legend:** 300 GEBURTSTAG FRIEDRICH II 1712-1786 **Rev:** Stylized eagle, stars, country name, denomination and date **Edge Lettering:** MICH MEINEN MITBÜRGERN NÜTZLICH ERWEISEN

| Date | Mintage | F12 | VF20 | XF40 | MS60 | MS63 |
|---|---|---|---|---|---|---|
| 2012 A | 230,000 | PF63 18.00 | PF65 20.00 | | | |

**KM# 309 10 EURO**
14.00 g., Copper-Nickel, 32.5 mm. **Subject:** German Argo Action, 50th Anniversary of **Obv:** Sprouting seedling **Obv. Legend:** 50 JAHRE DEUTSCHE WELTHUNGERHILFE **Rev:** Stylized eagle, stars, country name, denomination and date **Edge Lettering:** HILFE ZUR SELBSTHILFE

| Date | Mintage | F12 | VF20 | XF40 | MS60 | MS63 |
|---|---|---|---|---|---|---|
| 2012 G | Est. 1579000 | — | — | — | 14.50 | 15.00 |

**KM# 310 10 EURO**
16.00 g., 0.625 Silver 0.3215 oz. ASW, 32.5 mm. **Subject:** Brothers Grimm, 200th Anniversary **Obv:** Conjoined heads of Grimm Brothers facing left **Obv. Legend:** 200 JAHRE GRIMMS MARCHEN **Rev:** Stylized eagle, stars, country name, denomination and date **Edge Lettering:** UND WENN SIE NICHT GESTORBEN SIND...

| Date | Mintage | F12 | VF20 | XF40 | MS60 | MS63 |
|---|---|---|---|---|---|---|
| 2012 F | Est. 210000 | PF63 18.00 | PF65 20.00 | | | |

**KM# 311 10 EURO**
14.00 g., 0.925 Silver 0.4164 oz. ASW, 32.5 mm. **Subject:** German National Library, 100th Anniversary **Obv:** Head facing left, design **Obv. Legend:** DEUTSCHE NATIONAL BIBLIOTECK 100 JAHRE **Rev:** Stylized eagle, country name, denomination and date **Edge Lettering:** BÜCHER SIND DER EINGANG ZUR WELT

| Date | Mintage | F12 | VF20 | XF40 | MS60 | MS63 |
|---|---|---|---|---|---|---|
| 2012 D | 1,490,000 | PF63 18.00 | PF65 20.00 | | | |

**KM# 312 10 EURO**
14.00 g., Copper-Nickel, 32.5 mm. **Subject:** Gerhart Hauptmann, 150th Anniversary of Birth **Obv:** Head of Gerhart Hauptmann **Obv. Legend:** 150 GEBURTSTAG GERHART HAUPTMANN **Rev:** Stylized eagle, stars country name, denomination and date **Edge Lettering:** A JEDER MENSCH HAT HALT 'NE SEHNSUCHT

| Date | Mintage | F12 | VF20 | XF40 | MS60 | MS63 |
|---|---|---|---|---|---|---|
| 2012 J | 1,432,000 | — | — | — | 14.50 | 15.00 |

**KM# 316 10 EURO**
18.00 g., 0.925 Silver 0.5353 oz. ASW **Subject:** Richard Wagner, 200th Anniversary of Birth

| Date | Mintage | F12 | VF20 | XF40 | MS60 | MS63 |
|---|---|---|---|---|---|---|
| 2013 | — | — | — | — | — | 25.00 |
| 2013 | — | PF63 28.00 | PF65 30.00 | | | |

**KM# 317 10 EURO**
18.00 g., 0.925 Silver 0.5353 oz. ASW, 32.5 mm. **Subject:** Freidrich III

| Date | Mintage | F12 | VF20 | XF40 | MS60 | MS63 |
|---|---|---|---|---|---|---|
| 2013 | — | — | — | — | — | 25.00 |
| 2013 | — | PF63 28.00 | PF65 30.00 | | | |

**KM# 318 10 EURO**
16.00 g., 0.925 Silver 0.4758 oz. ASW, 32.5 mm. **Subject:** Georg Buchner, 200th Anniversary of Birth

| Date | Mintage | F12 | VF20 | XF40 | MS60 | MS63 |
|---|---|---|---|---|---|---|
| 2013 | — | — | — | — | — | 25.00 |
| 2013 | — | PF63 28.00 | PF65 30.00 | | | |

### KM# 319 10 EURO

16.00 g., 0.925 Silver 0.4758 oz. ASW, 32.5 mm. **Subject:** Heinrich Hertz, Electric Rays, 125th Anniversary

| Date | Mintage | F12 | VF20 | XF40 | MS60 | MS63 |
|---|---|---|---|---|---|---|
| 2013 | — | — | — | — | — | 25.00 |
| 2013 | — | **PF63** 28.00 | **PF65** 30.00 | | | |

### KM# 320 10 EURO

16.00 g., 0.925 Silver 0.4758 oz. ASW, 32.5 mm. **Subject:** Red Cross, 150th Anniversary

| Date | Mintage | F12 | VF20 | XF40 | MS60 | MS63 |
|---|---|---|---|---|---|---|
| 2013 | — | — | — | — | — | 25.00 |
| 2013 | — | **PF63** 28.00 | **PF65** 30.00 | | | |

### KM# 321 10 EURO

16.00 g., 0.925 Silver 0.4758 oz. ASW **Subject:** German Fairy Tales - Snow White

| Date | Mintage | F12 | VF20 | XF40 | MS60 | MS63 |
|---|---|---|---|---|---|---|
| 2013 | — | — | — | — | — | 25.00 |
| 2013 | — | **PF63** 28.00 | **PF65** 30.00 | | | |

### KM# 328 10 EURO

14.00 g., Copper-Nickel, 32.5 mm. **Obv:** Eagle **Rev:** Old lady with Hansel and Gretel

| Date | Mintage | F12 | VF20 | XF40 | MS60 | MS63 |
|---|---|---|---|---|---|---|
| 2014 G | — | — | — | — | — | 20.00 |

### KM# 328a 10 EURO

16.00 g., 0.625 Silver 0.3215 oz. ASW, 32.5 mm. **Obv:** Eagle **Rev:** Old lady with Hansel and Gretel

| Date | Mintage | F12 | VF20 | XF40 | MS60 | MS63 |
|---|---|---|---|---|---|---|
| 2014 G | — | **PF63** 38.00 | **PF65** 40.00 | | | |

### KM# 329 10 EURO

14.00 g., Copper-Nickel, 32.5 mm. **Subject:** Johann Gottfried Schadow, 250th Anniversary of Birth **Obv:** Eagle **Rev:** Portrait facing, two ladies at left

| Date | Mintage | F12 | VF20 | XF40 | MS60 | MS63 |
|---|---|---|---|---|---|---|
| 2014 A | — | — | — | — | — | 20.00 |

### KM# 329a 10 EURO

16.00 g., 0.625 Silver 0.3215 oz. ASW, 32.5 mm. **Subject:** Johann Gottfried Schadow, 250th Anniversary of Birth **Obv:** Eagle **Rev:** Bust facing, two women at left

| Date | Mintage | F12 | VF20 | XF40 | MS60 | MS63 |
|---|---|---|---|---|---|---|
| 2014 A | — | **PF63** 38.00 | **PF65** 40.00 | | | |

### KM# 330 10 EURO

14.00 g., Copper-Nickel, 32.5 mm. **Subject:** Richard Strauss, 150th Anniversary of Birth **Obv:** Eagle **Rev:** Head right

| Date | Mintage | F12 | VF20 | XF40 | MS60 | MS63 |
|---|---|---|---|---|---|---|
| 2014 | — | — | — | — | — | 20.00 |

### KM# 330a 10 EURO

16.00 g., 0.625 Silver 0.3215 oz. ASW, 32.5 mm. **Obv:** Eagle **Rev:** Richard Strauss, 150th Anniversary of Birth

| Date | Mintage | F12 | VF20 | XF40 | MS60 | MS63 |
|---|---|---|---|---|---|---|
| 2014 D | — | **PF63** 38.00 | **PF65** 40.00 | | | |

### KM# 331 10 EURO

14.00 g., Copper-Nickel, 32.5 mm. **Subject:** Chronicles of Ulrich Richental - King Sigismund, the Pope and Jan Hus, 600th Anniversary **Obv:** Eagle **Rev:** Council of Bishops

| Date | Mintage | F12 | VF20 | XF40 | MS60 | MS63 |
|---|---|---|---|---|---|---|
| 2014 F | — | — | — | — | — | 20.00 |

### KM# 331a 10 EURO

16.00 g., 0.625 Silver 0.3215 oz. ASW, 32.5 mm. **Subject:** Chronicles of Ulrich Richental on King Sigismund, the Pope and Jan Hus, 600th Anniversary **Obv:** Eagle **Rev:** Council of Bishops

| Date | Mintage | F12 | VF20 | XF40 | MS60 | MS63 |
|---|---|---|---|---|---|---|
| 2014 F | — | **PF63** 38.00 | **PF65** 40.00 | | | |

### KM# 332 10 EURO

14.00 g., Copper-Nickel, 32.5 mm. **Subject:** Daniel Gabriel Fahrenheit's invention of the mercury thermometer **Obv:** Eagle

| Date | Mintage | F12 | VF20 | XF40 | MS60 | MS63 |
|---|---|---|---|---|---|---|
| 2014 J | — | — | — | — | — | 20.00 |

### KM# 297 20 EURO

3.89 g., 0.9999 Gold 0.1251 oz. AGW, 17.5 mm. **Series:** German Forest **Subject:** Oak Tree **Obv:** Stylized eagle, stars, legend "BUNDERSREPUBLIK DEUTSCHLAND", date and value **Rev:** Oak leaf and legends "DEUTSCHER WALD" and "EICHE **Edge:** Reeded

| Date | Mintage | F12 | VF20 | XF40 | MS60 | MS63 |
|---|---|---|---|---|---|---|
| 2010 D | 40,000 | — | — | — | — | 225 |
| 2010 F | 40,000 | — | — | — | — | 225 |
| 2010 A | 40,000 | — | — | — | — | 225 |
| 2010 G | 40,000 | — | — | — | — | 225 |
| 2010 J | 40,000 | — | — | — | — | 225 |

### KM# 303 20 EURO

3.89 g., 0.9999 Gold 0.1251 oz. AGW, 17.5 mm. **Series:** German Forest **Subject:** Beech Tree **Obv:** Stylized eagle, stars, legend, date and value **Obv. Legend:** BUNDERSREPUBLIK DEUTSCHLAND **Rev:** Beech leaf and legends **Rev. Legend:** DEUTSCHER WALD / BUCHE **Edge:** Reeded

| Date | Mintage | F12 | VF20 | XF40 | MS60 | MS63 |
|---|---|---|---|---|---|---|
| 2011 A | 40,000 | — | — | — | — | 225 |
| 2011 D | 40,000 | — | — | — | — | 225 |
| 2011 F | 40,000 | — | — | — | — | 225 |
| 2011 G | 40,000 | — | — | — | — | 225 |
| 2011 J | 40,000 | — | — | — | — | 225 |

### KM# 307 20 EURO

3.89 g., 0.9999 Gold 0.1251 oz. AGW, 17.5 mm. **Series:** German Forest **Subject:** Spruce Tree **Obv:** Stylized eagle, stars, date and value **Obv. Legend:** BUNDESREPUBLIK DEUTSCHLAND **Rev:** Spruce branch end and legends **Rev. Legend:** DEUTSCHER WALD / FICHTE **Edge:** Reeded

| Date | Mintage | F12 | VF20 | XF40 | MS60 | MS63 |
|---|---|---|---|---|---|---|
| 2012 A | 40,000 | — | — | — | — | 225 |
| 2012 D | 40,000 | — | — | — | — | 225 |
| 2012 F | 40,000 | — | — | — | — | 225 |
| 2012 G | 40,000 | — | — | — | — | 225 |
| 2012 J | 40,000 | — | — | — | — | 225 |

### KM# 324 20 EURO

3.89 g., 0.9999 Gold 0.1251 oz. AGW, 17.5 mm. **Series:** German Forest **Subject:** Pine Tree **Obv:** Stylized eagle, stars, country name, date and denomination **Rev:** Pine needles **Rev. Legend:** DEUTSCHER WALD and KIEFER **Edge:** Reeded

| Date | Mintage | F12 | VF20 | XF40 | MS60 | MS63 |
|---|---|---|---|---|---|---|
| 2013 | — | — | — | — | — | 225 |
| 2013 | Est. 40000 | — | — | — | — | 225 |
| 2013 | — | — | — | — | — | 225 |
| 2013 | Est. 40000 | — | — | — | — | 225 |
| 2013 | Est. 40000 | — | — | — | — | 225 |

### KM# 220 100 EURO

15.55 g., 0.9999 Gold 0.4999 oz. AGW, 28 mm. **Subject:** Introduction of the Euro Currency **Obv:** Stylized round eagle **Rev:** Euro symbol and arches **Edge:** Reeded

| Date | Mintage | F12 | VF20 | XF40 | MS60 | MS63 |
|---|---|---|---|---|---|---|
| 2002 A | 100,000 | **PF63** 750 | **PF65** 800 | | | |
| 2002 D | 100,000 | **PF63** 750 | **PF65** 800 | | | |
| 2002 F | 100,000 | **PF63** 750 | **PF65** 800 | | | |
| 2002 G | 100,000 | **PF63** 750 | **PF65** 800 | | | |
| 2002 J | 100,000 | **PF63** 750 | **PF65** 800 | | | |

### KM# 228 100 EURO

15.55 g., 0.9999 Gold 0.4999 oz. AGW, 28 mm. **Obv:** Stylized eagle, denomination below **Rev:** Quedlinburg Abbey in monogram **Edge:** Reeded

| Date | Mintage | F12 | VF20 | XF40 | MS60 | MS63 |
|---|---|---|---|---|---|---|
| 2003D | 80,000 | **PF63** 750 | **PF65** 800 | | | |
| 2003F | 80,000 | **PF63** 750 | **PF65** 800 | | | |
| 2003J | 80,000 | **PF63** 750 | **PF65** 800 | | | |
| 2003 A | 80,000 | **PF63** 750 | **PF65** 800 | | | |
| 2003G | 80,000 | **PF63** 750 | **PF65** 800 | | | |

### KM# 235 100 EURO

15.55 g., 0.9999 Gold 0.4999 oz. AGW, 28 mm. **Obv:** Stylized eagle, denomination below **Rev:** Bamberg city view **Edge:** Reeded

| Date | Mintage | F12 | VF20 | XF40 | MS60 | MS63 |
|---|---|---|---|---|---|---|
| 2004 A | 80,000 | **PF63** 750 | **PF65** 800 | | | |
| 2004 F | 80,000 | **PF63** 750 | **PF65** 800 | | | |
| 2004 D | 80,000 | **PF63** 750 | **PF65** 800 | | | |
| 2004 J | 80,000 | **PF63** 750 | **PF65** 800 | | | |
| 2004 G | 80,000 | **PF63** 750 | **PF65** 800 | | | |

### KM# 236 100 EURO

15.55 g., 0.9999 Gold 0.4999 oz. AGW **Subject:** UNESCO - Weimar **Obv:** Stylized eagle **Rev:** Historical City of Weimar buildings **Edge:** Reeded

| Date | Mintage | F12 | VF20 | XF40 | MS60 | MS63 |
|---|---|---|---|---|---|---|
| 2006 A | 70,000 | **PF63** 750 | **PF65** 800 | | | |
| 2006 D | 70,000 | **PF63** 750 | **PF65** 800 | | | |
| 2006 F | 70,000 | **PF63** 750 | **PF65** 800 | | | |
| 2006 G | 70,000 | **PF63** 750 | **PF65** 800 | | | |
| 2006 J | 70,000 | **PF63** 750 | **PF65** 800 | | | |

### KM# 237 100 EURO

15.55 g., 0.9999 Gold 0.4999 oz. AGW, 28 mm. **Subject:** Soccer - Germany 2006 **Obv:** Round stylized eagle **Rev:** Aerial view of stadium

| Date | Mintage | VF20 | XF40 | MS60 | MS63 | MS65 |
|---|---|---|---|---|---|---|
| 2005 A | 70,000 | **PF63** 750 | **PF65** 800 | | | |
| 2005 D | 70,000 | **PF63** 750 | **PF65** 800 | | | |
| 2005 F | 70,000 | **PF63** 750 | **PF65** 800 | | | |
| 2005 G | 70,000 | **PF63** 750 | **PF65** 800 | | | |
| 2005 J | 70,000 | **PF63** 750 | **PF65** 800 | | | |

### KM# 267 100 EURO

15.55 g., 0.9999 Gold 0.4999 oz. AGW, 28 mm. **Subject:** Lubeck - UNESCO Heritage site **Obv:** Eagle **Rev:** City view

| Date | Mintage | F12 | VF20 | XF40 | MS60 | MS63 |
|---|---|---|---|---|---|---|
| 2007 A | 66,000 | **PF63** 750 | **PF65** 800 | | | |
| 2007 D | 66,000 | **PF63** 750 | **PF65** 800 | | | |
| 2007 F | 66,000 | **PF63** 750 | **PF65** 800 | | | |
| 2007 G | 66,000 | **PF63** 750 | **PF65** 800 | | | |
| 2007 J | 66,000 | **PF63** 750 | **PF65** 800 | | | |

### KM# 270 100 EURO

15.55 g., 0.9999 Gold 0.4999 oz. AGW, 28 mm. **Subject:** Goslar - UNESCO Heritage site **Obv:** Eagle **Edge:** Reeded

| Date | Mintage | F12 | VF20 | XF40 | MS60 | MS63 |
|---|---|---|---|---|---|---|
| 2008 A | 64,000 | **PF63** 750 | **PF65** 800 | | | |
| 2008 D | 64,000 | **PF63** 750 | **PF65** 800 | | | |
| 2008 F | 64,000 | **PF63** 750 | **PF65** 800 | | | |
| 2008 G | 64,000 | **PF63** 750 | **PF65** 800 | | | |
| 2008 J | 64,000 | **PF63** 750 | **PF65** 800 | | | |

### KM# 278 100 EURO

15.55 g., 0.9999 Gold 0.4999 oz. AGW, 28 mm. **Subject:** Trier - UNESCO Heritage site **Obv:** Eagle and denomination **Rev:** Riverside montage of buildings **Edge:** Reeded

| Date | Mintage | F12 | VF20 | XF40 | MS60 | MS63 |
|---|---|---|---|---|---|---|
| 2009 A | 64,000 | **PF63** 750 | **PF65** 800 | | | |
| 2009 D | 64,000 | **PF63** 750 | **PF65** 800 | | | |
| 2009 F | 64,000 | **PF63** 750 | **PF65** 800 | | | |
| 2009 G | 64,000 | **PF63** 750 | **PF65** 800 | | | |
| 2009 J | 64,000 | **PF63** 750 | **PF65** 800 | | | |

### KM# 286 100 EURO

15.55 g., 0.9999 Gold 0.4999 oz. AGW, 28 mm. **Subject:** Würzburg - UNESCO Heritage site **Rev:** Würzburg residence and court garden

| Date | Mintage | F12 | VF20 | XF40 | MS60 | MS63 |
|---|---|---|---|---|---|---|
| 2010 A | 64,000 | **PF63** 750 | **PF65** 800 | | | |
| 2010 D | 64,000 | **PF63** 750 | **PF65** 800 | | | |
| 2010 F | 64,000 | **PF63** 750 | **PF65** 800 | | | |
| 2010 G | 64,000 | **PF63** 750 | **PF65** 800 | | | |
| 2010 J | 64,000 | **PF63** 750 | **PF65** 800 | | | |

### KM# 304 100 EURO

15.55 g., 0.9999 Gold 0.4999 oz. AGW **Subject:** UNESCO World Heritage Site - Wartburg Castle **Obv:** Stylized eagle, stars, legend date and value **Obv. Legend:** BUNDERSREPUBLIK DEUTSCHLAND **Rev:** Wartburg Castle and legends **Rev. Legend:** UNESCO WELTERE WARTBURG / GEGR 1067 LUDWIG DER SPRINGER HERMANN I... **Edge:** Reeded

| Date | Mintage | F12 | VF20 | XF40 | MS60 | MS63 |
|---|---|---|---|---|---|---|
| 2011 A | 60,000 | **PF63** 750 | **PF65** 800 | | | |
| 2011 D | 60,000 | **PF63** 750 | **PF65** 800 | | | |
| 2011 F | 60,000 | **PF63** 750 | **PF65** 800 | | | |
| 2011 G | 60,000 | **PF63** 750 | **PF65** 800 | | | |
| 2011 J | 60,000 | **PF63** 750 | **PF65** 800 | | | |

### KM# 313 100 EURO

15.55 g., 0.9999 Gold 0.4999 oz. AGW, 28 mm. **Subject:** UNESCO - Aachen Cathedral **Obv:** Eagle **Rev:** Side view of Cathedral

| Date | Mintage | F12 | VF20 | XF40 | MS60 | MS63 |
|---|---|---|---|---|---|---|
| 2012 A | 54,000 | **PF63** 750 | **PF65** 800 | | | |
| 2012 D | 54,000 | **PF63** 750 | **PF65** 800 | | | |
| 2012 F | 54,000 | **PF63** 750 | **PF65** 800 | | | |
| 2012 G | 54,000 | **PF63** 750 | **PF65** 800 | | | |
| 2012 J | 54,000 | **PF63** 750 | **PF65** 800 | | | |

### KM# 322 100 EURO

15.55 g., 0.999 Gold 0.4994 oz. AGW, 28 mm. **Subject:** Aachen Cathedral, European Heritage Site.

| Date | Mintage | F12 | VF20 | XF40 | MS60 | MS63 |
|---|---|---|---|---|---|---|
| 2012 A | 44,000 | **PF63** 750 | **PF65** 800 | | | |
| 2012 D | 44,000 | **PF63** 750 | **PF65** 800 | | | |
| 2012 F | 44,000 | **PF63** 750 | **PF65** 800 | | | |
| 2012 G | 44,000 | **PF63** 750 | **PF65** 800 | | | |
| 2012 J | 44,000 | **PF63** 750 | **PF65** 800 | | | |

### KM# 333 100 EURO

15.55 g., 0.999 Gold 0.4994 oz. AGW, 28 mm. **Subject:** Lorsch Cloister **Obv:** Eagle

| Date | Mintage | F12 | VF20 | XF40 | MS60 | MS63 |
|---|---|---|---|---|---|---|
| 2014 A | — | **PF63** 950 | **PF65** 975 | | | |
| 2014 D | — | **PF63** 950 | **PF65** 975 | | | |
| 2014 F | — | **PF63** 950 | **PF65** 975 | | | |
| 2014 G | — | **PF63** 950 | **PF65** 975 | | | |
| 2014 J | — | **PF63** 950 | **PF65** 975 | | | |

### KM# 221 200 EURO

31.10 g., 0.9999 Gold 0.9998 oz. AGW, 32.5 mm. **Subject:** Introduction of the Euro Currency **Obv:** Stylized round eagle **Rev:** Euro symbol and arches **Edge Lettering:** IM ... ZEICHEN ... DER ... EINIGUNG ... EUROPAS

| Date | Mintage | F12 | VF20 | XF40 | MS60 | MS63 |
|---|---|---|---|---|---|---|
| 2002 A | 1,700 | **PF63** 1,450 | **PF65** 1,550 | | | |
| 2002 D | 1,700 | **PF63** 1,450 | **PF65** 1,550 | | | |
| 2002 F | 1,700 | **PF63** 1,450 | **PF65** 1,550 | | | |
| 2002 G | 1,700 | **PF63** 1,450 | **PF65** 1,550 | | | |
| 2002 J | 1,700 | **PF63** 1,450 | **PF65** 1,550 | | | |

## MINT SETS

| KM# | Date | Mintage | Identification | Issue Price | Mkt Val |
|---|---|---|---|---|---|
| MS119 | 2001A (10) | 130,000 | KM105, 106a, 107-108, 109.2, 110, 140.1, 170, 175, 183 | — | 40.00 |
| MS120 | 2001D (10) | 130,000 | KM105,1 06a, 107-108, 109.2, 110, 140.1, 170, 175, 183 | — | 40.00 |
| MS121 | 2001F (10) | 130,000 | KM105, 106a, 107-108, 109.2, 110, 140.1, 170, 175, 183 | — | 40.00 |
| MS122 | 2001G (10) | 130,000 | KM105, 106a, 107-108, 109.2, 110, 140.1, 170, 175, 183 | — | 40.00 |
| MS123 | 2001J (10) | 130,000 | KM105, 106a, 107-108, 109.2, 110, 140.1, 170, 175, 183 | — | 40.00 |
| MS124 | 2002A (8) | 90,000 | KM#207-214 | — | 20.00 |
| MS125 | 2002D (8) | 90,000 | KM#207-214 | — | 20.00 |
| MS126 | 2002F (8) | 90,000 | KM#207-214 | — | 20.00 |
| MS127 | 2002G (8) | 90,000 | KM#207-214 | — | 20.00 |
| MS128 | 2002J (8) | 90,000 | KM#207-214 | — | 20.00 |
| MS129 | 2003A (8) | 90,000 | KM#207-214 | — | 25.00 |
| MS130 | 2003D (8) | 90,000 | KM#207-214 | — | 27.50 |
| MS131 | 2003F (8) | 90,000 | KM#207-214 | — | 27.50 |
| MS132 | 2003G (8) | 90,000 | KM#207-214 | — | 27.50 |
| MS133 | 2003J (8) | 90,000 | KM#207-214 | — | 25.00 |
| MS134 | 2004A (8) | 90,000 | KM#207-214 | — | 24.00 |
| MS135 | 2004D (8) | 90,000 | KM#207-214 | — | 22.00 |
| MS136 | 2004F (8) | 90,000 | KM#207-214 | — | 24.00 |
| MS137 | 2004G (8) | 90,000 | KM#207-214 | — | 24.00 |
| MS138 | 2004J (8) | 90,000 | KM#207-214 | — | 28.00 |
| MS139 | 2005A (8) | 90,000 | KM#207-214 | — | 28.00 |
| MS140 | 2005D (8) | 90,000 | KM#207-214 | — | 28.00 |
| MS141 | 2005F (8) | 90,000 | KM#207-214 | — | 28.00 |
| MS142 | 2005G (8) | 90,000 | KM#207-214 | — | 28.00 |
| MS143 | 2005J (8) | 90,000 | KM#207-214 | — | 26.00 |
| MS144 | 2006A (9) | 90,000 | KM#207-214, 253 | — | 35.00 |
| MS145 | 2006D (9) | 90,000 | KM#207-214, 253 | — | 35.00 |
| MS146 | 2006F (9) | 90,000 | KM#207-214, 253 | — | 35.00 |
| MS147 | 2006G (9) | 90,000 | KM#207-214, 253 | — | 35.00 |
| MS148 | 2006J (9) | 90,000 | KM#207-214, 253 | — | 35.00 |
| MS149 | 2006 (5) | 80,000 | KM#253 (A, D, F, G and J) | — | 23.00 |
| MS150 | 2007A (9) | 90,000 | KM#207-209, 254-257, 259, 260 | — | 27.00 |
| MS151 | 2007D (9) | 90,000 | KM#207-209, 254-257, 259, 260 | — | 27.00 |
| MS152 | 2007F (9) | 90,000 | KM#207-209, 254-257, 259, 260 | — | 27.00 |
| MS153 | 2007G (9) | 90,000 | KM#207-209, 254-257, 259, 260 | — | 27.00 |
| MS154 | 2007J (9) | 90,000 | KM#207-209, 254-257, 259, 260 | — | 27.00 |
| MS155 | 2007 (5) | 80,000 | KM#260 (A, D, F, G and J) | — | 23.00 |
| MS156 | 2008A (9) | 80,000 | KM#207-209, 254-258, 261 | — | 27.00 |
| MS157 | 2008D (9) | 80,000 | KM#207-209, 254-258, 261 | — | 27.00 |
| MS158 | 2008F (9) | 80,000 | KM#207-209, 254-258, 261 | — | 27.00 |
| MS159 | 2008G (9) | 80,000 | KM#207-209, 254-258, 261 | — | 27.00 |
| MS160 | 2008J (9) | 80,000 | KM#207-209, 254-258, 261 | — | 27.00 |
| MS161 | 2008 (5) | 80,000 | KM#261 (A, D, F, G, J) | — | 23.00 |
| MS162 | 2009A (9) | 60,000 | KM#207-209, 254-257, 276, 277 | — | 27.00 |
| MS163 | 2009D (9) | 60,000 | KM#207-209, 254-257, 276, 277 | — | 27.00 |
| MS164 | 2009F (9) | 60,000 | KM#207-209, 254-257, 276, 277 | — | 27.00 |
| MS165 | 2009G (9) | 60,000 | KM#207-209, 254-257, 276, 277 | — | 27.00 |
| MS166 | 2009J (9) | 60,000 | KM#207-209, 254-257, 276, 277 | — | 27.00 |
| MS167 | 2009 (5) | 50,000 | KM#276 (A, D, F, G, J) | — | 23.00 |
| MS168 | 2010A (9) | 53,800 | KM#207-209, 254-258, 285 | — | 20.00 |
| MS169 | 2010D (9) | 46,800 | KM#207-209, 254-258, 285 | — | 20.00 |
| MS170 | 2010F (9) | 46,800 | KM#207-209, 254-258, 285 | — | 20.00 |
| MS171 | 2010G (9) | 46,800 | KM#207-209, 254-258, 285 | — | 20.00 |
| MS172 | 2010J (9) | 46,800 | KM#207-209, 254-258, 285 | — | 20.00 |
| MS173 | 2010 (5) | 45,000 | KM#285 (A, D, F, G, J) | — | 23.00 |
| MS174 | 2011A (9) | 48,000 | KM#207-209, 254-258, 293 | — | 20.00 |
| MS176 | 2011F (9) | 44,000 | KM#207-209, 254-258, 293 | — | 20.00 |
| MS177 | 2011G (9) | 44,000 | KM#207-209, 254-258, 293 | — | 20.00 |
| MS178 | 2011J (9) | 44,000 | KM#207-209, 254-258, 293 | — | 20.00 |
| MS179 | 2011 (5) | 147,000 | KM#293 (A, D, F, G, J) | — | 23.00 |
| MS180 | 2012A (9) | 50,000 | KM#207-209, 254-257, 305, 306 | — | 20.00 |
| MS181 | 2012D (9) | 50,000 | KM#207-209, 254-257, 305, 306 | — | 20.00 |
| MS182 | 2012G (9) | 50,000 | KM#207-209, 254-257, 305, 306 | — | 20.00 |
| MS183 | 2012G (9) | 50,000 | KM#207-209, 254-257, 305, 306 | — | 20.00 |
| MS184 | 2012J (9) | 50,000 | KM#207-209, 254-257, 305, 306 | — | 20.00 |
| MS185 | 2012 (5) | 45,000 | KM#305 (A, D, F, G and J) | — | 24.00 |
| MS186 | 2012 (6) | 45,000 | KM#306 (A, D, F, G and J) | — | 38.00 |

## PROOF SETS

| KM# | Date | Mintage | Identification | Issue Price | Mkt Val |
|---|---|---|---|---|---|
| PS150 | 2001A (10) | 78,000 | KM105, 106a, 107-108, 109.2, 110, 140.1, 170, 175, 183 | — | 45.00 |
| PS151 | 2001D (10) | 78,000 | KM105, 106a, 107-108, 109.2, 110, 140.1, 170, 175, 183 | — | 45.00 |
| PS152 | 2001F (10) | 78,000 | KM105, 106a, 107-108, 110, 140.1, 170, 175, 183 | — | 45.00 |
| PS153 | 2001G (10) | 78,000 | KM105, 106a, 107-108, 109.2, 110, 140.1, 170, 175, 183 | — | 45.00 |
| PS154 | 2001J (10) | 78,000 | KM105, 106a, 107-108, 109.2, 110, 140.1, 170, 175, 183 | — | 45.00 |
| PS155 | 2002A (8) | 75,000 | KM#207-214 | — | 20.00 |
| PS156 | 2002D (8) | 75,000 | KM#207-214 | — | 20.00 |
| PS157 | 2002F (8) | 75,000 | KM#207-214 | — | 20.00 |
| PS158 | 2002G (8) | 75,000 | KM#207-214 | — | 20.00 |
| PS159 | 2002J (8) | 75,000 | KM#207-214 | — | 20.00 |
| PS221 | 2002 (5) | 80,000 | KM#215-219 | — | 150 |
| PS160 | 2003A (8) | 75,000 | KM#207-214 | — | 20.00 |
| PS161 | 2003D (8) | 75,000 | KM#207-214 | — | 20.00 |
| PS162 | 2003F (8) | 75,000 | KM#207-214 | — | 20.00 |
| PS163 | 2003G (8) | 75,000 | KM#207-214 | — | 20.00 |

| | | | | | |
|---|---|---|---|---|---|
| PS164 | 2003J (8) | 75,000 | KM#207-214 | — | 20.00 |
| PS165 | 2004A (8) | 75,000 | KM#207-214 | — | 20.00 |
| PS166 | 2004D (8) | 75,000 | KM#207-214 | — | 20.00 |
| PS167 | 2004F (8) | 75,000 | KM#207-214 | — | 20.00 |
| PS168 | 2004G (8) | 75,000 | KM#207-214 | — | 20.00 |
| PS169 | 2004J (8) | 75,000 | KM#207-214 | — | 20.00 |
| PS223 | 2004 (6) | 80,000 | KM#229-234 | — | 180 |
| PS170 | 2005A (8) | 75,000 | KM#207-214 | — | 30.00 |
| PS171 | 2005D (8) | 75,000 | KM#207-214 | — | 30.00 |
| PS172 | 2005F (8) | 75,000 | KM#207-214 | — | 30.00 |
| PS173 | 2005G (8) | 75,000 | KM#207-214 | — | 30.00 |
| PS174 | 2005J (8) | 75,000 | KM#207-214 | — | 30.00 |
| PS224 | 2005 (6) | 80,000 | KM#238-243 | — | 200 |
| PS175 | 2006A (9) | 75,000 | KM#207-214, 253 | — | 35.00 |
| PS176 | 2006D (9) | 75,000 | KM#207-214, 253 | — | 35.00 |
| PS177 | 2006F (9) | 75,000 | KM#207-214, 253 | — | 35.00 |
| PS178 | 2006G (9) | 75,000 | KM#207-214, 253 | — | 35.00 |
| PS179 | 2006J (9) | 75,000 | KM#207-214, 253 | — | 35.00 |
| PS180 | 2006 (5) | 70,000 | KM#253 (A, D, F, G, J) | — | 30.00 |
| PS225 | 2006 (6) | 80,000 | KM#245-249 | — | 150 |
| PS181 | 2007A (9) | 70,000 | KM#207-209, 254-257, 259, 260 | — | 35.00 |
| PS182 | 2007D (9) | 70,000 | KM#207-209, 254-257, 259, 260 | — | 35.00 |
| PS183 | 2007F (9) | 70,000 | KM#207-209, 254-257, 259, 260 | — | 35.00 |
| PS184 | 2007G (9) | 75,000 | KM#207-209, 254-257, 259, 260 | — | 35.00 |
| PS185 | 2007J (9) | 75,000 | KM#207-209, 254-257, 259, 260 | — | 35.00 |
| PS186 | 2007 (5) | 70,000 | KM#260 (A, D, F, G, J) | — | 40.00 |
| PS226 | 2007 (5) | 50,000 | KM#259 (A, D, F, G and J) | — | 42.00 |
| PS227 | 2007 (5) | 80,000 | KM#263-266, 268 | — | 150 |
| PS187 | 2008A (9) | 70,000 | KM#207-209, 254-258, 261 | — | 35.00 |
| PS188 | 2008D (9) | 70,000 | KM#207-209, 254-258, 261 | — | 35.00 |
| PS189 | 2008F (9) | 70,000 | KM#207-209, 254-258, 261 | — | 35.00 |
| PS190 | 2008G (9) | 70,000 | KM#207-209, 254-258, 261 | — | 35.00 |
| PS191 | 2008J (9) | 70,000 | KM#207-209, 254-258, 261 | — | 35.00 |
| PS192 | 2008 (5) | 70,000 | KM#261 (A, D, F, G, J) | — | 40.00 |
| PS228 | 2008 (5) | 80,000 | KM#271-274, 294 | — | 150 |
| PS193 | 2009A (9) | 50,000 | KM#207-209, 254-258, 276 | — | 35.00 |
| PS194 | 2009D (9) | 50,000 | KM#207-209, 254-258, 276 | — | 35.00 |
| PS195 | 2009F (9) | 50,000 | KM#207-209, 254-258, 276 | — | 35.00 |
| PS196 | 2009G (9) | 50,000 | KM#207-209, 254-258, 276 | — | 35.00 |
| PS197 | 2009J (9) | 50,000 | KM#207-209, 254-258, 276 | — | 35.00 |
| PS198 | 2009 (5) | 50,000 | KM#276 (A, D, F, G, J) | — | 40.00 |
| PS229 | 2009 (5) | 20,000 | KM#277 (A, D, F, G and J) | — | 42.00 |
| PS230 | 2009 (6) | 60,000 | KM#279, 281, 281a, 282-284 | — | 180 |
| PS199 | 2010A (9) | 45,150 | KM#207-209, 254-258, 285 | — | 40.00 |
| PS200 | 2010D (9) | 40,120 | KM#207-209, 254-258, 285 | — | 40.00 |
| PS201 | 2010F (9) | 40,120 | KM#207-209, 254-258, 285 | — | 40.00 |
| PS202 | 2010G (9) | 40,120 | KM#207-209, 254-258, 285 | — | 40.00 |
| PS203 | 2010J (9) | 40,120 | KM#207-209, 254-258, 285 | — | 40.00 |
| PS204 | 2010 (5) | 45,000 | KM#285 (A, D, F, G, J) | — | 40.00 |
| PS231 | 2010 (5) | 57,900 | KM#287-291, 298a | — | 180 |
| PS215 | 2011A (9) | 43,000 | KM#207-209, 254-258, 293 | — | 40.00 |
| PS216 | 2011D (9) | 37,000 | KM#207-209, 254-258, 293 | — | 40.00 |
| PS217 | 2011F (9) | 37,000 | KM#207-209, 254-258, 293 | — | 40.00 |
| PS218 | 2011G (9) | 37,000 | KM#207-209, 254-258, 293 | — | 40.00 |
| PS219 | 2011J (9) | 37,000 | KM#207-209, 254-258, 293 | — | 40.00 |
| PS220 | 2011 (5) | 55,000 | KM#293 (A, D, F, G, J) | — | 40.00 |
| PS232 | 2011 (6) | 63,000 | KM#295, 296a, 299a-302a | — | 180 |
| PS233 | 2012A (9) | 40,000 | KM#207-209, 254-258, 305, 306 | — | 30.00 |
| PS234 | 2012D (9) | 32,000 | KM#207-209, 254-257, 305, 306 | — | 30.00 |
| PS235 | 2012F (9) | 32,000 | KM#207-209, 254-257, 305, 306 | — | 30.00 |
| PS236 | 2012G (9) | 40,000 | KM#207-209, 254-257, 305, 306 | — | 30.00 |
| PS237 | 2012J (10) | 32,000 | KM#207-209, 254-258, 305, 306 | — | 30.00 |
| PS238 | 2012 (5) | 55,000 | KM#306 (A, D, F, G and J) | — | 42.00 |
| PS239 | 2012 (0) | 60,000 | KM#308a-312a | — | 150 |

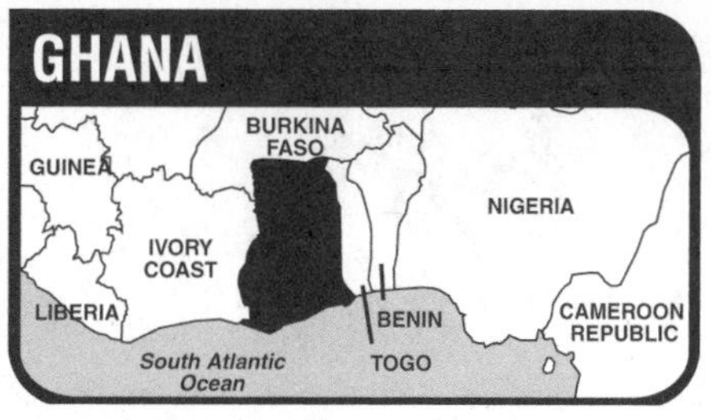


The Republic of Ghana, a member of the Commonwealth of Nations situated on the West Coast of Africa between Ivory Coast and Togo, has an area of 92,100 sq. mi. (238,540 sq. km.) and a population of 14 million, almost entirely African. Capital: Accra. Cocoa (the major crop), coconuts, palm kernels and coffee are exported. Mining, second in importance to agriculture, is concentrated on gold, manganese and industrial diamonds.

**MONETARY SYSTEM**

1 Cedi = 100 Pesewas, 1965-2007

1 (new) Cedi = 10,000 (old) Cedis, 2007-

# REPUBLIC

## DECIMAL COINAGE

**KM# 36 10 CEDIS**

4.41 g., Copper-Nickel, 22.9 mm. **Obv:** National arms divides date and denomination **Rev:** Gorilla family **Edge:** Plain

| Date | Mintage | VF20 | XF40 | MS60 | MS63 | MS65 |
|---|---|---|---|---|---|---|
| 2003 | — | — | — | 1.50 | 2.00 | 2.50 |

## REFORM COINAGE

2007-

**KM# 37 PESEWA**

1.82 g., Copper Plated Steel, 17 mm. **Obv:** National arms **Obv. Legend:** GHANA **Rev:** Adomi Bridge **Edge:** Plain

| Date | Mintage | VF20 | XF40 | MS60 | MS63 | MS65 |
|---|---|---|---|---|---|---|
| 2007 | — | — | — | — | 0.75 | 1.00 |

**KM# 38 5 PESEWAS**

2.50 g., Nickel Clad Steel, 18 mm. **Obv:** National arms **Obv. Legend:** GHANA **Rev:** Native male blowing horn **Edge:** Plain

| Date | Mintage | VF20 | XF40 | MS60 | MS63 | MS65 |
|---|---|---|---|---|---|---|
| 2007 | — | — | — | — | 1.25 | 1.50 |

**KM# 39 10 PESEWAS**

3.23 g., Nickel Clad Steel, 20.4 mm. **Obv:** National arms **Obv. Legend:** GHANA **Rev:** Open book, pen **Edge:** Reeded

| Date | Mintage | VF20 | XF40 | MS60 | MS63 | MS65 |
|---|---|---|---|---|---|---|
| 2007 | — | — | — | — | 2.50 | 3.00 |

**KM# 40 20 PESEWAS**

4.40 g., Nickel Plated Steel, 23.5 mm. **Obv:** National arms **Obv. Legend:** GHANA **Rev:** Split open cocoa pod **Edge:** Plain

| Date | Mintage | VF20 | XF40 | MS60 | MS63 | MS65 |
|---|---|---|---|---|---|---|
| 2007 | — | — | — | — | 3.50 | 4.00 |

**KM# 41 50 PESEWAS**

6.08 g., Nickel Plated Steel, 26.4 mm. **Obv:** National arms **Obv. Legend:** GHANA **Rev:** 1/2 length figure of market woman facing **Edge:** Reeded

| Date | Mintage | VF20 | XF40 | MS60 | MS63 | MS65 |
|---|---|---|---|---|---|---|
| 2007 | — | — | — | — | 6.00 | 7.00 |

**KM# 42 CEDI**

7.40 g., Bi-Metallic Brass center in Nickel Plated Steel ring, 28 mm. **Obv:** National arms **Obv. Legend:** GHANA **Rev:** Scale of Justice in sprays **Edge:** Segmented reeding

| Date | Mintage | VF20 | XF40 | MS60 | MS63 | MS65 |
|---|---|---|---|---|---|---|
| 2007 | — | — | — | — | 9.00 | 10.00 |

**KM# 43 5 CEDIS**

31.14 g., 0.999 Silver 1.000 oz. ASW, 40 mm. **Obv:** Elizabeth II **Rev:** Elephants

| Date | Mintage | VF20 | XF40 | MS60 | MS63 | MS65 |
|---|---|---|---|---|---|---|
| 2013 | 2,000 | **PF63** 65.00 | **PF65** 70.00 | | | |

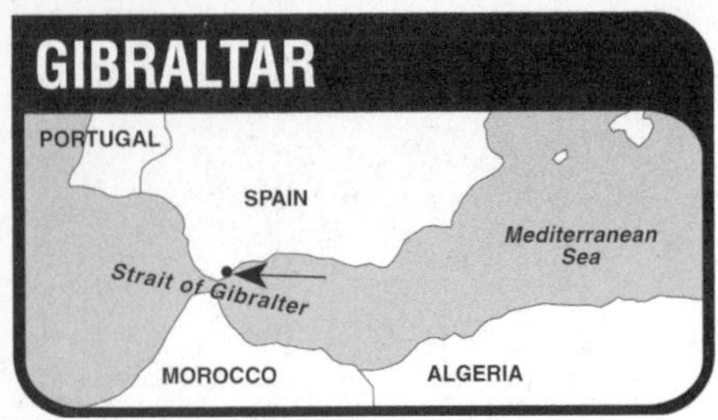


The British Colony of Gibraltar, located at the southernmost point of the Iberian Peninsula, has an area of 2.25 sq. mi. (6.5 sq. km.) and a population of 29,651. Capital (and only town): Gibraltar. Aside from its strategic importance as guardian of the western entrance to the Mediterranean Sea, Gibraltar is also a free port and a British naval base.

**RULERS**
British

**MINT MARKS**
PM - Pobjoy Mint
PMM – Pobjoy Mint (only appears on coins dated 2000)

**NOTE: ALL coins for 1988 –2003 include the PM mint mark except the 2000 dated circulation pieces which instead have PMM.**

**MINT PRIVY MARKS**
U - Unc finish

**MONETARY SYSTEM**
100Pence = 1 Pound

# BRITISH COLONY

## DECIMAL COINAGE

100 Pence = 1 Pound

### KM# 773 PENNY

3.56 g., Copper Plated Steel, 20.32 mm. **Ruler:** Elizabeth II **Obv:** Head with tiara right **Rev:** Barbary partridge left divides denomination

| Date | Mintage | VF20 | XF40 | MS60 | MS63 | MS65 |
|---|---|---|---|---|---|---|
| 2001 AA | — | — | — | 0.15 | 0.35 | 0.50 |
| 2002 AA | — | — | — | 0.15 | 0.35 | 0.50 |
| 2003 AA | — | — | — | 0.15 | 0.35 | 0.50 |

### KM# 1046 PENNY

3.56 g., Copper Plated Steel, 20.32 mm. **Ruler:** Elizabeth II **Subject:** 300th Anniversary **Obv:** Crowned bust right **Rev:** Monkey **Edge:** Plain

| Date | Mintage | VF20 | XF40 | MS60 | MS63 | MS65 |
|---|---|---|---|---|---|---|
| 2004 | — | — | — | 0.15 | 0.35 | 0.50 |

### KM# 1079 PENNY

3.56 g., Copper Plated Steel, 20.32 mm. **Ruler:** Elizabeth II **Obv:** Bust right **Rev:** Sceptre

| Date | Mintage | VF20 | XF40 | MS60 | MS63 | MS65 |
|---|---|---|---|---|---|---|
| 2005 | — | — | — | 0.15 | 0.35 | 0.50 |
| 2006 | — | — | — | 0.15 | 0.35 | 0.50 |
| 2007 | — | — | — | 0.15 | 0.35 | 0.50 |
| 2008 | — | — | — | 0.15 | 0.35 | 0.50 |
| 2009 | — | — | — | 0.15 | 0.35 | 0.50 |
| 2010 | — | — | — | 0.15 | 0.35 | 0.50 |
| 2011 | — | — | — | 0.15 | 0.35 | 0.50 |

### KM# 1098 PENNY

3.54 g., Bronze Plated Steel, 20.5 mm. **Ruler:** Elizabeth II **Rev:** Bird left

| Date | Mintage | VF20 | XF40 | MS60 | MS63 | MS65 |
|---|---|---|---|---|---|---|
| 2010 | — | — | — | 0.15 | 0.35 | 0.50 |

### KM# 1099 PENNY

3.56 g., Copper Plated Steel, 20.32 mm. **Ruler:** Elizabeth II **Obv:** Bust right **Obv. Legend:** ELIZABETH II QUEEN OF GIBRALTAR **Rev:** Bird left

| Date | Mintage | VF20 | XF40 | MS60 | MS63 | MS65 |
|---|---|---|---|---|---|---|
| 2012 | — | — | — | 0.15 | 0.35 | 0.50 |

### KM# 774 2 PENCE

7.12 g., Copper Plated Steel, 25.91 mm. **Ruler:** Elizabeth II **Obv:** Head with tiara right

| Date | Mintage | VF20 | XF40 | MS60 | MS63 | MS65 |
|---|---|---|---|---|---|---|
| 2001 AA | — | — | — | 0.20 | 0.50 | 0.85 |
| 2001 PM AB | — | — | — | 0.20 | 0.50 | 0.85 |
| 2002 | — | — | — | 0.20 | 0.50 | 0.85 |
| 2003 AA | — | — | — | 0.20 | 0.50 | 0.85 |

### KM# 1044 2 PENCE

7.12 g., Copper Plated Steel, 25.91 mm. **Ruler:** Elizabeth II **Subject:** 300th Anniversary **Obv:** Crowned bust right **Rev:** Four old keys **Edge:** Plain

| Date | Mintage | VF20 | XF40 | MS60 | MS63 | MS65 |
|---|---|---|---|---|---|---|
| 2004 | — | — | — | 0.20 | 0.50 | 0.65 |

### KM# 1065 2 PENCE

7.12 g., Copper Plated Steel, 25.91 mm. **Ruler:** Elizabeth II **Subject:** Operation Torch, 1942 **Rev:** Three soldiers

| Date | Mintage | VF20 | XF40 | MS60 | MS63 | MS65 |
|---|---|---|---|---|---|---|
| 2005 | — | — | — | 0.20 | 0.50 | 0.65 |
| 2006 | — | — | — | 0.20 | 0.50 | 0.65 |
| 2007 | — | — | — | 0.20 | 0.50 | 0.65 |
| 2008 | — | — | — | 0.20 | 0.50 | 0.65 |
| 2009 | — | — | — | 0.20 | 0.50 | 0.65 |
| 2010 | — | — | — | 0.20 | 0.50 | 0.65 |
| 2011 | — | — | — | 0.20 | 0.50 | 0.65 |

### KM# 1080 2 PENCE

7.12 g., Copper Plated Steel, 25.91 mm. **Ruler:** Elizabeth II **Subject:** Diamond Wedding **Rev:** Conjoined busts of Elizabeth II and Philip

| Date | Mintage | VF20 | XF40 | MS60 | MS63 | MS65 |
|---|---|---|---|---|---|---|
| 2007 | — | — | — | 0.20 | 0.50 | 0.65 |

### KM# 1100 2 PENCE

7.12 g., Copper Plated Steel, 25.91 mm. **Ruler:** Elizabeth II **Obv:** Bust right **Obv. Legend:** ELIZABETH II QUEEN OF GIBRALTAR

| Date | Mintage | VF20 | XF40 | MS60 | MS63 | MS65 |
|---|---|---|---|---|---|---|
| 2012 | — | — | — | 0.20 | 0.50 | 0.65 |

### KM# 775 5 PENCE

3.25 g., Copper-Nickel, 18 mm. **Ruler:** Elizabeth II **Obv:** Head with tiara right **Rev:** Barbary Ape left divides denomination **Edge:** Reeded

| Date | Mintage | VF20 | XF40 | MS60 | MS63 | MS65 |
|---|---|---|---|---|---|---|
| 2001 AB | — | — | — | 0.25 | 0.60 | 0.75 |
| 2002 AB | — | — | — | 0.25 | 0.60 | 0.75 |
| 2003 AA | — | — | — | 0.25 | 0.60 | 0.75 |

### KM# 1049 5 PENCE

3.25 g., Copper-Nickel, 18 mm. **Ruler:** Elizabeth II **Subject:** Tercentenary 1704-2004 **Obv:** Elizabeth II **Rev:** British Royal Sceptre **Edge:** Reeded

| Date | Mintage | VF20 | XF40 | MS60 | MS63 | MS65 |
|---|---|---|---|---|---|---|
| 2004 | — | — | — | — | — | 1.50 |

### KM# 1081 5 PENCE

3.25 g., Copper-Nickel, 18 mm. **Ruler:** Elizabeth II **Obv:** Bust in diadem right **Rev:** Barbary ape seated **Edge:** Reeded

| Date | Mintage | VF20 | XF40 | MS60 | MS63 | MS65 |
|---|---|---|---|---|---|---|
| 2005 | — | — | — | 0.25 | 0.60 | 0.75 |
| 2006 | — | — | — | 0.25 | 0.60 | 0.75 |
| 2007 | — | — | — | 0.25 | 0.60 | 0.75 |
| 2008 | — | — | — | 0.25 | 0.60 | 0.75 |
| 2009 | — | — | — | 0.25 | 0.60 | 0.75 |
| 2010 | — | — | — | 0.25 | 0.60 | 0.75 |
| 2011 | — | — | — | 0.25 | 0.60 | 0.75 |

### KM# 1207 5 PENCE

3.25 g., Copper-Nickel, 18 mm. **Ruler:** Elizabeth II **Rev:** Barbary ape seated

| Date | Mintage | VF20 | XF40 | MS60 | MS63 | MS65 |
|---|---|---|---|---|---|---|
| 2010 | — | — | — | 0.25 | 0.60 | 0.75 |
| 2011 | — | — | — | 0.25 | 0.60 | 0.75 |

### KM# 1101 5 PENCE

3.25 g., Copper-Nickel, 18 mm. **Ruler:** Elizabeth II **Obv:** Bust right **Obv. Legend:** ELIZABETH II QUEEN OF GIBRALTAR

| Date | Mintage | VF20 | XF40 | MS60 | MS63 | MS65 |
|---|---|---|---|---|---|---|
| 2012 | — | — | — | 0.25 | 0.60 | 0.75 |

### KM# 776 10 PENCE

6.50 g., Copper-Nickel, 24.5 mm. **Ruler:** Elizabeth II **Obv:** Head with tiara right, date below **Rev:** Denomination below building **Edge:** Reeded

| Date | Mintage | VF20 | XF40 | MS60 | MS63 | MS65 |
|---|---|---|---|---|---|---|
| 2001 AC | — | — | — | 0.50 | 1.00 | 1.25 |
| 2001 AB | — | — | — | 0.50 | 1.00 | 1.25 |
| 2001 AE | — | — | — | 0.50 | 1.00 | 1.25 |
| 2001 AA | — | — | — | 0.50 | 1.00 | 1.25 |
| 2002 AC | — | — | — | 0.50 | 1.00 | 1.25 |
| 2003 AA | — | — | — | 0.50 | 1.00 | 1.25 |

### KM# 1047 10 PENCE

6.50 g., Copper-Nickel, 24.5 mm. **Ruler:** Elizabeth II **Subject:** 300th Anniversary **Obv:** Elizabeth II **Rev:** Three military officers planning Operation Torch 1942 **Edge:** Reeded

| Date | Mintage | VF20 | XF40 | MS60 | MS63 | MS65 |
|---|---|---|---|---|---|---|
| 2004 | — | — | — | 0.35 | 0.75 | 1.00 |

**KM# 1082 10 PENCE**
6.50 g., Copper-Nickel, 24.5 mm. **Ruler:** Elizabeth II **Subject:** The Great Siege, 1779-1783 **Obv:** Bust in diadem right **Rev:** Cannon left **Edge:** Reeded

| Date | Mintage | VF20 | XF40 | MS60 | MS63 | MS65 |
|---|---|---|---|---|---|---|
| 2005 | — | — | — | 0.35 | 0.75 | 1.00 |
| 2006 | — | — | — | 0.35 | 0.75 | 1.00 |
| 2007 | — | — | — | 0.35 | 0.75 | 1.00 |
| 2008 | — | — | — | 0.35 | 0.75 | 1.00 |
| 2009 | — | — | — | 0.35 | 0.75 | 1.00 |
| 2010 | — | — | — | 0.35 | 0.75 | 1.00 |
| 2011 | — | — | — | 0.35 | 0.75 | 1.00 |

**KM# 1102 10 PENCE**
6.50 g., Copper-Nickel, 24.5 mm. **Ruler:** Elizabeth II **Obv:** Bust right **Obv. Legend:** ELIZABETH II QUEEN OF GIBRALTAR

| Date | Mintage | VF20 | XF40 | MS60 | MS63 | MS65 |
|---|---|---|---|---|---|---|
| 2012 | — | — | — | 0.35 | 0.75 | 1.00 |

**KM# 777 20 PENCE**
5.00 g., Copper-Nickel, 21.4 mm. **Ruler:** Elizabeth II **Obv:** Head with tiara right, date below **Rev:** Our Lady of Europa, denomination below and right **Shape:** 7-sided

| Date | Mintage | VF20 | XF40 | MS60 | MS63 | MS65 |
|---|---|---|---|---|---|---|
| 2001 AA | — | — | — | 0.70 | 1.50 | 2.00 |
| 2002 AA | — | — | — | 0.70 | 1.50 | 2.00 |
| 2003 AA | — | — | — | 0.70 | 1.50 | 2.00 |

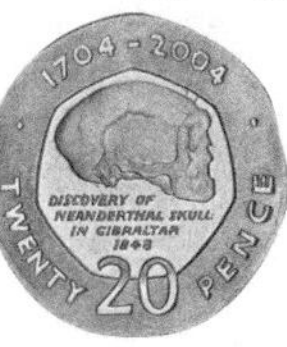


**KM# 1048 20 PENCE**
5.00 g., Copper-Nickel, 21.4 mm. **Ruler:** Elizabeth II **Subject:** 300th Anniversary **Obv:** Crowned buat right **Rev:** Neanderthal skull found in Gibraltar in 1848 **Edge:** Plain **Shape:** 7-sided

| Date | Mintage | VF20 | XF40 | MS60 | MS63 | MS65 |
|---|---|---|---|---|---|---|
| 2004 | — | — | — | 0.50 | 1.00 | 1.50 |

**KM# 1083 20 PENCE**
5.00 g., Copper-Nickel, 21.4 mm. **Ruler:** Elizabeth II **Obv:** Bust in diadem right **Rev:** Keyring with four keys **Shape:** 7-sided

| Date | Mintage | VF20 | XF40 | MS60 | MS63 | MS65 |
|---|---|---|---|---|---|---|
| 2005 | — | — | — | 0.70 | 1.50 | 2.00 |
| 2006 | — | — | — | 0.70 | 1.50 | 2.00 |
| 2007 | — | — | — | 0.70 | 1.50 | 2.00 |
| 2008 | — | — | — | 0.70 | 1.50 | 2.00 |
| 2009 | — | — | — | 0.70 | 1.50 | 2.00 |
| 2010 | — | — | — | 0.70 | 1.50 | 2.00 |
| 2011 | — | — | — | 0.70 | 1.50 | 2.00 |

**KM# 1103 20 PENCE**
5.00 g., Copper-Nickel, 21.4 mm. **Ruler:** Elizabeth II **Obv:** Bust right **Obv. Legend:** ELIZABETH II QUEEN OF GIBRALTAR

| Date | Mintage | VF20 | XF40 | MS60 | MS63 | MS65 |
|---|---|---|---|---|---|---|
| 2012 | — | — | — | 0.70 | 1.50 | 2.00 |

**KM# 778 50 PENCE**
8.00 g., Copper-Nickel, 27.3 mm. **Ruler:** Elizabeth II **Obv:** Head with tiara right **Rev:** Dolphins surround denomination **Edge:** Plain **Shape:** 7-sided

| Date | Mintage | VF20 | XF40 | MS60 | MS63 | MS65 |
|---|---|---|---|---|---|---|
| 2001 AA | — | — | — | — | 4.50 | 5.50 |
| 2001 AB | — | — | — | — | 4.50 | 5.50 |
| 2003 AB | — | — | — | — | 4.50 | 5.50 |

**KM# 971 50 PENCE**
8.00 g., Copper-Nickel, 27.3 mm. **Ruler:** Elizabeth II **Subject:** Christmas **Obv:** Head with tiara right, date below **Rev:** Three wise men **Edge:** Plain **Shape:** 7-sided

| Date | Mintage | VF20 | XF40 | MS60 | MS63 | MS65 |
|---|---|---|---|---|---|---|
| 2001 BB | 30,000 | — | — | — | 10.00 | 12.00 |

**KM# 971a 50 PENCE**
8.00 g., 0.925 Silver 0.2379 oz. ASW, 27.3 mm. **Ruler:** Elizabeth II **Obv:** Head with tiara right, date below **Rev:** Three wise men **Edge:** Plain **Shape:** 7-sided

| Date | Mintage | VF20 | XF40 | MS60 | MS63 | MS65 |
|---|---|---|---|---|---|---|
| 2001 | 5,000 | **PF63** 28.00 | **PF65** 35.00 | | | |

**KM# 971b 50 PENCE**
8.00 g., 0.9167 Gold 0.2358 oz. AGW, 27.3 mm. **Ruler:** Elizabeth II **Obv:** Head with tiara right, date below **Rev:** Three wise men **Edge:** Plain **Shape:** 7-sided

| Date | Mintage | VF20 | XF40 | MS60 | MS63 | MS65 |
|---|---|---|---|---|---|---|
| 2001 | 250 | **PF63** 625 | **PF65** 645 | | | |

**KM# 1026 50 PENCE**
8.00 g., Copper-Nickel, 27.3 mm. **Ruler:** Elizabeth II **Subject:** Christmas **Obv:** Head with tiara right, date below **Rev:** Shepherds **Edge:** Plain **Shape:** 7-sided

| Date | Mintage | VF20 | XF40 | MS60 | MS63 | MS65 |
|---|---|---|---|---|---|---|
| 2002 PM BB | 30,000 | — | — | — | 10.00 | 12.00 |

**KM# 1026a 50 PENCE**
8.00 g., 0.925 Silver 0.2379 oz. ASW, 27.3 mm. **Ruler:** Elizabeth II **Subject:** Christmas **Obv:** Head with tiara right, date below **Rev:** Two shepherds **Edge:** Plain **Shape:** 7-sided

| Date | Mintage | VF20 | XF40 | MS60 | MS63 | MS65 |
|---|---|---|---|---|---|---|
| 2002 PM | 2,002 | **PF63** 28.00 | **PF65** 35.00 | | | |

**KM# 1063 50 PENCE**
8.00 g., Copper-Nickel, 27.3 mm. **Ruler:** Elizabeth II **Series:** Christmas **Obv:** Head with tiara right, date below **Rev:** Joseph & Mary **Shape:** 7-sided

| Date | Mintage | VF20 | XF40 | MS60 | MS63 | MS65 |
|---|---|---|---|---|---|---|
| 2003 PM BB | — | — | — | — | 10.00 | 12.00 |

**KM# 1063a 50 PENCE**
8.00 g., 0.925 Silver 0.2379 oz. ASW, 27.3 mm. **Ruler:** Elizabeth II **Subject:** Christmas **Rev:** Joseph & Mary **Shape:** 7-sided

| Date | Mintage | VF20 | XF40 | MS60 | MS63 | MS65 |
|---|---|---|---|---|---|---|
| 2003 PM BB | — | — | — | — | 12.00 | 14.00 |

**KM# 1050 50 PENCE**
8.00 g., Copper-Nickel, 27.3 mm. **Ruler:** Elizabeth II **Subject:** Tercentenary 1704-2004 **Obv:** Elizabeth II **Rev:** HMS Victory sailing past Gibraltar **Edge:** Plain **Shape:** 7-sided

| Date | Mintage | VF20 | XF40 | MS60 | MS63 | MS65 |
|---|---|---|---|---|---|---|
| 2004 | — | — | — | — | — | 3.00 |

**KM# 1066 50 PENCE**
8.00 g., Copper-Nickel, 27.3 mm. **Ruler:** Elizabeth II **Subject:** Christmas **Rev:** Santa Claus walking left with sack over shoulder and waving **Shape:** 7-sided

| Date | Mintage | VF20 | XF40 | MS60 | MS63 | MS65 |
|---|---|---|---|---|---|---|
| 2004 | — | — | — | — | 10.00 | 12.00 |

**KM# 1084 50 PENCE**
8.00 g., Copper-Nickel, 27.3 mm. **Ruler:** Elizabeth II **Subject:** Glorious 1st of June, 1794 **Rev:** Marines firing from deck of Naval ship **Shape:** 7-sided

| Date | Mintage | VF20 | XF40 | MS60 | MS63 | MS65 |
|---|---|---|---|---|---|---|
| 2004 | — | — | — | — | 10.00 | 12.00 |

**KM# 1085 50 PENCE**
8.00 g., Copper-Nickel, 27.3 mm. **Ruler:** Elizabeth II **Subject:** Siege of Sebastopol, 1854 **Rev:** Troops in the Crimea **Shape:** 7-sided

| Date | Mintage | VF20 | XF40 | MS60 | MS63 | MS65 |
|---|---|---|---|---|---|---|
| 2004 | — | — | — | — | 10.00 | 12.00 |

**KM# 1086 50 PENCE**
8.00 g., Copper-Nickel, 27.3 mm. **Ruler:** Elizabeth II **Subject:** World War I **Rev:** Troops advancing right **Shape:** 7-sided

| Date | Mintage | VF20 | XF40 | MS60 | MS63 | MS65 |
|---|---|---|---|---|---|---|
| 2004 | — | — | — | — | 10.00 | 12.00 |

**KM# 1087 50 PENCE**
8.00 g., Copper-Nickel, 27.3 mm. **Ruler:** Elizabeth II **Subject:** World War II **Rev:** Troops in fox hole **Shape:** 7-sided

| Date | Mintage | VF20 | XF40 | MS60 | MS63 | MS65 |
|---|---|---|---|---|---|---|
| 2004 | — | — | — | — | 10.00 | 12.00 |

**KM# 1088 50 PENCE**
8.00 g., Copper-Nickel, 27.3 mm. **Ruler:** Elizabeth II **Subject:** The Falklands, 1982 **Rev:** Troops advancing forward **Shape:** 7-sided

| Date | Mintage | VF20 | XF40 | MS60 | MS63 | MS65 |
|---|---|---|---|---|---|---|
| 2004 | — | — | — | — | 10.00 | 12.00 |

**KM# 1142 50 PENCE**
8.00 g., Copper-Nickel, 27.3 mm. **Ruler:** Elizabeth II **Rev:** Royal Marines

| Date | Mintage | VF20 | XF40 | MS60 | MS63 | MS65 |
|---|---|---|---|---|---|---|
| 2004 | — | — | — | — | — | 17.50 |

**KM# 1142a 50 PENCE**
8.00 g., 0.925 Silver 0.2379 oz. ASW **Ruler:** Elizabeth II **Rev:** Royal Marines

| Date | Mintage | VF20 | XF40 | MS60 | MS63 | MS65 |
|---|---|---|---|---|---|---|
| 2004 | Est. 5000 | **PF65** 60.00 | | | | |

**KM# 1142b 50 PENCE**
15.50 g., 0.9167 Gold 0.4568 oz. AGW, 27.3 mm. **Ruler:** Elizabeth II **Rev:** Royal Marines

| Date | Mintage | VF20 | XF40 | MS60 | MS63 | MS65 |
|---|---|---|---|---|---|---|
| 2004 | Est. 100 | **PF65** 1,000 | | | | |

**KM# 1067 50 PENCE**
8.00 g., Copper-Nickel, 27.3 mm. **Ruler:** Elizabeth II **Subject:** Christmas **Rev:** Mary and child **Shape:** 7-sided

| Date | Mintage | VF20 | XF40 | MS60 | MS63 | MS65 |
|---|---|---|---|---|---|---|
| 2005 | — | — | — | — | 10.00 | 12.00 |

**KM# 1074 50 PENCE**
8.00 g., Copper-Nickel, 27.3 mm. **Ruler:** Elizabeth II **Subject:** Capture of Gibraltar **Rev:** Naval Battle **Shape:** 7-sided

| Date | Mintage | VF20 | XF40 | MS60 | MS63 | MS65 |
|---|---|---|---|---|---|---|
| 2005 | — | — | — | — | 7.50 | 10.00 |

**KM# 1068 50 PENCE**
8.00 g., Copper-Nickel, 27.3 mm. **Ruler:** Elizabeth II **Subject:** Christmas **Rev:** Tree **Shape:** 7-sided

| Date | Mintage | VF20 | XF40 | MS60 | MS63 | MS65 |
|---|---|---|---|---|---|---|
| 2006 | — | — | — | — | 10.00 | 12.00 |

**KM# 1089 50 PENCE**
8.00 g., Copper-Nickel, 27.3 mm. **Ruler:** Elizabeth II **Subject:** Capture of Gibraltar, 1704 **Rev:** Naval Battle **Shape:** 7-sided

| Date | Mintage | VF20 | XF40 | MS60 | MS63 | MS65 |
|---|---|---|---|---|---|---|
| 2006 | — | — | — | — | 4.50 | 5.50 |
| 2007 | — | — | — | — | 4.50 | 5.50 |
| 2008 | — | — | — | — | 4.50 | 5.50 |
| 2009 | — | — | — | — | 4.50 | 5.50 |
| 2010 | — | — | — | — | 4.50 | 5.50 |
| 2011 | — | — | — | — | 4.50 | 5.50 |

**KM# 1069 50 PENCE**
8.00 g., Copper-Nickel, 27.3 mm. **Ruler:** Elizabeth II **Subject:** Christmas **Rev:** Santa, large face **Shape:** 7-sided

| Date | Mintage | VF20 | XF40 | MS60 | MS63 | MS65 |
|---|---|---|---|---|---|---|
| 2007 | — | — | — | — | 10.00 | 12.00 |

**KM# 1070 50 PENCE**
8.00 g., Copper-Nickel, 27.3 mm. **Ruler:** Elizabeth II **Subject:** Christmas **Shape:** 7-sided

| Date | Mintage | VF20 | XF40 | MS60 | MS63 | MS65 |
|---|---|---|---|---|---|---|
| 2008 | — | — | — | — | 10.00 | 12.00 |

**KM# 1090 50 PENCE**
8.00 g., Copper-Nickel, 27.3 mm. **Ruler:** Elizabeth II **Subject:** Our Lady of Europe **Rev:** Madonna and Child seated **Shape:** 7-sided

| Date | Mintage | VF20 | XF40 | MS60 | MS63 | MS65 |
|---|---|---|---|---|---|---|
| 2008 | — | — | — | — | 7.50 | 9.00 |

**KM# 1071 50 PENCE**
8.00 g., Copper-Nickel, 27.3 mm. **Ruler:** Elizabeth II **Subject:** Christmas **Shape:** 7-sided

| Date | Mintage | VF20 | XF40 | MS60 | MS63 | MS65 |
|---|---|---|---|---|---|---|
| 2009 | — | — | — | — | 10.00 | 12.00 |

**KM# 229 50 PENCE**
8.00 g., Copper-Nickel, 27.3 mm. **Ruler:** Elizabeth II **Subject:** Christmas

| Date | Mintage | VF20 | XF40 | MS60 | MS63 | MS65 |
|---|---|---|---|---|---|---|
| 2010 | — | — | — | — | 10.00 | 12.00 |

**KM# 1479 50 PENCE**
8.00 g., Copper-Nickel, 27.3 mm. **Ruler:** Elizabeth II **Rev. Legend:** HAPPY CHRISTMAS

| Date | Mintage | VF20 | XF40 | MS60 | MS63 | MS65 |
|---|---|---|---|---|---|---|
| 2011 | — | — | — | — | 1.25 | 2.50 |

**KM# 1104 50 PENCE**
8.00 g., Copper-Nickel, 27.3 mm. **Ruler:** Elizabeth II **Obv:** Bust right **Obv. Legend:** ELIZABETH II QUEEN OF GIBRALTAR

| Date | Mintage | VF20 | XF40 | MS60 | MS63 | MS65 |
|---|---|---|---|---|---|---|
| 2012 | — | — | — | — | 4.50 | 5.50 |

**KM# 869 POUND**
9.50 g., Nickel-Brass, 22.5 mm. **Ruler:** Elizabeth II **Obv:** Head with tiara right **Rev:** Gibraltar coat of arms - castle and key

| Date | Mintage | VF20 | XF40 | MS60 | MS63 | MS65 |
|---|---|---|---|---|---|---|
| 2001 AA | — | — | — | 3.50 | 4.50 | 6.00 |
| 2001 AB | — | — | — | 3.50 | 4.50 | 6.00 |
| 2002 AC | — | — | — | 3.50 | 4.50 | 6.00 |

**KM# 1036 POUND**
9.50 g., Nickel-Brass, 22 mm. **Ruler:** Elizabeth II **Subject:** 1700th Anniversary - Death of St. George **Obv:** Bust with tiara right **Rev:** St. George and the dragon **Edge:** Reeded

| Date | Mintage | VF20 | XF40 | MS60 | MS63 | MS65 |
|---|---|---|---|---|---|---|
| 2003 | — | — | — | 9.00 | 10.00 | 12.00 |

**KM# 1051 POUND**
9.50 g., Nickel-Brass, 22.5 mm. **Ruler:** Elizabeth II **Subject:** Tercentenary 1704-2004 **Obv:** Elizabeth II **Rev:** Old cannon set for a downhill target **Edge:** Reeded

| Date | Mintage | VF20 | XF40 | MS60 | MS63 | MS65 |
|---|---|---|---|---|---|---|
| 2004 PM | — | — | — | 3.50 | 4.50 | 6.00 |

**KM# 1160 POUND**
7.98 g., 0.9167 Gold 0.2352 oz. AGW, 22 mm. **Ruler:** Elizabeth II **Subject:** Allied landing at Normandy, 1944

| Date | Mintage | VF20 | XF40 | MS60 | MS63 | MS65 |
|---|---|---|---|---|---|---|
| 2004 | Est. 1950 | **PF65** 450 | | | | |

**KM# 1091 POUND**
9.50 g., Nickel-Brass, 22.5 mm. **Ruler:** Elizabeth II **Obv:** Bust in diadem right **Rev:** Neanderthal Skull

| Date | Mintage | VF20 | XF40 | MS60 | MS63 | MS65 |
|---|---|---|---|---|---|---|
| 2005 | — | — | — | 3.50 | 4.50 | 6.00 |
| 2006 | — | — | — | 3.50 | 4.50 | 6.00 |

| Date | Mintage | VF20 | XF40 | MS60 | MS63 | MS65 |
|---|---|---|---|---|---|---|
| 2007 | — | — | — | 3.50 | 4.50 | 6.00 |
| 2008 | — | — | — | 3.50 | 4.50 | 6.00 |
| 2009 | — | — | — | 3.50 | 4.50 | 6.00 |
| 2010 | — | — | — | 3.50 | 4.50 | 6.00 |
| 2011 | — | — | — | 3.50 | 4.50 | 6.00 |

### KM# 1161 POUND

7.98 g., 0.9167 Gold 0.2352 oz. AGW **Ruler:** Elizabeth II **Subject:** Elizabeth II, 80th Birthday **Rev:** Old portrait

| Date | Mintage | VF20 | XF40 | MS60 | MS63 | MS65 |
|---|---|---|---|---|---|---|
| 2006 | Est. 250 | PF65 450 | | | | |

### KM# 1162 POUND

7.98 g., 0.9167 Gold 0.2352 oz. AGW **Ruler:** Elizabeth II **Subject:** Elizabeth II, 80th Birthday **Rev:** Elizabeth as a child

| Date | Mintage | VF20 | XF40 | MS60 | MS63 | MS65 |
|---|---|---|---|---|---|---|
| 2006 | Est. 250 | PF65 450 | | | | |

### KM# 1163 POUND

7.98 g., 0.9167 Gold 0.2352 oz. AGW **Ruler:** Elizabeth II **Subject:** Elizabeth II, 80th Birthday **Rev:** Elizabeth II as young lady

| Date | Mintage | VF20 | XF40 | MS60 | MS63 | MS65 |
|---|---|---|---|---|---|---|
| 2006 | Est. 250 | PF65 450 | | | | |

### KM# 1164 POUND

7.98 g., 0.9167 Gold 0.2352 oz. AGW **Ruler:** Elizabeth II **Subject:** Elizabeth II, 80th Birthday **Rev:** Elizabeth II with grandchildren

| Date | Mintage | VF20 | XF40 | MS60 | MS63 | MS65 |
|---|---|---|---|---|---|---|
| 2006 | Est. 250 | PF65 450 | | | | |

### KM# 1318 POUND

7.98 g., 0.9167 Gold 0.2352 oz. AGW **Ruler:** Elizabeth II **Subject:** Concord, 20th Anniversary **Rev:** Concord and the world

| Date | Mintage | VF20 | XF40 | MS60 | MS63 | MS65 |
|---|---|---|---|---|---|---|
| 2006 | Est. 1500 | PF65 450 | | | | |

### KM# 1335 POUND

7.98 g., 0.9167 Gold 0.2352 oz. AGW **Ruler:** Elizabeth II **Subject:** Elizabeth and Philip, 60th Wedding Anniversary **Rev:** Elizabeth and Philip busts

| Date | Mintage | VF20 | XF40 | MS60 | MS63 | MS65 |
|---|---|---|---|---|---|---|
| 2007 | Est. 250 | PF65 450 | | | | |

### KM# 1336 POUND

7.98 g., 0.9167 Gold 0.2352 oz. AGW **Ruler:** Elizabeth II **Subject:** Elizabeth and Philip, 60th Wedding Anniversary **Rev:** Wedding portrait, 1947

| Date | Mintage | VF20 | XF40 | MS60 | MS63 | MS65 |
|---|---|---|---|---|---|---|
| 2007 | Est. 995 | PF65 450 | | | | |

### KM# 1105 POUND

9.50 g., Nickel-Brass, 27.5 mm. **Ruler:** Elizabeth II **Obv:** Bust right **Obv. Legend:** ELIZABETH II QUEEN OF GIBRALTAR

| Date | Mintage | VF20 | XF40 | MS60 | MS63 | MS65 |
|---|---|---|---|---|---|---|
| 2012 | — | — | — | 3.50 | 4.50 | 6.00 |

### KM# 970 2 POUNDS

12.00 g., Bi-Metallic Copper-Nickel center in Nickel-Brass ring, 28.4 mm. **Ruler:** Elizabeth II **Subject:** Bicentennial of the Union Jack **Obv:** Head with tiara right **Rev:** Standing Britannia wearing flag as a cape **Edge:** Reeded

| Date | Mintage | VF20 | XF40 | MS60 | MS63 | MS65 |
|---|---|---|---|---|---|---|
| 2001 AA | — | — | — | 10.00 | 12.00 | 15.00 |

### KM# 970a 2 POUNDS

12.00 g., 0.999 Bi-Metallic 0.3854 oz. Silver center in Gold plated Silver ring, 28.4 mm. **Ruler:** Elizabeth II **Subject:** Bicentennial of the Union Jack **Obv:** Head with tiara right **Rev:** Standing Britannia wearing flag as a cape **Edge:** Reeded

| Date | Mintage | VF20 | XF40 | MS60 | MS63 | MS65 |
|---|---|---|---|---|---|---|
| 2001 | 7,500 | — | — | — | 35.00 | 40.00 |

### KM# 1043 2 POUNDS

12.00 g., Bi-Metallic Copper-Nickel center in Nickel-Brass ring, 28.4 mm. **Ruler:** Elizabeth II **Obv:** Head with tiara right **Rev:** Old cannon **Edge:** Reeded

| Date | Mintage | VF20 | XF40 | MS60 | MS63 | MS65 |
|---|---|---|---|---|---|---|
| 2003 PM | — | — | — | 10.00 | 12.00 | 15.00 |

### KM# 1057 2 POUNDS

12.00 g., Bi-Metallic Copper-Nickel center in Nickel-Brass ring, 28.4 mm. **Ruler:** Elizabeth II **Subject:** Tercentenary 1704-2004 **Obv:** Elizabeth II **Rev:** Naval Battle, capture of Gibraltar **Edge:** Reeded

| Date | Mintage | VF20 | XF40 | MS60 | MS63 | MS65 |
|---|---|---|---|---|---|---|
| 2004 PM | — | — | — | 10.00 | 12.00 | 15.00 |

### KM# 1072 2 POUNDS

12.00 g., Bi-Metallic, 28.4 mm. **Ruler:** Elizabeth II **Subject:** Capture of Gibraltar **Rev:** Sea Battle

| Date | Mintage | F12 | VF20 | XF40 | MS60 | MS63 |
|---|---|---|---|---|---|---|
| 2004 | — | — | — | — | 10.00 | 12.00 |

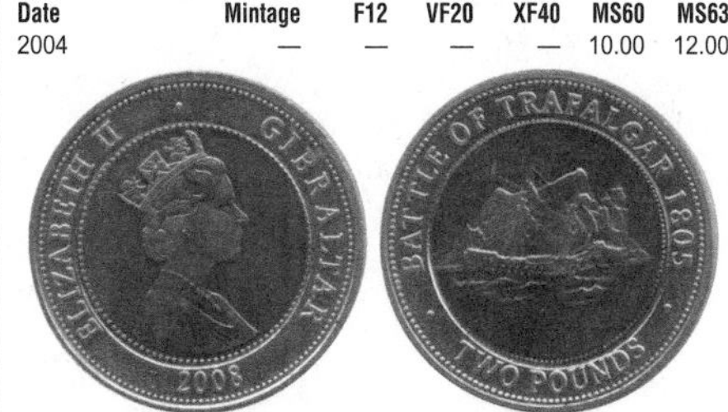

### KM# 1073 2 POUNDS

12.00 g., Bi-Metallic Copper-Nickel center in Nickel-Brass ring, 28.4 mm. **Ruler:** Elizabeth II **Subject:** Battle of Trafalgar **Rev:** Two Naval vessels and rock in backbround

| Date | Mintage | VF20 | XF40 | MS60 | MS63 | MS65 |
|---|---|---|---|---|---|---|
| 2005 | — | — | — | 10.00 | 12.00 | 15.00 |
| 2006 | — | — | — | 10.00 | 12.00 | 15.00 |
| 2007 | — | — | — | 10.00 | 12.00 | 15.00 |
| 2008 | — | — | — | 10.00 | 12.00 | 15.00 |
| 2009 | — | — | — | 10.00 | 12.00 | 15.00 |
| 2010 | — | — | — | 10.00 | 12.00 | 15.00 |
| 2011 | — | — | — | 10.00 | 12.00 | 15.00 |

### KM# 1092 2 POUNDS

12.00 g., Bi-Metallic, 28.4 mm. **Ruler:** Elizabeth II **Subject:** Battle of Trafalgar **Rev:** Two Naval vessels and rock in backbround

| Date | Mintage | F12 | VF20 | XF40 | MS60 | MS63 |
|---|---|---|---|---|---|---|
| 2005 | — | — | — | — | 10.00 | 12.00 |
| 2006 | — | — | — | — | 10.00 | 12.00 |
| 2007 | — | — | — | — | 10.00 | 12.00 |
| 2008 | — | — | — | — | 10.00 | 12.00 |
| 2009 | — | — | — | — | 10.00 | 12.00 |
| 2010 | — | — | — | — | 10.00 | 12.00 |
| 2011 | — | — | — | — | 10.00 | 12.00 |

### KM# 1093 2 POUNDS

12.00 g., Bi-Metallic Copper-Nickel center in Nickel-Brass ring, 28.4 mm. **Ruler:** Elizabeth II **Subject:** Diamond Wedding Anniversary **Obv:** Bust in diadem right **Rev:** Conjoined busts of Elizabeth and Philip

| Date | Mintage | VF20 | XF40 | MS60 | MS63 | MS65 |
|---|---|---|---|---|---|---|
| 2007 | — | — | — | 10.00 | 12.00 | 15.00 |

### KM# 1106 2 POUNDS

12.00 g., Bi-Metallic Copper-Nickel center in Nickel-Brass ring, 28.4 mm. **Ruler:** Elizabeth II **Obv:** Bust right **Obv. Legend:** ELIZABETH II QUEEN OF GIBRALTAR

| Date | Mintage | VF20 | XF40 | MS60 | MS63 | MS65 |
|---|---|---|---|---|---|---|
| 2012 | — | — | — | 10.00 | 12.00 | 15.00 |

### KM# 953 5 POUNDS

20.00 g., Virenium, 36.1 mm. **Ruler:** Elizabeth II **Subject:** Gibraltar Chronicle 200 Years **Obv:** Head with tiara right **Rev:** Naval battle scene with newspaper in background **Edge:** Reeded

| Date | Mintage | VF20 | XF40 | MS60 | MS63 | MS65 |
|---|---|---|---|---|---|---|
| 2001 | — | — | — | — | 17.00 | 22.00 |

### KM# 953a 5 POUNDS

23.50 g., 0.925 Silver 0.6989 oz. ASW, 36.1 mm. **Ruler:** Elizabeth II **Subject:** Gibraltar Chronicle 200 Years **Obv:** Head with tiara right **Rev:** Naval battle scene with newspaper in background **Edge:** Reeded

| Date | Mintage | VF20 | XF40 | MS60 | MS63 | MS65 |
|---|---|---|---|---|---|---|
| 2001 | 10,000 | PF63 50.00 | PF65 60.00 | | | |

### KM# 953b 5 POUNDS

39.83 g., 0.9167 Gold 1.1739 oz. AGW, 36.1 mm. **Ruler:** Elizabeth II **Subject:** Gibraltar Chronicle 200 Years **Obv:** Head with tiara right **Rev:** Naval battle scene with newspaper in background **Edge:** Reeded

| Date | Mintage | VF20 | XF40 | MS60 | MS63 | MS65 |
|---|---|---|---|---|---|---|
| 2001 | 850 | PF65 2,100 | | | | |

### KM# 1011 5 POUNDS

20.00 g., Virenium, 36.1 mm. **Ruler:** Elizabeth II **Subject:** Queen's Golden Jubilee **Obv:** Head with tiara right **Rev:** Coronation scene **Edge:** Reeded

| Date | Mintage | VF20 | XF40 | MS60 | MS63 | MS65 |
|---|---|---|---|---|---|---|
| 2002 | — | — | — | — | 17.00 | 22.00 |

**KM# 1011a 5 POUNDS**
23.50 g., 0.925 Silver 0.6989 oz. ASW, 36.1 mm. **Ruler:** Elizabeth II **Subject:** Queen's Golden Jubilee **Obv:** Head with tiara right **Rev:** Coronation scene **Edge:** Reeded

| Date | Mintage | VF20 | XF40 | MS60 | MS63 | MS65 |
|---|---|---|---|---|---|---|
| 2002 | 10,000 | PF63 50.00 PF65 60.00 | | | | |

**KM# 1011b 5 POUNDS**
39.83 g., 0.9166 Gold 1.1738 oz. AGW, 36.1 mm. **Ruler:** Elizabeth II **Subject:** Queen's Golden Jubilee **Obv:** Head with tiara right **Rev:** Coronation scene **Edge:** Reeded

| Date | Mintage | VF20 | XF40 | MS60 | MS63 | MS65 |
|---|---|---|---|---|---|---|
| 2002 | — | PF65 2,100 | | | | |

**KM# 1122 5 POUNDS**
20.00 g., Nickel-Copper, 36 mm. **Ruler:** Elizabeth II **Rev:** Pillars of Hercules and the defeat of the Spanish Armada

| Date | Mintage | VF20 | XF40 | MS60 | MS63 | MS65 |
|---|---|---|---|---|---|---|
| 2003 | — | — | — | — | 25.00 | 30.00 |

**KM# 1122a 5 POUNDS**
23.50 g., 0.925 Silver 0.6989 oz. ASW, 36 mm. **Ruler:** Elizabeth II **Rev:** Pillars of Hercules and the defeat of the Spanish Armada

| Date | Mintage | VF20 | XF40 | MS60 | MS63 | MS65 |
|---|---|---|---|---|---|---|
| 2003 | Est. 10000 | PF65 60.00 | | | | |

**KM# 1141 5 POUNDS**
28.28 g., 0.925 Silver 0.841 oz. ASW, 38.61 mm. **Ruler:** Elizabeth II **Rev:** Two children with Union Jack and Gibraltar flag

| Date | Mintage | VF20 | XF40 | MS60 | MS63 | MS65 |
|---|---|---|---|---|---|---|
| 2004 | Est. 2500 | PF65 60.00 | | | | |

**KM# 1141a 5 POUNDS**
39.94 g., 0.9167 Gold 1.1771 oz. AGW, 38.61 mm. **Ruler:** Elizabeth II **Rev:** Two children with Union Jack and Gibraltar flag

| Date | Mintage | VF20 | XF40 | MS60 | MS63 | MS65 |
|---|---|---|---|---|---|---|
| 2004 | Est. 50 | PF65 2,400 | | | | |

**KM# 1170 5 POUNDS**
28.28 g., 0.925 Silver 0.841 oz. ASW, 38.61 mm. **Ruler:** Elizabeth II **Rev:** Allied landing at Normandy, bluffs in color

| Date | Mintage | VF20 | XF40 | MS60 | MS63 | MS65 |
|---|---|---|---|---|---|---|
| 2004 | Est. 50000 | PF65 50.00 | | | | |

**KM# 1170a 5 POUNDS**
39.94 g., 0.9167 Gold 1.1771 oz. AGW, 38.61 mm. **Ruler:** Elizabeth II **Rev:** Allied landing at Normandy, 1944

| Date | Mintage | VF20 | XF40 | MS60 | MS63 | MS65 |
|---|---|---|---|---|---|---|
| 2004 | Est. 200 | PF65 2,400 | | | | |

**KM# 1171 5 POUNDS**
28.28 g., 0.925 Silver 0.841 oz. ASW, 38.61 mm. **Ruler:** Elizabeth II **Rev:** Battle of the Pegasus Bridge in Normandy

| Date | Mintage | VF20 | XF40 | MS60 | MS63 | MS65 |
|---|---|---|---|---|---|---|
| 2004 | Est. 19500 | PF65 60.00 | | | | |

**KM# 1172 5 POUNDS**
28.28 g., 0.925 Silver 0.841 oz. ASW, 38.61 mm. **Ruler:** Elizabeth II **Rev:** Construction of the Mulberry docks at Normandy

| Date | Mintage | VF20 | XF40 | MS60 | MS63 | MS65 |
|---|---|---|---|---|---|---|
| 2014 | Est. 19500 | PF65 60.00 | | | | |

**KM# 1173 5 POUNDS**
28.28 g., 0.925 Silver 0.841 oz. ASW, 38.61 mm. **Ruler:** Elizabeth II **Rev:** Winston Churchill giving V for Victory sign outside 10 Downing Street

| Date | Mintage | VF20 | XF40 | MS60 | MS63 | MS65 |
|---|---|---|---|---|---|---|
| 2004 | Est. 19500 | PF65 60.00 | | | | |

**KM# 1173a 5 POUNDS**
39.94 g., 0.9167 Gold 1.1771 oz. AGW, 38.61 mm. **Ruler:** Elizabeth II **Rev:** Winston Churchill giving V for victory sign outside of 10 Downing Street

| Date | Mintage | VF20 | XF40 | MS60 | MS63 | MS65 |
|---|---|---|---|---|---|---|
| 2004 | Est. 200 | PF65 2,400 | | | | |

**KM# 1174 5 POUNDS**
28.28 g., 0.925 Silver 0.841 oz. ASW, 38.61 mm. **Ruler:** Elizabeth II **Rev:** Battle of Britain

| Date | Mintage | VF20 | XF40 | MS60 | MS63 | MS65 |
|---|---|---|---|---|---|---|
| 2004 | Est. 19500 | PF65 60.00 | | | | |

**KM# 1174a 5 POUNDS**
39.94 g., 0.9167 Gold 1.1771 oz. AGW, 38.61 mm. **Ruler:** Elizabeth II **Rev:** Battle of Britain

| Date | Mintage | VF20 | XF40 | MS60 | MS63 | MS65 |
|---|---|---|---|---|---|---|
| 2004 | Est. 200 | PF65 2,400 | | | | |

**KM# 1175 5 POUNDS**
28.28 g., 0.9167 Silver 0.8335 oz. ASW, 38.61 mm. **Ruler:** Elizabeth II **Rev:** Sinking of the Bismarck

| Date | Mintage | VF20 | XF40 | MS60 | MS63 | MS65 |
|---|---|---|---|---|---|---|
| 2004 | Est. 19500 | PF65 60.00 | | | | |

**KM# 1176 5 POUNDS**
28.28 g., 0.925 Silver 0.841 oz. ASW, 38.61 mm. **Ruler:** Elizabeth II **Subject:** Battle of El Alamein

| Date | Mintage | VF20 | XF40 | MS60 | MS63 | MS65 |
|---|---|---|---|---|---|---|
| 2004 | Est. 19500 | PF65 60.00 | | | | |

**KM# 1176a 5 POUNDS**
39.94 g., 0.9167 Gold 1.1771 oz. AGW, 38.61 mm. **Ruler:** Elizabeth II **Subject:** Battle of El Alamein

| Date | Mintage | VF20 | XF40 | MS60 | MS63 | MS65 |
|---|---|---|---|---|---|---|
| 2004 | Est. 200 | PF65 2,400 | | | | |

**KM# 1177 5 POUNDS**
28.28 g., 0.925 Silver 0.841 oz. ASW, 38.61 mm. **Ruler:** Elizabeth II **Subject:** Allied troops preparing for the North African invasion (Operation Torch)

| Date | Mintage | VF20 | XF40 | MS60 | MS63 | MS65 |
|---|---|---|---|---|---|---|
| 2004 | Est. 19500 | PF65 60.00 | | | | |

**KM# 1178 5 POUNDS**
28.28 g., 0.925 Silver 0.841 oz. ASW, 38.61 mm. **Ruler:** Elizabeth II **Subject:** Battle for Stalingrad

| Date | Mintage | VF20 | XF40 | MS60 | MS63 | MS65 |
|---|---|---|---|---|---|---|
| 2004 | Est. 19500 | PF65 60.00 | | | | |

**KM# 1179 5 POUNDS**
28.28 g., 0.925 Silver 0.841 oz. ASW, 38.61 mm. **Ruler:** Elizabeth II **Subject:** Sabotage at the Norwegian Hard Water plants

| Date | Mintage | VF20 | XF40 | MS60 | MS63 | MS65 |
|---|---|---|---|---|---|---|
| 2004 | Est. 19500 | PF65 60.00 | | | | |

**KM# 1180 5 POUNDS**
28.28 g., 0.925 Silver 0.841 oz. ASW, 38.61 mm. **Ruler:** Elizabeth II **Subject:** Arc battle of Kursk

| Date | Mintage | VF20 | XF40 | MS60 | MS63 | MS65 |
|---|---|---|---|---|---|---|
| 2004 | — | PF65 60.00 | | | | |

**KM# 1189 5 POUNDS**
28.28 g., 0.925 Silver 0.841 oz. ASW, 38.61 mm. **Ruler:** Elizabeth II **Subject:** 2004 Summer Olympics, Athens **Rev:** Runner in Athens, Greek flag in color

| Date | Mintage | VF20 | XF40 | MS60 | MS63 | MS65 |
|---|---|---|---|---|---|---|
| 2004 | Est. 15000 | PF65 60.00 | | | | |

**KM# 1189a 5 POUNDS**
39.94 g., 0.9167 Gold 1.1771 oz. AGW, 38.61 mm. **Ruler:** Elizabeth II **Subject:** 2004 Summer Olympics, Athens **Rev:** Runner in Athens

| Date | Mintage | VF20 | XF40 | MS60 | MS63 | MS65 |
|---|---|---|---|---|---|---|
| 2004 | Est. 500 | PF65 2,400 | | | | |

**KM# 1190 5 POUNDS**
28.28 g., 0.925 Silver 0.841 oz. ASW, 38.61 mm. **Ruler:** Elizabeth II **Subject:** 2004 Summer Olympics, Athens **Rev:** Cyclist in Paris, French flag in color

| Date | Mintage | VF20 | XF40 | MS60 | MS63 | MS65 |
|---|---|---|---|---|---|---|
| 2004 | Est. 15000 | PF65 60.00 | | | | |

**KM# 1191 5 POUNDS**
28.28 g., 0.925 Silver 0.841 oz. ASW, 38.61 mm. **Ruler:** Elizabeth II **Subject:** 2004 Summer Olympics, Athens **Rev:** Basketball player and New York, US flag in color

| Date | Mintage | VF20 | XF40 | MS60 | MS63 | MS65 |
|---|---|---|---|---|---|---|
| 2004 | Est. 15000 | PF65 60.00 | | | | |

**KM# 1192.1 5 POUNDS**
28.28 g., 0.925 Silver 0.841 oz. ASW, 38.61 mm. **Ruler:** Elizabeth II **Subject:** 2004 Summer Olympics, Athens **Rev:** Rower on Thames, London. Union Jack in color **Rev. Inscription:** 1908 Great Britain 1948

| Date | Mintage | VF20 | XF40 | MS60 | MS63 | MS65 |
|---|---|---|---|---|---|---|
| 2004 | Est. 15000 | PF65 60.00 | | | | |

**KM# 1193 5 POUNDS**
28.28 g., 0.925 Silver 0.841 oz. ASW, 38.61 mm. **Ruler:** Elizabeth II **Subject:** 2004 Summer Olympics, Athens **Rev:** Canoeists in Stockholm, Swedish flag in color

| Date | Mintage | VF20 | XF40 | MS60 | MS63 | MS65 |
|---|---|---|---|---|---|---|
| 2004 | Est. 15000 | PF65 60.00 | | | | |

**KM# 1194 5 POUNDS**
28.28 g., 0.925 Silver 0.841 oz. ASW, 38.61 mm. **Ruler:** Elizabeth II **Subject:** 2004 Summer Olympics, Athens **Rev:** Judo fighter in Brussels, Belgian flag in color

| Date | Mintage | VF20 | XF40 | MS60 | MS63 | MS65 |
|---|---|---|---|---|---|---|
| 2005 | Est. 15000 | PF65 60.00 | | | | |

**KM# 1195 5 POUNDS**
28.28 g., 0.925 Silver 0.841 oz. ASW, 38.61 mm. **Ruler:** Elizabeth II **Subject:** 2004 Summer Olympics, Athens **Rev:** Sailboats in Holland, Dutch flag in color

| Date | Mintage | VF20 | XF40 | MS60 | MS63 | MS65 |
|---|---|---|---|---|---|---|
| 2005 | Est. 15000 | PF65 60.00 | | | | |

**KM# 1196 5 POUNDS**
28.28 g., 0.925 Silver 0.841 oz. ASW, 38.61 mm. **Ruler:** Elizabeth II **Subject:** 2004 Summer Olympics, Athens **Rev:** Dressage horsewoman before Brandenburg Gate, Berlin, German flag in color

| Date | Mintage | VF20 | XF40 | MS60 | MS63 | MS65 |
|---|---|---|---|---|---|---|
| 2004 | Est. 15000 | PF65 60.00 | | | | |

**KM# 1197 5 POUNDS**
28.28 g., 0.925 Silver 0.841 oz. ASW, 38.61 mm. **Ruler:** Elizabeth II **Subject:** 2004 Summer Olympics, Athens **Rev:** Javlin thrower in Helsinki, Finnish flag in color

| Date | Mintage | VF20 | XF40 | MS60 | MS63 | MS65 |
|---|---|---|---|---|---|---|
| 2004 | Est. 15000 | PF65 60.00 | | | | |

**KM# 1198 5 POUNDS**
28.28 g., 0.925 Silver 0.841 oz. ASW, 38.61 mm. **Ruler:** Elizabeth II **Subject:** 2004 Summer Olympics, Athens **Rev:** Swimmer, Australian flag in color

| Date | Mintage | VF20 | XF40 | MS60 | MS63 | MS65 |
|---|---|---|---|---|---|---|
| 2005 | Est. 15000 | PF65 60.00 | | | | |

**KM# 1200 5 POUNDS**
28.28 g., 0.925 Silver 0.841 oz. ASW, 38.61 mm. **Ruler:** Elizabeth II **Subject:** 2004 Summer Olympics, Athens **Rev:** Baseball player in Tokyo, Japanese flag in color

| Date | Mintage | VF20 | XF40 | MS60 | MS63 | MS65 |
|---|---|---|---|---|---|---|
| 2004 | Est. 15000 | PF65 60.00 | | | | |

**KM# 1064 5 POUNDS**
Silver, 38 mm. **Ruler:** Elizabeth II **Subject:** 200th Anniversary, Battle of Trafalgar **Rev:** Two naval vessels **Edge:** Reeded

| Date | Mintage | VF20 | XF40 | MS60 | MS63 | MS65 |
|---|---|---|---|---|---|---|
| 2005 | — | PF63 45.00 PF65 50.00 | | | | |

**KM# 1159 5 POUNDS**
28.28 g., 0.925 Silver 0.841 oz. ASW, 38.61 mm. **Ruler:** Elizabeth II **Subject:** Japanese surrender

| Date | Mintage | VF20 | XF40 | MS60 | MS63 | MS65 |
|---|---|---|---|---|---|---|
| 2005 | Est. 19500 | PF65 60.00 | | | | |

**KM# 1181 5 POUNDS**
28.28 g., 0.925 Silver 0.841 oz. ASW, 38.61 mm. **Ruler:** Elizabeth II **Subject:** Ruhr river dam roller bombs

| Date | Mintage | VF20 | XF40 | MS60 | MS63 | MS65 |
|---|---|---|---|---|---|---|
| 2005 | Est. 19500 | PF65 60.00 | | | | |

**KM# 1181a 5 POUNDS**
38.94 g., 0.9167 Gold 1.1477 oz. AGW, 38.61 mm. **Ruler:** Elizabeth II **Subject:** Ruhr river dam roller bombs

| Date | Mintage | VF20 | XF40 | MS60 | MS63 | MS65 |
|---|---|---|---|---|---|---|
| 2004 | Est. 200 | PF65 2,400 | | | | |

**KM# 1182 5 POUNDS**
28.28 g., 0.925 Silver 0.841 oz. ASW, 38.61 mm. **Ruler:** Elizabeth II **Subject:** Burma Campaign

| Date | Mintage | VF20 | XF40 | MS60 | MS63 | MS65 |
|---|---|---|---|---|---|---|
| 2005 | Est. 19500 | PF65 60.00 | | | | |

**KM# 1183 5 POUNDS**
28.28 g., 0.925 Silver 0.841 oz. ASW, 38.61 mm. **Ruler:** Elizabeth II **Subject:** Liberation of Paris

| Date | Mintage | VF20 | XF40 | MS60 | MS63 | MS65 |
|---|---|---|---|---|---|---|
| 2005 | Est. 19500 | PF65 60.00 | | | | |

**KM# 1184 5 POUNDS**
28.28 g., 0.925 Silver 0.841 oz. ASW, 38.61 mm. **Ruler:** Elizabeth II **Subject:** Yalta conference

| Date | Mintage | VF20 | XF40 | MS60 | MS63 | MS65 |
|---|---|---|---|---|---|---|
| 2005 | Est. 19500 | PF65 60.00 | | | | |

**KM# 1185 5 POUNDS**
28.28 g., 0.925 Silver 0.841 oz. ASW, 38.61 mm. **Ruler:** Elizabeth II **Subject:** Red Army soldier waving flag at Reichstag in Berlin

| Date | Mintage | VF20 | XF40 | MS60 | MS63 | MS65 |
|---|---|---|---|---|---|---|
| 2005 | Est. 19500 | PF65 60.00 | | | | |

**KM# 1186 5 POUNDS**
28.28 g., 0.925 Silver 0.841 oz. ASW, 38.61 mm. **Ruler:** Elizabeth II **Subject:** Winston Churchill at war end's service in St. Paul's Cathedral

| Date | Mintage | VF20 | XF40 | MS60 | MS63 | MS65 |
|---|---|---|---|---|---|---|
| 2005 | Est. 19500 | PF65 60.00 | | | | |

**KM# 1186a 5 POUNDS**
39.94 g., 0.9167 Gold 1.1771 oz. AGW, 38.61 mm. **Ruler:** Elizabeth II **Subject:** Winston Churchill at war's end service at St. Paul's Cathedral

| Date | Mintage | VF20 | XF40 | MS60 | MS63 | MS65 |
|---|---|---|---|---|---|---|
| 2005 | Est. 200 | PF65 2,400 | | | | |

**KM# 1187 5 POUNDS**
28.28 g., 0.925 Silver 0.841 oz. ASW, 38.61 mm. **Ruler:** Elizabeth II **Subject:** Japanese surrender

| Date | Mintage | VF20 | XF40 | MS60 | MS63 | MS65 |
|---|---|---|---|---|---|---|
| 2005 | Est. 19500 | PF65 60.00 | | | | |

**KM# 1192.2 5 POUNDS**
28.28 g., 0.925 Silver 0.841 oz. ASW, 38.61 mm. **Ruler:** Elizabeth II **Subject:** 2004 Summer Olympics, Athens **Rev:** Rower in Tames, London., Union Jack in color **Rev. Inscription:** 1908 Great Britain 1948 / 2012

| Date | Mintage | VF20 | XF40 | MS60 | MS63 | MS65 |
|---|---|---|---|---|---|---|
| 2005 | Est. 15000 | PF65 60.00 | | | | |

**KM# 1192.2a 5 POUNDS**
39.94 g., 0.9167 Gold 1.1771 oz. AGW, 38.61 mm. **Ruler:** Elizabeth II **Subject:** 2004 Summer Olympics, Athens **Rev:** Rower in Thames, London, Union Jack in color **Rev. Inscription:** 1908 Great Britain 1948 / 1912

| Date | Mintage | VF20 | XF40 | MS60 | MS63 | MS65 |
|---|---|---|---|---|---|---|
| 2005 | Est. 104 | PF65 2,400 | | | | |

**KM# 1199 5 POUNDS**
28.28 g., 0.925 Silver 0.841 oz. ASW, 38.61 mm. **Ruler:** Elizabeth II **Subject:** 2004 Summer Olympics, Athens **Rev:** Fencer in Rome, Italian flag in color

| Date | Mintage | VF20 | XF40 | MS60 | MS63 | MS65 |
|---|---|---|---|---|---|---|
| 2005 | Est. 15000 | PF65 60.00 | | | | |

**KM# 1201 5 POUNDS**
28.28 g., 0.925 Steel 0.841 oz., 38.61 mm. **Ruler:** Elizabeth II **Subject:** 2004 Summer Olympics, Athens **Rev:** Weightlifter, Mexico flag in color

| Date | Mintage | VF20 | XF40 | MS60 | MS63 | MS65 |
|---|---|---|---|---|---|---|
| 2005 | Est. 15000 | PF65 60.00 | | | | |

**KM# 1202 5 POUNDS**
28.28 g., 0.925 Silver 0.841 oz. ASW, 38.61 mm. **Ruler:** Elizabeth II **Subject:** 2004 Summer Olympics, Athens **Rev:** Relay runner and Montreal, Canadian flag in color

| Date | Mintage | VF20 | XF40 | MS60 | MS63 | MS65 |
|---|---|---|---|---|---|---|
| 2005 | Est. 15000 | PF65 60.00 | | | | |

**KM# 1203 5 POUNDS**
28.28 g., 0.925 Silver 0.841 oz. ASW, 38.61 mm. **Ruler:** Elizabeth II **Subject:** 2004 Summer Olympics, Athens **Rev:** Ribbon dancer, Moscow, Russian flag in color

| Date | Mintage | VF20 | XF40 | MS60 | MS63 | MS65 |
|---|---|---|---|---|---|---|
| 2005 | Est. 15000 | PF65 60.00 | | | | |

**KM# 1204 5 POUNDS**
28.28 g., 0.925 Silver 0.841 oz. ASW, 38.61 mm. **Ruler:** Elizabeth II **Subject:** 2004 Summer Olympics, Athens **Rev:** Archers and Seoul, South Korean flag in color

| Date | Mintage | VF20 | XF40 | MS60 | MS63 | MS65 |
|---|---|---|---|---|---|---|
| 2005 | Est. 15000 | PF65 60.00 | | | | |

**KM# 1205 5 POUNDS**
28.28 g., 0.925 Silver 0.841 oz. ASW, 38.61 mm. **Ruler:** Elizabeth II **Subject:** 2004 Summer Olympics, Athens **Rev:** Hockey player in Barcelona, Spanish flag in color

| Date | Mintage | VF20 | XF40 | MS60 | MS63 | MS65 |
|---|---|---|---|---|---|---|
| 2005 | Est. 15000 | PF65 60.00 | | | | |

**KM# 1206 5 POUNDS**
28.28 g., 0.925 Silver 0.841 oz. ASW, 38.61 mm. **Ruler:** Elizabeth II **Subject:** 2004 Summer Olympics, Athens **Rev:** Wrestler in Athens, Greek flag in color

| Date | Mintage | VF20 | XF40 | MS60 | MS63 | MS65 |
|---|---|---|---|---|---|---|
| 2005 | Est. 15000 | PF65 60.00 | | | | |

**KM# 1228 5 POUNDS**
28.28 g., 0.925 Silver 0.841 oz. ASW, 38.61 mm. **Ruler:** Elizabeth II **Subject:** Battle of Trafalgar, 200th Anniversary **Rev:** Horatio Nelson

| Date | Mintage | VF20 | XF40 | MS60 | MS63 | MS65 |
|---|---|---|---|---|---|---|
| 2005 | Est. 25000 | PF65 60.00 | | | | |

**KM# 1228a.1 5 POUNDS**
39.94 g., 0.9167 Gold 1.1771 oz. AGW, 38.61 mm. **Ruler:** Elizabeth II **Subject:** Battle of Trafalgar, 200th Anniversary **Rev:** Horatio Nelson, without 200

| Date | Mintage | VF20 | XF40 | MS60 | MS63 | MS65 |
|---|---|---|---|---|---|---|
| 2005 | Est. 150 | PF65 2,400 | | | | |

**KM# 1228a.2 5 POUNDS**
39.94 g., 0.9167 Gold 1.1771 oz. AGW, 38.61 mm. **Ruler:** Elizabeth II **Subject:** Battle of Trafalgar, 200th Anniversary **Rev:** Horatio Nelson with 200

| Date | Mintage | VF20 | XF40 | MS60 | MS63 | MS65 |
|---|---|---|---|---|---|---|
| 2005 | Est. 50 | PF65 2,400 | | | | |

**KM# 1229 5 POUNDS**
28.28 g., 0.925 Silver 0.841 oz. ASW, 38.61 mm. **Ruler:** Elizabeth II **Subject:** Battle of Trafalgar, 200th Anniversary **Rev:** Captain Hardy of the H.M.S. Victory

| Date | Mintage | VF20 | XF40 | MS60 | MS63 | MS65 |
|---|---|---|---|---|---|---|
| 2005 | — | PF65 60.00 | | | | |

**KM# 1230 5 POUNDS**
28.28 g., 0.925 Silver 0.841 oz. ASW, 38.61 mm. **Ruler:** Elizabeth II **Subject:** Battle of Trafalgar, 200th Anniversary **Rev:** Vice Admiral Cuthbert Collingswood

| Date | Mintage | VF20 | XF40 | MS60 | MS63 | MS65 |
|---|---|---|---|---|---|---|
| 2005 | — | PF65 60.00 | | | | |

**KM# 1231 5 POUNDS**
28.28 g., 0.925 Silver 0.841 oz. ASW, 38.61 mm. **Ruler:** Elizabeth II **Subject:** Battle of Trafalgar, 200th Anniversary **Rev:** Vice Admiral Pierre de Villeneuve

| Date | Mintage | VF20 | XF40 | MS60 | MS63 | MS65 |
|---|---|---|---|---|---|---|
| 2005 | — | PF65 60.00 | | | | |

**KM# 1232 5 POUNDS**
28.28 g., 0.925 Silver 0.841 oz. ASW, 38.61 mm. **Ruler:** Elizabeth II **Subject:** Battle of Trafalgar, 200th Anniversary **Rev:** Napoleon Bonapart

| Date | Mintage | VF20 | XF40 | MS60 | MS63 | MS65 |
|---|---|---|---|---|---|---|
| 2005 | — | PF65 60.00 | | | | |

**KM# 1233 5 POUNDS**
28.28 g., 0.925 Silver 0.841 oz. ASW, 38.61 mm. **Ruler:** Elizabeth II **Subject:** Battle of Trafalgar, 200th Anniversary **Rev:** Horatio Nelson reviewing the battle plans

| Date | Mintage | VF20 | XF40 | MS60 | MS63 | MS65 |
|---|---|---|---|---|---|---|
| 2005 | — | PF65 60.00 | | | | |

**KM# 1234 5 POUNDS**
28.28 g., 0.925 Silver 0.841 oz. ASW, 38.61 mm. **Ruler:** Elizabeth II **Subject:** Battle of Trafalgar, 200th Anniversary **Rev:** Battle plans

| Date | Mintage | VF20 | XF40 | MS60 | MS63 | MS65 |
|---|---|---|---|---|---|---|
| 2005 | — | PF65 60.00 | | | | |

**KM# 1235 5 POUNDS**
28.28 g., 0.925 Silver 0.841 oz. ASW, 38.61 mm. **Ruler:** Elizabeth II **Subject:** Battle of Trafalgar, 200th Anniversary **Rev:** Exchange of the first shots

| Date | Mintage | VF20 | XF40 | MS60 | MS63 | MS65 |
|---|---|---|---|---|---|---|
| 2005 | — | PF65 60.00 | | | | |

**KM# 1236 5 POUNDS**
28.28 g., 0.925 Silver 0.841 oz. ASW, 38.61 mm. **Ruler:** Elizabeth II **Subject:** Battle of Trafalgar, 200th Anniversary **Rev:** Break through the enemy's battle line

| Date | Mintage | VF20 | XF40 | MS60 | MS63 | MS65 |
|---|---|---|---|---|---|---|
| 2005 | — | PF65 60.00 | | | | |

**KM# 1237 5 POUNDS**
28.28 g., 0.925 Silver 0.841 oz. ASW, 38.61 mm. **Ruler:** Elizabeth II **Subject:** Battle of Trafalgar, 200th Anniversary **Rev:** Tracking the opponents

| Date | Mintage | VF20 | XF40 | MS60 | MS63 | MS65 |
|---|---|---|---|---|---|---|
| 2005 | — | PF65 60.00 | | | | |

**KM# 1238 5 POUNDS**
28.28 g., 0.925 Silver 0.841 oz. ASW, 38.61 mm. **Ruler:** Elizabeth II **Subject:** Battle of Trafalgar, 200th Anniversary **Rev:** Death of Nelson

| Date | Mintage | VF20 | XF40 | MS60 | MS63 | MS65 |
|---|---|---|---|---|---|---|
| 2005 | — | PF65 60.00 | | | | |

**KM# 1238a.1 5 POUNDS**
38.94 g., 0.9167 Gold 1.1477 oz. AGW, 38.61 mm. **Ruler:** Elizabeth II **Subject:** Battle of Trafalgar, 200th Anniversary **Rev:** Death of Nelson, without 200

| Date | Mintage | VF20 | XF40 | MS60 | MS63 | MS65 |
|---|---|---|---|---|---|---|
| 2005 | — | PF65 2,400 | | | | |

**KM# 1238a.2 5 POUNDS**
39.94 g., 0.9167 Gold 1.1771 oz. AGW, 38.61 mm. **Ruler:** Elizabeth II **Subject:** Battle of Trafalgar, 200th Anniversary **Rev:** Death of Nelson, with 200

| Date | Mintage | VF20 | XF40 | MS60 | MS63 | MS65 |
|---|---|---|---|---|---|---|
| 2005 | — | PF65 2,400 | | | | |

**KM# 1239 5 POUNDS**
28.28 g., 0.925 Silver 0.841 oz. ASW, 38.61 mm. **Ruler:** Elizabeth II **Subject:** Battle of Trafalgar, 200th Anniversary **Rev:** Signal flags

| Date | Mintage | VF20 | XF40 | MS60 | MS63 | MS65 |
|---|---|---|---|---|---|---|
| 2005 | Est. 14500 | PF65 60.00 | | | | |

**KM# 1240 5 POUNDS**
28.28 g., 0.925 Silver 0.841 oz. ASW, 38.61 mm. **Ruler:** Elizabeth II **Subject:** Battle of Trafalgar, 200th Anniversary **Rev:** Funeral procession for Horatio Nelson

| Date | Mintage | VF20 | XF40 | MS60 | MS63 | MS65 |
|---|---|---|---|---|---|---|
| 2005 | — | PF65 60.00 | | | | |

**KM# 1241 5 POUNDS**
28.28 g., 0.925 Silver 0.841 oz. ASW, 38.61 mm. **Ruler:** Elizabeth II **Subject:** Battle of Trafalgar, 200th Anniversary **Rev:** Nelson's Column in Trafalgar Square, London

| Date | Mintage | VF20 | XF40 | MS60 | MS63 | MS65 |
|---|---|---|---|---|---|---|
| 2005 | Est. 14500 | PF65 60.00 | | | | |

**KM# 1242 5 POUNDS**
28.28 g., 0.925 Silver 0.841 oz. ASW, 38.61 mm. **Ruler:** Elizabeth II **Subject:** Battle of Trafalgar, 200th Anniversary **Rev:** Horatio Nelson as young Captain

| Date | Mintage | VF20 | XF40 | MS60 | MS63 | MS65 |
|---|---|---|---|---|---|---|
| 2005 | Est. 14500 | PF65 60.00 | | | | |

**KM# 1243 5 POUNDS**
28.28 g., 0.925 Silver 0.841 oz. ASW, 38.61 mm. **Ruler:** Elizabeth II **Subject:** Battle of Trafalgar, 200th Anniversary **Rev:** Nelson dying

| Date | Mintage | VF20 | XF40 | MS60 | MS63 | MS65 |
|---|---|---|---|---|---|---|
| 2005 | Est. 14500 | PF65 60.00 | | | | |

**KM# 1244 5 POUNDS**
28.28 g., 0.925 Silver 0.841 oz. ASW, 38.61 mm. **Ruler:** Elizabeth II **Subject:** Battle of Trafalgar, 200th Anniversary **Rev:** H.M.S. Victory being towed to Gibraltar

| Date | Mintage | VF20 | XF40 | MS60 | MS63 | MS65 |
|---|---|---|---|---|---|---|
| 2005 | Est. 14500 | PF65 60.00 | | | | |

**KM# 1245 5 POUNDS**
28.28 g., 0.925 Silver 0.841 oz. ASW, 38.61 mm. **Ruler:** Elizabeth II **Subject:** Battle of Trafalgar, 200th Anniversary **Rev:** Horatio Nelson and Thomas Hardy on board the H.M.S. Victory

| Date | Mintage | VF20 | XF40 | MS60 | MS63 | MS65 |
|---|---|---|---|---|---|---|
| 2005 | Est. 14500 | PF65 60.00 | | | | |

**KM# 1246 5 POUNDS**
28.28 g., 0.925 Silver 0.841 oz. ASW, 38.61 mm. **Ruler:** Elizabeth II **Subject:** Battle of Trafalgar, 200th Anniversary **Rev:** H.M.S. Victory enters battle

| Date | Mintage | VF20 | XF40 | MS60 | MS63 | MS65 |
|---|---|---|---|---|---|---|
| 2005 | Est. 14500 | PF65 60.00 | | | | |

**KM# 1247 5 POUNDS**
28.28 g., 0.925 Silver 0.841 oz. ASW, 38.61 mm. **Ruler:** Elizabeth II **Subject:** Battle of Trafalgar, 200th Anniversary **Rev:** H.M.S. Agamemnon at Corsica and the Siege of Calvi

| Date | Mintage | VF20 | XF40 | MS60 | MS63 | MS65 |
|---|---|---|---|---|---|---|
| 2005 | Est. 14500 | PF65 60.00 | | | | |

**KM# 1248 5 POUNDS**
28.28 g., 0.925 Silver 0.841 oz. ASW, 38.61 mm. **Ruler:** Elizabeth II **Obv:** Siege of Cape St. Vincent **Rev:** Battle of Trafalgar, 200th Anniversary

| Date | Mintage | VF20 | XF40 | MS60 | MS63 | MS65 |
|---|---|---|---|---|---|---|
| 2005 | Est. 14500 | PF65 60.00 | | | | |

**KM# 1250 5 POUNDS**
28.28 g., 0.925 Silver 0.841 oz. ASW, 38.61 mm. **Ruler:** Elizabeth II **Subject:** Battle of Trafalgar, 200th Anniversary **Rev:** Battle of the Nile at Abukir

| Date | Mintage | VF20 | XF40 | MS60 | MS63 | MS65 |
|---|---|---|---|---|---|---|
| 2005 | Est. 14500 | PF65 60.00 | | | | |

**KM# 1263 5 POUNDS**
28.28 g., 0.925 Silver 0.841 oz. ASW, 38.61 mm. **Ruler:** Elizabeth II **Subject:** Elizabeth II, 79th Birthday **Rev:** Military parade

| Date | Mintage | VF20 | XF40 | MS60 | MS63 | MS65 |
|---|---|---|---|---|---|---|
| 2005 | Est. 20000 | PF65 60.00 | | | | |

**KM# 1264 5 POUNDS**
28.28 g., 0.925 Silver 0.841 oz. ASW, 38.61 mm. **Ruler:** Elizabeth II **Subject:** Elizabeth II, 79th Birthday **Rev:** Ceremony of the Garter

| Date | Mintage | VF20 | XF40 | MS60 | MS63 | MS65 |
|---|---|---|---|---|---|---|
| 2005 | Est. 20000 | PF65 60.00 | | | | |

**KM# 1265 5 POUNDS**
28.28 g., 0.925 Silver 0.841 oz. ASW, 38.61 mm. **Ruler:** Elizabeth II **Subject:** Elizabeth II, 79th Birthday **Rev:** Opening of Parlament

| Date | Mintage | VF20 | XF40 | MS60 | MS63 | MS65 |
|---|---|---|---|---|---|---|
| 2005 | Est. 14500 | PF65 60.00 | | | | |

**KM# 1266 5 POUNDS**
28.28 g., 0.925 Silver 0.841 oz. ASW, 38.61 mm. **Ruler:** Elizabeth II **Subject:** Elizabeth II, 79th Birthday **Rev:** Inauguration

| Date | Mintage | VF20 | XF40 | MS60 | MS63 | MS65 |
|---|---|---|---|---|---|---|
| 2005 | Est. 14500 | PF65 60.00 | | | | |

### KM# 1267 5 POUNDS

28.28 g., 0.925 Silver 0.841 oz. ASW, 38.61 mm. **Ruler:** Elizabeth II **Subject:** Elizabeth II, 79th Birthday **Rev:** Maundy Thursday

| Date | Mintage | VF20 | XF40 | MS60 | MS63 | MS65 |
|---|---|---|---|---|---|---|
| 2005 | Est. 14500 | **PF65** 60.00 | | | | |

### KM# 1268 5 POUNDS

28.28 g., 0.925 Silver 0.841 oz. ASW, 38.61 mm. **Ruler:** Elizabeth II **Subject:** Elizabeth II, 79th Birthday **Rev:** Country

| Date | Mintage | VF20 | XF40 | MS60 | MS63 | MS65 |
|---|---|---|---|---|---|---|
| 2005 | Est. 14500 | **PF65** 60.00 | | | | |

### KM# 1269 5 POUNDS

28.28 g., 0.925 Silver 0.841 oz. ASW, 38.61 mm. **Ruler:** Elizabeth II **Subject:** Elizabeth II, 79th Birthday **Rev:** Garden party at Buckingham Palace

| Date | Mintage | VF20 | XF40 | MS60 | MS63 | MS65 |
|---|---|---|---|---|---|---|
| 2005 | Est. 14500 | **PF65** 60.00 | | | | |

### KM# 1270 5 POUNDS

28.28 g., 0.925 Silver 0.841 oz. ASW, 38.61 mm. **Ruler:** Elizabeth II **Subject:** Elizabeth II, 79th Birthday **Rev:** Chelsea Flower Show

| Date | Mintage | VF20 | XF40 | MS60 | MS63 | MS65 |
|---|---|---|---|---|---|---|
| 2005 | Est. 14500 | **PF65** 60.00 | | | | |

### KM# 1271 5 POUNDS

28.28 g., 0.925 Silver 0.841 oz. ASW, 38.61 mm. **Ruler:** Elizabeth II **Subject:** Elizabeth II, 79th Birthday **Rev:** Horse races at Ascot

| Date | Mintage | VF20 | XF40 | MS60 | MS63 | MS65 |
|---|---|---|---|---|---|---|
| 2005 | Est. 14500 | **PF65** 60.00 | | | | |

### KM# 1272 5 POUNDS

28.28 g., 0.925 Silver 0.841 oz. ASW, 38.61 mm. **Ruler:** Elizabeth II **Subject:** Elizabeth II, 79th Birthday **Rev:** State visit

| Date | Mintage | VF20 | XF40 | MS60 | MS63 | MS65 |
|---|---|---|---|---|---|---|
| Elizabeth II 79th Birthday | Est. 14500 | **PF65** 60.00 | | | | |

### KM# 1274 5 POUNDS

28.28 g., 0.925 Silver 0.841 oz. ASW, 38.61 mm. **Ruler:** Elizabeth II **Subject:** Elizabeth II, 79th Birthday **Rev:** Christmas Speech

| Date | Mintage | VF20 | XF40 | MS60 | MS63 | MS65 |
|---|---|---|---|---|---|---|
| 2005 | Est. 14500 | **PF65** 60.00 | | | | |

### KM# 1284 5 POUNDS

28.28 g., 0.925 Silver 0.841 oz. ASW, 38.61 mm. **Ruler:** Elizabeth II **Subject:** Elizabeth II, 80th Birthday **Rev:** Older portrait

| Date | Mintage | VF20 | XF40 | MS60 | MS63 | MS65 |
|---|---|---|---|---|---|---|
| 2006 | Est. 30000 | **PF65** 60.00 | | | | |

### KM# 1284a 5 POUNDS

28.28 g., 0.999 Platinum 0.9083 oz. APW **Ruler:** Elizabeth II **Subject:** Elizabeth II, 80th Birthday **Rev:** Older portrait

| Date | Mintage | VF20 | XF40 | MS60 | MS63 | MS65 |
|---|---|---|---|---|---|---|
| 2006 | Est. 195 | **PF65** 1,500 | | | | |

### KM# 1285 5 POUNDS

28.28 g., 0.925 Silver 0.841 oz. ASW, 38.61 mm. **Ruler:** Elizabeth II **Subject:** Elizabeth II, 80th Birthday **Rev:** Elizabeth as child

| Date | Mintage | VF20 | XF40 | MS60 | MS63 | MS65 |
|---|---|---|---|---|---|---|
| 2006 | Est. 14500 | **PF65** 60.00 | | | | |

### KM# 1285a 5 POUNDS

28.28 g., 0.999 Platinum 0.9083 oz. APW **Ruler:** Elizabeth II **Obv:** Elizabeth II as a child **Rev:** Elizabeth II, 80th Birthday

| Date | Mintage | VF20 | XF40 | MS60 | MS63 | MS65 |
|---|---|---|---|---|---|---|
| 2006 | Est. 25 | **PF65** 1,700 | | | | |

### KM# 1286 5 POUNDS

28.28 g., 0.925 Silver 0.841 oz. ASW, 38.61 mm. **Ruler:** Elizabeth II **Subject:** Elizabeth II, 80th Birthday **Rev:** Elizabeth II as a young lady

| Date | Mintage | VF20 | XF40 | MS60 | MS63 | MS65 |
|---|---|---|---|---|---|---|
| 2006 | Est. 14500 | **PF65** 60.00 | | | | |

### KM# 1286a 5 POUNDS

28.28 g., 0.999 Platinum 0.9083 oz. APW **Ruler:** Elizabeth II **Subject:** Elizabeth II, 80th Birthday **Rev:** Elizabeth II as a young lady

| Date | Mintage | VF20 | XF40 | MS60 | MS63 | MS65 |
|---|---|---|---|---|---|---|
| 2006 | Est. 25 | **PF65** 1,700 | | | | |

### KM# 1287 5 POUNDS

28.28 g., 0.925 Silver 0.841 oz. ASW, 38.61 mm. **Ruler:** Elizabeth II **Subject:** Elizabeth II, 80th Birthday **Rev:** Elizabeth with grandchildren

| Date | Mintage | VF20 | XF40 | MS60 | MS63 | MS65 |
|---|---|---|---|---|---|---|
| 2006 | Est. 14500 | **PF65** 60.00 | | | | |

### KM# 1287a 5 POUNDS

28.28 g., 0.999 Platinum 0.9083 oz. APW **Ruler:** Elizabeth II **Subject:** Elizabeth II, 80th Birthday **Rev:** Elizabeth with grandchildren

| Date | Mintage | VF20 | XF40 | MS60 | MS63 | MS65 |
|---|---|---|---|---|---|---|
| 2006 | Est. 25 | **PF65** 1,700 | | | | |

### KM# 1297 5 POUNDS

28.28 g., Silver, 38.61 mm. **Ruler:** Elizabeth II **Subject:** Elizabeth II, 80th Birthday **Rev:** Baptism

| Date | Mintage | VF20 | XF40 | MS60 | MS63 | MS65 |
|---|---|---|---|---|---|---|
| 2006 | Est. 14500 | **PF65** 60.00 | | | | |

### KM# 1298 5 POUNDS

28.28 g., 0.925 Silver 0.841 oz. ASW, 38.61 mm. **Ruler:** Elizabeth II **Subject:** Elizabeth II, 80th Birthday **Rev:** Radio message

| Date | Mintage | VF20 | XF40 | MS60 | MS63 | MS65 |
|---|---|---|---|---|---|---|
| 2006 | Est. 14500 | **PF65** 60.00 | | | | |

### KM# 1299 5 POUNDS

28.28 g., 0.925 Silver 0.841 oz. ASW, 38.61 mm. **Ruler:** Elizabeth II **Subject:** Elizabeth II, 80th Birthday **Rev:** Coronation

| Date | Mintage | VF20 | XF40 | MS60 | MS63 | MS65 |
|---|---|---|---|---|---|---|
| 2006 | Est. 14500 | **PF65** 60.00 | | | | |

### KM# 1300 5 POUNDS

28.28 g., 0.925 Silver 0.841 oz. ASW, 38.61 mm. **Ruler:** Elizabeth II **Subject:** Elizabeth II, 80th Birthday **Rev:** Royal family

| Date | Mintage | VF20 | XF40 | MS60 | MS63 | MS65 |
|---|---|---|---|---|---|---|
| 2006 | Est. 14500 | **PF65** 60.00 | | | | |

### KM# 1301 5 POUNDS

28.28 g., 0.925 Silver 0.841 oz. ASW, 38.61 mm. **Ruler:** Elizabeth II **Subject:** Elizabeth II, 80th Birthday **Rev:** Investiture of Charles as Prince of Wales

| Date | Mintage | VF20 | XF40 | MS60 | MS63 | MS65 |
|---|---|---|---|---|---|---|
| 2006 | Est. 14500 | **PF65** 60.00 | | | | |

### KM# 1302 5 POUNDS

28.28 g., 0.925 Silver 0.841 oz. ASW, 38.61 mm. **Ruler:** Elizabeth II **Subject:** Elizabeth II, 80th Birthday **Rev:** Princes William and Harry

| Date | Mintage | VF20 | XF40 | MS60 | MS63 | MS65 |
|---|---|---|---|---|---|---|
| 2006 | Est. 14500 | **PF65** 60.00 | | | | |

### KM# 1303 5 POUNDS

28.28 g., 0.925 Silver 0.841 oz. ASW, 38.61 mm. **Ruler:** Elizabeth II **Subject:** Elizabeth II, 80th Birthday **Rev:** Military parade

| Date | Mintage | VF20 | XF40 | MS60 | MS63 | MS65 |
|---|---|---|---|---|---|---|
| 2006 | Est. 14500 | **PF65** 60.00 | | | | |

### KM# 1304 5 POUNDS

28.28 g., 0.925 Silver 0.841 oz. ASW, 38.61 mm. **Ruler:** Elizabeth II **Subject:** Elizabeth II, 80th Birthday **Rev:** Coronation Jubilee

| Date | Mintage | VF20 | XF40 | MS60 | MS63 | MS65 |
|---|---|---|---|---|---|---|
| 2006 | Est. 14500 | **PF65** 60.00 | | | | |

### KM# 1306 5 POUNDS

28.28 g., 0.925 Silver 0.841 oz. ASW, 38.61 mm. **Ruler:** Elizabeth II **Subject:** 1966 World Cup, England as Champions, 40th Anniversary **Rev:** Bobby Moore and trophy

| Date | Mintage | VF20 | XF40 | MS60 | MS63 | MS65 |
|---|---|---|---|---|---|---|
| 2006 | Est. 25000 | **PF65** 60.00 | | | | |

### KM# 1307 5 POUNDS

28.28 g., 0.925 Silver 0.841 oz. ASW, 38.61 mm. **Ruler:** Elizabeth II **Subject:** 1966 World Cup, England as Champions, 40th Anniversary **Rev:** Crowds

| Date | Mintage | VF20 | XF40 | MS60 | MS63 | MS65 |
|---|---|---|---|---|---|---|
| 2006 | Est. 20000 | **PF65** 60.00 | | | | |

### KM# 1308 5 POUNDS

28.28 g., 0.925 Silver 0.841 oz. ASW, 38.61 mm. **Ruler:** Elizabeth II **Subject:** 1966 World Cup, England as Champions, 40th Anniversary **Rev:** Wembley Stadium

| Date | Mintage | VF20 | XF40 | MS60 | MS63 | MS65 |
|---|---|---|---|---|---|---|
| 2006 | Est. 20000 | **PF65** 60.00 | | | | |

### KM# 1309 5 POUNDS

28.28 g., 0.925 Silver 0.841 oz. ASW, 38.61 mm. **Ruler:** Elizabeth II **Subject:** 1966 World Cup, England as Champions, 40th Anniversary **Rev:** Sir Alfred Ramsey and Bobby Moore

| Date | Mintage | VF20 | XF40 | MS60 | MS63 | MS65 |
|---|---|---|---|---|---|---|
| 2006 | Est. 20000 | **PF65** 60.00 | | | | |

### KM# 1310 5 POUNDS

28.28 g., 0.925 Silver 0.841 oz. ASW, 38.61 mm. **Ruler:** Elizabeth II **Subject:** 1966 World Cup, England as Champions, 40th Anniversary **Rev:** Elizabeth II and Bobby Moore

| Date | Mintage | VF20 | XF40 | MS60 | MS63 | MS65 |
|---|---|---|---|---|---|---|
| 2006 | Est. 20000 | **PF65** 60.00 | | | | |

### KM# 1311 5 POUNDS

28.28 g., 0.925 Silver 0.841 oz. ASW, 38.61 mm. **Ruler:** Elizabeth II **Subject:** 1966 World Cup, England as Champions, 40th Anniversary **Rev:** First round game with Flags of England and Uruguay in color

| Date | Mintage | VF20 | XF40 | MS60 | MS63 | MS65 |
|---|---|---|---|---|---|---|
| 2006 | Est. 20000 | **PF65** 60.00 | | | | |

### KM# 1312 5 POUNDS

28.28 g., 0.925 Silver 0.841 oz. ASW, 38.61 mm. **Ruler:** Elizabeth II **Subject:** 1966 World Cup, England as Champions, 40th Anniversary **Rev:** First round game with flags of England and Mexico in color

| Date | Mintage | VF20 | XF40 | MS60 | MS63 | MS65 |
|---|---|---|---|---|---|---|
| 2006 | Est. 20000 | **PF65** 60.00 | | | | |

### KM# 1313 5 POUNDS

28.28 g., 0.925 Silver 0.841 oz. ASW, 38.61 mm. **Ruler:** Elizabeth II **Subject:** 1966 World Cup, England as Champions, 40th Anniversary **Rev:** First round games with flags of England and France in color

| Date | Mintage | VF20 | XF40 | MS60 | MS63 | MS65 |
|---|---|---|---|---|---|---|
| 2006 | Est. 20000 | **PF65** 60.00 | | | | |

### KM# 1314 5 POUNDS

28.28 g., 0.925 Silver 0.841 oz. ASW, 38.61 mm. **Ruler:** Elizabeth II **Subject:** 1966 World Cup, England as Champions, 40th Anniversary **Rev:** Quarter Final games with flags of England and Argentina in color

| Date | Mintage | VF20 | XF40 | MS60 | MS63 | MS65 |
|---|---|---|---|---|---|---|
| 2006 | Est. 20000 | **PF65** 60.00 | | | | |

### KM# 1315 5 POUNDS

28.28 g., 0.925 Silver 0.841 oz. ASW, 38.61 mm. **Ruler:** Elizabeth II **Subject:** 1966 World Cup, England as Champions, 40th Anniversary **Rev:** Semi-final game with flags of England and Portugal in color

| Date | Mintage | VF20 | XF40 | MS60 | MS63 | MS65 |
|---|---|---|---|---|---|---|
| 2006 | Est. 20000 | **PF65** 60.00 | | | | |

### KM# 1316 5 POUNDS

28.28 g., 0.925 Silver 0.841 oz. ASW, 38.61 mm. **Ruler:** Elizabeth II **Subject:** 1966 World Cup, England as Champions, 40th Anniversary **Rev:** Final game with flags of England and Germany in color

| Date | Mintage | VF20 | XF40 | MS60 | MS63 | MS65 |
|---|---|---|---|---|---|---|
| 2006 | Est. 20000 | **PF65** 60.00 | | | | |

### KM# 1319 5 POUNDS

28.28 g., 0.925 Silver 0.841 oz. ASW, 38.61 mm. **Ruler:** Elizabeth II **Obv:** Concord over Toulouse, 1967 **Rev:** Concord, 40th Anniversary

| Date | Mintage | VF20 | XF40 | MS60 | MS63 | MS65 |
|---|---|---|---|---|---|---|
| 2006 | Est. 10000 | **PF65** 60.00 | | | | |

### KM# 1320 5 POUNDS

28.28 g., 0.925 Silver 0.841 oz. ASW, 38.61 mm. **Ruler:** Elizabeth II **Subject:** Concorde, 40th Anniversary **Rev:** First flight, 1969

| Date | Mintage | VF20 | XF40 | MS60 | MS63 | MS65 |
|---|---|---|---|---|---|---|
| 2006 | Est. 15000 | **PF65** 60.00 | | | | |

### KM# 1321 5 POUNDS

28.28 g., 0.925 Silver 0.841 oz. ASW, 38.61 mm. **Ruler:** Elizabeth II **Subject:** Concorde, 40th Anniversary **Rev:** Concorde breaking the sound barrier

| Date | Mintage | VF20 | XF40 | MS60 | MS63 | MS65 |
|---|---|---|---|---|---|---|
| 2006 | Est. 10000 | **PF65** 60.00 | | | | |

### KM# 1322 5 POUNDS

28.28 g., 0.925 Silver 0.841 oz. ASW, 38.61 mm. **Ruler:** Elizabeth II **Subject:** Concorde, 40th Anniversary **Rev:** Concord in record speed

| Date | Mintage | VF20 | XF40 | MS60 | MS63 | MS65 |
|---|---|---|---|---|---|---|
| 2006 | Est. 10000 | **PF65** 60.00 | | | | |

### KM# 1323 5 POUNDS

28.28 g., 0.925 Silver 0.841 oz. ASW, 38.61 mm. **Ruler:** Elizabeth II **Subject:** Concorde, 40th Anniversary **Rev:** Passenger operations

| Date | Mintage | VF20 | XF40 | MS60 | MS63 | MS65 |
|---|---|---|---|---|---|---|
| 2006 | Est. 10000 | **PF65** 60.00 | | | | |

### KM# 1324 5 POUNDS

28.28 g., 0.925 Silver 0.841 oz. ASW, 38.61 mm. **Ruler:** Elizabeth II **Subject:** Concorde, 40th Anniversary **Rev:** Elizabeth II flies on Concorde, 1977

| Date | Mintage | VF20 | XF40 | MS60 | MS63 | MS65 |
|---|---|---|---|---|---|---|
| 2006 | Est. 10000 | **PF65** 60.00 | | | | |

### KM# 1325 5 POUNDS

28.28 g., 0.925 Silver 0.841 oz. ASW, 38.61 mm. **Ruler:** Elizabeth II **Subject:** Concorde, 40th Anniversary **Rev:** London to Sydney service, 1985

| Date | Mintage | VF20 | XF40 | MS60 | MS63 | MS65 |
|---|---|---|---|---|---|---|
| 2006 | Est. 10000 | **PF65** 60.00 | | | | |

### KM# 1326 5 POUNDS

28.28 g., 0.925 Silver 0.841 oz. ASW, 38.61 mm. **Ruler:** Elizabeth II **Subject:** Concorde, 40th Anniversary **Rev:** Concord and globe

| Date | Mintage | VF20 | XF40 | MS60 | MS63 | MS65 |
|---|---|---|---|---|---|---|
| 2006 | Est. 15000 | **PF65** 60.00 | | | | |

### KM# 1327 5 POUNDS

28.28 g., 0.925 Silver 0.841 oz. ASW, 38.61 mm. **Ruler:** Elizabeth II **Subject:** Concorde, 40th Anniversary **Rev:** New York to London record flight, 1996

| Date | Mintage | VF20 | XF40 | MS60 | MS63 | MS65 |
|---|---|---|---|---|---|---|
| 2006 | Est. 15000 | **PF65** 60.00 | | | | |

### KM# 1328 5 POUNDS

28.28 g., 0.925 Silver 0.841 oz. ASW, 38.61 mm. **Ruler:** Elizabeth II **Subject:** Concorde, 40th Anniversary **Rev:** Fly-by over Buckingham Palace, 2002

| Date | Mintage | VF20 | XF40 | MS60 | MS63 | MS65 |
|---|---|---|---|---|---|---|
| 2006 | Est. 10000 | **PF65** 60.00 | | | | |

**KM# 1329 5 POUNDS**
28.28 g., 0.925 Silver 0.841 oz. ASW, 38.61 mm. **Ruler:** Elizabeth II **Subject:** Concorde, 40th Anniversary **Rev:** Adjustment of passenger operations, 2003

| Date | Mintage | VF20 | XF40 | MS60 | MS63 | MS65 |
|---|---|---|---|---|---|---|
| 2006 | Est. 10000 | **PF65** 60.00 | | | | |

**KM# 1330 5 POUNDS**
28.28 g., 0.925 Silver 0.841 oz. ASW, 38.61 mm. **Ruler:** Elizabeth II **Subject:** Concorde, 40th Anniversary **Rev:** Last flight, 2003

| Date | Mintage | VF20 | XF40 | MS60 | MS63 | MS65 |
|---|---|---|---|---|---|---|
| 2006 | Est. 15000 | **PF65** 60.00 | | | | |

**KM# 1095 5 POUNDS**
Silver, 38.6 mm. **Ruler:** Elizabeth II **Subject:** History fo the RAF - Flypast **Obv:** Bust in crown right **Rev:** Bomber and two planes in flight

| Date | Mintage | VF20 | XF40 | MS60 | MS63 | MS65 |
|---|---|---|---|---|---|---|
| 2007 | — | **PF63** 45.00 | **PF65** 50.00 | | | |

**KM# 1096 5 POUNDS**
Silver, 38.61 mm. **Ruler:** Elizabeth II **Subject:** History of the RAF - Avro Lancaster **Obv:** Bust in crown right **Rev:** Lancaster bomber flying right

| Date | Mintage | VF20 | XF40 | MS60 | MS63 | MS65 |
|---|---|---|---|---|---|---|
| 2007 | — | **PF63** 45.00 | **PF65** 50.00 | | | |

**KM# 1339 5 POUNDS**
28.28 g., 0.925 Silver 0.841 oz. ASW, 38.61 mm. **Ruler:** Elizabeth II **Subject:** Elizabeth and Philip, 60th Wedding Anniversary **Rev:** Elizabeth and Philips busts

| Date | Mintage | VF20 | XF40 | MS60 | MS63 | MS65 |
|---|---|---|---|---|---|---|
| 2007 | Est. 50000 | **PF65** 60.00 | | | | |

**KM# 1340 5 POUNDS**
28.28 g., 0.925 Silver 0.841 oz. ASW, 38.61 mm. **Ruler:** Elizabeth II **Subject:** Elizabeth and Philip, 60th Wedding Anniversary **Rev:** Wedding portrait, 1947

| Date | Mintage | VF20 | XF40 | MS60 | MS63 | MS65 |
|---|---|---|---|---|---|---|
| 2007 | Est. 50000 | **PF65** 60.00 | | | | |

**KM# 1341 5 POUNDS**
28.28 g., 0.925 Silver 0.841 oz. ASW, 38.61 mm. **Ruler:** Elizabeth II **Subject:** Elizabeth and Philip, 60th Wedding Anniversary **Rev:** State coach

| Date | Mintage | VF20 | XF40 | MS60 | MS63 | MS65 |
|---|---|---|---|---|---|---|
| 2007 | Est. 25000 | **PF65** 60.00 | | | | |

**KM# 1342 5 POUNDS**
28.28 g., 0.925 Silver 0.841 oz. ASW, 38.61 mm. **Ruler:** Elizabeth II **Subject:** Elizabeth and Philip, 60th Wedding Anniversary **Rev:** Westminster Abbey

| Date | Mintage | VF20 | XF40 | MS60 | MS63 | MS65 |
|---|---|---|---|---|---|---|
| 2007 | Est. 25000 | **PF65** 60.00 | | | | |

**KM# 1356 5 POUNDS**
28.28 g., 0.925 Silver 0.841 oz. ASW, 38.61 mm. **Ruler:** Elizabeth II **Subject:** Battle of Britain Memorial Flight **Rev:** Spitfire

| Date | Mintage | VF20 | XF40 | MS60 | MS63 | MS65 |
|---|---|---|---|---|---|---|
| 2007 | Est. 50000 | **PF65** 60.00 | | | | |

**KM# 1357 5 POUNDS**
28.28 g., 0.925 Silver 0.841 oz. ASW, 38.61 mm. **Ruler:** Elizabeth II **Subject:** Battle of Britain Memorial Flight **Rev:** Hawker Hurricane

| Date | Mintage | VF20 | XF40 | MS60 | MS63 | MS65 |
|---|---|---|---|---|---|---|
| 2007 | Est. 14500 | **PF65** 60.00 | | | | |

**KM# 1358 5 POUNDS**
28.28 g., 0.925 Silver 0.841 oz. ASW, 38.61 mm. **Ruler:** Elizabeth II **Subject:** Battle of Britain Memorial Flight **Rev:** Dakota C-47

| Date | Mintage | VF20 | XF40 | MS60 | MS63 | MS65 |
|---|---|---|---|---|---|---|
| 2007 | Est. 14500 | **PF65** 60.00 | | | | |

**KM# 1359 5 POUNDS**
28.28 g., 0.925 Silver 0.841 oz. ASW, 38.61 mm. **Ruler:** Elizabeth II **Subject:** Battle of Britain Memorial Flight **Rev:** DHC 1 Chipmunk

| Date | Mintage | VF20 | XF40 | MS60 | MS63 | MS65 |
|---|---|---|---|---|---|---|
| 2007 | Est. 14500 | **PF65** 60.00 | | | | |

**KM# 1379 5 POUNDS**
28.28 g., 0.925 Silver 0.841 oz. ASW, 38.61 mm. **Ruler:** Elizabeth II **Subject:** Royal Air Force, 90th Anniversary **Rev:** Hawker Hart

| Date | Mintage | VF20 | XF40 | MS60 | MS63 | MS65 |
|---|---|---|---|---|---|---|
| 2008 | Est. 25000 | **PF65** 60.00 | | | | |

**KM# 1380 5 POUNDS**
28.28 g., 0.925 Silver 0.841 oz. ASW, 38.61 mm. **Ruler:** Elizabeth II **Subject:** Royal Air Force, 90th Anniversary **Rev:** Eurofighter Typhoon

| Date | Mintage | VF20 | XF40 | MS60 | MS63 | MS65 |
|---|---|---|---|---|---|---|
| 2008 | Est. 25000 | **PF65** 60.00 | | | | |

**KM# 1381 5 POUNDS**
28.28 g., 0.925 Silver 0.841 oz. ASW, 38.61 mm. **Ruler:** Elizabeth II **Subject:** Royal Air Force, 90th Anniversary **Rev:** English Electric Canberra

| Date | Mintage | VF20 | XF40 | MS60 | MS63 | MS65 |
|---|---|---|---|---|---|---|
| 2008 | Est. 25000 | **PF65** 60.00 | | | | |

**KM# 1382 5 POUNDS**
28.28 g., 0.925 Silver 0.841 oz. ASW, 38.61 mm. **Ruler:** Elizabeth II **Subject:** Royal Air Force, 90th Anniversary **Rev:** Bristol Beaufighter

| Date | Mintage | VF20 | XF40 | MS60 | MS63 | MS65 |
|---|---|---|---|---|---|---|
| 2008 | Est. 25000 | **PF65** 60.00 | | | | |

**KM# 1383 5 POUNDS**
28.28 g., 0.925 Silver 0.841 oz. ASW, 38.61 mm. **Ruler:** Elizabeth II **Subject:** Royal Air Force, 90th Anniversary **Rev:** Vickers VC 10

| Date | Mintage | VF20 | XF40 | MS60 | MS63 | MS65 |
|---|---|---|---|---|---|---|
| 2008 | Est. 25000 | **PF65** 60.00 | | | | |

**KM# 1384 5 POUNDS**
28.28 g., 0.925 Silver 0.841 oz. ASW, 38.61 mm. **Ruler:** Elizabeth II **Subject:** Royal Air Force, 90th Anniversary **Rev:** Boeing C47 Chinook helicopter

| Date | Mintage | VF20 | XF40 | MS60 | MS63 | MS65 |
|---|---|---|---|---|---|---|
| 2008 | Est. 25000 | **PF65** 50.00 | | | | |

**KM# 1385 5 POUNDS**
28.28 g., 0.925 Silver 0.841 oz. ASW, 38.61 mm. **Ruler:** Elizabeth II **Subject:** Harrier GR 3

| Date | Mintage | VF20 | XF40 | MS60 | MS63 | MS65 |
|---|---|---|---|---|---|---|
| 2008 | Est. 25000 | **PF65** 60.00 | | | | |

**KM# 1386 5 POUNDS**
28.28 g., 0.925 Silver 0.841 oz. ASW, 38.61 mm. **Ruler:** Elizabeth II **Subject:** Hawker F6

| Date | Mintage | VF20 | XF40 | MS60 | MS63 | MS65 |
|---|---|---|---|---|---|---|
| 2008 | Est. 25000 | **PF65** 60.00 | | | | |

**KM# 1387 5 POUNDS**
28.28 g., 0.925 Silver 0.841 oz. ASW, 38.61 mm. **Ruler:** Elizabeth II **Subject:** Airco DH 9

| Date | Mintage | VF20 | XF40 | MS60 | MS63 | MS65 |
|---|---|---|---|---|---|---|
| 2008 | 25,000 | **PF65** 60.00 | | | | |

**KM# 1388 5 POUNDS**
28.28 g., 0.925 Silver 0.841 oz. ASW, 38.61 mm. **Ruler:** Elizabeth II **Subject:** Westland "Lysander"

| Date | Mintage | VF20 | XF40 | MS60 | MS63 | MS65 |
|---|---|---|---|---|---|---|
| 2008 | Est. 25000 | **PF65** 60.00 | | | | |

**KM# 1389 5 POUNDS**
28.28 g., 0.925 Silver 0.841 oz. ASW, 38.61 mm. **Ruler:** Elizabeth II **Subject:** Avro 504

| Date | Mintage | VF20 | XF40 | MS60 | MS63 | MS65 |
|---|---|---|---|---|---|---|
| 2008 | Est. 25000 | **PF65** 60.00 | | | | |

**KM# 1390 5 POUNDS**
28.28 g., 0.925 Silver 0.841 oz. ASW, 38.61 mm. **Ruler:** Elizabeth II **Subject:** English Electric "Lightning"

| Date | Mintage | VF20 | XF40 | MS60 | MS63 | MS65 |
|---|---|---|---|---|---|---|
| 2008 | Est. 25000 | **PF65** 60.00 | | | | |

**KM# 1391 5 POUNDS**
28.28 g., 0.925 Silver 0.841 oz. ASW, 38.61 mm. **Ruler:** Elizabeth II **Subject:** Short Sunderland

| Date | Mintage | VF20 | XF40 | MS60 | MS63 | MS65 |
|---|---|---|---|---|---|---|
| 2008 | Est. 25000 | **PF65** 60.00 | | | | |

**KM# 1392 5 POUNDS**
28.28 g., 0.925 Silver 0.841 oz. ASW, 38.61 mm. **Ruler:** Elizabeth II **Subject:** RAF "SE5a"

| Date | Mintage | VF20 | XF40 | MS60 | MS63 | MS65 |
|---|---|---|---|---|---|---|
| 2008 | Est. 25000 | **PF65** 60.00 | | | | |

**KM# 1393 5 POUNDS**
28.28 g., 0.925 Silver 0.841 oz. ASW, 38.61 mm. **Ruler:** Elizabeth II **Subject:** Hawker Typhoon

| Date | Mintage | VF20 | XF40 | MS60 | MS63 | MS65 |
|---|---|---|---|---|---|---|
| 2008 | Est. 25000 | **PF65** 60.00 | | | | |

**KM# 1394 5 POUNDS**
28.28 g., 0.925 Silver 0.841 oz. ASW, 38.61 mm. **Ruler:** Elizabeth II **Subject:** Sepecat Jaguar

| Date | Mintage | VF20 | XF40 | MS60 | MS63 | MS65 |
|---|---|---|---|---|---|---|
| 2008 | Est. 25000 | **PF65** 60.00 | | | | |

**KM# 1396 5 POUNDS**
28.28 g., 0.925 Silver 0.841 oz. ASW, 38.61 mm. **Ruler:** Elizabeth II **Subject:** DeHavilland Mosquito

| Date | Mintage | VF20 | XF40 | MS60 | MS63 | MS65 |
|---|---|---|---|---|---|---|
| 2008 | Est. 25000 | **PF65** 40.00 | | | | |

**KM# 1403 5 POUNDS**
28.28 g., 0.925 Silver 0.841 oz. ASW, 38.61 mm. **Ruler:** Elizabeth II **Subject:** End of WWI, 90th Anniversary **Rev:** British soldiers

| Date | Mintage | VF20 | XF40 | MS60 | MS63 | MS65 |
|---|---|---|---|---|---|---|
| 2008 | Est. 25000 | **PF65** 60.00 | | | | |

**KM# 1404 5 POUNDS**
28.28 g., 0.925 Silver 0.841 oz. ASW, 38.61 mm. **Ruler:** Elizabeth II **Subject:** End of WWI, 90th Anniversary **Rev:** Sopwith Camel biplane and British tank

| Date | Mintage | VF20 | XF40 | MS60 | MS63 | MS65 |
|---|---|---|---|---|---|---|
| 2008 | Est. 25000 | **PF65** 60.00 | | | | |

**KM# 1406 5 POUNDS**
28.28 g., 0.925 Silver 0.841 oz. ASW, 38.61 mm. **Ruler:** Elizabeth II **Subject:** End of WWI, 90th Anniversary **Rev:** Menin Gate Memorial

| Date | Mintage | VF20 | XF40 | MS60 | MS63 | MS65 |
|---|---|---|---|---|---|---|
| 2008 | Est. 25000 | **PF65** 60.00 | | | | |

**KM# 1407 5 POUNDS**
28.28 g., 0.925 Silver 0.841 oz. ASW, 38.61 mm. **Ruler:** Elizabeth II **Subject:** End of WWI, 90th Anniversary **Rev:** War grave

| Date | Mintage | VF20 | XF40 | MS60 | MS63 | MS65 |
|---|---|---|---|---|---|---|
| 2008 | Est. 25000 | **PF65** 60.00 | | | | |

**KM# 1408 5 POUNDS**
28.28 g., 0.925 Silver 0.841 oz. ASW, 38.61 mm. **Ruler:** Elizabeth II **Subject:** End of WWI, 90th Anniversary **Rev:** Poppies on the battlefield of the Somme

| Date | Mintage | VF20 | XF40 | MS60 | MS63 | MS65 |
|---|---|---|---|---|---|---|
| 2008 | Est. 25000 | **PF65** 60.00 | | | | |

**KM# 1409 5 POUNDS**
28.28 g., 0.925 Silver 0.841 oz. ASW, 38.61 mm. **Ruler:** Elizabeth II **Subject:** RMS Queen Elizabeth II sales to Dubai

| Date | Mintage | VF20 | XF40 | MS60 | MS63 | MS65 |
|---|---|---|---|---|---|---|
| 2008 | Est. 14500 | **PF65** 60.00 | | | | |

**KM# 1413 5 POUNDS**
28.28 g., 0.925 Silver 0.841 oz. ASW, 38.61 mm. **Ruler:** Elizabeth II **Subject:** British History **Rev:** Battle of Hastings

| Date | Mintage | VF20 | XF40 | MS60 | MS63 | MS65 |
|---|---|---|---|---|---|---|
| 2008 | Est. 25000 | **PF65** 60.00 | | | | |

**KM# 1414 5 POUNDS**
28.28 g., 0.925 Silver 0.841 oz. ASW, 38.61 mm. **Ruler:** Elizabeth II **Subject:** British History **Rev:** Signing of the Magna Carta

| Date | Mintage | VF20 | XF40 | MS60 | MS63 | MS65 |
|---|---|---|---|---|---|---|
| 2008 | Est. 25000 | **PF65** 60.00 | | | | |

**KM# 1415 5 POUNDS**
28.28 g., 0.925 Silver 0.841 oz. ASW, 38.61 mm. **Ruler:** Elizabeth II **Subject:** British History **Rev:** Bauer Rose

| Date | Mintage | VF20 | XF40 | MS60 | MS63 | MS65 |
|---|---|---|---|---|---|---|
| 2008 | Est. 25000 | **PF65** 60.00 | | | | |

**KM# 1416 5 POUNDS**
28.28 g., 0.925 Silver 0.841 oz. ASW, 38.61 mm. **Ruler:** Elizabeth II **Subject:** British History **Rev:** War of the Roses between the Houses of Lancaster and York

| Date | Mintage | VF20 | XF40 | MS60 | MS63 | MS65 |
|---|---|---|---|---|---|---|
| 2008 | Est. 25000 | **PF65** 60.00 | | | | |

**KM# 1417 5 POUNDS**
28.28 g., 0.925 Silver 0.841 oz. ASW, 38.61 mm. **Ruler:** Elizabeth II **Subject:** British History **Rev:** Henry VIII and the Mary Rose

| Date | Mintage | VF20 | XF40 | MS60 | MS63 | MS65 |
|---|---|---|---|---|---|---|
| 2008 | Est. 25000 | PF65 60.00 | | | | |

**KM# 1418 5 POUNDS**
28.28 g., 0.925 Silver 0.841 oz. ASW, 38.61 mm. **Ruler:** Elizabeth II **Subject:** British History **Rev:** Elizabeth I and the Spanish Armada

| Date | Mintage | VF20 | XF40 | MS60 | MS63 | MS65 |
|---|---|---|---|---|---|---|
| 2008 | Est. 25000 | PF65 60.00 | | | | |

**KM# 1419 5 POUNDS**
28.28 g., 0.925 Silver 0.841 oz. ASW, 38.61 mm. **Ruler:** Elizabeth II **Subject:** British History **Rev:** Charles I and Oliver Cromwell and the English Civil War

| Date | Mintage | VF20 | XF40 | MS60 | MS63 | MS65 |
|---|---|---|---|---|---|---|
| 2008 | Est. 25000 | PF65 60.00 | | | | |

**KM# 1420 5 POUNDS**
28.28 g., 0.925 Silver 0.841 oz. ASW, 38.61 mm. **Ruler:** Elizabeth II **Subject:** British History **Rev:** Great Fire in London, 1666

| Date | Mintage | VF20 | XF40 | MS60 | MS63 | MS65 |
|---|---|---|---|---|---|---|
| 2008 | Est. 25000 | PF65 60.00 | | | | |

**KM# 1421 5 POUNDS**
28.28 g., 0.925 Silver 0.841 oz. ASW, 38.61 mm. **Ruler:** Elizabeth II **Subject:** British History **Rev:** Horatio Nelson and the Battle of Trafalgar, 1805

| Date | Mintage | VF20 | XF40 | MS60 | MS63 | MS65 |
|---|---|---|---|---|---|---|
| 2008 | Est. 25000 | PF65 60.00 | | | | |

**KM# 1422 5 POUNDS**
28.28 g., 0.925 Silver 0.841 oz. ASW, 38.61 mm. **Ruler:** Elizabeth II **Subject:** British History **Rev:** Industrial Revolution

| Date | Mintage | VF20 | XF40 | MS60 | MS63 | MS65 |
|---|---|---|---|---|---|---|
| 2008 | Est. 25000 | PF65 60.00 | | | | |

**KM# 1423 5 POUNDS**
28.28 g., 0.925 Silver 0.841 oz. ASW, 38.61 mm. **Ruler:** Elizabeth II **Subject:** British History **Rev:** Britannia with shield and trident, Victoria as Empress of India

| Date | Mintage | VF20 | XF40 | MS60 | MS63 | MS65 |
|---|---|---|---|---|---|---|
| 2008 | Est. 25000 | PF65 60.00 | | | | |

**KM# 1424 5 POUNDS**
28.28 g., 0.925 Silver 0.841 oz. ASW, 38.61 mm. **Ruler:** Elizabeth II **Subject:** British History **Rev:** WWI advertising by Lord Kitchener

| Date | Mintage | VF20 | XF40 | MS60 | MS63 | MS65 |
|---|---|---|---|---|---|---|
| 2008 | Est. 25000 | PF65 60.00 | | | | |

**KM# 1425 5 POUNDS**
28.28 g., 0.925 Silver 0.841 oz. ASW, 38.61 mm. **Ruler:** Elizabeth II **Subject:** British History **Rev:** Thomas Becket, Archbishop of Canterbury

| Date | Mintage | VF20 | XF40 | MS60 | MS63 | MS65 |
|---|---|---|---|---|---|---|
| 2008 | Est. 25000 | PF65 80.00 | | | | |

**KM# 1426 5 POUNDS**
28.28 g., 0.925 Silver 0.841 oz. ASW, 38.61 mm. **Ruler:** Elizabeth II **Subject:** British History **Rev:** Battle of Agincourt, 1415

| Date | Mintage | VF20 | XF40 | MS60 | MS63 | MS65 |
|---|---|---|---|---|---|---|
| 2008 | Est. 25000 | PF65 60.00 | | | | |

**KM# 1427 5 POUNDS**
28.28 g., 0.925 Silver 0.841 oz. ASW, 38.61 mm. **Ruler:** Elizabeth II **Subject:** British History **Rev:** Thomas Cranmer, Reform Archbishop of Canterbury, 1533

| Date | Mintage | VF20 | XF40 | MS60 | MS63 | MS65 |
|---|---|---|---|---|---|---|
| 2009 | Est. 25000 | PF65 60.00 | | | | |

**KM# 1428 5 POUNDS**
28.28 g., 0.925 Silver 0.841 oz. ASW, 38.61 mm. **Ruler:** Elizabeth II **Subject:** British History **Rev:** Guy Fawkes, gunpowder conspiracy

| Date | Mintage | VF20 | XF40 | MS60 | MS63 | MS65 |
|---|---|---|---|---|---|---|
| 2009 | Est. 25000 | PF65 60.00 | | | | |

**KM# 1429 5 POUNDS**
28.28 g., 0.925 Silver 0.841 oz. ASW, 38.61 mm. **Ruler:** Elizabeth II **Subject:** British History **Rev:** Sir Isaac Newton

| Date | Mintage | VF20 | XF40 | MS60 | MS63 | MS65 |
|---|---|---|---|---|---|---|
| 2009 | Est. 25000 | PF65 60.00 | | | | |

**KM# 1430 5 POUNDS**
28.28 g., 0.925 Silver 0.841 oz. ASW, 38.61 mm. **Ruler:** Elizabeth II **Subject:** British History **Rev:** Charles E. Stewart, leader of the second Jacobean uprising, 1745

| Date | Mintage | VF20 | XF40 | MS60 | MS63 | MS65 |
|---|---|---|---|---|---|---|
| 2009 | Est. 25000 | PF65 60.00 | | | | |

**KM# 1431 5 POUNDS**
28.28 g., 0.925 Silver 0.841 oz. ASW, 38.61 mm. **Ruler:** Elizabeth II **Subject:** British History **Rev:** Battle of Waterloo, 1815

| Date | Mintage | VF20 | XF40 | MS60 | MS63 | MS65 |
|---|---|---|---|---|---|---|
| 2009 | Est. 25000 | PF65 60.00 | | | | |

**KM# 1432 5 POUNDS**
28.28 g., 0.925 Silver 0.841 oz. ASW, 38.61 mm. **Ruler:** Elizabeth II **Subject:** British History **Rev:** Industrial Revolution

| Date | Mintage | VF20 | XF40 | MS60 | MS63 | MS65 |
|---|---|---|---|---|---|---|
| 2009 | Est. 25000 | PF65 60.00 | | | | |

**KM# 1433 5 POUNDS**
28.28 g., 0.925 Silver 0.841 oz. ASW, 38.61 mm. **Ruler:** Elizabeth II **Subject:** British History **Rev:** Guglielmo Marconi

| Date | Mintage | VF20 | XF40 | MS60 | MS63 | MS65 |
|---|---|---|---|---|---|---|
| 2009 | Est. 25000 | PF65 60.00 | | | | |

**KM# 1434 5 POUNDS**
28.28 g., 0.925 Silver 0.841 oz. ASW, 38.61 mm. **Ruler:** Elizabeth II **Subject:** British History **Rev:** Woman suffrage movement

| Date | Mintage | VF20 | XF40 | MS60 | MS63 | MS65 |
|---|---|---|---|---|---|---|
| 2009 | Est. 25000 | PF65 60.00 | | | | |

**KM# 1435 5 POUNDS**
28.28 g., 0.925 Silver 0.841 oz. ASW, 38.61 mm. **Ruler:** Elizabeth II **Subject:** British History **Rev:** Great Depression, 1929

| Date | Mintage | VF20 | XF40 | MS60 | MS63 | MS65 |
|---|---|---|---|---|---|---|
| 2009 | Est. 25000 | PF65 60.00 | | | | |

**KM# 1436 5 POUNDS**
28.28 g., 0.925 Silver 0.841 oz. ASW, 38.61 mm. **Ruler:** Elizabeth II **Subject:** British History **Rev:** Churchill, Roosevelt and Stalin at Yalta Conference, 1945

| Date | Mintage | VF20 | XF40 | MS60 | MS63 | MS65 |
|---|---|---|---|---|---|---|
| 2009 | Est. 25000 | PF65 60.00 | | | | |

**KM# 1445 5 POUNDS**
28.28 g., 0.925 Silver 0.841 oz. ASW, 38.61 mm. **Ruler:** Elizabeth II **Subject:** World Explorers **Rev:** Sir Francis Drake and the Golden Hind

| Date | Mintage | VF20 | XF40 | MS60 | MS63 | MS65 |
|---|---|---|---|---|---|---|
| 2009 | Est. 25000 | PF65 60.00 | | | | |

**KM# 1446 5 POUNDS**
28.28 g., 0.925 Silver 0.841 oz. ASW, 38.61 mm. **Ruler:** Elizabeth II **Subject:** World Explorers **Rev:** Ferdinand Magellan and the Victoria

| Date | Mintage | VF20 | XF40 | MS60 | MS63 | MS65 |
|---|---|---|---|---|---|---|
| 2009 | Est. 25000 | PF65 60.00 | | | | |

**KM# 1447 5 POUNDS**
28.28 g., 0.925 Silver 0.841 oz. ASW, 38.61 mm. **Ruler:** Elizabeth II **Subject:** World Explorer **Rev:** Henry Hudson and the Halve Maen

| Date | Mintage | VF20 | XF40 | MS60 | MS63 | MS65 |
|---|---|---|---|---|---|---|
| 2009 | Est. 25000 | PF65 60.00 | | | | |

**KM# 1448 5 POUNDS**
28.28 g., 0.925 Silver 0.841 oz. ASW, 38.61 mm. **Ruler:** Elizabeth II **Subject:** World Explorers **Rev:** Sir Ernest Shackleton and the Endurance

| Date | Mintage | VF20 | XF40 | MS60 | MS63 | MS65 |
|---|---|---|---|---|---|---|
| 2009 | Est. 25000 | PF65 60.00 | | | | |

**KM# 1449 5 POUNDS**
28.28 g., 0.925 Silver 0.841 oz. ASW, 38.61 mm. **Ruler:** Elizabeth II **Subject:** World Explorer **Rev:** Abel Janszoon Tasman and sailing ship Heemskerck

| Date | Mintage | VF20 | XF40 | MS60 | MS63 | MS65 |
|---|---|---|---|---|---|---|
| 2009 | — | PF65 60.00 | | | | |

**KM# 1450 5 POUNDS**
28.28 g., 0.925 Silver 0.841 oz. ASW, 38.61 mm. **Ruler:** Elizabeth II **Subject:** World Explorer **Rev:** Marco Polo and Venetian galley

| Date | Mintage | VF20 | XF40 | MS60 | MS63 | MS65 |
|---|---|---|---|---|---|---|
| 2009 | Est. 25000 | PF65 60.00 | | | | |

**KM# 1465 5 POUNDS**
28.28 g., 0.925 Silver 0.841 oz. ASW, 38.61 mm. **Ruler:** Elizabeth II **Subject:** Navy Aviation **Rev:** Fairey Swordfish

| Date | Mintage | VF20 | XF40 | MS60 | MS63 | MS65 |
|---|---|---|---|---|---|---|
| 2009 | Est. 25000 | PF65 60.00 | | | | |

**KM# 1463 5 POUNDS**
28.28 g., 0.925 Silver 0.841 oz. ASW, 38.61 mm. **Ruler:** Elizabeth II **Subject:** Navy Aviation **Rev:** Submarine Scimitar

| Date | Mintage | VF20 | XF40 | MS60 | MS63 | MS65 |
|---|---|---|---|---|---|---|
| 2009 | Est. 25000 | PF65 60.00 | | | | |

**KM# 1464 5 POUNDS**
28.28 g., 0.925 Silver 0.841 oz. ASW, 38.61 mm. **Ruler:** Elizabeth II **Subject:** Navy Aviation **Rev:** Sopwith Pup

| Date | Mintage | VF20 | XF40 | MS60 | MS63 | MS65 |
|---|---|---|---|---|---|---|
| 2009 | Est. 25000 | PF65 60.00 | | | | |

**KM# 1466 5 POUNDS**
28.28 g., 0.925 Silver 0.841 oz. ASW, 38.61 mm. **Ruler:** Elizabeth II **Subject:** Navy Aviation **Rev:** Blackburn Dart

| Date | Mintage | VF20 | XF40 | MS60 | MS63 | MS65 |
|---|---|---|---|---|---|---|
| 2009 | Est. 25000 | PF65 60.00 | | | | |

**KM# 1467 5 POUNDS**
28.28 g., 0.925 Silver 0.841 oz. ASW, 38.61 mm. **Ruler:** Elizabeth II **Subject:** Navy Aviation **Rev:** BAE Sea Harrier

| Date | Mintage | VF20 | XF40 | MS60 | MS63 | MS65 |
|---|---|---|---|---|---|---|
| 2009 | Est. 25000 | PF65 60.00 | | | | |

**KM# 1468 5 POUNDS**
28.28 g., 0.925 Silver 0.841 oz. ASW, 38.61 mm. **Ruler:** Elizabeth II **Subject:** Navy Aviation **Rev:** Chance Vought Corsair

| Date | Mintage | VF20 | XF40 | MS60 | MS63 | MS65 |
|---|---|---|---|---|---|---|
| 2009 | Est. 25000 | PF65 60.00 | | | | |

**KM# 1469 5 POUNDS**
28.28 g., 0.925 Silver 0.841 oz. ASW, 38.61 mm. **Ruler:** Elizabeth II **Subject:** Navy Aviation **Rev:** Flexstowe F2A

| Date | Mintage | VF20 | XF40 | MS60 | MS63 | MS65 |
|---|---|---|---|---|---|---|
| 2009 | Est. 25000 | PF65 60.00 | | | | |

**KM# 1470 5 POUNDS**
28.28 g., 0.925 Silver 0.841 oz. ASW **Ruler:** Elizabeth II **Subject:** Navy Aviation **Rev:** Blackburn Buccaneer

| Date | Mintage | VF20 | XF40 | MS60 | MS63 | MS65 |
|---|---|---|---|---|---|---|
| 2009 | Est. 25000 | PF65 60.00 | | | | |

**KM# 1471 5 POUNDS**
28.28 g., 0.925 Silver 0.841 oz. ASW, 38.61 mm. **Ruler:** Elizabeth II **Subject:** Navy Aviation **Rev:** deHavilland DH 110 Sea Vixen

| Date | Mintage | VF20 | XF40 | MS60 | MS63 | MS65 |
|---|---|---|---|---|---|---|
| 2009 | Est. 25000 | PF65 60.00 | | | | |

**KM# 1472 5 POUNDS**
28.28 g., 0.925 Silver 0.841 oz. ASW, 38.61 mm. **Ruler:** Elizabeth II **Subject:** Navy Aviation **Rev:** Hawker Sea Fury

| Date | Mintage | VF20 | XF40 | MS60 | MS63 | MS65 |
|---|---|---|---|---|---|---|
| 2009 | Est. 25000 | PF65 60.00 | | | | |

**KM# 1473 5 POUNDS**
28.28 g., 0.925 Silver 0.841 oz. ASW, 38.61 mm. **Ruler:** Elizabeth II **Subject:** Navy Aviation **Rev:** Short 184

| Date | Mintage | VF20 | XF40 | MS60 | MS63 | MS65 |
|---|---|---|---|---|---|---|
| 2009 | Est. 25000 | PF65 60.00 | | | | |

**KM# 1474 5 POUNDS**
28.28 g., 0.925 Silver 0.841 oz. ASW, 38.61 mm. **Ruler:** Elizabeth II **Subject:** Navy Aviation **Rev:** Westland Whirlwind

| Date | Mintage | VF20 | XF40 | MS60 | MS63 | MS65 |
|---|---|---|---|---|---|---|
| 2009 | Est. 25000 | PF65 60.00 | | | | |

**KM# 1475 5 POUNDS**
11.70 g., Nickel-Brass, 32 mm. **Ruler:** Elizabeth II **Rev:** Rock of Gibraltar

| Date | Mintage | VF20 | XF40 | MS60 | MS63 | MS65 |
|---|---|---|---|---|---|---|
| 2010 | — | — | — | — | 9.00 | 15.00 |
| 2011 | — | — | — | — | 9.00 | 15.00 |

**KM# 1475A 5 POUNDS**
31.10 g., 0.999 Gold 0.9989 oz. AGW **Ruler:** Elizabeth II **Rev:** Rock of Gibraltar

| Date | Mintage | VF20 | XF40 | MS60 | MS63 | MS65 |
|---|---|---|---|---|---|---|
| 2010 | 29 | PF65 1,750 | | | | |

**KM# 1476 5 POUNDS**
8.00 g., Copper-Nickel, 27.3 mm. **Ruler:** Elizabeth II **Rev:** Partridge in a Pear tree **Rev. Legend:** CHRISTMAS **Shape:** 7-sided

| Date | Mintage | VF20 | XF40 | MS60 | MS63 | MS65 |
|---|---|---|---|---|---|---|
| 2010 | — | — | — | — | 1.50 | 2.50 |

### KM# 1478 5 POUNDS

28.28 g., 0.925 Silver 0.841 oz. ASW, 38.61 mm. **Ruler:** Elizabeth II **Subject:** Marriage of Prince William and Catherine Middleton

| Date | Mintage | VF20 | XF40 | MS60 | MS63 | MS65 |
|---|---|---|---|---|---|---|
| 2011 | Est. 50000 | PF65 60.00 | | | | |

### KM# 1481 5 POUNDS

28.28 g., 0.925 Silver 0.841 oz. ASW, 38.61 mm. **Ruler:** Elizabeth II **Subject:** Elizabeth II, 60th Anniversary of reign **Rev:** Elizabeth II young and old portraits

| Date | Mintage | VF20 | XF40 | MS60 | MS63 | MS65 |
|---|---|---|---|---|---|---|
| 2012 | — | PF65 60.00 | | | | |

### KM# 1188.1 10 POUNDS

155.50 g., 0.925 Silver 4.6245 oz. ASW, 65 mm. **Ruler:** Elizabeth II **Rev:** Landing scene surrounded by allied flags in color

| Date | Mintage | VF20 | XF40 | MS60 | MS63 | MS65 |
|---|---|---|---|---|---|---|
| 2004 | Est. 950 | PF65 300 | | | | |

### KM# 1188.1a 10 POUNDS

155.50 g., 0.9167 Gold 4.583 oz. AGW, 65 mm. **Ruler:** Elizabeth II **Rev:** Landing scene, allied flags around

| Date | Mintage | VF20 | XF40 | MS60 | MS63 | MS65 |
|---|---|---|---|---|---|---|
| 2004 | Est. 50 | PF65 9,500 | | | | |

### KM# 1188.2 10 POUNDS

155.50 g., 0.925 Silver 4.6245 oz. ASW, 65 mm. **Ruler:** Elizabeth II **Rev:** Landing scene with Allied flags around, all gilt

| Date | Mintage | VF20 | XF40 | MS60 | MS63 | MS65 |
|---|---|---|---|---|---|---|
| 2004 | Est. 500 | PF65 300 | | | | |

### KM# 1275 10 POUNDS

155.50 g., 0.925 Silver 4.6245 oz. ASW, 65 mm. **Ruler:** Elizabeth II **Subject:** Elizabeth II, 79th Birthday **Rev:** Flag in color

| Date | Mintage | VF20 | XF40 | MS60 | MS63 | MS65 |
|---|---|---|---|---|---|---|
| 2005 | Est. 950 | PF65 275 | | | | |

### KM# 1288 10 POUNDS

155.50 g., 0.925 Silver 4.6245 oz. ASW, 65 mm. **Ruler:** Elizabeth II **Subject:** Elizabeth II, 80th Birthday **Rev:** Four portraits **Note:** With crystal inserts

| Date | Mintage | VF20 | XF40 | MS60 | MS63 | MS65 |
|---|---|---|---|---|---|---|
| 2006 | Est. 1926 | PF65 300 | | | | |

### KM# 1288a 10 POUNDS

155.50 g., 0.9167 Gold 4.583 oz. AGW, 65 mm. **Ruler:** Elizabeth II **Subject:** Elizabeth II, 80th Birthday **Rev:** Four portraits **Note:** With crystal inserts

| Date | Mintage | VF20 | XF40 | MS60 | MS63 | MS65 |
|---|---|---|---|---|---|---|
| 2006 | Est. 80 | PF65 8,500 | | | | |

### KM# 1317 10 POUNDS

155.50 g., 0.925 Silver 4.6245 oz. ASW, 65 mm. **Ruler:** Elizabeth II **Subject:** 1966 World Cup, England as Champions, 40th Anniversary **Rev:** Bobby Moore and trophy

| Date | Mintage | VF20 | XF40 | MS60 | MS63 | MS65 |
|---|---|---|---|---|---|---|
| 2006 | Est. 1966 | PF65 275 | | | | |

### KM# 1343 10 POUNDS

155.50 g., 0.750 Gold 3.7496 oz. AGW, 65 mm. **Ruler:** Elizabeth II **Subject:** Elizabeth and Philip, 60th Wedding Anniversary **Rev:** Wedding portrait, 1947

| Date | Mintage | VF20 | XF40 | MS60 | MS63 | MS65 |
|---|---|---|---|---|---|---|
| 2007 | Est. 60 | PF65 7,000 | | | | |

### KM# 1360 10 POUNDS

155.50 g., 0.925 Silver 4.6245 oz. ASW, 65 mm. **Ruler:** Elizabeth II **Subject:** Battle of Britain Memorial Flight **Rev:** Air show

| Date | Mintage | VF20 | XF40 | MS60 | MS63 | MS65 |
|---|---|---|---|---|---|---|
| 2007 | Est. 1957 | PF65 300 | | | | |

### KM# 1360a 10 POUNDS

155.50 g., 0.925 Gold 4.6245 oz. AGW, 65 mm. **Ruler:** Elizabeth II **Subject:** Battle of Britain Memorial Flight **Rev:** Air show

| Date | Mintage | VF20 | XF40 | MS60 | MS63 | MS65 |
|---|---|---|---|---|---|---|
| 2007 | Est. 50 | PF65 7,000 | | | | |

### KM# 1410 10 POUNDS

155.50 g., 0.925 Silver 4.6245 oz. ASW, 65 mm. **Ruler:** Elizabeth II **Subject:** RMS Queen Elizabeth II sails to Dubai

| Date | Mintage | VF20 | XF40 | MS60 | MS63 | MS65 |
|---|---|---|---|---|---|---|
| 2008 | Est. 450 | PF65 275 | | | | |

### KM# 1437 10 POUNDS

155.50 g., 0.925 Silver 4.6245 oz. ASW, 65 mm. **Ruler:** Elizabeth II **Subject:** British History **Rev:** Nelson and Battle of Trafalgar

| Date | Mintage | VF20 | XF40 | MS60 | MS63 | MS65 |
|---|---|---|---|---|---|---|
| 2008 | Est. 995 | PF65 250 | | | | |

### KM# 1437a 10 POUNDS

155.50 g., 0.750 Gold 3.7496 oz. AGW, 65 mm. **Ruler:** Elizabeth II **Subject:** British History **Rev:** Nelson and Battle of Trafalgar

| Date | Mintage | VF20 | XF40 | MS60 | MS63 | MS65 |
|---|---|---|---|---|---|---|
| 2008 | Est. 50 | PF65 6,000 | | | | |

### KM# 1438 10 POUNDS

155.50 g., 0.925 Silver 4.6245 oz. ASW, 65 mm. **Ruler:** Elizabeth II **Subject:** British History **Rev:** Henry VIII and the Mary Rose

| Date | Mintage | VF20 | XF40 | MS60 | MS63 | MS65 |
|---|---|---|---|---|---|---|
| 2009 | Est. 995 | PF65 250 | | | | |

### KM# 1438a 10 POUNDS

155.50 g., 0.750 Gold 3.7496 oz. AGW, 65 mm. **Ruler:** Elizabeth II **Subject:** British History **Rev:** Henry VIII and the Mary Rose

| Date | Mintage | VF20 | XF40 | MS60 | MS63 | MS65 |
|---|---|---|---|---|---|---|
| 2009 | Est. 50 | PF65 6,000 | | | | |

## SOVEREIGN COINAGE

### KM# 1037 1/5 SOVEREIGN

1.22 g., 0.9999 Gold 0.0392 oz. AGW, 13.92 mm. **Ruler:** Elizabeth II **Subject:** Death of St. George **Obv:** Bust with tiara right **Rev:** St. George and the dragon **Edge:** Reeded

| Date | Mintage | VF20 | XF40 | MS60 | MS63 | MS65 |
|---|---|---|---|---|---|---|
| 2003 | 10,000 | PF63 75.00 | PF65 85.00 | | | |

### KM# 1118 SOVEREIGN

6.22 g., 0.375 Gold 0.075 oz. AGW, 22 mm. **Ruler:** Elizabeth II **Rev:** Treetops Hotel in Aberdare National Park in Kenya

| Date | Mintage | VF20 | XF40 | MS60 | MS63 | MS65 |
|---|---|---|---|---|---|---|
| 2002 | Est. 5000 | PF65 170 | | | | |

### KM# 1119 SOVEREIGN

6.22 g., 0.375 Gold 0.075 oz. AGW, 22 mm. **Ruler:** Elizabeth II **Rev:** Westminster Abby

| Date | Mintage | VF20 | XF40 | MS60 | MS63 | MS65 |
|---|---|---|---|---|---|---|
| 2002 | Est. 5000 | PF65 170 | | | | |

### KM# 1120 SOVEREIGN

6.22 g., 0.375 Gold 0.075 oz. AGW, 22 mm. **Ruler:** Elizabeth II **Rev:** Birth of Prince Charles, 1948

| Date | Mintage | VF20 | XF40 | MS60 | MS63 | MS65 |
|---|---|---|---|---|---|---|
| 2002 | Est. 5000 | PF65 170 | | | | |

### KM# 1121 SOVEREIGN

6.22 g., 0.375 Gold 0.075 oz. AGW, 22 mm. **Ruler:** Elizabeth II **Rev:** Royal Yacht Britannia under Tower Bridge

| Date | Mintage | VF20 | XF40 | MS60 | MS63 | MS65 |
|---|---|---|---|---|---|---|
| 2002 | Est. 5000 | PF65 170 | | | | |

### KM# 1038 SOVEREIGN

6.22 g., 0.9999 Gold 0.200 oz. AGW, 22 mm. **Ruler:** Elizabeth II **Subject:** Death of St. George **Obv:** Bust with tiara right **Rev:** St. George and the dragon **Edge:** Reeded

| Date | Mintage | VF20 | XF40 | MS60 | MS63 | MS65 |
|---|---|---|---|---|---|---|
| 2003 | 5,000 | PF63 350 | PF65 375 | | | |

## CROWN SERIES

1980 -

### KM# 988 1/25 CROWN

1.22 g., 0.999 Gold 0.0393 oz. AGW, 13.92 mm. **Ruler:** Elizabeth II **Subject:** Peter Rabbit Centennial **Obv:** Crowned bust right **Rev:** Peter Rabbit **Edge:** Reeded

| Date | Mintage | VF20 | XF40 | MS60 | MS63 | MS65 |
|---|---|---|---|---|---|---|
| 2002 | 5,000 | PF65 61.00 | | | | |

### KM# 988a 1/25 CROWN

1.22 g., 0.999 Platinum 0.0393 oz. APW, 13.92 mm. **Ruler:** Elizabeth II **Subject:** Peter Rabbit Centennial **Obv:** Crowned bust right **Rev:** Peter Rabbit **Edge:** Reeded

| Date | Mintage | VF20 | XF40 | MS60 | MS63 | MS65 |
|---|---|---|---|---|---|---|
| 2002 | 3,000 | PF65 61.00 | | | | |

### KM# 1016 1/25 CROWN

1.24 g., 0.9999 Gold 0.040 oz. AGW, 13.92 mm. **Ruler:** Elizabeth II **Subject:** Peter Pan **Obv:** Crowned bust right **Rev:** Peter Pan and Tinkerbell flying above city **Edge:** Reeded

| Date | Mintage | VF20 | XF40 | MS60 | MS63 | MS65 |
|---|---|---|---|---|---|---|
| 2002 | 10,000 | PF65 62.00 | | | | |

### KM# 1132 1/25 CROWN

1.24 g., 0.999 Gold 0.0398 oz. AGW, 13.92 mm. **Ruler:** Elizabeth II **Rev:** Peter rabbit holding carrot

| Date | Mintage | VF20 | XF40 | MS60 | MS63 | MS65 |
|---|---|---|---|---|---|---|
| 2003 | Est. 5000 | PF65 62.00 | | | | |

### KM# 1132a 1/25 CROWN

1.24 g., 0.999 Platinum 0.0398 oz. APW, 13.92 mm. **Ruler:** Elizabeth II **Rev:** Peter rabbit holding carrot

| Date | Mintage | VF20 | XF40 | MS60 | MS63 | MS65 |
|---|---|---|---|---|---|---|
| 2003 | Est. 3000 | PF65 62.00 | | | | |

### KM# 989 1/10 CROWN

3.11 g., 0.999 Gold 0.0999 oz. AGW, 17.95 mm. **Ruler:** Elizabeth II **Subject:** Peter Rabbit Centennial **Obv:** Crowned bust right **Rev:** Peter Rabbit **Edge:** Reeded

| Date | Mintage | VF20 | XF40 | MS60 | MS63 | MS65 |
|---|---|---|---|---|---|---|
| 2002 | 5,000 | PF65 156 | | | | |

### KM# 989a 1/10 CROWN

3.11 g., 0.999 Platinum 0.0999 oz. APW, 17.95 mm. **Ruler:** Elizabeth II **Subject:** Peter Rabbit Centennial **Obv:** Crowned bust right **Rev:** Peter Rabbit **Edge:** Reeded

| Date | Mintage | VF20 | XF40 | MS60 | MS63 | MS65 |
|---|---|---|---|---|---|---|
| 2002 | 2,000 | PF65 156 | | | | |

### KM# 1017 1/10 CROWN

3.11 g., 0.9999 Gold 0.100 oz. AGW, 17.95 mm. **Ruler:** Elizabeth II **Subject:** Peter Pan **Obv:** Crowned bust right **Rev:** Peter Pan and Tinkerbell flying above city **Edge:** Reeded

| Date | Mintage | VF20 | XF40 | MS60 | MS63 | MS65 |
|---|---|---|---|---|---|---|
| 2002 | — | PF65 156 | | | | |

### KM# 1133 1/10 CROWN

3.11 g., 0.999 Gold 0.0999 oz. AGW, 17.95 mm. **Ruler:** Elizabeth II **Rev:** Peter rabbit with carrot

| Date | Mintage | VF20 | XF40 | MS60 | MS63 | MS65 |
|---|---|---|---|---|---|---|
| 2003 | Est. 5000 | PF65 156 | | | | |

### KM# 1133a 1/10 CROWN

3.11 g., 0.999 Platinum 0.0999 oz. APW, 17.95 mm. **Ruler:** Elizabeth II **Rev:** Peter rabbit with carrot

| Date | Mintage | VF20 | XF40 | MS60 | MS63 | MS65 |
|---|---|---|---|---|---|---|
| 2003 | Est. 2000 | PF65 156 | | | | |

### KM# 909 1/5 CROWN

6.22 g., 0.9999 Gold 0.200 oz. AGW, 22 mm. **Ruler:** Elizabeth II **Series:** Victorian Era - Victoria's Coronation 1838 **Obv:** Bust with tiara right **Rev:** 1838 Coronation scene **Edge:** Reeded

| Date | Mintage | VF20 | XF40 | MS60 | MS63 | MS65 |
|---|---|---|---|---|---|---|
| 2001 | 5,000 | PF65 289 | | | | |

### KM# 909.1 1/5 CROWN

6.22 g., 0.9999 Gold 0.200 oz. AGW, 22 mm. **Ruler:** Elizabeth II **Series:** Victorian Era **Obv:** Bust with tiara right **Rev:** 1838 Coronation scene with a tiny emerald set in the field below the 1838 date **Edge:** Reeded

| Date | Mintage | VF20 | XF40 | MS60 | MS63 | MS65 |
|---|---|---|---|---|---|---|
| 2001 | 2,001 | PF65 289 | | | | |

### KM# 902 1/5 CROWN

6.22 g., 0.9999 Gold 0.200 oz. AGW, 22 mm. **Ruler:** Elizabeth II **Subject:** Queen Mother **Obv:** Bust with tiara right **Rev:** 1953 Coronation scene **Edge:** Reeded

| Date | Mintage | VF20 | XF40 | MS60 | MS63 | MS65 |
|---|---|---|---|---|---|---|
| 2001 | 5,000 | PF65 289 | | | | |

### KM# 903 1/5 CROWN

6.22 g., 0.9999 Gold 0.200 oz. AGW, 22 mm. **Ruler:** Elizabeth II **Obv:** Bust with tiara right **Rev:** Queen Mother and Prince Charles in 1954

| Date | Mintage | VF20 | XF40 | MS60 | MS63 | MS65 |
|---|---|---|---|---|---|---|
| 2001 | 5,000 | PF65 289 | | | | |

### KM# 911.1 1/5 CROWN

6.22 g., 0.9999 Gold 0.200 oz. AGW, 22 mm. **Ruler:** Elizabeth II **Series:** Victorian Era - Empress of India 1876 **Obv:** Bust with tiara right **Rev:** Crowned portrait of Victoria and two elephants **Edge:** Reeded

| Date | Mintage | VF20 | XF40 | MS60 | MS63 | MS65 |
|---|---|---|---|---|---|---|
| 2001 | 5,000 | PF65 289 | | | | |

### KM# 911.2 1/5 CROWN

6.22 g., 0.9999 Gold 0.200 oz. AGW, 22 mm. **Ruler:** Elizabeth II **Series:** Victorian Era - Empress of India 1876 **Obv:** Bust with tiara right **Rev:** Tiny ruby set in the field behind Victoria's head **Edge:** Reeded

| Date | Mintage | VF20 | XF40 | MS60 | MS63 | MS65 |
|---|---|---|---|---|---|---|
| 2001 | 2,001 | PF65 289 | | | | |

### KM# 913.1 1/5 CROWN

6.22 g., 0.9999 Gold 0.200 oz. AGW, 22 mm. **Ruler:** Elizabeth II **Series:** Victorian Era - Diamond Jubilee 1897 **Obv:** Bust with tiara right **Rev:** Victoria's cameo portrait above naval ships **Edge:** Reeded

| Date | Mintage | VF20 | XF40 | MS60 | MS63 | MS65 |
|---|---|---|---|---|---|---|
| 2001 | 5,000 | PF65 289 | | | | |

### KM# 913.2 1/5 CROWN

6.22 g., 0.9999 Gold 0.200 oz. AGW, 22 mm. **Ruler:** Elizabeth II **Series:** Victorian Era - Diamond Jubilee 1897 **Obv:** Bust with tiara right **Rev:** Tiny diamond set at the top of the fourth mast **Edge:** Reeded

| Date | Mintage | VF20 | XF40 | MS60 | MS63 | MS65 |
|---|---|---|---|---|---|---|
| 2001 | 2,001 | PF65 289 | | | | |

### KM# 915.1 1/5 CROWN

6.22 g., 0.9999 Gold 0.200 oz. AGW, 22 mm. **Ruler:** Elizabeth II **Series:** Victorian Era - Victoria's Death 1901 **Obv:** Bust with tiara right **Rev:** Victoria's cameo portrait and Osborne Manor **Edge:** Reeded

| Date | Mintage | VF20 | XF40 | MS60 | MS63 | MS65 |
|---|---|---|---|---|---|---|
| 2001 | 5,000 | PF65 289 | | | | |

### KM# 915.2 1/5 CROWN

6.22 g., 0.9999 Gold 0.200 oz. AGW, 22 mm. **Ruler:** Elizabeth II **Series:** Victorian Era - Victoria's Death 1901 **Obv:** Bust with tiara right **Rev:** Tiny sapphire set in the field between the towers **Edge:** Reeded

| Date | Mintage | VF20 | XF40 | MS60 | MS63 | MS65 |
|---|---|---|---|---|---|---|
| 2001 | 2,001 | PF65 289 | | | | |

### KM# 917 1/5 CROWN

6.22 g., 0.9999 Gold 0.200 oz. AGW, 22 mm. **Ruler:** Elizabeth II **Series:** Victorian Era - Prince Albert and the Great Exhibition 1851 **Obv:** Bust with tiara right **Rev:** Albert's cameo portrait and the exhibit hall **Edge:** Reeded

| Date | Mintage | VF20 | XF40 | MS60 | MS63 | MS65 |
|---|---|---|---|---|---|---|
| 2001 | 5,000 | PF65 289 | | | | |

### KM# 919 1/5 CROWN

6.22 g., 0.9999 Gold 0.200 oz. AGW, 22 mm. **Ruler:** Elizabeth II **Series:** Victorian Era - Isambard K. Brunel **Obv:** Bust with tiara right **Rev:** Portrait in top hat and railroad bridge **Edge:** Reeded

| Date | Mintage | VF20 | XF40 | MS60 | MS63 | MS65 |
|---|---|---|---|---|---|---|
| 2001 | 5,000 | PF65 289 | | | | |

### KM# 921 1/5 CROWN

6.22 g., 0.9999 Gold 0.200 oz. AGW, 22 mm. **Ruler:** Elizabeth II **Series:** Victorian Era - Charles Dickens **Obv:** Bust with tiara right **Rev:** Portrait and scene from "Oliver Twist **Edge:** Reeded

| Date | Mintage | VF20 | XF40 | MS60 | MS63 | MS65 |
|---|---|---|---|---|---|---|
| 2001 | 5,000 | PF65 289 | | | | |

### KM# 923 1/5 CROWN

6.22 g., 0.9999 Gold 0.200 oz. AGW, 22 mm. **Ruler:** Elizabeth II **Series:** Victorian Era - Charles Darwin **Obv:** Bust with tiara right **Rev:** Portrait, ship and a squatting aboriginal figure **Edge:** Reeded

| Date | Mintage | VF20 | XF40 | MS60 | MS63 | MS65 |
|---|---|---|---|---|---|---|
| 2001 | 5,000 | PF65 289 | | | | |

### KM# 925 1/5 CROWN

6.22 g., 0.9999 Gold 0.200 oz. AGW, 22 mm. **Ruler:** Elizabeth II **Series:** Mythology of the Solar System **Obv:** Queens portrait **Rev:** Standing goddess with snake basket **Edge:** Reeded

| Date | Mintage | VF20 | XF40 | MS60 | MS63 | MS65 |
|---|---|---|---|---|---|---|
| 2001 | 5,000 | PF65 289 | | | | |

### KM# 926 1/5 CROWN

Bi-Metallic 0.925 Silver center in 0.999 Gold ring, 32.25 mm. **Ruler:** Elizabeth II **Series:** Mythology of the Solar System **Obv:** Bust with tiara right **Rev:** Standing goddess with snake basket **Edge:** Reeded

| Date | Mintage | VF20 | XF40 | MS60 | MS63 | MS65 |
|---|---|---|---|---|---|---|
| 2001 In Proof sets only | 999 | PF65 500 | | | | |

### KM# 929.1 1/5 CROWN

6.22 g., 0.9999 Gold 0.200 oz. AGW, 22 mm. **Ruler:** Elizabeth II **Series:** Mythology of the Solar System - Sun **Obv:** Bust with tiara right **Rev:** Helios in chariot and the sun **Edge:** Reeded

| Date | Mintage | VF20 | XF40 | MS60 | MS63 | MS65 |
|---|---|---|---|---|---|---|
| 2001 | 5,000 | PF65 289 | | | | |

### KM# 929.2 1/5 CROWN

6.22 g., 0.9999 Gold 0.200 oz. AGW, 22 mm. **Ruler:** Elizabeth II **Series:** Mythology of the Solar System **Obv:** Bust with tiara right **Rev:** Fiery hologram in the sun **Edge:** Reeded

| Date | Mintage | VF20 | XF40 | MS60 | MS63 | MS65 |
|---|---|---|---|---|---|---|
| 2001 In Proof sets only | 999 | PF65 289 | | | | |

### KM# 931.1 1/5 CROWN

6.22 g., 0.9999 Gold 0.200 oz. AGW, 22 mm. **Ruler:** Elizabeth II **Series:** Mythology of the Solar System - Moon **Obv:** Bust with tiara right **Rev:** Goddess Diana and the moon **Edge:** Reeded

| Date | Mintage | VF20 | XF40 | MS60 | MS63 | MS65 |
|---|---|---|---|---|---|---|
| 2001 | 5,000 | PF65 289 | | | | |

### KM# 931.2 1/5 CROWN

6.22 g., 0.9999 Gold 0.200 oz. AGW, 22 mm. **Ruler:** Elizabeth II **Series:** Mythology of the Solar System - Moon **Obv:** Bust with tiara right **Rev:** Small pearl set in the moon **Edge:** Reeded

| Date | Mintage | VF20 | XF40 | MS60 | MS63 | MS65 |
|---|---|---|---|---|---|---|
| 2001 In Proof sets only | 999 | PF65 450 | | | | |

### KM# 933.1 1/5 CROWN

6.22 g., 0.9999 Gold 0.200 oz. AGW, 22 mm. **Ruler:** Elizabeth II **Series:** Mythology of the Solar System - Atlas **Obv:** Bust with tiara right **Rev:** Atlas carrying the earth **Edge:** Reeded

| Date | Mintage | VF20 | XF40 | MS60 | MS63 | MS65 |
|---|---|---|---|---|---|---|
| 2001 | 5,000 | PF65 289 | | | | |

### KM# 933.2 1/5 CROWN

6.22 g., 0.9999 Gold 0.200 oz. AGW, 22 mm. **Ruler:** Elizabeth II **Series:** Mythology of the Solar System - Atlas **Obv:** Bust with tiara right **Rev:** Tiny diamond set in the earth **Edge:** Reeded

| Date | Mintage | VF20 | XF40 | MS60 | MS63 | MS65 |
|---|---|---|---|---|---|---|
| 2001 In Proof sets only | 999 | PF65 354 | | | | |

### KM# 935 1/5 CROWN

6.22 g., 0.9999 Gold 0.200 oz. AGW, 22 mm. **Ruler:** Elizabeth II **Series:** Mythology of the Solar System - Neptune **Obv:** Bust with tiara right **Rev:** Seated god with trident and ringed planet **Edge:** Reeded

| Date | Mintage | VF20 | XF40 | MS60 | MS63 | MS65 |
|---|---|---|---|---|---|---|
| 2001 | 5,000 | PF65 289 | | | | |

### KM# 937 1/5 CROWN

6.22 g., 0.9999 Gold 0.200 oz. AGW, 22 mm. **Ruler:** Elizabeth II **Series:** Mythology of the Solar System - Jupiter **Obv:** Bust with tiara right **Rev:** Seated god with lightning bolts and a planet **Edge:** Reeded

| Date | Mintage | VF20 | XF40 | MS60 | MS63 | MS65 |
|---|---|---|---|---|---|---|
| 2001 | 5,000 | PF65 289 | | | | |

### KM# 939 1/5 CROWN

6.22 g., 0.9999 Gold 0.200 oz. AGW, 22 mm. **Ruler:** Elizabeth II **Series:** Mythology of the Solar System - Mars **Obv:** Bust with tiara right **Rev:** Standing Roman solider and a planet **Edge:** Reeded

| Date | Mintage | VF20 | XF40 | MS60 | MS63 | MS65 |
|---|---|---|---|---|---|---|
| 2001 | 5,000 | PF65 289 | | | | |

### KM# 941 1/5 CROWN

6.22 g., 0.9999 Gold 0.200 oz. AGW, 22 mm. **Ruler:** Elizabeth II **Series:** Mythology of the Solar System - Mercury **Obv:** Bust with tiara right **Rev:** Seated god with caduceus and a planet **Edge:** Reeded

| Date | Mintage | VF20 | XF40 | MS60 | MS63 | MS65 |
|---|---|---|---|---|---|---|
| 2001 | 5,000 | PF65 289 | | | | |

### KM# 943 1/5 CROWN

6.22 g., 0.9999 Gold 0.200 oz. AGW, 22 mm. **Ruler:** Elizabeth II **Series:** Mythology of the Solar System - Uranus **Obv:** Bust with tiara right **Rev:** Seated god with scepter **Edge:** Reeded

| Date | Mintage | VF20 | XF40 | MS60 | MS63 | MS65 |
|---|---|---|---|---|---|---|
| 2001 | 5,000 | PF65 289 | | | | |

### KM# 945 1/5 CROWN

6.22 g., 0.9999 Gold 0.200 oz. AGW, 22 mm. **Ruler:** Elizabeth II **Series:** Mythology of the Solar System - Saturn **Obv:** Bust with tiara right **Rev:** Seated god with long handled sickle and a ringed planet **Edge:** Reeded

| Date | Mintage | VF20 | XF40 | MS60 | MS63 | MS65 |
|---|---|---|---|---|---|---|
| 2001 | 5,000 | PF65 289 | | | | |

### KM# 947 1/5 CROWN

6.22 g., 0.9999 Gold 0.200 oz. AGW, 22 mm. **Ruler:** Elizabeth II **Series:** Mythology of the Solar System - Pluto **Obv:** Bust with tiara right **Rev:** Seated god with dogs and a planet **Edge:** Reeded

| Date | Mintage | VF20 | XF40 | MS60 | MS63 | MS65 |
|---|---|---|---|---|---|---|
| 2001 | 5,000 | PF65 289 | | | | |

### KM# 949 1/5 CROWN

6.22 g., 0.9999 Gold 0.200 oz. AGW, 22 mm. **Ruler:** Elizabeth II **Series:** Mythology of the Solar System - Venus **Obv:** Bust with tiara right **Rev:** Goddess seated on a half shell **Edge:** Reeded

| Date | Mintage | VF20 | XF40 | MS60 | MS63 | MS65 |
|---|---|---|---|---|---|---|
| 2001 | 5,000 | PF65 289 | | | | |

### KM# 951 1/5 CROWN

6.22 g., 0.9999 Gold 0.200 oz. AGW, 22 mm. **Ruler:** Elizabeth II **Subject:** Queen's 76th Birthday **Obv:** Bust with tiara right **Rev:** Queen in Order of the Garter robes with a tiny inset diamond **Edge:** Reeded

| Date | Mintage | VF20 | XF40 | MS60 | MS63 | MS65 |
|---|---|---|---|---|---|---|
| 2001 | 2,001 | PF65 289 | | | | |

### KM# 954 1/5 CROWN

6.22 g., 0.9999 Gold 0.200 oz. AGW, 22 mm. **Ruler:** Elizabeth II **Series:** Victorian Age Part II - Victoria's Accession to the Throne **Obv:** Bust with tiara right **Rev:** Victoria learning of her accession **Edge:** Reeded

| Date | Mintage | VF20 | XF40 | MS60 | MS63 | MS65 |
|---|---|---|---|---|---|---|
| 2001 | 5,000 | PF65 289 | | | | |

### KM# 956 1/5 CROWN

6.22 g., 0.9999 Gold 0.200 oz. AGW, 22 mm. **Ruler:** Elizabeth II **Series:** Victorian Age Part II - Royal Family **Rev:** Victoria and Albert seated with children **Edge:** Reeded

| Date | Mintage | VF20 | XF40 | MS60 | MS63 | MS65 |
|---|---|---|---|---|---|---|
| 2001 | 5,000 | PF65 289 | | | | |

### KM# 958 1/5 CROWN

6.22 g., 0.9999 Gold 0.200 oz. AGW, 22 mm. **Ruler:** Elizabeth II **Series:** Victorian Age Part II - Victoria in Scotland **Obv:** Bust with tiara right **Rev:** Victoria on horse and servant **Edge:** Reeded

| Date | Mintage | VF20 | XF40 | MS60 | MS63 | MS65 |
|---|---|---|---|---|---|---|
| 2001 | 5,000 | PF65 289 | | | | |

### KM# 960 1/5 CROWN

6.22 g., 0.9999 Gold 0.200 oz. AGW, 22 mm. **Ruler:** Elizabeth II **Series:** Victorian Age Part II **Obv:** Bust with tiara right **Rev:** Portraits of Gladstone and Disaraeli **Edge:** Reeded

| Date | Mintage | VF20 | XF40 | MS60 | MS63 | MS65 |
|---|---|---|---|---|---|---|
| 2001 | 5,000 | PF65 289 | | | | |

### KM# 962 1/5 CROWN

6.22 g., 0.9999 Gold 0.200 oz. AGW, 22 mm. **Ruler:** Elizabeth II **Series:** Victorian Age Part II **Obv:** Bust with tiara right **Rev:** Florence Nightingale holding lantern **Edge:** Reeded

| Date | Mintage | VF20 | XF40 | MS60 | MS63 | MS65 |
|---|---|---|---|---|---|---|
| 2001 | 5,000 | PF65 289 | | | | |

### KM# 964 1/5 CROWN

6.22 g., 0.9999 Gold 0.200 oz. AGW, 22 mm. **Ruler:** Elizabeth II **Series:** Victorian Age Part II **Obv:** Bust with tiara right **Rev:** Lord Tennyson with the Light Brigade in background **Edge:** Reeded

| Date | Mintage | VF20 | XF40 | MS60 | MS63 | MS65 |
|---|---|---|---|---|---|---|
| 2001 | 5,000 | PF65 289 | | | | |

### KM# 966 1/5 CROWN

6.22 g., 0.9999 Gold 0.200 oz. AGW, 22 mm. **Ruler:** Elizabeth II **Series:** Victorian Age Part II **Obv:** Bust with tiara right **Rev:** Stanley meeting Dr. Livingstone **Edge:** Reeded

| Date | Mintage | VF20 | XF40 | MS60 | MS63 | MS65 |
|---|---|---|---|---|---|---|
| 2001 | 5,000 | PF65 289 | | | | |

### KM# 968 1/5 CROWN

6.22 g., 0.9999 Gold 0.200 oz. AGW, 22 mm. **Ruler:** Elizabeth II **Series:** Victorian Age Part II **Obv:** Bust with tiara right **Rev:** Bronte sisters **Edge:** Reeded

| Date | Mintage | VF20 | XF40 | MS60 | MS63 | MS65 |
|---|---|---|---|---|---|---|
| 2001 | 5,000 | PF65 289 | | | | |

### KM# 978 1/5 CROWN

6.22 g., 0.999 Gold 0.1998 oz. AGW, 22 mm. **Ruler:** Elizabeth II **Subject:** Queen Mother's Life **Obv:** Bust right **Rev:** Prince William's christening scene **Edge:** Reeded

| Date | Mintage | VF20 | XF40 | MS60 | MS63 | MS65 |
|---|---|---|---|---|---|---|
| 2002 | 5,000 | PF65 288 | | | | |

### KM# 980 1/5 CROWN

6.22 g., 0.9999 Gold 0.200 oz. AGW, 22 mm. **Ruler:** Elizabeth II **Subject:** World Cup Soccer **Obv:** Bust right **Rev:** Two players about to collide **Edge:** Reeded

| Date | Mintage | VF20 | XF40 | MS60 | MS63 | MS65 |
|---|---|---|---|---|---|---|
| 2002 | — | PF65 289 | | | | |

### KM# 982 1/5 CROWN

6.22 g., 0.9999 Gold 0.200 oz. AGW, 22 mm. **Ruler:** Elizabeth II **Subject:** World Cup Soccer **Obv:** Bust right **Rev:** Two players facing viewer **Edge:** Reeded

| Date | Mintage | VF20 | XF40 | MS60 | MS63 | MS65 |
|---|---|---|---|---|---|---|
| 2002 | — | PF65 289 | | | | |

### KM# 984 1/5 CROWN

6.22 g., 0.9999 Gold 0.200 oz. AGW, 22 mm. **Ruler:** Elizabeth II **Subject:** World Cup Soccer **Obv:** Bust right **Rev:** Two horizontal players **Edge:** Reeded

| Date | Mintage | VF20 | XF40 | MS60 | MS63 | MS65 |
|---|---|---|---|---|---|---|
| 2002 | — | PF65 289 | | | | |

### KM# 986 1/5 CROWN

6.22 g., 0.9999 Gold 0.200 oz. AGW, 22 mm. **Ruler:** Elizabeth II **Subject:** World Cup Soccer **Obv:** Bust right **Rev:** Two players moving to the left **Edge:** Reeded

| Date | Mintage | VF20 | XF40 | MS60 | MS63 | MS65 |
|---|---|---|---|---|---|---|
| 2002 | — | PF65 289 | | | | |

### KM# 990 1/5 CROWN

6.22 g., 0.999 Gold 0.1998 oz. AGW, 22 mm. **Ruler:** Elizabeth II **Subject:** Peter Rabbit Centennial **Obv:** Bust right **Rev:** Peter Rabbit **Edge:** Reeded

| Date | Mintage | VF20 | XF40 | MS60 | MS63 | MS65 |
|---|---|---|---|---|---|---|
| 2002 | 3,500 | PF65 288 | | | | |

### KM# 990a 1/5 CROWN

6.22 g., 0.999 Platinum 0.1998 oz. APW, 22 mm. **Ruler:** Elizabeth II **Subject:** Peter Rabbit Centennial **Obv:** Bust right **Rev:** Peter Rabbit **Edge:** Reeded

| Date | Mintage | VF20 | XF40 | MS60 | MS63 | MS65 |
|---|---|---|---|---|---|---|
| 2002 | 1,500 | PF65 301 | | | | |

### KM# 993 1/5 CROWN

6.22 g., 0.375 Gold 0.075 oz. AGW, 22 mm. **Ruler:** Elizabeth II **Subject:** Queen's Golden Jubilee **Obv:** Bust with tiara right **Rev:** Royal couple and tree house **Edge:** Reeded

| Date | Mintage | VF20 | XF40 | MS60 | MS63 | MS65 |
|---|---|---|---|---|---|---|
| 2002 | — | PF65 108 | | | | |

### KM# 993a 1/5 CROWN

6.22 g., 0.9999 Gold 0.200 oz. AGW, 22 mm. **Ruler:** Elizabeth II **Subject:** Queen's Golden Jubilee **Obv:** Bust with tiara right **Rev:** Royal couple and tree house **Edge:** Reeded

| Date | Mintage | VF20 | XF40 | MS60 | MS63 | MS65 |
|---|---|---|---|---|---|---|
| 2002 | — | PF65 289 | | | | |

### KM# 995 1/5 CROWN

6.22 g., 0.375 Gold 0.075 oz. AGW, 22 mm. **Ruler:** Elizabeth II **Subject:** Queen's Golden Jubilee **Obv:** Bust with tiara right **Rev:** Royal coach **Edge:** Reeded

| Date | Mintage | VF20 | XF40 | MS60 | MS63 | MS65 |
|---|---|---|---|---|---|---|
| 2002 | — | PF65 108 | | | | |

### KM# 995a 1/5 CROWN

6.22 g., 0.9999 Gold 0.200 oz. AGW, 22 mm. **Ruler:** Elizabeth II **Subject:** Queen's Golden Jubilee **Obv:** Bust with tiara right **Rev:** Royal coach **Edge:** Reeded

| Date | Mintage | VF20 | XF40 | MS60 | MS63 | MS65 |
|---|---|---|---|---|---|---|
| 2002 | — | PF65 289 | | | | |

### KM# 997 1/5 CROWN

6.22 g., 0.375 Gold 0.075 oz. AGW, 22 mm. **Ruler:** Elizabeth II **Subject:** Queen's Golden Jubilee **Obv:** Bust with tiara right **Rev:** Queen holding baby **Edge:** Reeded

| Date | Mintage | VF20 | XF40 | MS60 | MS63 | MS65 |
|---|---|---|---|---|---|---|
| 2002 | — | PF65 108 | | | | |

### KM# 997a 1/5 CROWN

6.22 g., 0.9999 Gold 0.200 oz. AGW, 22 mm. **Ruler:** Elizabeth II **Subject:** Queen's Golden Jubilee **Obv:** Bust with tiara right **Rev:** Queen holding baby **Edge:** Reeded

| Date | Mintage | VF20 | XF40 | MS60 | MS63 | MS65 |
|---|---|---|---|---|---|---|
| 2002 | — | PF65 289 | | | | |

### KM# 999 1/5 CROWN

6.22 g., 0.375 Gold 0.075 oz. AGW, 22 mm. **Ruler:** Elizabeth II **Subject:** Queen's Golden Jubilee **Obv:** Bust with tiara right **Rev:** Yacht under Tower bridge **Edge:** Reeded

| Date | Mintage | VF20 | XF40 | MS60 | MS63 | MS65 |
|---|---|---|---|---|---|---|
| 2002 | — | PF65 108 | | | | |

### KM# 999a 1/5 CROWN

6.22 g., 0.9999 Gold 0.200 oz. AGW, 22 mm. **Ruler:** Elizabeth II **Subject:** Queen's Golden Jubilee **Obv:** Bust with tiara right **Rev:** Yacht under Tower bridge **Edge:** Reeded

| Date | Mintage | VF20 | XF40 | MS60 | MS63 | MS65 |
|---|---|---|---|---|---|---|
| 2002 | — | PF65 289 | | | | |

**KM# 1001 1/5 CROWN**
6.22 g., 0.9999 Gold 0.200 oz. AGW, 22 mm. **Ruler:** Elizabeth II **Subject:** Queen's Golden Jubilee **Obv:** Bust with tiara right **Rev:** Crown jewels inset with a tiny diamond, ruby, sapphire and emerald **Edge:** Reeded

| Date | Mintage | VF20 | XF40 | MS60 | MS63 | MS65 |
|---|---|---|---|---|---|---|
| 2002 | — | PF65 289 | | | | |

**KM# 1003 1/5 CROWN**
6.22 g., Electrum Special alloy of equal parts of gold and silver, 22 mm. **Ruler:** Elizabeth II **Series:** Ancient Coins **Obv:** Bust with tiara right **Rev:** Head of Athena left **Edge:** Reeded **Note:** From a Mysia electrum coin c.520BC.

| Date | Mintage | VF20 | XF40 | MS60 | MS63 | MS65 |
|---|---|---|---|---|---|---|
| 2002 | 3,500 | PF63 175 | PF65 185 | | | |

**KM# 1005 1/5 CROWN**
6.22 g., Electrum Special alloy of equal parts of gold and silver., 22 mm. **Ruler:** Elizabeth II **Series:** Ancient Coins **Obv:** Bust with tiara right **Rev:** Head of Hercules right **Edge:** Reeded **Note:** From a Lesbos coin c. 480-450 BC.

| Date | Mintage | VF20 | XF40 | MS60 | MS63 | MS65 |
|---|---|---|---|---|---|---|
| 2002 | 3,500 | PF63 175 | PF65 185 | | | |

**KM# 1007 1/5 CROWN**
6.22 g., 0.999 Electrum 0.1998 oz. Special alloy of equal parts of gold and silver., 22 mm. **Ruler:** Elizabeth II **Series:** Ancient Coins **Obv:** Bust with tiara right **Rev:** Pegasus **Edge:** Reeded **Note:** From a Lampsakos electrum coin c. 450 BC.

| Date | Mintage | VF20 | XF40 | MS60 | MS63 | MS65 |
|---|---|---|---|---|---|---|
| 2002 | 3,500 | PF63 175 | PF65 185 | | | |

**KM# 1009 1/5 CROWN**
6.22 g., Electrum Special Alloy of equal parts of gold and silver., 22 mm. **Ruler:** Elizabeth II **Series:** Ancient Coins **Obv:** Bust with tiara right **Rev:** Lion and bull facing **Edge:** Reeded **Note:** From a Kroisos "sic" coin c. 560-546 BC.

| Date | Mintage | VF20 | XF40 | MS60 | MS63 | MS65 |
|---|---|---|---|---|---|---|
| 2002 | 3,500 | PF63 175 | PF65 185 | | | |

**KM# 1012 1/5 CROWN**
6.22 g., 0.9999 Gold 0.200 oz. AGW, 22 mm. **Ruler:** Elizabeth II **Subject:** Queen Mother **Obv:** Bust with tiara right **Rev:** Queen Mother trout fishing **Edge:** Reeded

| Date | Mintage | VF20 | XF40 | MS60 | MS63 | MS65 |
|---|---|---|---|---|---|---|
| 2002 | — | PF65 289 | | | | |

**KM# 1014 1/5 CROWN**
6.22 g., 0.9999 Gold 0.200 oz. AGW, 22 mm. **Ruler:** Elizabeth II **Subject:** Princess Diana **Obv:** Bust right **Rev:** Diana's portrait **Edge:** Reeded

| Date | Mintage | VF20 | XF40 | MS60 | MS63 | MS65 |
|---|---|---|---|---|---|---|
| 2002 | — | PF65 289 | | | | |

**KM# 1018 1/5 CROWN**
6.22 g., 0.9999 Gold 0.200 oz. AGW, 22 mm. **Ruler:** Elizabeth II **Subject:** Peter Pan **Obv:** Bust right **Rev:** Peter Pan and Tinkerbell flying above city **Edge:** Reeded

| Date | Mintage | VF20 | XF40 | MS60 | MS63 | MS65 |
|---|---|---|---|---|---|---|
| 2002 | — | PF65 289 | | | | |

**KM# 1020 1/5 CROWN**
6.22 g., 0.9999 Gold 0.200 oz. AGW, 22 mm. **Ruler:** Elizabeth II **Subject:** Grand Masonic Lodge **Obv:** Bust right **Rev:** Masonic seal above Gibraltar **Edge:** Reeded

| Date | Mintage | VF20 | XF40 | MS60 | MS63 | MS65 |
|---|---|---|---|---|---|---|
| 2002 | — | PF65 289 | | | | |

**KM# 1130 1/5 CROWN**
6.22 g., 0.999 Gold 0.1998 oz. AGW, 22 mm. **Ruler:** Elizabeth II **Rev:** Elizabeth I in coronation robes

| Date | Mintage | VF20 | XF40 | MS60 | MS63 | MS65 |
|---|---|---|---|---|---|---|
| 2003 | Est. 5000 | PF65 333 | | | | |

**KM# 1131 1/5 CROWN**
6.22 g., 0.999 Gold 0.1998 oz. AGW, 22 mm. **Ruler:** Elizabeth II **Rev:** Elizabeth I in ship

| Date | Mintage | VF20 | XF40 | MS60 | MS63 | MS65 |
|---|---|---|---|---|---|---|
| 2003 | Est. 5000 | PF65 333 | | | | |

**KM# 1134.1 1/5 CROWN**
6.22 g., 0.999 Gold 0.1998 oz. AGW **Ruler:** Elizabeth II **Rev:** Peter rabbit with carrot

| Date | Mintage | VF20 | XF40 | MS60 | MS63 | MS65 |
|---|---|---|---|---|---|---|
| 2003 | Est. 3500 | PF65 400 | | | | |

**KM# 1134.2 1/5 CROWN**
6.22 g., 0.999 Gold 0.1998 oz. AGW, 22 mm. **Ruler:** Elizabeth II **Rev:** Peter rabbit with carrot in color

| Date | Mintage | VF20 | XF40 | MS60 | MS63 | MS65 |
|---|---|---|---|---|---|---|
| 2003 | Est. 1500 | PF65 400 | | | | |

**KM# 1136 1/5 CROWN**
6.22 g., 0.999 Gold 0.1998 oz. AGW, 22 mm. **Ruler:** Elizabeth II **Subject:** 2004 Summer Olympics, Athens **Rev:** Two Field Hockey players after a marble relief

| Date | Mintage | VF20 | XF40 | MS60 | MS63 | MS65 |
|---|---|---|---|---|---|---|
| 2003 | Est. 5000 | PF65 313 | | | | |

**KM# 1137 1/5 CROWN**
6.22 g., 0.999 Gold 0.1998 oz. AGW, 22 mm. **Ruler:** Elizabeth II **Subject:** 2004 Summer Olympics, Athens **Rev:** Bronze statue of horse race and jockeys

| Date | Mintage | VF20 | XF40 | MS60 | MS63 | MS65 |
|---|---|---|---|---|---|---|
| 2003 | Est. 5000 | PF65 313 | | | | |

**KM# 1138 1/5 CROWN**
6.22 g., 0.999 Gold 0.1998 oz. AGW, 22 mm. **Ruler:** Elizabeth II **Subject:** 2004 Summer Olympics, Athens **Rev:** Drinking cup with wrestler

| Date | Mintage | VF20 | XF40 | MS60 | MS63 | MS65 |
|---|---|---|---|---|---|---|
| 2003 | Est. 5000 | PF65 313 | | | | |

**KM# 1139 1/5 CROWN**
6.22 g., 0.999 Gold 0.1998 oz. AGW, 22 mm. **Ruler:** Elizabeth II **Subject:** 2004 Summer Olympics, Athens **Rev:** Red figure vase, speed runner

| Date | Mintage | VF20 | XF40 | MS60 | MS63 | MS65 |
|---|---|---|---|---|---|---|
| 2003 | Est. 5000 | PF65 313 | | | | |

**KM# 1134.1A 1/5 CROWN**
6.22 g., 0.999 Platinum 0.1998 oz. APW, 22 mm. **Ruler:** Elizabeth II **Rev:** Peter rabbit with carrot

| Date | Mintage | VF20 | XF40 | MS60 | MS63 | MS65 |
|---|---|---|---|---|---|---|
| 2003 | Est. 1500 | PF65 400 | | | | |

**KM# 1117 1/2 CROWN**
15.55 g., 0.999 Gold 0.4994 oz. AGW, 30 mm. **Ruler:** Elizabeth II **Subject:** Victoria, 100th Anniversary of Death **Rev:** Victoria as Empress of India

| Date | Mintage | VF20 | XF40 | MS60 | MS63 | MS65 |
|---|---|---|---|---|---|---|
| 2001 | Est. 999 | PF65 900 | | | | |

**KM# 991 1/2 CROWN**
15.55 g., 0.999 Gold 0.4994 oz. AGW, 30 mm. **Ruler:** Elizabeth II **Subject:** Peter Rabbit Centennial **Obv:** Bust right **Rev:** Peter Rabbit **Edge:** Reeded

| Date | Mintage | VF20 | XF40 | MS60 | MS63 | MS65 |
|---|---|---|---|---|---|---|
| 2002 | 1,000 | PF63 750 | PF65 800 | | | |

**KM# 1002 1/2 CROWN**
15.55 g., 0.9999 Gold 0.4999 oz. AGW, 30 mm. **Ruler:** Elizabeth II **Subject:** Queen's Golden Jubilee **Obv:** Bust with tiara right **Rev:** Crown jewels inset with a tiny diamond, ruby, sapphire and emerald **Edge:** Reeded

| Date | Mintage | VF20 | XF40 | MS60 | MS63 | MS65 |
|---|---|---|---|---|---|---|
| 2002 | — | PF63 750 | PF65 800 | | | |

**KM# 1004 1/2 CROWN**
15.55 g., Electrum Special alloy of equal parts of gold and silver., 32.2 mm. **Ruler:** Elizabeth II **Series:** Ancient Coins **Obv:** Bust with tiara right **Rev:** Head of Athena left **Edge:** Reeded **Note:** From a Mysia electrum coin c. 520 BC.

| Date | Mintage | VF20 | XF40 | MS60 | MS63 | MS65 |
|---|---|---|---|---|---|---|
| 2002 | 2,000 | PF63 300 | PF65 325 | | | |

**KM# 1006 1/2 CROWN**
15.55 g., Electrum Special alloy of equal parts of gold and silver., 32.2 mm. **Ruler:** Elizabeth II **Series:** Ancient Coins **Obv:** Bust with tiara right **Rev:** Head of Hercules right **Edge:** Reeded **Note:** From a Lesbos coin c. 480-450 BC.

| Date | Mintage | VF20 | XF40 | MS60 | MS63 | MS65 |
|---|---|---|---|---|---|---|
| 2002 | 2,000 | PF63 300 | PF65 325 | | | |

**KM# 1008 1/2 CROWN**
15.55 g., Gold with Silver Special alloy of equal parts of gold and silver., 32.2 mm. **Ruler:** Elizabeth II **Series:** Ancient Coins **Obv:** Bust with tiara right **Rev:** Pegasus **Edge:** Reeded **Note:** From a Lampsakos electrum coin c. 450 BC.

| Date | Mintage | VF20 | XF40 | MS60 | MS63 | MS65 |
|---|---|---|---|---|---|---|
| 2002 | 2,000 | PF63 300 | PF65 325 | | | |

**KM# 1010 1/2 CROWN**
15.55 g., Electrum Special alloy of equal parts of gold and silver., 32.2 mm. **Ruler:** Elizabeth II **Series:** Ancient Coins **Obv:** Bust with tiara right **Rev:** Lion and bull facing **Edge:** Reeded **Note:** From a Kroisos [sic] coin c. 560-546 BC.

| Date | Mintage | VF20 | XF40 | MS60 | MS63 | MS65 |
|---|---|---|---|---|---|---|
| 2002 | 2,000 | PF63 300 | PF65 325 | | | |

**KM# 1135 1/2 CROWN**
15.55 g., 0.999 Gold 0.4994 oz. AGW, 30 mm. **Ruler:** Elizabeth II **Rev:** Peter rabbit with carrot

| Date | Mintage | VF20 | XF40 | MS60 | MS63 | MS65 |
|---|---|---|---|---|---|---|
| 2003 | Est. 1000 | PF65 900 | | | | |

**KM# 904 CROWN**
28.28 g., Copper-Nickel, 38.6 mm. **Ruler:** Elizabeth II **Subject:** The Life of Queen Elizabeth - The Queen Mother **Obv:** Bust with tiara right **Rev:** 1953 Coronation scene **Edge:** Reeded

| Date | Mintage | VF20 | XF40 | MS60 | MS63 | MS65 |
|---|---|---|---|---|---|---|
| 2001 | — | — | — | — | 10.00 | 12.00 |

**KM# 904a CROWN**
28.28 g., 0.925 Silver 0.841 oz. ASW, 38.6 mm. **Ruler:** Elizabeth II **Subject:** The Life of Queen Elizabeth - The Queen Mother **Obv:** Bust with tiara right **Rev:** 1953 Coronation scene **Edge:** Reeded

| Date | Mintage | VF20 | XF40 | MS60 | MS63 | MS65 |
|---|---|---|---|---|---|---|
| 2001 | 10,000 | PF63 45.00 | PF65 47.00 | | | |

## KM# 905 CROWN

28.28 g., Copper-Nickel, 38.6 mm. **Ruler:** Elizabeth II **Subject:** The Life of Queen Elizabeth - The Queen Mother **Obv:** Bust with tiara right **Rev:** Queen Mother with Prince Charles in 1954 **Edge:** Reeded

| Date | Mintage | VF20 | XF40 | MS60 | MS63 | MS65 |
|---|---|---|---|---|---|---|
| 2001 | — | — | — | — | 10.00 | 12.00 |

## KM# 905a CROWN

28.28 g., 0.925 Silver 0.841 oz. ASW, 38.6 mm. **Ruler:** Elizabeth II **Subject:** The Life of Queen Elizabeth - The Queen Mother **Obv:** Bust with tiara right **Rev:** Queen Mother with Prince Charles in 1954 **Edge:** Reeded

| Date | Mintage | VF20 | XF40 | MS60 | MS63 | MS65 |
|---|---|---|---|---|---|---|
| 2001 | 10,000 | PF63 45.00 | PF65 47.00 | | | |

## KM# 906 CROWN

28.28 g., Copper-Nickel, 38.6 mm. **Ruler:** Elizabeth II **Subject:** 21st Century **Obv:** Crowned bust right, date below **Rev:** Celtic cross, Viking ship and modern technological items **Edge:** Reeded

| Date | Mintage | VF20 | XF40 | MS60 | MS63 | MS65 |
|---|---|---|---|---|---|---|
| 2001 | — | — | — | — | 10.00 | 12.00 |

## KM# 906a CROWN

31.10 g., 0.999 Silver 0.999 oz. ASW, 38.6 mm. **Ruler:** Elizabeth II **Subject:** 21st Century **Obv:** Crowned bust right, date below **Rev:** Celtic cross, Viking ship and modern technological items **Edge:** Reeded **Note:** 31.1035 .999 Silver, 1.000 ASW with a gold plated inner ring and a blackened outer ring.

| Date | Mintage | VF20 | XF40 | MS60 | MS63 | MS65 |
|---|---|---|---|---|---|---|
| 2001 | 2,001 | PF65 75.00 | | | | |

## KM# 906b CROWN

31.10 g., Tri-Metallic Center .9995 Platinum 5.2g. Inner Ring .9999 Gold 14.2g. Outer Ring .999 Silver 11.7g **Ruler:** Elizabeth II **Subject:** 21st Century **Obv:** Crowned bust right, date below **Rev:** Celtic cross, Viking ship and modern technological items

| Date | Mintage | VF20 | XF40 | MS60 | MS63 | MS65 |
|---|---|---|---|---|---|---|
| 2001 | 999 | PF65 750 | | | | |

## KM# 910 CROWN

28.28 g., Copper-Nickel, 38.6 mm. **Ruler:** Elizabeth II **Series:** The Victorian Age **Obv:** Bust with tiara right **Rev:** 1838 Coronation of Queen Victoria **Edge:** Reeded

| Date | Mintage | VF20 | XF40 | MS60 | MS63 | MS65 |
|---|---|---|---|---|---|---|
| 2001 | — | — | — | — | 10.00 | 12.00 |

## KM# 910a CROWN

28.28 g., 0.925 Silver 0.841 oz. ASW, 38.6 mm. **Ruler:** Elizabeth II **Series:** Victorian Era **Obv:** Bust with tiara right **Rev:** 1838 Coronation scene **Edge:** Reeded

| Date | Mintage | VF20 | XF40 | MS60 | MS63 | MS65 |
|---|---|---|---|---|---|---|
| 2001 | 10,000 | PF63 45.00 | PF65 47.00 | | | |

## KM# 912 CROWN

Copper-Nickel, 38.6 mm. **Ruler:** Elizabeth II **Series:** Victorian Era - Empress of India 1876 **Obv:** Bust with tiara right **Rev:** Crowned portrait of Victoria and two elephants

| Date | Mintage | VF20 | XF40 | MS60 | MS63 | MS65 |
|---|---|---|---|---|---|---|
| 2001 | — | — | — | — | 10.00 | 12.00 |

## KM# 912a CROWN

28.28 g., 0.925 Silver 0.841 oz. ASW **Ruler:** Elizabeth II **Series:** The Victorian Age - Empress of India 1876 **Obv:** Bust with tiara right **Rev:** Crowned portrait of Victoria and two elephants

| Date | Mintage | VF20 | XF40 | MS60 | MS63 | MS65 |
|---|---|---|---|---|---|---|
| 2001 | 10,000 | PF63 45.00 | PF65 47.00 | | | |

## KM# 914 CROWN

Copper-Nickel, 38.6 mm. **Ruler:** Elizabeth II **Series:** Victorian Era - Diamond Jubilee **Obv:** Bust with tiara right **Rev:** Victoria's cameo portrait above naval ships

| Date | Mintage | VF20 | XF40 | MS60 | MS63 | MS65 |
|---|---|---|---|---|---|---|
| 2001 | — | — | — | — | 10.00 | 12.00 |

## KM# 914a CROWN

28.28 g., 0.925 Silver 0.841 oz. ASW **Ruler:** Elizabeth II **Series:** The Victorian Age - Diamond Jubilee 1897 **Obv:** Bust with tiara right **Rev:** Victoria's cameo above naval ships, Spithead Review

| Date | Mintage | VF20 | XF40 | MS60 | MS63 | MS65 |
|---|---|---|---|---|---|---|
| 2001 | 10,000 | PF63 45.00 | PF65 47.00 | | | |

## KM# 916 CROWN

Copper-Nickel, 38.6 mm. **Ruler:** Elizabeth II **Series:** The Victorian Age - Victoria's Death 1901 **Obv:** Bust with tiara right **Rev:** Victoria's cameo portrait and Osborne Manor

| Date | Mintage | VF20 | XF40 | MS60 | MS63 | MS65 |
|---|---|---|---|---|---|---|
| 2001 | — | — | — | — | 10.00 | 12.00 |

## KM# 916a CROWN

28.28 g., 0.925 Silver 0.841 oz. ASW, 38.6 mm. **Ruler:** Elizabeth II **Series:** The Victorian Age - Victoria's Death 1901 **Obv:** Bust with tiara right **Rev:** Victoria's cameo portrait and Osborne Manor

| Date | Mintage | VF20 | XF40 | MS60 | MS63 | MS65 |
|---|---|---|---|---|---|---|
| 2001 | 10,000 | PF63 45.00 | PF65 47.00 | | | |

## KM# 918 CROWN

Copper-Nickel, 38.6 mm. **Ruler:** Elizabeth II **Series:** The Victorian Age - Prince Albert and the Great Exhibition 1851 **Obv:** Bust with tiara right **Rev:** Albert's cameo portrait and the exhibit hall

| Date | Mintage | VF20 | XF40 | MS60 | MS63 | MS65 |
|---|---|---|---|---|---|---|
| 2001 | 5,000 | PF63 175 | | | | |

## KM# 918a CROWN

28.28 g., 0.925 Silver 0.841 oz. ASW, 38.6 mm. **Ruler:** Elizabeth II **Series:** The Victorian Age - Prince Albert and the Great Exhibition 1851 **Obv:** Bust with tiara right **Rev:** Albert's cameo portrait and the exhibit hall

| Date | Mintage | VF20 | XF40 | MS60 | MS63 | MS65 |
|---|---|---|---|---|---|---|
| 2001 | 10,000 | PF63 45.00 | PF65 47.00 | | | |

## KM# 920 CROWN

Copper-Nickel, 38.6 mm. **Ruler:** Elizabeth II **Series:** The Victorian Age **Obv:** Bust with tiara right **Rev:** 1/2 bust of Isambard K. Brunel half left in front of railroad bridge

| Date | Mintage | VF20 | XF40 | MS60 | MS63 | MS65 |
|---|---|---|---|---|---|---|
| 2001 | — | — | — | — | 10.00 | 12.00 |

## KM# 920a CROWN

28.28 g., 0.925 Silver 0.841 oz. ASW, 38.6 mm. **Ruler:** Elizabeth II **Series:** Victorian Era **Obv:** Bust with tiara right **Rev:** 1/2 bust of Isambard K. Brunel half left in front of railroad bridge

| Date | Mintage | VF20 | XF40 | MS60 | MS63 | MS65 |
|---|---|---|---|---|---|---|
| 2001 | 10,000 | PF63 45.00 | PF65 47.00 | | | |

**KM# 922 CROWN**
Copper-Nickel, 38.6 mm. **Ruler:** Elizabeth II **Series:** The Victorian Age **Obv:** Bust with tiara right **Rev:** 1/2 length bust of Charles Dickens half left, scene from "Oliver Twist" in background

| Date | Mintage | VF20 | XF40 | MS60 | MS63 | MS65 |
|---|---|---|---|---|---|---|
| 2001 | — | — | — | — | 10.00 | 12.00 |

**KM# 922a CROWN**
28.28 g., 0.925 Silver 0.841 oz. ASW, 38.6 mm. **Series:** The Victorian Age **Obv:** Bust with tiara right **Rev:** 1/2 length bust of Charles Dickens half left, scene from "Oliver Twist" in background

| Date | Mintage | VF20 | XF40 | MS60 | MS63 | MS65 |
|---|---|---|---|---|---|---|
| 2001 | 10,000 | PF63 45.00 | PF65 47.00 | | | |

**KM# 924 CROWN**
Copper-Nickel, 38.6 mm. **Ruler:** Elizabeth II **Series:** The Victorian Age **Obv:** Bust with tiara right **Rev:** 3/4-length figure of Charles Darwin right, ship and a squatting aboriginal figure

| Date | Mintage | VF20 | XF40 | MS60 | MS63 | MS65 |
|---|---|---|---|---|---|---|
| 2001 | — | — | — | — | 10.00 | 12.00 |

**KM# 924a CROWN**
28.28 g., 0.925 Silver 0.841 oz. ASW, 38.6 mm. **Ruler:** Elizabeth II **Series:** The Victorian Age **Obv:** Bust with tiara right **Rev:** 3/4-length figure of Charles Darwin right, ship and a squatting aboriginal figure

| Date | Mintage | VF20 | XF40 | MS60 | MS63 | MS65 |
|---|---|---|---|---|---|---|
| 2001 | 10,000 | PF63 45.00 | PF65 47.00 | | | |

**KM# 927 CROWN**
28.28 g., Copper-Nickel, 38.6 mm. **Ruler:** Elizabeth II **Series:** Mythology of the Solar System **Obv:** Bust with tiara right **Rev:** Standing goddess with snake basket **Edge:** Reeded

| Date | Mintage | VF20 | XF40 | MS60 | MS63 | MS65 |
|---|---|---|---|---|---|---|
| 2001 | — | — | — | — | 10.00 | 12.00 |

**KM# 927a CROWN**
28.28 g., 0.925 Silver 0.841 oz. ASW, 38.6 mm. **Ruler:** Elizabeth II **Series:** Mythology of the Solar System **Obv:** Bust with tiara right **Rev:** Standing goddess with snake basket **Edge:** Reeded

| Date | Mintage | VF20 | XF40 | MS60 | MS63 | MS65 |
|---|---|---|---|---|---|---|
| 2001 | 10,000 | PF63 45.00 | PF65 47.00 | | | |

**KM# 928 CROWN**
Bi-Metallic Titanium center in Silver ring, 32.25 mm. **Ruler:** Elizabeth II **Series:** Mythology of the Solar System **Obv:** Bust with tiara right **Rev:** Standing goddess with snake basket **Edge:** Reeded

| Date | Mintage | VF20 | XF40 | MS60 | MS63 | MS65 |
|---|---|---|---|---|---|---|
| 2001 In Proof sets only | 2,001 | PF65 150 | | | | |

**KM# 930 CROWN**
Copper-Nickel, 38.6 mm. **Ruler:** Elizabeth II **Series:** Mythology of the Solar System - Sun **Obv:** Bust with tiara right **Rev:** Helios in chariot and the sun

| Date | Mintage | VF20 | XF40 | MS60 | MS63 | MS65 |
|---|---|---|---|---|---|---|
| 2001 | — | — | — | — | 10.00 | 12.00 |

**KM# 930a CROWN**
28.28 g., 0.925 Silver 0.841 oz. ASW, 38.6 mm. **Ruler:** Elizabeth II **Series:** Mythology of the Solar System - Sun **Obv:** Bust with tiara right **Rev:** Helios in chariot and the sun

| Date | Mintage | VF20 | XF40 | MS60 | MS63 | MS65 |
|---|---|---|---|---|---|---|
| 2001 | 10,000 | PF63 45.00 | PF65 47.00 | | | |

**KM# 930a.1 CROWN**
28.28 g., 0.925 Silver 0.841 oz. ASW **Ruler:** Elizabeth II **Series:** Mythology of the Solar System - Sun **Obv:** Bust with tiara right **Rev:** Fiery hologram in the sun

| Date | Mintage | VF20 | XF40 | MS60 | MS63 | MS65 |
|---|---|---|---|---|---|---|
| 2001 | 2,001 | PF65 90.00 | | | | |

**KM# 932 CROWN**
Copper-Nickel, 38.6 mm. **Ruler:** Elizabeth II **Series:** Mythology of the Solar System - Moon **Obv:** Bust with tiara right **Rev:** Goddess Diana and the moon

| Date | Mintage | VF20 | XF40 | MS60 | MS63 | MS65 |
|---|---|---|---|---|---|---|
| 2001 | — | — | — | — | 10.00 | 12.00 |

**KM# 932a CROWN**
28.28 g., 0.925 Silver 0.841 oz. ASW, 38.6 mm. **Ruler:** Elizabeth II **Series:** Mythology of the Solar System - Moon **Obv:** Bust with tiara right **Rev:** Goddess Diana and the moon

| Date | Mintage | VF20 | XF40 | MS60 | MS63 | MS65 |
|---|---|---|---|---|---|---|
| 2001 | 10,000 | PF63 45.00 | PF65 47.00 | | | |

**KM# 932a.1 CROWN**
28.28 g., 0.925 Silver 0.841 oz. ASW, 38.6 mm. **Ruler:** Elizabeth II **Series:** Mythology of the Solar System - Moon **Obv:** Bust with tiara right **Rev:** Small pearl set in the moon

| Date | Mintage | VF20 | XF40 | MS60 | MS63 | MS65 |
|---|---|---|---|---|---|---|
| 2001 | 2,001 | PF65 90.00 | | | | |

**KM# 934 CROWN**
Copper-Nickel **Ruler:** Elizabeth II **Series:** Mythology of the Solar System - Atlas **Obv:** Bust with tiara right **Rev:** Atlas carrying the earth

| Date | Mintage | VF20 | XF40 | MS60 | MS63 | MS65 |
|---|---|---|---|---|---|---|
| 2001 | — | — | — | — | 10.00 | 12.00 |

**KM# 934a CROWN**
28.28 g., 0.925 Silver 0.841 oz. ASW, 38.6 mm. **Ruler:** Elizabeth II **Series:** Mythology of the Solar System - Atlas **Obv:** Bust with tiara right **Rev:** Atlas carrying the earth

| Date | Mintage | VF20 | XF40 | MS60 | MS63 | MS65 |
|---|---|---|---|---|---|---|
| 2001 | 10,000 | PF63 45.00 | PF65 47.00 | | | |

**KM# 934a.1 CROWN**
28.28 g., 0.925 Silver 0.841 oz. ASW, 38.6 mm. **Ruler:** Elizabeth II **Series:** Mythology of the Solar System - Atlas **Obv:** Bust with tiara right **Rev:** Fancy diamond set in the earth

| Date | Mintage | VF20 | XF40 | MS60 | MS63 | MS65 |
|---|---|---|---|---|---|---|
| 2001 | 2,001 | PF65 90.00 | | | | |

**KM# 936 CROWN**
Copper-Nickel, 38.6 mm. **Ruler:** Elizabeth II **Series:** Mythology of the Solar System **Obv:** Bust with tiara right **Rev:** Seated Neptune with trident and ringed planet

| Date | Mintage | VF20 | XF40 | MS60 | MS63 | MS65 |
|---|---|---|---|---|---|---|
| 2001 | — | — | — | — | 10.00 | 12.00 |

**KM# 936a CROWN**
28.28 g., 0.925 Silver 0.841 oz. ASW, 38.6 mm. **Ruler:** Elizabeth II **Series:** Mythology of the Solar System **Obv:** Bust with tiara right **Rev:** Seated Neptune with trident and ringed planet

| Date | Mintage | VF20 | XF40 | MS60 | MS63 | MS65 |
|---|---|---|---|---|---|---|
| 2001 | 10,000 | PF63 45.00 | PF65 47.00 | | | |

**KM# 938 CROWN**
Copper-Nickel, 38.6 mm. **Ruler:** Elizabeth II **Series:** Mythology of the Solar System **Obv:** Bust with tiara right **Rev:** Seated Jupiter with lightening bolts and a planet

| Date | Mintage | VF20 | XF40 | MS60 | MS63 | MS65 |
|---|---|---|---|---|---|---|
| 2001 | — | — | — | — | 10.00 | 12.00 |

**KM# 938a CROWN**
28.28 g., 0.925 Silver 0.841 oz. ASW, 38.6 mm. **Ruler:** Elizabeth II **Series:** Mythology of the Solar System **Obv:** Bust with tiara right **Rev:** Seated Jupiter with lightening bolts and a planet

| Date | Mintage | VF20 | XF40 | MS60 | MS63 | MS65 |
|---|---|---|---|---|---|---|
| 2001 | 10,000 | PF63 45.00 | PF65 47.00 | | | |

**KM# 940 CROWN**
Copper-Nickel, 38.6 mm. **Ruler:** Elizabeth II **Series:** Mythology of the Solar System - Mars **Obv:** Bust with tiara right **Rev:** Standing Roman soldier and a planet

| Date | Mintage | VF20 | XF40 | MS60 | MS63 | MS65 |
|---|---|---|---|---|---|---|
| 2001 | — | — | — | — | 10.00 | 12.00 |

**KM# 940a CROWN**
28.28 g., 0.925 Silver 0.841 oz. ASW, 38.6 mm. **Ruler:** Elizabeth II **Series:** Mythology of the Solar System - Mars **Obv:** Bust with tiara right **Rev:** Standing Roman soldier and a planet

| Date | Mintage | VF20 | XF40 | MS60 | MS63 | MS65 |
|---|---|---|---|---|---|---|
| 2001 | 10,000 | PF63 45.00 | PF65 47.00 | | | |

**KM# 942 CROWN**
Copper-Nickel, 38.6 mm. **Ruler:** Elizabeth II **Series:** Mythology of the Solar System **Obv:** Bust with tiara right **Rev:** Seated Mercury with caduceus and a planet

| Date | Mintage | VF20 | XF40 | MS60 | MS63 | MS65 |
|---|---|---|---|---|---|---|
| 2001 | — | — | — | — | 10.00 | 12.00 |

**KM# 942a CROWN**
28.28 g., 0.925 Silver 0.841 oz. ASW, 38.6 mm. **Ruler:** Elizabeth II **Series:** Mythology of the Solar System **Obv:** Bust with tiara right **Rev:** Seated Mercury with caduceus and a planet

| Date | Mintage | VF20 | XF40 | MS60 | MS63 | MS65 |
|---|---|---|---|---|---|---|
| 2001 | 10,000 | **PF63** 45.00 | **PF65** 47.00 | | | |

**KM# 944 CROWN**
Copper-Nickel, 38.6 mm. **Ruler:** Elizabeth II **Series:** Mythology of the Solar System **Obv:** Bust with tiara right **Rev:** Seated Uranus with scepter

| Date | Mintage | VF20 | XF40 | MS60 | MS63 | MS65 |
|---|---|---|---|---|---|---|
| 2001 | — | — | — | — | 10.00 | 12.00 |

**KM# 944a CROWN**
28.28 g., 0.925 Silver 0.841 oz. ASW, 38.6 mm. **Ruler:** Elizabeth II **Series:** Mythology of the Solar System **Obv:** Bust with tiara right **Rev:** Seated Uranus with scepter

| Date | Mintage | VF20 | XF40 | MS60 | MS63 | MS65 |
|---|---|---|---|---|---|---|
| 2001 | 10,000 | **PF63** 45.00 | **PF65** 47.00 | | | |

**KM# 946 CROWN**
Copper-Nickel, 38.6 mm. **Ruler:** Elizabeth II **Series:** Mythology of the Solar System **Obv:** Bust with tiara right **Rev:** Seated Saturn with long handled sickle and a ringed planet

| Date | Mintage | VF20 | XF40 | MS60 | MS63 | MS65 |
|---|---|---|---|---|---|---|
| 2001 | — | — | — | — | 10.00 | 12.00 |

**KM# 946a CROWN**
28.28 g., 0.925 Silver 0.841 oz. ASW, 38.6 mm. **Ruler:** Elizabeth II **Series:** Mythology of the Solar System **Obv:** Bust with tiara right **Rev:** Seated Saturn with long handled sickle and a ringed planet

| Date | Mintage | VF20 | XF40 | MS60 | MS63 | MS65 |
|---|---|---|---|---|---|---|
| 2001 | 10,000 | **PF63** 45.00 | **PF65** 47.00 | | | |

**KM# 948 CROWN**
Copper-Nickel, 38.6 mm. **Ruler:** Elizabeth II **Series:** Mythology of the Solar System **Obv:** Bust with tiara right **Rev:** Seated Pluto with dogs and planet

| Date | Mintage | VF20 | XF40 | MS60 | MS63 | MS65 |
|---|---|---|---|---|---|---|
| 2001 | — | — | — | — | 10.00 | 12.00 |

**KM# 948a CROWN**
28.28 g., 0.925 Silver 0.841 oz. ASW, 38.6 mm. **Ruler:** Elizabeth II **Series:** Mythology of the Solar System **Obv:** Bust with tiara right **Rev:** Seated Pluto with dogs and planet

| Date | Mintage | VF20 | XF40 | MS60 | MS63 | MS65 |
|---|---|---|---|---|---|---|
| 2001 | 10,000 | **PF63** 45.00 | **PF65** 47.00 | | | |

**KM# 950 CROWN**
Copper-Nickel, 38.6 mm. **Ruler:** Elizabeth II **Series:** Mythology of the Solar System **Obv:** Bust with tiara right **Rev:** Venus seated on a half shell

| Date | Mintage | VF20 | XF40 | MS60 | MS63 | MS65 |
|---|---|---|---|---|---|---|
| 2001 | — | — | — | — | 10.00 | 12.00 |

**KM# 950a CROWN**
28.28 g., 0.925 Silver 0.841 oz. ASW, 38.6 mm. **Ruler:** Elizabeth II **Series:** Mythology of the Solar System **Obv:** Bust with tiara right **Rev:** Venus seated on a half shell

| Date | Mintage | VF20 | XF40 | MS60 | MS63 | MS65 |
|---|---|---|---|---|---|---|
| 2001 | 10,000 | **PF63** 45.00 | **PF65** 47.00 | | | |

**KM# 952 CROWN**
28.28 g., Copper-Nickel, 38.6 mm. **Ruler:** Elizabeth II **Subject:** Queen's 75th Birthday **Obv:** Bust with tiara right **Rev:** Queen in Order of Garter robes **Edge:** Reeded

| Date | Mintage | VF20 | XF40 | MS60 | MS63 | MS65 |
|---|---|---|---|---|---|---|
| 2001 | — | — | — | — | 10.00 | 12.00 |

**KM# 952a CROWN**
28.28 g., 0.925 Silver 0.841 oz. ASW, 38.6 mm. **Ruler:** Elizabeth II **Subject:** Queen's 75th Birthday **Obv:** Bust with tiara right **Rev:** Queen in Order of Garter robes **Edge:** Reeded

| Date | Mintage | VF20 | XF40 | MS60 | MS63 | MS65 |
|---|---|---|---|---|---|---|
| 2001 | 10,000 | **PF63** 45.00 | **PF65** 47.00 | | | |

**KM# 955 CROWN**
28.28 g., Copper-Nickel, 38.6 mm. **Ruler:** Elizabeth II **Series:** Victorian Age Part II **Obv:** Bust with tiara right **Rev:** Victoria learning of her accession **Edge:** Reeded

| Date | Mintage | VF20 | XF40 | MS60 | MS63 | MS65 |
|---|---|---|---|---|---|---|
| 2001 | — | — | — | — | 10.00 | 12.00 |

**KM# 955a CROWN**
28.28 g., 0.925 Silver 0.841 oz. ASW, 38.6 mm. **Ruler:** Elizabeth II **Series:** Victorian Age Part II **Obv:** Bust with tiara right **Rev:** Victoria learning of her accession **Edge:** Reeded

| Date | Mintage | VF20 | XF40 | MS60 | MS63 | MS65 |
|---|---|---|---|---|---|---|
| 2001 | 10,000 | **PF63** 45.00 | **PF65** 47.00 | | | |

**KM# 957 CROWN**
Copper-Nickel, 38.6 mm. **Ruler:** Elizabeth II **Series:** Victorian Age Part II - Royal Family **Obv:** Bust with tiara right **Rev:** Victoria and Albert seated with children **Edge:** Reeded

| Date | Mintage | VF20 | XF40 | MS60 | MS63 | MS65 |
|---|---|---|---|---|---|---|
| 2001 | — | — | — | — | 10.00 | 12.00 |

**KM# 957a CROWN**
28.28 g., 0.925 Silver 0.841 oz. ASW, 38.6 mm. **Ruler:** Elizabeth II **Series:** Victorian Age Part II - Royal Family **Obv:** Bust with tiara right **Rev:** Victoria and Albert seated with children **Edge:** Reeded

| Date | Mintage | VF20 | XF40 | MS60 | MS63 | MS65 |
|---|---|---|---|---|---|---|
| 2001 | 10,000 | **PF63** 45.00 | **PF65** 47.00 | | | |

**KM# 959 CROWN**
Copper-Nickel, 38.6 mm. **Ruler:** Elizabeth II **Series:** Victorian Age Part II - Victoria in Scotland **Obv:** Bust with tiara right **Rev:** Victoria on horse with servant **Edge:** Reeded

| Date | Mintage | VF20 | XF40 | MS60 | MS63 | MS65 |
|---|---|---|---|---|---|---|
| 2001 | 2,001 | — | — | — | 10.00 | 12.00 |

**KM# 959a CROWN**
28.28 g., 0.925 Silver 0.841 oz. ASW, 38.6 mm. **Ruler:** Elizabeth II **Series:** Victorian Age Part II - Victoria in Scotland **Obv:** Bust with tiara right **Rev:** Victoria on horse with servant **Edge:** Reeded

| Date | Mintage | VF20 | XF40 | MS60 | MS63 | MS65 |
|---|---|---|---|---|---|---|
| 2001 | 10,000 | **PF63** 45.00 | **PF65** 47.00 | | | |

**KM# 961 CROWN**
Copper-Nickel, 38.6 mm. **Ruler:** Elizabeth II **Series:** Victorian Age Part II - Gladstone and Disraeli **Obv:** Bust with tiara right **Rev:** Portraits of both politicians **Edge:** Reeded

| Date | Mintage | VF20 | XF40 | MS60 | MS63 | MS65 |
|---|---|---|---|---|---|---|
| 2001 | — | — | — | — | 10.00 | 12.00 |

**KM# 961a CROWN**
28.28 g., 0.925 Silver 0.841 oz. ASW, 38.6 mm. **Ruler:** Elizabeth II **Series:** Victorian Age Part II - Gladstone and Disraeli **Obv:** Bust with tiara right **Rev:** Portraits of both politicians **Edge:** Reeded

| Date | Mintage | VF20 | XF40 | MS60 | MS63 | MS65 |
|---|---|---|---|---|---|---|
| 2001 | 10,000 | **PF63** 45.00 | **PF65** 47.00 | | | |

**KM# 963 CROWN**
Copper-Nickel, 38.6 mm. **Ruler:** Elizabeth II **Series:** Victorian Age Part II **Obv:** Bust with tiara right **Rev:** Florence Nightingale holding lantern **Edge:** Reeded

| Date | Mintage | VF20 | XF40 | MS60 | MS63 | MS65 |
|---|---|---|---|---|---|---|
| 2001 | — | — | — | — | 10.00 | 12.00 |

**KM# 963a CROWN**
28.28 g., 0.925 Silver 0.841 oz. ASW, 38.6 mm. **Ruler:** Elizabeth II **Series:** Victorian Age Part II **Obv:** Bust with tiara right **Rev:** Florence Nightingale holding lantern **Edge:** Reeded

| Date | Mintage | VF20 | XF40 | MS60 | MS63 | MS65 |
|---|---|---|---|---|---|---|
| 2001 | 10,000 | **PF63** 45.00 | **PF65** 47.00 | | | |

**KM# 965 CROWN**
Copper-Nickel, 38.6 mm. **Ruler:** Elizabeth II **Series:** Victorian Age Part II **Obv:** Bust with tiara right **Rev:** Lord Tennyson with the Light Brigade in background **Edge:** Reeded

| Date | Mintage | VF20 | XF40 | MS60 | MS63 | MS65 |
|---|---|---|---|---|---|---|
| 2001 | — | — | — | — | 10.00 | 12.00 |

**KM# 965a CROWN**
28.28 g., 0.925 Silver 0.841 oz. ASW, 38.6 mm. **Ruler:** Elizabeth II **Series:** Victorian Age Part II **Obv:** Bust with tiara right **Rev:** Lord Tennyson with the Light Brigade in background **Edge:** Reeded

| Date | Mintage | VF20 | XF40 | MS60 | MS63 | MS65 |
|---|---|---|---|---|---|---|
| 2001 | 10,000 | **PF63** 45.00 | **PF65** 47.00 | | | |

**KM# 967 CROWN**
Copper-Nickel, 38.6 mm. **Ruler:** Elizabeth II **Series:** Victorian Age Part II **Obv:** Bust with tiara right **Rev:** Stanley meeting Dr. Livingstone **Edge:** Reeded

| Date | Mintage | VF20 | XF40 | MS60 | MS63 | MS65 |
|---|---|---|---|---|---|---|
| 2001 | — | — | — | — | 10.00 | 12.00 |

**KM# 967a CROWN**
28.28 g., 0.925 Silver 0.841 oz. ASW, 38.6 mm. **Ruler:** Elizabeth II **Series:** Victorian Age Part II **Obv:** Bust with tiara right **Rev:** Stanley meeting Dr. Livingstone **Edge:** Reeded

| Date | Mintage | VF20 | XF40 | MS60 | MS63 | MS65 |
|---|---|---|---|---|---|---|
| 2001 | 10,000 | **PF63** 45.00 | **PF65** 47.00 | | | |

**KM# 969 CROWN**
Copper-Nickel, 38.6 mm. **Ruler:** Elizabeth II **Series:** Victorian Age Part II **Obv:** Bust with tiara right **Rev:** Bronte sisters **Edge:** Reeded

| Date | Mintage | VF20 | XF40 | MS60 | MS63 | MS65 |
|---|---|---|---|---|---|---|
| 2001 | — | — | — | — | 10.00 | 12.00 |

**KM# 969a CROWN**
28.28 g., 0.925 Silver 0.841 oz. ASW, 38.6 mm. **Ruler:** Elizabeth II **Series:** Victorian Age Part II **Obv:** Bust with tiara right **Rev:** Bronte sisters **Edge:** Reeded

| Date | Mintage | VF20 | XF40 | MS60 | MS63 | MS65 |
|---|---|---|---|---|---|---|
| 2001 | 10,000 | **PF63** 45.00 | **PF65** 47.00 | | | |

**KM# 1056 CROWN**
31.10 g., 0.999 Tri-Metallic 0.9989 oz. Center: silver, Ring: silver-gilt, Outer ring: silver-pearl black, 38.60 mm. **Ruler:** Elizabeth II **Subject:** 21st Century **Obv:** Crowned bust right **Obv. Legend:** GIBRALTAR • ELIZABETH II **Rev:** Helmeted cross at center flanked by satellites, archaic sailing ship below **Rev. Legend:** 21st CENTURY **Edge:** Reeded

| Date | Mintage | VF20 | XF40 | MS60 | MS63 | MS65 |
|---|---|---|---|---|---|---|
| 2001 | 2,001 | **PF65** 700 | | | | |

**KM# 979 CROWN**
28.28 g., Copper-Nickel, 38.6 mm. **Ruler:** Elizabeth II **Subject:** Queen Mother's Life **Obv:** Bust with tiara right **Rev:** Christening of Prince William **Edge:** Reeded

| Date | Mintage | VF20 | XF40 | MS60 | MS63 | MS65 |
|---|---|---|---|---|---|---|
| 2002 | — | — | — | — | 10.00 | 12.00 |

**KM# 979a CROWN**
28.28 g., 0.925 Silver 0.841 oz. ASW, 38.6 mm. **Ruler:** Elizabeth II **Subject:** Queen Mother's Life **Obv:** Bust with tiara right **Rev:** Prince William's christening **Edge:** Reeded

| Date | Mintage | VF20 | XF40 | MS60 | MS63 | MS65 |
|---|---|---|---|---|---|---|
| 2002 | 10,000 | **PF63** 45.00 | **PF65** 47.00 | | | |

**KM# 981 CROWN**
28.28 g., Copper-Nickel, 38.6 mm. **Ruler:** Elizabeth II **Subject:** World Cup Soccer **Obv:** Bust with tiara right **Rev:** Two players about to collide **Edge:** Reeded

| Date | Mintage | VF20 | XF40 | MS60 | MS63 | MS65 |
|---|---|---|---|---|---|---|
| 2002 | — | — | — | — | 10.00 | 11.50 |

**KM# 981a CROWN**
28.28 g., 0.925 Silver 0.841 oz. ASW, 38.6 mm. **Ruler:** Elizabeth II **Subject:** World Cup Soccer **Obv:** Bust with tiara right **Rev:** Two players about to collide **Edge:** Reeded

| Date | Mintage | VF20 | XF40 | MS60 | MS63 | MS65 |
|---|---|---|---|---|---|---|
| 2002 | 10,000 | **PF63** 45.00 | **PF65** 47.00 | | | |

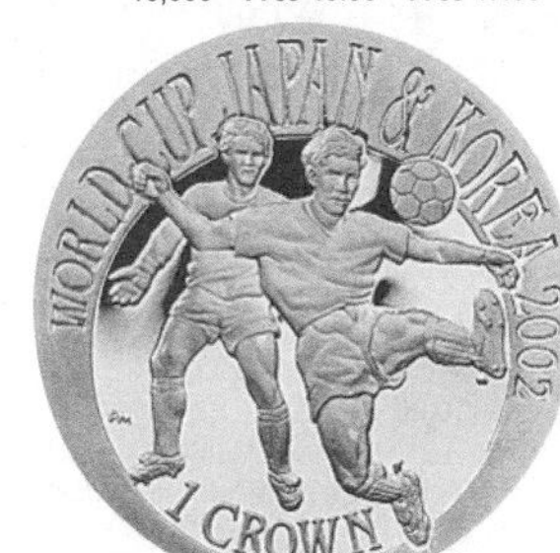


**KM# 983 CROWN**
28.28 g., Copper-Nickel, 38.6 mm. **Ruler:** Elizabeth II **Subject:** World Cup Soccer **Obv:** Bust with tiara right **Rev:** Two players facing viewer **Edge:** Reeded

| Date | Mintage | VF20 | XF40 | MS60 | MS63 | MS65 |
|---|---|---|---|---|---|---|
| 2002 | — | — | — | — | 10.00 | 11.50 |

**KM# 983a CROWN**
28.28 g., 0.925 Silver 0.841 oz. ASW, 38.6 mm. **Ruler:** Elizabeth II **Subject:** World Cup Soccer **Obv:** Bust with tiara right **Rev:** Two players facing viewer **Edge:** Reeded

| Date | Mintage | VF20 | XF40 | MS60 | MS63 | MS65 |
|---|---|---|---|---|---|---|
| 2002 | 10,000 | **PF63** 45.00 | **PF65** 47.00 | | | |

**KM# 985 CROWN**

28.28 g., Copper-Nickel, 38.6 mm. **Ruler:** Elizabeth II **Subject:** World Cup Soccer **Obv:** Bust with tiara right **Rev:** Two horizontal players **Edge:** Reeded

| Date | Mintage | VF20 | XF40 | MS60 | MS63 | MS65 |
|---|---|---|---|---|---|---|
| 2002 | — | — | — | — | 10.00 | 11.50 |

**KM# 985a CROWN**

28.28 g., 0.925 Silver 0.841 oz. ASW, 38.6 mm. **Ruler:** Elizabeth II **Subject:** World Cup Soccer **Obv:** Bust with tiara right **Rev:** Two horizontal players **Edge:** Reeded

| Date | Mintage | VF20 | XF40 | MS60 | MS63 | MS65 |
|---|---|---|---|---|---|---|
| 2002 | 10,000 | PF63 45.00 | PF65 47.00 | | | |

**KM# 987 CROWN**

28.28 g., Copper-Nickel, 38.6 mm. **Ruler:** Elizabeth II **Subject:** World Cup Soccer **Obv:** Bust with tiara right **Rev:** Two players moving to left **Edge:** Reeded

| Date | Mintage | VF20 | XF40 | MS60 | MS63 | MS65 |
|---|---|---|---|---|---|---|
| 2002 | — | — | — | — | 10.00 | 11.50 |

**KM# 987a CROWN**

28.28 g., 0.925 Silver 0.841 oz. ASW, 38.6 mm. **Ruler:** Elizabeth II **Subject:** World Cup Soccer **Obv:** Bust with tiara right **Rev:** Two players moving to left **Edge:** Reeded

| Date | Mintage | VF20 | XF40 | MS60 | MS63 | MS65 |
|---|---|---|---|---|---|---|
| 2002 | 10,000 | PF63 45.00 | PF65 47.00 | | | |

**KM# 992.1 CROWN**

28.28 g., Copper-Nickel, 38.6 mm. **Ruler:** Elizabeth II **Subject:** Peter Rabbit Centennial **Obv:** Bust with tiara right **Rev:** Peter Rabbit **Edge:** Reeded

| Date | Mintage | VF20 | XF40 | MS60 | MS63 | MS65 |
|---|---|---|---|---|---|---|
| 2002 | — | — | — | — | 10.00 | 12.00 |

**KM# 992.2 CROWN**

Copper-Nickel **Ruler:** Elizabeth II **Obv:** Bust with tiara right **Rev:** Peter Rabbit in multi-color

| Date | Mintage | VF20 | XF40 | MS60 | MS63 | MS65 |
|---|---|---|---|---|---|---|
| 2002 | — | — | — | — | 10.00 | 12.00 |

**KM# 992a CROWN**

28.28 g., 0.925 Silver 0.841 oz. ASW, 38.6 mm. **Ruler:** Elizabeth II **Subject:** Peter Rabbit Centennial **Obv:** Bust with tiara right **Rev:** Peter Rabbit **Edge:** Reeded

| Date | Mintage | VF20 | XF40 | MS60 | MS63 | MS65 |
|---|---|---|---|---|---|---|
| 2002 | 10,000 | PF63 45.00 | PF65 47.00 | | | |

**KM# 994 CROWN**

28.28 g., Copper-Nickel, 38.6 mm. **Ruler:** Elizabeth II **Subject:** Queen's Golden Jubilee **Obv:** Bust with tiara right **Rev:** Royal couple and tree house **Edge:** Reeded

| Date | Mintage | VF20 | XF40 | MS60 | MS63 | MS65 |
|---|---|---|---|---|---|---|
| 2002 | — | — | — | — | 10.00 | 12.00 |

**KM# 994a CROWN**

Yellow Brass, 38.6 mm. **Ruler:** Elizabeth II **Subject:** Queen's Golden Jubilee **Obv:** Bust with tiara right **Rev:** Royal couple and tree house **Edge:** Reeded

| Date | Mintage | VF20 | XF40 | MS60 | MS63 | MS65 |
|---|---|---|---|---|---|---|
| 2002 | 15,000 | PF63 20.00 | PF65 22.00 | | | |

**KM# 994b CROWN**

28.28 g., 0.925 Gold Clad Silver 0.841 oz., 38.6 mm. **Ruler:** Elizabeth II **Subject:** Queen's Golden Jubilee **Obv:** Bust with tiara right **Rev:** Royal couple and tree house **Edge:** Reeded

| Date | Mintage | VF20 | XF40 | MS60 | MS63 | MS65 |
|---|---|---|---|---|---|---|
| 2002 | 10,000 | PF65 55.00 | | | | |

**KM# 996 CROWN**

28.28 g., Copper-Nickel, 38.6 mm. **Ruler:** Elizabeth II **Subject:** Queen's Golden Jubilee **Obv:** Bust with tiara right **Rev:** Royal coach **Edge:** Reeded

| Date | Mintage | VF20 | XF40 | MS60 | MS63 | MS65 |
|---|---|---|---|---|---|---|
| 2002 | — | — | — | — | 10.00 | 12.00 |

**KM# 996a CROWN**

Yellow Brass, 38.6 mm. **Ruler:** Elizabeth II **Subject:** Queen's Golden Jubilee **Obv:** Bust with tiara right **Rev:** Royal coach **Edge:** Reeded

| Date | Mintage | VF20 | XF40 | MS60 | MS63 | MS65 |
|---|---|---|---|---|---|---|
| 2002 | 15,000 | PF63 20.00 | PF65 22.00 | | | |

**KM# 996b CROWN**

28.28 g., 0.925 Gold Clad Silver 0.841 oz., 38.6 mm. **Ruler:** Elizabeth II **Subject:** Queen's Golden Jubilee **Obv:** Bust with tiara right **Rev:** Royal coach **Edge:** Reeded

| Date | Mintage | VF20 | XF40 | MS60 | MS63 | MS65 |
|---|---|---|---|---|---|---|
| 2002 | 10,000 | PF65 55.00 | | | | |

**KM# 998 CROWN**

28.28 g., Copper-Nickel, 38.6 mm. **Ruler:** Elizabeth II **Subject:** Queen's Golden Jubilee **Obv:** Bust with tiara right **Rev:** Royal couple with baby **Edge:** Reeded

| Date | Mintage | VF20 | XF40 | MS60 | MS63 | MS65 |
|---|---|---|---|---|---|---|
| 2002 | — | — | — | — | 10.00 | 12.00 |

**KM# 998a CROWN**

Yellow Brass, 38.6 mm. **Ruler:** Elizabeth II **Subject:** Queen's Golden Jubilee **Obv:** Bust with tiara right **Rev:** Royal couple with baby **Edge:** Reeded

| Date | Mintage | VF20 | XF40 | MS60 | MS63 | MS65 |
|---|---|---|---|---|---|---|
| 2002 | 15,000 | PF63 20.00 | PF65 22.00 | | | |

**KM# 998b CROWN**

28.28 g., 0.925 Gold Clad Silver 0.841 oz., 38.6 mm. **Ruler:** Elizabeth II **Subject:** Queen's Golden Jubilee **Obv:** Bust with tiara right **Rev:** Royal couple with baby **Edge:** Reeded

| Date | Mintage | VF20 | XF40 | MS60 | MS63 | MS65 |
|---|---|---|---|---|---|---|
| 2002 | 1,000 | PF65 55.00 | | | | |

**KM# 1000 CROWN**

28.28 g., Copper-Nickel, 38.6 mm. **Ruler:** Elizabeth II **Subject:** Queen's Golden Jubilee **Obv:** Bust with tiara right **Rev:** Royal yacht under Tower bridge **Edge:** Reeded

| Date | Mintage | VF20 | XF40 | MS60 | MS63 | MS65 |
|---|---|---|---|---|---|---|
| 2002 | — | — | — | — | 10.00 | 12.00 |

**KM# 1000a CROWN**

Yellow Brass, 38.6 mm. **Ruler:** Elizabeth II **Subject:** Queen's Golden Jubilee **Obv:** Bust with tiara right **Rev:** Royal yacht under Tower bridge **Edge:** Reeded

| Date | Mintage | VF20 | XF40 | MS60 | MS63 | MS65 |
|---|---|---|---|---|---|---|
| 2002 | 15,000 | PF63 20.00 | PF65 22.00 | | | |

**KM# 1000b CROWN**

28.28 g., 0.925 Gold Clad Silver 0.841 oz., 38.6 mm. **Ruler:** Elizabeth II **Subject:** Queen's Golden Jubilee **Obv:** Bust with tiara right **Rev:** Royal yacht under Tower bridge **Edge:** Reeded

| Date | Mintage | VF20 | XF40 | MS60 | MS63 | MS65 |
|---|---|---|---|---|---|---|
| 2002 | 10,000 | PF65 55.00 | | | | |

**KM# 1013 CROWN**

28.28 g., Copper-Nickel dark patina, 38.6 mm. **Ruler:** Elizabeth II **Subject:** Death of Queen Mother **Obv:** Bust with tiara right **Rev:** Queen Mother trout fishing **Edge:** Reeded

| Date | Mintage | VF20 | XF40 | MS60 | MS63 | MS65 |
|---|---|---|---|---|---|---|
| 2002 | — | — | — | — | 10.00 | 12.00 |

**KM# 1013a CROWN**
28.28 g., 0.925 Silver 0.841 oz. ASW, 38.6 mm. **Ruler:** Elizabeth II **Subject:** Queen Mother **Obv:** Bust with tiara right **Rev:** Queen Mother trout fishing **Edge:** Reeded **Note:** Blackened legends on both sides.

| Date | Mintage | VF20 | XF40 | MS60 | MS63 | MS65 |
|---|---|---|---|---|---|---|
| 2002 | — | PF65 175 | | | | |

**KM# 1015 CROWN**
28.28 g., Copper-Nickel, 38.6 mm. **Ruler:** Elizabeth II **Subject:** Princess Diana **Obv:** Bust with tiara right **Rev:** Diana's portrait **Edge:** Reeded

| Date | Mintage | VF20 | XF40 | MS60 | MS63 | MS65 |
|---|---|---|---|---|---|---|
| 2002 | — | — | — | — | 10.00 | 12.00 |

**KM# 1015a CROWN**
28.28 g., 0.925 Silver 0.841 oz. ASW, 38.6 mm. **Ruler:** Elizabeth II **Subject:** Princess Diana **Obv:** Bust with tiara right **Rev:** Diana's portrait **Edge:** Reeded

| Date | Mintage | VF20 | XF40 | MS60 | MS63 | MS65 |
|---|---|---|---|---|---|---|
| 2002 | 10,000 | PF63 45.00 | PF65 47.00 | | | |

**KM# 1019 CROWN**
28.28 g., Copper-Nickel, 38.6 mm. **Ruler:** Elizabeth II **Subject:** Peter Pan **Obv:** Bust with tiara right **Rev:** Peter Pan and Tinkerbell flying above city **Edge:** Reeded

| Date | Mintage | VF20 | XF40 | MS60 | MS63 | MS65 |
|---|---|---|---|---|---|---|
| 2002 | — | — | — | — | 10.00 | 12.00 |

**KM# 1019a CROWN**
28.28 g., 0.925 Silver 0.841 oz. ASW, 38.6 mm. **Ruler:** Elizabeth II **Subject:** Peter Pan **Obv:** Bust with tiara right **Rev:** Peter Pan and Tinkerbell flying above city **Edge:** Reeded

| Date | Mintage | VF20 | XF40 | MS60 | MS63 | MS65 |
|---|---|---|---|---|---|---|
| 2002 | 10,000 | PF63 45.00 | PF65 47.00 | | | |

**KM# 1021 CROWN**
28.28 g., Copper-Nickel, 38.6 mm. **Ruler:** Elizabeth II **Subject:** Grand Masonic Lodge **Obv:** Bust with tiara right **Rev:** Masonic seal above Gibraltar **Edge:** Reeded

| Date | Mintage | VF20 | XF40 | MS60 | MS63 | MS65 |
|---|---|---|---|---|---|---|
| 2002 | — | PF63 12.00 | PF65 14.00 | | | |

**KM# 1021a CROWN**
28.28 g., 0.925 Silver 0.841 oz. ASW, 38.6 mm. **Ruler:** Elizabeth II **Subject:** Grand Masonic Lodge **Obv:** Bust with tiara right **Rev:** Masonic seal above Gibraltar **Edge:** Reeded

| Date | Mintage | VF20 | XF40 | MS60 | MS63 | MS65 |
|---|---|---|---|---|---|---|
| 2002 | 10,000 | PF63 45.00 | PF65 47.00 | | | |

**KM# 1025 CROWN**
28.28 g., Copper-Nickel, 38.6 mm. **Ruler:** Elizabeth II **Subject:** Calpe Conference **Obv:** Bust with tiara right **Rev:** Crossed flags and arms **Edge:** Reeded

| Date | Mintage | VF20 | XF40 | MS60 | MS63 | MS65 |
|---|---|---|---|---|---|---|
| 2002 PM | — | — | — | — | 10.00 | 12.00 |

**KM# 1025a CROWN**
28.28 g., 0.925 Silver 0.841 oz. ASW, 38.6 mm. **Ruler:** Elizabeth II **Subject:** Calpe Conference **Obv:** Bust with tiara right **Rev:** Crossed flags and arms **Edge:** Reeded

| Date | Mintage | VF20 | XF40 | MS60 | MS63 | MS65 |
|---|---|---|---|---|---|---|
| 2002 PM | 10,000 | PF63 45.00 | PF65 47.00 | | | |

**KM# 1058 CROWN**
31.10 g., 1.000 Electrum 0.9999 oz. Special alloy of equal parts of gold and silver. **Ruler:** Elizabeth II **Series:** Ancient Coins **Obv:** Crowned head right **Rev:** Head of Athena left **Note:** From a Mysia electrum coin c. 520 BC.

| Date | Mintage | VF20 | XF40 | MS60 | MS63 | MS65 |
|---|---|---|---|---|---|---|
| 2002 | — | PF65 700 | | | | |

**KM# 1059 CROWN**
31.10 g., Electrum Special alloy of equal parts of gold and silver. **Ruler:** Elizabeth II **Series:** Ancient Coins **Obv:** Crowned bust right **Rev:** Head of Hercules right **Note:** From a Lesbos coin c. 480-450

| Date | Mintage | VF20 | XF40 | MS60 | MS63 | MS65 |
|---|---|---|---|---|---|---|
| 2002 | — | PF65 700 | | | | |

**KM# 1060 CROWN**
31.10 g., Electrum Special alloy of equal parts of gold and silver. **Ruler:** Elizabeth II **Series:** Ancient Coins. **Obv:** Crowned bust right **Rev:** Lion and bull facing **Note:** From a Lampsakos electrum coin c. 450 BC.

| Date | Mintage | VF20 | XF40 | MS60 | MS63 | MS65 |
|---|---|---|---|---|---|---|
| 2002 | — | PF65 700 | | | | |

**KM# 1061 CROWN**
31.10 g., Electrum Special alloy of equal parts of gold and silver. **Ruler:** Elizabeth II **Series:** Ancient Coins **Obv:** Crowned bust right **Rev:** Lion and bull facing **Note:** From a Kroisos [sic] coin c. 560-546 BC.

| Date | Mintage | VF20 | XF40 | MS60 | MS63 | MS65 |
|---|---|---|---|---|---|---|
| 2002 | — | PF65 700 | | | | |

**KM# 1035 CROWN**
28.28 g., Nickel-Brass, 38.6 mm. **Ruler:** Elizabeth II **Subject:** 1700th Anniversary - Death of St. George **Obv:** Bust with tiara right **Rev:** St. George and the dragon **Edge:** Reeded

| Date | Mintage | VF20 | XF40 | MS60 | MS63 | MS65 |
|---|---|---|---|---|---|---|
| 2003 | — | — | — | — | 9.00 | 10.00 |

**KM# 1035a CROWN**
28.28 g., 0.925 Silver 0.841 oz. ASW, 38.6 mm. **Ruler:** Elizabeth II **Subject:** 1700th Anniversary - Death of St. George **Obv:** Bust with tiara right **Rev:** St. George and the dragon **Edge:** Reeded

| Date | Mintage | VF20 | XF40 | MS60 | MS63 | MS65 |
|---|---|---|---|---|---|---|
| 2003 | 10,000 | PF63 45.00 | PF65 47.00 | | | |

**KM# 1039 CROWN**
28.30 g., Copper-Nickel, 38.6 mm. **Ruler:** Elizabeth II **Subject:** Peter Rabbit **Obv:** Bust with tiara right **Rev:** Peter Rabbit holding carrot **Edge:** Reeded

| Date | Mintage | VF20 | XF40 | MS60 | MS63 | MS65 |
|---|---|---|---|---|---|---|
| 2003 PM | — | — | — | — | 9.00 | 10.00 |

### KM# 1040 CROWN

28.28 g., Copper-Nickel, 38.6 mm. **Ruler:** Elizabeth II **Subject:** Centennial of Powered Flight **Obv:** Queens portrait **Rev:** Stealth bomber within circles of WWI and WWII planes **Edge:** Reeded

| Date | Mintage | VF20 | XF40 | MS60 | MS63 | MS65 |
|---|---|---|---|---|---|---|
| 2003 PM | — | — | — | — | 10.00 | 12.00 |

### KM# 1040a CROWN

31.10 g., Tri-Metallic .9995 Platinum 5.2g center in .9999 Gold 14.2 g ring within .999 Silver 11.7 g outer ring, 38.6 mm. **Ruler:** Elizabeth II **Subject:** Centennial of Powered Flight **Obv:** Queens portrait **Rev:** Stealth bomber within circles of WWI and WWII planes **Edge:** Reeded

| Date | Mintage | VF20 | XF40 | MS60 | MS63 | MS65 |
|---|---|---|---|---|---|---|
| 2003 PM | 999 | PF65 1,750 | | | | |

### KM# 1041 CROWN

28.28 g., Copper-Nickel, 38.6 mm. **Ruler:** Elizabeth II **Subject:** 50th Anniversary of Coronation **Obv:** Queens portrait **Rev:** Buckingham Palace **Edge:** Reeded

| Date | Mintage | VF20 | XF40 | MS60 | MS63 | MS65 |
|---|---|---|---|---|---|---|
| 2003 PM | — | — | — | — | 10.00 | 12.00 |

### KM# 1052 CROWN

Copper-Nickel **Ruler:** Elizabeth II **Subject:** 2004 Athens Olympics **Rev:** Horse jumping left

| Date | Mintage | VF20 | XF40 | MS60 | MS63 | MS65 |
|---|---|---|---|---|---|---|
| 2003 | — | — | — | — | 10.00 | 12.00 |

### KM# 1053 CROWN

Copper-Nickel **Ruler:** Elizabeth II **Subject:** 2004 Athens Olympics **Rev:** Javelin thrower

| Date | Mintage | VF20 | XF40 | MS60 | MS63 | MS65 |
|---|---|---|---|---|---|---|
| 2003 | — | — | — | — | 10.00 | 12.00 |

### KM# 1054 CROWN

Copper-Nickel **Ruler:** Elizabeth II **Subject:** 2004 Athens Olympics **Rev:** Field Hockey

| Date | Mintage | VF20 | XF40 | MS60 | MS63 | MS65 |
|---|---|---|---|---|---|---|
| 2003 | — | — | — | — | 10.00 | 12.00 |

### KM# 1055 CROWN

Copper-Nickel **Ruler:** Elizabeth II **Subject:** 2004 Athens Olympics **Rev:** Wrestlers

| Date | Mintage | VF20 | XF40 | MS60 | MS63 | MS65 |
|---|---|---|---|---|---|---|
| 2003 | — | — | — | — | 10.00 | 12.00 |

### KM# 1123 CROWN

28.28 g., Copper-Nickel, 38.61 mm. **Ruler:** Elizabeth II **Rev:** Princess Elizabeth and ball game in garden at Hatfield Palace

| Date | Mintage | VF20 | XF40 | MS60 | MS63 | MS65 |
|---|---|---|---|---|---|---|
| 2003 | — | — | — | — | 10.00 | 12.00 |

### KM# 1123a CROWN

28.28 g., 0.925 Silver 0.841 oz. ASW, 38.61 mm. **Ruler:** Elizabeth II **Rev:** Princess Elizabeth and ball game in garden at Hatfield Palace

| Date | Mintage | VF20 | XF40 | MS60 | MS63 | MS65 |
|---|---|---|---|---|---|---|
| 2003 | Est. 10000 | PF65 60.00 | | | | |

### KM# 1124 CROWN

28.28 g., Copper-Nickel, 38.61 mm. **Ruler:** Elizabeth II **Rev:** Elizabeth I in coronation robes

| Date | Mintage | VF20 | XF40 | MS60 | MS63 | MS65 |
|---|---|---|---|---|---|---|
| 2003 | — | — | — | — | 10.00 | 12.00 |

### KM# 1124a CROWN

28.28 g., 0.925 Silver 0.841 oz. ASW, 38.61 mm. **Ruler:** Elizabeth II **Rev:** Elizabeth I in coronation robes

| Date | Mintage | VF20 | XF40 | MS60 | MS63 | MS65 |
|---|---|---|---|---|---|---|
| 2003 | Est. 10000 | PF65 60.00 | | | | |

### KM# 1125 CROWN

28.28 g., Copper-Nickel, 38.61 mm. **Ruler:** Elizabeth II **Rev:** Elizabeth I and Robert Dudley deer hunting

| Date | Mintage | VF20 | XF40 | MS60 | MS63 | MS65 |
|---|---|---|---|---|---|---|
| 2003 | — | — | — | — | 10.00 | 12.00 |

### KM# 1125a CROWN

28.28 g., 0.925 Silver 0.841 oz. ASW, 38.61 mm. **Ruler:** Elizabeth II **Rev:** Elizabeth I and Robert Dudley deer hunting

| Date | Mintage | VF20 | XF40 | MS60 | MS63 | MS65 |
|---|---|---|---|---|---|---|
| 2003 | Est. 10000 | PF65 60.00 | | | | |

### KM# 1126 CROWN

Copper-Nickel **Ruler:** Elizabeth II **Rev:** Address to the British forces in Tilbury to ward off the Spanish Armada

| Date | Mintage | VF20 | XF40 | MS60 | MS63 | MS65 |
|---|---|---|---|---|---|---|
| 2003 | — | — | — | — | 10.00 | 12.00 |

### KM# 1126a CROWN

28.28 g., 0.925 Silver 0.841 oz. ASW **Ruler:** Elizabeth II **Rev:** Address to the British forces in Tilbury to ward off the Spanish Armada

| Date | Mintage | VF20 | XF40 | MS60 | MS63 | MS65 |
|---|---|---|---|---|---|---|
| 2003 | Est. 10000 | PF65 60.00 | | | | |

### KM# 1127 CROWN

28.28 g., Copper-Nickel, 38.61 mm. **Ruler:** Elizabeth II **Rev:** Royal coin design

| Date | Mintage | VF20 | XF40 | MS60 | MS63 | MS65 |
|---|---|---|---|---|---|---|
| 2003 | — | — | — | — | 10.00 | 12.00 |

### KM# 1127a CROWN

28.28 g., 0.925 Silver 0.841 oz. ASW, 38.61 mm. **Ruler:** Elizabeth II **Rev:** Royal coin design

| Date | Mintage | VF20 | XF40 | MS60 | MS63 | MS65 |
|---|---|---|---|---|---|---|
| 2003 | — | PF65 60.00 | | | | |

### KM# 1128 CROWN

28.28 g., Copper-Nickel, 38.61 mm. **Ruler:** Elizabeth II **Rev:** Coat of Arms

| Date | Mintage | VF20 | XF40 | MS60 | MS63 | MS65 |
|---|---|---|---|---|---|---|
| 2003 | — | — | — | — | 10.00 | 12.00 |

### KM# 1128a CROWN

28.28 g., 0.925 Silver 0.841 oz. ASW, 38.61 mm. **Ruler:** Elizabeth II **Rev:** Coat of Arms

| Date | Mintage | VF20 | XF40 | MS60 | MS63 | MS65 |
|---|---|---|---|---|---|---|
| 2003 | Est. 10000 | PF65 60.00 | | | | |

### KM# 1129 CROWN

400.000 Silver 0.999, 75 mm. **Ruler:** Elizabeth II **Rev:** Pillars of Hercules and the Spanish Armada

| Date | Mintage | VF20 | XF40 | MS60 | MS63 | MS65 |
|---|---|---|---|---|---|---|
| 2003 | Est. 1000 | PF63 850 | | | | |
| 2003 | Est. 1000 | PF65 850 | | | | |

### KM# 1094 CROWN

28.28 g., Copper-Nickel, 38.6 mm. **Ruler:** Elizabeth II **Rev:** Battleship Bismark under fire, colored poppy below

| Date | Mintage | VF20 | XF40 | MS60 | MS63 | MS65 |
|---|---|---|---|---|---|---|
| 2004 | — | — | — | — | 10.00 | 12.00 |

### KM# 1140 CROWN

28.28 g., Copper-Nickel, 38.61 mm. **Ruler:** Elizabeth II **Rev:** Two children with Union Jack and Gibraltar flag

| Date | Mintage | VF20 | XF40 | MS60 | MS63 | MS65 |
|---|---|---|---|---|---|---|
| 2004 | — | — | — | — | 10.00 | 12.00 |

### KM# 1143 CROWN

28.28 g., Copper-Nickel, 38.61 mm. **Ruler:** Elizabeth II **Rev:** Normandy landing, bluffs in color

| Date | Mintage | VF20 | XF40 | MS60 | MS63 | MS65 |
|---|---|---|---|---|---|---|
| 2004 | — | — | — | — | 10.00 | 12.00 |

### KM# 1144 CROWN

28.28 g., Copper-Nickel, 38.61 mm. **Ruler:** Elizabeth II **Rev:** Battle for Pegasus Bridge in Normandy

| Date | Mintage | VF20 | XF40 | MS60 | MS63 | MS65 |
|---|---|---|---|---|---|---|
| 2004 | — | — | — | — | 10.00 | 12.00 |

### KM# 1145 CROWN

28.28 g., Copper-Nickel, 38.61 mm. **Ruler:** Elizabeth II **Rev:** Construction of the Mulberry ports at Normandy

| Date | Mintage | VF20 | XF40 | MS60 | MS63 | MS65 |
|---|---|---|---|---|---|---|
| 2004 | — | — | — | — | 10.00 | 12.00 |

### KM# 1146 CROWN

28.28 g., Copper-Nickel, 38.61 mm. **Ruler:** Elizabeth II **Rev:** Winston Churchill raises V sign in front of 10 Downing Street

| Date | Mintage | VF20 | XF40 | MS60 | MS63 | MS65 |
|---|---|---|---|---|---|---|
| 2004 | — | — | — | — | 10.00 | 12.00 |

### KM# 1147 CROWN

28.28 g., Copper-Nickel, 38.61 mm. **Ruler:** Elizabeth II **Subject:** Battle of Britain, 1940

| Date | Mintage | VF20 | XF40 | MS60 | MS63 | MS65 |
|---|---|---|---|---|---|---|
| 2004 | — | — | — | — | 10.00 | 12.00 |

### KM# 1148 CROWN

28.28 g., Copper-Nickel, 38.61 mm. **Ruler:** Elizabeth II **Subject:** Battle of El Alamein, 1942

| Date | Mintage | VF20 | XF40 | MS60 | MS63 | MS65 |
|---|---|---|---|---|---|---|
| 2004 | — | — | — | — | 10.00 | 12.00 |
| 2004 | — | — | — | — | 10.00 | 12.00 |

### KM# 1149 CROWN

28.28 g., Copper-Nickel, 38.61 mm. **Ruler:** Elizabeth II **Subject:** Allied troops in Gibraltar for invasion of North Africa (Operation Torch), 1942

| Date | Mintage | VF20 | XF40 | MS60 | MS63 | MS65 |
|---|---|---|---|---|---|---|
| 2004 | — | — | — | — | 10.00 | 12.00 |

### KM# 1150 CROWN

28.28 g., Copper-Nickel, 38.61 mm. **Ruler:** Elizabeth II **Subject:** Battle of Stalingrad, 1942

| Date | Mintage | VF20 | XF40 | MS60 | MS63 | MS65 |
|---|---|---|---|---|---|---|
| 2004 | — | — | — | — | 10.00 | 12.00 |

### KM# 1151 CROWN

28.28 g., Copper-Nickel, 38.61 mm. **Ruler:** Elizabeth II **Subject:** Norwegian sabotage of the Hard Water plant, 1943

| Date | Mintage | VF20 | XF40 | MS60 | MS63 | MS65 |
|---|---|---|---|---|---|---|
| 2004 | — | — | — | — | 10.00 | 12.00 |

### KM# 1152 CROWN

28.28 g., Copper-Nickel, 38.61 mm. **Ruler:** Elizabeth II **Subject:** Arc battle at Kirsk

| Date | Mintage | VF20 | XF40 | MS60 | MS63 | MS65 |
|---|---|---|---|---|---|---|
| 2004 | — | — | — | — | 10.00 | 12.00 |
| 2004 | — | — | — | — | 10.00 | 12.00 |

### KM# 1153 CROWN

28.28 g., Copper-Nickel, 38.61 mm. **Ruler:** Elizabeth II **Subject:** Ruhr river dam busting roller bombs, 1943

| Date | Mintage | VF20 | XF40 | MS60 | MS63 | MS65 |
|---|---|---|---|---|---|---|
| 2005 | — | — | — | — | 10.00 | 12.00 |

**KM# 1154 CROWN**
28.28 g., Copper-Nickel, 38.61 mm. **Ruler:** Elizabeth II **Subject:** Burma Campaign, 1943

| Date | Mintage | VF20 | XF40 | MS60 | MS63 | MS65 |
|---|---|---|---|---|---|---|
| 2005 | — | — | — | — | 10.00 | 12.00 |

**KM# 1155 CROWN**
28.28 g., Copper-Nickel, 38.61 mm. **Ruler:** Elizabeth II **Subject:** Liberation of Paris, 1944

| Date | Mintage | VF20 | XF40 | MS60 | MS63 | MS65 |
|---|---|---|---|---|---|---|
| 2005 | — | — | — | — | 10.00 | 12.00 |

**KM# 1075 CROWN**
28.28 g., Copper-Nickel, 38.6 mm. **Ruler:** Elizabeth II **Subject:** Trafalgar - First Shot **Rev:** Naval battle scene

| Date | Mintage | VF20 | XF40 | MS60 | MS63 | MS65 |
|---|---|---|---|---|---|---|
| 2005 | — | — | — | — | 10.00 | 12.00 |

**KM# 1076 CROWN**
28.28 g., Copper-Nickel, 38.6 mm. **Ruler:** Elizabeth II **Subject:** Trafalgar - Breaking the line **Rev:** Naval battle

| Date | Mintage | VF20 | XF40 | MS60 | MS63 | MS65 |
|---|---|---|---|---|---|---|
| 2005 | — | — | — | — | 10.00 | 12.00 |

**KM# 1077 CROWN**
28.28 g., Copper-Nickel, 38.6 mm. **Ruler:** Elizabeth II **Subject:** Trafalgar - Hardy **Rev:** Bust facing

| Date | Mintage | VF20 | XF40 | MS60 | MS63 | MS65 |
|---|---|---|---|---|---|---|
| 2005 | — | — | — | — | 10.00 | 12.00 |

**KM# 1078 CROWN**
28.28 g., Copper-Nickel, 38.6 mm. **Ruler:** Elizabeth II **Subject:** Trafalgar - Nelson **Rev:** Bust facing

| Date | Mintage | VF20 | XF40 | MS60 | MS63 | MS65 |
|---|---|---|---|---|---|---|
| 2005 | — | — | — | — | 10.00 | 12.00 |

**KM# 1156 CROWN**
28.28 g., Copper-Nickel, 38.61 mm. **Ruler:** Elizabeth II **Subject:** Yalta Conference, 1945

| Date | Mintage | VF20 | XF40 | MS60 | MS63 | MS65 |
|---|---|---|---|---|---|---|
| 2005 | — | — | — | — | 10.00 | 12.00 |

**KM# 1157 CROWN**
28.28 g., Copper-Nickel, 38.61 mm. **Ruler:** Elizabeth II **Rev:** Red Army soldier with flag on the Reichstag building in Berlin, 1945

| Date | Mintage | VF20 | XF40 | MS60 | MS63 | MS65 |
|---|---|---|---|---|---|---|
| 2005 | — | — | — | — | 10.00 | 12.00 |

**KM# 1158 CROWN**
28.28 g., Copper-Nickel, 38.61 mm. **Ruler:** Elizabeth II **Subject:** Winston Churchill at St. Paul's Cathedral War's end service

| Date | Mintage | VF20 | XF40 | MS60 | MS63 | MS65 |
|---|---|---|---|---|---|---|
| 2005 | — | — | — | — | 10.00 | 12.00 |

**KM# 1208 CROWN**
28.28 g., Copper-Nickel, 38.61 mm. **Ruler:** Elizabeth II **Subject:** Trafalgar, 200th Anniversary **Rev:** H.M.S. Victory

| Date | Mintage | VF20 | XF40 | MS60 | MS63 | MS65 |
|---|---|---|---|---|---|---|
| 2005 | — | — | — | — | 7.50 | 9.00 |

**KM# 1209 CROWN**
28.28 g., Copper-Nickel, 38.61 mm. **Ruler:** Elizabeth II **Subject:** Trafalgar, 200th Anniversary **Rev:** Vice-Admiral Cuthbert Collinswood

| Date | Mintage | VF20 | XF40 | MS60 | MS63 | MS65 |
|---|---|---|---|---|---|---|
| 2005 | — | — | — | — | 7.50 | 9.00 |

**KM# 1210 CROWN**
28.28 g., Copper-Nickel, 38.61 mm. **Ruler:** Elizabeth II **Subject:** Battle of Trafalgar, 200th Anniversary **Rev:** Vice-Admiral Pierre de Villeneuve

| Date | Mintage | VF20 | XF40 | MS60 | MS63 | MS65 |
|---|---|---|---|---|---|---|
| 2005 | — | — | — | — | 7.50 | 9.00 |

**KM# 1213 CROWN**
28.28 g., Copper-Nickel, 38.61 mm. **Ruler:** Elizabeth II **Subject:** Battle of Trafalgar, 200th Anniversary **Rev:** Nelson's battle plan

| Date | Mintage | VF20 | XF40 | MS60 | MS63 | MS65 |
|---|---|---|---|---|---|---|
| 2005 | — | — | — | — | 7.50 | 9.00 |

**KM# 1214 CROWN**
28.28 g., Copper-Nickel, 38.61 mm. **Ruler:** Elizabeth II **Subject:** Battle of Trafalgar, 200th Anniversary **Rev:** Tracking of the opponent

| Date | Mintage | VF20 | XF40 | MS60 | MS63 | MS65 |
|---|---|---|---|---|---|---|
| 2005 | — | — | — | — | 7.50 | 9.00 |

**KM# 1215 CROWN**
28.28 g., Copper-Nickel, 38.61 mm. **Ruler:** Elizabeth II **Subject:** Battle of Trafalgar, 200th Anniversary **Rev:** Death of Horatio Nelson

| Date | Mintage | VF20 | XF40 | MS60 | MS63 | MS65 |
|---|---|---|---|---|---|---|
| 2005 | — | — | — | — | 7.50 | 9.00 |

**KM# 1216 CROWN**
28.28 g., Copper-Nickel, 38.61 mm. **Ruler:** Elizabeth II **Subject:** Battle of Trafalgar, 200th Anniversary **Rev:** Signal flags

| Date | Mintage | VF20 | XF40 | MS60 | MS63 | MS65 |
|---|---|---|---|---|---|---|
| 2005 | — | — | — | — | 7.50 | 9.00 |

**KM# 1217 CROWN**
28.28 g., Copper-Nickel, 38.61 mm. **Ruler:** Elizabeth II **Subject:** Battle of Trafalgar, 200th Anniversary **Rev:** Funeral procession for Horatio Nelson

| Date | Mintage | VF20 | XF40 | MS60 | MS63 | MS65 |
|---|---|---|---|---|---|---|
| 2005 | — | — | — | — | 7.50 | 9.00 |

**KM# 1218 CROWN**
28.28 g., Copper-Nickel, 38.61 mm. **Ruler:** Elizabeth II **Subject:** Battle of Trafalgar, 200th Anniversary **Rev:** Nelson's column in Trafalgar Square, London

| Date | Mintage | VF20 | XF40 | MS60 | MS63 | MS65 |
|---|---|---|---|---|---|---|
| 2005 | — | — | — | — | 7.50 | 9.00 |

**KM# 1219 CROWN**
28.28 g., Copper-Nickel, 38.61 mm. **Ruler:** Elizabeth II **Subject:** Battle of Trafalgar, 200th Anniversary **Rev:** Nelson as young Captain

| Date | Mintage | VF20 | XF40 | MS60 | MS63 | MS65 |
|---|---|---|---|---|---|---|
| 2005 | — | — | — | — | 7.50 | 9.00 |

**KM# 1220 CROWN**
28.28 g., Copper-Nickel, 38.61 mm. **Ruler:** Elizabeth II **Subject:** Battle of Trafalgar, 200th Anniversary **Rev:** Nelson at work desk

| Date | Mintage | VF20 | XF40 | MS60 | MS63 | MS65 |
|---|---|---|---|---|---|---|
| 2005 | — | — | — | — | 7.50 | 9.00 |

**KM# 1221 CROWN**
28.28 g., Copper-Nickel, 38.61 mm. **Ruler:** Elizabeth II **Subject:** Battle of Trafalgar, 200th Anniversary **Rev:** H.M.S. Victory being towed to Gibraltar

| Date | Mintage | VF20 | XF40 | MS60 | MS63 | MS65 |
|---|---|---|---|---|---|---|
| 2005 | — | — | — | — | 7.50 | 9.00 |

**KM# 1222 CROWN**
28.28 g., Copper-Nickel, 38.61 mm. **Ruler:** Elizabeth II **Subject:** Battle of Trafalgar, 200th Anniversary **Rev:** Horatio Nelson and Thomas Hardy on board the H.M.S. Victory

| Date | Mintage | VF20 | XF40 | MS60 | MS63 | MS65 |
|---|---|---|---|---|---|---|
| 2005 | — | — | — | — | 7.50 | 9.00 |

**KM# 1223 CROWN**
28.28 g., Copper-Nickel, 38.61 mm. **Ruler:** Elizabeth II **Subject:** Battle of Trafalgar, 200th Anniversary **Rev:** H.M.S. Victory enters the battle

| Date | Mintage | VF20 | XF40 | MS60 | MS63 | MS65 |
|---|---|---|---|---|---|---|
| 2005 | — | — | — | — | 7.50 | 9.00 |

**KM# 1224 CROWN**
28.28 g., Copper-Nickel, 38.61 mm. **Ruler:** Elizabeth II **Subject:** Battle of Trafalgar, 200th Anniversary **Rev:** H.M.S. Agamemnon before Corsica at the Siege of Calvi (West Indies)

| Date | Mintage | VF20 | XF40 | MS60 | MS63 | MS65 |
|---|---|---|---|---|---|---|
| 2005 | — | — | — | — | 7.50 | 9.00 |

**KM# 1225 CROWN**
28.28 g., Copper-Nickel, 38.61 mm. **Ruler:** Elizabeth II **Subject:** Battle of Trafalgar, 200th Anniversary **Rev:** Naval battle at Cape St. Vincent

| Date | Mintage | VF20 | XF40 | MS60 | MS63 | MS65 |
|---|---|---|---|---|---|---|
| 2005 | — | — | — | — | 7.50 | 9.00 |

**KM# 1226 CROWN**
28.28 g., Copper-Nickel **Ruler:** Elizabeth II **Subject:** Battle of Trafalgar, 200th Anniversary **Rev:** Nelson wounded on the right arm at the expedition of Santa Cruz de Tenerife

| Date | Mintage | VF20 | XF40 | MS60 | MS63 | MS65 |
|---|---|---|---|---|---|---|
| 2005 | — | — | — | — | 7.50 | 9.00 |

**KM# 1227 CROWN**
28.28 g., Copper-Nickel, 38.61 mm. **Ruler:** Elizabeth II **Subject:** Battle of Trafalgar, 200th Anniversary **Rev:** Navy battle at the mouth of the Nile at Abukir

| Date | Mintage | VF20 | XF40 | MS60 | MS63 | MS65 |
|---|---|---|---|---|---|---|
| 2005 | — | — | — | — | 7.50 | 9.00 |

**KM# 1251 CROWN**
28.28 g., Copper-Nickel, 38.61 mm. **Ruler:** Elizabeth II **Subject:** Elizabeth II, 79th Birthday **Rev:** Military parade

| Date | Mintage | VF20 | XF40 | MS60 | MS63 | MS65 |
|---|---|---|---|---|---|---|
| 2005 | — | — | — | — | 7.50 | 9.00 |

**KM# 1252 CROWN**
28.28 g., Silver, 38.61 mm. **Ruler:** Elizabeth II **Subject:** Elizabeth II, 79th Birthday **Rev:** Ceremony of the Garter

| Date | Mintage | VF20 | XF40 | MS60 | MS63 | MS65 |
|---|---|---|---|---|---|---|
| 2005 | — | — | — | — | 7.50 | 9.00 |

**KM# 1253 CROWN**
28.28 g., Copper-Nickel, 38.61 mm. **Ruler:** Elizabeth II **Subject:** Elizabeth II, 79th Birthday **Rev:** Opening of Parlament

| Date | Mintage | VF20 | XF40 | MS60 | MS63 | MS65 |
|---|---|---|---|---|---|---|
| 2005 | — | — | — | — | 7.50 | 9.00 |

**KM# 1254 CROWN**
28.28 g., Copper-Nickel, 38.61 mm. **Ruler:** Elizabeth II **Subject:** Elizabeth II, 79th Birthday **Rev:** Investiture, 1953

| Date | Mintage | VF20 | XF40 | MS60 | MS63 | MS65 |
|---|---|---|---|---|---|---|
| 2005 Proof | — | — | — | — | 7.50 | 9.00 |

**KM# 1255 CROWN**
28.28 g., Copper-Nickel, 38.61 mm. **Ruler:** Elizabeth II **Subject:** Elizabeth II, 79th Birthday **Rev:** Maundy Thursday ceremony

| Date | Mintage | VF20 | XF40 | MS60 | MS63 | MS65 |
|---|---|---|---|---|---|---|
| 2005 | — | — | — | — | 7.50 | 9.00 |

**KM# 1256 CROWN**
28.28 g., Copper-Nickel, 38.61 mm. **Ruler:** Elizabeth II **Subject:** Elizabeth II, 79th Birthday **Rev:** In the country

| Date | Mintage | VF20 | XF40 | MS60 | MS63 | MS65 |
|---|---|---|---|---|---|---|
| 2005 | — | — | — | — | 7.50 | 9.00 |

**KM# 1257 CROWN**
28.28 g., Copper-Nickel, 38.61 mm. **Ruler:** Elizabeth II **Subject:** Elizabeth II, 79th Birthday **Rev:** Carnival in the gardens at Buckingham Palace

| Date | Mintage | VF20 | XF40 | MS60 | MS63 | MS65 |
|---|---|---|---|---|---|---|
| 2005 Proof | — | — | — | — | 7.50 | 9.00 |

**KM# 1258 CROWN**
28.28 g., Copper-Nickel, 38.61 mm. **Ruler:** Elizabeth II **Subject:** Elizabeth II, 79th Birthday **Rev:** Chelsea Flower show

| Date | Mintage | VF20 | XF40 | MS60 | MS63 | MS65 |
|---|---|---|---|---|---|---|
| 2005 | — | — | — | — | 7.50 | 9.00 |

**KM# 1259 CROWN**
28.28 g., Copper-Nickel, 38.61 mm. **Ruler:** Elizabeth II **Subject:** Elizabeth II, 79th Birthday **Rev:** Horse races at Ascot

| Date | Mintage | VF20 | XF40 | MS60 | MS63 | MS65 |
|---|---|---|---|---|---|---|
| 2005 | — | — | — | — | 7.50 | 9.00 |

**KM# 1260 CROWN**
28.28 g., Copper-Nickel, 38.61 mm. **Ruler:** Elizabeth II **Subject:** Elizabeth II, 79th Birthday **Rev:** State visit

| Date | Mintage | VF20 | XF40 | MS60 | MS63 | MS65 |
|---|---|---|---|---|---|---|
| 2005 | — | — | — | — | 7.50 | 9.00 |

**KM# 1261 CROWN**
28.28 g., Copper-Nickel, 38.61 mm. **Ruler:** Elizabeth II **Subject:** Elizabeth II, 79th Birthday **Rev:** Memorial Day

| Date | Mintage | VF20 | XF40 | MS60 | MS63 | MS65 |
|---|---|---|---|---|---|---|
| 2005 | — | — | — | — | 7.50 | 9.00 |

**KM# 1262 CROWN**
28.28 g., Copper-Nickel, 38.61 mm. **Ruler:** Elizabeth II **Subject:** Elizabeth II, 79th Birthday **Rev:** Christmas speach

| Date | Mintage | VF20 | XF40 | MS60 | MS63 | MS65 |
|---|---|---|---|---|---|---|
| 2005 | — | — | — | — | 7.50 | 9.00 |

**KM# 1211 CROWN**
28.28 g., Copper-Nickel, 38.61 mm. **Ruler:** Elizabeth II **Subject:** Battle of Trafalgar, 200th Anniversary **Rev:** Napoleon Bonaparte

| Date | Mintage | VF20 | XF40 | MS60 | MS63 | MS65 |
|---|---|---|---|---|---|---|
| 2005 | — | — | — | — | 7.50 | 9.00 |

**KM# 1212 CROWN**
28.28 g., Copper-Nickel, 38.61 mm. **Ruler:** Elizabeth II **Subject:** Battle of Trafalgar, 200th Anniversary **Rev:** Horatio Nelson explaining his battle plan

| Date | Mintage | VF20 | XF40 | MS60 | MS63 | MS65 |
|---|---|---|---|---|---|---|
| 2005 | — | — | — | — | 7.50 | 9.00 |

**KM# 1276 CROWN**
28.28 g., Copper-Nickel, 38.61 mm. **Ruler:** Elizabeth II **Subject:** Elizabeth II, 80th Birthday **Rev:** Older Effigy

| Date | Mintage | VF20 | XF40 | MS60 | MS63 | MS65 |
|---|---|---|---|---|---|---|
| 2006 | — | — | — | — | 7.50 | 9.00 |

**KM# 1277 CROWN**
28.28 g., Copper-Nickel, 38.61 mm. **Ruler:** Elizabeth II **Subject:** Elizabeth II, 80th Birthday **Rev:** Elizabeth II as a child

| Date | Mintage | VF20 | XF40 | MS60 | MS63 | MS65 |
|---|---|---|---|---|---|---|
| 2006 | — | — | — | — | 7.50 | 9.00 |

**KM# 1278 CROWN**
28.28 g., Copper-Nickel, 38.61 mm. **Ruler:** Elizabeth II **Subject:** Elizabeth II, 80th Birthday **Rev:** Elizabeth II as a young lady

| Date | Mintage | VF20 | XF40 | MS60 | MS63 | MS65 |
|---|---|---|---|---|---|---|
| 2006 | — | — | — | — | 7.50 | 9.00 |

**KM# 1279 CROWN**
28.28 g., Copper-Nickel, 38.61 mm. **Ruler:** Elizabeth II **Subject:** Elizabeth II, 80th Birthday **Rev:** Elizabeth II and grandchildren

| Date | Mintage | VF20 | XF40 | MS60 | MS63 | MS65 |
|---|---|---|---|---|---|---|
| 2006 | — | — | — | — | 7.50 | 9.00 |

**KM# 1280 CROWN**
28.28 g., Copper-Nickel, 38.61 mm. **Ruler:** Elizabeth II **Subject:** Elizabeth II, 80th Birthday **Rev:** Four portraits

| Date | Mintage | VF20 | XF40 | MS60 | MS63 | MS65 |
|---|---|---|---|---|---|---|
| 2006 | Est. 50000 | **PF65** 12.50 | | | | |

**KM# 1289 CROWN**
28.28 g., Copper-Nickel, 38.61 mm. **Ruler:** Elizabeth II **Subject:** Elizabeth II, 80th Birthday **Rev:** Baptism

| Date | Mintage | VF20 | XF40 | MS60 | MS63 | MS65 |
|---|---|---|---|---|---|---|
| 2006 | — | — | — | — | 7.50 | 9.00 |

**KM# 1290 CROWN**
28.28 g., Copper-Nickel, 38.61 mm. **Ruler:** Elizabeth II **Subject:** Elizabeth II, 80th Birthday **Rev:** Radio address

| Date | Mintage | VF20 | XF40 | MS60 | MS63 | MS65 |
|---|---|---|---|---|---|---|
| 2006 | — | — | — | — | 7.50 | 9.00 |

**KM# 1291 CROWN**
28.28 g., Copper-Nickel, 38.61 mm. **Ruler:** Elizabeth II **Subject:** Elizabeth II, 80th Birthday **Rev:** Coronation

| Date | Mintage | VF20 | XF40 | MS60 | MS63 | MS65 |
|---|---|---|---|---|---|---|
| 2006 | — | — | — | — | 7.50 | 9.00 |

**KM# 1292 CROWN**
28.28 g., Copper-Nickel, 38.61 mm. **Ruler:** Elizabeth II **Subject:** Elizabeth II, 80th Birthday **Rev:** Royal family

| Date | Mintage | VF20 | XF40 | MS60 | MS63 | MS65 |
|---|---|---|---|---|---|---|
| 2006 | — | — | — | — | 7.50 | 9.00 |

**KM# 1293 CROWN**
28.28 g., (No Composition), 38.61 mm. **Ruler:** Elizabeth II **Subject:** Elizabeth II, 80th Birthday **Rev:** Investiture of Charles as Prince of Wales

| Date | Mintage | VF20 | XF40 | MS60 | MS63 | MS65 |
|---|---|---|---|---|---|---|
| 2006 | — | — | — | — | 7.50 | 9.00 |

**KM# 1294 CROWN**
28.28 g., Copper-Nickel, 38.61 mm. **Ruler:** Elizabeth II **Subject:** Elizabeth II, 80th Birthday **Rev:** Princes William and Harry

| Date | Mintage | VF20 | XF40 | MS60 | MS63 | MS65 |
|---|---|---|---|---|---|---|
| 2006 | — | — | — | — | 7.50 | 9.00 |

**KM# 1295 CROWN**
28.28 g., Copper-Nickel, 38.61 mm. **Ruler:** Elizabeth II **Subject:** Elizabeth II, 80th Birthday **Rev:** Military parade

| Date | Mintage | VF20 | XF40 | MS60 | MS63 | MS65 |
|---|---|---|---|---|---|---|
| 2006 | — | — | — | — | 7.50 | 9.00 |

**KM# 1296 CROWN**
28.28 g., Copper-Nickel, 38.61 mm. **Ruler:** Elizabeth II **Subject:** Elizabeth II, 80th Birthday **Rev:** Coronation Jubilee

| Date | Mintage | VF20 | XF40 | MS60 | MS63 | MS65 |
|---|---|---|---|---|---|---|
| 2006 | — | — | — | — | 7.50 | 9.00 |

**KM# 1305 CROWN**
28.28 g., Copper-Nickel, 38.61 mm. **Ruler:** Elizabeth II **Subject:** 1966 World Cup, England as Champions, 40th Anniversary **Rev:** Bobby Moore and the trophy

| Date | Mintage | VF20 | XF40 | MS60 | MS63 | MS65 |
|---|---|---|---|---|---|---|
| 2006 | — | — | — | — | 7.50 | 9.00 |

**KM# 1331 CROWN**
28.28 g., Copper-Nickel, 38.61 mm. **Ruler:** Elizabeth II **Subject:** Elizabeth and Philip, 60th Wedding Anniversary **Rev:** Elizabeth and Philip busts

| Date | Mintage | VF20 | XF40 | MS60 | MS63 | MS65 |
|---|---|---|---|---|---|---|
| 2007 | — | — | — | — | 7.50 | 9.00 |

**KM# 1332 CROWN**
28.28 g., Copper-Nickel, 38.61 mm. **Ruler:** Elizabeth II **Subject:** Elizabeth and Philip, 60th Wedding Anniversary **Rev:** Wedding portrait

| Date | Mintage | VF20 | XF40 | MS60 | MS63 | MS65 |
|---|---|---|---|---|---|---|
| 2007 | — | — | — | — | 7.50 | 9.00 |

**KM# 1333 CROWN**
28.28 g., Copper-Nickel, 38.61 mm. **Ruler:** Elizabeth II **Subject:** Elizabeth and Philip, 60th Wedding Anniversary **Rev:** State coach

| Date | Mintage | VF20 | XF40 | MS60 | MS63 | MS65 |
|---|---|---|---|---|---|---|
| 2007 | — | — | — | — | 7.50 | 9.00 |

**KM# 1334 CROWN**
28.28 g., Copper-Nickel, 38.61 mm. **Ruler:** Elizabeth II **Subject:** Elizabeth and Philip, 60th Wedding Anniversary **Rev:** Westminster Abbey

| Date | Mintage | VF20 | XF40 | MS60 | MS63 | MS65 |
|---|---|---|---|---|---|---|
| 2007 | — | — | — | — | 7.50 | 9.00 |

**KM# 1337 CROWN**
7.98 g., 0.9167 Gold 0.2352 oz. AGW **Ruler:** Elizabeth II **Subject:** Elizabeth and Philip, 60th Wedding Anniversary **Rev:** State coach

| Date | Mintage | VF20 | XF40 | MS60 | MS63 | MS65 |
|---|---|---|---|---|---|---|
| 2007 | Est. 250 | **PF65** 450 | | | | |

**KM# 1338 CROWN**
7.98 g., 0.9167 Gold 0.2352 oz. AGW **Ruler:** Elizabeth II **Subject:** Elizabeth and Philip, 60th Wedding Anniversary **Rev:** Westminster Abbey

| Date | Mintage | VF20 | XF40 | MS60 | MS63 | MS65 |
|---|---|---|---|---|---|---|
| 2007 | Est. 250 | **PF65** 450 | | | | |

**KM# 1350 CROWN**
28.28 g., Copper-Nickel, 38.61 mm. **Ruler:** Elizabeth II **Subject:** Battle of Britain Memorial Flight, 50th Anniversary **Rev:** Spitfire

| Date | Mintage | VF20 | XF40 | MS60 | MS63 | MS65 |
|---|---|---|---|---|---|---|
| 2007 | — | — | — | — | 7.50 | 9.00 |
| 2007 | — | — | — | — | 7.50 | 9.00 |

**KM# 1351 CROWN**
28.28 g., Copper-Nickel, 38.61 mm. **Ruler:** Elizabeth II **Subject:** Battle of Britain Memorial Flight **Rev:** Hawker Hurricane

| Date | Mintage | VF20 | XF40 | MS60 | MS63 | MS65 |
|---|---|---|---|---|---|---|
| 2007 | — | — | — | — | 7.50 | 9.00 |

**KM# 1352 CROWN**
28.28 g., Copper-Nickel, 38.61 mm. **Ruler:** Elizabeth II **Subject:** Battle of Britain Memorial Flight **Rev:** Avro Lancaster

| Date | Mintage | VF20 | XF40 | MS60 | MS63 | MS65 |
|---|---|---|---|---|---|---|
| 2007 | — | — | — | — | 7.50 | 9.00 |
| 2007 | — | — | — | — | 7.50 | 9.00 |

**KM# 1353 CROWN**
28.28 g., Copper-Nickel, 38.61 mm. **Ruler:** Elizabeth II **Subject:** Battle of Britain Memorial Flight **Rev:** Dakota C-47

| Date | Mintage | VF20 | XF40 | MS60 | MS63 | MS65 |
|---|---|---|---|---|---|---|
| 2007 | — | — | — | — | 7.50 | 9.00 |

**KM# 1354 CROWN**
28.28 g., Copper-Nickel, 38.61 mm. **Ruler:** Elizabeth II **Subject:** Battle of Britain Memorial Flight **Rev:** DHC 1 Chipmunk

| Date | Mintage | VF20 | XF40 | MS60 | MS63 | MS65 |
|---|---|---|---|---|---|---|
| 2007 | — | — | — | — | 7.50 | 9.00 |

**KM# 1355 CROWN**
28.28 g., Copper-Nickel, 38.61 mm. **Ruler:** Elizabeth II **Subject:** Battle of Britain Memorial Flight **Rev:** Air show

| Date | Mintage | VF20 | XF40 | MS60 | MS63 | MS65 |
|---|---|---|---|---|---|---|
| 2007 | — | — | — | — | 7.50 | 9.00 |

**KM# 1355a CROWN**
28.28 g., Silver Plated Copper-Nickel, 38.61 mm. **Ruler:** Elizabeth II **Subject:** Battle of Britain Memorial Flight **Rev:** Air show

| Date | Mintage | VF20 | XF40 | MS60 | MS63 | MS65 |
|---|---|---|---|---|---|---|
| 2007 | Est. 50000 | **PF65** 12.50 | | | | |

**KM# 1322 CROWN**
28.28 g., Copper-Nickel, 38.61 mm. **Ruler:** Elizabeth II **Subject:** Royal Air Force, 90th Anniversary **Rev:** Bristol Beaufighter

| Date | Mintage | VF20 | XF40 | MS60 | MS63 | MS65 |
|---|---|---|---|---|---|---|
| 2008 | — | — | — | — | 7.50 | 9.00 |

**KM# 1361 CROWN**
28.28 g., Copper-Nickel, 38.61 mm. **Ruler:** Elizabeth II **Subject:** Royal Air Force, 90th Anniversary **Rev:** Hawker Hart

| Date | Mintage | VF20 | XF40 | MS60 | MS63 | MS65 |
|---|---|---|---|---|---|---|
| 2008 | — | — | — | — | 7.50 | 9.00 |

**KM# 1362 CROWN**
28.28 g., Copper-Nickel, 38.61 mm. **Ruler:** Elizabeth II **Subject:** Royal Air Force, 90th Anniversary **Rev:** Euro fighter Typhoon

| Date | Mintage | VF20 | XF40 | MS60 | MS63 | MS65 |
|---|---|---|---|---|---|---|
| 2008 | — | — | — | — | 7.50 | 9.00 |
| 2008 | — | **PF65** 60.00 | | | | |

**KM# 1363 CROWN**
28.28 g., Copper-Nickel, 38.61 mm. **Ruler:** Elizabeth II **Subject:** Royal Air Force, 90th Anniversary **Rev:** English Electric Canberra

| Date | Mintage | VF20 | XF40 | MS60 | MS63 | MS65 |
|---|---|---|---|---|---|---|
| 2008 | — | — | — | — | 7.50 | 9.00 |
| 2008 | — | **PF65** 60.00 | | | | |

**KM# 1364 CROWN**
28.28 g., Copper-Nickel, 38.61 mm. **Ruler:** Elizabeth II **Subject:** Royal Air Force, 90th Anniversary **Rev:** Bristol Beaufighter

| Date | Mintage | VF20 | XF40 | MS60 | MS63 | MS65 |
|---|---|---|---|---|---|---|
| 2008 | — | — | — | — | 7.50 | 9.00 |

**KM# 1365 CROWN**
28.28 g., Copper-Nickel, 38.61 mm. **Ruler:** Elizabeth II **Subject:** Royal Air Force, 90th Anniversary **Rev:** Vickers VC 10

| Date | Mintage | VF20 | XF40 | MS60 | MS63 | MS65 |
|---|---|---|---|---|---|---|
| 2008 | — | — | — | — | 7.50 | 9.00 |
| 2008 | — | **PF65** 60.00 | | | | |

**KM# 1366 CROWN**
28.28 g., Copper-Nickel, 38.61 mm. **Ruler:** Elizabeth II **Subject:** Royal Air Force, 90th Anniversary **Rev:** Boeing C 47 Chinook helicopter

| Date | Mintage | VF20 | XF40 | MS60 | MS63 | MS65 |
|---|---|---|---|---|---|---|
| 2008 | — | — | — | — | 7.50 | 9.00 |
| 2008 | — | — | — | — | 7.50 | 9.00 |

**KM# 1367 CROWN**
28.28 g., Copper-Nickel, 38.61 mm. **Ruler:** Elizabeth II **Subject:** Royal Air Force, 90th Anniversary **Rev:** BAE Harrier GR 3

| Date | Mintage | VF20 | XF40 | MS60 | MS63 | MS65 |
|---|---|---|---|---|---|---|
| 2008 | — | — | — | — | 7.50 | 9.00 |
| 2008 | — | — | — | — | 7.50 | 9.00 |

**KM# 1368 CROWN**
28.28 g., Copper-Nickel, 38.61 mm. **Ruler:** Elizabeth II **Subject:** Royal Air Force, 90th Anniversary **Rev:** Hawker Hunter F 6

| Date | Mintage | VF20 | XF40 | MS60 | MS63 | MS65 |
|---|---|---|---|---|---|---|
| 2008 | — | — | — | — | 7.50 | 9.00 |

**KM# 1369 CROWN**
28.28 g., Copper-Nickel, 38.61 mm. **Ruler:** Elizabeth II **Subject:** Royal Air Force, 90th Anniversary **Rev:** Airco DH9

| Date | Mintage | VF20 | XF40 | MS60 | MS63 | MS65 |
|---|---|---|---|---|---|---|
| 2008 | — | — | — | — | 7.50 | 9.00 |
| 2008 | — | — | — | — | 7.50 | 9.00 |

**KM# 1370 CROWN**
28.28 g., Copper-Nickel, 38.61 mm. **Ruler:** Elizabeth II **Subject:** Royal Air Force, 90th Anniversary **Rev:** Westland Lysander

| Date | Mintage | VF20 | XF40 | MS60 | MS63 | MS65 |
|---|---|---|---|---|---|---|
| 2008 | — | — | — | — | 7.50 | 9.00 |
| 2008 | — | — | — | — | 7.50 | 9.00 |

**KM# 1371 CROWN**
28.28 g., Copper-Nickel, 38.61 mm. **Ruler:** Elizabeth II **Subject:** Royal Air Force, 90th Anniversary **Rev:** Avro 504

| Date | Mintage | VF20 | XF40 | MS60 | MS63 | MS65 |
|---|---|---|---|---|---|---|
| 2008 | — | — | — | — | 7.50 | 9.00 |
| 2008 | — | — | — | — | 7.50 | 9.00 |

**KM# 1372 CROWN**
28.28 g., Copper-Nickel, 38.61 mm. **Ruler:** Elizabeth II **Subject:** Royal Air Force, 90th Anniversary **Rev:** English Electric Lightning

| Date | Mintage | VF20 | XF40 | MS60 | MS63 | MS65 |
|---|---|---|---|---|---|---|
| 2008 | — | — | — | — | 7.50 | 9.00 |
| 2008 | — | — | — | — | 7.50 | 9.00 |

**KM# 1373 CROWN**
28.28 g., Copper-Nickel, 38.61 mm. **Ruler:** Elizabeth II **Subject:** Royal Air Force, 90th Anniversary **Rev:** Short Sunderland

| Date | Mintage | VF20 | XF40 | MS60 | MS63 | MS65 |
|---|---|---|---|---|---|---|
| 2008 | — | — | — | — | 7.50 | 9.00 |

**KM# 1374 CROWN**
28.28 g., Copper-Nickel, 38.61 mm. **Ruler:** Elizabeth II **Subject:** Royal Air Force, 90th Anniversary **Rev:** RAF SE 5a

| Date | Mintage | VF20 | XF40 | MS60 | MS63 | MS65 |
|---|---|---|---|---|---|---|
| 2008 | — | — | — | — | 7.50 | 9.00 |

**KM# 1375 CROWN**
28.28 g., Copper-Nickel, 38.61 mm. **Ruler:** Elizabeth II **Subject:** Royal Air Force, 90th Anniversary **Rev:** Hawker Typhoon

| Date | Mintage | VF20 | XF40 | MS60 | MS63 | MS65 |
|---|---|---|---|---|---|---|
| 2008 | — | — | — | — | 7.50 | 9.00 |

**KM# 1376 CROWN**
28.28 g., Copper-Nickel, 38.61 mm. **Ruler:** Elizabeth II **Subject:** Royal Air Force, 90th Anniversary **Rev:** Sepecat Jaguar

| Date | Mintage | VF20 | XF40 | MS60 | MS63 | MS65 |
|---|---|---|---|---|---|---|
| 2008 | — | — | — | — | 7.50 | 9.00 |

**KM# 1377 CROWN**
28.28 g., Copper-Nickel, 38.61 mm. **Ruler:** Elizabeth II **Subject:** Royal Air Force, 90th Anniversary **Rev:** Vickers Vimy

| Date | Mintage | VF20 | XF40 | MS60 | MS63 | MS65 |
|---|---|---|---|---|---|---|
| 2008 | — | — | — | — | 7.50 | 9.00 |

**KM# 1378 CROWN**
28.28 g., Copper-Nickel, 38.61 mm. **Ruler:** Elizabeth II **Subject:** Royal Air Force, 90th Anniversary **Rev:** De Havilland Mosquito

| Date | Mintage | VF20 | XF40 | MS60 | MS63 | MS65 |
|---|---|---|---|---|---|---|
| 2008 | — | — | — | — | 7.50 | 9.00 |

**KM# 1397 CROWN**
28.28 g., Copper-Nickel, 38.61 mm. **Ruler:** Elizabeth II **Subject:** End of WWI, 90th Anniversary **Rev:** British soldiers

| Date | Mintage | VF20 | XF40 | MS60 | MS63 | MS65 |
|---|---|---|---|---|---|---|
| 2008 | — | — | — | — | 7.50 | — |

**KM# 1398 CROWN**
28.28 g., Copper-Nickel, 38.61 mm. **Ruler:** Elizabeth II **Subject:** End of WWI, 90th Anniversary **Rev:** Sopwith Camel biplane and British tank

| Date | Mintage | VF20 | XF40 | MS60 | MS63 | MS65 |
|---|---|---|---|---|---|---|
| 2008 | — | — | — | — | 7.50 | — |

**KM# 1399 CROWN**
28.28 g., Copper-Nickel, 38.61 mm. **Ruler:** Elizabeth II **Subject:** End of WWI, 90th Anniversary **Rev:** Truce

| Date | Mintage | VF20 | XF40 | MS60 | MS63 | MS65 |
|---|---|---|---|---|---|---|
| 2008 | — | — | — | — | 7.50 | — |

**KM# 1400 CROWN**
28.28 g., Copper-Nickel, 38.61 mm. **Ruler:** Elizabeth II **Subject:** End of WWI, 90th Anniversary **Rev:** Menin Gate memorial

| Date | Mintage | VF20 | XF40 | MS60 | MS63 | MS65 |
|---|---|---|---|---|---|---|
| 2008 | — | — | — | — | 7.50 | — |

**KM# 1401 CROWN**
28.28 g., Copper-Nickel, 38.61 mm. **Ruler:** Elizabeth II **Subject:** End of WWI, 90th Anniversary **Rev:** War graves

| Date | Mintage | VF20 | XF40 | MS60 | MS63 | MS65 |
|---|---|---|---|---|---|---|
| 2008 | — | — | — | — | 7.50 | — |

**KM# 1402 CROWN**
28.28 g., Copper-Nickel, 38.61 mm. **Ruler:** Elizabeth II **Subject:** End of WWI, 90th Anniversary **Rev:** Poppies on the Battlefield at the Somme

| Date | Mintage | VF20 | XF40 | MS60 | MS63 | MS65 |
|---|---|---|---|---|---|---|
| 2008 | — | — | — | — | 7.50 | — |

**KM# 1411 CROWN**
28.28 g., Copper-Nickel Silverplated, 38.61 mm. **Ruler:** Elizabeth II **Subject:** British History **Rev:** Elizabeth I and the Spanish Armada

| Date | Mintage | VF20 | XF40 | MS60 | MS63 | MS65 |
|---|---|---|---|---|---|---|
| 2008 | Est. 50000 | PF65 15.00 | | | | |

**KM# 1412 CROWN**
28.28 g., Copper-Nickel Silverplated, 38.61 mm. **Ruler:** Elizabeth II **Subject:** British History **Rev:** Henry VIII and the Mary Rose

| Date | Mintage | VF20 | XF40 | MS60 | MS63 | MS65 |
|---|---|---|---|---|---|---|
| 2009 | Est. 50000 | PF65 15.00 | | | | |

**KM# 1439 CROWN**
28.28 g., Copper-Nickel, 38.61 mm. **Ruler:** Elizabeth II **Subject:** World Explorers **Rev:** Sir Francis Drake and the Golden Hind

| Date | Mintage | VF20 | XF40 | MS60 | MS63 | MS65 |
|---|---|---|---|---|---|---|
| 2009 | — | — | — | — | 7.50 | 9.00 |

**KM# 1440 CROWN**
28.28 g., Copper-Nickel, 38.61 mm. **Ruler:** Elizabeth II **Subject:** World Explorers **Rev:** Ferdinand Magellan and the Victoria

| Date | Mintage | VF20 | XF40 | MS60 | MS63 | MS65 |
|---|---|---|---|---|---|---|
| 2009 | — | — | — | — | 7.50 | — |

**KM# 1441 CROWN**
28.28 g., Silver, 38.61 mm. **Ruler:** Elizabeth II **Subject:** World Explorers **Rev:** Henry Hudson and the Halve Maen

| Date | Mintage | VF20 | XF40 | MS60 | MS63 | MS65 |
|---|---|---|---|---|---|---|
| 2009 | — | — | — | — | 7.50 | — |

**KM# 1442 CROWN**
28.28 g., Copper-Nickel, 38.61 mm. **Ruler:** Elizabeth II **Subject:** World Explorers **Rev:** Sir Ernest Shackleton and the Endurance

| Date | Mintage | VF20 | XF40 | MS60 | MS63 | MS65 |
|---|---|---|---|---|---|---|
| 2009 | — | — | — | — | 7.50 | 9.00 |

**KM# 1443 CROWN**
28.28 g., Copper-Nickel, 38.61 mm. **Ruler:** Elizabeth II **Subject:** World Explorers **Rev:** Abel Janszoon Tasman and sailing ship Heemskerck

| Date | Mintage | VF20 | XF40 | MS60 | MS63 | MS65 |
|---|---|---|---|---|---|---|
| 2009 | — | — | — | — | 7.50 | — |

**KM# 1444 CROWN**
28.28 g., Copper-Nickel, 38.61 mm. **Ruler:** Elizabeth II **Subject:** World Explorers **Rev:** Marco Polo and Venetian galley

| Date | Mintage | VF20 | XF40 | MS60 | MS63 | MS65 |
|---|---|---|---|---|---|---|
| 2009 | — | — | — | — | 7.50 | — |

**KM# 1451 CROWN**
28.28 g., Copper-Nickel, 38.61 mm. **Ruler:** Elizabeth II **Subject:** Navy Aviation **Rev:** Supermarine Scimitar

| Date | Mintage | VF20 | XF40 | MS60 | MS63 | MS65 |
|---|---|---|---|---|---|---|
| 2009 | — | — | — | — | 7.50 | — |

**KM# 1452 CROWN**
28.28 g., Copper-Nickel, 38.61 mm. **Ruler:** Elizabeth II **Subject:** Navy Aviation **Rev:** Sopwith Pup

| Date | Mintage | VF20 | XF40 | MS60 | MS63 | MS65 |
|---|---|---|---|---|---|---|
| 2009 | — | — | — | — | 7.50 | — |

**KM# 1453 CROWN**
28.28 g., Copper-Nickel, 38.61 mm. **Ruler:** Elizabeth II **Subject:** Navy Aviation **Rev:** Fairey Swordfish

| Date | Mintage | VF20 | XF40 | MS60 | MS63 | MS65 |
|---|---|---|---|---|---|---|
| 2009 | — | — | — | — | 7.50 | — |

**KM# 1454 CROWN**
28.28 g., Copper-Nickel, 38.61 mm. **Ruler:** Elizabeth II **Subject:** Navy Aviation **Rev:** Blackburn Dart

| Date | Mintage | VF20 | XF40 | MS60 | MS63 | MS65 |
|---|---|---|---|---|---|---|
| 2009 | — | — | — | — | 7.50 | — |

**KM# 1455 CROWN**
28.28 g., Copper-Nickel, 38.61 mm. **Ruler:** Elizabeth II **Subject:** Navy Aviation **Rev:** BAE Sea Harrier

| Date | Mintage | VF20 | XF40 | MS60 | MS63 | MS65 |
|---|---|---|---|---|---|---|
| 2009 | — | — | — | — | 7.50 | — |

**KM# 1456 CROWN**
28.28 g., Copper-Nickel, 38.61 mm. **Ruler:** Elizabeth II **Subject:** Navy Aviation **Rev:** Chance Vought Corsair

| Date | Mintage | VF20 | XF40 | MS60 | MS63 | MS65 |
|---|---|---|---|---|---|---|
| 2009 | — | — | — | — | 7.50 | — |

**KM# 1457 CROWN**
28.28 g., Copper-Nickel, 38.61 mm. **Ruler:** Elizabeth II **Subject:** Navy Aviation **Rev:** Felixstowe F2A

| Date | Mintage | VF20 | XF40 | MS60 | MS63 | MS65 |
|---|---|---|---|---|---|---|
| 2009 | — | — | — | — | 7.50 | — |

**KM# 1458 CROWN**
28.28 g., Copper-Nickel, 38.61 mm. **Ruler:** Elizabeth II **Subject:** Navy Aviation **Rev:** Blackburn Buccaneer

| Date | Mintage | VF20 | XF40 | MS60 | MS63 | MS65 |
|---|---|---|---|---|---|---|
| 2009 | — | — | — | — | 7.50 | — |

**KM# 1459 CROWN**
28.28 g., Copper-Nickel, 38.61 mm. **Ruler:** Elizabeth II **Subject:** Navy Aviation **Rev:** deHavilland DH 110 Sea Vixen

| Date | Mintage | VF20 | XF40 | MS60 | MS63 | MS65 |
|---|---|---|---|---|---|---|
| 2009 | — | — | — | — | 7.50 | — |

**KM# 1460 CROWN**
28.28 g., Copper-Nickel, 38.61 mm. **Ruler:** Elizabeth II **Subject:** Navy Aviation **Rev:** Hawker Sea Fury

| Date | Mintage | VF20 | XF40 | MS60 | MS63 | MS65 |
|---|---|---|---|---|---|---|
| 2009 | — | — | — | — | 7.50 | — |

**KM# 1461 CROWN**
28.28 g., Copper-Nickel, 38.61 mm. **Ruler:** Elizabeth II **Subject:** Navy Aviation **Rev:** Short 184

| Date | Mintage | VF20 | XF40 | MS60 | MS63 | MS65 |
|---|---|---|---|---|---|---|
| 2009 | — | — | — | — | 7.50 | — |

**KM# 1462 CROWN**
28.28 g., Copper-Nickel, 38.61 mm. **Ruler:** Elizabeth II **Subject:** Navy Aviation **Rev:** Westland Whirlwind

| Date | Mintage | VF20 | XF40 | MS60 | MS63 | MS65 |
|---|---|---|---|---|---|---|
| 2009 | — | — | — | — | 7.50 | — |

**KM# 1477 CROWN**
28.28 g., Copper-Nickel, 38.61 mm. **Ruler:** Elizabeth II **Subject:** Marriage of Prince William and Catherine Middleton

| Date | Mintage | VF20 | XF40 | MS60 | MS63 | MS65 |
|---|---|---|---|---|---|---|
| 2011 Proof | — | — | — | — | 7.50 | 9.00 |

**KM# 1480 CROWN**
28.28 g., Copper-Nickel, 38.61 mm. **Ruler:** Elizabeth II **Subject:** Elizabeth II, 60th Anniversary of reign **Rev:** Elizabeth II young and older heads

| Date | Mintage | VF20 | XF40 | MS60 | MS63 | MS65 |
|---|---|---|---|---|---|---|
| 2012 | — | — | — | — | 7.50 | — |

**KM# 1034 2 CROWN**
41.50 g., Bi-Metallic .999 Silver 11.5g. star shaped center in Copper outer ring, 50 mm. **Ruler:** Elizabeth II **Subject:** Euro's First Anniversary **Obv:** Crowned bust right within star silhouette **Rev:** Europa riding a bull, stars and star silhouette in background **Edge:** Reeded

| Date | Mintage | VF20 | XF40 | MS60 | MS63 | MS65 |
|---|---|---|---|---|---|---|
| 2003 PM | 3,500 | PF63 125 | PF65 145 | | | |

**KM# 1034a 2 CROWN**
50.00 g., Bi-Metallic .9999 Gold 20g star shaped center in Copper outer ring, 50 mm. **Ruler:** Elizabeth II **Subject:** 1st Anniversary - Euro **Obv:** Crowned bust right within star silhouette **Rev:** Europa riding the bull, stars and star silhouette in background **Edge:** Reeded

| Date | Mintage | VF20 | XF40 | MS60 | MS63 | MS65 |
|---|---|---|---|---|---|---|
| 2003 PM | 2,003 | PF65 850 | | | | |

**KM# 1034b 2 CROWN**
56.30 g., Bi-Metallic .9999 Gold 20.8g star shaped center in a .999 Silver 35.5g outer ring, 50 mm. **Ruler:** Elizabeth II **Subject:** 1st Anniversary - Euro **Obv:** Crowned bust right within star silhouette **Rev:** Europa riding the bull, stars and star silhouette in background **Edge:** Reeded

| Date | Mintage | VF20 | XF40 | MS60 | MS63 | MS65 |
|---|---|---|---|---|---|---|
| 2003 PM | 2,003 | PF65 900 | | | | |

**KM# 907 5 CROWN**
Tri-Metallic Center .9995 Platinum 26.9g. Inner Ring .9999 Gold 73.41g. Outer Ring .999 Silver 55.19g, 50 mm. **Ruler:** Elizabeth II **Subject:** 21st Century **Obv:** Crowned bust right, date below **Rev:** Celtic cross, Viking ship and modern technological items **Edge:** Reeded

| Date | Mintage | VF20 | XF40 | MS60 | MS63 | MS65 |
|---|---|---|---|---|---|---|
| 2001 | 199 | PF65 6,500 | | | | |

**KM# 1042 5 CROWN**
155.55 g., 0.999 Silver 4.996 oz. ASW, 65 mm. **Ruler:** Elizabeth II **Subject:** 50th Anniversary of Coronation **Obv:** Queens portrait **Rev:** Buckingham Palace with tiny .01ct ruby, diamond and sapphire inserts above the main entrance **Edge:** Reeded

| Date | Mintage | VF20 | XF40 | MS60 | MS63 | MS65 |
|---|---|---|---|---|---|---|
| 2003 PM | 2,003 | PF63 200 | PF65 225 | | | |

**KM# 1045 32 CROWNS**
1000.00 g., 0.999 Silver 32.1186 oz. ASW **Ruler:** Elizabeth II **Subject:** Beatrix Potter's Peter Rabbit **Obv:** Bust with tiara right **Rev:** Multicolor Peter Rabbit holding carrot, with blue coat and red slippers

| Date | Mintage | VF20 | XF40 | MS60 | MS63 | MS65 |
|---|---|---|---|---|---|---|
| 2003 | 1,000 | PF63 1,000 | PF65 1,100 | | | |

**KM# 1405 5 POUNDS**
28.28 g., 0.925 Silver 0.841 oz. ASW, 38.61 mm. **Ruler:** Elizabeth II **Subject:** End of WWI, 90th Anniversary **Rev:** Truce

| Date | Mintage | VF20 | XF40 | MS60 | MS63 | MS65 |
|---|---|---|---|---|---|---|
| 2008 | Est. 25000 | PF65 60.00 | | | | |

## ROYAL COINAGE

**KM# 896 1/25 ROYAL**
1.24 g., 0.9999 Gold 0.040 oz. AGW, 13.92 mm. **Ruler:** Elizabeth II **Subject:** Bullion **Obv:** Bust with tiara right **Rev:** Two cherubs **Edge:** Reeded

| Date | Mintage | VF20 | XF40 | MS60 | MS63 | MS65 |
|---|---|---|---|---|---|---|
| 2001 | — | — | — | — | — | 75.00 |
| 2001 | 1,000 | PF65 77.50 | | | | |

**KM# 972 1/25 ROYAL**
1.24 g., 0.999 Gold 0.040 oz. AGW, 13.92 mm. **Ruler:** Elizabeth II **Subject:** Cherubs **Obv:** Bust with tiara right **Rev:** Two cherubs shooting arrrows **Edge:** Reeded

| Date | Mintage | VF20 | XF40 | MS60 | MS63 | MS65 |
|---|---|---|---|---|---|---|
| 2002 | — | — | — | — | — | 75.00 |
| 2002 | 1,000 | PF65 77.50 | | | | |

**KM# 1027 1/25 ROYAL**
1.24 g., 0.9999 Gold 0.040 oz. AGW, 13.92 mm. **Ruler:** Elizabeth II **Obv:** Bust with tiara right **Rev:** Cherub with crossed arms **Edge:** Reeded

| Date | Mintage | VF20 | XF40 | MS60 | MS63 | MS65 |
|---|---|---|---|---|---|---|
| 2003 PM | — | PF65 77.50 | | | | |
| 2003 PM | — | — | — | — | — | 75.00 |

**KM# 897 1/10 ROYAL**
3.11 g., 0.9999 Gold 0.100 oz. AGW, 18 mm. **Ruler:** Elizabeth II **Subject:** Bullion **Obv:** Bust with tiara right **Rev:** Two cherubs **Edge:** Reeded

| Date | Mintage | VF20 | XF40 | MS60 | MS63 | MS65 |
|---|---|---|---|---|---|---|
| 2001 | — | — | — | — | — | 175 |
| 2001 | 1,000 | PF65 180 | | | | |

**KM# 973 1/10 ROYAL**
3.11 g., 0.999 Gold 0.0999 oz. AGW, 17.95 mm. **Ruler:** Elizabeth II **Subject:** Cherubs **Obv:** Bust with tiara right **Rev:** Two cherubs shooting arrows **Edge:** Reeded

| Date | Mintage | VF20 | XF40 | MS60 | MS63 | MS65 |
|---|---|---|---|---|---|---|
| 2002 | 1,000 | PF65 180 | | | | |
| 2002 | — | — | — | — | — | 175 |

**KM# 1028 1/10 ROYAL**
3.11 g., 0.9999 Gold 0.100 oz. AGW, 17.95 mm. **Ruler:** Elizabeth II **Obv:** Bust with tiara right **Rev:** Cherub with crossed arms **Edge:** Reeded

| Date | Mintage | VF20 | XF40 | MS60 | MS63 | MS65 |
|---|---|---|---|---|---|---|
| 2003 PM | — | — | — | — | — | 175 |
| 2003 PM | — | PF65 180 | | | | |

**KM# 898 1/5 ROYAL**
6.22 g., 0.999 Gold 0.1998 oz. AGW, 22 mm. **Ruler:** Elizabeth II **Subject:** Bullion **Obv:** Bust with tiara right **Rev:** Two cherubs **Edge:** Reeded

| Date | Mintage | VF20 | XF40 | MS60 | MS63 | MS65 |
|---|---|---|---|---|---|---|
| 2001 | — | — | — | — | — | 350 |
| 2001 | 1,000 | PF65 355 | | | | |

**KM# 974 1/5 ROYAL**
6.22 g., 0.999 Gold 0.1998 oz. AGW, 22 mm. **Ruler:** Elizabeth II **Obv:** Bust with tiara right **Rev:** Two cherubs shooting arrows **Edge:** Reeded

| Date | Mintage | VF20 | XF40 | MS60 | MS63 | MS65 |
|---|---|---|---|---|---|---|
| 2002 | — | — | — | — | — | 350 |
| 2002 | 1,000 | PF65 355 | | | | |

**KM# 1029 1/5 ROYAL**
6.22 g., 0.9999 Gold 0.200 oz. AGW, 22 mm. **Ruler:** Elizabeth II **Obv:** Bust with tiara right **Rev:** Cherub with crossed arms **Edge:** Reeded

| Date | Mintage | VF20 | XF40 | MS60 | MS63 | MS65 |
|---|---|---|---|---|---|---|
| 2003 PM | — | — | — | — | — | 350 |
| 2003 PM | — | PF65 355 | | | | |

**KM# 899 1/2 ROYAL**
15.55 g., 0.9999 Gold 0.4999 oz. AGW, 30 mm. **Ruler:** Elizabeth II **Subject:** Bullion **Obv:** Bust with tiara right **Rev:** Two cherubs **Edge:** Reeded

| Date | Mintage | VF20 | XF40 | MS60 | MS63 | MS65 |
|---|---|---|---|---|---|---|
| 2001 | — | — | — | — | — | 875 |
| 2001 | 1,000 | PF65 880 | | | | |

**KM# 975 1/2 ROYAL**
15.55 g., 0.999 Gold 0.4995 oz. AGW, 30 mm. **Ruler:** Elizabeth II **Obv:** Bust with tiara right **Rev:** Two cherubs shooting arrows **Edge:** Reeded

| Date | Mintage | VF20 | XF40 | MS60 | MS63 | MS65 |
|---|---|---|---|---|---|---|
| 2002 | — | — | — | — | — | 875 |
| 2002 | 1,000 | PF65 880 | | | | |

**KM# 1030 1/2 ROYAL**
15.55 g., 0.9999 Gold 0.4999 oz. AGW, 30 mm. **Ruler:** Elizabeth II **Obv:** Bust with tiara right **Rev:** Cherub with crossed arms **Edge:** Reeded

| Date | Mintage | VF20 | XF40 | MS60 | MS63 | MS65 |
|---|---|---|---|---|---|---|
| 2003 PM | — | — | — | — | — | 875 |
| 2003 PM | — | PF65 880 | | | | |

**KM# 900 ROYAL**
28.28 g., Copper-Nickel, 38.6 mm. **Ruler:** Elizabeth II **Obv:** Bust with tiara right **Rev:** Two cherubs **Edge:** Reeded

| Date | Mintage | VF20 | XF40 | MS60 | MS63 | MS65 |
|---|---|---|---|---|---|---|
| 2001 | — | — | — | — | 10.00 | 12.00 |

**KM# 900a ROYAL**
31.10 g., 0.999 Silver 0.999 oz. ASW **Ruler:** Elizabeth II **Obv:** Bust with tiara right **Rev:** Two cherubs

| Date | Mintage | VF20 | XF40 | MS60 | MS63 | MS65 |
|---|---|---|---|---|---|---|
| 2001 | 10,000 | PF63 45.00 | PF65 47.00 | | | |

**KM# 901 ROYAL**
31.10 g., 0.9999 Gold 0.9999 oz. AGW, 32.7 mm. **Ruler:** Elizabeth II **Subject:** Bullion **Obv:** Bust with tiara right **Rev:** Two cherubs **Edge:** Reeded

| Date | Mintage | VF20 | XF40 | MS60 | MS63 | MS65 |
|---|---|---|---|---|---|---|
| 2001 | — | — | — | — | — | 1,750 |
| 2001 | 1,000 | PF65 1,800 | | | | |

**KM# 976 ROYAL**
28.28 g., Copper-Nickel, 38.6 mm. **Ruler:** Elizabeth II **Obv:** Bust with tiara right **Rev:** Two cherubs shooting arrows **Edge:** Reeded

| Date | Mintage | VF20 | XF40 | MS60 | MS63 | MS65 |
|---|---|---|---|---|---|---|
| 2002 | — | — | — | — | 10.00 | 12.00 |

**KM# 976a ROYAL**
31.10 g., 0.999 Silver 0.999 oz. ASW **Ruler:** Elizabeth II **Obv:** Bust with tiara right **Rev:** Two cherubs shooting arrows **Edge:** Reeded

| Date | Mintage | VF20 | XF40 | MS60 | MS63 | MS65 |
|---|---|---|---|---|---|---|
| 2002 | 1,000 | PF63 45.00 | PF65 47.00 | | | |

**KM# 977 ROYAL**
31.10 g., 0.999 Gold 0.999 oz. AGW, 32.7 mm. **Ruler:** Elizabeth II **Obv:** Bust with tiara right **Rev:** Two cherubs shooting arrows **Edge:** Reeded

| Date | Mintage | VF20 | XF40 | MS60 | MS63 | MS65 |
|---|---|---|---|---|---|---|
| 2002 | — | — | — | — | — | 1,750 |
| 2002 | 1,000 | PF65 1,800 | | | | |

**KM# 1031 ROYAL**
28.28 g., Copper-Nickel, 38.6 mm. **Ruler:** Elizabeth II **Obv:** Bust with tiara right **Rev:** Cherub with crossed arms **Edge:** Reeded

| Date | Mintage | VF20 | XF40 | MS60 | MS63 | MS65 |
|---|---|---|---|---|---|---|
| 2003 PM | — | — | — | — | 10.00 | 12.00 |

**KM# 1032 ROYAL**
31.10 g., 0.9999 Gold 0.9999 oz. AGW, 32.7 mm. **Ruler:** Elizabeth II **Obv:** Bust with tiara right **Rev:** Cherub with crossed arms **Edge:** Reeded

| Date | Mintage | VF20 | XF40 | MS60 | MS63 | MS65 |
|---|---|---|---|---|---|---|
| 2003 PM | — | PF65 1,800 | | | | |
| 2003 PM | — | — | — | — | — | 1,750 |

**KM# 1031a ROYAL**
28.28 g., 0.999 Silver 0.9083 oz. ASW, 38.6 mm. **Ruler:** Elizabeth II **Obv:** Bust with tiara right **Rev:** Cherub with crossed arms **Edge:** Reeded

| Date | Mintage | VF20 | XF40 | MS60 | MS63 | MS65 |
|---|---|---|---|---|---|---|
| 2003 PM | 10,000 | PF63 45.00 | PF65 47.00 | | | |

## PROOF SETS

| KM# | Date | Mintage | Identification | Issue Price | Mkt Val |
|---|---|---|---|---|---|
| PS29 | 2001 (5) | 1,000 | KM#896-899, 901 | — | 3,300 |
| PS30 | 2003 (5) | 1,000 | KM#1027-30, 1032 | — | 3,300 |

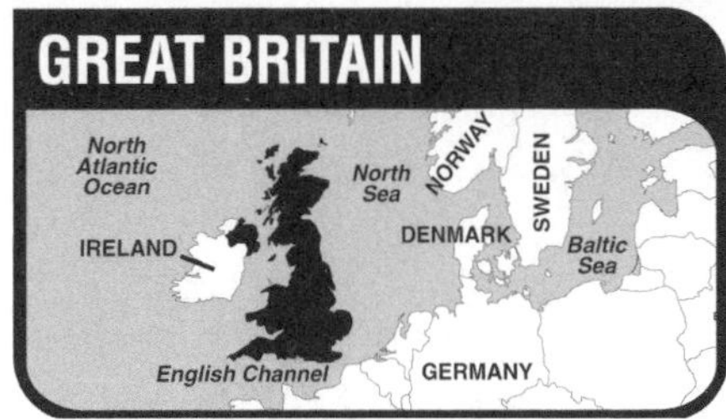


The United Kingdom of Great Britain and Northern Ireland, located off the northwest coast of the European continent, has an area of 94,227 sq. mi. (244,820 sq. km.) and a population of 54 million. Capital: London. The economy is based on industrial activity and trading. Machinery, motor vehicles, chemicals, and textile yarns and fabrics are exported.

By the mid-20th century, most of the territories formerly comprising the British Empire had gained independence, and the empire had evolved into the Commonwealth of Nations, an association of equal and autonomous states, which enjoy special trade interests. The Commonwealth is presently composed of 54 member nations, including the United Kingdom. All recognize the British monarch as head of the Commonwealth. Sixteen continue to recognize the British monarch as Head of State. They are: United Kingdom, Antigua and Barbuda, Australia, Bahamas, Barbados, Belize, Canada, Grenada, Jamaica, New Zealand, Papua New Guinea, St. Christopher & Nevis, Saint Lucia, Saint Vincent and the Grenadines, Solomon Islands, and Tuvalu. Elizabeth II is personally, and separately, the Queen of the sovereign, independent countries just mentioned. There is no other British connection between the several individual, national sovereignties, except that High Commissioners represent them each instead of ambassadors in each other's countries.

**RULERS**
Elizabeth II, 1952--

**MINT MARKS**
H - Heaton
KN - King's Norton

## KINGDOM

### PRE-DECIMAL COINAGE

**KM# 898 PENNY**
0.47 g., 0.925 Silver, 11 mm. **Ruler:** Elizabeth II **Obv:** Laureate bust right **Rev:** Crowned value in sprays divides date within wreath **Edge:** Reeded **Mint:** British Royal Mint

| Date | Mintage | F12 | VF20 | XF40 | MS60 | MS63 |
|---|---|---|---|---|---|---|
| 2001 Prooflike | 1,132 | — | — | — | 50.00 | 55.00 |
| 2002 Prooflike | 1,681 | — | — | — | 50.00 | 55.00 |
| 2003 Prooflike | 1,608 | — | — | — | 55.00 | 60.00 |
| 2004 Prooflike | 1,613 | — | — | — | 55.00 | 60.00 |
| 2005 Prooflike | 1,685 | — | — | — | 55.00 | 60.00 |
| 2006 Prooflike | 1,811 | — | — | — | 55.00 | 60.00 |
| 2006 Proof | 6,394 | — | — | — | — | — |
| 2007 Prooflike | 1,985 | — | — | — | 55.00 | 60.00 |
| 2008 Prooflike | 1,833 | — | — | — | 55.00 | 60.00 |
| 2009 Prooflike | 1,602 | — | — | — | 55.00 | 60.00 |
| 2010 Prooflike | 1,617 | — | — | — | 55.00 | 60.00 |
| 2011 Prooflike | — | — | — | — | 55.00 | 60.00 |
| 2012 Prooflike | — | — | — | — | 55.00 | 60.00 |
| 2013 Prooflike | — | — | — | — | 55.00 | 60.00 |
| 2014 Prooflike | — | — | — | — | 55.00 | 60.00 |

**KM# 898a PENNY**
0.9167 Gold, 11 mm. **Ruler:** Elizabeth II **Obv:** Laureate bust right **Rev:** Crowned denomination divides date within wreath **Mint:** British Royal Mint

| Date | Mintage | VF20 | XF40 | MS60 | MS63 | MS65 |
|---|---|---|---|---|---|---|
| 2002 | 2,002 | PF63 1,000 | | | | |

**KM# 899 2 PENCE**
0.94 g., 0.925 Silver, 13 mm. **Ruler:** Elizabeth II **Obv:** Laureate bust right **Obv. Legend:** Without BRITT OMN **Rev:** Crowned value in sprays divides date within wreath **Edge:** Reeded **Mint:** British Royal Mint

| Date | Mintage | F12 | VF20 | XF40 | MS60 | MS63 |
|---|---|---|---|---|---|---|
| 2001 Prooflike | 1,132 | — | — | — | 60.00 | 70.00 |
| 2002 Prooflike | 1,681 | — | — | — | 60.00 | 70.00 |
| 2003 Prooflike | 1,608 | — | — | — | 65.00 | 75.00 |
| 2004 Prooflike | 1,613 | — | — | — | 65.00 | 75.00 |
| 2005 Prooflike | 1,685 | — | — | — | 65.00 | 75.00 |
| 2006 Prooflike | 1,811 | — | — | — | 65.00 | 75.00 |
| 2006 Proof | 6,394 | — | — | — | — | — |
| 2007 Prooflike | 1,822 | — | — | — | 65.00 | 75.00 |
| 2008 Prooflike | 1,999 | — | — | — | 65.00 | 75.00 |
| 2009 Prooflike | 1,602 | — | — | — | 65.00 | 75.00 |
| 2010 Prooflike | 1,617 | — | — | — | 65.00 | 75.00 |
| 2011 Prooflike | — | — | — | — | 65.00 | 75.00 |
| 2012 Prooflike | — | — | — | — | 65.00 | 75.00 |
| 2014 Prooflike | — | — | — | — | 65.00 | 75.00 |
| 2014 Prooflike | — | — | — | — | 65.00 | 75.00 |

**KM# 899a 2 PENCE**
0.9167 Gold, 13 mm. **Ruler:** Elizabeth II **Series:** Maundy Sets **Obv:** Laureate bust right **Obv. Legend:** Without BRITT OMN **Rev:** Crowned denomination divides date within wreath **Mint:** British Royal Mint

| Date | Mintage | VF20 | XF40 | MS60 | MS63 | MS65 |
|---|---|---|---|---|---|---|
| 2002 | 2,002 | PF63 1,100 | | | | |

**KM# 901 3 PENCE**
1.41 g., 0.925 Silver 0.042 oz. ASW, 16 mm. **Ruler:** Elizabeth II **Obv:** Laureate bust right **Obv. Legend:** without BRITT OMN **Rev:** Crowned value in sprays divides date within wreath **Edge:** Reeded **Mint:** British Royal Mint

| Date | Mintage | F12 | VF20 | XF40 | MS60 | MS63 |
|---|---|---|---|---|---|---|
| 2001 Prooflike | 1,132 | — | — | — | 65.00 | 75.00 |
| 2002 Prooflike | 1,681 | — | — | — | 65.00 | 75.00 |
| 2003 Prooflike | 1,608 | — | — | — | 70.00 | 80.00 |
| 2004 Prooflike | 1,613 | — | — | — | 70.00 | 80.00 |
| 2005 Prooflike | 1,685 | — | — | — | 70.00 | 80.00 |
| 2006 Prooflike | 1,811 | — | — | — | 70.00 | 80.00 |
| 2006 Proof | 6,394 | — | — | — | — | — |
| 2007 Prooflike | 1,822 | — | — | — | 70.00 | 80.00 |
| 2008 Prooflike | 1,833 | — | — | — | 70.00 | 80.00 |
| 2009 Prooflike | 1,794 | — | — | — | 70.00 | 80.00 |
| 2010 Prooflike | 1,617 | — | — | — | 70.00 | 80.00 |
| 2011 Prooflike | — | — | — | — | 70.00 | 80.00 |
| 2012 Prooflike | — | — | — | — | 70.00 | 80.00 |
| 2013 Prooflike | — | — | — | — | 70.00 | 80.00 |
| 2014 Prooflike | — | — | — | — | 70.00 | 80.00 |

**KM# 901a 3 PENCE**
0.9167 Gold, 16 mm. **Ruler:** Elizabeth II **Obv:** Laureate bust right **Obv. Legend:** Without RITT OMN **Rev:** Crowned denomination divides date within wreath **Mint:** British Royal Mint

| Date | Mintage | VF20 | XF40 | MS60 | MS63 | MS65 |
|---|---|---|---|---|---|---|
| 2002 | 2,002 | PF63 1,150 | | | | |

**KM# 902 4 PENCE (GROAT)**
1.89 g., 0.925 Silver 0.0561 oz. ASW, 18 mm. **Ruler:** Elizabeth II **Obv:** Laureate bust right **Obv. Legend:** without BRITT OMN **Rev:** Crowned denomination divides date within wreath **Edge:** Reeded **Mint:** British Royal Mint

| Date | Mintage | F12 | VF20 | XF40 | MS60 | MS63 |
|---|---|---|---|---|---|---|
| 2001 Prooflike | 1,132 | — | — | — | 65.00 | 75.00 |
| 2002 Prooflike | 1,681 | — | — | — | 65.00 | 75.00 |
| 2003 Prooflike | 1,608 | — | — | — | 65.00 | 75.00 |
| 2004 Prooflike | 1,613 | — | — | — | 65.00 | 75.00 |
| 2005 Prooflike | 1,685 | — | — | — | 65.00 | 75.00 |
| 2006 Prooflike | 1,811 | — | — | — | 65.00 | 75.00 |
| 2006 Proof | 6,394 | — | — | — | — | — |
| 2007 Prooflike | 1,822 | — | — | — | 65.00 | 75.00 |
| 2008 Prooflike | 1,833 | — | — | — | 65.00 | 75.00 |
| 2009 Prooflike | 1,602 | — | — | — | 65.00 | 75.00 |
| 2010 Prooflike | 1,787 | — | — | — | 65.00 | 75.00 |
| 2011 Prooflike | — | — | — | — | 65.00 | 75.00 |
| 2012 Prooflike | — | — | — | — | 65.00 | 75.00 |
| 2013 Prooflike | — | — | — | — | 65.00 | 75.00 |
| 2014 Prooflike | — | — | — | — | 65.00 | 75.00 |

**KM# 902a 4 PENCE**
0.9167 Gold, 18 mm. **Ruler:** Elizabeth II **Obv:** Laureate bust right **Obv. Legend:** Without BRITT OMN **Rev:** Crowned denomination divides date within wreath **Mint:** British Royal Mint

| Date | Mintage | VF20 | XF40 | MS60 | MS63 | MS65 |
|---|---|---|---|---|---|---|
| 2002 | 2,002 | PF63 1,250 | | | | |

### DECIMAL COINAGE

1971-1981: 100 New Pence = 1 Pound;
1982-present: 100 Pence = 1 Pound

**KM# 986 PENNY**
3.56 g., Copper Plated Steel, 20.32 mm. **Ruler:** Elizabeth II **Subject:** Badge of Henry VII **Obv:** Head with tiara right **Rev:** Crowned portcullis with chains **Edge:** Plain

| Date | Mintage | VF20 | XF40 | MS60 | MS63 | MS65 |
|---|---|---|---|---|---|---|
| 2001 | 928,698,000 | — | 0.15 | 1.00 | 1.75 | 2.50 |
| 2001 | 49,372 | PF65 3.25 | | | | |
| 2002 | 601,446,000 | — | 0.15 | 1.00 | 1.75 | 2.50 |
| 2002 | 60,770 | PF65 3.25 | | | | |
| 2003 | 539,436,000 | — | 0.15 | 1.00 | 1.75 | 2.50 |
| 2003 | 43,513 | PF65 3.25 | | | | |
| 2004 | 739,764,000 | — | 0.15 | 1.00 | 1.75 | 2.50 |
| 2004 | 35,020 | PF65 3.25 | | | | |
| 2005 | 536,318,000 | — | 0.15 | 1.00 | 1.75 | 2.50 |
| 2005 | 40,563 | PF65 3.25 | | | | |
| 2006 | 524,605,000 | — | 0.15 | 1.00 | 1.75 | 2.50 |
| 2006 | 37,689 | PF65 3.25 | | | | |
| 2007 | 548,002,000 | — | 0.15 | 1.00 | 1.75 | 2.50 |
| 2007 | 38,215 | PF65 3.25 | | | | |
| 2008 | 180,600,000 | — | 0.25 | 2.00 | 2.50 | 3.00 |
| 2008 | 36,333 | PF65 3.25 | | | | |

**KM# 986b PENNY**
3.56 g., 0.925 Silver 0.1059 oz. ASW, 20.3 mm. **Ruler:** Elizabeth II **Obv:** Head with tiara right **Rev:** Crowned portcullis **Edge:** Plain **Mint:** British Royal Mint

| Date | Mintage | VF20 | XF40 | MS60 | MS63 | MS65 |
|---|---|---|---|---|---|---|
| 2008 | 10,000 | PF65 16.50 | | | | |

**KM# 986c PENNY**
0.9167 Gold, 20.3 mm. **Ruler:** Elizabeth II **Obv:** Head with tiara right **Rev:** Crowned portcullis **Mint:** British Royal Mint

| Date | Mintage | VF20 | XF40 | MS60 | MS63 | MS65 |
|---|---|---|---|---|---|---|
| 2002 | — | PF65 750 | | | | |
| 2008 | 2,008 | PF65 550 | | | | |

**KM# 1107 PENNY**
3.59 g., Copper Plated Steel, 20.3 mm. **Ruler:** Elizabeth II **Obv:** Head with tiara right **Rev:** Section of the Royal Arms - Lion and Harp

| Date | Mintage | VF20 | XF40 | MS60 | MS63 | MS65 |
|---|---|---|---|---|---|---|
| 2008 | 507,952,000 | — | — | — | 0.20 | 0.40 |
| 2008 | 56,333 | PF65 3.50 | | | | |
| 2009 | 556,412,000 | — | — | — | 0.20 | 0.40 |
| 2009 | 40,000 | PF65 3.50 | | | | |
| 2010 | 421,002,000 | — | — | — | 0.20 | 0.40 |
| 2010 | 40,000 | PF65 3.50 | | | | |
| 2011 | — | — | — | — | 0.20 | 0.40 |
| 2011 | 40,000 | PF65 3.50 | | | | |
| 2012 | — | — | — | — | 0.20 | 0.40 |
| 2012 | 33,500 | PF65 3.50 | | | | |
| 2013 | — | — | — | — | 0.20 | 0.40 |
| 2013 | 44,000 | PF65 3.50 | | | | |
| 2014 | — | — | — | — | 0.20 | 0.40 |
| 2014 | — | PF65 3.50 | | | | |

**KM# 1107a PENNY**
3.56 g., 0.925 Silver 0.1059 oz. ASW, 20.3 mm. **Ruler:** Elizabeth II **Obv:** Head with tiara right **Rev:** Section of the Royal Arms - Lion and Harp

| Date | Mintage | VF20 | XF40 | MS60 | MS63 | MS65 |
|---|---|---|---|---|---|---|
| 2008 | — | PF65 13.50 | | | | |
| 2009 | — | — | — | — | — | 25.00 |

| Date | Mintage | VF20 | XF40 | MS60 | MS63 | MS65 |
|---|---|---|---|---|---|---|
| 2009 | — | PF65 25.00 | | | | |
| 2010 | — | — | — | — | — | 25.00 |
| 2010 | 3,500 | PF65 25.00 | | | | |
| 2013 | 2,013 | PF65 25.00 | | | | |
| 2014 | 2,014 | PF65 25.00 | | | | |

### KM# 1107b PENNY

0.9167 Gold, 20.3 mm. **Ruler:** Elizabeth II **Obv:** Head with tiara right **Rev:** Section of the Royal Arms - Lion and Harp

| Date | Mintage | VF20 | XF40 | MS60 | MS63 | MS65 |
|---|---|---|---|---|---|---|
| 2008 | — | PF65 350 | | | | |

### KM# 1107c PENNY

Platinum APW, 20.3 mm. **Ruler:** Elizabeth II **Obv:** Head with tiara right **Rev:** Section of the Royal Arms - Lion and Harp

| Date | Mintage | VF20 | XF40 | MS60 | MS63 | MS65 |
|---|---|---|---|---|---|---|
| 2008 | — | PF65 600 | | | | |

### KM# 1107a.1 PENNY

3.56 g., 0.925 Silver 0.1059 oz. ASW partially gilt, 20.3 mm. **Ruler:** Elizabeth II **Obv:** Head with tiara right **Rev:** Section of the Royal Arms - Lion and Harp, gilt

| Date | Mintage | VF20 | XF40 | MS60 | MS63 | MS65 |
|---|---|---|---|---|---|---|
| 2012 | — | PF65 25.00 | | | | |

### KM# 987 2 PENCE

7.14 g., Copper Plated Steel, 25.86 mm. **Ruler:** Elizabeth II **Obv:** Head with tiara right **Rev:** Welsh plumes and crown **Edge:** Plain

| Date | Mintage | VF20 | XF40 | MS60 | MS63 | MS65 |
|---|---|---|---|---|---|---|
| 2001 | 551,880,000 | — | 0.15 | 1.00 | 1.75 | 2.50 |
| 2002 | 168,556,000 | — | 0.15 | 1.00 | 1.75 | 2.50 |
| 2003 | 260,225,000 | — | 0.15 | 1.00 | 1.75 | 2.50 |
| 2003 | 43,513 | PF65 3.25 | | | | |
| 2004 | 356,396,000 | — | 0.15 | 1.00 | 1.75 | 2.50 |
| 2004 | 35,020 | PF65 3.25 | | | | |
| 2005 | 280,396,000 | — | 0.15 | 1.00 | 1.75 | 2.50 |
| 2005 | 40,563 | PF65 3.25 | | | | |
| 2006 | 170,637,000 | — | 0.15 | 1.00 | 1.75 | 2.50 |
| 2006 | 37,689 | PF65 3.25 | | | | |
| 2007 | 254,500,000 | — | 0.15 | 1.00 | 1.75 | 2.50 |
| 2007 | 38,215 | PF65 3.25 | | | | |
| 2008 | 10,600,000 | — | 0.25 | 2.50 | 3.00 | 3.50 |

### KM# 987a 2 PENCE

Bronze, 25.91 mm. **Ruler:** Elizabeth II **Obv:** Head with tiara right **Rev:** Welsh plumes and crown

| Date | Mintage | VF20 | XF40 | MS60 | MS63 | MS65 |
|---|---|---|---|---|---|---|
| 2002 | 60,770 | PF65 2.50 | | | | |
| 2003 | 43,513 | PF65 2.50 | | | | |
| 2004 | 35,020 | PF65 2.50 | | | | |

### KM# 987b 2 PENCE

7.12 g., 0.925 Silver 0.2117 oz. ASW, 25.9 mm. **Ruler:** Elizabeth II **Obv:** Head with tiara right **Rev:** Welsh plumes and crown **Edge:** Plain **Mint:** British Royal Mint

| Date | Mintage | VF20 | XF40 | MS60 | MS63 | MS65 |
|---|---|---|---|---|---|---|
| 2008 | 10,000 | PF65 18.50 | | | | |

### KM# 987c 2 PENCE

0.9167 Gold, 25.91 mm. **Ruler:** Elizabeth II **Subject:** Queen's Golden Jubilee - 1952-2002 **Obv:** Head with tiara right **Rev:** Welsh plumes and crown **Mint:** British Royal Mint

| Date | Mintage | VF20 | XF40 | MS60 | MS63 | MS65 |
|---|---|---|---|---|---|---|
| 2002 | — | PF65 850 | | | | |
| 2008 | 2,008 | PF65 650 | | | | |

### KM# 1108 2 PENCE

7.10 g., Copper Plated Steel, 25.86 mm. **Ruler:** Elizabeth II **Obv:** Head with tiara right **Rev:** Section of the Royal Arms - Lion

| Date | Mintage | VF20 | XF40 | MS60 | MS63 | MS65 |
|---|---|---|---|---|---|---|
| 2008 | 241,679,000 | — | 0.15 | 1.00 | 1.75 | 2.50 |
| 2008 | 56,333 | PF65 3.25 | | | | |
| 2009 | 150,400,500 | — | 0.15 | 1.00 | 1.75 | 2.50 |
| 2009 | 40,000 | PF65 3.25 | | | | |
| 2010 | 38,000,000 | — | 0.15 | 1.00 | 1.75 | 2.50 |
| 2010 | 40,000 | PF65 3.25 | | | | |
| 2011 | — | — | 0.15 | 1.00 | 1.75 | 2.50 |
| 2011 | 40,000 | PF65 3.25 | | | | |
| 2012 | — | — | 0.15 | 1.00 | 1.75 | 2.50 |
| 2012 | 33,500 | PF65 3.25 | | | | |
| 2013 | — | — | 0.15 | 1.00 | 1.75 | 2.50 |
| 2013 | 44,000 | PF65 3.25 | | | | |
| 2014 | — | — | 0.15 | 1.00 | 1.75 | 2.50 |
| 2014 | — | PF65 3.25 | | | | |

### KM# 1108a 2 PENCE

7.12 g., 0.925 Silver 0.2117 oz. ASW, 25.91 mm. **Ruler:** Elizabeth II **Obv:** Head in tiara right **Rev:** Section of the Royal Arms - Lion

| Date | Mintage | VF20 | XF40 | MS60 | MS63 | MS65 |
|---|---|---|---|---|---|---|
| 2008 | — | PF65 17.50 | | | | |
| 2009 | — | PF65 17.50 | | | | |
| 2010 | 3,500 | PF65 17.50 | | | | |
| 2011 | — | PF65 25.00 | | | | |
| Note: Also exists as a Piedfort, P78. | | | | | | |
| 2013 | 2,013 | PF65 25.00 | | | | |

### KM# 1108b 2 PENCE

0.9167 Gold, 25.9 mm. **Ruler:** Elizabeth II **Obv:** Head in tiara right **Rev:** Section of the Royal Arms - Lion

| Date | Mintage | VF20 | XF40 | MS60 | MS63 | MS65 |
|---|---|---|---|---|---|---|
| 2008 | — | PF65 700 | | | | |

### KM# 1108c 2 PENCE

Platinum APW, 25.9 mm. **Ruler:** Elizabeth II **Obv:** Head in tiara right **Rev:** Section of Royal Arms - Lion

| Date | Mintage | VF20 | XF40 | MS60 | MS63 | MS65 |
|---|---|---|---|---|---|---|
| 2008 | — | PF65 1,100 | | | | |

### KM# 1108a.1 2 PENCE

7.12 g., 0.925 Silver 0.2117 oz. ASW partially gilt, 25.86 mm. **Ruler:** Elizabeth II **Obv:** Head with tiara right **Rev:** Section of the Royal Arms - Lion

| Date | Mintage | VF20 | XF40 | MS60 | MS63 | MS65 |
|---|---|---|---|---|---|---|
| 2012 | — | PF65 17.50 | | | | |

### KM# 988 5 PENCE

3.25 g., Copper-Nickel, 18 mm. **Ruler:** Elizabeth II **Obv:** Head with tiara right **Rev:** Crowned thistle

| Date | Mintage | VF20 | XF40 | MS60 | MS63 | MS65 |
|---|---|---|---|---|---|---|
| 2001 | 337,930,000 | — | 0.25 | 1.00 | 2.00 | 2.50 |
| 2001 | 49,372 | PF65 3.00 | | | | |
| 2002 | 219,258,000 | — | 0.25 | 1.00 | 2.00 | 2.50 |
| 2002 | 60,770 | PF65 3.00 | | | | |
| 2003 | 333,230,000 | — | 0.25 | 1.00 | 2.00 | 2.50 |
| 2003 | 43,513 | PF65 3.00 | | | | |
| 2004 | 271,810,000 | — | 0.25 | 1.00 | 2.00 | 2.50 |
| 2004 | 35,020 | PF65 3.00 | | | | |
| 2005 | 236,212,000 | — | 0.25 | 1.00 | 2.00 | 2.50 |
| 2005 | 40,563 | PF65 3.00 | | | | |
| 2006 | 317,697,000 | — | 0.25 | 1.00 | 2.00 | 2.50 |
| 2006 | 37,689 | PF65 3.00 | | | | |
| 2007 | 246,720,000 | — | 0.25 | 1.00 | 2.00 | 2.50 |
| 2007 | 38,215 | PF65 3.00 | | | | |
| 2008 | 92,880,000 | — | — | — | 4.50 | 5.00 |

### KM# 988a 5 PENCE

3.25 g., 0.925 Silver 0.0967 oz. ASW, 18 mm. **Ruler:** Elizabeth II **Obv:** Head with tiara right **Rev:** Crowned thistle **Edge:** Reeded **Mint:** British Royal Mint

| Date | Mintage | VF20 | XF40 | MS60 | MS63 | MS65 |
|---|---|---|---|---|---|---|
| 2008 | 10,000 | PF65 22.50 | | | | |

### KM# 988b 5 PENCE

0.9167 Gold, 18 mm. **Ruler:** Elizabeth II **Obv:** Head with tiara right **Rev:** Crowned thistle **Mint:** British Royal Mint

| Date | Mintage | VF20 | XF40 | MS60 | MS63 | MS65 |
|---|---|---|---|---|---|---|
| 2002 | — | PF65 450 | | | | |
| 2008 | — | PF65 400 | | | | |

### KM# 1109 5 PENCE

3.25 g., Copper-Nickel, 18 mm. **Ruler:** Elizabeth II **Obv:** Head with tiara right **Rev:** Section of the Royal Arms - Center of shield

| Date | Mintage | VF20 | XF40 | MS60 | MS63 | MS65 |
|---|---|---|---|---|---|---|
| 2008 | 165,172,000 | — | 0.25 | 1.00 | 2.00 | 2.50 |
| 2008 | 56,333 | PF65 3.00 | | | | |
| 2009 | 132,960,300 | — | 0.25 | 1.00 | 2.00 | 2.50 |
| 2009 | 40,000 | PF65 3.00 | | | | |
| 2010 | 180,250,500 | — | 0.25 | 1.00 | 2.00 | 2.50 |
| 2010 | 40,000 | PF65 3.00 | | | | |

### KM# 1109a 5 PENCE

3.25 g., 0.925 Silver 0.0967 oz. ASW, 18 mm. **Ruler:** Elizabeth II **Obv:** Head in tiara right **Rev:** Section of Royal Arms - Center of shield

| Date | Mintage | VF20 | XF40 | MS60 | MS63 | MS65 |
|---|---|---|---|---|---|---|
| 2008 | — | PF65 20.00 | | | | |
| 2009 | — | PF65 20.00 | | | | |
| 2010 | 3,500 | PF65 20.00 | | | | |
| 2011 | — | PF65 35.00 | | | | |
| Note: Also exists as a Piedfort, P79. | | | | | | |
| 2013 | 2,013 | PF65 35.00 | | | | |

### KM# 1109b 5 PENCE

0.9167 Gold, 18 mm. **Ruler:** Elizabeth II **Obv:** Head in tiara right **Rev:** Section of Royal Arms - Center

| Date | Mintage | VF20 | XF40 | MS60 | MS63 | MS65 |
|---|---|---|---|---|---|---|
| 2008 | — | PF65 500 | | | | |

### KM# 1109c 5 PENCE

Platinum APW, 18 mm. **Ruler:** Elizabeth II **Obv:** Head in tiara right **Rev:** Section of Royal Arms - Center

| Date | Mintage | VF20 | XF40 | MS60 | MS63 | MS65 |
|---|---|---|---|---|---|---|
| 2008 | — | PF65 800 | | | | |

### KM# 1109d 5 PENCE

3.25 g., Nickel Plated Steel, 18 mm. **Ruler:** Elizabeth II **Obv:** Head with tiara right **Rev:** Section of Royal Arms - Center of shield **Mint:** British Royal Mint

| Date | Mintage | VF20 | XF40 | MS60 | MS63 | MS65 |
|---|---|---|---|---|---|---|
| 2011 | — | — | 0.25 | 1.00 | 2.00 | 2.50 |
| 2011 | 40,000 | PF65 3.00 | | | | |
| 2012 | — | — | 0.25 | 1.00 | 2.00 | 2.50 |
| 2012 | 33,500 | PF65 3.00 | | | | |
| 2013 | — | — | 0.25 | 1.00 | 2.00 | 2.50 |
| 2013 | 44,000 | PF65 3.00 | | | | |
| 2014 | — | — | 0.25 | 1.00 | 2.00 | 2.50 |
| 2014 | — | PF65 3.00 | | | | |

### KM# 1109a.1 5 PENCE

3.25 g., 0.925 Silver 0.0967 oz. ASW with fully gilt reverse, 18 mm. **Ruler:** Elizabeth II **Obv:** Head with tiara right **Rev:** Section of the Royal Arms - Center of shield

| Date | Mintage | VF20 | XF40 | MS60 | MS63 | MS65 |
|---|---|---|---|---|---|---|
| 2012 | — | PF65 20.00 | | | | |

### KM# 989 10 PENCE

6.50 g., Copper-Nickel, 24.5 mm. **Ruler:** Elizabeth II **Obv:** Head with tiara right **Rev:** Crowned lion passant left

| Date | Mintage | VF20 | XF40 | MS60 | MS63 | MS65 |
|---|---|---|---|---|---|---|
| 2001 | 129,281,000 | — | 0.50 | 1.75 | 3.50 | 4.00 |
| 2001 | 45,617 | PF65 3.50 | | | | |

| Date | Mintage | VF20 | XF40 | MS60 | MS63 | MS65 |
|---|---|---|---|---|---|---|
| 2002 | 80,934,000 | — | 0.50 | 1.75 | 3.50 | 4.00 |
| 2002 | 60,770 | PF65 3.50 | | | | |
| 2003 | 88,118,000 | — | 0.50 | 1.75 | 3.50 | 4.00 |
| 2003 | 43,513 | PF65 3.50 | | | | |
| 2004 | 99,602,000 | — | 0.50 | 1.75 | 3.50 | 4.00 |
| 2004 | 35,020 | PF65 3.50 | | | | |
| 2005 | 69,604,000 | — | 0.50 | 1.75 | 3.50 | 4.00 |
| 2005 | 40,563 | PF65 3.50 | | | | |
| 2006 | 118,803,000 | — | 0.50 | 1.75 | 3.50 | 4.00 |
| 2006 | 37,689 | PF65 3.50 | | | | |
| 2007 | 72,720,000 | — | 0.50 | 1.75 | 3.50 | 4.00 |
| 2007 | 38,215 | PF65 3.50 | | | | |
| 2008 | 9,720,000 | — | 0.50 | 1.75 | 3.50 | 4.00 |

## KM# 989a 10 PENCE

6.50 g., 0.925 Silver 0.1933 oz. ASW, 24.5 mm. **Ruler:** Elizabeth II **Obv:** Head with tiara right **Rev:** Crowned lion prancing left **Edge:** Reeded **Mint:** British Royal Mint

| Date | Mintage | VF20 | XF40 | MS60 | MS63 | MS65 |
|---|---|---|---|---|---|---|
| 2008 | 10,000 | PF65 20.00 | | | | |

## KM# 989b 10 PENCE

0.9167 Gold, 24.5 mm. **Ruler:** Elizabeth II **Obv:** Head with tiara right **Rev:** Crowned lion prancing left **Mint:** British Royal Mint

| Date | Mintage | VF20 | XF40 | MS60 | MS63 | MS65 |
|---|---|---|---|---|---|---|
| 2002 | — | PF65 650 | | | | |
| 2008 | 2,008 | PF65 550 | | | | |

## KM# 1110 10 PENCE

6.50 g., Copper-Nickel, 24.5 mm. **Ruler:** Elizabeth II **Obv:** Head with tiara right **Rev:** Section of the Royal Arms - two lions

| Date | Mintage | VF20 | XF40 | MS60 | MS63 | MS65 |
|---|---|---|---|---|---|---|
| 2008 | 71,447,000 | — | 0.50 | 1.75 | 3.50 | 4.00 |
| 2008 | 36,333 | PF65 3.50 | | | | |
| 2009 | 84,360,000 | — | 0.50 | 1.75 | 3.50 | 4.00 |
| 2009 | 40,000 | PF65 3.50 | | | | |
| 2010 | 25,320,500 | — | 0.50 | 1.75 | 3.50 | 4.00 |
| 2010 | 40,000 | PF65 3.50 | | | | |

## KM# 1110a 10 PENCE

6.50 g., 0.925 Silver 0.1933 oz. ASW, 24.5 mm. **Ruler:** Elizabeth II **Obv:** Head with tiara right **Rev:** Section of the Royal Arms - two lions

| Date | Mintage | VF20 | XF40 | MS60 | MS63 | MS65 |
|---|---|---|---|---|---|---|
| 2008 | — | PF65 25.00 | | | | |
| 2009 proof | — | PF65 25.00 | | | | |
| 2010 | 3,500 | PF65 25.00 | | | | |
| 2011 | — | PF65 80.00 | | | | |
| Note: Also exists as a Piedfort, P80. | | | | | | |
| 2013 | 2,013 | PF65 80.00 | | | | |

## KM# 1110b 10 PENCE

0.9167 Gold, 24.5 mm. **Ruler:** Elizabeth II **Obv:** Head in tiara right **Rev:** Section of Royal Arms - two lions

| Date | Mintage | VF20 | XF40 | MS60 | MS63 | MS65 |
|---|---|---|---|---|---|---|
| 2008 | — | PF65 950 | | | | |

## KM# 1110c 10 PENCE

Platinum APW, 24.5 mm. **Ruler:** Elizabeth II **Obv:** Head in tiara right **Rev:** Section of Royal Arms - two lions

| Date | Mintage | VF20 | XF40 | MS60 | MS63 | MS65 |
|---|---|---|---|---|---|---|
| 2008 | — | PF65 1,600 | | | | |

## KM# 1110d 10 PENCE

6.50 g., Nickel Plated Steel, 24.5 mm. **Ruler:** Elizabeth II **Obv:** Head with tiara right **Rev:** Section of Royal Arms - two lions **Mint:** British Royal Mint

| Date | Mintage | VF20 | XF40 | MS60 | MS63 | MS65 |
|---|---|---|---|---|---|---|
| 2011 | — | — | 0.50 | 1.75 | 3.50 | 4.00 |
| 2011 | 40,000 | PF65 3.50 | | | | |
| 2012 | — | — | 0.50 | 1.75 | 3.50 | 4.00 |
| 2012 | 33,500 | PF65 3.50 | | | | |
| 2013 | — | — | 0.50 | 1.75 | 3.50 | 4.00 |
| 2013 | 44,000 | PF65 3.50 | | | | |
| 2014 | — | — | 0.50 | 1.75 | 3.50 | 4.00 |
| 2014 | — | PF65 3.50 | | | | |

## KM# 1110a.1 10 PENCE

6.50 g., 0.925 Silver 0.1933 oz. ASW, 24.5 mm. **Ruler:** Elizabeth II **Obv:** Head with tiara right **Rev:** Section of the Royal Arms - two lions

| Date | Mintage | VF20 | XF40 | MS60 | MS63 | MS65 |
|---|---|---|---|---|---|---|
| 2012 | — | PF65 25.00 | | | | |

## KM# 990 20 PENCE

5.00 g., Copper-Nickel, 21.4 mm. **Ruler:** Elizabeth II **Obv:** Head with tiara right **Rev:** Crowned double rose **Shape:** 7-sided

| Date | Mintage | VF20 | XF40 | MS60 | MS63 | MS65 |
|---|---|---|---|---|---|---|
| 2001 | 148,122,500 | — | 0.50 | 1.75 | 3.50 | 4.00 |
| 2001 | 45,617 | PF65 4.50 | | | | |
| 2002 | 93,360,000 | — | 0.50 | 1.75 | 3.50 | 4.00 |
| 2002 | 60,770 | PF65 4.50 | | | | |
| 2003 | 153,383,750 | — | 0.50 | 1.75 | 3.50 | 4.00 |
| 2003 | 43,513 | PF65 4.50 | | | | |
| 2004 | 120,212,500 | — | 0.50 | 1.75 | 3.50 | 4.00 |
| 2004 | 35,020 | PF65 4.50 | | | | |
| 2005 | 124,488,750 | — | 0.50 | 1.75 | 3.50 | 4.00 |
| 2005 | 40,563 | PF65 4.50 | | | | |
| 2006 | 114,800,000 | — | 0.50 | 1.75 | 3.50 | 4.00 |
| 2006 | 37,689 | PF65 4.50 | | | | |
| 2007 | 117,075,000 | — | 0.50 | 1.75 | 3.50 | 4.00 |
| 2007 | 38,215 | PF65 4.50 | | | | |
| 2008 | 11,900,000 | — | 0.50 | 1.75 | 3.50 | 4.00 |

## KM# 990a 20 PENCE

5.00 g., 0.925 Silver 0.1487 oz. ASW, 21.4 mm. **Ruler:** Elizabeth II **Obv:** Head with tiara right **Rev:** Crowned double rose **Edge:** Plain **Shape:** 7-sided **Mint:** British Royal Mint

| Date | Mintage | VF20 | XF40 | MS60 | MS63 | MS65 |
|---|---|---|---|---|---|---|
| 2008 | 10,000 | PF65 22.50 | | | | |

## KM# 990b 20 PENCE

0.9167 Gold, 21.4 mm. **Ruler:** Elizabeth II **Obv:** Head with tiara right **Rev:** Crowned double rose **Shape:** 7-sided **Mint:** British Royal Mint

| Date | Mintage | VF20 | XF40 | MS60 | MS63 | MS65 |
|---|---|---|---|---|---|---|
| 2002 | — | PF65 550 | | | | |
| 2008 | 2,008 | PF65 500 | | | | |

## KM# 1111 20 PENCE

5.00 g., Copper-Nickel, 21.4 mm. **Ruler:** Elizabeth II **Obv:** Head with tiara right **Rev:** Section of the Royal Arms - lion's tails **Shape:** 7-sided

| Date | Mintage | VF20 | XF40 | MS60 | MS63 | MS65 |
|---|---|---|---|---|---|---|
| 2008 | 115,022,000 | — | 0.50 | 1.75 | 3.50 | 4.00 |
| 2008 | 56,333 | PF65 4.50 | | | | |
| 2009 | 121,625,300 | — | 0.50 | 1.75 | 3.50 | 4.00 |
| 2009 | 40,000 | PF65 4.50 | | | | |
| 2010 | 91,700,500 | — | 0.50 | 1.75 | 3.50 | 4.00 |
| 2010 | 40,000 | PF65 4.50 | | | | |
| 2011 | — | — | 5.00 | 1.75 | 3.50 | 4.00 |
| 2011 | 40,000 | PF65 4.50 | | | | |
| 2012 | — | — | 0.50 | 1.75 | 3.50 | 4.00 |
| 2012 | 33,500 | PF65 4.50 | | | | |
| 2013 | — | — | 0.50 | 1.75 | 3.50 | 4.00 |
| 2013 | 44,000 | PF65 4.50 | | | | |
| 2014 | — | — | 0.50 | 1.50 | 3.00 | 4.00 |
| 2014 | — | PF65 4.50 | | | | |

## KM# 1111a 20 PENCE

5.00 g., 0.925 Silver 0.1487 oz. ASW, 21.4 mm. **Ruler:** Elizabeth II **Obv:** Head in tiara right **Rev:** Section of the Royal Arms - lion's tails **Shape:** 7-sided

| Date | Mintage | VF20 | XF40 | MS60 | MS63 | MS65 |
|---|---|---|---|---|---|---|
| 2008 | — | PF65 35.00 | | | | |
| 2009 | — | PF65 35.00 | | | | |
| 2010 | 3,500 | PF65 35.00 | | | | |
| 2011 | — | PF65 80.00 | | | | |
| Note: Also exists as a Piedfort, P81. | | | | | | |
| 2013 | 2,013 | PF65 80.00 | | | | |

## KM# 1111b 20 PENCE

0.9167 Gold, 21.4 mm. **Ruler:** Elizabeth II **Obv:** Head in tiara right **Rev:** Section of Royal Arms - lion's tails **Shape:** 7-sided

| Date | Mintage | VF20 | XF40 | MS60 | MS63 | MS65 |
|---|---|---|---|---|---|---|
| 2008 | — | PF65 700 | | | | |

## KM# 1111c 20 PENCE

Platinum APW, 21.4 mm. **Ruler:** Elizabeth II **Obv:** Head in tiara right **Rev:** Section of Royal Arms - lion's tails **Shape:** 7-sided

| Date | Mintage | VF20 | XF40 | MS60 | MS63 | MS65 |
|---|---|---|---|---|---|---|
| 2008 | — | PF65 1,200 | | | | |

## KM# 1122 20 PENCE

5.00 g., Copper-Nickel, 21.4 mm. **Ruler:** Elizabeth II **Obv:** Head right. Obverse of KM#990 **Rev:** Royal Arms part. Reverse of KM#1111 **Mint:** British Royal Mint **Note:** Mule.

| Date | Mintage | VF20 | XF40 | MS60 | MS63 | MS65 |
|---|---|---|---|---|---|---|
| ND-2008 | — | 30.00 | 40.00 | — | — | — |

## KM# 1111a.1 20 PENCE

5.00 g., 0.925 Silver 0.1487 oz. ASW partially gilt, 21.4 mm. **Ruler:** Elizabeth II **Obv:** Head with tiara right **Rev:** Section of Royal Arms - lion's tails

| Date | Mintage | VF20 | XF40 | MS60 | MS63 | MS65 |
|---|---|---|---|---|---|---|
| 2012 | — | PF65 35.00 | | | | |

## KM# 1266 20 PENCE

15.71 g., 0.999 Silver 0.5046 oz. ASW, 27 mm. **Ruler:** Elizabeth II **Obv:** Head with tiara right **Rev:** St. George slaying dragon **Mint:** Royal Mint

| Date | Mintage | VF20 | XF40 | MS60 | MS63 | MS65 |
|---|---|---|---|---|---|---|
| 2013 | 250,000 | — | — | — | — | 40.00 |

## KM# 991 50 PENCE

8.00 g., Copper-Nickel, 27.3 mm. **Ruler:** Elizabeth II **Obv:** Head with tiara right **Rev:** Britannia seated right with shield, spear and lion **Shape:** 7-sided

| Date | Mintage | VF20 | XF40 | MS60 | MS63 | MS65 |
|---|---|---|---|---|---|---|
| 2001 | 84,998,500 | — | 1.00 | 2.50 | 3.50 | 4.00 |
| 2001 | 45,617 | PF65 4.00 | | | | |
| 2002 | 23,907,500 | — | 1.00 | 2.50 | 3.50 | 4.00 |
| 2002 | 60,770 | PF65 4.00 | | | | |
| 2003 | 23,583,000 | — | 1.00 | 2.50 | 3.50 | 4.00 |
| 2003 | 43,513 | PF65 4.00 | | | | |
| 2004 | 35,315,500 | — | 1.00 | 2.50 | 3.50 | 4.00 |
| 2004 | 35,020 | PF65 4.00 | | | | |
| 2005 | 25,363,500 | — | 1.00 | 2.50 | 3.50 | 4.00 |
| 2005 | 40,563 | PF65 4.00 | | | | |
| 2006 | 24,567,000 | — | 1.00 | 2.50 | 3.50 | 4.00 |
| 2006 | 37,689 | PF65 4.00 | | | | |
| 2007 | 11,200,000 | — | 1.00 | 2.50 | 3.50 | 4.00 |
| 2007 | 38,215 | PF65 4.00 | | | | |
| 2008 | 3,500,000 | — | 1.50 | 3.50 | 5.00 | 6.00 |

## KM# 991b 50 PENCE

0.9167 Gold, 27.3 mm. **Ruler:** Elizabeth II **Obv:** Head with tiara right **Rev:** Britannia seated right with shield, spear and lion **Shape:** 7-sided **Mint:** British Royal Mint

| Date | Mintage | VF20 | XF40 | MS60 | MS63 | MS65 |
|---|---|---|---|---|---|---|
| 2002 | — | PF65 700 | | | | |
| 2008 | — | PF65 650 | | | | |

### KM# 1036 50 PENCE

8.00 g., Copper-Nickel, 27.3 mm. **Ruler:** Elizabeth II **Subject:** Woman's Social and Political Union, 100th Anniversary **Obv:** Head with tiara right **Rev:** Standing suffragette chained to railings and holding banner **Edge:** Plain **Shape:** 7-sided **Mint:** British Royal Mint

| Date | Mintage | VF20 | XF40 | MS60 | MS63 | MS65 |
|---|---|---|---|---|---|---|
| 2003 | 3,124,030 | — | 1.00 | 2.50 | 3.50 | 4.00 |
| 2003 | 35,513 | PF65 9.50 | | | | |

### KM# 1036a 50 PENCE

8.00 g., 0.925 Silver 0.2379 oz. ASW, 27.3 mm. **Ruler:** Elizabeth II **Subject:** Woman's Social and Political Union, 100th Anniversary **Obv:** Head with tiara right **Rev:** Standing suffragette chained to railings and holding banner **Edge:** Plain **Shape:** 7-sided **Mint:** British Royal Mint

| Date | Mintage | VF20 | XF40 | MS60 | MS63 | MS65 |
|---|---|---|---|---|---|---|
| 2003 | 6,267 | PF65 45.00 | | | | |

Note: Also exists as a Piefort, P40.

### KM# 1036b 50 PENCE

15.50 g., 0.9166 Gold 0.4568 oz. AGW, 27.3 mm. **Ruler:** Elizabeth II **Subject:** Woman's Social and Political Union, 100th Anniversary **Obv:** Head with tiara right **Rev:** Standing suffragette chained to railings and holding banner **Edge:** Plain **Shape:** 7-sided **Mint:** British Royal Mint

| Date | Mintage | VF20 | XF40 | MS60 | MS63 | MS65 |
|---|---|---|---|---|---|---|
| 2003 | 942 | PF65 800 | | | | |

### KM# 1047 50 PENCE

8.00 g., Copper-Nickel, 27.3 mm. **Ruler:** Elizabeth II **Subject:** Roger Bannister, 50th Anniversary of the four minute mile **Obv:** Head with tiara right **Rev:** Running legs, stop watch and value **Edge:** Plain **Mint:** British Royal Mint

| Date | Mintage | VF20 | XF40 | MS60 | MS63 | MS65 |
|---|---|---|---|---|---|---|
| 2004 | 35,020 | PF65 7.50 | | | | |
| 2004 | 9,032,500 | — | 1.50 | 3.50 | 5.00 | 6.00 |

### KM# 1047a 50 PENCE

8.00 g., 0.925 Silver 0.2379 oz. ASW, 27.3 mm. **Ruler:** Elizabeth II **Subject:** Roger Bannister, 50th Anniversary four minute mile **Obv:** Head with tiara right **Rev:** Running legs, stop watch and value **Shape:** 7-sided

| Date | Mintage | VF20 | XF40 | MS60 | MS63 | MS65 |
|---|---|---|---|---|---|---|
| 2004 | 4,924 | PF65 50.00 | | | | |

Note: Also exists as a Piedfort, P43.

### KM# 1050 50 PENCE

8.00 g., Copper-Nickel, 27.3 mm. **Ruler:** Elizabeth II **Subject:** Samuel Johnson's Dictonary of the English Language, 250th Anniversary **Obv:** Head with tiara right **Rev:** Dictonary entries for Fifty and Pence **Edge:** Plain **Shape:** 7-sided **Mint:** British Royal Mint

| Date | Mintage | VF20 | XF40 | MS60 | MS63 | MS65 |
|---|---|---|---|---|---|---|
| 2005 | 40,563 | PF65 6.00 | | | | |
| 2005 | 17,649,000 | — | 1.00 | 2.50 | 3.50 | 4.00 |

### KM# 1050a 50 PENCE

8.00 g., 0.925 Silver 0.2379 oz. ASW, 27.3 mm. **Ruler:** Elizabeth II **Subject:** Samuel Johnson's Dictonary of the English Language, 250th Anniversary **Obv:** Head with tiara right **Rev:** Dictonary entries for Fifty and Pence **Edge:** Plain **Shape:** 7-sided **Mint:** British Royal Mint

| Date | Mintage | VF20 | XF40 | MS60 | MS63 | MS65 |
|---|---|---|---|---|---|---|
| 2005 | 4,029 | PF65 45.00 | | | | |

Note: Also exists as a Piedfort, P48.

### KM# 1050b 50 PENCE

15.50 g., 0.9167 Gold 0.4568 oz. AGW, 27.3 mm. **Ruler:** Elizabeth II **Subject:** Samuel Johnson's Dictonary of the English Language, 250th Anniversary **Obv:** Head with tiara right **Rev:** Dictonary entries for Fifty and Pence **Edge:** Plain **Shape:** 7-sided **Mint:** British Royal Mint

| Date | Mintage | VF20 | XF40 | MS60 | MS63 | MS65 |
|---|---|---|---|---|---|---|
| 2005 | 1,000 | PF65 800 | | | | |

### KM# 1057 50 PENCE

8.00 g., Copper-Nickel, 27.3 mm. **Ruler:** Elizabeth II **Subject:** Victoria Cross, 150th Anniversary **Obv:** Head with tiara right **Rev:** Victoria Cross Medal, obverse and reverse views **Edge:** Plain **Shape:** 7-sided **Mint:** British Royal Mint

| Date | Mintage | VF20 | XF40 | MS60 | MS63 | MS65 |
|---|---|---|---|---|---|---|
| 2006 | 12,087,000 | — | 1.50 | 3.50 | 5.00 | 6.00 |
| 2006 | Est. 50000 | PF65 7.50 | | | | |
| 2007 | — | PF65 7.50 | | | | |

### KM# 1057a 50 PENCE

8.00 g., 0.925 Silver 0.2379 oz. ASW **Ruler:** Elizabeth II **Subject:** Victoria Cross, 150th Anniversary **Obv:** Head with tiara right **Rev:** Victoria Cross Medal, obverse and reverse views **Mint:** British Royal Mint

| Date | Mintage | VF20 | XF40 | MS60 | MS63 | MS65 |
|---|---|---|---|---|---|---|
| 2006 | 7,500 | PF65 40.00 | | | | |

Note: Also exists as a Piedfort, P53.

### KM# 1058 50 PENCE

8.00 g., Copper-Nickel, 27.3 mm. **Ruler:** Elizabeth II **Subject:** Victoria Cross, 150th Anniversary **Obv:** Head with tiara right **Rev:** Heroic Act scene of a soldier carring a wounded comrade with outline of the Victoria Cross in the background **Edge:** Plain **Shape:** 7-sided **Mint:** British Royal Mint

| Date | Mintage | VF20 | XF40 | MS60 | MS63 | MS65 |
|---|---|---|---|---|---|---|
| 2006 | 10,000,500 | — | 1.50 | 3.50 | 5.00 | 6.00 |
| 2006 | Est. 50000 | PF65 7.50 | | | | |

### KM# 1058a 50 PENCE

8.00 g., 0.925 Silver 0.2379 oz. ASW, 27.3 mm. **Ruler:** Elizabeth II **Subject:** Victoria Cross, 150th Anniversary **Obv:** Head with tiara right **Rev:** Heroic Act scene of a soldier carring a wounded comrade with outline of the Victoria Cross in the background **Shape:** 7-sided **Mint:** British Royal Mint

| Date | Mintage | VF20 | XF40 | MS60 | MS63 | MS65 |
|---|---|---|---|---|---|---|
| 2006 | — | PF65 40.00 | | | | |

Note: Also exists as a Piedfort, P-54.

### KM# 1073 50 PENCE

8.00 g., Copper-Nickel, 27.3 mm. **Ruler:** Elizabeth II **Subject:** Scouting Movement, 100th Anniversary **Obv:** Head with tiara right **Rev:** Fleur-de-lis emblem superimposed on globe **Edge:** Plain **Shape:** Seven sided **Mint:** British Royal Mint

| Date | Mintage | VF20 | XF40 | MS60 | MS63 | MS65 |
|---|---|---|---|---|---|---|
| 2007 | Est. 50000 | PF65 7.50 | | | | |
| 2007 | 7,710,750 | — | 1.50 | 3.50 | 5.00 | 6.00 |

### KM# 1073a 50 PENCE

8.00 g., 0.925 Silver 0.2379 oz. ASW, 27.3 mm. **Ruler:** Elizabeth II **Subject:** Scouting Movement, 100th Anniversary **Obv:** Head with tiara right **Rev:** Fleur-de-lis emblem superimposed on globe **Edge:** Plain **Shape:** 7-sided **Mint:** British Royal Mint

| Date | Mintage | VF20 | XF40 | MS60 | MS63 | MS65 |
|---|---|---|---|---|---|---|
| 2007 | 10,895 | PF65 60.00 | | | | |

Note: Also exists as a Piedfort, P-59.

### KM# 1073b 50 PENCE

15.50 g., 0.9166 Gold 0.4568 oz. AGW, 27.3 mm. **Ruler:** Elizabeth II **Subject:** Scouting Movement, 100th Anniversary **Obv:** Head with tiara right **Rev:** Fleur-de-lis emblem superimposed on globe **Edge:** Plain **Shape:** 7-sided **Mint:** British Royal Mint

| Date | Mintage | VF20 | XF40 | MS60 | MS63 | MS65 |
|---|---|---|---|---|---|---|
| 2007 | 1,250 | PF65 800 | | | | |

### KM# 1080a 50 PENCE

7.78 g., 0.999 Silver 0.2481 oz. ASW, 22 mm. **Ruler:** Elizabeth II **Obv:** Head with tiara right **Rev:** Britiannia standing **Edge Lettering:** SS GAIRSOPPA **Note:** Struck from recovered silver from WWII era shipwreck

| Date | Mintage | F12 | VF20 | XF40 | MS60 | MS63 |
|---|---|---|---|---|---|---|
| 2013 | Est. 500000 | — | — | — | — | 20.00 |

### KM# 1112 50 PENCE

8.00 g., Copper-Nickel, 27.3 mm. **Ruler:** Elizabeth II **Obv:** Head with tiara right **Rev:** Section of the Royal Arms - bottom center **Shape:** 7-sided

| Date | Mintage | VF20 | XF40 | MS60 | MS63 | MS65 |
|---|---|---|---|---|---|---|
| 2008 | 22,747,000 | — | 1.00 | 2.50 | 3.50 | 4.00 |
| 2008 | 56,333 | PF65 7.00 | | | | |
| 2009 Sets only | — | — | — | — | — | 4.00 |
| 2009 | 40,000 | PF65 7.00 | | | | |
| 2010 Sets only | — | — | — | — | — | 4.00 |
| 2010 | 40,000 | PF65 7.00 | | | | |
| 2011 Sets only | — | — | — | — | — | 4.00 |

| Date | Mintage | VF20 | XF40 | MS60 | MS63 | MS65 |
|---|---|---|---|---|---|---|
| 2011 | 40,000 | PF65 7.00 | | | | |
| 2012 | — | — | 1.00 | 2.50 | 3.50 | 4.00 |
| 2012 | 33,500 | PF65 7.00 | | | | |
| 2013 | — | — | 1.00 | 2.50 | 3.50 | 4.00 |
| 2013 | 44,000 | PF65 7.00 | | | | |
| 2014 | — | — | 1.00 | 2.50 | 3.50 | 4.00 |
| 2014 | — | PF65 7.00 | | | | |

### KM# 1112a 50 PENCE

8.00 g., 0.925 Silver 0.2379 oz. ASW, 27.3 mm. **Ruler:** Elizabeth II **Obv:** Head in tiara right **Rev:** Section of Royal Arms - bottom center **Shape:** 7-sided

| Date | Mintage | VF20 | XF40 | MS60 | MS63 | MS65 |
|---|---|---|---|---|---|---|
| 2008 | — | PF65 50.00 | | | | |
| Note: Also exists as a Piedfort, P-97. | | | | | | |
| 2009 | — | PF65 50.00 | | | | |
| 2010 | 3,500 | PF65 50.00 | | | | |
| 2011 | — | PF65 50.00 | | | | |
| Note: Also exists as a Piedfort, P-82. | | | | | | |
| 2013 | 2,013 | PF65 50.00 | | | | |

### KM# 1112b 50 PENCE

15.50 g., 0.9167 Gold 0.4568 oz. AGW, 27.3 mm. **Ruler:** Elizabeth II **Obv:** Head in tiara right **Rev:** Section of Royal Arms - bottom center **Shape:** 7-sided

| Date | Mintage | VF20 | XF40 | MS60 | MS63 | MS65 |
|---|---|---|---|---|---|---|
| 2008 | — | PF65 825 | | | | |
| 2009 | — | PF65 825 | | | | |

### KM# 1112C 50 PENCE

Platinum APW, 27.3 mm. **Ruler:** Elizabeth II **Obv:** Head in tiara right **Rev:** Section of Royal Arms - bottom center **Shape:** 7-sided

| Date | Mintage | VF20 | XF40 | MS60 | MS63 | MS65 |
|---|---|---|---|---|---|---|
| 2008 | — | PF65 1,350 | | | | |

### KM# 1114 50 PENCE

8.00 g., Copper-Nickel, 27.3 mm. **Ruler:** Elizabeth II **Subject:** Royal Botanical Gardens at Kew, 250th Anniversary **Obv:** Head with tiara right **Rev:** Pagoda and vine, 1759-2009 **Edge:** Plain **Shape:** 7-sided **Mint:** British Royal Mint

| Date | Mintage | VF20 | XF40 | MS60 | MS63 | MS65 |
|---|---|---|---|---|---|---|
| 2009 | — | PF65 7.50 | | | | |
| 2009 | 10,000 | — | 1.50 | 4.00 | 6.00 | 5.00 |

### KM# 1114a 50 PENCE

8.00 g., 0.925 Silver 0.2379 oz. ASW, 27.3 mm. **Ruler:** Elizabeth II **Subject:** Royal Botanical Gardens at Kew, 250th Anniversary **Obv:** Head right **Rev:** Pagoda and vine, 1759 2009 **Edge:** Plain **Shape:** 7-sided **Mint:** British Royal Mint

| Date | Mintage | VF20 | XF40 | MS60 | MS63 | MS65 |
|---|---|---|---|---|---|---|
| 2009 | 7,500 | PF65 50.00 | | | | |
| Note: Also exists as a Piedfort, P98 | | | | | | |

### KM# 1114b 50 PENCE

15.50 g., 0.916 Gold 0.4565 oz. AGW, 27.3 mm. **Ruler:** Elizabeth II **Subject:** Royal Botanical Gardens at Kew, 250th Anniversary **Obv:** Head right **Rev:** Pagoda and vine, 1759 2009 **Edge:** Plain **Shape:** 7-sided **Mint:** British Royal Mint

| Date | Mintage | VF20 | XF40 | MS60 | MS63 | MS65 |
|---|---|---|---|---|---|---|
| 2009 | 1,000 | PF65 800 | | | | |

### KM# 1150 50 PENCE

8.00 g., Copper-Nickel, 27.3 mm. **Ruler:** Elizabeth II **Subject:** London Olympics, 2012 - Athletics **Obv:** Head with tiara right **Rev:** Youth's drawing of kid going over vault **Edge:** Plain **Shape:** 7-sided **Mint:** British Royal Mint

| Date | Mintage | VF20 | XF40 | MS60 | MS63 | MS65 |
|---|---|---|---|---|---|---|
| 2009 | — | — | 1.00 | 2.50 | 3.50 | 4.00 |
| 2011 | 900,000 | — | — | 1.25 | 2.50 | 3.50 |

### KM# 1150a 50 PENCE

8.00 g., 0.925 Silver 0.2379 oz. ASW, 27.3 mm. **Ruler:** Elizabeth II **Subject:** London Olympics, 2012 **Obv:** Head with tiara right **Rev:** Youth drawing of high jumper **Mint:** British Royal Mint

| Date | Mintage | VF20 | XF40 | MS60 | MS63 | MS65 |
|---|---|---|---|---|---|---|
| 2009 | — | PF65 50.00 | | | | |

### KM# 1165 50 PENCE

8.00 g., Copper-Nickel, 27.3 mm. **Ruler:** Elizabeth II **Subject:** Girl Guides, 100th Anniversary **Obv:** Head with tiara right **Rev:** Circle of six trefoils **Edge:** Plain **Shape:** 7-sided **Mint:** British Royal Mint

| Date | Mintage | VF20 | XF40 | MS60 | MS63 | MS65 |
|---|---|---|---|---|---|---|
| 2010 | 510,090 | — | 1.50 | 2.50 | 4.00 | 5.00 |
| 2010 | — | PF65 10.00 | | | | |

### KM# 1165a 50 PENCE

8.00 g., 0.925 Silver 0.2379 oz. ASW, 27.3 mm. **Ruler:** Elizabeth II **Subject:** Girl Guides, 100th Anniversary **Obv:** Head with tiara right **Rev:** Circle of six trifoils **Edge:** Plain **Shape:** 7-sided **Mint:** British Royal Mint

| Date | Mintage | VF20 | XF40 | MS60 | MS63 | MS65 |
|---|---|---|---|---|---|---|
| 2010 | — | PF65 50.00 | | | | |
| Note: Also exists as a Piedfort, P99 | | | | | | |

### KM# 1166 50 PENCE

8.00 g., Copper-Nickel, 27.3 mm. **Ruler:** Elizabeth II **Subject:** 2012 London Olympics - Aquatics **Obv:** Head with tiara right **Edge:** Plain **Shape:** 7-sided **Mint:** British Royal Mint

| Date | Mintage | VF20 | XF40 | MS60 | MS63 | MS65 |
|---|---|---|---|---|---|---|
| 2011 | 1,000,000 | — | 1.50 | 3.50 | 5.00 | 6.00 |

### KM# 1166a 50 PENCE

8.00 g., 0.925 Silver 0.2379 oz. ASW, 27.3 mm. **Ruler:** Elizabeth II **Subject:** 2012 London Olympics - Aquatics **Obv:** Head with tiara right **Edge:** Plain **Shape:** 7-sided **Mint:** Royal Mint

| Date | Mintage | VF20 | XF40 | MS60 | MS63 | MS65 |
|---|---|---|---|---|---|---|
| 2011 | — | PF65 50.00 | | | | |

### KM# 1167 50 PENCE

8.00 g., Copper-Nickel, 27.3 mm. **Ruler:** Elizabeth II **Subject:** 2012 London Paralympics - Archery **Obv:** Head with tirara right **Edge:** Plain **Shape:** 7-sided **Mint:** British Royal Mint

| Date | Mintage | VF20 | XF40 | MS60 | MS63 | MS65 |
|---|---|---|---|---|---|---|
| 2011 | 800,000 | — | 1.50 | 3.50 | 5.00 | 6.00 |

### KM# 1167a 50 PENCE

8.00 g., 0.925 Silver 0.2379 oz. ASW, 27.3 mm. **Ruler:** Elizabeth II **Subject:** 2012 London Olympics - Archery **Obv:** Head with tiara right **Shape:** 7-sided **Mint:** Royal Mint

| Date | Mintage | VF20 | XF40 | MS60 | MS63 | MS65 |
|---|---|---|---|---|---|---|
| 2011 | — | PF65 50.00 | | | | |

### KM# 1168 50 PENCE

8.00 g., Copper-Nickel, 27.3 mm. **Ruler:** Elizabeth II **Subject:** 2012 London Olympics - Canoeing **Obv:** Head with tiara right **Edge:** Plain **Shape:** 7-sided **Mint:** British Royal Mint

| Date | Mintage | VF20 | XF40 | MS60 | MS63 | MS65 |
|---|---|---|---|---|---|---|
| 2011 | 800,000 | — | 1.50 | 3.50 | 5.00 | 6.00 |

### KM# 1168a 50 PENCE

8.00 g., 0.925 Silver 0.2379 oz. ASW, 27.3 mm. **Ruler:** Elizabeth II **Subject:** 2012 London Olympics - Canoeing **Obv:** Head with tiara right **Shape:** 7-sided **Mint:** Royal Mint

| Date | Mintage | VF20 | XF40 | MS60 | MS63 | MS65 |
|---|---|---|---|---|---|---|
| 2011 | — | PF65 50.00 | | | | |

### KM# 1169 50 PENCE

8.00 g., Copper-Nickel, 27.3 mm. **Ruler:** Elizabeth II **Subject:** 2012 London Olympics - Cycling **Obv:** Head with tiara right **Rev:** Cycle racing in a Velodrome **Edge:** Plain **Shape:** 7-sided **Mint:** British Royal Mint

| Date | Mintage | VF20 | XF40 | MS60 | MS63 | MS65 |
|---|---|---|---|---|---|---|
| 2011 | 400,000 | — | 1.50 | 3.50 | 5.00 | 6.00 |

### KM# 1169a 50 PENCE

8.00 g., 0.925 Silver 0.2379 oz. ASW, 27.3 mm. **Ruler:** Elizabeth II **Subject:** 2012 London Olympics - Cycling **Obv:** Head with tiara right **Rev:** Cycle racing in a velodrome **Shape:** 7-sided **Mint:** Royal Mint

| Date | Mintage | VF20 | XF40 | MS60 | MS63 | MS65 |
|---|---|---|---|---|---|---|
| 2012 Proof | — | PF65 50.00 | | | | |

### KM# 1170 50 PENCE

8.00 g., Copper-Nickel, 27.3 mm. **Ruler:** Elizabeth II **Subject:** 2012 London Olympics - Gymnastics **Obv:** Head with tiara right **Edge:** Plain **Shape:** 7-sided **Mint:** British Royal Mint

| Date | Mintage | VF20 | XF40 | MS60 | MS63 | MS65 |
|---|---|---|---|---|---|---|
| 2011 | 900,000 | — | 1.50 | 3.50 | 5.00 | 6.00 |

**KM# 1170a 50 PENCE**
8.00 g., 0.925 Silver 0.2379 oz. ASW, 27.3 mm. **Ruler:** Elizabeth II **Subject:** 2012 London Olympics - Gymnastics **Obv:** Head with tiara right **Shape:** 7-sided **Mint:** Royal Mint

| Date | Mintage | VF20 | XF40 | MS60 | MS63 | MS65 |
|---|---|---|---|---|---|---|
| 2013 | — | PF65 50.00 | | | | |

**KM# 1171 50 PENCE**
8.00 g., Copper-Nickel, 27.3 mm. **Ruler:** Elizabeth II **Subject:** 2012 London Olympics - Hockey **Obv:** Head with tiara right **Edge:** Plain **Shape:** 7-sided **Mint:** British Royal Mint

| Date | Mintage | VF20 | XF40 | MS60 | MS63 | MS65 |
|---|---|---|---|---|---|---|
| 2011 | 1,000,000 | — | 1.50 | 3.50 | 5.00 | 6.00 |

**KM# 1171a 50 PENCE**
8.00 g., 0.925 Silver 0.2379 oz. ASW, 27.3 mm. **Ruler:** Elizabeth II **Subject:** 2012 London Olympics - Hockey **Obv:** Head with tiara right **Shape:** 7-sided **Mint:** Royal Mint

| Date | Mintage | VF20 | XF40 | MS60 | MS63 | MS65 |
|---|---|---|---|---|---|---|
| 2011 | — | PF65 50.00 | | | | |

**KM# 1172 50 PENCE**
8.00 g., Copper-Nickel, 27.3 mm. **Ruler:** Elizabeth II **Subject:** 2012 London Olympics - Rowing **Obv:** Head with tiara right **Edge:** Plain **Shape:** 7-sided **Mint:** British Royal Mint

| Date | Mintage | VF20 | XF40 | MS60 | MS63 | MS65 |
|---|---|---|---|---|---|---|
| 2011 | 700,000 | — | 1.50 | 3.50 | 5.00 | 6.00 |

**KM# 1172a 50 PENCE**
8.00 g., 0.925 Silver 0.2379 oz. ASW, 27.3 mm. **Ruler:** Elizabeth II **Subject:** 2012 London Olympics - Rowing **Obv:** Head with tiara right **Shape:** 7-sided **Mint:** Royal Mint

| Date | Mintage | VF20 | XF40 | MS60 | MS63 | MS65 |
|---|---|---|---|---|---|---|
| 2011 | — | PF65 50.00 | | | | |

**KM# 1173 50 PENCE**
8.00 g., Copper-Nickel, 27.3 mm. **Ruler:** Elizabeth II **Subject:** 2012 London Olympics - Triathlon **Obv:** Head with tiara right **Edge:** Plain **Shape:** 7-sided **Mint:** British Royal Mint

| Date | Mintage | VF20 | XF40 | MS60 | MS63 | MS65 |
|---|---|---|---|---|---|---|
| 2011 | 1,000,000 | — | 1.50 | 3.50 | 5.00 | 6.00 |

**KM# 1173a 50 PENCE**
8.00 g., 0.925 Silver 0.2379 oz. ASW, 27.3 mm. **Ruler:** Elizabeth II **Subject:** 2012 London Olympics - Triathlon **Obv:** Head with tiara right **Shape:** 7-sided **Mint:** Royal Mint

| Date | Mintage | VF20 | XF40 | MS60 | MS63 | MS65 |
|---|---|---|---|---|---|---|
| 2011 | — | PF65 50.00 | | | | |

**KM# 1174 50 PENCE**
8.00 g., Copper-Nickel, 27.3 mm. **Ruler:** Elizabeth II **Subject:** 2012 London Olympics - Badminton **Obv:** Head with tiara right **Edge:** Plain **Shape:** 7-sided **Mint:** British Royal Mint

| Date | Mintage | VF20 | XF40 | MS60 | MS63 | MS65 |
|---|---|---|---|---|---|---|
| 2011 | 900,000 | — | 1.50 | 3.50 | 5.00 | 6.00 |

**KM# 1174a 50 PENCE**
8.00 g., 0.925 Silver 0.2379 oz. ASW, 27.3 mm. **Ruler:** Elizabeth II **Subject:** 2012 London Olympics - Badminton **Obv:** Head with tiara right **Shape:** 7-sided **Mint:** Royal Mint

| Date | Mintage | VF20 | XF40 | MS60 | MS63 | MS65 |
|---|---|---|---|---|---|---|
| 2011 | — | PF65 50.00 | | | | |

**KM# 1175 50 PENCE**
8.00 g., Copper-Nickel, 27.3 mm. **Ruler:** Elizabeth II **Subject:** 2012 London Olympics - Boxing **Obv:** Head with tiara right **Edge:** Plain **Shape:** 7-sided **Mint:** British Royal Mint

| Date | Mintage | VF20 | XF40 | MS60 | MS63 | MS65 |
|---|---|---|---|---|---|---|
| 2011 | 800,000 | — | 1.50 | 3.50 | 5.00 | 6.00 |

**KM# 1175a 50 PENCE**
8.00 g., 0.925 Silver 0.2379 oz. ASW, 27.3 mm. **Ruler:** Elizabeth II **Subject:** 2012 London Olympics - Boxing **Obv:** Head with tiara right **Shape:** 7-sided **Mint:** Royal Mint

| Date | Mintage | VF20 | XF40 | MS60 | MS63 | MS65 |
|---|---|---|---|---|---|---|
| 2011 | — | PF65 50.00 | | | | |

**KM# 1176 50 PENCE**
8.00 g., Copper-Nickel, 27.3 mm. **Ruler:** Elizabeth II **Subject:** 2012 London Olympics - Equestrian **Obv:** Head with tiara right **Edge:** Plain **Shape:** 7-sided **Mint:** British Royal Mint

| Date | Mintage | VF20 | XF40 | MS60 | MS63 | MS65 |
|---|---|---|---|---|---|---|
| 2011 | — | — | 1.50 | 3.50 | 5.00 | 6.00 |

**KM# 1176a 50 PENCE**
8.00 g., 0.925 Silver 0.2379 oz. ASW, 27.3 mm. **Ruler:** Elizabeth II **Subject:** 2012 London Olympics - Equestrian **Obv:** Head with tiara right **Shape:** 7-sided **Mint:** Royal Mint

| Date | Mintage | VF20 | XF40 | MS60 | MS63 | MS65 |
|---|---|---|---|---|---|---|
| 2011 | — | PF65 50.00 | | | | |

**KM# 1177 50 PENCE**
8.00 g., Copper-Nickel, 27.3 mm. **Ruler:** Elizabeth II **Subject:** 2012 London Olympics - Modern Pentathlon **Obv:** Head with tiara right **Edge:** Plain **Shape:** 7-sided **Mint:** British Royal Mint

| Date | Mintage | VF20 | XF40 | MS60 | MS63 | MS65 |
|---|---|---|---|---|---|---|
| 2011 | — | — | 1.50 | 3.50 | 5.00 | 6.00 |

**KM# 1177a 50 PENCE**
8.00 g., 0.925 Silver 0.2379 oz. ASW, 27.3 mm. **Ruler:** Elizabeth II **Subject:** 2012 London Olympics - Modern Pentathlon **Obv:** Head with tiara right **Shape:** 7-sided **Mint:** Royal Mint

| Date | Mintage | VF20 | XF40 | MS60 | MS63 | MS65 |
|---|---|---|---|---|---|---|
| 2011 | — | PF65 50.00 | | | | |

### KM# 1178 50 PENCE

8.00 g., Copper-Nickel, 27.3 mm. **Ruler:** Elizabeth II **Subject:** 2012 London Olympics - Sailing **Obv:** Head with tiara right **Edge:** Plain **Shape:** 7-sided **Mint:** British Royal Mint

| Date | Mintage | VF20 | XF40 | MS60 | MS63 | MS65 |
|---|---|---|---|---|---|---|
| 2011 | — | — | 1.50 | 3.50 | 5.00 | 6.00 |

### KM# 1178a 50 PENCE

8.00 g., 0.925 Silver 0.2379 oz. ASW, 27.3 mm. **Ruler:** Elizabeth II **Subject:** 2012 London Olympics - Sailing **Obv:** Head with tiara right **Shape:** 7-sided **Mint:** Royal Mint

| Date | Mintage | VF20 | XF40 | MS60 | MS63 | MS65 |
|---|---|---|---|---|---|---|
| 2011 | — | **PF65** 50.00 | | | | |

### KM# 1179 50 PENCE

8.00 g., Copper-Nickel, 27.3 mm. **Ruler:** Elizabeth II **Subject:** 2012 London Olympics - Shooting **Obv:** Head with tiara right **Edge:** Plain **Shape:** 7-sided **Mint:** British Royal Mint

| Date | Mintage | VF20 | XF40 | MS60 | MS63 | MS65 |
|---|---|---|---|---|---|---|
| 2011 | — | — | 1.50 | 3.50 | 5.00 | 6.00 |

### KM# 1179a 50 PENCE

8.00 g., 0.925 Silver 0.2379 oz. ASW, 27.3 mm. **Ruler:** Elizabeth II **Subject:** 2012 London Olympics - Shooting **Obv:** Head with tiara right **Shape:** 7-sided **Mint:** Royal Mint

| Date | Mintage | VF20 | XF40 | MS60 | MS63 | MS65 |
|---|---|---|---|---|---|---|
| 2011 | — | **PF65** 50.00 | | | | |

### KM# 1180 50 PENCE

8.00 g., Copper-Nickel, 27.3 mm. **Ruler:** Elizabeth II **Subject:** 2012 London Paralympics - Table Tennis **Obv:** Head with tiara right **Edge:** Plain **Shape:** 7-sided **Mint:** British Royal Mint

| Date | Mintage | VF20 | XF40 | MS60 | MS63 | MS65 |
|---|---|---|---|---|---|---|
| 2011 | 1,000,000 | — | 1.50 | 3.50 | 5.00 | 6.00 |

### KM# 1180a 50 PENCE

8.00 g., 0.925 Silver 0.2379 oz. ASW, 27.3 mm. **Ruler:** Elizabeth II **Subject:** 2012 London Olympics - Table Tennis **Obv:** Head with tiara right **Shape:** 7-sided **Mint:** Royal Mint

| Date | Mintage | VF20 | XF40 | MS60 | MS63 | MS65 |
|---|---|---|---|---|---|---|
| 2011 | — | **PF65** 63.00 | | | | |

### KM# 1181 50 PENCE

8.00 g., Copper-Nickel, 27.3 mm. **Ruler:** Elizabeth II **Subject:** 2012 London Olympics - Volleyball **Shape:** 7-sided **Mint:** British Royal Mint

| Date | Mintage | VF20 | XF40 | MS60 | MS63 | MS65 |
|---|---|---|---|---|---|---|
| 2011 | 1,000,000 | — | 1.50 | 3.50 | 5.00 | 6.00 |

### KM# 1181a 50 PENCE

8.00 g., 0.925 Silver 0.2379 oz. ASW, 27.3 mm. **Ruler:** Elizabeth II **Subject:** 2012 London Olympics - Volleyball **Obv:** Head with tiara right **Shape:** 7-sided **Mint:** Royal Mint

| Date | Mintage | VF20 | XF40 | MS60 | MS63 | MS65 |
|---|---|---|---|---|---|---|
| 2011 | — | **PF65** 50.00 | | | | |

### KM# 1182 50 PENCE

8.00 g., Copper-Nickel, 27.3 mm. **Ruler:** Elizabeth II **Subject:** 2012 London Olympics - Kyacking **Shape:** 7-sided **Mint:** British Royal Mint

| Date | Mintage | VF20 | XF40 | MS60 | MS63 | MS65 |
|---|---|---|---|---|---|---|
| 2011 | — | — | 1.50 | 3.50 | 5.00 | 6.00 |

### KM# 1182a 50 PENCE

8.00 g., 0.925 Silver 0.2379 oz. ASW, 27.3 mm. **Ruler:** Elizabeth II **Subject:** 2012 London Olympics - Kyacking **Obv:** Head with tiara right **Shape:** 7-sided **Mint:** Royal Mint

| Date | Mintage | VF20 | XF40 | MS60 | MS63 | MS65 |
|---|---|---|---|---|---|---|
| 2011 | — | **PF65** 50.00 | | | | |

### KM# 1183 50 PENCE

8.00 g., Copper-Nickel, 27.3 mm. **Ruler:** Elizabeth II **Subject:** 2012 London Paralympics - Goalball **Obv:** Head with tiara right **Edge:** Plain **Shape:** 7-sided **Mint:** British Royal Mint

| Date | Mintage | VF20 | XF40 | MS60 | MS63 | MS65 |
|---|---|---|---|---|---|---|
| 2011 | 900,000 | — | 1.50 | 3.50 | 5.00 | 6.00 |

### KM# 1183a 50 PENCE

8.00 g., 0.925 Silver 0.2379 oz. ASW, 27.3 mm. **Ruler:** Elizabeth II **Subject:** 2012 London Olympics - Goalball **Obv:** Head with tiara right **Shape:** 7-sided **Mint:** Royal Mint

| Date | Mintage | VF20 | XF40 | MS60 | MS63 | MS65 |
|---|---|---|---|---|---|---|
| 2011 | — | **PF65** 50.00 | | | | |

### KM# 1184 50 PENCE

8.00 g., Copper-Nickel, 24.3 mm. **Ruler:** Elizabeth II **Subject:** 2012 London Olympics - Judo **Obv:** Head with tiara right **Edge:** Plain **Shape:** 7-sided **Mint:** British Royal Mint

| Date | Mintage | VF20 | XF40 | MS60 | MS63 | MS65 |
|---|---|---|---|---|---|---|
| 2011 | — | — | 1.50 | 3.50 | 5.00 | 6.00 |

### KM# 1184a 50 PENCE

8.00 g., 0.925 Silver 0.2379 oz. ASW, 27.3 mm. **Ruler:** Elizabeth II **Subject:** 2012 London Olympics - Judo **Obv:** Head with tiara right **Shape:** 7-sided **Mint:** Royal Mint

| Date | Mintage | VF20 | XF40 | MS60 | MS63 | MS65 |
|---|---|---|---|---|---|---|
| 2011 | — | **PF65** 50.00 | | | | |

### KM# 1185 50 PENCE

8.00 g., Copper-Nickel, 27.3 mm. **Ruler:** Elizabeth II **Subject:** 2012 London Olympics - Taekwondo **Obv:** Head with tiara right **Edge:** Plain **Shape:** 7-sided **Mint:** British Royal Mint

| Date | Mintage | VF20 | XF40 | MS60 | MS63 | MS65 |
|---|---|---|---|---|---|---|
| 2011 | — | — | 1.50 | 3.50 | 5.00 | 6.00 |

### KM# 1185a 50 PENCE

8.00 g., 0.925 Silver 0.2379 oz. ASW, 27.3 mm. **Ruler:** Elizabeth II **Subject:** 2012 London Olympics - Taekwondo **Obv:** Head with tiara right **Shape:** 7-sided **Mint:** Royal Mint

| Date | Mintage | VF20 | XF40 | MS60 | MS63 | MS65 |
|---|---|---|---|---|---|---|
| 2011 | — | **PF65** 50.00 | | | | |

### KM# 1186 50 PENCE

8.00 g., Copper-Nickel, 27.3 mm. **Ruler:** Elizabeth II **Subject:** 2012 London Olympics - Weightlifting **Obv:** Head with tiara right **Edge:** Plain **Shape:** 7-sided **Mint:** British Royal Mint

| Date | Mintage | VF20 | XF40 | MS60 | MS63 | MS65 |
|---|---|---|---|---|---|---|
| 2011 | — | — | 1.50 | 3.50 | 5.00 | 6.00 |

### KM# 1186a 50 PENCE

8.00 g., 0.925 Silver 0.2379 oz. ASW, 27.3 mm. **Ruler:** Elizabeth II **Subject:** 2012 London Olympics - Weightlifting **Obv:** Head with tiara right **Shape:** 7-sided **Mint:** Royal Mint

| Date | Mintage | VF20 | XF40 | MS60 | MS63 | MS65 |
|---|---|---|---|---|---|---|
| 2011 | — | **PF65** 50.00 | | | | |

### KM# 1187 50 PENCE

8.00 g., Copper-Nickel, 27.3 mm. **Ruler:** Elizabeth II **Subject:** 2012 London Paralympics - Wheelchair Rugby **Obv:** Head with tiara right **Edge:** Plain **Shape:** 7-sided **Mint:** British Royal Mint

| Date | Mintage | VF20 | XF40 | MS60 | MS63 | MS65 |
|---|---|---|---|---|---|---|
| 2011 | — | — | 1.50 | 3.50 | 5.00 | 6.00 |

### KM# 1187a 50 PENCE

8.00 g., 0.925 Silver 0.2379 oz. ASW, 27.3 mm. **Ruler:** Elizabeth II **Subject:** 2012 London Olympics - Wheelchair Rugby **Obv:** Head with tiara right **Shape:** 7-sided **Mint:** Royal Mint

| Date | Mintage | VF20 | XF40 | MS60 | MS63 | MS65 |
|---|---|---|---|---|---|---|
| 2011 | — | **PF65** 50.00 | | | | |

### KM# 1188 50 PENCE

8.00 g., Copper-Nickel, 27.3 mm. **Ruler:** Elizabeth II **Subject:** 2012 Summer Olympics - Wrestling **Obv:** Head with tiara right **Edge:** Plain **Shape:** 7-sided **Mint:** British Royal Mint

| Date | Mintage | VF20 | XF40 | MS60 | MS63 | MS65 |
|---|---|---|---|---|---|---|
| 2011 | — | — | 1.50 | 3.50 | 5.00 | 6.00 |

### KM# 1188a 50 PENCE

8.00 g., 0.925 Silver 0.2379 oz. ASW, 27.3 mm. **Ruler:** Elizabeth II **Subject:** 2012 London Olympics - Wrestling **Obv:** Head with tiara right **Shape:** 7-sided **Mint:** Royal Mint

| Date | Mintage | VF20 | XF40 | MS60 | MS63 | MS65 |
|---|---|---|---|---|---|---|
| 2011 | — | **PF65** 50.00 | | | | |

### KM# 1189 50 PENCE

8.00 g., Copper-Nickel, 27.3 mm. **Ruler:** Elizabeth II **Subject:** 2012 London Paralympics - Boccia **Obv:** Head with tiara right **Edge:** Plain **Shape:** 7-sided **Mint:** British Royal Mint

| Date | Mintage | VF20 | XF40 | MS60 | MS63 | MS65 |
|---|---|---|---|---|---|---|
| 2011 | 900,000 | — | 1.50 | 3.50 | 5.00 | 6.00 |

### KM# 1189a 50 PENCE

8.00 g., 0.925 Silver 0.2379 oz. ASW, 27.3 mm. **Ruler:** Elizabeth II **Subject:** 2012 London Olympics - Boccia **Obv:** Head with tiara right **Shape:** 7-sided **Mint:** Royal Mint

| Date | Mintage | VF20 | XF40 | MS60 | MS63 | MS65 |
|---|---|---|---|---|---|---|
| 2011 | — | **PF65** 50.00 | | | | |

### KM# 1190 50 PENCE

8.00 g., Copper-Nickel, 27.3 mm. **Ruler:** Elizabeth II **Subject:** 2012 London Olympics - Basketball **Obv:** Head with tiara right **Edge:** Plain **Shape:** 7-sided **Mint:** British Royal Mint

| Date | Mintage | VF20 | XF40 | MS60 | MS63 | MS65 |
|---|---|---|---|---|---|---|
| 2011 | — | — | 1.50 | 3.50 | 5.00 | 6.00 |

### KM# 1190a 50 PENCE

8.00 g., 0.925 Silver 0.2379 oz. ASW, 27.3 mm. **Ruler:** Elizabeth II **Subject:** 2012 London Olympics - Basketball **Obv:** Head with tiara right **Shape:** 7-sided **Mint:** Royal Mint

| Date | Mintage | VF20 | XF40 | MS60 | MS63 | MS65 |
|---|---|---|---|---|---|---|
| 2011 | — | **PF65** 50.00 | | | | |

### KM# 1191 50 PENCE

8.00 g., Copper-Nickel, 27.3 mm. **Ruler:** Elizabeth II **Subject:** 2012 London Olympics - Fencing **Obv:** Head with tiara right **Edge:** Plain **Shape:** 7-sided **Mint:** British Royal Mint

| Date | Mintage | VF20 | XF40 | MS60 | MS63 | MS65 |
|---|---|---|---|---|---|---|
| 2011 | 1,000,000 | — | 1.50 | 3.50 | 5.00 | 6.00 |

### KM# 1191a 50 PENCE

8.00 g., 0.925 Silver 0.2379 oz. ASW, 27.3 mm. **Ruler:** Elizabeth II **Subject:** 2012 London Olympics - Fencing **Obv:** Head with tiara right **Shape:** 7-sided **Mint:** Royal Mint

| Date | Mintage | VF20 | XF40 | MS60 | MS63 | MS65 |
|---|---|---|---|---|---|---|
| 2011 | — | **PF65** 50.00 | | | | |

### KM# 1192 50 PENCE

8.00 g., Copper-Nickel, 27.3 mm. **Ruler:** Elizabeth II **Subject:** 2012 London Olympics - Handball **Obv:** Head with tiara right **Edge:** Plain **Shape:** 7-sided **Mint:** British Royal Mint

| Date | Mintage | VF20 | XF40 | MS60 | MS63 | MS65 |
|---|---|---|---|---|---|---|
| 2011 | — | — | 1.50 | 3.50 | 5.00 | 6.00 |

### KM# 1192a 50 PENCE

8.00 g., 0.925 Silver 0.2379 oz. ASW, 27.3 mm. **Ruler:** Elizabeth II **Subject:** 2012 London Olympics - Handball **Obv:** Head with tiara right **Shape:** 7-sided **Mint:** Royal Mint

| Date | Mintage | VF20 | XF40 | MS60 | MS63 | MS65 |
|---|---|---|---|---|---|---|
| 2011 | — | **PF65** 50.00 | | | | |

### KM# 1193 50 PENCE

8.00 g., Copper-Nickel, 27.3 mm. **Ruler:** Elizabeth II **Subject:** 2012 London Olympics - Football (Soccer) **Obv:** Head with tiara right **Edge:** Plain **Shape:** 7-sided **Mint:** British Royal Mint

| Date | Mintage | VF20 | XF40 | MS60 | MS63 | MS65 |
|---|---|---|---|---|---|---|
| 2011 | — | — | 1.50 | 3.50 | 5.00 | 6.00 |

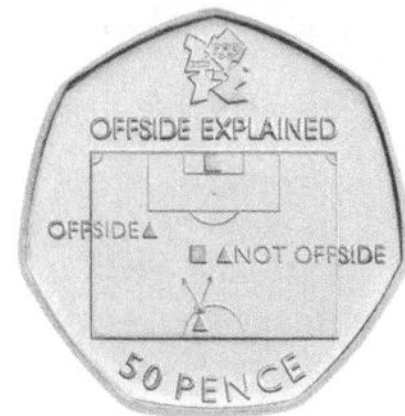


**KM# 1193a 50 PENCE**
8.00 g., 0.925 Silver 0.2379 oz. ASW, 27.3 mm. **Ruler:** Elizabeth II **Subject:** 2012 London Olympics - Football (Soccer) **Obv:** Head with tiara right **Shape:** 7-sided **Mint:** Royal Mint

| Date | Mintage | VF20 | XF40 | MS60 | MS63 | MS65 |
|---|---|---|---|---|---|---|
| 2011 | — | PF65 50.00 | | | | |

**KM# 1194 50 PENCE**
8.00 g., Copper-Nickel, 27.3 mm. **Ruler:** Elizabeth II **Subject:** 2012 London Olympics - Tennis **Obv:** Head with tiara right **Edge:** Plain **Shape:** 7-sided **Mint:** British Royal Mint

| Date | Mintage | VF20 | XF40 | MS60 | MS63 | MS65 |
|---|---|---|---|---|---|---|
| 2011 | — | — | 1.50 | 3.50 | 5.00 | 6.00 |

**KM# 1194a 50 PENCE**
8.00 g., 0.925 Silver 0.2379 oz. ASW, 27.3 mm. **Ruler:** Elizabeth II **Subject:** 2012 London Olympics - Tennis **Obv:** Head with tiara right **Shape:** 7-sided **Mint:** Royal Mint

| Date | Mintage | VF20 | XF40 | MS60 | MS63 | MS65 |
|---|---|---|---|---|---|---|
| 2011 | — | PF65 50.00 | | | | |

**KM# 1195 50 PENCE**
8.00 g., Copper-Nickel, 27.3 mm. **Ruler:** Elizabeth II **Subject:** London Olympics - Sailing **Obv:** Head with tiara right **Edge:** Plain **Shape:** 7-sided

| Date | Mintage | F12 | VF20 | XF40 | MS60 | MS63 |
|---|---|---|---|---|---|---|
| 2011 | — | — | — | 1.00 | 5.00 | 6.00 |

**KM# 1196 50 PENCE**
8.00 g., Copper-Nickel, 27.3 mm. **Ruler:** Elizabeth II **Subject:** World Wildlife Fund, 50th Anniversary **Obv:** Head with tiara right **Rev:** Panda in center of animal shaped blocks **Edge:** Plain **Shape:** 7-sided **Mint:** British Royal Mint

| Date | Mintage | VF20 | XF40 | MS60 | MS63 | MS65 |
|---|---|---|---|---|---|---|
| 2011 | — | PF65 8.50 | | | | |
| 2011 | — | — | 1.50 | 3.50 | 5.00 | 6.00 |

**KM# 1196a 50 PENCE**
8.00 g., 0.925 Silver 0.2379 oz. ASW, 27.3 mm. **Ruler:** Elizabeth II **Subject:** World Wildlife Fund, 50th Anniversary **Obv:** Head with tiara right **Rev:** Panda at center, animal shapes as blocks **Edge:** Plain **Shape:** 7-sided **Mint:** British Royal Mint

| Date | Mintage | VF20 | XF40 | MS60 | MS63 | MS65 |
|---|---|---|---|---|---|---|
| 2011 | — | PF65 50.00 | | | | |

Note: Also exists as a Piedfort, P86

**KM# 1112a.1 50 PENCE**
8.00 g., 0.925 Silver 0.2379 oz. ASW partially gilt, 27.3 mm. **Ruler:** Elizabeth II **Obv:** Head with tiara right **Rev:** Section of Royal Arms - bottom center

| Date | Mintage | VF20 | XF40 | MS60 | MS63 | MS65 |
|---|---|---|---|---|---|---|
| 2012 | — | PF65 50.00 | | | | |

**KM# 1246 50 PENCE**
8.00 g., Copper-Nickel, 27.3 mm. **Ruler:** Elizabeth II **Subject:** Christopher Ironside, 100th Anniversary of Birth **Obv:** Head with tiara right **Rev:** Royal Arms **Shape:** 7-sided

| Date | Mintage | VF20 | XF40 | MS60 | MS63 | MS65 |
|---|---|---|---|---|---|---|
| 2013 | — | — | — | — | — | 15.00 |
| 2013 | 44,000 | PF65 50.00 | | | | |

**KM# 1246a 50 PENCE**
8.00 g., 0.925 Silver 0.2379 oz. ASW, 27.3 mm. **Ruler:** Elizabeth II **Subject:** Christopher Ironside, 100th Anniversary of Birth **Obv:** Bust with tiara right **Rev:** Royal arms with supporters **Shape:** 7-sided

| Date | Mintage | VF20 | XF40 | MS60 | MS63 | MS65 |
|---|---|---|---|---|---|---|
| 2013 | 2,013 | PF65 50.00 | | | | |

**KM# 1253 50 PENCE**
8.00 g., Copper-Nickel, 27.3 mm. **Ruler:** Elizabeth II **Subject:** Benjamin Britten, 100th Anniversary of Birth **Obv:** Head with tiara right **Rev:** Quote from Tennyson: BLOW BUGLE BLOW: SET THE WILD ECHOES FLYING **Shape:** 7-sided **Mint:** British Royal Mint

| Date | Mintage | VF20 | XF40 | MS60 | MS63 | MS65 |
|---|---|---|---|---|---|---|
| 2013 | — | — | — | 2.50 | 3.50 | 4.00 |

**KM# 1253a 50 PENCE**
8.00 g., 0.925 Silver 0.2379 oz. ASW, 27.3 mm. **Ruler:** Elizabeth II **Subject:** Bnjamin Britten, 100th Anniversary of Birth **Obv:** Head with tiara right **Shape:** 7-sided **Mint:** British Royal Mint

| Date | Mintage | VF20 | XF40 | MS60 | MS63 | MS65 |
|---|---|---|---|---|---|---|
| 2013 | — | PF65 40.00 | | | | |

**KM# 1253b 50 PENCE**
15.50 g., 0.916 Gold 0.4565 oz. AGW, 27.3 mm. **Ruler:** Elizabeth II **Subject:** Benjamin Britten, 100th Anniversary of Birth **Obv:** Head with tiara right **Mint:** British Royal Mint

| Date | Mintage | VF20 | XF40 | MS60 | MS63 | MS65 |
|---|---|---|---|---|---|---|
| 2013 | — | PF65 850 | | | | |

Note: 1253.8

**KM# 993 POUND**
9.50 g., Nickel-Brass, 22.5 mm. **Ruler:** Elizabeth II **Subject:** United Kingdom **Obv:** Head with tiara right **Rev:** Royal Arms with supporters **Edge:** Reeded and lettered **Edge Lettering:** DECUS ET TUTAMEN

| Date | Mintage | VF20 | XF40 | MS60 | MS63 | MS65 |
|---|---|---|---|---|---|---|
| 2003 | 61,596,500 | — | 3.00 | 4.50 | 6.00 | 7.50 |
| 2003 | 43,513 | PF65 7.50 | | | | |
| 2008 | — | — | 3.00 | 4.50 | 6.00 | 7.50 |

**KM# 993a POUND**
9.50 g., 0.925 Silver 0.2825 oz. ASW, 22.5 mm. **Ruler:** Elizabeth II **Subject:** United Kingdom **Obv:** Head with tiara right **Rev:** Royal Arms with supporters **Edge:** Reeded and lettered **Edge Lettering:** DECUS ET TUTAMEN

| Date | Mintage | VF20 | XF40 | MS60 | MS63 | MS65 |
|---|---|---|---|---|---|---|
| 2003 | 15,830 | PF65 45.00 | | | | |

Note: Also exists as a Piedfort, P41

**KM# 1013 POUND**
9.50 g., Nickel-Brass, 22.5 mm. **Ruler:** Elizabeth II **Subject:** Northern Ireland **Obv:** Head with tiara right **Rev:** Celtic cross with a pimpernel flower at the center **Edge:** Reeded and lettered **Edge Lettering:** DECUS ET TUTAMEN **Mint:** British Royal Mint

| Date | Mintage | VF20 | XF40 | MS60 | MS63 | MS65 |
|---|---|---|---|---|---|---|
| 2001 | 63,968,065 | — | 3.00 | 4.50 | 6.00 | 7.50 |
| 2001 | 45,617 | PF65 7.50 | | | | |

**KM# 1013a POUND**
9.50 g., 0.925 Silver 0.2825 oz. ASW, 22.5 mm. **Ruler:** Elizabeth II **Subject:** Northern Ireland **Obv:** Head with tiara right **Rev:** Celtic cross with a pimpernel flower in the center **Edge:** Reeded and lettered **Edge Lettering:** DECUS ET TUTAMEN **Mint:** British Royal Mint

| Date | Mintage | VF20 | XF40 | MS60 | MS63 | MS65 |
|---|---|---|---|---|---|---|
| 2001 | 25,000 | PF65 45.00 | | | | |

Note: Also exists as a Piedfort, P101

**KM# 1030 POUND**
9.50 g., Nickel-Brass, 22.5 mm. **Ruler:** Elizabeth II **Subject:** England **Obv:** Head with tiara right **Rev:** Three lions passant left **Edge:** Reeded and lettered **Edge Lettering:** DECUS ET TUTAMEN **Mint:** British Royal Mint

| Date | Mintage | VF20 | XF40 | MS60 | MS63 | MS65 |
|---|---|---|---|---|---|---|
| 2002 | 60,770 | PF65 7.50 | | | | |
| 2002 | 77,818,000 | — | 3.00 | 4.50 | 6.00 | 7.00 |

**KM# 1030a POUND**
9.50 g., 0.925 Silver 0.2825 oz. ASW, 22.5 mm. **Ruler:** Elizabeth II **Subject:** England **Obv:** Head with tiara right **Rev:** Three lions passant left **Edge:** Reeded and lettered **Edge Lettering:** DECUS ET TUTAMEN **Mint:** British Royal Mint

| Date | Mintage | VF20 | XF40 | MS60 | MS63 | MS65 |
|---|---|---|---|---|---|---|
| 2002 | — | PF65 45.00 | | | | |

Note: Also exists as a Piedfort, P102

**KM# 1030b POUND**
0.9167 Gold, 22.5 mm. **Ruler:** Elizabeth II **Subject:** England **Obv:** Head with tiara right **Rev:** Three lions left passant left **Edge:** Reeded and lettered **Edge Lettering:** DECUS ET TUTAMEN **Mint:** British Royal Mint

| Date | Mintage | VF20 | XF40 | MS60 | MS63 | MS65 |
|---|---|---|---|---|---|---|
| 2002 | — | PF65 850 | | | | |

**KM# 1048 POUND**
9.50 g., Nickel-Brass, 22.5 mm. **Ruler:** Elizabeth II **Obv:** Head with tiara right **Rev:** Forth Rail Bridge in Scotland **Edge:** Reeded and ornamented **Mint:** British Royal Mint

| Date | Mintage | VF20 | XF40 | MS60 | MS63 | MS65 |
|---|---|---|---|---|---|---|
| 2004 | 39,162,000 | — | 3.50 | 5.00 | 7.50 | 9.00 |
| 2004 | 35,020 | PF65 9.00 | | | | |

**KM# 1048a POUND**
9.50 g., 0.925 Silver 0.2825 oz. ASW, 22.5 mm. **Ruler:** Elizabeth II **Obv:** Head with tiara right **Rev:** Forth Railway Bridge in Scotland **Edge:** Ornamented and reeded **Mint:** British Royal Mint

| Date | Mintage | VF20 | XF40 | MS60 | MS63 | MS65 |
|---|---|---|---|---|---|---|
| 2004 | Est. 20000 | PF65 45.00 | | | | |

Note: Also exists as a Piedfort, P44

**KM# 1048b POUND**
19.62 g., 0.9166 Gold 0.5782 oz. AGW, 22.5 mm. **Ruler:** Elizabeth II **Obv:** Head with tiara right **Rev:** Forth Railway Bridge in Scotland **Edge:** Reeded and ornamented **Mint:** British Royal Mint

| Date | Mintage | VF20 | XF40 | MS60 | MS63 | MS65 |
|---|---|---|---|---|---|---|
| 2004 | Est. 1500 | PF65 1,100 | | | | |

### KM# 1051 POUND

9.50 g., Nickel-Brass, 22.5 mm. **Ruler:** Elizabeth II **Obv:** Head with tiara right **Rev:** Menai Bridge to the Isle of Anglesey **Edge:** Reeded and ornamented **Mint:** British Royal Mint

| Date | Mintage | VF20 | XF40 | MS60 | MS63 | MS65 |
|---|---|---|---|---|---|---|
| 2005 | 40,563 | PF63 10.00 | PF65 12.00 | | | |
| 2005 | 99,429,500 | — | 3.00 | 4.50 | 6.00 | 7.50 |

### KM# 1051a.2 POUND

9.50 g., 0.925 Silver 0.2825 oz. ASW, 22.5 mm. **Ruler:** Elizabeth II **Obv:** Elizabeth II **Rev:** Menai Bridge to the Isle of Anglesey **Edge:** Reeded and ornamented **Mint:** British Royal Mint

| Date | Mintage | VF20 | XF40 | MS60 | MS63 | MS65 |
|---|---|---|---|---|---|---|
| 2005 | Est. 20000 | PF65 45.00 | | | | |

### KM# 1051a POUND

9.50 g., 0.925 Silver 0.2825 oz. ASW, 22.5 mm. **Ruler:** Elizabeth II **Obv:** Head with tiara right **Rev:** Menai Bridge to the Isle of Anglesey **Edge:** Reeded and lettered **Edge Lettering:** PLEIDOL WYF I'M GWLAD **Mint:** British Royal Mint

| Date | Mintage | VF20 | XF40 | MS60 | MS63 | MS65 |
|---|---|---|---|---|---|---|
| 2005 | Est. 15000 | PF65 45.00 | | | | |

Note: Also exists as a Piedfort, P50

### KM# 1051b.2 POUND

19.62 g., 0.9166 Gold 0.5782 oz. AGW, 22.5 mm. **Ruler:** Elizabeth II **Obv:** Head with tiara right **Rev:** Menai Bridge to the Isle of Anglesey **Edge:** Reeded and ornamented **Mint:** British Royal Mint

| Date | Mintage | VF20 | XF40 | MS60 | MS63 | MS65 |
|---|---|---|---|---|---|---|
| 2005 | Est. 1500 | PF65 1,000 | | | | |

### KM# 1051b POUND

19.62 g., 0.9167 Gold 0.5782 oz. AGW, 22.5 mm. **Ruler:** Elizabeth II **Obv:** Head with tiara right **Rev:** Menai Bridge to the Isle of Anglesey **Edge:** Reeded and lettered **Edge Lettering:** PLEIDOL WYF I'M GWLAD **Mint:** British Royal Mint

| Date | Mintage | VF20 | XF40 | MS60 | MS63 | MS65 |
|---|---|---|---|---|---|---|
| 2005 | Est. 1500 | PF65 1,000 | | | | |

### KM# 1059 POUND

9.60 g., Nickel-Brass, 22.5 mm. **Ruler:** Elizabeth II **Obv:** Head with tiara right **Rev:** Egyptian Arch Railway Bridge at Newry **Edge:** Reeded and lettered **Mint:** British Royal Mint

| Date | Mintage | VF20 | XF40 | MS60 | MS63 | MS65 |
|---|---|---|---|---|---|---|
| 2006 | 37,689 | PF65 10.00 | | | | |
| 2006 | 38,938,000 | — | 4.00 | 6.00 | 8.00 | 9.00 |
| 2007 | — | PF65 10.00 | | | | |

### KM# 1059a POUND

9.50 g., 0.925 Silver 0.2825 oz. ASW, 22.5 mm. **Ruler:** Elizabeth II **Obv:** Head with tiara right **Rev:** Egyptian Arch Railway Bridge at Newry **Edge:** Reeded and lettered **Edge Lettering:** DECUS ET TUTAMEN **Mint:** British Royal Mint

| Date | Mintage | VF20 | XF40 | MS60 | MS63 | MS65 |
|---|---|---|---|---|---|---|
| 2006 | Est. 20000 | PF65 50.00 | | | | |

Note: Also exists as a Piedfort, P55

### KM# 1059a.2 POUND

9.50 g., 0.925 Silver 0.2825 oz. ASW, 22.5 mm. **Ruler:** Elizabeth II **Obv:** Head with tiara right **Rev:** Egyptian Arch Railway Bridge at Newry **Edge:** Reeded and ornamented **Mint:** British Royal Mint

| Date | Mintage | VF20 | XF40 | MS60 | MS63 | MS65 |
|---|---|---|---|---|---|---|
| 2006 | Est. 20000 | PF65 45.00 | | | | |

### KM# 1059b.2 POUND

19.62 g., 0.9166 Gold 0.5782 oz. AGW, 22.5 mm. **Ruler:** Elizabeth II **Obv:** Head with tiara right **Rev:** Egyptian Arch Railway Bridge at Newry **Edge:** Reeded and ornamented **Mint:** British Royal Mint

| Date | Mintage | VF20 | XF40 | MS60 | MS63 | MS65 |
|---|---|---|---|---|---|---|
| 2006 | Est. 1500 | PF65 1,100 | | | | |

### KM# 1059b POUND

19.62 g., 0.9167 Gold 0.5782 oz. AGW, 22.5 mm. **Ruler:** Elizabeth II **Obv:** Head with tiara right **Rev:** Egyptian Arch Railway Bridge at Newry **Edge:** Reeded and lettered **Edge Lettering:** DECUS ET TUTAMEN **Mint:** British Royal Mint

| Date | Mintage | VF20 | XF40 | MS60 | MS63 | MS65 |
|---|---|---|---|---|---|---|
| 2006 | — | PF65 1,000 | | | | |

### KM# 1074 POUND

9.50 g., Nickel-Brass, 22.5 mm. **Ruler:** Elizabeth II **Obv:** Head with tiara right **Rev:** Millennium Bridge at Gateshead **Edge:** Reeded and ornamented **Mint:** British Royal Mint

| Date | Mintage | VF20 | XF40 | MS60 | MS63 | MS65 |
|---|---|---|---|---|---|---|
| 2007 | 26,180,160 | — | 4.00 | 6.00 | 8.00 | 9.00 |
| 2007 | 38,215 | PF65 10.00 | | | | |

### KM# 1074a POUND

9.50 g., 0.925 Silver 0.2825 oz. ASW, 22.5 mm. **Ruler:** Elizabeth II **Obv:** head with tiara right **Rev:** Millennium Bridge at Gateshead **Edge:** Reeded and ornamented **Mint:** British Royal Mint

| Date | Mintage | VF20 | XF40 | MS60 | MS63 | MS65 |
|---|---|---|---|---|---|---|
| 2007 | Est. 20000 | PF65 45.00 | | | | |

Note: Also exists as a Piedfort, P60

### KM# 1074b POUND

19.62 g., 0.9166 Gold 0.5782 oz. AGW, 22.5 mm. **Ruler:** Elizabeth II **Obv:** Head with tiara right **Rev:** Millennium Bridge at Gateshead **Edge:** Reeded and ornamented **Mint:** British Royal Mint

| Date | Mintage | VF20 | XF40 | MS60 | MS63 | MS65 |
|---|---|---|---|---|---|---|
| 2007 | Est. 1500 | PF65 1,000 | | | | |

### KM# 993b POUND

19.60 g., 0.9167 Gold 0.5777 oz. AGW, 22.5 mm. **Ruler:** Elizabeth II **Subject:** United Kingdom **Obv:** Head with tiara right **Rev:** Royal Arms with supporters **Edge Lettering:** DECUS ET TUTAMEN

| Date | Mintage | VF20 | XF40 | MS60 | MS63 | MS65 |
|---|---|---|---|---|---|---|
| 2008 | Est. 2008 | PF65 1,100 | | | | |
| 2013 | 100 | PF65 1,200 | | | | |

### KM# 1113 POUND

9.50 g., Nickel-Brass, 22.5 mm. **Ruler:** Elizabeth II **Obv:** Head with tiara right **Rev:** Shield of the Royal Arms **Edge:** Reeded and lettered **Edge Lettering:** DECUS ET TUTAMEN **Mint:** British Royal Mint

| Date | Mintage | VF20 | XF40 | MS60 | MS63 | MS65 |
|---|---|---|---|---|---|---|
| 2008 | 43,827,300 | — | 3.00 | 4.50 | 6.00 | 7.50 |
| 2008 | 56,333 | PF65 7.50 | | | | |
| 2009 | 27,625,600 | — | 4.00 | 6.00 | 8.00 | 9.00 |
| 2009 | 40,000 | PF65 9.00 | | | | |
| 2010 | 38,505,000 | — | 3.00 | 4.50 | 6.00 | 7.50 |
| 2010 | 40,000 | PF65 7.50 | | | | |
| 2011 | — | — | 3.00 | 4.50 | 6.00 | 7.50 |
| 2011 | 40,000 | PF65 7.50 | | | | |

| Date | Mintage | VF20 | XF40 | MS60 | MS63 | MS65 |
|---|---|---|---|---|---|---|
| 2012 | — | — | 3.00 | 4.50 | 6.00 | 7.50 |
| 2012 | 33,500 | PF65 7.50 | | | | |
| 2013 | — | — | 3.00 | 4.50 | 6.00 | 7.50 |
| 2013 | 44,000 | PF65 7.50 | | | | |
| 2014 | — | — | — | 4.50 | 6.00 | 7.50 |
| 2014 | — | PF65 7.50 | | | | |

### KM# 1113a POUND

9.50 g., 0.925 Silver 0.2825 oz. ASW, 22.5 mm. **Ruler:** Elizabeth II **Obv:** Head in tiara right **Rev:** Shield of the Royal Arms **Mint:** British Royal Mint

| Date | Mintage | VF20 | XF40 | MS60 | MS63 | MS65 |
|---|---|---|---|---|---|---|
| 2008 | 5,000 | PF65 50.00 | | | | |
| Note: Also exists as a Piedfort, P103 | | | | | | |
| 2009 | 50,000 | — | — | — | — | 50.00 |
| 2009 | 20,000 | PF65 60.00 | | | | |
| 2010 | 50,000 | — | — | — | — | 50.00 |
| 2010 | 20,000 | PF65 60.00 | | | | |

### KM# 1113b POUND

16.62 g., 0.9167 Gold 0.4898 oz. AGW, 22.5 mm. **Ruler:** Elizabeth II **Obv:** Head in tiara right **Rev:** Shield of the Royal Arms **Mint:** British Royal Mint

| Date | Mintage | VF20 | XF40 | MS60 | MS63 | MS65 |
|---|---|---|---|---|---|---|
| 2008 | 860 | PF65 1,100 | | | | |
| 2009 | 1,000 | PF65 1,000 | | | | |
| 2013 | 100 | PF65 1,250 | | | | |

### KM# 1113c POUND

Platinum APW, 22.5 mm. **Ruler:** Elizabeth II **Obv:** Head in tiara right **Rev:** Shield of the Royal Arms **Mint:** British Royal Mint

| Date | Mintage | VF20 | XF40 | MS60 | MS63 | MS65 |
|---|---|---|---|---|---|---|
| 2008 | — | PF65 1,650 | | | | |

### KM# 1158 POUND

9.50 g., Nickel-Brass, 22.5 mm. **Ruler:** Elizabeth II **Obv:** Head with tiara right **Rev:** City of London arms, three smaller arms below **Edge:** Reeded and lettered **Edge Lettering:** DOMINE DIRIGE NOS **Mint:** British Royal Mint

| Date | Mintage | VF20 | XF40 | MS60 | MS63 | MS65 |
|---|---|---|---|---|---|---|
| 2010 | — | PF63 10.00 | PF65 12.00 | | | |
| 2010 | — | — | 3.00 | 4.50 | 6.00 | 7.50 |

### KM# 1158a POUND

9.50 g., 0.925 Silver 0.2825 oz. ASW, 22.5 mm. **Ruler:** Elizabeth II **Obv:** Head with tiara right **Rev:** City of London arms, three smaller arms below **Mint:** British Royal Mint

| Date | Mintage | VF20 | XF40 | MS60 | MS63 | MS65 |
|---|---|---|---|---|---|---|
| 2010 | 20,000 | PF65 60.00 | | | | |

Note: Also exists as a Piedfort, P75

### KM# 1158b POUND

19.62 g., 0.9167 Gold 0.5782 oz. AGW, 22.5 mm. **Ruler:** Elizabeth II **Obv:** Head with tiara right **Rev:** City of London arms, three smaller arms below **Mint:** British Royal Mint

| Date | Mintage | VF20 | XF40 | MS60 | MS63 | MS65 |
|---|---|---|---|---|---|---|
| 2010 | 2,500 | PF65 1,100 | | | | |

### KM# 1159 POUND

9.50 g., Nickel-Brass, 22.5 mm. **Ruler:** Elizabeth II **Obv:** Head with tiara right **Rev:** City of Belfast arms, three smaller arms below **Edge:** Reeded and lettered **Edge Lettering:** PRO TANTO QUID RETRIBUAMUS **Mint:** British Royal Mint

| Date | Mintage | VF20 | XF40 | MS60 | MS63 | MS65 |
|---|---|---|---|---|---|---|
| 2010 | — | — | 3.00 | 4.50 | 6.00 | 7.50 |
| 2010 | — | PF63 10.00 | PF65 12.00 | | | |

### KM# 1159a POUND

9.50 g., 0.925 Silver 0.2825 oz. ASW, 22.5 mm. **Ruler:** Elizabeth II **Obv:** Head with tiara right **Rev:** City of Belfast arms, three smaller arms below **Mint:** British Royal Mint

| Date | Mintage | VF20 | XF40 | MS60 | MS63 | MS65 |
|---|---|---|---|---|---|---|
| 2010 | 20,000 | PF65 60.00 | | | | |

Note: Also exists as a Piedfort, P76

**KM# 1159b POUND**
19.62 g., 0.9167 Gold 0.5782 oz. AGW, 22.5 mm. **Ruler:** Elizabeth II **Obv:** Head with tiara right **Rev:** City of Belfast arms, three smaller arms below **Mint:** British Royal Mint

| Date | Mintage | VF20 | XF40 | MS60 | MS63 | MS65 |
|---|---|---|---|---|---|---|
| 2010 | 2,500 | PF65 1,100 | | | | |

**KM# 1197 POUND**
9.50 g., Nickel-Brass, 22.5 mm. **Ruler:** Elizabeth II **Obv:** Head with tiara right **Rev:** Edinburgh city arms, three smaller arms below **Edge:** Reeded and lettered **Edge Lettering:** NISI DOMINUS FRUSTRA **Mint:** British Royal Mint

| Date | Mintage | VF20 | XF40 | MS60 | MS63 | MS65 |
|---|---|---|---|---|---|---|
| 2011 | — | — | 3.00 | 4.50 | 6.00 | 7.50 |
| 2011 | — | PF63 10.00 | PF65 12.00 | | | |

**KM# 1197a POUND**
9.50 g., 0.925 Silver 0.2825 oz. ASW, 22.5 mm. **Ruler:** Elizabeth II **Obv:** Head with tiara right **Rev:** Edinburgh City arms, three smailer arms below **Mint:** British Royal Mint

| Date | Mintage | VF20 | XF40 | MS60 | MS63 | MS65 |
|---|---|---|---|---|---|---|
| 2011 | — | PF63 45.00 | PF65 45.00 | | | |

Note: Also exists as a Piedfort, P83

**KM# 1198 POUND**
9.50 g., Nickel-Brass, 22.5 mm. **Ruler:** Elizabeth II **Obv:** Head with tiara right **Rev:** Cardiff city arms, three smaller arms below **Edge:** Reeded and lettered **Edge Lettering:** DDRAIG GOCH DDYRY CYCHWYN **Mint:** British Royal Mint

| Date | Mintage | VF20 | XF40 | MS60 | MS63 | MS65 |
|---|---|---|---|---|---|---|
| 2011 | — | — | 3.00 | 4.50 | 6.00 | 7.50 |
| 2011 | — | PF63 10.00 | PF65 12.00 | | | |

**KM# 1198a POUND**
9.50 g., 0.925 Silver 0.2825 oz. ASW, 22.5 mm. **Ruler:** Elizabeth II **Obv:** Head with tiara right **Rev:** Cardiff city arms, three smaller arms below **Mint:** British Royal Mint

| Date | Mintage | VF20 | XF40 | MS60 | MS63 | MS65 |
|---|---|---|---|---|---|---|
| 2011 | — | PF65 45.00 | | | | |

Note: Also exists as a Piedfort, P84

**KM# 1113a.1 POUND**
9.50 g., 0.925 Silver 0.2825 oz. ASW partially gilt, 22.5 mm. **Ruler:** Elizabeth II **Obv:** Head with tiara right **Rev:** Shield of the Royal Arms

| Date | Mintage | VF20 | XF40 | MS60 | MS63 | MS65 |
|---|---|---|---|---|---|---|
| 2012 | — | PF65 60.00 | | | | |

**KM# 1237 POUND**
9.50 g., Nickel-Brass, 22.5 mm. **Ruler:** Elizabeth II **Obv:** Head with tiara right **Rev:** England flora - Rose and oak

| Date | Mintage | VF20 | XF40 | MS60 | MS63 | MS65 |
|---|---|---|---|---|---|---|
| 2013 | — | — | 3.00 | 4.50 | 6.00 | 7.50 |
| 2013 | — | PF63 10.00 | PF65 12.00 | | | |

**KM# 1237a POUND**
9.50 g., 0.925 Silver 0.2825 oz. ASW, 22.5 mm. **Ruler:** Elizabeth II **Obv:** Bust with tiara right **Rev:** England flora - Rose and oak

| Date | Mintage | VF20 | XF40 | MS60 | MS63 | MS65 |
|---|---|---|---|---|---|---|
| 2013 | 12,500 | PF65 40.00 | | | | |

**KM# 1237b POUND**
19.61 g., 0.9167 Gold 0.578 oz. AGW, 22.5 mm. **Ruler:** Elizabeth II **Obv:** Head with tiara right **Rev:** England Flora - oak and rose

| Date | Mintage | VF20 | XF40 | MS60 | MS63 | MS65 |
|---|---|---|---|---|---|---|
| 2013 | 560 | PF65 1,400 | | | | |

**KM# 1238 POUND**
9.50 g., Nickel-Brass, 22.5 mm. **Ruler:** Elizabeth II **Obv:** Head with tiara right **Rev:** Wales flora - Leek and daffodil

| Date | Mintage | VF20 | XF40 | MS60 | MS63 | MS65 |
|---|---|---|---|---|---|---|
| 2013 | — | PF63 10.00 | PF65 12.00 | | | |
| 2013 | — | — | 3.00 | 4.50 | 6.00 | 7.50 |

**KM# 1238a POUND**
9.50 g., 0.925 Silver 0.2825 oz. ASW, 22.5 mm. **Ruler:** Elizabeth II **Obv:** Head with tiara right **Rev:** Wales flora - leek and daffodil

| Date | Mintage | VF20 | XF40 | MS60 | MS63 | MS65 |
|---|---|---|---|---|---|---|
| 2013 | 12,500 | PF65 40.00 | | | | |

**KM# 1238b POUND**
19.61 g., 0.9167 Gold 0.578 oz. AGW, 22.5 mm. **Ruler:** Elizabeth II **Obv:** Head with tiara right **Rev:** Wales flora - leek and daffodil

| Date | Mintage | VF20 | XF40 | MS60 | MS63 | MS65 |
|---|---|---|---|---|---|---|
| 2013 | 560 | PF65 1,400 | | | | |

**KM# 1245 POUND**
16.62 g., 0.917 Gold 0.490 oz. AGW, 22.5 mm. **Ruler:** Elizabeth II **Obv:** Head with tiara right **Rev:** Crowned shield of the United Kingdom **Edge Lettering:** DECUS ET TUTAMEN

| Date | Mintage | VF20 | XF40 | MS60 | MS63 | MS65 |
|---|---|---|---|---|---|---|
| 2013 | 100 | PF65 1,200 | | | | |

**KM# 994 2 POUNDS**
12.00 g., Bi-Metallic Copper-Nickel center in Nickel-Brass ring, 28.4 mm. **Ruler:** Elizabeth II **Subject:** Technology **Obv:** Head with tiara right **Rev:** Symbolic depiction in concentric circles of technological development from the Iron Age to the Internet **Edge Lettering:** STANDING ON THE SHOULDERS OF GIANTS

| Date | Mintage | VF20 | XF40 | MS60 | MS63 | MS65 |
|---|---|---|---|---|---|---|
| 2001 | 34,984,750 | — | 5.00 | 7.00 | 9.50 | 12.00 |
| 2001 | — | PF65 12.00 | | | | |
| 2002 | 13,024,750 | — | 5.00 | 7.00 | 9.50 | 12.00 |
| 2002 | — | PF65 12.00 | | | | |
| 2003 | 17,531,250 | — | 5.00 | 7.00 | 9.50 | 12.00 |
| 2003 | 43,513 | PF65 12.00 | | | | |
| 2004 | 11,981,500 | — | 5.00 | 7.00 | 9.50 | 12.00 |
| 2004 | 35,020 | PF65 12.00 | | | | |
| 2005 | 3,837,250 | — | 5.00 | 7.00 | 9.50 | 12.00 |
| 2005 | 40,563 | PF65 12.00 | | | | |
| 2006 | 16,715,000 | — | 5.00 | 7.00 | 9.50 | 12.00 |
| 2006 | — | PF65 12.00 | | | | |
| 2007 | 10,270,000 | — | 5.00 | 7.00 | 9.50 | 12.00 |
| 2007 | — | PF65 12.00 | | | | |
| 2008 | 30,107,000 | — | 5.00 | 7.00 | 9.50 | 12.00 |
| 2008 | — | PF65 12.00 | | | | |
| 2009 | 8,775,000 | — | 5.00 | 7.00 | 9.50 | 12.00 |
| 2009 | — | PF65 12.00 | | | | |
| 2010 | 2,015,000 | — | 5.00 | 7.00 | 9.50 | 12.00 |
| 2010 | — | PF65 12.00 | | | | |
| 2011 | — | — | 5.00 | 7.00 | 9.50 | 12.00 |
| 2011 | — | PF65 12.00 | | | | |
| 2012 | — | — | 5.00 | 7.00 | 9.50 | 12.00 |
| 2012 | — | PF65 12.00 | | | | |
| 2013 | — | — | 5.00 | 7.00 | 9.50 | 12.00 |
| 2013 | — | PF65 12.00 | | | | |
| 2014 | — | — | 5.00 | 7.00 | 9.50 | 12.00 |
| 2014 | — | PF65 12.00 | | | | |

**KM# 994a 2 POUNDS**
12.00 g., 0.925 Silver 0.3569 oz. ASW, 28.35 mm. **Ruler:** Elizabeth II **Subject:** Technology **Obv:** Head with tiara right **Rev:** Symbolic depiction in concentric circles of technological development from the Iron Age to the Internet **Note:** Gold plated silver ring, silver center.

| Date | Mintage | VF20 | XF40 | MS60 | MS63 | MS65 |
|---|---|---|---|---|---|---|
| 2006 | — | PF65 45.00 | | | | |

**KM# 994c 2 POUNDS**
15.98 g., 0.9167 Gold 0.471 oz. AGW, 28.35 mm. **Ruler:** Elizabeth II **Subject:** Technology **Obv:** Head with tiara right **Rev:** Symbolic depiction in concentric circles of technological development from the Iron Age to the Internet

| Date | Mintage | VF20 | XF40 | MS60 | MS63 | MS65 |
|---|---|---|---|---|---|---|
| 2002 | — | PF65 900 | | | | |

**KM# 1014 2 POUNDS**
11.97 g., Bi-Metallic Copper-Nickel center in Nickel-Brass ring, 28.35 mm. **Ruler:** Elizabeth II **Subject:** First Transatlantic Radio Transmission **Obv:** Head with tiara right within circle **Rev:** Symbolic design **Edge:** Reeded and inscribed **Edge Lettering:** WIRELESS BRIDGES THE ATLANTIC... MARCONI... 1901 **Mint:** British Royal Mint

| Date | Mintage | VF20 | XF40 | MS60 | MS63 | MS65 |
|---|---|---|---|---|---|---|
| 2001 | 4,558,000 | — | 5.00 | 7.00 | 9.50 | 12.00 |
| 2001 | — | PF63 14.00 | PF65 16.00 | | | |

**KM# 1014a 2 POUNDS**
12.00 g., 0.925 Silver 0.3569 oz. ASW with gilt ring, 28.4 mm. **Ruler:** Elizabeth II **Subject:** First Transatlantic Radio Transmission **Obv:** Head with tiara right within circle **Rev:** Symbolic design **Edge Lettering:** WIRELESS BRIDGES THE ATLANTIC...MARCONI 1901...

| Date | Mintage | VF20 | XF40 | MS60 | MS63 | MS65 |
|---|---|---|---|---|---|---|
| 2001 | 11,488 | PF65 45.00 | | | | |

Note: Also exists as a Piefort, P106

**KM# 1014b 2 POUNDS**
15.97 g., 0.9166 Gold 0.4706 oz. AGW Yellow gold plated Red Gold center in Red Gold ring, 28.4 mm. **Ruler:** Elizabeth II **Subject:** First Transatlantic Radio Transmission **Obv:** Head with tiara right **Rev:** Symbolic design

| Date | Mintage | VF20 | XF40 | MS60 | MS63 | MS65 |
|---|---|---|---|---|---|---|
| 2001 | 1,658 | PF65 900 | | | | |

**KM# 1031 2 POUNDS**
12.00 g., Bi-Metallic Copper-Nickel center in Nickel-Brass ring, 28.4 mm. **Ruler:** Elizabeth II **Subject:** 17th Commonwealth Games - Manchester, England **Obv:** Head with tiara right **Rev:** Runner breaking ribbon at finish line, national flag of England in circle behind athlete **Edge:** Reeded and lettered **Edge Lettering:** SPIRIT OF FRIENDSHIP MANCHESTER 2002 **Mint:** British Royal Mint

| Date | Mintage | VF20 | XF40 | MS60 | MS63 | MS65 |
|---|---|---|---|---|---|---|
| 2002 | 650,500 | — | 6.00 | 9.00 | 12.00 | 15.00 |
| 2002 | — | **PF63** 16.00 | **PF65** 18.00 | | | |

**KM# 1031a 2 POUNDS**
12.00 g., 0.925 Silver 0.3569 oz. ASW Silver center in Gold plated ring, 28.4 mm. **Ruler:** Elizabeth II **Subject:** Commonwealth Games - England **Obv:** Head with tiara right **Rev:** Runner breaking ribbon at finish line **Edge:** Reeded and lettered **Mint:** British Royal Mint

| Date | Mintage | VF20 | XF40 | MS60 | MS63 | MS65 |
|---|---|---|---|---|---|---|
| 2002 | 10,000 | **PF65** 45.00 | | | | |

Note: Also exists as a Piefort, P107

**KM# 1031b 2 POUNDS**
15.98 g., 0.916 Gold 0.4706 oz. AGW Yellow gold center in Red Gold ring, 28.4 mm. **Ruler:** Elizabeth II **Subject:** Commonwealth Games - England **Obv:** Head with tiara right **Rev:** Runner breaking ribbon at finish line **Edge:** Reeded and lettered **Mint:** British Royal Mint

| Date | Mintage | VF20 | XF40 | MS60 | MS63 | MS65 |
|---|---|---|---|---|---|---|
| 2002 | 500 | **PF65** 950 | | | | |

**KM# 1032 2 POUNDS**
12.00 g., Bi-Metallic Copper-Nickel center in Nickel-Brass ring, 28.4 mm. **Ruler:** Elizabeth II **Subject:** 17th Commonwealth Games - Manchester, England **Obv:** Head with tiara right **Rev:** Runner breaking ribbon at finish line, national flag of Scotland in circle behind athlete **Edge:** Reeded and lettered **Mint:** British Royal Mint

| Date | Mintage | VF20 | XF40 | MS60 | MS63 | MS65 |
|---|---|---|---|---|---|---|
| 2002 | 771,750 | — | 6.00 | 9.00 | 12.00 | 15.00 |
| 2002 | — | **PF63** 16.00 | **PF65** 18.00 | | | |

**KM# 1032a 2 POUNDS**
12.00 g., 0.925 Silver 0.3569 oz. ASW Silver center with Gold plated ring, 28.4 mm. **Ruler:** Elizabeth II **Subject:** Commonwealth Games - Scotland **Obv:** Head with tiara right **Rev:** Runner breaking ribbon at finish line **Edge:** Reeded and lettered **Mint:** British Royal Mint

| Date | Mintage | VF20 | XF40 | MS60 | MS63 | MS65 |
|---|---|---|---|---|---|---|
| 2002 | 10,000 | **PF65** 35.00 | | | | |

Note: Also exists as a Piefort, P108

**KM# 1032b 2 POUNDS**
15.98 g., 0.916 Gold 0.4706 oz. AGW Yellow gold center in Red Gold ring, 28.4 mm. **Ruler:** Elizabeth II **Subject:** Commonwealth Games - Scotland **Obv:** Head with tiara right **Rev:** Runner breaking ribbon at finish line **Edge:** Reeded and lettered **Mint:** British Royal Mint

| Date | Mintage | VF20 | XF40 | MS60 | MS63 | MS65 |
|---|---|---|---|---|---|---|
| 2002 | 500 | **PF65** 950 | | | | |

**KM# 1033 2 POUNDS**
12.00 g., Bi-Metallic Copper-Nickel center in Nickel-Brass ring, 28.4 mm. **Ruler:** Elizabeth II **Subject:** 17th Commonwealth Games - Manchester, England **Obv:** Head with tiara right **Rev:** Runner breaking ribbon at finish line, national flag of Wales in circle behind athlete **Edge:** Reeded and lettered **Edge Lettering:** SPIRIT OF FRIENDSHIP MANCHESTER 2002 **Mint:** British Royal Mint

| Date | Mintage | VF20 | XF40 | MS60 | MS63 | MS65 |
|---|---|---|---|---|---|---|
| 2002 | 588,500 | — | 6.00 | 9.00 | 12.00 | 15.00 |
| 2002 | — | **PF63** 16.00 | **PF65** 18.00 | | | |

**KM# 1033a 2 POUNDS**
12.00 g., 0.925 Silver 0.3569 oz. ASW Silver center in Gold plated ring, 28.4 mm. **Ruler:** Elizabeth II **Subject:** Commonwealth Games - Wales **Obv:** Head with tiara right **Rev:** Runner breaking ribbon at finish line **Edge:** Reeded and lettered **Mint:** British Royal Mint

| Date | Mintage | VF20 | XF40 | MS60 | MS63 | MS65 |
|---|---|---|---|---|---|---|
| 2002 | 10,000 | **PF65** 35.00 | | | | |

Note: Also exists as a Piefort, P109

**KM# 1033b 2 POUNDS**
15.98 g., 0.916 Gold 0.4706 oz. AGW Yellow Gold center in Red Gold ring, 28.4 mm. **Ruler:** Elizabeth II **Subject:** Commonwealth Games - Wales **Obv:** Head with tiara right **Rev:** Runner breaking ribbon at finish line **Edge:** Reeded and lettered **Mint:** British Royal Mint

| Date | Mintage | VF20 | XF40 | MS60 | MS63 | MS65 |
|---|---|---|---|---|---|---|
| 2002 | 500 | **PF65** 950 | | | | |

**KM# 1034 2 POUNDS**
12.00 g., Bi-Metallic Copper-Nickel center in Nickel-Brass ring, 28.4 mm. **Ruler:** Elizabeth II **Subject:** 17th Commonwealth Games - Manchester, England **Obv:** Head with tiara right **Rev:** Runner breaking ribbon at finish line, national flag of Northern Ireland in circle behind athlete **Edge:** Reeded and lettered **Edge Lettering:** SPIRIT OF FRIENDSHIP MANCHESTER 2002 **Mint:** British Royal Mint

| Date | Mintage | VF20 | XF40 | MS60 | MS63 | MS65 |
|---|---|---|---|---|---|---|
| 2002 | 485,500 | — | 6.00 | 9.00 | 12.00 | 15.00 |
| 2002 | — | **PF63** 16.00 | **PF65** 18.00 | | | |

**KM# 1034a 2 POUNDS**
12.00 g., 0.925 Silver 0.3569 oz. ASW Silver center in Gold plated ring, 28.4 mm. **Ruler:** Elizabeth II **Subject:** Commonwealth Games - Northern Ireland **Obv:** Head with tiara right **Rev:** Runner breaking ribbon at finish line **Edge:** Reeded and lettered **Mint:** British Royal Mint

| Date | Mintage | VF20 | XF40 | MS60 | MS63 | MS65 |
|---|---|---|---|---|---|---|
| 2002 | 10,000 | **PF65** 35.00 | | | | |

Note: Also exists as a Piefort, P110

**KM# 1034b 2 POUNDS**
15.98 g., 0.916 Gold 0.4706 oz. AGW Yellow Gold center in Red Gold ring, 28.4 mm. **Ruler:** Elizabeth II **Subject:** Commonwealth Games - Northern Ireland **Obv:** Head with tiara right **Rev:** Runner breaking ribbon at finish line **Edge:** Reeded and lettered **Mint:** British Royal Mint

| Date | Mintage | VF20 | XF40 | MS60 | MS63 | MS65 |
|---|---|---|---|---|---|---|
| 2002 | 500 | **PF65** 950 | | | | |

**KM# 1037 2 POUNDS**
12.00 g., Bi-Metallic Copper-Nickel center in Nickel-Brass ring, 28.4 mm. **Ruler:** Elizabeth II **Subject:** 50th Anniversary of the Discovery of DNA **Obv:** Head with tiara right **Rev:** DNA Double Helix **Edge:** Reeded and inscribed **Edge Lettering:** DEOXYRIBONUCLEIC ACID **Mint:** British Royal Mint

| Date | Mintage | VF20 | XF40 | MS60 | MS63 | MS65 |
|---|---|---|---|---|---|---|
| ND(2003) | 4,299,000 | — | 6.00 | 9.00 | 12.00 | 15.00 |
| ND(2003) | 43,513 | **PF63** 16.00 | **PF65** 18.00 | | | |

**KM# 1037a 2 POUNDS**
12.00 g., 0.925 Silver 0.3569 oz. ASW Silver center in Gold plated ring, 28.4 mm. **Ruler:** Elizabeth II **Obv:** Head with tiara right **Rev:** DNA Double Helix **Edge:** Reeded and lettered **Mint:** British Royal Mint

| Date | Mintage | VF20 | XF40 | MS60 | MS63 | MS65 |
|---|---|---|---|---|---|---|
| ND(2003) | 11,204 | **PF65** 35.00 | | | | |

Note: Also exists as a Piefort, P42

**KM# 1037b 2 POUNDS**
15.98 g., 0.9167 Gold 0.471 oz. AGW Yellow gold center in Red gold ring, 28.4 mm. **Ruler:** Elizabeth II **Obv:** Head with tiara right **Rev:** DNA Double Helix **Edge:** Reeded and lettered **Mint:** British Royal Mint

| Date | Mintage | VF20 | XF40 | MS60 | MS63 | MS65 |
|---|---|---|---|---|---|---|
| ND2003 | 1,500 | **PF65** 900 | | | | |

**KM# 1049 2 POUNDS**
12.00 g., Bi-Metallic Copper-Nickel center in Nickel-Brass ring, 28.4 mm. **Ruler:** Elizabeth II **Subject:** Richard Trevithick, Inventor of the First Steam Locomotive **Obv:** Head with tiara right **Rev:** First steam locomotive **Rev. Legend:** 2004 R. TREVITHICK 1804 INVENTION-INDUSTRY-PROGRESS **Edge:** Incuse railway line motif **Mint:** British Royal Mint

| Date | Mintage | VF20 | XF40 | MS60 | MS63 | MS65 |
|---|---|---|---|---|---|---|
| 2004 | 5,004,500 | — | 6.00 | 9.00 | 12.00 | 15.00 |
| 2004 | 35,020 | **PF63** 16.00 | **PF65** 18.00 | | | |

**KM# 1049a 2 POUNDS**
12.00 g., 0.925 Silver 0.3569 oz. ASW Silver center in Gold plated ring, 28.4 mm. **Ruler:** Elizabeth II **Obv:** Head with tiara right **Rev:** First steam locomotive **Rev. Legend:** 2004 R. TREVITHICK 1804 INVENTION-INDUSTRY-PROGRESS **Edge:** Incuse railway line motif **Mint:** British Royal Mint

| Date | Mintage | VF20 | XF40 | MS60 | MS63 | MS65 |
|---|---|---|---|---|---|---|
| 2004 | 19,233 | **PF65** 35.00 | | | | |
| 2004 | 1,923 | — | — | — | — | 50.00 |

Note: Also exists as a Piefort, P45

### KM# 1049b 2 POUNDS

15.98 g., 0.9166 Gold 0.4709 oz. AGW Yellow Gold center in Red Gold ring, 28.4 mm. **Ruler:** Elizabeth II **Obv:** Head with tiara right **Rev:** First steam locomotive **Rev. Legend:** 2004 R. TREVITHICK 1804 INVENTION-INDUSTRY-PROGRESS **Edge:** Incuse railway line motif **Mint:** British Royal Mint

| Date | Mintage | VF20 | XF40 | MS60 | MS63 | MS65 |
|---|---|---|---|---|---|---|
| 2004 | 1,500 | PF65 900 | | | | |

### KM# 1052 2 POUNDS

12.00 g., Bi-Metallic Copper-Nickel center in Nickel-Brass ring, 28.4 mm. **Ruler:** Elizabeth II **Subject:** 400th Anniversary - The Gunpowder Plot **Obv:** Head with tiara right **Rev:** Circular design of Royal scepters, swords and crosiers **Edge:** Reeded and lettered **Edge Lettering:** REMEMBER REMEMBER THE FIFTH OF NOVEMBER **Mint:** British Royal Mint

| Date | Mintage | VF20 | XF40 | MS60 | MS63 | MS65 |
|---|---|---|---|---|---|---|
| ND-2005 | 5,140,500 | — | 6.00 | 9.00 | 12.00 | 15.00 |
| ND-2005 | 40,563 | PF63 16.00 | PF65 18.00 | | | |

Note: Also exists as a Piefort, P46

### KM# 1056 2 POUNDS

Bi-Metallic Copper-Nickel center in Nickel-Brass ring, 28.4 mm. **Ruler:** Elizabeth II **Subject:** 60th Anniversary of the End of WW II **Obv:** Head with tiara right **Rev:** St. Paul's Cathedral amid search light beams **Edge:** Reeded and lettered **Edge Lettering:** IN VICTORY MAGNANIMITY IN PEACE GOODWILL **Mint:** British Royal Mint

| Date | Mintage | VF20 | XF40 | MS60 | MS63 | MS65 |
|---|---|---|---|---|---|---|
| ND (2005) | 10,191,000 | — | 6.00 | 9.00 | 12.00 | 15.00 |

### KM# 1056a 2 POUNDS

12.00 g., 0.925 Silver 0.3569 oz. ASW center in Gold-plated ring, 28.4 mm. **Ruler:** Elizabeth II **Subject:** 60th Anniversary of the End of WWII **Obv:** Crowned head right **Rev:** St. Paul's Cathedral amid search light beams **Edge:** Reeded and lettered **Edge Lettering:** IN VICTORY MAGNANIMITY IN PEACE GOODWILL **Mint:** British Royal Mint

| Date | Mintage | VF20 | XF40 | MS60 | MS63 | MS65 |
|---|---|---|---|---|---|---|
| ND-2005 | 21,734 | PF65 35.00 | | | | |

Note: Also exists as a Piefort, P49

### KM# 1056b 2 POUNDS

15.97 g., 0.9167 Gold 0.4707 oz. AGW, 28.4 mm. **Ruler:** Elizabeth II **Subject:** 60th Anniversary of the End of WWII **Obv:** Crowned head right **Rev:** St. Paul's Cathedral amid search light beams **Edge:** Reeded and lettered **Edge Lettering:** IN VICTORY MAGNANIMITY IN PEACE GOODWILL

| Date | Mintage | VF20 | XF40 | MS60 | MS63 | MS65 |
|---|---|---|---|---|---|---|
| ND-2005 | 2,924 | PF65 900 | | | | |

### KM# 1060 2 POUNDS

12.00 g., Bi-Metallic Copper-Nickel center in Nickel-Brass ring, 28.4 mm. **Ruler:** Elizabeth II **Subject:** 200th Birthday of Engineer Isambard Kingdom Brunel **Obv:** Head with tiara right **Rev:** Isambard Brunel **Edge Lettering:** 1806-1859 ISAMBARD KINGDOM BRUNEL ENGINEER **Mint:** British Royal Mint

| Date | Mintage | VF20 | XF40 | MS60 | MS63 | MS65 |
|---|---|---|---|---|---|---|
| 2006 | 7,925,250 | — | — | 12.00 | 16.00 | 20.00 |
| 2006 | Est. 50000 | PF63 22.00 | PF65 24.00 | | | |

### KM# 1060a 2 POUNDS

12.00 g., 0.925 Silver 0.3569 oz. ASW with gilt ring, 28.4 mm. **Ruler:** Elizabeth II **Subject:** Brunel's 200th Birthday **Obv:** Head with tiara right **Rev:** Brunel and gears **Mint:** British Royal Mint

| Date | Mintage | VF20 | XF40 | MS60 | MS63 | MS65 |
|---|---|---|---|---|---|---|
| 2006 | — | PF65 55.00 | | | | |

Note: Also exists as a Piefort, P56

### KM# 1060b 2 POUNDS

15.98 g., 0.916 Gold 0.4706 oz. AGW Yellow Gold center in Red Gold ring, 28.4 mm. **Ruler:** Elizabeth II **Subject:** Brunel's 200th Birthday **Obv:** Head with tiara right **Rev:** Brunel and gears **Mint:** British Royal Mint

| Date | Mintage | VF20 | XF40 | MS60 | MS63 | MS65 |
|---|---|---|---|---|---|---|
| 2006 | — | PF65 900 | | | | |

### KM# 1061 2 POUNDS

12.00 g., Bi-Metallic Copper-Nickel center in Nickel-Brass ring, 28.4 mm. **Ruler:** Elizabeth II **Subject:** Engineering Achievements of Isambard Kingdom Brunel **Obv:** Head with tiara right **Rev:** Paddington Station structural supports **Edge Lettering:** SO MANY IRONS IN THE FIRE **Mint:** British Royal Mint

| Date | Mintage | VF20 | XF40 | MS60 | MS63 | MS65 |
|---|---|---|---|---|---|---|
| 2006 | 7,452,250 | — | — | 12.00 | 16.00 | 20.00 |
| 2006 | Est. 50000 | PF63 22.00 | PF65 24.00 | | | |

### KM# 1061a 2 POUNDS

12.00 g., 0.925 Silver 0.3569 oz. ASW center in gilt ring, 28.4 mm. **Ruler:** Elizabeth II **Subject:** Brunel's engineering achievements **Obv:** Head with tiara right **Rev:** Archways **Mint:** British Royal Mint

| Date | Mintage | VF20 | XF40 | MS60 | MS63 | MS65 |
|---|---|---|---|---|---|---|
| 2006 | — | PF65 55.00 | | | | |

Note: Also exists as a Piefort, P57

### KM# 1061b 2 POUNDS

15.98 g., 0.916 Gold 0.4706 oz. AGW Yellow Gold center in Red Gold ring, 28.4 mm. **Ruler:** Elizabeth II **Subject:** Brunel's engineering achievements **Obv:** Head with tiara right **Rev:** Archways **Mint:** British Royal Mint

| Date | Mintage | VF20 | XF40 | MS60 | MS63 | MS65 |
|---|---|---|---|---|---|---|
| 2006 | — | PF65 900 | | | | |

### KM# 1075 2 POUNDS

12.00 g., Bi-Metallic Copper-Nickel center in Nickel-Brass ring, 28.4 mm. **Ruler:** Elizabeth II **Subject:** 200th Anniversary of the Abolition of the Slave Trade **Obv:** Bust right **Rev:** Chain crossing 1807 date **Edge:** Reeded and lettered **Edge Lettering:** AM I NOT A MAN AND A BROTHER **Mint:** British Royal Mint

| Date | Mintage | VF20 | XF40 | MS60 | MS63 | MS65 |
|---|---|---|---|---|---|---|
| 2007 | 8,445,000 | — | 6.00 | 9.00 | 12.50 | 15.00 |
| 2007 | Est. 50000 | PF63 16.00 | PF65 18.00 | | | |

### KM# 1075a 2 POUNDS

12.00 g., 0.925 Silver 0.3569 oz. ASW center in Gold plated ring, 28.4 mm. **Ruler:** Elizabeth II **Subject:** Abolition of the Slave Trade **Obv:** Elizabeth II right **Rev:** Zero in 1807 date as a broken chain link **Edge:** Reeded and lettered **Edge Lettering:** AM I NOT A MAN AND A BROTHER **Mint:** British Royal Mint

| Date | Mintage | VF20 | XF40 | MS60 | MS63 | MS65 |
|---|---|---|---|---|---|---|
| 2007 | 7,095 | PF65 55.00 | | | | |

Note: Also exists as a Piefort, P61

### KM# 1075b 2 POUNDS

15.97 g., 0.9166 Gold 0.4706 oz. AGW Yellow Gold center in Red Gold ring, 28.4 mm. **Ruler:** Elizabeth II **Subject:** Abolition of the Slave Trade **Obv:** Head with tiara right **Rev:** Zero in 1807 date as a broken chain link **Edge:** Reeded and lettered **Edge Lettering:** AM I NOT A MAN AND A BROTHER **Mint:** British Royal Mint

| Date | Mintage | VF20 | XF40 | MS60 | MS63 | MS65 |
|---|---|---|---|---|---|---|
| 2007 | 1,000 | PF65 900 | | | | |

### KM# 1076 2 POUNDS

12.00 g., Bi-Metallic Copper-Nickel center in Nickel-Brass ring, 28.4 mm. **Ruler:** Elizabeth II **Subject:** 300th Anniversary of the Act of Union of England and Scotland **Obv:** Head with tiara right **Rev:** Combination of British and Scottish arms **Edge:** Reeded and lettered **Edge Lettering:** UNITED INTO ONE KINGDOM **Mint:** British Royal Mint

| Date | Mintage | VF20 | XF40 | MS60 | MS63 | MS65 |
|---|---|---|---|---|---|---|
| 2007 | 7,545,000 | — | 6.00 | 9.00 | 12.50 | 15.00 |
| 2007 | Est. 50000 | PF63 16.00 | PF65 18.00 | | | |

### KM# 1076a 2 POUNDS

12.00 g., 0.925 Silver 0.3569 oz. ASW center in Gold Plated ring, 28.4 mm. **Ruler:** Elizabeth II **Subject:** 300th Anniv. Union of Scotland and England **Obv:** Head with tiara right **Rev:** Combined English and Scottish arms **Edge:** Reeded and lettered **Mint:** British Royal Mint

| Date | Mintage | VF20 | XF40 | MS60 | MS63 | MS65 |
|---|---|---|---|---|---|---|
| 2007 | 8,310 | PF65 55.00 | | | | |

Note: Also exists as a Piefort, P62

### KM# 1076b 2 POUNDS

15.98 g., 0.9166 Gold 0.4709 oz. AGW Yellow Gold center in Red Gold ring, 28.4 mm. **Ruler:** Elizabeth II **Subject:** 300th Anniv. Union of Scotland and England **Obv:** Head with tiara right **Rev:** Combined English and Scottish arms **Edge:** Reeded and lettered **Mint:** British Royal Mint

| Date | Mintage | VF20 | XF40 | MS60 | MS63 | MS65 |
|---|---|---|---|---|---|---|
| 2007 | 750 | PF65 900 | | | | |

### KM# 1105 2 POUNDS

12.00 g., Bi-Metallic Copper-Nickel center in Nickel-Brass ring, 28.4 mm. **Ruler:** Elizabeth II **Subject:** London 1908 - Olympics **Obv:** Head with tiara right **Rev:** Sprint track **Edge:** Lettered and reeded **Edge Lettering:** THE 4TH OLYMPIAD LONDON

| Date | Mintage | VF20 | XF40 | MS60 | MS63 | MS65 |
|---|---|---|---|---|---|---|
| 2008 | 910,000 | — | 6.00 | 9.00 | 12.50 | 15.00 |
| 2008 | — | PF63 15.00 | PF65 17.00 | | | |

### KM# 1106 2 POUNDS

12.00 g., Bi-Metallic Copper-Nickel center in Nickel-Brass ring, 28.4 mm. **Ruler:** Elizabeth II **Subject:** Beijing - London Olympic Flag handoff **Obv:** Head with tiara right **Rev:** London 2012 Games Flag hand off **Edge Lettering:** I CALL UPON THE YOUTH OF THE WORLD

| Date | Mintage | VF20 | XF40 | MS60 | MS63 | MS65 |
|---|---|---|---|---|---|---|
| 2008 | 918,000 | — | — | 14.00 | 18.00 | 22.00 |
| 2008 | Est. 250000 | PF65 45.00 | | | | |

**KM# 1106a 2 POUNDS**

12.00 g., 0.925 Silver 0.3569 oz. ASW Silver center in Gilt ring, 28.4 mm. **Ruler:** Elizabeth II **Obv:** Head with tiara right **Rev:** Handoff of the Olympic Flag **Mint:** British Royal Mint

| Date | Mintage | VF20 | XF40 | MS60 | MS63 | MS65 |
|---|---|---|---|---|---|---|
| 2008 | — | PF65 55.00 | | | | |

Note: Also exists as a Piefort, P65

**KM# 1106b 2 POUNDS**

15.98 g., 0.916 Gold 0.4706 oz. AGW, 28.4 mm. **Ruler:** Elizabeth II **Subject:** Countdown to 2010 London Olympics **Obv:** Head right **Rev:** Handoff of the Olympic flag **Edge Lettering:** I CALL UPON THE YOUTH OF THE WORLD **Mint:** British Royal Mint

| Date | Mintage | VF20 | XF40 | MS60 | MS63 | MS65 |
|---|---|---|---|---|---|---|
| 2008 | 3,000 | PF65 875 | | | | |

**KM# 1115 2 POUNDS**

12.00 g., Bi-Metallic Copper-Nickel center in Nickel-Brass ring., 28.4 mm. **Ruler:** Elizabeth II **Subject:** Charles Darwin, 200th Anniversary of Birth **Obv:** Head with tiara right **Rev:** Darwin and ape heads facing **Edge Lettering:** ON THE ORIGIN OF SPECIES 1859

| Date | Mintage | VF20 | XF40 | MS60 | MS63 | MS65 |
|---|---|---|---|---|---|---|
| 2009 | 3,903,000 | — | — | 12.00 | 16.00 | 20.00 |
| 2009 | — | PF65 25.00 | | | | |

**KM# 1115a 2 POUNDS**

12.00 g., 0.925 Silver 0.3569 oz. ASW Silver center in Gilt ring, 28.4 mm. **Ruler:** Elizabeth II **Subject:** Charles Darwin, 200th Anniversary of Brith **Obv:** Head with tiara right **Rev:** Darwin and ape heads facing **Mint:** British Royal Mint

| Date | Mintage | VF20 | XF40 | MS60 | MS63 | MS65 |
|---|---|---|---|---|---|---|
| 2009 | — | PF65 55.00 | | | | |

Note: Also exists as a Piefort, P66

**KM# 1115b 2 POUNDS**

15.98 g., 0.916 Gold 0.4706 oz. AGW Yellow Gold center in Red Gold ring, 28.4 mm. **Ruler:** Elizabeth II **Subject:** Charles Darwin, 200th Anniversary of Birth **Obv:** Head with tiara right **Rev:** Darwin and ape heads facing **Mint:** British Royal Mint

| Date | Mintage | VF20 | XF40 | MS60 | MS63 | MS65 |
|---|---|---|---|---|---|---|
| 2009 | — | PF65 900 | | | | |

**KM# 1116 2 POUNDS**

12.00 g., Bi-Metallic Copper-Nickel center in Nickel-Brass ring, 28.4 mm. **Ruler:** Elizabeth II **Subject:** Robert Burns, 250th Anniversary of Birth **Obv:** Head with tiara right **Rev:** Text **Edge:** Reeded and lettered **Edge Lettering:** SHOULD AULD ACQUAINTANCE BE FORGOT

| Date | Mintage | VF20 | XF40 | MS60 | MS63 | MS65 |
|---|---|---|---|---|---|---|
| 2009 | 3,253,000 | — | — | 12.00 | 16.00 | 20.00 |
| 2009 | — | PF65 25.00 | | | | |

**KM# 1116a 2 POUNDS**

12.00 g., 0.925 Silver 0.3569 oz. ASW Sivler center in Gilt ring, 28.4 mm. **Ruler:** Elizabeth II **Subject:** Robert Burns, 250th Anniversary of Birth **Obv:** Head with tiara right **Rev:** Text **Mint:** British Royal Mint

| Date | Mintage | VF20 | XF40 | MS60 | MS63 | MS65 |
|---|---|---|---|---|---|---|
| 2009 | — | PF65 55.00 | | | | |

Note: Also exists as a Piefort, P

**KM# 1116b 2 POUNDS**

15.97 g., 0.9167 Gold 0.4707 oz. AGW Yellow Gold center in Red Gold ring, 28.4 mm. **Ruler:** Elizabeth II **Subject:** Robert Burns, 250th Anniversary of Birth **Obv:** Head with tiara right **Rev:** Text **Mint:** British Royal Mint

| Date | Mintage | VF20 | XF40 | MS60 | MS63 | MS65 |
|---|---|---|---|---|---|---|
| 2009 | 1,000 | PF65 900 | | | | |

**KM# 1160 2 POUNDS**

11.97 g., Bi-Metallic Copper-Nickel center in Nickel-Brass ring, 28.35 mm. **Ruler:** Elizabeth II **Subject:** Florence Nightengale, 100th Anniversary of Death **Obv:** Head with tiara right **Rev:** Hand taking pulse **Edge Lettering:** 150 YEARS OF NURSING **Mint:** British Royal Mint

| Date | Mintage | VF20 | XF40 | MS60 | MS63 | MS65 |
|---|---|---|---|---|---|---|
| 2010 | — | — | 6.00 | 9.00 | 12.00 | 15.00 |
| 2010 | — | PF63 16.00 | PF65 18.00 | | | |

**KM# 1199 2 POUNDS**

11.97 g., Bi-Metallic Copper-Nickel center in Nickel-Brass ring, 28.4 mm. **Ruler:** Elizabeth II **Subject:** Mary Rose, 500th Anniversary **Obv:** Head with tiara right **Rev:** H.M.S. Mary Rose under sail **Edge Lettering:** YOUR NOBLEST SHIPPE 1511 **Mint:** British Royal Mint

| Date | Mintage | VF20 | XF40 | MS60 | MS63 | MS65 |
|---|---|---|---|---|---|---|
| 2011 | — | — | 6.00 | 9.00 | 12.00 | 15.00 |
| 2011 | — | PF63 16.00 | PF65 18.00 | | | |

**KM# 1199a 2 POUNDS**

12.00 g., 0.925 Silver 0.3569 oz. ASW center in Gilt ring, 28.4 mm. **Ruler:** Elizabeth II **Subject:** Mary Rose, 500th Anniversary **Obv:** Head with tiara right **Rev:** H.M.S. Mary Rose under sail **Edge Lettering:** YOUR NOBLEST SHIPPE 1511 **Mint:** British Royal Mint

| Date | Mintage | VF20 | XF40 | MS60 | MS63 | MS65 |
|---|---|---|---|---|---|---|
| 2011 | — | PF65 55.00 | | | | |

Note: Also exists as a Piefort, P87

**KM# 1199b 2 POUNDS**

15.98 g., 0.9166 Gold 0.4709 oz. AGW Yellow Gold center in Red Gold ring, 28.4 mm. **Ruler:** Elizabeth II **Subject:** Mary Rose, 500th Anniversary **Obv:** Head with tiara right **Rev:** H.M.S. Mary Rose under sail **Edge Lettering:** YOUR NOBLEST SHIPPE 1511 **Mint:** British Royal Mint

| Date | Mintage | VF20 | XF40 | MS60 | MS63 | MS65 |
|---|---|---|---|---|---|---|
| 2011 | — | PF65 1,600 | | | | |

**KM# 1200 2 POUNDS**

11.97 g., Bi-Metallic Copper-Nickel center in Nickel-Brass ring, 28.4 mm. **Ruler:** Elizabeth II **Subject:** King James Bible, 400th Anniversary **Obv:** Head in tiara right **Rev:** Lead type and printed page of bible text **Edge:** Reeded and lettered **Edge Lettering:** THE AUTHORIZED VERSION **Mint:** British Royal Mint

| Date | Mintage | VF20 | XF40 | MS60 | MS63 | MS65 |
|---|---|---|---|---|---|---|
| 2011 | — | — | 6.00 | 9.00 | 12.00 | 15.00 |
| 2011 | — | PF63 16.00 | PF65 18.00 | | | |

**KM# 1200a 2 POUNDS**

12.00 g., 0.925 Silver 0.3569 oz. ASW center in Gilt ring, 28.4 mm. **Ruler:** Elizabeth II **Subject:** King James Bible, 500th Anniversary **Obv:** Head with tiara right **Rev:** Lead type and printed page **Mint:** British Royal Mint

| Date | Mintage | VF20 | XF40 | MS60 | MS63 | MS65 |
|---|---|---|---|---|---|---|
| 2011 | — | PF65 55.00 | | | | |

Note: Also exists as a Piefort, P88

**KM# 994a.1 2 POUNDS**

12.00 g., 0.925 Silver 0.3569 oz. ASW partially gilt, 28.35 mm. **Ruler:** Elizabeth II **Obv:** Head with tiara right **Rev:** Symbolic depictions of technological development

| Date | Mintage | VF20 | XF40 | MS60 | MS63 | MS65 |
|---|---|---|---|---|---|---|
| 2012 | — | PF65 50.00 | | | | |

**KM# 1224 2 POUNDS**

12.00 g., Bi-Metallic Copper-Nickel center in Nickel-Brass ring, 28.4 mm. **Ruler:** Elizabeth II **Subject:** Charles Dickens, 200th Anniversary of Birth **Rev:** Profile left of Dickens made up from titles of his works

| Date | Mintage | VF20 | XF40 | MS60 | MS63 | MS65 |
|---|---|---|---|---|---|---|
| 2012 | — | — | 6.00 | 9.00 | 12.00 | 15.00 |
| 2012 | — | PF63 16.00 | PF65 18.00 | | | |

**KM# 1224a 2 POUNDS**

12.00 g., 0.925 Silver 0.3569 oz. ASW center in Gold-Plated ring, 28.4 mm. **Ruler:** Elizabeth II **Rev:** Head of Charles Dickens left

| Date | Mintage | VF20 | XF40 | MS60 | MS63 | MS65 |
|---|---|---|---|---|---|---|
| 2012 | — | PF65 35.00 | | | | |

**KM# 1224b 2 POUNDS**

15.98 g., 0.916 Gold 0.4706 oz. AGW Yellow Gold center in Red Gold ring, 28.4 mm. **Ruler:** Elizabeth II **Rev:** Charles Dickens head left **Mint:** Royal Mint

| Date | Mintage | VF20 | XF40 | MS60 | MS63 | MS65 |
|---|---|---|---|---|---|---|
| 2012 | — | PF65 900 | | | | |

**KM# 1244 2 POUNDS**

12.00 g., Bi-Metallic Copper-Nickel center in Nickel-Brass ring, 28.4 mm. **Ruler:** Elizabeth II **Subject:** Olympic flag handoff to Brazil - Rio, 2016 **Obv:** Head with tiara right **Rev:** UK and Brazil flags **Edge Lettering:** I CALL UPON THE YOUTH OF THE WORLD

| Date | Mintage | VF20 | XF40 | MS60 | MS63 | MS65 |
|---|---|---|---|---|---|---|
| 2012 | — | — | 6.00 | 9.00 | 12.50 | 15.00 |
| 2012 | — | PF63 16.00 | PF65 18.00 | | | |

**KM# 1244a 2 POUNDS**

12.00 g., 0.925 Bi-Metallic 0.3569 oz. Silver center in Gold plated silver ring, 28.4 mm. **Ruler:** Elizabeth II

| Date | Mintage | VF20 | XF40 | MS60 | MS63 | MS65 |
|---|---|---|---|---|---|---|
| 2012 | 12,000 | PF65 145 | | | | |

**KM# 1244b 2 POUNDS**
15.97 g., 0.916 Gold 0.4703 oz. AGW, 28.4 mm. **Ruler:** Elizabeth II

| Date | Mintage | VF20 | XF40 | MS60 | MS63 | MS65 |
|---|---|---|---|---|---|---|
| 2012 | 1,200 | **PF65** 2,250 | | | | |

**KM# 1239 2 POUNDS**
12.00 g., Bi-Metallic Copper-nickel center in Nickel-Brass ring, 28.4 mm. **Ruler:** Elizabeth II **Subject:** London Subway, 150th Anniversary **Obv:** Head with tiara right **Rev:** London Subway train in tube **Edge:** Linear representation of the Tube map

| Date | Mintage | VF20 | XF40 | MS60 | MS63 | MS65 |
|---|---|---|---|---|---|---|
| 2013 | — | — | 6.00 | 9.00 | 12.00 | 15.00 |
| 2013 | — | **PF63** 16.00 | **PF65** 18.00 | | | |

**KM# 1239a 2 POUNDS**
12.00 g., 0.925 Silver 0.3569 oz. ASW center in Gilt ring, 28.4 mm. **Ruler:** Elizabeth II **Obv:** Head with tiara right **Rev:** London Subway in tube **Edge:** Linear representation of the Tube map

| Date | Mintage | VF20 | XF40 | MS60 | MS63 | MS65 |
|---|---|---|---|---|---|---|
| 2013 | 12,000 | **PF65** 75.00 | | | | |

**KM# 1239b 2 POUNDS**
15.97 g., 0.9167 Gold 0.4707 oz. AGW - Yellow gold center in Red Gold ring, 28.4 mm. **Ruler:** Elizabeth II **Obv:** Head with tiara right **Rev:** London Subway train in tube **Edge:** Linear representation of the Tube map

| Date | Mintage | VF20 | XF40 | MS60 | MS63 | MS65 |
|---|---|---|---|---|---|---|
| 2013 | 960 | **PF65** 1,600 | | | | |

**KM# 1240 2 POUNDS**
12.00 g., Bi-Metallic Copper-Nickel center in Nickel-Brass ring, 28.4 mm. **Ruler:** Elizabeth II **Subject:** London Subway, 150th Anniversary **Obv:** Head with tiara right **Rev:** Underground logo **Edge Lettering:** MIND THE GAP

| Date | Mintage | VF20 | XF40 | MS60 | MS63 | MS65 |
|---|---|---|---|---|---|---|
| 2013 | — | — | 6.00 | 9.00 | 12.00 | 15.00 |
| 2013 | — | **PF63** 16.00 | **PF65** 18.00 | | | |

**KM# 1240a 2 POUNDS**
12.00 g., 0.925 Silver 0.3569 oz. ASW center in Gilt ring, 28.4 mm. **Ruler:** Elizabeth II **Obv:** Head with tiara right **Rev:** Underground logo **Edge Lettering:** MIND THE GAP

| Date | Mintage | VF20 | XF40 | MS60 | MS63 | MS65 |
|---|---|---|---|---|---|---|
| 2013 | 12,000 | **PF65** 75.00 | | | | |

**KM# 1240b 2 POUNDS**
15.97 g., 0.9167 Gold 0.4707 oz. AGW - Yellow Gold center in Rose Gold ring, 28.4 mm. **Ruler:** Elizabeth II **Obv:** Head with tiara right **Rev:** London Underground logo **Edge Lettering:** MIND THE GAP

| Date | Mintage | VF20 | XF40 | MS60 | MS63 | MS65 |
|---|---|---|---|---|---|---|
| 2013 | 960 | **PF65** 1,600 | | | | |

**KM# 1241 2 POUNDS**
12.00 g., Bi-Metallic Copper-Nickel center in Nickel-Brass ring, 28.4 mm. **Ruler:** Elizabeth II **Subject:** Anniversary of the Spade Guinea coinage of George III **Obv:** Head with tiara right **Rev:** Spade shield crowned **Edge Lettering:** WHAT IS A GUINEA? 'TIS A SPLENDID THING

| Date | Mintage | VF20 | XF40 | MS60 | MS63 | MS65 |
|---|---|---|---|---|---|---|
| 2013 | — | — | 6.00 | 9.00 | 12.00 | 15.00 |
| 2013 | 44,000 | **PF63** 15.00 | **PF65** 18.00 | | | |

**KM# 1241a 2 POUNDS**
12.00 g., 0.925 Silver 0.3569 oz. ASW center in Gilt ring, 28.4 mm. **Ruler:** Elizabeth II **Obv:** Head with tiara right **Rev:** Spade shield crowned **Edge Lettering:** WHAT IS A GUINEA? 'TIS A SPLENDID THING

| Date | Mintage | VF20 | XF40 | MS60 | MS63 | MS65 |
|---|---|---|---|---|---|---|
| 2013 | 2,013 | **PF65** 55.00 | | | | |

**KM# 1015 5 POUNDS**
28.28 g., Copper-Nickel, 38.6 mm. **Ruler:** Elizabeth II **Subject:** Centennial of Queen Victoria's death **Obv:** Head with tiara right **Rev:** Young portrait from stamp, within industrial "V **Edge:** Reeded **Mint:** British Royal Mint

| Date | Mintage | VF20 | XF40 | MS60 | MS63 | MS65 |
|---|---|---|---|---|---|---|
| 2001 | 851,491 | — | — | 7.00 | 12.00 | 15.00 |
| 2001 | — | **PF63** 20.00 | **PF65** 22.00 | | | |

**KM# 1015a 5 POUNDS**
28.28 g., 0.925 Silver 0.841 oz. ASW, 38.6 mm. **Ruler:** Elizabeth II **Subject:** Centennial of Queen Victoria **Obv:** Head with tiara right **Rev:** Queen Victoria's portrait within "V **Mint:** British Royal Mint

| Date | Mintage | VF20 | XF40 | MS60 | MS63 | MS65 |
|---|---|---|---|---|---|---|
| 2001 | — | **PF65** 50.00 | | | | |

**KM# 1015b 5 POUNDS**
39.94 g., 0.9167 Gold 1.1771 oz. AGW **Ruler:** Elizabeth II **Subject:** Centennial of Queen Victoria **Obv:** Head with tiara right **Rev:** Queen Victoria's portrait within "V

| Date | Mintage | VF20 | XF40 | MS60 | MS63 | MS65 |
|---|---|---|---|---|---|---|
| 2001 | 1,000 | **PF65** 2,100 | | | | |

**KM# 1024 5 POUNDS**
28.28 g., Copper-Nickel, 38.6 mm. **Ruler:** Elizabeth II **Subject:** Queen's Golden Jubilee of Reign **Obv:** Crowned bust in royal garb right **Rev:** Queen on horse **Edge:** Reeded **Mint:** British Royal Mint

| Date | Mintage | VF20 | XF40 | MS60 | MS63 | MS65 |
|---|---|---|---|---|---|---|
| 2002 | 3,469,243 | — | — | 7.00 | 12.00 | 15.00 |
| Note: Mintage figure includes KM#1035 | | | | | | |
| 2002 | — | **PF63** 20.00 | **PF65** 22.00 | | | |

**KM# 1024A 5 POUNDS**
28.28 g., 0.925 Silver 0.841 oz. ASW, 38.6 mm. **Ruler:** Elizabeth II **Subject:** Queen's Golden Jubilee of Reign **Obv:** Crowned bust in royal garb right **Rev:** Queen on horse **Edge:** Reeded **Mint:** British Royal Mint

| Date | Mintage | VF20 | XF40 | MS60 | MS63 | MS65 |
|---|---|---|---|---|---|---|
| 2002 | — | **PF65** 50.00 | | | | |

**KM# 1024b 5 POUNDS**
39.94 g., 0.9167 Gold 1.1771 oz. AGW, 38.6 mm. **Ruler:** Elizabeth II **Subject:** Queen's Golden Jubilee of Reign **Obv:** Crowned bust in royal garb right **Rev:** Queen on horse left **Edge:** Reeded **Mint:** British Royal Mint

| Date | Mintage | VF20 | XF40 | MS60 | MS63 | MS65 |
|---|---|---|---|---|---|---|
| 2002 | — | **PF65** 2,100 | | | | |

**KM# 1035 5 POUNDS**
28.28 g., Copper-Nickel, 38.6 mm. **Ruler:** Elizabeth II **Subject:** Queen Mother **Obv:** Head with tiara right **Rev:** Queen Mother's portrait in wreath **Edge:** Reeded **Mint:** British Royal Mint

| Date | Mintage | VF20 | XF40 | MS60 | MS63 | MS65 |
|---|---|---|---|---|---|---|
| ND(2002) | — | — | — | 7.00 | 12.00 | 15.00 |
| Note: Mintage included with KM#1024. | | | | | | |
| ND(2002) | — | **PF63** 20.00 | **PF65** 22.00 | | | |

**KM# 1035a 5 POUNDS**
28.28 g., Silver, 38.6 mm. **Ruler:** Elizabeth II **Subject:** Queen Mother **Obv:** Head with tiara right **Rev:** Queen Mother's portrait in wreath **Edge:** Reeded **Mint:** British Royal Mint

| Date | Mintage | VF20 | XF40 | MS60 | MS63 | MS65 |
|---|---|---|---|---|---|---|
| ND(2002) | — | **PF65** 50.00 | | | | |

**KM# 1035b 5 POUNDS**
39.94 g., 0.9167 Gold 1.1771 oz. AGW, 38.6 mm. **Ruler:** Elizabeth II **Subject:** Queen Mother **Obv:** Head with tiara right **Rev:** Queen Mother's portrait in wreath **Edge:** Reeded **Mint:** British Royal Mint

| Date | Mintage | VF20 | XF40 | MS60 | MS63 | MS65 |
|---|---|---|---|---|---|---|
| ND(2002) | — | **PF65** 2,150 | | | | |

**KM# 1038 5 POUNDS**
28.28 g., Copper-Nickel, 38.6 mm. **Ruler:** Elizabeth II **Subject:** Queen's Golden Jubilee **Obv:** Queen's stylized portrait **Rev:** Childlike lettering **Edge:** Reeded **Mint:** British Royal Mint

| Date | Mintage | VF20 | XF40 | MS60 | MS63 | MS65 |
|---|---|---|---|---|---|---|
| 2003 | 1,307,147 | — | — | 7.00 | 12.00 | 15.00 |
| 2003 | 43,513 | **PF63** 20.00 | **PF65** 22.00 | | | |

**KM# 1038a 5 POUNDS**
28.28 g., 0.925 Silver 0.841 oz. ASW, 38.6 mm. **Ruler:** Elizabeth II **Subject:** Queen's Golden Jubilee **Obv:** Stylized Queens portrait **Rev:** Childlike lettering **Edge:** Reeded **Mint:** British Royal Mint

| Date | Mintage | VF20 | XF40 | MS60 | MS63 | MS65 |
|---|---|---|---|---|---|---|
| 2003 | 28,758 | **PF65** 50.00 | | | | |

**KM# 1038b 5 POUNDS**

39.94 g., 0.9166 Gold 1.177 oz. AGW, 38.6 mm. **Ruler:** Elizabeth II **Subject:** Queen's Golden Jubilee **Obv:** Stylized Queens portrait **Rev:** Childlike lettering **Edge:** Reeded **Mint:** British Royal Mint

| Date | Mintage | VF20 | XF40 | MS60 | MS63 | MS65 |
|---|---|---|---|---|---|---|
| 2003 | 1,896 | PF65 2,100 | | | | |

**KM# 1055 5 POUNDS**

28.28 g., Copper-Nickel, 38.6 mm. **Ruler:** Elizabeth II **Subject:** Entente Cordiale **Obv:** Head with tiara right **Rev:** Britannia and Marianne **Edge:** Reeded **Mint:** British Royal Mint

| Date | Mintage | VF20 | XF40 | MS60 | MS63 | MS65 |
|---|---|---|---|---|---|---|
| 2004 | 1,205,594 | — | — | 7.00 | 12.00 | 15.00 |
| 2004 | 51,527 | PF63 20.00 | PF65 22.00 | | | |

**KM# 1055a 5 POUNDS**

28.28 g., 0.925 Silver 0.841 oz. ASW, 38.6 mm. **Ruler:** Elizabeth II **Subject:** Entente Cordiale **Obv:** Head with tiara right **Rev:** Britannia and Marianne **Edge:** Reeded **Mint:** British Royal Mint

| Date | Mintage | VF20 | XF40 | MS60 | MS63 | MS65 |
|---|---|---|---|---|---|---|
| 2004 | 11,295 | PF65 50.00 | | | | |

Note: Also exists as a Piefort, P47

**KM# 1055b 5 POUNDS**

39.94 g., 0.9167 Gold 1.1771 oz. AGW, 38.6 mm. **Ruler:** Elizabeth II **Subject:** Entente Cordiale **Obv:** Head with tiara right **Rev:** Britannia and Marianne **Edge:** Reeded **Mint:** British Royal Mint

| Date | Mintage | VF20 | XF40 | MS60 | MS63 | MS65 |
|---|---|---|---|---|---|---|
| 2004 | 926 | PF65 2,150 | | | | |

**KM# 1055c 5 POUNDS**

94.20 g., 0.9995 Platinum 3.0271 oz. APW, 38.6 mm. **Ruler:** Elizabeth II **Subject:** Entente Cordiale **Obv:** Head with tiara right **Rev:** Britannia and Marianne **Edge:** Reeded **Mint:** British Royal Mint

| Date | Mintage | VF20 | XF40 | MS60 | MS63 | MS65 |
|---|---|---|---|---|---|---|
| 2004 | 501 | PF65 5,700 | | | | |

**KM# 1053 5 POUNDS**

28.28 g., Copper-Nickel, 38.6 mm. **Ruler:** Elizabeth II **Subject:** Battle of Trafalgar **Obv:** Head with tiara right **Obv. Legend:** ELIZABETH • II D • G • REG • F • D **Rev:** HMS Victory and HMS Temeraire at Trafalgar **Rev. Legend:** TRAFALGAR **Edge:** Reeded **Mint:** British Royal Mint

| Date | Mintage | VF20 | XF40 | MS60 | MS63 | MS65 |
|---|---|---|---|---|---|---|
| 2005 | 1,075,516 | — | — | 7.00 | 12.00 | 15.00 |
| 2005 | 40,563 | PF63 20.00 | PF65 22.00 | | | |

**KM# 1053a 5 POUNDS**

28.28 g., 0.925 Silver 0.841 oz. ASW, 38.6 mm. **Ruler:** Elizabeth II **Subject:** Battle of Trafalgar **Obv:** Head with tiara right **Obv. Legend:** ELIZABETH • II D • G • REG • F • D **Rev:** Ships HMS Victory and Temeraire at Trafalgar **Rev. Legend:** TRAFALGAR **Edge:** Reeded **Mint:** British Royal Mint

| Date | Mintage | VF20 | XF40 | MS60 | MS63 | MS65 |
|---|---|---|---|---|---|---|
| 2005 | 21,448 | PF65 50.00 | | | | |

Note: Also exists as a Piefort, P51

**KM# 1053b 5 POUNDS**

39.94 g., 0.9167 Gold 1.1771 oz. AGW, 38.6 mm. **Ruler:** Elizabeth II **Subject:** Battle of Trafalgar **Obv:** Head with tiara right **Obv. Legend:** ELIZABETH • II D • G • REG • F • D **Rev:** Ships HMS Victory and Temeraire at Trafalgar **Rev. Legend:** TRAFALGAR **Edge:** Reeded **Mint:** British Royal Mint

| Date | Mintage | VF20 | XF40 | MS60 | MS63 | MS65 |
|---|---|---|---|---|---|---|
| 2005 | 1,805 | PF63 2,000 | PF65 2,100 | | | |

**KM# 1054 5 POUNDS**

28.28 g., Copper-Nickel, 38.6 mm. **Ruler:** Elizabeth II **Obv:** Head with tiara right **Obv. Legend:** ELIZABETH • II D • G • REG • F • D **Rev:** Uniformed facing 1/2 bust of Admiral Horatio Nelson **Rev. Legend:** HORATIO NELSON **Edge:** Reeded **Mint:** British Royal Mint

| Date | Mintage | VF20 | XF40 | MS60 | MS63 | MS65 |
|---|---|---|---|---|---|---|
| 2005 | — | — | — | 7.00 | 12.00 | 15.00 |

Note: Mintage included with KM#1053b, 2005.

| Date | Mintage | VF20 | XF40 | MS60 | MS63 | MS65 |
|---|---|---|---|---|---|---|
| 2005 | 40,563 | PF63 20.00 | PF65 22.00 | | | |

**KM# 1054a 5 POUNDS**

28.28 g., 0.925 Silver 0.841 oz. ASW, 38.6 mm. **Ruler:** Elizabeth II **Obv:** Queen's head with tiara right **Obv. Legend:** ELIZABETH • II D • G • REG • F • D **Rev:** Uniformed facing 1/2 bust of Admiral Horatio Nelson **Rev. Legend:** HORATIO NELSON **Mint:** British Royal Mint

| Date | Mintage | VF20 | XF40 | MS60 | MS63 | MS65 |
|---|---|---|---|---|---|---|
| 2005 | 12,852 | PF65 50.00 | | | | |

Note: Also exists as a Piefort, P52

**KM# 1054b 5 POUNDS**

39.94 g., 0.9167 Gold 1.1771 oz. AGW, 38.6 mm. **Ruler:** Elizabeth II **Subject:** Battle of Trafalgar **Obv:** Queen's head with tiara right **Obv. Legend:** ELIZABETH • II D • G • REG • F • D **Rev:** Uniformed facing 1/2 bust of Admiral Horatio Nelson **Rev. Legend:** HORATIO NELSON **Mint:** British Royal Mint

| Date | Mintage | VF20 | XF40 | MS60 | MS63 | MS65 |
|---|---|---|---|---|---|---|
| 2005 | 1,700 | PF63 2,000 | PF65 2,100 | | | |

**KM# 1062 5 POUNDS**

28.28 g., Copper-Nickel, 38.6 mm. **Ruler:** Elizabeth II **Obv:** Head with tiara right **Rev:** Three bannered trumpets **Edge:** Reeded **Mint:** British Royal Mint

| Date | Mintage | VF20 | XF40 | MS60 | MS63 | MS65 |
|---|---|---|---|---|---|---|
| 2006 | — | — | — | — | 18.00 | 22.00 |
| 2006 | Est. 50000 | PF63 30.00 | PF65 32.00 | | | |

**KM# 1062a 5 POUNDS**

28.28 g., 0.925 Silver 0.841 oz. ASW **Ruler:** Elizabeth II **Subject:** Queen's 80th Birthday Celebration **Obv:** Queens head right **Obv. Legend:** ELIZABETH • II D • G • REG • F • D **Rev:** Three bannered trumpets **Rev. Legend:** VIVAT REGINA **Edge:** Reeded **Mint:** British Royal Mint

| Date | Mintage | VF20 | XF40 | MS60 | MS63 | MS65 |
|---|---|---|---|---|---|---|
| 2006 | — | PF65 50.00 | | | | |

Note: Also exists as a Piefort, P58

**KM# 1062b 5 POUNDS**

39.94 g., 0.9167 Gold 1.1771 oz. AGW, 38.6 mm. **Ruler:** Elizabeth II **Subject:** Queen's 80th Birthday Celebration **Obv:** Queen's head with tiara right **Obv. Legend:** ELIZABETH • II D • G • REG • F • D **Rev:** Three bannered trumpets **Rev. Legend:** VIVAT REGINA **Edge:** Reeded **Mint:** British Royal Mint

| Date | Mintage | VF20 | XF40 | MS60 | MS63 | MS65 |
|---|---|---|---|---|---|---|
| 2006 | — | PF65 2,150 | | | | |

**KM# 1077 5 POUNDS**

28.28 g., Copper-Nickel, 38.6 mm. **Ruler:** Elizabeth II **Subject:** Queen's 60th Wedding Anniversary **Obv:** Conjoined busts of Queen Elizabeth II and Prince Philip **Rev:** Westminster Abbey's North Rose Window **Edge:** Reeded **Mint:** British Royal Mint

| Date | Mintage | VF20 | XF40 | MS60 | MS63 | MS65 |
|---|---|---|---|---|---|---|
| 2007 | — | — | — | — | 18.00 | 22.00 |
| 2007 | Est. 50000 | PF63 30.00 | PF65 32.00 | | | |

**KM# 1077a 5 POUNDS**

28.28 g., 0.925 Silver 0.841 oz. ASW, 38.6 mm. **Ruler:** Elizabeth II **Subject:** 60th Wedding Anniversary **Obv:** Conjoined busts of Queen Elizabeth II and Prince Philip **Rev:** Westminster Abbey's North Rose Window **Edge Lettering:** MY STRENGTH AND STAY **Mint:** British Royal Mint

| Date | Mintage | VF20 | XF40 | MS60 | MS63 | MS65 |
|---|---|---|---|---|---|---|
| ND (2007) | Est. 35000 | PF65 50.00 | | | | |

Note: Also exists as a Piefort, P63

**KM# 1077b 5 POUNDS**

39.94 g., 0.9167 Gold 1.1771 oz. AGW, 28.4 mm. **Ruler:** Elizabeth II **Subject:** 60th Wedding Anniversary **Obv:** Conjoined busts of Queen Elizabeth II and Prince Philip **Rev:** Westminster Abbey's North Rose Window **Edge Lettering:** MY STRENGTH AND STAY **Mint:** British Royal Mint

| Date | Mintage | VF20 | XF40 | MS60 | MS63 | MS65 |
|---|---|---|---|---|---|---|
| ND (2007) | — | PF65 2,150 | | | | |

Note: Also exists as a Piefort, P64

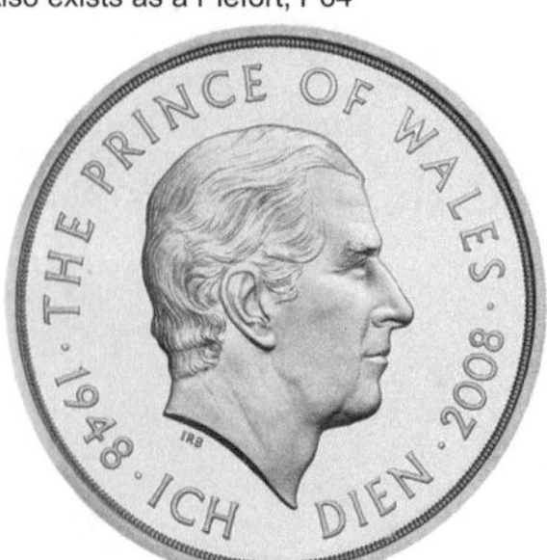

**KM# 1103 5 POUNDS**

28.28 g., Copper-Nickel, 38.6 mm. **Ruler:** Elizabeth II **Subject:** Charles, Prince of Wales 60th Birthday **Obv:** Head with tiara right **Rev:** Head right of Prince Charles

| Date | Mintage | VF20 | XF40 | MS60 | MS63 | MS65 |
|---|---|---|---|---|---|---|
| 2008 | 500,000 | — | — | 7.00 | 12.00 | 15.00 |
| 2008 | — | PF63 20.00 | PF65 22.00 | | | |

### KM# 1103a 5 POUNDS

28.28 g., 0.925 Silver 0.841 oz. ASW, 38.6 mm. **Ruler:** Elizabeth II **Subject:** Charles, Prince of Wales 60th Birthday **Obv:** Head with tiara right **Rev:** Head right of Prince Charles

| Date | Mintage | VF20 | XF40 | MS60 | MS63 | MS65 |
|---|---|---|---|---|---|---|
| 2008 | 10,398 | PF65 50.00 | | | | |

Note: Exists as a Piedfort, P113.

### KM# 1104 5 POUNDS

28.28 g., Copper-Nickel, 38.6 mm. **Ruler:** Elizabeth II **Subject:** Elizabeth I Accession 1558-2008 **Obv:** Head with tiara right **Rev:** Bust of Elizabeth I

| Date | Mintage | VF20 | XF40 | MS60 | MS63 | MS65 |
|---|---|---|---|---|---|---|
| 2008 | 500,000 | — | — | 7.00 | 12.00 | 15.00 |
| 2008 | — | PF63 20.00 | PF65 22.00 | | | |

### KM# 1104a 5 POUNDS

28.28 g., 0.925 Silver 0.841 oz. ASW, 38.6 mm. **Ruler:** Elizabeth II **Subject:** Elizabeth I Accession 1558-2008 **Obv:** Head with tiara right **Rev:** Bust of Elizabeth I

| Date | Mintage | VF20 | XF40 | MS60 | MS63 | MS65 |
|---|---|---|---|---|---|---|
| 2008 | 7,446 | PF65 2,100 | | | | |

Note: Exists as a Piedfort, P67

### KM# 1118 5 POUNDS

28.28 g., Copper-Nickel, 38.6 mm. **Ruler:** Elizabeth II **Obv:** Head with tiara right **Rev:** Henry VIII standing, HR flanking **Mint:** British Royal Mint

| Date | Mintage | VF20 | XF40 | MS60 | MS63 | MS65 |
|---|---|---|---|---|---|---|
| 2009 | — | PF65 40.00 | | | | |

### KM# 1118a 5 POUNDS

28.28 g., 0.925 Silver 0.841 oz. ASW, 38.6 mm. **Ruler:** Elizabeth II **Obv:** Head with tiara right **Rev:** Henry VIII standing, HR flanking **Mint:** British Royal Mint

| Date | Mintage | VF20 | XF40 | MS60 | MS63 | MS65 |
|---|---|---|---|---|---|---|
| 2009 | 20,000 | PF65 50.00 | | | | |

Note: Also exists as a Piedfort, P70

### KM# 1121 5 POUNDS

28.28 g., Copper-Nickel, 38.61 mm. **Ruler:** Elizabeth II **Subject:** Countdown to 2012 London Olympics **Obv:** Bust right **Rev:** Swimmer, stopwatch, 3 in center **Mint:** British Royal Mint

| Date | Mintage | VF20 | XF40 | MS60 | MS63 | MS65 |
|---|---|---|---|---|---|---|
| 2009 | 500,000 | — | — | — | 18.00 | 22.00 |
| 2009 | — | PF63 30.00 | PF65 32.00 | | | |

### KM# 1121a 5 POUNDS

28.28 g., 0.925 Silver 0.841 oz. ASW, 38.61 mm. **Ruler:** Elizabeth II **Subject:** Countdown to the 2010 London Olympics **Obv:** Bust right **Rev:** Swimmer, stopwatch, 3 in center **Mint:** British Royal Mint

| Date | Mintage | VF20 | XF40 | MS60 | MS63 | MS65 |
|---|---|---|---|---|---|---|
| 2009 | 30,000 | PF63 50.00 | PF65 55.00 | | | |

### KM# 1121b 5 POUNDS

39.94 g., 0.9167 Gold 1.1771 oz. AGW, 38.61 mm. **Ruler:** Elizabeth II **Subject:** Countdown to 2012 London Olympics **Rev:** 3 in large stopwatch, swimmer **Mint:** British Royal Mint

| Date | Mintage | VF20 | XF40 | MS60 | MS63 | MS65 |
|---|---|---|---|---|---|---|
| 2009 | — | PF65 2,100 | | | | |

### KM# 1140 5 POUNDS

28.28 g., 0.925 Silver 0.841 oz. ASW, 38.6 mm. **Ruler:** Elizabeth II **Subject:** London Olympics, 2012 **Obv:** Head with tiara right **Rev:** Angel of the North, blue logo **Mint:** British Royal Mint

| Date | Mintage | VF20 | XF40 | MS60 | MS63 | MS65 |
|---|---|---|---|---|---|---|
| 2009 | 95,000 | PF63 50.00 | PF65 55.00 | | | |

### KM# 1141 5 POUNDS

28.28 g., 0.925 Silver 0.841 oz. ASW, 38.6 mm. **Ruler:** Elizabeth II **Subject:** London Olympics, 2012 **Obv:** Head with tiara right **Rev:** Big Ben, blue logo **Mint:** British Royal Mint

| Date | Mintage | VF20 | XF40 | MS60 | MS63 | MS65 |
|---|---|---|---|---|---|---|
| 2009 | 95,000 | PF63 50.00 | PF65 55.00 | | | |

### KM# 1141a 5 POUNDS

28.28 g., Copper-Nickel, 38.6 mm. **Ruler:** Elizabeth II **Subject:** London Olympics, 2012 **Obv:** Head in tiara right **Rev:** Big Ben, blue logo **Mint:** British Royal Mint

| Date | Mintage | VF20 | XF40 | MS60 | MS63 | MS65 |
|---|---|---|---|---|---|---|
| 2009 | — | PF63 30.00 | PF65 32.00 | | | |

### KM# 1142 5 POUNDS

28.28 g., 0.925 Silver 0.841 oz. ASW, 38.6 mm. **Ruler:** Elizabeth II **Subject:** London Olympics, 2012 **Obv:** Head with tiara right **Rev:** Flying Scotsman, blue logo **Mint:** British Royal Mint

| Date | Mintage | VF20 | XF40 | MS60 | MS63 | MS65 |
|---|---|---|---|---|---|---|
| 2009 | 95,000 | PF63 50.00 | PF65 55.00 | | | |

### KM# 1143 5 POUNDS

28.28 g., 0.925 Silver 0.841 oz. ASW, 38.6 mm. **Ruler:** Elizabeth II **Subject:** London Olympics, 2012 **Obv:** Head with tiara right **Rev:** Globe Theatre, blue logo **Mint:** British Royal Mint

| Date | Mintage | VF20 | XF40 | MS60 | MS63 | MS65 |
|---|---|---|---|---|---|---|
| 2009 | 95,000 | PF63 50.00 | PF65 55.00 | | | |

### KM# 1144 5 POUNDS

28.28 g., 0.925 Silver 0.841 oz. ASW, 38.6 mm. **Ruler:** Elizabeth II **Subject:** London Olympics, 2012 **Obv:** Head with tiara right **Rev:** Man in leg braces, Issac Newton quote, blue logo **Mint:** British Royal Mint

| Date | Mintage | VF20 | XF40 | MS60 | MS63 | MS65 |
|---|---|---|---|---|---|---|
| 2009 | 95,000 | PF63 50.00 | PF65 55.00 | | | |

### KM# 1145 5 POUNDS

28.28 g., 0.925 Silver 0.841 oz. ASW, 38.6 mm. **Ruler:** Elizabeth II **Series:** London Olympics, 2012 **Obv:** Head with tiara right **Rev:** Stonehenge, blue logo **Mint:** British Royal Mint

| Date | Mintage | VF20 | XF40 | MS60 | MS63 | MS65 |
|---|---|---|---|---|---|---|
| 2009 | 95,000 | PF63 50.00 | PF65 55.00 | | | |

### KM# 1139 5 POUNDS

28.28 g., Copper-Nickel, 38.6 mm. **Ruler:** Elizabeth II **Obv:** Head with tiara right **Rev:** Runners and stopwatch, 2 in center **Mint:** British Royal Mint

| Date | Mintage | VF20 | XF40 | MS60 | MS63 | MS65 |
|---|---|---|---|---|---|---|
| 2010 | — | PF63 30.00 | PF65 32.00 | | | |
| 2010 | 500,000 | — | — | — | 18.00 | 22.00 |

### KM# 1139a 5 POUNDS

28.28 g., 0.925 Silver 0.841 oz. ASW, 38.6 mm. **Ruler:** Elizabeth II **Obv:** Head with tiara right **Rev:** Runners and stopwatch, 2 in center **Mint:** British Royal Mint

| Date | Mintage | VF20 | XF40 | MS60 | MS63 | MS65 |
|---|---|---|---|---|---|---|
| 2010 | — | PF63 50.00 | PF65 55.00 | | | |

### KM# 1139b 5 POUNDS

39.94 g., 0.9167 Gold 1.1771 oz. AGW, 38.61 mm. **Ruler:** Elizabeth II **Subject:** Countdown to the 2012 London Olympics **Obv:** Head with tiara right **Rev:** Runners and stopwatch, 2 in center **Mint:** British Royal Mint

| Date | Mintage | VF20 | XF40 | MS60 | MS63 | MS65 |
|---|---|---|---|---|---|---|
| 2010 | — | PF65 2,100 | | | | |

### KM# 1146 5 POUNDS

28.28 g., 0.925 Silver 0.841 oz. ASW, 38.6 mm. **Ruler:** Elizabeth II **Subject:** London Olympics, 2012 **Obv:** Head with tiara right **Rev:** Churchill figure and quote, blue logo **Mint:** British Royal Mint

| Date | Mintage | VF20 | XF40 | MS60 | MS63 | MS65 |
|---|---|---|---|---|---|---|
| 2010 | 95,000 | PF63 50.00 | PF65 55.00 | | | |

### KM# 1146a 5 POUNDS

28.28 g., Copper-Nickel, 38.6 mm. **Ruler:** Elizabeth II **Subject:** London Olympics, 2012 **Obv:** Head with tiara right **Rev:** Churchill figure and quote, blue logo **Mint:** British Royal Mint

| Date | Mintage | VF20 | XF40 | MS60 | MS63 | MS65 |
|---|---|---|---|---|---|---|
| 2010 | — | PF63 40.00 | | | | |

### KM# 1147 5 POUNDS

28.28 g., 0.925 Silver 0.841 oz. ASW, 38.6 mm. **Ruler:** Elizabeth II **Subject:** London Olympics, 2012 **Obv:** Head with tiara right **Rev:** Unity, flora, blue logo **Mint:** British Royal Mint

| Date | Mintage | VF20 | XF40 | MS60 | MS63 | MS65 |
|---|---|---|---|---|---|---|
| 2010 | 95,000 | PF63 50.00 | PF65 55.00 | | | |

### KM# 1148 5 POUNDS

28.28 g., 0.999 Silver 0.9083 oz. ASW, 38.6 mm. **Ruler:** Elizabeth II **Subject:** London Olympics, 2012 **Obv:** Head with tiara right **Rev:** Buckingham Palace and the Mall, blue logo **Mint:** British Royal Mint

| Date | Mintage | VF20 | XF40 | MS60 | MS63 | MS65 |
|---|---|---|---|---|---|---|
| 2010 | 95,000 | PF63 50.00 | PF65 55.00 | | | |

### KM# 1148a 5 POUNDS

28.28 g., Copper-Nickel, 38.6 mm. **Ruler:** Elizabeth II **Subject:** London Olympics, 2012 **Obv:** Head with tiara right **Rev:** Buckingham Palace and the Mall, blue logo **Mint:** British Royal Mint

| Date | Mintage | VF20 | XF40 | MS60 | MS63 | MS65 |
|---|---|---|---|---|---|---|
| 2010 | — | PF63 40.00 | PF65 42.00 | | | |

### KM# 1149 5 POUNDS

28.28 g., 0.925 Silver 0.841 oz. ASW, 38.6 mm. **Ruler:** Elizabeth II **Subject:** London Olympics, 2010 **Obv:** Head with tiara right **Rev:** Musical instruments, blue logo **Mint:** British Royal Mint

| Date | Mintage | VF20 | XF40 | MS60 | MS63 | MS65 |
|---|---|---|---|---|---|---|
| 2010 | 95,000 | PF63 50.00 | PF65 55.00 | | | |

### KM# 1151 5 POUNDS

28.28 g., Copper-Nickel, 38.6 mm. **Ruler:** Elizabeth II **Subject:** Restoration of the Monarchy, 1660 **Obv:** Head with tiara right **Mint:** British Royal Mint

| Date | Mintage | VF20 | XF40 | MS60 | MS63 | MS65 |
|---|---|---|---|---|---|---|
| 2010 | — | — | — | — | 18.00 | 22.00 |

### KM# 1151a 5 POUNDS

28.28 g., 0.925 Silver 0.841 oz. ASW, 38.6 mm. **Ruler:** Elizabeth II **Subject:** Restoration of the Monarchy, 1660 **Obv:** Head with tiara right **Mint:** British Royal Mint

| Date | Mintage | VF20 | XF40 | MS60 | MS63 | MS65 |
|---|---|---|---|---|---|---|
| 2010 | — | PF63 50.00 | PF65 55.00 | | | |

Note: Also exists as a Piedfort, P114

### KM# 1151b 5 POUNDS

39.94 g., 0.9167 Gold 1.1771 oz. AGW, 38.61 mm. **Ruler:** Elizabeth II **Subject:** Restoration of the Monarchy, 1660 **Obv:** Head with tiara right **Rev:** Crown above wreath **Mint:** British Royal Mint

| Date | Mintage | VF20 | XF40 | MS60 | MS63 | MS65 |
|---|---|---|---|---|---|---|
| 2010 | — | PF65 2,100 | | | | |

### KM# 1152 5 POUNDS

28.28 g., 0.925 Silver 0.841 oz. ASW, 38.6 mm. **Ruler:** Elizabeth II **Subject:** London Olympics, 2012 **Obv:** Head with tiara right **Rev:** Giants Causeway, orange logo **Mint:** British Royal Mint

| Date | Mintage | VF20 | XF40 | MS60 | MS63 | MS65 |
|---|---|---|---|---|---|---|
| 2010 | 95,000 | PF63 50.00 | PF65 55.00 | | | |

### KM# 1153 5 POUNDS

28.28 g., 0.925 Silver 0.841 oz. ASW, 38.6 mm. **Ruler:** Elizabeth II **Subject:** London Olympics, 2012 **Obv:** Head with tiara right **Rev:** Coastline, orange logo **Mint:** British Royal Mint

| Date | Mintage | VF20 | XF40 | MS60 | MS63 | MS65 |
|---|---|---|---|---|---|---|
| 2010 | 95,000 | PF63 50.00 | PF65 55.00 | | | |

### KM# 1154 5 POUNDS

28.28 g., 0.925 Silver 0.841 oz. ASW, 38.6 mm. **Ruler:** Elizabeth II **Subject:** London Olympics, 2012 **Obv:** Head with tiara right **Rev:** River Thames, orange logo **Mint:** British Royal Mint

| Date | Mintage | VF20 | XF40 | MS60 | MS63 | MS65 |
|---|---|---|---|---|---|---|
| 2010 | 95,000 | PF63 50.00 | PF65 55.00 | | | |

### KM# 1155 5 POUNDS

28.28 g., 0.925 Silver 0.841 oz. ASW, 38.6 mm. **Ruler:** Elizabeth II **Subject:** London Olympics, 2012 **Obv:** Head with tiara right **Rev:** British flora -oak leaves and acorn, orange logo **Mint:** British Royal Mint

| Date | Mintage | VF20 | XF40 | MS60 | MS63 | MS65 |
|---|---|---|---|---|---|---|
| 2010 | 95,000 | PF63 50.00 | PF65 55.00 | | | |

### KM# 1156 5 POUNDS

28.28 g., 0.925 Silver 0.841 oz. ASW, 38.6 mm. **Ruler:** Elizabeth II **Subject:** London Olympics, 2012 **Obv:** Head with tiara right **Rev:** Owl, orange logo **Mint:** British Royal Mint

| Date | Mintage | VF20 | XF40 | MS60 | MS63 | MS65 |
|---|---|---|---|---|---|---|
| 2010 | 95,000 | PF63 50.00 | PF65 55.00 | | | |

### KM# 1157 5 POUNDS

28.28 g., 0.925 Silver 0.841 oz. ASW, 38.6 mm. **Ruler:** Elizabeth II **Subject:** London Olympics, 2012 **Obv:** Head with tiara right **Rev:** Weather vane, orange logo **Mint:** British Royal Mint

| Date | Mintage | VF20 | XF40 | MS60 | MS63 | MS65 |
|---|---|---|---|---|---|---|
| 2010 | 95,000 | **PF63** 50.00 | **PF65** 55.00 | | | |

### KM# 1260 5 POUNDS

28.28 g., 0.925 Silver 0.841 oz. ASW, 38.6 mm. **Ruler:** Elizabeth II **Subject:** 2012 Summer Olympics, London **Obv:** Head with tiara right **Rev:** Beefeaters **Mint:** Royal Mint

| Date | Mintage | VF20 | XF40 | MS60 | MS63 | MS65 |
|---|---|---|---|---|---|---|
| 2010 | — | **PF63** 50.00 | **PF65** 55.00 | | | |

### KM# 1261 5 POUNDS

28.28 g., 0.925 Silver 0.841 oz. ASW, 38.6 mm. **Ruler:** Elizabeth II **Subject:** 2012 Summer Olympics, London **Obv:** Head with tiara right **Rev:** Rabbit

| Date | Mintage | VF20 | XF40 | MS60 | MS63 | MS65 |
|---|---|---|---|---|---|---|
| 2013 | — | **PF63** 50.00 | **PF65** 55.00 | | | |

### KM# 1201 5 POUNDS

28.28 g., Copper-Nickel, 38.6 mm. **Ruler:** Elizabeth II **Subject:** Prince Philip's 90th Birthday **Obv:** Head with tiara right **Rev:** Large head of Prince Philip in profile right **Mint:** British Royal Mint

| Date | Mintage | VF20 | XF40 | MS60 | MS63 | MS65 |
|---|---|---|---|---|---|---|
| 2011 | — | — | — | — | 18.00 | 22.00 |
| 2011 | — | **PF63** 30.00 | **PF65** 32.00 | | | |

### KM# 1201a 5 POUNDS

28.28 g., 0.925 Silver 0.841 oz. ASW, 38.6 mm. **Ruler:** Elizabeth II **Subject:** Prince Philip, 90th Birthday **Mint:** British Royal Mint

| Date | Mintage | VF20 | XF40 | MS60 | MS63 | MS65 |
|---|---|---|---|---|---|---|
| 2011 | — | **PF63** 50.00 | **PF65** 55.00 | | | |

Note: Also exists as a Piedfort, P89

### KM# 1201b 5 POUNDS

39.94 g., 0.9167 Gold 1.1771 oz. AGW, 38.61 mm. **Ruler:** Elizabeth II **Subject:** Prince Philip's 90th Birthday **Obv:** Head with tiara right **Rev:** Large head of Prince Philip in profile right **Mint:** British Royal Mint

| Date | Mintage | VF20 | XF40 | MS60 | MS63 | MS65 |
|---|---|---|---|---|---|---|
| 2011 | — | **PF65** 2,100 | | | | |

### KM# 1202 5 POUNDS

28.28 g., Copper-Nickel, 38.6 mm. **Ruler:** Elizabeth II **Subject:** Countdown to London Olympics, 2012 **Obv:** Head with tiara right **Rev:** 1 between wheels of cyclist traveling left **Mint:** British Royal Mint

| Date | Mintage | VF20 | XF40 | MS60 | MS63 | MS65 |
|---|---|---|---|---|---|---|
| 2011 | — | — | — | — | 18.00 | 22.00 |
| 2011 | — | **PF63** 30.00 | **PF65** 32.00 | | | |

### KM# 1202a 5 POUNDS

28.28 g., 0.925 Silver 0.841 oz. ASW, 38.6 mm. **Ruler:** Elizabeth II **Subject:** Countdown to London Olympics, 2012 **Obv:** Head with tiara right **Rev:** 1 between wheels of cyclist traveling left **Mint:** British Royal Mint

| Date | Mintage | VF20 | XF40 | MS60 | MS63 | MS65 |
|---|---|---|---|---|---|---|
| 2011 | — | **PF63** 50.00 | **PF65** 55.00 | | | |

### KM# 1202b 5 POUNDS

39.94 g., 0.9167 Gold 1.1771 oz. AGW, 38.61 mm. **Ruler:** Elizabeth II **Subject:** Countdown to London Olympics, 2012 **Obv:** Head with tiara right **Rev:** 1 between wheels of cyclists traveling left, logo in color **Mint:** Royal Mint

| Date | Mintage | VF20 | XF40 | MS60 | MS63 | MS65 |
|---|---|---|---|---|---|---|
| 2011 | — | **PF65** 2,100 | | | | |

### KM# 1203 5 POUNDS

28.28 g., Copper-Nickel, 38.6 mm. **Ruler:** Elizabeth II **Subject:** Royal Wedding - William and Katherine **Rev:** Heads facing

| Date | Mintage | VF20 | XF40 | MS60 | MS63 | MS65 |
|---|---|---|---|---|---|---|
| 2011 | — | — | — | — | 18.00 | 22.00 |

### KM# 1203a 5 POUNDS

28.28 g., 0.925 Silver 0.841 oz. ASW, 38.6 mm. **Ruler:** Elizabeth II **Subject:** Royal Wedding - William and Catherine

| Date | Mintage | VF20 | XF40 | MS60 | MS63 | MS65 |
|---|---|---|---|---|---|---|
| 2011 | — | **PF63** 50.00 | **PF65** 55.00 | | | |

### KM# 1216 5 POUNDS

28.28 g., Copper-Nickel, 38.61 mm. **Ruler:** Elizabeth II **Subject:** Elizabeth's 60th anniversary of reign **Obv:** Bust with tiara in robes of the Garter, right **Rev:** Young head portrait right

| Date | Mintage | VF20 | XF40 | MS60 | MS63 | MS65 |
|---|---|---|---|---|---|---|
| 2012 | — | **PF63** 25.00 | **PF65** 28.00 | | | |

### KM# 1242 5 POUNDS

28.28 g., Copper-Nickel, 38.61 mm. **Ruler:** Elizabeth II **Subject:** Elizabeth's coronation, 60th Anniversary **Obv:** Head with tiara right **Rev:** State Crown

| Date | Mintage | VF20 | XF40 | MS60 | MS63 | MS65 |
|---|---|---|---|---|---|---|
| 2013 | — | — | — | — | — | 25.00 |
| 2013 | 44,000 | **PF63** 35.00 | **PF65** 37.00 | | | |

### KM# 1242a 5 POUNDS

28.28 g., 0.925 Silver 0.841 oz. ASW, 38.61 mm. **Ruler:** Elizabeth II **Subject:** Elizabeth's coronation, 60th Anniversary **Obv:** Head with tiara right **Rev:** State Crown

| Date | Mintage | VF20 | XF40 | MS60 | MS63 | MS65 |
|---|---|---|---|---|---|---|
| 2013 | 60,000 | **PF65** 125 | | | | |

### KM# 1242b 5 POUNDS

28.28 g., 0.999 Silver 0.9083 oz. ASW gold plated, 38.61 mm. **Ruler:** Elizabeth II **Subject:** Elizabeth's coronation, 60th Anniversary **Obv:** Head with tiara right **Rev:** State Crown

| Date | Mintage | VF20 | XF40 | MS60 | MS63 | MS65 |
|---|---|---|---|---|---|---|
| 2013 | 12,500 | **PF65** 150 | | | | |

### KM# 1242c 5 POUNDS
39.94 g., 0.9167 Gold 1.1771 oz. AGW, 38.61 mm. **Ruler:** Elizabeth II **Subject:** Elizabeth's coronation, 60th Anniversary **Obv:** Head with tiara right **Rev:** State Crown

| Date | Mintage | VF20 | XF40 | MS60 | MS63 | MS65 |
|---|---|---|---|---|---|---|
| 2013 | 2,060 | **PF65** 3,500 | | | | |

### KM# 1242d 5 POUNDS
94.20 g., 0.9995 Platinum 3.0271 oz. APW, 38.61 mm. **Ruler:** Elizabeth II **Subject:** Elizabeth's coronation, 60th Anniversary **Obv:** Head with tiara right **Rev:** State Crown

| Date | Mintage | VF20 | XF40 | MS60 | MS63 | MS65 |
|---|---|---|---|---|---|---|
| 2013 | 150 | **PF65** 9,000 | | | | |

### KM# 1247 5 POUNDS
28.28 g., 0.925 Silver 0.841 oz. ASW, 38.61 mm. **Ruler:** Elizabeth II **Obv:** Young Head Portrait **Rev:** Royal Arms

| Date | Mintage | VF20 | XF40 | MS60 | MS63 | MS65 |
|---|---|---|---|---|---|---|
| 2013 | Est. 5000 | **PF65** 150 | | | | |

### KM# 1247a 5 POUNDS
39.95 g., 0.9167 Gold 1.1774 oz. AGW, 38.61 mm. **Ruler:** Elizabeth II **Obv:** Young bust right **Rev:** Royal Arms

| Date | Mintage | VF20 | XF40 | MS60 | MS63 | MS65 |
|---|---|---|---|---|---|---|
| 2013 | Est. 500 | **PF65** 3,000 | | | | |

### KM# 1248 5 POUNDS
28.28 g., 0.925 Silver 0.841 oz. ASW, 38.61 mm. **Ruler:** Elizabeth II **Obv:** Bust right by Arnold Machin **Rev:** Royal Arms

| Date | Mintage | VF20 | XF40 | MS60 | MS63 | MS65 |
|---|---|---|---|---|---|---|
| 2013 | Est. 5000 | **PF65** 150 | | | | |

### KM# 1248a 5 POUNDS
39.95 g., 0.9167 Gold 1.1774 oz. AGW, 38.61 mm. **Ruler:** Elizabeth II **Obv:** Bust with tiara right **Rev:** Royal Arms

| Date | Mintage | VF20 | XF40 | MS60 | MS63 | MS65 |
|---|---|---|---|---|---|---|
| 2013 | Est. 500 | **PF65** 3,000 | | | | |

### KM# 1249 5 POUNDS
28.28 g., 0.925 Silver 0.841 oz. ASW, 38.61 mm. **Ruler:** Elizabeth II **Obv:** Head with crown right **Rev:** Royal Arms

| Date | Mintage | VF20 | XF40 | MS60 | MS63 | MS65 |
|---|---|---|---|---|---|---|
| 2013 | — | **PF65** 150 | | | | |

### KM# 1249a 5 POUNDS
39.95 g., 0.9167 Gold 1.1774 oz. AGW, 38.61 mm. **Ruler:** Elizabeth II **Obv:** Head with crown right **Rev:** Royal Arms

| Date | Mintage | VF20 | XF40 | MS60 | MS63 | MS65 |
|---|---|---|---|---|---|---|
| 2013 | — | **PF65** 3,000 | | | | |

### KM# 1250 5 POUNDS
28.28 g., 0.925 Silver 0.841 oz. ASW, 38.61 mm. **Ruler:** Elizabeth II **Obv:** Head with tiara right **Rev:** Royal Arms

| Date | Mintage | VF20 | XF40 | MS60 | MS63 | MS65 |
|---|---|---|---|---|---|---|
| 2013 | Est. 5000 | **PF65** 150 | | | | |

### KM# 1250a 5 POUNDS
39.94 g., 0.9167 Gold 1.1771 oz. AGW, 38.61 mm. **Ruler:** Elizabeth II **Obv:** Head with tiara right **Rev:** Royal Arms

| Date | Mintage | VF20 | XF40 | MS60 | MS63 | MS65 |
|---|---|---|---|---|---|---|
| 2013 | Est. 500 | **PF65** 3,000 | | | | |

### KM# 1251 5 POUNDS
28.28 g., 0.925 Silver 0.841 oz. ASW, 38.61 mm. **Ruler:** Elizabeth II **Subject:** Birth of HRH George Alexander Louis, son of William and Katherine **Obv:** Head in tiara right **Rev:** St. George slaying dragon **Mint:** British Royal Mint

| Date | Mintage | VF20 | XF40 | MS60 | MS63 | MS65 |
|---|---|---|---|---|---|---|
| 2013 | 10,000 | **PF65** 185 | | | | |

### KM# 1259 5 POUNDS
28.28 g., Copper-Nickel, 38.61 mm. **Ruler:** Elizabeth II **Subject:** Christening of Prince George **Mint:** Royal Mint

| Date | Mintage | VF20 | XF40 | MS60 | MS63 | MS65 |
|---|---|---|---|---|---|---|
| 2013 | — | — | — | — | — | 25.00 |

### KM# 1091a 10 POUNDS
3.11 g., 0.9999 Platinum 0.0993 oz. APW, 16.5 mm. **Ruler:** Elizabeth II **Obv:** Head with tiara right **Rev:** Britannia seated with reclining lion right **Edge:** Reeded

| Date | Mintage | F12 | VF20 | XF40 | MS60 | MS63 |
|---|---|---|---|---|---|---|
| 2007 | 691 | **PF63** 300 | | | | |

### KM# 1227 10 POUNDS

155.50 g., 0.999 Silver 4.9944 oz. ASW **Ruler:** Elizabeth II **Obv:** Head with tiara right **Rev:** Pegasus right

| Date | Mintage | VF20 | XF40 | MS60 | MS63 | MS65 |
|---|---|---|---|---|---|---|
| 2012 | — | PF65 225 | | | | |

### KM# 1227a 10 POUNDS

155.50 g., 0.999 Gold 4.9944 oz. AGW **Ruler:** Elizabeth II **Obv:** Head with tiara right **Rev:** Pegasus right

| Date | Mintage | VF20 | XF40 | MS60 | MS63 | MS65 |
|---|---|---|---|---|---|---|
| 2012 | — | PF65 9,500 | | | | |

### KM# 1264 10 POUNDS

155.60 g., Silver, 65 mm. **Ruler:** Elizabeth II **Rev:** Coronation insignia and Westminster Abbey **Mint:** Royal Mint

| Date | Mintage | VF20 | XF40 | MS60 | MS63 | MS65 |
|---|---|---|---|---|---|---|
| 2013 | Est. 1953 | PF65 525 | | | | |

### KM# 1092a 25 POUNDS

0.9999 Platinum APW, 22 mm. **Ruler:** Elizabeth II **Obv:** Head with tiara right **Rev:** Britannia seated with reclining lion right **Edge:** Reeded

| Date | Mintage | F12 | VF20 | XF40 | MS60 | MS63 |
|---|---|---|---|---|---|---|
| 2007 | — | PF63 650 | | | | |

### KM# 1163 25 POUNDS

8.51 g., 0.9167 Gold 0.2508 oz. AGW, 22 mm. **Ruler:** Elizabeth II **Subject:** London Olympics, 2012 **Obv:** Head with tiara right **Rev:** Mercury and cyclists **Mint:** British Royal Mint

| Date | Mintage | VF20 | XF40 | MS60 | MS63 | MS65 |
|---|---|---|---|---|---|---|
| 2010 | 20,000 | PF65 800 | | | | |

### KM# 1164 25 POUNDS

8.51 g., 0.9167 Gold 0.2508 oz. AGW, 22 mm. **Ruler:** Elizabeth II **Subject:** London Olympics, 2012 **Obv:** Head with tiara right **Rev:** Diana and cyclists **Mint:** British Royal Mint

| Date | Mintage | VF20 | XF40 | MS60 | MS63 | MS65 |
|---|---|---|---|---|---|---|
| 2010 | 20,000 | PF65 800 | | | | |

### KM# 1218 25 POUNDS

8.51 g., 0.9167 Gold 0.2508 oz. AGW, 22 mm. **Ruler:** Elizabeth II **Subject:** London Olympics, 2012 **Obv:** Head with tiara right **Rev:** Juno

| Date | Mintage | VF20 | XF40 | MS60 | MS63 | MS65 |
|---|---|---|---|---|---|---|
| 2011 | — | PF65 800 | | | | |

### KM# 1219 25 POUNDS

8.51 g., 0.9167 Gold 0.2508 oz. AGW, 22 mm. **Ruler:** Elizabeth II **Obv:** Head with tiara right **Rev:** Apollo

| Date | Mintage | VF20 | XF40 | MS60 | MS63 | MS65 |
|---|---|---|---|---|---|---|
| 2011 | — | PF65 800 | | | | |

### KM# 1221 25 POUNDS

8.51 g., 0.9167 Gold 0.2508 oz. AGW, 22 mm. **Ruler:** Elizabeth II **Obv:** Head with tiara right **Rev:** Minervia

| Date | Mintage | VF20 | XF40 | MS60 | MS63 | MS65 |
|---|---|---|---|---|---|---|
| 2012 | — | PF65 800 | | | | |

### KM# 1222 25 POUNDS

8.51 g., 0.9167 Gold 0.2508 oz. AGW, 22 mm. **Ruler:** Elizabeth II **Obv:** Head with tiara right **Rev:** Vulcan

| Date | Mintage | VF20 | XF40 | MS60 | MS63 | MS65 |
|---|---|---|---|---|---|---|
| 2012 | — | PF65 800 | | | | |

### KM# 1162 100 POUNDS

32.69 g., 0.9167 Gold 0.9635 oz. AGW, 32.7 mm. **Ruler:** Elizabeth II **Subject:** London Olympics, 2012 **Obv:** Head with tiara right **Rev:** Neptune and sailing **Mint:** British Royal Mint

| Date | Mintage | VF20 | XF40 | MS60 | MS63 | MS65 |
|---|---|---|---|---|---|---|
| 2010 | 7,500 | PF65 1,850 | | | | |

### KM# 1220 100 POUNDS

32.69 g., 0.9167 Gold 0.9635 oz. AGW, 32.7 mm. **Ruler:** Elizabeth II **Obv:** Head with tiara right **Rev:** Jupiter

| Date | Mintage | VF20 | XF40 | MS60 | MS63 | MS65 |
|---|---|---|---|---|---|---|
| 2011 | — | PF65 1,850 | | | | |

### KM# 1223 100 POUNDS

32.69 g., 0.9167 Gold 0.9635 oz. AGW, 32.7 mm. **Ruler:** Elizabeth II **Obv:** Head with tiara right **Rev:** Mars

| Date | Mintage | VF20 | XF40 | MS60 | MS63 | MS65 |
|---|---|---|---|---|---|---|
| 2012 | — | PF65 1,850 | | | | |

### KM# 1235 500 POUNDS

1000.00 g., 0.9999 Silver 32.1475 oz. ASW **Ruler:** Elizabeth II **Subject:** London Olympics, 2012 **Rev:** Ring of Penants around central legend

| Date | Mintage | VF20 | XF40 | MS60 | MS63 | MS65 |
|---|---|---|---|---|---|---|
| 2012 | 2,012 | PF65 1,500 | | | | |

### KM# 1243 500 POUNDS

1000.00 g., 0.9999 Silver 32.1475 oz. ASW **Ruler:** Elizabeth II **Subject:** Elizabeth II, 60th Anniversary of reign **Obv:** Bust with tiara and in robes of the Garter right **Rev:** Royal Arms crowned and supported within wreath

| Date | Mintage | VF20 | XF40 | MS60 | MS63 | MS65 |
|---|---|---|---|---|---|---|
| 2012 | — | PF65 1,300 | | | | |

### KM# 1265 500 POUNDS

1000.00 g., 0.999 Gold 32.1186 oz. AGW, 100 mm. **Ruler:** Elizabeth II **Rev:** Coronation insignia on roses and laurel **Mint:** Royal Mint

| Date | Mintage | VF20 | XF40 | MS60 | MS63 | MS65 |
|---|---|---|---|---|---|---|
| 2013 | Est. 400 | PF65 2,600 | | | | |

### KM# 1236 1000 POUNDS

1000.00 g., 0.999 Gold 32.1186 oz. AGW **Ruler:** Elizabeth II **Rev:** Weight bar bell and wreath

| Date | Mintage | VF20 | XF40 | MS60 | MS63 | MS65 |
|---|---|---|---|---|---|---|
| 2012 | 60 | PF65 58,000 | | | | |

### KM# 1263 1000 POUNDS

1000.00 g., 0.999 Gold 32.1186 oz. AGW, 100 mm. **Ruler:** Elizabeth II **Obv:** Bust in robes of the Garter **Rev:** Shield before Buckingham palace **Mint:** Royal Mint

| Date | Mintage | VF20 | XF40 | MS60 | MS63 | MS65 |
|---|---|---|---|---|---|---|
| 2012 | Est. 60 | PF65 55,000 | | | | |

## SOVEREIGN COINAGE

### KM# 1117 1/4 SOVEREIGN

2.00 g., 0.917 Gold 0.059 oz. AGW, 13.5 mm. **Ruler:** Elizabeth II **Obv:** Head with tiara right **Rev:** St. George slaying dragon

| Date | Mintage | VF20 | XF40 | MS60 | MS63 | MS65 |
|---|---|---|---|---|---|---|
| 2009 | 50,000 | — | — | — | 115 | — |
| 2009 | 25,000 | PF63 135 | | | | |
| 2010 | 250,000 | — | — | — | 115 | — |
| 2010 | 25,000 | PF63 135 | | | | |
| 2011 | — | — | — | — | 115 | — |
| 2011 | 15,000 | PF63 135 | | | | |
| 2013 | — | — | — | — | 115 | — |
| 2013 | 5,645 | PF63 135 | | | | |
| 2014 | — | — | — | — | 115 | — |
| 2014 | 4,575 | PF63 82.00 | | | | |

### KM# 1205 1/4 SOVEREIGN

2.00 g., 0.917 Gold 0.059 oz. AGW, 13.5 mm. **Ruler:** Elizabeth II **Obv:** Head with tiara right **Rev:** St. George spearing dragon head

| Date | Mintage | VF20 | XF40 | MS60 | MS63 | MS65 |
|---|---|---|---|---|---|---|
| 2012 | — | PF63 135 | | | | |

### KM# 1001 1/2 SOVEREIGN

3.99 g., 0.917 Gold 0.1176 oz. AGW **Ruler:** Elizabeth II **Obv:** Head with tiara right **Rev:** St. George slaying the dragon

| Date | Mintage | VF20 | XF40 | MS60 | MS63 | MS65 |
|---|---|---|---|---|---|---|
| 2001 | 94,763 | — | — | — | 142 | — |
| 2001 | 10,000 | PF63 149 | | | | |
| 2002 | 61,347 | — | — | — | 142 | — |
| 2003 | 47,818 | — | — | — | 142 | — |
| 2003 | 14,750 | PF63 149 | | | | |
| 2004 | 34,924 | — | — | — | 142 | — |
| 2006 | 30,299 | — | — | — | 142 | — |
| 2006 | 8,500 | PF63 149 | | | | |
| 2007 | 75,000 | — | — | — | 142 | — |
| 2007 | 7,500 | PF63 149 | | | | |
| 2008 | 75,000 | — | — | — | 142 | — |
| 2008 | 7,500 | PF63 149 | | | | |

### KM# 1025 1/2 SOVEREIGN

3.99 g., 0.9167 Gold 0.1176 oz. AGW, 19.3 mm. **Ruler:** Elizabeth II **Subject:** Queen Elizabeth II's Golden Jubilee **Obv:** Head with tiara right **Rev:** Crowned arms within wreath, date below **Edge:** Reeded **Mint:** British Royal Mint

| Date | Mintage | VF20 | XF40 | MS60 | MS63 | MS65 |
|---|---|---|---|---|---|---|
| 2002 | 61,347 | — | — | — | 157 | — |
| 2002 | 10,000 | PF63 178 | | | | |

### KM# 1064 1/2 SOVEREIGN

3.99 g., 0.9167 Gold 0.1177 oz. AGW, 19.3 mm. **Ruler:** Elizabeth II **Obv:** Head with tiara right **Rev:** Knight fighting dragon with sword **Edge:** Reeded **Mint:** British Royal Mint

| Date | Mintage | VF20 | XF40 | MS60 | MS63 | MS65 |
|---|---|---|---|---|---|---|
| 2005 | 30,299 | — | — | — | 142 | — |
| 2005 | 5,011 | PF63 164 | | | | |

### KM# 1001.1 1/2 SOVEREIGN

3.99 g., 0.917 Gold 0.1176 oz. AGW, 19.3 mm. **Ruler:** Elizabeth II **Obv:** Head with tiara right **Rev:** St. George slaying the dragon **Mint:** British Royal Mint

| Date | Mintage | VF20 | XF40 | MS60 | MS63 | MS65 |
|---|---|---|---|---|---|---|
| 2009 | 50,000 | — | — | — | 149 | — |
| 2009 | 6,000 | PF63 164 | | | | |
| 2010 | 250,000 | — | — | — | 149 | — |
| 2010 | 7,000 | PF63 164 | | | | |
| 2011 | — | — | — | — | 149 | — |
| 2011 | — | PF63 164 | | | | |
| 2013 | — | — | — | — | 149 | — |
| 2013 | 4,795 | PF63 164 | | | | |
| 2014 | 9,900 | — | — | — | 149 | — |
| 2014 | 4,075 | PF63 164 | | | | |

### KM# 1206 1/2 SOVEREIGN

3.99 g., 0.917 Gold 0.1176 oz. AGW, 19.3 mm. **Ruler:** Elizabeth II **Obv:** Head with tiara right **Rev:** St. George spearing dragon head

| Date | Mintage | VF20 | XF40 | MS60 | MS63 | MS65 |
|---|---|---|---|---|---|---|
| 2012 | — | PF63 164 | | | | |

### KM# 1002 SOVEREIGN

7.99 g., 0.917 Gold 0.2355 oz. AGW **Ruler:** Elizabeth II **Obv:** Head with tiara right **Rev:** St. George slaying the dragon

| Date | Mintage | VF20 | XF40 | MS60 | MS63 | MS65 |
|---|---|---|---|---|---|---|
| 2001 | 49,462 | — | — | — | 285 | — |
| 2001 | 15,000 | PF63 425 | | | | |
| 2002 | 75,264 | — | — | — | 285 | — |
| 2003 | 43,230 | — | — | — | 285 | — |
| 2003 | 19,750 | PF63 425 | | | | |
| 2004 | 30,688 | — | — | — | 285 | — |
| 2006 | 45,542 | — | — | — | 285 | — |
| 2006 | 16,000 | PF63 425 | | | | |
| 2007 | 75,000 | — | — | — | 285 | — |
| 2007 | 12,500 | PF63 425 | | | | |
| 2008 | 75,000 | — | — | — | 285 | — |
| 2008 | 12,500 | PF63 425 | | | | |

### KM# 1026 SOVEREIGN

7.98 g., 0.9167 Gold 0.2352 oz. AGW, 22 mm. **Ruler:** Elizabeth II **Subject:** Queen Elizabeth II's Golden Jubilee **Obv:** Head with tiara right **Rev:** Crowned arms within wreath, date below **Edge:** Reeded **Mint:** British Royal Mint

| Date | Mintage | VF20 | XF40 | MS60 | MS63 | MS65 |
|---|---|---|---|---|---|---|
| 2002 | 75,264 | — | — | — | 285 | — |
| 2002 | 20,500 | PF63 425 | | | | |

### KM# 1065 SOVEREIGN

7.99 g., 0.9176 Gold 0.2357 oz. AGW, 22.05 mm. **Ruler:** Elizabeth II **Obv:** Head with tiara right **Rev:** Knight fighting dragon with sword **Edge:** Reeded **Mint:** British Royal Mint

| Date | Mintage | VF20 | XF40 | MS60 | MS63 | MS65 |
|---|---|---|---|---|---|---|
| 2005 | 17,500 | PF63 425 | | | | |
| 2005 | 45,542 | — | — | — | 285 | — |

### KM# 1002.1 SOVEREIGN

7.98 g., 0.917 Gold 0.2353 oz. AGW, 22.05 mm. **Ruler:** Elizabeth II **Obv:** Head with tiara right **Rev:** St. George slaying the dragon **Mint:** British Royal Mint

| Date | Mintage | VF20 | XF40 | MS60 | MS63 | MS65 |
|---|---|---|---|---|---|---|
| 2009 | 75,000 | — | — | — | 299 | — |
| 2009 | 12,500 | PF63 425 | | | | |
| 2010 | 250,000 | — | — | — | 299 | — |
| 2010 | 12,500 | PF63 425 | | | | |
| 2011 | — | — | — | — | 299 | — |
| 2011 | 12,500 | PF63 425 | | | | |
| 2013 | — | — | — | — | 299 | — |
| 2013 | 10,295 | PF63 425 | | | | |
| 2014 | 15,000 | — | — | — | 299 | — |
| 2014 | 9,725 | PF63 425 | | | | |

### KM# 1207 SOVEREIGN

7.99 g., 0.917 Gold 0.2355 oz. AGW, 22 mm. **Ruler:** Elizabeth II **Obv:** Head with tiara right **Rev:** St. George spearing dragon head

| Date | Mintage | VF20 | XF40 | MS60 | MS63 | MS65 |
|---|---|---|---|---|---|---|
| 2012 | — | PF63 425 | | | | |

### KM# 1027 2 POUNDS

15.97 g., 0.9167 Gold 0.4707 oz. AGW, 28.4 mm. **Ruler:** Elizabeth II **Subject:** Queen Elizabeth II's Golden Jubilee **Obv:** Head with tiara right **Rev:** Crowned arms within wreath, date below **Edge:** Reeded **Mint:** British Royal Mint

| Date | Mintage | VF20 | XF40 | MS60 | MS63 | MS65 |
|---|---|---|---|---|---|---|
| 2002 | 8,000 | PF63 850 | | | | |

### KM# 1066 2 POUNDS

15.98 g., 0.9167 Gold 0.4709 oz. AGW, 28.4 mm. **Ruler:** Elizabeth II **Obv:** Head with tiara right **Rev:** Knight fighting dragon with sword **Edge:** Reeded **Mint:** British Royal Mint

| Date | Mintage | VF20 | XF40 | MS60 | MS63 | MS65 |
|---|---|---|---|---|---|---|
| 2005 | 5,000 | PF63 850 | | | | |

### KM# 1072 2 POUNDS

15.97 g., 0.9167 Gold 0.4707 oz. AGW, 28.4 mm. **Ruler:** Elizabeth II **Obv:** Head with tiara right **Rev:** St. George slaying the Dragon **Edge:** Reeded **Mint:** British Royal Mint

| Date | Mintage | VF20 | XF40 | MS60 | MS63 | MS65 |
|---|---|---|---|---|---|---|
| 2006 | 3,500 | PF63 850 | | | | |
| 2007 | 2,500 | PF63 875 | | | | |
| 2008 | 2,500 | PF63 875 | | | | |

### KM# 1072.1 2 POUNDS

15.97 g., 0.917 Gold 0.4708 oz. AGW, 28.4 mm. **Ruler:** Elizabeth II **Obv:** Head with tiara right **Rev:** St. George slaying the dragon **Mint:** British Royal Mint

| Date | Mintage | VF20 | XF40 | MS60 | MS63 | MS65 |
|---|---|---|---|---|---|---|
| 2009 | 2,500 | PF63 875 | | | | |
| 2010 | 2,750 | PF63 875 | | | | |
| 2011 | 2,950 | PF63 875 | | | | |
| 2013 | 1,895 | PF63 875 | | | | |
| 2014 | 750 | PF63 875 | | | | |

### KM# 1208 2 POUNDS

15.97 g., 0.9167 Gold 0.4707 oz. AGW, 28.4 mm. **Ruler:** Elizabeth II **Obv:** Head with tiara right **Rev:** St. George spearing dragon's head

| Date | Mintage | VF20 | XF40 | MS60 | MS63 | MS65 |
|---|---|---|---|---|---|---|
| 2012 | — | PF63 875 | | | | |

### KM# 1003 5 POUNDS

39.94 g., 0.917 Gold 1.1775 oz. AGW, 36 mm. **Ruler:** Elizabeth II **Obv:** Head with tiara right **Rev:** St. George slaying dragon **Edge:** Reeded **Mint:** British Royal Mint

| Date | Mintage | VF20 | XF40 | MS60 | MS63 | MS65 |
|---|---|---|---|---|---|---|
| 2001 (u) | 1,000 | — | — | — | 2,100 | — |
| 2001 | 1,000 | PF63 2,250 | | | | |
| 2003 | 812 | — | — | — | 2,100 | — |
| 2003 | 2,250 | PF63 2,150 | | | | |
| 2004 | 1,000 | — | — | — | 2,100 | — |
| 2004 Proof | 1,750 | — | — | — | — | — |
| 2006 | 1,000 | — | — | — | 2,100 | — |
| 2006 | 1,750 | PF63 2,150 | | | | |
| 2007 | 768 | — | — | — | 2,100 | — |
| 2007 | 1,750 | PF63 2,150 | | | | |
| 2008 | 750 | — | — | — | 2,100 | — |
| 2008 | 1,750 | PF63 2,150 | | | | |

### KM# 1028 5 POUNDS

39.94 g., 0.9167 Gold 1.1771 oz. AGW, 36 mm. **Ruler:** Elizabeth II **Subject:** Queen Elizabeth II's Golden Jubilee **Obv:** Head with tiara right **Rev:** Crowned arms within wreath **Edge:** Reeded **Mint:** British Royal Mint

| Date | Mintage | VF20 | XF40 | MS60 | MS63 | MS65 |
|---|---|---|---|---|---|---|
| 2002 | 1,370 | — | — | — | 2,100 | — |
| 2002 | 3,000 | PF63 2,150 | | | | |

### KM# 1067 5 POUNDS

39.94 g., 0.9167 Gold 1.1771 oz. AGW, 36 mm. **Ruler:** Elizabeth II **Obv:** Head with tiara right **Rev:** Knight fighting dragon with sword **Edge:** Reeded **Mint:** British Royal Mint

| Date | Mintage | VF20 | XF40 | MS60 | MS63 | MS65 |
|---|---|---|---|---|---|---|
| 2005 | 936 | — | — | — | 2,100 | — |
| 2005 | 2,500 | PF63 2,150 | | | | |

### KM# 1003.1 5 POUNDS

39.94 g., 0.917 Gold 1.1775 oz. AGW **Ruler:** Elizabeth II **Obv:** Head with tiara right **Rev:** St. George slaying the dragon **Mint:** British Royal Mint

| Date | Mintage | VF20 | XF40 | MS60 | MS63 | MS65 |
|---|---|---|---|---|---|---|
| 2009 | 1,000 | — | — | — | 2,100 | — |
| 2009 | 1,750 | PF63 2,150 | | | | |
| 2010 | 1,000 | — | — | — | 2,100 | — |
| 2010 | 2,000 | PF63 2,150 | | | | |
| 2011 | — | PF63 2,150 | | | | |
| 2013 | 1,000 | PF63 2,150 | | | | |
| 2014 750 | 750 | PF63 2,150 | | | | |

### KM# 1209 5 POUNDS

39.94 g., 0.9167 Gold 1.1771 oz. AGW, 36 mm. **Ruler:** Elizabeth II **Obv:** Head with tiara right **Rev:** St. George spearing dragon's head

| Date | Mintage | VF20 | XF40 | MS60 | MS63 | MS65 |
|---|---|---|---|---|---|---|
| 2012 | — | PF63 2,250 | | | | |

## BULLION COINAGE

Until 1990, .917 Gold was commonly alloyed with copper by the British Royal Mint. Starting in 2013 the bullion coins have been struck at .999 fine.

All proof issues have designers name as P. Nathan. The uncirculated issues use only Nathan.

### KM# 1254 10 PENCE

1.58 g., 0.999 Silver 0.0507 oz. ASW, 12 mm. **Ruler:** Elizabeth II **Obv:** Head with tiara right **Rev:** Britannia seated with owl and trident **Mint:** British Royal Mint

| Date | Mintage | VF20 | XF40 | MS60 | MS63 | MS65 |
|---|---|---|---|---|---|---|
| 2013 | 12,000 | PF63 15.00 | | | | |

### KM# 1079 20 PENCE

3.24 g., 0.9584 Silver 0.0998 oz. ASW, 16.5 mm. **Ruler:** Elizabeth II **Obv:** Head with tiara right **Rev:** Britannia standing **Edge:** Reeded **Mint:** British Royal Mint

| Date | Mintage | VF20 | XF40 | MS60 | MS63 | MS65 |
|---|---|---|---|---|---|---|
| 2002 | — | PF63 25.00 | | | | |
| 2004 | — | PF63 25.00 | | | | |
| 2006 | — | PF63 25.00 | | | | |
| 2012 | — | PF63 25.00 | | | | |

### KM# 1016 20 PENCE

3.24 g., 0.9584 Silver 0.0998 oz. ASW, 16.5 mm. **Ruler:** Elizabeth II **Subject:** Britannia Bullion **Obv:** Head with tiara right **Rev:** Una and Lion **Edge:** Reeded **Mint:** British Royal Mint

| Date | Mintage | VF20 | XF40 | MS60 | MS63 | MS65 |
|---|---|---|---|---|---|---|
| 2001 | 15,000 | PF63 25.00 | | | | |

### KM# 1044 20 PENCE

3.24 g., 0.9584 Silver 0.0998 oz. ASW, 16.5 mm. **Ruler:** Elizabeth II **Obv:** Head with tiara right **Rev:** Britannia portrait behind wavy lines **Edge:** Reeded **Mint:** British Royal Mint

| Date | Mintage | VF20 | XF40 | MS60 | MS63 | MS65 |
|---|---|---|---|---|---|---|
| 2003 | 5,848 | PF63 35.00 | | | | |

### KM# 1085 20 PENCE

3.24 g., 0.9584 Silver 0.0998 oz. ASW, 16.5 mm. **Ruler:** Elizabeth II **Obv:** Head with tiara right **Rev:** Britannia seated with shield left **Edge:** Reeded **Mint:** British Royal Mint

| Date | Mintage | VF20 | XF40 | MS60 | MS63 | MS65 |
|---|---|---|---|---|---|---|
| 2005 | 3,273 | PF63 25.00 | | | | |

### KM# 1088 20 PENCE

3.24 g., 0.9584 Silver 0.0998 oz. ASW, 16.5 mm. **Ruler:** Elizabeth II **Obv:** Head with tiara right **Rev:** Britannia seated with reclining lion right **Edge:** Reeded **Mint:** British Royal Mint

| Date | Mintage | VF20 | XF40 | MS60 | MS63 | MS65 |
|---|---|---|---|---|---|---|
| 2007 | 3,401 | PF63 25.00 | | | | |

### KM# 1095 20 PENCE

3.24 g., 0.9584 Silver 0.0998 oz. ASW, 16.5 mm. **Ruler:** Elizabeth II **Obv:** Head with tiara right **Rev:** Britannia standing facing left with trident, flowing garment, shield **Edge:** Reeded **Mint:** British Royal Mint

| Date | Mintage | VF20 | XF40 | MS60 | MS63 | MS65 |
|---|---|---|---|---|---|---|
| 2008 | 5,000 | PF63 35.00 | | | | |

### KM# 1123 20 PENCE

3.24 g., 0.958 Silver 0.0998 oz. ASW, 16.5 mm. **Ruler:** Elizabeth II **Obv:** Head right **Rev:** Britania in chariot right

| Date | Mintage | VF20 | XF40 | MS60 | MS63 | MS65 |
|---|---|---|---|---|---|---|
| 2009 | 6,000 | PF63 35.00 | | | | |

### KM# 1131 20 PENCE

3.24 g., 0.958 Silver 0.0998 oz. ASW, 16.5 mm. **Ruler:** Elizabeth II **Obv:** Head right **Rev:** Britannia bust right

| Date | Mintage | VF20 | XF40 | MS60 | MS63 | MS65 |
|---|---|---|---|---|---|---|
| 2010 | 8,000 | PF63 35.00 | | | | |

### KM# 1262 20 PENCE

3.24 g., 0.958 Silver 0.0998 oz. ASW, 16.5 mm. **Ruler:** Elizabeth II **Obv:** Head with tiara right **Rev:** Britannia seated behind Union Jack veil **Mint:** Royal Mint

| Date | Mintage | VF20 | XF40 | MS60 | MS63 | MS65 |
|---|---|---|---|---|---|---|
| 2011 Proof | — | — | — | — | — | — |

### KM# 1255 20 PENCE

3.15 g., 0.999 Silver 0.1012 oz. ASW, 16.5 mm. **Ruler:** Elizabeth II **Obv:** Head with tiara right **Rev:** Britannia seated with owl and trident **Mint:** British Royal Mint

| Date | Mintage | VF20 | XF40 | MS60 | MS63 | MS65 |
|---|---|---|---|---|---|---|
| 2013 | 12,000 | PF63 25.00 | | | | |

### KM# 1080 50 PENCE

8.11 g., 0.9584 Silver 0.2499 oz. ASW, 22 mm. **Ruler:** Elizabeth II **Obv:** Head with tiara right **Rev:** Britannia standing **Edge:** Reeded **Mint:** British Royal Mint

| Date | Mintage | VF20 | XF40 | MS60 | MS63 | MS65 |
|---|---|---|---|---|---|---|
| 2002 | — | PF63 35.00 | | | | |
| 2004 | — | PF63 35.00 | | | | |
| 2006 | — | PF63 35.00 | | | | |
| 2012 | — | PF63 35.00 | | | | |

### KM# 1017 50 PENCE

8.11 g., 0.9584 Silver 0.2499 oz. ASW, 27.3 mm. **Ruler:** Elizabeth II **Subject:** Britannia Bullion **Obv:** Head with tiara right **Rev:** Una and Lion **Edge:** Reeded **Mint:** British Royal Mint

| Date | Mintage | VF20 | XF40 | MS60 | MS63 | MS65 |
|---|---|---|---|---|---|---|
| 2001 | 5,000 | PF63 35.00 | | | | |

### KM# 1045 50 PENCE

8.11 g., 0.9584 Silver 0.2499 oz. ASW, 22 mm. **Ruler:** Elizabeth II **Obv:** Head with tiara right **Rev:** Britannia portrait behind wavy lines **Edge:** Reeded **Mint:** British Royal Mint

| Date | Mintage | VF20 | XF40 | MS60 | MS63 | MS65 |
|---|---|---|---|---|---|---|
| 2003 | 3,669 | PF63 35.00 | | | | |

### KM# 1086 50 PENCE

8.11 g., 0.9584 Silver 0.2499 oz. ASW, 22 mm. **Ruler:** Elizabeth II **Obv:** Head with tiara right **Rev:** Britannia seated with shield left **Edge:** Reeded **Mint:** British Royal Mint

| Date | Mintage | VF20 | XF40 | MS60 | MS63 | MS65 |
|---|---|---|---|---|---|---|
| 2005 | 2,360 | PF63 35.00 | | | | |

### KM# 1089 50 PENCE

8.11 g., 0.9584 Silver 0.2499 oz. ASW, 22 mm. **Ruler:** Elizabeth II **Obv:** Head with tiara right **Rev:** Britannia seated with reclining lion right **Edge:** Reeded **Mint:** British Royal Mint

| Date | Mintage | VF20 | XF40 | MS60 | MS63 | MS65 |
|---|---|---|---|---|---|---|
| 2007 | 2,500 | PF63 35.00 | | | | |

### KM# 1096 50 PENCE

8.11 g., 0.9584 Silver 0.2499 oz. ASW, 22 mm. **Ruler:** Elizabeth II **Obv:** Head with tiara right **Rev:** Britannia standing facing left with trident, flowing garment, shield **Edge:** Reeded **Mint:** British Royal Mint

| Date | Mintage | VF20 | XF40 | MS60 | MS63 | MS65 |
|---|---|---|---|---|---|---|
| 2008 | 2,500 | PF63 45.00 | | | | |

### KM# 1124 50 PENCE

8.11 g., 0.958 Silver 0.2498 oz. ASW, 22 mm. **Ruler:** Elizabeth II **Obv:** Head right **Rev:** Britannia in chariot right

| Date | Mintage | VF20 | XF40 | MS60 | MS63 | MS65 |
|---|---|---|---|---|---|---|
| 2009 | 2,500 | PF63 50.00 | | | | |

### KM# 1132 50 PENCE

8.11 g., 0.958 Silver 0.2498 oz. ASW, 22 mm. **Ruler:** Elizabeth II **Obv:** Head right **Rev:** Britannia bust right

| Date | Mintage | VF20 | XF40 | MS60 | MS63 | MS65 |
|---|---|---|---|---|---|---|
| 2010 | 3,500 | **PF63** 50.00 | | | | |

### KM# 1228 50 PENCE

8.11 g., 0.9584 Silver 0.2499 oz. ASW, 22 mm. **Ruler:** Elizabeth II **Obv:** Head with tiara right **Rev:** Britannia seated behind Union Jack veil

| Date | Mintage | VF20 | XF40 | MS60 | MS63 | MS65 |
|---|---|---|---|---|---|---|
| 2011 | — | **PF63** 50.00 | | | | |

### KM# 1080.1 50 PENCE

7.78 g., 0.999 Silver 0.2498 oz. ASW, 22 mm. **Ruler:** Elizabeth II **Obv:** Head with tiara right **Rev:** Britiannia standing **Edge Lettering:** SS GAIRSOPPA **Mint:** British Royal Mint **Note:** Struck from recovered silver from WWII era shipwreck

| Date | Mintage | VF20 | XF40 | MS60 | MS63 | MS65 |
|---|---|---|---|---|---|---|
| 2013 | Est. 500000 | — | — | — | 20.00 | — |

### KM# 1256 50 PENCE

7.78 g., 0.999 Silver 0.2498 oz. ASW, 22 mm. **Ruler:** Elizabeth II **Obv:** Head with tiara right **Rev:** Britannia seated with owl and trident **Mint:** British Royal Mint

| Date | Mintage | VF20 | XF40 | MS60 | MS63 | MS65 |
|---|---|---|---|---|---|---|
| 2013 | 4,500 | **PF63** 35.00 | | | | |

### KM# 1081 POUND

16.22 g., 0.9584 Silver 0.4998 oz. ASW, 27 mm. **Ruler:** Elizabeth II **Obv:** Head with tiara right **Rev:** Britannia standing **Edge:** Reeded **Mint:** British Royal Mint

| Date | Mintage | VF20 | XF40 | MS60 | MS63 | MS65 |
|---|---|---|---|---|---|---|
| 2002 | — | **PF63** 50.00 | | | | |
| 2004 | — | **PF63** 50.00 | | | | |
| 2006 | — | **PF63** 50.00 | | | | |
| 2012 | 2,012 | **PF63** 115 | | | | |

### KM# 1084 POUND

16.22 g., 0.9584 Silver 0.4998 oz. ASW, 27 mm. **Ruler:** Elizabeth II **Obv:** Head with tiara right **Rev:** Britannia in chariot right **Edge:** Reeded **Mint:** British Royal Mint

| Date | Mintage | VF20 | XF40 | MS60 | MS63 | MS65 |
|---|---|---|---|---|---|---|
| 2012 | 2,012 | **PF63** 60.00 | | | | |

### KM# 1018 POUND

16.22 g., 0.9584 Silver 0.4998 oz. ASW, 27 mm. **Ruler:** Elizabeth II **Obv:** Head with tiara right **Rev:** Una and Lion **Edge:** Reeded **Mint:** British Royal Mint

| Date | Mintage | VF20 | XF40 | MS60 | MS63 | MS65 |
|---|---|---|---|---|---|---|
| 2001 | 5,000 | **PF63** 50.00 | | | | |
| 2012 | 2,012 | **PF63** 115 | | | | |

### KM# 1046 POUND

16.22 g., 0.9584 Silver 0.4998 oz. ASW, 27 mm. **Ruler:** Elizabeth II **Obv:** Head with tiara right **Rev:** Britannia portrait behind wavy lines **Edge:** Reeded **Mint:** British Royal Mint

| Date | Mintage | VF20 | XF40 | MS60 | MS63 | MS65 |
|---|---|---|---|---|---|---|
| 2003 | 3,669 | **PF63** 50.00 | | | | |
| 2012 | 2,012 | **PF63** 115 | | | | |

### KM# 1087 POUND

16.22 g., 0.9584 Silver 0.4998 oz. ASW, 27 mm. **Ruler:** Elizabeth II **Obv:** Head with tiara right **Rev:** Britannia seated with shield left **Edge:** Reeded **Mint:** British Royal Mint

| Date | Mintage | VF20 | XF40 | MS60 | MS63 | MS65 |
|---|---|---|---|---|---|---|
| 2005 | 2,360 | **PF63** 70.00 | | | | |
| 2012 | 2,012 | **PF63** 115 | | | | |

### KM# 1090 POUND

16.22 g., 0.9584 Silver 0.4998 oz. ASW, 27 mm. **Ruler:** Elizabeth II **Obv:** Head with tiara right **Rev:** Britannia seated with reclining lion right **Edge:** Reeded **Mint:** British Royal Mint

| Date | Mintage | VF20 | XF40 | MS60 | MS63 | MS65 |
|---|---|---|---|---|---|---|
| 2007 | 2,500 | **PF63** 70.00 | | | | |
| 2012 | 2,012 | **PF63** 115 | | | | |

### KM# 1097 POUND

16.22 g., 0.9584 Silver 0.4998 oz. ASW, 27 mm. **Ruler:** Elizabeth II **Obv:** Head with tiara right **Rev:** Britannia standing facing left with trident, flowing garment, shield **Edge:** Reeded **Mint:** British Royal Mint

| Date | Mintage | VF20 | XF40 | MS60 | MS63 | MS65 |
|---|---|---|---|---|---|---|
| 2008 | 2,500 | **PF63** 70.00 | | | | |
| 2012 | 2,012 | **PF63** 115 | | | | |

### KM# 1125 POUND

16.22 g., 0.958 Silver 0.4996 oz. ASW, 27 mm. **Ruler:** Elizabeth II **Obv:** Head right **Rev:** Britannia in chariot right

| Date | Mintage | VF20 | XF40 | MS60 | MS63 | MS65 |
|---|---|---|---|---|---|---|
| 2009 | 2,500 | **PF63** 70.00 | | | | |
| 2012 | 2,012 | **PF63** 115 | | | | |

### KM# 1133 POUND

16.22 g., 0.958 Silver 0.4996 oz. ASW, 27 mm. **Ruler:** Elizabeth II **Obv:** Head right **Rev:** Britannia bust right

| Date | Mintage | VF20 | XF40 | MS60 | MS63 | MS65 |
|---|---|---|---|---|---|---|
| 2010 | 3,500 | **PF63** 70.00 | | | | |
| 2012 | 2,012 | **PF63** 115 | | | | |

### KM# 1229 POUND

16.22 g., 0.9584 Silver 0.4998 oz. ASW, 27 mm. **Ruler:** Elizabeth II **Obv:** Head with tiara right **Rev:** Britannia seated behind Union Jack veil

| Date | Mintage | VF20 | XF40 | MS60 | MS63 | MS65 |
|---|---|---|---|---|---|---|
| 2011 | — | **PF63** 60.00 | | | | |
| 2012 | 2,012 | **PF63** 115 | | | | |

### KM# 1257 POUND

15.71 g., 0.999 Silver 0.5046 oz. ASW, 27 mm. **Ruler:** Elizabeth II **Obv:** Head with tiara right **Rev:** Britannia seated with owl and trident **Mint:** British Royal Mint

| Date | Mintage | VF20 | XF40 | MS60 | MS63 | MS65 |
|---|---|---|---|---|---|---|
| 2013 | 4,500 | **PF63** 40.00 | | | | |

### KM# 1269 POUND

1.57 g., 0.999 Gold 0.0503 oz. AGW, 12 mm. **Ruler:** Elizabeth II **Obv:** Head with tiara right **Rev:** Britannia seated left with owl **Mint:** Royal Mint

| Date | Mintage | VF20 | XF40 | MS60 | MS63 | MS65 |
|---|---|---|---|---|---|---|
| 2013 | Est. 5750 | **PF63** 95.00 | | | | |

### KM# 1029 2 POUNDS

32.54 g., 0.958 Silver 1.0022 oz. ASW, 40 mm. **Ruler:** Elizabeth II **Obv:** Head with tiara right **Rev:** Standing Britannia **Edge:** Reeded **Mint:** British Royal Mint

| Date | Mintage | VF20 | XF40 | MS60 | MS63 | MS65 |
|---|---|---|---|---|---|---|
| 2002 | 36,543 | — | — | — | 38.00 | — |
| 2002 | — | **PF63** 60.00 | | | | |
| 2004 | 100,000 | — | — | — | 38.00 | — |
| 2004 | 2,174 | **PF63** 60.00 | | | | |
| 2006 | 100,000 | — | — | — | 38.00 | — |
| 2006 | 2,529 | **PF63** 60.00 | | | | |
| 2012 | — | — | — | — | 38.00 | — |
| 2012 | — | **PF63** 60.00 | | | | |
| 2013 | — | — | — | — | 38.00 | — |
| 2013 Snake on edge | — | — | — | — | 50.00 | — |
| 2013 | — | **PF63** 60.00 | | | | |

### KM# 1000 2 POUNDS

32.54 g., 0.958 Silver 1.0022 oz. ASW, 40 mm. **Ruler:** Elizabeth II **Obv:** Head with tiara right **Rev:** Britannia in chariot **Edge:** Reeded **Mint:** British Royal Mint

| Date | Mintage | VF20 | XF40 | MS60 | MS63 | MS65 |
|---|---|---|---|---|---|---|
| 2009 | — | — | — | — | 40.00 | — |
| 2009 | — | PF63 60.00 | | | | |

### KM# 1019 2 POUNDS

32.45 g., 0.9584 Silver 0.9999 oz. ASW, 40 mm. **Ruler:** Elizabeth II **Subject:** Britannia Bullion **Obv:** Head with tiara right **Rev:** Una and Lion **Edge:** Reeded **Mint:** British Royal Mint

| Date | Mintage | VF20 | XF40 | MS60 | MS63 | MS65 |
|---|---|---|---|---|---|---|
| 2001 | 44,816 | — | — | 38.00 | 42.00 | — |
| 2001 | 3,047 | PF63 65.00 | | | | |

### KM# 1039 2 POUNDS

32.45 g., 0.958 Silver 0.9995 oz. ASW, 40 mm. **Ruler:** Elizabeth II **Subject:** Britannia Bullion **Obv:** Head with tiara right **Rev:** Britannia portrait behind wavy puzzle-like lines **Edge:** Reeded **Mint:** British Royal Mint

| Date | Mintage | VF20 | XF40 | MS60 | MS63 | MS65 |
|---|---|---|---|---|---|---|
| 2003 | 73,271 | — | — | — | 38.00 | — |
| 2003 | 2,016 | PF63 65.00 | | | | |

### KM# 1063 2 POUNDS

32.45 g., 0.958 Silver 0.9995 oz. ASW, 40 mm. **Ruler:** Elizabeth II **Obv:** Head with tiara right **Rev:** Seated Britannia **Edge:** Reeded **Mint:** British Royal Mint

| Date | Mintage | VF20 | XF40 | MS60 | MS63 | MS65 |
|---|---|---|---|---|---|---|
| 2005 | 100,000 | — | — | — | 38.00 | — |
| 2005 | 1,539 | PF63 70.00 | | | | |

### KM# 1000a 2 POUNDS

32.45 g., 0.958 Silver 0.9995 oz. ASW partially gilt, 40 mm. **Ruler:** Elizabeth II **Obv:** Head with tiara right **Rev:** Britannia in chariot, gilt **Edge:** Reeded **Mint:** British Royal Mint

| Date | Mintage | VF20 | XF40 | MS60 | MS63 | MS65 |
|---|---|---|---|---|---|---|
| 2006 | 3,000 | PF63 100 | | | | |

### KM# 1019a 2 POUNDS

32.45 g., 0.958 Silver 0.9995 oz. ASW, 40 mm. **Ruler:** Elizabeth II **Subject:** Golden Silhouette Britannias **Obv:** Head with tiara right **Rev:** Gold plated Britannia and Lion **Edge:** Reeded **Mint:** British Royal Mint

| Date | Mintage | VF20 | XF40 | MS60 | MS63 | MS65 |
|---|---|---|---|---|---|---|
| 2006 | 3,000 | PF63 100 | | | | |

### KM# 1029a 2 POUNDS

32.45 g., 0.958 Silver 0.9995 oz. ASW partially gilt, 40 mm. **Ruler:** Elizabeth II **Obv:** Head with tiara right **Rev:** Britannia standing with shield, gilt **Edge:** Reeded **Mint:** British Royal Mint

| Date | Mintage | VF20 | XF40 | MS60 | MS63 | MS65 |
|---|---|---|---|---|---|---|
| 2006 | 3,000 | PF63 100 | | | | |

### KM# 1039a 2 POUNDS

32.45 g., 0.958 Silver 0.9995 oz. ASW partially gilt, 40 mm. **Ruler:** Elizabeth II **Obv:** Head with tiara right **Rev:** Britannia head gilt **Edge:** Reeded **Mint:** British Royal Mint

| Date | Mintage | VF20 | XF40 | MS60 | MS63 | MS65 |
|---|---|---|---|---|---|---|
| 2006 | 3,000 | PF63 100 | | | | |

### KM# 1063a 2 POUNDS

32.45 g., 0.958 Silver 0.9995 oz. ASW partially gilt, 40 mm. **Ruler:** Elizabeth II **Obv:** Head with tiara right **Rev:** Britannia seated, gilt **Edge:** Reeded **Mint:** British Royal Mint

| Date | Mintage | VF20 | XF40 | MS60 | MS63 | MS65 |
|---|---|---|---|---|---|---|
| 2006 | 3,000 | PF63 100 | | | | |

### KM# 1078 2 POUNDS

32.45 g., 0.958 Silver 0.9995 oz. ASW, 40 mm. **Ruler:** Elizabeth II **Subject:** Britannia series **Obv:** Elizabeth II **Rev:** Seated, bareheaded Britannia with a recumbent lion at her feet **Edge:** Reeded **Mint:** British Royal Mint

| Date | Mintage | VF20 | XF40 | MS60 | MS63 | MS65 |
|---|---|---|---|---|---|---|
| 2007 | 100,000 | — | — | — | 40.00 | — |
| 2007 | 2,500 | PF63 65.00 | | | | |

### KM# 1098 2 POUNDS

32.45 g., 0.9584 Silver 0.9999 oz. ASW, 40 mm. **Ruler:** Elizabeth II **Obv:** Head with tiara right **Rev:** Britannia standing facing left with trident, flowing garment, shield **Edge:** Reeded **Mint:** British Royal Mint

| Date | Mintage | VF20 | XF40 | MS60 | MS63 | MS65 |
|---|---|---|---|---|---|---|
| 2008 | — | — | — | — | 40.00 | — |
| 2008 | — | PF63 80.00 | | | | |

### KM# 1134 2 POUNDS

32.45 g., 0.958 Silver 0.9995 oz. ASW, 40 mm. **Ruler:** Elizabeth II **Obv:** Head right **Rev:** Britannia bust right

| Date | Mintage | VF20 | XF40 | MS60 | MS63 | MS65 |
|---|---|---|---|---|---|---|
| 2010 | — | — | — | — | 38.00 | — |
| 2010 | 8,000 | PF63 90.00 | | | | |

### KM# 1230 2 POUNDS

32.54 g., 0.958 Silver 1.0022 oz. ASW, 40 mm. **Ruler:** Elizabeth II **Obv:** Head with tiara right **Rev:** Britannia seated behind Union Jack veil

| Date | Mintage | VF20 | XF40 | MS60 | MS63 | MS65 |
|---|---|---|---|---|---|---|
| 2011 | — | — | — | — | 40.00 | — |
| 2011 | — | PF63 80.00 | | | | |

### KM# 1258 2 POUNDS

31.21 g., 0.999 Silver 1.0024 oz. ASW, 38.61 mm. **Ruler:** Elizabeth II **Obv:** Head with tiara right **Rev:** Britannia seated with owl and trident **Mint:** British Royal Mint

| Date | Mintage | VF20 | XF40 | MS60 | MS63 | MS65 |
|---|---|---|---|---|---|---|
| 2013 | 8,500 | PF63 65.00 | | | | |

### KM# 1267 2 POUNDS

31.21 g., 0.9999 Silver 1.0033 oz. ASW, 38.61 mm. **Ruler:** Elizabeth II **Obv:** Head with tiara right **Rev:** Standing Britannia **Edge:** Reeded

| Date | Mintage | VF20 | XF40 | MS60 | MS63 | MS65 |
|---|---|---|---|---|---|---|
| 2013 | — | — | — | — | 45.00 | — |
| 2013 | — | PF63 60.00 | | | | |
| 2014 | — | — | — | — | 40.00 | — |
| 2014 | — | PF63 60.00 | | | | |

### KM# 1008 10 POUNDS

3.41 g., 0.9167 Gold 0.1005 oz. AGW, 16.5 mm. **Ruler:** Elizabeth II **Obv:** Head with tiara right **Rev:** Britannia standing **Edge:** Reeded **Mint:** British Royal Mint

| Date | Mintage | VF20 | XF40 | MS60 | MS63 | MS65 |
|---|---|---|---|---|---|---|
| 2002 | — | — | — | — | 141 | — |
| 2002 | 1,500 | PF63 210 | | | | |
| 2004 | 929 | PF63 225 | | | | |
| 2006 | 700 | PF63 225 | | | | |

### KM# 1020 10 POUNDS

3.41 g., 0.9167 Gold 0.1005 oz. AGW, 16.5 mm. **Ruler:** Elizabeth II **Subject:** Britannia Bullion **Obv:** Head with tiara right **Rev:** Stylized "Britannia and the Lion **Edge:** Reeded **Mint:** British Royal Mint

| Date | Mintage | VF20 | XF40 | MS60 | MS63 | MS65 |
|---|---|---|---|---|---|---|
| 2001 | 1,100 | — | — | — | 141 | — |
| 2001 | 1,557 | PF63 210 | | | | |

### KM# 1040 10 POUNDS

3.41 g., 0.9167 Gold 0.1005 oz. AGW, 16.5 mm. **Ruler:** Elizabeth II **Obv:** Head with tiara right **Rev:** Britannia portrait behind wavy lines **Edge:** Reeded **Mint:** British Royal Mint

| Date | Mintage | VF20 | XF40 | MS60 | MS63 | MS65 |
|---|---|---|---|---|---|---|
| 2003 | — | — | — | — | 141 | — |
| 2003 | 4,000 | PF63 210 | | | | |

### KM# 1068 10 POUNDS

3.41 g., 0.9167 Gold 0.1005 oz. AGW, 16.5 mm. **Ruler:** Elizabeth II **Obv:** Head with tiara right **Rev:** Seated Britannia **Edge:** Reeded **Mint:** British Royal Mint

| Date | Mintage | VF20 | XF40 | MS60 | MS63 | MS65 |
|---|---|---|---|---|---|---|
| 2005 | 1,225 | PF63 210 | | | | |

### KM# 1091 10 POUNDS

3.41 g., 0.9167 Gold 0.1005 oz. AGW, 16.5 mm. **Ruler:** Elizabeth II **Obv:** Head with tiara right **Rev:** Britannia seated with reclining lion right **Edge:** Reeded **Mint:** British Royal Mint

| Date | Mintage | VF20 | XF40 | MS60 | MS63 | MS65 |
|---|---|---|---|---|---|---|
| 2007 | — | PF63 141 | | | | |
| 2007 | 893 | PF63 225 | | | | |

### KM# 1275 10 POUNDS

3.14 g., 0.9995 Platinum 0.1009 oz. APW, 15 mm. **Ruler:** Elizabeth II **Obv:** Head with tiara right **Rev:** Britannia seated with reclining lion right **Edge:** Reeded **Mint:** British Royal Mint

| Date | Mintage | VF20 | XF40 | MS60 | MS63 | MS65 |
|---|---|---|---|---|---|---|
| 2007 | 691 | PF63 300 | | | | |

### KM# 1099 10 POUNDS

3.41 g., 0.9167 Gold 0.1005 oz. AGW, 16.5 mm. **Ruler:** Elizabeth II **Obv:** Head with tiara right **Rev:** Britannia standing facing left with trident, flowing garment, shield **Edge:** Reeded **Mint:** British Royal Mint

| Date | Mintage | VF20 | XF40 | MS60 | MS63 | MS65 |
|---|---|---|---|---|---|---|
| 2008 | — | PF63 210 | | | | |

### KM# 1099a 10 POUNDS

3.11 g., 0.9999 Platinum 0.100 oz. APW, 16.5 mm. **Ruler:** Elizabeth II **Obv:** Head with tiara right **Rev:** Britannia standing facing left with trident, flowing garment, shield **Edge:** Reeded **Mint:** British Royal Mint

| Date | Mintage | VF20 | XF40 | MS60 | MS63 | MS65 |
|---|---|---|---|---|---|---|
| 2008 | — | PF63 300 | | | | |

### KM# 1127 10 POUNDS

3.41 g., 0.916 Gold 0.1004 oz. AGW, 16.5 mm. **Ruler:** Elizabeth II **Obv:** Head right **Rev:** Britannia in chariot right

| Date | Mintage | VF20 | XF40 | MS60 | MS63 | MS65 |
|---|---|---|---|---|---|---|
| 2009 | 2,000 | PF63 210 | | | | |

### KM# 1135 10 POUNDS

3.41 g., 0.916 Gold 0.1004 oz. AGW, 16.5 mm. **Ruler:** Elizabeth II **Obv:** Head right **Rev:** Britannia bust right

| Date | Mintage | VF20 | XF40 | MS60 | MS63 | MS65 |
|---|---|---|---|---|---|---|
| 2010 | 750 | PF63 225 | | | | |

### KM# 1231 10 POUNDS

3.41 g., 0.9167 Gold 0.1005 oz. AGW, 22 mm. **Ruler:** Elizabeth II **Obv:** Head with tiara right **Rev:** Britannia seated behind Union Jack veil

| Date | Mintage | VF20 | XF40 | MS60 | MS63 | MS65 |
|---|---|---|---|---|---|---|
| 2011 | — | PF63 210 | | | | |

### KM# 1268 10 POUNDS

157.25 g., 0.999 Silver 5.0506 oz. ASW, 65 mm. **Ruler:** Elizabeth II **Obv:** Head with tiara right **Rev:** Britannia seated left with owl **Mint:** Royal Mint

| Date | Mintage | VF20 | XF40 | MS60 | MS63 | MS65 |
|---|---|---|---|---|---|---|
| 2013 | Est. 1150 | PF63 400 | | | | |

### KM# 1270 10 POUNDS

3.13 g., 0.999 Gold 0.1007 oz. AGW, 16.5 mm. **Ruler:** Elizabeth II **Obv:** Head with tiara right **Rev:** Britannia seated left with owl **Mint:** Royal Mint

| Date | Mintage | VF20 | XF40 | MS60 | MS63 | MS65 |
|---|---|---|---|---|---|---|
| 2013 | Est. 1125 | PF63 190 | | | | |

### KM# 1009 25 POUNDS

8.51 g., 0.9167 Gold 0.2508 oz. AGW, 22 mm. **Ruler:** Elizabeth II **Obv:** Head with tiara right **Rev:** Britannia standing **Edge:** Reeded **Mint:** British Royal Mint

| Date | Mintage | VF20 | XF40 | MS60 | MS63 | MS65 |
|---|---|---|---|---|---|---|
| 2002 | — | PF63 465 | | | | |
| 2004 | 750 | PF63 465 | | | | |
| 2006 | 1,000 | PF63 465 | | | | |

### KM# 1021 25 POUNDS

8.51 g., 0.9167 Gold 0.2508 oz. AGW, 22 mm. **Ruler:** Elizabeth II **Subject:** Britannia Bullion **Obv:** Head with tiara right **Rev:** Stylized "Britannia and the Lion **Edge:** Reeded **Mint:** British Royal Mint

| Date | Mintage | VF20 | XF40 | MS60 | MS63 | MS65 |
|---|---|---|---|---|---|---|
| 2001 | 1,100 | — | — | — | 379 | — |
| 2001 | 1,500 | PF63 450 | | | | |
| 2006 | — | PF63 450 | | | | |

### KM# 1041 25 POUNDS

8.51 g., 0.9167 Gold 0.2508 oz. AGW, 22 mm. **Ruler:** Elizabeth II **Obv:** Head with tiara right **Rev:** Britannia portrait behind wavy lines **Edge:** Reeded **Mint:** British Royal Mint

| Date | Mintage | VF20 | XF40 | MS60 | MS63 | MS65 |
|---|---|---|---|---|---|---|
| 2003 | 609 | PF63 465 | | | | |
| 2006 | — | PF63 465 | | | | |

### KM# 1069 25 POUNDS

8.51 g., 0.9167 Gold 0.2508 oz. AGW, 22 mm. **Ruler:** Elizabeth II **Obv:** Head with tiara right **Rev:** Seated Britannia **Edge:** Reeded **Mint:** British Royal Mint

| Date | Mintage | VF20 | XF40 | MS60 | MS63 | MS65 |
|---|---|---|---|---|---|---|
| 2005 | 750 | PF63 465 | | | | |
| 2006 | — | PF63 465 | | | | |

### KM# 1204 25 POUNDS

8.51 g., 0.9167 Gold 0.2508 oz. AGW **Ruler:** Elizabeth II **Rev:** Standing Britannia in horse drawn chariot

| Date | Mintage | VF20 | XF40 | MS60 | MS63 | MS65 |
|---|---|---|---|---|---|---|
| 2006 | — | PF63 465 | | | | |
| 2009 | — | PF63 465 | | | | |

### KM# 1092 25 POUNDS

8.51 g., 0.9167 Gold 0.2508 oz. AGW, 22 mm. **Ruler:** Elizabeth II **Obv:** Head with tiara right **Rev:** Britannia seated with reclining lion right **Edge:** Reeded **Mint:** British Royal Mint

| Date | Mintage | VF20 | XF40 | MS60 | MS63 | MS65 |
|---|---|---|---|---|---|---|
| 2007 | — | — | — | — | 379 | — |
| 2007 | 1,000 | PF63 465 | | | | |

### KM# 1276 25 POUNDS

7.85 g., 0.9995 Platinum 0.2521 oz. APW, 20 mm. **Ruler:** Elizabeth II **Obv:** Head with tiara right **Rev:** Britannia seated with reclining lion right **Edge:** Reeded **Mint:** British Royal Mint

| Date | Mintage | VF20 | XF40 | MS60 | MS63 | MS65 |
|---|---|---|---|---|---|---|
| 2007 | — | PF63 650 | | | | |

### KM# 1100 25 POUNDS

8.51 g., 0.9167 Gold 0.2508 oz. AGW, 22 mm. **Ruler:** Elizabeth II **Obv:** Head with tiara right **Rev:** Britannia standing facing left with trident, flowing garment, shield **Edge:** Reeded **Mint:** British Royal Mint

| Date | Mintage | VF20 | XF40 | MS60 | MS63 | MS65 |
|---|---|---|---|---|---|---|
| 2008 | 1,000 | PF63 465 | | | | |

### KM# 1100a 25 POUNDS

0.9999 Platinum APW, 22 mm. **Ruler:** Elizabeth II **Obv:** Head with tiara right **Rev:** Britannia standing facing left with trident, flowing garment, shield **Edge:** Reeded **Mint:** British Royal Mint

| Date | Mintage | VF20 | XF40 | MS60 | MS63 | MS65 |
|---|---|---|---|---|---|---|
| 2008 | — | PF63 650 | | | | |

### KM# 1128 25 POUNDS

8.51 g., 0.916 Gold 0.2506 oz. AGW, 22 mm. **Ruler:** Elizabeth II **Obv:** Head right **Rev:** Britannia in chariot right

| Date | Mintage | VF20 | XF40 | MS60 | MS63 | MS65 |
|---|---|---|---|---|---|---|
| 2009 | 2,250 | PF63 450 | | | | |

### KM# 1136 25 POUNDS

8.51 g., 0.916 Gold 0.2506 oz. AGW, 22 mm. **Ruler:** Elizabeth II **Obv:** Head right **Rev:** Britannia bust right

| Date | Mintage | VF20 | XF40 | MS60 | MS63 | MS65 |
|---|---|---|---|---|---|---|
| 2010 | 3,000 | PF63 450 | | | | |

### KM# 1232 25 POUNDS

8.51 g., 0.9167 Gold 0.2508 oz. AGW, 22 mm. **Ruler:** Elizabeth II **Obv:** Head with tiara right **Rev:** Britannia seated behind Union Jack veil

| Date | Mintage | VF20 | XF40 | MS60 | MS63 | MS65 |
|---|---|---|---|---|---|---|
| 2011 | — | PF63 450 | | | | |

### KM# 1271 25 POUNDS

7.81 g., 0.9999 Gold 0.2512 oz. AGW, 22 mm. **Ruler:** Elizabeth II **Obv:** Head with tiara right **Rev:** Britannia seated left with owl **Mint:** Royal Mint

| Date | Mintage | VF20 | XF40 | MS60 | MS63 | MS65 |
|---|---|---|---|---|---|---|
| 2013 | Est. 875 | PF63 450 | | | | |

### KM# 1010 50 POUNDS

17.03 g., 0.9167 Gold 0.5019 oz. AGW, 27 mm. **Ruler:** Elizabeth II **Obv:** Head with tiara right **Rev:** Britannia standing **Edge:** Reeded **Mint:** British Royal Mint

| Date | Mintage | VF20 | XF40 | MS60 | MS63 | MS65 |
|---|---|---|---|---|---|---|
| 2002 | 1,000 | PF63 668 | | | | |
| 2004 | — | PF63 698 | | | | |
| 2006 | — | PF63 698 | | | | |

### KM# 1022 50 POUNDS

17.02 g., 0.9167 Gold 0.5016 oz. AGW, 27 mm. **Ruler:** Elizabeth II **Subject:** Britannia Bullion **Obv:** Head with tiara right **Rev:** Stylized "Britannia and the Lion **Edge:** Reeded **Mint:** British Royal Mint

| Date | Mintage | VF20 | XF40 | MS60 | MS63 | MS65 |
|---|---|---|---|---|---|---|
| 2001 | 600 | — | — | — | 759 | — |
| 2001 | 1,000 | PF63 668 | | | | |

### KM# 1042 50 POUNDS

17.02 g., 0.9167 Gold 0.5016 oz. AGW, 27 mm. **Ruler:** Elizabeth II **Obv:** Head with tiara right **Rev:** Britannia portrait behind wavy lines **Edge:** Reeded **Mint:** British Royal Mint

| Date | Mintage | VF20 | XF40 | MS60 | MS63 | MS65 |
|---|---|---|---|---|---|---|
| 2003 | — | — | — | — | 698 | — |
| 2003 | 2,500 | PF63 637 | | | | |

### KM# 1070 50 POUNDS

17.03 g., 0.9167 Gold 0.5019 oz. AGW, 27 mm. **Ruler:** Elizabeth II **Obv:** Head with tiara right **Rev:** Seated Britannia **Edge:** Reeded **Mint:** British Royal Mint

| Date | Mintage | VF20 | XF40 | MS60 | MS63 | MS65 |
|---|---|---|---|---|---|---|
| 2005 | 2,000 | PF63 638 | | | | |

**KM# 1093 50 POUNDS**
17.03 g., 0.9167 Gold 0.5018 oz. AGW, 27 mm. **Ruler:** Elizabeth II **Obv:** Head with tiara right **Rev:** Britannia seated with reclining lion right **Edge:** Reeded **Mint:** British Royal Mint

| Date | Mintage | VF20 | XF40 | MS60 | MS63 | MS65 |
|---|---|---|---|---|---|---|
| 2007 | — | — | — | — | 698 | — |
| 2007 | — | PF63 668 | | | | |

**KM# 1093a 50 POUNDS**
0.9999 Platinum APW, 27 mm. **Ruler:** Elizabeth II **Obv:** Head with tiara right **Rev:** Britannia seated with reclining lion right **Edge:** Reeded

| Date | Mintage | F12 | VF20 | XF40 | MS60 | MS63 |
|---|---|---|---|---|---|---|
| 2007 | — | PF63 1,500 | | | | |

**KM# 1277 50 POUNDS**
15.69 g., 0.9995 Platinum 0.5043 oz. APW, 27 mm. **Ruler:** Elizabeth II **Obv:** Head with tiara right **Rev:** Britannia seated with reclining lion right **Edge:** Reeded **Mint:** British Royal Mint

| Date | Mintage | VF20 | XF40 | MS60 | MS63 | MS65 |
|---|---|---|---|---|---|---|
| 2007 | — | PF63 1,500 | | | | |

**KM# 1101 50 POUNDS**
17.03 g., 0.9167 Gold 0.5018 oz. AGW, 27 mm. **Ruler:** Elizabeth II **Obv:** Head with tiara right **Rev:** Britannia standing facing left with trident, flowing garment, shield **Edge:** Reeded **Mint:** British Royal Mint

| Date | Mintage | VF20 | XF40 | MS60 | MS63 | MS65 |
|---|---|---|---|---|---|---|
| 2008 | — | PF63 668 | | | | |

**KM# 1101a 50 POUNDS**
0.9999 Platinum APW, 27 mm. **Ruler:** Elizabeth II **Obv:** Head with tiara right **Rev:** Britannia standing facing left with trident, flowing garment, shield **Edge:** Reeded **Mint:** British Royal Mint

| Date | Mintage | VF20 | XF40 | MS60 | MS63 | MS65 |
|---|---|---|---|---|---|---|
| 2008 | — | PF63 1,500 | | | | |

**KM# 1129 50 POUNDS**
17.03 g., 0.916 Gold 0.5014 oz. AGW, 27 mm. **Ruler:** Elizabeth II **Obv:** Head right **Rev:** Britania in chariot right

| Date | Mintage | VF20 | XF40 | MS60 | MS63 | MS65 |
|---|---|---|---|---|---|---|
| 2009 | 1,250 | PF63 667 | | | | |
| 2009 | — | — | — | — | 698 | — |

**KM# 1137 50 POUNDS**
17.02 g., 0.916 Gold 0.5012 oz. AGW, 27 mm. **Ruler:** Elizabeth II **Obv:** Head right **Rev:** Britannia bust right

| Date | Mintage | VF20 | XF40 | MS60 | MS63 | MS65 |
|---|---|---|---|---|---|---|
| 2010 | 1,250 | PF63 667 | | | | |

**KM# 1233 50 POUNDS**
17.02 g., 0.9167 Gold 0.5016 oz. AGW, 27 mm. **Ruler:** Elizabeth II

| Date | Mintage | VF20 | XF40 | MS60 | MS63 | MS65 |
|---|---|---|---|---|---|---|
| 2011 | — | PF63 1,500 | | | | |

**KM# 1272 50 POUNDS**
15.61 g., 0.9999 Gold 0.5018 oz. AGW, 27 mm. **Ruler:** Elizabeth II **Obv:** Head with tiara right **Rev:** Britannia seated left with owl **Mint:** Royal Mint

| Date | Mintage | VF20 | XF40 | MS60 | MS63 | MS65 |
|---|---|---|---|---|---|---|
| 2013 | Est. 525 | PF63 900 | | | | |

**KM# 1011 100 POUNDS**
34.05 g., 0.9167 Gold 1.0035 oz. AGW, 32.7 mm. **Ruler:** Elizabeth II **Obv:** Head with tiara right **Rev:** Britannia standing **Edge:** Reeded **Mint:** British Royal Mint

| Date | Mintage | VF20 | XF40 | MS60 | MS63 | MS65 |
|---|---|---|---|---|---|---|
| 2002 | 1,000 | PF63 1,275 | | | | |
| 2004 | — | — | — | — | 1,396 | — |
| 2004 | — | PF63 1,275 | | | | |
| 2006 | — | PF63 1,275 | | | | |
| 2012 | — | PF63 1,275 | | | | |

**KM# 1023 100 POUNDS**
34.05 g., 0.9167 Gold 1.0035 oz. AGW, 32.7 mm. **Ruler:** Elizabeth II **Subject:** Britannia Bullion **Obv:** Head with tiara right **Rev:** Stylized "Britannia and the Lion **Edge:** Reeded **Mint:** British Royal Mint

| Date | Mintage | VF20 | XF40 | MS60 | MS63 | MS65 |
|---|---|---|---|---|---|---|
| 2001 | 900 | — | — | — | 1,396 | — |
| 2001 | 1,000 | PF63 1,275 | | | | |

**KM# 1043 100 POUNDS**
34.05 g., 0.9167 Gold 1.0035 oz. AGW, 32.7 mm. **Ruler:** Elizabeth II **Obv:** Head with tiara right **Rev:** Britannia portrait behind wavy lines **Edge:** Reeded **Mint:** British Royal Mint

| Date | Mintage | VF20 | XF40 | MS60 | MS63 | MS65 |
|---|---|---|---|---|---|---|
| 2003 | — | — | — | — | 1,396 | — |
| 2003 | 1,500 | PF63 1,275 | | | | |

**KM# 1071 100 POUNDS**
34.05 g., 0.9167 Gold 1.0035 oz. AGW, 32.7 mm. **Ruler:** Elizabeth II **Obv:** Head with tiara right **Rev:** Seated Britannia **Edge:** Reeded **Mint:** British Royal Mint

| Date | Mintage | VF20 | XF40 | MS60 | MS63 | MS65 |
|---|---|---|---|---|---|---|
| 2005 | 1,500 | PF63 1,275 | | | | |

**KM# 1094 100 POUNDS**
34.05 g., 0.9167 Gold 1.0035 oz. AGW, 32.7 mm. **Ruler:** Elizabeth II **Obv:** Head with tiara right **Rev:** Britannia seated with reclining lion right **Edge:** Reeded **Mint:** British Royal Mint

| Date | Mintage | VF20 | XF40 | MS60 | MS63 | MS65 |
|---|---|---|---|---|---|---|
| 2007 | — | — | — | — | 1,396 | — |
| 2007 | — | PF63 1,275 | | | | |

**KM# 1094a 100 POUNDS**
0.9999 Platinum APW, 32.7 mm. **Ruler:** Elizabeth II **Obv:** Head with tiara right **Rev:** Britannia seated with reclining lion right **Edge:** Reeded

| Date | Mintage | F12 | VF20 | XF40 | MS60 | MS63 |
|---|---|---|---|---|---|---|
| 2007 | — | PF63 2,900 | | | | |

**KM# 1278 100 POUNDS**
31.39 g., 0.9995 Platinum 1.0086 oz. APW, 32.7 mm. **Ruler:** Elizabeth II **Obv:** Head with tiara right **Rev:** Britannia seated with reclining lion right **Edge:** Reeded **Mint:** British Royal Mint

| Date | Mintage | VF20 | XF40 | MS60 | MS63 | MS65 |
|---|---|---|---|---|---|---|
| 2007 | — | PF63 2,900 | | | | |

**KM# 1102 100 POUNDS**
34.05 g., 0.9167 Gold 1.0035 oz. AGW, 32.7 mm. **Ruler:** Elizabeth II **Obv:** Head with tiara right **Rev:** Britannia standing facing left with trident, flowing garment, shield **Edge:** Reeded **Mint:** British Royal Mint

| Date | Mintage | VF20 | XF40 | MS60 | MS63 | MS65 |
|---|---|---|---|---|---|---|
| 2008 | — | — | — | — | 1,396 | — |
| 2008 | — | PF63 1,275 | | | | |
| 2013 | — | — | — | — | 1,396 | — |
| 2013 | — | PF63 1,275 | | | | |

**KM# 1102a 100 POUNDS**
0.9999 Platinum APW, 32.7 mm. **Ruler:** Elizabeth II **Obv:** Head with tiara right **Rev:** Britannia standing facing left with trident, flowing garment, shield **Edge:** Reeded **Mint:** British Royal Mint

| Date | Mintage | VF20 | XF40 | MS60 | MS63 | MS65 |
|---|---|---|---|---|---|---|
| 2008 | — | PF63 2,900 | | | | |

**KM# 1130 100 POUNDS**
32.69 g., 0.916 Gold 0.9627 oz. AGW, 32.6 mm. **Ruler:** Elizabeth II **Obv:** Head right **Rev:** Britannia in chariot right

| Date | Mintage | VF20 | XF40 | MS60 | MS63 | MS65 |
|---|---|---|---|---|---|---|
| 2009 | — | — | — | — | 1,340 | — |
| 2009 | 1,250 | PF63 1,223 | | | | |

**KM# 1138 100 POUNDS**
34.05 g., 0.916 Gold 1.0028 oz. AGW, 32.7 mm. **Ruler:** Elizabeth II **Obv:** Head right **Rev:** Britannia bust right

| Date | Mintage | VF20 | XF40 | MS60 | MS63 | MS65 |
|---|---|---|---|---|---|---|
| 2010 | — | — | — | — | 1,395 | — |
| 2010 | 1,250 | PF63 1,274 | | | | |

**KM# 1234 100 POUNDS**
34.05 g., 0.9167 Gold 1.0035 oz. AGW, 32.7 mm. **Ruler:** Elizabeth II **Obv:** Head with tiara right **Rev:** Britannia seated behind Union Jack veil

| Date | Mintage | VF20 | XF40 | MS60 | MS63 | MS65 |
|---|---|---|---|---|---|---|
| 2011 | — | PF63 1,275 | | | | |

**KM# 1011a 100 POUNDS**
31.11 g., 0.999 Gold 0.999 oz. AGW, 32.7 mm. **Ruler:** Elizabeth II **Obv:** Head with tiara right **Rev:** Britannia standing **Edge:** Reeded

| Date | Mintage | VF20 | XF40 | MS60 | MS63 | MS65 |
|---|---|---|---|---|---|---|
| 2013 | — | — | — | — | 1,390 | — |
| 2013 | — | PF63 1,269 | | | | |

**KM# 1266 100 POUNDS**
31.21 g., 0.9999 Gold 1.0033 oz. AGW, 38.61 mm. **Ruler:** Elizabeth II **Obv:** Head with tiara right **Rev:** Britannia standing **Mint:** Royal Mint

| Date | Mintage | VF20 | XF40 | MS60 | MS63 | MS65 |
|---|---|---|---|---|---|---|
| 2013 | — | PF63 1,396 | | | | |

**KM# 1273 100 POUNDS**
31.21 g., 0.9999 Gold 1.0033 oz. AGW, 38.61 mm. **Ruler:** Elizabeth II **Obv:** Head with tiara right **Rev:** Britannia seated left with owl **Mint:** Royal Mint

| Date | Mintage | VF20 | XF40 | MS60 | MS63 | MS65 |
|---|---|---|---|---|---|---|
| 2013 | Est. 400 | PF63 1,800 | | | | |

**KM# 1274 500 POUNDS**
156.29 g., 0.9999 Gold 5.0243 oz. AGW, 50 mm. **Ruler:** Elizabeth II **Obv:** Head with tiara right **Rev:** Britannia seated left with owl **Mint:** Royal Mint

| Date | Mintage | VF20 | XF40 | MS60 | MS63 | MS65 |
|---|---|---|---|---|---|---|
| 2013 | Est. 100 | PF63 8,500 | | | | |

## PIEDFORT

| KM# | Date | Mintage | Identification | Mkt Val |
|---|---|---|---|---|
| P101 | 2001 | 8,464 | Pound 0.925 Silver KM#1013a | 115 |
| P106 | 2001 | 6,759 | 2 Pounds 0.925 Silver KM#1014a | 115 |
| P102 | 2002 | 6,599 | Pound 0.925 Silver KM#1030a | 115 |
| P107 | 2002 | — | 2 Pounds 0.925 Silver KM#1031a | 125 |
| P108 | 2002 | — | 2 Pounds 0.925 Silver KM#1032a | 125 |
| P109 | 2002 | — | 2 Pounds 0.925 Silver KM#1033a | 125 |

| | | | | |
|---|---|---|---|---|
| P110 | 2002 | — | 2 Pounds 0.925 Silver Piedfort w/ color. KM#1034a. | 125 |
| P40 | 2003 | 6,795 | 50 Pence 0.925 Silver KM#1036a. | 110 |

Note: Also exists as a Piefort, P1004a.

| | | | | |
|---|---|---|---|---|
| P41 | 2003 | 9,871 | Pound 0.925 Silver KM#993a. | 115 |
| P42 | ND2003 | 8,728 | 2 Pounds 0.925 Silver KM#1037a. | 95.00 |
| P43 | 2004 | 4,054 | 50 Pence 0.925 Silver KM#1047a. | 110 |
| P44 | 2004 | 7,013 | Pound 0.925 Silver KM#1048a. | 115 |
| P45 | 2004 | 5,303 | 2 Pounds 0.925 Silver KM#1049a. | 125 |
| P47 | 2004 | 2,500 | 5 Pounds 0.925 Silver KM#1055a. | 150 |
| P46 | ND2005 | 4,585 | 2 Pounds 0.925 Silver KM#1052a. | 95.00 |
| P48 | 2005 | 3,808 | 50 Pence 0.925 Silver KM#1050a. | 110 |
| P49 | ND2005 | 4,798 | 2 Pounds 0.925 Silver KM#1056a. | 95.00 |
| P50 | 2005 | 6,007 | Pound 0.925 Silver KM#1051a. | 115 |
| P51 | 2005 | — | 5 Pounds 0.925 Silver KM#1053a. | 150 |
| P52 | 2005 | — | 5 Pounds 0.925 Silver KM#1054a. | 150 |
| P53 | 2006 | 3,532 | 50 Pence 0.925 Silver KM#1057a. | 110 |
| P54 | 2006 | 3,415 | 50 Pence 0.925 Silver KM#1058a. | 110 |
| P55 | 2006 | 7,500 | Pound 0.925 Silver KM#1051a. | 125 |
| P56 | 2006 | 3,199 | 2 Pounds 0.925 Silver KM#1060a. | 115 |
| P57 | 2006 | 3,018 | 2 Pounds 0.925 Silver KM#1061a. | 115 |
| P58 | 2006 | 5,000 | 5 Pounds 0.925 Silver KM#1062a. | 150 |
| P59 | 2007 | 1,555 | 50 Pence 0.925 Silver KM#1073a. | 135 |
| P60 | 2007 | 5,739 | Pound 0.925 Silver KM#1074a. | 95.00 |
| P61 | 2007 | 4,000 | 2 Pounds 0.925 Silver KM#1075a. | 115 |
| P62 | 2007 | 3,990 | 2 Pounds 0.925 Silver KM#1076a. | 115 |
| P63 | 2007 | 2,000 | 5 Pounds 0.925 Silver KM#1077a. | 150 |
| P64 | 2007 | 250 | 5 Pounds 0.9995 Platinum | 7,500 |
| P65 | 2008 | — | 2 Pounds 0.925 Silver KM#1106a. | 115 |
| P67 | 2008 | — | 5 Pounds 0.925 Silver KM#1104. | 150 |
| P68 | 2008 | — | 5 Pounds 0.925 Silver KM#1103. | 150 |
| P97 | 2008 | — | 50 Pence Silver KM#1112a | 125 |
| P103 | 2008 | 8,000 | Pound 0.925 Silver KM#1113a | 125 |
| P113 | 2008 | 5,000 | 5 Pounds Silver KM#1103a | 150 |
| P66 | 2009 | 3,500 | 2 Pounds 0.925 Silver KM#1115a. | 115 |
| P70 | 2009 | 4,009 | 5 Pounds 0.925 Silver KM#1118a. | 180 |
| P98 | 2009 | — | 50 Pence Silver KM#1114a | 125 |
| P111 | 2009 | 3,500 | 2 Pounds Silver | 115 |
| P75 | 2010 | 3,000 | Pound 0.925 Silver KM#1158a. | 110 |
| P76 | 2010 | 5,000 | Pound 0.925 Silver | 110 |
| P99 | 2010 | — | 50 Pence Silver KM#1165a | 125 |
| P114 | 2010 | — | 5 Pounds Silver KM#1151a | 160 |
| P77 | 2011 | — | Penny 0.925 Silver KM#1107a. | 15.00 |
| P78 | 2011 | — | 2 Pence 0.925 Silver KM#1108a. | 25.00 |
| P79 | 2011 | — | 5 Pence 0.925 Silver KM#1109a. | 35.00 |
| P80 | 2011 | — | 10 Pence 0.925 Silver KM#1110a. | 80.00 |
| P81 | 2011 | — | 20 Pence 0.925 Silver KM#1111a. | 80.00 |
| P82 | 2011 | — | 50 Pence 0.925 Silver KM#1112a. | 125 |
| P83 | 2011 | — | Pound 0.925 Silver KM#1113a. | 115 |
| P84 | 2011 | — | Pound 0.925 Silver KM#1197a. | 115 |
| P85 | 2011 | — | Pound 0.925 Silver KM#1198a. | 115 |
| P86 | 2011 | — | 50 Pence 0.925 Silver KM#1196a. | 125 |
| P87 | 2011 | — | 2 Pounds 0.925 Silver KM#1199a. | 115 |
| P88 | 2011 | — | 2 Pounds 0.925 Silver KM#1200a. | 115 |
| P89 | 2011 | — | 5 Pounds 0.925 Silver KM#1201a. | 150 |

## MAUNDY SETS

| KM# | Date | Mintage | Identification | Issue Price | Mkt Val |
|---|---|---|---|---|---|
| MDS260 | 2001 (4) | 1,132 | KM#898-899, 901-902. Westminster Abbey | — | 300 |
| MDS261 | 2002 (4) | 1,681 | KM#898-899, 901-902. Canterbury Cathedral | — | 300 |
| MDS262 | 2003 (4) | 1,608 | KM#898-899, 901-902. Gloucester Cathedral | — | 325 |
| MDS263 | 2004 (4) | 1,613 | KM#898-899, 901-902. Liverpool Cathedral | — | 325 |
| MDS264 | 2005 (4) | 1,685 | KM#898-899, 901-902. Wakefield Cathedral | — | 325 |
| MDS265 | 2006 (4) | 1,811 | KM#898-899, 901-902. Guilford Cathedral | — | 325 |
| MDS266 | 2007 (4) | 1,822 | KM#898-899, 901-902. Manchester Cathedral | — | 325 |
| MDS267 | 2008 (4) | 1,833 | KM#898-899, 901-902. St. Patrick's Cathedral | — | 325 |
| MDS268 | 2009 (4) | 1,602 | KM#898-899, 901-902. | — | 325 |
| MDS269 | 2010 (4) | 1,617 | KM#898-899, 901-902. | — | 325 |
| MDS270 | 2011 (4) | — | KM#898-899, 901-902. | — | 325 |

## MINT SETS

| KM# | Date | Mintage | Identification | Issue Price | Mkt Val |
|---|---|---|---|---|---|
| MS129 | 2001 (9) | 57,741 | KM#986-991, 994, 1013-1015 B.U. set | 22.50 | 25.00 |
| MS130 | 2001 (9) | — | KM#986-991, 994, 1013-1014 Wedding Collection | 27.50 | 25.00 |
| MS131 | 2001 (9) | — | KM#986-991, 994, 1013-1014 Baby Gift Set | 27.50 | 25.00 |
| MS132 | 2002 (8) | 60,539 | KM#986-991, 994, 1030 | 22.50 | 20.00 |
| MS133 | 2002 (8) | — | KM#986-991, 994, 1030 Wedding Collection | 27.50 | 20.00 |
| MS134 | 2002 (8) | — | KM#986-991, 994, 1030 Baby Gift Set | 27.50 | 20.00 |
| MSA135 | 2004 (10) | 46,032 | KM#986-991, 994, 1047-1049 BU Set | — | 35.00 |
| MSB135 | 2004 (10) | 4,214 | KM#986-991, 994, 1047-1049, 1055 Wedding Collection | — | 35.00 |
| MSC135 | 2004 (10) | 34,371 | KM#986-991, 994, 1047-1049, 1055 Baby Gift Set | — | 35.00 |
| MS135 | 2003 (10) | 62,741 | KM#986-991, 993, 994, 1036-1037 BU Set | 22.50 | 35.00 |
| MS136 | 2003 (10) | 7,130 | KM#986-991, 993, 994, 1036-1037 Wedding Collection | 27.50 | 30.00 |
| MS137 | 2003 (10) | 43,128 | KM#986-991, 993, 994, 1036-1037 Baby Gift Set | 27.50 | 30.00 |
| MS138 | 2005 (10) | 51,776 | KM#986-991, 994, 1050-1052 | 26.50 | 30.00 |
| MS139 | 2005 (10) | 29,924 | KM#986-991, 994, 1050-1052 Baby Gift Set | 36.50 | 35.00 |
| MS140 | 2005 (3) | — | KM#1050-1052 New Coinage Set | 16.25 | 17.50 |
| MS141 | 2005 (2) | — | KM#1053-1054 Trafalgar Set | 36.00 | 35.00 |
| MS142 | 2006 (10) | 74,231 | KM#986-990, 1057-1061, BV set | 30.00 | 60.00 |
| MS143 | 2006 (10) | 25,878 | KM#986-990, 1057-1061 Baby Gift Set | 38.50 | 60.00 |
| MS144 | 2007 (6) | — | KM#986-991 | — | 10.00 |

## PROOF SETS

| KM# | Date | Mintage | Identification | Issue Price | Mkt Val |
|---|---|---|---|---|---|
| PS116 | 2001 (3) | 1,500 | KM#1001-1002, 1014a | 795 | 525 |
| PS117 | 2001 (4) | 1,000 | KM#1001-1003,1014a | 1,645 | 2,250 |
| PS118 | 2001 (4) | 5,000 | KM#1016-1019 | — | 175 |
| PS119 | 2001 (4) | 1,000 | KM#1020-1023 | 1,595 | 3,200 |
| PSA119 | 2001 (3) | 1,500 | KM#1001, 1002, 1014b | — | 525 |
| PSB119 | 2001 (4) | 1,000 | KM#1001, 1002, 1014b, 1015b | — | 2,700 |
| PS120 | 2002 (3) | 5,000 | KM#1025-1027 | 795 | 1,275 |
| PS121 | 2002 (4) | 3,000 | KM#1025-1028 | 1,645 | 3,000 |
| PS122 | 2002 (4) | 3,358 | KM#1031-1034; Standard Set | 34.95 | 35.00 |
| PS123 | 2002 (4) | 673 | KM#1031-1034; Display Set | 44.95 | 40.00 |
| PS124 | 2002 (4) | 2,553 | KM#1031a-1034a; Display Set | 120 | 150 |
| PS125 | 2002 (4) | 315 | KM#1031b-1034b; Display Set | 1,675 | 3,000 |
| PS126 | 2002 (4) | 1,000 | KM#1008-1011 | 1,600 | 3,200 |
| PS127 | 2001 (10) | 10,000 | KM#986-991, 994, 1013-1015 Executive Proof Set in display case | 115 | 80.00 |
| PS128 | 2001 (10) | 30,000 | KM#986-991, 994, 1013-1015 Deluxe Proof Set in red leather case | 72.50 | 80.00 |
| PS129 | 2001 (10) | 28,244 | KM#986-991, 994, 1013-1015 Standard Proof Set in simple case | 50.00 | 65.00 |
| PS130 | 2001 (10) | 1,351 | KM#986-991, 994, 1013-1015 Gift Proof Set with a pack of occasion cards | 65.00 | 65.00 |
| PS131 | 2002 (9) | 5,000 | KM#986-991, 994, 1024, 1030 Executive Proof Set | 100 | 60.00 |
| PS132 | 2002 (9) | 30,000 | KM#986-991, 994, 1024, 1030 Deluxe Proof Set | 70.00 | 55.00 |
| PS133 | 2002 (9) | 30,884 | KM#986-991, 994, 1024, 1030 Standard Proof Set | 48.00 | 55.00 |
| PS134 | 2002 (9) | 1,544 | KM#986-991, 994, 1024, 1030 Gift Proof Set | 62.40 | 55.00 |
| PSA135 | 2002 (13) | — | KM#898a, 899a, 901a, 902a, 986c, 987c, 988b, 989b, 990b, 991b, 1030b, 994c, 1024b Queen Elizabeth II - Golden Jubilee 1952-2002, set is struck in gold (including Maundy set), in presentation box | — | 11,250 |
| PS135 | 2003 (11) | 5,000 | KM#986-991, 993, 994, 1036-1038 Executive Proof Set | 100 | 85.00 |
| PS136 | 2003 (11) | 14,863 | KM#986-991, 993, 994, 1036-1038 Deluxe Proof Set | 72.00 | 80.00 |
| PS137 | 2003 (11) | 23,650 | KM#986-991, 993, 994, 1036-1038 Standard Proof Set | 50.00 | 80.00 |
| PSA138 | 2003 (4) | 3,669 | KM#1039, 1044-1046 | — | 180 |
| PSB138 | 2004 (11) | 4,101 | KM#986-991, 994, 1047-1049, 1055 Executive Proof Set | — | 80.00 |
| PSC138 | 2004 (11) | 12,968 | KM#986-991, 994, 1047-1049, 1055 Deluxe Proof Set | — | 80.00 |
| PSD138 | 2004 (11) | 17,951 | KM#986-991, 994, 1047-1049, 1055 Standard Proof Set | — | 80.00 |
| PS138 | 2005 (12) | 4,290 | KM#986-991, 994, 1050-1054 Executive Set | 145 | 95.00 |
| PS139 | 2005 (12) | 14,899 | KM#986-991, 994, 1050-1054 Deluxe Proof Set | 80.00 | 95.00 |
| PS140 | 2005 (12) | 21,374 | KM#986-991, 994, 1050-1054, Standard Proof Set | 60.00 | 95.00 |
| PS141 | 2005 (3) | 417 | KM#1068-1070 | 850 | 1,350 |
| PS142 | 2005 (4) | 1,439 | KM#1068-1071 | 1,895 | 2,850 |
| PS143 | 2005 (3) | 2,500 | KM#1064-1066 | 820 | 1,100 |
| PS144 | 2005 (4) | 2,500 | KM#1064-1067 | 1,925 | 2,600 |
| PS145 | 2005 (2) | — | P39, P40 | — | 175 |
| PS146 | 2006 (13) | 5,000 | KM#986-991, 994, 1057-1062 Executive Proof Set, wooden case | — | 140 |
| PS147 | 2006 (13) | 15,000 | KM#986-991, 994, 1057-1062 Deluxe Proof Set | 82.50 | 140 |
| PS148 | 2006 (13) | 17,689 | KM#986-991, 994, 1057-1062 Standard Proof Set | 65.00 | 140 |
| PS149 | 2006 (5) | 3,000 | KM#1000a, 1012a, 1018a, 1039, 1063a | 475 | 525 |
| PS150 | 2006 (3) | 1,750 | KM#1001, 1002, 1072 | 1,015 | 1,150 |
| PS151 | 2006 (4) | 1,750 | KM#1001-1003, 1072 | 2,091 | 2,650 |
| PS152 | 2007 (13) | 18,215 | KM#986-991, 994, 1057-1062 | 65.00 | 140 |
| PS153 | 2007 (4) | 1,750 | KM#1001-1003, 1072 | — | 2,850 |
| PS154 | 2007 (3) | 750 | KM#1001-1002, 1072 | — | 1,200 |
| PS155 | 2007 (2) | 5,000 | KM#1001-1002 | — | 550 |
| PS156 | 2007 (5) | 3,000 | KM#P33, P35-P38 | 450 | 500 |
| PS160 | 2002 (4) | — | KM#1029, 1079-1081 | — | 175 |
| PS161 | 2003 (4) | 1,250 | KM#1040-1043 | — | 2,800 |
| PS162 | 2004 (4) | — | KM#1029, 1079-1081 | — | 175 |
| PS163 | 2004 (4) | 973 | KM#1008-1011 | — | 3,000 |
| PS164 | 2005 (4) | 2,360 | KM#1063, 1085-1087 | — | 185 |
| PS165 | 2006 (4) | — | KM#1029, 1079-1081 | — | 175 |
| PS166 | 2006 (4) | — | KM#1008-1011 | — | 2,900 |

| | | | | | |
|---|---|---|---|---|---|
| PS167 | 2007 (4) | — | KM#1078, 1088-1090 | — | 185 |
| PS168 | 2007 (4) | — | KM#1091-1094 | — | 2,950 |
| PS169 | 2007 (4) | — | KM#1091a-1094a | — | 5,850 |
| PS170 | 2008 (4) | — | KM#1095-1098 | — | 225 |
| PS171 | 2008 (4) | — | KM#1099-1102 | — | 3,000 |
| PS172 | 2008 (4) | — | KM#1099a-1102a | — | 5,850 |

The Hellenic (Greek) Republic is situated in southeastern Europe on the southern tip of the Balkan Peninsula. The republic includes many islands, the most important of which are Crete and the Ionian Islands. Greece (including islands) has an area of 50,944 sq. mi. (131,940 sq. km.) and a population of 10.3 million. Capital: Athens. Greece is still largely agricultural. Tobacco, cotton, fruit and wool are exported.

**MONETARY SYSTEM**

100 Euro Cent = 1 Euro

# REPUBLIC

## EURO COINAGE

The Greek Euro coinage series contains the denomination in Lepta as well.

European Union Issues

### KM# 181 EURO CENT

2.27 g., Copper Plated Steel, 16.2 mm. **Obv:** Ancient Athenian trireme **Rev:** Denomination and globe **Edge:** Plain

| Date | Mintage | VF20 | XF40 | MS60 | MS63 | MS65 |
|---|---|---|---|---|---|---|
| 2002 | 101,000,000 | — | — | 0.15 | 0.35 | 0.50 |
| 2002 F in star | 15,000,000 | — | — | 1.00 | 1.25 | 1.50 |
| 2003 | 35,200,000 | — | — | 0.15 | 0.35 | 0.50 |
| 2004 | 50,000,000 | — | — | 0.15 | 0.35 | 0.50 |
| 2005 | 15,000,000 | — | — | 0.15 | 0.35 | 0.50 |
| 2006 | 45,000,000 | — | — | 0.15 | 0.35 | 0.50 |
| 2007 | 60,000,000 | — | — | 0.15 | 0.35 | 0.50 |
| 2008 | 24,000,000 | — | — | 0.15 | 0.35 | 0.50 |
| 2009 | 50,000,000 | — | — | 0.15 | 0.35 | 0.50 |
| 2010 | 27,000,000 | — | — | 0.15 | 0.35 | 0.50 |
| 2011 | 35,000,000 | — | — | 0.15 | 0.35 | 0.50 |
| 2011 | 2,500 | **PF65** 15.00 | | | | |
| 2012 | 48,000,000 | — | — | 0.15 | 0.35 | 0.50 |
| 2012 | 2,500 | **PF65** 15.00 | | | | |
| 2013 | — | — | — | 0.15 | 0.35 | 0.50 |
| 2013 | 4,000 | **PF65** 15.00 | | | | |
| 2014 Sets only | — | — | — | — | — | 0.75 |
| 2014 | 2,500 | **PF65** 15.00 | | | | |

### KM# 182 2 EURO CENT

3.03 g., Copper Plated Steel, 18.7 mm. **Obv:** Corvette sailing ship **Rev:** Denomination and globe **Edge:** Grooved

| Date | Mintage | VF20 | XF40 | MS60 | MS63 | MS65 |
|---|---|---|---|---|---|---|
| 2002 | 176,000,000 | — | — | 0.25 | 0.50 | 0.75 |
| 2002 F in star | 18,000,000 | — | — | 0.50 | 1.00 | 1.50 |
| 2003 | 10,000,000 | — | — | 0.25 | 0.50 | 0.75 |
| 2004 | 25,000,000 | — | — | 0.25 | 0.50 | 0.75 |
| 2005 | 15,000,000 | — | — | 0.25 | 0.50 | 0.75 |
| 2006 | 45,000,000 | — | — | 0.25 | 0.50 | 0.75 |
| 2007 | 25,000,103 | — | — | 0.25 | 0.50 | 0.75 |
| 2008 | 68,000,000 | — | — | 0.25 | 0.50 | 0.75 |
| 2009 | 16,000,000 | — | — | 0.25 | 0.50 | 0.75 |
| 2010 | 32,000,000 | — | — | 0.25 | 0.50 | 0.75 |
| 2011 | 47,000,000 | — | — | 0.25 | 0.50 | 0.75 |
| 2011 | 2,500 | **PF65** 15.00 | | | | |
| 2012 | 34,000,000 | — | — | 0.25 | 0.50 | 0.75 |
| 2012 | 2,500 | **PF65** 15.00 | | | | |
| 2013 | — | — | — | 0.25 | 0.50 | 0.75 |
| 2013 | 4,000 | **PF65** 15.00 | | | | |
| 2014 Sets only | 13,000 | — | — | — | — | 1.00 |
| 2014 | 2,500 | **PF65** 15.00 | | | | |

### KM# 183 5 EURO CENT

3.86 g., Copper Plated Steel, 21.2 mm. **Obv:** Freighter **Rev:** Denomination and globe **Edge:** Plain

| Date | Mintage | VF20 | XF40 | MS60 | MS63 | MS65 |
|---|---|---|---|---|---|---|
| 2002 | 211,000,000 | — | — | 0.45 | 1.00 | 1.25 |
| 2002 F in star | 90,000,000 | — | — | 0.50 | 1.25 | 1.50 |
| 2003 | 750,000 | — | — | 0.45 | 1.00 | 1.25 |
| 2004 | 250,000 | — | — | 0.45 | 1.00 | 1.25 |
| 2005 | 1,000,000 | — | — | 0.45 | 1.00 | 1.25 |
| 2006 | 50,000,000 | — | — | 0.45 | 1.00 | 1.25 |
| 2007 | 55,005,598 | — | — | 0.45 | 1.00 | 1.25 |
| 2008 | 50,000,000 | — | — | 0.45 | 1.00 | 1.25 |
| 2009 | 38,000,000 | — | — | 0.45 | 1.00 | 1.25 |
| 2010 | 5,000,000 | — | — | 0.45 | 1.00 | 1.25 |
| 2011 | 2,500 | **PF65** 15.00 | | | | |
| 2011 | 34,000,000 | — | — | 0.45 | 1.00 | 1.25 |
| 2012 | 1,000,000 | — | — | 0.45 | 1.00 | 1.25 |
| 2012 | 2,500 | **PF65** 15.00 | | | | |
| 2013 | — | — | — | 0.45 | 1.00 | 1.25 |
| 2013 | 4,000 | **PF65** 15.00 | | | | |
| 2014 Sets only | 13,000 | — | — | — | — | 1.50 |
| 2014 | 2,500 | **PF65** 15.00 | | | | |

### KM# 184 10 EURO CENT

4.07 g., Brass, 19.7 mm. **Obv:** Bust of Rhgas Feriaou's half right **Rev:** Denomination and map **Edge:** Reeded

| Date | Mintage | VF20 | XF40 | MS60 | MS63 | MS65 |
|---|---|---|---|---|---|---|
| 2002 | 138,000,000 | — | — | 0.50 | 1.25 | 1.50 |
| 2002 F in star | 100,000,000 | — | — | 1.25 | 2.00 | 2.50 |
| 2003 | 600,000 | — | — | 0.50 | 1.25 | 1.50 |
| 2004 | 10,000,000 | — | — | 0.50 | 1.25 | 1.50 |
| 2005 | 25,000,000 | — | — | 0.50 | 1.25 | 1.50 |
| 2006 | 45,000,000 | — | — | 0.50 | 1.25 | 1.50 |

### KM# 211 10 EURO CENT

4.07 g., Brass, 19.25 mm. **Obv:** Bust of Rhgas Feriaou's half right **Rev:** Relief map of Western Europe, stars, lines and value **Edge:** Reeded

| Date | Mintage | VF20 | XF40 | MS60 | MS63 | MS65 |
|---|---|---|---|---|---|---|
| 2007 | 63,000,000 | — | — | 0.50 | 1.25 | 1.50 |
| 2008 | 40,000,000 | — | — | 0.50 | 1.25 | 1.50 |
| 2009 | 46,000,000 | — | — | 0.50 | 1.25 | 1.50 |
| 2010 | 5,000,000 | — | — | 0.50 | 1.25 | 1.50 |
| 2011 | 36,000,000 | — | — | 0.50 | 1.25 | 1.50 |
| 2011 | 2,500 | **PF65** 15.00 | | | | |
| 2012 | 1,000,000 | — | — | 0.50 | 1.25 | 1.50 |
| 2012 | 2,500 | **PF65** 15.00 | | | | |
| 2013 | 1,900,000 | — | — | 0.50 | 1.25 | 1.50 |
| 2013 | 4,000 | **PF65** 15.00 | | | | |
| 2014 Sets only | 13,000 | — | — | — | — | 2.00 |
| 2014 | 2,500 | **PF65** 15.00 | | | | |

### KM# 185 20 EURO CENT

5.73 g., Brass, 22.25 mm. **Obv:** Bust of John Kapodistrias half right **Rev:** Denomination and map **Edge:** Notched

| Date | Mintage | VF20 | XF40 | MS60 | MS63 | MS65 |
|---|---|---|---|---|---|---|
| 2002 | 209,000,000 | — | — | 0.50 | 1.25 | 1.50 |
| 2002 E in star | 120,000,000 | — | — | 1.25 | 2.25 | 3.50 |
| 2003 | 800,000 | — | — | 0.50 | 1.25 | 1.50 |
| 2004 | 500,000 | — | — | 0.50 | 1.25 | 1.50 |
| 2005 | 1,000,000 | — | — | 0.50 | 1.25 | 1.50 |
| 2006 | 1,000,000 | — | — | 0.50 | 1.25 | 1.50 |

### KM# 212 20 EURO CENT

5.73 g., Brass, 22.1 mm. **Obv:** Bust of John Kapodistrias' half right **Rev:** Relief map of Western Europe, stars, lines and value **Edge:** Notched

| Date | Mintage | VF20 | XF40 | MS60 | MS63 | MS65 |
|---|---|---|---|---|---|---|
| 2007 | 1,000,000 | — | — | 0.50 | 1.25 | 1.50 |
| 2008 | 20,000,000 | — | — | 0.50 | 1.25 | 1.50 |
| 2009 | 24,000,000 | — | — | 0.50 | 1.25 | 1.50 |
| 2010 | 12,000,000 | — | — | 0.50 | 1.25 | 1.50 |
| 2011 | 965,000 | — | — | 0.50 | 1.25 | 1.50 |
| 2011 | 2,500 | **PF65** 20.00 | | | | |
| 2012 Sets only | 30,000 | — | — | — | — | 2.00 |
| 2012 | 2,500 | **PF65** 20.00 | | | | |
| 2013 Sets only | 20,000 | — | — | — | — | 2.00 |
| 2013 | 4,000 | **PF65** 20.00 | | | | |
| 2014 | 2,500 | **PF65** 15.00 | | | | |
| 2014 Sets only | 13,000 | — | — | — | — | 2.00 |

### KM# 186 50 EURO CENT

7.81 g., Brass, 24.2 mm. **Obv:** Bust of El. Venizelos half left **Rev:** Denomination and map **Edge:** Reeded

| Date | Mintage | VF20 | XF40 | MS60 | MS63 | MS65 |
|---|---|---|---|---|---|---|
| 2002 | 93,000,000 | — | — | 1.00 | 1.50 | 2.00 |
| 2002 F in star | 70,000,000 | — | — | 2.00 | 2.50 | 3.00 |
| 2003 | 700,000 | — | — | 1.00 | 1.50 | 2.00 |
| 2004 | 500,000 | — | — | 1.00 | 1.50 | 2.00 |
| 2005 | 1,000,000 | — | — | 1.00 | 1.50 | 2.00 |
| 2006 | 1,000,000 | — | — | 1.00 | 1.50 | 2.00 |

### KM# 213 50 EURO CENT

7.81 g., Brass, 24.2 mm. **Obv:** Bust of El. Venizelos half left **Rev:** Relief map of Western Europe, stars, lines and value **Edge:** Reeded

| Date | Mintage | VF20 | XF40 | MS60 | MS63 | MS65 |
|---|---|---|---|---|---|---|
| 2007 | 1,000,000 | — | — | 0.75 | 1.00 | 1.50 |
| 2008 | 10,000,000 | — | — | 0.75 | 1.00 | 1.50 |
| 2009 | 7,000,000 | — | — | 0.75 | 1.00 | 1.50 |
| 2010 | 6,000,000 | — | — | 0.75 | 1.00 | 1.50 |
| 2011 | 7,000,000 | — | — | 0.75 | 1.00 | 1.50 |
| 2011 | 2,500 | **PF65** 25.00 | | | | |
| 2012 Sets only | 30,000 | — | — | — | — | 1.50 |
| 2012 | 2,500 | **PF65** 25.00 | | | | |
| 2013 Sets only | 20,000 | — | — | — | — | 1.50 |
| 2013 | 4,000 | **PF65** 25.00 | | | | |
| 2014 Sets only | 13,000 | — | — | — | — | 2.00 |
| 2014 | 2,500 | **PF65** 25.00 | | | | |

### KM# 187 EURO

7.50 g., Bi-Metallic Copper-Nickel center in Nickel-Brass ring, 23.25 mm. **Obv:** Ancient Athenian coin design **Rev:** Denomination and map **Edge:** Segmented reeding

| Date | Mintage | VF20 | XF40 | MS60 | MS63 | MS65 |
|---|---|---|---|---|---|---|
| 2002 | 61,500,000 | — | — | 2.00 | 4.00 | — |
| 2002 S in star | 50,000,000 | — | — | 3.00 | 6.00 | — |
| 2003 | 11,000,000 | — | — | 3.50 | 7.50 | — |
| 2004 | 10,000,000 | — | — | 2.50 | 5.00 | — |
| 2005 | 10,000,000 | — | — | 2.50 | 5.00 | — |
| 2006 | 10,000,000 | — | — | 2.50 | 5.00 | — |

## KM# 214 EURO

7.50 g., Bi-Metallic Copper-Nickel center in Nickel-Brass ring, 23.25 mm. **Obv:** Ancient Athenian coin design **Rev:** Relief map of Western Europe, stars, lines and value **Edge:** Segmented reeding

| Date | Mintage | VF20 | XF40 | MS60 | MS63 | MS65 |
|---|---|---|---|---|---|---|
| 2007 | 24,000,000 | — | — | 2.00 | 3.00 | 4.00 |
| 2008 | 4,000,000 | — | — | 2.00 | 3.00 | 4.00 |
| 2009 | 18,000,000 | — | — | 2.00 | 3.00 | 4.00 |
| 2010 | 11,000,000 | — | — | 2.00 | 3.00 | 4.00 |
| 2011 | 965,000 | — | — | 2.00 | 3.00 | 4.00 |
| 2011 | 2,500 | **PF65** 40.00 | | | | |
| 2012 Sets only | 30,000 | — | — | — | — | 4.00 |
| 2012 | 2,500 | **PF65** 40.00 | | | | |
| 2013 Sets only | 20,000 | — | — | — | — | 4.00 |
| 2013 | 4,000 | **PF65** 40.00 | | | | |
| 2014 | 2,500 | **PF65** 40.00 | | | | |
| 2014 Sets only | 13,000 | — | — | — | — | 8.00 |

## KM# 188 2 EURO

8.50 g., Bi-Metallic Nickel-Brass center in Copper-Nickel ring, 25.75 mm. **Obv:** Europa seated on a bull **Rev:** Denomination and map **Edge:** Reeded with Greek legend and stars

| Date | Mintage | VF20 | XF40 | MS60 | MS63 | MS65 |
|---|---|---|---|---|---|---|
| 2002 | 75,400,000 | — | — | 3.50 | 5.00 | 6.00 |
| 2002 S in star | 70,000,000 | — | — | — | 7.00 | 8.00 |
| 2003 | 550,000 | — | — | — | — | 20.00 |
| 2004 Sets only | 30,000 | — | — | — | — | 50.00 |
| 2005 | 1,000,000 | — | — | 3.50 | 5.00 | 6.00 |
| 2006 | 1,000,000 | — | — | 3.50 | 5.00 | 6.00 |

## KM# 209 2 EURO

8.50 g., Bi-Metallic Nickel-Brass center in Copper-Nickel ring., 25.75 mm. **Subject:** 2004 Olympics **Obv:** Discus thrower **Rev:** Denomination and map **Edge:** Reeded with Greek legend and stars

| Date | Mintage | VF20 | XF40 | MS60 | MS63 | MS65 |
|---|---|---|---|---|---|---|
| 2004 | 49,500,000 | — | — | 3.50 | 5.00 | 6.00 |
| 2004 Prooflike | 500,000 | — | — | — | — | 15.00 |

## KM# 215 2 EURO

8.50 g., Bi-Metallic Nickel-Brass center in Copper-Nickel ring, 25.75 mm. **Obv:** Europa seated on a bull **Rev:** Relief map of Western Europe, stars, lines and value **Edge:** Reeded with Greek legend and stars

| Date | Mintage | VF20 | XF40 | MS60 | MS63 | MS65 |
|---|---|---|---|---|---|---|
| 2007 Sets only | 15,000 | — | — | — | — | 25.00 |
| 2008 | 2,000,000 | — | — | — | 4.00 | 10.00 |
| 2009 | 982,000 | — | — | — | 3.50 | 5.00 |
| 2010 | 2,000,000 | — | — | — | 3.50 | 5.00 |
| 2011 | — | — | — | — | 3.50 | 5.00 |
| 2011 | 2,500 | **PF65** 50.00 | | | | |
| 2012 | 2,000,000 | — | — | — | 3.50 | 5.00 |
| 2012 | 2,500 | **PF65** 50.00 | | | | |
| 2013 | — | — | — | — | 3.50 | 5.00 |
| 2013 | — | **PF65** 50.00 | | | | |
| 2014 Sets only | 20,000 | — | — | — | — | 10.00 |
| 2014 | 2,500 | **PF65** 50.00 | | | | |

## KM# 216 2 EURO

8.50 g., Bi-Metallic Nickel-Brass center in Copper-Nickel ring, 25.75 mm. **Subject:** 50th Anniversary - Treaty of Rome **Obv:** Open treaty book **Rev:** Large value at left, modified outline of Europe at right **Edge:** Reeded with Greek legend and stars

| Date | Mintage | VF20 | XF40 | MS60 | MS63 | MS65 |
|---|---|---|---|---|---|---|
| 2007 | 4,000,000 | — | — | — | — | 9.00 |

## KM# 227 2 EURO

8.50 g., Bi-Metallic Nickel-Brass center in Copper-Nickel ring, 25.75 mm. **Subject:** European Monetary Union, 10th Anniversary **Obv:** Stick figure and Euro symbol **Edge:** Reeded with Greek legend and stars

| Date | Mintage | VF20 | XF40 | MS60 | MS63 | MS65 |
|---|---|---|---|---|---|---|
| 2009 | 4,000,000 | — | — | — | — | 7.00 |

## KM# 236 2 EURO

8.50 g., Bi-Metallic Nickel-Brass center in Copper-Nickel ring, 25.75 mm. **Subject:** Battle of Marathon, 2500th Anniversary **Obv:** Ancient Greek Warrior holding javelin running **Edge:** Reeded with Greek legend and stars

| Date | Mintage | VF20 | XF40 | MS60 | MS63 | MS65 |
|---|---|---|---|---|---|---|
| 2010 | 3,500,000 | — | — | — | 4.00 | 9.00 |

## KM# 239 2 EURO

8.50 g., Bi-Metallic Nickel-Brass center in Copper-Nickel ring, 25.75 mm. **Subject:** Special Olympics - Athens **Obv:** Figure standing in spiral, laureal weath at left

| Date | Mintage | VF20 | XF40 | MS60 | MS63 | MS65 |
|---|---|---|---|---|---|---|
| 2011 | 1,000,000 | — | — | — | 6.00 | 7.50 |

## KM# 245 2 EURO

8.50 g., Bi-Metallic Nickel-Brass center in Copper-Nickel ring, 25.75 mm. **Subject:** Euro coinage, 10th Anniversary **Obv:** Euro symbol on globe at center, child-like rendering around

| Date | Mintage | VF20 | XF40 | MS60 | MS63 | MS65 |
|---|---|---|---|---|---|---|
| 2012 Special Unc. | 5,000 | — | — | — | — | 15.00 |
| 2012 | 1,000,000 | — | — | — | 6.00 | 8.00 |
| 2012 Proof, Sets only | 2,500 | **PF65** 50.00 | | | | |

## KM# 252 2 EURO

8.50 g., Bi-Metallic Nickel-Brass center in Copper-Nickel ring, 25.75 mm. **Obv:** Plato, head left

| Date | Mintage | VF20 | XF40 | MS60 | MS63 | MS65 |
|---|---|---|---|---|---|---|
| 2013 | 750,000 | — | — | — | 4.00 | 6.00 |

## KM# 253 2 EURO

8.50 g., Bi-Metallic Nickel-Brass center in Copper-Nickel ring, 25.75 mm. **Subject:** 1913 Revolution **Obv:** Man with flag

| Date | Mintage | VF20 | XF40 | MS60 | MS63 | MS65 |
|---|---|---|---|---|---|---|
| 2013 | 750,000 | — | — | — | 4.00 | 6.00 |

## KM# 261 5 EURO

18.80 g., Copper-Nickel-Zinc, 30.5 mm. **Subject:** Konstantinos Kavafis, 150th Anniversary of Birth **Obv:** Sailing ship **Rev:** Bust facing

| Date | Mintage | VF20 | XF40 | MS60 | MS63 | MS65 |
|---|---|---|---|---|---|---|
| 2014 | 40,000 | — | — | — | — | 15.00 |
| 2014 Special Unc | 10,000 | — | — | — | — | 20.00 |

## KM# 190 10 EURO

34.00 g., 0.925 Silver 1.0111 oz. ASW, 40 mm. **Subject:** Olympics **Obv:** Olympic rings in wreath above value within circle of stars **Rev:** Ancient and modern runners **Edge:** Plain **Note:** Olympics

| Date | Mintage | VF20 | XF40 | MS60 | MS63 | MS65 |
|---|---|---|---|---|---|---|
| ND (2003) | 68,000 | **PF65** 50.00 | | | | |

## KM# 191 10 EURO

34.00 g., 0.925 Silver 1.0111 oz. ASW, 40 mm. **Subject:** Olympics **Obv:** Olympic rings in wreath above value within circle of stars **Rev:** Ancient and modern discus throwers **Edge:** Plain

| Date | Mintage | VF20 | XF40 | MS60 | MS63 | MS65 |
|---|---|---|---|---|---|---|
| ND(2003) | 68,000 | **PF65** 50.00 | | | | |

## KM# 193 10 EURO

34.00 g., 0.925 Silver 1.0111 oz. ASW, 40 mm. **Subject:** Olympics **Obv:** Olympic rings in wreath above value within circle of stars **Rev:** Ancient and modern javelin throwers **Edge:** Plain

| Date | Mintage | VF20 | XF40 | MS60 | MS63 | MS65 |
|---|---|---|---|---|---|---|
| ND(2003) | 68,000 | **PF65** 50.00 | | | | |

## KM# 194 10 EURO

34.00 g., 0.925 Silver 1.0111 oz. ASW, 40 mm. **Subject:** Olympics **Obv:** Olympic rings in wreath above value within circle of stars **Rev:** Ancient and modern long jumpers **Edge:** Plain

| Date | Mintage | VF20 | XF40 | MS60 | MS63 | MS65 |
|---|---|---|---|---|---|---|
| ND(2003) | 68,000 | **PF65** 50.00 | | | | |

## KM# 196 10 EURO

34.00 g., 0.925 Silver 1.0111 oz. ASW, 40 mm. **Subject:** Olympics **Obv:** Olympic rings in wreath above value within circle of stars **Rev:** Ancient and modern relay runners **Edge:** Plain

| Date | Mintage | VF20 | XF40 | MS60 | MS63 | MS65 |
|---|---|---|---|---|---|---|
| ND(2003) | 68,000 | **PF65** 50.00 | | | | |

## KM# 197 10 EURO

34.00 g., 0.925 Silver 1.0111 oz. ASW, 40 mm. **Subject:** Olympics **Obv:** Olympic rings in wreath above value within circle of stars **Rev:** Ancient and modern horsemen **Edge:** Plain

| Date | Mintage | VF20 | XF40 | MS60 | MS63 | MS65 |
|---|---|---|---|---|---|---|
| ND(2003) | 68,000 | **PF65** 50.00 | | | | |

## KM# 199 10 EURO

34.00 g., 0.925 Silver 1.0111 oz. ASW, 40 mm. **Subject:** Olympics **Obv:** Olympic rings in wreath above value within circle of stars **Rev:** Modern ribbon dancer and two ancient female acrobats **Edge:** Plain

| Date | Mintage | VF20 | XF40 | MS60 | MS63 | MS65 |
|---|---|---|---|---|---|---|
| ND(2003) | 68,000 | **PF65** 50.00 | | | | |

## KM# 200 10 EURO

34.00 g., 0.925 Silver 1.0111 oz. ASW, 40 mm. **Subject:** Olympics **Obv:** Olympic rings in wreath above value within a circle of stars **Rev:** Ancient and modern female swimmers **Edge:** Plain

| Date | Mintage | VF20 | XF40 | MS60 | MS63 | MS65 |
|---|---|---|---|---|---|---|
| ND(2003) | 68,000 | **PF65** 50.00 | | | | |

## KM# 208 10 EURO

9.75 g., 0.925 Silver 0.290 oz. ASW, 28.25 mm. **Subject:** Greek Presidency of E. U. **Obv:** National arms in wreath above value **Rev:** Stylized document design **Edge:** Notched

| Date | Mintage | VF20 | XF40 | MS60 | MS63 | MS65 |
|---|---|---|---|---|---|---|
| 2003 | 50,000 | **PF65** 70.00 | | | | |

## KM# 202 10 EURO

34.00 g., 0.925 Silver 1.0111 oz. ASW, 40 mm. **Subject:** Olympics **Obv:** Olympic rings in wreath above value within circle of stars **Rev:** Ancient and modern weight lifters **Edge:** Plain

| Date | Mintage | VF20 | XF40 | MS60 | MS63 | MS65 |
|---|---|---|---|---|---|---|
| ND(2004) | 68,000 | **PF65** 50.00 | | | | |

**KM# 203 10 EURO**

34.00 g., 0.925 Silver 1.0111 oz. ASW, 40 mm. **Subject:** Olympics **Obv:** Olympic rings in wreath above value within circle of stars **Rev:** Ancient and modern wrestlers **Edge:** Plain

| Date | Mintage | VF20 | XF40 | MS60 | MS63 | MS65 |
|---|---|---|---|---|---|---|
| ND(2004) | 68,000 | PF65 50.00 | | | | |

**KM# 205 10 EURO**

34.00 g., 0.925 Silver 1.0111 oz. ASW, 40 mm. **Subject:** Olympics **Obv:** Olympic rings in wreath above value within circle of stars **Rev:** Ancient and modern handball players **Edge:** Plain

| Date | Mintage | VF20 | XF40 | MS60 | MS63 | MS65 |
|---|---|---|---|---|---|---|
| ND(2004) | 68,000 | PF65 50.00 | | | | |

**KM# 206 10 EURO**

34.00 g., 0.925 Silver 1.0111 oz. ASW, 40 mm. **Subject:** Olympics **Obv:** Olympic rings in wreath above value within circle of stars **Rev:** Ancient and modern soccer players **Edge:** Plain

| Date | Mintage | VF20 | XF40 | MS60 | MS63 | MS65 |
|---|---|---|---|---|---|---|
| ND(2004) | 68,000 | PF65 50.00 | | | | |

**KM# 230 10 EURO**

34.00 g., 0.925 Silver 1.0111 oz. ASW, 40 mm. **Obv:** Wreath **Rev:** Torch runner and map of Australia

| Date | Mintage | VF20 | XF40 | MS60 | MS63 | MS65 |
|---|---|---|---|---|---|---|
| 2004 | 10,000 | PF63 90.00 | PF65 110 | | | |

**KM# 231 10 EURO**

34.00 g., 0.925 Silver 1.0111 oz. ASW, 40 mm. **Rev:** Torch runner and map of Asia

| Date | Mintage | VF20 | XF40 | MS60 | MS63 | MS65 |
|---|---|---|---|---|---|---|
| 2004 | 10,000 | PF63 90.00 | PF65 110 | | | |

**KM# 232 10 EURO**

34.00 g., 0.925 Silver 1.0111 oz. ASW, 40 mm. **Rev:** Torch runner and map of Africa

| Date | Mintage | VF20 | XF40 | MS60 | MS63 | MS65 |
|---|---|---|---|---|---|---|
| 2004 | 10,000 | PF63 90.00 | PF65 110 | | | |

**KM# 233 10 EURO**

34.00 g., 0.925 Silver 1.0111 oz. ASW, 40 mm. **Rev:** Torch runner and map of North and South America

| Date | Mintage | VF20 | XF40 | MS60 | MS63 | MS65 |
|---|---|---|---|---|---|---|
| 2004 | 10,000 | PF63 90.00 | PF65 110 | | | |

**KM# 217 10 EURO**

9.75 g., 0.925 Silver 0.290 oz. ASW **Subject:** Olympic National Park **Obv:** National arms above stylized flowers **Rev:** Four Titans above flowers in camp

| Date | Mintage | VF20 | XF40 | MS60 | MS63 | MS65 |
|---|---|---|---|---|---|---|
| 2005 | 25,000 | PF65 35.00 | | | | |

**KM# 218 10 EURO**

9.75 g., 0.925 Silver 0.290 oz. ASW, 28.25 mm. **Subject:** PATRA - European Capitol of Culture - Achaia **Obv:** National arms at upper right, stylized bridge below **Rev:** PATRA logo **Edge:** Plain

| Date | Mintage | VF20 | XF40 | MS60 | MS63 | MS65 |
|---|---|---|---|---|---|---|
| 2006 | — | PF65 40.00 | | | | |

**KM# 219 10 EURO**

34.00 g., 0.925 Silver 1.0111 oz. ASW, 40 mm. **Obv:** National arms above stylized flowers **Rev:** Outline of Greece at left, statue of Zeus, flowers at right **Edge:** Plain

| Date | Mintage | VF20 | XF40 | MS60 | MS63 | MS65 |
|---|---|---|---|---|---|---|
| 2006 | 5,000 | PF65 45.00 | | | | |

**KM# 220 10 EURO**

34.00 g., 0.925 Silver 1.0111 oz. ASW, 40 mm. **Subject:** National Parks - Mount Olympus - International Biosphere Reserve **Obv:** National arms above stylized flowers **Rev:** Archaeological outline of Dion City above landscape **Edge:** Plain

| Date | Mintage | VF20 | XF40 | MS60 | MS63 | MS65 |
|---|---|---|---|---|---|---|
| 2006 | 5,000 | PF65 45.00 | | | | |

**KM# 221 10 EURO**

34.00 g., 0.925 Silver 1.0111 oz. ASW, 40 mm. **Subject:** National Parks - Arkoudorema River in Southern Pindos - Valia Kalda **Obv:** National arms on stylized tree **Rev:** Outlined map at upper left, bird perched on stalk, flowers at center right **Edge:** Plain

| Date | Mintage | VF20 | XF40 | MS60 | MS63 | MS65 |
|---|---|---|---|---|---|---|
| 2007 | 5,000 | PF65 50.00 | | | | |

**KM# 222 10 EURO**

34.00 g., 0.925 Silver 1.0111 oz. ASW, 40 mm. **Subject:** National Parks - Valia Kalda - Southern Pindos **Obv:** National arms on stylized tree **Rev:** Tree line **Edge:** Plain

| Date | Mintage | VF20 | XF40 | MS60 | MS63 | MS65 |
|---|---|---|---|---|---|---|
| 2007 | 5,000 | PF65 50.00 | | | | |

**KM# 223 10 EURO**

9.75 g., 0.925 Silver 0.290 oz. ASW, 28.25 mm. **Subject:** 30th Anniversary Death of Maria Callas, Operatic Soprano **Obv:** National arms above denomination, facsimile signature below, music scores in background **Rev:** Bust of Maria Callas right **Edge:** Plain **Shape:** Spanish Flower

| Date | Mintage | VF20 | XF40 | MS60 | MS63 | MS65 |
|---|---|---|---|---|---|---|
| 2007 | 5,000 | PF65 40.00 | | | | |

**KM# 224 10 EURO**

9.75 g., 0.925 Silver 0.290 oz. ASW, 28.25 mm. **Subject:** 50th Anniversary death of Nikos Kazantzakis, Author **Obv:** National arms above denomination, facsimile signature below **Rev:** Head of N. Kazantzakis facing 3/4 left **Edge:** Plain **Shape:** Spanish Flower

| Date | Mintage | VF20 | XF40 | MS60 | MS63 | MS65 |
|---|---|---|---|---|---|---|
| 2007 | 5,000 | PF65 40.00 | | | | |

**KM# 225 10 EURO**

9.75 g., 0.925 Silver 0.290 oz. ASW, 28.25 mm. **Subject:** Acropolis Museum **Obv:** Panoramic view of the Acropolis **Rev:** Pediment sculpture

| Date | Mintage | VF20 | XF40 | MS60 | MS63 | MS65 |
|---|---|---|---|---|---|---|
| 2008 | 10,000 | — | — | — | — | 40.00 |

**KM# 226 10 EURO**

9.75 g., 0.925 Silver 0.290 oz. ASW, 28.25 mm. **Subject:** Yannis Ritsas

| Date | Mintage | VF20 | XF40 | MS60 | MS63 | MS65 |
|---|---|---|---|---|---|---|
| 2009 | — | PF65 40.00 | | | | |

**KM# 228 10 EURO**

9.75 g., 0.925 Silver 0.290 oz. ASW, 28.25 mm. **Subject:** International Year of Astronomy

| Date | Mintage | VF20 | XF40 | MS60 | MS63 | MS65 |
|---|---|---|---|---|---|---|
| 2009 | — | PF65 35.00 | | | | |

**KM# 237 10 EURO**

34.00 g., 0.925 Silver 1.0111 oz. ASW, 40 mm. **Subject:** Sofia Vempo, 100th Anniversary of Birth **Obv:** Sofia Vempo portrait **Rev:** Stave, national emblem and value **Shape:** Spanish flower

| Date | Mintage | VF20 | XF40 | MS60 | MS63 | MS65 |
|---|---|---|---|---|---|---|
| 2010 | 5,000 | PF65 55.00 | | | | |

**KM# 238 10 EURO**

9.75 g., 0.925 Silver 0.290 oz. ASW, 28.25 mm. **Subject:** International Year of Biodiversity **Obv:** Various species of Biodiversity **Rev:** Nature's species, national emblem and value **Shape:** Spanish flower

| Date | Mintage | VF20 | XF40 | MS60 | MS63 | MS65 |
|---|---|---|---|---|---|---|
| 2010 | 5,000 | PF65 40.00 | | | | |

**KM# 240 10 EURO**

9.75 g., 0.925 Silver 0.290 oz. ASW, 28.25 mm. **Subject:** XIII Special Olympics, Special Olympics Founder Declaration **Obv:** Declaration over the Acropolis of Athens, Radiant Sun **Rev:** Special Olympics emblem, National arms below value **Shape:** 5 double edge notches

| Date | Mintage | VF20 | XF40 | MS60 | MS63 | MS65 |
|---|---|---|---|---|---|---|
| 2011 Proof, Sets only | 7,500 | PF65 35.00 | | | | |
| 2011 | — | — | — | — | — | — |

**KM# 241 10 EURO**

9.75 g., 0.925 Silver 0.290 oz. ASW, 28.25 mm. **Subject:** XIII Special Olympics, Athletes in Union **Obv:** Stylized athletes around a radiant sun and olive branch **Rev:** Panathenaikon Stadium below the National Arms and value **Shape:** 5 double edge notches

| Date | Mintage | VF20 | XF40 | MS60 | MS63 | MS65 |
|---|---|---|---|---|---|---|
| 2011 | — | — | — | — | — | — |
| 2011 Proof, Sets only | 7,500 | PF65 35.00 | | | | |

**KM# 242 10 EURO**

34.10 g., 0.925 Silver 1.0141 oz. ASW, 40 mm. **Subject:** Special Olympics, Highlight **Obv:** Highlight from an event during the games **Rev:** Stylized elements from the XIII Special Olympics emblem in Athens, National Arms, value below

| Date | Mintage | VF20 | XF40 | MS60 | MS63 | MS65 |
|---|---|---|---|---|---|---|
| 2011 | 2,000 | PF65 135 | | | | |

**KM# 243 10 EURO**

34.10 g., 0.925 Silver 1.0141 oz. ASW, 40 mm. **Subject:** Special Olympics, Torch-bearer **Obv:** Torch-bearer **Rev:** Stylized elements from the XIII Special Olympics emblem in Athens, National Arms, value below

| Date | Mintage | VF20 | XF40 | MS60 | MS63 | MS65 |
|---|---|---|---|---|---|---|
| 2011 | 2,000 | PF65 135 | | | | |

**KM# 246 10 EURO**

9.75 g., 0.925 Silver 0.290 oz. ASW, 28.25 mm. **Subject:** Dr. George N. Papanicolaou **Obv:** Dr. Papanicolaou and a microscope **Rev:** Shaped human cells around the national emblem and value **Shape:** 5 double edge notches

| Date | Mintage | VF20 | XF40 | MS60 | MS63 | MS65 |
|---|---|---|---|---|---|---|
| 2012 Prooflike, Sets only | 10,000 | — | — | — | — | 60.00 |

**KM# 247 10 EURO**

34.10 g., 0.925 Silver 1.0141 oz. ASW, 40 mm. **Subject:** Greek Culture" - Poet: Aeschylus **Obv:** Aeschylus (524-455 B.C.) portrait. **Rev:** Ancient lyrics, national emblem, value and date

| Date | Mintage | VF20 | XF40 | MS60 | MS63 | MS65 |
|---|---|---|---|---|---|---|
| 2012 | 5,000 | PF65 125 | | | | |

**KM# 248 10 EURO**

34.10 g., 0.925 Silver 1.0141 oz. ASW, 40 mm. **Subject:** Greek Culture" - Socrates **Obv:** Socrates (469-399 B.C.) portrait facing left **Rev:** Ancient sayings, national emblem, value and date

| Date | Mintage | VF20 | XF40 | MS60 | MS63 | MS65 |
|---|---|---|---|---|---|---|
| 2012 | 5,000 | PF65 125 | | | | |

**KM# 254 10 EURO**

34.00 g., 0.925 Silver 1.0111 oz. ASW, 40 mm. **Subject:** Pythagoras of Samos

| Date | Mintage | VF20 | XF40 | MS60 | MS63 | MS65 |
|---|---|---|---|---|---|---|
| 2013 | 1,000 | PF65 135 | | | | |

### KM# 255 10 EURO

34.00 g., 0.925 Silver 1.0111 oz. ASW, 40 mm. **Subject:** Sophokles

| Date | Mintage | VF20 | XF40 | MS60 | MS63 | MS65 |
|---|---|---|---|---|---|---|
| 2013 | 1,000 | PF65 135 | | | | |

### KM# 210 20 EURO

24.00 g., 0.925 Silver 0.7137 oz. ASW, 37 mm. **Subject:** Bank of Greece 75th Anniversary **Obv:** Value **Rev:** Flag

| Date | Mintage | VF20 | XF40 | MS60 | MS63 | MS65 |
|---|---|---|---|---|---|---|
| 2003 | 15,000 | PF65 170 | | | | |

### KM# 251 50 EURO

1.00 g., 0.9999 Gold 0.0321 oz. AGW, 14 mm. **Subject:** Ancient Pella (Macedonia), Northern Greece. **Obv:** Wave and geometric pattern, ornaments of a stone slab table (Hellenistic era) found in Pella, capital of ancient Macedonia **Rev:** Wave shaped ornament of a stove slab table (Hellensitic era) found in Pella, capital of ancient Macedonia, Pella, and the national arms of Greece, value below

| Date | Mintage | VF20 | XF40 | MS60 | MS63 | MS65 |
|---|---|---|---|---|---|---|
| 2012 | 4,000 | PF65 95.00 | | | | |

### KM# 256 50 EURO

1.00 g., 0.999 Gold 0.0321 oz. AGW, 14 mm. **Obv:** State emblem within waves **Rev:** Mycenae shield

| Date | Mintage | VF20 | XF40 | MS60 | MS63 | MS65 |
|---|---|---|---|---|---|---|
| 2013 | 1,000 | PF65 200 | | | | |

### KM# 192 100 EURO

10.00 g., 0.9999 Gold 0.3215 oz. AGW, 25 mm. **Subject:** Olympics **Obv:** Olympic rings in wreath above value within circle of stars **Rev:** Knossos Palace **Edge:** Plain

| Date | Mintage | VF20 | XF40 | MS60 | MS63 | MS65 |
|---|---|---|---|---|---|---|
| ND(2003) | 28,000 | PF63 500 | PF65 550 | | | |

### KM# 195 100 EURO

10.00 g., 0.9999 Gold 0.3215 oz. AGW, 25 mm. **Subject:** Olympics **Obv:** Olympic rings in wreath above value within circle of stars **Rev:** Krypte archway **Edge:** Plain

| Date | Mintage | VF20 | XF40 | MS60 | MS63 | MS65 |
|---|---|---|---|---|---|---|
| ND(2003) | 28,000 | PF63 500 | PF65 550 | | | |

### KM# 198 100 EURO

10.00 g., 0.9999 Gold 0.3215 oz. AGW, 25 mm. **Subject:** Olympics **Obv:** Olympic rings in wreath above value within circle of stars **Rev:** Panathenean Stadium **Edge:** Plain

| Date | Mintage | VF20 | XF40 | MS60 | MS63 | MS65 |
|---|---|---|---|---|---|---|
| ND(2003) | 28,000 | PF63 500 | PF65 550 | | | |

### KM# 201 100 EURO

10.00 g., 0.9999 Gold 0.3215 oz. AGW, 25 mm. **Subject:** Olympics **Obv:** Olympic rings in wreath above value within circle of stars **Rev:** Zappeion Mansion **Edge:** Plain

| Date | Mintage | VF20 | XF40 | MS60 | MS63 | MS65 |
|---|---|---|---|---|---|---|
| ND(2003) | 28,000 | PF63 500 | PF65 550 | | | |

### KM# 204 100 EURO

10.00 g., 0.9999 Gold 0.3215 oz. AGW, 25 mm. **Subject:** Olympics **Obv:** Olympic rings in wreath above value within circle of stars **Rev:** Acropolis **Edge:** Plain

| Date | Mintage | VF20 | XF40 | MS60 | MS63 | MS65 |
|---|---|---|---|---|---|---|
| ND(2004) | 28,000 | PF63 500 | PF65 550 | | | |

### KM# 207 100 EURO

10.00 g., 0.9999 Gold 0.3215 oz. AGW, 25 mm. **Subject:** Olympics **Obv:** Olympic rings in wreath above value within circle of stars **Rev:** Academy of Athens **Edge:** Plain

| Date | Mintage | VF20 | XF40 | MS60 | MS63 | MS65 |
|---|---|---|---|---|---|---|
| ND(2004) | 28,000 | PF63 500 | PF65 550 | | | |

### KM# 234 100 EURO

10.00 g., 0.999 Gold 0.3212 oz. AGW, 25 mm. **Rev:** Classical female handing torch to kneeling runner

| Date | Mintage | VF20 | XF40 | MS60 | MS63 | MS65 |
|---|---|---|---|---|---|---|
| 2004 | 10,000 | PF63 525 | PF65 575 | | | |

### KM# 235 100 EURO

10.00 g., 0.999 Gold 0.3212 oz. AGW, 25 mm. **Rev:** Torch runner and flag

| Date | Mintage | VF20 | XF40 | MS60 | MS63 | MS65 |
|---|---|---|---|---|---|---|
| 2004 | 10,000 | PF63 525 | PF65 575 | | | |

### KM# 244 100 EURO

7.99 g., 0.9166 Gold 0.2354 oz. AGW, 22.1 mm. **Subject:** Special Olympics' Athletes in Union **Obv:** Stylized Athletes around a radiant sun and olive branch **Rev:** Panathenaikon Stadium below the National Arms and value

| Date | Mintage | VF20 | XF40 | MS60 | MS63 | MS65 |
|---|---|---|---|---|---|---|
| 2011 | 1,000 | PF63 1,250 | PF65 1,350 | | | |

### KM# 249 100 EURO

7.99 g., 0.9166 Gold 0.2354 oz. AGW, 22.1 mm. **Subject:** Liberation of Thessaloniki, 100th Anniversary **Obv:** Golden round ornament with rosette (480 B.C.) from an ancient tomb, flag of modern Greece background. **Rev:** The White Tower (symbol of Thewsaloniki) with the National Arms engraved and value, shaped laurels above

| Date | Mintage | VF20 | XF40 | MS60 | MS63 | MS65 |
|---|---|---|---|---|---|---|
| 2012 | 1,500 | PF63 750 | PF65 800 | | | |

### KM# 250 100 EURO

7.99 g., 0.916 Gold 0.2353 oz. AGW, 22.1 mm. **Subject:** Balkan Wars outbreak, 100th Anniversary **Obv:** Admiral Parlos Kountouriotis bust, the flag of Greece on the background **Rev:** The battleship "Averoph", national arms above left and value below

| Date | Mintage | VF20 | XF40 | MS60 | MS63 | MS65 |
|---|---|---|---|---|---|---|
| 2012 | 1,500 | PF63 750 | PF65 800 | | | |

### KM# 229 200 EURO

31.11 g., 0.999 Gold 0.999 oz. AGW, 37 mm. **Subject:** Bank of Greece, 75th Anniversary

| Date | Mintage | VF20 | XF40 | MS60 | MS63 | MS65 |
|---|---|---|---|---|---|---|
| 2003 | 1,000 | PF65 3,500 | | | | |

### KM# 258 200 EURO

7.98 g., 0.9167 Gold 0.2352 oz. AGW, 22 mm. **Subject:** Hippocrates

| Date | Mintage | VF20 | XF40 | MS60 | MS63 | MS65 |
|---|---|---|---|---|---|---|
| 2013 | 1,200 | PF65 750 | | | | |

### KM# 257 10 ECU

34.10 g., 0.925 Silver 1.0141 oz. ASW, 40 mm. **Subject:** Hippocrates

| Date | Mintage | VF20 | XF40 | MS60 | MS63 | MS65 |
|---|---|---|---|---|---|---|
| 2013 | 1,200 | PF65 225 | | | | |

## MINT SETS

| KM# | Date | Mintage | Identification | Issue Price | Mkt Val |
|---|---|---|---|---|---|
| MS6 | 2002 (8) | 50,000 | KM#181-188 | — | 30.00 |
| MS7 | 2002F (8) | 5,000 | KM#181-188 Issued by Ministry of Finance | — | 300 |
| MS8 | 2003 (8) | — | KM#181-188 | — | 40.00 |
| MS9 | 2003 (9) | — | KM#181-188, 208 | — | 80.00 |
| MS11 | 2004 (8) | 20,000 | KM#181-188 2004 Discobole commemo-rating Olympic Games in Athens | — | 65.00 |
| MS12 | 2005 (8) | 25,000 | KM#181-188 | — | 35.00 |
| MS13 | 2005 (9) | 25,000 | KM#181-188, 220 Mount Olympus as a National Park | — | 70.00 |
| MS14 | 2006 (9) | 25,000 | KM#181-188 (2005), 220 Aegina - Korinth set | 28.00 | 70.00 |
| MS15 | 2006 (9) | 25,000 | KM#181-188, 218 Patras - Cultural Capital of Europe | 50.00 | 70.00 |
| MS16 | 2007 (8) | 15,000 | KM#181-183, 211-215 Ancient Coins of the Aegean Sea | — | 50.00 |
| MS17 | 2007 (9) | 15,000 | KM#181-183, 211-215, 224 Nikos Kazantzakis | 50.00 | 75.00 |
| MS18 | 2007 (9) | 15,000 | KM#181-183, 211-215, 223 Maria Callas | 50.00 | 95.00 |
| MS19 | 2008 (8) | 15,000 | KM#181-183, 211-215 | 28.00 | 40.00 |
| MS20 | 2008 (9) | 10,000 | KM#181-183, 211-215, 225 | 45.00 | 55.00 |
| MS21 | 2009 (8) | 7,500 | KM#181-183, 211-215 | 28.00 | 45.00 |
| MS22 | 2009 (9) | 5,000 | KM#181-183, 211-215, 226 | 45.00 | 55.00 |
| MS23 | 2009 (9) | 5,000 | KM#181-183, 211-215, 228 | 45.00 | 55.00 |
| MS24 | 2010 (8) | 7,500 | KM#181-183, 211-215 | 28.00 | 30.00 |
| MS25 | 2010 (8) | 7,500 | KM#181-183, 211-214, 236 | 28.00 | 30.00 |
| MS26 | 2010 (9) | 5,000 | KM#181-183, 211-215, 237 Sofia Vempo 100th Anniversary of Birth | 45.00 | 80.00 |
| MS27 | 2010 (9) | 5,000 | KM#181-183, 211-215, 238 International Year of Biodiversity | 45.00 | 75.00 |
| MS28 | 2011 (8) | 15,000 | KM#181-183, 211-215 | 28.00 | 40.00 |
| MS29 | 2011 (9) | 5,000 | KM#181-183, 211-215, 239 | 28.00 | 45.00 |
| MS30 | 2011 (9) | 7,500 | KM#181-183, 211-215, 240 Special Olympics - Declaration | 45.00 | 70.00 |
| MS31 | 2011 (9) | 7,500 | KM#181-183, 211-215, 241 Special Olympics - Unity | 45.00 | 70.00 |
| MS32 | 2012 (9) | 10,000 | KM#181-183, 211-215, 246, Dr. George Papanicolaou | 45.00 | 65.00 |
| MS33 | 2012 (8) | 20,000 | KM#181-183, 211-215. Santorini, the Island of Lava | 28.00 | 40.00 |

## PROOF SETS

| KM# | Date | Mintage | Identification | Issue Price | Mkt Val |
|---|---|---|---|---|---|
| PS6 | 2011 (8) | 2,500 | KM#181-183, 211-215 | 115 | 300 |
| PS7 | 2012 (9) | 2,500 | KM#181-183, 211-215, 245 | — | 250 |

# GUATEMALA

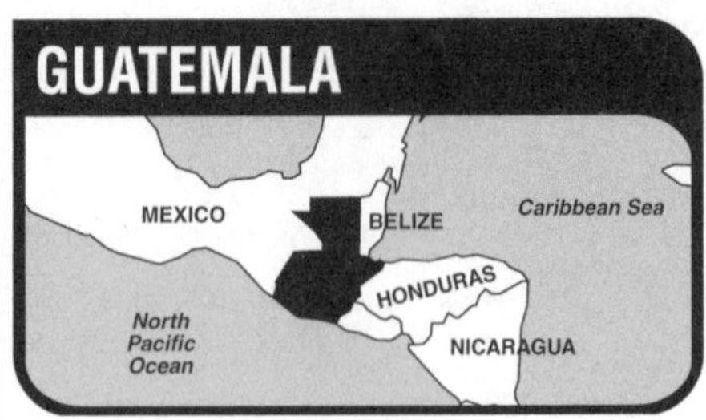


The Republic of Guatemala, the northernmost of the five Central American republics, has an area of 42,042 sq. mi. (108,890 sq. km.) and a population of 10.7 million. Capital: Guatemala City. The economy of Guatemala is heavily dependent on agriculture, however, the country is rich in nickel resources which are being developed. Coffee, cotton and bananas are exported.

Guatemala, once the site of an ancient Mayan civilization, was conquered by Pedro de Alvarado, the resourceful lieutenant of Cortes who undertook the conquest from Mexico. Cruel but strategically skillful, he progressed rapidly along the Pacific coastal lowlands to the highland plain of Quetzaltenango where the decisive battle for Guatemala was fought. After routing the Indian forces, he established the city of Guatemala in 1524. The Spanish Captaincy-General of Guatemala included all Central America but Panama. Guatemala declared its independence of Spain in 1821 and was absorbed into the Mexican empire of Augustin Iturbide (1822-23). From 1823 to 1839 Guatemala was a constituent state of the Central American Republic. Upon dissolution of that confederation, Guatemala proclaimed itself an independent republic. Like El Salvador, Guatemala suffered from internal strife between right-wing, US-backed military government and leftist indigenous peoples from ca. 1954 to ca. 1997.

**MINT MARKS**

(L) – London, Royal Mint

## REPUBLIC

## REFORM COINAGE

100 Centavos = 1 Quetzal

### KM# 282 CENTAVO (UN)

0.80 g., Aluminum, 19 mm. **Subject:** Fray Bartolome de las Casas **Obv:** National arms **Rev:** Bust left **Edge:** Plain **Note:** 7-sided interior field

| Date | Mintage | VF20 | XF40 | MS60 | MS63 | MS65 |
|---|---|---|---|---|---|---|
| 2007 | — | — | 0.15 | 0.25 | 0.30 | 0.45 |

### KM# 276.6 5 CENTAVOS

1.60 g., Copper-Nickel, 16 mm. **Obv:** National arms, smaller sized emblem, no dots by date **Obv. Legend:** REPUBLICA DE GUATEMALA 1997 **Rev:** Kapok tree center, value at right, ground below **Edge:** Reeded **Note:** Varieties exist.

| Date | Mintage | VF20 | XF40 | MS60 | MS63 | MS65 |
|---|---|---|---|---|---|---|
| 2006 | — | — | 0.15 | 0.30 | 0.40 | 0.50 |
| 2008 | — | — | 0.15 | 0.30 | 0.40 | 0.50 |
| 2009 | — | — | 0.15 | 0.30 | 0.40 | 0.50 |
| 2010 | — | — | 0.15 | 0.30 | 0.40 | 0.50 |

**KM# 277.6 10 CENTAVOS**
3.20 g., Copper-Nickel, 21 mm. **Obv:** National arms, small letters in legend **Obv. Legend:** REPUBLICA DE GUATEMALA **Rev:** Monolith **Rev. Legend:** MONOLITO DE QUIRIGUA **Edge:** Reeded **Note:** Varieties exist.

| Date | Mintage | VF20 | XF40 | MS60 | MS63 | MS65 |
|---|---|---|---|---|---|---|
| 2006 | — | 0.15 | 0.25 | 0.50 | 0.75 | 1.00 |
| 2008 | — | 0.15 | 0.25 | 0.50 | 0.75 | 1.00 |
| 2009 | — | 0.15 | 0.25 | 0.50 | 0.75 | 1.00 |

**KM# 277.6a 10 CENTAVOS**
2.40 g., Nickel Plated Steel, 21 mm. **Obv:** National arms, small letters in legend **Obv. Legend:** REPUBLICA DE GUATEMALA **Rev:** Monolith, smaller dots at rim **Rev. Legend:** MONOLITO DE QUIRIGUA **Edge:** Reeded

| Date | Mintage | VF20 | XF40 | MS60 | MS63 | MS65 |
|---|---|---|---|---|---|---|
| 2010 | — | 0.15 | 0.25 | 0.50 | 0.75 | 1.00 |

**KM# 283 50 CENTAVOS**
5.50 g., Nickel-Brass, 26.5 mm. **Obv:** National arms **Rev:** Whitenun orchid (lycaste skinneri var. alba orchidaceae) **Edge:** Reeded

| Date | Mintage | VF20 | XF40 | MS60 | MS63 | MS65 |
|---|---|---|---|---|---|---|
| 2001 | — | — | 0.50 | 1.00 | 1.25 | 1.50 |
| 2007 | — | — | 0.50 | 1.00 | 1.25 | 1.50 |

**KM# 284 QUETZAL**
11.00 g., Nickel-Brass, 29 mm. **Obv:** National arms **Obv. Legend:** REPUBLIC DE GUATEMALA **Rev:** PAZ above stylized dove **Rev. Legend:** Paz Firme y Duradera 29 de Diciembre de 1996 **Edge:** Reeded

| Date | Mintage | VF20 | XF40 | MS60 | MS63 | MS65 |
|---|---|---|---|---|---|---|
| 2001 Thick letters | — | — | 0.25 | 1.00 | 1.50 | 2.00 |
| 2006 Thin letters | — | — | 0.25 | 1.00 | 1.50 | 2.00 |
| 2008 | — | — | 0.25 | 1.00 | 1.50 | 2.00 |
| 2011 Thin letters | — | — | 0.25 | 1.00 | 1.50 | 2.00 |

**KM# 287 QUETZAL**
31.10 g., 0.9999 Silver 0.9999 oz. ASW, 30 mm. **Subject:** Canonization of Brother Pedro Betancourt **Obv:** National arms **Rev:** Standing monk **Edge:** Plain

| Date | Mintage | VF20 | XF40 | MS60 | MS63 | MS65 |
|---|---|---|---|---|---|---|
| ND(2002) | 6,000 | PF60 30.00 | PF63 45.00 | PF65 60.00 | | |

**KM# 288 QUETZAL**
31.10 g., 0.999 Silver 0.999 oz. ASW, 40 mm. **Subject:** Discovery of the Americas **Obv:** Shields around inner circle holding arms with date below **Rev:** Native peoples in canoe with fish

| Date | Mintage | VF20 | XF40 | MS60 | MS63 | MS65 |
|---|---|---|---|---|---|---|
| 2002 | — | PF60 30.00 | PF63 45.00 | PF65 60.00 | | |

**KM# 289 QUETZAL**
27.00 g., 0.925 Silver 0.803 oz. ASW, 40 mm. **Obv:** Arms at center surrounded by odler arms **Rev:** Ancient temple

| Date | Mintage | VF20 | XF40 | MS60 | MS63 | MS65 |
|---|---|---|---|---|---|---|
| 2005 | — | PF60 30.00 | PF63 45.00 | PF65 60.00 | | |

**KM# 290 QUETZAL**
27.00 g., 0.925 Silver 0.803 oz. ASW, 40 mm. **Obv:** Arms surrounded by older arms **Rev:** Female dancer and figures

| Date | Mintage | VF20 | XF40 | MS60 | MS63 | MS65 |
|---|---|---|---|---|---|---|
| 2007 | — | PF60 30.00 | PF63 45.00 | PF65 60.00 | | |

**KM# 291 QUETZAL**
27.00 g., 0.925 Silver 0.803 oz. ASW, 40 mm. **Subject:** Ibero-American series

| Date | Mintage | VF20 | XF40 | MS60 | MS63 | MS65 |
|---|---|---|---|---|---|---|
| 2010 | — | PF60 30.00 | PF63 45.00 | PF65 60.00 | | |

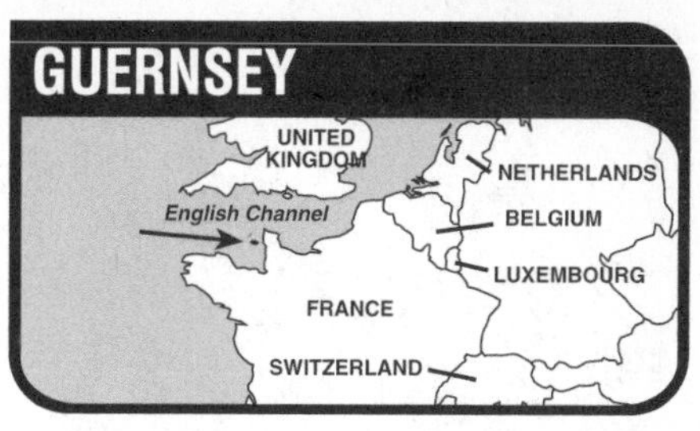


The Bailiwick of Guernsey, a British crown dependency located in the English Channel 30 miles (48 km.) west of Normandy, France, has an area of 30 sq. mi. (194 sq. km.) (including the isles of Alderney, Jethou, Herm, Brechou, and Sark), and a population of 54,000. Capital: St. Peter Port. Agriculture and cattle breeding are the main occupations.

Guernsey is administered by its own laws and customs. Unless the island is mentioned specifically, acts passed by the British Parliament are not applicable to Guernsey. During World War II, German troops occupied the island from June 30, 1940 till May 9,1945.

**RULER**
British

**MONETARY SYSTEM**
100 Pence = 1 Pound

# BRITISH DEPENDENCY

## DECIMAL COINAGE

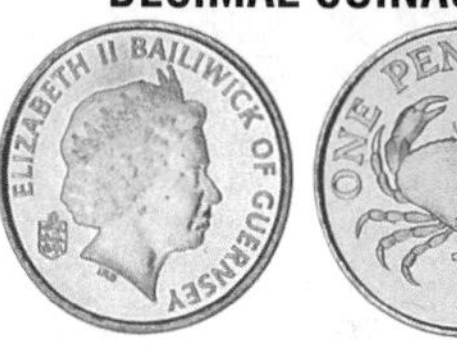

**KM# 89 PENNY**
3.56 g., Copper Plated Steel, 20.32 mm. **Ruler:** Elizabeth II **Obv:** Head with tiara right **Rev:** Edible crab **Edge:** Plain

| Date | Mintage | VF20 | XF40 | MS60 | MS63 | MS65 |
|---|---|---|---|---|---|---|
| 2003 | 1,302,600 | — | — | 0.20 | 0.35 | 1.00 |
| 2006 | 1,731,000 | — | — | 0.20 | 0.35 | 0.75 |
| 2012 | — | — | — | 0.20 | 0.35 | 0.75 |

**KM# 96 2 PENCE**
7.12 g., Copper Plated Steel, 25.91 mm. **Ruler:** Elizabeth II **Obv:** Head with tiara, shield at left **Rev:** Guernsey cows **Edge:** Plain

| Date | Mintage | VF20 | XF40 | MS60 | MS63 | MS65 |
|---|---|---|---|---|---|---|
| 2003 | 662,600 | — | — | 0.50 | 0.70 | 1.00 |
| 2006 | 1,322,000 | — | — | 0.50 | 0.70 | 1.00 |
| 2011 | — | — | — | 0.50 | 0.70 | 1.00 |
| 2012 | — | — | — | 0.50 | 0.70 | 1.00 |

**KM# 97 5 PENCE**
3.25 g., Copper-Nickel, 18 mm. **Ruler:** Elizabeth II **Obv:** Head with tiara right **Rev:** Sailboat **Edge:** Reeded

| Date | Mintage | VF20 | XF40 | MS60 | MS63 | MS65 |
|---|---|---|---|---|---|---|
| 2003 | 292,600 | — | — | 0.35 | 0.45 | 0.65 |
| 2006 | 1,217,000 | — | — | 0.35 | 0.45 | 0.65 |
| 2010 | — | — | — | 0.35 | 0.45 | 0.65 |

**KM# 97a 5 PENCE**
3.25 g., Nickel Plated Steel, 18 mm. **Ruler:** Elizabeth II **Obv:** Head with tiara right **Rev:** Sailboat **Edge:** Reeded

| Date | Mintage | VF20 | XF40 | MS60 | MS63 | MS65 |
|---|---|---|---|---|---|---|
| 2012 | — | — | — | 0.35 | 0.45 | 0.65 |

**KM# 149 10 PENCE**
6.50 g., Copper-Nickel, 24.5 mm. **Ruler:** Elizabeth II **Obv:** Crowned head right **Rev:** Tomato plant **Edge:** Reeded

| Date | Mintage | VF20 | XF40 | MS60 | MS63 | MS65 |
|---|---|---|---|---|---|---|
| 2003 | 32,600 | — | — | 0.40 | 0.60 | 0.85 |
| 2006 | 26,000 | — | — | 0.40 | 0.60 | 0.85 |

**KM# 149a 10 PENCE**
6.50 g., Nickel Plated Steel, 24.5 mm. **Ruler:** Elizabeth II **Obv:** Head with tiara right **Rev:** Tomato plant **Edge:** Reeded

| Date | Mintage | VF20 | XF40 | MS60 | MS63 | MS65 |
|---|---|---|---|---|---|---|
| 2012 | — | — | — | 0.40 | 0.60 | 0.85 |

**KM# 90 20 PENCE**
5.00 g., Copper-Nickel, 21.4 mm. **Ruler:** Elizabeth II **Obv:** Head with tiara right, small arms at left **Rev:** Island map within cogwheel **Shape:** 7-sided

| Date | Mintage | VF20 | XF40 | MS60 | MS63 | MS65 |
|---|---|---|---|---|---|---|
| 2003 | 732,600 | — | — | 0.65 | 0.90 | 1.25 |
| 2006 | 16,250 | — | — | 0.65 | 0.90 | 1.25 |
| 2009 | — | — | — | 0.65 | 0.90 | 1.25 |
| 2012 | — | — | — | 0.65 | 0.90 | 1.25 |

**KM# 145 50 PENCE**

8.00 g., Copper-Nickel, 27.3 mm. **Ruler:** Elizabeth II **Subject:** Coronation Jubilee **Obv:** Head with tiara right **Rev:** Queen on horseback **Edge:** Plain **Shape:** 7-sided

| Date | Mintage | VF20 | XF40 | MS60 | MS63 | MS65 |
|---|---|---|---|---|---|---|
| 2003 | — | — | — | 1.50 | 2.50 | 3.00 |

**KM# 145a 50 PENCE**

8.10 g., 0.925 Silver 0.2409 oz. ASW, 27.3 mm. **Ruler:** Elizabeth II **Subject:** Coronation Jubilee **Obv:** Head with tiara right **Rev:** Queen on horseback **Edge:** Plain **Shape:** 7-sided

| Date | Mintage | VF20 | XF40 | MS60 | MS63 | MS65 |
|---|---|---|---|---|---|---|
| 2003 | — | PF65 25.00 | | | | |

**KM# 146 50 PENCE**

8.00 g., Copper-Nickel, 27.3 mm. **Ruler:** Elizabeth II **Subject:** Coronation Jubilee **Obv:** Head with tiara right **Rev:** Queen on throne **Edge:** Plain **Shape:** 7-sided

| Date | Mintage | VF20 | XF40 | MS60 | MS63 | MS65 |
|---|---|---|---|---|---|---|
| 2003 | — | — | — | 1.50 | 2.50 | 3.00 |

**KM# 146a 50 PENCE**

8.10 g., 0.925 Silver 0.2409 oz. ASW, 27.3 mm. **Ruler:** Elizabeth II **Subject:** Coronation Jubilee **Obv:** Head with tiara right **Rev:** Queen on throne **Edge:** Plain **Shape:** 7-sided

| Date | Mintage | VF20 | XF40 | MS60 | MS63 | MS65 |
|---|---|---|---|---|---|---|
| 2003 | — | PF65 25.00 | | | | |

**KM# 147 50 PENCE**

8.00 g., Copper-Nickel, 27.3 mm. **Ruler:** Elizabeth II **Subject:** Coronation Jubilee **Obv:** Head with tiara right **Rev:** Crown **Edge:** Plain **Shape:** 7-sided

| Date | Mintage | VF20 | XF40 | MS60 | MS63 | MS65 |
|---|---|---|---|---|---|---|
| 2003 | — | — | — | 1.50 | 2.50 | 3.00 |

**KM# 147a 50 PENCE**

8.10 g., 0.925 Silver 0.2409 oz. ASW, 27.3 mm. **Ruler:** Elizabeth II **Subject:** Coronation Jubilee **Obv:** Head with tiara right **Rev:** Crown **Edge:** Plain **Shape:** 7-sided

| Date | Mintage | VF20 | XF40 | MS60 | MS63 | MS65 |
|---|---|---|---|---|---|---|
| 2003 | — | PF65 25.00 | | | | |

**KM# 148 50 PENCE**

8.00 g., Copper-Nickel, 27.3 mm. **Ruler:** Elizabeth II **Subject:** Coronation Jubilee **Obv:** Head with tiara right **Rev:** Crowned ERII monogram **Edge:** Plain **Shape:** 7-sided

| Date | Mintage | VF20 | XF40 | MS60 | MS63 | MS65 |
|---|---|---|---|---|---|---|
| 2003 | — | — | — | 1.50 | 2.50 | 3.00 |

**KM# 148a 50 PENCE**

8.10 g., 0.925 Silver 0.2409 oz. ASW, 27.3 mm. **Ruler:** Elizabeth II **Subject:** Coronation Jubilee **Obv:** Head with tiara right **Rev:** Crowned ERII monogram **Edge:** Plain **Shape:** 7-sided

| Date | Mintage | VF20 | XF40 | MS60 | MS63 | MS65 |
|---|---|---|---|---|---|---|
| 2003 | — | PF65 25.00 | | | | |

**KM# 156 50 PENCE**

8.00 g., Copper-Nickel, 27.3 mm. **Ruler:** Elizabeth II **Obv:** Head with tiara right **Rev:** Crossed flowers **Edge:** Plain **Shape:** 7-sided

| Date | Mintage | VF20 | XF40 | MS60 | MS63 | MS65 |
|---|---|---|---|---|---|---|
| 2003 | — | — | — | 1.75 | 2.75 | 3.25 |
| 2006 | 19,000 | — | — | 1.75 | 2.75 | 3.25 |
| 2008 | — | — | — | 1.75 | 2.75 | 3.25 |
| 2012 | — | — | — | 1.75 | 2.75 | 3.25 |

**KM# 110 POUND**

9.50 g., Nickel-Brass, 22.5 mm. **Ruler:** Elizabeth II **Subject:** Circulation Type **Obv:** Head with tiara right **Rev:** Denomination **Edge:** Reeded

| Date | Mintage | VF20 | XF40 | MS60 | MS63 | MS65 |
|---|---|---|---|---|---|---|
| 2001 | 175,000 | — | — | 2.50 | 3.50 | 4.00 |
| 2003 | 46,600 | — | — | 2.50 | 3.50 | 4.00 |
| 2006 | 11,000 | — | — | 2.50 | 3.50 | 4.00 |
| 2012 | — | — | — | 2.50 | 3.50 | 4.00 |

**KM# 111 POUND**

9.50 g., 0.925 Silver 0.2825 oz. ASW, 22.5 mm. **Ruler:** Elizabeth II **Subject:** Elizabeth II, 75th Birthday **Obv:** Head with tiara right **Rev:** Queen's portrait in wreath **Edge:** Reeded

| Date | Mintage | VF20 | XF40 | MS60 | MS63 | MS65 |
|---|---|---|---|---|---|---|
| 2001 | 50,000 | PF63 22.00 | PF65 27.00 | | | |

**KM# 142 POUND**

30.93 g., 0.925 Silver 0.9198 oz. ASW, 38.6 mm. **Ruler:** Elizabeth II **Obv:** Head with tiara right **Rev:** 1/2-bust of William, Duke of Normandy holding sword at left **Edge:** Reeded

| Date | Mintage | VF20 | XF40 | MS60 | MS63 | MS65 |
|---|---|---|---|---|---|---|
| 2002 | — | — | — | — | 40.00 | 50.00 |

**KM# 83 2 POUNDS**

12.00 g., Bi-Metallic Copper-Nickel center in Nickel-Brass ring, 28.4 mm. **Ruler:** Elizabeth II **Obv:** Head with tiara right **Rev:** Latent image arms on cross **Edge:** BAILIWICK OF GUERNSEY

| Date | Mintage | VF20 | XF40 | MS60 | MS63 | MS65 |
|---|---|---|---|---|---|---|
| 2003 | 19,600 | — | — | 5.00 | 7.00 | 9.00 |
| 2006 | 9,500 | — | — | 5.00 | 7.00 | 9.00 |

**KM# 106 5 POUNDS**

28.28 g., Copper-Nickel, 38.6 mm. **Ruler:** Elizabeth II **Subject:** Queen Victoria Centennial **Obv:** Head with tiara right **Rev:** Bust of Queen Victoria left **Edge:** Reeded

| Date | Mintage | VF20 | XF40 | MS60 | MS63 | MS65 |
|---|---|---|---|---|---|---|
| 2001 | 12,754 | — | — | 5.00 | 7.50 | 8.50 |
| 2001 | 30,000 | PF63 18.00 | PF65 20.00 | | | |

**KM# 106a 5 POUNDS**

28.28 g., 0.925 Silver 0.841 oz. ASW, 38.6 mm. **Ruler:** Elizabeth II **Subject:** Queen Victoria 1837-1901 **Obv:** Head with tiara right **Rev:** Bust of Queen Victoria left **Edge:** Reeded

| Date | Mintage | VF20 | XF40 | MS60 | MS63 | MS65 |
|---|---|---|---|---|---|---|
| 2001 | 10,000 | PF63 40.00 | PF65 50.00 | | | |

**KM# 106b 5 POUNDS**

39.94 g., 0.917 Gold 1.1775 oz. AGW, 38.61 mm. **Ruler:** Elizabeth II **Subject:** Queen Victoria 1837-1901 **Obv:** Head with tiara right **Rev:** Queen Victoria's portrait **Edge:** Reeded

| Date | Mintage | VF20 | XF40 | MS60 | MS63 | MS65 |
|---|---|---|---|---|---|---|
| 2001 | 300 | PF65 2,250 | | | | |

**KM# 108 5 POUNDS**

28.28 g., Copper-Nickel, 38.6 mm. **Ruler:** Elizabeth II **Subject:** Queen Elizabeth's 75th Birthday **Obv:** Head with tiara right **Rev:** Queen's portrait in wreath **Edge:** Reeded

| Date | Mintage | VF20 | XF40 | MS60 | MS63 | MS65 |
|---|---|---|---|---|---|---|
| 2001 | 14,000 | — | — | 4.00 | 6.00 | 7.00 |

**KM# 108a 5 POUNDS**

28.28 g., 0.925 Silver 0.841 oz. ASW, 38.6 mm. **Ruler:** Elizabeth II **Subject:** Queen's 75th Birthday **Obv:** Head with tiara right **Rev:** Queen's portrait in wreath **Edge:** Reeded

| Date | Mintage | VF20 | XF40 | MS60 | MS63 | MS65 |
|---|---|---|---|---|---|---|
| 2001 | 20,000 | PF63 45.00 | PF65 55.00 | | | |

**KM# 108b 5 POUNDS**

39.94 g., 0.917 Gold 1.1775 oz. AGW, 38.61 mm. **Ruler:** Elizabeth II **Subject:** Queen's 75th Birthday **Obv:** Head with tiara right **Rev:** Queen's portrait in wreath **Edge:** Reeded

| Date | Mintage | VF20 | XF40 | MS60 | MS63 | MS65 |
|---|---|---|---|---|---|---|
| 2001 | 250 | PF65 2,150 | | | | |

**KM# 114 5 POUNDS**

28.28 g., Copper-Nickel, 38.6 mm. **Ruler:** Elizabeth II **Subject:** 19th Century Monarchy **Obv:** Head with tiara right **Rev:** Four portraits **Edge:** Reeded

| Date | Mintage | VF20 | XF40 | MS60 | MS63 | MS65 |
|---|---|---|---|---|---|---|
| 2001 | 5,700 | — | — | 8.00 | 10.00 | 12.50 |

**KM# 114a 5 POUNDS**

28.28 g., 0.925 Silver 0.841 oz. ASW, 38.6 mm. **Ruler:** Elizabeth II **Obv:** Head with tiara right **Rev:** Four portraits **Edge:** Reeded

| Date | Mintage | VF20 | XF40 | MS60 | MS63 | MS65 |
|---|---|---|---|---|---|---|
| 2001 | 10,000 | PF63 45.00 | PF65 55.00 | | | |

**KM# 114b 5 POUNDS**

39.94 g., 0.9166 Gold 1.177 oz. AGW, 38.6 mm. **Ruler:** Elizabeth II **Subject:** 19th Century Monarchy **Obv:** Head with tiara right **Rev:** Four royal portraits **Edge:** Reeded

| Date | Mintage | VF20 | XF40 | MS60 | MS63 | MS65 |
|---|---|---|---|---|---|---|
| 2001 | 200 | PF65 2,200 | | | | |

**KM# 119 5 POUNDS**
27.71 g., Copper-Nickel, 38.6 mm. **Ruler:** Elizabeth II **Subject:** The Golden Jubilee **Obv:** Head with tiara right **Rev:** The queen in her coach **Edge:** Reeded

| Date | Mintage | VF20 | XF40 | MS60 | MS63 | MS65 |
|---|---|---|---|---|---|---|
| 2002 | 9,250 | — | — | 13.00 | 16.50 | 18.00 |

**KM# 119a 5 POUNDS**
28.28 g., Base Metal Gilt Gold plated copper-nickel, 38.6 mm. **Ruler:** Elizabeth II **Subject:** Golden Jubilee **Obv:** Head with tiara right **Rev:** Queen in coach **Edge:** Reeded

| Date | Mintage | VF20 | XF40 | MS60 | MS63 | MS65 |
|---|---|---|---|---|---|---|
| 2002 | 50,000 | — | — | 12.00 | 15.00 | 16.50 |

**KM# 119c 5 POUNDS**
39.94 g., 0.9166 Gold 1.177 oz. AGW, 38.6 mm. **Ruler:** Elizabeth II **Subject:** Golden Jubilee **Obv:** Head with tiara right **Rev:** Queen in coach **Edge:** Reeded

| Date | Mintage | VF20 | XF40 | MS60 | MS63 | MS65 |
|---|---|---|---|---|---|---|
| 2002 | 250 | **PF65** 2,200 | | | | |

**KM# 119b 5 POUNDS**
28.28 g., 0.925 Silver 0.841 oz. ASW, 38.6 mm. **Ruler:** Elizabeth II **Subject:** Queen's Golden Jubilee **Obv:** Head with tiara right **Rev:** Queen in her coach **Edge:** Reeded **Note:** Prev. KM#119a.

| Date | Mintage | VF20 | XF40 | MS60 | MS63 | MS65 |
|---|---|---|---|---|---|---|
| 2002 | — | **PF63** 40.00 | **PF65** 50.00 | | | |

**KM# 121 5 POUNDS**
27.71 g., Copper-Nickel, 38.6 mm. **Ruler:** Elizabeth II **Subject:** Queen's Golden Jubilee **Obv:** Head with tiara right **Rev:** Trooping the Colors scene **Edge:** Reeded

| Date | Mintage | VF20 | XF40 | MS60 | MS63 | MS65 |
|---|---|---|---|---|---|---|
| 2002 | 2,000 | — | — | 15.00 | 17.50 | 20.00 |

**KM# 121a 5 POUNDS**
28.28 g., 0.925 Silver 0.841 oz. ASW, 38.6 mm. **Ruler:** Elizabeth II **Subject:** Queen's Golden Jubilee **Obv:** Head with tiara right **Rev:** Trooping the Colors scene **Edge:** Reeded

| Date | Mintage | VF20 | XF40 | MS60 | MS63 | MS65 |
|---|---|---|---|---|---|---|
| 2002 | — | **PF63** 40.00 | **PF65** 50.00 | | | |

**KM# 121b 5 POUNDS**
39.94 g., 0.9166 Gold 1.177 oz. AGW, 38.6 mm. **Ruler:** Elizabeth II **Subject:** Golden Jubilee **Obv:** Head with tiara right **Rev:** Trooping the Colors scene **Edge:** Reeded

| Date | Mintage | VF20 | XF40 | MS60 | MS63 | MS65 |
|---|---|---|---|---|---|---|
| 2002 | 250 | **PF65** 2,200 | | | | |

**KM# 122 5 POUNDS**
28.28 g., Copper-Nickel, 38.6 mm. **Ruler:** Elizabeth II **Subject:** Princess Diana **Obv:** Head with tiara right **Rev:** World and children behind cameo portrait of Diana **Edge:** Reeded

| Date | Mintage | VF20 | XF40 | MS60 | MS63 | MS65 |
|---|---|---|---|---|---|---|
| 2002 | 4,231 | — | — | 10.00 | 12.00 | 15.00 |

**KM# 122a 5 POUNDS**
28.28 g., 0.925 Silver 0.841 oz. ASW, 38.61 mm. **Ruler:** Elizabeth II **Subject:** Princess Diana **Obv:** Head with tiara right **Rev:** World and children behind Diana's cameo portrait **Edge:** Reeded

| Date | Mintage | VF20 | XF40 | MS60 | MS63 | MS65 |
|---|---|---|---|---|---|---|
| 2002 | 20,000 | **PF63** 35.00 | **PF65** 45.00 | | | |

**KM# 122b 5 POUNDS**
39.94 g., 0.9167 Gold 1.1771 oz. AGW, 38.61 mm. **Ruler:** Elizabeth II **Subject:** Princess Diana **Obv:** Head with tiara right **Rev:** World and children behind Diana's cameo portrait **Edge:** Reeded

| Date | Mintage | VF20 | XF40 | MS60 | MS63 | MS65 |
|---|---|---|---|---|---|---|
| 2002 | 100 | **PF65** 2,250 | | | | |

**KM# 124 5 POUNDS**
28.28 g., Copper-Nickel, 38.6 mm. **Ruler:** Elizabeth II **Subject:** 18th Century British Monarchy **Obv:** Head with tiara right **Rev:** Five royal portraits **Edge:** Reeded

| Date | Mintage | VF20 | XF40 | MS60 | MS63 | MS65 |
|---|---|---|---|---|---|---|
| 2002 | 1,300 | — | — | 12.00 | 15.00 | 16.50 |

**KM# 124a 5 POUNDS**
28.28 g., 0.925 Silver 0.841 oz. ASW, 38.6 mm. **Ruler:** Elizabeth II **Subject:** 18th Century British Monarchy **Obv:** Head with tiara right **Rev:** Five royal portraits **Edge:** Reeded

| Date | Mintage | VF20 | XF40 | MS60 | MS63 | MS65 |
|---|---|---|---|---|---|---|
| 2002 | 10,000 | **PF63** 40.00 | **PF65** 50.00 | | | |

**KM# 124b 5 POUNDS**
39.94 g., 0.9166 Gold 1.177 oz. AGW, 38.6 mm. **Ruler:** Elizabeth II **Subject:** 18th Century British Monarchy **Obv:** Head with tiara right **Rev:** Five royal portraits **Edge:** Reeded

| Date | Mintage | VF20 | XF40 | MS60 | MS63 | MS65 |
|---|---|---|---|---|---|---|
| 2002 | 200 | **PF65** 2,200 | | | | |

**KM# 127 5 POUNDS**
28.28 g., Copper-Nickel, 38.6 mm. **Ruler:** Elizabeth II **Subject:** Queen Mother **Obv:** Head with tiara right **Rev:** The late Queen Mother's portrait **Edge:** Reeded

| Date | Mintage | VF20 | XF40 | MS60 | MS63 | MS65 |
|---|---|---|---|---|---|---|
| 2002 | 1,750 | — | — | 12.00 | 15.00 | 16.50 |
| 2002 | 1,680 | **PF63** 18.00 | **PF65** 20.00 | | | |

**KM# 127a 5 POUNDS**
28.28 g., 0.925 Silver 0.841 oz. ASW, 38.6 mm. **Ruler:** Elizabeth II **Subject:** Queen Mother **Obv:** Head with tiara right **Rev:** The late Queen Mother's portrait **Edge:** Reeded

| Date | Mintage | VF20 | XF40 | MS60 | MS63 | MS65 |
|---|---|---|---|---|---|---|
| 2002 | 15,000 | **PF63** 40.00 | **PF65** 50.00 | | | |

**KM# 127b 5 POUNDS**
39.94 g., 0.9166 Gold 1.177 oz. AGW, 38.6 mm. **Ruler:** Elizabeth II **Subject:** Queen Mother **Obv:** Head with tiara right **Rev:** Queen Mother's portrait **Edge:** Reeded

| Date | Mintage | VF20 | XF40 | MS60 | MS63 | MS65 |
|---|---|---|---|---|---|---|
| 2002 | 250 | **PF65** 2,200 | | | | |

**KM# 129 5 POUNDS**
28.28 g., Copper-Nickel, 38.6 mm. **Ruler:** Elizabeth II **Subject:** The Duke of Wellington **Obv:** Head with tiara right **Rev:** Portrait with mounted dragoons in background **Edge:** Reeded

| Date | Mintage | VF20 | XF40 | MS60 | MS63 | MS65 |
|---|---|---|---|---|---|---|
| 2002 | 675 | — | — | 20.00 | 22.50 | 25.00 |

**KM# 129a 5 POUNDS**
28.28 g., 0.925 Silver 0.841 oz. ASW, 38.6 mm. **Ruler:** Elizabeth II **Subject:** The Duke of Wellington **Obv:** Head with tiara right **Rev:** Portrait with multicolor mounted dragoons in background **Edge:** Reeded

| Date | Mintage | VF20 | XF40 | MS60 | MS63 | MS65 |
|---|---|---|---|---|---|---|
| 2002 | 15,000 | **PF63** 40.00 | **PF65** 50.00 | | | |

**KM# 129b 5 POUNDS**
39.94 g., 0.9166 Gold 1.177 oz. AGW, 38.6 mm. **Ruler:** Elizabeth II **Subject:** Duke of Wellington **Obv:** Head with tiara right **Rev:** Wellington's portrait with multicolor cavalry scene **Edge:** Reeded

| Date | Mintage | VF20 | XF40 | MS60 | MS63 | MS65 |
|---|---|---|---|---|---|---|
| 2002 | 200 | **PF65** 2,200 | | | | |

**KM# 143 5 POUNDS**
28.28 g., Copper-Nickel, 38.6 mm. **Ruler:** Elizabeth II **Obv:** Head with tiara right **Rev:** Prince William wearing sweater **Edge:** Reeded

| Date | Mintage | VF20 | XF40 | MS60 | MS63 | MS65 |
|---|---|---|---|---|---|---|
| 2003 | 3,700 | — | — | 15.00 | 17.50 | 20.00 |

**KM# 143a 5 POUNDS**
28.28 g., 0.925 Silver 0.841 oz. ASW, 38.6 mm. **Ruler:** Elizabeth II **Obv:** Head with tiara right **Rev:** Prince William wearing sweater **Edge:** Reeded

| Date | Mintage | VF20 | XF40 | MS60 | MS63 | MS65 |
|---|---|---|---|---|---|---|
| 2003 | 5,000 | **PF63** 40.00 | **PF65** 50.00 | | | |

**KM# 143b 5 POUNDS**
39.94 g., 0.9166 Gold 1.177 oz. AGW, 38.6 mm. **Ruler:** Elizabeth II **Obv:** Head with tiara right **Rev:** Prince William wearing sweater **Edge:** Reeded

| Date | Mintage | VF20 | XF40 | MS60 | MS63 | MS65 |
|---|---|---|---|---|---|---|
| 2003 | 200 | **PF65** 2,200 | | | | |

### KM# 158 5 POUNDS

28.28 g., Copper-Nickel, 38.7 mm. **Ruler:** Elizabeth II **Subject:** Golden Hind **Obv:** Head with tiara right **Rev:** The Golden Hind ship **Edge:** Reeded

| Date | Mintage | VF20 | XF40 | MS60 | MS63 | MS65 |
|---|---|---|---|---|---|---|
| 2003 | 300 | — | — | — | — | 25.00 |

### KM# 159 5 POUNDS

Copper-Nickel **Ruler:** Elizabeth II **Subject:** 17th Century Monarchs **Obv:** Head with tiara right

| Date | Mintage | VF20 | XF40 | MS60 | MS63 | MS65 |
|---|---|---|---|---|---|---|
| 2003 | 500 | — | — | — | — | 22.50 |

### KM# 160 5 POUNDS

Copper-Nickel **Ruler:** Elizabeth II **Subject:** Royal Navy - H. Nelson **Obv:** Head with tiara right

| Date | Mintage | VF20 | XF40 | MS60 | MS63 | MS65 |
|---|---|---|---|---|---|---|
| 2003 | 550 | — | — | — | — | 22.50 |

### KM# 160a 5 POUNDS

28.32 g., Nickel-Brass, 38 mm. **Ruler:** Elizabeth II **Subject:** History of the Royal Navy **Rev:** Two naval vessels and Horatio Nelson, flag in color

| Date | Mintage | VF20 | XF40 | MS60 | MS63 | MS65 |
|---|---|---|---|---|---|---|
| 2003 | — | PF63 35.00 | PF65 40.00 | | | |

### KM# 160b 5 POUNDS

39.94 g., 0.917 Gold 1.1775 oz. AGW, 38.61 mm. **Ruler:** Elizabeth II **Subject:** History of the Navy - Horatio Nelson

| Date | Mintage | VF20 | XF40 | MS60 | MS63 | MS65 |
|---|---|---|---|---|---|---|
| 2003 | — | PF65 2,150 | | | | |

### KM# 130 5 POUNDS

28.28 g., Copper-Nickel, 38.61 mm. **Ruler:** Elizabeth II **Subject:** Steam Locomotives **Rev:** Tower switchman at leavers

| Date | Mintage | VF20 | XF40 | MS60 | MS63 | MS65 |
|---|---|---|---|---|---|---|
| 2004 | — | — | — | — | — | 25.00 |

### KM# 130a 5 POUNDS

28.28 g., 0.925 Silver 0.841 oz. ASW, 38.61 mm. **Ruler:** Elizabeth II **Subject:** Steam Locomotives **Rev:** Tower switchman at leavers

| Date | Mintage | VF20 | XF40 | MS60 | MS63 | MS65 |
|---|---|---|---|---|---|---|
| 2004 | Est. 10000 | PF63 50.00 | PF65 60.00 | | | |

### KM# 133 5 POUNDS

28.28 g., Copper-Nickel, 38.61 mm. **Ruler:** Elizabeth II **Subject:** Steam Locomotives **Rev:** Two locomotives side-by-side view of tender being refilled with water, and fireman shoveling coal

| Date | Mintage | VF20 | XF40 | MS60 | MS63 | MS65 |
|---|---|---|---|---|---|---|
| 2004 | — | — | — | — | — | 25.00 |

### KM# 133a 5 POUNDS

28.28 g., 0.925 Silver 0.841 oz. ASW, 38.61 mm. **Ruler:** Elizabeth II **Subject:** Steam Locomotives **Rev:** Two locomotives side-by-side view of tender being refilled with water, and fireman shoveling coal

| Date | Mintage | VF20 | XF40 | MS60 | MS63 | MS65 |
|---|---|---|---|---|---|---|
| 2004 | Est. 10000 | PF63 50.00 | PF65 60.00 | | | |

### KM# 150 5 POUNDS

28.28 g., Copper-Nickel, 38.6 mm. **Ruler:** Elizabeth II **Subject:** D-Day **Obv:** Head with tiara right **Rev:** British troops storming ashore **Edge:** Reeded

| Date | Mintage | VF20 | XF40 | MS60 | MS63 | MS65 |
|---|---|---|---|---|---|---|
| 2004 | 65,611 | — | — | 12.00 | 15.00 | 16.50 |

### KM# 154 5 POUNDS

28.28 g., 0.925 Silver 0.841 oz. ASW, 38.6 mm. **Ruler:** Elizabeth II **Subject:** D-Day **Obv:** Head with tiara right **Rev:** British soldier advancing to left **Edge:** Reeded

| Date | Mintage | VF20 | XF40 | MS60 | MS63 | MS65 |
|---|---|---|---|---|---|---|
| 2004 | 10,000 | PF63 75.00 | PF65 85.00 | | | |

### KM# 154a 5 POUNDS

39.94 g., 0.9167 Gold 1.1771 oz. AGW, 38.6 mm. **Ruler:** Elizabeth II **Subject:** D-Day **Obv:** Head with tiara right **Rev:** British soldier advancing to left **Edge:** Reeded

| Date | Mintage | VF20 | XF40 | MS60 | MS63 | MS65 |
|---|---|---|---|---|---|---|
| 2004 | 500 | PF65 2,100 | | | | |

### KM# 155 5 POUNDS

28.28 g., Copper-Nickel, 38.6 mm. **Ruler:** Elizabeth II **Subject:** 150th Anniversary of the Crimean War **Obv:** Head with tiara right **Rev:** Sgt. Luke O'Connor , first army Victoria Cross winner, above Battle of Alma scene with multicolor flag **Edge:** Reeded

| Date | Mintage | VF20 | XF40 | MS60 | MS63 | MS65 |
|---|---|---|---|---|---|---|
| 2004 plain | — | — | — | — | 25.00 | 27.50 |
| 2004 partial color | 1,060 | — | — | — | 25.00 | 27.50 |

### KM# 155a 5 POUNDS

28.28 g., 0.925 Silver 0.841 oz. ASW, 38.6 mm. **Ruler:** Elizabeth II **Obv:** Head with tiara right **Rev:** Sgt. Luke O'Conner, first army Victoria Cross winner, above Battle of Alma scene with multicolor flag **Edge:** Reeded

| Date | Mintage | VF20 | XF40 | MS60 | MS63 | MS65 |
|---|---|---|---|---|---|---|
| 2004 | 10,000 | PF63 75.00 | PF65 85.00 | | | |

### KM# 155b 5 POUNDS

39.94 g., 0.9166 Gold 1.177 oz. AGW, 38.6 mm. **Ruler:** Elizabeth II **Obv:** Head with tiara right **Rev:** Sgt. Luke O'Connor, first army Victoria Cross winner, above Battle of Alma scene with multicolor flag **Edge:** Reeded

| Date | Mintage | VF20 | XF40 | MS60 | MS63 | MS65 |
|---|---|---|---|---|---|---|
| 2004 | 500 | PF65 2,100 | | | | |

### KM# 161 5 POUNDS

Copper-Nickel **Ruler:** Elizabeth II **Subject:** 16th Century Monarchs **Obv:** Head with tiara right

| Date | Mintage | VF20 | XF40 | MS60 | MS63 | MS65 |
|---|---|---|---|---|---|---|
| 2004 | 500 | — | — | — | — | 22.50 |

### KM# 162 5 POUNDS

Copper-Nickel **Ruler:** Elizabeth II **Subject:** Mallard Locomotive **Obv:** Head with tiara right

| Date | Mintage | VF20 | XF40 | MS60 | MS63 | MS65 |
|---|---|---|---|---|---|---|
| 2004 | 2,193 | — | — | — | — | 17.50 |

### KM# 163 5 POUNDS

Copper-Nickel **Ruler:** Elizabeth II **Subject:** City of Truro Train **Obv:** Head with tiara right

| Date | Mintage | VF20 | XF40 | MS60 | MS63 | MS65 |
|---|---|---|---|---|---|---|
| 2004 | 500 | — | — | — | — | 22.50 |

### KM# 164 5 POUNDS

Copper-Nickel **Ruler:** Elizabeth II **Subject:** The Boat Train **Obv:** Head with tiara right

| Date | Mintage | VF20 | XF40 | MS60 | MS63 | MS65 |
|---|---|---|---|---|---|---|
| 2004 | 250 | — | — | — | — | 25.00 |

### KM# 165 5 POUNDS

Copper-Nickel **Ruler:** Elizabeth II **Subject:** Train Spotter **Obv:** Head with tiara right

| Date | Mintage | VF20 | XF40 | MS60 | MS63 | MS65 |
|---|---|---|---|---|---|---|
| 2004 | 300 | — | — | — | — | 25.00 |

### KM# 166 5 POUNDS

Copper-Nickel **Ruler:** Elizabeth II **Subject:** Royal Navy - Henry VIII **Obv:** Head with tiara right

| Date | Mintage | VF20 | XF40 | MS60 | MS63 | MS65 |
|---|---|---|---|---|---|---|
| 2004 | 300 | — | — | — | — | 25.00 |

### KM# 167 5 POUNDS

Copper-Nickel **Ruler:** Elizabeth II **Subject:** Royal Navy - Invincible **Obv:** Head with tiara right

| Date | Mintage | VF20 | XF40 | MS60 | MS63 | MS65 |
|---|---|---|---|---|---|---|
| 2004 | 300 | — | — | — | — | 25.00 |

### KM# 176 5 POUNDS

28.32 g., Silver, 38 mm. **Ruler:** Elizabeth II **Subject:** History of the Royal Navy **Rev:** HMS Invincible, flag in color

| Date | Mintage | VF20 | XF40 | MS60 | MS63 | MS65 |
|---|---|---|---|---|---|---|
| 2004 | — | PF63 45.00 | PF65 50.00 | | | |

### KM# 168a 5 POUNDS

28.28 g., 0.925 Silver 0.841 oz. ASW, 38.6 mm. **Ruler:** Elizabeth II **Subject:** End of WWII **Obv:** Head with tiara right **Rev:** Churchill and George VI **Edge:** Reeded

| Date | Mintage | VF20 | XF40 | MS60 | MS63 | MS65 |
|---|---|---|---|---|---|---|
| 2005 | 5,000 | PF63 75.00 | PF65 85.00 | | | |

### KM# 168b 5 POUNDS

39.94 g., 0.9167 Gold 1.1771 oz. AGW, 38.6 mm. **Ruler:** Elizabeth II **Subject:** End of WWII **Obv:** Head with tiara right **Rev:** Churchill and George VI **Edge:** Reeded

| Date | Mintage | VF20 | XF40 | MS60 | MS63 | MS65 |
|---|---|---|---|---|---|---|
| 2005 | 150 | PF65 2,250 | | | | |

**KM# 169a 5 POUNDS**
39.94 g., 0.9167 Gold 1.1771 oz. AGW, 38.6 mm. **Ruler:** Elizabeth II **Subject:** WWII Liberation **Obv:** Head with tiara right **Rev:** Soldiers and waving crowd **Edge:** Reeded

| Date | Mintage | VF20 | XF40 | MS60 | MS63 | MS65 |
|---|---|---|---|---|---|---|
| 2005 | 150 | PF65 2,250 | | | | |

**KM# 186 5 POUNDS**
28.28 g., Copper-Nickel, 38.61 mm. **Ruler:** Elizabeth II **Subject:** Royal Navy - Sir John Jellicoe

| Date | Mintage | VF20 | XF40 | MS60 | MS63 | MS65 |
|---|---|---|---|---|---|---|
| 2005 | — | — | — | — | — | 17.50 |

**KM# 186a 5 POUNDS**
28.28 g., 0.925 Silver 0.841 oz. ASW, 38.61 mm. **Ruler:** Elizabeth II **Subject:** Royal Navy - Sir John Jellicoe **Rev:** Flag in color

| Date | Mintage | VF20 | XF40 | MS60 | MS63 | MS65 |
|---|---|---|---|---|---|---|
| 2005 | Est. 15000 | PF63 50.00 | PF65 60.00 | | | |

**KM# 187 5 POUNDS**
28.28 g., Copper-Nickel, 38.61 mm. **Ruler:** Elizabeth II **Subject:** Royal Navy **Rev:** H.M.S. Ark Royal

| Date | Mintage | VF20 | XF40 | MS60 | MS63 | MS65 |
|---|---|---|---|---|---|---|
| 2005 | — | — | — | — | — | 17.50 |

**KM# 187a 5 POUNDS**
28.28 g., 0.925 Silver 0.841 oz. ASW, 38.61 mm. **Ruler:** Elizabeth II **Subject:** Royal Navy **Rev:** H.M.S. Ark Royal, flag in color

| Date | Mintage | VF20 | XF40 | MS60 | MS63 | MS65 |
|---|---|---|---|---|---|---|
| 2005 | Est. 15000 | PF63 50.00 | PF65 60.00 | | | |

**KM# 189 5 POUNDS**
28.28 g., Copper-Nickel, 38.61 mm. **Ruler:** Elizabeth II **Subject:** Battle of Trafalgar, 200th Anniversary **Rev:** H.M.S. Victory

| Date | Mintage | VF20 | XF40 | MS60 | MS63 | MS65 |
|---|---|---|---|---|---|---|
| 2005 | — | — | — | — | — | 17.50 |

**KM# 189a 5 POUNDS**
28.28 g., 0.925 Silver 0.841 oz. ASW, 38.61 mm. **Ruler:** Elizabeth II **Subject:** Battle of Trafalgar, 200th Anniversary **Rev:** H.M.S. Victory

| Date | Mintage | VF20 | XF40 | MS60 | MS63 | MS65 |
|---|---|---|---|---|---|---|
| 2005 | — | PF63 50.00 | PF65 60.00 | | | |

**KM# 189b 5 POUNDS**
39.94 g., 0.917 Gold 1.1775 oz. AGW, 38.61 mm. **Ruler:** Elizabeth II **Subject:** Battle of Trafalgar, 200th Anniversary **Rev:** H.M.S. Victory

| Date | Mintage | VF20 | XF40 | MS60 | MS63 | MS65 |
|---|---|---|---|---|---|---|
| 2005 | — | PF65 2,250 | | | | |

**KM# 130b 5 POUNDS**
28.28 g., 0.925 Silver 0.841 oz. ASW selectively gilt, 38.61 mm. **Ruler:** Elizabeth II **Subject:** Steam Locomotives **Rev:** Tower Switchmen at leavers

| Date | Mintage | VF20 | XF40 | MS60 | MS63 | MS65 |
|---|---|---|---|---|---|---|
| 2006 | 25,000 | PF63 50.00 | PF65 60.00 | | | |

**KM# 133b 5 POUNDS**
28.28 g., 0.925 Silver 0.841 oz. ASW partially gilt, 38.61 mm. **Ruler:** Elizabeth II **Subject:** Steam Locomotives **Rev:** Two locomotives side-by-side view of tender being refilled with water, and fireman shoveling coal

| Date | Mintage | VF20 | XF40 | MS60 | MS63 | MS65 |
|---|---|---|---|---|---|---|
| 2006 | Est. 25000 | PF63 50.00 | PF65 60.00 | | | |

**KM# 170 5 POUNDS**
28.28 g., 0.925 Silver 0.841 oz. ASW, 38.6 mm. **Ruler:** Elizabeth II **Subject:** Queen's 80th Birthday **Obv:** Head with tiara right - gilt **Obv. Legend:** ELIZABETH II BAILIWICK OF GUERNSEY **Rev:** Bust at left looking upwards, tower and florals at upper right

| Date | Mintage | VF20 | XF40 | MS60 | MS63 | MS65 |
|---|---|---|---|---|---|---|
| 2006 | — | PF63 40.00 | PF65 45.00 | | | |

**KM# 173 5 POUNDS**
28.28 g., 0.925 Silver 0.841 oz. ASW, 22 mm. **Ruler:** Elizabeth II **Subject:** FIFA - XVIII World Football Championship - Germany 2006 **Rev:** Wembley Stadium

| Date | Mintage | VF20 | XF40 | MS60 | MS63 | MS65 |
|---|---|---|---|---|---|---|
| 2006 | 50,000 | PF63 55.00 | PF65 65.00 | | | |

**KM# 191 5 POUNDS**
28.28 g., Copper-Nickel, 38.61 mm. **Ruler:** Elizabeth II **Rev:** Horatio Nelson

| Date | Mintage | VF20 | XF40 | MS60 | MS63 | MS65 |
|---|---|---|---|---|---|---|
| 2006 | — | — | — | — | — | 15.00 |

**KM# 191a 5 POUNDS**
28.28 g., 0.925 Silver 0.841 oz. ASW, 38.61 mm. **Ruler:** Elizabeth II **Rev:** Horatio Nelson

| Date | Mintage | VF20 | XF40 | MS60 | MS63 | MS65 |
|---|---|---|---|---|---|---|
| 2006 | 25,000 | PF63 50.00 | PF65 60.00 | | | |

**KM# 192 5 POUNDS**
28.28 g., Copper-Nickel, 38.61 mm. **Ruler:** Elizabeth II **Rev:** Isambard Kingdom Brunel

| Date | Mintage | VF20 | XF40 | MS60 | MS63 | MS65 |
|---|---|---|---|---|---|---|
| 2006 | — | — | — | — | — | 15.00 |

**KM# 192a 5 POUNDS**
28.28 g., 0.925 Silver 0.841 oz. ASW, 38.61 mm. **Ruler:** Elizabeth II **Rev:** Isambard Kingdom Brunel

| Date | Mintage | VF20 | XF40 | MS60 | MS63 | MS65 |
|---|---|---|---|---|---|---|
| 2006 | 25,000 | PF63 50.00 | PF65 60.00 | | | |

**KM# 193 5 POUNDS**
28.28 g., 0.925 Silver 0.841 oz. ASW, 38.61 mm. **Ruler:** Elizabeth II **Rev:** Robert Falcon Scott

| Date | Mintage | VF20 | XF40 | MS60 | MS63 | MS65 |
|---|---|---|---|---|---|---|
| 2006 | 25,000 | PF63 50.00 | PF65 60.00 | | | |

**KM# 194 5 POUNDS**
28.28 g., 0.925 Silver 0.841 oz. ASW, 38.61 mm. **Ruler:** Elizabeth II **Rev:** Queen Victoria

| Date | Mintage | VF20 | XF40 | MS60 | MS63 | MS65 |
|---|---|---|---|---|---|---|
| 2006 | 25,000 | PF63 50.00 | PF65 60.00 | | | |

**KM# 195 5 POUNDS**
28.28 g., Copper-Nickel, 38.61 mm. **Ruler:** Elizabeth II **Subject:** Elizabeth II, 80th Birthday **Rev:** Elizabeth II and Queen Mother

| Date | Mintage | VF20 | XF40 | MS60 | MS63 | MS65 |
|---|---|---|---|---|---|---|
| 2006 | — | — | — | — | — | 15.00 |

**KM# 195a 5 POUNDS**
28.28 g., 0.925 Silver 0.841 oz. ASW partially gilt, 38.61 mm. **Ruler:** Elizabeth II **Subject:** Elizabeth II, 80th Birthday **Rev:** Elizabeth II and Queen Mother, gilt

| Date | Mintage | VF20 | XF40 | MS60 | MS63 | MS65 |
|---|---|---|---|---|---|---|
| 2006 | 25,000 | PF63 50.00 | PF65 60.00 | | | |

**KM# 196 5 POUNDS**
28.28 g., 0.925 Silver 0.841 oz. ASW, 38.61 mm. **Ruler:** Elizabeth II **Subject:** Elizabeth II, 80th Birthday **Rev:** Elizabeth II portrait by Mary Gillick

| Date | Mintage | VF20 | XF40 | MS60 | MS63 | MS65 |
|---|---|---|---|---|---|---|
| 2006 | — | PF63 50.00 | PF65 60.00 | | | |

**KM# 196a 5 POUNDS**
39.94 g., 0.917 Gold 1.1775 oz. AGW, 8.61 mm. **Ruler:** Elizabeth II **Subject:** Elizabeth II, 80th Birthday **Rev:** Elizabeth II portrait by Mary Gillick

| Date | Mintage | VF20 | XF40 | MS60 | MS63 | MS65 |
|---|---|---|---|---|---|---|
| 2006 | — | PF65 2,250 | | | | |

**KM# 197 5 POUNDS**
28.28 g., Copper-Nickel, 38.61 mm. **Ruler:** Elizabeth II **Subject:** Victoria Cross, 150th Anniversary **Rev:** Herbert Wallace le Patourel

| Date | Mintage | VF20 | XF40 | MS60 | MS63 | MS65 |
|---|---|---|---|---|---|---|
| 2006 | — | — | — | — | — | 15.00 |

**KM# 197a 5 POUNDS**
28.28 g., 0.925 Silver 0.841 oz. ASW, 38.61 mm. **Ruler:** Elizabeth II **Subject:** Victoria Cross, 150th Anniversary **Rev:** Herbert Wallace le Patourel

| Date | Mintage | VF20 | XF40 | MS60 | MS63 | MS65 |
|---|---|---|---|---|---|---|
| 2006 | Est. 30000 | PF63 50.00 | PF65 60.00 | | | |

**KM# 198 5 POUNDS**
28.28 g., 0.925 Silver 0.841 oz. ASW, 38.61 mm. **Ruler:** Elizabeth II **Subject:** Victoria Cross, 150th Anniversary **Rev:** Victor Buller Turner

| Date | Mintage | VF20 | XF40 | MS60 | MS63 | MS65 |
|---|---|---|---|---|---|---|
| 2006 | Est. 30000 | PF63 50.00 | PF65 60.00 | | | |

**KM# 199 5 POUNDS**
28.28 g., 0.925 Silver 0.841 oz. ASW, 38.61 mm. **Ruler:** Elizabeth II **Subject:** Victoria Cross, 150th Anniversary **Rev:** William Leefe Robinson

| Date | Mintage | VF20 | XF40 | MS60 | MS63 | MS65 |
|---|---|---|---|---|---|---|
| 2006 | 30,000 | PF63 50.00 | PF65 60.00 | | | |

**KM# 200 5 POUNDS**
28.28 g., 0.925 Silver 0.841 oz. ASW, 38.61 mm. **Ruler:** Elizabeth II **Subject:** Victoria Cross, 150th Anniversary **Rev:** Gerard Roope

| Date | Mintage | VF20 | XF40 | MS60 | MS63 | MS65 |
|---|---|---|---|---|---|---|
| 2006 | Est. 30000 | PF63 50.00 | PF65 60.00 | | | |

**KM# 201 5 POUNDS**
28.28 g., 0.925 Silver 0.841 oz. ASW, 38.61 mm. **Ruler:** Elizabeth II **Subject:** Victoria Cross, 150th Anniversary **Rev:** Robert Henry Cain

| Date | Mintage | VF20 | XF40 | MS60 | MS63 | MS65 |
|---|---|---|---|---|---|---|
| 2006 | Est. 30000 | PF63 50.00 | PF65 60.00 | | | |

**KM# 202 5 POUNDS**
28.28 g., 0.925 Silver 0.841 oz. ASW, 38.61 mm. **Ruler:** Elizabeth II **Subject:** Victoria Cross, 150th Anniversary **Rev:** Eugene Esmonde

| Date | Mintage | VF20 | XF40 | MS60 | MS63 | MS65 |
|---|---|---|---|---|---|---|
| 2006 | Est. 30000 | PF63 50.00 | PF65 60.00 | | | |

**KM# 203 5 POUNDS**
28.28 g., 0.925 Silver 0.841 oz. ASW, 38.61 mm. **Ruler:** Elizabeth II **Rev:** Sir Alexander Fleming

| Date | Mintage | VF20 | XF40 | MS60 | MS63 | MS65 |
|---|---|---|---|---|---|---|
| 2007 | 25,000 | PF63 45.00 | PF65 55.00 | | | |

**KM# 204 5 POUNDS**
28.28 g., 0.925 Silver 0.841 oz. ASW, 38.61 mm. **Ruler:** Elizabeth II **Rev:** Montgomery

| Date | Mintage | VF20 | XF40 | MS60 | MS63 | MS65 |
|---|---|---|---|---|---|---|
| 2007 | Est. 25000 | PF63 45.00 | PF65 55.00 | | | |

**KM# 205 5 POUNDS**
28.28 g., 0.925 Silver 0.841 oz. ASW, 38.61 mm. **Ruler:** Elizabeth II **Rev:** Oliver Cromwell

| Date | Mintage | VF20 | XF40 | MS60 | MS63 | MS65 |
|---|---|---|---|---|---|---|
| 2007 | Est. 25000 | PF63 45.00 | PF65 55.00 | | | |

**KM# 206 5 POUNDS**
28.28 g., 0.925 Silver 0.841 oz. ASW, 38.61 mm. **Ruler:** Elizabeth II **Rev:** Alexander Graham Bell

| Date | Mintage | VF20 | XF40 | MS60 | MS63 | MS65 |
|---|---|---|---|---|---|---|
| 2007 | — | PF63 45.00 | PF65 55.00 | | | |

**KM# 207 5 POUNDS**
28.28 g., Copper-Nickel, 38.61 mm. **Ruler:** Elizabeth II **Subject:** Elizabeth II and Prince Philip, 60th Wedding Anniversary **Rev:** Busts

| Date | Mintage | VF20 | XF40 | MS60 | MS63 | MS65 |
|---|---|---|---|---|---|---|
| 2007 | — | — | — | — | — | 15.00 |

**KM# 207a 5 POUNDS**
28.28 g., 0.925 Silver 0.841 oz. ASW, 38.61 mm. **Ruler:** Elizabeth II **Subject:** Elizabeth II and Prince Philip, 60th Wedding Anniversary **Rev:** Busts

| Date | Mintage | VF20 | XF40 | MS60 | MS63 | MS65 |
|---|---|---|---|---|---|---|
| 2007 | — | PF63 45.00 | PF65 55.00 | | | |

**KM# 208 5 POUNDS**
28.28 g., Copper-Nickel, 38.61 mm. **Ruler:** Elizabeth II **Subject:** Elizabeth II and Prince Philip, 60th Wedding Anniversary **Rev:** Honeymoon

| Date | Mintage | VF20 | XF40 | MS60 | MS63 | MS65 |
|---|---|---|---|---|---|---|
| 2007 | — | — | — | — | — | 15.00 |

**KM# 208a 5 POUNDS**
28.28 g., 0.925 Silver 0.841 oz. ASW, 38.61 mm. **Ruler:** Elizabeth II **Subject:** Elizabeth II and Prince Philip, 60th Wedding Anniversary **Rev:** Honeymoon

| Date | Mintage | VF20 | XF40 | MS60 | MS63 | MS65 |
|---|---|---|---|---|---|---|
| 2007 | — | PF63 45.00 | PF65 55.00 | | | |

### KM# 209 5 POUNDS

28.28 g., Copper-Nickel, 38.61 mm. **Ruler:** Elizabeth II **Subject:** Elizabeth II and Prince Philip, 60th Wedding Anniversary **Rev:** Bouquet

| Date | Mintage | VF20 | XF40 | MS60 | MS63 | MS65 |
|---|---|---|---|---|---|---|
| 2007 | — | — | — | — | — | 15.00 |

### KM# 209a 5 POUNDS

28.28 g., 0.925 Silver 0.841 oz. ASW, 38.61 mm. **Ruler:** Elizabeth II **Subject:** Elizabeth II and Prince Philip, 60th Wedding Anniversary **Rev:** Bouquet

| Date | Mintage | VF20 | XF40 | MS60 | MS63 | MS65 |
|---|---|---|---|---|---|---|
| 2007 | — | PF63 45.00 | PF65 55.00 | | | |

### KM# 210 5 POUNDS

28.28 g., 0.925 Copper-Nickel 0.841 oz., 38.61 mm. **Ruler:** Elizabeth II **Subject:** Elizabeth II and Prince Philip, 60th Wedding Anniversary **Rev:** Wedding scene

| Date | Mintage | VF20 | XF40 | MS60 | MS63 | MS65 |
|---|---|---|---|---|---|---|
| 2007 | — | — | — | — | — | 15.00 |

### KM# 210a 5 POUNDS

28.28 g., 0.925 Silver 0.841 oz. ASW, 38.61 mm. **Ruler:** Elizabeth II **Subject:** Elizabeth II and Prince Philip, 60th Wedding Anniversary **Rev:** Wedding scene

| Date | Mintage | VF20 | XF40 | MS60 | MS63 | MS65 |
|---|---|---|---|---|---|---|
| 2007 | — | PF63 45.00 | PF65 55.00 | | | |

### KM# 179 5 POUNDS

28.28 g., Copper-Nickel, 38.61 mm. **Ruler:** Elizabeth II **Subject:** Royal Air Force, 90th Anniversary **Obv:** Head with tiara right **Rev:** Air battle

| Date | Mintage | VF20 | XF40 | MS60 | MS63 | MS65 |
|---|---|---|---|---|---|---|
| 2008 | — | — | — | — | — | 15.00 |

### KM# 179a 5 POUNDS

28.28 g., 0.925 Silver 0.841 oz. ASW, 38.61 mm. **Ruler:** Elizabeth II **Subject:** Royal Air Force, 90th Anniversary **Rev:** Air battle

| Date | Mintage | VF20 | XF40 | MS60 | MS63 | MS65 |
|---|---|---|---|---|---|---|
| 2008 | Est. 25000 | PF63 45.00 | PF65 55.00 | | | |

### KM# 211 5 POUNDS

28.28 g., Copper-Nickel, 38.61 mm. **Ruler:** Elizabeth II **Subject:** Royal Air Force, 90th Anniversary **Rev:** Lancaster bomber

| Date | Mintage | VF20 | XF40 | MS60 | MS63 | MS65 |
|---|---|---|---|---|---|---|
| 2008 | — | — | — | — | — | 15.00 |

### KM# 211a 5 POUNDS

28.28 g., 0.925 Silver 0.841 oz. ASW, 38.61 mm. **Ruler:** Elizabeth II **Subject:** Royal Air Force, 90th Anniversary **Rev:** Lancaster bomber

| Date | Mintage | VF20 | XF40 | MS60 | MS63 | MS65 |
|---|---|---|---|---|---|---|
| 2008 | Est. 25000 | PF63 45.00 | PF65 55.00 | | | |

### KM# 212 5 POUNDS

28.28 g., 0.925 Silver 0.841 oz. ASW, 38.61 mm. **Ruler:** Elizabeth II **Subject:** Royal Air Force, 90th Anniversary **Rev:** Founding of the Air Force, 1918

| Date | Mintage | VF20 | XF40 | MS60 | MS63 | MS65 |
|---|---|---|---|---|---|---|
| 2008 | Est. 25000 | PF63 45.00 | PF65 55.00 | | | |

### KM# 213 5 POUNDS

28.28 g., 0.925 Silver 0.841 oz. ASW, 38.61 mm. **Ruler:** Elizabeth II **Subject:** Royal Air Force, 90th Anniversary **Rev:** Berlin Airlift, 1949

| Date | Mintage | VF20 | XF40 | MS60 | MS63 | MS65 |
|---|---|---|---|---|---|---|
| 2008 | Est. 25000 | PF63 45.00 | PF65 55.00 | | | |

### KM# 214 5 POUNDS

28.28 g., 0.925 Silver 0.841 oz. ASW, 38.61 mm. **Ruler:** Elizabeth II **Subject:** Royal Air Force, 90th Anniversary **Rev:** Monarchy

| Date | Mintage | VF20 | XF40 | MS60 | MS63 | MS65 |
|---|---|---|---|---|---|---|
| 2008 | Est. 25000 | PF63 45.00 | PF65 55.00 | | | |

### KM# 215 5 POUNDS

28.28 g., 0.925 Silver 0.841 oz. ASW, 38.61 mm. **Ruler:** Elizabeth II **Subject:** Royal Air Force, 90th Anniversary **Rev:** Schneider Trophy

| Date | Mintage | VF20 | XF40 | MS60 | MS63 | MS65 |
|---|---|---|---|---|---|---|
| 2008 | Est. 25000 | PF63 45.00 | PF65 55.00 | | | |

### KM# 216 5 POUNDS

28.28 g., 0.925 Silver 0.841 oz. ASW, 38.61 mm. **Ruler:** Elizabeth II **Subject:** Royal Air Force, 90th Anniversary **Rev:** Falkland Islands War, 1982

| Date | Mintage | VF20 | XF40 | MS60 | MS63 | MS65 |
|---|---|---|---|---|---|---|
| 2008 | — | PF63 45.00 | PF65 55.00 | | | |

### KM# 217 5 POUNDS

28.28 g., 0.925 Silver 0.841 oz. ASW, 38.61 mm. **Ruler:** Elizabeth II **Subject:** Royal Air Force, 90th Anniversary **Rev:** Gulf War

| Date | Mintage | VF20 | XF40 | MS60 | MS63 | MS65 |
|---|---|---|---|---|---|---|
| 2008 | Est. 25000 | PF63 45.00 | PF65 55.00 | | | |

### KM# 219 5 POUNDS

28.28 g., Copper-Nickel, 38.61 mm. **Ruler:** Elizabeth II **Subject:** British Warships **Rev:** H.M.S. Daring, drestoyer

| Date | Mintage | VF20 | XF40 | MS60 | MS63 | MS65 |
|---|---|---|---|---|---|---|
| 2009 | — | — | — | — | — | 15.00 |

### KM# 219a 5 POUNDS

28.28 g., 0.925 Silver 0.841 oz. ASW, 38.61 mm. **Ruler:** Elizabeth II **Subject:** British Warships **Rev:** H.M.S. Daring, destroyer

| Date | Mintage | VF20 | XF40 | MS60 | MS63 | MS65 |
|---|---|---|---|---|---|---|
| 2009 | Est. 25000 | PF63 45.00 | PF65 55.00 | | | |

### KM# 220 5 POUNDS

28.28 g., Copper-Nickel, 38.61 mm. **Ruler:** Elizabeth II **Subject:** British Warships **Rev:** H.M.S. Mary Rose, 1511

| Date | Mintage | VF20 | XF40 | MS60 | MS63 | MS65 |
|---|---|---|---|---|---|---|
| 2009 | — | — | — | — | — | 15.00 |

### KM# 220a 5 POUNDS

28.28 g., 0.925 Silver 0.841 oz. ASW, 38.61 mm. **Ruler:** Elizabeth II **Subject:** British Warships **Rev:** H.M.S. Mary Rose, 1511

| Date | Mintage | VF20 | XF40 | MS60 | MS63 | MS65 |
|---|---|---|---|---|---|---|
| 2009 | 25,000 | PF63 45.00 | PF65 55.00 | | | |

### KM# 222 5 POUNDS

28.28 g., Copper-Nickel, 38.61 mm. **Ruler:** Elizabeth II **Subject:** British Aircraft carriers, 100th Anniversary **Rev:** H.M.S. Ark Royal IV with combat aircraft

| Date | Mintage | VF20 | XF40 | MS60 | MS63 | MS65 |
|---|---|---|---|---|---|---|
| 2009 | — | — | — | — | — | 15.00 |

### KM# 222a 5 POUNDS

28.28 g., 0.925 Silver 0.841 oz. ASW, 38.61 mm. **Ruler:** Elizabeth II **Subject:** British Aircraft Carrier, 100th Anniversary **Rev:** H.M.S. Royal Ark VI and fighter aircraft

| Date | Mintage | VF20 | XF40 | MS60 | MS63 | MS65 |
|---|---|---|---|---|---|---|
| 2009 | — | PF63 45.00 | PF65 55.00 | | | |

### KM# 223 5 POUNDS

28.28 g., 0.925 Copper-Nickel 0.841 oz., 38.61 mm. **Ruler:** Elizabeth II **Subject:** Apollo 11 moon landing, 40th Anniversary **Rev:** Lunar Module Eagle and moon in color

| Date | Mintage | VF20 | XF40 | MS60 | MS63 | MS65 |
|---|---|---|---|---|---|---|
| 2009 | — | — | — | — | — | 15.00 |

### KM# 223a 5 POUNDS

28.28 g., 0.925 Silver 0.841 oz. ASW, 38.61 mm. **Ruler:** Elizabeth II **Subject:** Apollo 11 moon landing, 40th Anniversary **Rev:** Lunar module Eagle and moon

| Date | Mintage | VF20 | XF40 | MS60 | MS63 | MS65 |
|---|---|---|---|---|---|---|
| 2009 | — | PF63 45.00 | PF65 55.00 | | | |

### KM# 225 5 POUNDS

28.28 g., Copper-Nickel, 38.61 mm. **Ruler:** Elizabeth II **Subject:** Decimialization, 40th Anniversary **Rev:** Coins in color

| Date | Mintage | VF20 | XF40 | MS60 | MS63 | MS65 |
|---|---|---|---|---|---|---|
| 2011 | — | PF63 15.00 | PF65 17.50 | | | |

### KM# 226 5 POUNDS

28.28 g., Copper-Nickel, 38.61 mm. **Ruler:** Elizabeth II **Subject:** Royal Wedding **Rev:** Prince William and Catherine Middleton

| Date | Mintage | VF20 | XF40 | MS60 | MS63 | MS65 |
|---|---|---|---|---|---|---|
| 2011 | — | — | — | — | — | 15.00 |

### KM# 226a 5 POUNDS

28.28 g., 0.925 Silver 0.841 oz. ASW, 38.61 mm. **Ruler:** Elizabeth II **Subject:** Royal Wedding **Rev:** Prince William and Catherine Middleton

| Date | Mintage | VF20 | XF40 | MS60 | MS63 | MS65 |
|---|---|---|---|---|---|---|
| 2011 | — | PF63 45.00 | PF65 55.00 | | | |

### KM# 227 5 POUNDS

28.28 g., Copper-Nickel, 38.61 mm. **Ruler:** Elizabeth II **Subject:** Prince Philip, 90th Birthday

| Date | Mintage | VF20 | XF40 | MS60 | MS63 | MS65 |
|---|---|---|---|---|---|---|
| 2011 | — | — | — | — | — | 20.00 |

### KM# 228 5 POUNDS

28.28 g., Brass gilt, 38.61 mm. **Ruler:** Elizabeth II **Subject:** Royal British Legion, 90th Anniversary **Rev:** Poppies in color on the battlefield of the Somme

| Date | Mintage | VF20 | XF40 | MS60 | MS63 | MS65 |
|---|---|---|---|---|---|---|
| 2011 | Est. 19500 | — | — | — | — | 35.00 |

### KM# 116 10 POUNDS

141.75 g., 0.999 Silver 4.5528 oz. ASW, 65 mm. **Ruler:** Elizabeth II **Subject:** 19th Century Monarchy **Obv:** Head with tiara right **Rev:** Four portraits **Edge:** Reeded

| Date | Mintage | VF20 | XF40 | MS60 | MS63 | MS65 |
|---|---|---|---|---|---|---|
| 2001 | 950 | PF63 200 | PF65 225 | | | |

### KM# 126 10 POUNDS

155.52 g., 0.999 Silver 4.995 oz. ASW, 65 mm. **Ruler:** Elizabeth II **Subject:** British Monarchy 18th Century **Obv:** Head with tiara right **Rev:** Five royal portraits **Edge:** Reeded

| Date | Mintage | VF20 | XF40 | MS60 | MS63 | MS65 |
|---|---|---|---|---|---|---|
| 2002 | 950 | PF63 200 | PF65 225 | | | |

### KM# 125 10 POUNDS

155.50 g., 0.925 Silver 4.6245 oz. ASW, 65 mm. **Ruler:** Elizabeth II **Subject:** British Monarchs, 1700 years

| Date | Mintage | VF20 | XF40 | MS60 | MS63 | MS65 |
|---|---|---|---|---|---|---|
| 2003 | Est. 950 | PF63 225 | PF65 275 | | | |

### KM# 151 10 POUNDS

155.52 g., 0.925 Silver 4.625 oz. ASW, 65 mm. **Ruler:** Elizabeth II **Subject:** D-Day **Obv:** Head with tiara right **Rev:** British troops storming ashore **Edge:** Reeded

| Date | Mintage | VF20 | XF40 | MS60 | MS63 | MS65 |
|---|---|---|---|---|---|---|
| 2004 | 1,944 | PF63 375 | PF65 400 | | | |

### KM# 175 10 POUNDS

155.50 g., 0.925 Silver 4.6245 oz. ASW, 65 mm. **Ruler:** Elizabeth II **Subject:** British monarch of the 1500s **Rev:** Five portraits

| Date | Mintage | VF20 | XF40 | MS60 | MS63 | MS65 |
|---|---|---|---|---|---|---|
| 2004 | — | PF63 250 | PF65 275 | | | |

### KM# 180 10 POUNDS

155.50 g., 0.917 Gold 4.5845 oz. AGW, 65 mm. **Ruler:** Elizabeth II **Subject:** Crimea, 150th Anniversary

| Date | Mintage | VF20 | XF40 | MS60 | MS63 | MS65 |
|---|---|---|---|---|---|---|
| 2004 | — | PF65 11,000 | | | | |

### KM# 182 10 POUNDS

155.50 g., 0.925 Silver 4.6245 oz. ASW, 65 mm. **Ruler:** Elizabeth II **Subject:** End of WWII, 60th Anniversary

| Date | Mintage | VF20 | XF40 | MS60 | MS63 | MS65 |
|---|---|---|---|---|---|---|
| 2005 | — | PF63 250 | PF65 280 | | | |

### KM# 182a 10 POUNDS

155.50 g., 0.917 Gold 4.5845 oz. AGW, 65 mm. **Ruler:** Elizabeth II **Subject:** End of WWII, 60th Anniversary

| Date | Mintage | VF20 | XF40 | MS60 | MS63 | MS65 |
|---|---|---|---|---|---|---|
| 2005 | — | PF65 11,000 | | | | |

### KM# 182b 10 POUNDS

155.50 g., 0.9995 Platinum 4.9969 oz. APW, 65 mm. **Ruler:** Elizabeth II **Subject:** End of WWII, 60th Anniversary

| Date | Mintage | VF20 | XF40 | MS60 | MS63 | MS65 |
|---|---|---|---|---|---|---|
| 2005 | — | PF65 11,000 | | | | |

### KM# 184 10 POUNDS

155.50 g., 0.925 Silver 4.6245 oz. ASW, 65 mm. **Ruler:** Elizabeth II **Subject:** Return of the Islanders

| Date | Mintage | VF20 | XF40 | MS60 | MS63 | MS65 |
|---|---|---|---|---|---|---|
| 2005 | — | PF63 270 | PF65 300 | | | |

### KM# 184a 10 POUNDS

155.50 g., 0.917 Gold 4.5845 oz. AGW, 65 mm. **Ruler:** Elizabeth II **Subject:** Return of the Islanders

| Date | Mintage | VF20 | XF40 | MS60 | MS63 | MS65 |
|---|---|---|---|---|---|---|
| 2005 | — | PF65 11,000 | | | | |

### KM# 190 10 POUNDS

155.50 g., 0.917 Gold 4.5845 oz. AGW, 65 mm. **Ruler:** Elizabeth II **Subject:** Battle of Trafalgar, 200th Anniversary **Rev:** H.M.S. Victory

| Date | Mintage | VF20 | XF40 | MS60 | MS63 | MS65 |
|---|---|---|---|---|---|---|
| 2005 | — | PF65 9,500 | | | | |

### KM# 224 10 POUNDS

155.50 g., 0.999 Silver 4.9944 oz. ASW, 65 mm. **Ruler:** Elizabeth II **Subject:** Apollo 11 moon landing, 40th Anniversary **Rev:** Lunar module Eagle and moon

| Date | Mintage | VF20 | XF40 | MS60 | MS63 | MS65 |
|---|---|---|---|---|---|---|
| 2009 | — | PF63 245 | PF65 275 | | | |

### KM# 224a 10 POUNDS

155.50 g., 0.917 Gold 4.5845 oz. AGW, 65 mm. **Ruler:** Elizabeth II **Subject:** Apollo 11 moon landing, 40th Anniversary **Rev:** Lunar module Eagle and moon scape

| Date | Mintage | VF20 | XF40 | MS60 | MS63 | MS65 |
|---|---|---|---|---|---|---|
| 2009 | — | PF65 9,000 | | | | |

### KM# 107 25 POUNDS

7.81 g., 0.917 Gold 0.2303 oz. AGW, 22 mm. **Ruler:** Elizabeth II **Subject:** Queen Victoria Centennial **Obv:** Head with tiara right **Rev:** Queen Victoria's portrait **Edge:** Reeded

| Date | Mintage | VF20 | XF40 | MS60 | MS63 | MS65 |
|---|---|---|---|---|---|---|
| 2001 | 2,500 | PF63 425 | PF65 450 | | | |

### KM# 112 25 POUNDS
7.81 g., 0.917 Gold 0.2303 oz. AGW, 22 mm. **Ruler:** Elizabeth II **Subject:** Queen's 75th Birthday **Obv:** Head with tiara right **Rev:** Queen's portrait in wreath **Edge:** Reeded

| Date | Mintage | VF20 | XF40 | MS60 | MS63 | MS65 |
|---|---|---|---|---|---|---|
| 2001 | 5,000 | PF63 400 | PF65 425 | | | |

### KM# 123 25 POUNDS
7.98 g., 0.9167 Gold 0.2352 oz. AGW, 22.05 mm. **Ruler:** Elizabeth II **Subject:** Princess Diana **Obv:** Head with tiara right **Rev:** Diana's cameo portrait in wreath **Edge:** Reeded

| Date | Mintage | VF20 | XF40 | MS60 | MS63 | MS65 |
|---|---|---|---|---|---|---|
| 2002 | 2,500 | PF63 425 | PF65 450 | | | |

### KM# 131 25 POUNDS
7.81 g., 0.9166 Gold 0.2302 oz. AGW, 22 mm. **Ruler:** Elizabeth II **Subject:** The Duke of Wellington **Obv:** Head with tiara right **Rev:** Portrait with mounted dragoons in the background **Edge:** Reeded

| Date | Mintage | VF20 | XF40 | MS60 | MS63 | MS65 |
|---|---|---|---|---|---|---|
| 2002 | 2,500 | PF63 400 | PF65 425 | | | |

### KM# 139 25 POUNDS
7.98 g., 0.9166 Gold 0.2352 oz. AGW, 22 mm. **Ruler:** Elizabeth II **Subject:** Golden Jubilee **Obv:** Head with tiara right **Rev:** Queen in coach **Edge:** Reeded

| Date | Mintage | VF20 | XF40 | MS60 | MS63 | MS65 |
|---|---|---|---|---|---|---|
| 2002 | 5,000 | PF63 420 | PF65 445 | | | |

### KM# 140 25 POUNDS
7.98 g., 0.9166 Gold 0.2352 oz. AGW, 22 mm. **Ruler:** Elizabeth II **Subject:** Queen Mother **Obv:** Head with tiara right **Rev:** Queen Mother's portrait **Edge:** Reeded

| Date | Mintage | VF20 | XF40 | MS60 | MS63 | MS65 |
|---|---|---|---|---|---|---|
| 2002 | 2,500 | PF63 425 | PF65 450 | | | |

### KM# 128 25 POUNDS
7.98 g., 0.917 Gold 0.2353 oz. AGW, 22 mm. **Ruler:** Elizabeth II **Subject:** Royal Navy - Golden Hind and Sir Francis Drake

| Date | Mintage | VF20 | XF40 | MS60 | MS63 | MS65 |
|---|---|---|---|---|---|---|
| 2003 | — | PF63 475 | PF65 525 | | | |

### KM# 141 25 POUNDS
7.98 g., 0.9166 Gold 0.2352 oz. AGW, 22 mm. **Ruler:** Elizabeth II **Subject:** Golden Jubilee **Obv:** Head with tiara right **Rev:** Trooping the Colors scene **Edge:** Reeded

| Date | Mintage | VF20 | XF40 | MS60 | MS63 | MS65 |
|---|---|---|---|---|---|---|
| 2003 | 5,000 | PF63 420 | PF65 445 | | | |

### KM# 144 25 POUNDS
7.98 g., 0.917 Gold 0.2353 oz. AGW, 22 mm. **Ruler:** Elizabeth II **Subject:** Steam Locomotives **Rev:** Mallard Locomotive

| Date | Mintage | VF20 | XF40 | MS60 | MS63 | MS65 |
|---|---|---|---|---|---|---|
| 2004 | Est. 2500 | PF63 475 | PF65 525 | | | |

### KM# 152 25 POUNDS
7.98 g., 0.9167 Gold 0.2352 oz. AGW, 22 mm. **Ruler:** Elizabeth II **Subject:** D-Day **Obv:** Head with tiara right **Rev:** Advancing British soldier **Edge:** Reeded

| Date | Mintage | VF20 | XF40 | MS60 | MS63 | MS65 |
|---|---|---|---|---|---|---|
| 2004 | 500 | PF63 450 | PF65 475 | | | |

### KM# 172 25 POUNDS
7.98 g., 0.917 Gold 0.2353 oz. AGW, 22 mm. **Ruler:** Elizabeth II **Subject:** Steam Locomotives **Rev:** City of Truro locomotive

| Date | Mintage | VF20 | XF40 | MS60 | MS63 | MS65 |
|---|---|---|---|---|---|---|
| 2004 | Est. 2500 | PF63 475 | PF65 525 | | | |

### KM# 181 25 POUNDS
7.98 g., 0.917 Gold 0.2353 oz. AGW, 22 mm. **Ruler:** Elizabeth II **Subject:** Crimea, 150th Anniversary

| Date | Mintage | VF20 | XF40 | MS60 | MS63 | MS65 |
|---|---|---|---|---|---|---|
| 2004 | — | PF63 475 | PF65 525 | | | |

### KM# 183 25 POUNDS
7.98 g., 0.917 Gold 0.2353 oz. AGW, 22 mm. **Ruler:** Elizabeth II **Subject:** End of WWII, 60th Anniversary

| Date | Mintage | VF20 | XF40 | MS60 | MS63 | MS65 |
|---|---|---|---|---|---|---|
| 2005 | — | PF63 475 | PF65 525 | | | |

### KM# 185 25 POUNDS
7.98 g., 0.917 Gold 0.2353 oz. AGW, 22 mm. **Ruler:** Elizabeth II **Rev:** Return of the Islanders

| Date | Mintage | VF20 | XF40 | MS60 | MS63 | MS65 |
|---|---|---|---|---|---|---|
| 2005 | — | PF63 475 | PF65 525 | | | |

### KM# 188 25 POUNDS
7.98 g., 0.917 Gold 0.2353 oz. AGW, 22 mm. **Ruler:** Elizabeth II **Subject:** Royal Navy **Rev:** H.M.S. Ark Royal

| Date | Mintage | VF20 | XF40 | MS60 | MS63 | MS65 |
|---|---|---|---|---|---|---|
| 2005 | — | PF63 475 | PF65 525 | | | |

### KM# 174 25 POUNDS
7.98 g., 0.9166 Gold 0.2352 oz. AGW, 22 mm. **Ruler:** Elizabeth II **Subject:** FIFA - XVIII World Football Championship - Germany 2006 **Rev:** Wembley Stadium

| Date | Mintage | VF20 | XF40 | MS60 | MS63 | MS65 |
|---|---|---|---|---|---|---|
| 2006 | 2,500 | PF63 420 | PF65 445 | | | |

### KM# 218 25 POUNDS
7.98 g., 0.917 Gold 0.2353 oz. AGW, 22 mm. **Ruler:** Elizabeth II **Subject:** Royal Air Force, 90th Anniversary **Rev:** Lancaster

| Date | Mintage | VF20 | XF40 | MS60 | MS63 | MS65 |
|---|---|---|---|---|---|---|
| 2008 | — | PF63 450 | PF65 475 | | | |

### KM# 221 25 POUNDS
7.98 g., 0.917 Gold 0.2353 oz. AGW, 22 mm. **Ruler:** Elizabeth II **Subject:** British Warships **Rev:** H.M.S. Mary Rose, 1511

| Date | Mintage | VF20 | XF40 | MS60 | MS63 | MS65 |
|---|---|---|---|---|---|---|
| 2009 | Est. 995 | PF63 450 | PF65 475 | | | |

### KM# 177 50 POUNDS
1000.00 g., 0.916 Silver 29.4501 oz. ASW, 100 mm. **Ruler:** Elizabeth II **Subject:** Coronation, 50th Anniversary **Rev:** Buckingham Palace

| Date | Mintage | VF20 | XF40 | MS60 | MS63 | MS65 |
|---|---|---|---|---|---|---|
| 2003 | Est. 999 | PF63 950 | PF65 1,100 | | | |

### KM# 153 50 POUNDS
1000.00 g., 0.925 Silver 29.7394 oz. ASW, 100 mm. **Ruler:** Elizabeth II **Subject:** D-Day **Obv:** Head with tiara right **Rev:** British troops storming ashore **Edge:** Reeded

| Date | Mintage | VF20 | XF40 | MS60 | MS63 | MS65 |
|---|---|---|---|---|---|---|
| 2004 | 600 | PF63 1,100 | PF65 1,300 | | | |

### KM# 178 50 POUNDS
7.98 g., 0.916 Gold 0.235 oz. AGW, 22.05 mm. **Ruler:** Elizabeth II **Subject:** Royal Air Force, 90th Anniversary **Rev:** Pilots scrambling to planes, some in the sky **Edge:** Reeded

| Date | Mintage | VF20 | XF40 | MS60 | MS63 | MS65 |
|---|---|---|---|---|---|---|
| 2008 | — | PF63 450 | PF65 475 | | | |

## PIEDFORT

| KM# | Date | Mintage | Identification | Mkt Val |
|---|---|---|---|---|
| P3 | 2002 | 100 | 5 Pounds 0.9166 Gold Queen's portrait Queen in coach | 4,250 |

## MINT SETS

| KM# | Date | Mintage | Identification | Issue Price | Mkt Val |
|---|---|---|---|---|---|
| MS10 | 2003 (8) | — | KM#83, 89-90, 96-97, 110, 148-49 | — | 22.50 |
| MS11 | 2004 (1) | — | Guernsey KM#155, Alderney KM#43, Jersey KM#126, 150th Anniversary of the Crimean War | — | 80.00 |

# GUINEA

The Republic of Guinea, situated on the Atlantic Coast of Africa between Sierra Leone and Guinea-Bissau, has an area of 94,964 sq. mi. (245,860 sq. km.) and a population of 6.4 million. Capital: Conakry. Although Guinea contains one-third of the world's reserves of bauxite and significant deposits of iron ore, gold and diamonds, the economy is still dependent on agriculture, aluminum, bananas, copra and coffee are exported.

The coast of Guinea was known to Portuguese navigators of the 15th century but was seldom visited by European traders of the 16th-18th centuries because of its dangerous coastal waters. French penetration of the area began in the mid-19th century with the entering into of protectorate treaties with several of the coastal chiefs. After a long struggle with Guinea's native leader Samory Toure, France secured the area and until 1890 administered it as a part of Senegal. In 1895 the colony (Guinee Francais) became an autonomous part of the federation of French West Africa. The inhabitants were extended French citizenship in 1946 when the colony became an overseas territory of the French Union. Guinea became an independent republic on Oct. 2, 1958, when it declined to enter the new French Community.

**MONETARY SYSTEM**
100 Centimes = 1 Franc

## REPUBLIC
### REFORM COINAGE

### KM# 65 2000 FRANCS
22.20 g., 0.900 Silver 0.6424 oz. ASW, 37 mm. **Obv:** National Arms **Rev:** Map and female figure

| Date | Mintage | VF20 | XF40 | MS60 | MS63 | MS65 |
|---|---|---|---|---|---|---|
| 2002 | 500 | PF65 120 | | | | |

# GUYANA

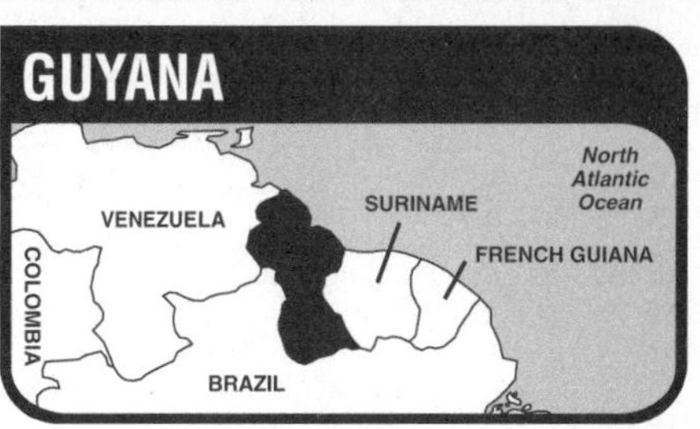


The Cooperative Republic of Guyana, is situated on the northeast coast of South America, has an area of 83,000 sq. mi. (214,970 sq. km.) and a population of 729,000. Capital: Georgetown. The economy is basically agrarian. Sugar, rice and bauxite are exported.

The original area of Essequibo and Demerary, which included present-day Suriname, French Guiana, and parts of Brazil and Venezuela was sighted by Columbus in 1498. Guyana became a republic on Feb. 23, 1970. It is a member of the Commonwealth of Nations. The president is the Chief of State. The prime minister is the Head of Government. Guyana is a member of the Caribbean Community and Common Market (CARICOM).

## REPUBLIC
### DECIMAL COINAGE

### KM# 50 DOLLAR
2.40 g., Copper Plated Steel, 17 mm. **Obv:** Helmeted and supported arms **Rev:** Hand gathering rice **Edge:** Reeded

| Date | Mintage | VF20 | XF40 | MS60 | MS63 | MS65 |
|---|---|---|---|---|---|---|
| 2001 | — | — | — | 0.35 | 0.50 | 0.65 |
| 2002 | — | — | — | 0.35 | 0.50 | 0.65 |
| 2005 | — | — | — | 0.35 | 0.50 | 0.65 |
| 2008 | — | — | — | 0.35 | 0.50 | 0.65 |
| 2011 | — | — | — | 0.35 | 0.50 | 0.65 |

### KM# 51 5 DOLLARS
3.78 g., Copper Plated Steel, 20.5 mm. **Obv:** Helmeted and supported arms **Rev:** Sugar cane **Edge:** Reeded

| Date | Mintage | VF20 | XF40 | MS60 | MS63 | MS65 |
|---|---|---|---|---|---|---|
| 2002 | — | — | — | 0.35 | 0.75 | 1.00 |
| 2005 | — | — | — | 0.35 | 0.75 | 1.00 |
| 2008 | — | — | — | 0.35 | 0.75 | 1.00 |
| 2009 | — | — | — | 0.35 | 0.75 | 1.00 |

### KM# 52 10 DOLLARS
5.00 g., Nickel Plated Steel, 23 mm. **Obv:** Helmeted and supported arms **Rev:** Gold mining scene **Edge:** Reeded **Shape:** 7-sided **Note:** Slightly different die for each date.

| Date | Mintage | VF20 | XF40 | MS60 | MS63 | MS65 |
|---|---|---|---|---|---|---|
| 2007 | — | — | — | 0.75 | 1.25 | 1.50 |
| 2009 | — | — | — | 0.75 | 1.25 | 1.50 |

### KM# 54 1000 DOLLARS
28.28 g., 0.925 Silver 0.841 oz. ASW partially gilt, 38.6 mm. **Subject:** Bank of Guyana, 40th Anniversary **Obv:** Arms **Rev:** Bank building, partially gilt

| Date | Mintage | VF20 | XF40 | MS60 | MS63 | MS65 |
|---|---|---|---|---|---|---|
| 2005 | 1,000 | PF65 85.00 | | | | |

### KM# 54a 1000 DOLLARS

28.28 g., Copper-Nickel, 38.61 mm. **Subject:** Central Bank, 40th Anniversary **Obv:** Supported arms **Rev:** Building

| Date | Mintage | VF20 | XF40 | MS60 | MS63 | MS65 |
|---|---|---|---|---|---|---|
| 2005 | — | — | — | — | 50.00 | 60.00 |

### KM# 55 2000 DOLLARS

28.28 g., 0.925 Silver 0.841 oz. ASW, 38.61 mm. **Obv:** National Arms **Rev:** National soccer stadium

| Date | Mintage | VF20 | XF40 | MS60 | MS63 | MS65 |
|---|---|---|---|---|---|---|
| 2007 | Est. 4000 | **PF63** 80.00 | **PF65** 90.00 | | | |

### KM# 56 2000 DOLLARS

25.00 g., Copper-Nickel, 39 mm. **Obv:** National Arms **Rev:** Face design

| Date | Mintage | VF20 | XF40 | MS60 | MS63 | MS65 |
|---|---|---|---|---|---|---|
| 2008 | — | — | — | — | 75.00 | 80.00 |

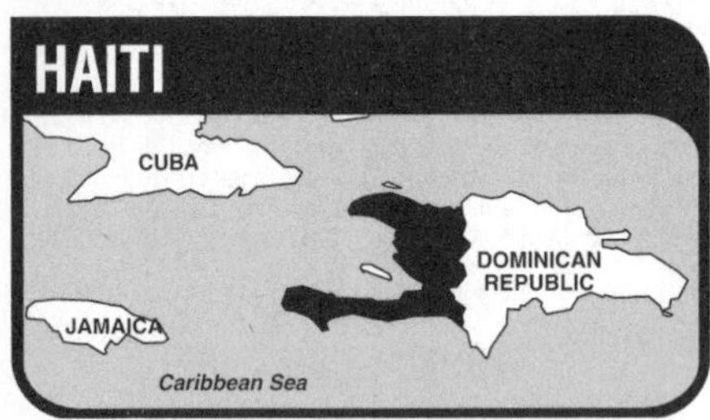


The Republic of Haiti, which occupies the western one-third of the island of Hispaniola in the Caribbean Sea between Puerto Rico and Cuba, has an area of 10,714 sq. mi. (27,750 sq. km.) and a population of 6.5 million. Capital: Port-au-Prince. The economy is based on agriculture; but light manufacturing and tourism are increasingly important. Coffee, bauxite, sugar, essential oils and handicrafts are exported.

The French language is used on Haitian coins although it is spoken by only about 10% of the populace. A form of Creole is the language of the Haitians.

**MONETARY SYSTEM**

100 Centimes = 1 Gourde

## REPUBLIC

### DECIMAL COINAGE

### KM# 155 GOURDE

6.30 g., Brass Plated Steel, 23 mm. **Obv:** Citadelle de Roi Christophe **Shape:** 7-sided

| Date | Mintage | VF20 | XF40 | MS60 | MS63 | MS65 |
|---|---|---|---|---|---|---|
| 2003 | — | — | — | 1.00 | 1.75 | 2.00 |
| 2009 | — | — | — | 1.00 | 1.75 | 2.00 |

### KM# 156 5 GOURDES

9.20 g., Brass Plated Steel, 28 mm. **Obv:** Four portraits in circle of Haitian statesmen top: Gen. Tonsaint Louverture, Left: Henri Christophe, Right: Jean Jacques Dessalines, Bottom: Alexandre Petion, date below **Rev:** National arms **Shape:** 7-sided

| Date | Mintage | VF20 | XF40 | MS60 | MS63 | MS65 |
|---|---|---|---|---|---|---|
| 2007 | — | — | — | — | 2.25 | 3.00 |

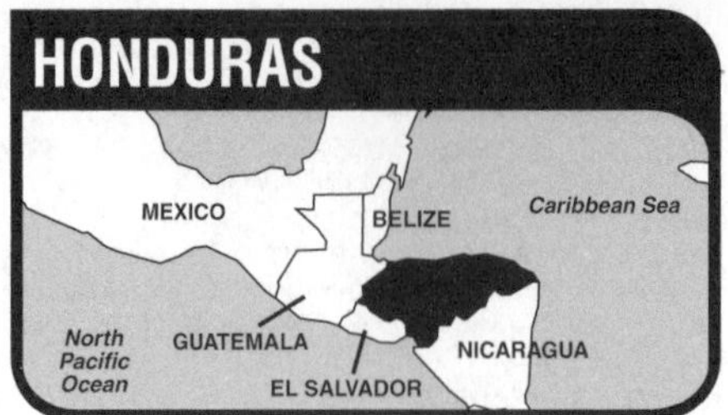


The Republic of Honduras, situated in Central America alongside El Salvador, between Nicaragua and Guatemala, has an area of 43,277 sq. mi. (112,090 sq. km.) and a population of 5.6 million. Capital: Tegucigalpa. Agriculture, mining (gold and silver), and logging are the major economic activities, with increasing tourism and emerging petroleum resource discoveries. Precious metals, bananas, timber and coffee are exported.

From 1933 to 1940 General Tiburcio Carias Andino was dictator president of the Republic. Since 1990 democratic practices have become more consistent.

**MINT MARKS**

T.G. - Yoro

T.L. – Comayagua

**MONETARY SYSTEM**

100 Centavos = 1 Lempira

## REPUBLIC

### REFORM COINAGE

### KM# 72.4 5 CENTAVOS

3.20 g., Brass, 21 mm. **Obv:** National arms **Rev:** Value in circle within sprays **Edge:** Plain

| Date | Mintage | VF20 | XF40 | MS60 | MS63 | MS65 |
|---|---|---|---|---|---|---|
| 2002 | — | — | 0.10 | 0.25 | 0.35 | 0.50 |
| 2003 | — | — | 0.10 | 0.25 | 0.35 | 0.50 |
| 2005 | — | — | 0.10 | 0.25 | 0.35 | 0.50 |
| 2006 | — | — | 0.10 | 0.25 | 0.35 | 0.50 |
| 2007 | — | — | 0.10 | 0.25 | 0.35 | 0.50 |

### KM# 76.3 10 CENTAVOS

6.00 g., Brass, 26 mm. **Obv:** National arms, without clouds behind pyramid **Rev:** Denomination within circle, wreath surrounds **Edge:** Plain

| Date | Mintage | VF20 | XF40 | MS60 | MS63 | MS65 |
|---|---|---|---|---|---|---|
| 2002 | — | — | 0.20 | 0.35 | 0.45 | 0.65 |
| 2003 | — | — | 0.20 | 0.35 | 0.45 | 0.65 |
| 2005 | — | — | 0.20 | 0.35 | 0.45 | 0.65 |
| 2006 | — | — | 0.20 | 0.35 | 0.45 | 0.65 |
| 2007 | — | — | 0.20 | 0.35 | 0.45 | 0.65 |

### KM# 76.4 10 CENTAVOS

6.00 g., Brass, 26 mm. **Obv:** National arms, slightly larger legend, large date **Rev:** Value in circle within wreath **Edge:** Plain

| Date | Mintage | VF20 | XF40 | MS60 | MS63 | MS65 |
|---|---|---|---|---|---|---|
| 2006 | — | — | 0.15 | 0.25 | 0.35 | 0.50 |
| 2007 | — | — | 0.15 | 0.25 | 0.35 | 0.50 |
| 2010 | — | — | 0.15 | 0.25 | 0.35 | 0.50 |

### KM# 83a.2 20 CENTAVOS

2.00 g., Nickel Plated Steel, 18 mm. **Obv:** National arms, without clouds **Rev:** Chief Lempira head left within circle **Edge:** Reeded

| Date | Mintage | VF20 | XF40 | MS60 | MS63 | MS65 |
|---|---|---|---|---|---|---|
| 2007 | — | — | 0.20 | 0.40 | 0.60 | 1.00 |
| 2010 | — | — | 0.20 | 0.40 | 0.60 | 1.00 |

### KM# 84a.2 50 CENTAVOS

5.00 g., Nickel Plated Steel, 24 mm. **Obv:** National arms above date **Rev:** Chief Lempira head left within circle **Edge:** Reeded

| Date | Mintage | VF20 | XF40 | MS60 | MS63 | MS65 |
|---|---|---|---|---|---|---|
| 2005 | — | 0.15 | 0.35 | 0.65 | 1.00 | 1.50 |
| 2007 | — | 0.15 | 0.35 | 0.65 | 1.00 | 1.50 |

### KM# 91 10 LEMPIRAS

27.00 g., 0.925 Silver 0.803 oz. ASW, 40 mm. **Obv:** State arms **Rev:** Bust of Jose Trinidad Cabanas Fiallos, president 1852-1855

| Date | Mintage | VF20 | XF40 | MS60 | MS63 | MS65 |
|---|---|---|---|---|---|---|
| 2005 | — | **PF60** 90.00 | **PF63** 100 | **PF65** 120 | | |

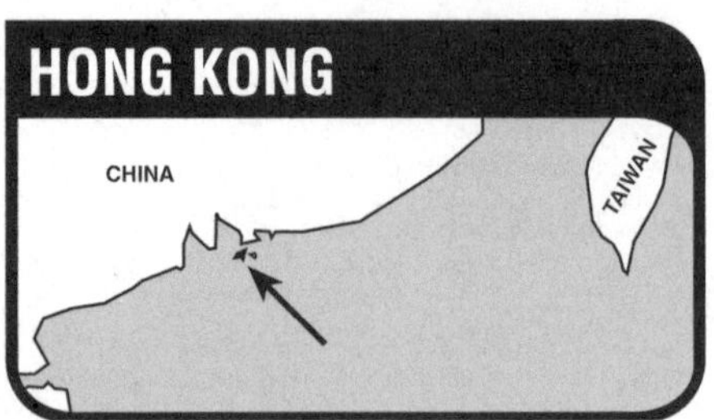


Hong Kong, a former British colony, reverted to control of the People's Republic of China on July 1, 1997 as a Special Administrative Region. It is situated at the mouth of the Canton or Pearl River 90 miles (145 km.) southeast of Canton, has an area of 403 sq. mi. (1,040 sq. km.) and an estimated population of 6.3 million. Capital: Victoria. The free port of Hong Kong, the commercial center of the Far East, is a trans-shipment point for goods destined for China and the countries of the Pacific Rim. Light manufacturing and tourism are important components of the economy.Special Administration Region (S.A.R.)

### DECIMAL COINAGE

### KM# 80 50 DOLLARS

35.43 g., 0.925 Silver 1.0537 oz. ASW Gold plated center, 40 mm. **Series:** Five Blessings **Obv:** Bauhinia flower **Rev:** Jade Ju-I

| Date | Mintage | VF20 | XF40 | MS60 | MS63 | MS65 |
|---|---|---|---|---|---|---|
| 2002 | 60,000 | **PF63** 75.00 | **PF65** 95.00 | | | |

**KM# 81 50 DOLLARS**
35.43 g., 0.925 Silver 1.0537 oz. ASW Gold plated center, 40 mm. **Series:** Five Blessings **Obv:** Bauhinia flower **Rev:** Fish

| Date | Mintage | VF20 | XF40 | MS60 | MS63 | MS65 |
|---|---|---|---|---|---|---|
| 2002 | 60,000 | **PF63** 75.00 | **PF65** 95.00 | | | |

**KM# 82 50 DOLLARS**
35.25 g., 0.925 Silver 1.0483 oz. ASW Gold plated center, 40 mm. **Series:** Five Blessings **Obv:** Bauhinia flower **Rev:** Horses

| Date | Mintage | VF20 | XF40 | MS60 | MS63 | MS65 |
|---|---|---|---|---|---|---|
| 2002 | 60,000 | **PF63** 75.00 | **PF65** 95.00 | | | |

**KM# 83 50 DOLLARS**
35.34 g., 0.925 Silver 1.051 oz. ASW Gold plated center, 40 mm. **Series:** Five Blessings **Obv:** Bauhinia flower **Rev:** Peony flower

| Date | Mintage | VF20 | XF40 | MS60 | MS63 | MS65 |
|---|---|---|---|---|---|---|
| 2002 | 60,000 | **PF63** 75.00 | **PF65** 95.00 | | | |

**KM# 84 50 DOLLARS**
35.14 g., 0.925 Silver 1.045 oz. ASW Gold plated center, 40 mm. **Series:** Five Blessings **Obv:** Bauhinia flower **Rev:** Windmills

| Date | Mintage | VF20 | XF40 | MS60 | MS63 | MS65 |
|---|---|---|---|---|---|---|
| 2002 | 60,000 | **PF63** 75.00 | **PF65** 95.00 | | | |

## PROOF SETS

| KM# | Date | Mintage | Identification | Issue Price | Mkt Val |
|---|---|---|---|---|---|
| PS8 | 2002 (5) | 60,000 | KM#80-84 plus 7.8g, .9999, AGW .2508, 25mm gold medal | 370 | 625 |

# HUNGARY

Hungary, located in central Europe, has an area of 35,929 sq. mi. (93,030 sq. km.) and a population of 10.7 million. Capital: Budapest. The economy is based on agriculture, bauxite and a rapidly expanding industrial sector. Machinery, chemicals, iron and steel, and fruits and vegetables are exported.

**MINT MARKS**
BP - Budapest

**MONETARY SYSTEM**
Commencing 1946
100 Filler = 1 Forint

## SECOND REPUBLIC

### DECIMAL COINAGE

**KM# 692 FORINT**
2.05 g., Nickel-Brass, 16.5 mm. **Obv:** Crowned shield **Rev:** Denomination **Mint:** Budapest

| Date | Mintage | VF20 | XF40 | MS60 | MS63 | MS65 |
|---|---|---|---|---|---|---|
| 2001 BP | 65,007,000 | — | — | 0.10 | 0.25 | 0.40 |
| 2001 BP | 3,000 | **PF65** 3.75 | | | | |
| 2002 BP | 70,007,000 | — | — | 0.10 | 0.25 | 0.40 |
| 2002 BP | 3,000 | **PF65** 3.75 | | | | |
| 2003 BP | 75,008,000 | — | — | 0.10 | 0.25 | 0.40 |
| 2003 BP | 7,000 | **PF65** 3.50 | | | | |
| 2004 BP | 96,008,000 | — | — | 0.10 | 0.25 | 0.40 |
| 2004 BP | 7,000 | **PF65** 3.50 | | | | |
| 2005 BP | 80,008,000 | — | — | 0.10 | 0.25 | 0.40 |
| 2005 BP | 7,000 | **PF65** 3.50 | | | | |
| 2006 BP | 67,008,000 | — | — | 0.10 | 0.25 | 0.40 |
| 2006 BP | 7,000 | **PF65** 3.50 | | | | |
| 2007 BP | 85,013,010 | — | — | 0.10 | 0.25 | 0.40 |
| 2007 BP | 7,000 | **PF65** 3.50 | | | | |
| 2008 BP Sets only | 8,010 | — | — | — | — | 3.50 |
| 2008 BP | 7,000 | **PF65** 3.50 | | | | |

**KM# 693 2 FORINT**
3.10 g., Copper-Nickel, 19.2 mm. **Obv:** Native flower: Colchicum Hungaricum **Rev:** Denomination **Edge:** Reeded

| Date | Mintage | VF20 | XF40 | MS60 | MS63 | MS65 |
|---|---|---|---|---|---|---|
| 2001 BP | 50,007,000 | — | — | 0.20 | 0.35 | 0.65 |
| 2001 BP | — | **PF65** 4.25 | | | | |
| 2002 BP | 60,007,000 | — | — | 0.20 | 0.35 | 0.65 |
| 2002 BP | 3,000 | **PF65** 4.25 | | | | |
| 2003 BP | 7,008,000 | — | — | 0.20 | 0.35 | 0.65 |
| 2003 BP | 7,000 | **PF65** 4.00 | | | | |
| 2004 BP | 88,008,000 | — | — | 0.20 | 0.35 | 0.65 |
| 2004 BP | 7,000 | **PF65** 4.00 | | | | |
| 2005 BP | 72,008,000 | — | — | 0.20 | 0.35 | 0.65 |
| 2005 BP | 7,000 | **PF65** 4.00 | | | | |
| 2006 BP | 54,008,000 | — | — | 0.20 | 0.35 | 0.65 |
| 2006 BP | 7,000 | **PF65** 4.00 | | | | |
| 2007 BP | 82,013,010 | — | — | 0.20 | 0.35 | 0.65 |
| 2007 BP | 7,000 | **PF65** 4.00 | | | | |
| 2008 BP Sets only | 8,010 | — | — | — | 4.00 | — |
| 2009 BP | 7,000 | **PF65** 4.00 | | | | |

**KM# 694 5 FORINT**
4.20 g., Nickel-Brass, 21.2 mm. **Obv:** Great White Egret **Rev:** Denomination **Mint:** Budapest

| Date | Mintage | VF20 | XF40 | MS60 | MS63 | MS65 |
|---|---|---|---|---|---|---|
| 2001 BP | 18,007,000 | — | — | 0.65 | 1.25 | 1.50 |
| 2001 BP | — | **PF65** 5.00 | | | | |
| 2002 BP | 11,007,000 | — | — | 0.65 | 1.25 | 1.50 |
| 2002 BP | 3,000 | **PF65** 5.00 | | | | |
| 2003 BP | 15,008,000 | — | — | 0.65 | 1.25 | 1.50 |
| 2003 BP | 7,000 | **PF65** 4.50 | | | | |
| 2004 BP | 40,008,000 | — | — | 0.65 | 1.25 | 1.50 |
| 2004 BP | 7,000 | **PF65** 4.50 | | | | |
| 2005 BP | 16,008,000 | — | — | 0.65 | 1.25 | 1.50 |
| 2005 BP | 7,000 | **PF65** 4.50 | | | | |
| 2006 BP | 21,008,000 | — | — | 0.65 | 1.25 | 1.50 |
| 2006 BP | 7,000 | **PF65** 4.50 | | | | |
| 2007 BP | 33,008,000 | — | — | 0.65 | 1.25 | 1.50 |
| 2007 BP | 7,000 | **PF65** 4.50 | | | | |
| 2008 BP | 34,038,005 | — | — | 0.65 | 1.25 | 1.50 |
| 2008 BP | 7,000 | **PF65** 4.50 | | | | |
| 2009 BP | 5,980,015 | — | — | 0.65 | 1.25 | 1.50 |
| 2009 BP | 7,000 | **PF65** 4.50 | | | | |
| 2010 BP | 45,015,520 | — | — | 0.65 | 1.25 | 1.50 |
| 2010 BP | 7,000 | **PF65** 4.50 | | | | |
| 2011 BP Sets only | 9,000 | — | — | 0.65 | 1.25 | 1.50 |
| 2011 BP | 7,000 | **PF65** 4.50 | | | | |
| 2012 BP | — | — | — | 0.65 | 1.25 | 1.50 |

**KM# 847 5 FORINT**
4.20 g., Nickel-Brass, 21.2 mm. **Obv:** Great White Egret **Obv. Legend:** MAGYARORSZAG **Rev:** Denomination **Mint:** Budapest

| Date | Mintage | VF20 | XF40 | MS60 | MS63 | MS65 |
|---|---|---|---|---|---|---|
| 2012 BP | 10,000,000 | — | — | 0.65 | 1.25 | 1.50 |
| 2012 BP | 4,000 | **PF65** 2.50 | | | | |
| 2013 BP | — | — | — | 0.65 | 1.25 | 1.50 |
| 2013 BP | — | **PF65** 2.50 | | | | |
| 2014 | — | — | — | 0.65 | 1.25 | 1.50 |
| 2014 | 2,000 | **PF65** 2.50 | | | | |

### KM# 695 10 FORINT

6.10 g., Copper-Nickel, 24.8 mm. **Obv:** Crowned shield **Rev:** Denomination **Edge:** Segmented reeding

| Date | Mintage | VF20 | XF40 | MS60 | MS63 | MS65 |
|---|---|---|---|---|---|---|
| 2001 BP | 12,007,000 | — | — | 1.00 | 1.25 | 2.00 |
| 2001 BP | — | PF65 5.50 | | | | |
| 2002 BP | 5,007,000 | — | — | 1.00 | 1.25 | 2.00 |
| 2002 BP | 3,000 | PF65 5.50 | | | | |
| 2003 BP | 1,008,000 | — | — | 1.00 | 1.25 | 2.00 |
| 2003 BP | 7,000 | PF65 5.00 | | | | |
| 2004 BP | 19,008,000 | — | — | 1.00 | 1.25 | 2.00 |
| 2004 BP | 7,000 | PF65 5.00 | | | | |
| 2005 BP | 8,981,000 | — | — | 1.00 | 1.25 | 2.00 |
| 2005 BP | 7,000 | PF65 5.00 | | | | |
| 2006 BP | 15,008,000 | — | — | 1.00 | 1.25 | 2.00 |
| 2006 BP | 7,000 | PF65 5.00 | | | | |
| 2007 | 25,008,000 | — | — | 1.00 | 1.25 | 2.00 |
| 2007 | 7,000 | PF65 5.00 | | | | |
| 2008 | 14,003,005 | — | — | 1.00 | 1.25 | 2.00 |
| 2008 | 7,000 | PF65 5.00 | | | | |
| 2009 | 2,015,015 | — | — | 1.00 | 1.25 | 2.00 |
| 2009 | 7,000 | PF65 5.00 | | | | |
| 2010 | 15,020 | — | — | 1.00 | 1.25 | 2.00 |
| 2010 | 7,000 | PF65 5.00 | | | | |
| 2011 Sets only | 9,000 | — | — | — | — | 2.50 |
| 2011 | 7,000 | PF65 5.00 | | | | |

### KM# 779 10 FORINT

6.10 g., Copper-Nickel, 24.8 mm. **Obv:** Attila Jozsef **Rev:** Value **Edge:** Segmented reeding

| Date | Mintage | VF20 | XF40 | MS60 | MS63 | MS65 |
|---|---|---|---|---|---|---|
| 2005 BP | 20,000 | — | — | 1.50 | 2.50 | 3.00 |
| 2005 BP | 7,000 | PF65 3.50 | | | | |

### KM# 848 10 FORINT

6.10 g., Copper-Nickel, 24.8 mm. **Obv:** Crowned shield **Obv. Legend:** MAGYARORSZAG **Rev:** Denomination **Edge:** Segmented reeding **Mint:** Budapest

| Date | Mintage | VF20 | XF40 | MS60 | MS63 | MS65 |
|---|---|---|---|---|---|---|
| 2012 BP | 10,000,000 | — | — | 1.00 | 1.25 | 2.00 |
| 2012 BP | 4,000 | PF65 5.00 | | | | |
| 2013 BP | — | — | — | 1.00 | 1.25 | 2.00 |
| 2013 BP | — | PF65 5.00 | | | | |
| 2014 | — | — | — | 1.00 | 1.25 | 2.00 |
| 2014 | — | PF65 5.00 | | | | |

### KM# 696 20 FORINT

6.90 g., Nickel-Brass, 26.3 mm. **Obv:** Hungarian Iris **Rev:** Denomination **Edge:** Reeded **Mint:** Budapest

| Date | Mintage | VF20 | XF40 | MS60 | MS63 | MS65 |
|---|---|---|---|---|---|---|
| 2001 BP | 7,000 | — | — | — | 2.00 | 3.00 |
| 2001 BP | 3,000 | PF65 4.50 | | | | |
| 2002 BP | 7,000 | — | — | — | 2.00 | 3.00 |
| 2002 BP | 3,000 | PF65 4.50 | | | | |
| 2003 BP | 8,000 | — | — | — | 2.00 | 3.00 |
| 2003 BP | 7,000 | PF65 4.00 | | | | |
| 2004 BP | 7,008,000 | — | — | 0.75 | 1.50 | 2.00 |
| 2004 BP | 7,000 | PF65 4.00 | | | | |
| 2005 BP | 11,008,000 | — | — | 0.75 | 1.50 | 2.00 |
| 2005 BP | 7,000 | PF65 4.00 | | | | |
| 2006 BP | 14,008,000 | — | — | 0.75 | 1.50 | 2.00 |
| 2006 BP | 7,000 | PF65 4.00 | | | | |
| 2007 BP | 18,008,010 | — | — | 0.75 | 1.50 | 2.00 |
| 2007 BP | 7,000 | PF65 4.00 | | | | |
| 2008 BP | 9,020,505 | — | — | 0.75 | 1.50 | 2.00 |
| 2008 BP | 7,000 | PF65 4.00 | | | | |
| 2009 BP | 4,997,515 | — | — | 0.75 | 1.50 | 2.00 |
| 2009 BP | 7,000 | PF65 4.00 | | | | |
| 2010 BP | 14,020 | — | — | — | 2.00 | 3.00 |
| 2010 BP | 7,000 | PF65 4.00 | | | | |
| 2011 BP | 9,000 | — | — | — | 2.00 | 3.00 |
| 2011 BP | 7,000 | PF65 4.00 | | | | |

### KM# 768 20 FORINT

6.90 g., Nickel-Brass, 26.3 mm. **Obv:** Ferenc Deak **Rev:** Denomination **Edge:** Reeded **Mint:** Budapest

| Date | Mintage | VF20 | XF40 | MS60 | MS63 | MS65 |
|---|---|---|---|---|---|---|
| 2003 BP | 993,000 | — | — | 0.75 | 1.50 | 2.00 |
| 2003 BP | 7,000 | PF65 4.00 | | | | |

### KM# 849 20 FORINT

6.90 g., Nickel-Brass, 26.3 mm. **Obv:** Hungarian Iris **Obv. Legend:** MAGYARORSZAG **Rev:** Denomination **Edge:** Reeded **Mint:** Budapest

| Date | Mintage | VF20 | XF40 | MS60 | MS63 | MS65 |
|---|---|---|---|---|---|---|
| 2012 BP | 10,000,000 | — | — | 0.75 | 1.50 | 2.50 |
| 2012 BP | 4,000 | PF65 5.00 | | | | |
| 2013 BP | — | — | — | 0.75 | 1.50 | 2.50 |
| 2013 BP | — | PF65 5.00 | | | | |
| 2014 | — | — | — | 0.75 | 1.50 | 2.50 |

### KM# 697 50 FORINT

7.60 g., Copper-Nickel, 27.5 mm. **Obv:** Saker falcon **Rev:** Denomination **Mint:** Budapest

| Date | Mintage | VF20 | XF40 | MS60 | MS63 | MS65 |
|---|---|---|---|---|---|---|
| 2001 BP | 15,007,000 | — | — | 1.50 | 3.00 | 4.00 |
| 2001 BP | — | PF65 6.00 | | | | |
| 2002 BP | 7,000 | — | — | — | 2.00 | 3.50 |
| 2002 BP | 3,000 | PF65 5.50 | | | | |
| 2003 BP | 7,008,000 | — | — | 1.25 | 2.00 | 3.50 |
| 2003 BP | 7,000 | PF65 5.00 | | | | |
| 2004 BP | 8,000 | — | — | — | 2.00 | 3.50 |
| 2004 BP | 7,000 | PF65 5.00 | | | | |
| 2005 BP | 9,007,000 | — | — | 1.25 | 2.00 | 3.50 |
| 2005 BP | 8,000 | PF65 5.00 | | | | |
| 2006 BP | 5,008,000 | — | — | 1.25 | 2.00 | 3.50 |
| 2006 BP | 7,000 | PF65 5.00 | | | | |
| 2007 BP | 13,008,000 | — | — | 1.25 | 2.00 | 3.50 |
| 2007 BP | 7,000 | PF65 5.00 | | | | |
| 2008 BP | 6,032,010 | — | — | 1.25 | 2.00 | 3.50 |
| 2008 BP | 7,000 | PF65 5.00 | | | | |
| 2009 BP | 1,986,010 | — | — | 1.25 | 2.00 | 3.50 |
| 2009 BP | 7,000 | PF65 5.00 | | | | |
| 2010 BP | 14,020 | — | — | — | 2.00 | 3.50 |
| 2010 BP | 7,000 | PF65 5.00 | | | | |
| 2011 BP | 9,000 | — | — | — | 2.00 | 3.50 |
| 2011 BP | 7,000 | PF65 5.00 | | | | |

### KM# 773 50 FORINT

7.70 g., Copper-Nickel, 27.5 mm. **Obv:** National arms above Euro Union star circle **Rev:** Denomination **Edge:** Plain **Mint:** Budapest

| Date | Mintage | VF20 | XF40 | MS60 | MS63 | MS65 |
|---|---|---|---|---|---|---|
| 2004 BP | 993,000 | — | — | 1.25 | 2.00 | 3.50 |
| 2004 BP | 7,000 | PF65 6.00 | | | | |

### KM# 780 50 FORINT

7.70 g., Copper-Nickel, 27.4 mm. **Subject:** International Childrens Safety Service **Obv:** Stylized crying child **Rev:** Denomination **Edge:** Plain **Mint:** Budapest

| Date | Mintage | VF20 | XF40 | MS60 | MS63 | MS65 |
|---|---|---|---|---|---|---|
| 2005 BP | 2,000,000 | — | — | 1.25 | 2.00 | 3.50 |

### KM# 788 50 FORINT

7.70 g., Copper-Nickel, 27.4 mm. **Obv:** Hungarian Red Cross 125th Anniversary seal above date and country name **Rev:** Value **Edge:** Plain **Mint:** Budapest

| Date | Mintage | VF20 | XF40 | MS60 | MS63 | MS65 |
|---|---|---|---|---|---|---|
| 2006 BP | 2,000,000 | — | — | 1.25 | 2.00 | 3.50 |

### KM# 789 50 FORINT

7.70 g., Copper-Nickel, 27.4 mm. **Subject:** 1956 Revolution **Obv:** Holed flag with Parliament building in background **Rev:** Value **Edge:** Plain **Mint:** Budapest

| Date | Mintage | VF20 | XF40 | MS60 | MS63 | MS65 |
|---|---|---|---|---|---|---|
| 2006 BP | 2,000,000 | — | — | 1.25 | 2.00 | 3.50 |

### KM# 805 50 FORINT

7.70 g., Copper-Nickel, 27.4 mm. **Subject:** Celebrating 50 years of the Treaty of Rome **Obv:** Book logo **Rev:** Value

| Date | Mintage | VF20 | XF40 | MS60 | MS63 | MS65 |
|---|---|---|---|---|---|---|
| 2007 | 2,000,000 | — | — | 1.25 | 2.00 | 3.50 |
| 2007 | 5,000 | PF65 3.50 | | | | |

### KM# 850 50 FORINT

7.60 g., Copper-Nickel, 27.5 mm. **Obv:** Saker falcon **Obv. Legend:** MAGYARORSZAG **Rev:** Denomination **Mint:** Budapest

| Date | Mintage | VF20 | XF40 | MS60 | MS63 | MS65 |
|---|---|---|---|---|---|---|
| 2012 BP | — | — | — | — | 2.00 | 3.50 |
| 2012 BP | 4,000 | PF65 7.00 | | | | |
| 2013 BP | — | — | — | — | 2.00 | 3.50 |

| Date | Mintage | VF20 | XF40 | MS60 | MS63 | MS65 |
|---|---|---|---|---|---|---|
| 2013 BP | — | PF65 7.00 | | | | |
| 2014 | — | — | — | — | 2.00 | 3.50 |
| 2014 | 2,000 | PF65 7.00 | | | | |

**KM# 721 100 FORINT**
8.00 g., Bi-Metallic Brass Plated Steel center in Stainless Steel ring, 23.8 mm. **Obv:** Crowned shield **Rev:** Denomination **Edge:** Reeded **Mint:** Budapest

| Date | Mintage | VF20 | XF40 | MS60 | MS63 | MS65 |
|---|---|---|---|---|---|---|
| 2001 BP | 7,000 | — | — | — | — | 5.00 |
| 2001 BP | 3,000 | PF65 8.00 | | | | |
| 2002 BP | 7,000 | — | — | — | — | 5.00 |
| 2002 BP | 3,000 | PF65 8.00 | | | | |
| 2003 BP | 8,000 | — | — | — | — | 5.00 |
| 2003 BP | 7,000 | PF65 7.50 | | | | |
| 2004 BP | 4,008,000 | — | — | — | 3.50 | 5.00 |
| 2004 BP | 7,000 | PF65 7.50 | | | | |
| 2005 BP | 8,000 | — | — | — | — | 5.00 |
| 2005 BP | 7,000 | PF65 7.50 | | | | |
| 2006 BP | 8,000 | — | — | — | — | 5.00 |
| 2006 BP | 7,000 | PF65 7.50 | | | | |
| 2007 BP | 7,008,010 | — | — | — | 3.50 | 5.00 |
| 2007 BP | 7,000 | PF65 7.50 | | | | |
| 2008 BP | 7,008,010 | — | — | — | 3.50 | 5.00 |
| 2008 BP | 7,000 | PF65 7.50 | | | | |
| 2009 BP | 11,210 | — | — | — | — | 5.00 |
| 2009 BP | 7,000 | PF65 7.50 | | | | |
| 2010 BP | 14,020 | — | — | — | — | 5.00 |
| 2010 BP | 7,000 | PF65 7.50 | | | | |
| 2011 BP | 9,000 | — | — | — | — | 5.00 |
| 2011 BP | 7,000 | PF65 7.50 | | | | |

**KM# 760 100 FORINT**
8.00 g., Bi-Metallic Brass Plated Steel center in Stainless Steel ring, 23.8 mm. **Subject:** Lajos Kossuth **Obv:** Head right within circle **Rev:** Denomination within circle **Edge:** Reeded **Mint:** Budapest

| Date | Mintage | VF20 | XF40 | MS60 | MS63 | MS65 |
|---|---|---|---|---|---|---|
| 2002 BP | 997,000 | — | — | — | 2.00 | 3.00 |
| 2002 BP | 3,000 | PF65 5.00 | | | | |

**KM# 844 100 FORINT**
10.00 g., Copper-Nickel, 30 mm. **Subject:** Hungarian Scout Association, 100th Anniversary **Obv:** Hungarian Scout emblem at right **Rev:** Scout in uniform blowing bugle towards left **Shape:** 12-sided **Mint:** Budapest

| Date | Mintage | VF20 | XF40 | MS60 | MS63 | MS65 |
|---|---|---|---|---|---|---|
| 2012 BP | 5,000 | — | — | — | — | 20.00 |
| 2012 BP | 10,000 | PF65 25.00 | | | | |

**KM# 851 100 FORINT**
8.00 g., Bi-Metallic Brass Plated Steel center in Stainless Steel ring, 23.6 mm. **Obv:** Crowned shield **Obv. Legend:** MAGYARORZAG **Rev:** Denomination **Mint:** Budapest

| Date | Mintage | VF20 | XF40 | MS60 | MS63 | MS65 |
|---|---|---|---|---|---|---|
| 2012 BP | — | — | — | — | 3.50 | 5.00 |
| 2012 BP | 4,000 | PF63 7.00 | PF65 10.00 | | | |
| 2013 BP | — | — | — | — | 3.50 | 5.00 |
| 2013 BP | — | PF63 7.00 | PF65 10.00 | | | |
| 2014 | — | — | — | — | 3.50 | 5.00 |
| 2014 | 2,000 | PF63 7.00 | PF65 10.00 | | | |

**KM# 754 200 FORINT**
9.40 g., Brass, 29.2 mm. **Subject:** Childrens Literature: Ludas Matyi **Obv:** Denomination **Rev:** Man holding a goose **Edge:** Plain **Mint:** Budapest

| Date | Mintage | VF20 | XF40 | MS60 | MS63 | MS65 |
|---|---|---|---|---|---|---|
| 2001 BP | 12,000 | — | — | — | 5.00 | 7.00 |
| 2001 BP | 5,000 | PF65 12.00 | | | | |

**KM# 755 200 FORINT**
Brass, 29.2 mm. **Subject:** Childrens Literature: Janos Vitez **Obv:** Denomination **Rev:** Soldier riding a flying bird **Edge:** Plain **Mint:** Budapest

| Date | Mintage | VF20 | XF40 | MS60 | MS63 | MS65 |
|---|---|---|---|---|---|---|
| 2001 BP | 12,000 | — | — | — | 5.00 | 7.00 |
| 2001 BP | 5,000 | PF65 12.00 | | | | |

**KM# 756 200 FORINT**
Brass, 29.2 mm. **Subject:** Childrens Literature: Toldi **Obv:** Denomination **Rev:** Knight kicking a boat off the shore **Edge:** Plain **Mint:** Budapest

| Date | Mintage | VF20 | XF40 | MS60 | MS63 | MS65 |
|---|---|---|---|---|---|---|
| 2001 BP | 12,000 | — | — | — | 5.00 | 7.00 |
| 2001 BP | 5,000 | PF65 12.00 | | | | |

**KM# 757 200 FORINT**
Brass, 29.2 mm. **Subject:** Childrens Literature: A Pal Utcai Fiuk **Obv:** Denomination **Rev:** Two men and cordwood **Edge:** Plain **Mint:** Budapest

| Date | Mintage | VF20 | XF40 | MS60 | MS63 | MS65 |
|---|---|---|---|---|---|---|
| 2001 | 12,000 | — | — | — | 5.00 | 7.00 |
| 2001 | 5,000 | PF65 12.00 | | | | |

**KM# 826 200 FORINT**
9.00 g., Bi-Metallic Copper-Nickel center in Nickel-Brass ring, 28.3 mm. **Obv:** Suspension Bridge over the Danube **Rev:** Value **Edge:** Segmented reeding **Mint:** Budapest

| Date | Mintage | VF20 | XF40 | MS60 | MS63 | MS65 |
|---|---|---|---|---|---|---|
| 2009 BP | 71,010,010 | — | — | — | 3.00 | 5.00 |
| 2009 BP Proof | 7,000 | — | — | — | — | — |
| 2010 BP | 25,014,020 | — | — | — | 3.00 | 5.00 |
| 2010 BP Proof | 7,000 | — | — | — | — | — |
| 2011 BP | 30,009,000 | — | — | — | 3.00 | 5.00 |
| 2011 BP Proof | 7,000 | — | — | — | — | — |

**KM# 852 200 FORINT**
9.00 g., Bi-Metallic Copper-Nickel center in Nickel-Brass ring, 28.3 mm. **Obv:** Suspension Bridge over the Danube **Obv. Legend:** MAGYARORSZAG **Rev:** Denomination **Edge:** Segmented reeding **Mint:** Budapest

| Date | Mintage | VF20 | XF40 | MS60 | MS63 | MS65 |
|---|---|---|---|---|---|---|
| 2012 BP | — | — | — | — | 3.00 | 5.00 |
| 2012 BP | 4,000 | PF65 8.00 | | | | |
| 2013 BP | — | — | — | — | 3.00 | 5.00 |
| 2013 BP | — | PF65 8.00 | | | | |
| 2014 | — | — | — | — | 3.00 | 5.00 |
| 2014 | 2,000 | PF65 8.00 | | | | |

**KM# 764 500 FORINT**
13.90 g., Copper-Nickel, 28.4x28.4 mm. **Subject:** Farkas Kempelen's Chess Machine **Obv:** Denomination, letters A-H and numbers 1-8 repeated along edges **Rev:** Robotic human form chess playing machine built in 1769 **Edge:** Plain **Shape:** Square **Mint:** Budapest

| Date | Mintage | VF20 | XF40 | MS60 | MS63 | MS65 |
|---|---|---|---|---|---|---|
| 2002 BP | 5,000 | — | — | — | 22.00 | 27.00 |
| 2002 BP | 5,000 | PF65 55.00 | | | | |

**KM# 765 500 FORINT**
13.80 g., Copper-Nickel, 28.4x28.4 mm. **Subject:** Rubik's Cube **Obv:** Inscription on Rubik's Cube design **Rev:** Rubik's Cube with inscription **Edge:** Plain **Shape:** Square **Mint:** Budapest

| Date | Mintage | VF20 | XF40 | MS60 | MS63 | MS65 |
|---|---|---|---|---|---|---|
| 2002 BP | 5,000 | — | — | — | 20.00 | 25.00 |
| 2002 BP | 5,000 | PF65 50.00 | | | | |

**KM# 781 500 FORINT**
14.00 g., Copper-Nickel, 28.4x28.4 mm. **Obv:** Old wheel **Rev:** First Hungarian Post Office motor vehicle **Edge:** Plain **Shape:** Square **Mint:** Budapest **Note:** 28.43 x 28.43mm

| Date | Mintage | VF20 | XF40 | MS60 | MS63 | MS65 |
|---|---|---|---|---|---|---|
| 2005 BP | 5,000 | — | — | — | 17.00 | 22.00 |
| 2005 BP | 10,000 | PF63 32.00 | PF65 35.00 | | | |

**KM# 766 1000 FORINT**
Bronze Hollow coin unscrews to open **Obv:** Denomination and satellite dish **Rev:** Mercury **Mint:** Budapest

| Date | Mintage | VF20 | XF40 | MS60 | MS63 | MS65 |
|---|---|---|---|---|---|---|
| 2002 | 15,000 | — | — | — | 15.00 | 16.50 |

**KM# 787 1000 FORINT**
13.81 g., Copper-Nickel, 28.3 mm. **Obv:** Value and partial front view of antique automobile **Rev:** Model T Ford **Edge:** Plain **Shape:** Square **Mint:** Budapest

| Date | Mintage | VF20 | XF40 | MS60 | MS63 | MS65 |
|---|---|---|---|---|---|---|
| 2006 BP | 10,000 | — | — | — | 17.00 | 20.00 |
| 2006 BP | 10,000 | PF63 28.00 | PF65 30.00 | | | |

**KM# 797 1000 FORINT**

14.00 g., Copper-Nickel, 28.43 x 28.43 mm. **Subject:** 125th Anniversary - Birth of János Adorján **Obv:** Early two cylinder aircraft motor with propeller **Obv. Legend:** MAGYAR / KOZTARSASAG **Rev:** Early monoplane **Rev. Legend:** ADORJAN JANOS / AZ ELSO SIKERES MAGYAR / REPULOGEP TERVEZOJE **Edge:** Plain **Shape:** Square **Mint:** Budapest

| Date | Mintage | VF20 | XF40 | MS60 | MS63 | MS65 |
|---|---|---|---|---|---|---|
| 2007 BP | 10,000 | — | — | — | 17.00 | 20.00 |
| 2007 BP | 10,000 | PF63 28.00 | PF65 30.00 | | | |

**KM# 809 1000 FORINT**

14.00 g., Copper-Nickel, 28.43 x 28.43 mm. **Subject:** Telephone Herald **Edge:** Plain **Shape:** Square

| Date | Mintage | VF20 | XF40 | MS60 | MS63 | MS65 |
|---|---|---|---|---|---|---|
| 2008 | 10,000 | — | — | — | 17.00 | 20.00 |
| 2008 | 15,000 | PF63 25.00 | PF65 27.00 | | | |

**KM# 813 1000 FORINT**

14.00 g., Copper-Nickel, 28.4 x 28.4 mm. **Subject:** Donat Banki, 150th Anniversary of Birth **Obv:** Denomination view of crossflow turbine **Rev:** Portrait facing in suit **Shape:** Square **Mint:** Budapest

| Date | Mintage | VF20 | XF40 | MS60 | MS63 | MS65 |
|---|---|---|---|---|---|---|
| 2009 BP | 10,000 | — | — | — | 16.00 | 18.00 |
| 2009 BP | 10,000 | PF63 22.00 | PF65 25.00 | | | |

**KM# 818 1000 FORINT**

14.00 g., Copper-Nickel, 28.4 x 28.4 mm. **Subject:** Laszlo Jozsef Biro, Inventor of the ball point pen **Obv:** Ball point pen schematic **Rev:** Bust facing **Shape:** Square **Mint:** Budapest

| Date | Mintage | VF20 | XF40 | MS60 | MS63 | MS65 |
|---|---|---|---|---|---|---|
| 2010 BP | 10,000 | — | — | — | 17.00 | 20.00 |
| 2010 BP | 10,000 | PF63 25.00 | PF65 28.00 | | | |

**KM# 829 1000 FORINT**

14.00 g., Copper-Nickel, 28.43x28.43 mm. **Subject:** Anyos Jedlik, principals of the dynamo, 1861 **Obv:** Dynamo **Rev:** Jedlik portrait **Mint:** Budapest

| Date | Mintage | VF20 | XF40 | MS60 | MS63 | MS65 |
|---|---|---|---|---|---|---|
| 2011 BP | 10,000 | — | — | — | 15.00 | 18.00 |
| 2011 BP | 10,000 | PF63 22.00 | PF65 25.00 | | | |

**KM# 840 1000 FORINT**

14.00 g., Copper-Nickel, 28.43x28.43 mm. **Subject:** Masat-1 satellite launch **Obv:** Land-based antenna **Rev:** Satellite above Eastern Europe map, Hungary highlighted **Mint:** Budapest

| Date | Mintage | VF20 | XF40 | MS60 | MS63 | MS65 |
|---|---|---|---|---|---|---|
| 2012 BP | 5,000 | — | — | — | — | 25.00 |
| 2012 BP | 5,000 | PF65 25.00 | | | | |

**KM# 752 3000 FORINT**

31.46 g., 0.925 Silver 0.9356 oz. ASW, 38.5 mm. **Subject:** Hungarian Silver Coinage Millennium **Obv:** Denomination in ornamental frame **Rev:** Thaler design circa 1500 portraying Ladislaus I (1077-95) with the title of saint **Edge:** Reeding over "1001-2001 **Edge Lettering:** BP • NX • KB • HX • GY • F • AF • MM • C + **Mint:** Budapest

| Date | Mintage | VF20 | XF40 | MS60 | MS63 | MS65 |
|---|---|---|---|---|---|---|
| 2001 BP | 5,000 | — | — | — | 40.00 | 45.00 |
| 2001 BP | 5,000 | PF65 50.00 | | | | |

**KM# 759 3000 FORINT**

31.80 g., 0.925 Silver 0.9457 oz. ASW, 38.7 mm. **Subject:** Centennial of First Hungarian Film "The Dance **Obv:** Denomination **Rev:** Two dancers on film **Edge:** Reeded **Mint:** Budapest

| Date | Mintage | VF20 | XF40 | MS60 | MS63 | MS65 |
|---|---|---|---|---|---|---|
| 2001 BP | 3,500 | — | — | — | 42.00 | 47.50 |
| 2001 BP | 3,500 | PF65 55.00 | | | | |

**KM# 761 3000 FORINT**

31.33 g., 0.925 Silver 0.9317 oz. ASW, 38.6 mm. **Subject:** Hortobagy National Park **Obv:** Landscape, denomination **Rev:** Hungarian Grey Longhorn bull **Edge:** Reeded **Mint:** Budapest

| Date | Mintage | VF20 | XF40 | MS60 | MS63 | MS65 |
|---|---|---|---|---|---|---|
| 2002 BP | 5,000 | — | — | — | 25.00 | 35.00 |
| 2002 BP | 5,000 | PF65 50.00 | | | | |

**KM# 762 3000 FORINT**

31.46 g., 0.925 Silver 0.9356 oz. ASW, 38.5 mm. **Subject:** 200th Anniversary - National Library **Obv:** Small coat of arms in ornate frame **Rev:** Interior view of library **Edge:** Reeded **Mint:** Budapest

| Date | Mintage | VF20 | XF40 | MS60 | MS63 | MS65 |
|---|---|---|---|---|---|---|
| 2002 BP | 3,000 | — | — | — | 40.00 | 45.00 |
| 2002 BP | 3,000 | PF65 50.00 | | | | |

**KM# 763 3000 FORINT**

31.46 g., 0.925 Silver 0.9356 oz. ASW, 38.5 mm. **Subject:** Janos Bolyai's publication of his "Appendix **Obv:** Circular graph **Rev:** Signature above 7-line inscription, name and dates **Edge:** Reeded **Mint:** Budapest

| Date | Mintage | VF20 | XF40 | MS60 | MS63 | MS65 |
|---|---|---|---|---|---|---|
| 2002 BP | 3,000 | — | — | — | 40.00 | 45.00 |
| 2002 BP | 3,000 | PF65 50.00 | | | | |

**KM# 767 3000 FORINT**

31.46 g., 0.925 Silver 0.9356 oz. ASW **Subject:** 100th Anniversary - Birth of Kovacs Margit (1902-1977) **Obv:** Denomination **Rev:** The "Trumpet of Judgement Day **Mint:** Budapest

| Date | Mintage | VF20 | XF40 | MS60 | MS63 | MS65 |
|---|---|---|---|---|---|---|
| 2002 | 4,000 | — | — | — | 40.00 | 45.00 |
| 2002 | — | PF65 55.00 | | | | |

**KM# 817 3000 FORINT**
10.00 g., 0.925 Silver 0.2974 oz. ASW **Subject:** Ferenc Kazinczy, 250th Anniversary of Birth **Obv:** Quill pen and rolled document **Rev:** Bust facing

| Date | Mintage | VF20 | XF40 | MS60 | MS63 | MS65 |
|---|---|---|---|---|---|---|
| 2009 | 5,000 | — | — | — | 17.00 | 20.00 |
| 2009 | 5,000 | PF65 40.00 | | | | |

**KM# 828 3000 FORINT**
10.00 g., 0.925 Silver 0.2974 oz. ASW, 30 mm. **Subject:** Hungary's EU Council Presidency, 2011 **Obv:** Crowned shield within grometric design **Rev:** Skyline view below EU star circle **Mint:** Budapest

| Date | Mintage | VF20 | XF40 | MS60 | MS63 | MS65 |
|---|---|---|---|---|---|---|
| 2011 BP | 3,000 | — | — | — | — | 30.00 |
| 2011 BP | 5,000 | PF65 45.00 | | | | |

**KM# 837 3000 FORINT**
20.00 g., 0.925 Silver 0.5948 oz. ASW, 34 mm. **Subject:** Imre Madach's The Tragedy of Man, 150th Anniversary **Obv:** Bust at left, large value **Rev:** Two figures standing on hilltop, guardian in background **Mint:** Budapest

| Date | Mintage | VF20 | XF40 | MS60 | MS63 | MS65 |
|---|---|---|---|---|---|---|
| 2012 BP | 2,000 | — | — | — | — | 45.00 |
| 2012 BP | 4,000 | PF65 50.00 | | | | |

**KM# 842 3000 FORINT**
24.00 g., 0.925 Silver 0.7137 oz. ASW, 30 mm. **Subject:** XXX Summer Olympics, London **Obv:** Two kayak paddles **Rev:** Three kayakers advancing right **Mint:** Budapest

| Date | Mintage | VF20 | XF40 | MS60 | MS63 | MS65 |
|---|---|---|---|---|---|---|
| 2012 BP | 3,000 | — | — | — | — | 45.00 |
| 2012 BP | 5,000 | PF65 50.00 | | | | |

**KM# 845 3000 FORINT**
10.00 g., 0.925 Silver 0.2974 oz. ASW, 30x25 mm. **Subject:** Albert Szent-Gyorgyi, Nobel prize winner **Obv:** Paprika, value at upper right **Rev:** Szent-Gyorgyi bust at left **Shape:** Horizontal oval **Mint:** Budapest

| Date | Mintage | VF20 | XF40 | MS60 | MS63 | MS65 |
|---|---|---|---|---|---|---|
| 2012 BP | 2,000 | — | — | — | — | 45.00 |
| 2012 BP | 5,000 | PF65 50.00 | | | | |

**KM# 846 3000 FORINT**
20.00 g., 0.925 Silver 0.5948 oz. ASW, 34 mm. **Subject:** Sandor Popovics, 150th Anniversary of Birth **Obv:** Architectural statuary group **Rev:** Popovics bust **Mint:** Budapest

| Date | Mintage | VF20 | XF40 | MS60 | MS63 | MS65 |
|---|---|---|---|---|---|---|
| 2012 BP | 2,000 | — | — | — | — | 45.00 |
| 2012 BP | 4,000 | PF65 50.00 | | | | |

**KM# 854 3000 FORINT**
12.50 g., 0.925 Silver 0.3717 oz. ASW, 30x25 mm. **Subject:** Albert Szenj-Gyorgyi Nobel in Physiology 1937 **Shape:** Horizontal oval **Mint:** Budapest

| Date | Mintage | VF20 | XF40 | MS60 | MS63 | MS65 |
|---|---|---|---|---|---|---|
| 2012 BP | 2,000 | — | — | — | — | 30.00 |
| 2012 BP | 5,000 | PF65 40.00 | | | | |

**KM# 853 3000 FORINT**
Silver **Subject:** Traditional dance **Obv:** Tulip **Rev:** Family dancing **Mint:** Budapest

| Date | Mintage | VF20 | XF40 | MS60 | MS63 | MS65 |
|---|---|---|---|---|---|---|
| 2013 | — | PF65 50.00 | | | | |

**KM# 856 3000 FORINT**
10.00 g., 0.925 Silver 0.2974 oz. ASW, 30x25 mm. **Subject:** Wigner Jeno, Nobel Prize 1963 **Shape:** Oval **Mint:** Budapest

| Date | Mintage | VF20 | XF40 | MS60 | MS63 | MS65 |
|---|---|---|---|---|---|---|
| 2013 | — | — | — | — | — | 45.00 |

**KM# 751 4000 FORINT**
31.46 g., 0.925 Silver 0.9356 oz. ASW, 26.4 x 39.6 mm. **Subject:** Godollo Artist Colony Centennial **Obv:** Denomination **Rev:** Sisters" stained glass window design **Edge:** Plain **Shape:** Vertical rectangle **Mint:** Budapest

| Date | Mintage | VF20 | XF40 | MS60 | MS63 | MS65 |
|---|---|---|---|---|---|---|
| 2001 BP | 4,000 | — | — | — | 40.00 | 45.00 |
| 2001 BP | 4,000 | PF65 50.00 | | | | |

**KM# 769 5000 FORINT**
31.46 g., 0.925 Silver 0.9356 oz. ASW, 38.6 mm. **Subject:** Budapest Philharmonic Orchestra **Obv:** Crowned arms in wreath **Rev:** Four coin-like portraits of Erkel, Dohnanyi, Bartók and Kodaly **Edge:** Reeded **Mint:** Budapest

| Date | Mintage | VF20 | XF40 | MS60 | MS63 | MS65 |
|---|---|---|---|---|---|---|
| 2003 BP | 4,000 | — | — | — | 37.50 | 42.50 |
| 2003 BP | 4,000 | PF65 50.00 | | | | |

**KM# 770 5000 FORINT**
31.46 g., 0.925 Silver 0.9356 oz. ASW, 38.6 mm. **Subject:** Janos Neumann, 100th Anniversary of Birth **Obv:** Denomination and binary number date **Rev:** Portrait and building **Edge:** Reeded **Mint:** Budapest

| Date | Mintage | VF20 | XF40 | MS60 | MS63 | MS65 |
|---|---|---|---|---|---|---|
| 2003 BP | 3,000 | — | — | — | 40.00 | 45.00 |
| 2003 BP | 3,000 | PF65 75.00 | | | | |

**KM# 771 5000 FORINT**
31.46 g., 0.925 Silver 0.9356 oz. ASW, 38.6 mm. **Subject:** Rakoczi's War of Liberation **Obv:** Transylvanian ducat design above country name, value and date **Rev:** Kuruc cavalryman with sword and trumpet **Edge:** Reeded **Mint:** Budapest

| Date | Mintage | VF20 | XF40 | MS60 | MS63 | MS65 |
|---|---|---|---|---|---|---|
| 2003 BP | 3,000 | — | — | — | 45.00 | 50.00 |
| 2003 BP | 3,000 | PF65 65.00 | | | | |

**KM# 772 5000 FORINT**
31.46 g., 0.925 Silver 0.9356 oz. ASW, 38.6 mm. **Subject:** World Heritage in Hungary - Holloko **Obv:** Holloko castle ruins above country name, value and date **Rev:** Village view behind woman in folk costume **Edge:** Reeded **Mint:** Budapest

| Date | Mintage | VF20 | XF40 | MS60 | MS63 | MS65 |
|---|---|---|---|---|---|---|
| 2003 BP | 5,000 | — | — | — | 42.50 | 45.00 |
| 2003 BP | 5,000 | PF65 60.00 | | | | |

**KM# 774 5000 FORINT**
31.46 g., 0.925 Silver 0.9356 oz. ASW, 38.6 mm. **Obv:** Value **Rev:** Two Olympic boxers **Edge:** Reeded **Mint:** Budapest

| Date | Mintage | VF20 | XF40 | MS60 | MS63 | MS65 |
|---|---|---|---|---|---|---|
| 2004 BP | 3,000 | — | — | — | 45.00 | 47.50 |
| 2004 BP | 9,000 | PF65 55.00 | | | | |

**KM# 775 5000 FORINT**
31.46 g., 0.925 Silver 0.9356 oz. ASW, 38.6 mm. **Obv:** Solomon Tower" above value **Rev:** Visegrad Castle with the Solomon Tower **Edge:** Reeded **Mint:** Budapest

| Date | Mintage | VF20 | XF40 | MS60 | MS63 | MS65 |
|---|---|---|---|---|---|---|
| 2004 BP | 4,000 | — | — | — | 45.00 | 50.00 |
| 2004 BP | 4,000 | PF65 60.00 | | | | |

**KM# 776 5000 FORINT**
31.46 g., 0.925 Silver 0.9356 oz. ASW, 38.6 mm. **Obv:** Value and country name above Euro Union stars **Rev:** Mythical stag seen through an ornate window **Edge:** Reeded **Mint:** Budapest

| Date | Mintage | VF20 | XF40 | MS60 | MS63 | MS65 |
|---|---|---|---|---|---|---|
| 2004 BP | 10,000 | PF63 50.00 | PF65 55.00 | | | |

**KM# 778 5000 FORINT**
31.46 g., 0.925 Silver 0.9356 oz. ASW, 38.6 mm. **Subject:** Ancient Christian Necropolis at Pecs **Obv:** Value and ancient artifact **Rev:** Interior view of tomb **Edge:** Reeded **Mint:** Budapest

| Date | Mintage | VF20 | XF40 | MS60 | MS63 | MS65 |
|---|---|---|---|---|---|---|
| 2004 BP | 5,000 | — | — | — | 40.00 | 45.00 |
| 2004 BP | 5,000 | PF65 50.00 | | | | |

**KM# 782 5000 FORINT**
31.46 g., 0.925 Silver 0.9356 oz. ASW, 38.6 mm. **Obv:** Bat flying above value **Rev:** Interior cave view **Edge:** Reeded **Mint:** Budapest

| Date | Mintage | VF20 | XF40 | MS60 | MS63 | MS65 |
|---|---|---|---|---|---|---|
| 2005 BP | 5,000 | — | — | — | 45.00 | 50.00 |
| 2005 BP | 5,000 | PF65 55.00 | | | | |

**KM# 783 5000 FORINT**
31.46 g., 0.925 Silver 0.9356 oz. ASW, 38.6 mm. **Obv:** Hungarian National Bank building **Rev:** Ignac Alpar and life dates **Edge:** Reeded **Mint:** Budapest

| Date | Mintage | VF20 | XF40 | MS60 | MS63 | MS65 |
|---|---|---|---|---|---|---|
| ND (2005) BP | 3,000 | — | — | — | 45.00 | 50.00 |
| ND (2005) BP | 3,000 | PF65 60.00 | | | | |

**KM# 784 5000 FORINT**
31.46 g., 0.925 Silver 0.9356 oz. ASW, 38.6 mm. **Obv:** Knight on horse with lance **Rev:** Diosgyor Castle **Edge:** Reeded **Mint:** Budapest

| Date | Mintage | VF20 | XF40 | MS60 | MS63 | MS65 |
|---|---|---|---|---|---|---|
| 2005 BP | 4,000 | — | — | — | 45.00 | 50.00 |
| 2005 BP | 4,000 | PF65 60.00 | | | | |

**KM# 785 5000 FORINT**
31.46 g., 0.925 Silver 0.9356 oz. ASW, 38.6 mm. **Obv:** Large building above value **Rev:** Karoli Gaspar Reformed (Calvinist) University seal **Edge:** Reeded **Mint:** Budapest

| Date | Mintage | VF20 | XF40 | MS60 | MS63 | MS65 |
|---|---|---|---|---|---|---|
| 2005 BP | 3,000 | — | — | — | 45.00 | 50.00 |
| 2005 BP | 3,000 | PF65 60.00 | | | | |

**KM# 786 5000 FORINT**
31.46 g., 0.925 Silver 0.9356 oz. ASW, 38.6 mm. **Obv:** Coin design of a Transylvanian KM-10 thaler reverse dated 1605 **Rev:** Stephan Bocskai (1557-1606) **Edge:** Reeded **Mint:** Budapest

| Date | Mintage | VF20 | XF40 | MS60 | MS63 | MS65 |
|---|---|---|---|---|---|---|
| 2005 BP | 3,000 | — | — | — | 45.00 | 50.00 |
| 2005 BP | 3,000 | PF65 55.00 | | | | |

**KM# 790 5000 FORINT**
31.46 g., 0.925 Silver 0.9356 oz. ASW, 38.61 mm. **Series:** Masterpieces of Ecclesiastical Architecture **Obv:** View of interior of dome **Obv. Legend:** MAGYAR KÖZTÁRSASÁG **Rev:** Basilica facade **Rev. Legend:** ESZTERGOMI BAZILIKA **Mint:** Budapest

| Date | Mintage | VF20 | XF40 | MS60 | MS63 | MS65 |
|---|---|---|---|---|---|---|
| 2006 BP | 2,500 | — | — | — | 50.00 | 55.00 |
| 2006 BP | 3,500 | PF65 65.00 | | | | |

**KM# 791 5000 FORINT**
31.46 g., 0.925 Silver 0.9356 oz. ASW, 38.61 mm. **Subject:** 125th Anniversary - Birth of Béla Bartók **Obv:** Transylvanian woodcarving **Obv. Legend:** MAGYAR KÖZTÁRSASÁG **Rev:** Bust of Bartók right, Euro star behind **Edge:** Reeded and lettered **Edge Lettering:** Bartók Béla repeated three times **Mint:** Budapest

| Date | Mintage | VF20 | XF40 | MS60 | MS63 | MS65 |
|---|---|---|---|---|---|---|
| 2006 BP | 25,000 | PF63 40.00 | PF65 45.00 | | | |

**KM# 792 5000 FORINT**
31.46 g., 0.925 Silver 0.9356 oz. ASW, 38.61 mm. **Series:** Heritage Sites **Obv:** Great White Egret in flight **Obv. Legend:** MAGYAR - KÖZTÁRSASÁG **Rev:** Landscape, Schneeberg Mountain above Esterházy palace facade **Mint:** Budapest

| Date | Mintage | VF20 | XF40 | MS60 | MS63 | MS65 |
|---|---|---|---|---|---|---|
| 2006 BP | 5,000 | — | — | — | 42.50 | 47.50 |
| 2006 BP | 5,000 | PF65 55.00 | | | | |

**KM# 793 5000 FORINT**
31.46 g., 0.925 Silver 0.9356 oz. ASW, 38.61 mm. **Series:** Hungarian Castles **Subject:** Hungarian Castles **Obv:** Portrait of Ilona Zrinyi **Obv. Legend:** MAGYAR KÖZTÁRSASÁG **Rev:** Munkács Castle **Mint:** Budapest

| Date | Mintage | VF20 | XF40 | MS60 | MS63 | MS65 |
|---|---|---|---|---|---|---|
| 2006 BP | 4,000 | — | — | — | 42.50 | 47.50 |
| 2006 BP | 4,000 | PF65 55.00 | | | | |

**KM# 794 5000 FORINT**
31.46 g., 0.925 Silver 0.9356 oz. ASW, 38.61 mm. **Subject:** 500th Anniversary - Victory in Nándorfehévár **Obv:** Decorative sword hilt **Obv. Legend:** MAGYAR KÖZTÁRSASÁG **Rev:** János Hunyadi in armor at left, John Capistrano in monk's garb at right **Rev. Inscription:** NÁNDORFEHÉRVÁRI / DIADAL **Mint:** Budapest

| Date | Mintage | VF20 | XF40 | MS60 | MS63 | MS65 |
|---|---|---|---|---|---|---|
| 2006 BP | 2,500 | — | — | — | 45.00 | 50.00 |
| 2006 BP | 3,500 | PF65 60.00 | | | | |

**KM# 795 5000 FORINT**
31.46 g., 0.925 Silver 0.9356 oz. ASW, 38.61 mm. **Subject:** 50th Anniversary - Hungarian Revolution **Obv:** 1956 repeated in stone blocks at right **Obv. Legend:** MAGYAR KÖZTÁRSASÁG **Rev:** 1956 repeated in stone blocks at left, freedom fighter's flag at center **Rev. Legend:** MAGYAR FORRADALOM ÉS SZABADSÁGHARC **Mint:** Budapest

| Date | Mintage | VF20 | XF40 | MS60 | MS63 | MS65 |
|---|---|---|---|---|---|---|
| 2006 BP | 5,000 | — | — | — | 42.50 | 47.50 |
| 2006 BP | 5,000 | PF65 55.00 | | | | |

**KM# 798 5000 FORINT**
31.46 g., 0.925 Silver 0.9356 oz. ASW, 38.61 mm. **Series:** Hungarian Castles **Obv:** Walled tower **Obv. Inscription:** MAGYAR / KÖZTÁRSASÁG **Rev:** Gyula castle **Rev. Inscription:** GYULAI / VÁR **Mint:** Budapest

| Date | Mintage | VF20 | XF40 | MS60 | MS63 | MS65 |
|---|---|---|---|---|---|---|
| 2007 BP | 4,000 | — | — | — | 55.00 | 60.00 |
| 2007 BP | 4,000 | PF65 75.00 | | | | |

**KM# 799 5000 FORINT**
31.46 g., 0.925 Silver 0.9356 oz. ASW, 38.61 mm. **Subject:** 200th Anniversary - Birth of Count Lajos Batthyány **Obv:** Seal dated 1848 with crowned arms above Batthyány's autograph **Obv. Legend:** MAGYAR KÖZTÁRASÁG **Rev:** 1/2 length figure of Batthyány facing **Rev. Legend:** BATTHYÁNY LAJOS **Mint:** Budapest

| Date | Mintage | VF20 | XF40 | MS60 | MS63 | MS65 |
|---|---|---|---|---|---|---|
| 2007 BP | 20,000 | PF63 40.00 | PF65 45.00 | | | |

**KM# 800 5000 FORINT**

31.46 g., 0.925 Silver 0.9356 oz. ASW, 38.61 mm. **Subject:** 125th Anniversary - Birth of Zoltán Kodály **Obv:** Gramaphone **Obv. Legend:** MAGYAR KÖZTÁRSASÁG **Rev:** Bust of Kodály facing 3/4 right **Mint:** Budapest

| Date | Mintage | VF20 | XF40 | MS60 | MS63 | MS65 |
|---|---|---|---|---|---|---|
| 2007 BP | 4,000 | — | — | — | 42.50 | 47.50 |
| 2007 BP | 6,000 | PF65 50.00 | | | | |

**KM# 802 5000 FORINT**

31.46 g., 0.925 Silver 0.9356 oz. ASW, 38.61 mm. **Subject:** 8ooth Anniversary - Birth of St. Elizabeth **Obv:** Stylized image of St. Elizabeth feeding the hungry **Obv. Inscription:** Magyar / Köztárszág **Rev:** 3/4 length figure of St. Elizabeth seated facing holding roses and bread rolls in her lap **Mint:** Budapest

| Date | Mintage | VF20 | XF40 | MS60 | MS63 | MS65 |
|---|---|---|---|---|---|---|
| 2007 BP | 4,000 | — | — | — | 52.50 | 55.00 |
| 2007 BP | 4,000 | PF65 65.00 | | | | |

**KM# 804 5000 FORINT**

31.46 g., 0.925 Silver 0.9356 oz. ASW, 38.61 mm. **Subject:** Great Reformed Church - Debrecen **Obv:** Church interior **Obv. Legend:** MAGYAR KOZTARSASAG **Rev:** Church facade **Rev. Legend:** DEBRECENI REFORMATUS NAGYTEMPLOM **Edge:** Plain **Shape:** 12-sided **Mint:** Budapest

| Date | Mintage | VF20 | XF40 | MS60 | MS63 | MS65 |
|---|---|---|---|---|---|---|
| 2007 BP | 4,000 | — | — | — | 42.50 | 47.50 |
| 2007 BP | 6,000 | PF65 50.00 | | | | |

**KM# 806 5000 FORINT**

31.46 g., 0.925 Silver 0.9356 oz. ASW, 38.61 mm. **Obv:** Grape wreath rim with denomination, legend & mintmark inside **Rev:** Tokaj hill, TV tower, grapefield with a village & church **Edge:** Milled

| Date | Mintage | VF20 | XF40 | MS60 | MS63 | MS65 |
|---|---|---|---|---|---|---|
| 2008 | 5,000 | — | — | — | — | 48.00 |
| 2008 | 15,000 | PF63 50.00 | PF65 55.00 | | | |

**KM# 807 5000 FORINT**

31.46 g., 0.925 Silver 0.9356 oz. ASW, 38.61 mm. **Subject:** Castle of the Siklós **Obv:** Castle, tower, Franciscan monastery & church **Rev:** Castle of the Siklós

| Date | Mintage | VF20 | XF40 | MS60 | MS63 | MS65 |
|---|---|---|---|---|---|---|
| 2008 | 4,000 | — | — | — | — | 45.00 |
| 2008 | 6,000 | PF65 50.00 | | | | |

**KM# 808 5000 FORINT**

31.46 g., 0.925 Silver 0.9356 oz. ASW, 38.61 mm. **Subject:** 29th Summer Olympics **Obv:** Coat of arms over water **Rev:** Water polo player **Edge:** Milled

| Date | Mintage | VF20 | XF40 | MS60 | MS63 | MS65 |
|---|---|---|---|---|---|---|
| 2008 | 4,000 | — | — | — | — | 40.00 |
| 2008 | 14,000 | PF63 42.00 | PF65 45.00 | | | |

**KM# 810 5000 FORINT**

31.46 g., 0.925 Silver 0.9356 oz. ASW, 38.61 mm. **Subject:** Centenery birth of Ede Teller **Obv:** Diagram of Deuterium-tritium fusion reaction **Rev:** Portrait Ede Teller

| Date | Mintage | VF20 | XF40 | MS60 | MS63 | MS65 |
|---|---|---|---|---|---|---|
| 2008 | 4,000 | — | — | — | — | 45.00 |
| 2008 | 6,000 | PF65 55.00 | | | | |

**KM# 811 5000 FORINT**

31.46 g., 0.925 Silver 0.9356 oz. ASW, 38.6 mm. **Subject:** Europa heritage site Tokaj Wine Region **Obv:** Value within grape wreath **Rev:** Tokaj Hill and TV tower **Edge:** Reeded **Mint:** Budapest

| Date | Mintage | VF20 | XF40 | MS60 | MS63 | MS65 |
|---|---|---|---|---|---|---|
| 2008 BP | 5,000 | — | — | — | — | 48.00 |
| 2008 BP | 15,000 | PF63 50.00 | PF65 55.00 | | | |

**KM# 812 5000 FORINT**

31.46 g., 0.925 Silver 0.9356 oz. ASW **Subject:** Miklós Badnóti, 100th Anniversary of Birth **Obv:** Value **Rev:** Bust in suit facing

| Date | Mintage | VF20 | XF40 | MS60 | MS63 | MS65 |
|---|---|---|---|---|---|---|
| 2009 | 4,000 | — | — | — | — | 50.00 |
| 2009 | 4,000 | PF65 65.00 | | | | |

**KM# 814 5000 FORINT**

31.46 g., 0.925 Silver 0.9356 oz. ASW, 38.6 mm. **Subject:** Dohany Street Synagogue, 150th Anniversary **Obv:** Stained glass window **Rev:** Synagogue facade **Shape:** 12-sided **Mint:** Budapest

| Date | Mintage | VF20 | XF40 | MS60 | MS63 | MS65 |
|---|---|---|---|---|---|---|
| 2009 BP | 4,000 | — | — | — | — | 50.00 |
| 2009 BP | 4,000 | PF65 65.00 | | | | |

**KM# 815 5000 FORINT**

31.46 g., 0.925 Silver 0.9356 oz. ASW, 38.61 mm. **Subject:** Budapest - World Heritage Site **Obv:** Street scene **Rev:** Panoramic view of Danube and Parliament

| Date | Mintage | VF20 | XF40 | MS60 | MS63 | MS65 |
|---|---|---|---|---|---|---|
| 2009 | 5,000 | — | — | — | — | 50.00 |
| 2009 | 5,000 | PF65 60.00 | | | | |

**KM# 827 5000 FORINT**
31.46 g., 0.925 Silver 0.9356 oz. ASW, 38.6 mm. **Subject:** John Calvin, 500th Anniversary **Mint:** Budapest

| Date | Mintage | VF20 | XF40 | MS60 | MS63 | MS65 |
|---|---|---|---|---|---|---|
| 2009 BP | — | PF65 75.00 | | | | |

**KM# 819 5000 FORINT**
31.46 g., 0.925 Silver 0.9356 oz. ASW, 38.61 mm. **Subject:** Kosztolanyi Dezso, 125th Anniversary of Birth **Obv:** Architectural element of stone **Rev:** Portrait **Mint:** Budapest

| Date | Mintage | VF20 | XF40 | MS60 | MS63 | MS65 |
|---|---|---|---|---|---|---|
| 2010 BP | 3,000 | — | — | — | 40.00 | 45.00 |
| 2010 BP | 5,000 | PF65 55.00 | | | | |

**KM# 820 5000 FORINT**
31.46 g., 0.925 Silver 0.9356 oz. ASW, 39.6x26.4 mm. **Subject:** Orseg National Park **Obv:** Butterfly **Rev:** Traditional rural buildings **Shape:** Rectangle **Mint:** Budapest

| Date | Mintage | VF20 | XF40 | MS60 | MS63 | MS65 |
|---|---|---|---|---|---|---|
| 2010 BP | 3,000 | — | — | — | 40.00 | 45.00 |
| 2010 BP | 5,000 | PF65 55.00 | | | | |

**KM# 821 5000 FORINT**
31.46 g., 0.925 Silver 0.9356 oz. ASW, 38.61 mm. **Subject:** European Watersports Championships **Obv:** Value and waves **Rev:** Swimmer with butterfly stroke **Mint:** Budapest

| Date | Mintage | VF20 | XF40 | MS60 | MS63 | MS65 |
|---|---|---|---|---|---|---|
| 2010 BP | 4,000 | — | — | — | 40.00 | 45.00 |
| 2010 BP | 6,000 | PF65 50.00 | | | | |

**KM# 822 5000 FORINT**
0.50 g., 0.999 Gold, 11 mm. **Subject:** Ferenc Erkel - 200th Anniversary of Birth **Obv:** Denomination **Rev:** Large bust facing **Mint:** Budapest

| Date | Mintage | VF20 | XF40 | MS60 | MS63 | MS65 |
|---|---|---|---|---|---|---|
| 2010 BP | 10,000 | PF63 45.00 | PF65 50.00 | | | |

**KM# 823 5000 FORINT**
31.46 g., 0.925 Silver 0.9356 oz. ASW, 38.61 mm. **Subject:** Ferenc Erkel, 200th Anniversary of Birth **Obv:** House **Rev:** Bust facing, signature below **Mint:** Budapest

| Date | Mintage | VF20 | XF40 | MS60 | MS63 | MS65 |
|---|---|---|---|---|---|---|
| 2010 BP | 5,000 | PF65 55.00 | | | | |

**KM# 830 5000 FORINT**
31.46 g., 0.925 Silver 0.9356 oz. ASW, 38.61 mm. **Subject:** Busojaras Carnival in Mohacs **Obv:** Standing figure in carnival costume **Rev:** Horned demon face **Mint:** Budapest

| Date | Mintage | VF20 | XF40 | MS60 | MS63 | MS65 |
|---|---|---|---|---|---|---|
| 2011 BP | 3,000 | — | — | — | — | 45.00 |
| 2011 BP | 5,000 | PF65 65.00 | | | | |

**KM# 831 5000 FORINT**
31.46 g., 0.925 Silver 0.9356 oz. ASW, 38.61 mm. **Subject:** Árpád Tóth, 125th Anniversary of Birth **Obv:** Handwritten poem at center **Rev:** Tóth bust **Mint:** Budapest

| Date | Mintage | VF20 | XF40 | MS60 | MS63 | MS65 |
|---|---|---|---|---|---|---|
| 2011 BP | 2,000 | — | — | — | — | 45.00 |
| 2011 BP | 4,000 | PF65 60.00 | | | | |

**KM# 832 5000 FORINT**
31.46 g., 0.925 Silver 0.9356 oz. ASW, 39.6x26.4 mm. **Subject:** Duna-Drava National Park **Obv:** Riverside scene **Rev:** Bird in flight **Mint:** Budapest

| Date | Mintage | VF20 | XF40 | MS60 | MS63 | MS65 |
|---|---|---|---|---|---|---|
| 2011 BP | 3,000 | — | — | — | — | 45.00 |
| 2011 BP | 5,000 | PF65 55.00 | | | | |

**KM# 833 5000 FORINT**
31.46 g., 0.925 Silver 0.9356 oz. ASW, 38.61 mm. **Subject:** Deak-Ter Evangelistic Church, Budapest **Obv:** Altar detail **Rev:** Church exterior **Shape:** Scalloped **Mint:** Budapest

| Date | Mintage | VF20 | XF40 | MS60 | MS63 | MS65 |
|---|---|---|---|---|---|---|
| 2011 BP | 3,000 | — | — | — | — | 45.00 |
| 2011 BP | 5,000 | PF65 55.00 | | | | |

**KM# 834 5000 FORINT**
31.46 g., 0.925 Silver 0.9356 oz. ASW, 38.61 mm. **Subject:** István Bibó, 100 Anniversary of Birth **Obv:** Value and legend **Rev:** Bibó seated, writing at table **Mint:** Budapest

| Date | Mintage | VF20 | XF40 | MS60 | MS63 | MS65 |
|---|---|---|---|---|---|---|
| 2011 BP | 6,000 | PF65 60.00 | | | | |

**KM# 835 5000 FORINT**
0.50 g., 0.999 Gold, 11 mm. **Subject:** Adam Clark, 200th Anniversary of Birth **Obv:** Large value **Rev:** Large portrait **Mint:** Budapest

| Date | Mintage | VF20 | XF40 | MS60 | MS63 | MS65 |
|---|---|---|---|---|---|---|
| 2011 BP Prooflike | 10,000 | — | — | — | — | 75.00 |

**KM# 838 5000 FORINT**
31.46 g., 0.925 Silver 0.9356 oz. ASW, 38.61 mm. **Subject:** Jozsef Remenyi, 125th Anniversary of Birth **Obv:** Kneeling nude female with vase on shoulder **Rev:** Remenyi profile left **Mint:** Budapest

| Date | Mintage | VF20 | XF40 | MS60 | MS63 | MS65 |
|---|---|---|---|---|---|---|
| 2012 BP | 6,000 | PF65 50.00 | | | | |

**KM# 839 5000 FORINT**
31.46 g., 0.925 Silver 0.9356 oz. ASW, 38.61 mm. **Subject:** István Örkény, 100th Anniversary of Birth **Obv:** Text forming rectangle at center **Rev:** Large portrait **Mint:** Budapest

| Date | Mintage | VF20 | XF40 | MS60 | MS63 | MS65 |
|---|---|---|---|---|---|---|
| 2012 BP | 2,000 | — | — | — | — | 45.00 |
| 2012 BP | 4,000 | PF65 60.00 | | | | |

**KM# 843 5000 FORINT**
0.50 g., 0.999 Gold, 11 mm. **Subject:** XXX Summer Olympics, London **Obv:** Paddle in water **Rev:** Canoeist advancing front **Mint:** Budapest

| Date | Mintage | VF20 | XF40 | MS60 | MS63 | MS65 |
|---|---|---|---|---|---|---|
| 2012 BP Prooflike | 10,000 | — | — | — | — | 75.00 |

**KM# 855 5000 FORINT**
20.00 g., 0.925 Silver 0.5948 oz. ASW, 38.61 mm. **Subject:** Sándor Weöres, 100th Anniversary of Birth **Mint:** Budapest

| Date | Mintage | VF20 | XF40 | MS60 | MS63 | MS65 |
|---|---|---|---|---|---|---|
| 2013 | — | PF65 50.00 | | | | |

**KM# 841 10000 FORINT (TIZEZER)**
13.96 g., 0.986 Gold 0.4427 oz. AGW, 20 mm. **Subject:** Charles I florin **Obv:** Old coin: Fleur-dis-lis at center **Rev:** Old coin: St. John standing **Mint:** Budapest

| Date | Mintage | VF20 | XF40 | MS60 | MS63 | MS65 |
|---|---|---|---|---|---|---|
| 2012 BP | 5,000 | PF65 800 | | | | |

Note: A piefort of this type exists with edge lettering

**KM# 753 20000 FORINT**
6.98 g., 0.986 Gold 0.2213 oz. AGW, 22 mm. **Subject:** Hungarian Coinage Millennium **Obv:** Denomination **Rev:** Hammered coinage minting scene above old coin design **Edge:** Plain **Mint:** Budapest

| Date | Mintage | VF20 | XF40 | MS60 | MS63 | MS65 |
|---|---|---|---|---|---|---|
| 2001 BP | 3,000 | PF65 425 | | | | |

**KM# 777 50000 FORINT**
13.96 g., 0.986 Gold 0.4427 oz. AGW, 25 mm. **Obv:** Value and country name above Euro Union stars **Rev:** Mythical stag seen through ornate window **Edge:** Reeded **Mint:** Budapest

| Date | Mintage | VF20 | XF40 | MS60 | MS63 | MS65 |
|---|---|---|---|---|---|---|
| 2004 BP | 7,000 | PF63 750 | PF65 800 | | | |

**KM# 803 50000 FORINT**
10.00 g., 0.986 Gold 0.317 oz. AGW, 25 mm. **Subject:** 550th Anniversary - Enthronement of Matthias Hunyadi **Obv:** Raven holding a ring in its beak **Rev:** Portrait of Mátyás Hunyadi based on a marble relief **Edge:** Smooth **Mint:** Budapest

| Date | Mintage | VF20 | XF40 | MS60 | MS63 | MS65 |
|---|---|---|---|---|---|---|
| 2008 | 5,000 | PF65 600 | | | | |

**KM# 816 50000 FORINT**
10.00 g., 0.986 Gold 0.317 oz. AGW, 25 mm. **Subject:** Ferenc Kazinczy, 250th Anniversary of Birth **Obv:** Value and classical facade **Rev:** Bust at left

| Date | Mintage | VF20 | XF40 | MS60 | MS63 | MS65 |
|---|---|---|---|---|---|---|
| 2009 | 5,000 | PF65 600 | | | | |

**KM# 825 50000 FORINT**
6.98 g., 0.986 Gold 0.2213 oz. AGW, 22 mm. **Subject:** St. Stephen and St. Emeric **Obv:** Medieval document **Rev:** St. Stephen and prince standing **Mint:** Budapest

| Date | Mintage | VF20 | XF40 | MS60 | MS63 | MS65 |
|---|---|---|---|---|---|---|
| 2010 BP | 5,000 | PF65 425 | | | | |

**KM# 836 50000 FORINT**
6.98 g., 0.986 Gold 0.2213 oz. AGW, 22 mm. **Subject:** Franz Liszt, 200th Anniversary of Birth **Obv:** Open piano case above musical score **Rev:** Bust right **Edge:** Plain **Mint:** Budapest

| Date | Mintage | VF20 | XF40 | MS60 | MS63 | MS65 |
|---|---|---|---|---|---|---|
| 2011 BP | 5,000 | PF65 450 | | | | |

Note: A piefort exists with edge lettering

**KM# 758 100000 FORINT**
31.10 g., 0.986 Gold 0.986 oz. AGW, 37 mm. **Subject:** Saint Stephen **Obv:** Angels crowning coat of arms **Rev:** King seated on throne **Edge:** Reeded **Mint:** Budapest

| Date | Mintage | VF20 | XF40 | MS60 | MS63 | MS65 |
|---|---|---|---|---|---|---|
| 2001 BP | 3,000 | PF65 1,750 | | | | |

**KM# 796 100000 FORINT**
20.95 g., 0.986 Gold 0.664 oz. AGW, 38.61 mm. **Subject:** 50th Anniversary - Hungarian Revolution **Obv:** 1956 repeated in cut out stone **Rev:** 1956 repeated in cut out stone with two freedom fighter's flags **Mint:** Budapest

| Date | Mintage | VF20 | XF40 | MS60 | MS63 | MS65 |
|---|---|---|---|---|---|---|
| 2006 BP | 5,000 | PF65 1,250 | | | | |

**KM# 824 500,000 FORINT**
62.84 g., 0.986 Gold 1.992 oz. AGW, 46 mm. **Subject:** St. Stephan and St. Emeric **Obv:** Medieval document **Rev:** King and prince standing **Mint:** Budapest **Note:** 18 Ducats

| Date | Mintage | VF20 | XF40 | MS60 | MS63 | MS65 |
|---|---|---|---|---|---|---|
| 2010 BP | 500 | PF65 3,750 | | | | |

## PIEDFORT

| KM# | Date | Mintage | Identification | Mkt Val |
|---|---|---|---|---|
| P27 | 2011BP | 1,500 | 50000 Forint 0.986 Gold KM#836. | 800 |
| P28 | 2012BP | 1,500 | 10000 Forint 0.986 Gold KM#341 | 900 |

## MINT SETS

| KM# | Date | Mintage | Identification | Issue Price | Mkt Val |
|---|---|---|---|---|---|
| MS32 | 2001 (7) | — | KM#692-697, 721 | — | 16.50 |
| MS33 | 2002 (8) | — | KM#692, 693, 694, 695, 696, 697, 721, 760 | — | 18.00 |
| MS34 | 2003 (8) | — | KM#692, 693, 694, 695, 696, 697, 721, 768 | — | 17.50 |
| MS35 | 2004 (8) | — | KM#692, 693, 694, 695, 696, 697, 721, 773 | — | 19.00 |
| MS36 | 2005 (8) | — | KM#692-697, 721, 779 Magyarorszag Penzemei | — | 20.00 |
| MS37 | 2006 (7) | — | KM#692-697, 721, plus silver 1946 KM532 | — | 17.50 |
| MS38 | 2009 (6) | — | KM#694-697, 721, 826 | — | 20.00 |
| MS39 | 2010 (6) | — | KM#694-697, 721, 826 | — | 20.00 |
| MS40 | 2011 (6) | — | KM#694-697, 721, 826 | — | 20.00 |
| MS41 | 2012 (6) | — | KM#847-852 | — | 20.00 |

## PROOF SETS

| KM# | Date | Mintage | Identification | Issue Price | Mkt Val |
|---|---|---|---|---|---|
| PS28 | 2001 (7) | — | KM#692-697, 721 | 35.00 | 37.50 |
| PS29 | 2002 (8) | — | KM#692-697, 721, 760 | — | 42.50 |
| PS30 | 2003 (8) | — | KM#692-697, 721, 768 | — | 40.00 |
| PS31 | 2004 (8) | — | KM#692-697, 721, 773 | — | 40.00 |
| PS32 | 2005 (8) | 7,000 | KM#692-697, 721, 779 | — | 37.50 |
| PS33 | 2006 (7) | — | KM#692-697, 721 | — | 35.00 |
| PS34 | 2007 (8) | — | KM#692-697, 721, 805 | — | 40.00 |
| PS35 | 2008 (7) | — | KM#692-697, 721 | — | 35.00 |
| PS36 | 2012 (6) | 4,000 | KM#847-852 | — | 40.00 |
| PS37 | 2009 (6) | — | KM#694-697, 721, 826 | — | 28.00 |
| PS38 | 2010 (6) | — | KM#694-697, 721, 826 | — | 28.00 |
| PS39 | 2011 (6) | — | KM#694-697, 721, 826 | — | 28.00 |
| PS40 | 2012 (6) | — | KM#847-852 | — | 40.00 |

# ICELAND

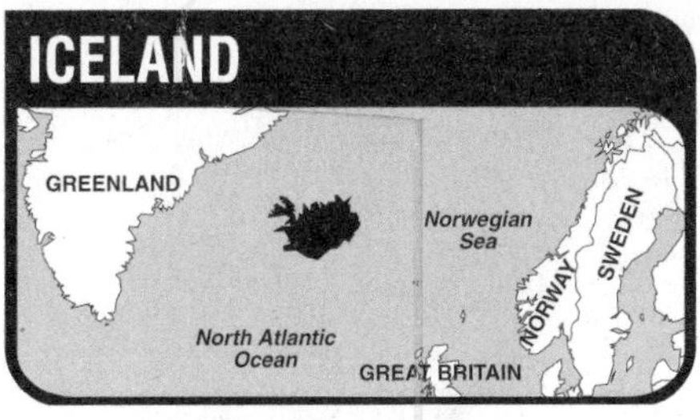


Iceland, an island of recent volcanic origin in the North Atlantic east of Greenland and immediately south of the Arctic Circle, has an area of 39,768 sq. mi. (103,000 sq. km.) and a population of just over 300,000. Capital: Reykjavik. Fishing is the chief industry and accounts for a little less than 60 percent of the exports.

## REPUBLIC

### REFORM COINAGE

100 Old Kronur = 1 New Krona

**KM# 27a KRÓNA**
4.00 g., Nickel Plated Steel, 21.5 mm. **Obv:** Giant facing **Rev:** Cod **Edge:** Reeded

| Date | Mintage | VF20 | XF40 | MS60 | MS63 | MS65 |
|---|---|---|---|---|---|---|
| 2003 | 5,144,000 | — | — | 0.40 | 0.85 | 1.70 |
| 2005 | 5,000,000 | — | — | 0.40 | 0.85 | 1.70 |
| 2006 | 10,000,000 | — | — | 0.40 | 0.85 | 1.70 |
| 2007 | 10,000,000 | — | — | 0.40 | 0.85 | 1.70 |
| 2011 | 5,000,000 | — | — | 0.40 | 0.85 | 1.70 |

**KM# 28a 5 KRÓNUR**
5.60 g., Nickel Plated Steel, 24.5 mm. **Obv:** Quartered design of Eagle, dragon, bull and giant **Rev:** Two dolphins leaping left **Edge:** Reeded

| Date | Mintage | VF20 | XF40 | MS60 | MS63 | MS65 |
|---|---|---|---|---|---|---|
| 2005 | 2,000,000 | — | — | 1.00 | 1.60 | 2.25 |
| 2006 | 2,000,000 | — | — | 1.00 | 1.60 | 2.25 |
| 2007 | 10,000,000 | — | — | 1.00 | 1.60 | 2.25 |
| 2008 | 1,900,000 | — | — | 1.00 | 1.60 | 2.25 |

**KM# 29.1a 10 KRÓNUR**
7.00 g., Nickel Plated Steel, 27.5 mm. **Obv:** Quartered design of Eagle, dragon, bull and giant **Rev:** Four capelins left **Edge:** Reeded

| Date | Mintage | VF20 | XF40 | MS60 | MS63 | MS65 |
|---|---|---|---|---|---|---|
| 2004 | 2,000,000 | — | — | 0.75 | 1.85 | 2.75 |
| 2005 | 4,505,000 | — | — | 0.75 | 1.85 | 2.75 |
| 2006 | 7,800,000 | — | — | 0.75 | 1.85 | 2.75 |
| 2008 | 1,520,000 | — | — | 1.00 | 2.00 | 3.00 |

**KM# 31 50 KRÓNUR**
8.25 g., Nickel-Brass, 23 mm. **Obv:** Quartered design of eagle, dragon, bull and giant **Rev:** Crab **Edge:** Reeded

| Date | Mintage | VF20 | XF40 | MS60 | MS63 | MS65 |
|---|---|---|---|---|---|---|
| 2001 | 2,000,000 | — | — | 1.50 | 3.50 | 5.00 |
| 2005 | 2,000,000 | — | — | 1.50 | 3.50 | 5.00 |

**KM# 35 100 KRÓNUR**
8.50 g., Nickel-Brass, 25.5 mm. **Obv:** Quartered design of Eagle, dragon, bull and giant **Rev:** Lumpfish left **Edge:** Reeded

| Date | Mintage | VF20 | XF40 | MS60 | MS63 | MS65 |
|---|---|---|---|---|---|---|
| 2001 | 2,140,000 | — | — | 4.50 | 6.50 | 7.75 |
| 2004 | 2,400,000 | — | — | 4.50 | 6.50 | 7.75 |
| 2006 | 2,000,000 | — | — | 4.50 | 6.50 | 7.75 |
| 2007 | 3,000,000 | — | — | 4.50 | 6.50 | 7.75 |
| 2011 | 3,000,000 | — | — | 4.50 | 6.50 | 7.75 |

# INDIA - REPUBLIC

The Republic of India, a subcontinent jutting southward from the mainland of Asia, has an area of 1,269,346 sq. mi. (3,287,590 sq. km.) and a population of over 900 million, second only to that of the People's Republic of China. Capital: New Delhi. India's economy is based on agriculture and industrial activity. Engineering goods, cotton apparel and fabrics, handicrafts, tea, iron and steel are exported.

The Republic of India is a member of the Common-wealth of Nations. The president is the Chief of State. The prime minister is the Head of Government.

**MINT MARKS**

(Mint marks usually appear directly below the date.)

B - Mumbai (Bombay), proof issues only
(B) - Mumbai (Bombay), diamond
(C) - Calcutta, no mint mark
(H) - Hyderabad, star (1963-- )
M - Mumbai (Bombay), proof only after 1996
(N) - Noida, dot
(T) - Taegu (Korea), star below first or last date digit

**KM# 54 25 PAISE**
2.82 g., Stainless Steel, 19 mm. **Obv:** Small Lion capitol of Ashoka Pillar above value **Rev:** Rhinoceros left **Edge:** Plain
**Note:** Varieties of date size exist.

| Date | Mintage | VF20 | XF40 | MS60 | MS63 | MS65 |
|---|---|---|---|---|---|---|
| 2001 (B) | — | 1.00 | 3.00 | 4.00 | 7.00 | — |
| 2001 (C) | — | 1.00 | 3.00 | 4.00 | 7.00 | — |
| 2001 (H) | — | 1.00 | 3.00 | 4.00 | 7.00 | — |
| 2002 (B) | — | 1.00 | 3.00 | 4.00 | 7.00 | — |
| 2002 (C) | — | 1.00 | 3.00 | 4.00 | 7.00 | — |
| 2002 (H) | — | 1.00 | 3.00 | 4.00 | 7.00 | — |

**KM# 69 50 PAISE**
3.80 g., Stainless Steel, 22 mm. **Subject:** Parliament Building in New Delhi **Obv:** Denomination **Rev:** Building

| Date | Mintage | VF20 | XF40 | MS60 | MS63 | MS65 |
|---|---|---|---|---|---|---|
| 2001 (B) | — | 1.00 | 1.50 | 2.00 | 4.00 | — |
| 2001 (C) | — | 1.00 | 1.50 | 2.00 | 4.00 | — |
| 2001 (H) | — | 1.00 | 1.50 | 2.00 | 4.00 | — |
| 2001 (N) | — | 1.00 | 1.50 | 2.00 | 4.00 | — |
| 2002 (B) | — | 1.00 | 1.50 | 2.00 | 4.00 | — |
| 2002 (C) | — | 1.00 | 1.50 | 2.00 | 4.00 | — |
| 2002 (H) | — | 1.00 | 1.50 | 2.00 | 4.00 | — |
| 2002 (N) | — | 1.00 | 1.50 | 2.00 | 4.00 | — |
| 2003 (B) | — | 4.00 | 5.00 | 6.00 | 10.00 | — |
| 2007 (C) | — | 6.00 | 7.00 | 8.00 | 10.00 | — |
| 2007 (N) | — | 6.00 | 7.00 | 8.00 | 10.00 | — |

**KM# 374 50 PAISE**
3.80 g., Stainless Steel, 23 mm. **Obv:** Lion capitol of Ashoka Pillar **Rev:** Clenched fist and value

| Date | Mintage | VF20 | XF40 | MS60 | MS63 | MS65 |
|---|---|---|---|---|---|---|
| 2008 (B) | — | 0.30 | 0.60 | 1.00 | 1.50 | — |
| 2008 (C) | — | 0.30 | 0.60 | 1.00 | 1.50 | — |
| 2008 (H) | — | 0.30 | 0.60 | 1.00 | 1.50 | — |
| 2008 (N) | — | 0.30 | 0.60 | 1.00 | 1.50 | — |
| 2009 (B) | — | 0.30 | 0.60 | 1.00 | 1.50 | — |
| 2009 (C) | — | 0.30 | 0.60 | 1.00 | 1.50 | — |
| 2010 (C) | — | 1.00 | 1.50 | 2.00 | 3.00 | — |

**KM# 398 50 PAISE**
Stainless Steel, 19 mm. **Obv:** Lion capitol of Ashoka Pillar **Rev:** Value flanked by flora **Edge:** Reeded

| Date | Mintage | VF20 | XF40 | MS60 | MS63 | MS65 |
|---|---|---|---|---|---|---|
| 2011 (B) | — | — | 1.00 | 3.00 | — | — |
| 2011 (H) | — | — | 0.50 | 1.50 | — | — |
| 2013 H | — | — | 0.50 | 1.50 | — | — |
| 2013 C | — | — | 0.50 | 1.50 | — | — |

**KM# 92.2 RUPEE**
4.90 g., Stainless Steel, 25 mm. **Obv:** Lion capitol of Ashoka Pillar **Rev:** Denomination and date, grain ears flank **Edge:** Plain
**Note:** Mint mark varieties exist.

| Date | Mintage | VF20 | XF40 | MS60 | MS63 | MS65 |
|---|---|---|---|---|---|---|
| 2001 (B) | — | 0.50 | 1.00 | 1.50 | — | — |
| 2001 (C) | — | 0.50 | 1.00 | 1.50 | — | — |
| 2001 (K) | — | 0.50 | 1.00 | 1.50 | — | — |
| 2001 (N) | — | 0.50 | 1.00 | 1.50 | — | — |
| 2001 (H) | — | 0.50 | 1.00 | 1.50 | — | — |

Note: Small and large mint mark exist, doubled left or right of wheat stalks

| Date | Mintage | VF20 | XF40 | MS60 | MS63 | MS65 |
|---|---|---|---|---|---|---|
| 2002 (B) | — | 0.50 | 1.00 | 1.50 | — | — |
| 2002 (N) | — | 0.50 | 1.00 | 1.50 | — | — |
| 2002 (C) | — | 0.50 | 1.00 | 1.50 | — | — |
| 2002 (H) | — | 0.50 | 1.00 | 1.50 | — | — |
| 2003 (B) | — | 0.50 | 1.00 | 1.50 | — | — |
| 2003 (C) | — | 0.50 | 1.00 | 1.50 | — | — |
| 2003 (H) | — | 0.50 | 1.00 | 1.50 | — | — |
| 2004 (B) | — | 1.50 | 2.00 | 3.00 | — | — |
| 2004 (C) | — | 1.50 | 2.00 | 3.00 | — | — |
| 2004 (H) | — | 1.50 | 2.00 | 3.00 | — | — |
| 2004 (N) | — | 1.50 | 2.00 | 3.00 | — | — |

**KM# 313 RUPEE**
4.95 g., Stainless Steel, 25 mm. **Subject:** 100th Anniversary - Birth of Jaya Prakash Narayan **Obv:** Lion capitol of Ashoka Pillar **Rev:** Bust of Jaya Prakash Narayan slightly left **Edge:** Plain

| Date | Mintage | VF20 | XF40 | MS60 | MS63 | MS65 |
|---|---|---|---|---|---|---|
| 2002 | — | 30.00 | 40.00 | 50.00 | — | — |

Note: B without mint mark

| Date | Mintage | VF20 | XF40 | MS60 | MS63 | MS65 |
|---|---|---|---|---|---|---|
| 2002 (B) | — | 4.00 | 5.00 | 6.00 | — | — |
| 2002 (B) | — | **PF63** 40.00 | | | | |
| 2002 (H) | — | 2.00 | 3.00 | 4.00 | — | — |

**KM# 314 RUPEE**
4.95 g., Stainless Steel, 25 mm. **Subject:** Maharana Pratap **Obv:** Lion capitol of Ashoka Pillar **Rev:** Bust left in national costume **Edge:** Plain

| Date | Mintage | VF20 | XF40 | MS60 | MS63 | MS65 |
|---|---|---|---|---|---|---|
| 2003 (B) | — | 4.00 | 7.00 | 10.00 | — | — |
| 2003 (B) | — | PF63 60.00 | | | | |
| 2003 (H) | — | 2.00 | 3.00 | 7.00 | — | — |

**KM# 316 RUPEE**
4.85 g., Stainless Steel, 25 mm. **Obv:** Lion capitol of Ashoka Pillar **Rev:** 3/4 length military figure Veer Durgadass with spear left **Edge:** Plain **Note:** Weak strike typical for 2003(H)

| Date | Mintage | VF20 | XF40 | MS60 | MS63 | MS65 |
|---|---|---|---|---|---|---|
| 2003 (B) | — | PF63 40.00 | | | | |
| 2003 (H) | — | 1.00 | 2.00 | 6.00 | — | — |

**KM# 321 RUPEE**
5.00 g., Stainless Steel, 24.9 mm. **Subject:** 150th Anniversary of the Indian Postal Service **Obv:** Lion capitol of Ashoka Pillar above value **Rev:** Partial postage stamp design **Edge:** Grooved

| Date | Mintage | VF20 | XF40 | MS60 | MS63 | MS65 |
|---|---|---|---|---|---|---|
| 2004 (C) | — | 6.00 | 8.00 | 10.00 | — | — |
| 2004 (C) | — | PF63 50.00 | | | | |
| 2004 (C) Proof, restrike | — | PF63 40.00 | | | | |

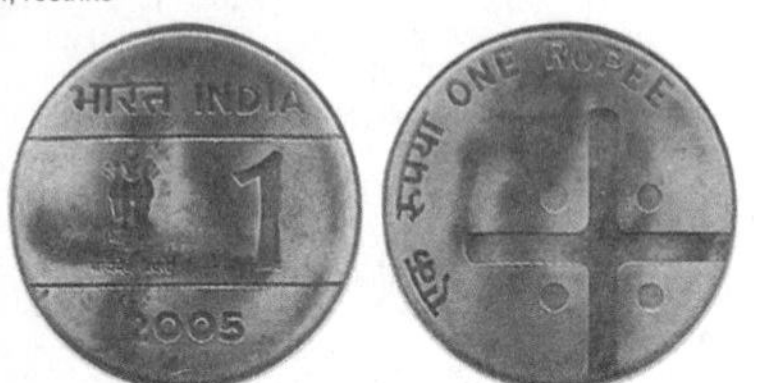

**KM# 322 RUPEE**
4.95 g., Stainless Steel, 24.8 mm. **Obv:** Lion capitol of Ashoka Pillar at left, value at right **Rev:** Cross dividing four dots **Edge:** Plain

| Date | Mintage | VF20 | XF40 | MS60 | MS63 | MS65 |
|---|---|---|---|---|---|---|
| 2004 (B) | — | 10.00 | 20.00 | 30.00 | — | — |
| 2005 (C) | — | 0.50 | 2.00 | 3.00 | — | — |
| 2005 (B) | — | 0.50 | 1.00 | 1.50 | — | — |
| 2005 (H) | — | 0.50 | 1.00 | 1.50 | — | — |
| 2005 (N) | — | 0.50 | 1.00 | 1.50 | — | — |
| 2006 (N) | — | 4.00 | 6.00 | 10.00 | — | — |

**KM# 331 RUPEE**
4.90 g., Stainless Steel, 25 mm. **Subject:** Bharata Natyam Dance Expressions **Obv:** Lion capitol of Ashoka Pillar **Rev:** Gesture of hand with thumb up **Edge:** Plain

| Date | Mintage | VF20 | XF40 | MS60 | MS63 | MS65 |
|---|---|---|---|---|---|---|
| 2007 (C) | — | 0.50 | 1.00 | 1.50 | — | — |
| 2007 (H) | — | 0.50 | 1.00 | 1.50 | — | — |
| 2007 (N) | — | 0.50 | 1.00 | 1.50 | — | — |
| 2008 (B) | — | 0.50 | 1.00 | 1.50 | — | — |
| 2008 (C) | — | 0.50 | 1.00 | 1.50 | — | — |
| 2008 (Hy) | — | 0.50 | 1.00 | 1.50 | — | — |
| 2008 (N) | — | 0.50 | 1.00 | 1.50 | — | — |
| 2009 (B) | — | 0.50 | 1.00 | 1.50 | — | — |
| 2009 (C) | — | 0.50 | 1.00 | 1.50 | — | — |
| 2009 (Hy) | — | 0.50 | 1.00 | 1.50 | — | — |
| 2009 (N) | — | 0.50 | 1.00 | 1.50 | — | — |
| 2010 (B) | — | 0.50 | 1.00 | 1.50 | — | — |
| 2010 (C) | — | 0.50 | 1.00 | 1.50 | — | — |
| 2010 (H) | — | 0.50 | 1.00 | 1.50 | — | — |
| 2010 (N) | — | 0.50 | 1.00 | 1.50 | — | — |
| 2011 (C) | — | 1.00 | 1.50 | 2.00 | — | — |
| 2011 (H) | — | 1.00 | 1.50 | 2.00 | — | — |
| 2011 (N) | — | 1.00 | 1.50 | 2.00 | — | — |

**KM# 385 RUPEE**
4.95 g., Stainless Steel, 24.8 mm. **Subject:** Reserve Bank of India, 75th Anniversary **Obv:** Lion capitol of Ashoka Pillar above value **Rev:** Lion advancing left, palm tree in background

| Date | Mintage | VF20 | XF40 | MS60 | MS63 | MS65 |
|---|---|---|---|---|---|---|
| 2010 (B) | — | PF63 20.00 | | | | |
| 2010 (H) | — | 1.00 | 1.50 | 2.00 | — | — |

**KM# 394 RUPEE**
4.95 g., Stainless Steel, 22 mm. **Obv:** Lion capitol of Ashoka Pillar **Rev:** New Rupee symbol above value

| Date | Mintage | VF20 | XF40 | MS60 | MS63 | MS65 |
|---|---|---|---|---|---|---|
| 2011 (B) | — | — | — | 0.40 | — | — |
| 2011 (C) | — | — | — | 0.40 | — | — |
| 2011 (H) | — | — | — | 0.40 | — | — |
| 2011 (N) | — | — | — | 0.40 | — | — |
| 2012 (B) | — | — | — | 0.40 | — | — |
| 2012 (C) | — | — | — | 0.40 | — | — |
| 2012 (H) | — | — | — | 0.40 | — | — |
| 2012 (N) | — | — | — | 0.40 | — | — |

**KM# 121.3 2 RUPEES**
6.00 g., Copper-Nickel, 26 mm. **Subject:** National Integration **Obv:** Type A Lion capitol of Ashoka Pillar **Rev:** Flag on map **Edge:** Plain **Shape:** 11-sided **Note:** Reduced size, non magnetic.

| Date | Mintage | VF20 | XF40 | MS60 | MS63 | MS65 |
|---|---|---|---|---|---|---|
| 2001 (B) | — | 1.00 | 1.50 | 2.00 | — | — |
| 2001 (C) | — | 1.00 | 1.50 | 2.00 | — | — |
| 2002 (C) | — | 1.00 | 1.50 | 2.00 | — | — |
| 2003 (C) | — | 1.00 | 1.50 | 2.00 | — | — |
| 2003 (H) | — | 1.00 | 1.50 | 2.00 | — | — |
| 2003 (N) | — | 1.00 | 1.50 | 2.00 | — | — |

**KM# 121.5 2 RUPEES**
6.06 g., Copper-Nickel, 26 mm. **Subject:** National Integration **Obv:** Type C Lion capitol of Ashoka Pillar **Rev:** Flag on map **Edge:** Plain **Note:** 11-sided

| Date | Mintage | VF20 | XF40 | MS60 | MS63 | MS65 |
|---|---|---|---|---|---|---|
| 2001 (B) | — | 0.60 | 0.80 | 1.20 | — | — |
| 2001 (C) | — | 0.60 | 0.80 | 1.20 | — | — |
| 2001 (H) | — | 0.60 | 0.80 | 1.20 | — | — |
| 2002 (B) | — | 0.60 | 0.80 | 1.20 | — | — |
| 2002 (C) | — | 0.60 | 0.80 | 1.20 | — | — |
| 2002 (H) | — | 0.60 | 0.80 | 1.20 | — | — |
| 2002 (N) | — | 0.60 | 0.80 | 1.20 | — | — |
| 2003 (B) | — | 0.60 | 0.80 | 1.20 | — | — |
| 2003 (C) | — | 0.60 | 0.80 | 1.20 | — | — |
| 2003 (H) | — | 0.60 | 0.80 | 1.20 | — | — |
| 2004 (B) | — | 1.00 | 1.50 | 2.00 | — | — |
| 2004 (C) | — | 4.00 | 20.00 | 40.00 | — | — |
| 2004 (H) | — | 2.00 | 3.00 | 4.00 | — | — |

**KM# 303 2 RUPEES**
6.24 g., Copper-Nickel, 25.7 mm. **Subject:** 100th Anniversary - Birth of Dr. Syama P. Mookerjee **Obv:** Type B Lion capitol of Ashoka Pillar above denomination **Rev:** Bust of Dr. Mookerjeeright **Edge:** Plain

| Date | Mintage | VF20 | XF40 | MS60 | MS63 | MS65 |
|---|---|---|---|---|---|---|
| 2001 (C) | — | 5.00 | 8.00 | 10.00 | — | — |
| 2001 (C) | — | PF63 40.00 | | | | |
| 2001 (H) | — | 1.00 | 1.50 | 2.00 | — | — |
| 2001 (N) | — | 1.00 | 1.50 | 2.00 | — | — |

**KM# 305 2 RUPEES**
6.10 g., Copper-Nickel, 25.7 mm. **Subject:** Sant Tukaram **Obv:** Lion capitol of Ashoka Pillar above value **Rev:** Seated musician **Shape:** 11-sided

| Date | Mintage | VF20 | XF40 | MS60 | MS63 | MS65 |
|---|---|---|---|---|---|---|
| 2002 (B) | — | 1.00 | 2.50 | 4.00 | — | — |
| 2002 (C) | — | 4.00 | 5.00 | 6.00 | — | — |
| 2002 (C) | — | PF63 60.00 | | | | |
| 2002 (H) | — | 1.00 | 1.50 | 2.00 | — | — |
| 2002 (N) | — | 4.00 | 7.00 | 10.00 | — | — |

**KM# 307 2 RUPEES**
6.05 g., Copper-Nickel **Subject:** 150th Anniversary - Indian Railways **Obv:** Lion capitol of Ashoka Pillar above value **Rev:** Cartoon elephant holding railroad lantern **Edge:** Plain **Shape:** 11-sided **Note:** Generally poor strike quality.

| Date | Mintage | VF20 | XF40 | MS60 | MS63 | MS65 |
|---|---|---|---|---|---|---|
| 2003 (B) | — | 1.50 | 2.50 | 4.00 | — | — |
| 2003 (C) | — | 1.50 | 2.50 | 4.00 | — | — |
| 2003 (C) | — | PF63 40.00 | | | | |
| 2003 (C) Proof, restrike | — | PF63 30.00 | | | | |
| 2003 (H) | — | 1.00 | 1.50 | 2.00 | — | — |
| 2003 (N) | — | 4.00 | 7.00 | 10.00 | — | — |

**KM# 334 2 RUPEES**
6.00 g., Copper-Nickel, 26 mm. **Subject:** 150th Anniversary - Telecommunications **Obv:** Lion capitol of Ashoka Pillar **Rev:** Cartoon bird standing holding cell phone **Edge:** Plain **Shape:** 11-sided

| Date | Mintage | VF20 | XF40 | MS60 | MS63 | MS65 |
|---|---|---|---|---|---|---|
| 2004 (C) | — | PF63 60.00 | | | | |
| Note: Issued only as part of a set. | | | | | | |
| 2004 (C) Proof, restrike | — | PF63 50.00 | | | | |

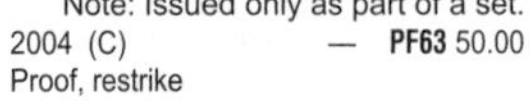

**KM# 326 2 RUPEES**
5.80 g., Stainless Steel **Obv:** Lion capitol of Ashoka Pillar at left and value at right **Rev:** Cross with U-shaped arms and dots **Edge:** Plain **Note:** Size varies 26.75 - 27.07 mm

| Date | Mintage | VF20 | XF40 | MS60 | MS63 | MS65 |
|---|---|---|---|---|---|---|
| 2005 (B) | — | 0.40 | 0.60 | 1.00 | — | — |
| 2005 (C) | — | 0.40 | 0.60 | 1.00 | — | — |
| 2005 (C) Reverse same as 2007 Calcutta | — | 10.00 | 20.00 | 30.00 | — | — |
| 2005 (H) | — | 0.40 | 0.60 | 1.00 | — | — |
| 2005 (N) | — | 0.40 | 0.60 | 1.00 | — | — |
| 2006 (B) small date | — | 0.40 | 0.60 | 1.00 | — | — |
| 2006 (B) large date | — | 0.40 | 0.60 | 1.00 | — | — |
| 2006 (H) | — | 0.40 | 0.60 | 1.00 | — | — |
| 2006 (N) | — | 0.40 | 0.60 | 1.00 | — | — |
| 2007 (B) | — | 0.40 | 0.60 | 1.00 | — | — |
| 2007 (C) | — | 0.40 | 0.60 | 1.00 | — | — |
| 2007 (C) Reverse same as 2005 Calcutta | — | 6.00 | 12.00 | 20.00 | — | — |
| 2007 (H) | — | 0.40 | 0.60 | 1.00 | — | — |
| 2007 (N) | — | 1.00 | 1.50 | 2.00 | — | — |

**KM# 327 2 RUPEES**

5.80 g., Stainless Steel, 27 mm. **Obv:** Lion capitol of Ashoka Pillar at center **Obv. Inscription:** INDIA in Hindi and English **Rev:** Hasta Mudra - hand gesture from the dance Bharata Natyam **Edge:** Plain

| Date | Mintage | VF20 | XF40 | MS60 | MS63 | MS65 |
|---|---|---|---|---|---|---|
| 2007 (B) | — | 0.40 | 0.60 | 1.00 | — | — |
| 2007 (C) | — | 0.40 | 0.60 | 1.00 | — | — |
| 2007 (H) | — | 0.40 | 0.60 | 1.00 | — | — |
| 2007 (N) | — | 0.40 | 0.60 | 1.00 | — | — |
| 2008 (B) | — | 0.40 | 0.60 | 1.00 | — | — |
| 2008 (C) | — | 0.40 | 0.60 | 1.00 | — | — |
| 2008 (H) | — | 0.40 | 0.60 | 1.00 | — | — |
| 2008 (N) | — | 0.40 | 0.60 | 1.00 | — | — |
| 2009 (B) | — | 0.40 | 0.60 | 1.00 | — | — |
| 2009 (C) | — | 0.40 | 0.60 | 1.00 | — | — |
| 2009 (H) | — | 0.40 | 0.60 | 1.00 | — | — |
| 2009 (N) | — | 0.40 | 0.60 | 1.00 | — | — |
| 2010 (B) | — | 0.40 | 0.60 | 1.00 | — | — |
| 2010 (C) | — | 0.40 | 0.60 | 1.00 | — | — |
| 2010 (H) | — | 0.40 | 0.60 | 1.00 | — | — |
| 2010 (N) | — | 0.40 | 0.60 | 1.00 | — | — |
| 2011 (H) | — | 0.40 | 0.60 | 1.00 | — | — |
| 2011 (N) | — | 0.40 | 0.60 | 1.00 | — | — |

**KM# 350 2 RUPEES**

6.00 g., Stainless Steel, 26.9 mm. **Subject:** 75th Anniversary Indian Air Force **Obv:** Lion capitol of Ashoka Pillar at left and value at right **Rev:** Planes in flight **Edge:** Plain **Shape:** 11-sided

| Date | Mintage | VF20 | XF40 | MS60 | MS63 | MS65 |
|---|---|---|---|---|---|---|
| 2007 (C) | — | — | 6.00 | 8.00 | 10.00 | — |
| 2007 (C) | — | **PF63** 40.00 | | | | |

**KM# 375 2 RUPEES**

5.80 g., Stainless Steel, 27 mm. **Subject:** Natya Mudra **Obv:** Lion capitol of Ashoka Pillar **Rev:** Hasta Mudra - hand gesture from the dance Bharata Natyam **Note:** Issued in Mule only

| Date | Mintage | VF20 | XF40 | MS60 | MS63 | MS65 |
|---|---|---|---|---|---|---|
| 2008 (N) | — | 200 | 350 | 500 | — | — |

**KM# 368 2 RUPEES**

5.80 g., Stainless Steel, 27 mm. **Subject:** Louis Braille, 200th Anniversary of Birth **Obv:** Lion capitol of Ashoka Pillar **Rev:** Facing portrait above Braille text

| Date | Mintage | VF20 | XF40 | MS60 | MS63 | MS65 |
|---|---|---|---|---|---|---|
| 2009 (B) | — | 1.00 | 1.50 | 2.00 | — | — |
| 2009 (C) | — | 1.00 | 1.50 | 2.00 | — | — |
| 2009 (C) Packaged | — | — | — | — | 5.00 | — |
| 2009 (C) | — | **PF63** 20.00 | | | | |
| 2009 (C) Proof, packaged | — | **PF63** 7.00 | | | | |
| 2009 (Hy) Packaged | — | — | — | — | 5.00 | — |

**KM# 386 2 RUPEES**

5.80 g., Stainless Steel, 27 mm. **Subject:** Reserve Bank of India, 75th Anniversary **Obv:** Lion capitol of Ashoka Pillar **Rev:** Lion advancing left, palm tree in background

| Date | Mintage | VF20 | XF40 | MS60 | MS63 | MS65 |
|---|---|---|---|---|---|---|
| 2010 (B) | — | **PF63** 20.00 | | | | |
| 2010 (C) | — | 1.00 | 1.50 | 3.50 | — | — |

**KM# 401 2 RUPEES**

5.75 g., Stainless Steel, 25 mm. **Subject:** 19th Commonwealth Games

| Date | Mintage | VF20 | XF40 | MS60 | MS63 | MS65 |
|---|---|---|---|---|---|---|
| 2010 (B) | — | — | — | 3.00 | — | — |
| 2010 (C) | — | — | — | 1.25 | — | — |
| 2010 (C) | — | **PF63** 5.00 | | | | |
| 2010 (Hy) | — | — | — | 3.00 | — | — |
| 2010 (Hy) Packaged | — | — | — | — | 4.00 | — |
| 2010 (N) | — | — | — | 1.25 | — | — |

**KM# 395 2 RUPEES**

4.85 g., Stainless Steel, 25 mm. **Obv:** Lion capitol of Ashoka Pillar **Rev:** New Rupee symbol above value **Edge:** Reeded **Note:** The spacing in the reeding is different at some mints.

| Date | Mintage | VF20 | XF40 | MS60 | MS63 | MS65 |
|---|---|---|---|---|---|---|
| 2011 (B) | — | 0.40 | 0.60 | 1.00 | — | — |
| 2011 (C) | — | 0.40 | 0.60 | 1.00 | — | — |
| 2011 (H) | — | 0.40 | 0.60 | 1.00 | — | — |
| 2011 (N) | — | 0.40 | 0.60 | 1.00 | — | — |
| 2012 (B) | — | 0.40 | 0.60 | 1.00 | — | — |
| 2012 (H) | — | 0.40 | 0.60 | 1.00 | — | — |

**KM# 154.1 5 RUPEES**

9.30 g., Copper-Nickel, 23.4 mm. **Obv:** Lion capitol of Ashoka Pillar. Type I **Rev:** Denomination flanked by flowers **Edge:** Security **Note:** (C) - Calcutta mint has issued 2 distinctly different security edge varieties every year 1992-2003 with large dots and thick center line, w/small dots and narrow center line.

| Date | Mintage | VF20 | XF40 | MS60 | MS63 | MS65 |
|---|---|---|---|---|---|---|
| 2001 (N) | — | 1.00 | 1.50 | 2.00 | — | — |
| 2001 (C) Plain 1 | — | 1.00 | 1.50 | 2.00 | — | — |
| 2001 (C) Serif 1 | — | 1.00 | 1.50 | 2.00 | — | — |
| 2001 (H) | — | 1.00 | 1.50 | 2.00 | — | — |
| 2001 (N) | — | 1.00 | 1.50 | 2.00 | — | — |
| 2002 (C) | — | 1.00 | 1.50 | 2.00 | — | — |
| 2002 (H) | — | 1.00 | 1.50 | 2.00 | — | — |
| 2002 (N) | — | 1.00 | 1.50 | 2.00 | — | — |
| 2003 (C) | — | 1.00 | 1.50 | 2.00 | — | — |
| 2003 (H) | — | 1.00 | 1.50 | 2.00 | — | — |
| 2003 (N) | — | 1.00 | 1.50 | 2.00 | — | — |
| 2004 (C) | — | 10.00 | 15.00 | 20.00 | — | — |
| 2004 (H) | — | 2.00 | 3.00 | 4.00 | — | — |
| 2004 (N) | — | 1.00 | 1.50 | 2.00 | — | — |
| 2005 (B) | — | 1.00 | 1.50 | 2.00 | — | — |

**KM# 154.2 5 RUPEES**

8.91 g., Copper-Nickel, 23 mm. **Obv:** Lion capitol of Ashoka Pillar **Rev:** Denomination flanked by flowers **Edge:** Reeded

| Date | Mintage | VF20 | XF40 | MS60 | MS63 | MS65 |
|---|---|---|---|---|---|---|
| 2001 (C) | — | 10.00 | 19.00 | 20.00 | — | — |
| 2002 (C) | — | 10.00 | 19.00 | 20.00 | — | — |
| 2003 (C) | — | 10.00 | 19.00 | 20.00 | — | — |

**KM# 154.4 5 RUPEES**

9.30 g., Copper-Nickel, 23.4 mm. **Obv:** Lion capitol of Ashoka Pillar, Type II, Small Lion **Rev:** Denomination flanked by flowers **Edge:** Security

| Date | Mintage | VF20 | XF40 | MS60 | MS63 | MS65 |
|---|---|---|---|---|---|---|
| 2001 (B) | — | 1.00 | 1.50 | 2.00 | — | — |
| 2002 (B) | — | 1.00 | 1.50 | 2.00 | — | — |
| 2003 (B) | — | 1.00 | 1.50 | 2.00 | — | — |
| 2004 (B) | — | 1.00 | 1.50 | 2.00 | — | — |

**KM# 304 5 RUPEES**

9.07 g., Copper-Nickel, 23.19 mm. **Subject:** 2600th Anniversary Birth of Bhagwan Mahavir **Obv:** Lion capitol of Ashoka Pillar above denomination **Rev:** Swastika above hand in irregular frame **Edge:** Security

| Date | Mintage | VF20 | XF40 | MS60 | MS63 | MS65 |
|---|---|---|---|---|---|---|
| 2001 (B) | — | 2.00 | 6.00 | 10.00 | — | — |
| 2001 (B) | — | **PF63** 70.00 | | | | |
| 2001 (N) | — | 2.00 | 6.00 | 10.00 | — | — |

**KM# 308 5 RUPEES**

8.92 g., Copper-Nickel, 23.1 mm. **Subject:** Dadabhai Naroji **Obv:** Lion capitol of Ashoka Pillar above value **Rev:** Bust of Naroji 3/4 right **Edge:** Security

| Date | Mintage | VF20 | XF40 | MS60 | MS63 | MS65 |
|---|---|---|---|---|---|---|
| ND(2003) (B) | — | 2.50 | 4.50 | 6.50 | — | — |
| ND-2003 (C) | — | 2.00 | 4.00 | 6.00 | — | — |
| ND-2003 (H) | — | 2.00 | 4.00 | 6.00 | — | — |

**KM# A308 5 RUPEES**

Copper-Nickel, 23.1 mm. **Subject:** Dadabhai Naroji **Obv:** Lion capital of Ashoka Pillar above denomination **Rev:** Bust of Naroji 3/4 right **Edge:** Security

| Date | Mintage | VF20 | XF40 | MS60 | MS63 | MS65 |
|---|---|---|---|---|---|---|
| ND-2003 (C) | — | 10.00 | 15.00 | 20.00 | — | — |
| ND-2003 (C) Reeded Edge | — | 10.00 | 18.00 | 30.00 | — | — |

**KM# 317.1 5 RUPEES**

8.80 g., Copper-Nickel, 23.1 mm. **Obv:** Lion capitol of Ashoka Pillar **Rev:** K. Kamaraj bust 3/4 left, dates below **Edge:** Security

| Date | Mintage | VF20 | XF40 | MS60 | MS63 | MS65 |
|---|---|---|---|---|---|---|
| ND-2003 (B) | — | 2.00 | 7.00 | 11.00 | — | — |
| ND-2003 (B) | — | **PF63** 40.00 | | | | |
| ND-2003 (B) Proof, restrike | — | **PF63** 30.00 | | | | |
| ND-2003 (H) | — | 2.00 | 4.00 | 6.00 | — | — |

### KM# 317.2 5 RUPEES

8.80 g., Copper-Nickel, 23.1 mm. **Obv:** Lion capitol of Ashoka Pillar **Rev:** K. Kamaraj 3/4 left, dates below **Edge:** Reeded

| Date | Mintage | VF20 | XF40 | MS60 | MS63 | MS65 |
|---|---|---|---|---|---|---|
| ND (2003) (H) | — | 10.00 | 15.00 | 20.00 | — | — |

### KM# 329 5 RUPEES

9.07 g., Copper-Nickel, 23.1 mm. **Obv:** Lion capitol of Ashoka Pillar, value below **Rev:** Shastri bust 3/4 left below **Rev. Legend:** LALBAHADUR SHASTRI BIRTH CENTENARY **Edge:** Security

| Date | Mintage | VF20 | XF40 | MS60 | MS63 | MS65 |
|---|---|---|---|---|---|---|
| ND-2004 (C) | — | 4.00 | 10.00 | 20.00 | — | — |
| ND-2004 (C) | — | PF63 40.00 | | | | |

### KM# 329a 5 RUPEES

6.03 g., Stainless Steel, 23 mm. **Obv:** Lion capital of Ashoka Pillar, value below **Rev:** Shastri bust 3/4 left **Rev. Legend:** LALBAHADUR SHASTRI BIRTH CENTENARY **Edge:** Security

| Date | Mintage | VF20 | XF40 | MS60 | MS63 | MS65 |
|---|---|---|---|---|---|---|
| 2004 (C) | — | 6.00 | 12.00 | 20.00 | — | — |

### KM# 325 5 RUPEES

8.85 g., Copper-Nickel, 23 mm. **Subject:** 75th Anniversary Dandi March **Obv:** Lion capitol of Ashoka Pillar **Rev:** Ghandi leading marchers **Edge:** Security type

| Date | Mintage | VF20 | XF40 | MS60 | MS63 | MS65 |
|---|---|---|---|---|---|---|
| ND-2005 (B) | — | 50.00 | 75.00 | 100 | — | — |
| ND-2005 (B) | — | PF63 125 | | | | |
| ND-2005 (B) Proof, restrike | — | PF63 100 | | | | |

### KM# 325a 5 RUPEES

6.03 g., Stainless Steel, 23 mm. **Subject:** 75th Anniversary Dandi March **Obv:** Lion capital of Ashoka Pillar **Rev:** Ghandi leading marchers **Edge:** Security

| Date | Mintage | VF20 | XF40 | MS60 | MS63 | MS65 |
|---|---|---|---|---|---|---|
| ND-2005 (B) | — | 2.00 | 3.00 | 4.00 | — | — |

### KM# A365 5 RUPEES

6.03 g., Stainless Steel, 23 mm. **Subject:** Dandi March, 75th Anniversary **Note:** New design

| Date | Mintage | VF20 | XF40 | MS60 | MS63 | MS65 |
|---|---|---|---|---|---|---|
| 2005 (B) | — | 1.00 | 1.50 | 2.00 | — | — |

### KM# 324 5 RUPEES

8.85 g., Copper-Nickel, 23 mm. **Obv:** Lion capitol of Ashoka Pillar **Rev:** Mahatma Basaveshwara bust 3/4 left **Edge:** Security

| Date | Mintage | VF20 | XF40 | MS60 | MS63 | MS65 |
|---|---|---|---|---|---|---|
| ND-2006 (B) | — | 4.00 | 6.00 | 10.00 | — | — |
| ND-2006 (B) | — | PF63 15.00 | | | | |
| ND-2006 (B) Proof, packaged | — | PF63 10.00 | | | | |

### KM# 324a 5 RUPEES

6.00 g., Stainless Steel **Subject:** Mahatma Basveshwara

| Date | Mintage | VF20 | XF40 | MS60 | MS63 | MS65 |
|---|---|---|---|---|---|---|
| ND-2006 (B) | — | — | — | 4.00 | — | — |

### KM# A324 5 RUPEES

6.03 g., Stainless Steel, 23 mm. **Obv:** Lion capital of Ashoka Pillar **Rev:** Mahatma Basaveshwara bust 3/4 left **Edge:** Security

| Date | Mintage | VF20 | XF40 | MS60 | MS63 | MS65 |
|---|---|---|---|---|---|---|
| ND-2006 (B) | — | 6.00 | 8.00 | 10.00 | — | — |

### KM# 354 5 RUPEES

6.03 g., Stainless Steel, 22.8 mm. **Subject:** O.N.G.C., 50th Anniversary **Obv:** Lion capitol of Ashoka Pillar, value below

| Date | Mintage | VF20 | XF40 | MS60 | MS63 | MS65 |
|---|---|---|---|---|---|---|
| ND-2006 (C) | — | — | — | 2.00 | — | — |
| ND-2006 (C) | — | PF63 20.00 | | | | |
| ND-2006 (H) | — | — | — | 2.00 | — | — |

### KM# 355 5 RUPEES

9.50 g., Copper-Nickel, 23.1 mm. **Subject:** Jagathguru Sree Narayana Gurudev **Obv:** Lion capitol of Ashoka Pillar **Rev:** Bust facing

| Date | Mintage | VF20 | XF40 | MS60 | MS63 | MS65 |
|---|---|---|---|---|---|---|
| ND-2006 (B) | — | 4.00 | 6.00 | 10.00 | — | — |
| ND-2006 (B) | — | PF63 40.00 | | | | |

### KM# 355a 5 RUPEES

6.03 g., Stainless Steel, 22.9 mm. **Subject:** Jagadguru Shree Narayan Guru **Obv:** Lion capitol of Ashoka Pilar **Rev:** Bust facing

| Date | Mintage | VF20 | XF40 | MS60 | MS63 | MS65 |
|---|---|---|---|---|---|---|
| ND-2006 (B) | — | — | — | 6.00 | — | — |

### KM# 357 5 RUPEES

6.03 g., Stainless Steel, 22.9 mm. **Subject:** State Bank of India, 200th Anniversary **Obv:** Lion capitol of Ashoka Pillar, value below **Edge:** Security

| Date | Mintage | VF20 | XF40 | MS60 | MS63 | MS65 |
|---|---|---|---|---|---|---|
| ND-2006 (C) | — | — | — | 2.00 | — | — |
| ND-2006 (C) | — | PF63 10.00 | | | | |
| ND-2006 (H) | — | — | — | 2.00 | — | — |
| ND-2006 (C) Proof, restrike | — | PF63 7.50 | | | | |

### KM# 330 5 RUPEES

6.03 g., Stainless Steel, 23 mm. **Subject:** Information Technology **Obv:** Lion capitol of Ashoka Pillar **Rev:** Waves below value **Edge:** Security

| Date | Mintage | VF20 | XF40 | MS60 | MS63 | MS65 |
|---|---|---|---|---|---|---|
| 2007 (B) | — | — | 1.00 | 4.00 | — | — |
| 2007 (C) | — | — | 1.00 | 4.00 | — | — |
| 2007 (H) | — | — | 1.00 | 4.00 | — | — |
| 2008 (B) | — | — | 1.00 | 4.00 | — | — |
| 2008 (C) | — | — | 1.00 | 4.00 | — | — |
| 2008 (H) | — | — | 1.00 | 4.00 | — | — |

### KM# A330 5 RUPEES

6.03 g., Stainless Steel, 23 mm. **Subject:** Information Technology **Obv:** Lion capitol of Ashoka Pillar **Rev:** Waves below value **Edge:** Security **Note:** Mule, Obv of 50 Paisa

| Date | Mintage | VF20 | XF40 | MS60 | MS63 | MS65 |
|---|---|---|---|---|---|---|
| 2008 (C) | — | 60.00 | 80.00 | 100 | — | — |

### KM# 356 5 RUPEES

6.03 g., Copper-Nickel, 22.9 mm. **Subject:** Lokmanya Bal Gangadhar Tilak, 150th Anniversary

| Date | Mintage | VF20 | XF40 | MS60 | MS63 | MS65 |
|---|---|---|---|---|---|---|
| 2007 (B) | — | PF63 20.00 | | | | |
| 2007 (N) | — | — | — | 100 | — | — |

Note: Withdrawn.

### KM# 359 5 RUPEES

6.03 g., Stainless Steel, 22.9 mm. **Subject:** First War of Independence **Obv:** Lion capitol of Ashoka Pillar, value below

| Date | Mintage | VF20 | XF40 | MS60 | MS63 | MS65 |
|---|---|---|---|---|---|---|
| ND-2007 (B) | — | — | — | 4.00 | — | — |
| ND-2007 (B) | — | PF63 20.00 | | | | |
| ND-2007 (B) Proof, restrike | — | PF63 10.00 | | | | |

### KM# 360.1 5 RUPEES

6.03 g., Stainless Steel, 23 mm. **Subject:** Khadi and Village Industries Commission, 50th Anniversary **Rev:** Ghandi seated facing

| Date | Mintage | VF20 | XF40 | MS60 | MS63 | MS65 |
|---|---|---|---|---|---|---|
| 2007 (B) | — | — | — | 10.00 | — | — |

### KM# 360.1a 5 RUPEES

9.50 g., Copper-Nickel, 23 mm. **Rev:** Ghandi seated facing

| Date | Mintage | VF20 | XF40 | MS60 | MS63 | MS65 |
|---|---|---|---|---|---|---|
| 2007 (B) | — | — | — | 100 | — | — |
| 2007 (B) | — | PF63 60.00 | | | | |

### KM# 360.2 5 RUPEES

6.03 g., Stainless Steel, 23 mm. **Rev:** Ghandi seated facing **Note:** Mint mark "M" in between 2007

| Date | Mintage | VF20 | XF40 | MS60 | MS63 | MS65 |
|---|---|---|---|---|---|---|
| 2007 (B) | — | — | — | 12.00 | — | — |

### KM# 390 5 RUPEES

6.03 g., Stainless Steel, 22.9 mm. **Obv:** Lion capitol of Ashoka Pillar **Rev:** Cross

| Date | Mintage | VF20 | XF40 | MS60 | MS63 | MS65 |
|---|---|---|---|---|---|---|
| 2007 (C) | — | — | — | 20.00 | — | — |

### KM# 406 5 RUPEES

6.00 g., Stainless Steel, 23 mm. **Subject:** Shaheed Bhagat Singh, 100th Anniversary of Birth **Obv:** Lion capital of Ashoka Pillar **Rev:** Bust facing wearing hat **Note:** Dated 2007, but released in 2012.

| Date | Mintage | VF20 | XF40 | MS60 | MS63 | MS65 |
|---|---|---|---|---|---|---|
| 1907-2007 (C) | — | PF63 40.00 | | | | |
| 1907-2007 (H) | — | — | 2.00 | 6.50 | — | — |
| 1907-2007 (H) | — | — | 2.00 | 6.50 | — | — |
| 1907-2007 (Hy) Packaged | — | — | — | — | 6.00 | — |

### KM# 409 5 RUPEES

Nickel-Brass, 23 mm. **Subject:** Kuka Movement, 150th Anniversary **Note:** Issued in 2013.

| Date | Mintage | VF20 | XF40 | MS60 | MS63 | MS65 |
|---|---|---|---|---|---|---|
| 1857-2007 | — | — | — | 1.00 | 3.00 | — |

### KM# 365 5 RUPEES

6.03 g., Nickel-Brass, 23 mm. **Subject:** St. Alphonsa, 100th Anniversary **Obv:** Lion capitol of Ashoka Pillar **Rev:** Bust facing in habit

| Date | Mintage | VF20 | XF40 | MS60 | MS63 | MS65 |
|---|---|---|---|---|---|---|
| 2009 (B) | — | — | — | 3.00 | — | — |
| 2009 (B) Packaged | — | — | — | — | 6.00 | — |
| 2009 (B) | — | PF63 40.00 | | | | |
| 2009 (C) | — | — | — | 4.00 | — | — |
| 2009 (H) | — | — | — | 4.50 | — | — |

### KM# 367 5 RUPEES

6.03 g., Nickel-Brass, 23 mm. **Subject:** C. N. Annadurai, 100th Anniversary of Birth **Obv:** Lion capitol of Ashoka Pillar **Rev:** Portrait, signature below

| Date | Mintage | VF20 | XF40 | MS60 | MS63 | MS65 |
|---|---|---|---|---|---|---|
| 2009 (B) | — | — | — | 3.00 | — | — |
| 2009 (C) | — | — | — | 2.00 | — | — |
| 2009 (C) | — | PF63 30.00 | | | | |
| 2009 (H) | — | — | — | 6.00 | — | — |

### KM# 373 5 RUPEES

6.00 g., Nickel-Brass, 23 mm. **Obv:** Lion capitol of Ashoka Pillar **Rev:** Value flanked by flowers

| Date | Mintage | VF20 | XF40 | MS60 | MS63 | MS65 |
|---|---|---|---|---|---|---|
| 2009 (B) | — | — | — | 1.00 | — | — |
| 2009 (C) | — | — | — | 1.00 | — | — |
| 2009 (H) | — | — | — | 1.00 | — | — |
| 2010 (B) | — | — | — | 1.00 | — | — |
| 2010 (C) | — | — | — | 1.00 | — | — |
| 2010 (H) | — | — | — | 1.00 | — | — |
| 2010 (N) | — | — | — | 2.00 | — | — |

### KM# 376 5 RUPEES

6.03 g., Nickel-Brass, 23 mm. **Subject:** 60th Anniversary of Commonwealth **Obv:** Lion capitol of Ashoka Pillar **Rev:** Building

| Date | Mintage | VF20 | XF40 | MS60 | MS63 | MS65 |
|---|---|---|---|---|---|---|
| 2009 (B) | — | — | — | 3.00 | — | — |
| 2009 (B) | — | PF63 30.00 | | | | |
| 2009 (C) | — | — | — | 2.00 | — | — |
| 2009 (H) | — | — | — | 4.00 | — | — |

### KM# 392 5 RUPEES

6.03 g., Nickel-Brass, 23 mm. **Subject:** Dr. Rajendra Prasad **Obv:** Lion capitol of Ashoka Pillar

| Date | Mintage | VF20 | XF40 | MS60 | MS63 | MS65 |
|---|---|---|---|---|---|---|
| 2009 (B) | — | — | 2.50 | 4.00 | — | — |
| 2009 (C) | — | — | — | 2.00 | — | — |
| 2009 (C) | — | PF63 30.00 | | | | |
| 2009 (Hy) | — | — | — | 2.00 | — | — |
| 2009 (Hy) Packaged | — | — | — | — | 5.00 | — |
| 2009 (N) | — | — | — | 2.00 | — | — |

### KM# 413 5 RUPEES

6.00 g., Nickel-Brass, 23 mm. **Subject:** Perarignar Anna, 100th Anniversary of Birth

| Date | Mintage | VF20 | XF40 | MS60 | MS63 | MS65 |
|---|---|---|---|---|---|---|
| 2009 (B) | — | — | — | — | 4.00 | — |
| 2009 (C) | — | — | — | — | 4.00 | — |
| 2009 (H) | — | — | — | — | 4.00 | — |
| 2009 | — | PF63 30.00 | | | | |

### KM# 377 5 RUPEES

6.00 g., Nickel-Brass, 23 mm. **Obv:** Lion capitol of Ashoka Pillar **Rev:** C. Subramaniam facing **Edge:** Reeded

| Date | Mintage | VF20 | XF40 | MS60 | MS63 | MS65 |
|---|---|---|---|---|---|---|
| 2010 | — | — | — | 3.00 | — | — |
| Note: (B)without mint mark | | | | | | |
| 2010 (B) | — | PF63 30.00 | | | | |
| 2010 (C) | — | — | — | 3.00 | — | — |
| 2010 (Hy) | — | — | — | 1.00 | — | — |
| 2010 (Hy) Packaged | — | — | — | — | 5.50 | — |
| 2010 (N) | — | — | — | 1.00 | — | — |

### KM# 378 5 RUPEES

6.00 g., Nickel-Brass, 23 mm. **Subject:** Brihadeeswarar Temple, 1000th Anniversary **Obv:** Lion capitol of Ashoka Pillar **Rev:** Statue of King Raja Rajan I before temple **Edge:** Reeded

| Date | Mintage | VF20 | XF40 | MS60 | MS63 | MS65 |
|---|---|---|---|---|---|---|
| 2010 (B) | — | — | — | 1.00 | — | — |
| 2010 (B) | — | PF63 30.00 | | | | |
| 2010 (C) | — | — | — | 2.00 | — | — |
| 2010 (Hy) | — | — | — | 1.00 | — | — |
| 2010 (Hy) Packaged | — | — | — | — | 5.50 | — |
| 2010 (N) | — | — | — | 1.00 | — | — |

### KM# 379 5 RUPEES

6.00 g., Nickel-Brass, 23 mm. **Subject:** Income Tax, 150th Anniversary **Obv:** Lion capitol of Ashoka Pillar **Rev:** Chanakya portrait at right **Edge:** Reeded

| Date | Mintage | VF20 | XF40 | MS60 | MS63 | MS65 |
|---|---|---|---|---|---|---|
| 2010 (B) | — | — | 1.00 | 4.00 | — | — |
| 2010 (C) | — | — | 1.00 | 4.00 | — | — |
| 2010 (C) | — | PF63 20.00 | | | | |
| 2010 (Hy) | — | — | 1.00 | 4.00 | — | — |
| 2010 (Hy) Packaged | — | — | — | — | 5.50 | — |

### KM# 381 5 RUPEES

6.03 g., Nickel-Brass, 23 mm. **Subject:** Mother Theresa, 100th Anniversary of Birth **Obv:** Lion capitol of Ashoka Pillar **Rev:** Bust facing

| Date | Mintage | VF20 | XF40 | MS60 | MS63 | MS65 |
|---|---|---|---|---|---|---|
| 2010 (B) | — | — | — | 3.00 | — | — |
| 2010 (C) | — | — | — | 4.00 | — | — |
| 2010 (C) | — | PF63 30.00 | | | | |
| 2010 (Hy) | — | — | — | 4.00 | — | — |
| 2010 (Hy) Packaged | — | — | — | — | 5.50 | — |
| 2010 (N) | — | — | — | 4.00 | — | — |

### KM# 387 5 RUPEES

6.03 g., Nickel-Brass, 23 mm. **Subject:** Reserve Bank of India, 75th Anniversary **Obv:** Lion capitol of Ashoka Pillar **Rev:** Lion advancing left, palm tree in background

| Date | Mintage | VF20 | XF40 | MS60 | MS63 | MS65 |
|---|---|---|---|---|---|---|
| 2010 (B) | — | 0.75 | 1.00 | 2.00 | — | — |
| 2010 (B) | — | PF63 30.00 | | | | |

### KM# 391 5 RUPEES

6.00 g., Nickel-Brass, 23 mm. **Subject:** 19th Commonwealth Games Delhi 2010 **Obv:** Lion capital of Ashoka Pillar **Rev:** Logo of commonwealth

| Date | Mintage | VF20 | XF40 | MS60 | MS63 | MS65 |
|---|---|---|---|---|---|---|
| 2010 (B) | — | — | 3.00 | 4.00 | — | — |
| 2010 (C) | — | — | — | 2.00 | — | — |
| 2010 (C) | — | PF63 30.00 | | | | |
| 2010 (Hy) | — | — | — | 2.00 | — | — |
| 2010 (Hy) Packaged | — | — | — | — | 5.50 | — |
| 2010 (N) | — | — | — | 2.00 | — | — |

### KM# A391 5 RUPEES

6.00 g., Nickel-Brass **Subject:** XIX Commonwealth Game Delhi 2010 **Obv:** Lion capital of Ashoka Pillar, KM#399.1 **Rev:** Logo of Commonwealth Games **Note:** Mule, without Denomination

| Date | Mintage | VF20 | XF40 | MS60 | MS63 | MS65 |
|---|---|---|---|---|---|---|
| 2010 (C) | — | 50.00 | 100 | 200 | — | — |

### KM# 403 5 RUPEES

Nickel-Brass, 23 mm. **Subject:** Comptroller & Auditor General of India, 150th Anniversary **Obv:** Lion capital of Ashoka Pillar **Rev:** Logo

| Date | Mintage | VF20 | XF40 | MS60 | MS63 | MS65 |
|---|---|---|---|---|---|---|
| 2010 (B) | — | — | 2.50 | 4.00 | — | — |
| 2010 (C) | — | — | 2.50 | 4.00 | — | — |
| 2010 (C) | — | PF63 30.00 | | | | |
| 2010 (H) | — | — | 2.50 | 4.00 | — | — |
| 2010 (N) | — | — | 2.50 | 4.00 | — | — |

### KM# 393 5 RUPEES

6.00 g., Nickel-Brass, 23 mm. **Subject:** Rabindranath Tagore, 150th Anniversary of Birth **Obv:** Lion capitol of Ashoka Pillar **Rev:** Bust facing **Edge:** Reeded

| Date | Mintage | VF20 | XF40 | MS60 | MS63 | MS65 |
|---|---|---|---|---|---|---|
| 2011 (B) | — | — | 4.00 | 5.00 | — | — |
| 2011 (C) | — | — | 3.00 | 4.00 | — | — |
| 2011 (C) | — | PF63 40.00 | | | | |
| 2011 (C) Proof, packaged | — | PF63 4.00 | | | | |
| 2011 (Hy) | — | — | 2.00 | 4.00 | — | — |
| 2011 (Hy) Packaged | — | — | — | — | 5.50 | — |
| 2011 (N) | — | — | 2.00 | 4.00 | — | — |

**KM# 396 5 RUPEES**

6.00 g., Nickel-Brass, 23 mm. **Subject:** Indian Council of Medical Research, 100th Anniversary **Obv:** Lion capitol of Ashoka Pillar **Rev:** Anniversary Logo

| Date | Mintage | VF20 | XF40 | MS60 | MS63 | MS65 |
|---|---|---|---|---|---|---|
| 2011 (B) | — | — | 1.00 | 4.00 | — | — |
| 2011 (B) | — | PF63 30.00 | | | | |
| 2011 (C) | — | — | 1.00 | 4.00 | — | — |
| 2011 (H) | — | — | 1.00 | 4.00 | — | — |
| 2011 (N) | — | — | 1.00 | 4.00 | — | — |

**KM# 397 5 RUPEES**

Nickel-Brass, 23 mm. **Subject:** Civil Aviation, 100th Anniversary **Obv:** Lion capitol of Ashoka Pillar **Rev:** Aircraft above 100

| Date | Mintage | VF20 | XF40 | MS60 | MS63 | MS65 |
|---|---|---|---|---|---|---|
| 2011 (B) | — | — | 1.00 | 4.00 | — | — |
| 2011 (B) | — | PF63 40.00 | | | | |
| 2011 (C) | — | — | 1.00 | 4.00 | — | — |
| 2011 (H) | — | — | 1.00 | 4.00 | — | — |
| 2011 (N) | — | — | 1.00 | 4.00 | — | — |

**KM# 399.1 5 RUPEES**

6.00 g., Nickel-Brass, 23 mm. **Obv:** Lion capitol of Ashoka Pillar **Rev:** New rupee value flanked by flora **Edge:** Reeded **Note:** Type I

| Date | Mintage | VF20 | XF40 | MS60 | MS63 | MS65 |
|---|---|---|---|---|---|---|
| 2011 (C) | — | — | — | 1.00 | — | — |
| 2011 (H) | — | — | — | 1.00 | — | — |
| 2011 (N) | — | — | — | 1.00 | — | — |
| 2012 (B) | — | — | — | 1.00 | — | — |
| 2012 (C) | — | — | — | 1.00 | — | — |
| 2012 (H) | — | — | — | 1.00 | — | — |
| 2012 (N) | — | — | — | 1.00 | — | — |

**KM# 399.2 5 RUPEES**

Nickel-Brass, 23 mm. **Obv:** Lion capital of Ashoka Pillar **Rev:** New rupee value flanked by flora **Edge:** Reeded **Note:** Type 2

| Date | Mintage | VF20 | XF40 | MS60 | MS63 | MS65 |
|---|---|---|---|---|---|---|
| 2011 (B) | — | — | — | 10.00 | — | — |

**KM# 399.3 5 RUPEES**

Nickel-Brass, 23 mm. **Obv:** Lion capitol of Ashoka Pillar **Rev:** New rupee value flanked by flora **Edge:** Reeded

| Date | Mintage | VF20 | XF40 | MS60 | MS63 | MS65 |
|---|---|---|---|---|---|---|
| 2011 (C) | — | — | — | 10.00 | — | — |
| 2012 (C) | — | — | — | 10.00 | — | — |

**KM# 405 5 RUPEES**

6.00 g., Nickel-Brass, 23 mm. **Subject:** Madan Mohan Malaviya, 150th Anniversary of Birth **Obv:** Lion capital of Ashoka Pillar **Rev:** Bust facing **Note:** Released in 2013.

| Date | Mintage | VF20 | XF40 | MS60 | MS63 | MS65 |
|---|---|---|---|---|---|---|
| 2011 (B) | — | — | — | 4.00 | 5.00 | — |

**KM# 429 5 RUPEES**

6.00 g., Nickel-Brass, 23 mm. **Subject:** Shri Mata Vaishmo Devi Shrine Board **Obv:** Asoka lion pedestal

| Date | Mintage | VF20 | XF40 | MS60 | MS63 | MS65 |
|---|---|---|---|---|---|---|
| (2012) 429 | — | — | — | 2.00 | 2.50 | — |

**KM# 404 5 RUPEES**

6.00 g., Nickel-Brass, 23 mm. **Subject:** Indian Parliament, 60th Anniversary **Obv:** Lion capital of Ashoka Pillar **Rev:** Building at center

| Date | Mintage | VF20 | XF40 | MS60 | MS63 | MS65 |
|---|---|---|---|---|---|---|
| 2012 (B) | — | 0.50 | 2.00 | 4.00 | — | — |
| 2012 (H) | — | 0.50 | 2.00 | 4.00 | — | — |

**KM# 425 5 RUPEES**

6.00 g., Nickel-Brass, 23 mm. **Subject:** Madan Mohan Malviya, 150th Anniversary of Birth

| Date | Mintage | VF20 | XF40 | MS60 | MS63 | MS65 |
|---|---|---|---|---|---|---|
| 2012 | — | — | — | 4.00 | 5.00 | — |

**KM# 423 5 RUPEES**

6.00 g., Nickel-Brass, 23 mm. **Subject:** Swami Vivekanad, 150th Anniversary of Birth

| Date | Mintage | VF20 | XF40 | MS60 | MS63 | MS65 |
|---|---|---|---|---|---|---|
| 2013 | — | — | — | 4.00 | 5.00 | — |
| 2013 | — | PF63 100 | | | | |

**KM# 431 5 RUPEES**

6.00 g., Nickel-Brass, 23 mm. **Subject:** Acharya Tulsi, 100th Anniversary of Birth

| Date | Mintage | VF20 | XF40 | MS60 | MS63 | MS65 |
|---|---|---|---|---|---|---|
| 2013 | — | — | — | 1.00 | — | — |

**KM# 432 5 RUPEES**

6.00 g., Nickel-Brass, 23 mm. **Subject:** Maulana Abul Kalam Azad, 125th Anniversary of Birth

| Date | Mintage | VF20 | XF40 | MS60 | MS63 | MS65 |
|---|---|---|---|---|---|---|
| 2013 | — | — | — | 2.00 | — | — |

**KM# 427 5 RUPEES**

6.00 g., Stainless Steel, 23 mm. **Subject:** Jamsetji Nusserwanji Tata, 175th Anniversary of Birth

| Date | Mintage | F12 | VF20 | XF40 | MS60 | MS63 |
|---|---|---|---|---|---|---|
| 2014 | — | — | — | — | 4.00 | 5.00 |

**KM# 309 10 RUPEES**

12.50 g., Copper-Nickel, 31 mm. **Subject:** 100th Anniversary Birth of Dr. Syama P. Mookerjee **Obv:** Lion capitol of Ashoka Pillar **Rev:** Bust of Dr. Mookerjee 1/2 right **Edge:** Reeded

| Date | Mintage | VF20 | XF40 | MS60 | MS63 | MS65 |
|---|---|---|---|---|---|---|
| 2001 (C) | — | — | — | 200 | 250 | — |
| 2001 (C) | — | PF65 350 | | | | |

**KM# 344 10 RUPEES**

12.50 g., Copper-Nickel, 31 mm. **Subject:** 100th Anniversary Birth of Jaya Prakash Narayan **Obv:** Lion capitol of Ashoka Pillar **Rev:** Bust of Jaya Prakash Narayan slightly left **Edge:** Reeded

| Date | Mintage | VF20 | XF40 | MS60 | MS63 | MS65 |
|---|---|---|---|---|---|---|
| 2002 (B) | — | — | — | 80.00 | 110 | — |
| 2002 (B) | — | PF65 175 | | | | |

**KM# 347 10 RUPEES**

12.50 g., Copper-Nickel, 31 mm. **Subject:** Sant Tukaram **Obv:** Lion capitol of Ashoka Pillar **Edge:** Reeded

| Date | Mintage | VF20 | XF40 | MS60 | MS63 | MS65 |
|---|---|---|---|---|---|---|
| 2002 (C) | — | — | — | 250 | 350 | — |
| 2002 (C) | — | PF65 500 | | | | |

**KM# 319 10 RUPEES**

12.50 g., Copper-Nickel, 31 mm. **Obv:** Lion capitol of Ashoka Pillar **Rev:** Bust of Maharana Pratap left

| Date | Mintage | VF20 | XF40 | MS60 | MS63 | MS65 |
|---|---|---|---|---|---|---|
| 2003 (B) | — | — | — | 80.00 | 100 | — |
| 2003 (B) | — | PF65 150 | | | | |

**KM# 332 10 RUPEES**

12.50 g., Copper-Nickel, 31 mm. **Obv:** Lion capitol of Ashoka Pillar **Rev:** 3/4 length military figure Veer Durgadass with spear left **Edge:** Reeded

| Date | Mintage | VF20 | XF40 | MS60 | MS63 | MS65 |
|---|---|---|---|---|---|---|
| 2003 (B) | — | — | — | 50.00 | 70.00 | — |
| 2003 (B) | — | PF65 100 | | | | |

**KM# 353 10 RUPEES**

7.70 g., Bi-Metallic Copper-Nickel center in Brass ring., 27 mm. **Subject:** Unity in Diversity **Obv:** Asoka Pillar **Rev:** Four heads sharing a common body

| Date | Mintage | VF20 | XF40 | MS60 | MS63 | MS65 |
|---|---|---|---|---|---|---|
| 2005 (N) | — | — | — | 9.00 | — | — |
| 2006 (N) | — | — | — | 4.00 | — | — |
| 2007 (N) | — | — | — | 6.00 | — | — |

Note: Poor strike quality

**KM# 363 10 RUPEES**

7.70 g., Bi-Metallic Copper-Nickel center in Brass ring, 27 mm. **Subject:** Connectivity and Information Technology **Obv:** Lion capitol of Ashoka Pillar **Rev:** Large 10, wide rays above

| Date | Mintage | VF20 | XF40 | MS60 | MS63 | MS65 |
|---|---|---|---|---|---|---|
| 2008 (N) | — | — | — | 2.00 | — | — |
| 2009 (N) | — | — | — | 4.00 | — | — |
| 2010 (B) | — | — | — | 12.00 | 15.00 | — |
| 2010 (N) | — | — | — | 2.00 | — | — |

**KM# 371 10 RUPEES**

7.70 g., Bi-Metallic Copper-Nickel center in Brass ring, 27 mm. **Subject:** Tercentenary of Gurta-Gaddi of Shri Guru Granth Sahibji **Obv:** Lion capitol of Ashoka Pillar and value

| Date | Mintage | VF20 | XF40 | MS60 | MS63 | MS65 |
|---|---|---|---|---|---|---|
| 2008 (Hy) Packaged | — | — | — | — | 7.00 | — |
| 2008 (M) Packaged | — | — | — | — | 7.00 | — |
| 2008 (M) | — | PF65 20.00 | | | | |

**KM# 372 10 RUPEES**

7.70 g., Bi-Metallic Copper-Nickel center in Brass ring, 27 mm. **Subject:** Dr. Homi Bhabha - 100th Anniversary of Birth **Obv:** Lion capitol of Ashoka Pillar and value **Rev:** Portrait

| Date | Mintage | VF20 | XF40 | MS60 | MS63 | MS65 |
|---|---|---|---|---|---|---|
| 2009 (B) | — | — | — | 9.00 | — | — |
| 2009 (B) | — | PF65 20.00 | | | | |
| 2009 (N) | — | — | — | 2.00 | — | — |

**KM# 388 10 RUPEES**
8.00 g., Bi-Metallic Copper-Nickel center in Aluminum-Bronze ring, 27 mm. **Subject:** Reserve Bank of India, 75th Anniversary **Obv:** Lion capitol of Ashoka Pillar **Rev:** Lion advancing left, palm tree in background

| Date | Mintage | VF20 | XF40 | MS60 | MS63 | MS65 |
|---|---|---|---|---|---|---|
| 2010 (B) | — | — | 2.00 | 6.00 | — | — |
| 2010 (B) | — | PF65 20.00 | | | | |
| 2010 (N) | — | — | 4.00 | 7.00 | — | — |

**KM# 400 10 RUPEES**
Bi-Metallic Copper-Nickel center in Aluminum-Bronze ring, 27 mm. **Obv:** Lion capitol of Ashoka Pillar **Rev:** New rupee symbol above value

| Date | Mintage | VF20 | XF40 | MS60 | MS63 | MS65 |
|---|---|---|---|---|---|---|
| 2011 (B) | — | — | — | 6.00 | — | — |
| 2011 (C) | — | — | — | 6.00 | — | — |
| 2011 (H) | — | — | — | 6.00 | — | — |
| 2011 (N) | — | — | — | 6.00 | — | — |
| 2012 (B) | — | — | — | 4.00 | — | — |
| 2012 (C) | — | — | — | 3.00 | — | — |
| 2012 (H) | — | — | — | 3.00 | — | — |
| 2012 (N) | — | — | — | 2.00 | — | — |

**KM# 407 10 RUPEES**
8.00 g., Bi-Metallic Copper-Nickel center in Aluminum-Bronze ring, 27 mm. **Subject:** Indian Parliament, 60th Anniversary **Obv:** Lion capital of Ashoka Pillar, value below **Rev:** Parliament Building

| Date | Mintage | VF20 | XF40 | MS60 | MS63 | MS65 |
|---|---|---|---|---|---|---|
| 2012 (B) | — | — | 4.00 | 6.00 | — | — |
| 2012 (N) | — | — | 4.00 | 6.00 | — | — |

**KM# 430 10 RUPEES**
Bi-Metallic Copper-Nickel center in Aluminum-Bronze ring **Subject:** Shri Mata Vaishno Devi Shrine Board **Obv:** Asoka lion pedestal

| Date | Mintage | VF20 | XF40 | MS60 | MS63 | MS65 |
|---|---|---|---|---|---|---|
| (2012) | — | — | — | 4.00 | 8.00 | — |

**KM# 433 10 RUPEES**
8.00 g., Bi-Metallic Copper-Nickel center in Aluminum-Bronze ring, 27 mm. **Subject:** Coir Board, 60th Anniversary

| Date | Mintage | VF20 | XF40 | MS60 | MS63 | MS65 |
|---|---|---|---|---|---|---|
| 2013 | — | — | — | 6.00 | — | — |

**KM# 310 50 RUPEES**
30.00 g., Copper-Nickel, 39 mm. **Subject:** 100th Anniversary Birth of Dr. Syama P. Mookerjee **Obv:** Lion capitol of Ashoka Pillar **Rev:** Bust of Dr. Mookerjee 1/2 right **Edge:** Reeded

| Date | Mintage | VF20 | XF40 | MS60 | MS63 | MS65 |
|---|---|---|---|---|---|---|
| 2001 (C) | — | — | — | 300 | 340 | — |
| 2001 (C) | — | PF65 450 | | | | |

**KM# 348 50 RUPEES**
30.00 g., Copper-Nickel, 39 mm. **Subject:** Sant Tukaram **Obv:** Lion capitol of Ashoka Pillar **Edge:** Reeded

| Date | Mintage | VF20 | XF40 | MS60 | MS63 | MS65 |
|---|---|---|---|---|---|---|
| 2002 (C) | — | — | — | 300 | 340 | — |
| 2002 (C) | — | PF65 450 | | | | |

**KM# 352 50 RUPEES**
30.00 g., Copper-Nickel, 39 mm. **Subject:** O.N.G.C., 50th Anniversary

| Date | Mintage | VF20 | XF40 | MS60 | MS63 | MS65 |
|---|---|---|---|---|---|---|
| 2006 | — | — | — | 20.00 | 30.00 | — |
| 2006 | — | PF65 50.00 | | | | |

**KM# 361 50 RUPEES**
30.00 g., Copper-Nickel, 39 mm. **Subject:** Khadi & Village Industries Commission, 50th Anniversary

| Date | Mintage | VF20 | XF40 | MS60 | MS63 | MS65 |
|---|---|---|---|---|---|---|
| 2007 | — | — | — | — | 50.00 | — |
| 2007 | — | PF65 100 | | | | |

**KM# 408 60 RUPEES**
Silver **Subject:** 60th Anniversary of Indian Parliament **Obv:** Lion capital of Ashoka Pillar

| Date | Mintage | VF20 | XF40 | MS60 | MS63 | MS65 |
|---|---|---|---|---|---|---|
| 2012 | — | PF65 50.00 | | | | |

**KM# 389 75 RUPEES**
35.00 g., 0.500 Silver 0.5626 oz. ASW, 42 mm. **Subject:** Reserve Bank of India, 75th Anniversary **Obv:** Lion capitol of Ashoka Pillar **Rev:** Lion advancing left, palm tree in background

| Date | Mintage | VF20 | XF40 | MS60 | MS63 | MS65 |
|---|---|---|---|---|---|---|
| 2010 (B) | — | — | — | 50.00 | 55.00 | — |
| 2010 B | — | PF65 85.00 | | | | |
| 2010 (C) | — | — | — | 50.00 | 55.00 | — |
| 2010 (N) | — | — | — | 50.00 | 55.00 | — |

**KM# 311 100 RUPEES**
35.00 g., 0.500 Silver 0.5626 oz. ASW, 44 mm. **Subject:** 10th Anniversary Dr, Syama P. Mookerjee **Obv:** Lion capitol of Ashoka Pillar **Rev:** Bust of Dr. Mookerjee 1/2 right **Edge:** Reeded

| Date | Mintage | VF20 | XF40 | MS60 | MS63 | MS65 |
|---|---|---|---|---|---|---|
| 2001 (C) | — | — | — | 325 | 400 | — |
| 2001 (C) | — | PF65 500 | | | | |

**KM# 312 100 RUPEES**
35.00 g., 0.500 Silver 0.5626 oz. ASW, 44 mm. **Subject:** 2600th Anniversary Birth of Bhagwan Mahavir **Obv:** Lion capitol of Ashoka Pillar **Rev:** Swastika above hand in irregular frame **Edge:** Reeded

| Date | Mintage | VF20 | XF40 | MS60 | MS63 | MS65 |
|---|---|---|---|---|---|---|
| 2001 (B) | — | — | — | 350 | 400 | — |
| 2001 (B) | — | PF65 500 | | | | |

**KM# 345 100 RUPEES**
35.00 g., 0.500 Silver 0.5626 oz. ASW, 44 mm. **Subject:** 100th Anniversary Birth of Jaya Prakash Narayan **Obv:** Lion capitol of Ashoka Pillar **Rev:** Bust of Jaya Prakash Narayan slightly left **Edge:** Reeded

| Date | Mintage | VF20 | XF40 | MS60 | MS63 | MS65 |
|---|---|---|---|---|---|---|
| 2002 (B) | — | — | — | 200 | 250 | — |
| 2002 (B) | — | PF65 325 | | | | |

**KM# 349 100 RUPEES**
35.00 g., 0.500 Silver 0.5626 oz. ASW, 44 mm. **Subject:** Sant Tukaram **Obv:** Lion capitol of Ashoka Pillar **Edge:** Reeded

| Date | Mintage | VF20 | XF40 | MS60 | MS63 | MS65 |
|---|---|---|---|---|---|---|
| 2002 (C) | — | — | — | 400 | 450 | — |
| 2002 (C) | — | PF65 60.00 | | | | |

**KM# 318 100 RUPEES**
35.00 g., 0.500 Silver 0.5626 oz. ASW, 44 mm. **Obv:** Lion capitol of Ashoka Pillar **Rev:** K. Kamaraj above life dates **Edge:** Reeded

| Date | Mintage | VF20 | XF40 | MS60 | MS63 | MS65 |
|---|---|---|---|---|---|---|
| ND-2003 (B) | — | — | — | 80.00 | 120 | — |
| ND-2003 (B) | — | PF65 150 | | | | |
| ND-2003 (B) Proof, restrike | — | PF65 80.00 | | | | |

**KM# 320 100 RUPEES**
35.00 g., 0.500 Silver 0.5626 oz. ASW, 44 mm. **Obv:** Lion capitol of Ashoka Pillar **Rev:** Bust of Maharana Pratap left **Edge:** Reeded

| Date | Mintage | VF20 | XF40 | MS60 | MS63 | MS65 |
|---|---|---|---|---|---|---|
| 2003 (B) | — | — | — | 120 | 140 | — |
| 2003 (B) | — | PF65 225 | | | | |

**KM# 333 100 RUPEES**
35.00 g., 0.500 Silver 0.5626 oz. ASW, 44 mm. **Obv:** Lion capitol of Ashoka Pillar **Rev:** 3/4 length military figure Veer Durgadass with spear left **Edge:** Reeded

| Date | Mintage | VF20 | XF40 | MS60 | MS63 | MS65 |
|---|---|---|---|---|---|---|
| 2003 (B) | — | — | — | 60.00 | 80.00 | — |
| 2003 (B) | — | PF65 120 | | | | |

**KM# 340 100 RUPEES**
35.00 g., 0.500 Silver 0.5626 oz. ASW, 44 mm. **Subject:** 150th Anniversary Indian Railways **Obv:** Lion capitol of Ashoka Pillar **Rev:** Cartoon elephant holding railroad lantern **Edge:** Reeded

| Date | Mintage | VF20 | XF40 | MS60 | MS63 | MS65 |
|---|---|---|---|---|---|---|
| 2003 (C) | — | — | — | 60.00 | 80.00 | — |
| 2003 (C) | — | PF65 120 | | | | |
| 2003 (C) Proof, restrike | — | PF65 80.00 | | | | |

### KM# 335 100 RUPEES

35.00 g., 0.500 Silver 0.5626 oz. ASW, 44 mm. **Subject:** 150th Anniversary Telecommunications **Obv:** Lion capitol of Ashoka Pillar **Rev:** Cartoon bird standing holding cell phone **Edge:** Reeded

| Date | Mintage | VF20 | XF40 | MS60 | MS63 | MS65 |
|---|---|---|---|---|---|---|
| 2004 (B) | — | — | — | 60.00 | 100 | — |
| 2004 (B) | — | **PF65** 120 | | | | |
| 2004 (B) Proof, restrike | — | **PF65** 80.00 | | | | |

### KM# 337 100 RUPEES

35.00 g., 0.500 Silver 0.5626 oz. ASW, 44 mm. **Subject:** 100th Anniversary Birth of Lal Bahadur Shasti **Obv:** Lion capitol of Ashoka Pillar **Rev:** Bust of Lal Bahadur Shastri 3/4 left **Edge:** Reeded

| Date | Mintage | VF20 | XF40 | MS60 | MS63 | MS65 |
|---|---|---|---|---|---|---|
| ND-2004 (C) | — | — | — | 60.00 | 80.00 | — |
| ND-2004 (C) | — | **PF65** 120 | | | | |

### KM# 343 100 RUPEES

35.00 g., 0.500 Silver 0.5626 oz. ASW, 44 mm. **Subject:** Indian Postal Service, 150th Anniversary **Obv:** Lion capitol of Ashoka Pillar **Rev:** Perforation corner of a postage stamp **Edge:** Reeded

| Date | Mintage | VF20 | XF40 | MS60 | MS63 | MS65 |
|---|---|---|---|---|---|---|
| 2004 (C) | — | — | — | 60.00 | 80.00 | — |
| 2004 (C) | — | **PF65** 120 | | | | |
| 2004 (C) Proof, restrike | — | **PF65** 80.00 | | | | |

### KM# 338 100 RUPEES

35.00 g., 0.500 Silver 0.5626 oz. ASW, 44 mm. **Subject:** 75th Anniversary Dandi March **Obv:** Lion capitol of Ashoka Pillar **Rev:** Ghandi leading marchers **Edge:** Reeded

| Date | Mintage | VF20 | XF40 | MS60 | MS63 | MS65 |
|---|---|---|---|---|---|---|
| ND-2005 (B) | — | — | — | 50.00 | 60.00 | — |
| ND-2005 (B) | — | **PF65** 80.00 | | | | |
| ND-2005 (B) Proof, restrike | — | **PF65** 75.00 | | | | |

### KM# 339 100 RUPEES

35.00 g., 0.500 Silver 0.5626 oz. ASW, 44 mm. **Obv:** Lion capitol of Ashoka Pillar **Rev:** Bust of Mahatma Basaveshwara slightly left **Edge:** Reeded

| Date | Mintage | VF20 | XF40 | MS60 | MS63 | MS65 |
|---|---|---|---|---|---|---|
| ND-2006 B | — | — | — | 50.00 | 60.00 | — |
| ND-2006 B | — | **PF65** 80.00 | | | | |

### KM# 358 100 RUPEES

35.00 g., 0.500 Silver 0.5626 oz. ASW, 44 mm. **Subject:** State Bank of India, 200th Anniversary

| Date | Mintage | VF20 | XF40 | MS60 | MS63 | MS65 |
|---|---|---|---|---|---|---|
| 2006 | — | — | — | — | 65.00 | — |
| 2006 (C) | — | **PF65** 90.00 | | | | |
| 2006 (C) Proof, restrike | — | **PF65** 75.00 | | | | |

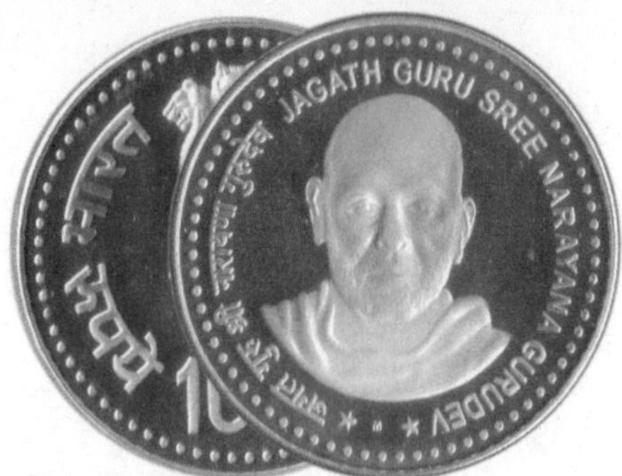


### KM# 364 100 RUPEES

35.00 g., 0.500 Silver 0.5626 oz. ASW, 44 mm. **Subject:** Jagatguru Shree Narayan Gurudev

| Date | Mintage | VF20 | XF40 | MS60 | MS63 | MS65 |
|---|---|---|---|---|---|---|
| 2006 | — | — | — | 40.00 | 50.00 | — |
| 2006 | — | **PF65** 100 | | | | |

### KM# 351 100 RUPEES

35.00 g., 0.500 Silver 0.5626 oz. ASW, 44 mm. **Subject:** 75th Anniversary Indian Air Force **Obv:** Lion capitol of Ashoka Pillar **Edge:** Reeded

| Date | Mintage | VF20 | XF40 | MS60 | MS63 | MS65 |
|---|---|---|---|---|---|---|
| 2007 (C) | — | — | — | 50.00 | 60.00 | — |
| 2007 (C) | — | **PF65** 80.00 | | | | |

### KM# 366 100 RUPEES

35.00 g., 0.500 Silver 0.5626 oz. ASW, 44 mm. **Subject:** Lokmanya Bal Gangadhar Tilak, 150th Anniversary

| Date | Mintage | VF20 | XF40 | MS60 | MS63 | MS65 |
|---|---|---|---|---|---|---|
| 2007 | — | — | — | — | 50.00 | — |
| 2007 | — | **PF65** 100 | | | | |

### KM# 384 100 RUPEES

35.00 g., 0.500 Silver 0.5626 oz. ASW, 44 mm. **Subject:** First War of Independence, 150th Anniversary

| Date | Mintage | VF20 | XF40 | MS60 | MS63 | MS65 |
|---|---|---|---|---|---|---|
| 2007 | — | — | — | — | 50.00 | — |
| 2007 | — | **PF65** 90.00 | | | | |
| 2007 Proof, restrike | — | **PF65** 70.00 | | | | |

**KM# 410 100 RUPEES**
35.00 g., 0.500 Silver 0.5626 oz. ASW, 44 mm. **Subject:** Kuka Movement, 150th Anniversary **Note:** Issued in 2012.

| Date | Mintage | VF20 | XF40 | MS60 | MS63 | MS65 |
|---|---|---|---|---|---|---|
| 1857-2007 | — | PF65 55.00 | | | | |

**KM# 370 100 RUPEES**
35.00 g., 0.500 Silver 0.5626 oz. ASW, 44 mm. **Subject:** Gur-Ta Gaddi, 300th Anniversary

| Date | Mintage | VF20 | XF40 | MS60 | MS63 | MS65 |
|---|---|---|---|---|---|---|
| 2008 | — | — | — | — | 75.00 | — |
| 2008 | — | PF65 100 | | | | |

**KM# 369 100 RUPEES**
35.00 g., 0.500 Silver 0.5626 oz. ASW, 44 mm. **Subject:** Louis Braille, 200th Anniversary of Birth **Obv:** Lion capitol of Ashoka Pillar

| Date | Mintage | VF20 | XF40 | MS60 | MS63 | MS65 |
|---|---|---|---|---|---|---|
| 2009 | — | — | — | 50.00 | 60.00 | — |
| 2009 | — | PF65 80.00 | | | | |

**KM# 383 100 RUPEES**
35.00 g., 0.500 Silver 0.5626 oz. ASW, 44 mm. **Subject:** Homi Bhamba **Obv:** Lion capitol of Ashoka Pillar

| Date | Mintage | VF20 | XF40 | MS60 | MS63 | MS65 |
|---|---|---|---|---|---|---|
| 2009 | — | — | — | 50.00 | 60.00 | — |
| 2009 | — | PF65 80.00 | | | | |

**KM# 411 100 RUPEES**
35.00 g., 0.500 Silver 0.5626 oz. ASW, 44 mm. **Subject:** Saint Alphanso, 100th Anniversary of Birth

| Date | Mintage | VF20 | XF40 | MS60 | MS63 | MS65 |
|---|---|---|---|---|---|---|
| 2009 | — | — | — | — | 50.00 | — |
| 2009 | — | PF65 75.00 | | | | |

**KM# 412 100 RUPEES**
35.00 g., 0.500 Silver 0.5626 oz. ASW, 44 mm. **Subject:** Perarignar Anna, 100th Anniversary

| Date | Mintage | VF20 | XF40 | MS60 | MS63 | MS65 |
|---|---|---|---|---|---|---|
| 2009 | — | — | — | — | 50.00 | — |
| 2009 | — | PF65 75.00 | | | | |

**KM# 414 100 RUPEES**
35.00 g., 0.500 Silver 0.5626 oz. ASW, 44 mm. **Subject:** Commonwealth, 60th Anniversary

| Date | Mintage | VF20 | XF40 | MS60 | MS63 | MS65 |
|---|---|---|---|---|---|---|
| 2009 | — | — | — | — | 50.00 | — |
| 2009 | — | PF65 75.00 | | | | |

**KM# 382 100 RUPEES**
35.00 g., 0.500 Silver 0.5626 oz. ASW, 44 mm. **Subject:** Mother Theresa, 100th Anniversary of birth **Obv:** Lion capitol of Ashoka Pillar **Rev:** Bust facing

| Date | Mintage | VF20 | XF40 | MS60 | MS63 | MS65 |
|---|---|---|---|---|---|---|
| 2010 | — | — | — | 50.00 | 60.00 | — |
| 2010 | — | PF65 80.00 | | | | |

**KM# 415 100 RUPEES**
35.00 g., 0.500 Silver 0.5626 oz. ASW, 44 mm. **Subject:** Dr. Rajendra Prasad, 125th Anniversary of Birth

| Date | Mintage | VF20 | XF40 | MS60 | MS63 | MS65 |
|---|---|---|---|---|---|---|
| 2010 | — | — | — | — | 50.00 | — |
| 2010 | — | PF65 75.00 | | | | |

**KM# 417 100 RUPEES**
35.00 g., 0.500 Silver 0.5626 oz. ASW, 44 mm. **Subject:** 19th Commonwealth Games, Delhi

| Date | Mintage | VF20 | XF40 | MS60 | MS63 | MS65 |
|---|---|---|---|---|---|---|
| 2010 | — | — | — | — | 50.00 | — |
| 2010 | — | PF65 75.00 | | | | |

**KM# 418 100 RUPEES**
35.00 g., 0.500 Silver 0.5626 oz. ASW, 44 mm. **Subject:** C. Subramaniam, 100th Anniversary of Birth

| Date | Mintage | VF20 | XF40 | MS60 | MS63 | MS65 |
|---|---|---|---|---|---|---|
| 2010 | — | — | — | — | 40.00 | — |
| 2010 | — | PF65 70.00 | | | | |

**KM# 420 100 RUPEES**
35.00 g., 0.500 Silver 0.5626 oz. ASW, 44 mm. **Subject:** Civil Aviation, 100th Anniversary

| Date | Mintage | VF20 | XF40 | MS60 | MS63 | MS65 |
|---|---|---|---|---|---|---|
| 2011 | — | — | — | — | 50.00 | — |
| 2011 | — | PF65 70.00 | | | | |

### KM# 421 100 RUPEES

35.00 g., 0.500 Silver 0.5626 oz. ASW, 44 mm. **Subject:** Council of Medical Research, 100th Anniversary

| Date | Mintage | VF20 | XF40 | MS60 | MS63 | MS65 |
|---|---|---|---|---|---|---|
| 2011 | — | — | — | — | 50.00 | — |
| 2011 | — | PF65 70.00 | | | | |

### KM# 380 150 RUPEES

35.00 g., 0.500 Silver 0.5626 oz. ASW, 44 mm. **Subject:** Income Tax, 150th Anniversary **Obv:** Lion capitol of Ashoka Pillar **Rev:** Chanakya portrait at right

| Date | Mintage | VF20 | XF40 | MS60 | MS63 | MS65 |
|---|---|---|---|---|---|---|
| 2010 (C) | — | — | — | 50.00 | 60.00 | — |
| 2010 (C) | — | PF65 80.00 | | | | |

### KM# 416 150 RUPEES

35.00 g., 0.500 Silver 0.5626 oz. ASW, 44 mm. **Subject:** Rabindranth Tagore, 150th Anniversary of Birth

| Date | Mintage | VF20 | XF40 | MS60 | MS63 | MS65 |
|---|---|---|---|---|---|---|
| 2010 | — | — | — | — | 50.00 | — |
| 2010 | — | PF65 80.00 | | | | |

### KM# 419 150 RUPEES

35.00 g., 0.500 Silver 0.5626 oz. ASW, 44 mm. **Subject:** Comptroller & Auditor General, 150th Anniversary

| Date | Mintage | VF20 | XF40 | MS60 | MS63 | MS65 |
|---|---|---|---|---|---|---|
| 2011 | — | — | — | — | 40.00 | — |
| 2011 | — | PF65 75.00 | | | | |

### KM# 426 150 RUPEES

35.00 g., 0.5626 Silver 0.6331 oz. ASW, 44 mm. **Subject:** Madan Mohan Malviya, 150th Anniversary of Birth

| Date | Mintage | VF20 | XF40 | MS60 | MS63 | MS65 |
|---|---|---|---|---|---|---|
| 2012 | — | — | — | — | 50.00 | — |
| 2012 | — | PF65 75.00 | | | | |

### KM# 424 150 RUPEES

0.50 g., 0.562 Silver ASW, 44 mm. **Subject:** Swami Vivekanad, 150th Anniversary of Birth

| Date | Mintage | VF20 | XF40 | MS60 | MS63 | MS65 |
|---|---|---|---|---|---|---|
| 2013 | — | — | — | — | 50.00 | — |
| 2013 | — | PF65 75.00 | | | | |

### KM# 422 1000 RUPEES

35.00 g., 0.500 Silver 0.5626 oz. ASW, 44 mm. **Subject:** Brihadeeswarar Temple, 1000th Anniversary

| Date | Mintage | VF20 | XF40 | MS60 | MS63 | MS65 |
|---|---|---|---|---|---|---|
| 2010 | — | — | — | — | 75.00 | — |
| 2010 | — | PF65 90.00 | | | | |

## MINT SETS

| KM# | Date | Mintage | Identification | Issue Price | Mkt Val |
|---|---|---|---|---|---|
| MS60 | 2002 (3) | — | KM#347, 348, 349 Saint Tukaram. | — | 780 |
| MS61 | 2001 (3) | — | KM#309, 310, 311. Shyama Prasad Mookherji. | — | 750 |
| MS62 | 2001 (2) | — | KM#304, 312 Bhagwan Mahavir. | — | 325 |
| MS63 | 2002 (3) | — | KM#313, 344, 345 Kok Nayak Jaiparakash Narayan. | — | 275 |
| MS64 | 2003 (3) | — | KM#314, 319, 320 Maharana Pratap. | — | 200 |
| MS66 | 2003 (2) | — | KM#316, 332, 333 Veer Durgadas. | — | 150 |
| MS66A | 2003 (2) | — | KM#307, 340 Railways, restrike 2010. | — | 80.00 |
| MS67 | 2004 (2) | — | KM#321, 343 India Post. | — | 110 |
| MS67A | 2004 (2) | — | KM#321, 343 India Post, restrike 2010. | — | 80.00 |
| MS68 | 2003 (2) | — | KM#317.1, 318 Bharat Ratna Shri K. Kamraj. | — | 130 |
| MS68A | 2003 (2) | — | KM#317.1, 318 Bharat Ratna K. Kamraj, reminted 2012. | — | 125 |
| MS69 | 2004 (2) | — | KM#334, 335 Telecommunications. | — | 110 |
| MS69A | 2004 (2) | — | KM#334, 335 Telecommunication, reminted 2010. | — | 100 |
| MS70 | 2005 (2) | — | KM#325, 338 Dandi march. | — | 150 |
| MS70A | 2005 (2) | — | KM#325, 338 Dandi march, reminted 2012. | — | 125 |
| MS71 | 2005 (2) | — | KM#329, 337 Lal Bahadur Shastri. | — | 120 |
| MS72 | 2006 (2) | — | KM#357, 358 State Bank of India. | — | 90.00 |
| MS72A | 2006 (2) | — | KM#357, 358 State Bank of India, restrike 2010. | — | 80.00 |
| MS73 | 2006 (2) | — | KM#324, 339 Mahatma Basveshwar. | — | 120 |
| MS74 | 2006 (2) | — | KM#352, 354 O.N.G.C. | — | 30.00 |
| MS75 | 2006 (2) | — | KM#355, 364 Jagatguru Shree Narayan Gurudev | — | 120 |
| MS76 | 2007 (2) | — | KM#356, 366 Lokmanya Bal Gangadhar Tilak | — | 120 |
| MS77 | 2007 (2) | — | KM#350, 351 Indian Air Force | — | 85.00 |
| MS78 | 2007 (2) | — | KM#361, 362 Khadi & Village Industies | — | 120 |
| MS79 | 2007 (2) | — | KM#359, 384 First War of Independence | — | 120 |
| MS79A | 2007 (2) | — | KM#359, 384 First War of Independence, restruck 2012 | — | 100 |
| MS80 | 2007 (2) | — | MK#402, 406 Shaheed Bhagat Singh | — | 100 |
| MS80A | 2007 (2) | — | KM#402, 406 Shaheed Shagat Singh | — | 110 |
| MS81 | 2008 (2) | — | KM#370, 371 Gaddi, front cover big gurudwara | — | 100 |
| MS81A | 2008 (2) | — | KM#370, 371 Gaddi, front cover small gurudwara | — | 100 |
| MS82 | 2009 (2) | — | KM#368, 369 Louis Braille | — | 70.00 |
| MS83 | 2009 (2) | — | KM#365, 411 Saint Alphanso | — | 100 |
| MS84 | 2009 (2) | — | KM#412, 413 Perarignar Anna | — | 100 |
| MS85 | 2009 (2) | — | KM#372, 383 Homi Bhabha | — | 100 |
| MS86 | 2009 (2) | — | KM#376, 414 Commonwealth | — | 100 |
| MS87 | 2010 (2) | — | KM#392, 415 Dr. Rajendra Prasad | — | 100 |
| MS88 | 2010 (2) | — | MS#393, 416 Rabindranath Tagore | — | 100 |
| MS89 | 2010 (5) | — | KM#385-389 Reserve Bank of India | — | 100 |
| MS90 | 2010 (3) | — | KM#391, 401, 417 XIX Commonwealth Games | — | 90.00 |
| MS91 | 2010 (2) | — | KM#381, 382 Teresa, back cover coin design | — | 70.00 |
| MS91A | 2010 (2) | — | KM#381, 382 Teresa, back cover mother with child | — | 70.00 |
| MS92 | 2010 (2) | — | KM#377, 418 Subramanian, 5 Rupee Z type | — | 70.00 |
| MS92A | 2010 (2) | — | KM#377, 418 Subramanian, 5 Rupee round type | — | 90.00 |
| MS93 | 2011 (5) | — | KM#394, 395, 398, 399.1, 400 New Rupee Logo | — | 11.00 |
| MS94 | 2011 (2) | — | KM#379, 380 Income Tax | — | 100 |
| MS95 | 2011 (2) | — | KM#403.1, 419 Comptroller & Auditor General | — | 90.00 |
| MS96 | 2011 (2) | — | KM#397, 420 Civil Aviation of India | — | 100 |
| MS97 | 2011 (2) | — | KM#396, 421 Council of Medical Research | — | 100 |
| MS98 | 2010 (2) | — | KM#378, 422, released 2011 Brihadeeswrar Temple | — | 90.00 |

## PROOF SETS

| KM# | Date | Mintage | Identification | Issue Price | Mkt Val |
|---|---|---|---|---|---|
| PS69 | 2002(C) (4) | — | KM#346-349 | — | 1,200 |
| PS70 | 2001 (4) | — | KM#303, 309, 310, 311 Dr. Syhama Prasad Mookherji. | — | 1,200 |

| KM# | Date | Mintage | Identification | Issue Price | Mkt Val |
|---|---|---|---|---|---|
| PS71 | 2001 (2) | — | KM#304, 312 Bhagwam Mahavir 2600th Janm Kalyanak. | — | 480 |
| PS72 | 2002B (3) | — | KM#313, 344, 345 Lok Nayak Jaiprakash Narayan. | — | 400 |
| PS73 | 2003 (3) | — | KM#314, 319, 320 Maharana Pratap. | — | 320 |
| PS74 | 2003B (3) | — | KM#316, 332, 333 Veer Durgdas. | — | 210 |
| PS75 | 2003(C) (2) | — | KM#307, 340 Railways. | — | 180 |
| PS76 | 2003 (2) | — | KM#307, 340 Railways, 2010 restrike. | — | 120 |
| PS77 | 2004 (2) | — | KM#321, 343 India Post. | — | 140 |
| PS78 | 2004 (2) | — | KM#324, 343 India Post, 2010 restrike. | — | 80.00 |
| PS79 | ND(2003) (2) | — | KM#317.1, 318 Bharat Ratna Shri K. Kamraj. | — | 150 |
| PS80 | 2004 (2) | — | KM#317.1, 318 Bharat Ratna Shri K. Kamraj, 2012 restrike. | — | 150 |
| PS81 | 2004 (2) | — | KM#317.1, 318 Bharat Ratna Shri K. Kamraj, Executive restrike. | — | 170 |
| PS82 | 2004B (2) | — | KM#334, 335 Telecommunications. | — | 150 |
| PS83 | 2005 (2) | — | KM#3334, 335 Telecommunications, restrike. | — | 140 |
| PS84 | 2005B (2) | — | KM#325, 338 Dandi march. | — | 150 |
| PS85 | 2005 (2) | — | KM#325, 338 Dandi march, restrike. | — | 140 |
| PS86 | 2005 (2) | — | KM#325, 338 Dandi march, Executive restrike. | — | 175 |
| PS87 | 2004(C) (2) | — | KM#336, 337 Lal Bahadur Shastri. | — | 160 |
| PS88 | 2006 (2) | — | KM#357, 358 State Bank | — | 110 |
| PS89 | 2006 (2) | — | KM#357, 358 State Bank, 2010 restrike. | — | 90.00 |
| PS90 | 2006B (2) | — | KM#324, 339 Mahatma Basveshwara. | — | 150 |
| PS91 | 2006 (2) | — | KM#352, 354 O.N.G.C. | — | 352 |
| PS92 | 2006 (2) | — | KM#355, 364 Jagatguru Shree Narayan Gurudev. | — | 150 |
| PS93 | 2007 (2) | — | KM#356, 366 Lokmanya Bal Gangadhar Tilak. | — | 150 |
| PS94 | 2007 (2) | — | KM#350, 351 Indian Air Force. | — | 100 |
| PS95 | 2007 (2) | — | KM#361, 362 Khadi & Village Industries Commission. | — | 150 |
| PS96 | 2007 (2) | — | KM#359, 384 First War of Independence. | — | 150 |
| PS97 | 2007 (2) | — | KM#359, 384 First War of Independence. 2012 Restrike. | — | 140 |
| PS98 | 2007 (2) | — | KM#402, 406 Shaheed Bhagat Singh. | — | 135 |
| PS99 | 2007 (2) | — | KM#402, 406 Spelled as Shagat Singh. | — | 140 |
| PS100 | 2008 (2) | — | KM#370, 371 Gur-Ta Gaddi, large image of Gurudwara (temple) on front cover. | — | 150 |
| PS101 | 2008 (2) | — | KM#370, 371 Gur-Ta Gaddi, small image of Gurudwara (temple) on front cover. | — | 140 |
| PS102 | 2009 (2) | — | KM#368, 369 Louis Braille. | — | 140 |
| PS103 | 2009 (2) | — | KM#365, 411 Saint Alphanso. | — | 150 |
| PS104 | 2009 (2) | — | KM#412, 413 Perarignar Anna | — | 140 |
| PS105 | 2009 (2) | — | KM#372, 383 Homi Bhabha. | — | 150 |
| PS106 | 2009 (2) | — | KM#376, 414 Commonwealth. | — | 150 |
| PS107 | 2010 (2) | — | KM#392, 415 Dr. Rajendra Prasad. | — | 135 |
| PS108 | 2010 (2) | — | KM#393, 416 Rabindranth Tagore. | — | 150 |
| PS109 | 2010 (5) | — | KM#385, 386, 387, 388, 389 Reserve Bank of India. | — | 140 |
| PS110 | 2010 (3) | — | KM#391, 401, 417 19th Commonwealth Games. | — | 135 |
| PS111 | 2010 (2) | — | KM#381, 382 Mother Teresa, Error Hindi "tursa" on package. | — | 110 |
| PS112 | 2010 (2) | — | KM#381, 382 Mother Teresa. | — | 80.00 |
| PS113 | 2010 (2) | — | KM#381, 382 Mother Teresa. Back cover Mother with child. | — | 80.00 |
| PS114 | 2010 (2) | — | KM#377, 418 C. Subramaniam. | — | 140 |
| PS115 | 2010 (2) | — | KM#377, 418 C. Subramaniam, executive package. | — | 155 |
| PS116 | 2011 (2) | — | KM#379, 380 Income tax. | — | 140 |
| PS117 | 2011 (2) | — | KM#403.1, 419 Comptroller & Auditor General. | — | 135 |
| PS118 | 2011 (2) | — | KM#397, 420 Civil Aviation. | — | 135 |
| PS119 | 2011 (2) | — | KM#396, 421 Council of Medical Research. | — | 135 |
| PS120 | 2010 (2) | — | KM#378, 422 Brihadeeswarar Temple. | — | 110 |
| PS121 | 2010 (2) | — | KM#378, 422 Brihadeeswarar Temple, executive set. | — | 150 |
| PS122 | 2010 (2) | — | KM#378, 422 Brihadeeswarar Temple, VIP set. | — | 180 |

The Republic of Indonesia, the world's largest archipelago, extends for more than 3,000 miles (4,827 km.) along the equator from the mainland of southeast Asia to Australia. The 17,508 islands comprising the archipelago have a combined area of 788,425 sq. mi. (1,919,440 sq. km.) and a population of 205 million, including East Timor. On August 30, 1999, the Timorese majority voted for independence. The Inter FET (International Forces for East Timor) is now in charge of controlling the chaotic situation. Capitol: Jakarta. Petroleum, timber, rubber, and coffee are exported.

Modern coinage issued by the Republic of Indonesia includes separate series for West Irian and for the Riau Archipelago, an area of small islands between Singapore and Sumatra.

**MONETARY SYSTEM**

100 Sen = 1 Rupiah

# REPUBLIC

## STANDARD COINAGE

### KM# 60 50 RUPIAH

1.35 g., Aluminum, 19.95 mm. **Obv:** National emblem **Rev:** Black-naped Oriole **Edge:** Plain

| Date | Mintage | VF20 | XF40 | MS60 | MS63 | MS65 |
|---|---|---|---|---|---|---|
| 2001 | — | — | — | 0.30 | 0.50 | 1.00 |
| 2002 | — | — | — | 0.30 | 0.50 | 1.00 |

### KM# 61 100 RUPIAH

1.79 g., Aluminum, 23 mm. **Obv:** National emblem **Rev:** Palm Cockatoo **Edge:** Plain

| Date | Mintage | VF20 | XF40 | MS60 | MS63 | MS65 |
|---|---|---|---|---|---|---|
| 2001 | — | — | — | 0.75 | 1.00 | 1.25 |
| 2002 | — | — | — | 0.75 | 1.00 | 1.25 |
| 2003 | — | — | — | 0.75 | 1.00 | 1.25 |
| 2004 | — | — | — | 0.75 | 1.00 | 1.25 |
| 2005 | — | — | — | 0.75 | 1.00 | 1.25 |

### KM# 66 200 RUPIAH

2.40 g., Aluminum, 25 mm. **Obv:** National arms **Rev:** Balinese starling bird above value **Edge:** Plain

| Date | Mintage | VF20 | XF40 | MS60 | MS63 | MS65 |
|---|---|---|---|---|---|---|
| 2003 | — | — | — | 1.00 | 1.25 | 1.50 |

Note: The typeface of the date often makes 2003 look like 2008

### KM# 59 500 RUPIAH

5.35 g., Aluminum-Bronze, 24 mm. **Obv:** National emblem **Rev:** Jasmine above denomination

| Date | Mintage | VF20 | XF40 | MS60 | MS63 | MS65 |
|---|---|---|---|---|---|---|
| 2001 | — | — | — | 1.75 | 2.00 | 2.25 |
| 2002 | — | — | — | 1.75 | 2.00 | 2.25 |
| 2003 | — | — | — | 1.75 | 2.00 | 2.25 |

### KM# 67 500 RUPIAH

3.05 g., Aluminum, 27.2 mm. **Obv:** National arms **Rev:** Jasmine flower above value **Edge:** Segmented reeding

| Date | Mintage | VF20 | XF40 | MS60 | MS63 | MS65 |
|---|---|---|---|---|---|---|
| 2003 | — | — | — | 2.00 | 2.25 | 2.50 |

Note: The typeface of the date often makes 2003 look like 2008.

### KM# 70 1000 RUPIAH

4.50 g., Nickel Plated Steel, 24 mm. **Obv:** National arms above value **Rev:** Angklung - a traditional bamboo musical instrument; West Java Provincial's Governor office in Bandung in background **Rev. Legend:** ANGKLUNG / date

| Date | Mintage | VF20 | XF40 | MS60 | MS63 | MS65 |
|---|---|---|---|---|---|---|
| 2010 | — | — | — | 0.75 | 1.00 | 1.50 |

### KM# 64 25000 RUPIAH

28.28 g., 0.925 Silver 0.841 oz. ASW, 38.6 mm. **Subject:** Centennial of Sukarno's Birth **Obv:** National arms **Rev:** Uniformed bust of Sukarno **Edge:** Reeded

| Date | Mintage | VF20 | XF40 | MS60 | MS63 | MS65 |
|---|---|---|---|---|---|---|
| 2001 | 500 | **PF63** 120 | **PF65** 150 | | | |

### KM# 68 25000 RUPIAH

28.28 g., 0.925 Silver 0.841 oz. ASW, 38.61 mm. **Subject:** Mohammas Hatta, vice-president (1945-1956) **Obv:** National Arms **Rev:** Bust facing

| Date | Mintage | VF20 | XF40 | MS60 | MS63 | MS65 |
|---|---|---|---|---|---|---|
| 2002 | 2,000 | **PF63** 120 | **PF65** 150 | | | |

**KM# 65 500,000 RUPIAH**
15.00 g., 0.999 Gold 0.4818 oz. AGW, 28.2 mm. **Subject:** Centennial of Sukarno's Birth **Obv:** National arms **Rev:** Head left **Edge:** Reeded

| Date | Mintage | VF20 | XF40 | MS60 | MS63 | MS65 |
|---|---|---|---|---|---|---|
| 2001 | 500 | **PF63** 1,000 | **PF65** 1,100 | | | |

**KM# 69 500,000 RUPIAH**
15.00 g., 0.999 Gold 0.4818 oz. AGW, 28.2 mm. **Subject:** Mohammad Hatta, vice-president (1945-1956) **Obv:** National Arms **Rev:** Bust facing

| Date | Mintage | VF20 | XF40 | MS60 | MS63 | MS65 |
|---|---|---|---|---|---|---|
| 2002 | 2,000 | **PF63** 850 | **PF65** 875 | | | |

# IRAN

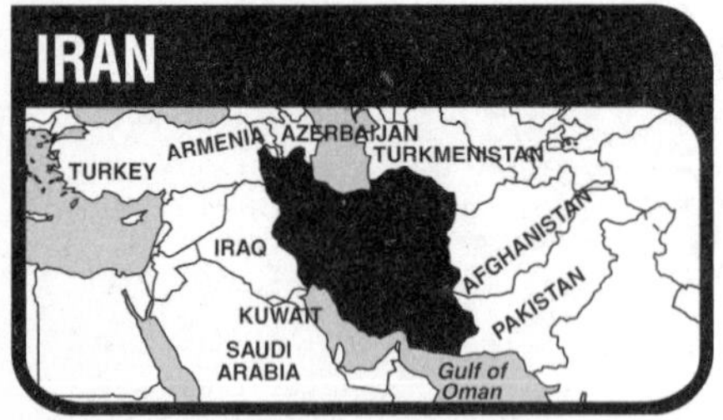


The Islamic Republic of Iran, located between the Caspian Sea and the Persian Gulf in southwestern Asia, has an area of 636,296 sq. mi. (1,648,000 sq. km.) and a population of 59.7 million. Capital: Tehran. Although predominantly an agricultural state, Iran depends heavily on oil for foreign exchange. Crude oil, carpets and agricultural products are exported.

On March 22, 1935 the Kingdom of Persia became the Kingdom of Iran. In 1979 the monarchy was toppled and an Islamic Republic proclaimed.

**TITLES**

دار الخلافة

Dar al-Khilafat

**RULERS**
Islamic Republic, SH1358-/1979-AD

**MINT NAME**

طهران

Tehran

تفليس

Tiflis

**MINT MARKS**
H - Heaton (Birmingham)
L - Leningrad (St. Petersburg)

**COIN DATING**

Iranian coins were dated according to the Moslem lunar calendar until March 21, 1925 (AD), when dating was switched to a new calendar based on the solar year, indicated by the notation SH. The monarchial calendar system was adopted in 1976 = MS2535 and was abandoned in 1978 = MS2537. The previously used solar year calendar was restored at that time.

**MONETARY SYSTEM**
20 Shahis = 1 Rial (100 Dinars)

## ISLAMIC REPUBLIC

### MILLED COINAGE

**KM# 1260 50 RIALS**
Copper-Nickel, 26 mm. **Subject:** Shrine of Hazrat Masumah **Obv:** Value and date **Rev:** Shrine within beaded circle **Edge:** Reeded

| Date | Mintage | F12 | VF20 | XF40 | MS60 | MS63 |
|---|---|---|---|---|---|---|
| SH1380 | — | — | 2.50 | 3.50 | 5.00 | — |
| SH1382 | — | — | 2.50 | 3.50 | 5.00 | — |

**KM# 1266 50 RIALS**
3.51 g., Aluminum-Bronze, 20.1 mm. **Obv:** Value and date **Rev:** Hazrat Masumah Shrine **Edge:** Reeded **Mint:** Tehran

| Date | Mintage | F12 | VF20 | XF40 | MS60 | MS63 |
|---|---|---|---|---|---|---|
| SH1382(2003) | — | — | — | — | 50.00 | — |
| SH1383(2004) | — | — | — | — | 2.50 | — |
| SH1384(2005) | — | — | — | — | 2.50 | — |
| SH1385(2006) | — | — | — | — | 2.50 | — |

**KM# 1261.2 100 RIALS**
Copper-Nickel, 29 mm. **Obv:** Value and date **Rev:** Shrine within designed border **Note:** Thick denomination and numerals

| Date | Mintage | F12 | VF20 | XF40 | MS60 | MS63 |
|---|---|---|---|---|---|---|
| SH1380 | — | — | — | — | 6.50 | — |
| SH1382 | — | — | — | — | 6.50 | — |

**KM# 1267 100 RIALS**
4.62 g., Aluminum-Bronze, 22.9 mm. **Obv:** Value, date divides wreath below **Rev:** Imam Reza Shrine **Edge:** Reeded **Mint:** Tehran

| Date | Mintage | F12 | VF20 | XF40 | MS60 | MS63 |
|---|---|---|---|---|---|---|
| SH1382(2003) | — | — | — | — | 50.00 | — |
| SH1383(2004) | — | — | — | — | 3.50 | — |
| SH1384(2005) | — | — | — | — | 3.50 | — |
| SH1385(2006) | — | — | — | — | 3.50 | — |

**KM# 1262 250 RIALS**
10.70 g., Bi-Metallic Copper-Nickel center in Brass ring, 28.3 mm. **Obv:** Value within circle, inscription and date divide wreath **Rev:** Stylized flower within circle and wreath

| Date | Mintage | F12 | VF20 | XF40 | MS60 | MS63 |
|---|---|---|---|---|---|---|
| SH1381 | — | — | — | — | 7.50 | — |
| SH1382 | — | — | — | — | 7.50 | — |

**KM# 1268 250 RIALS**
5.50 g., Copper-Nickel, 24.6 mm. **Obv:** Value, date below divides sprays **Rev:** Stylized flower within sprays **Edge:** Plain **Mint:** Tehran

| Date | Mintage | F12 | VF20 | XF40 | MS60 | MS63 |
|---|---|---|---|---|---|---|
| SH1382(2003) | — | — | — | — | 50.00 | — |
| SH1383(2004) | — | — | — | — | 4.50 | — |
| SH1384(2005) | — | — | — | — | 4.50 | — |
| SH1385(2006) | — | — | — | — | 4.50 | — |

**KM# 1282 250 RIALS**
5.00 g., Aluminum-Bronze, 24 mm. **Obv:** Value, date below divides sprays **Rev:** Stylized flower within sprays **Mint:** Tehran

| Date | Mintage | F12 | VF20 | XF40 | MS60 | MS63 |
|---|---|---|---|---|---|---|
| SH1386 (2007) | — | — | — | — | 0.75 | 1.75 |

**KM# 1269 500 RIALS**
8.91 g., Bi-Metallic Aluminum-Bronze center in Copper-Nickel ring, 27.1 mm. **Obv:** Value **Rev:** Bird and flowers **Edge:** Reeded **Mint:** Tehran

| Date | Mintage | F12 | VF20 | XF40 | MS60 | MS63 |
|---|---|---|---|---|---|---|
| SH1382(2003) | — | — | — | — | 50.00 | — |
| SH1383(2004) | — | — | — | — | 6.00 | — |
| SH1384(2005) | — | — | — | — | 6.00 | — |
| SH1385(2006) | — | — | — | — | 6.00 | — |
| SH1386 (2007) | — | — | — | — | — | 6.00 |

**KM# 1283 500 RIALS**
6.35 g., Aluminum-Bronze, 25.5 mm. **Obv:** Value in ornamental circle **Rev:** Bird and flowers **Mint:** Tehran

| Date | Mintage | F12 | VF20 | XF40 | MS60 | MS63 |
|---|---|---|---|---|---|---|
| SH1386(2007) | — | — | — | — | 1.50 | 3.00 |

### REFORM COINAGE

**KM# 1270 250 RIALS**
2.80 g., Aluminum-Bronze, 18.5 mm. **Rev:** Feyziyeh School

| Date | Mintage | F12 | VF20 | XF40 | MS60 | MS63 |
|---|---|---|---|---|---|---|
| AH1387 (2008) | — | — | — | — | 0.55 | 1.00 |
| SH1388 (2009) | — | — | — | — | 0.55 | 1.00 |
| SH1389 (2010) | — | — | — | — | 0.55 | 1.00 |
| SH1390 (2011) | — | — | — | — | 0.55 | 1.00 |

**KM# 1271 500 RIALS**
3.90 g., Copper-Nickel, 20.6 mm. **Rev:** Saadi Tomb

| Date | Mintage | F12 | VF20 | XF40 | MS60 | MS63 |
|---|---|---|---|---|---|---|
| SH1387 (2008) | — | — | — | — | — | 6.00 |
| SH1387 (2009) | — | — | — | — | — | 6.00 |
| SH1389 (2010) | — | — | — | — | — | 6.00 |
| SH1390 (2011) | — | — | — | — | — | 6.00 |

**KM# 1281 500 RIALS**
3.90 g., Copper-Nickel, 20.6 mm. **Subject:** Freedom of Khorramshahr **Obv:** Value in wreath **Rev:** Stylized flower

| Date | Mintage | F12 | VF20 | XF40 | MS60 | MS63 |
|---|---|---|---|---|---|---|
| SH1390 (2011) | — | — | — | — | 2.00 | 5.00 |

**KM# 1285 500 RIALS**
3.50 g., Aluminum-Bronze, 20.3 mm. **Obv:** Vlaue **Rev:** Dove shaped tulip **Mint:** Tehran

| Date | Mintage | F12 | VF20 | XF40 | MS60 | MS63 |
|---|---|---|---|---|---|---|
| SH1390 (2011) | 50,000,000 | — | — | — | 1.50 | 3.00 |

**KM# 1287 1000 RIALS**
4.60 g., Aluminum-Bronze, 23 mm. **Subject:** Shah Cheragh **Obv:** Value **Rev:** Shah Cheragh shrine

| Date | Mintage | F12 | VF20 | XF40 | MS60 | MS63 |
|---|---|---|---|---|---|---|
| SH1391 (2012) | — | — | — | — | 2.25 | 4.50 |

**KM# 1272 1000 RIALS**
5.80 g., Aluminum-Brass, 23.7 mm. **Rev:** Khajou Bridge in Isfahan

| Date | Mintage | F12 | VF20 | XF40 | MS60 | MS63 |
|---|---|---|---|---|---|---|
| SH1387 (2008) | — | — | — | — | — | 12.00 |
| SH1388 (2009) | — | — | — | — | — | 12.00 |
| SH1389 (2010) | — | — | — | — | — | 12.00 |

**KM# 1274 1000 RIALS**
5.80 g., Copper-Nickel, 23.7 mm. **Subject:** Eid al-Ghadeer **Rev:** Ali in star

| Date | Mintage | F12 | VF20 | XF40 | MS60 | MS63 |
|---|---|---|---|---|---|---|
| SH1389 (2010) | — | — | — | — | — | 6.00 |

**KM# 1275 1000 RIALS**
5.80 g., Brass, 23.7 mm. **Subject:** Eid al-Adha **Rev:** Kaaba Cubus

| Date | Mintage | F12 | VF20 | XF40 | MS60 | MS63 |
|---|---|---|---|---|---|---|
| SH1389(2010) | — | — | — | — | — | 6.00 |

**KM# 1284 1000 RIALS**
5.80 g., Aluminum-Bronze, 23.7 mm. **Subject:** National Statistical Office, 75th Anniversary **Obv:** Mountain above value **Rev:** Tile motif **Mint:** Tehran

| Date | Mintage | F12 | VF20 | XF40 | MS60 | MS63 |
|---|---|---|---|---|---|---|
| SH1389 (2010) | — | — | — | — | 2.25 | 4.50 |

**KM# 1286 1000 RIALS**
4.60 g., Aluminum-Bronze, 23.7 mm. **Subject:** 15 Shaaban **Obv:** Value **Rev:** Dafoldills **Mint:** Tehran

| Date | Mintage | F12 | VF20 | XF40 | MS60 | MS63 |
|---|---|---|---|---|---|---|
| SH1390 (2011) | 60,000,000 | — | — | — | 2.25 | 4.50 |

**KM# 1288 2000 RIALS**
6.80 g., Copper-Nickel, 26.3 mm. **Subject:** Master plan **Obv:** Value **Rev:** Stylized star

| Date | Mintage | F12 | VF20 | XF40 | MS60 | MS63 |
|---|---|---|---|---|---|---|
| SH1391 (2012) | — | — | — | — | — | 8.00 |

**KM# 1276 2000 RIALS**
6.80 g., Copper-Nickel, 23.7 mm. **Subject:** Central Bank of the Islamic Republic of Iran, 50th Anniversary

| Date | Mintage | F12 | VF20 | XF40 | MS60 | MS63 |
|---|---|---|---|---|---|---|
| SH1389(2010) | — | — | — | — | — | 8.00 |

**KM# 1278 2000 RIALS**
Copper-Nickel **Obv:** Value **Rev:** Mosque

| Date | Mintage | F12 | VF20 | XF40 | MS60 | MS63 |
|---|---|---|---|---|---|---|
| SH1389 (2010) | — | — | — | — | — | 8.00 |

**KM# 1289 5000 RIALS**
10.00 g., Copper-Nickel, 29.4 mm. **Obv:** Value **Rev:** Mosque

| Date | Mintage | F12 | VF20 | XF40 | MS60 | MS63 |
|---|---|---|---|---|---|---|
| SH1392 (2013) | — | — | — | — | — | 10.00 |

**KM# 1277 5000 RIALS**
10.20 g., Copper-Nickel, 29.4 mm. **Subject:** Central Bank, 50th Anniversary **Obv:** Value **Rev:** Commemorative calligraphy

| Date | Mintage | F12 | VF20 | XF40 | MS60 | MS63 |
|---|---|---|---|---|---|---|
| SH1389(2010) | — | — | — | — | — | 10.00 |

**KM# 1279 5000 RIALS**
10.20 g., Copper-Nickel, 29.4 mm. **Obv:** Value **Rev:** Calligraphy

| Date | Mintage | F12 | VF20 | XF40 | MS60 | MS63 |
|---|---|---|---|---|---|---|
| SH1389 (2010) | — | — | — | — | — | 10.00 |

**KM# 1280 5000 RIALS**
12.00 g., Aluminum-Bronze, 28.5 mm. **Subject:** Muslim Week **Obv:** Value **Rev:** Two roses

| Date | Mintage | F12 | VF20 | XF40 | MS60 | MS63 |
|---|---|---|---|---|---|---|
| SH1389 (2010) | — | — | — | — | — | 10.00 |

**KM# 1290 10000 RIALS**
Aluminum-Bronze **Obv:** Value **Rev:** Mosque **Mint:** Tehran

| Date | Mintage | F12 | VF20 | XF40 | MS60 | MS63 |
|---|---|---|---|---|---|---|
| SH1389 (2010) | — | — | — | — | — | 15.00 |

## BULLION COINAGE

Issued by the National Bank of Iran

**KM# 1250.2 1/2 AZADI**
4.07 g., 0.900 Gold 0.1177 oz. AGW **Obv:** Legend larger **Obv. Legend:** Spring of Freedom

| Date | Mintage | F12 | VF20 | XF40 | MS60 | MS63 |
|---|---|---|---|---|---|---|
| SH1381 | — | — | — | — | 215 | — |
| SH1383 | — | — | — | — | 215 | — |

# IRAQ

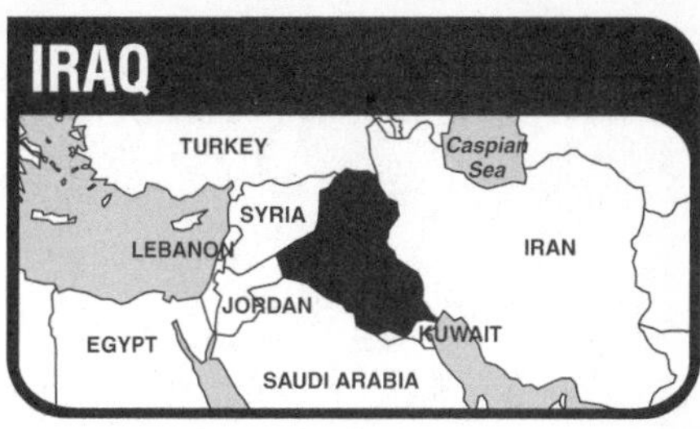


The Republic of Iraq, historically known as Mesopotamia, is located in the Near East and is bordered by Kuwait, Iran, Turkey, Syria, Jordan and Saudi Arabia. It has an area of 167,925 sq. mi. (434,920 sq. km.) and a population of 19 million. Capital: Baghdad. The economy of Iraq is based on agriculture and petroleum. Crude oil accounted for 94 percent of the exports before the war with Iran began in 1980.

Mesopotamia was the site of a number of flourishing civilizations of antiquity - Sumeria, Assyria, Babylonia, Parthia, Persia and the Biblical cities of Ur, Ninevehand and Babylon. Desired because of its favored location, which embraced the fertile alluvial plains of the Tigris and Euphrates Rivers, Mesopotamia - 'land between the rivers'- was conquered by Cyrus the Great of Persia, Alexander of Macedonia and by Arabs who made the legendary city of Baghdad the capital of the ruling caliphate. Suleiman the Magnificent conquered Mesopotamia for Turkey in1534, and it formed part of the Ottoman Empire until 1623, and from 1638 to 1917. Great Britain, given a League of Nations mandate over the territory in 1920, recognized Iraq as a kingdom in 1922. Iraq became an independent constitutional monarchy presided over by the Hashemite family, direct descendants of the prophet Mohammed, in 1932. In 1958, the army-led revolution of July 14 overthrew the monarchy and proclaimed a republic.

**MONETARY SYSTEM**

Falus, Fulus — Fals, Fils — Falsan

50 Fils = 1 Dirham
200 Fils = 1 Riyal
1000 Fils = 1 Dinar (Pound)

## REPUBLIC
### DECIMAL COINAGE

**KM# 175 25 DINARS**
2.50 g., Copper Plated Steel, 17.4 mm. **Obv:** Value **Rev:** Map **Edge:** Plain

| Date | Mintage | VF20 | XF40 | MS60 | MS63 | MS65 |
|---|---|---|---|---|---|---|
| AH1425-2004 | — | — | 0.30 | 0.75 | 1.00 | 1.25 |

**KM# 176 50 DINARS**
4.34 g., Brass Plated Steel, 22 mm. **Obv:** Value and legend **Rev:** Map **Edge:** Plain

| Date | Mintage | VF20 | XF40 | MS60 | MS63 | MS65 |
|---|---|---|---|---|---|---|
| AH1425-2004 | — | — | 0.50 | 1.00 | 1.25 | 1.50 |

**KM# 177 100 DINARS**
4.30 g., Stainless Steel, 22 mm. **Obv:** Value **Rev:** Map **Edge:** Reeded

| Date | Mintage | VF20 | XF40 | MS60 | MS63 | MS65 |
|---|---|---|---|---|---|---|
| AH1425-2004 | — | — | 0.65 | 1.00 | 1.25 | 1.50 |

# IRELAND REPUBLIC

Ireland, which occupies five-sixths of the island of Ireland located in the Atlantic Ocean west of Great Britain, has an area of 27,136 sq. mi. (70,280 sq. km.) and a population of 4.3 million. Capital: Dublin. Agriculture and dairy farming are the principal industries. Meat, livestock, dairy products and textiles are exported.

## REPUBLIC

## EURO COINAGE

European Union Issues

### KM# 32 EURO CENT

2.27 g., Copper Plated Steel, 16.25 mm. **Obv:** Harp **Rev:** Denomination and globe **Edge:** Plain

| Date | Mintage | VF20 | XF40 | MS60 | MS63 | MS65 |
|---|---|---|---|---|---|---|
| 2002 | 404,339,788 | — | — | 0.25 | 0.35 | 0.50 |
| 2003 | 67,902,182 | — | — | 0.25 | 0.35 | 0.50 |
| 2004 | 174,833,634 | — | — | 0.25 | 0.35 | 0.50 |
| 2005 | 126,964,391 | — | — | 0.25 | 0.35 | 0.50 |
| 2006 | 105,413,273 | — | — | 0.25 | 0.35 | 0.50 |
| 2006 | 5,000 | PF65 15.00 | | | | |
| 2007 | 18,515,843 | — | — | 0.25 | 0.35 | 0.50 |
| 2007 | 10,000 | PF65 12.00 | | | | |
| 2008 | 59,002,134 | — | — | 0.25 | 0.35 | 0.50 |
| 2009 | 42,109,347 | — | — | 0.25 | 0.35 | 0.50 |
| 2009 | 5,000 | PF65 12.00 | | | | |
| 2010 | 4,946,711 | — | — | 0.25 | 0.35 | 0.50 |
| 2010 | 5,000 | PF65 12.00 | | | | |
| 2011 | 23,261,567 | — | — | 0.25 | 0.35 | 0.50 |
| 2011 | 5,000 | PF65 12.00 | | | | |
| 2012 | — | — | — | 0.25 | 0.35 | 0.50 |
| 2012 | 5,000 | PF65 12.00 | | | | |
| 2013 | — | — | — | 0.25 | 0.35 | 0.50 |
| 2014 | — | — | — | 0.25 | 0.35 | 0.50 |

### KM# 33 2 EURO CENT

3.00 g., Copper Plated Steel, 18.75 mm. **Obv:** Harp **Rev:** Denomination and globe **Edge:** Plain with groove

| Date | Mintage | VF20 | XF40 | MS60 | MS63 | MS65 |
|---|---|---|---|---|---|---|
| 2002 | 354,643,386 | — | — | 0.30 | 0.50 | 0.65 |
| 2003 | 177,290,034 | — | — | 0.30 | 0.50 | 0.65 |
| 2004 | 143,004,694 | — | — | 0.30 | 0.50 | 0.65 |
| 2005 | 72,544,884 | — | — | 0.30 | 0.50 | 0.65 |
| 2006 | 26,568,597 | — | — | 0.30 | 0.50 | 0.65 |
| 2006 | 5,000 | PF65 15.00 | | | | |
| 2007 | 84,291,248 | — | — | 0.30 | 0.50 | 0.65 |
| 2007 | 10,000 | PF65 12.00 | | | | |
| 2008 | 42,116,152 | — | — | 0.30 | 0.50 | 0.65 |
| 2009 | 7,284,499 | — | — | 0.30 | 0.50 | 0.65 |
| 2009 | 5,000 | PF65 12.00 | | | | |
| 2010 | 3,496,511 | — | — | 0.30 | 0.50 | 0.60 |
| 2010 | 5,000 | PF65 12.00 | | | | |
| 2011 | 4,813,844 | — | — | 0.30 | 0.50 | 0.65 |
| 2011 | 5,000 | PF65 12.00 | | | | |
| 2012 | — | — | — | 0.30 | 0.50 | 0.65 |
| 2012 | 5,000 | PF65 12.00 | | | | |
| 2013 | — | — | — | 0.30 | 0.50 | 0.65 |
| 2014 | — | — | — | 0.30 | 0.50 | 0.65 |

### KM# 34 5 EURO CENT

4.00 g., Copper Plated Steel, 19.60 mm. **Obv:** Harp **Rev:** Denomination and globe **Edge:** Plain

| Date | Mintage | VF20 | XF40 | MS60 | MS63 | MS65 |
|---|---|---|---|---|---|---|
| 2002 | 456,270,848 | — | — | 0.45 | 0.75 | 1.00 |
| 2003 | 48,352,370 | — | — | 0.45 | 0.75 | 1.00 |
| 2004 | 80,354,322 | — | — | 0.45 | 0.75 | 1.00 |
| 2005 | 56,454,380 | — | — | 0.45 | 0.75 | 1.00 |
| 2006 | 88,003,370 | — | — | 0.45 | 0.75 | 1.00 |
| 2006 | 5,000 | PF65 18.00 | | | | |
| 2007 | 36,225,742 | — | — | 0.45 | 0.75 | 1.00 |
| 2007 | 10,000 | PF65 15.00 | | | | |
| 2008 | 61,844,008 | — | — | 0.45 | 0.75 | 1.00 |
| 2009 | 10,333,341 | — | — | 0.45 | 0.75 | 1.00 |
| 2009 | 5,000 | PF65 15.00 | | | | |
| 2010 | 1,023,881 | — | — | 0.45 | 0.75 | 1.00 |
| 2010 | 5,000 | PF65 15.00 | | | | |
| 2011 | 1,024,637 | — | — | 0.45 | 0.75 | 1.00 |
| 2011 | 5,000 | PF65 15.00 | | | | |
| 2012 | — | — | — | 0.45 | 0.75 | 1.00 |
| 2012 | 5,000 | PF65 15.00 | | | | |
| 2013 | — | — | — | 0.45 | 0.75 | 1.00 |
| 2014 | — | — | — | 0.45 | 0.75 | 1.00 |

### KM# 35 10 EURO CENT

4.07 g., Brass, 19.75 mm. **Obv:** Harp **Rev:** Denomination and map **Edge:** Reeded

| Date | Mintage | VF20 | XF40 | MS60 | MS63 | MS65 |
|---|---|---|---|---|---|---|
| 2002 | 275,913,000 | — | — | 0.60 | 1.00 | 1.25 |
| 2003 | 133,815,907 | — | — | 0.60 | 1.00 | 1.25 |
| 2004 | 36,732,778 | — | — | 0.60 | 1.00 | 1.25 |
| 2005 | 4,652,786 | — | — | 0.60 | 1.00 | 1.25 |
| 2006 | 9,208,411 | — | — | 0.60 | 1.00 | 1.25 |
| 2006 | 5,000 | PF65 18.00 | | | | |

### KM# 47 10 EURO CENT

4.07 g., Brass, 19.75 mm. **Obv:** Harp **Rev:** Relief map of Western Europe, stars, lines and value **Edge:** Reeded

| Date | Mintage | VF20 | XF40 | MS60 | MS63 | MS65 |
|---|---|---|---|---|---|---|
| 2007 | 54,434,307 | — | — | 0.60 | 1.00 | 1.25 |
| 2007 | 10,000 | PF65 15.00 | | | | |
| 2008 | 53,997,990 | — | — | 0.60 | 1.00 | 1.25 |
| 2009 | 10,850,328 | — | — | 0.60 | 1.00 | 1.25 |
| 2009 | 5,000 | PF65 15.00 | | | | |
| 2010 | 1,078,313 | — | — | 0.60 | 1.00 | 1.25 |
| 2010 | 5,000 | PF65 15.00 | | | | |
| 2011 | 1,030,118 | — | — | 0.60 | 1.00 | 1.25 |
| 2011 | 5,000 | PF65 15.00 | | | | |
| 2012 | — | — | — | 0.60 | 1.00 | 1.25 |
| 2012 | 5,000 | PF65 15.00 | | | | |
| 2013 | — | — | — | 0.60 | 1.00 | 1.25 |
| 2014 | — | — | — | 0.60 | 1.00 | 1.25 |

### KM# 36 20 EURO CENT

5.73 g., Brass, 22.25 mm. **Obv:** Harp **Rev:** Denomination and map **Edge:** Notched

| Date | Mintage | VF20 | XF40 | MS60 | MS63 | MS65 |
|---|---|---|---|---|---|---|
| 2002 | 234,575,562 | — | — | 0.75 | 1.25 | 1.50 |
| 2003 | 57,142,221 | — | — | 0.75 | 1.25 | 1.50 |
| 2004 | 32,421,447 | — | — | 0.75 | 1.25 | 1.50 |
| 2005 | 40,439,062 | — | — | 0.75 | 1.25 | 1.50 |
| 2006 | 10,357,229 | — | — | 0.75 | 1.25 | 1.50 |
| 2006 | 5,000 | PF65 20.00 | | | | |

### KM# 48 20 EURO CENT

5.73 g., Brass, 22.25 mm. **Obv:** Harp **Rev:** Relief map of Western Europe, stars, lines and value **Edge:** Notched

| Date | Mintage | VF20 | XF40 | MS60 | MS63 | MS65 |
|---|---|---|---|---|---|---|
| 2007 | 12,953,789 | — | — | 0.75 | 1.25 | 1.50 |
| 2007 | 10,000 | PF65 18.00 | | | | |
| 2008 | 45,990,533 | — | — | 0.75 | 1.25 | 1.50 |
| 2009 | 4,279,307 | — | — | 0.75 | 1.25 | 1.50 |
| 2009 | 5,000 | PF65 18.00 | | | | |
| 2010 | 1,027,059 | — | — | 0.75 | 1.25 | 1.50 |
| 2010 | 5,000 | PF65 18.00 | | | | |
| 2011 | 1,201,428 | — | — | 0.75 | 1.25 | 1.50 |
| 2011 | 5,000 | PF65 18.00 | | | | |
| 2012 | — | — | — | 0.75 | 1.25 | 1.50 |
| 2012 | 5,000 | PF65 18.00 | | | | |
| 2013 | — | — | — | 0.75 | 1.25 | 1.50 |
| 2014 | — | — | — | 0.75 | 1.25 | 1.50 |

### KM# 37 50 EURO CENT

7.81 g., Brass, 24.25 mm. **Obv:** Harp **Rev:** Denomination and map **Edge:** Reeded

| Date | Mintage | VF20 | XF40 | MS60 | MS63 | MS65 |
|---|---|---|---|---|---|---|
| 2002 | 144,144,592 | — | — | 1.00 | 1.50 | 1.75 |
| 2003 | 11,811,926 | — | — | 1.00 | 1.50 | 1.75 |
| 2004 | 6,748,912 | — | — | 1.00 | 1.50 | 1.75 |
| 2005 | 17,253,568 | — | — | 1.00 | 1.50 | 1.75 |
| 2006 | 966,138 | — | — | 1.00 | 1.50 | 1.75 |
| 2006 Proof | 5,000 | — | — | — | — | — |

### KM# 49 50 EURO CENT

7.81 g., Brass, 24.25 mm. **Obv:** Harp **Rev:** Relief map of Western Europe, stars, lines and value **Edge:** Reeded

| Date | Mintage | VF20 | XF40 | MS60 | MS63 | MS65 |
|---|---|---|---|---|---|---|
| 2007 | 4,991,002 | — | — | 1.00 | 1.50 | 1.75 |
| 2007 | 10,000 | PF65 20.00 | | | | |
| 2008 | 1,122,371 | — | — | 1.00 | 1.50 | 1.75 |
| 2009 | 1,876,011 | — | — | 1.00 | 1.50 | 1.75 |
| 2009 | 5,000 | PF65 20.00 | | | | |
| 2010 | 1,173,242 | — | — | 1.00 | 1.50 | 1.75 |
| 2010 | 5,000 | PF65 20.00 | | | | |
| 2011 | 1,096,961 | — | — | 1.00 | 1.50 | 1.75 |
| 2011 | 5,000 | PF65 20.00 | | | | |
| 2012 | — | — | — | 1.00 | 1.50 | 1.75 |
| 2012 | 5,000 | PF65 20.00 | | | | |
| 2013 | — | — | — | 1.00 | 1.50 | 1.75 |
| 2014 | — | — | — | 1.00 | 1.50 | 1.75 |

### KM# 38 EURO

7.50 g., Bi-Metallic Copper-Nickel center in Brass ring, 23.25 mm. **Obv:** Harp **Rev:** Denomination and map **Edge:** Reeded and plain sections

| Date | Mintage | VF20 | XF40 | MS60 | MS63 | MS65 |
|---|---|---|---|---|---|---|
| 2002 | 135,139,737 | — | — | 1.75 | 2.75 | 3.00 |
| 2003 | 2,520,000 | — | — | 1.75 | 2.75 | 3.00 |
| 2004 | 1,632,990 | — | — | 1.75 | 2.75 | 3.00 |
| 2005 | 6,769,777 | — | — | 1.75 | 2.75 | 3.00 |
| 2006 | 4,023,722 | — | — | 1.75 | 2.75 | 3.00 |
| 2006 | 5,000 | PF65 25.00 | | | | |

### KM# 50 EURO

7.50 g., Bi-Metallic Copper-Nickel center in Brass ring, 23.25 mm. **Obv:** Harp **Rev:** Relief map of Western Europe, stars, lines and value **Edge:** Reeded and plain sections

| Date | Mintage | VF20 | XF40 | MS60 | MS63 | MS65 |
|---|---|---|---|---|---|---|
| 2007 | 1,850,049 | — | — | 1.75 | 2.75 | 3.00 |
| 2007 | 10,000 | PF65 22.00 | | | | |
| 2008 | 2,609,757 | — | — | 1.75 | 2.75 | 3.00 |

| Date | Mintage | VF20 | XF40 | MS60 | MS63 | MS65 |
|---|---|---|---|---|---|---|
| 2009 | 3,314,828 | — | — | 1.75 | 2.75 | 3.00 |
| 2009 | 5,000 | PF65 22.00 | | | | |
| 2010 | 1,082,716 | — | — | 1.75 | 2.75 | 3.00 |
| 2010 | 5,000 | PF65 22.00 | | | | |
| 2011 | 1,104,965 | — | — | 1.75 | 2.75 | 3.00 |
| 2011 | 5,000 | PF65 22.00 | | | | |
| 2012 | — | — | — | 1.75 | 2.75 | 3.00 |
| 2012 | 5,000 | PF65 22.00 | | | | |
| 2013 | — | — | — | 1.75 | 2.75 | 3.00 |
| 2014 | — | — | — | 1.75 | 2.75 | 3.00 |

**KM# 39 2 EURO**

8.52 g., Bi-Metallic Nickel-Brass center in Copper-Nickel ring, 25.7 mm. **Obv:** Harp **Rev:** Denomination and map **Edge:** Reeded with 2's and stars

| Date | Mintage | VF20 | XF40 | MS60 | MS63 | MS65 |
|---|---|---|---|---|---|---|
| 2002 | 90,548,166 | — | — | 3.50 | 4.00 | 4.50 |
| 2003 | 2,631,076 | — | — | 3.50 | 4.00 | 4.50 |
| 2004 | 3,738,186 | — | — | 3.50 | 4.00 | 4.50 |
| 2005 | 11,982,981 | — | — | 3.50 | 4.00 | 4.50 |
| 2006 | 3,860,519 | — | — | 3.50 | 4.00 | 4.50 |
| 2006 | 5,000 | PF65 28.00 | | | | |

**KM# 51 2 EURO**

8.52 g., Bi-Metallic Nickel-Brass center in Copper-Nickel ring, 25.7 mm. **Obv:** Harp **Rev:** Relief map of Western Europe, stars, lines and value **Edge:** Reeded with 2's and stars

| Date | Mintage | VF20 | XF40 | MS60 | MS63 | MS65 |
|---|---|---|---|---|---|---|
| 2007 | 7,595,260 | — | — | 3.50 | 4.00 | 4.50 |
| 2007 | 10,000 | PF65 25.00 | | | | |
| 2008 | 5,792,003 | — | — | 3.50 | 4.00 | 4.50 |
| 2009 | 30,063 | — | — | 3.50 | 4.00 | 4.50 |
| 2009 | 5,000 | PF65 25.00 | | | | |
| 2010 | 1,448,746 | — | — | 3.50 | 4.00 | 4.50 |
| 2010 | 5,000 | PF65 25.00 | | | | |
| 2011 | 1,053,271 | — | — | 3.50 | 4.00 | 4.50 |
| 2011 | 5,000 | PF65 25.00 | | | | |
| 2012 | — | — | — | 3.50 | 4.00 | 4.50 |
| 2012 | 5,000 | PF65 25.00 | | | | |
| 2013 | — | — | — | 3.50 | 4.00 | 4.50 |
| 2014 | — | — | — | 3.50 | 4.00 | 4.50 |

**KM# 53 2 EURO**

8.45 g., Bi-Metallic Nickel-Brass center in Copper-Nickel ring, 25.72 mm. **Subject:** 50th Anniversary Treaty of Rome **Obv:** Open treaty book **Rev:** Large value at left, modified outline of Europe at right **Edge:** Reeded with stars and 2's

| Date | Mintage | VF20 | XF40 | MS60 | MS63 | MS65 |
|---|---|---|---|---|---|---|
| 2007 | 4,605,112 | — | — | 4.00 | 6.00 | 10.00 |
| 2007 Special Unc. | 35,000 | — | — | — | — | 20.00 |
| 2007 | 10,000 | PF65 25.00 | | | | |

**KM# 62 2 EURO**

8.52 g., Bi-Metallic Nickel-Brass center in Copper-Nickel ring, 25.72 mm. **Subject:** EMU, 10th Anniversary

| Date | Mintage | VF20 | XF40 | MS60 | MS63 | MS65 |
|---|---|---|---|---|---|---|
| 2009 | 5,000,000 | — | — | 5.00 | 8.00 | 10.00 |
| 2009 | 7,000 | PF65 115 | | | | |

**KM# 71 2 EURO**

8.50 g., Bi-Metallic Nickel-Brass center in Copper-Nickel ring, 25.75 mm. **Subject:** Euro Coinage, 10th Anniversary **Obv:** Euro symbol on globe at center, child-like rendering around

| Date | Mintage | VF20 | XF40 | MS60 | MS63 | MS65 |
|---|---|---|---|---|---|---|
| 2012 | 3,000,000 | — | — | 4.00 | 6.00 | 9.00 |
| 2012 | — | PF65 25.00 | | | | |

**KM# 40 5 EURO**

14.19 g., Copper-Nickel, 28.4 mm. **Subject:** Special Olympics **Obv:** Harp **Rev:** Multicolor games logo **Edge:** Reeded

| Date | Mintage | VF20 | XF40 | MS60 | MS63 | MS65 |
|---|---|---|---|---|---|---|
| 2003 | 35,000 | — | — | 12.00 | 15.00 | 18.00 |
| 2003 | 25,000 | PF63 25.00 | PF65 28.00 | | | |

**KM# 56 5 EURO**

8.52 g., 0.925 Silver 0.2534 oz. ASW, 28 mm. **Subject:** International Polar Year **Obv:** Harp within wreath **Rev:** Ernest Shackleton, Tom Crean and The Endurance in distance **Edge:** Reeded

| Date | Mintage | VF20 | XF40 | MS60 | MS63 | MS65 |
|---|---|---|---|---|---|---|
| 2008 | 5,000 | PF63 85.00 | PF65 95.00 | | | |

**KM# 41 10 EURO**

28.28 g., 0.925 Silver 0.841 oz. ASW, 38.61 mm. **Subject:** Special Olympics **Obv:** Gold highlighted harp, 2003, Eire **Rev:** Gold highlighted games logo **Edge:** Reeded

| Date | Mintage | VF20 | XF40 | MS60 | MS63 | MS65 |
|---|---|---|---|---|---|---|
| 2003 | 30,000 | PF63 50.00 | PF65 60.00 | | | |

**KM# 42 10 EURO**

28.28 g., 0.925 Silver 0.841 oz. ASW, 38.61 mm. **Subject:** EU Presidency **Obv:** 2004, Eire, Harp **Rev:** Stylized Celtic swan **Edge:** Reeded

| Date | Mintage | VF20 | XF40 | MS60 | MS63 | MS65 |
|---|---|---|---|---|---|---|
| 2004 | 50,000 | PF63 45.00 | PF65 55.00 | | | |

**KM# 44 10 EURO**

28.28 g., 0.925 Silver 0.841 oz. ASW, 38.6 mm. **Subject:** Sir William R. Hamilton **Obv:** Eire, 2005, Harp **Rev:** Triangle in circle of Greek letters used as math symbols **Edge:** Reeded

| Date | Mintage | VF20 | XF40 | MS60 | MS63 | MS65 |
|---|---|---|---|---|---|---|
| 2005 | 30,000 | PF63 55.00 | PF65 65.00 | | | |

**KM# 45 10 EURO**

28.28 g., 0.925 Silver 0.841 oz. ASW, 38.61 mm. **Subject:** Samuel Beckett 1906-1989 **Obv:** 2006, Eire, Harp **Rev:** Face, value and play scene **Edge:** Reeded

| Date | Mintage | VF20 | XF40 | MS60 | MS63 | MS65 |
|---|---|---|---|---|---|---|
| 2006 | 35,000 | PF63 50.00 | PF65 60.00 | | | |

**KM# 58 10 EURO**

28.28 g., 0.925 Silver 0.841 oz. ASW, 38.6 mm. **Subject:** European Culture - Ireland **Obv:** Irish Harp **Rev:** Celtic design

| Date | Mintage | VF20 | XF40 | MS60 | MS63 | MS65 |
|---|---|---|---|---|---|---|
| 2007 | 35,000 | PF63 55.00 | PF65 65.00 | | | |

**KM# 54 10 EURO**

28.28 g., 0.925 Silver 0.841 oz. ASW, 38.61 mm. **Subject:** Skellig Michael Island **Rev:** Birds and 12 stars above island **Rev. Legend:** SCEILIG MHICHIL

| Date | Mintage | VF20 | XF40 | MS60 | MS63 | MS65 |
|---|---|---|---|---|---|---|
| 2008 | 25,000 | PF63 65.00 | PF65 75.00 | | | |

**KM# 60 10 EURO**

28.28 g., 0.925 Silver 0.841 oz. ASW, 38.61 mm. **Subject:** First currency, 80th Anniversary **Obv:** Irish harp **Rev:** Ploughman design

| Date | Mintage | VF20 | XF40 | MS60 | MS63 | MS65 |
|---|---|---|---|---|---|---|
| 2009 | 15,000 | PF63 55.00 | PF65 65.00 | | | |

**KM# 65 10 EURO**
28.28 g., 0.925 Silver 0.841 oz. ASW, 38.61 mm. **Subject:** The President's Award - Gaisce

| Date | Mintage | VF20 | XF40 | MS60 | MS63 | MS65 |
|---|---|---|---|---|---|---|
| 2010 | 8,000 | PF63 65.00 | PF65 75.00 | | | |

**KM# 67 10 EURO**
28.28 g., 0.925 Silver 0.841 oz. ASW, 38.61 mm. **Subject:** St. Brendan the Navigator **Rev:** Medieval ship

| Date | Mintage | VF20 | XF40 | MS60 | MS63 | MS65 |
|---|---|---|---|---|---|---|
| 2011 | 15,000 | PF63 60.00 | PF65 70.00 | | | |

**KM# 70 10 EURO**
28.28 g., 0.925 Silver 0.841 oz. ASW, 38.61 mm. **Subject:** Jack B. Yates

| Date | Mintage | VF20 | XF40 | MS60 | MS63 | MS65 |
|---|---|---|---|---|---|---|
| 2012 | 12,000 | PF63 60.00 | PF65 70.00 | | | |

**KM# 75 10 EURO**
28.28 g., 0.925 Silver 0.841 oz. ASW, 38.61 mm. **Subject:** Micahel Collins **Rev:** Bust facing

| Date | Mintage | VF20 | XF40 | MS60 | MS63 | MS65 |
|---|---|---|---|---|---|---|
| 2012 | 14,000 | PF63 70.00 | PF65 80.00 | | | |

**KM# 78 10 EURO**
28.28 g., 0.925 Silver 0.841 oz. ASW, 38.61 mm. **Subject:** J.F. Kennedy, 50th Anniversary of Visit

| Date | Mintage | VF20 | XF40 | MS60 | MS63 | MS65 |
|---|---|---|---|---|---|---|
| 2013 | 25,000 | PF63 60.00 | PF65 70.00 | | | |

**KM# 80.1 10 EURO**
28.28 g., 0.925 Silver 0.841 oz. ASW, 38.61 mm. **Subject:** James Joyce **Note:** Incorrect quote on reverse.

| Date | Mintage | VF20 | XF40 | MS60 | MS63 | MS65 |
|---|---|---|---|---|---|---|
| 2013 | — | PF63 150 | | | | |

**KM# 80.2 10 EURO**
28.28 g., 0.925 Silver 0.841 oz. ASW, 38.61 mm. **Subject:** James Joyce **Note:** Corrected quote on reverse.

| Date | Mintage | VF20 | XF40 | MS60 | MS63 | MS65 |
|---|---|---|---|---|---|---|
| 2013 | 10,000 | PF63 65.00 | PF65 75.00 | | | |

**KM# 81 10 EURO**
28.28 g., 0.925 Silver 0.841 oz. ASW, 38.61 mm. **Subject:** John McCormack

| Date | Mintage | F12 | VF20 | XF40 | MS60 | MS63 |
|---|---|---|---|---|---|---|
| 2014 | 8,000 | PF63 65.00 | PF65 75.00 | | | |

**KM# 52 15 EURO**
28.28 g., 0.925 Silver 0.841 oz. ASW, 37 mm. **Obv:** Stylized clover with date and harp **Rev:** Ivan Mestroviae's Seated Woman with Harp design **Edge:** Plain **Note:** Illustration reduced.

| Date | Mintage | VF20 | XF40 | MS60 | MS63 | MS65 |
|---|---|---|---|---|---|---|
| 2007 | 10,000 | PF63 85.00 | PF65 100 | | | |

Note: 8,000 were sold in a single coin case. 1,000 were sold in a two coin set with the corresponding Croatian coin, as an Ireland set. An additional 1,000 were sold with the corresponding Croatian coin as a Croatia set. coins in both sets were the same but the packaging was different.

**KM# 63 15 EURO**
28.28 g., 0.925 Silver 0.841 oz. ASW, 38.61 mm. **Subject:** Gaelic Athletics, 125 years

| Date | Mintage | VF20 | XF40 | MS60 | MS63 | MS65 |
|---|---|---|---|---|---|---|
| 2009 | 10,000 | PF63 75.00 | PF65 85.00 | | | |

**KM# 64 15 EURO**
28.28 g., 0.925 Silver 0.841 oz. ASW, 38.61 mm. **Rev:** Foal and mare

| Date | Mintage | VF20 | XF40 | MS60 | MS63 | MS65 |
|---|---|---|---|---|---|---|
| 2010 | 15,000 | PF63 75.00 | PF65 85.00 | | | |

**KM# 68 15 EURO**
28.28 g., 0.925 Silver 0.841 oz. ASW, 38.61 mm. **Rev:** Salmon

| Date | Mintage | VF20 | XF40 | MS60 | MS63 | MS65 |
|---|---|---|---|---|---|---|
| 2011 | 12,000 | PF63 75.00 | PF65 85.00 | | | |

**KM# 72 15 EURO**
28.28 g., 0.925 Silver 0.841 oz. ASW, 38.61 mm. **Rev:** Wolfhounds

| Date | Mintage | VF20 | XF40 | MS60 | MS63 | MS65 |
|---|---|---|---|---|---|---|
| 2012 | 8,000 | PF63 75.00 | PF65 85.00 | | | |

**KM# 77 15 EURO**
28.28 g., 0.925 Silver 0.841 oz. ASW, 38.61 mm. **Subject:** Dublin Lockout, 100th Anniversary

| Date | Mintage | VF20 | XF40 | MS60 | MS63 | MS65 |
|---|---|---|---|---|---|---|
| 2013 | 10,000 | PF63 75.00 | PF65 85.00 | | | |

**KM# 83 15 EURO**
28.28 g., 0.925 Silver 0.841 oz. ASW, 38.61 mm. **Subject:** John Philip Holland, 100th Anniversary of Death

| Date | Mintage | F12 | VF20 | XF40 | MS60 | MS63 |
|---|---|---|---|---|---|---|
| 2014 | — | PF65 50.00 | | | | |

**KM# 46 20 EURO**
1.24 g., 0.999 Gold 0.0398 oz. AGW, 14 mm. **Subject:** Samuel Beckett 1906-1989 **Obv:** 2006, Eire, Harp **Rev:** Face, value and play **Edge:** Reeded

| Date | Mintage | VF20 | XF40 | MS60 | MS63 | MS65 |
|---|---|---|---|---|---|---|
| 2006 | 20,000 | PF63 75.00 | PF65 85.00 | | | |

**KM# 59 20 EURO**
1.24 g., 0.999 Gold 0.040 oz. AGW, 14 mm. **Subject:** European Culture - Ireland **Obv:** Map **Rev:** Celtic design

| Date | Mintage | VF20 | XF40 | MS60 | MS63 | MS65 |
|---|---|---|---|---|---|---|
| 2007 | 25,000 | PF63 95.00 | PF65 110 | | | |

**KM# 55 20 EURO**
1.24 g., 0.999 Gold 0.040 oz. AGW, 14 mm. **Subject:** Skellig Michael Island **Rev:** Birds and 12 stars above island **Rev. Legend:** SCEILIG MHICHIL

| Date | Mintage | VF20 | XF40 | MS60 | MS63 | MS65 |
|---|---|---|---|---|---|---|
| 2008 | 15,000 | PF63 90.00 | PF65 100 | | | |

**KM# 61 20 EURO**
1.24 g., 0.999 Gold 0.040 oz. AGW, 14 mm. **Subject:** First currency, 80th Anniversary

| Date | Mintage | VF20 | XF40 | MS60 | MS63 | MS65 |
|---|---|---|---|---|---|---|
| 2009 | 15,000 | PF63 80.00 | PF65 90.00 | | | |

**KM# 66 20 EURO**
1.24 g., 0.999 Gold 0.0398 oz. AGW, 14 mm. **Subject:** The President's Award - Gaisce

| Date | Mintage | VF20 | XF40 | MS60 | MS63 | MS65 |
|---|---|---|---|---|---|---|
| 2010 | 6,000 | PF63 90.00 | PF65 100 | | | |

### KM# 69 20 EURO

0.50 g., 0.999 Gold, 11 mm. **Rev:** Celtic Cross

| Date | Mintage | VF20 | XF40 | MS60 | MS63 | MS65 |
|---|---|---|---|---|---|---|
| 2011 | 12,000 | PF63 45.00 | PF65 50.00 | | | |

### KM# 73 20 EURO

0.50 g., 0.999 Gold, 11 mm. **Obv:** Irish Monastic Art **Rev:** Book of Kells

| Date | Mintage | VF20 | XF40 | MS60 | MS63 | MS65 |
|---|---|---|---|---|---|---|
| 2012 | 12,000 | PF63 55.00 | PF65 65.00 | | | |

### KM# 74 20 EURO

0.50 g., 0.999 Gold **Rev:** Michael Collins

| Date | Mintage | VF20 | XF40 | MS60 | MS63 | MS65 |
|---|---|---|---|---|---|---|
| 2012 | 18,000 | PF63 55.00 | PF65 65.00 | | | |

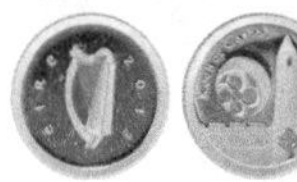

### KM# 76 20 EURO

0.50 g., 0.999 Gold AGW, 11 mm. **Subject:** Medieval Irish Architecture **Rev:** Rock of Cashel architectural elements

| Date | Mintage | VF20 | XF40 | MS60 | MS63 | MS65 |
|---|---|---|---|---|---|---|
| 2013 | 10,000 | PF63 55.00 | PF65 65.00 | | | |

### KM# 79 20 EURO

1.00 g., 0.999 Gold 0.0321 oz. AGW, 13.92 mm. **Subject:** J.F. Kennedy, 50th Anniversary of Visit

| Date | Mintage | VF20 | XF40 | MS60 | MS63 | MS65 |
|---|---|---|---|---|---|---|
| 2013 | — | PF63 55.00 | PF65 65.00 | | | |

### KM# 82 20 EURO

0.50 g., 0.999 Gold 0.0161 oz. AGW, 11 mm. **Subject:** Battle of Clontarf, 1000 Anniversary

| Date | Mintage | F12 | VF20 | XF40 | MS60 | MS63 |
|---|---|---|---|---|---|---|
| 2014 Proof | 12,000 | — | — | — | — | — |

### KM# 57 100 EURO

15.55 g., 0.999 Gold 0.4994 oz. AGW, 28 mm. **Subject:** International Polar Year **Obv:** Harp within wreath **Rev:** Ernest Shackleton, Tom Crean and The Endurance in distance **Edge:** Reeded

| Date | Mintage | VF20 | XF40 | MS60 | MS63 | MS65 |
|---|---|---|---|---|---|---|
| 2008 | 2,000 | PF65 950 | | | | |

## MINT SETS

| KM# | Date | Mintage | Identification | Issue Price | Mkt Val |
|---|---|---|---|---|---|
| MS10 | 2002 (8) | 20,000 | KM#32-39 | 16.00 | 200 |
| MS11 | 2003 (8) | 30,000 | KM#32-39 | 20.00 | 65.00 |
| MS12 | 2003 (9) | 35,000 | KM#32-40 Special Olympics | 25.00 | 90.00 |
| MS13 | 2004 (8) | 40,000 | KM#32-39 | 25.00 | 45.00 |
| MS14 | 2005 (8) | 50,000 | KM#32-39 Hey-wood Gardens | 29.00 | 40.00 |
| MS15 | 2006 (8) | 40,000 | KM#32-39 Glen-veagh National Park and Castle | 26.00 | 40.00 |
| MS16 | 2006 (8) | — | KM#32-39 Boy Baby Set | 35.00 | 42.50 |
| MS17 | 2006 (8) | — | KM#32-39 Girl Baby Set | 35.00 | 42.50 |
| MS18 | 2007 (8) | 20,000 | KM#32-34, 47-51 Aran Islands | 29.00 | 30.00 |
| MS19 | 2007 (8) | — | KM#32-34, 47-51 Boy Baby Set | — | 30.00 |
| MS20 | 2007 (8) | — | KM#32-34, 47-51 Girl Baby Set | — | 30.00 |
| MS21 | 2007 (9) | 20,000 | KM#32-34, 47-51, 53 | — | 30.00 |
| MS22 | 2008 (8) | 30,000 | KM#32-34, 47-51 Newgrange | — | 30.00 |
| MS23 | 2008 (8) | — | KM#32-34, 47-51 Boy Baby Set | — | 30.00 |
| MS24 | 2008 (8) | — | KM#32-34, 47-51 Girl Baby Set | — | 30.00 |
| MS25 | 2009 (8) | 25,000 | KM#32-34, 47-51 GAA 125th Anniversary | — | 30.00 |
| MS26 | 2009 (8) | — | KM#32-34, 47-51 Boy Baby Set | — | 30.00 |
| MS27 | 2009 (8) | — | KM#32-34, 47-51 Girl Baby Set | — | 30.00 |
| MS28 | 2010 (8) | 20,000 | KM#32-34, 47-51 Horse | 45.00 | 45.00 |
| MS29 | 2010 (8) | — | KM#32-34, 47-51 Baby Set | 45.00 | 45.00 |
| MS30 | 2011 (8) | 20,000 | KM#32-34, 47-51 | — | 45.00 |
| MS31 | 2012 (8) | 17,000 | KM#32-34, 47-51 | — | 45.00 |

## PROOF SETS

| KM# | Date | Mintage | Identification | Issue Price | Mkt Val |
|---|---|---|---|---|---|
| PS6 | 2006 (8) | 5,000 | KM#32-39 | 125 | 165 |
| PS7 | 2006 (2) | — | KM#45, 46 | — | 135 |
| PS8 | 2007 (9) | 10,000 | KM#32-34, 47-51, 53 | — | 165 |
| PS9 | 2007 (2) | — | KM#58-59 | — | 150 |
| PS10 | 2008 (2) | — | KM#54-55 | — | 165 |
| PS11 | 2008 (2) | — | KM#56-57 | — | 950 |
| PS12 | 2009 (9) | — | KM#32-34, 47-51, 58 GAA 125th Anniversary | — | 200 |
| PS13 | 2009 (9) | 5,000 | KM#32-34, 47-51, 61. | — | 225 |
| PS14 | 2009 (2) | 5,000 | KM#60, 61. Ploughman Bank Note | — | 160 |
| PS15 | 2010 (2) | — | KM#65-66 | — | 150 |
| PS16 | 2010 (8) | 5,000 | KM#32-34, 47-51 | — | 200 |
| PS17 | 2011 (8) | 5,000 | KM#32-34, 47-51 | — | 200 |
| PS18 | 2012 (9) | 5,000 | KM#32-34, 47-51, 71 | — | 125 |
| PS19 | 2012 (4) | 6,000 | KM#74, 75 | — | 150 |

# ISLE OF MAN

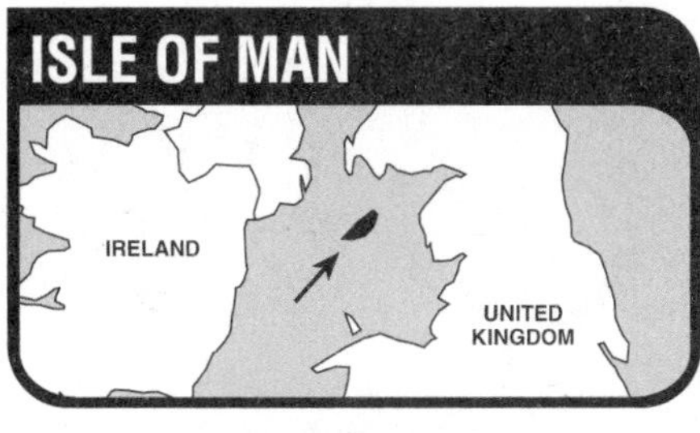


## BRITISH DEPENDENCY

### DECIMAL COINAGE

100 Pence = 1 Pound

### KM# 1036 PENNY

3.56 g., Copper Plated Steel, 20.32 mm. **Ruler:** Elizabeth II **Obv:** Head with tiara right with small triskeles dividing legend **Rev:** Ruins **Edge:** Plain

| Date | Mintage | VF20 | XF40 | MS60 | MS63 | MS65 |
|---|---|---|---|---|---|---|
| 2001 PM AA | — | — | — | 0.15 | 0.25 | 0.45 |
| 2001 PM AC | — | — | — | 0.15 | 0.25 | 0.45 |
| 2002 PM AA | — | — | — | 0.15 | 0.25 | 0.45 |
| 2002 PM AE | — | — | — | 0.15 | 0.25 | 0.45 |
| 2003 PM AA | — | — | — | 0.15 | 0.25 | 0.45 |
| 2003 PM AE | — | — | — | 0.15 | 0.25 | 0.45 |

### KM# 1253 PENNY

3.56 g., Copper Plated Steel, 20.3 mm. **Ruler:** Elizabeth II **Obv:** Head with tiara right **Rev:** Santon War Memorial

| Date | Mintage | VF20 | XF40 | MS60 | MS63 | MS65 |
|---|---|---|---|---|---|---|
| 2004 PM AA | — | — | — | 0.15 | 0.25 | 0.45 |
| 2004 PM AB | — | — | — | 0.15 | 0.25 | 0.45 |
| 2005 PM AA | — | — | — | 0.15 | 0.25 | 0.45 |
| 2005 PM AB | — | — | — | 0.15 | 0.25 | 0.45 |
| 2006 PM AA | — | — | — | 0.15 | 0.25 | 0.45 |
| 2006 PM AB | — | — | — | 0.15 | 0.25 | 0.45 |
| 2007 PM AA | — | — | — | 0.15 | 0.25 | 0.45 |
| 2007 PM AB | — | — | — | 0.15 | 0.25 | 0.45 |
| 2007 PM BA | — | — | — | 0.15 | 0.25 | 0.45 |
| 2008 PM AA | — | — | — | 0.15 | 0.25 | 0.45 |
| 2009 PM AA | — | — | — | 0.15 | 0.25 | 0.45 |
| 2010 PM AA | — | — | — | 0.15 | 0.25 | 0.45 |
| 2011 PM AA | — | — | — | 0.15 | 0.25 | 0.45 |
| 2012 PM AA | — | — | — | 0.15 | 0.25 | 0.45 |
| 2013 PM AA | — | — | — | 0.15 | 0.25 | 0.45 |

### KM# 1037 2 PENCE

7.12 g., Copper Plated Steel, 25.9 mm. **Ruler:** Elizabeth II **Obv:** Head with tiara right **Rev:** Sailboat **Edge:** Plain

| Date | Mintage | VF20 | XF40 | MS60 | MS63 | MS65 |
|---|---|---|---|---|---|---|
| 2001 PM AA | — | — | — | 0.20 | 0.40 | 0.60 |
| 2001 PM AB | — | — | — | 0.20 | 0.40 | 0.60 |
| 2001 PM AC | — | — | — | 0.20 | 0.40 | 0.60 |
| 2002 PM AA | — | — | — | 0.20 | 0.40 | 0.60 |
| 2002 PM AB | — | — | — | 0.20 | 0.40 | 0.60 |
| 2002 PM AC | — | — | — | 0.20 | 0.40 | 0.60 |
| 2002 PM AF | — | — | — | 0.20 | 0.40 | 0.60 |
| 2003 PM AA | — | — | — | 0.20 | 0.40 | 0.60 |
| 2003 PM AF | — | — | — | 0.20 | 0.40 | 0.60 |

### KM# 1254 2 PENCE

7.12 g., Copper Plated Steel, 25.9 mm. **Ruler:** Elizabeth II **Obv:** Head with tiara right **Rev:** Albert Tower

| Date | Mintage | VF20 | XF40 | MS60 | MS63 | MS65 |
|---|---|---|---|---|---|---|
| 2004 PM AA | — | — | — | 0.20 | 0.40 | 0.60 |
| 2004 PM AB | — | — | — | 0.20 | 0.40 | 0.60 |
| 2005 PM AA | — | — | — | 0.20 | 0.40 | 0.60 |
| 2005 PM AB | — | — | — | 0.20 | 0.40 | 0.60 |
| 2006 PM AA | — | — | — | 0.20 | 0.40 | 0.60 |
| 2006 PM AB | — | — | — | 0.20 | 0.40 | 0.60 |
| 2007 PM AA | — | — | — | 0.20 | 0.40 | 0.60 |
| 2007 PM AB | — | — | — | 0.20 | 0.40 | 0.60 |
| 2007 PM BA | — | — | — | 0.20 | 0.40 | 0.60 |
| 2008 PM AA | — | — | — | 0.20 | 0.40 | 0.60 |
| 2009 PM AA | — | — | — | 0.20 | 0.40 | 0.60 |
| 2010 PM AA | — | — | — | 0.20 | 0.40 | 0.60 |
| 2011 PM AA | — | — | — | 0.20 | 0.40 | 0.60 |
| 2012 PM AA | — | — | — | 0.20 | 0.40 | 0.60 |
| 2013 PM AA | — | — | — | 0.20 | 0.40 | 0.60 |

### KM# 1038 5 PENCE

3.25 g., Copper-Nickel, 18 mm. **Ruler:** Elizabeth II **Obv:** Head with tiara right **Rev:** Gaut's Cross **Edge:** Reeded

| Date | Mintage | VF20 | XF40 | MS60 | MS63 | MS65 |
|---|---|---|---|---|---|---|
| 2001 PM AA | — | — | — | 0.35 | 0.75 | 1.00 |
| 2002 PM AA | — | — | — | 0.35 | 0.75 | 1.00 |
| 2002 PM AC | — | — | — | 0.35 | 0.75 | 1.00 |
| 2002 PM AD | — | — | — | 0.35 | 0.75 | 1.00 |
| 2002 PM AE | — | — | — | 0.35 | 0.75 | 1.00 |
| 2003 PM AA | — | — | — | 0.35 | 0.75 | 1.00 |
| 2003 PM AB | — | — | — | 0.35 | 0.75 | 1.00 |
| 2003 PM AD | — | — | — | 0.35 | 0.75 | 1.00 |

### KM# 1255 5 PENCE

3.25 g., Copper-Nickel, 18 mm. **Ruler:** Elizabeth II **Obv:** Head with tiara right **Rev:** Tower of Refuge **Edge:** Reeded

| Date | Mintage | VF20 | XF40 | MS60 | MS63 | MS65 |
|---|---|---|---|---|---|---|
| 2004 PM AA | — | — | — | 0.35 | 0.75 | 1.00 |
| 2004 PM AB | — | — | — | 0.35 | 0.75 | 1.00 |
| 2005 PM AA | — | — | — | 0.35 | 0.75 | 1.00 |
| 2005 PM AB | — | — | — | 0.35 | 0.75 | 1.00 |
| 2006 PM AA | — | — | — | 0.35 | 0.75 | 1.00 |
| 2006 PM AB | — | — | — | 0.35 | 0.75 | 1.00 |
| 2007 PM AA | — | — | — | 0.35 | 0.75 | 1.00 |
| 2007 PM AB | — | — | — | 0.35 | 0.75 | 1.00 |
| 2008 PM AA | — | — | — | 0.35 | 0.75 | 1.00 |
| 2009 PM AA | — | — | — | 0.35 | 0.75 | 1.00 |
| 2010 PM AA | — | — | — | 0.35 | 0.75 | 1.00 |
| 2011 PM AA | — | — | — | 0.35 | 0.75 | 1.00 |
| 2012 PM AA | — | — | — | 0.35 | 0.75 | 1.00 |
| 2013 PM AA | — | — | — | 0.35 | 0.75 | 1.00 |

### KM# 1039 10 PENCE

6.50 g., Copper-Nickel, 24.5 mm. **Ruler:** Elizabeth II **Obv:** Head with tiara right **Rev:** Cathedral **Edge:** Reeded

| Date | Mintage | VF20 | XF40 | MS60 | MS63 | MS65 |
|---|---|---|---|---|---|---|
| 2001 PM AA | — | — | — | 0.50 | 1.00 | 1.50 |
| 2002 PM AA | — | — | — | 0.50 | 1.00 | 1.50 |
| 2003 PM AA | — | — | — | 0.50 | 1.00 | 1.50 |

### KM# 1256 10 PENCE

6.50 g., Copper-Nickel, 24.5 mm. **Ruler:** Elizabeth II **Obv:** Head with tiara right **Rev:** Chicken Rock Lighthouse **Edge:** Reeded

| Date | Mintage | VF20 | XF40 | MS60 | MS63 | MS65 |
|---|---|---|---|---|---|---|
| 2004 PM AA | — | — | — | 0.50 | 1.00 | 1.50 |
| 2004 PM AB | — | — | — | 0.50 | 1.00 | 1.50 |
| 2005 PM AA | — | — | — | 0.50 | 1.00 | 1.50 |
| 2005 PM AB | — | — | — | 0.50 | 1.00 | 1.50 |
| 2006 PM AA | — | — | — | 0.50 | 1.00 | 1.50 |
| 2006 PM AB | — | — | — | 0.50 | 1.00 | 1.50 |
| 2007 PM AA | — | — | — | 0.50 | 1.00 | 1.50 |
| 2007 PM AB | — | — | — | 0.50 | 1.00 | 1.50 |
| 2008 PM AA | — | — | — | 0.50 | 1.00 | 1.50 |
| 2009 PM AA | — | — | — | 0.50 | 1.00 | 1.50 |
| 2010 PM AA | — | — | — | 0.50 | 1.00 | 1.50 |
| 2011 PM AA | — | — | — | 0.50 | 1.00 | 1.50 |
| 2012 PM AA | — | — | — | 0.50 | 1.00 | 1.50 |
| 2013 PM AA | — | — | — | 0.50 | 1.00 | 1.50 |

### KM# 1040 20 PENCE

5.00 g., Copper-Nickel, 21.4 mm. **Ruler:** Elizabeth II **Subject:** Rushen Abbey **Obv:** Head with tiara right **Rev:** Monk writing **Edge:** Plain **Shape:** 7-sided

| Date | Mintage | VF20 | XF40 | MS60 | MS63 | MS65 |
|---|---|---|---|---|---|---|
| 2001 PM AA | — | — | — | 0.75 | 1.50 | 2.00 |
| 2001 PM AB | — | — | — | 0.75 | 1.50 | 2.00 |
| 2002 PM AA | — | — | — | 0.75 | 1.50 | 2.00 |
| 2002 PM AB | — | — | — | 0.75 | 1.50 | 2.00 |
| 2002 PM AC | — | — | — | 0.75 | 1.50 | 2.00 |
| 2003 PM AA | — | — | — | 0.75 | 1.50 | 2.00 |
| 2003 PM BA | — | — | — | 0.75 | 1.50 | 2.00 |

### KM# 1257 20 PENCE

5.00 g., Copper-Nickel, 21.4 mm. **Ruler:** Elizabeth II **Obv:** Head with tiara right **Rev:** Castle Rushen Clock **Edge:** Plain **Shape:** 7-sided

| Date | Mintage | VF20 | XF40 | MS60 | MS63 | MS65 |
|---|---|---|---|---|---|---|
| 2004 PM AA | — | — | — | 0.75 | 1.50 | 2.00 |
| 2004 PM AB | — | — | — | 0.75 | 1.50 | 2.00 |
| 2005 PM AA | — | — | — | 0.75 | 1.50 | 2.00 |
| 2005 PM AB | — | — | — | 0.75 | 1.50 | 2.00 |
| 2006 PM AA | — | — | — | 0.75 | 1.50 | 2.00 |
| 2006 PM AB | — | — | — | 0.75 | 1.50 | 2.00 |
| 2007 PM AA | — | — | — | 0.75 | 1.50 | 2.00 |
| 2007 PM AB | — | — | — | 0.75 | 1.50 | 2.00 |
| 2008 PM AA | — | — | — | 0.75 | 1.50 | 2.00 |
| 2009 PM AA | — | — | — | 0.75 | 1.50 | 2.00 |
| 2010 PM AA | — | — | — | 0.75 | 1.50 | 2.00 |
| 2011 PM AA | — | — | — | 0.75 | 1.50 | 2.00 |
| 2012 PM AA | — | — | — | 0.75 | 1.50 | 2.00 |
| 2013 PM AA | — | — | — | 0.75 | 1.50 | 2.00 |

### KM# 1041 50 PENCE

8.00 g., Copper-Nickel, 27.3 mm. **Ruler:** Elizabeth II **Obv:** Head with tiara right **Rev:** Stylized crucifix **Edge:** Plain **Shape:** 7-sided

| Date | Mintage | VF20 | XF40 | MS60 | MS63 | MS65 |
|---|---|---|---|---|---|---|
| 2001 PM AA | — | — | — | — | 2.25 | 2.75 |
| 2002 PM AA | — | — | — | — | 2.25 | 2.75 |
| 2003 PM AA | — | — | — | — | 2.25 | 2.75 |

### KM# 1105 50 PENCE

8.00 g., Copper-Nickel, 27.3 mm. **Ruler:** Elizabeth II **Subject:** Christmas **Obv:** Head with tiara right **Rev:** Postman and children **Edge:** Plain **Shape:** 7-sided

| Date | Mintage | VF20 | XF40 | MS60 | MS63 | MS65 |
|---|---|---|---|---|---|---|
| 2001 PM BB | 30,000 | — | — | 7.00 | 10.00 | — |

### KM# 1105a 50 PENCE

8.00 g., 0.925 Silver 0.2379 oz. ASW, 27.3 mm. **Ruler:** Elizabeth II **Obv:** Head with tiara right **Rev:** Postman and children **Edge:** Plain **Shape:** 7-sided

| Date | Mintage | VF20 | XF40 | MS60 | MS63 | MS65 |
|---|---|---|---|---|---|---|
| 2001 PM | 5,000 | **PF63** 35.00 | | | | |

### KM# 1105b 50 PENCE

8.00 g., 0.9167 Gold 0.2358 oz. AGW, 27.3 mm. **Ruler:** Elizabeth II **Obv:** Head with tiara right **Rev:** Postman and children **Edge:** Plain **Shape:** 7-sided

| Date | Mintage | VF20 | XF40 | MS60 | MS63 | MS65 |
|---|---|---|---|---|---|---|
| 2001 PM | 250 | **PF63** 450 | | | | |

### KM# 1160 50 PENCE

8.00 g., Copper-Nickel, 27.3 mm. **Ruler:** Elizabeth II **Subject:** Christmas **Obv:** Head with tiara right **Rev:** Scrooge in bed **Edge:** Plain **Shape:** 7-sided

| Date | Mintage | VF20 | XF40 | MS60 | MS63 | MS65 |
|---|---|---|---|---|---|---|
| 2002BB PM | 30,000 | — | — | 7.00 | 10.00 | — |

### KM# 1160a 50 PENCE

8.00 g., 0.925 Silver 0.2379 oz. ASW, 27.3 mm. **Ruler:** Elizabeth II **Subject:** Christmas **Obv:** Head with tiara right **Rev:** Scrooge in bed **Edge:** Plain **Shape:** 7-sided

| Date | Mintage | VF20 | XF40 | MS60 | MS63 | MS65 |
|---|---|---|---|---|---|---|
| 2002 PM | 5,000 | **PF63** 35.00 | | | | |

### KM# 1160b 50 PENCE

8.00 g., 0.9167 Gold 0.2358 oz. AGW, 27.3 mm. **Ruler:** Elizabeth II **Subject:** Christmas **Obv:** Head with tiara right **Rev:** Scrooge in bed **Edge:** Plain **Shape:** 7-sided

| Date | Mintage | VF20 | XF40 | MS60 | MS63 | MS65 |
|---|---|---|---|---|---|---|
| 2002 PM | 250 | **PF63** 450 | | | | |

### KM# 1183 50 PENCE

8.00 g., Copper-Nickel, 27.3 mm. **Ruler:** Elizabeth II **Obv:** Head with tiara right **Rev:** The Snowman and James **Edge:** Plain **Shape:** 7-sided

| Date | Mintage | VF20 | XF40 | MS60 | MS63 | MS65 |
|---|---|---|---|---|---|---|
| 2003 PM BB | 10,000 | — | — | 7.00 | 10.00 | — |
| 2008 PM | — | — | — | 7.00 | 10.00 | — |

### KM# 1183a 50 PENCE

8.00 g., 0.925 Silver 0.2379 oz. ASW, 27.3 mm. **Ruler:** Elizabeth II **Subject:** Christmas **Obv:** Head with tiara right **Rev:** The Snowman and James **Edge:** Plain **Shape:** 7-sided

| Date | Mintage | VF20 | XF40 | MS60 | MS63 | MS65 |
|---|---|---|---|---|---|---|
| 2003 PM | 3,000 | **PF63** 35.00 | | | | |

### KM# 1183b 50 PENCE

8.00 g., 0.9167 Gold 0.2358 oz. AGW, 27.3 mm. **Ruler:** Elizabeth II **Obv:** Head with tiara right **Rev:** The Snowman and James **Edge:** Plain **Shape:** 7-sided

| Date | Mintage | VF20 | XF40 | MS60 | MS63 | MS65 |
|---|---|---|---|---|---|---|
| 2003 PM | 100 | **PF63** 475 | | | | |

### KM# 1258 50 PENCE

8.00 g., Copper-Nickel, 27.3 mm. **Ruler:** Elizabeth II **Obv:** Head with tiara right **Rev:** Milner's Tower **Edge:** Plain **Shape:** 7-sided

| Date | Mintage | VF20 | XF40 | MS60 | MS63 | MS65 |
|---|---|---|---|---|---|---|
| 2004 PM AA | — | — | — | — | 2.25 | 2.75 |
| 2004 PM AB | — | — | — | — | 2.25 | 2.75 |
| 2005 PM AA | — | — | — | — | 2.25 | 2.75 |
| 2005 PM AB | — | — | — | — | 2.25 | 2.75 |
| 2006 PM AA | — | — | — | — | 2.25 | 2.75 |
| 2006 PM AB | — | — | — | — | 2.25 | 2.75 |
| 2007 PM AA | — | — | — | — | 2.25 | 2.75 |
| 2007 PM AB | — | — | — | — | 2.25 | 2.75 |
| 2008 PM AA | — | — | — | — | 2.25 | 2.75 |
| 2009 PM AA | — | — | — | — | 2.25 | 2.75 |
| 2010 PM AA | — | — | — | — | 2.25 | 2.75 |
| 2011 PM AA | — | — | — | — | 2.25 | 2.75 |
| 2012 PM AA | — | — | — | — | 2.25 | 2.75 |
| 2013 PM AA | — | — | — | — | 2.25 | 2.75 |

### KM# 1262 50 PENCE

8.00 g., Copper-Nickel, 27.3 mm. **Ruler:** Elizabeth II **Subject:** Christmas **Obv:** Head with tiara right **Rev:** Laxey Wheel **Edge:** Plain **Shape:** 7-sided

| Date | Mintage | VF20 | XF40 | MS60 | MS63 | MS65 |
|---|---|---|---|---|---|---|
| 2004 PM AA | — | — | — | 7.00 | 10.00 | — |
| 2004 PM BA | 30,000 | — | — | 7.00 | 10.00 | — |

### KM# 1262a 50 PENCE

9.19 g., 0.925 Silver 0.2732 oz. ASW, 27.3 mm. **Ruler:** Elizabeth II **Subject:** Christmas **Obv:** Head with tiara right **Rev:** Laxey Wheel **Edge:** Plain **Shape:** 7-sided

| Date | Mintage | VF20 | XF40 | MS60 | MS63 | MS65 |
|---|---|---|---|---|---|---|
| 2004 PM | 5,000 | **PF63** 35.00 | | | | |

### KM# 1262b 50 PENCE

15.41 g., 0.9167 Gold 0.4541 oz. AGW, 27.3 mm. **Ruler:** Elizabeth II **Subject:** Christmas **Obv:** Head with tiara right **Rev:** Laxey Wheel **Edge:** Plain **Shape:** 7-sided

| Date | Mintage | VF20 | XF40 | MS60 | MS63 | MS65 |
|---|---|---|---|---|---|---|
| 2004 PM | 250 | **PF63** 850 | | | | |

### KM# 1293 50 PENCE

8.00 g., Copper-Nickel, 27.3 mm. **Ruler:** Elizabeth II **Obv:** Queen's new portrait **Rev:** Tourist Trophy Races **Shape:** 7-sided

| Date | Mintage | VF20 | XF40 | MS60 | MS63 | MS65 |
|---|---|---|---|---|---|---|
| 2004 PM AA | — | — | — | 6.00 | 7.00 | — |
| 2007 PM AA | — | — | — | 6.00 | 7.00 | — |

### KM# 1294 50 PENCE

8.00 g., Copper-Nickel, 27.3 mm. **Ruler:** Elizabeth II **Obv:** Queen's new portrait **Rev:** Partridge in a pear tree **Shape:** 7-sided

| Date | Mintage | VF20 | XF40 | MS60 | MS63 | MS65 |
|---|---|---|---|---|---|---|
| 2005 | — | — | — | 7.00 | 10.00 | — |

### KM# 1320.1 50 PENCE

8.00 g., Copper-Nickel, 27.3 mm. **Ruler:** Elizabeth II **Series:** 12 Days of Christmas **Obv:** Head with tiara right **Obv. Legend:** ISLE OF MAN - ELIZABETH II **Rev:** Partridge in a Pear Tree **Rev. Legend:** CHRISTMAS **Edge:** Plain **Shape:** 7-sided

| Date | Mintage | VF20 | XF40 | MS60 | MS63 | MS65 |
|---|---|---|---|---|---|---|
| 2005 PM AA | 30,000 | — | — | — | 16.00 | — |

### KM# 1320.1a 50 PENCE

9.18 g., 0.925 Silver 0.2731 oz. ASW, 27.3 mm. **Ruler:** Elizabeth II **Series:** 12 Days of Christmas **Obv:** Head with tiara right **Obv. Legend:** ISLE OF MAN - ELIZABETH II **Rev:** Partridge in a Pear Tree **Rev. Legend:** CHRISTMAS **Edge:** Plain **Shape:** 7-sided

| Date | Mintage | VF20 | XF40 | MS60 | MS63 | MS65 |
|---|---|---|---|---|---|---|
| 2005 PM | — | PF63 35.00 | | | | |

### KM# 1320.2 50 PENCE

8.00 g., Copper-Nickel, 27.3 mm. **Ruler:** Elizabeth II **Series:** 12 Days of Christmas **Obv:** Head with tiara right **Obv. Legend:** ISLE OF MAN - ELIZABETH II **Rev:** Partidge in a Pear Tree multicolor **Rev. Legend:** CHRISTMAS **Edge:** Plain **Shape:** 7-sided

| Date | Mintage | VF20 | XF40 | MS60 | MS63 | MS65 |
|---|---|---|---|---|---|---|
| 2005 PM | Inc. above | — | — | — | 20.00 | — |

### KM# 1320.2a 50 PENCE

8.00 g., 0.925 Silver 0.2379 oz. ASW, 27.3 mm. **Ruler:** Elizabeth II **Series:** 12 Days of Christmas **Obv:** Head with tiara right **Obv. Legend:** ISLE OF MAN - ELIZABETH II **Rev:** Partridge in a Pear Tree multicolor **Rev. Legend:** CHRISTMAS **Edge:** Plain **Shape:** 7-sided

| Date | Mintage | VF20 | XF40 | MS60 | MS63 | MS65 |
|---|---|---|---|---|---|---|
| 2005 PM | — | PF63 35.00 | | | | |

### KM# 1320b 50 PENCE

0.9167 Gold, 27.3 mm. **Ruler:** Elizabeth II **Series:** 12 Days of Christmas **Obv:** Head with tiara right **Obv. Legend:** ISLE OF MAN - ELIZABETH II **Rev:** Partridge in a Pear Tree **Rev. Legend:** CHRISTMAS **Edge:** Plain **Shape:** 7-sided

| Date | Mintage | VF20 | XF40 | MS60 | MS63 | MS65 |
|---|---|---|---|---|---|---|
| 2005 PM | — | PF63 850 | | | | |

### KM# 1321.1 50 PENCE

8.00 g., Copper-Nickel, 27.3 mm. **Ruler:** Elizabeth II **Series:** 12 Days of Christmas **Obv:** Head with tiara right **Obv. Legend:** ISLE OF MAN - ELIZABETH II **Rev:** Two Turtle Doves **Rev. Legend:** CHRISTMAS **Edge:** Plain **Shape:** 7-sided

| Date | Mintage | VF20 | XF40 | MS60 | MS63 | MS65 |
|---|---|---|---|---|---|---|
| 2006 PM AA | — | — | — | 7.00 | 10.00 | — |

### KM# 1321.1a 50 PENCE

0.925 Silver, 27.3 mm. **Ruler:** Elizabeth II **Series:** 12 Days of Christmas **Obv:** Head with tiara right **Obv. Legend:** ISLE OF MAN - ELIZABETH II **Rev:** Two Turtle Doves **Rev. Legend:** CHRISTMAS **Edge:** Plain **Shape:** 7-sided

| Date | Mintage | VF20 | XF40 | MS60 | MS63 | MS65 |
|---|---|---|---|---|---|---|
| 2006 PM | — | PF63 35.00 | | | | |

### KM# 1321.2 50 PENCE

8.00 g., Copper-Nickel, 27.3 mm. **Ruler:** Elizabeth II **Series:** 12 Days of Christmas **Obv:** Head with tiara right **Obv. Legend:** ISLE OF MAN - ELIZABETH II **Rev:** 2 Turtle Doves multicolor **Rev. Legend:** CHRISTMAS **Edge:** Plain **Shape:** 7-sided

| Date | Mintage | VF20 | XF40 | MS60 | MS63 | MS65 |
|---|---|---|---|---|---|---|
| 2006 PM | — | — | — | 8.00 | 12.00 | — |

### KM# 1321.2a 50 PENCE

0.925 Silver, 27.3 mm. **Ruler:** Elizabeth II **Series:** 12 Days of Christmas **Obv:** Head with tiara right **Obv. Legend:** ISLE OF MAN - ELIZABETH II **Rev:** 2 Turtle Doves multicolor **Rev. Legend:** CHRISTMAS **Edge:** Plain **Shape:** 7-sided

| Date | Mintage | VF20 | XF40 | MS60 | MS63 | MS65 |
|---|---|---|---|---|---|---|
| 2006 PM | — | PF63 40.00 | | | | |

### KM# 1321b 50 PENCE

0.9167 Gold, 27.3 mm. **Ruler:** Elizabeth II **Series:** 12 Days of Christmas **Obv:** Head with tiara right **Obv. Legend:** ISLE OF MAN - ELIZABETH II **Rev:** 2 Turtle Doves **Rev. Legend:** CHRISTMAS **Edge:** Plain **Shape:** 7-sided

| Date | Mintage | VF20 | XF40 | MS60 | MS63 | MS65 |
|---|---|---|---|---|---|---|
| 2006 PM | — | PF63 850 | | | | |

### KM# 1322.1 50 PENCE

8.00 g., Copper-Nickel, 27.3 mm. **Ruler:** Elizabeth II **Series:** 12 Days of Christmas **Obv:** Head with tiara right **Obv. Legend:** ISLE OF MAN - ELIZABETH II **Rev:** 3 French Hens **Rev. Legend:** CHRISTMAS **Edge:** Plain **Shape:** 7-sided

| Date | Mintage | VF20 | XF40 | MS60 | MS63 | MS65 |
|---|---|---|---|---|---|---|
| 2007 PM AA | — | — | — | 7.00 | 10.00 | — |

### KM# 1322.1a 50 PENCE

0.925 Silver, 27.3 mm. **Ruler:** Elizabeth II **Series:** 12 Days of Christmas **Obv:** Head with tiara right **Obv. Legend:** ISLE OF MAN - ELIZABETH II **Rev:** 3 French Hens **Rev. Legend:** CHRISTMAS **Edge:** Plain **Shape:** 7-sided

| Date | Mintage | VF20 | XF40 | MS60 | MS63 | MS65 |
|---|---|---|---|---|---|---|
| 2007 PM | — | PF63 35.00 | | | | |

### KM# 1322.2 50 PENCE

8.00 g., Copper-Nickel, 27.3 mm. **Ruler:** Elizabeth II **Series:** 12 Days of Christmas **Obv:** Head with tiara right **Obv. Legend:** ISLE OF MAN - ELIZABETH II **Rev:** 3 French Hens multicolor **Rev. Legend:** CHRISTMAS **Edge:** Plain **Shape:** 7-sided

| Date | Mintage | VF20 | XF40 | MS60 | MS63 | MS65 |
|---|---|---|---|---|---|---|
| 2007 PM | — | — | — | 8.00 | 12.00 | — |

### KM# 1322.2a 50 PENCE

0.925 Silver, 27.3 mm. **Ruler:** Elizabeth II **Series:** 12 Days of Christmas **Obv:** Head with tiara right **Obv. Legend:** ISLE OF MAN - ELIZABETH II **Rev:** 3 French Hens multicolor **Rev. Legend:** CHRISTMAS **Edge:** Plain **Shape:** 7-sided

| Date | Mintage | VF20 | XF40 | MS60 | MS63 | MS65 |
|---|---|---|---|---|---|---|
| 2007 PM | — | PF63 40.00 | | | | |

### KM# 1322b 50 PENCE

0.9167 Gold, 27.3 mm. **Ruler:** Elizabeth II **Series:** 12 Days of Christmas **Obv:** Head with tiara right **Obv. Legend:** ISLE OF MAN - ELIZABETH II **Rev:** 3 French Hens **Rev. Legend:** CHRISTMAS **Edge:** Plain **Shape:** 7-sided

| Date | Mintage | VF20 | XF40 | MS60 | MS63 | MS65 |
|---|---|---|---|---|---|---|
| 2007 PM | 250 | PF63 850 | | | | |

### KM# 1425 50 PENCE

8.00 g., Copper-Nickel, 27.3 mm. **Ruler:** Elizabeth II **Subject:** TT Centennial **Obv:** Head with tiara right **Rev:** Two motorcyclists within wreath **Shape:** 7-sided

| Date | Mintage | VF20 | XF40 | MS60 | MS63 | MS65 |
|---|---|---|---|---|---|---|
| 2007 PM | — | — | — | 8.00 | 10.00 | — |

### KM# 1393.1 50 PENCE

8.00 g., Copper-Nickel, 27.3 mm. **Ruler:** Elizabeth II **Subject:** Christmas **Rev:** Snowman **Shape:** 7-sided

| Date | Mintage | VF20 | XF40 | MS60 | MS63 | MS65 |
|---|---|---|---|---|---|---|
| 2008 PM | — | — | — | 10.00 | 12.00 | — |

### KM# 1393.2 50 PENCE

8.00 g., Copper-Nickel, 27.3 mm. **Ruler:** Elizabeth II **Subject:** Christmas **Rev:** Snowman, multicolored **Shape:** 7-sided

| Date | Mintage | VF20 | XF40 | MS60 | MS63 | MS65 |
|---|---|---|---|---|---|---|
| 2008 PM | — | — | — | 10.00 | 12.00 | — |

### KM# 1487 50 PENCE

8.00 g., Copper-Nickel, 27.3 mm. **Ruler:** Elizabeth II **Subject:** Christmas **Rev:** 4 Calling Birds **Shape:** 7-sided

| Date | Mintage | VF20 | XF40 | MS60 | MS63 | MS65 |
|---|---|---|---|---|---|---|
| 2008 PM | — | — | — | 7.00 | 10.00 | — |

### KM# 1487a 50 PENCE

8.00 g., 0.925 Silver 0.2379 oz. ASW, 27.3 mm. **Ruler:** Elizabeth II **Subject:** Christmas **Rev:** 4 Calling birds **Shape:** 7-sided

| Date | Mintage | VF20 | XF40 | MS60 | MS63 | MS65 |
|---|---|---|---|---|---|---|
| 2008 PM | — | PF63 25.00 | | | | |

### KM# 1487b 50 PENCE

8.00 g., 0.9167 Gold 0.2358 oz. AGW, 27.3 mm. **Ruler:** Elizabeth II **Subject:** Christmas **Rev:** 4 Calling birds **Shape:** 7-sided

| Date | Mintage | VF20 | XF40 | MS60 | MS63 | MS65 |
|---|---|---|---|---|---|---|
| 2008 PM | — | PF63 500 | | | | |

### KM# 1372 50 PENCE

8.00 g., Copper-Nickel, 27.3 mm. **Ruler:** Elizabeth II **Subject:** Honda, 50th Anniversary TT **Shape:** 7-sided

| Date | Mintage | VF20 | XF40 | MS60 | MS63 | MS65 |
|---|---|---|---|---|---|---|
| 2009 PM AA | — | — | — | 7.00 | 10.00 | — |

### KM# 1431 50 PENCE

8.00 g., Copper-Nickel, 27.3 mm. **Ruler:** Elizabeth II **Subject:** Fifth day of Christmas **Rev:** Five rings **Shape:** 7-sided

| Date | Mintage | VF20 | XF40 | MS60 | MS63 | MS65 |
|---|---|---|---|---|---|---|
| 2009 PM | 30,000 | — | — | 7.00 | 10.00 | — |

### KM# 1431a 50 PENCE

8.00 g., 0.925 Silver 0.2379 oz. ASW, 27.3 mm. **Ruler:** Elizabeth II **Subject:** Fifth day of Christmas **Rev:** Five golden rings **Shape:** 7-sided

| Date | Mintage | VF20 | XF40 | MS60 | MS63 | MS65 |
|---|---|---|---|---|---|---|
| 2009 PM | 5,000 | PF63 20.00 | | | | |

### KM# 1431b 50 PENCE

8.00 g., 0.9167 Gold 0.2358 oz. AGW, 27.3 mm. **Ruler:** Elizabeth II **Subject:** Fifth day of Christmas **Rev:** Five golden rings **Shape:** 7-sided

| Date | Mintage | VF20 | XF40 | MS60 | MS63 | MS65 |
|---|---|---|---|---|---|---|
| 2009 PM | 250 | PF63 500 | | | | |

### KM# 1433.1a 50 PENCE

8.00 g., 0.925 Silver 0.2379 oz. ASW, 27.3 mm. **Ruler:** Elizabeth II **Subject:** Christmas **Rev:** Six geese a laying **Shape:** 7-sided

| Date | Mintage | VF20 | XF40 | MS60 | MS63 | MS65 |
|---|---|---|---|---|---|---|
| 2009 PM | 5,000 | PF63 15.00 | | | | |

### KM# 1433.1 50 PENCE

8.00 g., Copper-Nickel, 27.3 mm. **Ruler:** Elizabeth II **Rev:** Six Geese a laying **Shape:** 7-sided

| Date | Mintage | VF20 | XF40 | MS60 | MS63 | MS65 |
|---|---|---|---|---|---|---|
| 2010 PM | 30,000 | — | — | 7.00 | 10.00 | — |

**KM# 1433.1b 50 PENCE**
8.00 g., 0.9167 Gold 0.2358 oz. AGW, 27.3 mm. **Ruler:** Elizabeth II **Subject:** Christmas **Rev:** Six geese a laying **Shape:** 7-sided

| Date | Mintage | VF20 | XF40 | MS60 | MS63 | MS65 |
|---|---|---|---|---|---|---|
| 2010 PM | — | PF63 500 | | | | |

**KM# 1433.2 50 PENCE**
8.00 g., Copper-Nickel, 27.3 mm. **Ruler:** Elizabeth II **Subject:** Christmas **Rev:** Six geese a laying in color **Shape:** 7-sided

| Date | Mintage | VF20 | XF40 | MS60 | MS63 | MS65 |
|---|---|---|---|---|---|---|
| 2010 PM | — | — | — | 10.00 | 12.00 | — |

**KM# 1469 50 PENCE**
8.00 g., Copper-Nickel, 27.3 mm. **Ruler:** Elizabeth II **Subject:** Isle of Man TT race **Rev:** Suzuki driver left **Shape:** 7-sided

| Date | Mintage | VF20 | XF40 | MS60 | MS63 | MS65 |
|---|---|---|---|---|---|---|
| 2010 PM | — | — | — | 6.00 | 8.00 | — |

**KM# 1453.1 50 PENCE**
8.00 g., Copper-Nickel, 27.3 mm. **Ruler:** Elizabeth II **Subject:** Christmas **Rev:** Santa Claus **Shape:** 7-sided

| Date | Mintage | VF20 | XF40 | MS60 | MS63 | MS65 |
|---|---|---|---|---|---|---|
| 2011 PM | 30,000 | — | — | 7.00 | 10.00 | — |

**KM# 1453.1a 50 PENCE**
8.00 g., 0.925 Silver 0.2379 oz. ASW, 27.3 mm. **Ruler:** Elizabeth II **Subject:** Christmas **Rev:** Santa Claus **Shape:** 7-sided

| Date | Mintage | VF20 | XF40 | MS60 | MS63 | MS65 |
|---|---|---|---|---|---|---|
| 2011 PM | 5,000 | PF63 25.00 | | | | |

**KM# 1453.1b 50 PENCE**
8.00 g., 0.9167 Gold 0.2358 oz. AGW, 27.3 mm. **Ruler:** Elizabeth II **Subject:** Christmas **Rev:** Santa Claus **Shape:** 7-sided

| Date | Mintage | VF20 | XF40 | MS60 | MS63 | MS65 |
|---|---|---|---|---|---|---|
| 2011 PM proof | 250 | PF63 500 | | | | |

**KM# 1453.2 50 PENCE**
8.00 g., Copper-Nickel, 27.3 mm. **Ruler:** Elizabeth II **Subject:** Christmas **Rev:** Santa Claus in color **Shape:** 7-sided

| Date | Mintage | VF20 | XF40 | MS60 | MS63 | MS65 |
|---|---|---|---|---|---|---|
| 2011 PM | — | — | — | 10.00 | 12.00 | — |

**KM# 1454 50 PENCE**
8.00 g., Copper-Nickel, 27.3 mm. **Ruler:** Elizabeth II **Subject:** Isle of Man Tourist Trophy race **Rev:** Yamaha motorcycle and racer **Shape:** 7-sided

| Date | Mintage | VF20 | XF40 | MS60 | MS63 | MS65 |
|---|---|---|---|---|---|---|
| 2011 PM | — | — | — | 6.00 | 8.00 | — |

**KM# 1454a 50 PENCE**
8.00 g., 0.925 Silver 0.2379 oz. ASW, 27.3 mm. **Ruler:** Elizabeth II **Subject:** Isle of Man Tourist Trophy race **Rev:** Yamaha motorcycle and racer **Shape:** 7-sided

| Date | Mintage | VF20 | XF40 | MS60 | MS63 | MS65 |
|---|---|---|---|---|---|---|
| 2011 PM | 5,000 | PF63 25.00 | | | | |

**KM# 1488 50 PENCE**
8.00 g., Copper-Nickel, 27.3 mm. **Ruler:** Elizabeth II **Subject:** Diamond Jubilee

| Date | Mintage | VF20 | XF40 | MS60 | MS63 | MS65 |
|---|---|---|---|---|---|---|
| 2012 PM | — | — | — | — | 6.50 | — |

**KM# 1490.1 50 PENCE**
8.00 g., Copper-Nickel, 27.3 mm. **Ruler:** Elizabeth II **Subject:** Christmas **Rev:** Angel in flight

| Date | Mintage | VF20 | XF40 | MS60 | MS63 | MS65 |
|---|---|---|---|---|---|---|
| 2012 PM | Est. 30000 | — | — | 7.00 | 10.00 | — |

**KM# 1490.2 50 PENCE**
8.00 g., Copper-Nickel, 27.3 mm. **Ruler:** Elizabeth II **Subject:** Christmas **Rev:** Angel in color **Shape:** 7-sided

| Date | Mintage | VF20 | XF40 | MS60 | MS63 | MS65 |
|---|---|---|---|---|---|---|
| 2012 PM | — | — | — | 7.00 | 10.00 | — |

**KM# 1490a 50 PENCE**
0.925 Silver, 27.3 mm. **Ruler:** Elizabeth II **Rev:** Angel in flight **Shape:** 7-sided

| Date | Mintage | VF20 | XF40 | MS60 | MS63 | MS65 |
|---|---|---|---|---|---|---|
| 2012 PM | — | PF63 25.00 | | | | |

**KM# 1490b 50 PENCE**
0.917 Gold, 27.3 mm. **Ruler:** Elizabeth II **Rev:** Angel in flight **Shape:** 7-sided

| Date | Mintage | VF20 | XF40 | MS60 | MS63 | MS65 |
|---|---|---|---|---|---|---|
| 2012 PM | 250 | PF63 450 | | | | |

**KM# 1491 50 PENCE**
8.00 g., 0.925 Copper-Nickel 0.2379 oz., 27.3 mm. **Ruler:** Elizabeth II **Subject:** Mark Cavendish **Shape:** 7-sided

| Date | Mintage | VF20 | XF40 | MS60 | MS63 | MS65 |
|---|---|---|---|---|---|---|
| 2012 PM | — | — | — | — | 8.00 | 10.00 |

**KM# 1491a 50 PENCE**
0.925 Silver, 27.3 mm. **Ruler:** Elizabeth II **Subject:** Mark Cavendish **Shape:** 7-sided

| Date | Mintage | VF20 | XF40 | MS60 | MS63 | MS65 |
|---|---|---|---|---|---|---|
| 2012 PM | — | PF65 25.00 | | | | |

**KM# 1492 50 PENCE**
8.00 g., 0.925 Copper-Nickel 0.2379 oz., 27.3 mm. **Ruler:** Elizabeth II **Subject:** Enduro Motorcycle Sport - Dave Knight **Shape:** 7-sided

| Date | Mintage | VF20 | XF40 | MS60 | MS63 | MS65 |
|---|---|---|---|---|---|---|
| 2012 PM | Est. 5000 | — | — | — | 8.00 | 10.00 |

**KM# 1492a 50 PENCE**
0.925 Silver, 27.3 mm. **Ruler:** Elizabeth II **Subject:** Enduro Motorcucle Sport - Dave Knight **Shape:** 7-Sided

| Date | Mintage | VF20 | XF40 | MS60 | MS63 | MS65 |
|---|---|---|---|---|---|---|
| 2012 PM | — | PF65 25.00 | | | | |

**KM# 1542 50 PENCE**
8.00 g., Copper-Nickel, 27.3 mm. **Ruler:** Elizabeth II **Rev:** Christmas stocking within wreath **Shape:** 7-sided

| Date | Mintage | VF20 | XF40 | MS60 | MS63 | MS65 |
|---|---|---|---|---|---|---|
| 2013 | — | — | — | 7.00 | 10.00 | — |

**KM# 1542a 50 PENCE**
8.00 g., Copper-Nickel, 27.3 mm. **Ruler:** Elizabeth II **Rev:** Christmas stocking in wreath all in color **Shape:** 7-sided

| Date | Mintage | VF20 | XF40 | MS60 | MS63 | MS65 |
|---|---|---|---|---|---|---|
| 2013 | — | — | — | 10.00 | 12.00 | — |

**KM# 1941a 50 PENCE**
0.925 Silver, 27.3 mm. **Ruler:** Elizabeth II **Subject:** Mark Cavendish **Shape:** 7-sided

| Date | Mintage | VF20 | XF40 | MS60 | MS63 | MS65 |
|---|---|---|---|---|---|---|
| 2013 PM | — | PF63 25.00 | | | | |

**KM# 1128 60 PENCE**
Bi-Metallic Bronze finished base metal with a silver finished rotator on reverse., 38.6 mm. **Ruler:** Elizabeth II **Subject:** Euro Currency Converter **Obv:** Head with tiara right **Rev:** Rotating map with cut out arrow revealing the Euro equivalent of the country's currency to which the arrow is pointed **Edge:** Reeded

| Date | Mintage | VF20 | XF40 | MS60 | MS63 | MS65 |
|---|---|---|---|---|---|---|
| 2002 | 15,000 | — | — | 20.00 | 22.50 | — |

### KM# 1042 POUND

9.50 g., Nickel-Brass, 22.5 mm. **Ruler:** Elizabeth II **Subject:** Millennium Bells **Obv:** Head with tiara right **Rev:** Triskeles and three bells **Edge:** Segmented reeding

| Date | Mintage | VF20 | XF40 | MS60 | MS63 | MS65 |
|---|---|---|---|---|---|---|
| 2001 PM AA | — | — | — | — | 4.00 | 5.00 |
| 2002 PM AA | — | — | — | — | 4.00 | 5.00 |
| 2003 PM AA | — | — | — | — | 4.00 | 5.00 |
| 2003 PM BA | — | — | — | — | 4.00 | 5.00 |

### KM# 1259 POUND

9.50 g., Nickel-Brass, 22.5 mm. **Ruler:** Elizabeth II **Obv:** Head with tiara right **Rev:** St. John's Chapel **Edge:** Segmented reeding

| Date | Mintage | VF20 | XF40 | MS60 | MS63 | MS65 |
|---|---|---|---|---|---|---|
| 2004 PM | — | — | — | — | 4.00 | 5.00 |
| 2004 PM AA | — | — | — | — | 4.00 | 5.00 |
| 2004 PM AB | — | — | — | — | 4.00 | 5.00 |
| 2004 PM AC | — | — | — | — | 4.00 | 5.00 |
| 2005 PM AA | — | — | — | — | 4.00 | 5.00 |
| 2005 PM AB | — | — | — | — | 4.00 | 5.00 |
| 2006 PM AA | — | — | — | — | 4.00 | 5.00 |
| 2006 PM AB | — | — | — | — | 4.00 | 5.00 |
| 2007 PM AA | — | — | — | — | 4.00 | 5.00 |
| 2007 PM BA | — | — | — | — | 4.00 | 5.00 |
| 2007 PM AB | — | — | — | — | 4.00 | 5.00 |
| 2008 PM AA | — | — | — | — | 4.00 | 5.00 |
| 2008 PM BA | — | — | — | — | 4.00 | 5.00 |
| 2009 PM AA | — | — | — | — | 4.00 | 5.00 |
| 2010 PM AA | — | — | — | — | 4.00 | 5.00 |
| 2011 PM AA | — | — | — | — | 4.00 | 5.00 |
| 2012 PM AA | — | — | — | — | 4.00 | 5.00 |
| 2013 PM AA | — | — | — | — | — | 5.00 |

### KM# 1043 2 POUNDS

12.00 g., Bi-Metallic Copper-Nickel center in Nickel-Brass ring, 28.4 mm. **Ruler:** Elizabeth II **Subject:** Thorwald's Cross **Obv:** Head with tiara right within beaded circle **Rev:** Ancient drawing within circle **Edge:** Reeded

| Date | Mintage | VF20 | XF40 | MS60 | MS63 | MS65 |
|---|---|---|---|---|---|---|
| 2001 PM AA | — | — | — | — | 6.50 | 7.50 |
| 2002 PM AA | — | — | — | — | 6.50 | 7.50 |
| 2003 PM AA | — | — | — | — | 6.50 | 7.50 |
| 2003 PM AB | — | — | — | — | 6.50 | 7.50 |

### KM# 1260 2 POUNDS

12.00 g., Bi-Metallic Copper-Nickel center in Nickel-Brass ring, 28.4 mm. **Ruler:** Elizabeth II **Obv:** Head with tiara right **Rev:** Round Tower of Peel Castle **Edge:** Reeded

| Date | Mintage | VF20 | XF40 | MS60 | MS63 | MS65 |
|---|---|---|---|---|---|---|
| 2004 PM AA | — | — | — | — | 6.50 | 7.50 |
| 2005 PM AA | — | — | — | — | 6.50 | 7.50 |
| 2006 PM AA | — | — | — | — | 6.50 | 7.50 |
| 2007 PM AA | — | — | — | — | 6.50 | 7.50 |
| 2007 PM AB | — | — | — | — | 6.50 | 7.50 |
| 2008 PM AA | — | — | — | — | 6.50 | 7.50 |
| 2009 PM AA | — | — | — | — | 6.50 | 7.50 |
| 2010 PM AA | — | — | — | — | 6.50 | 7.50 |
| 2011 PM AA | — | — | — | — | 6.50 | 7.50 |
| 2012 PM AA | — | — | — | — | 6.50 | 7.50 |

### KM# 1476 2 POUNDS

12.00 g., Bi-Metallic Copper-Nickel center in Nickel-Brass ring, 28.4 mm. **Ruler:** Elizabeth II **Obv:** Head with tiara right **Rev:** Tosha the cat, games mascot and games logo

| Date | Mintage | VF20 | XF40 | MS60 | MS63 | MS65 |
|---|---|---|---|---|---|---|
| 2011 PM | — | — | — | — | 6.00 | 7.50 |

### KM# 1044 5 POUNDS

20.10 g., Virenium, 36.5 mm. **Ruler:** Elizabeth II **Subject:** St. Patrick's Hymn **Obv:** Head with tiara right **Rev:** Stylized cross design **Edge:** Segmented reeding

| Date | Mintage | VF20 | XF40 | MS60 | MS63 | MS65 |
|---|---|---|---|---|---|---|
| 2001 PM AA | — | — | — | — | 15.00 | 16.50 |
| 2002 PM AA | — | — | — | — | 15.00 | 16.50 |
| 2003 PM AA | — | — | — | — | 15.00 | 16.50 |

### KM# 1261 5 POUNDS

20.10 g., Virenium, 36 mm. **Ruler:** Elizabeth II **Obv:** Head with tiara right **Rev:** Laxey Wheel **Edge:** Reeded

| Date | Mintage | VF20 | XF40 | MS60 | MS63 | MS65 |
|---|---|---|---|---|---|---|
| 2004 PM AA | — | — | — | — | 15.00 | 16.50 |
| 2005 PM AA | — | — | — | — | 15.00 | 16.50 |
| 2006 PM AA | — | — | — | — | 15.00 | 16.50 |
| 2007 PM AA | — | — | — | — | 15.00 | 16.50 |
| 2007 PM AB | — | — | — | — | 15.00 | 16.50 |
| 2008 PM AA | — | — | — | — | 15.00 | 16.50 |
| 2009 PM AA | — | — | — | — | 15.00 | 16.50 |
| 2010 PM AA | — | — | — | — | 15.00 | 16.50 |
| 2011 PM AA | — | — | — | — | 15.00 | 16.50 |
| 2012 PM AA | — | — | — | — | 15.00 | 16.50 |

## CROWN SERIES

(M) MATTE - Normal circulation strike

(U) SPECIAL UNCIRCULATED - Polished or prooflike in appearance, slightly frosted features.

(P) PROOF - The highest quality obtainable having mirror-like fields and frosted features.

### KM# 1472 1/64 CROWN

0.49 g., 0.9999 Gold 0.0156 oz. AGW **Ruler:** Elizabeth II **Obv:** Bust in tiara right **Rev:** Buckingham Palace

| Date | Mintage | VF20 | XF40 | MS60 | MS63 | MS65 |
|---|---|---|---|---|---|---|
| 2010 PM | — | **PF65** 50.00 | | | | |

### KM# 1129 1/32 CROWN

1.00 g., 0.972 Gold 0.0313 oz. AGW, 9.8 mm. **Ruler:** Elizabeth II **Subject:** Queen's Golden Jubilee **Obv:** Head with tiara right **Rev:** Seated crowned Queen holding sceptre at her coronation **Edge:** Plain

| Date | Mintage | VF20 | XF40 | MS60 | MS63 | MS65 |
|---|---|---|---|---|---|---|
| 2002 Prooflike | — | — | — | — | — | 60.00 |

### KM# 1058 1/25 CROWN

1.24 g., 0.9999 Gold 0.040 oz. AGW, 13.92 mm. **Ruler:** Elizabeth II **Subject:** Year of the Snake **Obv:** Bust with tiara right **Rev:** Snake **Edge:** Reeded

| Date | Mintage | VF20 | XF40 | MS60 | MS63 | MS65 |
|---|---|---|---|---|---|---|
| 2001 | 20,000 | **PF65** 59.00 | | | | |

### KM# 1067 1/25 CROWN

1.24 g., 0.9999 Gold 0.040 oz. AGW, 13.9 mm. **Ruler:** Elizabeth II **Subject:** Somali Kittens **Obv:** Head with tiara right **Rev:** Two kittens **Edge:** Reeded

| Date | Mintage | VF20 | XF40 | MS60 | MS63 | MS65 |
|---|---|---|---|---|---|---|
| 2001 | — | — | — | — | — | 59.00 |
| 2001 | 1,000 | **PF63** 59.00 | **PF65** 69.00 | | | |

### KM# 1067a 1/25 CROWN

1.24 g., 0.9995 Platinum 0.040 oz. APW, 13.9 mm. **Ruler:** Elizabeth II **Subject:** Somali Kittens **Obv:** Head with tiara right **Rev:** Two kittens **Edge:** Reeded

| Date | Mintage | VF20 | XF40 | MS60 | MS63 | MS65 |
|---|---|---|---|---|---|---|
| 2001 | — | — | — | — | — | 64.00 |

### KM# 1086 1/25 CROWN

1.24 g., 0.9999 Gold 0.040 oz. AGW, 13.9 mm. **Ruler:** Elizabeth II **Subject:** Harry Potter **Obv:** Bust with tiara right **Rev:** Boy with magic wand **Edge:** Reeded

| Date | Mintage | VF20 | XF40 | MS60 | MS63 | MS65 |
|---|---|---|---|---|---|---|
| 2001 | 10,000 | **PF65** 59.00 | | | | |

### KM# 1088 1/25 CROWN

1.24 g., 0.9999 Gold 0.040 oz. AGW, 13.9 mm. **Ruler:** Elizabeth II **Series:** Harry Potter **Subject:** Journey to Hogwarts School **Obv:** Bust with tiara right **Rev:** Boat full of children going to Hogwarts School **Edge:** Reeded

| Date | Mintage | VF20 | XF40 | MS60 | MS63 | MS65 |
|---|---|---|---|---|---|---|
| 2001 | 10,000 | **PF65** 59.00 | | | | |

### KM# 1090 1/25 CROWN

1.24 g., 0.9999 Gold 0.040 oz. AGW, 13.9 mm. **Ruler:** Elizabeth II **Series:** Harry Potter **Subject:** First Quidditch Match **Obv:** Bust with tiara right **Rev:** Harry flying a broom **Edge:** Reeded

| Date | Mintage | VF20 | XF40 | MS60 | MS63 | MS65 |
|---|---|---|---|---|---|---|
| 2001 | 10,000 | **PF65** 59.00 | | | | |

### KM# 1092 1/25 CROWN

1.24 g., 0.9999 Gold 0.040 oz. AGW, 13.9 mm. **Ruler:** Elizabeth II **Series:** Harry Potter **Subject:** Birth of Norbert **Obv:** Bust with tiara right **Edge:** Reeded

| Date | Mintage | VF20 | XF40 | MS60 | MS63 | MS65 |
|---|---|---|---|---|---|---|
| 2001 | 10,000 | **PF65** 59.00 | | | | |

### KM# 1094 1/25 CROWN

1.24 g., 0.9999 Gold 0.040 oz. AGW, 13.9 mm. **Ruler:** Elizabeth II **Series:** Harry Potter **Subject:** School **Obv:** Bust with tiara right **Rev:** Harry in Potions class **Edge:** Reeded

| Date | Mintage | VF20 | XF40 | MS60 | MS63 | MS65 |
|---|---|---|---|---|---|---|
| 2001 | 10,000 | **PF65** 59.00 | | | | |

### KM# 1096 1/25 CROWN

1.24 g., 0.9999 Gold 0.040 oz. AGW, 13.9 mm. **Ruler:** Elizabeth II **Series:** Harry Potter **Subject:** Keys **Obv:** Bust with tiara right **Rev:** Harry chasing the golden snitch **Edge:** Reeded

| Date | Mintage | VF20 | XF40 | MS60 | MS63 | MS65 |
|---|---|---|---|---|---|---|
| 2001 | 10,000 | **PF65** 59.00 | | | | |

### KM# 1098 1/25 CROWN

1.24 g., 0.9999 Gold 0.040 oz. AGW, 13.9 mm. **Ruler:** Elizabeth II **Subject:** Year of the Horse **Obv:** Bust with tiara right **Rev:** Two horses **Edge:** Reeded

| Date | Mintage | VF20 | XF40 | MS60 | MS63 | MS65 |
|---|---|---|---|---|---|---|
| 2002 | 20,000 | **PF65** 59.00 | | | | |

### KM# 1107 1/25 CROWN

1.24 g., 0.999 Gold 0.040 oz. AGW, 13.92 mm. **Ruler:** Elizabeth II **Subject:** Bengal Cat **Obv:** Head with tiara right **Rev:** Cat and kitten **Edge:** Reeded

| Date | Mintage | VF20 | XF40 | MS60 | MS63 | MS65 |
|---|---|---|---|---|---|---|
| 2002 | — | — | — | — | — | 64.00 |
| 2002 | 1,000 | **PF65** 69.00 | | | | |

### KM# 1107a 1/25 CROWN

1.24 g., 0.999 Platinum 0.040 oz. APW, 13.92 mm. **Ruler:** Elizabeth II **Subject:** Bengal Cat **Obv:** Head with tiara right **Rev:** Cat and kitten **Edge:** Reeded

| Date | Mintage | VF20 | XF40 | MS60 | MS63 | MS65 |
|---|---|---|---|---|---|---|
| 2002 | — | **PF65** 69.00 | | | | |

### KM# 1143 1/25 CROWN

1.24 g., 0.9999 Gold 0.040 oz. AGW, 13.92 mm. **Ruler:** Elizabeth II **Subject:** Harry Potter **Obv:** Bust with tiara right **Rev:** Tom Riddle twirling Harry's magic wand **Edge:** Reeded

| Date | Mintage | VF20 | XF40 | MS60 | MS63 | MS65 |
|---|---|---|---|---|---|---|
| 2002 PM | 10,000 | **PF65** 59.00 | | | | |

### KM# 1145 1/25 CROWN

1.24 g., 0.9999 Gold 0.040 oz. AGW, 13.92 mm. **Ruler:** Elizabeth II **Subject:** Harry Potter Series **Obv:** Bust with tiara right **Rev:** Harry and friends making Polyjuice potion **Edge:** Reeded

| Date | Mintage | VF20 | XF40 | MS60 | MS63 | MS65 |
|---|---|---|---|---|---|---|
| 2002 PM | 10,000 | **PF65** 59.00 | | | | |

### KM# 1147 1/25 CROWN

1.24 g., 0.9999 Gold 0.040 oz. AGW, 13.92 mm. **Ruler:** Elizabeth II **Subject:** Harry Potter **Obv:** Bust with tiara right **Rev:** Harry arrives at the Burrow in a flying car **Edge:** Reeded

| Date | Mintage | VF20 | XF40 | MS60 | MS63 | MS65 |
|---|---|---|---|---|---|---|
| 2002 PM | 10,000 | **PF65** 59.00 | | | | |

### KM# 1149 1/25 CROWN

1.24 g., 0.9999 Gold 0.040 oz. AGW, 13.92 mm. **Ruler:** Elizabeth II **Subject:** Harry Potter Series **Obv:** Bust with tiara right **Rev:** Harry retrieves Gryffindor sword from snake **Edge:** Reeded

| Date | Mintage | VF20 | XF40 | MS60 | MS63 | MS65 |
|---|---|---|---|---|---|---|
| 2002 PM | 10,000 | **PF65** 59.00 | | | | |

### KM# 1151 1/25 CROWN

1.22 g., 0.9999 Gold 0.0393 oz. AGW, 13.92 mm. **Ruler:** Elizabeth II **Series:** Harry Potter **Obv:** Bust with tiara right **Rev:** Harry and Ron encounter the spider Aragog **Edge:** Reeded

| Date | Mintage | VF20 | XF40 | MS60 | MS63 | MS65 |
|---|---|---|---|---|---|---|
| 2002 PM | 10,000 | PF65 58.00 | | | | |

### KM# 1153 1/25 CROWN

1.24 g., 0.9999 Gold 0.040 oz. AGW, 13.92 mm. **Ruler:** Elizabeth II **Series:** Harry Potter **Obv:** Bust with tiara right **Rev:** Harry in hospital **Edge:** Reeded

| Date | Mintage | VF20 | XF40 | MS60 | MS63 | MS65 |
|---|---|---|---|---|---|---|
| 2002 PM | 10,000 | PF65 59.00 | | | | |

### KM# 1161 1/25 CROWN

1.24 g., 0.9999 Gold 0.040 oz. AGW, 13.92 mm. **Ruler:** Elizabeth II **Subject:** Cat **Obv:** Head with tiara right **Rev:** Two Balinese kittens **Edge:** Reeded

| Date | Mintage | VF20 | XF40 | MS60 | MS63 | MS65 |
|---|---|---|---|---|---|---|
| 2003 PM | — | — | — | — | — | 59.00 |
| 2003 PM | — | PF63 59.00 | PF65 69.00 | | | |

### KM# 1161a 1/25 CROWN

1.24 g., 0.9995 Platinum 0.040 oz. APW, 13.92 mm. **Ruler:** Elizabeth II **Subject:** Cat **Obv:** Head with tiara right **Rev:** Two Balinese kittens **Edge:** Reeded

| Date | Mintage | VF20 | XF40 | MS60 | MS63 | MS65 |
|---|---|---|---|---|---|---|
| 2003 PM | — | PF65 69.00 | | | | |

### KM# 1167 1/25 CROWN

1.24 g., 0.9999 Gold 0.040 oz. AGW, 13.9 mm. **Ruler:** Elizabeth II **Subject:** Year of the Goat **Obv:** Head with tiara right **Rev:** Three goats **Edge:** Reeded

| Date | Mintage | VF20 | XF40 | MS60 | MS63 | MS65 |
|---|---|---|---|---|---|---|
| 2003 PM | 20,000 | PF65 59.00 | | | | |

### KM# 1186 1/25 CROWN

1.24 g., 0.9999 Gold 0.040 oz. AGW, 13.9 mm. **Ruler:** Elizabeth II **Subject:** Lord of the Rings **Obv:** Bust with tiara right **Rev:** Frodo Baggins with short sword **Edge:** Reeded

| Date | Mintage | VF20 | XF40 | MS60 | MS63 | MS65 |
|---|---|---|---|---|---|---|
| 2003 PM | 6,000 | PF65 59.00 | | | | |

### KM# 1203 1/25 CROWN

1.24 g., 0.9999 Gold 0.040 oz. AGW, 14 mm. **Ruler:** Elizabeth II **Obv:** Bust with tiara right **Rev:** Harry Potter and patron fighting off a spectre **Edge:** Reeded

| Date | Mintage | VF20 | XF40 | MS60 | MS63 | MS65 |
|---|---|---|---|---|---|---|
| 2004 PM | 2,500 | PF65 59.00 | | | | |

### KM# 1205 1/25 CROWN

1.24 g., 0.9999 Gold 0.040 oz. AGW, 14 mm. **Ruler:** Elizabeth II **Obv:** Bust with tiara right **Rev:** Harry Potter in the shrieking shack **Edge:** Reeded

| Date | Mintage | VF20 | XF40 | MS60 | MS63 | MS65 |
|---|---|---|---|---|---|---|
| 2004 PM | 2,500 | PF65 59.00 | | | | |

### KM# 1207 1/25 CROWN

1.24 g., 0.9999 Gold 0.040 oz. AGW, 14 mm. **Ruler:** Elizabeth II **Obv:** Bust with tiara right **Rev:** Harry Potter and Professor Dumbledore **Edge:** Reeded

| Date | Mintage | VF20 | XF40 | MS60 | MS63 | MS65 |
|---|---|---|---|---|---|---|
| 2004 PM | 2,500 | PF65 59.00 | | | | |

### KM# 1209 1/25 CROWN

1.24 g., 0.9999 Gold 0.040 oz. AGW, 14 mm. **Ruler:** Elizabeth II **Obv:** Bust with tiara right **Rev:** Sirius Black on flying griffin **Edge:** Reeded

| Date | Mintage | VF20 | XF40 | MS60 | MS63 | MS65 |
|---|---|---|---|---|---|---|
| 2004 PM | 2,500 | PF65 59.00 | | | | |

### KM# 1211 1/25 CROWN

1.24 g., 0.9999 Gold 0.040 oz. AGW, 14 mm. **Ruler:** Elizabeth II **Obv:** Head with tiara right **Rev:** Three Olympic Swimmers **Edge:** Reeded

| Date | Mintage | VF20 | XF40 | MS60 | MS63 | MS65 |
|---|---|---|---|---|---|---|
| 2004 PM | 5,000 | PF65 59.00 | | | | |

### KM# 1213 1/25 CROWN

1.24 g., 0.9999 Gold 0.040 oz. AGW, 14 mm. **Ruler:** Elizabeth II **Obv:** Head with tiara right **Rev:** Three Olympic Cyclists **Edge:** Reeded

| Date | Mintage | VF20 | XF40 | MS60 | MS63 | MS65 |
|---|---|---|---|---|---|---|
| 2004 PM | 5,000 | PF65 59.00 | | | | |

### KM# 1215 1/25 CROWN

1.24 g., 0.9999 Gold 0.040 oz. AGW, 14 mm. **Ruler:** Elizabeth II **Obv:** Head with tiara right **Rev:** Three Olympic Runners **Edge:** Reeded

| Date | Mintage | VF20 | XF40 | MS60 | MS63 | MS65 |
|---|---|---|---|---|---|---|
| 2004 PM | 5,000 | PF65 59.00 | | | | |

### KM# 1217 1/25 CROWN

1.24 g., 0.9999 Gold 0.040 oz. AGW, 14 mm. **Ruler:** Elizabeth II **Obv:** Head with tiara right **Rev:** Three Olympic Sail Boarders **Edge:** Reeded

| Date | Mintage | VF20 | XF40 | MS60 | MS63 | MS65 |
|---|---|---|---|---|---|---|
| 2004 PM | 5,000 | PF65 59.00 | | | | |

### KM# 1240 1/25 CROWN

1.24 g., 0.9999 Gold 0.040 oz. AGW, 14 mm. **Ruler:** Elizabeth II **Obv:** Head with tiara right **Rev:** Monkey **Edge:** Reeded

| Date | Mintage | VF20 | XF40 | MS60 | MS63 | MS65 |
|---|---|---|---|---|---|---|
| 2004 PM | 20,000 | PF65 59.00 | | | | |

### KM# 1247 1/25 CROWN

1.24 g., 0.9999 Gold 0.040 oz. AGW, 14 mm. **Ruler:** Elizabeth II **Obv:** Head with tiara right **Rev:** Two Tonkinese cats **Edge:** Reeded

| Date | Mintage | VF20 | XF40 | MS60 | MS63 | MS65 |
|---|---|---|---|---|---|---|
| 2004 PM | — | — | — | — | — | 64.00 |
| 2004 PM | 1,000 | PF65 69.00 | | | | |

### KM# 1269 1/25 CROWN

1.24 g., 0.9999 Gold 0.040 oz. AGW, 13.92 mm. **Ruler:** Elizabeth II **Obv:** Bust with tiara right **Rev:** Himalayan cat and two kittens **Edge:** Reeded

| Date | Mintage | VF20 | XF40 | MS60 | MS63 | MS65 |
|---|---|---|---|---|---|---|
| 2005 PM | — | PF65 59.00 | | | | |

### KM# 1269a 1/25 CROWN

1.24 g., 0.995 Platinum 0.0398 oz. APW, 13.92 mm. **Ruler:** Elizabeth II **Obv:** Bust with tiara right **Rev:** Himalayan cat and two kittens **Edge:** Reeded

| Date | Mintage | VF20 | XF40 | MS60 | MS63 | MS65 |
|---|---|---|---|---|---|---|
| 2005 PM | — | PF65 69.00 | | | | |

### KM# 1340 1/25 CROWN

1.24 g., 0.9999 Gold 0.040 oz. AGW, 13.92 mm. **Ruler:** Elizabeth II **Obv:** Bust with tiara right **Rev:** Three Exotic Shorthair cats sitting facing **Edge:** Reeded

| Date | Mintage | VF20 | XF40 | MS60 | MS63 | MS65 |
|---|---|---|---|---|---|---|
| 2006 PM | — | — | — | — | — | 64.00 |

### KM# 1308 1/25 CROWN

1.24 g., 0.9999 Gold 0.040 oz. AGW, 13.92 mm. **Ruler:** Elizabeth II **Subject:** 100th Anniversary of Scouting **Obv:** Bust with tiara right **Obv. Legend:** ELIZABETH II - ISLE OF MAN **Rev:** 3/4 length figure of Robert Baden-Powell standing facing 3/4 left, Fleur-de-lys below, images of scouting at left and right **Rev. Legend:** CENTENARY OF SCOUTING **Edge:** Reeded

| Date | Mintage | VF20 | XF40 | MS60 | MS63 | MS65 |
|---|---|---|---|---|---|---|
| 2007 PM | — | PF65 59.00 | | | | |

### KM# 1314 1/25 CROWN

1.24 g., 0.9999 Gold 0.0399 oz. AGW, 13.92 mm. **Ruler:** Elizabeth II **Obv:** Bust with tiara right **Obv. Legend:** ELIZABETH II - ISLE OF MAN **Rev:** Two swans facing **Edge:** Reeded

| Date | Mintage | VF20 | XF40 | MS60 | MS63 | MS65 |
|---|---|---|---|---|---|---|
| 2007 | 10,000 | PF65 59.00 | | | | |

### KM# 1343 1/25 CROWN

1.24 g., 0.9999 Gold 0.040 oz. AGW, 13.92 mm. **Ruler:** Elizabeth II **Obv:** Bust with tiara right **Obv. Legend:** ELIZABETH II - ISLE OF MAN **Rev:** Ragdoll cat with two kittens sitting facing **Edge:** Reeded

| Date | Mintage | VF20 | XF40 | MS60 | MS63 | MS65 |
|---|---|---|---|---|---|---|
| 2007 PM | — | — | — | — | — | 64.00 |

### KM# 1349 1/25 CROWN

1.24 g., 0.9999 Gold 0.040 oz. AGW, 13.92 mm. **Ruler:** Elizabeth II **Subject:** The Tale of Peter Rabbit **Obv:** Bust with tiara right **Obv. Legend:** ELIZABETH II - ISLE OF MAN **Rev:** Peter walking with friends **Edge:** Reeded

| Date | Mintage | VF20 | XF40 | MS60 | MS63 | MS65 |
|---|---|---|---|---|---|---|
| 2007 PM | — | — | — | — | — | 59.00 |

### KM# 1383 1/25 CROWN

1.24 g., 0.9999 Gold 0.0399 oz. AGW, 13.92 mm. **Ruler:** Elizabeth II **Obv:** Bust right **Rev:** Chinchilla cat and kitten

| Date | Mintage | VF20 | XF40 | MS60 | MS63 | MS65 |
|---|---|---|---|---|---|---|
| 2009 | — | — | — | — | — | 64.00 |
| 2009 | 1,000 | PF65 69.00 | | | | |

### KM# 1387 1/25 CROWN

1.24 g., 0.995 Platinum 0.0397 oz. APW, 13.92 mm. **Ruler:** Elizabeth II **Obv:** Bust right **Rev:** Chinchilla cat and kitten

| Date | Mintage | VF20 | XF40 | MS60 | MS63 | MS65 |
|---|---|---|---|---|---|---|
| 2009 | — | — | — | — | — | 61.00 |

### KM# 1473 1/25 CROWN

1.24 g., 0.999 Gold 0.0398 oz. AGW, 13.92 mm. **Ruler:** Elizabeth II **Subject:** George F. Handel, 325th Anniversary of Birth **Obv:** Bust in tiara right **Rev:** Handel bust, music score in background

| Date | Mintage | VF20 | XF40 | MS60 | MS63 | MS65 |
|---|---|---|---|---|---|---|
| 2010 PM | — | PF65 69.00 | | | | |

### KM# 1435 1/25 CROWN

1.24 g., 0.9999 Gold 0.0399 oz. AGW, 13.92 mm. **Ruler:** Elizabeth II **Subject:** Turkish Angora cat

| Date | Mintage | VF20 | XF40 | MS60 | MS63 | MS65 |
|---|---|---|---|---|---|---|
| 2011 PM | 1,000 | PF65 69.00 | | | | |
| 2011 PM | — | — | — | — | — | 64.00 |

### KM# 1059 1/10 CROWN

3.11 g., 0.9999 Gold 0.100 oz. AGW, 17.95 mm. **Ruler:** Elizabeth II **Subject:** Year of the Snake **Obv:** Bust with tiara right **Rev:** Snake **Edge:** Reeded

| Date | Mintage | VF20 | XF40 | MS60 | MS63 | MS65 |
|---|---|---|---|---|---|---|
| 2001 | 15,000 | PF65 160 | | | | |

### KM# 1068 1/10 CROWN

3.11 g., 0.9999 Gold 0.100 oz. AGW, 18 mm. **Ruler:** Elizabeth II **Obv:** Head with tiara right **Rev:** Somali kittens **Edge:** Reeded

| Date | Mintage | VF20 | XF40 | MS60 | MS63 | MS65 |
|---|---|---|---|---|---|---|
| 2001 | — | — | — | — | — | 160 |
| 2001 | 1,000 | PF63 160 | PF65 165 | | | |

### KM# 1068a 1/10 CROWN

3.11 g., 0.9995 Platinum 0.0999 oz. APW, 18 mm. **Ruler:** Elizabeth II **Obv:** Head with tiara right **Rev:** Somali kittens **Edge:** Reeded

| Date | Mintage | VF20 | XF40 | MS60 | MS63 | MS65 |
|---|---|---|---|---|---|---|
| 2001 | — | PF65 165 | | | | |

### KM# 1328 1/10 CROWN

3.11 g., 0.999 Gold 0.0999 oz. AGW, 18 mm. **Ruler:** Elizabeth II **Subject:** Harry Potter **Obv:** Bust right **Rev:** Boy with magic wand **Edge:** Reeded

| Date | Mintage | VF20 | XF40 | MS60 | MS63 | MS65 |
|---|---|---|---|---|---|---|
| 2001 | 7,500 | PF63 160 | PF65 165 | | | |

### KM# 1329 1/10 CROWN

3.11 g., 0.999 Gold 0.0999 oz. AGW, 18 mm. **Ruler:** Elizabeth II **Subject:** Harry Potter - Journey to Hogwarts **Obv:** Bust right **Rev:** Boat full of children going to Hogwarts School **Edge:** Reeded

| Date | Mintage | VF20 | XF40 | MS60 | MS63 | MS65 |
|---|---|---|---|---|---|---|
| 2001 | 7,500 | PF63 160 | PF65 165 | | | |

### KM# 1330 1/10 CROWN

3.11 g., 0.999 Gold 0.0999 oz. AGW, 18 mm. **Ruler:** Elizabeth II **Subject:** Harry Potter **Obv:** Bust right **Rev:** Harry flying on a broomstick **Edge:** Reeded

| Date | Mintage | VF20 | XF40 | MS60 | MS63 | MS65 |
|---|---|---|---|---|---|---|
| 2001 | 7,500 | PF63 160 | PF65 165 | | | |

### KM# 1331 1/10 CROWN

3.11 g., 0.999 Gold 0.0999 oz. AGW, 18 mm. **Ruler:** Elizabeth II **Subject:** Harry Potter **Obv:** Bust right **Rev:** Birth of Norbert the dragon **Edge:** Reeded

| Date | Mintage | VF20 | XF40 | MS60 | MS63 | MS65 |
|---|---|---|---|---|---|---|
| 2001 | 7,500 | PF63 160 | PF65 165 | | | |

### KM# 1332 1/10 CROWN

3.11 g., 0.999 Gold 0.0999 oz. AGW, 18 mm. **Ruler:** Elizabeth II **Subject:** Harry Potter **Obv:** Bust right **Rev:** Harry in Potions class **Edge:** Reeded

| Date | Mintage | VF20 | XF40 | MS60 | MS63 | MS65 |
|---|---|---|---|---|---|---|
| 2001 | 7,500 | PF63 160 | PF65 165 | | | |

### KM# 1333 1/10 CROWN

3.11 g., 0.999 Gold 0.0999 oz. AGW, 18 mm. **Ruler:** Elizabeth II **Subject:** Harry Potter **Obv:** Bust right **Rev:** Harry chasing a snitch **Edge:** Reeded

| Date | Mintage | VF20 | XF40 | MS60 | MS63 | MS65 |
|---|---|---|---|---|---|---|
| 2001 | 7,500 | PF63 160 | PF65 165 | | | |

### KM# 1099 1/10 CROWN

3.11 g., 0.9999 Gold 0.100 oz. AGW, 17.95 mm. **Ruler:** Elizabeth II **Subject:** Year of the Horse **Obv:** Bust with tiara right **Rev:** Two horses **Edge:** Reeded

| Date | Mintage | VF20 | XF40 | MS60 | MS63 | MS65 |
|---|---|---|---|---|---|---|
| 2002 | 15,000 | PF65 165 | | | | |

**KM# 1108 1/10 CROWN**
3.11 g., 0.999 Gold 0.0999 oz. AGW, 17.95 mm. **Ruler:** Elizabeth II **Subject:** Bengal Cat **Obv:** Head with tiara right **Rev:** Cat and kitten **Edge:** Reeded

| Date | Mintage | VF20 | XF40 | MS60 | MS63 | MS65 |
|---|---|---|---|---|---|---|
| 2002 | — | — | — | — | — | 165 |
| 2002 | — | PF65 165 | | | | |

**KM# 1108a 1/10 CROWN**
3.11 g., 0.999 Platinum 0.0999 oz. APW, 17.95 mm. **Ruler:** Elizabeth II **Subject:** Bengal Cat **Obv:** Head with tiara right **Rev:** Cat and kitten **Edge:** Reeded

| Date | Mintage | VF20 | XF40 | MS60 | MS63 | MS65 |
|---|---|---|---|---|---|---|
| 2002 | — | — | — | — | — | 165 |

**KM# 1155 1/10 CROWN**
3.11 g., 0.999 Gold 0.0999 oz. AGW, 17.95 mm. **Ruler:** Elizabeth II **Subject:** Queen's Golden Jubilee **Obv:** Queen's portrait **Rev:** Queen on horse **Edge:** Reeded

| Date | Mintage | VF20 | XF40 | MS60 | MS63 | MS65 |
|---|---|---|---|---|---|---|
| 2002 PM | 500 | PF65 165 | | | | |

**KM# 1162 1/10 CROWN**
3.11 g., 0.9999 Gold 0.100 oz. AGW, 17.95 mm. **Ruler:** Elizabeth II **Subject:** Cat **Obv:** Head with tiara right **Rev:** Two Balinese kittens **Edge:** Reeded

| Date | Mintage | VF20 | XF40 | MS60 | MS63 | MS65 |
|---|---|---|---|---|---|---|
| 2003 PM | — | — | — | — | — | 148 |
| 2003 PM | — | PF63 160 | PF65 165 | | | |

**KM# 1162a 1/10 CROWN**
3.11 g., 0.9995 Platinum 0.0999 oz. APW, 17.95 mm. **Ruler:** Elizabeth II **Subject:** Cat **Obv:** Head with tiara right **Rev:** Two Balinese kittens **Edge:** Reeded

| Date | Mintage | VF20 | XF40 | MS60 | MS63 | MS65 |
|---|---|---|---|---|---|---|
| 2003 PM | — | — | — | — | — | 160 |

**KM# 1168 1/10 CROWN**
3.11 g., 0.9999 Gold 0.100 oz. AGW, 17.95 mm. **Ruler:** Elizabeth II **Subject:** Year of the Goat **Obv:** Bust with tiara right **Rev:** Three goats **Edge:** Reeded

| Date | Mintage | VF20 | XF40 | MS60 | MS63 | MS65 |
|---|---|---|---|---|---|---|
| 2003 PM | — | PF65 160 | | | | |

**KM# 1187 1/10 CROWN**
3.11 g., 0.9999 Gold 0.100 oz. AGW, 18 mm. **Ruler:** Elizabeth II **Subject:** Lord of the Rings **Obv:** Bust with tiara right **Rev:** Aragorn with broad sword **Edge:** Reeded

| Date | Mintage | VF20 | XF40 | MS60 | MS63 | MS65 |
|---|---|---|---|---|---|---|
| 2003 PM | 4,500 | PF65 160 | | | | |

**KM# 1241 1/10 CROWN**
3.11 g., 0.9999 Gold 0.100 oz. AGW, 18 mm. **Ruler:** Elizabeth II **Obv:** Head with tiara right **Rev:** Monkey **Edge:** Reeded

| Date | Mintage | VF20 | XF40 | MS60 | MS63 | MS65 |
|---|---|---|---|---|---|---|
| 2004 PM | 15,000 | PF65 160 | | | | |

**KM# 1248 1/10 CROWN**
3.11 g., 0.9999 Gold 0.100 oz. AGW, 18 mm. **Ruler:** Elizabeth II **Obv:** Head with tiara right **Rev:** Two Tonkinese cats **Edge:** Reeded

| Date | Mintage | VF20 | XF40 | MS60 | MS63 | MS65 |
|---|---|---|---|---|---|---|
| 2004 PM | — | — | — | — | — | 165 |
| 2004 PM | 1,000 | PF63 166 | PF65 171 | | | |

**KM# 1270 1/10 CROWN**
3.11 g., 0.9999 Gold 0.100 oz. AGW, 18 mm. **Ruler:** Elizabeth II **Obv:** Bust with tiara right **Rev:** Himalayan cat and two kittens **Edge:** Reeded

| Date | Mintage | VF20 | XF40 | MS60 | MS63 | MS65 |
|---|---|---|---|---|---|---|
| 2005 PM | — | PF65 166 | | | | |

**KM# 1270a 1/10 CROWN**
3.11 g., 0.995 Platinum 0.0995 oz. APW, 18 mm. **Ruler:** Elizabeth II **Obv:** Queen Elizabeth II **Rev:** Himalayan cat and two kittens **Edge:** Reeded

| Date | Mintage | VF20 | XF40 | MS60 | MS63 | MS65 |
|---|---|---|---|---|---|---|
| 2005 PM | — | PF65 165 | | | | |

**KM# 1341 1/10 CROWN**
3.11 g., 0.9999 Gold 0.100 oz. AGW, 18 mm. **Ruler:** Elizabeth II **Obv:** Bust with tiara right **Rev:** Three Exotic Shorthair cats sitting facing **Edge:** Reeded

| Date | Mintage | VF20 | XF40 | MS60 | MS63 | MS65 |
|---|---|---|---|---|---|---|
| 2006 PM | — | — | — | — | — | 160 |

**KM# 1344 1/10 CROWN**
3.11 g., 0.9999 Gold 0.100 oz. AGW, 18 mm. **Ruler:** Elizabeth II **Obv:** Bust with tiara right **Obv. Legend:** ELIZABETH II - ISLE OF MAN **Rev:** Ragdoll cat with two kittens sitting facing **Edge:** Reeded

| Date | Mintage | VF20 | XF40 | MS60 | MS63 | MS65 |
|---|---|---|---|---|---|---|
| 2007 PM | — | — | — | — | — | 165 |

**KM# 1350 1/10 CROWN**
3.11 g., 0.9999 Gold 0.100 oz. AGW, 18 mm. **Ruler:** Elizabeth II **Subject:** The Tale of Peter Rabbit **Obv:** Bust with tiara right **Obv. Legend:** ELIZABETH II - ISLE OF MAN **Rev:** Peter walking with friends **Edge:** Reeded

| Date | Mintage | VF20 | XF40 | MS60 | MS63 | MS65 |
|---|---|---|---|---|---|---|
| 2007 PM | — | — | — | — | — | 148 |

**KM# 1382 1/10 CROWN**
3.11 g., 0.9999 Gold 0.100 oz. AGW, 18 mm. **Ruler:** Elizabeth II **Obv:** Bust right **Rev:** Chinchilla cat and kitten

| Date | Mintage | VF20 | XF40 | MS60 | MS63 | MS65 |
|---|---|---|---|---|---|---|
| 2009 | — | — | — | — | — | 165 |
| 2009 | 1,000 | PF63 166 | PF65 171 | | | |

**KM# 1386 1/10 CROWN**
3.11 g., 0.995 Platinum 0.0995 oz. APW, 18 mm. **Ruler:** Elizabeth II **Obv:** Bust right **Rev:** Chinchilla cat and kitten

| Date | Mintage | VF20 | XF40 | MS60 | MS63 | MS65 |
|---|---|---|---|---|---|---|
| 2009 | — | — | — | — | — | 160 |

**KM# 1535 1/10 CROWN**
3.11 g., 0.999 Gold 0.0999 oz. AGW, 18 mm. **Ruler:** Elizabeth II **Rev:** Two cats

| Date | Mintage | VF20 | XF40 | MS60 | MS63 | MS65 |
|---|---|---|---|---|---|---|
| 2010 | — | PF65 170 | | | | |

**KM# 1436 1/10 CROWN**
3.11 g., 0.9999 Gold 0.100 oz. AGW, 18 mm. **Ruler:** Elizabeth II **Subject:** Turkish Angora Cat

| Date | Mintage | VF20 | XF40 | MS60 | MS63 | MS65 |
|---|---|---|---|---|---|---|
| 2011 PM | 1,000 | PF63 165 | PF65 171 | | | |
| 2011 PM | — | — | — | — | — | 165 |

**KM# 1537 1/10 CROWN**
3.11 g., 0.999 Gold 0.0999 oz. AGW, 18 mm. **Ruler:** Elizabeth II **Obv:** Conjoined busts rigth **Rev:** Elizabeth II in coronation regalia, diamond chip insert

| Date | Mintage | VF20 | XF40 | MS60 | MS63 | MS65 |
|---|---|---|---|---|---|---|
| 2012 | — | PF65 170 | | | | |

**KM# 1060 1/5 CROWN**
6.22 g., 0.9999 Gold 0.200 oz. AGW, 22 mm. **Ruler:** Elizabeth II **Subject:** Year of the Snake **Obv:** Bust with tiara right **Rev:** Snake **Edge:** Reeded

| Date | Mintage | VF20 | XF40 | MS60 | MS63 | MS65 |
|---|---|---|---|---|---|---|
| 2001 | 12,000 | PF65 296 | | | | |

**KM# 1069 1/5 CROWN**
6.22 g., 0.9999 Gold 0.200 oz. AGW, 22 mm. **Ruler:** Elizabeth II **Obv:** Head with tiara right **Rev:** Two Somali kittens **Edge:** Reeded

| Date | Mintage | VF20 | XF40 | MS60 | MS63 | MS65 |
|---|---|---|---|---|---|---|
| 2001 | — | — | — | — | — | 296 |
| 2001 | 1,000 | PF65 296 | | | | |

**KM# 1069a 1/5 CROWN**
6.22 g., 0.9995 Platinum 0.1999 oz. APW, 22 mm. **Ruler:** Elizabeth II **Obv:** Head with tiara right **Rev:** Somali kittens **Edge:** Reeded

| Date | Mintage | VF20 | XF40 | MS60 | MS63 | MS65 |
|---|---|---|---|---|---|---|
| 2001 | — | — | — | — | — | 314 |

**KM# 1074 1/5 CROWN**
6.22 g., 0.9999 Gold 0.200 oz. AGW, 22 mm. **Ruler:** Elizabeth II **Subject:** Queen Mother **Obv:** Head with tiara right **Rev:** 1948 Silver wedding anniversary **Edge:** Reeded

| Date | Mintage | VF20 | XF40 | MS60 | MS63 | MS65 |
|---|---|---|---|---|---|---|
| 2001 | 5,000 | PF65 296 | | | | |

**KM# 1075 1/5 CROWN**
6.22 g., 0.9999 Gold 0.200 oz. AGW, 22 mm. **Ruler:** Elizabeth II **Subject:** Queen Mother **Obv:** Head with tiara right **Rev:** 1948 holding baby Prince Charles **Edge:** Reeded

| Date | Mintage | VF20 | XF40 | MS60 | MS63 | MS65 |
|---|---|---|---|---|---|---|
| 2001 | 5,000 | PF65 296 | | | | |

**KM# 1078 1/5 CROWN**
6.22 g., 0.9999 Gold 0.200 oz. AGW, 22 mm. **Ruler:** Elizabeth II **Subject:** Martin Frobisher **Obv:** Head with tiara right **Rev:** Portrait, ship and map **Edge:** Reeded

| Date | Mintage | VF20 | XF40 | MS60 | MS63 | MS65 |
|---|---|---|---|---|---|---|
| 2001 | 5,000 | PF65 296 | | | | |

**KM# 1079 1/5 CROWN**
6.22 g., 0.9999 Gold 0.200 oz. AGW, 22 mm. **Ruler:** Elizabeth II **Subject:** Ronald Amundsen **Obv:** Head with tiara right **Rev:** Portrait, ship and dirigible **Edge:** Reeded

| Date | Mintage | VF20 | XF40 | MS60 | MS63 | MS65 |
|---|---|---|---|---|---|---|
| 2001 | 5,000 | PF65 296 | | | | |

**KM# 1082 1/5 CROWN**
6.22 g., 0.9999 Gold 0.200 oz. AGW, 22 mm. **Ruler:** Elizabeth II **Subject:** Queen's 75th Birthday **Obv:** Head with tiara right **Rev:** Flower bouquet with a tiny diamond mounted on the bow of the ribbon **Edge:** Reeded

| Date | Mintage | VF20 | XF40 | MS60 | MS63 | MS65 |
|---|---|---|---|---|---|---|
| 2001 | 2,000 | PF65 296 | | | | |

**KM# 1334 1/5 CROWN**
6.15 g., 0.999 Gold 0.1975 oz. AGW, 22 mm. **Ruler:** Elizabeth II **Subject:** Harry Potter **Obv:** Bust right **Rev:** Harry with magic wand **Edge:** Reeded

| Date | Mintage | VF20 | XF40 | MS60 | MS63 | MS65 |
|---|---|---|---|---|---|---|
| 2001 | 5,000 | PF65 292 | | | | |

**KM# 1335 1/5 CROWN**
6.15 g., 0.999 Gold 0.1975 oz. AGW, 22 mm. **Ruler:** Elizabeth II **Subject:** Harry Potter - Journey to Hogwarts School **Obv:** Bust right **Rev:** Boat full of children going to Hogwarts School **Edge:** Reeded

| Date | Mintage | VF20 | XF40 | MS60 | MS63 | MS65 |
|---|---|---|---|---|---|---|
| 2001 | 5,000 | PF65 292 | | | | |

**KM# 1336 1/5 CROWN**
6.15 g., 0.999 Gold 0.1975 oz. AGW, 22 mm. **Ruler:** Elizabeth II **Subject:** Harry Potter - First Quidditch Match **Obv:** Bust right **Rev:** Harry flying a broom in a quidditch match **Edge:** Reeded

| Date | Mintage | VF20 | XF40 | MS60 | MS63 | MS65 |
|---|---|---|---|---|---|---|
| 2001 | 5,000 | PF65 292 | | | | |

**KM# 1337 1/5 CROWN**
6.15 g., 0.999 Gold 0.1975 oz. AGW, 22 mm. **Ruler:** Elizabeth II **Subject:** Harry Potter **Obv:** Bust right **Rev:** Birth of Norbert, the dragon **Edge:** Reeded

| Date | Mintage | VF20 | XF40 | MS60 | MS63 | MS65 |
|---|---|---|---|---|---|---|
| 2001 | 5,000 | PF65 292 | | | | |

**KM# 1338 1/5 CROWN**
6.15 g., 0.999 Gold 0.1975 oz. AGW, 22 mm. **Ruler:** Elizabeth II **Subject:** Harry Potter **Obv:** Bust right **Rev:** Harry in Potions class **Edge:** Reeded

| Date | Mintage | VF20 | XF40 | MS60 | MS63 | MS65 |
|---|---|---|---|---|---|---|
| 2001 | 5,000 | PF65 292 | | | | |

**KM# 1339 1/5 CROWN**
6.15 g., 0.999 Gold 0.1975 oz. AGW, 22 mm. **Ruler:** Elizabeth II **Subject:** Harry Potter **Obv:** Bust right **Rev:** Harry chasing a jeweled snitch **Edge:** Reeded

| Date | Mintage | VF20 | XF40 | MS60 | MS63 | MS65 |
|---|---|---|---|---|---|---|
| 2001 | 5,000 | PF65 292 | | | | |

**KM# 1100 1/5 CROWN**
6.22 g., 0.9999 Gold 0.200 oz. AGW, 22 mm. **Ruler:** Elizabeth II **Subject:** Year of the Horse **Obv:** Bust with tiara right **Rev:** Two horses **Edge:** Reeded

| Date | Mintage | VF20 | XF40 | MS60 | MS63 | MS65 |
|---|---|---|---|---|---|---|
| 2002 | 12,000 | PF65 296 | | | | |

**KM# 1109 1/5 CROWN**
6.22 g., 0.999 Gold 0.1998 oz. AGW, 22 mm. **Ruler:** Elizabeth II **Subject:** Bengal Cat **Obv:** Head with tiara right **Rev:** Cat and kitten **Edge:** Reeded

| Date | Mintage | VF20 | XF40 | MS60 | MS63 | MS65 |
|---|---|---|---|---|---|---|
| 2002 | — | — | — | — | — | 300 |
| 2002 | 1,000 | PF65 310 | | | | |

### KM# 1109a 1/5 CROWN

6.22 g., 0.999 Platinum 0.1998 oz. APW, 22 mm. **Ruler:** Elizabeth II **Subject:** Bengal Cat **Obv:** Head with tiara right **Rev:** Cat and kitten **Edge:** Reeded

| Date | Mintage | VF20 | XF40 | MS60 | MS63 | MS65 |
|---|---|---|---|---|---|---|
| 2002 | — | — | — | — | — | 314 |

### KM# 1113 1/5 CROWN

6.22 g., 0.999 Gold 0.1998 oz. AGW, 22 mm. **Ruler:** Elizabeth II **Subject:** Olympics - Salt Lake City **Obv:** Bust with tiara right **Rev:** Skier, torch and flag **Edge:** Reeded

| Date | Mintage | VF20 | XF40 | MS60 | MS63 | MS65 |
|---|---|---|---|---|---|---|
| 2002 | 5,000 | PF65 295 | | | | |

### KM# 1114 1/5 CROWN

6.22 g., 0.999 Gold 0.1998 oz. AGW, 22 mm. **Ruler:** Elizabeth II **Subject:** Olympics - Salt Lake City **Obv:** Bust with tiara right **Rev:** Bobsled, torch and stadium **Edge:** Reeded

| Date | Mintage | VF20 | XF40 | MS60 | MS63 | MS65 |
|---|---|---|---|---|---|---|
| 2002 | 5,000 | PF65 295 | | | | |

### KM# 1117 1/5 CROWN

6.22 g., 0.999 Gold 0.1998 oz. AGW, 22 mm. **Ruler:** Elizabeth II **Subject:** Queen Mother's Love of Horses **Obv:** Bust with tiara right **Rev:** Queen Mother and horse **Edge:** Reeded

| Date | Mintage | VF20 | XF40 | MS60 | MS63 | MS65 |
|---|---|---|---|---|---|---|
| 2002 | 5,000 | PF65 295 | | | | |

### KM# 1120 1/5 CROWN

6.22 g., 0.999 Gold 0.1998 oz. AGW, 22 mm. **Ruler:** Elizabeth II **Subject:** World Cup 2002 Japan - Korea **Obv:** Bust with tiara right **Rev:** Player running right **Edge:** Reeded

| Date | Mintage | VF20 | XF40 | MS60 | MS63 | MS65 |
|---|---|---|---|---|---|---|
| 2002 | 5,000 | PF65 295 | | | | |

### KM# 1122 1/5 CROWN

6.22 g., 0.999 Gold 0.1998 oz. AGW, 22 mm. **Ruler:** Elizabeth II **Subject:** World Cup 2002 Japan - Korea **Obv:** Bust with tiara right **Rev:** Player kicking to right **Edge:** Reeded

| Date | Mintage | VF20 | XF40 | MS60 | MS63 | MS65 |
|---|---|---|---|---|---|---|
| 2002 | 5,000 | PF65 295 | | | | |

### KM# 1124 1/5 CROWN

6.22 g., 0.999 Gold 0.1998 oz. AGW, 22 mm. **Ruler:** Elizabeth II **Subject:** World Cup 2002 Japan - Korea **Obv:** Head with tiara right **Rev:** Player kicking to left **Edge:** Reeded

| Date | Mintage | VF20 | XF40 | MS60 | MS63 | MS65 |
|---|---|---|---|---|---|---|
| 2002 | 5,000 | PF65 295 | | | | |

### KM# 1126 1/5 CROWN

6.22 g., 0.999 Gold 0.1998 oz. AGW, 22 mm. **Ruler:** Elizabeth II **Subject:** World Cup 2002 Japan - Korea **Obv:** Head with tiara right **Rev:** Player running to left **Edge:** Reeded

| Date | Mintage | VF20 | XF40 | MS60 | MS63 | MS65 |
|---|---|---|---|---|---|---|
| 2002 | 5,000 | PF65 295 | | | | |

### KM# 1130 1/5 CROWN

6.22 g., 0.375 Gold 0.075 oz. AGW, 22 mm. **Ruler:** Elizabeth II **Subject:** Elizabeth II's Golden Jubilee **Obv:** Bust with tiara right **Rev:** Seated crowned Queen holding scepter at her coronation **Edge:** Reeded

| Date | Mintage | VF20 | XF40 | MS60 | MS63 | MS65 |
|---|---|---|---|---|---|---|
| 2002 | 2,002 | PF65 111 | | | | |

### KM# 1132 1/5 CROWN

6.22 g., 0.375 Gold 0.075 oz. AGW, 22 mm. **Ruler:** Elizabeth II **Subject:** Elizabeth II's Golden Jubilee **Obv:** Bust with tiara right **Rev:** Queen on horse **Edge:** Reeded

| Date | Mintage | VF20 | XF40 | MS60 | MS63 | MS65 |
|---|---|---|---|---|---|---|
| 2002 | 2,002 | PF65 111 | | | | |

### KM# 1134 1/5 CROWN

6.22 g., 0.375 Gold 0.075 oz. AGW, 22 mm. **Ruler:** Elizabeth II **Subject:** Elizabeth II's Golden Jubilee **Obv:** Head with tiara right **Rev:** Queen with dog **Edge:** Reeded

| Date | Mintage | VF20 | XF40 | MS60 | MS63 | MS65 |
|---|---|---|---|---|---|---|
| 2002 | 2,002 | PF65 111 | | | | |

### KM# 1136 1/5 CROWN

6.22 g., 0.375 Gold 0.075 oz. AGW, 22 mm. **Ruler:** Elizabeth II **Subject:** Elizabeth II's Golden Jubilee **Obv:** Bust with tiara right **Rev:** Queen at war memorial **Edge:** Reeded

| Date | Mintage | VF20 | XF40 | MS60 | MS63 | MS65 |
|---|---|---|---|---|---|---|
| 2002 | 2,002 | PF65 111 | | | | |

### KM# 1138 1/5 CROWN

6.22 g., 0.999 Gold 0.1998 oz. AGW, 22 mm. **Ruler:** Elizabeth II **Subject:** Queen Mother **Obv:** Bust with tiara right **Rev:** Queen Mother and Castle May **Edge:** Reeded

| Date | Mintage | VF20 | XF40 | MS60 | MS63 | MS65 |
|---|---|---|---|---|---|---|
| 2002 | 5,000 | PF65 295 | | | | |

### KM# 1140 1/5 CROWN

6.22 g., 0.9999 Gold 0.200 oz. AGW, 22 mm. **Ruler:** Elizabeth II **Subject:** Princess Diana **Obv:** Bust with tiara right **Rev:** Diana's portrait **Edge:** Reeded

| Date | Mintage | VF20 | XF40 | MS60 | MS63 | MS65 |
|---|---|---|---|---|---|---|
| 2002 | — | PF65 296 | | | | |

### KM# 1156 1/5 CROWN

6.22 g., 0.999 Gold 0.1998 oz. AGW, 22 mm. **Ruler:** Elizabeth II **Subject:** Queen's Golden Jubilee **Obv:** Queen's portrait **Rev:** Queen on horse **Edge:** Reeded

| Date | Mintage | VF20 | XF40 | MS60 | MS63 | MS65 |
|---|---|---|---|---|---|---|
| 2002 PM | 500 | PF65 295 | | | | |

### KM# 1163 1/5 CROWN

6.22 g., 0.9999 Gold 0.200 oz. AGW, 22 mm. **Ruler:** Elizabeth II **Subject:** Cat **Obv:** Head with tiara right **Rev:** Two Balinese kittens **Edge:** Reeded

| Date | Mintage | VF20 | XF40 | MS60 | MS63 | MS65 |
|---|---|---|---|---|---|---|
| 2003 PM | — | — | — | — | — | 296 |
| 2003 PM | — | PF65 296 | | | | |

### KM# 1163a 1/5 CROWN

6.22 g., 0.9995 Platinum 0.1999 oz. APW, 22 mm. **Ruler:** Elizabeth II **Subject:** Cat **Obv:** Head with tiara right **Rev:** Two Balinese kittens **Edge:** Reeded

| Date | Mintage | VF20 | XF40 | MS60 | MS63 | MS65 |
|---|---|---|---|---|---|---|
| 2003 PM | — | — | — | — | — | 314 |

### KM# 1169 1/5 CROWN

6.22 g., 0.9999 Gold 0.200 oz. AGW, 22 mm. **Ruler:** Elizabeth II **Subject:** Year of the Goat **Obv:** Bust with tiara right **Rev:** Three goats **Edge:** Reeded

| Date | Mintage | VF20 | XF40 | MS60 | MS63 | MS65 |
|---|---|---|---|---|---|---|
| 2003 PM | — | PF65 296 | | | | |

### KM# 1175 1/5 CROWN

6.22 g., 0.9999 Gold 0.200 oz. AGW, 22 mm. **Ruler:** Elizabeth II **Subject:** Olympics **Obv:** Bust with tiara right **Rev:** Swimmers **Edge:** Reeded

| Date | Mintage | VF20 | XF40 | MS60 | MS63 | MS65 |
|---|---|---|---|---|---|---|
| 2003 PM | 5,000 | PF65 296 | | | | |

### KM# 1177 1/5 CROWN

6.22 g., 0.9999 Gold 0.200 oz. AGW, 22 mm. **Ruler:** Elizabeth II **Subject:** Olympics **Obv:** Bust with tiara right **Rev:** Runners **Edge:** Reeded

| Date | Mintage | VF20 | XF40 | MS60 | MS63 | MS65 |
|---|---|---|---|---|---|---|
| 2003 PM | 5,000 | PF65 296 | | | | |

### KM# 1179 1/5 CROWN

6.22 g., 0.9999 Gold 0.200 oz. AGW, 22 mm. **Ruler:** Elizabeth II **Subject:** Olympics **Obv:** Bust with tiara right **Rev:** Bicyclists **Edge:** Reeded

| Date | Mintage | VF20 | XF40 | MS60 | MS63 | MS65 |
|---|---|---|---|---|---|---|
| 2003 PM | 5,000 | PF65 296 | | | | |

### KM# 1181 1/5 CROWN

6.22 g., 0.9999 Gold 0.200 oz. AGW, 22 mm. **Ruler:** Elizabeth II **Subject:** Olympics **Obv:** Head with tiara right **Rev:** Sail Boarders **Edge:** Reeded

| Date | Mintage | VF20 | XF40 | MS60 | MS63 | MS65 |
|---|---|---|---|---|---|---|
| 2003 PM | — | PF65 296 | | | | |

### KM# 1188 1/5 CROWN

6.22 g., 0.9999 Gold 0.200 oz. AGW, 22 mm. **Ruler:** Elizabeth II **Subject:** Lord of the Rings **Obv:** Bust with tiara right **Rev:** Legolas with bow and arrow **Edge:** Reeded

| Date | Mintage | VF20 | XF40 | MS60 | MS63 | MS65 |
|---|---|---|---|---|---|---|
| 2003 PM | 3,500 | PF65 296 | | | | |

### KM# 1198 1/5 CROWN

6.22 g., 0.999 Palladium 0.1998 oz. APW, 22 mm. **Ruler:** Elizabeth II **Subject:** Palladium Bicentennial **Obv:** Head with tiara right **Rev:** Athena **Edge:** Reeded

| Date | Mintage | VF20 | XF40 | MS60 | MS63 | MS65 |
|---|---|---|---|---|---|---|
| 2004 PM | 999 | PF65 195 | | | | |

### KM# 1223 1/5 CROWN

6.22 g., 0.9999 Gold 0.200 oz. AGW, 22 mm. **Ruler:** Elizabeth II **Obv:** Bust with tiara right **Rev:** D-Day Invasion Plan Map **Edge:** Reeded

| Date | Mintage | VF20 | XF40 | MS60 | MS63 | MS65 |
|---|---|---|---|---|---|---|
| 2004 PM | 5,000 | PF65 296 | | | | |

### KM# 1225 1/5 CROWN

6.22 g., 0.9999 Gold 0.200 oz. AGW, 22 mm. **Ruler:** Elizabeth II **Obv:** Bust with tiara right **Rev:** Victoria Cross and battle scene **Edge:** Reeded

| Date | Mintage | VF20 | XF40 | MS60 | MS63 | MS65 |
|---|---|---|---|---|---|---|
| 2004 PM | 5,000 | PF65 296 | | | | |

### KM# 1227 1/5 CROWN

6.22 g., 0.9999 Gold 0.200 oz. AGW, 22 mm. **Ruler:** Elizabeth II **Obv:** Bust with tiara right **Rev:** Silver Star and battle scene **Edge:** Reeded

| Date | Mintage | VF20 | XF40 | MS60 | MS63 | MS65 |
|---|---|---|---|---|---|---|
| 2004 PM | 5,000 | PF65 296 | | | | |

### KM# 1229 1/5 CROWN

6.22 g., 0.9999 Gold 0.200 oz. AGW, 22 mm. **Ruler:** Elizabeth II **Obv:** Bust with tiara right **Rev:** George Cross and rescue scene **Edge:** Reeded

| Date | Mintage | VF20 | XF40 | MS60 | MS63 | MS65 |
|---|---|---|---|---|---|---|
| 2004 PM | 5,000 | PF65 296 | | | | |

### KM# 1231 1/5 CROWN

6.22 g., 0.9999 Gold 0.200 oz. AGW, 22 mm. **Ruler:** Elizabeth II **Obv:** Bust with tiara right **Rev:** White Rose of Finland Medal and battle scene **Edge:** Reeded

| Date | Mintage | VF20 | XF40 | MS60 | MS63 | MS65 |
|---|---|---|---|---|---|---|
| 2004 PM | 5,000 | PF65 296 | | | | |

### KM# 1233 1/5 CROWN

6.22 g., 0.9999 Gold 0.200 oz. AGW, 22 mm. **Ruler:** Elizabeth II **Obv:** Bust with tiara right **Rev:** The Norwegian War Medal and naval battle scene **Edge:** Reeded

| Date | Mintage | VF20 | XF40 | MS60 | MS63 | MS65 |
|---|---|---|---|---|---|---|
| 2004 PM | 5,000 | PF65 296 | | | | |

### KM# 1235 1/5 CROWN

6.22 g., 0.9999 Gold 0.200 oz. AGW, 22 mm. **Ruler:** Elizabeth II **Obv:** Bust with tiara right **Rev:** French Croix de Guerre and Partisan battle scene **Edge:** Reeded

| Date | Mintage | VF20 | XF40 | MS60 | MS63 | MS65 |
|---|---|---|---|---|---|---|
| 2004 PM | 5,000 | PF65 296 | | | | |

### KM# 1249.1 1/5 CROWN

6.22 g., 0.9999 Gold 0.200 oz. AGW, 22 mm. **Ruler:** Elizabeth II **Obv:** Head with tiara right **Rev:** Two Tonkinese cats **Edge:** Reeded

| Date | Mintage | VF20 | XF40 | MS60 | MS63 | MS65 |
|---|---|---|---|---|---|---|
| 2004 PM | 1,000 | PF65 306 | | | | |
| 2004 PM | — | — | — | — | — | 301 |

### KM# 1249.2 1/5 CROWN

6.22 g., 0.9999 Gold 0.200 oz. AGW, 22 mm. **Ruler:** Elizabeth II **Obv:** Head with tiara right **Rev:** Two multicolor Tonkinese cats **Edge:** Reeded

| Date | Mintage | VF20 | XF40 | MS60 | MS63 | MS65 |
|---|---|---|---|---|---|---|
| 2004 PM | — | PF65 306 | | | | |

### KM# 1271.1 1/5 CROWN

6.22 g., 0.9999 Gold 0.200 oz. AGW, 22 mm. **Ruler:** Elizabeth II **Rev:** Two cats, colored

| Date | Mintage | VF20 | XF40 | MS60 | MS63 | MS65 |
|---|---|---|---|---|---|---|
| 2004 | — | — | — | — | — | — |

### KM# 1529 1/5 CROWN

6.22 g., 0.999 Gold 0.1998 oz. AGW, 22 mm. **Ruler:** Elizabeth II **Subject:** World Cup Soccer, Germany 2006 **Rev:** Player by soccer ball

| Date | Mintage | VF20 | XF40 | MS60 | MS63 | MS65 |
|---|---|---|---|---|---|---|
| 2004 | — | PF65 295 | | | | |

### KM# 1271 1/5 CROWN

6.22 g., 0.9999 Gold 0.200 oz. AGW, 22 mm. **Ruler:** Elizabeth II **Obv:** Bust with tiara right **Rev:** Himalayan cat and two kittens **Edge:** Reeded

| Date | Mintage | VF20 | XF40 | MS60 | MS63 | MS65 |
|---|---|---|---|---|---|---|
| 2005 PM | — | PF65 301 | | | | |

### KM# 1271a 1/5 CROWN

6.22 g., 0.995 Platinum 0.199 oz. APW, 22 mm. **Ruler:** Elizabeth II **Obv:** Bust with tiara right **Rev:** Himalayan cat and two kittens **Edge:** Reeded

| Date | Mintage | VF20 | XF40 | MS60 | MS63 | MS65 |
|---|---|---|---|---|---|---|
| 2005 PM | — | PF65 313 | | | | |

### KM# 1295 1/5 CROWN

6.22 g., 0.9999 Gold 0.200 oz. AGW, 22 mm. **Ruler:** Elizabeth II **Subject:** Battles that Changed the World **Obv:** Elizabeth II **Rev:** Trojan War scene **Edge:** Reeded

| Date | Mintage | VF20 | XF40 | MS60 | MS63 | MS65 |
|---|---|---|---|---|---|---|
| 2006 PM | 5,000 | PF65 296 | | | | |

### KM# 1297 1/5 CROWN

6.22 g., 0.9999 Gold 0.200 oz. AGW, 22 mm. **Ruler:** Elizabeth II **Subject:** Battles that Changed the World **Obv:** Elizabeth II **Rev:** Battle of Arbela scene **Edge:** Reeded

| Date | Mintage | VF20 | XF40 | MS60 | MS63 | MS65 |
|---|---|---|---|---|---|---|
| 2006 PM | 5,000 | PF65 296 | | | | |

### KM# 1299 1/5 CROWN

6.22 g., 0.9999 Gold 0.200 oz. AGW, 22 mm. **Ruler:** Elizabeth II **Subject:** Battles that Changed the World **Obv:** Elizabeth II **Rev:** Battle of Thapsus scene **Edge:** Reeded

| Date | Mintage | VF20 | XF40 | MS60 | MS63 | MS65 |
|---|---|---|---|---|---|---|
| 2006 PM | 5,000 | PF65 296 | | | | |

### KM# 1301 1/5 CROWN

6.22 g., 0.9999 Gold 0.200 oz. AGW, 22 mm. **Ruler:** Elizabeth II **Subject:** Battles that Changed the World **Obv:** Elizabeth II **Rev:** Battle of Cologne scene **Edge:** Reeded

| Date | Mintage | VF20 | XF40 | MS60 | MS63 | MS65 |
|---|---|---|---|---|---|---|
| 2006 PM | 5,000 | PF65 296 | | | | |

**KM# 1303 1/5 CROWN**
6.22 g., 0.9999 Gold 0.200 oz. AGW, 22 mm. **Ruler:** Elizabeth II **Subject:** Battles that Changed the World **Obv:** Elizabeth II **Rev:** Siege of Valencia scene **Edge:** Reeded

| Date | Mintage | VF20 | XF40 | MS60 | MS63 | MS65 |
|---|---|---|---|---|---|---|
| 2006 PM | 5,000 | PF65 296 | | | | |

**KM# 1305 1/5 CROWN**
6.22 g., 0.9999 Gold 0.200 oz. AGW, 22 mm. **Ruler:** Elizabeth II **Subject:** Battles that Changed the World **Obv:** Elizabeth II **Rev:** Battle of Agincourt scene **Edge:** Reeded

| Date | Mintage | VF20 | XF40 | MS60 | MS63 | MS65 |
|---|---|---|---|---|---|---|
| 2006 PM | 5,000 | PF65 296 | | | | |

**KM# 1342 1/5 CROWN**
6.22 g., 0.9999 Gold 0.200 oz. AGW, 22 mm. **Ruler:** Elizabeth II **Obv:** Bust with tiara right **Rev:** Three Exotic Shorthair cats sitting facing **Edge:** Reeded

| Date | Mintage | VF20 | XF40 | MS60 | MS63 | MS65 |
|---|---|---|---|---|---|---|
| 2006 PM | — | PF65 301 | | | | |

**KM# 1309 1/5 CROWN**
6.22 g., 0.9999 Gold 0.200 oz. AGW, 22 mm. **Ruler:** Elizabeth II **Subject:** 100th Anniversary of Scouting **Obv:** Bust with tiara right **Obv. Legend:** ELIZABETH II - ISLE OF MAN **Rev:** 3/4 length figure of Robert Baden-Powell standing facing 3/4 left, Fleur-de-lys below, images of scouting at left and right **Rev. Legend:** CENTERARY OF SCOUTING **Edge:** Reeded

| Date | Mintage | VF20 | XF40 | MS60 | MS63 | MS65 |
|---|---|---|---|---|---|---|
| 2007 | — | PF65 296 | | | | |

**KM# 1345 1/5 CROWN**
6.22 g., 0.9999 Gold 0.200 oz. AGW, 22 mm. **Ruler:** Elizabeth II **Obv:** Bust with tiara right **Obv. Legend:** ELIZABETH II - ISLE OF MAN **Rev:** Ragdoll cat with two kittens sitting facing **Edge:** Reeded

| Date | Mintage | VF20 | XF40 | MS60 | MS63 | MS65 |
|---|---|---|---|---|---|---|
| 2007 PM | — | — | — | — | — | 296 |

**KM# 1351.1 1/5 CROWN**
6.22 g., 0.9999 Gold 0.200 oz. AGW **Ruler:** Elizabeth II **Subject:** The Tale of Peter Rabbit **Obv:** Bust with tiara right **Obv. Legend:** ELIZABETH II - ISLE OF MAN **Rev:** Peter walking with friends **Edge:** Reeded

| Date | Mintage | VF20 | XF40 | MS60 | MS63 | MS65 |
|---|---|---|---|---|---|---|
| 2007 PM | — | — | — | — | — | 296 |

**KM# 1351.2 1/5 CROWN**
6.22 g., 0.9999 Gold 0.200 oz. AGW **Ruler:** Elizabeth II **Subject:** The Tale of Peter Rabbit **Obv:** Bust with tiara right **Obv. Legend:** ELIZABETH II - ISLE OF MAN **Rev:** Peter walking with friends **Edge:** Reeded

| Date | Mintage | VF20 | XF40 | MS60 | MS63 | MS65 |
|---|---|---|---|---|---|---|
| 2007 PM | — | — | — | — | — | 296 |

**KM# 1352 1/5 CROWN**
6.22 g., 0.9999 Gold 0.200 oz. AGW, 22 mm. **Ruler:** Elizabeth II **Subject:** Prince Charles 60th Birthday **Obv:** Bust with tiara right **Obv. Legend:** ELIZABETH II - ISLE OF MAN **Rev:** Heads of Charles, Princes William and Henry right **Edge:** Reeded

| Date | Mintage | VF20 | XF40 | MS60 | MS63 | MS65 |
|---|---|---|---|---|---|---|
| 2008 PM | 5,000 | PF65 296 | | | | |

**KM# 1534 1/5 CROWN**
6.22 g., 0.999 Gold 0.1998 oz. AGW, 22 mm. **Ruler:** Elizabeth II **Rev:** Two cats seated, in color

| Date | Mintage | VF20 | XF40 | MS60 | MS63 | MS65 |
|---|---|---|---|---|---|---|
| 2008 | — | PF65 295 | | | | |

**KM# 1375 1/5 CROWN**
6.22 g., 0.9999 Gold 0.200 oz. AGW, 22 mm. **Ruler:** Elizabeth II **Subject:** Terra Cotta Army **Obv:** Bust right **Rev:** Making of the Soldier

| Date | Mintage | VF20 | XF40 | MS60 | MS63 | MS65 |
|---|---|---|---|---|---|---|
| 2009 | 5,000 | PF65 296 | | | | |

**KM# 1377 1/5 CROWN**
6.22 g., 0.9999 Gold 0.200 oz. AGW, 22 mm. **Ruler:** Elizabeth II **Subject:** Terra Cotta Army **Obv:** Bust right **Rev:** Making of the Horse

| Date | Mintage | VF20 | XF40 | MS60 | MS63 | MS65 |
|---|---|---|---|---|---|---|
| 2009 | 5,000 | PF65 296 | | | | |

**KM# 1381 1/5 CROWN**
6.22 g., 0.9999 Gold 0.200 oz. AGW **Ruler:** Elizabeth II **Obv:** Bust right **Rev:** Chinchilla cat and kitten

| Date | Mintage | VF20 | XF40 | MS60 | MS63 | MS65 |
|---|---|---|---|---|---|---|
| 2009 | — | — | — | — | — | 301 |
| 2009 | 1,000 | PF65 301 | | | | |

**KM# 1536 1/5 CROWN**
6.22 g., 0.999 Gold 0.1998 oz. AGW, 22 mm. **Ruler:** Elizabeth II **Rev:** Two cats

| Date | Mintage | VF20 | XF40 | MS60 | MS63 | MS65 |
|---|---|---|---|---|---|---|
| 2010 | — | PF65 295 | | | | |

**KM# 1437 1/5 CROWN**
6.22 g., 0.9999 Gold 0.200 oz. AGW, 22 mm. **Ruler:** Elizabeth II **Subject:** Turkish Angora Cat

| Date | Mintage | VF20 | XF40 | MS60 | MS63 | MS65 |
|---|---|---|---|---|---|---|
| 2011 PM | 1,000 | PF65 311 | | | | |
| 2011 PM | — | — | — | — | — | 301 |

**KM# 1385 1/4 CROWN**
6.22 g., 0.995 Platinum 0.199 oz. APW, 22 mm. **Ruler:** Elizabeth II **Series:** Bust right **Obv:** Chinchilla cat and kitten

| Date | Mintage | VF20 | XF40 | MS60 | MS63 | MS65 |
|---|---|---|---|---|---|---|
| 2009 | — | — | — | — | — | 308 |

**KM# 1061 1/2 CROWN**
15.55 g., 0.9999 Gold 0.4999 oz. AGW, 30 mm. **Ruler:** Elizabeth II **Subject:** Year of the Snake **Obv:** Bust with tiara right **Rev:** Snake **Edge:** Reeded

| Date | Mintage | VF20 | XF40 | MS60 | MS63 | MS65 |
|---|---|---|---|---|---|---|
| 2001 | 6,000 | PF65 685 | | | | |

**KM# 1070 1/2 CROWN**
15.55 g., 0.9999 Gold 0.4999 oz. AGW, 30 mm. **Ruler:** Elizabeth II **Obv:** Head with tiara right **Rev:** Two Somali kittens **Edge:** Reeded

| Date | Mintage | VF20 | XF40 | MS60 | MS63 | MS65 |
|---|---|---|---|---|---|---|
| 2001 | — | — | — | — | — | 685 |
| 2001 | 1,000 | PF65 690 | | | | |

**KM# 1071 1/2 CROWN**
15.55 g., 0.9995 Platinum 0.4997 oz. APW, 27 mm. **Ruler:** Elizabeth II **Obv:** Head with tiara right **Rev:** Two Somali kittens **Edge:** Reeded

| Date | Mintage | VF20 | XF40 | MS60 | MS63 | MS65 |
|---|---|---|---|---|---|---|
| 2001 | — | — | — | — | — | 721 |

**KM# 1101 1/2 CROWN**
15.55 g., 0.9999 Gold 0.4999 oz. AGW, 30 mm. **Ruler:** Elizabeth II **Subject:** Year of the Horse **Obv:** Bust with tiara right **Rev:** Two horses **Edge:** Reeded

| Date | Mintage | VF20 | XF40 | MS60 | MS63 | MS65 |
|---|---|---|---|---|---|---|
| 2002 | 6,000 | PF65 685 | | | | |

**KM# 1110 1/2 CROWN**
15.55 g., 0.999 Gold 0.4995 oz. AGW, 30 mm. **Ruler:** Elizabeth II **Subject:** Bengal Cat **Obv:** Head with tiara right **Rev:** Cat and kitten **Edge:** Reeded

| Date | Mintage | VF20 | XF40 | MS60 | MS63 | MS65 |
|---|---|---|---|---|---|---|
| 2002 | — | — | — | — | — | 685 |
| 2002 | 1,000 | PF65 690 | | | | |

**KM# 1110a 1/2 CROWN**
6.22 g., 0.999 Platinum 0.1998 oz. APW, 30 mm. **Ruler:** Elizabeth II **Subject:** Bengal Cat **Obv:** Head with tiara right **Rev:** Cat and kitten **Edge:** Reeded

| Date | Mintage | VF20 | XF40 | MS60 | MS63 | MS65 |
|---|---|---|---|---|---|---|
| 2002 | — | — | — | — | — | 296 |

**KM# 1157 1/2 CROWN**
15.55 g., 0.999 Gold 0.4995 oz. AGW, 30 mm. **Ruler:** Elizabeth II **Subject:** Queen's Golden Jubilee **Obv:** Queen's portrait **Rev:** Queen on horse **Edge:** Reeded

| Date | Mintage | VF20 | XF40 | MS60 | MS63 | MS65 |
|---|---|---|---|---|---|---|
| 2002 PM | 500 | PF65 685 | | | | |

**KM# 1164 1/2 CROWN**
15.55 g., 0.9999 Gold 0.4999 oz. AGW, 30 mm. **Ruler:** Elizabeth II **Subject:** Cat **Obv:** Head with tiara right **Rev:** Two Balinese kittens **Edge:** Reeded

| Date | Mintage | VF20 | XF40 | MS60 | MS63 | MS65 |
|---|---|---|---|---|---|---|
| 2003 PM | — | — | — | — | — | 685 |
| 2003 PM | — | PF65 690 | | | | |

**KM# 1164a 1/2 CROWN**
15.55 g., 0.9995 Platinum 0.4997 oz. APW, 30 mm. **Ruler:** Elizabeth II **Subject:** Cat **Obv:** Head with tiara right **Rev:** Two Balinese kittens **Edge:** Reeded

| Date | Mintage | VF20 | XF40 | MS60 | MS63 | MS65 |
|---|---|---|---|---|---|---|
| 2003 PM | — | — | — | — | — | 721 |

**KM# 1170 1/2 CROWN**
15.55 g., 0.9999 Gold 0.4999 oz. AGW, 30 mm. **Ruler:** Elizabeth II **Subject:** Year of the Goat **Obv:** Bust with tiara right **Rev:** Three goats **Edge:** Reeded

| Date | Mintage | VF20 | XF40 | MS60 | MS63 | MS65 |
|---|---|---|---|---|---|---|
| 2003 PM | — | PF65 685 | | | | |

**KM# 1189 1/2 CROWN**
15.55 g., 0.9999 Gold 0.4999 oz. AGW, 30 mm. **Ruler:** Elizabeth II **Subject:** Lord of the Rings **Obv:** Bust with tiara right **Rev:** Gimli with two battle axes **Edge:** Reeded

| Date | Mintage | VF20 | XF40 | MS60 | MS63 | MS65 |
|---|---|---|---|---|---|---|
| 2003 PM | 1,000 | PF65 685 | | | | |

**KM# 1199 1/2 CROWN**
15.55 g., 0.999 Gold with Palladium 0.4994 oz. .999 Palladium 6.3g center in .9999 Gold 9.25 g ring, 30 mm. **Ruler:** Elizabeth II **Subject:** Palladium Bicentennial **Obv:** Bust with tiara right **Rev:** Athena **Edge:** Reeded

| Date | Mintage | VF20 | XF40 | MS60 | MS63 | MS65 |
|---|---|---|---|---|---|---|
| 2004 PM | 500 | PF65 1,050 | | | | |

**KM# 1243 1/2 CROWN**
15.55 g., 0.9999 Gold 0.500 oz. AGW, 30 mm. **Ruler:** Elizabeth II **Obv:** Head with tiara right **Rev:** Monkey **Edge:** Reeded

| Date | Mintage | VF20 | XF40 | MS60 | MS63 | MS65 |
|---|---|---|---|---|---|---|
| 2004 PM | 6,000 | PF65 685 | | | | |

**KM# 1250 1/2 CROWN**
15.55 g., 0.9999 Gold 0.500 oz. AGW, 30 mm. **Ruler:** Elizabeth II **Obv:** Head with tiara right **Rev:** Two Tonkinese cats **Edge:** Reeded

| Date | Mintage | VF20 | XF40 | MS60 | MS63 | MS65 |
|---|---|---|---|---|---|---|
| 2004 PM | — | — | — | — | — | 685 |
| 2004 PM | 1,000 | PF65 690 | | | | |

**KM# 1272 1/2 CROWN**
15.55 g., 0.9999 Gold 0.4999 oz. AGW, 27 mm. **Ruler:** Elizabeth II **Obv:** Bust with tiara right **Rev:** Himalayan cat and two kittens **Edge:** Reeded

| Date | Mintage | VF20 | XF40 | MS60 | MS63 | MS65 |
|---|---|---|---|---|---|---|
| 2005 PM | — | PF65 690 | | | | |

**KM# 1272a 1/2 CROWN**
15.55 g., 0.995 Platinum 0.4975 oz. APW, 27 mm. **Ruler:** Elizabeth II **Obv:** Bust with tiara right **Rev:** Himalayan cat and two kittens **Edge:** Reeded

| Date | Mintage | VF20 | XF40 | MS60 | MS63 | MS65 |
|---|---|---|---|---|---|---|
| 2005 PM | — | — | — | — | — | 718 |
| 2005 PM | — | PF65 723 | | | | |

**KM# 1346 1/2 CROWN**
15.55 g., 0.9999 Gold 0.4999 oz. AGW **Ruler:** Elizabeth II **Obv:** Bust with tiara right **Obv. Legend:** ELIZABETH II - ISLE OF MAN **Rev:** Ragdoll cat with two kittens sitting facing **Edge:** Reeded

| Date | Mintage | VF20 | XF40 | MS60 | MS63 | MS65 |
|---|---|---|---|---|---|---|
| 2007 PM | — | — | — | — | — | 690 |

**KM# 1396 1/2 CROWN**
6.22 g., 0.9999 Gold 0.200 oz. AGW, 30x20 mm. **Ruler:** Elizabeth II **Rev:** Tut's golden mask

| Date | Mintage | VF20 | XF40 | MS60 | MS63 | MS65 |
|---|---|---|---|---|---|---|
| 2008 PM | — | — | — | — | — | 296 |

### KM# 1399 1/2 CROWN

6.22 g., 0.9999 Gold 0.200 oz. AGW **Ruler:** Elizabeth II **Obv:** Bust with tiara right in Egyptian motif **Rev:** Statue standing **Shape:** Triangle

| Date | Mintage | VF20 | XF40 | MS60 | MS63 | MS65 |
|---|---|---|---|---|---|---|
| 2008 PM | — | PF65 306 | | | | |

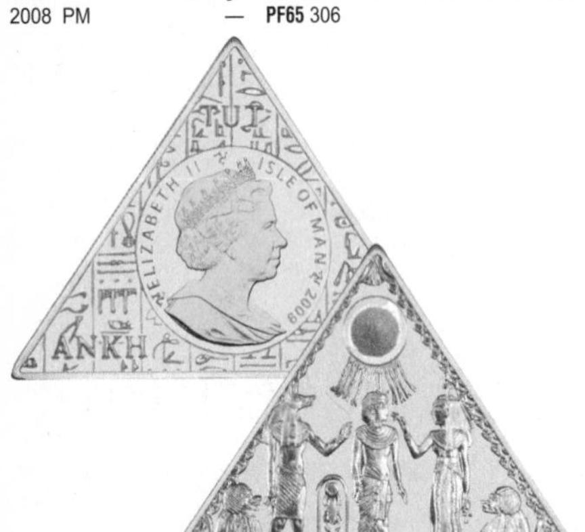


### KM# 1400 1/2 CROWN

6.22 g., 0.9999 Gold 0.200 oz. AGW **Ruler:** Elizabeth II **Obv:** Bust with tiara right in Egyptian motif **Rev:** Statue standing, vile of sand above **Shape:** Triangle

| Date | Mintage | VF20 | XF40 | MS60 | MS63 | MS65 |
|---|---|---|---|---|---|---|
| 2008 PM | — | PF65 306 | | | | |

### KM# 1380 1/2 CROWN

15.55 g., 0.9999 Gold 0.4999 oz. AGW, 30 mm. **Ruler:** Elizabeth II **Obv:** Bust right **Rev:** Chinchilla cat and kitten

| Date | Mintage | VF20 | XF40 | MS60 | MS63 | MS65 |
|---|---|---|---|---|---|---|
| 2009 | — | — | — | — | — | 685 |
| 2009 | 1,000 | PF65 690 | | | | |

### KM# 1384 1/2 CROWN

15.55 g., 0.995 Platinum 0.4974 oz. APW, 27 mm. **Ruler:** Elizabeth II **Obv:** Bust right **Rev:** Chinchilla cat and kitten

| Date | Mintage | VF20 | XF40 | MS60 | MS63 | MS65 |
|---|---|---|---|---|---|---|
| 2009 | — | — | — | — | — | 718 |

### KM# 1474 1/2 CROWN

Titanium **Ruler:** Elizabeth II **Subject:** George F. Handel, 325th Anniversary of Birth **Obv:** Bust in tiara right **Rev:** Fireworks above river barges **Note:** Blue in color.

| Date | Mintage | VF20 | XF40 | MS60 | MS63 | MS65 |
|---|---|---|---|---|---|---|
| 2010 PM | — | PF65 125 | | | | |

### KM# 1438 1/2 CROWN

15.55 g., 0.9999 Gold 0.4999 oz. AGW, 30 mm. **Ruler:** Elizabeth II **Subject:** Turkish Angora Cat

| Date | Mintage | VF20 | XF40 | MS60 | MS63 | MS65 |
|---|---|---|---|---|---|---|
| 2011 PM | 1,000 | PF65 690 | | | | |
| 2011 PM | — | — | — | — | — | 744 |

### KM# 1447 1/2 CROWN

12.00 g., 0.999 Silver 0.3854 oz. ASW, 38.6 mm. **Ruler:** Elizabeth II **Subject:** Olympics, London **Rev:** Horse jumper

| Date | Mintage | VF20 | XF40 | MS60 | MS63 | MS65 |
|---|---|---|---|---|---|---|
| 2012 PM | 10,000 | PF63 20.00 | PF65 22.00 | | | |

### KM# 1448 1/2 CROWN

12.00 g., 0.999 Silver 0.3854 oz. ASW, 38.6 mm. **Ruler:** Elizabeth II **Subject:** Olympics, London **Rev:** Track Cyclist, road cyclist in background

| Date | Mintage | VF20 | XF40 | MS60 | MS63 | MS65 |
|---|---|---|---|---|---|---|
| 2012 PM | 10,000 | PF63 20.00 | PF65 22.00 | | | |

### KM# 1449 1/2 CROWN

12.00 g., 0.999 Silver 0.3854 oz. ASW, 38.6 mm. **Ruler:** Elizabeth II **Subject:** Olympics, London **Rev:** Swimmer, two divers in background

| Date | Mintage | VF20 | XF40 | MS60 | MS63 | MS65 |
|---|---|---|---|---|---|---|
| 2012 PM | 10,000 | PF63 20.00 | PF65 22.00 | | | |

### KM# 1450 1/2 CROWN

12.00 g., 0.999 Silver 0.3854 oz. ASW, 38.6 mm. **Ruler:** Elizabeth II **Subject:** Olympics, London **Rev:** Canoeist, two rowers in background

| Date | Mintage | VF20 | XF40 | MS60 | MS63 | MS65 |
|---|---|---|---|---|---|---|
| 2012 PM | 10,000 | PF63 20.00 | PF65 22.00 | | | |

### KM# 1451 1/2 CROWN

12.00 g., 0.999 Silver 0.3854 oz. ASW, 38.6 mm. **Ruler:** Elizabeth II **Subject:** Olympics, London **Rev:** Judo players, two boxers in background

| Date | Mintage | VF20 | XF40 | MS60 | MS63 | MS65 |
|---|---|---|---|---|---|---|
| 2012 PM | 10,000 | PF63 20.00 | PF65 22.00 | | | |

### KM# 1452 1/2 CROWN

12.00 g., 0.999 Silver 0.3854 oz. ASW, 38.6 mm. **Ruler:** Elizabeth II **Subject:** Olympics, London **Rev:** Table tennis, Lawn tennis in background

| Date | Mintage | VF20 | XF40 | MS60 | MS63 | MS65 |
|---|---|---|---|---|---|---|
| 2012 PM | 10,000 | PF63 20.00 | PF65 22.00 | | | |

### KM# 1457 1/2 CROWN

12.00 g., 0.999 Silver 0.3854 oz. ASW, 38.6 mm. **Ruler:** Elizabeth II **Subject:** European Football Championships 2012 **Rev:** Player heading a football, Statue of Liberty in Lviv and Neptune's fountain in Gdansk

| Date | Mintage | VF20 | XF40 | MS60 | MS63 | MS65 |
|---|---|---|---|---|---|---|
| 2012 PM | 10,000 | PF63 20.00 | PF65 22.00 | | | |

### KM# 1458 1/2 CROWN

12.00 g., 0.999 Silver 0.3854 oz. ASW, 38.6 mm. **Ruler:** Elizabeth II **Subject:** European Football Championships 2012 **Rev:** Player passing the ball, Motherland statue in Kiev and King Sigismund's statue in Warsaw in background

| Date | Mintage | VF20 | XF40 | MS60 | MS63 | MS65 |
|---|---|---|---|---|---|---|
| 2012 PM | 10,000 | PF63 20.00 | PF65 22.00 | | | |

### KM# 1459 1/2 CROWN

12.00 g., 0.999 Silver 0.3854 oz. ASW, 38.6 mm. **Ruler:** Elizabeth II **Subject:** European Football Championships 2012 **Rev:** Footballer shooting, Cathedral of the Transfiguration in Donetsk and the Raclawice Panorama in Wroclaw in background

| Date | Mintage | VF20 | XF40 | MS60 | MS63 | MS65 |
|---|---|---|---|---|---|---|
| 2012 PM | 10,000 | PF63 20.00 | PF65 22.00 | | | |

### KM# 1460 1/2 CROWN

12.00 g., 0.999 Silver 0.3854 oz. ASW, 38.6 mm. **Ruler:** Elizabeth II **Subject:** European Football Championships 2012 **Rev:** Two footballers tackling, Cathedral of the Annunciation in Kharkiv and the Cathedral in Poznan in background

| Date | Mintage | VF20 | XF40 | MS60 | MS63 | MS65 |
|---|---|---|---|---|---|---|
| 2012 PM | 10,000 | PF63 20.00 | PF65 22.00 | | | |

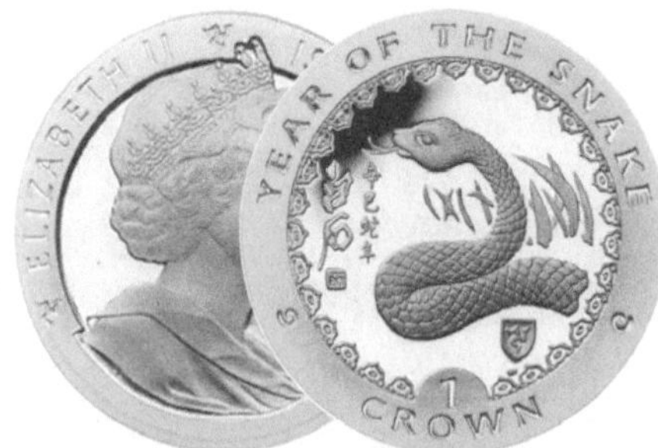


### KM# 1062 CROWN

28.28 g., Copper-Nickel, 38.6 mm. **Ruler:** Elizabeth II **Subject:** Year of the Snake **Obv:** Bust with tiara right **Rev:** Snake **Edge:** Reeded

| Date | Mintage | VF20 | XF40 | MS60 | MS63 | MS65 |
|---|---|---|---|---|---|---|
| 2001 | — | — | — | — | 10.00 | 15.00 |

### KM# 1062a CROWN

28.28 g., 0.925 Silver 0.841 oz. ASW, 38.6 mm. **Ruler:** Elizabeth II **Subject:** Year of the Snake **Obv:** Head with tiara right **Rev:** Snake **Edge:** Reeded

| Date | Mintage | VF20 | XF40 | MS60 | MS63 | MS65 |
|---|---|---|---|---|---|---|
| 2001 | 30,000 | PF63 42.00 | PF65 47.00 | | | |

### KM# 1063 CROWN

31.10 g., 0.9999 Gold 0.9999 oz. AGW, 32.7 mm. **Ruler:** Elizabeth II **Subject:** Year of the Snake **Obv:** Bust with tiara right **Rev:** Snake **Edge:** Reeded

| Date | Mintage | VF20 | XF40 | MS60 | MS63 | MS65 |
|---|---|---|---|---|---|---|
| 2001 | — | — | — | — | — | 1,800 |
| 2001 | 2,000 | PF63 1,825 | PF65 1,850 | | | |

### KM# 1072 CROWN

28.28 g., Copper-Nickel, 38.6 mm. **Ruler:** Elizabeth II **Subject:** Somali Kittens **Obv:** Bust with tiara right **Rev:** Two kittens **Edge:** Reeded

| Date | Mintage | VF20 | XF40 | MS60 | MS63 | MS65 |
|---|---|---|---|---|---|---|
| 2001 | — | — | — | — | 11.00 | 15.00 |

### KM# 1072a CROWN

31.10 g., 0.999 Silver 0.999 oz. ASW, 38.6 mm. **Ruler:** Elizabeth II **Subject:** Somali Kittens **Obv:** Bust with tiara right **Rev:** Two kittens **Edge:** Reeded

| Date | Mintage | VF20 | XF40 | MS60 | MS63 | MS65 |
|---|---|---|---|---|---|---|
| 2001 | 50,000 | PF63 42.00 | PF65 47.00 | | | |

### KM# 1073 CROWN

31.10 g., 0.9999 Gold 0.9999 oz. AGW, 32.7 mm. **Ruler:** Elizabeth II **Subject:** Somali Kittens **Obv:** Bust with tiara right **Rev:** Two kittens **Edge:** Reeded

| Date | Mintage | VF20 | XF40 | MS60 | MS63 | MS65 |
|---|---|---|---|---|---|---|
| 2001 | — | — | — | — | — | 1,825 |
| 2001 | 1,000 | PF63 1,850 | PF65 1,875 | | | |

### KM# 1076 CROWN

28.28 g., Copper-Nickel, 38.6 mm. **Ruler:** Elizabeth II **Subject:** Queen Mother **Obv:** Bust with tiara right **Rev:** 1948 Silver wedding anniversary **Edge:** Reeded

| Date | Mintage | VF20 | XF40 | MS60 | MS63 | MS65 |
|---|---|---|---|---|---|---|
| 2001 | — | — | — | — | 10.00 | 12.00 |

### KM# 1076a CROWN

28.28 g., 0.925 Silver 0.841 oz. ASW, 38.6 mm. **Ruler:** Elizabeth II **Subject:** Queen Mother **Obv:** Bust with tiara right **Rev:** 1948 Silver wedding anniversary **Edge:** Reeded

| Date | Mintage | VF20 | XF40 | MS60 | MS63 | MS65 |
|---|---|---|---|---|---|---|
| 2001 | 10,000 | PF63 42.00 | PF65 47.00 | | | |

### KM# 1077 CROWN

Copper-Nickel, 38.6 mm. **Ruler:** Elizabeth II **Subject:** Queen Mother **Obv:** Bust with tiara right **Rev:** 1948 holding infant Prince Charles **Edge:** Reeded

| Date | Mintage | VF20 | XF40 | MS60 | MS63 | MS65 |
|---|---|---|---|---|---|---|
| 2001 | — | — | — | — | 10.00 | 12.00 |

### KM# 1077a CROWN

28.28 g., 0.925 Silver 0.841 oz. ASW, 38.6 mm. **Ruler:** Elizabeth II **Subject:** Queen Mother **Obv:** Head with tiara right **Rev:** 1948 holding baby Prince Charles **Edge:** Reeded

| Date | Mintage | VF20 | XF40 | MS60 | MS63 | MS65 |
|---|---|---|---|---|---|---|
| 2001 | 10,000 | PF63 42.00 | PF65 47.00 | | | |

### KM# 1080 CROWN

Copper-Nickel, 38.6 mm. **Ruler:** Elizabeth II **Subject:** Martin Frobisher **Obv:** Bust with tiara right **Rev:** Bust at left, ship at right and map below **Edge:** Reeded

| Date | Mintage | VF20 | XF40 | MS60 | MS63 | MS65 |
|---|---|---|---|---|---|---|
| 2001 | — | — | — | — | 10.00 | 12.00 |

**KM# 1080a CROWN**
28.28 g., 0.925 Silver 0.841 oz. ASW, 38.6 mm. **Ruler:** Elizabeth II **Subject:** Martin Frobisher **Obv:** Bust of Queen Elizabeth II right **Edge:** Reeded

| Date | Mintage | VF20 | XF40 | MS60 | MS63 | MS65 |
|---|---|---|---|---|---|---|
| 2001 | 10,000 | **PF63** 42.00 | **PF65** 47.00 | | | |

**KM# 1081 CROWN**
Copper-Nickel, 38.6 mm. **Ruler:** Elizabeth II **Subject:** Roald Amundsen **Obv:** Bust with tiara right **Rev:** Bust at right, ship at center, dirigible above at left **Edge:** Reeded

| Date | Mintage | VF20 | XF40 | MS60 | MS63 | MS65 |
|---|---|---|---|---|---|---|
| 2001 | — | — | — | — | 10.00 | 12.00 |

**KM# 1081a CROWN**
28.28 g., 0.925 Silver 0.841 oz. ASW, 38.6 mm. **Ruler:** Elizabeth II **Subject:** Roald Amundsen **Obv:** Bust with tiara right **Rev:** Bust at right, ship at center, dirigible at upper left **Edge:** Reeded

| Date | Mintage | VF20 | XF40 | MS60 | MS63 | MS65 |
|---|---|---|---|---|---|---|
| 2001 | 10,000 | **PF63** 42.00 | **PF65** 47.00 | | | |

**KM# 1083 CROWN**
28.28 g., Copper-Nickel, 38.6 mm. **Ruler:** Elizabeth II **Subject:** Queen's 75th Birthday **Obv:** Bust with tiara right **Rev:** Flower bouquet **Edge:** Reeded

| Date | Mintage | VF20 | XF40 | MS60 | MS63 | MS65 |
|---|---|---|---|---|---|---|
| 2001 | — | — | — | — | 14.00 | 16.00 |

**KM# 1083a CROWN**
28.28 g., 0.925 Silver 0.841 oz. ASW, 38.6 mm. **Ruler:** Elizabeth II **Subject:** Queen's 75th Birthday **Obv:** Bust with tiara right **Rev:** Flower bouquet **Edge:** Reeded

| Date | Mintage | VF20 | XF40 | MS60 | MS63 | MS65 |
|---|---|---|---|---|---|---|
| 2001 | 10,000 | **PF63** 45.00 | **PF65** 50.00 | | | |

**KM# 1085 CROWN**
28.28 g., Copper-Nickel, 38.6 mm. **Ruler:** Elizabeth II **Subject:** Joey Dunlop (1952-2000) **Obv:** Bust with tiara right **Rev:** Motorcycle racer **Edge:** Reeded

| Date | Mintage | VF20 | XF40 | MS60 | MS63 | MS65 |
|---|---|---|---|---|---|---|
| 2001 Black finish | — | — | — | — | 10.00 | 12.00 |

**KM# 1085a CROWN**
28.28 g., 0.925 Silver 0.841 oz. ASW, 38.6 mm. **Ruler:** Elizabeth II **Subject:** Joey Dunlop (1952-2000) **Obv:** Bust with tiara right **Rev:** Motorcycle racer **Edge:** Reeded

| Date | Mintage | VF20 | XF40 | MS60 | MS63 | MS65 |
|---|---|---|---|---|---|---|
| 2001 | 10,000 | **PF63** 42.00 | **PF65** 47.00 | | | |

**KM# 1087 CROWN**
28.28 g., Copper-Nickel, 38.6 mm. **Ruler:** Elizabeth II **Series:** Harry Potter **Obv:** Bust with tiara right **Rev:** Harry with magic wand **Edge:** Reeded

| Date | Mintage | VF20 | XF40 | MS60 | MS63 | MS65 |
|---|---|---|---|---|---|---|
| 2001 | — | — | — | — | 10.00 | 12.00 |

**KM# 1087a CROWN**
28.28 g., 0.925 Silver 0.841 oz. ASW, 38.6 mm. **Ruler:** Elizabeth II **Series:** Harry Potter **Obv:** Bust with tiara right **Rev:** Harry with magic wand **Edge:** Reeded

| Date | Mintage | VF20 | XF40 | MS60 | MS63 | MS65 |
|---|---|---|---|---|---|---|
| 2001 | 15,000 | **PF63** 42.00 | **PF65** 47.00 | | | |

**KM# 1089 CROWN**
28.28 g., Copper-Nickel, 38.6 mm. **Ruler:** Elizabeth II **Series:** Harry Potter **Subject:** Journey to Hogwart's **Obv:** Bust with tiara right **Rev:** Boat full of children going to Hogwart's **Edge:** Reeded

| Date | Mintage | VF20 | XF40 | MS60 | MS63 | MS65 |
|---|---|---|---|---|---|---|
| 2001 | — | — | — | — | 10.00 | 12.00 |

**KM# 1089a CROWN**
28.28 g., 0.925 Silver 0.841 oz. ASW, 38.6 mm. **Ruler:** Elizabeth II **Series:** Harry Potter **Obv:** Bust with tiara right **Rev:** Boat full of children going to Hogwart's **Edge:** Reeded

| Date | Mintage | VF20 | XF40 | MS60 | MS63 | MS65 |
|---|---|---|---|---|---|---|
| 2001 | 15,000 | **PF63** 42.00 | **PF65** 47.00 | | | |

**KM# 1091 CROWN**
Copper-Nickel **Ruler:** Elizabeth II **Series:** Harry Potter **Subject:** First Quidditch Match **Obv:** Bust with tiara right **Rev:** Harry flying his Nimbus 2000

| Date | Mintage | VF20 | XF40 | MS60 | MS63 | MS65 |
|---|---|---|---|---|---|---|
| 2001 | — | — | — | — | 10.00 | 12.00 |

**KM# 1091a CROWN**
28.28 g., 0.925 Silver 0.841 oz. ASW **Ruler:** Elizabeth II **Series:** Harry Potter **Subject:** First Quidditch Match **Obv:** Bust with tiara right **Rev:** Harry flying his Nimbus 2000

| Date | Mintage | VF20 | XF40 | MS60 | MS63 | MS65 |
|---|---|---|---|---|---|---|
| 2001 | 15,000 | **PF63** 42.00 | **PF65** 47.00 | | | |

**KM# 1093 CROWN**
Copper-Nickel **Ruler:** Elizabeth II **Series:** Harry Potter **Subject:** Birth of Norbert **Obv:** Bust with tiara right **Rev:** Hagrid and children watching Norbert hatch

| Date | Mintage | VF20 | XF40 | MS60 | MS63 | MS65 |
|---|---|---|---|---|---|---|
| 2001 | — | — | — | — | 10.00 | 14.00 |

**KM# 1093a CROWN**
28.28 g., 0.925 Silver 0.841 oz. ASW **Ruler:** Elizabeth II **Series:** Harry Potter **Subject:** Birth of Norbert **Obv:** Bust with tiara right **Rev:** Hagrid and children watching Norbert hatch

| Date | Mintage | VF20 | XF40 | MS60 | MS63 | MS65 |
|---|---|---|---|---|---|---|
| 2001 | 15,000 | **PF63** 42.00 | **PF65** 47.00 | | | |

**KM# 1095 CROWN**
Copper-Nickel **Ruler:** Elizabeth II **Series:** Harry Potter **Subject:** School **Obv:** Bust with tiara right **Rev:** Harry in Potions class

| Date | Mintage | VF20 | XF40 | MS60 | MS63 | MS65 |
|---|---|---|---|---|---|---|
| 2001 | — | — | — | — | 10.00 | 12.00 |

**KM# 1095a CROWN**
28.28 g., 0.925 Silver 0.841 oz. ASW **Ruler:** Elizabeth II **Series:** Harry Potter **Subject:** School **Obv:** Bust with tiara right **Rev:** Harry in Potions class

| Date | Mintage | VF20 | XF40 | MS60 | MS63 | MS65 |
|---|---|---|---|---|---|---|
| 2001 | 15,000 | **PF63** 42.00 | **PF65** 47.00 | | | |

**KM# 1097 CROWN**
Copper-Nickel, 38.72 mm. **Ruler:** Elizabeth II **Series:** Harry Potter **Obv:** Bust with tiara right **Rev:** Harry catching the golden snitch **Edge:** Reeded

| Date | Mintage | VF20 | XF40 | MS60 | MS63 | MS65 |
|---|---|---|---|---|---|---|
| 2001 | — | — | — | — | 10.00 | 12.00 |

**KM# 1097a CROWN**
28.28 g., 0.925 Silver 0.841 oz. ASW, 38.71 mm. **Ruler:** Elizabeth II **Series:** Harry Potter **Obv:** Bust with tiara right **Rev:** Harry catching the golden snitch **Edge:** Reeded

| Date | Mintage | VF20 | XF40 | MS60 | MS63 | MS65 |
|---|---|---|---|---|---|---|
| 2001 | 15,000 | **PF63** 42.00 | **PF65** 47.00 | | | |

**KM# 1102 CROWN**
28.28 g., Copper-Nickel, 38.6 mm. **Ruler:** Elizabeth II **Subject:** Year of the Horse **Obv:** Bust with tiara right **Rev:** Two horses **Edge:** Reeded

| Date | Mintage | VF20 | XF40 | MS60 | MS63 | MS65 |
|---|---|---|---|---|---|---|
| 2002 | — | — | — | — | 12.00 | 15.00 |

**KM# 1102a CROWN**
28.28 g., 0.925 Silver 0.841 oz. ASW, 38.6 mm. **Ruler:** Elizabeth II **Subject:** Year of the Horse **Obv:** Bust with tiara right **Rev:** Two horses **Edge:** Reeded

| Date | Mintage | VF20 | XF40 | MS60 | MS63 | MS65 |
|---|---|---|---|---|---|---|
| 2002 | 30,000 | PF63 42.00 | PF65 47.00 | | | |

**KM# 1103 CROWN**
31.10 g., 0.9999 Gold 0.9998 oz. AGW **Ruler:** Elizabeth II **Subject:** Year of the Horse **Obv:** Bust with tiara right

| Date | Mintage | VF20 | XF40 | MS60 | MS63 | MS65 |
|---|---|---|---|---|---|---|
| 2002 | 2,000 | PF65 1,800 | | | | |

**KM# 1111 CROWN**
28.28 g., Copper-Nickel, 38.6 mm. **Ruler:** Elizabeth II **Subject:** Bengal Cat **Obv:** Bust with tiara right **Rev:** Cat and kitten **Edge:** Reeded

| Date | Mintage | VF20 | XF40 | MS60 | MS63 | MS65 |
|---|---|---|---|---|---|---|
| 2002 | — | — | — | — | 12.50 | 14.00 |

**KM# 1111a CROWN**
31.10 g., 0.999 Silver 0.999 oz. ASW, 38.6 mm. **Ruler:** Elizabeth II **Subject:** Bengal Cat **Obv:** Bust with tiara right **Rev:** Cat and kitten **Edge:** Reeded

| Date | Mintage | VF20 | XF40 | MS60 | MS63 | MS65 |
|---|---|---|---|---|---|---|
| 2002 | 10,000 | PF65 70.00 | | | | |

**KM# 1112 CROWN**
31.10 g., 0.999 Gold 0.999 oz. AGW, 33 mm. **Ruler:** Elizabeth II **Subject:** Bengal Cat **Obv:** Bust with tiara right **Rev:** Cat and kitten **Edge:** Reeded

| Date | Mintage | VF20 | XF40 | MS60 | MS63 | MS65 |
|---|---|---|---|---|---|---|
| 2002 | — | — | — | — | — | 1,800 |
| 2002 | 1,000 | PF63 1,825 | PF65 1,850 | | | |

**KM# 1115 CROWN**
28.28 g., Copper-Nickel, 38.6 mm. **Ruler:** Elizabeth II **Subject:** Olympics - Salt Lake City **Obv:** Bust with tiara right **Rev:** Skier, torch and flag **Edge:** Reeded

| Date | Mintage | VF20 | XF40 | MS60 | MS63 | MS65 |
|---|---|---|---|---|---|---|
| 2002 | — | — | — | — | 10.00 | 12.00 |

**KM# 1115a CROWN**
28.28 g., 0.925 Silver 0.841 oz. ASW, 38.6 mm. **Ruler:** Elizabeth II **Subject:** Olympics - Salt Lake City **Obv:** Bust with tiara right **Rev:** Skier, torch and flag **Edge:** Reeded

| Date | Mintage | VF20 | XF40 | MS60 | MS63 | MS65 |
|---|---|---|---|---|---|---|
| 2002 | 10,000 | PF63 42.00 | PF65 47.00 | | | |

**KM# 1116 CROWN**
28.28 g., Copper-Nickel, 38.6 mm. **Ruler:** Elizabeth II **Subject:** Olympics - Salt Lake City **Obv:** Bust with tiara right **Rev:** Bobsled, torch and stadium **Edge:** Reeded

| Date | Mintage | VF20 | XF40 | MS60 | MS63 | MS65 |
|---|---|---|---|---|---|---|
| 2002 | — | — | — | — | 10.00 | 12.00 |

**KM# 1116a CROWN**
28.28 g., 0.925 Silver 0.841 oz. ASW, 38.6 mm. **Ruler:** Elizabeth II **Subject:** Olympics - Salt Lake City **Obv:** Bust with tiara right **Rev:** Bobsled, torch and stadium **Edge:** Reeded

| Date | Mintage | VF20 | XF40 | MS60 | MS63 | MS65 |
|---|---|---|---|---|---|---|
| 2002 | 10,000 | PF63 42.00 | PF65 47.00 | | | |

**KM# 1118 CROWN**
28.28 g., Copper-Nickel, 38.6 mm. **Ruler:** Elizabeth II **Subject:** Queen Mother's Love of Horses **Obv:** Bust with tiara right **Rev:** Queen Mother and horse **Edge:** Reeded

| Date | Mintage | VF20 | XF40 | MS60 | MS63 | MS65 |
|---|---|---|---|---|---|---|
| 2002 | — | — | — | — | 10.00 | 12.00 |

**KM# 1118a CROWN**
28.28 g., 0.925 Silver 0.841 oz. ASW, 38.6 mm. **Ruler:** Elizabeth II **Subject:** Queen Mother's Love of Horses **Obv:** Bust with tiara right **Rev:** Queen Mother and horse **Edge:** Reeded

| Date | Mintage | VF20 | XF40 | MS60 | MS63 | MS65 |
|---|---|---|---|---|---|---|
| 2002 | 10,000 | PF63 42.00 | PF65 47.00 | | | |

**KM# 1119 CROWN**
35.00 g., 0.750 Gold 0.844 oz. AGW, 38.6 mm. **Ruler:** Elizabeth II **Subject:** Golden Jubilee **Obv:** Bust with tiara right **Rev:** Queen Elizabeth II's young laureate bust right **Edge:** Reeded **Note:** Red Gold center in a White Gold inner ring within a Yellow Gold outer ring.

| Date | Mintage | VF20 | XF40 | MS60 | MS63 | MS65 |
|---|---|---|---|---|---|---|
| 2002 | 999 | PF65 1,550 | | | | |

**KM# 1121 CROWN**
28.28 g., Copper-Nickel, 38.6 mm. **Ruler:** Elizabeth II **Subject:** World Cup 2002 Japan - Korea **Obv:** Bust with tiara right **Rev:** Player running right **Edge:** Reeded

| Date | Mintage | VF20 | XF40 | MS60 | MS63 | MS65 |
|---|---|---|---|---|---|---|
| 2002 | — | — | — | — | 10.00 | 12.00 |

**KM# 1121a CROWN**
28.28 g., 0.925 Silver 0.841 oz. ASW, 38.6 mm. **Ruler:** Elizabeth II **Subject:** World Cup 2002 Japan - Korea **Obv:** Bust with tiara right **Rev:** Player running right **Edge:** Reeded

| Date | Mintage | VF20 | XF40 | MS60 | MS63 | MS65 |
|---|---|---|---|---|---|---|
| 2002 | 10,000 | PF63 42.00 | PF65 47.00 | | | |

**KM# 1123 CROWN**
28.28 g., Copper-Nickel, 38.6 mm. **Ruler:** Elizabeth II **Subject:** World Cup 2002 Japan - Korea **Obv:** Bust with tiara right **Rev:** Player kicking to right **Edge:** Reeded

| Date | Mintage | VF20 | XF40 | MS60 | MS63 | MS65 |
|---|---|---|---|---|---|---|
| 2002 | — | — | — | — | 10.00 | 12.00 |

**KM# 1123a CROWN**
28.28 g., 0.925 Silver 0.841 oz. ASW, 38.6 mm. **Ruler:** Elizabeth II **Subject:** World Cup 2002 Japan - Korea **Obv:** Bust with tiara right **Rev:** Player kicking to right **Edge:** Reeded

| Date | Mintage | VF20 | XF40 | MS60 | MS63 | MS65 |
|---|---|---|---|---|---|---|
| 2002 | 10,000 | PF63 42.00 | PF65 47.00 | | | |

### KM# 1125 CROWN

28.28 g., Copper-Nickel, 38.6 mm. **Ruler:** Elizabeth II **Subject:** World Cup 2002 Japan - Korea **Obv:** Bust with tiara right **Rev:** Player kicking to left **Edge:** Reeded

| Date | Mintage | VF20 | XF40 | MS60 | MS63 | MS65 |
|---|---|---|---|---|---|---|
| 2002 | — | — | — | — | 10.00 | 12.00 |

### KM# 1125a CROWN

28.28 g., 0.925 Silver 0.841 oz. ASW, 38.6 mm. **Ruler:** Elizabeth II **Subject:** World Cup 2002 Japan - Korea **Obv:** Bust with tiara right **Rev:** Player kicking to left **Edge:** Reeded

| Date | Mintage | VF20 | XF40 | MS60 | MS63 | MS65 |
|---|---|---|---|---|---|---|
| 2002 | 10,000 | PF63 42.00 | PF65 47.00 | | | |

### KM# 1127 CROWN

28.28 g., Copper-Nickel, 38.6 mm. **Ruler:** Elizabeth II **Subject:** World Cup 2002 Japan - Korea **Obv:** Bust with tiara right **Rev:** Player running to left **Edge:** Reeded

| Date | Mintage | VF20 | XF40 | MS60 | MS63 | MS65 |
|---|---|---|---|---|---|---|
| 2002 | — | — | — | — | 10.00 | 12.00 |

### KM# 1127a CROWN

28.28 g., 0.925 Silver 0.841 oz. ASW, 38.6 mm. **Ruler:** Elizabeth II **Subject:** World Cup 2002 Japan - Korea **Obv:** Bust with tiara right **Rev:** Player running to left **Edge:** Reeded

| Date | Mintage | VF20 | XF40 | MS60 | MS63 | MS65 |
|---|---|---|---|---|---|---|
| 2002 | 10,000 | PF63 42.00 | PF65 47.00 | | | |

### KM# 1131 CROWN

28.28 g., Copper-Nickel, 38.6 mm. **Ruler:** Elizabeth II **Subject:** Queen Elizabeth II's Golden Jubilee **Obv:** Bust with tiara right **Rev:** Seated crowned Queen holding scepter at her coronation **Edge:** Reeded

| Date | Mintage | VF20 | XF40 | MS60 | MS63 | MS65 |
|---|---|---|---|---|---|---|
| 2002 | — | — | — | — | 10.00 | 12.00 |

### KM# 1131a CROWN

28.28 g., Gold Color Base Metal, 38.6 mm. **Ruler:** Elizabeth II **Subject:** Queen Elizabeth II's Golden Jubilee **Obv:** Bust with tiara right **Rev:** Seated crowned Queen holding scepter at her coronation **Edge:** Reeded

| Date | Mintage | VF20 | XF40 | MS60 | MS63 | MS65 |
|---|---|---|---|---|---|---|
| 2002 | 15,000 | — | — | — | 10.00 | 12.00 |

### KM# 1131b CROWN

28.28 g., 0.925 Gold Clad Silver 0.841 oz., 38.6 mm. **Ruler:** Elizabeth II **Subject:** Queen Elizabeth II's Golden Jubilee **Obv:** Bust with tiara right **Rev:** Seated crowned Queen holding scepter at her coronation **Edge:** Reeded

| Date | Mintage | VF20 | XF40 | MS60 | MS63 | MS65 |
|---|---|---|---|---|---|---|
| 2002 | 10,000 | PF63 42.00 | PF65 47.00 | | | |

### KM# 1133 CROWN

28.28 g., Copper-Nickel, 38.6 mm. **Ruler:** Elizabeth II **Subject:** Queen Elizabeth II's Golden Jubilee **Obv:** Bust with tiara right **Rev:** Queen on horse **Edge:** Reeded

| Date | Mintage | VF20 | XF40 | MS60 | MS63 | MS65 |
|---|---|---|---|---|---|---|
| 2002 | — | — | — | — | 10.00 | 12.00 |

### KM# 1133a CROWN

28.28 g., Gold Color Base Metal, 38.6 mm. **Ruler:** Elizabeth II **Subject:** Queen Elizabeth II's Golden Jubilee **Obv:** Bust with tiara right **Rev:** Queen on horse **Edge:** Reeded

| Date | Mintage | VF20 | XF40 | MS60 | MS63 | MS65 |
|---|---|---|---|---|---|---|
| 2002 | 15,000 | — | — | — | 10.00 | 12.00 |

### KM# 1133b CROWN

28.28 g., 0.925 Gold Clad Silver 0.841 oz., 38.6 mm. **Ruler:** Elizabeth II **Subject:** Queen Elizabeth II's Golden Jubilee **Obv:** Bust with tiara right **Rev:** Queen on horse half left **Edge:** Reeded

| Date | Mintage | VF20 | XF40 | MS60 | MS63 | MS65 |
|---|---|---|---|---|---|---|
| 2002 | 10,000 | PF63 42.00 | PF65 47.00 | | | |

### KM# 1135 CROWN

28.28 g., Copper-Nickel, 38.6 mm. **Ruler:** Elizabeth II **Subject:** Queen Elizabeth II's Golden Jubilee **Obv:** Bust with tiara right **Rev:** Queen with her pet Corgi **Edge:** Reeded

| Date | Mintage | VF20 | XF40 | MS60 | MS63 | MS65 |
|---|---|---|---|---|---|---|
| 2002 | — | — | — | — | 10.00 | 12.00 |

### KM# 1135a CROWN

28.28 g., Gold Color Base Metal, 38.6 mm. **Ruler:** Elizabeth II **Subject:** Queen Elizabeth II's Golden Jubilee **Obv:** Bust with tiara right **Rev:** Seated Queen with her pet Corgi **Edge:** Reeded

| Date | Mintage | VF20 | XF40 | MS60 | MS63 | MS65 |
|---|---|---|---|---|---|---|
| 2002 | 15,000 | — | — | — | 10.00 | 12.00 |

### KM# 1135b CROWN

28.28 g., 0.925 Gold Clad Silver 0.841 oz., 38.6 mm. **Ruler:** Elizabeth II **Subject:** Queen Elizabeth II's Golden Jubilee **Obv:** Bust with tiara right **Rev:** Queen with her pet Corgi **Edge:** Reeded

| Date | Mintage | VF20 | XF40 | MS60 | MS63 | MS65 |
|---|---|---|---|---|---|---|
| 2002 | 10,000 | PF63 42.00 | PF65 47.00 | | | |

### KM# 1137 CROWN

28.28 g., Copper-Nickel, 38.6 mm. **Ruler:** Elizabeth II **Subject:** Queen Elizabeth II's Golden Jubilee **Obv:** Bust with tiara right **Rev:** Queen at war memorial **Edge:** Reeded

| Date | Mintage | VF20 | XF40 | MS60 | MS63 | MS65 |
|---|---|---|---|---|---|---|
| 2002 | — | — | — | — | 10.00 | 12.00 |

### KM# 1137a CROWN

28.28 g., Gold Color Base Metal, 38.6 mm. **Ruler:** Elizabeth II **Subject:** Queen Elizabeth II's Golden Jubilee **Obv:** Bust with tiara right **Rev:** Queen at war memorial **Edge:** Reeded

| Date | Mintage | VF20 | XF40 | MS60 | MS63 | MS65 |
|---|---|---|---|---|---|---|
| 2002 | 15,000 | — | — | — | 10.00 | 12.00 |

### KM# 1137b CROWN

28.28 g., Gold Clad Silver, 38.6 mm. **Ruler:** Elizabeth II **Subject:** Queen Elizabeth II's Golden Jubilee **Obv:** Bust with tiara right **Rev:** Queen at war memorial **Edge:** Reeded

| Date | Mintage | VF20 | XF40 | MS60 | MS63 | MS65 |
|---|---|---|---|---|---|---|
| 2002 | 10,000 | PF63 42.00 | PF65 47.00 | | | |

### KM# 1139 CROWN

Copper-Nickel dark patina, 38.6 mm. **Ruler:** Elizabeth II **Subject:** Queen Mother **Obv:** Bust with tiara right **Rev:** Queen Mother and Castle May **Edge:** Reeded

| Date | Mintage | VF20 | XF40 | MS60 | MS63 | MS65 |
|---|---|---|---|---|---|---|
| 2002 | — | — | — | — | 10.00 | 12.00 |

### KM# 1139a CROWN

28.28 g., 0.925 Silver 0.841 oz. ASW, 38.6 mm. **Ruler:** Elizabeth II **Obv:** Head with tiara right with blackened legends **Rev:** Queen Mother standing at left in front of Castle May with blackened legends

| Date | Mintage | VF20 | XF40 | MS60 | MS63 | MS65 |
|---|---|---|---|---|---|---|
| 2002 | 10,000 | PF63 42.00 | PF65 47.00 | | | |

### KM# 1141 CROWN

28.28 g., Copper-Nickel, 38.6 mm. **Ruler:** Elizabeth II **Subject:** Princess Diana **Obv:** Bust with tiara right **Rev:** Diana's bust facing **Edge:** Reeded

| Date | Mintage | VF20 | XF40 | MS60 | MS63 | MS65 |
|---|---|---|---|---|---|---|
| 2002 | — | — | — | — | 10.00 | 12.00 |

### KM# 1141a CROWN

28.28 g., 0.925 Silver 0.841 oz. ASW, 38.6 mm. **Ruler:** Elizabeth II **Subject:** Princess Diana **Obv:** Bust with tiara right **Rev:** Diana facing **Edge:** Reeded

| Date | Mintage | VF20 | XF40 | MS60 | MS63 | MS65 |
|---|---|---|---|---|---|---|
| 2002 | 10,000 | PF63 42.00 | PF65 47.00 | | | |

### KM# 1144 CROWN

28.28 g., Copper-Nickel, 38.6 mm. **Ruler:** Elizabeth II **Series:** Harry Potter **Obv:** Bust with tiara right **Rev:** Tom Riddle twirling Harry's magic wand **Edge:** Reeded

| Date | Mintage | VF20 | XF40 | MS60 | MS63 | MS65 |
|---|---|---|---|---|---|---|
| 2002 PM | — | — | — | — | 10.00 | 12.00 |

### KM# 1144a CROWN

28.28 g., 0.925 Silver 0.841 oz. ASW, 28.6 mm. **Ruler:** Elizabeth II **Series:** Harry Potter **Obv:** Bust with tiara right **Rev:** Tom Riddle twirling Harry's magic wand **Edge:** Reeded

| Date | Mintage | VF20 | XF40 | MS60 | MS63 | MS65 |
|---|---|---|---|---|---|---|
| 2002 PM | 15,000 | PF63 45.00 | PF65 50.00 | | | |

### KM# 1146 CROWN

28.28 g., Copper-Nickel, 38.6 mm. **Ruler:** Elizabeth II **Series:** Harry Potter **Obv:** Bust with tiara right **Rev:** Harry and friends making Polyjuice potion **Edge:** Reeded

| Date | Mintage | VF20 | XF40 | MS60 | MS63 | MS65 |
|---|---|---|---|---|---|---|
| 2002 PM | — | — | — | — | 10.00 | 12.00 |

### KM# 1146a CROWN

28.28 g., 0.925 Silver 0.841 oz. ASW, 38.6 mm. **Ruler:** Elizabeth II **Series:** Harry Potter **Obv:** Bust with tiara right **Rev:** Harry Potter and friends making Polyjuice potion **Edge:** Reeded

| Date | Mintage | VF20 | XF40 | MS60 | MS63 | MS65 |
|---|---|---|---|---|---|---|
| 2002 PM | 15,000 | PF63 45.00 | PF65 50.00 | | | |

### KM# 1148 CROWN

28.28 g., Copper-Nickel, 38.6 mm. **Ruler:** Elizabeth II **Series:** Harry Potter **Obv:** Bust with tiara right **Rev:** Harry arrives at the Burrow in a flying car **Edge:** Reeded

| Date | Mintage | VF20 | XF40 | MS60 | MS63 | MS65 |
|---|---|---|---|---|---|---|
| 2002 PM | — | — | — | — | 10.00 | 12.00 |

### KM# 1148a CROWN

28.28 g., 0.925 Silver 0.841 oz. ASW, 38.6 mm. **Ruler:** Elizabeth II **Series:** Harry Potter **Obv:** Bust with tiara right **Rev:** Harry arrives at the Burrow in a flying car **Edge:** Reeded

| Date | Mintage | VF20 | XF40 | MS60 | MS63 | MS65 |
|---|---|---|---|---|---|---|
| 2002 PM | 15,000 | PF63 45.00 | PF65 50.00 | | | |

### KM# 1150 CROWN

28.28 g., Copper-Nickel, 38.6 mm. **Ruler:** Elizabeth II **Series:** Harry Potter **Obv:** Bust with tiara right **Rev:** Harry retrieves Gryffindor sword from sorting hat **Edge:** Reeded

| Date | Mintage | VF20 | XF40 | MS60 | MS63 | MS65 |
|---|---|---|---|---|---|---|
| 2002 PM | — | — | — | — | 10.00 | 12.00 |

### KM# 1150a CROWN

28.28 g., 0.925 Silver 0.841 oz. ASW, 38.6 mm. **Ruler:** Elizabeth II **Series:** Harry Potter **Obv:** Bust with tiara right **Rev:** Harry retrieves Gryffindor sword from sorting hat **Edge:** Reeded

| Date | Mintage | VF20 | XF40 | MS60 | MS63 | MS65 |
|---|---|---|---|---|---|---|
| 2002 PM | 15,000 | PF63 45.00 | PF65 50.00 | | | |

### KM# 1152 CROWN

28.28 g., Copper-Nickel, 38.6 mm. **Ruler:** Elizabeth II **Series:** Harry Potter **Obv:** Bust with tiara right **Rev:** Harry and Ron encounter the spider Aragog **Edge:** Reeded

| Date | Mintage | VF20 | XF40 | MS60 | MS63 | MS65 |
|---|---|---|---|---|---|---|
| 2002 PM | — | — | — | — | 10.00 | 12.00 |

### KM# 1152a CROWN

28.28 g., 0.925 Silver 0.841 oz. ASW, 38.6 mm. **Ruler:** Elizabeth II **Series:** Harry Potter **Obv:** Bust with tiara right **Rev:** Harry and Ron encounter the spider Aragog **Edge:** Reeded

| Date | Mintage | VF20 | XF40 | MS60 | MS63 | MS65 |
|---|---|---|---|---|---|---|
| 2002 PM | 15,000 | PF63 45.00 | PF65 50.00 | | | |

### KM# 1154 CROWN

28.28 g., Copper-Nickel, 38.6 mm. **Ruler:** Elizabeth II **Series:** Harry Potter **Obv:** Bust with tiara right **Rev:** Harry in hospital with Dobby **Edge:** Reeded

| Date | Mintage | VF20 | XF40 | MS60 | MS63 | MS65 |
|---|---|---|---|---|---|---|
| 2002 PM | — | — | — | — | 10.00 | 12.00 |

### KM# 1154a CROWN

28.28 g., 0.925 Silver 0.841 oz. ASW, 38.6 mm. **Ruler:** Elizabeth II **Series:** Harry Potter **Obv:** Bust with tiara right **Rev:** Harry in hospital with Dobby **Edge:** Reeded

| Date | Mintage | VF20 | XF40 | MS60 | MS63 | MS65 |
|---|---|---|---|---|---|---|
| 2002 PM | 15,000 | PF63 45.00 | PF65 50.00 | | | |

### KM# 1165 CROWN

28.28 g., Copper-Nickel, 38.6 mm. **Ruler:** Elizabeth II **Subject:** Cat **Obv:** Bust with tiara right **Rev:** Two Balinese kittens **Edge:** Reeded

| Date | Mintage | VF20 | XF40 | MS60 | MS63 | MS65 |
|---|---|---|---|---|---|---|
| 2003 PM | — | — | — | — | 12.00 | 14.00 |

### KM# 1165a CROWN

31.10 g., 0.999 Silver 0.999 oz. ASW, 38.6 mm. **Ruler:** Elizabeth II **Subject:** Cat **Obv:** Head with tiara right **Rev:** Two Balinese kittens **Edge:** Reeded

| Date | Mintage | VF20 | XF40 | MS60 | MS63 | MS65 |
|---|---|---|---|---|---|---|
| 2003 PM | 50,000 | PF65 70.00 | | | | |

### KM# 1166 CROWN

31.10 g., 0.9999 Gold 0.9999 oz. AGW, 32.7 mm. **Ruler:** Elizabeth II **Subject:** Cat **Obv:** Head with tiara right **Rev:** Two Balinese kittens **Edge:** Reeded

| Date | Mintage | VF20 | XF40 | MS60 | MS63 | MS65 |
|---|---|---|---|---|---|---|
| 2003 PM | — | — | — | — | — | 1,800 |
| 2003 PM | — | PF63 1,825 | PF65 1,850 | | | |

### KM# 1171 CROWN

28.28 g., Copper-Nickel, 38.6 mm. **Ruler:** Elizabeth II **Subject:** Year of the Goat **Obv:** Bust with tiara right **Rev:** Three goats **Edge:** Reeded

| Date | Mintage | VF20 | XF40 | MS60 | MS63 | MS65 |
|---|---|---|---|---|---|---|
| 2003 PM | — | — | — | — | 12.00 | 14.00 |

### KM# 1171a CROWN

28.28 g., 0.925 Silver 0.841 oz. ASW, 38.6 mm. **Ruler:** Elizabeth II **Subject:** Year of the Goat **Obv:** Bust with tiara right **Rev:** Three goats **Edge:** Reeded

| Date | Mintage | VF20 | XF40 | MS60 | MS63 | MS65 |
|---|---|---|---|---|---|---|
| 2003 PM | — | PF63 42.00 | PF65 47.00 | | | |

### KM# 1172 CROWN

31.10 g., 0.9999 Gold 0.9999 oz. AGW, 32.7 mm. **Ruler:** Elizabeth II **Subject:** Year of the Goat **Obv:** Bust with tiara right **Rev:** Three goats **Edge:** Reeded

| Date | Mintage | VF20 | XF40 | MS60 | MS63 | MS65 |
|---|---|---|---|---|---|---|
| 2003 PM | 2,000 | PF65 1,850 | | | | |

### KM# 1174 CROWN

28.53 g., Copper-Nickel, 38.6 mm. **Ruler:** Elizabeth II **Obv:** Bust with tiara right **Rev:** The Star of India sailing ship **Edge:** Reeded

| Date | Mintage | VF20 | XF40 | MS60 | MS63 | MS65 |
|---|---|---|---|---|---|---|
| 2003 PM | — | — | — | — | 10.00 | 12.00 |

## KM# 1176 CROWN

28.28 g., Copper-Nickel, 38.6 mm. **Ruler:** Elizabeth II **Subject:** Olympics **Obv:** Bust with tiara right **Rev:** Swimmers **Edge:** Reeded

| Date | Mintage | VF20 | XF40 | MS60 | MS63 | MS65 |
|---|---|---|---|---|---|---|
| 2003 PM | — | — | — | — | 10.00 | 12.00 |

## KM# 1176a CROWN

28.28 g., 0.925 Silver 0.841 oz. ASW, 38.6 mm. **Ruler:** Elizabeth II **Subject:** Olympics **Obv:** Bust with tiara right **Rev:** Swimmers **Edge:** Reeded

| Date | Mintage | VF20 | XF40 | MS60 | MS63 | MS65 |
|---|---|---|---|---|---|---|
| 2003 PM | 10,000 | PF63 42.00 | PF65 47.00 | | | |

## KM# 1178 CROWN

28.28 g., Copper-Nickel, 38.6 mm. **Ruler:** Elizabeth II **Subject:** Olympics **Obv:** Bust with tiara right **Rev:** Runners **Edge:** Reeded

| Date | Mintage | VF20 | XF40 | MS60 | MS63 | MS65 |
|---|---|---|---|---|---|---|
| 2003 PM | — | — | — | — | 10.00 | 12.00 |

## KM# 1178a CROWN

28.28 g., 0.925 Silver 0.841 oz. ASW, 38.6 mm. **Ruler:** Elizabeth II **Subject:** Olympics **Obv:** Bust with tiara right **Rev:** Runners **Edge:** Reeded

| Date | Mintage | VF20 | XF40 | MS60 | MS63 | MS65 |
|---|---|---|---|---|---|---|
| 2003 PM | 10,000 | PF63 42.00 | PF65 47.00 | | | |

## KM# 1180 CROWN

28.28 g., Copper-Nickel, 38.6 mm. **Ruler:** Elizabeth II **Subject:** Olympics **Obv:** Bust with tiara right **Rev:** Bicyclists **Edge:** Reeded

| Date | Mintage | VF20 | XF40 | MS60 | MS63 | MS65 |
|---|---|---|---|---|---|---|
| 2003 PM | — | — | — | — | 10.00 | 12.00 |

## KM# 1180a CROWN

28.28 g., 0.925 Silver 0.841 oz. ASW, 38.6 mm. **Ruler:** Elizabeth II **Subject:** Olympics **Obv:** Bust with tiara right **Rev:** Bicyclists **Edge:** Reeded

| Date | Mintage | VF20 | XF40 | MS60 | MS63 | MS65 |
|---|---|---|---|---|---|---|
| 2003 PM | 10,000 | PF63 42.00 | PF65 47.00 | | | |

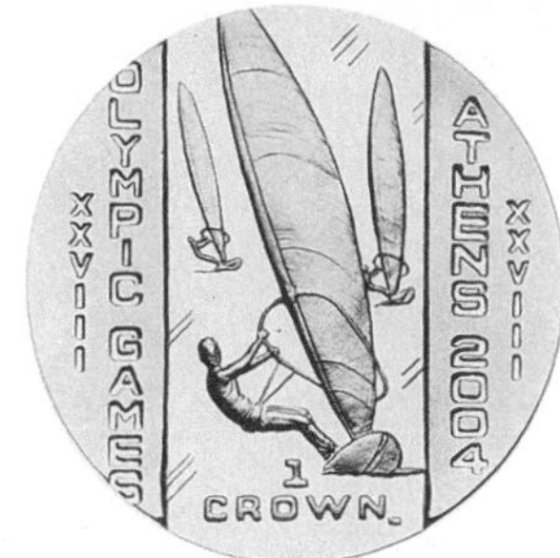

## KM# 1182 CROWN

28.28 g., Copper-Nickel, 38.6 mm. **Ruler:** Elizabeth II **Subject:** Olympics **Obv:** Bust with tiara right **Rev:** Sail Boarders **Edge:** Reeded

| Date | Mintage | VF20 | XF40 | MS60 | MS63 | MS65 |
|---|---|---|---|---|---|---|
| 2003 PM | — | — | — | — | 10.00 | 12.00 |

## KM# 1182a CROWN

28.28 g., 0.925 Silver 0.841 oz. ASW, 38.6 mm. **Ruler:** Elizabeth II **Subject:** Olympics **Obv:** Bust with tiara right **Rev:** Sail Boarders **Edge:** Reeded

| Date | Mintage | VF20 | XF40 | MS60 | MS63 | MS65 |
|---|---|---|---|---|---|---|
| 2003 PM | 10,000 | PF63 42.00 | PF65 47.00 | | | |

## KM# 1185 CROWN

28.28 g., Copper-Nickel, 38.6 mm. **Ruler:** Elizabeth II **Obv:** Bust with tiara right **Rev:** Lord of the Rings characters **Edge:** Reeded

| Date | Mintage | VF20 | XF40 | MS60 | MS63 | MS65 |
|---|---|---|---|---|---|---|
| 2003 PM | 100,000 | — | — | — | 12.50 | 14.50 |

## KM# 1185a CROWN

28.28 g., 0.925 Silver 0.841 oz. ASW, 38.6 mm. **Ruler:** Elizabeth II **Obv:** Bust with tiara right **Rev:** Lord of the Rings characters **Edge:** Reeded

| Date | Mintage | VF20 | XF40 | MS60 | MS63 | MS65 |
|---|---|---|---|---|---|---|
| 2003 PM | 10,000 | PF63 45.00 | PF65 50.00 | | | |

## KM# 1190 CROWN

31.10 g., 0.9999 Gold 0.9999 oz. AGW, 32.7 mm. **Ruler:** Elizabeth II **Subject:** Lord of the Rings **Obv:** Bust with tiara right **Rev:** Man on horse **Edge:** Reeded

| Date | Mintage | VF20 | XF40 | MS60 | MS63 | MS65 |
|---|---|---|---|---|---|---|
| 2003 PM | 1,000 | PF65 1,850 | | | | |

## KM# 1191 CROWN

28.28 g., 0.925 Silver 0.841 oz. ASW, 38.6 mm. **Ruler:** Elizabeth II **Subject:** Lord of the Rings **Obv:** Bust with tiara right **Rev:** Man with short sword **Edge:** Reeded

| Date | Mintage | VF20 | XF40 | MS60 | MS63 | MS65 |
|---|---|---|---|---|---|---|
| 2003 PM | 5,000 | PF65 47.50 | | | | |

## KM# 1192 CROWN

28.28 g., 0.925 Silver 0.841 oz. ASW, 38.6 mm. **Ruler:** Elizabeth II **Subject:** Lord of the Rings **Obv:** Bust with tiara right **Rev:** Aragorn with broadsword **Edge:** Reeded

| Date | Mintage | VF20 | XF40 | MS60 | MS63 | MS65 |
|---|---|---|---|---|---|---|
| 2003 PM | 5,000 | PF65 47.50 | | | | |

## KM# 1193 CROWN

28.28 g., 0.925 Silver 0.841 oz. ASW, 38.6 mm. **Ruler:** Elizabeth II **Subject:** Lord of the Rings **Obv:** Bust with tiara right **Rev:** Legolas **Edge:** Reeded

| Date | Mintage | VF20 | XF40 | MS60 | MS63 | MS65 |
|---|---|---|---|---|---|---|
| 2003 PM | 5,000 | PF65 47.50 | | | | |

## KM# 1194 CROWN

28.28 g., 0.925 Silver 0.841 oz. ASW, 38.6 mm. **Ruler:** Elizabeth II **Subject:** Lord of the Rings **Obv:** Bust with tiara right **Rev:** Gimli with two battle axes **Edge:** Reeded

| Date | Mintage | VF20 | XF40 | MS60 | MS63 | MS65 |
|---|---|---|---|---|---|---|
| 2003 PM | 5,000 | PF65 47.50 | | | | |

## KM# 1195 CROWN

28.28 g., 0.925 Silver 0.841 oz. ASW, 38.6 mm. **Ruler:** Elizabeth II **Subject:** Lord of the Rings **Obv:** Bust with tiara right **Rev:** Man on horse **Edge:** Reeded

| Date | Mintage | VF20 | XF40 | MS60 | MS63 | MS65 |
|---|---|---|---|---|---|---|
| 2003 PM | 5,000 | PF65 47.50 | | | | |

## KM# 1196 CROWN

28.44 g., Copper-Nickel, 38.6 mm. **Ruler:** Elizabeth II **Obv:** Bust with tiara right **Rev:** Four pre-1918 airplanes **Edge:** Reeded

| Date | Mintage | VF20 | XF40 | MS60 | MS63 | MS65 |
|---|---|---|---|---|---|---|
| 2003 PM | — | — | — | — | 10.00 | 12.00 |

## KM# 1197 CROWN

28.44 g., Copper-Nickel, 38.6 mm. **Obv:** Bust with tiara right **Rev:** Propeller plain, Zeppelin and two jet airliners **Edge:** Reeded

| Date | Mintage | VF20 | XF40 | MS60 | MS63 | MS65 |
|---|---|---|---|---|---|---|
| 2003 PM | — | — | — | — | 10.00 | 12.00 |

## KM# 1201 CROWN

28.28 g., Copper-Nickel, 38.6 mm. **Ruler:** Elizabeth II **Obv:** Bust with tiara right **Rev:** European Union map within hand held rope circle **Edge:** Reeded

| Date | Mintage | VF20 | XF40 | MS60 | MS63 | MS65 |
|---|---|---|---|---|---|---|
| 2004 PM | — | — | — | — | 10.00 | 12.00 |

## KM# 1201a CROWN

28.28 g., 0.925 Silver 0.841 oz. ASW, 38.6 mm. **Ruler:** Elizabeth II **Obv:** Bust with tiara right **Rev:** European Union map within a hand held rope circle **Edge:** Reeded

| Date | Mintage | VF20 | XF40 | MS60 | MS63 | MS65 |
|---|---|---|---|---|---|---|
| 2004 PM | 10,000 | PF63 45.00 | PF65 50.00 | | | |

## KM# 1202 CROWN

28.28 g., Copper-Nickel, 38.6 mm. **Ruler:** Elizabeth II **Obv:** Bust with tiara right **Rev:** Harry Potter and patron fighting off a Deventer **Edge:** Reeded

| Date | Mintage | VF20 | XF40 | MS60 | MS63 | MS65 |
|---|---|---|---|---|---|---|
| 2004 PM | — | — | — | — | 15.00 | 17.00 |

## KM# 1202a CROWN

28.28 g., 0.925 Silver 0.841 oz. ASW, 38.6 mm. **Ruler:** Elizabeth II **Obv:** Bust with tiara right **Rev:** Harry Potter and patron fighting off a Deventer **Edge:** Reeded

| Date | Mintage | VF20 | XF40 | MS60 | MS63 | MS65 |
|---|---|---|---|---|---|---|
| 2004 PM | 10,000 | PF63 45.00 | PF65 50.00 | | | |

## KM# 1204 CROWN

28.28 g., Copper-Nickel, 38.6 mm. **Ruler:** Elizabeth II **Obv:** Bust with tiara right **Rev:** Harry Potter in the shrieking shed **Edge:** Reeded

| Date | Mintage | VF20 | XF40 | MS60 | MS63 | MS65 |
|---|---|---|---|---|---|---|
| 2004 PM | — | — | — | — | 15.00 | 17.00 |

## KM# 1204a CROWN

28.28 g., 0.925 Silver 0.841 oz. ASW, 38.6 mm. **Ruler:** Elizabeth II **Obv:** Bust with tiara right **Rev:** Harry Potter in the shrieking shack **Edge:** Reeded

| Date | Mintage | VF20 | XF40 | MS60 | MS63 | MS65 |
|---|---|---|---|---|---|---|
| 2004 PM | 10,000 | PF63 45.00 | PF65 50.00 | | | |

### KM# 1206 CROWN

28.28 g., Copper-Nickel, 38.6 mm. **Ruler:** Elizabeth II **Obv:** Bust with tiara right **Rev:** Harry Potter and Professor Dumbledore **Edge:** Reeded

| Date | Mintage | VF20 | XF40 | MS60 | MS63 | MS65 |
|---|---|---|---|---|---|---|
| 2004 PM | — | — | — | — | 15.00 | 17.00 |

### KM# 1206a CROWN

28.28 g., 0.925 Silver 0.841 oz. ASW, 38.6 mm. **Ruler:** Elizabeth II **Obv:** Bust with tiara right **Rev:** Harry Potter and Professor Dumbledore **Edge:** Reeded

| Date | Mintage | VF20 | XF40 | MS60 | MS63 | MS65 |
|---|---|---|---|---|---|---|
| 2004 PM | 10,000 | PF63 45.00 | PF65 50.00 | | | |

### KM# 1208 CROWN

28.28 g., Copper-Nickel, 38.6 mm. **Ruler:** Elizabeth II **Obv:** Bust with tiara right **Rev:** Sirius Black on flying griffin **Edge:** Reeded

| Date | Mintage | VF20 | XF40 | MS60 | MS63 | MS65 |
|---|---|---|---|---|---|---|
| 2004 PM | — | — | — | — | 15.00 | 17.00 |

### KM# 1208a CROWN

28.28 g., 0.925 Silver 0.841 oz. ASW, 38.6 mm. **Ruler:** Elizabeth II **Obv:** Bust with tiara right **Rev:** Sirius Black on flying griffin **Edge:** Reeded

| Date | Mintage | VF20 | XF40 | MS60 | MS63 | MS65 |
|---|---|---|---|---|---|---|
| 2004 PM | 10,000 | PF63 45.00 | PF65 50.00 | | | |

### KM# 1210 CROWN

28.28 g., Copper-Nickel, 38.6 mm. **Ruler:** Elizabeth II **Obv:** Bust with tiara right **Rev:** Three Olympic Swimmers **Edge:** Reeded

| Date | Mintage | VF20 | XF40 | MS60 | MS63 | MS65 |
|---|---|---|---|---|---|---|
| 2004 PM | — | — | — | — | 10.00 | 12.00 |

### KM# 1210a CROWN

28.28 g., 0.925 Silver 0.841 oz. ASW, 38.6 mm. **Ruler:** Elizabeth II **Obv:** Bust with tiara right **Rev:** Three Olympic Swimmers **Edge:** Reeded

| Date | Mintage | VF20 | XF40 | MS60 | MS63 | MS65 |
|---|---|---|---|---|---|---|
| 2004 PM | 10,000 | PF63 45.00 | PF65 50.00 | | | |

### KM# 1212 CROWN

28.28 g., Copper-Nickel, 38.6 mm. **Ruler:** Elizabeth II **Obv:** Bust with tiara right **Rev:** Three Olympic Cyclists **Edge:** Reeded

| Date | Mintage | VF20 | XF40 | MS60 | MS63 | MS65 |
|---|---|---|---|---|---|---|
| 2004 PM | — | — | — | — | 10.00 | 12.00 |

### KM# 1212a CROWN

28.28 g., 0.925 Silver 0.841 oz. ASW, 38.6 mm. **Ruler:** Elizabeth II **Obv:** Bust with tiara right **Rev:** Three Olympic Cyclists **Edge:** Reeded

| Date | Mintage | VF20 | XF40 | MS60 | MS63 | MS65 |
|---|---|---|---|---|---|---|
| 2004 PM | 10,000 | PF63 45.00 | PF65 50.00 | | | |

### KM# 1214 CROWN

28.28 g., Copper-Nickel, 38.6 mm. **Ruler:** Elizabeth II **Obv:** Bust with tiara right **Rev:** Three Olympic Runners **Edge:** Reeded

| Date | Mintage | VF20 | XF40 | MS60 | MS63 | MS65 |
|---|---|---|---|---|---|---|
| 2004 PM | — | — | — | — | 10.00 | 12.00 |

### KM# 1214a CROWN

28.28 g., 0.925 Silver 0.841 oz. ASW, 38.6 mm. **Ruler:** Elizabeth II **Obv:** Bust with tiara right **Rev:** Three Olympic Runners **Edge:** Reeded

| Date | Mintage | VF20 | XF40 | MS60 | MS63 | MS65 |
|---|---|---|---|---|---|---|
| 2004 PM | 10,000 | PF63 45.00 | PF65 50.00 | | | |

### KM# 1216 CROWN

28.28 g., Copper-Nickel, 38.6 mm. **Ruler:** Elizabeth II **Obv:** Bust with tiara right **Rev:** Three Olympic Sail Boarders **Edge:** Reeded

| Date | Mintage | VF20 | XF40 | MS60 | MS63 | MS65 |
|---|---|---|---|---|---|---|
| 2004 PM | — | — | — | — | 10.00 | 12.00 |

### KM# 1216a CROWN

28.28 g., 0.925 Silver 0.841 oz. ASW, 38.6 mm. **Ruler:** Elizabeth II **Obv:** Bust with tiara right **Rev:** Three Olympic Sail Boarders **Edge:** Reeded

| Date | Mintage | VF20 | XF40 | MS60 | MS63 | MS65 |
|---|---|---|---|---|---|---|
| 2004 PM | 10,000 | PF63 45.00 | PF65 50.00 | | | |

### KM# 1218 CROWN

28.28 g., Copper-Nickel, 38.6 mm. **Ruler:** Elizabeth II **Obv:** Bust with tiara right **Rev:** Ocean Liner Queen Mary 2 **Edge:** Reeded

| Date | Mintage | VF20 | XF40 | MS60 | MS63 | MS65 |
|---|---|---|---|---|---|---|
| 2004 PM | — | — | — | — | 15.00 | 17.00 |

### KM# 1220 CROWN

28.28 g., Copper-Nickel, 38.6 mm. **Ruler:** Elizabeth II **Obv:** Bust with tiara right **Rev:** Lt. Quillan portrait above Battle of Trafalgar scene **Edge:** Reeded

| Date | Mintage | VF20 | XF40 | MS60 | MS63 | MS65 |
|---|---|---|---|---|---|---|
| 2004 PM | — | — | — | — | 15.00 | 17.00 |

### KM# 1220a CROWN

28.28 g., 0.925 Silver 0.841 oz. ASW, 38.6 mm. **Ruler:** Elizabeth II **Obv:** Bust with tiara right **Rev:** Lt. Quillan portrait above Battle of Trafalgar scene **Edge:** Reeded

| Date | Mintage | VF20 | XF40 | MS60 | MS63 | MS65 |
|---|---|---|---|---|---|---|
| 2004 PM | 10,000 | PF63 45.00 | PF65 50.00 | | | |

### KM# 1221 CROWN

28.28 g., Copper-Nickel, 38.6 mm. **Ruler:** Elizabeth II **Obv:** Bust with tiara right **Rev:** Napoleon and Nelson portraits above Battle of Trafalgar scene **Edge:** Reeded

| Date | Mintage | VF20 | XF40 | MS60 | MS63 | MS65 |
|---|---|---|---|---|---|---|
| 2004 PM | — | — | — | — | 15.00 | 17.00 |

### KM# 1222 CROWN

28.28 g., Copper-Nickel, 38.6 mm. **Ruler:** Elizabeth II **Obv:** Bust with tiara right **Rev:** D-Day Invasion Plan Map **Edge:** Reeded

| Date | Mintage | VF20 | XF40 | MS60 | MS63 | MS65 |
|---|---|---|---|---|---|---|
| 2004 PM | — | — | — | — | 15.00 | 17.00 |

### KM# 1222a CROWN

28.28 g., 0.925 Silver 0.841 oz. ASW, 38.6 mm. **Ruler:** Elizabeth II **Obv:** Bust with tiara right **Rev:** D-Day Invasion Plan Map **Edge:** Reeded

| Date | Mintage | VF20 | XF40 | MS60 | MS63 | MS65 |
|---|---|---|---|---|---|---|
| 2004 PM | 10,000 | PF63 45.00 | PF65 50.00 | | | |

### KM# 1224 CROWN

28.28 g., Copper-Nickel, 38.6 mm. **Ruler:** Elizabeth II **Obv:** Bust with tiara right **Rev:** Victoria Cross and battle scene **Edge:** Reeded

| Date | Mintage | VF20 | XF40 | MS60 | MS63 | MS65 |
|---|---|---|---|---|---|---|
| 2004 PM | — | — | — | — | 15.00 | 17.00 |

### KM# 1221a CROWN

28.28 g., 0.999 Silver 0.9083 oz. ASW, 38.6 mm. **Ruler:** Elizabeth II **Obv:** Bust with tiara right **Rev:** Napoleon and Nelson portraits above Battle of Trafalgar scene **Edge:** Reeded

| Date | Mintage | VF20 | XF40 | MS60 | MS63 | MS65 |
|---|---|---|---|---|---|---|
| 2004 PM | 10,000 | PF63 45.00 | PF65 50.00 | | | |

### KM# 1224a CROWN

28.28 g., 0.925 Silver 0.841 oz. ASW, 38.6 mm. **Ruler:** Elizabeth II **Obv:** Bust with tiara right **Rev:** Victoria Cross and battle scene **Edge:** Reeded

| Date | Mintage | VF20 | XF40 | MS60 | MS63 | MS65 |
|---|---|---|---|---|---|---|
| 2004 PM | 10,000 | PF63 45.00 | PF65 50.00 | | | |

**KM# 1226 CROWN**
28.28 g., Copper-Nickel, 38.6 mm. **Ruler:** Elizabeth II **Obv:** Bust with tiara right **Rev:** Silver Star and battle scene **Edge:** Reeded

| Date | Mintage | VF20 | XF40 | MS60 | MS63 | MS65 |
|---|---|---|---|---|---|---|
| 2004 PM | — | — | — | — | 15.00 | 17.00 |

**KM# 1226a CROWN**
28.28 g., 0.925 Silver 0.841 oz. ASW, 38.6 mm. **Ruler:** Elizabeth II **Obv:** Bust with tiara right **Rev:** Silver Star and battle scene **Edge:** Reeded

| Date | Mintage | VF20 | XF40 | MS60 | MS63 | MS65 |
|---|---|---|---|---|---|---|
| 2004 PM | 10,000 | **PF63** 45.00 | **PF65** 50.00 | | | |

**KM# 1228 CROWN**
28.28 g., Copper-Nickel, 38.6 mm. **Ruler:** Elizabeth II **Obv:** Bust with tiara right **Rev:** George Cross and rescue scene **Edge:** Reeded

| Date | Mintage | VF20 | XF40 | MS60 | MS63 | MS65 |
|---|---|---|---|---|---|---|
| 2004 PM | — | — | — | — | 15.00 | 17.00 |

**KM# 1228a CROWN**
28.28 g., 0.925 Silver 0.841 oz. ASW, 38.6 mm. **Ruler:** Elizabeth II **Obv:** Bust with tiara right **Rev:** George Cross and rescue scene **Edge:** Reeded

| Date | Mintage | VF20 | XF40 | MS60 | MS63 | MS65 |
|---|---|---|---|---|---|---|
| 2004 PM | 10,000 | **PF63** 45.00 | **PF65** 50.00 | | | |

**KM# 1230 CROWN**
28.28 g., Copper-Nickel, 38.6 mm. **Ruler:** Elizabeth II **Obv:** Bust with tiara right **Rev:** White Rose of Finland Medal and battle scene **Edge:** Reeded

| Date | Mintage | VF20 | XF40 | MS60 | MS63 | MS65 |
|---|---|---|---|---|---|---|
| 2004 PM | — | — | — | — | 15.00 | 17.00 |

**KM# 1230a CROWN**
28.28 g., 0.925 Silver 0.841 oz. ASW, 38.6 mm. **Ruler:** Elizabeth II **Obv:** Bust with tiara right **Rev:** White Rose of Finland Medal and battle scene **Edge:** Reeded

| Date | Mintage | VF20 | XF40 | MS60 | MS63 | MS65 |
|---|---|---|---|---|---|---|
| 2004 PM | 10,000 | **PF63** 45.00 | **PF65** 50.00 | | | |

**KM# 1232 CROWN**
28.28 g., Copper-Nickel, 38.6 mm. **Ruler:** Elizabeth II **Obv:** Bust with tiara right **Rev:** The Norwegian War Medal and naval battle scene **Edge:** Reeded

| Date | Mintage | VF20 | XF40 | MS60 | MS63 | MS65 |
|---|---|---|---|---|---|---|
| 2004 PM | — | — | — | — | 15.00 | 17.00 |

**KM# 1232a CROWN**
28.28 g., 0.925 Silver 0.841 oz. ASW, 38.6 mm. **Ruler:** Elizabeth II **Obv:** Bust with tiara right **Rev:** The Norwegian War Medal and a naval battle scene **Edge:** Reeded

| Date | Mintage | VF20 | XF40 | MS60 | MS63 | MS65 |
|---|---|---|---|---|---|---|
| 2004 PM | 10,000 | **PF63** 45.00 | **PF65** 50.00 | | | |

**KM# 1234 CROWN**
28.28 g., Copper-Nickel, 38.6 mm. **Ruler:** Elizabeth II **Obv:** Bust with tiara right **Rev:** French Croix de Guerre and partisan battle scene **Edge:** Reeded

| Date | Mintage | VF20 | XF40 | MS60 | MS63 | MS65 |
|---|---|---|---|---|---|---|
| 2004 PM | — | — | — | — | 15.00 | 17.00 |

**KM# 1234a CROWN**
28.28 g., 0.925 Silver 0.841 oz. ASW, 38.6 mm. **Ruler:** Elizabeth II **Obv:** Bust with tiara right **Rev:** French Croix de Guerre and partisan battle scene **Edge:** Reeded

| Date | Mintage | VF20 | XF40 | MS60 | MS63 | MS65 |
|---|---|---|---|---|---|---|
| 2004 PM | 10,000 | **PF63** 45.00 | **PF65** 50.00 | | | |

**KM# 1236 CROWN**
28.28 g., Copper-Nickel, 38.6 mm. **Ruler:** Elizabeth II **Obv:** Bust with tiara right **Rev:** Multicolor cartoon soccer player **Edge:** Reeded

| Date | Mintage | VF20 | XF40 | MS60 | MS63 | MS65 |
|---|---|---|---|---|---|---|
| 2004 PM | — | — | — | — | 10.00 | 12.00 |

**KM# 1236a CROWN**
28.28 g., 0.925 Silver 0.841 oz. ASW, 38.6 mm. **Ruler:** Elizabeth II **Obv:** Bust with tiara right **Rev:** Multicolor cartoon soccer player **Edge:** Reeded

| Date | Mintage | VF20 | XF40 | MS60 | MS63 | MS65 |
|---|---|---|---|---|---|---|
| 2004 PM | 7,500 | **PF63** 45.00 | **PF65** 50.00 | | | |

**KM# 1237 CROWN**
28.28 g., Copper-Nickel, 38.6 mm. **Ruler:** Elizabeth II **Obv:** Bust with tiara right **Rev:** Soccer ball in flight **Edge:** Reeded

| Date | Mintage | VF20 | XF40 | MS60 | MS63 | MS65 |
|---|---|---|---|---|---|---|
| 2004 PM | — | — | — | — | 10.00 | 12.00 |

**KM# 1237a CROWN**
28.28 g., 0.925 Silver 0.841 oz. ASW, 38.6 mm. **Ruler:** Elizabeth II **Obv:** Bust with tiara right **Rev:** Soccer ball in flight **Edge:** Reeded

| Date | Mintage | VF20 | XF40 | MS60 | MS63 | MS65 |
|---|---|---|---|---|---|---|
| 2004 PM | 7,500 | **PF63** 45.00 | **PF65** 50.00 | | | |

**KM# 1238 CROWN**
28.28 g., Copper-Nickel, 38.6 mm. **Ruler:** Elizabeth II **Obv:** Bust with tiara right **Rev:** Gibbon monkey **Edge:** Reeded

| Date | Mintage | VF20 | XF40 | MS60 | MS63 | MS65 |
|---|---|---|---|---|---|---|
| 2004 PM | — | — | — | — | 10.00 | 15.00 |

**KM# 1238a CROWN**
28.28 g., 0.925 Silver 0.841 oz. ASW, 38.6 mm. **Ruler:** Elizabeth II **Obv:** Bust with tiara right **Rev:** Monkey **Edge:** Reeded

| Date | Mintage | VF20 | XF40 | MS60 | MS63 | MS65 |
|---|---|---|---|---|---|---|
| 2004 PM | 30,000 | **PF63** 45.00 | **PF65** 50.00 | | | |

**KM# 1239 CROWN**
31.10 g., 0.9999 Gold 0.9999 oz. AGW, 32.7 mm. **Ruler:** Elizabeth II **Obv:** Bust with tiara right **Rev:** Monkey **Edge:** Reeded

| Date | Mintage | VF20 | XF40 | MS60 | MS63 | MS65 |
|---|---|---|---|---|---|---|
| 2004 PM | 2,000 | **PF65** 1,850 | | | | |

**KM# 1242 CROWN**
6.22 g., 0.9999 Gold 0.200 oz. AGW, 22 mm. **Ruler:** Elizabeth II **Obv:** Bust with tiara right **Rev:** Monkey **Edge:** Reeded

| Date | Mintage | VF20 | XF40 | MS60 | MS63 | MS65 |
|---|---|---|---|---|---|---|
| 2004 PM | 12,000 | **PF65** 375 | | | | |

**KM# 1245 CROWN**
28.28 g., Copper-Nickel, 38.6 mm. **Ruler:** Elizabeth II **Subject:** Lord of the Rings **Obv:** Bust with tiara right **Rev:** Nine characters **Edge:** Reeded

| Date | Mintage | VF20 | XF40 | MS60 | MS63 | MS65 |
|---|---|---|---|---|---|---|
| 2004 PM | 100,000 | — | — | — | 15.00 | 17.00 |

**KM# 1245a CROWN**
28.28 g., 0.925 Silver 0.841 oz. ASW, 38.6 mm. **Ruler:** Elizabeth II **Subject:** Lord of the Rings **Obv:** Bust with tiara right **Rev:** Nine characters **Edge:** Reeded

| Date | Mintage | VF20 | XF40 | MS60 | MS63 | MS65 |
|---|---|---|---|---|---|---|
| 2004 PM | 10,000 | **PF63** 45.00 | **PF65** 50.00 | | | |

**KM# 1246.1 CROWN**
28.28 g., Copper-Nickel, 38.6 mm. **Ruler:** Elizabeth II **Obv:** Head with tiara right **Rev:** Pair of Tonkinese cats **Edge:** Reeded

| Date | Mintage | VF20 | XF40 | MS60 | MS63 | MS65 |
|---|---|---|---|---|---|---|
| 2004 PM | — | — | — | — | 10.00 | 12.00 |

**KM# 1246.2 CROWN**
28.28 g., Copper-Nickel **Ruler:** Elizabeth II **Obv:** Head with tiara right **Rev:** Two multicolor Tonkinese cats **Edge:** Reeded

| Date | Mintage | VF20 | XF40 | MS60 | MS63 | MS65 |
|---|---|---|---|---|---|---|
| 2004 PM | — | — | — | — | 12.00 | 16.00 |

### KM# 1246a.1 CROWN

31.10 g., 0.999 Silver 0.999 oz. ASW, 38.6 mm. **Ruler:** Elizabeth II **Obv:** Head with tiara right **Rev:** Two Tonkinese cats **Edge:** Reeded

| Date | Mintage | VF20 | XF40 | MS60 | MS63 | MS65 |
|---|---|---|---|---|---|---|
| 2004 PM | 50,000 | **PF63** 65.00 | **PF65** 70.00 | | | |

### KM# 1246a.2 CROWN

31.10 g., 0.999 Silver 0.999 oz. ASW, 38.6 mm. **Ruler:** Elizabeth II **Obv:** Head with tiara right **Rev:** Two multicolor Tonkinese cats **Edge:** Reeded

| Date | Mintage | VF20 | XF40 | MS60 | MS63 | MS65 |
|---|---|---|---|---|---|---|
| 2004 PM | — | **PF63** 70.00 | **PF65** 75.00 | | | |

### KM# 1251 CROWN

31.10 g., 0.9999 Gold 0.9999 oz. AGW, 32.7 mm. **Ruler:** Elizabeth II **Obv:** Head with tiara right **Rev:** Two Tonkinese cats **Edge:** Reeded

| Date | Mintage | VF20 | XF40 | MS60 | MS63 | MS65 |
|---|---|---|---|---|---|---|
| 2004 PM | — | — | — | — | — | 1,800 |
| 2004 PM | 1,000 | **PF63** 1,825 | **PF65** 1,850 | | | |

### KM# 1266 CROWN

28.33 g., Copper-Nickel, 38.7 mm. **Ruler:** Elizabeth II **Obv:** Bust with tiara right **Rev:** Himalayan cat with two kittens **Edge:** Reeded

| Date | Mintage | VF20 | XF40 | MS60 | MS63 | MS65 |
|---|---|---|---|---|---|---|
| 2005 PM | — | — | — | — | 12.00 | 14.00 |

### KM# 1266a CROWN

31.10 g., 0.999 Silver 0.999 oz. ASW, 38.6 mm. **Ruler:** Elizabeth II **Obv:** Bust with tiara right **Rev:** Himalayan cat and two kittens **Edge:** Reeded

| Date | Mintage | VF20 | XF40 | MS60 | MS63 | MS65 |
|---|---|---|---|---|---|---|
| 2005 PM | 50,000 | **PF63** 65.00 | **PF65** 70.00 | | | |

### KM# 1268 CROWN

31.10 g., 0.9999 Gold 0.9999 oz. AGW, 32.7 mm. **Ruler:** Elizabeth II **Obv:** Bust with tiara right **Rev:** Himalayan cat and two kittens **Edge:** Reeded

| Date | Mintage | VF20 | XF40 | MS60 | MS63 | MS65 |
|---|---|---|---|---|---|---|
| 2005 PM | — | **PF65** 1,850 | | | | |

### KM# 1273 CROWN

28.28 g., Copper-Nickel, 38.6 mm. **Ruler:** Elizabeth II **Obv:** Bust with tiara right **Rev:** Harry Potter and the Hungarian Horn Tail, Tri-Wizard Tournament feat **Edge:** Reeded

| Date | Mintage | VF20 | XF40 | MS60 | MS63 | MS65 |
|---|---|---|---|---|---|---|
| 2005 PM | — | — | — | — | 12.00 | 14.00 |

### KM# 1274 CROWN

28.28 g., Copper-Nickel, 38.6 mm. **Ruler:** Elizabeth II **Subject:** 60th Anniversary - End of WW II **Obv:** Bust with tiara right **Rev:** Sir Winston Churchill

| Date | Mintage | VF20 | XF40 | MS60 | MS63 | MS65 |
|---|---|---|---|---|---|---|
| 2005 | — | — | — | — | 10.00 | 12.00 |

### KM# 1275 CROWN

28.28 g., Copper-Nickel, 38.6 mm. **Ruler:** Elizabeth II **Subject:** 400th Anniversary - Gunpowder plot **Obv:** Bust with tiara right **Rev:** Tower of London, Beefeaters

| Date | Mintage | VF20 | XF40 | MS60 | MS63 | MS65 |
|---|---|---|---|---|---|---|
| 2005 | — | — | — | — | 10.00 | 12.00 |

### KM# 1276 CROWN

28.28 g., Copper-Nickel, 38.6 mm. **Ruler:** Elizabeth II **Obv:** Bust with tiara right **Rev:** Harry Potter and Tri-Wizard Tournament feat - Underwater retrieval

| Date | Mintage | VF20 | XF40 | MS60 | MS63 | MS65 |
|---|---|---|---|---|---|---|
| 2005 | — | — | — | — | 12.00 | 14.00 |

### KM# 1277 CROWN

28.28 g., Copper-Nickel, 38.6 mm. **Ruler:** Elizabeth II **Obv:** Bust with tiara right **Rev:** Harry Potter and pensive

| Date | Mintage | VF20 | XF40 | MS60 | MS63 | MS65 |
|---|---|---|---|---|---|---|
| 2005 | — | — | — | — | 10.00 | 12.00 |

### KM# 1278 CROWN

28.28 g., Copper-Nickel, 38.6 mm. **Ruler:** Elizabeth II **Obv:** Bust with tiara right **Rev:** Harry Potter and portkey

| Date | Mintage | VF20 | XF40 | MS60 | MS63 | MS65 |
|---|---|---|---|---|---|---|
| 2005 | — | — | — | — | 10.00 | 12.00 |

### KM# 1279 CROWN

28.28 g., Copper-Nickel, 38.6 mm. **Ruler:** Elizabeth II **Subject:** The Battle of Cape St. Vincent **Obv:** Bust with tiara right **Rev:** Naval battle scene

| Date | Mintage | VF20 | XF40 | MS60 | MS63 | MS65 |
|---|---|---|---|---|---|---|
| 2005 | — | — | — | — | 10.00 | 12.00 |

### KM# 1280 CROWN

28.28 g., Copper-Nickel, 38.6 mm. **Ruler:** Elizabeth II **Subject:** Nelson Funeral Procession **Obv:** Bust with tiara right **Rev:** Thames and Greenwich view

| Date | Mintage | VF20 | XF40 | MS60 | MS63 | MS65 |
|---|---|---|---|---|---|---|
| 2005 | — | — | — | — | 10.00 | 12.00 |

**KM# 1281 CROWN**
Copper-Nickel **Ruler:** Elizabeth II **Subject:** Battle of the Nile **Obv:** Bust with tiara right **Rev:** Naval battle

| Date | Mintage | VF20 | XF40 | MS60 | MS63 | MS65 |
|---|---|---|---|---|---|---|
| 2005 | — | — | — | — | 10.00 | 12.00 |

**KM# 1282 CROWN**
28.28 g., Copper-Nickel, 38.6 mm. **Ruler:** Elizabeth II **Subject:** Norway Independence **Obv:** Bust with tiara right **Rev:** Three swords

| Date | Mintage | VF20 | XF40 | MS60 | MS63 | MS65 |
|---|---|---|---|---|---|---|
| 2005 | — | — | — | — | 10.00 | 12.00 |

**KM# 1283 CROWN**
28.28 g., Copper-Nickel, 38.6 mm. **Ruler:** Elizabeth II **Subject:** Nelson - Trafalgar 200th Anniversary **Rev:** Nelson portrait

| Date | Mintage | VF20 | XF40 | MS60 | MS63 | MS65 |
|---|---|---|---|---|---|---|
| 2005 | — | — | — | — | 10.00 | 12.00 |

**KM# 1284 CROWN**
28.28 g., Copper-Nickel, 38.6 mm. **Ruler:** Elizabeth II **Subject:** Battle of Trafalgar **Rev:** Naval battle scene

| Date | Mintage | VF20 | XF40 | MS60 | MS63 | MS65 |
|---|---|---|---|---|---|---|
| 2005 | — | — | — | — | 10.00 | 12.00 |

**KM# 1285 CROWN**
28.28 g., Copper-Nickel, 38.6 mm. **Ruler:** Elizabeth II **Subject:** Steam Packet - King Orry III **Obv:** Bust with tiara right **Rev:** Ship view

| Date | Mintage | VF20 | XF40 | MS60 | MS63 | MS65 |
|---|---|---|---|---|---|---|
| 2005 | — | — | — | — | 10.00 | 12.00 |

**KM# 1286 CROWN**
28.28 g., Copper-Nickel, 38.6 mm. **Ruler:** Elizabeth II **Subject:** Isle of Man Steam Packet Company - 175th Anniversary **Obv:** Bust with tiara right **Rev:** Modern and early ferry

| Date | Mintage | VF20 | XF40 | MS60 | MS63 | MS65 |
|---|---|---|---|---|---|---|
| 2005 | — | — | — | — | 10.00 | 12.00 |

**KM# 1287 CROWN**
28.28 g., Copper-Nickel, 38.6 mm. **Ruler:** Elizabeth II **Rev:** Motorcycle right

| Date | Mintage | VF20 | XF40 | MS60 | MS63 | MS65 |
|---|---|---|---|---|---|---|
| 2005 | — | — | — | — | 10.00 | 12.00 |

**KM# 1288 CROWN**
28.28 g., Copper-Nickel, 38.6 mm. **Ruler:** Elizabeth II **Rev:** Motorcycle forward

| Date | Mintage | VF20 | XF40 | MS60 | MS63 | MS65 |
|---|---|---|---|---|---|---|
| 2005 | — | — | — | — | 10.00 | 12.00 |

**KM# 1289 CROWN**
28.28 g., Copper-Nickel, 38.6 mm. **Ruler:** Elizabeth II **Subject:** Ugly Duckling story **Obv:** Bust with tiara right **Rev:** Farm animals

| Date | Mintage | VF20 | XF40 | MS60 | MS63 | MS65 |
|---|---|---|---|---|---|---|
| 2005 | — | — | — | — | 12.00 | 14.00 |

**KM# 1291 CROWN**
28.28 g., Copper-Nickel, 38.6 mm. **Ruler:** Elizabeth II **Subject:** Trafalgar - 200th Anniversary **Obv:** Bust with tiara right **Rev:** Nelson at Battle of Copenhagen

| Date | Mintage | VF20 | XF40 | MS60 | MS63 | MS65 |
|---|---|---|---|---|---|---|
| 2005 | — | — | — | — | 10.00 | 12.00 |

**KM# 1428 CROWN**
28.28 g., Copper-Nickel, 38.6 mm. **Ruler:** Elizabeth II **Subject:** Traflagar, 200th Anniversary **Rev:** Quillian portrait above naval battle scene

| Date | Mintage | VF20 | XF40 | MS60 | MS63 | MS65 |
|---|---|---|---|---|---|---|
| 2005 PM | — | — | — | — | 10.00 | 12.00 |

**KM# 1429 CROWN**
28.28 g., Copper-Nickel, 38.6 mm. **Ruler:** Elizabeth II **Subject:** Trafalgar, 200th Anniversary **Rev:** Napoleon and Nelson portraits above Naval battle scene

| Date | Mintage | VF20 | XF40 | MS60 | MS63 | MS65 |
|---|---|---|---|---|---|---|
| 2005 PM | — | — | — | — | 10.00 | 12.00 |

### KM# 1290a CROWN

28.28 g., Copper-Nickel, 38.6 mm. **Ruler:** Elizabeth II **Obv:** Bust with tiara right **Rev:** Three Exotic Shorthair cats sitting facing **Edge:** Reeded

| Date | Mintage | VF20 | XF40 | MS60 | MS63 | MS65 |
|---|---|---|---|---|---|---|
| 2006 PM | — | — | — | — | 12.00 | 14.00 |

### KM# 1290b CROWN

28.28 g., 0.925 Silver 0.841 oz. ASW, 38.6 mm. **Ruler:** Elizabeth II **Obv:** Bust with tiara right **Rev:** Three Exotic Shorthair cats sitting facing **Edge:** Reeded

| Date | Mintage | VF20 | XF40 | MS60 | MS63 | MS65 |
|---|---|---|---|---|---|---|
| 2006 PM | — | — | — | — | — | 70.00 |

### KM# 1290c CROWN

31.10 g., 0.9999 Gold 0.9999 oz. AGW **Ruler:** Elizabeth II **Obv:** Bust with tiara right **Rev:** Three Exotic Shorthair cats sitting facing, multicolor **Edge:** Reeded

| Date | Mintage | VF20 | XF40 | MS60 | MS63 | MS65 |
|---|---|---|---|---|---|---|
| 2006 PM | — | — | — | — | — | 1,825 |

### KM# 1296 CROWN

28.28 g., Copper-Nickel, 38.6 mm. **Ruler:** Elizabeth II **Subject:** Battles that Changed the World **Obv:** Elizabeth II **Rev:** Trojan War scene **Edge:** Reeded

| Date | Mintage | VF20 | XF40 | MS60 | MS63 | MS65 |
|---|---|---|---|---|---|---|
| 2006 PM | — | — | — | — | 10.00 | 12.00 |

### KM# 1296a CROWN

28.28 g., 0.925 Silver 0.841 oz. ASW, 38.6 mm. **Ruler:** Elizabeth II **Subject:** Battles that Changed the World **Obv:** Elizabeth II **Rev:** Trojan War scene **Edge:** Reeded

| Date | Mintage | VF20 | XF40 | MS60 | MS63 | MS65 |
|---|---|---|---|---|---|---|
| 2006 PM | 10,000 | **PF63** 42.00 | **PF65** 47.00 | | | |

### KM# 1298 CROWN

28.28 g., Copper-Nickel, 38.6 mm. **Ruler:** Elizabeth II **Subject:** Battles that Changed the World **Obv:** Elizabeth II **Rev:** Battle of Arbela scene **Edge:** Reeded

| Date | Mintage | VF20 | XF40 | MS60 | MS63 | MS65 |
|---|---|---|---|---|---|---|
| 2006 PM | — | — | — | — | 10.00 | 12.00 |

### KM# 1298a CROWN

28.28 g., 0.925 Silver 0.841 oz. ASW, 38.6 mm. **Ruler:** Elizabeth II **Subject:** Battles that Changed the World **Obv:** Elizabeth II **Rev:** Battle of Arbela scene **Edge:** Reeded

| Date | Mintage | VF20 | XF40 | MS60 | MS63 | MS65 |
|---|---|---|---|---|---|---|
| 2006 PM | 10,000 | **PF63** 42.00 | **PF65** 47.00 | | | |

### KM# 1300 CROWN

28.28 g., Copper-Nickel, 38.6 mm. **Ruler:** Elizabeth II **Subject:** Battles that Changed the World **Obv:** Elizabeth II **Rev:** Battle of Thapsus scene **Edge:** Reeded

| Date | Mintage | VF20 | XF40 | MS60 | MS63 | MS65 |
|---|---|---|---|---|---|---|
| 2006 PM | — | — | — | — | 10.00 | 12.00 |

### KM# 1300a CROWN

28.28 g., 0.925 Silver 0.841 oz. ASW, 38.6 mm. **Ruler:** Elizabeth II **Subject:** Battles that Changed the World **Obv:** Elizabeth II **Rev:** Battle of Thapsus scene **Edge:** Reeded

| Date | Mintage | VF20 | XF40 | MS60 | MS63 | MS65 |
|---|---|---|---|---|---|---|
| 2006 PM | 10,000 | **PF63** 42.00 | **PF65** 47.00 | | | |

### KM# 1302 CROWN

28.28 g., Copper-Nickel, 38.6 mm. **Ruler:** Elizabeth II **Subject:** Battles that Changed the World **Obv:** Elizabeth II **Rev:** Battle of Cologne scene **Edge:** Reeded

| Date | Mintage | VF20 | XF40 | MS60 | MS63 | MS65 |
|---|---|---|---|---|---|---|
| 2006 PM | — | — | — | — | 10.00 | 12.00 |

### KM# 1302a CROWN

28.28 g., 0.925 Silver 0.841 oz. ASW, 38.6 mm. **Ruler:** Elizabeth II **Subject:** Battles that Changed the World **Obv:** Elizabeth II **Rev:** Battle of Cologne scene **Edge:** Reeded

| Date | Mintage | VF20 | XF40 | MS60 | MS63 | MS65 |
|---|---|---|---|---|---|---|
| 2006 PM | 10,000 | **PF63** 42.00 | **PF65** 47.00 | | | |

### KM# 1304 CROWN

28.28 g., Copper-Nickel, 38.6 mm. **Ruler:** Elizabeth II **Subject:** Battles that Changed the World **Obv:** Elizabeth II **Rev:** Siege of Valencia scene **Edge:** Reeded

| Date | Mintage | VF20 | XF40 | MS60 | MS63 | MS65 |
|---|---|---|---|---|---|---|
| 2006 PM | — | — | — | — | 10.00 | 12.00 |

### KM# 1304a CROWN

28.28 g., 0.925 Silver 0.841 oz. ASW, 38.6 mm. **Ruler:** Elizabeth II **Subject:** Battles that Changed the World **Obv:** Elizabeth II **Rev:** Siege of Valencia scene **Edge:** Reeded

| Date | Mintage | VF20 | XF40 | MS60 | MS63 | MS65 |
|---|---|---|---|---|---|---|
| 2006 PM | 10,000 | **PF63** 42.00 | **PF65** 47.00 | | | |

### KM# 1306 CROWN

28.28 g., Copper-Nickel, 38.6 mm. **Ruler:** Elizabeth II **Subject:** Battles that Changed the World **Obv:** Elizabeth II **Rev:** Battle of Agincourt scene **Edge:** Reeded

| Date | Mintage | VF20 | XF40 | MS60 | MS63 | MS65 |
|---|---|---|---|---|---|---|
| 2006 PM | — | — | — | — | 10.00 | 12.00 |

### KM# 1306a CROWN

28.28 g., 0.925 Silver 0.841 oz. ASW, 38.6 mm. **Ruler:** Elizabeth II **Subject:** Battles that Changed the World **Obv:** Elizabeth II **Rev:** Battle of Agincourt scene **Edge:** Reeded

| Date | Mintage | VF20 | XF40 | MS60 | MS63 | MS65 |
|---|---|---|---|---|---|---|
| 2006 PM | 10,000 | **PF63** 42.00 | **PF65** 47.00 | | | |

### KM# 1323.1 CROWN

28.28 g., Copper-Nickel, 38.60 mm. **Ruler:** Elizabeth II **Subject:** Hans Christian Anderson's Fairy Tales **Obv:** Bust with tiarra right **Obv. Legend:** ELIZABETH II - ISLE OF MAN **Rev:** Three bears startling Goldilocks in bed **Rev. Legend:** Goldilocks and the Three Bears **Edge:** Reeded

| Date | Mintage | VF20 | XF40 | MS60 | MS63 | MS65 |
|---|---|---|---|---|---|---|
| 2006 PM | — | — | — | — | — | 35.00 |

### KM# 1323.1a CROWN

28.28 g., 0.925 Silver 0.841 oz. ASW, 38.60 mm. **Ruler:** Elizabeth II **Subject:** Hans Christian Anderson's Fairy Tales **Obv:** Bust with tiara right **Obv. Legend:** ELIZABETH II - ISLE OF MAN **Rev:** Three bears startling Goldilocks in bed **Rev. Legend:** Goldilocks and the Three Bears **Edge:** Reeded

| Date | Mintage | VF20 | XF40 | MS60 | MS63 | MS65 |
|---|---|---|---|---|---|---|
| 2006 PM | — | **PF65** 80.00 | | | | |

### KM# 1323.2 CROWN

28.28 g., Copper-Nickel, 38.60 mm. **Ruler:** Elizabeth II **Subject:** Hans Christian Anderson's Fairy Tales **Obv:** Bust with tiara right **Obv. Legend:** ELIZABETH II - ISLE OF MAN **Rev:** Three bears startling Goldilocks in bed multicolor **Rev. Legend:** Goldilocks and the Three Bears **Edge:** Reeded

| Date | Mintage | VF20 | XF40 | MS60 | MS63 | MS65 |
|---|---|---|---|---|---|---|
| 2006 PM | — | — | — | — | — | 40.00 |

**KM# 1323.2a CROWN**
28.28 g., 0.925 Silver 0.841 oz. ASW, 38.60 mm. **Ruler:** Elizabeth II **Subject:** Hans Christian Anderson's Fairy Tales **Obv:** Bust with tiara right **Obv. Legend:** ELIZABETH II - ISLE OF MAN **Rev:** Three bears startling Goldilocks in bed multicolor **Rev. Legend:** Goldilocks and the Three Bears **Edge:** Reeded

| Date | Mintage | VF20 | XF40 | MS60 | MS63 | MS65 |
|---|---|---|---|---|---|---|
| 2006 PM | — | PF65 100 | | | | |

**KM# 1423.1 CROWN**
28.28 g., Copper-Nickel, 38.6 mm. **Ruler:** Elizabeth II **Subject:** Concord, 30th Anniversary of transatlantic service **Obv:** Bust with tiara right **Rev:** Concord in flight, buildings below

| Date | Mintage | VF20 | XF40 | MS60 | MS63 | MS65 |
|---|---|---|---|---|---|---|
| 2006 PM | — | PF65 30.00 | | | | |
| 2006 PM P/L | — | — | — | — | — | 12.00 |

**KM# 1423.2 CROWN**
28.28 g., Copper-Nickel, 38.6 mm. **Ruler:** Elizabeth II **Subject:** Concorde, 30th Anniversary of transatlantic service **Obv:** Bust with tiara right **Rev:** Concorde in flight, multicolor

| Date | Mintage | VF20 | XF40 | MS60 | MS63 | MS65 |
|---|---|---|---|---|---|---|
| 2006 PM | — | PF65 50.00 | | | | |

**KM# 1307.1 CROWN**
28.28 g., Copper-Nickel, 38.6 mm. **Ruler:** Elizabeth II **Rev:** Ragdoll cat and kittens

| Date | Mintage | VF20 | XF40 | MS60 | MS63 | MS65 |
|---|---|---|---|---|---|---|
| 2007 | — | — | — | — | 15.00 | 18.00 |

**KM# 1307.2 CROWN**
28.28 g., Copper-Nickel, 38.6 mm. **Ruler:** Elizabeth II **Rev:** Three cats, multicolor

| Date | Mintage | VF20 | XF40 | MS60 | MS63 | MS65 |
|---|---|---|---|---|---|---|
| 2007 PM | — | — | — | — | — | 25.00 |

**KM# 1310 CROWN**
28.28 g., Copper-Nickel, 38.6 mm. **Ruler:** Elizabeth II **Subject:** 100th Anniversary of Scouting **Obv:** Bust with tiara right **Obv. Legend:** ELIZABETH II - ISLE OF MAN **Rev:** 3/4 length figure of Robert Baden-Powell standing facing 3/4 left, Fleur-de-lys below, images of scouting at left and right **Rev. Legend:** CENTENARY OF SCOUTING **Edge:** Reeded

| Date | Mintage | VF20 | XF40 | MS60 | MS63 | MS65 |
|---|---|---|---|---|---|---|
| 2007 | — | — | — | — | 17.00 | 20.00 |

**KM# 1311 CROWN**
28.28 g., 0.9167 Silver 0.8335 oz. ASW **Ruler:** Elizabeth II **Subject:** 100th Anniversary of Scouting **Obv:** Bust with tiara right **Obv. Legend:** ELIZABETH II - ISLE OF MAN **Rev:** 3/4 length figure of Robert Baden-Powell standing facing 3/4 left, Fleur-de-lys below, images of scouting at left and right **Rev. Legend:** CENTENARY OF SCOUTING **Edge:** Reeded

| Date | Mintage | VF20 | XF40 | MS60 | MS63 | MS65 |
|---|---|---|---|---|---|---|
| 2007 | — | PF65 50.00 | | | | |

**KM# 1312 CROWN**
0.750 Gold Yellow, white and red Gold **Ruler:** Elizabeth II **Subject:** Diamond Wedding Anniversary **Obv:** Bust with tiara right **Obv. Legend:** ELIZABETH II - ISLE OF MAN **Rev:** Crowned pair of doves surrounded by a leek, thistle, rose and shamrock **Edge:** Reeded

| Date | Mintage | VF20 | XF40 | MS60 | MS63 | MS65 |
|---|---|---|---|---|---|---|
| 2007 | — | PF65 2,000 | | | | |

**KM# 1313 CROWN**
28.28 g., Copper-Nickel, 38.60 mm. **Ruler:** Elizabeth II **Obv:** Bust with tiara right **Obv. Legend:** ELIZABETH II - ISLE OF MAN **Rev:** Two swans facing **Edge:** Reeded

| Date | Mintage | VF20 | XF40 | MS60 | MS63 | MS65 |
|---|---|---|---|---|---|---|
| 2007 | — | — | — | — | 15.00 | 18.00 |

**KM# 1315 CROWN**
28.28 g., 0.9167 Silver 0.8335 oz. ASW, 38.60 mm. **Ruler:** Elizabeth II **Obv:** Bust with tiara right **Obv. Legend:** ELIZABETH II - ISLE OF MAN **Rev:** Two swans facing **Edge:** Reeded

| Date | Mintage | VF20 | XF40 | MS60 | MS63 | MS65 |
|---|---|---|---|---|---|---|
| 2007 | 10,000 | PF65 50.00 | | | | |

**KM# 1316 CROWN**
28.28 g., Copper-Nickel, 38.6 mm. **Ruler:** Elizabeth II **Subject:** Diamond Wedding Anniversary **Obv:** Conjoined busts with Philip right **Obv. Legend:** ELIZABETH II - ISLE OF MAN **Rev:** Bridal bouquet of white orchids **Rev. Legend:** Diamond Wedding of H.M. Queen Elizabeth II & H.R.H. Prince Philip **Edge:** Reeded

| Date | Mintage | VF20 | XF40 | MS60 | MS63 | MS65 |
|---|---|---|---|---|---|---|
| 2007 | — | — | — | — | 15.00 | 18.00 |

**KM# 1316a CROWN**
28.28 g., 0.9167 Silver 0.8335 oz. ASW **Ruler:** Elizabeth II **Subject:** Diamond Wedding Anniversary **Obv:** Conjoined busts with Philip right **Obv. Legend:** ELIZABETH II - ISLE OF MAN **Rev:** Bridal bouquet of white orchids **Rev. Legend:** Diamond Wedding of H.M. Queen Elizabeth II & H.R.H. Prince Philip **Edge:** Reeded

| Date | Mintage | VF20 | XF40 | MS60 | MS63 | MS65 |
|---|---|---|---|---|---|---|
| 2007 | — | PF63 45.00 | PF65 50.00 | | | |

**KM# 1317 CROWN**
28.28 g., Copper-Nickel **Ruler:** Elizabeth II **Subject:** Diamond Wedding Anniversary **Obv:** Conjoined busts with Philip right **Obv. Legend:** ELIZABETH II - ISLE OF MAN **Rev:** Westminster Abbey **Rev. Legend:** Diamond Wedding of H.M. Queen Elizabeth II & H.R.H. Prince Philip **Edge:** Reeded

| Date | Mintage | VF20 | XF40 | MS60 | MS63 | MS65 |
|---|---|---|---|---|---|---|
| 2007 | — | — | — | — | 15.00 | 18.00 |

**KM# 1317a CROWN**
28.28 g., 0.9167 Silver 0.8335 oz. ASW **Ruler:** Elizabeth II **Subject:** Diamond Wedding Anniversary **Obv:** Conjoined busts with Philip right **Obv. Legend:** ELIZABETH II - ISLE OF MAN **Rev:** Westminster Abbey **Rev. Legend:** Diamond Wedding of H.M. Queen Elizabeth II & H.R.H. Prince Philip **Edge:** Reeded

| Date | Mintage | VF20 | XF40 | MS60 | MS63 | MS65 |
|---|---|---|---|---|---|---|
| 2007 | — | PF63 45.00 | PF65 50.00 | | | |

**KM# 1318 CROWN**
28.28 g., Copper-Nickel, 38.6 mm. **Ruler:** Elizabeth II **Subject:** Diamond Wedding Anniversary **Obv:** Conjoined busts with Philip right **Obv. Legend:** ELIZABETH II - ISLE OF MAN **Rev:** Royal Family of five standing facing **Rev. Legend:** Diamond Wedding of H.M. Queen Elizabeth II & H.R.H. Prince Philip **Edge:** Reeded

| Date | Mintage | VF20 | XF40 | MS60 | MS63 | MS65 |
|---|---|---|---|---|---|---|
| 2007 | — | — | — | — | 15.00 | 18.00 |

**KM# 1318a CROWN**
28.28 g., 0.9167 Silver 0.8335 oz. ASW, 38.6 mm. **Ruler:** Elizabeth II **Subject:** Diamond Wedding Anniversary **Obv:** Conjoined busts with Philip right **Obv. Legend:** ELIZABETH II - ISLE OF MAN **Rev:** Royal Family of five standing facing **Rev. Legend:** Diamond Wedding of H.M. Queen Elizabeth II & H.R.H. Prince Philip **Edge:** Reeded

| Date | Mintage | VF20 | XF40 | MS60 | MS63 | MS65 |
|---|---|---|---|---|---|---|
| 2007 | — | PF63 45.00 | PF65 50.00 | | | |

**KM# 1319 CROWN**
28.28 g., Copper-Nickel, 38.6 mm. **Ruler:** Elizabeth II **Subject:** Diamond Wedding Anniversary **Obv:** Conjoined busts with Philip right **Obv. Legend:** ELIZABETH II - ISLE OF MAN **Rev:** Bride and groom standing facing **Rev. Legend:** Diamond Wedding of H.M. Queen Elizabeth II & H.R.H. Prince Philip **Edge:** Reeded

| Date | Mintage | VF20 | XF40 | MS60 | MS63 | MS65 |
|---|---|---|---|---|---|---|
| 2007 | — | — | — | — | 15.00 | 18.00 |

**KM# 1319a CROWN**
28.28 g., 0.9167 Silver 0.8335 oz. ASW, 38.6 mm. **Ruler:** Elizabeth II **Subject:** Diamond Wedding Anniversary **Obv:** Conjoined busts with Philip right **Obv. Legend:** ELIZABETH II - ISLE OF MAN **Rev:** Bride and groom standing facing **Rev. Legend:** Diamond Wedding of H.M. Queen Elizabeth II & H.R.H. Prince Philip **Edge:** Reeded

| Date | Mintage | VF20 | XF40 | MS60 | MS63 | MS65 |
|---|---|---|---|---|---|---|
| 2007 | — | PF63 45.00 | PF65 50.00 | | | |

**KM# 1324.1 CROWN**
28.28 g., Copper-Nickel, 38.60 mm. **Ruler:** Elizabeth II **Subject:** Hans Christian Anderson's Fairy Tales **Obv:** Bust with tiara right **Obv. Legend:** ELIZABETH II - ISLE OF MAN **Rev:** Prince awakening Sleeping Beauty, castle in background **Rev. Legend:** Sleeping Beauty **Edge:** Reeded

| Date | Mintage | VF20 | XF40 | MS60 | MS63 | MS65 |
|---|---|---|---|---|---|---|
| 2007 PM | — | — | — | — | — | 25.00 |

**KM# 1324.1a CROWN**
28.28 g., 0.925 Silver 0.841 oz. ASW, 38.60 mm. **Ruler:** Elizabeth II **Subject:** Hans Christian Anderson's Fairy Tales **Obv:** Bust with tiara right **Obv. Legend:** ELIZABETH II - ISLE OF MAN **Rev:** Prince wakening Sleeping Beauty, castle in background **Rev. Legend:** Sleeping Beauty **Edge:** Reeded

| Date | Mintage | VF20 | XF40 | MS60 | MS63 | MS65 |
|---|---|---|---|---|---|---|
| 2007 PM | — | PF63 45.00 | PF65 50.00 | | | |

**KM# 1324.2 CROWN**
28.28 g., Copper-Nickel, 38.60 mm. **Ruler:** Elizabeth II **Subject:** Hans Christian Anderson's Fairy Tales **Obv:** Bust with tiara right **Obv. Legend:** ELIZABET II - ISLE OF MAN **Rev:** Prince awakening Sleeping Beauty, castle in background multicolor **Rev. Legend:** Sleeping Beauty **Edge:** Reeded

| Date | Mintage | VF20 | XF40 | MS60 | MS63 | MS65 |
|---|---|---|---|---|---|---|
| 2007 PM | — | — | — | — | — | 25.00 |

**KM# 1324.2a CROWN**
28.28 g., 0.925 Silver 0.841 oz. ASW, 38.60 mm. **Ruler:** Elizabeth II **Subject:** Hans Christian Anderson's Fairy Tales **Obv:** Bust with tiara right **Obv. Legend:** ELIZABETH II - ISLE OF MAN **Rev:** Prince awakening Sleeping Beauty, castle in background multicolor **Rev. Legend:** Sleeping Beauty **Edge:** Reeded

| Date | Mintage | VF20 | XF40 | MS60 | MS63 | MS65 |
|---|---|---|---|---|---|---|
| 2007 PM | — | PF63 45.00 | PF65 50.00 | | | |

**KM# 1325.1 CROWN**
28.28 g., Copper-Nickel, 38.60 mm. **Ruler:** Elizabeth II **Subject:** Hans Christian Anderson's Fairy Tales **Obv:** Bust with tiara right **Obv. Legend:** ELIZABETH II - ISLE OF MAN **Rev:** Wolf at right trying to blow pig's house down, two pigs fleeing above in background **Rev. Legend:** Three Little Pigs **Edge:** Reeded

| Date | Mintage | VF20 | XF40 | MS60 | MS63 | MS65 |
|---|---|---|---|---|---|---|
| 2007 PM | — | — | — | — | — | 35.00 |

**KM# 1325.1a CROWN**
28.28 g., 0.925 Silver 0.841 oz. ASW, 38.60 mm. **Ruler:** Elizabeth II **Subject:** Hans Christian Anderson's Fairy Tales **Obv:** Bust with tiara right **Obv. Legend:** ELIZABETH II - ISLE OF MAN **Rev:** Wolf at right trying to blow pig's house down, two pigs fleeing above in background **Rev. Legend:** Three Little Pigs **Edge:** Reeded

| Date | Mintage | VF20 | XF40 | MS60 | MS63 | MS65 |
|---|---|---|---|---|---|---|
| 2007 PM | — | PF63 45.00 | PF65 50.00 | | | |

**KM# 1325.2 CROWN**
28.28 g., Copper-Nickel, 38.60 mm. **Ruler:** Elizabeth II **Subject:** Hans Christian Anderson's Fairy Tales **Obv:** Bust with tiara right **Obv. Legend:** ELIZABETH II - ISLE OF MAN **Rev:** Wolf at right trying to blow pig's house down, two pigs fleeing above in backgound multicolor **Rev. Legend:** Three Little Pigs **Edge:** Reeded

| Date | Mintage | VF20 | XF40 | MS60 | MS63 | MS65 |
|---|---|---|---|---|---|---|
| 2007 PM | — | — | — | — | — | 40.00 |

**KM# 1325.2a CROWN**
28.28 g., 0.925 Silver 0.841 oz. ASW, 38.60 mm. **Ruler:** Elizabeth II **Subject:** Hans Christian Anderson's Fairy Tales **Obv:** Bust with tiara right **Obv. Legend:** ELIZABETH II - ISLE OF MAN **Rev:** Wolf at right trying to blow pig's house down, two pigs fleeing above in background multicolor **Rev. Legend:** Three Little Pigs **Edge:** Reeded

| Date | Mintage | VF20 | XF40 | MS60 | MS63 | MS65 |
|---|---|---|---|---|---|---|
| 2007 PM | — | PF65 75.00 | | | | |

**KM# 1347 CROWN**
31.10 g., 0.9999 Gold 0.9999 oz. AGW **Ruler:** Elizabeth II **Obv:** Bust with tiara right **Obv. Legend:** ELIZABETH II - ISLE OF MAN **Rev:** Ragdoll cat with two kittens sitting facing **Edge:** Reeded

| Date | Mintage | VF20 | XF40 | MS60 | MS63 | MS65 |
|---|---|---|---|---|---|---|
| 2007 PM | — | — | — | — | — | 1,825 |

**KM# 1348.1 CROWN**
Copper-Nickel **Ruler:** Elizabeth II **Subject:** The Tale of Peter Rabbit **Obv:** Bust with tiara right **Obv. Legend:** ELIZABETH II - ISLE OF MAN **Rev:** Peter walking with friends **Edge:** Reeded

| Date | Mintage | VF20 | XF40 | MS60 | MS63 | MS65 |
|---|---|---|---|---|---|---|
| 2007 PM | — | — | — | — | — | 30.00 |

**KM# 1348.1a CROWN**
0.925 Silver **Ruler:** Elizabeth II **Subject:** The Tale of Peter Rabbit **Obv:** Bust with tiara right **Obv. Legend:** ELIZABETH II - ISLE OF MAN **Rev:** Peter walking with friends **Edge:** Reeded

| Date | Mintage | VF20 | XF40 | MS60 | MS63 | MS65 |
|---|---|---|---|---|---|---|
| 2007 PM | — | PF63 45.00 | PF65 50.00 | | | |

**KM# 1348.2 CROWN**
Copper-Nickel **Ruler:** Elizabeth II **Subject:** The Tale of Peter Rabbit **Obv:** Bust with tiara right **Obv. Legend:** ELIZABETH II - ISLE OF MAN **Rev:** Peter walking with friends, multicolor **Edge:** Reeded

| Date | Mintage | VF20 | XF40 | MS60 | MS63 | MS65 |
|---|---|---|---|---|---|---|
| 2007 PM | — | — | — | — | — | 35.00 |

**KM# 1348.2a CROWN**
0.925 Silver **Ruler:** Elizabeth II **Subject:** The Tale of Peter Rabbit **Obv:** Bust with tiara right **Obv. Legend:** ELIZABETH II - ISLE OF MAN **Rev:** Peter walking with friends, multicolor **Edge:** Reeded

| Date | Mintage | VF20 | XF40 | MS60 | MS63 | MS65 |
|---|---|---|---|---|---|---|
| 2007 PM | — | PF65 75.00 | | | | |

**KM# 1418 CROWN**
28.28 g., Copper-Nickel, 38.6 mm. **Ruler:** Elizabeth II **Subject:** TT Centennial **Obv:** Bust with tiara right **Rev:** Motorcyclist left

| Date | Mintage | VF20 | XF40 | MS60 | MS63 | MS65 |
|---|---|---|---|---|---|---|
| 2007 PM | — | — | — | — | 10.00 | 12.00 |

**KM# 1419 CROWN**
28.28 g., Copper-Nickel, 38.6 mm. **Ruler:** Elizabeth II **Subject:** TT Centennial **Obv:** Bust with tiara right **Rev:** Motorcyclists Dunlop

| Date | Mintage | VF20 | XF40 | MS60 | MS63 | MS65 |
|---|---|---|---|---|---|---|
| 2007 PM | — | — | — | — | 10.00 | 12.00 |

**KM# 1420 CROWN**
28.28 g., Copper-Nickel, 38.6 mm. **Ruler:** Elizabeth II **Subject:** TT Centennial **Obv:** Bust with tiara right **Rev:** Motorcyclists Woods

| Date | Mintage | VF20 | XF40 | MS60 | MS63 | MS65 |
|---|---|---|---|---|---|---|
| 2007 PM | — | — | — | — | 10.00 | 12.00 |

**KM# 1421 CROWN**
28.28 g., Copper-Nickel, 38.6 mm. **Ruler:** Elizabeth II **Subject:** TT Centennial **Obv:** Bust with tiara right **Rev:** Motorcyclists Haliwood

| Date | Mintage | VF20 | XF40 | MS60 | MS63 | MS65 |
|---|---|---|---|---|---|---|
| 2007 PM | — | — | — | — | 10.00 | 12.00 |

**KM# 1422 CROWN**
28.28 g., Copper-Nickel, 38.6 mm. **Ruler:** Elizabeth II **Subject:** TT Centennial **Obv:** Bust with tiara right **Rev:** Motorcyclists Colier

| Date | Mintage | VF20 | XF40 | MS60 | MS63 | MS65 |
|---|---|---|---|---|---|---|
| 2007 PM | — | — | — | — | 10.00 | 12.00 |

**KM# 1530 CROWN**
28.28 g., Copper-Nickel, 38.61 mm. **Ruler:** Elizabeth II **Subject:** Christmas **Rev:** Two French hens

| Date | Mintage | VF20 | XF40 | MS60 | MS63 | MS65 |
|---|---|---|---|---|---|---|
| 2007 | — | — | — | — | — | 8.00 |

**KM# 1353 CROWN**
28.28 g., Copper-Nickel, 38.6 mm. **Ruler:** Elizabeth II **Subject:** Prince Charles 60th Birthday **Obv:** Bust with tiara right **Obv. Legend:** ELIZABETH II - ISLE OF MAN **Rev:** Heads of Charles, Princes William and Henry right **Edge:** Reeded

| Date | Mintage | VF20 | XF40 | MS60 | MS63 | MS65 |
|---|---|---|---|---|---|---|
| 2008 PM | — | — | — | — | 10.00 | 12.00 |

**KM# 1353a CROWN**
28.28 g., 0.925 Silver 0.841 oz. ASW, 38.6 mm. **Ruler:** Elizabeth II **Subject:** Prince Charles 60th Birthday **Obv:** Bust with tiara right **Obv. Legend:** ELIZABETH II - ISLE OF MAN **Rev:** Heads of Charles, Princes William and Henry right **Edge:** Reeded

| Date | Mintage | VF20 | XF40 | MS60 | MS63 | MS65 |
|---|---|---|---|---|---|---|
| 2008 PM | 10,000 | PF63 45.00 | PF65 50.00 | | | |

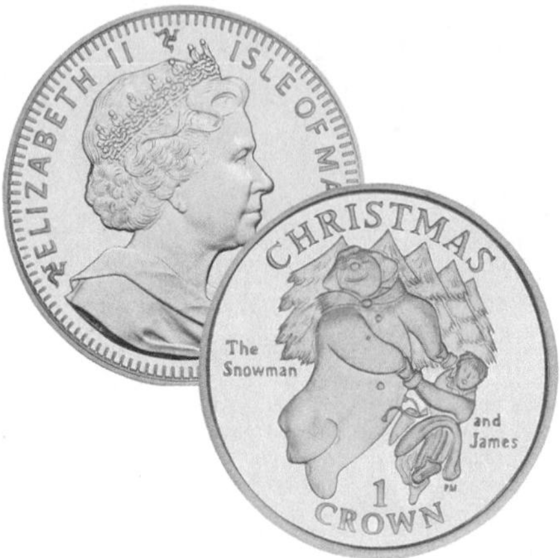


**KM# 1394 CROWN**
28.28 g., Copper-Nickel, 38.6 mm. **Ruler:** Elizabeth II **Rev:** Snowman and James

| Date | Mintage | VF20 | XF40 | MS60 | MS63 | MS65 |
|---|---|---|---|---|---|---|
| 2008 PM AA | — | — | — | — | — | 20.00 |

**KM# 1397 CROWN**
0.925 Silver, 56.2x40 mm. **Ruler:** Elizabeth II **Obv:** Bust with tiara right within Egyptian motif **Rev:** Seated figure and attendant **Shape:** Triangle

| Date | Mintage | VF20 | XF40 | MS60 | MS63 | MS65 |
|---|---|---|---|---|---|---|
| 2008 PM | 2,500 | PF65 75.00 | | | | |

**KM# 1398 CROWN**
0.925 Silver, 56.2x40 mm. **Ruler:** Elizabeth II **Obv:** Bust right in Tiaria within Egyptian motif **Rev:** Statue standing **Shape:** Triangle

| Date | Mintage | VF20 | XF40 | MS60 | MS63 | MS65 |
|---|---|---|---|---|---|---|
| 2008 PM | 2,500 | PF65 75.00 | | | | |

**KM# 1401 CROWN**
28.28 g., 0.925 Silver 0.841 oz. ASW, 38.6 mm. **Ruler:** Elizabeth II **Obv:** Bust with tiara right, multicolor band around **Rev:** Seated figures, multicolor band

| Date | Mintage | VF20 | XF40 | MS60 | MS63 | MS65 |
|---|---|---|---|---|---|---|
| 2008 PM | — | PF65 65.00 | | | | |

**KM# 1403 CROWN**
28.28 g., Copper-Nickel, 38.6 mm. **Ruler:** Elizabeth II **Subject:** Bejing Olympics **Obv:** Bust with tiara right **Rev:** Torch runner and Great Wall of China

| Date | Mintage | VF20 | XF40 | MS60 | MS63 | MS65 |
|---|---|---|---|---|---|---|
| 2008 PM | — | PF63 22.00 | PF65 25.00 | | | |

**KM# 1404 CROWN**
28.28 g., Copper-Nickel, 38.6 mm. **Ruler:** Elizabeth II **Obv:** Bust wiht tiara right **Rev:** Paddington Bear

| Date | Mintage | VF20 | XF40 | MS60 | MS63 | MS65 |
|---|---|---|---|---|---|---|
| 2008 PM | — | PF63 22.00 | PF65 25.00 | | | |

**KM# 1405 CROWN**
31.10 g., 0.999 Silver 0.999 oz. ASW, 56.2x40.7 mm. **Ruler:** Elizabeth II **Obv:** Bust with tiara right **Rev:** Three figures standing, vile of sand above **Shape:** Triangle

| Date | Mintage | VF20 | XF40 | MS60 | MS63 | MS65 |
|---|---|---|---|---|---|---|
| 2008 PM | 3,000 | PF65 75.00 | | | | |

**KM# 1424 CROWN**
28.28 g., Copper-Nickel, 38.6 mm. **Ruler:** Elizabeth II **Obv:** Bust with tiara right **Rev:** Two cats seated

| Date | Mintage | VF20 | XF40 | MS60 | MS63 | MS65 |
|---|---|---|---|---|---|---|
| 2008 PM | — | — | — | — | 15.00 | 17.00 |

**KM# 1424a CROWN**
31.11 g., 0.999 Silver 0.999 oz. ASW, 38.6 mm. **Ruler:** Elizabeth II **Obv:** Bust with tiara right **Rev:** Two cats seated

| Date | Mintage | VF20 | XF40 | MS60 | MS63 | MS65 |
|---|---|---|---|---|---|---|
| 2008 PM | — | PF65 70.00 | | | | |

**KM# 1373 CROWN**
28.28 g., Copper-Nickel, 38.6 mm. **Ruler:** Elizabeth II **Rev:** Berlin Wall and Brandenburg Gate statue group

| Date | Mintage | VF20 | XF40 | MS60 | MS63 | MS65 |
|---|---|---|---|---|---|---|
| 2009 | — | — | — | — | 15.00 | 18.00 |

**KM# 1373a CROWN**
28.28 g., 0.925 Silver 0.841 oz. ASW, 38.6 mm. **Ruler:** Elizabeth II **Rev:** Berlin Wall and Brandenberg Gate

| Date | Mintage | VF20 | XF40 | MS60 | MS63 | MS65 |
|---|---|---|---|---|---|---|
| 2009 | 10,000 | PF63 35.00 | PF65 40.00 | | | |

**KM# 1374 CROWN**
28.28 g., Copper-Nickel, 38.6 mm. **Ruler:** Elizabeth II **Subject:** Terra Cotta Army **Obv:** Bust right **Rev:** Making of the Soldier

| Date | Mintage | VF20 | XF40 | MS60 | MS63 | MS65 |
|---|---|---|---|---|---|---|
| 2009 | — | — | — | — | 12.00 | 15.00 |

**KM# 1374a CROWN**
28.28 g., 0.925 Silver 0.841 oz. ASW, 38.6 mm. **Ruler:** Elizabeth II **Subject:** Terra Cotta Army **Obv:** Bust right **Rev:** Making of the Soldier

| Date | Mintage | VF20 | XF40 | MS60 | MS63 | MS65 |
|---|---|---|---|---|---|---|
| 2009 | 10,000 | PF63 35.00 | PF65 40.00 | | | |

**KM# 1376 CROWN**
28.28 g., 0.925 Copper-Nickel 0.841 oz., 38.6 mm. **Ruler:** Elizabeth II **Subject:** Terra Cotta Army **Obv:** Bust right **Rev:** Making of the Horse

| Date | Mintage | VF20 | XF40 | MS60 | MS63 | MS65 |
|---|---|---|---|---|---|---|
| 2009 | — | — | — | — | 12.00 | 15.00 |

**KM# 1376a CROWN**
28.28 g., 0.925 Silver 0.841 oz. ASW, 38.6 mm. **Ruler:** Elizabeth II **Subject:** Terra Cotta Army **Obv:** Bust right **Rev:** Making of the Horse

| Date | Mintage | VF20 | XF40 | MS60 | MS63 | MS65 |
|---|---|---|---|---|---|---|
| 2009 | 10,000 | PF63 35.00 | PF65 40.00 | | | |

**KM# 1378.1 CROWN**
28.28 g., Copper-Nickel, 38.6 mm. **Ruler:** Elizabeth II **Obv:** Bust right **Rev:** Chinchilla cat and kitten

| Date | Mintage | VF20 | XF40 | MS60 | MS63 | MS65 |
|---|---|---|---|---|---|---|
| 2009 | — | — | — | — | 15.00 | 18.00 |

**KM# 1378.1a CROWN**
31.11 g., 0.999 Silver 0.999 oz. ASW, 38.6 mm. **Ruler:** Elizabeth II **Obv:** Bust with tiara right **Rev:** Two cats

| Date | Mintage | VF20 | XF40 | MS60 | MS63 | MS65 |
|---|---|---|---|---|---|---|
| 2009 PM | — | PF65 70.00 | | | | |

**KM# 1378.2 CROWN**
28.28 g., Copper-Nickel, 38.6 mm. **Ruler:** Elizabeth II **Obv:** Bust right **Rev:** Multicolor chinchilla cat and kitten

| Date | Mintage | VF20 | XF40 | MS60 | MS63 | MS65 |
|---|---|---|---|---|---|---|
| 2009 | — | — | — | — | — | 25.00 |

**KM# 1378.2a CROWN**
31.11 g., 0.999 Silver 0.999 oz. ASW, 38.6 mm. **Ruler:** Elizabeth II **Obv:** Bust with tiara right **Rev:** Two cats, multicolor

| Date | Mintage | VF20 | XF40 | MS60 | MS63 | MS65 |
|---|---|---|---|---|---|---|
| 2009 PM | — | **PF65** 80.00 | | | | |

**KM# 1379 CROWN**
31.11 g., 0.9999 Gold 0.9999 oz. AGW, 32.7 mm. **Ruler:** Elizabeth II **Obv:** Bust right **Rev:** Chinchilla cat and kitten

| Date | Mintage | VF20 | XF40 | MS60 | MS63 | MS65 |
|---|---|---|---|---|---|---|
| 2009 | — | — | — | — | — | 1,800 |
| 2009 | 1,000 | **PF63** 1,825 | **PF65** 1,850 | | | |

**KM# 1388 CROWN**
31.11 g., 0.9999 Gold 0.9999 oz. AGW, 45x31.1 mm. **Ruler:** Elizabeth II **Subject:** Howard Carter, 70th Anniversary of Death **Obv:** Bust right **Rev:** Pharoah and Anubis carving, encased with sand **Shape:** Triangle

| Date | Mintage | VF20 | XF40 | MS60 | MS63 | MS65 |
|---|---|---|---|---|---|---|
| 2009 | 250 | **PF65** 1,850 | | | | |

**KM# 1389 CROWN**
31.10 g., 0.999 Silver 0.999 oz. ASW, 56.2x40.7 mm. **Ruler:** Elizabeth II **Subject:** Howard Carter, 70th Anniversary of death **Obv:** Bust right **Rev:** Pharoah and Anubis, encased with sand **Shape:** Triangle

| Date | Mintage | VF20 | XF40 | MS60 | MS63 | MS65 |
|---|---|---|---|---|---|---|
| 2009 | 3,000 | **PF65** 125 | | | | |

**KM# 1390.1 CROWN**
28.28 g., Copper-Nickel, 38.6 mm. **Ruler:** Elizabeth II **Subject:** Concorde test flight, 40th Anniversary **Obv:** Bust right **Rev:** Concorde and five world landmarks

| Date | Mintage | VF20 | XF40 | MS60 | MS63 | MS65 |
|---|---|---|---|---|---|---|
| 2009 | — | — | — | — | 15.00 | 18.00 |

**KM# 1390.1a CROWN**
28.28 g., 0.925 Silver 0.841 oz. ASW, 38.6 mm. **Ruler:** Elizabeth II **Subject:** Corcorde test flight, 40th Anniversary **Obv:** Bust right **Rev:** Concorde and five world landmarks

| Date | Mintage | VF20 | XF40 | MS60 | MS63 | MS65 |
|---|---|---|---|---|---|---|
| 2009 | 10,000 | **PF63** 35.00 | **PF65** 40.00 | | | |

**KM# 1390.2 CROWN**
28.28 g., Copper-Nickel, 38.6 mm. **Ruler:** Elizabeth II **Subject:** 40th Anniversary of test flight **Rev:** Concorde in color

| Date | Mintage | VF20 | XF40 | MS60 | MS63 | MS65 |
|---|---|---|---|---|---|---|
| 2009 PM | — | — | — | — | — | 25.00 |

**KM# 1391 CROWN**
28.28 g., Copper-Nickel, 38.6 mm. **Ruler:** Elizabeth II **Obv:** Bust right **Rev:** Henry VIII and portraits of wives

| Date | Mintage | VF20 | XF40 | MS60 | MS63 | MS65 |
|---|---|---|---|---|---|---|
| 2009 | — | — | — | — | 15.00 | 18.00 |

**KM# 1391a CROWN**
28.28 g., 0.925 Silver 0.841 oz. ASW, 38.6 mm. **Ruler:** Elizabeth II **Obv:** Bust right **Rev:** Henry VIII

| Date | Mintage | VF20 | XF40 | MS60 | MS63 | MS65 |
|---|---|---|---|---|---|---|
| 2009 | 10,000 | **PF63** 35.00 | **PF65** 40.00 | | | |

**KM# 1392 CROWN**
28.28 g., Copper-Nickel, 38.6 mm. **Ruler:** Elizabeth II **Subject:** FIFA World Cup - South Africa **Obv:** Bust right **Rev:** Two soccer players

| Date | Mintage | VF20 | XF40 | MS60 | MS63 | MS65 |
|---|---|---|---|---|---|---|
| 2009 | — | — | — | — | 15.00 | 18.00 |

**KM# 1392a CROWN**
28.28 g., 0.925 Silver 0.841 oz. ASW, 38.6 mm. **Ruler:** Elizabeth II **Subject:** FIFA World Cup - South Africa **Obv:** Bust right

| Date | Mintage | VF20 | XF40 | MS60 | MS63 | MS65 |
|---|---|---|---|---|---|---|
| 2009 | 10,000 | **PF63** 35.00 | **PF65** 40.00 | | | |

**KM# 1406 CROWN**
28.28 g., Copper-Nickel, 38.6 mm. **Ruler:** Elizabeth II **Series:** London Olympics 2012 **Obv:** Bust wiht tiara right **Rev:** Three cyclists before Buckingham Palace

| Date | Mintage | VF20 | XF40 | MS60 | MS63 | MS65 |
|---|---|---|---|---|---|---|
| 2009 PM | — | **PF63** 22.00 | **PF65** 25.00 | | | |

**KM# 1406a CROWN**
28.28 g., 0.925 Silver 0.841 oz. ASW, 38.6 mm. **Ruler:** Elizabeth II **Series:** Olympics, London **Rev:** Three cyclists speeding past Buckingham Palace

| Date | Mintage | VF20 | XF40 | MS60 | MS63 | MS65 |
|---|---|---|---|---|---|---|
| 2009 PM | 10,000 | **PF63** 45.00 | **PF65** 50.00 | | | |

**KM# 1407 CROWN**
28.28 g., Copper-Nickel, 38.6 mm. **Ruler:** Elizabeth II **Subject:** London Olympics, 2012 **Obv:** Bust with tiara right **Rev:** Rowers before Big Ben and Parliament

| Date | Mintage | VF20 | XF40 | MS60 | MS63 | MS65 |
|---|---|---|---|---|---|---|
| 2009 PM | — | **PF63** 22.00 | **PF65** 25.00 | | | |

**KM# 1407a CROWN**
28.28 g., 0.925 Silver 0.841 oz. ASW, 38.6 mm. **Ruler:** Elizabeth II **Subject:** Olympics, London **Rev:** Skull of 4 rowers on Thames

| Date | Mintage | VF20 | XF40 | MS60 | MS63 | MS65 |
|---|---|---|---|---|---|---|
| 2009 PM | 10,000 | **PF63** 45.00 | **PF65** 50.00 | | | |

**KM# 1408 CROWN**
28.28 g., Copper-Nickel, 38.6 mm. **Ruler:** Elizabeth II **Subject:** London Olympics, 2012 **Obv:** Bust with tiara right **Rev:** Swimmer before Tower of London

| Date | Mintage | VF20 | XF40 | MS60 | MS63 | MS65 |
|---|---|---|---|---|---|---|
| 2009 PM | — | **PF63** 22.00 | **PF65** 25.00 | | | |

**KM# 1408a CROWN**
28.28 g., 0.925 Silver 0.841 oz. ASW, 38.6 mm. **Ruler:** Elizabeth II **Subject:** Olympics, London **Rev:** Swimmer in the Thames, Tower of London in background

| Date | Mintage | VF20 | XF40 | MS60 | MS63 | MS65 |
|---|---|---|---|---|---|---|
| 2009 PM | 10,000 | **PF63** 45.00 | **PF65** 50.00 | | | |

**KM# 1409 CROWN**
28.28 g., Copper-Nickel, 38.6 mm. **Ruler:** Elizabeth II **Subject:** London Olympics, 2012 **Obv:** Bust with tiara right **Rev:** Two runners before St. Paul's Cathedral

| Date | Mintage | VF20 | XF40 | MS60 | MS63 | MS65 |
|---|---|---|---|---|---|---|
| 2009 PM | — | **PF63** 22.00 | **PF65** 25.00 | | | |

**KM# 1409a CROWN**
28.28 g., 0.925 Silver 0.841 oz. ASW, 38.6 mm. **Ruler:** Elizabeth II **Subject:** Olympics, London **Rev:** Two female runners by St. Paul's Cathedral

| Date | Mintage | VF20 | XF40 | MS60 | MS63 | MS65 |
|---|---|---|---|---|---|---|
| 2009 PM | 10,000 | **PF63** 45.00 | **PF65** 50.00 | | | |

### KM# 1410 CROWN

28.28 g., Copper-Nickel, 38.6 mm. **Ruler:** Elizabeth II **Subject:** London Olympics, 2012 **Obv:** Bust with tiara right **Rev:** Two sailboats before Tower Bridge

| Date | Mintage | VF20 | XF40 | MS60 | MS63 | MS65 |
|---|---|---|---|---|---|---|
| 2009 PM | — | PF63 22.00 | PF65 25.00 | | | |

### KM# 1410a CROWN

28.28 g., 0.925 Silver 0.841 oz. ASW, 38.6 mm. **Ruler:** Elizabeth II **Subject:** Olympics, London **Rev:** Sailing on the Thames, Tower Bridge in background

| Date | Mintage | VF20 | XF40 | MS60 | MS63 | MS65 |
|---|---|---|---|---|---|---|
| 2009 PM | 10,000 | PF63 45.00 | PF65 50.00 | | | |

### KM# 1411 CROWN

28.28 g., Copper-Nickel, 38.6 mm. **Ruler:** Elizabeth II **Subject:** London Olympics, 2012 **Obv:** Bust with tiara right **Rev:** Two boxers before London Wheel and skyline

| Date | Mintage | VF20 | XF40 | MS60 | MS63 | MS65 |
|---|---|---|---|---|---|---|
| 2009 PM | — | PF63 22.00 | PF65 25.00 | | | |

### KM# 1411a CROWN

28.28 g., 0.925 Silver 0.841 oz. ASW, 38.6 mm. **Ruler:** Elizabeth II **Subject:** Olympics, London **Rev:** Boxers with London architecture in background

| Date | Mintage | VF20 | XF40 | MS60 | MS63 | MS65 |
|---|---|---|---|---|---|---|
| 2009 PM | 10,000 | PF63 45.00 | PF65 50.00 | | | |

### KM# 1412 CROWN

28.28 g., Copper-Nickel, 38.6 mm. **Ruler:** Elizabeth II **Subject:** Vancouver Olympics, 2010 **Obv:** Bust with tiara right **Rev:** Torch at center of four sports, hockey, sled, figure skating and bobsled

| Date | Mintage | VF20 | XF40 | MS60 | MS63 | MS65 |
|---|---|---|---|---|---|---|
| 2009 PM | — | PF63 22.00 | PF65 25.00 | | | |

### KM# 1413 CROWN

28.28 g., Copper-Nickel, 38.6 mm. **Ruler:** Elizabeth II **Subject:** Vancouver Olympics, 2010 **Obv:** Bust with tiara right **Rev:** Torch at center of four sports, ski jump, snoboardiong, biathlon and Salom

| Date | Mintage | VF20 | XF40 | MS60 | MS63 | MS65 |
|---|---|---|---|---|---|---|
| 2009 PM | — | PF63 22.00 | PF65 25.00 | | | |

### KM# 1414 CROWN

28.28 g., Copper-Nickel, 38.6 mm. **Ruler:** Elizabeth II **Subject:** Bee Gee's 50th Anniversary **Obv:** Bust with tiara right **Rev:** Band name at center

| Date | Mintage | VF20 | XF40 | MS60 | MS63 | MS65 |
|---|---|---|---|---|---|---|
| 2009 PM | — | PF63 22.00 | PF65 25.00 | | | |

### KM# 1415 CROWN

28.28 g., Copper-Nickel, 38.6 mm. **Ruler:** Elizabeth II **Subject:** First man on the Moon, 40th Anniversary **Obv:** Bust with tiara right **Rev:** Man in space suit with American Flag on moon

| Date | Mintage | VF20 | XF40 | MS60 | MS63 | MS65 |
|---|---|---|---|---|---|---|
| 2009 PM | — | PF63 22.00 | PF65 25.00 | | | |

### KM# 1465 CROWN

31.10 g., 0.9999 Gold 0.9999 oz. AGW with sand insert, 45x32.1 mm. **Ruler:** Elizabeth II **Subject:** Howard Carter, 70th Anniversary of Death **Shape:** Triangle

| Date | Mintage | VF20 | XF40 | MS60 | MS63 | MS65 |
|---|---|---|---|---|---|---|
| 2009 PM | 250 | PF65 1,850 | | | | |

### KM# 1417 CROWN

0.999 Silver **Ruler:** Elizabeth II **Obv:** Bust with tiara right within ornimentation **Rev:** Kubla Kahn standing **Shape:** Vertical rectangle

| Date | Mintage | VF20 | XF40 | MS60 | MS63 | MS65 |
|---|---|---|---|---|---|---|
| 2010 PM | — | PF65 50.00 | | | | |

### KM# 1426 CROWN

28.28 g., Copper-Nickel, 38.6 mm. **Ruler:** Elizabeth II **Obv:** Bust with tiara right **Rev:** Abyssinian Cat standing right over kitten **Edge:** Reeded

| Date | Mintage | VF20 | XF40 | MS60 | MS63 | MS65 |
|---|---|---|---|---|---|---|
| 2010 PM | — | — | — | — | 15.00 | 17.00 |

### KM# 1426a CROWN

31.11 g., 0.999 Silver 0.999 oz. ASW, 38.6 mm. **Ruler:** Elizabeth II **Obv:** Bust with tiara right **Rev:** Cat standing right

| Date | Mintage | VF20 | XF40 | MS60 | MS63 | MS65 |
|---|---|---|---|---|---|---|
| 2010 PM | — | PF65 70.00 | | | | |

### KM# 1471 CROWN

28.28 g., Copper-Nickel, 38.6 mm. **Ruler:** Elizabeth II **Obv:** Bust in tiara right **Rev:** Buckingham Palace

| Date | Mintage | VF20 | XF40 | MS60 | MS63 | MS65 |
|---|---|---|---|---|---|---|
| 2010 PM | — | — | — | — | — | 10.00 |

### KM# 1471a CROWN

28.28 g., 0.925 Silver 0.841 oz. ASW, 38.6 mm. **Ruler:** Elizabeth II **Obv:** Bust in tiara right **Rev:** Buckingham Palace

| Date | Mintage | VF20 | XF40 | MS60 | MS63 | MS65 |
|---|---|---|---|---|---|---|
| 2010 PM | — | PF63 45.00 | PF65 50.00 | | | |
| 2010 PM | — | PF63 50.00 | PF65 55.00 | | | |

Note: Script WK privy mark for engagement

**KM# 1439 CROWN**
31.11 g., 0.9999 Gold 0.9999 oz. AGW, 32.7 mm. **Ruler:** Elizabeth II **Subject:** Turkish Angora Cat

| Date | Mintage | VF20 | XF40 | MS60 | MS63 | MS65 |
|---|---|---|---|---|---|---|
| 2011 PM | 1,000 | PF63 1,875 | PF65 1,900 | | | |
| 2011 PM | — | — | — | — | — | 1,850 |

**KM# 1440 CROWN**
28.28 g., Copper-Nickel, 38.6 mm. **Ruler:** Elizabeth II **Subject:** Turkish Angora Cat

| Date | Mintage | VF20 | XF40 | MS60 | MS63 | MS65 |
|---|---|---|---|---|---|---|
| 2011 PM | — | — | — | — | — | 10.00 |

**KM# 1440a.1 CROWN**
31.11 g., 0.999 Silver 0.999 oz. ASW, 38.6 mm. **Ruler:** Elizabeth II **Subject:** Turkish Angora Cat

| Date | Mintage | VF20 | XF40 | MS60 | MS63 | MS65 |
|---|---|---|---|---|---|---|
| 2011 PM | 10,000 | PF65 70.00 | | | | |

**KM# 1440a.2 CROWN**
31.11 g., 0.999 Silver 0.999 oz. ASW, 38.6 mm. **Ruler:** Elizabeth II **Rev:** Two cats in color

| Date | Mintage | VF20 | XF40 | MS60 | MS63 | MS65 |
|---|---|---|---|---|---|---|
| 2011 PM | — | — | — | — | — | 75.00 |

**KM# 1455 CROWN**
28.28 g., Copper-Nickel, 38.6 mm. **Ruler:** Elizabeth II **Subject:** Isle of Man Tourist Trophy race **Rev:** Two racers and outline map of the Isle of Man

| Date | Mintage | VF20 | XF40 | MS60 | MS63 | MS65 |
|---|---|---|---|---|---|---|
| 2011 PM | — | — | — | — | — | 10.00 |

**KM# 1455a CROWN**
28.28 g., 0.925 Silver 0.841 oz. ASW, 38.6 mm. **Ruler:** Elizabeth II **Subject:** Isle of Man Tourist Trophy race **Rev:** Two racers and map of the Isle of Man

| Date | Mintage | VF20 | XF40 | MS60 | MS63 | MS65 |
|---|---|---|---|---|---|---|
| 2011 PM | 10,000 | PF63 45.00 | PF65 50.00 | | | |

**KM# 1456 CROWN**
31.10 g., 0.9999 Gold 0.9999 oz. AGW, 32.7 mm. **Ruler:** Elizabeth II **Subject:** Donatello's Chellini Madonna **Rev:** Mary and child in very high relief

| Date | Mintage | VF20 | XF40 | MS60 | MS63 | MS65 |
|---|---|---|---|---|---|---|
| 2011 PM | 999 | PF65 1,850 | | | | |

**KM# 1477 CROWN**
28.28 g., Copper-Nickel, 38.6 mm. **Ruler:** Elizabeth II **Rev:** Busts right of Elizabeth II and Prince Philip, flags flanking, royal shield below

| Date | Mintage | VF20 | XF40 | MS60 | MS63 | MS65 |
|---|---|---|---|---|---|---|
| 2011 PM | — | — | — | — | — | 10.00 |

**KM# 1477a CROWN**
28.28 g., 0.925 Silver 0.841 oz. ASW, 38.6 mm. **Ruler:** Elizabeth II **Rev:** Busts right of Elizabeth II and Prince Philip, flags flanking, royal shield below

| Date | Mintage | VF20 | XF40 | MS60 | MS63 | MS65 |
|---|---|---|---|---|---|---|
| 2011 PM | 10,000 | PF63 45.00 | PF65 50.00 | | | |

**KM# 1478 CROWN**
28.28 g., Copper-Nickel, 38.6 mm. **Ruler:** Elizabeth II **Subject:** Royal Wedding **Rev:** Busts left of Catherine Middleton in large hat and Prince William

| Date | Mintage | VF20 | XF40 | MS60 | MS63 | MS65 |
|---|---|---|---|---|---|---|
| 2011 PM | — | — | — | — | — | 10.00 |

**KM# 1478a CROWN**
28.28 g., 0.925 Silver 0.841 oz. ASW, 38.6 mm. **Ruler:** Elizabeth II **Subject:** Royal Wedding **Rev:** Busts left of Catherine Middleton in large hat and Prince William

| Date | Mintage | VF20 | XF40 | MS60 | MS63 | MS65 |
|---|---|---|---|---|---|---|
| 2011 PM | 10,000 | PF63 45.00 | PF65 50.00 | | | |

**KM# 1485 CROWN**
28.28 g., Copper-Nickel, 38.6 mm. **Ruler:** Elizabeth II **Subject:** Year of the Rabbit **Rev:** Image of Beatrix Potter's Peter Rabbit

| Date | Mintage | VF20 | XF40 | MS60 | MS63 | MS65 |
|---|---|---|---|---|---|---|
| 2011 PM | — | — | — | — | — | 10.00 |

**KM# 1485a CROWN**
28.28 g., 0.925 Silver 0.841 oz. ASW, 38.6 mm. **Ruler:** Elizabeth II **Subject:** Year of the Rabbit **Rev:** Beatrix Potter's Peter Rabbit

| Date | Mintage | VF20 | XF40 | MS60 | MS63 | MS65 |
|---|---|---|---|---|---|---|
| 2011 PM | 10,000 | PF63 45.00 | PF65 50.00 | | | |

**KM# 1441 CROWN**
28.28 g., Copper-Nickel, 38.6 mm. **Ruler:** Elizabeth II **Subject:** Olympics, London **Rev:** Horse Jumping

| Date | Mintage | VF20 | XF40 | MS60 | MS63 | MS65 |
|---|---|---|---|---|---|---|
| 2012 PM | — | — | — | — | — | 10.00 |

**KM# 1441a CROWN**
28.28 g., 0.925 Silver 0.841 oz. ASW, 38.6 mm. **Ruler:** Elizabeth II **Subject:** Olympics, London **Rev:** Horse jumping

| Date | Mintage | VF20 | XF40 | MS60 | MS63 | MS65 |
|---|---|---|---|---|---|---|
| 2012 PM | 10,000 | PF63 45.00 | PF65 50.00 | | | |

**KM# 1442 CROWN**
28.28 g., Copper-Nickel, 38.6 mm. **Ruler:** Elizabeth II **Subject:** Olympics, London **Rev:** Track cyclist

| Date | Mintage | VF20 | XF40 | MS60 | MS63 | MS65 |
|---|---|---|---|---|---|---|
| 2012 PM | — | — | — | — | — | 10.00 |

**KM# 1442a CROWN**
28.28 g., 0.925 Silver 0.841 oz. ASW, 38.6 mm. **Ruler:** Elizabeth II **Subject:** Olympics, London **Rev:** Track Cyclist

| Date | Mintage | VF20 | XF40 | MS60 | MS63 | MS65 |
|---|---|---|---|---|---|---|
| 2012 PM | 10,000 | PF63 45.00 | PF65 50.00 | | | |

**KM# 1443 CROWN**
28.28 g., Copper-Nickel, 38.6 mm. **Ruler:** Elizabeth II **Subject:** Olympics, London **Rev:** Swimmer with divers in background

| Date | Mintage | VF20 | XF40 | MS60 | MS63 | MS65 |
|---|---|---|---|---|---|---|
| 2012 PM | — | — | — | — | — | 10.00 |

**KM# 1443a CROWN**
28.28 g., 0.925 Silver 0.841 oz. ASW, 38.6 mm. **Ruler:** Elizabeth II **Subject:** Olympics, London **Rev:** Swimmer, divers in background

| Date | Mintage | VF20 | XF40 | MS60 | MS63 | MS65 |
|---|---|---|---|---|---|---|
| 2012 PM | 10,000 | PF63 45.00 | PF65 50.00 | | | |

**KM# 1444 CROWN**

28.28 g., Copper-Nickel, 38.6 mm. **Ruler:** Elizabeth II **Subject:** Olympics, London **Rev:** Canoeist, two rowers in background

| Date | Mintage | VF20 | XF40 | MS60 | MS63 | MS65 |
|---|---|---|---|---|---|---|
| 2012 PM | — | — | — | — | — | 10.00 |

**KM# 1444a CROWN**

28.28 g., 0.925 Silver 0.841 oz. ASW, 38.6 mm. **Ruler:** Elizabeth II **Subject:** Olympics, London **Rev:** Canoeist, two rowers in background

| Date | Mintage | VF20 | XF40 | MS60 | MS63 | MS65 |
|---|---|---|---|---|---|---|
| 2012 PM | 10,000 | PF63 45.00 | PF65 50.00 | | | |

**KM# 1445 CROWN**

28.28 g., Copper-Nickel, 38.6 mm. **Ruler:** Elizabeth II **Subject:** Olympics, London **Rev:** Judo players, two boxers in background

| Date | Mintage | VF20 | XF40 | MS60 | MS63 | MS65 |
|---|---|---|---|---|---|---|
| 2012 PM | — | — | — | — | — | 10.00 |

**KM# 1445a CROWN**

28.28 g., 0.925 Silver 0.841 oz. ASW, 38.6 mm. **Ruler:** Elizabeth II **Subject:** Olympics, London **Rev:** Judo players, two boxers in background

| Date | Mintage | VF20 | XF40 | MS60 | MS63 | MS65 |
|---|---|---|---|---|---|---|
| 2012 PM | 10,000 | PF63 45.00 | PF65 50.00 | | | |

**KM# 1446 CROWN**

28.28 g., Copper-Nickel, 38.6 mm. **Ruler:** Elizabeth II **Subject:** Olympics, London **Rev:** Table tennis players, Lawn Tennis players in background

| Date | Mintage | VF20 | XF40 | MS60 | MS63 | MS65 |
|---|---|---|---|---|---|---|
| 2012 PM | — | — | — | — | — | 10.00 |

**KM# 1446a CROWN**

28.28 g., 0.925 Silver 0.841 oz. ASW, 38.6 mm. **Ruler:** Elizabeth II **Subject:** Olympics, London **Rev:** Table tennis players, Lawn tennis players in background

| Date | Mintage | VF20 | XF40 | MS60 | MS63 | MS65 |
|---|---|---|---|---|---|---|
| 2012 PM | 10,000 | PF63 45.00 | PF65 50.00 | | | |

**KM# 1461 CROWN**

28.28 g., Copper-Nickel, 38.6 mm. **Ruler:** Elizabeth II **Subject:** European Football Championships 2012 **Obv:** Player heading a football, Sitting Statue of Liberty in Lviv and Neptune's fountain in Gdansk in background

| Date | Mintage | VF20 | XF40 | MS60 | MS63 | MS65 |
|---|---|---|---|---|---|---|
| 2012 PM | — | — | — | — | — | 10.00 |

**KM# 1461a CROWN**

28.28 g., 0.925 Silver 0.841 oz. ASW, 38.6 mm. **Ruler:** Elizabeth II **Subject:** European Football Championships 2012 **Rev:** Footballer heading ball, Sitting Statue of Liberty in Lviv and Neptune's fountain in Gdansk in background

| Date | Mintage | VF20 | XF40 | MS60 | MS63 | MS65 |
|---|---|---|---|---|---|---|
| 2012 PM | 10,000 | PF63 45.00 | PF65 50.00 | | | |

**KM# 1462 CROWN**

28.28 g., Copper-Nickel, 38.6 mm. **Ruler:** Elizabeth II **Subject:** European Football Championships 2012 **Rev:** Player passing ball, Motherland Statue in Kiev and King Sigismund's statue in Warsaw

| Date | Mintage | VF20 | XF40 | MS60 | MS63 | MS65 |
|---|---|---|---|---|---|---|
| 2012 PM | — | — | — | — | — | 10.00 |

**KM# 1462a CROWN**

28.28 g., 0.925 Silver 0.841 oz. ASW, 38.6 mm. **Ruler:** Elizabeth II **Subject:** European Football Championships 2012 **Rev:** Player passing the ball, Motherland Statue in Kiev and King Sigismund's statue in Warsaw in background

| Date | Mintage | VF20 | XF40 | MS60 | MS63 | MS65 |
|---|---|---|---|---|---|---|
| 2012 PM | 10,000 | PF63 45.00 | PF65 50.00 | | | |

**KM# 1463 CROWN**

28.28 g., Copper-Nickel, 38.6 mm. **Ruler:** Elizabeth II **Subject:** European Football Championships 2012 **Rev:** Footballer shooting, Cathedral of the Transfiguration in Donetsk and the Raclawice Panorama in Wroclaw in background

| Date | Mintage | VF20 | XF40 | MS60 | MS63 | MS65 |
|---|---|---|---|---|---|---|
| 2012 PM | — | — | — | — | — | 10.00 |

**KM# 1463a CROWN**

28.28 g., 0.925 Silver 0.841 oz. ASW, 38.6 mm. **Ruler:** Elizabeth II **Subject:** European Football Championships 2012 **Rev:** Footballer shooting, Cathedral of the Transfiguration in Donetsk and the Raclawice Panorama in Wroclaw in background

| Date | Mintage | VF20 | XF40 | MS60 | MS63 | MS65 |
|---|---|---|---|---|---|---|
| 2012 PM | 10,000 | PF63 45.00 | PF65 50.00 | | | |

**KM# 1464 CROWN**

28.28 g., Copper-Nickel, 38.6 mm. **Ruler:** Elizabeth II **Subject:** European Football Championships 2012 **Rev:** Two footballers tackling, Cathedral of the Annunciation in Kharkiv and the Cathedral in Poznan in background

| Date | Mintage | VF20 | XF40 | MS60 | MS63 | MS65 |
|---|---|---|---|---|---|---|
| 2012 PM | — | — | — | — | — | 10.00 |

**KM# 1464a CROWN**

28.28 g., 0.925 Silver 0.841 oz. ASW, 38.6 mm. **Ruler:** Elizabeth II **Subject:** European Football Championships 2012 **Rev:** Two footballers tackling, Catheral of the annunciation in Kharkiv and the Cathedral in Poznan in background

| Date | Mintage | VF20 | XF40 | MS60 | MS63 | MS65 |
|---|---|---|---|---|---|---|
| 2012 PM | 10,000 | PF63 45.00 | PF65 50.00 | | | |

**KM# 1480 CROWN**

28.28 g., Copper-Nickel, 38.6 mm. **Ruler:** Elizabeth II **Obv:** Conjoined busts right **Rev:** Elizabeth II at coronation with scepter, orb and state crown

| Date | Mintage | VF20 | XF40 | MS60 | MS63 | MS65 |
|---|---|---|---|---|---|---|
| 2012 PM | — | — | — | — | — | 10.00 |

**KM# 1480a CROWN**

28.28 g., 0.925 Silver 0.841 oz. ASW, 38.6 mm. **Ruler:** Elizabeth II **Obv:** Conjoined busts right **Rev:** Elizabeth II at coronation with sceptre, orb and state crown

| Date | Mintage | VF20 | XF40 | MS60 | MS63 | MS65 |
|---|---|---|---|---|---|---|
| 2012 PM | 10,000 | PF63 45.00 | PF65 50.00 | | | |

**KM# 1481 CROWN**

28.28 g., Copper-Nickel, 38.6 mm. **Ruler:** Elizabeth II **Obv:** Conjoined busts right **Rev:** Elizabeth II during 2010 visit to Canada

| Date | Mintage | VF20 | XF40 | MS60 | MS63 | MS65 |
|---|---|---|---|---|---|---|
| 2012 PM | — | — | — | — | — | 10.00 |

**KM# 1481a CROWN**

28.28 g., 0.925 Silver 0.841 oz. ASW, 38.6 mm. **Ruler:** Elizabeth II **Obv:** Conjoined busts right **Rev:** Elizabeth, the Queen Mother

| Date | Mintage | VF20 | XF40 | MS60 | MS63 | MS65 |
|---|---|---|---|---|---|---|
| 2012 PM | 10,000 | PF63 45.00 | PF65 50.00 | | | |

**KM# 1482 CROWN**
28.28 g., Copper-Nickel, 38.6 mm. **Ruler:** Elizabeth II **Obv:** Conjoined busts right **Rev:** Passengers boarding Titanic

| Date | Mintage | VF20 | XF40 | MS60 | MS63 | MS65 |
|---|---|---|---|---|---|---|
| 2012 PM | — | — | — | — | — | 10.00 |

**KM# 1482a CROWN**
28.28 g., 0.925 Silver 0.841 oz. ASW, 38.6 mm. **Ruler:** Elizabeth II **Obv:** Conjoined busts right **Rev:** Passengers boarding Titanic

| Date | Mintage | VF20 | XF40 | MS60 | MS63 | MS65 |
|---|---|---|---|---|---|---|
| 2012 PM | 10,000 | PF63 50.00 | PF65 55.00 | | | |

**KM# 1483 CROWN**
28.28 g., Copper-Nickel, 38.6 mm. **Ruler:** Elizabeth II **Obv:** Conjoined busts right **Rev:** Titanic sailing into icefield

| Date | Mintage | VF20 | XF40 | MS60 | MS63 | MS65 |
|---|---|---|---|---|---|---|
| 2012 PM | — | — | — | — | — | 10.00 |

**KM# 1483a CROWN**
28.28 g., 0.925 Silver 0.841 oz. ASW, 38.6 mm. **Ruler:** Elizabeth II **Obv:** Conjoined busts right **Rev:** Titanic sailing into icefield

| Date | Mintage | VF20 | XF40 | MS60 | MS63 | MS65 |
|---|---|---|---|---|---|---|
| 2012 PM | 10,000 | PF63 45.00 | PF65 50.00 | | | |

**KM# 1489 CROWN**
Copper-Nickel, 38.8 mm. **Ruler:** Elizabeth II **Obv:** Two busts right

| Date | Mintage | VF20 | XF40 | MS60 | MS63 | MS65 |
|---|---|---|---|---|---|---|
| 2012 PM Proof | — | — | — | — | — | 10.00 |

**KM# 1532 CROWN**
28.28 g., Copper-Nickel, 38.61 mm. **Ruler:** Elizabeth II **Rev:** Westminster Abbey and Trumpeter

| Date | Mintage | VF20 | XF40 | MS60 | MS63 | MS65 |
|---|---|---|---|---|---|---|
| 2012 | — | — | — | — | — | 10.00 |

**KM# 1532a CROWN**
28.28 g., 0.925 Silver 0.841 oz. ASW **Ruler:** Elizabeth II **Rev:** Westminster Abbey and Trumpeter **Shape:** 38.61

| Date | Mintage | VF20 | XF40 | MS60 | MS63 | MS65 |
|---|---|---|---|---|---|---|
| 2012 | Est. 10000 | PF65 50.00 | | | | |

**KM# 1538 CROWN**
28.28 g., Copper-Nickel, 38.61 mm. **Ruler:** Elizabeth II **Obv:** Conjoined head right **Rev:** Two cats

| Date | Mintage | VF20 | XF40 | MS60 | MS63 | MS65 |
|---|---|---|---|---|---|---|
| 2012 | — | — | — | — | — | 10.00 |

**KM# 1539 CROWN**
28.28 g., Copper-Nickel, 38.61 mm. **Ruler:** Elizabeth II **Obv:** Conjoined busts right **Rev:** Tower Bridge and Thames Jubilee pagent

| Date | Mintage | VF20 | XF40 | MS60 | MS63 | MS65 |
|---|---|---|---|---|---|---|
| 2012 | — | — | — | — | — | 10.00 |

**KM# 1540 CROWN**
28.28 g., Copper-Nickel **Ruler:** Elizabeth II **Obv:** Bust right within brick pattern **Rev:** Treasury at Petra and insert

| Date | Mintage | VF20 | XF40 | MS60 | MS63 | MS65 |
|---|---|---|---|---|---|---|
| 2012 | — | PF65 50.00 | | | | |

**KM# 1544 CROWN**
28.28 g., Copper-Nickel, 38.61 mm. **Ruler:** Elizabeth II **Obv:** Conjoined busts of Elizabeth II, young and mature **Rev:** Conjoined busts of Elizabeth II and Victoria

| Date | Mintage | VF20 | XF40 | MS60 | MS63 | MS65 |
|---|---|---|---|---|---|---|
| 2013 | — | — | — | — | — | 15.00 |

**KM# 1456a CROWN**
31.11 g., 0.999 Silver 0.999 oz. ASW, 32.7 mm. **Ruler:** Elizabeth II **Subject:** Conatello's Chellini Madonna **Rev:** Mary and child in very high relief

| Date | Mintage | VF20 | XF40 | MS60 | MS63 | MS65 |
|---|---|---|---|---|---|---|
| 2013 | — | PF65 125 | | | | |

**KM# 1494 CROWN**
28.28 g., Copper-Nickel, 38.60 mm. **Ruler:** Elizabeth II **Subject:** St. Patrick

| Date | Mintage | VF20 | XF40 | MS60 | MS63 | MS65 |
|---|---|---|---|---|---|---|
| 2013 | — | — | — | — | — | 10.00 |

**KM# 1494a CROWN**
28.28 g., Silver, 38.6 mm. **Ruler:** Elizabeth II **Subject:** St. Patrick

| Date | Mintage | VF20 | XF40 | MS60 | MS63 | MS65 |
|---|---|---|---|---|---|---|
| 2013 | Est. 10000 | PF63 45.00 | PF65 50.00 | | | |

**KM# 1494a CROWN**
28.28 g., 0.925 Silver 0.841 oz. ASW, 38.61 mm. **Ruler:** Elizabeth II **Rev:** St. Patrick

| Date | Mintage | VF20 | XF40 | MS60 | MS63 | MS65 |
|---|---|---|---|---|---|---|
| 2013 | — | PF65 60.00 | | | | |

**KM# 1533 CROWN**
28.28 g., Copper-Nickel, 38.61 mm. **Ruler:** Elizabeth II **Subject:** Coronation, 60th Anniversary **Rev:** Royal family on balcony of Buckingham Palace, 1953

| Date | Mintage | VF20 | XF40 | MS60 | MS63 | MS65 |
|---|---|---|---|---|---|---|
| 2013 | — | — | — | — | — | 10.00 |

**KM# 1533a CROWN**
28.28 g., 0.925 Silver 0.841 oz. ASW, 38.61 mm. **Ruler:** Elizabeth II **Subject:** Coronation, 60th Anniversary **Rev:** Royal family on balcony of Buckingham Palace, 1953

| Date | Mintage | VF20 | XF40 | MS60 | MS63 | MS65 |
|---|---|---|---|---|---|---|
| 2013 | Est. 10000 | PF65 50.00 | | | | |

**KM# 1543 CROWN**
28.28 g., Copper-Nickel, 38.61 mm. **Ruler:** Elizabeth II **Rev:** Two Siberian cats seated

| Date | Mintage | VF20 | XF40 | MS60 | MS63 | MS65 |
|---|---|---|---|---|---|---|
| 2013 | — | — | — | — | — | 10.00 |

**KM# 1543a CROWN**
31.11 g., 0.999 Silver 0.999 oz. ASW, 38.61 mm. **Ruler:** Elizabeth II **Rev:** Two Siberian cats seated

| Date | Mintage | VF20 | XF40 | MS60 | MS63 | MS65 |
|---|---|---|---|---|---|---|
| 2013 | — | PF65 27.50 | | | | |

**KM# 1544a CROWN**
28.28 g., 0.925 Silver 0.841 oz. ASW, 38.61 mm. **Ruler:** Elizabeth II **Obv:** Conjoined busts of Elizabeth II, young and mature **Rev:** Conjoined busts of Elizabeth II and Victoria

| Date | Mintage | VF20 | XF40 | MS60 | MS63 | MS65 |
|---|---|---|---|---|---|---|
| 2013 | — | PF65 50.00 | | | | |

**KM# 1545 CROWN**
28.28 g., Copper-Nickel, 38.61 mm. **Ruler:** Elizabeth II **Subject:** Winter Olympics 2014, Sochi **Rev:** Curling

| Date | Mintage | VF20 | XF40 | MS60 | MS63 | MS65 |
|---|---|---|---|---|---|---|
| 2013 | — | — | — | — | — | 15.00 |

**KM# 1545.1 CROWN**
28.28 g., Copper-Nickel, 38.61 mm. **Ruler:** Elizabeth II **Subject:** Winter Olympics 2014, Sochi **Rev:** Curling with color snowflakes

| Date | Mintage | VF20 | XF40 | MS60 | MS63 | MS65 |
|---|---|---|---|---|---|---|
| 2013 | — | — | — | — | — | 17.50 |

**KM# 1545a CROWN**
28.28 g., 0.925 Silver 0.841 oz. ASW, 38.61 mm. **Ruler:** Elizabeth II **Subject:** Winter Olympics 2014, Sochi **Rev:** Curling

| Date | Mintage | VF20 | XF40 | MS60 | MS63 | MS65 |
|---|---|---|---|---|---|---|
| 2013 | — | PF65 60.00 | | | | |

**KM# 1546 CROWN**

28.28 g., Copper-Nickel, 38.61 mm. **Ruler:** Elizabeth II **Subject:** Winter Olympics 2014, Sochi **Rev:** Luge

| Date | Mintage | VF20 | XF40 | MS60 | MS63 | MS65 |
|---|---|---|---|---|---|---|
| 2013 | — | — | — | — | — | 15.00 |

**KM# 1546.1 CROWN**

28.28 g., Copper-Nickel, 38.61 mm. **Ruler:** Elizabeth II **Subject:** Winter Olympics 2014, Sochi **Rev:** Luge and color snowflakes

| Date | Mintage | VF20 | XF40 | MS60 | MS63 | MS65 |
|---|---|---|---|---|---|---|
| 2013 | — | — | — | — | — | 17.50 |

**KM# 1546a CROWN**

28.28 g., 0.925 Silver 0.841 oz. ASW, 38.61 mm. **Ruler:** Elizabeth II **Subject:** Winter Olympics 2014, Sochi **Rev:** Luge

| Date | Mintage | VF20 | XF40 | MS60 | MS63 | MS65 |
|---|---|---|---|---|---|---|
| 2013 | — | PF65 60.00 | | | | |

**KM# 1545a.1 CROWN**

28.28 g., 0.925 Silver 0.841 oz. ASW, 38.61 mm. **Ruler:** Elizabeth II **Subject:** Winter Olympics 2014, Sochi **Rev:** Curling with snowflakes in color

| Date | Mintage | VF20 | XF40 | MS60 | MS63 | MS65 |
|---|---|---|---|---|---|---|
| 2013 | — | PF65 70.00 | | | | |

**KM# 1546a.1 CROWN**

28.28 g., 0.925 Silver 0.841 oz. ASW, 38.61 mm. **Ruler:** Elizabeth II **Subject:** Winter Olympics 2014, Sochi **Rev:** Luge with snowflakes in color

| Date | Mintage | VF20 | XF40 | MS60 | MS63 | MS65 |
|---|---|---|---|---|---|---|
| 2013 | — | PF65 70.00 | | | | |

**KM# 1547 CROWN**

28.28 g., Copper-Nickel, 38.61 mm. **Ruler:** Elizabeth II **Subject:** Winter Olympics 2014, Sochi **Rev:** Figure skating

| Date | Mintage | VF20 | XF40 | MS60 | MS63 | MS65 |
|---|---|---|---|---|---|---|
| 2013 | — | — | — | — | — | 15.00 |

**KM# 1547.1 CROWN**

28.28 g., Copper-Nickel, 38.61 mm. **Ruler:** Elizabeth II **Subject:** Winter Olympics 2014, Sochi **Rev:** Figure skating with color snowflakes

| Date | Mintage | VF20 | XF40 | MS60 | MS63 | MS65 |
|---|---|---|---|---|---|---|
| 2013 | — | — | — | — | — | 17.50 |

**KM# 1547a CROWN**

28.28 g., 0.925 Silver 0.841 oz. ASW, 38.61 mm. **Ruler:** Elizabeth II **Subject:** Winter Olympics 2014, Sochi **Rev:** Figure skating

| Date | Mintage | VF20 | XF40 | MS60 | MS63 | MS65 |
|---|---|---|---|---|---|---|
| 2013 | — | PF65 60.00 | | | | |

**KM# 1547a.1 CROWN**

28.28 g., 0.925 Silver 0.841 oz. ASW, 38.61 mm. **Ruler:** Elizabeth II **Subject:** Winter Olympics 2014, Sochi **Rev:** Figure skating with snowflakes in color

| Date | Mintage | VF20 | XF40 | MS60 | MS63 | MS65 |
|---|---|---|---|---|---|---|
| 2013 | — | PF65 70.00 | | | | |

**KM# 1548 CROWN**

28.28 g., Copper-Nickel, 38.61 mm. **Ruler:** Elizabeth II **Subject:** Winter Olympics 2014, Sochi **Rev:** Downhill Skiing

| Date | Mintage | VF20 | XF40 | MS60 | MS63 | MS65 |
|---|---|---|---|---|---|---|
| 2013 | — | — | — | — | — | 15.00 |

**KM# 1548.1 CROWN**

28.28 g., Copper-Nickel, 38.61 mm. **Ruler:** Elizabeth II **Subject:** Winter Olympics 2014, Sochi **Rev:** Downhill skier with snowflakes in color

| Date | Mintage | VF20 | XF40 | MS60 | MS63 | MS65 |
|---|---|---|---|---|---|---|
| 2013 | — | — | — | — | — | 17.50 |

**KM# 1548a CROWN**

28.28 g., 0.925 Silver 0.841 oz. ASW, 38.61 mm. **Ruler:** Elizabeth II **Subject:** Winter Olympics 2014, Sochi **Rev:** Downhill skiing

| Date | Mintage | VF20 | XF40 | MS60 | MS63 | MS65 |
|---|---|---|---|---|---|---|
| 2013 | — | PF65 60.00 | | | | |

**KM# 1548a.1 CROWN**

28.28 g., 0.925 Silver 0.841 oz. ASW, 38.61 mm. **Ruler:** Elizabeth II **Subject:** Winter Olympics 2014, Sochi **Rev:** Downhill skiing and snowflakes in color

| Date | Mintage | VF20 | XF40 | MS60 | MS63 | MS65 |
|---|---|---|---|---|---|---|
| 2013 | — | PF65 70.00 | | | | |

**KM# 1549 CROWN**

28.28 g., Copper-Nickel, 38.61 mm. **Ruler:** Elizabeth II **Rev:** Kermode bear and two cubs

| Date | Mintage | VF20 | XF40 | MS60 | MS63 | MS65 |
|---|---|---|---|---|---|---|
| 2013 | — | — | — | — | — | 15.00 |

**KM# 1549a CROWN**

28.28 g., 0.925 Silver 0.841 oz. ASW, 38.61 mm. **Ruler:** Elizabeth II **Rev:** Kermode bear and two cubs

| Date | Mintage | VF20 | XF40 | MS60 | MS63 | MS65 |
|---|---|---|---|---|---|---|
| 2013 | — | PF65 50.00 | | | | |

**KM# 1200 2 CROWNS**

62.20 g., 0.999 Palladium 1.9978 oz. APW, 40 mm. **Ruler:** Elizabeth II **Subject:** Discovery of Palladium Bicentennial **Obv:** Bust with tiara right **Rev:** Pallas Athena left **Edge:** Reeded

| Date | Mintage | VF20 | XF40 | MS60 | MS63 | MS65 |
|---|---|---|---|---|---|---|
| 2004 PM | 300 | PF65 1,650 | | | | |

**KM# 1402 2 CROWNS**

0.925 Silver, 40 mm. **Ruler:** Elizabeth II **Obv:** Bust with tiara right **Rev:** Seven Wonders of the World, multicolor central item

| Date | Mintage | VF20 | XF40 | MS60 | MS63 | MS65 |
|---|---|---|---|---|---|---|
| 2008 PM | — | PF65 100 | | | | |

**KM# 1064 5 CROWN**

155.52 g., 0.9999 Gold 4.9995 oz. AGW, 65 mm. **Ruler:** Elizabeth II **Subject:** Year of the Snake **Obv:** Bust with tiara right **Rev:** Snake **Edge:** Reeded

| Date | Mintage | VF20 | XF40 | MS60 | MS63 | MS65 |
|---|---|---|---|---|---|---|
| 2001 | 250 | PF60 7,500 | PF63 8,500 | PF65 9,500 | | |

**KM# 1104 5 CROWN**

155.51 g., 0.9999 Gold 4.9993 oz. AGW, 65 mm. **Ruler:** Elizabeth II **Subject:** Year of the Horse **Obv:** Bust with tiara right **Rev:** Two horses **Edge:** Reeded

| Date | Mintage | VF20 | XF40 | MS60 | MS63 | MS65 |
|---|---|---|---|---|---|---|
| 2002 | 250 | PF60 7,500 | PF63 8,500 | PF65 9,500 | | |

**KM# 1173 5 CROWN**

155.51 g., 0.9999 Gold 4.9993 oz. AGW, 65 mm. **Ruler:** Elizabeth II **Subject:** Year of the Goat **Obv:** Bust with tiara right **Rev:** Three goats **Edge:** Reeded

| Date | Mintage | VF20 | XF40 | MS60 | MS63 | MS65 |
|---|---|---|---|---|---|---|
| 2003 PM | 250 | PF60 7,500 | PF63 8,500 | PF65 9,500 | | |

**KM# 1244 5 CROWN**

155.52 g., 0.9999 Gold 4.9995 oz. AGW, 65 mm. **Ruler:** Elizabeth II **Obv:** Bust with tiara right **Rev:** Monkey **Edge:** Reeded

| Date | Mintage | VF20 | XF40 | MS60 | MS63 | MS65 |
|---|---|---|---|---|---|---|
| 2004 PM | 250 | PF60 7,500 | PF63 8,500 | PF65 9,500 | | |

**KM# 1541 5 CROWN**

155.50 g., 0.999 Silver 4.9944 oz. ASW **Ruler:** Elizabeth II **Rev:** Mary and child in high relief

| Date | Mintage | VF20 | XF40 | MS60 | MS63 | MS65 |
|---|---|---|---|---|---|---|
| 2013 | — | PF65 250 | | | | |

**KM# 1528 13 CROWNS**

404.30 g., 0.999 Silver 12.9855 oz. ASW **Ruler:** Elizabeth II **Subject:** World Cup Soccer, Germany, 2006 **Rev:** Torszene in Empire Stadium in Wembley (1966)

| Date | Mintage | VF20 | XF40 | MS60 | MS63 | MS65 |
|---|---|---|---|---|---|---|
| 2004 | — | PF65 400 | | | | |

**KM# 1219 64 CROWNS**

2000.00 g., 0.999 Silver 64.2371 oz. ASW, 140 mm. **Ruler:** Elizabeth II **Obv:** Bust with tiara right **Rev:** Ocean Liner Queen Mary 2 **Edge:** Reeded

| Date | Mintage | VF20 | XF40 | MS60 | MS63 | MS65 |
|---|---|---|---|---|---|---|
| 2004 PM | 500 | PF65 2,350 | | | | |

**KM# 1142 100 CROWNS**

3000.00 g., 0.9999 Silver 96.4425 oz. ASW, 130 mm. **Ruler:** Elizabeth II **Subject:** Queen's Golden Jubilee **Obv:** Bust with tiara right **Rev:** Queen on horse **Edge:** Reeded **Note:** Illustration reduced.

| Date | Mintage | VF20 | XF40 | MS60 | MS63 | MS65 |
|---|---|---|---|---|---|---|
| 2002 | — | PF65 3,500 | | | | |

**KM# 1184 130 CROWNS**

4000.00 g., 0.999 Silver 128.4743 oz. ASW, 130 mm. **Ruler:** Elizabeth II **Obv:** Bust with tiara right **Rev:** Gold clad cameo portrait of Elizabeth I with a .035ct ruby inset on her forehead all within a circle of portraits **Edge:** Reeded

| Date | Mintage | VF20 | XF40 | MS60 | MS63 | MS65 |
|---|---|---|---|---|---|---|
| 2003 PM | 500 | PF65 4,700 | | | | |

## SILVER BULLION COINAGE

Angel Series

**KM# 1475 ANGEL**

31.11 g., 0.999 Silver 0.999 oz. ASW **Ruler:** Elizabeth II **Subject:** 15th Anniversary of the Angel **Obv:** Bust in tiara right **Rev:** St. Michael slaying dragon

| Date | Mintage | VF20 | XF40 | MS60 | MS63 | MS65 |
|---|---|---|---|---|---|---|
| 2010 PM | — | PF65 50.00 | | | | |

Note: Privy mark: 15

## SILVER BULLION COINAGE

Nobel Series

**KM# 1484 NOBLE**

31.11 g., 0.9999 Silver 0.9999 oz. ASW, 38.6 mm. **Ruler:** Elizabeth II **Obv:** Bust with tiara right **Rev:** Viking ship

| Date | Mintage | VF20 | XF40 | MS60 | MS63 | MS65 |
|---|---|---|---|---|---|---|
| 2011 PM Prooflike | — | — | — | — | — | 50.00 |

## GOLD BULLION COINAGE

Angel Issues

**KM# 1479 1/64 ANGEL**

0.49 g., 0.9999 Gold 0.0156 oz. AGW **Ruler:** Elizabeth II **Rev:** St. Michael slaying dragon

| Date | Mintage | VF20 | XF40 | MS60 | MS63 | MS65 |
|---|---|---|---|---|---|---|
| 2011 PM | — | PF65 50.00 | | | | |

Note: Privy mark: Wedding bells and date

**KM# 393 1/20 ANGEL**
1.56 g., 0.9999 Gold 0.050 oz. AGW, 18 mm. **Ruler:** Elizabeth II **Obv:** Crowned bust right **Rev:** Archangel Michael slaying dragon right

| Date | Mintage | VF20 | XF40 | MS60 | MS63 | MS65 |
|---|---|---|---|---|---|---|
| 2001 | — | — | — | — | — | 90.00 |
| 2001 | — | PF65 90.00 | | | | |
| 2001 | — | PF65 95.00 | | | | |
| Note: Privy mark: 3 Kings | | | | | | |
| 2002 | — | — | — | — | — | 90.00 |
| 2002 | — | PF65 90.00 | | | | |
| 2002 | — | PF65 95.00 | | | | |
| Note: Privy mark: Candy cane | | | | | | |
| 2003 | — | — | — | — | — | 90.00 |
| 2003 | — | PF65 90.00 | | | | |
| 2003 | — | PF65 95.00 | | | | |
| Note: Privy mark: Candy | | | | | | |
| 2004 | — | — | — | — | — | 90.00 |
| 2004 | — | PF65 90.00 | | | | |
| 2004 | — | PF65 95.00 | | | | |
| Note: Privy mark: Partridge in a Pear Tree | | | | | | |
| 2005 | — | — | — | — | — | 90.00 |
| 2005 | — | PF65 90.00 | | | | |
| 2005 | — | PF65 95.00 | | | | |
| Note: Privy mark: 2 Turtle doves | | | | | | |
| 2006 | — | — | — | — | — | 90.00 |
| 2006 | — | PF65 90.00 | | | | |
| 2006 | — | PF65 95.00 | | | | |
| Note: Privy mark: 3 French hens | | | | | | |
| 2007 | — | — | — | — | — | 90.00 |
| 2007 | — | PF65 90.00 | | | | |
| 2007 | — | PF65 95.00 | | | | |
| Note: Privy mark: 4 Calling birds | | | | | | |

**KM# 1106 1/20 ANGEL**
1.56 g., 0.9999 Gold 0.050 oz. AGW, 18 mm. **Ruler:** Elizabeth II **Obv:** Bust with tiara right **Rev:** St. Michael slaying dragon, three crown privy mark at right **Edge:** Reeded

| Date | Mintage | VF20 | XF40 | MS60 | MS63 | MS65 |
|---|---|---|---|---|---|---|
| 2001 (3c) | 1,000 | PF65 95.00 | | | | |
| 2002 | — | PF65 95.00 | | | | |
| Note: With candy cane privy mark | | | | | | |

**KM# 1252 1/20 ANGEL**
1.56 g., 0.9999 Gold 0.050 oz. AGW, 18 mm. **Ruler:** Elizabeth II **Obv:** Bust with tiara right **Rev:** St. Michael and Christmas privy mark **Edge:** Reeded

| Date | Mintage | VF20 | XF40 | MS60 | MS63 | MS65 |
|---|---|---|---|---|---|---|
| 2004 PM | 1,000 | PF65 95.00 | | | | |

**KM# 1430 1/20 ANGEL**
1.55 g., 0.9999 Gold 0.0498 oz. AGW, 18 mm. **Ruler:** Elizabeth II **Rev:** St. Michael slaying the dragon

| Date | Mintage | VF20 | XF40 | MS60 | MS63 | MS65 |
|---|---|---|---|---|---|---|
| 2009 PM Six Geese a laying privy mark | 1,000 | PF65 125 | | | | |
| 2010 PM Seven swans a swimming privy mark | 1,000 | PF65 125 | | | | |
| 2011 PM Eight maids a milking privy mark | 1,000 | PF65 125 | | | | |

**KM# 394 1/10 ANGEL**
3.11 g., 0.9999 Gold 0.100 oz. AGW, 23 mm. **Ruler:** Elizabeth II **Obv:** Crowned bust right **Rev:** Archangel Michael

| Date | Mintage | VF20 | XF40 | MS60 | MS63 | MS65 |
|---|---|---|---|---|---|---|
| 2001 | — | PF65 180 | | | | |
| 2001 | — | — | — | — | — | 175 |
| 2002 | — | — | — | — | — | 175 |
| 2002 | — | PF65 180 | | | | |
| 2003 | — | — | — | — | — | 175 |
| 2003 | — | PF65 180 | | | | |
| 2004 | — | — | — | — | — | 175 |
| 2004 | — | PF65 180 | | | | |
| 2005 | — | — | — | — | — | 175 |
| 2005 | — | PF65 180 | | | | |

**KM# 395 1/4 ANGEL**
7.78 g., 0.9999 Gold 0.250 oz. AGW **Ruler:** Elizabeth II **Obv:** Crowned bust right **Rev:** Archangel Michael slaying dragon

| Date | Mintage | VF20 | XF40 | MS60 | MS63 | MS65 |
|---|---|---|---|---|---|---|
| 2001 | — | — | — | — | — | 450 |
| 2001 | — | PF65 455 | | | | |
| 2002 | — | PF65 455 | | | | |
| 2002 | — | — | — | — | — | 450 |
| 2003 | — | PF65 455 | | | | |
| 2003 | — | — | — | — | — | 450 |
| 2004 | — | — | — | — | — | 450 |
| 2004 | — | PF65 455 | | | | |
| 2005 | — | — | — | — | — | 450 |
| 2005 | — | PF65 455 | | | | |

**KM# 397 ANGEL**
31.10 g., 0.9999 Gold 0.9999 oz. AGW **Ruler:** Elizabeth II **Obv:** Crowned bust right **Rev:** Archangel Michael slaying dragon right

| Date | Mintage | VF20 | XF40 | MS60 | MS63 | MS65 |
|---|---|---|---|---|---|---|
| 2001 | — | — | — | — | — | 1,725 |
| 2001 | — | PF65 1,750 | | | | |
| 2002 | — | — | — | — | — | 1,725 |
| 2002 | — | PF65 1,750 | | | | |
| 2003 | — | — | — | — | — | 1,725 |
| 2003 | — | PF65 1,750 | | | | |
| 2004 | — | PF65 1,750 | | | | |
| 2004 | — | — | — | — | — | 1,725 |
| 2005 | — | PF65 1,750 | | | | |
| 2005 | — | — | — | — | — | 1,725 |
| 2006 | 500 | PF65 1,750 | | | | |
| 2006 | — | — | — | — | — | 1,725 |
| 2007 | — | PF65 1,750 | | | | |
| 2007 | — | — | — | — | — | 1,725 |

**KM# 397.1 ANGEL**
31.10 g., 0.999 Gold 0.999 oz. AGW **Ruler:** Elizabeth II **Obv:** Crowned bust right **Rev:** Archangel Michael slaying dragon right

| Date | Mintage | VF20 | XF40 | MS60 | MS63 | MS65 |
|---|---|---|---|---|---|---|
| 2006 Proof, High Relief | Est. 1000 | PF65 1,725 | | | | |
| 2007 Proof, High Relief | Est. 1000 | PF65 1,725 | | | | |

**KM# 1466 ANGEL**
31.11 g., 0.9999 Gold 0.9999 oz. AGW, 33 mm. **Ruler:** Elizabeth II **Obv:** Bust in tiara right **Rev:** St. Michael slaying dragon

| Date | Mintage | VF20 | XF40 | MS60 | MS63 | MS65 |
|---|---|---|---|---|---|---|
| 2008 PM | — | — | — | — | — | 1,850 |
| 2008 PM | — | PF63 1,860 | PF65 1,875 | | | |

**KM# 1467 ANGEL**
31.11 g., 0.9999 Gold 0.9999 oz. AGW, 33 mm. **Ruler:** Elizabeth II **Obv:** Bust with tiara right **Rev:** St. Michael lunging right with spear

| Date | Mintage | VF20 | XF40 | MS60 | MS63 | MS65 |
|---|---|---|---|---|---|---|
| 2009 PM | — | PF63 1,860 | PF65 1,875 | | | |

**KM# 1468 ANGEL**
31.11 g., 0.9999 Gold 0.9999 oz. AGW, 33 mm. **Ruler:** Elizabeth II **Obv:** Bust with tiara right **Rev:** Dragon receiving spear wound

| Date | Mintage | VF20 | XF40 | MS60 | MS63 | MS65 |
|---|---|---|---|---|---|---|
| 2009 PM | — | PF63 1,860 | PF65 1,875 | | | |

## BI-METALLIC BULLION COINAGE

**KM# 1486 NOBLE**
39.10 g., Bi-Metallic 31.105 .999 Gold center in 9.39 .999 Silver ring, 36.7 mm. **Ruler:** Elizabeth II **Rev:** Viking ship, 15 in left field

| Date | Mintage | VF20 | XF40 | MS60 | MS63 | MS65 |
|---|---|---|---|---|---|---|
| 2009 PM | 3,000 | PF65 1,900 | | | | |

## CROWN SERIES

| KM# | Date | Mintage | Identification | Mkt Val |
|---|---|---|---|---|
| | 2002 PM pcs. Proof | 500 | | |

## MINT SETS

| KM# | Date | Mintage | Identification | Issue Price | Mkt Val |
|---|---|---|---|---|---|
| MS30 | 2001 (8) | — | KM#1036-1043 | — | 22.50 |
| MS31 | 2001 (9) | — | KM#1036-1044 | — | 40.00 |
| MS32 | 2002 (8) | — | KM#1036-1043 | — | 22.50 |
| MS33 | 2002 (9) | — | KM#1036-1044 | — | 40.00 |
| MS34 | 2003 (8) | — | KM#1036-1043 | — | 22.50 |
| MS35 | 2003 (9) | — | KM#1036-1044 | — | 40.00 |
| MS36 | 2004 (8) | — | KM#1253-1260 | — | 25.00 |
| MS37 | 2004 (9) | — | KM#1253-1261 | — | 40.00 |
| MS38 | 2005 (8) | — | KM#1253-1260 | — | 22.50 |
| MS39 | 2005 (9) | — | KM#1253-1261 | — | 40.00 |
| MS40 | 2006 (8) | — | MS#1253-1260 | 35.00 | 25.00 |
| MS41 | 2006 (9) | — | KM1253-1261 | 42.50 | 40.00 |
| MS42 | 2007 (8) | — | KM#1253-1260 | 35.00 | 22.50 |
| MS43 | 2007 (9) | — | KM1253-1261 | 42.50 | 40.00 |

## PROOF SETS

| KM# | Date | Mintage | Identification | Issue Price | Mkt Val |
|---|---|---|---|---|---|
| PS59 | 2001 (5) | 1,000 | KM#1067-1070, 1073 | — | 3,350 |
| PS60 | 2003 (3) | — | KM#1186, 1187, 1188 | — | 650 |
| PS61 | 2003 (5) | — | KM#1186, 1187, 1188, 1189, 1190 w/gold ring | — | 3,300 |
| PS62 | 2003 (5) | — | KM#1191-1195 w/gold-plated silver ring | — | 245 |
| PS63 | 2004 (5) | 1,000 | KM#1247, 1248, 1249.1, 1250, 1251 | — | 3,375 |

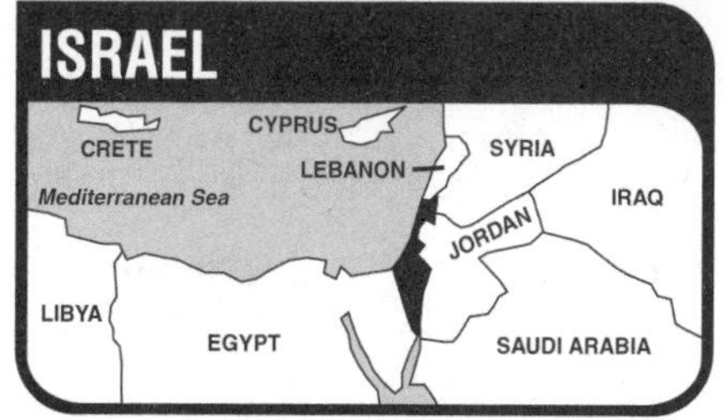


The state of Israel, a Middle Eastern republic at the eastern end of the Mediterranean Sea, bounded by Lebanon on the north, Syria on the northeast, Jordan on the east, and Egypt on the southwest, has an area of 9,000sq. mi. (20,770 sq. km.) and a population of 6 million. Capital: Jerusalem. Finished diamonds, chemicals, citrus, textiles, minerals, electronic and transportation equipment are exported.

**HEBREW COIN DATING**

Israeli coins are dated according to the Christian year (AD). The JE New Year falls in September or during the first few days of October. In the case of dual-dated coins, with some exceptions, the JE date is 3,760 years greater than the AD date. Thus, for example, JE5735 is equivalent to AD1975. Exceptions are almost all of the Hanukka (Festival of Lights) commemorative coins because Hanukka falls early in the JE year and late in the AD year (late November or December) and certain other commemorative coins issued early in the JE year. In the case of the dual-dated Hanukka coins (other than the JE5720 coin) and certain others, the difference is 3,761 years. However, for ease of reference, except in the case of such dual-dated coins, the AD date given is always 3,760 years greater than the JE date (including the Hanukka coins bearing only a JE date). In the case of Hanukka mint sets, however, where the packaging gives an AD date that differs from the JE date by 3,761 years, the AD date on the packaging is indicated by the issued date in brackets.

Israel's coins carry Hebrew dating formed from a combination of the 22 consonant letters of the Hebrew alphabet and read from right to left. The Jewish calendar dates back more than 5700 years; but five millenniums are assumed in the dating of coins (until 1981). Thus, the year 5735 (1975AD) appears as 735, with the first two characters from the right indicating the number of years in hundreds; tav (400), plus shin (300). The next is lamedh (30), followed by a separation mark which has the appearance of double quotation marks, then heh (5).

The separation mark - generally similar to a single quotation mark through 5718 (1958 AD), and like a double quotation mark thereafter - serves the purpose of indicating that the letters form a number, not a word, and on some issues can be confused with the character yodh (10), which in a stylized rendering can appear similar, although slightly larger and thicker. The separation mark does not appear in either form on a few commemorative issues.

The Star of David is not a mintmark. It appears only on some coins sold by the Israel Government Coins and Medals Corporation Ltd., which is owned by the Israel government, and is a division of the Prime Minister's office and sole distributor to collectors. The Star of David was first used in 1971 on the science coin to signify that it was minted in Jerusalem, but was later used by different mint facilities.

| AD DATE | JEWISH ERA | |
|---|---|---|
| 2001 | התשס"א | 5761 |
| 2002 | התשס"ב | 5762 |
| 2003 | התשס"ג | 5763 |
| 2004 | התשס"ד | 5764 |
| 2005 | התשס"ה | 5765 |
| 2006 | התשס"ו | 5766 |
| 2007 | התשס"ז | 5767 |
| 2008 | התשס"ח | 5768 |
| 2009 | התשס"ט | 5769 |
| 2010 | התש"ע | 5770 |
| 2011 | התשע"א | 5771 |
| 2012 | התשע"ב | 5772 |
| 2013 | התשע"ג | 5773 |
| 2014 | התשע"ד | 5774 |
| 2015 | התשע"ה | 5775 |

**MINT MARKS**

מ

(m) - Mem
(o) - Ottawa
(s) - San Francisco
None - Jerusalem

# REPUBLIC

## REFORM COINAGE

100 Agorot = 1 New Sheqel
1,000 Sheqalim = 1 New Sheqel;
September 4, 1985-present

### KM# 157 5 AGOROT

3.00 g., Aluminum-Bronze, 19.5 mm. **Obv:** Ancient coin **Rev:** Value within lined square **Edge:** Plain

| Date | Mintage | F12 | VF20 | XF40 | MS60 | MS63 |
|---|---|---|---|---|---|---|
| JE5761 (2001) (dj) | 6,144,000 | — | — | — | 0.15 | — |
| JE5762 (2002) (dj) | 6,144,000 | — | — | — | 0.15 | — |
| JE5764 (2004) | — | — | — | — | 0.15 | — |
| JE5765 (2005) | — | — | — | — | 0.15 | — |
| JE5766 (2006) | — | — | — | — | 0.15 | — |
| JE5767 (2007) | — | — | — | — | 0.15 | — |

### KM# 172 5 AGOROT

3.00 g., Aluminum-Bronze, 19.5 mm. **Subject:** Hanukka **Obv:** Ancient coin **Rev:** Value within lined square **Note:** JE5754-5768 coins contain the Star of David mint mark; the JE5747-5753 coins do not.

| Date | Mintage | F12 | VF20 | XF40 | MS60 | MS63 |
|---|---|---|---|---|---|---|
| JE5761 (2001) (u) Sets only | 4,000 | — | — | — | — | 2.50 |
| JE5762 (2002) (u) Sets only | 4,000 | — | — | — | — | 2.50 |
| JE5763 (2003) (u) Sets only | 3,000 | — | — | — | — | 3.00 |
| JE5764 (2004) (u) Sets only | 3,000 | — | — | — | — | 3.00 |
| JE5765 (2005) (u) Sets only | 2,500 | — | — | — | — | 3.00 |
| JE5766 (2006) (u) Sets only | 3,000 | — | — | — | — | 3.00 |
| JE5767 (2007) (u) Sets only | 3,000 | — | — | — | — | 3.00 |
| JE5768 (2008) (u) Sets only | 3,000 | — | — | — | — | 3.00 |

### KM# 158 10 AGOROT

4.00 g., Aluminum-Bronze, 22 mm. **Obv:** Menorah **Rev:** Value within lined square **Edge:** Plain

| Date | Mintage | F12 | VF20 | XF40 | MS60 | MS63 |
|---|---|---|---|---|---|---|
| JE5761 (2001) (dj) | 46,140,000 | — | — | — | 0.20 | — |
| Note: Sides of central part of zero are rounded. | | | | | | |
| JE5761 (2001) (so) | 32,256,000 | — | — | — | 0.20 | — |
| Note: Sides of central part of zero are straight. | | | | | | |
| JE5762 (2002) (w) | 4,608,000 | — | — | — | 0.20 | — |
| JE5763 (2003) (dj) | 22,980,000 | — | — | — | 0.20 | — |
| JE5764 (2004) | — | — | — | — | 0.20 | — |
| JE5765 (2005) | — | — | — | — | 0.20 | — |
| JE5766 (2006) | — | — | — | — | 0.20 | — |
| JE5767 (2007) (dj) | — | — | — | — | 0.20 | — |
| JE5768 (2008) (dj) | — | — | — | — | 0.20 | — |
| JE5769 (2009) (dj) | — | — | — | — | 0.20 | — |
| JE5770 (2010) (dj) | — | — | — | — | 0.20 | — |
| JE5771 (2011) (dj) | — | — | — | — | 0.20 | — |
| JE5772 (2012) (dj) | — | — | — | — | 0.20 | — |
| 5773 (2013) | — | — | — | — | 0.20 | — |
| 5774 (2014) | — | — | — | — | 0.20 | — |

### KM# 173 10 AGOROT

4.00 g., Aluminum-Bronze, 22 mm. **Subject:** Hanukka **Obv:** Menorah **Rev:** Value within lined square **Edge:** Plain **Note:** JE5754-5770 have the Star of David mint mark, JE5747-5753 coins do not.

| Date | Mintage | F12 | VF20 | XF40 | MS60 | MS63 |
|---|---|---|---|---|---|---|
| JE5761 (2001) (u) Sets only | 4,000 | — | — | — | — | 3.00 |
| JE5762 (2002) (u) Sets only | 4,000 | — | — | — | — | 3.00 |
| JE5763 (2003) (u) Sets only | 3,000 | — | — | — | — | 3.00 |
| JE5764 (2004) (u) Sets only | 3,000 | — | — | — | — | 3.00 |
| JE5765 (2005) (u) Sets only | 2,500 | — | — | — | — | 3.00 |
| JE5766 (2006) (u) Sets only | 3,000 | — | — | — | — | 3.00 |
| JE5767 (2007) (u) Sets only | 3,000 | — | — | — | — | 3.00 |
| JE5768 (2008) (u) Sets only | 3,000 | — | — | — | — | 3.00 |
| JE5769 (2009) (u) Sets only | 1,800 | — | — | — | — | 3.50 |
| JE5770 (2010) (u) Sets only | 1,800 | — | — | — | — | 3.50 |

### KM# 159 1/2 NEW SHEQEL

6.50 g., Aluminum-Bronze, 26 mm. **Obv:** Value **Rev:** Lyre **Edge:** Plain

| Date | Mintage | F12 | VF20 | XF40 | MS60 | MS63 |
|---|---|---|---|---|---|---|
| JE5762 (2002) (so) | 2,880,000 | — | — | — | 0.75 | — |
| JE5762 (2002) (v) | 5,760,000 | — | — | — | 0.75 | — |
| Note: Length of fraction line is 4 or 4.5 mm. but which mint produced which coin is not known. | | | | | | |
| JE5763 (2003) | — | — | — | — | 0.75 | — |
| JE5764 (2004) (so) | 2,640,000 | — | — | — | 0.75 | — |
| JE5765 (2005) | — | — | — | — | 0.75 | — |
| JE5766 (2006) | — | — | — | — | 0.75 | — |
| JE5767 (2007) | — | — | — | — | 0.75 | — |
| JE5768 (2008) (dj) | — | — | — | — | 0.75 | — |
| JE5769 (2009) (dj) | — | — | — | — | 0.60 | — |
| JE5770 (2010) (dj) | — | — | — | — | 0.60 | — |
| JE5771 (2011) (v) | — | — | — | — | 0.60 | — |
| JE5772 (dj) | — | — | — | — | 0.50 | — |
| 5774 (2014) | — | — | — | — | 0.50 | — |

### KM# 174 1/2 NEW SHEQEL

6.50 g., Aluminum-Bronze, 26 mm. **Subject:** Hanukka **Obv:** Value **Rev:** Lyre **Note:** Coins dated JE5754-5770 have the Star of David mint mark; the coins dated JE5747-5753 do not.

| Date | Mintage | F12 | VF20 | XF40 | MS60 | MS63 |
|---|---|---|---|---|---|---|
| JE5761 (2001) (u) Sets only | 4,000 | — | — | — | — | 3.50 |
| JE5762 (2002) (u) Sets only | 4,000 | — | — | — | — | 3.50 |
| JE5763 (2003) (u) Sets only | 3,000 | — | — | — | — | 3.50 |
| JE5764 (2004) (u) Sets only | 3,000 | — | — | — | — | 3.50 |
| JE5765 (2005) (u) Sets only | 2,500 | — | — | — | — | 3.50 |

| Date | Mintage | F12 | VF20 | XF40 | MS60 | MS63 |
|---|---|---|---|---|---|---|
| JE5766 (2006) (u) Sets only | 3,000 | — | — | — | — | 3.50 |
| JE5767 (2007) (u) Sets only | 3,000 | — | — | — | — | 3.50 |
| JE5768 (2008) (u) Sets only | 3,000 | — | — | — | — | 3.50 |
| JE5769 (2009) (u) Sets only | 1,800 | — | — | — | — | 3.50 |
| JE5770 (2010) (u) Sets only | 1,800 | — | — | — | — | 3.50 |

## KM# 354 1/2 NEW SHEQEL

6.50 g., Aluminum-Bronze, 26 mm. **Subject:** Hanukka **Obv:** Denomination **Rev:** Curacao Hanukka lamp **Edge:** Plain **Shape:** 12-sided **Note:** Struck for sets only

| Date | Mintage | F12 | VF20 | XF40 | MS60 | MS63 |
|---|---|---|---|---|---|---|
| JE5761 (2001) (u) | 4,000 | — | — | — | 11.00 | — |

## KM# 355 1/2 NEW SHEQEL

6.50 g., Aluminum-Bronze, 26 mm. **Obv:** Value **Rev:** Yemenite Hanukka Lamp **Edge:** Twelve plain sections **Note:** Struck for sets only

| Date | Mintage | F12 | VF20 | XF40 | MS60 | MS63 |
|---|---|---|---|---|---|---|
| JE5762 (2002) (u) | 4,000 | — | — | — | 11.00 | — |

## KM# 389 1/2 NEW SHEQEL

6.50 g., Aluminum-Bronze, 26 mm. **Obv:** Value **Rev:** Polish Hanukka Lamp **Edge:** Plain **Shape:** 12-sided **Note:** Struck for sets only

| Date | Mintage | F12 | VF20 | XF40 | MS60 | MS63 |
|---|---|---|---|---|---|---|
| JE5763 (2003) (u) | 3,000 | — | — | — | 12.00 | — |

Note: Even though not a proof, the coin has a mem

## KM# 390 1/2 NEW SHEQEL

6.50 g., Aluminum-Bronze, 26 mm. **Obv:** Value **Rev:** Iraqi Hanukka Lamp **Edge:** Plain **Shape:** 12-sided **Note:** Struck for sets only

| Date | Mintage | F12 | VF20 | XF40 | MS60 | MS63 |
|---|---|---|---|---|---|---|
| JE5764 (2004) (u) | 3,000 | — | — | — | 12.00 | — |

## KM# 391 1/2 NEW SHEQEL

6.50 g., Aluminum-Bronze, 26 mm. **Obv:** Value **Rev:** Syrian Hanukka Lamp **Edge:** Plain **Shape:** 12-sided **Note:** Struck for sets only

| Date | Mintage | F12 | VF20 | XF40 | MS60 | MS63 |
|---|---|---|---|---|---|---|
| JE5765 (2005) (u) | 2,500 | — | — | — | 12.00 | — |

## KM# 415 1/2 NEW SHEQEL

6.50 g., Aluminum-Bronze, 26 mm. **Obv:** Value and mini-Hanukka Lamp **Rev:** Dutch Hanukka Lamp **Edge:** Plain **Shape:** 12-sided **Note:** Struck for sets only

| Date | Mintage | F12 | VF20 | XF40 | MS60 | MS63 |
|---|---|---|---|---|---|---|
| JE5766 (2006) (u) | 3,000 | — | — | — | 12.00 | — |

## KM# 422 1/2 NEW SHEQEL

6.50 g., Aluminum-Bronze, 26 mm. **Obv:** Value and mini-Hanukka Lamp **Rev:** Corfu (Greek) Hanukka Lamp **Edge:** Plain **Shape:** 12-sided **Note:** Struck for sets only

| Date | Mintage | F12 | VF20 | XF40 | MS60 | MS63 |
|---|---|---|---|---|---|---|
| JE5767 (2007) (u) | 3,000 | — | — | — | 12.00 | — |

## KM# 434 1/2 NEW SHEQEL

6.50 g., Aluminum-Bronze, 26 mm. **Subject:** Hanukka **Obv:** Value, date, inscriptions and menorah **Rev:** Egyptian Hanukka lamp **Shape:** 12-sided **Note:** Struck for sets only

| Date | Mintage | F12 | VF20 | XF40 | MS60 | MS63 |
|---|---|---|---|---|---|---|
| JE5768 (2008) (u) | 3,000 | — | — | — | 12.00 | — |

## KM# 436 1/2 NEW SHEQEL

6.50 g., Aluminum-Bronze, 26 mm. **Subject:** Hanukka **Obv:** Value, date, inscriptions and menorah **Rev:** Prague Hanukka Lamp **Shape:** 12-sided **Note:** Struck for sets only

| Date | Mintage | F12 | VF20 | XF40 | MS60 | MS63 |
|---|---|---|---|---|---|---|
| JE5769 (2009) (u) | 1,800 | — | — | — | 12.00 | — |

## KM# 466 1/2 NEW SHEQEL

6.50 g., Aluminum-Bronze, 26 mm. **Subject:** Hanukka **Obv:** Value, date, inscriptions and menorah **Rev:** Algerian Hanukka Lamp **Edge:** Plain **Note:** Struck for sets only

| Date | Mintage | F12 | VF20 | XF40 | MS60 | MS63 |
|---|---|---|---|---|---|---|
| JE5770 (2010) (u) | 1,800 | — | — | — | 12.00 | — |

## KM# 163 NEW SHEQEL

4.00 g., Copper-Nickel, 18 mm. **Subject:** Hanukka **Obv:** Value **Rev:** Lily, state emblem and ancient Hebrew inscription. **Note:** Coins dated JE5754-5769 have the Star of David mint mark; the JE5746-5753 coins do not.

| Date | Mintage | F12 | VF20 | XF40 | MS60 | MS63 |
|---|---|---|---|---|---|---|
| JE5761 (2001) (u) Sets only | 4,000 | — | — | — | — | 4.00 |
| JE5770 (2010) | 1,800 | — | — | — | — | 4.00 |
| JE5762 (2002) (u) Sets only | 4,000 | — | — | — | — | 4.00 |
| JE5763 (2003) (u) Sets only | 3,000 | — | — | — | — | 4.00 |

| Date | Mintage | F12 | VF20 | XF40 | MS60 | MS63 |
|---|---|---|---|---|---|---|
| JE5764 (2004) (u) Sets only | 3,000 | — | — | — | — | 4.00 |
| JE5765 (2005) (u) Sets only | 2,500 | — | — | — | — | 4.00 |
| JE5766 (2006) (u) Sets only | 3,000 | — | — | — | — | 4.00 |
| JE5767 (2007) (u) Sets only | 3,000 | — | — | — | — | 4.00 |
| JE5769 (2009) (u) Sets only | 1,800 | — | — | — | — | 4.00 |
| JE5770 (2010) (u) Sets only | — | — | — | — | — | 4.00 |

## KM# 160a NEW SHEQEL

3.45 g., Nickel Plated Steel, 17.97 mm. **Obv:** Value **Rev:** Lily, state emblem and ancient Hebrew inscription **Edge:** Plain

| Date | Mintage | F12 | VF20 | XF40 | MS60 | MS63 |
|---|---|---|---|---|---|---|
| JE5761 (2001) (h) | 9,648,000 | — | — | — | 1.00 | — |
| JE5762 (2002) (h) | 18,816,000 | — | — | — | 1.00 | — |
| JE5763 (2003) (v) | 10,198,500 | — | — | — | 1.00 | — |
| JE5765 (2005) | — | — | — | — | 1.00 | — |
| JE5766 (2006) | — | — | — | — | 1.00 | — |
| Note: Coin alignment error exists. Value: $80 in Unc, $40 in XF. | | | | | | |
| JE5767 (2007) | — | — | — | — | 1.00 | — |
| JE5769 (2009) | — | — | — | — | 1.00 | — |
| JE5771 (2011) (h and v) | — | — | — | — | 0.75 | — |
| JE5772 (2012) | — | — | — | — | 0.75 | — |
| JE5773(2013) | — | — | — | — | 0.75 | — |
| 5774 (2014) | — | — | — | — | 0.75 | — |

## KM# 163a NEW SHEQEL

4.00 g., Nickel Plated Steel, 18 mm. **Subject:** Hanukka **Obv:** Value, small menorah, country name in Hebrew, English and Arabic and inscription "HANUKKA" in Hebrew and English **Rev:** Lily, state emblem, ancient Hebrew inscription and Star of David mintmark **Note:** Non-magnetic.

| Date | Mintage | F12 | VF20 | XF40 | MS60 | MS63 |
|---|---|---|---|---|---|---|
| 5761 (2001) (u) | 4,000 | — | — | — | — | 4.00 |
| Note: Sets only. | | | | | | |
| 5762 (2002) (u) | 4,000 | — | — | — | — | 4.00 |
| Note: Sets only. | | | | | | |
| 5763 (2003) (u) | 3,000 | — | — | — | — | 4.00 |
| Note: Sets only. | | | | | | |
| 5764 (2004) (u) | 3,000 | — | — | — | — | 4.00 |
| Note: Sets only. | | | | | | |
| 5765 (2005) (u) | 2,500 | — | — | — | — | 4.00 |
| Note: Sets only. | | | | | | |
| 5766 (2006) (u) | 3,000 | — | — | — | — | 4.00 |
| Note: Sets only. | | | | | | |
| 5767 (2007) (u) | 3,000 | — | — | — | — | 4.00 |
| Note: Sets only. | | | | | | |
| JE5768 (2008) (u) | 3,000 | — | — | — | — | 4.00 |
| Note: Sets only. | | | | | | |
| 5769 (2009) (u) | 1,800 | — | — | — | — | 4.00 |
| Note: Sets only. | | | | | | |
| 5770 (2010) (u) | — | — | — | — | — | 4.00 |
| Note: Sets only. | | | | | | |

## KM# 163b NEW SHEQEL

3.50 g., Nickel Bonded Steel, 18 mm. **Subject:** Hanukka **Obv:** Value, small menorah, country name in Hebrew, English and Arabic and inscription "HANUKKA" in Hebrew and English **Rev:** Lily, state emblem, ancient Hebrew inscription and Star of David mintmark **Edge:** Plain

| Date | Mintage | F12 | VF20 | XF40 | MS60 | MS63 |
|---|---|---|---|---|---|---|
| JE5761 (2001) (u) | 4,000 | — | — | — | — | 4.00 |
| Note: Sets only | | | | | | |
| JE5762 (2002) (u) | 4,000 | — | — | — | — | 4.00 |
| Note: Sets only | | | | | | |
| JE5763 (2003) (u) | 3,000 | — | — | — | — | 4.00 |
| Note: Sets only | | | | | | |
| JE5764 (2004) (u) | 3,000 | — | — | — | — | 4.00 |
| Note: Sets only | | | | | | |
| JE5765 (2005) (u) | 2,500 | — | — | — | — | 4.00 |
| Note: Sets only | | | | | | |
| JE5766 (2006) (u) | 3,000 | — | — | — | — | 4.00 |
| Note: Sets only | | | | | | |
| JE5767 (2007) (u) | 3,000 | — | — | — | — | 4.00 |
| Note: Sets only | | | | | | |
| JE5769 (2009) (u) | 1,800 | — | — | — | — | 4.00 |
| Note: Sets only | | | | | | |
| JE5770 (2010) (u) | 1,800 | — | — | — | — | 4.00 |
| Note: Sets only | | | | | | |

## KM# 344 NEW SHEQEL

14.40 g., 0.925 Silver 0.4282 oz. ASW, 30 mm. **Series:** Independence Day **Subject:** Education **Obv:** Denomination **Rev:** Pomegranate full of symbols - Hebrew 'ABC-123', etc. **Edge:** Plain

| Date | Mintage | F12 | VF20 | XF40 | MS60 | MS63 |
|---|---|---|---|---|---|---|
| JE5761-2001 (u) Prooflike | 1,653 | — | — | — | — | 30.00 |

## KM# 351 NEW SHEQEL

14.40 g., 0.925 Silver 0.4282 oz. ASW, 30 mm. **Series:** Art and Culture in Israel **Subject:** Music **Obv:** National arms and denomination **Rev:** Musical instruments **Edge:** Plain

| Date | Mintage | F12 | VF20 | XF40 | MS60 | MS63 |
|---|---|---|---|---|---|---|
| JE5761-2001 (u) Prooflike | 1,182 | — | — | — | — | 35.00 |

## KM# 356 NEW SHEQEL

14.40 g., 0.925 Silver 0.4282 oz. ASW, 30 mm. **Series:** Independence Day **Subject:** Volunteering **Obv:** Denomination **Rev:** Heart in hands **Edge:** Plain

| Date | Mintage | F12 | VF20 | XF40 | MS60 | MS63 |
|---|---|---|---|---|---|---|
| JE5762-2002 (o) Prooflike | 1,364 | — | — | — | — | 30.00 |

## KM# 359 NEW SHEQEL

14.40 g., 0.925 Silver 0.4282 oz. ASW, 30 mm. **Series:** Biblical Art **Subject:** Tower of Babel **Obv:** National arms in spiral inscription **Rev:** Tower of Hebrew verses **Edge:** Plain

| Date | Mintage | F12 | VF20 | XF40 | MS60 | MS63 |
|---|---|---|---|---|---|---|
| JE5762 (2002) (o) Prooflike | 1,312 | — | — | — | — | 55.00 |

## KM# 371 NEW SHEQEL

14.40 g., 0.925 Silver 0.4282 oz. ASW, 30 mm. **Series:** Independence Day **Subject:** Space Exploration **Obv:** Ofeq" satellite in orbit **Rev:** Shavit" rocket **Edge Lettering:** Hebrew: "In memory of Ilan Ramon and his colleagues in the Columbia

| Date | Mintage | F12 | VF20 | XF40 | MS60 | MS63 |
|---|---|---|---|---|---|---|
| JE5763-2003 (v) Prooflike | 1,233 | — | — | — | — | 40.00 |

## KM# 374 NEW SHEQEL

14.40 g., 0.925 Silver 0.4282 oz. ASW, 30 mm. **Series:** Biblical Art **Subject:** Jacob and Rachel **Obv:** Value **Rev:** Jacob and Rachel floating in air **Edge:** Plain

| Date | Mintage | F12 | VF20 | XF40 | MS60 | MS63 |
|---|---|---|---|---|---|---|
| JE5763-2003 (u) Prooflike | 1,661 | — | — | — | — | 55.00 |

## KM# 377 NEW SHEQEL

14.40 g., 0.925 Silver 0.4282 oz. ASW, 30 mm. **Series:** Art and Culture in Israel **Subject:** Architecture and design **Obv:** Value **Rev:** Architecture and design **Edge:** Plain **Note:** With enamel.

| Date | Mintage | F12 | VF20 | XF40 | MS60 | MS63 |
|---|---|---|---|---|---|---|
| JE5764-2004 (u) Prooflike | 930 | — | — | — | — | 35.00 |

## KM# 380 NEW SHEQEL

14.40 g., 0.925 Silver 0.4282 oz. ASW, 30 mm. **Series:** Independence Day **Subject:** Children of Israel **Obv:** Value **Rev:** Parent and child **Edge:** Plain

| Date | Mintage | F12 | VF20 | XF40 | MS60 | MS63 |
|---|---|---|---|---|---|---|
| JE5764-2004 | 1,446 | — | — | — | — | 35.00 |
| (u) Prooflike | | | | | | |

## KM# 383 NEW SHEQEL

14.40 g., 0.925 Silver 0.4282 oz. ASW, 30 mm. **Subject:** 2004 Summer Olympics **Obv:** Four windsurfers, value and national arms **Rev:** Eight windsurfers **Edge:** Plain

| Date | Mintage | F12 | VF20 | XF40 | MS60 | MS63 |
|---|---|---|---|---|---|---|
| JE5764-2004 | 2,800 | — | — | — | — | 40.00 |
| (v) Prooflike | | | | | | |

## KM# 386 NEW SHEQEL

14.40 g., 0.925 Silver 0.4282 oz. ASW, 30 mm. **Series:** Biblical Art **Subject:** Burning Bush **Obv:** Burning twig and value **Rev:** Burning Bush **Edge:** Plain

| Date | Mintage | F12 | VF20 | XF40 | MS60 | MS63 |
|---|---|---|---|---|---|---|
| JE5764-2004 | 1,274 | — | — | — | — | 55.00 |
| (v) Prooflike | | | | | | |

## KM# 405.1 NEW SHEQEL

1.24 g., 0.999 Gold 0.040 oz. AGW, 13.92 mm. **Series:** Biblical Art **Subject:** Jacob and Rachel **Obv:** Value **Rev:** Jacob and Rachel floating in air **Edge:** Reeded

| Date | Mintage | F12 | VF20 | XF40 | MS60 | MS63 |
|---|---|---|---|---|---|---|
| JE5764 (2004) (u) | 6,057 | **PF65** 150 | | | | |

## KM# 405.2 NEW SHEQEL

1.24 g., 0.999 Gold 0.040 oz. AGW, 13.92 mm. **Series:** Biblical Art **Subject:** Jacob and Rachel **Obv:** Value **Rev:** Jacob and Rachel floating in air. Arabic legend Israel is mispelled **Edge:** Reeded

| Date | Mintage | F12 | VF20 | XF40 | MS60 | MS63 |
|---|---|---|---|---|---|---|
| JE5764 (2004) (u) | 682 | **PF65** 225 | | | | |

## KM# 406 NEW SHEQEL

14.40 g., 0.925 Silver 0.4282 oz. ASW, 30 mm. **Subject:** FIFA 2006 World Cup **Obv:** Value and soccer ball **Rev:** Map and soccer ball **Edge:** Plain

| Date | Mintage | F12 | VF20 | XF40 | MS60 | MS63 |
|---|---|---|---|---|---|---|
| JE5764-2004 | Est. 1200 | — | — | — | — | 40.00 |
| (u) Prooflike | | | | | | |

Note: Issued in 2006

## KM# 396 NEW SHEQEL

14.40 g., 0.925 Silver 0.4282 oz. ASW, 30 mm. **Subject:** Einstein's Relativity Theory **Obv:** Concentric circles above equation **Rev:** Value above signature

| Date | Mintage | F12 | VF20 | XF40 | MS60 | MS63 |
|---|---|---|---|---|---|---|
| JE5765-2005 | 1,100 | — | — | — | — | 48.00 |
| (v) Prooflike | | | | | | |

## KM# 399 NEW SHEQEL

14.40 g., 0.925 Silver 0.4282 oz. ASW, 30 mm. **Series:** Biblical Art **Subject:** Moses and the Ten Commandments **Obv:** Ten Commandments and value **Rev:** Moses and the Ten Commandments

| Date | Mintage | F12 | VF20 | XF40 | MS60 | MS63 |
|---|---|---|---|---|---|---|
| JE5765-2005 | 1,400 | — | — | — | — | 55.00 |
| (u) Prooflike | | | | | | |

## KM# 402 NEW SHEQEL

14.40 g., 0.925 Silver 0.4282 oz. ASW, 30 mm. **Series:** Independence Day **Subject:** Israel 57th Anniversary The Golden Years **Obv:** Value and olive branch **Rev:** Twisted olive tree

| Date | Mintage | F12 | VF20 | XF40 | MS60 | MS63 |
|---|---|---|---|---|---|---|
| JE5765-2005 | 1,100 | — | — | — | — | 40.00 |
| (u) Prooflike | | | | | | |

## KM# 412 NEW SHEQEL

14.40 g., 0.925 Silver 0.4282 oz. ASW, 30 mm. **Series:** Art and Culture in Israel **Subject:** Naomi Shemer **Obv:** Value **Rev:** Portrait of Naomi Shemer **Edge:** Plain

| Date | Mintage | F12 | VF20 | XF40 | MS60 | MS63 |
|---|---|---|---|---|---|---|
| JE5765-2005 | 1,100 | — | — | — | — | 35.00 |
| (u) Prooflike | | | | | | |

## KM# 409 NEW SHEQEL

14.40 g., 0.925 Silver 0.4282 oz. ASW, 30 mm. **Series:** Biblical Art **Subject:** Abraham and the Three Angels **Obv:** Value and stars **Rev:** Abraham and the three angels **Edge:** Reeded

| Date | Mintage | F12 | VF20 | XF40 | MS60 | MS63 |
|---|---|---|---|---|---|---|
| JE5766-2006 | 1,075 | — | — | — | — | 55.00 |
| (ig) Prooflike | | | | | | |

## KM# 416 NEW SHEQEL

14.40 g., 0.925 Silver 0.4282 oz. ASW, 30 mm. **Series:** Independence Day **Subject:** Higher Education in Israel **Obv:** Value and design **Rev:** Symbols of Science, Humanities, Technology and Mathematics **Edge:** Plain

| Date | Mintage | F12 | VF20 | XF40 | MS60 | MS63 |
|---|---|---|---|---|---|---|
| JE5766-2006 | 737 | — | — | — | — | 45.00 |
| (ig) Prooflike | | | | | | |

## KM# 419 NEW SHEQEL

14.40 g., 0.925 Silver 0.4282 oz. ASW, 30 mm. **Series:** UNESCO World Heritage Sites in Israel **Subject:** White City of Tel Aviv **Obv:** Value and Bauhaus building **Rev:** Fall of Bauhaus style building and UNESCO symbol **Edge:** Plain

| Date | Mintage | F12 | VF20 | XF40 | MS60 | MS63 |
|---|---|---|---|---|---|---|
| JE5766-2006 | 844 | — | — | — | — | 50.00 |
| (ig) Prooflike | | | | | | |

## KM# 423 NEW SHEQEL

14.40 g., 0.925 Silver 0.4282 oz. ASW, 30 mm. **Series:** Independence Day **Subject:** Performing Arts in Israel **Obv:** Value, state emblem and inscriptions **Rev:** Stylized actor, dancer and musician and inscription in Hebrew, English and Arabic, Performing Arts in Israel **Edge:** Plain

| Date | Mintage | F12 | VF20 | XF40 | MS60 | MS63 |
|---|---|---|---|---|---|---|
| JE5767-2007 | 765 | — | — | — | — | 50.00 |
| (ig) Prooflike | | | | | | |

## KM# 426 NEW SHEQEL

14.40 g., 0.925 Silver 0.4282 oz. ASW, 30 mm. **Subject:** 2008 Olympics - Judo **Obv:** Value, state emblem, judo belt and inscriptions **Rev:** 2 judo athletes and inscriptions in Hebrew, English and Arabic **Edge:** Plain

| Date | Mintage | F12 | VF20 | XF40 | MS60 | MS63 |
|---|---|---|---|---|---|---|
| JE5767-2007 | 1,160 | — | — | — | — | 50.00 |
| (u) Prooflike | | | | | | |

## KM# 429 NEW SHEQEL

14.40 g., 0.925 Silver 0.4282 oz. ASW, 30 mm. **Series:** Biblical Art **Subject:** Isaiah, Wolf with the Lamb **Obv:** Value, state emblem and inscriptions in Hebrew, English and Arabic **Obv. Inscription:** And the Wolf shall dwell with the Lamb **Rev:** Wolf and lamb lying together under a tree **Edge:** Plain

| Date | Mintage | F12 | VF20 | XF40 | MS60 | MS63 |
|---|---|---|---|---|---|---|
| JE5767-2007 | 1,363 | — | — | — | — | 55.00 |
| (v) Prooflike | | | | | | |

## KM# 437 NEW SHEQEL

1.24 g., 0.999 Gold 0.040 oz. AGW, 13.92 mm. **Series:** Biblical Art **Subject:** Abraham and the Angels **Obv:** Value, state emblem and Moses in Hebrew, English and Arabic **Rev:** Abraham greeting three angels **Edge:** Reeded

| Date | Mintage | F12 | VF20 | XF40 | MS60 | MS63 |
|---|---|---|---|---|---|---|
| JE5767-2007 | 1,500 | PF65 150 | | | | |
| (v) | | | | | | |

## KM# 438 NEW SHEQEL

1.24 g., 0.999 Gold 0.040 oz. AGW, 13.92 mm. **Series:** Biblical Art **Subject:** Moses and the Ten Commandments **Obv:** Value, state emblem and Moses in Hebrew **Rev:** Moses holding the Ten Commandments **Edge:** Reeded

| Date | Mintage | F12 | VF20 | XF40 | MS60 | MS63 |
|---|---|---|---|---|---|---|
| JE5767-2007 | 2,467 | PF65 150 | | | | |

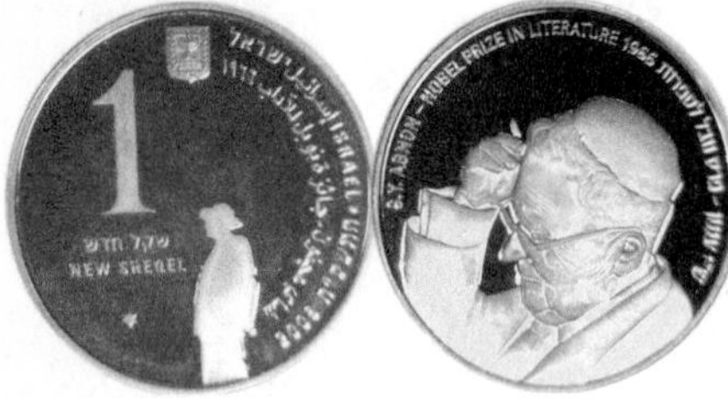

## KM# 439 NEW SHEQEL

14.40 g., 0.925 Silver 0.4282 oz. ASW, 30 mm. **Series:** Israeli Nobel Prize Laureates **Subject:** Shmuel Yosef Agnon **Obv:** Value, state emblem, outline of Agnon **Rev:** Portrait of Agnon **Edge:** Plain

| Date | Mintage | F12 | VF20 | XF40 | MS60 | MS63 |
|---|---|---|---|---|---|---|
| JE5768-2008 | 666 | — | — | — | — | 60.00 |
| (ig) Prooflike | | | | | | |

## KM# 440 NEW SHEQEL

1.24 g., 0.999 Gold 0.040 oz. AGW, 13.92 mm. **Series:** Biblical Art **Subject:** Isaiah, Wolf with the Lamb **Obv:** Value, state emblem, and inscriptions **Rev:** Wolf and lamb lying under tree **Edge:** Reeded

| Date | Mintage | F12 | VF20 | XF40 | MS60 | MS63 |
|---|---|---|---|---|---|---|
| JE5768-2008 | 3,302 | PF65 150 | | | | |
| (v) | | | | | | |

## KM# 441 NEW SHEQEL

14.40 g., 0.925 Silver 0.4282 oz. ASW, 30 mm. **Series:** Independence Day **Subject:** Israel's Sixtieth Anniversary **Obv:** Value, state emblem and inscriptions including "Independence Day **Rev:** 60" the zero is shaped like a pomegranite and a dove

| Date | Mintage | F12 | VF20 | XF40 | MS60 | MS63 |
|---|---|---|---|---|---|---|
| JE5768-2008 | 1,800 | — | — | — | — | 60.00 |
| (v) Prooflike | | | | | | |

## KM# 442 NEW SHEQEL

14.40 g., 0.925 Silver 0.4282 oz. ASW, 30 mm. **Subject:** Israel Defense Forces Reserves **Obv:** Triangle, state emblem and inscription **Rev:** Teddy bear pendant over soldier's ID tag

| Date | Mintage | F12 | VF20 | XF40 | MS60 | MS63 |
|---|---|---|---|---|---|---|
| JE5768-2008 | 492 | — | — | — | — | 60.00 |
| (ig) Prooflike | | | | | | |

## KM# 444 NEW SHEQEL

14.40 g., 0.925 Silver 0.4282 oz. ASW, 30 mm. **Series:** Biblical Art **Subject:** Parting of the Red Sea **Obv:** Value, state emblem and inscriptions **Rev:** Israelites passing through the Red Sea

| Date | Mintage | F12 | VF20 | XF40 | MS60 | MS63 |
|---|---|---|---|---|---|---|
| JE5769-2008 | Est. 987 | — | — | — | — | 60.00 |
| (v) Prooflike | | | | | | |

## KM# 453 NEW SHEQEL

14.40 g., 0.925 Silver 0.4282 oz. ASW, 30 mm. **Series:** UNESCO World Heritage Sites in Israel **Subject:** Masada **Obv:** Value, state emblem, image of Masada **Rev:** View of Masada, UNESCO emblem, World Heritage Site emblem **Edge:** Plain

| Date | Mintage | F12 | VF20 | XF40 | MS60 | MS63 |
|---|---|---|---|---|---|---|
| JE5769 (2009) | Est. 783 | — | — | — | — | 60.00 |
| (u) Prooflike | | | | | | |

## KM# 456 NEW SHEQEL

14.40 g., 0.925 Silver 0.4282 oz. ASW, 30 mm. **Series:** Independence Day **Subject:** Israel's Sixty-first Anniversary Birds of Israel **Obv:** Value, state emblem, finch **Rev:** Three birds, hoopoe, warbler and finch **Edge:** Plain

| Date | Mintage | F12 | VF20 | XF40 | MS60 | MS63 |
|---|---|---|---|---|---|---|
| JE5769 (2009) | Est. 790 | — | — | — | — | 60.00 |
| (u) Prooflike | | | | | | |

## KM# 459 NEW SHEQEL

14.40 g., 0.925 Silver 0.4282 oz. ASW, 30 mm. **Subject:** 2010 FIFA World Cup South Africa **Obv:** Soccer Player, ball, outline of globe, value, state emblem **Rev:** Soccer ball with design **Edge:** Plain

| Date | Mintage | F12 | VF20 | XF40 | MS60 | MS63 |
|---|---|---|---|---|---|---|
| JE5769 (2009) | 771 | — | — | — | — | 60.00 |
| (u) Prooflike | | | | | | |

## KM# 462 NEW SHEQEL

1.24 g., 0.999 Gold 0.040 oz. AGW, 13.92 mm. **Series:** Biblical Art **Subject:** Samson and the Lion **Obv:** Small stylized palm tree, value, state emblem **Rev:** Stylized Samson wrestling a lion and small stylized palm tree **Edge:** Reeded

| Date | Mintage | F12 | VF20 | XF40 | MS60 | MS63 |
|---|---|---|---|---|---|---|
| JE5769 (2009) | Est. 5000 | PF65 125 | | | | |
| (u) | | | | | | |

## KM# 463 NEW SHEQEL

14.40 g., 0.925 Silver 0.4282 oz. ASW, 30 mm. **Series:** Biblical Art **Subject:** Samson and the Lion **Obv:** Small stylized palm tree, value, state emblem **Rev:** Stylized Samson wrestling a lion and small stylized palm tree **Edge:** Plain

| Date | Mintage | F12 | VF20 | XF40 | MS60 | MS63 |
|---|---|---|---|---|---|---|
| JE5769 (2009) | Est. 1800 | — | — | — | — | 60.00 |
| (u) Prooflike | | | | | | |

## KM# 468 NEW SHEQEL

14.40 g., 0.925 Silver 0.4282 oz. ASW, 30 mm. **Series:** UNESCO World Heritage Sites in Israel **Subject:** Old Akko (Acre) **Obv:** Fortress of Akko as seen agains backdrop of Mediterranean Sea, state emblem, value UNESCO logo **Rev:** Ancient fortress walls, Khan-el-Undan caravanseraie and its clock tower, underground Crussader Knights' hall, White Mosque and other buildings **Edge:** Plain

| Date | Mintage | F12 | VF20 | XF40 | MS60 | MS63 |
|---|---|---|---|---|---|---|
| JE5770 (2010) | Est. 1800 | — | — | — | — | 60.00 |
| (h) Prooflike | | | | | | |

**KM# 471 NEW SHEQEL**
14.40 g., 0.925 Silver 0.4282 oz. ASW, 30 mm. **Series:** Independence Day **Subject:** Israeli National Trail 62nd Anniversary **Obv:** Trail forming stylized 62, state emblem **Rev:** Map of Isreal highlighting trail, boot, flowers **Edge:** Plain

| Date | Mintage | F12 | VF20 | XF40 | MS60 | MS63 |
|---|---|---|---|---|---|---|
| JE5770-2010 (h) Prooflike | Est. 1800 | — | — | — | — | 60.00 |

**KM# 474 NEW SHEQEL**
1.24 g., 0.999 Gold 0.040 oz. AGW, 13.92 mm. **Series:** Biblical Art **Subject:** Jonah in the Whale **Obv:** Small image of Jonah, value, state emblem **Rev:** Stylized Jonah in belly of whale **Edge:** Reeded

| Date | Mintage | F12 | VF20 | XF40 | MS60 | MS63 |
|---|---|---|---|---|---|---|
| JE5770-2010 (v) | Est. 5000 | PF65 140 | | | | |

**KM# 475 NEW SHEQEL**
14.40 g., 0.925 Silver 0.4282 oz. ASW, 30 mm. **Series:** Biblical Art **Subject:** Jonah in the Whale **Obv:** Small image of Jonah, value, state emblem **Rev:** Stylized Jonah in belly of whale **Edge:** Plain

| Date | Mintage | F12 | VF20 | XF40 | MS60 | MS63 |
|---|---|---|---|---|---|---|
| JE5770-2010 (v) Prooflike | Est. 1800 | — | — | — | — | 70.00 |

**KM# 478 NEW SHEQEL**
14.40 g., 0.925 Silver 0.4282 oz. ASW, 30 mm. **Series:** Israeli Nobel Prize Laureates **Subject:** Menachem Begin **Obv:** Menachem Begin, Jimmy Carter and Anwar Sadat in triple handshake on White House lawn **Rev:** Portrait of Begin **Edge:** Plain

| Date | Mintage | F12 | VF20 | XF40 | MS60 | MS63 |
|---|---|---|---|---|---|---|
| JE5771-2010 (u) Prooflike | Est. 2800 | — | — | — | — | 65.00 |

**KM# 481 NEW SHEQEL**
14.40 g., 0.925 Silver 0.4282 oz. ASW, 30 mm. **Series:** Independence Day **Subject:** Israel's sixty-third anniversary, Dead Sea **Obv:** Image of Dead Sea region, ibex and legend "DEAD SEA" in Hebrew, English and Arabic **Rev:** Value, mirror image of value, state emblem, dates, country name in Hebrew, English and Arabic and legend "INDEPENDENCE DAY" in Hebrew and English

| Date | Mintage | F12 | VF20 | XF40 | MS60 | MS63 |
|---|---|---|---|---|---|---|
| JE5771-2011 (u) Prooflike | Est. 1800 | — | — | — | — | 75.00 |

**KM# 484 NEW SHEQEL**
14.40 g., 0.925 Silver 0.4282 oz. ASW, 30 mm. **Subject:** 2012 London Olympics, Gymnastics **Obv:** Stlyized gymnast holding a ribbon in the shape of the Star of David and legends "THE OLYMPIC DELEGATION OF ISRAEL 2012" and "gymnastics" in Hebrew, English and Arabic **Rev:** Ribbon representation of Israeli flag, statem emblem, value, dates, country name in Hebrew, English and Arabic and inscription

| Date | Mintage | F12 | VF20 | XF40 | MS60 | MS63 |
|---|---|---|---|---|---|---|
| JE5771-2011 (u) Prooflike | Est. 1800 | PF65 75.00 | | | | |

**KM# 487 NEW SHEQEL**
14.40 g., 0.925 Silver 0.4282 oz. ASW, 30 mm. **Series:** Biblical Art **Subject:** Elijah in the Whirlwind **Obv:** State emblem, dates, country name in Hebrew, English and Arabic and inscription "ELIJAH WENT UP BY A WHIRLWIND INTO HEAVEN" in Hebrew, English and Arabic **Rev:** Stylized Elijah ascending to heaven in a horse-drawn chariot of fire in a whilrwind with Elisha below

| Date | Mintage | F12 | VF20 | XF40 | MS60 | MS63 |
|---|---|---|---|---|---|---|
| JE5771-2011 (v) Prooflike | Est. 1800 | — | — | — | — | 75.00 |

**KM# 488 NEW SHEQEL**
1.24 g., 0.999 Gold 0.040 oz. AGW, 13.92 mm. **Series:** Biblical Art **Subject:** Elijah in the Whirlwind **Obv:** State emblem dates, country name in Hebrew, English Arabic **Rev:** Stylized Elijah ascending to heaven in a horse-drawn chariot of fire **Edge:** Reeded

| Date | Mintage | F12 | VF20 | XF40 | MS60 | MS63 |
|---|---|---|---|---|---|---|
| JE5771-2011 (v) | Est. 5000 | PF65 125 | | | | |

**KM# 495 NEW SHEQEL**
14.40 g., 0.925 Silver 0.4282 oz. ASW, 30 mm. **Subject:** Yitzhak Rabin **Rev:** Bust left

| Date | Mintage | F12 | VF20 | XF40 | MS60 | MS63 |
|---|---|---|---|---|---|---|
| JE5772-2012 (u) Prooflike | Est. 1800 | — | — | — | — | 70.00 |

**KM# 492 NEW SHEQEL**
14.40 g., 0.925 Silver 0.4282 oz. ASW, 30 mm. **Subject:** Tel Megiddo, UNESCO Heritage site

| Date | Mintage | F12 | VF20 | XF40 | MS60 | MS63 |
|---|---|---|---|---|---|---|
| JE5772-2012 (u) Prooflike | Est. 1800 | — | — | — | — | 70.00 |

**KM# 501 NEW SHEQEL**
14.40 g., 0.925 Silver 0.4282 oz. ASW, 30 mm. **Subject:** Biblical Art - Daniel and the lion's den **Obv:** State emblem **Rev:** Daniel with two lions **Edge:** Plain

| Date | Mintage | F12 | VF20 | XF40 | MS60 | MS63 |
|---|---|---|---|---|---|---|
| 2012 | — | — | — | — | — | 60.00 |

**KM# 504 NEW SHEQEL**
14.40 g., 0.925 Silver 0.4282 oz. ASW, 30 mm. **Subject:** Eilat - Coral reef **Obv:** State emblem and two tropical sea fish **Rev:** Dolphin and tropical fish in coral reef **Edge:** Plain

| Date | Mintage | F12 | VF20 | XF40 | MS60 | MS63 |
|---|---|---|---|---|---|---|
| 2012 | — | — | — | — | — | 60.00 |

**KM# 498 NEW SHEQEL**
14.40 g., 0.925 Silver 0.4282 oz. ASW, 30 mm. **Subject:** Independence, 60th Anniversary

| Date | Mintage | F12 | VF20 | XF40 | MS60 | MS63 |
|---|---|---|---|---|---|---|
| 2013 | — | PF65 60.00 | | | | |

**KM# 508 NEW SHEQEL**
14.40 g., 0.925 Silver 0.4282 oz. ASW, 30 mm. **Subject:** Yad Vashem, 60th Anniversary **Obv:** State emblem and star of David **Rev:** Large Star of David and a Concentration Camp uniform **Edge:** Plain

| Date | Mintage | F12 | VF20 | XF40 | MS60 | MS63 |
|---|---|---|---|---|---|---|
| 2013 | — | — | — | — | — | 60.00 |

**KM# 345 2 NEW SHEQALIM**
28.80 g., 0.925 Silver 0.8565 oz. ASW, 38.7 mm. **Series:** Independence Day **Subject:** Education **Obv:** Denomination **Rev:** Pomegranate full of symbols **Edge:** Reeded

| Date | Mintage | F12 | VF20 | XF40 | MS60 | MS63 |
|---|---|---|---|---|---|---|
| JE5761-2001 (u) | 1,847 | PF65 60.00 | | | | |

**KM# 349 2 NEW SHEQALIM**
28.80 g., 0.925 Silver 0.8565 oz. ASW, 38.7 mm. **Series:** Wildlife **Subject:** Wild goat and acacia tree **Obv:** Acacia tree **Rev:** Ibex **Edge:** Reeded

| Date | Mintage | F12 | VF20 | XF40 | MS60 | MS63 |
|---|---|---|---|---|---|---|
| JE5761-2000 (u) | 2,000 | PF65 70.00 | | | | |

**KM# 352 2 NEW SHEQALIM**
28.80 g., 0.925 Silver 0.8565 oz. ASW, 38.7 mm. **Series:** Art and Culture in Israel **Subject:** Music **Obv:** National arms and denomination **Rev:** Musical instruments **Edge:** Reeded

| Date | Mintage | F12 | VF20 | XF40 | MS60 | MS63 |
|---|---|---|---|---|---|---|
| JE5761-2001 (u) | 1,747 | PF65 60.00 | | | | |

**KM# 357 2 NEW SHEQALIM**
28.80 g., 0.925 Silver 0.8565 oz. ASW, 38.7 mm. **Series:** Independence Day **Subject:** Volunteering **Obv:** Denomination **Rev:** Heart in hands **Edge:** Reeded

| Date | Mintage | F12 | VF20 | XF40 | MS60 | MS63 |
|---|---|---|---|---|---|---|
| JE5762-2002 (o) | 1,426 | PF65 50.00 | | | | |

**KM# 360 2 NEW SHEQALIM**
28.80 g., 0.925 Silver 0.8565 oz. ASW, 38.7 mm. **Series:** Biblical Art **Subject:** Tower of Babel **Obv:** National arms in spiral inscription **Rev:** Tower of Hebrew verses **Edge:** Reeded

| Date | Mintage | F12 | VF20 | XF40 | MS60 | MS63 |
|---|---|---|---|---|---|---|
| JE5762-2002 (o) | 1,295 | PF65 100 | | | | |

**KM# 372 2 NEW SHEQALIM**
28.80 g., 0.925 Silver 0.8565 oz. ASW, 38.7 mm. **Subject:** Space Exploration **Obv:** Amos" satellite in orbit **Rev:** Shavit" rocket **Edge Lettering:** Hebrew: "In memory of Ilan Ramon and his colleagues in the Columbia

| Date | Mintage | F12 | VF20 | XF40 | MS60 | MS63 |
|---|---|---|---|---|---|---|
| JE5763-2003 (v) | 1,249 | PF65 60.00 | | | | |

**KM# 375 2 NEW SHEQALIM**
28.80 g., 0.925 Silver 0.8565 oz. ASW, 38.7 mm. **Series:** Biblical Art **Subject:** Jacob and Rachel **Obv:** Value **Rev:** Figures floating in air above flower and sheep **Edge:** Reeded

| Date | Mintage | F12 | VF20 | XF40 | MS60 | MS63 |
|---|---|---|---|---|---|---|
| JE5763-2003 (u) | 1,377 | PF65 100 | | | | |

**KM# 378 2 NEW SHEQALIM**
28.80 g., 0.925 Silver 0.8565 oz. ASW, 38.7 mm. **Series:** Art and Culture in Israel **Subject:** Architecture and design **Obv:** Value and enameled shapes **Rev:** Architectural design **Edge:** Reeded

| Date | Mintage | F12 | VF20 | XF40 | MS60 | MS63 |
|---|---|---|---|---|---|---|
| JE5764-2004 (u) | 1,084 | PF65 60.00 | | | | |

**KM# 381 2 NEW SHEQALIM**
28.80 g., 0.925 Silver 0.8565 oz. ASW, 38.7 mm. **Series:** Independence Day **Subject:** Children of Israel **Obv:** Value and stylized human shapes **Rev:** Stylized parent and child **Edge:** Reeded

| Date | Mintage | F12 | VF20 | XF40 | MS60 | MS63 |
|---|---|---|---|---|---|---|
| JE5764-2004 (u) | 1,182 | PF65 50.00 | | | | |

**KM# 384 2 NEW SHEQALIM**
28.80 g., 0.925 Silver 0.8565 oz. ASW, 38.7 mm. **Subject:** 2004 Summer Olympics **Obv:** Four windsurfers, value and national arms **Rev:** Eight windsurfers **Edge:** Reeded

| Date | Mintage | F12 | VF20 | XF40 | MS60 | MS63 |
|---|---|---|---|---|---|---|
| JE5764-2004 (v) | 2,800 | PF65 60.00 | | | | |

**KM# 387 2 NEW SHEQALIM**
28.80 g., 0.925 Silver 0.8565 oz. ASW, 38.7 mm. **Series:** Biblical Art **Subject:** Burning Bush **Obv:** Burning twig and value **Rev:** Burning Bush **Edge:** Reeded

| Date | Mintage | F12 | VF20 | XF40 | MS60 | MS63 |
|---|---|---|---|---|---|---|
| JE5764-2004 (v) | 1,354 | PF65 100 | | | | |

**KM# 407 2 NEW SHEQALIM**
28.80 g., 0.925 Silver 0.8565 oz. ASW, 38.7 mm. **Subject:** FIFA 2006 World Cup **Obv:** Value and soccer ball **Rev:** Map and soccer ball **Edge:** Reeded

| Date | Mintage | F12 | VF20 | XF40 | MS60 | MS63 |
|---|---|---|---|---|---|---|
| JE5764-2004 (u) | Est. 5000 | PF65 60.00 | | | | |

Note: Issued in 2006

**KM# 397 2 NEW SHEQALIM**
28.80 g., 0.925 Silver 0.8565 oz. ASW, 38.7 mm. **Subject:** Einstein's Relativity Theory **Obv:** Concentric circles above equation **Rev:** Value above signature

| Date | Mintage | F12 | VF20 | XF40 | MS60 | MS63 |
|---|---|---|---|---|---|---|
| JE5765-2005 (v) | 1,600 | PF65 85.00 | | | | |

**KM# 400 2 NEW SHEQALIM**
28.80 g., 0.925 Silver 0.8565 oz. ASW, 38.7 mm. **Series:** Biblical Art **Subject:** Moses and the Ten Commandments **Obv:** Ten Commandments and value **Rev:** Moses and Ten Commandments

| Date | Mintage | F12 | VF20 | XF40 | MS60 | MS63 |
|---|---|---|---|---|---|---|
| JE5765-2005 (u) | 1,400 | PF65 100 | | | | |

**KM# 403 2 NEW SHEQALIM**
28.80 g., 0.925 Silver 0.8565 oz. ASW, 38.7 mm. **Series:** Independence Day **Subject:** Israel 57th Anniversary - The Golden Years **Obv:** Value and olive branch **Rev:** Twisted olive tree **Edge:** Reeded

| Date | Mintage | F12 | VF20 | XF40 | MS60 | MS63 |
|---|---|---|---|---|---|---|
| JE5765-2005 (u) | 1,100 | PF65 50.00 | | | | |

**KM# 413 2 NEW SHEQALIM**
28.80 g., 0.925 Silver 0.8565 oz. ASW, 38.7 mm. **Series:** Art and Culture in Israel **Subject:** Naomi Shemer **Obv:** Value **Rev:** Portrait of Naomi Shemer **Edge:** Reeded

| Date | Mintage | F12 | VF20 | XF40 | MS60 | MS63 |
|---|---|---|---|---|---|---|
| JE5765-2005 (u) | 1,100 | PF65 60.00 | | | | |

**KM# 410 2 NEW SHEQALIM**
28.80 g., 0.925 Silver 0.8565 oz. ASW, 38.7 mm. **Series:** Biblical Art **Subject:** Abraham and the Three Angels **Obv:** Value and stars **Rev:** Abraham and the three angels **Edge:** Reeded

| Date | Mintage | F12 | VF20 | XF40 | MS60 | MS63 |
|---|---|---|---|---|---|---|
| JE5766-2006 (ig) | 967 | PF65 110 | | | | |

**KM# 417 2 NEW SHEQALIM**
28.80 g., 0.925 Silver 0.8565 oz. ASW, 38.7 mm. **Series:** Independence Day **Subject:** Higher Education in Israel **Obv:** Value and design **Rev:** Symbols of Science, Humanities, Technology and Mathematics **Edge:** Reeded

| Date | Mintage | F12 | VF20 | XF40 | MS60 | MS63 |
|---|---|---|---|---|---|---|
| JE5766-2006 (ig) | 846 | PF65 60.00 | | | | |

**KM# 420 2 NEW SHEQALIM**
28.80 g., 0.925 Silver 0.8565 oz. ASW, 38.7 mm. **Series:** UNESCO World Heritage Sites in Israel **Subject:** White City of Tel Aviv **Obv:** Value and Bauhaus building **Rev:** Fall of Bauhaus building and UNESCO symbol **Edge:** Reeded

| Date | Mintage | F12 | VF20 | XF40 | MS60 | MS63 |
|---|---|---|---|---|---|---|
| JE5766-2006 (ig) | 837 | PF65 75.00 | | | | |

**KM# 424 2 NEW SHEQALIM**
28.80 g., 0.925 Silver 0.8565 oz. ASW, 38.7 mm. **Series:** Independence Day **Subject:** Performing Arts in Israel **Obv:** Value, state emblem and inscriptions **Rev:** Stylized actor, dancer and musician and inscription in Hebrew, English and Arabiv **Edge:** Reeded

| Date | Mintage | F12 | VF20 | XF40 | MS60 | MS63 |
|---|---|---|---|---|---|---|
| JE5767-2007 (ig) | 756 | **PF65** 75.00 | | | | |

**KM# 427 2 NEW SHEQALIM**
28.80 g., 0.925 Silver 0.8565 oz. ASW, 38.7 mm. **Subject:** 2008 Olympics - Judo **Obv:** Value, state emblem, judo belt and inscriptions **Rev:** 2 judo athletes and inscriptions **Edge:** Reeded

| Date | Mintage | F12 | VF20 | XF40 | MS60 | MS63 |
|---|---|---|---|---|---|---|
| JE5767-2007 (u) | 5,211 | **PF65** 75.00 | | | | |

**KM# 430 2 NEW SHEQALIM**
28.80 g., 0.925 Silver 0.8565 oz. ASW, 38.7 mm. **Series:** Biblical Art **Subject:** Isaiah, Wolf with the Lamb **Obv:** Value, state emblem and inscriptions in Hebrew, English and Arabic **Obv. Inscription:** And the Wolf shall dwell with the Lamb **Rev:** Wolf and lamb lying together under a tree **Edge:** Reeded

| Date | Mintage | F12 | VF20 | XF40 | MS60 | MS63 |
|---|---|---|---|---|---|---|
| JE5767-2007 (v) | 1,734 | **PF65** 100 | | | | |

**KM# 432 2 NEW SHEQALIM**
5.70 g., Nickel Plated Steel, 21.6 mm. **Subject:** Hanukka **Obv:** Value, date, inscriptions and menorah **Rev:** Double cornucopiae (horns of plenty) draped in ribbons and filled with fruit and grain including a pomegranate **Edge:** Plain with 4 notches

| Date | Mintage | F12 | VF20 | XF40 | MS60 | MS63 |
|---|---|---|---|---|---|---|
| JE5768 (2008) (u) Sets only | 3,000 | — | — | — | — | 5.00 |
| JE5769 (2009) (u) Sets only | 1,800 | — | — | — | — | 5.00 |
| JE5770 (2010) (u) Sets only | 1,800 | — | — | — | — | 5.00 |

**KM# 433 2 NEW SHEQALIM**
5.70 g., Nickel Plated Steel, 21.6 mm. **Obv:** Value, date and inscriptions **Rev:** Double cornucopiae (horns of plenty) draped in ribbons and filled with fruit and grain including a pomegranate **Edge:** Plain with 4 notches

| Date | Mintage | F12 | VF20 | XF40 | MS60 | MS63 |
|---|---|---|---|---|---|---|
| JE5768 (2008) (u) | Est. 26000000 | — | — | — | 1.25 | — |
| JE5769 (2009) (u) | — | — | — | — | 1.25 | — |
| JE5770 (2010) (u) | — | — | — | — | 1.25 | — |
| JE5771 (2011) (v) | — | — | — | — | 1.25 | — |

**KM# 443 2 NEW SHEQALIM**
1.24 g., 0.999 Gold 0.040 oz. AGW, 13.92 mm. **Series:** Biblical Art **Subject:** Parting of the Red Sea **Obv:** Value, state emblem and inscriptions **Rev:** Israelites passing through the Red Sea **Edge:** Reeded

| Date | Mintage | F12 | VF20 | XF40 | MS60 | MS63 |
|---|---|---|---|---|---|---|
| JE5769-2008 (v) | 1,896 | **PF65** 125 | | | | |

**KM# 445 2 NEW SHEQALIM**
28.80 g., 0.925 Silver 0.8565 oz. ASW, 38.7 mm. **Series:** Israeli Nobel Prize Laureates **Subject:** Shmuel Yosef Agnon **Obv:** Value, state emblem and outline of Agnon **Rev:** Portrait of Agnon **Edge:** Reeded

| Date | Mintage | F12 | VF20 | XF40 | MS60 | MS63 |
|---|---|---|---|---|---|---|
| JE5768-2008 (ig) | 666 | **PF65** 90.00 | | | | |

**KM# 446 2 NEW SHEQALIM**
28.80 g., 0.925 Silver 0.8565 oz. ASW, 38.7 mm. **Series:** Independence Day **Subject:** Israel's 60th Anniversary **Obv:** Value, state emblem and inscription "Independence Day **Rev:** 60" the zero is shaped like a pomegranate and a dove

| Date | Mintage | F12 | VF20 | XF40 | MS60 | MS63 |
|---|---|---|---|---|---|---|
| JE5768-2008 (v) | 1,800 | **PF65** 110 | | | | |

**KM# 447 2 NEW SHEQALIM**
28.80 g., 0.925 Silver 0.8565 oz. ASW, 38.7 mm. **Subject:** Israel Defense Forces Reserves **Obv:** Triangle, state emblem and inscription **Rev:** Teddy bear pendant over a soldier's ID tag **Edge:** Reeded

| Date | Mintage | F12 | VF20 | XF40 | MS60 | MS63 |
|---|---|---|---|---|---|---|
| JE5768-2008 (ig) | 481 | **PF65** 95.00 | | | | |

**KM# 448 2 NEW SHEQALIM**
28.80 g., 0.925 Silver 0.8565 oz. ASW, 38.7 mm. **Series:** Biblical Art **Subject:** Parting of the Red Sea **Obv:** Value, state emblem and inscriptions **Rev:** Israelites passing through the Red Sea **Edge:** Reeded

| Date | Mintage | F12 | VF20 | XF40 | MS60 | MS63 |
|---|---|---|---|---|---|---|
| JE5769-2008 (v) | 1,800 | **PF65** 100 | | | | |

**KM# 454 2 NEW SHEQALIM**
28.80 g., 0.925 Silver 0.8565 oz. ASW, 38.7 mm. **Series:** UNESCO World Heritage Sites in Israel **Subject:** Masada **Obv:** Value, state emblem, image of Masada **Rev:** View of Masada, UNESCO emblem, World Heritage Site emblem **Edge:** Reeded

| Date | Mintage | F12 | VF20 | XF40 | MS60 | MS63 |
|---|---|---|---|---|---|---|
| JE5769 (2009) (u) | Est. 1037 | **PF65** 90.00 | | | | |

**KM# 457 2 NEW SHEQALIM**
28.80 g., 0.925 Silver 0.8565 oz. ASW, 38.7 mm. **Series:** Independence Day **Subject:** Israel's Sixty-first Anniversary-Birds of Israel **Obv:** Value, state emblem, hoopoe **Rev:** Three birds, hoopoe, warbler and finch **Edge:** Reeded

| Date | Mintage | F12 | VF20 | XF40 | MS60 | MS63 |
|---|---|---|---|---|---|---|
| JE5769 (2009) (u) | 2,800 | **PF65** 110 | | | | |

**KM# 460 2 NEW SHEQALIM**
28.80 g., 0.925 Silver 0.8565 oz. ASW, 38.7 mm. **Subject:** 2010 FIFA World Cup South Africa **Obv:** Soccer Player, ball, outline of globe **Rev:** Soccer player with design **Edge:** Reeded

| Date | Mintage | F12 | VF20 | XF40 | MS60 | MS63 |
|---|---|---|---|---|---|---|
| JE5769 (2009) (u) | 1,767 | **PF65** 90.00 | | | | |

**KM# 464 2 NEW SHEQALIM**
28.80 g., 0.925 Silver 0.8565 oz. ASW, 38.7 mm. **Series:** Biblical Art **Subject:** Samson and the Lion **Obv:** Small stylized palm tree, value, state emblem **Rev:** Stylized Samson wrestling with a lion and small stylized palm tree **Edge:** Reeded

| Date | Mintage | F12 | VF20 | XF40 | MS60 | MS63 |
|---|---|---|---|---|---|---|
| JE5769 (2009) (u) | — | PF65 100 | | | | |

**KM# 469 2 NEW SHEQALIM**
28.80 g., 0.925 Silver 0.8565 oz. ASW, 38.7 mm. **Series:** UNESCO World Heritage Sites in Israel **Subject:** Old Akko (Acre) **Obv:** Fortress of Akko as seen against backdrop of Mediterranean Sea, state emblem, value **Rev:** Ancient fortress walls, Khan-el-Umdan caravanseraie and its clock tower, underground Crusader Knights' Hall, White Mosque and other buildings **Edge:** Reeded

| Date | Mintage | F12 | VF20 | XF40 | MS60 | MS63 |
|---|---|---|---|---|---|---|
| JE5770 (2010) (h) | Est. 2800 | PF65 90.00 | | | | |

**KM# 472 2 NEW SHEQALIM**
28.80 g., 0.925 Silver 0.8565 oz. ASW, 38.7 mm. **Series:** Independence Day **Subject:** Israel National Trail **Obv:** Trail forming stylized 62, state emblem **Rev:** Map of Israel highlighting national trail, boot, flowers **Edge:** Reeded

| Date | Mintage | F12 | VF20 | XF40 | MS60 | MS63 |
|---|---|---|---|---|---|---|
| JE5770-2010 (h) | Est. 1800 | PF65 90.00 | | | | |

**KM# 476 2 NEW SHEQALIM**
28.80 g., 0.925 Silver 0.8565 oz. ASW, 38.7 mm. **Series:** Biblical Art **Subject:** Jonah in the Whale **Obv:** Small image of Jonah, value, state emblem **Rev:** Stylized Jonah in belly of whale **Edge:** Reeded

| Date | Mintage | F12 | VF20 | XF40 | MS60 | MS63 |
|---|---|---|---|---|---|---|
| JE5770-2010 (v) | Est. 2800 | PF65 120 | | | | |

**KM# 479 2 NEW SHEQALIM**
28.80 g., 0.925 Silver 0.8565 oz. ASW, 38.7 mm. **Series:** Israeli Nobel Pize Laureates **Subject:** Menachem Begin **Obv:** Menachem Begin, Jimmy Carter and Anwar Sadat in triple handshake on White House lawn, state emblem **Rev:** Portrait of Menachem Begin **Edge:** Reeded

| Date | Mintage | F12 | VF20 | XF40 | MS60 | MS63 |
|---|---|---|---|---|---|---|
| JE5771-2010 (u) | — | PF65 120 | | | | |

**KM# 482 2 NEW SHEQALIM**
28.80 g., 0.925 Silver 0.8565 oz. ASW, 38.7 mm. **Series:** Independence Day **Subject:** Israel's sixty-third anniversary, Dead Sea **Obv:** Image of Dead Sea region, ibex and legend "DEAD SEA" in Hebrew, English and Arabic **Rev:** Value, mirror image of value, state emblem, dates, country name in Hebrew, English and Arabic and legend "INDEPENDENCE DAY" in Hebrew and English **Edge:** Reeded

| Date | Mintage | F12 | VF20 | XF40 | MS60 | MS63 |
|---|---|---|---|---|---|---|
| JE5771-2011 | — | PF65 120 | | | | |

**KM# 485 2 NEW SHEQALIM**
28.80 g., 0.925 Silver 0.8565 oz. ASW, 38.7 mm. **Subject:** 2012 London Olympics, Gymnastics **Obv:** Stylized gymnast holding a ribbon in the shape of the Star of David and legends "THE OLYMPIC DELEGATION OF ISRAEL 2012" and "gymnastics" in Hebrew, English and Arabic **Rev:** Ribbon representation of Israeli flag, state emblem, value, dates, country name in Hebrew, English and Arabic and inscription **Edge:** Reeded

| Date | Mintage | F12 | VF20 | XF40 | MS60 | MS63 |
|---|---|---|---|---|---|---|
| JE5771-2011 (u) | Est. 5000 | PF65 120 | | | | |

**KM# 489 2 NEW SHEQALIM**
28.80 g., 0.925 Silver 0.8565 oz. ASW, 38.7 mm. **Series:** Biblical Art **Subject:** Elijah caught up in the firestorm **Obv:** State emblem, dates, country name in Hebrew, English and Arabic and inscription "ELIJAH WENT UP BY A WHIRLWIND INTO HEAVEN" in Hebrew, English and Arabic **Rev:** Stylized Elijah ascending to heaven in a horse-drawn chariot of fire in a whirlwind with Elisha below **Edge:** Reeded

| Date | Mintage | F12 | VF20 | XF40 | MS60 | MS63 |
|---|---|---|---|---|---|---|
| JE5771-2011 (v) | Est. 2800 | PF65 120 | | | | |

**KM# 496 2 NEW SHEQALIM**
28.28 g., 0.925 Silver 0.841 oz. ASW, 38.7 mm. **Subject:** Yitzhak Rabin **Rev:** Bust left **Edge:** Reeded

| Date | Mintage | F12 | VF20 | XF40 | MS60 | MS63 |
|---|---|---|---|---|---|---|
| JE5772-2011 (u) | Est. 2800 | PF65 110 | | | | |

**KM# 493 2 NEW SHEQALIM**
28.80 g., 0.925 Silver 0.8565 oz. ASW, 38.7 mm. **Subject:** Tel Megiddo, UNESCO Heritage site **Edge:** Reeded

| Date | Mintage | F12 | VF20 | XF40 | MS60 | MS63 |
|---|---|---|---|---|---|---|
| JE5772-2012 (u) | Est. 2800 | PF65 110 | | | | |

**KM# 502 2 NEW SHEQALIM**
28.28 g., 0.925 Silver 0.841 oz. ASW **Subject:** Biblical Arts - Daniel and the lion's den **Obv:** State emblem **Rev:** Daniel and two lions

| Date | Mintage | F12 | VF20 | XF40 | MS60 | MS63 |
|---|---|---|---|---|---|---|
| 2012 | — | PF65 120 | | | | |

**KM# 505 2 NEW SHEQALIM**
28.28 g., 0.925 Silver 0.841 oz. ASW, 38.7 mm. **Subject:** Eilat - Coral reef **Obv:** State emblem and two tropical fish **Rev:** Dolphin and tropical fish in coral reef **Edge:** Reeded

| Date | Mintage | F12 | VF20 | XF40 | MS60 | MS63 |
|---|---|---|---|---|---|---|
| 2013 | — | PF65 120 | | | | |

**KM# 499 2 NEW SHEQALIM**
28.28 g., 0.925 Silver 0.841 oz. ASW, 38.7 mm. **Subject:** Independence, 60th Anniversary

| Date | Mintage | F12 | VF20 | XF40 | MS60 | MS63 |
|---|---|---|---|---|---|---|
| 2013 | — | PF65 100 | | | | |

**KM# 509 2 NEW SHEQALIM**
28.28 g., 0.925 Silver 0.841 oz. ASW, 38.7 mm. **Subject:** Yad Vashem, 60th Anniversary **Obv:** State emblem and Star of David **Rev:** Large Star of David and a Concentration Camp uniform **Edge:** Reeded

| Date | Mintage | F12 | VF20 | XF40 | MS60 | MS63 |
|---|---|---|---|---|---|---|
| 2013 | — | — | — | — | — | 120 |

**KM# 207 5 NEW SHEQALIM**
8.20 g., Copper-Nickel, 24 mm. **Obv:** Value **Rev:** Ancient column capitol **Edge:** Plain **Shape:** 12-sided

| Date | Mintage | F12 | VF20 | XF40 | MS60 | MS63 |
|---|---|---|---|---|---|---|
| JE5762 (2002) (wg) | 4,464,000 | — | — | — | 3.75 | — |
| Note: The JE5762 coins are practically round. | | | | | | |
| JE5765 (2005) | — | — | — | — | 3.00 | — |
| JE5766 (2006) | — | — | — | — | 3.00 | — |
| JE5768 (2008) (dj) | — | — | — | — | 3.00 | — |
| JE5769 (2009) (dj) | — | — | — | — | 3.00 | — |
| JE5771 (2011) (dj) | — | — | — | — | 3.00 | — |
| JE5772 (2012) (dj) | — | — | — | — | 3.00 | — |
| JE5773 (2013) | — | PF63 3.00 | | | | |

**KM# 217 5 NEW SHEQALIM**
8.20 g., Copper-Nickel, 24 mm. **Obv:** Value, small menorah and inscription Hanukka **Rev:** Ancient column capitol **Edge:** Plain **Shape:** 12-sided **Note:** Coins dated JE5754-5770 have the Star of David mint mark; the JE5751-5753 coins do not.

| Date | Mintage | F12 | VF20 | XF40 | MS60 | MS63 |
|---|---|---|---|---|---|---|
| JE5762 (2002) (u) Sets only | 4,000 | — | — | — | — | 7.00 |
| JE5763 (2003) (u) Sets only | 3,000 | — | — | — | — | 8.00 |
| JE5764 (2004) (u) Sets only | 3,000 | — | — | — | — | 8.00 |
| JE5765 (2005) (u) Sets only | 2,500 | — | — | — | — | 8.00 |
| JE5766 (2006) (u) Sets only | 3,000 | — | — | — | — | 8.00 |
| JE5767 (2007) (u) Sets only | 3,000 | — | — | — | — | 8.00 |
| JE5768 (2008) (u) Sets only | 3,000 | — | — | — | — | 8.00 |
| JE5769 (2009) (u) Sets only | 1,800 | — | — | — | — | 8.00 |
| JE5770 (2010) (u) Sets only | 1,800 | — | — | — | — | 8.00 |

**KM# 408 5 NEW SHEQALIM**
7.78 g., 0.999 Gold 0.2498 oz. AGW, 27 mm. **Subject:** FIFA 2006 World Cup **Obv:** Value and soccer ball **Rev:** Map and soccer ball **Edge:** Reeded **Note:** Issued in 2006

| Date | Mintage | F12 | VF20 | XF40 | MS60 | MS63 |
|---|---|---|---|---|---|---|
| JE5764-2004 (u) | Est. 655 | PF65 500 | | | | |

**KM# 461 5 NEW SHEQALIM**
7.77 g., 0.999 Gold 0.2496 oz. AGW, 27 mm. **Subject:** 2010 FIFA World Cup South Africa **Obv:** Soccer Player, ball, outline of globe **Rev:** Soccer ball with design **Edge:** Reeded

| Date | Mintage | F12 | VF20 | XF40 | MS60 | MS63 |
|---|---|---|---|---|---|---|
| JE5769 (2009) (u) | 391 | PF65 550 | | | | |

**KM# 270 10 NEW SHEQALIM**
7.00 g., Bi-Metallic Aureate Bonded Bronze center in Nickel Bonded Steel ring, 23 mm. **Obv:** Value, vertical lines and text within circle **Rev:** Palm tree and baskets within half beaded circle **Edge:** Reeded

| Date | Mintage | F12 | VF20 | XF40 | MS60 | MS63 |
|---|---|---|---|---|---|---|
| JE5762 (2002) (h) | 4,749,000 | — | — | — | 5.00 | — |
| JE5765 (2005) | — | — | — | — | 5.00 | — |
| Note: Coin alignment error exists. Value: $200 in Unc, $100 in XF. | | | | | | |
| JE5766 (2006) | — | — | — | — | 5.00 | — |
| JE5769 (2009) | — | — | — | — | 5.00 | — |
| JE5770 (2010) | — | — | — | — | 5.00 | — |
| JE5771 (2011) (h) | — | — | — | — | 5.00 | — |
| JE5772 (2012) (v) | — | — | — | — | 5.00 | — |
| JE5773 (2013) | — | — | — | — | 5.00 | — |
| 5774 (2014) | — | — | — | — | 5.00 | — |

**KM# 315 10 NEW SHEQALIM**
7.00 g., Bi-Metallic Aureate Bonded Bronze center in Nickel Bonded Steel ring, 23 mm. **Subject:** Hanukka **Obv:** Value, text and menorah within circle and vertical lines **Rev:** Palm tree and baskets within half beaded circle **Edge:** Reeded

| Date | Mintage | F12 | VF20 | XF40 | MS60 | MS63 |
|---|---|---|---|---|---|---|
| JE5761 (2001) (u) Sets only | 4,000 | — | — | — | — | 9.00 |
| JE5762 (2002) (u) Sets only | 4,000 | — | — | — | — | 9.00 |
| JE5763 (2003) (u) Sets only | 3,000 | — | — | — | — | 10.00 |
| JE5764 (2004) (u) Sets only | 3,000 | — | — | — | — | 10.00 |
| JE5765 (2005) (u) Sets only | 2,500 | — | — | — | — | 10.00 |
| JE5766 (2006) (u) Sets only | 3,000 | — | — | — | — | 10.00 |
| JE5767 (2007) (u) Sets only | 3,000 | — | — | — | — | 10.00 |
| JE5768 (2008) (u) Sets only | 3,000 | — | — | — | — | 10.00 |
| JE5769 (2009) (u) Sets only | 1,800 | — | — | — | — | 10.00 |
| JE5770 (2010) (u) Sets only | 1,800 | — | — | — | — | 10.00 |

**KM# 346 10 NEW SHEQALIM**
16.96 g., 0.917 Gold 0.500 oz. AGW, 30 mm. **Series:** Independence Day **Subject:** Education **Obv:** Value **Rev:** Pomegranate full of symbols - Hebrew for 'ABC - 123', etc. **Edge:** Reeded

| Date | Mintage | F12 | VF20 | XF40 | MS60 | MS63 |
|---|---|---|---|---|---|---|
| JE5761-2001 (u) | 660 | PF65 1,100 | | | | |

**KM# 353 10 NEW SHEQALIM**
16.96 g., 0.917 Gold 0.500 oz. AGW, 30 mm. **Series:** Art and Culture in Israel **Subject:** Music **Obv:** National arms and value **Rev:** Musical instruments **Edge:** Reeded

| Date | Mintage | F12 | VF20 | XF40 | MS60 | MS63 |
|---|---|---|---|---|---|---|
| JE5761-2001 (u) | 766 | PF65 1,000 | | | | |

**KM# 358 10 NEW SHEQALIM**
16.96 g., 0.9166 Gold 0.4998 oz. AGW, 30 mm. **Series:** Independence Day **Subject:** Volunteering **Obv:** Value **Rev:** Heart in hands **Edge:** Reeded

| Date | Mintage | F12 | VF20 | XF40 | MS60 | MS63 |
|---|---|---|---|---|---|---|
| JE5762-2002 (o) | 617 | PF65 1,100 | | | | |

**KM# 361 10 NEW SHEQALIM**
16.96 g., 0.917 Gold 0.500 oz. AGW, 30 mm. **Series:** Biblical Art **Subject:** Tower of Babel **Obv:** National arms in spiral inscription **Rev:** Tower of Hebrew verses **Edge:** Reeded

| Date | Mintage | F12 | VF20 | XF40 | MS60 | MS63 |
|---|---|---|---|---|---|---|
| JE5762-2002 (o) | 750 | PF65 1,150 | | | | |

**KM# 373 10 NEW SHEQALIM**
16.96 g., 0.917 Gold 0.500 oz. AGW, 30 mm. **Series:** Independence Day **Subject:** Space Exploration **Obv:** Eros" satellite in orbit **Rev:** Shavit" rocket **Edge Lettering:** Hebrew: In memory of Ilan Ramon and his colleagues in the Columbia

| Date | Mintage | F12 | VF20 | XF40 | MS60 | MS63 |
|---|---|---|---|---|---|---|
| JE5763-2003 (v) | 573 | PF65 1,125 | | | | |

**KM# 376 10 NEW SHEQALIM**
16.96 g., 0.917 Gold 0.500 oz. AGW, 30 mm. **Series:** Biblical Art **Subject:** Jacob and Rachel **Obv:** Value **Rev:** Jacob and Rachel floating in air above tree and sheep **Edge:** Reeded

| Date | Mintage | F12 | VF20 | XF40 | MS60 | MS63 |
|---|---|---|---|---|---|---|
| JE5763-2003 (u) | 686 | PF65 1,150 | | | | |

**KM# 379 10 NEW SHEQALIM**
16.96 g., 0.917 Gold 0.500 oz. AGW, 30 mm. **Series:** Art and Culture in Israel **Subject:** Architecture and Design **Obv:** Value **Rev:** Architectural design **Edge:** Reeded

| Date | Mintage | F12 | VF20 | XF40 | MS60 | MS63 |
|---|---|---|---|---|---|---|
| JE5764-2004 (u) | 555 | PF65 1,100 | | | | |

**KM# 382 10 NEW SHEQALIM**
16.96 g., 0.917 Gold 0.500 oz. AGW, 30 mm. **Series:** Independence Day **Subject:** Children of Israel **Obv:** Value **Rev:** Stylized parent and child **Edge:** Reeded

| Date | Mintage | F12 | VF20 | XF40 | MS60 | MS63 |
|---|---|---|---|---|---|---|
| JE5764-2004 (u) | 539 | PF65 1,100 | | | | |

**KM# 385 10 NEW SHEQALIM**
16.96 g., 0.917 Gold 0.500 oz. AGW, 30 mm. **Subject:** 2004 Summer Olympics **Obv:** Four windsurfers, value and national arms **Rev:** Eight windsurfers **Edge:** Reeded

| Date | Mintage | F12 | VF20 | XF40 | MS60 | MS63 |
|---|---|---|---|---|---|---|
| JE5764-2004 (v) | 540 | PF65 1,100 | | | | |

**KM# 388 10 NEW SHEQALIM**
16.96 g., 0.917 Gold 0.500 oz. AGW, 30 mm. **Series:** Biblical Art **Subject:** Burning Bush **Obv:** Burning twig and value **Rev:** Burning Bush **Edge:** Reeded

| Date | Mintage | F12 | VF20 | XF40 | MS60 | MS63 |
|---|---|---|---|---|---|---|
| JE5764-2004 (v) | 555 | PF65 1,150 | | | | |

**KM# 398 10 NEW SHEQALIM**
16.96 g., 0.9166 Gold 0.4998 oz. AGW, 30 mm. **Subject:** Einstein's Relativity Theory **Obv:** Concentric circles above equation **Rev:** Value above signature **Edge:** Reeded

| Date | Mintage | F12 | VF20 | XF40 | MS60 | MS63 |
|---|---|---|---|---|---|---|
| JE5765-2005 (v) | 555 | PF65 1,200 | | | | |

**KM# 401 10 NEW SHEQALIM**
16.96 g., 0.9166 Gold 0.4998 oz. AGW, 30 mm. **Series:** Biblical Art **Subject:** Moses and the Ten Commandments **Obv:** The Ten Commandments and value **Rev:** Moses and the Ten Commandments **Edge:** Reeded

| Date | Mintage | F12 | VF20 | XF40 | MS60 | MS63 |
|---|---|---|---|---|---|---|
| JE5765-2005 (u) | 555 | PF65 1,150 | | | | |

**KM# 404 10 NEW SHEQALIM**
16.96 g., 0.9166 Gold 0.4998 oz. AGW, 30 mm. **Series:** Independence Day **Subject:** Israel 57th Anniversary - Golden years **Obv:** Value and olive branch **Rev:** Twisted olive tree **Edge:** Reeded

| Date | Mintage | F12 | VF20 | XF40 | MS60 | MS63 |
|---|---|---|---|---|---|---|
| JE5765-2005 (u) | 485 | PF65 1,100 | | | | |

### KM# 414 10 NEW SHEQALIM

16.96 g., 0.917 Gold 0.500 oz. AGW, 30 mm. **Series:** Art and Culture in Israel **Subject:** Naomi Shemer **Obv:** Value **Rev:** Portrait of Naomi Shemer **Edge:** Reeded

| Date | Mintage | F12 | VF20 | XF40 | MS60 | MS63 |
|---|---|---|---|---|---|---|
| JE5765-2005 (u) | 455 | PF65 1,175 | | | | |

### KM# 411 10 NEW SHEQALIM

16.96 g., 0.917 Gold 0.500 oz. AGW, 30 mm. **Series:** Biblical Art **Subject:** Abraham and the Three Angels **Obv:** Value and stars **Rev:** Abraham and the three angels **Edge:** Reeded

| Date | Mintage | F12 | VF20 | XF40 | MS60 | MS63 |
|---|---|---|---|---|---|---|
| JE5766-2006 (ig) | 555 | PF65 1,150 | | | | |

### KM# 418 10 NEW SHEQALIM

16.96 g., 0.917 Gold 0.500 oz. AGW, 30 mm. **Series:** Independence Day **Subject:** Higher Education in Israel **Obv:** Value and design **Rev:** Symbols of Science, Humanities, Technology and Mathematics **Edge:** Reeded

| Date | Mintage | F12 | VF20 | XF40 | MS60 | MS63 |
|---|---|---|---|---|---|---|
| JE5766-2006 (ig) | 444 | PF65 1,100 | | | | |

### KM# 421 10 NEW SHEQALIM

16.96 g., 0.917 Gold 0.500 oz. AGW, 30 mm. **Series:** UNESCO World Heritage Sites in Israel **Subject:** White City of Tel Aviv **Obv:** Value and Bauhaus building **Rev:** Face of Bauhaus building and UNESCO symbol **Edge:** Reeded

| Date | Mintage | F12 | VF20 | XF40 | MS60 | MS63 |
|---|---|---|---|---|---|---|
| JE5766-2006 (ig) | 383 | PF65 1,150 | | | | |

### KM# 425 10 NEW SHEQALIM

16.96 g., 0.917 Gold 0.500 oz. AGW, 30 mm. **Series:** Independence Day **Subject:** Performing Arts in Israel **Obv:** Value, state emblem and inscriptions **Rev:** Stylized actor, dancer and musician and inscription in Hebrew, English and Arabic, "Performing Arts in Israel **Edge:** Reeded

| Date | Mintage | F12 | VF20 | XF40 | MS60 | MS63 |
|---|---|---|---|---|---|---|
| JE5767-2007 (ig) | 332 | PF65 1,200 | | | | |

### KM# 428 10 NEW SHEQALIM

16.96 g., 0.917 Gold 0.500 oz. AGW, 30 mm. **Subject:** 2008 Olympics - Judo **Obv:** Value, state emblem, judo belt and inscriptions **Rev:** 2 judo athletes and inscriptions in Hebrew, English and Arabic **Edge:** Reeded

| Date | Mintage | F12 | VF20 | XF40 | MS60 | MS63 |
|---|---|---|---|---|---|---|
| JE5767 (2007) (u) | 548 | PF65 1,050 | | | | |

### KM# 431 10 NEW SHEQALIM

16.96 g., 0.917 Gold 0.500 oz. AGW, 30 mm. **Series:** Biblical Art **Subject:** Isaiah, Wolf with the Lamb **Obv:** Value, state emblem and inscriptions in Hebrew, English and Arabic **Obv. Inscription:** And the Wolf shall dwell with the Lamb **Rev:** Wolf and lamb lying together under a tree **Edge:** Reeded

| Date | Mintage | F12 | VF20 | XF40 | MS60 | MS63 |
|---|---|---|---|---|---|---|
| JE5767-2007 (v) | 553 | PF65 1,150 | | | | |

### KM# 449 10 NEW SHEQALIM

16.96 g., 0.917 Gold 0.500 oz. AGW, 30 mm. **Series:** Israeli Nobel Prize Laureates **Subject:** Shmuel Yosef Agnon **Obv:** Value, state emblem and outline of Agnon **Rev:** Portrait of Agnon **Edge:** Reeded

| Date | Mintage | F12 | VF20 | XF40 | MS60 | MS63 |
|---|---|---|---|---|---|---|
| JE5768-2008 (ig) | 322 | PF65 1,200 | | | | |

### KM# 450 10 NEW SHEQALIM

16.96 g., 0.917 Gold 0.500 oz. AGW, 30 mm. **Series:** Independence Day **Subject:** Israel's 60th Anniversary **Obv:** Value, state emblem and inscription "Independence Day **Rev:** 60" the zero is shaped like a pomegranite and a dove **Edge:** Reeded

| Date | Mintage | F12 | VF20 | XF40 | MS60 | MS63 |
|---|---|---|---|---|---|---|
| JE5768-2008 (v) | 444 | PF65 1,150 | | | | |

### KM# 451 10 NEW SHEQALIM

16.96 g., 0.917 Gold 0.500 oz. AGW, 30 mm. **Subject:** Israel Defense Force Reserves **Obv:** Value over a triangle, state emblem and inscriptions **Rev:** Teddy bear pendant over a soldier's ID tag **Edge:** Reeded

| Date | Mintage | F12 | VF20 | XF40 | MS60 | MS63 |
|---|---|---|---|---|---|---|
| JE5768-2008 | 262 | PF65 1,200 | | | | |

### KM# 452 10 NEW SHEQALIM

16.96 g., 0.917 Gold 0.500 oz. AGW, 30 mm. **Series:** Biblical Art **Subject:** Parting of the Red Sea **Obv:** Value, state emblem and inscriptions **Rev:** Israelites passing through the Red Sea **Edge:** Reeded

| Date | Mintage | F12 | VF20 | XF40 | MS60 | MS63 |
|---|---|---|---|---|---|---|
| JE5769-2008 (v) | 491 | PF65 1,150 | | | | |

### KM# 455 10 NEW SHEQALIM

16.96 g., 0.917 Gold 0.500 oz. AGW, 30 mm. **Series:** UNESCO World Heritage Sites in Israel **Subject:** Masada **Obv:** Value, state emblem, image of Masada **Rev:** View of Masada, UNESCO emblem, World Heritage Site Emblem **Edge:** Reeded

| Date | Mintage | F12 | VF20 | XF40 | MS60 | MS63 |
|---|---|---|---|---|---|---|
| JE5769 (2009) (u) | Est. 548 | PF65 1,150 | | | | |

### KM# 458 10 NEW SHEQALIM

16.96 g., 0.917 Gold 0.500 oz. AGW, 30 mm. **Series:** Independence Day **Subject:** Israel's Sixty-first Anniversary Birds of Israel **Obv:** Value, state emblem, warbler **Rev:** Three birds, hoopoe, warbler and finch **Edge:** Reeded

| Date | Mintage | F12 | VF20 | XF40 | MS60 | MS63 |
|---|---|---|---|---|---|---|
| JE5769 (2009) (u) | Est. 445 | PF65 1,250 | | | | |

### KM# 465 10 NEW SHEQALIM

16.96 g., 0.917 Gold 0.500 oz. AGW, 30 mm. **Series:** Biblical Art **Subject:** Samson and the Lion **Obv:** Small stylized palm tree, value, state emblem **Rev:** Stylized Samson wrestling a lion, stylized palm tree **Edge:** Reeded

| Date | Mintage | F12 | VF20 | XF40 | MS60 | MS63 |
|---|---|---|---|---|---|---|
| JE5769 (2009) (u) | 555 | PF65 1,150 | | | | |

### KM# 470 10 NEW SHEQALIM

16.96 g., 0.917 Gold 0.500 oz. AGW, 30 mm. **Series:** UNESCO World Heritage Sites in Israel **Subject:** Old Akko (Acre) **Obv:** Fortress of Akko as seen against backdrop of Mediterranean Sea, state emblem, value **Rev:** Ancient fortress walls, Khan-el-Umdan caravanseraie and its clock tower, underground Crusader Knights' hall, White Mosque and other buildings **Edge:** Reeded

| Date | Mintage | F12 | VF20 | XF40 | MS60 | MS63 |
|---|---|---|---|---|---|---|
| JE5770 (2010) (h) | Est. 555 | PF65 1,150 | | | | |

### KM# 473 10 NEW SHEQALIM

16.95 g., 0.917 Gold 0.4997 oz. AGW, 30 mm. **Series:** Independence Day **Subject:** Israel National Trail **Obv:** Trail forming stylized 62, state emblem **Rev:** Map of Israel highlighting trail, boot, flowers **Edge:** Reeded

| Date | Mintage | F12 | VF20 | XF40 | MS60 | MS63 |
|---|---|---|---|---|---|---|
| JE5770-2010 (h) | Est. 555 | PF65 1,175 | | | | |

**KM# 477 10 NEW SHEQALIM**
16.96 g., 0.917 Gold 0.500 oz. AGW, 30 mm. **Series:** Biblical Art **Subject:** Jonah in the Whale **Obv:** Small image of Jonah, value, state emblem **Rev:** Stylized Jonah in belly of whale **Edge:** Reeded

| Date | Mintage | F12 | VF20 | XF40 | MS60 | MS63 |
|---|---|---|---|---|---|---|
| JE5770-2010 | Est. 555 | PF65 1,200 | | | | |

**KM# 480 10 NEW SHEQALIM**
16.96 g., 0.917 Gold 0.500 oz. AGW, 30 mm. **Series:** Israeli Nobel Prize Laureates **Subject:** Menachem Begin **Obv:** Menachem Begin, Jimmy Carter adn Anwar Sadat in triple handshake on White House lawn, state emblem **Rev:** Portrait of Menachem Begin **Edge:** Reeded

| Date | Mintage | F12 | VF20 | XF40 | MS60 | MS63 |
|---|---|---|---|---|---|---|
| JE5771-2010 (u) | Est. 888 | PF65 1,250 | | | | |

**KM# 483 10 NEW SHEQALIM**
16.96 g., 0.917 Gold 0.500 oz. AGW, 30 mm. **Series:** Independence Day **Subject:** Israel's sixty-third anniversary, Dead Sea **Obv:** Image of Dead Sea region, ibex and legend "DEAD SEA" in Hebrew, English and Arabic **Rev:** Value, mirror image of value, state emblem, dates, country name in Hebrew. **Rev. Legend:** "INDEPENDENCE DAY" in Hebrew and English **Edge:** Reeded

| Date | Mintage | F12 | VF20 | XF40 | MS60 | MS63 |
|---|---|---|---|---|---|---|
| JE5771-2011 (u) | Est. 555 | PF65 1,200 | | | | |

**KM# 486 10 NEW SHEQALIM**
16.96 g., 0.917 Gold 0.500 oz. AGW, 30 mm. **Subject:** 2012 London Olympics, Gymnastics **Obv:** Stylized gymnast holding a ribbon in the shape of the Star of David and legends "THE OLYMPIC DELEGATION OF ISRAEL 2012" and "gymnastics" in Hebrew, English and Arabic **Rev:** Ribbon represenatation of Israeli flag, state emblem, value, dates, country name in Hebrew, English and Arabic and inscription **Edge:** Reeded

| Date | Mintage | F12 | VF20 | XF40 | MS60 | MS63 |
|---|---|---|---|---|---|---|
| JE5771-2011 (u) | Est. 555 | PF65 1,200 | | | | |

**KM# 490 10 NEW SHEQALIM**
16.96 g., 0.917 Gold 0.500 oz. AGW, 30 mm. **Series:** Biblical Art **Subject:** Elijah in the Whirlwind **Obv:** State emblem, dates, country name in Hebrew, English and Arabic and inscription "ELIJAH WENT UP BY A WHIRLWIND INTO HEAVEN" in Hebrew, English and Arabic **Rev:** Stylized Elijah ascending to heaven in a horse-drawn chariot of fire in a whirlwind with Elisha below **Edge:** Reeded

| Date | Mintage | F12 | VF20 | XF40 | MS60 | MS63 |
|---|---|---|---|---|---|---|
| JE5771-2011 (v) | Est. 555 | PF65 1,200 | | | | |

**KM# 497 10 NEW SHEQALIM**
16.90 g., 0.917 Gold 0.4982 oz. AGW, 30 mm. **Subject:** Yitzhak Rabin **Rev:** Bust left **Edge:** Reeded

| Date | Mintage | F12 | VF20 | XF40 | MS60 | MS63 |
|---|---|---|---|---|---|---|
| JE5772-2011 | Est. 888 | PF65 1,100 | | | | |

**KM# 494 10 NEW SHEQALIM**
16.96 g., 0.917 Gold 0.500 oz. AGW, 30 mm. **Subject:** Tel Megiddo, UNESCO Heritage site **Edge:** Reeded

| Date | Mintage | F12 | VF20 | XF40 | MS60 | MS63 |
|---|---|---|---|---|---|---|
| JE5772-2012 (u) | Est. 555 | PF65 1,100 | | | | |

**KM# 503 10 NEW SHEQALIM**
16.96 g., 0.917 Gold 0.500 oz. AGW, 30 mm. **Subject:** Biblical art - Daniel and the lion's den **Obv:** State emblem **Rev:** Daniel and two lions **Edge:** Reeded

| Date | Mintage | F12 | VF20 | XF40 | MS60 | MS63 |
|---|---|---|---|---|---|---|
| 2012 | — | PF65 1,100 | | | | |

**KM# 506 10 NEW SHEQALIM**
16.96 g., 0.917 Gold 0.500 oz. AGW, 30 mm. **Subject:** Eilat - Coral reef **Obv:** State emblem and two tropical fish **Rev:** Dolphin and tropical fish in coral reef **Edge:** Reeded

| Date | Mintage | F12 | VF20 | XF40 | MS60 | MS63 |
|---|---|---|---|---|---|---|
| 2012 | — | PF65 1,100 | | | | |

**KM# 500 10 NEW SHEQALIM**
16.90 g., 0.917 Gold 0.4982 oz. AGW, 30 mm. **Subject:** Independence, 60th Anniversary

| Date | Mintage | F12 | VF20 | XF40 | MS60 | MS63 |
|---|---|---|---|---|---|---|
| 2013 | — | PF65 1,200 | | | | |

**KM# 510 10 NEW SHEQALIM**
16.96 g., 0.917 Gold 0.500 oz. AGW, 30 mm. **Subject:** Yad Vashem, 60th Anniversary **Obv:** State emblem, Star of David **Rev:** Large Star of David and a Concentration Camp uniform **Edge:** Reeded

| Date | Mintage | F12 | VF20 | XF40 | MS60 | MS63 |
|---|---|---|---|---|---|---|
| 2013 | — | PF65 1,100 | | | | |

## BULLION COINAGE

**KM# 467 20 NEW SHEQALIM**
31.10 g., 0.999 Gold 0.9989 oz. AGW, 32 mm. **Series:** Jerusalem of Gold **Subject:** Tower of David **Obv:** State emblem above lion of Megiddo and country name in Hebrew, English and Arabic **Rev:** Tower of David near the Jaffa Gate in Jerusalem **Edge:** Plain

| Date | Mintage | F12 | VF20 | XF40 | MS60 | MS63 |
|---|---|---|---|---|---|---|
| JE5770 (2010) (u) | 3,600 | — | — | — | — | 1,450 |

**KM# 491 20 NEW SHEQALIM**
31.10 g., 0.999 Gold 0.9989 oz. AGW, 32 mm. **Series:** Jerusalem of Gold **Subject:** Western Wall of the Temple **Obv:** State emblem above lion of Megiddo **Rev:** Sestern wall of the Temple, dates and legends "JERUSALEM" in Hebrew, English and Arabic and "1 OZ FINE GOLD .9999" in English and Hebrew

| Date | Mintage | F12 | VF20 | XF40 | MS60 | MS63 |
|---|---|---|---|---|---|---|
| JE5771 (2011) (u) | Est. 3600 | — | — | — | — | 1,450 |

**KM# 507 20 NEW SHEQALIM**
31.11 g., 0.999 Gold 0.999 oz. AGW, 32 mm. **Rev:** Menorah and the Knesset building **Edge:** Plain

| Date | Mintage | F12 | VF20 | XF40 | MS60 | MS63 |
|---|---|---|---|---|---|---|
| 2012 | — | — | — | — | — | 1,451 |

**KM# 511 20 NEW SHEQALIM**
31.10 g., 0.999 Gold 0.9989 oz. AGW, 32 mm. **Rev:** Shrine of the Book in the Israel Museum **Edge:** Plain

| Date | Mintage | F12 | VF20 | XF40 | MS60 | MS63 |
|---|---|---|---|---|---|---|
| 2013 | — | — | — | — | — | 1,450 |

## MINT SETS

| KM# | Date | Mintage | Identification | Issue Price | Mkt Val |
|---|---|---|---|---|---|
| MS86 | JE5761 (2001) (7) | 4,000 | KM#163b, 172-174, 217, 315, 354 (plastic case) 350th Anniversary of the Jewish Community of Curacao | 24.00 | 37.00 |
| MS88 | JE5762 (2002) (7) | 4,000 | KM#163b, 172-174, 217, 315, 355 (plastic case) Yemenite Jewry (issued 2001) | 27.00 | 40.00 |
| MS89 | JE5761-5762 (2001-2002) (9) | 3,000 | KM#157, 158, 160a (JE5761), 157-159, 160a, 207, 270 (JE5762) plus Twin Towers medal (folder) Israel - New York | — | 30.00 |
| MS91 | JE5763 (2003) (7) | 3,000 | KM#163b, 172-174, 217, 315, 389 (plastic case) The March of the Living into Poland (issued 2002) | 30.00 | 42.00 |
| MS93 | JE5764 (2004) (7) | 3,000 | KM#163b, 172-174, 217, 315, 390 (plastic case) Iraqi Jewry (issued 2003) | — | 40.00 |
| MS94 | JE5761-5763 (2001-2003) (6) | 3,000 | KM#157-159, 160a, 207, 270 (various dates) (folder) Bank of Israel Jubilee; (given or sold to Bank of Israel employees and VIP guests, not to the general public; issued 2004) | — | 45.00 |
| MS96 | JE5765 (2005) (7) | 2,500 | KM#163b, 172-174, 217, 315, 391 (plastic case) Syrian Jewry (issued 2004) | — | 42.00 |
| MS97 | JE5764-5765 (2004-2005) (6) | 3,000 | KM#158, 159 (JE5764), 157, 160a, 207, 270 (JE5765) (folder) Israel Today | 37.00 | 35.00 |
| MS98 | JE5766 (2006) (7) | 2,700 | KM#163b, 172-174, 217, 315, 415 (folder) Dutch Jewry (issued 2005) | 45.00 | 45.00 |
| MS99 | JE5766 (2006) (7) | 300 | KM#163b, 172-174, 217, 315, 415 (plastic case) Dutch Jewry (issued 2005) | — | 45.00 |
| MS100 | JE5766 (2006) (6) | 2,000 | KM#157-159, 160a, 207, 270 (folder) To the North With Love | 37.00 | 35.00 |
| MS101 | JE5767 (2007) (7) | 3,000 | KM#163b, 172-174, 217, 315, 422 (folder) Greek Jewry (issued 2006) | 43.00 | 42.00 |
| MS102 | JE5768 (2008) (8) | 3,000 | KM#163a, 172-174, 217, 315, 432, 434 (folder) Egyptian Jewry (issued 2007) | 43.00 | 45.00 |
| MS103 | JE5767-5768 (2007-2008) (8) | 1,000 | KM#157-159, 160a (JE5767), 158, 159, 207, 433 (JE5768) (folder) The Negev Shall Blossom | 37.00 | 46.00 |
| MS104 | JE5769 (2009) (7) | 1,800 | KM#163b, 173, 174, 217, 315, 432, 436 (folder) Glorious Prague (issued 2008) | 43.00 | 45.00 |
| MS105 | JE5770 (2010) (7) | 1,800 | KM#163b, 173, 174, 217, 315, 432, 466 (folder) Jews of Algeria | 43.00 | 45.00 |
| MS106 | JE5766-5770 (2006-10) (7) | — | KM#270 (JE5766), 160a (JE5767), 207 (JE5768), 158, 433 (JE5769), 159 (JE5770) (folder) 2010 coin set, Type I | 29.95 | 30.00 |
| MS107 | JE5769-5770 (2009-10) (6) | — | KM#160a, 207, 433 (JE5769), 158, 159, 270 (JE5770) (folder) 2010 coin set, Type II | 29.95 | 30.00 |
| MS108 | JE5770-5771 (2010-2011) (5) | — | KM#433 (JE5770), 158, 159, 160a, 207, 270 (JE5771) The Western Wall, 2011 Uncirculated Coin Set | 36.00 | 36.00 |

## MINT SETS NON-STANDARD METALS

| KM# | Date | Mintage | Identification | Issue Price | Mkt Val |
|---|---|---|---|---|---|
| MS85 | JE5761 (2001) (7) | 4,000 | KM#163b, 172-174, 217, 315, 354 (folder) 350th Anniversary of the Jewish Community of Curacao (issued 2000) | 32.00 | 38.00 |
| MS87 | JE5762 (2002) (7) | 4,000 | KM#163b, 172-174, 217, 315, 355 (folder) Yemenite Jewry (issued 2001) | 32.00 | 40.00 |
| MS90 | JE5763 (2003) (7) | 3,000 | KM#163b, 172-174, 217, 315, 389 (folder) The March of the Living into Poland (issued 2002) | 33.00 | 39.00 |
| MS92 | JE5764 (2004) (7) | 3,000 | KM#163b, 172-174, 217, 315, 390 (folder) Iraqi Jewry (issued 2003) | 39.00 | 40.00 |
| MS95 | JE5765 (2005) (7) | 2,500 | KM#163b, 172-174, 217, 315, 391 (folder) Syrian Jewry (issued 2004) | 39.00 | 40.00 |

The Italian Republic, a 700-mile-long peninsula extending into the heart of the Mediterranean Sea, has an area of 116,304 sq. mi. (301,230 sq. km.) and a population of 60 million. Capital: Rome. The economy centers around agriculture, manufacturing, forestry and fishing. Machinery, textiles, clothing and motor vehicles are exported.

**MINT**

R - Rome

## REPUBLIC

### DECIMAL COINAGE

**KM# 91 LIRA**

0.62 g., Aluminum, 17 mm. **Obv:** Balance scales **Rev:** Cornucopia, value and date **Note:** The 1968-1969 and 1982-2001 dates were issued in sets only.

| Date | Mintage | F12 | VF20 | XF40 | MS60 | MS63 |
|---|---|---|---|---|---|---|
| 2001 R | 100,000 | — | — | — | 10.00 | — |
| 2001 R | 10,000 | PF60 70.00 | | | | |

**KM# 219 LIRA**

11.00 g., 0.835 Silver 0.2953 oz. ASW, 29 mm. **Subject:** History of the Lira - Lira of 1946 (KM#87) **Obv:** Head with laureate left within circle **Rev:** Apple on branch within circle flanked by sprigs **Edge:** Reeded **Note:** This is a Lira Series reproducing an old coin design in the center of each coin.

| Date | Mintage | F12 | VF20 | XF40 | MS60 | MS63 |
|---|---|---|---|---|---|---|
| 2001 R | 50,000 | — | — | — | — | 40.00 |
| 2001 R | 6,100 | PF63 100 | | | | |

**KM# 220 LIRA**

6.00 g., 0.835 Silver 0.1611 oz. ASW, 24 mm. **Subject:** History of the Lira - Lira of 1951 (KM#91) **Obv:** Balance scale within circle **Rev:** Value and cornucopia within circle **Edge:** Reeded **Note:** This is a Lira Series reproducing an old coin design in the center of each coin.

| Date | Mintage | F12 | VF20 | XF40 | MS60 | MS63 |
|---|---|---|---|---|---|---|
| 2001 R | 50,000 | — | — | — | — | 40.00 |
| 2001 R | 6,100 | PF63 100 | | | | |

**KM# 87a LIRA**

8.00 g., 0.900 Gold 0.2315 oz. AGW, 21.6 mm. **Obv:** Ceres **Rev:** Orange on branch **Edge:** Plain **Note:** Official Restrike

| Date | Mintage | F12 | VF20 | XF40 | MS60 | MS63 |
|---|---|---|---|---|---|---|
| 1946 (2006) R | 1,999 | PF63 750 | | | | |

**KM# 91a LIRA**

4.00 g., 0.900 Gold 0.1157 oz. AGW, 17.2 mm. **Obv:** Balance scale **Rev:** Cornucopia, date and value **Edge:** Plain **Note:** Official Restrike

| Date | Mintage | F12 | VF20 | XF40 | MS60 | MS63 |
|---|---|---|---|---|---|---|
| 1951 (2006) R | 1,999 | PF63 400 | | | | |

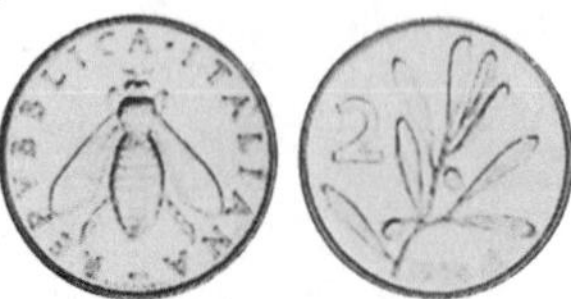

**KM# 94 2 LIRE**

0.80 g., Aluminum, 18 mm. **Obv:** Honey bee **Rev:** Olive branch and value **Edge:** Reeded **Note:** The 1968-1969 and 1982-2001 dates were issued in sets only.

| Date | Mintage | F12 | VF20 | XF40 | MS60 | MS63 |
|---|---|---|---|---|---|---|
| 2001 R | 100,000 | — | — | — | 10.00 | — |
| 2001 R | 10,000 | PF60 70.00 | | | | |

**KM# 88a 2 LIRE**

11.00 g., 0.900 Gold 0.3183 oz. AGW, 24.1 mm. **Obv:** Farmer plowing field **Rev:** Wheat ear **Edge:** Plain **Note:** Official Restrike

| Date | Mintage | F12 | VF20 | XF40 | MS60 | MS63 |
|---|---|---|---|---|---|---|
| 1946 (2006) R | 1,999 | PF63 900 | | | | |

**KM# 94a 2 LIRE**

5.00 g., 0.900 Gold 0.1447 oz. AGW, 18.3 mm. **Obv:** Honey bee **Rev:** Olive branch **Edge:** Reeded **Note:** Official Restrike

| Date | Mintage | F12 | VF20 | XF40 | MS60 | MS63 |
|---|---|---|---|---|---|---|
| 1953 (2006) R | 1,999 | PF63 550 | | | | |

**KM# 92 5 LIRE**

1.04 g., Aluminum, 20.12 mm. **Obv:** Rudder **Rev:** Dolphin and value **Edge:** Plain

| Date | Mintage | F12 | VF20 | XF40 | MS60 | MS63 |
|---|---|---|---|---|---|---|
| 2001 R | 100,000 | — | — | — | 12.00 | — |
| 2001 R | 10,000 | PF60 25.00 | | | | |

**KM# 89a 5 LIRE**

16.00 g., 0.900 Gold 0.463 oz. AGW, 26.7 mm. **Obv:** Italia with torch **Rev:** Bunch of grapes **Edge:** Reeded **Note:** Official Restrike

| Date | Mintage | F12 | VF20 | XF40 | MS60 | MS63 |
|---|---|---|---|---|---|---|
| 1946 (2006) R | 1,999 | PF63 1,200 | | | | |

**KM# 92a 5 LIRE**

6.00 g., 0.900 Gold 0.1736 oz. AGW, 20.2 mm. **Obv:** Rudder **Rev:** Dolphin and value **Edge:** Plain **Note:** Official Restrike

| Date | Mintage | F12 | VF20 | XF40 | MS60 | MS63 |
|---|---|---|---|---|---|---|
| 1951 (2006) R | 1,999 | PF63 650 | | | | |

## KM# 93 10 LIRE

1.60 g., Aluminum, 23.25 mm. **Obv:** Plow **Rev:** Value within wheat ears **Edge:** Plain

| Date | Mintage | F12 | VF20 | XF40 | MS60 | MS63 |
|---|---|---|---|---|---|---|
| 2001 R | 100,000 | — | — | — | 12.00 | — |
| 2001 R | 10,000 | PF60 30.00 | | | | |

## KM# 90a 10 LIRE

19.00 g., 0.900 Gold 0.5498 oz. AGW, 29 mm. **Obv:** Pegasus **Rev:** Olive branch **Edge:** Lettered **Edge Lettering:** REPVBBLICA ITALIANA **Note:** Official Restrike

| Date | Mintage | F12 | VF20 | XF40 | MS60 | MS63 |
|---|---|---|---|---|---|---|
| 1946 (2006) R | 1,999 | PF63 1,400 | | | | |

## KM# 93a 10 LIRE

10.00 g., 0.900 Gold 0.2894 oz. AGW, 23.3 mm. **Obv:** Plow **Rev:** Value within wheat ears **Edge:** Plain **Note:** Official Restrike

| Date | Mintage | F12 | VF20 | XF40 | MS60 | MS63 |
|---|---|---|---|---|---|---|
| 1951 (2006) R | 1,999 | PF63 800 | | | | |

## KM# 97.2 20 LIRE

3.60 g., Aluminum-Bronze, 21.25 mm. **Obv:** Wheat sprigs within head left **Rev:** Oak leaves divide value and date **Edge:** Plain

| Date | Mintage | F12 | VF20 | XF40 | MS60 | MS63 |
|---|---|---|---|---|---|---|
| 2001 R | 100,000 | — | — | — | 10.00 | — |
| 2001 R | 10,000 | PF60 25.00 | | | | |

## KM# 97.1a 20 LIRE

8.00 g., 0.900 Gold 0.2315 oz. AGW, 21.3 mm. **Obv:** Head laureate left **Rev:** Oak leaves divides date and value **Edge:** Reeded **Note:** Official Restrike

| Date | Mintage | F12 | VF20 | XF40 | MS60 | MS63 |
|---|---|---|---|---|---|---|
| 1957 (2006) R | 1,999 | PF63 800 | | | | |

## KM# 183 50 LIRE

4.50 g., Copper-Nickel, 19 mm. **Obv:** Turreted head left **Rev:** Large value within wreath of produce

| Date | Mintage | F12 | VF20 | XF40 | MS60 | MS63 |
|---|---|---|---|---|---|---|
| 2001 R | 100,000 | — | — | — | 10.00 | — |
| 2001 R | 10,000 | PF60 20.00 | | | | |

## KM# 95.1a 50 LIRE

14.00 g., 0.900 Gold 0.4051 oz. AGW, 24.8 mm. **Obv:** Italia **Rev:** Vulcan **Edge:** Reeded **Note:** Official Restrike

| Date | Mintage | F12 | VF20 | XF40 | MS60 | MS63 |
|---|---|---|---|---|---|---|
| 1954 (2006) R | 1,999 | PF63 1,000 | | | | |

## KM# 183a 50 LIRE

9.00 g., 0.900 Gold 0.2604 oz. AGW, 19.2 mm. **Obv:** Roma **Rev:** Value within wreath **Edge:** Plain **Note:** Official Restrike

| Date | Mintage | F12 | VF20 | XF40 | MS60 | MS63 |
|---|---|---|---|---|---|---|
| 1996 (2006) R | 1,999 | PF63 700 | | | | |

## KM# 159 100 LIRE

4.50 g., Copper-Nickel, 22 mm. **Obv:** Turreted head left **Rev:** Large value within circle flanked by sprigs **Edge:** Segmented reeding

| Date | Mintage | F12 | VF20 | XF40 | MS60 | MS63 |
|---|---|---|---|---|---|---|
| 2001 R | 100,000 | — | — | — | 12.00 | — |
| 2001 R | 10,000 | PF60 20.00 | | | | |

## KM# 96.1a 100 LIRE

18.00 g., 0.900 Gold 0.5208 oz. AGW, 27.8 mm. **Obv:** Ancient athlete **Rev:** Minerva standing **Edge:** Reeded **Note:** Official Restrike

| Date | Mintage | F12 | VF20 | XF40 | MS60 | MS63 |
|---|---|---|---|---|---|---|
| 1955 (2006) R | 1,999 | PF63 1,300 | | | | |

## KM# 159a 100 LIRE

9.00 g., 0.900 Gold 0.2604 oz. AGW, 22 mm. **Obv:** Turreted head left **Rev:** Large value within circle flanked by sprigs **Edge:** Segmented reeding **Note:** Official Restrike

| Date | Mintage | F12 | VF20 | XF40 | MS60 | MS63 |
|---|---|---|---|---|---|---|
| 1993 (2006) R | 1,999 | PF63 700 | | | | |

## KM# 105 200 LIRE

5.00 g., Aluminum-Bronze, 24 mm. **Obv:** Head right **Rev:** Value within gear **Edge:** Reeded

| Date | Mintage | F12 | VF20 | XF40 | MS60 | MS63 |
|---|---|---|---|---|---|---|
| 2001 R | 100,000 | — | — | — | 12.00 | — |
| 2001 R | 10,000 | PF60 30.00 | | | | |

## KM# 105a 200 LIRE

11.00 g., 0.900 Gold 0.3183 oz. AGW, 24 mm. **Obv:** Head right **Rev:** Value within gear **Edge:** Reeded **Note:** Official Restrike

| Date | Mintage | F12 | VF20 | XF40 | MS60 | MS63 |
|---|---|---|---|---|---|---|
| 1977 (2006) R | 1,999 | PF63 900 | | | | |

## KM# 98 500 LIRE

11.00 g., 0.835 Silver 0.2953 oz. ASW, 29.3 mm. **Obv:** Columbus' ships **Rev:** Bust left within wreath **Edge:** Dates in raised lettering

| Date | Mintage | F12 | VF20 | XF40 | MS60 | MS63 |
|---|---|---|---|---|---|---|
| 2001 R | 100,000 | — | — | — | 30.00 | — |
| 2001 R | 10,000 | PF63 160 | | | | |

## KM# 111 500 LIRE

6.80 g., Bi-Metallic Aluminum-Bronze center in Stainless Steel ring, 25.8 mm. **Obv:** Head left within circle **Rev:** Plaza within circle flanked by sprigs **Edge:** Segmented reeding

| Date | Mintage | F12 | VF20 | XF40 | MS60 | MS63 |
|---|---|---|---|---|---|---|
| 2001 R | 100,000 | — | — | — | 12.00 | — |
| 2001 R | 10,000 | PF60 30.00 | | | | |

## KM# 98a 500 LIRE

18.00 g., 0.900 Gold 0.5208 oz. AGW, 29 mm. **Obv:** Columbus' ships **Rev:** Bust left within wreath **Edge:** Lettered **Edge Lettering:** REPVBBLICA ITALIANA *** 1958*** **Note:** Official Restrike

| Date | Mintage | F12 | VF20 | XF40 | MS60 | MS63 |
|---|---|---|---|---|---|---|
| 1958 (2006) R | 1,999 | PF63 1,300 | | | | |

## KM# 99a 500 LIRE

18.00 g., 0.900 Gold 0.5208 oz. AGW, 29 mm. **Obv:** Seated Italia **Rev:** Lady **Edge:** Lettered **Edge Lettering:** 1 CENTENARIO VNITA'D'ITALIA * 1861-1961* **Note:** Official Restrike

| Date | Mintage | F12 | VF20 | XF40 | MS60 | MS63 |
|---|---|---|---|---|---|---|
| 1961 (2006) R | 1,999 | PF63 1,300 | | | | |

## KM# 100a 500 LIRE

18.00 g., 0.900 Gold 0.5208 oz. AGW, 29 mm. **Obv:** Dante **Rev:** Hell **Edge:** Lettered **Edge Lettering:** 7 CENTENARIO DELLA NASCITA DI DANTE **Note:** Official Restrike

| Date | Mintage | F12 | VF20 | XF40 | MS60 | MS63 |
|---|---|---|---|---|---|---|
| 1965 (2006) R | 1,999 | PF63 1,300 | | | | |

## KM# 111a 500 LIRE

14.00 g., Bi-Metallic .750 Gold center in .900 Gold ring, 25.8 mm. **Obv:** Head left within circle **Rev:** Plaza within circle flanked by sprigs **Edge:** Segmented reeding **Note:** Official Restrike

| Date | Mintage | F12 | VF20 | XF40 | MS60 | MS63 |
|---|---|---|---|---|---|---|
| 1982 (2006) R | 1,999 | PF63 1,000 | | | | |

## KM# 194 1000 LIRE

8.80 g., Bi-Metallic Copper-Nickel center in Aluminum-Bronze ring, 27 mm. **Subject:** European Union **Obv:** Head left within circle **Rev:** Corrected map with United Germany within globe design **Edge:** Segmented reeding

| Date | Mintage | F12 | VF20 | XF40 | MS60 | MS63 |
|---|---|---|---|---|---|---|
| 2001 R | 100,000 | — | — | — | 10.00 | 12.00 |
| 2001 R | 10,000 | PF63 40.00 | | | | |

## KM# 236 1000 LIRE

14.60 g., 0.835 Silver 0.3919 oz. ASW, 31.4 mm. **Obv:** Giuseppe Verdi **Rev:** Building

| Date | Mintage | F12 | VF20 | XF40 | MS60 | MS63 |
|---|---|---|---|---|---|---|
| 2001 R | 115,000 | — | — | — | — | 50.00 |
| 2001 R | 10,000 | PF63 80.00 | | | | |

## KM# 101a 1000 LIRE

24.00 g., 0.900 Gold 0.6945 oz. AGW, 31.2 mm. **Obv:** Concordia **Rev:** Geometric shape above value **Edge Lettering:** REPVBBLICA ITALIANA **Note:** Official restrike.

| Date | Mintage | F12 | VF20 | XF40 | MS60 | MS63 |
|---|---|---|---|---|---|---|
| 1970 (2006) R | 1,999 | PF63 1,500 | | | | |

## KM# 190a 1000 LIRE

17.00 g., 0.900 Gold 0.4919 oz. AGW, 27 mm. **Obv:** Roma **Rev:** European map **Edge:** Segmented reeding **Note:** Official Restrike

| Date | Mintage | F12 | VF20 | XF40 | MS60 | MS63 |
|---|---|---|---|---|---|---|
| 1997 (2006) R | 1,999 | PF63 1,250 | | | | |

## KM# 234 50000 LIRE

7.50 g., 0.900 Gold 0.217 oz. AGW, 20 mm. **Subject:** 250th Anniversary - Palace of Caserta **Obv:** Front view of palace **Rev:** Fountain, date and denomination

| Date | Mintage | F12 | VF20 | XF40 | MS60 | MS63 |
|---|---|---|---|---|---|---|
| 2001 R | 6,200 | PF63 800 | | | | |

## KM# 233 100000 LIRE

15.00 g., 0.900 Gold 0.434 oz. AGW, 25 mm. **Subject:** 700th Anniversary - Pulpit at the Church of St. Andrea a Pistoia **Obv:** Full pulpit **Rev:** Enlarged detail of the pulpit

| Date | Mintage | F12 | VF20 | XF40 | MS60 | MS63 |
|---|---|---|---|---|---|---|
| 2001 R | 4,500 | PF63 1,400 | | | | |

# EURO COINAGE

European Union Issues

## KM# 210 EURO CENT

2.30 g., Copper Plated Steel, 16.25 mm. **Obv:** Castle del Monte **Rev:** Value and globe **Edge:** Plain

| Date | Mintage | VF20 | XF40 | MS60 | MS63 | MS65 |
|---|---|---|---|---|---|---|
| 2002 R | 1,348,899,500 | — | — | 0.25 | 0.35 | — |
| 2003 R | 9,629,000 | — | — | 0.35 | 0.50 | — |
| 2003 R | 12,000 | PF63 10.00 | | | | |
| 2004 R | 100,000,000 | — | — | 0.25 | 0.35 | — |
| 2004 R | 12,000 | PF63 7.00 | | | | |
| 2005 R | 180,000,000 | — | — | 0.25 | 0.35 | — |
| 2005 R | 12,000 | PF63 5.00 | | | | |
| 2006 R | 159,000,000 | — | — | 0.25 | 0.35 | — |
| 2006 R | 12,000 | PF63 5.00 | | | | |
| 2007 R | 215,000,000 | — | — | 0.25 | 0.35 | — |
| 2007 R | 12,000 | PF63 5.00 | | | | |
| 2008 R | 180,000,000 | — | — | 0.25 | 0.35 | — |
| 2008 R | 5,000 | PF63 5.00 | | | | |
| 2009 R | 174,951,500 | — | — | 0.25 | 0.35 | — |
| 2009 R | 5,500 | PF63 5.00 | | | | |
| 2010 R | 42,000,000 | — | — | 0.25 | 0.35 | — |
| 2010 R | 5,000 | PF63 5.00 | | | | |
| 2011 R | 134,000,000 | — | — | 0.25 | 0.35 | — |
| 2011 R | 5,000 | PF63 5.00 | | | | |
| 2012 R | 217,959,500 | — | — | 0.25 | 0.35 | — |
| 2012 R | — | PF63 5.00 | | | | |
| 2013 R | — | — | — | 0.25 | 0.35 | — |
| 2013 R | — | PF63 5.00 | | | | |
| 2014 | — | — | — | 0.25 | 0.35 | — |
| 2014 | — | PF63 5.00 | | | | |

## KM# 211 2 EURO CENT

3.06 g., Copper Plated Steel, 18.75 mm. **Obv:** Observation tower in Turin **Rev:** Value and globe **Edge:** Grooved

| Date | Mintage | VF20 | XF40 | MS60 | MS63 | MS65 |
|---|---|---|---|---|---|---|
| 2002 R | 1,099,166,250 | — | — | 0.25 | 0.35 | — |
| 2003 R | 21,817,000 | — | — | 0.25 | 0.35 | — |
| 2003 R | 12,000 | PF63 10.00 | | | | |
| 2004 R | 120,000,000 | — | — | 0.25 | 0.35 | — |
| 2004 R | 12,000 | PF63 7.00 | | | | |
| 2005 R | 120,000,000 | — | — | 0.25 | 0.35 | — |
| 2005 R | 12,000 | PF63 5.00 | | | | |
| 2006 R | 196,000,000 | — | — | 0.25 | 0.35 | — |
| 2006 R | 12,000 | PF63 5.00 | | | | |
| 2007 R | 140,000,000 | — | — | 0.25 | 0.35 | — |
| 2007 R | 12,000 | PF63 5.00 | | | | |
| 2008 R | 135,000,000 | — | — | 0.25 | 0.35 | — |
| 2008 R | 5,000 | PF63 5.00 | | | | |
| 2009 R | 184,951,500 | — | — | 0.25 | 0.35 | — |
| 2009 R | 5,500 | PF63 5.00 | | | | |
| 2010 R | 115,000,000 | — | — | 0.25 | 0.35 | — |
| 2010 R | 5,000 | PF63 5.00 | | | | |
| 2011 R | 109,000,000 | — | — | 0.25 | 0.35 | — |
| 2011 R | 5,000 | PF63 5.00 | | | | |
| 2012 R | 79,959,500 | — | — | 0.25 | 0.35 | — |
| 2012 R | — | PF63 5.00 | | | | |
| 2013 R | — | — | — | 0.25 | 0.35 | — |
| 2013 R | — | PF63 5.00 | | | | |
| 2014 | — | — | — | 0.25 | 0.35 | — |
| 2014 | — | PF63 5.00 | | | | |

## KM# 212 5 EURO CENT

3.92 g., Copper Plated Steel, 21.25 mm. **Obv:** Colosseum **Rev:** Value and globe **Edge:** Plain

| Date | Mintage | VF20 | XF40 | MS60 | MS63 | MS65 |
|---|---|---|---|---|---|---|
| 2002 R | 1,341,742,204 | — | — | 0.25 | 0.35 | — |
| 2003 R | 1,960,000 | — | — | 10.00 | 14.00 | — |
| 2003 R | 12,000 | PF63 20.00 | | | | |
| 2004 R | 10,000,000 | — | — | 0.25 | 0.35 | — |
| 2004 R | 12,000 | PF63 8.00 | | | | |
| 2005 R | 70,000,000 | — | — | 0.25 | 0.35 | — |
| 2005 R | 12,000 | PF63 6.00 | | | | |
| 2006 R | 119,000,000 | — | — | 0.25 | 0.35 | — |
| 2006 R | 12,000 | PF63 6.00 | | | | |
| 2007 R | 85,000,000 | — | — | 0.25 | 0.35 | — |
| 2007 R | 12,000 | PF63 6.00 | | | | |
| 2008 R | 90,000,000 | — | — | 0.25 | 0.35 | — |
| 2008 R | 5,000 | PF63 6.00 | | | | |
| 2009 R | 84,955,000 | — | — | 0.25 | 0.35 | — |
| 2009 R | 5,500 | PF63 6.00 | | | | |
| 2010 R | 32,000,000 | — | — | 0.25 | 0.35 | — |
| 2010 R | 5,000 | PF63 6.00 | | | | |
| 2011 R | 37,000,000 | — | — | 0.25 | 0.35 | — |
| 2011 R | 5,000 | PF63 6.00 | | | | |
| 2012 R | 75,959,500 | — | — | 0.25 | 0.35 | — |
| 2012 R | — | PF63 6.00 | | | | |
| 2013 R | — | — | — | 0.25 | 0.35 | — |
| 2013 R | — | PF63 6.00 | | | | |
| 2014 | — | — | — | 0.25 | 0.35 | — |
| 2014 | — | PF63 6.00 | | | | |

## KM# 247 10 EURO CENT

4.10 g., Brass, 19.75 mm. **Obv:** Venus by Botticelli **Rev:** Relief Map of Western Europe, stars, lines and value **Edge:** Reeded

| Date | Mintage | VF20 | XF40 | MS60 | MS63 | MS65 |
|---|---|---|---|---|---|---|
| 2008 R | 104,955,000 | — | — | 0.25 | 0.35 | — |
| 2008 R | 5,000 | PF63 7.00 | | | | |
| 2009 R | 105,951,500 | — | — | 0.25 | 0.35 | — |
| 2009 R | 5,500 | PF63 7.00 | | | | |
| 2010 R | 57,000,000 | — | — | 0.25 | 0.35 | — |
| 2010 R | 5,000 | PF63 7.00 | | | | |
| 2011 R | 76,000,000 | — | — | 0.25 | 0.35 | — |
| 2011 R | 5,000 | PF63 7.00 | | | | |
| 2012 R | 99,959,500 | — | — | 0.25 | 0.35 | — |
| 2012 R | — | PF63 7.00 | | | | |
| 2013 R | — | — | — | 0.25 | 0.35 | — |
| 2013 R | — | PF63 7.00 | | | | |
| 2014 | — | — | — | 0.25 | 0.35 | — |
| 2014 | — | PF63 7.00 | | | | |

## KM# 213 10 EURO CENT

4.10 g., Brass, 19.75 mm. **Obv:** Venus by Botticelli **Rev:** Value and map **Edge:** Reeded

| Date | Mintage | VF20 | XF40 | MS60 | MS63 | MS65 |
|---|---|---|---|---|---|---|
| 2002 R | 1,142,383,000 | — | — | 0.25 | 0.35 | — |
| Note: Three varieties in size of the obverse designer's name | | | | | | |
| 2003 R | 29,976,000 | — | — | 0.25 | 0.35 | — |
| 2003 R | 12,000 | PF63 15.00 | | | | |
| 2004 R | 5,000,000 | — | — | 5.00 | 7.00 | — |
| 2004 R | 12,000 | PF63 10.00 | | | | |
| 2005 R | 100,000,000 | — | — | 0.25 | 0.35 | — |
| 2005 R | 12,000 | PF63 7.00 | | | | |
| 2006 R | 180,000,000 | — | — | 0.25 | 0.35 | — |
| 2006 R | 12,000 | PF63 7.00 | | | | |
| 2007 R | 105,000,000 | — | — | 0.25 | 0.35 | — |
| 2007 R | 12,000 | PF63 7.00 | | | | |

## KM# 214 20 EURO CENT

5.74 g., Brass, 22.25 mm. **Obv:** Futuristic sculpture by Boccioni **Rev:** Value and map **Edge:** Notched

| Date | Mintage | VF20 | XF40 | MS60 | MS63 | MS65 |
|---|---|---|---|---|---|---|
| 2002 R | 1,411,836,000 | — | — | 0.30 | 0.50 | — |
| 2003 R | 26,155,000 | — | — | 0.30 | 0.50 | — |
| 2003 R | 12,000 | PF63 16.00 | | | | |
| 2004 R | 5,000,000 | — | — | 0.30 | 0.50 | — |
| 2004 R | 12,000 | PF63 14.00 | | | | |
| 2005 R | 5,000,000 | — | — | 0.30 | 0.50 | — |
| 2005 R | 12,000 | PF63 8.00 | | | | |
| 2006 R | 5,000,000 | — | — | 0.30 | 0.50 | — |
| 2006 R | 12,000 | PF63 8.00 | | | | |
| 2007 R | 5,000,000 | — | — | 0.30 | 0.50 | — |
| 2007 R | 12,000 | PF63 8.00 | | | | |

## KM# 248 20 EURO CENT

5.74 g., Brass, 22.25 mm. **Obv:** Futuristic sculpture **Rev:** Relief map of Western Europe, stars, lines and value **Edge:** Notched

| Date | Mintage | VF20 | XF40 | MS60 | MS63 | MS65 |
|---|---|---|---|---|---|---|
| 2008 R | 4,955,000 | — | — | 0.30 | 0.50 | — |
| 2008 R | 5,000 | PF63 8.00 | | | | |
| 2009 R | 59,951,500 | — | — | 0.30 | 0.50 | — |
| 2009 R | 5,500 | PF63 8.00 | | | | |
| 2010 R | 23,000,000 | — | — | 0.30 | 0.50 | — |
| 2010 R | 5,000 | PF63 8.00 | | | | |
| 2011 R | 67,000,000 | — | — | 0.30 | 0.50 | — |
| 2011 R | 5,000 | PF63 8.00 | | | | |
| 2012 R | 4,959,500 | — | — | 0.30 | 0.50 | — |
| 2012 R | — | PF63 8.00 | | | | |
| 2013 R | — | — | — | 0.30 | 0.50 | — |
| 2013 R | — | PF63 8.00 | | | | |
| 2014 | — | — | — | 0.30 | 0.50 | — |
| 2014 | — | PF63 8.00 | | | | |

## KM# 215 50 EURO CENT

7.80 g., Brass, 24.25 mm. **Obv:** Sculpture of Marcus Aurelius on horseback **Rev:** Value and map **Edge:** Reeded

| Date | Mintage | VF20 | XF40 | MS60 | MS63 | MS65 |
|---|---|---|---|---|---|---|
| 2002 R | 1,136,718,000 | — | — | 0.80 | 1.00 | — |
| 2003 R | 44,825,000 | — | — | 1.00 | 1.25 | — |
| 2003 R | 12,000 | PF63 18.00 | | | | |
| 2004 R | 5,000,000 | — | — | 1.00 | 1.25 | — |
| 2004 R | 12,000 | PF63 16.00 | | | | |
| 2005 R | 5,000,000 | — | — | 1.00 | 1.25 | — |
| 2005 R | 12,000 | PF63 10.00 | | | | |
| 2006 R | 5,000,000 | — | — | 1.00 | 1.25 | — |
| 2006 R | 12,000 | PF63 10.00 | | | | |
| 2007 R | 5,000,000 | — | — | 1.00 | 1.25 | — |
| 2007 R | 12,000 | PF63 10.00 | | | | |

## KM# 249 50 EURO CENT

7.80 g., Brass, 24.25 mm. **Obv:** Sculpture of Marcus Aurelius on horseback **Rev:** Relief map of Western Europe, stars, lines and value **Edge:** Reeded

| Date | Mintage | VF20 | XF40 | MS60 | MS63 | MS65 |
|---|---|---|---|---|---|---|
| 2008 R | 4,955,000 | — | — | 1.00 | 1.25 | — |
| 2008 R | 5,000 | PF63 10.00 | | | | |
| 2009 R | 2,451,500 | — | — | 1.00 | 1.25 | — |
| 2009 R | 5,500 | PF63 10.00 | | | | |
| 2010 R | 9,000,000 | — | — | 1.00 | 1.25 | — |
| 2010 R | 5,000 | PF63 10.00 | | | | |
| 2011 R | 5,000,000 | — | — | 1.00 | 1.25 | — |
| 2011 R | 5,000 | PF63 10.00 | | | | |
| 2012 R | 4,959,500 | — | — | 1.00 | 1.25 | — |
| 2012 R | — | PF63 10.00 | | | | |
| 2013 R | — | — | — | 1.00 | 1.25 | — |
| 2013 R | — | PF63 10.00 | | | | |
| 2014 | — | — | — | 1.00 | 1.25 | — |
| 2014 | — | PF63 10.00 | | | | |

## KM# 216 EURO

7.50 g., Bi-Metallic Copper-Nickel center in Nickel-Brass ring, 23.25 mm. **Obv:** Male figure drawing by Leonardo da Vinci within circle of stars **Rev:** Value and map within circle **Edge:** Segmented reeding

| Date | Mintage | VF20 | XF40 | MS60 | MS63 | MS65 |
|---|---|---|---|---|---|---|
| 2002 R | 966,025,300 | — | — | 1.50 | 1.75 | — |
| Note: A variety exists which lacks the artist's signature | | | | | | |
| 2003 R | 66,474,000 | — | — | 1.50 | 1.75 | — |
| 2003 R | 12,000 | PF63 20.00 | | | | |
| 2004 R | 5,000,000 | — | — | 1.50 | 1.75 | — |
| 2004 R | 12,000 | PF63 18.00 | | | | |
| 2005 R | 5,000,000 | — | — | 1.50 | 1.75 | — |
| 2005 R | 12,000 | PF63 15.00 | | | | |
| 2006 R | 108,000,000 | — | — | 1.50 | 1.75 | — |
| 2006 R | 12,000 | PF63 15.00 | | | | |
| 2007 R | 135,000,000 | — | — | 1.50 | 1.75 | — |
| 2007 R | 12,000 | PF63 15.00 | | | | |

## KM# 250 EURO

7.50 g., Bi-Metallic Copper-Nickel center in Nickel-Brass ring, 23.25 mm. **Obv:** Male figure drawing by Leonardo da Vinci **Rev:** Relief map of Western Europe, stars, lines and value **Edge:** Segmented reeding

| Date | Mintage | VF20 | XF40 | MS60 | MS63 | MS65 |
|---|---|---|---|---|---|---|
| 2008 R | 134,955,000 | — | — | 1.50 | 1.75 | — |
| 2008 R | 5,000 | PF63 15.00 | | | | |
| 2009 R | 144,951,500 | — | — | 1.50 | 1.75 | — |
| 2009 R | 5,500 | PF63 15.00 | | | | |
| 2010 R | 50,000,000 | — | — | 1.50 | 1.75 | — |
| 2010 R | 5,000 | PF63 15.00 | | | | |
| 2011 R | 88,000,000 | — | — | 1.50 | 1.75 | — |
| 2011 R | 5,000 | PF63 15.00 | | | | |
| 2012 R | 4,959,500 | — | — | 1.50 | 1.75 | — |
| 2012 R | — | PF63 15.00 | | | | |
| 2013 R | — | — | — | 1.50 | 1.75 | — |
| 2013 R | — | PF63 15.00 | | | | |
| 2014 | — | — | — | 1.50 | 1.75 | — |
| 2014 | — | PF63 18.00 | | | | |

**KM# 217 2 EURO**
8.50 g., Bi-Metallic Nickel-Brass center in Copper-Nickel ring, 25.75 mm. **Obv:** Bust of Dante Aligheri left **Rev:** Value and map within circle **Edge:** Reeded **Edge Lettering:** 2's and stars

| Date | Mintage | VF20 | XF40 | MS60 | MS63 | MS65 |
|---|---|---|---|---|---|---|
| 2002 R | 463,702,000 | — | — | 3.00 | 3.50 | — |
| 2003 R | 36,160,000 | — | — | 3.00 | 3.50 | — |
| 2003 R | 12,000 | **PF63** 25.00 | | | | |
| 2004 R | 7,000,000 | — | — | 3.00 | 3.50 | — |
| 2004 R | 12,000 | **PF63** 22.00 | | | | |
| 2005 R | 62,000,000 | — | — | 3.00 | 3.50 | — |
| 2005 R | 12,000 | **PF63** 20.00 | | | | |
| 2006 R | 10,000,000 | — | — | 3.00 | 3.50 | — |
| 2006 R | 12,000 | **PF63** 20.00 | | | | |
| 2007 R | 5,000,000 | — | — | 3.00 | 3.50 | — |
| 2007 R | 12,000 | **PF63** 20.00 | | | | |

**KM# 237 2 EURO**
8.50 g., Bi-Metallic Nickel-Brass center in Copper-Nickel ring, 25.75 mm. **Obv:** World Food Program globe within circle **Rev:** Value and map within circle **Edge:** Reeded and lettered **Edge Lettering:** 2's and stars

| Date | Mintage | VF20 | XF40 | MS60 | MS63 | MS65 |
|---|---|---|---|---|---|---|
| 2004 R | 16,000,000 | — | — | 3.00 | 3.50 | — |

**KM# 245 2 EURO**
8.50 g., Bi-Metallic Nickel-Brass center in Copper-Nickel ring, 25.75 mm. **Subject:** European Constitution **Obv:** Europa holding an open book while sitting on a bull within circle **Rev:** Value and map within circle **Edge:** Reeding over stars and 2's

| Date | Mintage | VF20 | XF40 | MS60 | MS63 | MS65 |
|---|---|---|---|---|---|---|
| 2005 R | 18,000,000 | — | — | 3.00 | 3.50 | — |

**KM# 246 2 EURO**
8.50 g., Bi-Metallic Nickel-Brass center in Copper-Nickel ring, 25.75 mm. **Subject:** Torino Winter Olympics **Obv:** Skier and other designs within circle **Rev:** Value and map within circle **Edge:** Reeded with stars and 2's

| Date | Mintage | VF20 | XF40 | MS60 | MS63 | MS65 |
|---|---|---|---|---|---|---|
| 2006 R | 40,000,000 | — | — | 3.00 | 3.50 | — |

**KM# 311 2 EURO**
8.50 g., Bi-Metallic Nickel-Brass center in Copper-Nickel ring, 25.75 mm. **Subject:** Treaty of Rome, 50th Anniversary **Obv:** Open treaty

| Date | Mintage | VF20 | XF40 | MS60 | MS63 | MS65 |
|---|---|---|---|---|---|---|
| 2007 R | 5,000,000 | — | — | 3.00 | 3.50 | — |

**KM# 251 2 EURO**
8.50 g., Bi-Metallic Nickel-Brass center in Copper-Nickel ring, 25.75 mm. **Obv:** Bust of Dante Aligheri **Rev:** Relief map of Western Europe, stars, lines and value **Edge:** Reeded **Edge Lettering:** 2's and stars

| Date | Mintage | VF20 | XF40 | MS60 | MS63 | MS65 |
|---|---|---|---|---|---|---|
| 2008 R | 2,455,000 | — | — | 3.00 | 3.50 | — |
| 2008 R | 5,000 | **PF63** 10.00 | | | | |
| 2009 R | 1,951,500 | — | — | 3.00 | 3.50 | — |
| 2009 R | 5,500 | **PF63** 10.00 | | | | |
| 2010 R | 6,000,000 | — | — | 3.00 | 3.50 | — |
| 2010 R | 5,000 | **PF63** 10.00 | | | | |
| 2011 R | 20,000,000 | — | — | 3.00 | 3.50 | — |
| 2011 R | 5,000 | **PF63** 10.00 | | | | |
| 2012 R | 26,959,500 | — | — | 3.00 | 3.50 | — |
| 2012 R | — | **PF63** 10.00 | | | | |
| 2013 R | — | — | — | 3.00 | 3.50 | — |
| 2013 R | — | **PF63** 10.00 | | | | |
| 2014 | — | — | — | 3.00 | 3.50 | — |
| 2014 | — | **PF63** 15.00 | | | | |

**KM# 301 2 EURO**
8.50 g., Bi-Metallic Nickel-Brass center in Copper-Nickel ring, 25.75 mm. **Subject:** Declaration of Rights **Obv:** Nude male and female figures

| Date | Mintage | VF20 | XF40 | MS60 | MS63 | MS65 |
|---|---|---|---|---|---|---|
| 2008 R | 5,000,000 | — | — | 3.00 | 3.50 | — |

**KM# 310 2 EURO**
8.50 g., Bi-Metallic Nickel-Brass center in Copper-Nickel ring, 25.75 mm. **Subject:** Louis Braille **Obv:** Hand reading book in braille font

| Date | Mintage | VF20 | XF40 | MS60 | MS63 | MS65 |
|---|---|---|---|---|---|---|
| 2009 R | 2,000,000 | — | — | 6.00 | 7.00 | — |

**KM# 312 2 EURO**
8.50 g., Bi-Metallic Nickel-Brass center in Copper-Nickel ring, 25.75 mm. **Subject:** European Monetrary Union, 10th Anniversary **Obv:** Stick figure and Euro symbol

| Date | Mintage | VF20 | XF40 | MS60 | MS63 | MS65 |
|---|---|---|---|---|---|---|
| 2009 R | 2,000,000 | — | — | 6.00 | 7.00 | — |
| 2009 R | 5,500 | **PF63** 25.00 | | | | |

**KM# 328 2 EURO**
8.50 g., Bi-Metallic Nickel-Brass center in Copper-Nickel ring., 25.75 mm. **Subject:** Camillo Benso Count of Cavour **Obv:** Bust 3/4 right

| Date | Mintage | VF20 | XF40 | MS60 | MS63 | MS65 |
|---|---|---|---|---|---|---|
| 2010 R | 4,000,000 | — | — | 5.00 | 6.00 | — |
| 2010 R Special Unc. | 16,000 | — | — | — | 15.00 | — |
| 2010 R | 5,000 | **PF63** 25.00 | | | | |

**KM# 338 2 EURO**
8.50 g., Bi-Metallic Nickel-Brass center in Copper-Nickel ring, 25.75 mm. **Subject:** Italian Unification, 150th Anniversary **Obv:** Three banners

| Date | Mintage | VF20 | XF40 | MS60 | MS63 | MS65 |
|---|---|---|---|---|---|---|
| 2011 R | 10,000,000 | — | — | 4.00 | 5.00 | — |
| 2011 R Special Unc. | 20,000 | — | — | — | 15.00 | — |
| 2011 R | 5,000 | **PF63** 25.00 | | | | |

**KM# 350 2 EURO**
8.50 g., Bi-Metallic Nickel-Brass center in Copper-Nickel ring, 25.75 mm. **Subject:** Eurocoinage, 10th Anniversary **Obv:** Euro symbol on globe at center, child-like drawings around

| Date | Mintage | VF20 | XF40 | MS60 | MS63 | MS65 |
|---|---|---|---|---|---|---|
| 2012 R | 15,000,000 | — | — | 5.00 | 6.00 | — |

**KM# 355 2 EURO**
8.50 g., Bi-Metallic Nickel-Brass plated Nickel center in Copper-Nickel ring, 25.75 mm. **Subject:** Giovanni Pascoli, 100th Anniversary of Death **Obv:** Giovanni Pascoli bust **Edge:** Reeded with 2's and stars

| Date | Mintage | VF20 | XF40 | MS60 | MS63 | MS65 |
|---|---|---|---|---|---|---|
| 2012 Special Unc | — | — | — | — | 15.00 | — |
| 2012 R | 15,000,000 | — | — | 5.00 | 6.00 | — |

**KM# 357 2 EURO**
8.50 g., Bi-Metallic Nickel-Brass center in Copper-Nickel ring, 25.75 mm. **Subject:** Verdi, 200th Anniversary of Birth **Obv:** Giuseppe Verdi bust facing

| Date | Mintage | VF20 | XF40 | MS60 | MS63 | MS65 |
|---|---|---|---|---|---|---|
| 2013 | 10,000,000 | — | — | 5.00 | 6.00 | — |

**KM# 358 2 EURO**
8.50 g., Bi-Metallic Nickel-Brass center in Copper-Nickel ring, 25.75 mm. **Subject:** Boccaccio, 700th Anniversary of Birth **Obv:** Giovanni Boccaccio head facing

| Date | Mintage | VF20 | XF40 | MS60 | MS63 | MS65 |
|---|---|---|---|---|---|---|
| 2013 | 10,000,000 | — | — | — | 6.00 | — |

**KM# 367 2 EURO**
8.50 g., Bi-Metallic, 25.75 mm. **Subject:** Carabinieri, 150th Anniversary

| Date | Mintage | F12 | VF20 | XF40 | MS60 | MS63 |
|---|---|---|---|---|---|---|
| 2014 | — | — | — | — | — | 5.00 |

**KM# 252 5 EURO**
18.00 g., 0.925 Silver 0.5353 oz. ASW, 32 mm. **Subject:** People in Europe

| Date | Mintage | VF20 | XF40 | MS60 | MS63 | MS65 |
|---|---|---|---|---|---|---|
| 2003 R | 25,000 | — | — | — | 35.00 | — |
| Special Unc | | | | | | |
| 2003 R | 8,000 | **PF63** 60.00 | | | | |

**KM# 253 5 EURO**
18.00 g., 0.925 Silver 0.5353 oz. ASW, 32 mm. **Subject:** Work in Europe

| Date | Mintage | VF20 | XF40 | MS60 | MS63 | MS65 |
|---|---|---|---|---|---|---|
| 2003 R | 50,000 | — | — | — | 35.00 | — |
| 2003 R | 12,000 | **PF63** 65.00 | | | | |

**KM# 302 5 EURO**
18.00 g., 0.925 Silver 0.5353 oz. ASW, 32 mm. **Subject:** Antonia Meucci - 200th Birthday

| Date | Mintage | VF20 | XF40 | MS60 | MS63 | MS65 |
|---|---|---|---|---|---|---|
| 2003 R | — | **PF63** 55.00 | | | | |

**KM# 238 5 EURO**
18.00 g., 0.925 Silver 0.5353 oz. ASW, 32 mm. **Subject:** World Cup Soccer - Germany 2006 **Obv:** Santa Croce Square in Florence **Rev:** Soccer ball and world globe design

| Date | Mintage | VF20 | XF40 | MS60 | MS63 | MS65 |
|---|---|---|---|---|---|---|
| 2004 R | 35,000 | **PF63** 90.00 | | | | |

**KM# 239 5 EURO**
18.00 g., 0.925 Silver 0.5353 oz. ASW, 32 mm. **Subject:** Madam Butterfly **Obv:** La Scala Opera House, where Madam Butterfly was first performed there in 1904 **Rev:** Geisha

| Date | Mintage | VF20 | XF40 | MS60 | MS63 | MS65 |
|---|---|---|---|---|---|---|
| 2004 R | 30,000 | — | — | — | 35.00 | — |
| 2004 R | 12,000 | **PF63** 40.00 | | | | |

**KM# 254 5 EURO**
18.00 g., 0.925 Silver 0.5353 oz. ASW, 32 mm. **Subject:** 50th Anniversary of Italian Television

| Date | Mintage | VF20 | XF40 | MS60 | MS63 | MS65 |
|---|---|---|---|---|---|---|
| 2004 R | 40,000 | — | — | — | 40.00 | — |
| 2004 R | 15,000 | **PF63** 80.00 | | | | |

**KM# 255 5 EURO**
18.00 g., 0.925 Silver 0.5353 oz. ASW, 32 mm. **Subject:** 85th Birthday of Federico Fellini

| Date | Mintage | VF20 | XF40 | MS60 | MS63 | MS65 |
|---|---|---|---|---|---|---|
| 2005 R | 35,000 | — | — | — | 65.00 | — |
| 2005 R | 22,000 | **PF63** 140 | | | | |

**KM# 256 5 EURO**
18.00 g., 0.925 Silver 0.5353 oz. ASW, 32 mm. **Subject:** 2006 Olympic Winter Games Torino Ski Jump

| Date | Mintage | VF20 | XF40 | MS60 | MS63 | MS65 |
|---|---|---|---|---|---|---|
| 2005 R | 35,000 | **PF63** 55.00 | | | | |

**KM# 257 5 EURO**
18.00 g., 0.925 Silver 0.5353 oz. ASW, 32 mm. **Subject:** 2006 Olympic Winter Games Cross Country Skiing

| Date | Mintage | VF20 | XF40 | MS60 | MS63 | MS65 |
|---|---|---|---|---|---|---|
| 2005 R | 35,000 | **PF63** 55.00 | | | | |

**KM# 266 5 EURO**
18.00 g., 0.925 Silver 0.5353 oz. ASW, 32 mm. **Subject:** 2006 Olympic Games Torino Figure Skating

| Date | Mintage | VF20 | XF40 | MS60 | MS63 | MS65 |
|---|---|---|---|---|---|---|
| 2005 | 35,000 | **PF63** 55.00 | | | | |

**KM# 282 5 EURO**
18.00 g., 0.925 Silver 0.5353 oz. ASW, 32 mm. **Subject:** FIFA World Cup 12

| Date | Mintage | VF20 | XF40 | MS60 | MS63 | MS65 |
|---|---|---|---|---|---|---|
| 2006 R | 25,000 | **PF63** 65.00 | | | | |

**KM# 291 5 EURO**
18.00 g., 0.925 Silver 0.5353 oz. ASW, 32 mm. **Subject:** Kyoto Agreement - 5th Anniversary **Obv:** Allegorical representation of nature rebelling against pollution **Rev:** Allegorical representation of clear air with a spiral of vital energy

| Date | Mintage | VF20 | XF40 | MS60 | MS63 | MS65 |
|---|---|---|---|---|---|---|
| 2007 R | 20,000 | — | — | — | 50.00 | — |
| Special Unc | | | | | | |
| 2007 R | 7,000 | **PF63** 85.00 | | | | |

**KM# 292 5 EURO**
18.00 g., 0.925 Silver 0.5353 oz. ASW, 32 mm. **Subject:** Giuseppe Garibaldi - 200th Anniversary Birth **Obv:** Portrait facing **Rev:** Harbor Lympia in Nice

| Date | Mintage | VF20 | XF40 | MS60 | MS63 | MS65 |
|---|---|---|---|---|---|---|
| 2007 R | 8,000 | — | — | — | 120 | — |
| Special Unc. | | | | | | |

**KM# 293 5 EURO**
18.00 g., 0.925 Silver 0.5353 oz. ASW, 32 mm. **Subject:** Aitero Spinelini 100th Birthday **Obv:** Bust 3/4 facing **Rev:** Representation of Ventotene island and Parliament hemicycle

| Date | Mintage | VF20 | XF40 | MS60 | MS63 | MS65 |
|---|---|---|---|---|---|---|
| 2007 R | 7,000 | — | — | — | 120 | — |
| Special Unc. | | | | | | |

**KM# 294 5 EURO**
18.00 g., 0.925 Silver 0.5353 oz. ASW, 32 mm. **Subject:** Arturo Toscani - 50th Aniversary Death

| Date | Mintage | VF20 | XF40 | MS60 | MS63 | MS65 |
|---|---|---|---|---|---|---|
| 2007 R | 7,000 | — | — | — | 50.00 | — |

**KM# 323 5 EURO**
18.00 g., 0.925 Silver 0.5353 oz. ASW, 32 mm. **Subject:** Arturo Toscanini. 50th Death Anniversary **Obv:** Profile left **Rev:** Hand with baton, and musical instruments

| Date | Mintage | VF20 | XF40 | MS60 | MS63 | MS65 |
|---|---|---|---|---|---|---|
| 2007 R | 7,000 | — | — | — | 125 | — |
| Special Unc. | | | | | | |

**KM# 281 5 EURO**
18.00 g., 0.925 Silver 0.5353 oz. ASW, 32 mm. **Subject:** Italian Republic - 60th Anniversary

| Date | Mintage | VF20 | XF40 | MS60 | MS63 | MS65 |
|---|---|---|---|---|---|---|
| 2008 R | — | — | — | — | 65.00 | — |

**KM# 303 5 EURO**
18.00 g., 0.925 Silver 0.5353 oz. ASW, 32 mm. **Subject:** Anna Magnani, 100th Anniversary of Birth

| Date | Mintage | VF20 | XF40 | MS60 | MS63 | MS65 |
|---|---|---|---|---|---|---|
| (2008) | 9,000 | **PF63** 75.00 | | | | |

**KM# 304 5 EURO**
18.00 g., 0.925 Silver 0.5353 oz. ASW, 32 mm. **Subject:** Italian Constitution - 60th Anniversary

| Date | Mintage | VF20 | XF40 | MS60 | MS63 | MS65 |
|---|---|---|---|---|---|---|
| 2008 | 9,000 | — | — | — | 65.00 | — |

**KM# 325 5 EURO**
18.00 g., 0.925 Silver 0.5353 oz. ASW, 32 mm. **Series:** IFAD, 30th Anniversary

| Date | Mintage | VF20 | XF40 | MS60 | MS63 | MS65 |
|---|---|---|---|---|---|---|
| 2008 R | 20,000 | — | — | — | 60.00 | — |
| 2008 R | 5,000 | **PF63** 130 | | | | |

**KM# 326 5 EURO**
18.00 g., 0.925 Silver 0.5353 oz. ASW, 32 mm. **Subject:** Antonio Meucci **Obv:** Bust 3/4 facing right

| Date | Mintage | VF20 | XF40 | MS60 | MS63 | MS65 |
|---|---|---|---|---|---|---|
| 2008 R | 9,000 | **PF63** 75.00 | | | | |

**KM# 313 5 EURO**
18.00 g., 0.925 Silver 0.5353 oz. ASW, 32 mm. **Subject:** Giro d'Italy - Cycling Race Centennial **Obv:** Two cyclists **Rev:** Bicycle and map of Italy

| Date | Mintage | VF20 | XF40 | MS60 | MS63 | MS65 |
|---|---|---|---|---|---|---|
| 2009 R | 14,000 | — | — | — | 60.00 | — |
| Special Unc. | | | | | | |

**KM# 314 5 EURO**
18.00 g., 0.925 Silver 0.5353 oz. ASW, 32 mm. **Subject:** World Aquatics Championships **Obv:** River God reclining **Rev:** Two swimmers

| Date | Mintage | VF20 | XF40 | MS60 | MS63 | MS65 |
|---|---|---|---|---|---|---|
| 2009 R | 21,000 | — | — | — | 50.00 | — |
| 2009 R | 7,500 | — | — | — | — | — |

**KM# 315 5 EURO**
18.00 g., 0.925 Silver 0.5353 oz. ASW, 32 mm. **Subject:** Herculaneum Discovery, 300th Anniversary **Obv:** Four dogs nipping at horse **Rev:** Marble relief of nymph drawing water with a horn

| Date | Mintage | VF20 | XF40 | MS60 | MS63 | MS65 |
|---|---|---|---|---|---|---|
| 2009 R | 9,000 | — | — | — | 55.00 | — |

**KM# 327 5 EURO**
18.00 g., 0.925 Silver 0.5353 oz. ASW, 32 mm. **Subject:** FINA, 13th Anniversary **Obv:** Sculpture Allegory of the Tiber River **Rev:** Swimmer Mosaics decorating the Foro Italico

| Date | Mintage | VF20 | XF40 | MS60 | MS63 | MS65 |
|---|---|---|---|---|---|---|
| 2009 R | 21,000 | — | — | — | 65.00 | — |
| 2009 R | 5,500 | **PF63** 110 | | | | |

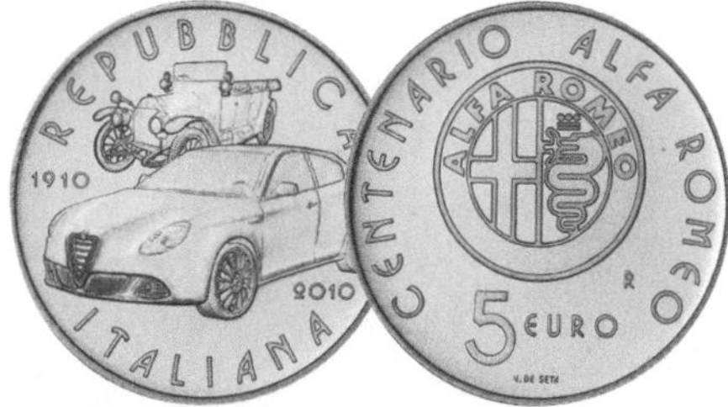

**KM# 329 5 EURO**
18.00 g., 0.925 Silver 0.5353 oz. ASW, 32 mm. **Subject:** Alfa Romeo 100th Anniversary **Obv:** Two Automobiles: 24HP in back, new Giulietta in front **Rev:** Company logo

| Date | Mintage | VF20 | XF40 | MS60 | MS63 | MS65 |
|---|---|---|---|---|---|---|
| 2010 R | 17,000 | — | — | — | 65.00 | — |
| 2010 R | 5,500 | **PF63** 110 | | | | |

**KM# 330 5 EURO**
18.00 g., 0.925 Silver 0.5353 oz. ASW, 32 mm. **Subject:** Confindustria 100th Anniversary **Obv:** Female head left, mechanical gears within spiral at right **Rev:** Linear eagle and 100 logo

| Date | Mintage | VF20 | XF40 | MS60 | MS63 | MS65 |
|---|---|---|---|---|---|---|
| 2010 R | 7,500 | — | — | — | 65.00 | — |

**KM# 331 5 EURO**
18.00 g., 0.925 Silver 0.5353 oz. ASW, 32 mm. **Subject:** Santa Chiara in Naples **Obv:** Church facade **Rev:** Cloister interior

| Date | Mintage | VF20 | XF40 | MS60 | MS63 | MS65 |
|---|---|---|---|---|---|---|
| 2010 R | 7,500 | **PF63** 80.00 | | | | |

**KM# 341 5 EURO**
18.00 g., 0.925 Silver 0.5353 oz. ASW, 32 mm. **Subject:** Italian unification, 150th Anniversary

| Date | Mintage | VF20 | XF40 | MS60 | MS63 | MS65 |
|---|---|---|---|---|---|---|
| 2011 R | 18,000 | — | — | — | 65.00 | — |
| 2011 R | 5,000 | **PF63** 100 | | | | |

**KM# 343 5 EURO**
18.00 g., 0.925 Silver 0.5353 oz. ASW, 32 mm. **Subject:** Italian Council of State, 180th Anniversary

| Date | Mintage | VF20 | XF40 | MS60 | MS63 | MS65 |
|---|---|---|---|---|---|---|
| 2011 R | 7,000 | **PF63** 85.00 | | | | |

**KM# 344 5 EURO**
18.00 g., 0.925 Silver 0.5353 oz. ASW, 32 mm. **Subject:** Historical Building of the Italian Mint, 100th Anniversary

| Date | Mintage | VF20 | XF40 | MS60 | MS63 | MS65 |
|---|---|---|---|---|---|---|
| 2011 R | 7,000 | — | — | — | 70.00 | — |

**KM# 345 5 EURO**
18.00 g., 0.925 Silver 0.5353 oz. ASW, 32 mm. **Subject:** Art in Italy - Anagini

| Date | Mintage | VF20 | XF40 | MS60 | MS63 | MS65 |
|---|---|---|---|---|---|---|
| 2011 R | 7,000 | **PF63** 85.00 | | | | |

**KM# 353 5 EURO**
18.00 g., 0.925 Silver 0.5353 oz. ASW, 32 mm. **Subject:** Italian Monetary Unification, 150th Anniversary **Obv:** Italia head in vertical oval **Rev:** Alegory and fruits

| Date | Mintage | VF20 | XF40 | MS60 | MS63 | MS65 |
|---|---|---|---|---|---|---|
| 2012 R | 7,000 | — | — | — | 70.00 | — |

**KM# 359 5 EURO**
18.00 g., 0.925 Silver 0.5353 oz. ASW, 32 mm. **Subject:** Sistine Chapel, 500th Anniversary **Obv:** Female head right **Rev:** Statue seated facing right

| Date | Mintage | VF20 | XF40 | MS60 | MS63 | MS65 |
|---|---|---|---|---|---|---|
| 2012 | — | — | — | — | 25.00 | — |
| 2012 | — | **PF65** 60.00 | | | | |

**KM# 360 5 EURO**
18.00 g., 0.925 Silver 0.5353 oz. ASW, 32 mm. **Subject:** Giuseppe Gioachino Belli, 150th Anniversary of Death **Obv:** Bust facing **Rev:** Temple of Hercules and Basilica of Santa Maria in Cosmedin

| Date | Mintage | VF20 | XF40 | MS60 | MS63 | MS65 |
|---|---|---|---|---|---|---|
| 2013 | — | — | — | — | 65.00 | — |

**KM# 361 5 EURO**
18.00 g., 0.925 Silver 0.5353 oz. ASW, 32 mm. **Obv:** Temple of Hera in Salinas **Rev:** Statue of Perseus and Medusa **Edge:** Reeded

| Date | Mintage | VF20 | XF40 | MS60 | MS63 | MS65 |
|---|---|---|---|---|---|---|
| 2013 | 7,000 | **PF63** 75.00 | | | | |

**KM# 362 5 EURO**
18.00 g., 0.925 Silver 0.5353 oz. ASW, 32 mm. **Obv:** Mosaic from Hadrian's villa **Rev:** Detail of the Maritime Theatre of Hadrian's villa in Tivoli **Edge:** Reeded

| Date | Mintage | VF20 | XF40 | MS60 | MS63 | MS65 |
|---|---|---|---|---|---|---|
| 2013 | 7,000 | **PF63** 75.00 | | | | |

**KM# 258 10 EURO**
22.00 g., 0.925 Silver 0.6543 oz. ASW, 34 mm. **Subject:** People In Europe

| Date | Mintage | VF20 | XF40 | MS60 | MS63 | MS65 |
|---|---|---|---|---|---|---|
| 2003 | 25,000 | — | — | — | 40.00 | — |
| 2003 R | 8,000 | **PF63** 60.00 | | | | |

**KM# 259 10 EURO**
22.00 g., 0.925 Silver 0.6543 oz. ASW, 34 mm. **Subject:** Italian Presidency of E.U.

| Date | Mintage | VF20 | XF40 | MS60 | MS63 | MS65 |
|---|---|---|---|---|---|---|
| 2003 R | 40,000 | — | — | — | 50.00 | — |
| 2003 R | 8,000 | **PF63** 140 | | | | |

**KM# 240 10 EURO**
22.00 g., 0.925 Silver 0.6543 oz. ASW, 34 mm. **Subject:** City of Genoa **Obv:** Sculpture and art works **Rev:** Tower and harbor map

| Date | Mintage | VF20 | XF40 | MS60 | MS63 | MS65 |
|---|---|---|---|---|---|---|
| 2004 R | 10,500 | **PF63** 110 | | | | |
| 2004 R | 20,000 | — | — | — | 60.00 | — |

**KM# 241 10 EURO**
22.00 g., 0.925 Silver 0.6543 oz. ASW, 34 mm. **Subject:** Giacomo Puccini **Obv:** Puccini wearing hat **Rev:** Stage, music and quill

| Date | Mintage | VF20 | XF40 | MS60 | MS63 | MS65 |
|---|---|---|---|---|---|---|
| 2004 R | 13,500 | — | — | — | 40.00 | — |
| 2004 R | 8,000 | **PF63** 60.00 | | | | |

**KM# 260 10 EURO**
22.00 g., 0.925 Silver 0.6543 oz. ASW, 34 mm. **Subject:** 2006 Olympic Winter Games Torino Alpine Skiing

| Date | Mintage | VF20 | XF40 | MS60 | MS63 | MS65 |
|---|---|---|---|---|---|---|
| 2005 R | 40,000 | **PF63** 80.00 | | | | |

**KM# 261 10 EURO**
22.00 g., 0.925 Silver 0.6543 oz. ASW, 34 mm. **Subject:** 2006 Olympic Winter Games Torino Ice Hockey

| Date | Mintage | VF20 | XF40 | MS60 | MS63 | MS65 |
|---|---|---|---|---|---|---|
| 2005 R | 35,000 | **PF63** 80.00 | | | | |

**KM# 262 10 EURO**
22.00 g., 0.925 Silver 0.6543 oz. ASW, 34 mm. **Subject:** 2006 Olympic Winter Games Torino Speed Skating

| Date | Mintage | VF20 | XF40 | MS60 | MS63 | MS65 |
|---|---|---|---|---|---|---|
| 2005 R | 35,000 | **PF63** 80.00 | | | | |

**KM# 268 10 EURO**
22.00 g., 0.925 Silver 0.6543 oz. ASW, 34 mm. **Subject:** 60th Anniversary UN "ONU

| Date | Mintage | VF20 | XF40 | MS60 | MS63 | MS65 |
|---|---|---|---|---|---|---|
| 2005 | 25,000 | — | — | — | 65.00 | — |

**KM# 271 10 EURO**
22.00 g., 0.925 Silver 0.6543 oz. ASW, 34 mm. **Subject:** Peace and Freedom In Europe

| Date | Mintage | VF20 | XF40 | MS60 | MS63 | MS65 |
|---|---|---|---|---|---|---|
| 2005 | 22,000 | PF63 100 | | | | |

**KM# 283 10 EURO**
22.00 g., 0.925 Silver 0.6543 oz. ASW, 34 mm. **Subject:** FIFA World Cup - Germany

| Date | Mintage | VF20 | XF40 | MS60 | MS63 | MS65 |
|---|---|---|---|---|---|---|
| 2006 R | 20,000 | — | — | — | 65.00 | — |

**KM# 284 10 EURO**
22.00 g., 0.925 Silver 0.6543 oz. ASW **Subject:** Andre Martenga - 500th Anniversary

| Date | Mintage | VF20 | XF40 | MS60 | MS63 | MS65 |
|---|---|---|---|---|---|---|
| 2006 R | 8,000 | PF63 150 | | | | |

**KM# 285 10 EURO**
22.00 g., 0.925 Silver 0.6543 oz. ASW, 34 mm. **Subject:** Leonardo da Vinci

| Date | Mintage | VF20 | XF40 | MS60 | MS63 | MS65 |
|---|---|---|---|---|---|---|
| 2006 R | 25,000 | PF63 85.00 | | | | |

**KM# 286 10 EURO**
22.00 g., 0.925 Silver 0.6543 oz. ASW, 34 mm. **Subject:** UNICEF 60th Anniversary

| Date | Mintage | VF20 | XF40 | MS60 | MS63 | MS65 |
|---|---|---|---|---|---|---|
| 2006 R | 15,000 | — | — | — | 70.00 | — |

**KM# 295 10 EURO**
22.00 g., 0.925 Silver 0.6543 oz. ASW, 34 mm. **Subject:** Treaty of Rome, 50th Anniversary

| Date | Mintage | VF20 | XF40 | MS60 | MS63 | MS65 |
|---|---|---|---|---|---|---|
| 2007 R | 20,504 | PF63 100 | | | | |

**KM# 296 10 EURO**
22.00 g., 0.925 Silver 0.6543 oz. ASW, 34 mm. **Subject:** Antonia Canova - 250th Anniversary Birth **Obv:** Portrait facing **Rev:** Sculpture Eros and Psyche

| Date | Mintage | VF20 | XF40 | MS60 | MS63 | MS65 |
|---|---|---|---|---|---|---|
| 2007 R | 8,000 | PF63 100 | | | | |

**KM# 297 10 EURO**
22.00 g., 0.925 Silver 0.6543 oz. ASW, 34 mm. **Subject:** Mint of Rome's School of Medallic Art - 100th Anniversary **Obv:** Sculptor designing medal, from a medal by Giuseppe Romagnoli **Rev:** School logo

| Date | Mintage | VF20 | XF40 | MS60 | MS63 | MS65 |
|---|---|---|---|---|---|---|
| 2007 R | 8,000 | PF63 65.00 | | | | |

**KM# 324 10 EURO**
22.00 g., 0.925 Silver 0.6543 oz. ASW, 34 mm. **Subject:** Treaty of Rome, 50th Anniversary **Obv:** Pavement pattern from Capitol Square in Rome **Rev:** Steps leading up to Capitol

| Date | Mintage | VF20 | XF40 | MS60 | MS63 | MS65 |
|---|---|---|---|---|---|---|
| 2008 R | 22,000 | PF63 85.00 | | | | |

**KM# 305 10 EURO**
22.00 g., 0.925 Silver 0.6543 oz. ASW, 34 mm. **Subject:** Andrea Palladio - 500th Birthday

| Date | Mintage | VF20 | XF40 | MS60 | MS63 | MS65 |
|---|---|---|---|---|---|---|
| 2008 | 16,000 | PF63 90.00 | | | | |

**KM# 306 10 EURO**
22.00 g., 0.925 Silver 0.6543 oz. ASW, 34 mm. **Subject:** University of Perugia - 700th Anniversary

| Date | Mintage | VF20 | XF40 | MS60 | MS63 | MS65 |
|---|---|---|---|---|---|---|
| 2008 | 9,000 | PF63 90.00 | | | | |

**KM# 316 10 EURO**
22.00 g., 0.925 Silver 0.6543 oz. ASW, 34 mm. **Subject:** International Year of Astronomy **Obv:** Head right, astrolabe at left **Rev:** Galilei's telescope, details of an astrolabe and sky

| Date | Mintage | VF20 | XF40 | MS60 | MS63 | MS65 |
|---|---|---|---|---|---|---|
| 2009 R | 9,000 | PF63 80.00 | | | | |

**KM# 317 10 EURO**
22.00 g., 0.925 Silver 0.6543 oz. ASW, 34 mm. **Subject:** Guglielmo Maroni's Nobel Prize in Physics **Obv:** Bust and yacht Elettra **Rev:** Radio receiver and antenna and radio waves

| Date | Mintage | VF20 | XF40 | MS60 | MS63 | MS65 |
|---|---|---|---|---|---|---|
| 2009 R | 18,000 | PF63 85.00 | | | | |

**KM# 318 10 EURO**
22.00 g., 0.925 Silver 0.6543 oz. ASW, 34 mm. **Subject:** Annibale Carracci, 400th Anniversary **Obv:** 1/2 length figure standing **Rev:** Historical cart

| Date | Mintage | VF20 | XF40 | MS60 | MS63 | MS65 |
|---|---|---|---|---|---|---|
| 2009 R | 9,000 | PF63 80.00 | | | | |

**KM# 319 10 EURO**
22.00 g., 0.925 Silver 0.6543 oz. ASW, 34 mm. **Subject:** Futurist movement, 100th Anniversary **Obv:** Building design **Rev:** Round sculpture

| Date | Mintage | VF20 | XF40 | MS60 | MS63 | MS65 |
|---|---|---|---|---|---|---|
| 2009 R | 9,000 | PF63 85.00 | | | | |

**KM# 337 10 EURO**
22.00 g., 0.925 Silver 0.6543 oz. ASW, 34 mm. **Subject:** L'Aquila Earthquake, reconstruction

| Date | Mintage | VF20 | XF40 | MS60 | MS63 | MS65 |
|---|---|---|---|---|---|---|
| 2009 R | 5,000 | PF63 130 | | | | |

**KM# 332 10 EURO**
22.00 g., 0.925 Silver 0.6543 oz. ASW, 34 mm. **Subject:** Caravaggio 400th Death Anniversary **Obv:** Bust 3/4 facing left, basket of fruit below **Rev:** Medussa head painting detail

| Date | Mintage | VF20 | XF40 | MS60 | MS63 | MS65 |
|---|---|---|---|---|---|---|
| 2010 R | 7,500 | PF63 85.00 | | | | |

**KM# 333 10 EURO**
22.00 g., 0.925 Silver 0.6543 oz. ASW, 34 mm. **Subject:** Giorgione, 500th Death Anniverdary **Obv:** Bust 3/4 left **Rev:** Detail from the painting "La Tempesta

| Date | Mintage | VF20 | XF40 | MS60 | MS63 | MS65 |
|---|---|---|---|---|---|---|
| 2010 R | 7,500 | PF63 85.00 | | | | |

**KM# 334 10 EURO**
22.00 g., 0.925 Silver 0.6543 oz. ASW, 34 mm. **Subject:** Arts of Italy, Aquileia **Obv:** Basilica and architechtural floorplan **Rev:** Interpertation from the "Tabula Peuntigeriana

| Date | Mintage | VF20 | XF40 | MS60 | MS63 | MS65 |
|---|---|---|---|---|---|---|
| 2010 R | 7,500 | PF63 85.00 | | | | |

**KM# 339 10 EURO**
22.00 g., 0.925 Silver 0.6543 oz. ASW, 34 mm. **Subject:** Amerigo Vespucci

| Date | Mintage | VF20 | XF40 | MS60 | MS63 | MS65 |
|---|---|---|---|---|---|---|
| 2011 R | 7,000 | PF63 95.00 | | | | |

**KM# 340 10 EURO**
22.00 g., 0.925 Silver 0.6543 oz. ASW, 34 mm. **Subject:** Alcide de Gasperi, 130th Anniversary of Birth

| Date | Mintage | VF20 | XF40 | MS60 | MS63 | MS65 |
|---|---|---|---|---|---|---|
| 2011 R | 7,000 | PF63 95.00 | | | | |

**KM# 342 10 EURO**
22.00 g., 0.925 Silver 0.6543 oz. ASW, 34 mm. **Subject:** Giorgio Vasari, 500th Anniversary of Birth

| Date | Mintage | VF20 | XF40 | MS60 | MS63 | MS65 |
|---|---|---|---|---|---|---|
| 2011 R | 7,000 | PF63 95.00 | | | | |

**KM# 346 10 EURO**
22.00 g., 0.925 Silver 0.6543 oz. ASW, 34 mm. **Subject:** Art in Italy - Torino

| Date | Mintage | VF20 | XF40 | MS60 | MS63 | MS65 |
|---|---|---|---|---|---|---|
| 2011 R | 7,000 | PF63 95.00 | | | | |

**KM# 349 10 EURO**
22.00 g., 0.925 Silver 0.6543 oz. ASW, 34 mm. **Subject:** Bari **Obv:** St. Nicolas Church

| Date | Mintage | VF20 | XF40 | MS60 | MS63 | MS65 |
|---|---|---|---|---|---|---|
| 2011 R | 7,000 | PF63 95.00 | | | | |

**KM# 354 10 EURO**
22.00 g., 0.925 Silver 0.6543 oz. ASW, 34 mm. **Subject:** Francesco Guardi, 300th anniversary of Birth **Obv:** Venice from the lagoon **Rev:** Guardi bust

| Date | Mintage | VF20 | XF40 | MS60 | MS63 | MS65 |
|---|---|---|---|---|---|---|
| 2012 R | 7,000 | PF63 100 | | | | |

**KM# 356 10 EURO**
22.00 g., 0.925 Silver 0.6543 oz. ASW, 34 mm. **Obv:** Bust right, signature below **Rev:** Head of David statue at left, Holy Year Door at right

| Date | Mintage | VF20 | XF40 | MS60 | MS63 | MS65 |
|---|---|---|---|---|---|---|
| 2012 R | 9,000 | PF63 100 | | | | |

**KM# 363 10 EURO**
22.00 g., 0.925 Silver 0.6543 oz. ASW, 34 mm. **Obv:** Half-length figure left, seated, hand holding head **Rev:** Stone figure from theater scene

| Date | Mintage | VF20 | XF40 | MS60 | MS63 | MS65 |
|---|---|---|---|---|---|---|
| 2013 | — | PF63 85.00 | | | | |

**KM# 364 10 EURO**
22.00 g., 0.925 Silver 0.6543 oz. ASW, 34 mm. **Obv:** Fenis castle **Rev:** Fresco of St. George slaying dragon

| Date | Mintage | VF20 | XF40 | MS60 | MS63 | MS65 |
|---|---|---|---|---|---|---|
| 2013 | 7,000 | PF63 85.00 | | | | |

**KM# 368 10 EURO**
22.00 g., 0.925 Silver 0.6543 oz. ASW, 34 mm. **Subject:** Gioachino Rossini

| Date | Mintage | VF20 | XF40 | MS60 | MS63 | MS65 |
|---|---|---|---|---|---|---|
| 2014 | — | PF63 85.00 | | | | |

**KM# 263 20 EURO**
6.45 g., 0.900 Gold 0.1866 oz. AGW, 21 mm. **Subject:** Arts in Europe - Italy

| Date | Mintage | VF20 | XF40 | MS60 | MS63 | MS65 |
|---|---|---|---|---|---|---|
| 2003 R | 6,000 | PF63 550 | | | | |

**KM# 242 20 EURO**
6.45 g., 0.900 Gold 0.1866 oz. AGW, 21 mm. **Obv:** Arts In Europe: Belgium **Rev:** Flying bird obscuring a man's face

| Date | Mintage | VF20 | XF40 | MS60 | MS63 | MS65 |
|---|---|---|---|---|---|---|
| 2004 R | 6,000 | PF63 550 | | | | |

**KM# 243 20 EURO**
6.45 g., 0.900 Gold 0.1866 oz. AGW, 21 mm. **Subject:** World Cup Soccer - Germany 2006 **Obv:** Mascot **Rev:** Soccer ball and world globe

| Date | Mintage | VF20 | XF40 | MS60 | MS63 | MS65 |
|---|---|---|---|---|---|---|
| 2004 R | 7,500 | PF63 550 | | | | |

**KM# 265 20 EURO**
6.45 g., 0.900 Gold 0.1866 oz. AGW, 21 mm. **Subject:** 2006 Olympic Winter Games Torino Porte Palatine Gate

| Date | Mintage | VF20 | XF40 | MS60 | MS63 | MS65 |
|---|---|---|---|---|---|---|
| 2005 R | 10,000 | PF63 500 | | | | |

**KM# 267 20 EURO**
6.45 g., 0.900 Gold 0.1866 oz. AGW, 21 mm. **Subject:** 2006 Olympic Games Torino Madama Palace

| Date | Mintage | VF20 | XF40 | MS60 | MS63 | MS65 |
|---|---|---|---|---|---|---|
| 2005 R | 10,000 | PF63 500 | | | | |

**KM# 269 20 EURO**
6.45 g., 0.900 Gold 0.1866 oz. AGW, 21 mm. **Subject:** 2006 Olympic Games Torino Stupinigi Palace

| Date | Mintage | VF20 | XF40 | MS60 | MS63 | MS65 |
|---|---|---|---|---|---|---|
| 2005 R | 10,000 | PF63 500 | | | | |

**KM# 272 20 EURO**
6.45 g., 0.900 Gold 0.1866 oz. AGW, 21 mm. **Subject:** Art In Europe - Finland **Obv:** Sailing ship

| Date | Mintage | VF20 | XF40 | MS60 | MS63 | MS65 |
|---|---|---|---|---|---|---|
| 2005 R | 5,000 | PF63 550 | | | | |

**KM# 287 20 EURO**
6.45 g., 0.900 Gold 0.1866 oz. AGW, 21 mm. **Subject:** FIFA World Cup

| Date | Mintage | VF20 | XF40 | MS60 | MS63 | MS65 |
|---|---|---|---|---|---|---|
| 2006 R | 4,350 | PF63 550 | | | | |

**KM# 288 20 EURO**
6.45 g., 0.900 Gold 0.1866 oz. AGW, 21 mm. **Subject:** European Arts - Germany

| Date | Mintage | VF20 | XF40 | MS60 | MS63 | MS65 |
|---|---|---|---|---|---|---|
| 2006 R | 3,100 | PF63 600 | | | | |

**KM# 298 20 EURO**
6.45 g., 0.900 Gold 0.1866 oz. AGW, 21 mm. **Subject:** Treaty of Rome - 50th Anniversary **Obv:** Pavement pattern in Capital Square in Rome **Rev:** Steps leading to Capital Building

| Date | Mintage | VF20 | XF40 | MS60 | MS63 | MS65 |
|---|---|---|---|---|---|---|
| 2007 R | 4,000 | PF63 550 | | | | |

**KM# 299 20 EURO**
6.45 g., 0.900 Gold 0.1866 oz. AGW, 21 mm. **Subject:** European Art - Ireland **Obv:** Sailing ship **Rev:** Tara Brooch

| Date | Mintage | VF20 | XF40 | MS60 | MS63 | MS65 |
|---|---|---|---|---|---|---|
| 2007 R | 3,500 | PF63 600 | | | | |

**KM# 307 20 EURO**
6.45 g., 0.900 Gold 0.1866 oz. AGW, 21 mm. **Subject:** Andrea Palladio - 500th Birthday **Obv:** Head left **Rev:** Building façade and floorplans

| Date | Mintage | VF20 | XF40 | MS60 | MS63 | MS65 |
|---|---|---|---|---|---|---|
| 2008 R | 5,500 | PF63 550 | | | | |

**KM# 308 20 EURO**
6.45 g., 0.900 Gold 0.1866 oz. AGW, 21 mm. **Subject:** Arts in Europe - Netherlands **Obv:** Sailing ship

| Date | Mintage | VF20 | XF40 | MS60 | MS63 | MS65 |
|---|---|---|---|---|---|---|
| 2008 R | 2,011 | PF63 550 | | | | |

### KM# 320 20 EURO

6.45 g., 0.900 Gold 0.1866 oz. AGW, 21 mm. **Subject:** Guglielmo Marconi, 100th Anniversary of Nobel in Physics **Obv:** Bust and yacht Elettra **Rev:** Radio receiver with antenna and radio waves

| Date | Mintage | VF20 | XF40 | MS60 | MS63 | MS65 |
|---|---|---|---|---|---|---|
| 2009 R | 5,000 | PF63 550 | | | | |

### KM# 321 20 EURO

6.45 g., 0.900 Gold 0.1866 oz. AGW, 21 mm. **Subject:** Arts in Europe - Great Britain **Obv:** Sailing ship **Rev:** Venus by Edward B. Jones

| Date | Mintage | VF20 | XF40 | MS60 | MS63 | MS65 |
|---|---|---|---|---|---|---|
| 2009 R | 3,000 | PF63 550 | | | | |

### KM# 335 20 EURO

6.45 g., 0.900 Gold 0.1866 oz. AGW, 21 mm. **Subject:** Arts of Europe - Sweden **Obv:** Sailing ship **Rev:** Viking Helmet

| Date | Mintage | VF20 | XF40 | MS60 | MS63 | MS65 |
|---|---|---|---|---|---|---|
| 2010 R | 2,000 | PF63 650 | | | | |

### KM# 347 20 EURO

6.45 g., 0.900 Gold 0.1866 oz. AGW, 21 mm. **Subject:** Flora in art

| Date | Mintage | VF20 | XF40 | MS60 | MS63 | MS65 |
|---|---|---|---|---|---|---|
| 2011 R | 1,500 | PF63 650 | | | | |

### KM# 352 20 EURO

6.45 g., 0.900 Gold 0.1867 oz. AGW, 21 mm. **Subject:** Flora in Art - Middle ages **Obv:** Face at center of triskles **Rev:** Two peacocks face-to-face

| Date | Mintage | VF20 | XF40 | MS60 | MS63 | MS65 |
|---|---|---|---|---|---|---|
| 2012 R | 1,500 | PF63 650 | | | | |

### KM# 365 20 EURO

6.45 g., 0.900 Gold 0.1867 oz. AGW, 21 mm. **Obv:** Lis from Florence's state emblem **Rev:** Female head detail from Botticelli's painting Primavera, allegory of Spring **Edge:** Reeded

| Date | Mintage | VF20 | XF40 | MS60 | MS63 | MS65 |
|---|---|---|---|---|---|---|
| 2013 | 1,500 | PF63 550 | | | | |

### KM# 369 20 EURO

6.45 g., 0.900 Gold 0.1866 oz. AGW, 21 mm. **Subject:** Baroque art **Rev:** Female statue

| Date | Mintage | VF20 | XF40 | MS60 | MS63 | MS65 |
|---|---|---|---|---|---|---|
| 2013 | — | PF63 550 | | | | |

### KM# 264 50 EURO

16.13 g., 0.900 Gold 0.4667 oz. AGW, 28 mm. **Subject:** Arts in Europe - Austria

| Date | Mintage | VF20 | XF40 | MS60 | MS63 | MS65 |
|---|---|---|---|---|---|---|
| 2003 R | 6,000 | PF63 1,200 | | | | |

### KM# 244 50 EURO

16.13 g., 0.900 Gold 0.4667 oz. AGW, 28 mm. **Obv:** Arts In Europe: Denmark **Rev:** Angel carrying away two children

| Date | Mintage | VF20 | XF40 | MS60 | MS63 | MS65 |
|---|---|---|---|---|---|---|
| 2004 R | 6,000 | PF63 1,200 | | | | |

### KM# 270 50 EURO

16.13 g., 0.900 Gold 0.4667 oz. AGW, 28 mm. **Subject:** 2006 Olympic Games Torino Emanuele Filiberto

| Date | Mintage | VF20 | XF40 | MS60 | MS63 | MS65 |
|---|---|---|---|---|---|---|
| 2005 R | 6,000 | PF63 1,200 | | | | |

### KM# 273 50 EURO

16.13 g., 0.900 Gold 0.4667 oz. AGW, 28 mm. **Subject:** Art In Europe - France

| Date | Mintage | VF20 | XF40 | MS60 | MS63 | MS65 |
|---|---|---|---|---|---|---|
| 2005 R | 5,000 | PF63 1,200 | | | | |

### KM# 274 50 EURO

16.13 g., 0.900 Gold 0.4667 oz. AGW, 28 mm. **Subject:** 2006 Olympic Games Torino Olympic Torch

| Date | Mintage | VF20 | XF40 | MS60 | MS63 | MS65 |
|---|---|---|---|---|---|---|
| 2006 R | 5,000 | PF63 1,200 | | | | |

### KM# 289 50 EURO

16.13 g., 0.900 Gold 0.4667 oz. AGW, 28 mm. **Subject:** European Arts - Greece

| Date | Mintage | VF20 | XF40 | MS60 | MS63 | MS65 |
|---|---|---|---|---|---|---|
| 2006 R | 1,792 | PF63 1,200 | | | | |

### KM# 300 50 EURO

16.13 g., 0.900 Gold 0.4667 oz. AGW, 28 mm. **Subject:** European Art - Norway **Obv:** Sailing ship **Rev:** Painting "The Scream" by Edvard Munch

| Date | Mintage | VF20 | XF40 | MS60 | MS63 | MS65 |
|---|---|---|---|---|---|---|
| 2007 R | 2,000 | PF63 1,250 | | | | |

### KM# 309 50 EURO

16.13 g., 0.900 Gold 0.4667 oz. AGW, 28 mm. **Subject:** Arts in Europe - Portugal

| Date | Mintage | VF20 | XF40 | MS60 | MS63 | MS65 |
|---|---|---|---|---|---|---|
| 2008 R | 2,000 | PF63 1,250 | | | | |

### KM# 322 50 EURO

16.13 g., 0.900 Gold 0.4667 oz. AGW, 28 mm. **Subject:** Arts in Europe - Spain **Obv:** Sailing ship **Rev:** Sagrada Familia of Antoni Gaudí

| Date | Mintage | VF20 | XF40 | MS60 | MS63 | MS65 |
|---|---|---|---|---|---|---|
| 2009 R | 2,000 | PF63 1,250 | | | | |

### KM# 336 50 EURO

16.13 g., 0.900 Gold 0.4667 oz. AGW, 28 mm. **Subject:** Arts of Europe - Hungary **Obv:** Sailing ship **Rev:** Detail of painting "Rozsi Szinyei Merse" by Pal Szinyel Merse

| Date | Mintage | VF20 | XF40 | MS60 | MS63 | MS65 |
|---|---|---|---|---|---|---|
| 2010 R | 1,500 | PF63 1,300 | | | | |

### KM# 348 50 EURO

16.13 g., 0.900 Gold 0.4667 oz. AGW, 28 mm. **Subject:** Fauna in art

| Date | Mintage | VF20 | XF40 | MS60 | MS63 | MS65 |
|---|---|---|---|---|---|---|
| 2011 R | 1,000 | PF63 1,800 | | | | |

### KM# 351 50 EURO

16.13 g., 0.900 Gold 0.4667 oz. AGW, 28 mm. **Subject:** Fauna in Art - Middle ages **Obv:** Stylized animal's head facing **Rev:** Statue of lions confronted

| Date | Mintage | VF20 | XF40 | MS60 | MS63 | MS65 |
|---|---|---|---|---|---|---|
| 2012 R | — | PF63 1,600 | | | | |

### KM# 366 50 EURO

16.13 g., 0.900 Gold 0.4667 oz. AGW, 28 mm. **Obv:** Statue of Marzocco, the lion holding shield of Florence by Donatello **Rev:** Statue of Gianfrancesco Gonzaga of Mantua on horseback by Pisanello **Edge:** Reeded

| Date | Mintage | VF20 | XF40 | MS60 | MS63 | MS65 |
|---|---|---|---|---|---|---|
| 2013 | 1,500 | PF63 1,300 | | | | |

## MINT SETS

| KM# | Date | Mintage | Identification | Issue Price | Mkt Val |
|---|---|---|---|---|---|
| MS39 | 2001 (12) | 125,200 | KM#91-94, 97.2, 98, 105, 111, 159, 183, 194, 236 | — | 70.00 |
| MS40 | 2002 (8) | 50,000 | KM#210-217 | — | 25.00 |
| MS41 | 2003 (8) | 50,000 | KM#210-217 | — | 45.00 |
| MS42 | 2003 (9) | 50,000 | KM#210-217, 253 | — | 70.00 |
| MS43 | 2004 (8) | 40,000 | KM#210-217 | — | 35.00 |
| MS44 | 2004 (9) | 40,000 | KM#210-217, 254 | — | 75.00 |
| MS45 | 2005 (8) | 35,000 | KM#210-217 | — | 45.00 |
| MS46 | 2005 (9) | 35,000 | KM#210-217, 255 | — | 100 |
| MS47 | 2006 (8) | 25,000 | KM#210-217 | — | 40.00 |
| MS48 | 2007 (8) | 20,000 | KM#210-217 | — | 60.00 |
| MS49 | 2008 (8) | 20,000 | KM#210-216, 301 | — | 50.00 |
| MS50 | 2008 (9) | 22,000 | KM#210-217, 281 | — | 100 |
| MS51 | 2009 (9) | 22,000 | KM#210-212; 247-251 | — | 50.00 |
| MS52 | 2010 (9) | 21,000 | KM#210-212; 247-251 | — | 60.00 |

## PROOF SETS

| KM# | Date | Mintage | Identification | Issue Price | Mkt Val |
|---|---|---|---|---|---|
| PS25 | 2001 (12) | 10,000 | KM#91-94, 97.2, 98, 105, 111, 159, 183, 194, 236 | — | 470 |
| PS26 | 2003 (9) | 12,000 | KM#210-217, 253 | — | 180 |
| PS27 | 2004 (9) | 15,000 | KM#210-217, 254 | — | 100 |
| PS28 | 2005 (9) | 12,000 | KM#210-217, 255 | — | 140 |
| PS29 | 2006 (9) | 10,000 | KM#210-217 | — | 150 |
| PS30 | 2007 (9) | 7,000 | KM#210-217 | — | 160 |
| PS31 | 2008 (9) | 5,000 | KM#210-212, 247-251, 325 | — | 200 |
| PS32 | 2009 (10) | 5,500 | KM#210-212, 247-251, 312, 327 | — | 200 |
| PS33 | 2010 (10) | 5,000 | KM#210-212, 247-251, 328, 329 | — | 200 |
| PS34 | 2011 (10) | 5,000 | KM#210-212, 247-251, 338, 341 | — | 200 |

# IVORY COAST

The Republic of the Ivory Coast, (Cote d'Ivoire), a former French Overseas territory located on the south side of the African bulge between Liberia and Ghana, has an area of 124,504 sq. mi. (322,463 sq. km.) and a population of 11.8 million. Capital: Yamoussoukro. The predominantly agricultural economy is one of Africa's most prosperous. Coffee, tropical woods, cocoa, and bananas are exported.

## REPUBLIC

### DECIMAL COINAGE

**KM# 14 1000 CFA FRANCS**
31.11 g., 0.999 Silver 0.999 oz. ASW **Rev:** Young Chimpanzee

| Date | Mintage | F12 | VF20 | XF40 | MS60 | MS63 |
|---|---|---|---|---|---|---|
| 2013 Antique patina | 750 | — | — | — | — | 40.00 |

**KM# 10 100 FRANCS**
25.00 g., Silver Plated Copper-Nickel, 38.61 mm. **Subject:** The Big Five **Obv:** Coat of Arms **Rev:** Elephants in color

| Date | Mintage | F12 | VF20 | XF40 | MS60 | MS63 |
|---|---|---|---|---|---|---|
| 2010 | 2,500 | PF63 40.00 | PF65 45.00 | | | |

**KM# 11 100 FRANCS**
27.00 g., Silver Plated Copper-Nickel, 38.61 mm. **Subject:** The Big Five **Obv:** Coat of Arms **Rev:** Leopard in color

| Date | Mintage | F12 | VF20 | XF40 | MS60 | MS63 |
|---|---|---|---|---|---|---|
| Proof | 1,000 | PF63 40.00 | PF65 45.00 | | | |

**KM# 6 1000 FRANCS**
25.00 g., 0.925 Silver 0.7435 oz. ASW, 38.6 mm. **Obv:** National arms **Rev:** Mamouth and embedded tooth fragment

| Date | Mintage | F12 | VF20 | XF40 | MS60 | MS63 |
|---|---|---|---|---|---|---|
| 2010 | 2,500 | PF63 75.00 | PF65 85.00 | | | |

**KM# 8 1000 FRANCS**
25.00 g., 0.925 Silver 0.7435 oz. ASW, 38.61 mm. **Obv:** National arms **Rev:** Map of Africa with montage of animals, blue field

| Date | Mintage | F12 | VF20 | XF40 | MS60 | MS63 |
|---|---|---|---|---|---|---|
| 2010 | 2,500 | PF63 75.00 | PF65 85.00 | | | |

**KM# 9 1000 FRANCS**
20.00 g., 0.925 Silver 0.5948 oz. ASW, 38.61 mm. **Rev:** Sabre-Tooth Tiger

| Date | Mintage | F12 | VF20 | XF40 | MS60 | MS63 |
|---|---|---|---|---|---|---|
| 2011 Proof | Est. 1000 | PF65 75.00 | | | | |

**KM# 12 1001 FRANCS CFA**
25.00 g., 0.999 Silver 0.803 oz. ASW, 38.61 mm. **Obv:** National arms **Rev:** Lord Ganesha (elephant) in color

| Date | Mintage | F12 | VF20 | XF40 | MS60 | MS63 |
|---|---|---|---|---|---|---|
| 2013 | 1,001 | PF63 75.00 | PF65 85.00 | | | |

**KM# 13 1500 FRANCS**
1.00 g., 0.917 Gold 0.0295 oz. AGW, 16 mm. **Subject:** Eurosoccer 2008 **Obv:** Coat of Arms **Rev:** Football stadium

| Date | Mintage | F12 | VF20 | XF40 | MS60 | MS63 |
|---|---|---|---|---|---|---|
| 2007 | — | PF63 125 | PF65 135 | | | |

**KM# 7 1500 FRANCS**
273.00 g., 0.925 Silver 8.1189 oz. ASW, 50 mm. **Subject:** Qibia Compass **Obv:** National arms **Rev:** Legend and design around center disc for compass spoon

| Date | Mintage | F12 | VF20 | XF40 | MS60 | MS63 |
|---|---|---|---|---|---|---|
| 2010 Antique patina | — | — | — | — | 500 | — |

# JAMAICA

Jamaica is situated in the Caribbean Sea 90 miles south of Cuba, has an area of 4,244 sq. mi. (10,990 sq. km.) and a population of 2.1 million. Capital: Kingston. The economy is founded chiefly on mining, tourism and agriculture. Aluminum, bauxite, sugar, rum and molasses are exported.

Jamaica is a member of the Commonwealth of Nations. Elizabeth II is the Head of State, as Queen of Jamaica.

**MONETARY SYSTEM**
100 Cents = 1 Dollar

## COMMONWEALTH

### DECIMAL COINAGE

**KM# 64 CENT**
1.22 g., Aluminum, 21.08 mm. **Ruler:** Elizabeth II **Series:** F.A.O. **Obv:** National arms, country named spaced beyond supporters **Obv. Legend:** JAMAICA **Rev:** Ackee fruit above value **Edge:** Plain **Shape:** 12-sided

| Date | Mintage | VF20 | XF40 | MS60 | MS63 | MS65 |
|---|---|---|---|---|---|---|
| 2002 | — | — | 0.25 | 0.35 | 0.50 | 0.75 |
| 2002 | 500 | PF65 1.00 | | | | |

**KM# 146.2 10 CENTS**
2.40 g., Copper Plated Steel, 17 mm. **Ruler:** Elizabeth II **Series:** National Heroes **Subject:** Paul Bogle **Obv:** National arms **Obv. Legend:** JAMAICA **Rev:** Bust facing **Edge:** Plain **Note:** Reduced size.

| Date | Mintage | VF20 | XF40 | MS60 | MS63 | MS65 |
|---|---|---|---|---|---|---|
| 2002 | — | — | 0.15 | 0.25 | 0.50 | 0.75 |
| 2002 | 500 | PF65 2.00 | | | | |
| 2003 | — | — | 0.15 | 0.25 | 0.50 | 0.75 |
| 2008 | — | — | 0.15 | 0.25 | 0.50 | 0.75 |

**KM# 167 25 CENTS**
3.60 g., Copper Plated Steel, 20 mm. **Ruler:** Elizabeth II **Series:** National Heroes **Subject:** Marcus Garvey **Obv:** National arms **Obv. Legend:** JAMAICA **Rev:** Head 1/4 right **Edge:** Plain

| Date | Mintage | VF20 | XF40 | MS60 | MS63 | MS65 |
|---|---|---|---|---|---|---|
| 2002 | — | — | — | — | 0.50 | 0.75 |
| 2002 | 500 | PF65 3.00 | | | | |
| 2003 | — | — | — | — | 0.50 | 0.75 |

**KM# 164 DOLLAR**
2.91 g., Nickel Plated Steel, 18.5 mm. **Ruler:** Elizabeth II **Series:** National Heroes **Subject:** Sir Alexander Bustamante **Obv:** National arms **Obv. Legend:** JAMAICA **Rev:** Bust facing **Edge:** Plain **Shape:** 7-sided

| Date | Mintage | VF20 | XF40 | MS60 | MS63 | MS65 |
|---|---|---|---|---|---|---|
| 2002 | — | — | — | 0.50 | 0.75 | 1.25 |
| 2002 | 500 | PF65 4.00 | | | | |
| 2003 | — | — | — | 0.50 | 0.75 | 1.25 |
| 2005 | — | — | — | 0.50 | 0.75 | 1.25 |
| 2006 | — | — | — | 0.50 | 0.75 | 1.25 |
| 2008 | — | — | — | 0.50 | 0.75 | 1.25 |

**KM# 189 DOLLAR**
2.90 g., Nickel Plated Steel, 18.5 mm. **Ruler:** Elizabeth II **Rev:** Sir Alexander Bustamante

| Date | Mintage | VF20 | XF40 | MS60 | MS63 | MS65 |
|---|---|---|---|---|---|---|
| 2008 | — | — | — | 0.50 | 0.75 | 1.25 |
| 2009 | — | — | — | 0.50 | 0.75 | 1.25 |

**KM# 163 5 DOLLARS**
4.30 g., Nickel Plated Steel, 21.5 mm. **Ruler:** Elizabeth II **Series:** National Heroes **Subject:** Norman Manley **Obv:** National arms **Obv. Legend:** JAMAICA **Rev:** Head left **Edge:** Reeded

| Date | Mintage | VF20 | XF40 | MS60 | MS63 | MS65 |
|---|---|---|---|---|---|---|
| 2002 | — | — | 0.75 | 1.50 | 2.00 | 2.50 |
| 2002 | 500 | PF65 5.00 | | | | |
| 2006 | — | — | 0.75 | 1.50 | 2.00 | 2.50 |

**KM# 181 10 DOLLARS**
5.94 g., Nickel Plated Steel **Ruler:** Elizabeth II **Series:** National Heroes **Subject:** George William Gordon **Obv:** National arms **Obv. Legend:** JAMAICA / TEN DOLLARS - (date) **Rev:** Bust facing **Edge:** Plain **Shape:** Scalloped **Note:** Diameter varies: 24-24.6.

| Date | Mintage | VF20 | XF40 | MS60 | MS63 | MS65 |
|---|---|---|---|---|---|---|
| 2002 | — | — | — | — | 2.50 | 3.50 |
| 2002 | 500 | PF65 9.00 | | | | |
| 2005 | — | — | — | — | 2.50 | 3.50 |

**KM# 197 10 DOLLARS**
28.28 g., 0.925 Silver 0.841 oz. ASW, 38.61 mm. **Ruler:** Elizabeth II **Subject:** UNICEF, 55th Anniversary

| Date | Mintage | VF20 | XF40 | MS60 | MS63 | MS65 |
|---|---|---|---|---|---|---|
| 2001 | — | PF65 95.00 | | | | |

**KM# 190 10 DOLLARS**
6.00 g., Nickel Plated Steel, 24.5 mm. **Ruler:** Elizabeth II **Obv:** Arms **Obv. Legend:** JAMAICA / TEN DOLLARS (date) **Rev:** George William Gordon

| Date | Mintage | VF20 | XF40 | MS60 | MS63 | MS65 |
|---|---|---|---|---|---|---|
| 2008 | — | — | — | — | 6.00 | 7.50 |
| 2009 | — | — | — | — | 6.00 | 7.50 |

**KM# 182 20 DOLLARS**
7.80 g., Bi-Metallic Copper-Nickel center in Nickel-Brass ring, 23 mm. **Ruler:** Elizabeth II **Series:** National Heroes **Subject:** Marcus Garvey **Obv:** Value above national arms within circle **Obv. Legend:** JAMAICA **Rev:** Head 1/4 right within circle **Edge:** Segmented reeding

| Date | Mintage | VF20 | XF40 | MS60 | MS63 | MS65 |
|---|---|---|---|---|---|---|
| 2001 | — | — | — | — | 2.50 | 3.50 |
| 2002 | — | — | — | — | 2.50 | 3.50 |
| 2002 | 500 | PF65 7.00 | | | | |

**KM# 186 25 DOLLARS**
28.28 g., 0.925 Silver 0.841 oz. ASW, 38.6 mm. **Ruler:** Elizabeth II **Subject:** UNICEF **Obv:** Arms with supporters **Rev:** Two boys above "Pals **Edge:** Reeded

| Date | Mintage | VF20 | XF40 | MS60 | MS63 | MS65 |
|---|---|---|---|---|---|---|
| 2001 | — | PF63 60.00 | PF65 70.00 | | | |

**KM# 185 25 DOLLARS**
28.28 g., 0.925 Silver 0.841 oz. ASW, 38.6 mm. **Ruler:** Elizabeth II **Subject:** IAAF World Junior Championships **Obv:** Arms with supporters and value **Rev:** Female runner **Edge:** Reeded

| Date | Mintage | VF20 | XF40 | MS60 | MS63 | MS65 |
|---|---|---|---|---|---|---|
| 2002 | 5,500 | PF63 55.00 | PF65 65.00 | | | |

**KM# 198 25 DOLLARS**
28.28 g., 0.925 Silver 0.841 oz. ASW with Integrated Diamond, 38.61 mm. **Ruler:** Elizabeth II **Subject:** Diamond Jubilee of Queen Elizabeth II **Rev:** St. Edward's Crown and trumpants

| Date | Mintage | VF20 | XF40 | MS60 | MS63 | MS65 |
|---|---|---|---|---|---|---|
| 2011 | Est. 10000 | PF63 60.00 | PF65 70.00 | | | |

**KM# 199 25 DOLLARS**
28.28 g., 0.925 Silver 0.841 oz. ASW, 38.61 mm. **Ruler:** Elizabeth II **Obv:** National arms **Rev:** Crown and trumpets

| Date | Mintage | VF20 | XF40 | MS60 | MS63 | MS65 |
|---|---|---|---|---|---|---|
| 2011 | — | PF65 90.00 | | | | |

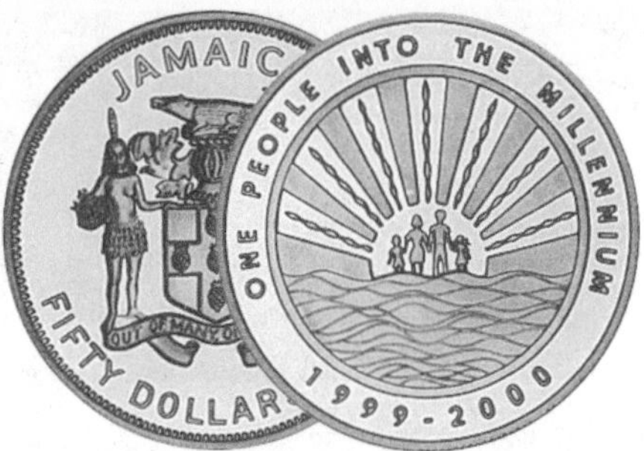

**KM# 184 50 DOLLARS**
28.45 g., 0.925 Silver 0.8461 oz. ASW, 38.6 mm. **Ruler:** Elizabeth II **Subject:** Millennium **Obv:** Arms with supporters **Rev:** Family within radiant sun **Edge:** Reeded

| Date | Mintage | VF20 | XF40 | MS60 | MS63 | MS65 |
|---|---|---|---|---|---|---|
| ND-2002 | 5,000 | PF63 60.00 | PF65 70.00 | | | |

## PROOF SETS

| KM# | Date | Mintage | Identification | Issue Price | Mkt Val |
|---|---|---|---|---|---|
| PS33 | 2002 (8) | 500 | KM#64, 146.2, 163, 164, 167, 181, 182, 185 | 99.00 | 110 |

# JAPAN

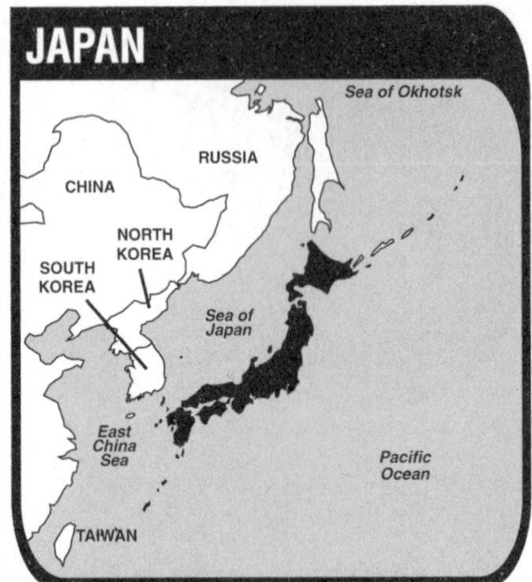


Japan, a constitutional monarchy situated off the east coast of Asia, has an area of 145,809 sq. mi. (377,835 sq. km.) and a population of 123.2 million. Capital: Tokyo. Japan, one of the major industrial nations of the world, exports machinery, motor vehicles, electronics and chemicals.

Japanese coinage of concern to this catalog includes those issued for the Ryukyu Islands (also called Liuchu), a chain of islands extending southwest from Japan toward Taiwan (Formosa), before the Japanese government converted the islands into a prefecture under the name Okinawa. Many of the provinces of Japan issued their own definitive coinage under the Shogunate.

**RULERS**

Emperors

Akihito (Heisei), 1989-

平成

Years 1 -

**NOTE:** The personal name of the emperor is followed by the name that he chose for his regnal era.

**MONETARY UNITS**

円 or 圓 or 圓

Yen

## EMPIRE

## REFORM COINAGE

**Y# 95.2 YEN**
1.00 g., Aluminum, 20 mm. **Ruler:** Akihito **Obv:** Sprouting branch divides authority and value **Rev:** Value within circles above date **Edge:** Plain

| Date | Mintage | VF20 | XF40 | MS60 | MS63 | MS65 |
|---|---|---|---|---|---|---|
| Yr13(2001) | 7,786,000 | — | 0.70 | 1.25 | 1.50 | — |
| Yr.13(2001) | 238,000 | PF63 3.00 | | | | |

| Date | Mintage | VF20 | XF40 | MS60 | MS63 | MS65 |
|---|---|---|---|---|---|---|
| Yr.14(2002) | 9,428,000 | — | 0.70 | 1.25 | 1.50 | — |
| Yr.14(2002) | 239,000 | PF63 5.00 | | | | |
| Yr.15(2003) | 117,131,000 | — | — | — | 0.50 | — |
| Yr.15(2003) | 275,000 | PF63 3.00 | | | | |
| Yr.16(2004) | 52,620,000 | — | — | — | 0.50 | — |
| Yr.16(2004) | 283,000 | PF63 3.00 | | | | |
| Yr.17(2005) | 29,771,000 | — | — | — | 0.50 | — |
| Yr.17(2005) | 258,000 | PF63 3.00 | | | | |
| Yr.18(2006) | 129,347,000 | — | — | — | 0.25 | — |
| Yr.18(2006) | 247,000 | PF63 3.00 | | | | |
| Yr.19(2007) | 223,702,200 | — | — | — | 0.25 | — |
| Yr.19(2007) | 201,800 | PF63 4.00 | | | | |
| Yr.20(2008) | 134,642,800 | — | — | — | 0.25 | — |
| Yr.20(2008) | 168,200 | PF63 4.00 | | | | |
| Yr.21(2009) | 47,871,000 | — | 0.25 | 1.00 | 3.00 | — |
| Yr.21(2009) | 132,000 | PF63 4.00 | | | | |
| Yr.22(2010) | 7,775,000 | — | 1.00 | 5.00 | 8.00 | — |
| Yr.22(2010) | 130,000 | PF63 15.00 | | | | |
| Yr.23(2011) | 348,000 | — | 5.00 | 20.00 | 30.00 | — |
| Yr.23(2011) | 108,000 | PF63 35.00 | | | | |
| Yr.24 (2012) | 556,000 | — | 5.00 | 20.00 | 30.00 | — |
| Yr.24 (2012) | 103,000 | PF63 35.00 | | | | |
| Yr.25 (2013) | 452,000 | — | 5.00 | 20.00 | 30.00 | — |
| Yr.25 (2013) | 102,000 | PF63 35.00 | | | | |
| Yr.26(2014) | — | — | — | 3.50 | 5.00 | — |
| Yr.26(2014) | — | PF63 9.00 | | | | |
| Yr.27(2015) | — | — | — | 3.50 | 5.00 | — |
| Yr.27(2015) | — | PF63 9.00 | | | | |

### Y# 96.2 5 YEN

3.75 g., Brass, 22 mm. **Ruler:** Akihito **Obv:** Hole in center flanked by a seed leaf with authority on top and date below **Rev:** Gear design around center hole with bending rice stalk above value in horizontal lines below

| Date | Mintage | VF20 | XF40 | MS60 | MS63 | MS65 |
|---|---|---|---|---|---|---|
| Yr.13(2001) | 77,787,000 | — | — | 0.20 | 0.35 | — |
| Yr.13(2001) | 238,000 | PF63 3.50 | | | | |
| Yr.14(2002) | 143,423,000 | — | — | 0.20 | 0.35 | — |
| Yr.14(2002) | 239,000 | PF63 3.50 | | | | |
| Yr.15(2003) | 102,031,000 | — | — | 0.20 | 0.35 | — |
| Yr.15(2003) | — | PF63 3.50 | | | | |
| Yr.16(2004) | 70,620,000 | — | — | 0.20 | 0.35 | — |
| Yr.16(2004) | 283,000 | PF63 3.50 | | | | |
| Yr.17(2005) | 15,771,000 | — | 1.00 | 2.00 | 3.00 | — |
| Yr.17(2005) | 258,000 | PF63 6.00 | | | | |
| Yr.18(2006) | 9,347,000 | — | 1.00 | 2.50 | 3.50 | — |
| Yr.18(2006) | 247,000 | PF63 6.00 | | | | |
| Yr.19(2007) | 9,702,200 | — | 1.00 | 2.50 | 3.50 | — |
| Yr.19(2007) | 201,800 | PF63 9.00 | | | | |
| Yr.20(2008) | 9,642,800 | — | 1.00 | 2.50 | 3.50 | — |
| Yr.20(2008) | 168,200 | PF63 6.00 | | | | |
| Yr.21(2009) | 3,871,000 | — | 2.00 | 5.00 | 7.00 | — |
| Yr.21(2009) | 132,000 | PF63 12.00 | | | | |
| Yr.22(2010) | 380,000 | — | 20.00 | 30.00 | 35.00 | — |
| Yr.22(2010) | 130,000 | PF63 35.00 | | | | |
| Yr.23(2011) | 348,000 | — | 20.00 | 30.00 | 35.00 | — |
| Yr.23(2011) | 108,000 | PF63 35.00 | | | | |
| Yr.24 (2012) | 556,000 | — | 20.00 | 30.00 | 35.00 | — |
| Yr.24 (2012) | 103,000 | PF63 35.00 | | | | |
| Yr.25 (2013) | 452,000 | — | 20.00 | 30.00 | 35.00 | — |
| Yr.25 (2013) | 102,000 | PF63 35.00 | | | | |
| Yr.26(2014) | — | — | 1.25 | 1.75 | 2.00 | — |
| Yr.26(2014) | — | PF63 8.00 | | | | |
| Yr.27(2015) | — | — | — | 1.75 | 2.00 | — |
| Yr.27(2015) | — | PF63 8.00 | | | | |

### Y# 97.2 10 YEN

4.50 g., Bronze, 23.5 mm. **Ruler:** Akihito **Obv:** Temple divides authority and value **Rev:** Value within wreath

| Date | Mintage | VF20 | XF40 | MS60 | MS63 | MS65 |
|---|---|---|---|---|---|---|
| Yr.13(2001) | 541,786,000 | — | — | 0.35 | 0.45 | — |
| Yr.13(2001) | 238,000 | PF63 10.00 | | | | |
| Yr.14(2002) | 445,428,000 | — | — | 0.35 | 0.45 | — |
| Yr.14(2002) | 239,000 | PF63 10.00 | | | | |
| Yr.15(2003) | 551,131,000 | — | — | 0.35 | 0.45 | — |
| Yr.15(2003) | 275,000 | PF63 10.00 | | | | |
| Yr.16(2004) | 592,620,000 | — | — | 0.35 | 0.45 | — |
| Yr.16(2004) | 283,000 | PF63 10.00 | | | | |
| Yr.17(2005) | 503,771,000 | — | — | 0.35 | 0.45 | — |
| Yr.17(2005) | 258,000 | PF63 10.00 | | | | |
| Yr.18(2006) | 440,347,000 | — | — | 0.35 | 0.45 | — |

| Date | Mintage | VF20 | XF40 | MS60 | MS63 | MS65 |
|---|---|---|---|---|---|---|
| Yr.18(2006) | 247,000 | PF63 10.00 | | | | |
| Yr.19(2007) | 388,702,200 | — | — | 0.35 | 0.45 | — |
| Yr.19(2007) | 201,800 | PF63 10.00 | | | | |
| Yr.20(2008) | 362,642,800 | — | — | 0.35 | 0.45 | — |
| Yr.20(2008) | 168,200 | PF63 10.00 | | | | |
| Yr.21(2009) | 337,871,000 | — | — | 0.35 | 0.45 | — |
| Yr.21(2009) | 132,000 | PF63 10.00 | | | | |
| Yr.22(2010) | 328,775,000 | — | — | 0.35 | 0.45 | — |
| Yr.22(2010) | 130,000 | PF63 10.00 | | | | |
| Yr.23(2011) | 255,828,000 | — | — | 0.35 | 0.45 | — |
| Yr.23(2011) | 108,000 | PF63 10.00 | | | | |
| Yr.24(2012) | 279,108,000 | — | — | 0.35 | 0.45 | — |
| Yr.24(2012) | 103,000 | PF63 10.00 | | | | |
| Yr.25 (2013) | 100,790,000 | — | — | 0.35 | 0.45 | — |
| Yr.25 (2013) | 102,000 | PF63 10.00 | | | | |
| Yr.26(2014) | — | — | — | 0.35 | 0.45 | — |
| Yr.26(2014) | — | PF63 10.00 | | | | |
| Yr.27(2015) | — | — | — | 0.35 | 0.45 | — |
| Yr.27(2015) | — | PF63 10.00 | | | | |

### Y# 101.2 50 YEN

4.00 g., Copper-Nickel, 21 mm. **Ruler:** Akihito **Obv:** Center hole flanked by chrysanthemums, authority at top and value below **Rev:** Value above hole in center **Edge:** Reeded

| Date | Mintage | VF20 | XF40 | MS60 | MS63 | MS65 |
|---|---|---|---|---|---|---|
| Yr.13(2001) | 7,786,000 | — | 1.75 | 3.50 | 5.00 | — |
| Yr.13(2001) | 238,000 | PF63 7.50 | | | | |
| Yr.14(2002) | 11,428,000 | — | 2.50 | 5.00 | 9.00 | — |
| Yr.14(2002) | 239,000 | PF63 10.00 | | | | |
| Yr.15(2003) | 10,131,000 | — | 2.50 | 5.00 | 9.00 | — |
| Yr.15(2003) | 275,000 | PF63 10.00 | | | | |
| Yr.16(2004) | 9,620,000 | — | 2.50 | 5.00 | 9.00 | — |
| Yr.16(2004) | 283,000 | PF63 10.00 | | | | |
| Yr.17(2005) | 9,771,000 | — | 2.50 | 5.00 | 9.00 | — |
| Yr.17(2005) | 258,000 | PF63 10.00 | | | | |
| Yr.18(2006) | 10,347,000 | — | 2.50 | 5.00 | 9.00 | — |
| Yr.18(2006) | 247,000 | PF63 10.00 | | | | |
| Yr.19(2007) | 9,702,200 | — | 2.50 | 5.00 | 9.00 | — |
| Yr.19(2007) | 201,800 | PF63 10.00 | | | | |
| Yr.20(2008) | 8,642,800 | — | 2.50 | 5.00 | 9.00 | — |
| Yr.20(2008) | 168,200 | PF63 10.00 | | | | |
| Yr.21(2009) | 4,871,000 | — | 2.50 | 7.50 | 12.00 | — |
| Yr.21(2009) | 132,000 | PF63 12.00 | | | | |
| Yr.22(2010) | 380,000 | — | 15.00 | 20.00 | 30.00 | — |
| Yr.22(2010) | 130,000 | PF63 35.00 | | | | |
| Yr.23(2011) | 348,000 | — | 15.00 | 20.00 | 30.00 | — |
| Yr.23(2011) | 108,000 | PF63 35.00 | | | | |
| Yr.24(2012) | 556,000 | — | 15.00 | 20.00 | 30.00 | — |
| Yr.24(2012) | 103,000 | PF63 35.00 | | | | |
| Yr.25(2013) | 452,000 | — | 15.00 | 20.00 | 30.00 | — |
| Yr.25(2013) | 102,000 | PF63 35.00 | | | | |
| Yr.26(2014) | — | — | — | 5.00 | 6.00 | — |
| Yr.26(2014) | — | PF63 15.00 | | | | |
| Yr.27(2015) | — | — | — | 4.00 | 5.00 | — |
| Yr.27(2015) | — | PF63 15.00 | | | | |

### Y# 98.2 100 YEN

4.80 g., Copper-Nickel, 22.6 mm. **Ruler:** Akihito **Obv:** Cherry blossoms **Rev:** Large numeral 100, date in western numerals **Edge:** Reeded

| Date | Mintage | VF20 | XF40 | MS60 | MS63 | MS65 |
|---|---|---|---|---|---|---|
| Yr.13(2001) | 7,786,000 | — | — | 5.00 | 7.50 | — |
| Yr.13(2001) | 238,000 | PF63 12.00 | | | | |
| Yr.14(2002) | 10,428,000 | — | — | 4.00 | 5.00 | — |
| Yr.14(2002) | 239,000 | PF63 12.00 | | | | |
| Yr.15(2003) | 98,131,000 | — | — | 2.00 | 2.50 | — |
| Yr.15(2003) | 275,000 | PF63 12.00 | | | | |
| Yr.16(2004) | 204,620,000 | — | — | 2.00 | 2.50 | — |
| Yr.16(2004) | 283,000 | PF63 15.00 | | | | |
| Yr.17(2005) | 299,771,000 | — | — | 2.00 | 2.50 | — |
| Yr.17(2005) | 258,000 | PF63 15.00 | | | | |
| Yr.18(2006) | 216,347,000 | — | — | 1.75 | 2.00 | — |
| Yr.18(2006) | 247,000 | PF63 15.00 | | | | |
| Yr.19(2007) | 129,702,200 | — | — | 1.75 | 2.00 | — |
| Yr.19(2007) | 201,800 | PF63 15.00 | | | | |
| Yr.20(2008) | 93,642,800 | — | — | 1.75 | 2.00 | — |
| Yr.20(2008) | 168,200 | PF63 18.00 | | | | |
| Yr.21(2009) | 114,871,000 | — | — | 1.75 | 2.00 | — |
| Yr.21(2009) | 132,000 | PF63 18.00 | | | | |
| Yr.22(2010) | 67,775,000 | — | — | 1.75 | 2.00 | — |
| Yr.22(2010) | 130,000 | PF63 18.00 | | | | |

| Date | Mintage | VF20 | XF40 | MS60 | MS63 | MS65 |
|---|---|---|---|---|---|---|
| Yr.23(2011) | 178,828,000 | — | — | 1.75 | 2.00 | — |
| Yr.23(2011) | 108,000 | PF63 18.00 | | | | |
| Yr.24(2012) | 402,108,000 | — | — | 1.75 | 2.00 | — |
| Yr.24(2012) | 103,000 | PF63 18.00 | | | | |
| Yr.25 (2013) | 608,790,000 | — | — | 1.75 | 2.00 | — |
| Yr.25 (2013) | 102,000 | PF63 18.00 | | | | |
| Yr.26(2014) | — | — | — | 1.75 | 2.00 | — |
| Yr.26(2014) | — | PF63 18.00 | | | | |
| Yr.27(2015) | — | — | — | 1.75 | 2.00 | — |
| Yr.27(2015) | — | PF63 18.00 | | | | |

### Y# 125 500 YEN

7.00 g., Nickel-Brass, 26.5 mm. **Ruler:** Akihito **Obv:** Pawlownia flower and highlighted legends **Rev:** Value with latent zeros **Edge:** Slanted reeding

| Date | Mintage | VF20 | XF40 | MS60 | MS63 | MS65 |
|---|---|---|---|---|---|---|
| Yr.13(2001) | 607,813,000 | — | — | 7.00 | 9.00 | — |
| Yr.13(2001) | 238,000 | PF63 22.00 | | | | |
| Yr.14(2002) | 504,422,000 | — | — | 7.00 | 9.00 | — |
| Yr.14(2002) | 239,000 | PF63 22.00 | | | | |
| Yr.15(2003) | 438,130,000 | — | — | 7.00 | 9.00 | — |
| Yr.15(2003) | 275,000 | PF63 22.00 | | | | |
| Yr.16(2004) | 356,620,000 | — | — | 7.00 | 9.00 | — |
| Yr.16(2004) | 283,000 | PF63 22.00 | | | | |
| Yr.17(2005) | 344,772,000 | — | — | 7.00 | 9.00 | — |
| Yr.17(2005) | 258,000 | PF63 22.00 | | | | |
| Yr.18(2006) | 381,346,000 | — | — | 7.00 | 9.00 | — |
| Yr.18(2006) | 247,000 | PF63 22.00 | | | | |
| Yr.19(2007) | 409,701,200 | — | — | 7.00 | 9.00 | — |
| Yr.19(2007) | 201,800 | PF63 30.00 | | | | |
| Yr.20(2008) | 432,642,800 | — | — | 7.00 | 9.00 | — |
| Yr.20(2008) | 168,200 | PF63 30.00 | | | | |
| Yr.21(2009) | 342,871,000 | — | — | 7.00 | 9.00 | — |
| Yr.21(2009) | 132,000 | PF63 30.00 | | | | |
| Yr.22(2010) | 130,000 | — | — | 7.00 | 9.00 | — |
| Yr.22(2010) | 406,775,000 | PF63 30.00 | | | | |
| Yr.23(2011) | 301,828,000 | — | — | 7.00 | 9.00 | — |
| Yr.23(2011) | 108,000 | PF63 30.00 | | | | |
| Yr.24(2012) | 267,108,000 | — | — | 7.00 | 9.00 | — |
| Yr.24(2012) | 103,000 | PF63 30.00 | | | | |
| Yr.25(2013) | 137,790,000 | — | — | 7.00 | 9.00 | — |
| Yr.25(2013) | 102,000 | PF63 30.00 | | | | |
| Yr.26(2014) | — | — | — | 7.00 | 9.00 | — |
| Yr26(2014) | — | PF63 30.00 | | | | |
| Yr.27(2015) | — | — | — | 7.00 | 9.00 | — |
| Yr.27(2015) | — | PF63 30.00 | | | | |

### Y# 126 500 YEN

7.00 g., Copper-Nickel-Zinc, 26.5 mm. **Ruler:** Akihito **Subject:** World Cup Soccer - Europe & Africa **Obv:** Four players and map background **Rev:** Games logo within shooting star wreath **Edge:** Reeded

| Date | Mintage | VF20 | XF40 | MS60 | MS63 | MS65 |
|---|---|---|---|---|---|---|
| Yr.14(2002) | 10,000,000 | — | 7.50 | 8.50 | 10.00 | — |

### Y# 127 500 YEN

7.00 g., Copper-Nickel-Zinc, 26.5 mm. **Ruler:** Akihito **Subject:** World Cup Soccer - Asia & Oceania **Obv:** Three players and map background **Rev:** Games logo within shooting star wreath **Edge:** Reeded

| Date | Mintage | VF20 | XF40 | MS60 | MS63 | MS65 |
|---|---|---|---|---|---|---|
| Yr. 14(2002) | 10,000,000 | — | 7.50 | 8.50 | 10.00 | — |

### Y# 128 500 YEN

7.00 g., Copper-Nickel-Zinc, 26.5 mm. **Ruler:** Akihito **Subject:** World Cup Soccer - North & South America **Obv:** Four players and map background **Rev:** Games logo **Edge:** Reeded

| Date | Mintage | VF20 | XF40 | MS60 | MS63 | MS65 |
|---|---|---|---|---|---|---|
| Yr. 14 (2002) | 10,000,000 | — | 7.50 | 8.50 | 10.00 | — |

**Y# 133 500 YEN**

7.00 g., Copper-Nickel-Zinc, 26.5 mm. **Ruler:** Akihito **Subject:** Expo 2005 - Aichi, Japan **Obv:** Pacific map an globe **Rev:** Circular Expo logo

| Date | Mintage | VF20 | XF40 | MS60 | MS63 | MS65 |
|---|---|---|---|---|---|---|
| Yr. 17(2005) | 8,241,000 | — | 7.50 | 8.50 | 10.00 | — |

**Y# 134 500 YEN**

15.60 g., 0.999 Silver 0.501 oz. ASW, 28 mm. **Ruler:** Akihito **Subject:** Chubu International Airport **Obv:** Aircraft wing in flight over airport **Rev:** Aircraft silhouettes over maps

| Date | Mintage | VF20 | XF40 | MS60 | MS63 | MS65 |
|---|---|---|---|---|---|---|
| Yr. 17(2005) | 50,000 | PF65 85.00 | | | | |

**Y# 137 500 YEN**

7.00 g., Copper-Nickel-Zinc, 26.5 mm. **Ruler:** Akihito **Subject:** 50th Anniversary of Japanese Antarctic Research **Obv:** Ship and two dogs **Rev:** Map of Antarctica **Edge:** Helical ridges

| Date | Mintage | VF20 | XF40 | MS60 | MS63 | MS65 |
|---|---|---|---|---|---|---|
| Yr.19(2007) | 6,600,000 | — | 9.00 | 10.00 | 12.00 | — |

**Y# 139 500 YEN**

7.00 g., Copper-Nickel-Zinc, 26.5 mm. **Ruler:** Akihito **Subject:** Centenary of Japanese immigration to Brazil/Japan-Brazil year of exchange **Obv:** Ship **Rev:** Crossed sprigs of cherry and coffee **Note:** Prev. #Y143.

| Date | Mintage | VF20 | XF40 | MS60 | MS63 | MS65 |
|---|---|---|---|---|---|---|
| Yr. 20 (2008) | 4,800,000 | — | 11.00 | 13.00 | 15.00 | — |

**Y# 141 500 YEN**

7.10 g., Bi-Metallic Copper-Nickel center in Nickel-Brass ring, 26.5 mm. **Ruler:** Akihito **Subject:** Local Autonomy - Hokkaido Prefecture **Obv:** Lake Toya and the former Hokkaido Government Building **Rev:** Legend for 47 prefectures coin program, and ancient coin design reading "local autonomy

| Date | Mintage | VF20 | XF40 | MS60 | MS63 | MS65 |
|---|---|---|---|---|---|---|
| Yr.20(2008) | 2,070,000 | — | 8.00 | 15.00 | 17.50 | — |
| Yr.20(2008) | 30,000 | PF63 45.00 | PF65 50.00 | | | |

**Y# 143 500 YEN**

7.10 g., Bi-Metallic Copper-Nickel center in Nickel-Brass ring, 26.5 mm. **Ruler:** Akihito **Subject:** Local Autonomy - Kyoto Prefecture **Obv:** Scene from an antique illustrated version of the Tale of Genji **Rev:** Legend for 47 prefectures coin program, and ancient coin design reading "local autonomy

| Date | Mintage | VF20 | XF40 | MS60 | MS63 | MS65 |
|---|---|---|---|---|---|---|
| Yr.20(2008) | 2,020,000 | — | 8.00 | 15.00 | 17.50 | — |
| Yr.20(2008) | 30,000 | PF63 45.00 | PF65 50.00 | | | |

**Y# 145 500 YEN**

7.10 g., Bi-Metallic Copper-Nickel center in Nickel-Brass ring, 26.5 mm. **Ruler:** Akihito **Subject:** Local Autonomy - Shimane Prefecture **Obv:** Bell shaped bronze vessel, artifact from Kamoiwakura **Rev:** Legend for 47 prefectures coin program, and ancient coin design reading "local autonomy

| Date | Mintage | VF20 | XF40 | MS60 | MS63 | MS65 |
|---|---|---|---|---|---|---|
| Yr.20(2008) | 1,940,000 | — | 8.00 | 15.00 | 17.50 | — |
| Yr.20(2008) | 30,000 | PF63 45.00 | PF65 50.00 | | | |

**Y# 147 500 YEN**

7.10 g., Bi-Metallic Copper-Nickel center in Nickel-Brass ring, 26.5 mm. **Ruler:** Akihito **Subject:** Local Autonomy - Nagano Prefecture **Obv:** Zenkoji Temple and ox **Rev:** Legend for 47 prefectures coin program, and ancient coin design reading "local autonomy

| Date | Mintage | VF20 | XF40 | MS60 | MS63 | MS65 |
|---|---|---|---|---|---|---|
| Yr.21(2009) | 1,800,000 | — | 8.00 | 15.00 | 17.50 | — |
| Yr.21(2009) | 30,000 | PF63 45.00 | PF65 50.00 | | | |

**Y# 149 500 YEN**

7.10 g., Bi-Metallic Copper-Nickel center in Nickel-Brass ring, 26.5 mm. **Ruler:** Akihito **Subject:** Local Autonomy - Niigata Prefecture **Obv:** Two Japanese crested ibises and rice terrace **Rev:** Legend for 47 prefectures coin program, and ancient coin design reading "local autonomy

| Date | Mintage | VF20 | XF40 | MS60 | MS63 | MS65 |
|---|---|---|---|---|---|---|
| Yr.21(2009) | 1,800,000 | — | 8.00 | 15.00 | 17.50 | — |
| Yr.21(2009) | 30,000 | PF63 45.00 | PF65 50.00 | | | |

**Y# 153 500 YEN**

7.10 g., Bi-Metallic Copper-Nickel center in Nickel-Brass ring, 26.5 mm. **Ruler:** Akihito **Subject:** Local Autonomy - Ibaraki Prefecture **Obv:** Kairakuen Garden and plum tree **Rev:** Legend for 47 prefectures coin program, and ancient coin design reading "local autonomy

| Date | Mintage | VF20 | XF40 | MS60 | MS63 | MS65 |
|---|---|---|---|---|---|---|
| Yr.21(2009) | 1,840,000 | — | 8.00 | 15.00 | 17.50 | — |
| Yr.21(2009) | 30,000 | PF63 45.00 | PF65 50.00 | | | |

**Y# 155 500 YEN**

7.10 g., Bi-Metallic Copper-Nickel center in Nickel-Brass ring, 26.5 mm. **Ruler:** Akihito **Subject:** Local Autonomy - Nara Prefecture **Obv:** Kentoshi-sen, ship of the Japanese envoy to China in Tang Dynasty **Rev:** Legend for 47 prefectures coin program, and ancient coin design reading "local autonomy

| Date | Mintage | VF20 | XF40 | MS60 | MS63 | MS65 |
|---|---|---|---|---|---|---|
| Yr.21(2009) | 1,770,000 | — | 8.00 | 15.00 | 17.50 | — |
| Yr.21(2009) | 30,000 | PF63 45.00 | PF65 50.00 | | | |

**Y# 157 500 YEN**

7.00 g., Nickel-Brass, 26.5 mm. **Ruler:** Akihito **Subject:** 20th Anniversary of Emperor's Enthronement **Obv:** Imperial chrysthantem crest **Rev:** Chrysthantem blosums

| Date | Mintage | VF20 | XF40 | MS60 | MS63 | MS65 |
|---|---|---|---|---|---|---|
| Yr.21(2009) | 50,000 | PF63 25.00 | PF65 30.00 | | | |
| Yr.21(2009) | 9,950,000 | — | 8.00 | 10.00 | 12.50 | — |

**Y# 159 500 YEN**

7.10 g., Bi-Metallic Copper-Nickel center in Nickel-Brass ring, 26.5 mm. **Ruler:** Akihito **Subject:** Local Autonomy commemorative - Kochi Prefecture **Obv:** SAKAMOTO Ryoma **Rev:** Legend for 47 prefectures coin program, and ancient coin design reading "local autonomy

| Date | Mintage | VF20 | XF40 | MS60 | MS63 | MS65 |
|---|---|---|---|---|---|---|
| Yr.22(2010) | 1,930,000 | — | 8.00 | 15.00 | 17.50 | — |
| Yr.22(2010) | 30,000 | PF63 45.00 | PF65 50.00 | | | |

**Y# 161 500 YEN**

7.10 g., Bi-Metallic Copper-Nickel center in Nickel-Brass ring, 26.5 mm. **Ruler:** Akihito **Subject:** Local Autonomy commemorative - Gifu Prefecture **Obv:** Shirakawa village and Chinese milk vetch **Rev:** Legend for 47 prefectures coin program, and ancient coin design reading "local autonomy

| Date | Mintage | VF20 | XF40 | MS60 | MS63 | MS65 |
|---|---|---|---|---|---|---|
| Yr.22(2010) | 1,830,000 | — | 8.00 | 15.00 | 17.50 | — |
| Yr.22(2010) | 30,000 | PF63 45.00 | PF65 50.00 | | | |

**Y# 163 500 YEN**

7.10 g., Bi-Metallic Copper-Nickel center in Nickel-Brass ring, 26.5 mm. **Ruler:** Akihito **Subject:** Local Autonomy commemorative - Fukui Prefecture **Obv:** Fukuiraptor (foreground) and Fukuisaurus **Rev:** Legend for 47 prefectures coin program, and ancient coin design reading "local autonomy

| Date | Mintage | VF20 | XF40 | MS60 | MS63 | MS65 |
|---|---|---|---|---|---|---|
| Yr.22(2010) | 30,000 | PF63 45.00 | PF65 50.00 | | | |
| Yr.22(2010) | 1,800,000 | — | 8.00 | 15.00 | 17.50 | — |

**Y# 165 500 YEN**

7.10 g., Bi-Metallic Copper-Nickel center in Nickel-Brass ring, 26.5 mm. **Ruler:** Akihito **Subject:** Local Autonomy commemorative - Aichi Prefecture **Obv:** Prefectural capitol building and rabbit-ear iris **Rev:** Legend for 47 prefectures coin program, and ancient coin design reading "local autonomy

| Date | Mintage | VF20 | XF40 | MS60 | MS63 | MS65 |
|---|---|---|---|---|---|---|
| Yr.22 (2010) | 30,000 | PF63 45.00 | PF65 50.00 | | | |
| Yr.22 (2010) | 1,920,000 | — | 8.00 | 15.00 | 17.50 | — |

**Y# 167 500 YEN**

7.10 g., Bi-Metallic Copper-Nickel center in Nickel-Brass ring, 26.5 mm. **Ruler:** Akihito **Subject:** Local Autonomy commemorative - Aomori Prefecture **Obv:** Jomon period structure and figurines **Rev:** Legend for 47 prefectures coin program and ancient coin design reading "local autonomy

| Date | Mintage | VF20 | XF40 | MS60 | MS63 | MS65 |
|---|---|---|---|---|---|---|
| Yr.22 (2010) | 30,000 | PF63 45.00 | PF65 50.00 | | | |
| Yr.22 (2010) | 1,870,000 | — | 8.00 | 15.00 | 17.50 | — |

**Y# 169 500 YEN**

7.10 g., Bi-Metallic Copper-Nickel center in Nickel-Brass ring, 26.5 mm. **Ruler:** Akihito **Subject:** Local Autonomy commemorative - Saga Prefecture **Obv:** OKUMA Shigenobu and Saga Nishiki fabric **Rev:** Legend for 47 prefectures coin program, and ancient coin design reading "local autonomy

| Date | Mintage | VF20 | XF40 | MS60 | MS63 | MS65 |
|---|---|---|---|---|---|---|
| Yr.22 (2010) | 30,000 | PF63 45.00 | PF65 50.00 | | | |
| Yr.22 (2010) | 1,880,000 | — | 8.00 | 15.00 | 17.50 | — |

**Y# 171 500 YEN**

7.10 g., Bi-Metallic Copper-Nickel center in Nickel-Brass ring, 26.5 mm. **Ruler:** Akihito **Subject:** Local Autonomy commemorative - Toyama Prefecture **Obv:** Owara Kaze-no-bon Festival dancers **Rev:** Legend for 47 prefectures coin program and ancient coin design reading "local autonomy

| Date | Mintage | VF20 | XF40 | MS60 | MS63 | MS65 |
|---|---|---|---|---|---|---|
| Yr. 23 (2011) | 1,770,000 | — | 8.00 | 15.00 | 17.50 | — |
| Yr. 23 (2011) | 30,000 | PF63 45.00 | PF65 50.00 | | | |

**Y# 173 500 YEN**

7.10 g., Bi-Metallic Copper-Nickel center in Nickel-Brass ring, 26.5 mm. **Ruler:** Akihito **Subject:** Local Autonomy commemorative - Tottori Prefecture **Obv:** Nageiredo Hall at Mitokusan Sanbutsuji Temple **Rev:** Legend for 47 prefectures coin program and ancient coin design reading "local autonomy

| Date | Mintage | VF20 | XF40 | MS60 | MS63 | MS65 |
|---|---|---|---|---|---|---|
| Yr. 23 (2011) | 1,740,000 | — | 8.00 | 15.00 | 17.50 | — |
| Yr. 23 (2011) | 30,000 | PF63 45.00 | PF65 50.00 | | | |

**Y# 175 500 YEN**

7.10 g., Bi-Metallic Copper-Nickel center in Nickel-Brass ring, 26.5 mm. **Ruler:** Akihito **Subject:** Local Autonomy commemorative - Kumamoto Prefecture **Obv:** Kumamoto Castle **Rev:** Legend for 47 prefectures con program and ancient coin design reading "local autonomy

| Date | Mintage | VF20 | XF40 | MS60 | MS63 | MS65 |
|---|---|---|---|---|---|---|
| Yr. 23 (2011) | 1,840,000 | — | 8.00 | 15.00 | 17.50 | — |
| Yr. 23 (2011) | 30,000 | PF63 45.00 | PF65 50.00 | | | |

**Y# 177 500 YEN**

7.10 g., Bi-Metallic Copper-Nickel center in Nickel-Brass ring, 26.5 mm. **Ruler:** Akihito **Subject:** Local Autonomy - Shiga Prefecture **Obv:** Biwa catfish and Round Crucian carp **Rev:** Legend for 47 prefectures coin program, and ancient coin design reading "local autonomy

| Date | Mintage | VF20 | XF40 | MS60 | MS63 | MS65 |
|---|---|---|---|---|---|---|
| Yr. 23 (2011) | 1,740,000 | — | 8.00 | 15.00 | 17.50 | — |
| Yr. 23 (2011) | 30,000 | PF63 45.00 | PF65 50.00 | | | |

**Y# 179 500 YEN**

7.10 g., Bi-Metallic Copper-Nickel center in Nickel-Brass ring, 26.5 mm. **Ruler:** Akihito **Subject:** Local Autonomy - Iwate Prefecture **Obv:** Water Poetry Party at Môtsû-ji **Rev:** Legend for 47 prefectures coin program, and ancient coin design reading "local autonomy

| Date | Mintage | VF20 | XF40 | MS60 | MS63 | MS65 |
|---|---|---|---|---|---|---|
| Yr. 23 (2011) | 1,760,000 | — | 8.00 | 15.00 | 17.50 | — |
| Yr. 23 (2011) | 30,000 | PF63 45.00 | PF65 50.00 | | | |

**Y# 181 500 YEN**

7.10 g., Bi-Metallic Copper-Nickel center in Nickel-Brass ring, 26.5 mm. **Ruler:** Akihito **Subject:** Local Autonomy - Akita Prefecture **Obv:** Nobu Shirase (explorer) and Kanto festival **Rev:** Legend for 47 prefectures coin program, and ancient coin design reading "local autonomy

| Date | Mintage | VF20 | XF40 | MS60 | MS63 | MS65 |
|---|---|---|---|---|---|---|
| Yr. 23 (2011) | 1,710,000 | — | 8.00 | 15.00 | 17.50 | — |
| Yr. 23 (2011) | 30,000 | PF63 45.00 | PF65 50.00 | | | |

**Y# 183 500 YEN**

7.10 g., Bi-Metallic Copper-Nickel center in Nickel-Brass ring, 26.5 mm. **Ruler:** Akihito **Subject:** Local Autonomy - Okinawa Prefecture **Obv:** Naha Giant Tug-of-war and Eisa folk dance **Rev:** Legend for 47 prefectures coin program, and ancient coin design reading "local autonomy

| Date | Mintage | VF20 | XF40 | MS60 | MS63 | MS65 |
|---|---|---|---|---|---|---|
| Yr.24(2012) | 30,000 | PF63 45.00 | PF65 50.00 | | | |
| Yr.24(2012) | 1,780,000 | — | 8.00 | 15.00 | 17.50 | — |

**Y# 185 500 YEN**

7.10 g., Bi-Metallic Copper-Nickel center in Nickel-Brass ring, 26.5 mm. **Ruler:** Akihito **Subject:** Local Autonomy - Kanagawa Prefecture **Obv:** Great Buddah of Kamakura **Rev:** Legend for 47 prefectures coin program, and ancient coin design reading "local autonomy

| Date | Mintage | VF20 | XF40 | MS60 | MS63 | MS65 |
|---|---|---|---|---|---|---|
| Yr.24(2012) | 30,000 | PF63 45.00 | PF65 50.00 | | | |
| Yr.24(2012) | 1,860,000 | — | 8.00 | 15.00 | 17.50 | — |

**Y# 187 500 YEN**

7.10 g., Bi-Metallic Copper-Nickel center in Nickel-Brass ring, 26.5 mm. **Ruler:** Akihito **Subject:** Local Autonomy - Miyazaki Prefecture **Obv:** Miyazaki Prefectural Government Building **Rev:** Legend for 47 prefectures coin program, and ancient coin design reading "local autonomy

| Date | Mintage | VF20 | XF40 | MS60 | MS63 | MS65 |
|---|---|---|---|---|---|---|
| Yr.24(2012) | 30,000 | PF63 45.00 | PF65 50.00 | | | |
| Yr.24(2012) | 1,710,000 | — | 8.00 | 15.00 | 17.50 | — |

**Y# 189 500 YEN**

7.10 g., Bi-Metallic Copper-Nickel center in Nickel-Brass ring, 26.5 mm. **Ruler:** Akihito **Subject:** Local Autonomy - Tochigi Prefecture **Obv:** Sleeping cat in flora **Rev:** Legend for 47 prefectures coin program, and ancient coin design reading "local autonomy

| Date | Mintage | VF20 | XF40 | MS60 | MS63 | MS65 |
|---|---|---|---|---|---|---|
| Yr. 24 (2012) | 1,770,000 | — | 8.00 | 15.00 | 17.50 | — |
| Yr. 24 (2012) | 30,000 | PF63 45.00 | PF65 50.00 | | | |

**Y# 191 500 YEN**

7.10 g., Bi-Metallic Copper-Nickel center in Nickel-Brass ring, 26.5 mm. **Ruler:** Akihito **Subject:** Hyogo **Obv:** Two black beak storks **Rev:** Legend for 47 prefectures coin program, and ancient coin design reading "local autonomy

| Date | Mintage | VF20 | XF40 | MS60 | MS63 | MS65 |
|---|---|---|---|---|---|---|
| Yr.24 (2012) | 1,770,000 | — | 8.00 | 15.00 | 17.50 | — |
| Yr.24 (2012) | 30,000 | PF63 45.00 | PF65 50.00 | | | |

**Y# 193 500 YEN**

7.10 g., Bi-Metallic Copper-Nickel center in Nickel-Brass ring, 26.5 mm. **Ruler:** Akihito **Subject:** Oita **Obv:** Buddha statue **Rev:** Legend for 47 prefectures coin program, and ancient coin design reading "local autonomy

| Date | Mintage | VF20 | XF40 | MS60 | MS63 | MS65 |
|---|---|---|---|---|---|---|
| Yr.24 (2012) | 1,760,000 | — | 8.00 | 15.00 | 17.50 | — |
| Yr.24 (2012) | 30,000 | PF63 45.00 | PF65 50.00 | | | |

**Y# 196 500 YEN**
Bi-Metallic, 26.5 mm. **Ruler:** Akihito **Subject:** Miyagi Prefecture **Obv:** Sendai Tanabata festival decorations **Rev:** Legend for 47 prefectures coin program, and ancient coin design reading "local autonomy

| Date | Mintage | VF20 | XF40 | MS60 | MS63 | MS65 |
|---|---|---|---|---|---|---|
| yr.25 (2013) | 30,000 | PF63 45.00 | PF65 50.00 | | | |
| yr.25 (2013) | 1,670,000 | — | 8.00 | 15.00 | 17.50 | — |

**Y# 198 500 YEN**
7.10 g., Bi-Metallic, 26.5 mm. **Ruler:** Akihito **Subject:** Hiroshima Prefecture **Obv:** Peace commemorative monument **Rev:** Legend for 47 prefectures coin program, and ancient coin design reading "local autonomy

| Date | Mintage | VF20 | XF40 | MS60 | MS63 | MS65 |
|---|---|---|---|---|---|---|
| yr.25 (2013) | 30,000 | PF63 45.00 | PF65 50.00 | | | |
| yr.25 (2013) | 1,670,000 | — | 8.00 | 15.00 | 17.50 | — |

**Y# 200 500 YEN**
7.10 g., Bi-Metallic, 26.5 mm. **Ruler:** Akihito **Subject:** Gunma Prefecture **Obv:** Keystone of the East (silk) Cocoon Warehouse **Rev:** Legend for 47 prefectures coin program, and ancient coin design reading "local autonomy

| Date | Mintage | VF20 | XF40 | MS60 | MS63 | MS65 |
|---|---|---|---|---|---|---|
| yr. 25 (2013) | 1,690,000 | — | 8.00 | 15.00 | 17.50 | — |
| yr. 25 (2013) | 30,000 | PF63 45.00 | PF65 50.00 | | | |

**Y# 202 500 YEN**
7.10 g., Bi-Metallic, 26.5 mm. **Ruler:** Akihito **Subject:** Yamanashi Prefecture **Obv:** Mt. Fuji and grapes **Rev:** Legend for 47 prefectures coin program, and ancient coin design reading "local autonomy

| Date | Mintage | VF20 | XF40 | MS60 | MS63 | MS65 |
|---|---|---|---|---|---|---|
| yr. 25 (2013) | 30,000 | PF63 45.00 | PF65 50.00 | | | |
| yr. 25 (2013) | 1,640,000 | — | 8.00 | 15.00 | 17.50 | — |

**Y# 204 500 YEN**
7.10 g., Bi-Metallic, 26.5 mm. **Ruler:** Akihito **Subject:** Shizuoka Prefecture **Obv:** Mt. Fuji and tea plantation **Rev:** Legend for 47 prefectures coin program, and ancient coin design reading "local autonomy

| Date | Mintage | VF20 | XF40 | MS60 | MS63 | MS65 |
|---|---|---|---|---|---|---|
| yr. 25 (2013) | 1,670,000 | — | 8.00 | 15.00 | 17.50 | — |
| yr. 25 (2013) | 30,000 | PF63 45.00 | PF65 50.00 | | | |

**Y# 206 500 YEN**
7.10 g., Bi-Metallic, 26.5 mm. **Ruler:** Akihito **Subject:** Okayama Prefecture **Obv:** Okayama Kōrakuen garden **Rev:** Legend for 47 prefectures coin program, and ancient coin design reading "local autonomy

| Date | Mintage | VF20 | XF40 | MS60 | MS63 | MS65 |
|---|---|---|---|---|---|---|
| yr. 25 (2013) | 1,630,000 | — | 8.00 | 15.00 | 17.50 | — |
| yr. 25 (2013) | 30,000 | PF63 45.00 | PF65 50.00 | | | |

**Y# 208 500 YEN**
7.10 g., Bi-Metallic, 26.5 mm. **Ruler:** Akihito **Subject:** Kagoshima Prefecture **Obv:** Mt. Sakurajima **Rev:** Legend for 47 prefectures coin program, and ancient coin design reading "local autonomy

| Date | Mintage | VF20 | XF40 | MS60 | MS63 | MS65 |
|---|---|---|---|---|---|---|
| yr. 25 (2013) | 1,630,000 | — | 8.00 | 15.00 | 17.50 | — |
| yr. 25 (2013) | 30,000 | PF63 45.00 | PF65 50.00 | | | |

**Y# 129 1000 YEN**
31.10 g., 0.999 Silver 0.9989 oz. ASW, 40 mm. **Ruler:** Akihito **Subject:** World Cup Soccer **Obv:** Trophy within flower sprigs **Rev:** Games logo flanked by players **Edge:** Reeded

| Date | Mintage | VF20 | XF40 | MS60 | MS63 | MS65 |
|---|---|---|---|---|---|---|
| Yr. 14 (2002) | 100,000 | PF65 200 | | | | |

**Y# 131 1000 YEN**
31.10 g., 0.999 Silver 0.9989 oz. ASW, 40 mm. **Ruler:** Akihito **Subject:** 5th Winter Asian Games, Aomori **Obv:** Skier and skater **Rev:** Three red apples and multicolor games logo

| Date | Mintage | VF20 | XF40 | MS60 | MS63 | MS65 |
|---|---|---|---|---|---|---|
| Yr.15 (2003) | 50,000 | PF65 625 | | | | |

**Y# 132 1000 YEN**
31.10 g., 0.999 Silver 0.9989 oz. ASW, 40 mm. **Ruler:** Akihito **Subject:** 50th Anniversary of the reversion of the Amami Islands **Obv:** Lily and bird in multicolor enamel **Rev:** Map of the Amami-shoto

| Date | Mintage | VF20 | XF40 | MS60 | MS63 | MS65 |
|---|---|---|---|---|---|---|
| Yr. 15 (2003) | 50,000 | PF65 220 | | | | |

**Y# 135 1000 YEN**
31.10 g., 0.999 Silver 0.9989 oz. ASW, 40 mm. **Ruler:** Akihito **Subject:** Expo 2005 **Obv:** Blue and white enamel Pacific map in wreath **Rev:** Expo logo

| Date | Mintage | VF20 | XF40 | MS60 | MS63 | MS65 |
|---|---|---|---|---|---|---|
| Yr. 16(2004) | 70,000 | PF65 165 | | | | |

**Y# 138 1000 YEN**
31.10 g., 1.000 Silver 0.9999 oz. ASW, 40 mm. **Ruler:** Akihito **Subject:** 50th Anniversary of Japan's Entry into the United Nations **Obv:** Globe and plum blossom wreath (enameled blue, pink and green) **Rev:** UN emblem

| Date | Mintage | VF20 | XF40 | MS60 | MS63 | MS65 |
|---|---|---|---|---|---|---|
| Yr.18(2006) | 70,000 | PF65 165 | | | | |

**Y# 140 1000 YEN**
31.10 g., 0.999 Silver 0.9989 oz. ASW, 40 mm. **Ruler:** Akihito **Obv:** Dual multicolor rainbows **Obv. Inscription:** SKILLS / 2007 **Rev:** Mount Fuji **Rev. Legend:** International Skills Festival for All, Japan **Edge:** Helical ridges **Note:** Prev. #Y142.

| Date | Mintage | VF20 | XF40 | MS60 | MS63 | MS65 |
|---|---|---|---|---|---|---|
| Yr.19(2007) | 80,000 | PF65 75.00 | | | | |

**Y# 142 1000 YEN**
31.10 g., 0.999 Silver 0.9989 oz. ASW, 40 mm. **Ruler:** Akihito **Subject:** Local Autonomy - Hokkaido Prefecture **Obv:** Lake Toya and two multicolor red-crowned cranes in flight **Rev:** Snowflakes, cherry blossoms and crescent

| Date | Mintage | VF20 | XF40 | MS60 | MS63 | MS65 |
|---|---|---|---|---|---|---|
| Yr.20(2008) | 100,000 | PF65 135 | | | | |

**Y# 144 1000 YEN**
31.10 g., 0.999 Silver 0.9989 oz. ASW, 40 mm. **Ruler:** Akihito **Subject:** Local Autonomy - Kyoto Prefecture **Obv:** Multicolor scene from an antique illustrated version of the Tale of Genji **Rev:** Snowflakes, cherry blossoms and crescent **Edge:** Reeded

| Date | Mintage | VF20 | XF40 | MS60 | MS63 | MS65 |
|---|---|---|---|---|---|---|
| Yr.20(2008) | 100,000 | PF65 120 | | | | |

**Y# 146 1000 YEN**
31.10 g., 0.999 Silver 0.9989 oz. ASW, 40 mm. **Ruler:** Akihito **Subject:** Local Autonomy - Shimane Prefecture **Obv:** Multicolor peony flowers and Otoriosame chogin coin **Rev:** Snowflakes, cherry blossoms and crescent **Edge:** Reeded

| Date | Mintage | VF20 | XF40 | MS60 | MS63 | MS65 |
|---|---|---|---|---|---|---|
| Yr.20(2008) | 100,000 | PF65 115 | | | | |

**Y# 154 1000 YEN**
31.10 g., 0.999 Silver 0.9989 oz. ASW **Ruler:** Akihito **Subject:** Local Autonomy - Ibaraki Prefecture **Obv:** Multicolor H-II launch vehicle and Mt. Tsukuba **Rev:** Snowflakes, cherry blossoms and crescent **Edge:** Reeded

| Date | Mintage | VF20 | XF40 | MS60 | MS63 | MS65 |
|---|---|---|---|---|---|---|
| Yr.21(2008) | 100,000 | PF65 100 | | | | |

**Y# 156 1000 YEN**
31.10 g., 0.999 Silver 0.9989 oz. ASW **Ruler:** Akihito **Subject:** Local Autonomy - Nara Prefecture **Obv:** Daigokuden Audience Hall in multicolor, cherry blossoms and Kemari (ancient ball players) **Rev:** Snowflakes, cherry blossoms and crescent **Edge:** Reeded

| Date | Mintage | VF20 | XF40 | MS60 | MS63 | MS65 |
|---|---|---|---|---|---|---|
| Yr.21(2008) | 100,000 | PF65 115 | | | | |

**Y# 148 1000 YEN**
31.10 g., 0.999 Silver 0.9989 oz. ASW, 40 mm. **Ruler:** Akihito **Subject:** Local Autonomy - Nagano Prefecture **Obv:** Multicolor Japan Alps and Kamikochi **Rev:** Snowflakes, cherry blossoms and crescent **Edge:** Reeded

| Date | Mintage | VF20 | XF40 | MS60 | MS63 | MS65 |
|---|---|---|---|---|---|---|
| Yr.21(2009) | 100,000 | PF65 115 | | | | |

**Y# 150 1000 YEN**
31.10 g., 0.999 Silver 0.9989 oz. ASW, 40 mm. **Ruler:** Akihito **Subject:** Local Autonomy - Niigata Prefecture **Obv:** Two Japanese crested ibis and Sado Island **Rev:** Snowflakes, cherry blossoms and crescent **Edge:** Reeded

| Date | Mintage | VF20 | XF40 | MS60 | MS63 | MS65 |
|---|---|---|---|---|---|---|
| Yr.21(2009) | 100,000 | PF65 100 | | | | |

**Y# 160 1000 YEN**
31.10 g., 0.999 Silver 0.9989 oz. ASW, 40 mm. **Ruler:** Akihito **Subject:** Local Autonomy commemorative - Kochi Prefecture **Obv:** SAKAMOTO Ryoma and Katsurahama Beach **Rev:** Snowflakes, cherry blossoms and crescent **Rev. Legend:** Local Autonomy 60 Years **Edge:** Reeded

| Date | Mintage | VF20 | XF40 | MS60 | MS63 | MS65 |
|---|---|---|---|---|---|---|
| Yr.22(2010) Proof; colorized | 100,000 | PF65 130 | | | | |

**Y# 162 1000 YEN**
31.10 g., 0.999 Silver 0.9989 oz. ASW, 40 mm. **Ruler:** Akihito **Subject:** Local Autonomy commemorative - Gifu Prefecture **Obv:** Cormorant fishing on the Nagara River **Rev:** Snowflakes, cherry blossoms, and crescent moon with legend **Rev. Legend:** Local Autonomy 60 Years **Edge:** Reeded

| Date | Mintage | VF20 | XF40 | MS60 | MS63 | MS65 |
|---|---|---|---|---|---|---|
| Yr.22(2010) Proof; colorized | 100,000 | PF65 130 | | | | |

**Y# 164 1000 YEN**
31.10 g., 0.999 Silver 0.9989 oz. ASW, 40 mm. **Ruler:** Akihito **Subject:** Local Autonomy commemorative - Fukui Prefecture **Obv:** Fukuiraptor and Tojinbo Cliffs **Rev:** Snowflakes, cherry blossoms, and crescent moon with legend **Rev. Legend:** Local Autonomy 60 Years **Edge:** Reeded

| Date | Mintage | VF20 | XF40 | MS60 | MS63 | MS65 |
|---|---|---|---|---|---|---|
| Yr.22(2010) Proof; colorized | 100,000 | PF65 130 | | | | |

**Y# 166 1000 YEN**
31.10 g., 1.000 Silver 0.9999 oz. ASW, 40 mm. **Ruler:** Akihito **Subject:** Local Autonomy commemorative - Aichi Prefecture **Obv:** Golden dolphin, rabbit-ear iris and the Atsumi Peninsula **Rev:** Snowflakes, cherry blossoms and crescent moon with legend reading "local autonomy 60 years **Edge:** Reeded

| Date | Mintage | VF20 | XF40 | MS60 | MS63 | MS65 |
|---|---|---|---|---|---|---|
| Yr.22 (2010) | 100,000 | PF65 130 | | | | |

**Y# 168 1000 YEN**
31.10 g., 1.000 Silver 0.9999 oz. ASW, 40 mm. **Ruler:** Akihito **Subject:** Local Autonomy commemorative - Aomori Prefecture **Obv:** Traditional parade floats and apples **Rev:** Snowflakes, cherry blossoms and crescent moon with legend reading "local autonomy 60 years **Edge:** Reeded

| Date | Mintage | VF20 | XF40 | MS60 | MS63 | MS65 |
|---|---|---|---|---|---|---|
| Yr.22 (2010) | 100,000 | PF65 130 | | | | |

**Y# 170 1000 YEN**
31.10 g., 1.000 Silver 0.9999 oz. ASW, 40 mm. **Ruler:** Akihito **Subject:** Local Autonomy commemorative - Saga Prefecture **Obv:** OKUMA Shigenobu and Imari - Arita ware **Rev:** Snowflakes, cherry blossoms and crescent moon with legend reading "local autonomy 60 years **Edge:** Reeded

| Date | Mintage | VF20 | XF40 | MS60 | MS63 | MS65 |
|---|---|---|---|---|---|---|
| Yr.22 (2010) | 100,000 | **PF65** 130 | | | | |

**Y# 172 1000 YEN**
31.11 g., 1.000 Silver 1.000 oz. ASW, 40 mm. **Ruler:** Akihito **Subject:** Local Autonomy commemorative - Toyama Prefecture **Obv:** Tateyama mountain range rising from the sea **Rev:** Snowflakes, cherry blossoms and crescent moon with legend reading "local autonomy 60 years **Edge:** Reeded

| Date | Mintage | VF20 | XF40 | MS60 | MS63 | MS65 |
|---|---|---|---|---|---|---|
| Yr. 23 (2011) | 100,000 | **PF65** 130 | | | | |

**Y# 174 1000 YEN**
31.10 g., 1.000 Silver 0.9999 oz. ASW, 40 mm. **Ruler:** Akihito **Subject:** Local Autonomy commemorative - Tottori Prefecture **Obv:** Tottori Sand Dunes and San'in Kaigan Coast **Rev:** Snowflakes, cherry blossoms and crescent moon with legend reading "local autonomy 60 years **Edge:** Reeded

| Date | Mintage | VF20 | XF40 | MS60 | MS63 | MS65 |
|---|---|---|---|---|---|---|
| Yr. 23 (2011) | 100,000 | **PF65** 130 | | | | |

**Y# 176 1000 YEN**
31.10 g., 1.000 Silver 0.9999 oz. ASW, 40 mm. **Ruler:** Akihito **Subject:** Local Autonomy commemorative - Kumamoto Prefecture **Obv:** Mount Aso **Rev:** Snowflakes, cherry blossoms and crescent moon with legend reading "local autonomy 60 years **Edge:** Reeded

| Date | Mintage | VF20 | XF40 | MS60 | MS63 | MS65 |
|---|---|---|---|---|---|---|
| Yr. 23 (2011) | 100,000 | **PF65** 130 | | | | |

**Y# 178 1000 YEN**
31.11 g., 0.999 Silver 0.999 oz. ASW, 40 mm. **Ruler:** Akihito **Subject:** Local Autonomy - Shiga Prefecture **Obv:** Lake Biwa, family of little grebe birds and Ukimido temple **Rev:** Crescent moon, flora and snowflake **Edge:** Reeded

| Date | Mintage | VF20 | XF40 | MS60 | MS63 | MS65 |
|---|---|---|---|---|---|---|
| Yr. 23 (2011) | 100,000 | **PF65** 115 | | | | |

**Y# 180 1000 YEN**
31.11 g., 0.999 Silver 0.999 oz. ASW, 40 mm. **Ruler:** Akihito **Subject:** Local Autonomy - Iwate Prefecture **Obv:** Konjiko-do, the golden hall of Chuson-ji Temple, lotus and Pure Land Garden of Motsu-ji temple **Rev:** Crescent moon, flora and snowflake **Edge:** Reeded

| Date | Mintage | VF20 | XF40 | MS60 | MS63 | MS65 |
|---|---|---|---|---|---|---|
| Yr. 23 (2011) | 100,000 | **PF65** 110 | | | | |

**Y# 182 1000 YEN**
31.11 g., 0.999 Silver 0.999 oz. ASW, 40 mm. **Ruler:** Akihito **Subject:** Local Autonomy - Akita Prefecture **Obv:** Nobu Shirase, Antartic explorer, Namahage folk ritual **Rev:** Crescent moon, flora and snowflake **Edge:** Reeded

| Date | Mintage | VF20 | XF40 | MS60 | MS63 | MS65 |
|---|---|---|---|---|---|---|
| Yr. 23 (2011) | 100,000 | **PF65** 110 | | | | |

**Y# 184 1000 YEN**
31.10 g., 0.999 Silver 0.9989 oz. ASW, 40 mm. **Ruler:** Akihito **Subject:** Local Autonomy - Okinawa Prefecture **Obv:** State Hall in Suri and Kumidori dancer **Rev:** Crescent moon, flora and snowflake **Edge:** Reeded

| Date | Mintage | VF20 | XF40 | MS60 | MS63 | MS65 |
|---|---|---|---|---|---|---|
| Yr.24(2012) | 100,000 | **PF65** 100 | | | | |

**Y# 186 1000 YEN**
31.10 g., 0.999 Silver 0.9989 oz. ASW, 40 mm. **Ruler:** Akihito **Subject:** Local Autonomy - Kanagawa Prefecture **Obv:** Tsurugaoka Hachimangu Shrine and horseback archery - Yabusame **Rev:** Crescent moon, flora and snowflake **Edge:** Reeded

| Date | Mintage | VF20 | XF40 | MS60 | MS63 | MS65 |
|---|---|---|---|---|---|---|
| Yr.24(2012) | 100,000 | **PF65** 100 | | | | |

**Y# 188 1000 YEN**
31.10 g., 0.999 Silver 0.9989 oz. ASW, 40 mm. **Ruler:** Akihito **Subject:** Local Autonomy - Miyazaki Prefecture **Obv:** Miyazaki Prefectural Government Building and Takachiho Yokagura dancer **Rev:** Crescent moon, flora and snowflake **Edge:** Reeded

| Date | Mintage | VF20 | XF40 | MS60 | MS63 | MS65 |
|---|---|---|---|---|---|---|
| Yr.24(2012) | 100,000 | **PF65** 100 | | | | |

**Y# 190 1000 YEN**
31.13 g., 0.999 Silver 0.9999 oz. ASW, 40 mm. **Ruler:** Akihito **Subject:** Tochigi **Obv:** Tokugawa Ieyasu Mausoleum in Nikko in color **Rev:** Crescent moon, flora and snowflake

| Date | Mintage | VF20 | XF40 | MS60 | MS63 | MS65 |
|---|---|---|---|---|---|---|
| Yr.24 (2012) | 100,000 | **PF65** 95.00 | | | | |

**Y# 192 1000 YEN**
31.13 g., 0.999 Silver 0.9999 oz. ASW, 40 mm. **Ruler:** Akihito **Subject:** Hyogo **Obv:** Black beaked stork in flight over Himeji temple **Rev:** Crescent moon, flora and snowflake

| Date | Mintage | VF20 | XF40 | MS60 | MS63 | MS65 |
|---|---|---|---|---|---|---|
| Yr. 24 (2012) | 100,000 | **PF65** 95.00 | | | | |

**Y# 194 1000 YEN**
31.13 g., 0.999 Silver 0.9999 oz. ASW, 40 mm. **Ruler:** Akihito **Subject:** Oita **Obv:** Sumo wrestler Akiyoski Sadaji, and Usa shrine **Rev:** Crescent moon, flora and snowflake

| Date | Mintage | VF20 | XF40 | MS60 | MS63 | MS65 |
|---|---|---|---|---|---|---|
| Yr.24 (2012) | 100,000 | **PF65** 95.00 | | | | |

**Y# 195 1000 YEN**
31.13 g., 0.999 Silver 0.9999 oz. ASW, 40 mm. **Ruler:** Akihito **Subject:** International Monatary Fund Meeting, Toyko **Obv:** Mt. Fuji and traditional pesants in color **Rev:** Pan-Pacific map

| Date | Mintage | VF20 | XF40 | MS60 | MS63 | MS65 |
|---|---|---|---|---|---|---|
| Yr.24 (2012) | 50,000 | **PF65** 95.00 | | | | |

**Y# 197 1000 YEN**
31.10 g., Silver, 40 mm. **Ruler:** Akihito **Subject:** Miyagi Prefecture **Obv:** Statue of DATE Masamune at Sendai Castle, and ship used by the Keicho Embassy to Europe in 1613 **Rev:** Crescent moon, flora and snowflake

| Date | Mintage | VF20 | XF40 | MS60 | MS63 | MS65 |
|---|---|---|---|---|---|---|
| yr.25 (2013) | 100,000 | **PF65** 100 | | | | |

**Y# 199 1000 YEN**
31.10 g., Silver, 40 mm. **Ruler:** Akihito **Subject:** Hiroshima Prefecture **Obv:** Itsukushima Shintō Shrine, Bugaku dancer, and red maple leaves **Rev:** Crescent moon, flora and snowflake

| Date | Mintage | VF20 | XF40 | MS60 | MS63 | MS65 |
|---|---|---|---|---|---|---|
| yr. 25 (2013) | 100,000 | **PF65** 100 | | | | |

**Y# 201 1000 YEN**
31.10 g., Silver, 40 mm. **Ruler:** Akihito **Subject:** Gunma Prefecture **Obv:** Tomioka silk mill and a mill worker **Rev:** Crescent moon, flora and snowflake

| Date | Mintage | VF20 | XF40 | MS60 | MS63 | MS65 |
|---|---|---|---|---|---|---|
| yr. 25 (2013) | 100,000 | **PF65** 100 | | | | |

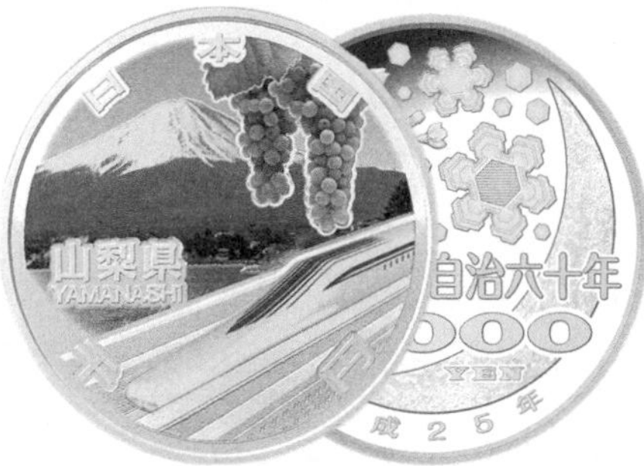


**Y# 203 1000 YEN**
31.10 g., Silver, 40 mm. **Ruler:** Akihito **Subject:** Yamanashi Prefecture **Obv:** Mt. Fuji, the Yamanashi mag-lev test train, and Kōshu grapes **Rev:** Crescent moon, flora and snowflake

| Date | Mintage | VF20 | XF40 | MS60 | MS63 | MS65 |
|---|---|---|---|---|---|---|
| yr. 25 (2013) | 100,000 | **PF65** 100 | | | | |

**Y# 205 1000 YEN**
31.10 g., Silver, 40 mm. **Ruler:** Akihito **Subject:** Shizuoka Prefecture **Obv:** Ultramarine Mt. Fuji" or "Gunjō Fuji" by YOKOYAMA Taikan **Rev:** Crescent moon, flora and snowflake

| Date | Mintage | VF20 | XF40 | MS60 | MS63 | MS65 |
|---|---|---|---|---|---|---|
| yr. 25 (2013) | 100,000 | **PF65** 100 | | | | |

**Y# 207 1000 YEN**
31.10 g., Silver, 40 mm. **Ruler:** Akihito **Subject:** Okayama Prefecture **Obv:** Kōrakuen Garden and Momotarō (a folklore hero) **Rev:** Crescent moon, flora and snowflake

| Date | Mintage | VF20 | XF40 | MS60 | MS63 | MS65 |
|---|---|---|---|---|---|---|
| yr. 25 (2013) | 100,000 | **PF65** 100 | | | | |

**Y# 209 1000 YEN**
31.10 g., Silver, 40 mm. **Ruler:** Akihito **Subject:** Kagoshima Prefecture **Obv:** Jōmonsugi Cedar Tree, Mt. Nagatadake, and Yakushima rhododendron on Yakushima Island **Rev:** Crescent moon, flora and snowflake

| Date | Mintage | VF20 | XF40 | MS60 | MS63 | MS65 |
|---|---|---|---|---|---|---|
| yr. 25 (2013) | — | **PF65** 100 | | | | |

**Y# 130 10000 YEN**
15.60 g., 0.999 Gold 0.501 oz. AGW, 26 mm. **Ruler:** Akihito **Subject:** World Cup Soccer **Obv:** Two soccer players **Rev:** Games logo **Edge:** Reeded

| Date | Mintage | VF20 | XF40 | MS60 | MS63 | MS65 |
|---|---|---|---|---|---|---|
| Yr.14(2002) | 100,000 | **PF65** 950 | | | | |

**Y# 136 10000 YEN**
15.60 g., 0.999 Gold 0.501 oz. AGW, 26 mm. **Ruler:** Akihito **Subject:** Expo 2005 **Obv:** Two owls on globe **Rev:** Expo logo

| Date | Mintage | VF20 | XF40 | MS60 | MS63 | MS65 |
|---|---|---|---|---|---|---|
| Yr. 16(2004) | 70,000 | **PF65** 950 | | | | |

**Y# 158 10000 YEN**
20.00 g., 0.999 Gold 0.6424 oz. AGW, 28 mm. **Ruler:** Akihito **Subject:** 20th Anniversary of Emperor's enthronment **Obv:** Imperial christaniumn crest **Rev:** Phoenix, an auspicious cloud, Niju-bashi bridge

| Date | Mintage | VF20 | XF40 | MS60 | MS63 | MS65 |
|---|---|---|---|---|---|---|
| Yr.21(2009) | 100,000 | **PF65** 1,050 | | | | |

## MINT SETS

| KM# | Date | Mintage | Identification | Issue Price | Mkt Val |
|---|---|---|---|---|---|
| MS125 | 2001 (6) | 8,000 | Y#95.2-98.2, 101.2, 125 Mint exhibition in Fukuoka | 16.00 | 30.00 |
| MS126 | 2001 (6) | 85,000 | Y#95.2-98.2, 101.2, 125 Osaka cherry blossoms box | 17.00 | 30.00 |
| MS127 | 2001 (6) | 10,000 | Y#95.2-98.2, 101.2, 125 Hiroshima cherry blossoms box | 17.00 | 33.00 |
| MS128 | 2001 (6) | 10,000 | Y#95.2-98.2, 101.2, 125 12th Tokyo International Coin Convention | 17.00 | 30.00 |
| MS129 | 2001 (6) | 5,000 | Y#95.2-98.2, 101.2, 125 Beautiful Future Exposition | 17.00 | 30.00 |
| MS130 | 2001 (6) | 8,000 | Y#95.2-98.2, 101.2, 125 Kagoshima Coin and Stamp Show | 17.00 | 30.00 |
| MS131 | 2001 (6) | 5,000 | Y#95.2-98.2, 101.2, 125 Tokyo Mint Fair | 17.00 | 33.00 |
| MS132 | 2001 (6) | 5,000 | Y#95.2-98.2, 101.2, 125 Yamaguchi Exposition | 17.00 | 40.00 |
| MS133 | 2001 (6) | 193,600 | Y#95.2-98.2, 101.2, 125 21st Century Commemorative Respect for the Aged | 17.00 | 27.00 |
| MS134 | 2001 (6) | 190,300 | Y#95.2-98.2, 101.2, 125 Ryukyu World Cultural Sites | 17.00 | 27.00 |
| MS135 | 2001 (6) | 8,300 | Y#95.2-98.2, 101.2, 125 "Anniversary" folder | 18.00 | 33.00 |
| MS136 | 2001 (1) | 4,000 | Y#125 Mint Visit Commemorative | 8.00 | 10.00 |
| MS137 | 2001 (6) | 224,000 | Y#95.2-98.2, 101.2, 125 Mint Bureau Box | 15.00 | 27.00 |
| MS138 | 2001 (6) | 7,300 | Y#95.2-98.2, 101.2, 125 "Japan Coins" | 17.00 | 30.00 |
| MS139 | 2001 (2) | 5,000 | Y#96.2, 125 "Japan Coins" (short set) | 8.50 | 13.00 |
| MS140 | 2001 (6) | 128,700 | Y#95.2-98.2, 101.2, 125 World Intangible Heritage - Nogaku | 17.00 | 27.00 |
| MSA141 | 2002 (3) | 50,000 | Y#126-128 World Cup soccer | 26.00 | 35.00 |
| MS141 | 2002 (1) | 3,000 | Y#125 Mint Visit Commemorative | 7.50 | 10.00 |
| MS142 | 2002 (6) | 7,000 | Y#95.2-98.2, 102.2, 125 "Anniversary" folder | 18.00 | 27.00 |
| MS143 | 2002 (2) | 4,000 | Y#96.2, 125. "Japan Coins" (short set) | 8.50 | 13.00 |
| MS144 | 2002 (6) | 6,000 | Y#95.2-98.2, 101.2, 125 "Japan Coins" | 17.00 | 23.00 |
| MS145 | 2002 (6) | 4,000 | Y#95.2-98.2, 101.2, 125 Mint exhibition in Takamatsu | 16.00 | 33.00 |
| MS146 | 2002 (6) | 80,000 | Y#95.2-98.2, 101.2, 125 Osaka cherry blossoms | 16.00 | 20.00 |
| MS147 | 2002 (6) | 10,000 | Y#95.2-98.2, 101.2, 125 Hiroshima cherry blossoms | 16.00 | 23.00 |
| MS148 | 2002 (6) | 10,000 | Y#95.2-98.2, 101.2, 125 13th Tokyo Int'l Coin Convention | 16.00 | 20.00 |
| MS149 | 2002 (6) | 6,000 | Y#95.2-98.2, 101.2, 125 Mint exhibition in Sendai | 16.00 | 23.00 |
| MS150 | 2002 (6) | 194,000 | Y#95.2-98.2, 101.2, 125 Respect for the Aged | 19.00 | 20.00 |
| MS151 | 2002 (6) | 6,000 | Y#95.2-98.2, 101.2, 125 Matsuyama Coin and Stamp Show | 16.00 | 23.00 |
| MS152 | 2002 (6) | 3,000 | Y395.2-98.2, 101.2, 125 Tokyo Mint Fair | 16.00 | 120 |
| MS153 | 2002 (6) | 2,000 | Y#95.2-98.2, 101,2, 125 Birthday folder (with sound recording function) | 25.00 | 40.00 |
| MS154 | 2002 (6) | 214,800 | Y395.2-98.2, 101.2, 125 Mint Bureau box | 15.00 | 20.00 |
| MS155 | 2003 (6) | 8,000 | Y#95.2-98.2, 101,2, 125 "Japan Coins" | 17.00 | 20.00 |
| MS156 | 2003 (6) | 7,000 | Y#95.2-98.2, 101.2, 125 "Anniversary" folder | 18.00 | 20.00 |
| MS157 | 2003 (6) | 3,000 | Y#95.2-98.2, 101.2, 125 "Anniversary" folder (with sound recording function) | 25.00 | 27.00 |
| MS158 | 2003 (6) | 6,000 | Y#95.2-98.2, 101.2, 125 Mint exhibition in Okayama | 16.00 | 30.00 |
| MS159 | 2003 (6) | 80,000 | Y#95.2-98.2, 101.2, 125 Osaka cherry blossoms | 16.00 | 20.00 |
| MS160 | 2003 (6) | 10,000 | Y#95.2-98.2, 101.2, 125 Hiroshima cherry blossoms | 16.00 | 20.00 |
| MS161 | 2003 (6) | 10,000 | Y#95.2-98.2, 101.2, 125 14th Tokyo Int'l Coin Convention | 16.00 | 20.00 |
| MS162 | 2003 (6) | 6,000 | Y#95.2-98.2, 101.2, 125 First Osaka Coin Show | 16.00 | 20.00 |
| MS163 | 2003 (6) | 235,000 | Y#95.2-98.2, 101.2, 125 Birth of Astro Boy | 19.00 | 20.00 |
| MS164 | 2003 (6) | 130,000 | Y#95.2-98.2, 101.2, 125 Respect for the Aged | 19.00 | 17.00 |
| MS165 | 2003 (6) | 5,000 | Y#95.2-98.2, 101.2, 125 Tokyo Mint Fair - Mint Collection in Omote-sando | 17.00 | 30.00 |
| MS166 | 2003 (6) | 5,000 | Y#95.2-98.2, 101.2, 125 Mint exhibition in Sapporo | 17.00 | 27.00 |
| MS167 | 2003 (6) | 5,000 | Y#95.2-98.2, 101.2, 125 Yonago Coin and Stamp Show | 17.00 | 23.00 |
| MS168 | 2003 (6) | 205,000 | Y#95.2-98.2, 101.2, 125 Mint Bureau box | 17.00 | 16.00 |
| MS169 | 2003 (6) | 100,000 | Y#95.2-98.2, 101.2, 125 2003 Central League Champions - Hanshin Tigers | 22.00 | 27.00 |
| MS170 | 2003 (6) | 100,000 | Y#95.2-98.2, 101.2, 125 2003 Pacific league Champions - Fukuoka Daiei Hawks | 22.00 | 16.00 |
| MS171 | 2003 (6) | 5,000 | Y#95.2-98.2, 101.2, 126 400th Anniversary of the Establishment of Government in Edo | 22.00 | 200 |
| MS172 | 2004 (6) | 8,000 | Y#95.2-98.2, 101.2, 125 Japan Coin Set | 19.00 | 20.00 |
| MS173 | 2004 (6) | 5,000 | Y#95.2-98.2, 101.2, 125 Anniversary folder | 20.00 | 22.00 |
| MS174 | 2004 (6) | 5,000 | Y#95.2-98.2, 101.2, 125 Anniversary folder (with sound recording function) | 28.50 | 27.00 |
| MS175 | 2004 (6) | 4,000 | Y#95.2-98.2, 101.2, 125 Mint exhibition in Fukui | 18.00 | 53.00 |
| MS176 | 2004 (6) | 70,000 | Y#95.2-98.2, 101.2, 125 Osaka cherry blossoms | 18.00 | 20.00 |
| MS177 | 2004 (6) | 10,000 | Y#95.2-98.2, 101.2, 125 Hiroshima cherry blossoms | 18.00 | 20.00 |
| MS178 | 2004 (6) | 10,000 | Y#95.2-98.2, 101.2, 125 15th Tokyo Int'l Coin Convention | 18.00 | 20.00 |
| MS179 | 2004 (6) | 6,000 | Y#95.2-98.2, 101.2, 125 Second Osaka Coin Show | 18.00 | 20.00 |
| MS180 | 2004 (6) | 100,000 | Y#95.2-98.2, 101.2, 125 World Intangible Heritage series: Bunraku puppets | 19.00 | 20.00 |
| MS181 | 2004 (6) | 122,500 | Y#95.2-98.2, 101.2, 125 Respect for the Aged | 20.00 | 20.00 |
| MS182 | 2004 (6) | 5,000 | Y#95.2-98.2, 101.2, 125 Mint exhibition in Tosu | 18.00 | 23.00 |
| MS183 | 2004 (6) | 189,000 | Y#95.2-98.2, 101.2, 125 Mint Bureau box | 16.00 | 17.00 |
| MS184 | 2004 (6) | 5,000 | Y#95.2-98.2, 101.2, 125 Gifu Coin and Stamp Show | 17.00 | 23.00 |
| MS185 | 2004 (6) | 226,000 | Y#95.2-98.2, 101.2, 125 30th Birthday of Hello Kitty (cartoon character) | 22.00 | 23.00 |
| MS186 | 2004 (6) | 5,000 | Y#95.2-98.2, 101.2, 125 Tokyo Mint Fair - 40th Anniversary - Issue of Commemorative Coins | 17.00 | 33.00 |
| MS187 | 2004 (6) | 44,000 | Y#95.2-98.2, 101.2, 125 2004 Central League Champions - Chunichi Dragons | 21.00 | 17.00 |
| MS188 | 2004 (6) | 38,500 | Y#95.2-98.2, 101.2, 125 2004 Pacific League Champions - Seibu Lions | 21.00 | 17.00 |
| MSA189 | 2005 (6) | 1,000 | Y#95.2-98.2, 101.2, 125 34th International Coin Convention, Basel | — | — |
| MS189 | 2005 (6) | 200,000 | Y#95.2-98.2, 101.2, 133 Expo 2005, Aichi | 22.00 | 23.00 |
| MS190 | 2005 (6) | 8,000 | Y#95.2-98.2, 101.2, 125 "Japan Coin Set" | 17.00 | 16.00 |
| MS191 | 2005 (6) | 5,000 | Y#95.2-98.2, 101.2, 125 "Anniversary" folder | 19.00 | 20.00 |
| MS192 | 2005 (6) | 2,000 | Y#95.2-98.2, 101.2, 125 Anniversary folder (with sound recording function) | 27.50 | 27.00 |
| MS193 | 2005 (6) | 5,000 | Y#95.2-98.2, 101.2, 125 Mint exhibition in Shizuoka | 17.00 | 33.00 |
| MS194 | 2005 (6) | 60,000 | Y#95.2-98.2, 101.2, 125 Osaka cherry blossoms | 17.00 | 23.00 |
| MS195 | 2005 (6) | 10,000 | Y#95.2-98.2, 101.2, 125 Hiroshima Flower Tour | 17.00 | 20.00 |
| MS196 | 2005 (6) | 10,000 | Y#95.2-98.2, 101.2, 125 16th Tokyo International Coin Convention | 17.00 | 20.00 |
| MS197 | 2005 (6) | 5,000 | Y#95.2-98.2, 101.2, 125 Third Osaka Coin Show | 17.00 | 20.00 |
| MS198 | 2005 (6) | 126,500 | Y#95.2-98.2, 101.2, 125 World Cultural Heritage Series: Kii Hills Sacred Places and Pilgrimage Trails | 18.00 | 20.00 |
| MS199 | 2005 (6) | 104,500 | Y#95.2-98.2, 101.2, 125 Respect for the Aged | 19.00 | 20.00 |
| MS200 | 2005 (6) | 5,000 | Y#95.2-98.2, 101.2, 125 Mint Exhibition in Morioka | 18.00 | 23.00 |
| MS201 | 2005 (6) | 5,000 | Y#95.2-98.2, 101.2, 125 Koriyama Coin and Stamp Show | 17.00 | 23.00 |
| MS202 | 2005 (6) | 182,000 | Y#95.2-98.2, 101.2, 125 35th Anniversary of Doraemon (cartoon character) | 17.00 | 30.00 |
| MS203 | 2005 (6) | 141,000 | Y#95.2-98.2, 101.2, 125 Mint Bureau Box | 16.00 | 18.00 |
| MS204 | 2005 (6) | 75,800 | Y#95.2-98.2, 101.2, 125 World Natural Heritage | 18.00 | 20.00 |
| MS205 | 2005 (6) | 5,000 | Y#95.2-98.2, 101.2, 125 Mint Bureau Tokyo Fair / 50th Anniversary of One-Yen Aluminum Coin | 17.00 | 40.00 |
| MS206 | 2005 (6) | 83,600 | Y#95.2-98.2, 101.2, 125 2005 Central League Champions - Hanshin Tigers | 21.00 | 20.00 |
| MS207 | 2005 (6) | 56,600 | Y#95.2-98.2, 101.2, 125 2005 Pacific League Champions - Chiba Lotte Marines | 21.00 | 20.00 |
| MS208 | 2006 (6) | 5,000 | Y#95.2-98.2, 101.2, 125 Mint exhibition in Oita | 17.00 | 17.50 |
| MS209 | 2006 (6) | 9,000 | Y#95.2-98.2, 101.2, 125 "Japan Coin Set" | 18.00 | 18.00 |
| MS210 | 2006 (6) | 5,000 | Y#95.2-98.2, 101.2, 125 "Anniversary" Folder | 19.00 | 20.00 |
| MS211 | 2006 (6) | 189,400 | Y#95.2-98.2, 101.2, 125 Mint Bureau box | 16.00 | 17.00 |
| MS212 | 2006 (6) | 66,000 | Y#95.2-98.2, 101.2, 125 World Intangible Heritage Series: Kabuki Theater | 18.00 | 18.00 |
| MS213 | 2006 (6) | 60,000 | Y#95.2-98.2, 101.2, 125 Osaka Cherry Blossoms | 17.00 | 17.50 |
| MS214 | 2006 (6) | 8,000 | Y#95.2-98.2, 101.2, 125 Hiroshima Flower Tour | 17.00 | 17.50 |
| MS215 | 2006 (6) | 8,000 | Y#95.2-98.2, 101.2, 125 17th Tokyo International Coin Convention | 17.00 | 18.50 |
| MS216 | 2006 (6) | 85,500 | Y#95.2-98.2, 101.2, 125 Respect for the Aged | 19.00 | 20.00 |

| KM# | Date | Mintage | Identification | Issue Price | Mkt Val |
|---|---|---|---|---|---|
| MS217 | 2006 (6) | 4,000 | Y#95.2-98.2, 101.2, 125 Third Osaka Coin Show | 17.00 | 18.50 |
| MS218 | 2006 (6) | 4,000 | Y#95.2-98.2, 101.2, 125 Mint Exhibition in Kofu | 17.00 | 17.50 |
| MS219 | 2006 (6) | 105,200 | Y#95.2-98.2, 101.2, 125 80th Anniversary of Pooh-Bear | 22.00 | 22.50 |
| MS220 | 2006 (6) | 3,500 | Y#95.2-98.2, 101.2, 125 Nagasaki Coin and Stamp Show | 17.00 | 17.50 |
| MS221 | 2006 (6) | 4,000 | Y#95.2-98.2, 101.2, 125 Mint Bureau Tokyo Fair/"The Dawn of Modern Japan" | 17.00 | 50.00 |
| MS222 | 2006 (6) | 49,600 | Y#95.2-98.2, 101.2, 125 2006 Central League Champions - Chunichi Dragons | 21.00 | 27.00 |
| MS223 | 2006 (6) | 52,800 | Y#95.2-98.2, 101.2, 125 2006 Pacific League Champions - Japan Hamfighters | 21.00 | 27.00 |
| MS224 | 2007 (6) | 180,000 | Y#95.2-98.2, 101.2, 137 50th Anniversary of Japanese Antarctic Research | 23.00 | 30.00 |
| MS225 | 2007 (6) | 4,000 | Y#95.2-98.2, 101.2, 125 Mint exhibition in Tsukuba | 17.00 | 18.00 |
| MS226 | 2007 (6) | 8,000 | Y#95.2-98.2, 101.2, 125 "Japan Coin Set" | 18.00 | 20.00 |
| MS227 | 2007 (6) | 5,700 | Y#95.2-98.2, 101.2, 125 "Anniversary" folder | 19.00 | 20.00 |
| MS228 | 2007 (6) | 142,680 | Y#95.2-98.2, 101.2, 125 Mint Bureau box | 16.00 | 18.00 |
| MS229 | 2007 (6) | 70,000 | Y#95.2-98.2, 101.2, 125 "Gongitsune" 75th Anniversary of Publication | 22.00 | 25.00 |
| MS230 | 2007 (6) | 7,000 | Y#95.2-98.2, 101.2, 125 Hiroshima Flower Tour | 18.00 | 20.00 |
| MS231 | 2007 (6) | 60,000 | Y#95.2-98.2, 101.2, 125 Osaka cherry blossoms | 17.00 | 18.00 |
| MS232 | 2007 (6) | 6,000 | Y#95.2-98.2, 101.2, 125 18th Tokyo International Coin Convention | 17.00 | 18.00 |
| MS233 | 2007 (6) | 4,000 | Y#95.2-98.2, 101.2, 125 Fifth Osaka Coin Show | 17.00 | 18.00 |
| MS234 | 2007 (6) | 100,000 | Y#95.2-98.2, 101.2, 125 Rose of Versailles, Lady Oscar | 22.00 | 25.00 |
| MS235 | 2007 (6) | 4,000 | Y#95.2-98.2, 101.2, 125 Mint exhibition in Matsue | 17.00 | 18.00 |
| MS236 | 2007 (6) | 4,000 | Y#95.2-98.2, 101.2, 125 Nagoya Coin and Stamp Show | 17.00 | 18.00 |
| MS237 | 2007 (6) | 69,000 | Y#95.2-98.2, 101.2, 125 Respect for the Aged | 19.00 | 20.00 |
| MS238 | 2007 (6) | 4,000 | Y#95.2-98.2, 101.2, 125 Mint Bureau Tokyo Fair/50th anniversary of introduction of the 100-yen coin | 17.00 | 18.00 |
| MS239 | 2007 (6) | 45,200 | Y#95.2-98.2, 101.2, 125 2007 Central League Champions - Yomiuri Giants | 21.00 | 22.00 |
| MS240 | 2007 (6) | 36,500 | Y#95.2-98.2, 101.2, 125 2007 Pacific League Champions - Japan Hamfighters | 21.00 | 22.00 |
| MS241 | 2007 (6) | 74,500 | Y#95.2-98.2, 101.2, 125 World Cultural Heritage Series: Iwami Silver Mines Ruins and Cultural Landscape | 18.00 | 20.00 |
| MS243 | 2008 (6) | 11,500 | Y95.2-98.2, 101.2, 125, "Japan Coin Set" | 19.00 | 20.00 |
| MS244 | 2008 (6) | 7,650 | Y95.2-98.2, 101.2, 125, "Anniversary" folder | 20.00 | 20.00 |
| MS245 | 2008 (6) | 154,022 | Y95.2-98.2, 101.2, 125, Mint Bureau Box | 17.00 | 20.00 |
| MS246 | 2008 (6) | 4,500 | Y95.2-98.2, 101.2, 125, Hiroshima Flower Tour | 18.00 | 20.00 |
| MS247 | 2008 (6) | 60,000 | Y95.2-98.2, 101.2, 125, Osaka cherry blossoms | 18.00 | 20.00 |
| MS248 | 2008 (6) | 5,500 | Y95.2-98.2, 101.2, 125, 19th Tokyo International Coin Convention | 18.00 | 20.00 |
| MS249 | 2008 (6) | 4,000 | Y25.2-98.2, 101.2, 125, G8 Finance Ministers' meeting, Osaka | 18.00 | 18.00 |
| MS250 | 2008 (6) | 3,500 | Y95.2-98.2, 101.2, 125, Sixth Osaka Coin Show. | 18.00 | 20.00 |
| MS251 | 2008 (6) | 4,000 | Y95.2-98.2, 101.2, 125, Kobe Coin and Stamp Exposition. | 18.00 | 18.00 |
| MS252 | 2008 (6) | 142,000 | Y95.2-98.2, 101.2, 125, Japan-Brazil Year of Exchange and Centenary of Japanese Immigration to Brazil | 24.00 | 25.00 |
| MS253 | 2008 (6) | 64,300 | Y95.2-98.2, 101.2, 125, Children's song coin set, Red Dragonfly. | 23.00 | 25.00 |
| MS254 | 2009 (6) | 4,000 | Y95.2-98.2, 101.2, 125 Mint Bureau Tokyo Fair/"Japan's Attractions" | 20.00 | 20.00 |
| MS255 | 2009 (6) | 3,950 | Y95.2-Y98.2, 101.2, 125 32nd World Money Festival, Nagoya | 20.00 | 21.00 |
| MS256 | 2009 (6) | 11,500 | Y95.2-Y98.2, 101.2, 125 Japan Coin Set | 21.00 | 22.00 |
| MS257 | 2009 (6) | 7,650 | Y95.2-Y98.2, 101.2, 125 Anniversary folder | 22.00 | 22.00 |
| MS258 | 2009 (6) | 4,500 | Y95.2-Y98.2, 101.2, 125 Hiroshima Flower Tour | 20.00 | 20.00 |
| MS259 | 2009 (6) | 60,000 | Y95.2-Y98.2, 101.2, 125 Osaka cherry blossoms | 20.00 | 20.00 |
| MS260 | 2009 (6) | 5,500 | Y95.2-Y98.2, 101.2, 125 20th Toyko International Coin Convention | 20.00 | 20.00 |
| MS261 | 2009 (6) | 152,637 | Y95.2-Y98.2, 101.2, 125 Mint Bureau box | 19.00 | 20.00 |
| MS262 | 2009 (6) | 4,850 | Y95.2-Y98.2, 101.2, 125 Mint exhibition in Niigata | 20.00 | 20.00 |
| MS263 | 2009 (6) | 4,000 | Y95.2-Y98.2, 101.2, 125 Seventh Osaka Coin Show | 20.00 | 20.00 |
| MS264 | 2009 (6) | 5,300 | Y95.2-Y98.2, 101.2, 125 Aqua Metropolis Osaka 2009 | 20.00 | 20.00 |
| MS265 | 2009 (6) | 4,000 | Y95.2-Y98.2, 101.2, 125 Yamagata Coin and Stamp Exibition | 20.00 | 20.00 |
| MS266 | 2009 (6) | 7,413 | Y95.2-98.2, 101.2, 125 2009 Niigata Sports Festival | 19.00 | 20.00 |
| MS267 | 2009 (6) | 70,000 | Y95.2-98.2, 101.2, 125 Music box set, "My Home Town" | 25.00 | 25.00 |
| MS268 | 2009 (6) | 4,000 | Y95.2-98.2, 101.2, 125 Mint Future Fair, "Hallmark" case | 20.00 | 20.00 |
| MS269 | 2010 (6) | 152,500 | Y95.2-98.2, 101.2, 125 "Mint Set 2010" | 19.00 | 25.00 |
| MS270 | 2010 (6) | 7,900 | Y95.2-98.2, 101.2, 125 33rd World Money Festival | 20.00 | 20.00 |
| MS271 | 2010 (6) | 10,500 | Y95.2-98.2, 101.2, 125 "Japan Coin Set" | 20.00 | 21.00 |
| MS272 | 2010 (6) | 6,700 | Y95.2-98.2, 101.2, 125 "Anniversary" folder | 22.00 | 22.00 |
| MS273 | 2010 (6) | 4,748 | Y95.2-98.2, 101.2, 125 Toshima Monozukuri set | 20.00 | 20.00 |
| MS274 | 2010 (6) | 5,000 | Y95.2-98.2, 101.2, 125 Hiroshima Flower Tour | 20.00 | 20.00 |
| MS275 | 2010 (6) | 60,000 | Y95.2-98.2, 101.2, 125 Osaka cherry blossoms | 20.00 | 20.00 |
| MS276 | 2010 (6) | 6,000 | Y95.2-98.2, 101.2, 125 21st Tokyo International Coin Convention | 20.00 | 20.00 |
| MS277 | 2010 (6) | 5,245 | Y95.2-98.2, 101.2, 125 Mint Exhibition in Gifu | 20.00 | 20.00 |
| MS278 | 2010 (6) | 4,572 | Y95.2-98.2, 101.2, 125 Eighth Osaka Coin Show | 20.00 | 20.00 |
| MS279 | 2010 (6) | 4,267 | Y95.2-98.2, 101.2, 125 Kumamoto Coin and Stamp Exhibition | 20.00 | 20.00 |
| MS280 | 2010 (6) | 42,300 | Y95.2-98.2, 101.2, 125 Intangible Cultural Heritage (2009 enrollments) | 22.00 | 22.00 |
| MS281 | 2010 (6) | 8,012 | Y95.2-98.2, 101.2, 125 2010 Chiba Sports Festival | 20.00 | 20.00 |
| MS282 | 2010 (6) | 58,001 | Y95.2-98.2, 101.2, 125 Music box set, "Snow" | 26.00 | 28.00 |
| MS283 | 2010 (6) | 4,000 | Y95.2-98.2, 101.2, 125 Tokyo Mint Fair 2010 | 20.00 | 20.00 |
| MS284 | 2011 (6) | 168,291 | Y95.2-98.2, 101.2, 125 "Mint Set 2011" | 19.00 | 20.00 |
| MS285 | 2011 (6) | 8,000 | Y95.2-98.2, 101.2, 125 34th World Money Festival | 20.00 | 20.00 |
| MS286 | 2011 (6) | 9,614 | Y95.2-98.2, 101.2, 125 "Anniversary" folder | 22.00 | 20.00 |
| MS287 | 2011 (6) | 10,000 | Y95.2-98.2, 101.2, 125 "Japan" mint set | 21.00 | 20.00 |
| MS288 | 2011 (6) | 5,186 | Y95.2-98.2, 101.2, 125 4th Toshima Monozukuri set | 20.00 | 20.00 |
| MS289 | 2011 (6) | 6,000 | Y95.2-98.2, 101.2, 125 Hiroshima Flower Tour | 20.00 | 20.00 |
| MS290 | 2011 (6) | 60,000 | Y95.2-98.2, 101.2, 125 Osaka cherry blossoms | 20.00 | 20.00 |
| MS291 | 2011 (6) | 6,000 | Y95.2-98.2, 101.2, 125 22nd Tokyo International Coin Convention | 20.00 | 20.00 |
| MS292 | 2011 (6) | 4,272 | Y95.2-98.2, 101.2, 125 Ninth Osaka Coin Show | 20.00 | 20.00 |
| MS293 | 2011 (6) | 4,151 | Y95.2-98.2, 101.2, 125 Mint Exhibition in Tottori | 20.00 | 20.00 |
| MS294 | 2011 (6) | 4,377 | Y95.2-98.2, 101.2, 125 Morioka Coin and Stamp Exhibition | 20.00 | 20.00 |
| MS295 | 2011 (6) | 8,109 | Y95.2-98.2, 101.2, 125 Yamaguchi Expo | 20.00 | 20.00 |
| MS296 | 2011 (6) | 4,000 | Y95.2-98.2, 101.2, 125 Tokyo Mint Fair 2011 | 20.00 | 23.00 |
| MS297 | 2011 (6) | 50,000 | Y95.2-98.2, 101.2, 125 Children's Songs, "A Poetry Book of Misuzu Kaneko" | 26.00 | 20.00 |
| MS298 | 2012 (6) | 8,923 | Y95.2-98.2, 101.2, 125 35th World Money Festival | 20.00 | 20.00 |
| MS299 | 2012 (6) | 158,500 | Y95.2-98.2, 101.2, 125 "Mint Set 2012" | 19.00 | 20.00 |
| MS300 | 2012 (6) | 8,633 | Y95.2-98.2, 101.2, 125 "Anniversary" folder | 22.00 | 20.00 |
| MS301 | 2012 (6) | 15,000 | Y95.2-98.2, 101.2, 125 "Japan" mint set | 21.00 | 20.00 |
| MS302 | 2012 (6) | 5,435 | Y95.2-98.2, 101.2, 125 5th Toshima Monozukuri set | 20.00 | 20.00 |
| MS303 | 2012 (6) | 8,000 | Y95.2-98.2, 101.2, 125 Hiroshima Flower Tour | 20.00 | 20.00 |
| MS304 | 2012 (6) | 60,000 | Y95.2-98.2, 101.2, 125 Osaka cherry blossoms | 20.00 | 20.00 |
| MS305 | 2012 (6) | 6,000 | Y95.2-98.2, 101.2, 125 23rd Tokyo International Coin Convention | 20.00 | 20.00 |
| MS306 | 2012 (6) | 67,000 | Y95.2-98.2, 101.2, 125 Ogasawara World Cultural Heritage site | 22.00 | 20.00 |
| MS307 | 2012 (6) | 72,000 | Y95.2-98.2, 101.2, 125 Hiraizumi World Cultural Heritage site | 22.00 | 20.00 |
| MS308 | 2012 (6) | 4,500 | Y95.2-98.2, 101.2, 125 Tenth Osaka Coin Show | 20.00 | 20.00 |
| MS309 | 2012 (6) | 5,000 | Y95.2-98.2, 101.2, 125 Mint Exhibition in Miyazaki | 20.00 | 20.00 |

| KM# | Date | Mintage | Identification | Issue Price | Mkt Val |
|---|---|---|---|---|---|
| MS310 | 2012 (6) | 72,000 | Y95.2-98.2, 101.2, 125 1300th Anniversary of the Kojiki | 26.00 | 20.00 |
| MS311 | 2012 (6) | 5,000 | Y95.2-98.2, 101.2, 125 Coin and Stamp Exhibition in Kagoshima | 20.00 | 20.00 |
| MS312 | 2012 (6) | 46,000 | Y95.2-98.2, 101.2, 125 Music box set, "Shiki" (Song of Four Seasons) | 26.00 | 20.00 |
| MS313 | 2012 (6) | 10,009 | Y95.2-98.2, 101.2, 125 Gifu Kokutai | 20.00 | 20.00 |
| MS314 | 2012 (6) | 4,000 | Y95.2-98.2, 101.2, 125 Tokyo Mint Fair 2012 | 20.00 | 23.00 |
| MS315 | 2013 (6) | 8,000 | Y95.2-98.2, 101.2, 125 36th World Money Festival | 18.00 | 18.00 |
| MS316 | 2013 (6) | 150,000 | Y95.2-98.2, 101.2, 125 "Mint Set 2013" | 17.00 | 17.00 |
| MS317 | 2013 (6) | 12,500 | Y95.2-98.2, 101.2, 125 "Japan" mint set | 19.00 | 19.00 |
| MS318 | 2013 (6) | 8,000 | Y95.2-98.2, 101.2, 125 "Anniversary" folder | 20.00 | 20.00 |
| MS318 | 2013 (6) | 8,000 | Y95.2-98.2, 101.2, 125 "Anniversary" folder | 20.00 | 20.00 |
| MS319 | 2013 (6) | 5,000 | Y95.2-98.2, 101.2, 125 6th Toshima Monozukuri set | 18.00 | 18.00 |
| MS320 | 2013 (6) | 60,000 | Y95.2-98.2, 101.2, 125 Osaka cherry blossoms | 18.00 | 18.00 |
| MS321 | 2013 (6) | 8,000 | Y95.2-98.2, 101.2, 125 Hiroshima Flower Tour | 18.00 | 18.00 |
| MS322 | 2013 (6) | 5,000 | Y95.2-98.2, 101.2, 125 Mint Exhibition in Hiroshima | 18.00 | 18.00 |
| MS323 | 2013 (6) | 6,000 | Y95.2-98.2, 101.2, 125 24th Tokyo International Coin Convention | 18.00 | 18.00 |
| MS324 | 2013 (6) | 50,000 | Y95.2-98.2, 101.2, 125 Music box set, "Memories of Summer" | 23.00 | 23.00 |
| MS325 | 2013 (6) | 4,500 | Y95.2-98.2, 101.2, 125 Eleventh Osaka Coin Show | 18.00 | 18.00 |
| MS326 | 2013 (6) | 50,000 | Y95.2-98.2, 101.2, 125 Music box set, "Buying Mittens" | 23.00 | 23.00 |
| MS327 | 2013 (6) | 4,000 | Y95.2-98.2, 101.2, 125 Coin and Stamp Exhibition in Sendai | 18.00 | 18.00 |
| MS328 | 2013 (6) | 8,000 | Y95.2-98.2, 101.2, 125 Sports Festival Tokyo | 18.00 | 18.00 |
| MS329 | 2013 (6) | 4,000 | Y95.2-98.2, 101.2, 125 Mint Exhibition in Tokyo | 18.00 | 18.00 |
| MS330 | 2013 (6) | 4,000 | Y95.2-98.2, 101.2, 125 Mint Saitama Criterium | 18.00 | 18.00 |
| MS331 | 2014 (6) | 8,000 | Y95.2-98.2, 101.2, 125 37th World Coin Festival | 18.00 | 18.00 |
| MS332 | 2014 (6) | est 145000 | Y95.2-98.2, 101.2, 125 "Mint Set 2014" | 17.00 | 17.00 |
| MS333 | 2014 (6) | est 12500 | Y95.2-98.2, 101.2, 125 "Japan" Coin Set | 19.00 | 19.00 |
| MS334 | 2014 (6) | est 8000 | Y95.2-98.2, 101.2, 125 "Anniversary" folder | 20.00 | 20.00 |
| MS335 | 2014 (6) | 5,000 | Y95.2-98.2, 101.2, 125 Toshima Monozukuri set | 18.00 | 18.00 |
| MS336 | 2014 (6) | 60,000 | Y95.2-98.2, 101.2, 125 Osaka cherry blossoms | 18.00 | 18.00 |
| MS337 | 2014 (6) | 7,000 | Y95.2-98.2, 101.2, 125 Hiroshima Flower Tour | 18.00 | 18.00 |
| MS338 | 2014 (6) | 70,000 | Y95.2-98.2, 101.2, 125 Mt. Fuji Cultural Heritage set | 22.00 | 22.00 |
| MS339 | 2014 (6) | 6,000 | Y95.2-98.2, 101.2, 125 25th Tokyo International Coin Convention | 18.00 | 18.00 |
| MS340 | 2014 (6) | 4,500 | Y95.2-98.2, 101.2, 125 Twelfth Osaka Coin Show | 18.00 | 18.00 |
| MS341 | 2014 (6) | 4,000 | Y95.2-98.2, 101.2, 125 Okayama Festival set | 18.00 | 18.00 |
| MS342 | 2014 (2) | 50,000 | Y125 and Bangladesh 2 taka coin set | 18.00 | 18.00 |
| MS343 | 2014 (6) | 4,000 | Y95.2-98.2, 101.2, 125 Mint Exhibition in Kawagoe | 18.00 | 18.00 |
| MS344 | 2014 (6) | 8,000 | Y95.2-98.2, 101.2, 125 Nagasaki National Polity Tournament set | 18.00 | 18.00 |

## PIEFORT PROOF SETS (PPS)

| KM# | Date | Mintage | Identification | Issue Price | Mkt Val |
|---|---|---|---|---|---|
| PS85 | 2010 (7) | 20,000 | Y95.2-98.2, 101.2, 125 120 years of Japan-Turkey Amity (with 50 lira Turkish coin on same subject included) | 144 | 150 |

## PROOF SETS

| KM# | Date | Mintage | Identification | Issue Price | Mkt Val |
|---|---|---|---|---|---|
| PS32 | 2001 (6) | 138,000 | Y#95.2-98.2, 101.2, 125 Mint Bureau Box | 62.50 | 47.00 |
| PS33 | 2001 (6) | 100,000 | Y#95.2-98.2, 101.2, 125 Old Type Coin Series (Trade dollar medallet) | 62.50 | 53.00 |
| PS34 | 2002 (6) | 141,000 | Y#95.2-98.2, 101.2, 125 Mint Bureau box | 62.50 | 53.00 |
| PS35 | 2002 (6) | 3,000 | Y#95.2-98.2, 101.2, 125 15th Anniversary of Proof Sets | 62.50 | 100 |
| PS36 | 2002 (6) | 95,000 | Y#95.2-98.2, 101.2, 125 Techno medal set | 62.50 | 53.00 |
| PS38 | 2002 (2) | 50,000 | Y#129, 130 World Cup | 385 | 550 |
| PS39 | 2003 (6) | 98,400 | Y#95.2-98.2, 101.2, 125 Mint Bureau box, with date plaquette | 67.50 | 53.00 |
| PSA40 | 2003 (6) | 6,600 | Y#95.2-98.2, 101.2, 125 Mint Bureau Box without Date Plaquette | 66.00 | 100 |
| PS40 | 2003 (6) | 90,000 | Y#95.2-98.2, 101.2, 125 Astro Boy | 115 | 100 |
| PS41 | 2003 (6) | 5,000 | Y#95.2-98.2, 101.2, 125 Tokyo Mint Fair - Mint Collection in Omote-Sando | 67.50 | 100 |
| PS42 | 2003 (6) | 70,000 | Y#95.2-98.2, 101.2, 125 Mickey Mouse | 125 | 120 |
| PS43 | 2003 (6) | 5,000 | Y#95.2-98.2, 101.2, 125 400th Anniversary - Establishment of Government in Edo | 67.50 | 165 |
| PS44 | 2004 (6) | 94,900 | Y#95.2-98.2, 101.2, 125 Mint Bureau box with date plaquette | 71.00 | 60.00 |
| PS45 | 2004 (6) | 13,100 | Y#95.2-98.2, 101.2, 125 Mint Bureau box without date plaquette | 70.00 | 100 |
| PS46 | 2004 (6) | 60,000 | Y#95.2-98.2, 101.2, 125 70h Anniversary - Pro Baseball | 120 | 145 |
| PS47 | 2004 (6) | 60,000 | Y#95.2-98.2, 101.2, 125 Techno Medal Series 2 | 71.00 | 60.00 |
| PS48 | 2004 (6) | 50,000 | Y#95.2-98.2, 101.2, 125 30th Birthday of Hello Kitty (cartoon character) | 120 | 150 |
| PS49 | 2004 (6) | 5,000 | Y#95.2-98.2, 101.2, 125 Tokyo Mint Fair - 40th Anniversary - Issue of Commemorative Coins | 71.00 | 100 |
| PS50 | 2004 (2) | 35,000 | Y#135-136 Expo 2005, Aichi | 425 | 500 |
| PS51 | 2005 (6) | 76,700 | Y#95.2-98.2, 101.2, 125 Mint Bureau Box with date plaquette | 71.00 | 65.00 |
| PS52 | 2005 (6) | 10,000 | Y#95.2-98.2, 101.2, 125 Mint Bureau Box without date plaquette | 70.00 | 100 |
| PS53 | 2005 (6) | 60,000 | Y#95.2-98.2, 101.2, 125 35th Anniversary of Doraemon (cartoon character) | 125 | 170 |
| PS54 | 2005 (6) | 34,000 | Y#95.2-98.2, 101.2, 125 50th Anniversary of One-Yen Aluminum Coin | 125 | 170 |
| PS55 | 2005 (6) | 30,000 | Y#95.2-98.2, 101.2, 125 50th Anniversary of the Pencil Rocket | 125 | 100 |
| PS56 | 2005 (6) | 47,300 | Y#95.2-98.2, 101.2, 125 Techno Medal Series #3 | 71.00 | 65.00 |
| PS57 | 2006 (6) | 63,400 | Y#95.2-98.2, 101.2, 125 Mint Bureau box with date plaquette | 71.00 | 65.00 |
| PS58 | 2006 (6) | 8,700 | Y#95.2-98.2, 101.2, 125 Mint Bureau Box without date plaquette | 70.00 | 65.00 |
| PS59 | 2006 (6) | 35,000 | Y#95.2-98.2, 101.2, 125 120th Anniversary of Cherry Blossom Viewing at the Mint | 125 | 125 |
| PS60 | 2006 (6) | 46,000 | Y#95.2-98.2, 101.2, 125 Australia-Japan Year of Exchange; includes Australian 1oz Silver coin KM#838 | 128 | 145 |
| PS61 | 2006 (6) | 49,900 | Y#95.2-98.2, 101.2, 125 50th Anniversary of Debut of Ishihara Yujiro (film actor) | 125 | 120 |
| PS62 | 2006 (6) | 4,000 | Y#95.2-98.2, 101.2, 125 Mint Bureau Tokyo Fair/"The Dawn of Modern Japan" | 71.00 | 150 |
| PS63 | 2006 (6) | 40,000 | Y#95.2-98.2, 101.2, 125 20-yen Gold Coin Memorial | 125 | 150 |
| PS64 | 2007 (6) | 53,200 | Y#95.2-98.2, 101.2, 125 Mint Bureau box, with date plaquette | 71.00 | 75.00 |
| PS65 | 2007 (6) | 7,000 | Y#95.2-98.2, 101.2, 125 Mint Bureau box, without date plaquette | 70.00 | 75.00 |
| PS66 | 2007 (6) | 35,000 | Y#95.2-98.2, 101.2, 125 60th Anniversary of Resumption of Cherry Blossom Viewing (at the Mint) | 125 | 125 |
| PS67 | 2007 (6) | 40,100 | Y#95.2-98.2, 101.2, 125 Sakamoto Ryohma (pre-Meiji loyalist, assassinated 1867) | 125 | 125 |
| PS68 | 2007 (6) | 33,500 | Y#95.2-98.2, 101.2, 125 11th IAAF World Championships in Athletics, Osaka (plus silver medal) | 125 | 125 |
| PS69 | 2007 (6) | 3,000 | Y#95.2-98.2, 101.2, 125 Mint Bureau Tokyo Fair/50th anniversary of introduction of the 100-yen coin | 71.00 | 75.00 |
| PS70 | 2007 (7) | 30,000 | Y#95.2-98.2, 101.2, 125 Japan-New Zealand Friendship (with NZ KM#232 coin) | 125 | 120 |
| PS71 | 2008 (6) | 55,200 | Y95.2-95.2, 101.2, 125 Mint Bureau box with date plaquette | 75.00 | 75.00 |
| PS72 | 2008 (6) | 6,000 | Y95.2-98.2, 101.2, 125 Mint Bureau box without date plaquette | 73.50 | 75.00 |
| PS73 | 2008 (6) | 27,000 | Y95.2-98.2, 101.2, 125 Cherry blossom viewing (at the mint) | 130 | 130 |
| PS74 | 2008 (7) | 44,000 | Y95.2-Y98.2, 101.2, 125 150th Anniversary of Japanese-French relations (with French 1.5 euro coin KM1550.) | 130 | 110 |
| PS75 | 2008 (6) | 33,000 | Y95.2-98.2, 101.2, 125 1300th Anniversary of the Wado Kaichin coin (with a silver replica) | 100 | 100 |
| PS76 | 2008 (6) | 3,000 | Y95.2-Y98.2, 101.2, 125 Mint Bureau Tokyo Fair - Japan Attractions | 79.00 | 75.00 |
| PS77 | 2009 (6) | 48,400 | Y95.2-Y98.2, 101.2, 125 Mint Bureau box with date plaquette | 79.00 | 70.00 |
| PS78 | 2009 (6) | 5,600 | Y95.2-Y98.2, 101.2, 125 Mint Bureau box without date plaquette | 77.50 | 80.00 |
| PS79 | 2009 (6) | 25,000 | Y95.2-Y98.2, 101.2, 125 Cherry blossom viewing (at the mint) | 136 | 135 |
| PS80 | 2009 (7) | 25,000 | Y95.2-Y98.2, 101.2, 125 80 years of Japan/Canada Amity (with $5 Canadian coin KM#1036 included) | 136 | 135 |
| PS81 | 2009 (7) | 30,000 | Y95.2-Y98.2, 101.2, 125 400 years of Japan/Dutch Commerce (with Dutch €5 coin, KM287 included) | 136 | 135 |
| PS82 | 2009 (6) | 3,000 | Y95.2-98.2, 101.2, 125 Mint Bureau Tokyo Fair/"Hallmark 80 years" | 83.00 | 85.00 |
| PS83 | 2010 (6) | 41,687 | Y95.2-98.2, 101.2, 125 Mint Bureau box, with date plaquette | 83.00 | 80.00 |
| PS84 | 2010 (6) | 20,000 | Y95.2-98.2, 101.2, 125 Cherry blossom viewing (at the Mint) | 144 | 150 |

| | | | | | |
|---|---|---|---|---|---|
| PS86 | 2010 (6) | 20,000 | Y95.2-98.2, 101.2, 125 Techno set, with medal included showing iridescent features (new mint technology) | 111 | 115 |
| PS87 | 2010 (7) | 20,000 | Y95.2-98.2, 101.2, 125 "A Dog of Flanders" set, with Belgian €20 KM#305 proof coin included | 144 | 150 |
| PS88 | 2010 (6) | 5,500 | Y95.2-98.2, 101.2, 125 Mint Bureau box, without date plaquette | 88.00 | 100 |
| PS89 | 2010 (6) | 3,000 | Y95.2-98.2, 101.2, 125 Tokyo Mint Fair, celebrating coin designers | 90.00 | 100 |
| PS90 | 2011 (6) | 40,100 | Y95.2-98.2, 101.2, 125 Mint Bureau box, with date plaquette | 90.00 | 75.00 |
| PS91 | 2011 (6) | 5,500 | Y95.2-98.2, 101.2, 125 Mint Bureau box, without date plaquette | 88.00 | 100 |
| PS92 | 2011 (6) | 19,400 | Y95.2-98.2, 101.2, 125 Cherry blossom viewing (at the Mint) | 156 | 90.00 |
| PS93 | 2011 (6) | 3,000 | Y95.2-98.2, 101.2, 125 Tokyo Mint Fair, with extra medal for 60th anniv of the 10-yen coin | 156 | 100 |
| PS94 | 2011 (6) | 20,000 | Y95.2-98.2, 101.2, 125 Techno set, with medal included showing new mint technology | 120 | 85.00 |
| PS95 | 2011 (7) | 20,000 | Y95.2-98.2, 101.2, 125 World Wildlife Fund 50th Anniversary, with Gt Britain 50 pence KM1196 | 156 | 100 |
| PS96 | 2012 (6) | 38,220 | Y95.2-98.2, 101.2, 125 Mint Bureau box, with date plaquette | 83.00 | 75.00 |
| PS97 | 2012 (6) | 5,000 | Y95.2-98.2, 101.2, 125 Mint Bureau box, without date plaquette | 82.00 | 100 |
| PS98 | 2012 (6) | 20,000 | Y95.2-98.2, 101.2, 125 Cherry blossom viewing (at the Mint) | 144 | 90.00 |
| PS99 | 2012 (6) | 22,000 | Y95.2-98.2, 101.2, 125 with medal for 30th anniversary of 500 yen coin | 144 | 100 |
| PS100 | 2012 (6) | 2,780 | Y95.2-98.2, 101.2, 125 Tokyo Mint Fair | 144 | 75.00 |
| PS101 | 2012 (7) | 15,000 | Y95.2-98.2, 101.2, 125 60th Aniversary of Sri Lanka-Japan Diplomatic Relations (with 1000 rupee Sri Lanka silver coin on same subject) | 144 | 100 |
| PS102 | 2013 (6) | 37,500 | Y95.2-98.2, 101.2, 125 Mint Bureau box, with date plaquette | 80.00 | 80.00 |
| PS103 | 2013 (6) | 5,000 | Y95.2-98.2, 101.2, 125 Mint Bureau box, without date plaquette | 75.00 | 78.00 |
| PS104 | 2013 (6) | 20,000 | Y95.2-98.2, 101.2, 125 Cherry blossom viewing (at the Mint) | 130 | 140 |
| PS105 | 2013 (7) | 18,000 | Y95.2-98.2, 101.2, 125 400th Anniversary of Japan-Spain Relations, with Spanish €10 silver coin commemorating the same relations | 135 | 140 |
| PS106 | 2013 (6) | 20,000 | Y95.2-98.2, 101.2, 125 Nostalgic Small Coins set (commemorating 60 years since sen, rin, and mon coinage was abolished) | 130 | 140 |
| PS107 | 2013 (6) | 3,000 | Y95.2-98.2, 101.2, 125 Mint Fair at Tokyo (commemorating 25 years of the Heisei Era) | 75.00 | 78.00 |
| PS108 | 2014 (6) | | Y95.2-98.2, 101.2, 125 Mint Bureau box, with date plaquette | 75.00 | 75.00 |
| PS109 | 2014 (6) | | Y95.2-98.2, 101.2, 125 Mint Bureau box, without date plaquette | 75.00 | 75.00 |
| PS110 | 2014 (6) | 16,000 | Y95.2-98.2, 101.2, 125 Cherry blossom viewing (at the Mint) | 133 | 135 |
| PS111 | 2014 (6) | 15,000 | Y95.2-98.2, 101.2, 125 Commemorating 50 years of coinage | 133 | 135 |

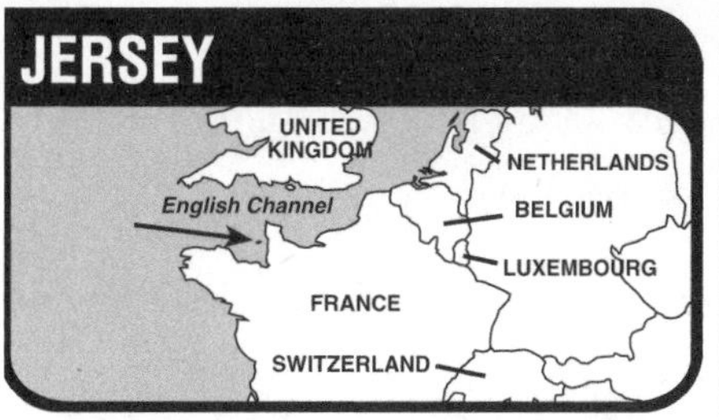


The Bailiwick of Jersey, a British Crown dependency located in the English Channel 12 miles (19 km.) west of Normandy, France, has an area of 45 sq. mi. (117 sq. km.) and a population of 74,000. Capital: St. Helier. The economy is based on agriculture and cattle breeding – the importation of cattle is prohibited to protect the purity of the island's world-famous strain of milk cows.

The island together with the Bailiwick of Guernsey, is the only part of the Dutchy of Normandy belonging to the British Crown, has been a possession of Britain since the Norman conquest of 1066. Jersey is administered by its own laws and customs. Unless the island is mentioned specifically, acts passed by the British Parliament are not applicable to Jersey. During WW II, German troops occupied the island from 1940 to 1945.

**RULER**

British

**MINT MARK**

H - Heaton, Birmingham

# BRITISH DEPENDENCY

## DECIMAL COINAGE

100 New Pence = 1 Pound

### KM# 103 PENNY

3.56 g., Copper Plated Steel, 20.3 mm. **Ruler:** Elizabeth II **Obv:** Crowned head right **Rev:** Le Hoeq Watchtower, St. Clement **Edge:** Plain

| Date | Mintage | VF20 | XF40 | MS60 | MS63 | MS65 |
|---|---|---|---|---|---|---|
| 2002 | 1,520,000 | — | 0.15 | 0.45 | 0.65 | 1.25 |
| 2003 | 1,575,000 | — | 0.15 | 0.45 | 0.65 | 1.25 |
| 2005 | — | — | 0.15 | 0.45 | 0.65 | 1.25 |
| 2006 | 585,000 | — | 0.15 | 0.45 | 0.65 | 1.25 |
| 2008 | 4,800,000 | — | 0.15 | 0.45 | 0.65 | 1.25 |
| 2012 | — | — | 0.15 | 0.45 | 0.65 | 1.25 |

### KM# 104 2 PENCE

7.12 g., Copper Plated Steel, 25.91 mm. **Ruler:** Elizabeth II **Obv:** Head with tiara right **Rev:** L'Hermitage, St. Helier **Edge:** Plain

| Date | Mintage | VF20 | XF40 | MS60 | MS63 | MS65 |
|---|---|---|---|---|---|---|
| 2002 | 1,259,000 | — | 0.20 | 0.40 | 0.75 | 1.50 |
| 2003 | 10,000 | — | 0.20 | 0.40 | 0.75 | 1.50 |
| 2005 | 400,000 | — | 0.20 | 0.40 | 0.75 | 1.50 |
| 2006 | 1,200,000 | — | 0.20 | 0.40 | 0.75 | 1.50 |
| 2008 | 2,459,000 | — | 0.20 | 0.40 | 0.75 | 1.50 |
| 2013 | — | — | 0.20 | 0.40 | 0.75 | 1.50 |

### KM# 105 5 PENCE

3.25 g., Copper-Nickel, 18 mm. **Ruler:** Elizabeth II **Obv:** Head with tiara right **Rev:** Seymour Tower, Grouville, L'Avathigon **Edge:** Reeded

| Date | Mintage | VF20 | XF40 | MS60 | MS63 | MS65 |
|---|---|---|---|---|---|---|
| 2002 | 1,200,000 | — | 0.20 | 0.40 | 0.80 | 1.50 |
| 2003 | 1,005,000 | — | 0.20 | 0.40 | 0.80 | 1.50 |
| 2006 | 1,200,000 | — | 0.20 | 0.40 | 0.80 | 1.50 |
| 2008 | 3,600,000 | — | 0.20 | 0.40 | 0.80 | 1.50 |
| 2012 | — | — | 0.20 | 0.40 | 0.80 | 1.50 |

### KM# 106 10 PENCE

6.50 g., Copper-Nickel, 24.5 mm. **Ruler:** Elizabeth II **Obv:** Head with tiara right **Rev:** La Hougne Bie, Faldouet, St. Martin

| Date | Mintage | VF20 | XF40 | MS60 | MS63 | MS65 |
|---|---|---|---|---|---|---|
| 2002 | 500,000 | — | — | — | 1.25 | 1.50 |
| 2003 | 10,000 | — | — | — | 1.25 | 1.50 |
| 2005 | — | — | — | — | 1.25 | 1.50 |
| 2006 | — | — | — | — | 1.25 | 1.50 |
| 2007 | 630,000 | — | — | — | 1.25 | 1.50 |
| 2010 | — | — | — | — | 1.25 | 1.50 |
| 2012 | — | — | — | — | 1.25 | 1.50 |

### KM# 107 20 PENCE

5.00 g., Copper-Nickel, 21.4 mm. **Ruler:** Elizabeth II **Obv:** Head with tiara right

| Date | Mintage | VF20 | XF40 | MS60 | MS63 | MS65 |
|---|---|---|---|---|---|---|
| 2002 | 975,500 | — | — | 0.75 | 1.25 | 2.00 |
| 2003 | 10,000 | — | — | 0.75 | 1.25 | 2.00 |
| 2005 | 500,000 | — | — | 0.75 | 1.25 | 2.00 |
| 2006 | 500,000 | — | — | 0.75 | 1.25 | 2.00 |
| 2007 | 780,000 | — | — | 0.75 | 1.25 | 2.00 |
| 2009 | 1,500,000 | — | — | 0.75 | 1.25 | 2.00 |
| 2012 | — | — | — | 0.75 | 1.25 | 2.00 |

### KM# 108 50 PENCE

8.00 g., Copper-Nickel, 27.3 mm. **Ruler:** Elizabeth II **Obv:** Crowned bust right **Rev:** Gothic gate arch **Edge:** Plain **Shape:** 7-sided

| Date | Mintage | VF20 | XF40 | MS60 | MS63 | MS65 |
|---|---|---|---|---|---|---|
| 2003 | 10,000 | — | 0.75 | 1.00 | 2.00 | 3.00 |
| 2005 | 200,000 | — | 0.75 | 1.00 | 2.00 | 3.00 |
| 2006 | 300,000 | — | 0.75 | 1.00 | 2.00 | 3.00 |
| 2009 | 480,000 | — | 0.75 | 1.00 | 2.00 | 3.00 |

### KM# 123 50 PENCE

8.00 g., Copper-Nickel, 27.3 mm. **Ruler:** Elizabeth II **Subject:** Coronation, 50th Anniversary **Obv:** Crowned head right **Rev:** Archbishop crowning Queen **Edge:** Plain **Shape:** 7-sided

| Date | Mintage | VF20 | XF40 | MS60 | MS63 | MS65 |
|---|---|---|---|---|---|---|
| 2003 | 10,000 | — | — | — | 2.50 | 3.00 |

### KM# 123a 50 PENCE

8.00 g., 0.925 Silver 0.2379 oz. ASW, 27.3 mm. **Ruler:** Elizabeth II **Subject:** Coronation, 50th Anniversary **Obv:** Crowned head right **Rev:** Archbishop crowning Queen **Edge:** Plain **Shape:** 7-sided

| Date | Mintage | VF20 | XF40 | MS60 | MS63 | MS65 |
|---|---|---|---|---|---|---|
| 2003 | 15,000 | PF63 | 18.00 | PF65 | 22.00 | |

**KM# 148 50 PENCE**

8.00 g., Copper-Nickel, 27.3 mm. **Ruler:** Elizabeth II **Subject:** Coronation, 50th Anniversary **Rev:** Regalia in quatrilobe **Shape:** 7-sided

| Date | Mintage | VF20 | XF40 | MS60 | MS63 | MS65 |
|---|---|---|---|---|---|---|
| 2003 | — | — | — | — | 2.50 | 3.50 |

**KM# 148a 50 PENCE**

8.00 g., 0.925 Silver 0.2379 oz. ASW, 27.3 mm. **Ruler:** Elizabeth II **Subject:** Coronation, 50th Anniversary **Rev:** Regalia in quatrilobe **Shape:** 7-sided

| Date | Mintage | VF20 | XF40 | MS60 | MS63 | MS65 |
|---|---|---|---|---|---|---|
| 2003 | 15,000 | PF63 18.00 | PF65 22.00 | | | |

**KM# 149 50 PENCE**

8.00 g., Copper-Nickel, 27.3 mm. **Ruler:** Elizabeth II **Subject:** Coronation, 50th Anniversary **Rev:** Queen facing, seated on throne **Shape:** 7-sided

| Date | Mintage | VF20 | XF40 | MS60 | MS63 | MS65 |
|---|---|---|---|---|---|---|
| 2003 | 10,000 | — | — | — | 2.50 | 3.50 |

**KM# 149a 50 PENCE**

8.00 g., 0.925 Silver 0.2379 oz. ASW, 27.3 mm. **Ruler:** Elizabeth II **Subject:** Coronation, 50th Anniversary **Rev:** Queen facing, seated on throne **Shape:** 7-sided

| Date | Mintage | VF20 | XF40 | MS60 | MS63 | MS65 |
|---|---|---|---|---|---|---|
| 2003 | 15,000 | PF63 18.00 | PF65 22.00 | | | |

**KM# 150 50 PENCE**

8.00 g., Copper-Nickel, 27.3 mm. **Ruler:** Elizabeth II **Subject:** Coronation, 50th Anniversary **Rev:** Crown, scepter and shield **Shape:** 7-sided

| Date | Mintage | VF20 | XF40 | MS60 | MS63 | MS65 |
|---|---|---|---|---|---|---|
| 2003 | 10,000 | — | — | — | 2.50 | 3.50 |

**KM# 150a 50 PENCE**

8.00 g., 0.925 Silver 0.2379 oz. ASW, 27.3 mm. **Ruler:** Elizabeth II **Subject:** Coronation, 50th Anniversary **Rev:** Crown, sceptre and shield **Shape:** 7-sided

| Date | Mintage | VF20 | XF40 | MS60 | MS63 | MS65 |
|---|---|---|---|---|---|---|
| 2003 | 15,000 | PF63 18.00 | PF65 22.00 | | | |

**KM# 101 POUND**

9.50 g., Nickel-Brass, 22.5 mm. **Ruler:** Elizabeth II **Obv:** Head with tiara right **Rev:** Schooner, Resolute **Edge Lettering:** CAESAREA INSULA

| Date | Mintage | VF20 | XF40 | MS60 | MS63 | MS65 |
|---|---|---|---|---|---|---|
| 2003 | 10,000 | — | — | — | 4.00 | 4.50 |
| 2005 | 200,000 | — | — | — | 4.00 | 4.50 |
| 2006 | 93,000 | — | — | — | 4.00 | 4.50 |

**KM# 160 POUND**

1.24 g., 0.999 Gold 0.0398 oz. AGW, 13.92 mm. **Ruler:** Elizabeth II **Subject:** Trafalgar, 200th Anniversary

| Date | Mintage | VF20 | XF40 | MS60 | MS63 | MS65 |
|---|---|---|---|---|---|---|
| 2005 | — | PF65 100 | | | | |

**KM# 173 POUND**

1.24 g., 0.999 Gold 0.0398 oz. AGW, 13.92 mm. **Ruler:** Elizabeth II **Subject:** Princess Diana

| Date | Mintage | VF20 | XF40 | MS60 | MS63 | MS65 |
|---|---|---|---|---|---|---|
| 2007 | — | PF65 100 | | | | |

**KM# 102 2 POUNDS**

12.00 g., Bi-Metallic Copper-Nickel center in Nickel-Brass ring, 28.4 mm. **Ruler:** Elizabeth II **Obv:** Head with tiara right **Rev:** Latent image value within circle of assorted shields **Edge Lettering:** CAESAREA INSULA

| Date | Mintage | VF20 | XF40 | MS60 | MS63 | MS65 |
|---|---|---|---|---|---|---|
| 2002 | — | — | — | — | 8.00 | 10.00 |
| 2003 | 10,000 | — | — | — | 8.00 | 10.00 |
| 2006 | 3,500 | — | — | — | 8.00 | 10.00 |

**KM# 111 5 POUNDS**

28.28 g., Copper-Nickel, 38.6 mm. **Ruler:** Elizabeth II **Subject:** Princess Diana **Obv:** Crowned head right **Rev:** Diana's cameo above people **Edge:** Reeded

| Date | Mintage | VF20 | XF40 | MS60 | MS63 | MS65 |
|---|---|---|---|---|---|---|
| 2002 | — | — | — | — | 12.00 | 14.00 |

**KM# 111a 5 POUNDS**

28.28 g., 0.925 Silver 0.841 oz. ASW, 38.6 mm. **Ruler:** Elizabeth II **Subject:** Princess Diana **Obv:** Crowned head right **Rev:** Diana's cameo above people **Edge:** Reeded

| Date | Mintage | VF20 | XF40 | MS60 | MS63 | MS65 |
|---|---|---|---|---|---|---|
| 2002 | 20,000 | PF63 40.00 | PF65 45.00 | | | |

**KM# 111b 5 POUNDS**

39.94 g., 0.9167 Gold 1.1771 oz. AGW, 38.6 mm. **Ruler:** Elizabeth II **Subject:** Princess Diana **Obv:** Crowned head right **Rev:** Diana's cameo above people **Edge:** Reeded

| Date | Mintage | VF20 | XF40 | MS60 | MS63 | MS65 |
|---|---|---|---|---|---|---|
| 2002 | 100 | PF65 2,150 | | | | |

**KM# 113 5 POUNDS**

28.28 g., Copper-Nickel, 38.6 mm. **Ruler:** Elizabeth II **Subject:** Queen Mother **Obv:** Crowned head right **Rev:** Queen Mother's bust right (circa 1918) **Rev. Legend:** HER MAJESTY QUEEN ELIZABETH THE QUEEN MOTHER **Edge:** Reeded

| Date | Mintage | VF20 | XF40 | MS60 | MS63 | MS65 |
|---|---|---|---|---|---|---|
| 2002 | — | — | — | — | 12.00 | 14.00 |

**KM# 113a 5 POUNDS**

28.28 g., 0.925 Silver 0.841 oz. ASW, 38.6 mm. **Ruler:** Elizabeth II **Subject:** Queen Mother **Obv:** Crowned head right **Rev:** Queen Mother's bust right, (circa 1918) **Rev. Legend:** HER MAJESTY QUEEN ELIZABETH THE QUEEN MOTHER **Edge:** Reeded

| Date | Mintage | VF20 | XF40 | MS60 | MS63 | MS65 |
|---|---|---|---|---|---|---|
| 2002 | 15,000 | PF63 45.00 | PF65 50.00 | | | |

**KM# 113b 5 POUNDS**

39.94 g., 0.9166 Gold 1.177 oz. AGW, 38.6 mm. **Ruler:** Elizabeth II **Subject:** Queen Mother **Obv:** Crowned head right **Rev:** Queen Mother's bust right, (circa 1918) **Rev. Legend:** HER MAJESTY QUEEN ELIZABETH THE QUEEN MOTHER **Edge:** Reeded

| Date | Mintage | VF20 | XF40 | MS60 | MS63 | MS65 |
|---|---|---|---|---|---|---|
| 2002 | 250 | PF65 2,100 | | | | |

**KM# 115 5 POUNDS**

28.28 g., Copper-Nickel, 38.6 mm. **Ruler:** Elizabeth II **Subject:** Golden Jubilee **Obv:** Crowned head right **Rev:** Abbey procession scene **Edge:** Reeded

| Date | Mintage | VF20 | XF40 | MS60 | MS63 | MS65 |
|---|---|---|---|---|---|---|
| 2002 | — | — | — | — | 12.00 | 14.00 |

**KM# 115a 5 POUNDS**

28.28 g., 0.925 Silver 0.841 oz. ASW, 38.6 mm. **Ruler:** Elizabeth II **Subject:** Golden Jubilee **Obv:** Crowned head right **Rev:** Abbey procession scene **Edge:** Reeded

| Date | Mintage | VF20 | XF40 | MS60 | MS63 | MS65 |
|---|---|---|---|---|---|---|
| 2002 | 20,000 | PF63 45.00 | PF65 50.00 | | | |

**KM# 115b 5 POUNDS**

39.94 g., 0.9166 Gold 1.177 oz. AGW, 38.6 mm. **Ruler:** Elizabeth II **Subject:** Golden Jubilee **Obv:** Crowned head right **Rev:** Abbey procession scene **Edge:** Reeded

| Date | Mintage | VF20 | XF40 | MS60 | MS63 | MS65 |
|---|---|---|---|---|---|---|
| 2002 | 100 | PF65 2,150 | | | | |

**KM# 117 5 POUNDS**

28.28 g., Copper-Nickel, 38.6 mm. **Ruler:** Elizabeth II **Subject:** Duke of Wellington **Obv:** Crowned head right **Rev:** Wellington's portrait with multicolor infantry scene **Edge:** Reeded

| Date | Mintage | VF20 | XF40 | MS60 | MS63 | MS65 |
|---|---|---|---|---|---|---|
| 2002 | — | — | — | — | 12.00 | 14.00 |

**KM# 117a 5 POUNDS**

28.28 g., 0.925 Silver 0.841 oz. ASW, 38.6 mm. **Ruler:** Elizabeth II **Subject:** Duke of Wellington **Obv:** Crowned head right **Rev:** Wellington's portrait with multicolor infantry scene **Edge:** Reeded

| Date | Mintage | VF20 | XF40 | MS60 | MS63 | MS65 |
|---|---|---|---|---|---|---|
| 2002 | 15,000 | PF63 45.00 | PF65 50.00 | | | |

**KM# 117b 5 POUNDS**

39.94 g., 0.9166 Gold 1.177 oz. AGW, 38.6 mm. **Ruler:** Elizabeth II **Subject:** Duke of Wellington **Obv:** Crowned head right **Rev:** Wellington's portrait with multicolor infantry scene **Edge:** Reeded

| Date | Mintage | VF20 | XF40 | MS60 | MS63 | MS65 |
|---|---|---|---|---|---|---|
| 2002 | 200 | PF65 2,100 | | | | |

**KM# 119 5 POUNDS**

28.28 g., Copper-Nickel, 38.6 mm. **Ruler:** Elizabeth II **Subject:** Golden Jubilee **Obv:** Crowned head right **Rev:** Honor guard and memorial **Edge:** Reeded

| Date | Mintage | VF20 | XF40 | MS60 | MS63 | MS65 |
|---|---|---|---|---|---|---|
| 2003 | — | — | — | — | 12.00 | 14.00 |

**KM# 119a 5 POUNDS**

28.28 g., 0.925 Silver 0.841 oz. ASW, 38.6 mm. **Ruler:** Elizabeth II **Subject:** Golden Jubilee **Obv:** Crowned head right **Rev:** Honor guard and monument **Edge:** Reeded

| Date | Mintage | VF20 | XF40 | MS60 | MS63 | MS65 |
|---|---|---|---|---|---|---|
| 2003 | 20,000 | PF63 45.00 | PF65 50.00 | | | |

**KM# 119b 5 POUNDS**

39.94 g., 0.9166 Gold 1.177 oz. AGW, 38.6 mm. **Ruler:** Elizabeth II **Subject:** Golden Jubilee **Obv:** Crowned head right **Rev:** Honor guard and monument **Edge:** Reeded

| Date | Mintage | VF20 | XF40 | MS60 | MS63 | MS65 |
|---|---|---|---|---|---|---|
| 2003 | 250 | PF65 2,100 | | | | |

**KM# 121 5 POUNDS**
28.28 g., Copper-Nickel, 38.6 mm. **Ruler:** Elizabeth II **Obv:** Crowned head right **Rev:** Bust of Prince William facing and crowned arms with supporters **Edge:** Reeded

| Date | Mintage | VF20 | XF40 | MS60 | MS63 | MS65 |
|---|---|---|---|---|---|---|
| 2003 | — | — | — | — | 15.00 | 18.00 |

**KM# 121a 5 POUNDS**
28.28 g., 0.925 Silver 0.841 oz. ASW, 38.6 mm. **Ruler:** Elizabeth II **Obv:** Crowned head right **Rev:** Bust of Prince William facing and crowned arms with supporters **Edge:** Reeded

| Date | Mintage | VF20 | XF40 | MS60 | MS63 | MS65 |
|---|---|---|---|---|---|---|
| 2003 | 5,000 | PF63 42.00 | PF65 47.00 | | | |

**KM# 121b 5 POUNDS**
39.94 g., 0.9166 Gold 1.177 oz. AGW, 38.6 mm. **Ruler:** Elizabeth II **Obv:** Crowned head right **Rev:** Bust of Prince William facing and crowned arms with supporters **Edge:** Reeded

| Date | Mintage | VF20 | XF40 | MS60 | MS63 | MS65 |
|---|---|---|---|---|---|---|
| 2003 | 200 | PF65 2,100 | | | | |

**KM# 130 5 POUNDS**
28.28 g., Copper-Nickel, 38.6 mm. **Ruler:** Elizabeth II **Subject:** Sir Francis Drake **Obv:** Crowned head right

| Date | Mintage | VF20 | XF40 | MS60 | MS63 | MS65 |
|---|---|---|---|---|---|---|
| 2003 | — | — | — | — | 12.00 | 14.00 |

**KM# 130a 5 POUNDS**
28.28 g., 0.925 Silver 0.841 oz. ASW, 38.6 mm. **Ruler:** Elizabeth II **Subject:** Drake **Obv:** Crowned head right **Rev:** Naval leader Sir Francis Drake

| Date | Mintage | VF20 | XF40 | MS60 | MS63 | MS65 |
|---|---|---|---|---|---|---|
| 2003 | — | PF63 65.00 | PF65 75.00 | | | |

**KM# 131 5 POUNDS**
28.28 g., Copper-Nickel, 38.6 mm. **Ruler:** Elizabeth II **Subject:** Sovereign of the Seas **Obv:** Crowned head right **Rev:** Sailing ship

| Date | Mintage | VF20 | XF40 | MS60 | MS63 | MS65 |
|---|---|---|---|---|---|---|
| 2003 | — | — | — | — | 12.00 | 14.00 |

**KM# 131a 5 POUNDS**
28.28 g., 0.925 Silver 0.841 oz. ASW, 38.6 mm. **Ruler:** Elizabeth II **Subject:** Sovereign Of The Seas **Obv:** Crowned head right **Rev:** The Sovereign of the Seas ship

| Date | Mintage | VF20 | XF40 | MS60 | MS63 | MS65 |
|---|---|---|---|---|---|---|
| 2003 | — | PF63 65.00 | PF65 75.00 | | | |

**KM# 132 5 POUNDS**
28.28 g., Copper-Nickel, 38.6 mm. **Ruler:** Elizabeth II **Obv:** Crowned head right **Rev:** WWI naval leader Sir John Fisher

| Date | Mintage | VF20 | XF40 | MS60 | MS63 | MS65 |
|---|---|---|---|---|---|---|
| 2003 | — | — | — | — | 12.00 | 14.00 |

**KM# 132a 5 POUNDS**
28.28 g., 0.925 Silver 0.841 oz. ASW, 38.6 mm. **Ruler:** Elizabeth II **Subject:** John Fisher **Obv:** Crowned head right **Rev:** WWI Naval leader Sir John Fisher

| Date | Mintage | VF20 | XF40 | MS60 | MS63 | MS65 |
|---|---|---|---|---|---|---|
| 2003 | — | PF63 65.00 | PF65 75.00 | | | |

**KM# 133 5 POUNDS**
28.28 g., Copper-Nickel, 38.6 mm. **Ruler:** Elizabeth II **Subject:** HMS Victory **Obv:** Crowned head right **Rev:** Nelson's flagship HMS Victory

| Date | Mintage | VF20 | XF40 | MS60 | MS63 | MS65 |
|---|---|---|---|---|---|---|
| 2003 | — | — | — | — | 12.00 | 14.00 |

**KM# 133a 5 POUNDS**
28.28 g., 0.925 Silver 0.841 oz. ASW, 38.6 mm. **Ruler:** Elizabeth II **Subject:** HMS Victory **Obv:** Crowned head right **Rev:** Nelson's flag ship HMS Victory, multicolor flag at top

| Date | Mintage | VF20 | XF40 | MS60 | MS63 | MS65 |
|---|---|---|---|---|---|---|
| 2004 | — | PF63 65.00 | PF65 75.00 | | | |

**KM# 134 5 POUNDS**
28.28 g., Copper-Nickel, 38.6 mm. **Ruler:** Elizabeth II **Obv:** Crowned head right **Rev:** WWII Admiral Andrew B. Cunningham

| Date | Mintage | VF20 | XF40 | MS60 | MS63 | MS65 |
|---|---|---|---|---|---|---|
| 2003 | — | — | — | — | 12.00 | 14.00 |

**KM# 134a 5 POUNDS**
28.28 g., 0.925 Silver 0.841 oz. ASW, 38.6 mm. **Ruler:** Elizabeth II **Subject:** Cunningham **Obv:** Crowned head right **Rev:** WWII Admiral Andrew B. Cunningham

| Date | Mintage | VF20 | XF40 | MS60 | MS63 | MS65 |
|---|---|---|---|---|---|---|
| 2003 | — | PF63 65.00 | PF65 75.00 | | | |

**KM# 135 5 POUNDS**
28.28 g., Copper-Nickel, 38.6 mm. **Ruler:** Elizabeth II **Subject:** HMS Conqueror **Obv:** Crowned head right **Rev:** Submarine HMS Conqueror

| Date | Mintage | VF20 | XF40 | MS60 | MS63 | MS65 |
|---|---|---|---|---|---|---|
| 2003 | — | — | — | — | 12.00 | 14.00 |

**KM# 135a 5 POUNDS**
28.28 g., 0.925 Silver 0.841 oz. ASW, 38.6 mm. **Ruler:** Elizabeth II **Subject:** Conqueror **Obv:** Crowned head right **Rev:** Submarine HMS Conqueror

| Date | Mintage | VF20 | XF40 | MS60 | MS63 | MS65 |
|---|---|---|---|---|---|---|
| 2003 | — | PF63 65.00 | PF65 75.00 | | | |

**KM# 144 5 POUNDS**
28.28 g., Copper-Nickel, 38.6 mm. **Ruler:** Elizabeth II **Subject:** History of the Royal Navy **Rev:** Five heads, four ships and a sub

| Date | Mintage | VF20 | XF40 | MS60 | MS63 | MS65 |
|---|---|---|---|---|---|---|
| 2003 | — | — | — | — | 12.00 | 14.00 |

**KM# 144a 5 POUNDS**
28.28 g., 0.925 Silver 0.841 oz. ASW, 38.61 mm. **Ruler:** Elizabeth II **Subject:** History of the Royal Navy **Obv:** Head left with tiarra **Obv. Legend:** ELIZABETH II BALIWICK - OF JERSEY **Rev:** Five heads of King Alfred the Great, Sir Francis Drake, Admirals Horatio Nelson, John Fisher and John Woodward at five ships, colored flag at top **Edge:** Reeded

| Date | Mintage | VF20 | XF40 | MS60 | MS63 | MS65 |
|---|---|---|---|---|---|---|
| 2003 | — | PF63 65.00 | PF65 75.00 | | | |

**KM# 124 5 POUNDS**
28.28 g., Copper-Nickel, 38.6 mm. **Ruler:** Elizabeth II **Obv:** Crowned head right **Rev:** British Horsa gliders in flight **Edge:** Reeded **Note:** D-Day

| Date | Mintage | VF20 | XF40 | MS60 | MS63 | MS65 |
|---|---|---|---|---|---|---|
| 2004 | — | — | — | — | 15.00 | 17.00 |

**KM# 124a 5 POUNDS**
28.28 g., 0.925 Silver 0.841 oz. ASW, 38.6 mm. **Ruler:** Elizabeth II **Obv:** Crowned head right **Rev:** British Horsa gliders in flight

| Date | Mintage | VF20 | XF40 | MS60 | MS63 | MS65 |
|---|---|---|---|---|---|---|
| 2004 | 10,000 | PF63 75.00 | PF65 85.00 | | | |

**KM# 124b 5 POUNDS**
39.94 g., 0.9167 Gold 1.1771 oz. AGW, 38.6 mm. **Ruler:** Elizabeth II **Obv:** Crowned head right **Rev:** British Horsa gliders in flight

| Date | Mintage | VF20 | XF40 | MS60 | MS63 | MS65 |
|---|---|---|---|---|---|---|
| 2004 | 500 | PF65 2,100 | | | | |

**KM# 126 5 POUNDS**
28.28 g., Copper-Nickel, 38.6 mm. **Ruler:** Elizabeth II **Subject:** 150th Anniversary of the Crimean War **Obv:** Crowned head right **Rev:** Charge of the Light Brigade scene with one blue uniform behind the Earl of Cardigan **Edge:** Reeded

| Date | Mintage | VF20 | XF40 | MS60 | MS63 | MS65 |
|---|---|---|---|---|---|---|
| 2004 plain | — | — | — | — | 22.00 | 25.00 |

**KM# 126a 5 POUNDS**
28.28 g., 0.925 Silver 0.841 oz. ASW, 38.6 mm. **Ruler:** Elizabeth II **Obv:** Crowned head right **Rev:** Charge of the Light Brigade scene with one blue uniform behind the Earl of Cardigan **Edge:** Reeded

| Date | Mintage | VF20 | XF40 | MS60 | MS63 | MS65 |
|---|---|---|---|---|---|---|
| 2004 | 10,000 | PF63 75.00 | PF65 85.00 | | | |

**KM# 126b 5 POUNDS**
39.94 g., 0.9166 Gold 1.177 oz. AGW, 38.6 mm. **Ruler:** Elizabeth II **Obv:** Crowned head right **Rev:** Charge of the Light Brigade scene with one blue uniform behind the Earl of Cardigan **Edge:** Reeded

| Date | Mintage | VF20 | XF40 | MS60 | MS63 | MS65 |
|---|---|---|---|---|---|---|
| 2004 | 500 | PF65 2,100 | | | | |

**KM# 136 5 POUNDS**
28.28 g., Copper-Nickel, 38.6 mm. **Ruler:** Elizabeth II **Subject:** Steam Locomotive - Coronation **Obv:** Crowned head right **Rev:** The Pacific class (4-6-2) Coronation

| Date | Mintage | VF20 | XF40 | MS60 | MS63 | MS65 |
|---|---|---|---|---|---|---|
| 2004 | — | — | — | — | 12.00 | 14.00 |

**KM# 136a 5 POUNDS**
28.28 g., 0.925 Silver 0.841 oz. ASW, 38.6 mm. **Ruler:** Elizabeth II **Subject:** Coronation **Obv:** Crowned head right **Rev:** The Pacific Class Coronation

| Date | Mintage | VF20 | XF40 | MS60 | MS63 | MS65 |
|---|---|---|---|---|---|---|
| 2004 | — | PF63 65.00 | PF65 75.00 | | | |

**KM# 137 5 POUNDS**
28.28 g., Copper-Nickel, 38.6 mm. **Ruler:** Elizabeth II **Subject:** Steam Locomotive - Flying Scotsman **Obv:** Crowned head right **Rev:** Sir Nigel Gresley's Flying Scotsman

| Date | Mintage | VF20 | XF40 | MS60 | MS63 | MS65 |
|---|---|---|---|---|---|---|
| 2004 | — | — | — | — | 12.00 | 14.00 |

**KM# 137a 5 POUNDS**
28.28 g., 0.925 Silver 0.841 oz. ASW, 38.6 mm. **Ruler:** Elizabeth II **Subject:** Flying Scotsman **Obv:** Crowned head right **Rev:** Famous Flying Scotsman Locomotive, designed by Sir Nigel Gresley

| Date | Mintage | VF20 | XF40 | MS60 | MS63 | MS65 |
|---|---|---|---|---|---|---|
| 2004 | — | PF63 65.00 | PF65 75.00 | | | |

**KM# 138 5 POUNDS**
28.28 g., Copper-Nickel, 38.6 mm. **Ruler:** Elizabeth II **Subject:** Steam Locomotive - The Golden Arrow **Obv:** Crowned head right **Rev:** The Golden Arrow, London-Dover to Paris service

| Date | Mintage | VF20 | XF40 | MS60 | MS63 | MS65 |
|---|---|---|---|---|---|---|
| 2004 | — | — | — | — | 12.00 | 14.00 |

**KM# 138a 5 POUNDS**
28.28 g., 0.925 Silver 0.841 oz. ASW, 38.6 mm. **Ruler:** Elizabeth II **Subject:** Golden Arrow **Obv:** Crowned head right **Rev:** The Golden Arrow, which ran from London to Dover en route to Paris

| Date | Mintage | VF20 | XF40 | MS60 | MS63 | MS65 |
|---|---|---|---|---|---|---|
| 2004 | — | PF63 65.00 | PF65 75.00 | | | |

**KM# 139 5 POUNDS**
28.28 g., Copper-Nickel, 38.6 mm. **Ruler:** Elizabeth II **Subject:** Steam Locomotive driver and fireman **Obv:** Crowned head right **Rev:** Driver and Fireman

| Date | Mintage | VF20 | XF40 | MS60 | MS63 | MS65 |
|---|---|---|---|---|---|---|
| 2004 | — | — | — | — | 12.00 | 14.00 |

**KM# 139a 5 POUNDS**
28.28 g., 0.925 Silver 0.841 oz. ASW, 38.6 mm. **Ruler:** Elizabeth II **Subject:** Driver and Fireman **Obv:** Crowned head right **Rev:** Familiar image from the Golden Age of Steam: the driver and fireman

| Date | Mintage | VF20 | XF40 | MS60 | MS63 | MS65 |
|---|---|---|---|---|---|---|
| 2004 | — | PF63 65.00 | PF65 75.00 | | | |

**KM# 140 5 POUNDS**
28.28 g., Copper-Nickel, 38.6 mm. **Ruler:** Elizabeth II **Subject:** Tunnel **Obv:** Crowned head right **Rev:** Steam locomotive exiting tunnel

| Date | Mintage | VF20 | XF40 | MS60 | MS63 | MS65 |
|---|---|---|---|---|---|---|
| 2004 | — | — | — | — | 12.00 | 14.00 |

**KM# 140a 5 POUNDS**
28.28 g., 0.925 Silver 0.841 oz. ASW, 38.6 mm. **Ruler:** Elizabeth II **Subject:** Tunnel **Obv:** Crowned head right **Rev:** Steam locomotive exiting from tunnel

| Date | Mintage | VF20 | XF40 | MS60 | MS63 | MS65 |
|---|---|---|---|---|---|---|
| 2004 | — | PF63 65.00 | PF65 75.00 | | | |

**KM# 141 5 POUNDS**
28.28 g., Copper-Nickel, 38.6 mm. **Ruler:** Elizabeth II **Subject:** The Evening Star **Obv:** Crowned head right **Rev:** The Evening Star, representing the last British Steam Locomotive

| Date | Mintage | VF20 | XF40 | MS60 | MS63 | MS65 |
|---|---|---|---|---|---|---|
| 2004 | — | — | — | — | 12.00 | 14.00 |

**KM# 141a 5 POUNDS**
28.28 g., 0.925 Silver 0.841 oz. ASW, 38.6 mm. **Ruler:** Elizabeth II **Subject:** Evening Star **Obv:** Crowned head right **Rev:** The Evening Star - representing the last British Rail Steam Locomotive

| Date | Mintage | VF20 | XF40 | MS60 | MS63 | MS65 |
|---|---|---|---|---|---|---|
| 2004 | — | PF63 65.00 | PF65 75.00 | | | |

**KM# 127 5 POUNDS**
28.28 g., Copper-Nickel, 38.61 mm. **Ruler:** Elizabeth II **Subject:** Battle of Trafalgar **Obv:** Crowned head right

| Date | Mintage | VF20 | XF40 | MS60 | MS63 | MS65 |
|---|---|---|---|---|---|---|
| 2005 | — | — | — | — | 7.50 | 10.00 |

**KM# 127a 5 POUNDS**
28.28 g., 0.925 Silver 0.841 oz. ASW, 38.6 mm. **Ruler:** Elizabeth II **Subject:** Nelson Trafalger **Obv:** Crowned head right **Rev:** 200th Anniversary of the Battle of Trafalgar, image of Nelson with a gilded ship in the background

| Date | Mintage | VF20 | XF40 | MS60 | MS63 | MS65 |
|---|---|---|---|---|---|---|
| 2005 | — | PF63 65.00 | PF65 75.00 | | | |

**KM# 128 5 POUNDS**
28.28 g., Copper-Nickel, 38.61 mm. **Ruler:** Elizabeth II **Subject:** 60th Anniversary - End of WW II **Obv:** Crowned head right **Rev:** Big Ben Tower

| Date | Mintage | VF20 | XF40 | MS60 | MS63 | MS65 |
|---|---|---|---|---|---|---|
| 2005 | — | — | — | — | 7.50 | 10.00 |

**KM# 128a 5 POUNDS**
28.28 g., 0.925 Silver 0.841 oz. ASW, 38.6 mm. **Ruler:** Elizabeth II **Subject:** WWII Liberation **Obv:** Crowned head right **Rev:** Big Ben Tower **Edge:** Reeded

| Date | Mintage | VF20 | XF40 | MS60 | MS63 | MS65 |
|---|---|---|---|---|---|---|
| 2005 | 5,000 | PF63 75.00 | PF65 85.00 | | | |

**KM# 128b 5 POUNDS**
39.94 g., 0.9167 Gold 1.1771 oz. AGW, 38.6 mm. **Ruler:** Elizabeth II **Subject:** WWII Liberation **Obv:** Crowned head right **Rev:** Big Ben Tower **Edge:** Reeded

| Date | Mintage | VF20 | XF40 | MS60 | MS63 | MS65 |
|---|---|---|---|---|---|---|
| 2005 | 150 | PF65 2,150 | | | | |

**KM# 129 5 POUNDS**
28.28 g., Copper-Nickel, 38.61 mm. **Ruler:** Elizabeth II **Subject:** WW II Liberation **Obv:** Crowned head right **Rev:** Returning evacuees **Edge:** Reeded

| Date | Mintage | VF20 | XF40 | MS60 | MS63 | MS65 |
|---|---|---|---|---|---|---|
| 2005 | — | — | — | — | 7.50 | 10.00 |

**KM# 129a 5 POUNDS**
39.94 g., 0.9167 Gold 1.1771 oz. AGW, 38.6 mm. **Ruler:** Elizabeth II **Subject:** WWII Liberation **Obv:** Crowned head right **Rev:** Returning evacuees **Edge:** Reeded

| Date | Mintage | VF20 | XF40 | MS60 | MS63 | MS65 |
|---|---|---|---|---|---|---|
| 2005 | 150 | PF65 2,150 | | | | |

**KM# 164 5 POUNDS**
28.28 g., 0.925 Silver 0.841 oz. ASW, 38.61 mm. **Ruler:** Elizabeth II **Subject:** Charles Robert Darwin

| Date | Mintage | VF20 | XF40 | MS60 | MS63 | MS65 |
|---|---|---|---|---|---|---|
| 2005 | — | PF63 50.00 | PF65 55.00 | | | |

**KM# 142 5 POUNDS**
28.28 g., 0.925 Silver 0.841 oz. ASW, 38.6 mm. **Ruler:** Elizabeth II **Subject:** Queen's 80th Birthday **Obv:** Head with tiara right - gilt **Obv. Legend:** ELIZABETH II BAILIWICK - OF JERSEY **Rev:** Queen horseback facing

| Date | Mintage | VF20 | XF40 | MS60 | MS63 | MS65 |
|---|---|---|---|---|---|---|
| 2006 | — | PF63 40.00 | PF65 45.00 | | | |

**KM# 142a 5 POUNDS**
28.28 g., 0.925 Silver 0.841 oz. ASW partially gilt, 38.6 mm. **Ruler:** Elizabeth II **Subject:** Elizabeth II's 80th Birthday **Obv:** Head with tiara right **Obv. Legend:** ELIZABETH II BAILIWICK - OF JERSEY **Rev:** Queen on horseback **Edge:** Reeded

| Date | Mintage | VF20 | XF40 | MS60 | MS63 | MS65 |
|---|---|---|---|---|---|---|
| 2006 | — | PF63 40.00 | PF65 45.00 | | | |

**KM# 145 5 POUNDS**
28.28 g., Copper-Nickel, 38.61 mm. **Ruler:** Elizabeth II **Subject:** Elizabeth II's 80th Birthday **Rev:** Bobby Moore and Wembley's Royal Box

| Date | Mintage | VF20 | XF40 | MS60 | MS63 | MS65 |
|---|---|---|---|---|---|---|
| 2006 | — | — | — | — | — | 15.00 |

**KM# 145a 5 POUNDS**
28.28 g., 0.925 Silver 0.841 oz. ASW, 38.61 mm. **Ruler:** Elizabeth II **Subject:** Elizabeth II, 80th Birthday **Rev:** Bobby Moor and Wembley's Royal Box

| Date | Mintage | VF20 | XF40 | MS60 | MS63 | MS65 |
|---|---|---|---|---|---|---|
| 2006 | — | PF63 50.00 | PF65 55.00 | | | |

**KM# 163 5 POUNDS**
28.28 g., 0.925 Silver 0.841 oz. ASW **Ruler:** Elizabeth II **Subject:** Sir Winston Churchill

| Date | Mintage | VF20 | XF40 | MS60 | MS63 | MS65 |
|---|---|---|---|---|---|---|
| 2006 | Est. 25000 | PF63 50.00 | PF65 55.00 | | | |

**KM# 165 5 POUNDS**
28.28 g., 0.925 Silver 0.841 oz. ASW, 38.61 mm. **Ruler:** Elizabeth II **Subject:** Robert (Bobby) Moore, soccerplayer

| Date | Mintage | VF20 | XF40 | MS60 | MS63 | MS65 |
|---|---|---|---|---|---|---|
| 2006 | Est. 25000 | PF63 50.00 | PF65 55.00 | | | |

**KM# 166 5 POUNDS**
28.28 g., 0.925 Silver 0.841 oz. ASW, 38.61 mm. **Ruler:** Elizabeth II **Subject:** Florence Nightingale

| Date | Mintage | VF20 | XF40 | MS60 | MS63 | MS65 |
|---|---|---|---|---|---|---|
| 2006 | 25,000 | PF63 50.00 | PF65 55.00 | | | |

**KM# 167 5 POUNDS**
28.28 g., Copper-Nickel, 38.61 mm. **Ruler:** Elizabeth II **Subject:** Guy Penrose Gibson, Victoria Cross

| Date | Mintage | VF20 | XF40 | MS60 | MS63 | MS65 |
|---|---|---|---|---|---|---|
| 2006 | — | — | — | — | — | 15.00 |

**KM# 167a 5 POUNDS**
28.28 g., 0.925 Silver 0.841 oz. ASW, 38.61 mm. **Ruler:** Elizabeth II **Subject:** Guy Penrose Gibson, Victoria Cross

| Date | Mintage | VF20 | XF40 | MS60 | MS63 | MS65 |
|---|---|---|---|---|---|---|
| 2006 | Est. 30000 | PF63 45.00 | PF65 50.00 | | | |

**KM# 168 5 POUNDS**
28.28 g., 0.925 Silver 0.841 oz. ASW, 38.61 mm. **Ruler:** Elizabeth II **Subject:** Nicholson

| Date | Mintage | VF20 | XF40 | MS60 | MS63 | MS65 |
|---|---|---|---|---|---|---|
| 2006 | — | PF63 45.00 | PF65 50.00 | | | |

**KM# 169 5 POUNDS**
28.28 g., 0.925 Silver 0.841 oz. ASW, 38.61 mm. **Ruler:** Elizabeth II **Subject:** Hook, Char and Bro

| Date | Mintage | VF20 | XF40 | MS60 | MS63 | MS65 |
|---|---|---|---|---|---|---|
| 2006 | — | PF63 45.00 | PF65 50.00 | | | |

**KM# 170 5 POUNDS**
28.28 g., 0.925 Silver 0.841 oz. ASW, 38.61 mm. **Ruler:** Elizabeth II **Subject:** First Lanc Fusiliers

| Date | Mintage | VF20 | XF40 | MS60 | MS63 | MS65 |
|---|---|---|---|---|---|---|
| 2006 | — | PF63 45.00 | PF65 50.00 | | | |

**KM# 171 5 POUNDS**
28.28 g., 0.925 Silver 0.841 oz. ASW, 38.61 mm. **Ruler:** Elizabeth II **Subject:** Noel Godfrey Chavasse

| Date | Mintage | VF20 | XF40 | MS60 | MS63 | MS65 |
|---|---|---|---|---|---|---|
| 2006 | — | PF63 45.00 | PF65 50.00 | | | |

**KM# 172 5 POUNDS**
28.28 g., 0.925 Silver 0.841 oz. ASW, 38.61 mm. **Ruler:** Elizabeth II **Subject:** David MacKay

| Date | Mintage | VF20 | XF40 | MS60 | MS63 | MS65 |
|---|---|---|---|---|---|---|
| 2006 | — | PF63 45.00 | PF65 50.00 | | | |

### KM# 174 5 POUNDS

28.28 g., 0.925 Silver 0.841 oz. ASW, 38.61 mm. **Ruler:** Elizabeth II **Subject:** Elizabeth, the Queen Mother

| Date | Mintage | VF20 | XF40 | MS60 | MS63 | MS65 |
|---|---|---|---|---|---|---|
| 2007 | Est. 2500 | PF63 50.00 | PF65 55.00 | | | |

### KM# 175 5 POUNDS

28.28 g., 0.925 Silver 0.841 oz. ASW, 38.61 mm. **Ruler:** Elizabeth II **Subject:** Henry VIII

| Date | Mintage | VF20 | XF40 | MS60 | MS63 | MS65 |
|---|---|---|---|---|---|---|
| 2007 | Est. 25000 | PF63 50.00 | PF65 55.00 | | | |

### KM# 176 5 POUNDS

28.28 g., 0.925 Silver 0.841 oz. ASW, 38.61 mm. **Ruler:** Elizabeth II **Subject:** Diana, Princess of Wales

| Date | Mintage | VF20 | XF40 | MS60 | MS63 | MS65 |
|---|---|---|---|---|---|---|
| 2007 | Est. 25000 | PF63 50.00 | PF65 55.00 | | | |

### KM# 177 5 POUNDS

28.28 g., 0.925 Silver 0.841 oz. ASW, 38.61 mm. **Ruler:** Elizabeth II **Subject:** Christopher Wren

| Date | Mintage | VF20 | XF40 | MS60 | MS63 | MS65 |
|---|---|---|---|---|---|---|
| 2007 | Est. 25000 | PF63 50.00 | PF65 55.00 | | | |

### KM# 178 5 POUNDS

28.28 g., Copper-Nickel, 38.61 mm. **Ruler:** Elizabeth II **Subject:** Elizabeth II and Prince Philip, 60th Wedding Anniversary **Rev:** Elizabeth and Philip, 1947

| Date | Mintage | VF20 | XF40 | MS60 | MS63 | MS65 |
|---|---|---|---|---|---|---|
| 2007 | — | — | — | — | — | 15.00 |

### KM# 178a 5 POUNDS

28.28 g., 0.925 Silver 0.841 oz. ASW, 38.61 mm. **Ruler:** Elizabeth II **Subject:** Elizabeth II and Prince Philip, 60th Wedding Anniversary **Rev:** Elizabeth and Philip, 1947

| Date | Mintage | VF20 | XF40 | MS60 | MS63 | MS65 |
|---|---|---|---|---|---|---|
| 2007 | — | PF63 50.00 | PF65 55.00 | | | |

### KM# 179 5 POUNDS

28.28 g., Copper-Nickel, 38.61 mm. **Ruler:** Elizabeth II **Subject:** Elizabeth II and Prince Philip, 60th Wedding Anniversary **Rev:** Westminster Abbey

| Date | Mintage | VF20 | XF40 | MS60 | MS63 | MS65 |
|---|---|---|---|---|---|---|
| 2007 | — | — | — | — | — | 15.00 |

### KM# 179a 5 POUNDS

28.28 g., 0.925 Silver 0.841 oz. ASW, 38.61 mm. **Ruler:** Elizabeth II **Subject:** Elizabeth II and Prince Philip, 60th Wedding Anniversary **Rev:** Westminster Abbey

| Date | Mintage | VF20 | XF40 | MS60 | MS63 | MS65 |
|---|---|---|---|---|---|---|
| 2007 | — | PF63 50.00 | PF65 55.00 | | | |

### KM# 180 5 POUNDS

28.28 g., Copper-Nickel, 38.61 mm. **Ruler:** Elizabeth II **Subject:** Elizabeth II and Prince Philip, 60th Wedding Anniversary **Rev:** Wedding cake

| Date | Mintage | VF20 | XF40 | MS60 | MS63 | MS65 |
|---|---|---|---|---|---|---|
| 2007 | — | — | — | — | — | 15.00 |

### KM# 180a 5 POUNDS

28.28 g., 0.925 Silver 0.841 oz. ASW, 38.61 mm. **Ruler:** Elizabeth II **Subject:** Elizabeth II and Prince Philip, 60th Wedding Anniversary **Rev:** Wedding cake

| Date | Mintage | VF20 | XF40 | MS60 | MS63 | MS65 |
|---|---|---|---|---|---|---|
| 2007 | — | PF63 50.00 | PF65 55.00 | | | |

### KM# 181 5 POUNDS

28.28 g., Copper-Nickel, 38.61 mm. **Ruler:** Elizabeth II **Subject:** Elizabeth II and Prince Philip, 60th Wedding Anniversary **Rev:** Elizabeth and Prince Philip, 2007

| Date | Mintage | VF20 | XF40 | MS60 | MS63 | MS65 |
|---|---|---|---|---|---|---|
| 2007 | — | — | — | — | — | 15.00 |

### KM# 181a 5 POUNDS

28.28 g., 0.925 Silver 0.841 oz. ASW, 38.61 mm. **Ruler:** Elizabeth II **Subject:** Elizabeth II and Prince Philip, 60th Wedding Anniversary **Rev:** Elizabeth and Philip, 2007

| Date | Mintage | VF20 | XF40 | MS60 | MS63 | MS65 |
|---|---|---|---|---|---|---|
| 2007 | — | PF63 50.00 | PF65 55.00 | | | |

### KM# 182 5 POUNDS

28.28 g., Copper-Nickel, 38.61 mm. **Ruler:** Elizabeth II **Subject:** Royal Air Force **Rev:** Barnes Wallis, Roy Chadwick, Guy Penrose Gibson

| Date | Mintage | VF20 | XF40 | MS60 | MS63 | MS65 |
|---|---|---|---|---|---|---|
| 2008 | — | — | — | — | — | 15.00 |

### KM# 182a 5 POUNDS

26.00 g., Brass, 38.61 mm. **Ruler:** Elizabeth II **Subject:** Royal Air Force **Rev:** Barnes Wallis, Roy Chadwick, Guy Penrose Gibson

| Date | Mintage | VF20 | XF40 | MS60 | MS63 | MS65 |
|---|---|---|---|---|---|---|
| 2008 | Est. 25000 | PF63 25.00 | PF65 30.00 | | | |

### KM# 182b 5 POUNDS

28.28 g., 0.925 Silver 0.841 oz. ASW, 38.61 mm. **Ruler:** Elizabeth II **Subject:** Royal Air Force **Rev:** Barnes Wallis, Roy Chadwick, Guy Penrose Gibson

| Date | Mintage | VF20 | XF40 | MS60 | MS63 | MS65 |
|---|---|---|---|---|---|---|
| 2008 | Est. 25000 | PF63 50.00 | PF65 55.00 | | | |

### KM# 183 5 POUNDS

28.28 g., Copper-Nickel, 38.61 mm. **Ruler:** Elizabeth II **Subject:** Royal Air Force **Rev:** Reginald Joseph MItchell, Spitfire

| Date | Mintage | VF20 | XF40 | MS60 | MS63 | MS65 |
|---|---|---|---|---|---|---|
| 2008 | — | — | — | — | — | 15.00 |

### KM# 183a 5 POUNDS

28.28 g., 0.925 Silver 0.841 oz. ASW, 38.61 mm. **Ruler:** Elizabeth II **Subject:** Royal Air Force **Rev:** Reginald Joseph MItchell, Spitfire

| Date | Mintage | VF20 | XF40 | MS60 | MS63 | MS65 |
|---|---|---|---|---|---|---|
| 2008 | — | PF63 50.00 | PF65 55.00 | | | |

### KM# 184 5 POUNDS

28.28 g., Copper-Nickel, 38.61 mm. **Ruler:** Elizabeth II **Subject:** Royal Air Force **Rev:** Battle of Britain

| Date | Mintage | VF20 | XF40 | MS60 | MS63 | MS65 |
|---|---|---|---|---|---|---|
| 2008 | — | — | — | — | — | 15.00 |

### KM# 185 5 POUNDS

28.28 g., Copper-Nickel, 38.61 mm. **Ruler:** Elizabeth II **Subject:** Royal Air Force **Rev:** Frank Whittle

| Date | Mintage | VF20 | XF40 | MS60 | MS63 | MS65 |
|---|---|---|---|---|---|---|
| 2008 | — | — | — | — | — | 15.00 |

### KM# 186 5 POUNDS

28.28 g., Copper-Nickel, 38.61 mm. **Ruler:** Elizabeth II **Subject:** Royal Air Force **Rev:** Hugh Trenchard, founder of the British Air Force

| Date | Mintage | VF20 | XF40 | MS60 | MS63 | MS65 |
|---|---|---|---|---|---|---|
| 2008 | — | — | — | — | — | 15.00 |

### KM# 186a 5 POUNDS

28.28 g., 0.925 Silver 0.841 oz. ASW, 38.61 mm. **Ruler:** Elizabeth II **Subject:** Royal Air Force **Rev:** Hugh Trenchard, founder of the British Air Force

| Date | Mintage | VF20 | XF40 | MS60 | MS63 | MS65 |
|---|---|---|---|---|---|---|
| 2008 | — | PF63 50.00 | PF65 55.00 | | | |

### KM# 187 5 POUNDS

28.28 g., Copper-Nickel, 38.61 mm. **Ruler:** Elizabeth II **Subject:** British Air Force

| Date | Mintage | VF20 | XF40 | MS60 | MS63 | MS65 |
|---|---|---|---|---|---|---|
| 2008 | — | — | — | — | — | 15.00 |

### KM# 188 5 POUNDS

28.28 g., Copper-Nickel, 38.61 mm. **Ruler:** Elizabeth II **Subject:** Royal Air Force

| Date | Mintage | VF20 | XF40 | MS60 | MS63 | MS65 |
|---|---|---|---|---|---|---|
| 2008 | — | — | — | — | — | 15.00 |

### KM# 189 5 POUNDS

28.28 g., Copper-Nickel, 38.61 mm. **Ruler:** Elizabeth II **Subject:** Royal Air Force

| Date | Mintage | VF20 | XF40 | MS60 | MS63 | MS65 |
|---|---|---|---|---|---|---|
| 2008 | — | — | — | — | — | 15.00 |

### KM# 190 5 POUNDS

28.28 g., Copper-Nickel, 38.61 mm. **Ruler:** Elizabeth II **Subject:** Royal Air Force

| Date | Mintage | VF20 | XF40 | MS60 | MS63 | MS65 |
|---|---|---|---|---|---|---|
| 2008 | — | — | — | — | — | 15.00 |

### KM# 191 5 POUNDS

28.28 g., Copper-Nickel, 38.61 mm. **Ruler:** Elizabeth II **Subject:** Royal Air Force

| Date | Mintage | VF20 | XF40 | MS60 | MS63 | MS65 |
|---|---|---|---|---|---|---|
| 2008 | — | — | — | — | — | 15.00 |

### KM# 193a 5 POUNDS

28.00 g., 0.925 Silver 0.8327 oz. ASW, 38.61 mm. **Ruler:** Elizabeth II **Subject:** End of World War I **Obv:** Head with tiara right **Rev:** Sundial motif **Shape:** Number 8

| Date | Mintage | VF20 | XF40 | MS60 | MS63 | MS65 |
|---|---|---|---|---|---|---|
| 2008 | 9,500 | PF63 50.00 | PF65 55.00 | | | |

### KM# 193b 5 POUNDS

28.00 g., 0.916 Gold 0.8246 oz. AGW, 38.61 mm. **Ruler:** Elizabeth II **Subject:** End of World War I **Obv:** Head with tiara right **Rev:** Sundial motif **Shape:** Numeral 8

| Date | Mintage | VF20 | XF40 | MS60 | MS63 | MS65 |
|---|---|---|---|---|---|---|
| 2008 | Est. 450 | PF65 1,500 | | | | |

### KM# 193.1 5 POUNDS

Copper-Nickel, 38.61 mm. **Ruler:** Elizabeth II **Subject:** End of World War I **Obv:** Head in tiara right **Rev:** Sundial motif **Shape:** Number 8

| Date | Mintage | VF20 | XF40 | MS60 | MS63 | MS65 |
|---|---|---|---|---|---|---|
| 2008 | — | — | — | — | — | 18.00 |

### KM# 193.2 5 POUNDS

Copper-Nickel, 38.61 mm. **Ruler:** Elizabeth II **Subject:** End of World War I **Obv:** Head in tiara right **Rev:** Sundial motif in color **Shape:** Number 8

| Date | Mintage | VF20 | XF40 | MS60 | MS63 | MS65 |
|---|---|---|---|---|---|---|
| 2008 | — | — | — | — | — | 25.00 |

### KM# 194 5 POUNDS

Silver **Ruler:** Elizabeth II **Rev:** St. George slaying the dragon

| Date | Mintage | VF20 | XF40 | MS60 | MS63 | MS65 |
|---|---|---|---|---|---|---|
| 2008 | — | — | — | — | — | — |

### KM# 146 5 POUNDS

28.28 g., 0.925 Silver 0.841 oz. ASW, 38.6 mm. **Ruler:** Elizabeth II **Subject:** Battle of Agincourt, 1415 **Obv:** Head right **Rev:** Archers and horsemen

| Date | Mintage | VF20 | XF40 | MS60 | MS63 | MS65 |
|---|---|---|---|---|---|---|
| 2009 | 2,500 | PF63 50.00 | PF65 55.00 | | | |

### KM# 147 5 POUNDS

155.50 g., 0.925 Silver 4.6245 oz. ASW partially gilt, 65 mm. **Ruler:** Elizabeth II **Obv:** Head right **Rev:** St. George slaying dragon, partially gilt

| Date | Mintage | VF20 | XF40 | MS60 | MS63 | MS65 |
|---|---|---|---|---|---|---|
| 2009 | 450 | PF65 350 | | | | |

### KM# 195 5 POUNDS

28.28 g., Copper-Nickel, 38.61 mm. **Ruler:** Elizabeth II **Subject:** Henry VIII, 500th Anniversary of reign

| Date | Mintage | VF20 | XF40 | MS60 | MS63 | MS65 |
|---|---|---|---|---|---|---|
| 2009 | — | — | — | — | — | 15.00 |

### KM# 195a 5 POUNDS

28.28 g., 0.925 Silver 0.841 oz. ASW, 38.61 mm. **Ruler:** Elizabeth II **Subject:** Henry VIII, 500th Anniversary of reign

| Date | Mintage | VF20 | XF40 | MS60 | MS63 | MS65 |
|---|---|---|---|---|---|---|
| 2009 | — | PF63 50.00 | PF65 55.00 | | | |

### KM# 195b 5 POUNDS

39.94 g., 0.916 Gold 1.1762 oz. AGW, 38.91 mm. **Ruler:** Elizabeth II **Subject:** Henry VIII, 500th Anniversary of reign

| Date | Mintage | VF20 | XF40 | MS60 | MS63 | MS65 |
|---|---|---|---|---|---|---|
| 2009 | — | PF65 2,150 | | | | |

### KM# 197 5 POUNDS

28.28 g., 0.925 Silver 0.841 oz. ASW, 38.61 mm. **Ruler:** Elizabeth II **Subject:** British Battles - Agincourt

| Date | Mintage | VF20 | XF40 | MS60 | MS63 | MS65 |
|---|---|---|---|---|---|---|
| 2009 | 25,000 | PF63 50.00 | PF65 55.00 | | | |

### KM# 198 5 POUNDS

28.28 g., 0.925 Silver 0.841 oz. ASW, 38.61 mm. **Ruler:** Elizabeth II **Subject:** British Battles - Somme

| Date | Mintage | VF20 | XF40 | MS60 | MS63 | MS65 |
|---|---|---|---|---|---|---|
| 2009 | Est. 25000 | PF63 50.00 | PF65 55.00 | | | |

### KM# 199 5 POUNDS

28.28 g., 0.925 Silver 0.841 oz. ASW, 38.61 mm. **Ruler:** Elizabeth II **Subject:** British Battles - Normandie

| Date | Mintage | VF20 | XF40 | MS60 | MS63 | MS65 |
|---|---|---|---|---|---|---|
| 2009 | Est. 25000 | PF63 50.00 | PF65 55.00 | | | |

### KM# 200 5 POUNDS

28.28 g., 0.925 Silver 0.841 oz. ASW, 38.61 mm. **Ruler:** Elizabeth II **Subject:** British Battles - El Alamein

| Date | Mintage | VF20 | XF40 | MS60 | MS63 | MS65 |
|---|---|---|---|---|---|---|
| 2009 | Est. 25000 | PF63 50.00 | PF65 55.00 | | | |

### KM# 201 5 POUNDS

28.28 g., 0.925 Silver 0.841 oz. ASW, 38.61 mm. **Ruler:** Elizabeth II **Subject:** British Battles - Hastings

| Date | Mintage | VF20 | XF40 | MS60 | MS63 | MS65 |
|---|---|---|---|---|---|---|
| 2009 | Est. 25000 | PF63 50.00 | PF65 55.00 | | | |

### KM# 202 5 POUNDS

28.28 g., 0.925 Silver 0.841 oz. ASW, 38.61 mm. **Ruler:** Elizabeth II **Subject:** British Battles - Bosworth

| Date | Mintage | VF20 | XF40 | MS60 | MS63 | MS65 |
|---|---|---|---|---|---|---|
| 2009 | Est. 25000 | PF63 50.00 | PF65 55.00 | | | |

### KM# 203 5 POUNDS

28.28 g., 0.925 Silver 0.841 oz. ASW, 38.61 mm. **Ruler:** Elizabeth II **Subject:** British Battles - Naseby

| Date | Mintage | VF20 | XF40 | MS60 | MS63 | MS65 |
|---|---|---|---|---|---|---|
| 2009 | Est. 25000 | PF63 50.00 | PF65 55.00 | | | |

### KM# 204 5 POUNDS

28.28 g., 0.925 Silver 0.841 oz. ASW, 38.61 mm. **Ruler:** Elizabeth II **Subject:** British Battles - Culloden

| Date | Mintage | VF20 | XF40 | MS60 | MS63 | MS65 |
|---|---|---|---|---|---|---|
| 2009 | Est. 25000 | PF63 50.00 | PF65 55.00 | | | |

### KM# 205 5 POUNDS

28.28 g., 0.925 Silver 0.841 oz. ASW, 38.61 mm. **Ruler:** Elizabeth II **Subject:** British Battles - Waterloo

| Date | Mintage | VF20 | XF40 | MS60 | MS63 | MS65 |
|---|---|---|---|---|---|---|
| 2009 | — | PF63 50.00 | PF65 55.00 | | | |

### KM# 206 5 POUNDS

28.28 g., 0.925 Silver 0.841 oz. ASW, 38.61 mm. **Ruler:** Elizabeth II **Subject:** British Battles - Alma

| Date | Mintage | VF20 | XF40 | MS60 | MS63 | MS65 |
|---|---|---|---|---|---|---|
| 2009 | Est. 25000 | PF63 50.00 | PF65 55.00 | | | |

### KM# 207 5 POUNDS

28.28 g., 0.925 Silver 0.841 oz. ASW, 38.61 mm. **Ruler:** Elizabeth II **Subject:** British Battles - Rorkes Drift

| Date | Mintage | VF20 | XF40 | MS60 | MS63 | MS65 |
|---|---|---|---|---|---|---|
| 2009 | Est. 25000 | PF63 50.00 | PF65 55.00 | | | |

### KM# 208 5 POUNDS

28.28 g., 0.925 Silver 0.841 oz. ASW, 38.61 mm. **Ruler:** Elizabeth II **Subject:** British Battles - Mafeking

| Date | Mintage | VF20 | XF40 | MS60 | MS63 | MS65 |
|---|---|---|---|---|---|---|
| 2009 | Est. 25000 | PF63 50.00 | PF65 55.00 | | | |

### KM# 211 5 POUNDS

28.28 g., Copper-Nickel, 38.61 mm. **Ruler:** Elizabeth II **Subject:** James Cook

| Date | Mintage | VF20 | XF40 | MS60 | MS63 | MS65 |
|---|---|---|---|---|---|---|
| 2009 | — | — | — | — | — | 15.00 |

### KM# 211a 5 POUNDS

28.28 g., 0.925 Silver 0.841 oz. ASW, 38.61 mm. **Ruler:** Elizabeth II **Subject:** James Cook

| Date | Mintage | VF20 | XF40 | MS60 | MS63 | MS65 |
|---|---|---|---|---|---|---|
| 2009 | — | PF63 50.00 | PF65 55.00 | | | |

### KM# 212 5 POUNDS
28.28 g., Copper-Nickel, 38.61 mm. **Ruler:** Elizabeth II **Subject:** Robert F. Scott

| Date | Mintage | VF20 | XF40 | MS60 | MS63 | MS65 |
|---|---|---|---|---|---|---|
| 2009 | — | — | — | — | — | 15.00 |

### KM# 212a 5 POUNDS
28.28 g., 0.925 Silver 0.841 oz. ASW, 38.61 mm. **Ruler:** Elizabeth II **Subject:** Robert F. Scott

| Date | Mintage | VF20 | XF40 | MS60 | MS63 | MS65 |
|---|---|---|---|---|---|---|
| 2009 | — | PF63 50.00 | PF65 55.00 | | | |

### KM# 213 5 POUNDS
28.28 g., Copper-Nickel, 38.61 mm. **Ruler:** Elizabeth II **Subject:** Naval Airforce

| Date | Mintage | VF20 | XF40 | MS60 | MS63 | MS65 |
|---|---|---|---|---|---|---|
| 2009 | — | — | — | — | — | 15.00 |

### KM# 213a 5 POUNDS
28.28 g., 0.925 Silver 0.841 oz. ASW, 38.61 mm. **Ruler:** Elizabeth II **Subject:** Naval Airforce

| Date | Mintage | VF20 | XF40 | MS60 | MS63 | MS65 |
|---|---|---|---|---|---|---|
| 2009 | — | PF63 50.00 | PF65 55.00 | | | |

### KM# 214 5 POUNDS
28.28 g., Copper-Nickel, 38.61 mm. **Ruler:** Elizabeth II **Subject:** Falkland War

| Date | Mintage | VF20 | XF40 | MS60 | MS63 | MS65 |
|---|---|---|---|---|---|---|
| 2009 | — | — | — | — | — | 15.00 |

### KM# 214a 5 POUNDS
28.28 g., 0.925 Copper-Nickel 0.841 oz., 38.61 mm. **Ruler:** Elizabeth II **Subject:** Falkland War

| Date | Mintage | VF20 | XF40 | MS60 | MS63 | MS65 |
|---|---|---|---|---|---|---|
| 2009 | — | PF63 50.00 | PF65 55.00 | | | |

### KM# 215 5 POUNDS
28.28 g., Copper-Nickel, 38.61 mm. **Ruler:** Elizabeth II **Subject:** H.M.S. Ark Royal

| Date | Mintage | VF20 | XF40 | MS60 | MS63 | MS65 |
|---|---|---|---|---|---|---|
| 2009 | — | — | — | — | — | 15.00 |

### KM# 216 5 POUNDS
28.28 g., 0.925 Silver 0.841 oz. ASW, 38.61 mm. **Ruler:** Elizabeth II **Subject:** H.M.S. Ark Royal

| Date | Mintage | VF20 | XF40 | MS60 | MS63 | MS65 |
|---|---|---|---|---|---|---|
| 2009 | — | PF63 50.00 | PF65 55.00 | | | |

### KM# 217 5 POUNDS
28.28 g., 0.925 Silver 0.841 oz. ASW, 38.6 mm. **Ruler:** Elizabeth II **Obv:** Head with tiara right **Rev:** Katherine Middleton and Prince WIlliam facing

| Date | Mintage | VF20 | XF40 | MS60 | MS63 | MS65 |
|---|---|---|---|---|---|---|
| 2011 | — | PF63 75.00 | PF65 85.00 | | | |

### KM# 143 10 POUNDS
155.50 g., 0.925 Silver 4.6245 oz. ASW partially gilt, 65 mm. **Ruler:** Elizabeth II **Subject:** 50th Anniversary of Coronation **Obv:** Queens silver portrait on gold plated fields **Rev:** Crown and scepter above arms, gold plated

| Date | Mintage | VF20 | XF40 | MS60 | MS63 | MS65 |
|---|---|---|---|---|---|---|
| 2003 | 2,000 | — | — | — | 135 | 150 |

### KM# 154 10 POUNDS
155.50 g., 0.916 Gold 4.5795 oz. AGW, 65 mm. **Ruler:** Elizabeth II **Subject:** Crimean War, 150th anniversary **Rev:** Light Brigade, Earl of Cardigan

| Date | Mintage | VF20 | XF40 | MS60 | MS63 | MS65 |
|---|---|---|---|---|---|---|
| 2004 | — | PF65 8,500 | | | | |

### KM# 159 10 POUNDS
155.50 g., 0.925 Silver 4.6245 oz. ASW, 65 mm. **Ruler:** Elizabeth II **Subject:** End of World War II, 60th Anniversary **Rev:** Parlament buildings

| Date | Mintage | VF20 | XF40 | MS60 | MS63 | MS65 |
|---|---|---|---|---|---|---|
| 2005 | — | PF63 175 | PF65 200 | | | |

### KM# 161 10 POUNDS
155.50 g., 0.916 Gold 4.5795 oz. AGW, 65 mm. **Ruler:** Elizabeth II **Subject:** Trafalgar, 200th Anniversary

| Date | Mintage | VF20 | XF40 | MS60 | MS63 | MS65 |
|---|---|---|---|---|---|---|
| 2005 | — | PF65 8,500 | | | | |

### KM# 192 10 POUNDS
155.50 g., 0.925 Silver 4.6245 oz. ASW, 65 mm. **Ruler:** Elizabeth II **Subject:** Royal Air Force **Rev:** Reginald Joseph Mitchell, founder of the Royal Air Force

| Date | Mintage | VF20 | XF40 | MS60 | MS63 | MS65 |
|---|---|---|---|---|---|---|
| 2008 | Est. 1943 | PF65 200 | | | | |

### KM# 112 25 POUNDS
7.98 g., 0.9167 Gold 0.2352 oz. AGW, 22.05 mm. **Ruler:** Elizabeth II **Subject:** Princess Diana **Obv:** Crowned head right **Rev:** Diana's portrait **Edge:** Reeded

| Date | Mintage | VF20 | XF40 | MS60 | MS63 | MS65 |
|---|---|---|---|---|---|---|
| 2002 | 2,500 | PF63 425 | PF65 450 | | | |

### KM# 114 25 POUNDS
7.98 g., 0.9166 Gold 0.2352 oz. AGW, 22 mm. **Ruler:** Elizabeth II **Subject:** Queen Mother **Obv:** Crowned head right **Rev:** Queen Mother's portrait circa 1918 **Edge:** Reeded

| Date | Mintage | VF20 | XF40 | MS60 | MS63 | MS65 |
|---|---|---|---|---|---|---|
| 2002 | 2,500 | PF63 425 | PF65 450 | | | |

### KM# 116 25 POUNDS
7.98 g., 0.9166 Gold 0.2352 oz. AGW, 22 mm. **Ruler:** Elizabeth II **Subject:** Golden Jubilee **Obv:** Crowned head right **Rev:** Abbey procession scene **Edge:** Reeded

| Date | Mintage | VF20 | XF40 | MS60 | MS63 | MS65 |
|---|---|---|---|---|---|---|
| 2002 | 2,500 | PF63 425 | PF65 450 | | | |

### KM# 118 25 POUNDS
7.98 g., 0.9166 Gold 0.2352 oz. AGW, 22 mm. **Ruler:** Elizabeth II **Subject:** Duke of Wellington **Obv:** Crowned head right **Rev:** Wellington's portrait with infantry scene **Edge:** Reeded

| Date | Mintage | VF20 | XF40 | MS60 | MS63 | MS65 |
|---|---|---|---|---|---|---|
| 2002 | 2,500 | PF63 425 | PF65 450 | | | |

### KM# 120 25 POUNDS
7.98 g., 0.9166 Gold 0.2352 oz. AGW, 22 mm. **Ruler:** Elizabeth II **Subject:** Golden Jubilee **Obv:** Crowned head right **Rev:** Honor guard and monument **Edge:** Reeded

| Date | Mintage | VF20 | XF40 | MS60 | MS63 | MS65 |
|---|---|---|---|---|---|---|
| 2003 | 5,000 | PF63 425 | PF65 450 | | | |

### KM# 151 25 POUNDS
7.98 g., 0.916 Gold 0.235 oz. AGW, 22.05 mm. **Ruler:** Elizabeth II **Rev:** Multipe portraits of Alfred, Drake, Nelson, Fisher and Woodward and the Mary Rose, Visctory, Warspite, Ark Royal and Conqueror

| Date | Mintage | VF20 | XF40 | MS60 | MS63 | MS65 |
|---|---|---|---|---|---|---|
| 2003 | — | PF63 425 | PF65 450 | | | |

### KM# 125 25 POUNDS
7.98 g., 0.9167 Gold 0.2352 oz. AGW, 22 mm. **Ruler:** Elizabeth II **Subject:** D-Day **Obv:** Crowned head right **Rev:** British Horsa gliders in flight **Edge:** Reeded

| Date | Mintage | VF20 | XF40 | MS60 | MS63 | MS65 |
|---|---|---|---|---|---|---|
| 2004 | 500 | PF63 425 | PF65 450 | | | |

### KM# 152 25 POUNDS
7.98 g., 0.916 Gold 0.235 oz. AGW, 22.05 mm. **Ruler:** Elizabeth II **Rev:** Locomotive 6220 Coronation, and LMSR Pacific

| Date | Mintage | VF20 | XF40 | MS60 | MS63 | MS65 |
|---|---|---|---|---|---|---|
| 2004 | Est. 2500 | PF63 425 | PF65 450 | | | |

### KM# 153 25 POUNDS
7.98 g., 0.916 Gold 0.235 oz. AGW, 22.05 mm. **Ruler:** Elizabeth II **Rev:** British Railway's locomotive 92229 Evening Star

| Date | Mintage | VF20 | XF40 | MS60 | MS63 | MS65 |
|---|---|---|---|---|---|---|
| 2004 | Est. 2500 | PF63 425 | PF65 450 | | | |

### KM# 155 25 POUNDS
7.98 g., 0.916 Gold 0.235 oz. AGW, 22.05 mm. **Ruler:** Elizabeth II **Subject:** Crimean War, 150th anniversary **Rev:** Light Brigade, Earl of Cardigan

| Date | Mintage | VF20 | XF40 | MS60 | MS63 | MS65 |
|---|---|---|---|---|---|---|
| 2004 | — | PF63 425 | PF65 450 | | | |

### KM# 156 25 POUNDS
7.98 g., 0.916 Gold 0.235 oz. AGW, 22.05 mm. **Ruler:** Elizabeth II **Subject:** Royal Navy **Rev:** H.M.S. Vicotry

| Date | Mintage | VF20 | XF40 | MS60 | MS63 | MS65 |
|---|---|---|---|---|---|---|
| 2004 | — | PF63 425 | PF65 450 | | | |

### KM# 157 25 POUNDS
7.98 g., 0.916 Gold 0.235 oz. AGW, 22.05 mm. **Ruler:** Elizabeth II **Subject:** Royal Navy **Rev:** Admiral Andrew B. Cunningham

| Date | Mintage | VF20 | XF40 | MS60 | MS63 | MS65 |
|---|---|---|---|---|---|---|
| 2004 | — | PF63 425 | PF65 450 | | | |

### KM# 158 25 POUNDS
7.98 g., 0.916 Gold 0.235 oz. AGW, 22.05 mm. **Ruler:** Elizabeth II **Subject:** Royal Navy **Rev:** Submarine H.M.S. Conqueror

| Date | Mintage | VF20 | XF40 | MS60 | MS63 | MS65 |
|---|---|---|---|---|---|---|
| 2004 | — | PF63 425 | PF65 450 | | | |

### KM# 162 25 POUNDS
7.98 g., 0.916 Gold 0.235 oz. AGW, 22.05 mm. **Ruler:** Elizabeth II **Subject:** Trafalgar, 200th Anniversary

| Date | Mintage | VF20 | XF40 | MS60 | MS63 | MS65 |
|---|---|---|---|---|---|---|
| 2005 | — | PF63 425 | PF65 450 | | | |

### KM# 196 25 POUNDS
7.98 g., 0.916 Gold 0.235 oz. AGW, 22.05 mm. **Ruler:** Elizabeth II **Subject:** Henry VIII, 500th Anniversary of reign

| Date | Mintage | VF20 | XF40 | MS60 | MS63 | MS65 |
|---|---|---|---|---|---|---|
| 2009 | Est. 995 | PF63 425 | PF65 450 | | | |

### KM# 209 25 POUNDS
7.98 g., 0.916 Gold 0.235 oz. AGW, 22.05 mm. **Ruler:** Elizabeth II **Subject:** British Battles - Agincourt

| Date | Mintage | VF20 | XF40 | MS60 | MS63 | MS65 |
|---|---|---|---|---|---|---|
| 2009 | Est. 995 | PF63 425 | PF65 450 | | | |

### KM# 210 25 POUNDS
7.98 g., 0.916 Gold 0.235 oz. AGW, 22.05 mm. **Ruler:** Elizabeth II **Subject:** British Battles - Somme

| Date | Mintage | VF20 | XF40 | MS60 | MS63 | MS65 |
|---|---|---|---|---|---|---|
| 2009 | Est. 995 | PF63 425 | PF65 450 | | | |

### KM# 122 50 POUNDS
1000.00 g., 0.925 Silver 29.7394 oz. ASW, 100 mm. **Ruler:** Elizabeth II **Obv:** Crowned head right **Rev:** Bust facing and crowned arms with supporters **Edge:** Reeded

| Date | Mintage | VF20 | XF40 | MS60 | MS63 | MS65 |
|---|---|---|---|---|---|---|
| 2003 | 500 | PF63 1,000 | PF65 1,150 | | | |

## PIEDFORT

| KM# | Date | Mintage | Identification | Mkt Val |
|---|---|---|---|---|
| P3 | 2002 | 100 | 5 Pounds 0.9166 Gold Queen's portrait Abbey procession scene Underweight piefort | 1,900 |
| P4 | 2009 | Est. 450 | 5 Pounds 0.925 Silver KM#195a but with enamel | 125 |

## MINT SETS

| KM# | Date | Mintage | Identification | Issue Price | Mkt Val |
|---|---|---|---|---|---|
| MS7 | 2004 (1) | — | Jersey KM#126, Guernsey KM#155, Alderney KM#43, 150th Anniversary of the Crimean War | — | 100 |

# JORDAN

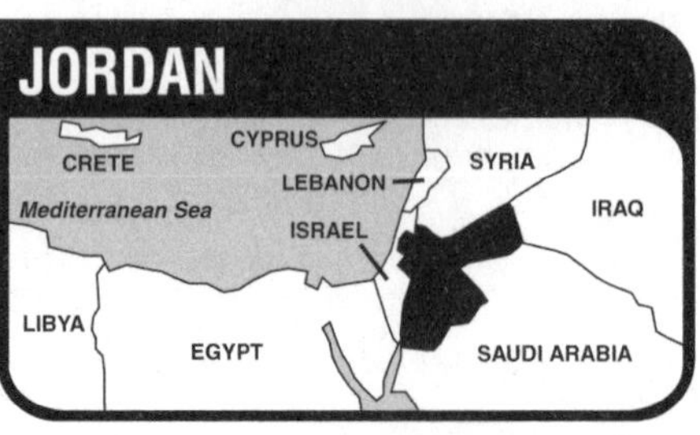


The Hashemite Kingdom of Jordan, a constitutional monarchy in southwest Asia, has an area of 37,738 sq. mi.(91,880 sq. km.) and a population of 3.5 million. Capital: Amman. Agriculture and tourism comprise Jordan's economic base. Chief exports are phosphates, tomatoes and oranges.

**RULER**

Abdullah Ibn Al-Hussein, 1999-

**MONETARY SYSTEM**

100 Piastres = 1 Dinar

## KINGDOM

## DECIMAL COINAGE

### KM# 78.1 QIRSH (Piastre)
5.47 g., Copper Plated Steel, 25 mm. **Ruler:** Abdullah II **Obv:** King Abdullah II **Rev:** Christian date left, Islamic date right **Edge:** Plain

| Date | Mintage | VF20 | XF40 | MS60 | MS63 | MS65 |
|---|---|---|---|---|---|---|
| AH1430-2009 | — | 0.35 | 0.45 | 0.75 | 1.00 | 1.25 |
| AH1432-2011 | — | 0.35 | 0.45 | 0.75 | 1.00 | 1.25 |

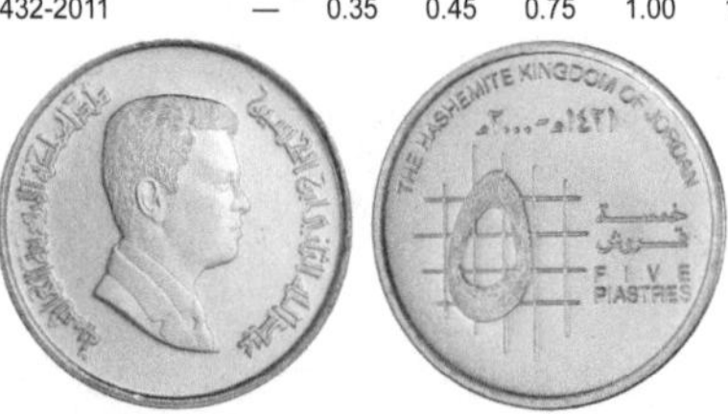

### KM# 73 5 PIASTRES
5.00 g., Nickel Plated Steel, 25.8 mm. **Ruler:** Abdullah II **Obv:** Bust right **Rev:** Value to left within lines below date with written value at lower right **Edge:** Milled

| Date | Mintage | VF20 | XF40 | MS60 | MS63 | MS65 |
|---|---|---|---|---|---|---|
| AH1427-2006 | — | 0.50 | 0.70 | 1.50 | 2.00 | 2.50 |
| AH1429-2008 | — | 0.50 | 0.70 | 1.50 | 2.00 | 2.50 |
| AH1430-2009 | — | 0.50 | 0.70 | 1.50 | 2.00 | 2.50 |
| AH1433-2012 | — | 0.50 | 0.70 | 1.50 | 2.00 | 2.50 |

**KM# 74 10 PIASTRES**
8.00 g., Nickel Plated Steel, 28 mm. **Ruler:** Abdullah II **Obv:** Bust right **Rev:** Value at left within lines below date with written value at lower right **Edge:** Milled

| Date | Mintage | VF20 | XF40 | MS60 | MS63 | MS65 |
|---|---|---|---|---|---|---|
| AH1425-2004 | — | 0.35 | 0.50 | 1.00 | 1.50 | 3.00 |
| AH1427-2006 | — | 0.35 | 0.50 | 1.00 | 2.00 | 5.00 |
| AH1429-2008 | — | 0.35 | 0.50 | 1.00 | 1.50 | 3.00 |
| AH1430-2009 | — | 0.35 | 0.50 | 1.00 | 1.50 | 3.00 |
| AH1433-2012 | — | 0.35 | 0.50 | 1.00 | 1.50 | 3.00 |

**KM# 83 1/4 DINAR**
7.40 g., Nickel-Brass, 26.5 mm. **Ruler:** Abdullah II **Obv:** Bust right **Edge:** Plain **Shape:** 7-sided

| Date | Mintage | VF20 | XF40 | MS60 | MS63 | MS65 |
|---|---|---|---|---|---|---|
| AH1425-2004 | — | 0.75 | 1.00 | 2.00 | 3.00 | 4.00 |
| AH1427-2006 | — | 0.75 | 1.00 | 2.00 | 3.00 | 4.00 |
| AH1429-2008 | — | 0.75 | 1.00 | 2.00 | 3.00 | 4.00 |
| AH1430-2009 | — | 0.75 | 1.00 | 2.00 | 3.00 | 4.00 |

**KM# 79 1/2 DINAR**
9.67 g., Bi-Metallic Copper-Nickel center in Brass ring, 29 mm. **Ruler:** Abdullah II **Obv:** Bust right within circle **Rev:** Value in center of circled wreath **Edge:** Plain **Shape:** 7-sided

| Date | Mintage | VF20 | XF40 | MS60 | MS63 | MS65 |
|---|---|---|---|---|---|---|
| AH1427-2006 | — | 1.00 | 2.00 | 3.00 | 4.00 | 5.00 |
| AH1429-2008 | — | 1.00 | 2.00 | 3.00 | 4.00 | 5.00 |
| AH1430-2009 | — | 1.00 | 2.00 | 3.00 | 4.00 | 5.00 |

**KM# 75 3 DINARS**
28.50 g., Brass, 40 mm. **Ruler:** Abdullah II **Subject:** Amman: Arabic Culture Capital **Obv:** Bust right **Rev:** Building **Edge:** Milled

| Date | Mintage | VF20 | XF40 | MS60 | MS63 | MS65 |
|---|---|---|---|---|---|---|
| AH1423//2002 | 2,000 | 100 | 130 | 150 | | |

Note: Only 500 sold to collectors. Rest were taken by Amman municipality as official gifts

**KM# 86 5 DINARS**
120.00 g., Bronze, 60 mm. **Ruler:** Abdullah **Subject:** Selection of Petra as one of the new Seven Wonders of the World **Obv:** King Abdullah II and Queen Rania **Rev:** Petra **Edge:** Milled

| Date | Mintage | VF20 | XF40 | MS60 | MS63 | MS65 |
|---|---|---|---|---|---|---|
| AH1428-2008 | 500 | PF60 150 | PF63 160 | PF65 175 | | |

**KM# 84 10 DINARS**
120.00 g., 0.999 Silver 3.8542 oz. ASW, 60 mm. **Ruler:** Abdullah **Subject:** 60th Anniversary of Jordan's Independence **Obv:** King Abdullah I and Independence speech **Rev:** The National Assembly building **Edge:** Milled

| Date | Mintage | VF20 | XF40 | MS60 | MS63 | MS65 |
|---|---|---|---|---|---|---|
| 2006 | 250 | PF60 325 | PF63 335 | PF65 350 | | |

**KM# 88 10 DINARS**
31.11 g., 0.999 Silver 0.999 oz. ASW, 40 mm. **Ruler:** Abdullah II **Subject:** Accession, 10th Anniversary **Obv:** Bust facing **Rev:** Crowned and mantled shield

| Date | Mintage | VF20 | XF40 | MS60 | MS63 | MS65 |
|---|---|---|---|---|---|---|
| 2009 | 2,250 | PF60 130 | PF63 140 | PF65 150 | | |

**KM# 87 20 DINARS**
120.00 g., 0.999 Silver 3.8542 oz. ASW, 60 mm. **Ruler:** Abdullah **Subject:** Selection of Petra as one of the new Seven Wonders of the World **Obv:** King Abdullah II and Queen Rania **Rev:** Petra **Edge:** Milled

| Date | Mintage | VF20 | XF40 | MS60 | MS63 | MS65 |
|---|---|---|---|---|---|---|
| AH1428-2008 | 500 | PF60 300 | PF63 325 | PF65 350 | | |

**KM# 89 50 DINARS**
16.96 g., 0.999 Gold 0.5447 oz. AGW, 30 mm. **Ruler:** Abdullah II **Subject:** Accession, 10th Anniversary **Obv:** Bust **Rev:** Arms

| Date | Mintage | VF20 | XF40 | MS60 | MS63 | MS65 |
|---|---|---|---|---|---|---|
| 2009 | 1,750 | PF60 900 | PF63 950 | PF65 975 | | |

**KM# 85 60 DINARS**
72.75 g., 0.917 Gold 2.1448 oz. AGW, 40 mm. **Ruler:** Abdullah **Subject:** 60th Anniversary of Jordan's Independence **Obv:** King Abdullah II **Rev:** Treasury in Petra **Edge:** Milled

| Date | Mintage | VF20 | XF40 | MS60 | MS63 | MS65 |
|---|---|---|---|---|---|---|
| 2006 | 250 | PF60 3,500 | PF63 3,650 | PF65 3,750 | | |

## MINT SETS

| KM# | Date | Mintage | Identification | Issue Price | Mkt Val |
|---|---|---|---|---|---|
| MS4 | 2000-2004 (5) | — | KM#73-74, 78.1, 79, 83, mixed dates | — | 20.00 |

## PROOF SETS

| KM# | Date | Mintage | Identification | Issue Price | Mkt Val |
|---|---|---|---|---|---|
| PS14 | 2006 (2) | 250 | KM#84-85 | — | 3,500 |
| PS15 | 2008 (2) | — | KM#86-87 | — | 425 |

The Republic of Kazakhstan (formerly Kazakhstan S.S.R.) is bordered to the west by the Caspian Sea and Russia, to the north by Russia, in the east by the Peoples Republic of China and in the south by Uzbekistan and Kirghizia. It has an area of 1,049,155 sq. mi. (2,717,300 sq. km.) and a population of 16.7 million. Capital: Astana. Rich in mineral resources including coal, tungsten, copper, lead, zinc and manganese with huge oil and natural gas reserves. Agriculture is very important, (it previously represented 20 percent of the total arable acreage of the combined U.S.S.R.) Non-ferrous metallurgy, heavy engineering and chemical industries are leaders in its economy.

**MONETARY SYSTEM**

100 Tyin = 1 Tenge

# REPUBLIC

## DECIMAL COINAGE

### KM# 23 TENGE

1.60 g., Nickel-Brass, 15 mm. **Obv:** National emblem **Rev:** Value flanked by designs **Edge:** Plain

| Date | Mintage | VF20 | XF40 | MS60 | MS63 | MS65 |
|---|---|---|---|---|---|---|
| 2002 | — | — | — | 0.25 | 0.50 | 0.85 |
| 2004 | — | — | — | 0.25 | 0.50 | 0.85 |
| 2005 | — | — | — | 0.25 | 0.50 | 0.85 |
| 2011 | — | — | — | 0.25 | 0.50 | 0.85 |
| 2012 | — | — | — | 0.25 | 0.50 | 0.85 |

### KM# 64 2 TENGE

1.82 g., Nickel-Brass, 16 mm. **Obv:** National emblem **Rev:** Value flanked by designs **Edge:** Plain

| Date | Mintage | VF20 | XF40 | MS60 | MS63 | MS65 |
|---|---|---|---|---|---|---|
| 2005 | — | — | — | 0.30 | 0.65 | 1.20 |
| 2006 | — | — | — | 0.30 | 0.65 | 1.20 |

### KM# 24 5 TENGE

2.20 g., Nickel-Brass, 17.3 mm. **Obv:** National emblem **Rev:** Value flanked by designs

| Date | Mintage | VF20 | XF40 | MS60 | MS63 | MS65 |
|---|---|---|---|---|---|---|
| 2002 | — | — | — | 0.25 | 0.50 | 0.85 |
| 2004 | — | — | — | 0.25 | 0.50 | 0.85 |
| 2005 | — | — | — | 0.25 | 0.50 | 0.85 |
| 2006 | — | — | — | 0.25 | 0.50 | 0.85 |
| 2010 | — | — | — | 0.25 | 0.50 | 0.85 |
| 2011 | — | — | — | 0.25 | 0.50 | 0.85 |
| 2012 | — | — | — | 0.25 | 0.50 | 0.85 |

### KM# 25 10 TENGE

2.80 g., Nickel-Brass, 19.6 mm. **Obv:** National emblem **Rev:** Value above design

| Date | Mintage | VF20 | XF40 | MS60 | MS63 | MS65 |
|---|---|---|---|---|---|---|
| 2002 | — | — | — | 0.35 | 0.75 | 1.25 |
| 2004 | — | — | — | 0.35 | 0.75 | 1.25 |
| 2005 | — | — | — | 0.35 | 0.75 | 1.25 |
| 2006 | — | — | — | 0.35 | 0.75 | 1.25 |
| 2010 | — | — | — | 0.35 | 0.75 | 1.25 |
| 2011 | — | — | — | 0.35 | 0.75 | 1.25 |
| 2012 | — | — | — | 0.35 | 0.75 | 1.25 |

### KM# 26 20 TENGE

2.90 g., Copper-Nickel-Zinc, 18.3 mm. **Obv:** National emblem **Rev:** Value above design **Edge:** Segmented reeding **Edge Lettering:** * CTO TENGE * Y 3 TENGE

| Date | Mintage | VF20 | XF40 | MS60 | MS63 | MS65 |
|---|---|---|---|---|---|---|
| 2002 | — | — | — | 0.50 | 1.00 | 1.75 |
| 2004 | — | — | — | 0.50 | 1.00 | 1.75 |
| 2006 | — | — | — | 0.50 | 1.00 | 1.75 |
| 2010 | — | — | — | 0.50 | 1.00 | 1.75 |
| 2011 | — | — | — | 0.50 | 1.00 | 1.75 |
| 2012 | — | — | — | 0.50 | 1.00 | 1.75 |

### KM# 27 50 TENGE

4.70 g., Copper-Nickel-Zinc, 23 mm. **Obv:** National emblem **Rev:** Value above design

| Date | Mintage | VF20 | XF40 | MS60 | MS63 | MS65 |
|---|---|---|---|---|---|---|
| 2002 | — | — | — | 1.00 | 2.00 | 3.50 |

### KM# 40 50 TENGE

11.50 g., Copper-Nickel, 31 mm. **Obv:** Eagle superimposed on ornate 10 **Edge:** Reeded and plain sections

| Date | Mintage | VF20 | XF40 | MS60 | MS63 | MS65 |
|---|---|---|---|---|---|---|
| 2001 | — | — | — | 2.00 | 3.50 | 5.50 |

### KM# 41 50 TENGE

11.20 g., Copper-Nickel, 31.1 mm. **Subject:** Gabiden Mustafin **Obv:** National emblem above value **Rev:** Bust 1/4 left **Edge:** Segmented reeding

| Date | Mintage | VF20 | XF40 | MS60 | MS63 | MS65 |
|---|---|---|---|---|---|---|
| ND(2002) | — | — | — | 2.00 | 3.50 | 5.50 |

### KM# 69 50 TENGE

Copper-Nickel, 31 mm. **Subject:** Gabit Mosrepov **Obv:** Symbol and value **Rev:** Bust facing

| Date | Mintage | VF20 | XF40 | MS60 | MS63 | MS65 |
|---|---|---|---|---|---|---|
| 2002 | — | — | — | 2.00 | 3.50 | 5.50 |

### KM# 70 50 TENGE

Copper-Nickel, 31 mm. **Subject:** 200th Anniversary of Makhambet Utemisov **Obv:** Symbol and value

| Date | Mintage | VF20 | XF40 | MS60 | MS63 | MS65 |
|---|---|---|---|---|---|---|
| 2003 | — | — | — | 5.00 | 7.00 | 9.00 |

### KM# 54 50 TENGE

11.50 g., Copper-Nickel, 31.1 mm. **Obv:** National emblem above value **Rev:** Painter Abylichan Kasteev (1904-1973) **Edge:** Reeded and plain sections

| Date | Mintage | VF20 | XF40 | MS60 | MS63 | MS65 |
|---|---|---|---|---|---|---|
| 2004 | — | — | — | 5.00 | 7.00 | 9.00 |

### KM# 65 50 TENGE

11.50 g., Copper-Nickel, 31.1 mm. **Subject:** Alken Margulan **Obv:** National emblem above value **Rev:** Bust facing **Edge:** Segmented reeding

| Date | Mintage | VF20 | XF40 | MS60 | MS63 | MS65 |
|---|---|---|---|---|---|---|
| 2004 | — | — | — | 5.00 | 7.00 | 9.00 |

### KM# 58 50 TENGE

11.50 g., Copper-Nickel, 31.1 mm. **Subject:** 10th Anniversary of the Constitution **Obv:** National emblem above value **Rev:** National emblem within circle above book **Edge:** Segmented reeding

| Date | Mintage | VF20 | XF40 | MS60 | MS63 | MS65 |
|---|---|---|---|---|---|---|
| 2005 | — | — | — | 5.00 | 7.00 | 9.00 |

### KM# 71 50 TENGE

10.95 g., Copper-Nickel, 31 mm. **Subject:** 60 Years Victory WWII **Obv:** Symbol and value

| Date | Mintage | VF20 | XF40 | MS60 | MS63 | MS65 |
|---|---|---|---|---|---|---|
| 2005 | — | — | — | 5.00 | 7.00 | 9.00 |

### KM# 73 50 TENGE

11.37 g., Copper-Nickel, 31 mm. **Obv:** Human figure and solar system **Rev:** Astronaut and solar system **Edge:** Segmented reeding

| Date | Mintage | VF20 | XF40 | MS60 | MS63 | MS65 |
|---|---|---|---|---|---|---|
| 2006 | 50,000 | — | — | 5.00 | 7.00 | 9.00 |

**KM# 74 50 TENGE**
11.37 g., Copper-Nickel, 31 mm. **Obv:** National arms on tapestry **Rev:** Woman with baby in cradle **Edge:** Segmented reeding

| Date | Mintage | VF20 | XF40 | MS60 | MS63 | MS65 |
|---|---|---|---|---|---|---|
| 2006 | — | — | — | 5.00 | 7.00 | 9.00 |

**KM# 75 50 TENGE**
11.37 g., Copper-Nickel, 31 mm. **Obv:** National arms **Rev:** Altai Snowcock **Edge:** Segmented reeding

| Date | Mintage | VF20 | XF40 | MS60 | MS63 | MS65 |
|---|---|---|---|---|---|---|
| 2006 | 50,000 | — | — | 5.00 | 7.00 | 9.00 |

**KM# 77 50 TENGE**
11.37 g., Copper-Nickel, 31 mm. **Obv:** National arms **Rev:** Altyn Kyran Order Breast Star **Edge:** Segmented reeding

| Date | Mintage | VF20 | XF40 | MS60 | MS63 | MS65 |
|---|---|---|---|---|---|---|
| 2006 | 50,000 | — | — | 5.00 | 7.00 | 9.00 |

**KM# 78 50 TENGE**
11.37 g., Copper-Nickel, 31 mm. **Obv:** National arms **Rev:** Zhubanov bust and music score **Edge:** Segmented reeding

| Date | Mintage | VF20 | XF40 | MS60 | MS63 | MS65 |
|---|---|---|---|---|---|---|
| 2006 | 50,000 | — | — | 5.00 | 7.00 | 9.00 |

**KM# 79 50 TENGE**
11.22 g., Copper-Nickel, 31 mm. **Subject:** 20th Anniversary **Obv:** National arms above value **Rev:** Happy woman **Edge:** Segmented reeding

| Date | Mintage | VF20 | XF40 | MS60 | MS63 | MS65 |
|---|---|---|---|---|---|---|
| 1986-2006 | — | — | — | 5.00 | 7.00 | 9.00 |

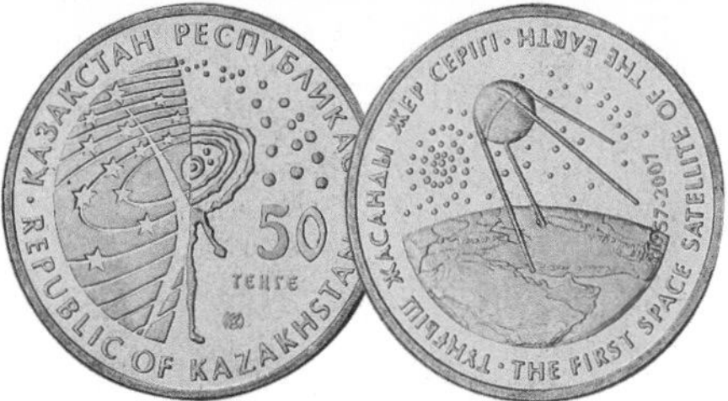


**KM# 80 50 TENGE**
10.89 g., Copper-Nickel, 31.10 mm. **Subject:** 50th Anniversary Launch of Sputnik I **Obv:** Stylized view of solar system **Obv. Legend:** REPUBLIC OF KAZAKHSTAN **Rev:** Sputnik I in space, earth in background **Rev. Legend:** THE FIRST SPACE SATELLITE OF THE EARTH **Edge:** Segmented reeding

| Date | Mintage | VF20 | XF40 | MS60 | MS63 | MS65 |
|---|---|---|---|---|---|---|
| 1957-2007 | — | — | — | 5.00 | 7.00 | 9.00 |

**KM# 81 50 TENGE**
11.11 g., Copper-Nickel, 31 mm. **Obv:** National arms, value below **Obv. Legend:** КАЗАКСТАН.... **Rev:** Eurasian Spoonbill standing left **Rev. Legend:** ... • PLATALEA LEUCORODIA **Edge:** Segmented reeding

| Date | Mintage | VF20 | XF40 | MS60 | MS63 | MS65 |
|---|---|---|---|---|---|---|
| 2007 | — | — | — | 5.00 | 7.00 | 9.00 |

**KM# 164 50 TENGE**
11.37 g., Copper-Nickel, 31 mm. **Obv:** National arms on tapestry **Rev:** Child and two men

| Date | Mintage | VF20 | XF40 | MS60 | MS63 | MS65 |
|---|---|---|---|---|---|---|
| 2007 | — | — | — | 5.00 | 7.00 | 9.00 |

**KM# 165 50 TENGE**
11.37 g., Copper-Nickel, 31 mm. **Obv:** National arms above value **Rev:** Otan badge

| Date | Mintage | VF20 | XF40 | MS60 | MS63 | MS65 |
|---|---|---|---|---|---|---|
| 2007 | — | — | — | 5.00 | 7.00 | 9.00 |

**KM# 86 50 TENGE**
Copper-Nickel, 31 mm. **Obv:** National Arms

| Date | Mintage | VF20 | XF40 | MS60 | MS63 | MS65 |
|---|---|---|---|---|---|---|
| 2008 Prooflike | — | — | — | — | — | 14.00 |

**KM# 169 50 TENGE**
11.37 g., Copper-Nickel, 31 mm. **Obv:** National arms on tapersry background **Rev:** Two horsemen

| Date | Mintage | VF20 | XF40 | MS60 | MS63 | MS65 |
|---|---|---|---|---|---|---|
| 2008 | — | — | — | 5.00 | 7.00 | 9.00 |

**KM# 170 50 TENGE**
11.37 g., Copper-Nickel, 31 mm. **Obv:** National arms above vlaue **Rev:** Dank Order Star

| Date | Mintage | VF20 | XF40 | MS60 | MS63 | MS65 |
|---|---|---|---|---|---|---|
| 2008 | — | — | — | 5.00 | 7.00 | 9.00 |

**KM# 171 50 TENGE**
11.37 g., Copper-Nickel, 31 mm. **Obv:** National arms **Rev:** Aibyn Order Star

| Date | Mintage | VF20 | XF40 | MS60 | MS63 | MS65 |
|---|---|---|---|---|---|---|
| 2008 | — | — | — | 5.00 | 7.00 | 9.00 |

**KM# 172 50 TENGE**
11.37 g., Copper-Nickel, 31 mm. **Subject:** Astana capital, 10th Anniversary **Obv:** National arms **Rev:** Architecture

| Date | Mintage | VF20 | XF40 | MS60 | MS63 | MS65 |
|---|---|---|---|---|---|---|
| 2008 | — | — | — | 5.00 | 7.00 | 9.00 |

**KM# 201 50 TENGE**
11.37 g., Copper-Nickel, 31 mm. **Obv:** National emblem **Rev:** Building views

| Date | Mintage | VF20 | XF40 | MS60 | MS63 | MS65 |
|---|---|---|---|---|---|---|
| 2008 | 50,000 | — | — | 5.00 | 7.00 | 9.00 |

**KM# 202 50 TENGE**
11.37 g., Copper-Nickel, 31 mm. **Obv:** Human figure and solar system **Rev:** Spaceship Vostok

| Date | Mintage | VF20 | XF40 | MS60 | MS63 | MS65 |
|---|---|---|---|---|---|---|
| 2008 | 50,000 | — | — | 5.00 | 7.00 | 9.00 |

**KM# 132 50 TENGE**
Copper-Nickel, 31 mm. **Subject:** Betashar **Obv:** Arms **Rev:** Two figures standing

| Date | Mintage | VF20 | XF40 | MS60 | MS63 | MS65 |
|---|---|---|---|---|---|---|
| 2009 | 50,000 | — | — | 5.00 | 7.00 | 9.00 |

**KM# 135 50 TENGE**
0.50 g., 0.999 Gold AGW, 11 mm. **Obv:** Value **Rev:** Cat head sculpture

| Date | Mintage | VF20 | XF40 | MS60 | MS63 | MS65 |
|---|---|---|---|---|---|---|
| 2009 | 14,000 | PF63 40.00 | PF65 50.00 | | | |

**KM# 140 50 TENGE**
Copper-Nickel, 31 mm. **Obv:** Arms **Rev:** Parassat medal insignia

| Date | Mintage | VF20 | XF40 | MS60 | MS63 | MS65 |
|---|---|---|---|---|---|---|
| 2009 | 50,000 | — | — | 5.00 | 7.00 | 9.00 |

**KM# 141 50 TENGE**
Copper-Nickel **Obv:** Arms **Rev:** Porcupine advancing right **Shape:** 31

| Date | Mintage | VF20 | XF40 | MS60 | MS63 | MS65 |
|---|---|---|---|---|---|---|
| 2009 | 50,000 | — | — | 6.00 | 8.00 | 12.00 |

**KM# 144 50 TENGE**
Copper-Nickel, 31 mm. **Obv:** Man standing in solar system **Rev:** Apollo-Soyoz space craft

| Date | Mintage | VF20 | XF40 | MS60 | MS63 | MS65 |
|---|---|---|---|---|---|---|
| 2009 | 50,000 | — | — | 5.00 | 7.00 | 9.00 |

**KM# 145 50 TENGE**
Copper-Nickel, 31 mm. **Obv:** Arms **Rev:** Star of the Order of Dostyk

| Date | Mintage | VF20 | XF40 | MS60 | MS63 | MS65 |
|---|---|---|---|---|---|---|
| 2009 | 50,000 | — | — | 5.00 | 7.00 | 9.00 |

**KM# 146 50 TENGE**
Copper-Nickel, 31 mm. **Subject:** T. Bassenov, 100th Anniversary of Birth **Obv:** Arms **Rev:** Bust at right, architectural column

| Date | Mintage | VF20 | XF40 | MS60 | MS63 | MS65 |
|---|---|---|---|---|---|---|
| 2009 | 50,000 | — | — | 5.00 | 7.00 | 9.00 |

**KM# 152 50 TENGE**
0.50 g., 0.999 Gold AGW, 11 mm. **Subject:** Ahalavlinky Treasure **Obv:** Value **Rev:** Historical jewlery design

| Date | Mintage | VF20 | XF40 | MS60 | MS63 | MS65 |
|---|---|---|---|---|---|---|
| 2009 | 14,000 | PF63 35.00 | PF65 45.00 | | | |

**KM# 174 50 TENGE**
Copper-Nickel, 31 mm. **Subject:** Moon Exploration, 40th Anniversary **Obv:** Figure standing within solar system design **Rev:** Lunar Rover vehicle

| Date | Mintage | VF20 | XF40 | MS60 | MS63 | MS65 |
|---|---|---|---|---|---|---|
| 2010 | — | — | — | 5.00 | 7.00 | 9.00 |

**KM# 175 50 TENGE**
Copper-Nickel, 31 mm. **Subject:** Great Victory, 65th Anniversary **Obv:** National Emblem, value below **Rev:** Order star, 1945 above

| Date | Mintage | VF20 | XF40 | MS60 | MS63 | MS65 |
|---|---|---|---|---|---|---|
| 2010 | — | — | — | 5.00 | 7.00 | 9.00 |

**KM# 224 50 TENGE**
Copper-Nickel, 31 mm. **Obv:** Arms **Rev:** Star of the Order of Kormet

| Date | Mintage | VF20 | XF40 | MS60 | MS63 | MS65 |
|---|---|---|---|---|---|---|
| 2010 | — | — | — | 5.00 | 7.00 | 9.00 |

**KM# 239 50 TENGE**
11.37 g., Copper-Nickel, 31 mm. **Rev:** Curly head pelican

| Date | Mintage | VF20 | XF40 | MS60 | MS63 | MS65 |
|---|---|---|---|---|---|---|
| 2010 Proof | 50,000 | — | — | — | 6.00 | 8.00 |

**KM# 240 50 TENGE**
11.37 g., Copper-Nickel, 31 mm. **Subject:** Qurmet Civilian Award

| Date | Mintage | VF20 | XF40 | MS60 | MS63 | MS65 |
|---|---|---|---|---|---|---|
| 2010 | 50,000 | — | — | — | 6.00 | 8.00 |

**KM# 241 50 TENGE**
11.37 g., Copper-Nickel, 31 mm. **Rev:** Horseman with Yerts Cross

| Date | Mintage | VF20 | XF40 | MS60 | MS63 | MS65 |
|---|---|---|---|---|---|---|
| 2010 | 50,000 | — | — | — | 6.00 | 8.00 |

**KM# 206 50 TENGE**
Copper-Nickel, 31 mm. **Subject:** Aktobe **Rev:** Griffin seal

| Date | Mintage | VF20 | XF40 | MS60 | MS63 | MS65 |
|---|---|---|---|---|---|---|
| 2011 | — | — | — | 2.25 | 3.50 | 7.50 |

**KM# 207 50 TENGE**
4.71 g., Copper-Nickel, 31 mm. **Subject:** Aitys **Obv:** National arms **Rev:** Celebration

| Date | Mintage | VF20 | XF40 | MS60 | MS63 | MS65 |
|---|---|---|---|---|---|---|
| 2011 | 50,000 | — | — | 2.25 | 3.50 | 7.50 |

**KM# 208 50 TENGE**
4.71 g., Copper-Nickel, 31 mm. **Subject:** Ust Kamenogorsk **Obv:** Shield **Rev:** Value

| Date | Mintage | VF20 | XF40 | MS60 | MS63 | MS65 |
|---|---|---|---|---|---|---|
| 2011 | 50,000 | — | — | 2.25 | 3.50 | 7.50 |

**KM# 209 50 TENGE**
4.71 g., Copper-Nickel **Subject:** Karaganda **Obv:** Shield **Rev:** Value

| Date | Mintage | VF20 | XF40 | MS60 | MS63 | MS65 |
|---|---|---|---|---|---|---|
| 2011 | 50,000 | — | — | 2.25 | 3.50 | 7.50 |

**KM# 210 50 TENGE**
11.37 g., Copper-Nickel, 31 mm. **Subject:** Independence, 20th Anniversary **Obv:** Arms **Rev:** Anniversary logo

| Date | Mintage | VF20 | XF40 | MS60 | MS63 | MS65 |
|---|---|---|---|---|---|---|
| 2011 | — | — | — | — | 5.00 | 10.00 |

**KM# 253 50 TENGE**
11.37 g., Copper-Nickel, 31 mm. **Subject:** Manned space flight, 50th Anniversary **Rev:** Juri A. Gagarin

| Date | Mintage | VF20 | XF40 | MS60 | MS63 | MS65 |
|---|---|---|---|---|---|---|
| 2011 | 50,000 | — | — | — | 4.00 | 8.00 |

**KM# 256 50 TENGE**
11.37 g., Copper-Nickel, 31 mm. **Rev:** Hawk owl

| Date | Mintage | VF20 | XF40 | MS60 | MS63 | MS65 |
|---|---|---|---|---|---|---|
| 2011 | 50,000 | — | — | — | 4.00 | 8.00 |

**KM# 39 100 TENGE**
6.23 g., Bi-Metallic Copper-Nickel-Zinc center in Nickel-Brass ring, 24.4 mm. **Obv:** National emblem **Rev:** Value within lined circle flanked by designs **Edge:** Reeding over incuse value

| Date | Mintage | VF20 | XF40 | MS60 | MS63 | MS65 |
|---|---|---|---|---|---|---|
| 2002 | — | — | — | 2.00 | 3.50 | 5.50 |
| 2004 | — | — | — | 2.00 | 3.50 | 5.50 |
| 2005 | — | — | — | 2.00 | 3.50 | 5.50 |
| 2006 | — | — | — | 2.00 | 3.50 | 5.50 |
| 2007 | — | — | — | 2.00 | 3.50 | 5.50 |

**KM# 49 100 TENGE**
6.40 g., Bi-Metallic Copper-Nickel-Zinc center in Nickel-Brass ring, 24.5 mm. **Obv:** Stylized chicken **Rev:** Value within lined circle flanked by designs **Edge:** Reeded and lettered

| Date | Mintage | VF20 | XF40 | MS60 | MS63 | MS65 |
|---|---|---|---|---|---|---|
| 2003 | 100,000 | — | — | 2.50 | 4.00 | 6.50 |

**KM# 50 100 TENGE**
6.40 g., Bi-Metallic Copper-Nickel-Zinc center in Nickel-Brass ring, 24.5 mm. **Obv:** Stylized panther **Rev:** Value within lined circle flanked by designs **Edge:** Reeded and lettered

| Date | Mintage | VF20 | XF40 | MS60 | MS63 | MS65 |
|---|---|---|---|---|---|---|
| 2003 | 100,000 | — | — | 2.50 | 4.00 | 6.50 |

**KM# 51 100 TENGE**
6.40 g., Bi-Metallic Copper-Nickel-Zinc center in Nickel-Brass ring, 24.5 mm. **Obv:** Stylized wolf's head **Rev:** Value within lined circle flanked by designs **Edge:** Reeded and lettered

| Date | Mintage | VF20 | XF40 | MS60 | MS63 | MS65 |
|---|---|---|---|---|---|---|
| 2003 | 100,000 | — | — | 2.50 | 4.00 | 6.50 |

**KM# 52 100 TENGE**
6.40 g., Bi-Metallic Copper-Nickel-Zinc center in Nickel-Brass ring, 24.5 mm. **Obv:** Stylized sheep's head **Rev:** Value within lined circle flanked by designs **Edge:** Reeded and lettered

| Date | Mintage | VF20 | XF40 | MS60 | MS63 | MS65 |
|---|---|---|---|---|---|---|
| 2003 | 100,000 | — | — | 2.50 | 4.00 | 6.50 |

**KM# 116 100 TENGE**
31.10 g., 0.925 Silver 0.9249 oz. ASW, 37 mm. **Subject:** Olympics **Obv:** Arms and stylized stadium **Rev:** Two cyclists

| Date | Mintage | VF20 | XF40 | MS60 | MS63 | MS65 |
|---|---|---|---|---|---|---|
| 2004 | — | PF65 55.00 | | | | |

**KM# 119 100 TENGE**
31.10 g., 0.925 Silver 0.9249 oz. ASW, 37 mm. **Subject:** FIFA World Cup, Germany **Obv:** Arms and stylized stadium **Rev:** Two soccer players and large ball

| Date | Mintage | VF20 | XF40 | MS60 | MS63 | MS65 |
|---|---|---|---|---|---|---|
| 2004 | — | PF65 55.00 | | | | |

**KM# 120 100 TENGE**
1.24 g., 0.999 Gold 0.0398 oz. AGW, 13.92 mm. **Subject:** King Kroisos **Obv:** Arms **Rev:** Head left, coin, temple

| Date | Mintage | VF20 | XF40 | MS60 | MS63 | MS65 |
|---|---|---|---|---|---|---|
| 2004 | — | PF63 75.00 | PF65 85.00 | | | |

**KM# 121 100 TENGE**
1.24 g., 0.999 Gold 0.0398 oz. AGW, 13.92 mm. **Subject:** King Midas **Rev:** King Midas reclining on bench

| Date | Mintage | VF20 | XF40 | MS60 | MS63 | MS65 |
|---|---|---|---|---|---|---|
| 2004 | — | PF63 75.00 | PF65 85.00 | | | |

**KM# 122 100 TENGE**
1.24 g., 0.999 Gold 0.0398 oz. AGW, 13.92 mm. **Subject:** Ancient Turkestan **Obv:** Arms **Rev:** Camel caravan and building

| Date | Mintage | VF20 | XF40 | MS60 | MS63 | MS65 |
|---|---|---|---|---|---|---|
| 2004 | — | PF63 75.00 | PF65 85.00 | | | |

**KM# 188 100 TENGE**
1.24 g., 0.999 Gold 0.0398 oz. AGW, 13.92 mm. **Rev:** Marco Polo

| Date | Mintage | VF20 | XF40 | MS60 | MS63 | MS65 |
|---|---|---|---|---|---|---|
| 2004 | 15,000 | PF63 85.00 | PF65 100 | | | |

**KM# 57 100 TENGE**
6.40 g., Bi-Metallic Copper-Nickel-Zinc center in Nickel-Brass ring, 24.5 mm. **Subject:** 60th Anniversary of the UN **Obv:** UN logo as part of the number 60 **Rev:** Value within lined circle flanked by designs **Edge:** Reeded and lettered

| Date | Mintage | VF20 | XF40 | MS60 | MS63 | MS65 |
|---|---|---|---|---|---|---|
| 2005 | — | — | — | 3.00 | 5.00 | 7.50 |

**KM# 191 100 TENGE**
31.11 g., 0.925 Silver 0.925 oz. ASW, 38.61 mm. **Subject:** Torino Winter Olympics **Rev:** Three stone cross-country skiers

| Date | Mintage | VF20 | XF40 | MS60 | MS63 | MS65 |
|---|---|---|---|---|---|---|
| 2005 | 10,000 | PF63 50.00 | PF65 60.00 | | | |

**KM# 95 100 TENGE**
31.11 g., 0.925 Silver 0.925 oz. ASW, 38.61 mm. **Subject:** Baiturramman Mosque **Rev:** Mosque and reflecting pool

| Date | Mintage | VF20 | XF40 | MS60 | MS63 | MS65 |
|---|---|---|---|---|---|---|
| 2006 (2008) | 6,000 | PF65 80.00 | | | | |

**KM# 98 100 TENGE**
31.11 g., 0.925 Silver 0.925 oz. ASW, 38.61 mm. **Subject:** Zahir Mosque **Rev:** Mosque

| Date | Mintage | VF20 | XF40 | MS60 | MS63 | MS65 |
|---|---|---|---|---|---|---|
| 2006 | 6,000 | PF65 80.00 | | | | |

**KM# 195 100 TENGE**
31.11 g., 0.925 Silver 0.925 oz. ASW, 38.61 mm. **Subject:** Olympics 2008 **Obv:** National emblem in stadium **Rev:** Boxers

| Date | Mintage | VF20 | XF40 | MS60 | MS63 | MS65 |
|---|---|---|---|---|---|---|
| 2006 | 4,000 | PF65 75.00 | | | | |

**KM# 200 100 TENGE**
1.24 g., 0.999 Gold 0.0398 oz. AGW, 13.92 mm. **Obv:** National emblem **Rev:** Decoration

| Date | Mintage | VF20 | XF40 | MS60 | MS63 | MS65 |
|---|---|---|---|---|---|---|
| 2006 | 18,000 | PF63 85.00 | PF65 100 | | | |

**KM# 166 100 TENGE**
31.10 g., 0.925 Silver 0.9249 oz. ASW, 37 mm. **Subject:** Olympics - Pentathlon **Obv:** National arms and stylized stadium **Rev:** Five sports

| Date | Mintage | VF20 | XF40 | MS60 | MS63 | MS65 |
|---|---|---|---|---|---|---|
| 2007 | — | PF65 55.00 | | | | |

**KM# 96 100 TENGE**
31.11 g., 0.925 Silver 0.925 oz. ASW, 38.61 mm. **Subject:** Faisal Mosque, Islamabad **Rev:** Mosque

| Date | Mintage | VF20 | XF40 | MS60 | MS63 | MS65 |
|---|---|---|---|---|---|---|
| 2006 (2008) | 6,000 | PF65 80.00 | | | | |

**KM# 97 100 TENGE**
31.11 g., 0.925 Silver 0.925 oz. ASW, 38.61 mm. **Subject:** Hodja Akhmed Yassavi Mausoleum Turkestan **Rev:** Mausoleum

| Date | Mintage | VF20 | XF40 | MS60 | MS63 | MS65 |
|---|---|---|---|---|---|---|
| 2006 (2008) | 6,000 | PF65 80.00 | | | | |

**KM# 110 100 TENGE**
31.11 g., 0.925 Silver 0.925 oz. ASW, 38.61 mm. **Subject:** Chingis Khan **Rev:** Khan on horseback facing

| Date | Mintage | VF20 | XF40 | MS60 | MS63 | MS65 |
|---|---|---|---|---|---|---|
| 2008 | 13,000 | PF63 55.00 | PF65 65.00 | | | |

**KM# 125 100 TENGE**
31.11 g., 0.925 Silver 0.925 oz. ASW, 38.61 mm. **Subject:** Attila the Hun **Rev:** Medallic Profile right

| Date | Mintage | VF20 | XF40 | MS60 | MS63 | MS65 |
|---|---|---|---|---|---|---|
| 2009 | 13,000 | PF63 65.00 | PF65 75.00 | | | |

**KM# 126 100 TENGE**
31.11 g., 0.925 Silver 0.925 oz. ASW, 38.61 mm. **Subject:** 2010 Olympics **Rev:** Ski jumper over Vancouver skyline

| Date | Mintage | VF20 | XF40 | MS60 | MS63 | MS65 |
|---|---|---|---|---|---|---|
| 2009 | 12,000 | PF63 45.00 | PF65 55.00 | | | |

**KM# 134 100 TENGE**
31.10 g., 0.925 Silver 0.9249 oz. ASW partially gilt **Obv:** Arms **Rev:** Western Lynx head facing, partially gilt

| Date | Mintage | VF20 | XF40 | MS60 | MS63 | MS65 |
|---|---|---|---|---|---|---|
| 2009 | 13,000 | PF63 45.00 | PF65 55.00 | | | |

**KM# 136 100 TENGE**
1.24 g., 0.999 Gold 0.0398 oz. AGW, 13.92 mm. **Obv:** Value **Rev:** Cat head sculpture

| Date | Mintage | VF20 | XF40 | MS60 | MS63 | MS65 |
|---|---|---|---|---|---|---|
| 2009 | 9,500 | PF63 75.00 | PF65 85.00 | | | |

**KM# 147 100 TENGE**
31.10 g., 0.925 Silver 0.9249 oz. ASW, 38.6 mm. **Obv:** Arms **Rev:** Tiger advancing right

| Date | Mintage | VF20 | XF40 | MS60 | MS63 | MS65 |
|---|---|---|---|---|---|---|
| 2009 | 13,000 | PF63 55.00 | PF65 65.00 | | | |

**KM# 151 100 TENGE**
31.10 g., 0.999 Silver 0.9989 oz. ASW, 38.61 mm. **Subject:** World Cup, South Africa **Obv:** Arms and stadium **Rev:** Soccer Player, gilt ball

| Date | Mintage | VF20 | XF40 | MS60 | MS63 | MS65 |
|---|---|---|---|---|---|---|
| 2009 | — | PF65 50.00 | | | | |

**KM# 153 100 TENGE**
1.24 g., 0.999 Gold 0.0398 oz. AGW, 13.92 mm. **Subject:** Zhalavlinky Treasure **Obv:** Arms **Rev:** Historic jewelery design

| Date | Mintage | VF20 | XF40 | MS60 | MS63 | MS65 |
|---|---|---|---|---|---|---|
| 2009 | 9,500 | PF63 75.00 | PF65 85.00 | | | |

**KM# 220 100 TENGE**
1.24 g., 0.999 Gold 0.0398 oz. AGW, 13.92 mm. **Rev:** Two lions on rock

| Date | Mintage | VF20 | XF40 | MS60 | MS63 | MS65 |
|---|---|---|---|---|---|---|
| 2009 | — | PF63 110 | PF65 125 | | | |

**KM# 227 100 TENGE**
1.24 g., 0.999 Gold 0.0398 oz. AGW, 13.92 mm. **Subject:** Snow Leopard

| Date | Mintage | VF20 | XF40 | MS60 | MS63 | MS65 |
|---|---|---|---|---|---|---|
| 2009 | Est. 9500 | PF63 75.00 | PF65 85.00 | | | |

**KM# 228 100 TENGE**
31.10 g., 0.925 Silver 0.9249 oz. ASW, 38.61 mm. **Subject:** Snow Leopard

| Date | Mintage | VF20 | XF40 | MS60 | MS63 | MS65 |
|---|---|---|---|---|---|---|
| 2009 | Est. 7000 | PF65 55.00 | | | | |

**KM# 176 100 TENGE**
31.10 g., 0.925 Silver 0.9249 oz. ASW, 38.61 mm. **Obv:** State Emblem, gilt horsemen at right **Rev:** Queen Tomris

| Date | Mintage | VF20 | XF40 | MS60 | MS63 | MS65 |
|---|---|---|---|---|---|---|
| 2010 | — | PF65 70.00 | | | | |

**KM# 245 100 TENGE**
1.24 g., 0.999 Gold 0.0398 oz. AGW, 13.92 mm. **Subject:** Asian Winter Games in Astana and Almaty **Obv:** Fir in the Sky Mountains **Rev:** Games logo

| Date | Mintage | VF20 | XF40 | MS60 | MS63 | MS65 |
|---|---|---|---|---|---|---|
| 2010 | 8,000 | PF65 90.00 | | | | |

**KM# 248 100 TENGE**
31.10 g., 0.925 Silver 0.9249 oz. ASW, 38.61 mm. **Subject:** XXX Summer Olympics - London **Rev:** Wrestlers

| Date | Mintage | VF20 | XF40 | MS60 | MS63 | MS65 |
|---|---|---|---|---|---|---|
| 2010 | 12,000 | PF63 55.00 | PF65 65.00 | | | |

**KM# 249 100 TENGE**
31.10 g., 0.925 Silver 0.9249 oz. ASW, 38.61 mm. **Subject:** XXX Summer Olympics - London **Rev:** Weightlifter

| Date | Mintage | VF20 | XF40 | MS60 | MS63 | MS65 |
|---|---|---|---|---|---|---|
| 2010 | 12,000 | PF63 55.00 | PF65 65.00 | | | |

**KM# 211 100 TENGE**
31.11 g., 0.925 Silver 0.925 oz. ASW, 38.61 mm. **Subject:** Olympics, 2014 **Rev:** Speed Skating

| Date | Mintage | VF20 | XF40 | MS60 | MS63 | MS65 |
|---|---|---|---|---|---|---|
| 2011 | — | PF65 75.00 | | | | |

**KM# 234 100 TENGE**
31.11 g., 0.925 Silver 0.925 oz. ASW partially gilt, 38.61 mm. **Subject:** Sultan Baybars **Obv:** Sultan on horseback at left, National Arms gilt at right **Rev:** Sultan on horseback

| Date | Mintage | VF20 | XF40 | MS60 | MS63 | MS65 |
|---|---|---|---|---|---|---|
| 2012 | — | PF65 75.00 | | | | |

**KM# 263 100 TENGE**
24.00 g., 0.925 Silver 0.7137 oz. ASW, 37 mm. **Subject:** 2016 Olympics - Pole Vault

| Date | Mintage | VF20 | XF40 | MS60 | MS63 | MS65 |
|---|---|---|---|---|---|---|
| 2013 | Est. 8000 | PF63 65.00 | PF65 75.00 | | | |

**KM# 226 100 TENGE**
31.10 g., 0.925 Silver 0.9249 oz. ASW, 38.61 mm. **Subject:** Sotchi Olympic Games - Skating

| Date | Mintage | VF20 | XF40 | MS60 | MS63 | MS65 |
|---|---|---|---|---|---|---|
| 2014 | Est. 8000 | PF63 45.00 | PF65 55.00 | | | |

**KM# 237 200 TENGE**
62.20 g., 0.9999 Gold 1.9996 oz. AGW, 38.61 mm. **Rev:** Irbis

| Date | Mintage | VF20 | XF40 | MS60 | MS63 | MS65 |
|---|---|---|---|---|---|---|
| 2010 | — | — | — | — | — | 2,700 |

**KM# 37 500 TENGE**
23.90 g., 0.925 Silver 0.7108 oz. ASW, 37 mm. **Subject:** Wildlife **Obv:** Value **Rev:** Female Saiga with two calves **Edge:** Plain

| Date | Mintage | VF20 | XF40 | MS60 | MS63 | MS65 |
|---|---|---|---|---|---|---|
| 2001 | 3,000 | PF65 90.00 | | | | |

**KM# 38 500 TENGE**
23.81 g., 0.925 Silver 0.7081 oz. ASW, 36.9 mm. **Subject:** 10 Years of Independence **Obv:** Monument and flag **Rev:** National emblem within design above value **Edge:** Plain

| Date | Mintage | VF20 | XF40 | MS60 | MS63 | MS65 |
|---|---|---|---|---|---|---|
| 2001 | — | PF65 125 | | | | |

**KM# 55 500 TENGE**
24.00 g., 0.925 Silver 0.7137 oz. ASW, 37 mm. **Obv:** Value **Rev:** Altai Mountain petroglyph **Edge:** Plain

| Date | Mintage | VF20 | XF40 | MS60 | MS63 | MS65 |
|---|---|---|---|---|---|---|
| 2001 | 3,000 | PF65 175 | | | | |

**KM# 66 500 TENGE**
24.00 g., 0.925 Silver 0.7137 oz. ASW, 37 mm. **Obv:** Man seated under tree playing stringed instrument **Rev:** Stringed instrument, musical notes

| Date | Mintage | VF20 | XF40 | MS60 | MS63 | MS65 |
|---|---|---|---|---|---|---|
| 2001 | — | PF65 50.00 | | | | |

**KM# 112 500 TENGE**
24.00 g., 0.925 Silver 0.7137 oz. ASW **Subject:** Applied art, stringed instrument **Obv:** Man seated under tree **Rev:** Stringed instrument and notes

| Date | Mintage | VF20 | XF40 | MS60 | MS63 | MS65 |
|---|---|---|---|---|---|---|
| 2001 | — | PF65 42.00 | | | | |

**KM# 42 500 TENGE**
23.90 g., 0.925 Silver 0.7108 oz. ASW, 37 mm. **Subject:** Music **Obv:** Musician and value divided by tree **Rev:** Musical instruments **Edge:** Plain

| Date | Mintage | VF20 | XF40 | MS60 | MS63 | MS65 |
|---|---|---|---|---|---|---|
| 2002 | — | PF65 165 | | | | |

**KM# 43 500 TENGE**
23.90 g., 0.925 Silver 0.7108 oz. ASW, 37 mm. **Subject:** Prehistoric Art **Obv:** Value **Rev:** Prehistoric cave art **Edge:** Plain

| Date | Mintage | VF20 | XF40 | MS60 | MS63 | MS65 |
|---|---|---|---|---|---|---|
| 2002 | 3,000 | PF65 140 | | | | |

**KM# 44 500 TENGE**
23.90 g., 0.925 Silver 0.7108 oz. ASW, 37 mm. **Subject:** Bighorn Sheep **Obv:** Value **Rev:** Kazakhstan Argali Ram **Edge:** Plain

| Date | Mintage | VF20 | XF40 | MS60 | MS63 | MS65 |
|---|---|---|---|---|---|---|
| 2002 | 3,000 | PF65 120 | | | | |

**KM# 113 500 TENGE**
24.00 g., 0.925 Silver 0.7137 oz. ASW, 37 mm. **Subject:** Petroglyph **Obv:** Value on traditional weave pattern **Rev:** Horse petroglyph

| Date | Mintage | VF20 | XF40 | MS60 | MS63 | MS65 |
|---|---|---|---|---|---|---|
| 2002 | — | PF65 60.00 | | | | |

**KM# 183 500 TENGE**
24.00 g., 0.925 Silver 0.7137 oz. ASW, 36. mm. **Obv:** Large value within brick arch design **Rev:** Byzantine church and floor plan

| Date | Mintage | VF20 | XF40 | MS60 | MS63 | MS65 |
|---|---|---|---|---|---|---|
| 2002 | 3,000 | PF65 75.00 | | | | |

**KM# 53 500 TENGE**
24.00 g., 0.925 Silver 0.7137 oz. ASW, 37 mm. **Obv:** Value **Rev:** Great Bustard bird standing on ground **Edge:** Plain

| Date | Mintage | VF20 | XF40 | MS60 | MS63 | MS65 |
|---|---|---|---|---|---|---|
| 2003 | 3,000 | PF65 75.00 | | | | |

**KM# 56 500 TENGE**
24.00 g., 0.925 Silver 0.7137 oz. ASW, 37 mm. **Subject:** Applied Arts **Obv:** Folk Dancer **Rev:** Cultural artifacts **Edge:** Plain

| Date | Mintage | VF20 | XF40 | MS60 | MS63 | MS65 |
|---|---|---|---|---|---|---|
| 2003 | 3,000 | PF65 80.00 | | | | |

**KM# 184 500 TENGE**
24.00 g., 0.925 Silver 0.7137 oz. ASW **Rev:** Warriors in a cave

| Date | Mintage | VF20 | XF40 | MS60 | MS63 | MS65 |
|---|---|---|---|---|---|---|
| 2003 | 3,000 | PF65 60.00 | | | | |

### KM# 185 500 TENGE

24.00 g., 0.925 Silver 0.7137 oz. ASW, 36 mm. **Obv:** Intricate tile design **Rev:** View of Kecensci Mausoleum

| Date | Mintage | VF20 | XF40 | MS60 | MS63 | MS65 |
|---|---|---|---|---|---|---|
| 2003 | 3,000 | PF65 50.00 | | | | |

### KM# 59 500 TENGE

31.10 g., 0.925 Bi-Metallic 0.9249 oz. Blackend silver center in proof silver ring, 38.6 mm. **Subject:** Denga **Obv:** Black square holed coin design above value **Rev:** Black square holed coin design and metal content statement **Edge:** Reeded

| Date | Mintage | VF20 | XF40 | MS60 | MS63 | MS65 |
|---|---|---|---|---|---|---|
| 2004 | 5,000 | PF65 90.00 | | | | |

### KM# 117 500 TENGE

31.10 g., 0.925 Silver 0.9249 oz. ASW partially gilt, 38.6 mm. **Obv:** Three riders **Rev:** Golden deer ornament **Shape:** 12-sided

| Date | Mintage | VF20 | XF40 | MS60 | MS63 | MS65 |
|---|---|---|---|---|---|---|
| 2004 | — | PF65 100 | | | | |

### KM# 186 500 TENGE

24.00 g., 0.925 Silver 0.7137 oz. ASW **Rev:** Saker Falcon

| Date | Mintage | VF20 | XF40 | MS60 | MS63 | MS65 |
|---|---|---|---|---|---|---|
| 2004 | 3,000 | PF65 75.00 | | | | |

### KM# 187 500 TENGE

24.00 g., 0.925 Silver 0.7137 oz. ASW, 37 mm. **Rev:** Cave painting of a Shaman in Tamgaly

| Date | Mintage | VF20 | XF40 | MS60 | MS63 | MS65 |
|---|---|---|---|---|---|---|
| 2004 | 3,000 | PF65 75.00 | | | | |

### KM# 189 500 TENGE

24.00 g., 0.925 Silver 0.7137 oz. ASW, 36 mm. **Obv:** Tree of Life **Rev:** Three stone figures

| Date | Mintage | VF20 | XF40 | MS60 | MS63 | MS65 |
|---|---|---|---|---|---|---|
| 2004 | 3,000 | PF65 75.00 | | | | |

### KM# 190 500 TENGE

24.00 g., 0.925 Silver 0.7137 oz. ASW, 36 mm. **Obv:** Woman in national costume playing the zither **Rev:** Zither and musical notes

| Date | Mintage | VF20 | XF40 | MS60 | MS63 | MS65 |
|---|---|---|---|---|---|---|
| 2004 | 3,000 | PF65 75.00 | | | | |

### KM# 60 500 TENGE

24.00 g., 0.925 Silver 0.7137 oz. ASW, 37 mm. **Obv:** Value **Rev:** Prehistoric art horseman **Edge:** Plain

| Date | Mintage | VF20 | XF40 | MS60 | MS63 | MS65 |
|---|---|---|---|---|---|---|
| 2005 | 3,000 | PF65 70.00 | | | | |

### KM# 61 500 TENGE

24.00 g., 0.925 Silver 0.7137 oz. ASW, 37 mm. **Obv:** Value **Rev:** Two Goitered Gazelles **Edge:** Plain

| Date | Mintage | VF20 | XF40 | MS60 | MS63 | MS65 |
|---|---|---|---|---|---|---|
| 2005 | 3,000 | PF65 70.00 | | | | |

### KM# 62 500 TENGE

31.10 g., 0.925 Silver 0.9249 oz. ASW, 38.6 mm. **Obv:** Horse race and value **Rev:** Gold plated tiger **Edge:** Plain **Shape:** 12-sided

| Date | Mintage | VF20 | XF40 | MS60 | MS63 | MS65 |
|---|---|---|---|---|---|---|
| 2005 | 5,000 | PF65 120 | | | | |

### KM# 63 500 TENGE

31.10 g., 0.925 Bi-Metallic 0.9249 oz. Blackened Silver center in proof Silver ring, 38.6 mm. **Subject:** Drakhma" coin **Obv:** Old coin design **Rev:** Old coin design **Edge:** Reeded

| Date | Mintage | VF20 | XF40 | MS60 | MS63 | MS65 |
|---|---|---|---|---|---|---|
| 2005 | 5,000 | PF65 65.00 | | | | |

### KM# 72 500 TENGE

31.10 g., 0.925 Silver 0.9249 oz. ASW, 38.6 mm. **Obv:** Horse race and value **Rev:** Gold plated rider **Edge:** Plain

| Date | Mintage | VF20 | XF40 | MS60 | MS63 | MS65 |
|---|---|---|---|---|---|---|
| 2005 | 5,000 | PF65 100 | | | | |

### KM# 124 500 TENGE

24.00 g., 0.925 Silver 0.7137 oz. ASW, 37 mm. **Subject:** Zhoshi Khan Mausoleum **Rev:** 3/4 view of building facade

| Date | Mintage | VF20 | XF40 | MS60 | MS63 | MS65 |
|---|---|---|---|---|---|---|
| 2005 | — | PF65 50.00 | | | | |

### KM# 192 500 TENGE

24.00 g., 0.925 Silver 0.7137 oz. ASW, 36 mm. **Obv:** Man seated with stringed musical instrument **Rev:** two string musical instruments, musical notes at right

| Date | Mintage | VF20 | XF40 | MS60 | MS63 | MS65 |
|---|---|---|---|---|---|---|
| 2005 | 3,000 | PF65 55.00 | | | | |

### KM# 193 500 TENGE

7.78 g., 0.999 Gold 0.2499 oz. AGW, 25 mm. **Obv:** State shield **Rev:** head of a dhole

| Date | Mintage | VF20 | XF40 | MS60 | MS63 | MS65 |
|---|---|---|---|---|---|---|
| 2005 | — | PF65 750 | | | | |

### KM# 76 500 TENGE

31.10 g., 0.925 Silver 0.9249 oz. ASW **Series:** Flora **Rev:** Tulopa Regeli in multicolor

| Date | Mintage | VF20 | XF40 | MS60 | MS63 | MS65 |
|---|---|---|---|---|---|---|
| 2006 | — | PF65 150 | | | | |

### KM# 83 500 TENGE

24.00 g., 0.925 Silver 0.7137 oz. ASW, 38.7 mm. **Obv:** Value at center **Rev:** Tetraogallus Altalcus, Altai Snowcock

| Date | Mintage | VF20 | XF40 | MS60 | MS63 | MS65 |
|---|---|---|---|---|---|---|
| 2006 | 3,000 | PF65 100 | | | | |

### KM# 84 500 TENGE

31.10 g., 0.925 Bi-Metallic 0.9249 oz. Blackened Silver center in proof Silver ring., 38.6 mm. **Subject:** Dirkhem" coin **Obv:** Old coin design **Rev:** Old coin design **Edge:** Reeded

| Date | Mintage | VF20 | XF40 | MS60 | MS63 | MS65 |
|---|---|---|---|---|---|---|
| 2006 | 5,000 | PF65 65.00 | | | | |

### KM# 162 500 TENGE

0.999 Gold **Obv:** Archway **Rev:** Al-Baram Mosque in Mecca

| Date | Mintage | VF20 | XF40 | MS60 | MS63 | MS65 |
|---|---|---|---|---|---|---|
| 2006 | — | PF65 500 | | | | |

### KM# 163 500 TENGE

0.999 Gold **Obv:** Archway **Rev:** Al-Nabawi Mosque in Medina

| Date | Mintage | VF20 | XF40 | MS60 | MS63 | MS65 |
|---|---|---|---|---|---|---|
| 2006 | — | PF65 500 | | | | |

**KM# 194 500 TENGE**
24.00 g., 0.925 Silver 0.7137 oz. ASW **Rev:** Triumph cars

| Date | Mintage | VF20 | XF40 | MS60 | MS63 | MS65 |
|---|---|---|---|---|---|---|
| 2006 | 3,000 | PF65 75.00 | | | | |

**KM# 196 500 TENGE**
31.11 g., 0.925 Silver 0.925 oz. ASW, 38.61 mm. **Obv:** National emblem **Rev:** Figure seated at loom

| Date | Mintage | VF20 | XF40 | MS60 | MS63 | MS65 |
|---|---|---|---|---|---|---|
| 2006 | 4,000 | PF65 75.00 | | | | |

**KM# 197 500 TENGE**
31.11 g., 0.925 Silver 0.925 oz. ASW, 38.61 mm. **Obv:** State emblem **Rev:** Central Mosque in Almati

| Date | Mintage | VF20 | XF40 | MS60 | MS63 | MS65 |
|---|---|---|---|---|---|---|
| 2006 | 4,000 | PF65 75.00 | | | | |

**KM# 198 500 TENGE**
31.11 g., 0.925 Silver 0.925 oz. ASW, 38.61 mm. **Rev:** female with apples, a drawing by Sidorkin

| Date | Mintage | VF20 | XF40 | MS60 | MS63 | MS65 |
|---|---|---|---|---|---|---|
| 2006 | 4,000 | PF65 75.00 | | | | |

**KM# 199 500 TENGE**
41.00 g., Bi-Metallic Silver and Tantalium, 38.61 mm. **Obv:** Figure standing within solar system **Rev:** Spaceman and orbits of planets

| Date | Mintage | VF20 | XF40 | MS60 | MS63 | MS65 |
|---|---|---|---|---|---|---|
| 2006 | 4,000 | PF65 135 | | | | |

**KM# 82 500 TENGE**
41.40 g., Bi-Metallic Tantalum center in .925 Silver ring., 38.61 mm. **Subject:** 50th Anniversary Launch of Sputnik I **Obv:** Stylized view of our solar system, multicolor **Obv. Legend:** REPUBLIC OF KAZAKHSTAN **Rev:** Sputnik I in space, earth in background, multicolor **Rev. Legend:** THE FIRST SPACE SATELLITE OF THE EARTH **Edge:** Reeded

| Date | Mintage | VF20 | XF40 | MS60 | MS63 | MS65 |
|---|---|---|---|---|---|---|
| ND(2007) | 4,000 | PF65 100 | | | | |

**KM# 85 500 TENGE**
31.10 g., 0.925 Bi-Metallic 0.9249 oz. Blackened Silver center in proof Silver ring., 38.6 mm. **Subject:** Otyrar" coin **Obv:** Old coin design **Rev:** Old coin design **Edge:** Reeded

| Date | Mintage | VF20 | XF40 | MS60 | MS63 | MS65 |
|---|---|---|---|---|---|---|
| 2007 | 4,000 | PF65 75.00 | | | | |

**KM# 87 500 TENGE**
24.00 g., 0.925 Silver 0.7137 oz. ASW, 38.6 mm. **Obv:** Value **Rev:** Terekin Valley - noble deer petraglyph

| Date | Mintage | VF20 | XF40 | MS60 | MS63 | MS65 |
|---|---|---|---|---|---|---|
| 2007 | 3,000 | PF65 90.00 | | | | |

**KM# 88 500 TENGE**
31.10 g., 0.925 Silver 0.9249 oz. ASW **Subject:** Movement series - myth **Obv:** Value within square **Rev:** Design

| Date | Mintage | VF20 | XF40 | MS60 | MS63 | MS65 |
|---|---|---|---|---|---|---|
| 2007 | 4,000 | PF65 80.00 | | | | |

**KM# 89 500 TENGE**
31.10 g., 0.925 Silver 0.9249 oz. ASW, 38.6 mm. **Subject:** Gold of the Romans **Obv:** Four horseman **Rev:** Gilt Roman seal ring **Shape:** 12-sided

| Date | Mintage | VF20 | XF40 | MS60 | MS63 | MS65 |
|---|---|---|---|---|---|---|
| 2007 | 5,000 | PF65 100 | | | | |

**KM# 90 500 TENGE**
31.10 g., 0.925 Silver 0.9249 oz. ASW, 38.6 mm. **Obv:** State emblem **Rev:** Church

| Date | Mintage | VF20 | XF40 | MS60 | MS63 | MS65 |
|---|---|---|---|---|---|---|
| 2007 | 4,000 | PF65 75.00 | | | | |

**KM# 91 500 TENGE**
31.10 g., 0.925 Silver 0.9249 oz. ASW, 38.6 mm. **Obv:** State emblem **Rev:** Traditional family

| Date | Mintage | VF20 | XF40 | MS60 | MS63 | MS65 |
|---|---|---|---|---|---|---|
| 2007 | 4,000 | PF65 70.00 | | | | |

**KM# 92 500 TENGE**
31.10 g., 0.925 Silver 0.9249 oz. ASW, 38.6 mm. **Obv:** Leaves **Rev:** Tree growth rings, multicolor seeds

| Date | Mintage | VF20 | XF40 | MS60 | MS63 | MS65 |
|---|---|---|---|---|---|---|
| 2007 | 4,000 | PF65 75.00 | | | | |

**KM# 93 500 TENGE**
24.00 g., 0.925 Silver 0.7137 oz. ASW, 38.6 mm. **Subject:** Spoon billed duck **Obv:** Value **Rev:** Duck in reeds

| Date | Mintage | VF20 | XF40 | MS60 | MS63 | MS65 |
|---|---|---|---|---|---|---|
| 2007 | 3,000 | PF65 85.00 | | | | |

**KM# 167 500 TENGE**
7.78 g., 0.999 Gold 0.2499 oz. AGW, 25 mm. **Subject:** Olympics, high jump **Obv:** Arms and stylized stadium **Rev:** Female high jump

| Date | Mintage | VF20 | XF40 | MS60 | MS63 | MS65 |
|---|---|---|---|---|---|---|
| 2007 | — | PF65 460 | | | | |

**KM# 168 500 TENGE**
7.77 g., 0.999 Gold 0.2496 oz. AGW, 25 mm. **Obv:** Arms **Rev:** Lynx, crystal eyes **Rev. Legend:** FELIS LYNX

| Date | Mintage | VF20 | XF40 | MS60 | MS63 | MS65 |
|---|---|---|---|---|---|---|
| 2007 | — | PF65 475 | | | | |

**KM# 94 500 TENGE**
31.11 g., 0.925 Silver 0.925 oz. ASW, 38.6 mm. **Subject:** National currency, 15th Anniversary **Obv:** Three coin designs

| Date | Mintage | VF20 | XF40 | MS60 | MS63 | MS65 |
|---|---|---|---|---|---|---|
| 2008 | 5,000 | PF65 75.00 | | | | |

**KM# 99 500 TENGE**
31.11 g., 0.925 Silver 0.925 oz. ASW, 38.61 mm. **Subject:** Eurasic Capitals - Astana **Rev:** Skyline montage

| Date | Mintage | VF20 | XF40 | MS60 | MS63 | MS65 |
|---|---|---|---|---|---|---|
| 2008 | 5,000 | **PF65** 75.00 | | | | |

**KM# 100 500 TENGE**
24.00 g., 0.925 Silver 0.7137 oz. ASW, 38.61 mm. **Subject:** Tien Shan - Brown Bear **Rev:** Bear seated

| Date | Mintage | VF20 | XF40 | MS60 | MS63 | MS65 |
|---|---|---|---|---|---|---|
| 2008 | 3,000 | **PF65** 85.00 | | | | |

**KM# 101 500 TENGE**
31.11 g., 0.925 Silver 0.925 oz. ASW, 38.61 mm. **Subject:** Nomad Gold **Rev:** Diadem fragment **Shape:** 12-sided

| Date | Mintage | VF20 | XF40 | MS60 | MS63 | MS65 |
|---|---|---|---|---|---|---|
| 2008 | 5,000 | **PF65** 115 | | | | |

**KM# 102 500 TENGE**
31.11 g., 0.925 Silver 0.925 oz. ASW, 38.61 mm. **Subject:** Kalmykov **Rev:** Fantasy scene

| Date | Mintage | VF20 | XF40 | MS60 | MS63 | MS65 |
|---|---|---|---|---|---|---|
| 2008 | 4,000 | **PF65** 80.00 | | | | |

**KM# 103 500 TENGE**
31.11 g., 0.925 Silver 0.925 oz. ASW, 38.61 mm. **Subject:** Kyz Kuu **Rev:** Two horseback riders

| Date | Mintage | VF20 | XF40 | MS60 | MS63 | MS65 |
|---|---|---|---|---|---|---|
| 2008 | 4,000 | **PF65** 80.00 | | | | |

**KM# 104 500 TENGE**
31.11 g., 0.925 Silver 0.925 oz. ASW, 38.61 mm. **Subject:** Linum Olgae **Rev:** Flowers

| Date | Mintage | VF20 | XF40 | MS60 | MS63 | MS65 |
|---|---|---|---|---|---|---|
| 2008 | 4,000 | **PF65** 100 | | | | |

**KM# 106 500 TENGE**
24.00 g., 0.925 Silver 0.7137 oz. ASW, 38.6x28.8 mm. **Subject:** Papilio Alexanor **Rev:** Two butterflies **Shape:** oval

| Date | Mintage | VF20 | XF40 | MS60 | MS63 | MS65 |
|---|---|---|---|---|---|---|
| 2008 | 4,000 | **PF65** 115 | | | | |

**KM# 107 500 TENGE**
31.11 g., 0.925 Silver 0.925 oz. ASW, 38.61 mm. **Subject:** Saraichik Coin **Rev:** Coin of the 14th Century

| Date | Mintage | VF20 | XF40 | MS60 | MS63 | MS65 |
|---|---|---|---|---|---|---|
| 2008 | 5,000 | **PF65** 65.00 | | | | |

**KM# 108 500 TENGE**
41.40 g., Bi-Metallic Tantalum center in .925 Silver ring., 38.61 mm. **Subject:** Vostok **Rev:** Space ship

| Date | Mintage | VF20 | XF40 | MS60 | MS63 | MS65 |
|---|---|---|---|---|---|---|
| 2008 | 4,000 | **PF65** 110 | | | | |

**KM# 109 500 TENGE**
31.11 g., 0.925 Silver 0.925 oz. ASW, 38.61 mm. **Subject:** Zharkent Mosque **Rev:** Mosque

| Date | Mintage | VF20 | XF40 | MS60 | MS63 | MS65 |
|---|---|---|---|---|---|---|
| 2008 | 400 | **PF65** 145 | | | | |

**KM# 118 500 TENGE**
24.00 g., 0.925 Silver 0.7137 oz. ASW, 37 mm. **Subject:** Kazakhstan Railroads, 100th Anniversary **Obv:** Arms **Rev:** Modern train and Steam locomotive, country route map in background

| Date | Mintage | VF20 | XF40 | MS60 | MS63 | MS65 |
|---|---|---|---|---|---|---|
| 2008 | — | **PF65** 55.00 | | | | |

**KM# 127 500 TENGE**
7.78 g., 0.999 Gold 0.2499 oz. AGW, 25 mm. **Subject:** Olympics - Biathlon **Obv:** Arms and stylized stadium **Rev:** Biathlon, 2 cross country skiers and shooter

| Date | Mintage | VF20 | XF40 | MS60 | MS63 | MS65 |
|---|---|---|---|---|---|---|
| 2009 | 5,000 | **PF65** 445 | | | | |

**KM# 128 500 TENGE**
31.10 g., 0.999 Silver 0.9989 oz. ASW, 38.6 mm. **Subject:** Almaty Aport **Obv:** Value and leaves **Rev:** Apples and flower

| Date | Mintage | VF20 | XF40 | MS60 | MS63 | MS65 |
|---|---|---|---|---|---|---|
| 2009 | 4,000 | PF65 65.00 | | | | |

**KM# 129 500 TENGE**
31.10 g., 0.925 Silver 0.9249 oz. ASW, 36.6 mm. **Subject:** Eurasian Economic Community **Obv:** Arms **Rev:** Alpamys Batyr

| Date | Mintage | VF20 | XF40 | MS60 | MS63 | MS65 |
|---|---|---|---|---|---|---|
| 2009 | 5,000 | PF65 55.00 | | | | |

**KM# 130 500 TENGE**
41.40 g., Bi-Metallic Tantalum center in .925 Silver ring., 38.61 mm. **Subject:** Apollo - Soyoz Missions **Rev:** Spacecraft docked in orbit above the earth

| Date | Mintage | VF20 | XF40 | MS60 | MS63 | MS65 |
|---|---|---|---|---|---|---|
| 2009 | 4,000 | PF65 115 | | | | |

**KM# 131 500 TENGE**
31.11 g., 0.925 Silver 0.925 oz. ASW, 38.61 mm. **Subject:** Almaty Aport **Rev:** Apple tree branch and flower

| Date | Mintage | VF20 | XF40 | MS60 | MS63 | MS65 |
|---|---|---|---|---|---|---|
| 2009 | 4,000 | PF65 80.00 | | | | |

**KM# 133 500 TENGE**
31.11 g., 0.999 Silver 0.999 oz. ASW, 38.61 mm. **Subject:** Betashar **Rev:** Two figures standing

| Date | Mintage | VF20 | XF40 | MS60 | MS63 | MS65 |
|---|---|---|---|---|---|---|
| 2009 | 4,000 | PF65 75.00 | | | | |

**KM# 137 500 TENGE**
31.11 g., 0.925 Silver 0.925 oz. ASW, 38.61 mm. **Subject:** Coin of Almaty **Rev:** 13th Century coin

| Date | Mintage | VF20 | XF40 | MS60 | MS63 | MS65 |
|---|---|---|---|---|---|---|
| 2009 | 4,000 | PF65 100 | | | | |

**KM# 138 500 TENGE**
24.00 g., 0.925 Silver 0.7137 oz. ASW, 28.61x28.81 mm. **Subject:** Flamingo **Obv:** Partial butterfly **Rev:** Pair of flamings standing in holographic water **Shape:** Vertical oval

| Date | Mintage | VF20 | XF40 | MS60 | MS63 | MS65 |
|---|---|---|---|---|---|---|
| 2009 | 4,000 | PF65 80.00 | | | | |

**KM# 139 500 TENGE**
31.11 g., 0.925 Silver 0.925 oz. ASW, 38.6 mm. **Subject:** Nur-Astana Mosque **Rev:** Mosque

| Date | Mintage | VF20 | XF40 | MS60 | MS63 | MS65 |
|---|---|---|---|---|---|---|
| 2009 | 4,000 | PF65 75.00 | | | | |

**KM# 142 500 TENGE**
24.00 g., 0.925 Silver 0.7137 oz. ASW, 38.61 mm. **Rev:** Porcupine left with quills raised

| Date | Mintage | VF20 | XF40 | MS60 | MS63 | MS65 |
|---|---|---|---|---|---|---|
| 2009 | 3,000 | PF65 90.00 | | | | |

**KM# 143 500 TENGE**
31.11 g., 0.999 Silver 0.999 oz. ASW, 38.61 mm. **Rev:** Satir head facing **Shape:** 12-sided

| Date | Mintage | VF20 | XF40 | MS60 | MS63 | MS65 |
|---|---|---|---|---|---|---|
| 2009 | 5,000 | PF65 100 | | | | |

**KM# 148 500 TENGE**
7.78 g., 0.999 Gold 0.2499 oz. AGW, 21.87 mm. **Rev:** Tiger walking right

| Date | Mintage | VF20 | XF40 | MS60 | MS63 | MS65 |
|---|---|---|---|---|---|---|
| 2009 | 3,000 | PF65 450 | | | | |

**KM# 149 500 TENGE**
31.11 g., 0.925 Silver 0.925 oz. ASW, 38.61 mm. **Subject:** Balkhash Tiger **Rev:** Tiger on the hunt

| Date | Mintage | VF20 | XF40 | MS60 | MS63 | MS65 |
|---|---|---|---|---|---|---|
| 2009 | 5,000 | PF65 75.00 | | | | |

**KM# 150 500 TENGE**
7.78 g., 0.999 Gold 0.2499 oz. AGW, 25 mm. **Subject:** Uncia **Obv:** Arms **Rev:** Snow Leopard head left

| Date | Mintage | VF20 | XF40 | MS60 | MS63 | MS65 |
|---|---|---|---|---|---|---|
| 2009 | 5,000 | PF65 445 | | | | |

**KM# 225 500 TENGE**
7.78 g., 0.999 Gold 0.2499 oz. AGW, 25 mm. **Subject:** Biathlon Gold with 3 Diamonds

| Date | Mintage | VF20 | XF40 | MS60 | MS63 | MS65 |
|---|---|---|---|---|---|---|
| 2012 | Est. 5000 | PF65 550 | | | | |

**KM# 230 500 TENGE**
31.10 g., 0.999 Gold 0.9989 oz. AGW, 32 mm. **Subject:** Snow Leopard

| Date | Mintage | VF20 | XF40 | MS60 | MS63 | MS65 |
|---|---|---|---|---|---|---|
| 2009 | Est. 1500 | PF65 2,150 | | | | |

**KM# 231 500 TENGE**
7.78 g., 0.999 Gold 0.2499 oz. AGW, 25 mm. **Subject:** Snow Leopard with 2 Diamonds

| Date | Mintage | VF20 | XF40 | MS60 | MS63 | MS65 |
|---|---|---|---|---|---|---|
| 2009 | Est. 5000 | PF65 550 | | | | |

**KM# 177 500 TENGE**
31.10 g., 0.925 Silver 0.9249 oz. ASW **Obv:** Outline of three pelicans **Rev:** Pelecanus Crispus, pelican standing

| Date | Mintage | VF20 | XF40 | MS60 | MS63 | MS65 |
|---|---|---|---|---|---|---|
| 2010 | 5,000 | PF65 65.00 | | | | |

**KM# 178 500 TENGE**
31.10 g., 0.925 Silver 0.9249 oz. ASW, 38.6 mm. **Subject:** Otau Koteru **Obv:** National Emblem **Rev:** Horseman and large ceremonial umbrella

| Date | Mintage | VF20 | XF40 | MS60 | MS63 | MS65 |
|---|---|---|---|---|---|---|
| 2010 | 5,000 | PF65 90.00 | | | | |

**KM# 179 500 TENGE**
31.10 g., 0.925 Silver 0.9249 oz. ASW, 38.6 mm. **Obv:** Three horsemen **Rev:** Buckle, gilt pair of seated raindeer **Shape:** 12-sided

| Date | Mintage | VF20 | XF40 | MS60 | MS63 | MS65 |
|---|---|---|---|---|---|---|
| 2010 | 5,000 | PF65 85.00 | | | | |

**KM# 180 500 TENGE**
31.10 g., 0.925 Silver 0.9249 oz. ASW **Subject:** Flora **Rev:** Papaver Pavoninum in color

| Date | Mintage | VF20 | XF40 | MS60 | MS63 | MS65 |
|---|---|---|---|---|---|---|
| 2010 | 4,000 | PF65 90.00 | | | | |

**KM# 181 500 TENGE**
3.11 g., 0.999 Gold 0.0999 oz. AGW, 16 mm. **Obv:** Archway **Rev:** Dome of the Rock, Jerusalem

| Date | Mintage | VF20 | XF40 | MS60 | MS63 | MS65 |
|---|---|---|---|---|---|---|
| 2010 | — | PF65 200 | | | | |

**KM# 182 500 TENGE**
31.10 g., 0.925 Silver 0.9249 oz. ASW **Rev:** Musical instrument

| Date | Mintage | VF20 | XF40 | MS60 | MS63 | MS65 |
|---|---|---|---|---|---|---|
| 2010 | — | PF65 75.00 | | | | |

**KM# 238 500 TENGE**
155.50 g., 0.999 Gold 4.9944 oz. AGW **Rev:** Irbis

| Date | Mintage | VF20 | XF40 | MS60 | MS63 | MS65 |
|---|---|---|---|---|---|---|
| 2010 | — | — | — | — | — | 7,500 |

**KM# 242 500 TENGE**
26.80 g., 0.925 Silver 0.797 oz. ASW, 38.61 mm. **Subject:** 40th anniversary of Lunar rover **Obv:** Man within universe **Rev:** Moon vehicle

| Date | Mintage | VF20 | XF40 | MS60 | MS63 | MS65 |
|---|---|---|---|---|---|---|
| 2010 | — | PF65 135 | | | | |

**KM# 243 500 TENGE**
24.00 g., 0.925 Silver 0.7137 oz. ASW, 38.61x28.81 mm. **Subject:** Flora and Fauna **Rev:** Phrynocephalus mystaceus - Agamidae **Shape:** Oval

| Date | Mintage | VF20 | XF40 | MS60 | MS63 | MS65 |
|---|---|---|---|---|---|---|
| 2010 | 4,000 | PF65 75.00 | | | | |

**KM# 244 500 TENGE**
31.10 g., 0.925 Silver 0.9249 oz. ASW, 38.61 mm. **Subject:** Asia Winter Games in Astana and Almaty **Obv:** Drawing of Sun Gog Tengi in Mountains **Rev:** Games logo in kinegram

| Date | Mintage | VF20 | XF40 | MS60 | MS63 | MS65 |
|---|---|---|---|---|---|---|
| 2010 | 13,000 | PF63 65.00 | PF65 75.00 | | | |

**KM# 250 500 TENGE**
31.10 g., 0.925 Silver 0.9249 oz. ASW, 38.61 mm. **Subject:** Euroasian Economic Community, 10th Anniversary

| Date | Mintage | VF20 | XF40 | MS60 | MS63 | MS65 |
|---|---|---|---|---|---|---|
| 2010 | 5,000 | PF65 65.00 | | | | |

**KM# 251 500 TENGE**
3.11 g., 0.999 Gold 0.0999 oz. AGW, 16 mm. **Subject:** Mosques **Rev:** Ka'aba in Mecca

| Date | Mintage | VF20 | XF40 | MS60 | MS63 | MS65 |
|---|---|---|---|---|---|---|
| 2010 | 3,000 | PF65 200 | | | | |

**KM# 252 500 TENGE**
3.11 g., 0.999 Gold 0.0999 oz. AGW, 16 mm. **Subject:** Mosques **Rev:** Masjid Sultan in Singapore

| Date | Mintage | VF20 | XF40 | MS60 | MS63 | MS65 |
|---|---|---|---|---|---|---|
| 2010 | 3,000 | PF65 200 | | | | |

**KM# 205 500 TENGE**
24.00 g., 0.925 Silver 0.7137 oz. ASW, 38.61 mm. **Obv:** Stylized hawk at right **Rev:** Hawk on branch

| Date | Mintage | VF20 | XF40 | MS60 | MS63 | MS65 |
|---|---|---|---|---|---|---|
| 2011 | — | PF65 85.00 | | | | |

**KM# 212 500 TENGE**
31.11 g., 0.925 Silver 0.925 oz. ASW partially gilt, 38.61 mm. **Subject:** Independence, 20th Anniversary **Obv:** Map **Rev:** Architecture

| Date | Mintage | VF20 | XF40 | MS60 | MS63 | MS65 |
|---|---|---|---|---|---|---|
| 2011 | — | PF65 75.00 | | | | |

**KM# 213 500 TENGE**
31.11 g., 0.925 Silver 0.925 oz. ASW, 38.61 mm. **Subject:** Issyk Chieftain **Rev:** Standing figure, gilt **Shape:** 8-sided

| Date | Mintage | VF20 | XF40 | MS60 | MS63 | MS65 |
|---|---|---|---|---|---|---|
| 2011 | — | PF65 100 | | | | |

**KM# 214 500 TENGE**
24.00 g., 0.925 Silver 0.7137 oz. ASW partially gilt, 38.61x28.8 mm. **Subject:** Sturgen **Shape:** Oval

| Date | Mintage | VF20 | XF40 | MS60 | MS63 | MS65 |
|---|---|---|---|---|---|---|
| 2011 | 5,000 | PF65 75.00 | | | | |

**KM# 215 500 TENGE**
31.10 g., 0.925 Silver 0.9249 oz. ASW, 38.61 mm. **Subject:** Aldar Rose **Obv:** Arms **Rev:** Figure riding donkey

| Date | Mintage | VF20 | XF40 | MS60 | MS63 | MS65 |
|---|---|---|---|---|---|---|
| 2011 | — | PF65 75.00 | | | | |

**KM# 217 500 TENGE**
31.11 g., 0.925 Silver 0.925 oz. ASW partially gilt, 38.61 mm. **Subject:** Gold of the Nomads - Elk's head **Rev:** Artistic elk's head gilt **Shape:** 12-sided

| Date | Mintage | VF20 | XF40 | MS60 | MS63 | MS65 |
|---|---|---|---|---|---|---|
| 2011 | — | PF65 100 | | | | |

**KM# 218 500 TENGE**
40.70 g., Bi-Metallic .925 Silver center in Tantalum ring, 38.61 mm. **Obv:** Stylized view of solar system, man standing at center **Rev:** First astronaut at right, spacecraft at left

| Date | Mintage | VF20 | XF40 | MS60 | MS63 | MS65 |
|---|---|---|---|---|---|---|
| 2011 | — | PF65 100 | | | | |

**KM# 219 500 TENGE**
31.11 g., 0.925 Silver 0.925 oz. ASW, 38.61 mm. **Subject:** Year of the Rabbit **Obv:** Zodiac constelations of the Milky Way **Rev:** Rabbit in center of 12-year sysle of animals **Shape:** 12-sided

| Date | Mintage | VF20 | XF40 | MS60 | MS63 | MS65 |
|---|---|---|---|---|---|---|
| 2011 | — | PF65 100 | | | | |

**KM# 221 500 TENGE**
7.77 g., 0.999 Gold 0.2496 oz. AGW, 25 mm. **Rev:** Eagle owl head, crystal eye

| Date | Mintage | VF20 | XF40 | MS60 | MS63 | MS65 |
|---|---|---|---|---|---|---|
| 2011 | — | PF65 550 | | | | |

**KM# 232 500 TENGE**
7.78 g., 0.999 Gold 0.2499 oz. AGW, 25 mm. **Subject:** Eagle Owl

| Date | Mintage | VF20 | XF40 | MS60 | MS63 | MS65 |
|---|---|---|---|---|---|---|
| 2011 | Est. 5000 | PF65 550 | | | | |

**KM# 254 500 TENGE**
31.10 g., 0.925 Silver 0.9249 oz. ASW, 38.61 mm. **Subject:** Shanghai Cooperation Organization, 10th Anniversary **Obv:** National arms **Rev:** Logo

| Date | Mintage | VF20 | XF40 | MS60 | MS63 | MS65 |
|---|---|---|---|---|---|---|
| 2011 | 4,000 | PF65 65.00 | | | | |

**KM# 255 500 TENGE**
7.78 g., 0.999 Gold 0.2499 oz. AGW, 21.87 mm. **Subject:** Year of the Rabbit **Obv:** Constellations **Rev:** Rabbit in center of Zodiac

| Date | Mintage | VF20 | XF40 | MS60 | MS63 | MS65 |
|---|---|---|---|---|---|---|
| 2011 | 3,000 | PF65 550 | | | | |

**KM# 257 500 TENGE**
3.11 g., 0.999 Gold 0.0999 oz. AGW, 16 mm. **Subject:** Mosques **Obv:** Archway **Rev:** Alabaster Mosque of Mohammed Ali in Cairo

| Date | Mintage | VF20 | XF40 | MS60 | MS63 | MS65 |
|---|---|---|---|---|---|---|
| 2011 | 3,000 | PF65 250 | | | | |

**KM# 258 500 TENGE**
3.11 g., 0.999 Gold 0.0999 oz. AGW **Subject:** Mosques **Obv:** Archway **Rev:** Sultan Omar Ali Saifuddien mosque in Brunei

| Date | Mintage | VF20 | XF40 | MS60 | MS63 | MS65 |
|---|---|---|---|---|---|---|
| 2011 | 3,000 | PF65 250 | | | | |

**KM# 259 500 TENGE**
3.11 g., 0.999 Gold 0.0999 oz. AGW **Subject:** Mosques **Obv:** Archway **Rev:** Taj ul Masajid Mosque in Bhopal **Shape:** 16

| Date | Mintage | VF20 | XF40 | MS60 | MS63 | MS65 |
|---|---|---|---|---|---|---|
| 2011 | 3,000 | PF65 250 | | | | |

**KM# 260 500 TENGE**
7.78 g., 0.999 Gold 0.2499 oz. AGW **Rev:** Abu Nasir Muhammad bin Muhammad al Farabi, 1 Tenge bank note

| Date | Mintage | VF20 | XF40 | MS60 | MS63 | MS65 |
|---|---|---|---|---|---|---|
| 2011 | 4,000 | PF65 550 | | | | |

**KM# 222 500 TENGE**
31.10 g., 0.999 Silver 0.9989 oz. ASW, 38.6 mm. **Subject:** Kolobuk **Rev:** Fairy tale characters

| Date | Mintage | VF20 | XF40 | MS60 | MS63 | MS65 |
|---|---|---|---|---|---|---|
| 2012 | — | PF65 95.00 | | | | |

**KM# 223 500 TENGE**
0.93 g., 31.105 Silver, 38.61 mm. **Obv:** Soviet and Kazakhstan arms **Rev:** Portrait of D. Kunaev facing **Shape:** 8-sided

| Date | Mintage | VF20 | XF40 | MS60 | MS63 | MS65 |
|---|---|---|---|---|---|---|
| 2012 | — | PF65 75.00 | | | | |

**KM# 233 500 TENGE**
31.11 g., 0.925 Silver 0.925 oz. ASW, 38.61 mm. **Subject:** Security: 20th Anniversary **Obv:** National arms **Rev:** Four-pronged device in circle

| Date | Mintage | VF20 | XF40 | MS60 | MS63 | MS65 |
|---|---|---|---|---|---|---|
| 2012 | — | PF65 75.00 | | | | |

**KM# 235 500 TENGE**
8.00 g., Bi-Metallic, 31 mm. **Subject:** Mir

| Date | Mintage | VF20 | XF40 | MS60 | MS63 | MS65 |
|---|---|---|---|---|---|---|
| 2012 | — | PF65 100 | | | | |

**KM# 236 500 TENGE**
7.78 g., 0.999 Gold 0.2499 oz. AGW, 21.87 mm. **Obv:** Year of the Dragon **Shape:** 12-Sided

| Date | Mintage | VF20 | XF40 | MS60 | MS63 | MS65 |
|---|---|---|---|---|---|---|
| 2012 | — | PF65 675 | | | | |

**KM# 68 1000 TENGE**
7.78 g., 0.999 Gold 0.2499 oz. AGW, 20 mm. **Obv:** Two winged ibexes **Rev:** Ancient warrior **Edge:** Reeded

| Date | Mintage | VF20 | XF40 | MS60 | MS63 | MS65 |
|---|---|---|---|---|---|---|
| 2001 | — | PF65 445 | | | | |

**KM# 114 1000 TENGE**
67.25 g., 0.925 Silver 2.000 oz. ASW, 50 mm. **Subject:** National Currency, 10th Anniversary **Obv:** Flag, multicolor **Rev:** Coin and bank note designs

| Date | Mintage | VF20 | XF40 | MS60 | MS63 | MS65 |
|---|---|---|---|---|---|---|
| 2003 | — | PF65 150 | | | | |

**KM# 115 1000 TENGE**
67.25 g., 0.925 Silver 2.000 oz. ASW, 50 mm. **Subject:** National Currency, 10th Anniversary **Obv:** Arms, gilt and blue enamel **Rev:** Coin montage

| Date | Mintage | VF20 | XF40 | MS60 | MS63 | MS65 |
|---|---|---|---|---|---|---|
| 2003 | — | PF65 170 | | | | |

**KM# 67 5000 TENGE**
1000.00 g., 0.925 Silver 29.7394 oz. ASW, 100 mm. **Subject:** 10th Anniversary of Independence **Obv:** National arms above value **Rev:** Monument statue

| Date | Mintage | VF20 | XF40 | MS60 | MS63 | MS65 |
|---|---|---|---|---|---|---|
| 2001 | — | PF65 1,150 | | | | |

**KM# 173 5000 TENGE**
1000.00 g., 0.925 Silver 29.7394 oz. ASW, 100 mm. **Subject:** Astana capitol, 10th anniversary **Obv:** National arms **Rev:** Architectural elements

| Date | Mintage | VF20 | XF40 | MS60 | MS63 | MS65 |
|---|---|---|---|---|---|---|
| 2008 | — | PF65 1,250 | | | | |

**KM# 229 5000 TENGE**
1000.00 g., 0.925 Silver 29.7394 oz. ASW, 100 mm. **Subject:** Snow Leopard

| Date | Mintage | VF20 | XF40 | MS60 | MS63 | MS65 |
|---|---|---|---|---|---|---|
| 2009 | Est. 700 | PF65 1,150 | | | | |

**KM# 245 5000 TENGE**
1000.00 g., 0.925 Silver 29.7394 oz. ASW, 100 mm. **Subject:** Asian Winter games in Astana and Almaty **Obv:** Fir in the Sky mountains **Rev:** Games logo

| Date | Mintage | VF20 | XF40 | MS60 | MS63 | MS65 |
|---|---|---|---|---|---|---|
| 2010 | 225 | PF65 1,350 | | | | |

Note: Proof

**KM# 105 50000 TENGE**
1000.00 g., 0.9999 Gold 32.1475 oz. AGW, 100 mm. **Subject:** National Currency, 15th Anniversary **Rev:** Coin and bank note montage

| Date | Mintage | VF20 | XF40 | MS60 | MS63 | MS65 |
|---|---|---|---|---|---|---|
| 2008 | 100 | PF65 60,000 | | | | |

**KM# 247 50000 TENGE**
1000.00 g., 0.999 Gold 32.1186 oz. AGW, 100 mm. **Subject:** Asian Winter Games in Astana and Almaty **Obv:** Sun god and snowflakes **Rev:** Games logo

| Date | Mintage | VF20 | XF40 | MS60 | MS63 | MS65 |
|---|---|---|---|---|---|---|
| 2010 | 145 | PF65 65,000 | | | | |

**KM# 216 50000 TENGE**
1000.00 g., 0.999 Gold 32.1186 oz. AGW, 100 mm. **Subject:** Independence, 20th Anniversary **Obv:** Map and national arms **Rev:** Architecture montage

| Date | Mintage | VF20 | XF40 | MS60 | MS63 | MS65 |
|---|---|---|---|---|---|---|
| 2011 | — | PF65 60,000 | | | | |

## BULLION COINAGE

**KM# 161 TENGE**
31.11 g., 0.999 Silver 0.999 oz. ASW, 38.61 mm. **Obv:** Arms **Rev:** Snow Leopard standing right on rock

| Date | Mintage | VF20 | XF40 | MS60 | MS63 | MS65 |
|---|---|---|---|---|---|---|
| 2009 | — | — | — | — | — | 65.00 |

**KM# 160 2 TENGE**
64.21 g., 0.999 Silver 2.0623 oz. ASW, 50 mm. **Obv:** Arms **Rev:** Snow Leopard standing right on rock

| Date | Mintage | VF20 | XF40 | MS60 | MS63 | MS65 |
|---|---|---|---|---|---|---|
| 2009 | — | — | — | — | — | 125 |

**KM# 159 5 TENGE**
155.00 g., 0.999 Silver 4.9784 oz. ASW, 65 mm. **Obv:** Arms **Rev:** Snow Leopard standing right on rock

| Date | Mintage | VF20 | XF40 | MS60 | MS63 | MS65 |
|---|---|---|---|---|---|---|
| 2009 | — | — | — | — | — | 250 |

**KM# 157 10 TENGE**
3.11 g., 0.999 Gold 0.0999 oz. AGW **Obv:** Arms **Rev:** Snow Leopard standing right on rock

| Date | Mintage | VF20 | XF40 | MS60 | MS63 | MS65 |
|---|---|---|---|---|---|---|
| 2009 | — | — | — | — | — | 225 |

**KM# 158 10 TENGE**
311.05 g., 0.999 Silver 9.9905 oz. ASW **Obv:** Arms **Rev:** Snow Leopard standing right on rock

| Date | Mintage | VF20 | XF40 | MS60 | MS63 | MS65 |
|---|---|---|---|---|---|---|
| 2009 | — | — | — | — | — | 550 |

**KM# 156 20 TENGE**
7.78 g., 0.999 Gold 0.2499 oz. AGW **Obv:** Arms **Rev:** Snow Leopard standing right on rock

| Date | Mintage | VF20 | XF40 | MS60 | MS63 | MS65 |
|---|---|---|---|---|---|---|
| 2009 | — | — | — | — | — | 450 |

**KM# 155 50 TENGE**
15.55 g., 0.999 Gold 0.4994 oz. AGW, 25 mm. **Obv:** Arms **Rev:** Snow Leopard standing right on rock

| Date | Mintage | VF20 | XF40 | MS60 | MS63 | MS65 |
|---|---|---|---|---|---|---|
| 2009 | — | — | — | — | — | 900 |

**KM# 154 100 TENGE**
31.11 g., 0.999 Gold 0.999 oz. AGW, 32 mm. **Obv:** Arms **Rev:** Snow Leopard standing right on rock

| Date | Mintage | VF20 | XF40 | MS60 | MS63 | MS65 |
|---|---|---|---|---|---|---|
| 2009 | — | — | — | — | — | 1,750 |

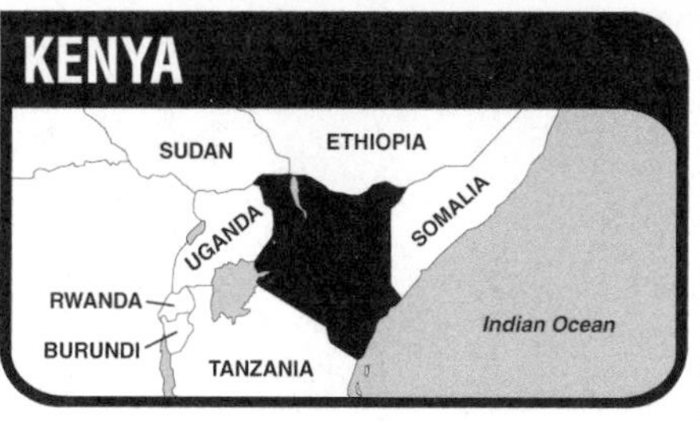


The Republic of Kenya, located on the east coast of Central Africa, has an area of 224,961 sq. mi (582,650 sq. km.) and a population of 20.1 million. Capital: Nairobi. The predominantly agricultural country exports coffee, tea and petroleum products.

Independence was attained on Dec. 12, 1963. Kenya became a republic in 1964. It is a member of the Commonwealth of Nations. The president is Chief of State and Head of Government.

**MONETARY SYSTEM**
100 Cents = 1 Shilling

# REPUBLIC

## STANDARD COINAGE

**KM# 39 5 CENTS**
Copper Clad Steel **Subject:** First President **Obv:** National arms **Rev:** Bust of Mzee Jomo Kenyatta left **Note:** Initially a planned issue, abandoned prior to release for circulation.

| Date | Mintage | VF20 | XF40 | MS60 | MS63 | MS65 |
|---|---|---|---|---|---|---|
| 2005 | — | — | — | — | — | — |

**KM# 40 10 CENTS**
Copper Clad Steel **Subject:** First President **Obv:** National arms **Rev:** Bust of Mzee Jomo Kenyatta left **Note:** Initially a planned issue, abandoned prior to release for circulation.

| Date | Mintage | VF20 | XF40 | MS60 | MS63 | MS65 |
|---|---|---|---|---|---|---|
| 2005 | — | — | — | — | — | — |

**KM# 41 50 CENTS**
4.50 g., Nickel Plated Steel, 21.9 mm. **Subject:** First President **Obv:** National arms, value **Rev:** Bust of Mwee Jomo Kenyatta left

| Date | Mintage | VF20 | XF40 | MS60 | MS63 | MS65 |
|---|---|---|---|---|---|---|
| 2005 | — | — | — | 0.30 | 0.60 | 0.80 |
| 2009 | — | — | — | 0.30 | 0.60 | 0.80 |

**KM# 34 SHILLING**
5.46 g., Nickel Plated Steel, 23.9 mm. **Subject:** First President **Obv:** Value above national arms **Rev:** Bust of President Mzee Jomo Kenyata left **Edge:** Segmented reeding

| Date | Mintage | VF20 | XF40 | MS60 | MS63 | MS65 |
|---|---|---|---|---|---|---|
| 2005 | — | — | — | 0.45 | 0.80 | 1.20 |
| 2009 | — | — | — | 0.45 | 0.80 | 1.20 |
| 2010 | — | — | — | 0.45 | 0.80 | 1.20 |

**KM# 37.1 5 SHILLINGS**
3.75 g., Bi-Metallic Aluminum-Bronze center in Copper-Nickel ring, 19.5 mm. **Subject:** First President **Obv:** Value above national arms **Obv. Legend:** REPUBLIC OF KENYA **Rev:** Bust of President Mzee Jomo Kenyatta left **Edge:** Reeded

| Date | Mintage | VF20 | XF40 | MS60 | MS63 | MS65 |
|---|---|---|---|---|---|---|
| 2005 | — | — | 0.60 | 1.00 | 1.50 | 2.00 |
| 2009 | — | — | 0.60 | 1.00 | 1.50 | 2.00 |

**KM# 37.2 5 SHILLINGS**
3.75 g., Bi-Metallic Aluminum-Bronze center in Copper-Nickel ring, 19.5 mm. **Obv:** Value above national arms **Rev:** Bust of President Mzee Jomo Kenyatta **Edge:** Reeded **Note:** Larger numeral and smaller shield.

| Date | Mintage | VF20 | XF40 | MS60 | MS63 | MS65 |
|---|---|---|---|---|---|---|
| 2010 | — | — | 0.60 | 1.00 | 1.50 | 2.00 |

**KM# 35.1 10 SHILLINGS**
5.00 g., Bi-Metallic Copper-Nickel center in Aluminum-Bronze ring, 23 mm. **Subject:** First President **Obv:** Value above national arms **Obv. Legend:** REPUBLIC OF KENYA **Rev:** Bust of President Mzee Jomo Kenyatta left **Edge:** Reeded

| Date | Mintage | VF20 | XF40 | MS60 | MS63 | MS65 |
|---|---|---|---|---|---|---|
| 2005 | — | — | 0.90 | 1.25 | 2.25 | 3.00 |
| 2009 | — | — | 0.90 | 1.25 | 2.25 | 3.00 |

**KM# 35.2 10 SHILLINGS**
5.00 g., Bi-Metallic Copper-Nickel center in Aluminum-Bronze ring, 23 mm. **Obv:** Value above national arms **Rev:** Bust of President Mzee Jomo Kenyatta left **Edge:** Reeded **Note:** Larger value and smaller shield.

| Date | Mintage | VF20 | XF40 | MS60 | MS63 | MS65 |
|---|---|---|---|---|---|---|
| 2010 | — | — | 0.90 | 1.25 | 2.25 | 3.00 |

**KM# 36.1 20 SHILLINGS**
9.00 g., Bi-Metallic Aluminum-Bronze center in Copper-Nickel ring, 26 mm. **Subject:** First President **Obv:** Large value above national arms **Obv. Legend:** REPUBLIC OF KENYA **Rev:** Bust of President Mzee Jomo Kenyatta left **Edge:** Segmented reeding

| Date | Mintage | VF20 | XF40 | MS60 | MS63 | MS65 |
|---|---|---|---|---|---|---|
| 2005 | — | — | 1.20 | 2.00 | 3.00 | 4.00 |
| 2009 | — | — | 1.20 | 2.00 | 3.00 | 4.00 |

**KM# 36.2 20 SHILLINGS**
9.00 g., Bi-Metallic Aluminum-Bronze center in Copper-Nickel ring, 26 mm. **Obv:** Value above shield **Rev:** Bust of President Mzee Jomo Kenyatta **Note:** Larger value and smaller shield than 36.1.

| Date | Mintage | VF20 | XF40 | MS60 | MS63 | MS65 |
|---|---|---|---|---|---|---|
| 2010 | — | — | — | 2.00 | 3.00 | 4.00 |

**KM# 33 40 SHILLINGS**
11.00 g., Bi-Metallic Copper-Nickel center in Nickel-Brass ring, 27.5 mm. **Obv:** Bust of H. E. Mwai Kibaki facing **Rev:** National arms, value below **Edge:** Reeded and lettered **Edge Lettering:** 40 YEARS OF INDEPENDENCE **Note:** Issued December 11, 2003.

| Date | Mintage | VF20 | XF40 | MS60 | MS63 | MS65 |
|---|---|---|---|---|---|---|
| ND(2003) | — | — | — | 6.00 | 7.50 | 9.00 |

**KM# 38 1000 SHILLINGS**

28.28 g., 0.925 Silver 0.841 oz. ASW, 38.61 mm. **Subject:** 40th Anniversary Independence **Obv:** National arms **Rev:** Bust of President H. E. Mwai Kibaki facing

| Date | Mintage | VF20 | XF40 | MS60 | MS63 | MS65 |
|---|---|---|---|---|---|---|
| 1963-2003 | — | PF63 55.00 | PF65 65.00 | | | |

**KM# 43 5000 SHILLINGS**

39.94 g., 0.9167 Gold 1.1771 oz. AGW, 27.5 mm. **Obv:** National arms **Rev:** H.E. Mwai Kibaki, 3rd president **Edge:** Reeded

| Date | Mintage | VF20 | XF40 | MS60 | MS63 | MS65 |
|---|---|---|---|---|---|---|
| 1963-2003 | — | PF63 2,000 | PF65 2,200 | | | |

**KM# 44 50 SHILLINGS**

Nickel-Brass gold plated, 38.61 mm. **Obv:** National arms **Rev:** Map and flag **Note:** Set in lucite block

| Date | Mintage | VF20 | XF40 | MS60 | MS63 | MS65 |
|---|---|---|---|---|---|---|
| 2013 | — | — | — | — | 50.00 | — |

**KM# 44a 50 SHILLINGS**

28.28 g., 0.925 Silver 0.841 oz. ASW gilt, 38.61 mm. **Obv:** National arms **Rev:** Map and flag

| Date | Mintage | VF20 | XF40 | MS60 | MS63 | MS65 |
|---|---|---|---|---|---|---|
| 2013 | — | PF63 50.00 | | | | |

**KM# 44b 50 SHILLINGS**

31.21 g., 0.999 Gold 1.0024 oz. AGW, 38.61 mm. **Obv:** National arms **Rev:** Map and flag

| Date | Mintage | VF20 | XF40 | MS60 | MS63 | MS65 |
|---|---|---|---|---|---|---|
| 2013 | — | PF63 1,400 | | | | |

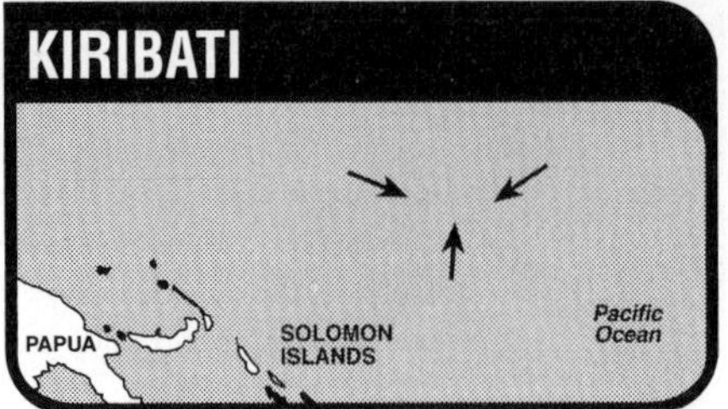


The Republic of Kiribati (formerly the Gilbert Islands), consists of 30 coral atolls and islands spread over more than one million sq. mi. (2,590,000 sq. km.) of the southwest Pacific Ocean, has an area of 332 sq. mi. (717 sq. km.) and a population of 64,200. Capital: Bairiki, on Tarawa. In addition to the Gilbert Islands proper, Kiribati includes Ocean Island, the Central and Southern Line Islands, and the Phoenix Islands, though possession of Canton and Enderbury of the Phoenix Islands is disputed with the United States. Most families engage in subsistence fishing. Copra and phosphates are exported, mostly to Australia and New Zealand.

Kiribati is a member of the Commonwealth of Nations. The President is the Head of State and Head of Government.

**MONETARY SYSTEM**

100 Cents = 1 Dollar

## REPUBLIC

### DECIMAL COINAGE

**KM# 40 5 CENTS**

4.24 g., Brass, 22.9 mm. **Obv:** National arms **Rev:** Gorilla **Edge:** Reeded

| Date | Mintage | VF20 | XF40 | MS60 | MS63 | MS65 |
|---|---|---|---|---|---|---|
| 2003 | — | — | — | 0.50 | 1.00 | 1.50 |

**KM# 60 DOLLAR**

26.00 g., Silver Plated Copper, 38.61 mm. **Subject:** London Olympics, 2012 **Obv:** Shield **Rev:** Weightlifter and sunrise

| Date | Mintage | VF20 | XF40 | MS60 | MS63 | MS65 |
|---|---|---|---|---|---|---|
| 2011 | Est. 10000 | PF63 18.00 | PF65 20.00 | | | |

**KM# 62 DOLLAR**

0.50 g., 0.999 Gold 0.0161 oz. AGW, 11 mm. **Obv:** Shield **Rev:** Mary, Child Jesus and Joseph, in manger with cattle

| Date | Mintage | VF20 | XF40 | MS60 | MS63 | MS65 |
|---|---|---|---|---|---|---|
| 2011 | — | PF65 55.00 | | | | |

**KM# 68 DOLLAR**

0.50 g., 0.585 Gold 0.0094 oz. AGW 24K Gold Plated, 11 mm. **Obv:** Shield **Rev:** Mother and child

| Date | Mintage | VF20 | XF40 | MS60 | MS63 | MS65 |
|---|---|---|---|---|---|---|
| 2012 | — | PF65 215 | | | | |

**KM# 78 DOLLAR**

0.50 g., 0.585 Gold 0.0094 oz. AGW with 24Kt gold plating, 11 mm. **Subject:** Holy Family

| Date | Mintage | VF20 | XF40 | MS60 | MS63 | MS65 |
|---|---|---|---|---|---|---|
| 2013 | Est. 5000 | PF63 45.00 | PF65 50.00 | | | |

**KM# 69 5 DOLLARS**

12.00 g., 0.925 Silver 0.3569 oz. ASW, 38.61 mm. **Obv:** Shield **Rev:** Santa in sled in color

| Date | Mintage | VF20 | XF40 | MS60 | MS63 | MS65 |
|---|---|---|---|---|---|---|
| 2012 | — | PF65 50.00 | | | | |

**KM# 70 5 DOLLARS**

12.00 g., 0.925 Silver 0.3569 oz. ASW, 38.61 mm. **Obv:** Shield **Rev:** Rudolph gilt, crystal red nose

| Date | Mintage | VF20 | XF40 | MS60 | MS63 | MS65 |
|---|---|---|---|---|---|---|
| 2012 | Est. 7500 | PF63 50.00 | PF65 55.00 | | | |

**KM# 74 5 DOLLARS**

20.00 g., 0.925 Silver 0.5948 oz. ASW partially gilt with ruby, 38.61 mm. **Subject:** Rudolph the red-nose reindeer

| Date | Mintage | VF20 | XF40 | MS60 | MS63 | MS65 |
|---|---|---|---|---|---|---|
| 2013 | Est. 5000 | PF63 65.00 | PF65 75.00 | | | |

**KM# 75 5 DOLLARS**

20.00 g., 0.925 Silver 0.5948 oz. ASW with color, 38.61 mm. **Subject:** Jingle Bells

| Date | Mintage | VF20 | XF40 | MS60 | MS63 | MS65 |
|---|---|---|---|---|---|---|
| 2013 | Est. 5000 | PF63 65.00 | PF65 75.00 | | | |

**KM# 54 10 DOLLARS**

1.25 g., 0.999 Gold 0.0401 oz. AGW, 13.92 mm. **Obv:** Shield **Rev:** Angel with horn

| Date | Mintage | VF20 | XF40 | MS60 | MS63 | MS65 |
|---|---|---|---|---|---|---|
| 2005 | Est. 15000 | PF63 75.00 | PF65 85.00 | | | |

**KM# 55 10 DOLLARS**

1.24 g., 0.999 Gold 0.0398 oz. AGW, 13.92 mm. **Obv:** Shield **Rev:** Angel

| Date | Mintage | VF20 | XF40 | MS60 | MS63 | MS65 |
|---|---|---|---|---|---|---|
| 2006 | Est. 15000 | PF63 75.00 | PF65 85.00 | | | |

**KM# 58 10 DOLLARS**

31.11 g., 0.999 Silver 0.999 oz. ASW, 38.61 mm. **Obv:** Shield **Rev:** The Magi

| Date | Mintage | VF20 | XF40 | MS60 | MS63 | MS65 |
|---|---|---|---|---|---|---|
| 2011 | 10,000 | PF63 45.00 | PF65 50.00 | | | |

**KM# 59 10 DOLLARS**
28.28 g., 0.925 Silver 0.841 oz. ASW, 38.61 mm. **Subject:** London Olympics, 2012 **Obv:** Shield **Rev:** Weightlifting and sunrise

| Date | Mintage | VF20 | XF40 | MS60 | MS63 | MS65 |
|---|---|---|---|---|---|---|
| 2011 | Est. 10000 | PF63 35.00 | PF65 40.00 | | | |

**KM# 61 10 DOLLARS**
28.28 g., 0.925 Silver 0.841 oz. ASW, 38.61 mm. **Subject:** Ships and explorers **Obv:** Shield **Rev:** Mayflower, 1620

| Date | Mintage | VF20 | XF40 | MS60 | MS63 | MS65 |
|---|---|---|---|---|---|---|
| 2011 | Est. 5000 | PF65 45.00 | | | | |

**KM# 63 10 DOLLARS**
28.28 g., 0.925 Silver 0.841 oz. ASW, 38.61 mm. **Subject:** Elizabeth II 60th Anniversary of reign, 90th Birthday of Prince Philip **Obv:** Shield **Rev:** Prince Philip at right, Philip and Elizabeth at right

| Date | Mintage | VF20 | XF40 | MS60 | MS63 | MS65 |
|---|---|---|---|---|---|---|
| 2011 | 10,000 | PF63 35.00 | PF65 40.00 | | | |

**KM# 65 10 DOLLARS**
1.24 g., 0.999 Gold 0.0398 oz. AGW, 13.92 mm. **Obv:** Shield **Rev:** Joseph, Jesus and Mary, in manger, with cattle

| Date | Mintage | VF20 | XF40 | MS60 | MS63 | MS65 |
|---|---|---|---|---|---|---|
| 2011 | Est. 7500 | PF63 75.00 | PF65 85.00 | | | |

**KM# 66 10 DOLLARS**
12.00 g., 0.925 Silver 0.3569 oz. ASW, 38.61 mm. **Obv:** Shield **Rev:** Water Scene - Dark blue sky

| Date | Mintage | VF20 | XF40 | MS60 | MS63 | MS65 |
|---|---|---|---|---|---|---|
| 2012 | Est. 5000 | PF63 55.00 | PF65 65.00 | | | |

**KM# 71 10 DOLLARS**
20.00 g., 0.925 Silver 0.5948 oz. ASW, 38.61 mm. **Subject:** 2016 Olympics - Sailing

| Date | Mintage | VF20 | XF40 | MS60 | MS63 | MS65 |
|---|---|---|---|---|---|---|
| 2013 | Est. 10000 | PF63 65.00 | PF65 75.00 | | | |

**KM# 72 10 DOLLARS**
10.00 g., 0.500 Silver 0.1608 oz. ASW, 25 mm. **Subject:** ANZAC Day - Trumpet

| Date | Mintage | VF20 | XF40 | MS60 | MS63 | MS65 |
|---|---|---|---|---|---|---|
| 2013 | Est. 150000 | PF63 40.00 | PF65 50.00 | | | |

**KM# 73 10 DOLLARS**
10.00 g., 0.500 Silver 0.1608 oz. ASW, 25 mm. **Subject:** ANZAC Day - Rifle

| Date | Mintage | VF20 | XF40 | MS60 | MS63 | MS65 |
|---|---|---|---|---|---|---|
| 2013 | Est. 150000 | PF63 40.00 | PF65 50.00 | | | |

**KM# 67 20 DOLLARS**
62.21 g., 0.925 Silver 1.8501 oz. ASW, 55 mm. **Obv:** Shield **Rev:** Christmas tree cut out, gilt highlights

| Date | Mintage | VF20 | XF40 | MS60 | MS63 | MS65 |
|---|---|---|---|---|---|---|
| 2012 | Est. 999 | PF65 200 | | | | |

**KM# 76 20 DOLLARS**
62.20 g., 0.925 Silver 1.8498 oz. ASW with gold plating and crystal, 55 mm. **Subject:** Christmas Bells

| Date | Mintage | VF20 | XF40 | MS60 | MS63 | MS65 |
|---|---|---|---|---|---|---|
| 2013 | Est. 999 | PF65 125 | | | | |

**KM# 53 50 DOLLARS**
3.11 g., 0.999 Gold 0.0999 oz. AGW, 18.5 mm. **Obv:** Shield **Rev:** Jesus and Mary riding donkey, Joseph walking beside

| Date | Mintage | VF20 | XF40 | MS60 | MS63 | MS65 |
|---|---|---|---|---|---|---|
| 2005 | 1,500 | PF65 185 | | | | |

**KM# 56 50 DOLLARS**
3.11 g., 0.999 Gold 0.0999 oz. AGW, 18.5 mm. **Obv:** Shield **Rev:** Holy family in manger

| Date | Mintage | VF20 | XF40 | MS60 | MS63 | MS65 |
|---|---|---|---|---|---|---|
| 2006 | 1,500 | PF65 185 | | | | |

**KM# 64 50 DOLLARS**
7.77 g., 0.999 Gold 0.2496 oz. AGW, 25 mm. **Obv:** Shield **Rev:** Angel, facing hands in prayer

| Date | Mintage | VF20 | XF40 | MS60 | MS63 | MS65 |
|---|---|---|---|---|---|---|
| 2011 | Est. 1500 | PF65 475 | | | | |

**KM# 77 150 DOLLARS**
0.50 g., 0.999 Gold 0.0161 oz. AGW, 11 mm. **Subject:** Holy Family

| Date | Mintage | VF20 | XF40 | MS60 | MS63 | MS65 |
|---|---|---|---|---|---|---|
| 2013 | Est. 5000 | PF63 45.00 | PF65 50.00 | | | |

**KM# 52 200 DOLLARS**
31.11 g., 0.999 Gold 0.999 oz. AGW, 40 mm. **Obv:** Shield **Rev:** The Holy Family - Joseph, Mary and Jesus

| Date | Mintage | VF20 | XF40 | MS60 | MS63 | MS65 |
|---|---|---|---|---|---|---|
| 2005 | 500 | PF65 1,800 | | | | |

**KM# 57 200 DOLLARS**
31.11 g., 0.999 Gold 0.999 oz. AGW, 40 mm. **Obv:** Shield **Rev:** Holy Family and shepards in manger

| Date | Mintage | VF20 | XF40 | MS60 | MS63 | MS65 |
|---|---|---|---|---|---|---|
| 2006 | 500 | PF65 1,800 | | | | |

# NORTH KOREA

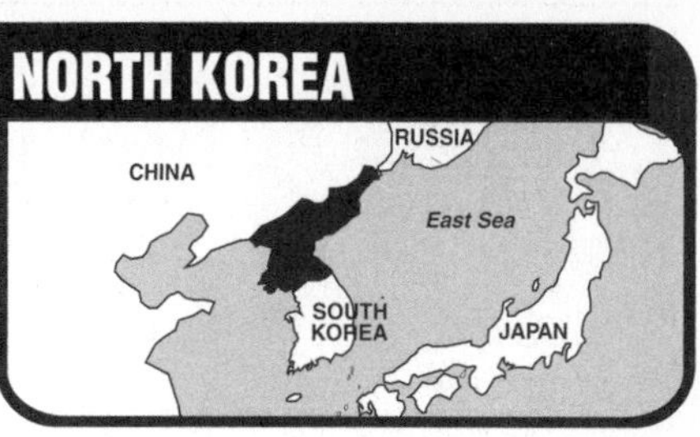


The Democratic Peoples Republic of Korea, situated in northeastern Asia on the northern half of the Korean peninsula between the Peoples Republic of China and the Republic of Korea, has an area of 46,540 sq. mi. (120,540 sq. km.) and a population of 20 million. Capital: Pyongyang. The economy is based on heavy industry and agriculture. Metals, minerals and farm produce are exported.

**MONETARY SYSTEM**
100 Chon = 1 Won

**MINT**
Pyongyang

**DATING**
In the year 2001 the North Korean adopted the "Juche" dating system which is based on the birth year of Kim Il Sung, founder of North Korea. He was born in 1911. "Quel" refers to month and "Quil" refers to day. 9 Quel 3 Quil refers to September 3rd. The western dates on these coins follow the "Juche" date in parenthesis.

## PEOPLES REPUBLIC

### DECIMAL COINAGE

**KM# 183 1/2 CHON**
2.16 g., Aluminum, 27.02 mm. **Obv:** State arms **Rev:** Horse **Edge:** Plain

| Date | Mintage | F12 | VF20 | XF40 | MS60 | MS63 |
|---|---|---|---|---|---|---|
| 2002 | — | — | — | — | 1.25 | 1.50 |

**KM# 184 1/2 CHON**
2.16 g., Aluminum, 27.02 mm. **Obv:** State arms **Rev:** Orangutan **Edge:** Plain

| Date | Mintage | F12 | VF20 | XF40 | MS60 | MS63 |
|---|---|---|---|---|---|---|
| 2002 | — | — | — | — | 1.25 | 1.50 |

**KM# 185 1/2 CHON**
2.16 g., Aluminum, 27.02 mm. **Obv:** State arms **Rev:** Leopard **Edge:** Plain

| Date | Mintage | F12 | VF20 | XF40 | MS60 | MS63 |
|---|---|---|---|---|---|---|
| 2002 | — | — | — | — | 1.25 | 1.50 |

**KM# 186 1/2 CHON**
2.16 g., Aluminum, 27.02 mm. **Obv:** State arms **Rev:** Two giraffes **Edge:** Plain

| Date | Mintage | F12 | VF20 | XF40 | MS60 | MS63 |
|---|---|---|---|---|---|---|
| 2002 | — | — | — | — | 1.25 | 1.50 |

**KM# 187 1/2 CHON**
2.16 g., Aluminum, 27.02 mm. **Obv:** State arms **Rev:** Helmeted guineafowl **Edge:** Plain

| Date | Mintage | F12 | VF20 | XF40 | MS60 | MS63 |
|---|---|---|---|---|---|---|
| 2002 | — | — | — | — | 1.25 | 1.50 |

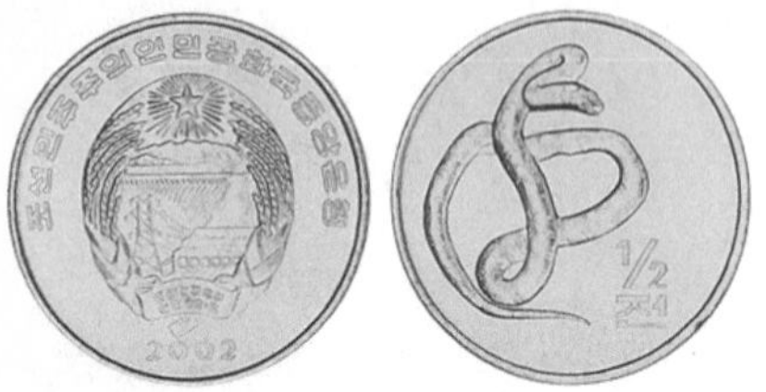

**KM# 188 1/2 CHON**
2.16 g., Aluminum, 27.02 mm. **Obv:** State arms **Rev:** Mamushi pit viper **Edge:** Plain

| Date | Mintage | F12 | VF20 | XF40 | MS60 | MS63 |
|---|---|---|---|---|---|---|
| 2002 | — | — | — | — | 1.25 | 1.50 |

**KM# 189 1/2 CHON**
2.16 g., Aluminum, 27.02 mm. **Obv:** State arms **Rev:** Bighorn sheep **Edge:** Plain

| Date | Mintage | F12 | VF20 | XF40 | MS60 | MS63 |
|---|---|---|---|---|---|---|
| 2002 | — | — | — | — | 1.25 | 1.50 |

**KM# 190 1/2 CHON**
2.16 g., Aluminum, 27.02 mm. **Obv:** State arms **Rev:** Hippopotamus **Edge:** Plain

| Date | Mintage | F12 | VF20 | XF40 | MS60 | MS63 |
|---|---|---|---|---|---|---|
| 2002 | — | — | — | — | 1.25 | 1.50 |

**KM# 191 1/2 CHON**
2.16 g., Aluminum, 27.02 mm. **Subject:** FAO **Obv:** State arms **Rev:** Ancient ship **Edge:** Plain

| Date | Mintage | F12 | VF20 | XF40 | MS60 | MS63 |
|---|---|---|---|---|---|---|
| 2002 | — | — | — | — | 1.25 | 1.50 |

**KM# 192 1/2 CHON**
2.16 g., Aluminum, 27.02 mm. **Subject:** FAO **Obv:** State arms **Rev:** Archaic ship **Edge:** Plain

| Date | Mintage | F12 | VF20 | XF40 | MS60 | MS63 |
|---|---|---|---|---|---|---|
| 2002 | — | — | — | — | 1.25 | 1.50 |

**KM# 193 1/2 CHON**
2.16 g., Aluminum, 27.02 mm. **Subject:** FAO **Obv:** State arms **Rev:** Modern train **Edge:** Plain

| Date | Mintage | F12 | VF20 | XF40 | MS60 | MS63 |
|---|---|---|---|---|---|---|
| 2002 | — | — | — | — | 1.25 | 1.50 |

**KM# 194 1/2 CHON**
2.16 g., Aluminum, 27.02 mm. **Subject:** FAO **Obv:** State arms **Rev:** Jet airliner **Edge:** Plain

| Date | Mintage | F12 | VF20 | XF40 | MS60 | MS63 |
|---|---|---|---|---|---|---|
| 2002 | — | — | — | — | 1.25 | 1.50 |

**KM# 195 CHON**
4.63 g., Brass, 21.7 mm. **Subject:** FAO **Obv:** State arms **Rev:** Antique steam locomotive **Edge:** Plain

| Date | Mintage | F12 | VF20 | XF40 | MS60 | MS63 |
|---|---|---|---|---|---|---|
| 2002 | — | — | — | — | 1.50 | 1.75 |

**KM# 196 CHON**
4.63 g., Brass, 21.7 mm. **Subject:** FAO **Obv:** State arms **Rev:** Antique automobile **Edge:** Plain

| Date | Mintage | F12 | VF20 | XF40 | MS60 | MS63 |
|---|---|---|---|---|---|---|
| 2002 | — | — | — | — | 1.50 | 1.75 |

**KM# 197 2 CHON**
6.04 g., Copper-Nickel, 24.2 mm. **Subject:** FAO **Obv:** State arms **Rev:** Antique touring car **Edge:** Plain

| Date | Mintage | F12 | VF20 | XF40 | MS60 | MS63 |
|---|---|---|---|---|---|---|
| 2002 | — | — | — | — | 2.00 | 2.50 |

**KM# 499 50 CHON**
Aluminum, 27 mm. **Rev:** Two bicyclists

| Date | Mintage | F12 | VF20 | XF40 | MS60 | MS63 |
|---|---|---|---|---|---|---|
| 2001 Proof, rare | — | — | — | — | — | — |

**KM# 157 WON**
6.70 g., Aluminum, 40 mm. **Subject:** Seafaring Ships **Obv:** State arms **Rev:** Cruise ship below stylized head left profile **Edge:** Plain

| Date | Mintage | F12 | VF20 | XF40 | MS60 | MS63 |
|---|---|---|---|---|---|---|
| JU90-2001 | — | **PF65** 10.00 | | | | |

**KM# 157a WON**
29.05 g., Brass, 40.2 mm. **Obv:** State arms **Rev:** Cruise ship below stylized head profile left **Edge:** Plain

| Date | Mintage | F12 | VF20 | XF40 | MS60 | MS63 |
|---|---|---|---|---|---|---|
| 2001 | — | **PF65** 17.50 | | | | |

**KM# 158 WON**
17.00 g., Copper-Nickel, 35 mm. **Subject:** First Nobel Prize Winner in Literature - Sully Prudhomme **Obv:** State arms **Rev:** Half length seated bust left flanked by shelves and books **Edge:** Plain

| Date | Mintage | F12 | VF20 | XF40 | MS60 | MS63 |
|---|---|---|---|---|---|---|
| ND-2001 | 2,000 | **PF65** 100 | | | | |

**KM# 158a WON**
5.00 g., Aluminum, 35 mm. **Subject:** Nobel prize in literature, Sully Prudhomme

| Date | Mintage | F12 | VF20 | XF40 | MS60 | MS63 |
|---|---|---|---|---|---|---|
| 2001 | — | **PF65** 6.00 | | | | |

**KM# 158b WON**
16.20 g., Brass, 35 mm. **Subject:** First Nobel Prize Winner in Literature - Sully Prudhomme **Obv:** State arms **Rev:** Half length seated bust left flanked by shelves and books **Edge:** Plain

| Date | Mintage | F12 | VF20 | XF40 | MS60 | MS63 |
|---|---|---|---|---|---|---|
| ND-2001 | — | **PF65** 10.00 | | | | |

### KM# 159 WON

17.00 g., Copper-Nickel, 35 mm. **Subject:** First Nobel Prize Winner in Physics - Wilhelm C. Roentgen **Obv:** State arms **Rev:** Bust 3/4 right at left with same person seated in lab at right **Edge:** Plain

| Date | Mintage | F12 | VF20 | XF40 | MS60 | MS63 |
|---|---|---|---|---|---|---|
| ND-2001 | 2,000 | **PF65** 100 | | | | |

### KM# 159a WON

5.00 g., Aluminum, 35 mm. **Subject:** Nobel in Physics, Wilhelm C. Rontgen

| Date | Mintage | F12 | VF20 | XF40 | MS60 | MS63 |
|---|---|---|---|---|---|---|
| 2001 | — | **PF65** 6.00 | | | | |

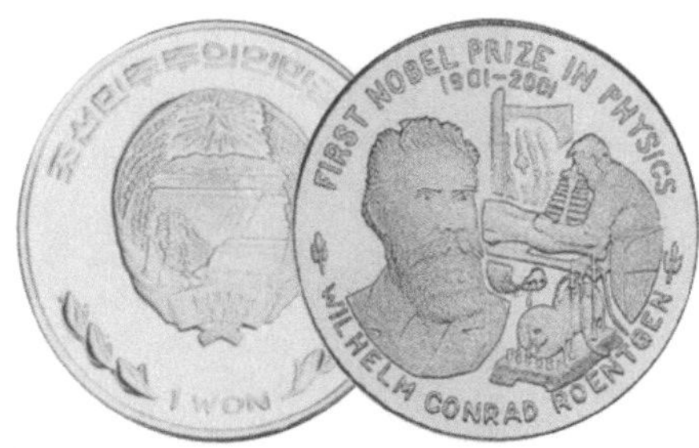


### KM# 159b WON

16.20 g., Brass, 35 mm. **Subject:** First Nobel Prize in Physics - Wiliam C. Rontgen **Obv:** State arms **Rev:** Bust 3/4 right at left with same person seated in lab at right **Edge:** Plain

| Date | Mintage | F12 | VF20 | XF40 | MS60 | MS63 |
|---|---|---|---|---|---|---|
| ND-2001 | — | **PF65** 10.00 | | | | |

### KM# 160 WON

16.20 g., Brass, 35 mm. **Subject:** Nipponia Nippon **Obv:** State arms **Rev:** Two nest building Japanese ibis **Edge:** Plain

| Date | Mintage | F12 | VF20 | XF40 | MS60 | MS63 |
|---|---|---|---|---|---|---|
| JU90-2001 | — | **PF65** 15.00 | | | | |

### KM# 160a WON

17.00 g., Copper-Nickel, 35 mm. **Subject:** Wildlife **Obv:** State arms **Rev:** Two nesting Japanese Ibis birds **Edge:** Plain

| Date | Mintage | F12 | VF20 | XF40 | MS60 | MS63 |
|---|---|---|---|---|---|---|
| JU2001 | 200 | **PF65** 100 | | | | |

### KM# 160b WON

5.35 g., Aluminum, 35.1 mm. **Obv:** State arms **Rev:** Two nest building Japanese Ibis birds **Edge:** Plain

| Date | Mintage | F12 | VF20 | XF40 | MS60 | MS63 |
|---|---|---|---|---|---|---|
| JU90-2001 | — | **PF65** 15.00 | | | | |

### KM# 162.2 WON

7.00 g., Aluminum, 40 mm. **Obv:** State arms, date above value **Rev:** Radiant Korean map and landmarks **Edge:** Plain

| Date | Mintage | F12 | VF20 | XF40 | MS60 | MS63 |
|---|---|---|---|---|---|---|
| 2001 | — | **PF65** 15.00 | | | | |

### KM# 202 WON

17.00 g., Copper-Nickel, 35 mm. **Subject:** School Ships **Obv:** State arms **Rev:** SS Krusenstern **Edge:** Plain

| Date | Mintage | F12 | VF20 | XF40 | MS60 | MS63 |
|---|---|---|---|---|---|---|
| ND-2001 | 200 | **PF65** 100 | | | | |

### KM# 204 WON

17.00 g., Copper-Nickel, 35 mm. **Subject:** Wildlife **Obv:** State arms **Rev:** Two standing Japanese Ibis birds **Edge:** Plain

| Date | Mintage | F12 | VF20 | XF40 | MS60 | MS63 |
|---|---|---|---|---|---|---|
| JU90-2001 | 100 | **PF65** 150 | | | | |

### KM# 207 WON

17.00 g., Copper-Nickel, 35 mm. **Subject:** Wildlife **Obv:** State arms **Rev:** Two Korean Longtail Gorals **Edge:** Plain

| Date | Mintage | F12 | VF20 | XF40 | MS60 | MS63 |
|---|---|---|---|---|---|---|
| JU90-2001 | 200 | **PF65** 100 | | | | |

### KM# 207a WON

16.05 g., Brass, 35 mm. **Obv:** State arms **Rev:** Two Longtail Gorals **Edge:** Plain

| Date | Mintage | F12 | VF20 | XF40 | MS60 | MS63 |
|---|---|---|---|---|---|---|
| JU90-2001 | — | **PF65** 12.50 | | | | |

### KM# 207b WON

5.35 g., Aluminum, 35.1 mm. **Obv:** State arms **Rev:** Two Longtail Gorals **Edge:** Plain

| Date | Mintage | F12 | VF20 | XF40 | MS60 | MS63 |
|---|---|---|---|---|---|---|
| JU90-2001 | — | **PF65** 10.00 | | | | |

### KM# 209 WON

17.00 g., Copper-Nickel, 35 mm. **Subject:** First Nobel Prize Winner in Medicine - Emil A. von Behring **Obv:** State arms **Rev:** Lab beaker divides half length figures facing each other **Edge:** Plain

| Date | Mintage | F12 | VF20 | XF40 | MS60 | MS63 |
|---|---|---|---|---|---|---|
| ND-2001 | 2,000 | **PF65** 100 | | | | |

### KM# 209a WON

5.00 g., Aluminum, 35 mm. **Subject:** Nobel prize in Medicine, Emil von Behring

| Date | Mintage | F12 | VF20 | XF40 | MS60 | MS63 |
|---|---|---|---|---|---|---|
| 2001 | — | **PF65** 6.00 | | | | |

### KM# 209b WON

16.00 g., Brass, 35 mm. **Subject:** Nobel prize in Medicine, Emil von Behring

| Date | Mintage | F12 | VF20 | XF40 | MS60 | MS63 |
|---|---|---|---|---|---|---|
| 2001 | — | **PF65** 7.00 | | | | |

### KM# 210 WON

17.00 g., Copper-Nickel, 35 mm. **Subject:** First Nobel Prize Winner in Peace - Henri Dunant **Obv:** State arms **Rev:** Bust facing at left, war wounded at right **Edge:** Plain

| Date | Mintage | F12 | VF20 | XF40 | MS60 | MS63 |
|---|---|---|---|---|---|---|
| ND-2001 | 2,000 | **PF65** 100 | | | | |

### KM# 210a WON

5.00 g., Aluminum, 35 mm. **Subject:** Nobel Peace Prize, Jean H. Dunant

| Date | Mintage | F12 | VF20 | XF40 | MS60 | MS63 |
|---|---|---|---|---|---|---|
| 2001 | — | **PF65** 6.00 | | | | |

**KM# 210b WON**

5.00 g., Aluminum, 35 mm. **Subject:** Nobel Peace prize, Jean H. Dunant

| Date | Mintage | F12 | VF20 | XF40 | MS60 | MS63 |
|---|---|---|---|---|---|---|
| 2001 | — | PF65 7.00 | | | | |

**KM# 211 WON**

17.00 g., Copper-Nickel, 35 mm. **Subject:** First Nobel Prize Winner in Chemistry - Jacobus Van't Hoff **Obv:** State arms **Rev:** Standing figures in lab scene **Edge:** Plain

| Date | Mintage | F12 | VF20 | XF40 | MS60 | MS63 |
|---|---|---|---|---|---|---|
| ND-2001 | 2,000 | PF65 100 | | | | |

**KM# 211a WON**

5.00 g., Aluminum, 35 mm. **Subject:** Nobel in Chemistry, Jacob van't Hoff

| Date | Mintage | F12 | VF20 | XF40 | MS60 | MS63 |
|---|---|---|---|---|---|---|
| 2001 | — | PF65 6.00 | | | | |

**KM# 211b WON**

16.00 g., Brass, 35 mm. **Subject:** Nobel prize in Chemistry, Jabob van't Hoff

| Date | Mintage | F12 | VF20 | XF40 | MS60 | MS63 |
|---|---|---|---|---|---|---|
| 2001 | — | PF65 7.00 | | | | |

**KM# 212 WON**

17.00 g., Copper-Nickel, 35 mm. **Subject:** First Nobel Prize Winner in Peace - Frederic Passy **Obv:** State arms **Rev:** Head left at right with allegorical scene at left **Edge:** Plain

| Date | Mintage | F12 | VF20 | XF40 | MS60 | MS63 |
|---|---|---|---|---|---|---|
| ND-2001 | 2,000 | PF65 100 | | | | |

**KM# 212a WON**

5.00 g., Aluminum, 35 mm. **Subject:** Nobel Peace Prize, Frederic Passy

| Date | Mintage | F12 | VF20 | XF40 | MS60 | MS63 |
|---|---|---|---|---|---|---|
| 2001 | — | PF65 6.00 | | | | |

**KM# 212b WON**

16.00 g., Brass, 35 mm. **Subject:** Nobel Peace Prize, Frederic Passy

| Date | Mintage | F12 | VF20 | XF40 | MS60 | MS63 |
|---|---|---|---|---|---|---|
| 2001 | — | PF65 7.00 | | | | |

**KM# 232 WON**

28.11 g., Brass, 40 mm. **Obv:** State arms **Rev:** White-bellied woodpecker **Edge:** Plain

| Date | Mintage | F12 | VF20 | XF40 | MS60 | MS63 |
|---|---|---|---|---|---|---|
| 2001 | — | PF65 27.50 | | | | |

**KM# 233 WON**

28.11 g., Brass, 40 mm. **Obv:** State arms **Rev:** Black grouse **Edge:** Plain

| Date | Mintage | F12 | VF20 | XF40 | MS60 | MS63 |
|---|---|---|---|---|---|---|
| 2001 | — | PF65 27.50 | | | | |

**KM# 234 WON**

28.11 g., Brass, 40 mm. **Obv:** State arms **Rev:** Sand grouse **Edge:** Plain

| Date | Mintage | F12 | VF20 | XF40 | MS60 | MS63 |
|---|---|---|---|---|---|---|
| 2001 | — | PF65 27.50 | | | | |

**KM# 235 WON**

28.11 g., Brass, 40 mm. **Obv:** State arms **Rev:** Fairy Pitta bird **Edge:** Plain

| Date | Mintage | F12 | VF20 | XF40 | MS60 | MS63 |
|---|---|---|---|---|---|---|
| 2001 | — | PF65 27.50 | | | | |

**KM# 236 WON**

28.11 g., Brass, 40 mm. **Obv:** State arms **Rev:** Mythical "Hyonmu **Edge:** Plain

| Date | Mintage | F12 | VF20 | XF40 | MS60 | MS63 |
|---|---|---|---|---|---|---|
| 2001 | — | PF65 27.50 | | | | |

**KM# 236a WON**

7.00 g., Aluminum, 40 mm. **Obv:** State arms **Rev:** Hyonmu **Edge:** Plain

| Date | Mintage | F12 | VF20 | XF40 | MS60 | MS63 |
|---|---|---|---|---|---|---|
| 2001 | — | PF65 17.50 | | | | |

**KM# 237 WON**

28.11 g., Brass, 40 mm. **Obv:** State arms **Rev:** Blue Dragon **Edge:** Plain

| Date | Mintage | F12 | VF20 | XF40 | MS60 | MS63 |
|---|---|---|---|---|---|---|
| 2001 | — | PF65 27.50 | | | | |

**KM# 238 WON**

28.11 g., Brass, 40 mm. **Obv:** State arms **Rev:** Two tigers **Edge:** Plain

| Date | Mintage | F12 | VF20 | XF40 | MS60 | MS63 |
|---|---|---|---|---|---|---|
| 2001 | — | PF65 27.50 | | | | |

**KM# 238a WON**

7.14 g., Aluminum, 40.1 mm. **Obv:** State arms **Rev:** Tiger and cub **Edge:** Plain

| Date | Mintage | F12 | VF20 | XF40 | MS60 | MS63 |
|---|---|---|---|---|---|---|
| 2001 | — | PF65 17.00 | | | | |

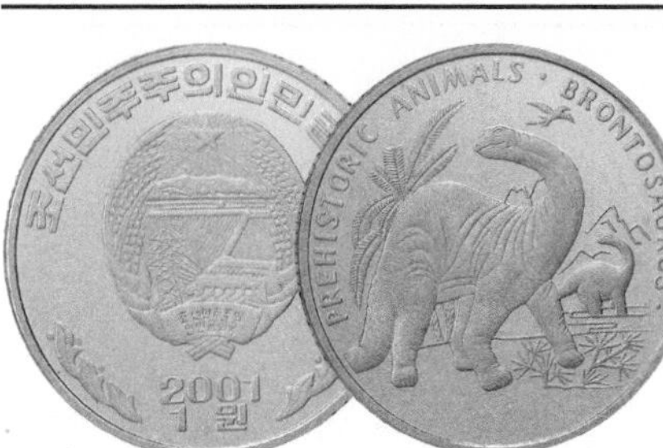


**KM# 239 WON**
28.11 g., Brass, 40 mm. **Obv:** State arms **Rev:** Brontosaurus **Edge:** Plain

| Date | Mintage | F12 | VF20 | XF40 | MS60 | MS63 |
|---|---|---|---|---|---|---|
| 2001 | — | PF65 27.50 | | | | |

**KM# 247 WON**
26.95 g., Brass, 40 mm. **Obv:** State arms **Rev:** Soldier watching an air raid on a Yalu River bridge **Edge:** Plain

| Date | Mintage | F12 | VF20 | XF40 | MS60 | MS63 |
|---|---|---|---|---|---|---|
| 2001 | — | PF65 20.00 | | | | |

**KM# 248 WON**
7.00 g., Aluminum, 40 mm. **Obv:** State arms **Rev:** Multicolor rabbit and hearts **Edge:** Plain **Note:** Year of the Rabbit

| Date | Mintage | F12 | VF20 | XF40 | MS60 | MS63 |
|---|---|---|---|---|---|---|
| 2001 | — | PF65 20.00 | | | | |

**KM# 290 WON**
28.20 g., Brass, 40.1 mm. **Obv:** State arms **Rev:** Bust of Kim Johg-Il facing above flower sprigs **Edge:** Plain

| Date | Mintage | F12 | VF20 | XF40 | MS60 | MS63 |
|---|---|---|---|---|---|---|
| JU90-2001 | — | PF65 20.00 | | | | |

**KM# 291 WON**
28.20 g., Brass, 40.1 mm. **Obv:** State arms **Rev:** Bust of Kim Jung-Suk facing, 1917-1949 flanking, flower sprigs below **Edge:** Plain

| Date | Mintage | F12 | VF20 | XF40 | MS60 | MS63 |
|---|---|---|---|---|---|---|
| JU90-2001 | — | PF65 20.00 | | | | |

**KM# 293 WON**
28.20 g., Brass, 40.2 mm. **Obv:** State arms **Rev:** Olympic runners **Edge:** Crude reeding

| Date | Mintage | F12 | VF20 | XF40 | MS60 | MS63 |
|---|---|---|---|---|---|---|
| 2001 | — | PF65 20.00 | | | | |

**KM# 294 WON**
28.20 g., Brass, 40.2 mm. **Obv:** State arms **Rev:** Antique porcelain objects **Edge:** Plain

| Date | Mintage | F12 | VF20 | XF40 | MS60 | MS63 |
|---|---|---|---|---|---|---|
| 2001 | — | PF65 20.00 | | | | |

**KM# 294a WON**
6.75 g., Aluminum, 40 mm. **Obv:** State arms **Rev:** Antique ceramics **Edge:** Plain

| Date | Mintage | F12 | VF20 | XF40 | MS60 | MS63 |
|---|---|---|---|---|---|---|
| 2001 | — | PF65 15.00 | | | | |

**KM# 310 WON**
Aluminum **Obv:** State arms **Rev:** Tomb of King Tongmyong

| Date | Mintage | F12 | VF20 | XF40 | MS60 | MS63 |
|---|---|---|---|---|---|---|
| 2001 | — | PF65 12.00 | | | | |

**KM# 351 WON**
7.00 g., Aluminum, 40 mm. **Obv:** State arms, date and value below **Rev:** North Korean Arch of Triumph **Edge:** Plain

| Date | Mintage | F12 | VF20 | XF40 | MS60 | MS63 |
|---|---|---|---|---|---|---|
| 2001 | — | PF65 12.00 | | | | |

**KM# 352 WON**
28.60 g., Brass, 40.1 mm. **Obv:** State arms, value below **Rev:** North Korean Arch of Triumph **Edge:** Plain

| Date | Mintage | F12 | VF20 | XF40 | MS60 | MS63 |
|---|---|---|---|---|---|---|
| 2001 | — | PF65 15.00 | | | | |

**KM# 353 WON**
6.45 g., Aluminum, 40 mm. **Obv:** State arms, value below **Rev:** N. Korean landmarks and tourists above ship **Edge:** Plain

| Date | Mintage | F12 | VF20 | XF40 | MS60 | MS63 |
|---|---|---|---|---|---|---|
| 2001 | — | PF65 12.00 | | | | |

**KM# 354 WON**
27.63 g., Brass, 40 mm. **Obv:** State arms, date and value below **Rev:** N. Korean landmarks and tourists above ship **Edge:** Plain

| Date | Mintage | F12 | VF20 | XF40 | MS60 | MS63 |
|---|---|---|---|---|---|---|
| 2001 | — | PF65 15.00 | | | | |

**KM# 355 WON**
6.75 g., Aluminum, 40 mm. **Obv:** State arms, value below **Rev:** Temple of Heaven above Hong Kong city view below **Edge:** Plain

| Date | Mintage | F12 | VF20 | XF40 | MS60 | MS63 |
|---|---|---|---|---|---|---|
| ND | — | PF65 12.00 | | | | |

**KM# 356 WON**
28.10 g., Brass, 40 mm. **Obv:** State arms, date and value below **Rev:** Temple of Heaven above, Hong Kong city view below **Edge:** Plain

| Date | Mintage | F12 | VF20 | XF40 | MS60 | MS63 |
|---|---|---|---|---|---|---|
| 2001 | — | PF65 15.00 | | | | |

**KM# 358 WON**
6.75 g., Aluminum, 40 mm. **Obv:** State arms **Rev:** Old fort **Edge:** Plain

| Date | Mintage | F12 | VF20 | XF40 | MS60 | MS63 |
|---|---|---|---|---|---|---|
| 2001 | — | PF65 12.00 | | | | |

**KM# 358a WON**
28.10 g., Brass, 40 mm. **Obv:** State arms **Rev:** Old fort **Edge:** Plain

| Date | Mintage | F12 | VF20 | XF40 | MS60 | MS63 |
|---|---|---|---|---|---|---|
| 2001 | — | PF65 15.00 | | | | |

**KM# 359 WON**
7.00 g., Aluminum, 40.1 mm. **Obv:** State arms **Rev:** Old couple above dates1945-2000 **Edge:** Plain

| Date | Mintage | F12 | VF20 | XF40 | MS60 | MS63 |
|---|---|---|---|---|---|---|
| 2001 | — | PF65 12.00 | | | | |

**KM# 359a WON**
27.80 g., Brass, 40.1 mm. **Obv:** State arms **Rev:** Old couple above dates 1945-2000 **Edge:** Plain

| Date | Mintage | F12 | VF20 | XF40 | MS60 | MS63 |
|---|---|---|---|---|---|---|
| 2001 | — | PF65 15.00 | | | | |

**KM# 360 WON**
27.80 g., Brass, 40.1 mm. **Obv:** State arms **Rev:** Blue Dragon **Edge:** Plain

| Date | Mintage | F12 | VF20 | XF40 | MS60 | MS63 |
|---|---|---|---|---|---|---|
| 2001 | — | PF65 20.00 | | | | |

### KM# 361 WON

7.00 g., Aluminum, 40.1 mm. **Obv:** State arms **Rev:** Head of Deng Zio Ping 3/4 left, 1904-1997 flanking, sprigs below **Edge:** Plain

| Date | Mintage | F12 | VF20 | XF40 | MS60 | MS63 |
|---|---|---|---|---|---|---|
| 2001 | — | PF65 12.00 | | | | |

### KM# 361a WON

27.80 g., Brass, 40.1 mm. **Obv:** State arms **Rev:** Head 3/4 left divides dates(1904-1997) flanked by sprigs **Edge:** Plain

| Date | Mintage | F12 | VF20 | XF40 | MS60 | MS63 |
|---|---|---|---|---|---|---|
| 2001 | — | PF65 15.00 | | | | |

### KM# 362 WON

7.00 g., Aluminum, 40.1 mm. **Obv:** State arms **Rev:** Children flying a kite **Edge:** Plain

| Date | Mintage | F12 | VF20 | XF40 | MS60 | MS63 |
|---|---|---|---|---|---|---|
| 2001 | — | PF65 15.00 | | | | |

### KM# 362a WON

27.80 g., Brass, 40.1 mm. **Obv:** State arms **Rev:** Children flying a kite **Edge:** Plain

| Date | Mintage | F12 | VF20 | XF40 | MS60 | MS63 |
|---|---|---|---|---|---|---|
| 2001 | — | PF65 17.50 | | | | |

### KM# 363 WON

7.00 g., Aluminum, 40.1 mm. **Obv:** State arms **Rev:** Children on seesaw **Edge:** Plain

| Date | Mintage | F12 | VF20 | XF40 | MS60 | MS63 |
|---|---|---|---|---|---|---|
| 2001 | — | PF65 15.00 | | | | |

### KM# 363a WON

27.80 g., Brass, 40.1 mm. **Obv:** State arms **Rev:** Children on seesaw **Edge:** Plain

| Date | Mintage | F12 | VF20 | XF40 | MS60 | MS63 |
|---|---|---|---|---|---|---|
| 2001 | — | PF65 17.50 | | | | |

### KM# 364 WON

7.00 g., Aluminum, 40.1 mm. **Obv:** State arms **Rev:** Children wrestling **Edge:** Plain

| Date | Mintage | F12 | VF20 | XF40 | MS60 | MS63 |
|---|---|---|---|---|---|---|
| 2001 | — | PF65 15.00 | | | | |

### KM# 364a WON

27.80 g., Brass, 40.1 mm. **Obv:** State arms **Rev:** Children wrestling **Edge:** Plain

| Date | Mintage | F12 | VF20 | XF40 | MS60 | MS63 |
|---|---|---|---|---|---|---|
| 2001 | — | PF65 17.50 | | | | |

### KM# 365 WON

7.00 g., Aluminum, 40.1 mm. **Obv:** State arms **Rev:** Girl on swing **Edge:** Plain

| Date | Mintage | F12 | VF20 | XF40 | MS60 | MS63 |
|---|---|---|---|---|---|---|
| 2001 | — | PF65 15.00 | | | | |

### KM# 365a WON

27.80 g., Brass, 40.1 mm. **Obv:** State arms **Rev:** Girl on swing **Edge:** Plain

| Date | Mintage | F12 | VF20 | XF40 | MS60 | MS63 |
|---|---|---|---|---|---|---|
| 2001 | — | PF65 17.50 | | | | |

### KM# 366 WON

7.00 g., Aluminum, 40.1 mm. **Obv:** State arms **Rev:** Girls jumping rope **Edge:** Plain

| Date | Mintage | F12 | VF20 | XF40 | MS60 | MS63 |
|---|---|---|---|---|---|---|
| 2001 | — | PF65 15.00 | | | | |

### KM# 366a WON

27.80 g., Brass, 40.1 mm. **Obv:** State arms **Rev:** Girls jumping rope **Edge:** Plain

| Date | Mintage | F12 | VF20 | XF40 | MS60 | MS63 |
|---|---|---|---|---|---|---|
| 2001 | — | PF65 17.50 | | | | |

### KM# 367 WON

8.70 g., Aluminum, 40.4 mm. **Obv:** State arms **Rev:** Kumdang-2 Injection" in center square on leaves **Edge:** Plain

| Date | Mintage | F12 | VF20 | XF40 | MS60 | MS63 |
|---|---|---|---|---|---|---|
| 2001 | — | PF65 15.00 | | | | |

### KM# 367a WON

26.54 g., Brass, 40.2 mm. **Obv:** State arms **Rev:** Kumdang-2 Injection" in center square on leaves **Edge:** Plain

| Date | Mintage | F12 | VF20 | XF40 | MS60 | MS63 |
|---|---|---|---|---|---|---|
| 2001 | — | PF65 17.50 | | | | |

### KM# 368 WON

27.61 g., Brass, 40.2 mm. **Obv:** State arms **Rev:** Bust of Kim Il-Sung, 1912-1994 flanking, sprigs below **Edge:** Plain

| Date | Mintage | F12 | VF20 | XF40 | MS60 | MS63 |
|---|---|---|---|---|---|---|
| JU90-2001 | — | PF65 17.50 | | | | |

### KM# 369 WON

6.55 g., Aluminum, 40.4 mm. **Obv:** State arms **Rev:** Train at left, couple below jet plane at right **Edge:** Plain

| Date | Mintage | F12 | VF20 | XF40 | MS60 | MS63 |
|---|---|---|---|---|---|---|
| 2001 | — | PF65 15.00 | | | | |

**KM# 370 WON**
27.56 g., Brass, 40.1 mm. **Obv:** State arms **Rev:** Train at left, couple below jet plane at right **Edge:** Plain

| Date | Mintage | F12 | VF20 | XF40 | MS60 | MS63 |
|---|---|---|---|---|---|---|
| 2001 | — | PF65 17.50 | | | | |

**KM# 371 WON**
5.05 g., Aluminum, 35 mm. **Obv:** State arms **Rev:** Hong Kong city view **Edge:** Plain

| Date | Mintage | F12 | VF20 | XF40 | MS60 | MS63 |
|---|---|---|---|---|---|---|
| 2001 | — | PF65 10.00 | | | | |

**KM# 372 WON**
6.40 g., Aluminum, 40 mm. **Obv:** State arms **Rev:** Bust with beard facing flanked by text **Edge:** Plain

| Date | Mintage | F12 | VF20 | XF40 | MS60 | MS63 |
|---|---|---|---|---|---|---|
| 2001 | — | PF65 12.00 | | | | |

**KM# 372a WON**
27.70 g., Brass, 40 mm. **Obv:** State arms **Rev:** Bust with beard facing flanked by text **Edge:** Plain

| Date | Mintage | F12 | VF20 | XF40 | MS60 | MS63 |
|---|---|---|---|---|---|---|
| 2001 | — | PF65 15.00 | | | | |

**KM# 373 WON**
6.90 g., Aluminum, 40 mm. **Subject:** 1996 Olympics **Obv:** State arms **Rev:** Two green gymnasts and multicolor flame **Edge:** Plain

| Date | Mintage | F12 | VF20 | XF40 | MS60 | MS63 |
|---|---|---|---|---|---|---|
| 2001 | — | PF65 15.00 | | | | |

**KM# 374 WON**
7.00 g., Aluminum, 40 mm. **Obv:** State arms **Rev:** Taedong Gatehouse **Edge:** Plain

| Date | Mintage | F12 | VF20 | XF40 | MS60 | MS63 |
|---|---|---|---|---|---|---|
| 2001 | — | PF65 15.00 | | | | |

**KM# 375 WON**
8.50 g., Aluminum, 40.2 mm. **Obv:** State arms **Rev:** Logo above Baektn Mountain volcano crater **Edge:** Plain

| Date | Mintage | F12 | VF20 | XF40 | MS60 | MS63 |
|---|---|---|---|---|---|---|
| JU90-2001 | — | PF65 10.00 | | | | |

**KM# 376 WON**
7.10 g., Aluminum, 40.1 mm. **Subject:** 1996 Olympics **Obv:** State arms **Rev:** Horse jumping **Edge:** Plain

| Date | Mintage | F12 | VF20 | XF40 | MS60 | MS63 |
|---|---|---|---|---|---|---|
| 2001 | — | PF65 15.00 | | | | |

**KM# 377 WON**
7.00 g., Aluminum, 40.1 mm. **Subject:** 1996 Olympics **Obv:** State arms **Rev:** Four runners **Edge:** Plain

| Date | Mintage | F12 | VF20 | XF40 | MS60 | MS63 |
|---|---|---|---|---|---|---|
| 2001 | — | PF65 15.00 | | | | |

**KM# 378 WON**
6.84 g., Aluminum, 40.1 mm. **Obv:** State arms **Rev:** Monument flanked by multicolor flags and flowers **Edge:** Plain

| Date | Mintage | F12 | VF20 | XF40 | MS60 | MS63 |
|---|---|---|---|---|---|---|
| 2001 | — | PF65 12.00 | | | | |

**KM# 379 WON**
6.60 g., Aluminum, 40.1 mm. **Obv:** State arms **Rev:** Olympic diver **Edge:** Plain

| Date | Mintage | F12 | VF20 | XF40 | MS60 | MS63 |
|---|---|---|---|---|---|---|
| 2001 | — | PF65 15.00 | | | | |

**KM# 380 WON**
6.91 g., Aluminum, 40.1 mm. **Obv:** State arms **Rev:** Olympic handball player **Edge:** Plain

| Date | Mintage | F12 | VF20 | XF40 | MS60 | MS63 |
|---|---|---|---|---|---|---|
| 2001 | — | PF65 15.00 | | | | |

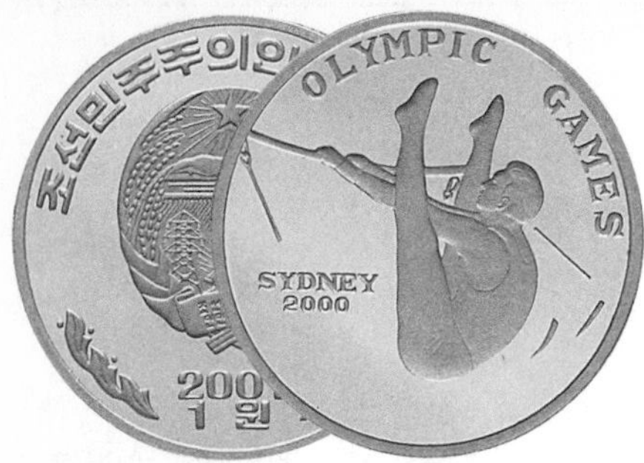


**KM# 381 WON**
7.11 g., Aluminum, 40.2 mm. **Obv:** State arms **Rev:** Olympic high bar gymnast **Edge:** Plain

| Date | Mintage | F12 | VF20 | XF40 | MS60 | MS63 |
|---|---|---|---|---|---|---|
| 2001 | — | PF65 15.00 | | | | |

**KM# 381a WON**
28.82 g., Brass, 40.1 mm. **Obv:** State arms **Rev:** Olympic high bar gymnast **Edge:** Plain

| Date | Mintage | F12 | VF20 | XF40 | MS60 | MS63 |
|---|---|---|---|---|---|---|
| 2001 | — | PF65 17.50 | | | | |

**KM# 382 WON**
6.50 g., Aluminum, 40.1 mm. **Obv:** State arms **Rev:** Olympic archer **Edge:** Plain

| Date | Mintage | F12 | VF20 | XF40 | MS60 | MS63 |
|---|---|---|---|---|---|---|
| 2001 | — | PF65 15.00 | | | | |

**KM# 382a WON**
27.41 g., Brass, 40.2 mm. **Obv:** State arms **Rev:** Olympic archer **Edge:** Plain

| Date | Mintage | F12 | VF20 | XF40 | MS60 | MS63 |
|---|---|---|---|---|---|---|
| 2001 | — | PF65 17.50 | | | | |

**KM# 383 WON**
7.10 g., Aluminum, 40.1 mm. **Obv:** State arms **Rev:** Olympic hurdler **Edge:** Plain

| Date | Mintage | F12 | VF20 | XF40 | MS60 | MS63 |
|---|---|---|---|---|---|---|
| 2001 | — | PF65 15.00 | | | | |

**KM# 383a WON**
28.00 g., Brass, 40.1 mm. **Obv:** State arms **Rev:** Olympic hurdler **Edge:** Plain

| Date | Mintage | F12 | VF20 | XF40 | MS60 | MS63 |
|---|---|---|---|---|---|---|
| 2001 | — | PF65 17.50 | | | | |

**KM# 384 WON**
7.15 g., Aluminum, 40.1 mm. **Obv:** State arms **Rev:** Kim Il Sung's birthplace side view **Edge:** Plain

| Date | Mintage | F12 | VF20 | XF40 | MS60 | MS63 |
|---|---|---|---|---|---|---|
| JU90-2001 | — | PF65 15.00 | | | | |

**KM# 385 WON**
7.00 g., Aluminum, 40.1 mm. **Obv:** State arms **Rev:** Mt. Kumgang Fairy playing flute **Edge:** Plain

| Date | Mintage | F12 | VF20 | XF40 | MS60 | MS63 |
|---|---|---|---|---|---|---|
| 2001 | — | PF65 12.00 | | | | |

**KM# 385a WON**
28.16 g., Brass, 40.2 mm. **Obv:** State arms **Rev:** Mt. Kumgang Fairy playing flute **Edge:** Plain

| Date | Mintage | F12 | VF20 | XF40 | MS60 | MS63 |
|---|---|---|---|---|---|---|
| 2001 | — | PF65 15.00 | | | | |

**KM# 452 WON**
27.44 g., Brass, 40 mm. **Obv:** State arms **Rev:** Early sailing ship **Rev. Legend:** • HISTORY OF SEAFARING • MERCHANTMAN - THE DPR KOREA . KORYO PERIOD . 918-1392 **Edge:** Plain

| Date | Mintage | F12 | VF20 | XF40 | MS60 | MS63 |
|---|---|---|---|---|---|---|
| 2001 | — | PF65 9.00 | | | | |

**KM# 458 WON**
5.00 g., Aluminum, 35 mm. **Obv:** National arms, Country name **Rev:** Krugenstern

| Date | Mintage | F12 | VF20 | XF40 | MS60 | MS63 |
|---|---|---|---|---|---|---|
| 2001 | — | PF65 7.00 | | | | |

**KM# 458a WON**
16.00 g., Brass, 35 mm. **Subject:** Tall ships **Obv:** Arms **Rev:** Krugenstern

| Date | Mintage | F12 | VF20 | XF40 | MS60 | MS63 |
|---|---|---|---|---|---|---|
| 2001 | — | PF65 8.00 | | | | |

**KM# 459 WON**
Brass, 35 mm. **Subject:** Return of Hong Kong **Obv:** Arms **Rev:** Architecture

| Date | Mintage | F12 | VF20 | XF40 | MS60 | MS63 |
|---|---|---|---|---|---|---|
| 2001 | — | PF65 6.50 | | | | |

**KM# 460 WON**
Brass, 35 mm. **Subject:** Return of Hong Kong **Obv:** Skyline **Rev:** Dragon boat

| Date | Mintage | F12 | VF20 | XF40 | MS60 | MS63 |
|---|---|---|---|---|---|---|
| 2001 | — | PF65 12.00 | | | | |

**KM# 461 WON**
6.00 g., Aluminum, 38 mm. **Obv:** National arms, Central Bank name **Rev:** Speed skater

| Date | Mintage | F12 | VF20 | XF40 | MS60 | MS63 |
|---|---|---|---|---|---|---|
| 2001 Proof | — | — | — | — | — | — |

**KM# 461a WON**
25.00 g., Brass **Subject:** 2002 Olympics **Obv:** Arms **Rev:** Speedskater

| Date | Mintage | F12 | VF20 | XF40 | MS60 | MS63 |
|---|---|---|---|---|---|---|
| 2001 | — | PF65 10.00 | | | | |

**KM# 462 WON**
Aluminum, 40 mm. **Subject:** Tae Kwon do **Obv:** Arms **Rev:** Two sportsmen

| Date | Mintage | F12 | VF20 | XF40 | MS60 | MS63 |
|---|---|---|---|---|---|---|
| 2001 | — | PF65 8.00 | | | | |

### KM# 462a WON
28.00 g., Brass, 40 mm. **Obv:** National arms, Country name **Rev:** Two Taekwondo players

| Date | Mintage | F12 | VF20 | XF40 | MS60 | MS63 |
|---|---|---|---|---|---|---|
| 2001 | — | PF65 7.00 | | | | |

### KM# 463 WON
Aluminum, 40 mm. **Obv:** Arms **Rev:** Multicolor flowers

| Date | Mintage | F12 | VF20 | XF40 | MS60 | MS63 |
|---|---|---|---|---|---|---|
| 2001 | — | PF65 8.00 | | | | |

### KM# 464 WON
Aluminum, 40 mm. **Obv:** Arms **Rev:** Woodpecker on branch (Dryocopus Javensis)

| Date | Mintage | F12 | VF20 | XF40 | MS60 | MS63 |
|---|---|---|---|---|---|---|
| 2001 | — | PF65 8.00 | | | | |

### KM# 465 WON
Aluminum, 35 mm. **Obv:** Arms **Rev:** Zhou Enlai portrait facing

| Date | Mintage | F12 | VF20 | XF40 | MS60 | MS63 |
|---|---|---|---|---|---|---|
| 2001 | — | PF65 8.00 | | | | |

### KM# 466 WON
Aluminum, 40 mm. **Obv:** Arms **Rev:** Buddha seated, facing

| Date | Mintage | F12 | VF20 | XF40 | MS60 | MS63 |
|---|---|---|---|---|---|---|
| 2001 | — | PF65 7.00 | | | | |

### KM# 467 WON
Brass **Obv:** Arms **Rev:** Buddha seated, facing

| Date | Mintage | F12 | VF20 | XF40 | MS60 | MS63 |
|---|---|---|---|---|---|---|
| 2001 | — | PF65 10.00 | | | | |

### KM# 468 WON
Brass **Obv:** Arms **Rev:** Couple embracing, 1945-2000

| Date | Mintage | F12 | VF20 | XF40 | MS60 | MS63 |
|---|---|---|---|---|---|---|
| ND-2001 | — | PF65 10.00 | | | | |

### KM# 504 WON
7.00 g., Aluminum, 40 mm. **Obv:** National arms **Rev:** Rainbow lori in color

| Date | Mintage | F12 | VF20 | XF40 | MS60 | MS63 |
|---|---|---|---|---|---|---|
| 2001 | — | PF65 8.50 | | | | |

### KM# 505 WON
28.00 g., Brass **Obv:** National arms **Rev:** Rainbow lori

| Date | Mintage | F12 | VF20 | XF40 | MS60 | MS63 |
|---|---|---|---|---|---|---|
| 2001 | — | PF65 8.50 | | | | |

### KM# 506 WON
7.00 g., Aluminum **Rev:** Mandarian Ducks in color

| Date | Mintage | F12 | VF20 | XF40 | MS60 | MS63 |
|---|---|---|---|---|---|---|
| 2001 | — | PF65 8.50 | | | | |

### KM# 507 WON
Brass **Rev:** Mandarin Ducks

| Date | Mintage | F12 | VF20 | XF40 | MS60 | MS63 |
|---|---|---|---|---|---|---|
| 2001 | — | PF65 9.00 | | | | |

### KM# 535 WON
7.00 g., Aluminum, 40 mm. **Obv:** National arms **Rev:** Power in teh frowing area of Kaeseong in color

| Date | Mintage | F12 | VF20 | XF40 | MS60 | MS63 |
|---|---|---|---|---|---|---|
| 2001 Proof | — | — | — | — | — | — |

### KM# 539 WON
7.00 g., Aluminum, 40 mm. **Obv:** National arms **Rev:** Panda seated in color, eating

| Date | Mintage | F12 | VF20 | XF40 | MS60 | MS63 |
|---|---|---|---|---|---|---|
| 2001 | — | PF65 7.50 | | | | |

### KM# 541 WON
7.00 g., Aluminum, 40 mm. **Obv:** National arms **Rev:** Two pandas in color

| Date | Mintage | F12 | VF20 | XF40 | MS60 | MS63 |
|---|---|---|---|---|---|---|
| 2001 | — | PF65 7.50 | | | | |

### KM# 542 WON
28.00 g., Brass **Obv:** National arms, name of the Central Bank **Rev:** Two pandas

| Date | Mintage | F12 | VF20 | XF40 | MS60 | MS63 |
|---|---|---|---|---|---|---|
| 2001 | — | PF65 8.00 | | | | |

### KM# 548 WON
7.00 g., Aluminum, 40 mm. **Obv:** National arms, name of the Central Bank **Rev:** Rainbow lori in color

| Date | Mintage | F12 | VF20 | XF40 | MS60 | MS63 |
|---|---|---|---|---|---|---|
| 2001 | — | PF65 7.50 | | | | |

### KM# 549 WON
7.00 g., Aluminum, 40 mm. **Obv:** National arms, name of the Central Bank **Rev:** Manderin duck in color

| Date | Mintage | F12 | VF20 | XF40 | MS60 | MS63 |
|---|---|---|---|---|---|---|
| 2001 | — | PF65 7.50 | | | | |

### KM# 556 WON
Brass **Rev:** Show jumper

| Date | Mintage | F12 | VF20 | XF40 | MS60 | MS63 |
|---|---|---|---|---|---|---|
| 2001 | — | PF65 8.00 | | | | |

### KM# 557 WON
7.00 g., Aluminum, 40 mm. **Obv:** National arms, name of the Central Bank **Rev:** Rythem dancers and logo in color

| Date | Mintage | F12 | VF20 | XF40 | MS60 | MS63 |
|---|---|---|---|---|---|---|
| 2001 | — | PF65 7.50 | | | | |

### KM# 558 WON
7.00 g., Aluminum, 40 mm. **Obv:** National arms, name of the Central Bank **Rev:** Chinese Peony

| Date | Mintage | F12 | VF20 | XF40 | MS60 | MS63 |
|---|---|---|---|---|---|---|
| 2001 | — | PF65 7.50 | | | | |

### KM# 559 WON
7.00 g., Aluminum, 40 mm. **Obv:** National arms, name of the Central Bank **Rev:** Panda seated in color eating

| Date | Mintage | F12 | VF20 | XF40 | MS60 | MS63 |
|---|---|---|---|---|---|---|
| 2001 | — | PF65 7.50 | | | | |

### KM# 560 WON
Brass, 28 mm. **Obv:** National arms, name of the Central Bank **Rev:** Panda seated eating

| Date | Mintage | F12 | VF20 | XF40 | MS60 | MS63 |
|---|---|---|---|---|---|---|
| 2001 | — | PF65 8.00 | | | | |

### KM# 561 WON
28.00 g., Brass, 40 mm. **Obv:** National arms, name of the Central Bank **Rev:** Soldiers attack bridge over the Yalu river at Dandong (1951)

| Date | Mintage | F12 | VF20 | XF40 | MS60 | MS63 |
|---|---|---|---|---|---|---|
| 2001 | — | PF65 7.50 | | | | |

### KM# 562 WON
28.00 g., Brass, 40 mm. **Obv:** National arms **Rev:** Soldiers attack bridge over the Yalu river at Dandong (1951)

| Date | Mintage | F12 | VF20 | XF40 | MS60 | MS63 |
|---|---|---|---|---|---|---|
| 2001 | — | PF65 7.50 | | | | |

### KM# 563 WON
28.00 g., Brass, 40 mm. **Obv:** National arms, name of the Central Bank **Rev:** Tower of Friendship in Pyeongyang with North Korean and P.R.C. flags

| Date | Mintage | F12 | VF20 | XF40 | MS60 | MS63 |
|---|---|---|---|---|---|---|
| 2001 | — | PF65 8.00 | | | | |

### KM# 568 WON
7.00 g., Aluminum, 40 mm. **Obv:** National arms **Rev:** Rocket and satelite

| Date | Mintage | F12 | VF20 | XF40 | MS60 | MS63 |
|---|---|---|---|---|---|---|
| 2001 | — | PF65 6.50 | | | | |

### KM# 568a WON
28.00 g., Brass, 40 mm. **Obv:** National arms **Rev:** Rocket and satellite

| Date | Mintage | F12 | VF20 | XF40 | MS60 | MS63 |
|---|---|---|---|---|---|---|
| 2001 | — | PF65 7.50 | | | | |

### KM# 572 WON
28.00 g., Brass, 40 mm. **Obv:** National arms, country name **Rev:** Dragon rising

| Date | Mintage | F12 | VF20 | XF40 | MS60 | MS63 |
|---|---|---|---|---|---|---|
| 2001 | — | PF65 7.50 | | | | |

### KM# 573 WON
28.00 g., Brass, 40 mm. **Obv:** National arms, name of the Central Bank **Rev:** Dragon rising

| Date | Mintage | F12 | VF20 | XF40 | MS60 | MS63 |
|---|---|---|---|---|---|---|
| 2001 | — | PF65 7.50 | | | | |

### KM# 574 WON
Brass **Obv:** National arms, country name **Rev:** Two girls on the seasaw

| Date | Mintage | F12 | VF20 | XF40 | MS60 | MS63 |
|---|---|---|---|---|---|---|
| 2001 | — | PF65 7.50 | | | | |

### KM# 575 WON
Brass **Obv:** National arms, Central Bank name **Rev:** Two girls on the seasaw

| Date | Mintage | F12 | VF20 | XF40 | MS60 | MS63 |
|---|---|---|---|---|---|---|
| 2001 | — | PF65 7.50 | | | | |

### KM# 576 WON
Brass **Obv:** National arms, country name **Rev:** Korean struggle

| Date | Mintage | F12 | VF20 | XF40 | MS60 | MS63 |
|---|---|---|---|---|---|---|
| 2001 | — | PF65 7.50 | | | | |

### KM# 577 WON
Brass **Obv:** National arms, Central Bank name **Rev:** Korean struggle

| Date | Mintage | F12 | VF20 | XF40 | MS60 | MS63 |
|---|---|---|---|---|---|---|
| 2001 | — | PF65 7.50 | | | | |

### KM# 578 WON
Brass **Obv:** National arms, country name **Rev:** Child on swing

| Date | Mintage | F12 | VF20 | XF40 | MS60 | MS63 |
|---|---|---|---|---|---|---|
| 2001 | — | PF65 7.50 | | | | |

### KM# 579 WON
Brass **Obv:** National arms, Central Bank name **Rev:** Child on swing

| Date | Mintage | F12 | VF20 | XF40 | MS60 | MS63 |
|---|---|---|---|---|---|---|
| 2001 | — | PF65 7.50 | | | | |

### KM# 580 WON
Brass **Obv:** National arms, country name **Rev:** Children skipping

| Date | Mintage | F12 | VF20 | XF40 | MS60 | MS63 |
|---|---|---|---|---|---|---|
| 2001 | — | PF65 7.50 | | | | |

### KM# 581 WON
28.00 g., Brass, 40 mm. **Obv:** National arms, Central Bank name **Rev:** Children skipping

| Date | Mintage | F12 | VF20 | XF40 | MS60 | MS63 |
|---|---|---|---|---|---|---|
| 2001 | — | PF65 7.50 | | | | |

### KM# 608 WON
7.00 g., Aluminum, 40 mm. **Obv:** National arms, Central Bank name **Rev:** Rabbit in color

| Date | Mintage | F12 | VF20 | XF40 | MS60 | MS63 |
|---|---|---|---|---|---|---|
| 2001 | — | PF65 7.50 | | | | |

### KM# 609 WON
28.00 g., Brass, 40 mm. **Obv:** National arms, country name **Rev:** Rabbit

| Date | Mintage | F12 | VF20 | XF40 | MS60 | MS63 |
|---|---|---|---|---|---|---|
| 2001 | — | PF65 7.50 | | | | |

### KM# 616 WON
7.00 g., Aluminum, 40 mm. **Obv:** National arms, Central Bank name **Rev:** White bellied woodpecker

| Date | Mintage | F12 | VF20 | XF40 | MS60 | MS63 |
|---|---|---|---|---|---|---|
| 2001 | — | PF65 6.00 | | | | |

### KM# 617 WON
7.00 g., Aluminum, 40 mm. **Obv:** National arms, Country name **Rev:** Black grouse

| Date | Mintage | F12 | VF20 | XF40 | MS60 | MS63 |
|---|---|---|---|---|---|---|
| 2001 | — | PF65 6.00 | | | | |

### KM# 618 WON
7.00 g., Aluminum, 40 mm. **Obv:** National arms, Country name **Rev:** Sand grouse

| Date | Mintage | F12 | VF20 | XF40 | MS60 | MS63 |
|---|---|---|---|---|---|---|
| 2001 | — | PF65 6.00 | | | | |

### KM# 619 WON
7.00 g., Aluminum, 40 mm. **Obv:** National arms, Country name **Rev:** Indian Pitta bird

| Date | Mintage | F12 | VF20 | XF40 | MS60 | MS63 |
|---|---|---|---|---|---|---|
| 2001 | — | PF65 6.00 | | | | |

### KM# 636 WON
28.00 g., Brass, 40 mm. **Obv:** National arms, Country name **Rev:** Two siberian tigers

| Date | Mintage | F12 | VF20 | XF40 | MS60 | MS63 |
|---|---|---|---|---|---|---|
| 2001 | — | PF65 7.00 | | | | |

### KM# 641 WON
7.00 g., Aluminum, 40 mm. **Obv:** National arms, Country name **Rev:** Gojumong, first king

| Date | Mintage | F12 | VF20 | XF40 | MS60 | MS63 |
|---|---|---|---|---|---|---|
| 2001 | — | PF65 6.00 | | | | |

### KM# 642 WON
28.00 g., Brass, 40 mm. **Obv:** National arms, Country name **Rev:** Gojumong, 1st king

| Date | Mintage | F12 | VF20 | XF40 | MS60 | MS63 |
|---|---|---|---|---|---|---|
| 2001 | — | PF65 7.00 | | | | |

### KM# 643 WON
28.00 g., Brass, 40 mm. **Obv:** National arms, Central Bank name **Rev:** Gojumong, 1st king

| Date | Mintage | F12 | VF20 | XF40 | MS60 | MS63 |
|---|---|---|---|---|---|---|
| 2001 | — | PF65 7.00 | | | | |

### KM# 644 WON
7.00 g., Aluminum, 40 mm. **Obv:** National arms, Country name **Rev:** Buddha figure as Myogilsand as rock relief in inner diamond mountain

| Date | Mintage | F12 | VF20 | XF40 | MS60 | MS63 |
|---|---|---|---|---|---|---|
| 2001 | — | PF65 6.00 | | | | |

### KM# 645 WON
28.00 g., Brass, 40 mm. **Obv:** National arms, Country name **Rev:** Buddha figure Myogilsang as rock relief in inner diamond mountain

| Date | Mintage | F12 | VF20 | XF40 | MS60 | MS63 |
|---|---|---|---|---|---|---|
| 2001 | — | PF65 7.00 | | | | |

### KM# 646 WON
Aluminum **Obv:** Dragon and country name **Rev:** King Gojoseon

| Date | Mintage | F12 | VF20 | XF40 | MS60 | MS63 |
|---|---|---|---|---|---|---|
| 2001 | — | PF65 6.00 | | | | |

### KM# 647 WON
28.00 g., Brass, 40 mm. **Obv:** Dragon and country name **Rev:** King Gojoseon

| Date | Mintage | F12 | VF20 | XF40 | MS60 | MS63 |
|---|---|---|---|---|---|---|
| 2001 | — | PF65 7.00 | | | | |

### KM# 648 WON
28.00 g., Brass, 40 mm. **Obv:** Dragon, Central Bank name **Rev:** King Gojoseon

| Date | Mintage | F12 | VF20 | XF40 | MS60 | MS63 |
|---|---|---|---|---|---|---|
| 2001 | — | PF65 7.00 | | | | |

### KM# 663 WON
7.00 g., Aluminum, 40 mm. **Obv:** National arms, Central Bank name **Rev:** Map of Korea in circle

| Date | Mintage | F12 | VF20 | XF40 | MS60 | MS63 |
|---|---|---|---|---|---|---|
| 2001 | — | PF65 6.00 | | | | |

**KM# 664 WON**
28.00 g., Brass, 40 mm. **Obv:** National arms, Country name **Rev:** Map of Korea in circle

| Date | Mintage | F12 | VF20 | XF40 | MS60 | MS63 |
|---|---|---|---|---|---|---|
| 2001 | — | PF65 7.00 | | | | |

**KM# 666 WON**
28.00 g., Brass, 40 mm. **Obv:** National arms, Country name **Rev:** First married couple to see again after the 1945 seperation

| Date | Mintage | F12 | VF20 | XF40 | MS60 | MS63 |
|---|---|---|---|---|---|---|
| 2001 | — | PF65 7.00 | | | | |

**KM# 670 WON**
28.00 g., Brass, 40 mm. **Obv:** National arms, Central Bank name **Rev:** Kim Jeongil and Kim Daejung embrace

| Date | Mintage | F12 | VF20 | XF40 | MS60 | MS63 |
|---|---|---|---|---|---|---|
| 2001 | — | PF65 7.00 | | | | |

**KM# 671 WON**
28.00 g., Brass, 40 mm. **Obv:** National arms, Central bank name **Rev:** Picture pose of Kim Jeongil and Kim Daejung

| Date | Mintage | F12 | VF20 | XF40 | MS60 | MS63 |
|---|---|---|---|---|---|---|
| 2001 | — | PF65 7.00 | | | | |

**KM# 672 WON**
28.00 g., Brass, 40 mm. **Obv:** National arms, Central Bank name **Rev:** Kim Jeongil and Kim Daejung sign joint agreement

| Date | Mintage | F12 | VF20 | XF40 | MS60 | MS63 |
|---|---|---|---|---|---|---|
| 2001 | — | PF65 7.00 | | | | |

**KM# 674 WON**
28.00 g., Brass, 40 mm. **Subject:** Sydney Olympics, 2000 **Obv:** National arms, Country name **Rev:** Archer

| Date | Mintage | F12 | VF20 | XF40 | MS60 | MS63 |
|---|---|---|---|---|---|---|
| 2001 | — | PF65 7.00 | | | | |

**KM# 675 WON**
28.00 g., Brass, 40 mm. **Obv:** National arms, Country name **Rev:** Handball player

| Date | Mintage | F12 | VF20 | XF40 | MS60 | MS63 |
|---|---|---|---|---|---|---|
| 2001 | — | PF65 7.00 | | | | |

**KM# 676 WON**
7.00 g., Aluminum, 40 mm. **Obv:** National arms, Country name **Rev:** Korean ringer

| Date | Mintage | F12 | VF20 | XF40 | MS60 | MS63 |
|---|---|---|---|---|---|---|
| 2001 | — | PF65 6.00 | | | | |

**KM# 677 WON**
28.00 g., Brass, 40 mm. **Subject:** Sydney Olympics **Obv:** National arms, Country name **Rev:** Korean ringer

| Date | Mintage | F12 | VF20 | XF40 | MS60 | MS63 |
|---|---|---|---|---|---|---|
| 2001 | — | PF65 7.00 | | | | |

**KM# 691 WON**
28.00 g., Brass, 40 mm. **Subject:** Kim Ilseong's 90th birthday **Obv:** National arms, Central Bank name **Rev:** Kim Ilseong

| Date | Mintage | F12 | VF20 | XF40 | MS60 | MS63 |
|---|---|---|---|---|---|---|
| 2001 | — | PF65 7.00 | | | | |

**KM# 692 WON**
28.00 g., Brass, 40 mm. **Obv:** National arms, Central Bank name **Rev:** Kim Jeongil

| Date | Mintage | F12 | VF20 | XF40 | MS60 | MS63 |
|---|---|---|---|---|---|---|
| 2001 | — | PF65 7.00 | | | | |

**KM# 693 WON**
28.00 g., Brass, 40 mm. **Obv:** National arms, Central Bank name **Rev:** Kim Jeongsuk

| Date | Mintage | F12 | VF20 | XF40 | MS60 | MS63 |
|---|---|---|---|---|---|---|
| 2001 | — | PF65 7.00 | | | | |

**KM# 698 WON**
7.00 g., Aluminum, 40 mm. **Obv:** National arms, Country name **Rev:** House where Kim Ilseong was born

| Date | Mintage | F12 | VF20 | XF40 | MS60 | MS63 |
|---|---|---|---|---|---|---|
| 2001 | — | PF65 6.00 | | | | |

**KM# 699 WON**
28.00 g., Brass, 40 mm. **Obv:** National arms, Country name **Rev:** House were Kim Ilseong was born

| Date | Mintage | F12 | VF20 | XF40 | MS60 | MS63 |
|---|---|---|---|---|---|---|
| 2001 | — | PF65 7.00 | | | | |

**KM# 700 WON**
28.00 g., Brass, 40 mm. **Obv:** National arms, Central Bank name **Rev:** House where Kim Ilseong was born

| Date | Mintage | F12 | VF20 | XF40 | MS60 | MS63 |
|---|---|---|---|---|---|---|
| 2001 | — | PF65 7.00 | | | | |

**KM# 701 WON**
28.00 g., Brass, 40 mm. **Obv:** National arms **Rev:** Mountain hut

| Date | Mintage | F12 | VF20 | XF40 | MS60 | MS63 |
|---|---|---|---|---|---|---|
| 2001 Proof | — | — | — | — | — | — |

**KM# 702 WON**
7.00 g., Aluminum, 40 mm. **Obv:** National arms **Rev:** House where Kim Jeongsuk was born

| Date | Mintage | F12 | VF20 | XF40 | MS60 | MS63 |
|---|---|---|---|---|---|---|
| 2001 Proof | — | — | — | — | — | — |

**KM# 703 WON**
28.00 g., Brass, 40 mm. **Obv:** National arms **Rev:** House where Kim Jeongsuk was born

| Date | Mintage | F12 | VF20 | XF40 | MS60 | MS63 |
|---|---|---|---|---|---|---|
| 2001 Proof | — | — | — | — | — | — |

**KM# 706 WON**
7.00 g., Aluminum, 40 mm. **Obv:** National arms, Country name **Rev:** East gate of Pyeongyang

| Date | Mintage | F12 | VF20 | XF40 | MS60 | MS63 |
|---|---|---|---|---|---|---|
| 2001 | — | PF65 6.00 | | | | |

**KM# 707 WON**
28.00 g., Brass, 40 mm. **Obv:** National arms, Country name **Rev:** East gate of Pyeongyang

| Date | Mintage | F12 | VF20 | XF40 | MS60 | MS63 |
|---|---|---|---|---|---|---|
| 2001 | — | PF65 7.00 | | | | |

**KM# 708 WON**
28.00 g., Brass, 40 mm. **Obv:** National arms, Central Bank name **Rev:** East gate of Pyeongyang

| Date | Mintage | F12 | VF20 | XF40 | MS60 | MS63 |
|---|---|---|---|---|---|---|
| 2001 | — | PF65 7.00 | | | | |

**KM# 709 WON**
7.00 g., Aluminum, 40 mm. **Obv:** National arms, Country name **Rev:** North gate of Pyeongyang reconstructed

| Date | Mintage | F12 | VF20 | XF40 | MS60 | MS63 |
|---|---|---|---|---|---|---|
| 2001 | — | PF65 6.00 | | | | |

**KM# 710 WON**
28.00 g., Brass, 40 mm. **Obv:** National arms, Country name **Rev:** North gate of Pyeongyang reconstructed

| Date | Mintage | F12 | VF20 | XF40 | MS60 | MS63 |
|---|---|---|---|---|---|---|
| 2001 | — | PF65 7.00 | | | | |

**KM# 711 WON**
28.00 g., Brass, 40 mm. **Obv:** National arms, Central Bank name **Rev:** North gate of Pyeongyang reconstructed

| Date | Mintage | F12 | VF20 | XF40 | MS60 | MS63 |
|---|---|---|---|---|---|---|
| 2001 | — | PF65 7.00 | | | | |

**KM# 712 WON**
28.00 g., Brass, 40 mm. **Obv:** National arms, Country name with date **Rev:** Celadon pottery

| Date | Mintage | F12 | VF20 | XF40 | MS60 | MS63 |
|---|---|---|---|---|---|---|
| 2001 | — | PF65 7.00 | | | | |

**KM# 713 WON**
28.00 g., Brass, 40 mm. **Obv:** National arms, Country name **Rev:** Celadon pottery

| Date | Mintage | F12 | VF20 | XF40 | MS60 | MS63 |
|---|---|---|---|---|---|---|
| 2001 | — | PF65 7.00 | | | | |

**KM# 714 WON**
28.00 g., Brass, 40 mm. **Obv:** National arms, Central bank name **Rev:** Celadon pottery

| Date | Mintage | F12 | VF20 | XF40 | MS60 | MS63 |
|---|---|---|---|---|---|---|
| 2001 | — | PF65 7.00 | | | | |

**KM# 718 WON**
Aluminum, 40 mm. **Obv:** National arms, Central Bank name **Rev:** Ginsing plant

| Date | Mintage | F12 | VF20 | XF40 | MS60 | MS63 |
|---|---|---|---|---|---|---|
| 2001 | — | PF65 7.00 | | | | |

**KM# 719 WON**
28.00 g., Brass, 40 mm. **Obv:** National arms, Central Bank name **Rev:** Ginsing plant

| Date | Mintage | F12 | VF20 | XF40 | MS60 | MS63 |
|---|---|---|---|---|---|---|
| 2001 | — | PF65 7.00 | | | | |

**KM# 721 WON**
7.00 g., Aluminum, 40 mm. **Obv:** National arms, Central Bank name **Rev:** Fairwell to the steam railway, 1945 and again in 2001

| Date | Mintage | F12 | VF20 | XF40 | MS60 | MS63 |
|---|---|---|---|---|---|---|
| 2001 | — | PF65 6.00 | | | | |

**KM# 722 WON**
28.00 g., Brass, 40 mm. **Obv:** National arms, Central Bank name **Rev:** Fairwell to the steam train, 1945, and then again, 2001

| Date | Mintage | F12 | VF20 | XF40 | MS60 | MS63 |
|---|---|---|---|---|---|---|
| 2001 | — | PF65 7.00 | | | | |

**KM# 724 WON**
7.00 g., Aluminum, 40 mm. **Obv:** National arms. Central Bank name **Rev:** Married couple in front of Pyongyang attractions with national flag and ferryboat

| Date | Mintage | F12 | VF20 | XF40 | MS60 | MS63 |
|---|---|---|---|---|---|---|
| 2001 | — | PF65 6.00 | | | | |

**KM# 725 WON**
28.00 g., Brass, 40 mm. **Obv:** National arms, Country name **Rev:** Married couple in front of Pyongyang attractions with national flag and ferryboat

| Date | Mintage | F12 | VF20 | XF40 | MS60 | MS63 |
|---|---|---|---|---|---|---|
| 2001 | — | PF65 7.00 | | | | |

**KM# 726 WON**
7.00 g., Aluminum, 40 mm. **Obv:** National arms, Central Bank name **Rev:** Ferryboat from Koreans in Japan on the route from Niigata to Wonsan

| Date | Mintage | F12 | VF20 | XF40 | MS60 | MS63 |
|---|---|---|---|---|---|---|
| 2001 | — | PF65 6.00 | | | | |

**KM# 727 WON**
28.00 g., Brass, 40 mm. **Obv:** National arms, Central Bank name **Rev:** Ferryboat from Koreans in Japan on the route from Niigata to Wonsan

| Date | Mintage | F12 | VF20 | XF40 | MS60 | MS63 |
|---|---|---|---|---|---|---|
| 2001 | — | PF65 7.00 | | | | |

**KM# 728 WON**
7.00 g., Aluminum, 40 mm. **Obv:** National arms, Country name **Rev:** Arch of Triumph on Moranbong in Pyeongyang

| Date | Mintage | F12 | VF20 | XF40 | MS60 | MS63 |
|---|---|---|---|---|---|---|
| 2001 | — | PF65 6.00 | | | | |

**KM# 729 WON**
28.00 g., Brass, 40 mm. **Obv:** National arms, Central Bank name **Rev:** Arch of Triumph on Moranbong in Pyeongyang

| Date | Mintage | F12 | VF20 | XF40 | MS60 | MS63 |
|---|---|---|---|---|---|---|
| 2001 | — | PF65 7.00 | | | | |

**KM# 730 WON**
7.00 g., Aluminum, 40 mm. **Obv:** National arms, Central Bank name **Rev:** Chonji crater on the Paektusan

| Date | Mintage | F12 | VF20 | XF40 | MS60 | MS63 |
|---|---|---|---|---|---|---|
| 2001 | — | PF65 6.00 | | | | |

**KM# 731 WON**
28.00 g., Brass, 40 mm. **Obv:** National arms, Central Bank name **Rev:** Chonji crater on the Paektusan

| Date | Mintage | F12 | VF20 | XF40 | MS60 | MS63 |
|---|---|---|---|---|---|---|
| 2001 | — | PF65 7.00 | | | | |

**KM# 746 WON**
28.00 g., Brass, 40 mm. **Obv:** National arms **Rev:** Kim Jeongill in Pudong industrial area of Shanghai

| Date | Mintage | F12 | VF20 | XF40 | MS60 | MS63 |
|---|---|---|---|---|---|---|
| 2001 Proof | — | — | — | — | — | — |

**KM# 749 WON**
28.00 g., Brass, 40 mm. **Obv:** National arms, Central Bank name **Rev:** Deng Xiaoping between peonies

| Date | Mintage | F12 | VF20 | XF40 | MS60 | MS63 |
|---|---|---|---|---|---|---|
| 2001 | — | PF65 7.00 | | | | |

**KM# 750 WON**
17.00 g., Copper-Nickel, 35 mm. **Obv:** National arms **Rev:** Orca before tourist boat

| Date | Mintage | F12 | VF20 | XF40 | MS60 | MS63 |
|---|---|---|---|---|---|---|
| 2001 | — | PF65 14.00 | | | | |

**KM# 751 WON**
5.00 g., Aluminum, 35 mm. **Obv:** National arms, Central Bank name **Rev:** Orca before tourist boat

| Date | Mintage | F12 | VF20 | XF40 | MS60 | MS63 |
|---|---|---|---|---|---|---|
| 2001 | — | PF65 6.00 | | | | |

**KM# 751a WON**
16.00 g., Brass, 35 mm. **Obv:** National arms, Central Bank name **Rev:** Orca before tourist boat

| Date | Mintage | F12 | VF20 | XF40 | MS60 | MS63 |
|---|---|---|---|---|---|---|
| 2001 | — | PF65 7.00 | | | | |

**KM# 752 WON**
17.00 g., Copper-Nickel, 35 mm. **Obv:** National arms, Country name **Rev:** Humpback whale

| Date | Mintage | F12 | VF20 | XF40 | MS60 | MS63 |
|---|---|---|---|---|---|---|
| 2001 | — | PF65 14.00 | | | | |

**KM# 753 WON**
5.00 g., Aluminum, 35 mm. **Obv:** National arms, Central Bank name **Rev:** Humpback whale

| Date | Mintage | F12 | VF20 | XF40 | MS60 | MS63 |
|---|---|---|---|---|---|---|
| 2001 | — | PF65 6.00 | | | | |

**KM# 753a WON**
16.00 g., Brass, 35 mm. **Obv:** National arms, Central Bank name **Rev:** Humpback whale

| Date | Mintage | F12 | VF20 | XF40 | MS60 | MS63 |
|---|---|---|---|---|---|---|
| 2001 | — | PF65 7.00 | | | | |

**KM# 754 WON**
17.00 g., Copper-Nickel, 35 mm. **Obv:** National arms, Country name **Rev:** Sperm whale

| Date | Mintage | F12 | VF20 | XF40 | MS60 | MS63 |
|---|---|---|---|---|---|---|
| 2001 | — | PF65 14.00 | | | | |

**KM# 755 WON**
5.00 g., Aluminum, 35 mm. **Obv:** National arms, Central Bank name **Rev:** Sperm whale

| Date | Mintage | F12 | VF20 | XF40 | MS60 | MS63 |
|---|---|---|---|---|---|---|
| 2001 | — | PF65 6.00 | | | | |

**KM# 755a WON**
16.00 g., Brass, 35 mm. **Obv:** National arms, Central Bank name **Rev:** Sperm whale

| Date | Mintage | F12 | VF20 | XF40 | MS60 | MS63 |
|---|---|---|---|---|---|---|
| 2001 | — | PF65 7.00 | | | | |

**KM# 756 WON**
17.00 g., Copper-Nickel, 35 mm. **Obv:** National arms, Country name **Rev:** Pilot whale

| Date | Mintage | F12 | VF20 | XF40 | MS60 | MS63 |
|---|---|---|---|---|---|---|
| 2001 | — | PF65 14.00 | | | | |

**KM# 757 WON**
5.00 g., Aluminum, 35 mm. **Obv:** National arms, Central Bank name **Rev:** Pilot whale

| Date | Mintage | F12 | VF20 | XF40 | MS60 | MS63 |
|---|---|---|---|---|---|---|
| 2001 | — | PF65 6.00 | | | | |

**KM# 757a WON**
16.00 g., Brass, 35 mm. **Obv:** National arms, Central Bank name **Rev:** Pilot whale

| Date | Mintage | F12 | VF20 | XF40 | MS60 | MS63 |
|---|---|---|---|---|---|---|
| 2001 | — | PF65 7.00 | | | | |

**KM# 758 WON**
17.00 g., Copper-Nickel, 35 mm. **Obv:** National arms, Country name **Rev:** Northern Right Whale

| Date | Mintage | F12 | VF20 | XF40 | MS60 | MS63 |
|---|---|---|---|---|---|---|
| 2001 | — | PF65 14.00 | | | | |

**KM# 759 WON**
5.00 g., Aluminum, 35 mm. **Obv:** National arms, Central Bank name **Rev:** Northern Right Whale

| Date | Mintage | F12 | VF20 | XF40 | MS60 | MS63 |
|---|---|---|---|---|---|---|
| 2001 | — | PF65 14.00 | | | | |

**KM# 759a WON**
16.00 g., Brass, 35 mm. **Obv:** National arms, Central Bank name **Rev:** Northern Right Whale

| Date | Mintage | F12 | VF20 | XF40 | MS60 | MS63 |
|---|---|---|---|---|---|---|
| 2001 | — | PF65 10.00 | | | | |

**KM# 760 WON**
17.00 g., Copper-Nickel, 35 mm. **Obv:** National arms, Country name **Rev:** Blue whale

| Date | Mintage | F12 | VF20 | XF40 | MS60 | MS63 |
|---|---|---|---|---|---|---|
| 2001 | — | PF65 14.00 | | | | |

**KM# 761 WON**
5.00 g., Aluminum, 35 mm. **Obv:** National arms, Central Bank name **Rev:** Blue Whale

| Date | Mintage | F12 | VF20 | XF40 | MS60 | MS63 |
|---|---|---|---|---|---|---|
| 2001 | — | PF65 6.00 | | | | |

**KM# 761a WON**
16.00 g., Brass, 35 mm. **Obv:** National arms, Central Bank name **Rev:** Blue whale

| Date | Mintage | F12 | VF20 | XF40 | MS60 | MS63 |
|---|---|---|---|---|---|---|
| 2001 | — | PF65 7.00 | | | | |

**KM# 762 WON**
17.00 g., Copper-Nickel, 35 mm. **Obv:** National arms, Country name **Rev:** Bowhead whale

| Date | Mintage | F12 | VF20 | XF40 | MS60 | MS63 |
|---|---|---|---|---|---|---|
| 2001 | — | PF65 14.00 | | | | |

**KM# 763 WON**
5.00 g., Aluminum, 35 mm. **Obv:** National arms, Central Bank name **Rev:** Bowhead whale

| Date | Mintage | F12 | VF20 | XF40 | MS60 | MS63 |
|---|---|---|---|---|---|---|
| 2001 | — | PF65 6.00 | | | | |

**KM# 763a WON**
16.00 g., Brass, 35 mm. **Obv:** National arms, Central Bank name **Rev:** Bowhead whale

| Date | Mintage | F12 | VF20 | XF40 | MS60 | MS63 |
|---|---|---|---|---|---|---|
| 2001 | — | PF65 7.00 | | | | |

**KM# 764 WON**
17.00 g., Copper-Nickel, 35 mm. **Obv:** National arms, Country name **Rev:** Killer whale off the coast

| Date | Mintage | F12 | VF20 | XF40 | MS60 | MS63 |
|---|---|---|---|---|---|---|
| 2001 | — | PF65 14.00 | | | | |

**KM# 765 WON**
5.00 g., Aluminum, 35 mm. **Obv:** Naitonal arms, Central Bank name **Rev:** Killer whale off the coast

| Date | Mintage | F12 | VF20 | XF40 | MS60 | MS63 |
|---|---|---|---|---|---|---|
| 2001 | — | PF65 6.00 | | | | |

**KM# 765a WON**
16.00 g., Brass, 35 mm. **Obv:** National arms, Central Bank name **Rev:** Killer whale off the coast

| Date | Mintage | F12 | VF20 | XF40 | MS60 | MS63 |
|---|---|---|---|---|---|---|
| 2001 | — | PF65 7.00 | | | | |

**KM# 766 WON**
15.00 g., 0.999 Silver 0.4818 oz. ASW, 35 mm. **Obv:** National arms, Country name **Rev:** Northern Right Whale

| Date | Mintage | F12 | VF20 | XF40 | MS60 | MS63 |
|---|---|---|---|---|---|---|
| 2001 | — | PF65 35.00 | | | | |

**KM# 767 WON**
5.00 g., Aluminum, 35 mm. **Obv:** National arms, Country name **Rev:** Chinese dragon boat

| Date | Mintage | F12 | VF20 | XF40 | MS60 | MS63 |
|---|---|---|---|---|---|---|
| 2001 | — | PF65 6.00 | | | | |

**KM# 767a WON**
Brass, 35 mm. **Obv:** National arms, Country name **Rev:** Chinese dragon boat

| Date | Mintage | F12 | VF20 | XF40 | MS60 | MS63 |
|---|---|---|---|---|---|---|
| 2001 | — | PF65 7.00 | | | | |

**KM# 769 WON**
16.00 g., Brass, 35 mm. **Obv:** East gate of Pyeongyang **Rev:** Krusenstern

| Date | Mintage | F12 | VF20 | XF40 | MS60 | MS63 |
|---|---|---|---|---|---|---|
| 2001 | — | PF65 7.00 | | | | |

**KM# 771 WON**
6.00 g., Aluminum, 38 mm. **Obv:** National arms, Central Bank name **Rev:** White-tailed sea eagle

| Date | Mintage | F12 | VF20 | XF40 | MS60 | MS63 |
|---|---|---|---|---|---|---|
| 2001 | — | PF65 8.00 | | | | |

**KM# 771a WON**
25.00 g., Brass, 38 mm. **Obv:** National arms, Central Bank name **Rev:** White-tailed sea eagle

| Date | Mintage | F12 | VF20 | XF40 | MS60 | MS63 |
|---|---|---|---|---|---|---|
| 2001 Proof | — | — | — | — | — | — |

**KM# 772 WON**
7.00 g., Aluminum, 40 mm. **Obv:** National arms, Country name **Rev:** Taekwondo kicker

| Date | Mintage | F12 | VF20 | XF40 | MS60 | MS63 |
|---|---|---|---|---|---|---|
| 2001 | — | PF65 6.00 | | | | |

**KM# 772a WON**
28.00 g., Brass, 40 mm. **Obv:** National arms, Country name **Rev:** Taekwondo kicker

| Date | Mintage | F12 | VF20 | XF40 | MS60 | MS63 |
|---|---|---|---|---|---|---|
| 2001 | — | PF65 7.00 | | | | |

**KM# 773 WON**
7.00 g., Aluminum, 40 mm. **Obv:** National arms, Country name **Rev:** Taekwondo kicker

| Date | Mintage | F12 | VF20 | XF40 | MS60 | MS63 |
|---|---|---|---|---|---|---|
| 2001 Proof | — | — | — | — | — | — |

**KM# 774 WON**
Aluminum, 40 mm. **Obv:** National arms, Central Bank name **Rev:** Two taekwondo players

| Date | Mintage | F12 | VF20 | XF40 | MS60 | MS63 |
|---|---|---|---|---|---|---|
| 2001 | — | PF65 6.00 | | | | |

**KM# 305 WON**
7.00 g., Aluminum, 40 mm. **Obv:** Arms **Rev:** Tomb of King Kong Min

| Date | Mintage | F12 | VF20 | XF40 | MS60 | MS63 |
|---|---|---|---|---|---|---|
| 2002 | — | PF65 7.50 | | | | |

**KM# 305a WON**
28.20 g., Brass, 40.2 mm. **Obv:** State arms **Rev:** Tomb of King Kong Min **Edge:** Plain

| Date | Mintage | F12 | VF20 | XF40 | MS60 | MS63 |
|---|---|---|---|---|---|---|
| JU91-2002 | — | PF65 20.00 | | | | |

**KM# 306 WON**
7.10 g., Aluminum, 40 mm. **Obv:** State arms **Rev:** Two horses within circle of Asian zodiac animals **Edge:** Plain **Note:** Prev. KM#398.

| Date | Mintage | F12 | VF20 | XF40 | MS60 | MS63 |
|---|---|---|---|---|---|---|
| 2002 | — | PF65 20.00 | | | | |

**KM# 306a WON**
28.20 g., Brass, 40.2 mm. **Obv:** State arms **Rev:** Two horses within circle of Asian zodiac animals **Edge:** Plain

| Date | Mintage | F12 | VF20 | XF40 | MS60 | MS63 |
|---|---|---|---|---|---|---|
| 2002 | — | PF65 20.00 | | | | |

**KM# 308 WON**
6.90 g., Aluminum, 40 mm. **Obv:** State arms **Rev:** Arirang dancer with cranes flying above **Edge:** Plain **Note:** Prev. KM#390.

| Date | Mintage | F12 | VF20 | XF40 | MS60 | MS63 |
|---|---|---|---|---|---|---|
| JU91-(2002) | — | PF65 15.00 | | | | |

**KM# 308a WON**
28.20 g., Brass, 40.2 mm. **Subject:** Arirang **Obv:** State arms **Rev:** Performers and flying cranes **Edge:** Plain

| Date | Mintage | F12 | VF20 | XF40 | MS60 | MS63 |
|---|---|---|---|---|---|---|
| JU91-(2002) | — | PF65 20.00 | | | | |

**KM# 310a WON**
28.20 g., Brass, 40.2 mm. **Obv:** State arms **Rev:** Tomb of King Tongmyong **Edge:** Plain

| Date | Mintage | F12 | VF20 | XF40 | MS60 | MS63 |
|---|---|---|---|---|---|---|
| JU91-2002 | — | PF65 15.00 | | | | |

**KM# 313 WON**
6.70 g., Aluminum, 40 mm. **Obv:** State arms **Rev:** Arirang dancer **Edge:** Plain **Note:** Prev. KM#389.

| Date | Mintage | F12 | VF20 | XF40 | MS60 | MS63 |
|---|---|---|---|---|---|---|
| JU91-(2002) | — | PF65 15.00 | | | | |

**KM# 313a WON**
28.20 g., Brass, 40.2 mm. **Subject:** Arirang **Obv:** State arms **Rev:** Dancer with upheld arms **Edge:** Plain

| Date | Mintage | F12 | VF20 | XF40 | MS60 | MS63 |
|---|---|---|---|---|---|---|
| JU91-(2002) | — | PF65 20.00 | | | | |

**KM# 388 WON**
7.10 g., Aluminum, 40 mm. **Obv:** State arms **Rev:** Arirang dancer Silhouette **Edge:** Plain

| Date | Mintage | F12 | VF20 | XF40 | MS60 | MS63 |
|---|---|---|---|---|---|---|
| 2002 | — | PF65 15.00 | | | | |

**KM# 391 WON**
7.10 g., Aluminum, 40 mm. **Obv:** State arms **Rev:** Arirang ribbon dancer **Edge:** Plain

| Date | Mintage | F12 | VF20 | XF40 | MS60 | MS63 |
|---|---|---|---|---|---|---|
| JU91-2002 | — | PF65 15.00 | | | | |

**KM# 392 WON**
7.00 g., Aluminum, 40 mm. **Obv:** State arms **Rev:** May Day Stadium **Edge:** Plain

| Date | Mintage | F12 | VF20 | XF40 | MS60 | MS63 |
|---|---|---|---|---|---|---|
| JU91-2002 | — | PF65 12.00 | | | | |

**KM# 392a WON**
28.50 g., Brass, 40.1 mm. **Obv:** State arms **Rev:** May Day Stadium **Edge:** Plain

| Date | Mintage | F12 | VF20 | XF40 | MS60 | MS63 |
|---|---|---|---|---|---|---|
| JU91-2002 | — | PF65 15.00 | | | | |

**KM# 393 WON**
7.10 g., Aluminum, 40 mm. **Obv:** State arms **Rev:** Woman floating above stadium **Edge:** Plain

| Date | Mintage | F12 | VF20 | XF40 | MS60 | MS63 |
|---|---|---|---|---|---|---|
| JU91-2002 | — | PF65 15.00 | | | | |

**KM# 393a WON**
28.20 g., Brass, 40 mm. **Obv:** State arms **Rev:** Woman floating above stadium **Edge:** Plain

| Date | Mintage | F12 | VF20 | XF40 | MS60 | MS63 |
|---|---|---|---|---|---|---|
| JU91-2002 | — | PF65 17.50 | | | | |

**KM# 394 WON**
27.50 g., Brass, 40 mm. **Obv:** State arms **Rev:** Ribbon dancer with Korea shaped ribbon **Edge:** Plain

| Date | Mintage | F12 | VF20 | XF40 | MS60 | MS63 |
|---|---|---|---|---|---|---|
| JU91-2002 | — | PF65 17.50 | | | | |

**KM# 395 WON**
27.50 g., Brass, 40 mm. **Obv:** State arms **Rev:** Dancer in the shape of Korea **Edge:** Plain

| Date | Mintage | F12 | VF20 | XF40 | MS60 | MS63 |
|---|---|---|---|---|---|---|
| JU91-2002 | — | PF65 17.50 | | | | |

**KM# 396 WON**
7.00 g., Aluminum, 40 mm. **Obv:** State arms **Rev:** Bust with hat facing divides dates(1337-1392) above building foundation **Edge:** Plain

| Date | Mintage | F12 | VF20 | XF40 | MS60 | MS63 |
|---|---|---|---|---|---|---|
| JU91-2002 | — | PF65 15.00 | | | | |

**KM# 397 WON**

7.00 g., Aluminum, 40 mm. **Obv:** State arms **Rev:** Victorious athletes hugging **Edge:** Plain

| Date | Mintage | F12 | VF20 | XF40 | MS60 | MS63 |
|---|---|---|---|---|---|---|
| JU91-(2002) | — | PF65 10.00 | | | | |

**KM# 397a WON**

28.24 g., Brass, 40 mm. **Obv:** State arms **Rev:** Victorious athletes hugging **Edge:** Plain

| Date | Mintage | F12 | VF20 | XF40 | MS60 | MS63 |
|---|---|---|---|---|---|---|
| JU91-(2002) | — | PF65 12.50 | | | | |

**KM# 399 WON**

4.86 g., Aluminum, 35 mm. **Obv:** State arms **Rev:** Cantering horse **Edge:** Plain

| Date | Mintage | F12 | VF20 | XF40 | MS60 | MS63 |
|---|---|---|---|---|---|---|
| JU91-(2002) | — | PF65 15.00 | | | | |

**KM# 399a WON**

16.93 g., Brass, 35 mm. **Obv:** State arms **Rev:** Cantering horse **Edge:** Plain

| Date | Mintage | F12 | VF20 | XF40 | MS60 | MS63 |
|---|---|---|---|---|---|---|
| JU91-(2002) | — | PF65 15.00 | | | | |

**KM# 400 WON**

5.10 g., Aluminum, 35 mm. **Obv:** State arms **Rev:** Two wrestlers **Edge:** Plain

| Date | Mintage | F12 | VF20 | XF40 | MS60 | MS63 |
|---|---|---|---|---|---|---|
| JU91-(2002) | — | PF65 12.50 | | | | |

**KM# 400a WON**

16.50 g., Brass, 35 mm. **Obv:** State arms **Rev:** Two wrestlers **Edge:** Plain

| Date | Mintage | F12 | VF20 | XF40 | MS60 | MS63 |
|---|---|---|---|---|---|---|
| JU91-(2002) | — | PF65 15.00 | | | | |

**KM# 470 WON**

Brass, 35 mm. **Subject:** 2004 Olympics **Obv:** Arms **Rev:** Three Karate Sportsmen

| Date | Mintage | F12 | VF20 | XF40 | MS60 | MS63 |
|---|---|---|---|---|---|---|
| 2002 | — | PF65 6.50 | | | | |

**KM# 471 WON**

Brass **Obv:** Arms **Rev:** Bridge

| Date | Mintage | F12 | VF20 | XF40 | MS60 | MS63 |
|---|---|---|---|---|---|---|
| 2002 (91) | — | PF65 7.50 | | | | |

**KM# 474 WON**

Brass **Obv:** Arms **Rev:** Family about to hug

| Date | Mintage | F12 | VF20 | XF40 | MS60 | MS63 |
|---|---|---|---|---|---|---|
| 2002 | — | PF65 10.00 | | | | |

**KM# 475 WON**

Brass, 40 mm. **Obv:** Arms **Rev:** Three people in group hug

| Date | Mintage | F12 | VF20 | XF40 | MS60 | MS63 |
|---|---|---|---|---|---|---|
| 2002 | — | PF65 10.00 | | | | |

**KM# 476 WON**

Brass **Obv:** Arms **Rev:** Four dragons around map of North Korea

| Date | Mintage | F12 | VF20 | XF40 | MS60 | MS63 |
|---|---|---|---|---|---|---|
| 2002 | — | PF65 10.00 | | | | |

**KM# 786 WON**

5.00 g., Aluminum, 35 mm. **Subject:** Year of the Horse **Obv:** National arms, Country name **Rev:** Horse head

| Date | Mintage | F12 | VF20 | XF40 | MS60 | MS63 |
|---|---|---|---|---|---|---|
| 2002 | — | PF65 6.00 | | | | |

**KM# 786a WON**

16.00 g., Brass, 35 mm. **Obv:** National arms, Country name **Rev:** Horse head

| Date | Mintage | F12 | VF20 | XF40 | MS60 | MS63 |
|---|---|---|---|---|---|---|
| 2002 | — | PF65 7.00 | | | | |

**KM# 794 WON**

7.00 g., Aluminum, 40 mm. **Obv:** National arms **Rev:** Reconstruction of the Mausoleums for King Dangun

| Date | Mintage | F12 | VF20 | XF40 | MS60 | MS63 |
|---|---|---|---|---|---|---|
| 2002 | — | PF65 6.00 | | | | |

**KM# 795 WON**

28.00 g., Brass, 40 mm. **Obv:** Naitonal arms, Country name **Rev:** Reconstruction of the mausoleum for King Dangun

| Date | Mintage | F12 | VF20 | XF40 | MS60 | MS63 |
|---|---|---|---|---|---|---|
| 2002 | — | PF65 7.00 | | | | |

**KM# 796 WON**

7.00 g., Aluminum, 40 mm. **Obv:** National arms **Rev:** Dongmyeong, 1st King of Goguryeo

| Date | Mintage | F12 | VF20 | XF40 | MS60 | MS63 |
|---|---|---|---|---|---|---|
| 2002 | — | PF65 6.00 | | | | |

**KM# 797 WON**

28.00 g., Brass, 40 mm. **Obv:** National arms **Rev:** Dongmyeong, 1st King of Goguryeo

| Date | Mintage | F12 | VF20 | XF40 | MS60 | MS63 |
|---|---|---|---|---|---|---|
| 2002 | — | PF65 7.00 | | | | |

**KM# 798 WON**

7.00 g., Aluminum, 40 mm. **Obv:** National arms, Central Bank name **Rev:** Wanggeon, 1st King of Goryeo dynasty

| Date | Mintage | F12 | VF20 | XF40 | MS60 | MS63 |
|---|---|---|---|---|---|---|
| 2002 | — | PF65 6.00 | | | | |

**KM# 799 WON**

28.00 g., Brass, 40 mm. **Obv:** National arms, Central Bank name **Rev:** Wanggeon, 1st King of Goryeo dynasty

| Date | Mintage | F12 | VF20 | XF40 | MS60 | MS63 |
|---|---|---|---|---|---|---|
| 2002 | — | PF65 7.00 | | | | |

**KM# 800 WON**

7.00 g., Aluminum, 40 mm. **Obv:** National arms **Rev:** Jeon Bongjun

| Date | Mintage | F12 | VF20 | XF40 | MS60 | MS63 |
|---|---|---|---|---|---|---|
| 2002 | — | PF65 6.00 | | | | |

**KM# 801 WON**

28.00 g., Brass, 40 mm. **Obv:** National arms, Central Bank name **Rev:** Jeon Bongjun

| Date | Mintage | F12 | VF20 | XF40 | MS60 | MS63 |
|---|---|---|---|---|---|---|
| 2002 | — | PF65 7.00 | | | | |

**KM# 821 WON**

7.00 g., Aluminum, 40 mm. **Obv:** National arms **Rev:** Prince Hodong and Princess Nakrang on horseback

| Date | Mintage | F12 | VF20 | XF40 | MS60 | MS63 |
|---|---|---|---|---|---|---|
| 2002 | — | PF65 6.00 | | | | |

**KM# 821a WON**

28.00 g., Brass, 40 mm. **Obv:** National arms **Rev:** Prince Hodong and Princess Nakrang on horseback

| Date | Mintage | F12 | VF20 | XF40 | MS60 | MS63 |
|---|---|---|---|---|---|---|
| 2002 | — | PF65 7.00 | | | | |

**KM# 822 WON**

7.00 g., Aluminum, 40 mm. **Obv:** National arms **Rev:** Half-length figures of Prince Hodong and Princess Nakrang

| Date | Mintage | F12 | VF20 | XF40 | MS60 | MS63 |
|---|---|---|---|---|---|---|
| 2002 | — | PF65 6.00 | | | | |

**KM# 822a WON**

28.00 g., Brass, 40 mm. **Obv:** National arms **Rev:** Half-length figures of Prince Hodong and Princess Nakrang

| Date | Mintage | F12 | VF20 | XF40 | MS60 | MS63 |
|---|---|---|---|---|---|---|
| 2002 | — | PF65 8.00 | | | | |

**KM# 836 WON**

4.00 g., Aluminum, 35 mm. **Obv:** National arms, Central Bank and Country name **Rev:** Ariang inscription

| Date | Mintage | F12 | VF20 | XF40 | MS60 | MS63 |
|---|---|---|---|---|---|---|
| 2002 | Est. 1000 | PF65 6.00 | | | | |

**KM# 837 WON**

4.00 g., Aluminum, 35 mm. **Obv:** National arms, Central Bank and Country name **Rev:** Three soldiers

| Date | Mintage | F12 | VF20 | XF40 | MS60 | MS63 |
|---|---|---|---|---|---|---|
| 2002 | — | PF65 7.00 | | | | |

**KM# 838 WON**

4.00 g., Aluminum, 35 mm. **Obv:** Naitonal arms, Central Bank and Country name **Rev:** Princess fairy paying flute

| Date | Mintage | F12 | VF20 | XF40 | MS60 | MS63 |
|---|---|---|---|---|---|---|
| 2002 | — | PF65 7.00 | | | | |

**KM# 839 WON**

4.00 g., Aluminum, 35 mm. **Obv:** National arms, Central Bank and Country name **Rev:** Bronze statue

| Date | Mintage | F12 | VF20 | XF40 | MS60 | MS63 |
|---|---|---|---|---|---|---|
| 2002 | — | PF65 6.00 | | | | |

**KM# 840 WON**

4.00 g., Aluminum, 35 mm. **Obv:** National arms, Central Bank and Country name **Rev:** Women in the worship of the Sun

| Date | Mintage | F12 | VF20 | XF40 | MS60 | MS63 |
|---|---|---|---|---|---|---|
| 2002 | — | PF65 6.00 | | | | |

**KM# 841 WON**

4.00 g., Aluminum, 35 mm. **Obv:** National arms, Central Bank and Country name **Rev:** Three principals of unification

| Date | Mintage | F12 | VF20 | XF40 | MS60 | MS63 |
|---|---|---|---|---|---|---|
| 2002 | — | PF65 6.00 | | | | |

**KM# 842 WON**

4.00 g., Aluminum, 35 mm. **Obv:** National arms, Central Bank and Country name **Rev:** Dancing children

| Date | Mintage | F12 | VF20 | XF40 | MS60 | MS63 |
|---|---|---|---|---|---|---|
| 2002 | — | PF65 6.00 | | | | |

**KM# 843 WON**

31.11 g., 0.999 Gold 0.999 oz. AGW, 35 mm. **Obv:** National arms, Central Bank and Country name **Rev:** Arirang inscription

| Date | Mintage | F12 | VF20 | XF40 | MS60 | MS63 |
|---|---|---|---|---|---|---|
| 2002 | — | PF65 1,600 | | | | |

**KM# 882 WON**

Copper-Nickel, 38 mm. **Obv:** National arms, Central Bank name **Rev:** World cup tophy, player and Brandenburg gate

| Date | Mintage | F12 | VF20 | XF40 | MS60 | MS63 |
|---|---|---|---|---|---|---|
| 2002 | — | PF65 14.00 | | | | |

### KM# 882a WON

6.00 g., Aluminum, 38 mm. **Obv:** National arms, Central Bank name **Rev:** World cup, player and Brandenburg Gate

| Date | Mintage | F12 | VF20 | XF40 | MS60 | MS63 |
|---|---|---|---|---|---|---|
| 2002 | — | PF65 6.00 | | | | |

### KM# 882b WON

25.00 g., Brass, 38 mm. **Obv:** National arms, Central Bank name **Rev:** World cup, player and Brandenberg Gate

| Date | Mintage | F12 | VF20 | XF40 | MS60 | MS63 |
|---|---|---|---|---|---|---|
| 2002 | — | PF65 7.00 | | | | |

### KM# 264 WON

7.00 g., Aluminum, 40 mm. **Obv:** National arms **Rev:** Sheep in center of Asian Zodiac animals

| Date | Mintage | F12 | VF20 | XF40 | MS60 | MS63 |
|---|---|---|---|---|---|---|
| 2003 | — | PF65 6.00 | | | | |

### KM# 264a WON

28.47 g., Brass, 40 mm. **Obv:** State arms **Rev:** Sheep within circle of Asian Zodiac animals **Edge:** Plain

| Date | Mintage | F12 | VF20 | XF40 | MS60 | MS63 |
|---|---|---|---|---|---|---|
| 2003 | — | PF65 22.00 | | | | |

### KM# 319 WON

9.62 g., Aluminum, 40 mm. **Obv:** State arms **Rev:** Helmeted head with two antenna-like horns on the helmet **Edge:** Plain

| Date | Mintage | F12 | VF20 | XF40 | MS60 | MS63 |
|---|---|---|---|---|---|---|
| JU92-2003 | — | PF65 15.00 | | | | |

### KM# 319a WON

28.20 g., Brass, 40.2 mm. **Obv:** State arms **Rev:** Helmeted head with two antenna-like horns on helmet **Edge:** Plain

| Date | Mintage | F12 | VF20 | XF40 | MS60 | MS63 |
|---|---|---|---|---|---|---|
| JU92-2003 | — | PF65 17.50 | | | | |

### KM# 323 WON

6.94 g., Aluminum, 40 mm. **Obv:** State arms **Rev:** Turtle shaped armoured ship of 1592 **Edge:** Plain

| Date | Mintage | F12 | VF20 | XF40 | MS60 | MS63 |
|---|---|---|---|---|---|---|
| JU92-2003 | — | PF65 15.00 | | | | |

### KM# 323a WON

28.10 g., Brass, 40.2 mm. **Obv:** State arms **Rev:** Turtle-shaped armoured ship of 1592 **Edge:** Plain

| Date | Mintage | F12 | VF20 | XF40 | MS60 | MS63 |
|---|---|---|---|---|---|---|
| JU92-2003 | — | PF65 20.00 | | | | |

### KM# 403 WON

7.00 g., Aluminum, 40 mm. **Obv:** National arms, Central Bank name **Rev:** Kang Kam-cheo bust facing

| Date | Mintage | F12 | VF20 | XF40 | MS60 | MS63 |
|---|---|---|---|---|---|---|
| 2003 | — | PF65 7.00 | | | | |

### KM# 403a WON

22.10 g., Brass, 40 mm. **Obv:** State arms **Rev:** Kang Kam-cheo bust facing **Edge:** Plain

| Date | Mintage | F12 | VF20 | XF40 | MS60 | MS63 |
|---|---|---|---|---|---|---|
| JU92-2003 | — | PF65 17.50 | | | | |

### KM# 404 WON

9.63 g., Aluminum, 40 mm. **Obv:** State arms **Rev:** Armored bust wearing a horned helmet **Edge:** Plain

| Date | Mintage | F12 | VF20 | XF40 | MS60 | MS63 |
|---|---|---|---|---|---|---|
| JU92-2003 | — | PF65 15.00 | | | | |

### KM# 404a WON

22.25 g., Brass, 40 mm. **Obv:** State arms **Rev:** Armored bust wearing a horned helmet **Edge:** Plain

| Date | Mintage | F12 | VF20 | XF40 | MS60 | MS63 |
|---|---|---|---|---|---|---|
| JU92-2003 | — | PF65 17.50 | | | | |

### KM# 405 WON

7.00 g., Aluminum, 40 mm. **Obv:** State arms **Rev:** Ram within circle of Asian Zodiac animals **Edge:** Plain

| Date | Mintage | F12 | VF20 | XF40 | MS60 | MS63 |
|---|---|---|---|---|---|---|
| 2003 | — | PF65 15.00 | | | | |

### KM# 405a WON

28.44 g., Brass, 40 mm. **Obv:** State arms **Rev:** Ram within circle of Asian Zodiac animals **Edge:** Plain

| Date | Mintage | F12 | VF20 | XF40 | MS60 | MS63 |
|---|---|---|---|---|---|---|
| 2003 | — | PF65 17.50 | | | | |

### KM# 406 WON

10.15 g., Aluminum, 40 mm. **Obv:** State arms **Rev:** Children kicking a shuttlecock **Edge:** Plain

| Date | Mintage | F12 | VF20 | XF40 | MS60 | MS63 |
|---|---|---|---|---|---|---|
| JU92-2003 | — | PF65 15.00 | | | | |

**KM# 406a WON**

24.63 g., Brass, 40 mm. **Obv:** State arms **Rev:** Children kicking a shuttlecock **Edge:** Plain

| Date | Mintage | F12 | VF20 | XF40 | MS60 | MS63 |
|---|---|---|---|---|---|---|
| JU92-2003 | — | PF65 17.50 | | | | |

**KM# 407a WON**

23.10 g., Brass, 40 mm. **Obv:** State arms **Rev:** Children playing jacks **Edge:** Plain

| Date | Mintage | F12 | VF20 | XF40 | MS60 | MS63 |
|---|---|---|---|---|---|---|
| JU92-2003 | — | PF65 17.50 | | | | |

**KM# 408a WON**

24.56 g., Brass, 40 mm. **Obv:** State arms **Rev:** Children spinning tops **Edge:** Plain

| Date | Mintage | F12 | VF20 | XF40 | MS60 | MS63 |
|---|---|---|---|---|---|---|
| JU92-2003 | — | PF65 17.50 | | | | |

**KM# 410a WON**

24.64 g., Brass, 40 mm. **Obv:** State arms **Rev:** Large dome building **Edge:** Plain

| Date | Mintage | F12 | VF20 | XF40 | MS60 | MS63 |
|---|---|---|---|---|---|---|
| JU92-2003 | — | PF65 17.50 | | | | |

**KM# 904 WON**

31.11 g., 0.999 Silver 0.999 oz. ASW, 40 mm. **Subject:** Athens olympics **Obv:** National arms, Central Bank name **Rev:** Wrestlers

| Date | Mintage | F12 | VF20 | XF40 | MS60 | MS63 |
|---|---|---|---|---|---|---|
| 2003 | Est. 1000 | PF65 45.00 | | | | |

**KM# 918 WON**

25.00 g., Brass, 38 mm. **Obv:** National arms, Central Bank name **Rev:** Steamship Princess Charlotte of Prussia

| Date | Mintage | F12 | VF20 | XF40 | MS60 | MS63 |
|---|---|---|---|---|---|---|
| 2003 | Est. 500 | PF65 45.00 | | | | |

**KM# 919 WON**

25.00 g., Brass, 35 mm. **Obv:** National arms, Central Bank name **Rev:** Ship Queen Maria

| Date | Mintage | F12 | VF20 | XF40 | MS60 | MS63 |
|---|---|---|---|---|---|---|
| 2003 | — | PF65 45.00 | | | | |

**KM# 920 WON**

25.00 g., Brass, 38 mm. **Obv:** National arms **Rev:** Trans-atlantic sail steamship Helena Sloman

| Date | Mintage | F12 | VF20 | XF40 | MS60 | MS63 |
|---|---|---|---|---|---|---|
| 2003 | — | PF65 45.00 | | | | |

**KM# 924 WON**

25.00 g., Brass, 38 mm. **Obv:** National arms, Central Bank name **Rev:** Alder, 1835 steam locomotive

| Date | Mintage | F12 | VF20 | XF40 | MS60 | MS63 |
|---|---|---|---|---|---|---|
| 2003 | Est. 500 | PF65 45.00 | | | | |

**KM# 925 WON**

25.00 g., Silver, 38 mm. **Obv:** National arms, Central Bank name **Rev:** Saxonia, 1838 steam locomotive

| Date | Mintage | F12 | VF20 | XF40 | MS60 | MS63 |
|---|---|---|---|---|---|---|
| 2003 | — | PF65 45.00 | | | | |

**KM# 926 WON**

25.00 g., Brass, 38 mm. **Obv:** National arms, Central Bank name **Rev:** Rheingold, 1928 Steam locomotive

| Date | Mintage | F12 | VF20 | XF40 | MS60 | MS63 |
|---|---|---|---|---|---|---|
| 2003 | — | PF65 45.00 | | | | |

**KM# 930 WON**

25.00 g., Brass, 38 mm. **Obv:** National arms, Central Bank name **Rev:** Gorch Fock 1 sailing ship

| Date | Mintage | F12 | VF20 | XF40 | MS60 | MS63 |
|---|---|---|---|---|---|---|
| 2003 | — | PF65 45.00 | | | | |

**KM# 265 WON**

17.70 g., Brass, 23.2 x 40.1 mm. **Obv:** State arms **Rev:** White-tufted-ear Marmoset **Edge:** Plain

| Date | Mintage | F12 | VF20 | XF40 | MS60 | MS63 |
|---|---|---|---|---|---|---|
| 2004 | — | PF65 27.50 | | | | |

**KM# 266 WON**

17.70 g., Brass, 23.2 x 40.1 mm. **Obv:** State arms **Rev:** Cercopjthecus Mitis monkey **Edge:** Plain

| Date | Mintage | F12 | VF20 | XF40 | MS60 | MS63 |
|---|---|---|---|---|---|---|
| 2004 | — | PF65 27.50 | | | | |

**KM# 267 WON**

17.70 g., Brass, 23.2 x 40.1 mm. **Obv:** State arms **Rev:** Two Saguinus Midas monkeys **Edge:** Plain

| Date | Mintage | F12 | VF20 | XF40 | MS60 | MS63 |
|---|---|---|---|---|---|---|
| 2004 | — | PF65 27.50 | | | | |

**KM# 330 WON**

9.92 g., Aluminum, 45 mm. **Obv:** State arms **Rev:** Mountain cabin **Edge:** Plain **Note:** Prev. KM#411.

| Date | Mintage | F12 | VF20 | XF40 | MS60 | MS63 |
|---|---|---|---|---|---|---|
| JU93-2004 | — | PF65 15.00 | | | | |

**KM# 330a WON**

26.45 g., Brass, 45 mm. **Obv:** State arms **Rev:** Mountain cabin **Edge:** Plain

| Date | Mintage | F12 | VF20 | XF40 | MS60 | MS63 |
|---|---|---|---|---|---|---|
| JU93-2004 | — | PF65 20.00 | | | | |

### KM# 331 WON

10.00 g., Aluminum, 45 mm. **Obv:** State arms **Rev:** Kim Il Sung's birthplace, front view **Edge:** Plain **Note:** Prev. KM#412.

| Date | Mintage | F12 | VF20 | XF40 | MS60 | MS63 |
|---|---|---|---|---|---|---|
| JU93-2004 | — | PF65 15.00 | | | | |

### KM# 331a WON

26.45 g., Brass, 45 mm. **Obv:** State arms **Rev:** Sung's birth place, front view **Edge:** Plain

| Date | Mintage | F12 | VF20 | XF40 | MS60 | MS63 |
|---|---|---|---|---|---|---|
| JU93-2004 | — | PF65 20.00 | | | | |

### KM# 332 WON

10.00 g., Aluminum, 45 mm. **Obv:** State arms **Rev:** Kim Il Sung's birthplace, side view **Edge:** Plain **Note:** Prev. KM#413.

| Date | Mintage | F12 | VF20 | XF40 | MS60 | MS63 |
|---|---|---|---|---|---|---|
| JU93-2004 | — | PF65 15.00 | | | | |

### KM# 332a WON

26.45 g., Brass, 45 mm. **Obv:** State arms **Rev:** Sung's birthplace, side view **Edge:** Plain

| Date | Mintage | F12 | VF20 | XF40 | MS60 | MS63 |
|---|---|---|---|---|---|---|
| JU93-2004 | — | PF65 20.00 | | | | |

### KM# 333 WON

10.00 g., Aluminum, 45 mm. **Obv:** Naitonal arms, Central Bank name **Rev:** Kim Jeongsuk

| Date | Mintage | F12 | VF20 | XF40 | MS60 | MS63 |
|---|---|---|---|---|---|---|
| 2004 | — | PF65 8.00 | | | | |

### KM# 333a WON

26.45 g., Brass, 45 mm. **Obv:** State arms **Rev:** Kim Jung Sook facing **Edge:** Plain

| Date | Mintage | F12 | VF20 | XF40 | MS60 | MS63 |
|---|---|---|---|---|---|---|
| JU93-2004 | — | PF65 22.50 | | | | |

### KM# 334 WON

10.00 g., Aluminum, 45 mm. **Obv:** National arms, Central Bank name **Rev:** Kim Jeong-il bust facing

| Date | Mintage | F12 | VF20 | XF40 | MS60 | MS63 |
|---|---|---|---|---|---|---|
| 2004 | — | PF65 8.00 | | | | |

### KM# 334a WON

26.45 g., Brass, 45 mm. **Obv:** State arms **Rev:** Kim Jong-il bust facing **Edge:** Plain

| Date | Mintage | F12 | VF20 | XF40 | MS60 | MS63 |
|---|---|---|---|---|---|---|
| JU93-2004 | — | PF65 22.50 | | | | |

### KM# 335 WON

10.00 g., Aluminum, 45 mm. **Obv:** National arms, Central Bank name **Rev:** Kim Il-seong bust facing

| Date | Mintage | F12 | VF20 | XF40 | MS60 | MS63 |
|---|---|---|---|---|---|---|
| 2004 | — | PF65 8.00 | | | | |

### KM# 335a WON

26.45 g., Brass, 45 mm. **Obv:** State arms **Rev:** Kim Il-seong bust facing **Edge:** Plain

| Date | Mintage | F12 | VF20 | XF40 | MS60 | MS63 |
|---|---|---|---|---|---|---|
| JU93-2004 | — | PF65 22.50 | | | | |

### KM# 336 WON

10.10 g., Aluminum, 45 mm. **Obv:** State arms **Rev:** Kim Il-sung flower, orchid **Edge:** Plain **Note:** Prev. KM#414.

| Date | Mintage | F12 | VF20 | XF40 | MS60 | MS63 |
|---|---|---|---|---|---|---|
| JU93-2004 | — | PF65 15.00 | | | | |

### KM# 336a WON

26.45 g., Brass, 45 mm. **Obv:** State arms **Rev:** Kim Il-sung flower, orchid **Edge:** Plain

| Date | Mintage | F12 | VF20 | XF40 | MS60 | MS63 |
|---|---|---|---|---|---|---|
| JU93-2004 | — | PF65 20.00 | | | | |

**KM# 337 WON**
10.10 g., Aluminum, 45 mm. **Obv:** State arms **Rev:** Kim Jong-Il flower, peony **Edge:** Plain **Note:** Prev. KM#415.

| Date | Mintage | F12 | VF20 | XF40 | MS60 | MS63 |
|---|---|---|---|---|---|---|
| JU93-2004 | — | PF65 15.00 | | | | |

**KM# 337a WON**
26.45 g., Brass, 45 mm. **Obv:** State arms **Rev:** Kim Jong-Il flower, peony **Edge:** Plain

| Date | Mintage | F12 | VF20 | XF40 | MS60 | MS63 |
|---|---|---|---|---|---|---|
| JU93-2004 | — | PF65 20.00 | | | | |

**KM# 338 WON**
9.93 g., Aluminum, 45 mm. **Obv:** State arms **Rev:** Jin Dal Lae flower, Rose of Sharon **Edge:** Plain **Note:** Prev. KM#416.

| Date | Mintage | F12 | VF20 | XF40 | MS60 | MS63 |
|---|---|---|---|---|---|---|
| JU93-2004 | — | PF65 15.00 | | | | |

**KM# 338a WON**
26.45 g., Brass, 45 mm. **Obv:** State arms **Rev:** Rose of Sharon flowers **Edge:** Plain

| Date | Mintage | F12 | VF20 | XF40 | MS60 | MS63 |
|---|---|---|---|---|---|---|
| JU93-2004 | — | PF65 20.00 | | | | |

**KM# 410 WON**
20.00 g., Aluminum, 40 mm. **Obv:** National arms, Central bank name **Rev:** Sports hall in Pyeongyang

| Date | Mintage | F12 | VF20 | XF40 | MS60 | MS63 |
|---|---|---|---|---|---|---|
| 2004 | — | PF65 16.00 | | | | |

**KM# 939 WON**
7.00 g., Aluminum, 40 mm. **Obv:** National arms, Central Bank arms **Rev:** Monkey in the center of the Zodiac

| Date | Mintage | F12 | VF20 | XF40 | MS60 | MS63 |
|---|---|---|---|---|---|---|
| 2004 | — | PF65 10.00 | | | | |

**KM# 939a WON**
28.00 g., Brass, 35 mm. **Obv:** National arms, Central Bank name **Rev:** Monkey in center of Zodiac

| Date | Mintage | F12 | VF20 | XF40 | MS60 | MS63 |
|---|---|---|---|---|---|---|
| 2004 | — | PF65 30.00 | | | | |

**KM# 994 WON**
25.00 g., Brass, 38 mm. **Obv:** National arms, Central Bank name **Rev:** Statsraad Lehmkuhl sailing ship

| Date | Mintage | F12 | VF20 | XF40 | MS60 | MS63 |
|---|---|---|---|---|---|---|
| 2004 | — | PF65 45.00 | | | | |

**KM# 995 WON**
25.00 g., Brass, 38 mm. **Obv:** Naitonal arms, Central Bank name **Rev:** Henry Hudson's Halve Maen

| Date | Mintage | F12 | VF20 | XF40 | MS60 | MS63 |
|---|---|---|---|---|---|---|
| 2004 | — | PF65 45.00 | | | | |

**KM# 1016 WON**
7.00 g., Aluminum, 40 mm. **Obv:** National arms, Central Bank name **Rev:** Rooster within Zodiac circle

| Date | Mintage | F12 | VF20 | XF40 | MS60 | MS63 |
|---|---|---|---|---|---|---|
| 2005 | — | PF65 17.50 | | | | |

**KM# 1016a WON**
28.00 g., Brass, 40 mm. **Obv:** National arms, Central Bank name **Rev:** Rooster in Zodiac circle

| Date | Mintage | F12 | VF20 | XF40 | MS60 | MS63 |
|---|---|---|---|---|---|---|
| 2005 | — | PF65 20.00 | | | | |

**KM# 1019 WON**
28.00 g., 0.999 Brass 0.8993 oz., 40 mm. **Obv:** National arms, Central Bank name **Rev:** Timber and tap in color

| Date | Mintage | F12 | VF20 | XF40 | MS60 | MS63 |
|---|---|---|---|---|---|---|
| 2005 | — | PF65 30.00 | | | | |

**KM# 1020 WON**
7.00 g., Aluminum, 40 mm. **Obv:** National arms, Central Bank name **Rev:** Hae Mosu in the sky with the five dragons

| Date | Mintage | F12 | VF20 | XF40 | MS60 | MS63 |
|---|---|---|---|---|---|---|
| 2005 | — | PF65 17.50 | | | | |

**KM# 1020a WON**
28.00 g., Brass, 40 mm. **Obv:** National arms, Central Bank name **Rev:** Hae Mosu in flight with the five dragons

| Date | Mintage | F12 | VF20 | XF40 | MS60 | MS63 |
|---|---|---|---|---|---|---|
| 2005 | — | PF65 20.00 | | | | |

**KM# 1024 WON**
7.00 g., Aluminum, 40 mm. **Obv:** National arms, Central Bank name **Rev:** Admiral Yi Sunsin and turtle boat

| Date | Mintage | F12 | VF20 | XF40 | MS60 | MS63 |
|---|---|---|---|---|---|---|
| 2005 | — | PF65 10.00 | | | | |

**KM# 1024a WON**
28.00 g., Brass, 40 mm. **Obv:** National arms, Central Bank name **Rev:** Admiral Yi Sunsin and turtle boat

| Date | Mintage | F12 | VF20 | XF40 | MS60 | MS63 |
|---|---|---|---|---|---|---|
| 2005 | — | PF65 15.00 | | | | |

**KM# 1025 WON**
7.00 g., Aluminum, 40 mm. **Obv:** National arms, Central Bank name **Rev:** General Hong Beomdo

| Date | Mintage | F12 | VF20 | XF40 | MS60 | MS63 |
|---|---|---|---|---|---|---|
| 2005 | — | PF65 14.00 | | | | |

**KM# 1025a WON**
28.00 g., Brass, 40 mm. **Obv:** National arms, Central Bank name **Rev:** General Hong Beomdo

| Date | Mintage | F12 | VF20 | XF40 | MS60 | MS63 |
|---|---|---|---|---|---|---|
| 2005 | — | PF65 20.00 | | | | |

**KM# 1034 WON**
25.00 g., Brass, 40 mm. **Obv:** National arms, Central Bank name **Rev:** Rally in front of the monument ot the three principals of reunification

| Date | Mintage | F12 | VF20 | XF40 | MS60 | MS63 |
|---|---|---|---|---|---|---|
| 2005 | — | PF65 20.00 | | | | |

**KM# 1035 WON**
28.00 g., Brass, 40 mm. **Obv:** National arms, Central Bank name **Rev:** Demonstration on the crater lake

| Date | Mintage | F12 | VF20 | XF40 | MS60 | MS63 |
|---|---|---|---|---|---|---|
| 2005 | — | PF65 20.00 | | | | |

**KM# 1036 WON**
28.00 g., Brass, 40 mm. **Obv:** National arms, Central Bank name **Rev:** Three drum dance

| Date | Mintage | F12 | VF20 | XF40 | MS60 | MS63 |
|---|---|---|---|---|---|---|
| 2005 | — | PF65 20.00 | | | | |

**KM# 1040 WON**
28.00 g., Brass, 40 mm. **Obv:** National arms, Central Bank name **Rev:** Map of Korea, pair of peace doves, rainbow

| Date | Mintage | F12 | VF20 | XF40 | MS60 | MS63 |
|---|---|---|---|---|---|---|
| 2005 | — | PF65 10.00 | | | | |

**KM# 1043 WON**
28.00 g., Brass **Obv:** National arms, Central Bank name **Rev:** Tomb of the Unknown Soldier in Moscow, Russian legend **Edge Lettering:** 40

| Date | Mintage | F12 | VF20 | XF40 | MS60 | MS63 |
|---|---|---|---|---|---|---|
| 2005 | — | PF65 14.00 | | | | |

**KM# 1044 WON**
28.00 g., Brass, 40 mm. **Obv:** National arms, Central Bank name **Rev:** Memorial to mothers in St. Petersburg, Russian legend

| Date | Mintage | F12 | VF20 | XF40 | MS60 | MS63 |
|---|---|---|---|---|---|---|
| 2005 | — | PF65 14.00 | | | | |

**KM# 1074 WON**
6.00 g., Aluminum, 38 mm. **Subject:** Torino Winter Olympics, 2006 **Obv:** National arms, Central Bank name **Rev:** Bobsled

| Date | Mintage | F12 | VF20 | XF40 | MS60 | MS63 |
|---|---|---|---|---|---|---|
| 2005 | — | PF65 12.00 | | | | |

**KM# 1074a WON**
25.00 g., Brass, 38 mm. **Subject:** Torino Winter Olympics, 2006 **Obv:** National arms, Central Bank name **Rev:** Bobsled

| Date | Mintage | F12 | VF20 | XF40 | MS60 | MS63 |
|---|---|---|---|---|---|---|
| 2005 | — | PF65 30.00 | | | | |

**KM# 1088 WON**
28.00 g., Brass, 40 mm. **Obv:** National arms, Central Bank name **Rev:** Dog in color

| Date | Mintage | F12 | VF20 | XF40 | MS60 | MS63 |
|---|---|---|---|---|---|---|
| 2006 | — | PF65 30.00 | | | | |

**KM# 1089 WON**
7.00 g., Aluminum, 40 mm. **Obv:** National arms, Central Bank name **Rev:** Ryuhwa, Mother of King Dongmyeong

| Date | Mintage | F12 | VF20 | XF40 | MS60 | MS63 |
|---|---|---|---|---|---|---|
| 2006 | — | PF65 10.00 | | | | |

**KM# 1089a WON**
28.00 g., Brass, 40 mm. **Obv:** National arms, Central Bank name **Rev:** Ryuhwa, Mother of King Dongmyeong

| Date | Mintage | F12 | VF20 | XF40 | MS60 | MS63 |
|---|---|---|---|---|---|---|
| 2006 | — | PF65 14.00 | | | | |

**KM# 1109 WON**
28.00 g., Brass, 40 mm. **Obv:** National arms, Central Bank name **Rev:** Pig in color

| Date | Mintage | F12 | VF20 | XF40 | MS60 | MS63 |
|---|---|---|---|---|---|---|
| 2007 | — | PF65 30.00 | | | | |

**KM# 483 WON**
Copper-Nickel **Subject:** Uzgn Monument **Obv:** Arms **Rev:** Map and building

| Date | Mintage | F12 | VF20 | XF40 | MS60 | MS63 |
|---|---|---|---|---|---|---|
| 2008 | — | PF65 15.00 | | | | |

**KM# 781 2 WON**
7.00 g., 0.999 Silver 0.2248 oz. ASW, 30 mm. **Obv:** National arms, Central Bank name **Rev:** Panda in color

| Date | Mintage | F12 | VF20 | XF40 | MS60 | MS63 |
|---|---|---|---|---|---|---|
| 2001 | Est. 5000 | PF65 30.00 | | | | |

**KM# 892 2 WON**
7.00 g., 0.999 Silver 0.2248 oz. ASW, 30 mm. **Obv:** National arms, Central Bank name **Rev:** Two panda in color

| Date | Mintage | F12 | VF20 | XF40 | MS60 | MS63 |
|---|---|---|---|---|---|---|
| 2002 | Est. 5000 | PF65 30.00 | | | | |

**KM# 249 2 WON**
7.00 g., 0.999 Silver 0.2248 oz. ASW, 30 mm. **Obv:** State arms **Rev:** Two multicolor pandas **Edge:** Plain

| Date | Mintage | F12 | VF20 | XF40 | MS60 | MS63 |
|---|---|---|---|---|---|---|
| 2003 | — | PF65 30.00 | | | | |

**KM# 933 2 WON**
7.00 g., 0.999 Silver 0.2248 oz. ASW, 30 mm. **Obv:** National arms, Central Bank name **Rev:** High speed train in Aichi

| Date | Mintage | F12 | VF20 | XF40 | MS60 | MS63 |
|---|---|---|---|---|---|---|
| 2003 | — | PF65 30.00 | | | | |

**KM# 934 2 WON**
7.00 g., 0.999 Silver 0.2248 oz. ASW, 30 mm. **Obv:** National Arms, Central Bank name **Rev:** Two soccer players in color

| Date | Mintage | F12 | VF20 | XF40 | MS60 | MS63 |
|---|---|---|---|---|---|---|
| 2003 | — | PF65 30.00 | | | | |

**KM# 417 2 WON**
24.66 g., Brass, 31.6x45.75 mm. **Obv:** State arms **Rev:** Half length uniformed figure standing in land rover saluting below dates 1904-2004 **Edge:** Plain **Shape:** Rectangle

| Date | Mintage | F12 | VF20 | XF40 | MS60 | MS63 |
|---|---|---|---|---|---|---|
| ND(2004) | — | PF65 25.00 | | | | |

**KM# 969 2 WON**
25.00 g., Brass, 40 mm. **Obv:** Dokdo, rocky islands, Central Bank name **Rev:** Map of the Island group

| Date | Mintage | F12 | VF20 | XF40 | MS60 | MS63 |
|---|---|---|---|---|---|---|
| 2004 | — | PF65 25.00 | | | | |

**KM# 970 2 WON**
25.00 g., Brass, 40 mm. **Obv:** Dokdo, rocky islands, Central Bank name **Rev:** Fisher Ahn Yongbok

| Date | Mintage | F12 | VF20 | XF40 | MS60 | MS63 |
|---|---|---|---|---|---|---|
| 2004 | — | PF65 25.00 | | | | |

**KM# 971 2 WON**
25.00 g., Brass, 40 mm. **Obv:** Dokdo, rocky islands, Central Bank name **Rev:** Seodo, western island

| Date | Mintage | F12 | VF20 | XF40 | MS60 | MS63 |
|---|---|---|---|---|---|---|
| 2004 | — | PF65 25.00 | | | | |

**KM# 972 2 WON**
25.00 g., Brass, 40 mm. **Obv:** Dokdo, rocky islands, Central Bank name **Rev:** Eastern island, Dongdo

| Date | Mintage | F12 | VF20 | XF40 | MS60 | MS63 |
|---|---|---|---|---|---|---|
| 2004 | — | PF65 25.00 | | | | |

**KM# 973 2 WON**
25.00 g., Brass, 40 mm. **Obv:** Dokdo, rocky islands, Central Bank name **Rev:** Three brother islands

| Date | Mintage | F12 | VF20 | XF40 | MS60 | MS63 |
|---|---|---|---|---|---|---|
| 2004 | — | PF65 25.00 | | | | |

**KM# 974 2 WON**
25.00 g., Brass, 40 mm. **Obv:** Dokdo, rocky islands, Central Bank name **Rev:** Chicken island

| Date | Mintage | F12 | VF20 | XF40 | MS60 | MS63 |
|---|---|---|---|---|---|---|
| 2004 | — | PF65 25.00 | | | | |

**KM# 975 2 WON**
25.00 g., Brass, 40 mm. **Obv:** Dokdo, rocky islands, Central Bank name **Rev:** Candle island

| Date | Mintage | F12 | VF20 | XF40 | MS60 | MS63 |
|---|---|---|---|---|---|---|
| 2004 | — | PF65 25.00 | | | | |

**KM# 976 2 WON**
25.00 g., Brass, 40 mm. **Obv:** Dokdo, rocky islands, Central Bank name **Rev:** Dome island

| Date | Mintage | F12 | VF20 | XF40 | MS60 | MS63 |
|---|---|---|---|---|---|---|
| 2004 | — | PF65 25.00 | | | | |

**KM# 1008 2 WON**
7.00 g., 0.999 Silver 0.2248 oz. ASW, 30 mm. **Obv:** National arms, Central Bank name **Rev:** Three pandas in color

| Date | Mintage | F12 | VF20 | XF40 | MS60 | MS63 |
|---|---|---|---|---|---|---|
| 2004 | Est. 5000 | PF65 30.00 | | | | |

**KM# 1078 2 WON**
7.00 g., Silver, 30 mm. **Obv:** National arms, Central Bank name **Rev:** Panda in color

| Date | Mintage | F12 | VF20 | XF40 | MS60 | MS63 |
|---|---|---|---|---|---|---|
| 2005 | Est. 5000 | PF65 30.00 | | | | |

**KM# 1079 2 WON**
7.00 g., 0.999 Silver 0.2248 oz. ASW partially gilt, 30 mm. **Subject:** Battle of Trafalgar, 200th Anniversary **Obv:** National arms, Central Bank name **Rev:** Horatio Nelson and the H.M.S. Victory, partially gilt

| Date | Mintage | F12 | VF20 | XF40 | MS60 | MS63 |
|---|---|---|---|---|---|---|
| 2005 | Est. 5000 | PF65 30.00 | | | | |

**KM# 1101 2 WON**
7.00 g., 0.999 Silver 0.2248 oz. ASW, 30 mm. **Obv:** National arms, Central Bank name **Rev:** Two pandas in color

| Date | Mintage | F12 | VF20 | XF40 | MS60 | MS63 |
|---|---|---|---|---|---|---|
| 2006 | Est. 5000 | PF65 30.00 | | | | |

**KM# 1124 2 WON**
7.00 g., 0.999 Silver 0.2248 oz. ASW, 30 mm. **Obv:** National arms, Central Bank name **Rev:** Panda in color

| Date | Mintage | F12 | VF20 | XF40 | MS60 | MS63 |
|---|---|---|---|---|---|---|
| 2007 | Est. 5000 | PF65 30.00 | | | | |

**KM# 339 3 WON**
12.55 g., Aluminum, 50.1 mm. **Obv:** Korean map **Rev:** Huh Jun Chosun doctor at left, books at right **Edge:** Plain

| Date | Mintage | F12 | VF20 | XF40 | MS60 | MS63 |
|---|---|---|---|---|---|---|
| JU93-2004 | — | PF65 20.00 | | | | |

**KM# 339a 3 WON**
40.53 g., Brass, 50.2 mm. **Obv:** Korean map **Rev:** Huh Jun Chosun doctor at left, books at right **Edge:** Plain

| Date | Mintage | F12 | VF20 | XF40 | MS60 | MS63 |
|---|---|---|---|---|---|---|
| JU93-2004 | — | PF65 25.00 | | | | |

**KM# 203 5 WON**
15.00 g., 0.999 Silver 0.4818 oz. ASW, 35 mm. **Subject:** School Ships **Obv:** State arms **Rev:** SS Krusenstern **Edge:** Plain

| Date | Mintage | F12 | VF20 | XF40 | MS60 | MS63 |
|---|---|---|---|---|---|---|
| ND-2001 | 500 | PF65 75.00 | | | | |

**KM# 205 5 WON**
15.00 g., 0.999 Silver 0.4818 oz. ASW, 35 mm. **Subject:** Wildlife **Obv:** State arms **Rev:** Two standing Japanese Ibis birds **Edge:** Plain

| Date | Mintage | F12 | VF20 | XF40 | MS60 | MS63 |
|---|---|---|---|---|---|---|
| JU90-2001 | 100 | PF65 200 | | | | |

**KM# 206 5 WON**
15.00 g., 0.999 Silver 0.4818 oz. ASW, 35 mm. **Subject:** Wildlife **Obv:** State arms **Rev:** Two nesting Japanese Ibis birds **Edge:** Plain

| Date | Mintage | F12 | VF20 | XF40 | MS60 | MS63 |
|---|---|---|---|---|---|---|
| JU90-2001 | 3,000 | PF65 50.00 | | | | |

**KM# 208 5 WON**
15.00 g., 0.999 Silver 0.4818 oz. ASW, 35 mm. **Subject:** Wildlife **Obv:** State arms **Rev:** Two Korean Longtail Gorals **Edge:** Plain

| Date | Mintage | F12 | VF20 | XF40 | MS60 | MS63 |
|---|---|---|---|---|---|---|
| JU90-2001 | 3,000 | PF65 50.00 | | | | |

**KM# 219 5 WON**
14.96 g., 0.999 Silver 0.4805 oz. ASW, 35 mm. **Obv:** State arms **Rev:** Dragon ship **Edge:** Plain

| Date | Mintage | F12 | VF20 | XF40 | MS60 | MS63 |
|---|---|---|---|---|---|---|
| 2001 | — | PF65 35.00 | | | | |

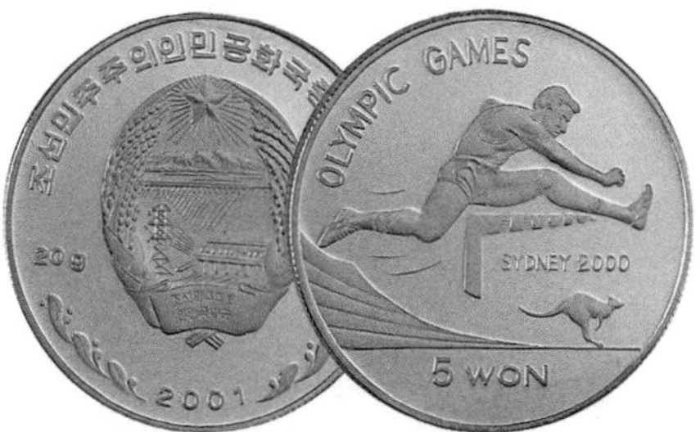


**KM# 226 5 WON**
20.00 g., 0.999 Silver 0.6424 oz. ASW, 33.8 mm. **Subject:** Olympics **Obv:** State arms **Rev:** Hurdler **Edge:** Reeded

| Date | Mintage | F12 | VF20 | XF40 | MS60 | MS63 |
|---|---|---|---|---|---|---|
| 2001 | — | PF65 35.00 | | | | |

**KM# 240 5 WON**
14.94 g., 0.999 Silver 0.4799 oz. ASW, 35 mm. **Obv:** State arms **Rev:** Orca" (Killer Whale) **Edge:** Plain

| Date | Mintage | F12 | VF20 | XF40 | MS60 | MS63 |
|---|---|---|---|---|---|---|
| 2001 | — | PF65 60.00 | | | | |

**KM# 241 5 WON**
14.92 g., 0.999 Silver 0.4792 oz. ASW, 35 mm. **Obv:** State arms **Rev:** Orca and Eco-Tourists in boat **Edge:** Plain

| Date | Mintage | F12 | VF20 | XF40 | MS60 | MS63 |
|---|---|---|---|---|---|---|
| 2001 | — | PF65 60.00 | | | | |

**KM# 242 5 WON**
14.87 g., 0.999 Silver 0.4776 oz. ASW, 35 mm. **Obv:** State arms **Rev:** Pottwal" (Sperm Whale) **Edge:** Plain

| Date | Mintage | F12 | VF20 | XF40 | MS60 | MS63 |
|---|---|---|---|---|---|---|
| 2001 | — | PF65 60.00 | | | | |

**KM# 243 5 WON**
14.95 g., 0.999 Silver 0.4802 oz. ASW, 35 mm. **Obv:** State arms **Rev:** Buckelwal" (Humpback Whale) **Edge:** Plain

| Date | Mintage | F12 | VF20 | XF40 | MS60 | MS63 |
|---|---|---|---|---|---|---|
| 2001 | — | PF65 60.00 | | | | |

**KM# 244 5 WON**
14.93 g., 0.999 Silver 0.4795 oz. ASW, 35 mm. **Obv:** State arms **Rev:** Groenlandwal" (Greenland Right Whale) **Edge:** Plain

| Date | Mintage | F12 | VF20 | XF40 | MS60 | MS63 |
|---|---|---|---|---|---|---|
| 2001 | — | PF65 60.00 | | | | |

**KM# 245 5 WON**
14.95 g., 0.999 Silver 0.4802 oz. ASW, 35 mm. **Obv:** State arms **Rev:** Blauwal" (Blue Whale) **Edge:** Plain

| Date | Mintage | F12 | VF20 | XF40 | MS60 | MS63 |
|---|---|---|---|---|---|---|
| 2001 | — | PF65 60.00 | | | | |

**KM# 246 5 WON**
14.96 g., 0.999 Silver 0.4805 oz. ASW, 35 mm. **Obv:** State arms **Rev:** Grindwal" (Pilot Whale) **Edge:** Plain

| Date | Mintage | F12 | VF20 | XF40 | MS60 | MS63 |
|---|---|---|---|---|---|---|
| 2001 | — | PF65 60.00 | | | | |

**KM# 250 5 WON**
14.96 g., 0.999 Silver 0.4805 oz. ASW, 35 mm. **Subject:** Return of Hong Kong to China **Obv:** State arms **Rev:** City view **Edge:** Plain

| Date | Mintage | F12 | VF20 | XF40 | MS60 | MS63 |
|---|---|---|---|---|---|---|
| 2001 | — | PF65 20.00 | | | | |

**KM# 694 5 WON**
27.00 g., 0.999 Silver 0.8672 oz. ASW, 40 mm. **Obv:** National arms, Country name **Rev:** Kim Ilseong

| Date | Mintage | F12 | VF20 | XF40 | MS60 | MS63 |
|---|---|---|---|---|---|---|
| 2001 | — | PF65 70.00 | | | | |

**KM# 695 5 WON**
Silver, 40 mm. **Obv:** National arms, Country name **Rev:** Kim Jeongil

| Date | Mintage | F12 | VF20 | XF40 | MS60 | MS63 |
|---|---|---|---|---|---|---|
| 2001 | — | PF65 75.00 | | | | |

**KM# 696 5 WON**
27.00 g., 0.999 Silver 0.8672 oz. ASW, 40 mm. **Obv:** National arms, Central Bank name **Rev:** Kim Jeongsuk

| Date | Mintage | F12 | VF20 | XF40 | MS60 | MS63 |
|---|---|---|---|---|---|---|
| 2001 | — | PF65 75.00 | | | | |

**KM# 747 5 WON**
27.00 g., Silver, 40 mm. **Obv:** National arms, Country name **Rev:** Confucius

| Date | Mintage | F12 | VF20 | XF40 | MS60 | MS63 |
|---|---|---|---|---|---|---|
| 2001 | — | PF65 135 | | | | |

**KM# 770 5 WON**
15.00 g., 0.999 Silver 0.4818 oz. ASW, 35 mm. **Obv:** National arms, Central Bank name **Rev:** Krusenstern

| Date | Mintage | F12 | VF20 | XF40 | MS60 | MS63 |
|---|---|---|---|---|---|---|
| 2001 | — | PF65 32.00 | | | | |

**KM# 782 5 WON**
15.00 g., Silver, 35 mm. **Obv:** National arms, Central Bank name **Rev:** Two pandas

| Date | Mintage | F12 | VF20 | XF40 | MS60 | MS63 |
|---|---|---|---|---|---|---|
| 2001 | Est. 5000 | PF65 32.00 | | | | |

**KM# 783 5 WON**
15.00 g., 0.999 Silver 0.4818 oz. ASW, 35 mm. **Obv:** National arms, Central Bank name **Rev:** Titanic

| Date | Mintage | F12 | VF20 | XF40 | MS60 | MS63 |
|---|---|---|---|---|---|---|
| 2001 | Est. 5000 | PF65 32.00 | | | | |

**KM# 784 5 WON**
Silver **Obv:** National arms, Central Bank name **Rev:** Five masted ship, Royal Clipper

| Date | Mintage | F12 | VF20 | XF40 | MS60 | MS63 |
|---|---|---|---|---|---|---|
| 2001 | — | PF65 32.00 | | | | |

**KM# 785 5 WON**
15.00 g., 0.999 Silver 0.4818 oz. ASW, 35 mm. **Subject:** 2002 Soccer - Korea and Japan **Obv:** National arms, Central Bank name **Rev:** Player and stadium

| Date | Mintage | F12 | VF20 | XF40 | MS60 | MS63 |
|---|---|---|---|---|---|---|
| 2001 | Est. 5000 | PF65 32.00 | | | | |

**KM# 251 5 WON**
14.90 g., 0.999 Silver 0.4786 oz. ASW, 35 mm. **Subject:** Year of the Horse **Obv:** State arms **Rev:** Cantering horse **Edge:** Plain

| Date | Mintage | F12 | VF20 | XF40 | MS60 | MS63 |
|---|---|---|---|---|---|---|
| 2002 | — | PF65 30.00 | | | | |

**KM# 252 5 WON**
14.92 g., 0.999 Silver 0.4792 oz. ASW, 35 mm. **Subject:** Korean Games **Obv:** State arms **Rev:** Two wrestlers **Edge:** Plain

| Date | Mintage | F12 | VF20 | XF40 | MS60 | MS63 |
|---|---|---|---|---|---|---|
| JU91-2002 | — | PF65 20.00 | | | | |

**KM# 303 5 WON**
15.00 g., 0.999 Silver 0.4818 oz. ASW, 35 mm. **Obv:** State arms **Rev:** Janggo dancer **Edge:** Segmented reeding

| Date | Mintage | F12 | VF20 | XF40 | MS60 | MS63 |
|---|---|---|---|---|---|---|
| JU91-2002 | — | PF65 30.00 | | | | |

**KM# 304 5 WON**
15.00 g., 0.999 Silver 0.4818 oz. ASW, 35 mm. **Obv:** State arms **Rev:** Armored Knight **Edge:** Segmented reeding

| Date | Mintage | F12 | VF20 | XF40 | MS60 | MS63 |
|---|---|---|---|---|---|---|
| JU91-2002 | — | PF65 30.00 | | | | |

**KM# 790 5 WON**
15.00 g., 0.999 Silver 0.4818 oz. ASW **Obv:** National arms, Country name **Rev:** Horse head **Shape:** 35

| Date | Mintage | F12 | VF20 | XF40 | MS60 | MS63 |
|---|---|---|---|---|---|---|
| 2002 | — | PF65 35.00 | | | | |

**KM# 877 5 WON**
15.00 g., 0.999 Silver 0.4818 oz. ASW, 35 mm. **Obv:** National arms, Central Bank name **Rev:** Map of Korea

| Date | Mintage | F12 | VF20 | XF40 | MS60 | MS63 |
|---|---|---|---|---|---|---|
| 2002 | — | PF65 45.00 | | | | |

**KM# 878 5 WON**
15.00 g., 0.999 Silver 0.4818 oz. ASW, 35 mm. **Obv:** National arms, Central Bank name **Rev:** Traditional Korean wedding

| Date | Mintage | F12 | VF20 | XF40 | MS60 | MS63 |
|---|---|---|---|---|---|---|
| 2002 | — | PF65 35.00 | | | | |

**KM# 879 5 WON**
15.00 g., 0.999 Silver 0.4818 oz. ASW, 35 mm. **Obv:** National arms, Central Bank name **Rev:** Trasitional wedding procession

| Date | Mintage | F12 | VF20 | XF40 | MS60 | MS63 |
|---|---|---|---|---|---|---|
| 2002 | — | PF65 35.00 | | | | |

**KM# 893 5 WON**
20.00 g., 0.999 Silver 0.6424 oz. ASW, 38 mm. **Obv:** Naitonal arms, Central Bank name **Rev:** Asian wild ox

| Date | Mintage | F12 | VF20 | XF40 | MS60 | MS63 |
|---|---|---|---|---|---|---|
| 2002 | — | PF65 60.00 | | | | |

**KM# 894 5 WON**
20.00 g., 0.999 Silver 0.6424 oz. ASW, 38 mm. **Obv:** National arms, Central Bank name **Rev:** Two scocer players with flag

| Date | Mintage | F12 | VF20 | XF40 | MS60 | MS63 |
|---|---|---|---|---|---|---|
| 2002 | Est. 5000 | PF65 35.00 | | | | |

**KM# 895 5 WON**
20.00 g., 0.999 Silver 0.6424 oz. ASW, 38 mm. **Obv:** National arms, Central Bank name **Rev:** Celebrating player in Yokohama stadium

| Date | Mintage | F12 | VF20 | XF40 | MS60 | MS63 |
|---|---|---|---|---|---|---|
| 2002 | — | PF65 60.00 | | | | |

**KM# 327 5 WON**
20.00 g., 0.999 Silver 0.6424 oz. ASW, 35 mm. **Obv:** State arms **Rev:** Turtle Boat " of 1592 **Edge:** Segmented reeding

| Date | Mintage | F12 | VF20 | XF40 | MS60 | MS63 |
|---|---|---|---|---|---|---|
| JU92-2003 | — | PF65 35.00 | | | | |

**KM# 328 5 WON**
20.00 g., 0.999 Silver 0.6424 oz. ASW, 35 mm. **Obv:** State arms **Rev:** Olympic fencers **Edge:** Segmented reeding

| Date | Mintage | F12 | VF20 | XF40 | MS60 | MS63 |
|---|---|---|---|---|---|---|
| JU92-2003 | — | PF65 35.00 | | | | |

**KM# 329 5 WON**
20.00 g., 0.999 Silver 0.6424 oz. ASW, 35 mm. **Obv:** State arms **Rev:** Three wild horses **Edge:** Segmented reeding

| Date | Mintage | F12 | VF20 | XF40 | MS60 | MS63 |
|---|---|---|---|---|---|---|
| JU92-2003 | — | PF65 35.00 | | | | |

**KM# 900 5 WON**
20.00 g., 0.999 Silver 0.6424 oz. ASW, 35 mm. **Obv:** National arms, Central Bank name **Rev:** Swan

| Date | Mintage | F12 | VF20 | XF40 | MS60 | MS63 |
|---|---|---|---|---|---|---|
| 2003 | Est. 1000 | PF65 45.00 | | | | |

**KM# 901 5 WON**
20.00 g., 0.999 Silver 0.6424 oz. ASW, 35 mm. **Obv:** National arms, Central Bank name **Rev:** Pelican

| Date | Mintage | F12 | VF20 | XF40 | MS60 | MS63 |
|---|---|---|---|---|---|---|
| 2003 | — | PF65 45.00 | | | | |

**KM# 902 5 WON**
20.00 g., 0.999 Silver 0.6424 oz. ASW, 35 mm. **Obv:** National arms, **Rev:** Stone eagle

| Date | Mintage | F12 | VF20 | XF40 | MS60 | MS63 |
|---|---|---|---|---|---|---|
| 2003 | — | PF65 45.00 | | | | |

**KM# 903 5 WON**
31.11 g., 0.999 Silver 0.999 oz. ASW, 40 mm. **Obv:** National arms, Central Bank name **Rev:** Chinese pangolin and young

| Date | Mintage | F12 | VF20 | XF40 | MS60 | MS63 |
|---|---|---|---|---|---|---|
| 2003 | Est. 1000 | PF65 60.00 | | | | |

**KM# 935 5 WON**
15.00 g., 0.999 Silver 0.4818 oz. ASW, 30 mm. **Subject:** Franz Schubert, 175th anniversary of death **Obv:** National arms, Central Bank name **Rev:** Franz Schubert

| Date | Mintage | F12 | VF20 | XF40 | MS60 | MS63 |
|---|---|---|---|---|---|---|
| 2003 | — | PF65 45.00 | | | | |

**KM# 936 5 WON**
20.00 g., 0.999 Silver 0.6424 oz. ASW, 38 mm. **Obv:** National arms, Central Bank name **Rev:** Horatio Nelson and H.M.S. Victory

| Date | Mintage | F12 | VF20 | XF40 | MS60 | MS63 |
|---|---|---|---|---|---|---|
| 2003 | — | PF65 45.00 | | | | |

**KM# 937 5 WON**
20.00 g., 0.999 Silver 0.6424 oz. ASW, 38 mm. **Obv:** National arms, Central Bank name **Rev:** Leopard

| Date | Mintage | F12 | VF20 | XF40 | MS60 | MS63 |
|---|---|---|---|---|---|---|
| 2003 | Est. 5000 | PF65 40.00 | | | | |

**KM# 1009 5 WON**
15.00 g., 0.999 Silver 0.4818 oz. ASW, 35 mm. **Obv:** National arms, Central Bank name **Rev:** Red deer in forest glade in color

| Date | Mintage | F12 | VF20 | XF40 | MS60 | MS63 |
|---|---|---|---|---|---|---|
| 2004 | — | PF65 60.00 | | | | |

**KM# 1010 5 WON**
15.00 g., 0.999 Silver 0.4818 oz. ASW, 35 mm. **Obv:** National arms, Central Bank name **Rev:** Kingfisher in color

| Date | Mintage | F12 | VF20 | XF40 | MS60 | MS63 |
|---|---|---|---|---|---|---|
| 2004 | — | PF65 60.00 | | | | |

**KM# 1011 5 WON**
31.11 g., 0.999 Silver 0.999 oz. ASW, 35 mm. **Obv:** National arms, Central Bank name **Rev:** Bewick's swan in flight in color

| Date | Mintage | F12 | VF20 | XF40 | MS60 | MS63 |
|---|---|---|---|---|---|---|
| 2004 | — | PF65 60.00 | | | | |

**KM# 1012 5 WON**
15.00 g., 0.999 Silver 0.4818 oz. ASW, 35 mm. **Obv:** National arms, Central Bank name **Rev:** Two blue whales and iceberg in color

| Date | Mintage | F12 | VF20 | XF40 | MS60 | MS63 |
|---|---|---|---|---|---|---|
| 2004 | — | PF65 60.00 | | | | |

**KM# 1013 5 WON**
15.00 g., 0.999 Silver 0.4818 oz. ASW, 35 mm. **Obv:** National arms, Central Bank name **Rev:** Lion in color

| Date | Mintage | F12 | VF20 | XF40 | MS60 | MS63 |
|---|---|---|---|---|---|---|
| 2004 | — | PF65 60.00 | | | | |

**KM# 1014 5 WON**
20.00 g., 0.999 Silver 0.6424 oz. ASW, 38 mm. **Obv:** National arms, Central Bank name **Rev:** Leopard

| Date | Mintage | F12 | VF20 | XF40 | MS60 | MS63 |
|---|---|---|---|---|---|---|
| 2004 | — | PF65 45.00 | | | | |

**KM# 1015 5 WON**
1.15 g., Aluminum, 21 mm. **Obv:** National arms, Central Bank name **Rev:** Large numeral 5

| Date | Mintage | F12 | VF20 | XF40 | MS60 | MS63 |
|---|---|---|---|---|---|---|
| 2005 | — | — | — | — | 3.00 | 5.00 |

**KM# 1080 5 WON**
15.00 g., 0.999 Silver 0.4818 oz. ASW, 35 mm. **Subject:** Tschaikowsky, 165 Birthday **Obv:** National arms, Central Bank name **Rev:** Peter Tschaikowsky

| Date | Mintage | F12 | VF20 | XF40 | MS60 | MS63 |
|---|---|---|---|---|---|---|
| 2005 | — | PF65 45.00 | | | | |

**KM# 1081 5 WON**
15.00 g., 0.999 Silver 0.4818 oz. ASW, 35 mm. **Obv:** National arms, Central Bank name **Rev:** Squirel in color

| Date | Mintage | F12 | VF20 | XF40 | MS60 | MS63 |
|---|---|---|---|---|---|---|
| 2005 | — | PF65 30.00 | | | | |

**KM# 1082 5 WON**
15.00 g., 0.999 Silver 0.4818 oz. ASW, 35 mm. **Obv:** National arms, Central Bank name **Rev:** Firefox in color

| Date | Mintage | F12 | VF20 | XF40 | MS60 | MS63 |
|---|---|---|---|---|---|---|
| 2005 | — | PF65 30.00 | | | | |

**KM# 1083 5 WON**
20.00 g., 0.999 Silver 0.6424 oz. ASW, 38 mm. **Obv:** National arms, Central Bank name **Rev:** Saiga antelope

| Date | Mintage | F12 | VF20 | XF40 | MS60 | MS63 |
|---|---|---|---|---|---|---|
| 2005 | — | PF65 45.00 | | | | |

**KM# 1084 5 WON**
20.00 g., 0.999 Silver 0.6424 oz. ASW, 38 mm. **Obv:** National arms, Central Bank name **Rev:** Malayian Tapir and young

| Date | Mintage | F12 | VF20 | XF40 | MS60 | MS63 |
|---|---|---|---|---|---|---|
| 2005 | Est. 5000 | PF65 45.00 | | | | |

**KM# 1085 5 WON**
20.00 g., 0.999 Silver 0.6424 oz. ASW, 38 mm. **Obv:** National arms, Central Bank name **Rev:** Sedov sailing ship

| Date | Mintage | F12 | VF20 | XF40 | MS60 | MS63 |
|---|---|---|---|---|---|---|
| 2005 | Est. 5000 | PF65 45.00 | | | | |

**KM# 1102 5 WON**
15.00 g., 0.999 Silver 0.4818 oz. ASW, 35 mm. **Obv:** National arms, Central Bank name **Rev:** Orca whale in color

| Date | Mintage | F12 | VF20 | XF40 | MS60 | MS63 |
|---|---|---|---|---|---|---|
| 2006 | — | PF65 60.00 | | | | |

**KM# 1103 5 WON**
15.00 g., 0.999 Silver 0.4818 oz. ASW, 35 mm. **Obv:** National arms, Central Bank name **Rev:** javanese flying frog in color

| Date | Mintage | F12 | VF20 | XF40 | MS60 | MS63 |
|---|---|---|---|---|---|---|
| 2006 | — | PF65 60.00 | | | | |

**KM# 1104 5 WON**
15.00 g., 0.999 Silver 0.4818 oz. ASW, 35 mm. **Obv:** National arms, Central Bank name **Rev:** Hymalayian Pheasant in color

| Date | Mintage | F12 | VF20 | XF40 | MS60 | MS63 |
|---|---|---|---|---|---|---|
| 2006 | — | PF65 60.00 | | | | |

**KM# 1105 5 WON**
15.00 g., 0.999 Silver 0.4818 oz. ASW, 35 mm. **Obv:** National arms, Central Bank name **Rev:** Karl Marx bust left

| Date | Mintage | F12 | VF20 | XF40 | MS60 | MS63 |
|---|---|---|---|---|---|---|
| 2006 | — | PF65 45.00 | | | | |

**KM# 1106 5 WON**
20.00 g., 0.999 Silver 0.6424 oz. ASW, 38 mm. **Obv:** National arms, Central Bank name **Rev:** Mir sailing ship

| Date | Mintage | F12 | VF20 | XF40 | MS60 | MS63 |
|---|---|---|---|---|---|---|
| 2006 | Est. 5000 | PF65 45.00 | | | | |

**KM# 1107 5 WON**
20.00 g., 0.999 Silver 0.6424 oz. ASW, 38 mm. **Subject:** Bejing Summer Olympics, 2008 **Obv:** National arms, Central Bank name **Rev:** Handball player making shot

| Date | Mintage | F12 | VF20 | XF40 | MS60 | MS63 |
|---|---|---|---|---|---|---|
| 2006 | Est. 5000 | PF65 35.00 | | | | |

**KM# 1108 5 WON**
20.00 g., 0.999 Silver 0.6424 oz. ASW, 38 mm. **Subject:** Bejing Summer Olympics, 2008 **Obv:** National arms, Central Bank name **Rev:** Archer before target

| Date | Mintage | F12 | VF20 | XF40 | MS60 | MS63 |
|---|---|---|---|---|---|---|
| 2006 | Est. 5000 | PF65 35.00 | | | | |

**KM# 1125 5 WON**
15.00 g., 0.999 Silver 0.4818 oz. ASW, 35 mm. **Obv:** National arms, Central Bank name **Rev:** Japanese snow money in color

| Date | Mintage | F12 | VF20 | XF40 | MS60 | MS63 |
|---|---|---|---|---|---|---|
| 2007 | — | PF65 60.00 | | | | |

**KM# 1126 5 WON**
20.00 g., 0.999 Silver 0.6424 oz. ASW, 38 mm. **Obv:** National arms, Central Bank name **Rev:** Siberian musk deer

| Date | Mintage | F12 | VF20 | XF40 | MS60 | MS63 |
|---|---|---|---|---|---|---|
| 2007 | Est. 5000 | PF65 60.00 | | | | |

**KM# 1127 5 WON**
20.00 g., 0.999 Silver 0.6424 oz. ASW, 38 mm. **Obv:** National arms, Central Bank name **Rev:** Ming treasure ship

| Date | Mintage | F12 | VF20 | XF40 | MS60 | MS63 |
|---|---|---|---|---|---|---|
| 2007 | Est. 5000 | PF65 45.00 | | | | |

**KM# 220 7 WON**
20.00 g., 0.999 Silver 0.6424 oz. ASW, 38 mm. **Subject:** 2002 Olympics **Obv:** State arms **Rev:** Two speed skaters **Edge:** Plain

| Date | Mintage | F12 | VF20 | XF40 | MS60 | MS63 |
|---|---|---|---|---|---|---|
| 2001 | 10,000 | PF63 35.00 | PF65 40.00 | | | |

**KM# 221 7 WON**
20.00 g., 0.999 Silver 0.6424 oz. ASW, 38 mm. **Subject:** Endangered Wildlife **Obv:** State arms **Rev:** White-tailed sea Eagle **Edge:** Plain

| Date | Mintage | F12 | VF20 | XF40 | MS60 | MS63 |
|---|---|---|---|---|---|---|
| 2001 | 10,000 | PF63 30.00 | PF65 35.00 | | | |

**KM# 881 7 WON**
20.00 g., 0.999 Silver 0.6424 oz. ASW **Obv:** Naitonal arms, Central Bank name **Rev:** Taekwondo **Shape:** 38

| Date | Mintage | F12 | VF20 | XF40 | MS60 | MS63 |
|---|---|---|---|---|---|---|
| 2002 | — | PF65 35.00 | | | | |

**KM# 883 7 WON**
20.00 g., 0.999 Silver 0.6424 oz. ASW, 38 mm. **Obv:** National arms, Central Bank name **Rev:** World Cup, player and Brandenburg Gate

| Date | Mintage | F12 | VF20 | XF40 | MS60 | MS63 |
|---|---|---|---|---|---|---|
| 2002 | — | PF65 30.00 | | | | |

**KM# 921 7 WON**
20.00 g., 0.999 Silver 0.6424 oz. ASW, 38 mm. **Obv:** National arms, Central Bank name **Rev:** Steamer Princess Charlotte of Prussia

| Date | Mintage | F12 | VF20 | XF40 | MS60 | MS63 |
|---|---|---|---|---|---|---|
| 2003 | Est. 500 | PF65 70.00 | | | | |

**KM# 922 7 WON**
20.00 g., 0.999 Silver 0.6424 oz. ASW, 35 mm. **Obv:** National arms, Central Bank name **Rev:** Steamship Queen Maria

| Date | Mintage | F12 | VF20 | XF40 | MS60 | MS63 |
|---|---|---|---|---|---|---|
| 2003 | — | PF65 75.00 | | | | |

**KM# 923 7 WON**
20.00 g., 0.999 Silver 0.6424 oz. ASW, 38 mm. **Obv:** National arms, Central Bank name **Rev:** Transatlantic sail steamship Helena Sloman

| Date | Mintage | F12 | VF20 | XF40 | MS60 | MS63 |
|---|---|---|---|---|---|---|
| 2003 | Est. 500 | PF65 75.00 | | | | |

**KM# 927 7 WON**
20.00 g., 0.999 Silver 0.6424 oz. ASW, 38 mm. **Obv:** National arms, Central Bank name **Rev:** Adler, 1835 steam locomotive

| Date | Mintage | F12 | VF20 | XF40 | MS60 | MS63 |
|---|---|---|---|---|---|---|
| 2003 | — | PF65 60.00 | | | | |

**KM# 928 7 WON**
20.00 g., 0.999 Silver 0.6424 oz. ASW, 38 mm. **Obv:** National arms, Central Bank name **Rev:** Saxonia, 1838 steam locomotive

| Date | Mintage | F12 | VF20 | XF40 | MS60 | MS63 |
|---|---|---|---|---|---|---|
| 2003 | — | PF65 60.00 | | | | |

**KM# 929 7 WON**
20.00 g., 0.999 Silver 0.6424 oz. ASW, 38 mm. **Obv:** National arms, Central Bank name **Rev:** Rheingold, 1928 steam locomotive

| Date | Mintage | F12 | VF20 | XF40 | MS60 | MS63 |
|---|---|---|---|---|---|---|
| 2003 | — | PF65 60.00 | | | | |

**KM# 931 7 WON**
20.00 g., 0.999 Silver 0.6424 oz. ASW, 38 mm. **Obv:** National arms, Central Bank name **Rev:** Gorch Fock I, sailing ship

| Date | Mintage | F12 | VF20 | XF40 | MS60 | MS63 |
|---|---|---|---|---|---|---|
| 2003 | — | PF65 60.00 | | | | |

**KM# 932 7 WON**
20.00 g., 0.999 Silver 0.6424 oz. ASW, 38 mm. **Obv:** National arms, Central Bank name **Rev:** Skier

| Date | Mintage | F12 | VF20 | XF40 | MS60 | MS63 |
|---|---|---|---|---|---|---|
| 2003 | Est. 5000 | PF65 40.00 | | | | |

**KM# 477 7 WON**
20.00 g., Bi-Metallic Silver center in Brass ring. **Obv:** Arms **Rev:** Stadium along river

| Date | Mintage | F12 | VF20 | XF40 | MS60 | MS63 |
|---|---|---|---|---|---|---|
| 2004 | — | PF65 55.00 | | | | |

**KM# 945 7 WON**
20.00 g., Silver, 23x40 mm. **Obv:** East gate of Pyeongyang **Rev:** Mormoset **Shape:** Rectangle

| Date | Mintage | F12 | VF20 | XF40 | MS60 | MS63 |
|---|---|---|---|---|---|---|
| 2004 | — | PF65 35.00 | | | | |

**KM# 946 7 WON**
20.00 g., 0.999 Silver 0.6424 oz. ASW, 23x40 mm. **Obv:** East gate of Pyeongyang **Rev:** Blue monkey **Shape:** Rectangle

| Date | Mintage | F12 | VF20 | XF40 | MS60 | MS63 |
|---|---|---|---|---|---|---|
| 2004 | — | PF65 35.00 | | | | |

**KM# 947 7 WON**
20.00 g., Silver, 23x40 mm. **Obv:** East gate of Pyeongyang **Rev:** Monkies **Shape:** Rectangle

| Date | Mintage | F12 | VF20 | XF40 | MS60 | MS63 |
|---|---|---|---|---|---|---|
| 2004 | — | PF65 35.00 | | | | |

**KM# 996 7 WON**
20.00 g., 0.999 Silver 0.6424 oz. ASW, 38 mm. **Obv:** National arms, Central Bank name **Rev:** Statsraad Lehmkuhl sailing ship

| Date | Mintage | F12 | VF20 | XF40 | MS60 | MS63 |
|---|---|---|---|---|---|---|
| 2004 | Est. 3000 | PF65 60.00 | | | | |

**KM# 997 7 WON**
20.00 g., 0.999 Silver 0.6424 oz. ASW, 38 mm. **Obv:** National arms, Central Bank name **Rev:** Henry Hudson's Halve Maen

| Date | Mintage | F12 | VF20 | XF40 | MS60 | MS63 |
|---|---|---|---|---|---|---|
| 2004 | Est. 3000 | PF65 60.00 | | | | |

**KM# 998 7 WON**
20.00 g., 0.999 Silver 0.6424 oz. ASW, 38 mm. **Subject:** 1980 Lake PLacid Olympics **Obv:** National arms, Central Bank name **Rev:** Speed skater

| Date | Mintage | F12 | VF20 | XF40 | MS60 | MS63 |
|---|---|---|---|---|---|---|
| 2004 | Est. 5000 | PF65 35.00 | | | | |

**KM# 1071 7 WON**
20.00 g., 0.999 Silver 0.6424 oz. ASW, 38 mm. **Subject:** Squaw Valley 1960 Winter Olympics **Obv:** National arms, Central Bank name **Rev:** Ice Dancing

| Date | Mintage | F12 | VF20 | XF40 | MS60 | MS63 |
|---|---|---|---|---|---|---|
| 2005 | Est. 5000 | PF65 45.00 | | | | |

**KM# 1072 7 WON**
20.00 g., 0.999 Silver 0.6424 oz. ASW, 38 mm. **Subject:** Calgary Winter Olympics, 1988 **Obv:** National arms, Central Bank name

| Date | Mintage | F12 | VF20 | XF40 | MS60 | MS63 |
|---|---|---|---|---|---|---|
| 2005 | — | PF65 45.00 | | | | |

**KM# 1073 7 WON**
20.00 g., 0.999 Silver 0.6424 oz. ASW, 38 mm. **Subject:** Nagano Winter Olympics, 1998 **Obv:** National arms, Central Bank name **Rev:** Snowboarder

| Date | Mintage | F12 | VF20 | XF40 | MS60 | MS63 |
|---|---|---|---|---|---|---|
| 2005 | — | PF65 45.00 | | | | |

**KM# 1075 7 WON**
20.00 g., 0.999 Silver 0.6424 oz. ASW, 38 mm. **Subject:** Torino Winter Olympics, 2006 **Obv:** National arms, Central Bank name **Rev:** bobsled

| Date | Mintage | F12 | VF20 | XF40 | MS60 | MS63 |
|---|---|---|---|---|---|---|
| 2005 | — | PF65 45.00 | | | | |

**KM# 1076 7 WON**
20.00 g., 0.999 Silver 0.6424 oz. ASW, 38 mm. **Obv:** National arms, Central Bank name **Rev:** Black faced spoonbill

| Date | Mintage | F12 | VF20 | XF40 | MS60 | MS63 |
|---|---|---|---|---|---|---|
| 2005 | — | PF65 60.00 | | | | |

**KM# 1077 7 WON**
20.00 g., 0.999 Silver 0.6424 oz. ASW, 38 mm. **Obv:** National arms, Central Bank name **Rev:** Flying dog

| Date | Mintage | F12 | VF20 | XF40 | MS60 | MS63 |
|---|---|---|---|---|---|---|
| 2005 | Est. 5000 | PF65 60.00 | | | | |

**KM# 152 10 WON**
31.00 g., 0.999 Silver 0.9957 oz. ASW, 39.8 mm. **Subject:** Asian Money Fair **Obv:** State arms **Rev:** Two snakes **Edge:** Reeded and plain sections

| Date | Mintage | F12 | VF20 | XF40 | MS60 | MS63 |
|---|---|---|---|---|---|---|
| 2001 | — | PF65 60.00 | | | | |

**KM# 153 10 WON**
31.00 g., 0.999 Silver 0.9957 oz. ASW, 39.8 mm. **Subject:** Tortoise-Serpent **Obv:** State arms **Rev:** Mythical creature **Edge:** Reeded and plain sections

| Date | Mintage | F12 | VF20 | XF40 | MS60 | MS63 |
|---|---|---|---|---|---|---|
| 2001 | — | PF65 55.00 | | | | |

**KM# 227 10 WON**
31.06 g., 0.925 Silver 0.9237 oz. ASW, 39.9 mm. **Subject:** General Ri Sun Sin **Obv:** State arms **Rev:** Helmeted head 1/4 left **Edge:** Reeded

| Date | Mintage | F12 | VF20 | XF40 | MS60 | MS63 |
|---|---|---|---|---|---|---|
| 2001 | — | PF65 47.50 | | | | |

**KM# 253 10 WON**
31.11 g., 0.999 Silver 0.9992 oz. ASW, 40.2 mm. **Obv:** State arms **Rev:** Deng Xio Ping head 3/4 left, 1904-1997 flanking, sprigs below **Edge:** Plain

| Date | Mintage | F12 | VF20 | XF40 | MS60 | MS63 |
|---|---|---|---|---|---|---|
| 2001 | — | **PF65** 45.00 | | | | |

**KM# 292 10 WON**
31.00 g., 0.999 Silver 0.9957 oz. ASW, 40.2 mm. **Obv:** State arms **Rev:** Kim Il-Seung bust facing, 1912-1994 flanking, sprigs below **Edge:** Plain

| Date | Mintage | F12 | VF20 | XF40 | MS60 | MS63 |
|---|---|---|---|---|---|---|
| JU90-2001 | — | **PF65** 45.00 | | | | |

**KM# 295 10 WON**
31.00 g., 0.999 Silver 0.9957 oz. ASW, 40.2 mm. **Obv:** State arms **Rev:** Mountain cabin **Edge:** Plain

| Date | Mintage | F12 | VF20 | XF40 | MS60 | MS63 |
|---|---|---|---|---|---|---|
| JU90-2001 | — | **PF65** 45.00 | | | | |

**KM# 296 10 WON**
31.00 g., 0.999 Silver 0.9957 oz. ASW, 40.2 mm. **Obv:** State arms **Rev:** KUMDANG - 2 INJECTION" in center of leaves **Edge:** Plain

| Date | Mintage | F12 | VF20 | XF40 | MS60 | MS63 |
|---|---|---|---|---|---|---|
| 2001 | — | **PF65** 50.00 | | | | |

**KM# 297 10 WON**
31.00 g., 0.999 Silver 0.9957 oz. ASW, 40.2 mm. **Obv:** State arms **Rev:** Train scene and a couple below a jet liner **Rev. Legend:** ...1945 - 2001... **Edge:** Plain

| Date | Mintage | F12 | VF20 | XF40 | MS60 | MS63 |
|---|---|---|---|---|---|---|
| ND-2001 | — | **PF65** 45.00 | | | | |

**KM# 298 10 WON**
31.00 g., 0.999 Silver 0.9957 oz. ASW, 40.2 mm. **Obv:** State arms **Rev:** Cruise ship below stylized head left profile **Edge:** Plain

| Date | Mintage | F12 | VF20 | XF40 | MS60 | MS63 |
|---|---|---|---|---|---|---|
| JU90-2001 | — | **PF65** 50.00 | | | | |

**KM# 299 10 WON**
31.00 g., 0.999 Silver 0.9957 oz. ASW, 40.2 mm. **Obv:** State arms **Rev:** Old fortress **Edge:** Plain

| Date | Mintage | F12 | VF20 | XF40 | MS60 | MS63 |
|---|---|---|---|---|---|---|
| JU90-2001 | — | **PF65** 47.50 | | | | |

**KM# 300 10 WON**
31.00 g., 0.999 Silver 0.9957 oz. ASW, 40.2 mm. **Obv:** State arms **Rev:** Landmarks, flag and tourist couple above cruise ship **Edge:** Plain

| Date | Mintage | F12 | VF20 | XF40 | MS60 | MS63 |
|---|---|---|---|---|---|---|
| JU90-2001 | — | **PF65** 45.00 | | | | |

**KM# 301 10 WON**
31.00 g., 0.999 Silver 0.9957 oz. ASW, 40.2 mm. **Obv:** State arms **Rev:** 2 facing half length men shaking hands **Edge:** Plain

| Date | Mintage | F12 | VF20 | XF40 | MS60 | MS63 |
|---|---|---|---|---|---|---|
| JU90-2001 | — | **PF65** 45.00 | | | | |

**KM# 302 10 WON**
31.00 g., 0.999 Silver 0.9957 oz. ASW, 40.1 mm. **Obv:** State arms **Rev:** Great East Gate **Edge:** Plain

| Date | Mintage | F12 | VF20 | XF40 | MS60 | MS63 |
|---|---|---|---|---|---|---|
| JU90-2001 | — | **PF65** 47.50 | | | | |

**KM# 357 10 WON**
31.00 g., 0.999 Silver 0.9957 oz. ASW, 40.2 mm. **Obv:** State arms **Rev:** Antique ceramic items **Edge:** Plain

| Date | Mintage | F12 | VF20 | XF40 | MS60 | MS63 |
|---|---|---|---|---|---|---|
| 2001 | — | **PF65** 45.00 | | | | |

**KM# 386 10 WON**
30.76 g., 0.999 Silver 0.988 oz. ASW, 40.1 mm. **Obv:** State arms **Rev:** Kim Jung Sook facing flanked by dates (1917-1949) above flower sprigs **Edge:** Plain

| Date | Mintage | F12 | VF20 | XF40 | MS60 | MS63 |
|---|---|---|---|---|---|---|
| JU90-2001 | — | **PF65** 47.50 | | | | |

**KM# 387 10 WON**
30.76 g., 0.999 Silver 0.988 oz. ASW, 40.1 mm. **Obv:** State arms **Rev:** Kim Jung-Il bust facing, sprigs below **Edge:** Plain

| Date | Mintage | F12 | VF20 | XF40 | MS60 | MS63 |
|---|---|---|---|---|---|---|
| JU90-2001 | — | PF65 47.50 | | | | |

**KM# 697 10 WON**
27.00 g., 0.999 Silver 0.8672 oz. ASW, 40 mm. **Obv:** National arms, value in English **Rev:** Kim Jeongsuk

| Date | Mintage | F12 | VF20 | XF40 | MS60 | MS63 |
|---|---|---|---|---|---|---|
| 2001 | — | PF65 60.00 | | | | |

**KM# 704 10 WON**
31.11 g., Silver, 40 mm. **Obv:** National arms, Country name **Rev:** House where Kim Ilseong was born

| Date | Mintage | F12 | VF20 | XF40 | MS60 | MS63 |
|---|---|---|---|---|---|---|
| 2001 Proof | — | — | — | — | — | — |

**KM# 705 10 WON**
31.11 g., 0.999 Silver 0.999 oz. ASW, 40 mm. **Obv:** National arms, Country name **Rev:** House where Kim Jeongsuk was born

| Date | Mintage | F12 | VF20 | XF40 | MS60 | MS63 |
|---|---|---|---|---|---|---|
| 2001 Proof | — | — | — | — | — | — |

**KM# 732 10 WON**
7.00 g., Aluminum, 40 mm. **Obv:** East gate of Pyeongyang **Rev:** Married couple before flag and ferryboat

| Date | Mintage | F12 | VF20 | XF40 | MS60 | MS63 |
|---|---|---|---|---|---|---|
| 2001 Proof | — | — | — | — | — | — |

**KM# 733 10 WON**
7.00 g., Aluminum, 40 mm. **Obv:** East gate of Pyeongyang **Rev:** Ferryboat between Korea and Japan

| Date | Mintage | F12 | VF20 | XF40 | MS60 | MS63 |
|---|---|---|---|---|---|---|
| 2001 Proof | — | — | — | — | — | — |

**KM# 734 10 WON**
7.00 g., Aluminum, 40 mm. **Obv:** East gate of Pyeongyang **Rev:** Triumphial arch of Moranbong in Pyeongyang

| Date | Mintage | F12 | VF20 | XF40 | MS60 | MS63 |
|---|---|---|---|---|---|---|
| 2001 Proof | — | — | — | — | — | — |

**KM# 735 10 WON**
Aluminum, 40 mm. **Obv:** East gate of Pyeongyang **Rev:** Chonji crater in Paektusan

| Date | Mintage | F12 | VF20 | XF40 | MS60 | MS63 |
|---|---|---|---|---|---|---|
| 2001 Proof | — | — | — | — | — | — |

**KM# 740 10 WON**
Silver, 40 mm. **Obv:** National arms, Country name **Rev:** Triumphial arch of Moranbong in Pyeongyang

| Date | Mintage | F12 | VF20 | XF40 | MS60 | MS63 |
|---|---|---|---|---|---|---|
| 2001 Proof | — | — | — | — | — | — |

**KM# 741 10 WON**
Silver, 40 mm. **Obv:** National arms, Country name **Rev:** Chonji crater in Paektusan

| Date | Mintage | F12 | VF20 | XF40 | MS60 | MS63 |
|---|---|---|---|---|---|---|
| 2001 Proof | — | — | — | — | — | — |

**KM# 775 10 WON**
7.00 g., Aluminum, 40 mm. **Obv:** East gate in Pyeongyang **Rev:** Taekwondo player

| Date | Mintage | F12 | VF20 | XF40 | MS60 | MS63 |
|---|---|---|---|---|---|---|
| 2001 | — | PF65 6.00 | | | | |

**KM# 776 10 WON**
7.00 g., Aluminum, 40 mm. **Obv:** National arms, Country name **Rev:** Two taekwondo players

| Date | Mintage | F12 | VF20 | XF40 | MS60 | MS63 |
|---|---|---|---|---|---|---|
| 2001 | — | PF65 6.00 | | | | |
| 2007 | — | PF65 6.00 | | | | |

**KM# 779 10 WON**
31.11 g., 0.999 Silver 0.999 oz. ASW, 40 mm. **Obv:** National arms, Central Bank name **Rev:** Taewankdo kicker

| Date | Mintage | F12 | VF20 | XF40 | MS60 | MS63 |
|---|---|---|---|---|---|---|
| 2001 | — | PF65 60.00 | | | | |

**KM# 780 10 WON**
31.11 g., 0.999 Silver 0.999 oz. ASW, 40 mm. **Obv:** National arms, Central Bank name **Rev:** Two taekwondo players

| Date | Mintage | F12 | VF20 | XF40 | MS60 | MS63 |
|---|---|---|---|---|---|---|
| 2001 | — | PF65 60.00 | | | | |

**KM# 231 10 WON**
31.00 g., 0.999 Silver 0.9957 oz. ASW, 39.9 mm. **Subject:** Kim Il Sung **Obv:** State arms **Rev:** Bust facing **Edge:** Segmented reeding

| Date | Mintage | F12 | VF20 | XF40 | MS60 | MS63 |
|---|---|---|---|---|---|---|
| JU91-2002 | — | PF65 50.00 | | | | |

**KM# 254 10 WON**
30.77 g., 0.999 Silver 0.9883 oz. ASW, 40.15 mm. **Obv:** State arms **Rev:** Tangun bust facing and his tomb **Edge:** Plain

| Date | Mintage | F12 | VF20 | XF40 | MS60 | MS63 |
|---|---|---|---|---|---|---|
| JU91-2002 | — | PF65 42.50 | | | | |

**KM# 255 10 WON**
30.94 g., 0.999 Silver 0.9937 oz. ASW, 40.2 mm. **Subject:** Jongmongju and Sonjukgyo **Obv:** State arms **Rev:** Head with hat facing above building foundation **Edge:** Plain

| Date | Mintage | F12 | VF20 | XF40 | MS60 | MS63 |
|---|---|---|---|---|---|---|
| JU91-2002 | — | PF65 42.50 | | | | |

**KM# 307 10 WON**
31.00 g., 0.999 Silver 0.9957 oz. ASW, 40.1 mm. **Obv:** State arms **Rev:** Two horses within a circle of Asian Zodiac animals **Edge:** Plain

| Date | Mintage | F12 | VF20 | XF40 | MS60 | MS63 |
|---|---|---|---|---|---|---|
| 2002 | — | PF65 45.00 | | | | |

**KM# 309 10 WON**
31.00 g., 0.999 Silver 0.9957 oz. ASW, 40.2 mm. **Subject:** Arirang **Obv:** State arms **Rev:** Performers and flying cranes **Edge:** Plain

| Date | Mintage | F12 | VF20 | XF40 | MS60 | MS63 |
|---|---|---|---|---|---|---|
| JU91-2002 | — | PF65 45.00 | | | | |

**KM# 311 10 WON**
31.00 g., 0.999 Silver 0.9957 oz. ASW, 40.2 mm. **Obv:** State arms **Rev:** Tomb of King Tongmyong **Edge:** Plain

| Date | Mintage | F12 | VF20 | XF40 | MS60 | MS63 |
|---|---|---|---|---|---|---|
| JU91-2002 | — | PF65 45.00 | | | | |

**KM# 312 10 WON**
31.00 g., 0.999 Silver 0.9957 oz. ASW, 40.2 mm. **Obv:** State arms **Rev:** Tomb of King Kong Min **Edge:** Plain

| Date | Mintage | F12 | VF20 | XF40 | MS60 | MS63 |
|---|---|---|---|---|---|---|
| JU91-2002 | — | PF65 45.00 | | | | |

**KM# 314 10 WON**
31.00 g., 0.999 Silver 0.9957 oz. ASW, 40.2 mm. **Subject:** Arirang **Obv:** State arms **Rev:** Stylized dancer **Edge:** Plain

| Date | Mintage | F12 | VF20 | XF40 | MS60 | MS63 |
|---|---|---|---|---|---|---|
| 2002 | — | PF65 45.00 | | | | |

**KM# 315 10 WON**
31.00 g., 0.999 Silver 0.9957 oz. ASW, 40.2 mm. **Obv:** State arms **Rev:** Korean map shaped dancer **Edge:** Plain

| Date | Mintage | F12 | VF20 | XF40 | MS60 | MS63 |
|---|---|---|---|---|---|---|
| JU91-2002 | — | PF65 47.50 | | | | |

**KM# 316 10 WON**
31.00 g., 0.999 Silver 0.9957 oz. ASW, 40.2 mm. **Obv:** State arms **Rev:** Korean map shaped ribbon dancer **Edge:** Plain

| Date | Mintage | F12 | VF20 | XF40 | MS60 | MS63 |
|---|---|---|---|---|---|---|
| JU91-2002 | — | PF65 47.50 | | | | |

**KM# 317 10 WON**
31.00 g., 0.999 Silver 0.9957 oz. ASW, 40.2 mm. **Obv:** State arms **Rev:** Victorious athletes hugging **Edge:** Plain

| Date | Mintage | F12 | VF20 | XF40 | MS60 | MS63 |
|---|---|---|---|---|---|---|
| JU91-2002 | — | PF65 45.00 | | | | |

**KM# 318 10 WON**
31.00 g., 0.999 Silver 0.9957 oz. ASW, 40.2 mm. **Obv:** State arms **Rev:** Woman floating above arena **Edge:** Plain

| Date | Mintage | F12 | VF20 | XF40 | MS60 | MS63 |
|---|---|---|---|---|---|---|
| JU91-2002 | — | PF65 45.00 | | | | |

**KM# 401 10 WON**
31.00 g., 0.999 Silver 0.9957 oz. ASW, 40.1 mm. **Obv:** State arms **Rev:** Arirang dancer **Edge:** Plain

| Date | Mintage | F12 | VF20 | XF40 | MS60 | MS63 |
|---|---|---|---|---|---|---|
| JU91-2002 | — | PF65 45.00 | | | | |

**KM# 402 10 WON**
31.00 g., 0.999 Silver 0.9957 oz. ASW, 40.1 mm. **Obv:** State arms **Rev:** Arirang ribbon dancer **Edge:** Plain

| Date | Mintage | F12 | VF20 | XF40 | MS60 | MS63 |
|---|---|---|---|---|---|---|
| JU91-2002 | — | PF65 45.00 | | | | |

**KM# 812 10 WON**
31.11 g., 0.999 Silver 0.999 oz. ASW, 40 mm. **Obv:** National arms, Central Bank name **Rev:** Dongmyeong, 1st King of Goguryeo

| Date | Mintage | F12 | VF20 | XF40 | MS60 | MS63 |
|---|---|---|---|---|---|---|
| 2002 | — | PF65 60.00 | | | | |

**KM# 813 10 WON**
31.11 g., 0.999 Silver 0.999 oz. ASW, 40 mm. **Obv:** National arms, Central Bank name **Rev:** Wanggeon, 1st King of Goryeo dynasty

| Date | Mintage | F12 | VF20 | XF40 | MS60 | MS63 |
|---|---|---|---|---|---|---|
| 2002 | — | PF65 60.00 | | | | |

**KM# 814 10 WON**
31.11 g., 0.999 Silver 0.999 oz. ASW, 40 mm. **Obv:** National arms, Central Bank name **Rev:** Jeon Bongjun

| Date | Mintage | F12 | VF20 | XF40 | MS60 | MS63 |
|---|---|---|---|---|---|---|
| 2002 | — | PF65 60.00 | | | | |

**KM# 823 10 WON**
31.11 g., 0.999 Silver 0.999 oz. ASW, 40 mm. **Obv:** National arms **Rev:** Prince Hodong and Princess Nakrang on horseback

| Date | Mintage | F12 | VF20 | XF40 | MS60 | MS63 |
|---|---|---|---|---|---|---|
| 2002 | — | PF65 60.00 | | | | |

**KM# 824 10 WON**
31.11 g., 0.999 Silver 0.999 oz. ASW, 40 mm. **Obv:** National arms **Rev:** Half-length figures of Prince Hodong and Princess Nakrang

| Date | Mintage | F12 | VF20 | XF40 | MS60 | MS63 |
|---|---|---|---|---|---|---|
| 2002 | — | PF65 60.00 | | | | |

**KM# 827 10 WON**
7.00 g., Aluminum, 40 mm. **Obv:** East gate of Pyeongyang **Rev:** Reconstruction of the Mausoleum of King Dongmyeong

| Date | Mintage | F12 | VF20 | XF40 | MS60 | MS63 |
|---|---|---|---|---|---|---|
| 2002 | — | PF65 7.00 | | | | |

**KM# 828 10 WON**
7.00 g., Aluminum, 40 mm. **Obv:** East gate in Pyeongyang **Rev:** Mausoleum for Gongmin

| Date | Mintage | F12 | VF20 | XF40 | MS60 | MS63 |
|---|---|---|---|---|---|---|
| 2002 | — | PF65 7.00 | | | | |

**KM# 829 10 WON**
7.00 g., Aluminum, 40 mm. **Obv:** East gate in Pyeongyang **Rev:** Stadium

| Date | Mintage | F12 | VF20 | XF40 | MS60 | MS63 |
|---|---|---|---|---|---|---|
| 2002 | — | PF65 7.00 | | | | |

**KM# 833 10 WON**
31.11 g., 0.999 Silver 0.999 oz. ASW, 40 mm. **Obv:** National arms, Central Bank name **Rev:** Stadium

| Date | Mintage | F12 | VF20 | XF40 | MS60 | MS63 |
|---|---|---|---|---|---|---|
| 2002 | — | PF65 60.00 | | | | |

**KM# 860 10 WON**
7.00 g., Aluminum, 40 mm. **Obv:** East gate of Pyeongyang **Rev:** The family

| Date | Mintage | F12 | VF20 | XF40 | MS60 | MS63 |
|---|---|---|---|---|---|---|
| 2002 | — | PF65 7.00 | | | | |

**KM# 861 10 WON**
7.00 g., Aluminum, 40 mm. **Obv:** East gate of Pyeongyang **Rev:** Map of Korea with the four cardinal compass points

| Date | Mintage | F12 | VF20 | XF40 | MS60 | MS63 |
|---|---|---|---|---|---|---|
| 2002 | — | PF65 7.00 | | | | |

**KM# 862 10 WON**
7.00 g., Aluminum, 40 mm. **Obv:** East gate of Pyeongyang **Rev:** Ryhmathic dancing and map of Korea

| Date | Mintage | F12 | VF20 | XF40 | MS60 | MS63 |
|---|---|---|---|---|---|---|
| 2002 | — | PF65 7.00 | | | | |

**KM# 863 10 WON**
7.00 g., Aluminum, 40 mm. **Obv:** East gate of Pyeongyang **Rev:** Drum dancer in form of the map of Korea

| Date | Mintage | F12 | VF20 | XF40 | MS60 | MS63 |
|---|---|---|---|---|---|---|
| 2002 | — | PF65 7.00 | | | | |

**KM# 864 10 WON**
7.00 g., Aluminum, 40 mm. **Obv:** East gate of Pyeongyang **Rev:** Victory celebration of Korean Teammates

| Date | Mintage | F12 | VF20 | XF40 | MS60 | MS63 |
|---|---|---|---|---|---|---|
| 2002 | — | PF65 7.00 | | | | |

**KM# 865 10 WON**
28.00 g., Brass, 40 mm. **Obv:** East gate of Pyeongyang **Rev:** Family

| Date | Mintage | F12 | VF20 | XF40 | MS60 | MS63 |
|---|---|---|---|---|---|---|
| 2002 | — | PF65 7.00 | | | | |

**KM# 870 10 WON**
31.11 g., 0.999 Silver 0.999 oz. ASW, 40 mm. **Obv:** National arms, Central Bank name **Rev:** Family

| Date | Mintage | F12 | VF20 | XF40 | MS60 | MS63 |
|---|---|---|---|---|---|---|
| 2002 | — | PF65 60.00 | | | | |

**KM# 871 10 WON**
31.11 g., 0.999 Silver 0.999 oz. ASW, 40 mm. **Obv:** National arms, Central Bank name **Rev:** Map of Korea with the four cardinal points

| Date | Mintage | F12 | VF20 | XF40 | MS60 | MS63 |
|---|---|---|---|---|---|---|
| 2002 | — | PF65 60.00 | | | | |

**KM# 884 10 WON**
31.11 g., 0.999 Silver 0.999 oz. ASW, 40 mm. **Subject:** Final issue of the German Mark **Obv:** National arms, Central Bank name **Rev:** Mark coin and Brandenburg Gate in color

| Date | Mintage | F12 | VF20 | XF40 | MS60 | MS63 |
|---|---|---|---|---|---|---|
| 2002 | Est. 2001 | PF65 85.00 | | | | |

**KM# 885 10 WON**
31.11 g., 0.999 Silver 0.999 oz. ASW, 40 mm. **Subject:** Final issue of the Belgian franc **Obv:** National arms, Central Bank name **Rev:** Franc and Axon in Brussels

| Date | Mintage | F12 | VF20 | XF40 | MS60 | MS63 |
|---|---|---|---|---|---|---|
| 2002 | Est. 2001 | PF65 85.00 | | | | |

**KM# 886 10 WON**
31.11 g., 0.999 Silver 0.999 oz. ASW, 40 mm. **Subject:** Final issue of the Greek Drachma **Obv:** National arms, Central Bank name **Rev:** Drachma and Acropolis in color

| Date | Mintage | F12 | VF20 | XF40 | MS60 | MS63 |
|---|---|---|---|---|---|---|
| 2002 | Est. 2001 | PF65 85.00 | | | | |

**KM# 887 10 WON**
31.11 g., 0.999 Silver 0.999 oz. ASW, 40 mm. **Subject:** Final issue of the Austrian schilling **Obv:** National arms, Central bank name **Rev:** Schilling and St. Stephen's in Vienna in color

| Date | Mintage | F12 | VF20 | XF40 | MS60 | MS63 |
|---|---|---|---|---|---|---|
| 2002 | Est. 2001 | PF65 85.00 | | | | |

**KM# 888 10 WON**
31.11 g., 0.999 Silver 0.999 oz. ASW, 40 mm. **Subject:** Final issue of the Netherland Gulden **Obv:** National arms, Central Bank name **Rev:** Gulden and Windmill in color

| Date | Mintage | F12 | VF20 | XF40 | MS60 | MS63 |
|---|---|---|---|---|---|---|
| 2002 | Est. 2001 | PF65 85.00 | | | | |

**KM# 889 10 WON**
31.11 g., 0.999 Silver 0.999 oz. ASW, 40 mm. **Subject:** Final issue of the San Marino Lira **Obv:** National arms, Central Bank name **Rev:** Lira and Mount Titano in color

| Date | Mintage | F12 | VF20 | XF40 | MS60 | MS63 |
|---|---|---|---|---|---|---|
| 2002 | Est. 2001 | PF65 85.00 | | | | |

**KM# 890 10 WON**
31.11 g., 0.999 Silver 0.999 oz. ASW, 40 mm. **Subject:** Final Vatican Lira **Obv:** National arms, Central Bank name **Rev:** Lira coin and St. Peter's in color

| Date | Mintage | F12 | VF20 | XF40 | MS60 | MS63 |
|---|---|---|---|---|---|---|
| 2002 | Est. 2001 | PF65 85.00 | | | | |

**KM# 320 10 WON**
31.00 g., 0.999 Silver 0.9957 oz. ASW, 40.2 mm. **Obv:** State arms **Rev:** Helmeted head with two antenna-like horns on helmet **Edge:** Plain

| Date | Mintage | F12 | VF20 | XF40 | MS60 | MS63 |
|---|---|---|---|---|---|---|
| JU92-2003 | — | PF65 47.50 | | | | |

**KM# 321 10 WON**
31.00 g., 0.999 Silver 0.9957 oz. ASW, 40.2 mm. **Obv:** State arms **Rev:** Helmeted head with horns **Edge:** Plain

| Date | Mintage | F12 | VF20 | XF40 | MS60 | MS63 |
|---|---|---|---|---|---|---|
| JU92-2003 | — | PF65 47.50 | | | | |

**KM# 322 10 WON**
31.00 g., 0.999 Silver 0.9957 oz. ASW, 40.2 mm. **Obv:** State arms **Rev:** Armored bust of Kang Kam-cheon facing (948-1031) wearing winged helmet **Edge:** Plain

| Date | Mintage | F12 | VF20 | XF40 | MS60 | MS63 |
|---|---|---|---|---|---|---|
| JU92-2003 | — | PF65 47.50 | | | | |

**KM# 324 10 WON**
31.00 g., 0.999 Silver 0.9957 oz. ASW, 40.2 mm. **Obv:** State arms **Rev:** Turtle-shaped armored ship of 1592 **Edge:** Plain

| Date | Mintage | F12 | VF20 | XF40 | MS60 | MS63 |
|---|---|---|---|---|---|---|
| JU92-2003 | — | PF65 45.00 | | | | |

**KM# 325 10 WON**
31.00 g., 0.999 Silver 0.9957 oz. ASW, 40.2 mm. **Obv:** State arms **Rev:** Children playing jacks **Edge:** Plain

| Date | Mintage | F12 | VF20 | XF40 | MS60 | MS63 |
|---|---|---|---|---|---|---|
| JU92-2003 | — | PF65 45.00 | | | | |

**KM# 326 10 WON**
31.00 g., 0.999 Silver 0.9957 oz. ASW, 40.2 mm. **Obv:** State arms **Rev:** Children kicking a shuttlecock **Edge:** Plain

| Date | Mintage | F12 | VF20 | XF40 | MS60 | MS63 |
|---|---|---|---|---|---|---|
| JU92-2003 | — | PF65 45.00 | | | | |

**KM# 409 10 WON**
30.94 g., 0.999 Silver 0.9937 oz. ASW, 40 mm. **Obv:** State arms **Rev:** Children spinning tops **Edge:** Plain

| Date | Mintage | F12 | VF20 | XF40 | MS60 | MS63 |
|---|---|---|---|---|---|---|
| JU92-2003 | — | PF65 45.00 | | | | |

**KM# 453 10 WON**
31.00 g., 0.999 Silver 0.9957 oz. ASW **Subject:** FIFA World Championship - Germany 2006 **Obv:** National arms **Rev:** Two hands holding up cup in rays at lower right, two smallplayers at left. **Rev. Legend:** WORLD CUP **Rev. Inscription:** FIFA

| Date | Mintage | F12 | VF20 | XF40 | MS60 | MS63 |
|---|---|---|---|---|---|---|
| JU92-2003 | — | PF65 60.00 | | | | |

**KM# 896 10 WON**
7.00 g., Aluminum, 40 mm. **Obv:** East gate of Pyeongand **Rev:** Sheep in center of Zodac

| Date | Mintage | F12 | VF20 | XF40 | MS60 | MS63 |
|---|---|---|---|---|---|---|
| 2003 | — | PF65 7.00 | | | | |

**KM# 898 10 WON**
31.11 g., 0.999 Silver 0.999 oz. ASW, 40 mm. **Obv:** Naitonal arms **Rev:** Sheep at center of Zodiac

| Date | Mintage | F12 | VF20 | XF40 | MS60 | MS63 |
|---|---|---|---|---|---|---|
| 2003 | — | PF65 60.00 | | | | |

**KM# 905 10 WON**
31.11 g., 0.999 Silver 0.999 oz. ASW, 40 mm. **Obv:** National arms, Central Bank name **Rev:** Highway and vehicles, train

| Date | Mintage | F12 | VF20 | XF40 | MS60 | MS63 |
|---|---|---|---|---|---|---|
| 2003 | Est. 1000 | PF65 70.00 | | | | |

**KM# 906 10 WON**
7.00 g., Aluminum, 40 mm. **Obv:** East gate of Pyeongyang **Rev:** Eulji Mundeok

| Date | Mintage | F12 | VF20 | XF40 | MS60 | MS63 |
|---|---|---|---|---|---|---|
| 2003 | — | PF65 7.00 | | | | |

**KM# 907 10 WON**
7.00 g., Aluminum, 40 mm. **Obv:** East gate of Pyrongyang **Rev:** Yeon Gaesomun

| Date | Mintage | F12 | VF20 | XF40 | MS60 | MS63 |
|---|---|---|---|---|---|---|
| 2003 | — | PF65 7.00 | | | | |

**KM# 908 10 WON**
7.00 g., Aluminum, 40 mm. **Obv:** East gate of Pyeongyang **Rev:** Gang Gaesomun

| Date | Mintage | F12 | VF20 | XF40 | MS60 | MS63 |
|---|---|---|---|---|---|---|
| 2003 | — | PF65 7.00 | | | | |

**KM# 911 10 WON**
28.00 g., Brass, 40 mm. **Obv:** East gate of Pyeongyang **Rev:** Gang Camchan

| Date | Mintage | F12 | VF20 | XF40 | MS60 | MS63 |
|---|---|---|---|---|---|---|
| 2003 | — | PF65 7.00 | | | | |

**KM# 915 10 WON**
7.00 g., Aluminum, 40 mm. **Obv:** East gate of Pyeongyang **Rev:** Turtle boat

| Date | Mintage | F12 | VF20 | XF40 | MS60 | MS63 |
|---|---|---|---|---|---|---|
| 2003 | — | PF65 7.00 | | | | |

**KM# 342 10 WON**
31.00 g., 0.999 Silver 0.9957 oz. ASW, 40 mm. **Obv:** State arms **Rev:** Domed building **Edge:** Plain

| Date | Mintage | F12 | VF20 | XF40 | MS60 | MS63 |
|---|---|---|---|---|---|---|
| JU93-2004 | — | PF65 47.50 | | | | |

**KM# 343 10 WON**
31.00 g., 0.999 Silver 0.9957 oz. ASW, 40 mm. **Obv:** State arms **Rev:** Pigeon on branch **Edge:** Segmented reeding

| Date | Mintage | F12 | VF20 | XF40 | MS60 | MS63 |
|---|---|---|---|---|---|---|
| JU93-2004 | — | PF65 45.00 | | | | |

**KM# 344 10 WON**
31.00 g., 0.999 Silver 0.9957 oz. ASW, 40 mm. **Obv:** State arms **Rev:** Two Leiothrix birds **Edge:** Segmented reeding

| Date | Mintage | F12 | VF20 | XF40 | MS60 | MS63 |
|---|---|---|---|---|---|---|
| JU93-2004 | — | PF65 45.00 | | | | |

**KM# 345 10 WON**
31.00 g., 0.999 Silver 0.9957 oz. ASW, 40 mm. **Obv:** State arms **Rev:** Two cranes standing in water **Edge:** Segmented reeding

| Date | Mintage | F12 | VF20 | XF40 | MS60 | MS63 |
|---|---|---|---|---|---|---|
| JU93-2004 | — | PF65 47.50 | | | | |

**KM# 346 10 WON**
31.00 g., 0.999 Silver 0.9957 oz. ASW, 40 mm. **Obv:** State arms **Rev:** Curlew bird **Edge:** Segmented reeding

| Date | Mintage | F12 | VF20 | XF40 | MS60 | MS63 |
|---|---|---|---|---|---|---|
| JU93-2004 | — | PF65 45.00 | | | | |

**KM# 347 10 WON**
31.00 g., 0.999 Silver 0.9957 oz. ASW, 40 mm. **Obv:** State arms **Rev:** Goshawk on branch **Edge:** Segmented reeding

| Date | Mintage | F12 | VF20 | XF40 | MS60 | MS63 |
|---|---|---|---|---|---|---|
| JU93-2004 | — | PF65 45.00 | | | | |

**KM# 418 10 WON**
31.00 g., 0.999 Silver 0.9957 oz. ASW, 39.7 mm. **Obv:** State arms **Rev:** Ibis standing in water **Edge:** Segmented reeding

| Date | Mintage | F12 | VF20 | XF40 | MS60 | MS63 |
|---|---|---|---|---|---|---|
| JU93-2004 | — | PF65 50.00 | | | | |

**KM# 938 10 WON**
31.11 g., 0.999 Silver 0.999 oz. ASW, 40 mm. **Obv:** National arms, Central Bank name **Rev:** Monkey King Sun Wukong from Journey to the West

| Date | Mintage | F12 | VF20 | XF40 | MS60 | MS63 |
|---|---|---|---|---|---|---|
| 2004 | — | PF65 70.00 | | | | |

**KM# 940 10 WON**
31.11 g., 0.999 Silver 0.999 oz. ASW, 40 mm. **Obv:** National arms, Central Bank name **Rev:** Monkey in center of Zodiac

| Date | Mintage | F12 | VF20 | XF40 | MS60 | MS63 |
|---|---|---|---|---|---|---|
| 2004 | — | PF65 60.00 | | | | |

**KM# 948 10 WON**
Silver, 32x46 mm. **Subject:** Deng Xiaoping, 100th Birth Anniversary **Obv:** National arms **Rev:** Deng Xiaoping saluting **Shape:** Vertical rectangle

| Date | Mintage | F12 | VF20 | XF40 | MS60 | MS63 |
|---|---|---|---|---|---|---|
| 2004 | — | PF65 60.00 | | | | |

**KM# 951 10 WON**
31.11 g., 0.999 Silver 0.999 oz. ASW, 40 mm. **Obv:** Naitonal arms, Central Bank name **Rev:** Broad throaded bird

| Date | Mintage | F12 | VF20 | XF40 | MS60 | MS63 |
|---|---|---|---|---|---|---|
| 2004 | — | PF65 45.00 | | | | |

**KM# 952 10 WON**
31.11 g., 0.999 Silver 0.999 oz. ASW, 40 mm. **Obv:** Naitonal arms, Central Bank name **Rev:** Imperial eagle

| Date | Mintage | F12 | VF20 | XF40 | MS60 | MS63 |
|---|---|---|---|---|---|---|
| 2004 | — | PF65 45.00 | | | | |

**KM# 953 10 WON**
31.11 g., 0.999 Silver 0.999 oz. ASW, 40 mm. **Obv:** National arms, Central Bank name **Rev:** Bittern

| Date | Mintage | F12 | VF20 | XF40 | MS60 | MS63 |
|---|---|---|---|---|---|---|
| 2004 | — | PF65 45.00 | | | | |

**KM# 954 10 WON**
31.11 g., 0.999 Silver 0.999 oz. ASW, 40 mm. **Obv:** National arms, Central Bank name **Rev:** Pheasant

| Date | Mintage | F12 | VF20 | XF40 | MS60 | MS63 |
|---|---|---|---|---|---|---|
| 2004 | — | PF65 45.00 | | | | |

**KM# 999 10 WON**
31.11 g., 0.999 Silver 0.999 oz. ASW, 40 mm. **Obv:** National arms, Central Bank name **Rev:** Tallinn castle in color, Estonian Krone

| Date | Mintage | F12 | VF20 | XF40 | MS60 | MS63 |
|---|---|---|---|---|---|---|
| 2004 | Est. 2004 | PF65 85.00 | | | | |

**KM# 1000 10 WON**
31.11 g., 0.999 Silver 0.999 oz. ASW, 40 mm. **Obv:** National arms, Central Bank name **Rev:** Malta's lira and Fort St. Angelo in color

| Date | Mintage | F12 | VF20 | XF40 | MS60 | MS63 |
|---|---|---|---|---|---|---|
| 2004 | — | PF65 85.00 | | | | |

**KM# 1001 10 WON**
31.11 g., 0.999 Silver 0.999 oz. ASW, 40 mm. **Obv:** National arms, Central Bank name **Rev:** Polish zloty and Danzig Grain Tower in color

| Date | Mintage | F12 | VF20 | XF40 | MS60 | MS63 |
|---|---|---|---|---|---|---|
| 2004 | — | PF65 85.00 | | | | |

**KM# 1002 10 WON**
31.11 g., 0.999 Silver 0.999 oz. ASW, 40 mm. **Obv:** National arms, Central Bank name **Rev:** Slovakian Korun and Bratislava castle in color

| Date | Mintage | F12 | VF20 | XF40 | MS60 | MS63 |
|---|---|---|---|---|---|---|
| 2004 | Est. 2004 | PF65 85.00 | | | | |

**KM# 1003 10 WON**
31.11 g., 0.999 Silver 0.999 oz. ASW, 40 mm. **Obv:** National arms, Central Bank name **Rev:** Czech Korun and Prague castle in color

| Date | Mintage | F12 | VF20 | XF40 | MS60 | MS63 |
|---|---|---|---|---|---|---|
| 2004 | Est. 2004 | PF65 85.00 | | | | |

**KM# 1004 10 WON**
31.11 g., 0.999 Silver 0.999 oz. ASW, 40 mm. **Obv:** National arms, Central Bank name **Rev:** Hungarian Forint and St. Stephan statue in Budapest castle in color

| Date | Mintage | F12 | VF20 | XF40 | MS60 | MS63 |
|---|---|---|---|---|---|---|
| 2004 | Est. 2004 | PF65 85.00 | | | | |

**KM# 1005 10 WON**
31.11 g., 0.999 Silver 0.999 oz. ASW, 40 mm. **Obv:** National arms, Central Bank name **Rev:** Cypriot Pound and Temple of Apollo

| Date | Mintage | F12 | VF20 | XF40 | MS60 | MS63 |
|---|---|---|---|---|---|---|
| 2004 | — | PF65 85.00 | | | | |

**KM# 1006 10 WON**
31.11 g., 0.999 Silver 0.999 oz. ASW, 40 mm. **Subject:** Athens olympics **Obv:** National arms, Central Bank name **Rev:** Discus thrower in color

| Date | Mintage | F12 | VF20 | XF40 | MS60 | MS63 |
|---|---|---|---|---|---|---|
| 2004 | — | PF65 115 | | | | |

**KM# 1007 10 WON**
31.11 g., 0.999 Silver 0.999 oz. ASW, 40 mm. **Obv:** National arms, Central Bank name **Rev:** Gorch Fock II sailing ship in color

| Date | Mintage | F12 | VF20 | XF40 | MS60 | MS63 |
|---|---|---|---|---|---|---|
| 2004 | Est. 2004 | PF65 115 | | | | |

**KM# 420 10 WON**
30.91 g., 0.999 Silver 0.9928 oz. ASW, 40 mm. **Subject:** End of WWII 60th Anniversary **Obv:** State arms **Rev:** Multicolor radiant map, doves, rainbow and inscription **Edge:** Plain

| Date | Mintage | F12 | VF20 | XF40 | MS60 | MS63 |
|---|---|---|---|---|---|---|
| JU94-2005 | — | PF65 45.00 | | | | |

**KM# 425 10 WON**
1.67 g., Aluminum, 23 mm. **Obv:** State arms **Rev:** Value

| Date | Mintage | F12 | VF20 | XF40 | MS60 | MS63 |
|---|---|---|---|---|---|---|
| JU94(2005) | — | — | — | — | 1.00 | 1.25 |

**KM# 1017 10 WON**
31.11 g., 0.999 Silver 0.999 oz. ASW, 40 mm. **Obv:** National arms, Central Bank name **Rev:** Rooster within Zodiac circle

| Date | Mintage | F12 | VF20 | XF40 | MS60 | MS63 |
|---|---|---|---|---|---|---|
| 2005 | — | PF65 50.00 | | | | |

**KM# 1021 10 WON**
7.00 g., Aluminum, 40 mm. **Obv:** East gate in Pyeongyang **Rev:** Hae Mosu in flight with the five dragons

| Date | Mintage | F12 | VF20 | XF40 | MS60 | MS63 |
|---|---|---|---|---|---|---|
| 2005 | — | PF65 20.00 | | | | |

**KM# 1023 10 WON**
31.11 g., 0.999 Silver 0.999 oz. ASW, 40 mm. **Obv:** National arms, Central Bank name **Rev:** Hae Mosu in flight with the five dragons

| Date | Mintage | F12 | VF20 | XF40 | MS60 | MS63 |
|---|---|---|---|---|---|---|
| 2005 | — | PF65 50.00 | | | | |

**KM# 1026 10 WON**
7.00 g., Aluminum, 40 mm. **Obv:** East gate of Pyeongyang **Rev:** Admiral Yi Sunsin and turtle boat

| Date | Mintage | F12 | VF20 | XF40 | MS60 | MS63 |
|---|---|---|---|---|---|---|
| 2005 | — | PF65 20.00 | | | | |

**KM# 1027 10 WON**
7.00 g., Aluminum, 40 mm. **Obv:** East gate of Pyeongyang **Rev:** General Hong Beomdo

| Date | Mintage | F12 | VF20 | XF40 | MS60 | MS63 |
|---|---|---|---|---|---|---|
| 2005 | — | PF65 20.00 | | | | |

**KM# 1030 10 WON**
31.11 g., 0.999 Silver 0.999 oz. ASW, 40 mm. **Obv:** National arms, Central Bank name **Rev:** Admiral Yi Sunsin and turtle boat

| Date | Mintage | F12 | VF20 | XF40 | MS60 | MS63 |
|---|---|---|---|---|---|---|
| 2005 | — | PF65 50.00 | | | | |

**KM# 1031 10 WON**
31.11 g., 0.999 Silver 0.999 oz. ASW, 40 mm. **Obv:** National arms, Central Bank name **Rev:** General Hong Beomdo

| Date | Mintage | F12 | VF20 | XF40 | MS60 | MS63 |
|---|---|---|---|---|---|---|
| 2005 | — | PF65 85.00 | | | | |

**KM# 1037 10 WON**
31.11 g., 0.999 Silver 0.999 oz. ASW, 40 mm. **Obv:** National arms, Central Bank name **Rev:** March before the monument of the three principals of reunification

| Date | Mintage | F12 | VF20 | XF40 | MS60 | MS63 |
|---|---|---|---|---|---|---|
| 2005 | — | PF65 50.00 | | | | |

**KM# 1038 10 WON**
31.11 g., 0.999 Silver 0.999 oz. ASW, 40 mm. **Obv:** National arms, Central Bank name **Rev:** Demonstrations before crater lake

| Date | Mintage | F12 | VF20 | XF40 | MS60 | MS63 |
|---|---|---|---|---|---|---|
| 2005 | — | PF65 50.00 | | | | |

**KM# 1039 10 WON**
31.11 g., 0.999 Silver 0.999 oz. ASW, 40 mm. **Obv:** National arms, Central Bank name **Rev:** Three drum dance

| Date | Mintage | F12 | VF20 | XF40 | MS60 | MS63 |
|---|---|---|---|---|---|---|
| 2005 | — | PF65 50.00 | | | | |

**KM# 1045 10 WON**
31.11 g., 0.999 Silver 0.999 oz. ASW, 40 mm. **Obv:** National arms, Central Bank name **Rev:** Tomb of the unknown solder in Moscow

| Date | Mintage | F12 | VF20 | XF40 | MS60 | MS63 |
|---|---|---|---|---|---|---|
| 2005 | — | PF65 85.00 | | | | |

**KM# 1046 10 WON**
31.11 g., 0.999 Silver 0.999 oz. ASW, 40 mm. **Obv:** National arms, Central Bank name **Rev:** Monument to mothers in St. Petersburg, Russian legend

| Date | Mintage | F12 | VF20 | XF40 | MS60 | MS63 |
|---|---|---|---|---|---|---|
| 2005 | — | PF65 85.00 | | | | |

**KM# 1090 10 WON**
7.00 g., Aluminum, 40 mm. **Obv:** East gate of Pyeongyang **Rev:** Ryuhwa, mother of King Dongmyeong

| Date | Mintage | F12 | VF20 | XF40 | MS60 | MS63 |
|---|---|---|---|---|---|---|
| 2006 | — | PF65 15.00 | | | | |

**KM# 1091 10 WON**
31.11 g., 0.999 Silver 0.999 oz. ASW, 40 mm. **Obv:** National arms, Central Bank name **Rev:** Ryuhwa, mother of King Dongmyeong

| Date | Mintage | F12 | VF20 | XF40 | MS60 | MS63 |
|---|---|---|---|---|---|---|
| 2006 proof | — | PF65 50.00 | | | | |

**KM# 496 10 WON**
7.00 g., Aluminum, 40 mm. **Rev:** Eastern City Gate in Pyeongyang

| Date | Mintage | F12 | VF20 | XF40 | MS60 | MS63 |
|---|---|---|---|---|---|---|
| 2007 | — | PF65 7.50 | | | | |

**KM# 501 10 WON**
7.00 g., Aluminum, 40 mm. **Obv:** Eastern city gate in Pyeongyang **Rev:** Brontosaurus

| Date | Mintage | F12 | VF20 | XF40 | MS60 | MS63 |
|---|---|---|---|---|---|---|
| 2007 | — | PF65 6.50 | | | | |

**KM# 508 10 WON**
7.00 g., Aluminum, 40 mm. **Obv:** Eastern gate in Pyeongyang **Rev:** Rainbow lori in color

| Date | Mintage | F12 | VF20 | XF40 | MS60 | MS63 |
|---|---|---|---|---|---|---|
| 2007 | — | PF65 8.50 | | | | |

**KM# 509 10 WON**
7.00 g., Aluminum **Obv:** Eastern Gate in Pyeongyang **Rev:** Manderian Duck in color

| Date | Mintage | F12 | VF20 | XF40 | MS60 | MS63 |
|---|---|---|---|---|---|---|
| 2007 | — | PF65 8.50 | | | | |

**KM# 514 10 WON**
7.00 g., Aluminum, 40 mm. **Obv:** East gate in Pyeoongyang **Rev:** Sports gym and emblem in color

| Date | Mintage | F12 | VF20 | XF40 | MS60 | MS63 |
|---|---|---|---|---|---|---|
| 2007 | — | PF65 8.50 | | | | |

**KM# 536 10 WON**
7.00 g., Aluminum, 40 mm. **Obv:** Eastern gate in Pyeongyang **Rev:** Growth in the Kaeseong area

| Date | Mintage | F12 | VF20 | XF40 | MS60 | MS63 |
|---|---|---|---|---|---|---|
| 2007 | — | PF65 7.50 | | | | |

**KM# 540 10 WON**
7.00 g., Aluminum, 40 mm. **Obv:** Eastern gate of Pyeongyang **Rev:** Panda seated eating

| Date | Mintage | F12 | VF20 | XF40 | MS60 | MS63 |
|---|---|---|---|---|---|---|
| 2007 | — | PF65 7.50 | | | | |

**KM# 543 10 WON**
7.00 g., Aluminum, 40 mm. **Obv:** Eastern gate in Pyeongyang **Rev:** Two pandas

| Date | Mintage | F12 | VF20 | XF40 | MS60 | MS63 |
|---|---|---|---|---|---|---|
| 2007 | — | PF65 7.50 | | | | |

**KM# 569 10 WON**
7.00 g., Aluminum, 40 mm. **Obv:** Eastern gate in Pyeongyang **Rev:** Rocket and satellite

| Date | Mintage | F12 | VF20 | XF40 | MS60 | MS63 |
|---|---|---|---|---|---|---|
| 2007 | — | PF65 6.50 | | | | |

**KM# 582 10 WON**
7.00 g., Aluminum, 40 mm. **Obv:** Eastern gate in Pyeongyang **Rev:** Dragon rising

| Date | Mintage | F12 | VF20 | XF40 | MS60 | MS63 |
|---|---|---|---|---|---|---|
| 2007 | — | PF65 6.00 | | | | |

**KM# 583 10 WON**
7.00 g., Aluminum, 40 mm. **Obv:** Eastern gate in Pyeongyang **Rev:** Two girls on seasaw

| Date | Mintage | F12 | VF20 | XF40 | MS60 | MS63 |
|---|---|---|---|---|---|---|
| 2007 | — | PF65 6.00 | | | | |

**KM# 584 10 WON**
7.00 g., Aluminum, 40 mm. **Obv:** Eastern gate in Pyeongyang **Rev:** Korean struggle

| Date | Mintage | F12 | VF20 | XF40 | MS60 | MS63 |
|---|---|---|---|---|---|---|
| 2007 | — | PF65 6.00 | | | | |

**KM# 585 10 WON**
7.00 g., Aluminum, 40 mm. **Obv:** Eastern gate in Pyeongyang **Rev:** Girl on swing

| Date | Mintage | F12 | VF20 | XF40 | MS60 | MS63 |
|---|---|---|---|---|---|---|
| 2007 | — | PF65 6.00 | | | | |

**KM# 586 10 WON**
7.00 g., Aluminum, 40 mm. **Obv:** Eastern gate in Pyeongyang **Rev:** Girls skipping

| Date | Mintage | F12 | VF20 | XF40 | MS60 | MS63 |
|---|---|---|---|---|---|---|
| 2007 | — | PF65 6.00 | | | | |

**KM# 610 10 WON**
7.00 g., Aluminum, 40 mm. **Obv:** Eastern gate in Pyeongyang **Rev:** Rabbit

| Date | Mintage | F12 | VF20 | XF40 | MS60 | MS63 |
|---|---|---|---|---|---|---|
| 2007 | — | PF65 7.50 | | | | |

**KM# 620 10 WON**
7.00 g., Aluminum, 40 mm. **Obv:** Eastern gate in Pyeongyang **Rev:** White bellied woodpecker

| Date | Mintage | F12 | VF20 | XF40 | MS60 | MS63 |
|---|---|---|---|---|---|---|
| 2007 | — | PF65 6.00 | | | | |

**KM# 621 10 WON**
7.00 g., Aluminum, 40 mm. **Obv:** Eastern gate in Pyeongyang **Rev:** Black grouse

| Date | Mintage | F12 | VF20 | XF40 | MS60 | MS63 |
|---|---|---|---|---|---|---|
| 2007 | — | PF65 6.00 | | | | |

**KM# 622 10 WON**
7.00 g., Aluminum, 40 mm. **Obv:** Eastern gate in Pyeongyang **Rev:** Sand Grouse

| Date | Mintage | F12 | VF20 | XF40 | MS60 | MS63 |
|---|---|---|---|---|---|---|
| 2007 | — | PF65 6.00 | | | | |

**KM# 623 10 WON**
7.00 g., Aluminum, 40 mm. **Obv:** Eastern gate in Pyeongyang **Rev:** Indian Pitta bird

| Date | Mintage | F12 | VF20 | XF40 | MS60 | MS63 |
|---|---|---|---|---|---|---|
| 2007 | — | PF65 6.00 | | | | |

**KM# 632 10 WON**
7.00 g., Aluminum, 40 mm. **Obv:** Eastern gate in Pyeongyang **Rev:** Blue dragon right

| Date | Mintage | F12 | VF20 | XF40 | MS60 | MS63 |
|---|---|---|---|---|---|---|
| 2007 | — | PF65 15.00 | | | | |

**KM# 637 10 WON**
7.00 g., Aluminum, 40 mm. **Obv:** Eastern gate in Pyeongyang **Rev:** Two siberian tigers

| Date | Mintage | F12 | VF20 | XF40 | MS60 | MS63 |
|---|---|---|---|---|---|---|
| 2007 | — | PF65 6.00 | | | | |

**KM# 649 10 WON**
Aluminum, 40 mm. **Obv:** Eastern gate in Pyeongyang **Rev:** King Goguryeo

| Date | Mintage | F12 | VF20 | XF40 | MS60 | MS63 |
|---|---|---|---|---|---|---|
| 2007 | — | PF65 15.00 | | | | |

**KM# 650 10 WON**
Aluminum, 40 mm. **Obv:** Eastern gate in Pyeongyang **Rev:** Buddha figure

| Date | Mintage | F12 | VF20 | XF40 | MS60 | MS63 |
|---|---|---|---|---|---|---|
| 2007 | — | PF65 15.00 | | | | |

**KM# 651 10 WON**
Aluminum, 40 mm. **Obv:** Eastern gate in Pyeongyang **Rev:** King Gojoseon

| Date | Mintage | F12 | VF20 | XF40 | MS60 | MS63 |
|---|---|---|---|---|---|---|
| 2007 | — | PF65 6.00 | | | | |

**KM# 667 10 WON**
7.00 g., Aluminum, 40 mm. **Obv:** Eastern gate in Pyeongyang **Rev:** First married couple to see again since the 1945 division

| Date | Mintage | F12 | VF20 | XF40 | MS60 | MS63 |
|---|---|---|---|---|---|---|
| 2007 | — | PF65 15.00 | | | | |

**KM# 715 10 WON**
7.00 g., Aluminum, 40 mm. **Obv:** East gate of Pyeongyang **Rev:** Celadon pottery

| Date | Mintage | F12 | VF20 | XF40 | MS60 | MS63 |
|---|---|---|---|---|---|---|
| 2007 | — | PF65 6.00 | | | | |

**KM# 802 10 WON**
7.00 g., Aluminum, 40 mm. **Obv:** East gate in Pyeongyang **Rev:** Reconstruction of the mausoleum for King Dangun

| Date | Mintage | F12 | VF20 | XF40 | MS60 | MS63 |
|---|---|---|---|---|---|---|
| 2007 | — | PF65 10.00 | | | | |

**KM# 803 10 WON**
7.00 g., Aluminum, 40 mm. **Obv:** East gatet in Pyeongyang **Rev:** Dongmyeong, 1st King of Goguryeb

| Date | Mintage | F12 | VF20 | XF40 | MS60 | MS63 |
|---|---|---|---|---|---|---|
| 2007 | — | PF65 10.00 | | | | |

**KM# 804 10 WON**
7.00 g., Aluminum, 40 mm. **Obv:** East gate in Pyeongyang **Rev:** Wanggeon, 1st king of Goryeo dynasty

| Date | Mintage | F12 | VF20 | XF40 | MS60 | MS63 |
|---|---|---|---|---|---|---|
| 2007 | — | PF65 10.00 | | | | |

**KM# 805 10 WON**
7.00 g., Aluminum, 40 mm. **Obv:** East gate in Pyeongyang **Rev:** Jeong Mongju

| Date | Mintage | F12 | VF20 | XF40 | MS60 | MS63 |
|---|---|---|---|---|---|---|
| 2007 | — | PF65 10.00 | | | | |

**KM# 806 10 WON**
7.00 g., Aluminum, 40 mm. **Obv:** East gate in Pyeongyang **Rev:** Jeon Bongjun

| Date | Mintage | F12 | VF20 | XF40 | MS60 | MS63 |
|---|---|---|---|---|---|---|
| 2007 | — | PF65 10.00 | | | | |

**KM# 850 10 WON**
7.00 g., Aluminum, 40 mm. **Obv:** East gate of Pyeongyang **Rev:** Dancer

| Date | Mintage | F12 | VF20 | XF40 | MS60 | MS63 |
|---|---|---|---|---|---|---|
| 2007 | — | PF65 6.00 | | | | |

**KM# 851 10 WON**
7.00 g., Aluminum, 40 mm. **Obv:** East gate of Pyeongyang **Rev:** Dancer

| Date | Mintage | F12 | VF20 | XF40 | MS60 | MS63 |
|---|---|---|---|---|---|---|
| 2007 | — | PF65 7.00 | | | | |

**KM# 852 10 WON**
7.00 g., Aluminum, 40 mm. **Obv:** National arms, Central Bank name **Rev:** Female in national costume

| Date | Mintage | F12 | VF20 | XF40 | MS60 | MS63 |
|---|---|---|---|---|---|---|
| 2007 | — | PF65 7.00 | | | | |

**KM# 853 10 WON**
7.00 g., Aluminum, 40 mm. **Obv:** National arms, Central Bank name **Rev:** Crane dancer

| Date | Mintage | F12 | VF20 | XF40 | MS60 | MS63 |
|---|---|---|---|---|---|---|
| 2007 | — | PF65 7.00 | | | | |

**KM# 854 10 WON**
7.00 g., Aluminum, 40 mm. **Obv:** National arms, Central Bank name **Rev:** Fairy princess

| Date | Mintage | F12 | VF20 | XF40 | MS60 | MS63 |
|---|---|---|---|---|---|---|
| 2007 | — | PF65 7.00 | | | | |

**KM# 880 10 WON**
6.00 g., 0.999 Aluminum 0.1927 oz., 38 mm. **Obv:** East gate of Pyeongyang **Rev:** Taekwando

| Date | Mintage | F12 | VF20 | XF40 | MS60 | MS63 |
|---|---|---|---|---|---|---|
| 2007 | — | PF65 6.00 | | | | |

**KM# 736 20 WON**
28.00 g., Brass, 40 mm. **Obv:** East gate of Pyeongyang **Rev:** Married couple before Korean flag and ferryboat

| Date | Mintage | F12 | VF20 | XF40 | MS60 | MS63 |
|---|---|---|---|---|---|---|
| 2001 | — | PF65 20.00 | | | | |

**KM# 737 20 WON**
28.00 g., Brass, 40 mm. **Obv:** East gate of Pyeongyang **Rev:** Ferryboat between Korea and Japan

| Date | Mintage | F12 | VF20 | XF40 | MS60 | MS63 |
|---|---|---|---|---|---|---|
| 2001 | — | PF65 7.00 | | | | |

**KM# 738 20 WON**
28.00 g., Brass, 40 mm. **Obv:** East gate in Pyeongyang **Rev:** Triumphial arch of Moranbong in Pyeongyang

| Date | Mintage | F12 | VF20 | XF40 | MS60 | MS63 |
|---|---|---|---|---|---|---|
| 2001 | — | PF65 20.00 | | | | |

**KM# 739 20 WON**
28.00 g., Brass, 40 mm. **Obv:** East gate in Pyeongyang **Rev:** Chonji crater in Paektusan

| Date | Mintage | F12 | VF20 | XF40 | MS60 | MS63 |
|---|---|---|---|---|---|---|
| 2001 | — | PF65 20.00 | | | | |

**KM# 768 20 WON**
16.00 g., Brass, 35 mm. **Obv:** East gate of Pyeongyang **Rev:** Chinese Dragon boat

| Date | Mintage | F12 | VF20 | XF40 | MS60 | MS63 |
|---|---|---|---|---|---|---|
| 2001 | — | PF65 7.00 | | | | |

**KM# 777 20 WON**
28.00 g., Brass, 40 mm. **Obv:** East gate of Pyeongyang **Rev:** Taekwondo kicker

| Date | Mintage | F12 | VF20 | XF40 | MS60 | MS63 |
|---|---|---|---|---|---|---|
| 2001 | — | PF65 7.00 | | | | |

**KM# 778 20 WON**
28.00 g., Brass, 40 mm. **Obv:** East gate of Pyeongyang **Rev:** Two taekwondo players

| Date | Mintage | F12 | VF20 | XF40 | MS60 | MS63 |
|---|---|---|---|---|---|---|
| 2001 | — | PF65 7.00 | | | | |

**KM# 787 20 WON**
16.00 g., Brass, 35 mm. **Obv:** East gate of Pyeongyang **Rev:** Horse head

| Date | Mintage | F12 | VF20 | XF40 | MS60 | MS63 |
|---|---|---|---|---|---|---|
| 2002 | — | PF65 7.00 | | | | |

**KM# 788 20 WON**
16.00 g., Brass, 35 mm. **Obv:** East gate of Pyeongyang **Rev:** Horse right

| Date | Mintage | F12 | VF20 | XF40 | MS60 | MS63 |
|---|---|---|---|---|---|---|
| 2002 | — | PF65 20.00 | | | | |

**KM# 789 20 WON**
28.00 g., Brass, 40 mm. **Obv:** East gate of Pyeongyang **Rev:** Two horses

| Date | Mintage | F12 | VF20 | XF40 | MS60 | MS63 |
|---|---|---|---|---|---|---|
| 2002 | — | PF65 7.00 | | | | |

**KM# 809 20 WON**
28.00 g., Brass, 40 mm. **Obv:** East gate of Pyeongyang **Rev:** Wanggeon, 1st King of Goryeo dynasty

| Date | Mintage | F12 | VF20 | XF40 | MS60 | MS63 |
|---|---|---|---|---|---|---|
| 2002 | — | PF65 7.00 | | | | |

**KM# 810 20 WON**
28.00 g., Brass, 40 mm. **Obv:** East gate of Pyeongyang **Rev:** Jeong Mongju

| Date | Mintage | F12 | VF20 | XF40 | MS60 | MS63 |
|---|---|---|---|---|---|---|
| 2002 | — | PF65 7.00 | | | | |

**KM# 830 20 WON**
28.00 g., Brass, 40 mm. **Obv:** East gate of Pyeongyang **Rev:** Resconstruction of the Mausoleums of King Dongmyeong

| Date | Mintage | F12 | VF20 | XF40 | MS60 | MS63 |
|---|---|---|---|---|---|---|
| 2002 | — | PF65 7.00 | | | | |

**KM# 831 20 WON**
28.00 g., Brass, 40 mm. **Obv:** East gate of Pyeongyang **Rev:** Mausoleum of King Gongmin

| Date | Mintage | F12 | VF20 | XF40 | MS60 | MS63 |
|---|---|---|---|---|---|---|
| 2002 | — | PF65 7.00 | | | | |

**KM# 832 20 WON**
28.00 g., Brass, 40 mm. **Obv:** East gate of Pyeongyang **Rev:** Stadium

| Date | Mintage | F12 | VF20 | XF40 | MS60 | MS63 |
|---|---|---|---|---|---|---|
| 2002 | — | PF65 7.00 | | | | |

**KM# 866 20 WON**
28.00 g., Brass, 40 mm. **Obv:** East gate of Pyeongyang **Rev:** Map of Korea with the four cardinal directions

| Date | Mintage | F12 | VF20 | XF40 | MS60 | MS63 |
|---|---|---|---|---|---|---|
| 2002 | — | PF65 7.00 | | | | |

**KM# 867 20 WON**
28.00 g., Brass, 40 mm. **Obv:** East gate of Pyeongyeong **Rev:** Rythem dancers and map of Korea

| Date | Mintage | F12 | VF20 | XF40 | MS60 | MS63 |
|---|---|---|---|---|---|---|
| 2002 | — | PF65 7.00 | | | | |

**KM# 897 20 WON**
28.00 g., Brass, 40 mm. **Obv:** East gate of Pyeongyang **Rev:** Sheep in center of Zodiac

| Date | Mintage | F12 | VF20 | XF40 | MS60 | MS63 |
|---|---|---|---|---|---|---|
| 2003 | — | PF65 7.00 | | | | |

**KM# 909 20 WON**
28.00 g., Brass, 40 mm. **Obv:** East gate of Pyeongyang **Rev:** Eulji Mundeok

| Date | Mintage | F12 | VF20 | XF40 | MS60 | MS63 |
|---|---|---|---|---|---|---|
| 2003 | — | PF65 7.00 | | | | |

**KM# 910 20 WON**
28.00 g., Brass, 40 mm. **Obv:** East gate in Pyeongyang **Rev:** Yeon Gaesomun

| Date | Mintage | F12 | VF20 | XF40 | MS60 | MS63 |
|---|---|---|---|---|---|---|
| 2003 | — | PF65 7.00 | | | | |

**KM# 916 20 WON**
28.00 g., Brass, 40 mm. **Obv:** East gate of Pyeongyang **Rev:** Turtle boat

| Date | Mintage | F12 | VF20 | XF40 | MS60 | MS63 |
|---|---|---|---|---|---|---|
| 2003 | — | PF65 7.00 | | | | |

**KM# 256 20 WON**
42.06 g., 0.999 Silver 1.3509 oz. ASW, 45.1 mm. **Obv:** State arms **Rev:** Rose of sharon flower **Edge:** Plain

| Date | Mintage | F12 | VF20 | XF40 | MS60 | MS63 |
|---|---|---|---|---|---|---|
| JU93-2004 | — | PF65 65.00 | | | | |

### KM# 257 20 WON

42.22 g., 0.999 Silver 1.3559 oz. ASW, 45.1 mm. **Obv:** State arms **Rev:** Kim Jong-Il, Peony flower **Edge:** Plain

| Date | Mintage | F12 | VF20 | XF40 | MS60 | MS63 |
|---|---|---|---|---|---|---|
| JU93-2004 | — | PF65 65.00 | | | | |

### KM# 258 20 WON

41.92 g., 0.999 Silver 1.3464 oz. ASW, 45.1 mm. **Obv:** State arms **Rev:** Kim Il-seung, Orchid flowers **Edge:** Plain

| Date | Mintage | F12 | VF20 | XF40 | MS60 | MS63 |
|---|---|---|---|---|---|---|
| JU93-2004 | — | PF65 65.00 | | | | |

### KM# 259 20 WON

42.00 g., 0.999 Silver 1.349 oz. ASW, 45.1 mm. **Obv:** State arms **Rev:** Kim Il Sung's birth place, side view **Edge:** Plain

| Date | Mintage | F12 | VF20 | XF40 | MS60 | MS63 |
|---|---|---|---|---|---|---|
| JU93-2004 | — | PF65 65.00 | | | | |

### KM# 260 20 WON

41.62 g., 0.999 Silver 1.3368 oz. ASW, 45.1 mm. **Obv:** State arms **Rev:** Mountain cabin **Edge:** Plain

| Date | Mintage | F12 | VF20 | XF40 | MS60 | MS63 |
|---|---|---|---|---|---|---|
| JU93-2004 | — | PF65 65.00 | | | | |

### KM# 261 20 WON

41.91 g., 0.999 Silver 1.3461 oz. ASW, 45.1 mm. **Obv:** State arms **Rev:** Kim Il Sung's birth place, front view **Edge:** Plain

| Date | Mintage | F12 | VF20 | XF40 | MS60 | MS63 |
|---|---|---|---|---|---|---|
| JU93-2004 | — | PF65 65.00 | | | | |

### KM# 340 20 WON

31.00 g., 0.999 Silver 0.9957 oz. ASW, 39.8 mm. **Obv:** State arms **Rev:** Kim Jong-Il and Vladimir Putin clasping hands **Edge:** Segmented reeding

| Date | Mintage | F12 | VF20 | XF40 | MS60 | MS63 |
|---|---|---|---|---|---|---|
| 2004 | — | PF65 50.00 | | | | |

### KM# 341 20 WON

31.00 g., 0.999 Silver 0.9957 oz. ASW, 39.8 mm. **Obv:** State arms **Rev:** Bust facing **Edge:** Segmented reeding

| Date | Mintage | F12 | VF20 | XF40 | MS60 | MS63 |
|---|---|---|---|---|---|---|
| 2004 | — | PF65 50.00 | | | | |

### KM# 419 20 WON

31.00 g., 0.999 Silver 0.9957 oz. ASW, 39.75 mm. **Subject:** Historic Pyongyang Meeting **Obv:** State arms **Rev:** Kim Jong-Il and Kim Dae-Jung clasping hands, English legend **Edge:** Segmented reeding

| Date | Mintage | F12 | VF20 | XF40 | MS60 | MS63 |
|---|---|---|---|---|---|---|
| 2004 | — | PF65 50.00 | | | | |

### KM# 942 20 WON

19.00 g., Copper, 23x40 mm. **Obv:** East gate of Pyeongyang **Rev:** Marmoset **Shape:** Rectangle

| Date | Mintage | F12 | VF20 | XF40 | MS60 | MS63 |
|---|---|---|---|---|---|---|
| 2004 | — | PF65 8.00 | | | | |

### KM# 943 20 WON

19.00 g., Copper, 23x40 mm. **Obv:** East gate of Pyeongyang **Rev:** Blue monkey

| Date | Mintage | F12 | VF20 | XF40 | MS60 | MS63 |
|---|---|---|---|---|---|---|
| 2004 | — | PF65 8.00 | | | | |

### KM# 944 20 WON

19.00 g., Copper, 23x40 mm. **Obv:** East gate of Pyeongyang **Rev:** two monkies

| Date | Mintage | F12 | VF20 | XF40 | MS60 | MS63 |
|---|---|---|---|---|---|---|
| 2004 | — | PF65 8.00 | | | | |

### KM# 949 20 WON

Brass, 40 mm. **Obv:** East gate of Pyeongyang **Rev:** Sports hall in Pyeongyang

| Date | Mintage | F12 | VF20 | XF40 | MS60 | MS63 |
|---|---|---|---|---|---|---|
| 2004 | — | PF65 14.00 | | | | |

### KM# 955 20 WON

42.22 g., 0.999 Silver 1.3559 oz. ASW, 45 mm. **Obv:** National arms, Central Bank name **Rev:** Kim Ilseong

| Date | Mintage | F12 | VF20 | XF40 | MS60 | MS63 |
|---|---|---|---|---|---|---|
| 2004 | — | PF65 70.00 | | | | |

### KM# 956 20 WON

42.22 g., 0.999 Silver 1.3559 oz. ASW, 45 mm. **Obv:** National arms, Central Bank name **Rev:** Kim Jeongil

| Date | Mintage | F12 | VF20 | XF40 | MS60 | MS63 |
|---|---|---|---|---|---|---|
| 2004 | — | PF65 70.00 | | | | |

### KM# 957 20 WON

42.22 g., 0.999 Silver 1.3559 oz. ASW, 45 mm. **Obv:** Naitonal arms, Central Bank name **Rev:** Kim Jeongsuk

| Date | Mintage | F12 | VF20 | XF40 | MS60 | MS63 |
|---|---|---|---|---|---|---|
| 2004 | — | PF65 70.00 | | | | |

### KM# 966 20 WON

31.11 g., 0.999 Silver 0.999 oz. ASW, 40 mm. **Obv:** National arms, Central Bank name **Rev:** Kim Jeongil and Hu Jintao

| Date | Mintage | F12 | VF20 | XF40 | MS60 | MS63 |
|---|---|---|---|---|---|---|
| 2004 | — | PF65 60.00 | | | | |

**KM# 977 20 WON**
31.11 g., 0.999 Silver 0.999 oz. ASW, 40 mm. **Obv:** Dokdo, rocky islands, Central Bank name **Rev:** Map of the island group

| Date | Mintage | F12 | VF20 | XF40 | MS60 | MS63 |
|---|---|---|---|---|---|---|
| 2004 | — | PF65 70.00 | | | | |

**KM# 978 20 WON**
31.11 g., 0.999 Silver 0.999 oz. ASW, 40 mm. **Obv:** Dokdo, rocky islands, Central Bank name **Rev:** Fisher Ahn Yongbok

| Date | Mintage | F12 | VF20 | XF40 | MS60 | MS63 |
|---|---|---|---|---|---|---|
| 2004 | — | PF65 70.00 | | | | |

**KM# 979 20 WON**
31.11 g., 0.999 Silver 0.999 oz. ASW, 40 mm. **Obv:** Dokdo, rocky islands, Central Bank name **Rev:** West island

| Date | Mintage | F12 | VF20 | XF40 | MS60 | MS63 |
|---|---|---|---|---|---|---|
| 2004 | — | PF65 70.00 | | | | |

**KM# 980 20 WON**
31.11 g., 0.999 Silver 0.999 oz. ASW, 40 mm. **Obv:** Dokdo, rocky islands, Central Bank name **Rev:** East island

| Date | Mintage | F12 | VF20 | XF40 | MS60 | MS63 |
|---|---|---|---|---|---|---|
| 2004 | — | PF65 70.00 | | | | |

**KM# 981 20 WON**
31.11 g., 0.999 Silver 0.999 oz. ASW, 40 mm. **Obv:** Dokdo, rocky islands, Central Bank name **Rev:** Three brother island

| Date | Mintage | F12 | VF20 | XF40 | MS60 | MS63 |
|---|---|---|---|---|---|---|
| 2004 | — | PF65 70.00 | | | | |

**KM# 982 20 WON**
31.11 g., 0.999 Silver 0.999 oz. ASW, 40 mm. **Obv:** Dokdo, rocky islands, Central Bank name **Rev:** Chicken island

| Date | Mintage | F12 | VF20 | XF40 | MS60 | MS63 |
|---|---|---|---|---|---|---|
| 2004 | — | PF65 70.00 | | | | |

**KM# 983 20 WON**
31.11 g., 0.999 Silver 0.999 oz. ASW, 40 mm. **Obv:** Dokdo, rocky islands, Central Bank name **Rev:** Candle island

| Date | Mintage | F12 | VF20 | XF40 | MS60 | MS63 |
|---|---|---|---|---|---|---|
| 2004 | — | PF65 70.00 | | | | |

**KM# 984 20 WON**
31.11 g., 0.999 Silver 0.999 oz. ASW, 40 mm. **Obv:** Dokdo, rocky islands, Central Bank name **Rev:** Dome island

| Date | Mintage | F12 | VF20 | XF40 | MS60 | MS63 |
|---|---|---|---|---|---|---|
| 2004 | — | PF65 70.00 | | | | |

**KM# 478 20 WON**
27.30 g., Brass, 40 mm. **Obv:** Temple **Rev:** Multicolor rooster right

| Date | Mintage | F12 | VF20 | XF40 | MS60 | MS63 |
|---|---|---|---|---|---|---|
| 2005 | — | PF65 10.00 | | | | |

**KM# 479 20 WON**
31.11 g., 0.999 Silver 0.999 oz. ASW **Obv:** Arms **Rev:** A puppy, dog's head facing

| Date | Mintage | F12 | VF20 | XF40 | MS60 | MS63 |
|---|---|---|---|---|---|---|
| 2005 | — | PF65 45.00 | | | | |

**KM# 1022 20 WON**
28.00 g., Brass, 40 mm. **Obv:** East gate of Pyeongyang **Rev:** Hae Mosu in flight with the five dragons

| Date | Mintage | F12 | VF20 | XF40 | MS60 | MS63 |
|---|---|---|---|---|---|---|
| 2005 | — | PF65 20.00 | | | | |

**KM# 1028 20 WON**
28.00 g., Brass, 40 mm. **Obv:** East gate of Pyeongyang **Rev:** Admiral Yi Sunsin and turtle boat

| Date | Mintage | F12 | VF20 | XF40 | MS60 | MS63 |
|---|---|---|---|---|---|---|
| 2005 | — | PF65 12.50 | | | | |

**KM# 1029 20 WON**
28.00 g., Brass, 40 mm. **Obv:** East gate of Pyeongyong **Rev:** General Hong Beomdo

| Date | Mintage | F12 | VF20 | XF40 | MS60 | MS63 |
|---|---|---|---|---|---|---|
| 2005 | — | PF65 12.50 | | | | |

**KM# 1041 20 WON**
28.00 g., Brass, 40 mm. **Obv:** East gate of Pyeongyang **Rev:** Map of Korea, pair of peace doves, rainbow

| Date | Mintage | F12 | VF20 | XF40 | MS60 | MS63 |
|---|---|---|---|---|---|---|
| 2005 | — | PF65 12.50 | | | | |

**KM# 1049 20 WON**
31.11 g., 0.999 Silver 0.999 oz. ASW, 40 mm. **Obv:** National arms, Central Bank name **Rev:** Dongmyeong, 1st king of Goguryeo

| Date | Mintage | F12 | VF20 | XF40 | MS60 | MS63 |
|---|---|---|---|---|---|---|
| 2005 | — | PF65 65.00 | | | | |

**KM# 1050 20 WON**
31.11 g., 0.999 Silver 0.999 oz. ASW, 40 mm. **Obv:** National arms, Central Bank name **Rev:** Blue dragon, Cheongryong, of the East

| Date | Mintage | F12 | VF20 | XF40 | MS60 | MS63 |
|---|---|---|---|---|---|---|
| 2005 | — | PF65 45.00 | | | | |

**KM# 1051 20 WON**
31.11 g., 0.999 Silver 0.999 oz. ASW, 40 mm. **Obv:** National arms, Central Bank name **Rev:** Red bird, Jujak, of the South

| Date | Mintage | F12 | VF20 | XF40 | MS60 | MS63 |
|---|---|---|---|---|---|---|
| 2005 | — | PF65 45.00 | | | | |

**KM# 1052 20 WON**
31.11 g., 0.999 Silver 0.999 oz. ASW, 40 mm. **Obv:** National arms, Central Bank name **Rev:** White tiger, Baekho, of the West

| Date | Mintage | F12 | VF20 | XF40 | MS60 | MS63 |
|---|---|---|---|---|---|---|
| 2005 | — | PF65 45.00 | | | | |

**KM# 1053 20 WON**
31.11 g., 0.999 Silver 0.999 oz. ASW, 40 mm. **Obv:** National arms, Central Bank name **Rev:** Black snake, Hyeonmu, of the North

| Date | Mintage | F12 | VF20 | XF40 | MS60 | MS63 |
|---|---|---|---|---|---|---|
| 2005 | — | PF65 45.00 | | | | |

**KM# 1054 20 WON**
31.11 g., 0.999 Silver 0.999 oz. ASW, 40 mm. **Obv:** National arms, Central Bank name **Rev:** Horse and rider

| Date | Mintage | F12 | VF20 | XF40 | MS60 | MS63 |
|---|---|---|---|---|---|---|
| 2005 | — | PF65 45.00 | | | | |

**KM# 1055 20 WON**
31.11 g., 0.999 Silver 0.999 oz. ASW, 40 mm. **Obv:** National arms, Central Bank name **Rev:** Horse drummers

| Date | Mintage | F12 | VF20 | XF40 | MS60 | MS63 |
|---|---|---|---|---|---|---|
| 2005 | — | PF65 45.00 | | | | |

**KM# 1056 20 WON**
31.11 g., 0.999 Silver 0.999 oz. ASW, 40 mm. **Obv:** National arms, Central Bank name **Rev:** Bugler to horse

| Date | Mintage | F12 | VF20 | XF40 | MS60 | MS63 |
|---|---|---|---|---|---|---|
| 2005 | — | PF65 45.00 | | | | |

**KM# 1057 20 WON**
31.11 g., 0.999 Silver 0.999 oz. ASW, 40 mm. **Obv:** National arms, Central Bank name **Rev:** Horseback hunter

| Date | Mintage | F12 | VF20 | XF40 | MS60 | MS63 |
|---|---|---|---|---|---|---|
| 2005 | — | PF65 45.00 | | | | |

**KM# 1058 20 WON**
31.11 g., 0.999 Silver 0.999 oz. ASW, 40 mm. **Obv:** National arms, Central Bank name **Rev:** Crane and bamboo image by Yi Kyeongyun

| Date | Mintage | F12 | VF20 | XF40 | MS60 | MS63 |
|---|---|---|---|---|---|---|
| 2005 | — | PF65 65.00 | | | | |

**KM# 1059 20 WON**
31.11 g., 0.999 Silver 0.999 oz. ASW, 40 mm. **Obv:** National arms, Central Bank name **Rev:** Ibis, image by Kim Sik

| Date | Mintage | F12 | VF20 | XF40 | MS60 | MS63 |
|---|---|---|---|---|---|---|
| 2005 | — | PF65 65.00 | | | | |

**KM# 1060 20 WON**
31.11 g., 0.999 Silver 0.999 oz. ASW, 40 mm. **Obv:** National arms, Central Bank name **Rev:** Pheasant by Jang Seungeop

| Date | Mintage | F12 | VF20 | XF40 | MS60 | MS63 |
|---|---|---|---|---|---|---|
| 2005 | — | PF65 65.00 | | | | |

**KM# 1061 20 WON**
31.11 g., 0.999 Silver 0.999 oz. ASW, 40 mm. **Obv:** National arms, Central Bank name **Rev:** Fairy princess of the diamond mountain

| Date | Mintage | F12 | VF20 | XF40 | MS60 | MS63 |
|---|---|---|---|---|---|---|
| 2005 | — | PF65 65.00 | | | | |

**KM# 1062 20 WON**
31.11 g., 0.999 Silver 0.999 oz. ASW, 40 mm. **Obv:** National arms, Central Bank name **Rev:** Big stone in the diamond mountain

| Date | Mintage | F12 | VF20 | XF40 | MS60 | MS63 |
|---|---|---|---|---|---|---|
| 2005 | — | PF65 65.00 | | | | |

**KM# 1063 20 WON**
31.11 g., 0.999 Silver 0.999 oz. ASW, 40 mm. **Obv:** National arms, Central Bank name **Rev:** Two rabbits

| Date | Mintage | F12 | VF20 | XF40 | MS60 | MS63 |
|---|---|---|---|---|---|---|
| 2005 | Est. 2000 | PF65 45.00 | | | | |

**KM# 1064 20 WON**
31.11 g., 0.999 Silver 0.999 oz. ASW, 40 mm. **Obv:** National arms, Central Bank name **Rev:** Cat

| Date | Mintage | F12 | VF20 | XF40 | MS60 | MS63 |
|---|---|---|---|---|---|---|
| 2005 | Est. 2000 | PF65 45.00 | | | | |

**KM# 1065 20 WON**
31.11 g., 0.999 Silver 0.999 oz. ASW, 40 mm. **Subject:** North-South Railway connection **Obv:** National arms, Central Bank name **Rev:** Map of Korea and railway line

| Date | Mintage | F12 | VF20 | XF40 | MS60 | MS63 |
|---|---|---|---|---|---|---|
| 2005 | — | PF65 65.00 | | | | |

**KM# 1066 20 WON**
31.11 g., 0.999 Silver 0.999 oz. ASW, 40 mm. **Obv:** National arms, Central Bank name **Rev:** FIFA World Cup trophy

| Date | Mintage | F12 | VF20 | XF40 | MS60 | MS63 |
|---|---|---|---|---|---|---|
| 2005 | — | PF65 45.00 | | | | |

**KM# 480 20 WON**
23.70 g., Brass, 40 mm. **Obv:** Temple **Rev:** Multicolor German shepard

| Date | Mintage | F12 | VF20 | XF40 | MS60 | MS63 |
|---|---|---|---|---|---|---|
| 2006 | — | PF65 10.00 | | | | |

**KM# 481 20 WON**
Brass **Obv:** Arms **Rev:** Bejeweled female head

| Date | Mintage | F12 | VF20 | XF40 | MS60 | MS63 |
|---|---|---|---|---|---|---|
| 2006 | — | PF65 10.00 | | | | |

**KM# 482 20 WON**
27.30 g., Brass, 40 mm. **Obv:** Temple **Rev:** Multicolor pig and pigletts

| Date | Mintage | F12 | VF20 | XF40 | MS60 | MS63 |
|---|---|---|---|---|---|---|
| 2007 | — | PF65 10.00 | | | | |

**KM# 497 20 WON**
28.00 g., Brass, 40 mm. **Rev:** Eastern city gate of Pyeongyang

| Date | Mintage | F12 | VF20 | XF40 | MS60 | MS63 |
|---|---|---|---|---|---|---|
| 2007 | — | PF65 8.50 | | | | |

**KM# 502 20 WON**
28.00 g., Brass, 40 mm. **Obv:** Eastern city gate of Pyeongyang **Rev:** Brontosaurus

| Date | Mintage | F12 | VF20 | XF40 | MS60 | MS63 |
|---|---|---|---|---|---|---|
| 2007 | — | PF65 8.50 | | | | |

**KM# 570 20 WON**
28.00 g., Brass, 40 mm. **Obv:** Eastern gate in Pyeongyang **Rev:** Rocket and satellite

| Date | Mintage | F12 | VF20 | XF40 | MS60 | MS63 |
|---|---|---|---|---|---|---|
| 2007 | — | PF65 7.50 | | | | |

**KM# 587 20 WON**
28.00 g., Brass, 40 mm. **Obv:** Eastern gate in Pyeongyang **Rev:** Dragon rising

| Date | Mintage | F12 | VF20 | XF40 | MS60 | MS63 |
|---|---|---|---|---|---|---|
| 2007 | — | PF65 7.50 | | | | |

**KM# 588 20 WON**
28.00 g., Brass, 40 mm. **Obv:** Eastern gate in Pyeongyang **Rev:** Two girls on seasaw

| Date | Mintage | F12 | VF20 | XF40 | MS60 | MS63 |
|---|---|---|---|---|---|---|
| 2007 | — | PF65 7.50 | | | | |

**KM# 589 20 WON**
28.00 g., Brass, 40 mm. **Obv:** Eastern gate in Pyeongyang **Rev:** Korean struggle

| Date | Mintage | F12 | VF20 | XF40 | MS60 | MS63 |
|---|---|---|---|---|---|---|
| 2007 | — | PF65 7.50 | | | | |

**KM# 590 20 WON**
28.00 g., Brass, 40 mm. **Obv:** Eastern gate in Pyeongyang **Rev:** Girl on swing

| Date | Mintage | F12 | VF20 | XF40 | MS60 | MS63 |
|---|---|---|---|---|---|---|
| 2007 | — | PF65 7.50 | | | | |

**KM# 591 20 WON**
28.00 g., Brass, 40 mm. **Obv:** Eastern gate in Pyeongyang **Rev:** Children Skipping

| Date | Mintage | F12 | VF20 | XF40 | MS60 | MS63 |
|---|---|---|---|---|---|---|
| 2007 | — | PF65 7.50 | | | | |

**KM# 624 20 WON**
28.00 g., Brass, 40 mm. **Obv:** Eastern gate in Pyeongyang **Rev:** White bellied woodpecker

| Date | Mintage | F12 | VF20 | XF40 | MS60 | MS63 |
|---|---|---|---|---|---|---|
| 2007 | — | PF65 7.00 | | | | |

**KM# 625 20 WON**
28.00 g., Brass, 40 mm. **Obv:** Eastern gate in Pyeongyang **Rev:** Black grouse

| Date | Mintage | F12 | VF20 | XF40 | MS60 | MS63 |
|---|---|---|---|---|---|---|
| 2007 | — | PF65 7.00 | | | | |

**KM# 626 20 WON**
28.00 g., Brass, 40 mm. **Obv:** Eastern gate in Pyeongyang **Rev:** Sand Grouse

| Date | Mintage | F12 | VF20 | XF40 | MS60 | MS63 |
|---|---|---|---|---|---|---|
| 2007 | — | PF65 7.00 | | | | |

**KM# 627 20 WON**
28.00 g., Brass, 40 mm. **Obv:** Eastern gate in Pyeongyang **Rev:** Indian Pitta bird

| Date | Mintage | F12 | VF20 | XF40 | MS60 | MS63 |
|---|---|---|---|---|---|---|
| 2007 | — | PF65 7.00 | | | | |

**KM# 633 20 WON**
28.00 g., Brass, 40 mm. **Obv:** Eastern gate in Pyeongyang **Rev:** Blue dragon right

| Date | Mintage | F12 | VF20 | XF40 | MS60 | MS63 |
|---|---|---|---|---|---|---|
| 2007 | — | PF65 7.00 | | | | |

**KM# 638 20 WON**
28.00 g., Brass, 40 mm. **Obv:** Eastern gate in Pyeongyang **Rev:** Two siberian tigers

| Date | Mintage | F12 | VF20 | XF40 | MS60 | MS63 |
|---|---|---|---|---|---|---|
| 2007 | — | PF65 7.00 | | | | |

**KM# 652 20 WON**
28.00 g., Brass, 40 mm. **Obv:** Eastern gate in Pyeongyang **Rev:** Dongmyeong, King of Goguryeo

| Date | Mintage | F12 | VF20 | XF40 | MS60 | MS63 |
|---|---|---|---|---|---|---|
| 2007 | — | PF65 7.00 | | | | |

**KM# 653 20 WON**
28.00 g., Brass, 40 mm. **Obv:** Eastern gate in Pyeongyang **Rev:** Buddha figure

| Date | Mintage | F12 | VF20 | XF40 | MS60 | MS63 |
|---|---|---|---|---|---|---|
| 2007 | — | PF65 7.00 | | | | |

**KM# 654 20 WON**
28.00 g., Brass, 40 mm. **Obv:** Eastern gate in Pyeongyang **Rev:** Dangun, King of Gojoseon

| Date | Mintage | F12 | VF20 | XF40 | MS60 | MS63 |
|---|---|---|---|---|---|---|
| 2007 | — | PF65 7.00 | | | | |

**KM# 668 20 WON**
28.00 g., Brass, 40 mm. **Obv:** Eastern gate in Pyeongyang **Rev:** First married couple to meet again after the 1945 division

| Date | Mintage | F12 | VF20 | XF40 | MS60 | MS63 |
|---|---|---|---|---|---|---|
| 2007 | — | PF65 7.00 | | | | |

**KM# 690 20 WON**
28.00 g., Brass, 40 mm. **Obv:** East gate of Pyeongyang **Rev:** Hyonmu

| Date | Mintage | F12 | VF20 | XF40 | MS60 | MS63 |
|---|---|---|---|---|---|---|
| 2007 | — | PF65 7.00 | | | | |

**KM# 716 20 WON**
28.00 g., Brass, 40 mm. **Obv:** East gate of Pyeongyang **Rev:** Celadon pottery

| Date | Mintage | F12 | VF20 | XF40 | MS60 | MS63 |
|---|---|---|---|---|---|---|
| 2007 | — | PF65 7.00 | | | | |

**KM# 807 20 WON**
28.00 g., Brass, 40 mm. **Obv:** East gate in Pyeongyang **Rev:** Reconstruction of the mausoleum of King Dangun

| Date | Mintage | F12 | VF20 | XF40 | MS60 | MS63 |
|---|---|---|---|---|---|---|
| 2007 | — | PF65 7.00 | | | | |

**KM# 808 20 WON**
28.00 g., Brass, 40 mm. **Obv:** East gate of Pyeongyang **Rev:** Dongmyeong, 1st King of Goguryeo

| Date | Mintage | F12 | VF20 | XF40 | MS60 | MS63 |
|---|---|---|---|---|---|---|
| 2007 | — | PF65 7.00 | | | | |

**KM# 811 20 WON**
28.00 g., Brass, 40 mm. **Obv:** East gate of Pyeongyang **Rev:** Jeon Bongjun

| Date | Mintage | F12 | VF20 | XF40 | MS60 | MS63 |
|---|---|---|---|---|---|---|
| 2007 | — | PF65 7.00 | | | | |

**KM# 855 20 WON**
28.00 g., Brass, 40 mm. **Obv:** East gate of Pyeongyang **Rev:** Dancer

| Date | Mintage | F12 | VF20 | XF40 | MS60 | MS63 |
|---|---|---|---|---|---|---|
| 2007 | — | PF65 7.00 | | | | |

**KM# 856 20 WON**
28.00 g., Brass, 40 mm. **Obv:** East gate of Pyeongyang **Rev:** Dancer

| Date | Mintage | F12 | VF20 | XF40 | MS60 | MS63 |
|---|---|---|---|---|---|---|
| 2007 | — | PF65 7.00 | | | | |

**KM# 857 20 WON**
28.00 g., Brass, 40 mm. **Obv:** East gate of Pyeongyang **Rev:** Woman in national costume

| Date | Mintage | F12 | VF20 | XF40 | MS60 | MS63 |
|---|---|---|---|---|---|---|
| 2007 | — | PF65 7.00 | | | | |

**KM# 858 20 WON**
28.00 g., Brass, 40 mm. **Obv:** East gate of Pyeongyang **Rev:** Crane dancer

| Date | Mintage | F12 | VF20 | XF40 | MS60 | MS63 |
|---|---|---|---|---|---|---|
| 2007 | — | PF65 7.00 | | | | |

**KM# 859 20 WON**
28.00 g., Brass, 40 mm. **Obv:** East gate of Pyeongyang **Rev:** Fairy princess

| Date | Mintage | F12 | VF20 | XF40 | MS60 | MS63 |
|---|---|---|---|---|---|---|
| 2007 | — | PF65 7.00 | | | | |

**KM# 868 20 WON**
28.00 g., Brass, 40 mm. **Obv:** East gate of Pyeongyang **Rev:** Drum dancers in shape of Korean map

| Date | Mintage | F12 | VF20 | XF40 | MS60 | MS63 |
|---|---|---|---|---|---|---|
| 2007 | — | PF65 7.00 | | | | |

**KM# 869 20 WON**
28.00 g., Brass, 40 mm. **Obv:** East gate of Pyeongyang **Rev:** Korean team victory celebration

| Date | Mintage | F12 | VF20 | XF40 | MS60 | MS63 |
|---|---|---|---|---|---|---|
| 2007 | — | PF65 7.00 | | | | |

**KM# 1128 20 WON**
28.00 g., Brass, 40 mm. **Obv:** National arms, Central Bank name **Rev:** Hoopoe

| Date | Mintage | F12 | VF20 | XF40 | MS60 | MS63 |
|---|---|---|---|---|---|---|
| 2007 | — | PF65 17.50 | | | | |

**KM# 1129 20 WON**
28.00 g., Brass, 40 mm. **Obv:** National arms, Central Bank name **Rev:** Ural owl

| Date | Mintage | F12 | VF20 | XF40 | MS60 | MS63 |
|---|---|---|---|---|---|---|
| 2007 | Est. 2000 | PF65 17.50 | | | | |

**KM# 1130 20 WON**
28.00 g., Brass, 40 mm. **Obv:** National arms, Central Bank name **Rev:** Eagle

| Date | Mintage | F12 | VF20 | XF40 | MS60 | MS63 |
|---|---|---|---|---|---|---|
| 2007 | Est. 2000 | PF65 17.50 | | | | |

**KM# 1131 20 WON**
28.00 g., Brass, 40 mm. **Obv:** National arms, Central Bank name **Rev:** White rhino

| Date | Mintage | F12 | VF20 | XF40 | MS60 | MS63 |
|---|---|---|---|---|---|---|
| 2007 | Est. 2000 | PF65 17.50 | | | | |

**KM# 1132 20 WON**
28.00 g., Brass, 40 mm. **Obv:** National arms, Central Bank name **Rev:** African elephant family

| Date | Mintage | F12 | VF20 | XF40 | MS60 | MS63 |
|---|---|---|---|---|---|---|
| 2007 | Est. 2000 | PF65 17.50 | | | | |

**KM# 1133 20 WON**
28.00 g., Brass, 40 mm. **Obv:** National arms, Central Bank name **Rev:** Lion family

| Date | Mintage | F12 | VF20 | XF40 | MS60 | MS63 |
|---|---|---|---|---|---|---|
| 2007 | Est. 2000 | PF65 17.50 | | | | |

**KM# 1134 20 WON**
28.00 g., Brass, 40 mm. **Obv:** National arms, Central Bank name **Rev:** Cape Buffalo

| Date | Mintage | F12 | VF20 | XF40 | MS60 | MS63 |
|---|---|---|---|---|---|---|
| 2007 | Est. 2000 | PF65 17.50 | | | | |

**KM# 1135 20 WON**
28.00 g., Brass **Obv:** National arms, Central Bank name **Rev:** Marine turtle

| Date | Mintage | F12 | VF20 | XF40 | MS60 | MS63 |
|---|---|---|---|---|---|---|
| 2007 | Est. 2000 | PF65 17.50 | | | | |

**KM# 1136 20 WON**
28.00 g., Brass, 40 mm. **Obv:** National arms, Central Bank name **Rev:** Penguin

| Date | Mintage | F12 | VF20 | XF40 | MS60 | MS63 |
|---|---|---|---|---|---|---|
| 2007 | Est. 2000 | PF65 17.50 | | | | |

**KM# 1137 20 WON**
28.00 g., Brass, 40 mm. **Obv:** National arms, Central Bank name **Rev:** Emu

| Date | Mintage | F12 | VF20 | XF40 | MS60 | MS63 |
|---|---|---|---|---|---|---|
| 2007 | — | PF65 17.50 | | | | |

**KM# 1138 20 WON**
28.00 g., Brass, 40 mm. **Obv:** National arms, Central Bank name **Rev:** Eagle owl

| Date | Mintage | F12 | VF20 | XF40 | MS60 | MS63 |
|---|---|---|---|---|---|---|
| 2007 | Est. 2000 | PF65 17.50 | | | | |

**KM# 1139 20 WON**
28.00 g., Brass, 40 mm. **Obv:** National arms, Central Bank name **Rev:** Lemur

| Date | Mintage | F12 | VF20 | XF40 | MS60 | MS63 |
|---|---|---|---|---|---|---|
| 2007 | Est. 2000 | PF65 17.50 | | | | |

**KM# 1140 20 WON**
28.00 g., Brass, 40 mm. **Obv:** National arms, Central Bank name **Rev:** Lion

| Date | Mintage | F12 | VF20 | XF40 | MS60 | MS63 |
|---|---|---|---|---|---|---|
| 2007 | Est. 2000 | PF65 17.50 | | | | |

**KM# 1141 20 WON**
28.00 g., Brass, 40 mm. **Obv:** National arms, Central Bank name **Rev:** Two Arfican elephants

| Date | Mintage | F12 | VF20 | XF40 | MS60 | MS63 |
|---|---|---|---|---|---|---|
| 2007 | — | PF65 17.50 | | | | |

**KM# 484 20 WON**
27.30 g., Brass, 40 mm. **Obv:** Temple **Rev:** Multicolor goat left

| Date | Mintage | F12 | VF20 | XF40 | MS60 | MS63 |
|---|---|---|---|---|---|---|
| 2008 | — | PF65 10.00 | | | | |

**KM# 485 20 WON**
27.30 g., Brass, 40 mm. **Obv:** Temple **Rev:** Multicolor snake and flowers

| Date | Mintage | F12 | VF20 | XF40 | MS60 | MS63 |
|---|---|---|---|---|---|---|
| 2008 | — | PF65 10.00 | | | | |

**KM# 486 20 WON**
27.30 g., Brass, 40 mm. **Obv:** Temple **Rev:** Multicolor, two rabbits

| Date | Mintage | F12 | VF20 | XF40 | MS60 | MS63 |
|---|---|---|---|---|---|---|
| 2008 | — | PF65 10.00 | | | | |

**KM# 487 20 WON**
27.30 g., Brass, 40 mm. **Obv:** Temple **Rev:** Multicolor two white rats

| Date | Mintage | F12 | VF20 | XF40 | MS60 | MS63 |
|---|---|---|---|---|---|---|
| 2008 | — | PF65 10.00 | | | | |

**KM# 488 20 WON**
27.30 g., Brass, 40 mm. **Obv:** Temple **Rev:** Multicolor monkey seated on branch

| Date | Mintage | F12 | VF20 | XF40 | MS60 | MS63 |
|---|---|---|---|---|---|---|
| 2008 | — | PF65 10.00 | | | | |

**KM# 489 20 WON**
27.30 g., Brass, 40 mm. **Obv:** Temple **Rev:** Multicolor tiger

| Date | Mintage | F12 | VF20 | XF40 | MS60 | MS63 |
|---|---|---|---|---|---|---|
| 2008 | — | PF65 10.00 | | | | |

**KM# 490 20 WON**
27.30 g., Brass, 40 mm. **Obv:** Temple **Rev:** Multicolor horse prancing right

| Date | Mintage | F12 | VF20 | XF40 | MS60 | MS63 |
|---|---|---|---|---|---|---|
| 2008 | — | PF65 10.00 | | | | |

**KM# 491 20 WON**
27.30 g., Brass, 40 mm. **Obv:** Temple **Rev:** Multicolor two oxen

| Date | Mintage | F12 | VF20 | XF40 | MS60 | MS63 |
|---|---|---|---|---|---|---|
| 2009 | — | PF65 10.00 | | | | |

**KM# 495 20 WON**
Aluminum, 45 mm. **Obv:** Raised Pagoda in ornamental loop **Rev:** Tiger with color inlay **Edge:** Plain

| Date | Mintage | F12 | VF20 | XF40 | MS60 | MS63 |
|---|---|---|---|---|---|---|
| 2010 | — | — | — | — | — | 20.00 |

**KM# 891 50 WON**
155.00 g., 0.999 Silver 4.9784 oz. ASW, 65 mm. **Obv:** National arms, Central Bank name **Rev:** Orca whale

| Date | Mintage | F12 | VF20 | XF40 | MS60 | MS63 |
|---|---|---|---|---|---|---|
| 2002 | Est. 500 | PF65 400 | | | | |

**KM# 815 50 WON**
1.24 g., 0.999 Gold 0.0398 oz. AGW, 14 mm. **Obv:** Naitonal arms, Central Bank name **Rev:** Wanggeon, 1st King of Goryeo Dynasty

| Date | Mintage | F12 | VF20 | XF40 | MS60 | MS63 |
|---|---|---|---|---|---|---|
| 2003 | Est. 20000 | PF63 75.00 | PF65 90.00 | | | |

**KM# 262 50 WON**
70.00 g., 0.999 Silver 2.2483 oz. ASW, 50 mm. **Obv:** Korean map **Rev:** Huh Jun Chosun doctor at left, books at right **Edge:** Plain

| Date | Mintage | F12 | VF20 | XF40 | MS60 | MS63 |
|---|---|---|---|---|---|---|
| JU93-2004 | — | PF65 100 | | | | |

**KM# 426 50 WON**
2.01 g., Aluminum, 25 mm. **Obv:** State arms **Rev:** Value

| Date | Mintage | F12 | VF20 | XF40 | MS60 | MS63 |
|---|---|---|---|---|---|---|
| JU94-2005 | — | — | — | — | 1.20 | 1.50 |

**KM# 427 100 WON**
2.27 g., Aluminum, 27 mm. **Obv:** State arms **Rev:** Value

| Date | Mintage | F12 | VF20 | XF40 | MS60 | MS63 |
|---|---|---|---|---|---|---|
| JU94-2005 | — | — | — | — | 1.35 | 1.75 |

**KM# 445 200 WON**
5.19 g., 0.999 Silver 0.1667 oz. ASW, 30 mm. **Series:** Endangered Wildlife **Obv:** Fortress Gate **Rev:** Polar Bear standing facing **Rev. Legend:** URSUS MARITIMUS **Edge:** Plain

| Date | Mintage | F12 | VF20 | XF40 | MS60 | MS63 |
|---|---|---|---|---|---|---|
| 2007 | 5,000 | PF65 15.00 | | | | |

**KM# 1110 200 WON**
25.00 g., Brass, 38 mm. **Subject:** Railways in Russia, 170th Anniversary **Obv:** East gate of Pyeongyang **Rev:** Steam train

| Date | Mintage | F12 | VF20 | XF40 | MS60 | MS63 |
|---|---|---|---|---|---|---|
| 2007 | Est. 200 | PF65 70.00 | | | | |

**KM# 1111 200 WON**
25.00 g., Brass, 35 mm. **Obv:** East gate of Pyeongyang **Rev:** Constantine Eduardovic and Sputnik

| Date | Mintage | F12 | VF20 | XF40 | MS60 | MS63 |
|---|---|---|---|---|---|---|
| 2007 | — | PF65 25.00 | | | | |

**KM# 1086 250 WON**
26.96 g., 0.900 Silver 0.7801 oz. ASW **Obv:** Old coins and Central Bank name

| Date | Mintage | F12 | VF20 | XF40 | MS60 | MS63 |
|---|---|---|---|---|---|---|
| 2005 | Est. 1000 | — | — | — | — | 25.00 |

**KM# 835 400 WON**
20.00 g., 0.999 Gold 0.6424 oz. AGW, 35 mm. **Obv:** National arms, Central Bank name **Rev:** Korean folk games, wrestling

| Date | Mintage | F12 | VF20 | XF40 | MS60 | MS63 |
|---|---|---|---|---|---|---|
| 2002 | — | PF65 1,200 | | | | |

**KM# 441 500 WON**
12.00 g., 0.999 Silver 0.3854 oz. ASW, 38 mm. **Subject:** 170th Anniversary First Public Railway St. Petersburg - Zarskoje Selo **Obv:** Fortress Gate **Rev:** First train arriving **Edge:** Plain

| Date | Mintage | F12 | VF20 | XF40 | MS60 | MS63 |
|---|---|---|---|---|---|---|
| ND(2007) | 5,000 | PF65 70.00 | | | | |

**KM# 447 500 WON**
12.00 g., 0.999 Silver 0.3854 oz. ASW, 38 mm. **Subject:** 150th Anniversay Birth of Ziolkowski and 50th Anniversary Launch of Sputnik I **Obv:** Fortress Gate **Rev:** Bust of Ziolkowski facing 3/4 right at lower left, Sputnik circling earth at upper right **Edge:** Plain

| Date | Mintage | F12 | VF20 | XF40 | MS60 | MS63 |
|---|---|---|---|---|---|---|
| ND(2007) | 5,000 | PF65 65.00 | | | | |

**KM# 1112 500 WON**
12.00 g., Silver, 38 mm. **Obv:** East gate of Pyeongyong **Rev:** Great Wall and Temple of Heaven in Bejing

| Date | Mintage | F12 | VF20 | XF40 | MS60 | MS63 |
|---|---|---|---|---|---|---|
| 2007 | — | PF65 35.00 | | | | |

**KM# 1113 500 WON**
12.00 g., 0.999 Silver 0.3854 oz. ASW, 38 mm. **Subject:** Bejing Olympics, 2008 **Obv:** East gate of Pyeongyong **Rev:** Fencing

| Date | Mintage | F12 | VF20 | XF40 | MS60 | MS63 |
|---|---|---|---|---|---|---|
| 2007 | Est. 5000 | PF65 35.00 | | | | |

**KM# 1114 500 WON**
12.00 g., 0.999 Silver 0.3854 oz. ASW, 38 mm. **Subject:** Bejing Olympics, 2008 **Obv:** East gate of Pyeongyong **Rev:** Boxing

| Date | Mintage | F12 | VF20 | XF40 | MS60 | MS63 |
|---|---|---|---|---|---|---|
| 2007 | — | PF65 35.00 | | | | |

**KM# 1115 500 WON**
12.00 g., 0.999 Silver 0.3854 oz. ASW, 38 mm. **Subject:** Bejing Olympics, 2008 **Obv:** East gate of Pyeongyong **Rev:** Swimming

| Date | Mintage | F12 | VF20 | XF40 | MS60 | MS63 |
|---|---|---|---|---|---|---|
| 2007 | — | PF65 35.00 | | | | |

**KM# 1116 500 WON**
12.00 g., 0.999 Silver 0.3854 oz. ASW, 38 mm. **Subject:** Bejing Olympics, 2008 **Obv:** East gate of Pyeongyong **Rev:** Weightlifting

| Date | Mintage | F12 | VF20 | XF40 | MS60 | MS63 |
|---|---|---|---|---|---|---|
| 2007 | Est. 5000 | PF65 35.00 | | | | |

**KM# 1117 500 WON**
12.00 g., 0.999 Silver 0.3854 oz. ASW, 38 mm. **Subject:** Bejing Olympics, 2008 **Obv:** East gate of Pyeongyong **Rev:** Baseball

| Date | Mintage | F12 | VF20 | XF40 | MS60 | MS63 |
|---|---|---|---|---|---|---|
| 2007 | Est. 5000 | PF65 35.00 | | | | |

**KM# 1118 500 WON**
12.00 g., 0.999 Silver 0.3854 oz. ASW, 38 mm. **Subject:** Bejing Olympics, 2008 **Obv:** East gate of Pyeongyong **Rev:** Wrestlers

| Date | Mintage | F12 | VF20 | XF40 | MS60 | MS63 |
|---|---|---|---|---|---|---|
| 2007 | — | PF65 35.00 | | | | |

**KM# 1119 500 WON**
12.00 g., 0.999 Silver 0.3854 oz. ASW, 38 mm. **Subject:** Bejing Olympics, 2008 **Obv:** East gate of Pyeongyong **Rev:** Gymnast

| Date | Mintage | F12 | VF20 | XF40 | MS60 | MS63 |
|---|---|---|---|---|---|---|
| 2007 | — | PF65 35.00 | | | | |

**KM# 1120 500 WON**
12.00 g., 0.999 Silver 0.3854 oz. ASW, 28 mm. **Subject:** Bejing Olympics, 2008 **Obv:** East gate of Pyeongyong **Rev:** Kayakers

| Date | Mintage | F12 | VF20 | XF40 | MS60 | MS63 |
|---|---|---|---|---|---|---|
| 2007 | Est. 5000 | PF65 35.00 | | | | |

**KM# 1121 500 WON**
12.00 g., 0.999 Silver 0.3854 oz. ASW, 38 mm. **Subject:** Bejing Olympics, 2008 **Obv:** East gate of Pyeongyong **Rev:** Hurdler

| Date | Mintage | F12 | VF20 | XF40 | MS60 | MS63 |
|---|---|---|---|---|---|---|
| 2007 | Est. 5000 | PF65 35.00 | | | | |

**KM# 1122 500 WON**
12.00 g., 0.999 Silver 0.3854 oz. ASW, 38 mm. **Subject:** Bejing Olympics, 2008 **Obv:** East gate of Pyeongyong **Rev:** Taekwondo

| Date | Mintage | F12 | VF20 | XF40 | MS60 | MS63 |
|---|---|---|---|---|---|---|
| 2007 | Est. 5000 | PF65 35.00 | | | | |

**KM# 1123 500 WON**
12.00 g., 0.999 Silver 0.3854 oz. ASW, 38 mm. **Subject:** Bejing Olympics, 2008 **Obv:** East gate of Pyeongyong **Rev:** Olympic Sport

| Date | Mintage | F12 | VF20 | XF40 | MS60 | MS63 |
|---|---|---|---|---|---|---|
| 2007 | Est. 5000 | PF65 35.00 | | | | |

**KM# 443 500 WON**
12.00 g., 0.999 Silver 0.3854 oz. ASW, 38.00 mm. **Subject:** Lunar Year of the Rat **Obv:** Fortress Gate **Rev:** Two rats within circle of Lunar figures **Edge:** Plain

| Date | Mintage | F12 | VF20 | XF40 | MS60 | MS63 |
|---|---|---|---|---|---|---|
| 2008 | — | — | — | — | — | 50.00 |
| 2008 | 5,000 | PF65 70.00 | | | | |

**KM# 1178 500 WON**
12.00 g., 0.999 Silver 0.3854 oz. ASW, 38 mm. **Subject:** Bejing Summer Olympics, 2008 **Obv:** East gate of Pyeongyang **Rev:** Great Wall, Temple of Heaven and Soccer player

| Date | Mintage | F12 | VF20 | XF40 | MS60 | MS63 |
|---|---|---|---|---|---|---|
| 2008 | Est. 5000 | PF65 35.00 | | | | |

**KM# 1179 500 WON**
12.00 g., 0.999 Silver 0.3854 oz. ASW, 38 mm. **Subject:** Bejing Summer Olympics, 2008 **Obv:** East gate of Pyeongyang **Rev:** Hockey player

| Date | Mintage | F12 | VF20 | XF40 | MS60 | MS63 |
|---|---|---|---|---|---|---|
| 2008 | — | PF65 35.00 | | | | |

**KM# 1180 500 WON**
12.00 g., 0.999 Silver 0.3854 oz. ASW, 38 mm. **Subject:** Bejing Summer Olympics, 2008 **Obv:** East gate of Pyeongyang **Rev:** Basketball player

| Date | Mintage | F12 | VF20 | XF40 | MS60 | MS63 |
|---|---|---|---|---|---|---|
| 2008 | — | PF65 35.00 | | | | |

**KM# 1181 500 WON**
12.00 g., 0.999 Silver 0.3854 oz. ASW, 38 mm. **Subject:** Bejing Summer Olympics, 2008 **Obv:** East gate of Pyeongyang **Rev:** Archer

| Date | Mintage | F12 | VF20 | XF40 | MS60 | MS63 |
|---|---|---|---|---|---|---|
| 2008 | Est. 5000 | PF65 35.00 | | | | |

**KM# 1182 500 WON**
12.00 g., 0.999 Silver 0.3854 oz. ASW, 38 mm. **Subject:** Bejing Summer Olympics, 2008 **Obv:** East gate of Pyeongyang **Rev:** Volleyball

| Date | Mintage | F12 | VF20 | XF40 | MS60 | MS63 |
|---|---|---|---|---|---|---|
| 2008 | Est. 5000 | PF65 35.00 | | | | |

**KM# 1183 500 WON**
12.00 g., 0.999 Silver 0.3854 oz. ASW, 38 mm. **Subject:** Bejing Summer Olympics, 2008 **Obv:** East gate of Pyeongyang **Rev:** Table tennis

| Date | Mintage | F12 | VF20 | XF40 | MS60 | MS63 |
|---|---|---|---|---|---|---|
| 2008 | — | PF65 35.00 | | | | |

**KM# 1184 500 WON**
12.00 g., 0.999 Silver 0.3854 oz. ASW, 38 mm. **Subject:** Bejing Summer Olympics, 2008 **Obv:** East gate of Pyeongyang **Rev:** Rowers

| Date | Mintage | F12 | VF20 | XF40 | MS60 | MS63 |
|---|---|---|---|---|---|---|
| 2008 | Est. 5000 | PF65 35.00 | | | | |

**KM# 717 700 WON**
31.11 g., 0.999 Gold 0.999 oz. AGW **Obv:** National arms **Rev:** Caledon pottery

| Date | Mintage | F12 | VF20 | XF40 | MS60 | MS63 |
|---|---|---|---|---|---|---|
| 2001 | — | PF65 1,800 | | | | |

**KM# 720 700 WON**
31.11 g., 0.999 Gold 0.999 oz. AGW, 40 mm. **Obv:** National arms, Central Bank name **Rev:** Ginsing plant

| Date | Mintage | F12 | VF20 | XF40 | MS60 | MS63 |
|---|---|---|---|---|---|---|
| 2001 | — | PF65 1,800 | | | | |

**KM# 723 700 WON**
31.11 g., 0.999 Gold 0.999 oz. AGW, 40 mm. **Obv:** National arms **Rev:** End of the steam train in 1945 and again in 2001

| Date | Mintage | F12 | VF20 | XF40 | MS60 | MS63 |
|---|---|---|---|---|---|---|
| 2001 | — | PF65 1,800 | | | | |

**KM# 742 700 WON**
31.11 g., 0.999 Gold 0.999 oz. AGW, 40 mm. **Obv:** National arms, Central Bank name **Rev:** Ferryboat, married couple and flag

| Date | Mintage | F12 | VF20 | XF40 | MS60 | MS63 |
|---|---|---|---|---|---|---|
| 2001 | — | PF65 1,800 | | | | |

**KM# 743 700 WON**
31.11 g., 0.9999 Gold 0.9999 oz. AGW, 40 mm. **Obv:** National arms, Central Bank name **Rev:** Ferryboat between Korea and Japan

| Date | Mintage | F12 | VF20 | XF40 | MS60 | MS63 |
|---|---|---|---|---|---|---|
| 2001 | — | PF65 1,800 | | | | |

**KM# 744 700 WON**
31.11 g., 0.999 Gold 0.999 oz. AGW, 40 mm. **Obv:** National arms, Central Bank name **Rev:** Triumphial arch of Moranbong in Pyeongyang

| Date | Mintage | F12 | VF20 | XF40 | MS60 | MS63 |
|---|---|---|---|---|---|---|
| 2001 | — | PF65 1,800 | | | | |

**KM# 745 700 WON**
31.11 g., 0.999 Gold 0.999 oz. AGW, 40 mm. **Obv:** National arms, Central Bank name **Rev:** Chonji crater in Paektusan

| Date | Mintage | F12 | VF20 | XF40 | MS60 | MS63 |
|---|---|---|---|---|---|---|
| 2001 | — | PF65 1,800 | | | | |

**KM# 748 700 WON**
31.11 g., 0.999 Gold 0.999 oz. AGW, 40 mm. **Obv:** National arms, Central Bank name **Rev:** Kim Jeongil and Jiang Zemin clasping hands

| Date | Mintage | F12 | VF20 | XF40 | MS60 | MS63 |
|---|---|---|---|---|---|---|
| 2001 | — | PF65 1,800 | | | | |

### KM# 503 700 WON

31.11 g., 0.999 Gold 0.999 oz. AGW, 40 mm. **Obv:** National arms **Rev:** Brontosaurus

| Date | Mintage | F12 | VF20 | XF40 | MS60 | MS63 |
|---|---|---|---|---|---|---|
| 2002 | — | PF65 1,800 | | | | |

### KM# 537 700 WON

31.11 g., 0.999 Gold 0.999 oz. AGW **Obv:** National arms **Rev:** Zhou Enlai, president of the P.R.C.

| Date | Mintage | F12 | VF20 | XF40 | MS60 | MS63 |
|---|---|---|---|---|---|---|
| 2002 | — | PF65 1,800 | | | | |

### KM# 612 700 WON

31.11 g., 0.999 Gold 0.999 oz. AGW **Obv:** National arms **Rev:** Chinese Junk at sail

| Date | Mintage | F12 | VF20 | XF40 | MS60 | MS63 |
|---|---|---|---|---|---|---|
| 2002 | — | PF65 1,800 | | | | |

### KM# 634 700 WON

31.11 g., 0.999 Gold 0.999 oz. AGW **Obv:** National arms, Central Bank name **Rev:** Blue dragon right

| Date | Mintage | F12 | VF20 | XF40 | MS60 | MS63 |
|---|---|---|---|---|---|---|
| 2002 | — | PF65 1,800 | | | | |

### KM# 640 700 WON

31.11 g., 0.999 Gold 0.999 oz. AGW **Obv:** National arms, Country name **Rev:** Two siberian tigers

| Date | Mintage | F12 | VF20 | XF40 | MS60 | MS63 |
|---|---|---|---|---|---|---|
| 2002 | — | PF65 1,800 | | | | |

### KM# 655 700 WON

31.11 g., 0.999 Gold 0.999 oz. AGW, 40 mm. **Obv:** National arms, Central Bank name **Rev:** Dongmyeong, King of Goguryeo

| Date | Mintage | F12 | VF20 | XF40 | MS60 | MS63 |
|---|---|---|---|---|---|---|
| 2002 | — | PF65 1,800 | | | | |

### KM# 656 700 WON

31.11 g., 0.999 Gold 0.999 oz. AGW, 40 mm. **Obv:** National arms, Central Bank name **Rev:** Buddha figure

| Date | Mintage | F12 | VF20 | XF40 | MS60 | MS63 |
|---|---|---|---|---|---|---|
| 2002 | — | PF65 1,800 | | | | |

### KM# 657 700 WON

31.11 g., 0.999 Gold 0.999 oz. AGW, 40 mm. **Obv:** National arms, Central Bank name **Rev:** Dangun, King of Gojoseon

| Date | Mintage | F12 | VF20 | XF40 | MS60 | MS63 |
|---|---|---|---|---|---|---|
| 2002 | — | PF65 1,800 | | | | |

### KM# 791 700 WON

31.11 g., 0.999 Gold 0.999 oz. AGW, 35 mm. **Obv:** National arms **Rev:** Horse head

| Date | Mintage | F12 | VF20 | XF40 | MS60 | MS63 |
|---|---|---|---|---|---|---|
| 2002 | — | PF65 1,800 | | | | |

### KM# 792 700 WON

31.11 g., 0.999 Gold 0.999 oz. AGW, 35 mm. **Obv:** National arms **Rev:** Horse to the right

| Date | Mintage | F12 | VF20 | XF40 | MS60 | MS63 |
|---|---|---|---|---|---|---|
| 2002 | — | PF65 1,800 | | | | |

### KM# 793 700 WON

31.11 g., 0.999 Gold 0.999 oz. AGW, 35 mm. **Obv:** National arms **Rev:** Two horses in center of the Zodiac

| Date | Mintage | F12 | VF20 | XF40 | MS60 | MS63 |
|---|---|---|---|---|---|---|
| 2002 | — | PF65 1,800 | | | | |

### KM# 816 700 WON

31.11 g., 0.999 Gold 0.999 oz. AGW, 40 mm. **Obv:** National arms, Central Bank name **Rev:** Reconstruction of the Mousoleum for King Dangun

| Date | Mintage | F12 | VF20 | XF40 | MS60 | MS63 |
|---|---|---|---|---|---|---|
| 2002 | — | PF65 1,800 | | | | |

### KM# 817 700 WON

**31.11 g., 0.999 Gold 0.999 oz. AGW, 40 mm. Obv: National arms, Central Bank name Rev: Dongmyeong, 1st King of Goguryeo**

| Date | Mintage | F12 | VF20 | XF40 | MS60 | MS63 |
|---|---|---|---|---|---|---|
| 2002 | — | PF65 1,800 | | | | |

### KM# 818 700 WON

31.11 g., 0.999 Gold 0.999 oz. AGW, 40 mm. **Obv:** National arms, Central Bank name **Rev:** Wanggeon, 1st King of Boryeo Dynasty

| Date | Mintage | F12 | VF20 | XF40 | MS60 | MS63 |
|---|---|---|---|---|---|---|
| 2002 | — | PF65 1,800 | | | | |

### KM# 819 700 WON

31.11 g., 0.999 Gold 0.999 oz. AGW, 40 mm. **Obv:** National arms, Central Bank name **Rev:** Jeong Mongju

| Date | Mintage | F12 | VF20 | XF40 | MS60 | MS63 |
|---|---|---|---|---|---|---|
| 2002 | — | PF65 1,800 | | | | |

### KM# 820 700 WON

31.11 g., 0.999 Gold 0.999 oz. AGW, 40 mm. **Obv:** National arms, Central Bank name **Rev:** Jeon Bongjun

| Date | Mintage | F12 | VF20 | XF40 | MS60 | MS63 |
|---|---|---|---|---|---|---|
| 2002 | — | PF65 1,800 | | | | |

### KM# 825 700 WON

31.11 g., 0.999 Gold 0.999 oz. AGW, 40 mm. **Obv:** National arms **Rev:** Prince Hodong and Princess Nakrang on horseback

| Date | Mintage | F12 | VF20 | XF40 | MS60 | MS63 |
|---|---|---|---|---|---|---|
| 2002 | — | PF65 1,800 | | | | |

### KM# 826 700 WON

31.11 g., 0.999 Gold 0.999 oz. AGW, 40 mm. **Obv:** National arms **Rev:** Half-length figures of Prince Hodong and Princess Nakrang

| Date | Mintage | F12 | VF20 | XF40 | MS60 | MS63 |
|---|---|---|---|---|---|---|
| 2002 | — | PF65 1,800 | | | | |

### KM# 834 700 WON

31.11 g., 0.999 Gold 0.999 oz. AGW, 35 mm. **Obv:** National Arms, Central Bank name **Rev:** Bust of Kim Ilseong

| Date | Mintage | F12 | VF20 | XF40 | MS60 | MS63 |
|---|---|---|---|---|---|---|
| 2002 | — | PF65 1,800 | | | | |

### KM# 844 700 WON

31.11 g., 0.999 Gold 0.999 oz. AGW, 35 mm. **Obv:** National arms, Central Bank and Country name **Rev:** The soldiers

| Date | Mintage | F12 | VF20 | XF40 | MS60 | MS63 |
|---|---|---|---|---|---|---|
| 2002 | — | PF65 1,800 | | | | |

### KM# 845 700 WON

31.11 g., 0.999 Gold 0.999 oz. AGW, 35 mm. **Obv:** National arms, Central Bank and Country name **Rev:** Fairy princess

| Date | Mintage | F12 | VF20 | XF40 | MS60 | MS63 |
|---|---|---|---|---|---|---|
| 2002 | — | PF65 1,800 | | | | |

### KM# 846 700 WON

31.11 g., 0.999 Gold 0.999 oz. AGW, 35 mm. **Obv:** National arms, Central Bank and Country name **Rev:** Bronze statue

| Date | Mintage | F12 | VF20 | XF40 | MS60 | MS63 |
|---|---|---|---|---|---|---|
| 2002 | — | PF65 1,800 | | | | |

### KM# 847 700 WON

31.11 g., 0.999 Gold 0.999 oz. AGW, 35 mm. **Obv:** National arms, Central Bank and Country name **Rev:** Female worshipers of the sun

| Date | Mintage | F12 | VF20 | XF40 | MS60 | MS63 |
|---|---|---|---|---|---|---|
| 2002 | — | PF65 1,800 | | | | |

### KM# 848 700 WON

31.11 g., 0.999 Gold 0.999 oz. AGW, 35 mm. **Obv:** National arms, Central Bank and Country name **Rev:** Trhee prinicpals of re-unification

| Date | Mintage | F12 | VF20 | XF40 | MS60 | MS63 |
|---|---|---|---|---|---|---|
| 2002 | — | PF65 1,800 | | | | |

### KM# 849 700 WON

31.11 g., 0.999 Gold 0.999 oz. AGW, 35 mm. **Obv:** National arms, Central Bank and Country name **Rev:** Dancing children

| Date | Mintage | F12 | VF20 | XF40 | MS60 | MS63 |
|---|---|---|---|---|---|---|
| 2002 | — | PF65 1,800 | | | | |

### KM# 872 700 WON

31.11 g., 0.999 Gold 0.999 oz. AGW, 40 mm. **Obv:** National arms, Central bank name **Rev:** Family

| Date | Mintage | F12 | VF20 | XF40 | MS60 | MS63 |
|---|---|---|---|---|---|---|
| 2002 | — | PF65 1,800 | | | | |

### KM# 873 700 WON

31.11 g., 0.999 Gold 0.999 oz. AGW, 40 mm. **Obv:** National arms, Central Bank name **Rev:** Map of Korea with four cardinal compass points

| Date | Mintage | F12 | VF20 | XF40 | MS60 | MS63 |
|---|---|---|---|---|---|---|
| 2002 | — | PF65 1,800 | | | | |

### KM# 874 700 WON

31.11 g., 0.999 Gold 0.999 oz. AGW, 40 mm. **Obv:** Naitonal arms, Central Bank name **Rev:** Rythem dancer and map of Korea

| Date | Mintage | F12 | VF20 | XF40 | MS60 | MS63 |
|---|---|---|---|---|---|---|
| 2002 | — | PF65 1,800 | | | | |

### KM# 875 700 WON

31.11 g., 0.999 Gold 0.999 oz. AGW, 40 mm. **Obv:** National arms, Central Bank name **Rev:** Drum dancers and map of Korea

| Date | Mintage | F12 | VF20 | XF40 | MS60 | MS63 |
|---|---|---|---|---|---|---|
| 2002 | — | PF65 1,800 | | | | |

### KM# 876 700 WON

31.11 g., 0.999 Gold 0.999 oz. AGW, 40 mm. **Obv:** National arms, Central Bank name **Rev:** Korean team victory celebration

| Date | Mintage | F12 | VF20 | XF40 | MS60 | MS63 |
|---|---|---|---|---|---|---|
| 2002 | — | PF65 1,800 | | | | |

### KM# 899 700 WON

31.11 g., 0.999 Gold 0.999 oz. AGW, 40 mm. **Obv:** East gate of Pyeongyang **Rev:** Sheep at center of Zodiac

| Date | Mintage | F12 | VF20 | XF40 | MS60 | MS63 |
|---|---|---|---|---|---|---|
| 2003 | — | PF65 1,800 | | | | |

### KM# 912 700 WON

31.11 g., 0.999 Gold 0.999 oz. AGW, 40 mm. **Obv:** National arms, Central Bank name **Rev:** Eulji Mundeok

| Date | Mintage | F12 | VF20 | XF40 | MS60 | MS63 |
|---|---|---|---|---|---|---|
| 2003 | — | PF65 1,800 | | | | |

### KM# 913 700 WON

31.11 g., 0.999 Gold 0.999 oz. AGW, 40 mm. **Obv:** National arms, Central Bank name **Rev:** Yeon Gaesomun

| Date | Mintage | F12 | VF20 | XF40 | MS60 | MS63 |
|---|---|---|---|---|---|---|
| 2003 | — | PF65 1,800 | | | | |

### KM# 914 700 WON

31.11 g., 0.999 Gold 0.999 oz. AGW, 40 mm. **Obv:** National arms, Central Bank name **Rev:** Gang Camchan

| Date | Mintage | F12 | VF20 | XF40 | MS60 | MS63 |
|---|---|---|---|---|---|---|
| 2003 | — | PF65 1,800 | | | | |

### KM# 917 700 WON

31.11 g., 0.999 Gold 0.999 oz. AGW, 40 mm. **Obv:** National arms, Central Bank name **Rev:** Turtle boat

| Date | Mintage | F12 | VF20 | XF40 | MS60 | MS63 |
|---|---|---|---|---|---|---|
| 2003 | — | PF65 1,800 | | | | |

### KM# 941 700 WON

31.11 g., 0.999 Gold 0.999 oz. AGW, 40 mm. **Obv:** Naitonal arms, Central Bank name **Rev:** Monkey at center of Zodiac

| Date | Mintage | F12 | VF20 | XF40 | MS60 | MS63 |
|---|---|---|---|---|---|---|
| 2004 | — | PF65 1,800 | | | | |

### KM# 1018 700 WON

31.11 g., 0.999 Gold 0.999 oz. AGW, 40 mm. **Obv:** National arms, Central Bank name **Rev:** Rooster within Zodiac circle

| Date | Mintage | F12 | VF20 | XF40 | MS60 | MS63 |
|---|---|---|---|---|---|---|
| 2005 | — | PF65 1,800 | | | | |

### KM# 1032 700 WON

31.11 g., 0.999 Gold 0.999 oz. AGW, 40 mm. **Obv:** National arms, Central Bank name **Rev:** Admiral Yi Sunsin and turtle boat

| Date | Mintage | F12 | VF20 | XF40 | MS60 | MS63 |
|---|---|---|---|---|---|---|
| 2005 | — | PF65 1,800 | | | | |

### KM# 1033 700 WON

31.11 g., 0.999 Gold 0.999 oz. AGW, 40 mm. **Obv:** National arms, Central Bank name **Rev:** General Hong Beomdo

| Date | Mintage | F12 | VF20 | XF40 | MS60 | MS63 |
|---|---|---|---|---|---|---|
| 2005 | — | PF65 1,800 | | | | |

### KM# 1042 700 WON

31.11 g., 0.999 Gold 0.999 oz. AGW, 40 mm. **Obv:** National arms, Central Bank name **Rev:** Map of Korea, two peace doves, rainbow

| Date | Mintage | F12 | VF20 | XF40 | MS60 | MS63 |
|---|---|---|---|---|---|---|
| 2005 | — | PF65 1,800 | | | | |

### KM# 1047 700 WON

31.11 g., 0.999 Gold 0.999 oz. AGW, 40 mm. **Obv:** National arms, Central Bank name **Rev:** Tomb of the unknown soldier in Moscow, Russian legend

| Date | Mintage | F12 | VF20 | XF40 | MS60 | MS63 |
|---|---|---|---|---|---|---|
| 2005 | — | PF65 1,800 | | | | |

### KM# 1048 700 WON

31.11 g., 0.999 Gold 0.999 oz. AGW, 40 mm. **Obv:** National arms, Central Bank name **Rev:** Memorial to mothers in St. Petersburg

| Date | Mintage | F12 | VF20 | XF40 | MS60 | MS63 |
|---|---|---|---|---|---|---|
| 2005 | — | PF65 1,800 | | | | |

### KM# 428 700 WON

15.55 g., 0.999 Silver 0.4994 oz. ASW, 30 mm. **Series:** European Union Euro Commemoratives **Obv:** National arms **Rev:** Schleswig-Holstein City gate in relief in tiger's-eye **Edge:** Plain

| Date | Mintage | F12 | VF20 | XF40 | MS60 | MS63 |
|---|---|---|---|---|---|---|
| 2006 | 3,000 | PF65 70.00 | | | | |

### KM# 429 700 WON

15.55 g., 0.999 Silver 0.4994 oz. ASW, 30 mm. **Series:** European Union Euro Commemoratives **Obv:** National arms **Rev:** Vatican in relief in tiger's-eye **Edge:** Plain

| Date | Mintage | F12 | VF20 | XF40 | MS60 | MS63 |
|---|---|---|---|---|---|---|
| 2006 | 3,000 | PF65 70.00 | | | | |

**KM# 430 700 WON**
15.55 g., 0.999 Silver 0.4994 oz. ASW, 30 mm. **Series:** European Union Euro Commemoratives **Obv:** National arms **Rev:** Male Olympic statue - discus - Athens in relief in tiger's-eye **Edge:** Plain

| Date | Mintage | F12 | VF20 | XF40 | MS60 | MS63 |
|---|---|---|---|---|---|---|
| 2006 | 3,000 | PF65 70.00 | | | | |

**KM# 431 700 WON**
15.55 g., 0.999 Silver 0.4994 oz. ASW, 30 mm. **Series:** European Union Euro Commemoratives **Obv:** National arms **Rev:** 50th Anniversary Austrian States Treaty in relief in tiger's-eye **Edge:** Plain

| Date | Mintage | F12 | VF20 | XF40 | MS60 | MS63 |
|---|---|---|---|---|---|---|
| 2006 | 3,000 | PF65 70.00 | | | | |

**KM# 432 700 WON**
15.55 g., 0.999 Silver 0.4994 oz. ASW, 30 mm. **Series:** European Union Euro Commemoratives **Obv:** National arms **Rev:** Don Quixote in relief in tiger's-eye **Edge:** Plain

| Date | Mintage | F12 | VF20 | XF40 | MS60 | MS63 |
|---|---|---|---|---|---|---|
| 2006 | 3,000 | PF65 70.00 | | | | |

**KM# 433 700 WON**
15.55 g., 0.999 Silver 0.4994 oz. ASW, 30 mm. **Series:** European Union Euro Commemoratives **Obv:** National arms **Rev:** Head of Henri, Grand Duke of Luxembourg at left facing right, crowned H at right in relief in tiger's-eye **Edge:** Plain

| Date | Mintage | F12 | VF20 | XF40 | MS60 | MS63 |
|---|---|---|---|---|---|---|
| 2006 | 3,000 | PF65 70.00 | | | | |

**KM# 434 700 WON**
15.55 g., 0.999 Silver 0.4994 oz. ASW, 30 mm. **Series:** European Union Euro Commemoratives **Obv:** National arms **Rev:** Italian FAO logo in relief in tiger's-eye **Edge:** Plain

| Date | Mintage | F12 | VF20 | XF40 | MS60 | MS63 |
|---|---|---|---|---|---|---|
| 2006 | 3,000 | PF65 70.00 | | | | |

**KM# 435 700 WON**
15.55 g., 0.999 Silver 0.4994 oz. ASW, 30 mm. **Series:** European Union Euro Commemoratives **Obv:** National arms **Rev:** Finland - stylized flower in relief in tiger's-eye **Edge:** Plain

| Date | Mintage | F12 | VF20 | XF40 | MS60 | MS63 |
|---|---|---|---|---|---|---|
| 2006 | 3,000 | PF65 70.00 | | | | |

**KM# 436 700 WON**
15.55 g., 0.999 Silver 0.4994 oz. ASW, 30 mm. **Series:** European Union Euro Commemoratives **Obv:** National arms **Rev:** Conjoined heads of Grand Duke Henri of Luxembourg and King Albert of Belgium left in relief in tiger's-eye **Edge:** Plain

| Date | Mintage | F12 | VF20 | XF40 | MS60 | MS63 |
|---|---|---|---|---|---|---|
| 2006 | 3,000 | PF65 70.00 | | | | |

**KM# 437 700 WON**
15.55 g., 0.999 Silver 0.4994 oz. ASW, 30 mm. **Series:** European Union Euro Commemoratives **Obv:** National arms **Rev:** San Marino - bust of Bartolomeo Borghesi slightly right in relief in tiger's-eye **Edge:** Plain

| Date | Mintage | F12 | VF20 | XF40 | MS60 | MS63 |
|---|---|---|---|---|---|---|
| 2006 | 3,000 | PF65 70.00 | | | | |

**KM# 438 700 WON**
15.55 g., 0.999 Silver 0.4994 oz. ASW tigereye colored center, 30 mm. **Series:** European Union Euro Commemoratives **Obv:** National arms **Rev:** Vatican - World Youth Day in Cologne **Edge:** Plain

| Date | Mintage | F12 | VF20 | XF40 | MS60 | MS63 |
|---|---|---|---|---|---|---|
| 2006 | 3,000 | PF65 70.00 | | | | |

**KM# 439 700 WON**
15.55 g., 0.999 Silver 0.4994 oz. ASW, 30 mm. **Series:** European Union Euro Commemoratives **Obv:** National arms **Rev:** San Marino - Year of Physics design in relief in tiger's-eye **Edge:** Plain

| Date | Mintage | F12 | VF20 | XF40 | MS60 | MS63 |
|---|---|---|---|---|---|---|
| 2006 | 3,000 | PF65 70.00 | | | | |

**KM# 958 1000 WON**
42.22 g., 0.999 Gold 1.3559 oz. AGW, 45 mm. **Obv:** National arms, Central Bank name **Rev:** Kim Ilseong

| Date | Mintage | F12 | VF20 | XF40 | MS60 | MS63 |
|---|---|---|---|---|---|---|
| 2004 | — | PF65 2,450 | | | | |

**KM# 959 1000 WON**
42.22 g., 0.999 Gold 1.3559 oz. AGW, 45 mm. **Obv:** National arms, Central Bank name **Rev:** Kim Jeongil

| Date | Mintage | F12 | VF20 | XF40 | MS60 | MS63 |
|---|---|---|---|---|---|---|
| 2004 | — | PF65 2,500 | | | | |

**KM# 960 1000 WON**
42.22 g., 0.999 Gold 1.3559 oz. AGW, 45 mm. **Obv:** National arms, Central Bank name **Rev:** Kim Jeongsuk

| Date | Mintage | F12 | VF20 | XF40 | MS60 | MS63 |
|---|---|---|---|---|---|---|
| 2004 | — | PF65 2,500 | | | | |

**KM# 961 1000 WON**
42.22 g., 0.999 Gold 1.3559 oz. AGW, 45 mm. **Obv:** National arms, Central Bank name **Rev:** Kim Ilseong's birthplace

| Date | Mintage | F12 | VF20 | XF40 | MS60 | MS63 |
|---|---|---|---|---|---|---|
| 2004 | — | PF65 2,500 | | | | |

**KM# 962 1000 WON**
42.22 g., 0.999 Gold 1.3559 oz. AGW, 45 mm. **Obv:** National arms, Central Bank name **Rev:** Mountain cottage of Kim Jeongil

| Date | Mintage | F12 | VF20 | XF40 | MS60 | MS63 |
|---|---|---|---|---|---|---|
| 2004 | — | PF65 2,500 | | | | |

**KM# 963 1000 WON**
42.22 g., 0.999 Gold 1.3559 oz. AGW, 45 mm. **Obv:** National arms, Central Bank name **Rev:** House where Kim Jeongsuk was born

| Date | Mintage | F12 | VF20 | XF40 | MS60 | MS63 |
|---|---|---|---|---|---|---|
| 2004 | — | PF65 2,500 | | | | |

**KM# 1097 1000 WON**
20.00 g., 0.999 Silver 0.6424 oz. ASW, 38 mm. **Subject:** Lake Placid Winter Olympics, 1936 **Obv:** National arms, Central Bank name **Rev:** Bobsled

| Date | Mintage | F12 | VF20 | XF40 | MS60 | MS63 |
|---|---|---|---|---|---|---|
| 2006 | Est. 5000 | PF65 45.00 | | | | |

**KM# 1098 1000 WON**
20.00 g., 0.999 Silver 0.6424 oz. ASW, 38 mm. **Subject:** Sarajevo Winter Olympics, 1984 **Obv:** National arms, Central Bank name **Rev:** Ice Hockey player

| Date | Mintage | F12 | VF20 | XF40 | MS60 | MS63 |
|---|---|---|---|---|---|---|
| 2006 | Est. 5000 | PF65 45.00 | | | | |

**KM# 1099 1000 WON**
20.00 g., 0.999 Silver 0.6424 oz. ASW, 38 mm. **Obv:** National arms, Central Bank name **Rev:** Soccer player and Brazil flag and map

| Date | Mintage | F12 | VF20 | XF40 | MS60 | MS63 |
|---|---|---|---|---|---|---|
| 2006 | Est. 5000 | PF65 45.00 | | | | |

**KM# 1100 1000 WON**
20.00 g., 0.999 Silver 0.6424 oz. ASW, 38 mm. **Subject:** Bejing Summer Olympics, 2008 **Obv:** National arms, Central Bank name **Rev:** Gymnast on pommel horse

| Date | Mintage | F12 | VF20 | XF40 | MS60 | MS63 |
|---|---|---|---|---|---|---|
| 2006 | — | PF65 35.00 | | | | |

**KM# 440 1000 WON**
20.00 g., 0.999 Silver 0.6424 oz. ASW, 38 mm. **Obv:** National arms **Rev:** Arctic animals with map of North Pole in background **Rev. Legend:** INTERNATIONAL POLAR YEAR / ARCTIC ANIMALS **Edge:** Plain

| Date | Mintage | F12 | VF20 | XF40 | MS60 | MS63 |
|---|---|---|---|---|---|---|
| ND(2007) | — | PF65 85.00 | | | | |

**KM# 446 1000 WON**
20.00 g., 0.999 Silver 0.6424 oz. ASW, 38 mm. **Series:** Endangered Wildlife **Obv:** Fortress Gate **Rev:** Polar Bear standing facing **Rev. Legend:** URSUS MAITIMUS **Edge:** Plain

| Date | Mintage | F12 | VF20 | XF40 | MS60 | MS63 |
|---|---|---|---|---|---|---|
| 2007 | 5,000 | PF65 70.00 | | | | |

**KM# 1186 1000 WON**
20.00 g., 0.999 Silver 0.6424 oz. ASW, 38 mm. **Subject:** Vancouver Winter Olympics, 2010 **Obv:** East gate of Pyeongyang **Rev:** Nordic Combine and triumphial arch

| Date | Mintage | F12 | VF20 | XF40 | MS60 | MS63 |
|---|---|---|---|---|---|---|
| 2008 | — | PF65 45.00 | | | | |

**KM# 1187 1000 WON**
20.00 g., 0.999 Silver 0.6424 oz. ASW, 38 mm. **Subject:** Wold Cup Soccer, South Africa, 2010 **Obv:** East gate of Pyeongyang **Rev:** Soccer foul play

| Date | Mintage | F12 | VF20 | XF40 | MS60 | MS63 |
|---|---|---|---|---|---|---|
| 2008 | — | PF65 35.00 | | | | |

**KM# 993 1500 WON**
70.00 g., 0.999 Gold 2.2483 oz. AGW, 50 mm. **Obv:** Map of Korea, Central Bank name **Rev:** Court physician Heo Jun

| Date | Mintage | F12 | VF20 | XF40 | MS60 | MS63 |
|---|---|---|---|---|---|---|
| 2004 | — | PF65 4,000 | | | | |

**KM# 1067 1500 WON**
31.11 g., 0.999 Silver 0.999 oz. ASW, 40 mm. **Obv:** Trumpeter, Central Bank name **Rev:** Triumphial arch in Pyeongyang

| Date | Mintage | F12 | VF20 | XF40 | MS60 | MS63 |
|---|---|---|---|---|---|---|
| 2005 | — | PF65 115 | | | | |

**KM# 1069 1500 WON**
31.11 g., 0.999 Silver 0.999 oz. ASW, 40 mm. **Subject:** Worker's Party, 60th Anniversary **Obv:** National arms, Central Bank name **Rev:** Party emblem

| Date | Mintage | F12 | VF20 | XF40 | MS60 | MS63 |
|---|---|---|---|---|---|---|
| 2005 | — | PF65 115 | | | | |

**KM# 1070 1500 WON**
31.11 g., 0.999 Gold 0.999 oz. AGW, 40 mm. **Subject:** Worker's Party,60th Anniversary **Obv:** National arms, Central Bank name **Rev:** Party emblem

| Date | Mintage | F12 | VF20 | XF40 | MS60 | MS63 |
|---|---|---|---|---|---|---|
| 2005 | — | PF65 1,800 | | | | |

**KM# 1092 1500 WON**
31.11 g., 0.999 Silver 0.999 oz. ASW, 40 mm. **Obv:** National arms, Central Bank name **Rev:** Two dogs

| Date | Mintage | F12 | VF20 | XF40 | MS60 | MS63 |
|---|---|---|---|---|---|---|
| 2006 | — | PF65 60.00 | | | | |

**KM# 1093 1500 WON**
31.11 g., 0.999 Silver 0.999 oz. ASW, 40 mm. **Obv:** National arms, Central Bank name **Rev:** Bronze staue of flying horse

| Date | Mintage | F12 | VF20 | XF40 | MS60 | MS63 |
|---|---|---|---|---|---|---|
| 2006 | — | PF65 115 | | | | |

**KM# 1094 1500 WON**
31.11 g., 0.999 Silver 0.999 oz. ASW, 40 mm. **Obv:** National arms, Central Bank name **Rev:** Triumphial arch

| Date | Mintage | F12 | VF20 | XF40 | MS60 | MS63 |
|---|---|---|---|---|---|---|
| 2006 | — | PF65 115 | | | | |

**KM# 1142 1500 WON**
31.11 g., 0.999 Silver 0.999 oz. ASW, 40 mm. **Obv:** National arms, Central Bank name **Rev:** Hoopoe

| Date | Mintage | F12 | VF20 | XF40 | MS60 | MS63 |
|---|---|---|---|---|---|---|
| 2007 | Est. 500 | PF65 60.00 | | | | |

**KM# 1143 1500 WON**
31.11 g., 0.999 Silver 0.999 oz. ASW, 40 mm. **Obv:** National arms, Central Bank name **Rev:** Ural owl

| Date | Mintage | F12 | VF20 | XF40 | MS60 | MS63 |
|---|---|---|---|---|---|---|
| 2007 | Est. 500 | PF65 100 | | | | |

**KM# 1144 1500 WON**
31.11 g., 0.999 Silver 0.999 oz. ASW, 40 mm. **Obv:** National arms, Central Bank name **Rev:** Eagle

| Date | Mintage | F12 | VF20 | XF40 | MS60 | MS63 |
|---|---|---|---|---|---|---|
| 2007 | — | PF65 60.00 | | | | |

**KM# 1145 1500 WON**
31.11 g., 0.999 Silver 0.999 oz. ASW, 40 mm. **Obv:** National arms, Central Bank name **Rev:** White Rhino

| Date | Mintage | F12 | VF20 | XF40 | MS60 | MS63 |
|---|---|---|---|---|---|---|
| 2007 | — | PF65 60.00 | | | | |

**KM# 1146 1500 WON**
31.11 g., 0.999 Silver 0.999 oz. ASW, 40 mm. **Obv:** National arms, Central Bank name **Rev:** African elephant family

| Date | Mintage | F12 | VF20 | XF40 | MS60 | MS63 |
|---|---|---|---|---|---|---|
| 2007 | Est. 500 | PF65 60.00 | | | | |

**KM# 1147 1500 WON**
31.11 g., 0.999 Silver 0.999 oz. ASW, 40 mm. **Obv:** National arms, Central Bank name **Rev:** Lion family

| Date | Mintage | F12 | VF20 | XF40 | MS60 | MS63 |
|---|---|---|---|---|---|---|
| 2007 | Est. 500 | PF65 60.00 | | | | |

**KM# 1148 1500 WON**
31.11 g., 0.999 Silver 0.999 oz. ASW, 40 mm. **Obv:** National arms, Central Bank name **Rev:** Cape buffalo

| Date | Mintage | F12 | VF20 | XF40 | MS60 | MS63 |
|---|---|---|---|---|---|---|
| 2007 | Est. 500 | PF65 60.00 | | | | |

**KM# 1149 1500 WON**
31.11 g., 0.999 Silver 0.999 oz. ASW, 40 mm. **Obv:** National arms, Central Bank name **Rev:** Marine turtle

| Date | Mintage | F12 | VF20 | XF40 | MS60 | MS63 |
|---|---|---|---|---|---|---|
| 2007 | Est. 500 | PF65 60.00 | | | | |

**KM# 1150 1500 WON**
31.11 g., 0.999 Silver 0.999 oz. ASW, 40 mm. **Obv:** National arms, Central Bank name **Rev:** Penguin

| Date | Mintage | F12 | VF20 | XF40 | MS60 | MS63 |
|---|---|---|---|---|---|---|
| 2007 | Est. 500 | PF65 60.00 | | | | |

**KM# 1151 1500 WON**
31.11 g., 0.999 Silver 0.999 oz. ASW, 40 mm. **Obv:** National arms, Central Bank name **Rev:** Emu

| Date | Mintage | F12 | VF20 | XF40 | MS60 | MS63 |
|---|---|---|---|---|---|---|
| 2007 | Est. 500 | PF65 60.00 | | | | |

**KM# 1152 1500 WON**
31.11 g., 0.999 Silver 0.999 oz. ASW, 40 mm. **Obv:** National arms, Central Bank name **Rev:** Eagle owl

| Date | Mintage | F12 | VF20 | XF40 | MS60 | MS63 |
|---|---|---|---|---|---|---|
| 2007 | Est. 500 | PF65 60.00 | | | | |

**KM# 1153 1500 WON**
31.11 g., 0.999 Silver 0.999 oz. ASW, 40 mm. **Obv:** National arms, Central Bank name **Rev:** Lemur

| Date | Mintage | F12 | VF20 | XF40 | MS60 | MS63 |
|---|---|---|---|---|---|---|
| 2007 | — | PF65 60.00 | | | | |

**KM# 1154 1500 WON**
31.11 g., 0.999 Silver 0.999 oz. ASW, 40 mm. **Obv:** National arms, Central Bank name **Rev:** Lion

| Date | Mintage | F12 | VF20 | XF40 | MS60 | MS63 |
|---|---|---|---|---|---|---|
| 2007 | Est. 500 | PF65 60.00 | | | | |

**KM# 1155 1500 WON**
31.11 g., 0.999 Silver 0.999 oz. ASW, 40 mm. **Obv:** National arms, Central Bank name **Rev:** Two African elephants

| Date | Mintage | F12 | VF20 | XF40 | MS60 | MS63 |
|---|---|---|---|---|---|---|
| 2007 | Est. 500 | PF65 60.00 | | | | |

**KM# 1176 1500 WON**
31.11 g., 0.999 Silver 0.999 oz. ASW, 40 mm. **Subject:** Nationhood, 60th Anniversary **Obv:** National arms, Central Bank name **Rev:** National flag, star above

| Date | Mintage | F12 | VF20 | XF40 | MS60 | MS63 |
|---|---|---|---|---|---|---|
| 2008 | — | PF65 115 | | | | |

**KM# 1185 1500 WON**
31.11 g., 0.999 Silver 0.999 oz. ASW, 40 mm. **Subject:** Bejing Summer Olympics, 2008 **Obv:** East gate of Pyeongyang **Rev:** Ancient ring gymnast

| Date | Mintage | F12 | VF20 | XF40 | MS60 | MS63 |
|---|---|---|---|---|---|---|
| 2008 | Est. 5000 | PF65 60.00 | | | | |

**KM# 950 2000 WON**
31.11 g., 0.999 Bi-Metallic 0.999 oz. Gold center in Silver ring, 40 mm. **Obv:** National arms, Central Bank name **Rev:** Sports hall in Pyeongyang

| Date | Mintage | F12 | VF20 | XF40 | MS60 | MS63 |
|---|---|---|---|---|---|---|
| 2004 | — | PF65 2,200 | | | | |

**KM# 964 2000 WON**
31.11 g., 0.999 Gold 0.999 oz. AGW, 35 mm. **Subject:** 10th Anniversary of the takeover **Obv:** National arms, Central Bank name **Rev:** Kim Jeongil

| Date | Mintage | F12 | VF20 | XF40 | MS60 | MS63 |
|---|---|---|---|---|---|---|
| 2004 | — | PF65 2,100 | | | | |

**KM# 965 2000 WON**
31.11 g., 0.999 Gold 0.999 oz. AGW, 35 mm. **Obv:** National arms, Central Bank name **Rev:** Kim Jeongil and Kim Daejung

| Date | Mintage | F12 | VF20 | XF40 | MS60 | MS63 |
|---|---|---|---|---|---|---|
| 2004 | — | PF65 2,000 | | | | |

**KM# 967 2000 WON**
31.11 g., 0.999 Gold 0.999 oz. AGW, 35 mm. **Obv:** National arms, Central Bank name **Rev:** Kim Jeongil and Hu Jintao

| Date | Mintage | F12 | VF20 | XF40 | MS60 | MS63 |
|---|---|---|---|---|---|---|
| 2004 | — | PF65 2,000 | | | | |

**KM# 968 2000 WON**
31.11 g., 0.999 Gold 0.999 oz. AGW, 35 mm. **Obv:** National arms, Central Bank name **Rev:** Kim Jeongil and Vladimir Putin

| Date | Mintage | F12 | VF20 | XF40 | MS60 | MS63 |
|---|---|---|---|---|---|---|
| 2004 | — | PF65 2,100 | | | | |

**KM# 985 2000 WON**
31.11 g., 0.999 Gold 0.999 oz. AGW, 40 mm. **Obv:** Dokdo, rocky islands, Central Bank name **Rev:** Island group map

| Date | Mintage | F12 | VF20 | XF40 | MS60 | MS63 |
|---|---|---|---|---|---|---|
| 2004 | — | PF65 2,000 | | | | |

**KM# 986 2000 WON**
31.11 g., 0.999 Gold 0.999 oz. AGW, 40 mm. **Obv:** Dokdo, rocky islands, Central Bank name **Rev:** Fisher Ahn Yongbok

| Date | Mintage | F12 | VF20 | XF40 | MS60 | MS63 |
|---|---|---|---|---|---|---|
| 2004 | — | PF65 2,100 | | | | |

**KM# 987 2000 WON**
31.11 g., 0.999 Gold 0.999 oz. AGW, 40 mm. **Obv:** Dokdo, rocky islands, Central Bank name **Rev:** West Island

| Date | Mintage | F12 | VF20 | XF40 | MS60 | MS63 |
|---|---|---|---|---|---|---|
| 2004 | — | PF65 2,100 | | | | |

**KM# 988 2000 WON**
31.11 g., 0.999 Gold 0.999 oz. AGW, 40 mm. **Obv:** Dokdo, rocky islands, Central Bank name **Rev:** East island

| Date | Mintage | F12 | VF20 | XF40 | MS60 | MS63 |
|---|---|---|---|---|---|---|
| 2004 | — | PF65 2,100 | | | | |

**KM# 989 2000 WON**
31.11 g., 0.999 Gold 0.999 oz. AGW, 40 mm. **Obv:** Dokdo, rocky islands, Central Bank name **Rev:** Three brothers islands

| Date | Mintage | F12 | VF20 | XF40 | MS60 | MS63 |
|---|---|---|---|---|---|---|
| 2004 | — | PF65 2,100 | | | | |

**KM# 990 2000 WON**
31.11 g., 0.999 Gold 0.999 oz. AGW, 40 mm. **Obv:** Dokdo, rocky islands, Central Bank name **Rev:** Chicken island

| Date | Mintage | F12 | VF20 | XF40 | MS60 | MS63 |
|---|---|---|---|---|---|---|
| 2004 | — | PF65 2,100 | | | | |

**KM# 991 2000 WON**
31.11 g., 0.999 Gold 0.999 oz. AGW, 40 mm. **Obv:** Dokdo, rocky islands, Central Bank name **Rev:** Candle island

| Date | Mintage | F12 | VF20 | XF40 | MS60 | MS63 |
|---|---|---|---|---|---|---|
| 2004 | — | PF65 2,100 | | | | |

**KM# 1087 2500 WON**
33.33 g., 0.900 Gold 0.9644 oz. AGW **Obv:** Old coins and Central Bank name

| Date | Mintage | F12 | VF20 | XF40 | MS60 | MS63 |
|---|---|---|---|---|---|---|
| 2005 | Est. 200 | — | — | — | — | 2,050 |

**KM# 1290 3000 WON**
62.21 g., 0.999 Silver 1.9981 oz. ASW **Subject:** Stone Lamp **Obv:** Temple **Rev:** Stone Lamp

| Date | Mintage | F12 | VF20 | XF40 | MS60 | MS63 |
|---|---|---|---|---|---|---|
| 2012 Proof | — | — | — | — | — | — |

**KM# 442 15000 WON**
7.78 g., 0.999 Gold 0.2499 oz. AGW, 26 mm. **Subject:** 170th Anniversary First Public Railway St. Petersburg - Zarskoje Selo **Obv:** Fortress Gate **Rev:** First train arriving **Edge:** Plain

| Date | Mintage | F12 | VF20 | XF40 | MS60 | MS63 |
|---|---|---|---|---|---|---|
| ND(2007) | 2,000 | PF65 550 | | | | |

**KM# 448 15000 WON**
7.78 g., 0.999 Gold 0.2499 oz. AGW, 26 mm. **Subject:** 150th Anniversary Birth of Ziolkowski and 50th Anniversary Launch of Sputnik I **Obv:** Fortress Gate **Rev:** Bust of Ziolkowski facing 3/4 right at lower left, Sputnik circling earth at top right **Edge:** Plain

| Date | Mintage | F12 | VF20 | XF40 | MS60 | MS63 |
|---|---|---|---|---|---|---|
| ND(2007) | 2,000 | PF65 550 | | | | |

**KM# 444 15000 WON**
7.78 g., 0.999 Gold 0.2499 oz. AGW, 26 mm. **Subject:** Lunar Year of the Rat **Obv:** Fortress Gate **Rev:** Two rats within circle of Lunar figures **Edge:** Plain

| Date | Mintage | F12 | VF20 | XF40 | MS60 | MS63 |
|---|---|---|---|---|---|---|
| 2008 | 2,000 | PF65 550 | | | | |

**KM# 1068 60000 WON**
31.11 g., 0.999 Gold 0.999 oz. AGW, 35 mm. **Obv:** Trumpeter, Central Bank name **Rev:** Triumphia arch in Pyeongyang

| Date | Mintage | F12 | VF20 | XF40 | MS60 | MS63 |
|---|---|---|---|---|---|---|
| 2005 | — | PF65 1,800 | | | | |

**KM# 1095 60000 WON**
31.11 g., 0.999 Gold 0.999 oz. AGW, 35 mm. **Obv:** National arms, Central Bank name **Rev:** Bronze statue of flying horse

| Date | Mintage | F12 | VF20 | XF40 | MS60 | MS63 |
|---|---|---|---|---|---|---|
| 2006 | — | PF65 2,100 | | | | |

**KM# 1096 60000 WON**
31.11 g., 0.999 Gold 0.999 oz. AGW, 35 mm. **Obv:** National arms, Central Bank name **Rev:** Triumphial arch

| Date | Mintage | F12 | VF20 | XF40 | MS60 | MS63 |
|---|---|---|---|---|---|---|
| 2006 | — | PF65 2,100 | | | | |

**KM# 1156 60000 WON**
31.11 g., 0.999 Gold 0.999 oz. AGW, 35 mm. **Obv:** National arms, Central Bank name **Rev:** Hoopoe

| Date | Mintage | F12 | VF20 | XF40 | MS60 | MS63 |
|---|---|---|---|---|---|---|
| 2007 | Est. 500 | PF65 2,100 | | | | |

**KM# 1157 60000 WON**
31.11 g., 0.999 Gold 0.999 oz. AGW, 35 mm. **Obv:** National arms, Central Bank name **Rev:** Ural owl

| Date | Mintage | F12 | VF20 | XF40 | MS60 | MS63 |
|---|---|---|---|---|---|---|
| 2007 | Est. 500 | PF65 2,100 | | | | |

**KM# 1158 60000 WON**
31.11 g., 0.999 Gold 0.999 oz. AGW, 35 mm. **Obv:** National arms, Central Bank name **Rev:** Eagle

| Date | Mintage | F12 | VF20 | XF40 | MS60 | MS63 |
|---|---|---|---|---|---|---|
| 2007 | Est. 500 | PF65 2,100 | | | | |

**KM# 1159 60000 WON**
31.11 g., 0.999 Gold 0.999 oz. AGW, 35 mm. **Obv:** National arms, Central Bank name **Rev:** White rhino

| Date | Mintage | F12 | VF20 | XF40 | MS60 | MS63 |
|---|---|---|---|---|---|---|
| 2007 | Est. 500 | PF65 2,100 | | | | |

**KM# 1160 60000 WON**
31.11 g., 0.999 Gold 0.999 oz. AGW, 35 mm. **Obv:** National arms, Central Bank name **Rev:** African elephant family

| Date | Mintage | F12 | VF20 | XF40 | MS60 | MS63 |
|---|---|---|---|---|---|---|
| 2007 | Est. 500 | PF65 2,100 | | | | |

**KM# 1161 60000 WON**
31.11 g., 0.999 Gold 0.999 oz. AGW, 35 mm. **Obv:** National arms, Central Bank name **Rev:** Lion family

| Date | Mintage | F12 | VF20 | XF40 | MS60 | MS63 |
|---|---|---|---|---|---|---|
| 2007 | Est. 500 | PF65 2,100 | | | | |

**KM# 1162 60000 WON**
31.11 g., 0.999 Gold 0.999 oz. AGW, 35 mm. **Obv:** National arms, Central Bank name **Rev:** Cape buffalo

| Date | Mintage | F12 | VF20 | XF40 | MS60 | MS63 |
|---|---|---|---|---|---|---|
| 2007 | — | PF65 2,100 | | | | |

**KM# 1163 60000 WON**
31.11 g., 0.999 Gold 0.999 oz. AGW, 35 mm. **Obv:** National arms, Central Bank name **Rev:** Marine turtle

| Date | Mintage | F12 | VF20 | XF40 | MS60 | MS63 |
|---|---|---|---|---|---|---|
| 2007 | — | PF65 2,100 | | | | |

**KM# 1164 60000 WON**
31.11 g., 0.999 Gold 0.999 oz. AGW, 35 mm. **Obv:** National arms, Central Bank name **Rev:** Penguin

| Date | Mintage | F12 | VF20 | XF40 | MS60 | MS63 |
|---|---|---|---|---|---|---|
| 2007 | Est. 500 | PF65 2,100 | | | | |

**KM# 1165 60000 WON**
31.11 g., 0.999 Gold 0.999 oz. AGW, 35 mm. **Obv:** National arms, Central Bank name **Rev:** Emu

| Date | Mintage | F12 | VF20 | XF40 | MS60 | MS63 |
|---|---|---|---|---|---|---|
| 2007 | Est. 500 | PF65 2,100 | | | | |

**KM# 1166 60000 WON**
31.11 g., 0.999 Gold 0.999 oz. AGW, 35 mm. **Obv:** National arms, Central Bank name **Rev:** Eagle owl

| Date | Mintage | F12 | VF20 | XF40 | MS60 | MS63 |
|---|---|---|---|---|---|---|
| 2007 | Est. 500 | PF65 2,100 | | | | |

**KM# 1167 60000 WON**
31.11 g., 0.999 Gold 0.999 oz. AGW, 35 mm. **Obv:** National arms, Central Bank name **Rev:** Lemur

| Date | Mintage | F12 | VF20 | XF40 | MS60 | MS63 |
|---|---|---|---|---|---|---|
| 2007 | — | PF65 2,100 | | | | |

**KM# 1168 60000 WON**
31.11 g., 0.999 Gold 0.999 oz. AGW, 35 mm. **Obv:** National arms, Central Bank name **Rev:** Lion

| Date | Mintage | F12 | VF20 | XF40 | MS60 | MS63 |
|---|---|---|---|---|---|---|
| 2007 | — | PF65 2,100 | | | | |

**KM# 1169 60000 WON**
31.11 g., 0.999 Gold 0.999 oz. AGW, 35 mm. **Obv:** National arms, Central Bank name **Rev:** Two African elephants

| Date | Mintage | F12 | VF20 | XF40 | MS60 | MS63 |
|---|---|---|---|---|---|---|
| 2007 | — | PF65 2,100 | | | | |

**KM# 1177 60000 WON**
31.11 g., 0.999 Gold 0.999 oz. AGW, 35 mm. **Subject:** Nationhood, 60th Anniversary **Obv:** National arms, Central Bank name **Rev:** National flag, star above

| Date | Mintage | F12 | VF20 | XF40 | MS60 | MS63 |
|---|---|---|---|---|---|---|
| 2008 | — | PF65 2,100 | | | | |

## REFORM COINAGE

100 (Old) Won = 1 (new) Won

**KM# 1170 CHON**
Aluminum, 18 mm. **Obv:** National arms, Central Bank name

| Date | Mintage | F12 | VF20 | XF40 | MS60 | MS63 |
|---|---|---|---|---|---|---|
| 2008 | — | — | — | — | 3.00 | 5.00 |

**KM# 1171 5 CHON**
Aluminum, 19 mm. **Obv:** National arms, Central Bank name **Rev:** Magnolia

| Date | Mintage | F12 | VF20 | XF40 | MS60 | MS63 |
|---|---|---|---|---|---|---|
| 2008 | — | — | — | — | 3.00 | 5.00 |

**KM# 1172 10 CHON**
1.00 g., Aluminum, 20 mm. **Obv:** National arms, Central Bank name **Rev:** Rhododendron

| Date | Mintage | F12 | VF20 | XF40 | MS60 | MS63 |
|---|---|---|---|---|---|---|
| 2002 | — | — | — | — | 1.00 | 1.75 |

**KM# 1173 50 CHON**
1.50 g., Aluminum, 22 mm. **Obv:** National arms, Central Bank name **Rev:** Begonia

| Date | Mintage | F12 | VF20 | XF40 | MS60 | MS63 |
|---|---|---|---|---|---|---|
| 2002 | — | — | — | — | 1.00 | 2.00 |

**KM# 1174 WON**
1.80 g., Aluminum, 24 mm. **Obv:** National arms, Central Bank name **Rev:** Beognia

| Date | Mintage | F12 | VF20 | XF40 | MS60 | MS63 |
|---|---|---|---|---|---|---|
| 2002 | — | — | — | — | 1.50 | 2.50 |

**KM# 1188 2 WON**
7.00 g., 0.999 Silver 0.2248 oz. ASW, 30 mm. **Obv:** National arms, Central Bank name **Rev:** Panda in color

| Date | Mintage | F12 | VF20 | XF40 | MS60 | MS63 |
|---|---|---|---|---|---|---|
| 2008 | Est. 5000 | PF65 30.00 | | | | |

**KM# 1217 2 WON**
7.00 g., 0.999 Silver 0.2248 oz. ASW, 30 mm. **Obv:** National arms, Central Bank name **Rev:** Panda in color

| Date | Mintage | F12 | VF20 | XF40 | MS60 | MS63 |
|---|---|---|---|---|---|---|
| 2009 | Est. 5000 | PF65 30.00 | | | | |

**KM# 1220 2 WON**
7.00 g., 0.999 Silver 0.2248 oz. ASW, 30 mm. **Obv:** National arms, Central Bank name **Rev:** Corwn gate of the Dresden Zwingers

| Date | Mintage | F12 | VF20 | XF40 | MS60 | MS63 |
|---|---|---|---|---|---|---|
| 2009 | — | PF65 30.00 | | | | |

**KM# 1221 2 WON**
7.00 g., 0.999 Silver 0.2248 oz. ASW, 30 mm. **Obv:** National arms, Central Bank name **Rev:** Acropolis in Athens

| Date | Mintage | F12 | VF20 | XF40 | MS60 | MS63 |
|---|---|---|---|---|---|---|
| 2009 | — | PF65 30.00 | | | | |

**KM# 1222 2 WON**
7.00 g., 0.999 Silver 0.2248 oz. ASW, 30 mm. **Obv:** National arms, Central Bank name **Rev:** Sydney Opera House

| Date | Mintage | F12 | VF20 | XF40 | MS60 | MS63 |
|---|---|---|---|---|---|---|
| 2009 | — | PF65 30.00 | | | | |

**KM# 1223 2 WON**
7.00 g., 0.999 Silver 0.2248 oz. ASW, 30 mm. **Obv:** National arms, Central Bank name **Rev:** Angkor Wat temple complex

| Date | Mintage | F12 | VF20 | XF40 | MS60 | MS63 |
|---|---|---|---|---|---|---|
| 2009 | — | PF65 30.00 | | | | |

**KM# 1224 2 WON**
7.00 g., 0.999 Silver 0.2248 oz. ASW, 30 mm. **Obv:** National arms, Central Bank name **Rev:** Minakshi and Sundareshwara temples in Madurai

| Date | Mintage | F12 | VF20 | XF40 | MS60 | MS63 |
|---|---|---|---|---|---|---|
| 2009 | — | PF65 30.00 | | | | |

**KM# 1225 2 WON**
7.00 g., 0.999 Silver 0.2248 oz. ASW, 30 mm. **Obv:** National arms, Central Bank name **Rev:** Kremlin in Moscow

| Date | Mintage | F12 | VF20 | XF40 | MS60 | MS63 |
|---|---|---|---|---|---|---|
| 2009 | — | PF65 30.00 | | | | |

**KM# 1226 2 WON**
7.00 g., 0.999 Silver 0.2248 oz. ASW, 30 mm. **Obv:** National arms, Central Bank name **Rev:** Abu Simbel

| Date | Mintage | F12 | VF20 | XF40 | MS60 | MS63 |
|---|---|---|---|---|---|---|
| 2009 | — | PF65 30.00 | | | | |

**KM# 1227 2 WON**
7.00 g., 0.999 Silver 0.2248 oz. ASW, 30 mm. **Obv:** National arms, Central Bank name **Rev:** Eiffel Tower in Paris

| Date | Mintage | F12 | VF20 | XF40 | MS60 | MS63 |
|---|---|---|---|---|---|---|
| 2009 | — | PF65 30.00 | | | | |

**KM# 1228 2 WON**
7.00 g., 0.999 Silver 0.2248 oz. ASW, 30 mm. **Obv:** National arms, Central Bank name **Rev:** Dalai Lama's Palace in Lhasa

| Date | Mintage | F12 | VF20 | XF40 | MS60 | MS63 |
|---|---|---|---|---|---|---|
| 2009 | — | PF65 30.00 | | | | |

**KM# 1229 2 WON**
7.00 g., 0.999 Silver 0.2248 oz. ASW, 30 mm. **Obv:** National arms, Central Bank name **Rev:** Terracotta warriors of King Qin Shihuangdi in China

| Date | Mintage | F12 | VF20 | XF40 | MS60 | MS63 |
|---|---|---|---|---|---|---|
| 2009 | — | PF65 30.00 | | | | |

**KM# 1230 2 WON**
7.00 g., 0.999 Silver 0.2248 oz. ASW, 30 mm. **Obv:** National arms, Central Bank name **Rev:** Palace at Versailles

| Date | Mintage | F12 | VF20 | XF40 | MS60 | MS63 |
|---|---|---|---|---|---|---|
| 2009 | — | PF65 30.00 | | | | |

**KM# 1231 2 WON**
7.00 g., 0.999 Silver 0.2248 oz. ASW, 30 mm. **Obv:** National arms, Central Bank name **Rev:** Aachen Cathedral

| Date | Mintage | F12 | VF20 | XF40 | MS60 | MS63 |
|---|---|---|---|---|---|---|
| 2010 | — | PF65 30.00 | | | | |

**KM# 1232 2 WON**
7.00 g., 0.999 Silver 0.2248 oz. ASW, 30 mm. **Obv:** National arms, Central Bank name **Rev:** Leaning Tower of Pisa

| Date | Mintage | F12 | VF20 | XF40 | MS60 | MS63 |
|---|---|---|---|---|---|---|
| 2010 | — | PF65 30.00 | | | | |

**KM# 1233 2 WON**
7.00 g., 0.999 Silver 0.2248 oz. ASW, 30 mm. **Obv:** National arms, Central Bank name **Rev:** Chapel in Luzern

| Date | Mintage | F12 | VF20 | XF40 | MS60 | MS63 |
|---|---|---|---|---|---|---|
| 2010 | — | PF65 30.00 | | | | |

**KM# 1272 2 WON**
7.00 g., 0.999 Silver 0.2248 oz. ASW, 30 mm. **Obv:** National arms, Central Bank name **Rev:** Three pandas in color

| Date | Mintage | F12 | VF20 | XF40 | MS60 | MS63 |
|---|---|---|---|---|---|---|
| 2010 | Est. 5000 | PF65 30.00 | | | | |

**KM# 1276 2 WON**
7.00 g., 0.999 Silver 0.2248 oz. ASW, 30 mm. **Obv:** National arms, Central Bank name **Rev:** Great Mosque of Cordoba

| Date | Mintage | F12 | VF20 | XF40 | MS60 | MS63 |
|---|---|---|---|---|---|---|
| 2010 | — | PF65 30.00 | | | | |

**KM# 1277 2 WON**
7.00 g., 0.999 Silver 0.2248 oz. ASW, 30 mm. **Obv:** National arms, Central Bank name **Rev:** Cathedral of Santiago de Compostela

| Date | Mintage | F12 | VF20 | XF40 | MS60 | MS63 |
|---|---|---|---|---|---|---|
| 2010 | — | PF65 30.00 | | | | |

**KM# 1278 2 WON**
7.00 g., 0.999 Silver 0.2248 oz. ASW, 30 mm. **Obv:** National arms, Central Bank name **Rev:** Timbuktu

| Date | Mintage | F12 | VF20 | XF40 | MS60 | MS63 |
|---|---|---|---|---|---|---|
| 2010 | — | PF65 30.00 | | | | |

**KM# 1279 2 WON**
7.00 g., 0.999 Silver 0.2248 oz. ASW, 30 mm. **Obv:** National arms, Central Bank name **Rev:** London's Big Ben clock tower

| Date | Mintage | F12 | VF20 | XF40 | MS60 | MS63 |
|---|---|---|---|---|---|---|
| 2010 | — | PF65 30.00 | | | | |

**KM# 1280 2 WON**
7.00 g., 0.999 Silver 0.2248 oz. ASW, 30 mm. **Obv:** National arms, Central Bank name **Rev:** Prague castle

| Date | Mintage | F12 | VF20 | XF40 | MS60 | MS63 |
|---|---|---|---|---|---|---|
| 2010 | — | PF65 30.00 | | | | |

**KM# 1281 2 WON**
7.00 g., 0.999 Silver 0.2248 oz. ASW, 30 mm. **Obv:** National arms, Central Bank name **Rev:** Teoihuacan pyramid

| Date | Mintage | F12 | VF20 | XF40 | MS60 | MS63 |
|---|---|---|---|---|---|---|
| 2010 | — | PF65 30.00 | | | | |

**KM# 1282 2 WON**
7.00 g., 0.999 Silver 0.2248 oz. ASW, 30 mm. **Obv:** National arms, Central Bank name **Rev:** Forbidden city

| Date | Mintage | F12 | VF20 | XF40 | MS60 | MS63 |
|---|---|---|---|---|---|---|
| 2010 | — | PF65 30.00 | | | | |

**KM# 1189 5 WON**
20.00 g., 0.999 Silver 0.6424 oz. ASW, 38 mm. **Obv:** National arms, Central Bank name **Rev:** Sailing ship Grand Duchess Elizabeth

| Date | Mintage | F12 | VF20 | XF40 | MS60 | MS63 |
|---|---|---|---|---|---|---|
| 2008 | Est. 5000 | PF65 45.00 | | | | |

**KM# 1191 5 WON**
20.00 g., 0.999 Silver 0.6424 oz. ASW, 38 mm. **Obv:** National arms, Central Bank name **Rev:** Four-masted schooner Elizabeth Bandi and three-masted bark Seute Deern

| Date | Mintage | F12 | VF20 | XF40 | MS60 | MS63 |
|---|---|---|---|---|---|---|
| 2008 | Est. 5000 | PF65 45.00 | | | | |

**KM# 1219 5 WON**
20.00 g., 0.999 Silver 0.6424 oz. ASW, 38 mm. **Obv:** National arms, Central Bank name **Rev:** U.S.C.G. Barque Eagle

| Date | Mintage | F12 | VF20 | XF40 | MS60 | MS63 |
|---|---|---|---|---|---|---|
| 2008 | — | PF65 45.00 | | | | |

**KM# 1190 5 WON**
20.00 g., 0.999 Silver 0.6424 oz. ASW, 38 mm. **Obv:** National arms, Central Bank name **Rev:** Three-masted sailing ship Passat

| Date | Mintage | F12 | VF20 | XF40 | MS60 | MS63 |
|---|---|---|---|---|---|---|
| 2009 | Est. 5000 | PF65 45.00 | | | | |

**KM# 1192 5 WON**
20.00 g., 0.999 Silver 0.6424 oz. ASW, 38 mm. **Obv:** National arms, Central Bank name **Rev:** Sail training ship Deutschland

| Date | Mintage | F12 | VF20 | XF40 | MS60 | MS63 |
|---|---|---|---|---|---|---|
| 2009 | Est. 5000 | PF65 45.00 | | | | |

**KM# 1193 5 WON**
20.00 g., 0.999 Silver 0.6424 oz. ASW, 38 mm. **Obv:** National arms, Central Bank name **Rev:** Three-masted sailing ship Gorch Fock II

| Date | Mintage | F12 | VF20 | XF40 | MS60 | MS63 |
|---|---|---|---|---|---|---|
| 2009 | Est. 5000 | PF65 45.00 | | | | |

**KM# 1218 5 WON**
20.00 g., 0.999 Silver 0.6424 oz. ASW, 38 mm. **Obv:** National arms, Central Bank name **Rev:** Sailing ship Dar Mlodziezy

| Date | Mintage | F12 | VF20 | XF40 | MS60 | MS63 |
|---|---|---|---|---|---|---|
| 2009 | — | PF65 45.00 | | | | |

**KM# 1273 5 WON**
20.00 g., 0.999 Silver 0.6424 oz. ASW, 38 mm. **Obv:** National arms, Central Bank name **Rev:** Philippine hood eagle

| Date | Mintage | F12 | VF20 | XF40 | MS60 | MS63 |
|---|---|---|---|---|---|---|
| 2010 | — | PF65 60.00 | | | | |

**KM# 1274 5 WON**
20.00 g., 0.999 Silver 0.6424 oz. ASW, 38 mm. **Obv:** National arms, Central Bank name **Rev:** Tibetian ox

| Date | Mintage | F12 | VF20 | XF40 | MS60 | MS63 |
|---|---|---|---|---|---|---|
| 2010 | — | PF65 60.00 | | | | |

**KM# 1194 10 WON**
1.00 g., 0.916 Gold 0.0295 oz. AGW, 16 mm. **Obv:** National arms, Central Bank name **Rev:** Rickmer Rickmers

| Date | Mintage | F12 | VF20 | XF40 | MS60 | MS63 |
|---|---|---|---|---|---|---|
| 2008 | 7,500 | — | — | — | 65.00 | 75.00 |

**KM# 1195 10 WON**
1.00 g., 0.916 Gold 0.0295 oz. AGW, 16 mm. **Obv:** National arms, Central Bank name **Rev:** Prussen

| Date | Mintage | F12 | VF20 | XF40 | MS60 | MS63 |
|---|---|---|---|---|---|---|
| 2008 | Est. 7500 | — | — | — | 65.00 | 75.00 |

**KM# 1196.1 10 WON**
1.00 g., 0.916 Gold 0.0295 oz. AGW, 16 mm. **Obv:** National arms, Central Bank name **Rev:** Alexander von Humboldt **Rev. Legend:** ...Humoldt **Note:** Error spelling of ship's name

| Date | Mintage | F12 | VF20 | XF40 | MS60 | MS63 |
|---|---|---|---|---|---|---|
| 2008 | 401 | — | — | — | 80.00 | 90.00 |

**KM# 1196.2 10 WON**
1.00 g., 0.916 Gold 0.0295 oz. AGW, 16 mm. **Obv:** National arms, Central Bank name **Rev:** Alexander von Humbolt **Rev. Legend:** ...Humboldt **Note:** Ship's name corrected.

| Date | Mintage | F12 | VF20 | XF40 | MS60 | MS63 |
|---|---|---|---|---|---|---|
| 2008 | 7,100 | — | — | — | 65.00 | 75.00 |

**KM# 1197 10 WON**
1.00 g., 0.916 Gold 0.0295 oz. AGW, 16 mm. **Obv:** National arms, Central Bank name **Rev:** Grand Duchess Elizabeth

| Date | Mintage | F12 | VF20 | XF40 | MS60 | MS63 |
|---|---|---|---|---|---|---|
| 2008 | Est. 7500 | — | — | — | 65.00 | 75.00 |

**KM# 1198 10 WON**
1.00 g., 0.916 Gold 0.0295 oz. AGW, 16 mm. **Obv:** National arms, Central Bank name **Rev:** Three masted training ship Passat

| Date | Mintage | F12 | VF20 | XF40 | MS60 | MS63 |
|---|---|---|---|---|---|---|
| 2008 | 7,500 | — | — | — | 65.00 | 75.00 |

**KM# 1199 10 WON**
1.00 g., 0.916 Gold 0.0295 oz. AGW, 16 mm. **Obv:** National arms, Central Bank name **Rev:** Four-masted schoner Elizabeth Bandi and three-masted bark Seute Deern

| Date | Mintage | F12 | VF20 | XF40 | MS60 | MS63 |
|---|---|---|---|---|---|---|
| 2008 | 7,500 | — | — | — | 65.00 | 75.00 |

**KM# 1200 10 WON**
1.00 g., 0.916 Gold 0.0295 oz. AGW, 16 mm. **Obv:** National arms, Central Bank name **Rev:** Sail training ship Deutschland

| Date | Mintage | F12 | VF20 | XF40 | MS60 | MS63 |
|---|---|---|---|---|---|---|
| 2008 | Est. 7500 | — | — | — | 65.00 | 75.00 |

**KM# 1201 10 WON**
1.00 g., 0.916 Gold 0.0295 oz. AGW, 16 mm. **Obv:** National arms, Central Bank name **Rev:** Three-masted barque Gorch Fock II

| Date | Mintage | F12 | VF20 | XF40 | MS60 | MS63 |
|---|---|---|---|---|---|---|
| 2008 | Est. 7500 | — | — | — | 65.00 | 75.00 |

**KM# 1234 10 WON**
0.50 g., 0.999 Gold, 11 mm. **Obv:** National arms, Central Bank name **Rev:** Cathedral of the Holy Family in Barcelona

| Date | Mintage | F12 | VF20 | XF40 | MS60 | MS63 |
|---|---|---|---|---|---|---|
| 2009 | — | PF65 45.00 | | | | |

**KM# 1235 10 WON**
0.50 g., 0.999 Gold, 11 mm. **Obv:** National arms, Central Bank name **Rev:** Alhambra in Granada

| Date | Mintage | F12 | VF20 | XF40 | MS60 | MS63 |
|---|---|---|---|---|---|---|
| 2009 | — | PF65 45.00 | | | | |

**KM# 1236 10 WON**
1.00 g., 0.999 Gold 0.0321 oz. AGW, 14 mm. **Obv:** National arms, Central Bank name **Rev:** Crown tower in Dresden Zwigers

| Date | Mintage | F12 | VF20 | XF40 | MS60 | MS63 |
|---|---|---|---|---|---|---|
| 2009 | — | PF65 75.00 | | | | |

**KM# 1237 10 WON**
1.00 g., 0.999 Gold 0.0321 oz. AGW, 14 mm. **Obv:** National arms, Central Bank name **Rev:** Acropolis in Athens

| Date | Mintage | F12 | VF20 | XF40 | MS60 | MS63 |
|---|---|---|---|---|---|---|
| 2009 | — | PF65 75.00 | | | | |

**KM# 1238 10 WON**
1.00 g., 0.999 Silver 0.0321 oz. ASW, 14 mm. **Obv:** National arms, Central Bank name **Rev:** Sydney Opera House

| Date | Mintage | F12 | VF20 | XF40 | MS60 | MS63 |
|---|---|---|---|---|---|---|
| 2009 | — | PF65 75.00 | | | | |

**KM# 1239 10 WON**
1.00 g., 0.999 Gold 0.0321 oz. AGW, 14 mm. **Obv:** National arms, Central Bank name **Rev:** Angkor Wat temple complex

| Date | Mintage | F12 | VF20 | XF40 | MS60 | MS63 |
|---|---|---|---|---|---|---|
| 2009 | — | PF65 75.00 | | | | |

**KM# 1240 10 WON**
1.00 g., 0.999 Gold 0.0321 oz. AGW, 14 mm. **Obv:** National arms, Central Bank name **Rev:** Minaksji and Sundareshwara Temples in Madurai

| Date | Mintage | F12 | VF20 | XF40 | MS60 | MS63 |
|---|---|---|---|---|---|---|
| 2009 | — | PF65 75.00 | | | | |

**KM# 1241 10 WON**
1.00 g., 0.999 Gold 0.0321 oz. AGW, 14 mm. **Obv:** National arms, Central Bank name **Rev:** Kremlin in Moscow

| Date | Mintage | F12 | VF20 | XF40 | MS60 | MS63 |
|---|---|---|---|---|---|---|
| 2009 | — | PF65 75.00 | | | | |

**KM# 1242 10 WON**
1.00 g., 0.999 Gold 0.0321 oz. AGW, 14 mm. **Obv:** National arms, Central Bank name **Rev:** Abu Simbel

| Date | Mintage | F12 | VF20 | XF40 | MS60 | MS63 |
|---|---|---|---|---|---|---|
| 2009 | — | PF65 75.00 | | | | |

**KM# 1243 10 WON**
1.00 g., 0.999 Gold 0.0321 oz. AGW, 14 mm. **Obv:** National arms, Central Bank name **Rev:** Eiffel Tower in Paris

| Date | Mintage | F12 | VF20 | XF40 | MS60 | MS63 |
|---|---|---|---|---|---|---|
| 2009 | — | PF65 75.00 | | | | |

**KM# 1244 10 WON**
1.00 g., 0.999 Gold 0.0321 oz. AGW, 14 mm. **Obv:** National arms, Central Bank name **Rev:** Dali Lama's Palace in Lhasa

| Date | Mintage | F12 | VF20 | XF40 | MS60 | MS63 |
|---|---|---|---|---|---|---|
| 2009 | — | PF65 75.00 | | | | |

**KM# 1245 10 WON**
1.00 g., 0.999 Gold 0.0321 oz. AGW, 14 mm. **Obv:** National arms, Central Bank name **Rev:** Terra Cotta Warriors

| Date | Mintage | F12 | VF20 | XF40 | MS60 | MS63 |
|---|---|---|---|---|---|---|
| 2009 | — | PF65 75.00 | | | | |

**KM# 1246 10 WON**
1.00 g., 0.999 Gold 0.0321 oz. AGW, 14 mm. **Obv:** National arms, Central Bank name **Rev:** Palace in Versalles

| Date | Mintage | F12 | VF20 | XF40 | MS60 | MS63 |
|---|---|---|---|---|---|---|
| 2009 | — | PF65 75.00 | | | | |

**KM# 1247 10 WON**
1.00 g., 0.999 Gold 0.0321 oz. AGW, 14 mm. **Obv:** National arms, Central Bank name **Rev:** Aachen Cathedral

| Date | Mintage | F12 | VF20 | XF40 | MS60 | MS63 |
|---|---|---|---|---|---|---|
| 2009 | — | PF65 75.00 | | | | |

**KM# 1248 10 WON**
1.00 g., 0.999 Gold 0.0321 oz. AGW, 14 mm. **Obv:** National arms, Central Bank name **Rev:** Leaning tower of Pisa

| Date | Mintage | F12 | VF20 | XF40 | MS60 | MS63 |
|---|---|---|---|---|---|---|
| 2009 | — | PF65 75.00 | | | | |

**KM# 1249 10 WON**
1.00 g., 0.999 Gold 0.0321 oz. AGW, 14 mm. **Obv:** National arms, Central Bank name **Rev:** Chapel in Luzern

| Date | Mintage | F12 | VF20 | XF40 | MS60 | MS63 |
|---|---|---|---|---|---|---|
| 2009 | — | PF65 75.00 | | | | |

**KM# 1262 10 WON**
Brass, 40 mm. **Obv:** National arms, Central Bank name **Rev:** South tower in Kaeseong

| Date | Mintage | F12 | VF20 | XF40 | MS60 | MS63 |
|---|---|---|---|---|---|---|
| 2010 | — | PF65 7.00 | | | | |

**KM# 1263 10 WON**
Brass, 40 mm. **Obv:** National arms, Central Bank name **Rev:** Mausoleum of King Wanggeon

| Date | Mintage | F12 | VF20 | XF40 | MS60 | MS63 |
|---|---|---|---|---|---|---|
| 2010 | — | PF65 7.00 | | | | |

**KM# 1264 10 WON**
Brass, 40 mm. **Obv:** National arms, Central Bank name **Rev:** Birthplace of Pyochung

| Date | Mintage | F12 | VF20 | XF40 | MS60 | MS63 |
|---|---|---|---|---|---|---|
| 2010 | — | PF65 7.00 | | | | |

**KM# 1265 10 WON**
Brass, 40 mm. **Obv:** National arms, Central Bank name **Rev:** Stone pagoda of Hyunhwa in Seongkyunkwan

| Date | Mintage | F12 | VF20 | XF40 | MS60 | MS63 |
|---|---|---|---|---|---|---|
| 2010 | — | PF65 7.00 | | | | |

**KM# 1266 10 WON**
Brass, 40 mm. **Obv:** National arms, Central Bank name **Rev:** Seongkyunkwan

| Date | Mintage | F12 | VF20 | XF40 | MS60 | MS63 |
|---|---|---|---|---|---|---|
| 2010 | — | PF65 7.00 | | | | |

**KM# 1267 10 WON**
Brass, 40 mm. **Obv:** National arms, Central Bank name **Rev:** Anhwa Temple

| Date | Mintage | F12 | VF20 | XF40 | MS60 | MS63 |
|---|---|---|---|---|---|---|
| 2010 | — | PF65 7.00 | | | | |

**KM# 1268 10 WON**
Brass, 40 mm. **Obv:** National arms, Central Bank name **Rev:** Nahanjun in Anhwa Temple

| Date | Mintage | F12 | VF20 | XF40 | MS60 | MS63 |
|---|---|---|---|---|---|---|
| 2010 | — | PF65 7.00 | | | | |

**KM# 1269 10 WON**
Brass, 40 mm. **Obv:** National arms, Central Bank name **Rev:** Turned wheel in Yungtong Temple

| Date | Mintage | F12 | VF20 | XF40 | MS60 | MS63 |
|---|---|---|---|---|---|---|
| 2010 | — | PF65 7.00 | | | | |

**KM# 1270 10 WON**
Brass, 40 mm. **Obv:** National arms, Central Bank name **Rev:** Shrine in Sungyang Sowon

| Date | Mintage | F12 | VF20 | XF40 | MS60 | MS63 |
|---|---|---|---|---|---|---|
| 2010 | — | PF65 7.00 | | | | |

**KM# 1271 10 WON**
Brass, 40 mm. **Obv:** National arms, Central Bank name **Rev:** Waterfall in Pakyeon

| Date | Mintage | F12 | VF20 | XF40 | MS60 | MS63 |
|---|---|---|---|---|---|---|
| 2010 | — | PF65 7.00 | | | | |

**KM# 1275 10 WON**
0.50 g., 0.999 Gold, 11 mm. **Obv:** National arms, Central Bank name **Rev:** Ernesto "Che" Guevara

| Date | Mintage | F12 | VF20 | XF40 | MS60 | MS63 |
|---|---|---|---|---|---|---|
| 2010 | — | PF65 50.00 | | | | |

**KM# 1283 10 WON**
1.00 g., 0.999 Gold 0.0321 oz. AGW, 14 mm. **Obv:** National arms, Central Bank name **Rev:** Grand Mosque in Cordoba

| Date | Mintage | F12 | VF20 | XF40 | MS60 | MS63 |
|---|---|---|---|---|---|---|
| 2010 | — | PF65 75.00 | | | | |

**KM# 1284 10 WON**
1.00 g., 0.999 Gold 0.0321 oz. AGW, 14 mm. **Obv:** National arms, Central Bank name **Rev:** Cathedral of Santiago de Compostela

| Date | Mintage | F12 | VF20 | XF40 | MS60 | MS63 |
|---|---|---|---|---|---|---|
| 2010 | — | PF65 75.00 | | | | |

**KM# 1285 10 WON**
1.00 g., 0.999 Gold 0.0321 oz. AGW, 14 mm. **Obv:** National arms, Central Bank name **Rev:** Timbuktu

| Date | Mintage | F12 | VF20 | XF40 | MS60 | MS63 |
|---|---|---|---|---|---|---|
| 2010 | — | PF65 75.00 | | | | |

**KM# 1286 10 WON**
1.00 g., 0.999 Gold 0.0321 oz. AGW, 14 mm. **Obv:** National arms, Central Bank name **Rev:** London's Big Ben tower

| Date | Mintage | F12 | VF20 | XF40 | MS60 | MS63 |
|---|---|---|---|---|---|---|
| 2010 | — | PF65 75.00 | | | | |

**KM# 1287 10 WON**
1.00 g., 0.999 Gold 0.0321 oz. AGW, 14 mm. **Obv:** National arms, Central Bank name **Rev:** Prague castle

| Date | Mintage | F12 | VF20 | XF40 | MS60 | MS63 |
|---|---|---|---|---|---|---|
| 2010 | — | PF65 75.00 | | | | |

**KM# 1288 10 WON**
1.00 g., 0.999 Gold 0.0321 oz. AGW, 14 mm. **Obv:** National arms, Central Bank name **Rev:** Teotihuacan pyramid

| Date | Mintage | F12 | VF20 | XF40 | MS60 | MS63 |
|---|---|---|---|---|---|---|
| 2010 | — | PF65 75.00 | | | | |

**KM# 1289 10 WON**
1.00 g., 0.999 Gold 0.0321 oz. AGW, 14 mm. **Obv:** National arms, Central Bank name **Rev:** Forbidden City

| Date | Mintage | F12 | VF20 | XF40 | MS60 | MS63 |
|---|---|---|---|---|---|---|
| 2010 | — | PF65 75.00 | | | | |

**KM# 1175 20 WON**
28.00 g., Brass, 40 mm. **Obv:** East gate of Pyeongyang **Rev:** Dragon in color

| Date | Mintage | F12 | VF20 | XF40 | MS60 | MS63 |
|---|---|---|---|---|---|---|
| 2008 | — | PF65 7.50 | | | | |

**KM# 1202 20 WON**
Brass, 30 mm. **Obv:** East gate of Pyeongyang **Rev:** Rat in color

| Date | Mintage | F12 | VF20 | XF40 | MS60 | MS63 |
|---|---|---|---|---|---|---|
| 2009 | — | PF65 6.00 | | | | |

**KM# 1203 20 WON**
Brass, 30 mm. **Obv:** East gate of Pyeongyang **Rev:** Ox in color

| Date | Mintage | F12 | VF20 | XF40 | MS60 | MS63 |
|---|---|---|---|---|---|---|
| 2009 | — | PF65 6.00 | | | | |

**KM# 1204 20 WON**
Brass, 30 mm. **Obv:** East gate of Pyeongyang **Rev:** Tiger in color

| Date | Mintage | F12 | VF20 | XF40 | MS60 | MS63 |
|---|---|---|---|---|---|---|
| 2009 | — | PF65 6.00 | | | | |

**KM# 1205 20 WON**
Brass, 30 mm. **Obv:** East gate of Pyeongyang **Rev:** Rabbit in color

| Date | Mintage | F12 | VF20 | XF40 | MS60 | MS63 |
|---|---|---|---|---|---|---|
| 2009 | — | PF65 6.00 | | | | |

**KM# 1206 20 WON**
Brass, 30 mm. **Obv:** East gate of Pyeongyang **Rev:** Dragon in color

| Date | Mintage | F12 | VF20 | XF40 | MS60 | MS63 |
|---|---|---|---|---|---|---|
| 2009 | — | PF65 6.00 | | | | |

**KM# 1207 20 WON**
Brass, 30 mm. **Obv:** East gate of Pyeongyang **Rev:** Snake in color

| Date | Mintage | F12 | VF20 | XF40 | MS60 | MS63 |
|---|---|---|---|---|---|---|
| 2009 | — | PF65 6.00 | | | | |

**KM# 1208 20 WON**
Brass, 30 mm. **Obv:** East gate of Pyeongyang **Rev:** Horse in color

| Date | Mintage | F12 | VF20 | XF40 | MS60 | MS63 |
|---|---|---|---|---|---|---|
| 2009 | — | PF65 6.00 | | | | |

**KM# 1209 20 WON**
Brass, 30 mm. **Obv:** East gate of Pyeongyang **Rev:** Goat in color

| Date | Mintage | F12 | VF20 | XF40 | MS60 | MS63 |
|---|---|---|---|---|---|---|
| 2009 | — | PF65 6.00 | | | | |

**KM# 1210 20 WON**
Brass, 30 mm. **Obv:** East gate of Pyeongyang **Rev:** Monkey in color

| Date | Mintage | F12 | VF20 | XF40 | MS60 | MS63 |
|---|---|---|---|---|---|---|
| 2009 | — | PF65 6.00 | | | | |

**KM# 1211 20 WON**
Brass, 30 mm. **Obv:** East gate of Pyeongyang **Rev:** Rooster in color

| Date | Mintage | F12 | VF20 | XF40 | MS60 | MS63 |
|---|---|---|---|---|---|---|
| 2009 | — | PF65 6.00 | | | | |

**KM# 1212 20 WON**
Brass, 30 mm. **Obv:** East gate of Pyeongyang **Rev:** Dog in color

| Date | Mintage | F12 | VF20 | XF40 | MS60 | MS63 |
|---|---|---|---|---|---|---|
| 2009 | — | PF65 6.00 | | | | |

**KM# 1213 20 WON**
Brass, 30 mm. **Obv:** East gate of Pyeongyang **Rev:** Pin in color

| Date | Mintage | F12 | VF20 | XF40 | MS60 | MS63 |
|---|---|---|---|---|---|---|
| 2009 | — | PF65 6.00 | | | | |

**KM# 492 20 WON**
Aluminum, 45 mm. **Obv:** Raised Pagoda in ornamental loop **Rev:** Hippopotamus with color inlay **Rev. Legend:** Hippopotamus amphibius **Edge:** Plain

| Date | Mintage | F12 | VF20 | XF40 | MS60 | MS63 |
|---|---|---|---|---|---|---|
| 2010 | — | — | — | — | — | 20.00 |

**KM# 493 20 WON**
Aluminum, 45 mm. **Obv:** Raised Pagoda with ornamental loop **Rev:** Rabbit with color inlay **Edge:** Plain

| Date | Mintage | F12 | VF20 | XF40 | MS60 | MS63 |
|---|---|---|---|---|---|---|
| 2010 | — | — | — | — | — | 20.00 |

**KM# 494 20 WON**
Aluminum, 45 mm. **Obv:** Raised Pagoda in ornamental loop **Rev:** Deer with color inlay **Edge:** Plain

| Date | Mintage | F12 | VF20 | XF40 | MS60 | MS63 |
|---|---|---|---|---|---|---|
| 2010 | — | — | — | — | — | 20.00 |

**KM# 1250 20 WON**
Brass, 45 mm. **Obv:** East gate in Pyeongyang **Rev:** Rat in center of Zodiac

| Date | Mintage | F12 | VF20 | XF40 | MS60 | MS63 |
|---|---|---|---|---|---|---|
| 2010 Proof | — | — | — | — | — | 7.00 |

**KM# 1251 20 WON**
Brass, 45 mm. **Obv:** East gate in Pyeongyang **Rev:** Buffalo at center of Zodiac

| Date | Mintage | F12 | VF20 | XF40 | MS60 | MS63 |
|---|---|---|---|---|---|---|
| 2010 | — | PF65 7.00 | | | | |

**KM# 1252 20 WON**
Brass, 45 mm. **Obv:** East gate in Pyeongyang **Rev:** Tiger at center of Zodiac

| Date | Mintage | F12 | VF20 | XF40 | MS60 | MS63 |
|---|---|---|---|---|---|---|
| 2010 | — | PF65 7.00 | | | | |

**KM# 1253 20 WON**
Brass, 45 mm. **Obv:** East gate in Pyeongyang **Rev:** Rabbit in center of Zodiac

| Date | Mintage | F12 | VF20 | XF40 | MS60 | MS63 |
|---|---|---|---|---|---|---|
| 2010 | — | PF65 7.00 | | | | |

**KM# 1254 20 WON**
Brass, 45 mm. **Obv:** East gate in Pyeongyang **Rev:** Dragon at center of Zodiac

| Date | Mintage | F12 | VF20 | XF40 | MS60 | MS63 |
|---|---|---|---|---|---|---|
| 2010 | — | PF65 7.00 | | | | |

**KM# 1255 20 WON**
Brass, 45 mm. **Obv:** East gate in Pyeongyang **Rev:** Snake in center of Zodiac

| Date | Mintage | F12 | VF20 | XF40 | MS60 | MS63 |
|---|---|---|---|---|---|---|
| 2010 | — | PF65 7.00 | | | | |

**KM# 1256 20 WON**
Brass, 45 mm. **Obv:** East gate in Pyeongyang **Rev:** Horse in center of Zodiac

| Date | Mintage | F12 | VF20 | XF40 | MS60 | MS63 |
|---|---|---|---|---|---|---|
| 2010 | — | PF65 7.00 | | | | |

**KM# 1257 20 WON**
Brass, 45 mm. **Obv:** East gate in Pyeongyang **Rev:** Goat in center of Zodiac

| Date | Mintage | F12 | VF20 | XF40 | MS60 | MS63 |
|---|---|---|---|---|---|---|
| 2010 | — | PF65 7.00 | | | | |

**KM# 1258 20 WON**
Brass, 45 mm. **Obv:** East gate in Pyeongyang **Rev:** Monkey in center of Zodiac

| Date | Mintage | F12 | VF20 | XF40 | MS60 | MS63 |
|---|---|---|---|---|---|---|
| 2010 | — | PF65 7.00 | | | | |

**KM# 1259 20 WON**
Brass, 45 mm. **Obv:** East gate in Pyeongyang **Rev:** Rooster in center of Zodiac

| Date | Mintage | F12 | VF20 | XF40 | MS60 | MS63 |
|---|---|---|---|---|---|---|
| 2010 | — | PF65 7.00 | | | | |

**KM# 1260 20 WON**
Brass, 45 mm. **Obv:** East gate in Pyeongyang **Rev:** Dog in center of Zodiac

| Date | Mintage | F12 | VF20 | XF40 | MS60 | MS63 |
|---|---|---|---|---|---|---|
| 2010 | — | PF65 7.00 | | | | |

**KM# 1261 20 WON**
Brass, 45 mm. **Obv:** East gate in Pyeongyang **Rev:** Pig in center of Zodiac

| Date | Mintage | F12 | VF20 | XF40 | MS60 | MS63 |
|---|---|---|---|---|---|---|
| 2010 | — | PF65 7.00 | | | | |

**KM# 1214 350 WON**
6.20 g., 0.999 Silver 0.1991 oz. ASW, 35 mm. **Obv:** East gate of Pyeongyang **Rev:** Chinese Junk, Marco Polo

| Date | Mintage | F12 | VF20 | XF40 | MS60 | MS63 |
|---|---|---|---|---|---|---|
| 2009 | — | PF65 25.00 | | | | |

**KM# 1215 350 WON**
6.20 g., 0.999 Silver 0.1991 oz. ASW, 35 mm. **Obv:** East gate of Pyeongyang **Rev:** Viking ship and map of the Atlantic, Leif Eriksson

| Date | Mintage | F12 | VF20 | XF40 | MS60 | MS63 |
|---|---|---|---|---|---|---|
| 2009 | Est. 5000 | PF65 25.00 | | | | |

**KM# 1216 1000 WON**
20.00 g., 0.999 Silver 0.6424 oz. ASW, 38 mm. **Subject:** World Cup Soccer, South Africa, 2010 **Obv:** East gate of Pyeongyang **Rev:** Two soccer players

| Date | Mintage | F12 | VF20 | XF40 | MS60 | MS63 |
|---|---|---|---|---|---|---|
| 2009 | Est. 10000 | PF63 27.00 | PF65 35.00 | | | |

# SOUTH KOREA

The Republic of Korea, situated in northeastern Asia on the southern half of the Korean peninsula between North Korea and the Korean Strait, has an area of 38,025 sq. mi. (98,480 sq. km.) and a population of 42.5 million. Capital: Seoul. The economy is based on agriculture and light and medium industry. Some of the world's largest oil tankers are built here. Automobiles, plywood, electronics, and textile products are exported.

**NOTE:** For earlier coinage see Korea.

**MINT**

KOMSCO - Korea Minting and Security Printing Corporation

## REPUBLIC

### REFORM COINAGE

10 Hwan = 1 Won

**KM# 31 WON**

0.73 g., Aluminum, 17.2 mm. **Obv:** Rose of Sharon **Rev:** Value and date

| Date | Mintage | F12 | VF20 | XF40 | MS60 | MS63 |
|---|---|---|---|---|---|---|
| 2001 | 130,000 | — | — | — | 0.15 | 0.25 |
| 2002 | 122,000 | — | — | — | 0.15 | 0.25 |
| 2003 | 20,000 | — | — | — | 0.15 | 0.25 |
| 2004 | 25,500 | — | — | — | 0.15 | 0.25 |
| 2005 | 38,000 | — | — | — | 0.15 | 0.25 |
| 2006 | 53,000 | — | — | — | 0.15 | 0.25 |
| 2007 | 53,000 | — | — | — | 0.15 | 0.25 |
| 2008 | — | — | — | — | 0.15 | 0.25 |
| 2009 | — | — | — | — | 0.15 | 0.25 |
| 2010 | — | — | — | — | 0.15 | 0.25 |
| 2011 | — | — | — | — | 0.15 | 0.25 |
| 2012 | — | — | — | — | 0.15 | 0.25 |

**KM# 32 5 WON**

2.95 g., Brass, 20.4 mm. **Obv:** Iron-clad turtle boat **Rev:** Value and date **Edge:** Plain

| Date | Mintage | F12 | VF20 | XF40 | MS60 | MS63 |
|---|---|---|---|---|---|---|
| 2001 | 130,000 | — | — | 0.10 | 0.20 | 0.30 |
| 2002 | 120,000 | — | — | 0.10 | 0.20 | 0.30 |
| 2003 | 20,000 | — | — | 0.10 | 0.20 | 0.30 |
| 2004 | 25,500 | — | — | 0.10 | 0.20 | 0.30 |
| 2005 | 38,000 | — | — | 0.10 | 0.20 | 0.30 |
| 2006 | 53,000 | — | — | 0.10 | 0.20 | 0.30 |
| 2007 | 53,000 | — | — | 0.10 | 0.20 | 0.30 |
| 2008 | — | — | — | 0.10 | 0.20 | 0.30 |
| 2009 | — | — | — | 0.10 | 0.20 | 0.30 |
| 2010 | — | — | — | 0.10 | 0.20 | 0.30 |
| 2011 | — | — | — | 0.10 | 0.20 | 0.30 |
| 2012 | — | — | — | 0.10 | 0.20 | 0.30 |

**KM# 33.2 10 WON**

4.06 g., Brass **Obv:** Pagoda at Pul Guk Temple **Rev:** Thicker value below date

| Date | Mintage | F12 | VF20 | XF40 | MS60 | MS63 |
|---|---|---|---|---|---|---|
| 2001 | 345,000,000 | — | — | — | 0.35 | 0.50 |
| 2002 | 100,000,000 | — | — | — | 0.35 | 0.50 |
| 2003 | 128,000,000 | — | — | — | 0.35 | 0.50 |
| 2004 | 135,000,000 | — | — | — | 0.35 | 0.50 |
| 2005 | 250,000,000 | — | — | — | 0.35 | 0.50 |

**KM# 33.2a 10 WON**

1.22 g., Aluminum-Bronze, 18 mm. **Obv:** Pagoda at Pul Guk Temple **Rev:** Value below date

| Date | Mintage | F12 | VF20 | XF40 | MS60 | MS63 |
|---|---|---|---|---|---|---|
| 2006 | 109,200,000 | — | — | — | 0.10 | 0.35 |
| 2007 | — | — | — | — | 0.10 | 0.35 |
| 2008 | — | — | — | — | 0.10 | 0.35 |
| 2009 | — | — | — | — | 0.10 | 0.35 |

**KM# 103 10 WON**

1.22 g., Copper Clad Aluminum, 18 mm. **Obv:** Pagoda at Pul Guk Temple **Rev:** Value below date **Edge:** Plain **Note:** Prev. KM #106.

| Date | Mintage | F12 | VF20 | XF40 | MS60 | MS63 |
|---|---|---|---|---|---|---|
| 2006 | 40,800,000 | — | — | 0.10 | 0.20 | 0.25 |
| 2007 | 210,000,000 | — | — | 0.10 | 0.20 | 0.25 |
| 2008 | — | — | — | 0.10 | 0.20 | 0.25 |
| 2009 | — | — | — | 0.10 | 0.20 | 0.25 |
| 2010 | — | — | — | 0.10 | 0.20 | 0.25 |
| 2011 | — | — | — | 0.10 | 0.20 | 0.25 |
| 2012 | — | — | — | 0.10 | 0.20 | 0.25 |
| 2013 | — | — | — | 0.10 | 0.20 | 0.25 |

**KM# 34 50 WON**

4.16 g., Copper-Nickel-Zinc, 21.6 mm. **Series:** F.A.O. **Obv:** Text below sagging oat sprig **Rev:** Value and date **Edge:** Reeded **Note:** Die varieties exist.

| Date | Mintage | F12 | VF20 | XF40 | MS60 | MS63 |
|---|---|---|---|---|---|---|
| 2001 | 102,000,000 | — | — | 0.10 | 0.35 | 1.00 |
| 2002 | 100,000,000 | — | — | 0.10 | 0.35 | 0.50 |
| 2003 | 169,000,000 | — | — | 0.10 | 0.35 | 0.50 |
| 2004 | 100,000,000 | — | — | 0.10 | 0.45 | 1.00 |
| 2005 | 90,000,000 | — | — | 0.10 | 0.35 | 0.50 |
| 2006 | 120,000,000 | — | — | 0.10 | 0.35 | 0.50 |
| 2007 | 50,000,000 | — | — | 0.10 | 0.35 | 0.50 |
| 2008 | — | — | — | 0.10 | 0.35 | 0.50 |
| 2009 | — | — | — | 0.10 | 0.35 | 0.50 |
| 2010 | — | — | — | 0.10 | 0.35 | 0.50 |
| 2011 | — | — | — | 0.10 | 0.35 | 0.50 |
| 2012 | — | — | — | 0.10 | 0.35 | 0.50 |

**KM# 35.2 100 WON**

5.42 g., Copper-Nickel, 24 mm. **Obv:** Admiral Yi-Sun-Sin, large bust with hat facing **Rev:** Value and date **Edge:** Reeded

| Date | Mintage | F12 | VF20 | XF40 | MS60 | MS63 |
|---|---|---|---|---|---|---|
| 2001 | 470,000,000 | — | 0.25 | 0.50 | 1.00 | 3.00 |
| 2002 | 490,000,000 | — | 0.15 | 0.25 | 0.55 | 1.00 |
| 2003 | 415,000,000 | — | 0.15 | 0.25 | 0.55 | 1.00 |
| 2004 | 250,000,000 | — | 0.15 | 0.25 | 0.55 | 1.00 |
| 2005 | 205,000,000 | — | 0.15 | 0.25 | 0.55 | 1.00 |
| 2006 | 310,000,000 | — | 0.15 | 0.25 | 0.55 | 0.75 |
| 2007 | 240,000,000 | — | 0.15 | 0.25 | 0.55 | 0.75 |
| 2008 | — | — | 0.15 | 0.25 | 0.55 | 0.75 |
| 2009 | — | — | 0.15 | 0.25 | 0.55 | 0.75 |
| 2010 | — | — | 0.15 | 0.25 | 0.55 | 0.75 |
| 2011 | — | — | 0.15 | 0.25 | 0.55 | 0.75 |
| 2012 | — | — | 0.15 | 0.25 | 0.55 | 0.75 |

**KM# 27 500 WON**

7.70 g., Copper-Nickel, 26.5 mm. **Obv:** Manchurian crane **Rev:** Value and date **Edge:** Reeded

| Date | Mintage | F12 | VF20 | XF40 | MS60 | MS63 |
|---|---|---|---|---|---|---|
| 2001 | 113,000,000 | — | — | 1.00 | 2.50 | 5.00 |
| 2002 | 110,000,000 | — | — | 1.00 | 2.50 | 5.00 |
| 2003 | 122,000,000 | — | — | 1.00 | 2.50 | 5.00 |
| 2004 | 45,000,000 | — | — | 1.00 | 2.50 | 5.00 |
| 2005 | 105,000,000 | — | — | 1.00 | 2.50 | 5.00 |
| 2006 | 170,000,000 | — | — | 1.00 | 2.50 | 5.00 |
| 2007 | 70,000,000 | — | — | 1.00 | 2.50 | 5.00 |
| 2008 | — | — | — | 1.00 | 2.50 | 5.00 |
| 2009 | — | — | — | 1.00 | 2.50 | 5.00 |
| 2010 | — | — | — | 1.00 | 2.50 | 5.00 |
| 2011 | — | — | — | 1.00 | 2.50 | 5.00 |
| 2012 | — | — | — | 1.00 | 2.50 | 5.00 |

**KM# 89 1000 WON**

12.00 g., Brass, 32 mm. **Series:** World Cup Soccer **Obv:** FIFA World Cup logo **Rev:** Mascot soccer player **Edge:** Reeded

| Date | Mintage | F12 | VF20 | XF40 | MS60 | MS63 |
|---|---|---|---|---|---|---|
| 2001 | 102,000 | — | — | — | 10.00 | 12.00 |

**KM# 112 1000 WON**

12.00 g., Aluminum-Bronze, 32 mm. **Rev:** Soccer player

| Date | Mintage | F12 | VF20 | XF40 | MS60 | MS63 |
|---|---|---|---|---|---|---|
| 2002 | 102,002 | — | — | — | — | 12.50 |

**KM# 127 1000 WON**

10.10 g., Tri-Metallic Copper center in Copper-Nickel inner ring in Copper-Nickel-Zinc outer ring, 28.2 mm. **Subject:** Expo 2012 **Obv:** Mascots Yeony and Suny **Rev:** Expo logo

| Date | Mintage | F12 | VF20 | XF40 | MS60 | MS63 |
|---|---|---|---|---|---|---|
| 2012 | 137,512 | — | — | — | — | 20.00 |

**KM# 115 2000 WON**

26.00 g., Copper, 40 mm. **Subject:** 14th Asian Games, Busan **Rev:** Bird sanctuary

| Date | Mintage | F12 | VF20 | XF40 | MS60 | MS63 |
|---|---|---|---|---|---|---|
| 2002 | — | PF63 15.00 | PF65 20.00 | | | |

**KM# 116 2000 WON**

26.00 g., Copper-Nickel, 40 mm. **Rev:** Torch and sport images

| Date | Mintage | F12 | VF20 | XF40 | MS60 | MS63 |
|---|---|---|---|---|---|---|
| 2002 | — | PF63 25.00 | | | | |

**KM# 124 5000 WON**

15.50 g., 0.999 Silver 0.4978 oz. ASW, 32 mm. **Subject:** Expo 2012 **Obv:** Korean Pavilion with latent image **Rev:** Expo logo in color

| Date | Mintage | F12 | VF20 | XF40 | MS60 | MS63 |
|---|---|---|---|---|---|---|
| 2012 | 20,000 | PF63 35.00 | PF65 45.00 | | | |

**KM# 125 5000 WON**

15.50 g., 0.999 Silver 0.4978 oz. ASW, 32 mm. **Subject:** Expo 2012 **Obv:** Theme Pavilion and latent image **Rev:** Expo logo in color

| Date | Mintage | F12 | VF20 | XF40 | MS60 | MS63 |
|---|---|---|---|---|---|---|
| 2012 | 20,000 | PF63 30.00 | PF65 40.00 | | | |

**KM# 90 10000 WON**
31.10 g., 0.999 Silver 0.999 oz. ASW, 35 mm. **Series:** World Cup Soccer **Subject:** Gwangju Stadium **Obv:** Multicolor soccer logo **Rev:** Player heading the ball **Edge:** Reeded

| Date | Mintage | F12 | VF20 | XF40 | MS60 | MS63 |
|---|---|---|---|---|---|---|
| 2001 | 37,000 | PF63 40.00 | PF65 50.00 | | | |

**KM# 91 10000 WON**
31.10 g., 0.999 Silver 0.999 oz. ASW, 35 mm. **Series:** World Sup Soccer **Subject:** Busan Stadium **Obv:** Multicolor soccer logo **Rev:** Player kicking the ball **Edge:** Reeded

| Date | Mintage | F12 | VF20 | XF40 | MS60 | MS63 |
|---|---|---|---|---|---|---|
| 2001 | 37,000 | PF63 40.00 | PF65 50.00 | | | |

**KM# 92 10000 WON**
31.10 g., 0.999 Silver 0.999 oz. ASW, 35 mm. **Series:** World Cup Soccer **Subject:** Daegu Stadium **Obv:** Multicolor soccer logo **Rev:** Player controlling the ball **Edge:** Reeded

| Date | Mintage | F12 | VF20 | XF40 | MS60 | MS63 |
|---|---|---|---|---|---|---|
| 2001 | 37,000 | PF63 40.00 | PF65 50.00 | | | |

**KM# 93 10000 WON**
31.10 g., 0.999 Silver 0.999 oz. ASW, 35 mm. **Series:** World Cup Soccer **Subject:** Suwon Stadium **Obv:** Multicolor soccer logo **Rev:** Player kicking the ball **Edge:** Reeded

| Date | Mintage | F12 | VF20 | XF40 | MS60 | MS63 |
|---|---|---|---|---|---|---|
| 2001 | 37,000 | PF63 40.00 | PF65 50.00 | | | |

**KM# 98 10000 WON**
31.10 g., 0.999 Silver 0.999 oz. ASW, 35 mm. **Obv:** Multi-color FIFA World Cup logo **Rev:** Player "Heading" ball **Edge:** Reeded

| Date | Mintage | F12 | VF20 | XF40 | MS60 | MS63 |
|---|---|---|---|---|---|---|
| 2002 | — | PF63 45.00 | PF65 50.00 | | | |

**KM# 99 10000 WON**
31.10 g., 0.999 Silver 0.999 oz. ASW, 35 mm. **Obv:** Multi-color FIFA World Cup logo **Rev:** Goalie catching ball **Edge:** Reeded

| Date | Mintage | F12 | VF20 | XF40 | MS60 | MS63 |
|---|---|---|---|---|---|---|
| 2002 | — | PF63 45.00 | PF65 50.00 | | | |

**KM# 100 10000 WON**
31.10 g., 0.999 Silver 0.999 oz. ASW, 35 mm. **Obv:** Multi-color FIFA World Cup logo **Rev:** Player's leg kicking ball **Edge:** Reeded

| Date | Mintage | F12 | VF20 | XF40 | MS60 | MS63 |
|---|---|---|---|---|---|---|
| 2002 | — | PF63 45.00 | PF65 50.00 | | | |

**KM# 101 10000 WON**
31.10 g., 0.999 Silver 0.999 oz. ASW, 35 mm. **Obv:** Multi-color FIFA World Cup logo **Rev:** Two players' legs and ball **Edge:** Reeded

| Date | Mintage | F12 | VF20 | XF40 | MS60 | MS63 |
|---|---|---|---|---|---|---|
| 2002 | — | PF63 45.00 | PF65 50.00 | | | |

**KM# 118 10000 WON**
Silver, 38.61 mm. **Subject:** 14th Asian Games, Busan **Obv:** Multicolor games logo **Rev:** Two dancers

| Date | Mintage | F12 | VF20 | XF40 | MS60 | MS63 |
|---|---|---|---|---|---|---|
| 2002 | — | PF63 80.00 | PF65 90.00 | | | |

**KM# 117 10000 WON**
31.11 g., 0.999 Silver 0.999 oz. ASW, 40 mm. **Rev:** Stadium, mascott at top

| Date | Mintage | F12 | VF20 | XF40 | MS60 | MS63 |
|---|---|---|---|---|---|---|
| 2005 | — | PF63 80.00 | PF65 90.00 | | | |

**KM# 126 10000 WON**
31.11 g., 0.999 Silver 0.999 oz. ASW, 40 mm. **Subject:** Expo 2012 **Obv:** Exposition's Sky Tower and sea image **Rev:** Expo logo in color

| Date | Mintage | F12 | VF20 | XF40 | MS60 | MS63 |
|---|---|---|---|---|---|---|
| 2012 | 20,000 | PF63 50.00 | PF65 60.00 | | | |

**KM# 128 15000 WON**
7.77 g., 0.999 Gold 0.2496 oz. AGW, 22 mm. **Subject:** Expo 2012 **Obv:** The Big-O maine stage **Rev:** Expo logo

| Date | Mintage | F12 | VF20 | XF40 | MS60 | MS63 |
|---|---|---|---|---|---|---|
| 2012 | 10,000 | PF63 425 | PF65 500 | | | |

**KM# 94 20000 WON**
15.55 g., 0.999 Gold 0.4995 oz. AGW, 28 mm. **Series:** World Cup Soccer **Obv:** Soccer logo **Rev:** World Cup soccer trophy **Edge:** Reeded

| Date | Mintage | F12 | VF20 | XF40 | MS60 | MS63 |
|---|---|---|---|---|---|---|
| 2001 | 20,000 | PF63 850 | PF65 900 | | | |

**KM# 113 20000 WON**
15.55 g., 0.999 Gold 0.4994 oz. AGW, 28 mm. **Rev:** World Cup venues on map

| Date | Mintage | F12 | VF20 | XF40 | MS60 | MS63 |
|---|---|---|---|---|---|---|
| 2002 | 19,502 | PF63 875 | PF65 925 | | | |

**KM# 119 20000 WON**
15.55 g., 0.999 Gold 0.4994 oz. AGW **Subject:** 14th Asian Games, Busan **Obv:** Games logo **Rev:** Crown

| Date | Mintage | F12 | VF20 | XF40 | MS60 | MS63 |
|---|---|---|---|---|---|---|
| 2002 | — | PF63 875 | PF65 925 | | | |

**KM# 97 20000 WON**
20.70 g., Silver, 35 mm. **Obv:** Blue circle with APEC, 2005 Korea at bottom at upper center, Vista Pacific Economic Cooperation and value below **Rev:** APEC on World map at upper center, building below with Korean words below it

| Date | Mintage | F12 | VF20 | XF40 | MS60 | MS63 |
|---|---|---|---|---|---|---|
| 2005 | 10,000 | PF63 55.00 | PF65 65.00 | | | |

**KM# 102 20000 WON**
20.70 g., 0.999 Silver 0.6649 oz. ASW **Subject:** 60th Anniversary of Independence **Obv:** Adult hand reaching out towards child's hand **Note:** Prev. KM #103.

| Date | Mintage | F12 | VF20 | XF40 | MS60 | MS63 |
|---|---|---|---|---|---|---|
| 2005 | 10,000 | PF63 55.00 | PF65 65.00 | | | |

**KM# 104 20000 WON**
19.00 g., 0.999 Silver 0.6103 oz. ASW **Subject:** 560th Year of Hangeul - Alphabet **Obv:** Early alphabet characters **Obv. Legend:** THE BANK OF KOREA **Rev:** Modern alphabet characters **Shape:** Round with square center hole

| Date | Mintage | F12 | VF20 | XF40 | MS60 | MS63 |
|---|---|---|---|---|---|---|
| 2006 | — | PF63 65.00 | PF65 75.00 | | | |

**KM# 105 20000 WON**
19.00 g., 0.999 Silver 0.6103 oz. ASW, 33.00 mm. **Series:** Traditional Folk Dance **Subject:** Talchum - Mask Dances **Obv:** Mask at center surrounded by 6 other masks **Obv. Legend:** THE BANK OF KOREA **Rev:** Mask dancer at left center **Edge:** Plain **Shape:** 12-sided **Note:** Prev. KM #102.

| Date | Mintage | F12 | VF20 | XF40 | MS60 | MS63 |
|---|---|---|---|---|---|---|
| 2007 | 50,000 | PF63 65.00 | PF65 75.00 | | | |

**KM# 106 20000 WON**
19.00 g., 0.999 Silver 0.6103 oz. ASW, 33 mm. **Subject:** Mask dance **Rev:** Ganggangsullae ("Circle dance") **Shape:** 12-sided

| Date | Mintage | F12 | VF20 | XF40 | MS60 | MS63 |
|---|---|---|---|---|---|---|
| 2008 | 50,000 | PF63 65.00 | PF65 75.00 | | | |

**KM# 108 20000 WON**
19.00 g., 0.900 Silver 0.5498 oz. ASW, 33 mm. **Subject:** Mask dance **Rev:** Youngsan Juldarigi (Tug of War)

| Date | Mintage | F12 | VF20 | XF40 | MS60 | MS63 |
|---|---|---|---|---|---|---|
| 2009 | 50,000 | PF63 65.00 | PF65 75.00 | | | |

**KM# 109 20000 WON**
19.00 g., 0.999 Silver 0.6103 oz. ASW, 33 mm. **Subject:** Traditional Folk Games - Yeongsan Juldarigi (Tug of war)

| Date | Mintage | F12 | VF20 | XF40 | MS60 | MS63 |
|---|---|---|---|---|---|---|
| 2009 | 50,000 | PF63 45.00 | PF65 55.00 | | | |

**KM# 129 20000 WON**
15.55 g., 0.999 Gold 0.4994 oz. AGW, 28 mm. **Subject:** Expo 2012 **Obv:** International Pavilion **Rev:** Expo logo

| Date | Mintage | F12 | VF20 | XF40 | MS60 | MS63 |
|---|---|---|---|---|---|---|
| 2012 | 6,000 | PF63 900 | PF65 950 | | | |

### KM# 95 30000 WON

31.10 g., 0.999 Gold 0.999 oz. AGW, 35 mm. **Series:** World Cup Soccer **Obv:** Soccer logo **Rev:** Nude soccer player flanked by other players **Edge:** Reeded

| Date | Mintage | F12 | VF20 | XF40 | MS60 | MS63 |
|---|---|---|---|---|---|---|
| 2001 | 12,000 | PF63 1,675 | PF65 1,775 | | | |

### KM# 114 30000 WON

31.11 g., 0.999 Gold 0.999 oz. AGW, 35 mm. **Obv:** World Cup soccer trophy **Rev:** Stadium, fireworks, soccer ball

| Date | Mintage | F12 | VF20 | XF40 | MS60 | MS63 |
|---|---|---|---|---|---|---|
| 2002 | 12,002 | PF63 1,700 | PF65 1,800 | | | |

### KM# 120 30000 WON

31.11 g., 0.999 Gold 0.999 oz. AGW, 35 mm. **Subject:** 14th Asian Games, Busan **Obv:** Games logo **Rev:** Many hands reaching upwards

| Date | Mintage | F12 | VF20 | XF40 | MS60 | MS63 |
|---|---|---|---|---|---|---|
| 2002 | — | PF63 1,750 | PF65 1,850 | | | |

### KM# 107 30000 WON

Silver **Subject:** Flag, 60th Anniversary **Obv:** Flag **Rev:** Multicolor 60 logo

| Date | Mintage | F12 | VF20 | XF40 | MS60 | MS63 |
|---|---|---|---|---|---|---|
| 2008 | — | PF63 65.00 | PF65 75.00 | | | |

### KM# 110 30000 WON

19.00 g., 0.999 Silver 0.6103 oz. ASW, 33 mm. **Subject:** UNESCO World Heritage Site - Jongmyo Shrine **Obv:** Main Hall of the Jongmyo Shrine **Rev:** Scene of the Royal Ancestral Ritual in the shrine **Edge:** Reeded

| Date | Mintage | F12 | VF20 | XF40 | MS60 | MS63 |
|---|---|---|---|---|---|---|
| 2010 | 50,000 | PF63 50.00 | PF65 60.00 | | | |

### KM# 111 30000 WON

19.00 g., 0.999 Silver 0.6103 oz. ASW, 33 mm. **Subject:** G-20 Summit in Seoul **Obv:** Gwang-Hwa-Mun restored on Independence Day **Rev:** Multicolor lantern in national colors **Edge:** Reeded

| Date | Mintage | F12 | VF20 | XF40 | MS60 | MS63 |
|---|---|---|---|---|---|---|
| 2010 | 50,000 | PF63 45.00 | PF65 55.00 | | | |

### KM# 121 50000 WON

19.00 g., 0.999 Silver 0.6103 oz. ASW, 33 mm. **Subject:** Jeju Volcanic Island and Lava Tubes - UNESCO World Heritage Site **Obv:** Volcano Crater **Rev:** Lava tubes

| Date | Mintage | F12 | VF20 | XF40 | MS60 | MS63 |
|---|---|---|---|---|---|---|
| 2011 | 30,000 | PF63 45.00 | PF65 55.00 | | | |

### KM# 122 50000 WON

19.00 g., 0.999 Silver 0.6103 oz. ASW, 33 mm. **Subject:** International Association of Athletics Federations Championships **Obv:** High Jumping athlete **Rev:** Athlete running thru finish line tape in color

| Date | Mintage | F12 | VF20 | XF40 | MS60 | MS63 |
|---|---|---|---|---|---|---|
| 2011 | 30,000 | PF63 90.00 | PF65 100 | | | |

### KM# 123 50000 WON

19.00 g., 0.999 Silver 0.6103 oz. ASW, 33 mm. **Subject:** Nuclear Security Summit **Obv:** Five hands raising up globe **Rev:** Summit logo in color

| Date | Mintage | F12 | VF20 | XF40 | MS60 | MS63 |
|---|---|---|---|---|---|---|
| 2012 | 20,000 | PF63 30.00 | PF65 40.00 | | | |

### KM# 130 50000 WON

19.00 g., 0.999 Silver 0.6103 oz. ASW, 33 mm. **Subject:** UNESCO World Heritage Site - Seokguram Grotto and Bulguksa Temple

| Date | Mintage | F12 | VF20 | XF40 | MS60 | MS63 |
|---|---|---|---|---|---|---|
| 2012 | — | PF63 60.00 | PF65 70.00 | | | |

### KM# 131 50000 WON

19.00 g., 0.999 Silver 0.6103 oz. ASW, 33 mm. **Subject:** World Conservation Congress **Rev:** Logo in color

| Date | Mintage | F12 | VF20 | XF40 | MS60 | MS63 |
|---|---|---|---|---|---|---|
| 2012 | 20,000 | PF63 75.00 | PF65 85.00 | | | |

## MINT SETS

| KM# | Date | Mintage | Identification | Issue Price | Mkt Val |
|---|---|---|---|---|---|
| MS8 | 2001 (7) | — | KM#27, 31, 32, 33.2, 34, 35.2, 89 | 10.00 | 22.50 |

## PROOF SETS

| KM# | Date | Mintage | Identification | Issue Price | Mkt Val |
|---|---|---|---|---|---|
| PS10 | 2001 (6) | 2,002 | KM#90-95 | — | 2,500 |

# KUWAIT

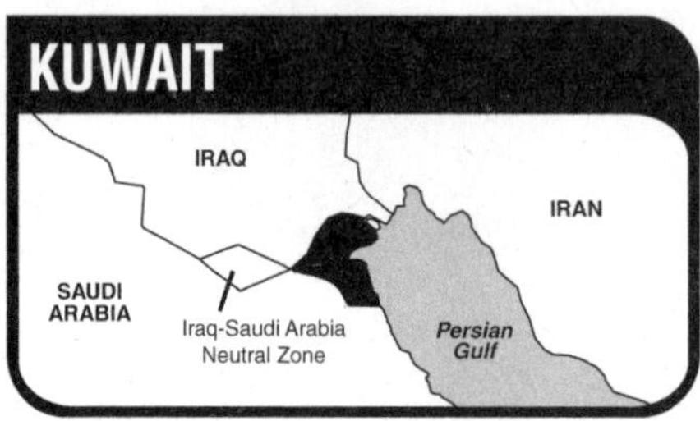


The State of Kuwait, a constitutional monarchy located on the Arabian Peninsula at the northwestern corner of the Persian Gulf, has an area of 6,880 sq. mi. (17,820 sq. km.) and a population of 1.7 million. Capital: Kuwait. Petroleum, the basis of the economy, provides 95 percent of the exports.

**RULERS**

**Al Sabah Dynasty**

Jabir Ibn Ahmad, 1977-2006
Sabah Al Ahmad Al Sabah, 2006-

**MONETARY SYSTEM**

1000 Fils = 1 Dinar

## SOVEREIGN EMIRATE

## MODERN COINAGE

### KM# 9a FILS

2.41 g., 0.925 Silver 0.0717 oz. ASW, 17 mm. **Ruler:** Jabir Ibn Ahmad **Obv:** Value within circle **Rev:** Ship with sails

| Date | Mintage | VF20 | XF40 | MS60 | MS63 | MS65 |
|---|---|---|---|---|---|---|
| AH1429-2008 | — | PF63 65.00 | | | | |

### KM# 9c FILS

2.41 g., 0.925 Silver Gilt 0.0717 oz., 17 mm. **Obv:** Value within circle **Rev:** Dhow, dates below

| Date | Mintage | VF20 | XF40 | MS60 | MS63 | MS65 |
|---|---|---|---|---|---|---|
| AH1429-2008 | — | PF63 75.00 | | | | |

### KM# 10 5 FILS

2.50 g., Nickel-Brass, 19.5 mm. **Ruler:** Jabir Ibn Ahmad **Obv:** Value within circle **Rev:** Dhow, dates below

| Date | Mintage | VF20 | XF40 | MS60 | MS63 | MS65 |
|---|---|---|---|---|---|---|
| AH1422-2001 | — | 0.10 | 0.20 | 0.50 | 0.70 | — |
| AH1424-2003 | — | 0.10 | 0.20 | 0.50 | 0.70 | — |
| AH1426-2005 | — | 0.10 | 0.20 | 0.50 | 0.70 | — |
| AH1427-2006 | — | 0.10 | 0.20 | 0.50 | 0.70 | — |
| AH1427-2007 | — | 0.10 | 0.20 | 0.50 | 0.70 | — |
| AH1428-2008 | — | 0.10 | 0.20 | 0.50 | 0.70 | — |
| AH1429-2008 | — | 0.10 | 0.20 | 0.50 | 0.70 | — |
| AH1430-2009 | — | 0.10 | 0.20 | 0.50 | 0.70 | — |
| AH1431-2010 | — | 0.10 | 0.20 | 0.50 | 0.70 | — |

### KM# 10a 5 FILS

3.01 g., 0.925 Silver 0.0895 oz. ASW, 19.5 mm. **Ruler:** Jabir Ibn Ahmad **Obv:** Value within circle **Rev:** Ship with sails

| Date | Mintage | VF20 | XF40 | MS60 | MS63 | MS65 |
|---|---|---|---|---|---|---|
| AH1429-2008 | — | PF63 70.00 | | | | |

### KM# 10c 5 FILS

3.01 g., 0.925 Silver Gilt 0.0895 oz., 19.5 mm. **Obv:** Value in circle **Rev:** Dhow, dates below

| Date | Mintage | VF20 | XF40 | MS60 | MS63 | MS65 |
|---|---|---|---|---|---|---|
| AH1429-2008 | — | PF63 80.00 | | | | |

### KM# 11 10 FILS

3.75 g., Nickel-Brass, 21 mm. **Ruler:** Jabir Ibn Ahmad **Obv:** Value within circle **Rev:** Dhow, dates below

| Date | Mintage | VF20 | XF40 | MS60 | MS63 | MS65 |
|---|---|---|---|---|---|---|
| AH1422-2001 | — | — | 0.25 | 0.75 | 1.25 | — |
| AH1424-2003 | — | — | 0.25 | 0.75 | 1.25 | — |
| AH1426-2005 | — | — | 0.25 | 0.75 | 1.25 | — |
| AH1427-2006 | — | — | 0.25 | 0.75 | 1.25 | — |
| AH1428-2007 | — | — | 0.25 | 0.75 | 1.25 | — |
| AH1429-2008 | — | — | 0.25 | 0.75 | 1.25 | — |
| AH1430-2009 | — | — | 0.25 | 0.75 | 1.25 | — |
| AH1431-2010 | — | — | 0.25 | 0.75 | 1.25 | — |

### KM# 11a 10 FILS

4.35 g., 0.925 Silver 0.1294 oz. ASW, 21 mm. **Ruler:** Jabir Ibn Ahmad **Obv:** Value within circle **Rev:** Ship with sails

| Date | Mintage | VF20 | XF40 | MS60 | MS63 | MS65 |
|---|---|---|---|---|---|---|
| AH1429-2008 | — | PF63 75.00 | | | | |

### KM# 11c 10 FILS

4.35 g., 0.925 Silver Gilt 0.1294 oz., 21 mm. **Obv:** Value within circle **Rev:** Dhow, dates below

| Date | Mintage | VF20 | XF40 | MS60 | MS63 | MS65 |
|---|---|---|---|---|---|---|
| AH1429-2008 | — | PF63 85.00 | | | | |

### KM# 12 20 FILS

3.00 g., Copper-Nickel, 20 mm. **Ruler:** Jabir Ibn Ahmad **Obv:** Value within circle **Rev:** Dhow, dates below **Edge:** Reeded **Note:** Varieties exist.

| Date | Mintage | VF20 | XF40 | MS60 | MS63 | MS65 |
|---|---|---|---|---|---|---|
| AH1422-2001 | — | 0.20 | 0.45 | 1.00 | 2.00 | — |
| AH1423-2002 | — | 0.20 | 0.45 | 1.00 | 2.00 | — |
| AH1424-2002 | — | 0.20 | 0.45 | 1.00 | 2.00 | — |
| AH1424-2003 | — | 0.20 | 0.45 | 1.00 | 2.00 | — |
| AH1426-2005 | — | 0.20 | 0.45 | 1.00 | 2.00 | — |
| AH1427-2006 | — | 0.20 | 0.45 | 1.00 | 2.00 | — |
| AH1428-2007 | — | 0.20 | 0.45 | 1.00 | 2.00 | — |
| AH1429-2008 | — | 0.20 | 0.45 | 1.00 | 2.00 | — |
| AH1430-2009 | — | 0.20 | 0.45 | 1.00 | 2.00 | — |
| AH1431-2010 | — | 0.20 | 0.45 | 1.00 | 2.00 | — |

### KM# 12a 20 FILS

3.37 g., 0.925 Silver 0.1002 oz. ASW, 20 mm. **Ruler:** Jabir Ibn Ahmad **Obv:** Value within circle **Rev:** Dhow, dates below

| Date | Mintage | VF20 | XF40 | MS60 | MS63 | MS65 |
|---|---|---|---|---|---|---|
| AH1429-2008 | — | PF63 80.00 | | | | |

### KM# 12c 20 FILS

Stainless Steel, 20 mm. **Ruler:** Jabir Ibn Ahmad **Obv:** Value **Rev:** Dhow, dates below

| Date | Mintage | VF20 | XF40 | MS60 | MS63 | MS65 |
|---|---|---|---|---|---|---|
| AH1422-2001 | — | 0.20 | 0.35 | 0.60 | 1.00 | — |
| AH1424-2003 | — | 0.20 | 0.35 | 0.60 | 1.00 | — |
| AH1426-2005 | — | 0.20 | 0.35 | 0.60 | 1.00 | — |

**KM# 12d 20 FILS**
3.37 g., 0.925 Silver Gilt 0.1002 oz., 20 mm. **Obv:** Value within cricle **Rev:** Dhow, dates below

| Date | Mintage | VF20 | XF40 | MS60 | MS63 | MS65 |
|---|---|---|---|---|---|---|
| AH1429-2008 | — | PF63 90.00 | | | | |

**KM# 13 50 FILS**
4.50 g., Copper-Nickel, 23 mm. **Ruler:** Jabir Ibn Ahmad **Obv:** Value within circle **Rev:** Dhow, dates below **Edge:** Reeded

| Date | Mintage | VF20 | XF40 | MS60 | MS63 | MS65 |
|---|---|---|---|---|---|---|
| AH1422-2001 | — | 0.25 | 0.35 | 0.75 | 1.50 | — |
| AH1424-2003 | — | 0.25 | 0.35 | 0.65 | 1.25 | — |
| AH1426-2005 | — | 0.25 | 0.35 | 0.65 | 1.25 | — |
| AH1427-2006 | — | 0.25 | 0.35 | 0.65 | 1.25 | — |
| AH1428-2007 | — | 0.25 | 0.35 | 0.65 | 1.25 | — |
| AH1429-2008 | — | 0.25 | 0.35 | 0.65 | 1.25 | — |
| AH1430-2009 | — | 0.25 | 0.35 | 0.65 | 1.25 | — |
| AH1431-2010 | — | 0.25 | 0.35 | 0.65 | 1.25 | — |
| AH1432-2011 | — | 0.25 | 0.35 | 0.65 | 1.25 | — |

**KM# 13a 50 FILS**
5.07 g., 0.925 Silver 0.1508 oz. ASW, 23 mm. **Ruler:** Jabir Ibn Ahmad **Obv:** Value within circle **Rev:** Ship with sails

| Date | Mintage | VF20 | XF40 | MS60 | MS63 | MS65 |
|---|---|---|---|---|---|---|
| AH1429-2008 | — | PF63 85.00 | | | | |

**KM# 13c 50 FILS**
5.07 g., 0.925 Silver Gilt 0.1508 oz., 23 mm. **Obv:** Value within circle **Rev:** Dhow, dates below

| Date | Mintage | VF20 | XF40 | MS60 | MS63 | MS65 |
|---|---|---|---|---|---|---|
| AH1429-2008 | — | PF63 100 | | | | |

**KM# 14 100 FILS**
6.50 g., Copper-Nickel, 26 mm. **Ruler:** Jabir Ibn Ahmad **Obv:** Value within circle **Rev:** Dhow, dates below **Edge:** Reeded

| Date | Mintage | VF20 | XF40 | MS60 | MS63 | MS65 |
|---|---|---|---|---|---|---|
| AH1424-2003 | — | 0.50 | 0.75 | 1.75 | — | — |
| AH1426-2005 | — | 0.50 | 0.75 | 1.75 | — | — |
| AH1427-2006 | — | 0.50 | 0.75 | 1.75 | — | — |
| AH1428-2007 | — | 0.50 | 0.75 | 1.75 | — | — |
| AH1429-2008 | — | 0.50 | 0.75 | 1.75 | — | — |
| AH1430-2009 | — | 0.50 | 0.75 | 1.75 | — | — |
| AH1431-2010 | — | 0.50 | 0.75 | 1.75 | — | — |

**KM# 14a 100 FILS**
7.34 g., 0.925 Silver 0.2183 oz. ASW, 26 mm. **Ruler:** Jabir Ibn Ahmad **Obv:** Value within circle **Rev:** Ship with sails

| Date | Mintage | VF20 | XF40 | MS60 | MS63 | MS65 |
|---|---|---|---|---|---|---|
| AH1429-2008 | — | PF63 90.00 | | | | |

**KM# 14c 100 FILS**
7.34 g., 0.925 Silver Gilt 0.2183 oz., 26 mm. **Obv:** Value within circle **Rev:** Dhow, dates below

| Date | Mintage | VF20 | XF40 | MS60 | MS63 | MS65 |
|---|---|---|---|---|---|---|
| AH1429-2008 | — | PF63 110 | | | | |

## PROOF SETS

| KM# | Date | Mintage | Identification | Issue Price | Mkt Val |
|---|---|---|---|---|---|
| PS5 | 2008 (6) | — | KM#9a-14a | — | 475 |
| PS6 | 2008 (6) | — | KM#9c-11c, 12d, 13c-14c | — | 500 |

# KYRGYZSTAN

The Kyrgyz Republic, (formerly Kirghiz S.S.R., a Union Republic of the U.S.S.R.), is an independent state since Aug. 31, 1991, a member of the United Nations and of the C.I.S. It was the last state of the Union Republics to declare its sovereignty. Capital: Bishkek (formerly Frunze).

**MONETARY SYSTEM**
100 Tiyin = 1 Som

## REPUBLIC

### STANDARD COINAGE

**KM# 11 TIYIN**
1.00 g., Aluminum-Bronze, 13.98 mm. **Obv:** National arms **Rev:** Flower at left of value **Edge:** Reeded **Note:** Prev. KM #8.

| Date | Mintage | VF20 | XF40 | MS60 | MS63 | MS65 |
|---|---|---|---|---|---|---|
| 2008 Sets only | 95,000 | — | — | — | — | 1.25 |

**KM# 12 10 TIYIN**
1.30 g., Brass Plated Steel, 15 mm. **Obv:** National arms **Rev:** Flower at left of value **Edge:** Plain **Note:** Prev. KM #9.

| Date | Mintage | VF20 | XF40 | MS60 | MS63 | MS65 |
|---|---|---|---|---|---|---|
| 2008 | — | — | — | 0.45 | 0.85 | 1.50 |

**KM# 13 50 TIYIN**
1.80 g., Brass Plated Steel, 17 mm. **Obv:** National arms **Rev:** Flower at left of value **Edge:** Plain **Note:** Prev. KM #10.

| Date | Mintage | VF20 | XF40 | MS60 | MS63 | MS65 |
|---|---|---|---|---|---|---|
| 2008 | — | — | — | 0.65 | 1.25 | 2.00 |

**KM# 14 SOM**
2.50 g., Nickel Plated Steel, 19 mm. **Obv:** National arms **Rev:** Symbol at left of denomination **Edge:** Reeded **Note:** Prev. KM #11.

| Date | Mintage | VF20 | XF40 | MS60 | MS63 | MS65 |
|---|---|---|---|---|---|---|
| 2008 | — | — | — | 0.75 | 1.50 | 2.25 |

**KM# 19 SOM**
12.00 g., Copper-Nickel, 30 mm. **Series:** Great Silk Road **Subject:** Tashrabat **Obv:** Arms **Rev:** Fortress

| Date | Mintage | VF20 | XF40 | MS60 | MS63 | MS65 |
|---|---|---|---|---|---|---|
| 2008 Prooflike | 5,000 | — | — | — | 10.00 | 15.00 |

**KM# 21 SOM**
12.00 g., Copper-Nickel, 30 mm. **Subject:** Uzgen Architectural Complex **Obv:** Arms **Rev:** Tower and building - map above

| Date | Mintage | VF20 | XF40 | MS60 | MS63 | MS65 |
|---|---|---|---|---|---|---|
| 2008 Prooflike | 5,000 | — | — | — | 10.00 | 15.00 |

**KM# 35 SOM**
12.00 g., Copper-Nickel, 30 mm. **Series:** Great Silk Road **Subject:** Burana Tower **Rev:** Tower and map

| Date | Mintage | VF20 | XF40 | MS60 | MS63 | MS65 |
|---|---|---|---|---|---|---|
| 2008 Prooflike | 5,000 | — | — | — | 10.00 | 15.00 |

**KM# 31 SOM**
12.00 g., Copper-Nickel, 30 mm. **Series:** Great Silk Road **Subject:** Suilaman Mountain

| Date | Mintage | VF20 | XF40 | MS60 | MS63 | MS65 |
|---|---|---|---|---|---|---|
| 2009 Prooflike | 5,000 | — | — | — | 10.00 | 15.00 |

**KM# 33 SOM**
12.00 g., Copper-Nickel, 30 mm. **Series:** Great Silk Road **Subject:** Lake Issykkul

| Date | Mintage | VF20 | XF40 | MS60 | MS63 | MS65 |
|---|---|---|---|---|---|---|
| 2009 Prooflike | 5,000 | — | — | — | 10.00 | 15.00 |

**KM# 45 SOM**
12.00 g., Copper-Nickel, 30 mm. **Subject:** Pobeda Peak **Obv:** National arms above stylized peaks **Rev:** Mountian range

| Date | Mintage | VF20 | XF40 | MS60 | MS63 | MS65 |
|---|---|---|---|---|---|---|
| 2011 | 5,000 | — | — | — | 25.00 | 30.00 |

**KM# 47 SOM**
12.00 g., Copper-Nickel, 30 mm. **Obv:** National arms **Rev:** Khan-Tengri Peak

| Date | Mintage | VF20 | XF40 | MS60 | MS63 | MS65 |
|---|---|---|---|---|---|---|
| 2011 | 5,000 | — | — | — | 25.00 | 30.00 |

**KM# 51 SOM**
12.00 g., Copper-Nickel, 30 mm. **Subject:** Saimaluu-Tash **Obv:** Rock carvings **Rev:** Rock drawings

| Date | Mintage | VF20 | XF40 | MS60 | MS63 | MS65 |
|---|---|---|---|---|---|---|
| 2013 | 5,000 | — | — | — | 25.00 | 30.00 |

**KM# 55 SOM**
28.28 g., 0.925 Silver 0.841 oz. ASW, 38.6 mm. **Subject:** Saimaluu-Tash **Obv:** Rock carvings **Rev:** Rock drawings

| Date | Mintage | VF20 | XF40 | MS60 | MS63 | MS65 |
|---|---|---|---|---|---|---|
| 2013 | 3,000 | PF65 110 | | | | |

**KM# 15 3 SOM**
3.20 g., Nickel Plated Steel, 21 mm. **Obv:** National arms **Rev:** Symbol above right of denomination **Edge:** Reeded **Note:** Prev. KM #12.

| Date | Mintage | VF20 | XF40 | MS60 | MS63 | MS65 |
|---|---|---|---|---|---|---|
| 2008 | — | — | — | 0.65 | 1.25 | 2.00 |

**KM# 16 5 SOM**
4.20 g., Nickel Plated Steel, 23 mm. **Obv:** National arms **Rev:** Symbol at right of value **Edge:** Reeded **Note:** Prev. KM #13.

| Date | Mintage | VF20 | XF40 | MS60 | MS63 | MS65 |
|---|---|---|---|---|---|---|
| 2008 | — | — | — | 0.75 | 1.50 | 2.50 |

**KM# 52 5 SOM**
14.35 g., Copper-Nickel, 33 mm. **Obv:** National arms and traditional musical instruments **Rev:** Man with Komuz

| Date | Mintage | VF20 | XF40 | MS60 | MS63 | MS65 |
|---|---|---|---|---|---|---|
| 2012 | 3,000 | — | — | — | 25.00 | 30.00 |

**KM# 4 10 SOM**
28.28 g., 0.925 Silver 0.841 oz. ASW, 38.6 mm. **Subject:** Tenth Anniversary of Republic **Obv:** National arms within circle **Rev:** Value and Khan Tengri mountain **Edge:** Reeded **Note:** Prev. KM #3.

| Date | Mintage | VF20 | XF40 | MS60 | MS63 | MS65 |
|---|---|---|---|---|---|---|
| 2001 | 1,000 | PF65 175 | | | | |

**KM# 5 10 SOM**
28.28 g., 0.925 Silver 0.841 oz. ASW, 38.6 mm. **Subject:** International Year of the mountains **Obv:** National arms **Rev:** Edelweiss flower and mountain **Edge:** Reeded **Note:** Prev. KM #4.

| Date | Mintage | VF20 | XF40 | MS60 | MS63 | MS65 |
|---|---|---|---|---|---|---|
| 2002 | 1,000 | PF65 125 | | | | |

**KM# 6 10 SOM**
28.28 g., 0.925 Silver 0.841 oz. ASW, 38.6 mm. **Subject:** International Year of the Mountains **Obv:** National arms **Rev:** Argali Ram head and mountain **Edge:** Reeded **Note:** Prev. KM #5.

| Date | Mintage | VF20 | XF40 | MS60 | MS63 | MS65 |
|---|---|---|---|---|---|---|
| 2002 | 1,000 | PF65 125 | | | | |

**KM# 36 10 SOM**
28.28 g., 0.925 Silver 0.841 oz. ASW partially gilt, 38.6 mm. **Subject:** Som, 10th Anniversary **Obv:** National arms **Rev:** Som coin designs, some gilt

| Date | Mintage | VF20 | XF40 | MS60 | MS63 | MS65 |
|---|---|---|---|---|---|---|
| 2003 | — | PF65 150 | | | | |

**KM# 7 10 SOM**
28.28 g., 0.925 Silver 0.841 oz. ASW partially gilt, 38.6 mm. **Subject:** Genesis of the Kyrgyz Statehood **Obv:** Arms **Rev:** Classical designs

| Date | Mintage | VF20 | XF40 | MS60 | MS63 | MS65 |
|---|---|---|---|---|---|---|
| 2003 | 1,000 | PF65 250 | | | | |

**KM# 8 10 SOM**
28.28 g., 0.925 Silver 0.841 oz. ASW, 38.6 mm. **Subject:** 60 Years of Great Victory **Rev:** Figure of a mother, eternal light, Victory Memorial complex **Note:** Prev. KM #6.

| Date | Mintage | VF20 | XF40 | MS60 | MS63 | MS65 |
|---|---|---|---|---|---|---|
| 2005 | 1,000 | PF65 110 | | | | |

**KM# 9 10 SOM**
28.28 g., 0.825 Silver 0.7501 oz. ASW partially gilt, 38.6 mm. **Series:** Great Silk Road **Subject:** Tashrabat **Note:** Prev. KM #7.

| Date | Mintage | VF20 | XF40 | MS60 | MS63 | MS65 |
|---|---|---|---|---|---|---|
| 2005 | 1,500 | PF65 100 | | | | |

**KM# 10 10 SOM**
28.28 g., 0.925 Silver 0.841 oz. ASW, 38.6 mm. **Subject:** Shanghai Cooperation **Obv:** Arms **Rev:** Multicolor logo of the Shanghai Cooperation Organization

| Date | Mintage | VF20 | XF40 | MS60 | MS63 | MS65 |
|---|---|---|---|---|---|---|
| 2007 | 1,000 | PF65 180 | | | | |

**KM# 22 10 SOM**
28.28 g., 0.925 Silver 0.841 oz. ASW partially gilt, 38.6 mm. **Series:** Great Silk Road **Subject:** Uzgen Architectural Complex

| Date | Mintage | VF20 | XF40 | MS60 | MS63 | MS65 |
|---|---|---|---|---|---|---|
| 2007 | 1,500 | PF65 120 | | | | |

**KM# 18 10 SOM**
28.28 g., 0.925 Silver 0.841 oz. ASW partially gilt, 38.6 mm. **Series:** Great Silk Road **Subject:** Burana Tower **Rev:** Buildings with partial gilting

| Date | Mintage | VF20 | XF40 | MS60 | MS63 | MS65 |
|---|---|---|---|---|---|---|
| 2008 | 1,500 | PF65 110 | | | | |

**KM# 23 10 SOM**
28.28 g., 0.925 Silver 0.841 oz. ASW, 38.6 mm. **Series:** Capitals of the Eurasia Economic Community **Subject:** City of Bishkek **Obv:** National emblem **Rev:** Horseman statue, multicolor logo

| Date | Mintage | VF20 | XF40 | MS60 | MS63 | MS65 |
|---|---|---|---|---|---|---|
| 2008 | 2,500 | PF65 90.00 | | | | |

**KM# 24 10 SOM**
28.28 g., 0.925 Silver 0.841 oz. ASW, 38.6 mm. **Rev:** Chynqyz Aytmatov

| Date | Mintage | VF20 | XF40 | MS60 | MS63 | MS65 |
|---|---|---|---|---|---|---|
| 2009 | 2,000 | PF65 75.00 | | | | |

**KM# 25 10 SOM**
28.28 g., 0.925 Silver 0.841 oz. ASW, 38.6 mm. **Series:** Chinqiz Aitmatov's work's **Rev:** Jamila

| Date | Mintage | VF20 | XF40 | MS60 | MS63 | MS65 |
|---|---|---|---|---|---|---|
| 2009 | 3,000 | PF65 75.00 | | | | |

**KM# 26 10 SOM**
28.28 g., 0.925 Silver 0.841 oz. ASW, 38.6 mm. **Series:** Chingiz Aitmatov's works **Rev:** Duishen

| Date | Mintage | VF20 | XF40 | MS60 | MS63 | MS65 |
|---|---|---|---|---|---|---|
| 2009 | 3,000 | PF65 75.00 | | | | |

**KM# 27 10 SOM**
28.28 g., 0.925 Silver 0.841 oz. ASW, 38.6 mm. **Series:** Chinqiz Aitmatov's works **Rev:** Mother field

| Date | Mintage | VF20 | XF40 | MS60 | MS63 | MS65 |
|---|---|---|---|---|---|---|
| 2009 | 3,000 | PF65 75.00 | | | | |

**KM# 28 10 SOM**
28.28 g., 0.925 Silver 0.841 oz. ASW, 38.5 mm. **Series:** Chinqiz Aitmatov's works **Rev:** Farewell, Gulsary!

| Date | Mintage | VF20 | XF40 | MS60 | MS63 | MS65 |
|---|---|---|---|---|---|---|
| 2009 | 3,000 | PF65 75.00 | | | | |

**KM# 29 10 SOM**
28.28 g., 0.925 Silver 0.841 oz. ASW, 38.5 mm. **Series:** Chinqiz Aitmatov's works **Rev:** The white ship

| Date | Mintage | VF20 | XF40 | MS60 | MS63 | MS65 |
|---|---|---|---|---|---|---|
| 2009 | 3,000 | PF65 75.00 | | | | |

**KM# 32 10 SOM**
28.28 g., 0.925 Silver 0.841 oz. ASW Partially gilt, 38.6 mm. **Series:** Great Silk Road **Subject:** Suliman Mountain

| Date | Mintage | VF20 | XF40 | MS60 | MS63 | MS65 |
|---|---|---|---|---|---|---|
| 2009 | 1,500 | PF65 110 | | | | |

**KM# 34 10 SOM**
28.28 g., 0.925 Silver 0.841 oz. ASW partially gilt, 38.6 mm. **Series:** Great Silk Road **Subject:** Lake Issykkul

| Date | Mintage | VF20 | XF40 | MS60 | MS63 | MS65 |
|---|---|---|---|---|---|---|
| 2009 | 1,500 | PF65 110 | | | | |

**KM# 38 10 SOM**
31.10 g., 0.925 Silver 0.9249 oz. ASW, 38.6 mm. **Obv:** National arms at top of repeating motif **Rev:** Eagle in flight right, multicolor logo below

| Date | Mintage | VF20 | XF40 | MS60 | MS63 | MS65 |
|---|---|---|---|---|---|---|
| 2009 | 3,000 | PF65 90.00 | | | | |

**KM# 41 10 SOM**
31.10 g., 0.925 Silver 0.9249 oz. ASW, 38.6 mm. **Obv:** National emblem and linear design **Rev:** Two people riding deer, as in a cave painting; multicolor logo below

| Date | Mintage | VF20 | XF40 | MS60 | MS63 | MS65 |
|---|---|---|---|---|---|---|
| 2009 | 3,000 | PF65 95.00 | | | | |

**KM# 43 10 SOM**
5.40 g., Nickel Plated Steel, 24.5 mm. **Obv:** National Arms **Rev:** Symbol above value

| Date | Mintage | VF20 | XF40 | MS60 | MS63 | MS65 |
|---|---|---|---|---|---|---|
| 2009 | — | — | — | 4.50 | 6.00 | — |

**KM# 39 10 SOM**
31.10 g., 0.925 Silver 0.9249 oz. ASW, 38.6 mm. **Obv:** National Arms, multicolor design **Rev:** Frame construction of a Yurta

| Date | Mintage | VF20 | XF40 | MS60 | MS63 | MS65 |
|---|---|---|---|---|---|---|
| 2010 | 3,000 | PF65 75.00 | | | | |

**KM# 40 10 SOM**
31.10 g., 0.925 Silver 0.9249 oz. ASW, 38.6 mm. **Subject:** EurAsEC 10th Anniversary **Obv:** National arms and globe **Rev:** Five world sites, multicolor logo at center

| Date | Mintage | VF20 | XF40 | MS60 | MS63 | MS65 |
|---|---|---|---|---|---|---|
| 2010 | 2,000 | PF65 75.00 | | | | |

**KM# 44 10 SOM**
28.28 g., Silver partially gilt, 38.6 mm. **Subject:** Independence, 20th Anniversary **Obv:** National arms **Rev:** Colored flag above map with Manas on horseback right **Edge:** Reeded

| Date | Mintage | VF20 | XF40 | MS60 | MS63 | MS65 |
|---|---|---|---|---|---|---|
| 2011 | 2,000 | PF65 75.00 | | | | |

**KM# 46 10 SOM**
28.28 g., 0.925 Silver 0.841 oz. ASW, 38.6 mm. **Subject:** Pobeda Peak **Obv:** National arms above stylized mountains **Rev:** Mountian range **Edge:** Reeded

| Date | Mintage | VF20 | XF40 | MS60 | MS63 | MS65 |
|---|---|---|---|---|---|---|
| 2011 | 3,000 | PF65 75.00 | | | | |

**KM# 48 10 SOM**
31.10 g., 0.925 Silver 0.9249 oz. ASW partially gilt, 38.6 mm. **Subject:** Great Silk Road **Obv:** National arms above caravan riding right **Rev:** Skyline views and Silk Road map of Eurasia, color logo at top **Edge:** Reeded

| Date | Mintage | VF20 | XF40 | MS60 | MS63 | MS65 |
|---|---|---|---|---|---|---|
| 2011 | Est. 2000 | PF65 75.00 | | | | |

**KM# 49 10 SOM**
33.94 g., 0.925 Silver 1.0094 oz. ASW, 38.6 mm. **Subject:** World of our Children **Obv:** National arms and six flowers **Rev:** Child's drawing in color of sun, girl and medow **Edge:** Reeded

| Date | Mintage | VF20 | XF40 | MS60 | MS63 | MS65 |
|---|---|---|---|---|---|---|
| 2011 | — | PF65 75.00 | | | | |

**KM# 50 10 SOM**
28.28 g., 0.925 Silver 0.841 oz. ASW, 38.6 mm. **Subject:** Kumranjan Datka, 200th Anniversary **Obv:** Arms, horseman below **Rev:** Female head wearing turban, facing

| Date | Mintage | VF20 | XF40 | MS60 | MS63 | MS65 |
|---|---|---|---|---|---|---|
| 2012 | — | PF65 110 | | | | |

**KM# 53 10 SOM**
28.28 g., 0.925 Silver 0.841 oz. ASW, 38.6 mm. **Obv:** Arms, stylized animals below **Rev:** Resting leopard, crystal inserts

| Date | Mintage | VF20 | XF40 | MS60 | MS63 | MS65 |
|---|---|---|---|---|---|---|
| 2012 | 3,000 | PF65 110 | | | | |

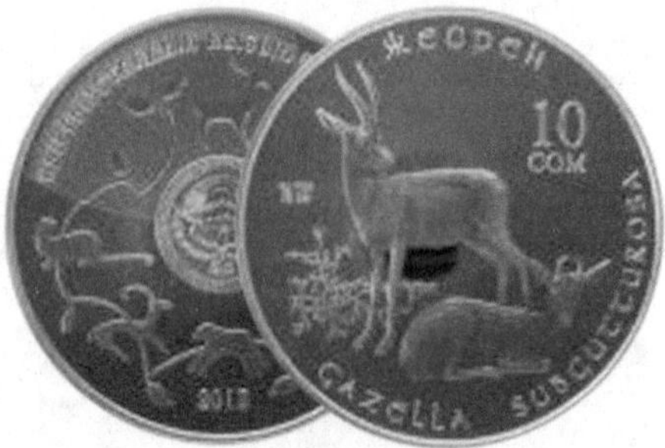


**KM# 54 10 SOM**
28.28 g., 0.925 Silver 0.841 oz. ASW, 38.6 mm. **Obv:** Arms, stylized animals below **Rev:** Gazelle, crystal inserts

| Date | Mintage | VF20 | XF40 | MS60 | MS63 | MS65 |
|---|---|---|---|---|---|---|
| 2012 | 3,000 | PF65 110 | | | | |

**KM# 37 100 SOM**
6.22 g., 0.999 Gold 0.1998 oz. AGW, 22 mm. **Rev:** Two horsemen

| Date | Mintage | VF20 | XF40 | MS60 | MS63 | MS65 |
|---|---|---|---|---|---|---|
| 2008 | — | PF65 375 | | | | |

**KM# 42 100 SOM**
31.10 g., 0.925 Silver 0.9249 oz. ASW, 38.61 mm. **Rev:** Panthera Tigris, gilt tiger

| Date | Mintage | VF20 | XF40 | MS60 | MS63 | MS65 |
|---|---|---|---|---|---|---|
| 2009 | 13,000 | PF63 85.00 | PF65 100 | | | |

## MINT SETS

| KM# | Date | Mintage | Identification | Issue Price | Mkt Val |
|---|---|---|---|---|---|
| MS1 | 2008 (6) | — | KM#11-16 | — | 30.00 |

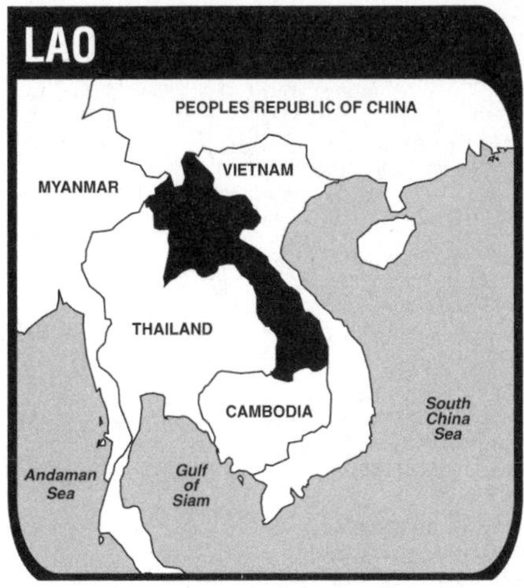


The Lao Peoples Democratic Republic, located on the Indo-Chinese Peninsula between the Socialist Republic of Vietnam and the Kingdom of Thailand, has an area of 91,428 sq. mi. (236,800 km.) and a population of 3.6 million. Capital Vientiane. Agriculture employs 95 per cent of the people. Tin, lumber and coffee are exported.

**MONETARY SYSTEM**

100 Att = 1 Kip

# PEOPLES DEMOCRATIC REPUBLIC

## STANDARD COINAGE

**KM# 159 500 KIP**

0.50 g., 0.999 Gold 0.0161 oz. AGW, 11 mm. **Obv:** National emblem **Rev:** Peacock

| Date | Mintage | VF20 | XF40 | MS60 | MS63 | MS65 |
|---|---|---|---|---|---|---|
| 2008 | 15,000 | PF63 50.00 | | PF65 60.00 | | |

**KM# 160 500 KIP**

0.50 g., 0.999 Gold 0.0161 oz. AGW, 11 mm. **Obv:** National emblem **Rev:** Victory Gate, Patouxai

| Date | Mintage | VF20 | XF40 | MS60 | MS63 | MS65 |
|---|---|---|---|---|---|---|
| 2008 | 10,000 | PF63 50.00 | | PF65 60.00 | | |

**KM# 151 500 KIP**

0.50 g., 0.999 Gold 0.0161 oz. AGW, 11 mm. **Rev:** Lion's head

| Date | Mintage | VF20 | XF40 | MS60 | MS63 | MS65 |
|---|---|---|---|---|---|---|
| 2009 | — | PF65 50.00 | | | | |

**KM# 152 500 KIP**

0.50 g., 0.999 Gold 0.0161 oz. AGW, 11 mm. **Subject:** Year of the Tiger **Rev:** Tiger

| Date | Mintage | VF20 | XF40 | MS60 | MS63 | MS65 |
|---|---|---|---|---|---|---|
| 2010 | Est. 5000 | PF65 50.00 | | | | |

**KM# 162 500 KIP**

0.50 g., 0.999 Gold 0.0161 oz. AGW, 11 mm. **Obv:** National emblem **Rev:** Buddha seated in archway

| Date | Mintage | VF20 | XF40 | MS60 | MS63 | MS65 |
|---|---|---|---|---|---|---|
| 2010 | — | PF65 60.00 | | | | |

**KM# 165 500 KIP**

0.50 g., 0.999 Gold 0.0161 oz. AGW, 11 mm. **Subject:** Year of the Rabbit **Obv:** National emblem **Rev:** Rabbit seated upright right, head looking left

| Date | Mintage | VF20 | XF40 | MS60 | MS63 | MS65 |
|---|---|---|---|---|---|---|
| 2011 | Est. 5000 | PF65 50.00 | | | | |

**KM# 168 500 KIP**

0.50 g., 0.585 Gold 0.0094 oz. AGW with 24K Goldplated, 11 mm. **Subject:** Golden Pha - That Luang

| Date | Mintage | VF20 | XF40 | MS60 | MS63 | MS65 |
|---|---|---|---|---|---|---|
| 2012 | Est. 5000 | PF65 70.00 | | | | |

**KM# 85 1000 KIP**

31.50 g., 0.999 Silver 1.0117 oz. ASW, 38.5 mm. **Subject:** Olympics **Obv:** State emblem **Rev:** Freestyle skier **Edge:** Reeded

| Date | Mintage | VF20 | XF40 | MS60 | MS63 | MS65 |
|---|---|---|---|---|---|---|
| 2001 | — | PF63 45.00 | | PF65 50.00 | | |

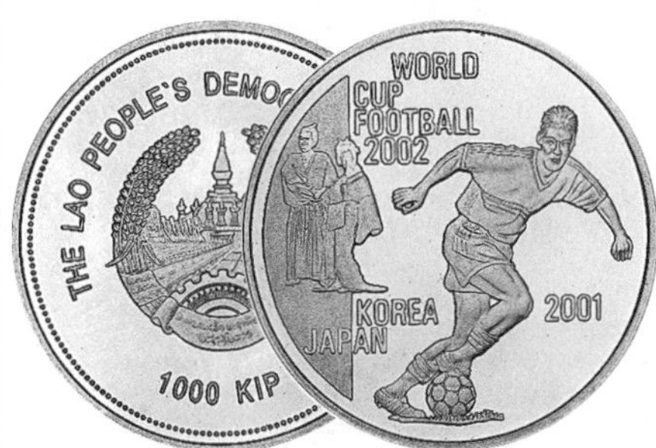

**KM# 96 1000 KIP**

31.45 g., 0.999 Silver 1.0101 oz. ASW, 38.5 mm. **Obv:** State emblem **Rev:** Soccer player **Edge:** Reeded

| Date | Mintage | VF20 | XF40 | MS60 | MS63 | MS65 |
|---|---|---|---|---|---|---|
| 2001 | — | PF65 50.00 | | | | |

**KM# 122 1000 KIP**

1.24 g., 0.999 Gold 0.0398 oz. AGW, 13.92 mm. **Rev:** Tiger head

| Date | Mintage | VF20 | XF40 | MS60 | MS63 | MS65 |
|---|---|---|---|---|---|---|
| 2003 | Est. 15000 | PF63 75.00 | | PF65 90.00 | | |

**KM# 126 1000 KIP**

Silver **Subject:** Beijing olympics, 2008 **Rev:** Torch relay between Parthenon in Athens and Temple of Heaven in Beijing

| Date | Mintage | VF20 | XF40 | MS60 | MS63 | MS65 |
|---|---|---|---|---|---|---|
| 2004 | — | PF65 35.00 | | | | |

**KM# 136 1000 KIP**

1.24 g., 0.999 Gold 0.0398 oz. AGW, 13.92 mm. **Rev:** Wat Phu Champasak

| Date | Mintage | VF20 | XF40 | MS60 | MS63 | MS65 |
|---|---|---|---|---|---|---|
| 2005 | — | PF65 90.00 | | | | |

**KM# 161 1000 KIP**

1.24 g., 0.999 Gold 0.0398 oz. AGW, 13.92 mm. **Subject:** Rennes le Chateau **Obv:** National emblem **Rev:** Town gate and menorah

| Date | Mintage | VF20 | XF40 | MS60 | MS63 | MS65 |
|---|---|---|---|---|---|---|
| 2007 | Est. 15000 | PF63 75.00 | | PF65 85.00 | | |

**KM# 150 1000 KIP**

28.28 g., 0.925 Silver 0.841 oz. ASW, 38.61 mm. **Subject:** Qinghai - Tibet Railway **Obv:** National emblem **Rev:** Train and map of the railroad from Zining to Lhasa

| Date | Mintage | VF20 | XF40 | MS60 | MS63 | MS65 |
|---|---|---|---|---|---|---|
| 2008 | — | PF65 75.00 | | | | |

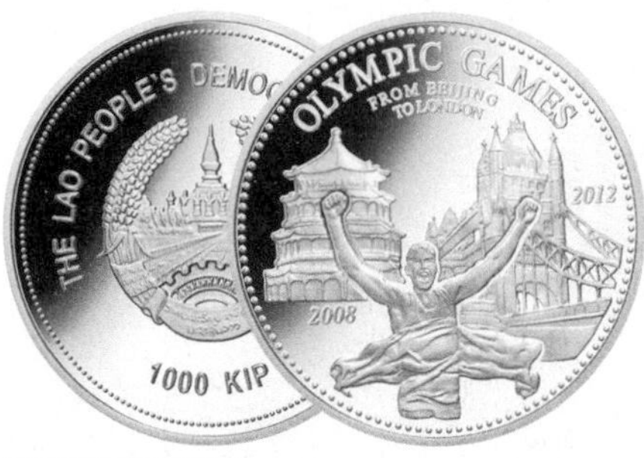

**KM# 157 1000 KIP**

28.28 g., 0.925 Silver 0.841 oz. ASW, 38.61 mm. **Subject:** Beijing to London Olympic transfer **Obv:** National emblem **Rev:** Temple of Heaven, Tower Bridge and athlete

| Date | Mintage | VF20 | XF40 | MS60 | MS63 | MS65 |
|---|---|---|---|---|---|---|
| 2008 | Est. 10000 | PF63 65.00 | | PF65 75.00 | | |

**KM# 104 1000 KIP**

36.47 g., 0.925 Silver 1.0846 oz. ASW, 38.6 mm. **Subject:** Terra Cotta Warriors **Obv:** Arms **Rev:** Gilt warrior standing, background warriors face right **Note:** Central gilt warrior is detachable and stands upright.

| Date | Mintage | VF20 | XF40 | MS60 | MS63 | MS65 |
|---|---|---|---|---|---|---|
| 2009 | 5,000 | PF63 85.00 | | PF65 100 | | |

**KM# 105 1000 KIP**

36.47 g., 0.925 Silver 1.0846 oz. ASW, 38.61 mm. **Subject:** Terra Cotta Warrior **Obv:** Arms **Rev:** Gilt standing warrior, warriors in background facing **Note:** Central gilt warrior is detachable and stands upright.

| Date | Mintage | VF20 | XF40 | MS60 | MS63 | MS65 |
|---|---|---|---|---|---|---|
| 2009 | 5,000 | PF63 85.00 | | PF65 100 | | |

### KM# 106 1000 KIP

36.47 g., 0.925 Silver 1.0846 oz. ASW, 38.6 mm. **Subject:** Terra Cotta Warrior **Obv:** Arms **Rev:** Archer kneeling **Note:** Central gilt warrior is detachable and stands upright.

| Date | Mintage | VF20 | XF40 | MS60 | MS63 | MS65 |
|---|---|---|---|---|---|---|
| 2009 | 1,000 | **PF63** 85.00 | **PF65** 100 | | | |

### KM# 107 1000 KIP

36.47 g., 0.925 Silver 1.0846 oz. ASW **Subject:** Terra Cotta Warrior **Obv:** Arms **Rev:** Gilt horse **Note:** Central gilt warrior is detachable and stands upright.

| Date | Mintage | VF20 | XF40 | MS60 | MS63 | MS65 |
|---|---|---|---|---|---|---|
| 2009 | 1,000 | **PF63** 85.00 | **PF65** 100 | | | |

### KM# 153 1000 KIP

28.28 g., 0.925 Silver 0.841 oz. ASW, 38.61 mm. **Subject:** World Cup 2010 in South Africa **Rev:** Sculpture of soccer players

| Date | Mintage | VF20 | XF40 | MS60 | MS63 | MS65 |
|---|---|---|---|---|---|---|
| 2010 | — | **PF65** 60.00 | | | | |

### KM# 163 1000 KIP

1.00 g., 0.999 Gold 0.0321 oz. AGW, 13.92 mm. **Obv:** National emblem **Rev:** Buddha Park, stone staute head

| Date | Mintage | VF20 | XF40 | MS60 | MS63 | MS65 |
|---|---|---|---|---|---|---|
| 2010 | Est. 10000 | **PF63** 65.00 | **PF65** 75.00 | | | |

### KM# 167 1000 KIP

28.35 g., 0.999 Silver 0.9106 oz. ASW, 40 mm. **Subject:** Lunar Series - Year of the Dragon, Colorized

| Date | Mintage | VF20 | XF40 | MS60 | MS63 | MS65 |
|---|---|---|---|---|---|---|
| 2012 | Est. 8888 | **PF65** 90.00 | | | | |

### KM# 164 2000 KIP

62.21 g., 0.999 Silver 1.9981 oz. ASW selective gilt and with jade inlay, 55 mm. **Subject:** Year of the Rabbit **Obv:** Naitonal emblem **Rev:** Rabbit and jade inlay

| Date | Mintage | VF20 | XF40 | MS60 | MS63 | MS65 |
|---|---|---|---|---|---|---|
| 2011 | Est. 2888 | **PF65** 200 | | | | |

### KM# 155 2000 KIP

62.20 g., 0.999 Silver 1.9978 oz. ASW, 55 mm. **Subject:** Year of the Dragon **Obv:** National arms **Rev:** Dragon with jade ring

| Date | Mintage | VF20 | XF40 | MS60 | MS63 | MS65 |
|---|---|---|---|---|---|---|
| 2012 | 2,888 | **PF65** 140 | | | | |

### KM# 166 2000 KIP

56.70 g., 0.999 Silver 1.8211 oz. ASW Gilt with Jade Insert, 55 mm. **Subject:** Lunar Series - Year of the Dragon

| Date | Mintage | VF20 | XF40 | MS60 | MS63 | MS65 |
|---|---|---|---|---|---|---|
| 2012 | Est. 2888 | **PF65** 225 | | | | |

### KM# 169 2000 KIP

62.20 g., 0.999 Silver 1.9978 oz. ASW partially gilt, 55 mm. **Subject:** Year of the Horse **Rev:** Gilt horse prancing left within jade insert

| Date | Mintage | F12 | VF20 | XF40 | MS60 | MS63 |
|---|---|---|---|---|---|---|
| 2014 | 2,888 | **PF65** 225 | | | | |

### KM# 119 5000 KIP

0.30 g., 0.999 Gold 0.0096 oz. AGW, 7 mm. **Rev:** Cichlasoma fish

| Date | Mintage | VF20 | XF40 | MS60 | MS63 | MS65 |
|---|---|---|---|---|---|---|
| 2003 | — | — | — | — | — | 50.00 |

### KM# 124 5000 KIP

0.30 g., 0.999 Gold 0.0096 oz. AGW, 7 mm. **Rev:** Rhino

| Date | Mintage | VF20 | XF40 | MS60 | MS63 | MS65 |
|---|---|---|---|---|---|---|
| 2004 | — | — | — | — | — | 50.00 |

### KM# 127 5000 KIP

37.00 g., Gold Plated Bronze, 45 mm. **Rev:** Majextic rooster as a laser engraving

| Date | Mintage | VF20 | XF40 | MS60 | MS63 | MS65 |
|---|---|---|---|---|---|---|
| 2005 | Est. 28000 | — | — | — | — | 35.00 |

### KM# 129 5000 KIP

0.30 g., 0.999 Gold 0.0096 oz. AGW, 7 mm. **Rev:** Majestic rooster in pose

| Date | Mintage | VF20 | XF40 | MS60 | MS63 | MS65 |
|---|---|---|---|---|---|---|
| 2005 | — | **PF65** 50.00 | | | | |

### KM# 139 5000 KIP

0.30 g., 0.999 Gold 0.0096 oz. AGW, 7 mm. **Subject:** Year of the Dog **Rev:** Dog with kinegram background

| Date | Mintage | VF20 | XF40 | MS60 | MS63 | MS65 |
|---|---|---|---|---|---|---|
| 2006 | — | — | — | — | — | 50.00 |

### KM# 158 5000 KIP

7.77 g., 0.583 Gold 0.1456 oz. AGW, 25 mm. **Subject:** Beijing to London Olympic transfer **Obv:** National emblem **Rev:** Temple of Heaven, Tower Bridge and athlete

| Date | Mintage | VF20 | XF40 | MS60 | MS63 | MS65 |
|---|---|---|---|---|---|---|
| 2008 | Est. 1000 | **PF65** 450 | | | | |

### KM# 113 10000 KIP

1.24 g., 0.999 Gold 0.0398 oz. AGW, 13.92 mm. **Rev:** Two redshank dress apes

| Date | Mintage | VF20 | XF40 | MS60 | MS63 | MS65 |
|---|---|---|---|---|---|---|
| 2001 | — | **PF65** 90.00 | | | | |

### KM# 114 10000 KIP

1.24 g., 0.999 Gold 0.0398 oz. AGW, 13.92 mm. **Rev:** Horse drawing in color by Xu Beihong

| Date | Mintage | VF20 | XF40 | MS60 | MS63 | MS65 |
|---|---|---|---|---|---|---|
| 2002 | — | — | — | — | — | 90.00 |

### KM# 120 10000 KIP

1.24 g., 0.999 Gold 0.0398 oz. AGW, 13.92 mm. **Rev:** Cichlasoma fish

| Date | Mintage | VF20 | XF40 | MS60 | MS63 | MS65 |
|---|---|---|---|---|---|---|
| 2003 | — | — | — | — | — | 90.00 |

### KM# 125 10000 KIP

1.24 g., 0.999 Gold 0.0398 oz. AGW, 13.92 mm. **Rev:** Black crested gibbon

| Date | Mintage | VF20 | XF40 | MS60 | MS63 | MS65 |
|---|---|---|---|---|---|---|
| 2004 | — | — | — | — | — | 90.00 |

### KM# 130 10000 KIP

1.24 g., 0.999 Gold 0.0398 oz. AGW, 13.92 mm. **Obv:** National Arms **Rev:** Majestic rooster right

| Date | Mintage | VF20 | XF40 | MS60 | MS63 | MS65 |
|---|---|---|---|---|---|---|
| 2005 | — | — | — | — | — | 80.00 |

### KM# 133 10000 KIP

1.24 g., 0.999 Gold 0.0398 oz. AGW, 13.92 mm. **Obv:** National arms **Rev:** Mazu seated, waves in background

| Date | Mintage | VF20 | XF40 | MS60 | MS63 | MS65 |
|---|---|---|---|---|---|---|
| 2005 | Est. 6888 | **PF63** 75.00 | **PF65** 90.00 | | | |

### KM# 140 10000 KIP

1.24 g., 0.999 Gold 0.0398 oz. AGW, 13.92 mm. **Subject:** Year of the Dog **Rev:** Don seated

| Date | Mintage | VF20 | XF40 | MS60 | MS63 | MS65 |
|---|---|---|---|---|---|---|
| 2006 | — | — | — | — | — | 90.00 |

### KM# 142 10000 KIP

1.24 g., 0.999 Gold 0.0398 oz. AGW, 13.92 mm. **Rev:** Mazu standing

| Date | Mintage | VF20 | XF40 | MS60 | MS63 | MS65 |
|---|---|---|---|---|---|---|
| 2006 | — | — | — | — | — | 90.00 |

### KM# 146 10000 KIP

1.24 g., 0.999 Gold 0.0398 oz. AGW **Rev:** Buddha in meditation **Shape:** 13.92

| Date | Mintage | VF20 | XF40 | MS60 | MS63 | MS65 |
|---|---|---|---|---|---|---|
| 2006 | Est. 6888 | **PF63** 75.00 | **PF65** 90.00 | | | |

### KM# 149 10000 KIP

1.24 g., 0.999 Gold 0.0398 oz. AGW, 13.92 mm. **Subject:** Year of the Pig **Obv:** National arms **Rev:** Pig

| Date | Mintage | VF20 | XF40 | MS60 | MS63 | MS65 |
|---|---|---|---|---|---|---|
| 2007 | — | — | — | — | — | 90.00 |

### KM# 154 10000 KIP

1.00 g., 0.999 Gold 0.0321 oz. AGW, 13.92 mm. **Subject:** World Cup Soccer, South Africa **Rev:** Sculpture of soccer players

| Date | Mintage | VF20 | XF40 | MS60 | MS63 | MS65 |
|---|---|---|---|---|---|---|
| 2010 | — | PF65 90.00 | | | | |

### KM# 86 15000 KIP

20.00 g., 0.925 Silver 0.5948 oz. ASW, 38.7 mm. **Subject:** Year of the Horse **Obv:** State emblem **Rev:** Multicolor horse **Edge:** Reeded

| Date | Mintage | VF20 | XF40 | MS60 | MS63 | MS65 |
|---|---|---|---|---|---|---|
| 2002 | 9,500 | PF63 45.00 | PF65 50.00 | | | |

### KM# 87 15000 KIP

20.00 g., 0.925 Silver 0.5948 oz. ASW, 38.7 mm. **Subject:** Year of the Horse **Obv:** State emblem **Rev:** Horse with multicolor holographic background **Edge:** Reeded

| Date | Mintage | VF20 | XF40 | MS60 | MS63 | MS65 |
|---|---|---|---|---|---|---|
| 2002 | 9,500 | PF63 50.00 | PF65 55.00 | | | |

### KM# 116 15000 KIP

20.00 g., 0.925 Silver 0.5948 oz. ASW **Obv:** National arms **Rev:** Shoulder-spot cichlid in color

| Date | Mintage | VF20 | XF40 | MS60 | MS63 | MS65 |
|---|---|---|---|---|---|---|
| 2003 | Est. 2300 | PF65 60.00 | | | | |

### KM# 117 15000 KIP

20.00 g., 0.925 Silver 0.5948 oz. ASW, 38 mm. **Rev:** Chilasoma flower horn fish swimming left

| Date | Mintage | VF20 | XF40 | MS60 | MS63 | MS65 |
|---|---|---|---|---|---|---|
| 2003 | — | PF65 60.00 | | | | |

### KM# 118 15000 KIP

20.00 g., 0.925 Silver 0.5948 oz. ASW, 38 mm. **Rev:** Fish in color kinegram

| Date | Mintage | VF20 | XF40 | MS60 | MS63 | MS65 |
|---|---|---|---|---|---|---|
| 2003 | — | PF65 60.00 | | | | |

### KM# 94 15000 KIP

20.00 g., 0.999 Silver 0.6424 oz. ASW, 38.7 mm. **Obv:** State emblem **Rev:** Multicolor Golden Monkey **Edge:** Reeded

| Date | Mintage | VF20 | XF40 | MS60 | MS63 | MS65 |
|---|---|---|---|---|---|---|
| 2004 | 2,300 | PF65 55.00 | | | | |

### KM# 123 15000 KIP

20.00 g., 0.999 Silver 0.6424 oz. ASW **Rev:** Black crested gibbon

| Date | Mintage | VF20 | XF40 | MS60 | MS63 | MS65 |
|---|---|---|---|---|---|---|
| 2004 | Est. 3800 | PF65 60.00 | | | | |

### KM# 128 15000 KIP

20.00 g., 0.999 Silver 0.6424 oz. ASW **Rev:** Majestic Rooster with kinegram background

| Date | Mintage | VF20 | XF40 | MS60 | MS63 | MS65 |
|---|---|---|---|---|---|---|
| 2005 | Est. 3800 | PF65 60.00 | | | | |

### KM# 132 15000 KIP

20.00 g., 0.925 Silver 0.5948 oz. ASW, 38 mm. **Obv:** National arms **Rev:** Mazu seated, waves in background

| Date | Mintage | VF20 | XF40 | MS60 | MS63 | MS65 |
|---|---|---|---|---|---|---|
| 2005 | Est. 6888 | PF63 50.00 | PF65 60.00 | | | |

### KM# 98 15000 KIP

Silver, 38.7 mm. **Issuer:** Bank of Lao PDR **Obv:** National arms **Obv. Legend:** THE LAO PEOPLE'S DEMOCRATIC REPUBLIC **Rev:** Statue of Mazu with stylized Phoenix at left and right **Rev. Legend:** GODDESS OF THE SEA **Edge:** Reeded

| Date | Mintage | VF20 | XF40 | MS60 | MS63 | MS65 |
|---|---|---|---|---|---|---|
| 2006 | 6,888 | PF63 60.00 | PF65 65.00 | | | |

### KM# 137 15000 KIP

20.00 g., 0.999 Silver 0.6424 oz. ASW, 38 mm. **Subject:** Year of the Dog **Rev:** Three dogs

| Date | Mintage | VF20 | XF40 | MS60 | MS63 | MS65 |
|---|---|---|---|---|---|---|
| 2006 | — | PF65 60.00 | | | | |

### KM# 138 15000 KIP

Silver **Subject:** Year of the Dog **Rev:** Dog with kinegram background

| Date | Mintage | VF20 | XF40 | MS60 | MS63 | MS65 |
|---|---|---|---|---|---|---|
| 2006 | — | PF65 60.00 | | | | |

### KM# 145 15000 KIP

20.00 g., 0.925 Silver 0.5948 oz. ASW, 38 mm. **Rev:** Buddha head facing

| Date | Mintage | VF20 | XF40 | MS60 | MS63 | MS65 |
|---|---|---|---|---|---|---|
| 2006 | Est. 6888 | PF63 50.00 | PF65 60.00 | | | |

### KM# 148 15000 KIP

20.00 g., 0.999 Silver 0.6424 oz. ASW, 38 mm. **Subject:** Year of the Pig **Obv:** National arms **Rev:** Pig with kinegram background

| Date | Mintage | VF20 | XF40 | MS60 | MS63 | MS65 |
|---|---|---|---|---|---|---|
| 2007 | — | PF65 60.00 | | | | |

### KM# 115 50000 KIP

7.78 g., 0.999 Gold 0.2499 oz. AGW, 22 mm. **Obv:** National arms **Rev:** Horse advancing right

| Date | Mintage | VF20 | XF40 | MS60 | MS63 | MS65 |
|---|---|---|---|---|---|---|
| 2002 | — | — | — | — | — | 475 |

### KM# 170 50000 KIP

31.11 g., 0.999 Silver 0.999 oz. ASW **Subject:** That Luang Vietrane elephants, 450th Anniversary

| Date | Mintage | VF20 | XF40 | MS60 | MS63 | MS65 |
|---|---|---|---|---|---|---|
| 2010 | 10,000 | PF63 140 | PF65 150 | | | |

### KM# 88 60000 KIP

155.52 g., 0.925 Silver 4.625 oz. ASW, 65 mm. **Subject:** Year of the Horse **Obv:** State emblem **Rev:** Multicolor horse **Edge:** Reeded

| Date | Mintage | VF20 | XF40 | MS60 | MS63 | MS65 |
|---|---|---|---|---|---|---|
| 2002 | 1,000 | PF65 225 | | | | |

### KM# 89 100000 KIP

15.55 g., 0.9999 Gold 0.500 oz. AGW, 27 mm. **Subject:** Year of the Horse **Obv:** State emblem **Rev:** Horse **Edge:** Reeded

| Date | Mintage | VF20 | XF40 | MS60 | MS63 | MS65 |
|---|---|---|---|---|---|---|
| 2002 | 2,000 | PF65 925 | | | | |

### KM# 121 100000 KIP

15.55 g., 0.999 Gold 0.4994 oz. AGW, 27 mm. **Rev:** Cichlasoma fish left

| Date | Mintage | VF20 | XF40 | MS60 | MS63 | MS65 |
|---|---|---|---|---|---|---|
| 2003 | Est. 888 | PF65 950 | | | | |

### KM# 95 100000 KIP

15.55 g., 0.999 Gold 0.4995 oz. AGW, 27 mm. **Obv:** State emblem **Rev:** Black Gibbon on holographic background **Edge:** Reeded

| Date | Mintage | VF20 | XF40 | MS60 | MS63 | MS65 |
|---|---|---|---|---|---|---|
| 2004 | 888 | PF65 950 | | | | |

### KM# 131 100000 KIP

15.55 g., 0.999 Gold 0.4994 oz. AGW, 27 mm. **Rev:** Majestic rooster right , kinegram background

| Date | Mintage | VF20 | XF40 | MS60 | MS63 | MS65 |
|---|---|---|---|---|---|---|
| 2005 | Est. 888 | PF65 950 | | | | |

### KM# 134 100000 KIP

15.55 g., 0.999 Gold 0.4994 oz. AGW **Rev:** Mazu seated, waves in background

| Date | Mintage | VF20 | XF40 | MS60 | MS63 | MS65 |
|---|---|---|---|---|---|---|
| 2005 | 688 | PF65 950 | | | | |

### KM# 141 100000 KIP

15.55 g., 0.999 Gold 0.4994 oz. AGW **Subject:** Year of the Dog

| Date | Mintage | VF20 | XF40 | MS60 | MS63 | MS65 |
|---|---|---|---|---|---|---|
| 2006 | Est. 888 | PF65 950 | | | | |

### KM# 143 100000 KIP

15.55 g., 0.999 Gold 0.4994 oz. AGW, 27 mm. **Rev:** Mazu half lenght left

| Date | Mintage | VF20 | XF40 | MS60 | MS63 | MS65 |
|---|---|---|---|---|---|---|
| 2006 | — | PF65 950 | | | | |

### KM# 147 100000 KIP

15.55 g., 0.999 Gold 0.4994 oz. AGW, 27 mm. **Rev:** Buddha in meditation

| Date | Mintage | VF20 | XF40 | MS60 | MS63 | MS65 |
|---|---|---|---|---|---|---|
| 2006 | Est. 688 | PF65 950 | | | | |

### KM# 102 100000 KIP

38.50 g., 0.925 Silver 1.145 oz. ASW, 36.5 mm. **Subject:** President Print Souphanouvong, 100th Anniversary of Birth **Obv:** Bust facing **Rev:** Presidential Palace

| Date | Mintage | VF20 | XF40 | MS60 | MS63 | MS65 |
|---|---|---|---|---|---|---|
| ND (2009) | 1,000 | PF65 100 | | | | |

### KM# 103 100000 KIP

7.78 g., 0.999 Gold 0.2497 oz. AGW, 27 mm. **Subject:** President Print Souphanouvong, 100th Anniversary of Birth **Obv:** Bust facing **Rev:** Presidential Palace

| Date | Mintage | VF20 | XF40 | MS60 | MS63 | MS65 |
|---|---|---|---|---|---|---|
| ND (2009) | 1,000 | PF65 475 | | | | |

### KM# 90 1000000 KIP

155.52 g., 0.9999 Gold 4.9995 oz. AGW, 55 mm. **Subject:** Year of the Horse **Obv:** State emblem **Rev:** Horse with multicolor holographic background **Edge:** Reeded

| Date | Mintage | VF20 | XF40 | MS60 | MS63 | MS65 |
|---|---|---|---|---|---|---|
| 2002 | 500 | PF65 9,250 | | | | |

### KM# 135 1000000 KIP

155.50 g., 0.999 Gold 4.9944 oz. AGW **Rev:** Mazu seated, waves in background

| Date | Mintage | VF20 | XF40 | MS60 | MS63 | MS65 |
|---|---|---|---|---|---|---|
| 2005 | 99 | PF65 9,750 | | | | |

### KM# 99 1000000 KIP

155.52 g., 0.9999 Gold 4.9994 oz. AGW, 55.0 mm. **Issuer:** Bank of Lao PDR **Obv:** National arms **Obv. Legend:** THE LAO PEOPLE'S DEMOCRATIC REPUBLIC **Rev:** Multi-latent color bust of Lord Buddha "Fo Guang Pu Zhao" facing with diamond insert in forehead **Edge:** Reeded

| Date | Mintage | VF20 | XF40 | MS60 | MS63 | MS65 |
|---|---|---|---|---|---|---|
| 2006 | 99 | PF65 9,750 | | | | |

### KM# 144 1000000 KIP

155.50 g., 0.999 Gold 4.9944 oz. AGW **Rev:** Mazu standing

| Date | Mintage | VF20 | XF40 | MS60 | MS63 | MS65 |
|---|---|---|---|---|---|---|
| 2006 | — | PF65 9,750 | | | | |

## PROOF SETS

| KM# | Date | Mintage | Identification | Issue Price | Mkt Val |
|---|---|---|---|---|---|
| PS7 | 2000-01 (3) | 3,500 | KM#74-76 | 138 | 200 |
| PS8 | 2000-01 (3) | 500 | KM#74-76 | 213 | 300 |
| PS9 | 2000-01 (2) | 500 | KM#78. 83 | — | 1,100 |

# LATVIA

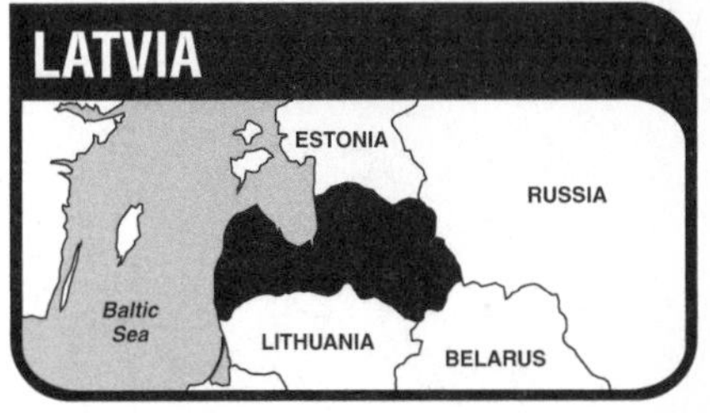


The Republic of Latvia, the central Baltic state in east Europe, has an area of 24,749 sq. mi. (43,601 sq. km.) and a population of 2.6 million. Capital: Riga. Livestock raising and manufacturing are the chief industries. Butter, bacon, fertilizers and telephone equipment are exported.

**MONETARY SYSTEM**

100 Santimu = 1 Lats

## MODERN REPUBLIC

1991-present

## STANDARD COINAGE

### KM# 15 SANTIMS

1.60 g., Copper Clad Steel, 15.65 mm. **Obv:** National arms **Rev:** Value flanked by diamonds below lined arch **Edge:** Plain

| Date | Mintage | VF20 | XF40 | MS60 | MS63 | MS65 |
|---|---|---|---|---|---|---|
| 2003 | 30,000,000 | — | 0.10 | 0.20 | 0.30 | 0.50 |
| 2005 | 20,000,000 | — | 0.10 | 0.20 | 0.30 | 0.50 |
| 2007 | 25,000,000 | — | 0.10 | 0.20 | 0.30 | 0.50 |
| 2008 | 75,000,000 | — | 0.10 | 0.20 | 0.30 | 0.50 |

### KM# 21 2 SANTIMI

1.90 g., Copper Clad Steel, 17 mm. **Obv:** National arms **Rev:** Lined arch above value flanked by diamonds **Edge:** Plain

| Date | Mintage | VF20 | XF40 | MS60 | MS63 | MS65 |
|---|---|---|---|---|---|---|
| 2006 | 18,000,000 | — | 0.20 | 0.30 | 0.50 | 0.75 |
| 2007 | 30,000,000 | — | 0.20 | 0.30 | 0.50 | 0.75 |
| 2009 | 50,000,000 | — | 0.20 | 0.30 | 0.50 | 0.75 |

### KM# 16 5 SANTIMI

2.50 g., Nickel-Brass, 18.5 mm. **Obv:** National arms **Obv. Legend:** LATVIJAS REPUBLIKA **Rev:** Lined arch above value flanked by diamonds **Edge:** Plain

| Date | Mintage | VF20 | XF40 | MS60 | MS63 | MS65 |
|---|---|---|---|---|---|---|
| 2006 | 8,000,000 | — | 0.30 | 0.50 | 0.75 | 1.00 |
| 2007 | 15,000,000 | — | 0.30 | 0.50 | 0.75 | 1.00 |
| 2009 | 10,000,000 | — | 0.30 | 0.50 | 0.75 | 1.00 |

**KM# 17 10 SANTIMU**
3.25 g., Nickel-Brass, 19.9 mm. **Obv:** National arms **Rev:** Lined arch above value flanked by diamonds **Edge:** Plain

| Date | Mintage | VF20 | XF40 | MS60 | MS63 | MS65 |
|---|---|---|---|---|---|---|
| 2008 | 15,000,000 | — | 0.35 | 0.50 | 1.00 | 1.50 |

**KM# 22.1 20 SANTIMU**
4.00 g., Nickel-Brass, 21.5 mm. **Obv:** National arms **Rev:** Lined arch above value flanked by diamonds **Edge:** Plain **Note:** 1.5mm thick.

| Date | Mintage | VF20 | XF40 | MS60 | MS63 | MS65 |
|---|---|---|---|---|---|---|
| 2007 | 7,000,000 | — | 0.25 | 0.50 | 1.00 | 2.00 |
| 2009 | 10,000,000 | — | 0.25 | 0.50 | 1.00 | 2.00 |

**KM# 13 50 SANTIMU**
3.50 g., Copper-Nickel, 18.8 mm. **Obv:** National arms **Rev:** Triple sprig above value **Edge:** Reeded

| Date | Mintage | VF20 | XF40 | MS60 | MS63 | MS65 |
|---|---|---|---|---|---|---|
| 2007 | 4,000,000 | — | 1.00 | 1.50 | 3.00 | 4.00 |
| 2009 | 5,000,000 | — | 1.00 | 1.50 | 3.00 | 4.00 |

**KM# 70 100 SANTIMU**
31.47 g., 0.925 Silver 0.9359 oz. ASW, 38.6 mm. **Obv:** Baron von Muenchausen with chain of birds around a dog with a lantern hanging from its tail. **Rev:** Baron von Muenchausen and dog hunting a circle of animals **Edge Lettering:** LATVIJAS BANKA LATVIJAS REPUBLIKA

| Date | Mintage | VF20 | XF40 | MS60 | MS63 | MS65 |
|---|---|---|---|---|---|---|
| 2005 | Est. 5000 | PF65 150 | | | | |

**KM# 12 LATS**
4.80 g., Copper-Nickel, 21.75 mm. **Obv:** Arms with supporters **Rev:** Salmon above value **Edge Lettering:** LATVIJAS BANKA • LATVIJAS BANKA

| Date | Mintage | VF20 | XF40 | MS60 | MS63 | MS65 |
|---|---|---|---|---|---|---|
| 2007 | 7,000,000 | — | 1.50 | 2.50 | 3.50 | 6.00 |
| 2008 | 25,000,000 | — | 1.50 | 2.50 | 3.50 | 6.00 |

**KM# 49 LATS**
31.47 g., 0.925 Silver 0.9359 oz. ASW, 38.6 mm. **Subject:** Hanseatic City of Cesis **Obv:** City arms **Rev:** Sailing ship above, inverted walled city view below **Edge Lettering:** LATVIJAS REPUBLIKA • LATVIJAS BANKA

| Date | Mintage | VF20 | XF40 | MS60 | MS63 | MS65 |
|---|---|---|---|---|---|---|
| 2001 | Est. 15000 | PF63 55.00 | PF65 75.00 | | | |

**KM# 50 LATS**
31.47 g., 0.925 Silver 0.9359 oz. ASW **Series:** Ice Hockey **Obv:** Arms with supporters **Rev:** Hockey player

| Date | Mintage | VF20 | XF40 | MS60 | MS63 | MS65 |
|---|---|---|---|---|---|---|
| 2001 | Est. 15000 | PF65 90.00 | | | | |

**KM# 51 LATS**
31.47 g., 0.925 Silver 0.9359 oz. ASW, 38.6 mm. **Subject:** Heaven **Obv:** Stylized design **Rev:** Stylized woman holding sun **Edge:** Plain

| Date | Mintage | VF20 | XF40 | MS60 | MS63 | MS65 |
|---|---|---|---|---|---|---|
| 2001 | — | PF65 125 | | | | |

**KM# 54 LATS**
4.80 g., Copper-Nickel, 21.75 mm. **Obv:** Arms with supporters **Rev:** Nesting stork above value **Edge Lettering:** LATVIJAS BANKA • LATVIJAS BANKA

| Date | Mintage | VF20 | XF40 | MS60 | MS63 | MS65 |
|---|---|---|---|---|---|---|
| 2001 | 250,000 | — | 4.00 | 7.00 | 12.00 | 15.00 |

**KM# 52 LATS**
31.47 g., 0.925 Silver 0.9359 oz. ASW, 38.6 mm. **Subject:** Destiny **Obv:** Stylized design **Rev:** Apple tree and landscape **Edge:** Plain

| Date | Mintage | VF20 | XF40 | MS60 | MS63 | MS65 |
|---|---|---|---|---|---|---|
| 2002 | Est. 5000 | PF65 150 | | | | |

**KM# 53 LATS**
31.47 g., 0.925 Silver 0.9359 oz. ASW, 38.6 mm. **Subject:** Hanseatic City of Kuldiga **Obv:** City arms **Rev:** City view and ships **Edge:** Lettered

| Date | Mintage | VF20 | XF40 | MS60 | MS63 | MS65 |
|---|---|---|---|---|---|---|
| 2002 | Est. 15000 | PF63 65.00 | PF65 75.00 | | | |

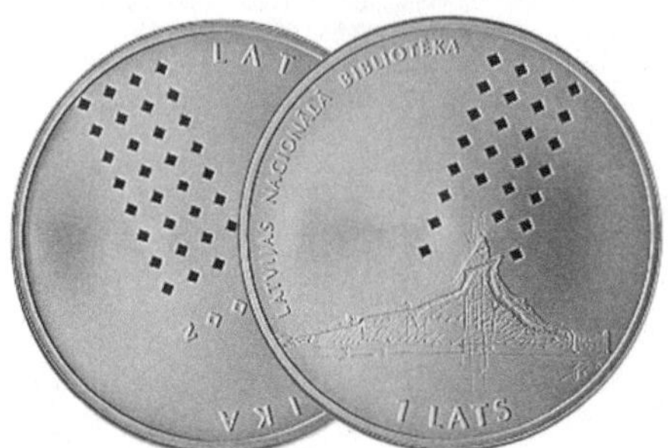

**KM# 55 LATS**
31.47 g., 0.925 Silver 0.9359 oz. ASW, 38.6 mm. **Subject:** National Library **Obv:** Country name and diamonds pattern **Rev:** Library building sketch and diamonds design **Edge Lettering:** GAISMU SAUCA • GAISMA AUSA

| Date | Mintage | VF20 | XF40 | MS60 | MS63 | MS65 |
|---|---|---|---|---|---|---|
| 2002 | Est. 5000 | PF63 65.00 | PF65 75.00 | | | |

**KM# 56 LATS**
15.00 g., 0.925 Silver 0.4461 oz. ASW with gilt obverse, 28 mm. **Subject:** Coin of Fortune **Obv:** Totally gold plated sun above country name **Rev:** Waning moon, date and value **Edge:** Plain

| Date | Mintage | VF20 | XF40 | MS60 | MS63 | MS65 |
|---|---|---|---|---|---|---|
| 2002 | Est. 5000 | PF65 250 | | | | |

**KM# 57 LATS**

31.47 g., 0.925 Silver 0.9359 oz. ASW, 38.6 mm. **Subject:** Olympics 2004 **Obv:** Arms with supporters **Rev:** Ancient wrestlers **Edge Lettering:** LATVIJAS BANKA • LATVIJAS BANKA

| Date | Mintage | VF20 | XF40 | MS60 | MS63 | MS65 |
|---|---|---|---|---|---|---|
| 2002 | Est. 26000 | PF63 60.00 | PF65 70.00 | | | |

**KM# 58 LATS**

4.80 g., Copper-Nickel, 21.75 mm. **Obv:** Arms with supporters **Rev:** Ant above value **Edge Lettering:** LATVIJAS BANKA • LATVIJAS BANKA

| Date | Mintage | VF20 | XF40 | MS60 | MS63 | MS65 |
|---|---|---|---|---|---|---|
| 2003 | 250,000 | — | 3.00 | 5.00 | 6.50 | 8.00 |

**KM# 60 LATS**

31.47 g., 0.925 Silver 0.9359 oz. ASW, 38.6 mm. **Subject:** Courland **Obv:** Crowned arms above partially built ship **Rev:** Hemp weighing scene with Iron foundry and brick wall in background **Edge Lettering:** LATVIJAS REPUBLIKA • LATVIJAS BANKA

| Date | Mintage | VF20 | XF40 | MS60 | MS63 | MS65 |
|---|---|---|---|---|---|---|
| 2003 | Est. 5000 | PF65 80.00 | | | | |

**KM# 71 LATS**

31.47 g., 0.925 Silver 0.9359 oz. ASW, 38.6 mm. **Subject:** Vidzeme **Obv:** Crowned arms above horse drawn wagon **Rev:** Two men sawing wood **Edge Lettering:** LATVIJAS BANKA • LATVIJAS REPUBLIKA

| Date | Mintage | VF20 | XF40 | MS60 | MS63 | MS65 |
|---|---|---|---|---|---|---|
| ND (2003) | — | PF65 75.00 | | | | |
| 2004 | — | PF65 75.00 | | | | |

**KM# 72 LATS**

31.47 g., 0.925 Silver 0.9359 oz. ASW, 38.6 mm. **Subject:** Latgale **Obv:** Madonna and Child above landscape **Rev:** Man sowing seeds and an angel **Edge Lettering:** LATVIJAS BANKA • LATVIJAS REPUBLIKA

| Date | Mintage | VF20 | XF40 | MS60 | MS63 | MS65 |
|---|---|---|---|---|---|---|
| ND (2003) | — | PF65 75.00 | | | | |
| 2004 | Est. 5000 | PF65 75.00 | | | | |

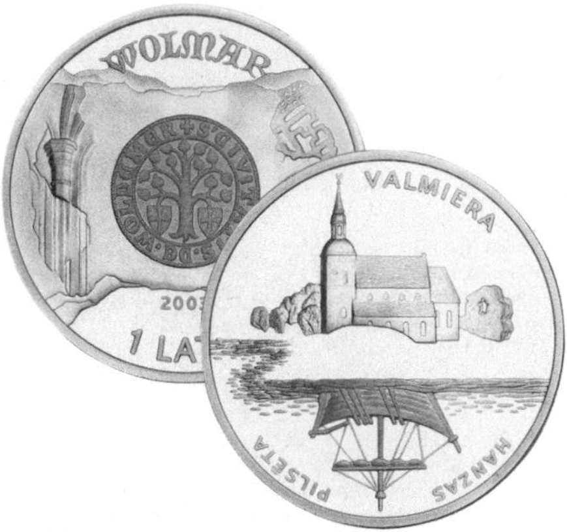

**KM# 75 LATS**

31.47 g., 0.925 Silver 0.9359 oz. ASW, 38.61 mm. **Subject:** Hanseatic City of Valmiera **Obv:** Coat of arms **Rev:** St. Simanis Church with VALMIERA and reflection of sailing ship **Edge:** LATVIJAS REPUBLIKA • LATVIJAS BANKA

| Date | Mintage | VF20 | XF40 | MS60 | MS63 | MS65 |
|---|---|---|---|---|---|---|
| 2003 | Est. 15000 | PF63 55.00 | PF65 65.00 | | | |

**KM# 61 LATS**

4.80 g., Copper-Nickel, 21.75 mm. **Obv:** Arms with supporters **Rev:** Spriditis with shovel above value **Edge Lettering:** LATVIJAS BANKA • LATVIJAS BANKA

| Date | Mintage | VF20 | XF40 | MS60 | MS63 | MS65 |
|---|---|---|---|---|---|---|
| 2004 | 500,000 | — | 2.00 | 3.00 | 4.00 | 6.00 |

**KM# 62 LATS**

17.15 g., Bi-Metallic Dark Blue Niobium 7.15g center in .900 Silver 10g ring, 34 mm. **Subject:** Coin of Time **Obv:** Heraldic Rose **Rev:** Clock dial in center, rings of hours, minutes, months and days around **Edge:** Plain

| Date | Mintage | VF20 | XF40 | MS60 | MS63 | MS65 |
|---|---|---|---|---|---|---|
| 2004 | Est. 5000 | — | — | — | 450 | 550 |

**KM# 63 LATS**

31.47 g., 0.925 Silver 0.9359 oz. ASW, 38.6 mm. **Obv:** Arms with supporters **Rev:** World Cup Soccer player **Edge Lettering:** LATVIJA three times

| Date | Mintage | VF20 | XF40 | MS60 | MS63 | MS65 |
|---|---|---|---|---|---|---|
| 2004 | Est. 50000 | PF63 60.00 | PF65 70.00 | | | |

**KM# 64 LATS**

31.47 g., 0.925 Silver 0.9359 oz. ASW, 38.6 mm. **Subject:** Latvian European Union Membership **Obv:** Arms with supporters **Rev:** P.S. LATVIJA-ES 2004 above value **Edge Lettering:** LATVIJAS BANKA • LATVIJAS BANKA

| Date | Mintage | VF20 | XF40 | MS60 | MS63 | MS65 |
|---|---|---|---|---|---|---|
| 2004 | Est. 15000 | PF63 75.00 | PF65 85.00 | | | |

**KM# 67 LATS**

4.80 g., Copper-Nickel, 21.75 mm. **Obv:** National arms **Obv. Legend:** LATVIJAS REPUBLIKA **Rev:** Mushroom above value **Edge Lettering:** LATVIJAS BANKA • LATVIJAS BANKA

| Date | Mintage | VF20 | XF40 | MS60 | MS63 | MS65 |
|---|---|---|---|---|---|---|
| 2004 | 500,000 | — | 2.00 | 3.00 | 4.00 | 6.00 |

**KM# 65 LATS**

4.80 g., Copper-Nickel, 21.75 mm. **Obv:** Arms with supporters **Rev:** Weathercock (from the spire of Riga's St. Peter Church) above value **Edge Lettering:** LATVIJAS BANKA • LATVIJAS BANKA

| Date | Mintage | VF20 | XF40 | MS60 | MS63 | MS65 |
|---|---|---|---|---|---|---|
| 2005 | 500,000 | — | 2.00 | 3.00 | 6.00 | 8.00 |

**KM# 66 LATS**

4.80 g., Copper-Nickel, 21.75 mm. **Obv:** National arms **Obv. Legend:** LATVIJAS REPUBLIKA **Rev:** Pretzel above value **Edge Lettering:** LATVIJAS BANKA • LATVIJAS BANKA

| Date | Mintage | VF20 | XF40 | MS60 | MS63 | MS65 |
|---|---|---|---|---|---|---|
| 2005 | 500,000 | — | 2.00 | 3.00 | 4.00 | 6.00 |

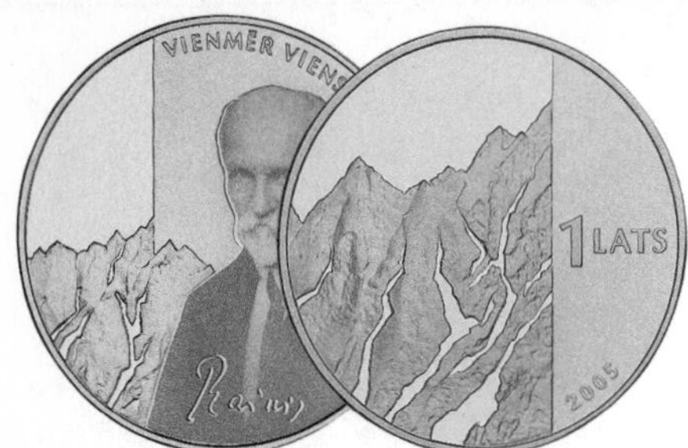

**KM# 68 LATS**

31.47 g., 0.925 Silver 0.9359 oz. ASW, 38.6 mm. **Subject:** Janis Plieksans "Rainis **Obv:** Mountains and value **Rev:** Laser picture of Rainis the mountain climbing poet, dramatist and patriot. **Edge Lettering:** LATVIJAS BANKA • LATVIJAS REPUBLIKA

| Date | Mintage | VF20 | XF40 | MS60 | MS63 | MS65 |
|---|---|---|---|---|---|---|
| 2005 | Est. 5000 | **PF65** 55.00 | | | | |

**KM# 69 LATS**

31.47 g., 0.925 Silver 0.9359 oz. ASW, 38.6 mm. **Obv:** National arms **Rev:** Bobsled **Edge Lettering:** LATVIJA (three times)

| Date | Mintage | VF20 | XF40 | MS60 | MS63 | MS65 |
|---|---|---|---|---|---|---|
| 2005 | Est. 15000 | **PF65** 50.00 | | | | |

**KM# 76 LATS**

31.47 g., 0.925 Silver 0.9359 oz. ASW, 38.61 mm. **Subject:** Ice Hockey World Championship **Obv:** Large coat of arms, date below **Rev:** Two hockey players viewed from above, RIGA 2006 on either side with hockey puck in center **Edge Lettering:** LATVIJA (three times)

| Date | Mintage | VF20 | XF40 | MS60 | MS63 | MS65 |
|---|---|---|---|---|---|---|
| 2005 | — | **PF65** 65.00 | | | | |

**KM# 77 LATS**

31.47 g., 0.925 Silver 0.9359 oz. ASW, 38.61 mm. **Subject:** Hanseatic City of Koknese **Obv:** Coat of arms **Rev:** Koknese castle on top with moon and sun on sides, reflection of Hanseatic Castle and ship on bottom **Edge Lettering:** LATVIJAS REPUBLIKA • LATVIJAS BANKA

| Date | Mintage | VF20 | XF40 | MS60 | MS63 | MS65 |
|---|---|---|---|---|---|---|
| 2005 | Est. 15000 | **PF63** 55.00 | **PF65** 75.00 | | | |

**KM# 81 LATS**

1.24 g., 0.9999 Gold 0.040 oz. AGW, 13.92 mm. **Subject:** Art Nouveau **Obv:** Ribbon design **Obv. Legend:** RIGAS / LATVIJAS REPUBLIKA **Rev:** Stone face **Edge:** Reeded

| Date | Mintage | VF20 | XF40 | MS60 | MS63 | MS65 |
|---|---|---|---|---|---|---|
| 2005 | Est. 20000 | **PF65** 100 | | | | |

**KM# 73 LATS**

4.80 g., Copper-Nickel, 21.75 mm. **Subject:** Summer Solstice **Obv:** National arms **Rev:** Head wearing Ligo wreath above value **Edge Lettering:** LATVIJAS BANKA • LATVIJAS BANKA

| Date | Mintage | VF20 | XF40 | MS60 | MS63 | MS65 |
|---|---|---|---|---|---|---|
| 2006 | 500,000 | — | 2.00 | 3.00 | 4.00 | 6.00 |

**KM# 74 LATS**

4.80 g., Copper-Nickel, 21.75 mm. **Obv:** National arms **Rev:** Pine cone above value **Edge Lettering:** LATVIJAS BANKA • LATVIJAS BANKA

| Date | Mintage | VF20 | XF40 | MS60 | MS63 | MS65 |
|---|---|---|---|---|---|---|
| 2006 | 1,000,000 | — | 2.00 | 3.00 | 5.00 | 6.00 |

**KM# 78 LATS**

31.47 g., 0.925 Silver 0.9359 oz. ASW, 38.61 mm. **Subject:** The Barricades of January 1991 **Obv:** Stylized bonfire flames **Obv. Legend:** janvāris 1991 **Rev:** Latvian mythological hero with raised sword against the background of concrete block barricades, rising sun behind **Edge Lettering:** LATVIJAS BANKA (twice)

| Date | Mintage | VF20 | XF40 | MS60 | MS63 | MS65 |
|---|---|---|---|---|---|---|
| 2006 | Est. 5000 | **PF65** 65.00 | | | | |

**KM# 79 LATS**

31.47 g., 0.925 Silver 0.9359 oz. ASW, 38.61 mm. **Subject:** Krisjanis Barons **Obv:** Starry sky on left with value on right side **Rev:** Portrait of Barons on right side and starry sky on left **Edge Lettering:** LATVIJAS BANKA • LATVIJAS REPUBLIKA

| Date | Mintage | VF20 | XF40 | MS60 | MS63 | MS65 |
|---|---|---|---|---|---|---|
| 2006 | Est. 5000 | **PF65** 65.00 | | | | |

**KM# 80 LATS**

31.47 g., 0.925 Silver 0.9359 oz. ASW, 38.61 mm. **Subject:** Krishjanis Valdemars **Obv:** Seagul flying above water on left, value on right **Rev:** Portrait of Valdemars on right with sea on left **Edge Lettering:** LATVIJAS BANKA • LATVIJAS REPUBLIKA

| Date | Mintage | VF20 | XF40 | MS60 | MS63 | MS65 |
|---|---|---|---|---|---|---|
| 2006 | — | **PF65** 65.00 | | | | |

**KM# 82 LATS**

31.47 g., 0.925 Silver 0.9359 oz. ASW, 38.61 mm. **Subject:** Fight for Freedom **Obv:** Outline of Latvia with three stars above **Obv. Inscription:** LATVIJAS REPUBLIKA **Rev:** Two crossed swords outlined against the sun **Rev. Inscription:** NO ZOBENA SAULE LECA **Edge:** Plain

| Date | Mintage | VF20 | XF40 | MS60 | MS63 | MS65 |
|---|---|---|---|---|---|---|
| 2006 | Est. 5000 | **PF65** 65.00 | | | | |

**KM# 83 LATS**

31.47 g., 0.925 Silver 0.9359 oz. ASW, 38.61 mm. **Subject:** Hanseatic City of Straupe **Obv:** Coat of arms, date and value below **Obv. Inscription:** ROOP / 1 LATS **Rev:** Lielstraupe castle church top, reflection of Hanseatic ship with trees on both sides on bottom **Edge Lettering:** LATVIJAS REPUBLIKA • LATVIJAS BANKA

| Date | Mintage | VF20 | XF40 | MS60 | MS63 | MS65 |
|---|---|---|---|---|---|---|
| 2006 | Est. 15000 | **PF65** 55.00 | | | | |

**KM# 84 LATS**

27.00 g., 0.999 Silver 0.8672 oz. ASW, 38.61 mm. **Subject:** Coin of Digits **Obv:** Arabic O at center against an oriental background **Rev:** Roman I at center **Shape:** 7-sided

| Date | Mintage | VF20 | XF40 | MS60 | MS63 | MS65 |
|---|---|---|---|---|---|---|
| 2006 | 2,007 | **PF65** 550 | | | | |

**KM# 85 LATS**

4.80 g., Copper-Nickel, 21.75 mm. **Obv:** National arms **Obv. Legend:** LATVIJAS REPUBLIKA **Rev:** Snowman **Edge Lettering:** LATVIJAS BANKA • LATVIJAS BANKA

| Date | Mintage | VF20 | XF40 | MS60 | MS63 | MS65 |
|---|---|---|---|---|---|---|
| 2007 | 1,000,000 | — | 2.00 | 3.00 | 4.00 | 6.00 |

**KM# 86 LATS**

4.80 g., Copper-Nickel, 21.75 mm. **Obv:** National arms **Obv. Legend:** LATVIJAS REPUBLIKA **Rev:** Medieval owl figurine **Edge Lettering:** LATVIJAS BANKA • LATVIJAS BANKA

| Date | Mintage | VF20 | XF40 | MS60 | MS63 | MS65 |
|---|---|---|---|---|---|---|
| 2007 | 1,000,000 | — | 2.00 | 3.00 | 5.00 | 7.00 |

**KM# 87 LATS**

31.47 g., 0.925 Silver 0.9359 oz. ASW, 38.6 mm. **Subject:** Foreign Rulers **Obv:** Fragment of a large coat of arms **Rev:** Large coat of arms broken into fragments **Edge:** Plain

| Date | Mintage | VF20 | XF40 | MS60 | MS63 | MS65 |
|---|---|---|---|---|---|---|
| 2007 | — | **PF65** 65.00 | | | | |

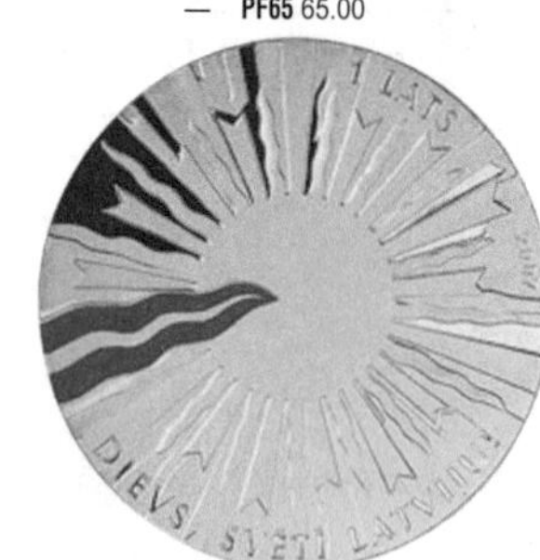

**KM# 88 LATS**

31.47 g., 0.925 Silver 0.9359 oz. ASW, 38.6 mm. **Subject:** Rebirth of the State **Obv:** Large coat of arms **Rev:** Sun with its rays forming the red-white-red flag of the Republic **Edge:** Plain

| Date | Mintage | VF20 | XF40 | MS60 | MS63 | MS65 |
|---|---|---|---|---|---|---|
| 2007 | Est. 5000 | **PF65** 65.00 | | | | |

**KM# 89 LATS**

31.47 g., 0.925 Silver 0.9359 oz. ASW, 38.6 mm. **Subject:** Sigulda **Obv:** Horse and sword within pendant **Rev:** Gauja Valley with the Turaida Castle and Sigulda Castle **Edge Lettering:** LATVIJAS REPUBLIKA • LATVIJAS BANKA

| Date | Mintage | VF20 | XF40 | MS60 | MS63 | MS65 |
|---|---|---|---|---|---|---|
| 2007 | Est. 5000 | **PF65** 55.00 | | | | |

**KM# 90 LATS**
17.15 g., Bi-Metallic Dark Purple, 34 mm. **Subject:** Coin of Time II **Obv:** Heraldic rose at center **Rev:** Outer ring signs of the zodiac, inner circle different evolutionary stages of the plant world **Edge:** Plain

| Date | Mintage | VF20 | XF40 | MS60 | MS63 | MS65 |
|---|---|---|---|---|---|---|
| 2007 | 7,000 | — | — | — | 175 | 200 |

**KM# 91 LATS**
1.24 g., 0.999 Gold 0.040 oz. AGW, 13.92 mm. **Obv:** Small coat of arms **Rev:** Logo of the publishing house Zelta abele **Edge:** Reeded

| Date | Mintage | VF20 | XF40 | MS60 | MS63 | MS65 |
|---|---|---|---|---|---|---|
| 2007 | Est. 15000 | PF63 95.00 | PF65 125 | | | |

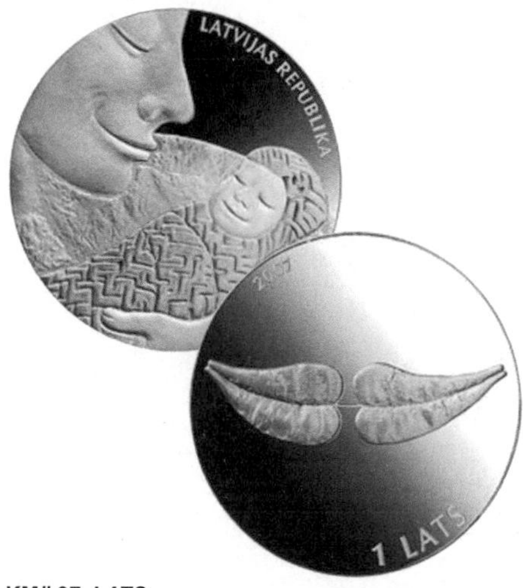

**KM# 97 LATS**
31.47 g., 0.925 Silver 0.9359 oz. ASW, 38.6 mm. **Subject:** Coin of life **Obv:** Mother holding gilt wrapped child **Rev:** Golden heart-shaped leaves **Edge:** Plain

| Date | Mintage | VF20 | XF40 | MS60 | MS63 | MS65 |
|---|---|---|---|---|---|---|
| 2007 | 5,000 | PF65 185 | | | | |

**KM# 92 LATS**
4.80 g., Copper-Nickel, 21.75 mm. **Obv:** National arms **Obv. Legend:** LATVIJAS REPUBLIKA **Rev:** Water Lily **Edge Lettering:** LATVIJAS BANKA • LATVIJAS BANKA

| Date | Mintage | VF20 | XF40 | MS60 | MS63 | MS65 |
|---|---|---|---|---|---|---|
| 2008 | 1,000,000 | — | 2.00 | 3.00 | 4.00 | 6.00 |

**KM# 93 LATS**
12.40 g., Copper-Nickel, 30 mm. **Obv:** Woman walking holding wheat **Rev:** Man walking holding flowers **Edge Lettering:** DZIESMAI SODIEN LIELA DIENA

| Date | Mintage | VF20 | XF40 | MS60 | MS63 | MS65 |
|---|---|---|---|---|---|---|
| 2008 | 30,000 | — | 3.00 | 4.00 | 7.00 | 9.00 |

**KM# 93a LATS**
31.47 g., 0.925 Silver 0.9359 oz. ASW, 38.61 mm. **Obv:** Woman walking holding wheat **Rev:** Man walking holding flowers **Edge Lettering:** DZIESMAI SODIEN LIELA DIENA

| Date | Mintage | VF20 | XF40 | MS60 | MS63 | MS65 |
|---|---|---|---|---|---|---|
| 2008 | 10,000 | PF65 75.00 | | | | |

**KM# 94 LATS**
31.47 g., 0.925 Silver 0.9359 oz. ASW, 38.61 mm. **Subject:** Hanseatic City of Limbazi **Obv:** Hanseatic city seal with coat of arms **Rev:** Limbazi Castle ruins and St. Johns Church with reflection of Hanseatic Ship on lower half **Edge Lettering:** LATVIJAS REPUBLIKA • LATVIJAS BANKA

| Date | Mintage | VF20 | XF40 | MS60 | MS63 | MS65 |
|---|---|---|---|---|---|---|
| 2008 | 15,000 | PF65 65.00 | | | | |

**KM# 95 LATS**
31.47 g., 0.925 Silver 0.9359 oz. ASW, 38.6 mm. **Subject:** Basketball **Obv:** Three stars and stylized basket ball design **Rev:** Two basketball players and a jump shot **Edge Lettering:** LATVIJAS BANKA • LATVIJAS REPUBLIKA

| Date | Mintage | VF20 | XF40 | MS60 | MS63 | MS65 |
|---|---|---|---|---|---|---|
| 2008 | 5,000 | PF65 80.00 | | | | |

**KM# 98 LATS**
22.00 g., 0.925 Silver 0.6543 oz. ASW, 35 mm. **Subject:** Lucky Coin **Obv:** Cat pearched on rooftop peak **Rev:** Chimney-sweep with ladder and rope coil with bruch and weight. **Edge Lettering:** LATVIJAS BANKA • LATVIJAS BANKA

| Date | Mintage | VF20 | XF40 | MS60 | MS63 | MS65 |
|---|---|---|---|---|---|---|
| 2008 | 5,000 | PF65 65.00 | | | | |

**KM# 99 LATS**
31.47 g., 0.925 Silver 0.9359 oz. ASW, 38.6 mm. **Subject:** 90th Anniversary of Statehood **Obv:** First Arms of the Republic **Rev:** Two children holding multicolor flag **Edge Lettering:** LATVIJAS BANKA (twice)

| Date | Mintage | VF20 | XF40 | MS60 | MS63 | MS65 |
|---|---|---|---|---|---|---|
| 2008 | 5,000 | PF65 95.00 | | | | |

**KM# 107 LATS**
4.80 g., Copper-Nickel, 21.75 mm. **Obv:** National arms **Rev:** Chimney sweep standing with brush and ladder **Edge Lettering:** LATVIJAS BANKA • LATVIJAS BANKA

| Date | Mintage | VF20 | XF40 | MS60 | MS63 | MS65 |
|---|---|---|---|---|---|---|
| 2008 | 1,000,000 | — | 2.00 | 3.00 | 5.00 | 6.00 |

**KM# 100 LATS**
20.00 g., 0.925 Silver 0.5948 oz. ASW, 34 mm. **Subject:** Children's drawing contest - My Dream Coin **Obv:** State Arms **Rev:** Piglet right **Edge Lettering:** LATVIJAS BANKA • LATVIJAS BANKA

| Date | Mintage | VF20 | XF40 | MS60 | MS63 | MS65 |
|---|---|---|---|---|---|---|
| 2009 | 5,000 | PF65 70.00 | | | | |

**KM# 101 LATS**
4.80 g., Copper-Nickel, 21.75 mm. **Obv:** National Arms **Rev:** Namejs ring **Edge Lettering:** LATVIJAS BANKA • LATVIJAS BANKA

| Date | Mintage | VF20 | XF40 | MS60 | MS63 | MS65 |
|---|---|---|---|---|---|---|
| 2009 | 1,000,000 | — | 2.00 | 3.00 | 5.00 | 6.00 |

**KM# 102 LATS**
31.47 g., 0.925 Silver 0.9359 oz. ASW, 38.6 mm. **Subject:** Time of the Land-Surveyors, Novel's 130th Anniversary **Obv:** Brali Kaudzites standing **Rev:** Six figures form novel, forming spokes of wheel **Edge Lettering:** LATVIJAS REPUBLICA • LATVIJAS BANKA

| Date | Mintage | VF20 | XF40 | MS60 | MS63 | MS65 |
|---|---|---|---|---|---|---|
| 2009 | 7,000 | PF65 60.00 | | | | |

**KM# 103 LATS**
31.47 g., 0.925 Silver 0.9359 oz. ASW, 38.6 mm. **Subject:** University of Latvia **Obv:** Oak tree within wreath, partially minted photo image **Rev:** Owl standing on open book, University building in background **Edge Lettering:** VIVAT • CRESCAT • FLOREAT

| Date | Mintage | VF20 | XF40 | MS60 | MS63 | MS65 |
|---|---|---|---|---|---|---|
| 2009 | 7,000 | PF65 70.00 | | | | |

**KM# 104 LATS**
26.00 g., 0.925 Silver 0.7732 oz. ASW, 32x32 mm. **Subject:** Coin of Water **Obv:** Water droplets **Rev:** Snowflake crystal **Edge:** Plain **Shape:** Square

| Date | Mintage | VF20 | XF40 | MS60 | MS63 | MS65 |
|---|---|---|---|---|---|---|
| 2009 | 7,000 | PF65 125 | | | | |

**KM# 105 LATS**
22.00 g., 0.925 Silver 0.6543 oz. ASW, 35 mm. **Subject:** Christmas Tree, 500th Anniversary **Obv:** Three children in folktale costumes **Rev:** Man walking with cut tree in moonlight, squirrel jumping from tree **Edge Lettering:** LATVIJAS BANKA • LATVIJAS REPUBLIKA

| Date | Mintage | VF20 | XF40 | MS60 | MS63 | MS65 |
|---|---|---|---|---|---|---|
| 2009 | 20,000 | PF65 60.00 | | | | |

**KM# 106 LATS**
4.80 g., Copper-Nickel, 21.75 mm. **Obv:** National Arms **Rev:** Christmas tree, heart as ornament **Edge Lettering:** LATVIJAS BANKA • LATVIJAS BANKA

| Date | Mintage | VF20 | XF40 | MS60 | MS63 | MS65 |
|---|---|---|---|---|---|---|
| 2009 | 1,000,000 | — | 2.00 | 3.00 | 4.00 | 6.00 |

**KM# 108 LATS**
4.80 g., Copper-Nickel, 21.75 mm. **Obv:** National arms **Rev:** Toad **Edge Lettering:** LATVIJAS BANKA • LATVIJAS BANKA

| Date | Mintage | VF20 | XF40 | MS60 | MS63 | MS65 |
|---|---|---|---|---|---|---|
| 2010 | 1,000,000 | — | 2.00 | 3.00 | 4.00 | 5.00 |

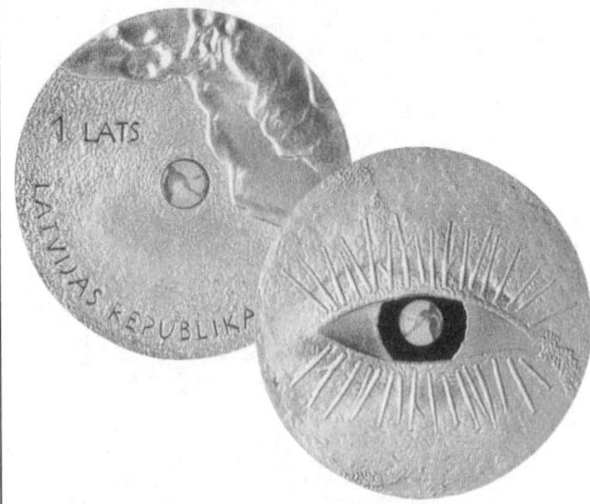

**KM# 109 LATS**
20.70 g., 0.925 Silver 0.6156 oz. ASW with amber insert, 35 mm. **Subject:** Amber Coin **Obv:** Amber stone on seashore **Rev:** Eye with amber as pupil **Edge:** Plain

| Date | Mintage | VF20 | XF40 | MS60 | MS63 | MS65 |
|---|---|---|---|---|---|---|
| 2010 | 7,000 | PF65 150 | | | | |

**KM# 110 LATS**
12.40 g., Copper-Nickel, 30 mm. **Subject:** The Latvian ABC Book **Obv:** Cock **Rev:** Teacher with students **Edge Lettering:** LATVIJAS BANKA • LATVIJAS REPUBLIKA

| Date | Mintage | VF20 | XF40 | MS60 | MS63 | MS65 |
|---|---|---|---|---|---|---|
| 2010 | 10,000 | — | — | — | — | 10.00 |

**KM# 111 LATS**
31.47 g., 0.925 Silver 0.9359 oz. ASW, 38.61 mm. **Subject:** Latvian ABC Book **Obv:** Cock **Rev:** Teacher and students **Edge Lettering:** LATVIJAS BANKA • LATVIJAS REPUBLIKA

| Date | Mintage | VF20 | XF40 | MS60 | MS63 | MS65 |
|---|---|---|---|---|---|---|
| 2010 | 5,000 | PF65 80.00 | | | | |

**KM# 112 LATS**
31.47 g., 0.925 Silver 0.9359 oz. ASW, 38.61 mm. **Subject:** Duke Jacob, 400th Anniversary of birth **Obv:** Bust right, value at bottom **Rev:** Arms **Edge Lettering:** LATVIJAS REPUBLIKA • LATVIJAS BANKA

| Date | Mintage | VF20 | XF40 | MS60 | MS63 | MS65 |
|---|---|---|---|---|---|---|
| 2010 | 5,000 | PF65 70.00 | | | | |

**KM# 113 LATS**
31.47 g., 0.925 Silver 0.9359 oz. ASW, 38.61 mm. **Subject:** Declaration of Independence, 20th Anniversary **Obv:** Three small buds, red in color **Rev:** Elderly female with yoke of oppression **Edge Lettering:** LATVIJAS BANKA (twice)

| Date | Mintage | VF20 | XF40 | MS60 | MS63 | MS65 |
|---|---|---|---|---|---|---|
| 2010 | 7,000 | PF65 60.00 | | | | |

**KM# 114 LATS**
17.15 g., Bi-Metallic Niobium center within 10g of .900 Silver ring, 34 mm. **Subject:** Coin of Time III **Obv:** Heraldic Rose **Rev:** Forests, fields, rocks and water in center, eight lunar phases around **Edge:** Plain

| Date | Mintage | VF20 | XF40 | MS60 | MS63 | MS65 |
|---|---|---|---|---|---|---|
| 2010 | 7,000 | — | — | — | 100 | 125 |

**KM# 117 LATS**
4.80 g., Copper-Nickel, 21.75 mm. **Obv:** National arms **Rev:** Horseshoe with open end upwards **Edge Lettering:** LATVIJAS BANKA • LATVIJAS BANKA

| Date | Mintage | VF20 | XF40 | MS60 | MS63 | MS65 |
|---|---|---|---|---|---|---|
| 2010 | 500,000 | — | — | 3.00 | 5.00 | 6.00 |

**KM# 118 LATS**
4.80 g., Copper-Nickel, 21.75 mm. **Obv:** Naitonal arms **Rev:** Horseshoe with open end downwards **Edge Lettering:** LATVIJAS BANKA • LATVIJAS BANKA

| Date | Mintage | VF20 | XF40 | MS60 | MS63 | MS65 |
|---|---|---|---|---|---|---|
| 2010 | 500,000 | — | — | 3.00 | 5.00 | 6.00 |

**KM# 119 LATS**
4.80 g., Copper-Nickel, 21.75 mm. **Obv:** National arms **Rev:** Beer stein **Edge Lettering:** LATVIJAS BANKA • LATVIJAS BANKA

| Date | Mintage | VF20 | XF40 | MS60 | MS63 | MS65 |
|---|---|---|---|---|---|---|
| 2011 | 1,000,000 | — | — | 3.00 | 5.00 | 6.00 |

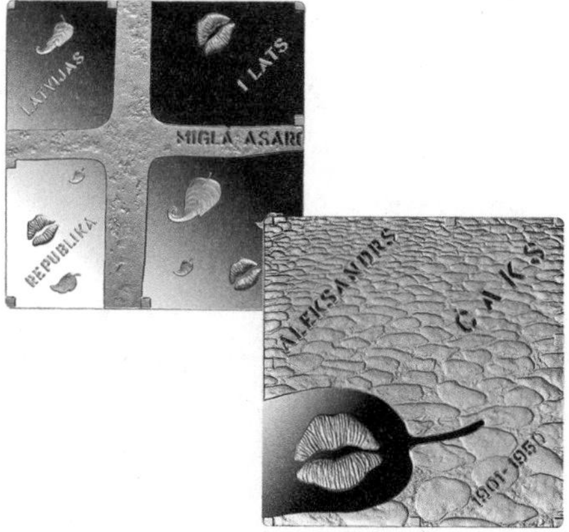

**KM# 120 LATS**
26.00 g., 0.925 Silver 0.7732 oz. ASW, 32x32 mm. **Subject:** Aleksandris Caks **Obv:** Window, glass with imprints of lips and leaves **Rev:** Cobble-stone paving, leave with lips imprint

| Date | Mintage | VF20 | XF40 | MS60 | MS63 | MS65 |
|---|---|---|---|---|---|---|
| 2011 | 7,000 | PF65 85.00 | | | | |

**KM# 121 LATS**
31.47 g., 0.925 Silver 0.9359 oz. ASW, 38.61 mm. **Subject:** Rundale Palace **Obv:** Arms of Earl Ernst Johann von Biron **Rev:** Ariel view of the palace and gardens

| Date | Mintage | VF20 | XF40 | MS60 | MS63 | MS65 |
|---|---|---|---|---|---|---|
| 2011 | 5,000 | PF63 45.00 | PF65 65.00 | | | |

**KM# 122 LATS**
31.47 g., 0.925 Silver 0.9359 oz. ASW, 38.61 mm. **Subject:** Hansa Cities - Riga **Obv:** Riga arms, gothic ornaments flanking **Rev:** Riga city view at top, Hanseatic ship inverted below

| Date | Mintage | VF20 | XF40 | MS60 | MS63 | MS65 |
|---|---|---|---|---|---|---|
| 2011 | 15,000 | PF63 45.00 | PF65 65.00 | | | |

**KM# 123 LATS**
22.00 g., 0.925 Silver 0.6543 oz. ASW, 35 mm. **Subject:** Riga Cathedral **Obv:** Angel at left **Rev:** Cross at left, cathedral exterior at right

| Date | Mintage | VF20 | XF40 | MS60 | MS63 | MS65 |
|---|---|---|---|---|---|---|
| 2011 | 5,000 | PF65 70.00 | | | | |

**KM# 124 LATS**
12.50 g., 0.925 Silver 0.3717 oz. ASW, 28 mm. **Subject:** Riga coinage, 800th Anniversary **Obv:** Pfennig of Bishop Albert (1198-1229) - Bishop in mitre **Rev:** Pfennig of Bishop Albert on frosted surface

| Date | Mintage | VF20 | XF40 | MS60 | MS63 | MS65 |
|---|---|---|---|---|---|---|
| 2011 | 5,000 | PF65 55.00 | | | | |

**KM# 125 LATS**
22.00 g., 0.925 Silver 0.6543 oz. ASW, 35 mm. **Subject:** Railways in Latvia, 50th Anniversary **Obv:** Steam locomotive's drive wheel **Rev:** Steam locomotive profile

| Date | Mintage | VF20 | XF40 | MS60 | MS63 | MS65 |
|---|---|---|---|---|---|---|
| 2011 | 5,000 | PF65 60.00 | | | | |

**KM# 126 LATS**
Bi-Metallic Granite center in .925 Silver ring, 35 mm. **Subject:** Granite Stone **Obv:** Country name at top, denomination at bottom **Rev:** National folk ornamentation

| Date | Mintage | VF20 | XF40 | MS60 | MS63 | MS65 |
|---|---|---|---|---|---|---|
| 2011 | 7,000 | PF65 75.00 | | | | |

**KM# 127 LATS**
4.80 g., Copper-Nickel, 21.75 mm. **Obv:** National arms with supporters **Rev:** Gingerbread heart **Edge Lettering:** LATVIJAS BANKA • LATVIJAS BANKA

| Date | Mintage | VF20 | XF40 | MS60 | MS63 | MS65 |
|---|---|---|---|---|---|---|
| 2011 | 1,000,000 | — | — | 3.00 | 5.00 | 6.00 |

**KM# 128 LATS**
22.00 g., 0.925 Silver 0.6543 oz. ASW, 35 mm. **Subject:** Latvia's participation in the 2012 London Olympics **Obv:** Three Latvian runners right **Rev:** Three ancient Greek runners right

| Date | Mintage | VF20 | XF40 | MS60 | MS63 | MS65 |
|---|---|---|---|---|---|---|
| 2012 | 5,000 | PF65 65.00 | | | | |

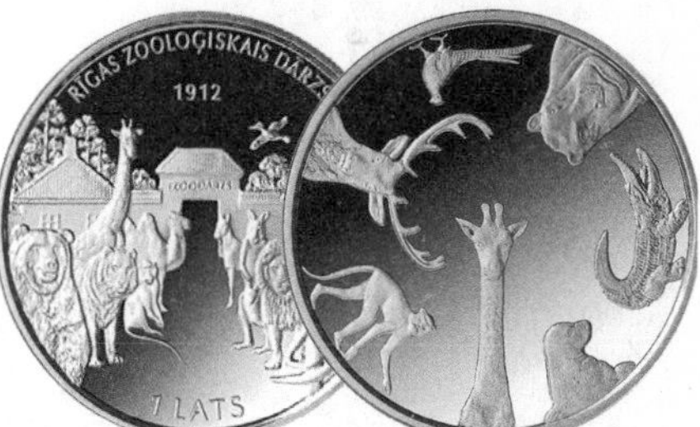

**KM# 129 LATS**
22.00 g., 0.925 Silver 0.6543 oz. ASW, 35 mm. **Subject:** Riga Zoo, 100th Anniversary **Obv:** Zoo entrance gate and exotic animals **Rev:** Seven animal figures **Edge Lettering:** LATVIJAS BANKA • LATVIJAS REPUBLIKA • 2012

| Date | Mintage | VF20 | XF40 | MS60 | MS63 | MS65 |
|---|---|---|---|---|---|---|
| 2012 | 5,000 | PF65 75.00 | | | | |

**KM# 131 LATS**
26.00 g., 0.925 Silver 0.7732 oz. ASW, 32x32 mm. **Subject:** Riga Technical University, 150th Anniversary **Obv:** Curved guage and mm scale **Rev:** Town view, gilt dividers and drafting triangle **Note:** Two-part.

| Date | Mintage | VF20 | XF40 | MS60 | MS63 | MS65 |
|---|---|---|---|---|---|---|
| 2012 | 3,000 | PF65 175 | | | | |

**KM# 132 LATS**
22.00 g., 0.925 Silver 0.6543 oz. ASW, 35 mm. **Subject:** K. Zale **Obv:** Head left **Rev:** Sculpture: Dying Horseman I **Edge Lettering:** LATVIJAS BANKA • LATVIJAS REPUBLIKA • 2012

| Date | Mintage | VF20 | XF40 | MS60 | MS63 | MS65 |
|---|---|---|---|---|---|---|
| 2012 | 7,000 | **PF65** 65.00 | | | | |

**KM# 133 LATS**
22.00 g., 0.925 Silver 0.6543 oz. ASW, 35 mm. **Subject:** Latvian National Traditions

| Date | Mintage | VF20 | XF40 | MS60 | MS63 | MS65 |
|---|---|---|---|---|---|---|
| 2012 | 5,000 | **PF65** 65.00 | | | | |

**KM# 134 LATS**
22.00 g., 0.925 Silver 0.6543 oz. ASW, 35 mm. **Subject:** K. Blaumanis

| Date | Mintage | VF20 | XF40 | MS60 | MS63 | MS65 |
|---|---|---|---|---|---|---|
| 2012 | 3,000 | **PF65** 70.00 | | | | |

**KM# 135 LATS**
4.80 g., Copper-Nickel, 21.75 mm. **Obv:** National arms **Rev:** Hedgehog **Edge Lettering:** LATVIJAS BANKA • LATVIJAS BANKA

| Date | Mintage | VF20 | XF40 | MS60 | MS63 | MS65 |
|---|---|---|---|---|---|---|
| 2012 | 1,000,000 | — | — | 3.00 | 4.00 | 5.00 |

**KM# 136 LATS**
4.80 g., Copper-Nickel, 21.75 mm. **Obv:** National arms **Rev:** Christmas bells **Edge Lettering:** LATVIJAS BANKA • LATVIJAS BANKA

| Date | Mintage | VF20 | XF40 | MS60 | MS63 | MS65 |
|---|---|---|---|---|---|---|
| 2012 | 1,000,000 | — | — | 3.00 | 4.00 | 5.00 |

**KM# 137 LATS**
22.00 g., 0.925 Silver 0.6543 oz. ASW, 35 mm. **Subject:** Rudolfs Blaumanis - 150th Anniversary of Birth **Obv:** Horse in the woods **Rev:** Portrait and writing

| Date | Mintage | VF20 | XF40 | MS60 | MS63 | MS65 |
|---|---|---|---|---|---|---|
| 2013 | Est. 7000 | **PF65** 30.00 | | | | |

**KM# 139 LATS**
22.00 g., 0.925 Silver 0.6543 oz. ASW, 35 mm. **Obv:** bird holding basket with baby **Rev:** Mouse pulling a cart **Edge:** Lettered

| Date | Mintage | VF20 | XF40 | MS60 | MS63 | MS65 |
|---|---|---|---|---|---|---|
| 2013 | — | **PF65** 25.00 | | | | |

**KM# 140 LATS**
22.00 g., 0.925 Silver 0.6543 oz. ASW, 35 mm. **Subject:** Richard Wagner, 200th Anniversary of Birth **Obv:** Profile left, horn flowing into flower **Rev:** Ship in stormy seas **Edge:** Lettered

| Date | Mintage | VF20 | XF40 | MS60 | MS63 | MS65 |
|---|---|---|---|---|---|---|
| 2013 | — | **PF65** 25.00 | | | | |

**KM# 141 LATS**
22.00 g., 0.925 Silver 0.6543 oz. ASW, 35 mm. **Subject:** Jazeps Vitols, 150th Anniversary of Birth **Obv:** Profile bust left **Rev:** Group of five rays of light **Edge:** Lettered

| Date | Mintage | VF20 | XF40 | MS60 | MS63 | MS65 |
|---|---|---|---|---|---|---|
| 2013 | — | **PF65** 25.00 | | | | |

**KM# 142 LATS**
4.80 g., Copper-Nickel, 21.75 mm. **Obv:** National Arms **Rev:** Kokle, folk instrument

| Date | Mintage | VF20 | XF40 | MS60 | MS63 | MS65 |
|---|---|---|---|---|---|---|
| 2013 | — | — | — | 3.00 | 4.00 | 5.00 |

**KM# 143 LATS**
16.40 g., 0.925 Silver 0.4877 oz. ASW, 30 mm. **Subject:** Last Lats

| Date | Mintage | VF20 | XF40 | MS60 | MS63 | MS65 |
|---|---|---|---|---|---|---|
| 2013 | 5,000 | **PF65** 45.00 | | | | |

**KM# 144 LATS**
1.24 g., 0.9999 Gold 0.040 oz. AGW, 13.92 mm. **Subject:** Oh Holy Listene **Obv:** Acanthus leaf design from the side décor of altar of the Lestene church **Rev:** Head of an angel from the altar of the Lestene church

| Date | Mintage | VF20 | XF40 | MS60 | MS63 | MS65 |
|---|---|---|---|---|---|---|
| 2013 | 5,000 | **PF65** 85.00 | | | | |

**KM# 145 LATS**
4.76 g., Copper-Nickel, 21.76 mm. **Subject:** Lats and Euro parity **Obv:** National arms **Rev:** Large 1 **Rev. Inscription:** 1 LATS .42 EURO

| Date | Mintage | VF20 | XF40 | MS60 | MS63 | MS65 |
|---|---|---|---|---|---|---|
| 2013 | — | — | — | 3.00 | 4.00 | 5.00 |

**KM# 38 2 LATI**
9.50 g., Bi-Metallic Nickel-Brass center in Copper-Nickel ring, 26.3 mm. **Obv:** Arms with supporters within circle **Rev:** Cow above value within circle **Edge Lettering:** LATVIJAS BANKA

| Date | Mintage | VF20 | XF40 | MS60 | MS63 | MS65 |
|---|---|---|---|---|---|---|
| 2003 Sets only | 30,000 | — | — | — | — | 12.00 |
| 2009 | 2,000,000 | — | 3.00 | 5.00 | 7.00 | 9.00 |

**KM# 59 5 LATI**
1.24 g., 0.9999 Gold 0.040 oz. AGW, 13.92 mm. **Obv:** Bust right **Rev:** Arms with supporters above value **Edge:** Reeded **Note:** Remake of the popular KM-9 design

| Date | Mintage | VF20 | XF40 | MS60 | MS63 | MS65 |
|---|---|---|---|---|---|---|
| 2003 | Est. 20000 | **PF65** 125 | | | | |

**KM# 130 5 LATI**
25.00 g., 0.925 Silver 0.7435 oz. ASW, 37 mm. **Subject:** Bank of Latvia and national currency, 90th Anniversary **Obv:** Female head in national costume right **Rev:** National arms **Edge Lettering:** DIEVS SVETI LATVIJS

| Date | Mintage | VF20 | XF40 | MS60 | MS63 | MS65 |
|---|---|---|---|---|---|---|
| 2012 | Est. 10000 | **PF65** 125 | | | | |

**KM# 138 20 LATU**
11.00 g., 0.925 Silver 0.3271 oz. ASW, 21.75 mm. **Subject:** 20th Anniversary of the return of Lats coinage **Obv:** National arms **Rev:** Salmon **Edge:** Lettered

| Date | Mintage | VF20 | XF40 | MS60 | MS63 | MS65 |
|---|---|---|---|---|---|---|
| 2013 | — | **PF65** 15.00 | | | | |

**KM# 96 20 LATI**
10.00 g., 0.999 Gold 0.3212 oz. AGW, 22 mm. **Obv:** Woman's head covered with scarf **Rev:** Vessel with a milk bottle, apple, jug of milk, bread & knife on table

| Date | Mintage | VF20 | XF40 | MS60 | MS63 | MS65 |
|---|---|---|---|---|---|---|
| 2008 | 5,000 | — | — | — | 750 | 850 |

## EURO COINAGE

**KM# 150 EURO CENT**
2.30 g., Copper Plated Steel, 16.25 mm. **Obv:** National shield, three stars above **Rev:** Value and globe **Edge:** Plain

| Date | Mintage | VF20 | XF40 | MS60 | MS63 | MS65 |
|---|---|---|---|---|---|---|
| 2014 | — | — | — | 0.25 | 0.35 | 0.50 |
| 2014 | 5,000 | **PF65** 12.00 | | | | |

**KM# 151 2 EURO CENT**
3.06 g., Copper Plated Steel, 18.75 mm. **Obv:** National shield, three stars above **Rev:** Value and globe

| Date | Mintage | VF20 | XF40 | MS60 | MS63 | MS65 |
|---|---|---|---|---|---|---|
| 2014 | — | — | — | 0.25 | 0.35 | 0.50 |
| 2014 | 5,000 | **PF65** 12.00 | | | | |

**KM# 152 5 EURO CENT**
3.92 g., Copper Plated Steel, 21.25 mm. **Obv:** National shield, three stars above **Rev:** Value and globe

| Date | Mintage | VF20 | XF40 | MS60 | MS63 | MS65 |
|---|---|---|---|---|---|---|
| 2014 | — | — | — | 0.25 | 0.35 | 0.50 |
| 2014 | 5,000 | **PF65** 12.00 | | | | |

**KM# 153 10 EURO CENT**
4.10 g., Brass, 19.75 mm. **Obv:** National arms **Rev:** Relief map of Western Europe; stars, lines and value **Edge:** Reeded

| Date | Mintage | VF20 | XF40 | MS60 | MS63 | MS65 |
|---|---|---|---|---|---|---|
| 2014 | — | — | — | 0.75 | 1.00 | 1.50 |
| 2014 | 5,000 | **PF65** 12.00 | | | | |

**KM# 154 20 EURO CENT**
5.74 g., Brass, 22.25 mm. **Obv:** National arms **Rev:** Relief map of Western Europe; stars, lines and value **Edge:** Notched

| Date | Mintage | VF20 | XF40 | MS60 | MS63 | MS65 |
|---|---|---|---|---|---|---|
| 2014 | — | — | — | 0.75 | 1.00 | 1.50 |
| 2014 | 5,000 | **PF65** 15.00 | | | | |

**KM# 155 50 EURO CENT**
7.80 g., Brass, 24.25 mm. **Obv:** National arms **Rev:** Relief map of Western Europe; stars, lines and value

| Date | Mintage | VF20 | XF40 | MS60 | MS63 | MS65 |
|---|---|---|---|---|---|---|
| 2014 | — | — | — | 0.75 | 1.00 | 1.50 |
| 2014 | 5,000 | **PF65** 15.00 | | | | |

**KM# 156 EURO**
7.50 g., Bi-Metallic Copper-Nickel cetner in Nickel-Brass ring., 23.25 mm. **Obv:** Female head in national costume right **Rev:** Value and map; stars and lines **Edge:** Segmented reeding

| Date | Mintage | VF20 | XF40 | MS60 | MS63 | MS65 |
|---|---|---|---|---|---|---|
| 2014 | — | — | — | 1.75 | 2.50 | 3.50 |
| 2014 | 5,000 | **PF65** 20.00 | | | | |

**KM# 157 2 EURO**
8.50 g., Bi-Metallic Nickel-Brass center in Copper-Nickel ring., 25.75 mm. **Obv:** Female head in national costume right **Rev:** Value and map, stars and lines. **Edge Lettering:** 2's and stars

| Date | Mintage | VF20 | XF40 | MS60 | MS63 | MS65 |
|---|---|---|---|---|---|---|
| 2014 | — | — | — | 4.00 | 5.00 | 7.00 |
| 2014 Proof | 5,000 | — | — | — | — | — |

# LEBANON

The Lebanese Republic, situated on the eastern shore of the Mediterranean Sea between Syria and Israel, has an area of 4,015 sq. mi. (10,400 sq. km.) and a population of 3.5 million. Capital: Beirut. The economy is based on agriculture, trade and tourism. Fruit, other foodstuffs and textiles are exported.

**MONETARY SYSTEM**
100 Piastres = 1 Livre (Pound)

## REPUBLIC

## STANDARD COINAGE

**KM# 41 LIVRE**
28.28 g., Silver **Subject:** Amin Maalouf to French Academy **Obv:** Cypress tree

| Date | Mintage | VF20 | XF40 | MS60 | MS63 | MS65 |
|---|---|---|---|---|---|---|
| 2012 proof | Est. 1000 | — | — | — | 550 | 600 |

**KM# 40 25 LIVRES**
2.82 g., Nickel Plated Steel, 20.5 mm. **Obv:** Large value on cedar tree **Rev:** Value within square design **Rev. Legend:** BANQUE DU LIBAN **Edge:** Plain

| Date | Mintage | VF20 | XF40 | MS60 | MS63 | MS65 |
|---|---|---|---|---|---|---|
| 2002 (c) | — | — | 0.30 | 0.50 | 0.80 | 1.20 |
| 2009 (v) | — | — | 0.30 | 0.50 | 0.80 | 1.20 |

**KM# 37a 50 LIVRES**
Nickel, 18.35 mm. **Obv:** Cedar tree with Arabic value superimposed. Arabic legend above, date below. **Rev:** Value in center.

| Date | Mintage | VF20 | XF40 | MS60 | MS63 | MS65 |
|---|---|---|---|---|---|---|
| 2006 | — | — | 0.50 | 0.70 | 1.20 | 1.80 |

**KM# 38 100 LIVRES**
4.00 g., Brass, 22.5 mm. **Obv:** Arabic legend above large value on cedar tree **Rev:** Stylized flag above large value "100" **Rev. Legend:** BANQUE DU LIBAN **Edge:** Plain

| Date | Mintage | VF20 | XF40 | MS60 | MS63 | MS65 |
|---|---|---|---|---|---|---|
| 2006 (c) | — | — | 0.65 | 0.85 | 1.50 | 2.00 |

**KM# 38a 100 LIVRES**
4.05 g., Stainless Steel, 22.48 mm. **Obv:** Arabic legend above large value on cedar tree **Rev:** Stylized flag above large value "100 **Rev. Legend:** BANQUE DU LIBAN **Edge:** Plain

| Date | Mintage | VF20 | XF40 | MS60 | MS63 | MS65 |
|---|---|---|---|---|---|---|
| 2003 (c) | — | — | 0.60 | 0.85 | 1.50 | 2.00 |

**KM# 38b 100 LIVRES**
4.07 g., Copper Plated Steel, 22.5 mm. **Obv:** Arabic legend above large value on cedar tree **Rev:** Stylized flag above large value "100" **Rev. Legend:** BANQUE DU LIBAN **Edge:** Plain

| Date | Mintage | VF20 | XF40 | MS60 | MS63 | MS65 |
|---|---|---|---|---|---|---|
| 2006 | — | — | 0.60 | 0.85 | 1.50 | 2.00 |
| 2009 | — | — | 0.60 | 0.85 | 1.50 | 2.00 |

**KM# 36 250 LIVRES**
5.00 g., Aluminum-Bronze, 23.5 mm. **Obv:** Arabic legend above large value on cedar tree **Rev:** Large 250 within eliptical border design **Edge:** Reeded

| Date | Mintage | VF20 | XF40 | MS60 | MS63 | MS65 |
|---|---|---|---|---|---|---|
| 2003 (c) | — | — | 0.75 | 0.95 | 1.85 | 2.50 |
| 2006 (a) | — | — | 0.75 | 0.95 | 1.85 | 2.50 |
| 2009 (v) | — | — | 0.75 | 0.95 | 1.85 | 2.50 |
| 2012 | — | — | 0.75 | 0.95 | 1.85 | 2.50 |

**KM# 36a 250 LIVRES**
5.00 g., Aluminum-Bronze with selective rhodium plating, 23.5 mm. **Obv:** Arabic legend above rhodium plated large value and cedar tree **Rev:** Large 250 within elliptical border design **Edge:** Reeded

| Date | Mintage | VF20 | XF40 | MS60 | MS63 | MS65 |
|---|---|---|---|---|---|---|
| 2012 | 100,000 | — | — | — | — | 15.00 |

**KM# 39 500 LIVRES**
6.06 g., Nickel Plated Steel, 24.5 mm. **Obv:** Arabic legend above large value on cedar tree **Rev:** Large value "500", thick segmented circular border **Rev. Legend:** BANQUE DU LIBAN **Edge:** Plain

| Date | Mintage | VF20 | XF40 | MS60 | MS63 | MS65 |
|---|---|---|---|---|---|---|
| 2003 (c) | — | — | 0.90 | 2.25 | 3.00 | — |
| 2006 (a) | — | — | 0.90 | 2.25 | 3.00 | — |
| 2009 (v) (2012) | — | — | 0.90 | 2.25 | 3.00 | — |

**KM# 39a 500 LIVRES**
6.06 g., Nickel Plated Steel, 24.5 mm. **Obv:** Arabic legend above large value on cedar tree **Rev:** Large value 500, thick segmented circular border, two cedars in security motif at top

| Date | Mintage | VF20 | XF40 | MS60 | MS63 | MS65 |
|---|---|---|---|---|---|---|
| 2012 | — | — | — | 2.25 | 3.00 | — |

# LESOTHO

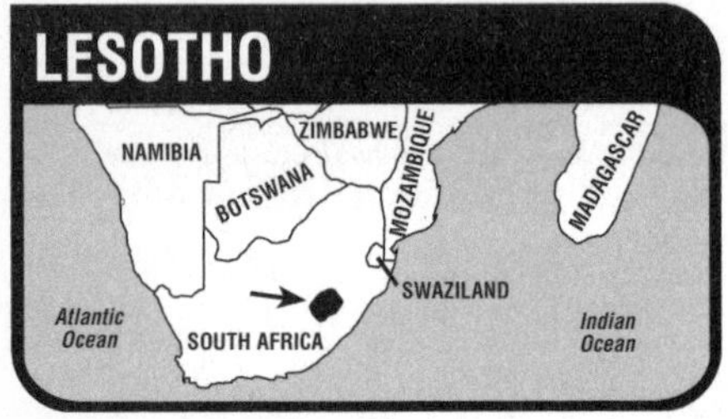


The Kingdom of Lesotho, a constitutional monarchy located within the east-central part of the Republic of South Africa, has an area of 11,720 sq. mi. (30,350 sq. km.) and a population of 1.5 million. Capital: Maseru. The economy is based on subsistence agriculture and livestock raising. Wool, mohair, and cattle are exported.

Lesotho (formerly Basutoland) was sparsely populated until the end of the 16th century. Between the 16th and 19th centuries an influx of refugees from tribal wars led to the development of a distinct Basotho group. During the reign of tribal chief Mashoeshoe I (1823-70), a series of wars with the Orange Free State resulted in the loss of large areas of territory to South Africa. Mashoeshoe appealed to the British for help, and Basutoland was constituted a native state under British protection. In 1871 it was annexed to Cape Colony, but was restored to direct control by the Crown in 1884. From 1884 to 1959 legislative and executive authority was vested in a British High Commissioner. The constitution of 1959 recognized the expressed wish of the people for independence, which was attained on Oct.4, 1966.

Lesotho is a member of the Commonwealth of Nations. The king is Head of State.

**RULERS**
Moshoeshoe II, 1966-1990
Letsie III, 1990-1995
Moshoeshoe II, 1995-

**MONETARY SYSTEM**
100 Licente/Lisente = 1 Maloti/Loti

## KINGDOM

### STANDARD COINAGE

100 Licente / Lisente = 1 Maloti / Loti

**KM# 62 5 LICENTE (Lisente)**
1.64 g., Brass Plated Steel, 15 mm. **Ruler:** Letsie III **Obv:** Arms with supporters **Rev:** Two pine trees among grass, hills and value

| Date | Mintage | VF20 | XF40 | MS60 | MS63 | MS65 |
|---|---|---|---|---|---|---|
| 2006 | — | — | 0.35 | 0.75 | 1.00 | 2.00 |

**KM# 63 10 LICENTE (Lisente)**
1.96 g., Brass Plated Steel, 16 mm. **Ruler:** Moshoeshoe II **Obv:** Arms with supporters **Rev:** Angora goat

| Date | Mintage | VF20 | XF40 | MS60 | MS63 | MS65 |
|---|---|---|---|---|---|---|
| 2010 | — | — | — | 1.00 | 1.50 | 3.00 |

**KM# 66 LOTI**
3.88 g., Nickel Plated Steel, 21 mm. **Ruler:** Letsie III **Obv:** Native seated right **Rev:** Value at left of arms with supporters

| Date | Mintage | VF20 | XF40 | MS60 | MS63 | MS65 |
|---|---|---|---|---|---|---|
| 2010 | — | — | — | 1.50 | 2.00 | 3.00 |

**KM# 59 5 MALOTI**
6.37 g., Nickel Plated Steel, 25 mm. **Ruler:** Moshoeshoe II **Obv:** Arms with supporters **Rev:** Wheat sprigs and value

| Date | Mintage | VF20 | XF40 | MS60 | MS63 | MS65 |
|---|---|---|---|---|---|---|
| 2010 | — | — | — | 4.50 | 5.00 | 6.50 |

**KM# 73 25 MALOTI**
Silver **Ruler:** Moshoeshoe II **Subject:** Central Bank, 25th Anniversary

| Date | Mintage | VF20 | XF40 | MS60 | MS63 | MS65 |
|---|---|---|---|---|---|---|
| 2005 | — | PF63 65.00 | PF65 75.00 | | | |

# LIBERIA

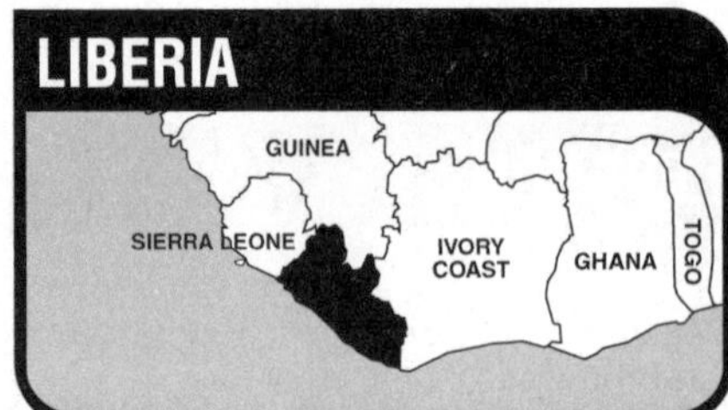


The Republic of Liberia, located on the southern side of the West African bulge between Sierra Leone and Ivory Coast, has an area of 38,250 sq. mi. (111,370 sq. km) and a population of 2.2 million. Capital: Monrovia. The major industries are agriculture, mining and lumbering. Iron ore, diamonds, rubber, coffee and coca are exported.

**MINT MARKS**
PM - Pobjoy Mint

**MONETARY SYSTEM**
100 Cents = 1 Dollar

## REPUBLIC

### STANDARD COINAGE

100 Cen ts = 1 Dollar

**KM# 618 5 CENTS**
5.02 g., Copper-Nickel, 23.8 mm. **Obv:** National arms **Rev:** Chimpanzee family **Edge:** Plain

| Date | Mintage | VF20 | XF40 | MS60 | MS63 | MS65 |
|---|---|---|---|---|---|---|
| 2003 | — | — | — | 1.00 | 1.50 | 2.00 |

**KM# 1033 DOLLAR**
Silver ASW, 50 mm. **Subject:** Euro Currency **Obv:** Europa on a bull and map **Rev:** French coin

| Date | Mintage | VF20 | XF40 | MS60 | MS63 | MS65 |
|---|---|---|---|---|---|---|
| 2002 | — | PF63 25.00 | PF65 30.00 | | | |

**KM# 1034 DOLLAR**
Silver ASW, 50 mm. **Subject:** Euro Currency **Obv:** Europa on a bull and map **Rev:** Belgian coin

| Date | Mintage | VF20 | XF40 | MS60 | MS63 | MS65 |
|---|---|---|---|---|---|---|
| 2002 | — | PF63 25.00 | PF65 30.00 | | | |

**KM# 1035 DOLLAR**
Silver ASW, 50 mm. **Subject:** Euro currency **Obv:** Europa on a bull and map **Rev:** Irish coin

| Date | Mintage | VF20 | XF40 | MS60 | MS63 | MS65 |
|---|---|---|---|---|---|---|
| 2002 | — | PF63 25.00 | PF65 30.00 | | | |

**KM# 1036 DOLLAR**
Copper-Nickel, 25 mm. **Obv:** National arms **Rev:** Ordination of a priest

| Date | Mintage | VF20 | XF40 | MS60 | MS63 | MS65 |
|---|---|---|---|---|---|---|
| 2005 | — | — | — | — | — | 15.00 |

**KM# 1037 DOLLAR**
15.57 g., 0.999 Silver 0.5001 oz. ASW, 33.02 mm. **Subject:** Merry Christmas & Happy New Year **Obv:** National arms **Rev:** Angel

| Date | Mintage | VF20 | XF40 | MS60 | MS63 | MS65 |
|---|---|---|---|---|---|---|
| 2009 | 5,000 | PF63 30.00 | PF65 35.00 | | | |

**KM# 1003 2 DOLLARS**
15.55 g., 0.999 Silver 0.4994 oz. ASW, 38.6 mm. **Obv:** National arms **Rev:** Santa in sleigh in color

| Date | Mintage | VF20 | XF40 | MS60 | MS63 | MS65 |
|---|---|---|---|---|---|---|
| 2011 | — | PF65 45.00 | | | | |

**KM# 1004 2 DOLLARS**
15.55 g., 0.999 Silver 0.4994 oz. ASW, 38.6 mm. **Obv:** National arms **Rev:** Christmas toys in color

| Date | Mintage | VF20 | XF40 | MS60 | MS63 | MS65 |
|---|---|---|---|---|---|---|
| 2011 | — | PF65 45.00 | | | | |

**KM# 1005 2 DOLLARS**
15.55 g., 0.999 Silver 0.4994 oz. ASW, 38.6 mm. **Obv:** National arms **Rev:** Christmas Angel in color

| Date | Mintage | VF20 | XF40 | MS60 | MS63 | MS65 |
|---|---|---|---|---|---|---|
| 2011 | — | PF65 45.00 | | | | |

**KM# 1006 2 DOLLARS**
15.55 g., 0.999 Silver 0.4994 oz. ASW, 38.6 mm. **Obv:** National arms **Rev:** Christmas - Drummer in color

| Date | Mintage | VF20 | XF40 | MS60 | MS63 | MS65 |
|---|---|---|---|---|---|---|
| 2011 | — | PF65 45.00 | | | | |

**KM# 1007 2 DOLLARS**
15.55 g., 0.999 Silver 0.4994 oz. ASW, 38.6 mm. **Obv:** National arms **Rev:** Christmas - bells in color

| Date | Mintage | VF20 | XF40 | MS60 | MS63 | MS65 |
|---|---|---|---|---|---|---|
| 2011 | — | PF65 45.00 | | | | |

**KM# 1008 2 DOLLARS**
15.55 g., 0.999 Silver 0.4994 oz. ASW, 38.6 mm. **Obv:** National arms **Rev:** Christmas Nutcracker in color

| Date | Mintage | VF20 | XF40 | MS60 | MS63 | MS65 |
|---|---|---|---|---|---|---|
| 2011 | — | PF65 45.00 | | | | |

**KM# 568 5 DOLLARS**
14.63 g., Copper-Nickel, 33.1 mm. **Subject:** Battle of Gettysburg **Obv:** National arms **Rev:** Cannon and crossed flags divides busts facing **Edge:** Reeded **Note:** This also exists in an obverse denominated type for $2,000. Also see KM828.

| Date | Mintage | VF20 | XF40 | MS60 | MS63 | MS65 |
|---|---|---|---|---|---|---|
| 2001 B | — | — | — | — | 12.00 | 14.00 |

**KM# 651 5 DOLLARS**
14.56 g., Copper-Nickel, 38 mm. **Obv:** National arms **Rev:** Japanese "Zero" flying over Pearl Harbor **Edge:** Reeded

| Date | Mintage | VF20 | XF40 | MS60 | MS63 | MS65 |
|---|---|---|---|---|---|---|
| 2001 | — | — | — | — | 10.00 | 12.00 |

**KM# 494 5 DOLLARS**
8.50 g., 0.9999 Silver 0.2733 oz. ASW, 30 mm. **Subject:** Soccer **Obv:** National arms **Rev:** Soccer player divides circle **Edge:** Reeded

| Date | Mintage | VF20 | XF40 | MS60 | MS63 | MS65 |
|---|---|---|---|---|---|---|
| 2002 | 3,000 | PF63 20.00 | PF65 25.00 | | | |

**KM# 829 5 DOLLARS**
14.94 g., Copper-Nickel, 32.9 mm. **Subject:** 12th Anniversary Columbia Space Shuttle **Obv:** National arms **Rev:** Astronaut, space shuttle **Edge:** Reeded

| Date | Mintage | VF20 | XF40 | MS60 | MS63 | MS65 |
|---|---|---|---|---|---|---|
| 2003 | — | — | — | — | 7.00 | 9.00 |

**KM# 831 5 DOLLARS**
15.55 g., 0.999 Niobium 0.4962 oz., 38 mm. **Series:** From ancient to Modern Sports **Obv:** National arms **Rev:** Discus throwers **Edge:** Plain

| Date | Mintage | F12 | VF20 | XF40 | MS60 | MS63 |
|---|---|---|---|---|---|---|
| 2004 | 2,004 | — | — | — | — | 30.00 |

**KM# 832 5 DOLLARS**
15.55 g., 0.999 Niobium 0.4962 oz., 38 mm. **Series:** From Ancient to Modern Sports **Obv:** National arms **Rev:** Javelin throwers **Edge:** Plain

| Date | Mintage | F12 | VF20 | XF40 | MS60 | MS63 |
|---|---|---|---|---|---|---|
| 2004 | 2,004 | — | — | — | — | 30.00 |

**KM# 833 5 DOLLARS**
15.55 g., 0.999 Niobium 0.4962 oz., 38 mm. **Series:** From ancient to Modern Sports **Obv:** National arms **Rev:** Broad jumpers **Edge:** Plain

| Date | Mintage | F12 | VF20 | XF40 | MS60 | MS63 |
|---|---|---|---|---|---|---|
| 2004 | 2,004 | — | — | — | — | 30.00 |

**KM# 834 5 DOLLARS**
15.55 g., 0.999 Niobium 0.4962 oz., 38 mm. **Series:** From Ancient to Modern Sports **Obv:** National arms **Rev:** Runners **Edge:** Plain

| Date | Mintage | F12 | VF20 | XF40 | MS60 | MS63 |
|---|---|---|---|---|---|---|
| 2004 | 2,004 | — | — | — | — | 30.00 |

**KM# 835 5 DOLLARS**
15.55 g., 0.999 Niobium 0.4962 oz., 38 mm. **Series:** From Ancient to Modern Sports **Obv:** National arms **Rev:** Wrestlers **Edge:** Plain

| Date | Mintage | F12 | VF20 | XF40 | MS60 | MS63 |
|---|---|---|---|---|---|---|
| 2004 | 2,004 | — | — | — | — | 30.00 |

**KM# 664 5 DOLLARS**
6.40 g., Bi-Metallic Brass center in Copper-Nickel ring, 25.7 mm. **Obv:** National arms **Rev:** Pope and cathedral within circle **Edge:** Reeded

| Date | Mintage | VF20 | XF40 | MS60 | MS63 | MS65 |
|---|---|---|---|---|---|---|
| 2005 | — | — | — | — | 10.00 | 12.00 |

**KM# 809 5 DOLLARS**
25.95 g., Silver Plated Copper-Nickel, 39.97 mm. **Subject:** Papal visits to Africa **Obv:** National arms **Rev:** 1/2 length multicolor figure of Pope John Paul II at center left, outlined map of Africa at center right in background **Edge:** Reeded

| Date | Mintage | VF20 | XF40 | MS60 | MS63 | MS65 |
|---|---|---|---|---|---|---|
| 2005 | — | PF65 35.00 | | | | |

**KM# 810 5 DOLLARS**
25.72 g., Silver, 39.92 mm. **Obv:** National arms **Rev:** St. Peter's square in background, multicolor bust of Pope Benedict XVI in oval frame at upper right **Edge:** Reeded

| Date | Mintage | VF20 | XF40 | MS60 | MS63 | MS65 |
|---|---|---|---|---|---|---|
| 2005 | — | PF65 40.00 | | | | |

**KM# 865 5 DOLLARS**
7.78 g., Niobium partially gilt, 35 mm. **Subject:** 10th Anniversary of the Euro - San Marino **Rev:** Castle

| Date | Mintage | VF20 | XF40 | MS60 | MS63 | MS65 |
|---|---|---|---|---|---|---|
| 2006 | 10,000 | PF65 50.00 | | | | |

**KM# 866 5 DOLLARS**
7.78 g., Niobium partially gilt, 35 mm. **Subject:** 10th Anniversary of the Euro - Slovakia **Rev:** Bratislava Castle

| Date | Mintage | VF20 | XF40 | MS60 | MS63 | MS65 |
|---|---|---|---|---|---|---|
| 2006 | 10,000 | PF65 50.00 | | | | |

**KM# 867 5 DOLLARS**
7.78 g., Niobium partially gilt, 35 mm. **Subject:** 10th Anniversary of the Euro - Latvia **Rev:** Old Buildings

| Date | Mintage | VF20 | XF40 | MS60 | MS63 | MS65 |
|---|---|---|---|---|---|---|
| 2006 | 10,000 | PF65 50.00 | | | | |

**KM# 868 5 DOLLARS**
7.78 g., Niobium partially gilt, 35 mm. **Subject:** 10th Anniversary of the Euro - Monaco **Rev:** Ariel view of Principality

| Date | Mintage | VF20 | XF40 | MS60 | MS63 | MS65 |
|---|---|---|---|---|---|---|
| 2006 | 10,000 | PF65 50.00 | | | | |

**KM# 869 5 DOLLARS**
7.78 g., Niobium partially gilt, 35 mm. **Subject:** 10th Anniversary of the Euro - Slovenia **Rev:** Hill-top buildings

| Date | Mintage | VF20 | XF40 | MS60 | MS63 | MS65 |
|---|---|---|---|---|---|---|
| 2006 | 10,000 | PF65 50.00 | | | | |

**KM# 724 5 DOLLARS**
26.30 g., Silver Plated Bronze, 38.6 mm. **Obv:** National arms **Rev:** Multicolor Pope John Paul II with cross **Edge:** Reeded

| Date | Mintage | VF20 | XF40 | MS60 | MS63 | MS65 |
|---|---|---|---|---|---|---|
| 2007 | — | PF65 30.00 | | | | |

**KM# 733 5 DOLLARS**
27.00 g., Copper-Nickel Silvered and Gilt, 38.61 mm. **Subject:** The Black Madonna of Czestochowa **Obv:** Arms **Obv. Legend:** REPUBLIC OF LIBERIA **Rev:** 1/2 length figure of Madonna facing with child

| Date | Mintage | VF20 | XF40 | MS60 | MS63 | MS65 |
|---|---|---|---|---|---|---|
| 2007 | 1,000 | PF65 40.00 | | | | |

**KM# 1022 5 DOLLARS**
28.28 g., 0.999 Silver 0.9083 oz. ASW, 38.6 mm. **Obv:** National arms **Rev:** Christ at center, apostles in 12 segments around

| Date | Mintage | VF20 | XF40 | MS60 | MS63 | MS65 |
|---|---|---|---|---|---|---|
| 2008 | — | PF63 32.00 | PF65 37.00 | | | |

**KM# 1024 5 DOLLARS**
28.28 g., 0.999 Silver 0.9083 oz. ASW, 38.6 mm. **Subject:** Tanks of WWII **Obv:** National arms **Rev:** T-34 in color applique

| Date | Mintage | VF20 | XF40 | MS60 | MS63 | MS65 |
|---|---|---|---|---|---|---|
| 2008 | — | PF65 32.00 | | | | |

**KM# 1025 5 DOLLARS**
28.28 g., 0.999 Silver 0.9083 oz. ASW, 38.6 mm. **Subject:** Tanks of WWII **Obv:** National arms **Rev:** Mark IV Churchill

| Date | Mintage | VF20 | XF40 | MS60 | MS63 | MS65 |
|---|---|---|---|---|---|---|
| 2008 | — | PF65 32.00 | | | | |

**KM# 1026 5 DOLLARS**
28.28 g., 0.999 Silver 0.9083 oz. ASW, 38.6 mm. **Subject:** Tanks of WWII **Obv:** National arms **Rev:** M4 Sherman

| Date | Mintage | VF20 | XF40 | MS60 | MS63 | MS65 |
|---|---|---|---|---|---|---|
| 2008 | — | PF65 32.00 | | | | |

**KM# 1027 5 DOLLARS**
28.28 g., 0.999 Silver 0.9083 oz. ASW, 38.6 mm. **Subject:** Tanks of WWII **Obv:** National arms **Rev:** VI Tiger

| Date | Mintage | VF20 | XF40 | MS60 | MS63 | MS65 |
|---|---|---|---|---|---|---|
| 2008 | — | PF65 32.00 | | | | |

**KM# 1028 5 DOLLARS**
28.28 g., 0.999 Silver 0.9083 oz. ASW, 38.6 mm. **Subject:** Tanks of WWII **Obv:** National arms **Rev:** Type 95

| Date | Mintage | VF20 | XF40 | MS60 | MS63 | MS65 |
|---|---|---|---|---|---|---|
| 2008 | — | PF65 32.00 | | | | |

**KM# 951 5 DOLLARS**
31.11 g., Copper-Nickel Silver plated **Rev:** George Washington multicolor applique

| Date | Mintage | VF20 | XF40 | MS60 | MS63 | MS65 |
|---|---|---|---|---|---|---|
| 2009 | — | — | — | — | 3.00 | 5.00 |

**KM# 952 5 DOLLARS**
31.11 g., Copper-Nickel Silver plated **Rev:** John Adams multicolor applique

| Date | Mintage | VF20 | XF40 | MS60 | MS63 | MS65 |
|---|---|---|---|---|---|---|
| 2009 | — | — | — | — | 3.00 | 5.00 |

**KM# 953 5 DOLLARS**
31.11 g., Copper-Nickel Silver plated **Rev:** Thomas Jefferson multicolor applique

| Date | Mintage | VF20 | XF40 | MS60 | MS63 | MS65 |
|---|---|---|---|---|---|---|
| 2009 | — | — | — | — | 3.00 | 5.00 |

**KM# 954 5 DOLLARS**
31.11 g., Copper-Nickel Silver plated **Rev:** James Madison multicolor applique

| Date | Mintage | VF20 | XF40 | MS60 | MS63 | MS65 |
|---|---|---|---|---|---|---|
| 2009 | — | — | — | — | 3.00 | 5.00 |

**KM# 955 5 DOLLARS**
31.11 g., Copper-Nickel Silver plated **Rev:** James Monroe multicolor applique

| Date | Mintage | VF20 | XF40 | MS60 | MS63 | MS65 |
|---|---|---|---|---|---|---|
| 2009 | — | — | — | — | 3.00 | 5.00 |

**KM# 956 5 DOLLARS**
31.11 g., Copper-Nickel Silver plated **Rev:** John Quincey Adams multicolor applique

| Date | Mintage | VF20 | XF40 | MS60 | MS63 | MS65 |
|---|---|---|---|---|---|---|
| 2009 | — | — | — | — | 3.00 | 5.00 |

**KM# 957 5 DOLLARS**
31.11 g., Copper-Nickel Silver plated **Rev:** Andrew Jackson multicolor applique

| Date | Mintage | VF20 | XF40 | MS60 | MS63 | MS65 |
|---|---|---|---|---|---|---|
| 2009 | — | — | — | — | 3.00 | 5.00 |

**KM# 958 5 DOLLARS**
31.11 g., Copper-Nickel Silver plated **Rev:** Martin van Buren multicolor applique

| Date | Mintage | VF20 | XF40 | MS60 | MS63 | MS65 |
|---|---|---|---|---|---|---|
| 2009 | — | — | — | — | 3.00 | 5.00 |

**KM# 959 5 DOLLARS**
31.11 g., Copper-Nickel Silver plated **Rev:** William Henry Harrison multicolor applique

| Date | Mintage | VF20 | XF40 | MS60 | MS63 | MS65 |
|---|---|---|---|---|---|---|
| 2009 | — | — | — | — | 3.00 | 5.00 |

**KM# 960 5 DOLLARS**
31.11 g., Copper-Nickel Silver plated **Rev:** John Tyler multicolor applique

| Date | Mintage | VF20 | XF40 | MS60 | MS63 | MS65 |
|---|---|---|---|---|---|---|
| 2009 | — | — | — | — | 3.00 | 5.00 |

**KM# 961 5 DOLLARS**
31.11 g., Copper-Nickel Silver plated **Rev:** James K. Polk multicolor applique

| Date | Mintage | VF20 | XF40 | MS60 | MS63 | MS65 |
|---|---|---|---|---|---|---|
| 2009 | — | — | — | — | 3.00 | 5.00 |

**KM# 962 5 DOLLARS**
31.11 g., Copper-Nickel Silver plated **Rev:** Zachary Taylor multicolor applique

| Date | Mintage | VF20 | XF40 | MS60 | MS63 | MS65 |
|---|---|---|---|---|---|---|
| 2009 | — | — | — | — | 3.00 | 5.00 |

**KM# 963 5 DOLLARS**
31.11 g., Copper-Nickel Silver plated **Rev:** Millard Filmore multicolor applique

| Date | Mintage | VF20 | XF40 | MS60 | MS63 | MS65 |
|---|---|---|---|---|---|---|
| 2009 | — | — | — | — | 3.00 | 5.00 |

**KM# 964 5 DOLLARS**
31.11 g., Copper-Nickel Silver plated **Rev:** Franklin Pierce multicolor applique

| Date | Mintage | VF20 | XF40 | MS60 | MS63 | MS65 |
|---|---|---|---|---|---|---|
| 2009 | — | — | — | — | 3.00 | 5.00 |

**KM# 965 5 DOLLARS**
31.11 g., Copper-Nickel Silver plated **Rev:** James Buchanan multicolor applique

| Date | Mintage | VF20 | XF40 | MS60 | MS63 | MS65 |
|---|---|---|---|---|---|---|
| 2009 | — | — | — | — | 3.00 | 5.00 |

**KM# 966 5 DOLLARS**
31.11 g., Copper-Nickel Silver plated **Rev:** Abraham Lincoln multicolor applique

| Date | Mintage | VF20 | XF40 | MS60 | MS63 | MS65 |
|---|---|---|---|---|---|---|
| 2009 | — | — | — | — | 3.00 | 5.00 |
| 2009 | — | — | — | — | 3.00 | 5.00 |

**KM# 967 5 DOLLARS**
31.11 g., Copper-Nickel Silver plated **Rev:** Andrew Johnson multicolor applique

| Date | Mintage | VF20 | XF40 | MS60 | MS63 | MS65 |
|---|---|---|---|---|---|---|
| 2009 | — | — | — | — | 3.00 | 5.00 |

**KM# 968 5 DOLLARS**
31.11 g., Copper-Nickel Silver plated **Rev:** Ulysses S. Grant multicolor applique

| Date | Mintage | VF20 | XF40 | MS60 | MS63 | MS65 |
|---|---|---|---|---|---|---|
| 2009 | — | — | — | — | 3.00 | 5.00 |

**KM# 969 5 DOLLARS**
31.11 g., Copper-Nickel Silver plated **Rev:** Rutherford B. Hayes multicolor applique

| Date | Mintage | VF20 | XF40 | MS60 | MS63 | MS65 |
|---|---|---|---|---|---|---|
| 2009 | — | — | — | — | 3.00 | 5.00 |

**KM# 970 5 DOLLARS**
31.11 g., Copper-Nickel Silver plated **Rev:** James A. Garfield multicolor applique

| Date | Mintage | VF20 | XF40 | MS60 | MS63 | MS65 |
|---|---|---|---|---|---|---|
| 2009 | — | — | — | — | 3.00 | 5.00 |

**KM# 971 5 DOLLARS**
31.11 g., Copper-Nickel Silver plated **Rev:** Chester Arthur multicolor underprint

| Date | Mintage | VF20 | XF40 | MS60 | MS63 | MS65 |
|---|---|---|---|---|---|---|
| 2009 | — | — | — | — | 3.00 | 5.00 |

**KM# 972 5 DOLLARS**
31.11 g., Copper-Nickel Silver plated **Rev:** Grover Cleveland multicolor applique

| Date | Mintage | VF20 | XF40 | MS60 | MS63 | MS65 |
|---|---|---|---|---|---|---|
| 2009 | — | — | — | — | 3.00 | 5.00 |

**KM# 973 5 DOLLARS**
31.11 g., Copper-Nickel Silver plated **Rev:** Benjamin Harrison multicolor applique

| Date | Mintage | VF20 | XF40 | MS60 | MS63 | MS65 |
|---|---|---|---|---|---|---|
| 2009 | — | — | — | — | 3.00 | 5.00 |

**KM# 974 5 DOLLARS**
31.11 g., Copper-Nickel Silver plated **Rev:** William McKinley multicolor applique

| Date | Mintage | VF20 | XF40 | MS60 | MS63 | MS65 |
|---|---|---|---|---|---|---|
| 2009 | — | — | — | — | 3.00 | 5.00 |

**KM# 975 5 DOLLARS**
31.11 g., Copper-Nickel Silver plated **Rev:** Theodore Roosevelt multicolor applique

| Date | Mintage | VF20 | XF40 | MS60 | MS63 | MS65 |
|---|---|---|---|---|---|---|
| 2009 | — | — | — | — | 3.00 | 5.00 |

**KM# 976 5 DOLLARS**
31.11 g., Copper-Nickel Silver plated **Rev:** William Howard Taft multicolor applique

| Date | Mintage | VF20 | XF40 | MS60 | MS63 | MS65 |
|---|---|---|---|---|---|---|
| 2009 | — | — | — | — | 3.00 | 5.00 |

### KM# 977 5 DOLLARS

31.11 g., Copper-Nickel Silver plated **Rev:** Woodrow Wilson multicolor applique

| Date | Mintage | VF20 | XF40 | MS60 | MS63 | MS65 |
|---|---|---|---|---|---|---|
| 2009 | — | — | — | — | 3.00 | 5.00 |

### KM# 978 5 DOLLARS

31.11 g., Copper-Nickel Silver plated **Rev:** Warren G. Harding multicolor applique

| Date | Mintage | VF20 | XF40 | MS60 | MS63 | MS65 |
|---|---|---|---|---|---|---|
| 2009 | — | — | — | — | 3.00 | 5.00 |

### KM# 979 5 DOLLARS

31.11 g., Copper-Nickel Silver plated **Rev:** Calvin Collidge multicolor applique

| Date | Mintage | VF20 | XF40 | MS60 | MS63 | MS65 |
|---|---|---|---|---|---|---|
| 2009 | — | — | — | — | 3.00 | 5.00 |

### KM# 980 5 DOLLARS

31.11 g., Copper-Nickel Silver plated **Rev:** Herbert Hoover multicolor applique

| Date | Mintage | VF20 | XF40 | MS60 | MS63 | MS65 |
|---|---|---|---|---|---|---|
| 2009 | — | — | — | — | 3.00 | 5.00 |

### KM# 981 5 DOLLARS

31.11 g., Copper-Nickel Silver plated **Rev:** Franklin D. Roosevelt multicolor applique

| Date | Mintage | VF20 | XF40 | MS60 | MS63 | MS65 |
|---|---|---|---|---|---|---|
| 2009 | — | — | — | — | 3.00 | 5.00 |

### KM# 982 5 DOLLARS

31.11 g., Copper-Nickel Silver plated **Rev:** Harry S Truman multicolor applique

| Date | Mintage | VF20 | XF40 | MS60 | MS63 | MS65 |
|---|---|---|---|---|---|---|
| 2009 | — | — | — | — | 3.00 | 5.00 |

### KM# 983 5 DOLLARS

31.11 g., Copper-Nickel Silver plated **Rev:** Swight D. Eisenhower multicolor applique

| Date | Mintage | VF20 | XF40 | MS60 | MS63 | MS65 |
|---|---|---|---|---|---|---|
| 2009 | — | — | — | — | 3.00 | 5.00 |

### KM# 984 5 DOLLARS

31.11 g., Copper-Nickel Silver plated **Rev:** John F. Kennedy multicolor applique

| Date | Mintage | VF20 | XF40 | MS60 | MS63 | MS65 |
|---|---|---|---|---|---|---|
| 2009 | — | — | — | — | 3.00 | 5.00 |

### KM# 985 5 DOLLARS

31.11 g., Copper-Nickel Silver plated **Rev:** Lyndon B. Johnson multicolor applique

| Date | Mintage | VF20 | XF40 | MS60 | MS63 | MS65 |
|---|---|---|---|---|---|---|
| 2009 | — | — | — | — | 3.00 | 5.00 |

### KM# 986 5 DOLLARS

31.11 g., Copper-Nickel Silver plated **Rev:** Richard M. Nixon multicolor applique

| Date | Mintage | VF20 | XF40 | MS60 | MS63 | MS65 |
|---|---|---|---|---|---|---|
| 2009 | — | — | — | — | 3.00 | 5.00 |

### KM# 987 5 DOLLARS

31.11 g., Copper-Nickel Silver plated **Rev:** Gerald R. Ford multicolor applique

| Date | Mintage | VF20 | XF40 | MS60 | MS63 | MS65 |
|---|---|---|---|---|---|---|
| 2009 | — | — | — | — | 3.00 | 5.00 |

### KM# 988 5 DOLLARS

31.11 g., Copper-Nickel Silver plated **Rev:** Jimmy Carter multicolor applique

| Date | Mintage | VF20 | XF40 | MS60 | MS63 | MS65 |
|---|---|---|---|---|---|---|
| 2009 | — | — | — | — | 3.00 | 5.00 |

### KM# 989 5 DOLLARS

31.11 g., Copper-Nickel Silver plated **Rev:** Ronald Reagan multicolor applique

| Date | Mintage | VF20 | XF40 | MS60 | MS63 | MS65 |
|---|---|---|---|---|---|---|
| 2009 | — | — | — | — | 3.00 | 5.00 |

### KM# 990 5 DOLLARS

31.11 g., Copper-Nickel Silver plated **Rev:** George H. W. Bush multicolor applique

| Date | Mintage | VF20 | XF40 | MS60 | MS63 | MS65 |
|---|---|---|---|---|---|---|
| 2009 | — | — | — | — | 3.00 | 5.00 |

### KM# 991 5 DOLLARS

31.11 g., Copper-Nickel Silver plated **Rev:** Bill Clinton multicolor applique

| Date | Mintage | VF20 | XF40 | MS60 | MS63 | MS65 |
|---|---|---|---|---|---|---|
| 2009 | — | — | — | — | 3.00 | 5.00 |

### KM# 992 5 DOLLARS

31.11 g., Copper-Nickel Silver plated **Rev:** George W. Bush multicolor applique

| Date | Mintage | VF20 | XF40 | MS60 | MS63 | MS65 |
|---|---|---|---|---|---|---|
| 2009 | — | — | — | — | 3.00 | 5.00 |

### KM# 993 5 DOLLARS

31.11 g., Copper-Nickel Silver plated **Rev:** Barack Obama multicolor applique

| Date | Mintage | VF20 | XF40 | MS60 | MS63 | MS65 |
|---|---|---|---|---|---|---|
| 2009 | — | — | — | — | 3.00 | 5.00 |

### KM# 1023 5 DOLLARS

28.28 g., 0.999 Silver 0.9083 oz. ASW, 38.6 mm. **Obv:** National arms **Rev:** Saint standing at center, 12 segments of artibutes around

| Date | Mintage | VF20 | XF40 | MS60 | MS63 | MS65 |
|---|---|---|---|---|---|---|
| 2009 | — | PF63 32.00 | PF65 37.00 | | | |

### KM# 997 5 DOLLARS

28.28 g., 0.999 Silver 0.9083 oz. ASW, 38.6 mm. **Obv:** National arms **Rev:** Kremlin - Tsar Canon, gilt shield

| Date | Mintage | VF20 | XF40 | MS60 | MS63 | MS65 |
|---|---|---|---|---|---|---|
| 2011 | — | PF65 90.00 | | | | |

### KM# 998 5 DOLLARS

28.28 g., 0.999 Silver 0.9083 oz. ASW, 38.6 mm. **Obv:** National arms **Rev:** Kremlin - Tsar bell, gilt shield

| Date | Mintage | VF20 | XF40 | MS60 | MS63 | MS65 |
|---|---|---|---|---|---|---|
| 2011 | — | PF65 90.00 | | | | |

### KM# 999 5 DOLLARS

28.28 g., 0.999 Silver 0.9083 oz. ASW, 38.6 mm. **Obv:** National arms **Rev:** Kremlin - Golden Cap, gilt shield

| Date | Mintage | VF20 | XF40 | MS60 | MS63 | MS65 |
|---|---|---|---|---|---|---|
| 2011 | — | PF65 90.00 | | | | |

### KM# 1000 5 DOLLARS

28.28 g., 0.999 Silver 0.9083 oz. ASW, 38.6 mm. **Obv:** National arms **Rev:** Kremlin - Palace, gilt shield

| Date | Mintage | VF20 | XF40 | MS60 | MS63 | MS65 |
|---|---|---|---|---|---|---|
| 2011 | — | PF65 90.00 | | | | |

### KM# 1001 5 DOLLARS

28.28 g., 0.999 Silver 0.9083 oz. ASW, 38.6 mm. **Obv:** National arms **Rev:** Kremlin - Uspenski Cathedral, gilt shield

| Date | Mintage | VF20 | XF40 | MS60 | MS63 | MS65 |
|---|---|---|---|---|---|---|
| 2011 | — | PF65 90.00 | | | | |

### KM# 1002 5 DOLLARS

28.28 g., 0.999 Silver 0.9083 oz. ASW, 38.6 mm. **Obv:** National arms **Rev:** Kremlin - Spasski tower, gilt shield

| Date | Mintage | VF20 | XF40 | MS60 | MS63 | MS65 |
|---|---|---|---|---|---|---|
| 2011 | — | PF65 90.00 | | | | |

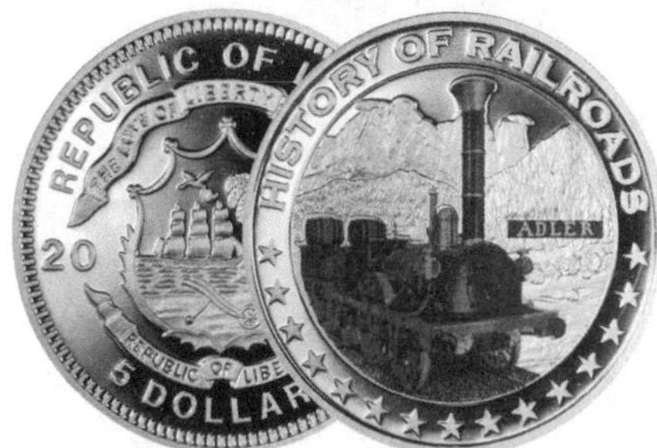


### KM# 1010 5 DOLLARS

20.00 g., 0.999 Silver 0.6424 oz. ASW, 38.6 mm. **Subject:** Trains **Obv:** National arms **Rev:** Adler in color

| Date | Mintage | VF20 | XF40 | MS60 | MS63 | MS65 |
|---|---|---|---|---|---|---|
| 2011 | — | PF65 70.00 | | | | |

**KM# 1011 5 DOLLARS**
20.00 g., 0.999 Silver 0.6424 oz. ASW, 38.6 mm. **Subject:** Trains **Obv:** National arms **Rev:** KKSTB 310.23

| Date | Mintage | VF20 | XF40 | MS60 | MS63 | MS65 |
|---|---|---|---|---|---|---|
| 2011 | — | PF65 70.00 | | | | |

**KM# 1012 5 DOLLARS**
20.00 g., 0.999 Silver 0.6424 oz. ASW, 38.6 mm. **Subject:** Trains **Obv:** National arms **Rev:** Mallard locomotive in color

| Date | Mintage | VF20 | XF40 | MS60 | MS63 | MS65 |
|---|---|---|---|---|---|---|
| 2011 | — | PF65 70.00 | | | | |

**KM# 1013 5 DOLLARS**
20.00 g., 0.999 Silver 0.6424 oz. ASW, 38.6 mm. **Subject:** Trains **Obv:** National arms **Rev:** Flying Scottsman locomotive in color

| Date | Mintage | VF20 | XF40 | MS60 | MS63 | MS65 |
|---|---|---|---|---|---|---|
| 2011 | — | PF65 70.00 | | | | |

**KM# 1014 5 DOLLARS**
20.00 g., 0.999 Silver 0.6424 oz. ASW, 38.6 mm. **Subject:** Trains **Obv:** National arms **Rev:** Trans-Siberian Express in color

| Date | Mintage | VF20 | XF40 | MS60 | MS63 | MS65 |
|---|---|---|---|---|---|---|
| 2011 | — | PF65 70.00 | | | | |

**KM# 1015 5 DOLLARS**
20.00 g., 0.999 Silver 0.6424 oz. ASW, 38.6 mm. **Subject:** Trains **Obv:** National arms **Rev:** Blue Train in color

| Date | Mintage | VF20 | XF40 | MS60 | MS63 | MS65 |
|---|---|---|---|---|---|---|
| 2011 | — | PF65 70.00 | | | | |

**KM# 491 10 DOLLARS**
25.25 g., 0.925 Silver 0.7509 oz. ASW, 36.8 mm. **Subject:** Illusion **Obv:** National arms **Rev:** Styilized head with glasses facing **Edge:** Plain **Shape:** 10-sided

| Date | Mintage | VF20 | XF40 | MS60 | MS63 | MS65 |
|---|---|---|---|---|---|---|
| 2001 | 5,000 | PF63 30.00 | PF65 32.00 | | | |

**KM# 493 10 DOLLARS**
770.00 g., Copper, 100 mm. **Subject:** Wreck of the Princess Louisa **Obv:** National arms **Rev:** Sailing ship **Edge:** Reeded **Note:** Illustration reduced. With an encased glass shard recovered from the wreck site of the Princess Louisa.

| Date | Mintage | VF20 | XF40 | MS60 | MS63 | MS65 |
|---|---|---|---|---|---|---|
| 2001 | 2,000 | — | — | — | — | 225 |

**KM# 510 10 DOLLARS**
33.24 g., Copper Gilt, 40.1 mm. **Obv:** National arms **Rev:** Multicolor holographic bald eagle **Edge:** Reeded

| Date | Mintage | VF20 | XF40 | MS60 | MS63 | MS65 |
|---|---|---|---|---|---|---|
| 2001 | 20,000 | — | — | — | — | 32.00 |

**KM# 513 10 DOLLARS**
28.50 g., Copper-Nickel, 38.6 mm. **Series:** Moments of Freedom **Subject:** Hungarian Revolution of 1848 **Obv:** National arms **Rev:** Multicolor heroic scene **Edge:** Reeded

| Date | Mintage | VF20 | XF40 | MS60 | MS63 | MS65 |
|---|---|---|---|---|---|---|
| 2001 | 9,999 | PF65 12.00 | | | | |

**KM# 537 10 DOLLARS**
28.50 g., Copper-Nickel, 38.6 mm. **Subject:** Moments of Freedom **Obv:** National arms **Rev:** Multicolor Buddha, spelled "Budha" on the coin **Edge:** Reeded

| Date | Mintage | VF20 | XF40 | MS60 | MS63 | MS65 |
|---|---|---|---|---|---|---|
| 2001 | — | PF65 12.00 | | | | |

**KM# 538 10 DOLLARS**
28.50 g., Copper-Nickel, 38.6 mm. **Subject:** Moments of Freedom **Obv:** National arms **Rev:** Multicolor Battle of Marathon scene **Edge:** Reeded

| Date | Mintage | VF20 | XF40 | MS60 | MS63 | MS65 |
|---|---|---|---|---|---|---|
| 2001 | — | PF65 12.00 | | | | |

**KM# 539 10 DOLLARS**
28.50 g., Copper-Nickel, 38.6 mm. **Series:** Moments of Freedom **Obv:** National arms **Rev:** Multicolor founding of Liberia design **Edge:** Reeded

| Date | Mintage | VF20 | XF40 | MS60 | MS63 | MS65 |
|---|---|---|---|---|---|---|
| 2001 | — | **PF65** 12.00 | | | | |

**KM# 540 10 DOLLARS**
28.50 g., Copper-Nickel, 38.6 mm. **Series:** Moments of Freedom **Obv:** National arms **Rev:** Multicolor portrait of Constantine I **Edge:** Reeded

| Date | Mintage | VF20 | XF40 | MS60 | MS63 | MS65 |
|---|---|---|---|---|---|---|
| 2001 | — | **PF65** 12.00 | | | | |

**KM# 541 10 DOLLARS**
28.50 g., Copper-Nickel, 38.6 mm. **Series:** Moments of Freedom **Obv:** National arms **Rev:** Multicolor William Tell statue **Edge:** Reeded

| Date | Mintage | VF20 | XF40 | MS60 | MS63 | MS65 |
|---|---|---|---|---|---|---|
| 2001 | — | **PF65** 12.00 | | | | |

**KM# 542 10 DOLLARS**
28.50 g., Copper-Nickel, 38.6 mm. **Series:** Moments of Freedom **Obv:** National arms **Rev:** Multicolor bust facing **Edge:** Reeded

| Date | Mintage | VF20 | XF40 | MS60 | MS63 | MS65 |
|---|---|---|---|---|---|---|
| 2001 | — | **PF65** 12.00 | | | | |

**KM# 543 10 DOLLARS**
28.50 g., Copper-Nickel, 38.6 mm. **Series:** Moments of Freedom **Obv:** National arms **Rev:** Multicolor head with headdress and battle scene **Edge:** Reeded

| Date | Mintage | VF20 | XF40 | MS60 | MS63 | MS65 |
|---|---|---|---|---|---|---|
| 2001 | — | **PF65** 12.00 | | | | |

**KM# 544 10 DOLLARS**
28.50 g., Copper-Nickel, 38.6 mm. **Series:** Moments of Freedom **Obv:** National arms **Rev:** Multicolor Brandenburg Gate scene **Edge:** Reeded

| Date | Mintage | VF20 | XF40 | MS60 | MS63 | MS65 |
|---|---|---|---|---|---|---|
| 2001 | — | **PF65** 12.00 | | | | |

**KM# 545 10 DOLLARS**
28.50 g., Copper-Nickel, 38.6 mm. **Series:** Moments of Freedom **Obv:** National arms **Rev:** Multicolor half length figure facing **Edge:** Reeded

| Date | Mintage | VF20 | XF40 | MS60 | MS63 | MS65 |
|---|---|---|---|---|---|---|
| 2001 | — | **PF65** 12.00 | | | | |

**KM# 546 10 DOLLARS**
28.50 g., Copper-Nickel, 38.6 mm. **Series:** Moments of Freedom **Obv:** National arms **Rev:** Multicolor Sitting Bull portrait **Edge:** Reeded

| Date | Mintage | VF20 | XF40 | MS60 | MS63 | MS65 |
|---|---|---|---|---|---|---|
| 2001 | — | **PF65** 12.00 | | | | |

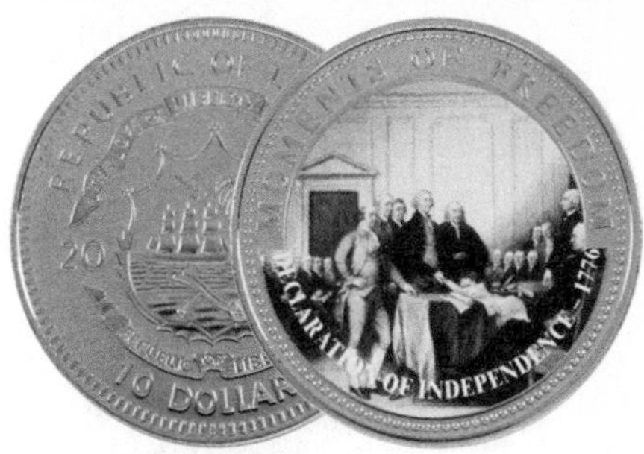

**KM# 547 10 DOLLARS**
28.50 g., Copper-Nickel, 38.6 mm. **Series:** Moments of Freedom **Obv:** National arms **Rev:** Multicolor Declaration of Independence scene **Edge:** Reeded

| Date | Mintage | VF20 | XF40 | MS60 | MS63 | MS65 |
|---|---|---|---|---|---|---|
| 2001 | — | **PF65** 12.00 | | | | |

**KM# 548 10 DOLLARS**
28.50 g., Copper-Nickel, 38.6 mm. **Series:** Moments of Freedom **Obv:** National arms **Rev:** Multicolor allegorical woman **Edge:** Reeded

| Date | Mintage | VF20 | XF40 | MS60 | MS63 | MS65 |
|---|---|---|---|---|---|---|
| 2001 | — | **PF65** 12.00 | | | | |

**KM# 549 10 DOLLARS**
28.50 g., Copper-Nickel, 38.6 mm. **Series:** Moments of Freedom **Obv:** National arms **Rev:** Multicolor bust of Gandhi looking down **Edge:** Reeded

| Date | Mintage | VF20 | XF40 | MS60 | MS63 | MS65 |
|---|---|---|---|---|---|---|
| 2001 | — | **PF65** 12.00 | | | | |

**KM# 550 10 DOLLARS**
28.50 g., Copper-Nickel, 38.6 mm. **Series:** Moments of Freedom **Obv:** National arms **Rev:** Multicolor picture of a soldier at the moment he is shot in battle **Edge:** Reeded

| Date | Mintage | VF20 | XF40 | MS60 | MS63 | MS65 |
|---|---|---|---|---|---|---|
| 2001 | — | **PF65** 12.00 | | | | |

### KM# 551 10 DOLLARS

28.50 g., Copper-Nickel, 38.6 mm. **Series:** Moments of Freedom **Obv:** National arms **Rev:** Multicolor inmates behind wire fence scene **Edge:** Reeded

| Date | Mintage | VF20 | XF40 | MS60 | MS63 | MS65 |
|---|---|---|---|---|---|---|
| 2001 | — | PF65 12.00 | | | | |

### KM# 552 10 DOLLARS

28.50 g., Copper-Nickel, 38.6 mm. **Series:** Moments of Freedom **Obv:** National arms **Rev:** Multicolor Iwo Jima flag raising scene **Edge:** Reeded

| Date | Mintage | VF20 | XF40 | MS60 | MS63 | MS65 |
|---|---|---|---|---|---|---|
| 2001 | — | PF65 12.00 | | | | |

### KM# 553 10 DOLLARS

28.50 g., Copper-Nickel, 38.6 mm. **Series:** Moments of Freedom **Obv:** National arms **Rev:** Multicolor UN logo and dove **Edge:** Reeded

| Date | Mintage | VF20 | XF40 | MS60 | MS63 | MS65 |
|---|---|---|---|---|---|---|
| 2001 | — | PF65 12.00 | | | | |

### KM# 554 10 DOLLARS

28.50 g., Copper-Nickel, 38.6 mm. **Series:** Moments of Freedom **Obv:** National arms **Rev:** Multicolor Solzhenitsyn portrait **Edge:** Reeded

| Date | Mintage | VF20 | XF40 | MS60 | MS63 | MS65 |
|---|---|---|---|---|---|---|
| 2001 | — | PF65 12.00 | | | | |

### KM# 555 10 DOLLARS

28.50 g., Copper-Nickel, 38.6 mm. **Series:** Moments of Freedom **Obv:** National arms **Rev:** Multicolor Spartacus and troops **Edge:** Reeded

| Date | Mintage | VF20 | XF40 | MS60 | MS63 | MS65 |
|---|---|---|---|---|---|---|
| 2001 | — | PF65 12.00 | | | | |

### KM# 556 10 DOLLARS

28.50 g., Copper-Nickel, 38.6 mm. **Series:** Moments of Freedom **Obv:** National arms **Rev:** Multicolor Soviet tank in Prague **Edge:** Reeded

| Date | Mintage | VF20 | XF40 | MS60 | MS63 | MS65 |
|---|---|---|---|---|---|---|
| 2001 | — | PF65 12.00 | | | | |

### KM# 557 10 DOLLARS

28.50 g., Copper-Nickel, 38.6 mm. **Series:** Moments of Freedom **Obv:** National arms **Rev:** Multicolor Bastille scene **Edge:** Reeded

| Date | Mintage | VF20 | XF40 | MS60 | MS63 | MS65 |
|---|---|---|---|---|---|---|
| 2001 | — | PF65 12.00 | | | | |

### KM# 558 10 DOLLARS

28.50 g., Copper-Nickel, 38.6 mm. **Series:** Moments of Freedom **Obv:** National arms **Rev:** Multicolor Nelson Mandela and fist **Edge:** Reeded

| Date | Mintage | VF20 | XF40 | MS60 | MS63 | MS65 |
|---|---|---|---|---|---|---|
| 2001 | — | PF65 12.00 | | | | |

### KM# 559 10 DOLLARS

28.50 g., Copper-Nickel, 38.6 mm. **Series:** Moments of Freedom **Obv:** National arms **Rev:** Multicolor circuit board and world globe **Edge:** Reeded

| Date | Mintage | VF20 | XF40 | MS60 | MS63 | MS65 |
|---|---|---|---|---|---|---|
| 2001 | — | PF65 12.00 | | | | |

### KM# 777 10 DOLLARS

14.55 g., Copper-Nickel, 32 mm. **Subject:** 43rd President of USA **Obv:** National arms **Obv. Legend:** REPUBLIC OF LIBERIA **Rev:** George W. Bush, flag in background

| Date | Mintage | VF20 | XF40 | MS60 | MS63 | MS65 |
|---|---|---|---|---|---|---|
| 2001 | — | PF65 12.00 | | | | |

### KM# 822 10 DOLLARS

1.24 g., Gold, 13.68 mm. **Obv:** National arms **Rev:** Bust of Marlene Dietrich facing **Edge:** Reeded

| Date | Mintage | VF20 | XF40 | MS60 | MS63 | MS65 |
|---|---|---|---|---|---|---|
| 2001 | — | PF65 75.00 | | | | |

### KM# 994 10 DOLLARS

0.999 Gold, 12 mm. **Obv:** National Arms **Rev:** Franklin, Jefferson, Adams and Declaration of Independence

| Date | Mintage | VF20 | XF40 | MS60 | MS63 | MS65 |
|---|---|---|---|---|---|---|
| 2001 | — | PF65 70.00 | | | | |

### KM# 654 10 DOLLARS

15.33 g., Copper-Nickel, 33.2 mm. **Obv:** National arms **Rev:** GEORGE W. BUSH..." No value at bottom **Edge:** Reeded

| Date | Mintage | VF20 | XF40 | MS60 | MS63 | MS65 |
|---|---|---|---|---|---|---|
| 2002 | — | — | — | — | 5.00 | 7.00 |

### KM# 705 10 DOLLARS

31.10 g., 0.999 Silver 0.999 oz. ASW, 38.6 mm. **Subject:** 2002 World Football Championship - Japan - South Korea **Obv:** National arms **Rev:** Pagoda superimposed on a soccer ball, legend around **Edge:** Reeded

| Date | Mintage | VF20 | XF40 | MS60 | MS63 | MS65 |
|---|---|---|---|---|---|---|
| 2002 | — | PF65 45.00 | | | | |

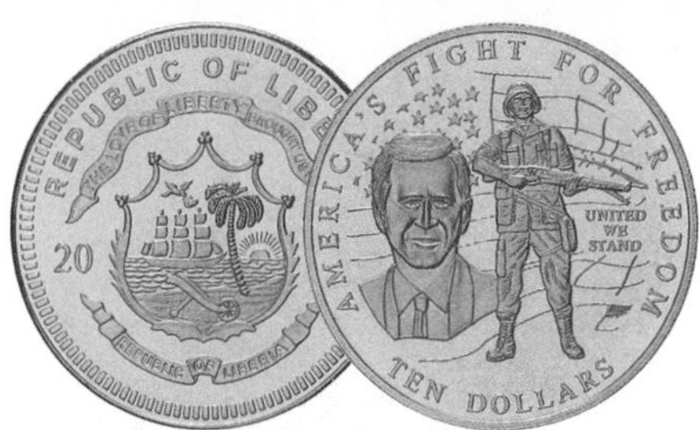

**KM# 806 10 DOLLARS**
14.30 g., Copper-Nickel, 33.11 mm. **Obv:** National arms **Rev:** Bust of President Bush facing at left, soldier standing at right facing, flag in background **Rev. Legend:** America's Fight For Freedom **Edge:** Reeded

| Date | Mintage | VF20 | XF40 | MS60 | MS63 | MS65 |
|---|---|---|---|---|---|---|
| 2002 | — | — | — | — | 5.00 | 7.00 |

**KM# 1016 10 DOLLARS**
Copper-Nickel **Obv:** National arms **Rev:** San Francisco cablecar hologram

| Date | Mintage | VF20 | XF40 | MS60 | MS63 | MS65 |
|---|---|---|---|---|---|---|
| 2002 | — | PF63 30.00 | PF65 35.00 | | | |

**KM# 602 10 DOLLARS**
25.00 g., 0.925 Silver 0.7435 oz. ASW, 38.6 mm. **Obv:** National arms **Rev:** Icarus and Daedalus in flight **Edge:** Reeded

| Date | Mintage | VF20 | XF40 | MS60 | MS63 | MS65 |
|---|---|---|---|---|---|---|
| 2003 | — | PF63 30.00 | PF65 35.00 | | | |

**KM# 603 10 DOLLARS**
25.00 g., 0.925 Silver 0.7435 oz. ASW, 38.6 mm. **Obv:** National arms **Rev:** First parachute **Edge:** Reeded

| Date | Mintage | VF20 | XF40 | MS60 | MS63 | MS65 |
|---|---|---|---|---|---|---|
| 2003 | — | PF63 30.00 | PF65 35.00 | | | |

**KM# 604 10 DOLLARS**
25.00 g., 0.925 Silver 0.7435 oz. ASW, 38.6 mm. **Obv:** National arms **Rev:** Montgolfier ballon **Edge:** Reeded

| Date | Mintage | VF20 | XF40 | MS60 | MS63 | MS65 |
|---|---|---|---|---|---|---|
| 2003 | — | PF63 30.00 | PF65 35.00 | | | |

**KM# 605 10 DOLLARS**
25.00 g., 0.925 Silver 0.7435 oz. ASW, 38.6 mm. **Obv:** National arms **Rev:** Otto v. Lillenthal **Edge:** Reeded

| Date | Mintage | VF20 | XF40 | MS60 | MS63 | MS65 |
|---|---|---|---|---|---|---|
| 2003 | — | PF63 30.00 | PF65 35.00 | | | |

**KM# 606 10 DOLLARS**
25.00 g., 0.925 Silver 0.7435 oz. ASW, 38.6 mm. **Obv:** National arms **Rev:** Wright Brothers **Edge:** Reeded

| Date | Mintage | VF20 | XF40 | MS60 | MS63 | MS65 |
|---|---|---|---|---|---|---|
| 2003 | — | PF63 30.00 | PF65 35.00 | | | |

**KM# 607 10 DOLLARS**
25.00 g., 0.925 Silver 0.7435 oz. ASW, 38.6 mm. **Obv:** National arms **Rev:** Mach 1- Bell X **Edge:** Reeded

| Date | Mintage | VF20 | XF40 | MS60 | MS63 | MS65 |
|---|---|---|---|---|---|---|
| 2003 | — | PF63 30.00 | PF65 35.00 | | | |

**KM# 608 10 DOLLARS**
25.00 g., 0.925 Silver 0.7435 oz. ASW, 38.6 mm. **Obv:** National arms **Rev:** The Concorde **Edge:** Reeded

| Date | Mintage | VF20 | XF40 | MS60 | MS63 | MS65 |
|---|---|---|---|---|---|---|
| 2003 | — | PF63 30.00 | PF65 35.00 | | | |

**KM# 708 10 DOLLARS**
25.10 g., 0.925 Silver 0.7465 oz. ASW, 38.6 mm. **Obv:** National arms **Rev:** Clipper ship "Flying Cloud **Edge:** Reeded

| Date | Mintage | VF20 | XF40 | MS60 | MS63 | MS65 |
|---|---|---|---|---|---|---|
| 2003 | — | PF65 35.00 | | | | |

**KM# 807 10 DOLLARS**
26.30 g., Copper-Nickel, 40.36 mm. **Subject:** America's First Ladies **Obv:** National arms **Rev:** Bust of Jacqueline Kennedy facing, small oval portrait of President John F. Kennedy at right **Edge:** Reeded

| Date | Mintage | VF20 | XF40 | MS60 | MS63 | MS65 |
|---|---|---|---|---|---|---|
| 2003 | — | PF65 15.00 | | | | |

**KM# 824 10 DOLLARS**
14.60 g., Copper-Nickel, 33 mm. **Subject:** Abraham Lincoln **Obv:** National arms **Rev:** Bust facing at left, Lincoln Memorial in background **Edge:** Reeded

| Date | Mintage | VF20 | XF40 | MS60 | MS63 | MS65 |
|---|---|---|---|---|---|---|
| 2003 | 20,000 | PF65 12.00 | | | | |

**KM# 1030 10 DOLLARS**
Silver **Subject:** Hapag 1848 Deutschland **Rev:** Sailing ship left

| Date | Mintage | VF20 | XF40 | MS60 | MS63 | MS65 |
|---|---|---|---|---|---|---|
| 2003 | — | PF65 50.00 | | | | |

**KM# 611 10 DOLLARS**
62.21 g., 0.999 Silver 1.998 oz. ASW, 50 mm. **Obv:** National arms left of window design with Tiffany Glass inlay **Rev:** Window design with Tiffany Glass inlay **Edge:** Plain

| Date | Mintage | VF20 | XF40 | MS60 | MS63 | MS65 |
|---|---|---|---|---|---|---|
| 2004 | 999 | — | — | — | — | 200 |

**KM# 740 10 DOLLARS**
20.00 g., 0.999 Silver 0.6424 oz. ASW partially gilt, 38.00 mm. **Series:** Endangered Wildlife **Obv:** National arms **Obv. Legend:** REPUBLIC OF LIBERIA **Rev:** Gilt Siberian Tiger with diamonds inset in eyes **Rev. Legend:** RUSSIA **Edge:** Plain

| Date | Mintage | VF20 | XF40 | MS60 | MS63 | MS65 |
|---|---|---|---|---|---|---|
| 2004 | 5,000 | PF65 115 | | | | |

**KM# 741 10 DOLLARS**
20.00 g., 0.999 Silver 0.6424 oz. ASW partially gilt, 38.00 mm. **Series:** Endangered Wildlife **Obv:** National arms **Obv. Legend:** REPUBLIC OF LIBERIA **Rev:** Two gilt Hyacinth Macaws perched on branch with diamond insets in eyes **Rev. Legend:** BRAZIL **Edge:** Plain

| Date | Mintage | VF20 | XF40 | MS60 | MS63 | MS65 |
|---|---|---|---|---|---|---|
| 2004 | 5,000 | PF65 115 | | | | |

**KM# 742 10 DOLLARS**
20.00 g., 0.999 Silver 0.6424 oz. ASW partially gilt, 38.00 mm. **Series:** Endangered Wildlife **Obv:** National arms **Obv. Legend:** REPUBLIC OF LIBERIA **Rev:** Gilt young Giant Panda seated eating bamboo shoots **Rev. Legend:** CHINA **Edge:** Plain

| Date | Mintage | VF20 | XF40 | MS60 | MS63 | MS65 |
|---|---|---|---|---|---|---|
| 2004 | 5,000 | PF65 115 | | | | |

**KM# 743 10 DOLLARS**
20.00 g., 0.999 Silver 0.6424 oz. ASW partially gilt, 38.00 mm. **Subject:** Endangered Wildlife **Obv:** National arms **Obv. Legend:** REPUBLIC OF LIBERIA **Rev:** Two gilt Bald Eagles. one perched at left, one alighting at center right **Rev. Legend:** USA **Edge:** Plain

| Date | Mintage | VF20 | XF40 | MS60 | MS63 | MS65 |
|---|---|---|---|---|---|---|
| 2004 | 5,000 | PF65 115 | | | | |

**KM# 744 10 DOLLARS**
20.00 g., 0.999 Silver 0.6424 oz. ASW partially gilt, 38 mm. **Series:** Endangered Wildlife **Obv:** National arms **Obv. Legend:** REPUBLIC OF LIBERIA **Rev:** Gilt Puma standing with diamonds inset in eyes **Rev. Legend:** MEXICO **Edge:** Plain

| Date | Mintage | VF20 | XF40 | MS60 | MS63 | MS65 |
|---|---|---|---|---|---|---|
| 2004 | 5,000 | PF65 115 | | | | |

**KM# 745 10 DOLLARS**
20.00 g., 0.999 Silver 0.6424 oz. ASW partially gilt, 38 mm. **Series:** Endangered Wildlife **Obv:** National arms **Obv. Legend:** REPUBLIC OF LIBERIA **Rev:** Gilt Red-ruffed Lemur on branch with diamonds inset in eyes **Rev. Legend:** MADAGASCAR **Edge:** Plain

| Date | Mintage | VF20 | XF40 | MS60 | MS63 | MS65 |
|---|---|---|---|---|---|---|
| 2004 | 5,000 | PF65 115 | | | | |

**KM# 746 10 DOLLARS**
20.00 g., 0.999 Silver 0.6424 oz. ASW partially gilt, 38 mm. **Series:** Endangered Wildlife **Obv:** National arms **Obv. Legend:** REPUBLIC OF LIBERIA **Rev:** Two gilt Andean Condors, one lifting off at center, one perched at right **Rev. Legend:** CHILE **Edge:** Plain

| Date | Mintage | VF20 | XF40 | MS60 | MS63 | MS65 |
|---|---|---|---|---|---|---|
| 2004 | 5,000 | PF65 115 | | | | |

**KM# 747 10 DOLLARS**
20.00 g., 0.999 Silver 0.6424 oz. ASW partially gilt, 38 mm. **Series:** Endangered Wildlife **Obv:** National arms **Obv. Legend:** REPUBLIC OF LIBERIA **Rev:** Two gilt Yellow-eyed Penguins standing facing with diamonds inset in eyes **Rev. Legend:** NEW ZEALAND **Edge:** Plain

| Date | Mintage | VF20 | XF40 | MS60 | MS63 | MS65 |
|---|---|---|---|---|---|---|
| 2004 | 5,000 | PF65 115 | | | | |

**KM# 748 10 DOLLARS**
20.00 g., 0.999 Silver 0.6424 oz. ASW partially gilt, 38 mm. **Series:** Endangered Wildlife **Obv:** National arms **Obv. Legend:** REPUBLIC OF LIBERIA **Rev:** Gilt African lion standing facing with diamonds inset in eyes **Rev. Legend:** SOUTH AFRICA **Edge:** Plain

| Date | Mintage | VF20 | XF40 | MS60 | MS63 | MS65 |
|---|---|---|---|---|---|---|
| 2004 | 5,000 | PF65 115 | | | | |

**KM# 749 10 DOLLARS**
20.00 g., 0.999 Silver 0.6424 oz. ASW partially gilt, 38 mm. **Series:** Endangered Wildlife **Obv:** National arms **Obv. Legend:** REPUBLIC OF LIBERIA **Rev:** Two gilt perched Kookaburras with diamonds inset in eyes **Rev. Legend:** AUSTRALIA **Edge:** Plain

| Date | Mintage | VF20 | XF40 | MS60 | MS63 | MS65 |
|---|---|---|---|---|---|---|
| 2004 | 5,000 | PF65 115 | | | | |

**KM# 750 10 DOLLARS**
20.00 g., 0.999 Silver 0.6424 oz. ASW partially gilt, 38 mm. **Series:** Endangered Wildlife **Obv:** National arms **Obv. Legend:** REPUBLIC OF LIBERIA **Rev:** Gilt Polar Bear standing facing with diamonds inset in eyes **Rev. Legend:** CANADA **Edge:** Plain

| Date | Mintage | VF20 | XF40 | MS60 | MS63 | MS65 |
|---|---|---|---|---|---|---|
| 2004 | 5,000 | PF65 115 | | | | |

**KM# 751 10 DOLLARS**
20.00 g., 0.999 Silver 0.6424 oz. ASW partially gilt **Series:** Endangered Wildlife **Obv:** National arms **Obv. Legend:** REPUBLIC OF LIBERIA **Rev:** Gilt perched Blakiston's Fish-owl with diamonds inset in eyes **Rev. Legend:** JAPAN

| Date | Mintage | VF20 | XF40 | MS60 | MS63 | MS65 |
|---|---|---|---|---|---|---|
| 2004 | 5,000 | PF65 115 | | | | |

**KM# 808 10 DOLLARS**
14.58 g., Copper-Nickel, 32.98 mm. **Obv:** National arms **Rev:** Bust of President Ronald Reagon facing, flag in background **Edge:** Reeded

| Date | Mintage | VF20 | XF40 | MS60 | MS63 | MS65 |
|---|---|---|---|---|---|---|
| 2004 | — | — | — | — | 7.00 | 9.00 |

**KM# 823 10 DOLLARS**
1.23 g., Gold, 13.88 mm. **Subject:** 2006 World Football championship Gernany **Obv:** National arms **Rev:** Football at lower left, stadium at center **Rev. Legend:** DEUTSCHLAND 2006 **Edge:** Reeded

| Date | Mintage | VF20 | XF40 | MS60 | MS63 | MS65 |
|---|---|---|---|---|---|---|
| 2004 | — | PF65 75.00 | | | | |

**KM# 830 10 DOLLARS**
15.62 g., Copper-Nickel, 33.3 mm. **Obv:** National arms **Rev:** Flag at left, bust of 43rd President George W. Bush facing at right **Edge:** Reeded

| Date | Mintage | VF20 | XF40 | MS60 | MS63 | MS65 |
|---|---|---|---|---|---|---|
| 2004 | — | — | — | — | 10.00 | 12.00 |

**KM# 738 10 DOLLARS**
27.19 g., Copper-Nickel, 43 mm. **Subject:** Death of Pope John-Paul II **Edge:** Reeded

| Date | Mintage | VF20 | XF40 | MS60 | MS63 | MS65 |
|---|---|---|---|---|---|---|
| 2005 | — | — | — | — | 12.00 | 14.00 |

**KM# 739.1 10 DOLLARS**
25.00 g., 0.925 Silver 0.7435 oz. ASW **Subject:** Death of Pope John-Paul II **Rev:** Silhouette of John-Paul gilt, backgound in Ruthenium

| Date | Mintage | VF20 | XF40 | MS60 | MS63 | MS65 |
|---|---|---|---|---|---|---|
| 2005 | 7,500 | — | — | — | — | 60.00 |

**KM# 739.2 10 DOLLARS**
25.00 g., 0.925 Silver 0.7435 oz. ASW **Subject:** Death of Pope John-Paul II **Rev:** Silhouette of John-Paul gilt, blackened background

| Date | Mintage | VF20 | XF40 | MS60 | MS63 | MS65 |
|---|---|---|---|---|---|---|
| 2005 | 7,500 | — | — | — | — | 42.00 |

**KM# 752 10 DOLLARS**
20.00 g., 0.999 Silver 0.6424 oz. ASW partially gilt, 38 mm. **Series:** Endangered Wildlife **Obv:** National arms **Obv. Legend:** REPUBLIC OF LIBERIA **Rev:** Gilt Koala perched on branch with diamonds inset in eyes **Rev. Legend:** AUSTRALIA **Edge:** Plain

| Date | Mintage | VF20 | XF40 | MS60 | MS63 | MS65 |
|---|---|---|---|---|---|---|
| 2005 | 5,000 | PF65 115 | | | | |

**KM# 753 10 DOLLARS**
20.00 g., 0.999 Silver 0.6424 oz. ASW partially gilt, 38 mm. **Series:** Endangered Wildlife **Obv:** National arms **Obv. Legend:** REPUBLIC OF LIBERIA **Rev:** Two perched gilt Yellow-eared Conures with diamonds inset in eyes **Rev. Legend:** COLOMBIA **Edge:** Plain

| Date | Mintage | VF20 | XF40 | MS60 | MS63 | MS65 |
|---|---|---|---|---|---|---|
| 2005 | 5,000 | PF65 115 | | | | |

**KM# 754 10 DOLLARS**
20.00 g., 0.999 Silver 0.6424 oz. ASW partially gilt, 38 mm. **Series:** Endangered Wildlife **Obv:** National arms **Obv. Legend:** REPUBLIC OF LIBERIA **Rev:** Gilt Iberian Lynx standing facing with diamonds inset in eyes **Rev. Legend:** SPAIN **Edge:** Plain

| Date | Mintage | VF20 | XF40 | MS60 | MS63 | MS65 |
|---|---|---|---|---|---|---|
| 2005 | 5,000 | PF65 115 | | | | |

**KM# 755 10 DOLLARS**
20.00 g., 0.999 Silver 0.6424 oz. ASW partially gilt, 38 mm. **Series:** Endangered Wildlife **Obv:** National arms **Obv. Legend:** REPUBLIC OF LIBERIA **Rev:** Two perched gilt Yellow-crested Cockatoos **Rev. Legend:** INDONESIA **Edge:** Plain

| Date | Mintage | VF20 | XF40 | MS60 | MS63 | MS65 |
|---|---|---|---|---|---|---|
| 2005 | 5,000 | PF65 115 | | | | |

**KM# 756 10 DOLLARS**
20.00 g., 0.999 Silver 0.6424 oz. ASW partially gilt, 38 mm. **Series:** Endangered Wildlife **Obv:** National arms **Obv. Legend:** REPUBLIC OF LIBERIA **Rev:** Gilt Jaguar resting on branch with diamonds inset in eyes **Rev. Legend:** BELIZE **Edge:** Plain

| Date | Mintage | VF20 | XF40 | MS60 | MS63 | MS65 |
|---|---|---|---|---|---|---|
| 2005 | 5,000 | PF65 115 | | | | |

**KM# 757 10 DOLLARS**
20.00 g., 0.999 Silver 0.6424 oz. ASW partially gilt, 38 mm. **Series:** Endangered Wildlife **Obv:** National arms **Obv. Legend:** REPUBLIC OF LIBERIA **Rev:** Two perched gilt Plate-billed Mountain Toucans with diamonds inset in eyes **Rev. Legend:** ECUADOR **Edge:** Plain

| Date | Mintage | VF20 | XF40 | MS60 | MS63 | MS65 |
|---|---|---|---|---|---|---|
| 2005 | 5,000 | PF65 115 | | | | |

**KM# 758 10 DOLLARS**
20.00 g., 0.999 Silver 0.6424 oz. ASW partially gilt, 38 mm. **Series:** Endangered Wildlife **Obv:** National arms **Obv. Legend:** REPUBLIC OF LIBERIA **Rev:** Gilt Red Panda resting facing with diamonds inset in eyes **Rev. Legend:** INDIA **Edge:** Plain

| Date | Mintage | VF20 | XF40 | MS60 | MS63 | MS65 |
|---|---|---|---|---|---|---|
| 2005 | 5,000 | PF65 115 | | | | |

**KM# 759 10 DOLLARS**
20.00 g., 0.999 Silver 0.6424 oz. ASW partially gilt, 38 mm. **Series:** Endangered Wildlife **Obv:** National arms **Obv. Legend:** REPUBLIC OF LIBERIA **Rev:** Two perched gilt Resplendent Quetzals with diamonds inset in eyes **Rev. Legend:** GUATEMALA **Edge:** Plain

| Date | Mintage | VF20 | XF40 | MS60 | MS63 | MS65 |
|---|---|---|---|---|---|---|
| 2005 | 5,000 | PF65 115 | | | | |

**KM# 760 10 DOLLARS**
20.00 g., 0.999 Silver 0.6424 oz. ASW partially gilt, 38 mm. **Series:** Endangered Wildlife **Obv:** National arms **Obv. Legend:** REPUBLIC OF LIBERIA **Rev:** Gilt Snow Leopard standing left looking back with diamonds inset in eyes **Rev. Legend:** NEPAL **Edge:** Plain

| Date | Mintage | VF20 | XF40 | MS60 | MS63 | MS65 |
|---|---|---|---|---|---|---|
| 2005 | 5,000 | PF65 115 | | | | |

**KM# 761 10 DOLLARS**
20.00 g., 0.999 Silver 0.6424 oz. ASW partially gilt, 38 mm. **Series:** Endangered Wildlife **Obv:** National arms **Obv. Legend:** REPUBLIC OF LIBERIA **Rev:** Gilt Fossa standing right on branch facing with diamonds inset in eyes **Rev. Legend:** MADAGASCAR **Edge:** Plain

| Date | Mintage | VF20 | XF40 | MS60 | MS63 | MS65 |
|---|---|---|---|---|---|---|
| 2005 | 5,000 | PF65 115 | | | | |

**KM# 762 10 DOLLARS**
20.00 g., 0.999 Silver 0.6424 oz. ASW partially gilt, 38 mm. **Series:** Endangered Wildlife **Obv:** National arms **Obv. Legend:** REPUBLIC OF LIBERIA **Rev:** Two gilt Chilean Flamingos standing left with diamonds inset in eyes **Rev. Legend:** ARGENTINA **Edge:** Plain

| Date | Mintage | VF20 | XF40 | MS60 | MS63 | MS65 |
|---|---|---|---|---|---|---|
| 2005 | 5,000 | PF65 115 | | | | |

**KM# 763 10 DOLLARS**
20.00 g., 0.999 Silver 0.6424 oz. ASW partially gilt, 38 mm. **Series:** Endangered Wildlife **Obv:** National arms **Obv. Legend:** REPUBLIC OF LIBERIA **Rev:** Two gilt White-winged ducks, one standing, one swimming right with diamonds inset in eyes **Rev. Legend:** THAILAND **Edge:** Plain

| Date | Mintage | VF20 | XF40 | MS60 | MS63 | MS65 |
|---|---|---|---|---|---|---|
| 2005 | 5,000 | PF65 115 | | | | |

**KM# 860 10 DOLLARS**
25.00 g., 0.925 Silver 0.7435 oz. ASW, 38.6 mm. **Subject:** Poison frogs **Rev:** Green Frog, multicolor

| Date | Mintage | VF20 | XF40 | MS60 | MS63 | MS65 |
|---|---|---|---|---|---|---|
| 2005 | 2,500 | PF65 50.00 | | | | |

**KM# 861 10 DOLLARS**
25.00 g., 0.925 Silver 0.7435 oz. ASW, 38.6 mm. **Subject:** Poison frogs **Rev:** Red frog, multicolor

| Date | Mintage | VF20 | XF40 | MS60 | MS63 | MS65 |
|---|---|---|---|---|---|---|
| 2005 | 2,500 | PF65 50.00 | | | | |

**KM# 862 10 DOLLARS**
25.00 g., 0.925 Silver 0.7435 oz. ASW, 38.6 mm. **Subject:** Poison frogs **Rev:** Blue frog, multicolor

| Date | Mintage | VF20 | XF40 | MS60 | MS63 | MS65 |
|---|---|---|---|---|---|---|
| 2005 | 2,500 | PF65 50.00 | | | | |

**KM# 864 10 DOLLARS**
0.50 g., 0.585 Gold 0.0094 oz. AGW, 11 mm. **Subject:** 25th Anniversary of the Krugerrand **Obv:** Shield **Rev:** Paul Krueger bust left

| Date | Mintage | VF20 | XF40 | MS60 | MS63 | MS65 |
|---|---|---|---|---|---|---|
| 2005 | — | PF65 35.00 | | | | |

**KM# 996 10 DOLLARS**
62.20 g., 0.999 Silver 1.9978 oz. ASW, 50 mm. **Subject:** Romanesque Architecture **Rev:** Facade, Tiffany Glass insert

| Date | Mintage | VF20 | XF40 | MS60 | MS63 | MS65 |
|---|---|---|---|---|---|---|
| 2005 Antique finish | 999 | — | — | — | — | 125 |

**KM# 1017 10 DOLLARS**
Silver **Subject:** Election of Pope Benedict XVI **Rev:** Pope with outstretched arms, St. Peter's in background

| Date | Mintage | VF20 | XF40 | MS60 | MS63 | MS65 |
|---|---|---|---|---|---|---|
| 2005 | — | PF63 30.00 | PF65 35.00 | | | |

**KM# 1018 10 DOLLARS**
Silver **Subject:** Moric Benovsky **Obv:** Naitonal arms **Rev:** Sailing ship right

| Date | Mintage | VF20 | XF40 | MS60 | MS63 | MS65 |
|---|---|---|---|---|---|---|
| 2005 | — | PF63 30.00 | PF65 35.00 | | | |

**KM# 1019 10 DOLLARS**
Silver, oval mm. **Obv:** National arms **Rev:** Titanic with recovered coal insert

| Date | Mintage | VF20 | XF40 | MS60 | MS63 | MS65 |
|---|---|---|---|---|---|---|
| 2005 | — | PF63 30.00 | PF65 35.00 | | | |

**KM# 764 10 DOLLARS**
20.00 g., 0.999 Silver 0.6424 oz. ASW partially gilt, 38 mm. **Series:** Endangered Wildlife **Obv:** National arms **Obv. Legend:** REPUBLIC OF LIBERIA **Rev:** Gilt Crested Genet on branch facing with diamonds inset in eyes **Rev. Legend:** CAMEROON **Edge:** Plain

| Date | Mintage | VF20 | XF40 | MS60 | MS63 | MS65 |
|---|---|---|---|---|---|---|
| 2006 | 5,000 | PF65 115 | | | | |

**KM# 765 10 DOLLARS**
20.00 g., 0.999 Silver 0.6424 oz. ASW partially gilt, 38 mm. **Series:** Endangered Wildlife **Obv:** National arms **Obv. Legend:** REPUBLIC OF LIBERIA **Rev:** Two gilt Dalmatian Pelicans, one swimming, one standing with diamonds inset in eyes **Rev. Legend:** MONTENEGRO **Edge:** Plain

| Date | Mintage | VF20 | XF40 | MS60 | MS63 | MS65 |
|---|---|---|---|---|---|---|
| 2006 | 5,000 | PF65 115 | | | | |

**KM# 766 10 DOLLARS**
20.00 g., 0.999 Silver 0.6424 oz. ASW partially gilt, 38 mm. **Series:** Endangered Wildlife **Obv:** National arms **Obv. Legend:** REPUBLIC OF LIBERIA **Rev:** Gilt Hairy-bared Dwarf Lemue standing on branch with diamonds inset in eyes **Rev. Legend:** MADAGASCAR **Edge:** Plain

| Date | Mintage | VF20 | XF40 | MS60 | MS63 | MS65 |
|---|---|---|---|---|---|---|
| 2006 | 5,000 | PF65 115 | | | | |

**KM# 767 10 DOLLARS**
20.00 g., 0.999 Silver 0.6424 oz. ASW partially gilt, 38 mm. **Series:** Endangered Wildlife **Obv:** National arms **Obv. Legend:** REPUBLIC OF LIBERIA **Rev:** Two gilt Visayan Tarictics perched on branches with diamonds inset in eyes **Rev. Legend:** Philippines **Edge:** Plain

| Date | Mintage | VF20 | XF40 | MS60 | MS63 | MS65 |
|---|---|---|---|---|---|---|
| 2006 | 5,000 | PF65 115 | | | | |

**KM# 768 10 DOLLARS**
20.00 g., 0.999 Silver 0.6424 oz. ASW partially gilt, 38 mm. **Series:** Endangered Wildlife **Obv:** National arms **Obv. Legend:** REPUBLIC OF LIBERIA **Rev:** Two gilt Ethiopian Wolves, one seated, one laying with diamonds inset in eyes **Rev. Legend:** ETHIOPIA **Edge:** Plain

| Date | Mintage | VF20 | XF40 | MS60 | MS63 | MS65 |
|---|---|---|---|---|---|---|
| 2006 | 5,000 | PF65 115 | | | | |

**KM# 769 10 DOLLARS**
20.00 g., 0.999 Silver 0.6424 oz. ASW partially gilt, 38 mm. **Series:** Endangered Wildlife **Obv:** National arms **Obv. Legend:** REPUBLIC OF LIBERIA **Rev:** Two gilt Kakapos perched on a branch with diamonds inset in eyes **Rev. Legend:** NEW ZEALAND **Edge:** Plain

| Date | Mintage | VF20 | XF40 | MS60 | MS63 | MS65 |
|---|---|---|---|---|---|---|
| 2006 | 5,000 | PF65 115 | | | | |

**KM# 770 10 DOLLARS**
20.00 g., 0.999 Silver 0.6424 oz. ASW partially gilt, 38 mm. **Series:** Endangered Wildlife **Obv:** National arms **Obv. Legend:** REPUBLIC OF LIBERIA **Rev:** Gilt Spectacled Bear standing with diamonds inset in eyes **Rev. Legend:** BOLIVIA **Edge:** Plain

| Date | Mintage | VF20 | XF40 | MS60 | MS63 | MS65 |
|---|---|---|---|---|---|---|
| 2006 | 5,000 | PF65 115 | | | | |

**KM# 771 10 DOLLARS**
20.00 g., 0.999 Silver 0.6424 oz. ASW partially gilt, 38 mm. **Series:** Endangered Wildlife **Obv:** National arms **Obv. Legend:** REPUBLIC OF LIBERIA **Rev:** Two gilt Mauritius Kestrels perched on branch with diamonds inset in eyes **Rev. Legend:** MAURITIUS **Edge:** Plain

| Date | Mintage | VF20 | XF40 | MS60 | MS63 | MS65 |
|---|---|---|---|---|---|---|
| 2006 | 5,000 | PF65 115 | | | | |

**KM# 772 10 DOLLARS**
20.00 g., 0.999 Silver 0.6424 oz. ASW Partially gilt, 38 mm. **Series:** Endangered Wildlife **Obv:** National arms **Obv. Legend:** REPUBLIC OF LIBERIA **Rev:** Two gilt Mhorr Gazelles, one standing, one resting with diamonds inset in eyes **Rev. Legend:** MALI **Edge:** Plain

| Date | Mintage | VF20 | XF40 | MS60 | MS63 | MS65 |
|---|---|---|---|---|---|---|
| 2006 | 5,000 | PF65 115 | | | | |

**KM# 773 10 DOLLARS**
20.00 g., 0.999 Silver 0.6424 oz. ASW partially gilt, 38 mm. **Series:** Endangered Wildlife **Obv:** National arms **Obv. Legend:** REPUBLIC OF LIBERIA **Rev:** Two gilt Blue Lorikeets perched on branches with diamonds inset in eyes **Rev. Legend:** FRENCH POLYNESIA **Edge:** Plain

| Date | Mintage | VF20 | XF40 | MS60 | MS63 | MS65 |
|---|---|---|---|---|---|---|
| 2006 | 5,000 | PF65 115 | | | | |

**KM# 774 10 DOLLARS**
20.00 g., 0.999 Silver 0.6424 oz. ASW partially gilt, 38 mm. **Series:** Endangered Wildlife **Obv:** National arms **Obv. Legend:** REPUBLIC OF LIBERIA **Rev:** Gilt resting Arabian Leopard with diamonds inset in eyes **Rev. Legend:** SAUDI ARABIA **Edge:** Plain

| Date | Mintage | VF20 | XF40 | MS60 | MS63 | MS65 |
|---|---|---|---|---|---|---|
| 2006 | 5,000 | PF65 115 | | | | |

**KM# 775 10 DOLLARS**
20.00 g., 0.999 Silver 0.6424 oz. ASW partially gilt, 38 mm. **Series:** Endangered Wildlife **Obv:** National arms **Obv. Legend:** REPUBLIC OF LIBERIA **Rev:** Two gilt Hawaiian Geese standing with diamonds inset in eyes **Rev. Legend:** USA **Edge:** Plain

| Date | Mintage | VF20 | XF40 | MS60 | MS63 | MS65 |
|---|---|---|---|---|---|---|
| 2006 | 5,000 | PF65 115 | | | | |

**KM# 827 10 DOLLARS**
14.60 g., Copper-Nickel, 33 mm. **Subject:** Abraham Lincoln **Obv:** National arms **Rev:** Bust facing 3/4 right **Edge:** Reeded

| Date | Mintage | VF20 | XF40 | MS60 | MS63 | MS65 |
|---|---|---|---|---|---|---|
| 2006 | 50,000 | PF65 10.00 | | | | |

**KM# 843 10 DOLLARS**
0.73 g., 0.999 Gold 0.0234 oz. AGW, 11 mm. **Obv:** Arms **Rev:** John F. Kennedy head left

| Date | Mintage | VF20 | XF40 | MS60 | MS63 | MS65 |
|---|---|---|---|---|---|---|
| 2006 | 20,000 | PF63 55.00 | PF65 60.00 | | | |

**KM# 725 10 DOLLARS**
3.11 g., 0.999 Gold 0.0999 oz. AGW, 16 mm. **Obv:** National arms **Rev:** Leopard head **Edge:** Reeded

| Date | Mintage | VF20 | XF40 | MS60 | MS63 | MS65 |
|---|---|---|---|---|---|---|
| 2007 | 120 | PF65 200 | | | | |

**KM# 734 10 DOLLARS**
25.00 g., 0.925 Silver 0.7435 oz. ASW, 38.61 mm. **Subject:** The Black Madonna of Czestochowa **Obv:** Arms **Obv. Legend:** REPUBLIC OF LIBERIA **Rev:** 1/2 length figure of Madonna facing with child

| Date | Mintage | VF20 | XF40 | MS60 | MS63 | MS65 |
|---|---|---|---|---|---|---|
| 2007 | 1,000 | PF65 70.00 | | | | |

**KM# 1009 10 DOLLARS**
62.21 g., 0.999 Silver 1.9981 oz. ASW **Obv:** National arms **Rev:** Christmas tree in color

| Date | Mintage | VF20 | XF40 | MS60 | MS63 | MS65 |
|---|---|---|---|---|---|---|
| 2010 | — | PF65 150 | | | | |

**KM# 1029 12 DOLLARS**
0.62 g., 0.999 Gold 0.0199 oz. AGW, 10 mm. **Rev:** Christ at center, apostles in 12 segments around

| Date | Mintage | VF20 | XF40 | MS60 | MS63 | MS65 |
|---|---|---|---|---|---|---|
| 2007 | — | PF65 70.00 | | | | |

**KM# 514 20 DOLLARS**
31.10 g., 0.999 Silver 0.999 oz. ASW, 38.2 mm. **Subject:** Bush-Cheney Inauguration **Obv:** White House **Rev:** Conjoined busts right **Edge:** Reeded

| Date | Mintage | VF20 | XF40 | MS60 | MS63 | MS65 |
|---|---|---|---|---|---|---|
| 2001 | — | PF65 45.00 | | | | |

**KM# 643 20 DOLLARS**
15.55 g., 0.999 Silver 0.4994 oz. ASW, 30.4 mm. **Obv:** St. Peter's Basilica **Rev:** Bust of Pope facing **Edge:** Reeded

| Date | Mintage | VF20 | XF40 | MS60 | MS63 | MS65 |
|---|---|---|---|---|---|---|
| 2001S | — | PF65 28.00 | | | | |

**KM# 650 20 DOLLARS**
19.91 g., 0.999 Silver 0.6395 oz. ASW, 40 mm. **Obv:** National arms **Rev:** Bust of Charles Lindbergh facing and Spirit of St. Louis in background **Edge:** Reeded

| Date | Mintage | VF20 | XF40 | MS60 | MS63 | MS65 |
|---|---|---|---|---|---|---|
| 2001 | — | PF65 40.00 | | | | |

**KM# 715 20 DOLLARS**
20.00 g., 0.999 Silver 0.6424 oz. ASW, 40.3 mm. **Series:** American History **Obv:** National arms **Rev:** First Continental Congress in prayer **Edge:** Reeded

| Date | Mintage | VF20 | XF40 | MS60 | MS63 | MS65 |
|---|---|---|---|---|---|---|
| 2001 | 20,000 | PF65 32.00 | | | | |

**KM# 716 20 DOLLARS**
20.00 g., 0.999 Silver 0.6424 oz. ASW, 40.3 mm. **Series:** American History **Obv:** National arms **Rev:** U.S. Constitution Ratification, text in stars of folded flag **Edge:** Reeded

| Date | Mintage | VF20 | XF40 | MS60 | MS63 | MS65 |
|---|---|---|---|---|---|---|
| 2001 | 20,000 | PF65 32.00 | | | | |

**KM# 717 20 DOLLARS**
20.00 g., 0.999 Silver 0.6424 oz. ASW, 40.3 mm. **Series:** American History **Obv:** National arms **Rev:** Washington's Inauguration scene **Edge:** Reeded

| Date | Mintage | VF20 | XF40 | MS60 | MS63 | MS65 |
|---|---|---|---|---|---|---|
| 2001 | 20,000 | PF65 32.00 | | | | |

**KM# 718 20 DOLLARS**
20.00 g., 0.925 Silver 0.5948 oz. ASW, 40.3 mm. **Series:** American History **Obv:** National arms **Rev:** Appomattox Courthouse surrender scene with Lee and Grant **Edge:** Reeded

| Date | Mintage | VF20 | XF40 | MS60 | MS63 | MS65 |
|---|---|---|---|---|---|---|
| 2001 | 20,000 | PF65 32.00 | | | | |

**KM# 719 20 DOLLARS**
20.00 g., 0.999 Silver 0.6424 oz. ASW, 40.3 mm. **Series:** American History **Obv:** National arms **Rev:** Prohibition, hatchet, barrels and bottles destruction **Edge:** Reeded

| Date | Mintage | VF20 | XF40 | MS60 | MS63 | MS65 |
|---|---|---|---|---|---|---|
| 2001 | 20,000 | PF65 32.00 | | | | |

**KM# 720 20 DOLLARS**
20.00 g., 0.999 Silver 0.6424 oz. ASW, 40.3 mm. **Series:** American History **Obv:** National arms **Rev:** Cuban Missile Crisis, Castro, Khrushchev, Kennedy, missiles and map **Edge:** Reeded

| Date | Mintage | VF20 | XF40 | MS60 | MS63 | MS65 |
|---|---|---|---|---|---|---|
| 2001 | 20,000 | PF65 32.00 | | | | |

**KM# 721 20 DOLLARS**
20.00 g., 0.999 Silver 0.6424 oz. ASW, 40.3 mm. **Series:** American History **Obv:** National arms **Rev:** First Man on Moon, Armstrong and Lander **Edge:** Reeded

| Date | Mintage | VF20 | XF40 | MS60 | MS63 | MS65 |
|---|---|---|---|---|---|---|
| 2001 | 20,000 | PF65 32.00 | | | | |

**KM# 722 20 DOLLARS**
20.00 g., 0.999 Silver 0.6424 oz. ASW, 40.3 mm. **Series:** American History **Obv:** National arms **Rev:** Desert Storm, soldier, helicopter, rocket launcher etc. **Edge:** Reeded

| Date | Mintage | VF20 | XF40 | MS60 | MS63 | MS65 |
|---|---|---|---|---|---|---|
| 2001 | 20,000 | PF65 32.00 | | | | |

**KM# 616 20 DOLLARS**
31.20 g., 0.999 Silver 1.0021 oz. ASW gilt, 38.7 mm. **Obv:** National arms **Rev:** Diamond studded scorpion (Scorpio) **Edge:** Reeded

| Date | Mintage | VF20 | XF40 | MS60 | MS63 | MS65 |
|---|---|---|---|---|---|---|
| 2002 | — | PF65 60.00 | | | | |

**KM# 617 20 DOLLARS**
31.20 g., 0.999 Silver 1.0021 oz. ASW gilt, 38.7 mm. **Obv:** National arms **Rev:** Diamond studded archer (Sagittarius) **Edge:** Reeded

| Date | Mintage | VF20 | XF40 | MS60 | MS63 | MS65 |
|---|---|---|---|---|---|---|
| 2002 | — | PF65 60.00 | | | | |

**KM# 825 20 DOLLARS**
20.00 g., Silver, 40 mm. **Series:** America's First Ladies **Subject:** Mary Todd Lincoln **Obv:** National arms **Rev:** Bust facing slightly left at center left, oval portrait of Abraham Lincoln at right **Edge:** Reeded

| Date | Mintage | VF20 | XF40 | MS60 | MS63 | MS65 |
|---|---|---|---|---|---|---|
| 2003 | 20,000 | PF65 32.50 | | | | |

**KM# 826 20 DOLLARS**
20.00 g., Silver, 40 mm. **Series:** History of America **Subject:** Emancipation Proclamation **Obv:** National arms **Rev:** Lincoln seated with seven politicians gathered **Edge:** Reeded

| Date | Mintage | VF20 | XF40 | MS60 | MS63 | MS65 |
|---|---|---|---|---|---|---|
| 2004 | 20,000 | PF65 37.50 | | | | |

**KM# 1020 20 DOLLARS**
Silver **Subject:** U.S. Constitution

| Date | Mintage | VF20 | XF40 | MS60 | MS63 | MS65 |
|---|---|---|---|---|---|---|
| 2006 | — | PF63 30.00 | PF65 35.00 | | | |

**KM# 1021 20 DOLLARS**
1.25 g., 0.999 Gold 0.0234 oz. AGW, 14 mm. **Subject:** World Cup Soccer, Germany **Obv:** National arms **Rev:** Soccer player heading ball

| Date | Mintage | VF20 | XF40 | MS60 | MS63 | MS65 |
|---|---|---|---|---|---|---|
| 2006 | — | PF65 80.00 | | | | |

**KM# 634 25 DOLLARS**
0.73 g., 0.999 Gold 0.0234 oz. AGW, 11.1 mm. **Obv:** National arms **Rev:** Joan of Arc **Edge:** Reeded

| Date | Mintage | VF20 | XF40 | MS60 | MS63 | MS65 |
|---|---|---|---|---|---|---|
| 2001 | — | PF65 60.00 | | | | |

**KM# 666 25 DOLLARS**
1.52 g., Gold, 13.68 mm. **Subject:** Abraham Lincoln **Obv:** National arms **Rev:** Statue of Lincoln seated **Edge:** Reeded

| Date | Mintage | VF20 | XF40 | MS60 | MS63 | MS65 |
|---|---|---|---|---|---|---|
| 2001 | — | PF65 95.00 | | | | |

**KM# 667 25 DOLLARS**
0.73 g., 0.999 Gold 0.0234 oz. AGW, 11 mm. **Obv:** National arms **Rev:** Mount Rushmore **Edge:** Reeded

| Date | Mintage | VF20 | XF40 | MS60 | MS63 | MS65 |
|---|---|---|---|---|---|---|
| 2001 | 20,000 | PF65 65.00 | | | | |

**KM# 995 25 DOLLARS**
0.73 g., 0.999 Gold 0.0234 oz. AGW, 11 mm. **Obv:** National Arms **Rev:** Martin Luther King and Washington Monument

| Date | Mintage | VF20 | XF40 | MS60 | MS63 | MS65 |
|---|---|---|---|---|---|---|
| 2001 | — | PF65 70.00 | | | | |

**KM# 669 25 DOLLARS**
0.73 g., 0.999 Gold 0.0234 oz. AGW, 11 mm. **Subject:** Abraham Lincoln **Obv:** National arms **Rev:** Bust facing at right, Lincoln Memorial in background **Edge:** Reeded

| Date | Mintage | VF20 | XF40 | MS60 | MS63 | MS65 |
|---|---|---|---|---|---|---|
| 2002 | 20,000 | PF65 65.00 | | | | |

**KM# 730 25 DOLLARS**
0.02 g., 0.999 Gold 0.0008 oz. AGW **Obv:** Shield **Rev:** Map of Germany and stars

| Date | Mintage | VF20 | XF40 | MS60 | MS63 | MS65 |
|---|---|---|---|---|---|---|
| 2003 B | — | PF65 35.00 | | | | |

**KM# 804 25 DOLLARS**
1.25 g., 0.999 Gold 0.0401 oz. AGW, 14.5 x 9 mm. **Subject:** R. M. S. Titanic - Expedition 2000 **Obv:** National arms **Obv. Legend:** REPUBLIC OF LIBERIA **Rev:** Titanic with small piece of recovered coal embedded in hull. **Edge:** Reeded **Shape:** Oval

| Date | Mintage | VF20 | XF40 | MS60 | MS63 | MS65 |
|---|---|---|---|---|---|---|
| 2005 | — | PF65 80.00 | | | | |

**KM# 495 50 DOLLARS**
907.00 g., 0.999 Silver 29.1315 oz. ASW, 100 mm. **Subject:** Wreck of the Princess Louisa **Obv:** National arms and value **Rev:** Ship under sail **Edge:** Reeded **Note:** Each coin has a cob coin recovered from the wreck site encased in a hole with clear resin. Illustration reduced.

| Date | Mintage | VF20 | XF40 | MS60 | MS63 | MS65 |
|---|---|---|---|---|---|---|
| 2001 | 500 | — | — | — | — | 1,150 |

**KM# 731 50 DOLLARS**
222.08 g., 0.999 Silver 7.1329 oz. ASW, 80.04 mm. **Subject:** Japanese Attack on Pearl Harbor **Obv:** National arms **Obv. Legend:** REPUBLIC OF LIBERIA **Rev:** USA flag hologram at upper left, bust of Franklin D. Roosevelt facing above Japanese aircraft attacking ship in harbor **Rev. Legend:** REMEMBERING PEARL HARBOR - DECEMBER 7, 1941

| Date | Mintage | VF20 | XF40 | MS60 | MS63 | MS65 |
|---|---|---|---|---|---|---|
| 2001 | — | PF65 275 | | | | |

**KM# 776 50 DOLLARS**
93.30 g., 0.999 Silver 2.9967 oz. ASW partially gilt, 65.00 mm. **Series:** Endangered Wildlife **Obv:** National arms **Obv. Legend:** REPUBLIC OF LIBERIA **Rev:** Two gilt Cheetahs, one sitting, one resting with diamonds inset in eyes **Rev. Legend:** TANZANIA **Edge:** Plain

| Date | Mintage | VF20 | XF40 | MS60 | MS63 | MS65 |
|---|---|---|---|---|---|---|
| 2005 | 999 | PF65 450 | | | | |

**KM# 726 50 DOLLARS**
62.21 g., 0.999 Silver 1.998 oz. ASW, 50 mm. **Obv:** National arms **Rev:** Leopard lying across a map of Africa **Edge:** Reeded

| Date | Mintage | VF20 | XF40 | MS60 | MS63 | MS65 |
|---|---|---|---|---|---|---|
| 2007 | 500 | PF65 125 | | | | |

**KM# 844 100 DOLLARS**
1000.00 g., 0.999 Silver 32.1186 oz. ASW **Subject:** Tanks of World War II - T-34

| Date | Mintage | VF20 | XF40 | MS60 | MS63 | MS65 |
|---|---|---|---|---|---|---|
| 2008 | 1,000 | PF65 1,500 | | | | |

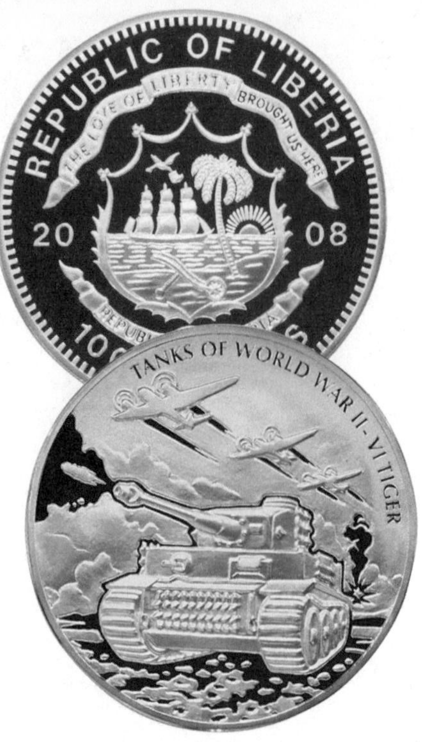


**KM# 845 100 DOLLARS**
1000.00 g., 0.999 Silver 32.1186 oz. ASW **Subject:** Tanks of World War II - VI-Tiger

| Date | Mintage | VF20 | XF40 | MS60 | MS63 | MS65 |
|---|---|---|---|---|---|---|
| 2008 | 1,000 | PF65 1,500 | | | | |

**KM# 846 100 DOLLARS**
1000.00 g., 0.999 Silver 32.1186 oz. ASW, 120 mm. **Obv:** Arms **Rev:** St. Paul standing, events of his life around

| Date | Mintage | VF20 | XF40 | MS60 | MS63 | MS65 |
|---|---|---|---|---|---|---|
| 2008 | 1,000 | PF65 2,000 | | | | |

**KM# 847 100 DOLLARS**

1000.00 g., 0.999 Silver 32.1186 oz. ASW, 120 mm. **Obv:** National shield **Rev:** Christ at center, apostles around

| Date | Mintage | VF20 | XF40 | MS60 | MS63 | MS65 |
|---|---|---|---|---|---|---|
| 2008 | 1,000 | **PF65** 2,000 | | | | |

**KM# 727 2500 DOLLARS**

155.52 g., 0.999 Gold 4.995 oz. AGW, 60 mm. **Obv:** National arms **Rev:** Leopard lying across a map of Africa **Edge:** Reeded

| Date | Mintage | VF20 | XF40 | MS60 | MS63 | MS65 |
|---|---|---|---|---|---|---|
| 2007 | 48 | **PF65** 9,500 | | | | |

## PATTERNS

Including off metal strikes

| KM# | Date | Mintage | Identification | Mkt Val |
|---|---|---|---|---|
| Pn58 | 2001 | — | 10 Dollars Copper-Nickel National arms 9-11" Flag raising scene | 250 |
| Pn59 | 2001 | — | 20 Dollars Silver Plated Base Metal National arms 9-11" Flag raising scene | 150 |
| Pn60 | 2001 | — | 100 Dollars Base Metal Gilt National arms 9-11" Flag raising scene | 125 |

# LIBYA

The Socialist People's Libyan Arab Jamahariya, located on the north-central coast of Africa between Tunisia and Egypt, has an area of 679,358 sq. mi. (1,759,540 sq. km.) and a population of 3.9 million. Capital: Tripoli. Crude oil, which accounts for 90 per cent of the export earnings, is the mainstay of the economy.

**TITLES**

المملكة الليبية

al-Mamlaka(t) al-Libiya(t)

الجمهورية اليبية

al-Jomhuriya(t) al-Arabiya(t) al-Libiya(t)

# GREAT SOCIALIST PEOPLE'S LIBYAN ARAB JAMAHIRIYA

## STANDARD COINAGE

1000 Dirhams = 1 Dinar

**KM# 28 50 DIRHAMS**

6.25 g., Copper-Nickel, 25 mm. **Obv:** Armored equestrian **Rev:** Value at center **Shape:** Scalloped

| Date | Mintage | F12 | VF20 | XF40 | MS60 | MS63 |
|---|---|---|---|---|---|---|
| MD1377-2009 | — | — | — | 2.50 | 5.00 | 7.00 |

**KM# 29 100 DIRHAMS**

Copper-Nickel, 27 mm. **Obv:** Armored Equestrian **Rev:** Value at center

| Date | Mintage | F12 | VF20 | XF40 | MS60 | MS63 |
|---|---|---|---|---|---|---|
| MD1377-2009 | — | — | — | 3.50 | 6.00 | 9.00 |

**KM# 26 1/4 DINAR**

11.15 g., Nickel-Brass, 28 mm. **Obv:** Libyan knight on horse with gun 1/2 left surrounded by name of Libyan Arab Jamahiriya, ornamental legend with date **Rev:** Value in Arabic script above wheat ears in ornamented frame **Edge:** Ten alternating reeded and plain flat sections **Shape:** 10-sided

| Date | Mintage | F12 | VF20 | XF40 | MS60 | MS63 |
|---|---|---|---|---|---|---|
| MD1369 | — | — | — | 5.00 | 8.00 | 10.00 |

Note: Restruck in 2001-2002

**KM# 30 1/4 DINAR**

11.50 g., Nickel-Brass, 28 mm. **Obv:** Armored horseman **Rev:** Value at center **Shape:** 10-sided

| Date | Mintage | F12 | VF20 | XF40 | MS60 | MS63 |
|---|---|---|---|---|---|---|
| MD1377-2009 | — | — | — | 8.00 | 10.00 | 12.00 |

**KM# 27 1/2 DINAR**

11.50 g., Bi-Metallic Aluminumn bronze center in Copper-Nickel ring., 30 mm. **Obv:** Man on horse with gun 1/2 left, ornamental legend with date **Rev:** Value in Arabic script above wheat ears in ornamented frame **Edge:** Reeded

| Date | Mintage | F12 | VF20 | XF40 | MS60 | MS63 |
|---|---|---|---|---|---|---|
| MD1372 (2004) | — | — | — | 9.00 | 11.00 | 13.00 |

**KM# 31 1/2 DINAR**

11.50 g., Bi-Metallic Aluminum-Bronze center in Copper-Nickel ring, 30 mm. **Obv:** Armored horseman **Rev:** Value at center **Edge:** Reeded

| Date | Mintage | F12 | VF20 | XF40 | MS60 | MS63 |
|---|---|---|---|---|---|---|
| MD1377-2009 | — | — | — | 10.00 | 12.00 | 15.00 |

# LIECHTENSTEIN

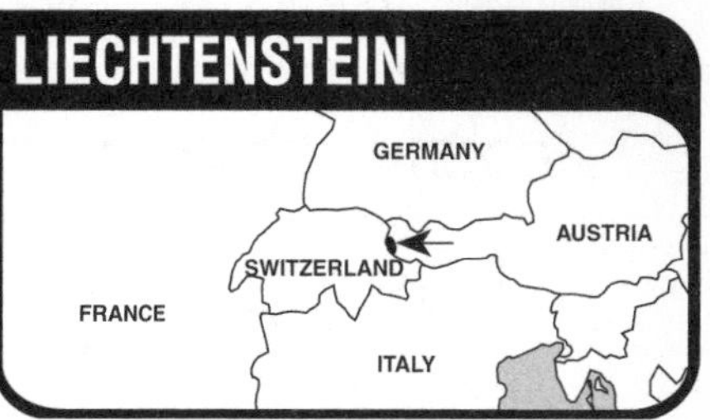


The Principality of Liechtenstein, located in central Europe on the east bank of the Rhine between Austria and Switzerland, has an area of 62 sq. mi. (160 sq. km.) and a population of 27,200. Capital: Vaduz. The economy is based on agriculture and light manufacturing. Canned goods, textiles, ceramics and precision instruments are exported.

**RULERS**

Prince Hans Adam II, 1990-

**MINT MARKS**

B - Bern

# PRINCIPALITY

## REFORM COINAGE

100 Rappen = 1 Frank

**Y# 24 10 FRANKEN**

29.95 g., 0.900 Silver 0.8666 oz. ASW, 37.3 mm. **Ruler:** Prince Hans Adam II **Subject:** 200 Years of Sovereignty **Obv:** Vertical inscription between crowned arms and value **Rev:** Johann I (1760-1836) **Edge:** Reeded

| Date | Mintage | F12 | VF20 | XF40 | MS60 | MS63 |
|---|---|---|---|---|---|---|
| ND (2006) B | — | **PF63** 45.00 | **PF65** 55.00 | | | |

**Y# 25 50 FRANKEN**

8.88 g., 0.999 Gold 0.2852 oz. AGW **Ruler:** Prince Hans Adam II **Subject:** 200th Anniversary of Sovereignty

| Date | Mintage | F12 | VF20 | XF40 | MS60 | MS63 |
|---|---|---|---|---|---|---|
| ND (2006) B | — | **PF63** 500 | **PF65** 525 | | | |

The Republic of Lithuania, southernmost of the Baltic states in east Europe, has an area of 25,174 sq. mi.(65,201 sq. km.) and a population of *3.6 million. Capital: Vilnius. The economy is based on livestock raising and manufacturing. Hogs, cattle, hides and electric motors are exported.

Lithuania declared its independence March 11, 1990 and it was recognized by the United States on Sept. 2, 1991, followed by the Soviet government in Moscow on Sept. 6. They were seated in the UN General Assembly on Sept. 17, 1991.

# MODERN REPUBLIC

1991-present

## REFORM COINAGE

100 Centas = 1 Litas

### KM# 106 10 CENTŲ

2.60 g., Nickel-Brass, 17 mm. **Obv:** National arms **Rev:** Value **Edge:** Reeded

| Date | Mintage | VF20 | XF40 | MS60 | MS63 | MS65 |
|---|---|---|---|---|---|---|
| 2003 Prooflike | 10,000 | — | — | — | — | 4.00 |
| 2006 | — | — | — | — | 0.25 | 0.40 |
| 2006 | 2,000 | PF63 45.00 | | | | |
| 2007 | — | — | — | — | 0.25 | 0.40 |
| 2008 | — | — | — | — | 0.25 | 0.40 |
| 2008 Prooflike | 200 | — | — | — | — | 5.00 |
| 2009 | — | — | — | — | 0.25 | 0.40 |
| 2009 Prooflike | 500 | — | — | — | — | 16.00 |
| 2010 | — | — | — | — | 0.25 | 0.40 |
| 2011 In sets only | 4,500 | — | — | — | — | 0.75 |
| 2012 In sets only | 4,000 | — | — | — | — | 0.75 |
| 2013 In sets only | 7,000 | — | — | — | — | 0.75 |

### KM# 107 20 CENTŲ

4.80 g., Nickel-Brass, 20.5 mm. **Obv:** National arms **Rev:** Value **Edge:** Reeded

| Date | Mintage | VF20 | XF40 | MS60 | MS63 | MS65 |
|---|---|---|---|---|---|---|
| 2003 In sets only | — | — | — | — | — | 1.50 |
| 2003 | 10,000 | PF65 2.00 | | | | |
| 2007 | — | — | — | — | — | 1.00 |
| 2008 | — | — | — | — | — | 1.00 |
| 2008 Prooflike | 200 | — | — | — | — | 5.00 |
| 2009 | — | — | — | — | — | 1.00 |
| 2009 Prooflike | 500 | — | — | — | — | 3.00 |
| 2010 | — | — | — | — | — | 1.00 |
| 2011 In sets only | 4,500 | — | — | — | — | 2.00 |
| 2012 In sets only | 4,000 | — | — | — | — | 2.00 |
| 2013 In sets only | 7,500 | — | — | — | — | 2.00 |

### KM# 108 50 CENTŲ

6.00 g., Nickel-Brass, 23 mm. **Obv:** National arms **Rev:** Value within designed circle **Edge:** Reeded

| Date | Mintage | VF20 | XF40 | MS60 | MS63 | MS65 |
|---|---|---|---|---|---|---|
| 2003 In sets only | — | — | — | — | — | 4.00 |
| 2003 | 10,000 | PF65 2.00 | | | | |
| 2008 In sets only | 4,000 | — | — | — | — | 4.00 |
| 2008 Prooflike | 200 | — | — | — | — | 30.00 |
| 2009 In sets only | 5,000 | — | — | — | — | 10.00 |
| 2009 Prooflike | 500 | — | — | — | — | 4.00 |
| 2010 In sets only | 3,500 | — | — | — | — | 10.00 |
| 2011 In sets only | 4,500 | — | — | — | — | 4.00 |
| 2012 In sets only | 4,000 | — | — | — | — | 4.00 |
| 2013 In sets only | 7,500 | — | — | — | — | 4.00 |

### KM# 111 LITAS

6.25 g., Copper-Nickel, 22.3 mm. **Obv:** National arms **Rev:** Value within circle above lined designs **Edge:** Reeded

| Date | Mintage | VF20 | XF40 | MS60 | MS63 | MS65 |
|---|---|---|---|---|---|---|
| 2001 | — | — | — | — | 1.50 | 2.00 |
| 2002 | — | — | — | — | 1.50 | 2.00 |
| 2003 In sets only | — | — | — | — | — | 5.00 |
| 2003 | 10,000 | PF65 8.00 | | | | |
| 2008 | — | — | — | — | 1.50 | 2.00 |
| 2008 Prooflike | 200 | — | — | — | — | 6.00 |
| 2009 | — | — | — | — | 1.50 | 2.00 |
| 2009 Prooflike | 500 | — | — | — | — | 4.00 |
| 2010 | — | — | — | — | 1.50 | 2.00 |
| 2011 In sets only | 4,500 | — | — | — | — | 3.00 |
| 2012 In sets only | 4,000 | — | — | — | — | 3.00 |
| 2013 In sets only | 7,500 | — | — | — | — | 3.00 |

### KM# 137 LITAS

6.25 g., Copper-Nickel, 22.3 mm. **Subject:** 425th Anniversary - University of Vilnius **Obv:** Knight on horse within rope wreath **Rev:** Building within court yard **Edge:** Segmented reeding

| Date | Mintage | VF20 | XF40 | MS60 | MS63 | MS65 |
|---|---|---|---|---|---|---|
| 2004 | 200,000 | — | — | — | 5.00 | 8.00 |

### KM# 142 LITAS

6.25 g., Copper-Nickel, 22.3 mm. **Obv:** Knight on horse within circle **Rev:** Palace **Edge:** Segmented reeding

| Date | Mintage | VF20 | XF40 | MS60 | MS63 | MS65 |
|---|---|---|---|---|---|---|
| 2005 | 1,000,000 | — | — | — | 2.00 | 3.00 |

### KM# 162 LITAS

6.25 g., Copper-Nickel, 22.3 mm. **Subject:** Vilnius - European Culture Capital **Obv:** National Arms **Rev:** Female figure standing at easel **Edge:** Segmented reeding

| Date | Mintage | VF20 | XF40 | MS60 | MS63 | MS65 |
|---|---|---|---|---|---|---|
| 2009 | 1,000,000 | — | — | — | 3.00 | 4.00 |

### KM# 172 LITAS

6.25 g., Copper-Nickel, 22.3 mm. **Subject:** Battle of Grunwald, 600th Anniversary **Obv:** National arms **Rev:** Long spears attacking each other **Edge:** Segmented reeding

| Date | Mintage | VF20 | XF40 | MS60 | MS63 | MS65 |
|---|---|---|---|---|---|---|
| 2010 | 1,000,000 | — | — | — | 3.00 | 4.00 |

### KM# 177 LITAS

6.25 g., Copper-Nickel, 22.3 mm. **Subject:** European Basketball Championship **Obv:** National arms **Rev:** Basketball **Rev. Legend:** EUROPOS KREPSINIO CEMPIONATAS **Edge:** Reeded

| Date | Mintage | VF20 | XF40 | MS60 | MS63 | MS65 |
|---|---|---|---|---|---|---|
| 2011 | 1,000,000 | — | — | — | 3.00 | 7.00 |

### KM# 182 LITAS

6.25 g., Copper-Nickel, 22.3 mm. **Subject:** Presidency of the EU **Obv:** Stylized map of Europe with stars **Rev:** Stylized Vytis with stars

| Date | Mintage | VF20 | XF40 | MS60 | MS63 | MS65 |
|---|---|---|---|---|---|---|
| 2013 | 100,000 | — | — | — | 3.00 | 7.00 |

### KM# 112 2 LITAI

7.50 g., Bi-Metallic Copper-Nickel center in Aluminum-Bronze ring, 25 mm. **Obv:** National arms within circle **Rev:** Value within circle **Edge:** Segmented reeding

| Date | Mintage | VF20 | XF40 | MS60 | MS63 | MS65 |
|---|---|---|---|---|---|---|
| 2001 | — | — | — | 1.50 | 2.50 | 4.50 |
| 2002 | — | — | — | 1.50 | 2.50 | 4.50 |
| 2003 | 10,000 | PF65 3.50 | | | | |
| 2008 | — | — | — | 1.25 | 2.25 | 3.00 |
| 2008 Prooflike | 200 | — | — | — | — | 30.00 |
| 2009 | — | — | — | 1.50 | 2.50 | 4.50 |
| 2009 Prooflike | 500 | — | — | — | — | 25.00 |
| 2010 | — | — | — | 1.50 | 2.50 | 4.50 |
| 2011 In sets only | 4,500 | — | — | — | — | 5.00 |
| 2012 In sets only | 4,000 | — | — | — | — | 5.00 |
| 2013 In sets only | 7,500 | — | — | — | — | 5.00 |

### KM# 183.1 2 LITAI

7.50 g., Bi-Metallic Copper-Nickel center in Aluminum-Bronze ring, 25 mm. **Subject:** Resorts - Birstonas **Obv:** National arms **Rev:** Arms of Birstonas

| Date | Mintage | VF20 | XF40 | MS60 | MS63 | MS65 |
|---|---|---|---|---|---|---|
| 2012 | 100,000 | — | — | 1.50 | 2.50 | 4.50 |

### KM# 183.2 2 LITAI

7.50 g., Bi-Metallic Copper-Nickel center in Aluminum-Bronze ring, 25 mm. **Subject:** Resorts - Birstonas **Obv:** National arms **Rev:** Arms of Birstonas in color

| Date | Mintage | VF20 | XF40 | MS60 | MS63 | MS65 |
|---|---|---|---|---|---|---|
| 2012 | 2,500 | PF65 25.00 | | | | |

**KM# 184.1 2 LITAI**
7.50 g., Bi-Metallic Copper-Nickel center in Aluminum-Bronze ring, 25 mm. **Subject:** Resorts - Druskininkai **Obv:** National arms **Rev:** Arms of Druskininkai

| Date | Mintage | VF20 | XF40 | MS60 | MS63 | MS65 |
|---|---|---|---|---|---|---|
| 2012 | 100,000 | — | — | 1.50 | 2.50 | 4.50 |

**KM# 184.2 2 LITAI**
7.50 g., Bi-Metallic Copper-Nickel center in Aluminum-Bronze ring, 25 mm. **Subject:** Resorts - Druskininkai **Obv:** National arms **Rev:** Arms of Druskininkai in color

| Date | Mintage | VF20 | XF40 | MS60 | MS63 | MS65 |
|---|---|---|---|---|---|---|
| 2012 | 2,500 | PF65 25.00 | | | | |

**KM# 185.1 2 LITAI**
7.50 g., Bi-Metallic Copper-Nickel center in Aluminum-Bronze ring, 25 mm. **Subject:** Resorts - Neringa **Obv:** National arms **Rev:** Arms of Neringa

| Date | Mintage | VF20 | XF40 | MS60 | MS63 | MS65 |
|---|---|---|---|---|---|---|
| 2012 | 100,000 | — | — | 1.50 | 2.50 | 4.50 |

**KM# 185.2 2 LITAI**
7.50 g., Bi-Metallic Copper-Nickel center in Aluminum-Bronze ring, 25 mm. **Subject:** Resorts - Neringa **Obv:** National arms **Rev:** Arms of Neringa in color

| Date | Mintage | VF20 | XF40 | MS60 | MS63 | MS65 |
|---|---|---|---|---|---|---|
| 2012 | 2,500 | PF65 25.00 | | | | |

**KM# 186.1 2 LITAI**
7.50 g., Bi-Metallic Copper-Nickel center in Aluminum-Bronze ring, 25 mm. **Subject:** Resorts - Palanga **Obv:** National arms **Rev:** Arms of Palanga

| Date | Mintage | VF20 | XF40 | MS60 | MS63 | MS65 |
|---|---|---|---|---|---|---|
| 2012 | 100,000 | — | — | 1.50 | 2.50 | 4.50 |

**KM# 186.2 2 LITAI**
7.50 g., Bi-Metallic Copper-Nickel center in Aluminum-Bronze ring, 25 mm. **Subject:** Resorts - Palanga **Obv:** National arms **Rev:** Arms of Palanga

| Date | Mintage | VF20 | XF40 | MS60 | MS63 | MS65 |
|---|---|---|---|---|---|---|
| 2012 | 2,500 | PF65 25.00 | | | | |

**KM# 191 2 LITAI**
1.24 g., 0.999 Gold 0.040 oz. AGW, 13.92 mm. **Subject:** Science **Obv:** Vytis **Rev:** Heart surgery

| Date | Mintage | VF20 | XF40 | MS60 | MS63 | MS65 |
|---|---|---|---|---|---|---|
| 2012 | 5,000 | PF65 50.00 | | | | |

**KM# 187 2 LITAI**
7.50 g., Bi-Metallic Copper-Nickel center in Aluminum-Bronze ring, 25 mm. **Obv:** National arms **Rev:** Distaff (spinning tool)

| Date | Mintage | VF20 | XF40 | MS60 | MS63 | MS65 |
|---|---|---|---|---|---|---|
| 2013 | 100,000 | — | — | 1.50 | 2.50 | 4.50 |

**KM# 188 2 LITAI**
7.50 g., Bi-Metallic Copper-Nickel center in Aluminum-Bronze ring, 25 mm. **Obv:** National arms **Rev:** Kurenas (traditional wooden boat)

| Date | Mintage | VF20 | XF40 | MS60 | MS63 | MS65 |
|---|---|---|---|---|---|---|
| 2013 | 100,000 | — | — | 1.50 | 2.50 | 4.50 |

**KM# 189 2 LITAI**
7.50 g., Bi-Metallic Copper-Nickel center in Aluminum-Bronze ring, 25 mm. **Obv:** National arms **Rev:** Puntukas stone

| Date | Mintage | VF20 | XF40 | MS60 | MS63 | MS65 |
|---|---|---|---|---|---|---|
| 2013 | 100,000 | — | — | 1.50 | 2.50 | 4.50 |

**KM# 190 2 LITAI**
7.50 g., Bi-Metallic Copper-Nickel center in Aluminum-Bronze ring, 25 mm. **Obv:** National arms **Rev:** Stelmuze oak

| Date | Mintage | VF20 | XF40 | MS60 | MS63 | MS65 |
|---|---|---|---|---|---|---|
| 2013 | 100,000 | — | — | 1.50 | 2.50 | 4.50 |

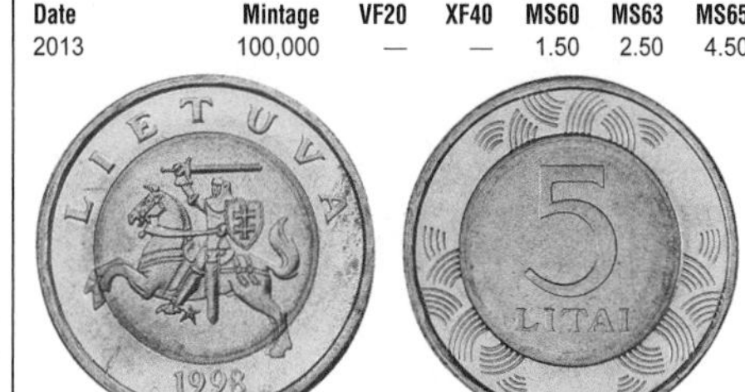

**KM# 113 5 LITAI**
10.10 g., Bi-Metallic Aluminum-Bronze center in Copper-Nickel ring, 27.5 mm. **Obv:** National arms within circle **Rev:** Value within circle **Edge Lettering:** PENKI LITAI

| Date | Mintage | VF20 | XF40 | MS60 | MS63 | MS65 |
|---|---|---|---|---|---|---|
| 2003 In sets only | — | — | — | — | — | 12.00 |
| 2003 | 10,000 | PF65 15.00 | | | | |
| 2008 In sets only | 3,800 | — | — | — | — | 14.00 |
| 2008 Prooflike | 200 | — | — | — | — | 30.00 |
| 2009 | — | — | — | 2.00 | 4.00 | 6.00 |
| 2009 Prooflike | 500 | — | — | — | — | 20.00 |
| 2010 In sets only | 3,500 | — | — | — | — | 15.00 |
| 2011 In sets only | 4,500 | — | — | — | — | 10.00 |
| 2012 In sets only | 4,000 | — | — | — | — | 10.00 |
| 2013 In sets only | 7,500 | — | — | — | — | 10.00 |

**KM# 132 5 LITAI**
28.28 g., 0.925 Silver 0.841 oz. ASW, 38.6 mm. **Series:** Endangered Wildlife **Obv:** Knight on horse **Rev:** Barn owl in flight **Edge Lettering:** LIETUVOS BANKAS

| Date | Mintage | VF20 | XF40 | MS60 | MS63 | MS65 |
|---|---|---|---|---|---|---|
| 2002 | 3,000 | PF65 150 | | | | |

**KM# 131 10 LITŲ**
13.15 g., Copper-Nickel, 28.7 mm. **Obv:** Knight on horse on shield within aerial harbor view **Rev:** Shield within city view **Edge Lettering:** KLAIPEDAI - 75 (twice)

| Date | Mintage | VF20 | XF40 | MS60 | MS63 | MS65 |
|---|---|---|---|---|---|---|
| 2002 | 5,000 | PF63 25.00 | PF65 35.00 | | | |

**KM# 160 10 LITŲ**
1.24 g., 0.999 Gold 0.0398 oz. AGW, 13.92 mm. **Obv:** Castle gate **Rev:** Geometric design

| Date | Mintage | VF20 | XF40 | MS60 | MS63 | MS65 |
|---|---|---|---|---|---|---|
| 2007 LMK | 7,000 | PF63 85.00 | PF65 95.00 | | | |

**KM# 169 10 LITŲ**
11.40 g., 0.925 Silver 0.339 oz. ASW, 28.7 mm. **Subject:** Lithuanian Culture - Music **Obv:** Vilnus **Rev:** Two chello and musical notations

| Date | Mintage | VF20 | XF40 | MS60 | MS63 | MS65 |
|---|---|---|---|---|---|---|
| 2010 | 10,000 | PF63 45.00 | PF65 50.00 | | | |

**KM# 175 10 LITŲ**
12.44 g., 0.925 Silver 0.370 oz. ASW, 28.7 mm. **Subject:** Lithuanian Culture - Theatre **Obv:** State emblem **Rev:** Theatre motif, two half faces **Edge Lettering:** LIETUVOS KULTURA * TEATRAS (twice)

| Date | Mintage | VF20 | XF40 | MS60 | MS63 | MS65 |
|---|---|---|---|---|---|---|
| 2011 | 10,000 | PF63 45.00 | PF65 50.00 | | | |

**KM# 179 10 LITŲ**
12.44 g., 0.925 Silver 0.370 oz. ASW, 28.7 mm. **Subject:** Artist's pallete

| Date | Mintage | VF20 | XF40 | MS60 | MS63 | MS65 |
|---|---|---|---|---|---|---|
| 2012 | 4,000 | PF63 45.00 | PF65 50.00 | | | |

**KM# 180 10 LITŲ**
1.24 g., 0.999 Gold 0.0398 oz. AGW, 13.92 mm. **Subject:** Science - Heart operation

| Date | Mintage | VF20 | XF40 | MS60 | MS63 | MS65 |
|---|---|---|---|---|---|---|
| 2012 | — | PF63 135 | PF65 155 | | | |

**KM# 201 10 LITŲ**
1.24 g., 0.999 Silver 0.0398 oz. ASW, 13.92 mm. **Obv:** Stylized Vytis left **Rev:** Neolithic period stylized amber disc

| Date | Mintage | F12 | VF20 | XF40 | MS60 | MS63 |
|---|---|---|---|---|---|---|
| 2014 | 5,000 | PF65 75.00 | | | | |

**KM# 203 10 LITŲ**
12.44 g., 0.925 Silver 0.370 oz. ASW, 28.7 mm. **Subject:** Lithuanian Culture - Cinema **Obv:** Vytis left **Rev:** Reel of film

| Date | Mintage | F12 | VF20 | XF40 | MS60 | MS63 |
|---|---|---|---|---|---|---|
| 2014 | 4,000 | PF65 75.00 | | | | |

**KM# 129 50 LITŲ**
28.28 g., 0.925 Silver 0.841 oz. ASW, 38.61 mm. **Subject:** Motiejus Valancius' 200th Birthday **Obv:** Knight on horse within shield above church and landscape **Rev:** Bust facing **Edge Lettering:** LIETUVISKAS ZODIS RASTAS IR TIKEJMAS TAUTOS GYVASTIS

| Date | Mintage | VF20 | XF40 | MS60 | MS63 | MS65 |
|---|---|---|---|---|---|---|
| 2001 | 2,000 | PF65 200 | | | | |

**KM# 130 50 LITŲ**
28.28 g., 0.925 Silver 0.841 oz. ASW, 38.61 mm. **Subject:** Jonas Basanavicius (1851-1927) **Obv:** Knight on horse **Rev:** Jonas Basanavlcius **Edge Lettering:** KAD AUSRAI AUSTANT PRAVISTU IR LIETUVOS DVASIA

| Date | Mintage | VF20 | XF40 | MS60 | MS63 | MS65 |
|---|---|---|---|---|---|---|
| 2001 | — | PF65 200 | | | | |

**KM# 133 50 LITŲ**
28.28 g., 0.925 Silver 0.841 oz. ASW, 38.61 mm. **Series:** Historical Architecture **Obv:** Republic of Lithuania coat of arms **Rev:** Trakai Island Castle **Edge Lettering:** ISTORIJOS IR ARCHITEKTUROS PAMINKLAI

| Date | Mintage | VF20 | XF40 | MS60 | MS63 | MS65 |
|---|---|---|---|---|---|---|
| 2002 | 1,500 | PF65 200 | | | | |

**KM# 134 50 LITŲ**
28.28 g., 0.925 Silver 0.841 oz. ASW, 38.6 mm. **Obv:** Knight on horse above value **Rev:** Vilnius Cathedral **Edge Lettering:** ISTORIJOS IR ARCHITEKTUROS PAMINKLAI

| Date | Mintage | VF20 | XF40 | MS60 | MS63 | MS65 |
|---|---|---|---|---|---|---|
| 2003 | 1,500 | PF65 175 | | | | |

**KM# 135 50 LITŲ**
28.28 g., 0.925 Silver 0.841 oz. ASW, 38.6 mm. **Subject:** Olympics **Obv:** Knight on horse above value **Rev:** Stylized cyclists **Edge Lettering:** XXVIII OLIMPIADOS ZAIDYNEMS

| Date | Mintage | VF20 | XF40 | MS60 | MS63 | MS65 |
|---|---|---|---|---|---|---|
| 2003 | 2,000 | PF65 150 | | | | |

**KM# 138 50 LITŲ**
28.28 g., 0.925 Silver 0.841 oz. ASW, 38.6 mm. **Series:** Historical Architecture **Subject:** 425th Anniversary - University of Vilnius **Obv:** Knight on horse **Rev:** Old university buildings **Edge:** Lettered **Edge Lettering:** ISTORIJOS IR ARCHITEKTUROS PAMINKLAI

| Date | Mintage | VF20 | XF40 | MS60 | MS63 | MS65 |
|---|---|---|---|---|---|---|
| 2004 | 2,000 | PF65 150 | | | | |

**KM# 139 50 LITŲ**
28.28 g., 0.925 Silver 0.841 oz. ASW, 38.6 mm. **Obv:** Knight on horse **Rev:** Pazaislis Monastery **Edge:** Lettered **Edge Lettering:** ISTORIJOS IR ARCHITEKTUROS PAMINKLAI

| Date | Mintage | VF20 | XF40 | MS60 | MS63 | MS65 |
|---|---|---|---|---|---|---|
| 2004 | 1,500 | PF65 150 | | | | |

**KM# 140 50 LITŲ**
28.28 g., 0.925 Silver 0.841 oz. ASW, 38.6 mm. **Subject:** First Lithuanian Statute of 1529 **Obv:** Knight on horse **Rev:** Seated and kneeling figures **Edge:** Lettered **Edge Lettering:** BUKIME TEISES VERGAI, KAD GALETUME NAUDOTIS LAISVEMIS

| Date | Mintage | VF20 | XF40 | MS60 | MS63 | MS65 |
|---|---|---|---|---|---|---|
| 2004 | 1,000 | PF65 200 | | | | |

**KM# 141 50 LITŲ**
28.28 g., 0.925 Silver 0.841 oz. ASW, 38.6 mm. **Subject:** Curonian Spit **Obv:** Knight on horse **Rev:** Shifting sand dunes design **Edge:** Ornamented pattern from Neringa emblem

| Date | Mintage | VF20 | XF40 | MS60 | MS63 | MS65 |
|---|---|---|---|---|---|---|
| 2004 | 2,000 | PF65 175 | | | | |

**KM# 143 50 LITŲ**
28.28 g., 0.925 Silver 0.841 oz. ASW, 38.61 mm. **Series:** Historical Architecture **Obv:** Denar coin with Knight on horse **Rev:** Kernavé hill fort **Edge Lettering:** ISTORIJOS IR ARCHITEKTUROS PAMINKLAI

| Date | Mintage | VF20 | XF40 | MS60 | MS63 | MS65 |
|---|---|---|---|---|---|---|
| 2005 | 2,000 | PF65 150 | | | | |

**KM# 144 50 LITŲ**
28.28 g., 0.925 Silver 0.841 oz. ASW, 38.6 mm. **Subject:** 150th Anniversary - National Museum **Obv:** Trio of ancient Lithuanian coins **Rev:** Man blowing horn **Edge Lettering:** PRO PUBLICO BONO

| Date | Mintage | VF20 | XF40 | MS60 | MS63 | MS65 |
|---|---|---|---|---|---|---|
| 2005 | 1,500 | PF65 275 | | | | |

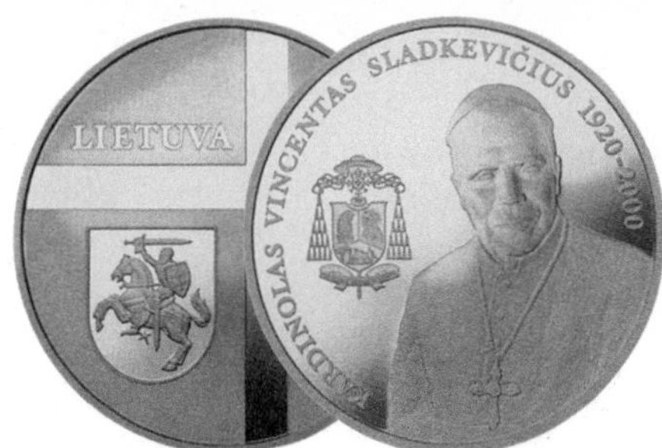


**KM# 145 50 LITŲ**
28.28 g., 0.925 Silver 0.841 oz. ASW, 38.6 mm. **Subject:** Knight on horse and cross **Rev:** Cardinal Vincentas Sladkevicius **Edge Lettering:** LET OUR LIFE BE BUILT ON GOODNESS AND HOPE

| Date | Mintage | VF20 | XF40 | MS60 | MS63 | MS65 |
|---|---|---|---|---|---|---|
| 2005 | 2,000 | **PF65** 175 | | | | |

**KM# 147 50 LITŲ**
28.28 g., 0.925 Silver 0.841 oz. ASW, 38.6 mm. **Subject:** 1905 Lithuanian Congress **Obv:** Knight on horse **Rev:** Legend and inscription **Edge:** Ornamented

| Date | Mintage | VF20 | XF40 | MS60 | MS63 | MS65 |
|---|---|---|---|---|---|---|
| 2005 | 1,500 | **PF65** 225 | | | | |

**KM# 148 50 LITŲ**
28.28 g., 0.925 Silver 0.841 oz. ASW, 38.6 mm. **Obv:** National arms on forest background **Rev:** Lynx prowling **Edge:** Stylized lynx paw prints

| Date | Mintage | VF20 | XF40 | MS60 | MS63 | MS65 |
|---|---|---|---|---|---|---|
| 2006 | 3,000 | **PF65** 175 | | | | |

**KM# 149 50 LITŲ**
28.28 g., 0.925 Silver 0.841 oz. ASW, 38.6 mm. **Obv:** National arms against castle wall background **Rev:** Medininkai Castle **Edge Lettering:** ISTORIJOS IR ARCHITEKTUROS PAMINKLAI

| Date | Mintage | VF20 | XF40 | MS60 | MS63 | MS65 |
|---|---|---|---|---|---|---|
| 2006 | 2,500 | **PF65** 200 | | | | |

**KM# 151 50 LITŲ**
28.28 g., 0.925 Silver 0.841 oz. ASW, 38.61 mm. **Subject:** 1831 Uprising **Obv:** Small national arms above battle scene **Obv. Legend:** LIETUVA **Rev:** Bust of Pliaterytė facing **Rev. Legend:** EMILIJA PLIATERYTĖ **Edge Lettering:** 1831 * SUKILIMAS

| Date | Mintage | VF20 | XF40 | MS60 | MS63 | MS65 |
|---|---|---|---|---|---|---|
| 2006 | 2,500 | **PF65** 200 | | | | |

**KM# 152 50 LITŲ**
28.28 g., 0.925 Silver 0.841 oz. ASW, 38.6 mm. **Subject:** XXIX Olympics 2008 - Beijing **Obv:** National arms **Obv. Legend:** LIETUVA **Rev:** Stylized swimmer right **Rev. Legend:** PEKINAS

| Date | Mintage | VF20 | XF40 | MS60 | MS63 | MS65 |
|---|---|---|---|---|---|---|
| 2007 | 5,000 | **PF65** 150 | | | | |

**KM# 161 50 LITŲ**
28.28 g., 0.925 Silver 0.841 oz. ASW, 38.6 mm. **Subject:** Panemune Castle **Obv:** Shield and fortress detail **Rev:** Castle towers

| Date | Mintage | VF20 | XF40 | MS60 | MS63 | MS65 |
|---|---|---|---|---|---|---|
| 2007 LMK | 5,000 | **PF65** 150 | | | | |

**KM# 153 50 LITŲ**
28.28 g., 0.925 Silver 0.841 oz. ASW, 38.6 mm. **Series:** European Cultural Heritage **Obv:** National arms surrounded by seven archaic crosses **Obv. Legend:** LIETUVA **Rev:** Circular latent image surrounded by seven archaic crosses

| Date | Mintage | VF20 | XF40 | MS60 | MS63 | MS65 |
|---|---|---|---|---|---|---|
| 2008 | 10,000 | **PF63** 120 | **PF65** 150 | | | |

**KM# 154 50 LITŲ**
28.28 g., 0.925 Silver 0.841 oz. ASW, 38.6 mm. **Subject:** 550th Anniversary Birth of St. Casimer **Obv:** National arms on shield **Obv. Legend:** LIETUVA **Rev:** St. Casimer standing holding flowers **Rev. Legend:** SV. KAZIMIERAS

| Date | Mintage | VF20 | XF40 | MS60 | MS63 | MS65 |
|---|---|---|---|---|---|---|
| 2008 | 5,000 | **PF65** 175 | | | | |

**KM# 155 50 LITŲ**
28.28 g., 0.925 Silver 0.841 oz. ASW, 38.6 mm. **Obv:** National arms **Obv. Legend:** LIETUVA **Rev:** Partial castle wall, towers **Rev. Legend:** KAUNO PILIS

| Date | Mintage | VF20 | XF40 | MS60 | MS63 | MS65 |
|---|---|---|---|---|---|---|
| 2008 | 10,000 | **PF63** 120 | **PF65** 150 | | | |

**KM# 159 50 LITŲ**
28.28 g., 0.925 Silver 0.841 oz. ASW, 38.6 mm. **Subject:** Lithuania Nature **Obv:** National Arms **Rev:** Bee

| Date | Mintage | VF20 | XF40 | MS60 | MS63 | MS65 |
|---|---|---|---|---|---|---|
| 2008 | 10,000 | **PF63** 120 | **PF65** 150 | | | |

**KM# 163 50 LITŲ**
28.28 g., 0.925 Silver 0.841 oz. ASW, 38.6 mm. **Subject:** Vilnius - European Culture Capital **Obv:** National Arms **Rev:** Female figure standing at easle

| Date | Mintage | VF20 | XF40 | MS60 | MS63 | MS65 |
|---|---|---|---|---|---|---|
| 2009 | 10,000 | **PF63** 120 | **PF65** 150 | | | |

**KM# 164 50 LITŲ**
28.28 g., 0.925 Silver 0.841 oz. ASW, 38.6 mm. **Subject:** Tytuvenai **Obv:** National Arms in Shield **Rev:** Tytuvenai Church facade at left

| Date | Mintage | VF20 | XF40 | MS60 | MS63 | MS65 |
|---|---|---|---|---|---|---|
| 2009 | 10,000 | **PF63** 120 | **PF65** 150 | | | |

**KM# 165 50 LITŲ**
28.28 g., 0.925 Silver 0.841 oz. ASW, 38.6 mm. **Subject:** Nature, Naktiziede **Obv:** Knight on horseback left **Rev:** Flowers

| Date | Mintage | VF20 | XF40 | MS60 | MS63 | MS65 |
|---|---|---|---|---|---|---|
| 2009 LMK | — | **PF63** 120 | **PF65** 150 | | | |

**KM# 170 50 LITŲ**
28.28 g., 0.925 Silver 0.841 oz. ASW, 38.61 mm. **Subject:** Biržai Castle **Obv:** Viltus in shield **Rev:** Castle view and ariel plan

| Date | Mintage | VF20 | XF40 | MS60 | MS63 | MS65 |
|---|---|---|---|---|---|---|
| 2010 | 10,000 | **PF63** 75.00 | **PF65** 85.00 | | | |

**KM# 171 50 LITŲ**
28.28 g., 0.925 Silver 0.841 oz. ASW, 38.61 mm. **Obv:** Vilnus **Rev:** Misgurnus Fossilis - European Weather Loach **Edge Lettering:** LIETUVOS GAMTA

| Date | Mintage | VF20 | XF40 | MS60 | MS63 | MS65 |
|---|---|---|---|---|---|---|
| 2010 | 10,000 | **PF63** 75.00 | **PF65** 85.00 | | | |

**KM# 181 50 LITŲ**
28.28 g., 0.925 Silver 0.841 oz. ASW, 38.6 mm. **Subject:** Battle of Grunwald

| Date | Mintage | VF20 | XF40 | MS60 | MS63 | MS65 |
|---|---|---|---|---|---|---|
| 2010 | — | **PF63** 75.00 | **PF65** 80.00 | | | |

**KM# 174 50 LITŲ**
28.28 g., 0.925 Silver 0.841 oz. ASW, 38.61 mm. **Subject:** Gabriele Petkevicaite-Bite, 150th Anniversary of Birth **Obv:** State emblem **Rev:** Portrait **Edge Lettering:** AD ASTRA (repeated 3 times)

| Date | Mintage | VF20 | XF40 | MS60 | MS63 | MS65 |
|---|---|---|---|---|---|---|
| 2011 | 10,000 | **PF63** 85.00 | **PF65** 100 | | | |

**KM# 176 50 LITŲ**
3.10 g., 0.9999 Gold 0.0997 oz. AGW, 16.25 mm. **Subject:** European Basketball Championship **Obv:** State emblem **Rev:** Basketball **Rev. Legend:** EUROPOS KREPSINIO CEMPIONATAS **Edge:** Reeded

| Date | Mintage | VF20 | XF40 | MS60 | MS63 | MS65 |
|---|---|---|---|---|---|---|
| 2011 | 5,000 | **PF63** 265 | **PF65** 285 | | | |

**KM# 178 50 LITŲ**
28.28 g., 0.925 Silver 0.841 oz. ASW, 38.61 mm. **Rev:** Balinis Vezlys - Emysorbicularis - Turtle **Edge Lettering:** LIETUVOS GAMTA

| Date | Mintage | VF20 | XF40 | MS60 | MS63 | MS65 |
|---|---|---|---|---|---|---|
| 2012 | 3,000 | **PF65** 90.00 | | | | |

**KM# 192 50 LITŲ**
28.28 g., 0.925 Silver 0.841 oz. ASW, 38.61 mm. **Subject:** Maironis, 150th Anniversary of Birth **Obv:** Vytis **Rev:** Maironis and text

| Date | Mintage | VF20 | XF40 | MS60 | MS63 | MS65 |
|---|---|---|---|---|---|---|
| 2012 | 3,000 | **PF65** 100 | | | | |

**KM# 193 50 LITŲ**
28.28 g., 0.925 Silver 0.841 oz. ASW, 38.61 mm. **Obv:** Vytis **Rev:** Dionizas Poska's "Baubliai"

| Date | Mintage | VF20 | XF40 | MS60 | MS63 | MS65 |
|---|---|---|---|---|---|---|
| 2012 | 4,000 | **PF65** 100 | | | | |

**KM# 194 50 LITŲ**
28.28 g., 0.925 Silver 0.841 oz. ASW, 38.61 mm. **Obv:** Vytis **Rev:** Christening of Samogitia

| Date | Mintage | VF20 | XF40 | MS60 | MS63 | MS65 |
|---|---|---|---|---|---|---|
| 2013 | 3,000 | **PF65** 100 | | | | |

**KM# 195 50 LITŲ**
28.28 g., 0.925 Silver 0.841 oz. ASW, 38.61 mm. **Subject:** Sajudis Independence demonstration, 125th Anniversary **Obv:** Vytis

| Date | Mintage | VF20 | XF40 | MS60 | MS63 | MS65 |
|---|---|---|---|---|---|---|
| 2013 | 4,000 | **PF65** 100 | | | | |

**KM# 196 50 LITŲ**
28.28 g., 0.925 Silver 0.841 oz. ASW, 38.61 mm. **Subject:** Presidency of the EU Council **Obv:** Stylized map of Europe with stars **Rev:** Vytis with stars

| Date | Mintage | VF20 | XF40 | MS60 | MS63 | MS65 |
|---|---|---|---|---|---|---|
| 2013 | 4,000 | **PF65** 100 | | | | |

**KM# 197 50 LITŲ**
28.28 g., 0.925 Silver 0.841 oz. ASW, 38.61 mm. **Subject:** Uprising of 1863-64 **Obv:** Three shields **Rev:** Swords

| Date | Mintage | VF20 | XF40 | MS60 | MS63 | MS65 |
|---|---|---|---|---|---|---|
| 2013 | 3,000 | PF65 100 | | | | |

**KM# 199 50 LITŲ**
28.28 g., 0.925 Silver 0.841 oz. ASW, 38.61 mm. **Subject:** Battle of Orsha, 500th Anniversary **Obv:** National shield **Rev:** Konstantinas Ostrogiskis and battle scene

| Date | Mintage | F12 | VF20 | XF40 | MS60 | MS63 |
|---|---|---|---|---|---|---|
| 2014 | 3,000 | PF65 75.00 | | | | |

**KM# 200 50 LITŲ**
28.28 g., 0.925 Silver 0.841 oz. ASW, 38.61 mm. **Subject:** Lithuania's road to independence, 25th Anniversary **Obv:** Vytis left **Rev:** Map of three Baltic States and vine

| Date | Mintage | F12 | VF20 | XF40 | MS60 | MS63 |
|---|---|---|---|---|---|---|
| 2014 | 4,000 | PF65 75.00 | | | | |

**KM# 202 50 LITŲ**
28.28 g., 0.925 Silver 0.841 oz. ASW, 38.61 mm. **Subject:** Vytautas Magnus University, 25th Anniversary of re-establishment **Obv:** Vytis left **Rev:** Open book

| Date | Mintage | F12 | VF20 | XF40 | MS60 | MS63 |
|---|---|---|---|---|---|---|
| 2014 | 3,000 | PF65 75.00 | | | | |

**KM# 204 50 LITŲ**
28.28 g., 0.925 Silver 0.841 oz. ASW, 38.61 mm. **Subject:** Kristijonas Donelaitis, 300th Anniversary of Birth **Obv:** Vytis left, Lithuanian peasant life around edge **Rev:** Works and activities of peasant life around edge, Sun at center

| Date | Mintage | F12 | VF20 | XF40 | MS60 | MS63 |
|---|---|---|---|---|---|---|
| 2014 | 3,000 | PF65 60.00 | | | | |

**KM# 158 100 LITŲ**
7.78 g., 0.999 Gold 0.2499 oz. AGW, 22.3 mm. **Subject:** Use of the Name Lithuania Millenium **Obv:** Linear National Arms **Rev:** Circular Legend

| Date | Mintage | VF20 | XF40 | MS60 | MS63 | MS65 |
|---|---|---|---|---|---|---|
| 2007 | 5,000 | PF65 600 | | | | |

**KM# 156 100 LITŲ**
7.78 g., 0.9999 Gold 0.2501 oz. AGW, 22.3 mm. **Subject:** Millennium of name "Lithuania **Obv:** Stylized national arms **Obv. Legend:** LIETUVA **Rev:** Partial parchment **Rev. Legend:** LIETUVOS DIDZIOJI KUNIGAIKSTYSTS

| Date | Mintage | VF20 | XF40 | MS60 | MS63 | MS65 |
|---|---|---|---|---|---|---|
| 2008 | 10,000 | PF63 500 | PF65 550 | | | |

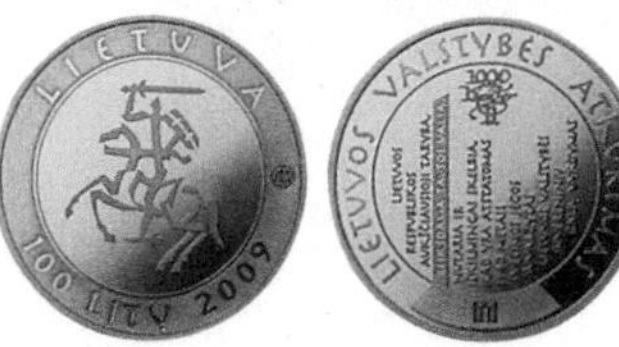

**KM# 166 100 LITŲ**
7.78 g., 0.999 Gold 0.2499 oz. AGW, 22.3 mm. **Subject:** 1000th Anniversary of Name Lithuania **Obv:** Linear knight **Rev:** Timeline

| Date | Mintage | VF20 | XF40 | MS60 | MS63 | MS65 |
|---|---|---|---|---|---|---|
| 2009 LMK | 10,000 | PF63 500 | PF65 550 | | | |

**KM# 198 100 LITŲ**
56.56 g., 0.925 Silver 1.6821 oz. ASW, 42 mm. **Subject:** First map, 400th Anniversary **Shape:** Square

| Date | Mintage | VF20 | XF40 | MS60 | MS63 | MS65 |
|---|---|---|---|---|---|---|
| 2013 | 4,000 | PF65 150 | | | | |

**KM# 136 200 LITŲ**
15.00 g., Bi-Metallic .900 Gold 7.9g. center in a .925 Silver 7.1g. ring, 27 mm. **Subject:** 750th Anniversary - King Mindaugas **Obv:** Knight on horse **Obv. Legend:** LIETUVA **Rev:** Seated King **Rev. Legend:** MINDAUGO KARUNAVIMAS **Edge Lettering:** LIETUVOS KARALYSTE 1253

| Date | Mintage | VF20 | XF40 | MS60 | MS63 | MS65 |
|---|---|---|---|---|---|---|
| 2003 | 2,000 | PF65 550 | | | | |

**KM# 146 500 LITŲ**
31.10 g., 0.9999 Gold 0.9998 oz. AGW, 32.5 mm. **Obv:** Knight on horse **Rev:** Palace **Edge:** Plain

| Date | Mintage | VF20 | XF40 | MS60 | MS63 | MS65 |
|---|---|---|---|---|---|---|
| 2005 | 1,000 | PF65 1,500 | | | | |

**KM# 173 500 LITŲ**
31.10 g., 0.999 Gold 0.9989 oz. AGW, 32.5 mm. **Subject:** Battle of Grunwald **Obv:** Shield around seated king **Rev:** Knights on horseback, warriors on foot

| Date | Mintage | VF20 | XF40 | MS60 | MS63 | MS65 |
|---|---|---|---|---|---|---|
| 2010 | 1,000 | PF65 1,500 | | | | |

## EURO COINAGE

**KM# 205 EURO CENT**
2.30 g., Copper Plated Steel, 16.25 mm. **Obv:** Vytis left **Rev:** Value and globe

| Date | Mintage | VF20 | XF40 | MS60 | MS63 | MS65 |
|---|---|---|---|---|---|---|
| 2015 | — | — | — | — | 0.50 | 1.00 |

**KM# 206 2 EURO CENT**
3.06 g., Copper Plated Steel, 16.25 mm. **Obv:** Vytis left **Rev:** Value and globe

| Date | Mintage | VF20 | XF40 | MS60 | MS63 | MS65 |
|---|---|---|---|---|---|---|
| 2015 | — | — | — | — | 0.75 | 1.50 |

**KM# 207 5 EURO CENT**
3.92 g., Copper Plated Steel, 21.25 mm. **Obv:** Vytis left **Rev:** Value and globe

| Date | Mintage | VF20 | XF40 | MS60 | MS63 | MS65 |
|---|---|---|---|---|---|---|
| 2015 | — | — | — | — | 1.00 | 2.00 |

**KM# 208 10 EURO CENT**
4.10 g., Brass, 19.75 mm. **Obv:** Vytis left **Rev:** Relief map of Western Europe, stars, lines and value

| Date | Mintage | VF20 | XF40 | MS60 | MS63 | MS65 |
|---|---|---|---|---|---|---|
| 2015 | — | — | — | — | 1.00 | 2.00 |

**KM# 209 20 EURO CENT**
5.74 g., Brass, 22.25 mm. **Obv:** Vytis left **Rev:** Relief map of Western Europe, stars, lines and value

| Date | Mintage | VF20 | XF40 | MS60 | MS63 | MS65 |
|---|---|---|---|---|---|---|
| 2015 | — | — | — | — | 1.25 | 2.50 |

**KM# 210 50 EURO CENT**
7.80 g., Brass, 24.25 mm. **Obv:** Vytis left **Rev:** Relief map of Western Europe, stars, lines and value

| Date | Mintage | VF20 | XF40 | MS60 | MS63 | MS65 |
|---|---|---|---|---|---|---|
| 2015 | — | — | — | — | 1.50 | 3.00 |

**KM# 211 EURO**
7.50 g., Bi-Metallic Copper-Nickel plated Nickel center in Copper-Nickel-Zinc ring, 23.25 mm. **Obv:** Vytis left **Rev:** Relief map of Western Europe, stars, lines and value

| Date | Mintage | VF20 | XF40 | MS60 | MS63 | MS65 |
|---|---|---|---|---|---|---|
| 2015 | — | — | — | — | 3.00 | 5.00 |

**KM# 212 2 EURO**
8.50 g., Bi-Metallic Copper-Nickel plated Nickel center in Copper-Nickel-Zinc ring, 25.75 mm. **Obv:** Vytis left **Rev:** Relief map of Western Europe, stars, lines and value

| Date | Mintage | VF20 | XF40 | MS60 | MS63 | MS65 |
|---|---|---|---|---|---|---|
| 2015 | — | — | — | — | 6.00 | 9.00 |

## MINT SETS

| KM# | Date | Mintage | Identification | Issue Price | Mkt Val |
|---|---|---|---|---|---|
| MS4 | 2003 (6) | 10,000 | KM#106-108, 111-113 | 7.50 | 35.00 |
| MS5 | 2008 (9) | 4,000 | KM#85-87 (dated 1991), 106-108, 111-113 | 30.00 | 30.00 |
| MS6 | 2009 (9) | 5,000 | KM#85-87, 106-108, 111-113 | — | 30.00 |
| MS7 | 2010 (7) | 3,500 | KM#106-108, 111-113 plus medal | — | 35.00 |
| MS8 | 2011 (7) | 4,500 | KM#106-108, 111-113 plus medal | — | 25.00 |
| MS9 | 2012 (7) | 4,000 | KM#106-108, 111-113 plus medal | — | 25.00 |
| MS10 | 2013 (7) | 3,500 | KM#106-108, 111-113 plus medal. Victorious battles of the Grand Duchy of Lithuania. | — | 25.00 |
| MS11 | 2013 (7) | 3,500 | KM#106-108, 111-113 plus medal. Transatlantic flight anniversary. | — | 25.00 |

## PROOF-LIKE SETS (PL)

| KM# | Date | Mintage | Identification | Issue Price | Mkt Val |
|---|---|---|---|---|---|
| PL1 | 2008 (6) | 200 | KM#106-108, 111-113 | — | 115 |
| PL2 | 2009 (6) | 500 | KM#106-108, 111-113 | — | 75.00 |

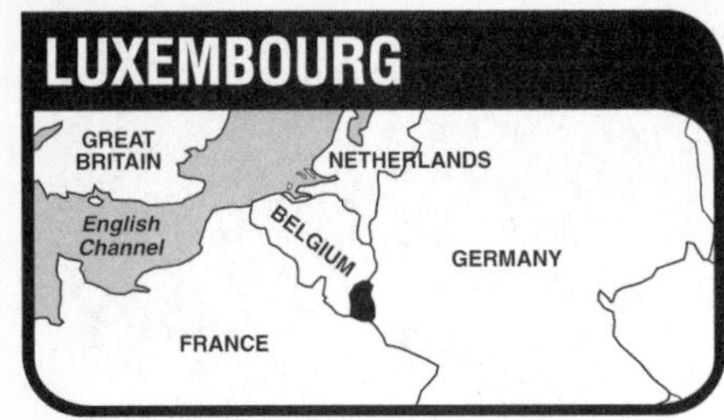


The Grand Duchy of Luxembourg is located in western Europe between Belgium, Germany and France, has an area of 1,103 sq. mi. (2,586 sq. km.) and a population of 377,100. Capital: Luxembourg. The economy is based on steel.

**RULER**
Henri, 2000-

**MINT MARKS**
A - Paris
(b) - Brussels, privy marks only
H – Gunzburg
(n) – lion - Namur
(u) - Utrecht, privy marks only
Grand Duchy

## EURO COINAGE

European Economic Community Issues

### KM# 75 EURO CENT

2.30 g., Copper Plated Steel, 16.25 mm. **Ruler:** Henri **Obv:** Head right **Rev:** Value and globe **Edge:** Plain

| Date | Mintage | VF20 | XF40 | MS60 | MS63 | MS65 |
|---|---|---|---|---|---|---|
| 2002 (u) | 34,557,500 | — | — | 0.35 | 0.50 | 0.75 |
| 2002 (u) | 1,500 | PF65 3.00 | | | | |
| 2003 (u) | 1,500,000 | — | — | 0.50 | 0.75 | 1.00 |
| 2003 (u) | 1,500 | PF65 3.00 | | | | |
| 2004 (u) | 21,001,000 | — | — | 0.35 | 0.50 | 0.75 |
| 2004 (u) | 1,500 | PF65 3.00 | | | | |
| 2005 (u) | 7,000,000 | — | — | 0.35 | 0.50 | 0.75 |
| 2005 (u) | 1,500 | PF65 3.00 | | | | |
| 2006 (u) | 4,000,000 | — | — | 0.35 | 0.50 | 0.75 |
| 2006 (u) | 2,000 | PF65 4.00 | | | | |
| 2007 (a) | 6,000,000 | — | — | 0.35 | 0.50 | 0.75 |
| 2007 (a) | 2,500 | PF65 4.00 | | | | |
| 2008 (a) | 10,000,000 | — | — | 0.35 | 0.50 | 0.75 |
| 2008 (a) | 2,500 | PF65 4.00 | | | | |
| 2009 (u) | 4,000,000 | — | — | 0.35 | 0.50 | 0.75 |
| 2009 (u) | 2,500 | PF65 4.00 | | | | |
| 2010 (u) | 6,000,000 | — | — | 0.35 | 0.50 | 0.75 |
| 2010 (u) | 1,500 | PF65 4.00 | | | | |
| 2011 (u) | 7,600,000 | — | — | 0.35 | 0.50 | 0.75 |
| 2011 (u) | 1,500 | PF65 4.00 | | | | |
| 2012 (u) | 9,200,000 | — | — | 0.35 | 0.50 | 0.75 |
| 2012 (u) | — | PF65 4.00 | | | | |
| 2013 | — | — | — | 0.35 | 0.50 | 0.75 |
| 2013 | — | PF65 4.00 | | | | |
| 2014 | — | — | — | 0.35 | 0.50 | 0.75 |
| 2014 | — | PF65 4.00 | | | | |

### KM# 76 2 EURO CENT

3.06 g., Copper Plated Steel, 18.75 mm. **Ruler:** Henri **Obv:** Head right **Rev:** Value and globe **Edge:** Grooved

| Date | Mintage | VF20 | XF40 | MS60 | MS63 | MS65 |
|---|---|---|---|---|---|---|
| 2002 (u) | 35,917,500 | — | — | 0.50 | 0.75 | 1.00 |
| 2002 (u) | 1,500 | PF65 5.00 | | | | |
| 2003 (u) | 1,500,000 | — | — | 0.65 | 0.85 | 1.25 |
| 2003 (u) | 1,500 | PF65 5.00 | | | | |
| 2004 (u) | 20,001,000 | — | — | 0.50 | 0.75 | 1.00 |
| 2004 (u) | 1,500 | PF65 5.00 | | | | |
| 2005 (u) | 13,000,000 | — | — | 0.50 | 0.75 | 1.00 |
| 2005 (u) | 1,500 | PF65 5.00 | | | | |
| 2006 (u) | 4,000,000 | — | — | 0.50 | 0.75 | 1.00 |
| 2006 (u) | 2,000 | PF65 6.00 | | | | |
| 2007 (a) | 8,000,000 | — | — | 0.50 | 0.75 | 1.00 |
| 2007 (a) | 2,500 | PF65 6.00 | | | | |
| 2008 (a) | 12,000,000 | — | — | 0.50 | 0.75 | 1.00 |
| 2008 (a) | 2,500 | PF65 6.00 | | | | |
| 2009 (u) | 3,000,000 | — | — | 0.50 | 0.75 | 1.00 |
| 2009 (u) | 2,500 | PF65 6.00 | | | | |
| 2010 (u) | 8,000,000 | — | — | 0.50 | 0.75 | 1.00 |
| 2010 (u) | 1,500 | PF65 6.00 | | | | |
| 2011 (u) | 6,200,000 | — | — | 0.50 | 0.75 | 1.00 |
| 2011 (u) | 1,500 | PF65 6.00 | | | | |
| 2012 (u) | 7,200,000 | — | — | 0.50 | 0.75 | 1.00 |
| 2012 (u) | — | PF65 6.00 | | | | |
| 2013 | — | — | — | 0.50 | 0.75 | 1.00 |
| 2013 | — | PF65 6.00 | | | | |
| 2014 | — | — | — | 0.50 | 0.75 | 1.00 |
| 2014 | — | PF65 6.00 | | | | |

### KM# 77 5 EURO CENT

3.92 g., Copper Plated Steel, 21.25 mm. **Ruler:** Henri **Obv:** Head right **Rev:** Value and globe **Edge:** Plain

| Date | Mintage | VF20 | XF40 | MS60 | MS63 | MS65 |
|---|---|---|---|---|---|---|
| 2002 (u) | 28,917,500 | — | — | 0.75 | 1.00 | 1.50 |
| 2002 (u) | 1,500 | PF65 7.00 | | | | |
| 2003 (u) | 4,500,000 | — | — | 1.00 | 1.25 | 2.00 |
| 2003 (u) | 1,500 | PF65 7.00 | | | | |
| 2004 (u) | 16,001,000 | — | — | 0.75 | 1.00 | 1.50 |
| 2004 (u) | 1,500 | PF65 7.00 | | | | |
| 2005 (u) | 6,000,000 | — | — | 0.75 | 1.00 | 1.50 |
| 2005 (u) | 1,500 | PF65 7.00 | | | | |
| 2006 (u) | 5,000,000 | — | — | 0.75 | 1.00 | 1.50 |
| 2006 (u) | 2,000 | PF65 8.00 | | | | |
| 2007 (a) | 5,000,000 | — | — | 0.75 | 1.00 | 1.50 |
| 2007 (a) | 2,500 | PF65 9.00 | | | | |
| 2008 (a) | 9,000,000 | — | — | 0.75 | 1.00 | 1.50 |
| 2008 (a) | 2,500 | PF65 9.00 | | | | |
| 2009 (u) | 6,000,000 | — | — | 0.75 | 1.00 | 1.50 |
| 2009 (u) | 2,500 | PF65 9.00 | | | | |
| 2010 (u) | 6,000,000 | — | — | 0.75 | 1.00 | 1.50 |
| 2010 (u) | 1,500 | PF65 9.00 | | | | |
| 2011 (u) | 6,700,000 | — | — | 0.75 | 1.00 | 1.50 |
| 2011 (u) | 1,500 | PF65 9.00 | | | | |
| 2012 (u) | 5,200,000 | — | — | 0.75 | 1.00 | 1.50 |
| 2012 (u) | — | PF65 9.00 | | | | |
| 2013 | — | — | — | 0.75 | 1.00 | 1.50 |
| 2013 | — | PF65 9.00 | | | | |
| 2014 | — | — | — | 0.75 | 1.00 | 1.50 |
| 2014 | — | PF65 9.00 | | | | |

### KM# 78 10 EURO CENT

4.10 g., Brass, 19.75 mm. **Ruler:** Henri **Obv:** Grand Duke's portrait **Rev:** Value and map **Edge:** Reeded

| Date | Mintage | VF20 | XF40 | MS60 | MS63 | MS65 |
|---|---|---|---|---|---|---|
| 2002 (u) | 25,117,500 | — | — | 0.75 | 1.00 | 1.50 |
| 2002 (u) | 1,500 | PF65 14.00 | | | | |
| 2003 (u) | 1,500,000 | — | — | 0.75 | 1.00 | 1.50 |
| 2003 (u) | 1,500 | PF65 14.00 | | | | |
| 2004 (u) | 12,001,000 | — | — | 0.75 | 1.00 | 1.50 |
| 2004 (u) | 1,500 | PF65 14.00 | | | | |
| 2005 (u) | 2,000,000 | — | — | 0.75 | 1.00 | 1.50 |
| 2005 (u) | 1,500 | PF65 14.00 | | | | |
| 2006 (u) | 4,000,000 | — | — | 0.75 | 1.00 | 1.50 |
| 2006 (u) | 2,000 | PF65 14.00 | | | | |

### KM# 89 10 EURO CENT

4.10 g., Brass, 19.75 mm. **Ruler:** Henri **Obv:** Prince's portrait **Rev:** Relief map of Western Europe, stars, lines and value **Edge:** Reeded

| Date | Mintage | VF20 | XF40 | MS60 | MS63 | MS65 |
|---|---|---|---|---|---|---|
| 2007 (a) | 5,000,000 | — | — | 0.75 | 1.00 | 1.50 |
| 2007 (a) | 2,500 | PF65 14.00 | | | | |
| 2008 (a) | 5,000,000 | — | — | 0.75 | 1.00 | 1.50 |
| 2008 (a) | 2,500 | PF65 14.00 | | | | |
| 2009 (u) | 4,000,000 | — | — | 0.75 | 1.00 | 1.50 |
| 2009 (u) | 2,500 | PF65 14.00 | | | | |
| 2010 (u) | 4,000,000 | — | — | 0.75 | 1.00 | 1.50 |
| 2010 (u) | 1,500 | PF65 14.00 | | | | |
| 2011 (u) | 4,800,000 | — | — | 0.75 | 1.00 | 1.50 |
| 2011 (u) | 1,500 | PF65 14.00 | | | | |
| 2012 (u) | 2,200,000 | — | — | 0.75 | 1.00 | 1.50 |
| 2012 (u) | — | PF65 14.00 | | | | |
| 2013 | — | — | — | 0.75 | 1.00 | 1.50 |
| 2013 | — | PF65 14.00 | | | | |
| 2014 | — | — | — | 0.75 | 1.00 | 1.50 |
| 2014 | — | PF65 14.00 | | | | |

### KM# 79 20 EURO CENT

5.74 g., Brass, 22.25 mm. **Ruler:** Henri **Obv:** Grand Duke's portrait **Rev:** Value and map **Edge:** Notched

| Date | Mintage | VF20 | XF40 | MS60 | MS63 | MS65 |
|---|---|---|---|---|---|---|
| 2002 (u) | 25,717,500 | — | — | 1.00 | 1.25 | 1.75 |
| 2002 (u) | 1,500 | PF65 16.00 | | | | |
| 2003 (u) | 1,500,000 | — | — | 1.25 | 1.50 | 2.00 |
| 2003 (u) | 1,500 | PF65 16.00 | | | | |
| 2004 (u) | 14,001,000 | — | — | 1.00 | 1.25 | 1.75 |
| 2004 (u) | 1,500 | PF65 16.00 | | | | |
| 2005 (u) | 6,000,000 | — | — | 1.00 | 1.25 | 1.75 |
| 2005 (u) | 1,500 | PF65 16.00 | | | | |
| 2006 (u) | 7,000,000 | — | — | 1.00 | 1.25 | 1.75 |
| 2006 (u) | 2,000 | PF65 16.00 | | | | |

### KM# 90 20 EURO CENT

5.74 g., Brass, 22.25 mm. **Ruler:** Henri **Obv:** Prince's portrait **Rev:** Relief map of Western Europe, stars, lines and value **Edge:** Notched

| Date | Mintage | VF20 | XF40 | MS60 | MS63 | MS65 |
|---|---|---|---|---|---|---|
| 2007 (a) | 8,000,000 | — | — | 1.00 | 1.25 | 1.75 |
| 2007 (a) | 2,500 | PF65 16.00 | | | | |
| 2008 (a) | 6,000,000 | — | — | 1.00 | 1.25 | 1.75 |
| 2008 (a) | 2,500 | PF65 16.00 | | | | |
| 2009 (u) | 5,000,000 | — | — | 1.00 | 1.25 | 1.75 |
| 2009 (u) | 2,500 | PF65 16.00 | | | | |
| 2010 (u) | 8,000,000 | — | — | 1.00 | 1.25 | 1.75 |
| 2010 (u) | 1,500 | PF65 16.00 | | | | |
| 2011 (u) | 5,300,000 | — | — | 1.00 | 1.25 | 1.75 |
| 2011 (u) | 1,500 | PF65 16.00 | | | | |
| 2012 (u) | 5,200,000 | — | — | 1.00 | 1.25 | 1.75 |
| 2012 (u) | — | PF65 16.00 | | | | |
| 2013 | — | — | — | 1.00 | 1.25 | 1.75 |
| 2013 | — | PF65 16.00 | | | | |
| 2014 | — | — | — | 1.00 | 1.25 | 1.75 |
| 2014 | — | PF65 16.00 | | | | |

### KM# 80 50 EURO CENT

7.80 g., Brass, 24.25 mm. **Ruler:** Henri **Obv:** Grand Duke's portrait **Rev:** Value and map **Edge:** Reeded

| Date | Mintage | VF20 | XF40 | MS60 | MS63 | MS65 |
|---|---|---|---|---|---|---|
| 2002 (u) | 21,917,500 | — | — | 1.25 | 1.50 | 2.00 |
| 2002 (u) | 1,500 | PF65 18.00 | | | | |
| 2003 (u) | 2,500,000 | — | — | 1.50 | 1.75 | 2.25 |
| 2003 (u) | 1,500 | PF65 18.00 | | | | |
| 2004 (u) | 10,001,000 | — | — | 1.25 | 1.50 | 2.00 |
| 2004 (u) | 1,500 | PF65 18.00 | | | | |
| 2005 (u) | 3,000,000 | — | — | 1.25 | 1.50 | 2.00 |
| 2005 (u) | 1,500 | PF65 18.00 | | | | |
| 2006 (u) | 3,000,000 | — | — | 1.25 | 1.50 | 2.00 |
| 2006 (u) | 2,000 | PF65 18.00 | | | | |

### KM# 91 50 EURO CENT

7.80 g., Brass, 24.25 mm. **Ruler:** Henri **Obv:** Prince's portrait **Rev:** Relief map of Western Europe, stars, lines and value **Edge:** Reeded

| Date | Mintage | VF20 | XF40 | MS60 | MS63 | MS65 |
|---|---|---|---|---|---|---|
| 2007 (a) | 4,000,000 | — | — | 1.25 | 1.50 | 2.00 |
| 2007 (a) | 2,500 | PF65 18.00 | | | | |
| 2008 (a) | 4,000,000 | — | — | 1.25 | 1.50 | 2.00 |
| 2008 (a) | 2,500 | PF65 18.00 | | | | |
| 2009 (u) | 2,000,000 | — | — | 1.25 | 1.50 | 2.00 |

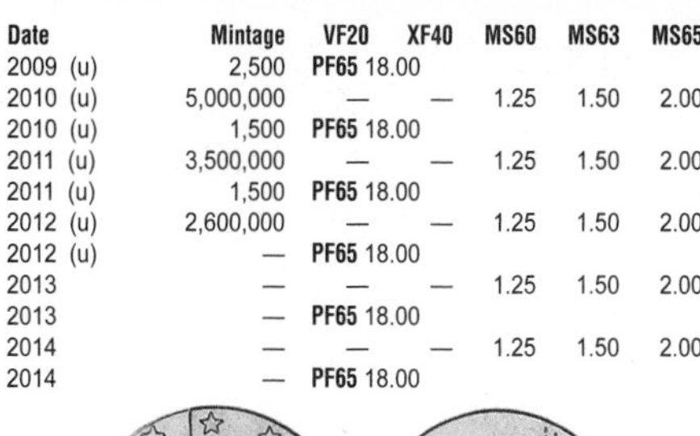

| Date | Mintage | VF20 | XF40 | MS60 | MS63 | MS65 |
|---|---|---|---|---|---|---|
| 2009 (u) | 2,500 | PF65 18.00 | | | | |
| 2010 (u) | 5,000,000 | — | — | 1.25 | 1.50 | 2.00 |
| 2010 (u) | 1,500 | PF65 18.00 | | | | |
| 2011 (u) | 3,500,000 | — | — | 1.25 | 1.50 | 2.00 |
| 2011 (u) | 1,500 | PF65 18.00 | | | | |
| 2012 (u) | 2,600,000 | — | — | 1.25 | 1.50 | 2.00 |
| 2012 (u) | — | PF65 18.00 | | | | |
| 2013 | — | — | — | 1.25 | 1.50 | 2.00 |
| 2013 | — | PF65 18.00 | | | | |
| 2014 | — | — | — | 1.25 | 1.50 | 2.00 |
| 2014 | — | PF65 18.00 | | | | |

### KM# 81 EURO

7.50 g., Bi-Metallic Copper-Nickel center in Nickel-Brass ring, 23.25 mm. **Ruler:** Henri **Obv:** Grand Duke's portrait **Rev:** Value and map within divided circle **Edge:** Segmented reeding

| Date | Mintage | VF20 | XF40 | MS60 | MS63 | MS65 |
|---|---|---|---|---|---|---|
| 2002 (u) | 21,318,525 | — | — | 2.50 | 3.00 | 3.50 |
| 2002 (u) | 1,500 | PF65 18.00 | | | | |
| 2003 (u) | 1,500,000 | — | — | 2.75 | 3.25 | 3.75 |
| 2003 (u) | 1,500 | PF65 18.00 | | | | |
| 2004 (u) | 9,001,000 | — | — | 2.50 | 3.00 | 3.50 |
| 2004 (u) | 1,500 | PF65 18.00 | | | | |
| 2005 (u) | 2,000,000 | — | — | 2.50 | 3.00 | 3.50 |
| 2005 (u) | 1,500 | PF65 18.00 | | | | |
| 2006 (u) | 1,000,000 | — | — | 2.50 | 3.00 | 3.50 |
| 2006 (u) | 2,000 | PF65 18.00 | | | | |

### KM# 92 EURO

7.50 g., Bi-Metallic Copper-Nickel center in Nickel-Brass ring, 23.25 mm. **Ruler:** Henri **Obv:** Prince's portrait **Rev:** Relief map of Western Europe, stars, lines and value **Edge:** Segmented reeding

| Date | Mintage | VF20 | XF40 | MS60 | MS63 | MS65 |
|---|---|---|---|---|---|---|
| 2007 (a) | 480,000 | — | — | 2.25 | 2.75 | 3.00 |
| 2007 (a) | 2,500 | PF65 24.00 | | | | |
| 2008 (a) | 480,000 | — | — | 2.25 | 2.75 | 3.00 |
| 2008 (a) | 2,500 | PF65 24.00 | | | | |
| 2009 (u) | 240,000 | — | — | 2.25 | 2.75 | 3.00 |
| 2009 (u) | 2,500 | PF65 24.00 | | | | |
| 2010 (u) | 1,000,000 | — | — | 2.25 | 2.75 | 3.00 |
| 2010 (u) | 1,500 | PF65 24.00 | | | | |
| 2011 (u) | 1,520,000 | — | — | 2.25 | 2.75 | 3.00 |
| 2011 (u) | 1,500 | PF65 24.00 | | | | |
| 2012 (u) | 2,240,000 | — | — | 2.25 | 2.75 | 3.00 |
| 2012 (u) | — | PF65 24.00 | | | | |
| 2013 | — | — | — | 2.25 | 2.75 | 3.00 |
| 2013 | — | PF65 24.00 | | | | |
| 2014 | — | — | — | 2.25 | 2.75 | 3.00 |
| 2014 | — | PF65 24.00 | | | | |

### KM# 82 2 EURO

8.50 g., Bi-Metallic Nickel-Brass center in Copper-Nickel ring, 25.75 mm. **Ruler:** Henri **Obv:** Grand Duke's portrait **Rev:** Value and map within divided circle **Edge:** Reeded with 2's and stars

| Date | Mintage | VF20 | XF40 | MS60 | MS63 | MS65 |
|---|---|---|---|---|---|---|
| 2002 (u) | 18,517,500 | — | — | — | 3.75 | 5.50 |
| 2002 (u) | 1,500 | PF65 28.00 | | | | |
| 2003 (u) | 3,500,000 | — | — | — | 4.50 | 7.00 |
| 2003 (u) | 1,500 | PF65 28.00 | | | | |
| 2004 (u) | 7,553,200 | — | — | — | 4.00 | 6.00 |
| 2004 (u) | 1,500 | PF65 28.00 | | | | |
| 2005 (u) | 3,500,000 | — | — | — | 4.00 | 6.00 |
| 2005 (u) | 1,500 | PF65 28.00 | | | | |
| 2006 (u) | 2,000,000 | — | — | — | 4.00 | 6.00 |
| 2006 (u) | 2,000 | PF65 28.00 | | | | |

### KM# 85 2 EURO

8.50 g., Bi-Metallic Nickel-Brass center in Copper-Nickel ring, 25.75 mm. **Ruler:** Henri **Obv:** Head right and crowned monogram within 1/2 star circle **Rev:** Value and map within divided circle **Edge:** Reeded with 2's and stars

| Date | Mintage | VF20 | XF40 | MS60 | MS63 | MS65 |
|---|---|---|---|---|---|---|
| 2004 (u) | 2,447,800 | — | — | — | 7.00 | 10.00 |
| 2004 (u) | 10,000 | — | — | — | — | 50.00 |
| Special Unc. | | | | | | |
| 2004 (u) | 4,000 | PF65 50.00 | | | | |

### KM# 87 2 EURO

8.50 g., Bi-Metallic Nickel-Brass center in Copper-Nickel ring, 25.75 mm. **Ruler:** Henri **Obv:** Conjoined heads right within circle **Rev:** Value and map within divided circle **Edge:** Reeded with 2's and stars

| Date | Mintage | VF20 | XF40 | MS60 | MS63 | MS65 |
|---|---|---|---|---|---|---|
| 2005 | 2,720,000 | — | — | — | 7.00 | 10.00 |
| 2005 Special Unc. | 10,000 | — | — | — | — | 75.00 |
| 2005 | 4,000 | PF65 50.00 | | | | |

### KM# 88 2 EURO

8.50 g., Bi-Metallic Nickel-Brass center in Copper-Nickel ring, 25.75 mm. **Ruler:** Henri **Obv:** Conjoined heads right within circle and star border **Rev:** Value and map within divided circle **Edge:** Reeded with 2's and stars

| Date | Mintage | VF20 | XF40 | MS60 | MS63 | MS65 |
|---|---|---|---|---|---|---|
| 2006 | 1,030,000 | — | — | — | 7.00 | 10.00 |
| 2006 Special Unc. | 15,000 | — | — | — | — | 32.00 |
| 2006 | 4,500 | PF65 50.00 | | | | |

### KM# 93 2 EURO

8.50 g., Bi-Metallic Nickel-Brass center in Copper-Nickel ring, 25.75 mm. **Ruler:** Henri **Obv:** Prince's portrait **Rev:** Relief map of Western Europe, stars, lines and value **Edge:** Reeded with 2's and stars

| Date | Mintage | VF20 | XF40 | MS60 | MS63 | MS65 |
|---|---|---|---|---|---|---|
| 2007 (a) | 4,000,000 | — | — | — | 4.00 | 5.00 |
| 2007 (a) | 2,500 | PF65 28.00 | | | | |
| 2008 (a) | 6,000,000 | — | — | — | 4.00 | 5.00 |
| 2008 (a) | 2,500 | PF65 28.00 | | | | |
| 2009 (u) | 240,000 | — | — | — | 6.00 | 8.00 |
| 2009 (u) | 2,500 | PF65 30.00 | | | | |
| 2010 (u) | 3,500,000 | — | — | — | 4.00 | 5.00 |
| 2010 (u) | 1,500 | PF65 30.00 | | | | |
| 2011 (u) | 2,320,000 | — | — | — | 4.00 | 5.00 |
| 2011 (u) | 1,500 | PF65 30.00 | | | | |
| 2012 (u) | 3,760,000 | — | — | — | 4.00 | 5.00 |
| 2012 (u) | — | PF65 30.00 | | | | |
| 2013 | — | — | — | — | 4.00 | 5.00 |
| 2013 | — | PF65 30.00 | | | | |
| 2014 | — | — | — | — | 4.00 | 5.00 |
| 2014 | — | PF65 30.00 | | | | |

### KM# 94 2 EURO

8.50 g., Bi-Metallic Nickel-Brass center in Copper-Nickel ring, 25.75 mm. **Ruler:** Henri **Subject:** 50th Anniversary Treaty of Rome **Obv:** Open treaty book with latent image on left hand page **Obv. Legend:** LËTZEBUERG **Rev:** Large value at left, modified outline of Europe at right **Edge:** Reeded with 2's and stars

| Date | Mintage | VF20 | XF40 | MS60 | MS63 | MS65 |
|---|---|---|---|---|---|---|
| 2007 (a) | 2,026,000 | — | — | — | 6.50 | 10.00 |
| 2007 (a) | 15,000 | — | — | — | — | 25.00 |
| Special Unc. | | | | | | |
| 2007 (a) | 5,000 | PF65 30.00 | | | | |

### KM# 95 2 EURO

8.50 g., Bi-Metallic Nickel-Brass center in Copper-Nickel ring, 25.75 mm. **Ruler:** Henri **Obv:** Palace in background at left, head 3/4 left at right **Obv. Legend:** LETZEBUERG **Rev:** Large value at left, modified outline of Europe at right **Edge:** Reeded with 2's and stars

| Date | Mintage | VF20 | XF40 | MS60 | MS63 | MS65 |
|---|---|---|---|---|---|---|
| 2007 (a) | 1,011,000 | — | — | — | 6.50 | 10.00 |
| 2007 (a) | 15,000 | — | — | — | — | 25.00 |
| Special Unc. | | | | | | |
| 2007 (a) | 5,000 | PF65 40.00 | | | | |

### KM# 96 2 EURO

8.50 g., Bi-Metallic Nickel-Brass center in Copper-Nickel ring, 25.75 mm. **Ruler:** Henri **Obv:** Head at left, Chateau de Berg at right **Obv. Legend:** LETZEBUERG **Rev:** Large value at left, modified outline of Europe at right **Edge:** Reeded with 2's and stars

| Date | Mintage | VF20 | XF40 | MS60 | MS63 | MS65 |
|---|---|---|---|---|---|---|
| 2008 (a) | 1,000,000 | — | 4.00 | — | 5.00 | 6.25 |
| 2008 (a) | 15,000 | — | — | — | — | 30.00 |
| Special Unc. | | | | | | |
| 2008 (a) | 5,000 | PF65 15.00 | | | | |

### KM# 106 2 EURO

8.50 g., Bi-Metallic Nickel-Brass center in Copper-Nickel ring, 25.75 mm. **Ruler:** Henri **Subject:** 90th Anniversary of Grand Duchess Charlotte **Obv:** Conjoined busts of Charlotte and Henri **Edge:** Reeded with 2's and stars

| Date | Mintage | VF20 | XF40 | MS60 | MS63 | MS65 |
|---|---|---|---|---|---|---|
| 2009 | 822,500 | — | — | — | 7.00 | 9.00 |
| 2009 Special Unc. | 10,000 | — | — | — | — | 30.00 |
| 2009 | 2,500 | PF65 15.00 | | | | |

### KM# 107 2 EURO

8.50 g., Bi-Metallic Nickel-Brass center in Copper-Nickel ring, 25.75 mm. **Ruler:** Henri **Subject:** European Monetary Union - 10th Anniversary **Obv:** Alternating stick figure with Euro emblem design or Head of Grand-Duke **Edge:** Reeded with 2's and stars

| Date | Mintage | VF20 | XF40 | MS60 | MS63 | MS65 |
|---|---|---|---|---|---|---|
| 2009 | 812,500 | — | — | — | 5.00 | 6.00 |
| 2009 Special Unc. | 10,000 | — | — | — | — | 30.00 |
| 2009 | 2,500 | **PF65** 15.00 | | | | |

### KM# 115 2 EURO

8.50 g., Bi-Metallic Nickel-Brass center in Copper-Nickel ring, 25.75 mm. **Ruler:** Henri **Obv:** Henry head facing, crowned shield **Rev:** Large value at left, modified outline mape of Europe at right **Edge:** Reeded with 2's and stars

| Date | Mintage | VF20 | XF40 | MS60 | MS63 | MS65 |
|---|---|---|---|---|---|---|
| 2010 (a) Special Unc. | 7,500 | — | — | — | — | 30.00 |
| 2010 (a) | 500,000 | — | — | — | 6.50 | 9.00 |
| 2010 (a) | 1,500 | **PF65** 20.00 | | | | |

### KM# 116 2 EURO

8.50 g., Bi-Metallic Nickel-Brass center in Copper-Nickel ring, 25.75 mm. **Ruler:** Henri **Subject:** Jean of Luxembourg - Nassau, 50th Anniversary of his appointment as Grand Duke **Obv:** Conjoined head left of Charlotte, Jean and Henri **Edge:** Reeded with 2's and stars

| Date | Mintage | VF20 | XF40 | MS60 | MS63 | MS65 |
|---|---|---|---|---|---|---|
| 2011 Special Unc. | 7,500 | — | — | — | — | 30.00 |
| 2011 | 707,500 | — | — | — | 7.00 | 9.00 |
| 2011 | 1,500 | **PF65** 15.00 | | | | |

### KM# 119 2 EURO

8.50 g., Bi-Metallic Nickel-Brass center in Copper-Nickel ring, 25.75 mm. **Ruler:** Henri **Subject:** Euro coinage, 10th Anniversary **Obv:** Euro symbol on globe, child-like rendering around

| Date | Mintage | VF20 | XF40 | MS60 | MS63 | MS65 |
|---|---|---|---|---|---|---|
| 2012 | 1,400,000 | — | — | — | 6.00 | 8.00 |

### KM# 120 2 EURO

8.50 g., Bi-Metallic Nickel-Brass center in Copper-Nickel ring, 25.75 mm. **Subject:** Royal Wedding **Obv:** Three portraits

| Date | Mintage | VF20 | XF40 | MS60 | MS63 | MS65 |
|---|---|---|---|---|---|---|
| 2012 | — | — | — | — | — | 8.00 |

### KM# 121 2 EURO

8.50 g., Bi-Metallic Nickel-Brass center in Copper-Nickel ring, 25.75 mm. **Subject:** 100th anniversary of the death of William IV

| Date | Mintage | VF20 | XF40 | MS60 | MS63 | MS65 |
|---|---|---|---|---|---|---|
| 2012 | — | — | — | — | — | 8.00 |

### KM# 125 2 EURO

8.50 g., Bi-Metallic Nickel-Brass plated nickel in Copper-Nickel ring, 25.75 mm. **Ruler:** Henri **Obv:** National anthem at left, profile at right

| Date | Mintage | VF20 | XF40 | MS60 | MS63 | MS65 |
|---|---|---|---|---|---|---|
| 2013 | 722,000 | — | — | — | 4.00 | 5.00 |
| 2013 Special Unc. | — | — | — | — | — | 30.00 |
| 2013 | — | **PF65** 20.00 | | | | |

### KM# 129 2 EURO

Bi-Metallic Nickel-Brass center in Copper-Nickel ring, 25.75 mm. **Ruler:** Henri **Subject:** 175th Anniversary

| Date | Mintage | F12 | VF20 | XF40 | MS60 | MS63 |
|---|---|---|---|---|---|---|
| 2014 | — | — | — | — | 6.50 | 9.00 |

### KM# 84 5 EURO

6.22 g., 0.999 Gold 0.1998 oz. AGW, 20 mm. **Ruler:** Henri **Subject:** European Central Bank **Obv:** Grand Duke Henri **Rev:** Building

| Date | Mintage | VF20 | XF40 | MS60 | MS63 | MS65 |
|---|---|---|---|---|---|---|
| 2003 (u) | 20,000 | **PF63** 350 | **PF65** 375 | | | |

### KM# 108 5 EURO

16.60 g., Bi-Metallic Niobium center in .925 Silver ring, 34 mm. **Ruler:** Henri **Subject:** Vianden Castle **Obv:** Head right **Rev:** Castle view

| Date | Mintage | VF20 | XF40 | MS60 | MS63 | MS65 |
|---|---|---|---|---|---|---|
| 2009 | 7,500 | — | — | — | — | 150 |

### KM# 109 5 EURO

Bi-Metallic Nordic Gold center in .925 Silver ring, 34 mm. **Ruler:** Henri **Subject:** Common Kestrel **Obv:** Head right **Rev:** Bird

| Date | Mintage | VF20 | XF40 | MS60 | MS63 | MS65 |
|---|---|---|---|---|---|---|
| 2009 | 3,000 | **PF63** 60.00 | **PF65** 70.00 | | | |

### KM# 111 5 EURO

16.60 g., Bi-Metallic Niobium center in .925 Silver ring, 34 mm. **Ruler:** Henri **Subject:** Chateau d'Esch-Sur-Sûre **Obv:** Head right **Rev:** Chateau view

| Date | Mintage | VF20 | XF40 | MS60 | MS63 | MS65 |
|---|---|---|---|---|---|---|
| 2010 Prooflike | 3,000 | — | — | — | — | 100 |

### KM# 112 5 EURO

Bi-Metallic Nordic Gold center in .925 Silver ring, 34 mm. **Ruler:** Henri **Subject:** Flora and Fauna - Arnica Montana **Obv:** Head right **Rev:** Flowers

| Date | Mintage | VF20 | XF40 | MS60 | MS63 | MS65 |
|---|---|---|---|---|---|---|
| 2010 | 3,000 | **PF63** 50.00 | **PF65** 60.00 | | | |

### KM# 117 5 EURO

16.60 g., Bi-Metallic Niobium center in .925 Silver ring, 34 mm. **Ruler:** Henri **Subject:** Mersch Castle **Obv:** Head right **Rev:** Castle vie

| Date | Mintage | VF20 | XF40 | MS60 | MS63 | MS65 |
|---|---|---|---|---|---|---|
| 2011 Prooflike | 3,000 | — | — | — | — | 100 |

### KM# 118 5 EURO

16.15 g., Bi-Metallic Nordic Gold center in .925 Silver ring, 34 mm. **Ruler:** Henri **Subject:** Flora and Fauna - Otter

| Date | Mintage | VF20 | XF40 | MS60 | MS63 | MS65 |
|---|---|---|---|---|---|---|
| 2011 | 3,000 | **PF63** 50.00 | **PF65** 60.00 | | | |

### KM# 123 5 EURO

16.60 g., Bi-Metallic Niobium center in .925 silver ring, 34 mm. **Ruler:** Henri **Obv:** Profile right **Rev:** Bourscheid castle

| Date | Mintage | VF20 | XF40 | MS60 | MS63 | MS65 |
|---|---|---|---|---|---|---|
| 2012 | 3,000 | **PF65** 135 | | | | |

### KM# 124 5 EURO

15.00 g., Bi-Metallic Aluminum-Bronze center in .925 Silver ring, 34 mm. **Ruler:** Henri **Rev:** Ophrys orchid

| Date | Mintage | VF20 | XF40 | MS60 | MS63 | MS65 |
|---|---|---|---|---|---|---|
| 2012 | 3,000 | **PF65** 120 | | | | |

### KM# 126 5 EURO

16.60 g., Bi-Metallic Niobium center in .925 Silver ring, 34 mm. **Ruler:** Henri **Obv:** Profile right **Rev:** Beaufort castle

| Date | Mintage | VF20 | XF40 | MS60 | MS63 | MS65 |
|---|---|---|---|---|---|---|
| 2013 | 3,000 | **PF65** 135 | | | | |

### KM# 127 5 EURO

16.00 g., Bi-Metallic Aluminum-Bronze center in .925 Silver ring, 34 mm. **Ruler:** Henri **Rev:** European honey bee flower

| Date | Mintage | VF20 | XF40 | MS60 | MS63 | MS65 |
|---|---|---|---|---|---|---|
| 2013 | 3,000 | **PF65** 120 | | | | |

### KM# 113 700 EURO CENTS

20.00 g., 0.925 Silver 0.5948 oz. ASW, 34 mm. **Ruler:** Henri **Subject:** 700th Anniversary - Marriage of John of Luxembourg

| Date | Mintage | VF20 | XF40 | MS60 | MS63 | MS65 |
|---|---|---|---|---|---|---|
| 2010 | 3,000 | PF63 75.00 | PF65 85.00 | | | |

### KM# 97 10 EURO

3.11 g., 0.999 Gold 0.0999 oz. AGW, 25.71 mm. **Ruler:** Henri **Subject:** Culture **Obv:** Head right **Rev:** Hellenic sculpture head

| Date | Mintage | VF20 | XF40 | MS60 | MS63 | MS65 |
|---|---|---|---|---|---|---|
| 2004 | 5,000 | PF63 175 | PF65 200 | | | |

### KM# 99 10 EURO

8.00 g., Bi-Metallic Titanium center in .925 Silver ring, 26 mm. **Ruler:** Henri **Subject:** State Bank 150th Anniversary **Obv:** Head right **Rev:** Bank Plaza

| Date | Mintage | VF20 | XF40 | MS60 | MS63 | MS65 |
|---|---|---|---|---|---|---|
| 2006 | 7,500 | — | — | — | — | 150 |

### KM# 101 10 EURO

3.11 g., 0.999 Gold 0.0999 oz. AGW, 16 mm. **Ruler:** Henri **Obv:** Head right **Rev:** Wild pig of Titelberg

| Date | Mintage | VF20 | XF40 | MS60 | MS63 | MS65 |
|---|---|---|---|---|---|---|
| 2006 | 5,000 | PF63 175 | PF65 200 | | | |

### KM# 104 10 EURO

10.37 g., 0.999 Gold 0.3331 oz. AGW, 23 mm. **Ruler:** Henri **Subject:** Banque Central - 10th Anniversary **Obv:** Head right **Rev:** Old and new bank buildings

| Date | Mintage | VF20 | XF40 | MS60 | MS63 | MS65 |
|---|---|---|---|---|---|---|
| 2008 | 1,250 | PF63 575 | PF65 600 | | | |

### KM# 110 10 EURO

3.11 g., 0.999 Gold 0.0999 oz. AGW, 16 mm. **Ruler:** Henri **Subject:** Deer of Orval's Refuge **Obv:** Head right **Rev:** Stag seated, flower in background

| Date | Mintage | VF20 | XF40 | MS60 | MS63 | MS65 |
|---|---|---|---|---|---|---|
| 2009 | 3,000 | PF63 175 | PF65 200 | | | |

### KM# 114 10 EURO

13.50 g., Bi-Metallic Titanium center in .925 Silver ring, 34 mm. **Ruler:** Henri **Subject:** Schengen Accord, 25th Anniversary **Obv:** Head right **Rev:** Building

| Date | Mintage | VF20 | XF40 | MS60 | MS63 | MS65 |
|---|---|---|---|---|---|---|
| 2010 Prooflike | 3,000 | — | — | — | — | 125 |

### KM# 122 10 EURO

3.11 g., 0.999 Gold 0.0999 oz. AGW, 16 mm. **Ruler:** Henri **Obv:** Profile right **Rev:** Renert the fox

| Date | Mintage | VF20 | XF40 | MS60 | MS63 | MS65 |
|---|---|---|---|---|---|---|
| 2011 | 3,000 | PF65 225 | | | | |

### KM# 128 10 EURO

3.11 g., 0.999 Gold 0.0999 oz. AGW, 16 mm. **Ruler:** Henri **Rev:** Golden Frau statue

| Date | Mintage | VF20 | XF40 | MS60 | MS63 | MS65 |
|---|---|---|---|---|---|---|
| 2013 | 3,000 | PF65 220 | | | | |

### KM# 130 15 EURO

6.22 g., 0.999 Gold 0.1998 oz. AGW, 20 mm. **Ruler:** Henri **Subject:** Central Bank, 15th Anniversary **Obv:** Head left **Rev:** Central Bank building

| Date | Mintage | VF20 | XF40 | MS60 | MS63 | MS65 |
|---|---|---|---|---|---|---|
| 2013 | 2,000 | PF65 350 | | | | |

### KM# 102 20 EURO

13.50 g., Bi-Metallic Titanium center in .925 Silver ring, 34 mm. **Ruler:** Henri **Obv:** Three heads facing **Rev:** Council D'Etat building

| Date | Mintage | VF20 | XF40 | MS60 | MS63 | MS65 |
|---|---|---|---|---|---|---|
| 2006 | 4,000 | — | — | — | — | 120 |

### KM# 83 25 EURO

22.85 g., 0.925 Silver 0.6795 oz. ASW, 37 mm. **Ruler:** Henri **Subject:** European Court System **Obv:** Grand Duke Henri **Rev:** Sword scale on law book

| Date | Mintage | VF20 | XF40 | MS60 | MS63 | MS65 |
|---|---|---|---|---|---|---|
| 2002 (u) | 20,000 | PF63 80.00 | PF65 100 | | | |

### KM# 86 25 EURO

22.85 g., 0.925 Silver 0.6795 oz. ASW, 37 mm. **Ruler:** Henri **Subject:** European Parliament **Obv:** Grand Duke Henri **Rev:** Parliament

| Date | Mintage | VF20 | XF40 | MS60 | MS63 | MS65 |
|---|---|---|---|---|---|---|
| 2004 (u) | 20,000 | PF63 80.00 | PF65 100 | | | |

### KM# 98 25 EURO

22.80 g., 0.925 Silver 0.6781 oz. ASW, 37 mm. **Ruler:** Henri **Subject:** EU Presidency **Obv:** Head right **Rev:** Conseil de l'Union building in Brussels

| Date | Mintage | VF20 | XF40 | MS60 | MS63 | MS65 |
|---|---|---|---|---|---|---|
| 2005 | 10,000 | PF63 80.00 | PF65 100 | | | |

### KM# 100 25 EURO

22.80 g., 0.925 Silver 0.6781 oz. ASW, 37 mm. **Ruler:** Henri **Obv:** Head right **Rev:** European Commission building "Berlaymont" in Brussels

| Date | Mintage | VF20 | XF40 | MS60 | MS63 | MS65 |
|---|---|---|---|---|---|---|
| 2006 | 5,000 | PF63 85.00 | PF65 110 | | | |

### KM# 103 25 EURO

22.85 g., 0.925 Silver 0.6795 oz. ASW, 37 mm. **Ruler:** Henri **Subject:** European Court of Auditors 30th Anniversary

| Date | Mintage | VF20 | XF40 | MS60 | MS63 | MS65 |
|---|---|---|---|---|---|---|
| 2007 | 3,000 | PF63 80.00 | PF65 100 | | | |

### KM# 105 25 EURO

22.85 g., 0.925 Silver 0.6795 oz. ASW, 37 mm. **Ruler:** Henri **Subject:** European Investment Bank

| Date | Mintage | VF20 | XF40 | MS60 | MS63 | MS65 |
|---|---|---|---|---|---|---|
| 2008 | 4,000 | PF65 275 | | | | |

## MINT SETS

| KM# | Date | Mintage | Identification | Issue Price | Mkt Val |
|---|---|---|---|---|---|
| MS7 | 2002 (8) | 35,000 | KM#75-82 | — | 20.00 |
| MS8 | 2002 (8) | — | KM#75-82 | — | 20.00 |
| MS9 | 2003 (8) | 50,000 | KM#75-82, Adolph Brucke | — | 30.00 |
| MS10 | 2003 (8) | 3,500 | KM#75-82 plus stamps | — | 75.00 |
| MS11 | 2004 (8) | 40,000 | KM#75-82 | — | 50.00 |
| MS12 | 2004 (8) | 6,400 | KM#75-82 plus stamps | — | 50.00 |
| MS13 | 2004 (8) | 500 | KM#75-82, Grand Duke | — | — |
| MS14 | 2004 (8) | 500 | KM#75-82, Ducal Palace | — | — |
| MS15 | 2005 (9) | 20,000 | KM#75-82, 87 | 40.00 | 65.00 |
| MS16 | 2005 (8) | 6,500 | KM#75-82 plus stamps | — | 55.00 |
| MS17 | 2005 (8) | 2,000 | KM#75-82, Women and Myth, signed by Gastauer | — | 75.00 |
| MS18 | 2006 (9) | 15,000 | KM#75-82, 88 | 40.00 | 65.00 |
| MS19 | 2006 (8) | 2,000 | KM#75-82 plus stamps | — | 75.00 |
| MS20 | 2007 (9) | 11,000 | KM#75-78, 89-93, 94 | 37.50 | 50.00 |
| MS21 | 2008 (9) | 10,000 | KM#75-77, 89-93, 96 | 37.50 | 40.00 |
| MS22 | 2009 (9) | 10,000 | KM#75-77, 89-93, 106 | 37.50 | 40.00 |
| MS23 | 2010 (9) | 7,500 | KM#75-77, 89-93, 115 | 37.50 | 40.00 |
| MS24 | 2011 (9) | 7,500 | KM#75-77, 89-93, 116 | 37.50 | 40.00 |

## PROOF SETS

| KM# | Date | Mintage | Identification | Issue Price | Mkt Val |
|---|---|---|---|---|---|
| PS2 | 2002 (8) | 1,500 | KM#75-82 | 100 | 300 |
| PS3 | 2003 (8) | 1,500 | KM#75-82 | 100 | 300 |
| PS4 | 2004 (9) | 1,500 | KM#75-82, 85 | 105 | 300 |
| PS5 | 2005 (9) | 1,500 | KM#75-82, 87 | 105 | 250 |
| PS6 | 2006 (9) | 2,000 | KM#75-82, 88 | 120 | 200 |
| PS7 | 2007 (10) | 2,500 | KM#75-77, 89-95 | 125 | 200 |
| PS8 | 2008 (9) | 2,500 | KM#75-77, 89-93, 96 | 125 | 250 |
| PS9 | 2004-2008 (6) | 2,500 | KM#85, 87, 88, 94, 95, 96 | 105 | 200 |
| PS10 | 2009 (10) | 2,000 | KM#75-77, 89-93, 106, 107 | 125 | 250 |
| PS11 | 2010 (9) | 2,500 | KM#75-77, 89-93, 115 | 125 | 250 |
| PS12 | 2011 (9) | 1,500 | KM#75-77, 89-93, 116 | 125 | 200 |

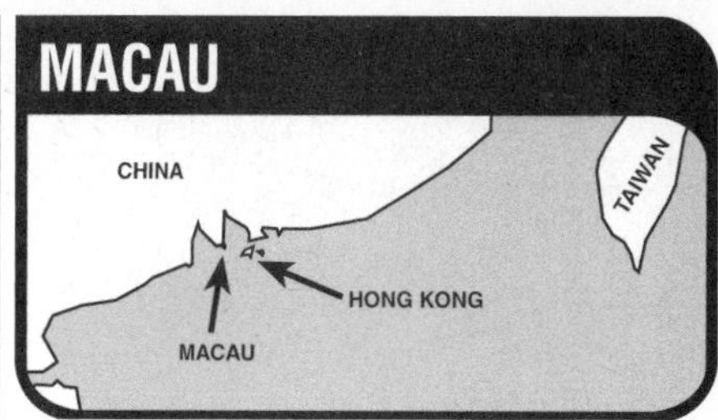


The Province of Macau, a Portuguese overseas province located in the South China Sea 40 miles southwest of Hong Kong, consists of the peninsula of Macau and the islands of Taipa and Coloane. It has an area of 6.2 sq. mi.(16 sq. km.) and a population of 500,000. Capital: Macau. Macau's economy is based on light industry, commerce, tourism, fishing, and gold trading - Macau is one of the entirely free markets for gold in the world. Cement, textiles, fireworks, vegetable oils, and metal products are exported.

In 1987, Portugal and China agreed that Macau would become a Chinese Territory in 1999. In December of 1999, Macau became a special administrative zone of China.

**MINT MARKS**

(p) - Pobjoy Mint

(s) - Singapore Mint

Pobjoy Mint

Singapore Mint

# SPECIAL ADMINISTRATIVE REGION (S.A.R.)

## STANDARD COINAGE

100 Avos = 1 Pataca

### KM# 70 10 AVOS

1.38 g., Brass, 17 mm. **Obv:** MACAU written at center with date below **Rev:** Crowned lion dance scene above value flanked by mint marks

| Date | Mintage | VF20 | XF40 | MS60 | MS63 | MS65 |
|---|---|---|---|---|---|---|
| 2005 | — | — | — | — | 0.75 | 1.25 |
| 2007 | — | — | — | — | 0.75 | 1.25 |

### KM# 72 50 AVOS

4.59 g., Brass, 23 mm. **Obv:** MACAU written across center of globe with date below **Rev:** The dragon dance led by a man

| Date | Mintage | VF20 | XF40 | MS60 | MS63 | MS65 |
|---|---|---|---|---|---|---|
| 2003 | — | — | — | 1.00 | 1.50 | 2.50 |
| 2005 | — | — | — | 1.00 | 1.50 | 2.50 |

### KM# 57 PATACA

9.18 g., Copper-Nickel, 25.98 mm. **Obv:** MACAU written across center of globe with date below **Rev:** Guia Fortress and Chapel of Our Lady of Guia **Edge:** Reeded

| Date | Mintage | VF20 | XF40 | MS60 | MS63 | MS65 |
|---|---|---|---|---|---|---|
| 2003 | — | — | 0.60 | 1.00 | 1.50 | 2.00 |
| 2005 | — | — | 0.60 | 1.00 | 1.50 | 2.00 |
| 2007 | — | — | 0.60 | 1.00 | 1.50 | 2.00 |

### KM# 56 5 PATACAS

10.10 g., Copper-Nickel **Obv:** MACAU written across center of globe with date below **Rev:** Chinese junk, ruins of St. Paul's Cathedral in background **Edge:** Plain **Shape:** 12-sided

| Date | Mintage | VF20 | XF40 | MS60 | MS63 | MS65 |
|---|---|---|---|---|---|---|
| 2003 | — | — | — | — | 3.00 | 5.00 |
| 2005 | — | — | — | — | 3.00 | 5.00 |
| 2007 | — | — | — | — | 3.00 | 5.00 |

### KM# 153 10 PATACAS

0.30 g., 0.999 Gold, 7 mm. **Obv:** A Ma statue **Rev:** Lotus flower

| Date | Mintage | VF20 | XF40 | MS60 | MS63 | MS65 |
|---|---|---|---|---|---|---|
| 2009 | Est. 5000 | PF63 22.00 PF65 25.00 | | | | |

### KM# 165 10 PATACAS

31.11 g., 0.999 Silver 0.999 oz. ASW, 40.7 mm. **Subject:** Year of the Snake **Obv:** Snake, color at right **Rev:** Ruins of St. Pauls

| Date | Mintage | VF20 | XF40 | MS60 | MS63 | MS65 |
|---|---|---|---|---|---|---|
| 2013 | Est. 6000 | PF63 75.00 PF65 85.00 | | | | |

### KM# 142 20 PATACAS

31.11 g., 0.999 Silver 0.999 oz. ASW, 40.7 mm. **Subject:** Year of the Rat **Obv:** A Ma Temple **Rev:** Rat, multicolor flowers at right

| Date | Mintage | VF20 | XF40 | MS60 | MS63 | MS65 |
|---|---|---|---|---|---|---|
| 2008 | 6,000 | PF65 130 | | | | |

### KM# 145 20 PATACAS

31.11 g., 0.999 Silver 0.999 oz. ASW, 40.7 mm. **Subject:** Year of the Ox **Obv:** Moorish Barracks **Rev:** Ox, multicolor flowers at right

| Date | Mintage | VF20 | XF40 | MS60 | MS63 | MS65 |
|---|---|---|---|---|---|---|
| 2009 | — | PF65 60.00 | | | | |

### KM# 151 20 PATACAS

31.11 g., 0.999 Silver 0.999 oz. ASW, 40.7 mm. **Obv:** A Ma statue **Rev:** Lotus flower

| Date | Mintage | VF20 | XF40 | MS60 | MS63 | MS65 |
|---|---|---|---|---|---|---|
| 2009 | Est. 5600 | PF63 65.00 PF65 75.00 | | | | |

### KM# 156 20 PATACAS

31.11 g., 0.999 Silver 0.999 oz. ASW, 40.7 mm. **Subject:** Year of the Tiger **Rev:** Tiger in color

| Date | Mintage | VF20 | XF40 | MS60 | MS63 | MS65 |
|---|---|---|---|---|---|---|
| 2010 | Est. 6000 | PF63 65.00 PF65 75.00 | | | | |

### KM# 159 20 PATACAS

31.11 g., 0.999 Silver 0.999 oz. ASW, 40.7 mm. **Obv:** Rabbit in color **Rev:** Dom Pedro V theater

| Date | Mintage | VF20 | XF40 | MS60 | MS63 | MS65 |
|---|---|---|---|---|---|---|
| 2011 | — | PF65 75.00 | | | | |

### KM# 162 20 PATACAS

28.28 g., 0.925 Silver 0.841 oz. ASW, 40.7 mm. **Subject:** Year of the Dragon **Obv:** Dragon in color

| Date | Mintage | VF20 | XF40 | MS60 | MS63 | MS65 |
|---|---|---|---|---|---|---|
| 2012 | — | PF65 150 | | | | |

### KM# 128 50 PATACAS

28.28 g., 0.925 Silver 0.841 oz. ASW partially gilt **Subject:** 1st World Championship Grand Prix **Rev:** Two race cars - gilt

| Date | Mintage | VF20 | XF40 | MS60 | MS63 | MS65 |
|---|---|---|---|---|---|---|
| 2003 | 5,000 | PF65 75.00 | | | | |

### KM# 154 50 PATACAS

1.24 g., 0.999 Gold 0.0398 oz. AGW, 13.92 mm. **Obv:** A Ma statue **Rev:** Lotus flower

| Date | Mintage | VF20 | XF40 | MS60 | MS63 | MS65 |
|---|---|---|---|---|---|---|
| 2009 | Est. 5000 | PF63 75.00 PF65 90.00 | | | | |

### KM# 102 100 PATACAS

28.28 g., 0.925 Silver 0.841 oz. ASW **Subject:** Year of the Snake **Obv:** Church façade **Rev:** Snake

| Date | Mintage | VF20 | XF40 | MS60 | MS63 | MS65 |
|---|---|---|---|---|---|---|
| 2001 | 4,000 | PF65 55.00 | | | | |

### KM# 107 100 PATACAS

28.28 g., 0.925 Silver 0.841 oz. ASW, 38.6 mm. **Subject:** Year of the Horse **Obv:** Church façade flanked by stars **Rev:** Horse above value **Edge:** Reeded

| Date | Mintage | VF20 | XF40 | MS60 | MS63 | MS65 |
|---|---|---|---|---|---|---|
| 2002 | — | PF65 45.00 | | | | |

### KM# 122 100 PATACAS

28.28 g., 0.925 Silver 0.841 oz. ASW **Subject:** 5th Anniversary Return of Macao to China

| Date | Mintage | VF20 | XF40 | MS60 | MS63 | MS65 |
|---|---|---|---|---|---|---|
| 2004 | 10,000 | PF63 50.00 PF65 60.00 | | | | |

### KM# 130 100 PATACAS

28.28 g., 0.925 Silver 0.841 oz. ASW **Series:** Lunar **Subject:** Year of the Monkey

| Date | Mintage | VF20 | XF40 | MS60 | MS63 | MS65 |
|---|---|---|---|---|---|---|
| 2004 | 4,000 | PF65 75.00 | | | | |
| 2004 | 1,000 | — | — | — | 50.00 | 60.00 |

### KM# 134 100 PATACAS

28.28 g., 0.925 Silver 0.841 oz. ASW **Series:** Lunar **Subject:** Year of the Rooster **Rev:** Stylized rooster walking left

| Date | Mintage | VF20 | XF40 | MS60 | MS63 | MS65 |
|---|---|---|---|---|---|---|
| 2005 | — | PF65 90.00 | | | | |

### KM# 137 100 PATACAS

28.28 g., 0.925 Silver 0.841 oz. ASW **Subject:** IV East Asian Games - FRIENDSHIP

| Date | Mintage | VF20 | XF40 | MS60 | MS63 | MS65 |
|---|---|---|---|---|---|---|
| 2005 | 6,000 | PF63 65.00 PF65 75.00 | | | | |

### KM# 139 100 PATACAS

28.28 g., 0.925 Silver 0.841 oz. ASW **Series:** Lunar **Subject:** Year of the Dog **Rev:** Stylized dog standing left

| Date | Mintage | VF20 | XF40 | MS60 | MS63 | MS65 |
|---|---|---|---|---|---|---|
| 2006 | — | PF65 90.00 | | | | |

### KM# 148 100 PATACAS

31.11 g., 0.925 Silver 0.925 oz. ASW, 40 mm. **Subject:** Year of the Pig **Rev:** Pig in color

| Date | Mintage | VF20 | XF40 | MS60 | MS63 | MS65 |
|---|---|---|---|---|---|---|
| 2007 | Est. 15000 | PF63 75.00 PF65 90.00 | | | | |

**KM# 143 100 PATACAS**
155.50 g., 0.999 Silver 4.9944 oz. ASW, 65 mm. **Subject:** Year of the Rat **Obv:** A Ma Temple **Rev:** Rat, multicolor flowers at right **Note:** Illustration reduced.

| Date | Mintage | VF20 | XF40 | MS60 | MS63 | MS65 |
|---|---|---|---|---|---|---|
| 2008 | 500 | PF65 250 | | | | |

**KM# 146 100 PATACAS**
155.50 g., 0.999 Silver 4.9944 oz. ASW, 65 mm. **Subject:** Year of the Ox **Obv:** Moorish Barracks **Rev:** Ox, multicolor flowers at right **Note:** Illustration reduced.

| Date | Mintage | VF20 | XF40 | MS60 | MS63 | MS65 |
|---|---|---|---|---|---|---|
| 2009 | 500 | PF65 250 | | | | |

**KM# 152 100 PATACAS**
155.50 g., 0.999 Silver 4.9944 oz. ASW, 65 mm. **Obv:** A Ma statue **Rev:** Lotus flower

| Date | Mintage | VF20 | XF40 | MS60 | MS63 | MS65 |
|---|---|---|---|---|---|---|
| 2009 | Est. 1000 | PF65 275 | | | | |

**KM# 157 100 PATACAS**
155.50 g., 0.999 Silver 4.9944 oz. ASW, 65 mm. **Subject:** Year of the Tiger **Rev:** Tiger in color

| Date | Mintage | VF20 | XF40 | MS60 | MS63 | MS65 |
|---|---|---|---|---|---|---|
| 2010 | — | PF65 450 | | | | |

**KM# 160 100 PATACAS**
155.50 g., 0.999 Silver 4.9944 oz. ASW, 65 mm. **Subject:** Year of the Rabbit **Obv:** Rabbit in color **Rev:** Dom Pedro V theater

| Date | Mintage | VF20 | XF40 | MS60 | MS63 | MS65 |
|---|---|---|---|---|---|---|
| 2011 | 500 | PF65 400 | | | | |

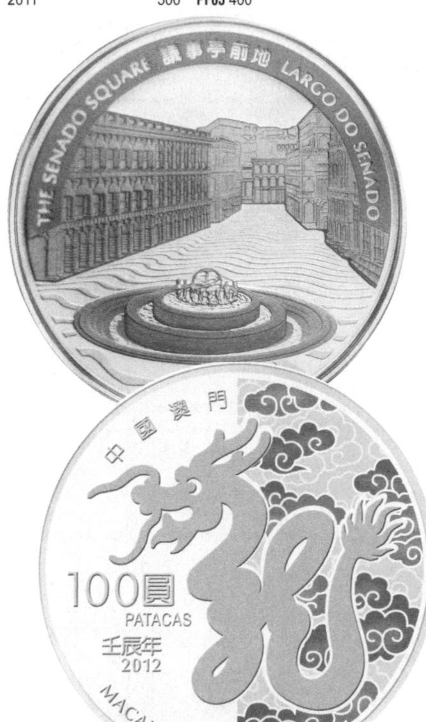


**KM# 163 100 PATACAS**
155.50 g., 0.999 Silver 4.9944 oz. ASW, 65 mm. **Subject:** Year of the Dragon **Obv:** Dragon in color

| Date | Mintage | VF20 | XF40 | MS60 | MS63 | MS65 |
|---|---|---|---|---|---|---|
| 2012 | — | PF65 750 | | | | |

**KM# 166 100 PATACAS**
155.52 g., 0.950 Silver 4.7501 oz. ASW, 65 mm. **Subject:** Year of the Snake **Obv:** Snake at right - color **Rev:** Ruins of St. Pauls

| Date | Mintage | VF20 | XF40 | MS60 | MS63 | MS65 |
|---|---|---|---|---|---|---|
| 2013 | — | PF65 540 | | | | |

**KM# 123 200 PATACAS**
28.28 g., 0.925 Silver 0.841 oz. ASW partially gilt. **Subject:** 5th Anniversary Return of Macao to China

| Date | Mintage | VF20 | XF40 | MS60 | MS63 | MS65 |
|---|---|---|---|---|---|---|
| 2004 | 10,000 | PF63 65.00 | PF65 75.00 | | | |

**KM# 138 200 PATACAS**
28.28 g., 0.925 Silver 0.841 oz. ASW partially gilt **Subject:** IV East Asian Games **Rev:** U-N-I-T-Y in blocks at left - bottom. logo at upper right

| Date | Mintage | VF20 | XF40 | MS60 | MS63 | MS65 |
|---|---|---|---|---|---|---|
| 2005 | 6,000 | PF65 120 | | | | |

**KM# 103 250 PATACAS**
3.99 g., 0.9167 Gold 0.1176 oz. AGW **Subject:** Year of the Snake **Obv:** Church façade **Rev:** Snake

| Date | Mintage | VF20 | XF40 | MS60 | MS63 | MS65 |
|---|---|---|---|---|---|---|
| 2001 | 2,500 | PF65 240 | | | | |

**KM# 108 250 PATACAS**
3.99 g., 0.9167 Gold 0.1176 oz. AGW, 19.3 mm. **Subject:** Year of the Horse **Obv:** Church of St. Paul façade **Rev:** Horse above value **Edge:** Reeded

| Date | Mintage | VF20 | XF40 | MS60 | MS63 | MS65 |
|---|---|---|---|---|---|---|
| 2002 | 2,500 | PF65 240 | | | | |

**KM# 119 250 PATACAS**
3.99 g., 0.9167 Gold 0.1176 oz. AGW, 19.3 mm. **Subject:** Year of the Goat **Obv:** Church façade **Rev:** Goat above value **Edge:** Reeded

| Date | Mintage | VF20 | XF40 | MS60 | MS63 | MS65 |
|---|---|---|---|---|---|---|
| 2003 | 2,500 | PF65 240 | | | | |

**KM# 131 250 PATACAS**
3.99 g., 0.9167 Gold 0.1176 oz. AGW **Series:** Lunar **Subject:** Year of the Monkey

| Date | Mintage | VF20 | XF40 | MS60 | MS63 | MS65 |
|---|---|---|---|---|---|---|
| 2004 | 2,500 | PF65 280 | | | | |

**KM# 135 250 PATACAS**
2.83 g., 0.999 Gold 0.0909 oz. AGW **Series:** Lunar **Subject:** Year of the Rooster **Rev:** Stylized rooster walking left

| Date | Mintage | VF20 | XF40 | MS60 | MS63 | MS65 |
|---|---|---|---|---|---|---|
| 2005 | — | PF65 280 | | | | |

**KM# 140 250 PATACAS**
3.11 g., 0.999 Gold 0.0999 oz. AGW **Series:** Lunar **Subject:** Year of the Dog **Rev:** Stylized dog standing left - multicolor

| Date | Mintage | VF20 | XF40 | MS60 | MS63 | MS65 |
|---|---|---|---|---|---|---|
| 2006 | — | PF65 280 | | | | |

### KM# 149 250 PATACAS

3.11 g., 0.999 Gold 0.0999 oz. AGW, 18 mm. **Subject:** Year of the Pig **Rev:** Pig in color

| Date | Mintage | VF20 | XF40 | MS60 | MS63 | MS65 |
|---|---|---|---|---|---|---|
| 2007 | — | PF65 220 | | | | |

### KM# 144 250 PATACAS

7.79 g., 0.999 Gold 0.2502 oz. AGW **Subject:** Year of the Rat **Obv:** Temple **Rev:** Rat and multicolor flowers at right

| Date | Mintage | VF20 | XF40 | MS60 | MS63 | MS65 |
|---|---|---|---|---|---|---|
| 2008 | — | PF65 525 | | | | |

### KM# 147 250 PATACAS

7.77 g., 0.999 Gold 0.2496 oz. AGW **Subject:** Year of the Ox **Obv:** Moorish Barracks **Rev:** Ox, multicolor flowers at right

| Date | Mintage | VF20 | XF40 | MS60 | MS63 | MS65 |
|---|---|---|---|---|---|---|
| 2009 | — | PF65 550 | | | | |

### KM# 155 250 PATACAS

7.78 g., 0.999 Gold 0.2499 oz. AGW, 22 mm. **Obv:** A Ma statue **Rev:** Lotus flower

| Date | Mintage | VF20 | XF40 | MS60 | MS63 | MS65 |
|---|---|---|---|---|---|---|
| 2009 | Est. 1600 | PF65 550 | | | | |

### KM# 158 250 PATACAS

7.78 g., 0.999 Gold 0.2499 oz. AGW, 22 mm. **Subject:** Year of the Tiger **Rev:** Tiger in color

| Date | Mintage | VF20 | XF40 | MS60 | MS63 | MS65 |
|---|---|---|---|---|---|---|
| 2010 | Est. 3000 | PF65 700 | | | | |

### KM# 161 250 PATACAS

7.78 g., 0.999 Gold 0.2499 oz. AGW, 22 mm. **Subject:** Year of the Rabbit **Obv:** Rabbit in color **Rev:** Dom Pedro V theater

| Date | Mintage | VF20 | XF40 | MS60 | MS63 | MS65 |
|---|---|---|---|---|---|---|
| 2011 (s) | — | PF65 700 | | | | |

### KM# 167 250 PATACAS

7.77 g., 0.999 Gold 0.2496 oz. AGW, 22 mm. **Subject:** Year of the Snake **Obv:** Snake at right, color **Rev:** Ruins of St. Pauls

| Date | Mintage | VF20 | XF40 | MS60 | MS63 | MS65 |
|---|---|---|---|---|---|---|
| 2013 | Est. 3000 | PF65 575 | | | | |

### KM# 104 500 PATACAS

7.99 g., 0.9167 Gold 0.2355 oz. AGW **Subject:** Year of the Snake **Obv:** Church façade **Rev:** Snake

| Date | Mintage | VF20 | XF40 | MS60 | MS63 | MS65 |
|---|---|---|---|---|---|---|
| 2001 | 2,500 | PF65 550 | | | | |

### KM# 109 500 PATACAS

7.98 g., 0.9167 Gold 0.2352 oz. AGW, 22.05 mm. **Subject:** Year of the Horse **Obv:** Church façade **Rev:** Horse above value **Edge:** Reeded

| Date | Mintage | VF20 | XF40 | MS60 | MS63 | MS65 |
|---|---|---|---|---|---|---|
| 2002 | 2,500 | PF65 550 | | | | |

### KM# 120 500 PATACAS

7.98 g., 0.9167 Gold 0.2352 oz. AGW, 22 mm. **Subject:** Year of the Goat **Obv:** Church façade **Rev:** Goat above value **Edge:** Reeded

| Date | Mintage | VF20 | XF40 | MS60 | MS63 | MS65 |
|---|---|---|---|---|---|---|
| 2003 | 2,500 | PF65 550 | | | | |

### KM# 129 500 PATACAS

7.96 g., 0.9167 Gold 0.2346 oz. AGW **Subject:** 1st World Championship Grand Prix **Rev:** Two race cars

| Date | Mintage | VF20 | XF40 | MS60 | MS63 | MS65 |
|---|---|---|---|---|---|---|
| 2003 | 2,000 | PF65 550 | | | | |

### KM# 124 500 PATACAS

62.21 g., 0.999 Silver 1.998 oz. ASW partially gilt **Subject:** 5th Anniversary Return of Macao to China

| Date | Mintage | VF20 | XF40 | MS60 | MS63 | MS65 |
|---|---|---|---|---|---|---|
| 2004 | 1,000 | PF65 120 | | | | |

### KM# 132 500 PATACAS

7.98 g., 0.9167 Gold 0.2352 oz. AGW **Series:** Lunar **Subject:** Year of the Monkey

| Date | Mintage | VF20 | XF40 | MS60 | MS63 | MS65 |
|---|---|---|---|---|---|---|
| 2004 | 2,500 | PF65 525 | | | | |

### KM# 136 500 PATACAS

7.96 g., 0.999 Gold 0.2557 oz. AGW **Series:** Lunar **Subject:** Year of the Rooster **Rev:** Stylized rooster walking left

| Date | Mintage | VF20 | XF40 | MS60 | MS63 | MS65 |
|---|---|---|---|---|---|---|
| 2005 | — | PF65 550 | | | | |

### KM# 141 500 PATACAS

7.96 g., 0.999 Gold 0.2557 oz. AGW **Series:** Lunar **Subject:** Year of the Dog **Rev:** Stylized dog standing left

| Date | Mintage | VF20 | XF40 | MS60 | MS63 | MS65 |
|---|---|---|---|---|---|---|
| 2006 | — | PF65 550 | | | | |

### KM# 150 500 PATACAS

7.96 g., 0.999 Gold 0.2557 oz. AGW, 22 mm. **Subject:** Year of the Pig **Rev:** Pig in color

| Date | Mintage | VF20 | XF40 | MS60 | MS63 | MS65 |
|---|---|---|---|---|---|---|
| 2007 | Est. 4000 | PF65 600 | | | | |

### KM# 164 500 PATACAS

7.78 g., 0.999 Gold 0.2499 oz. AGW, 22 mm. **Subject:** Year of the Dragon **Obv:** Dragon in color

| Date | Mintage | VF20 | XF40 | MS60 | MS63 | MS65 |
|---|---|---|---|---|---|---|
| 2012 | — | PF65 950 | | | | |

### KM# 105 1000 PATACAS

16.98 g., 0.9167 Gold 0.5003 oz. AGW **Subject:** Year of the Snake **Obv:** Church façade flanked by stars **Rev:** Snake

| Date | Mintage | VF20 | XF40 | MS60 | MS63 | MS65 |
|---|---|---|---|---|---|---|
| 2001 | 4,000 | PF65 1,000 | | | | |

### KM# 110 1000 PATACAS

15.97 g., 0.9167 Gold 0.4707 oz. AGW, 28.4 mm. **Subject:** Year of the Horse **Obv:** Church façade **Rev:** Horse above value **Edge:** Reeded

| Date | Mintage | VF20 | XF40 | MS60 | MS63 | MS65 |
|---|---|---|---|---|---|---|
| 2002 | — | PF65 1,000 | | | | |

### KM# 118 1000 PATACAS

28.28 g., 0.925 Silver 0.841 oz. ASW, 38.6 mm. **Subject:** Year of the Goat **Obv:** Church façade **Rev:** Goat above value **Edge:** Reeded

| Date | Mintage | VF20 | XF40 | MS60 | MS63 | MS65 |
|---|---|---|---|---|---|---|
| 2003 | 4,000 | PF65 45.00 | | | | |

### KM# 121 1000 PATACAS

15.98 g., 0.917 Gold 0.471 oz. AGW **Subject:** Year of the Goat **Obv:** Church façade flanked by stars **Rev:** Goat above value **Edge:** Reeded

| Date | Mintage | VF20 | XF40 | MS60 | MS63 | MS65 |
|---|---|---|---|---|---|---|
| 2003 | 4,000 | PF65 1,000 | | | | |

### KM# 125 1000 PATACAS

155.52 g., 0.999 Silver 4.9949 oz. ASW **Subject:** 5th Anniversary Return of Macao to China

| Date | Mintage | VF20 | XF40 | MS60 | MS63 | MS65 |
|---|---|---|---|---|---|---|
| 2004 | 3,000 | PF65 320 | | | | |

### KM# 133 1000 PATACAS

15.98 g., 0.9167 Gold 0.471 oz. AGW **Series:** Lunar **Subject:** Year of the Monkey

| Date | Mintage | VF20 | XF40 | MS60 | MS63 | MS65 |
|---|---|---|---|---|---|---|
| 2004 | 4,000 | PF65 1,000 | | | | |
| 2004 | 500 | — | — | — | 900 | 950 |

### KM# 126 2000 PATACAS

155.52 g., 0.999 Silver 4.9949 oz. ASW partially gilt **Subject:** 5th Anniversary Return of Macao to China

| Date | Mintage | VF20 | XF40 | MS60 | MS63 | MS65 |
|---|---|---|---|---|---|---|
| 2004 | 1,500 | PF65 300 | | | | |

## PROOF SETS

| KM# | Date | Mintage | Identification | Issue Price | Mkt Val |
|---|---|---|---|---|---|
| PS16 | 2001 (3) | 2,500 | KM#103-105 | 849 | 1,800 |
| PS17 | 2002 (3) | 4,000 | KM#108-110 | 849 | 1,800 |
| PS18 | 2003 (3) | 2,500 | KM#119-121 | 849 | 1,800 |
| PS19 | 2004 (4) | — | KM#130-133 | — | 2,000 |
| PS20 | 2005 (3) | — | KM#134-136 | — | 925 |
| PS21 | 2006 (3) | — | KM#139-141 | — | 925 |
| PS22 | 2007 (3) | — | KM#148-150 | — | 925 |
| PS23 | 2008 (3) | — | KM#142-144 | — | 925 |
| PS25 | 2010 (3) | — | KM#156-158 | — | 1,225 |
| PS26 | 2011 (3) | — | KM#159-161 | — | 1,175 |
| PS27 | 2012 (3) | — | KM#162-164 | — | 1,850 |

# MACEDONIA

The Republic of Macedonia is land-locked, and is bordered in the north by Yugoslavia, to the east by Bulgaria, in the south by Greece and to the west by Albania and has an area of 9,781 sq. mi. (25,713 sq. km.) and a population at the 1991 census was 2,038,847, of which the predominating ethnic groups were Macedonians. The capital is Skopje.

On Nov. 20, 1991 parliament promulgated a new constitution, and declared its independence on Nov.20, 1992, but failed to secure EC and US recognition owing to Greek objections to use of the name Macedonia. On Dec. 11, 1992, the UN Security Council authorized the expedition of a small peacekeeping force to prevent hostilities spreading into Macedonia.

There is a 120-member single-chamber National Assembly.

## REPUBLIC

### STANDARD COINAGE

### KM# 2 DENAR

5.15 g., Brass, 23.7 mm. **Obv:** Macedonian sheepdog **Obv. Legend:** РЕПУБЛИКА МАКЕДОНИЈА **Rev:** Radiant value **Edge:** Plain

| Date | Mintage | VF20 | XF40 | MS60 | MS63 | MS65 |
|---|---|---|---|---|---|---|
| 2001 | 12,874,000 | 0.20 | 0.35 | 0.75 | 1.50 | 3.00 |
| 2006 | — | — | — | 0.75 | 1.50 | 2.50 |
| 2008 | — | — | — | 0.75 | 1.50 | 2.50 |

**KM# 3 2 DENARI**
5.15 g., Brass, 23.7 mm. **Obv:** Trout above water **Obv. Legend:** РЕПУБЛИКА МАКЕДОНИЈА **Rev:** Radiant value **Edge:** Plain

| Date | Mintage | VF20 | XF40 | MS60 | MS63 | MS65 |
|---|---|---|---|---|---|---|
| 2001 | 11,672,000 | — | 0.50 | 0.75 | 1.50 | 3.00 |
| 2006 | — | — | 0.40 | 0.65 | 1.25 | 2.50 |
| 2008 | — | — | 0.40 | 0.65 | 1.25 | 2.50 |

**KM# 4 5 DENARI**
7.25 g., Brass, 27.5 mm. **Obv:** European lynx **Obv. Legend:** РЕПУБЛИКА МАКЕДОНИЈА **Rev:** Radiant value **Edge:** Plain

| Date | Mintage | VF20 | XF40 | MS60 | MS63 | MS65 |
|---|---|---|---|---|---|---|
| 2001 | 6,921,000 | 0.35 | 0.50 | 0.85 | 1.75 | 3.50 |
| 2006 | — | — | — | 0.75 | 1.50 | 3.00 |
| 2008 | — | — | — | 0.75 | 1.50 | 3.00 |

**KM# 13 10 DENARI**
10.00 g., 0.916 Gold 0.2945 oz. AGW, 27 mm. **Subject:** 10th Anniversary of Independence **Obv:** Value in circle within radiant map **Rev:** Grape vine

| Date | Mintage | VF20 | XF40 | MS60 | MS63 | MS65 |
|---|---|---|---|---|---|---|
| 2001 | 1,000 | — | — | — | 525 | 575 |

**KM# 31 10 DENARI**
6.60 g., Copper-Nickel-Zinc, 24.5 mm. **Obv:** Peacock **Rev:** Value within rays

| Date | Mintage | VF20 | XF40 | MS60 | MS63 | MS65 |
|---|---|---|---|---|---|---|
| 2008 | — | — | — | — | 1.50 | 3.00 |

**KM# 32 50 DENARI**
7.70 g., Copper-Nickel-Zinc, 26.5 mm. **Obv:** Classical female bust right **Rev:** Value within rays

| Date | Mintage | VF20 | XF40 | MS60 | MS63 | MS65 |
|---|---|---|---|---|---|---|
| 2008 | — | — | — | — | 1.50 | 3.00 |

**KM# 22 60 DENARI**
6.00 g., 0.916 Gold 0.1767 oz. AGW, 23.8 mm. **Subject:** 100th Anniversary - Statehood **Obv:** Monument above value within circle **Rev:** Djorce Petrov

| Date | Mintage | VF20 | XF40 | MS60 | MS63 | MS65 |
|---|---|---|---|---|---|---|
| 2003 | 500 | — | — | — | 350 | 400 |

**KM# 23 60 DENARI**
6.00 g., 0.916 Gold 0.1767 oz. AGW, 23.8 mm. **Subject:** 100th Anniversary - Statehood **Obv:** Monument above value within circle **Rev:** Krste Petkov-Misirkov

| Date | Mintage | VF20 | XF40 | MS60 | MS63 | MS65 |
|---|---|---|---|---|---|---|
| 2003 | 500 | — | — | — | 350 | 400 |

**KM# 24 60 DENARI**
6.00 g., 0.916 Gold 0.1767 oz. AGW, 23.8 mm. **Subject:** 100th Anniversary - Statehood **Obv:** Monument above value within circle **Rev:** Metodije Andonov

| Date | Mintage | VF20 | XF40 | MS60 | MS63 | MS65 |
|---|---|---|---|---|---|---|
| 2003 | 500 | — | — | — | 350 | 400 |

**KM# 25 60 DENARI**
6.00 g., 0.916 Gold 0.1767 oz. AGW, 23.8 mm. **Subject:** 100th Anniversary - Statehood **Obv:** Monument above value within circle **Rev:** Mihailo Apostolski

| Date | Mintage | VF20 | XF40 | MS60 | MS63 | MS65 |
|---|---|---|---|---|---|---|
| 2003 | 500 | — | — | — | 350 | 400 |

**KM# 26 60 DENARI**
6.00 g., 0.916 Gold 0.1767 oz. AGW, 23.8 mm. **Subject:** 100th Anniversary - Statehood **Obv:** Monument above value within circle **Rev:** Blaze Koneski

| Date | Mintage | VF20 | XF40 | MS60 | MS63 | MS65 |
|---|---|---|---|---|---|---|
| 2003 | 500 | — | — | — | 350 | 400 |

**KM# 21 60 DENARI**
8.00 g., 0.916 Gold 0.2356 oz. AGW, 23.8 mm. **Subject:** 50th Anniversary of separation from Greece **Obv:** The Monifest **Rev:** Monastery

| Date | Mintage | VF20 | XF40 | MS60 | MS63 | MS65 |
|---|---|---|---|---|---|---|
| 2004 | 500 | — | — | — | 400 | 450 |

**KM# 14 100 DENARI**
6.00 g., 0.916 Gold 0.1767 oz. AGW, 23.8 mm. **Subject:** 100th Anniversary of Statehood **Obv:** Monument above value within circle **Rev:** Cherry tree cannon divides circle

| Date | Mintage | VF20 | XF40 | MS60 | MS63 | MS65 |
|---|---|---|---|---|---|---|
| 2003 | 500 | PF65 400 | | | | |

**KM# 15 100 DENARI**
6.00 g., 0.916 Gold 0.1767 oz. AGW, 23.8 mm. **Subject:** 100th Anniversary of Statehood - Goce Delcev **Obv:** Monument above value within circle **Rev:** Bust facing within circle

| Date | Mintage | VF20 | XF40 | MS60 | MS63 | MS65 |
|---|---|---|---|---|---|---|
| 2003 | 500 | PF65 400 | | | | |

**KM# 16 100 DENARI**
6.00 g., 0.916 Gold 0.1767 oz. AGW, 23.8 mm. **Subject:** 100th Anniversary of Statehood - Pitu Guli **Obv:** Monument above value within circle **Rev:** Head with hat facing within circle

| Date | Mintage | VF20 | XF40 | MS60 | MS63 | MS65 |
|---|---|---|---|---|---|---|
| 2003 | 500 | PF65 400 | | | | |

**KM# 17 100 DENARI**
6.00 g., 0.916 Gold 0.1767 oz. AGW, 23.8 mm. **Subject:** 100th Anniversary of Statehood - Jane Sandanski **Obv:** Monument above value within circle **Rev:** Head facing within circle

| Date | Mintage | VF20 | XF40 | MS60 | MS63 | MS65 |
|---|---|---|---|---|---|---|
| 2003 | 500 | PF65 400 | | | | |

**KM# 18 100 DENARI**
6.00 g., 0.916 Gold 0.1767 oz. AGW, 23.8 mm. **Subject:** 100th Anniversary of Statehood - Dame Gruev **Obv:** Monument above value within circle **Rev:** Bust left within circle

| Date | Mintage | VF20 | XF40 | MS60 | MS63 | MS65 |
|---|---|---|---|---|---|---|
| 2003 | 500 | PF65 400 | | | | |

**KM# 19 100 DENARI**
6.00 g., 0.916 Gold 0.1767 oz. AGW, 23.8 mm. **Subject:** 100th Anniversary of Statehood - Nikola Karev **Obv:** Monument above value within circle **Rev:** Bust right within circle

| Date | Mintage | VF20 | XF40 | MS60 | MS63 | MS65 |
|---|---|---|---|---|---|---|
| 2003 | 500 | PF65 400 | | | | |

**KM# 28 100 DENARI**
6.00 g., 0.916 Gold 0.1767 oz. AGW **Subject:** 100th Anniversary of Statehood - Djorce Petrov **Obv:** Monument **Rev:** Bust facing

| Date | Mintage | VF20 | XF40 | MS60 | MS63 | MS65 |
|---|---|---|---|---|---|---|
| 2003 | 500 | PF65 400 | | | | |

**KM# 29 100 DENARI**
6.00 g., 0.916 Gold 0.1767 oz. AGW **Subject:** 100th Anniversary of Statehood - Krste Petkov-Misirkov **Obv:** Monument **Rev:** Bust facing

| Date | Mintage | VF20 | XF40 | MS60 | MS63 | MS65 |
|---|---|---|---|---|---|---|
| 2003 | 500 | PF65 400 | | | | |

**KM# 30 100 DENARI**
6.00 g., 0.916 Gold 0.1767 oz. AGW **Subject:** 100th Anniversary of statehood - Metodije Adamov-Cengo **Obv:** Monument **Rev:** Bust facing

| Date | Mintage | VF20 | XF40 | MS60 | MS63 | MS65 |
|---|---|---|---|---|---|---|
| 2003 | 500 | PF65 400 | | | | |

**KM# 33 100 DENARI**
6.00 g., 0.916 Gold 0.1767 oz. AGW, 23.8 mm. **Subject:** 100th Anniversary of Statehood - Mihailo Apostolski **Obv:** Monument **Rev:** Bust facing in field cap

| Date | Mintage | VF20 | XF40 | MS60 | MS63 | MS65 |
|---|---|---|---|---|---|---|
| 2003 | 500 | PF65 400 | | | | |

**KM# 34 100 DENARI**
6.00 g., 0.916 Gold 0.1767 oz. AGW, 23.8 mm. **Subject:** 100th Anniversary of Statehood - Blaze Koneski **Obv:** Monument **Rev:** Bust facing, wearing glasses

| Date | Mintage | VF20 | XF40 | MS60 | MS63 | MS65 |
|---|---|---|---|---|---|---|
| 2003 | 500 | PF65 400 | | | | |

## PATTERNS

(Including off-metal strikes)

| KM# | Date | Mintage | Identification | Mkt Val |
|---|---|---|---|---|
| Pn1 | 2003 | 50 | 100 Denari 0.925 Silver KM#14 | 150 |
| Pn2 | 2003 | 50 | 100 Denari 0.926 Silver KM#15. | 150 |
| Pn3 | 2003 | 50 | 100 Denari 0.925 Silver KM#16. | 150 |
| Pn4 | 2003 | 50 | 100 Denari 0.925 Silver KM#17. | 150 |
| Pn5 | 2003 | 50 | 100 Denari 0.925 Silver KM#18. | 150 |
| Pn6 | 2003 | 50 | 100 Denari 0.925 Silver KM#19. | 150 |
| Pn7 | 2003 | 50 | 100 Denari 0.925 Silver | 150 |
| Pn8 | 2003 | 50 | 100 Denari 0.925 Silver KM#29. | 150 |
| Pn9 | 2003 | 50 | 100 Denari 0.925 Silver KM#30. | 150 |
| Pn10 | 2003 | 50 | 100 Denari 0.925 Silver KM#33. | 150 |
| Pn11 | 2003 | 50 | 100 Denari 0.925 Silver | 100 |

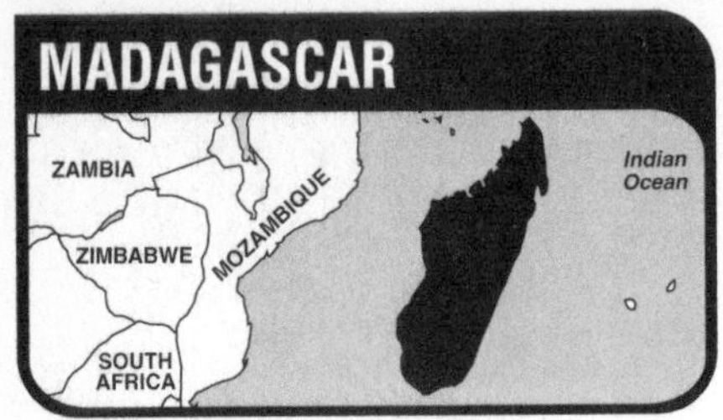


The Republic of Madagascar, an independent member of the French Community located in the Indian Ocean 250 miles (402 km.) off the southeast coast of Africa, has an area of 226,656 sq. mi. (587,040 sq. km.) and a population of 10 million. Capital: Antananarivo. The economy is primarily agricultural; large bauxite deposits are being developed. Coffee, vanilla, graphite, and rice are exported.

**MONETARY SYSTEM**
100 Centimes = 1 Franc

**MINT MARKS**
(a) - Paris, privy marks only
SA - Pretoria

# MALAGASY REPUBLIC

## STANDARD COINAGE

1 Ariary = 100 Iraimbilanja

**KM# 8 FRANC**
2.40 g., Stainless Steel **Obv:** Poinsettia **Rev:** Value within horns of ox head above sprigs

| Date | Mintage | VF20 | XF40 | MS60 | MS63 | MS65 |
|---|---|---|---|---|---|---|
| 2002 (a) | — | 0.20 | 0.40 | 0.75 | 1.45 | 2.25 |

# MADAGASIKARA REPUBLIC

**KM# 28 10 FRANCS (2 Ariary)**
4.34 g., Bronze (Red to Yellow), 21.9 mm. **Obv:** Monkey **Obv. Legend:** BANKY FOIBEN'I MADAGASIKARA **Rev:** Value within steer horns flanked by sprigs **Edge:** Plain

| Date | Mintage | VF20 | XF40 | MS60 | MS63 | MS65 |
|---|---|---|---|---|---|---|
| 2003 | — | — | 1.00 | 1.50 | 2.50 | 3.50 |

**KM# 29 ARIARY**
4.93 g., Stainless Steel, 22 mm. **Obv:** Flower **Obv. Legend:** BANKY FOIBEN'I MADAGASIKARA **Rev:** Value within steer horns above sprigs **Edge:** Plain

| Date | Mintage | VF20 | XF40 | MS60 | MS63 | MS65 |
|---|---|---|---|---|---|---|
| 2004 (a) | — | — | 0.90 | 1.25 | 2.25 | 3.00 |

**KM# 30 2 ARIARY**
3.23 g., Copper Plated Steel, 21 mm. **Obv:** Plant **Obv. Legend:** BANKY FOIBEN'I MADAGASIKARA **Rev:** Value within steer horns flanked by sprigs **Edge:** Reeded

| Date | Mintage | VF20 | XF40 | MS60 | MS63 | MS65 |
|---|---|---|---|---|---|---|
| 2003 | — | — | 0.90 | 1.25 | 2.25 | 3.00 |

**KM# 25.2 50 ARIARY**
10.15 g., Stainless Steel, 30 mm. **Obv:** Star above value within sprays **Rev:** Avenue of the Baobabs **Rev. Inscription:** Motto C **Edge:** Plain **Shape:** 11-sided

| Date | Mintage | VF20 | XF40 | MS60 | MS63 | MS65 |
|---|---|---|---|---|---|---|
| 2005 | — | — | 2.00 | 3.00 | 5.00 | 7.00 |

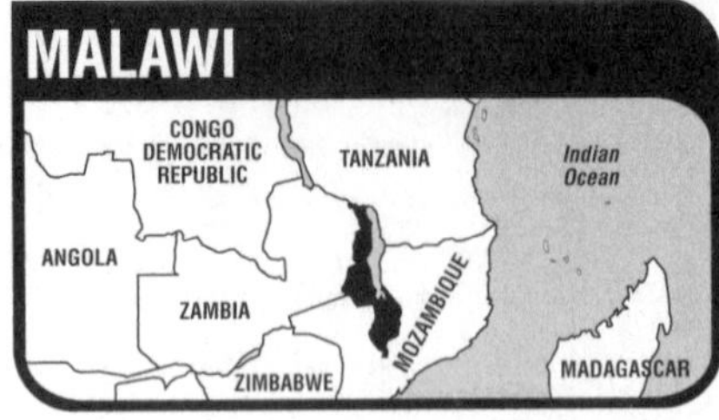


The Republic of Malawi (formerly Nyasaland), located in southeastern Africa to the west of Lake Malawi (Nyasa), has an area of 45,745 sq. mi. (118,480 sq. km.) and a population of 7 million. Capital: Lilongwe. The economy is predominantly agricultural. Tobacco, tea, peanuts and cotton are exported. Republic

## DECIMAL COINAGE

100 Tambala = 1 Kwacha

**KM# 33a TAMBALA**
Copper Plated Steel, 17.3 mm. **Obv:** Arms with supporters **Rev:** 2 Talapia fish **Edge:** Plain

| Date | Mintage | VF20 | XF40 | MS60 | MS63 | MS65 |
|---|---|---|---|---|---|---|
| 2003 | — | — | — | 0.50 | 1.00 | 1.50 |

**KM# 34a 2 TAMBALA**
Copper Plated Steel, 20.3 mm. **Obv:** Arms with supporters **Rev:** Paradise whydah bird divides date and value, designer's initials "P.V. **Edge:** Plain

| Date | Mintage | VF20 | XF40 | MS60 | MS63 | MS65 |
|---|---|---|---|---|---|---|
| 2003 | — | — | — | 0.50 | 1.00 | 1.50 |

**KM# 32.2 5 TAMBALA**
Nickel Plated Steel, 19.35 mm. **Obv:** Arms with supporters **Rev:** Purple heron, value, designer's initials "P.V.

| Date | Mintage | VF20 | XF40 | MS60 | MS63 | MS65 |
|---|---|---|---|---|---|---|
| 2003 | — | — | — | 0.75 | 1.25 | 2.50 |

**KM# 27 10 TAMBALA**
5.62 g., Nickel Plated Steel, 23.6 mm. **Obv:** Bust right **Rev:** Bundled corn cobs divide date and value

| Date | Mintage | VF20 | XF40 | MS60 | MS63 | MS65 |
|---|---|---|---|---|---|---|
| 2003 | — | — | — | 1.25 | 2.25 | 3.00 |

**KM# 29 20 TAMBALA**
7.52 g., Nickel Clad Steel, 26.5 mm. **Obv:** Bust right **Rev:** Elephants

| Date | Mintage | VF20 | XF40 | MS60 | MS63 | MS65 |
|---|---|---|---|---|---|---|
| 2003 | — | — | — | 2.50 | 4.00 | 6.00 |

**KM# 30 50 TAMBALA**
4.40 g., Brass Plated Steel, 22 mm. **Obv:** Bust right **Rev:** Arms with supporters **Shape:** 7-sided

| Date | Mintage | VF20 | XF40 | MS60 | MS63 | MS65 |
|---|---|---|---|---|---|---|
| 2003 | — | — | — | 2.00 | 3.50 | 5.00 |
| 2004 | — | — | — | 2.00 | 3.50 | 5.00 |

**KM# 66 50 TAMBALA**
4.40 g., Brass Plated Steel, 22 mm. **Obv:** State arms and supporters with country name below **Rev:** Zebras with date above and value below **Shape:** 7-sided

| Date | Mintage | VF20 | XF40 | MS60 | MS63 | MS65 |
|---|---|---|---|---|---|---|
| 2004 | — | — | — | 2.00 | 3.50 | 5.00 |

**KM# 28 KWACHA**
9.00 g., Brass Plated Steel, 26 mm. **Obv:** Bust right **Rev:** Fish eagle

| Date | Mintage | VF20 | XF40 | MS60 | MS63 | MS65 |
|---|---|---|---|---|---|---|
| 2003 | — | — | — | 3.00 | 7.00 | 10.00 |

**KM# 65 KWACHA**
9.50 g., Brass Plated Steel, 26 mm. **Obv:** State arms, country name **Rev:** Fish eagle, date

| Date | Mintage | VF20 | XF40 | MS60 | MS63 | MS65 |
|---|---|---|---|---|---|---|
| 2004 | — | — | — | 1.50 | 2.50 | 3.50 |

**KM# 201 KWACHA**
31.11 g., 0.999 Silver 0.999 oz. ASW, 47x27 mm. **Rev:** Impalla

| Date | Mintage | VF20 | XF40 | MS60 | MS63 | MS65 |
|---|---|---|---|---|---|---|
| 2009 | 100 | **PF65** 55.00 | | | | |

Note: Individually numbered

**KM# 202 KWACHA**
0.62 g., 0.999 Gold, 11 mm. **Rev:** Impalla

| Date | Mintage | VF20 | XF40 | MS60 | MS63 | MS65 |
|---|---|---|---|---|---|---|
| 2009 | 100 | **PF65** 50.00 | | | | |

**KM# 203 KWACHA**
3.11 g., 0.999 Gold 0.0999 oz. AGW, 18 mm. **Rev:** Impalla

| Date | Mintage | VF20 | XF40 | MS60 | MS63 | MS65 |
|---|---|---|---|---|---|---|
| 2009 | 100 | **PF65** 250 | | | | |

**KM# 204 KWACHA**
7.78 g., 0.999 Gold 0.2499 oz. AGW, 25 mm. **Rev:** Impalla

| Date | Mintage | VF20 | XF40 | MS60 | MS63 | MS65 |
|---|---|---|---|---|---|---|
| 2009 | 100 | **PF65** 550 | | | | |

**KM# 205 KWACHA**
15.55 g., 0.999 Gold 0.4994 oz. AGW, 30 mm. **Rev:** Impalla

| Date | Mintage | VF20 | XF40 | MS60 | MS63 | MS65 |
|---|---|---|---|---|---|---|
| 2009 | 100 | **PF65** 1,150 | | | | |

**KM# 212 KWACHA**
3.00 g., Stainless Steel, 20 mm. **Obv:** National arms, MALAWI below **Rev:** Flying eagle with date above and value below **Edge:** Reeded

| Date | Mintage | VF20 | XF40 | MS60 | MS63 | MS65 |
|---|---|---|---|---|---|---|
| 2012 | — | — | — | 1.00 | 1.50 | 2.00 |

**KM# 44 5 KWACHA**
22.00 g., Silver Plated Copper-Nickel, 40 mm. **Subject:** Asian Zodiac Animals **Obv:** Queen Elizabeth II above Zambian arms **Rev:** Multicolor stylized rat **Edge:** Reeded

| Date | Mintage | VF20 | XF40 | MS60 | MS63 | MS65 |
|---|---|---|---|---|---|---|
| 2005 Prooflike | 835 | — | — | — | — | 17.50 |

**KM# 45 5 KWACHA**
22.00 g., Silver Plated Copper-Nickel, 40 mm. **Subject:** Asian Zodiac Animals **Obv:** Queen Elizabeth II above Zambian arms **Rev:** Multicolor stylized ox **Edge:** Reeded

| Date | Mintage | VF20 | XF40 | MS60 | MS63 | MS65 |
|---|---|---|---|---|---|---|
| 2005 Prooflike | 835 | — | — | — | — | 17.50 |

**KM# 46 5 KWACHA**
22.00 g., Silver Plated Copper-Nickel, 40 mm. **Subject:** Asian Zodiac Animals **Obv:** Queen Elizabeth II above Zambian arms **Rev:** Multicolor stylized tiger **Edge:** Reeded

| Date | Mintage | VF20 | XF40 | MS60 | MS63 | MS65 |
|---|---|---|---|---|---|---|
| 2005 Prooflike | 835 | — | — | — | — | 17.50 |

**KM# 47 5 KWACHA**
22.00 g., Silver Plated Copper-Nickel, 40 mm. **Subject:** Asian Zodiac Animals **Obv:** Queen Elizabeth II above Zambian arms **Rev:** Multicolor stylized rabbit **Edge:** Reeded

| Date | Mintage | VF20 | XF40 | MS60 | MS63 | MS65 |
|---|---|---|---|---|---|---|
| 2005 Prooflike | 835 | — | — | — | — | 17.50 |

**KM# 48 5 KWACHA**
22.00 g., Silver Plated Copper-Nickel, 40 mm. **Subject:** Asian Zodiac Animals **Obv:** Queen Elizabeth II above Zambian arms **Rev:** Multicolor stylized dragon **Edge:** Reeded

| Date | Mintage | VF20 | XF40 | MS60 | MS63 | MS65 |
|---|---|---|---|---|---|---|
| 2005 Prooflike | 835 | — | — | — | — | 17.50 |

**KM# 49 5 KWACHA**
22.00 g., Silver Plated Copper-Nickel, 40 mm. **Subject:** Asian Zodiac Animals **Obv:** Que en Elizabeth II above Zambian arms **Rev:** Multicolor stylized snake **Edge:** Reeded

| Date | Mintage | VF20 | XF40 | MS60 | MS63 | MS65 |
|---|---|---|---|---|---|---|
| 2005 Prooflike | 835 | — | — | — | — | 17.50 |

**KM# 50 5 KWACHA**
22.00 g., Silver Plated Copper-Nickel, 40 mm. **Subject:** Asian Zodiac Animals **Obv:** Queen Elizabeth II above Zambian arms **Rev:** Multicolor stylized horse **Edge:** Reeded

| Date | Mintage | VF20 | XF40 | MS60 | MS63 | MS65 |
|---|---|---|---|---|---|---|
| 2005 Prooflike | 835 | — | — | — | — | 17.50 |

**KM# 51 5 KWACHA**
22.00 g., Silver Plated Copper-Nickel, 40 mm. **Subject:** Asian Zodiac Animals **Obv:** Queen Elizabeth II above Zambian arms **Rev:** Multicolor stylized goat **Edge:** Reeded

| Date | Mintage | VF20 | XF40 | MS60 | MS63 | MS65 |
|---|---|---|---|---|---|---|
| 2005 Prooflike | 835 | — | — | — | — | 17.50 |

**KM# 52 5 KWACHA**
22.00 g., Silver Plated Copper-Nickel, 40 mm. **Subject:** Asian Zodiac Animals **Obv:** Queen Elizabeth II above Zambian arms **Rev:** Multicolor stylized monkey **Edge:** Reeded

| Date | Mintage | VF20 | XF40 | MS60 | MS63 | MS65 |
|---|---|---|---|---|---|---|
| 2005 Proolike | 835 | — | — | — | — | 17.50 |

**KM# 53 5 KWACHA**
22.00 g., Silver Plated Copper-Nickel, 40 mm. **Subject:** Asian Zodiac Animals **Obv:** Queen Elizabeth II above Zambian arms **Rev:** Multicolor stylized rooster **Edge:** Reeded

| Date | Mintage | VF20 | XF40 | MS60 | MS63 | MS65 |
|---|---|---|---|---|---|---|
| 2005 Prooflike | 835 | — | — | — | — | 17.50 |

**KM# 54 5 KWACHA**
22.00 g., Silver Plated Copper-Nickel, 40 mm. **Subject:** Asian Zodiac Animals **Obv:** Queen Elizabeth II above Zambian arms **Rev:** Multicolor stylized dog **Edge:** Reeded

| Date | Mintage | VF20 | XF40 | MS60 | MS63 | MS65 |
|---|---|---|---|---|---|---|
| 2005 Prooflike | 835 | — | — | — | — | 17.50 |

**KM# 55 5 KWACHA**
22.00 g., Silver Plated Copper-Nickel, 40 mm. **Subject:** Asian Zodiac Animals **Obv:** Queen Elizabeth II above Zambian arms **Rev:** Multicolor stylized pig **Edge:** Reeded

| Date | Mintage | VF20 | XF40 | MS60 | MS63 | MS65 |
|---|---|---|---|---|---|---|
| 2005 Prooflike | 835 | — | — | — | — | 17.50 |

**KM# 59 5 KWACHA**
Brass, 45x27.5 mm. **Obv:** National arms, date and value **Rev:** USS Coral Sea aircraft carrier **Edge:** Plain

| Date | Mintage | VF20 | XF40 | MS60 | MS63 | MS65 |
|---|---|---|---|---|---|---|
| 2005 | — | PF63 20.00 | PF65 22.50 | | | |

**KM# 62 5 KWACHA**
Brass, 45x27.5 mm. **Obv:** National arms,date and value **Rev:** Ship USSR Molotov **Edge:** Plain

| Date | Mintage | VF20 | XF40 | MS60 | MS63 | MS65 |
|---|---|---|---|---|---|---|
| 2005 | — | PF63 20.00 | PF65 22.50 | | | |

**KM# 63 5 KWACHA**
Brass, 45x27.5 mm. **Obv:** National arms,date and value **Rev:** Ship USS Missouri **Edge:** Plain

| Date | Mintage | VF20 | XF40 | MS60 | MS63 | MS65 |
|---|---|---|---|---|---|---|
| 2005 | — | PF63 20.00 | PF65 22.50 | | | |

**KM# 64 5 KWACHA**
Brass, 45x27.5 mm. **Obv:** National arms,date and value **Rev:** Ship HMS Hood **Edge:** Plain

| Date | Mintage | VF20 | XF40 | MS60 | MS63 | MS65 |
|---|---|---|---|---|---|---|
| 2005 | — | PF63 20.00 | PF65 22.50 | | | |

**KM# 98 5 KWACHA**
29.10 g., Copper-Nickel, 38.7 mm. **Obv:** Arms **Rev:** Pope John Paul II holding child

| Date | Mintage | VF20 | XF40 | MS60 | MS63 | MS65 |
|---|---|---|---|---|---|---|
| 2005 | — | PF63 22.00 | PF65 25.00 | | | |

**KM# 57 5 KWACHA**
10.25 g., Bi-Metallic Copper-Nickel ring and Nickel-Brass center, 27 mm. **Obv:** State arms and supporters with country name below **Obv. Legend:** MALAWI **Rev:** Fisherman at work with date above and value below **Edge:** Reeded

| Date | Mintage | VF20 | XF40 | MS60 | MS63 | MS65 |
|---|---|---|---|---|---|---|
| 2006 | — | — | — | 2.00 | 3.50 | 5.00 |

**KM# 159 5 KWACHA**
28.28 g., 0.925 Silver 0.841 oz. ASW, 38.61 mm. **Subject:** Journey through Africa **Obv:** National arms **Rev:** Lion

| Date | Mintage | VF20 | XF40 | MS60 | MS63 | MS65 |
|---|---|---|---|---|---|---|
| 2006 | Est. 15000 | PF63 50.00 | PF65 60.00 | | | |

**KM# 160 5 KWACHA**
28.28 g., 0.925 Silver 0.841 oz. ASW, 38.61 mm. **Subject:** Journey through Africa **Obv:** National arms **Rev:** African elephant

| Date | Mintage | VF20 | XF40 | MS60 | MS63 | MS65 |
|---|---|---|---|---|---|---|
| 2006 | Est. 15000 | PF63 50.00 | PF65 60.00 | | | |

**KM# 161 5 KWACHA**
28.28 g., 0.925 Silver 0.841 oz. ASW, 38.61 mm. **Subject:** Journey through Africa **Obv:** National Arms **Rev:** Lake Malawi

| Date | Mintage | VF20 | XF40 | MS60 | MS63 | MS65 |
|---|---|---|---|---|---|---|
| 2006 | Est. 15000 | PF63 50.00 | PF65 60.00 | | | |

**KM# 162 5 KWACHA**
28.28 g., 0.925 Silver 0.841 oz. ASW, 38.61 mm. **Subject:** Journey through Africa **Obv:** National arms **Rev:** Sahara lizard

| Date | Mintage | VF20 | XF40 | MS60 | MS63 | MS65 |
|---|---|---|---|---|---|---|
| 2006 | Est. 15000 | PF63 50.00 | PF65 60.00 | | | |

**KM# 163 5 KWACHA**
28.28 g., 0.925 Silver 0.841 oz. ASW, 38.61 mm. **Subject:** Journey through Arfica **Obv:** National arms **Rev:** Mt. Kilimanjaro

| Date | Mintage | VF20 | XF40 | MS60 | MS63 | MS65 |
|---|---|---|---|---|---|---|
| 2006 | Est. 15000 | PF63 50.00 | PF65 60.00 | | | |

**KM# 164 5 KWACHA**
28.28 g., 0.925 Silver 0.841 oz. ASW, 38.61 mm. **Subject:** Journey through Africa **Obv:** National arms **Rev:** Tribal life

| Date | Mintage | VF20 | XF40 | MS60 | MS63 | MS65 |
|---|---|---|---|---|---|---|
| 2006 | Est. 15000 | PF63 50.00 | PF65 60.00 | | | |

**KM# 165 5 KWACHA**
28.28 g., 0.925 Silver 0.841 oz. ASW, 38.61 mm. **Rev:** Safari in color

| Date | Mintage | VF20 | XF40 | MS60 | MS63 | MS65 |
|---|---|---|---|---|---|---|
| 2006 | Est. 15000 | PF63 50.00 | PF65 60.00 | | | |

**KM# 166 5 KWACHA**
31.11 g., 0.925 Silver 0.925 oz. ASW, 38.61 mm. **Rev:** Victoria Falls in color

| Date | Mintage | VF20 | XF40 | MS60 | MS63 | MS65 |
|---|---|---|---|---|---|---|
| 2006 | Est. 15000 | PF63 50.00 | PF65 60.00 | | | |

**KM# 167 5 KWACHA**
28.28 g., 0.925 Silver 0.841 oz. ASW, 38.61 mm. **Rev:** Table top mountain in Cape town

| Date | Mintage | VF20 | XF40 | MS60 | MS63 | MS65 |
|---|---|---|---|---|---|---|
| 2006 | Est. 15000 | PF63 50.00 | PF65 60.00 | | | |

**KM# 168 5 KWACHA**
28.28 g., 0.925 Silver 0.841 oz. ASW, 38.61 mm. **Rev:** Nile in color

| Date | Mintage | VF20 | XF40 | MS60 | MS63 | MS65 |
|---|---|---|---|---|---|---|
| 2006 | Est. 15000 | PF63 50.00 | PF65 60.00 | | | |

**KM# 169 5 KWACHA**
28.28 g., 0.925 Silver 0.841 oz. ASW, 38.61 mm. **Rev:** Pyramids in color

| Date | Mintage | VF20 | XF40 | MS60 | MS63 | MS65 |
|---|---|---|---|---|---|---|
| 2006 | Est. 15000 | PF63 50.00 | PF65 60.00 | | | |

**KM# 170 5 KWACHA**
28.28 g., 0.925 Silver 0.841 oz. ASW, 38.61 mm. **Rev:** Great Sphinx in color

| Date | Mintage | VF20 | XF40 | MS60 | MS63 | MS65 |
|---|---|---|---|---|---|---|
| 2006 | Est. 15000 | PF63 50.00 | PF65 60.00 | | | |

**KM# 195 5 KWACHA**
27.00 g., Copper-Nickel, 40 mm. **Subject:** 2000th Anniversary of the ambush in the forest against the legions of Varus **Rev:** Arminius

| Date | Mintage | VF20 | XF40 | MS60 | MS63 | MS65 |
|---|---|---|---|---|---|---|
| 2009 | Est. 5000 | — | — | — | — | 20.00 |

**KM# 196 5 KWACHA**
27.00 g., Copper-Nickel, 40 mm. **Subject:** 2000th Anniversary of the ambush in the forest against the legions of Varus **Rev:** Centopah of Marcus Caelius and the 18th Legion

| Date | Mintage | VF20 | XF40 | MS60 | MS63 | MS65 |
|---|---|---|---|---|---|---|
| 2009 | — | — | — | — | — | 20.00 |

**KM# 197 5 KWACHA**
20.00 g., Silver Plated Copper, 40 mm. **Rev:** Battleship Bismarck in color

| Date | Mintage | VF20 | XF40 | MS60 | MS63 | MS65 |
|---|---|---|---|---|---|---|
| 2009 | Est. 5000 | — | — | — | — | 30.00 |

**KM# 198 5 KWACHA**
20.00 g., Silver Plated Copper, 40 mm. **Rev:** Ship Tirpitz in color

| Date | Mintage | VF20 | XF40 | MS60 | MS63 | MS65 |
|---|---|---|---|---|---|---|
| 2009 | Est. 5000 | — | — | — | — | 30.00 |

**KM# 199 5 KWACHA**
20.00 g., Silver Plated Copper, 40 mm. **Rev:** Ship Gneisenau in color

| Date | Mintage | VF20 | XF40 | MS60 | MS63 | MS65 |
|---|---|---|---|---|---|---|
| 2009 | Est. 5000 | — | — | — | — | 30.00 |

**KM# 200 5 KWACHA**
20.00 g., Silver Plated Copper, 40 mm. **Rev:** Ship Scharnhorst in color

| Date | Mintage | VF20 | XF40 | MS60 | MS63 | MS65 |
|---|---|---|---|---|---|---|
| 2009 | Est. 5000 | — | — | — | — | 30.00 |

**KM# 207 5 KWACHA**
30.70 g., Silver, 38.6 mm. **Subject:** John Paul II, 10th Anniversary of visits to Kazakistan and Armenia **Obv:** National arms **Rev:** John Paul II

| Date | Mintage | VF20 | XF40 | MS60 | MS63 | MS65 |
|---|---|---|---|---|---|---|
| 2011 | 1,000 | PF65 75.00 | | | | |

**KM# 213 5 KWACHA**
4.50 g., Stainless Steel plated iron, 22 mm. **Obv:** National arms, MALAWI below **Rev:** Standing heron, date above, value below

| Date | Mintage | VF20 | XF40 | MS60 | MS63 | MS65 |
|---|---|---|---|---|---|---|
| 2012 | — | — | — | — | 3.00 | 5.00 |

**KM# 39 10 KWACHA**
29.10 g., Copper-Nickel, 38.7 mm. **Subject:** Soccer World Championship **Obv:** Arms with supporters **Rev:** Soccer players **Edge:** Reeded

| Date | Mintage | VF20 | XF40 | MS60 | MS63 | MS65 |
|---|---|---|---|---|---|---|
| 2002 | — | PF65 50.00 | | | | |

**KM# 117 10 KWACHA**
Silver **Rev:** U.S.S. Nimitz

| Date | Mintage | VF20 | XF40 | MS60 | MS63 | MS65 |
|---|---|---|---|---|---|---|
| 2002 | — | PF65 40.00 | | | | |

**KM# 42 10 KWACHA**
19.74 g., 0.999 Silver 0.634 oz. ASW, 29.9 mm. **Subject:** XXVII Olympic Games - Athens 2004 **Obv:** Arms with supporters divides date **Obv. Legend:** REPUBLIC OF MALAWI **Rev:** Two rowers within circle flanked by sprigs **Edge:** Reeded

| Date | Mintage | VF20 | XF40 | MS60 | MS63 | MS65 |
|---|---|---|---|---|---|---|
| 2003 | — | PF65 40.00 | | | | |

**KM# 80 10 KWACHA**
24.00 g., 0.999 Silver 0.7708 oz. ASW, 38.5 mm. **Obv:** Arms **Rev:** Pope John Paul II in mitre and vestments

| Date | Mintage | VF20 | XF40 | MS60 | MS63 | MS65 |
|---|---|---|---|---|---|---|
| 2003 | — | PF65 30.00 | | | | |

**KM# 102 10 KWACHA**
19.30 g., Silver, 38 mm. **Subject:** Antelopes of Africa **Obv:** National arms **Rev:** Eland

| Date | Mintage | VF20 | XF40 | MS60 | MS63 | MS65 |
|---|---|---|---|---|---|---|
| 2003 | — | PF63 22.00 | PF65 25.00 | | | |

**KM# 103 10 KWACHA**
19.30 g., Silver, 38 mm. **Subject:** Antelopes of Africa **Obv:** National Arms **Rev:** Nyala

| Date | Mintage | VF20 | XF40 | MS60 | MS63 | MS65 |
|---|---|---|---|---|---|---|
| 2003 | — | PF63 22.00 | PF65 25.00 | | | |

**KM# 104 10 KWACHA**
19.30 g., Silver, 38 mm. **Subject:** Antelopes of Africa **Obv:** National Arms **Rev:** Springbok

| Date | Mintage | VF20 | XF40 | MS60 | MS63 | MS65 |
|---|---|---|---|---|---|---|
| 2003 | — | PF63 22.00 | PF65 25.00 | | | |

**KM# 105 10 KWACHA**
19.30 g., Silver, 38 mm. **Subject:** Antelopes of Africa **Obv:** National Arms **Rev:** Kudu

| Date | Mintage | VF20 | XF40 | MS60 | MS63 | MS65 |
|---|---|---|---|---|---|---|
| 2003 | — | PF63 22.00 | PF65 25.00 | | | |

**KM# 106 10 KWACHA**
19.30 g., Silver, 38 mm. **Subject:** Antelopes of Africa **Obv:** National Arms **Rev:** Sable pair

| Date | Mintage | VF20 | XF40 | MS60 | MS63 | MS65 |
|---|---|---|---|---|---|---|
| 2003 | — | PF63 22.00 | PF65 25.00 | | | |

**KM# 107 10 KWACHA**
Bronze gilt **Obv:** National Arms **Rev:** John Paul II in mitre and vestments

| Date | Mintage | VF20 | XF40 | MS60 | MS63 | MS65 |
|---|---|---|---|---|---|---|
| 2003 | — | PF65 7.50 | | | | |

**KM# 118 10 KWACHA**
Silver **Subject:** Elizabeth, the Queen Mother, First anniversary of death

| Date | Mintage | VF20 | XF40 | MS60 | MS63 | MS65 |
|---|---|---|---|---|---|---|
| 2003 | — | PF65 30.00 | | | | |

**KM# 119 10 KWACHA**
0.925 Silver, 38.6 mm. **Rev:** Trans-Siberian Railway

| Date | Mintage | VF20 | XF40 | MS60 | MS63 | MS65 |
|---|---|---|---|---|---|---|
| 2003 | — | PF63 35.00 | PF65 45.00 | | | |

**KM# 120 10 KWACHA**
Silver **Subject:** Los Angeles Olympics, 1984 **Rev:** Ribbon dancer

| Date | Mintage | VF20 | XF40 | MS60 | MS63 | MS65 |
|---|---|---|---|---|---|---|
| 2003 | — | PF63 35.00 | PF65 45.00 | | | |

**KM# 60 10 KWACHA**
29.15 g., Copper-Nickel silver plated, 38.7 mm. **Subject:** Endangered Wildlife **Obv:** National arms **Rev:** Multicolor Zebra and colt **Edge:** Reeded

| Date | Mintage | VF20 | XF40 | MS60 | MS63 | MS65 |
|---|---|---|---|---|---|---|
| 2004 | — | PF65 17.00 | | | | |

**KM# 61 10 KWACHA**
29.15 g., Copper-Nickel silver plated, 38.7 mm. **Subject:** Endangered Wildlife **Obv:** National arms **Rev:** Multicolor Leopard with cub **Edge:** Reeded

| Date | Mintage | VF20 | XF40 | MS60 | MS63 | MS65 |
|---|---|---|---|---|---|---|
| 2004 | — | PF65 17.00 | | | | |

**KM# 84 10 KWACHA**
29.14 g., Copper-Nickel, 38.7 mm. **Obv:** National arms **Rev:** Multicolor elephant and calf **Edge:** Reeded

| Date | Mintage | VF20 | XF40 | MS60 | MS63 | MS65 |
|---|---|---|---|---|---|---|
| 2004 | — | PF65 17.00 | | | | |

**KM# 86 10 KWACHA**
29.15 g., Copper-Nickel silver plated, 38.7 mm. **Subject:** Endangered Wildlife **Obv:** National arms **Rev:** Multicolor Lion and cub **Edge:** Reeded

| Date | Mintage | VF20 | XF40 | MS60 | MS63 | MS65 |
|---|---|---|---|---|---|---|
| 2004 | — | PF65 17.00 | | | | |

**KM# 89 10 KWACHA**

29.15 g., Copper-Nickel silver plated, 38.7 mm. **Obv:** National arms **Rev:** Multicolor Deer and fawn **Edge:** Reeded

| Date | Mintage | VF20 | XF40 | MS60 | MS63 | MS65 |
|---|---|---|---|---|---|---|
| 2004 | — | PF65 17.00 | | | | |

**KM# 90 10 KWACHA**

29.15 g., Copper-Nickel silver plated, 38.7 mm. **Obv:** National arms **Rev:** Multicolor Giraffe and her calf **Edge:** Reeded

| Date | Mintage | VF20 | XF40 | MS60 | MS63 | MS65 |
|---|---|---|---|---|---|---|
| 2004 | — | PF65 17.00 | | | | |

**KM# 71 10 KWACHA**

23.50 g., Silver Plated Copper-Nickel, 39 mm. **Subject:** Endangered wildlife **Obv:** National arms **Rev:** Tree pangolin (Manis Tricuspis)

| Date | Mintage | VF20 | XF40 | MS60 | MS63 | MS65 |
|---|---|---|---|---|---|---|
| 2005 | — | PF65 17.00 | | | | |

**KM# 81 10 KWACHA**

Copper-Nickel silver plated **Obv:** Arms **Rev:** Chevrotain advancing left

| Date | Mintage | VF20 | XF40 | MS60 | MS63 | MS65 |
|---|---|---|---|---|---|---|
| 2005 | — | PF65 17.00 | | | | |

**KM# 82 10 KWACHA**

Copper-Nickel silver plated **Obv:** Arms **Rev:** Lemur on branch

| Date | Mintage | VF20 | XF40 | MS60 | MS63 | MS65 |
|---|---|---|---|---|---|---|
| 2005 | — | PF65 17.00 | | | | |

**KM# 83 10 KWACHA**

Copper-Nickel silver plated **Obv:** Arms **Rev:** Pigmy Hippo

| Date | Mintage | VF20 | XF40 | MS60 | MS63 | MS65 |
|---|---|---|---|---|---|---|
| 2005 | — | PF65 17.00 | | | | |

**KM# 87 10 KWACHA**

Copper-Nickel **Obv:** Arms **Rev:** Monkies in photo insert

| Date | Mintage | VF20 | XF40 | MS60 | MS63 | MS65 |
|---|---|---|---|---|---|---|
| 2005 | — | PF65 17.50 | | | | |

**KM# 88 10 KWACHA**

Copper-Nickel **Obv:** Arms **Rev:** Oryx in photo insert

| Date | Mintage | VF20 | XF40 | MS60 | MS63 | MS65 |
|---|---|---|---|---|---|---|
| 2005 | — | — | — | — | 18.00 | 20.00 |

**KM# 130 10 KWACHA**

24.50 g., Silver Plated Brass, 38.6 mm. **Obv:** State shield **Rev:** Crocodile

| Date | Mintage | VF20 | XF40 | MS60 | MS63 | MS65 |
|---|---|---|---|---|---|---|
| 2005 | Est. 1000 | PF65 15.00 | | | | |

**KM# 131 10 KWACHA**

24.50 g., Silver Plated Brass, 38.6 mm. **Rev:** Pygmy Chimpanzie

| Date | Mintage | VF20 | XF40 | MS60 | MS63 | MS65 |
|---|---|---|---|---|---|---|
| 2005 | — | PF65 15.00 | | | | |

**KM# 132 10 KWACHA**

24.50 g., Silver Plated Brass, 38.6 mm. **Rev:** Corner

| Date | Mintage | VF20 | XF40 | MS60 | MS63 | MS65 |
|---|---|---|---|---|---|---|
| 2005 | 1,000 | PF65 15.00 | | | | |

**KM# 58 10 KWACHA**

15.10 g., Bi-Metallic Copper-Nickel center with Nickel-Brass ring, 28 mm. **Obv:** State arms and supporters with country name below **Obv. Legend:** MALAWI **Rev:** Farm worker harvesting **Edge:** Coarse reeding

| Date | Mintage | VF20 | XF40 | MS60 | MS63 | MS65 |
|---|---|---|---|---|---|---|
| 2006 | — | — | — | — | 4.50 | 6.00 |

**KM# 157 10 KWACHA**

Silver Plated **Subject:** World Cup Soccer 2006 **Obv:** National arms **Rev:** Soccer player in the stadium

| Date | Mintage | VF20 | XF40 | MS60 | MS63 | MS65 |
|---|---|---|---|---|---|---|
| 2006 | — | PF65 15.00 | | | | |

**KM# 158 10 KWACHA**

28.28 g., 0.925 Silver 0.841 oz. ASW, 38.6 mm. **Subject:** Elizabeth II, 80th Birthday **Obv:** National arms **Rev:** Elizabeth II

| Date | Mintage | VF20 | XF40 | MS60 | MS63 | MS65 |
|---|---|---|---|---|---|---|
| 2006 | — | PF65 37.50 | | | | |

**KM# 99 10 KWACHA**

0.999 Silver, 20x40 mm. **Obv:** Arms **Rev:** deRutter painting of ships

| Date | Mintage | VF20 | XF40 | MS60 | MS63 | MS65 |
|---|---|---|---|---|---|---|
| 2007 | — | PF65 45.00 | | | | |

**KM# 100 10 KWACHA**

Silver, 38.6 mm. **Obv:** Arms **Rev:** Puccini colorized

| Date | Mintage | VF20 | XF40 | MS60 | MS63 | MS65 |
|---|---|---|---|---|---|---|
| 2007 | — | PF65 40.00 | | | | |

**KM# 185 10 KWACHA**

Silver Plated Copper-Nickel, 45x30 mm. **Obv:** State arms **Rev:** Treaty of Rome anniversary in color

| Date | Mintage | VF20 | XF40 | MS60 | MS63 | MS65 |
|---|---|---|---|---|---|---|
| 2007 | — | PF65 15.00 | | | | |

**KM# 186 10 KWACHA**

Silver Plated Copper-Nickel, 45x30 mm. **Rev:** Mother Theresa in color

| Date | Mintage | VF20 | XF40 | MS60 | MS63 | MS65 |
|---|---|---|---|---|---|---|
| 2007 | — | PF65 15.00 | | | | |

**KM# 187 10 KWACHA**

Silver Plated Copper-Nickel, 45x30 mm. **Rev:** Verdespaleis Centennial

| Date | Mintage | VF20 | XF40 | MS60 | MS63 | MS65 |
|---|---|---|---|---|---|---|
| 2007 | — | PF65 15.00 | | | | |

**KM# 188 10 KWACHA**

Silver Plated Copper-Nickel, 45x30 mm. **Rev:** Ship painting of Michiel de Ruyter

| Date | Mintage | VF20 | XF40 | MS60 | MS63 | MS65 |
|---|---|---|---|---|---|---|
| 2007 | — | PF65 15.00 | | | | |

**KM# 189 10 KWACHA**

Silver Plated Copper-Nickel, 45x30 mm. **Rev:** Tulips in color

| Date | Mintage | VF20 | XF40 | MS60 | MS63 | MS65 |
|---|---|---|---|---|---|---|
| 2007 | — | PF65 15.00 | | | | |

**KM# 190 10 KWACHA**

Silver Plated Copper-Nickel **Rev:** 60th Anniversary, treaty of Rome, color

| Date | Mintage | VF20 | XF40 | MS60 | MS63 | MS65 |
|---|---|---|---|---|---|---|
| 2007 | — | PF65 15.00 | | | | |

**KM# 191 10 KWACHA**

Silver Plated Copper-Nickel **Rev:** Love and Psyche, in color

| Date | Mintage | VF20 | XF40 | MS60 | MS63 | MS65 |
|---|---|---|---|---|---|---|
| 2007 | — | PF65 15.00 | | | | |

**KM# 192 10 KWACHA**

Silver Plated Copper-Nickel **Rev:** Giuseppe Garibaldi in color

| Date | Mintage | VF20 | XF40 | MS60 | MS63 | MS65 |
|---|---|---|---|---|---|---|
| 2007 | — | PF65 15.00 | | | | |

**KM# 110 10 KWACHA**

62.20 g., 0.999 Silver 1.9978 oz. ASW, 42x42 mm. **Rev:** Lion with two crystal eyes

| Date | Mintage | VF20 | XF40 | MS60 | MS63 | MS65 |
|---|---|---|---|---|---|---|
| 2009 | 2,500 | PF65 135 | | | | |

**KM# 91 10 KWACHA**
23.50 g., Silver Plated Copper-Nickel, 39 mm. **Subject:** Endangered Frogs - Blue Poison Arrowfrog **Rev:** Multicolor blue frog right

| Date | Mintage | VF20 | XF40 | MS60 | MS63 | MS65 |
|---|---|---|---|---|---|---|
| 2010 | — | PF65 24.00 | | | | |

**KM# 92 10 KWACHA**
23.50 g., Silver Plated Copper-Nickel, 39 mm. **Subject:** Endangered Frogs - Dyeing Poison Arrow frog **Rev:** Multicolor blue frog left

| Date | Mintage | VF20 | XF40 | MS60 | MS63 | MS65 |
|---|---|---|---|---|---|---|
| 2010 | — | PF65 24.00 | | | | |

**KM# 93 10 KWACHA**
23.50 g., Silver Plated Copper-Nickel, 39 mm. **Subject:** Endangered Frogs - Darwin Frog **Rev:** Multicolor green frog right

| Date | Mintage | VF20 | XF40 | MS60 | MS63 | MS65 |
|---|---|---|---|---|---|---|
| 2010 | — | PF65 24.00 | | | | |

**KM# 94 10 KWACHA**
23.50 g., Silver Plated Copper-Nickel, 39 mm. **Subject:** Endangered Frogs - Panamanian Spotted frog **Rev:** Multicolor orange and black frog

| Date | Mintage | VF20 | XF40 | MS60 | MS63 | MS65 |
|---|---|---|---|---|---|---|
| 2010 | — | PF65 24.00 | | | | |

**KM# 95 10 KWACHA**
23.50 g., Silver Plated Copper-Nickel, 39 mm. **Subject:** Endangered Frogs - Purple frog **Rev:** Multicolor purple frog left

| Date | Mintage | VF20 | XF40 | MS60 | MS63 | MS65 |
|---|---|---|---|---|---|---|
| 2010 | — | PF65 24.00 | | | | |

**KM# 96 10 KWACHA**
23.50 g., Silver Plated Copper-Nickel, 39 mm. **Subject:** Endangered Frogs - Carnileri Harlequin **Rev:** Multicolor red frog left

| Date | Mintage | VF20 | XF40 | MS60 | MS63 | MS65 |
|---|---|---|---|---|---|---|
| 2010 | — | PF65 24.00 | | | | |

**KM# 97 10 KWACHA**
23.50 g., Silver Plated Copper-Nickel, 39 mm. **Subject:** Endangered Frogs - Tree frog **Rev:** Multicolor tree frog

| Date | Mintage | VF20 | XF40 | MS60 | MS63 | MS65 |
|---|---|---|---|---|---|---|
| 2010 | — | PF65 24.00 | | | | |

**KM# 214 10 KWACHA**
5.70 g., Stainless Steel plated iron, 22 mm. **Obv:** National arms, MALAWI below **Rev:** Elephant and calf walking right

| Date | Mintage | VF20 | XF40 | MS60 | MS63 | MS65 |
|---|---|---|---|---|---|---|
| 2012 | — | — | — | — | 4.00 | 6.00 |

**KM# 184 15 KWACHA**
20.00 g., 0.999 Silver 0.6424 oz. ASW, 38 mm. **Rev:** Brandenburg gate in color, map of Germany

| Date | Mintage | VF20 | XF40 | MS60 | MS63 | MS65 |
|---|---|---|---|---|---|---|
| 2006 | Est. 1000 | PF65 90.00 | | | | |

**KM# 56 20 KWACHA**
31.10 g., 0.999 Silver 0.9989 oz. ASW, 38.6 mm. **Series:** The Big Five **Obv:** National arms **Rev:** Two water buffalo on green malachite center insert **Edge:** Plain

| Date | Mintage | VF20 | XF40 | MS60 | MS63 | MS65 |
|---|---|---|---|---|---|---|
| 2004 | 3,000 | PF63 50.00 | PF65 55.00 | | | |

**KM# 67 20 KWACHA**
31.10 g., 0.999 Silver 0.9989 oz. ASW, 38.6 mm. **Series:** The Big Five **Obv:** National arms **Rev:** Elephant family on Haematite (blood stone) center insert **Edge:** Plain

| Date | Mintage | VF20 | XF40 | MS60 | MS63 | MS65 |
|---|---|---|---|---|---|---|
| 2004 | 3,000 | PF63 50.00 | PF65 55.00 | | | |

**KM# 68 20 KWACHA**
31.10 g., 0.999 Silver 0.9989 oz. ASW, 38.6 mm. **Series:** The Big Five **Obv:** National arms **Rev:** Leopard family on hawk or falcon-eye center insert **Edge:** Plain

| Date | Mintage | VF20 | XF40 | MS60 | MS63 | MS65 |
|---|---|---|---|---|---|---|
| 2004 | 3,000 | PF63 50.00 | PF65 55.00 | | | |

**KM# 69 20 KWACHA**
31.10 g., 0.999 Silver 0.9989 oz. ASW, 38.6 mm. **Series:** The Big Five **Obv:** National arms **Rev:** Lion family on tiger-eye center insert **Edge:** Plain

| Date | Mintage | VF20 | XF40 | MS60 | MS63 | MS65 |
|---|---|---|---|---|---|---|
| 2004 | 3,000 | PF63 50.00 | PF65 55.00 | | | |

**KM# 70 20 KWACHA**
31.10 g., 0.999 Silver 0.9989 oz. ASW, 38.6 mm. **Series:** The Big Five **Obv:** National arms **Rev:** Rhinoceros family on heliotrope center insert **Edge:** Plain

| Date | Mintage | VF20 | XF40 | MS60 | MS63 | MS65 |
|---|---|---|---|---|---|---|
| 2004 | 3,000 | PF63 50.00 | PF65 55.00 | | | |

**KM# 133 20 KWACHA**
Acrylic, 65 mm. **Subject:** Year of the Dog

| Date | Mintage | VF20 | XF40 | MS60 | MS63 | MS65 |
|---|---|---|---|---|---|---|
| 2006 | Est. 2000 | — | — | — | 65.00 | 75.00 |

**KM# 134 20 KWACHA**
31.11 g., 0.999 Silver 0.999 oz. ASW, 31x25 mm. **Subject:** Year of the Rat **Obv:** Temple of Heaven

| Date | Mintage | VF20 | XF40 | MS60 | MS63 | MS65 |
|---|---|---|---|---|---|---|
| 2006 | Est. 2000 | PF63 65.00 | PF65 75.00 | | | |

**KM# 135 20 KWACHA**
31.11 g., 0.999 Silver 0.999 oz. ASW, 31x25 mm. **Subject:** Year of the Ox **Obv:** Temple of Heaven

| Date | Mintage | VF20 | XF40 | MS60 | MS63 | MS65 |
|---|---|---|---|---|---|---|
| 2006 | Est. 2000 | PF63 65.00 | PF65 75.00 | | | |

**KM# 136 20 KWACHA**
31.11 g., 0.999 Silver 0.999 oz. ASW, 31x25 mm. **Subject:** Year of the Tiger **Obv:** Temple of Heaven

| Date | Mintage | VF20 | XF40 | MS60 | MS63 | MS65 |
|---|---|---|---|---|---|---|
| 2006 | — | PF63 65.00 | PF65 75.00 | | | |

**KM# 137 20 KWACHA**
31.11 g., 0.999 Silver 0.999 oz. ASW, 31x25 mm. **Subject:** Year of the Hare **Obv:** Temple of Heaven

| Date | Mintage | VF20 | XF40 | MS60 | MS63 | MS65 |
|---|---|---|---|---|---|---|
| 2006 | — | PF63 65.00 | PF65 75.00 | | | |

**KM# 138 20 KWACHA**
31.11 g., 0.999 Silver 0.999 oz. ASW, 31x25 mm. **Subject:** Year of the dragon **Obv:** Temple of Heaven

| Date | Mintage | VF20 | XF40 | MS60 | MS63 | MS65 |
|---|---|---|---|---|---|---|
| 2006 | Est. 2000 | PF63 65.00 | PF65 75.00 | | | |

**KM# 139 20 KWACHA**
31.11 g., 0.999 Silver 0.999 oz. ASW, 31x25 mm. **Subject:** Year of the Snake **Obv:** Temple of Heaven

| Date | Mintage | VF20 | XF40 | MS60 | MS63 | MS65 |
|---|---|---|---|---|---|---|
| 2006 | Est. 2000 | PF63 65.00 | PF65 75.00 | | | |

**KM# 140 20 KWACHA**
31.11 g., 0.999 Silver 0.999 oz. ASW, 31x25 mm. **Subject:** Year of the Horse **Obv:** Temple of Heaven

| Date | Mintage | VF20 | XF40 | MS60 | MS63 | MS65 |
|---|---|---|---|---|---|---|
| 2006 | Est. 2000 | PF63 65.00 | PF65 75.00 | | | |

**KM# 141 20 KWACHA**
31.11 g., 0.999 Silver 0.999 oz. ASW, 31x25 mm. **Subject:** Year of the goat **Obv:** Temple of Heaven

| Date | Mintage | VF20 | XF40 | MS60 | MS63 | MS65 |
|---|---|---|---|---|---|---|
| 2006 | Est. 2000 | PF63 65.00 | PF65 75.00 | | | |

**KM# 142 20 KWACHA**
31.11 g., 0.999 Silver 0.999 oz. ASW, 31x25 mm. **Subject:** Year of the monkey **Obv:** Temple of Heaven

| Date | Mintage | VF20 | XF40 | MS60 | MS63 | MS65 |
|---|---|---|---|---|---|---|
| 2006 | Est. 2000 | PF63 65.00 | PF65 75.00 | | | |

**KM# 143 20 KWACHA**
31.11 g., 0.999 Silver 0.999 oz. ASW, 31x25 mm. **Subject:** Year of the Rooster **Obv:** Temple of Heaven

| Date | Mintage | VF20 | XF40 | MS60 | MS63 | MS65 |
|---|---|---|---|---|---|---|
| 2006 | — | PF63 65.00 | PF65 75.00 | | | |

**KM# 144 20 KWACHA**
31.11 g., 0.999 Silver 0.999 oz. ASW, 31x25 mm. **Subject:** Year of the Dog **Obv:** Temple of Heaven

| Date | Mintage | VF20 | XF40 | MS60 | MS63 | MS65 |
|---|---|---|---|---|---|---|
| 2006 | Est. 2000 | PF63 65.00 | PF65 75.00 | | | |

**KM# 145 20 KWACHA**
31.11 g., 0.999 Silver 0.999 oz. ASW, 31x25 mm. **Subject:** Year of the pig **Obv:** Temple of Heaven

| Date | Mintage | VF20 | XF40 | MS60 | MS63 | MS65 |
|---|---|---|---|---|---|---|
| 2006 | Est. 2000 | PF63 65.00 | PF65 75.00 | | | |

**KM# 147 20 KWACHA**
31.11 g., 0.999 Silver 0.999 oz. ASW **Rev:** Sitting panda, city view of Moscow and flag in color

| Date | Mintage | VF20 | XF40 | MS60 | MS63 | MS65 |
|---|---|---|---|---|---|---|
| 2006 | Est. 5000 | PF65 60.00 | | | | |

**KM# 148 20 KWACHA**
31.11 g., 0.999 Silver 0.999 oz. ASW **Rev:** Sitting panda, city view of Osaka and flag in color

| Date | Mintage | VF20 | XF40 | MS60 | MS63 | MS65 |
|---|---|---|---|---|---|---|
| 2006 | Est. 5000 | PF65 60.00 | | | | |

**KM# 149 20 KWACHA**
31.11 g., 0.999 Silver 0.999 oz. ASW **Rev:** Sitting panda, city view of Paris and flag in color

| Date | Mintage | VF20 | XF40 | MS60 | MS63 | MS65 |
|---|---|---|---|---|---|---|
| 2006 | Est. 5000 | PF65 60.00 | | | | |

**KM# 150 20 KWACHA**
31.11 g., 0.999 Silver 0.999 oz. ASW **Rev:** Sitting panda, city view of Mexico City and flag in color

| Date | Mintage | VF20 | XF40 | MS60 | MS63 | MS65 |
|---|---|---|---|---|---|---|
| 2006 | — | PF65 60.00 | | | | |

**KM# 151 20 KWACHA**
31.11 g., 0.999 Silver 0.999 oz. ASW **Rev:** Sitting panda, city view of Madrid and flag in color

| Date | Mintage | VF20 | XF40 | MS60 | MS63 | MS65 |
|---|---|---|---|---|---|---|
| 2006 | Est. 5000 | PF65 60.00 | | | | |

**KM# 152 20 KWACHA**
31.11 g., 0.999 Silver 0.999 oz. ASW **Rev:** Panda on rock, city view of Pyeongyang and flag in color

| Date | Mintage | VF20 | XF40 | MS60 | MS63 | MS65 |
|---|---|---|---|---|---|---|
| 2006 | 5,000 | PF65 60.00 | | | | |

**KM# 153 20 KWACHA**
31.11 g., 0.999 Silver 0.999 oz. ASW

| Date | Mintage | VF20 | XF40 | MS60 | MS63 | MS65 |
|---|---|---|---|---|---|---|
| 2006 | Est. 5000 | PF65 60.00 | | | | |

**KM# 154 20 KWACHA**
31.11 g., 0.999 Silver 0.999 oz. ASW **Rev:** Panda on rock, city view of Berlin and flag in color

| Date | Mintage | VF20 | XF40 | MS60 | MS63 | MS65 |
|---|---|---|---|---|---|---|
| 2006 | — | PF65 60.00 | | | | |

**KM# 155 20 KWACHA**
31.11 g., 0.999 Silver 0.999 oz. ASW **Rev:** Panda on rock, city view of London and flag in color

| Date | Mintage | VF20 | XF40 | MS60 | MS63 | MS65 |
|---|---|---|---|---|---|---|
| 2006 | 5,000 | PF65 60.00 | | | | |

**KM# 156 20 KWACHA**
31.11 g., 0.999 Silver 0.999 oz. ASW **Rev:** Panda on rock, city view of Hong Kong and flag in color

| Date | Mintage | VF20 | XF40 | MS60 | MS63 | MS65 |
|---|---|---|---|---|---|---|
| 2006 | Est. 5000 | PF65 60.00 | | | | |

**KM# 74 20 KWACHA**
0.50 g., 0.999 Gold **Subject:** Springbnok, 40 years, first design

| Date | Mintage | VF20 | XF40 | MS60 | MS63 | MS65 |
|---|---|---|---|---|---|---|
| 2007 | — | PF63 65.00 | PF65 70.00 | | | |

**KM# 75 20 KWACHA**
0.50 g., 0.999 Gold **Subject:** Springbok, 40th Anniversary, second desgin

| Date | Mintage | VF20 | XF40 | MS60 | MS63 | MS65 |
|---|---|---|---|---|---|---|
| 2007 | — | PF63 65.00 | PF65 70.00 | | | |

**KM# 76 20 KWACHA**
0.50 g., 0.999 Gold **Subject:** Springbok, 40th Anniversary, third design

| Date | Mintage | VF20 | XF40 | MS60 | MS63 | MS65 |
|---|---|---|---|---|---|---|
| 2007 | — | PF63 65.00 | PF65 70.00 | | | |

**KM# 111 20 KWACHA**
28.28 g., 0.925 Silver 0.841 oz. ASW, 38.61 mm. **Subject:** Biosphere Reserves **Obv:** National Arms **Rev:** Goat on hillside, multicolor flower

| Date | Mintage | VF20 | XF40 | MS60 | MS63 | MS65 |
|---|---|---|---|---|---|---|
| 2010 | 8,000 | PF65 60.00 | | | | |

**KM# 208 20 KWACHA**
50.00 g., Silver Plated Base Metal, 65 mm. **Obv:** John Paul II and St. Peter's **Rev:** John Paul II hand raised in benidiction

| Date | Mintage | VF20 | XF40 | MS60 | MS63 | MS65 |
|---|---|---|---|---|---|---|
| 2011 | 2,000 | PF65 100 | | | | |

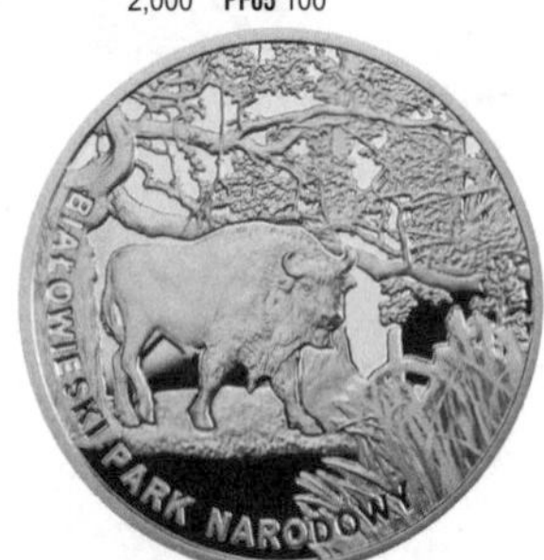


**KM# 209 20 KWACHA**
28.28 g., 0.925 Silver 0.841 oz. ASW, 38.61 mm. **Obv:** National arms **Rev:** Bison Zubr and grass in color

| Date | Mintage | VF20 | XF40 | MS60 | MS63 | MS65 |
|---|---|---|---|---|---|---|
| 2011 | 5,000 | PF65 150 | | | | |

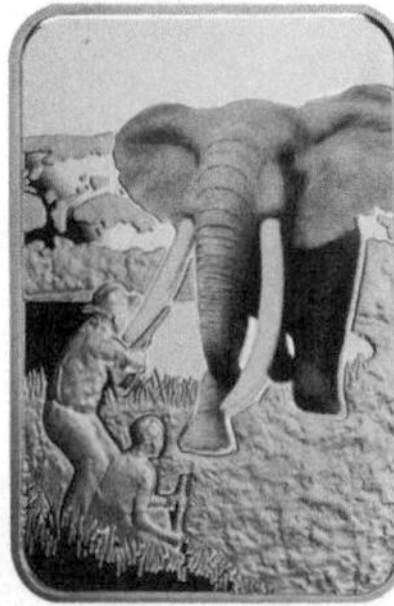

**KM# 210 20 KWACHA**
28.28 g., 0.925 Silver 0.841 oz. ASW, 28x40 mm. **Rev:** Elephant hunt in color **Shape:** Vertical rectangle

| Date | Mintage | VF20 | XF40 | MS60 | MS63 | MS65 |
|---|---|---|---|---|---|---|
| 2011 | 3,000 | PF65 150 | | | | |

**KM# 211 20 KWACHA**
28.28 g., 0.925 Silver 0.841 oz. ASW, 28x40 mm. **Rev:** Duck hunt in color **Shape:** Vertical rectangle

| Date | Mintage | VF20 | XF40 | MS60 | MS63 | MS65 |
|---|---|---|---|---|---|---|
| 2011 | — | PF65 150 | | | | |

**KM# 77 40 KWACHA**
1.00 g., 0.999 Gold 0.0321 oz. AGW **Rev:** Springbok

| Date | Mintage | VF20 | XF40 | MS60 | MS63 | MS65 |
|---|---|---|---|---|---|---|
| 2008 | — | PF65 100 | | | | |

**KM# 78 40 KWACHA**
1.00 g., 0.999 Palladium 0.0321 oz. APW **Rev:** Springbok

| Date | Mintage | VF20 | XF40 | MS60 | MS63 | MS65 |
|---|---|---|---|---|---|---|
| 2008 | — | PF65 75.00 | | | | |

**KM# 79 40 KWACHA**
1.00 g., 0.999 Platinum 0.0321 oz. APW **Rev:** Springbok

| Date | Mintage | VF20 | XF40 | MS60 | MS63 | MS65 |
|---|---|---|---|---|---|---|
| 2008 | — | PF65 125 | | | | |

**KM# 43 50 KWACHA**
141.21 g., Bronze with Gold Plated center and Silver Plated ring, 65 mm. **Subject:** Republic of China **Obv:** Large building above value within circle **Rev:** Conjoined busts facing within circle **Edge:** Reeded **Note:** Illustration reduced.

| Date | Mintage | VF20 | XF40 | MS60 | MS63 | MS65 |
|---|---|---|---|---|---|---|
| 2004 | 1,000 | PF63 85.00 | PF65 100 | | | |

**KM# 108 50 KWACHA**
Silver **Obv:** National Arms **Rev:** Soccer ball in flight from Germany to South Africa

| Date | Mintage | VF20 | XF40 | MS60 | MS63 | MS65 |
|---|---|---|---|---|---|---|
| 2006 | — | PF65 45.00 | | | | |

### KM# 109 50 KWACHA

Silver **Obv:** National Arms **Rev:** Two female hurdlers

| Date | Mintage | VF20 | XF40 | MS60 | MS63 | MS65 |
|---|---|---|---|---|---|---|
| 2008 | — | PF65 45.00 | | | | |

### KM# 193 50 KWACHA

27.00 g., Silver Plated Brass with sterling silver inlay, 38.6 mm. **Rev:** Springbock

| Date | Mintage | VF20 | XF40 | MS60 | MS63 | MS65 |
|---|---|---|---|---|---|---|
| 2008 | Est. 4444 | — | — | — | 60.00 | 70.00 |

### KM# 194 50 KWACHA

1.00 g., 0.999 Silver 0.0321 oz. ASW, 8.5x15 mm. **Rev:** Springbock

| Date | Mintage | VF20 | XF40 | MS60 | MS63 | MS65 |
|---|---|---|---|---|---|---|
| 2008 | Est. 5000 | PF65 15.00 | | | | |

### KM# 85 50 KWACHA

62.21 g., 0.999 Silver 1.9981 oz. ASW, 42x42 mm. **Obv:** Arms **Rev:** White lion with crystal inserts in eyes **Shape:** Square

| Date | Mintage | VF20 | XF40 | MS60 | MS63 | MS65 |
|---|---|---|---|---|---|---|
| 2009 | 2,500 | PF65 175 | | | | |

### KM# 215 50 KWACHA

31.31 g., 0.999 Silver 1.0056 oz. ASW, 40 mm. **Obv:** National arms **Rev:** Gazelle

| Date | Mintage | VF20 | XF40 | MS60 | MS63 | MS65 |
|---|---|---|---|---|---|---|
| 2010 | — | PF65 65.00 | | | | |

### KM# 146 75 KWACHA

4.00 g., 0.999 Gold 0.1285 oz. AGW, 20 mm. **Obv:** Temple of Mazu **Rev:** Mazu, goddess of protection

| Date | Mintage | VF20 | XF40 | MS60 | MS63 | MS65 |
|---|---|---|---|---|---|---|
| 2006 | Est. 3000 | PF63 225 | PF65 275 | | | |

### KM# 171 100 KWACHA

Gold **Subject:** 2008 Bejing Olympics **Rev:** Two hurdlers

| Date | Mintage | VF20 | XF40 | MS60 | MS63 | MS65 |
|---|---|---|---|---|---|---|
| 2006 Proof | — | — | — | — | — | — |

### KM# 216 100 KWACHA

62.21 g., 0.999 Gold 1.9981 oz. AGW, 44x44 mm. **Obv:** National arms **Rev:** White lion with crystal inserts in eyes **Shape:** Square

| Date | Mintage | VF20 | XF40 | MS60 | MS63 | MS65 |
|---|---|---|---|---|---|---|
| 2009 | 99 | PF65 2,700 | | | | |

## PATTERNS

Including off metal strikes

| KM# | Date | Mintage | Identification | Mkt Val |
|---|---|---|---|---|
| Pn2 | 2002 | — | 10 Kwacha Copper-Nickel National arms Alexander the Great | — |
| Pn3 | 2002 | — | 10 Kwacha Copper-Nickel National arms Olympic torch under two world globes | — |
| Pn4 | 2002 | — | 10 Kwacha Copper-Nickel National arms MILLENNIUM" above Mona Lisa like portrait | — |
| Pn5 | 2003 | — | 10 Kwacha Silver Plated National arms Trans-Siberian Express train | — |
| Pn6 | 2003 | — | 10 Kwacha Silver Plated National arms Blesbok antelope | — |
| Pn7 | 2003 | — | 10 Kwacha Copper-Nickel National arms Eland antelope | — |
| Pn8 | 2003 | — | 10 Kwacha Copper-Nickel National arms Kudu antelope | — |
| Pn9 | 2003 | — | 10 Kwacha Silver Plated Nyala antelope | — |
| Pn15 | ND (2004) | — | 10 Kwacha Silver Plated National arms Multicolor pair of birds with chick | 15.00 |

# MALAYSIA

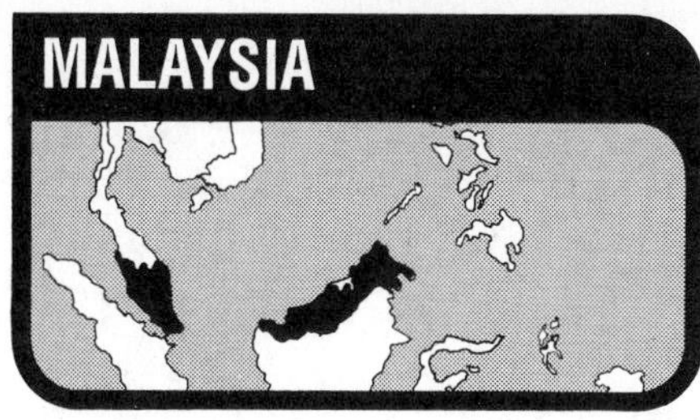

The independent limited constitutional monarchy of Malaysia, which occupies the southern part of the Malay Peninsula in Southeast Asia and the northern part of the island of Borneo, has an area of 127,316 sq. mi. (329,750 sq. km.) and a population of 15.4 million. Capital: Kuala Lumpur. The economy is based on agriculture, mining and forestry. Rubber, tin, timber and palm oil are exported.

Malaysia came into being on Sept. 16, 1963, as a federation of Malaya (Johore, Kelantan, Kedah, Perlis, Trengganu, Negri-Sembilan, Pahang, Perak, Selangor, Penang, Malacca), Singapore, Sabah (British North Borneo) and Sarawak. Following two serious racial riots involving Malays and Chinese, Singapore withdrew from the federation on Aug. 9, 1965. Malaysia is a member of the Commonwealth of Nations.

**MINT MARK**

FM - Franklin Mint, U.S.A.

## CONSTITUTIONAL MONARCHY

## STANDARD COINAGE

100 Sen = 1 Ringgit (Dollar)

### KM# 49 SEN

1.80 g., Bronze Clad Steel, 17.66 mm. **Obv:** Value divides date below flower blossom **Obv. Legend:** BANK NEGARA MALAYSIA **Rev:** Drum **Edge:** Plain

| Date | Mintage | VF20 | XF40 | MS60 | MS63 | MS65 |
|---|---|---|---|---|---|---|
| 2001 | 213,645,000 | — | — | 0.15 | 0.25 | 0.40 |
| 2002 | 185,220,000 | — | — | 0.15 | 0.25 | 0.40 |
| 2003 | 235,350,000 | — | — | 0.15 | 0.25 | 0.40 |
| 2004 | 227,700,000 | — | — | 0.15 | 0.25 | 0.40 |
| 2005 | 437,400,000 | — | — | 0.15 | 0.25 | 0.40 |
| 2006 | 328,050,000 | — | — | 0.15 | 0.25 | 0.40 |
| 2007 | — | — | — | 0.15 | 0.25 | 0.40 |

### KM# 50 5 SEN

1.40 g., Copper-Nickel, 16.25 mm. **Obv:** Value divides date below flower blossom **Obv. Legend:** BANK NEGARA MALAYSIA **Rev:** Top with string **Edge:** Reeded

| Date | Mintage | VF20 | XF40 | MS60 | MS63 | MS65 |
|---|---|---|---|---|---|---|
| 2001 | 94,617,472 | — | — | 0.15 | 0.25 | 0.45 |
| 2002 | 85,316,000 | — | — | 0.15 | 0.25 | 0.45 |
| 2003 | 75,690,000 | — | — | 0.15 | 0.25 | 0.45 |
| 2004 | 11,520,000 | — | — | 0.15 | 0.25 | 0.45 |
| 2005 | 119,520,000 | — | — | 0.15 | 0.25 | 0.45 |
| 2006 | 87,120,000 | — | — | 0.15 | 0.25 | 0.45 |
| 2007 | 97,200,338 | — | — | 0.15 | 0.25 | 0.45 |
| 2008 | 91,440,000 | — | — | 0.15 | 0.25 | 0.45 |
| 2009 | 125,172,842 | — | — | 0.15 | 0.25 | 0.45 |
| 2010 | — | — | — | 0.15 | 0.25 | 0.45 |
| 2011 | — | — | — | 0.15 | 0.25 | 0.45 |

### KM# 201 5 SEN

1.72 g., Stainless Steel, 17.78 mm. **Obv:** Flower, date and value **Obv. Legend:** BANK NEGARA MALAYSIA **Rev:** Geometric pattern

| Date | Mintage | VF20 | XF40 | MS60 | MS63 | MS65 |
|---|---|---|---|---|---|---|
| 2011 | — | — | — | 0.15 | 0.25 | 0.45 |
| 2012 | — | — | — | 0.15 | 0.25 | 0.45 |
| 2013 | — | — | — | 0.15 | 0.25 | 0.45 |

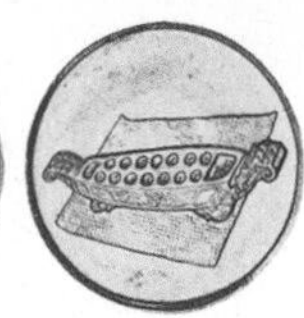

### KM# 51 10 SEN

2.82 g., Copper-Nickel, 19.4 mm. **Obv:** Value divides date below flower blossom **Obv. Legend:** BANK NEGARA MALAYSIA **Rev:** Ceremonial table **Edge:** Reeded

| Date | Mintage | VF20 | XF40 | MS60 | MS63 | MS65 |
|---|---|---|---|---|---|---|
| 2001 | 313,422,000 | — | — | 0.25 | 0.40 | 0.60 |
| 2002 | 290,451,948 | — | — | 0.25 | 0.40 | 0.60 |
| 2003 | 8,640,000 | — | — | 0.25 | 0.40 | 0.60 |
| 2004 | 170,640,000 | — | — | 0.25 | 0.40 | 0.60 |
| 2005 | 316,800,000 | — | — | 0.25 | 0.40 | 0.60 |
| 2006 | 304,560,000 | — | — | 0.25 | 0.40 | 0.60 |
| 2007 | 237,967,970 | — | — | 0.25 | 0.40 | 0.60 |
| 2008 | 241,560,000 | — | — | 0.25 | 0.40 | 0.60 |
| 2009 | 336,150,800 | — | — | 0.25 | 0.40 | 0.60 |
| 2010 | — | — | — | 0.25 | 0.40 | 0.60 |
| 2011 | — | — | — | 0.25 | 0.40 | 0.60 |

### KM# 202 10 SEN

2.98 g., Stainless Steel, 18.8 mm. **Obv:** Flower, date and value **Obv. Legend:** BANK NEGARA MALAYSIA **Rev:** Star-like geometric pattern **Edge:** Reeded

| Date | Mintage | VF20 | XF40 | MS60 | MS63 | MS65 |
|---|---|---|---|---|---|---|
| 2011 | — | — | — | 0.25 | 0.40 | 0.60 |
| 2012 | — | — | — | 0.25 | 0.40 | 0.60 |
| 2013 | — | — | — | 0.25 | 0.40 | 0.60 |

### KM# 52 20 SEN

5.66 g., Copper-Nickel, 23.6 mm. **Obv:** Value divides date below flower blossom **Obv. Legend:** BANK NEGARA MALAYSIA **Rev:** Basket with food and utensils **Edge:** Reeded

| Date | Mintage | VF20 | XF40 | MS60 | MS63 | MS65 |
|---|---|---|---|---|---|---|
| 2001 | 278,802,000 | — | — | 0.35 | 0.50 | 0.85 |
| 2002 | 131,279,881 | — | — | 0.35 | 0.50 | 0.85 |
| 2003 | — | — | — | 0.35 | 0.50 | 0.85 |
| 2004 | 96,840,000 | — | — | 0.35 | 0.50 | 0.85 |
| 2005 | 209,700,000 | — | — | 0.35 | 0.50 | 0.85 |
| Note: Obverse varieties exist with thick or thin lettering | | | | | | |
| 2006 | 155,880,000 | — | — | 0.35 | 0.50 | 0.85 |
| 2007 | 212,897,236 | — | — | 0.35 | 0.50 | 0.85 |
| 2008 | 19,764,000 | — | — | 0.35 | 0.50 | 0.85 |
| 2009 | — | — | — | 0.35 | 0.50 | 0.85 |
| 2010 | — | — | — | 0.35 | 0.50 | 0.85 |
| 2011 | — | — | — | 0.35 | 0.50 | 0.85 |

### KM# 203 20 SEN

4.18 g., Nickel-Brass, 20.6 mm. **Obv:** Flower, date and value **Obv. Legend:** BANK NEGARA MALAYSIA **Rev:** flowers on patterned background

| Date | Mintage | VF20 | XF40 | MS60 | MS63 | MS65 |
|---|---|---|---|---|---|---|
| 2011 | — | — | — | 0.35 | 0.50 | 0.85 |
| 2012 | — | — | — | 0.35 | 0.50 | 0.85 |
| 2013 | — | — | — | 0.35 | 0.50 | 0.85 |

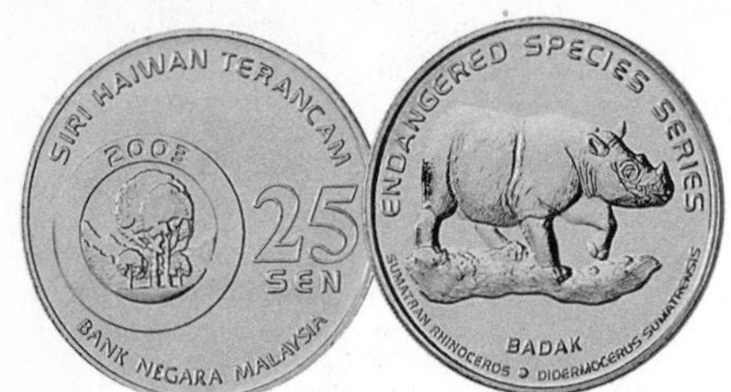


**KM# 77 25 SEN**

9.14 g., Brass, 30 mm. **Series:** Endangered Species **Obv:** Logo left, value right **Rev:** Sumatran Rhinoceros **Edge:** Reeded

| Date | Mintage | VF20 | XF40 | MS60 | MS63 | MS65 |
|---|---|---|---|---|---|---|
| 2003 | 100,000 | — | — | — | 5.00 | 6.00 |

**KM# 78 25 SEN**

9.14 g., Brass, 30 mm. **Series:** Endangered Species **Obv:** Logo left, value right **Rev:** Elephant **Edge:** Reeded

| Date | Mintage | VF20 | XF40 | MS60 | MS63 | MS65 |
|---|---|---|---|---|---|---|
| 2003 | 100,000 | — | — | — | 7.00 | 8.00 |

**KM# 79 25 SEN**

9.14 g., Brass, 30 mm. **Series:** Endangered Species **Obv:** Logo left, value right **Rev:** Orangutan **Edge:** Reeded

| Date | Mintage | VF20 | XF40 | MS60 | MS63 | MS65 |
|---|---|---|---|---|---|---|
| 2003 | 100,000 | — | — | — | 5.00 | 6.00 |

**KM# 80 25 SEN**

9.14 g., Brass, 30 mm. **Series:** Endangered Species **Obv:** Logo left, value right **Rev:** Sumatran Tiger **Edge:** Reeded

| Date | Mintage | VF20 | XF40 | MS60 | MS63 | MS65 |
|---|---|---|---|---|---|---|
| 2003 | 100,000 | — | — | — | 5.00 | 6.00 |

**KM# 81 25 SEN**

9.14 g., Brass, 30 mm. **Series:** Endangered Species **Obv:** Logo left, value right **Rev:** Slow Loris on branch **Edge:** Reeded

| Date | Mintage | VF20 | XF40 | MS60 | MS63 | MS65 |
|---|---|---|---|---|---|---|
| 2003 | 100,000 | — | — | — | 5.00 | 6.00 |

**KM# 82 25 SEN**

9.14 g., Brass, 30 mm. **Series:** Endangered Species **Obv:** Logo left, value right **Rev:** Barking Deer **Edge:** Reeded

| Date | Mintage | VF20 | XF40 | MS60 | MS63 | MS65 |
|---|---|---|---|---|---|---|
| 2003 | 100,000 | — | — | — | 5.00 | 6.00 |

**KM# 83 25 SEN**

9.14 g., Brass, 30 mm. **Series:** Endangered Species **Obv:** Logo left, value right **Rev:** Malayan Tapir **Edge:** Reeded

| Date | Mintage | VF20 | XF40 | MS60 | MS63 | MS65 |
|---|---|---|---|---|---|---|
| 2003 | 100,000 | — | — | — | 5.00 | 6.00 |

**KM# 84 25 SEN**

9.14 g., Brass, 30 mm. **Series:** Endangered Species **Obv:** Logo left, value right **Rev:** Serow **Edge:** Reeded

| Date | Mintage | VF20 | XF40 | MS60 | MS63 | MS65 |
|---|---|---|---|---|---|---|
| 2003 | 100,000 | — | — | — | 5.00 | 6.00 |

**KM# 85 25 SEN**

9.14 g., Brass, 30 mm. **Series:** Endangered Species **Obv:** Logo left, value right **Rev:** Sambar Deer **Edge:** Reeded

| Date | Mintage | VF20 | XF40 | MS60 | MS63 | MS65 |
|---|---|---|---|---|---|---|
| 2003 | 100,000 | — | — | — | 5.00 | 6.00 |

**KM# 86 25 SEN**

9.14 g., Brass, 30 mm. **Series:** Endangered Species **Obv:** Logo left, value right **Rev:** Seated Proboscis Monkey flanked by sprigs **Edge:** Reeded

| Date | Mintage | VF20 | XF40 | MS60 | MS63 | MS65 |
|---|---|---|---|---|---|---|
| 2003 | 100,000 | — | — | — | 5.00 | 6.00 |

**KM# 87 25 SEN**

9.14 g., Brass, 30 mm. **Series:** Endangered Species **Obv:** Logo left, value right **Rev:** Gaur **Edge:** Reeded

| Date | Mintage | VF20 | XF40 | MS60 | MS63 | MS65 |
|---|---|---|---|---|---|---|
| 2003 | 100,000 | — | — | — | 5.00 | 6.00 |

**KM# 88 25 SEN**

9.14 g., Brass, 30 mm. **Series:** Endangered Species **Obv:** Logo left, value right **Rev:** Clouded Leopard **Edge:** Reeded

| Date | Mintage | VF20 | XF40 | MS60 | MS63 | MS65 |
|---|---|---|---|---|---|---|
| 2003 | 100,000 | — | — | — | 5.00 | 6.00 |

**KM# 89 25 SEN**

9.14 g., Brass, 30 mm. **Series:** Endangered Species **Obv:** Logo left, value right **Obv. Legend:** BANK NEGARA MALAYSIA - SIRI HAIWAN TERANCAM **Rev:** Straw-headed Bulbul bird (Barau-Barau) **Edge:** Reeded

| Date | Mintage | VF20 | XF40 | MS60 | MS63 | MS65 |
|---|---|---|---|---|---|---|
| 2005 | — | — | — | — | 5.00 | 6.00 |

**KM# 90 25 SEN**

9.14 g., Brass, 30 mm. **Series:** Endangered Species **Obv:** Logo left, value right **Obv. Legend:** BANK NEGARA MALAYSIA - SIRI HAIWAN TERANCAM **Rev:** Great Argus Pheasant (Kuang Raya) **Edge:** Reeded

| Date | Mintage | VF20 | XF40 | MS60 | MS63 | MS65 |
|---|---|---|---|---|---|---|
| 2005 | 40,000 | — | — | — | 5.00 | 6.00 |

**KM# 91 25 SEN**

9.14 g., Brass, 30 mm. **Series:** Endangered Species **Obv:** Logo left, value right **Obv. Legend:** BANK NEGARA MALAYSIA - SIRI HAIWAN TERANCAM **Rev:** White-collared Kingfisher (Pekaka Sungai) **Edge:** Reeded

| Date | Mintage | VF20 | XF40 | MS60 | MS63 | MS65 |
|---|---|---|---|---|---|---|
| 2005 | 40,000 | — | — | — | 5.00 | 6.00 |

**KM# 92 25 SEN**

9.14 g., Brass, 30 mm. **Series:** Endangered Species **Obv:** Logo left, value right **Obv. Legend:** BANK NEGARA MALAYSIA - SIRI HAIWAN TERANCAM **Rev:** White-bellied Sea Eagle (Lang Siput) perched on branch **Edge:** Reeded

| Date | Mintage | VF20 | XF40 | MS60 | MS63 | MS65 |
|---|---|---|---|---|---|---|
| 2005 | 40,000 | — | — | — | 5.00 | 6.00 |

**KM# 93 25 SEN**

9.16 g., Brass, 30 mm. **Series:** Endangered Species **Obv:** Logo left, value right **Obv. Legend:** BANK NEGARA MALAYSIA - SIRI HAIWAN TERANCAM **Rev:** Asian Fairy Bluebird (Dendang Gajah) **Edge:** Reeded

| Date | Mintage | VF20 | XF40 | MS60 | MS63 | MS65 |
|---|---|---|---|---|---|---|
| 2005 | 40,000 | — | — | — | 5.00 | 6.00 |

**KM# 94 25 SEN**

9.16 g., Brass, 30 mm. **Series:** Endangered Species **Obv:** Logo left, value right **Obv. Legend:** BANK NEGARA MALAYSIA - SIRI HAIWAN TERANCAM **Rev:** Rhinoceros Hornbill bird (Enggang Badak) **Edge:** Reeded

| Date | Mintage | VF20 | XF40 | MS60 | MS63 | MS65 |
|---|---|---|---|---|---|---|
| 2005 | 40,000 | — | — | — | 5.00 | 6.00 |

**KM# 95 25 SEN**

9.16 g., Brass, 30 mm. **Series:** Endangered Species **Obv:** Logo left, value right **Obv. Legend:** BANK NEGARA MALAYSIA - SIRI HAIWAN TERANCAM **Rev:** Nicobar Pigeon (Merpati Emas) **Edge:** Reeded

| Date | Mintage | VF20 | XF40 | MS60 | MS63 | MS65 |
|---|---|---|---|---|---|---|
| 2005 | 40,000 | — | — | — | 5.00 | 6.00 |

**KM# 96 25 SEN**

9.16 g., Brass, 30 mm. **Series:** Endangered Species **Obv:** Logo left, value right **Obv. Legend:** BANK NEGARA MALAYSIA - SIRI HAIWAN TERANCAM **Rev:** Two Crested Wood Partridges (Siul Berjambul) **Edge:** Reeded

| Date | Mintage | VF20 | XF40 | MS60 | MS63 | MS65 |
|---|---|---|---|---|---|---|
| 2005 | 40,000 | — | — | — | 5.00 | 6.00 |

**KM# 97 25 SEN**

9.16 g., Brass, 30 mm. **Series:** Endangered Species **Obv:** Logo left, value right **Obv. Legend:** BANK NEGARA MALAYSIA - SIRI HAIWAN TERANCAM **Rev:** Black and Red Broadbill bird (Takau Rakit) **Edge:** Reeded

| Date | Mintage | VF20 | XF40 | MS60 | MS63 | MS65 |
|---|---|---|---|---|---|---|
| 2005 | 40,000 | — | — | — | 5.00 | 6.00 |

**KM# 98 25 SEN**

9.16 g., Brass, 30 mm. **Series:** Endangered Species **Obv:** Logo left, value right **Obv. Legend:** BANK NEGARA MALAYSIA - SIRI HAIWAN TERANCAM **Rev:** Green Imperial Pigeon (Pergam Besar) on branch **Edge:** Reeded

| Date | Mintage | VF20 | XF40 | MS60 | MS63 | MS65 |
|---|---|---|---|---|---|---|
| 2005 | 40,000 | — | — | — | 5.00 | 6.00 |

### KM# 99 25 SEN

9.16 g., Brass, 30 mm. **Series:** Endangered Species **Obv:** Logo left, value right **Obv. Legend:** BANK NEGARA MALAYSIA - SIRI HAIWAN TERANCAM **Rev:** Great Egret (Bangau Besar) **Edge:** Reeded

| Date | Mintage | VF20 | XF40 | MS60 | MS63 | MS65 |
|---|---|---|---|---|---|---|
| 2005 | 40,000 | — | — | — | 5.00 | 6.00 |

### KM# 100 25 SEN

9.16 g., Brass, 30 mm. **Series:** Endangered Species **Obv:** Logo left, value right **Obv. Legend:** BANK NEGARA MALAYSIA - SIRI HAIWAN TERANCAM **Rev:** Brown Shrike (Tirjup Tanah) on branch **Edge:** Reeded

| Date | Mintage | VF20 | XF40 | MS60 | MS63 | MS65 |
|---|---|---|---|---|---|---|
| 2005 | 40,000 | — | — | — | 5.00 | 6.00 |

### KM# 101 25 SEN

Brass, 34 mm. **Series:** Endangered Species **Obv:** Logo and value **Obv. Legend:** BANK NEGARA MALAYSIA - SIRI HAIWAN TERANCAM **Rev:** Olive Ridley Turtle (Pengu Lipas)

| Date | Mintage | VF20 | XF40 | MS60 | MS63 | MS65 |
|---|---|---|---|---|---|---|
| 2006 | 40,000 | — | — | — | 5.00 | 6.00 |

### KM# 102 25 SEN

Brass, 34 mm. **Series:** Endangered Species **Obv:** Logo and value **Obv. Legend:** BANK NEGARA MALAYSIA - SIRI HAIWAN TERANCAM **Rev:** Leatherback turtle (Penyu Belimbing)

| Date | Mintage | VF20 | XF40 | MS60 | MS63 | MS65 |
|---|---|---|---|---|---|---|
| 2006 | 40,000 | — | — | — | 5.00 | 6.00 |

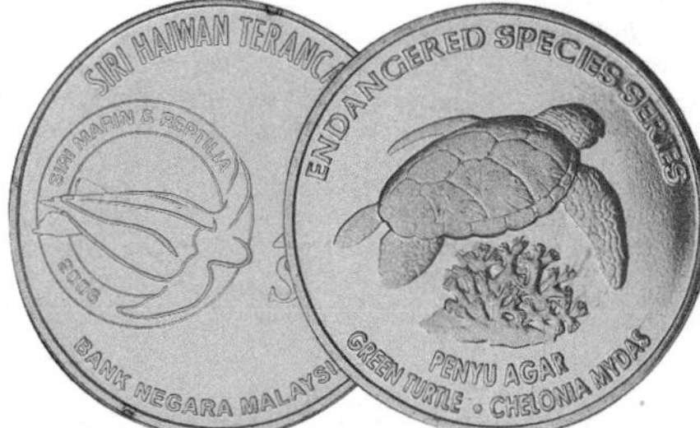


### KM# 103 25 SEN

Brass, 34 mm. **Series:** Endangered Species **Obv:** Logo and value **Obv. Legend:** BANK NEGARA MALAYSIA - SIRI HAIWAN TERANCAM **Rev:** Green turtle (Penyu Agar)

| Date | Mintage | VF20 | XF40 | MS60 | MS63 | MS65 |
|---|---|---|---|---|---|---|
| 2006 | 40,000 | — | — | — | 5.00 | 6.00 |

### KM# 104 25 SEN

Brass, 34 mm. **Series:** Endangered Species **Obv:** Logo and value **Obv. Legend:** BANK NEGARA MALAYSIA - SIRI HAIWAN TERANCAM **Rev:** Hawksbill turtle (Penyu Karah)

| Date | Mintage | VF20 | XF40 | MS60 | MS63 | MS65 |
|---|---|---|---|---|---|---|
| 2006 | 40,000 | — | — | — | 5.00 | 6.00 |

### KM# 105 25 SEN

15.50 g., Brass, 34 mm. **Series:** Endangered Species **Obv:** Logo and value **Obv. Legend:** BANK NEGARA MALAYSIA - SIRI HAIWAN TERANCAM **Rev:** Dugong **Edge:** Reeded

| Date | Mintage | VF20 | XF40 | MS60 | MS63 | MS65 |
|---|---|---|---|---|---|---|
| 2006 | 40,000 | — | — | — | 7.00 | 8.00 |

### KM# 106 25 SEN

15.50 g., Brass, 34 mm. **Series:** Endangered Species **Obv:** Logo and value **Obv. Legend:** BANK NEGARA MALAYSIA - SIRI HAIWAN TERANCAM **Rev:** Whale Shark (Jerung Paus) **Edge:** Reeded

| Date | Mintage | VF20 | XF40 | MS60 | MS63 | MS65 |
|---|---|---|---|---|---|---|
| 2006 | 40,000 | — | — | — | 5.00 | 6.00 |

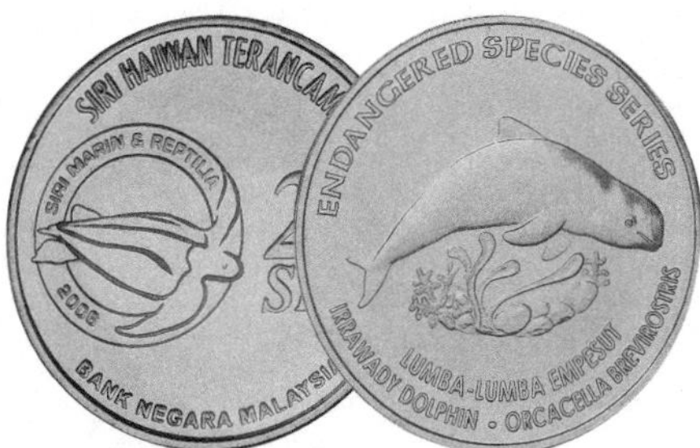


### KM# 107 25 SEN

15.50 g., Brass, 34 mm. **Series:** Endangered Species **Obv:** Logo and value **Obv. Legend:** BANK NEGARA MALAYSIA - SIRI HAIWAN TERANCAM **Rev:** Irraddy Dolphin (Lumba-Lumba Empesut) **Edge:** Reeded

| Date | Mintage | VF20 | XF40 | MS60 | MS63 | MS65 |
|---|---|---|---|---|---|---|
| 2006 | 40,000 | — | — | — | 5.00 | 6.00 |

### KM# 108 25 SEN

15.50 g., Brass, 34 mm. **Series:** Endangered Species **Obv:** Logo and value **Obv. Legend:** BANK NEGARA MALAYSIA - SIRI HAIWAN TERANCAM **Rev:** Bottlenose Dolphin (Lumba Lumba) **Edge:** Reeded

| Date | Mintage | VF20 | XF40 | MS60 | MS63 | MS65 |
|---|---|---|---|---|---|---|
| 2006 | 40,000 | — | — | — | 5.00 | 6.00 |

### KM# 109 25 SEN

15.50 g., Brass, 34 mm. **Series:** Endangered Species **Obv:** Logo and value **Obv. Legend:** BANK NEGARA MALAYSIA - SIRI HAIWAN TERANCAM **Rev:** Siamese Crocodile (Buaya Siam) **Edge:** Reeded

| Date | Mintage | VF20 | XF40 | MS60 | MS63 | MS65 |
|---|---|---|---|---|---|---|
| 2006 | 40,000 | — | — | — | 5.00 | 6.00 |

### KM# 110 25 SEN

15.50 g., Brass, 34 mm. **Series:** Endangered Species **Obv:** Logo and value **Obv. Legend:** BANK NEGARA MALAYSIA - SIRI HAIWAN TERANCAM **Rev:** Indopacific Crocodile (Buaya Tembaga) **Edge:** Reeded

| Date | Mintage | VF20 | XF40 | MS60 | MS63 | MS65 |
|---|---|---|---|---|---|---|
| 2006 | 40,000 | — | — | — | 5.00 | 6.00 |

### KM# 111 25 SEN

15.50 g., Brass, 34 mm. **Series:** Endangered Species **Obv:** Logo and value **Obv. Legend:** BANK NEGARA MALAYSIA - SIRI HAIWAN TERANCAM **Rev:** Malayan Gharial (Buaya Julong) **Edge:** Reeded

| Date | Mintage | VF20 | XF40 | MS60 | MS63 | MS65 |
|---|---|---|---|---|---|---|
| 2006 | 40,000 | — | — | — | 5.00 | 6.00 |

### KM# 112 25 SEN

15.50 g., Brass, 34 mm. **Series:** Endangered Species **Obv:** Logo and value **Obv. Legend:** BANK NEGARA MALAYSIA - SIRI HAIWAN TERANCAM **Rev:** Painted Terrapin turtle (Tuntung Laut) **Edge:** Reeded

| Date | Mintage | VF20 | XF40 | MS60 | MS63 | MS65 |
|---|---|---|---|---|---|---|
| 2006 | 40,000 | — | — | — | 5.00 | 6.00 |

### KM# 53 50 SEN

9.33 g., Copper-Nickel, 27.75 mm. **Obv:** Value divides date below flower blossom **Obv. Legend:** BANK NEGARA MALAYSIA **Rev:** Ceremonial kite **Edge Lettering:** BANK NEGARA MALAYSIA (twice)

| Date | Mintage | VF20 | XF40 | MS60 | MS63 | MS65 |
|---|---|---|---|---|---|---|
| 2001 | 67,371,000 | — | — | 0.50 | 0.75 | 1.00 |
| 2002 | 61,928,000 | — | — | 0.50 | 0.75 | 1.00 |
| 2003 | 32,580,000 | — | — | 0.50 | 0.75 | 1.00 |
| 2004 | 37,890,000 | — | — | 0.50 | 0.75 | 1.00 |
| 2005 | 691,680,006 | — | — | 0.50 | 0.75 | 1.00 |
| 2006 | 19,480,006 | — | — | 0.50 | 0.75 | 1.00 |
| 2007 | — | — | — | 0.50 | 0.75 | 1.00 |
| 2008 | 61,380,000 | — | — | 0.50 | 0.75 | 1.00 |
| 2009 | 94,691,783 | — | — | 0.50 | 0.75 | 1.00 |
| 2010 | — | — | — | 0.50 | 0.75 | 1.00 |
| 2011 | — | — | — | 0.50 | 0.75 | 1.00 |

### KM# 204 50 SEN

5.66 g., Nickel-Brass Plated Copper, 22.65 mm. **Obv:** Flower, date and value **Obv. Legend:** BANK NEGARA MALAYSIA **Rev:** Vine on patterned circle **Edge:** Notched

| Date | Mintage | VF20 | XF40 | MS60 | MS63 | MS65 |
|---|---|---|---|---|---|---|
| 2011 | — | — | — | 0.50 | 0.75 | 1.00 |
| 2012 | — | — | — | 0.50 | 0.75 | 1.00 |
| 2013 | — | — | — | 0.50 | 0.75 | 1.00 |

### KM# 71 RINGGIT

16.80 g., Copper-Nickel, 33.7 mm. **Subject:** XXI SEA Games **Obv:** Games logo **Rev:** Cartoon mascot **Edge:** Reeded

| Date | Mintage | VF20 | XF40 | MS60 | MS63 | MS65 |
|---|---|---|---|---|---|---|
| 2001 | 200,000 | — | — | 3.00 | 5.00 | 6.00 |

### KM# 74 RINGGIT

16.80 g., Copper-Nickel, 33.7 mm. **Subject:** Coronation of Agong XII **Obv:** Head with headdress facing **Rev:** Arms with supporters within sprigs **Edge:** Reeded **Note:** Prev. KM#72.

| Date | Mintage | VF20 | XF40 | MS60 | MS63 | MS65 |
|---|---|---|---|---|---|---|
| ND(2002) | 100,000 | — | — | 3.50 | 6.00 | 7.00 |

### KM# 165 RINGGIT

10.40 g., Copper Plated Zinc, 26 mm. **Subject:** 10th Men's Hockey World Cup **Obv:** Logo **Obv. Legend:** BANK NEGARA MALAYSIA **Rev:** 2 stylized players **Rev. Legend:** KEJOHANAN HOKI LELAKI PIALA DUNIA **Edge:** Reeded

| Date | Mintage | VF20 | XF40 | MS60 | MS63 | MS65 |
|---|---|---|---|---|---|---|
| 2002 | 100,000 | — | — | — | — | 12.00 |

### KM# 168 RINGGIT

Brass **Subject:** 45th National Day **Obv:** Buildings, tower, metro liner **Obv. Legend:** BANK NEGARA MALAYSIA **Rev:** Stylized waving flag **Rev. Legend:** 45 TAHUN MERDEKA

| Date | Mintage | VF20 | XF40 | MS60 | MS63 | MS65 |
|---|---|---|---|---|---|---|
| 2002 | 10,000 | — | — | — | — | 10.00 |

### KM# 171 RINGGIT

Brass **Subject:** XIII NAM Summit **Obv:** Modern building, plaza **Obv. Legend:** MALAYSIA - BANK NEGARA MALAYSIA **Rev:** Stylized dove in rays **Rev. Legend:** XIII CONFERENCE OF HEADS OF STATE OR GOVERNMENT OF THE NON-ALIGNED MOVEMENT

| Date | Mintage | VF20 | XF40 | MS60 | MS63 | MS65 |
|---|---|---|---|---|---|---|
| 2003 | 9,400 | PF65 10.00 | | | | |

### KM# 174 RINGGIT

Brass **Subject:** LIMA - 7th Bi-annual Langkawi Island Trade Fair **Obv:** Jet fighter plane above naval missile corvette **Obv. Legend:** BANK NEGARA MALAYSIA **Rev:** Logo **Rev. Legend:** LANGKAWI INTERNATIONAL MARITIME & AEROSPACE

| Date | Mintage | VF20 | XF40 | MS60 | MS63 | MS65 |
|---|---|---|---|---|---|---|
| 2003 | 25,000 | — | — | — | — | 10.00 |

### KM# 177 RINGGIT

Brass **Subject:** 10th Session Islamic Summit Conference **Obv:** Circular Arabic text **Obv. Legend:** BANK NEGARA MALAYSIA **Rev:** Symmetrical design **Rev. Legend:** PERSIDANGAN KETUA-KETUA NEGARASLAM

| Date | Mintage | VF20 | XF40 | MS60 | MS63 | MS65 |
|---|---|---|---|---|---|---|
| 2003 | 25,000 | — | — | — | — | 10.00 |

### KM# 200 RINGGIT

8.15 g., Bi-Metallic Copper-Nickel center in Nickel-Brass ring, 26.5 mm. **Subject:** 46th Anniversary of Independence **Rev:** Group of four people

| Date | Mintage | VF20 | XF40 | MS60 | MS63 | MS65 |
|---|---|---|---|---|---|---|
| 2003 | — | — | — | — | — | 10.00 |

### KM# 114 RINGGIT

Copper-Nickel **Subject:** Century of Tunku Abdul Rahman **Obv:** National arms **Obv. Legend:** BANK NEGARA MALAYSIA - BAPA KEMERDEKAAN **Rev:** 3/4 length figure of Tunku Abdul Rahman left with right hand raised **Rev. Legend:** Y. T. M. TUNKU ABDUL RAHMAN PUTRA AL-HAJ

| Date | Mintage | VF20 | XF40 | MS60 | MS63 | MS65 |
|---|---|---|---|---|---|---|
| 2005 | 25,000 | — | — | — | — | 10.00 |

### KM# 132 RINGGIT

Brass **Subject:** 30th Annual Meeting Islamic Development Bank **Obv:** Circular Arabic text **Obv. Legend:** BANK NEGARA MALYSIA - MESYUARAT TAHUNAN BANK PEMBANCUNAN ISLAM KE - 30 **Rev:** Logo

| Date | Mintage | VF20 | XF40 | MS60 | MS63 | MS65 |
|---|---|---|---|---|---|---|
| 2005 | 20,000 | — | — | — | — | 10.00 |

### KM# 135 RINGGIT

Copper-Nickel **Subject:** 11th ASEAN Summit **Obv:** Twin towers center right **Obv. Legend:** BANK NEGARA MALAYSIA - SIDANG KEMUNCAK ASEAN KE-11 **Rev:** Logo

| Date | Mintage | VF20 | XF40 | MS60 | MS63 | MS65 |
|---|---|---|---|---|---|---|
| 2005 | 20,000 | — | — | — | — | 8.00 |

### KM# 138 RINGGIT

Bi-Metallic **Subject:** Songket - The Regal Heritage **Obv:** Stylized flower - Bunga Ketola **Obv. Legend:** BANK NEGARA MALAYSIA **Rev:** Floral pattern below inscription

| Date | Mintage | VF20 | XF40 | MS60 | MS63 | MS65 |
|---|---|---|---|---|---|---|
| 2005 | 20,000 | — | — | — | — | 8.00 |

### KM# 141 RINGGIT

Brass **Subject:** 50th Anniversary Mara Technology University **Obv:** Large "50" with horizontal lines in background **Obv. Legend:** BANK NEGARA MALAYSIA - JUBLI EMAS UITM **Rev:** Logo **Rev. Legend:** Universiti Teknologi Mara

| Date | Mintage | VF20 | XF40 | MS60 | MS63 | MS65 |
|---|---|---|---|---|---|---|
| ND-2006 | 12,050 | — | — | — | — | 8.00 |

### KM# 144 RINGGIT

Brass **Subject:** 50th Anniversary P. Felda **Obv:** 1/2 length figure of Felda 3/4 right **Obv. Legend:** BANK NEGARA MALYSIA **Rev:** Two opposed hands holding symbol **Rev. Legend:** MENEMPA KEJAYAAN

| Date | Mintage | VF20 | XF40 | MS60 | MS63 | MS65 |
|---|---|---|---|---|---|---|
| 2006 | 10,000 | — | — | — | — | 8.00 |

### KM# 147 RINGGIT

Brass **Subject:** 9th Malaysian Plan **Obv:** Bust 3/4 right **Obv. Legend:** BANK NEGARA MALAYSIA - CEMERLANG GEMILANG TERBILANg **Rev:** Globe logo **Rev. Legend:** RANCANGAN MALAYSIA KE SEMBILAN

| Date | Mintage | VF20 | XF40 | MS60 | MS63 | MS65 |
|---|---|---|---|---|---|---|
| 2006 | 10,000 | — | — | — | — | 8.00 |

### KM# 162 RINGGIT

Brass **Subject:** 200th Anniversary Malaysian Police Force **Obv:** Police badge **Obv. Legend:** BANK NEGARA MALAYSIA **Rev:** Two hands clasped in sprays

| Date | Mintage | VF20 | XF40 | MS60 | MS63 | MS65 |
|---|---|---|---|---|---|---|
| 2007 | 20,000 | — | — | — | — | 7.00 |

### KM# 182 RINGGIT

8.80 g., Aluminum-Bronze, 30 mm. **Subject:** Installation of Agong XIII **Obv:** National arms within wreath **Rev:** Facing portrait

| Date | Mintage | VF20 | XF40 | MS60 | MS63 | MS65 |
|---|---|---|---|---|---|---|
| 2007 | 10,000 | — | — | — | — | 10.00 |
| 2007 Proof | 600 | — | — | — | — | — |

### KM# 185 RINGGIT

8.80 g., Aluminum-Bronze, 30 mm. **Subject:** Independence, 50th Anniversary **Obv:** National Arms **Rev:** 50 above city skyline

| Date | Mintage | VF20 | XF40 | MS60 | MS63 | MS65 |
|---|---|---|---|---|---|---|
| 2007 | 10,000 | — | — | — | — | 10.00 |
| 2007 Proof | 2,000 | — | — | — | — | — |

### KM# 188 RINGGIT

8.80 g., Aluminum-Bronze, 30 mm. **Subject:** Royal Malaysian Air Force, 50th Anniversary **Obv:** Air Force insignia **Rev:** Old and modern plane

| Date | Mintage | VF20 | XF40 | MS60 | MS63 | MS65 |
|---|---|---|---|---|---|---|
| 2008 Proof | 350 | — | — | — | — | — |
| 2008 | 10,000 | — | — | — | — | 10.00 |

### KM# 191 RINGGIT

8.80 g., Aluminum-Bronze, 30 mm. **Subject:** St. John's Ambulance, 100th Anniversary **Obv:** St. John's insignia in wreath above valye **Rev:** Client being loaded into ambulance

| Date | Mintage | VF20 | XF40 | MS60 | MS63 | MS65 |
|---|---|---|---|---|---|---|
| 2008 | 10,000 | — | — | — | — | 10.00 |
| 2008 Proof | 350 | — | — | — | — | — |

### KM# 155 RINGGIT

8.80 g., Brass, 30 mm. **Subject:** Bank Negara Malaysia, 50th Anniversary **Obv:** Bank logo **Rev:** 14-pointed star

| Date | Mintage | VF20 | XF40 | MS60 | MS63 | MS65 |
|---|---|---|---|---|---|---|
| 2009 | 13,700 | — | — | — | — | 10.00 |
| 2009 Proof | 3,300 | — | — | — | — | — |

### KM# 159 RINGGIT

8.00 g., Brass, 30 mm. **Subject:** Parliament, 50th Anniversary **Obv:** National Arms and 2 maces **Rev:** Parliament Building

| Date | Mintage | VF20 | XF40 | MS60 | MS63 | MS65 |
|---|---|---|---|---|---|---|
| 2009 | 10,000 | — | — | — | — | 10.00 |
| 2009 Proof | 450 | — | — | — | — | — |

### KM# 194 RINGGIT

8.80 g., Aluminum-Bronze, 30 mm. **Subject:** International Year of Astronomy **Obv:** Adult and Child looking to the heavens **Rev:** Langkawi National Observatory

| Date | Mintage | VF20 | XF40 | MS60 | MS63 | MS65 |
|---|---|---|---|---|---|---|
| 2009 | 10,000 | — | — | — | — | 10.00 |
| 2009 Proof | 350 | — | — | — | — | — |

### KM# 197 RINGGIT

8.80 g., Aluminum-Bronze, 30 mm. **Subject:** Royal Malaysian Navy, 75th Anniversary **Obv:** Submarine **Rev:** Navy insignia

| Date | Mintage | VF20 | XF40 | MS60 | MS63 | MS65 |
|---|---|---|---|---|---|---|
| 2009 | 10,000 | — | — | — | — | 10.00 |
| 2009 Proof | 450 | — | — | — | — | — |

### KM# 209 RINGGIT

8.80 g., Nordic Gold, 30 mm. **Subject:** Girl Guides

| Date | Mintage | VF20 | XF40 | MS60 | MS63 | MS65 |
|---|---|---|---|---|---|---|
| 2012 | Est. 15000 | — | — | — | — | 12.00 |

### KM# 72 10 RINGGIT

21.70 g., 0.925 Silver 0.6453 oz. ASW, 35.7 mm. **Subject:** XXI SEA Games **Obv:** Games logo **Rev:** Cartoon mascot **Edge:** Reeded

| Date | Mintage | VF20 | XF40 | MS60 | MS63 | MS65 |
|---|---|---|---|---|---|---|
| 2001 | 3,000 | PF65 65.00 | | | | |

### KM# 75 10 RINGGIT

21.70 g., 0.925 Silver 0.6453 oz. ASW, 35.7 mm. **Subject:** Coronation of Agong XII **Obv:** Head with headdress facing **Rev:** Arms with supporters within sprigs **Edge:** Reeded

| Date | Mintage | VF20 | XF40 | MS60 | MS63 | MS65 |
|---|---|---|---|---|---|---|
| ND(2002) | 10,000 | PF63 100 | PF65 120 | | | |

### KM# 166 10 RINGGIT

16.80 g., 0.925 Silver 0.4996 oz. ASW, 32 mm. **Subject:** 10th Men's Hockey World Cup **Obv:** Official logo of the World Cup games **Obv. Legend:** BANK NEGARA MALAYSIA **Rev:** 2 stylized players in front of the Kuala Lumpur skyline **Rev. Legend:** KEJOHANAN HOKI LELAKI PIALA

| Date | Mintage | VF20 | XF40 | MS60 | MS63 | MS65 |
|---|---|---|---|---|---|---|
| 2002 | 3,000 | PF63 140 | PF65 160 | | | |

### KM# 169 10 RINGGIT

0.925 Silver **Subject:** 45th National Day **Obv:** Buildings, tower, metro liner **Obv. Legend:** BANK NEGARA MALAYSIA **Rev:** Stylized waving flag **Rev. Legend:** 45 TAHUN MERDEKA

| Date | Mintage | VF20 | XF40 | MS60 | MS63 | MS65 |
|---|---|---|---|---|---|---|
| 2002 | 1,800 | PF63 110 | PF65 125 | | | |

### KM# 172 10 RINGGIT

0.925 Silver **Subject:** XIII NAM Summit **Obv:** Modern building, plaza **Obv. Legend:** MALAYSIA - BANK NEGARA MALAYSIA **Rev:** Stylized dove in rays **Rev. Legend:** XIII CONFERENCE OF HEADS OF STATE OR GOVERNMENT OF THE NON-ALIGNED MOVEMENT

| Date | Mintage | VF20 | XF40 | MS60 | MS63 | MS65 |
|---|---|---|---|---|---|---|
| 2003 | 2,400 | PF63 110 | PF65 125 | | | |

**KM# 175 10 RINGGIT**
0.925 Silver **Subject:** LIMA - 7th bi-annual Langkawi Island Trade Fair **Obv:** Jet fighter plane above naval missile corvette **Obv. Legend:** BANK NEGARA MALAYSIA **Rev:** Logo **Rev. Legend:** LANGKAWI INTERNATIONAL MARITIME & SPACE

| Date | Mintage | VF20 | XF40 | MS60 | MS63 | MS65 |
|---|---|---|---|---|---|---|
| 2003 | — | PF63 100 | PF65 120 | | | |

**KM# 178 10 RINGGIT**
0.925 Silver **Subject:** 10th Session Islamic Summit Conference **Obv:** Circular Arabic Text **Obv. Legend:** BANK NEGARA MALAYSIA **Rev:** Symmetrical pattern **Rev. Legend:** PERSIDANGAN KETUA - KETUA NEGARA ISLAM

| Date | Mintage | VF20 | XF40 | MS60 | MS63 | MS65 |
|---|---|---|---|---|---|---|
| 2003 | 300 | PF65 120 | | | | |

**KM# 115 10 RINGGIT**
0.925 Silver **Subject:** Century of Tunku Abdul Rahman **Obv:** National arms **Obv. Legend:** BANK NEGARA MALAYSIA - BAPA KEMERDEKAAN **Rev:** 3/4 length figure of Tunku Abdul Rahman left with right hand raised **Rev. Legend:** Y. T. M. TUNKU ABDUL RAHMAN PUTRA AL-HAJ

| Date | Mintage | VF20 | XF40 | MS60 | MS63 | MS65 |
|---|---|---|---|---|---|---|
| 2005 | 200 | PF65 120 | | | | |

**KM# 136 10 RINGGIT**
21.70 g., Silver, 35.7 mm. **Subject:** 11th ASEAN Summit **Obv:** Twin towers center right **Obv. Legend:** BANK NEGARA MALAYSIA - SIDANG KEMUNCAK ASEAN KE-11 **Rev:** Logo

| Date | Mintage | VF20 | XF40 | MS60 | MS63 | MS65 |
|---|---|---|---|---|---|---|
| 2005 | 250 | PF65 120 | | | | |

**KM# 139 10 RINGGIT**
21.70 g., Silver, 35.7 mm. **Subject:** Songket - The Regal Heritage **Obv:** Uniform pattern - Bunga Bintang **Obv. Legend:** BANK NEGARA MALAYSIA **Rev:** Floral pattern below inscription

| Date | Mintage | VF20 | XF40 | MS60 | MS63 | MS65 |
|---|---|---|---|---|---|---|
| 2005 | 250 | PF65 120 | | | | |

**KM# 142 10 RINGGIT**
21.70 g., Silver, 35.7 mm. **Subject:** 50th Anniversary Mara Technology Universit **Obv:** Large "50" with horizontal lines in background **Obv. Legend:** BANK NEGARA MALAYSIA - JUBLI EMAS UITM **Rev:** Logo **Rev. Legend:** Universiti Teknologi Mara

| Date | Mintage | VF20 | XF40 | MS60 | MS63 | MS65 |
|---|---|---|---|---|---|---|
| ND-2006 | 500 | PF65 110 | | | | |

**KM# 145 10 RINGGIT**
31.11 g., Silver, 40 mm. **Subject:** 50th Anniversary P. Felda **Obv:** Outlined map of South East Asia above logo **Obv. Legend:** BANK NEGARA MALAYSIA **Rev:** Monument at left, Felda with 4 others at right **Rev. Legend:** MENEMPA KEJAYAAN

| Date | Mintage | VF20 | XF40 | MS60 | MS63 | MS65 |
|---|---|---|---|---|---|---|
| 2006 | 300 | PF65 110 | | | | |

**KM# 148 10 RINGGIT**
21.00 g., Silver, 35.7 mm. **Subject:** 9th Malaysian Plan **Obv:** Bust 3/4 right **Obv. Legend:** BANK NEGARA MALAYSIA - CEMERLANG GEMILANG TERBILANG **Rev:** Globe logo **Rev. Legend:** RANCANGAN MALAYSIA KE SEMBILAN

| Date | Mintage | VF20 | XF40 | MS60 | MS63 | MS65 |
|---|---|---|---|---|---|---|
| 2006 | 300 | PF65 110 | | | | |

**KM# 163 10 RINGGIT**
21.00 g., Silver, 35.70 mm. **Subject:** 200th Anniversary Malaysian Police Force **Obv:** Police badge **Obv. Legend:** BANK NEGARA MALAYSIA **Rev:** Two hands clasped in sprays

| Date | Mintage | VF20 | XF40 | MS60 | MS63 | MS65 |
|---|---|---|---|---|---|---|
| 2007 | 500 | PF65 110 | | | | |

**KM# 183 10 RINGGIT**
21.00 g., 0.925 Silver 0.6245 oz. ASW, 35.7 mm. **Subject:** Installation of Agong XIII **Obv:** National arms in wreath **Rev:** Portrait facing

| Date | Mintage | VF20 | XF40 | MS60 | MS63 | MS65 |
|---|---|---|---|---|---|---|
| 2007 | 200 | PF65 100 | | | | |

**KM# 186 10 RINGGIT**
21.00 g., 0.925 Silver 0.6245 oz. ASW, 35.7 mm. **Subject:** Independence, 50th Anniversary **Obv:** National Arms **Rev:** 50 above city skyline

| Date | Mintage | VF20 | XF40 | MS60 | MS63 | MS65 |
|---|---|---|---|---|---|---|
| 2007 | 200 | PF65 110 | | | | |

**KM# 189 10 RINGGIT**
21.00 g., 0.925 Silver 0.6245 oz. ASW, 35.7 mm. **Subject:** Royal Malaysian Air Force, 50th Anniversary **Obv:** Air Force insignia **Rev:** Old and new plane

| Date | Mintage | VF20 | XF40 | MS60 | MS63 | MS65 |
|---|---|---|---|---|---|---|
| 2008 | 350 | PF65 100 | | | | |

**KM# 192 10 RINGGIT**
21.00 g., 0.925 Silver 0.6245 oz. ASW, 35.7 mm. **Subject:** St. John's Ambulance **Obv:** St. John's emblem in wreath above vlaue **Rev:** Client being loaded into ambulance

| Date | Mintage | VF20 | XF40 | MS60 | MS63 | MS65 |
|---|---|---|---|---|---|---|
| 2008 | 350 | PF65 100 | | | | |

**KM# 156 10 RINGGIT**
21.00 g., 0.925 Silver 0.6245 oz. ASW, 35.7 mm. **Subject:** Bank Negara Malaysia, 50th Anniversary **Obv:** Bank logo **Rev:** 14-pointed star

| Date | Mintage | VF20 | XF40 | MS60 | MS63 | MS65 |
|---|---|---|---|---|---|---|
| 2009 | 400 | PF65 100 | | | | |

**KM# 160 10 RINGGIT**
21.00 g., 0.925 Silver 0.6245 oz. ASW, 35.7 mm. **Subject:** Parliament, 50th Anniversary **Obv:** National Arms and 2 maces **Rev:** Parliament Building

| Date | Mintage | VF20 | XF40 | MS60 | MS63 | MS65 |
|---|---|---|---|---|---|---|
| 2009 | 300 | PF65 120 | | | | |

**KM# 195 10 RINGGIT**
21.00 g., 0.925 Silver 0.6245 oz. ASW, 35.7 mm. **Subject:** International Year of Astronomy **Obv:** Adult and child looking to the heavens **Rev:** Langkawi Naitonal Observatory

| Date | Mintage | VF20 | XF40 | MS60 | MS63 | MS65 |
|---|---|---|---|---|---|---|
| 2009 | 350 | PF65 120 | | | | |

**KM# 198 10 RINGGIT**
21.00 g., 0.925 Silver 0.6245 oz. ASW, 35.7 mm. **Subject:** Royal Malaysian navy, 75th Anniversary **Obv:** Submarine **Rev:** Navy insignia

| Date | Mintage | VF20 | XF40 | MS60 | MS63 | MS65 |
|---|---|---|---|---|---|---|
| 2009 | 300 | PF65 120 | | | | |

**KM# 206 10 RINGGIT**
Silver **Rev:** Belia flower

| Date | Mintage | VF20 | XF40 | MS60 | MS63 | MS65 |
|---|---|---|---|---|---|---|
| 2011 | — | PF65 125 | | | | |

**KM# 207 10 RINGGIT**
0.999 Silver **Rev:** Wanita flower

| Date | Mintage | VF20 | XF40 | MS60 | MS63 | MS65 |
|---|---|---|---|---|---|---|
| 2011 | — | PF65 125 | | | | |

**KM# 208 10 RINGGIT**
31.00 g., 0.925 Silver 0.9219 oz. ASW, 35.7 mm. **Subject:** Girl Guides

| Date | Mintage | VF20 | XF40 | MS60 | MS63 | MS65 |
|---|---|---|---|---|---|---|
| 2012 | Est. 600 | PF65 55.00 | | | | |

**KM# 133 20 RINGGIT**
31.10 g., Silver, 40 mm. **Subject:** 30th Annual Meeting Islamic Development Bank **Obv:** Mosque **Obv. Legend:** BANK NEGARA MALAYSIA **Rev:** Logo

| Date | Mintage | VF20 | XF40 | MS60 | MS63 | MS65 |
|---|---|---|---|---|---|---|
| 2005 | 1,000 | PF65 100 | | | | |

**KM# 157 50 RINGGIT**
10.07 g., 0.999 Gold 0.3234 oz. AGW, 25 mm. **Subject:** Bank Negara Malaysia, 50th Anniversary **Obv:** Bank logo **Rev:** 14-pointed star

| Date | Mintage | VF20 | XF40 | MS60 | MS63 | MS65 |
|---|---|---|---|---|---|---|
| 2009 | 300 | PF65 1,000 | | | | |

**KM# 73 100 RINGGIT**
8.60 g., 0.916 Gold 0.2533 oz. AGW, 22 mm. **Subject:** XXI SEA Games **Obv:** Games logo **Rev:** Cartoon mascot **Edge:** Reeded

| Date | Mintage | VF20 | XF40 | MS60 | MS63 | MS65 |
|---|---|---|---|---|---|---|
| 2001 | 500 | PF65 800 | | | | |

**KM# 76 100 RINGGIT**
8.60 g., 0.916 Gold 0.2533 oz. AGW, 22 mm. **Subject:** Coronation of Agong XII **Obv:** Head with headdress facing **Rev:** Arms with supporters within sprigs **Edge:** Reeded

| Date | Mintage | VF20 | XF40 | MS60 | MS63 | MS65 |
|---|---|---|---|---|---|---|
| ND(2002) | 300 | PF65 900 | | | | |

**KM# 167 100 RINGGIT**
9.00 g., 0.900 Gold 0.2604 oz. AGW, 22 mm. **Subject:** 10th Men's Hockey World Cup **Obv:** Logo **Obv. Legend:** BANK NEGARA MALAYSIA **Rev:** 2 stylized players in front of Kuala Lumpur skyline **Rev. Legend:** KEJOHANAN HOKI LELAKI PIALA

| Date | Mintage | VF20 | XF40 | MS60 | MS63 | MS65 |
|---|---|---|---|---|---|---|
| 2002 | 1,000 | PF63 600 | PF65 700 | | | |

**KM# 170 100 RINGGIT**
8.60 g., 0.9999 Gold 0.2765 oz. AGW **Subject:** 45th National Day **Obv:** Buildings, tower, metro liner **Obv. Legend:** BANK NEGARA MALAYSIA **Rev:** Stylized waving flag **Rev. Legend:** 45 TAHUN MERDEKA

| Date | Mintage | VF20 | XF40 | MS60 | MS63 | MS65 |
|---|---|---|---|---|---|---|
| 2002 | 300 | PF65 900 | | | | |

**KM# 173 100 RINGGIT**
8.60 g., 0.9999 Gold 0.2765 oz. AGW, 22 mm. **Subject:** XIII NAM Summit **Obv:** Modern building, plaza **Obv. Legend:** MALAYSIA - BANK NEGARA MALAYSIA **Rev:** Stylized dove in rays **Rev. Legend:** XIII CONFERENCE OF HEADS OF STATE OR GOVERNMENT OF THE NON-ALIGNED MOVEMENT

| Date | Mintage | VF20 | XF40 | MS60 | MS63 | MS65 |
|---|---|---|---|---|---|---|
| 2003 | 300 | PF65 900 | | | | |

**KM# 176 100 RINGGIT**
8.60 g., 0.9999 Gold 0.2765 oz. AGW, 22 mm. **Subject:** LIMA - 7th bi-annual Langkawi Island Trade Fair **Obv:** Jet fighter plane above naval missile corvette **Obv. Legend:** BANK NEGARA MALAYSIA **Rev:** Logo **Rev. Legend:** LANGKAWI INTERNATIONAL MARITIME & AEROSPACE

| Date | Mintage | VF20 | XF40 | MS60 | MS63 | MS65 |
|---|---|---|---|---|---|---|
| 2003 | 50 | PF65 1,400 | | | | |

**KM# 179 100 RINGGIT**
8.60 g., 0.9999 Gold 0.2765 oz. AGW, 22 mm. **Obv:** Circular Arabic text **Obv. Legend:** BANK NEGARA MALAYSIA **Rev:** Symmetrical design **Rev. Legend:** PERSIDANGAN KETUA - KETUA NEGARA ISLAM

| Date | Mintage | VF20 | XF40 | MS60 | MS63 | MS65 |
|---|---|---|---|---|---|---|
| 2003 | 200 | PF65 900 | | | | |

**KM# 116 100 RINGGIT**
0.9999 Gold **Subject:** Century of Tunku Abdul Rahman **Obv:** National arms **Obv. Legend:** BANK NEGARA MALAYSIA - BAPA KEMERDEKAAN **Rev:** 3/4 length figure of Tunku Abdul Rahman left with right hand raised **Rev. Legend:** Y. T. M. TUNKU ABDUL RAHMAN PUTRA AL-HAJ

| Date | Mintage | VF20 | XF40 | MS60 | MS63 | MS65 |
|---|---|---|---|---|---|---|
| 2005 | 100 | PF65 900 | | | | |

**KM# 137 100 RINGGIT**
8.60 g., Gold, 22 mm. **Subject:** 11th ASEAN Summit **Obv:** Twin towers center right **Obv. Legend:** BANK NEGARA MALAYSIA - SIDANG KEMUNCAK ASEAN KE-11 **Rev:** Logo

| Date | Mintage | VF20 | XF40 | MS60 | MS63 | MS65 |
|---|---|---|---|---|---|---|
| 2005 | 200 | PF65 900 | | | | |

**KM# 140 100 RINGGIT**
8.60 g., Gold, 22 mm. **Subject:** Songket - The Regal Heritage **Obv:** Uniform pattern - Tampur Kesemak **Obv. Legend:** BANK NEGARA MALAYSIA **Rev:** Floral pattern below inscription

| Date | Mintage | VF20 | XF40 | MS60 | MS63 | MS65 |
|---|---|---|---|---|---|---|
| 2005 | 150 | PF65 900 | | | | |

**KM# 143 100 RINGGIT**
8.60 g., Gold, 22 mm. **Subject:** 50th Anniversary Mara Technology University **Obv:** Large "50" with horizontal lines in background **Obv. Legend:** BANK NEGARA MALAYSIA - JUBLI EMAS UITM **Rev:** Logo **Rev. Legend:** Universiti Teknologi Mara

| Date | Mintage | VF20 | XF40 | MS60 | MS63 | MS65 |
|---|---|---|---|---|---|---|
| ND-2006 | 300 | PF65 900 | | | | |

**KM# 146 100 RINGGIT**
9.00 g., Gold, 22 mm. **Subject:** 50th Anniversary P. Felda **Obv:** 1/2 length figure of Felda 3/4 right **Obv. Legend:** BANK NEGARA MALAYSIA **Rev:** Stylized palm tree at left, rubber tree trunk at right **Rev. Legend:** MENEMPA KEJAYAAN

| Date | Mintage | VF20 | XF40 | MS60 | MS63 | MS65 |
|---|---|---|---|---|---|---|
| 2006 | 200 | PF65 900 | | | | |

**KM# 149 100 RINGGIT**
7.96 g., Gold, 22 mm. **Subject:** 9th Malaysian Plan **Obv:** Bust 3/4 right **Obv. Legend:** BANK NEGARA MALAYSIA - CEMERLANG GEMILANG TERBILANG **Rev:** Globe logo **Rev. Legend:** RANCANGAN MALAYSIA KE SEMBILAN

| Date | Mintage | VF20 | XF40 | MS60 | MS63 | MS65 |
|---|---|---|---|---|---|---|
| 2006 | 500 | PF65 900 | | | | |

**KM# 164 100 RINGGIT**
7.96 g., Gold, 22 mm. **Subject:** 200th Anniversary Malaysian Police Force **Obv:** Police badge **Obv. Legend:** BANK NEGARA MALAYSIA **Rev:** Two hands clasped in sprays

| Date | Mintage | VF20 | XF40 | MS60 | MS63 | MS65 |
|---|---|---|---|---|---|---|
| 2007 | 500 | PF65 900 | | | | |

**KM# 184 100 RINGGIT**
7.96 g., 0.9999 Gold 0.2559 oz. AGW, 22 mm. **Subject:** Installation of the King **Obv:** National Arms within wreath **Rev:** Facing portrait

| Date | Mintage | VF20 | XF40 | MS60 | MS63 | MS65 |
|---|---|---|---|---|---|---|
| 2007 | 100 | PF65 900 | | | | |

**KM# 187 100 RINGGIT**
7.96 g., 0.9999 Gold 0.2559 oz. AGW, 22 mm. **Subject:** Independence, 50th Anniversary **Obv:** National Arms **Rev:** 50 above city skyline

| Date | Mintage | VF20 | XF40 | MS60 | MS63 | MS65 |
|---|---|---|---|---|---|---|
| 2007 | 100 | PF65 900 | | | | |

**KM# 190 100 RINGGIT**
7.96 g., 0.9999 Gold 0.2559 oz. AGW, 22 mm. **Subject:** Royal Malaysian Air Force, 50th Anniversary **Obv:** Royal Airforce insignia **Rev:** Old and new plane

| Date | Mintage | VF20 | XF40 | MS60 | MS63 | MS65 |
|---|---|---|---|---|---|---|
| 2008 | 100 | PF65 900 | | | | |

**KM# 193 100 RINGGIT**
7.96 g., 0.9999 Gold 0.2559 oz. AGW, 22 mm. **Subject:** St. John's Ambulance, 100th Anniversary **Obv:** St. John's insignia in wreath above value **Rev:** Client being loaded into ambulance

| Date | Mintage | VF20 | XF40 | MS60 | MS63 | MS65 |
|---|---|---|---|---|---|---|
| 2008 | 100 | PF65 900 | | | | |

**KM# 158 100 RINGGIT**
7.96 g., 0.999 Gold 0.2557 oz. AGW, 22 mm. **Subject:** Bank Negara Malaysia, 50th Anniversary **Obv:** Bank logo **Rev:** 14-pointed star

| Date | Mintage | VF20 | XF40 | MS60 | MS63 | MS65 |
|---|---|---|---|---|---|---|
| 2009 | 300 | PF65 1,000 | | | | |

**KM# 180 100 RINGGIT**
7.96 g., 0.9999 Gold 0.2559 oz. AGW, 22 mm. **Subject:** Parliament, 50th Anniversary **Obv:** National arms above mace and sceptre **Rev:** Parliament buildings, sunburst

| Date | Mintage | VF20 | XF40 | MS60 | MS63 | MS65 |
|---|---|---|---|---|---|---|
| 2009 | 100 | PF65 800 | | | | |

### KM# 196 100 RINGGIT

7.96 g., 0.9999 Gold 0.2559 oz. AGW, 22 mm. **Subject:** International Year of Astronomy **Obv:** Adult and child looking to the ehavens **Rev:** Langkawi National Observatory

| Date | Mintage | VF20 | XF40 | MS60 | MS63 | MS65 |
|---|---|---|---|---|---|---|
| 2009 | 100 | **PF65** 900 | | | | |

### KM# 199 100 RINGGIT

7.96 g., 0.9999 Gold 0.2559 oz. AGW, 22 mm. **Subject:** Royal Malaysian Navy, 75th Anniversary **Obv:** Submarine **Rev:** Navy insignia

| Date | Mintage | VF20 | XF40 | MS60 | MS63 | MS65 |
|---|---|---|---|---|---|---|
| 2009 | 100 | **PF65** 900 | | | | |

### KM# 134 200 RINGGIT

15.55 g., Gold, 28 mm. **Subject:** 30th Annual Meeting Islamic Development Bank **Obv:** Mosque in rays **Obv. Legend:** BANK NEGARA MALAYSIA **Rev:** Logo

| Date | Mintage | VF20 | XF40 | MS60 | MS63 | MS65 |
|---|---|---|---|---|---|---|
| 2005 | 500 | **PF65** 600 | | | | |

## PROOF SETS

| KM# | Date | Mintage | Identification | Issue Price | Mkt Val |
|---|---|---|---|---|---|
| PS19 | 2003 (2) | 300 | KM#171, 172 | — | 150 |
| PS20 | 2003 (3) | 300 | KM#171-173 | — | 1,200 |
| PS21 | 2003 (2) | 300 | KM#174, 175 | — | 200 |
| PS22 | 2003 (3) | 100 | KM#174-176 | — | 1,800 |
| PS23 | 2003 (2) | 500 | KM#177, 178 | — | 150 |
| PS24 | 2003 (3) | 250 | KM#177-179 | — | 1,100 |
| PS25 | 2005 (2) | 300 | KM#114, 115 | — | 150 |
| PS26 | 2005 (3) | 100 | KM#114-116 | — | 1,400 |
| PS27 | 2005 (2) | 1,000 | KM#132, 133 | — | 150 |
| PS28 | 2005 (3) | 500 | KM#132-134 | — | 1,200 |
| PS29 | 2005 (2) | 200 | KM#135, 136 | — | 150 |
| PS30 | 2005 (3) | 150 | KM#135-137 | — | 1,200 |
| PS31 | 2006 (2) | 150 | KM#138, 139 | — | 150 |
| PS32 | 2005 (3) | 150 | KM#138-140 | — | 1,200 |
| PS33 | 2006 (2) | 300 | KM#141, 142 | — | 150 |
| PS34 | 2006 (3) | 300 | KM#141-143 | — | 1,200 |
| PS35 | 2006 (2) | 500 | KM#144, 145 | — | 150 |
| PS36 | 2006 (3) | 500 | KM#144-146 | — | 1,100 |
| PS37 | 2006 (2) | 300 | KM#147, 148 | — | 150 |
| PS38 | 2006 (3) | 500 | KM#147-149 | — | 1,000 |
| PS39 | 2007 (2) | 200 | KM#162, 163 | — | 150 |
| PS40 | 2007 (3) | 200 | KM#162-164 | — | 1,000 |

# MALDIVE ISLANDS

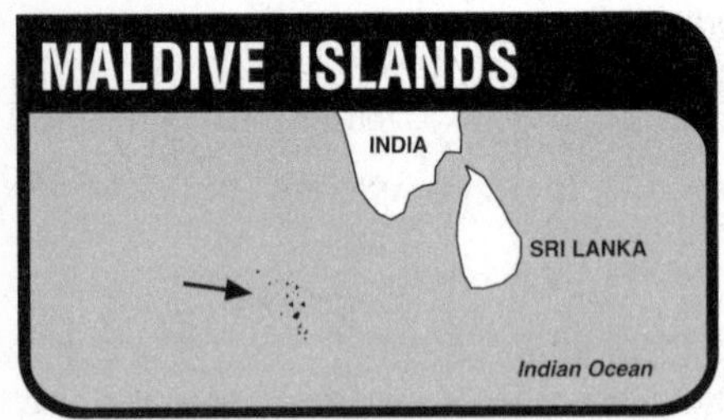


The Republic of Maldives, an archipelago of 2,000 coral islets in the northern Indian Ocean 417 miles (671 km.) west of Ceylon, has an area of 116 sq. mi. (298 sq. km.)and a population of 189,000. Capital: Male. Fishing employs 95% of the male work force. Dried fish, copra and coir yarn are exported.

The Maldive Islands were visited by Arab traders and converted to Islam in 1153. After being harassed in the16th and 17th centuries by Mopla pirates of the Malabar coast and Portuguese raiders, the Maldivians voluntarily placed themselves under the suzerainty of Ceylon. In 1887 the islands became an internally self-governing British protectorate and a nominal dependency of Ceylon. Traditionally a sultanate, the Maldives became a republic in 1953 but restored the sultanate in 1954. The Sultanate of the Maldive Islands attained complete internal and external autonomy on July 26, 1965, and on Nov. 11, 1968, again became a republic. The Maldives is a member of the Commonwealth of Nations.

**MONETARY SYSTEM**

100 Lari = 1 Rupee (Rufiyaa)

## 2ND REPUBLIC

## STANDARD COINAGE

100 Laari = 1 Rufiyaa

### KM# 68 LAARI

0.46 g., Aluminum, 15 mm. **Obv:** Value **Rev:** Palm tree within circle **Edge:** Plain

| Date | Mintage | VF20 | XF40 | MS60 | MS63 | MS65 |
|---|---|---|---|---|---|---|
| AH1423-2002 | — | — | 0.10 | 0.15 | 0.25 | 0.35 |
| AH1433-2012 | — | — | 0.10 | 0.15 | 0.25 | 0.35 |

### KM# 70 10 LAARI

1.95 g., Aluminum, 23.11 mm. **Obv:** Value **Rev:** Maldivian sailing ship - Odi **Shape:** Scalloped

| Date | Mintage | VF20 | XF40 | MS60 | MS63 | MS65 |
|---|---|---|---|---|---|---|
| AH1422-2001 | — | — | 0.10 | 0.20 | 0.30 | 0.50 |

### KM# 71a 25 LAARI

Brass Plated Steel, 20.2 mm. **Obv:** Value **Rev:** Mosque and minaret at Male

| Date | Mintage | VF20 | XF40 | MS60 | MS63 | MS65 |
|---|---|---|---|---|---|---|
| AH1429-2008 | — | — | 0.15 | 0.25 | 0.35 | 0.50 |

### KM# 72a 50 LAARI

Brass Plated Steel, 23.6 mm. **Obv:** Value **Rev:** Loggerhead sea turtle

| Date | Mintage | VF20 | XF40 | MS60 | MS63 | MS65 |
|---|---|---|---|---|---|---|
| AH1429-2008 | — | — | — | 0.75 | 1.50 | 2.50 |

### KM# 73b RUFIYAA

6.54 g., Nickel Plated Steel, 25.8 mm. **Obv:** Value **Obv. Legend:** REPUBLIC OF MALDIVES **Rev:** National arms **Edge:** Reeded

| Date | Mintage | VF20 | XF40 | MS60 | MS63 | MS65 |
|---|---|---|---|---|---|---|
| AH1428-2007 | — | — | 0.50 | 1.00 | 2.00 | 3.00 |
| 2012 | — | — | 0.50 | 1.00 | 2.00 | 3.00 |

### KM# 105 RUFIYAA

26.00 g., Silver Plated Copper, 38.61 mm. **Subject:** London Olympics **Obv:** National emblem **Rev:** Soccer

| Date | Mintage | VF20 | XF40 | MS60 | MS63 | MS65 |
|---|---|---|---|---|---|---|
| 2011 | Est. 10000 | **PF63** 22.00 | **PF65** 25.00 | | | |

### KM# 88 2 RUFIYAA

11.70 g., Nickel-Brass, 25.5 mm. **Obv:** Value **Rev:** Pacific triton sea shell **Edge:** Reeded and lettered **Edge Lettering:** REPUBLIC OF MALDIVES

| Date | Mintage | VF20 | XF40 | MS60 | MS63 | MS65 |
|---|---|---|---|---|---|---|
| AH1428-2007 | — | — | 2.25 | 3.50 | 5.50 | 7.50 |

### KM# 103 10 RUFIYAA

6.22 g., 0.999 Gold 0.1998 oz. AGW, 35 mm. **Subject:** Ships and Explorers **Obv:** National emblem **Rev:** Cutty Sark and map

| Date | Mintage | VF20 | XF40 | MS60 | MS63 | MS65 |
|---|---|---|---|---|---|---|
| 2011 | Est. 5000 | **PF63** 475 | **PF65** 550 | | | |

### KM# 104 20 RUFIYAA

28.28 g., 0.925 Silver 0.841 oz. ASW, 38.61 mm. **Subject:** London Olympics **Obv:** National emblem **Rev:** Soccer

| Date | Mintage | VF20 | XF40 | MS60 | MS63 | MS65 |
|---|---|---|---|---|---|---|
| 2011 | — | **PF63** 35.00 | **PF65** 45.00 | | | |

### KM# 107 20 RUFIYAA

0.50 g., 0.999 Gold, 11 mm. **Obv:** National emblem **Rev:** Two Anemonefish left

| Date | Mintage | VF20 | XF40 | MS60 | MS63 | MS65 |
|---|---|---|---|---|---|---|
| 2011 | Est. 5000 | **PF63** 50.00 | **PF65** 55.00 | | | |

### KM# 109 20 RUFIYAA

28.28 g., 0.925 Silver 0.841 oz. ASW, 38.61 mm. **Subject:** Elizabeth II, 60th Anniversary of reign **Obv:** National emblem **Rev:** Windsor castle

| Date | Mintage | VF20 | XF40 | MS60 | MS63 | MS65 |
|---|---|---|---|---|---|---|
| 2011 | 10,000 | **PF63** 35.00 | **PF65** 45.00 | | | |

### KM# 113 20 RUFIYAA

28.28 g., 0.925 Silver 0.841 oz. ASW, 38.61 mm. **Obv:** National emblem **Rev:** Windsor Castle, Elizabeth II and Philip

| Date | Mintage | VF20 | XF40 | MS60 | MS63 | MS65 |
|---|---|---|---|---|---|---|
| 2011 | — | **PF63** 85.00 | **PF65** 100 | | | |

**KM# 110 20 RUFIYAA**
20.00 g., 0.925 Silver 0.5948 oz. ASW, 38.61 mm. **Subject:** 2014 FIFA World Cup, Brazil **Obv:** National emblem **Rev:** Soccer field and ball in color

| Date | Mintage | VF20 | XF40 | MS60 | MS63 | MS65 |
|---|---|---|---|---|---|---|
| 2012 | Est. 10000 | PF63 35.00 | PF65 45.00 | | | |

**KM# 111 20 RUFIYAA**
0.50 g., 0.585 Gold with 24kt plating, 11 mm. **Obv:** National emblem **Rev:** Picasso Triggerfish

| Date | Mintage | VF20 | XF40 | MS60 | MS63 | MS65 |
|---|---|---|---|---|---|---|
| 2012 | Est. 5000 | PF63 30.00 | PF65 35.00 | | | |

**KM# 112 20 RUFIYAA**
20.00 g., 0.925 Silver 0.5948 oz. ASW, 38.61 mm. **Subject:** 2016 Olympics - Beach Volleyball

| Date | Mintage | VF20 | XF40 | MS60 | MS63 | MS65 |
|---|---|---|---|---|---|---|
| 2013 | Est. 10000 | PF63 65.00 | PF65 75.00 | | | |

**KM# 108 50 RUFIYAA**
1.24 g., 0.999 Gold 0.0398 oz. AGW, 13.92 mm. **Obv:** National emblem **Rev:** Two anemonefish left

| Date | Mintage | VF20 | XF40 | MS60 | MS63 | MS65 |
|---|---|---|---|---|---|---|
| 2011 | Est. 5000 | PF63 75.00 | PF65 85.00 | | | |

**KM# 106 500 RUFIYAA**
7.78 g., 0.585 Gold 0.1463 oz. AGW plated with 24Kt., 25 mm. **Subject:** London Olympics **Obv:** National emblem **Rev:** Soccer players

| Date | Mintage | VF20 | XF40 | MS60 | MS63 | MS65 |
|---|---|---|---|---|---|---|
| 2011 | Est. 1000 | PF65 300 | | | | |

# MALTA

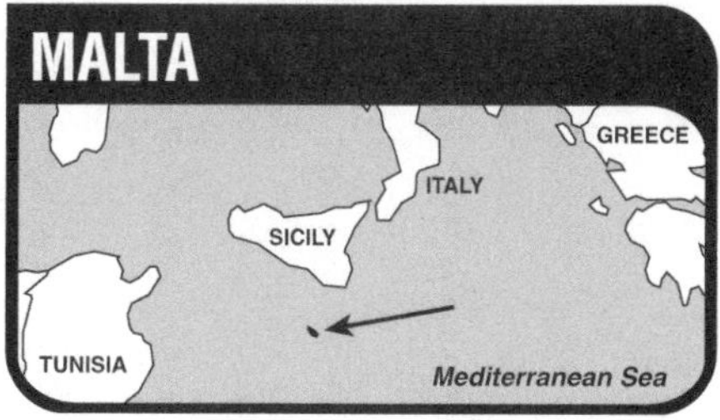


The Republic of Malta, an independent parliamentary democracy, is situated in the Mediterranean Sea between Sicily and North Africa. With the islands of Gozo and Comino, Malta has an area of 124 sq. mi. (320 sq. km.) and a population of 386,000.Capital: Valletta. Malta has no proven mineral resources, agriculture insufficient to its needs, and a small, but expanding, manufacturing facility. Clothing, textile yarns and fabrics, and knitted wear are exported.

Malta became a republic on Dec. 13, 1974, but remained a member of the Commonwealth of Nations. The president is Chief of State. The prime minister is the Head of Government. Malta is also a member of the European Union since May 2004.

## REPUBLIC

### DECIMAL COINAGE

10 Mils = 1 Cent; 100 Cents = 1 Pound

**KM# 5 2 MILS**
0.95 g., Aluminum, 20.3 mm. **Obv:** Maltese cross **Rev:** Value within 3/4 wreath **Shape:** Scalloped

| Date | Mintage | F12 | VF20 | XF40 | MS60 | MS63 |
|---|---|---|---|---|---|---|
| 2005 Sets only | — | — | — | — | — | 4.00 |
| 2006 Sets only | — | — | — | — | — | 4.00 |
| 2007 Sets only | — | — | — | — | — | 4.00 |

### REFORM COINAGE

1982 - Present;
10 Mils = 1 Cent; 100 Cents = 1 Lira

**KM# 93 CENT**
2.81 g., Nickel-Brass, 18.51 mm. **Obv:** Crowned shield within sprigs **Rev:** Common Weasel (ballottra) below value **Edge:** Plain

| Date | Mintage | F12 | VF20 | XF40 | MS60 | MS63 |
|---|---|---|---|---|---|---|
| 2001 | — | — | 0.40 | 0.50 | 1.00 | 1.25 |
| 2002 Sets only | — | — | — | — | 1.00 | 1.25 |
| 2004 | — | — | 0.40 | 0.50 | 0.75 | 1.00 |
| 2005 Sets only | — | — | — | — | — | 1.25 |
| 2006 Sets only | — | — | — | — | — | 1.25 |
| 2007 Sets only | — | — | — | — | — | 1.25 |

**KM# 94 2 CENTS**
2.26 g., Copper-Nickel, 17.78 mm. **Obv:** Crowned shield within sprigs **Rev:** Zebbuga branch and value **Edge:** Reeded

| Date | Mintage | F12 | VF20 | XF40 | MS60 | MS63 |
|---|---|---|---|---|---|---|
| 2002 | — | — | 0.75 | 1.00 | 1.25 | 1.50 |
| 2004 | — | — | 0.75 | 1.00 | 1.25 | 1.50 |
| 2005 | — | — | — | — | 1.25 | 1.50 |
| 2006 Sets only | — | — | — | — | — | 1.50 |
| 2007 Sets only | — | — | — | — | — | 1.50 |

**KM# 95 5 CENTS**
3.51 g., Copper-Nickel, 19.78 mm. **Obv:** Crowned shield within sprigs **Rev:** Freshwater Crab (il-Qobru) and value **Edge:** Reeded

| Date | Mintage | F12 | VF20 | XF40 | MS60 | MS63 |
|---|---|---|---|---|---|---|
| 2001 | — | — | 0.75 | 1.00 | 1.25 | 2.00 |
| 2005 Sets only | — | — | — | — | — | 2.00 |
| 2006 Sets only | — | — | — | — | — | 2.00 |
| 2007 Sets only | — | — | — | — | — | 2.00 |

**KM# 96 10 CENTS**
5.01 g., Copper-Nickel, 21.78 mm. **Obv:** Crowned shield within sprigs **Rev:** Lampuka and value **Edge:** Reeded

| Date | Mintage | F12 | VF20 | XF40 | MS60 | MS63 |
|---|---|---|---|---|---|---|
| 2005 | — | — | 1.25 | 1.50 | 2.00 | 2.50 |
| 2006 Sets only | — | — | — | — | — | 2.50 |
| 2007 Sets only | — | — | — | — | — | 2.50 |

**KM# 97 25 CENTS**
6.19 g., Copper-Nickel, 24.95 mm. **Obv:** Crowned shield within sprigs **Rev:** Ghirlanda flower and value

| Date | Mintage | F12 | VF20 | XF40 | MS60 | MS63 |
|---|---|---|---|---|---|---|
| 2001 | — | — | 2.25 | 2.50 | 3.00 | 3.50 |
| 2005 | — | — | 2.25 | 2.50 | 3.00 | 3.50 |
| 2006 Sets only | — | — | — | — | — | 3.50 |
| 2007 Sets only | — | — | — | — | — | 3.50 |

**KM# 98 50 CENTS**
8.00 g., Copper-Nickel, 27 mm. **Obv:** Crowned shield within sprigs **Rev:** Tulliera plant and value **Edge Lettering:** BANK CENTRALI TA' MALTA

| Date | Mintage | F12 | VF20 | XF40 | MS60 | MS63 |
|---|---|---|---|---|---|---|
| 2001 | — | — | 2.50 | 5.00 | 7.00 | 8.00 |
| 2005 Sets only | — | — | — | — | — | 8.00 |
| 2006 Sets only | — | — | — | — | — | 8.00 |
| 2007 Sets only | — | — | — | — | — | 8.00 |

**KM# 99 LIRA**
13.00 g., Nickel, 29.82 mm. **Obv:** Crowned shield within sprigs **Rev:** Merill bird and value **Edge Lettering:** BANK CENTRALI TA' MALTA

| Date | Mintage | F12 | VF20 | XF40 | MS60 | MS63 |
|---|---|---|---|---|---|---|
| 2005 | — | — | — | 4.50 | 6.50 | 10.00 |
| 2006 Sets only | — | — | — | — | — | 10.00 |
| 2007 Sets only | — | — | — | — | — | 10.00 |

**KM# 117 5 LIRI**
28.28 g., 0.925 Silver 0.841 oz. ASW, 38.6 mm. **Obv:** Crowned shield within sprigs **Rev:** Enrico Mizzi right **Edge:** Reeded

| Date | Mintage | F12 | VF20 | XF40 | MS60 | MS63 |
|---|---|---|---|---|---|---|
| 2001 | 2,000 | PF65 80.00 | | | | |

**KM# 118 5 LIRI**
28.28 g., 0.925 Silver 0.841 oz. ASW, 38.6 mm. **Obv:** Crowned shield within sprigs **Rev:** Nicolo Isouard left **Edge:** Reeded

| Date | Mintage | F12 | VF20 | XF40 | MS60 | MS63 |
|---|---|---|---|---|---|---|
| 2002 | 2,000 | PF65 80.00 | | | | |

**KM# 120 5 LIRI**
28.28 g., 0.925 Silver 0.841 oz. ASW, 38.6 mm. **Obv:** Crowned shield within sprigs **Rev:** Sir Adriano Dingli as Grand Commander of the St. Michael and George Order **Edge:** Reeded

| Date | Mintage | F12 | VF20 | XF40 | MS60 | MS63 |
|---|---|---|---|---|---|---|
| 2003 | 2,000 | PF65 80.00 | | | | |

**KM# 121 5 LIRI**
28.28 g., 0.925 Silver 0.841 oz. ASW, 38.6 mm. **Obv:** Crowned shield within sprigs **Rev:** Painter Giuseppe Cali with palette **Edge:** Reeded

| Date | Mintage | F12 | VF20 | XF40 | MS60 | MS63 |
|---|---|---|---|---|---|---|
| 2004 | 2,000 | PF65 120 | | | | |

**KM# 138 5 LIRI**
Silver, 39 mm. **Subject:** Zammit **Edge:** Reeded

| Date | Mintage | F12 | VF20 | XF40 | MS60 | MS63 |
|---|---|---|---|---|---|---|
| 2006 | — | PF63 70.00 | PF65 75.00 | | | |

**KM# 123 5 LIRI**
28.28 g., 0.925 Silver 0.841 oz. ASW, 38.61 mm. **Subject:** 450th Anniversary of Jean de la Valette appointed Grand master **Rev:** de la Vallete standing facing left, city of Valletta map at lower left

| Date | Mintage | F12 | VF20 | XF40 | MS60 | MS63 |
|---|---|---|---|---|---|---|
| ND(2007) | 25,000 | PF63 65.00 | PF65 75.00 | | | |

**KM# 119 10 LIRI**
1.24 g., 0.999 Gold 0.0398 oz. AGW, 13.92 mm. **Obv:** Crowned shield within sprigs **Rev:** Xprunara sailboat **Edge:** Reeded

| Date | Mintage | F12 | VF20 | XF40 | MS60 | MS63 |
|---|---|---|---|---|---|---|
| 2002 Prooflike | Est. 25000 | — | — | — | — | 130 |

**KM# 122 25 LIRI**
3.99 g., 0.9167 Gold 0.1177 oz. AGW, 19.3 mm. **Subject:** Accession to the European Union **Obv:** Crowned shield within sprigs **Rev:** Maltese flag under European Union star circle **Edge:** Reeded

| Date | Mintage | F12 | VF20 | XF40 | MS60 | MS63 |
|---|---|---|---|---|---|---|
| 2004 | 6,000 | PF65 290 | | | | |

**KM# 124 25 LIRI**
6.50 g., 0.920 Gold 0.1923 oz. AGW, 21 mm. **Subject:** 450th Anniversary Jean de la Valette Appointed as Grand Master **Rev:** de la Valette standing facing left, city of Valletta map at lower left

| Date | Mintage | F12 | VF20 | XF40 | MS60 | MS63 |
|---|---|---|---|---|---|---|
| ND(2007) | 2,500 | **PF65** 375 | | | | |

## EURO COINAGE

**KM# 125 EURO CENT**
2.30 g., Copper Plated Steel, 16.25 mm. **Obv:** Doorway **Rev:** Denomination and globe **Edge:** Plain

| Date | Mintage | F12 | VF20 | XF40 | MS60 | MS63 |
|---|---|---|---|---|---|---|
| 2008 | 14,960,000 | — | — | — | — | 1.00 |
| 2008 | 40,000 | **PF65** 5.00 | | | | |
| 2009 Sets only | 40,000 | — | — | — | — | 1.50 |
| 2010 Sets only | 30,000 | — | — | — | — | 1.50 |
| 2011 Sets only | 50,000 | — | — | — | — | 1.50 |
| 2012 Sets only | 50,000 | — | — | — | — | 1.50 |
| 2013 | 35,000 | — | — | — | — | 1.50 |
| 2013 Sets only | | | | | | |
| 2014 Sets only | 25,000 | — | — | — | — | 1.50 |

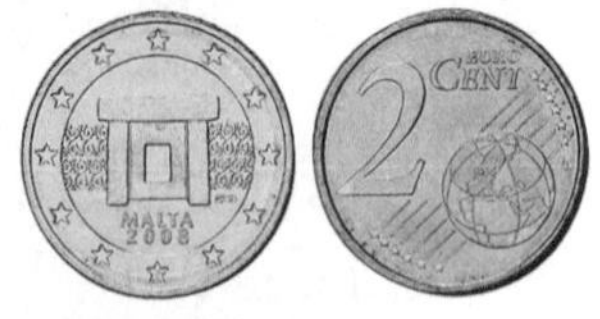

**KM# 126 2 EURO CENT**
3.06 g., Copper Plated Steel, 18.75 mm. **Obv:** Doorway **Rev:** Denomination and globe **Edge:** Grooved

| Date | Mintage | F12 | VF20 | XF40 | MS60 | MS63 |
|---|---|---|---|---|---|---|
| 2008 | 35,960,000 | — | — | — | — | 0.70 |
| 2008 | 40,000 | **PF65** 5.00 | | | | |
| 2009 Sets only | 40,000 | — | — | — | — | 2.00 |
| 2010 Sets only | 30,000 | — | — | — | — | 2.00 |
| 2011 Sets only | 50,000 | — | — | — | — | 2.00 |
| 2012 Sets only | 50,000 | — | — | — | — | 2.00 |
| 2013 Sets only | 35,000 | — | — | — | — | 2.00 |
| 2014 Sets only | 25,000 | — | — | — | — | 2.00 |

**KM# 127 5 EURO CENT**
3.92 g., Copper Plated Steel, 21.25 mm. **Obv:** Doorway **Rev:** Denomination and globe

| Date | Mintage | F12 | VF20 | XF40 | MS60 | MS63 |
|---|---|---|---|---|---|---|
| 2008 | 33,960,000 | — | — | — | — | 0.70 |
| 2008 | 40,000 | **PF65** 5.00 | | | | |
| 2009 Sets only | 40,000 | — | — | — | — | 2.50 |
| 2010 Sets only | 30,000 | — | — | — | — | 2.50 |
| 2011 Sets only | 50,000 | — | — | — | — | 2.50 |
| 2012 Sets only | 50,000 | — | — | — | — | 2.50 |
| 2013 Sets only | 35,000 | — | — | — | — | 2.50 |
| 2014 Sets only | 25,000 | — | — | — | — | 2.50 |

**KM# 128 10 EURO CENT**
4.10 g., Brass, 19.75 mm. **Obv:** Crowned shield within wreath **Rev:** Value and relief map of Europe **Edge:** Notched

| Date | Mintage | F12 | VF20 | XF40 | MS60 | MS63 |
|---|---|---|---|---|---|---|
| 2008 | 40,960,000 | — | — | — | — | 1.00 |
| 2008 | 40,000 | **PF65** 7.50 | | | | |
| 2009 Sets only | 40,000 | — | — | — | — | 3.00 |
| 2010 Sets only | 30,000 | — | — | — | — | 3.00 |
| 2011 Sets only | 50,000 | — | — | — | — | 3.00 |
| 2012 Sets only | 50,000 | — | — | — | — | 3.00 |

**KM# 129 20 EURO CENT**
5.75 g., Brass, 22.25 mm. **Obv:** Crowned shield within wreath **Rev:** Denomination and Map of Western Europe **Edge:** Notched

| Date | Mintage | F12 | VF20 | XF40 | MS60 | MS63 |
|---|---|---|---|---|---|---|
| 2008 | 39,960,000 | — | — | — | — | 1.50 |
| 2008 | 40,000 | **PF65** 7.50 | | | | |
| 2009 Sets only | 40,000 | — | — | — | — | 4.00 |
| 2010 Sets only | 30,000 | — | — | — | — | 4.00 |
| 2011 Sets only | 50,000 | — | — | — | — | 4.00 |
| 2012 Sets only | 50,000 | — | — | — | — | 4.00 |
| 2013 In set only | 35,000 | — | — | — | — | 3.00 |
| 2014 Sets only | 25,000 | — | — | — | — | 3.00 |

**KM# 130 50 EURO CENT**
7.80 g., Brass, 24.25 mm. **Obv:** Crowned shield within wreath **Rev:** Relief map of Western Europe **Edge:** Reeded

| Date | Mintage | F12 | VF20 | XF40 | MS60 | MS63 |
|---|---|---|---|---|---|---|
| 2008 | 14,960,000 | — | — | — | — | 2.00 |
| 2008 | 40,000 | **PF65** 7.50 | | | | |
| 2009 Sets only | 40,000 | — | — | — | — | 5.00 |
| 2010 Sets only | 30,000 | — | — | — | — | 5.00 |
| 2011 Sets only | 50,000 | — | — | — | — | 5.00 |
| 2012 Sets only | 50,000 | — | — | — | — | 5.00 |
| 2013 Sets only | 35,000 | — | — | — | — | 4.00 |
| 2014 Sets only | 25,000 | — | — | — | — | 4.00 |

**KM# 131 EURO**
7.50 g., Bi-Metallic Copper-Nickel center in Nickel-Brass ring, 23.25 mm. **Obv:** Maltese Cross **Rev:** Value and relief map of Europe **Edge:** Segmented reeding

| Date | Mintage | F12 | VF20 | XF40 | MS60 | MS63 |
|---|---|---|---|---|---|---|
| 2008 | 13,960,000 | — | — | — | — | 4.00 |
| 2008 | 40,000 | **PF65** 15.00 | | | | |
| 2009 Sets only | — | — | — | — | — | 5.00 |
| 2010 Sets only | — | — | — | — | — | 5.00 |
| 2011 Sets only | — | — | — | — | — | 5.00 |
| 2012 Sets only | 50,000 | — | — | — | — | 5.00 |
| 2013 Sets only | 35,000 | — | — | — | — | 5.00 |
| 2014 Sets only | 35,000 | — | — | — | — | 5.00 |

**KM# 132 2 EURO**
8.50 g., Bi-Metallic Nickel-Brass center in Copper-Nickel ring, 25.75 mm. **Obv:** Maltese Cross **Rev:** Value and Relief Map of Western Europe **Edge:** Reeded with 2s and Maltese Crosses

| Date | Mintage | F12 | VF20 | XF40 | MS60 | MS63 |
|---|---|---|---|---|---|---|
| 2008 | 9,960,000 | — | — | — | — | 6.00 |
| 2008 | 40,000 | **PF65** 25.00 | | | | |
| 2009 Sets only | — | — | — | — | — | 8.00 |
| 2010 | 19,990,000 | — | — | — | — | 8.00 |
| 2011 Sets only | — | — | — | — | — | 8.00 |
| 2012 Sets only | 50,000 | — | — | — | — | 8.00 |
| 2013 Sets only | 35,000 | — | — | — | — | 8.00 |
| 2014 Sets only | 25,000 | — | — | — | — | 8.00 |

**KM# 134 2 EURO**
8.50 g., Bi-Metallic Nickel-Brass center in Copper-Nickel ring, 25.75 mm. **Subject:** E.M.U., 10th Anniversary **Obv:** Stick figure and large E symbol **Rev:** Value and relief map of Western Europe **Edge:** Segmented reeding

| Date | Mintage | F12 | VF20 | XF40 | MS60 | MS63 |
|---|---|---|---|---|---|---|
| 2009 | 7,000,000 | — | — | — | — | 6.00 |

**KM# 144 2 EURO**
8.50 g., Bi-Metallic Nickel-Brass center in Copper-Nickel ring, 25.75 mm. **Subject:** First Elected Representatives of 1849 **Obv:** Hand placing ballot in slot

| Date | Mintage | F12 | VF20 | XF40 | MS60 | MS63 |
|---|---|---|---|---|---|---|
| 2011 | 375,000 | — | — | — | 6.00 | 8.00 |
| 2011 Special Unc. | 50,000 | — | — | — | — | 15.00 |
| 2011 | 5,000 | **PF65** 25.00 | | | | |

**KM# 139 2 EURO**
8.50 g., Bi-Metallic Nickel-Brass center in Copper-Nickel ring, 25.75 mm. **Subject:** Euro Coinage, 10th Anniversary **Obv:** Euro symbol on globe, child-like rendering around

| Date | Mintage | F12 | VF20 | XF40 | MS60 | MS63 |
|---|---|---|---|---|---|---|
| 2012 | 500,000 | — | — | — | 6.00 | 8.00 |
| 2012 | — | **PF65** 25.00 | | | | |

**KM# 145 2 EURO**
8.50 g., Bi-Metallic Nickel-Brass center in Copper-Nickel ring, 25.75 mm. **Subject:** Majority representation **Obv:** Jubilee crowd at Governor's Palace in Valletta

| Date | Mintage | F12 | VF20 | XF40 | MS60 | MS63 |
|---|---|---|---|---|---|---|
| 2012 | 400,000 | — | — | — | — | 15.00 |
| 2012 Special Unc | 5,000 | — | — | — | — | 20.00 |

**KM# 167 2 EURO**
8.50 g., Bi-Metallic Brass center in Copper-Nickel ring, 25.75 mm. **Subject:** Constitution History **Obv:** Document

| Date | Mintage | F12 | VF20 | XF40 | MS60 | MS63 |
|---|---|---|---|---|---|---|
| 2015 | — | — | — | — | — | 15.00 |

**KM# 155 5 EURO**
0.50 g., 0.585 Gold AGW, 11 mm. **Subject:** Picciolo of Jean de la Valette, 49th Grandmaster of the Order of Malta **Obv:** Crowned shield **Rev:** Old coin design

| Date | Mintage | F12 | VF20 | XF40 | MS60 | MS63 |
|---|---|---|---|---|---|---|
| 2013 | 10,000 | **PF65** 45.00 | | | | |

**KM# 136 10 EURO**
28.28 g., 0.925 Silver 0.841 oz. ASW, 38.6 mm. **Subject:** Auberge de Castille **Rev:** Building tower

| Date | Mintage | F12 | VF20 | XF40 | MS60 | MS63 |
|---|---|---|---|---|---|---|
| 2008 | 18,000 | PF63 55.00 | PF65 60.00 | | | |

**KM# 133 10 EURO**
28.28 g., 0.925 Silver 0.841 oz. ASW, 38.6 mm. **Rev:** La Castellania, Merchant's Street, Valletta

| Date | Mintage | F12 | VF20 | XF40 | MS60 | MS63 |
|---|---|---|---|---|---|---|
| 2009 | 15,000 | PF63 55.00 | PF65 60.00 | | | |

**KM# 140 10 EURO**
28.28 g., 0.925 Silver 0.841 oz. ASW, 38.61 mm. **Subject:** Valetta - Auberge d'Italie **Obv:** Crowned shield **Rev:** Architectural detail

| Date | Mintage | F12 | VF20 | XF40 | MS60 | MS63 |
|---|---|---|---|---|---|---|
| 2010 | 12,500 | PF63 60.00 | PF65 65.00 | | | |

**KM# 142 10 EURO**
28.28 g., 0.925 Silver 0.841 oz. ASW, 38.61 mm. **Subject:** Phoenicians in Malta **Obv:** Crowned shield **Rev:** Ancient Phoenician boat

| Date | Mintage | F12 | VF20 | XF40 | MS60 | MS63 |
|---|---|---|---|---|---|---|
| 2011 | 10,000 | PF63 70.00 | PF65 75.00 | | | |

**KM# 152 10 EURO**
28.28 g., 0.925 Silver 0.841 oz. ASW, 38.61 mm. **Subject:** Antonio Sciortino, sculpture of "Les Gavroches" **Obv:** Crowned shield **Rev:** Three figures

| Date | Mintage | F12 | VF20 | XF40 | MS60 | MS63 |
|---|---|---|---|---|---|---|
| 2012 | 10,000 | PF65 65.00 | | | | |

**KM# 147 10 EURO**
28.28 g., 0.925 Silver 0.841 oz. ASW, 38.6 mm. **Subject:** Fr. Karm Psaila, composer of the National Amthem **Rev:** Portrait looking left

| Date | Mintage | F12 | VF20 | XF40 | MS60 | MS63 |
|---|---|---|---|---|---|---|
| 2013 | — | PF63 60.00 | PF65 65.00 | | | |

**KM# 148 10 EURO**
28.28 g., 0.925 Silver 0.841 oz. ASW, 38.6 mm. **Subject:** Sir Paul Boffa, Prime Minister **Obv:** Crowned shield **Rev:** Bust facing

| Date | Mintage | F12 | VF20 | XF40 | MS60 | MS63 |
|---|---|---|---|---|---|---|
| 2013 | — | PF63 55.00 | PF65 60.00 | | | |

**KM# 154 10 EURO**
20.00 g., 0.925 Silver 0.5948 oz. ASW, 38.61 mm. **Subject:** Manuel Pinto, 68th Grandmaster of the Order of Malta **Obv:** Crowned shield **Rev:** Bust at left, map and crowned shield at right

| Date | Mintage | F12 | VF20 | XF40 | MS60 | MS63 |
|---|---|---|---|---|---|---|
| 2013 | 2,500 | PF65 65.00 | | | | |
| 2013 Star 15 | 5,000 | PF65 65.00 | | | | |

**KM# 156 10 EURO**
18.75 g., 0.925 Silver 0.5576 oz. ASW, 33 mm. **Obv:** Crowned shield **Rev:** Order Hostel in Valletta, now National Archaeology Museum

| Date | Mintage | F12 | VF20 | XF40 | MS60 | MS63 |
|---|---|---|---|---|---|---|
| 2013 | 5,000 | PF65 55.00 | | | | |

**KM# 157 15 EURO**
1.25 g., 0.999 Gold 0.0401 oz. AGW, 14 mm. **Obv:** Crowned shield **Rev:** Order Hostel in Valletta, now National Archaeology Museum

| Date | Mintage | F12 | VF20 | XF40 | MS60 | MS63 |
|---|---|---|---|---|---|---|
| 2013 | 2,500 | PF65 100 | | | | |

**KM# 137 50 EURO**
6.50 g., 0.916 Gold 0.1914 oz. AGW, 21 mm. **Subject:** Auberge de Castille **Rev:** Building tower

| Date | Mintage | F12 | VF20 | XF40 | MS60 | MS63 |
|---|---|---|---|---|---|---|
| 2008 | 3,000 | PF65 375 | | | | |

**KM# 135 50 EURO**
6.50 g., 0.916 Gold 0.1914 oz. AGW, 21 mm. **Rev:** La Castellania, Merchant's Street, Valletta

| Date | Mintage | F12 | VF20 | XF40 | MS60 | MS63 |
|---|---|---|---|---|---|---|
| 2009 | 3,000 | PF65 375 | | | | |

**KM# 141 50 EURO**
6.50 g., 0.916 Gold 0.1914 oz. AGW, 21 mm. **Subject:** Valetta - Auberge d'Italie **Obv:** Crowned shield **Rev:** Archetectural detail

| Date | Mintage | F12 | VF20 | XF40 | MS60 | MS63 |
|---|---|---|---|---|---|---|
| 2010 | 3,000 | PF65 400 | | | | |

**KM# 143 50 EURO**
6.50 g., 0.916 Gold 0.1914 oz. AGW, 21 mm. **Subject:** Phoenicians in Malta **Obv:** Crowned shield **Rev:** Ancient Phoenician boat

| Date | Mintage | F12 | VF20 | XF40 | MS60 | MS63 |
|---|---|---|---|---|---|---|
| 2011 | 2,000 | PF65 385 | | | | |

**KM# 146 50 EURO**
6.50 g., 0.916 Gold 0.1914 oz. AGW, 21 mm. **Subject:** Antonio Sciortino **Obv:** National arms **Rev:** Three figures

| Date | Mintage | F12 | VF20 | XF40 | MS60 | MS63 |
|---|---|---|---|---|---|---|
| 2012 | — | PF65 400 | | | | |

**KM# 153 50 EURO**
6.50 g., 0.9167 Gold 0.1916 oz. AGW, 21 mm. **Subject:** Composer of National Anthem **Obv:** Crowned shield

| Date | Mintage | F12 | VF20 | XF40 | MS60 | MS63 |
|---|---|---|---|---|---|---|
| 2013 | 2,000 | PF65 400 | | | | |

## MINT SETS

| KM# | Date | Mintage | Identification | Issue Price | Mkt Val |
|---|---|---|---|---|---|
| MS26 | 2005 (8) | — | KM#5, 93-99 | — | 35.00 |
| MS27 | 2006 (8) | — | KM#5, 93-99 | — | 37.50 |
| MS28 | 2007 (8) | — | KM#5, 93-99 | — | 45.00 |
| MS29 | 2008 (8) | 40,000 | KM#125-132, wooden box | — | 70.00 |
| MS30 | 2008 (8) | 30,000 | KM#125-132, Malta Post and Lombard Bank card | — | 45.00 |

## PROOF SETS

| KM# | Date | Mintage | Identification | Issue Price | Mkt Val |
|---|---|---|---|---|---|
| PS12 | 2008 (9) | 40,000 | KM#125-132, plus ingot | — | 80.00 |

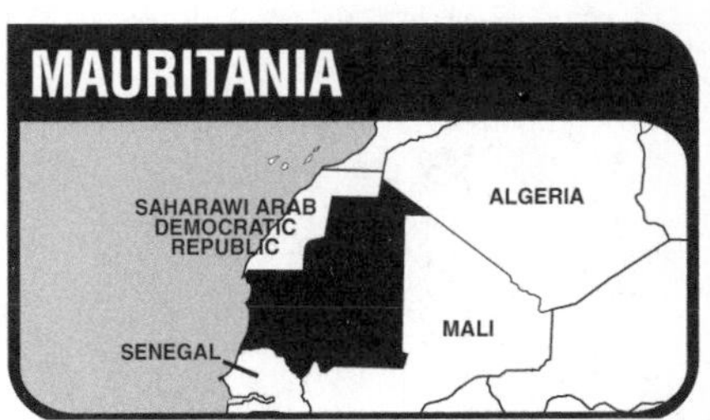


The Islamic Republic of Mauritania, located in northwest Africa bounded by Western Sahara, Mali, Algeria, Senegal and the Atlantic Ocean, has an area of 397,955 sq. mi.(1,030,700 sq. km.) and a population of 1.9 million. Capital: Nouakchott. The economy centers on herding, agriculture, fishing and mining. Iron ore, copper concentrates and fish products are exported.

On June 28, 1973, in a move designed to emphasize its non-alignment with France, Mauritania converted its currency from the old French-supported C.F.A. franc unit to a new unit called the Ouguiya.

**MONETARY SYSTEM**
5 Khoums = 1 Ouguiya

# REPUBLIC

## STANDARD COINAGE

**KM# 6 OUGUIYA**
3.60 g., Aluminum-Bronze, 21 mm. **Obv:** National emblem divides date above value **Obv. Legend:** BANQUE CENTRALE DE MAURITANIE **Rev:** Star and crescent divide sprigs with legend below value, all within circle **Edge:** Reeded

| Date | Mintage | VF20 | XF40 | MS60 | MS63 | MS65 |
|---|---|---|---|---|---|---|
| AH1423//2003 | — | — | 0.50 | 1.25 | 2.00 | 3.50 |

**KM# 10 OUGUIYA**
3.60 g., Steel, 21 mm. **Obv:** National arms **Rev:** Star and crescent

| Date | Mintage | VF20 | XF40 | MS60 | MS63 | MS65 |
|---|---|---|---|---|---|---|
| AH1430//2009 | — | — | 0.50 | 1.25 | 2.00 | 3.50 |

**KM# 3 5 OUGUIYA**
5.88 g., Aluminum-Bronze, 25 mm. **Obv:** National emblem divides date above value **Obv. Legend:** BANQUE CENTRALE DE MAURITANIE **Rev:** Star and crescent divide sprigs below value within circle **Edge:** Plain

| Date | Mintage | VF20 | XF40 | MS60 | MS63 | MS65 |
|---|---|---|---|---|---|---|
| AH1423//2003 | — | — | 1.75 | 3.50 | 5.00 | 7.00 |
| AH1425//2004 | — | — | 1.75 | 3.50 | 5.00 | 7.00 |

**KM# 3a 5 OUGUIYA**
6.00 g., Copper Plated Steel, 25 mm. **Obv:** National emblem divides date above value **Obv. Legend:** BANQUE CENTRALE DE MAURITANIE **Rev:** Star and crescent divides sprigs below value within circle **Edge:** Plain

| Date | Mintage | VF20 | XF40 | MS60 | MS63 | MS65 |
|---|---|---|---|---|---|---|
| AH1425//2004 | — | — | 1.00 | 2.00 | 3.00 | 5.00 |
| AH1426//2005 | — | — | 1.00 | 2.00 | 3.00 | 5.00 |
| AH1430//2009 | — | — | 1.00 | 2.00 | 3.00 | 5.00 |
| AH1434//2013 | — | — | 1.00 | 2.00 | 3.00 | 5.00 |

**KM# 4 10 OUGUIYA**
6.00 g., Copper-Nickel, 25 mm. **Obv:** National emblem divides date above value **Obv. Legend:** BANQUE CENTRALE DE MAURITANIE **Rev:** Crescent and star divide sprigs below value within circle **Edge:** Reeded

| Date | Mintage | VF20 | XF40 | MS60 | MS63 | MS65 |
|---|---|---|---|---|---|---|
| AH1423//2003 | — | — | 2.00 | 4.00 | 5.50 | 9.00 |
| AH1425//2004 | — | — | 2.00 | 4.00 | 5.50 | 9.00 |

**KM# 4a 10 OUGUIYA**
5.80 g., Nickel Plated Steel, 24.5 mm. **Obv:** National emblem divides date above value **Obv. Legend:** BANQUE CENTRALE DE MAURITANIE **Rev:** Crescent and star divides sprigs below value within circle **Edge:** Reeded

| Date | Mintage | VF20 | XF40 | MS60 | MS63 | MS65 |
|---|---|---|---|---|---|---|
| AH1425//2004 | — | — | 1.25 | 3.00 | 4.50 | 8.00 |
| AH1426//2005 | — | — | 1.25 | 3.00 | 4.50 | 8.00 |
| AH1430//2009 | — | — | 1.25 | 3.00 | 4.50 | 8.00 |
| AH1434//2013 | — | — | 1.25 | 3.00 | 4.50 | 8.00 |

**KM# 5 20 OUGUIYA**
8.00 g., Copper-Nickel, 28 mm. **Obv:** National emblem divides date above value **Obv. Legend:** BANQUE CENTRALE DE MAURITANIE **Rev:** Star and crescent divide sprigs below value within circle **Edge:** Reeded

| Date | Mintage | VF20 | XF40 | MS60 | MS63 | MS65 |
|---|---|---|---|---|---|---|
| AH1423//2003 | — | — | 3.00 | 5.00 | 8.00 | 12.00 |
| AH1425//2004 | — | — | 3.00 | 5.00 | 8.00 | 12.00 |

**KM# 5a 20 OUGUIYA**
7.80 g., Nickel Plated Steel, 28 mm. **Obv:** National emblem divides date above value **Obv. Legend:** BANQUE CENTRALE DE MAURITANIE **Rev:** Star and crescent divide sprigs below value within circle **Edge:** Reeded

| Date | Mintage | VF20 | XF40 | MS60 | MS63 | MS65 |
|---|---|---|---|---|---|---|
| AH1425//2004 | — | — | 2.00 | 4.00 | 6.00 | 9.00 |
| AH1426//2005 | — | — | 2.00 | 4.00 | 6.00 | 9.00 |
| AH1430//2009 | — | — | 2.00 | 4.00 | 6.00 | 9.00 |

**KM# 8 20 OUGUIYA**
Bi-Metallic Copper-Nickel center in Brass ring **Obv:** National arms above value **Rev:** Value within wreath

| Date | Mintage | VF20 | XF40 | MS60 | MS63 | MS65 |
|---|---|---|---|---|---|---|
| 2009 | — | — | — | 5.00 | 7.50 | 10.00 |
| 2010 | — | — | — | 5.00 | 7.50 | 10.00 |

**KM# 9 50 OUGUIYA**
Bi-Metallic Nickel-Brass center in Copper-Nickel ring **Obv:** National arms above value **Rev:** Value within wreath

| Date | Mintage | VF20 | XF40 | MS60 | MS63 | MS65 |
|---|---|---|---|---|---|---|
| 2010 | — | — | — | 5.00 | 7.50 | 10.00 |

# MAURITIUS

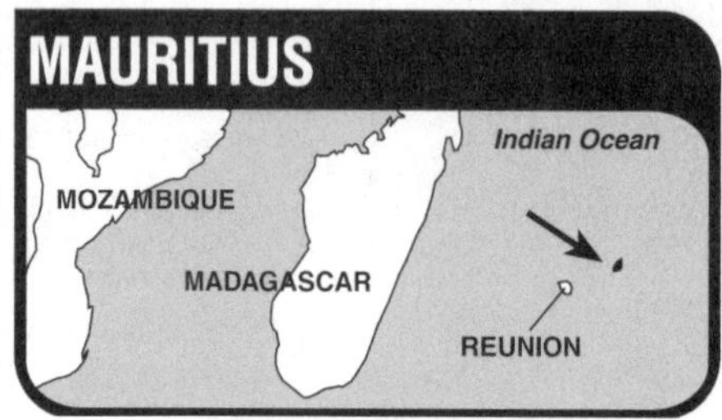


The Republic of Mauritius, is located in the Indian Ocean 500 miles (805 km.) east of Madagascar, has an area of 790 sq. mi. (1,860 sq. km.) and a population of 1 million. Capital: Port Louis. Sugar provides 90 percent of the export revenue.

Mauritius became independent on March 12, 1968. It is a member of the Commonwealth of Nations.

**MONETARY SYSTEM**
100 Cents = 1 Rupee

## REPUBLIC
### STANDARD COINAGE

**KM# 52 5 CENTS**
3.00 g., Copper Plated Steel **Obv:** Value within beaded circle **Rev:** Bust of Sir Seewoosagur Ramgoolam 3/4 right

| Date | Mintage | VF20 | XF40 | MS60 | MS63 | MS65 |
|---|---|---|---|---|---|---|
| 2003 | — | — | 0.10 | 0.35 | 0.50 | 1.00 |
| 2004 | — | — | 0.10 | 0.35 | 0.50 | 1.00 |
| 2005 | — | — | 0.10 | 0.35 | 0.50 | 1.00 |
| 2007 | — | — | 0.10 | 0.35 | 0.50 | 1.00 |
| 2010 | — | — | 0.10 | 0.35 | 0.50 | 1.00 |
| 2012 | — | — | 0.10 | 0.35 | 0.50 | 1.00 |

**KM# 53 20 CENTS**
3.00 g., Nickel Plated Steel, 19 mm. **Obv:** Value within beaded circle **Rev:** Bust of Sir Seewoosagur Ramgoolam 3/4 right

| Date | Mintage | VF20 | XF40 | MS60 | MS63 | MS65 |
|---|---|---|---|---|---|---|
| 2001 | — | — | 0.20 | 0.50 | 0.75 | 1.25 |
| 2003 | — | — | 0.20 | 0.50 | 0.75 | 1.25 |
| 2004 | — | — | 0.20 | 0.50 | 0.75 | 1.25 |
| 2005 | — | — | 0.20 | 0.50 | 0.75 | 1.25 |
| 2007 | — | — | 0.20 | 0.50 | 0.75 | 1.25 |
| 2010 | — | — | 0.20 | 0.50 | 0.75 | 1.25 |
| 2012 | — | — | 0.20 | 0.50 | 0.75 | 1.25 |

**KM# 54 1/2 RUPEE**
5.90 g., Nickel Plated Steel, 23.6 mm. **Obv:** Stag left **Rev:** Bust of Sir Seewoosagur Ramgoolam 3/4 right

| Date | Mintage | VF20 | XF40 | MS60 | MS63 | MS65 |
|---|---|---|---|---|---|---|
| 2002 | — | — | 0.60 | 1.25 | 2.00 | 2.50 |
| 2003 | — | — | 0.60 | 1.25 | 2.00 | 2.50 |
| 2004 | — | — | 0.60 | 1.25 | 2.00 | 2.50 |
| 2005 | — | — | 0.60 | 1.25 | 2.00 | 2.50 |
| 2007 | — | — | 0.60 | 1.25 | 2.00 | 2.50 |
| 2009 | — | — | 0.60 | 1.25 | 2.00 | 2.50 |
| 2010 | — | — | 0.60 | 1.25 | 2.00 | 2.50 |

**KM# 55 RUPEE**
7.50 g., Copper-Nickel, 26.6 mm. **Obv:** Shield divides date above value **Rev:** Bust of Sir Seewoosagur Ramgoolam 3/4 right **Edge:** Reeded

| Date | Mintage | VF20 | XF40 | MS60 | MS63 | MS65 |
|---|---|---|---|---|---|---|
| 2002 | — | — | 0.65 | 1.25 | 2.25 | 2.75 |
| 2004 | — | — | 0.65 | 1.25 | 2.25 | 2.75 |
| 2005 | — | — | 0.65 | 1.25 | 2.25 | 2.75 |
| 2007 | — | — | 0.65 | 1.25 | 2.25 | 2.75 |
| 2008 | — | — | 0.65 | 1.25 | 2.25 | 2.75 |
| 2009 | — | — | 0.65 | 1.25 | 2.25 | 2.75 |
| 2010 | — | — | 0.65 | 1.25 | 2.25 | 2.75 |

**KM# 55a RUPEE**
Nickel Plated Steel, 26.6 mm. **Obv:** Shield **Rev:** Sir Seewoosagur Ramgoolam 3/4 right

| Date | Mintage | VF20 | XF40 | MS60 | MS63 | MS65 |
|---|---|---|---|---|---|---|
| 2012 | — | — | — | 1.25 | 2.25 | 2.75 |

**KM# 56 5 RUPEES**
12.40 g., Copper-Nickel, 31 mm. **Obv:** Value within palm trees **Rev:** Bust of Sir Seewoosagur Ramgoolam 3/4 right

| Date | Mintage | VF20 | XF40 | MS60 | MS63 | MS65 |
|---|---|---|---|---|---|---|
| 2009 | — | — | — | 1.75 | 3.00 | 5.00 |
| 2010 | — | — | — | 1.75 | 3.00 | 5.00 |
| 2012 | — | — | — | 1.75 | 3.00 | 5.00 |

**KM# 66 20 RUPEES**
10.10 g., Bi-Metallic Copper-Nickel center in Aluminum-Bronze ring, 27.96 mm. **Obv:** Bank of Mauritius tower **Rev:** Bust of Sir Seewoosagur Ramgoolam KT 3/4 right **Edge:** Reeded

| Date | Mintage | VF20 | XF40 | MS60 | MS63 | MS65 |
|---|---|---|---|---|---|---|
| 2007 | — | — | 2.00 | 3.00 | 5.00 | 7.00 |

**KM# 65 100 RUPEES**
36.57 g., 0.925 Silver 1.0876 oz. ASW, 43.9 mm. **Obv:** National arms, date below **Obv. Legend:** MAURITIUS ONE HUNDRED RUPEES **Rev:** Bust of Gandhi 3/4 right **Rev. Legend:** MAHATMA GANDHI CENTENARY OF ARRIVAL IN MAURITIUS **Edge:** Reeded

| Date | Mintage | VF20 | XF40 | MS60 | MS63 | MS65 |
|---|---|---|---|---|---|---|
| 2001 | — | **PF63** 100 | **PF65** 125 | | | |

**KM# 67 1500 RUPEES**
7.78 g., 0.999 Platinum 0.2499 oz. APW, 25 mm. **Subject:** Sir Seewoosagur Ramgoolan **Obv:** Portrait **Rev:** State House **Edge:** Plain

| Date | Mintage | VF20 | XF40 | MS60 | MS63 | MS65 |
|---|---|---|---|---|---|---|
| 2009 | — | **PF63** 450 | **PF65** 500 | | | |

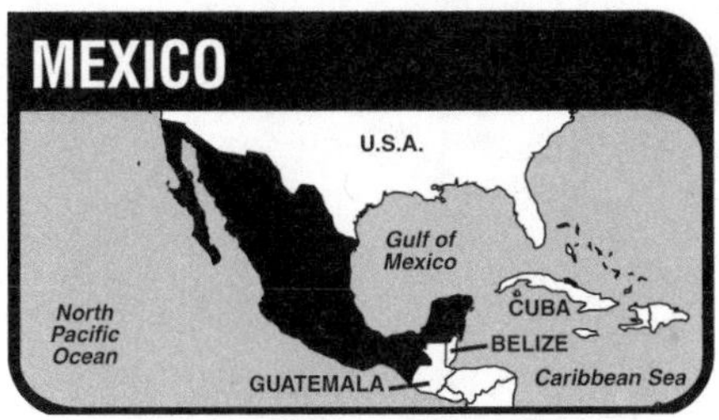


The United Mexican States, located immediately south of the United States has an area of 759,529 sq. mi. (1,967,183 sq. km.) and an estimated population of 100 million. Capital: Mexico City. The economy is based on agriculture, manufacturing and mining. Oil, cotton, silver, coffee, and shrimp are exported.

# ESTADOS UNIDOS MEXICANOS

## REFORM COINAGE

1 New Peso = 1000 Old Pesos;
100 centavos = 1 New Peso; 100 Centavos = 1 Peso

**KM# 546 5 CENTAVOS**
1.58 g., Stainless Steel, 15.5 mm. **Obv:** National arms **Rev:** Large value **Edge:** Plain

| Date | Mintage | VF20 | XF40 | MS60 | MS63 | MS65 |
|---|---|---|---|---|---|---|
| 2001 Mo | 34,811,000 | — | 0.15 | 0.20 | 0.50 | — |
| 2002 Mo | 14,901,000 | — | 0.20 | 0.75 | 1.00 | — |

**KM# 547 10 CENTAVOS**
2.08 g., Stainless Steel, 17 mm. **Obv:** National arms, eagle left **Rev:** Large value

| Date | Mintage | VF20 | XF40 | MS60 | MS63 | MS65 |
|---|---|---|---|---|---|---|
| 2001 Mo | 618,061,000 | — | 0.20 | 0.25 | 0.30 | — |
| 2002 Mo | 463,968,000 | — | 0.20 | 0.25 | 0.30 | — |
| 2003 Mo | 378,938,000 | — | 0.20 | 0.25 | 0.30 | — |
| 2004 Mo | 393,705,000 | — | 0.20 | 0.25 | 0.30 | — |
| 2005 Mo | 488,594,000 | — | 0.20 | 0.25 | 0.30 | — |
| 2006 Mo | 473,261,000 | — | 0.20 | 0.25 | 0.30 | — |
| 2007 Mo | 498,735,000 | — | 0.20 | 0.25 | 0.30 | — |
| 2008 Mo | 433,951,000 | — | 0.20 | 0.25 | 0.30 | — |
| 2009 Mo | 90,968,000 | — | 0.20 | 0.25 | 0.30 | — |

**KM# 934 10 CENTAVOS**
1.75 g., Stainless Steel, 14 mm. **Obv:** National arms **Rev:** Large value **Edge:** Grooved

| Date | Mintage | VF20 | XF40 | MS60 | MS63 | MS65 |
|---|---|---|---|---|---|---|
| 2009 Mo | 343,772,000 | — | — | 0.10 | 0.25 | — |
| 2010 Mo | 453,849,000 | — | — | 0.10 | 0.25 | — |
| 2011 Mo | 463,960,000 | — | — | 0.10 | 0.25 | — |
| 2012 Mo | 419,017,000 | — | — | 0.10 | 0.25 | — |
| 2013 Mo | Est. 399143000 | — | — | 0.10 | 0.25 | — |
| (2014) Mo | — | — | — | 0.10 | 0.25 | — |

**KM# 548 20 CENTAVOS**
3.04 g., Aluminum-Bronze, 19.5 mm. **Obv:** National arms, eagle left **Rev:** Value and date within 3/4 wreath **Shape:** 12-sided

| Date | Mintage | VF20 | XF40 | MS60 | MS63 | MS65 |
|---|---|---|---|---|---|---|
| 2001 Mo | 234,360,000 | — | 0.25 | 0.35 | 0.40 | — |
| 2002 Mo | 229,256,000 | — | 0.25 | 0.35 | 0.40 | — |
| 2003 Mo | 149,518,000 | — | 0.25 | 0.35 | 0.40 | — |
| 2004 Mo | 174,351,000 | — | 0.25 | 0.35 | 0.40 | — |
| 2005 Mo | 204,426,000 | — | 0.25 | 0.35 | 0.40 | — |
| 2006 Mo | 234,263,000 | — | 0.25 | 0.35 | 0.40 | — |
| 2007 Mo | 234,301,000 | — | 0.25 | 0.35 | 0.40 | — |
| 2008 Mo | 214,313,000 | — | 0.25 | 0.35 | 0.40 | — |
| 2009 Mo | 41,167,000 | — | 0.25 | 0.35 | 0.40 | — |

**KM# 935 20 CENTAVOS**
2.26 g., Stainless Steel, 15.3 mm. **Obv:** National arms **Rev:** Value and date within wreath **Edge:** Segmented reeding

| Date | Mintage | VF20 | XF40 | MS60 | MS63 | MS65 |
|---|---|---|---|---|---|---|
| 2009 Mo | 164,362,000 | — | — | 0.25 | 0.35 | — |
| 2010 Mo | 224,359,000 | — | — | 0.25 | 0.35 | — |
| 2011 Mo | 239,362,000 | — | — | 0.25 | 0.35 | — |
| 2012 Mo | 209,434,000 | — | — | 0.25 | 0.35 | — |
| 2013 Mo | Est. 194429000 | — | — | 0.25 | 0.35 | — |
| (2014) Mo | — | — | — | 0.25 | 0.35 | — |

**KM# 549 50 CENTAVOS**
4.39 g., Aluminum-Bronze, 22 mm. **Obv:** National arms, eagle left **Rev:** Value and date within 1/2 designed wreath **Shape:** 12-sided

| Date | Mintage | VF20 | XF40 | MS60 | MS63 | MS65 |
|---|---|---|---|---|---|---|
| 2001 Mo | 199,006,000 | — | 0.45 | 0.75 | 1.00 | — |
| 2002 Mo | 94,552,000 | — | 0.45 | 0.75 | 1.00 | — |
| 2003 Mo | 124,522,000 | — | 0.45 | 0.75 | 1.00 | — |
| 2004 Mo | 154,434,000 | — | 0.45 | 0.75 | 1.00 | — |
| 2005 Mo | 179,296,000 | — | 0.45 | 0.75 | 1.00 | — |
| 2006 Mo | 234,142,000 | — | 0.45 | 0.75 | 1.00 | — |
| 2007 Mo | 253,634,000 | — | 0.45 | 0.75 | 1.00 | — |
| 2008 Mo | 249,279,000 | — | 0.45 | 0.75 | 1.00 | — |
| 2009 Mo | 90,602,000 | — | 0.45 | 0.75 | 1.00 | — |

**KM# 936 50 CENTAVOS**
3.10 g., Stainless Steel, 17 mm. **Obv:** National arms **Rev:** Value and date within wreath **Edge:** Reeded

| Date | Mintage | VF20 | XF40 | MS60 | MS63 | MS65 |
|---|---|---|---|---|---|---|
| 2009 Mo | 19,910,000 | — | — | 0.75 | 1.00 | — |
| 2010 Mo | 114,567,000 | — | — | 0.75 | 1.00 | — |
| 2011 Mo | 194,480,000 | — | — | 0.75 | 1.00 | — |
| 2012 Mo | 359,183,000 | — | — | 0.60 | 0.75 | — |
| 2013 Mo | Est. 359338000 | — | — | 0.60 | 0.75 | — |
| (2014) Mo | — | — | — | 0.50 | 0.60 | — |

**KM# 603 PESO**
3.95 g., Bi-Metallic Aluminum-Bronze center in Stainless Steel ring, 21 mm. **Obv:** National arms, eagle left within circle **Rev:** Value and date within circle **Note:** Similar to KM#550 but without N.

| Date | Mintage | VF20 | XF40 | MS60 | MS63 | MS65 |
|---|---|---|---|---|---|---|
| 2001 Mo | 208,576,000 | — | — | 1.25 | 2.75 | — |
| 2002 Mo | 119,514,000 | — | — | 1.25 | 2.75 | — |
| 2003 Mo | 169,320,000 | — | — | 1.25 | 2.75 | — |
| 2004 Mo | 208,611,000 | — | — | 1.25 | 2.75 | — |
| 2005 Mo | 253,923,000 | — | — | 1.25 | 2.75 | — |
| 2006 Mo | 289,834,000 | — | — | 1.25 | 2.75 | — |
| 2007 Mo | 368,408,000 | — | — | 1.25 | 2.75 | — |
| 2008 Mo | 363,878,000 | — | — | 1.25 | 2.75 | — |
| 2009 Mo | 239,229,000 | — | — | 1.25 | 2.75 | — |
| 2010 Mo | 209,313,000 | — | — | 0.75 | 1.25 | — |
| 2011 Mo | 199,283,000 | — | — | 0.75 | 1.00 | — |
| 2012 Mo | 383,908,000 | — | — | 0.75 | 1.00 | — |
| 2013 Mo | Est. 264288000 | — | — | 0.75 | 1.00 | — |
| 2014 Mo | — | — | — | 0.60 | 0.75 | — |

**KM# 604 2 PESOS**
5.19 g., Bi-Metallic Aluminum-Bronze center in Stainless Steel ring, 23 mm. **Obv:** National arms, eagle left within circle **Rev:** Value and date within center circle of assorted emblems **Note:** Similar to KM#551, but denomination without N.

| Date | Mintage | VF20 | XF40 | MS60 | MS63 | MS65 |
|---|---|---|---|---|---|---|
| 2001 Mo | 74,563,000 | — | — | 2.35 | 4.00 | — |
| 2002 Mo | 74,547,000 | — | — | 2.35 | 4.00 | — |
| 2003 Mo | 39,814,000 | — | — | 2.35 | 4.00 | — |
| 2004 Mo | 89,496,000 | — | — | 2.35 | 4.00 | — |
| 2005 Mo | 94,532,000 | — | — | 2.35 | 4.00 | — |
| 2006 Mo | 144,123,000 | — | — | 2.35 | 4.00 | — |
| 2007 Mo | 129,422,000 | — | — | 2.35 | 4.00 | — |
| 2008 Mo | 134,235,000 | — | — | 2.35 | 4.00 | — |
| 2009 Mo | 64,650,000 | — | — | 2.35 | 4.00 | — |
| 2010 Mo | 34,878,000 | — | — | 1.00 | 1.50 | — |
| 2011 Mo | 114,522,000 | — | — | 1.00 | 1.50 | — |
| 2012 Mo | 134,445,000 | — | — | 1.00 | 1.25 | — |
| 2013 Mo | Est. 104596000 | — | — | 1.00 | 1.25 | — |

**KM# 605 5 PESOS**
7.07 g., Bi-Metallic Aluminum-Bronze center in Stainless Steel ring, 25.5 mm. **Obv:** National arms, eagle left within circle **Rev:** Value within circle **Note:** Similar to KM#552 but denomination without N.

| Date | Mintage | VF20 | XF40 | MS60 | MS63 | MS65 |
|---|---|---|---|---|---|---|
| 2001 Mo | 79,169,000 | — | 2.00 | 3.50 | 8.00 | — |
| 2002 Mo | 34,754,000 | — | 2.00 | 3.50 | 6.00 | — |
| 2003 Mo | 54,676,000 | — | 2.00 | 3.50 | 6.00 | — |
| 2004 Mo | 89,518,000 | — | 2.00 | 3.50 | 6.00 | — |
| 2005 Mo | 94,482,000 | — | 2.00 | 3.50 | 6.00 | — |
| 2006 Mo | 89,447,000 | — | 2.00 | 3.50 | 6.00 | — |
| 2007 Mo | 123,382,000 | — | 2.00 | 3.50 | 6.00 | — |
| 2008 Mo | 9,939,000 | — | 2.50 | 4.00 | 6.00 | — |
| 2009 Mo | 9,898,000 | — | 2.50 | 4.00 | 6.00 | — |
| 2010 Mo | 6,929,000 | — | 2.50 | 3.00 | 3.50 | — |
| 2011 Mo | 209,214,000 | — | 1.00 | 2.00 | 2.50 | — |
| 2012 Mo | 159,398,000 | — | — | 2.00 | 2.50 | — |
| 2013 Mo | Est. 129464000 | — | — | 2.00 | 2.50 | — |
| 2014 Mo | — | — | — | 1.50 | 2.00 | — |

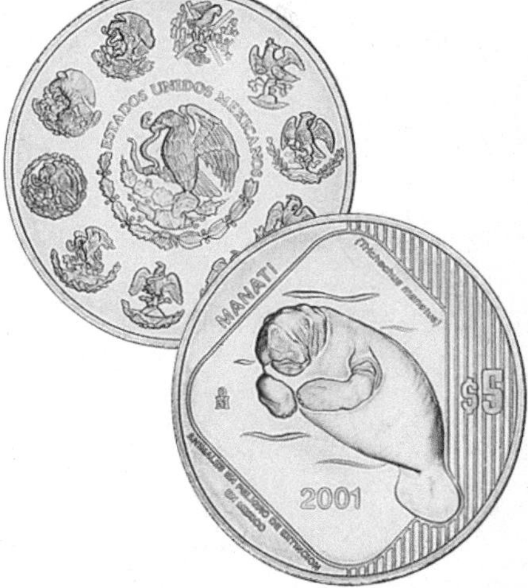

**KM# 651 5 PESOS**
31.10 g., 0.999 Silver 0.999 oz. ASW, 40 mm. **Subject:** Endangered Wildlife - Manatee **Obv:** National arms in center of past and present arms **Rev:** Manatee, value and date **Edge:** Reeded

| Date | Mintage | VF20 | XF40 | MS60 | MS63 | MS65 |
|---|---|---|---|---|---|---|
| 2001 Mo | 30,000 | — | — | — | 45.00 | 50.00 |

## KM# 653 5 PESOS

31.10 g., 0.999 Silver 0.999 oz. ASW, 40 mm. **Series:** Endangered Wildlife **Subject:** Harpy Eagle (Aguila Arpia) **Obv:** National arms in center of past and present arms **Rev:** Crowned Harpy Eagle perched on branch, value and date

| Date | Mintage | VF20 | XF40 | MS60 | MS63 | MS65 |
|---|---|---|---|---|---|---|
| 2001 Mo | 30,000 | — | — | — | 45.00 | 50.00 |

## KM# 654 5 PESOS

31.10 g., 0.999 Silver 0.999 oz. ASW, 40 mm. **Series:** Endangered Wildlife **Subject:** Black Bear (Oso Negro) **Obv:** National arms in center of past and present arms **Rev:** Black bear, value and date

| Date | Mintage | VF20 | XF40 | MS60 | MS63 | MS65 |
|---|---|---|---|---|---|---|
| 2001 Mo | 30,000 | — | — | — | 45.00 | 50.00 |

## KM# 658 5 PESOS

31.10 g., 0.999 Silver 0.999 oz. ASW, 40 mm. **Subject:** Endangered Wildlife - Jaguar **Obv:** National arms in center of past and present arms **Rev:** Jaguar, value and date

| Date | Mintage | VF20 | XF40 | MS60 | MS63 | MS65 |
|---|---|---|---|---|---|---|
| 2001 Mo | 30,000 | — | — | — | 45.00 | 50.00 |

## KM# 659 5 PESOS

31.10 g., 0.999 Silver 0.999 oz. ASW, 40 mm. **Subject:** Endangered Wildlife - Prairie Dog **Obv:** National arms in center of past and present arms **Rev:** Prairie dog, value and date

| Date | Mintage | VF20 | XF40 | MS60 | MS63 | MS65 |
|---|---|---|---|---|---|---|
| 2001 Mo | 30,000 | — | — | — | 45.00 | 50.00 |

## KM# 660 5 PESOS

31.10 g., 0.999 Silver 0.999 oz. ASW, 40 mm. **Subject:** Endangered Wildlife - Volcano Rabbit **Obv:** National arms in center of past and present arms **Rev:** Volcano rabbit, value and date

| Date | Mintage | VF20 | XF40 | MS60 | MS63 | MS65 |
|---|---|---|---|---|---|---|
| 2001 Mo | 30,000 | — | — | — | 45.00 | 50.00 |

## KM# 678 5 PESOS

27.00 g., 0.925 Silver 0.803 oz. ASW, 40 mm. **Series:** Ibero-America **Subject:** Acapulco Galleon **Obv:** National arms in center of past and present arms **Rev:** Spanish galleon with Pacific Ocean background and trading scene in foreground **Edge:** Reeded

| Date | Mintage | VF20 | XF40 | MS60 | MS63 | MS65 |
|---|---|---|---|---|---|---|
| 2003 Mo | 17,015 | PF65 60.00 | | | | |

## KM# 765 5 PESOS

31.10 g., 0.925 Silver 0.925 oz. ASW, 40 mm. **Series:** Ibero-America **Subject:** Palacio de Bellas Artes **Obv:** Mexican Eagle and Snake **Rev:** Palace of Fine Arts **Edge:** Reeded

| Date | Mintage | VF20 | XF40 | MS60 | MS63 | MS65 |
|---|---|---|---|---|---|---|
| 2005 Mo | 8,005 | PF65 90.00 | | | | |

## KM# 769 5 PESOS

15.55 g., 0.999 Silver 0.4995 oz. ASW, 33 mm. **Subject:** Monetary Reform of 1905 **Obv:** Mexican Eagle and Snake **Rev:** Cap and rays coin design

| Date | Mintage | VF20 | XF40 | MS60 | MS63 | MS65 |
|---|---|---|---|---|---|---|
| 2005 Mo | 1,505 | PF65 40.00 | | | | |

## KM# 770 5 PESOS

31.10 g., 0.999 Silver 0.999 oz. ASW, 40 mm. **Subject:** World Cup Soccer **Obv:** Mexican Eagle and Snake **Rev:** Mayan Pelota player and soccer ball

| Date | Mintage | VF20 | XF40 | MS60 | MS63 | MS65 |
|---|---|---|---|---|---|---|
| 2006 Mo | 40,005 | PF65 90.00 | | | | |

## KM# 805 5 PESOS

31.11 g., 0.925 Silver 0.925 oz. ASW, 40 mm. **Series:** Ibero-America **Obv:** Eagle on cactus within shields **Rev:** Mayan ball game

| Date | Mintage | VF20 | XF40 | MS60 | MS63 | MS65 |
|---|---|---|---|---|---|---|
| 2008 Mo | 8,013 | PF65 75.00 | | | | |

## KM# 894 5 PESOS

7.07 g., Bi-Metallic Aluminum-bronze center in stainless steel ring, 25.5 mm. **Series:** Mexican Independence, 200th Anniversary **Subject:** Ignacio Rayon **Obv:** National Arms - Eagle left **Rev:** Ignacio Rayon bust left

| Date | Mintage | VF20 | XF40 | MS60 | MS63 | MS65 |
|---|---|---|---|---|---|---|
| 2008 Mo | 9,934,397 | — | 0.75 | 1.50 | — | — |
| 2008 Mo Prooflike | 4,267 | — | — | — | 7.50 | — |

## KM# 895 5 PESOS

7.07 g., Bi-Metallic Aluminum-bronze center in stainless steel ring, 25.5 mm. **Series:** Mexican Revolution 100th Anniversary **Subject:** Alvaro Obregon **Obv:** National Arms - Eagle left **Rev:** Alvaro Obregon bust 3/4 facing left

| Date | Mintage | VF20 | XF40 | MS60 | MS63 | MS65 |
|---|---|---|---|---|---|---|
| 2008 Mo | 9,948,722 | — | 0.75 | 1.50 | — | — |
| 2008 Mo Prooflike | 4,727 | — | — | — | 7.50 | — |

## KM# 896 5 PESOS

7.07 g., Bi-Metallic Aluninum-bronze center in stainless steel ring, 25.5 mm. **Series:** Mexican Independence 200th Anniversary **Subject:** Carlos Maria de Bustamante **Obv:** National Arms - Eagle left **Rev:** Carlos Maria de Bustamante bust left

| Date | Mintage | VF20 | XF40 | MS60 | MS63 | MS65 |
|---|---|---|---|---|---|---|
| 2008 Mo | 9,941,302 | — | 0.75 | 1.50 | — | — |
| 2008 Mo Prooflike | 4,852 | — | — | — | 7.50 | — |

## KM# 897 5 PESOS

7.07 g., Bi-Metallic Aluminum-bronze center in stainless steel ring, 25.5 mm. **Series:** Mexican Revolution 100th Anniversary **Subject:** Jose Vasconcelos **Obv:** National Arms - Eagle left **Rev:** Jose Vasconcelos bust left

| Date | Mintage | VF20 | XF40 | MS60 | MS63 | MS65 |
|---|---|---|---|---|---|---|
| 2008 Mo | 9,939,839 | — | 0.75 | 1.50 | — | — |
| 2008 Mo Prooflike | 4,767 | — | — | — | 7.50 | — |

### KM# 898 5 PESOS

7.07 g., Bi-Metallic Aluminum-bronze center in stainless steel ring, 25.5 mm. **Series:** Mexican Independence 200th Anniversary **Subject:** Francisco Xavier Mina **Obv:** National Arms - Eagle left **Rev:** Francisco Mina bust 3/4 facing left

| Date | Mintage | VF20 | XF40 | MS60 | MS63 | MS65 |
|---|---|---|---|---|---|---|
| 2008 Mo | 9,914,938 | — | 0.75 | 1.50 | — | — |
| 2008 Mo Prooflike | 4,523 | — | — | — | 7.50 | — |

### KM# 899 5 PESOS

7.07 g., Bi-Metallic Aluminum-bronze center in stainless steel ring, 25.5 mm. **Series:** Mexican Revolution 100th Anniversary **Subject:** Francisco Villa **Obv:** National Arms - Eagle left **Rev:** Francisco Villa on horseback left

| Date | Mintage | VF20 | XF40 | MS60 | MS63 | MS65 |
|---|---|---|---|---|---|---|
| 2008 Mo | 9,917,084 | — | 0.75 | 1.50 | — | — |
| 2008 Mo Prooflike | 4,866 | — | — | — | 7.50 | — |

### KM# 900.1 5 PESOS

7.07 g., Bi-Metallic Aluminum-Bronze center in Stainless Steel ring, 25.5 mm. **Series:** Mexican Independence 200th Anniversary **Subject:** Francisco Primo de Verdad y Ramos **Obv:** National Arms - Eagle left **Rev:** Francisco Primode Verdad y Ramos bust right **Note:** Pellets at 4 and 7 o'clock in legend.

| Date | Mintage | VF20 | XF40 | MS60 | MS63 | MS65 |
|---|---|---|---|---|---|---|
| 2008 Mo | 9,937,000 | — | 0.75 | 1.50 | — | — |
| 2008 Mo Prooflike | 4,279 | — | — | — | 7.50 | — |

### KM# 900.2 5 PESOS

7.07 g., Bi-Metallic Aluminum-Bronze center in Stainless Steel ring, 25.5 mm. **Series:** Mexican Independence 200th Anniversary **Subject:** Francisco Primode Verdad y Ramos **Obv:** National arms - Eagle left **Rev:** Francisco Primode Verdad y Ramos bust right **Note:** No pellets at 4 and 7 o'clock in legend.

| Date | Mintage | VF20 | XF40 | MS60 | MS63 | MS65 |
|---|---|---|---|---|---|---|
| 2008 Mo | Inc. above | — | — | 10.00 | 15.00 | — |

### KM# 901 5 PESOS

7.07 g., Bi-Metallic Aluminum-Bronze center in Stainless Steel ring, 25.5 mm. **Series:** Mexican Revolution 100th Anniversary **Subject:** Heriberto Jara **Obv:** National Arms - Eagle left **Rev:** Heriberto Jara bust 3/4 left

| Date | Mintage | VF20 | XF40 | MS60 | MS63 | MS65 |
|---|---|---|---|---|---|---|
| 2008 Mo | 9,936,333 | — | 0.75 | 1.50 | — | — |
| 2008 Mo Prooflike | 4,870 | — | — | — | 7.50 | — |

### KM# 902 5 PESOS

7.07 g., Bi-Metallic Aluminum-Bronze center in Stainless Steel ring, 25.5 mm. **Series:** Mexican Independence 200th Anniversary **Subject:** Mariano Matamoros **Obv:** National Arms - Eagle left **Rev:** Mariano Matamoros bust 3/4 facing right

| Date | Mintage | VF20 | XF40 | MS60 | MS63 | MS65 |
|---|---|---|---|---|---|---|
| 2008 Mo | 9,947,802 | — | 0.75 | 1.50 | — | — |
| 2008 Mo Prooflike | 4,820 | — | — | — | 7.50 | — |

### KM# 903 5 PESOS

7.07 g., Bi-Metallic Aluminum-Bronze center in Stainless Steel ring, 25.5 mm. **Series:** Mexican Revolution 100th Anniversary **Subject:** Ricardo Magon **Obv:** National Arms - Eagle left **Rev:** Ricardo Magon bust right

| Date | Mintage | VF20 | XF40 | MS60 | MS63 | MS65 |
|---|---|---|---|---|---|---|
| 2008 Mo | 9,940,278 | — | 0.75 | 1.50 | — | — |
| 2008 Mo Prooflike | 4,690 | — | — | — | 7.50 | — |

### KM# 904 5 PESOS

7.07 g., Bi-Metallic Aluminum-Bronze center in Stainless Steel ring, 25.5 mm. **Series:** Mexican Independence 200th Anniversary **Subject:** Miguel Ramos Arizpe **Obv:** National Arms - Eagle left **Rev:** Miguel Ramos Arizpe bust right

| Date | Mintage | VF20 | XF40 | MS60 | MS63 | MS65 |
|---|---|---|---|---|---|---|
| 2008 Mo | 9,927,433 | — | 0.75 | 1.50 | — | — |
| 2008 Mo Prooflike | 4,863 | — | — | — | 7.50 | — |

### KM# 905 5 PESOS

7.07 g., Bi-Metallic Aluminum-Bronze center in Stainless Steel ring, 25.5 mm. **Series:** Mexican Revolution 100th Anniversary **Subject:** Francisco J. Mugica **Obv:** National arms, eagle left **Rev:** Francisco J. Mugica bust 3/4 facing left

| Date | Mintage | VF20 | XF40 | MS60 | MS63 | MS65 |
|---|---|---|---|---|---|---|
| 2008 Mo | 9,926,537 | — | 0.75 | 1.50 | — | — |
| 2008 Mo Prooflike | 4,588 | — | — | — | 7.50 | — |

### KM# 906 5 PESOS

7.07 g., Bi-Metallic Aluminum-Bronze center in Stainless Steel ring, 25.5 mm. **Series:** Mexican Independence 200th Anniversary **Subject:** Hermenegildo Galeana **Obv:** National Arms, eagle left **Rev:** Hermenegildo Galeana bust 3/4 facing left

| Date | Mintage | VF20 | XF40 | MS60 | MS63 | MS65 |
|---|---|---|---|---|---|---|
| 2008 Mo | 9,935,901 | — | 0.75 | 1.50 | — | — |
| 2008 Mo Prooflike | 4,966 | — | — | — | 7.50 | — |

### KM# 907 5 PESOS

7.07 g., Bi-Metallic Aluminum-Bronze center in Stainless Steel ring, 25.5 mm. **Series:** Mexican Revolution, 100th Anniversary **Subject:** Filomeno Mata **Obv:** National arms, eagle left **Rev:** Filomeno Mata bust facing left

| Date | Mintage | VF20 | XF40 | MS60 | MS63 | MS65 |
|---|---|---|---|---|---|---|
| 2009 Mo | 9,935,689 | — | 0.75 | 1.50 | — | — |
| 2009 Mo Prooflike | 4,920 | — | — | — | 7.50 | — |

### KM# 908 5 PESOS

7.07 g., Bi-Metallic Aluminum-Bronze cetner in Stainless Steel ring, 25.5 mm. **Series:** Mexican Independence 200th Anniversary **Subject:** Jose Maria Cos **Obv:** National arms, eagle left. **Rev:** Jose Maria Cos bust right

| Date | Mintage | VF20 | XF40 | MS60 | MS63 | MS65 |
|---|---|---|---|---|---|---|
| 2009 Mo | 9,935,040 | — | 0.75 | 1.50 | — | — |
| 2009 Mo Prooflike | 4,950 | — | — | — | 7.50 | — |

### KM# 909 5 PESOS

7.07 g., Bi-Metallic Aluminum-Bronze center in Stainless Steel ring, 25.5 mm. **Series:** Mexican Revolution 100th Anniversary **Subject:** Carmen Serdan **Obv:** National Amrs, Eagle left **Rev:** Carmen Serdan bust facing slightly right

| Date | Mintage | VF20 | XF40 | MS60 | MS63 | MS65 |
|---|---|---|---|---|---|---|
| 2009 Mo | 7,160,841 | — | 0.75 | 1.50 | — | — |
| 2009 Mo Prooflike | 4,787 | — | — | — | 7.50 | — |

### KM# 910 5 PESOS

7.07 g., Bi-Metallic Aluminum-Bronze center in Stainless Steel ring, 25.5 mm. **Series:** Mexican Independence, 200th Anniversary **Subject:** Pedro Moreno **Obv:** National arms, eagle left **Rev:** Pedro Moreno bust 3/4 right

| Date | Mintage | VF20 | XF40 | MS60 | MS63 | MS65 |
|---|---|---|---|---|---|---|
| 2009 Mo | 6,942,480 | — | 0.75 | 1.50 | — | — |
| 2009 Mo Prooflike | 4,940 | — | — | — | 7.50 | — |

### KM# 911 5 PESOS

7.07 g., Bi-Metallic Aluminum-Bronze center in Stainless Steel ring, 25.5 mm. **Series:** Mexican Revolution 100th Anniversary **Subject:** Andres Molina Enriquez **Obv:** National arms, eagle left **Rev:** Andres Molina Enriquez, bust 3/4 right

| Date | Mintage | VF20 | XF40 | MS60 | MS63 | MS65 |
|---|---|---|---|---|---|---|
| 2009 Mo | 6,942,763 | — | 0.75 | 1.50 | — | — |
| 2009 Mo Prooflike | 4,666 | — | — | — | 7.50 | — |

### KM# 912 5 PESOS

7.07 g., Bi-Metallic Aluminum-Bronze center in Stainless Steel ring, 25.5 mm. **Series:** Mexican Independence, 200th Anniversary **Subject:** Agustin de Iturbide **Obv:** National arms, eagle left **Rev:** Agustin de Iturbide bust left

| Date | Mintage | VF20 | XF40 | MS60 | MS63 | MS65 |
|---|---|---|---|---|---|---|
| 2009 Mo | 6,944,222 | — | 0.75 | 1.50 | — | — |
| 2009 Mo Prooflike | 4,838 | — | — | — | 7.50 | — |

### KM# 913 5 PESOS

7.07 g., Bi-Metallic Aluminumn-Bronze center in Stainless Steel ring, 25.5 mm. **Series:** Mexican Revolution 100th Anniversary **Subject:** Luis Cabrera **Obv:** National Arms, eagle left **Rev:** Luis Cabrera bust 3/4 facing left

| Date | Mintage | VF20 | XF40 | MS60 | MS63 | MS65 |
|---|---|---|---|---|---|---|
| 2009 Mo | 6,902,593 | — | 0.75 | 1.50 | — | — |
| 2009 Mo Prooflike | 4,656 | — | — | — | 7.50 | — |

### KM# 914 5 PESOS

7.07 g., Bi-Metallic Aluminum-Bronze center Stainless Steel ring, 25.5 mm. **Series:** Mexican Independence 200th Anniversary **Subject:** Nicolas Bravo **Obv:** National Arms, Eagle left **Rev:** Nicolas Bravo bust 3/4 facing left

| Date | Mintage | VF20 | XF40 | MS60 | MS63 | MS65 |
|---|---|---|---|---|---|---|
| 2009 Mo | 6,930,174 | — | 0.75 | 0.50 | — | — |
| 2009 Mo Prooflike | 4,780 | — | — | — | 7.50 | — |

### KM# 915 5 PESOS

7.07 g., Bi-Metallic Aluminum-bronze center in Stainless steel ring, 25.5 mm. **Series:** Mexican Revolution 100th Anniversary **Subject:** Eulalio Gutierrez **Obv:** National Arms, eagle left **Rev:** Eulalio Gutierrez bust 3/4 right

| Date | Mintage | VF20 | XF40 | MS60 | MS63 | MS65 |
|---|---|---|---|---|---|---|
| 2009 Mo | 6,908,760 | — | 0.75 | 1.50 | — | — |
| 2009 Mo Prooflike | 4,862 | — | — | — | 7.50 | — |

### KM# 916 5 PESOS

7.07 g., Bi-Metallic Aluminum-Bronze center in Stainless Steel ring, 25.5 mm. **Series:** Mexican Independence 200th Anniversary **Subject:** Servando Teresa de Mier **Obv:** National Arms, eagle left **Rev:** Servando Teresa de Mier bust left

| Date | Mintage | VF20 | XF40 | MS60 | MS63 | MS65 |
|---|---|---|---|---|---|---|
| 2009 Mo | 6,937,421 | — | 0.75 | 1.50 | — | — |
| 2009 Mo Prooflike | 4,675 | — | — | — | 7.50 | — |

### KM# 917 5 PESOS

7.07 g., Bi-Metallic Aluminum-Bronze center in Stainless Steel ring, 25.5 mm. **Series:** Mexican Revolution 100th Anniversary **Subject:** Otilio Montano **Obv:** National Arms, eagle left **Rev:** Otilio Montano bust left

| Date | Mintage | VF20 | XF40 | MS60 | MS63 | MS65 |
|---|---|---|---|---|---|---|
| 2009 Mo | 6,890,052 | — | 0.75 | 1.50 | — | — |
| 2009 Mo Prooflike | 4,923 | — | — | — | 7.50 | — |

### KM# 918 5 PESOS

7.07 g., Bi-Metallic Aluminum-Bronze center in Stainless Steel ring, 25.5 mm. **Series:** Mexican Revolution 100th Anniversary **Subject:** Belisario Dominguez **Obv:** National Arms, eagle left **Rev:** Belisario Dominguez bust 3/4 left

| Date | Mintage | VF20 | XF40 | MS60 | MS63 | MS65 |
|---|---|---|---|---|---|---|
| 2009 Mo | 6,926,606 | — | 0.75 | 1.50 | — | — |
| 2009 Mo Prooflike | 4,773 | — | — | — | 7.50 | — |

### KM# 919 5 PESOS

7.07 g., Bi-Metallic Aluminum-Bronze center in Stainless Steel ring, 25.5 mm. **Series:** Mexican Independence 200th Anniversary **Subject:** Leona Vicario **Obv:** National Arms, eagle left **Rev:** Leona Vicario bust left

| Date | Mintage | VF20 | XF40 | MS60 | MS63 | MS65 |
|---|---|---|---|---|---|---|
| 2009 Mo | 6,937,872 | — | 0.75 | 1.50 | — | — |
| 2009 Mo Prooflike | 4,730 | — | — | — | 7.50 | — |

### KM# 920 5 PESOS

7.07 g., Bi-Metallic Aluminum-Bronze center in Stainless Steel ring, 25.5 mm. **Series:** Mexican Independence 200th Anniversary **Subject:** Miguel Hidalgo y Costilla **Obv:** National Arms, eagle left **Rev:** Miguel Hidalgo y Costilla bust

| Date | Mintage | VF20 | XF40 | MS60 | MS63 | MS65 |
|---|---|---|---|---|---|---|
| 2010 Mo | 6,932,486 | — | 0.75 | 1.50 | — | — |
| 2010 Mo Prooflike | 4,763 | — | — | — | 7.50 | — |

### KM# 922 5 PESOS

7.07 g., Bi-Metallic Aluminum-Bronze center in Stainless Steel ring, 25.5 mm. **Series:** Mexican Revolution 100th Anniversary **Subject:** Francisco I. Madero **Rev:** Francisco I. Madero head facing 1/4 left

| Date | Mintage | VF20 | XF40 | MS60 | MS63 | MS65 |
|---|---|---|---|---|---|---|
| 2010 Mo | 6,930,998 | — | 0.75 | 1.50 | — | — |
| 2010 Mo Prooflike | 4,750 | — | — | — | 7.50 | — |

### KM# 923 5 PESOS

7.07 g., Bi-Metallic Aluminum-Bronze center in Stainless Steel ring, 25.5 mm. **Series:** Mexican Independence 200th Anniversary **Subject:** Jose Maria Morelos y Pavon **Rev:** Jose Maria Morelos y Pavon head facing 1/2 right

| Date | Mintage | VF20 | XF40 | MS60 | MS63 | MS65 |
|---|---|---|---|---|---|---|
| 2010 Mo | 6,927,961 | — | 0.75 | 1.50 | — | — |
| 2010 Mo Prooflike | 4,725 | — | — | — | 7.50 | — |

### KM# 924 5 PESOS

7.07 g., Bi-Metallic Aluminum-Bronze center in Stainless Steel ring, 25.5 mm. **Series:** Mexican Revolution 100th Anniversary **Subject:** Emiliano Zapata **Rev:** Emiliano Zapata head 1/4 facing left

| Date | Mintage | VF20 | XF40 | MS60 | MS63 | MS65 |
|---|---|---|---|---|---|---|
| 2010 Mo | 6,921,306 | — | 0.75 | 1.50 | — | — |
| 2010 Mo Prooflike | 4,810 | — | — | — | 7.50 | — |

### KM# 925 5 PESOS

7.07 g., Bi-Metallic Aluminum-Bronze center in Stainless Steel ring, 25.5 mm. **Series:** Mexican Independence 200th Anniversary **Subject:** Vicente Guerrero **Rev:** Vicente Guerrero head facing 1/4 left

| Date | Mintage | VF20 | XF40 | MS60 | MS63 | MS65 |
|---|---|---|---|---|---|---|
| 2010 Mo | 6,929,709 | — | 0.75 | 1.50 | — | — |
| 2010 Mo Prooflike | 4,716 | — | — | — | 7.50 | — |

### KM# 926 5 PESOS

7.07 g., Bi-Metallic Aluminum-Bronze center in Stainless Steel ring, 25.5 mm. **Series:** Mexican Revolution 100th Anniversary **Subject:** Venustiano Carranza **Rev:** Venustiano Carranza head 1/4 facing left

| Date | Mintage | VF20 | XF40 | MS60 | MS63 | MS65 |
|---|---|---|---|---|---|---|
| 2010 Mo | 6,936,993 | — | 0.75 | 1.50 | — | — |
| 2010 Mo Prooflike | 4,837 | — | — | — | 7.50 | — |

### KM# 927 5 PESOS

7.07 g., Bi-Metallic Aluminum-Bronze center in Stainless Steel ring, 25.5 mm. **Series:** Mexican Independence 200th Anniversary **Subject:** Ignacio Allende **Rev:** Ignacio Allende head facing 1/2 left

| Date | Mintage | VF20 | XF40 | MS60 | MS63 | MS65 |
|---|---|---|---|---|---|---|
| 2010 Mo | 6,939,957 | — | 0.75 | 1.50 | — | — |
| 2010 Mo Prooflike | 4,752 | — | — | — | 7.50 | — |

### KM# 928 5 PESOS

7.07 g., Bi-Metallic Aluminum-Bronze center in Stainless Steel ring, 25.5 mm. **Series:** Mexican Revolution 100th Anniversary **Subject:** La Soldadera **Rev:** Female soldier's head facing 1/4 left

| Date | Mintage | VF20 | XF40 | MS60 | MS63 | MS65 |
|---|---|---|---|---|---|---|
| 2010 Mo | 6,936,336 | — | 0.75 | 1.50 | — | — |
| 2010 Mo Prooflike | 4,730 | — | — | — | 7.50 | — |

### KM# 929 5 PESOS

7.07 g., Bi-Metallic Aluminum-Bronze center in Stainless Steel ring, 25.5 mm. **Series:** Mexican Indpendence 200th Anniversary **Subject:** Guadalupe Victoria **Rev:** Guadalupe Victoria head 1/4 facing left

| Date | Mintage | VF20 | XF40 | MS60 | MS63 | MS65 |
|---|---|---|---|---|---|---|
| 2010 Mo | 6,934,638 | — | 0.75 | 1.50 | — | — |
| 2010 Mo Prooflike | 4,767 | — | — | — | 7.50 | — |

### KM# 930 5 PESOS

7.07 g., Bi-Metallic Aluminum-Bronze center in Stainless Steel ring, 25.5 mm. **Series:** Mexican Revolution 100th Anniversary **Subject:** Jose Mario Pino Suarez **Rev:** Jose Mario Pino Suarez head

| Date | Mintage | VF20 | XF40 | MS60 | MS63 | MS65 |
|---|---|---|---|---|---|---|
| 2010 Mo | 6,930,255 | — | 0.75 | 1.50 | — | — |
| 2010 Mo Prooflike | 4,752 | — | — | — | 7.50 | — |

### KM# 931 5 PESOS

7.07 g., Bi-Metallic Aluminum-Bronze center in Stainless Steel ring, 25.5 mm. **Series:** Mexican Independence 200th Anniversary **Subject:** Josefa Ortiz de Dominguez **Rev:** Josefa Ortiz de Dominguez head right

| Date | Mintage | VF20 | XF40 | MS60 | MS63 | MS65 |
|---|---|---|---|---|---|---|
| 2010 Mo | 6,936,400 | — | 0.75 | 1.50 | — | — |
| 2010 Mo Prooflike | 4,743 | — | — | — | 7.50 | — |

### KM# 944 5 PESOS

27.01 g., 0.925 Silver 0.8031 oz. ASW, 40 mm. **Series:** Ibero-American **Subject:** Ibero-American Historical Coins **Obv:** National arms (eagle and snake facing left), legend **Obv. Legend:** ESTADOS UNIDOS MEXICANOS **Rev:** Mexican Cabillito Peso, legend **Rev. Legend:** MONEDAS HISTORICAS IBEROAMERICANAS

| Date | Mintage | VF20 | XF40 | MS60 | MS63 | MS65 |
|---|---|---|---|---|---|---|
| 2010 Mo | 8,000 | PF65 70.00 | | | | |

### KM# 945 5 PESOS

31.10 g., 0.999 Silver 0.9989 oz. ASW, 40 mm. **Subject:** Chichen Itza, the Nunnery **Obv:** National arms (eagle and snake facing left), legend **Obv. Legend:** ESTADOS UNIDOS MEXICANOS **Rev:** Nunnery of Chichen Itza, legend

| Date | Mintage | VF20 | XF40 | MS60 | MS63 | MS65 |
|---|---|---|---|---|---|---|
| ND-2011 Mo | 10,000 | PF65 90.00 | | | | |

### KM# 946 5 PESOS

31.10 g., 0.999 Silver 0.9989 oz. ASW, 40 mm. **Subject:** Chichen Itza, the Observatory **Obv:** National arms (eagle and snake facing left) legend **Obv. Legend:** ESTADOS UNIDOS MEXICANOS **Rev:** Observatory of Chichen Itza, legend **Rev. Legend:** OBSRVATORIO

| Date | Mintage | VF20 | XF40 | MS60 | MS63 | MS65 |
|---|---|---|---|---|---|---|
| ND-2011 | 10,000 | PF65 90.00 | | | | |

### KM# 947 5 PESOS

31.10 g., 0.999 Silver 0.999 oz. ASW, 40 mm. **Subject:** Chichen Itza, the Church **Obv:** National Arms (eagle and snake facing left) legend **Obv. Legend:** ESTADOS UNIDOS MEXICANOS **Rev:** Churcy of Chichen Itza, legend **Rev. Legend:** CHICHEN ITZA, LA IGLESIA 070707

| Date | Mintage | VF20 | XF40 | MS60 | MS63 | MS65 |
|---|---|---|---|---|---|---|
| ND-2011 Mo | 3,000 | PF65 80.00 | | | | |

### KM# 962 5 PESOS

27.00 g., 0.925 Silver 0.803 oz. ASW, 40 mm. **Series:** Ibero-American Series **Obv:** National arms within circle of other national arms **Rev:** Horse Peso

| Date | Mintage | VF20 | XF40 | MS60 | MS63 | MS65 |
|---|---|---|---|---|---|---|
| 2011 Mo | 8,000 | PF65 80.00 | | | | |

### KM# 616 10 PESOS

10.33 g., Bi-Metallic Copper-Nickel-Zinc center in Aluminum-Bronze ring, 28 mm. **Obv:** National arms **Obv. Legend:** ESTADOS UNIDOS MEXICANOS **Rev:** Aztec design of Tonatiuh with the Fire Mask

| Date | Mintage | VF20 | XF40 | MS60 | MS63 | MS65 |
|---|---|---|---|---|---|---|
| 2002 Mo | 44,721,000 | — | 2.50 | 4.00 | 8.00 | — |
| 2004 Mo | 74,739,000 | — | 2.50 | 4.00 | 8.00 | — |
| 2005 Mo | 64,616,000 | — | 2.50 | 4.00 | 8.00 | — |
| 2006 Mo | 84,575,000 | — | 2.50 | 4.00 | 8.00 | — |
| 2007 Mo | 89,678,000 | — | 2.50 | 4.00 | 8.00 | — |
| 2008 Mo | 64,744,000 | — | 2.50 | 4.00 | 8.00 | — |
| 2009 Mo | 54,812,000 | — | 2.00 | 3.00 | 6.00 | — |
| 2010 Mo | 54,822,000 | — | 2.00 | 3.00 | 6.00 | — |
| 2011 Mo | 69,731,000 | — | — | 3.00 | 6.00 | — |
| 2012 Mo | 89,732,000 | — | — | 3.00 | 6.00 | — |
| 2013 Mo | Est. 44769000 | — | — | 2.50 | 3.00 | — |
| 2014 Mo | — | — | — | 2.00 | 2.50 | — |

### KM# 636 10 PESOS

10.33 g., Bi-Metallic Copper-Nickel-Zinc center in Aluminum-Bronze ring, 28 mm. **Series:** Millennium **Obv:** National arms **Obv. Legend:** ESTADOS UNIDOS MEXICANOS **Rev:** Aztec carving **Edge Lettering:** ANO (year) repeated 3 times

| Date | Mintage | VF20 | XF40 | MS60 | MS63 | MS65 |
|---|---|---|---|---|---|---|
| 2001 Mo | 44,768,000 | — | 3.00 | 4.00 | 8.00 | — |

### KM# 679 10 PESOS

31.10 g., 0.999 Silver 0.999 oz. ASW, 39.9 mm. **Series:** First **Subject:** 180th Anniversary of Federation **Obv:** National arms **Obv. Legend:** ESTADOS UNIDOS MEXICANOS **Rev:** State Arms **Rev. Legend:** ESTADO DE ZACATECAS **Edge:** Reeded

| Date | Mintage | VF20 | XF40 | MS60 | MS63 | MS65 |
|---|---|---|---|---|---|---|
| 2003 Mo | 10,000 | PF65 70.00 | | | | |

### KM# 680 10 PESOS

31.10 g., 0.999 Silver 0.999 oz. ASW, 39.9 mm. **Series:** First **Subject:** 180th Anniversary of Federation **Obv:** National arms **Obv. Legend:** ESTADO UNIDOS MEXICANOS **Rev:** State arms **Rev. Legend:** ESTADO DE YUCATÁN **Edge:** Reeded

| Date | Mintage | VF20 | XF40 | MS60 | MS63 | MS65 |
|---|---|---|---|---|---|---|
| 2003 Mo | 10,000 | PF65 60.00 | | | | |

### KM# 681 10 PESOS

31.10 g., 0.999 Silver 0.999 oz. ASW, 39.9 mm. **Series:** First **Subject:** 180th Anniversary of Federation **Obv:** National arms **Obv. Legend:** ESTADOS UNIDOS MEXICANOS **Rev:** State arms **Rev. Legend:** ESTADO DE VERACRUZ-LLAVE **Edge:** Reeded

| Date | Mintage | VF20 | XF40 | MS60 | MS63 | MS65 |
|---|---|---|---|---|---|---|
| 2003 Mo | 10,000 | PF65 60.00 | | | | |

### KM# 682 10 PESOS

31.10 g., 0.999 Silver 0.999 oz. ASW, 39.9 mm. **Series:** First **Subject:** 180th Anniversary of Frederation **Obv:** National arms **Obv. Legend:** ESTADOS UNIDOS MEXICANOS **Rev:** State arms **Rev. Legend:** ESTADO DE TLAXCALA **Edge:** Reeded

| Date | Mintage | VF20 | XF40 | MS60 | MS63 | MS65 |
|---|---|---|---|---|---|---|
| 2003 Mo | 10,000 | PF65 60.00 | | | | |

### KM# 683 10 PESOS

31.10 g., 0.999 Silver 0.999 oz. ASW, 39.9 mm. **Series:** First **Subject:** 180th Anniversary of Federation **Obv:** National arms **Obv. Legend:** ESTADOS UNIDOS MEXICANOS **Rev:** State arms **Rev. Legend:** ESTADO DE TAMAULIPAS **Edge:** Reeded

| Date | Mintage | VF20 | XF40 | MS60 | MS63 | MS65 |
|---|---|---|---|---|---|---|
| 2004 Mo | 10,000 | PF65 60.00 | | | | |

### KM# 684 10 PESOS

31.10 g., 0.999 Silver 0.999 oz. ASW, 39.9 mm. **Series:** First **Subject:** 180th Anniversary of Federation **Obv:** National arms **Obv. Legend:** ESTADOS UNIDOS DE MEXICANOS **Rev:** State arms **Rev. Legend:** ESTADO DE TABASCO **Edge:** Reeded

| Date | Mintage | VF20 | XF40 | MS60 | MS63 | MS65 |
|---|---|---|---|---|---|---|
| 2004 Mo | 10,000 | PF65 60.00 | | | | |

**KM# 685 10 PESOS**
31.10 g., 0.999 Silver 0.999 oz. ASW, 39.9 mm. **Series:** First **Subject:** 180th Anniversary of Federation **Obv:** National arms **Obv. Legend:** ESTADOS UNIDOS MEXICANOS **Rev:** State arms **Rev. Legend:** ESTADO DE SONORA **Edge:** Reeded **Note:** Mexican States: Sonora

| Date | Mintage | VF20 | XF40 | MS60 | MS63 | MS65 |
|---|---|---|---|---|---|---|
| 2004 Mo | 10,000 | PF65 60.00 | | | | |

**KM# 686 10 PESOS**
31.10 g., 0.999 Silver 0.999 oz. ASW, 39.9 mm. **Series:** First **Subject:** 180th Anniversary of Federation **Obv:** National arms **Obv. Legend:** ESTADOS UNIDOS DE MEXICANOS **Rev:** State arms **Rev. Legend:** ESTADO DE SINALOA **Edge:** Reeded **Note:** Mexican States: Sinaloa

| Date | Mintage | VF20 | XF40 | MS60 | MS63 | MS65 |
|---|---|---|---|---|---|---|
| 2004 Mo | 10,000 | PF65 60.00 | | | | |

**KM# 687 10 PESOS**
31.10 g., 0.999 Silver 0.999 oz. ASW, 39.9 mm. **Series:** First **Subject:** 180th Anniversary of Federation **Obv:** National arms **Obv. Legend:** ESTADOS UNIDOS MEXICANOS **Rev:** State arms **Rev. Legend:** ESTADO DE SAN LUIS POTOSÍ **Edge:** Reeded

| Date | Mintage | VF20 | XF40 | MS60 | MS63 | MS65 |
|---|---|---|---|---|---|---|
| 2004 Mo | 10,000 | PF65 60.00 | | | | |

**KM# 733 10 PESOS**
31.10 g., 0.999 Silver 0.999 oz. ASW, 39.9 mm. **Series:** First **Subject:** 180th Anniversary of Federation **Obv:** National arms **Obv. Legend:** ESTADOS UNIDOS MEXICANOS **Rev:** State arms **Rev. Legend:** ESTADO DE QUERÉTARO ARTEAGA **Edge:** Reeded

| Date | Mintage | VF20 | XF40 | MS60 | MS63 | MS65 |
|---|---|---|---|---|---|---|
| 2004 Mo | 10,000 | PF65 60.00 | | | | |

**KM# 735 10 PESOS**
31.10 g., 0.999 Silver 0.999 oz. ASW, 39.9 mm. **Series:** First **Subject:** 180th Anniversary of Federation **Obv:** National arms **Obv. Legend:** ESTADOS UNIDOS MEXICANOS **Rev:** State arms **Rev. Legend:** ESTADO DE QUINTANA ROO

| Date | Mintage | VF20 | XF40 | MS60 | MS63 | MS65 |
|---|---|---|---|---|---|---|
| 2004 Mo | 10,000 | PF65 60.00 | | | | |

**KM# 737 10 PESOS**
31.10 g., 0.999 Silver 0.999 oz. ASW, 39.9 mm. **Series:** First **Subject:** 180th Anniversary of Federation **Obv:** National arms **Obv. Legend:** ESTADOS UNIDOS MEXICANOS **Rev:** State arms **Rev. Legend:** ESTADO DE PUEBLA **Edge:** Reeded

| Date | Mintage | VF20 | XF40 | MS60 | MS63 | MS65 |
|---|---|---|---|---|---|---|
| 2004 Mo | 10,000 | PF65 60.00 | | | | |

**KM# 739 10 PESOS**
31.10 g., 0.999 Bi-Metallic 0.999 oz., 39.9 mm. **Series:** First **Subject:** 180th Anniversary of Federation **Obv:** National arms **Obv. Legend:** ESTADOS UNIDOS MEXICANOS **Rev:** State arms **Rev. Legend:** ESTADO DE OAXACA **Edge:** Reeded

| Date | Mintage | VF20 | XF40 | MS60 | MS63 | MS65 |
|---|---|---|---|---|---|---|
| 2004 Mo | 10,000 | PF65 60.00 | | | | |

**KM# 741 10 PESOS**
31.10 g., 0.999 Silver 0.999 oz. ASW, 39.9 mm. **Series:** First **Subject:** 180th Anniversary of Federation **Obv:** National arms **Obv. Legend:** ESTADOS UNIDOS MEXICANOS **Rev:** State arms **Rev. Legend:** ESTADO DE NUEVO LEÓN **Edge:** Reeded

| Date | Mintage | VF20 | XF40 | MS60 | MS63 | MS65 |
|---|---|---|---|---|---|---|
| 2004 Mo | 10,000 | PF65 60.00 | | | | |

**KM# 743 10 PESOS**
31.10 g., 0.999 Silver 0.999 oz. ASW, 39.9 mm. **Series:** First **Subject:** 180th Anniversary of Federation **Obv:** National arms **Obv. Legend:** ESTADOS UNIDOS MEXICANOS **Rev:** State arms **Rev. Legend:** ESTADO DE NAYARIT **Edge:** Reeded

| Date | Mintage | VF20 | XF40 | MS60 | MS63 | MS65 |
|---|---|---|---|---|---|---|
| 2004 Mo | 10,000 | PF65 60.00 | | | | |

**KM# 745 10 PESOS**
31.10 g., 0.999 Silver 0.999 oz. ASW, 39.9 mm. **Series:** First **Subject:** 180th Anniversary of Federation **Obv:** National arms **Obv. Legend:** ESTADOS UNIDOS MEXICANOS **Rev:** State arms **Rev. Legend:** ESTADO DE MORELOS **Edge:** Reeded

| Date | Mintage | VF20 | XF40 | MS60 | MS63 | MS65 |
|---|---|---|---|---|---|---|
| 2004 Mo | 10,000 | PF65 60.00 | | | | |

**KM# 747 10 PESOS**
31.10 g., 0.999 Silver 0.999 oz. ASW, 39.9 mm. **Series:** First **Subject:** 180th Anniversary of Federation **Obv:** National arms **Obv. Legend:** ESTADOS UNIDOS MEXICANOS **Rev:** State arms **Rev. Legend:** ESTADO DE MÉXICO **Edge:** Reeded

| Date | Mintage | VF20 | XF40 | MS60 | MS63 | MS65 |
|---|---|---|---|---|---|---|
| 2004 Mo | 10,000 | PF65 60.00 | | | | |

**KM# 749 10 PESOS**
31.10 g., 0.999 Silver 0.999 oz. ASW, 39.9 mm. **Series:** First **Subject:** 180th Anniversary of Federation **Obv:** National arms **Obv. Legend:** ESTADOS UNIDOS MEXICANOS **Rev:** State arms **Rev. Legend:** ESTADO DE JALISCO **Edge:** Reeded

| Date | Mintage | VF20 | XF40 | MS60 | MS63 | MS65 |
|---|---|---|---|---|---|---|
| 2004 Mo | 10,000 | PF65 60.00 | | | | |

**KM# 796 10 PESOS**

31.10 g., 0.999 Silver 0.999 oz. ASW, 39.9 mm. **Series:** First **Subject:** 180th Anniversary of Federation **Obv:** National arms **Obv. Legend:** ESTADOS UNIDOS MEXICANOS **Rev:** State arms **Rev. Legend:** ESTADO DE MICHOACÁN DE OCAMPO **Edge:** Reeded

| Date | Mintage | VF20 | XF40 | MS60 | MS63 | MS65 |
|---|---|---|---|---|---|---|
| 2004 Mo | 10,000 | PF65 60.00 | | | | |

**KM# 961 10 PESOS**

31.10 g., 0.999 Silver 0.9989 oz. ASW, 40 mm. **Subject:** National University, 75th Anniversary

| Date | Mintage | VF20 | XF40 | MS60 | MS63 | MS65 |
|---|---|---|---|---|---|---|
| 2010 | — | PF65 100 | | | | |

**KM# 706 10 PESOS**

31.10 g., 0.999 Silver 0.999 oz. ASW, 39.9 mm. **Series:** First **Subject:** 180th Anniversary of Federation **Obv:** National arms **Obv. Legend:** ESTADOS UNIDOS MEXICANOS **Rev:** State arms **Rev. Legend:** ESTADO DE CHIAPAS **Edge:** Reeded

| Date | Mintage | VF20 | XF40 | MS60 | MS63 | MS65 |
|---|---|---|---|---|---|---|
| 2005 Mo | 10,000 | PF65 60.00 | | | | |

**KM# 707 10 PESOS**

31.10 g., 0.999 Silver 0.999 oz. ASW, 39.9 mm. **Series:** First **Subject:** 180th Anniversary of Federation **Obv:** National arms **Obv. Legend:** ESTADOS UNIDOS MEXICANOS **Rev:** Federal District arms **Rev. Legend:** DISTRITO FEDERAL **Edge:** Reeded

| Date | Mintage | VF20 | XF40 | MS60 | MS63 | MS65 |
|---|---|---|---|---|---|---|
| 2005 Mo | 10,000 | PF65 60.00 | | | | |

**KM# 708 10 PESOS**

31.10 g., 0.999 Silver 0.999 oz. ASW, 39.9 mm. **Series:** First **Subject:** 180th Anniversary of Federation **Obv:** National arms **Obv. Legend:** ESTADOS UNIDOS MEXICANOS **Rev:** State arms **Rev. Legend:** ESTADO DE DURANGO **Edge:** Reeded

| Date | Mintage | VF20 | XF40 | MS60 | MS63 | MS65 |
|---|---|---|---|---|---|---|
| 2005 Mo | 10,000 | PF65 60.00 | | | | |

**KM# 709 10 PESOS**

31.10 g., 0.999 Silver 0.999 oz. ASW, 39.9 mm. **Series:** First **Subject:** 180th Anniversary of Federation **Obv:** National arms **Obv. Legend:** ESTADOS UNIDOS MEXICANOS **Rev:** State arms **Rev. Legend:** ESTADO DE GUANAJUATO **Edge:** Reeded

| Date | Mintage | VF20 | XF40 | MS60 | MS63 | MS65 |
|---|---|---|---|---|---|---|
| 2005 Mo | 10,000 | PF65 60.00 | | | | |

**KM# 710 10 PESOS**

31.10 g., 0.999 Silver 0.999 oz. ASW, 39.9 mm. **Series:** First **Subject:** 180th Anniversary of Federation **Obv:** National arms **Obv. Legend:** ESTADOS UNIDOS MEXICANOS **Rev:** State arms **Rev. Legend:** ESTADO DE GUERRERO **Edge:** Reeded

| Date | Mintage | VF20 | XF40 | MS60 | MS63 | MS65 |
|---|---|---|---|---|---|---|
| 2005 Mo | 10,000 | PF65 60.00 | | | | |

**KM# 711 10 PESOS**

31.10 g., 0.999 Silver 0.999 oz. ASW, 39.9 mm. **Series:** First **Subject:** 180th Anniversary of Federation **Obv:** National arms **Obv. Legend:** ESTADOS UNIDOS MEXICANOS **Rev:** State arms **Rev. Legend:** ESTADO DE HIDALGO **Edge:** Reeded

| Date | Mintage | VF20 | XF40 | MS60 | MS63 | MS65 |
|---|---|---|---|---|---|---|
| 2005 Mo | 10,000 | PF65 60.00 | | | | |

**KM# 718 10 PESOS**

31.10 g., 0.999 Silver 0.999 oz. ASW, 40 mm. **Series:** Second **Obv:** National arms **Obv. Legend:** ESTADOS UNIDOS MEXICANOS **Rev:** Facade of the San Marcos garden above sculpture of national emblem at left, San Antonio Temple at right **Rev. Legend:** AGUASCALIENTES **Edge:** Reeded

| Date | Mintage | VF20 | XF40 | MS60 | MS63 | MS65 |
|---|---|---|---|---|---|---|
| 2005 Mo | 6,000 | PF65 65.00 | | | | |

**KM# 720 10 PESOS**

31.10 g., 0.999 Silver 0.999 oz. ASW, 39.9 mm. **Series:** First **Subject:** 180th Anniversary of Federation **Obv:** National arms **Obv. Legend:** ESTADOS UNIDOS MEXICANOS **Rev:** State arms **Rev. Legend:** ESTADO DE AGUASCALIENTES **Edge:** Reeded

| Date | Mintage | VF20 | XF40 | MS60 | MS63 | MS65 |
|---|---|---|---|---|---|---|
| 2005 Mo | 10,000 | PF65 60.00 | | | | |

**KM# 722 10 PESOS**

31.10 g., 0.999 Silver 0.999 oz. ASW, 39.9 mm. **Series:** First **Subject:** 180th Anniversary of Federation **Obv:** National arms **Obv. Legend:** ESTADOS UNIDOS MEXICANOS **Rev:** State arms **Rev. Legend:** ESTADO DE BAJA CALIFORNIA **Edge:** Reeded

| Date | Mintage | VF20 | XF40 | MS60 | MS63 | MS65 |
|---|---|---|---|---|---|---|
| 2005 Mo | 10,000 | PF65 60.00 | | | | |

**KM# 724 10 PESOS**

31.10 g., 0.999 Silver 0.999 oz. ASW, 39.9 mm. **Series:** First **Subject:** 180th Anniversary of Federation **Obv:** National arms **Obv. Legend:** ESTADOS UNIDOS MEXICANOS **Rev:** State arms **Rev. Legend:** ESTADO DE BAJA CALIFORNIA SUR **Edge:** Reeded

| Date | Mintage | VF20 | XF40 | MS60 | MS63 | MS65 |
|---|---|---|---|---|---|---|
| 2005 Mo | 10,000 | PF65 60.00 | | | | |

**KM# 726 10 PESOS**

31.10 g., 0.999 Silver 0.999 oz. ASW, 39.9 mm. **Series:** First **Subject:** 180th Anniversary of Federation **Obv:** National arms **Obv. Legend:** ESTADOS UNIDOS MEXICANOS **Rev:** State arms **Rev. Legend:** ESTADO DE CAMPECHE **Edge:** Reeded

| Date | Mintage | VF20 | XF40 | MS60 | MS63 | MS65 |
|---|---|---|---|---|---|---|
| 2005 Mo | 10,000 | PF65 60.00 | | | | |

**KM# 728 10 PESOS**

31.10 g., 0.999 Silver 0.999 oz. ASW, 39.9 mm. **Series:** First **Subject:** 180th Anniversary of Federation **Obv:** National arms **Obv. Legend:** ESTADOS UNIDOS MEXICANOS **Rev:** State arms **Rev. Legend:** ESTADO DE COLIMA **Edge:** Reeded

| Date | Mintage | VF20 | XF40 | MS60 | MS63 | MS65 |
|---|---|---|---|---|---|---|
| 2005 Mo | 10,000 | PF65 60.00 | | | | |

**KM# 751 10 PESOS**

31.10 g., 0.999 Silver 0.999 oz. ASW, 39.9 mm. **Series:** First **Subject:** 180th Anniversary of Federation **Obv:** National arms **Obv. Legend:** ESTADOS UNIDOS MEXICANOS **Rev:** State arms **Rev. Legend:** ESTADO DE COAHUILA DE ZARAGOZA **Edge:** Reeded

| Date | Mintage | VF20 | XF40 | MS60 | MS63 | MS65 |
|---|---|---|---|---|---|---|
| 2005 Mo | 10,000 | PF65 60.00 | | | | |

**KM# 753 10 PESOS**

31.10 g., 0.999 Silver 0.999 oz. ASW, 39.9 mm. **Series:** First **Subject:** 180th Anniversary of Federation **Obv:** National arms **Obv. Legend:** ESTADOS UNIDOS MEXICANOS **Rev:** State arms **Rev. Legend:** ESTADO DE CHIHUAHUA **Edge:** Reeded

| Date | Mintage | VF20 | XF40 | MS60 | MS63 | MS65 |
|---|---|---|---|---|---|---|
| 2005 Mo | 10,000 | PF65 60.00 | | | | |

**KM# 755 10 PESOS**

31.10 g., 0.999 Silver 0.999 oz. ASW, 40 mm. **Obv:** National arms **Rev:** Baja California del Norte arms

| Date | Mintage | VF20 | XF40 | MS60 | MS63 | MS65 |
|---|---|---|---|---|---|---|
| 2005 Mo | — | PF65 75.00 | | | | |

**KM# 757 10 PESOS**

31.10 g., 0.999 Silver 0.999 oz. ASW, 40 mm. **Series:** Second **Obv:** National arms **Obv. Legend:** ESTADOS UNIDOS MEXICANOS **Rev:** Rams head, mountain outline in background **Rev. Legend:** BAJA CALIFORNIA - GOBIERNO DEL ESTADO **Edge:** Reeded

| Date | Mintage | VF20 | XF40 | MS60 | MS63 | MS65 |
|---|---|---|---|---|---|---|
| 2005 Mo | 6,000 | PF65 65.00 | | | | |

**KM# 766 10 PESOS**

31.10 g., 0.999 Silver 0.999 oz. ASW, 40 mm. **Subject:** Cervantes Festival **Obv:** Mexican Eagle and Snake **Rev:** Don Quixote **Edge:** Reeded

| Date | Mintage | VF20 | XF40 | MS60 | MS63 | MS65 |
|---|---|---|---|---|---|---|
| 2005 Mo | 1,205 | PF65 75.00 | | | | |

**KM# 768 10 PESOS**

31.10 g., 0.999 Silver 0.999 oz. ASW, 40 mm. **Subject:** 470th Anniversary - Mexico City Mint **Obv:** Mexican Eagle and Snake **Rev:** Antique coin press

| Date | Mintage | VF20 | XF40 | MS60 | MS63 | MS65 |
|---|---|---|---|---|---|---|
| 2005 Mo | 2,005 | PF65 55.00 | | | | |

**KM# 759 10 PESOS**

31.10 g., 0.999 Silver 0.999 oz. ASW, 40 mm. **Series:** Second **Obv:** National arms **Obv. Legend:** ESTADOS UNIDOS MEXICANOS **Rev:** Jade mask - Calakmul, Campeche **Rev. Legend:** ESTADO DE CAMPECHE **Edge:** Reeded

| Date | Mintage | VF20 | XF40 | MS60 | MS63 | MS65 |
|---|---|---|---|---|---|---|
| 2006 Mo | 6,000 | PF65 65.00 | | | | |

**KM# 761 10 PESOS**

31.10 g., 0.999 Silver 0.999 oz. ASW, 40 mm. **Series:** Second **Obv:** National arms **Obv. Legend:** ESTADOS UNIDOS MEXICANOS **Rev:** Outlined map of peninsula at center, cave painting of deer behind, cactus at right **Rev. Legend:** ESTADO DE BAJA CALIFORNIA SUR **Edge:** Reeded

| Date | Mintage | VF20 | XF40 | MS60 | MS63 | MS65 |
|---|---|---|---|---|---|---|
| 2006 Mo | 6,000 | PF65 65.00 | | | | |

**KM# 763 10 PESOS**

31.10 g., 0.999 Silver 0.999 oz. ASW, 40 mm. **Obv:** National arms **Rev:** Benito Juarez **Edge:** Reeded

| Date | Mintage | VF20 | XF40 | MS60 | MS63 | MS65 |
|---|---|---|---|---|---|---|
| 2006 Mo | — | PF65 75.00 | | | | |

**KM# 772 10 PESOS**

31.10 g., 0.999 Silver 0.999 oz. ASW, 40 mm. **Series:** Second **Obv:** National arms **Obv. Legend:** ESTADOS UNIDOS MEXICANOS **Rev:** Head of Pakal, ancient Mayan king, Palenque **Rev. Legend:** ESTADO DE CHIAPAS - CABEZA MAYA DEL REY PAKAL, PALENQUE **Edge:** Reeded

| Date | Mintage | VF20 | XF40 | MS60 | MS63 | MS65 |
|---|---|---|---|---|---|---|
| 2006 Mo | 6,000 | PF65 65.00 | | | | |

**KM# 774 10 PESOS**

31.10 g., 0.999 Silver 0.999 oz. ASW, 40 mm. **Series:** Second **Obv:** National arms **Obv. Legend:** ESTADOS UNIDOS MEXICANOS **Rev:** Angel of Liberty **Rev. Legend:** MÉXICO - ANGEL DE LA LIBERTAD, CHIHUAHUA **Edge:** Reeded

| Date | Mintage | VF20 | XF40 | MS60 | MS63 | MS65 |
|---|---|---|---|---|---|---|
| 2006 Mo | 6,000 | PF65 65.00 | | | | |

**KM# 776 10 PESOS**

31.10 g., 0.999 Silver 0.999 oz. ASW, 40 mm. **Series:** Second **Obv:** National arms **Obv. Legend:** ESTADOS UNIDOS MEXICANOS **Rev:** State arms at lower center, Nevado de Colima and Volcan de Fuego volcanos in background **Rev. Legend:** Colima **Rev. Inscription:** GENEROSO **Edge:** Reeded

| Date | Mintage | VF20 | XF40 | MS60 | MS63 | MS65 |
|---|---|---|---|---|---|---|
| 2006 Mo | 6,000 | PF65 65.00 | | | | |

**KM# 778 10 PESOS**

31.10 g., 0.999 Silver 0.999 oz. ASW, 40 mm. **Series:** Second **Obv:** National arms **Obv. Legend:** ESTADOS UNIDOS MEXICANOS **Rev:** National Palace **Rev. Legend:** DISTRITO FEDERAL - ANTIGUO AYUNTAMIENTO **Edge:** Reeded

| Date | Mintage | VF20 | XF40 | MS60 | MS63 | MS65 |
|---|---|---|---|---|---|---|
| 2006 Mo | 6,000 | PF65 65.00 | | | | |

**KM# 780 10 PESOS**
31.10 g., 0.999 Silver 0.999 oz. ASW, 40 mm. **Series:** Second **Obv:** National arms **Obv. Legend:** ESTADOS UNIDOS MEXICANOS **Rev:** Outlined map with turtle, mine cart above grapes at center, Friendship dam above Christ of the Nodas at left, chimneys above crucibles and bell tower of Santiago's cathedral at right **Rev. Inscription:** COAHUILA DE ZARAGOZA **Edge:** Reeded

| Date | Mintage | VF20 | XF40 | MS60 | MS63 | MS65 |
|---|---|---|---|---|---|---|
| 2006 Mo | 6,000 | PF65 65.00 | | | | |

**KM# 786 10 PESOS**
31.10 g., 0.999 Silver 0.999 oz. ASW, 40 mm. **Series:** Second **Obv:** National arms **Obv. Legend:** ESTADOS UNIDOS MEXICANOS **Rev:** Tree **Rev. Legend:** PRIMERA RESERVA NACIONAL FORESTAL - DURANGO **Edge:** Reeded

| Date | Mintage | VF20 | XF40 | MS60 | MS63 | MS65 |
|---|---|---|---|---|---|---|
| 2006 Mo | 6,000 | PF65 65.00 | | | | |

**KM# 788 10 PESOS**
31.10 g., 0.999 Silver 0.999 oz. ASW, 40 mm. **Series:** Second **Obv:** National arms **Obv. Legend:** ESTADOS UNIDOS MEXICANOS **Rev:** State arms at center, statue of Miguel Hidalgo at left, monument to Pípila at lower right **Rev. Inscription:** Guanajuato **Edge:** Reeded

| Date | Mintage | VF20 | XF40 | MS60 | MS63 | MS65 |
|---|---|---|---|---|---|---|
| 2006 Mo | 6,000 | PF65 65.00 | | | | |

**KM# 790 10 PESOS**
31.10 g., 0.999 Silver 0.999 oz. ASW, 40 mm. **Series:** Second **Obv:** National arms **Obv. Legend:** ESTADOS UNIDOS MEXICANOS **Rev:** Stylized portrait of Vicente Guerrero at left, church of Taxco at upper center, Acapulco's la Quebrada with diver above Christmas Eve flower and mask **Rev. Legend:** GUERRERO **Edge:** Reeded

| Date | Mintage | VF20 | XF40 | MS60 | MS63 | MS65 |
|---|---|---|---|---|---|---|
| 2006 Mo | 6,000 | PF65 65.00 | | | | |

**KM# 792 10 PESOS**
31.10 g., 0.999 Silver 0.999 oz. ASW, 40 mm. **Series:** Second **Obv:** National arms **Obv. Legend:** ESTADOS UNIDOS MEXICANOS **Rev:** Monument of Pachuca Hidalgo **Rev. Inscription:** RELOJ / MONUMENTAL / DE / PACHUCA / HIDALGO - La / Bella / Airosa **Edge:** Reeded

| Date | Mintage | VF20 | XF40 | MS60 | MS63 | MS65 |
|---|---|---|---|---|---|---|
| 2006 Mo | 6,000 | PF65 65.00 | | | | |

**KM# 794 10 PESOS**
31.10 g., 0.999 Silver 0.999 oz. ASW, 40 mm. **Series:** Second **Obv:** National arms **Obv. Legend:** ESTADOS UNIDOS MEXICANOS **Rev:** Hospicio Cabañas orphanage **Rev. Legend:** ESTADO DE JALISCCO **Edge:** Reeded

| Date | Mintage | VF20 | XF40 | MS60 | MS63 | MS65 |
|---|---|---|---|---|---|---|
| 2006 Mo | 6,000 | PF65 65.00 | | | | |

**KM# 830 10 PESOS**
31.10 g., 0.999 Silver 0.999 oz. ASW, 40 mm. **Series:** Second **Obv:** National arms **Obv. Legend:** ESTADOS UNIDOS MEXICANOS **Rev:** Pyramid de la Loona (Moon) **Rev. Legend:** ESTADO DE MÉXICO **Edge:** Reeded

| Date | Mintage | VF20 | XF40 | MS60 | MS63 | MS65 |
|---|---|---|---|---|---|---|
| 2006 Mo | 6,000 | PF65 65.00 | | | | |

**KM# 831 10 PESOS**
31.10 g., 0.999 Silver 0.999 oz. ASW, 40 mm. **Series:** Second **Obv:** National arms **Obv. Legend:** ESTADOS UNIDOS MEXICANOS **Rev:** Four Monarch butterflies **Rev. Legend:** ESTADO DE MICHOACÁN **Edge:** Reeded

| Date | Mintage | VF20 | XF40 | MS60 | MS63 | MS65 |
|---|---|---|---|---|---|---|
| 2006 Mo | 6,000 | PF65 65.00 | | | | |

**KM# 832 10 PESOS**
31.10 g., 0.999 Silver 0.999 oz. ASW, 40 mm. **Series:** Second **Obv:** National arms **Obv. Legend:** ESTADOS UNIDOS MEXICANOS **Rev:** 1/2 length figure of Chinelo (local dancer) at right, Palacio de Cortes in background **Rev. Inscription:** ESTADO DE / MORELOS **Edge:** Reeded

| Date | Mintage | VF20 | XF40 | MS60 | MS63 | MS65 |
|---|---|---|---|---|---|---|
| 2006 Mo | 6,000 | PF65 65.00 | | | | |

**KM# 833 10 PESOS**
31.10 g., 0.999 Silver 0.999 oz. ASW, 40 mm. **Series:** Second **Obv:** National arms **Obv. Legend:** ESTADOS UNIDOS MEXICANOS **Rev:** Isle de Mexcaltitlán **Rev. Legend:** ESTADO DE NAYARIT **Edge:** Reeded

| Date | Mintage | VF20 | XF40 | MS60 | MS63 | MS65 |
|---|---|---|---|---|---|---|
| 2007 Mo | 6,000 | PF65 65.00 | | | | |

**KM# 834 10 PESOS**
31.10 g., 0.999 Silver 0.999 oz. ASW, 40 mm. **Series:** Second **Obv:** National arms **Obv. Legend:** ESTADOS UNIDOS MEXICANOS **Rev:** Old foundry in Pargue Fundidora (public park) at right, Cerro de la Silla (Saddle Hill) in background **Rev. Legend:** ESTADO DE NUEVO LEÓN **Edge:** Reeded

| Date | Mintage | VF20 | XF40 | MS60 | MS63 | MS65 |
|---|---|---|---|---|---|---|
| 2007 Mo | 6,000 | PF65 65.00 | | | | |

**KM# 835 10 PESOS**
31.10 g., 0.999 Silver 0.999 oz. ASW, 40 mm. **Series:** Second **Obv:** National arms **Obv. Legend:** ESTADOS UNIDOS MEXICANOS **Rev:** Teatro Macedonio Alcala (theater) **Rev. Legend:** OAXACA **Edge:** Reeded

| Date | Mintage | VF20 | XF40 | MS60 | MS63 | MS65 |
|---|---|---|---|---|---|---|
| 2007 Mo | 6,000 | PF65 65.00 | | | | |

**KM# 836 10 PESOS**
31.10 g., 0.999 Silver 0.999 oz. ASW, 40 mm. **Series:** Second **Obv:** National arms **Obv. Legend:** ESTADOS UNIDOS MEXICANOS **Rev:** Talavera porcelain dish **Rev. Legend:** ESTADO DE PUEBLA **Edge:** Reeded

| Date | Mintage | VF20 | XF40 | MS60 | MS63 | MS65 |
|---|---|---|---|---|---|---|
| 2007 Mo | 6,000 | PF65 65.00 | | | | |

**KM# 837 10 PESOS**
31.10 g., 0.999 Silver 0.999 oz. ASW, 40 mm. **Series:** Second **Obv:** National arms **Obv. Legend:** ESTADOS UNIDOS MEXICANOS **Rev:** Mask at left, rays above state arms at center, Mayan ruins at right **Rev. Legend:** QUINTANA ROO **Edge:** Reeded

| Date | Mintage | VF20 | XF40 | MS60 | MS63 | MS65 |
|---|---|---|---|---|---|---|
| 2007 Mo | 6,000 | PF65 65.00 | | | | |

**KM# 838 10 PESOS**
31.10 g., 0.999 Silver 0.999 oz. ASW, 40 mm. **Series:** Second **Obv:** National arms **Obv. Legend:** ESTADOS UNIDOS MEXICANOS **Rev:** Acqueduct of Querétaro at left, church of Santa Rosa de Viterbo at right **Rev. Legend:** ESTADO DE QUERÉTARO ARTEAGA **Edge:** Reeded

| Date | Mintage | VF20 | XF40 | MS60 | MS63 | MS65 |
|---|---|---|---|---|---|---|
| 2007 Mo | 6,000 | PF65 65.00 | | | | |

**KM# 839 10 PESOS**
31.10 g., Silver, 40 mm. **Series:** Second **Obv:** National arms **Obv. Legend:** ESTADOS UNIDOS MEXICANOS **Rev:** Facade of Caja Real **Rev. Legend:** • SAN LUIS POTOSÍ • **Edge:** Reeded

| Date | Mintage | VF20 | XF40 | MS60 | MS63 | MS65 |
|---|---|---|---|---|---|---|
| 2007 Mo | 6,000 | PF65 65.00 | | | | |

**KM# 840 10 PESOS**
31.10 g., 0.999 Silver 0.999 oz. ASW, 40 mm. **Series:** Second **Obv:** National arms **Obv. Legend:** ESTADOS UNIDOS MEXICANOS **Rev:** Shield on pile of cactus fruits **Rev. Legend:** ESTADO DE SINALOA - LUGAR DE PITAHAYAS **Edge:** Reeded

| Date | Mintage | VF20 | XF40 | MS60 | MS63 | MS65 |
|---|---|---|---|---|---|---|
| 2007 Mo | 6,000 | PF65 65.00 | | | | |

**KM# 841 10 PESOS**
31.10 g., 0.999 Silver 0.999 oz. ASW, 40 mm. **Series:** Second **Obv:** National arms **Obv. Legend:** ESTADOS UNIDOS MEXICANOS **Rev:** Local in Dance of the Deer at left, cactus at right, mountains in background **Rev. Legend:** ESTADO DE SONORA **Edge:** Reeded

| Date | Mintage | VF20 | XF40 | MS60 | MS63 | MS65 |
|---|---|---|---|---|---|---|
| 2007 Mo | 6,000 | PF65 65.00 | | | | |

**KM# 842 10 PESOS**
31.10 g., 0.999 Silver 0.999 oz. ASW, 40 mm. **Series:** Second **Obv:** National arms **Obv. Legend:** ESTADOS UNIDOS MEXICANOS **Rev:** Fuente de los Pescadores (fisherman fountain) at lower left, giant head from the Olmec-pre-Hispanic culture at right, Planetario Tabasco in background **Rev. Legend:** TABASCO **Edge:** Reeded

| Date | Mintage | VF20 | XF40 | MS60 | MS63 | MS65 |
|---|---|---|---|---|---|---|
| 2007 Mo | 6,000 | PF65 65.00 | | | | |

**KM# 843 10 PESOS**
31.10 g., 0.999 Silver 0.999 oz. ASW, 40 mm. **Series:** Second **Obv:** National arms **Obv. Legend:** ESTADOS UNIDOS MEXICANOS **Rev:** Ridge - Cerro Del Bernal, Gonzáles **Rev. Legend:** TAMAULIPAS **Edge:** Reeded

| Date | Mintage | VF20 | XF40 | MS60 | MS63 | MS65 |
|---|---|---|---|---|---|---|
| 2007 Mo | 6,000 | PF65 65.00 | | | | |

**KM# 844 10 PESOS**
31.10 g., 0.999 Silver 0.999 oz. ASW, 40 mm. **Series:** Second **Obv:** National arms **Obv. Legend:** ESTADOS UNIDOS MEXICANOS **Rev:** Basilica de Ocotlán at left, state arms above Capilla Abierta, Plaza de Toros Ranchero Aguilar below, Exconvento de San Francisco at right **Rev. Legend:** ESTADO DE TLAXCALA **Edge:** Reeded

| Date | Mintage | VF20 | XF40 | MS60 | MS63 | MS65 |
|---|---|---|---|---|---|---|
| 2007 Mo | 6,000 | PF65 65.00 | | | | |

**KM# 845 10 PESOS**
31.10 g., 0.999 Silver 0.999 oz. ASW, 40 mm. **Series:** Second **Obv:** National arms **Obv. Legend:** ESTADOS UNIDOS MEXICANOS **Rev:** Pyramid of El Tajín **Rev. Legend:** • VERACRUZ • - • DE IGNACIO DE LA LLAVE • **Edge:** Reeded

| Date | Mintage | VF20 | XF40 | MS60 | MS63 | MS65 |
|---|---|---|---|---|---|---|
| 2007 Mo | 6,000 | PF65 65.00 | | | | |

**KM# 846 10 PESOS**
31.10 g., 0.999 Silver 0.999 oz. ASW, 40 mm. **Series:** Second **Obv:** National arms **Obv. Legend:** ESTADOS UNIDOS MEXICANOS **Rev:** Stylized pyramid of Chichén-Itzá **Rev. Legend:** Castillo de Chichén Itzá **Rev. Inscription:** YUCATÁN **Edge:** Reeded

| Date | Mintage | VF20 | XF40 | MS60 | MS63 | MS65 |
|---|---|---|---|---|---|---|
| 2007 Mo | 6,000 | PF65 65.00 | | | | |

**KM# 847 10 PESOS**
31.10 g., 0.999 Silver 0.999 oz. ASW, 40 mm. **Series:** Second **Obv:** National arms **Obv. Legend:** ESTADOS UNIDOS MEXICANOS **Rev:** Cable car above Monumento al Minero at left, Cathedral de Zacatecas at center right **Rev. Legend:** Zacatecas **Edge:** Reeded

| Date | Mintage | VF20 | XF40 | MS60 | MS63 | MS65 |
|---|---|---|---|---|---|---|
| 2007 Mo | 6,000 | PF65 65.00 | | | | |

**KM# 937 10 PESOS**
62.20 g., 0.999 Silver 1.9978 oz. ASW, 48 mm. **Series:** Mexican Revolution 100th Anniversary **Subject:** Revolutionary woman **Obv:** National arms (eagle and snake facing left) and legend **Obv. Legend:** ESTRADOS UNIDOS MEXICANOS **Rev:** Adelita on a railroad car, denomination and legend **Rev. Legend:** REVOLUCION MEXICANA

| Date | Mintage | VF20 | XF40 | MS60 | MS63 | MS65 |
|---|---|---|---|---|---|---|
| 2010 Mo | 20,000 | PF65 120 | | | | |

**KM# 938 10 PESOS**
62.20 g., 0.999 Silver 1.9978 oz. ASW, 48 mm. **Series:** Mexican Revolution 100th Anniversary **Subject:** Railroad **Obv:** National arms (eagle and snake facing left) and legend **Obv. Legend:** ESTADOS UNIDOS MEXICANOS **Rev:** Four seated armed revolutionaries on locomotive **Rev. Legend:** REVOLUCION MEXICANA

| Date | Mintage | VF20 | XF40 | MS60 | MS63 | MS65 |
|---|---|---|---|---|---|---|
| 2010 Mo | 20,000 | PF65 120 | | | | |

**KM# 942 10 PESOS**
31.10 g., 0.999 Silver 0.9989 oz. ASW, 40 mm. **Subject:** 100th Anniversary of the National Autonomous University of Mexico **Obv:** National arms (eagle and snake facing left) and legend **Obv. Legend:** ESTADOS UNIDOS MEXICANOS **Rev:** University buildings, sculpture and legend **Rev. Legend:** UNIVERSIDAD NACIONAL AUTONOMIA DE MEXICO

| Date | Mintage | VF20 | XF40 | MS60 | MS63 | MS65 |
|---|---|---|---|---|---|---|
| 2010 Mo Prooflike | 5,000 | — | — | — | 60.00 | — |

**KM# 948 10 PESOS**
62.20 g., 0.999 Silver 1.9978 oz. ASW, 65 mm. **Subject:** Chichen Itza, Temple of Warriors **Obv:** National arms (eagle and snake facing left), legend **Obv. Legend:** ESTADOS UNIDOS MEXICANOS **Rev:** Temple of Warriors of Chichen Itza **Rev. Legend:** CHICHEN ITZA, TEMPLO DE LOS GUERROS

| Date | Mintage | VF20 | XF40 | MS60 | MS63 | MS65 |
|---|---|---|---|---|---|---|
| ND-2011 Mo | 3,000 | PF65 150 | | | | |

**KM# 956 10 PESOS**
10.33 g., Bi-Metallic Copper-nickel-zinc center in aluminum-bronze ring, 28 mm. **Subject:** Battle of Puebla 150th Anniversary **Obv:** National arms (eagle and snake facing left) and legend **Obv. Legend:** ESTADOS UNIDOS MEXICANOS **Rev:** Head of General Zaragoza facing left, legends **Rev. Legend:** 150 ANNIVERSARIO DE LA BATALLA DE PUEBLA, 5 DE MAYO **Edge:** Reeded

| Date | Mintage | VF20 | XF40 | MS60 | MS63 | MS65 |
|---|---|---|---|---|---|---|
| 2012 Mo | 29,871,000 | — | — | 2.00 | 2.50 | — |

**KM# 637 20 PESOS**
Bi-Metallic Copper-Nickel center within Brass ring, 32 mm. **Subject:** Xiuhtecuhtli **Obv:** National arms, eagle left within circle **Rev:** Aztec with torch within spiked circle

| Date | Mintage | VF20 | XF40 | MS60 | MS63 | MS65 |
|---|---|---|---|---|---|---|
| 2001 Mo | 2,478,000 | 2.50 | 3.50 | 16.00 | 18.00 | — |

**KM# 638 20 PESOS**
Bi-Metallic Copper-Nickel center within Brass ring, 32 mm. **Subject:** Octavio Paz **Obv:** National arms, eagle left within circle **Rev:** Head 1/4 right within circle

| Date | Mintage | VF20 | XF40 | MS60 | MS63 | MS65 |
|---|---|---|---|---|---|---|
| 2001 Mo | 2,515,000 | 2.50 | 3.50 | 16.00 | 18.50 | — |

**KM# 704 20 PESOS**
62.40 g., 0.999 Silver 2.0042 oz. ASW, 48.1 mm. **Subject:** 400th Anniversary of Don Quijote de la Manchia **Obv:** National arms **Rev:** Skeletal figure horseback with spear galloping right **Edge:** Plain

| Date | Mintage | VF20 | XF40 | MS60 | MS63 | MS65 |
|---|---|---|---|---|---|---|
| ND-2005 Mo | 3,605 | PF65 85.00 | | | | |

**KM# 767 20 PESOS**
62.40 g., 0.999 Silver 2.0042 oz. ASW, 48 mm. **Subject:** 80th Anniversary - Bank of Mexico **Obv:** National arms **Rev:** 100 Peso banknote design of 1925

| Date | Mintage | VF20 | XF40 | MS60 | MS63 | MS65 |
|---|---|---|---|---|---|---|
| 2005 Mo | — | — | — | — | 75.00 | 80.00 |
| 2005 Mo | 3,005 | PF65 90.00 | | | | |

**KM# 939 20 PESOS**
62.20 g., 0.999 Silver 1.9978 oz. ASW, 48 mm. **Series:** Mexican Independence 200th Anniversary **Subject:** Dolores Parrish Church **Obv:** National arms (eagle and snake facing left) and legend **Obv. Legend:** ESTADOS UNIDOS MEXICANOS **Rev:** Dolores Parrish church, Independence Bell **Rev. Legend:** Bicentenario de la Independencia de Mexico

| Date | Mintage | VF20 | XF40 | MS60 | MS63 | MS65 |
|---|---|---|---|---|---|---|
| 2010 Mo | 15,000 | PF65 100 | | | | |

## KM# 940 20 PESOS

62.21 g., 0.999 Silver 1.998 oz. ASW, 48 mm. **Series:** Mexican Independence 200th Anniversary **Obv:** National arms (eagle and snake facing left) and legend **Obv. Legend:** ESTADOS UNIDOS MEXICANOS **Rev:** Miguel Hidalgo y Costilla and Jose Maria Morelos y Pavon standing clasping hands, denomination and legend **Rev. Legend:** BICENTENARIO DE LA INDEPENDENCIA

| Date | Mintage | VF20 | XF40 | MS60 | MS63 | MS65 |
|---|---|---|---|---|---|---|
| 2010 Mo | 15,000 | PF65 100 | | | | |

## KM# 943 20 PESOS

15.95 g., Bi-Metallic Cupro-nickel center in aluminum-bronze ring, 32 mm. **Subject:** 20th Anniversary of Octavio Paz **Obv:** National arms (eagle and snake facing left) and legend **Obv. Legend:** ESTADOS UNIDOS MEXICANOS **Rev:** Bust of Octavio Paz facing right and Legend **Rev. Legend:** Premio Nobel de Lieteratura **Edge:** Segmented reeding

| Date | Mintage | VF20 | XF40 | MS60 | MS63 | MS65 |
|---|---|---|---|---|---|---|
| 2010 Mo | 4,954,000 | — | — | 3.50 | 4.00 | — |

Note: Minted in 2011

## KM# 949 20 PESOS

155.15 g., 0.999 Silver 4.9832 oz. ASW, 65 mm. **Subject:** Chichen Itza, Pyramid of Kukulcan **Obv:** National arms (eagle and snake facing left), legend **Obv. Legend:** ESTADOS UNIDOS MEXICANOS **Rev:** Pyramid of Kukulcan of Chichen Itza, legends **Rev. Legend:** CHICHEN ITZA, PIRAMID DE KUKULCAN and 070707 and denomination

| Date | Mintage | VF20 | XF40 | MS60 | MS63 | MS65 |
|---|---|---|---|---|---|---|
| ND-2011 Mo | 3,000 | PF65 260 | | | | |

## KM# 969 20 PESOS

15.95 g., Bi-Metallic Copper-Nickel center in Aluminum-Bronze ring, 32 mm. **Subject:** Armed Forces, 100th Anniversary **Obv:** National arms **Rev:** Silhouette of soldier with a helmet **Edge:** Segmented reeding

| Date | Mintage | VF20 | XF40 | MS60 | MS63 | MS65 |
|---|---|---|---|---|---|---|
| 2013 Mo | Est. 4956000 | — | — | 3.50 | 4.00 | — |

## KM# 970 20 PESOS

15.95 g., Bi-Metallic Copper-Nickel center in Aluminum-Bronze ring, 32 mm. **Subject:** Belisario Dominguez Palencia, 150th Anniversary of Birth and 100th Anniversary of Death **Obv:** National arms **Rev:** Bust 1/4 right **Edge:** Segmented reeding

| Date | Mintage | VF20 | XF40 | MS60 | MS63 | MS65 |
|---|---|---|---|---|---|---|
| 2013 Mo | Est. 985000 | — | — | 4.50 | 5.00 | — |

## KM# 688 100 PESOS

33.94 g., Bi-Metallic .925 Silver 16.812g center in Aluminum-Bronze ring, 39.04 mm. **Series:** First **Subject:** 180th Anniversary of Federation **Obv:** National arms **Obv. Legend:** ESTADOS UNIDOS MEXICANOS **Rev:** State arms **Rev. Legend:** ESTADO DE ZACATECAS **Edge:** Segmented reeding

| Date | Mintage | VF20 | XF40 | MS60 | MS63 | MS65 |
|---|---|---|---|---|---|---|
| 2003 Mo | 244,900 | — | — | 40.00 | 50.00 | — |

## KM# 689 100 PESOS

33.94 g., Bi-Metallic .925 Silver 16.812g center in Aluminum-Bronze ring, 39.04 mm. **Series:** First **Subject:** 180th Anniversary of Federation **Obv:** National arms **Obv. Legend:** ESTADOS UNIDOS MEXICANOS **Rev:** State arms **Rev. Legend:** ESTADO DE YUCATÁN **Edge:** Segmented reeding

| Date | Mintage | VF20 | XF40 | MS60 | MS63 | MS65 |
|---|---|---|---|---|---|---|
| 2003 Mo | 235,763 | — | — | 40.00 | 50.00 | — |

## KM# 690 100 PESOS

33.94 g., Bi-Metallic .925 Silver 16.812g center in Aluminum-Bronze ring, 39.04 mm. **Series:** First **Subject:** 180th Anniversary of Federation **Obv:** National arms **Obv. Legend:** ESTADOS UNIDOS MEXICANOS **Rev:** State arms **Rev. Legend:** ESTADO DE VERACRUZ-LLAVE **Edge:** Segmented reeding

| Date | Mintage | VF20 | XF40 | MS60 | MS63 | MS65 |
|---|---|---|---|---|---|---|
| 2003 Mo | 248,810 | — | — | 40.00 | 50.00 | — |

## KM# 691 100 PESOS

33.94 g., Bi-Metallic .925 Silver 16.812g center in Aluminum-Bronze ring, 39.9 mm. **Series:** First **Subject:** 180th Anniversary of Federation **Obv:** National arms **Obv. Legend:** ESTADOS UNIDOS MEXICANOS **Rev:** State arms **Rev. Legend:** ESTADO DE TLAXCALA **Edge:** Segmented reeding

| Date | Mintage | VF20 | XF40 | MS60 | MS63 | MS65 |
|---|---|---|---|---|---|---|
| 2003 Mo | 248,976 | — | — | 35.00 | 40.00 | — |

## KM# 696 100 PESOS

29.17 g., Bi-Metallic .999 Gold 17.154g center in .999 Silver 12.015g ring, 34.5 mm. **Series:** First **Subject:** 180th Anniversary of Federation **Obv:** National arms **Obv. Legend:** ESTADOS UNIDOS MEXICANOS **Rev:** State arms **Rev. Legend:** ESTADO DE ZACATECAS **Edge:** Segmented reeding

| Date | Mintage | VF20 | XF40 | MS60 | MS63 | MS65 |
|---|---|---|---|---|---|---|
| 2003 Mo | 1,000 | PF65 1,200 | | | | |

## KM# 697 100 PESOS

29.17 g., Bi-Metallic .999 Gold 17.154g center in .999 Silver 12.015g ring, 34.5 mm. **Series:** First **Subject:** 180th Anniversary of Federation **Obv:** National arms **Obv. Legend:** ESTADOS UNIDOS MEXICANOS **Rev:** State arms **Rev. Legend:** ESTADO DE YUCATÁN **Edge:** Segmented reeding

| Date | Mintage | VF20 | XF40 | MS60 | MS63 | MS65 |
|---|---|---|---|---|---|---|
| 2003 Mo | 1,000 | PF65 1,200 | | | | |

## KM# 698 100 PESOS

29.17 g., Bi-Metallic .999 Gold 17.154g center in .999 Silver 12.015g ring, 34.5 mm. **Series:** First **Subject:** 180th Anniversary of Federation **Obv:** National arms **Obv. Legend:** ESTADOS UNIDOS MEXICANOS **Rev:** State arms **Rev. Legend:** ESTADO DE VERACRUZ-LLAVE **Edge:** Segmented reeding

| Date | Mintage | VF20 | XF40 | MS60 | MS63 | MS65 |
|---|---|---|---|---|---|---|
| 2003 Mo | 1,000 | PF65 1,200 | | | | |

## KM# 699 100 PESOS

29.17 g., Bi-Metallic .999 Gold 17.154g center in .999 Silver 12.015g ring, 34.5 mm. **Series:** First **Subject:** 180th Anniversary of Federation **Obv:** National arms **Obv. Legend:** ESTADOS UNIDOS MEXICANOS **Rev:** State arms **Rev. Legend:** ESTADO DE TLAXCALA **Edge:** Segmented reeding

| Date | Mintage | VF20 | XF40 | MS60 | MS63 | MS65 |
|---|---|---|---|---|---|---|
| 2003 Mo | 1,000 | PF65 1,200 | | | | |

## KM# 692 100 PESOS

33.94 g., Bi-Metallic .925 Silver 16.812g center in Aluminum-Bronze ring, 39.04 mm. **Series:** First **Subject:** 180th Anniversay of Federation **Obv:** National arms **Obv. Legend:** ESTADOS UNIDOS MEXICANOS **Rev:** State arms **Rev. Legend:** ESTADO DE TAMAULIPAS **Edge:** Segmented reeding

| Date | Mintage | VF20 | XF40 | MS60 | MS63 | MS65 |
|---|---|---|---|---|---|---|
| 2004 Mo | 249,398 | — | — | 35.00 | 40.00 | — |

## KM# 693 100 PESOS

33.94 g., Bi-Metallic .925 Silver 16.812g center in Aluminum-Bronze ring, 39.04 mm. **Series:** First **Subject:** 180th Anniversary of Federation **Obv:** National arms **Obv. Legend:** ESTADOS UNIDOS MEXICANOS **Rev:** State arms **Rev. Legend:** ESTADO DE TABASCO **Edge:** Segmented reeding

| Date | Mintage | VF20 | XF40 | MS60 | MS63 | MS65 |
|---|---|---|---|---|---|---|
| 2004 Mo | 249,318 | — | — | 35.00 | 40.00 | — |

## KM# 694 100 PESOS

33.94 g., Bi-Metallic .925 Silver 16.812g center in Aluminum-Bronze ring, 39.04 mm. **Series:** First **Subject:** 180th Anniversary of Federation **Obv:** National arms **Obv. Legend:** ESTADOS UNIDOS MEXICANOS **Rev:** State arms **Rev. Legend:** ESTADO DE SONORA **Edge:** Segmented reeding

| Date | Mintage | VF20 | XF40 | MS60 | MS63 | MS65 |
|---|---|---|---|---|---|---|
| 2004 Mo | 249,300 | — | — | 35.00 | 40.00 | — |

**KM# 695 100 PESOS**
33.94 g., Bi-Metallic .925 Silver 16.812g center in Aluminum-Bronze ring, 39.04 mm. **Series:** First **Subject:** 180th Anniversary of Federation **Obv:** National arms **Obv. Legend:** ESTADOS UNIDOS MEXICANOS **Rev:** State arms **Rev. Legend:** ESTADO DE SINALOA **Edge:** Segmented reeding

| Date | Mintage | VF20 | XF40 | MS60 | MS63 | MS65 |
|---|---|---|---|---|---|---|
| 2004 Mo | 244,722 | — | — | 35.00 | 40.00 | — |

**KM# 700 100 PESOS**
29.17 g., Bi-Metallic .999 Gold 17.154g center in .999 Silver 12.015g ring, 34.5 mm. **Series:** First **Subject:** 180th Anniversary of Federation **Obv:** National arms **Obv. Legend:** ESTADOS UNIDOS MEXICANOS **Rev:** State arms **Rev. Legend:** ESTADO DE TAMAULIPAS **Edge:** Segmented reeding

| Date | Mintage | VF20 | XF40 | MS60 | MS63 | MS65 |
|---|---|---|---|---|---|---|
| 2004 Mo | 1,000 | **PF65** 1,200 | | | | |

**KM# 701 100 PESOS**
29.17 g., Bi-Metallic .999 Gold 17.154g center in .999 Silver 12.015g ring, 34.5 mm. **Series:** First **Subject:** 180th Anniversary of Federation **Obv:** National arms **Obv. Legend:** ESTADOS UNIDOS MEXICANOS **Rev:** State arms **Rev. Legend:** ESTADO DE TABASCO **Edge:** Segmented reeding

| Date | Mintage | VF20 | XF40 | MS60 | MS63 | MS65 |
|---|---|---|---|---|---|---|
| 2004 Mo | 1,000 | **PF65** 1,200 | | | | |

**KM# 702 100 PESOS**
29.17 g., Bi-Metallic .999 Gold 17.154g center in .999 Silver 12.015g ring, 34.5 mm. **Series:** First **Subject:** 180th Anniversary of Federation **Obv:** National arms **Obv. Legend:** ESTADOS UNIDOS MEXICANOS **Rev:** State arms **Rev. Legend:** ESTADO DE SONORA **Edge:** Segmented reeding

| Date | Mintage | VF20 | XF40 | MS60 | MS63 | MS65 |
|---|---|---|---|---|---|---|
| 2004 Mo | 1,000 | **PF65** 1,200 | | | | |

**KM# 703 100 PESOS**
29.17 g., Bi-Metallic .999 Gold 17.154g center in .999 Silver 12.015g ring, 34.5 mm. **Series:** First **Subject:** 180th Anniversary of Federation **Obv:** National arms **Obv. Legend:** ESTADOS UNIDOS MEXICANOS **Rev:** State arms **Rev. Legend:** ESTADO DE SINALOA **Edge:** Segmented reeding

| Date | Mintage | VF20 | XF40 | MS60 | MS63 | MS65 |
|---|---|---|---|---|---|---|
| 2004 Mo | 1,000 | **PF65** 1,200 | | | | |

**KM# 734 100 PESOS**
33.94 g., Bi-Metallic .925 Silver 16.812g center in Aluminum-Bronze ring, 39.04 mm. **Series:** First **Subject:** 180th Anniversary of Federation **Obv:** National arms **Obv. Legend:** ESTADOS UNIDOS MEXICANOS **Rev:** State arms **Rev. Legend:** ESTADO DE QUERÉTARO ARTEAGA **Edge:** Segmented reeding

| Date | Mintage | VF20 | XF40 | MS60 | MS63 | MS65 |
|---|---|---|---|---|---|---|
| 2004 Mo | 249,263 | — | — | 35.00 | 40.00 | — |

**KM# 736 100 PESOS**
33.94 g., Bi-Metallic .925 Silver 16.812g center in Aluminum-Bronze ring, 39.04 mm. **Series:** First **Subject:** 180th Anniversary of Federation **Obv:** National arms **Obv. Legend:** ESTADOS UNIDOS MEXICANOS **Rev:** State arms **Rev. Legend:** ESTADO DE QUINTANA ROO **Edge:** Segmented reeding

| Date | Mintage | VF20 | XF40 | MS60 | MS63 | MS65 |
|---|---|---|---|---|---|---|
| 2004 Mo | 249,134 | — | — | 35.00 | 40.00 | — |

**KM# 738 100 PESOS**
33.94 g., Bi-Metallic .925 Silver 16.812g center in Aluminum-Bronze ring, 39.04 mm. **Series:** First **Subject:** 180th Anniversary of Federation **Obv:** National arms **Obv. Legend:** ESTADOS UNIDOS MEXICANOS **Rev:** State arms **Rev. Legend:** ESTADO DE PUEBLA **Edge:** Segmented reeding

| Date | Mintage | VF20 | XF40 | MS60 | MS63 | MS65 |
|---|---|---|---|---|---|---|
| 2004 Mo | 248,850 | — | — | 35.00 | 40.00 | — |

**KM# 740 100 PESOS**
33.94 g., Bi-Metallic .925 Silver 16.812g center in Aluminum-Bronze ring, 39.04 mm. **Series:** First **Subject:** 180th Anniversary of Federation **Obv:** National arms **Obv. Legend:** ESTADOS UNIDOS MEXICANOS **Rev:** State arms **Rev. Legend:** ESTADO DE OAXACA **Edge:** Segmented reeding

| Date | Mintage | VF20 | XF40 | MS60 | MS63 | MS65 |
|---|---|---|---|---|---|---|
| 2004 Mo | 249,589 | — | — | 35.00 | 40.00 | — |

**KM# 742 100 PESOS**
33.94 g., Bi-Metallic .925 Silver 16.812g center in Aluminum-Bronze ring, 39.04 mm. **Series:** First **Subject:** 180th Anniversary of Federation **Obv:** National arms **Obv. Legend:** ESTADOS UNIDOS MEXICANOS **Rev:** State arms **Rev. Legend:** ESTADO DE NUEVO LEÓN **Edge:** Segmented reeding

| Date | Mintage | VF20 | XF40 | MS60 | MS63 | MS65 |
|---|---|---|---|---|---|---|
| 2004 Mo | 249,199 | — | — | 35.00 | 40.00 | — |

**KM# 744 100 PESOS**
33.94 g., Bi-Metallic .925 Silver 16.812g center in Aluminum-Bronze ring, 39.04 mm. **Series:** First **Subject:** 180th Anniversary of Federation **Obv:** National arms **Obv. Legend:** ESTADOS UNIDOS MEXICANOS **Rev:** State arms **Rev. Legend:** ESTADO DE NAYARIT **Edge:** Segmented reeding

| Date | Mintage | VF20 | XF40 | MS60 | MS63 | MS65 |
|---|---|---|---|---|---|---|
| 2004 Mo | 248,305 | — | — | 35.00 | 40.00 | — |

**KM# 746 100 PESOS**
33.94 g., Bi-Metallic .925 Silver 16.812g center in Aluminum-Bronze ring, 39.04 mm. **Series:** First **Subject:** 180th Anniversary of Federation **Obv:** National arms **Obv. Legend:** ESTADOS UNIDOS MEXICANOS **Rev:** State arms **Rev. Legend:** ESTADO DE MORELOS **Edge:** Segmented reeding

| Date | Mintage | VF20 | XF40 | MS60 | MS63 | MS65 |
|---|---|---|---|---|---|---|
| 2004 Mo | 249,260 | — | — | 35.00 | 40.00 | — |

**KM# 748 100 PESOS**
33.94 g., Bi-Metallic .925 Silver 16.812g center in Aluminum-Bronze ring, 39.04 mm. **Series:** First **Subject:** 180th Anniversary of Federation **Obv:** National arms **Obv. Legend:** ESTADOS UNIDOS MEXICANOS **Rev:** State arms **Rev. Legend:** ESTADO DE MÉXICO **Edge:** Segmented reeding

| Date | Mintage | VF20 | XF40 | MS60 | MS63 | MS65 |
|---|---|---|---|---|---|---|
| 2004 Mo | 249,800 | — | — | 35.00 | 40.00 | — |

**KM# 750 100 PESOS**
33.94 g., Bi-Metallic .925 Silver 16.812g center in Aluminum-Bronze ring, 39.04 mm. **Series:** First **Subject:** 180th Anniversary of Federation **Obv:** National arms **Obv. Legend:** ESTADOS UNIDOS MEXICANOS **Rev:** State arms **Rev. Legend:** ESTADO DE JALISCO **Edge:** Segmented reeding

| Date | Mintage | VF20 | XF40 | MS60 | MS63 | MS65 |
|---|---|---|---|---|---|---|
| 2004 Mo | 249,115 | — | — | 35.00 | 40.00 | — |

**KM# 803 100 PESOS**
33.94 g., Bi-Metallic .925 Silver 16.812g center in Aluminum-Bronze ring, 39.04 mm. **Series:** First **Subject:** 180th Anniversary of Federation **Obv:** National arms **Obv. Legend:** ESTADOS UNIDOS MEXICANOS **Rev:** State arms **Rev. Legend:** ESTADO DE SAN LUIS POTOSÍ **Edge:** Segmented reeding

| Date | Mintage | VF20 | XF40 | MS60 | MS63 | MS65 |
|---|---|---|---|---|---|---|
| 2004 Mo | 249,662 | — | — | 35.00 | 40.00 | — |

**KM# 804 100 PESOS**
33.94 g., Bi-Metallic .925 Silver 16.812g center in Aluminum-Bronze ring, 39.04 mm. **Series:** First **Subject:** 180th Anniversary of Federation **Obv:** National arms **Obv. Legend:** ESTADOS UNIDOS MEXICANOS **Rev:** State arms **Rev. Legend:** ESTADO DE MICHOACÁN DE OCAMPO **Edge:** Segmented reeding

| Date | Mintage | VF20 | XF40 | MS60 | MS63 | MS65 |
|---|---|---|---|---|---|---|
| 2004 Mo | 249,492 | — | — | 35.00 | 40.00 | — |

**KM# 806 100 PESOS**
29.17 g., Bi-Metallic .999 Gold 17.154g center in .999 silver 12.015 ring, 34.5 mm. **Series:** First **Subject:** 180th Anniversary of Federation **Obv:** National arms **Obv. Legend:** ESTADOS UNIDOS MEXICANOS **Rev:** State arms **Rev. Legend:** ESTADO DE SAN LUIS POTOSÍ **Edge:** Segmented reeding

| Date | Mintage | VF20 | XF40 | MS60 | MS63 | MS65 |
|---|---|---|---|---|---|---|
| 2004 Mo | 1,000 | PF65 1,200 | | | | |

**KM# 807 100 PESOS**
29.17 g., Bi-Metallic .999 Gold 17.154g center in .999 Silver 12.015g ring, 34.5 mm. **Series:** First **Subject:** 180th Anniversary of Federation **Obv:** National arms **Obv. Legend:** ESTADOS UNIDOS MEXICANOS **Rev:** State arms **Rev. Legend:** ESTADO DE QUINTANA ROO **Edge:** Segmented reeding

| Date | Mintage | VF20 | XF40 | MS60 | MS63 | MS65 |
|---|---|---|---|---|---|---|
| 2004 Mo | 1,000 | PF65 1,200 | | | | |

**KM# 808 100 PESOS**
29.17 g., Bi-Metallic .999 Gold 17.154g center in .999 Silver 12.015g ring, 34.5 mm. **Series:** First **Subject:** 180th Anniversary of Federation **Obv:** National arms **Obv. Legend:** ESTADOS UNIDOS MEXICANOS **Rev:** State arms **Rev. Legend:** ESTADO DE QUERÉTARO ARTEAGA **Edge:** Segmented reeding

| Date | Mintage | VF20 | XF40 | MS60 | MS63 | MS65 |
|---|---|---|---|---|---|---|
| 2004 Mo | 1,000 | PF65 1,200 | | | | |

**KM# 809 100 PESOS**
29.17 g., Bi-Metallic .999 Gold 17.154g center in .999 Silver 12.015g ring, 34.5 mm. **Series:** First **Subject:** 180th Anniversary of Federation **Obv:** National arms **Obv. Legend:** ESTADOS UNIDOS MEXICANOS **Rev:** State arms **Rev. Legend:** ESTADO DE PUEBLA **Edge:** Segmented reeding

| Date | Mintage | VF20 | XF40 | MS60 | MS63 | MS65 |
|---|---|---|---|---|---|---|
| 2004 Mo | 1,000 | PF65 1,200 | | | | |

**KM# 810 100 PESOS**
29.17 g., Bi-Metallic .999 Gold 17.154g center in .999 Silver 12.015g ring, 34.5 mm. **Series:** First **Subject:** 180th Anniversary of Federation **Obv:** National arms **Obv. Legend:** ESTADOS UNIDOS MEXICANOS **Rev:** State arms **Rev. Legend:** ESTADO DE OAXACA **Edge:** Segmented reeding

| Date | Mintage | VF20 | XF40 | MS60 | MS63 | MS65 |
|---|---|---|---|---|---|---|
| 2004 Mo | 1,000 | PF65 1,200 | | | | |

**KM# 811 100 PESOS**
29.17 g., Bi-Metallic .999 Gold 17.154g center in .999 Silver 12.015g ring, 34.5 mm. **Series:** First **Subject:** 180th Anniversary of Federation **Obv:** National arms **Obv. Legend:** ESTADOS UNIDOS MEXICANOS **Rev:** State arms **Rev. Legend:** ESTADO DE NUEVO LEÓN **Edge:** Segmented reeding

| Date | Mintage | VF20 | XF40 | MS60 | MS63 | MS65 |
|---|---|---|---|---|---|---|
| 2004 Mo | 1,000 | PF65 1,200 | | | | |

**KM# 812 100 PESOS**
29.17 g., Bi-Metallic .999 Gold 17.154g center in .999 Silver 12.015g ring, 34.5 mm. **Series:** First **Subject:** 180th Anniversary of Federation **Obv:** National arms **Obv. Legend:** ESTADOS UNIDOS MEXICANOS **Rev:** State arms **Rev. Legend:** ESTADO DE NAYARIT **Edge:** Segmented reeding

| Date | Mintage | VF20 | XF40 | MS60 | MS63 | MS65 |
|---|---|---|---|---|---|---|
| 2004 Mo | 1,000 | PF65 1,200 | | | | |

**KM# 813 100 PESOS**
29.17 g., Bi-Metallic .999 Gold 17.154g center in .999 Silver 12.015g ring, 34.5 mm. **Series:** First **Subject:** 180th Anniversary of Federation **Obv:** National arms **Obv. Legend:** ESTADOS UNIDOS MEXICANOS **Rev:** State arms **Rev. Legend:** ESTADO DE MORELOS **Edge:** Segmented reeding

| Date | Mintage | VF20 | XF40 | MS60 | MS63 | MS65 |
|---|---|---|---|---|---|---|
| 2004 Mo | 1,000 | PF65 1,200 | | | | |

**KM# 814 100 PESOS**
29.17 g., Bi-Metallic .999 Gold 17.154g center in .999 12.015g ring, 34.5 mm. **Series:** First **Subject:** 180th Anniversary of Federation **Obv:** National arms **Obv. Legend:** ESTADOS UNIDOS MEXICANOS **Rev:** State arms **Rev. Legend:** ESTADO DE MICHOACÁN DE OCAMPO **Edge:** Segmented reeding

| Date | Mintage | VF20 | XF40 | MS60 | MS63 | MS65 |
|---|---|---|---|---|---|---|
| 2004 Mo | 1,000 | PF65 1,200 | | | | |

**KM# 815 100 PESOS**
29.17 g., Bi-Metallic .999 Gold 17.154 center in .999 Silver 12.015 ring, 34.5 mm. **Series:** First **Subject:** 180th Anniversary of Federation **Obv:** National arms **Obv. Legend:** ESTADOS UNIDOS MEXICANOS **Rev:** State arms **Rev. Legend:** ESTADO DE MÉXICO **Edge:** Segmented reeding

| Date | Mintage | VF20 | XF40 | MS60 | MS63 | MS65 |
|---|---|---|---|---|---|---|
| 2004 Mo | 1,000 | PF65 1,200 | | | | |

**KM# 816 100 PESOS**
29.17 g., Bi-Metallic .999 Gold 17.154g center in .999 Silver 12.015g ring, 34.5 mm. **Series:** First **Subject:** 180th Anniversary of Federation **Obv:** National arms **Obv. Legend:** ESTADOS UNIDOS MEXICANOS **Rev:** State arms **Rev. Legend:** ESTADO DE JALISCO **Edge:** Segmented reeding

| Date | Mintage | VF20 | XF40 | MS60 | MS63 | MS65 |
|---|---|---|---|---|---|---|
| 2004 Mo | 1,000 | PF65 1,200 | | | | |

**KM# 705 100 PESOS**
33.74 g., Bi-Metallic .925 16.812g Silver center in Aluminum-Bronze ring, 39 mm. **Subject:** 400th Anniversary of Don Quijote de la Manchia **Obv:** National arms **Obv. Legend:** ESTADOS UNIDOS MEXICANOS **Rev:** Skeletal figure on horseback with spear galloping right **Edge:** Segmented reeding

| Date | Mintage | VF20 | XF40 | MS60 | MS63 | MS65 |
|---|---|---|---|---|---|---|
| 2005 Mo | 726,833 | — | — | 25.00 | 32.00 | — |
| 2005 Mo Prooflike | 3,761 | — | — | — | 75.00 | — |
| 2006 Mo Prooflike | 5,201 | — | — | — | 60.00 | — |

**KM# 712 100 PESOS**
33.94 g., Bi-Metallic .925 Silver 16.812g center in Brass ring, 39.04 mm. **Series:** First **Subject:** 180th Anniversary of Federation **Obv:** National arms **Obv. Legend:** ESTADOS UNIDOS MEXICANOS **Rev:** State arms **Rev. Legend:** ESTADO DE CHIAPAS **Edge:** Segmented reeding

| Date | Mintage | VF20 | XF40 | MS60 | MS63 | MS65 |
|---|---|---|---|---|---|---|
| 2005 Mo | 249,417 | — | — | 35.00 | 40.00 | — |

**KM# 713 100 PESOS**
33.94 g., Bi-Metallic .925 Silver 16.812g center in Brass ring, 39.04 mm. **Series:** First **Subject:** 180th Anniversary of Federation **Obv:** National arms **Obv. Legend:** ESTADOS UNIDOS MEXICANOS **Rev:** Federal District arms **Rev. Legend:** DISTRITO FEDERAL **Edge:** Segmented reeding

| Date | Mintage | VF20 | XF40 | MS60 | MS63 | MS65 |
|---|---|---|---|---|---|---|
| 2005 Mo | 249,461 | — | — | 35.00 | 40.00 | — |

**KM# 714 100 PESOS**
33.94 g., Bi-Metallic .925 Silver 16.812g center in Brass ring, 39.04 mm. **Series:** First **Subject:** 180th Anniversary of Federation **Obv:** National arms **Obv. Legend:** ESTADOS UNIDOS MEXICANOS **Rev:** State arms **Rev. Legend:** ESTADO DE DURANGO **Edge:** Segmented reeding

| Date | Mintage | VF20 | XF40 | MS60 | MS63 | MS65 |
|---|---|---|---|---|---|---|
| 2005 Mo | 249,774 | — | — | 35.00 | 40.00 | — |

**KM# 715 100 PESOS**
33.94 g., Bi-Metallic .925 Silver 16.812g center in Brass ring, 39.04 mm. **Series:** First **Subject:** 180th Anniversary of Federation **Obv:** National arms **Obv. Legend:** ESTADOS UNIDOS MEXICANOS **Rev:** State arms **Rev. Legend:** ESTADO DE GUANAJUATO **Edge:** Segmented reeding

| Date | Mintage | VF20 | XF40 | MS60 | MS63 | MS65 |
|---|---|---|---|---|---|---|
| 2005 Mo | 249,489 | — | — | 35.00 | 40.00 | — |

## KM# 716 100 PESOS

33.94 g., Bi-Metallic .925 Silver 16.812g center in Brass ring, 39.04 mm. **Series:** First **Subject:** 180th Anniversary of Federation **Obv:** National arms **Obv. Legend:** ESTADOS UNIDOS MEXICANOS **Rev:** State arms **Rev. Legend:** ESTADO DE GUERRERO **Edge:** Segmented reeding

| Date | Mintage | VF20 | XF40 | MS60 | MS63 | MS65 |
|---|---|---|---|---|---|---|
| 2005 Mo | 248,850 | — | — | 35.00 | 40.00 | — |

## KM# 717 100 PESOS

33.94 g., Bi-Metallic .925 Silver 16.812g center in Brass ring, 39.04 mm. **Series:** First **Subject:** 180th Anniversary of Federation **Obv:** National arms **Obv. Legend:** ESTADOS UNIDOS MEXICANOS **Rev:** State arms **Rev. Legend:** ESTADO DE HIDALGO **Edge:** Segmented reeding

| Date | Mintage | VF20 | XF40 | MS60 | MS63 | MS65 |
|---|---|---|---|---|---|---|
| 2005 Mo | 249,820 | — | — | 35.00 | 40.00 | — |

## KM# 719 100 PESOS

33.83 g., Bi-Metallic .925 Silver 16.812g center in Aluminum-Bronze ring, 39.04 mm. **Series:** Second **Obv:** National arms **Obv. Legend:** ESTADOS UNIDOS MEXICANOS **Rev:** Facade of the San Marcos garden above sculpture of national emblem at left, San Antonio Temple at right **Rev. Legend:** AGUASCALIENTES **Edge:** Segmented reeding

| Date | Mintage | VF20 | XF40 | MS60 | MS63 | MS65 |
|---|---|---|---|---|---|---|
| 2005 Mo | 149,705 | — | — | 25.00 | 30.00 | — |

## KM# 721 100 PESOS

33.94 g., Bi-Metallic .925 Silver 16.812g center in Aluminum-Bronze ring, 39.04 mm. **Series:** First **Subject:** 180th Anniversary of Federation **Obv:** National arms **Obv. Legend:** ESTADOS UNIDOS MEXICANOS **Rev:** Estados de Aguascalientes state arms **Rev. Legend:** ESTADO DE AGUASCALIENTES **Edge:** Segmented reeding

| Date | Mintage | VF20 | XF40 | MS60 | MS63 | MS65 |
|---|---|---|---|---|---|---|
| 2005 Mo | 248,410 | — | — | 35.00 | 40.00 | — |

## KM# 723 100 PESOS

33.94 g., Bi-Metallic .925 Silver 16.812g center in Aluminum-Bronze ring, 39.04 mm. **Series:** First **Subject:** 180th Anniversary of Federation **Obv:** National arms **Obv. Legend:** ESTADOS UNIDOS MEXICANOS **Rev:** State arms **Rev. Legend:** ESTADO DE BAJA CALIFORNIA **Edge:** Segmented reeding

| Date | Mintage | VF20 | XF40 | MS60 | MS63 | MS65 |
|---|---|---|---|---|---|---|
| 2005 Mo | 249,263 | — | — | 35.00 | 40.00 | — |

## KM# 725 100 PESOS

33.94 g., Bi-Metallic .925 Silver 16.812g center in Aluminum-Bronze ring, 39.04 mm. **Series:** First **Subject:** 180th Anniversary of Federation **Obv:** National arms **Obv. Legend:** ESTADOS UNIDOS MEXICANOS **Rev:** State arms **Rev. Legend:** ESTADO DE BAJA CALIFORNIA SUR **Edge:** Segmented reeding

| Date | Mintage | VF20 | XF40 | MS60 | MS63 | MS65 |
|---|---|---|---|---|---|---|
| 2005 Mo | 249,585 | — | — | 35.00 | 40.00 | — |

## KM# 727 100 PESOS

33.94 g., Bi-Metallic .925 Silver 16.812g center in Aluminum-Bronze ring, 39.04 mm. **Series:** First **Subject:** 180th Anniversary of Federation **Obv:** National arms **Obv. Legend:** ESTADOS UNIDOS MEXICANOS **Rev:** State arms **Rev. Legend:** ESTADO DE CAMPECHE **Edge:** Segmented reeding

| Date | Mintage | VF20 | XF40 | MS60 | MS63 | MS65 |
|---|---|---|---|---|---|---|
| 2005 Mo | 249,040 | — | — | 35.00 | 40.00 | — |

## KM# 729 100 PESOS

33.83 g., Bi-Metallic .925 Silver 16.812g center in Aluminum-Bronze ring, 39.04 mm. **Series:** First **Subject:** 180th Anniversary of Federation **Obv:** National arms **Obv. Legend:** ESTADOS UNIDOS MEXICANOS **Rev:** State arms **Rev. Legend:** ESTADO DE COLIMA **Edge:** Segmented reeding

| Date | Mintage | VF20 | XF40 | MS60 | MS63 | MS65 |
|---|---|---|---|---|---|---|
| 2005 Mo | 248,850 | — | — | 35.00 | 40.00 | — |

## KM# 730 100 PESOS

33.83 g., Bi-Metallic .925 Silver 16.812g center in Aluminum-Bronze ring, 39.9 mm. **Subject:** Monetary Reform Centennial **Obv:** National arms **Rev:** Radiant Liberty Cap divides date above value within circle **Edge:** Segmented reeding

| Date | Mintage | VF20 | XF40 | MS60 | MS63 | MS65 |
|---|---|---|---|---|---|---|
| 2005 Mo | 49,716 | — | — | 40.00 | 45.00 | — |
| 2005 Mo | — | PF65 75.00 | | | | |

## KM# 731 100 PESOS

33.83 g., Bi-Metallic .925 Silver 16.812g center in Aluminum-Bronze ring, 39.9 mm. **Subject:** Mexico City Mint's 470th Anniversary **Obv:** National arms **Rev:** Screw press, value and date within circle **Edge:** Segmented reeding

| Date | Mintage | VF20 | XF40 | MS60 | MS63 | MS65 |
|---|---|---|---|---|---|---|
| 2005 Mo | 49,895 | — | — | 40.00 | 45.00 | — |
| 2005 Mo | — | PF65 95.00 | | | | |

**KM# 732 100 PESOS**
33.83 g., Bi-Metallic .925 Silver 16.812g center in Aluminum-Bronze ring, 39.9 mm. **Subject:** Bank of Mexico's 80th Anniversary **Obv:** National arms **Rev:** Back design of the 1925 hundred peso note **Edge:** Segmented reeding

| Date | Mintage | VF20 | XF40 | MS60 | MS63 | MS65 |
|---|---|---|---|---|---|---|
| 2005 Mo | 49,712 | — | — | 40.00 | 45.00 | — |
| 2005 Mo | — | PF65 95.00 | | | | |

**KM# 752 100 PESOS**
33.94 g., Bi-Metallic .925 Silver 16.812g center in Aluminum-Bronze ring, 39.04 mm. **Series:** First **Subject:** 180th Anniversary of Federation **Obv:** National arms **Obv. Legend:** ESTADOS UNIDOS MEXICANOS **Rev:** State arms **Rev. Legend:** ESTADO DE COAHUILA DE ZARAGOZA **Edge:** Segmented reeding

| Date | Mintage | VF20 | XF40 | MS60 | MS63 | MS65 |
|---|---|---|---|---|---|---|
| 2005 Mo | 247,991 | — | — | 35.00 | 40.00 | — |

**KM# 754 100 PESOS**
33.94 g., Bi-Metallic .925 Silver 16.812g center in Aluminum-Bronze ring, 39.04 mm. **Series:** First **Subject:** 180th Anniversary of Federation **Obv:** National arms **Obv. Legend:** ESTADOS UNIDOS MEXICANOS **Rev:** State arms **Rev. Legend:** ESTADO DE CHIHUAHUA **Edge:** Segmented reeding

| Date | Mintage | VF20 | XF40 | MS60 | MS63 | MS65 |
|---|---|---|---|---|---|---|
| 2005 Mo | 249,102 | — | — | 35.00 | 40.00 | — |

**KM# 758 100 PESOS**
33.94 g., Bi-Metallic .925 Silver 16.812g center in Aluminum-Bronze ring, 39.04 mm. **Series:** Second **Obv:** National arms **Obv. Legend:** ESTADOS UNIDOS MEXICANOS **Rev:** Ram's head and value within circle **Rev. Legend:** BAJA CALIFORNIA - GOBIERNO DEL ESTADO **Edge:** Segmented reeding

| Date | Mintage | VF20 | XF40 | MS60 | MS63 | MS65 |
|---|---|---|---|---|---|---|
| 2005 Mo | 149,771 | — | — | 25.00 | 30.00 | — |

**KM# 762 100 PESOS**
33.94 g., Bi-Metallic .925 Silver 16.812g center in Aluminum-Bronze ring, 39.04 mm. **Series:** Second **Obv:** National arms **Obv. Legend:** ESTADOS UNIDOS MEXICANOS **Rev:** Outlined map of peninsula at center, cave painting of deer behind, cactus at right **Rev. Legend:** ESTADO DE BAJA CALIFORNIA SUR **Edge:** Segmented reeding

| Date | Mintage | VF20 | XF40 | MS60 | MS63 | MS65 |
|---|---|---|---|---|---|---|
| 2005 Mo | 149,152 | — | — | 25.00 | 30.00 | — |

**KM# 817 100 PESOS**
29.17 g., Bi-Metallic .999 Gold 17.154g center in .999 Silver 12.015g ring, 34.5 mm. **Series:** First **Subject:** 180th Anniversary of Federation **Obv:** National arms **Obv. Legend:** ESTADOS UNIDOS MEXICANOS **Rev:** State arms **Rev. Legend:** ESTADO DE HIDALGO **Edge:** Segmented reeding

| Date | Mintage | VF20 | XF40 | MS60 | MS63 | MS65 |
|---|---|---|---|---|---|---|
| 2005 Mo | 1,000 | PF65 1,200 | | | | |

**KM# 818 100 PESOS**
29.17 g., Bi-Metallic .999 Gold 17.154g center in .999 Silver 12.015 ring, 34.5 mm. **Series:** First **Subject:** 180th Anniversary of Federation **Obv:** National arms **Obv. Legend:** ESTADOS UNIDOS MEXICANOS **Rev:** State arms **Rev. Legend:** ESTADO DE GUERRERO **Edge:** Segmented reeding

| Date | Mintage | VF20 | XF40 | MS60 | MS63 | MS65 |
|---|---|---|---|---|---|---|
| 2005 Mo | 1,000 | PF65 1,200 | | | | |

**KM# 819 100 PESOS**
29.17 g., Bi-Metallic .999 Gold 17.154g center in .999 Silver 12.015g ring, 34.5 mm. **Series:** First **Subject:** 180th Anniversary of Federation **Obv:** National arms **Obv. Legend:** ESTADOS UNIDOS MEXICANOS **Rev:** State arms **Rev. Legend:** ESTADO DE GUANAJUATO **Edge:** Segmented reeding

| Date | Mintage | VF20 | XF40 | MS60 | MS63 | MS65 |
|---|---|---|---|---|---|---|
| 2005 Mo | 1,000 | PF65 1,200 | | | | |

**KM# 820 100 PESOS**
29.17 g., Bi-Metallic .999 Gold 17.154g center in .999 silver 12.015g ring, 34.5 mm. **Series:** First **Subject:** 180th Anniversary of Federation **Obv:** National arms **Obv. Legend:** ESTADOS UNIDOS MEXICANOS **Rev:** State arms **Rev. Legend:** ESTADO DE DURANGO **Edge:** Segmented reeding

| Date | Mintage | VF20 | XF40 | MS60 | MS63 | MS65 |
|---|---|---|---|---|---|---|
| 2005 Mo | 1,000 | PF65 1,200 | | | | |

**KM# 821 100 PESOS**
29.17 g., Bi-Metallic .999 Gold 17.154g center in .999 Silver 12.015g ring, 34.5 mm. **Series:** First **Subject:** 180th Anniversary of Federation **Obv:** National arms **Obv. Legend:** ESTADOS UNIDOS MEXICANOS **Rev:** Federal District arms **Rev. Legend:** DISTRITO FEDERAL **Edge:** Segmented reeding

| Date | Mintage | VF20 | XF40 | MS60 | MS63 | MS65 |
|---|---|---|---|---|---|---|
| 2005 Mo | 1,000 | PF65 1,200 | | | | |

**KM# 822 100 PESOS**
29.17 g., Bi-Metallic .999 Gold 17.154g center in .999 Silver 12.015g ring, 34.5 mm. **Series:** First **Subject:** 180th Anniversary of Federation **Obv:** National arms **Obv. Legend:** ESTADOS UNIDOS MEXICANOS **Rev:** State arms **Rev. Legend:** ESTADO DE CHIHUAHUA **Edge:** Segmented reeding

| Date | Mintage | VF20 | XF40 | MS60 | MS63 | MS65 |
|---|---|---|---|---|---|---|
| 2005 Mo | 1,000 | PF65 1,200 | | | | |

**KM# 823 100 PESOS**
29.17 g., Bi-Metallic .999 Gold 17.154g center in .999 Silver 12.015g ring, 34.5 mm. **Series:** First **Subject:** 180th Anniversary of Federation **Obv:** National arms **Obv. Legend:** ESTADOS UNIDOS MEXICANOS **Rev:** State arms **Rev. Legend:** ESTADO DE CHIAPAS **Edge:** Segmented reeding

| Date | Mintage | VF20 | XF40 | MS60 | MS63 | MS65 |
|---|---|---|---|---|---|---|
| 2005 Mo | 1,000 | PF65 1,200 | | | | |

**KM# 824 100 PESOS**
29.17 g., Bi-Metallic .999 Gold 17.154g center in .999 Silver 12.015g ring, 34.5 mm. **Series:** First **Subject:** 180th Anniversary of Federation **Obv:** National arms **Obv. Legend:** ESTADOS UNIDOS MEXICANOS **Rev:** State arms **Rev. Legend:** ESTADO DE COLIMA **Edge:** Segmented reeding

| Date | Mintage | VF20 | XF40 | MS60 | MS63 | MS65 |
|---|---|---|---|---|---|---|
| 2005 Mo | 1,000 | PF65 1,200 | | | | |

**KM# 825 100 PESOS**
29.17 g., Bi-Metallic .999 Gold 17.154g center in .999 Silver 12.015g ring, 34.5 mm. **Series:** First **Subject:** 180th Anniversary of Federation **Obv:** National arms **Obv. Legend:** ESTADOS UNIDOS MEXICANOS **Rev:** State arms **Rev. Legend:** ESTADO DE COAHUILA DE ZARAGOZA **Edge:** Segmented reeding

| Date | Mintage | VF20 | XF40 | MS60 | MS63 | MS65 |
|---|---|---|---|---|---|---|
| 2005 Mo | 1,000 | PF65 1,200 | | | | |

**KM# 826 100 PESOS**
29.17 g., Bi-Metallic .999 Gold 17.154g center in .999 Silver 12.015g ring, 34.5 mm. **Series:** First **Subject:** 180th Anniversary of Federation **Obv:** National arms **Obv. Legend:** ESTADOS UNIDOS MEXICANOS **Rev:** State arms **Rev. Legend:** ESTADO DE CAMPECHE **Edge:** Segmented reeding

| Date | Mintage | VF20 | XF40 | MS60 | MS63 | MS65 |
|---|---|---|---|---|---|---|
| 2005 Mo | 1,000 | PF65 1,200 | | | | |

**KM# 827 100 PESOS**
29.17 g., Bi-Metallic .999 Gold 17.154g center in .999 Silver 12.015g ring, 34.5 mm. **Series:** First **Subject:** 180th Anniversary of Federation **Obv:** National arms **Obv. Legend:** ESTADOS UNIDOS MEXICANOS **Rev:** State arms **Rev. Legend:** ESTADO DE BAJA CALIFORNIA SUR **Edge:** Segmented reeding

| Date | Mintage | VF20 | XF40 | MS60 | MS63 | MS65 |
|---|---|---|---|---|---|---|
| 2005 Mo | 1,000 | PF65 1,200 | | | | |

**KM# 828 100 PESOS**
29.17 g., Bi-Metallic .999 Gold 17.154g center in .999 Silver 12.015g ring, 34.5 mm. **Series:** First **Subject:** 180th Anniversary of Federation **Obv:** National arms **Obv. Legend:** ESTADOS UNIDOS MEXICANOS **Rev:** State arms **Rev. Legend:** ESTADO DE BAJA CALIFORNIA **Edge:** Segmented reeding

| Date | Mintage | VF20 | XF40 | MS60 | MS63 | MS65 |
|---|---|---|---|---|---|---|
| 2005 Mo | 1,000 | PF65 1,200 | | | | |

**KM# 829 100 PESOS**
29.17 g., Bi-Metallic .999 Gold 17.154g center in .999 Silver 12.015g ring, 34.5 mm. **Series:** First **Subject:** 180th Anniversary of Federation **Obv:** National arms **Obv. Legend:** ESTADOS UNIDOS MEXICANOS **Rev:** State arms **Rev. Legend:** ESTADO DE AGUASCALIENTES **Edge:** Segmented reeding

| Date | Mintage | VF20 | XF40 | MS60 | MS63 | MS65 |
|---|---|---|---|---|---|---|
| 2005 Mo | 1,000 | PF65 1,200 | | | | |

**KM# 862 100 PESOS**
29.17 g., Bi-Metallic .999 Gold 17.154g center in .999 Silver 12.015g ring, 34.5 mm. **Series:** Second **Obv:** National arms **Obv. Legend:** ESTADOS UNIDOS MEXICANOS **Rev:** Facade of the San Marcos garden above sculpture of national emblem at left, San Antonio temple at right **Rev. Legend:** AGUASCALIENTES **Edge:** Segmented reeding

| Date | Mintage | VF20 | XF40 | MS60 | MS63 | MS65 |
|---|---|---|---|---|---|---|
| 2005 Mo | 600 | PF65 1,200 | | | | |

**KM# 863 100 PESOS**
29.17 g., Bi-Metallic .999 Gold 17.154g center in .999 Silver 12.015g ring, 34.5 mm. **Series:** Second **Obv:** National arms **Obv. Legend:** ESTTADOS UNIDOS MEXICANOS **Rev:** Ram's head, mountain outline in background **Rev. Legend:** BAJA CALIFORNIA - GOBIERNO DEL ESTADO **Edge:** Segmented reeding

| Date | Mintage | VF20 | XF40 | MS60 | MS63 | MS65 |
|---|---|---|---|---|---|---|
| 2005 Mo | 600 | PF65 1,200 | | | | |

**KM# 760 100 PESOS**
33.94 g., Bi-Metallic .925 Silver 16.812g center in Aluminum-Bronze ring, 39.04 mm. **Series:** Second **Subject:** Estado de Campeche **Obv:** National arms **Obv. Legend:** ESTADOS UNIDOS MEXICANOS **Rev:** Jade mask - Calakmul, Campeche **Rev. Legend:** ESTADO DE CAMPECHE **Edge:** Segmented reeding

| Date | Mintage | VF20 | XF40 | MS60 | MS63 | MS65 |
|---|---|---|---|---|---|---|
| 2006 Mo | 149,803 | — | — | 25.00 | 30.00 | — |

**KM# 764 100 PESOS**

33.70 g., Bi-Metallic .925 Silver 16.812g center in Aluminum-Bronze ring **Subject:** 200th Anniversary Birth of Benito Juarez Garcia **Obv:** National arms **Rev:** Bust 1/4 left within circle

| Date | Mintage | VF20 | XF40 | MS60 | MS63 | MS65 |
|---|---|---|---|---|---|---|
| 2006 Mo | 49,913 | — | — | 40.00 | 45.00 | — |

**KM# 773 100 PESOS**

33.94 g., Bi-Metallic .925 Silver 16.812g center in Aluminum-Bronze ring, 39.04 mm. **Series:** Second **Obv:** National arms **Obv. Legend:** ESTADOS UNIDOS MEXICANOS **Rev:** Head of Pakal, ancient Mayan king, Palenque **Rev. Legend:** ESTADO DE CHIAPAS - CABEZA MAYA DEL REY PAKAL, PALENQUE **Edge:** Segmented reeding

| Date | Mintage | VF20 | XF40 | MS60 | MS63 | MS65 |
|---|---|---|---|---|---|---|
| 2006 Mo | 149,491 | — | — | 25.00 | 30.00 | — |

**KM# 775 100 PESOS**

33.94 g., Bi-Metallic .925 Silver 16.812g center in Aluminum-Bronze ring, 39.04 mm. **Series:** Second **Obv:** National arms **Obv. Legend:** ESTADOS UNIDOS MEXICANOS **Rev:** Angel of Liberty **Rev. Legend:** MÉXICO - ANGEL DE LA LIBERTAD, CHIHUAHUA **Edge:** Segmented reeding

| Date | Mintage | VF20 | XF40 | MS60 | MS63 | MS65 |
|---|---|---|---|---|---|---|
| 2006 Mo | 149,557 | — | — | 25.00 | 30.00 | — |

**KM# 777 100 PESOS**

33.94 g., Bi-Metallic .925 Silver 16.812g center in Aluminum-Bronze ring, 39.04 mm. **Series:** Second **Obv:** National arms **Obv. Legend:** ESTADOS UNIDOS MEXICANOS **Rev:** State arms at lower center, Nevado de Colima and Volcan de Fuego volcanos in background **Rev. Legend:** Colima **Rev. Inscription:** GENEROSO **Edge:** Segmented reeding

| Date | Mintage | VF20 | XF40 | MS60 | MS63 | MS65 |
|---|---|---|---|---|---|---|
| 2006 Mo | 149,041 | — | — | 25.00 | 30.00 | — |

**KM# 779 100 PESOS**

33.94 g., Bi-Metallic .925 Silver 16.812g center in Aluminum-Bronze ring, 39.04 mm. **Series:** Second **Obv:** National arms **Obv. Legend:** ESTADOS UNIDOS MEXICANOS **Rev:** National Palace **Rev. Legend:** DISTRITO FEDERAL - ANTIGUO AYUNTAMIENTO **Edge:** Segmented reeding

| Date | Mintage | VF20 | XF40 | MS60 | MS63 | MS65 |
|---|---|---|---|---|---|---|
| 2006 Mo | 149,525 | — | — | 25.00 | 30.00 | — |

**KM# 781 100 PESOS**

33.70 g., Bi-Metallic .925 Silver 16.812g center in Aluminum-Bronze ring, 39.04 mm. **Series:** Second **Obv:** National arms **Obv. Legend:** ESTADOS UNIDOS MEXICANOS **Rev:** Outlined map with turtle, mine cart above grapes at center, Friendship Dam above Christ of the Nodas at left, chimneys above crucibles and bell tower of Santiago's cathedral at right **Rev. Legend:** COAHUILA DE ZARAGOZA **Edge:** Segmented reeding

| Date | Mintage | VF20 | XF40 | MS60 | MS63 | MS65 |
|---|---|---|---|---|---|---|
| 2006 Mo | 149,560 | — | — | 25.00 | 30.00 | — |

**KM# 785 100 PESOS**

33.94 g., Bi-Metallic .925 Silver 16.812g center in Aluminum-Bronze ring, 39.04 mm. **Series:** Second **Obv:** National arms **Obv. Legend:** ESTADOS UNIDOS MEXICANOS **Rev:** Four Monarch butterflies **Rev. Legend:** ESTADO DE MICHOACÁN **Edge:** Segmented reeding

| Date | Mintage | VF20 | XF40 | MS60 | MS63 | MS65 |
|---|---|---|---|---|---|---|
| 2006 Mo | 149,730 | — | — | 25.00 | 30.00 | — |

**KM# 787 100 PESOS**

33.94 g., Bi-Metallic .925 Silver 16.812g center in Brass ring, 39.04 mm. **Series:** Second **Obv:** National arms **Obv. Legend:** ESTADOS UNIDOS MEXICANOS **Rev:** Tree **Rev. Legend:** PRIMERA RESERVA NACIONAL FORESTAL - DURANGO **Edge:** Segmented reeding

| Date | Mintage | VF20 | XF40 | MS60 | MS63 | MS65 |
|---|---|---|---|---|---|---|
| 2006 Mo | 149,034 | — | — | 25.00 | 30.00 | — |

**KM# 789 100 PESOS**

33.94 g., Bi-Metallic .925 Silver 16.812g center in Brass ring, 39.04 mm. **Series:** Second **Obv:** National arms **Obv. Legend:** ESTADOS UNIDOS MEXICANOS **Rev:** State arms at center, statue of Miguel Hidalgo at left, monument to Pipla at lower right **Rev. Inscription:** Guanajuato **Edge:** Segmented reeding

| Date | Mintage | VF20 | XF40 | MS60 | MS63 | MS65 |
|---|---|---|---|---|---|---|
| 2006 Mo | 149,921 | — | — | 25.00 | 30.00 | — |

**KM# 791 100 PESOS**

33.94 g., Bi-Metallic .925 Silver 16.812g center in Brass ring, 39.04 mm. **Series:** Second **Obv:** National arms **Obv. Legend:** ESTADOS UNIDOS MEXICANOS **Rev:** Stylized portrait of Vicente Guerrero at left, church of Taxco at upper center, Acapulco's la Quebrada with diver above Christmas Eve flower and mask **Rev. Legend:** GUERRERO **Edge:** Segmented reeding

| Date | Mintage | VF20 | XF40 | MS60 | MS63 | MS65 |
|---|---|---|---|---|---|---|
| 2006 Mo | 149,675 | — | — | 25.00 | 30.00 | — |

**KM# 793 100 PESOS**

33.94 g., Bi-Metallic .925 Silver 16.812g center in Aluminum-Bronze ring, 39.04 mm. **Series:** Second **Obv:** National arms **Obv. Legend:** ESTADOS UNIDOS MEXICANOS **Rev:** Monument of Pachuca Hidalgo **Rev. Inscription:** RELOJ / MONUMENTAL / DE / PACHUCA / HIDALGO - La / Bella / Airosa **Edge:** Segmented reeding

| Date | Mintage | VF20 | XF40 | MS60 | MS63 | MS65 |
|---|---|---|---|---|---|---|
| 2006 Mo | 149,273 | — | — | 25.00 | 30.00 | — |

**KM# 795 100 PESOS**

33.94 g., Bi-Metallic .925 Silver 16.812g center in Brass ring, 39.04 mm. **Series:** Second **Obv:** National arms **Obv. Legend:** ESTADOS UNIDOS MEXICANOS **Rev:** Hospicio Cabañas orphanage **Rev. Legend:** ESTADO DE JALISCO **Edge:** Segmented reeding

| Date | Mintage | VF20 | XF40 | MS60 | MS63 | MS65 |
|---|---|---|---|---|---|---|
| 2006 Mo | 149,750 | — | — | 25.00 | 30.00 | — |

**KM# 800 100 PESOS**
33.94 g., Bi-Metallic .925 Silver 16.812g center in Aluminum-Bronze ring, 39.04 mm. **Series:** Second **Obv:** National arms **Obv. Legend:** ESTADOS UNIDOS MEXICANOS **Rev:** 1/2 length figure of Chinelo (local dancer) at right, Palacio de Cortes in background **Rev. Inscription:** ESTADO DE / MORELOS **Edge:** Segmented reeding

| Date | Mintage | VF20 | XF40 | MS60 | MS63 | MS65 |
|---|---|---|---|---|---|---|
| 2006 Mo | 149,648 | — | — | 25.00 | 30.00 | — |

**KM# 802 100 PESOS**
33.94 g., Bi-Metallic .925 Silver 16.812g center in Aluminum-Bronze ring, 39.04 mm. **Series:** Second **Obv:** National arms **Obv. Legend:** ESTADOS UNIDOS MEXICANOS **Rev:** Pyramid de la Loona (moon) **Rev. Legend:** ESTADO DE MÉXICO **Edge:** Segmented reeding

| Date | Mintage | VF20 | XF40 | MS60 | MS63 | MS65 |
|---|---|---|---|---|---|---|
| 2006 Mo | 149,377 | — | — | 25.00 | 30.00 | — |

**KM# 864 100 PESOS**
29.17 g., Bi-Metallic .999 Gold 17.154g center in .999 Silver 12.015g ring, 34.5 mm. **Series:** Second **Obv:** National arms **Obv. Legend:** ESTADOS UNIDOS MEXICANOS **Rev:** Outlined map of peninsula at center, cave painting of deer behind, cactus at right **Rev. Legend:** ESTADO DE BAJA CALIFORNIA SUR **Edge:** Segmented reeding

| Date | Mintage | VF20 | XF40 | MS60 | MS63 | MS65 |
|---|---|---|---|---|---|---|
| 2006 Mo | 600 | PF65 1,200 | | | | |

**KM# 865 100 PESOS**
29.17 g., Bi-Metallic .999 Gold 17.154g center in .999 Silver 12.015g ring, 34.5 mm. **Series:** Second **Obv:** National arms **Obv. Legend:** ESTADOS UNIDOS MEXICANOS **Rev:** Jade mask - Calakmul, Campeche **Rev. Legend:** ESTADO DE CAMPECHE **Edge:** Segmented reeding

| Date | Mintage | VF20 | XF40 | MS60 | MS63 | MS65 |
|---|---|---|---|---|---|---|
| 2006 Mo | 600 | PF65 1,200 | | | | |

**KM# 866 100 PESOS**
29.17 g., Bi-Metallic .999 Gold 17.154g center in .999 Silver 12.015g ring, 34.5 mm. **Series:** Second **Obv:** National arms **Obv. Legend:** ESTADOS UNIDOS MEXICANOS **Rev:** Outlined map with turtle, mine cart above grapes at center, Friendship dam above Christ of the Nodas at left, chimneys above crucibles and bell tower of Santiago's cathedral at right **Rev. Inscription:** COAHUILA DE ZARAGOZA **Edge:** Segmented reeding

| Date | Mintage | VF20 | XF40 | MS60 | MS63 | MS65 |
|---|---|---|---|---|---|---|
| 2006 Mo | 600 | PF65 1,200 | | | | |

**KM# 867 100 PESOS**
29.17 g., Bi-Metallic .999 Gold 17.154g center in .999 Silver 12.015 ring, 34.5 mm. **Series:** Second **Obv:** National arms **Obv. Legend:** ESTADOS UNIDOS MEXICANOS **Rev:** State arms at lower center, Nevado de Colima and Volcan de Fuego volcanos in background **Rev. Legend:** Colima **Rev. Inscription:** GENEROSO **Edge:** Segmented reeding

| Date | Mintage | VF20 | XF40 | MS60 | MS63 | MS65 |
|---|---|---|---|---|---|---|
| 2006 Mo | 600 | PF65 1,200 | | | | |

**KM# 868 100 PESOS**
29.17 g., Bi-Metallic .999 Gold 17.154g center in .999 Silver 12.015g ring, 34.5 mm. **Series:** Second **Obv:** National arms **Obv. Legend:** ESTADOS UNIDOS MEXICANOS **Rev:** Head of Pakal, ancient Mayan king, Palenque **Rev. Legend:** ESTADO DE CHIAPAS - CABEZA MAYA DEL REY PAKAL, PALENQUE **Edge:** Segmented reeding

| Date | Mintage | VF20 | XF40 | MS60 | MS63 | MS65 |
|---|---|---|---|---|---|---|
| 2006 Mo | 600 | PF65 1,200 | | | | |

**KM# 869 100 PESOS**
29.17 g., Bi-Metallic .999 Gold 17.154g center in .999 Silver 12.015g ring, 34.5 mm. **Series:** Second **Obv:** National arms **Obv. Legend:** ESTADOS UNIDOS MEXICANOS **Rev:** Angel of Liberty **Rev. Legend:** MÉXICO - ANGEL DE LA LIBERTAD, CHIHUAHUA **Edge:** Segmented reeding

| Date | Mintage | VF20 | XF40 | MS60 | MS63 | MS65 |
|---|---|---|---|---|---|---|
| 2006 Mo | 600 | PF65 1,200 | | | | |

**KM# 870 100 PESOS**
29.17 g., Bi-Metallic .999 Gold 17.154g center in .999 Silver 12.015g ring, 34.5 mm. **Series:** Second **Obv:** National arms **Obv. Legend:** ESTADOS UNIDOS MEXICANOS **Rev:** National palace **Rev. Legend:** DISTRITO FEDERAL - ANTIGUO AYUNTAMIENTO **Edge:** Segmented reeding

| Date | Mintage | VF20 | XF40 | MS60 | MS63 | MS65 |
|---|---|---|---|---|---|---|
| 2006 Mo | 600 | PF65 1,200 | | | | |

**KM# 871 100 PESOS**
29.17 g., Bi-Metallic .999 Gold 17.154g center in .999 Silver 12.015g ring, 34.5 mm. **Series:** Second **Obv:** National arms **Obv. Legend:** ESYADOS UNIDOS MEXICANOS **Rev:** Tree **Rev. Legend:** PRIMERA RESERVA NACIONAL RORESTAL - DURANGO **Edge:** Segmented reeding

| Date | Mintage | VF20 | XF40 | MS60 | MS63 | MS65 |
|---|---|---|---|---|---|---|
| 2006 Mo | 600 | PF65 1,200 | | | | |

**KM# 872 100 PESOS**
29.17 g., Bi-Metallic .999 Gold 17.154g center in .999 Silver 12.015g ring, 34.50 mm. **Series:** Second **Obv:** National arms **Obv. Legend:** ESTADOS UNIDOS MEXICANOS **Rev:** State arms at lower center, statue of Miguel Hidalgo at left, monument to Pipila at lower right **Rev. Inscription:** Guanajauto **Edge:** Segmented reeding

| Date | Mintage | VF20 | XF40 | MS60 | MS63 | MS65 |
|---|---|---|---|---|---|---|
| 2006 Mo | 600 | PF65 1,200 | | | | |

**KM# 873 100 PESOS**
29.17 g., Bi-Metallic .999 Gold 17.154g center in .999 Silver 12.015g ring, 34.5 mm. **Series:** Second **Obv:** National arms **Obv. Legend:** ESTADOS UNIDOS MEXICANOS **Rev:** Stylized portrait of Vicente Guerrero at left, church of Taxco at upper center, Acapulco's la Quebrada with diver over Christmas Eve flower and mask **Rev. Legend:** GUERRERO **Edge:** Segmented reeding

| Date | Mintage | VF20 | XF40 | MS60 | MS63 | MS65 |
|---|---|---|---|---|---|---|
| 2006 Mo | 600 | PF65 1,200 | | | | |

**KM# 874 100 PESOS**
29.17 g., Bi-Metallic .999 Gold 17.154g center in .999 Silver 12.015g ring, 34.5 mm. **Series:** Second **Obv:** National arms **Obv. Legend:** ESTADOS UNIDOS MEXICANOS **Rev:** Monument of Pachuca Hidalgo **Rev. Inscription:** RELOJ / MONUMENTAL / DE / PACHUCA / HIDALGO **Edge:** Segmented reeding

| Date | Mintage | VF20 | XF40 | MS60 | MS63 | MS65 |
|---|---|---|---|---|---|---|
| 2006 Mo | 600 | PF65 1,200 | | | | |

**KM# 875 100 PESOS**
29.17 g., Bi-Metallic .999 Gold 17.154g center in .999 Silver 12.015g ring, 34.5 mm. **Series:** Second **Obv:** National arms **Obv. Legend:** ESTADOS UNIDOS MEXICANOS **Rev:** Hospicio Cabañas orphanage **Rev. Legend:** ESTADO DE JALISCO **Edge:** Segmented reeding

| Date | Mintage | VF20 | XF40 | MS60 | MS63 | MS65 |
|---|---|---|---|---|---|---|
| 2006 Mo | 600 | PF65 1,200 | | | | |

**KM# 876 100 PESOS**
29.17 g., Bi-Metallic .999 Gold 17.154g center in .999 Silver 12.015g ring, 34.5 mm. **Series:** Second **Obv:** National arms **Obv. Legend:** ESTADOS UNIDOS MEXICANOS **Rev:** Pyramid de la Looona (moon) **Rev. Legend:** ESTADO DE MÉXICO **Edge:** Segmented reeding

| Date | Mintage | VF20 | XF40 | MS60 | MS63 | MS65 |
|---|---|---|---|---|---|---|
| 2006 Mo | 600 | PF65 1,200 | | | | |

**KM# 877 100 PESOS**
29.17 g., Bi-Metallic .999 Gold 17.154g center in .999 Silver 12.015g ring, 34.5 mm. **Series:** Second **Obv:** National arms **Obv. Legend:** ESTADOS UNIDOS MEXICANOS **Rev:** Four Monarch butterflies **Rev. Legend:** ESTADO DE MICHOACÁN **Edge:** Segmented reeding

| Date | Mintage | VF20 | XF40 | MS60 | MS63 | MS65 |
|---|---|---|---|---|---|---|
| 2006 Mo | 600 | PF65 1,200 | | | | |

**KM# 878 100 PESOS**
29.17 g., Bi-Metallic .999 Gold 17.154g center in .999 Silver 12.015g ring, 34.5 mm. **Series:** Second **Obv:** National arms **Obv. Legend:** ESTADOS UNIDOS MEXICANOS **Rev:** 1/2 length figure of Chinelo (local dancer) at right, Palacio de Cortes in background **Rev. Inscription:** ESTADO DE / MORELOS **Edge:** Segmented reeding

| Date | Mintage | VF20 | XF40 | MS60 | MS63 | MS65 |
|---|---|---|---|---|---|---|
| 2006 Mo | 600 | PF65 1,200 | | | | |

**KM# 798 100 PESOS**
33.94 g., Bi-Metallic .925 Silver 16.812g center in Aluminum-Bronze ring, 39.04 mm. **Series:** Second **Obv:** National arms **Obv. Legend:** ESTADOS UNIDOS MEXICANOS **Rev:** Isle de Mexcaltitlán **Rev. Legend:** ESTADO DE NAYARIT **Edge:** Segmented reeding

| Date | Mintage | VF20 | XF40 | MS60 | MS63 | MS65 |
|---|---|---|---|---|---|---|
| 2007 Mo | 149,560 | — | — | 25.00 | 30.00 | — |

**KM# 848 100 PESOS**
33.94 g., Bi-Metallic .925 Silver 20.1753 center in Aluminum-Bronze ring, 39.04 mm. **Series:** Second **Obv:** National arms **Obv. Legend:** ESTADOS UNIDOS MEXICANOE **Rev:** Old foundry in Parque Fundidora (public park) at right, Cerro de la Silla (Saddle Hill) in background **Rev. Legend:** ESTADO DE NUEVO LÉON **Edge:** Segmented reeding

| Date | Mintage | VF20 | XF40 | MS60 | MS63 | MS65 |
|---|---|---|---|---|---|---|
| 2007 Mo | 149,425 | — | — | 25.00 | 30.00 | — |

**KM# 849 100 PESOS**
33.94 g., Bi-Metallic .925 Silver 20.1753g center in Aluminum-Bronze ring, 39.04 mm. **Series:** Second **Obv:** National arms **Obv. Legend:** ESTADOS UNIDOS MEXICANOS **Rev:** Teatro Macedonio Alcala (theater) **Rev. Legend:** OAXACA **Edge:** Segmented reeding

| Date | Mintage | VF20 | XF40 | MS60 | MS63 | MS65 |
|---|---|---|---|---|---|---|
| 2007 Mo | 149,892 | — | — | 25.00 | 30.00 | — |

**KM# 850 100 PESOS**
33.94 g., Bi-Metallic .925 Silver 20.1753g center in Aluminum-Bronze ring, 39.04 mm. **Series:** Second **Obv:** National arms **Obv. Legend:** ESTADOS UNIDOS MEXICANOS **Rev:** Talavera porcelain dish **Rev. Legend:** ESTADO DE PUEBLA **Edge:** Segmented reeding

| Date | Mintage | VF20 | XF40 | MS60 | MS63 | MS65 |
|---|---|---|---|---|---|---|
| 2007 Mo | 149,474 | — | — | 25.00 | 30.00 | — |

**KM# 851 100 PESOS**
33.94 g., Bi-Metallic .925 Silver 20.1753g center in Aluminum-Bronze ring, 39.04 mm. **Series:** Second **Obv:** National arms **Obv. Legend:** ESTADOS UNIDOS MEXICANOS **Rev:** Mask at left, rays above state arms at center, Mayan ruins at right **Rev. Legend:** QUINTANA ROO **Edge:** Segmented reeding

| Date | Mintage | VF20 | XF40 | MS60 | MS63 | MS65 |
|---|---|---|---|---|---|---|
| 2007 Mo | 149,582 | — | — | 25.00 | 30.00 | — |

**KM# 852 100 PESOS**

33.94 g., Bi-Metallic .925 Silver 20.1753 center in Aluminum-Bronze ring, 39.04 mm. **Series:** Second **Obv:** National arms **Obv. Legend:** ESTADOS UNIDOS MEXICANOS **Rev:** Aqueduct of Querétaro at left, church of Santa Rosa de Viterbo at right **Rev. Legend:** ESTADO DE QUERÉTARO ARTEAGA **Edge:** Segmented reeding

| Date | Mintage | VF20 | XF40 | MS60 | MS63 | MS65 |
|---|---|---|---|---|---|---|
| 2007 Mo | 149,127 | — | — | 25.00 | 30.00 | — |

**KM# 853 100 PESOS**

33.94 g., Bi-Metallic .925 Silver 20.1753g center in Aluminum-Bronze ring, 39.04 mm. **Series:** Second **Obv:** National arms **Obv. Legend:** ESTADOS UNIDOS MEXICANOS **Rev:** Facade of Caja Real **Rev. Legend:** • SAN LUIS POTOSÍ • **Edge:** Segmented reeding

| Date | Mintage | VF20 | XF40 | MS60 | MS63 | MS65 |
|---|---|---|---|---|---|---|
| 2007 Mo | 148,750 | — | — | 25.00 | 30.00 | — |

**KM# 854 100 PESOS**

33.94 g., Bi-Metallic .925 Silver 20.1753g center in Aluminum-Bronze ring, 39.04 mm. **Series:** Second **Obv:** National arms **Obv. Legend:** ESTADOS UNIDOS MEXICANOS **Rev:** Shield on pile of cactus fruits **Rev. Legend:** ESTADO DE SINALOA - LUGAR DE PITAHAYAS **Edge:** Segmented reeding

| Date | Mintage | VF20 | XF40 | MS60 | MS63 | MS65 |
|---|---|---|---|---|---|---|
| 2007 Mo | 149,032 | — | — | 25.00 | 30.00 | — |

**KM# 855 100 PESOS**

33.94 g., Bi-Metallic .925 Silver 20.1753g center in Aluminum-Bronze ring, 39.04 mm. **Series:** Second **Obv:** National arms **Obv. Legend:** ESTADOS UNIDOS MEXICANOS **Rev:** Local in Dance of the Deer at left, cactus at right, mountains in background **Rev. Legend:** ESTADO DE SONORA **Edge:** Segmented reeding

| Date | Mintage | VF20 | XF40 | MS60 | MS63 | MS65 |
|---|---|---|---|---|---|---|
| 2007 Mo | 149,891 | — | — | 25.00 | 30.00 | — |

**KM# 856 100 PESOS**

33.94 g., Bi-Metallic .925 Silver 20.1753 center in Aluminum-Bronze ring, 39.04 mm. **Series:** Second **Obv:** National arms **Obv. Legend:** ESTADOS UNIDOS MEXICANOS **Rev:** Fuente de los Pescadores (fisherman fountain) at lower left, giant head from the Olmec-pre-Hispanic culture at right, Planetario Tabasco in background **Rev. Legend:** TABASCO **Edge:** Segmented reeding

| Date | Mintage | VF20 | XF40 | MS60 | MS63 | MS65 |
|---|---|---|---|---|---|---|
| 2007 Mo | 149,715 | — | — | 25.00 | 30.00 | — |

**KM# 857 100 PESOS**

33.94 g., Bi-Metallic .925 Silver 20.1753g center in Aluminum-Bronze ring, 39.04 mm. **Series:** Second **Obv:** National arms **Obv. Legend:** ESTADOS UNIDOS MEXICANOS **Rev:** Ridge - Cerro Del Bermal, Gonzáles **Rev. Legend:** TAMAULIPAS **Edge:** Segmented reeding

| Date | Mintage | VF20 | XF40 | MS60 | MS63 | MS65 |
|---|---|---|---|---|---|---|
| 2007 Mo | 149,776 | — | — | 25.00 | 30.00 | — |

**KM# 858 100 PESOS**

33.94 g., Bi-Metallic .925 Silver 20.1753g center in Aluminum-Bronze ring, 39.04 mm. **Series:** Second **Obv:** National arms **Obv. Legend:** ESTADOS UNIDOS MEXICANOS **Rev:** Basilica de Ocotlán at left, state arms above Capilla Abierta, Plaza de Toros Ranchero Aguilar below, Exconvento de San Francisco at right **Rev. Legend:** ESTADO DE TLAXCALA **Edge:** Segmented reeding

| Date | Mintage | VF20 | XF40 | MS60 | MS63 | MS65 |
|---|---|---|---|---|---|---|
| 2007 Mo | 149,465 | — | — | 25.00 | 30.00 | — |

**KM# 859 100 PESOS**

33.94 g., Bi-Metallic .912 Silver 20.1753g center in Aluminum-Bronze ring, 39.04 mm. **Series:** Second **Obv:** National arms **Obv. Legend:** ESTADOS UNIDOS MEXICANOS **Rev:** Pyramid of El Tajín **Rev. Legend:** • VERACRUZ • - • DE IGNACIO DE LA LLAVE • **Edge:** Segmented reeding

| Date | Mintage | VF20 | XF40 | MS60 | MS63 | MS65 |
|---|---|---|---|---|---|---|
| 2007 Mo | 149,703 | — | — | 25.00 | 30.00 | — |

**KM# 860 100 PESOS**

33.94 g., Bi-Metallic .925 Silver 20.1753 center in Aluminum-Bronze ring, 39.04 mm. **Series:** Second **Obv:** National arms **Obv. Legend:** ESTADOS UNIDOS MEXICANOS **Rev:** Stylized pyramid of Chichén Itzá **Rev. Legend:** Castillo de Chichén Itzá **Edge:** Segmented reeding

| Date | Mintage | VF20 | XF40 | MS60 | MS63 | MS65 |
|---|---|---|---|---|---|---|
| 2007 Mo | 149,579 | — | — | 25.00 | 30.00 | — |

**KM# 861 100 PESOS**

33.94 g., Bi-Metallic .925 Silver 20.1753g center in Aluminum-Bronze ring, 39.04 mm. **Series:** Second **Obv:** National arms **Obv. Legend:** ESTADOS UNIDOS MEXICANOS **Rev:** Cable car above Monumento al Minero at left, Cathedral de Zacatecas at center right **Rev. Legend:** ZACATECAS **Edge:** Segmented reeding

| Date | Mintage | VF20 | XF40 | MS60 | MS63 | MS65 |
|---|---|---|---|---|---|---|
| 2007 Mo | 148,833 | — | — | 25.00 | 30.00 | — |

**KM# 879 100 PESOS**

29.17 g., Bi-Metallic .999 Gold 17.154g center in .999 12.015g ring, 34.5 mm. **Series:** Second **Obv:** National arms **Obv. Legend:** ESTADOS UNIDOS MEXICANOS **Rev:** Isle de Mexcaltitlán **Rev. Legend:** ESTADO DE NAYARIT **Edge:** Segmented reeding

| Date | Mintage | VF20 | XF40 | MS60 | MS63 | MS65 |
|---|---|---|---|---|---|---|
| 2007 Mo | 600 | **PF65** 1,200 | | | | |

**KM# 880 100 PESOS**

29.17 g., Bi-Metallic .999 Gold 17.154g center in .999 Silver 12.015g ring, 34.5 mm. **Series:** Second **Obv:** National arms **Obv. Legend:** ESTADOS UNIDOS MEXICANOS **Rev:** Old foundry in Parque Fundidora (public park) at right, Cerro de la Silla (Saddle hill) in background **Rev. Legend:** ESTADO DE NUEVO LEÓN **Edge:** Segmented reeding

| Date | Mintage | VF20 | XF40 | MS60 | MS63 | MS65 |
|---|---|---|---|---|---|---|
| 2007 Mo | 600 | **PF65** 1,200 | | | | |

**KM# 881 100 PESOS**

29.17 g., Bi-Metallic .999 Gold 17.154g center in .999 Silver 12.015g ring, 34.50 mm. **Series:** Second **Obv:** National arms **Obv. Legend:** ESTADOS UNIDOS MEXICANOS **Rev:** Teatro Macedonio Alcala (theater) **Rev. Legend:** OAXACA **Edge:** Segmented reeding

| Date | Mintage | VF20 | XF40 | MS60 | MS63 | MS65 |
|---|---|---|---|---|---|---|
| 2007 Mo | 600 | **PF65** 1,200 | | | | |

### KM# 882 100 PESOS

29.17 g., Bi-Metallic .999 Gold 17.154g center in .999 Silver 12.015g ring, 34.5 mm. **Series:** Second **Obv:** National arms **Obv. Legend:** ESTADOS UNIDOS MEXICANOS **Rev:** Talavera porcelain dish **Rev. Legend:** ESTADO DE PUEBLA **Edge:** Segmented reeding

| Date | Mintage | VF20 | XF40 | MS60 | MS63 | MS65 |
|---|---|---|---|---|---|---|
| 2007 Mo | 600 | PF65 1,200 | | | | |

### KM# 883 100 PESOS

29.17 g., Bi-Metallic .999 Gold 17.154g center in .999 Silver 12.015g ring, 34.5 mm. **Series:** Second **Obv:** National arms **Obv. Legend:** ESTADOS UNIDOS MEXICANOS **Rev:** Mask at left, rays above state arms at center, Mayan ruins at right **Rev. Legend:** QUINTANA ROO **Edge:** Segmented reeding

| Date | Mintage | VF20 | XF40 | MS60 | MS63 | MS65 |
|---|---|---|---|---|---|---|
| 2007 Mo | 600 | PF65 1,200 | | | | |

### KM# 884 100 PESOS

29.17 g., Bi-Metallic .999 Gold 17.154g center in .999 Silver 12.015g ring, 34.5 mm. **Series:** Second **Obv:** National arms **Obv. Legend:** ESTADOS UNIDOS MEXICANOS **Rev:** Aqueduct of Querétaro at left, church of Santa Rosa de Viterbo at right **Rev. Legend:** ESTADO DE QUERÉTARO ARTEAGA **Edge:** Segmented reeding

| Date | Mintage | VF20 | XF40 | MS60 | MS63 | MS65 |
|---|---|---|---|---|---|---|
| 2007 Mo | 600 | PF65 1,200 | | | | |

### KM# 885 100 PESOS

29.17 g., Bi-Metallic .999 Gold 17.154g center in .999 Silver 12.015 ring, 34.5 mm. **Series:** Second **Obv:** National arms **Obv. Legend:** ESTADOS UNIDOS MEXICANOS **Rev:** Facade of Caja Real **Rev. Legend:** • SAN LUIS POTOSÍ • **Edge:** Segmented reeding

| Date | Mintage | VF20 | XF40 | MS60 | MS63 | MS65 |
|---|---|---|---|---|---|---|
| 2007 Mo | 600 | PF65 1,200 | | | | |

### KM# 886 100 PESOS

29.17 g., Bi-Metallic .999 Gold 17.154 center in .999 Silver 12.015g ring, 34.5 mm. **Series:** Second **Obv:** National arms **Obv. Legend:** ESTADOS UNIDOS MEXICANOS **Rev:** Shield on pile of cactus fruits **Rev. Legend:** ESTADO DE SINALOA - LUGAR DE PITAHAYES **Edge:** Segmented reeding

| Date | Mintage | VF20 | XF40 | MS60 | MS63 | MS65 |
|---|---|---|---|---|---|---|
| 2007 Mo | 600 | PF65 1,200 | | | | |

### KM# 887 100 PESOS

29.17 g., Bi-Metallic .999 Gold 17.154g center in .999 Silver 12.015g ring, 34.5 mm. **Series:** Second **Obv:** National arms **Obv. Legend:** ESTADOS UNIDOS MEXICANOS **Rev:** Local in Dance of the Deer at left, cactus at right, mountains in background **Rev. Legend:** ESTADO DE SONORA **Edge:** Segmented reeding

| Date | Mintage | VF20 | XF40 | MS60 | MS63 | MS65 |
|---|---|---|---|---|---|---|
| 2007 Mo | 600 | PF65 1,200 | | | | |

### KM# 888 100 PESOS

29.17 g., Bi-Metallic .999 Gold 17.154g center in .999 Silver 12.015g ring, 34.5 mm. **Series:** Second **Obv:** National arms **Obv. Legend:** ESTADOS UNIDOS MEXICANOS **Rev:** Fuente de los Pescadores (fisherman fountain) at lower left, giant head from the Olmec-pre-Hispanic culture at right, Planetario Tabasco in background **Rev. Legend:** TABASCO **Edge:** Segmented reeding

| Date | Mintage | VF20 | XF40 | MS60 | MS63 | MS65 |
|---|---|---|---|---|---|---|
| 2007 Mo | 600 | PF65 1,200 | | | | |

### KM# 889 100 PESOS

29.17 g., Bi-Metallic .999 Gold 17.154g center in .999 Silver 12.015g ring, 34.5 mm. **Series:** Second **Obv:** National arms **Obv. Legend:** ESTADOS DE MEXICANOS **Rev:** Ridge - Cerro Del Bemal, Gonzáles **Rev. Legend:** TAMAULIPAS **Edge:** Segmented reeding

| Date | Mintage | VF20 | XF40 | MS60 | MS63 | MS65 |
|---|---|---|---|---|---|---|
| 2007 Mo | 600 | PF65 1,200 | | | | |

### KM# 890 100 PESOS

29.17 g., Bi-Metallic .999 Gold 17.154g center in .999 Silver 12.015g ring, 34.5 mm. **Series:** Second **Obv:** National arms **Obv. Legend:** ESTADOS UNIDOS MEXICANOS **Rev:** Basilica de Ocotlán at left, state arms above Capilla Abierta, Plaza de Toros Ranchero Aguilar below, Exconvento de San Francisco at right **Rev. Legend:** ESTADO DE TLAXCALA **Edge:** Segmented reeding

| Date | Mintage | VF20 | XF40 | MS60 | MS63 | MS65 |
|---|---|---|---|---|---|---|
| 2007 Mo | 600 | PF65 1,200 | | | | |

### KM# 891 100 PESOS

29.17 g., Bi-Metallic .999 Gold 17.154g center in .999 Silver 12.015g ring, 34.5 mm. **Series:** Second **Obv:** National arms **Obv. Legend:** ESTADOS UNIDOS MEXICANOS **Rev:** Pyramid of El Tajin **Rev. Legend:** • VERACRUZ • - • DE IGNACIO DE LA LLAVE • **Edge:** Segmented reeding

| Date | Mintage | VF20 | XF40 | MS60 | MS63 | MS65 |
|---|---|---|---|---|---|---|
| 2007 Mo | 600 | PF65 1,200 | | | | |

### KM# 892 100 PESOS

29.17 g., Bi-Metallic .999 Gold 17.154g center in .999 Silver 12.015g ring, 34.5 mm. **Series:** Second **Obv:** National arms **Obv. Legend:** ESTADOS UNIDOS MEXICANOS **Rev:** Stylized pyramid of Chichén-Itzá **Rev. Inscription:** YUCATÁN **Edge:** Segmented reeding

| Date | Mintage | VF20 | XF40 | MS60 | MS63 | MS65 |
|---|---|---|---|---|---|---|
| 2007 Mo | 600 | PF65 1,200 | | | | |

### KM# 893 100 PESOS

29.17 g., Bi-Metallic .999 Gold 17.154g center in .999 Silver 12.015g ring, 34.5 mm. **Series:** Second **Obv:** National arms **Obv. Legend:** ESTADOS UNIDOS MEXICANOS **Rev:** Cable car above Monumento al Minero at left, Cathedral de Zacatecas at center right **Rev. Legend:** Zacatecas **Edge:** Segmented reeding

| Date | Mintage | VF20 | XF40 | MS60 | MS63 | MS65 |
|---|---|---|---|---|---|---|
| 2007 Mo | 600 | PF65 1,200 | | | | |

### KM# 950 100 PESOS

33.97 g., Bi-Metallic 16.812g .925 Silver 0.500 oz. ASW center in aluminum-bronze ring, 39 mm. **Series:** Numismatic Heritage of Mexico **Subject:** 1732 Pillar Dollar **Obv:** National arms (eagle and snake facing left) and legend **Obv. Legend:** ESTADOS UNIDOS MEXICANOS **Rev:** Obverse of 1732 Pillar Dollar, legend **Rev. Legend:** HERENCIA NUMISMATICA DE MEXICO **Edge:** Segmented reeding

| Date | Mintage | VF20 | XF40 | MS60 | MS63 | MS65 |
|---|---|---|---|---|---|---|
| 2011 Mo Prooflike | 8,000 | — | — | — | 40.00 | — |

### KM# 951 100 PESOS

33.97 g., Bi-Metallic 16.812g .925 Silver 0.500 oz. ASW center in aluminum-bronze ring, 39 mm. **Series:** Numismatic Heritage of Mexico **Subject:** 1783 Coin with bust of Carlos III **Obv:** National arms (eagle and snake facing left), legend **Obv. Legend:** ESTADOS UNIDOS MEXICANOS **Rev:** Obverse of 1783 coin with bust of Carlos III **Rev. Legend:** HERENCIA NUMISMATICA DE MEXICO **Edge:** Segmented reeding

| Date | Mintage | VF20 | XF40 | MS60 | MS63 | MS65 |
|---|---|---|---|---|---|---|
| 2011 Mo Prooflike | 8,000 | — | — | — | 40.00 | — |

### KM# 952 100 PESOS

33.97 g., Bi-Metallic 16.812g .925 Silver 0.500 oz. ASW center in aluminum-bronze ring, 39 mm. **Series:** Numismatic Heritage of Mexico **Subject:** SUD 8 Reales **Obv:** National arms (eagle and snake facing left), legend **Obv. Legend:** ESTADOS UNIDOS MEXICANOS **Rev:** Obverse of SUD 8 Rales, legend **Rev. Legend:** HERENCIA NUMISMATICA DE MEXICO **Edge:** Segmented reeding

| Date | Mintage | VF20 | XF40 | MS60 | MS63 | MS65 |
|---|---|---|---|---|---|---|
| 2011 Mo Prooflike | 8,000 | — | — | — | 40.00 | — |

### KM# 953 100 PESOS

33.97 g., Bi-Metallic 16.812g .925 Silver 0.500 ASW oz. center in aluminum-bronze ring, 39 mm. **Series:** Numismatic Heritage of Mexico **Subject:** 1824DO 8 Reales **Obv:** National arms (eagle and snake facing left), legend **Obv. Legend:** ESTADOS UNIDOS MEXICANOS **Rev:** Reverse of 1824Do * reales, legend **Rev. Legend:** HERENCIA NUMISMATICA DE MEXICO **Edge:** Segmented reeding

| Date | Mintage | VF20 | XF40 | MS60 | MS63 | MS65 |
|---|---|---|---|---|---|---|
| 2011 Mo Prooflike | 8,000 | — | — | — | 40.00 | — |

### KM# 954 100 PESOS

33.97 g., Bi-Metallic 16.812g .925 Silver .500 ASW center in aluminum-bronze ring, 39 mm. **Series:** Numismatic Heritage of Mexico **Subject:** 1913 Parral Bolita Peso **Obv:** National arms (eagle and snake facing left) and legend **Obv. Legend:** ESTADOS UNIDOS MEXICANOS **Rev:** Obverse of 1913 Parral Bolita Peso, legend **Rev. Legend:** HERENCIA NUMISMATICA DE MEXICO **Edge:** Segmented reeding

| Date | Mintage | VF20 | XF40 | MS60 | MS63 | MS65 |
|---|---|---|---|---|---|---|
| 2011 Mo Prooflike | 8,000 | — | — | — | 40.00 | — |

### KM# 955 100 PESOS

33.97 g., Bi-Metallic 16.812g .925 Silver .500 ASW center in aluminum-bronze ring, 39 mm. **Series:** Numismatic Heritage of Mexico **Subject:** 1910 Caballito Peso **Obv:** National arms (eagle and snake facing left) and legend **Obv. Legend:** ESTADOS UNIDOS MEXICANOS **Rev:** Reverse of 1910 Caballito Peso, legend **Rev. Legend:** HERENCIA NUMISMATICA DE MEXICO **Edge:** Segmented reeding

| Date | Mintage | VF20 | XF40 | MS60 | MS63 | MS65 |
|---|---|---|---|---|---|---|
| 2011 Mo Prooflike | 8,000 | — | — | — | 40.00 | — |

### KM# 963 100 PESOS

33.97 g., Bi-Metallic .925 Silver .500 ASW center in Aluminum-Bronze ring, 39 mm. **Subject:** Numismatic Heritage of Mexico **Obv:** National arms **Rev:** Obverse of 1804Mo 8 Reale coin with chopmarks **Edge:** Segmented reeding

| Date | Mintage | VF20 | XF40 | MS60 | MS63 | MS65 |
|---|---|---|---|---|---|---|
| 2012 Mo Prooflike | 8,000 | — | — | — | 40.00 | — |

### KM# 964 100 PESOS

Bi-Metallic .925 Silver .500 ASW center in Aluminum-Bronze ring, 39 mm. **Subject:** Numismatic Heritage of Mexico **Obv:** National arms **Rev:** 1608Mo 8 Reales Cob coin of Philip III **Edge:** Segmented reeding

| Date | Mintage | VF20 | XF40 | MS60 | MS63 | MS65 |
|---|---|---|---|---|---|---|
| 2012 Mo Prooflike | 8,000 | — | — | — | 40.00 | — |

### KM# 965 100 PESOS

33.97 g., Bi-Metallic .925 Silver .500 ASW center in Aluminum-Bronze ring, 39 mm. **Subject:** Numismatic Heritage of Mexico **Obv:** National arms **Rev:** 1811Zs 8 Reale Royalist Provisional Coin **Edge:** Segmented reeding

| Date | Mintage | VF20 | XF40 | MS60 | MS63 | MS65 |
|---|---|---|---|---|---|---|
| 2012 Mo Prooflike | 8,000 | — | — | — | 40.00 | — |

### KM# 966 100 PESOS

33.97 g., Bi-Metallic .925 Silver .500 ASW center in Aluminum-Bronze ring, 39 mm. **Subject:** Numismatic Heritage of Mexico **Obv:** National arms **Rev:** 1866Mo 1 Peso coin **Edge:** Segmented reeding

| Date | Mintage | VF20 | XF40 | MS60 | MS63 | MS65 |
|---|---|---|---|---|---|---|
| 2012 Mo Prooflike | 8,000 | — | — | — | 40.00 | — |

### KM# 967 100 PESOS

33.97 g., Bi-Metallic .925 Silver .500 ASW center in Aluminum-Bronze ring, 39 mm. **Subject:** Numismatic Heritage of Mexico **Obv:** National arms **Rev:** 1828Mo 8 Escudo coin **Edge:** Segmented reeding

| Date | Mintage | VF20 | XF40 | MS60 | MS63 | MS65 |
|---|---|---|---|---|---|---|
| 2012 Mo Prooflike | 8,000 | — | — | — | 40.00 | — |

### KM# 968 100 PESOS

33.97 g., Bi-Metallic .925 Silver .500 ASW center in Aluminum-Bronze ring, 39 mm. **Subject:** Numismatic Heritage of Mexico **Obv:** National arms **Rev:** 1950Mo 5 Peso Southeast Railway Inauguration coin **Edge:** Segmented reeding

| Date | Mintage | VF20 | XF40 | MS60 | MS63 | MS65 |
|---|---|---|---|---|---|---|
| 2012 Mo Prooflike | 8,000 | — | — | — | 40.00 | — |

### KM# 971 100 PESOS

33.97 g., Bi-Metallic .925 Silver .500 ASW center in Aluminum-Bronze ring, 39 mm. **Subject:** Numismatic Heritage of Mexico **Obv:** National arms **Rev:** 1915Gro. 2 Peso Zapatista coin from Suriana **Edge:** Segmented reeding

| Date | Mintage | VF20 | XF40 | MS60 | MS63 | MS65 |
|---|---|---|---|---|---|---|
| 2013 Mo Prooflike | — | — | — | — | 40.00 | — |

### KM# 972 100 PESOS

33.97 g., Bi-Metallic .925 Silver .500 ASW center in Aluminum-Bronze ring, 39 mm. **Subject:** Numismatic Heritage of Mexico **Obv:** National arms **Rev:** Early MoR Charles and Joanna 3 Reale coin **Edge:** Segmented reeding

| Date | Mintage | VF20 | XF40 | MS60 | MS63 | MS65 |
|---|---|---|---|---|---|---|
| 2013 Mo Prooflike | — | — | — | — | 40.00 | — |

### KM# 973 100 PESOS

33.97 g., Bi-Metallic .925 Silver .500 ASW center in Aluminum-Bronze ring, 39 mm. **Subject:** Numismatic Heritage of Mexico **Obv:** National arms **Rev:** Zs 1 Peso Scale of Justice coin

| Date | Mintage | VF20 | XF40 | MS60 | MS63 | MS65 |
|---|---|---|---|---|---|---|
| 2013 Mo Prooflike | — | — | — | — | 40.00 | — |

### KM# 974 100 PESOS

33.97 g., Bi-Metallic .925 Silver .500 ASW center in Aluminum-Bronze ring, 39 mm. **Subject:** Numismatic Heritage of Mexico **Obv:** National arms **Rev:** Ca M.M. 8 Reale Republican coin with counterstamp **Edge:** Segmented reeding

| Date | Mintage | VF20 | XF40 | MS60 | MS63 | MS65 |
|---|---|---|---|---|---|---|
| 2013 Mo Prooflike | — | — | — | — | 40.00 | — |

### KM# 975 100 PESOS

33.97 g., Bi-Metallic .925 Silver .500 ASW center in Aluminum-Bronze ring, 39 mm. **Subject:** Numismatic Heritage of Mexico **Obv:** National arms **Rev:** 1811 8 Reale insurgent coin of the Supreme American Governing Board **Edge:** Segmented reeding

| Date | Mintage | VF20 | XF40 | MS60 | MS63 | MS65 |
|---|---|---|---|---|---|---|
| 2013 Mo Prooflike | — | — | — | — | 40.00 | — |

### KM# 976 100 PESOS

33.97 g., Bi-Metallic .925 Silver .500 ASW center in Aluminum-Bronze ring, 39 mm. **Subject:** Numismatic Heritage of Mexico **Obv:** National arms **Rev:** 1822Mo 8 Escudo **Edge:** Segmented reeding

| Date | Mintage | VF20 | XF40 | MS60 | MS63 | MS65 |
|---|---|---|---|---|---|---|
| 2013 Mo Prooflike | — | — | — | — | 40.00 | — |

### KM# 932 200 PESOS

41.67 g., 0.900 Gold 1.2057 oz. AGW, 37 mm. **Series:** Mexico Independence 200th Anniversary **Subject:** Winged Victory **Obv:** National Arms **Obv. Legend:** Bicentenario **Rev:** Winged Victory **Edge Lettering:** Independence y Liberted

| Date | Mintage | VF20 | XF40 | MS60 | MS63 | MS65 |
|---|---|---|---|---|---|---|
| 2010 Mo | 50,000 | — | — | 1,800 | — | — |
| 2010 Mo | 5,000 | PF65 2,000 | | | | |

### KM# 941 200 PESOS

1000.00 g., 0.999 Gold 32.1186 oz. AGW, 90 mm. **Series:** Mexican Independence 200th Anniversary **Subject:** Winged Victory **Obv:** National arms (eagle and snake facing left), legend **Obv. Legend:** ESTADOS UNIDOS MEXICANOS **Rev:** Winged Victory, legend **Rev. Legend:** BICENTENARIO **Edge Lettering:** Independencia y Libertad

| Date | Mintage | VF20 | XF40 | MS60 | MS63 | MS65 |
|---|---|---|---|---|---|---|
| 2010 Mo | 200 | PF65 50,000 | | | | |

### KM# 771 50000 PESOS

7.77 g., 0.999 Gold 0.2496 oz. AGW, 23 mm. **Subject:** World Cup Soccer **Obv:** Mexican Eagle and Snake **Rev:** Kneeling Mayan Pelota player and soccer ball

| Date | Mintage | VF20 | XF40 | MS60 | MS63 | MS65 |
|---|---|---|---|---|---|---|
| 2006 Mo | 9,505 | PF65 600 | | | | |

## SILVER BULLION COINAGE

Libertad Series

**KM# 609 1/20 ONZA (1/20 Troy Ounce of Silver)**
1.56 g., 0.999 Silver 0.0499 oz. ASW, 16 mm. **Obv:** National arms, eagle left **Rev:** Winged Victory

| Date | Mintage | VF20 | XF40 | MS60 | MS63 | MS65 |
|---|---|---|---|---|---|---|
| 2001 Mo | 4,500 | — | — | — | 25.00 | — |
| 2001 Mo | 1,500 | PF63 30.00 | | | | |
| 2002 Mo | 50,000 | — | — | — | 16.00 | — |
| 2002 Mo | 2,800 | PF63 25.00 | | | | |
| 2003 Mo | 30,000 | — | — | — | 16.00 | — |
| 2003 Mo | 4,400 | PF63 25.00 | | | | |
| 2004 Mo | 30,000 | — | — | — | 16.00 | — |
| 2004 Mo | 2,700 | PF63 25.00 | | | | |
| 2005 Mo | 15,000 | — | — | — | 16.00 | — |
| 2005 Mo | 2,600 | PF63 25.00 | | | | |
| 2006 Mo | 20,000 | — | — | — | 16.00 | — |
| 2006 Mo | 3,300 | PF63 25.00 | | | | |
| 2007 Mo | 3,500 | — | — | — | 16.00 | — |
| 2007 Mo | 4,000 | PF63 25.00 | | | | |
| 2008 Mo | 7,000 | — | — | — | 16.00 | — |
| 2008 Mo | 3,300 | PF63 25.00 | | | | |
| 2009 Mo | 10,000 | — | — | — | 10.00 | — |
| 2009 Mo | 5,000 | PF63 12.00 | | | | |
| 2010 Mo | 12,000 | — | — | — | 10.00 | — |
| 2010 Mo | 10,000 | PF63 12.00 | | | | |
| 2011 Mo | 15,000 | — | — | — | 10.00 | — |
| 2011 Mo | 10,000 | PF63 12.00 | | | | |
| 2013 Mo | 13,500 | — | — | — | 8.00 | — |
| 2013 Mo | 4,200 | PF63 12.00 | | | | |

**KM# 610 1/10 ONZA (1/10 Troy Ounce of Silver)**
3.11 g., 0.999 Silver 0.0999 oz. ASW, 20 mm. **Obv:** National arms, eagle left **Rev:** Winged Victory

| Date | Mintage | VF20 | XF40 | MS60 | MS63 | MS65 |
|---|---|---|---|---|---|---|
| 2001 Mo | 25,000 | — | — | — | 27.50 | — |
| 2001 Mo | 1,500 | PF63 36.00 | | | | |
| 2002 Mo | 35,000 | — | — | — | 20.00 | — |
| 2002 Mo | 2,800 | PF63 30.00 | | | | |
| 2003 Mo | 20,000 | — | — | — | 20.00 | — |
| 2003 Mo | 4,900 | PF63 30.00 | | | | |
| 2004 Mo | 15,000 | — | — | — | 20.00 | — |
| 2004 Mo | 2,500 | PF63 30.00 | | | | |
| 2005 Mo | 9,277 | — | — | — | 20.00 | — |
| 2005 Mo | 3,000 | PF63 27.50 | | | | |
| 2006 Mo | 15,000 | — | — | — | 20.00 | — |
| 2006 Mo | 3,000 | PF63 27.50 | | | | |
| 2007 Mo | 3,500 | — | — | — | 20.00 | — |
| 2007 Mo | 4,000 | PF63 27.50 | | | | |
| 2008 Mo | 10,000 | — | — | — | 20.00 | — |
| 2008 Mo | 5,000 | PF63 27.50 | | | | |
| 2009 Mo | 10,000 | — | — | — | 20.00 | — |
| 2009 Mo | 5,000 | PF63 27.50 | | | | |
| 2010 Mo | 12,000 | — | — | — | 12.00 | — |
| 2010 Mo | 10,000 | PF63 15.00 | | | | |
| 2011 Mo | 15,000 | — | — | — | 12.00 | — |
| 2011 Mo | 10,000 | PF63 15.00 | | | | |
| 2012 Mo | 3,300 | — | — | — | 15.00 | — |
| 2013 Mo | 18,900 | — | — | — | 10.00 | — |
| 2013 Mo | 4,100 | PF63 15.00 | | | | |

**KM# 611 1/4 ONZA (1/4 Troy Ounce of Silver)**
7.78 g., 0.999 Silver 0.2497 oz. ASW, 27 mm. **Obv:** National arms, eagle left **Rev:** Winged Victory

| Date | Mintage | VF20 | XF40 | MS60 | MS63 | MS65 |
|---|---|---|---|---|---|---|
| 2001 Mo | 25,000 | — | — | — | 36.00 | — |
| 2001 Mo | 1,000 | PF63 44.00 | | | | |
| 2002 Mo | 35,000 | — | — | — | 27.50 | — |
| 2002 Mo | 2,800 | PF63 40.00 | | | | |
| 2003 Mo | 22,000 | — | — | — | 27.50 | — |
| 2003 Mo | 3,900 | PF63 40.00 | | | | |
| 2004 Mo | 15,000 | — | — | — | 27.50 | — |
| 2004 Mo | 2,500 | PF63 40.00 | | | | |
| 2005 Mo | 15,000 | — | — | — | 27.50 | — |
| 2005 Mo | 2,400 | PF63 37.00 | | | | |
| 2006 Mo | 15,000 | — | — | — | 25.00 | — |
| 2006 Mo | 2,900 | PF63 37.00 | | | | |
| 2007 Mo | 3,500 | — | — | — | 25.00 | — |
| 2007 Mo | 3,000 | PF63 37.00 | | | | |
| 2008 Mo | 9,000 | — | — | — | 25.00 | — |
| 2008 Mo | 2,900 | PF63 37.00 | | | | |
| 2009 Mo | 10,000 | — | — | — | 25.00 | — |
| 2009 Mo | 3,000 | PF63 37.00 | | | | |
| 2010 Mo | 15,500 | — | — | — | 25.00 | — |
| 2010 Mo | 5,000 | PF63 37.00 | | | | |
| 2011 Mo | 15,500 | — | — | — | 25.00 | — |
| 2011 Mo | 5,000 | PF63 37.00 | | | | |
| 2012 Mo | 16,700 | — | — | — | 25.00 | — |
| 2013 Mo | 9,600 | — | — | — | 12.00 | — |
| 2013 Mo | 3,200 | PF63 30.00 | | | | |

**KM# 612 1/2 ONZA (1/2 Troy Ounce of Silver)**
15.55 g., 0.999 Silver 0.4995 oz. ASW, 33 mm. **Obv:** National arms, eagle left **Rev:** Winged Victory

| Date | Mintage | VF20 | XF40 | MS60 | MS63 | MS65 |
|---|---|---|---|---|---|---|
| 2001 Mo | 20,000 | — | — | — | 45.00 | — |
| 2001 Mo | 1,000 | PF63 60.00 | | | | |
| 2002 Mo | 35,000 | — | — | — | 37.00 | — |
| 2002 Mo | 2,800 | PF63 50.00 | | | | |
| 2003 Mo | 28,000 | — | — | — | 37.00 | — |
| 2003 Mo | 3,400 | PF63 50.00 | | | | |
| 2004 Mo | 20,000 | — | — | — | 37.00 | — |
| 2004 Mo | 2,500 | PF63 50.00 | | | | |
| 2005 Mo | 10,000 | — | — | — | 37.00 | — |
| 2005 Mo | 2,800 | PF63 45.00 | | | | |
| 2006 Mo | 15,000 | — | — | — | 37.00 | — |
| 2006 Mo | 2,900 | PF63 45.00 | | | | |
| 2007 Mo | 3,500 | — | — | — | 37.00 | — |
| 2007 Mo | 1,500 | PF63 45.00 | | | | |
| 2008 Mo | 9,000 | — | — | — | 37.00 | — |
| 2008 Mo | 2,500 | PF63 45.00 | | | | |
| 2009 Mo | 10,000 | — | — | — | 37.00 | — |
| 2009 Mo | 3,000 | PF63 45.00 | | | | |
| 2010 Mo | 20,000 | — | — | — | 37.00 | — |
| 2010 Mo | 5,000 | PF63 45.00 | | | | |
| 2011 Mo | 30,000 | — | — | — | 37.00 | — |
| 2011 Mo | 5,000 | PF63 45.00 | | | | |
| 2012 Mo | 17,000 | — | — | — | 37.00 | — |
| 2013 Mo | 24,500 | — | — | — | 20.00 | — |
| 2013 Mo Proof | 3,000 | — | — | — | — | — |

**KM# 639 ONZA (Troy Ounce of Silver)**
31.10 g., 0.999 Silver 0.9989 oz. ASW, 40 mm. **Subject:** Libertad **Obv:** National arms, eagle left within center of past and present arms **Rev:** Winged Victory **Edge:** Reeded

| Date | Mintage | VF20 | XF40 | MS60 | MS63 | MS65 |
|---|---|---|---|---|---|---|
| 2001 Mo | 725,000 | — | — | — | 55.00 | — |
| 2001 Mo | 2,000 | PF63 140 | | | | |
| 2002 Mo | 854,000 | — | — | — | 55.00 | — |
| 2002 Mo | 3,800 | PF63 150 | | | | |
| 2003 Mo | 805,000 | — | — | — | 60.00 | — |
| 2003 Mo | 5,400 | PF63 130 | | | | |
| 2004 Mo | 450,000 | — | — | — | 50.00 | — |
| 2004 Mo | 3,000 | PF63 130 | | | | |
| 2005 Mo | 698,281 | — | — | — | 50.00 | — |
| 2005 Mo | 3,300 | PF63 150 | | | | |
| 2006 Mo | 300,000 | — | — | — | 50.00 | — |
| 2006 Mo | 4,000 | PF63 140 | | | | |
| 2007 Mo | 200,000 | — | — | — | 100 | — |
| 2007 Mo | 5,800 | PF63 150 | | | | |
| 2008 Mo | 950,000 | — | — | — | 60.00 | — |
| 2008 Mo | 11,000 | PF63 150 | | | | |
| 2009 Mo | 1,650,000 | — | — | — | 40.00 | — |
| 2009 Mo | 10,000 | PF63 100 | | | | |
| 2010 Mo | 1,000,000 | — | — | — | 50.00 | — |
| 2010 Mo | 10,000 | PF63 140 | | | | |
| 2011 Mo | 1,200,000 | — | — | — | 30.00 | — |
| 2011 Mo | 10,000 | PF63 80.00 | | | | |
| 2012 Mo | 746,400 | — | — | — | 30.00 | — |
| 2012 Mo | 4,200 | PF63 80.00 | | | | |
| 2013 Mo | 777,100 | — | — | — | 80.00 | — |
| 2013 Mo | 9,100 | PF63 40.00 | | | | |

**KM# 614 2 ONZAS (2 Troy Ounces of Silver)**
62.21 g., 0.999 Silver 1.998 oz. ASW, 48 mm. **Subject:** Libertad **Obv:** National arms, eagle left within center of past and present arms **Rev:** Winged Victory **Edge:** Reeded

| Date | Mintage | VF20 | XF40 | MS60 | MS63 | MS65 |
|---|---|---|---|---|---|---|
| 2001 Mo | 6,700 | — | — | — | 120 | — |
| 2001 Mo | 500 | PF63 300 | | | | |
| 2002 Mo | 8,700 | — | — | — | 110 | — |
| 2002 Mo | 1,000 | PF63 225 | | | | |
| 2003 Mo | 9,500 | — | — | — | 110 | — |
| 2003 Mo | 800 | PF63 225 | | | | |
| 2004 Mo | 8,000 | — | — | — | 100 | — |
| 2004 Mo | 1,000 | PF63 175 | | | | |
| 2005 Mo | 3,549 | — | — | — | 100 | — |
| 2005 Mo | 600 | PF63 500 | | | | |
| 2006 Mo | 5,800 | — | — | — | 100 | — |
| 2006 Mo | 1,100 | PF63 175 | | | | |
| 2007 Mo | 8,000 | — | — | — | 100 | — |
| 2007 Mo | 500 | PF63 250 | | | | |
| 2008 Mo | 17,000 | — | — | — | 110 | — |
| 2008 Mo | 1,000 | PF63 170 | | | | |
| 2009 Mo | 46,000 | — | — | — | 90.00 | — |
| 2009 Mo | 6,200 | PF63 100 | | | | |
| 2010 Mo | 14,000 | — | — | — | 75.00 | — |
| 2010 Mo | 1,300 | PF63 120 | | | | |
| 2011 Mo | 14,000 | — | — | — | 110 | — |
| 2011 Mo | 1,000 | PF63 140 | | | | |
| 2012 Mo | 18,600 | — | — | — | 70.00 | — |
| 2013 Mo | 17,400 | — | — | — | 60.00 | — |
| 2013 Mo | 1,300 | PF63 110 | | | | |

### KM# 615 5 ONZAS (5 Troy Ounces of Silver)

155.52 g., 0.999 Silver 4.995 oz. ASW, 65 mm. **Subject:** Libertad **Obv:** National arms, eagle left within center of past and present arms **Rev:** Winged Victory **Edge:** Reeded **Note:** Illustration reduced.

| Date | Mintage | VF20 | XF40 | MS60 | MS63 | MS65 |
|---|---|---|---|---|---|---|
| 2001 Mo | 4,000 | — | — | — | 190 | — |
| 2001 Mo | 600 | **PF63** 325 | | | | |
| 2002 Mo | 5,200 | — | — | — | 190 | — |
| 2002 Mo | 1,000 | **PF63** 325 | | | | |
| 2003 Mo | 6,000 | — | — | — | 180 | — |
| 2003 Mo | 1,500 | **PF63** 250 | | | | |
| 2004 Mo | 3,923 | — | — | — | 180 | — |
| 2004 Mo | 800 | **PF63** 225 | | | | |
| 2005 Mo | 2,401 | — | — | — | 205 | — |
| 2005 Mo | 1,000 | **PF63** 225 | | | | |
| 2006 Mo | 3,000 | — | — | — | 180 | — |
| 2006 Mo | 700 | **PF63** 265 | | | | |
| 2007 Mo | 3,000 | — | — | — | 180 | — |
| 2007 Mo | 500 | **PF63** 205 | | | | |
| 2008 Mo | 9,000 | — | — | — | 205 | — |
| 2008 Mo | 900 | **PF63** 270 | | | | |
| 2009 Mo | 21,000 | — | — | — | 250 | — |
| 2009 Mo | 5,000 | **PF63** 270 | | | | |
| 2010 Mo | 9,500 | — | — | — | 220 | — |
| 2010 Mo | 2,000 | **PF63** 230 | | | | |
| 2011 Mo | 10,000 | — | — | — | 220 | — |
| 2011 Mo | 2,000 | **PF63** 230 | | | | |
| 2012 Mo | 9,500 | — | — | — | 220 | — |
| 2013 Mo | 10,400 | — | — | — | 150 | — |
| 2013 Mo | 1,600 | **PF63** 220 | | | | |

### KM# 677 KILO (32.15 Troy Ounces of Silver)

999.98 g., 0.999 Silver 32.1178 oz. ASW, 110 mm. **Subject:** Collector Bullion **Obv:** National arms in center of past and present arms **Rev:** Winged Victory **Edge:** Reeded

| Date | Mintage | VF20 | XF40 | MS60 | MS63 | MS65 |
|---|---|---|---|---|---|---|
| 2001 Mo Prooflike | — | — | — | — | 2,200 | — |
| 2002 Mo Prooflike | 1,820 | — | — | — | 1,750 | — |
| 2003 Mo Prooflike | 1,514 | — | — | — | 1,650 | — |
| 2004 Mo Prooflike | 1,501 | — | — | — | 1,800 | — |
| 2005 Mo Prooflike | 500 | — | — | — | 1,750 | — |
| 2006 Mo Prooflike | 874 | — | — | — | 1,650 | — |
| 2007 Mo Prooflike | 700 | — | — | — | 1,650 | — |
| 2008 Mo | 2,003 | — | — | — | 1,200 | — |
| 2008 Mo Prooflike | 1,700 | — | — | — | 1,500 | — |
| 2009 Mo | 4,000 | — | — | — | 1,200 | — |
| 2009 Mo Prooflike | 1,700 | — | — | — | 1,500 | — |
| 2010 Mo | 4,000 | — | — | — | 1,200 | — |
| 2010 Mo Prooflike | 1,500 | — | — | — | 1,500 | — |
| 2011 Mo | 6,000 | — | — | — | 1,200 | — |
| 2011 Mo Prooflike | 1,000 | — | — | — | 1,500 | — |
| 2013 Mo | 2,300 | — | — | — | 1,200 | — |
| 2012 Mo Prooflike | 500 | — | — | — | 1,500 | — |
| 2013 Mo Prooflike | 400 | — | — | — | 1,500 | — |

Pre-Columbian Aztec Series

### KM# 921 100 PESOS

1000.00 g., 0.999 Silver 32.1186 oz. ASW, 110 mm. **Obv:** National arms in center of past and present arms **Rev:** Aztec Calendar **Edge:** Plain

| Date | Mintage | VF20 | XF40 | MS60 | MS63 | MS65 |
|---|---|---|---|---|---|---|
| 2007 Mo Prooflike | 303 | — | — | — | 2,000 | — |
| 2008 Mo Prooflike | 1,000 | — | — | — | 1,800 | — |
| 2009 Mo Prooflike | 1,500 | — | — | — | 1,500 | — |
| 2010 Mo Prooflike | 1,500 | — | — | — | 1,500 | — |
| 2011 Mo Prooflike | 1,500 | — | — | — | 1,500 | — |
| 2012 Mo Prooflike | 1,500 | — | — | — | 1,800 | — |
| 2013 Mo Prooflike | 500 | — | — | — | 1,500 | — |

## GOLD BULLION COINAGE

### KM# 957 1.25 GRAMS

1.67 g., 0.0402 Gold 0.0022 oz. AGW, 13 mm. **Series:** Cultural Fusion **Subject:** Architecture **Obv:** National arms (eagle and snake facing left) and legend **Obv. Legend:** ESTADOS UNIDOS MEXICANOS **Rev:** Heads in profile, mail, woman with a plume **Rev. Legend:** FUSIÓN CULTURAL and 1.25 g DE ORO PURO LEY 0.750

| Date | Mintage | VF20 | XF40 | MS60 | MS63 | MS65 |
|---|---|---|---|---|---|---|
| 2011 Mo | 2,000 | **PF63** 110 | | | | |

### KM# 958 1.25 GRAMS

1.67 g., 0.750 Gold 0.0402 oz. AGW, 13 mm. **Series:** Cultural fusion **Subject:** Architecture **Obv:** Natioan arms (eagle and snake facing left) and legend **Obv. Legend:** ESTADOS UNIDOS MEXICANOS **Rev:** Pyramid, aquedect, church dome and cacao fruit **Rev. Legend:** FUSIÓN CULTURAL and 1.25 g DE ORO PURO LEY 0.750

| Date | Mintage | VF20 | XF40 | MS60 | MS63 | MS65 |
|---|---|---|---|---|---|---|
| 2011 Mo | 2,000 | **PF63** 110 | | | | |

### KM# 959 1.25 GRAMS

1.67 g., 0.750 Gold 0.0402 oz. AGW, 13 mm. **Series:** Cultural Fusion **Subject:** Cacao **Obv:** National arms (eagle and snake facing left) and legend **Obv. Legend:** ESTADOS UNIDOS MEXICANOS **Rev:** Aztec sculpture of a man carrying a cacao husk, legend **Rev. Legend:** XOCOLATL PARA EL MUNDS, EL CACAO and 1.25 g DE ORO PURO LEY

| Date | Mintage | VF20 | XF40 | MS60 | MS63 | MS65 |
|---|---|---|---|---|---|---|
| 2011 Mo 2000 | — | **PF63** 110 | | | | |

### KM# 960 1.25 GRAMS

1.67 g., 0.750 Gold 0.0402 oz. AGW, 13 mm. **Series:** Cultural Fusion **Subject:** Merchandise **Obv:** National arms (eagle and snake facing left) and legend **Obv. Legend:** ESTADOS UNIDOS MEXICANOS **Rev:** Allegory of Mesoamerican and Spanish cultural fusion. **Rev. Legend:** FUSIÒN CULTURAL and 1.25 g DE ORO PURO LEY

| Date | Mintage | VF20 | XF40 | MS60 | MS63 | MS65 |
|---|---|---|---|---|---|---|
| 2011 Mo | 2,000 | **PF63** 110 | | | | |

### KM# 671 1/20 ONZA (1/20 Ounce of Pure Gold)

1.56 g., 0.999 Gold 0.0499 oz. AGW, 13 mm. **Obv:** National arms, eagle left **Rev:** Winged Victory **Edge:** Reeded **Note:** Design similar to KM#609. Value estimates do not include the high taxes and surcharges added to the issue prices by the Mexican Government.

| Date | Mintage | VF20 | XF40 | MS60 | MS63 | MS65 |
|---|---|---|---|---|---|---|
| 2002 Mo | 5,000 | — | — | — | 79.00 | — |
| 2003 Mo | 800 | — | — | — | 80.00 | — |
| 2004 Mo | 4,000 | — | — | — | 79.00 | — |
| 2005 Mo | 3,200 | — | — | — | 79.00 | — |
| 2005 Mo | 400 | **PF63** 82.00 | | | | |
| 2006 Mo | 3,000 | — | — | — | 79.00 | — |
| 2006 Mo | 520 | **PF63** 82.00 | | | | |
| 2007 Mo | 500 | **PF63** 82.00 | | | | |
| 2007 Mo | 1,200 | — | — | — | 79.00 | — |
| 2008 Mo | 500 | **PF63** 82.00 | | | | |
| 2008 Mo | 800 | — | — | — | 79.00 | — |
| 2009 Mo | 2,000 | — | — | — | 79.00 | — |
| 2009 Mo | 600 | **PF63** 82.00 | | | | |
| 2010 Mo | 1,500 | — | — | — | 79.00 | — |
| 2010 Mo | 600 | **PF63** 82.00 | | | | |
| 2011 Mo | 2,500 | — | — | — | 79.00 | — |
| 2011 Mo | 1,100 | **PF63** 82.00 | | | | |
| 2013 Mo | 650 | — | — | — | 79.00 | — |
| 2013 Mo | 300 | **PF63** 82.00 | | | | |

### KM# 672 1/10 ONZA (1/10 Ounce of Pure Gold)

3.11 g., 0.999 Gold 0.0999 oz. AGW, 16 mm. **Obv:** National arms, eagle left **Rev:** Winged Victory **Edge:** Reeded **Note:** Design similar to KM#610. Value estimates do not include the high taxes and surcharges added to the issue prices by the Mexican Government.

| Date | Mintage | VF20 | XF40 | MS60 | MS63 | MS65 |
|---|---|---|---|---|---|---|
| 2002 Mo | 5,000 | — | — | — | 146 | — |
| 2003 Mo | 300 | — | — | — | 148 | — |
| 2004 Mo | 2,000 | — | — | — | 146 | — |
| 2005 Mo | 500 | — | — | — | 146 | — |
| 2005 Mo | 400 | **PF63** 148 | | | | |
| 2006 Mo | 2,500 | — | — | — | 146 | — |
| 2006 Mo | 520 | **PF63** 148 | | | | |
| 2007 Mo | 1,200 | — | — | — | 146 | — |
| 2007 Mo | 500 | **PF63** 148 | | | | |
| 2008 Mo | 2,500 | — | — | — | 146 | — |
| 2008 Mo | 500 | **PF63** 148 | | | | |
| 2009 Mo | 9,000 | — | — | — | 146 | — |
| 2009 Mo | 600 | **PF63** 148 | | | | |
| 2010 Mo | 4,500 | — | — | — | 146 | — |
| 2010 Mo | 600 | **PF63** 148 | | | | |
| 2011 Mo | 6,500 | — | — | — | 146 | — |
| 2011 Mo | 1,100 | **PF63** 148 | | | | |
| 2013 Mo | 2,150 | — | — | — | 146 | — |
| 2013 Mo | 300 | **PF63** 148 | | | | |

### KM# 673 1/4 ONZA (1/4 Ounce of Pure Gold)

7.78 g., 0.999 Gold 0.2497 oz. AGW, 23 mm. **Obv:** National arms, eagle left **Rev:** Winged Victory **Edge:** Reeded **Note:** Design similar to KM#611. Value estimates do not include the high taxes and surcharges added to the issue prices by the Mexican Government.

| Date | Mintage | VF20 | XF40 | MS60 | MS63 | MS65 |
|---|---|---|---|---|---|---|
| 2002 Mo | 5,000 | — | — | — | 340 | — |
| 2003 Mo | 300 | — | — | — | 346 | — |
| 2004 Mo | 1,500 | — | — | — | 340 | — |
| 2004 Mo | 1,000 | **PF63** 349 | | | | |
| 2005 Mo | 500 | — | — | — | 346 | — |
| 2005 Mo | 2,600 | **PF63** 349 | | | | |
| 2006 Mo | 1,500 | — | — | — | 340 | — |
| 2006 Mo | 2,120 | **PF63** 349 | | | | |
| 2007 Mo | 500 | — | — | — | 346 | — |
| 2007 Mo | 1,500 | **PF63** 349 | | | | |
| 2008 Mo | 800 | — | — | — | 346 | — |
| 2008 Mo | 800 | **PF63** 349 | | | | |
| 2009 Mo | 3,000 | — | — | — | 340 | — |
| 2009 Mo | 1,700 | **PF63** 349 | | | | |
| 2010 Mo | 1,500 | — | — | — | 340 | — |
| 2010 Mo | 1,000 | **PF63** 349 | | | | |
| 2011 Mo | 1,500 | — | — | — | 340 | — |
| 2011 Mo | 2,000 | **PF63** 349 | | | | |
| 2013 Mo | 750 | — | — | — | 340 | — |
| 2013 Mo | 600 | **PF63** 349 | | | | |

### KM# 674 1/2 ONZA (1/2 Ounce of Pure Gold)

15.55 g., 0.999 Gold 0.4995 oz. AGW, 29 mm. **Obv:** National arms, eagle left **Rev:** Winged Victory **Edge:** Reeded **Note:** Design similar to KM#612. Value estimates do not include the high taxes and surcharges added to the issue prices by the Mexican Government.

| Date | Mintage | VF20 | XF40 | MS60 | MS63 | MS65 |
|---|---|---|---|---|---|---|
| 2002 Mo | 5,000 | — | — | — | 656 | — |
| 2003 Mo | 300 | — | — | — | 668 | — |
| 2004 Mo | 500 | — | — | — | 656 | — |
| 2005 Mo | 500 | — | — | — | 668 | — |
| 2005 Mo | 400 | **PF63** 680 | | | | |
| 2006 Mo | 500 | — | — | — | 668 | — |
| 2006 Mo | 520 | **PF63** 680 | | | | |
| 2007 Mo | 500 | — | — | — | 668 | — |
| 2007 Mo | 500 | **PF63** 680 | | | | |
| 2008 Mo | 300 | — | — | — | 668 | — |
| 2008 Mo | 500 | **PF63** 680 | | | | |
| 2009 Mo | 3,000 | — | — | — | 656 | — |
| 2009 Mo | 600 | **PF63** 680 | | | | |
| 2010 Mo | 1,500 | — | — | — | 656 | — |
| 2010 Mo | 600 | **PF63** 680 | | | | |
| 2011 Mo | 1,500 | — | — | — | 656 | — |
| 2011 Mo | 1,100 | **PF63** 680 | | | | |
| 2013 Mo | 500 | — | — | — | 656 | — |
| 2013 Mo | 300 | **PF63** 680 | | | | |

### KM# 675 ONZA (Ounce of Pure Gold)

31.10 g., 0.999 Gold 0.999 oz. AGW, 34.5 mm. **Obv:** National arms, eagle left **Rev:** Winged Victory **Edge:** Reeded **Note:** Design similar to KM#639. Value estimates do not include the high taxes and surcharges added to the issue prices by the Mexican Government.

| Date | Mintage | VF20 | XF40 | MS60 | MS63 | MS65 |
|---|---|---|---|---|---|---|
| 2002 Mo | 15,000 | — | — | — | 1,251 | — |
| 2003 Mo | 500 | — | — | — | 1,263 | — |
| 2004 Mo | 3,000 | — | — | — | 1,251 | — |
| 2005 Mo | 3,000 | — | — | — | 1,251 | — |
| 2005 Mo | 250 | **PF63** 1,276 | | | | |
| 2006 Mo | 4,000 | — | — | — | 1,251 | — |
| 2006 Mo | 520 | **PF63** 1,276 | | | | |
| 2007 Mo | 2,500 | — | — | — | 1,251 | — |
| 2007 Mo | 500 | **PF63** 1,276 | | | | |
| 2008 Mo | 800 | — | — | — | 1,251 | — |
| 2008 Mo | 500 | **PF63** 1,276 | | | | |
| 2009 Mo | 6,200 | — | — | — | 1,251 | — |
| 2009 Mo | 600 | **PF63** 1,276 | | | | |
| 2010 Mo | 4,000 | — | — | — | 1,251 | — |
| 2010 Mo | 600 | **PF63** 1,276 | | | | |
| 2011 Mo | 3,000 | — | — | — | 1,251 | — |
| 2011 Mo | 1,100 | **PF63** 1,276 | | | | |
| 2012 Mo | 3,000 | — | — | — | 1,251 | — |
| 2013 Mo | 2,350 | — | — | — | 1,251 | — |
| 2013 Mo | 400 | **PF63** 1,276 | | | | |

## BANK SETS

| KM# | Date | Mintage | Identification | Issue Price | Mkt Val |
|---|---|---|---|---|---|
| BS38 | 2001 (10) | — | KM#546-549, 603-605, 636-638 Set in folder | — | 65.00 |
| BS39 | 2002 (8) | — | KM#546-549, 603-605, 616 Set in folder | — | 30.00 |
| BS40 | 2003 (6) | — | KM#547-549, 603-605 Set in folder | — | 30.00 |

The Republic of Moldova (formerly the Moldavian S.S.R.) is bordered in the north, east and south by the Ukraine and on the west by Romania. It has an area of 13,000 sq.mi. (33,700 sq.km.) and a population of 4.4 million. The capital is Chisinau. Agricultural products are mainly cereals, grapes, tobacco, sugar beets and fruits. Food processing, clothing, building materials and agricultural machinery manufacturing dominate industry.

**MONETARY SYSTEM**
100 Bani = 1 Leu

# REPUBLIC

## DECIMAL COINAGE

### KM# 1 BAN

0.67 g., Aluminum, 14.5 mm. **Obv:** National arms **Rev:** Value divides date above monogram **Edge:** Plain

| Date | Mintage | VF20 | XF40 | MS60 | MS63 | MS65 |
|---|---|---|---|---|---|---|
| 2004 | — | — | — | 0.15 | 0.25 | 0.50 |
| 2006 | — | — | — | 0.15 | 0.25 | 0.50 |

### KM# 2 5 BANI

0.75 g., Aluminum, 16 mm. **Obv:** National arms **Rev:** Monogram divides sprigs below value and date **Edge:** Plain

| Date | Mintage | VF20 | XF40 | MS60 | MS63 | MS65 |
|---|---|---|---|---|---|---|
| 2001 | — | — | — | 0.20 | 0.35 | 0.50 |
| 2002 | — | — | — | 0.20 | 0.35 | 0.50 |
| 2003 | — | — | — | 0.20 | 0.35 | 0.50 |
| 2004 | — | — | — | 0.20 | 0.35 | 0.50 |
| 2005 | — | — | — | 0.20 | 0.35 | 0.50 |
| 2006 | — | — | — | 0.20 | 0.35 | 0.50 |
| 2008 | — | — | — | 0.20 | 0.35 | 0.50 |
| 2010 | — | — | — | 0.20 | 0.35 | 0.50 |
| 2011 | — | — | — | 0.20 | 0.35 | 0.50 |
| 2012 | — | — | — | 0.20 | 0.35 | 0.50 |
| 2013 | — | — | — | 0.20 | 0.35 | 0.50 |

### KM# 7 10 BANI

0.85 g., Aluminum, 16.6 mm. **Obv:** National arms **Rev:** Value, date and monogram **Edge:** Plain

| Date | Mintage | VF20 | XF40 | MS60 | MS63 | MS65 |
|---|---|---|---|---|---|---|
| 2001 | — | — | — | 0.25 | 0.40 | 0.60 |
| 2002 | — | — | — | 0.25 | 0.40 | 0.60 |
| 2003 | — | — | — | 0.25 | 0.40 | 0.60 |
| 2004 | — | — | — | 0.25 | 0.40 | 0.60 |
| 2005 | — | — | — | 0.25 | 0.40 | 0.60 |
| 2006 | — | — | — | 0.25 | 0.40 | 0.60 |
| 2008 | — | — | — | 0.25 | 0.40 | 0.60 |
| 2010 | — | — | — | 0.25 | 0.40 | 0.60 |
| 2011 | — | — | — | 0.25 | 0.40 | 0.60 |
| 2013 | — | — | — | 0.25 | 0.40 | 0.60 |

### KM# 3 25 BANI

0.95 g., Aluminum, 17.5 mm. **Obv:** National arms **Rev:** Monogram divides sprigs below value and date **Edge:** Plain

| Date | Mintage | VF20 | XF40 | MS60 | MS63 | MS65 |
|---|---|---|---|---|---|---|
| 2001 | — | — | 0.20 | 0.30 | 0.50 | 0.75 |
| 2002 | — | — | 0.20 | 0.30 | 0.50 | 0.75 |
| 2003 | — | — | 0.20 | 0.30 | 0.50 | 0.75 |
| 2004 | — | — | 0.20 | 0.30 | 0.50 | 0.75 |
| 2005 | — | — | 0.20 | 0.30 | 0.50 | 0.75 |
| 2006 | — | — | 0.20 | 0.30 | 0.50 | 0.75 |
| 2008 | — | — | 0.20 | 0.30 | 0.50 | 0.75 |
| 2010 | — | — | 0.20 | 0.30 | 0.50 | 0.75 |
| 2011 | — | — | 0.20 | 0.30 | 0.50 | 0.75 |
| 2012 | — | — | 0.20 | 0.30 | 0.50 | 0.75 |
| 2013 | — | — | 0.20 | 0.30 | 0.50 | 0.75 |

### KM# 10 50 BANI

3.10 g., Brass Clad Steel, 19 mm. **Obv:** National arms **Rev:** Value and date within grapevine **Edge:** Reeded

| Date | Mintage | VF20 | XF40 | MS60 | MS63 | MS65 |
|---|---|---|---|---|---|---|
| 2003 | — | — | — | 0.75 | 1.50 | 2.00 |
| 2005 | — | — | — | 0.75 | 1.50 | 2.00 |
| 2008 | — | — | — | 0.75 | 1.50 | 2.00 |

### KM# 12 10 LEI

13.50 g., 0.925 Silver 0.4015 oz. ASW, 24.5 mm. **Obv:** National arms above value **Rev:** European wildcat within circle **Edge:** Plain

| Date | Mintage | VF20 | XF40 | MS60 | MS63 | MS65 |
|---|---|---|---|---|---|---|
| 2001 | 1,000 | PF63 55.00 | PF65 65.00 | | | |

### KM# 13 10 LEI

13.50 g., 0.925 Silver 0.4015 oz. ASW, 24.5 mm. **Obv:** National arms above value **Rev:** Green Woodpecker on tree within circle **Edge:** Plain

| Date | Mintage | VF20 | XF40 | MS60 | MS63 | MS65 |
|---|---|---|---|---|---|---|
| 2001 | 1,000 | PF63 50.00 | PF65 60.00 | | | |

### KM# 19 10 LEI

13.45 g., 0.925 Silver 0.400 oz. ASW, 24.5 mm. **Obv:** National arms above value **Rev:** European Mink within circle **Edge:** Plain

| Date | Mintage | VF20 | XF40 | MS60 | MS63 | MS65 |
|---|---|---|---|---|---|---|
| 2003 | 500 | PF65 65.00 | | | | |

### KM# 20 10 LEI

13.45 g., 0.925 Silver 0.400 oz. ASW, 24.5 mm. **Obv:** National arms above value **Rev:** Black Storks within circle **Edge:** Plain

| Date | Mintage | VF20 | XF40 | MS60 | MS63 | MS65 |
|---|---|---|---|---|---|---|
| 2003 | 500 | PF65 65.00 | | | | |

### KM# 25 10 LEI

25.00 g., Nickel Plated Brass, 30 mm. **Subject:** Wine Holiday **Obv:** National arms above value **Rev:** Wine grapes, goblet and flask **Edge:** Plain

| Date | Mintage | VF20 | XF40 | MS60 | MS63 | MS65 |
|---|---|---|---|---|---|---|
| 2003 | — | PF65 12.50 | | | | |

### KM# 22 10 LEI

13.50 g., 0.925 Silver 0.4015 oz. ASW, 24.5 mm. **Obv:** National arms above value **Rev:** Pine Marten within circle **Edge:** Plain

| Date | Mintage | VF20 | XF40 | MS60 | MS63 | MS65 |
|---|---|---|---|---|---|---|
| 2004 | 500 | PF65 65.00 | | | | |

### KM# 29 10 LEI

25.00 g., Nickel Plated Brass, 30 mm. **Subject:** European Women's Chess Championship **Obv:** Arms, date at top, value at bottom **Obv. Legend:** REPUBLICA - 2005 - MOLDOVA **Rev:** 2 chess figures on board at left, map at right **Rev. Inscription:** 2005 CHISINAU **Edge:** Plain

| Date | Mintage | VF20 | XF40 | MS60 | MS63 | MS65 |
|---|---|---|---|---|---|---|
| 2005 | — | PF65 12.50 | | | | |

### KM# 30 10 LEI

13.50 g., 0.925 Silver 0.4015 oz. ASW, 24.5 mm. **Obv:** Arms, value below **Obv. Legend:** REPUBLICA MOLDOVA **Rev:** Imperial eagle on branch, legend follows the coin circumference **Edge:** Plain

| Date | Mintage | VF20 | XF40 | MS60 | MS63 | MS65 |
|---|---|---|---|---|---|---|
| 2005 | 500 | PF65 65.00 | | | | |

### KM# 33 10 LEI

13.50 g., 0.925 Silver 0.4015 oz. ASW, 24.5 mm. **Obv:** Arms, value below **Obv. Legend:** REPUBLICA - 2006 - MOLDOVA **Rev:** Bird in grass, legend around circumference using Latin name **Edge:** Plain

| Date | Mintage | VF20 | XF40 | MS60 | MS63 | MS65 |
|---|---|---|---|---|---|---|
| 2006 | 500 | PF65 65.00 | | | | |

### KM# 38 10 LEI

13.50 g., 0.925 Silver 0.4015 oz. ASW, 24.5 mm. **Rev:** Common ground squirrel

| Date | Mintage | VF20 | XF40 | MS60 | MS63 | MS65 |
|---|---|---|---|---|---|---|
| 2006 | 500 | PF65 65.00 | | | | |

### KM# 43 10 LEI

13.50 g., 0.925 Silver 0.4015 oz. ASW, 24.5 mm. **Rev:** White water lilly

| Date | Mintage | VF20 | XF40 | MS60 | MS63 | MS65 |
|---|---|---|---|---|---|---|
| 2008 | 500 | PF65 60.00 | | | | |

### KM# 47 20 LEI

13.50 g., 0.925 Silver 0.4015 oz. ASW, 22 mm. **Subject:** Assumption of the Virgin Mary

| Date | Mintage | VF20 | XF40 | MS60 | MS63 | MS65 |
|---|---|---|---|---|---|---|
| 2009 | 1,000 | PF63 35.00 | PF65 40.00 | | | |

**KM# 17 50 LEI**

16.50 g., 0.925 Silver 0.4907 oz. ASW, 30 mm. **Obv:** National arms above value **Rev:** Constantin Brancusi and building **Edge:** Plain

| Date | Mintage | VF20 | XF40 | MS60 | MS63 | MS65 |
|---|---|---|---|---|---|---|
| 2001 | 1,000 | PF63 50.00 | PF65 60.00 | | | |

**KM# 18 50 LEI**

16.50 g., 0.925 Silver 0.4907 oz. ASW, 30 mm. **Obv:** National arms above value **Rev:** Vasile Alecsandri with book and landscape **Edge:** Plain

| Date | Mintage | VF20 | XF40 | MS60 | MS63 | MS65 |
|---|---|---|---|---|---|---|
| 2001 | 1,000 | PF63 50.00 | PF65 60.00 | | | |

**KM# 36 50 LEI**

16.50 g., 0.925 Silver 0.4907 oz. ASW, 30 mm. **Subject:** Vazile Alecsandri, 180th Anniversary **Obv:** Arms **Rev:** Bust and landscape

| Date | Mintage | VF20 | XF40 | MS60 | MS63 | MS65 |
|---|---|---|---|---|---|---|
| 2001 | 1,000 | PF63 35.00 | PF65 40.00 | | | |

**KM# 14 50 LEI**

16.55 g., 0.925 Silver 0.4922 oz. ASW, 29.9 mm. **Subject:** Effigy of Miron Costin **Obv:** National arms above value **Rev:** Bust with hat 1/4 right flanked by dates and books **Edge:** Plain

| Date | Mintage | VF20 | XF40 | MS60 | MS63 | MS65 |
|---|---|---|---|---|---|---|
| 2003 | 500 | PF65 165 | | | | |

**KM# 21 50 LEI**

16.50 g., 0.925 Silver 0.4907 oz. ASW, 29.8 mm. **Subject:** Effigy of Dimitrie Cantemir **Obv:** National arms above value **Rev:** Bust facing flanked by dates and scroll **Edge:** Plain

| Date | Mintage | VF20 | XF40 | MS60 | MS63 | MS65 |
|---|---|---|---|---|---|---|
| 2003 | 500 | PF65 165 | | | | |

**KM# 23 50 LEI**

16.50 g., 0.925 Silver 0.4907 oz. ASW, 30 mm. **Obv:** National arms above value **Rev:** Bust of Bishop facing holding scepter **Edge:** Plain

| Date | Mintage | VF20 | XF40 | MS60 | MS63 | MS65 |
|---|---|---|---|---|---|---|
| 2004 | 500 | PF65 90.00 | | | | |

**KM# 31 50 LEI**

16.50 g., 0.925 Silver 0.4907 oz. ASW, 30 mm. **Subject:** 415th Anniversary - Birth of Grigore Ureche **Obv:** Arms, date divides legend at top, value below, **Obv. Legend:** REPUBLICA MOLDOVA **Rev:** Bust faces right, scroll with feather pen at right, inscription on scroll **Rev. Legend:** GRIGORE URECHE **Rev. Inscription:** Letopisetul Tarii Moldovei **Edge:** Plain

| Date | Mintage | VF20 | XF40 | MS60 | MS63 | MS65 |
|---|---|---|---|---|---|---|
| 2005 | — | PF65 120 | | | | |

**KM# 34 50 LEI**

16.50 g., 0.925 Silver 0.4907 oz. ASW, 30 mm. **Subject:** 200th Anniversary - Birth of Alexandru Donici **Obv:** Arms, date divides legend above, value below **Obv. Legend:** REPUBLICA MOLDOVA **Rev:** Bust of Donici facing, life dates on ribbon below **Rev. Legend:** ALEXANDRU DONICI

| Date | Mintage | VF20 | XF40 | MS60 | MS63 | MS65 |
|---|---|---|---|---|---|---|
| 2006 | — | PF65 120 | | | | |

**KM# 40 50 LEI**

16.50 g., 0.925 Silver 0.4907 oz. ASW, 30 mm. **Subject:** Metropolitian Varilaam **Rev:** Bust 3/4 right

| Date | Mintage | VF20 | XF40 | MS60 | MS63 | MS65 |
|---|---|---|---|---|---|---|
| 2007 | 500 | PF65 120 | | | | |

**KM# 41 50 LEI**

16.50 g., 0.925 Silver 0.4907 oz. ASW, 30 mm. **Subject:** Pottery Tradition **Rev:** Hand modeling clay vessel on pottery wheel

| Date | Mintage | VF20 | XF40 | MS60 | MS63 | MS65 |
|---|---|---|---|---|---|---|
| 2007 | 500 | PF65 60.00 | | | | |

**KM# 44 50 LEI**

16.50 g., 0.925 Silver 0.4907 oz. ASW, 30 mm. **Subject:** Oak tree in Stefan **Rev:** Oak tree

| Date | Mintage | VF20 | XF40 | MS60 | MS63 | MS65 |
|---|---|---|---|---|---|---|
| 2008 | 500 | PF65 75.00 | | | | |

**KM# 45 50 LEI**

16.50 g., 0.925 Silver 0.4907 oz. ASW, 30 mm. **Subject:** Cooper Trade **Rev:** Barrell maker

| Date | Mintage | VF20 | XF40 | MS60 | MS63 | MS65 |
|---|---|---|---|---|---|---|
| 2008 | 500 | PF65 55.00 | | | | |

**KM# 48 50 LEI**

16.50 g., 0.925 Silver 0.4907 oz. ASW, 30 mm. **Subject:** Geodezic arc of Struve **Rev:** Map

| Date | Mintage | VF20 | XF40 | MS60 | MS63 | MS65 |
|---|---|---|---|---|---|---|
| 2009 | 500 | PF65 75.00 | | | | |

**KM# 49 50 LEI**

16.50 g., 0.925 Silver 0.4907 oz. ASW, 30 mm. **Subject:** Rule of Vasile Lupu **Rev:** Open book and coat-of-arms

| Date | Mintage | VF20 | XF40 | MS60 | MS63 | MS65 |
|---|---|---|---|---|---|---|
| 2009 | 500 | PF65 75.00 | | | | |

**KM# 50 50 LEI**

16.50 g., 0.925 Silver 0.4907 oz. ASW, 30 mm. **Subject:** Traditional weaving **Rev:** Woman seated at weaving frame

| Date | Mintage | VF20 | XF40 | MS60 | MS63 | MS65 |
|---|---|---|---|---|---|---|
| 2009 | 500 | PF65 70.00 | | | | |

**KM# 53 50 LEI**

16.50 g., 0.999 Silver 0.530 oz. ASW, 30 mm. **Subject:** Traditional Musical Instruments **Obv:** National arms **Rev:** Violin, bagpipe, pan pipe and flute

| Date | Mintage | VF20 | XF40 | MS60 | MS63 | MS65 |
|---|---|---|---|---|---|---|
| 2010 | 500 | PF65 40.00 | | | | |

**KM# 54 50 LEI**

16.50 g., 0.999 Silver 0.530 oz. ASW, 30 mm. **Obv:** National arms **Rev:** Archeological complex of Old Orhei

| Date | Mintage | VF20 | XF40 | MS60 | MS63 | MS65 |
|---|---|---|---|---|---|---|
| 2010 | 500 | **PF65** 45.00 | | | | |

**KM# 55 50 LEI**

13.00 g., 0.999 Silver 0.4175 oz. ASW, 28 mm. **Subject:** Maria Cebotari, 100th Anniversary of Birth **Obv:** National arms **Rev:** Cebotari bust left

| Date | Mintage | VF20 | XF40 | MS60 | MS63 | MS65 |
|---|---|---|---|---|---|---|
| 2010 | 500 | **PF65** 45.00 | | | | |

**KM# 56 50 LEI**

13.00 g., 0.999 Silver 0.4175 oz. ASW, 28 mm. **Subject:** Doina and Ion Aldea-Teodorovici **Obv:** National arms **Rev:** Conjoined busts right

| Date | Mintage | VF20 | XF40 | MS60 | MS63 | MS65 |
|---|---|---|---|---|---|---|
| 2010 | 500 | **PF65** 45.00 | | | | |

**KM# 58 50 LEI**

16.50 g., 0.999 Silver 0.530 oz. ASW, 30 mm. **Subject:** Moldovan Football, 100th Anniversary **Obv:** National Arms **Rev:** Soccer player

| Date | Mintage | VF20 | XF40 | MS60 | MS63 | MS65 |
|---|---|---|---|---|---|---|
| 2010 | 300 | **PF65** 45.00 | | | | |

**KM# 59 50 LEI**

16.50 g., 0.999 Silver 0.530 oz. ASW, 30 mm. **Subject:** Annunciation Church in Chisinau, 200th Anniversary **Obv:** National Arms **Rev:** Church façade

| Date | Mintage | VF20 | XF40 | MS60 | MS63 | MS65 |
|---|---|---|---|---|---|---|
| 2010 | 500 | **PF65** 45.00 | | | | |

**KM# 60 50 LEI**

13.00 g., 0.999 Silver 0.4175 oz. ASW, 28 mm. **Subject:** Grigore Vieru **Obv:** National Arms **Rev:** Profile bust right

| Date | Mintage | VF20 | XF40 | MS60 | MS63 | MS65 |
|---|---|---|---|---|---|---|
| 2010 | 500 | **PF65** 45.00 | | | | |

**KM# 65 50 LEI**

13.00 g., 0.999 Silver 0.4175 oz. ASW, 28 mm. **Subject:** Bogdan Petriceicu Hasdeu **Obv:** National arms **Rev:** Bust **Edge:** Reeded

| Date | Mintage | VF20 | XF40 | MS60 | MS63 | MS65 |
|---|---|---|---|---|---|---|
| 2011 | 500 | **PF65** 50.00 | | | | |

**KM# 67 50 LEI**

13.00 g., 0.999 Silver 0.4175 oz. ASW, 28 mm. **Subject:** Alexandru Bernardazzi, 180th Anniversary of Birth **Obv:** National arms **Rev:** Portrait **Edge:** Reeded

| Date | Mintage | VF20 | XF40 | MS60 | MS63 | MS65 |
|---|---|---|---|---|---|---|
| 2011 | 500 | **PF65** 50.00 | | | | |

**KM# 68 50 LEI**

16.50 g., 0.999 Silver 0.530 oz. ASW, 30 mm. **Obv:** National arms **Rev:** Spoonbill standing left, oval background **Edge:** Reeded

| Date | Mintage | VF20 | XF40 | MS60 | MS63 | MS65 |
|---|---|---|---|---|---|---|
| 2011 | 500 | **PF65** 50.00 | | | | |

**KM# 69 50 LEI**

16.50 g., 0.999 Silver 0.530 oz. ASW, 30 mm. **Subject:** Holiday Traditions **Obv:** National arms **Rev:** Carolers **Edge:** Reeded

| Date | Mintage | VF20 | XF40 | MS60 | MS63 | MS65 |
|---|---|---|---|---|---|---|
| 2011 | 1,000 | **PF63** 45.00 | **PF65** 50.00 | | | |

**KM# 71 50 LEI**

16.50 g., 0.999 Silver 0.530 oz. ASW, 30 mm. **Subject:** London Olympics **Rev:** Runner breaking tape at finish line

| Date | Mintage | VF20 | XF40 | MS60 | MS63 | MS65 |
|---|---|---|---|---|---|---|
| 2012 | — | **PF63** 45.00 | **PF65** 50.00 | | | |

**KM# 72 50 LEI**

16.50 g., 0.999 Silver 0.530 oz. ASW, 30 mm. **Subject:** Ivo Creanga, 175th Anniversary of Birth

| Date | Mintage | VF20 | XF40 | MS60 | MS63 | MS65 |
|---|---|---|---|---|---|---|
| 2012 | — | **PF63** 45.00 | **PF65** 50.00 | | | |

**KM# 73 50 LEI**

16.50 g., 0.999 Silver 0.530 oz. ASW, 30 mm. **Subject:** Soroka Fortress

| Date | Mintage | VF20 | XF40 | MS60 | MS63 | MS65 |
|---|---|---|---|---|---|---|
| 2012 | — | **PF63** 45.00 | **PF65** 50.00 | | | |

**KM# 74 50 LEI**

16.50 g., 0.999 Silver 0.530 oz. ASW, 30 mm. **Subject:** Mid-Summer's Day **Obv:** Arms **Rev:** Female head with wheat wreath

| Date | Mintage | VF20 | XF40 | MS60 | MS63 | MS65 |
|---|---|---|---|---|---|---|
| 2012 | — | **PF63** 45.00 | **PF65** 50.00 | | | |

**KM# 16 100 LEI**

31.10 g., 0.925 Silver 0.9249 oz. ASW, 37 mm. **Subject:** 10th Anniversary of Independence **Obv:** National arms above value **Rev:** Arch monument within circle above value and sprigs **Edge:** Plain

| Date | Mintage | VF20 | XF40 | MS60 | MS63 | MS65 |
|---|---|---|---|---|---|---|
| 2001 | 1,000 | **PF65** 220 | | | | |

**KM# 26 100 LEI**
7.80 g., 0.9999 Gold 0.2508 oz. AGW, 24 mm. **Obv:** National arms above value **Rev:** King Stephan the Great (1456-1504) **Edge:** Plain

| Date | Mintage | VF20 | XF40 | MS60 | MS63 | MS65 |
|---|---|---|---|---|---|---|
| 2004 | — | PF65 450 | | | | |

**KM# 32 100 LEI**
31.10 g., 0.925 Silver 0.9249 oz. ASW, 37 mm. **Subject:** Burebista - King of Dacians **Obv:** Arms, date divides legend at top, value below **Obv. Legend:** REPUBLICA MOLDOVA **Rev:** Bust of Burebista at left, battle scene of Geto-Dacians with Romans at right **Rev. Legend:** BUREBISTA REGELE DACILOR **Edge:** Plain

| Date | Mintage | VF20 | XF40 | MS60 | MS63 | MS65 |
|---|---|---|---|---|---|---|
| 2005 | 500 | PF65 300 | | | | |

**KM# 35 100 LEI**
31.10 g., 0.925 Silver 0.9249 oz. ASW, 37 mm. **Subject:** 15th Anniversary - Independence Proclamation of the Republic of Moldova **Obv:** Arms, date divides legend above, value below **Obv. Legend:** REPUBLICA MOLDOVA **Rev:** Map of Moldova within stars in inner circle, legend around **Rev. Legend:** PROCLAMAREA INDEPENDENTEI / 1991-2006 **Edge:** Plain

| Date | Mintage | VF20 | XF40 | MS60 | MS63 | MS65 |
|---|---|---|---|---|---|---|
| 2006 | 500 | PF65 500 | | | | |

**KM# 39 100 LEI**
31.11 g., 0.925 Silver 0.925 oz. ASW, 37 mm. **Subject:** National Bank, 15th Anniversary **Rev:** Bank building

| Date | Mintage | VF20 | XF40 | MS60 | MS63 | MS65 |
|---|---|---|---|---|---|---|
| 2006 | 500 | PF65 140 | | | | |

**KM# 42 100 LEI**
31.11 g., 0.925 Silver 0.925 oz. ASW, 37 mm. **Subject:** Petru Rares **Rev:** Bust 3/4 right

| Date | Mintage | VF20 | XF40 | MS60 | MS63 | MS65 |
|---|---|---|---|---|---|---|
| 2007 | 500 | PF65 450 | | | | |

**KM# 37 100 LEI**
7.78 g., 0.999 Gold 0.2499 oz. AGW, 24 mm. **Subject:** Dimitrie Cantemir

| Date | Mintage | VF20 | XF40 | MS60 | MS63 | MS65 |
|---|---|---|---|---|---|---|
| 2008 | Est. 1000 | PF63 550 | PF65 600 | | | |

**KM# 46 100 LEI**
31.10 g., 0.925 Silver 0.9249 oz. ASW, 37 mm. **Subject:** Antioh Cantemir **Rev:** Half-length figure standing 3/4 left

| Date | Mintage | VF20 | XF40 | MS60 | MS63 | MS65 |
|---|---|---|---|---|---|---|
| 2008 | 1,000 | PF63 95.00 | PF65 100 | | | |

**KM# 52 100 LEI**
15.50 g., 0.999 Gold 0.4978 oz. AGW, 28 mm. **Subject:** Dimitrie Cantemir **Obv:** National Arms **Rev:** Cantemir seated at desk

| Date | Mintage | VF20 | XF40 | MS60 | MS63 | MS65 |
|---|---|---|---|---|---|---|
| 2008 | 300 | PF65 950 | | | | |

**KM# 51 100 LEI**
22.50 g., 0.925 Silver 0.6691 oz. ASW, 34 mm. **Subject:** Moldovan Chronicals, 15-18 Centuries **Rev:** Man seated writing

| Date | Mintage | VF20 | XF40 | MS60 | MS63 | MS65 |
|---|---|---|---|---|---|---|
| 2009 | 1,000 | PF63 85.00 | PF65 90.00 | | | |

**KM# 57 100 LEI**
15.50 g., 0.999 Gold 0.4978 oz. AGW, 28 mm. **Subject:** Doina and Ion Aldea-Teodorovici **Obv:** National arms **Rev:** Conjoined busts right

| Date | Mintage | VF20 | XF40 | MS60 | MS63 | MS65 |
|---|---|---|---|---|---|---|
| 2010 | 300 | PF65 950 | | | | |

**KM# 61 100 LEI**
15.50 g., 0.999 Gold 0.4978 oz. AGW, 28 mm. **Subject:** Grigore Vieru **Obv:** National Arms **Rev:** Profile bust left

| Date | Mintage | VF20 | XF40 | MS60 | MS63 | MS65 |
|---|---|---|---|---|---|---|
| 2010 | 300 | PF65 950 | | | | |

**KM# 62 100 LEI**
31.10 g., 0.999 Silver 0.9989 oz. ASW, 37 mm. **Subject:** National Bank of Moldova, 20th Anniversary **Obv:** National arms **Rev:** National Bank logo **Edge:** Reeded

| Date | Mintage | VF20 | XF40 | MS60 | MS63 | MS65 |
|---|---|---|---|---|---|---|
| 2011 | 500 | PF65 80.00 | | | | |

**KM# 63 100 LEI**
31.10 g., 0.999 Silver 0.9989 oz. ASW, 37 mm. **Subject:** Independence, 20th Anniversary **Obv:** National arms **Rev:** Father and son holding Moldovian flag **Edge:** Reeded

| Date | Mintage | VF20 | XF40 | MS60 | MS63 | MS65 |
|---|---|---|---|---|---|---|
| 2011 | 1,000 | PF63 70.00 | PF65 75.00 | | | |

**KM# 64 100 LEI**
31.10 g., 0.999 Silver 0.9989 oz. ASW, 37 mm. **Subject:** Chisinau, 575th Anniversary of Founding of the City **Obv:** National arms **Rev:** Mazarachi Hill **Edge:** Reeded

| Date | Mintage | VF20 | XF40 | MS60 | MS63 | MS65 |
|---|---|---|---|---|---|---|
| 2011 | 1,000 | PF63 70.00 | PF65 75.00 | | | |

**KM# 66 100 LEI**
7.80 g., 0.999 Gold 0.2505 oz. AGW, 24 mm. **Subject:** Bogdan Petriceicu Hasdeu **Obv:** National arms **Rev:** Bust **Edge:** Reeded

| Date | Mintage | VF20 | XF40 | MS60 | MS63 | MS65 |
|---|---|---|---|---|---|---|
| 2011 | 300 | PF65 475 | | | | |

**KM# 70 100 LEI**
16.50 g., 0.999 Gold 0.530 oz. AGW, 28 mm. **Subject:** Stefan Cel Mare, 555th Anniversary of Accession **Rev:** Half-length bust facing right

| Date | Mintage | VF20 | XF40 | MS60 | MS63 | MS65 |
|---|---|---|---|---|---|---|
| 2012 | — | PF65 950 | | | | |

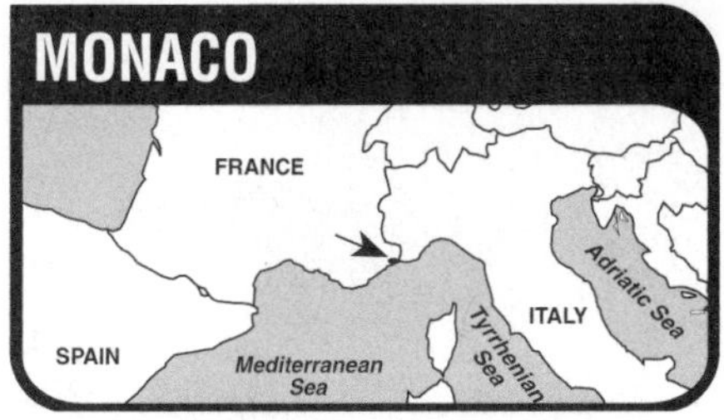


The Principality of Monaco, located on the Mediterranean coast nine miles from Nice, has an area of 0.58 sq. mi. (1.9 sq. km.) and a population of 26,000. Capital: Monaco-Ville. The economy is based on tourism and the manufacture of cosmetics, gourmet foods and highly specialized electronics. Monaco also derives its revenue from a tobacco monopoly and the sale of postage stamps for philatelic purpose. Gambling in Monte Carlo accounts for only a small fraction of the country's revenue.

**RULERS**

Rainier III, 1949-2005
Albert II, 2005-

**MINT PRIVY MARKS**

(a) - Paris (privy marks only)
Horseshoe - 2001 and 2002
Heart – 2002-2003
French Horn with starfish in water – 2003-
(p) - Thunderbolt - Poissy

**MONETARY SYSTEM**

100 Euro Cents = 1 Euro

# PRINCIPALITY

## EURO COINAGE

### KM# 167 EURO CENT

2.30 g., Copper Plated Steel, 16.25 mm. **Ruler:** Rainier III **Obv:** Crowned arms **Rev:** Value and globe **Edge:** Plain

| Date | Mintage | VF20 | XF40 | MS60 | MS63 | MS65 |
|---|---|---|---|---|---|---|
| 2001 (a) | 327,200 | — | — | 12.00 | 20.00 | 35.00 |
| 2001 (a) | 3,500 | PF65 75.00 | | | | |
| 2002 (a) In sets only | 40,000 | — | — | — | — | 75.00 |
| 2003 (a) | — | — | — | — | — | 10.00 |
| 2004 (a) | 14,999 | PF65 25.00 | | | | |
| 2005 (a) | 35,000 | PF65 50.00 | | | | |

### KM# 188 EURO CENT

2.30 g., Copper Plated Steel, 16.25 mm. **Ruler:** Albert II **Obv:** Crowned arms within circle of stars **Rev:** Value and globe

| Date | Mintage | VF20 | XF40 | MS60 | MS63 | MS65 |
|---|---|---|---|---|---|---|
| 2006 | 11,180 | PF65 30.00 | | | | |
| 2007 | — | — | — | — | — | 30.00 |
| 2009 In sets only | 8,020 | — | — | — | — | 30.00 |

### KM# 168 2 EURO CENT

3.06 g., Copper Plated Steel, 18.75 mm. **Ruler:** Rainier III **Obv:** Crowned arms **Rev:** Value and globe **Edge:** Grooved

| Date | Mintage | VF20 | XF40 | MS60 | MS63 | MS65 |
|---|---|---|---|---|---|---|
| 2001 (a) | 393,400 | — | — | 9.00 | 15.00 | 30.00 |
| 2001 (a) | 3,500 | PF65 85.00 | | | | |
| 2002 (a) In sets only | 40,000 | — | — | — | — | 85.00 |
| 2003 (a) | — | — | — | — | — | 10.00 |
| 2004 (a) | 14,999 | PF65 35.00 | | | | |
| 2005 (a) | 35,000 | PF65 50.00 | | | | |

### KM# 189 2 EURO CENT

3.06 g., Copper Plated Steel, 18.75 mm. **Ruler:** Albert II **Obv:** Crowned arms within circle of stars **Rev:** Value and globe **Edge:** Grooved

| Date | Mintage | VF20 | XF40 | MS60 | MS63 | MS65 |
|---|---|---|---|---|---|---|
| 2006 | 11,260 | PF65 25.00 | | | | |
| 2009 In sets only | 8,020 | — | — | — | — | 25.00 |
| 2007 | — | — | — | — | — | 25.00 |

### KM# 169 5 EURO CENT

3.92 g., Copper Plated Steel, 21.25 mm. **Ruler:** Rainier III **Obv:** Crowned arms **Rev:** Value and globe **Edge:** Plain

| Date | Mintage | VF20 | XF40 | MS60 | MS63 | MS65 |
|---|---|---|---|---|---|---|
| 2001 (a) | 320,000 | — | — | 12.00 | 20.00 | 35.00 |
| 2001 (a) | 3,500 | PF65 95.00 | | | | |
| 2002 (a) In sets only | 40,000 | — | — | — | — | 85.00 |
| 2003 (a) | — | — | — | — | — | 15.00 |
| 2004 (a) | 14,999 | PF65 45.00 | | | | |
| 2005 (a) | 35,000 | PF65 55.00 | | | | |

### KM# 190 5 EURO CENT

3.92 g., Copper Plated Steel, 21.25 mm. **Ruler:** Albert II **Obv:** Crowned arms within circle of stars **Rev:** Value and globe

| Date | Mintage | VF20 | XF40 | MS60 | MS63 | MS65 |
|---|---|---|---|---|---|---|
| 2006 | 11,180 | PF65 30.00 | | | | |
| 2007 | — | — | — | — | — | 30.00 |
| 2009 In sets only | 8,020 | — | — | — | — | 30.00 |
| 2011 In sets only | 7,000 | — | — | — | — | 30.00 |

### KM# 170 10 EURO CENT

4.10 g., Brass, 19.75 mm. **Ruler:** Rainier III **Obv:** Knight on horse **Rev:** Value and map **Edge:** Reeded

| Date | Mintage | VF20 | XF40 | MS60 | MS63 | MS65 |
|---|---|---|---|---|---|---|
| 2001 (a) | 320,000 | — | — | 9.00 | 15.00 | 25.00 |
| 2001 (a) | 3,500 | PF65 110 | | | | |
| 2002 (a) | 407,200 | — | — | 5.00 | 8.00 | 12.00 |
| 2003 (a) | 100,800 | — | — | 7.00 | 12.00 | 16.00 |
| 2004 (a) | 14,999 | PF65 50.00 | | | | |

### KM# 181 10 EURO CENT

4.10 g., Brass, 19.75 mm. **Ruler:** Albert II **Obv:** Crowned AA monogram **Rev:** Relief map of Western Europe, stars, lines and value **Edge:** Reeded

| Date | Mintage | VF20 | XF40 | MS60 | MS63 | MS65 |
|---|---|---|---|---|---|---|
| 2006 (a) | 11,180 | PF65 50.00 | | | | |

### KM# 191 10 EURO CENT

4.10 g., Brass, 19.75 mm. **Ruler:** Albert II **Obv:** Crowned AA monogram **Rev:** Relief map of western Europe, stars, lines and value **Edge:** Reeded

| Date | Mintage | VF20 | XF40 | MS60 | MS63 | MS65 |
|---|---|---|---|---|---|---|
| 2007 (a) | — | — | — | — | — | 30.00 |
| 2009 (a) In sets only | 8,020 | — | — | — | — | 30.00 |
| 2011 (a) In sets only | 7,000 | — | — | — | — | 30.00 |

### KM# 171 20 EURO CENT

5.74 g., Brass, 22.25 mm. **Ruler:** Rainier III **Obv:** Knight on horse **Rev:** Value and map **Edge:** Notched

| Date | Mintage | VF20 | XF40 | MS60 | MS63 | MS65 |
|---|---|---|---|---|---|---|
| 2001 (a) | 386,400 | — | — | 9.00 | 15.00 | 20.00 |
| 2001 (a) | 3,500 | PF65 120 | | | | |
| 2002 (a) | 376,000 | — | — | 7.00 | 12.00 | 16.00 |
| 2003 (a) | 100,000 | — | — | 7.00 | 12.00 | 16.00 |
| 2004 (a) | 14,999 | PF65 60.00 | | | | |

### KM# 182 20 EURO CENT

5.74 g., Brass, 22.25 mm. **Ruler:** Albert II **Obv:** Crowned AA monogram **Rev:** Relief map of Western Europe, stars, lines and value **Edge:** Notched

| Date | Mintage | VF20 | XF40 | MS60 | MS63 | MS65 |
|---|---|---|---|---|---|---|
| 2006 (a) | 11,180 | PF65 60.00 | | | | |

### KM# 192 20 EURO CENT

5.74 g., Brass, 22.25 mm. **Ruler:** Albert II **Obv:** Crowned AA monogram **Rev:** Relief map of western Europe, stars, lines and value **Edge:** Notched

| Date | Mintage | VF20 | XF40 | MS60 | MS63 | MS65 |
|---|---|---|---|---|---|---|
| 2007 (a) | — | — | — | — | — | 30.00 |
| 2009 (a) In sets only | 8,020 | — | — | — | — | 30.00 |
| 2011 (a) In sets only | 7,000 | — | — | — | — | 30.00 |

### KM# 172 50 EURO CENT

7.80 g., Brass, 24.25 mm. **Ruler:** Rainier III **Obv:** Knight on horse **Rev:** Value and map **Edge:** Reeded

| Date | Mintage | VF20 | XF40 | MS60 | MS63 | MS65 |
|---|---|---|---|---|---|---|
| 2001 (a) | 320,000 | — | — | 9.00 | 15.00 | 30.00 |
| 2001 (a) | 3,500 | PF65 130 | | | | |
| 2002 (a) | 364,000 | — | — | 5.00 | 8.00 | 12.00 |
| 2003 (a) | 100,000 | — | — | 7.00 | 12.00 | 16.00 |
| 2004 (a) | 14,999 | PF65 65.00 | | | | |

### KM# 183 50 EURO CENT

7.80 g., Brass, 24.25 mm. **Ruler:** Albert II **Obv:** Crowned AA monogram **Rev:** Relief map of Western Europe, stars, lines and value **Edge:** Reeded

| Date | Mintage | VF20 | XF40 | MS60 | MS63 | MS65 |
|---|---|---|---|---|---|---|
| 2006 (a) | 11,180 | PF65 65.00 | | | | |

### KM# 193 50 EURO CENT

7.80 g., Brass, 24.25 mm. **Ruler:** Albert II **Obv:** Crowned AA monogram **Rev:** Relief map of western Europe, stars, lines and values **Edge:** Reeded

| Date | Mintage | VF20 | XF40 | MS60 | MS63 | MS65 |
|---|---|---|---|---|---|---|
| 2007 (a) | — | — | — | — | — | 30.00 |
| 2009 (a) In sets only | 8,020 | — | — | — | — | 30.00 |
| 2011 (a) In sets only | 7,000 | — | — | — | — | 30.00 |

### KM# 173 EURO

7.50 g., Bi-Metallic Copper-Nickel center in Nickel-Brass ring, 23.25 mm. **Ruler:** Rainier III **Obv:** Conjoined heads of Prince Ranier and Crown Prince Albert right within circle **Rev:** Value and map **Edge:** Segmented reeding

| Date | Mintage | VF20 | XF40 | MS60 | MS63 | MS65 |
|---|---|---|---|---|---|---|
| 2001 (a) | 991,100 | — | — | 6.00 | 10.00 | 12.00 |
| 2001 (a) | 3,500 | PF65 145 | | | | |
| 2002 (a) | 512,500 | — | — | 6.50 | 11.00 | 14.00 |
| 2003 (a) | 135,000 | — | — | 8.00 | 13.50 | 18.50 |
| 2004 (a) | 14,999 | PF65 75.00 | | | | |

### KM# 184 EURO

7.50 g., Bi-Metallic Copper-Nickel center in Nickel-Brass ring, 23.25 mm. **Ruler:** Albert II **Obv:** Head right of Prince Albert **Rev:** Relief map of Western Europe, stars, lines and value **Edge:** Segmented reeding

| Date | Mintage | VF20 | XF40 | MS60 | MS63 | MS65 |
|---|---|---|---|---|---|---|
| 2006 (a) | 11,180 | PF65 75.00 | | | | |

**KM# 194 EURO**

7.50 g., Bi-Metallic Copper-Nickel center in Nickel-Brass ring, 23.25 mm. **Ruler:** Albert II **Obv:** Head right **Rev:** Relief map of western Europe, stars, lines and value **Edge:** Segmented reeding

| Date | Mintage | VF20 | XF40 | MS60 | MS63 | MS65 |
|---|---|---|---|---|---|---|
| 2007 (a) | 100,000 | — | — | — | — | 18.00 |
| 2009 (a) In sets only | 8,020 | — | — | — | — | 30.00 |
| 2011 (a) In sets only | 7,000 | — | — | — | — | 30.00 |

**KM# 174 2 EURO**

8.50 g., Bi-Metallic Nickel-Brass center in Copper-Nickel ring, 25.75 mm. **Ruler:** Rainier III **Obv:** Head right within circle flanked by stars **Rev:** Value and map **Edge:** Reeded with 2s and stars

| Date | Mintage | VF20 | XF40 | MS60 | MS63 | MS65 |
|---|---|---|---|---|---|---|
| 2001 (a) | 919,800 | — | — | 8.50 | 14.00 | 25.00 |
| 2001 (a) | 3,500 | PF65 165 | | | | |
| 2002 (a) | 496,000 | — | — | 9.00 | 15.00 | 18.00 |
| 2003 (a) | 228,000 | — | — | — | 17.50 | 22.50 |
| 2004 (a) | 14,999 | PF65 100 | | | | |

**KM# 185 2 EURO**

8.50 g., Bi-Metallic Nickel-Brass center in Copper-Nickel ring, 25.75 mm. **Ruler:** Albert II **Obv:** Prince Albert's head right **Rev:** Relief map of Western Europe, stars, lines and value **Edge:** Reeded with 2's and stars

| Date | Mintage | VF20 | XF40 | MS60 | MS63 | MS65 |
|---|---|---|---|---|---|---|
| 2006 (a) | 11,180 | PF65 130 | | | | |

**KM# 186 2 EURO**

8.50 g., Bi-Metallic Nickel-Brass center in Copper-Nickel ring., 25.75 mm. **Ruler:** Albert II **Subject:** Princess Grace, 25th Anniversary of Death **Obv:** Head of Princess Grace left **Rev:** Relief map of Western Europe, stars, lines and value **Edge:** Reeded with 2s and stars

| Date | Mintage | VF20 | XF40 | MS60 | MS63 | MS65 |
|---|---|---|---|---|---|---|
| 2007 (a) | 20,000 | — | — | — | 850 | 1,250 |

**KM# 195 2 EURO**

8.50 g., Bi-Metallic Nickel-Brass center in Copper-Nickel ring, 25.75 mm. **Ruler:** Albert II **Obv:** Head right **Rev:** Relief map of western Europe, stars, lines and values **Edge:** Reeded with 2's and stars

| Date | Mintage | VF20 | XF40 | MS60 | MS63 | MS65 |
|---|---|---|---|---|---|---|
| 2007 (a) | — | — | — | — | 65.00 | — |
| 2009 (a) | 250,000 | — | — | — | 35.00 | — |
| 2009 (a) In sets only | 8,000 | — | — | — | — | 150 |
| 2010 (a) | 25,000 | PF65 300 | | | | |
| 2011 (a) | 1,039,052 | — | — | — | 35.00 | 150 |
| 2012 (a) | — | — | — | — | 35.00 | 150 |

**KM# 196 2 EURO**

8.50 g., Bi-Metallic Nickel-Brass center in Copper-Nickel ring, 25.75 mm. **Ruler:** Albert II **Subject:** Royal Wedding of Prince Albert II and Princess Charlène **Obv:** Conjoined heads left

| Date | Mintage | VF20 | XF40 | MS60 | MS63 | MS65 |
|---|---|---|---|---|---|---|
| 2011 A | 147,877 | — | — | — | — | 75.00 |

**KM# 199 2 EURO**

8.50 g., Bi-Metallic Nickel-Brass center in Copper-Nickel ring **Ruler:** Albert II **Subject:** 500th Anniversary **Obv:** Lucien I bust left

| Date | Mintage | VF20 | XF40 | MS60 | MS63 | MS65 |
|---|---|---|---|---|---|---|
| 2012 (a) | 100,000 | — | — | — | — | 75.00 |

**KM# 200 2 EURO**

8.50 g., Bi-Metallic Nickel plated Brass center in Copper-Nickel ring, 25.75 mm. **Ruler:** Albert II **Subject:** UN Membership, 20th Anniversary **Obv:** Dove and hemisphere map

| Date | Mintage | VF20 | XF40 | MS60 | MS63 | MS65 |
|---|---|---|---|---|---|---|
| 2013 | 1,239,131 | — | — | — | — | 50.00 |
| 2013 | 10,000 | PF65 100 | | | | |

**KM# 180 5 EURO**

12.00 g., 0.900 Silver 0.3472 oz. ASW, 29 mm. **Ruler:** Rainier III **Obv:** Bust right **Rev:** Saint standing

| Date | Mintage | VF20 | XF40 | MS60 | MS63 | MS65 |
|---|---|---|---|---|---|---|
| 2004 (a) | 14,999 | PF65 150 | | | | |

**KM# 197 5 EURO**

12.00 g., 0.900 Silver 0.3472 oz. ASW, 29 mm. **Ruler:** Albert II **Subject:** Prince Albert II, 50th Birthday **Obv:** Bust right **Rev:** Crowned and mantled arms

| Date | Mintage | VF20 | XF40 | MS60 | MS63 | MS65 |
|---|---|---|---|---|---|---|
| 2008 (a) Prooflike | 9,000 | — | — | — | — | 185 |

**KM# 178 10 EURO**

25.00 g., 0.925 Silver 0.7435 oz. ASW, 37 mm. **Ruler:** Rainier III **Obv:** Conjoined busts of Prince Ranier and Crown Prince Albert right **Rev:** Arms

| Date | Mintage | VF20 | XF40 | MS60 | MS63 | MS65 |
|---|---|---|---|---|---|---|
| 2003 (a) | 4,000 | PF63 450 | PF65 475 | | | |

**KM# 187 10 EURO**

3.22 g., 0.900 Gold 0.0932 oz. AGW **Ruler:** Albert II **Subject:** Death of Rainier III **Obv:** Principality arms **Rev:** Head of Rainier III right

| Date | Mintage | VF20 | XF40 | MS60 | MS63 | MS65 |
|---|---|---|---|---|---|---|
| 2005 (a) | 3,313 | PF63 500 | PF65 550 | | | |

**KM# 201 10 EURO**

25.00 g., 0.900 Silver 0.7234 oz. ASW, 37 mm. **Ruler:** Albert II **Subject:** Albert II and Charlene Wittstock, 2nd Wedding Anniversary **Obv:** Conjoined busts left **Rev:** Crown above value at left and AC monogram at right

| Date | Mintage | VF20 | XF40 | MS60 | MS63 | MS65 |
|---|---|---|---|---|---|---|
| 2011 | 4,000 | PF65 600 | | | | |

**KM# 177 20 EURO**

18.00 g., 0.925 Gold 0.5353 oz. AGW, 32 mm. **Ruler:** Rainier III **Obv:** Bust right **Rev:** Arms

| Date | Mintage | VF20 | XF40 | MS60 | MS63 | MS65 |
|---|---|---|---|---|---|---|
| 2002 (a) | 10,000 | PF63 1,000 | PF65 1,100 | | | |

**KM# 198 20 EURO**

6.45 g., 0.900 Gold 0.1866 oz. AGW, 21 mm. **Ruler:** Albert II **Subject:** Prince Albert II, 50th Birthday **Obv:** Bust right **Rev:** Crowned and mantled arms

| Date | Mintage | VF20 | XF40 | MS60 | MS63 | MS65 |
|---|---|---|---|---|---|---|
| 2008 (a) | 3,000 | PF63 550 | PF65 600 | | | |

**KM# 179 100 EURO**

29.00 g., 0.900 Gold 0.8391 oz. AGW **Ruler:** Rainier III **Obv:** Bust right **Rev:** Knight on horse

| Date | Mintage | VF20 | XF40 | MS60 | MS63 | MS65 |
|---|---|---|---|---|---|---|
| 2003 (a) | 1,000 | PF63 3,000 | PF65 3,250 | | | |

## MINT SETS

| KM# | Date | Mintage | Identification | Issue Price | Mkt Val |
|---|---|---|---|---|---|
| MS1 | 2001 (8) | 20,000 | KM#167-174, exercise caution, privately packaged and deceptively false sets exist | 35.00 | 250 |
| MS2 | 2002 (8) | 40,000 | KM#167-174, exercise caution, privately packaged and deceptively false sets exist | 35.00 | 350 |
| MS3 | 2009 (8) | 8,000 | KM#188-195 | — | 600 |

## PROOF SETS

| KM# | Date | Mintage | Identification | Issue Price | Mkt Val |
|---|---|---|---|---|---|
| PS1 | 2001 (8) | 3,500 | KM#167-174 | — | 1,100 |
| PS2 | 2004 (9) | 14,999 | KM#167-174, 180 | — | 700 |
| PS3 | 2005 (3) | 35,000 | KM#167-169 | — | 160 |
| PS4 | 2006 (8) | 11,180 | KM#181-185, 188-190 | — | 475 |

# MONGOLIA

Mongolia, (formerly the Mongolian Peoples Republic) a landlocked country in central Asia between Russia and the People's Republic of China, has an area of 604,250 sq. mi. (1,565,000 sq. km.) and a population of 2.26 million. Capital: Ulaan Baator. Animal herds and flocks are the chief economic asset. Wool, cattle, butter, meat and hides are exported.

For earlier issues see Russia - Tannu Tuva.

**MONETARY SYSTEM**

100 Mongo = 1 Tugrik

## STATE

### DECIMAL COINAGE

**KM# 302 100 TUGRIK**

25.00 g., Copper-Nickel, 30 mm. **Subject:** XXVI Summer Olympics, Atlanta **Obv:** Arms **Rev:** 1904 St. Louis World's Fair Program Cover

| Date | Mintage | VF20 | XF40 | MS60 | MS63 | MS65 |
|---|---|---|---|---|---|---|
| 2002 | — | PF65 25.00 | | | | |

**KM# 303 100 TUGRIK**

Copper-Nickel, 38 mm. **Obv:** National emblem **Rev:** Two soccer players

| Date | Mintage | VF20 | XF40 | MS60 | MS63 | MS65 |
|---|---|---|---|---|---|---|
| 2003 Prooflike | 2,000 | — | — | — | 10.00 | 12.00 |

**KM# 254 100 TUGRIK**

25.00 g., Copper-Nickel Silver plated, 30 mm. **Obv:** National emblem **Rev:** Yin-Yang symbol

| Date | Mintage | VF20 | XF40 | MS60 | MS63 | MS65 |
|---|---|---|---|---|---|---|
| 2007 | 3,000 | PF65 20.00 | | | | |

**KM# 254a 100 TUGRIK**

25.00 g., Copper-Nickel Gilt **Obv:** Arms **Rev:** Yin-Yang symbol

| Date | Mintage | VF20 | XF40 | MS60 | MS63 | MS65 |
|---|---|---|---|---|---|---|
| 2007 | — | PF65 25.00 | | | | |

**KM# 306 100 TUGRIK**

27.00 g., Copper Plated Silver, 38.61 mm. **Subject:** Wonders of the World **Obv:** National emblem **Rev:** Rome's Colosseum

| Date | Mintage | VF20 | XF40 | MS60 | MS63 | MS65 |
|---|---|---|---|---|---|---|
| 2008 Prooflike | — | — | — | — | — | 25.00 |

**KM# 306a 100 TUGRIK**

27.00 g., Copper Plated Silver with color, 38.61 mm. **Rev:** Coliseum in color

| Date | Mintage | VF20 | XF40 | MS60 | MS63 | MS65 |
|---|---|---|---|---|---|---|
| 2008 Prooflike | — | — | — | — | — | 25.00 |

**KM# 307 100 TUGRIK**

27.00 g., Copper Plated Silver, 38.61 mm. **Subject:** Wonders of the World **Obv:** National Emblem **Rev:** Chichen Itza pyramid

| Date | Mintage | VF20 | XF40 | MS60 | MS63 | MS65 |
|---|---|---|---|---|---|---|
| 2008 Prooflike | — | — | — | — | — | 25.00 |

**KM# 307a 100 TUGRIK**

27.00 g., Copper Plated Silver with color, 38.61 mm. **Rev:** Chichen Itza in color

| Date | Mintage | VF20 | XF40 | MS60 | MS63 | MS65 |
|---|---|---|---|---|---|---|
| 2008 Prooflike | — | — | — | — | — | 25.00 |

**KM# 308 100 TUGRIK**

27.00 g., Copper Plated Silver, 38.61 mm. **Obv:** National emblem **Rev:** Treasury at Petra

| Date | Mintage | VF20 | XF40 | MS60 | MS63 | MS65 |
|---|---|---|---|---|---|---|
| 2008 Prooflike | — | — | — | — | — | 25.00 |

**KM# 308a 100 TUGRIK**

27.00 g., Copper Plated Silver with color, 38.61 mm. **Rev:** Treasury at Petra in color

| Date | Mintage | VF20 | XF40 | MS60 | MS63 | MS65 |
|---|---|---|---|---|---|---|
| 2008 Prooflike | — | — | — | — | — | 25.00 |

**KM# 317 100 TUGRIK**

27.00 g., Copper Plated Silver, 38.6 mm. **Subject:** Machu Picchu

| Date | Mintage | VF20 | XF40 | MS60 | MS63 | MS65 |
|---|---|---|---|---|---|---|
| 2008 Prooflike | — | — | — | — | — | 25.00 |

**KM# 317a 100 TUGRIK**

27.00 g., Copper Plated Silver with color, 38.61 mm. **Rev:** Machu Picchu in color

| Date | Mintage | VF20 | XF40 | MS60 | MS63 | MS65 |
|---|---|---|---|---|---|---|
| 2008 Prooflike | — | — | — | — | — | 25.00 |

**KM# 321 100 TUGRIK**

27.00 g., Copper Plated Silver, 38.6 mm. **Subject:** Taj Mahal

| Date | Mintage | VF20 | XF40 | MS60 | MS63 | MS65 |
|---|---|---|---|---|---|---|
| 2008 Prooflike | — | — | — | — | — | 25.00 |

**KM# 346 100 TUGRIK**

27.00 g., Copper Plated Silver, 38.61 mm. **Rev:** Christ the Redeemer

| Date | Mintage | VF20 | XF40 | MS60 | MS63 | MS65 |
|---|---|---|---|---|---|---|
| 2008 Prooflike | 5,000 | — | — | — | — | 25.00 |

**KM# 346a 100 TUGRIK**

27.00 g., Copper Plated Silver with color, 38.61 mm. **Rev:** Christ the Redeemer in color

| Date | Mintage | VF20 | XF40 | MS60 | MS63 | MS65 |
|---|---|---|---|---|---|---|
| 2008 Prooflike | 5,000 | — | — | — | — | 25.00 |

**KM# 347 100 TUGRIK**

27.00 g., Copper Plated Silver, 38.61 mm. **Rev:** Great Wall of China

| Date | Mintage | VF20 | XF40 | MS60 | MS63 | MS65 |
|---|---|---|---|---|---|---|
| 2008 Prooflike | 5,000 | — | — | — | — | 25.00 |

**KM# 282 250 TUGRIK**

15.50 g., 0.925 Silver 0.461 oz. ASW, 33 mm. **Subject:** Zodiac - Capricorn **Rev:** Seated goat left, partially gilt

| Date | Mintage | VF20 | XF40 | MS60 | MS63 | MS65 |
|---|---|---|---|---|---|---|
| 2007 | 7,000 | — | — | — | 25.00 | 28.00 |

**KM# 283 250 TUGRIK**

15.50 g., 0.925 Silver 0.461 oz. ASW, 33 mm. **Subject:** Zodiac - Aquarius **Rev:** Man pouring water, partially gilt

| Date | Mintage | VF20 | XF40 | MS60 | MS63 | MS65 |
|---|---|---|---|---|---|---|
| 2007 | 7,000 | — | — | — | 25.00 | 28.00 |

**KM# 284 250 TUGRIK**

15.50 g., 0.925 Silver 0.461 oz. ASW, 33 mm. **Subject:** Zodiac - Piceis **Rev:** Two fish partially gilt

| Date | Mintage | VF20 | XF40 | MS60 | MS63 | MS65 |
|---|---|---|---|---|---|---|
| 2007 | 7,000 | — | — | — | 25.00 | 28.00 |

**KM# 285 250 TUGRIK**

15.50 g., 0.925 Silver 0.461 oz. ASW, 33 mm. **Subject:** Zodiac - Aries **Rev:** Ram seated partially gilt

| Date | Mintage | VF20 | XF40 | MS60 | MS63 | MS65 |
|---|---|---|---|---|---|---|
| 2007 | 7,000 | — | — | — | 25.00 | 28.00 |

**KM# 286 250 TUGRIK**

15.50 g., 0.925 Silver 0.461 oz. ASW, 33 mm. **Subject:** Zodiac - Taurus **Rev:** Bull, partially gilt

| Date | Mintage | VF20 | XF40 | MS60 | MS63 | MS65 |
|---|---|---|---|---|---|---|
| 2007 | 7,000 | — | — | — | 25.00 | 28.00 |

**KM# 287 250 TUGRIK**

15.50 g., 0.925 Silver 0.461 oz. ASW, 33 mm. **Subject:** Zodiac - Gemini **Rev:** Twins, partially gilt

| Date | Mintage | VF20 | XF40 | MS60 | MS63 | MS65 |
|---|---|---|---|---|---|---|
| 2007 | 7,000 | — | — | — | 25.00 | 28.00 |

**KM# 288 250 TUGRIK**

15.50 g., 0.925 Silver 0.461 oz. ASW, 33 mm. **Subject:** Zodiac - Cancer **Rev:** Crab - partially gilt

| Date | Mintage | VF20 | XF40 | MS60 | MS63 | MS65 |
|---|---|---|---|---|---|---|
| 2007 | 7,000 | — | — | — | 25.00 | 28.00 |

**KM# 289 250 TUGRIK**

15.50 g., 0.925 Silver 0.461 oz. ASW, 33 mm. **Subject:** Zodiac - Leo **Rev:** Lion walking left, partially gilt

| Date | Mintage | VF20 | XF40 | MS60 | MS63 | MS65 |
|---|---|---|---|---|---|---|
| 2007 | 7,000 | — | — | — | 25.00 | 28.00 |

**KM# 290 250 TUGRIK**
15.50 g., 0.925 Silver 0.461 oz. ASW, 33 mm. **Subject:** Zodiac - Virgo **Rev:** Female, partially gilt

| Date | Mintage | VF20 | XF40 | MS60 | MS63 | MS65 |
|---|---|---|---|---|---|---|
| 2007 | 7,000 | — | — | — | 25.00 | 28.00 |

**KM# 291 250 TUGRIK**
15.50 g., 0.925 Silver 0.461 oz. ASW, 33 mm. **Subject:** Zodiac - Libra **Rev:** Scales, partially gilt

| Date | Mintage | VF20 | XF40 | MS60 | MS63 | MS65 |
|---|---|---|---|---|---|---|
| 2007 | 7,000 | — | — | — | 25.00 | 28.00 |

**KM# 292 250 TUGRIK**
15.50 g., 0.925 Silver 0.461 oz. ASW, 33 mm. **Subject:** Zodiac - Scorpio **Rev:** Scorpion, partially gilt

| Date | Mintage | VF20 | XF40 | MS60 | MS63 | MS65 |
|---|---|---|---|---|---|---|
| 2007 | 7,000 | — | — | — | 25.00 | 28.00 |

**KM# 293 250 TUGRIK**
15.50 g., 0.925 Silver 0.461 oz. ASW, 33 mm. **Subject:** Zodiac - Sagittarius **Rev:** Centar, partaillly gilt

| Date | Mintage | VF20 | XF40 | MS60 | MS63 | MS65 |
|---|---|---|---|---|---|---|
| 2007 | 7,000 | — | — | — | 25.00 | 28.00 |

**KM# 300 250 TUGRIK**
15.50 g., 0.999 Silver 0.4978 oz. ASW, 33 mm. **Subject:** Moscow Waterworks **Rev:** Building in multicolor, aqueduct in background

| Date | Mintage | VF20 | XF40 | MS60 | MS63 | MS65 |
|---|---|---|---|---|---|---|
| 2007 | 1,000 | — | — | — | — | 45.00 |

**KM# 301 250 TUGRIK**
15.50 g., 0.999 Silver 0.4978 oz. ASW, 33 mm. **Subject:** Moscow Metro **Rev:** Subway train, multicolor

| Date | Mintage | VF20 | XF40 | MS60 | MS63 | MS65 |
|---|---|---|---|---|---|---|
| 2007 | 1,000 | — | — | — | — | 45.00 |

**KM# 270 250 TUGRIK**
15.55 g., 0.925 Silver 0.4624 oz. ASW, 37 mm. **Subject:** Baby Boy **Obv:** Arms **Rev:** Baby seated on flower, multicolor **Shape:** Heart

| Date | Mintage | VF20 | XF40 | MS60 | MS63 | MS65 |
|---|---|---|---|---|---|---|
| 2008 | 2,500 | PF65 40.00 | | | | |

**KM# 271 250 TUGRIK**
15.55 g., 0.925 Silver 0.4624 oz. ASW, 37 mm. **Subject:** Baby Girl **Obv:** Arms **Rev:** Baby Girl on flower **Shape:** Heart

| Date | Mintage | VF20 | XF40 | MS60 | MS63 | MS65 |
|---|---|---|---|---|---|---|
| 2008 | 2,500 | PF65 40.00 | | | | |

**KM# 189 500 TUGRIK**
25.00 g., 0.925 Silver 0.7435 oz. ASW, 38.7 mm. **Obv:** National emblem above value **Rev:** Protoceratops Andrewsi **Edge:** Reeded

| Date | Mintage | VF20 | XF40 | MS60 | MS63 | MS65 |
|---|---|---|---|---|---|---|
| 2001 | 2,500 | PF63 42.00 | PF65 45.00 | | | |

**KM# 190 500 TUGRIK**
25.00 g., 0.925 Silver 0.7435 oz. ASW **Obv:** National emblem above value **Rev:** Velociraptor Mongoliensis

| Date | Mintage | VF20 | XF40 | MS60 | MS63 | MS65 |
|---|---|---|---|---|---|---|
| 2001 | 2,500 | PF63 42.00 | PF65 45.00 | | | |

**KM# 191 500 TUGRIK**
25.00 g., 0.925 Silver 0.7435 oz. ASW **Series:** Olympics **Obv:** National emblem above value **Rev:** Speed skater

| Date | Mintage | VF20 | XF40 | MS60 | MS63 | MS65 |
|---|---|---|---|---|---|---|
| 2001 | 15,000 | PF63 30.00 | PF65 35.00 | | | |

**KM# 192 500 TUGRIK**
25.00 g., 0.925 Silver 0.7435 oz. ASW **Series:** Olympics **Obv:** National emblem above value **Rev:** Cross-country skiers

| Date | Mintage | VF20 | XF40 | MS60 | MS63 | MS65 |
|---|---|---|---|---|---|---|
| 2001 | 20,000 | PF63 28.00 | PF65 32.00 | | | |

**KM# 195 500 TUGRIK**
Copper-Nickel, 22.1 mm. **Subject:** Sukhe-Bataar **Obv:** National emblem and value **Rev:** Crowned head facing **Edge:** Plain

| Date | Mintage | VF20 | XF40 | MS60 | MS63 | MS65 |
|---|---|---|---|---|---|---|
| 2001 | — | — | — | 1.50 | 2.50 | 3.00 |

**KM# 238 500 TUGRIK**
20.00 g., 0.925 Silver 0.5948 oz. ASW **Subject:** Gobi Desert Brown Bear **Obv:** Arms **Rev:** Bear standing on rock in stream

| Date | Mintage | VF20 | XF40 | MS60 | MS63 | MS65 |
|---|---|---|---|---|---|---|
| 2001 | — | PF65 28.00 | | | | |

**KM# 239 500 TUGRIK**
31.11 g., 0.999 Silver 0.999 oz. ASW, 38.5 mm. **Subject:** Year of the Snake **Rev:** Snake

| Date | Mintage | VF20 | XF40 | MS60 | MS63 | MS65 |
|---|---|---|---|---|---|---|
| 2001 | — | PF65 65.00 | | | | |

**KM# 239a 500 TUGRIK**
31.11 g., 0.999 Silver 0.999 oz. ASW partially gilt **Subject:** Year of the Snake **Obv:** Arms **Rev:** Snake, gilt

| Date | Mintage | VF20 | XF40 | MS60 | MS63 | MS65 |
|---|---|---|---|---|---|---|
| 2001 | — | PF65 75.00 | | | | |

**KM# 241 500 TUGRIK**
31.11 g., 0.999 Silver 0.999 oz. ASW, 38.5 mm. **Subject:** Year of the Horse **Obv:** Arms **Rev:** Horse

| Date | Mintage | VF20 | XF40 | MS60 | MS63 | MS65 |
|---|---|---|---|---|---|---|
| 2002 | — | PF65 65.00 | | | | |

**KM# 241a 500 TUGRIK**
31.11 g., 0.999 Silver 0.999 oz. ASW partially gilt, 38.5 mm. **Subject:** Year of the Horse **Rev:** Horse, gilt

| Date | Mintage | VF20 | XF40 | MS60 | MS63 | MS65 |
|---|---|---|---|---|---|---|
| 2002 | — | PF65 75.00 | | | | |

**KM# 200 500 TUGRIK**
25.57 g., 0.925 Silver 0.7604 oz. ASW, 38.5 mm. **Subject:** Marco Polo, Homeward **Obv:** National emblem above value **Rev:** Five-masted sailing junk **Edge:** Reeded

| Date | Mintage | VF20 | XF40 | MS60 | MS63 | MS65 |
|---|---|---|---|---|---|---|
| 2003 | 5,000 | PF65 45.00 | | | | |

**KM# 204 500 TUGRIK**
25.00 g., 0.925 Silver 0.7435 oz. ASW, 38 mm. **Obv:** National emblem above value **Rev:** Wolf within full moon **Edge:** Reeded

| Date | Mintage | VF20 | XF40 | MS60 | MS63 | MS65 |
|---|---|---|---|---|---|---|
| 2003 | 10,000 | PF65 90.00 | | | | |

**KM# 205 500 TUGRIK**
25.00 g., 0.925 Silver 0.7435 oz. ASW, 38.6 mm. **Obv:** National emblem above value **Rev:** Medallion divides busts **Edge:** Reeded

| Date | Mintage | VF20 | XF40 | MS60 | MS63 | MS65 |
|---|---|---|---|---|---|---|
| 2003 | 5,000 | PF65 65.00 | | | | |

**KM# 206 500 TUGRIK**
1.24 g., 0.9999 Gold 0.040 oz. AGW, 13.92 mm. **Obv:** National emblem above value **Rev:** Five masted sailing junk **Edge:** Reeded

| Date | Mintage | VF20 | XF40 | MS60 | MS63 | MS65 |
|---|---|---|---|---|---|---|
| 2003 | 25,000 | PF63 65.00 | PF65 70.00 | | | |

**KM# 207 500 TUGRIK**
1.24 g., 0.9999 Gold 0.040 oz. AGW, 13.92 mm. **Obv:** National emblem above value **Rev:** Medallion divides busts **Edge:** Reeded

| Date | Mintage | VF20 | XF40 | MS60 | MS63 | MS65 |
|---|---|---|---|---|---|---|
| 2003 | 25,000 | PF63 65.00 | PF65 70.00 | | | |

**KM# 229 500 TUGRIK**
31.11 g., 0.999 Silver 0.999 oz. ASW **Obv:** Arms above legend **Rev:** Ram standing left

| Date | Mintage | VF20 | XF40 | MS60 | MS63 | MS65 |
|---|---|---|---|---|---|---|
| 2003 | — | — | — | — | — | 65.00 |

**KM# 229a 500 TUGRIK**
31.11 g., 0.999 Silver 0.999 oz. ASW partialy gilt, 38.5 mm. **Subject:** Year of the Ram **Obv:** Arms **Rev:** Ram standing left, gilt

| Date | Mintage | VF20 | XF40 | MS60 | MS63 | MS65 |
|---|---|---|---|---|---|---|
| 2003 | — | PF65 75.00 | | | | |

**KM# 208 500 TUGRIK**
25.00 g., 0.925 Silver 0.7435 oz. ASW, 38 mm. **Obv:** National emblem above value **Rev:** Holographic Osprey catching fish **Edge:** Reeded

| Date | Mintage | VF20 | XF40 | MS60 | MS63 | MS65 |
|---|---|---|---|---|---|---|
| 2004 | 5,000 | PF65 45.00 | | | | |

**KM# 218 500 TUGRIK**
31.24 g., 0.999 Silver 1.0034 oz. ASW, 38.59 mm. **Series:** Chinese Lunar **Subject:** Year of the Monkey **Obv:** National emblem **Rev:** Monkey seated on branch - gilt, border of scampering monkeys **Edge:** Reeded

| Date | Mintage | VF20 | XF40 | MS60 | MS63 | MS65 |
|---|---|---|---|---|---|---|
| ND-2004 | 20,000 | PF65 45.00 | | | | |

**KM# 219 500 TUGRIK**
1.24 g., 0.9999 Gold 0.0399 oz. AGW **Series:** Chinese Lunar **Subject:** Year of the Monkey **Obv:** National emblem **Rev:** Monkey seated on branch

| Date | Mintage | VF20 | XF40 | MS60 | MS63 | MS65 |
|---|---|---|---|---|---|---|
| ND-2004 | — | PF63 60.00 | PF65 70.00 | | | |

**KM# 244 500 TUGRIK**
31.11 g., 0.999 Silver 0.999 oz. ASW, 38.5 mm. **Subject:** Year of the Monkey **Obv:** Arms **Rev:** Monkey

| Date | Mintage | VF20 | XF40 | MS60 | MS63 | MS65 |
|---|---|---|---|---|---|---|
| 2004 | — | PF65 65.00 | | | | |

**KM# 244a 500 TUGRIK**
31.11 g., 0.999 Silver 0.999 oz. ASW partially gilt, 38.5 mm. **Subject:** Year of the Monkey **Obv:** Arms **Rev:** Monkey, gilt

| Date | Mintage | VF20 | XF40 | MS60 | MS63 | MS65 |
|---|---|---|---|---|---|---|
| 2004 | — | PF65 75.00 | | | | |

**KM# 318 500 TUGRIK**
25.00 g., 0.925 Silver 0.7435 oz. ASW, 38.6 mm. **Subject:** Osprey

| Date | Mintage | VF20 | XF40 | MS60 | MS63 | MS65 |
|---|---|---|---|---|---|---|
| 2004 | Est. 5000 | PF65 45.00 | | | | |

**KM# 209 500 TUGRIK**
24.93 g., 0.925 Bi-Metallic 0.7414 oz. with .925 Silver oval in center, 30 mm. **Obv:** National emblem above value, niobium leopard in oval center **Rev:** Snow Leopard **Edge:** Reeded **Shape:** Oval

| Date | Mintage | VF20 | XF40 | MS60 | MS63 | MS65 |
|---|---|---|---|---|---|---|
| 2005 | 5,000 | PF65 95.00 | | | | |

**KM# 210 500 TUGRIK**
31.10 g., 0.999 Silver 0.999 oz. ASW, 35x35 mm. **Obv:** Bronze plated horse and rider on antiqued silver with national emblem and value **Rev:** Bronze plated horse and rider on antiqued silver above date **Edge:** Reeded **Shape:** Square

| Date | Mintage | VF20 | XF40 | MS60 | MS63 | MS65 |
|---|---|---|---|---|---|---|
| 2005 | 2,500 | — | — | — | 70.00 | 75.00 |

**KM# 210a 500 TUGRIK**
31.10 g., 0.999 Silver 0.999 oz. ASW, 35x35 mm. **Obv:** Gold plated horse and rider with national emblem and value **Rev:** Gold plated horse and rider above date **Edge:** Reeded

| Date | Mintage | VF20 | XF40 | MS60 | MS63 | MS65 |
|---|---|---|---|---|---|---|
| 2005 | 2,500 | PF65 85.00 | | | | |

### KM# 246 500 TUGRIK

31.11 g., 0.999 Silver 0.999 oz. ASW, 38.5 mm. **Subject:** Year of the Rooster **Obv:** Arms **Rev:** Rooster standing right

| Date | Mintage | VF20 | XF40 | MS60 | MS63 | MS65 |
|---|---|---|---|---|---|---|
| 2005 | — | PF65 70.00 | | | | |

### KM# 246a 500 TUGRIK

31.11 g., 0.999 Silver 0.999 oz. ASW, 38.5 mm. **Subject:** Year of the Rooster **Obv:** Arms **Rev:** Rooster, gilt

| Date | Mintage | VF20 | XF40 | MS60 | MS63 | MS65 |
|---|---|---|---|---|---|---|
| 2005 | — | PF65 80.00 | | | | |

### KM# 304 500 TUGRIK

31.10 g., 0.999 Silver 0.9989 oz. ASW, 38.5 mm. **Obv:** National emblem **Rev:** Sumo Wrestler Yokozuna Ounomatsu in color

| Date | Mintage | VF20 | XF40 | MS60 | MS63 | MS65 |
|---|---|---|---|---|---|---|
| 2005 | — | PF65 125 | | | | |

### KM# 319 500 TUGRIK

25.00 g., 0.925 Silver 0.7435 oz. ASW, 38.6 mm. **Subject:** Shiranui **Rev:** Classical wrestler in color

| Date | Mintage | VF20 | XF40 | MS60 | MS63 | MS65 |
|---|---|---|---|---|---|---|
| 2005 | — | PF65 100 | | | | |

### KM# 320 500 TUGRIK

25.00 g., 0.925 Silver 0.7435 oz. ASW, 38.6 mm. **Subject:** Tanikaze **Rev:** Classical wrestler in color

| Date | Mintage | VF20 | XF40 | MS60 | MS63 | MS65 |
|---|---|---|---|---|---|---|
| 2005 | — | PF65 100 | | | | |

### KM# 230 500 TUGRIK

25.00 g., 0.925 Silver 0.7435 oz. ASW **Rev:** Swan with crystal insert

| Date | Mintage | VF20 | XF40 | MS60 | MS63 | MS65 |
|---|---|---|---|---|---|---|
| 2006 | — | PF65 95.00 | | | | |

### KM# 231 500 TUGRIK

25.00 g., 0.925 Silver 0.7435 oz. ASW **Rev:** Gobi bear head with crystal inserts

| Date | Mintage | VF20 | XF40 | MS60 | MS63 | MS65 |
|---|---|---|---|---|---|---|
| 2006 | — | PF65 150 | | | | |

### KM# 248 500 TUGRIK

25.00 g., 0.925 Silver 0.7435 oz. ASW **Subject:** Long Eared Jerboa **Obv:** Arms **Rev:** Long eared jerboa, crystal eyes **Shape:** 38.6

| Date | Mintage | VF20 | XF40 | MS60 | MS63 | MS65 |
|---|---|---|---|---|---|---|
| 2006 | 2,500 | PF65 145 | | | | |

### KM# 249 500 TUGRIK

25.00 g., 0.925 Silver 0.7435 oz. ASW, 38.6 mm. **Obv:** Arms **Rev:** Scorpion, crystal tail point

| Date | Mintage | VF20 | XF40 | MS60 | MS63 | MS65 |
|---|---|---|---|---|---|---|
| 2006 | 2,500 | PF65 185 | | | | |

### KM# 250 500 TUGRIK

25.00 g., 0.925 Silver 0.7435 oz. ASW, 38.6 mm. **Rev:** Tiger, head facing, crystal eyes

| Date | Mintage | VF20 | XF40 | MS60 | MS63 | MS65 |
|---|---|---|---|---|---|---|
| 2006 | 2,500 | PF65 135 | | | | |

### KM# 251 500 TUGRIK

31.11 g., 0.999 Silver 0.999 oz. ASW, 38.5 mm. **Subject:** Year of the Dog **Obv:** Arms **Rev:** Dog standing

| Date | Mintage | VF20 | XF40 | MS60 | MS63 | MS65 |
|---|---|---|---|---|---|---|
| 2006 | — | PF65 60.00 | | | | |

### KM# 251a 500 TUGRIK

31.11 g., 0.999 Silver 0.999 oz. ASW, 38.5 mm. **Subject:** Year of the Dog **Obv:** Arms **Rev:** Dog standing, gilt

| Date | Mintage | VF20 | XF40 | MS60 | MS63 | MS65 |
|---|---|---|---|---|---|---|
| 2006 | — | PF65 70.00 | | | | |

### KM# 260 500 TUGRIK

25.00 g., 0.925 Silver 0.7435 oz. ASW, 38.6 mm. **Subject:** Great Mongolian State, 800th Anniversary **Obv:** Arms **Rev:** Chinggis Khan and black pennant

| Date | Mintage | VF20 | XF40 | MS60 | MS63 | MS65 |
|---|---|---|---|---|---|---|
| 2006 | 2,500 | PF65 75.00 | | | | |

### KM# 261 500 TUGRIK

25.00 g., 0.925 Silver 0.7435 oz. ASW, 38.61 mm. **Subject:** Great Mongolian State, 800th Anniversary **Obv:** Arms **Rev:** Nine white pennants

| Date | Mintage | VF20 | XF40 | MS60 | MS63 | MS65 |
|---|---|---|---|---|---|---|
| 2006 | 2,500 | PF65 75.00 | | | | |

### KM# 316 500 TUGRIK

25.00 g., 0.925 Silver 0.7435 oz. ASW, 38.5 mm. **Subject:** Ice skating

| Date | Mintage | VF20 | XF40 | MS60 | MS63 | MS65 |
|---|---|---|---|---|---|---|
| 2006 | — | PF63 45.00 | PF65 50.00 | | | |

**KM# 212 500 TUGRIK**
31.11 g., 0.999 Silver 0.999 oz. ASW, 38 mm. **Obv:** Arms and value **Rev:** Wolverine head facing with small sharp Swarovski crystals in eyes **Rev. Inscription:** WILDLIFE PROTECTION GULO GULO

| Date | Mintage | VF20 | XF40 | MS60 | MS63 | MS65 |
|---|---|---|---|---|---|---|
| 2007 | 2,500 | — | — | — | — | 1,350 |

**KM# 265 500 TUGRIK**
31.11 g., 0.999 Silver 0.999 oz. ASW, 38.61 mm. **Subject:** Society Space exploration **Obv:** Arms **Rev:** Sputnik, rocket, three figures

| Date | Mintage | VF20 | XF40 | MS60 | MS63 | MS65 |
|---|---|---|---|---|---|---|
| 2007 | 1,000 | PF65 75.00 | | | | |

**KM# 266 500 TUGRIK**
31.11 g., 0.999 Silver 0.999 oz. ASW, 38.61 mm. **Subject:** Soviet Space Exploration **Rev:** Laika, first dog in space

| Date | Mintage | VF20 | XF40 | MS60 | MS63 | MS65 |
|---|---|---|---|---|---|---|
| 2007 | 500 | PF65 85.00 | | | | |

**KM# 267 500 TUGRIK**
31.11 g., 0.999 Silver 0.999 oz. ASW, 38.61 mm. **Subject:** Soviet Space Exploration **Obv:** Arms **Rev:** Sputnik

| Date | Mintage | VF20 | XF40 | MS60 | MS63 | MS65 |
|---|---|---|---|---|---|---|
| 2007 | 500 | PF65 85.00 | | | | |

**KM# 268 500 TUGRIK**
31.11 g., 0.999 Silver 0.999 oz. ASW, 38.61 mm. **Subject:** Soviet Space Exploration **Obv:** Arms **Rev:** Yuri Gagarian

| Date | Mintage | VF20 | XF40 | MS60 | MS63 | MS65 |
|---|---|---|---|---|---|---|
| 2007 | 500 | PF65 85.00 | | | | |

**KM# 269 500 TUGRIK**
31.11 g., 0.999 Silver 0.999 oz. ASW, 38.61 mm. **Subject:** Soviet Space Exploration **Obv:** Arms **Rev:** Mir space station

| Date | Mintage | VF20 | XF40 | MS60 | MS63 | MS65 |
|---|---|---|---|---|---|---|
| 2007 | 1,000 | PF65 85.00 | | | | |

**KM# 322 500 TUGRIK**
31.11 g., 0.999 Silver 0.999 oz. ASW, 38.6 mm. **Subject:** Year of the Pig

| Date | Mintage | VF20 | XF40 | MS60 | MS63 | MS65 |
|---|---|---|---|---|---|---|
| 2007 | — | PF65 80.00 | | | | |

**KM# 322a 500 TUGRIK**
31.11 g., 0.999 Silver 0.999 oz. ASW partially gilt, 38.6 mm. **Subject:** Year of the Pig

| Date | Mintage | VF20 | XF40 | MS60 | MS63 | MS65 |
|---|---|---|---|---|---|---|
| 2007 | — | PF65 100 | | | | |

**KM# 325 500 TUGRIK**
25.00 g., 0.925 Silver 0.7435 oz. ASW, 38.6 mm. **Rev:** John F. Kennedy at microphone

| Date | Mintage | VF20 | XF40 | MS60 | MS63 | MS65 |
|---|---|---|---|---|---|---|
| 2007 | — | PF65 125 | | | | |

**KM# 213 500 TUGRIK**
31.10 g., 0.999 Silver 0.9989 oz. ASW, 39mm mm. **Subject:** Year of the Rat **Obv:** National emblem, value below **Rev:** Three rats in grass **Edge:** Reeded

| Date | Mintage | VF20 | XF40 | MS60 | MS63 | MS65 |
|---|---|---|---|---|---|---|
| 2008 | 20,000 | — | — | — | 45.00 | 50.00 |

**KM# 213a 500 TUGRIK**
31.10 g., 0.999 Silver 0.9989 oz. ASW, 39.0 mm. **Subject:** Year of the Rat **Obv:** National emblem, value below **Rev:** Three gilt rats in grass **Edge:** Reeded

| Date | Mintage | VF20 | XF40 | MS60 | MS63 | MS65 |
|---|---|---|---|---|---|---|
| 2008 | 5,000 | PF65 60.00 | | | | |

**KM# 222 500 TUGRIK**
25.00 g., 0.925 Silver 0.7435 oz. ASW, 38.61 mm. **Subject:** Wonders of the World **Obv:** Arms **Rev:** Multicolor Chichen Itza

| Date | Mintage | VF20 | XF40 | MS60 | MS63 | MS65 |
|---|---|---|---|---|---|---|
| 2008 | 2,500 | — | — | — | — | 75.00 |

**KM# 223 500 TUGRIK**
25.00 g., 0.925 Silver 0.7435 oz. ASW, 38.6 mm. **Subject:** Wonders of the World **Obv:** Arms **Rev:** Multicolor Treasury at Petra

| Date | Mintage | VF20 | XF40 | MS60 | MS63 | MS65 |
|---|---|---|---|---|---|---|
| 2008 | 2,500 | — | — | — | — | 95.00 |

**KM# 224 500 TUGRIK**
25.00 g., 0.925 Silver 0.7435 oz. ASW, 38.61 mm. **Subject:** Wonders of the World **Obv:** Arms **Rev:** Multicolor Taj Mahal

| Date | Mintage | VF20 | XF40 | MS60 | MS63 | MS65 |
|---|---|---|---|---|---|---|
| 2008 | 2,500 | — | — | — | — | 75.00 |

**KM# 225 500 TUGRIK**
25.00 g., 0.925 Silver 0.7435 oz. ASW, 38.61 mm. **Subject:** Wonders of the World **Obv:** Arms **Rev:** Multicolor Machu Picchu

| Date | Mintage | VF20 | XF40 | MS60 | MS63 | MS65 |
|---|---|---|---|---|---|---|
| 2008 | 2,500 | — | — | — | — | 85.00 |

**KM# 226 500 TUGRIK**
25.00 g., 0.925 Silver 0.7435 oz. ASW, 38.61 mm. **Subject:** Wonders of the World **Obv:** Arms **Rev:** Multicolor Great Wall of China

| Date | Mintage | VF20 | XF40 | MS60 | MS63 | MS65 |
|---|---|---|---|---|---|---|
| 2008 | 2,500 | — | — | — | — | 85.00 |

### KM# 227 500 TUGRIK

25.00 g., 0.925 Silver 0.7435 oz. ASW, 38.61 mm. **Subject:** Wonders of the World **Obv:** Arms **Rev:** Multicolor Colosseum in Rome

| Date | Mintage | VF20 | XF40 | MS60 | MS63 | MS65 |
|---|---|---|---|---|---|---|
| 2008 | 2,500 | — | — | — | — | 75.00 |

### KM# 228 500 TUGRIK

25.00 g., 0.925 Silver 0.7435 oz. ASW, 38.61 mm. **Subject:** Wonders of the World **Obv:** Arms **Rev:** Multicolor Christ the Redeemer statue in Rio

| Date | Mintage | VF20 | XF40 | MS60 | MS63 | MS65 |
|---|---|---|---|---|---|---|
| 2008 | 2,500 | — | — | — | — | 65.00 |

### KM# 255 500 TUGRIK

25.00 g., 0.925 Silver 0.7435 oz. ASW, 38.6 mm. **Subject:** Frederic Chopin **Obv:** Arms **Rev:** Bust right, color keyboard vertical in center

| Date | Mintage | VF20 | XF40 | MS60 | MS63 | MS65 |
|---|---|---|---|---|---|---|
| 2008 | 1,000 | PF65 90.00 | | | | |

### KM# 256 500 TUGRIK

31.11 g., 0.999 Silver 0.999 oz. ASW, 38.6 mm. **Subject:** Year of the Rat **Obv:** Arms **Rev:** Two mice

| Date | Mintage | VF20 | XF40 | MS60 | MS63 | MS65 |
|---|---|---|---|---|---|---|
| 2008 | — | PF65 55.00 | | | | |

### KM# 256a 500 TUGRIK

31.11 g., 0.999 Silver 0.999 oz. ASW partially gilt, 38.6 mm. **Subject:** Year of the Rat **Obv:** Arms **Rev:** Two mice, gilt

| Date | Mintage | VF20 | XF40 | MS60 | MS63 | MS65 |
|---|---|---|---|---|---|---|
| 2008 | — | PF65 65.00 | | | | |

### KM# 272 500 TUGRIK

25.00 g., 0.925 Silver 0.7435 oz. ASW, 38.6 mm. **Series:** Mongolian Olympians, Baatarjav **Obv:** Arms

| Date | Mintage | VF20 | XF40 | MS60 | MS63 | MS65 |
|---|---|---|---|---|---|---|
| 2008 | 2,500 | PF65 45.00 | | | | |

### KM# 273 500 TUGRIK

25.00 g., 0.925 Silver 0.7435 oz. ASW, 38.61 mm. **Subject:** Mongolian Olympians - Badar-Uugan

| Date | Mintage | VF20 | XF40 | MS60 | MS63 | MS65 |
|---|---|---|---|---|---|---|
| 2008 | 2,500 | PF65 45.00 | | | | |

### KM# 274 500 TUGRIK

25.00 g., 0.999 Silver 0.803 oz. ASW, 38.61 mm. **Subject:** Mongolian Olympians - Serdamba

| Date | Mintage | VF20 | XF40 | MS60 | MS63 | MS65 |
|---|---|---|---|---|---|---|
| 2008 | 2,500 | PF65 45.00 | | | | |

### KM# 275 500 TUGRIK

25.00 g., 0.925 Silver 0.7435 oz. ASW, 38.61 mm. **Subject:** Mongolian Olympians - Tuvshinbayar

| Date | Mintage | VF20 | XF40 | MS60 | MS63 | MS65 |
|---|---|---|---|---|---|---|
| 2008 | 2,500 | PF65 45.00 | | | | |

### KM# 276 500 TUGRIK

25.00 g., 0.925 Silver 0.7435 oz. ASW, 38.61 mm. **Subject:** Mongolian Olympians - Gundegmaa

| Date | Mintage | VF20 | XF40 | MS60 | MS63 | MS65 |
|---|---|---|---|---|---|---|
| 2008 | 2,500 | PF65 45.00 | | | | |

### KM# 279 500 TUGRIK

0.50 g., 0.999 Gold 0.0161 oz. AGW, 11 mm. **Subject:** Mongolian Olympic Sports - Archery

| Date | Mintage | VF20 | XF40 | MS60 | MS63 | MS65 |
|---|---|---|---|---|---|---|
| 2008 Proof | 15,000 | — | — | — | 50.00 | 60.00 |

### KM# 280 500 TUGRIK

25.00 g., 0.925 Silver 0.7435 oz. ASW, 38.61 mm. **Obv:** Arms **Rev:** Two snow leopards, multicolor

| Date | Mintage | VF20 | XF40 | MS60 | MS63 | MS65 |
|---|---|---|---|---|---|---|
| 2008 | 2,500 | PF65 75.00 | | | | |

### KM# 281 500 TUGRIK

25.00 g., 0.925 Silver 0.7435 oz. ASW, 38.61 mm. **Obv:** Arms **Rev:** The Almas, multicolor changing insert

| Date | Mintage | VF20 | XF40 | MS60 | MS63 | MS65 |
|---|---|---|---|---|---|---|
| 2008 | 2,500 | PF65 55.00 | | | | |

### KM# 305 500 TUGRIK

25.00 g., 0.925 Silver 0.7435 oz. ASW, 38.61 mm. **Subject:** Frederic Chopin **Obv:** National emblem **Rev:** Piano keys in color, bust at right

| Date | Mintage | VF20 | XF40 | MS60 | MS63 | MS65 |
|---|---|---|---|---|---|---|
| 2008 | — | PF65 75.00 | | | | |

### KM# 312 500 TUGRIK

31.11 g., 0.999 Silver 0.999 oz. ASW, 38.61 mm. **Subject:** Year of the Rat **Rev:** Mouse in multicolor

| Date | Mintage | VF20 | XF40 | MS60 | MS63 | MS65 |
|---|---|---|---|---|---|---|
| 2008 | — | PF65 65.00 | | | | |

### KM# 258 500 TUGRIK

31.11 g., 0.999 Silver 0.999 oz. ASW, 38.6 mm. **Subject:** Year of the Ox **Obv:** Arms **Rev:** Ox in color

| Date | Mintage | VF20 | XF40 | MS60 | MS63 | MS65 |
|---|---|---|---|---|---|---|
| 2009 | — | PF65 60.00 | | | | |

### KM# 258a 500 TUGRIK

31.11 g., 0.999 Silver 0.999 oz. ASW partially gilt, 38.6 mm. **Subject:** Year of the Ox **Obv:** Arms **Rev:** Ox, gilt

| Date | Mintage | VF20 | XF40 | MS60 | MS63 | MS65 |
|---|---|---|---|---|---|---|
| 2009 | — | PF65 70.00 | | | | |

### KM# 309 500 TUGRIK

31.10 g., 0.925 Silver 0.9249 oz. ASW, 38.6 mm. **Subject:** Endangered Wildlife **Obv:** National Emblem **Rev:** Owl's head facing (Strix Uralensis) crystal insert eyes

| Date | Mintage | VF20 | XF40 | MS60 | MS63 | MS65 |
|---|---|---|---|---|---|---|
| 2011 Antique finish | 2,500 | — | — | — | 650 | |

### KM# 310 500 TUGRIK

0.50 g., 0.999 Gold 0.0161 oz. AGW, 11 mm. **Subject:** Endangered Wildlife **Obv:** National emblem **Rev:** Ural Owl (Strix Uralersis) standing left

| Date | Mintage | VF20 | XF40 | MS60 | MS63 | MS65 |
|---|---|---|---|---|---|---|
| 2011 Proof | 15,000 | — | — | — | 60.00 | 70.00 |

### KM# 314 500 TUGRIK

25.00 g., 0.925 Silver 0.7435 oz. ASW, 38.61 mm. **Subject:** Joint Societ - mongolian space flight, 30th Anniversary

| Date | Mintage | VF20 | XF40 | MS60 | MS63 | MS65 |
|---|---|---|---|---|---|---|
| 2011 | — | PF65 70.00 | | | | |

### KM# 315 500 TUGRIK

25.00 g., 0.925 Silver 0.7435 oz. ASW, 38.61 mm. **Rev:** Saiga Tatarica in color

| Date | Mintage | VF20 | XF40 | MS60 | MS63 | MS65 |
|---|---|---|---|---|---|---|
| 2011 | 2,500 | PF65 70.00 | | | | |

### KM# 329 500 TUGRIK

0.50 g., 0.9999 Gold 0.0161 oz. AGW, 11 mm. **Obv:** National emblem **Rev:** Saiga Tatarica left

| Date | Mintage | VF20 | XF40 | MS60 | MS63 | MS65 |
|---|---|---|---|---|---|---|
| 2011 | — | PF65 65.00 | | | | |

### KM# 324 500 TUGRIK

31.11 g., 0.999 Silver 0.999 oz. ASW, 38.61 mm. **Rev:** Baby hedgehog with crystal eyes

| Date | Mintage | VF20 | XF40 | MS60 | MS63 | MS65 |
|---|---|---|---|---|---|---|
| 2012 Antique patina | — | — | — | — | — | 450 |

### KM# 326 500 TUGRIK

31.11 g., 0.999 Silver 0.9992 oz. ASW, 38.61 mm. **Obv:** National emblem **Rev:** Argali sheep with crystal eyes

| Date | Mintage | VF20 | XF40 | MS60 | MS63 | MS65 |
|---|---|---|---|---|---|---|
| 2013 Antique patina | — | — | — | — | — | 350 |

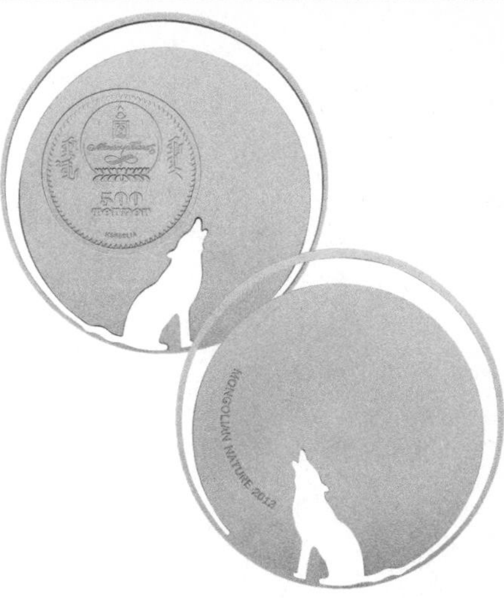

### KM# 327 500 TUGRIK

16.81 g., 0.925 Silver 0.4999 oz. ASW Gilt, 38.61 mm. **Obv:** Howling wolf seated right, crescent above, State emblem at left **Note:** Laser cut-out

| Date | Mintage | VF20 | XF40 | MS60 | MS63 | MS65 |
|---|---|---|---|---|---|---|
| 2013 Matte proof | 2,500 | PF65 200 | | | | |

### KM# 328 500 TUGRIK

0.50 g., 0.9999 Gold 0.0161 oz. AGW, 11 mm. **Obv:** National emblem **Rev:** Howling wolf seated right

| Date | Mintage | VF20 | XF40 | MS60 | MS63 | MS65 |
|---|---|---|---|---|---|---|
| 2013 | — | PF65 65.00 | | | | |

### KM# 330 500 TUGRIK

0.50 g., 0.9999 Gold 0.0161 oz. AGW, 11 mm. **Obv:** National emblem **Rev:** Argali sheep standing left

| Date | Mintage | VF20 | XF40 | MS60 | MS63 | MS65 |
|---|---|---|---|---|---|---|
| 2013 | — | PF65 65.00 | | | | |

### KM# 331 500 TUGRIK

0.50 g., 0.9999 Gold 0.0161 oz. AGW, 11 mm. **Obv:** National emblem **Rev:** Eagle head left, eagle in flight at top left

| Date | Mintage | VF20 | XF40 | MS60 | MS63 | MS65 |
|---|---|---|---|---|---|---|
| 2013 | — | PF65 65.00 | | | | |

### KM# 332 500 TUGRIK

25.00 g., 0.925 Silver 0.7435 oz. ASW, 38.61 mm. **Obv:** National emblem **Rev:** Eagle in flight above mountains in color

| Date | Mintage | VF20 | XF40 | MS60 | MS63 | MS65 |
|---|---|---|---|---|---|---|
| 2013 | — | PF65 70.00 | | | | |

**KM# 336 500 TUGRIK**
0.50 g., 0.9999 Gold 0.0161 oz. AGW, 11 mm. **Obv:** National emblem **Rev:** Horse rearing-up left

| Date | Mintage | F12 | VF20 | XF40 | MS60 | MS63 |
|---|---|---|---|---|---|---|
| 2014 | — | PF65 75.00 | | | | |

**KM# 338 500 TUGRIK**
0.50 g., 0.9999 Gold 0.0161 oz. AGW, 11 mm. **Obv:** National emblem **Rev:** Manul advancing left

| Date | Mintage | F12 | VF20 | XF40 | MS60 | MS63 |
|---|---|---|---|---|---|---|
| 2014 | — | PF65 85.00 | | | | |

**KM# 199 1000 TUGRIK**
31.11 g., 0.925 Silver 0.9252 oz. ASW, 38.6 mm. **Obv:** National emblem above value **Obv. Inscription:** Denomination spelled "TOGROG" **Rev:** Head facing **Edge:** Reeded

| Date | Mintage | VF20 | XF40 | MS60 | MS63 | MS65 |
|---|---|---|---|---|---|---|
| 2002 | 17,000 | — | — | — | 40.00 | 45.00 |

**KM# 233 1000 TUGRIK**
Gold **Rev:** Snow leopard

| Date | Mintage | VF20 | XF40 | MS60 | MS63 | MS65 |
|---|---|---|---|---|---|---|
| 2005 | — | PF63 85.00 | PF65 95.00 | | | |

**KM# 253 1000 TUGRIK**
1.24 g., 0.999 Gold 0.0398 oz. AGW, 13.92 mm. **Subject:** Mozart **Obv:** Arms **Rev:** Portrait and profile heads above building

| Date | Mintage | VF20 | XF40 | MS60 | MS63 | MS65 |
|---|---|---|---|---|---|---|
| 2006 | — | PF63 70.00 | PF65 80.00 | | | |

**KM# 262 1000 TUGRIK**
1.24 g., 0.999 Gold 0.0398 oz. AGW, 13.92 mm. **Obv:** Arms **Rev:** Scorpion

| Date | Mintage | VF20 | XF40 | MS60 | MS63 | MS65 |
|---|---|---|---|---|---|---|
| 2006 | 25,000 | PF63 85.00 | PF65 95.00 | | | |

**KM# 263 1000 TUGRIK**
1.24 g., 0.999 Silver 0.0398 oz. ASW, 13.9 mm. **Obv:** Arms **Rev:** Long-eared Jerboa

| Date | Mintage | VF20 | XF40 | MS60 | MS63 | MS65 |
|---|---|---|---|---|---|---|
| 2006 | — | PF63 85.00 | PF65 95.00 | | | |

**KM# 264 1000 TUGRIK**
1.24 g., 0.999 Gold 0.0398 oz. AGW, 13.9 mm. **Obv:** Arms **Rev:** Gobi Bear

| Date | Mintage | VF20 | XF40 | MS60 | MS63 | MS65 |
|---|---|---|---|---|---|---|
| 2006 | 25,000 | PF63 85.00 | PF65 95.00 | | | |

**KM# 294 1000 TUGRIK**
62.20 g., 0.999 Silver 1.9978 oz. ASW, 50 mm. **Rev:** Tsarina Catherina multicolor

| Date | Mintage | VF20 | XF40 | MS60 | MS63 | MS65 |
|---|---|---|---|---|---|---|
| 2007 | 500 | PF65 165 | | | | |

**KM# 295 1000 TUGRIK**
62.20 g., 0.999 Silver 1.9978 oz. ASW, 50 mm. **Rev:** Tsar Nicholas I, multicolor

| Date | Mintage | VF20 | XF40 | MS60 | MS63 | MS65 |
|---|---|---|---|---|---|---|
| 2007 | 500 | PF65 165 | | | | |

**KM# 296 1000 TUGRIK**
62.20 g., 0.999 Silver 1.9978 oz. ASW, 50 mm. **Rev:** Tsar Nicholas II

| Date | Mintage | VF20 | XF40 | MS60 | MS63 | MS65 |
|---|---|---|---|---|---|---|
| 2007 | 500 | PF65 165 | | | | |

**KM# 297 1000 TUGRIK**
62.20 g., 0.999 Silver 1.9978 oz. ASW, 50 mm. **Rev:** Tsar Ivan IV, multicolor

| Date | Mintage | VF20 | XF40 | MS60 | MS63 | MS65 |
|---|---|---|---|---|---|---|
| 2007 | 500 | PF65 165 | | | | |

**KM# 298 1000 TUGRIK**
62.20 g., 0.999 Silver 1.9978 oz. ASW, 50 mm. **Rev:** Tsar Peter I, multicolor

| Date | Mintage | VF20 | XF40 | MS60 | MS63 | MS65 |
|---|---|---|---|---|---|---|
| 2007 | 500 | PF65 165 | | | | |

**KM# 299 1000 TUGRIK**
62.20 g., 0.999 Silver 1.9978 oz. ASW, 50 mm. **Rev:** Tsar Yuri

| Date | Mintage | VF20 | XF40 | MS60 | MS63 | MS65 |
|---|---|---|---|---|---|---|
| 2007 | 500 | PF65 165 | | | | |

**KM# 214 1000 TUGRIK**
1.24 g., 0.999 Gold 0.0398 oz. AGW, 13.92 mm. **Subject:** Year of the Rat **Obv:** National emblem, value below **Edge:** Reeded

| Date | Mintage | VF20 | XF40 | MS60 | MS63 | MS65 |
|---|---|---|---|---|---|---|
| 2008 Proof, center emblem frosted | 10,000 | PF63 65.00 | PF65 75.00 | | | |
| 2008 Proof, center rays and emblem and background frosted | — | PF63 65.00 | PF65 70.00 | | | |

**KM# 277 1000 TUGRIK**
1.24 g., 0.999 Gold 0.0398 oz. AGW, 13.92 mm. **Subject:** Mongolian Olympic Sports - Boxing **Rev:** Two fighters in the ring

| Date | Mintage | VF20 | XF40 | MS60 | MS63 | MS65 |
|---|---|---|---|---|---|---|
| 2008 | 15,000 | PF63 75.00 | PF65 85.00 | | | |

**KM# 278 1000 TUGRIK**
1.24 g., 0.999 Gold 0.0398 oz. AGW, 13.92 mm. **Subject:** Mongolian Olympic Sports - Judo **Rev:** Judo athlete getting fliped

| Date | Mintage | VF20 | XF40 | MS60 | MS63 | MS65 |
|---|---|---|---|---|---|---|
| 2008 | 15,000 | PF63 75.00 | PF65 85.00 | | | |

**KM# 339 1000 TUGRIK**
1.00 g., 0.9999 Gold 0.0321 oz. AGW, 13.92 mm. **Rev:** Coliseum

| Date | Mintage | VF20 | XF40 | MS60 | MS63 | MS65 |
|---|---|---|---|---|---|---|
| 2008 | 15,000 | PF65 75.00 | | | | |

**KM# 340 1000 TUGRIK**
1.00 g., 0.9999 Gold 0.0321 oz. AGW, 13.92 mm. **Rev:** Chichen Itza

| Date | Mintage | VF20 | XF40 | MS60 | MS63 | MS65 |
|---|---|---|---|---|---|---|
| 2008 | 15,000 | PF65 75.00 | | | | |

**KM# 341 1000 TUGRIK**
1.00 g., 0.9999 Gold 0.0321 oz. AGW, 13.92 mm. **Rev:** Treasury at Petra

| Date | Mintage | VF20 | XF40 | MS60 | MS63 | MS65 |
|---|---|---|---|---|---|---|
| 2008 | 15,000 | PF65 75.00 | | | | |

**KM# 342 1000 TUGRIK**
1.00 g., 0.9999 Gold 0.0321 oz. AGW, 13.92 mm. **Rev:** Machu Picchu

| Date | Mintage | VF20 | XF40 | MS60 | MS63 | MS65 |
|---|---|---|---|---|---|---|
| 2008 | 15,000 | PF65 75.00 | | | | |

**KM# 343 1000 TUGRIK**
1.00 g., 0.9999 Gold 0.0321 oz. AGW, 13.92 mm. **Rev:** Taj Mahal

| Date | Mintage | VF20 | XF40 | MS60 | MS63 | MS65 |
|---|---|---|---|---|---|---|
| 2008 | 15,000 | PF65 75.00 | | | | |

**KM# 344 1000 TUGRIK**
1.00 g., 0.9999 Gold 0.0321 oz. AGW, 13.92 mm. **Rev:** Christ the Redeemer statue

| Date | Mintage | VF20 | XF40 | MS60 | MS63 | MS65 |
|---|---|---|---|---|---|---|
| 2008 | 15,000 | PF65 75.00 | | | | |

**KM# 345 1000 TUGRIK**
1.00 g., 0.9999 Gold 0.0321 oz. AGW, 13.92 mm. **Rev:** Great Wall of China

| Date | Mintage | VF20 | XF40 | MS60 | MS63 | MS65 |
|---|---|---|---|---|---|---|
| 2008 | 15,000 | PF65 75.00 | | | | |

**KM# 311 1000 TUGRIK**
1.24 g., 0.999 Gold 0.0398 oz. AGW, 13.92 mm. **Subject:** Frederic Chopin **Obv:** National Emblem **Rev:** Piano keyboard vertical at left, bust at right

| Date | Mintage | VF20 | XF40 | MS60 | MS63 | MS65 |
|---|---|---|---|---|---|---|
| 2011 | — | PF65 100 | | | | |

**KM# 333.1 1000 TUGRIK**
31.11 g., 0.999 Silver 0.999 oz. ASW, 38.61 mm. **Obv:** National emblem **Rev:** Ghinggis Khan facing at left

| Date | Mintage | VF20 | XF40 | MS60 | MS63 | MS65 |
|---|---|---|---|---|---|---|
| 2014 | — | PF65 75.00 | | | | |

**KM# 333.2 1000 TUGRIK**
31.11 g., 0.999 Silver 0.999 oz. ASW, 38.61 mm. **Obv:** National emblem **Rev:** Ghinggis Khan at left facing, dark patina

| Date | Mintage | VF20 | XF40 | MS60 | MS63 | MS65 |
|---|---|---|---|---|---|---|
| 2014 Proof, antique patina | 1,000 | PF65 100 | | | | |

**KM# 334 1000 TUGRIK**
0.50 g., 0.9999 Gold 0.0161 oz. AGW, 11 mm. **Obv:** National emblem **Rev:** Ghinggis Khan at left facing

| Date | Mintage | VF20 | XF40 | MS60 | MS63 | MS65 |
|---|---|---|---|---|---|---|
| 2014 | — | PF65 85.00 | | | | |

**KM# 240 2500 TUGRIK**
7.77 g., 0.999 Gold 0.2496 oz. AGW **Subject:** Year of the Snake **Obv:** Arms **Rev:** Snake

| Date | Mintage | VF20 | XF40 | MS60 | MS63 | MS65 |
|---|---|---|---|---|---|---|
| 2001 | 2,000 | PF65 500 | | | | |

**KM# 242 2500 TUGRIK**
7.70 g., 0.999 Gold 0.2473 oz. AGW **Subject:** Year of the Horse **Obv:** Arms **Rev:** Year of the Horse

| Date | Mintage | VF20 | XF40 | MS60 | MS63 | MS65 |
|---|---|---|---|---|---|---|
| 2002 | — | PF65 500 | | | | |

**KM# 243 2500 TUGRIK**
155.50 g., 0.999 Silver 4.9944 oz. ASW partially gilt, 65 mm. **Subject:** Year of the Ram **Obv:** Arms **Rev:** Ram standing left, gilt

| Date | Mintage | VF20 | XF40 | MS60 | MS63 | MS65 |
|---|---|---|---|---|---|---|
| 2003 | 4,000 | PF65 325 | | | | |

**KM# 220 2500 TUGRIK**
7.78 g., 0.9999 Gold 0.2501 oz. AGW **Series:** Chinese Lunar **Subject:** Year of the Monkey **Obv:** National emblem **Rev:** Monkey seated on branch **Edge:** Reeded

| Date | Mintage | VF20 | XF40 | MS60 | MS63 | MS65 |
|---|---|---|---|---|---|---|
| ND-2004 | 2,000 | PF65 525 | | | | |

**KM# 245 2500 TUGRIK**
155.50 g., 0.999 Silver 4.9944 oz. ASW partially gilt, 65 mm. **Subject:** Year of the Monkey **Obv:** Arms **Rev:** Monkey, gilt

| Date | Mintage | VF20 | XF40 | MS60 | MS63 | MS65 |
|---|---|---|---|---|---|---|
| 2004 | 4,000 | PF65 325 | | | | |

**KM# 247 2500 TUGRIK**
155.50 g., 0.999 Silver 4.9944 oz. ASW partially gilt, 65 mm. **Subject:** Year of the Rooster **Obv:** Arms **Rev:** Rooster, gilt

| Date | Mintage | VF20 | XF40 | MS60 | MS63 | MS65 |
|---|---|---|---|---|---|---|
| 2005 | 4,000 | PF65 325 | | | | |

**KM# 252 2500 TUGRIK**
155.50 g., 0.999 Silver 4.9944 oz. ASW partially gilt, 65 mm. **Subject:** Year of the Dog **Obv:** Arms **Rev:** Dog standing, gilt

| Date | Mintage | VF20 | XF40 | MS60 | MS63 | MS65 |
|---|---|---|---|---|---|---|
| 2006 | — | PF65 325 | | | | |

**KM# 257 2500 TUGRIK**
155.50 g., 0.999 Silver 4.9944 oz. ASW partially gilt, 65 mm. **Subject:** Year of the Rat **Obv:** Arms **Rev:** Two mice, gilt

| Date | Mintage | VF20 | XF40 | MS60 | MS63 | MS65 |
|---|---|---|---|---|---|---|
| 2008 | — | PF65 325 | | | | |

**KM# 259 2500 TUGRIK**
155.50 g., 0.999 Silver 4.9944 oz. ASW partially gilt, 65 mm. **Subject:** Year of the Ox **Obv:** Arms **Rev:** Ox, gilt

| Date | Mintage | VF20 | XF40 | MS60 | MS63 | MS65 |
|---|---|---|---|---|---|---|
| 2009 | — | PF65 325 | | | | |

**KM# 198 5000 TUGRIK**
155.50 g., 0.999 Silver 4.9944 oz. ASW, 40x90 mm. **Subject:** Year of the Horse **Obv:** National emblem above value to left of Palace Museum **Rev:** Five multicolor running horses **Edge:** Plain **Note:** Round-cornered rectangle. Photo reduced.

| Date | Mintage | VF20 | XF40 | MS60 | MS63 | MS65 |
|---|---|---|---|---|---|---|
| 2002 | — | PF65 350 | | | | |

**KM# 232 5000 TUGRIK**
155.50 g., 0.999 Silver 4.9944 oz. ASW, 40x90 mm. **Rev:** Three sumo wrestlers, multicolor **Shape:** Rectangle **Note:** Illustration reduced.

| Date | Mintage | VF20 | XF40 | MS60 | MS63 | MS65 |
|---|---|---|---|---|---|---|
| 2005 | — | PF65 400 | | | | |

**KM# 221 100000 TUGRIK**
3000.00 g., 0.999 Silver 96.3557 oz. ASW **Series:** Chinese Lunar **Subject:** Year of the Monkey **Obv:** National emblem **Rev:** Monkey seated on branch

| Date | Mintage | VF20 | XF40 | MS60 | MS63 | MS65 |
|---|---|---|---|---|---|---|
| ND-2004 | — | PF65 3,750 | | | | |

**KM# 215 100000 TUGRIK**
3000.00 g., 0.999 Silver 96.3557 oz. ASW, 130.0 mm. **Subject:** Year of the Rat **Obv:** National emblem, value below **Rev:** Three rats in grass **Edge:** Reeded **Note:** Serial number on edge.

| Date | Mintage | VF20 | XF40 | MS60 | MS63 | MS65 |
|---|---|---|---|---|---|---|
| 2008 | 500 | PF65 3,750 | | | | |

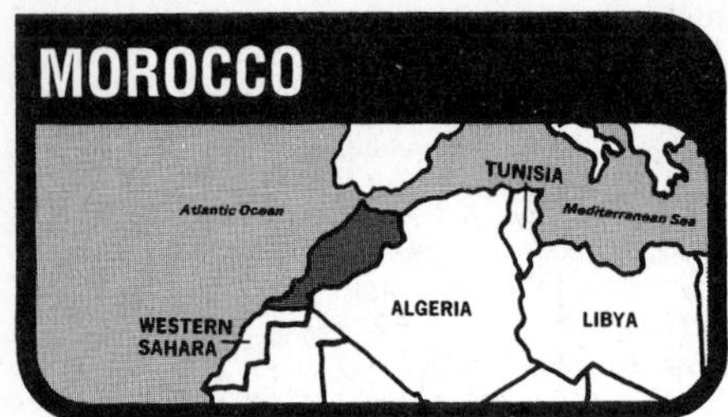


The Kingdom of Morocco, situated on the northwest corner of Africa, has an area of 432,620 sq. mi. (710,850 sq. km.) and a population of 36 million. Capital: Rabat. The economy is essentially agricultural. Phosphates, fresh and preserved vegetables, canned fish, and raw materials are exported.

# KINGDOM

## REFORM COINAGE

100 Santimat = 1 Dirham

### Y# 112 5 SANTIMAT

2.00 g., Aluminum-Bronze, 17.5 mm. **Ruler:** Mohammed VI **Obv:** Crowned arms with supporters **Rev:** Value, flower and dates **Edge:** Plain

| Date | Mintage | F12 | VF20 | XF40 | MS60 | MS63 |
|---|---|---|---|---|---|---|
| AH1423-2002 | — | — | — | — | 0.50 | 1.00 |

### Y# 158 5 SANTIMAT

Brass Plated Iron **Ruler:** Mohammed VI **Rev:** National arms

| Date | Mintage | F12 | VF20 | XF40 | MS60 | MS63 |
|---|---|---|---|---|---|---|
| 2011 | — | — | — | — | — | 0.70 |

### Y# 114 10 SANTIMAT

3.00 g., Aluminum-Bronze, 20 mm. **Ruler:** Mohammed VI **Obv:** Crowned arms with supporters **Rev:** Value, design of "sport and solidarity **Edge:** Reeded

| Date | Mintage | F12 | VF20 | XF40 | MS60 | MS63 |
|---|---|---|---|---|---|---|
| AH1423-2002 | — | — | — | — | 1.00 | 2.00 |

### Y# 136 10 SANTIMAT

3.00 g., Brass Plated Steel, 20 mm. **Ruler:** Mohammed VI **Rev:** Bee and flower

| Date | Mintage | F12 | VF20 | XF40 | MS60 | MS63 |
|---|---|---|---|---|---|---|
| AH1432-2011 | — | — | — | — | 1.00 | 2.00 |
| AH1433-2012 | — | — | — | — | 1.00 | 3.00 |
| AH1434-2013 | — | — | — | — | 1.00 | 3.00 |
| AH1435-2014 | — | — | — | — | 1.00 | 3.00 |

### Y# 115 20 SANTIMAT

4.00 g., Aluminum-Bronze, 23 mm. **Ruler:** Mohammed VI **Obv:** Crowned arms with supporters **Rev:** Value, design of "tourist and craftsmen trade **Edge:** Reeded

| Date | Mintage | F12 | VF20 | XF40 | MS60 | MS63 |
|---|---|---|---|---|---|---|
| AH1423-2002 | — | — | — | — | 1.50 | 3.00 |

### Y# 137 20 SANTIMAT

4.00 g., Brass Plated Steel, 23 mm. **Ruler:** Mohammed VI **Rev:** Lotus flower and globe **Edge:** Reeded

| Date | Mintage | F12 | VF20 | XF40 | MS60 | MS63 |
|---|---|---|---|---|---|---|
| AH1432-2011 | — | — | — | — | 1.50 | 3.00 |
| AH1433-2012 | — | — | — | — | 1.50 | 3.00 |
| AH1434-2013 | — | — | — | — | 1.50 | 3.00 |
| AH1435-2014 | — | — | — | — | 1.50 | 3.00 |

### Y# 116 1/2 DIRHAM

4.00 g., Copper-Nickel, 21 mm. **Ruler:** Mohammed VI **Obv:** Crowned arms with supporters **Rev:** Value, design theme "telecommunications and new technologies **Edge:** Reeded

| Date | Mintage | F12 | VF20 | XF40 | MS60 | MS63 |
|---|---|---|---|---|---|---|
| AH1423-2002 | — | — | — | — | 2.00 | 3.00 |

### Y# 138 1/2 DIRHAM

4.00 g., Nickel Plated Steel, 21 mm. **Ruler:** Mohammed VI **Obv:** Crowned national arms with supporters **Rev:** Two fish and large value **Edge:** Reeded

| Date | Mintage | F12 | VF20 | XF40 | MS60 | MS63 |
|---|---|---|---|---|---|---|
| AH1432-2011 | — | — | — | — | 3.00 | 5.00 |
| AH1433-2012 | — | — | — | — | 3.00 | 5.00 |
| AH1434-2013 | — | — | — | — | 3.00 | 5.00 |
| AH1435-2014 | — | — | — | — | 3.00 | 5.00 |

### Y# 117 DIRHAM

6.00 g., Copper-Nickel, 24 mm. **Ruler:** Mohammed VI **Obv:** Head 3/4 left **Rev:** Crowned arms with supporters above value **Edge:** Reeded

| Date | Mintage | F12 | VF20 | XF40 | MS60 | MS63 |
|---|---|---|---|---|---|---|
| AH1423-2002 | — | — | — | — | 3.00 | 5.00 |

### Y# 139 DIRHAM

6.00 g., Nickel Plated Steel, 24 mm. **Ruler:** Mohammed VI **Obv:** Head left **Rev:** Crowned national arms with supporters, value below **Edge:** Reeded

| Date | Mintage | F12 | VF20 | XF40 | MS60 | MS63 |
|---|---|---|---|---|---|---|
| AH1432-2011 | — | — | — | — | 3.50 | 5.00 |
| AH1433-2012 | — | — | — | — | 3.50 | 5.00 |
| AH1434-2013 | — | — | — | — | 3.50 | 5.00 |

### Y# 149 25 CENTIMES

0.70 g., Aluminum, 17 mm. **Ruler:** Mohammed VI **Subject:** F.A.O. **Obv:** National arms **Rev:** Tuna in net

| Date | Mintage | F12 | VF20 | XF40 | MS60 | MS63 |
|---|---|---|---|---|---|---|
| 2002 | — | — | — | — | — | — |

### Y# 118 2 DIRHAMS

7.00 g., Copper-Nickel, 26 mm. **Ruler:** Mohammed VI **Obv:** Head 3/4 left within octagon shape **Rev:** Crowned arms with supporters above value within octagon shape **Edge:** Reeded

| Date | Mintage | F12 | VF20 | XF40 | MS60 | MS63 |
|---|---|---|---|---|---|---|
| AH1423-2002 | — | — | — | — | 4.00 | 6.00 |

### Y# 109 5 DIRHAMS

7.50 g., Bi-Metallic Nickel-Brass center in Copper-Nickel ring, 25 mm. **Ruler:** Mohammed VI **Obv:** Head 3/4 left **Rev:** Crowned arms with supporters above value **Edge:** Segmented reeding

| Date | Mintage | F12 | VF20 | XF40 | MS60 | MS63 |
|---|---|---|---|---|---|---|
| AH1423-2002 | — | — | — | — | 6.00 | 9.00 |

### Y# 140 5 DIRHAMS

7.50 g., Bi-Metallic Nordic Gold center in Copper-Nickel ring, 25 mm. **Ruler:** Mohammed VI **Obv:** Head left **Rev:** Hassan II Mosque in Casablanca **Edge:** Segmented reeding

| Date | Mintage | F12 | VF20 | XF40 | MS60 | MS63 |
|---|---|---|---|---|---|---|
| AH1432-2011 | — | — | — | — | 6.00 | 9.00 |
| AH1434-2013 | — | — | — | — | 6.00 | 9.00 |

### Y# 110 10 DIRHAMS

9.00 g., Bi-Metallic Copper-Nickel center in Brass ring, 26.9 mm. **Ruler:** Mohammed VI **Obv:** Head 3/4 left **Rev:** Crowned arms with supporters above value **Edge:** Reeded

| Date | Mintage | F12 | VF20 | XF40 | MS60 | MS63 |
|---|---|---|---|---|---|---|
| AH1423-2002 | — | — | — | — | 10.00 | 15.00 |

### Y# 141 10 DIRHAMS

9.00 g., Bi-Metallic Copper-Nickel center in Nordic Gold ring, 27 mm. **Ruler:** Mohammed VI **Obv:** Head left **Rev:** Boumalne-du-Dades Fortress, palm tree at left, large value at right

| Date | Mintage | F12 | VF20 | XF40 | MS60 | MS63 |
|---|---|---|---|---|---|---|
| AH1432-2011 | — | — | — | — | 10.00 | 15.00 |
| AH1434-2013 | — | — | — | — | 10.00 | 15.00 |
| AH1435-2014 | — | — | — | — | 10.00 | 15.00 |

### Y# 148 100 DIRHAMS

25.00 g., 0.900 Gold 0.7234 oz. AGW, 37 mm. **Ruler:** Mohammed VI **Subject:** Mohammed VI, 38th Birthday **Rev:** National arms

| Date | Mintage | F12 | VF20 | XF40 | MS60 | MS63 |
|---|---|---|---|---|---|---|
| 2001 | — | **PF65** 1,500 | | | | |

### Y# 160 100 DIRHAMS

12.00 g., Bi-Metallic Nickel-Brass center in Copper-Nickel ring, 28.4 mm. **Ruler:** Mohammed VI **Subject:** UNESCO sites in Rabat **Rev:** Hassan tower and Mohammed V's mausoleum

| Date | Mintage | F12 | VF20 | XF40 | MS60 | MS63 |
|---|---|---|---|---|---|---|
| AH1433-2012 | — | **PF65** 30.00 | | | | |

### Y# 161 100 DIRHAMS

12.00 g., Bi-Metallic Nickel-Brass center in Copper-Nickel ring, 28.4 mm. **Ruler:** Mohammed VI **Subject:** UNESCO sites in Rabat **Rev:** Chellah door

| Date | Mintage | F12 | VF20 | XF40 | MS60 | MS63 |
|---|---|---|---|---|---|---|
| AH1433-2012 | — | **PF65** 30.00 | | | | |

### Y# 162 100 DIRHAMS

12.00 g., Bi-Metallic Nickel-Brass center in Copper-Nickel ring, 28.4 mm. **Ruler:** Mohammed VI **Subject:** UNESCO sites in Rabat **Rev:** Udayas Kasbah

| Date | Mintage | F12 | VF20 | XF40 | MS60 | MS63 |
|---|---|---|---|---|---|---|
| AH1433-2012 | — | **PF65** 30.00 | | | | |

### Y# 95 250 DIRHAMS

25.00 g., 0.925 Silver 0.7435 oz. ASW, 37 mm. **Ruler:** Mohammed VI **Subject:** World Children's Day **Obv:** Head 3/4 left **Rev:** Children standing on open book within globe **Edge:** Reeded

| Date | Mintage | F12 | VF20 | XF40 | MS60 | MS63 |
|---|---|---|---|---|---|---|
| AH1422-2001 | — | **PF65** 100 | | | | |
| AH1422-2001 | — | — | — | — | 60.00 | 80.00 |

**Y# 95a 250 DIRHAMS**
25.00 g., 0.9999 Gold 0.8037 oz. AGW, 37 mm. **Ruler:** Mohammed VI **Subject:** World Children's Day **Obv:** Head 3/4 left **Rev:** Two children standing on an open book within globe **Edge:** Reeded **Note:** Prev. Y#95.

| Date | Mintage | F12 | VF20 | XF40 | MS60 | MS63 |
|---|---|---|---|---|---|---|
| AH1422-2001 | 2,800 | PF63 1,400 | PF65 1,500 | | | |

**Y# 107 250 DIRHAMS**
25.00 g., 0.925 Silver 0.7435 oz. ASW, 37 mm. **Ruler:** Mohammed VI **Subject:** Inauguration of Mohammed VI 2nd Anniversary **Obv:** Head 3/4 left **Rev:** Crowned arms with supporters above value **Edge:** Reeded

| Date | Mintage | F12 | VF20 | XF40 | MS60 | MS63 |
|---|---|---|---|---|---|---|
| AH1422-2001 | — | — | — | — | 55.00 | 70.00 |

**Y# 108 250 DIRHAMS**
25.00 g., 0.925 Silver 0.7435 oz. ASW, 37 mm. **Ruler:** Mohammed VI **Subject:** Mohammed VI's Inauguration 3rd Anniversary **Obv:** Head 3/4 left **Rev:** Crowned arms with supporters above value **Edge:** Reeded **Note:** Slightly different legend of Y-107

| Date | Mintage | F12 | VF20 | XF40 | MS60 | MS63 |
|---|---|---|---|---|---|---|
| AH1423-2002 | — | PF65 100 | | | | |
| AH1423-2002 | — | — | — | — | 60.00 | 80.00 |

**Y# 113 250 DIRHAMS**
25.00 g., 0.925 Silver 0.7435 oz. ASW, 37 mm. **Ruler:** Mohammed VI **Subject:** Marriage of King Mohammed VI, July 12, 2002 **Obv:** Head 3/4 left **Rev:** Crown above radiant flowers **Edge:** Reeded

| Date | Mintage | F12 | VF20 | XF40 | MS60 | MS63 |
|---|---|---|---|---|---|---|
| ND (2002) | — | PF65 100 | | | | |

**Y# 111 250 DIRHAMS**
25.00 g., 0.925 Silver 0.7435 oz. ASW, 37 mm. **Ruler:** Mohammed VI **Subject:** Mohammed VI's Inauguration 4th Anniversary **Obv:** Head 3/4 left **Rev:** Crowned arms with supporters above value **Edge:** Reeded **Note:** Virtually identical to Y-107 and Y-108.

| Date | Mintage | F12 | VF20 | XF40 | MS60 | MS63 |
|---|---|---|---|---|---|---|
| AH1424-2003 | — | — | — | — | 60.00 | 80.00 |

**Y# 119 250 DIRHAMS**
25.00 g., 0.925 Silver 0.7435 oz. ASW, 37 mm. **Ruler:** Mohammed VI **Subject:** Birth of Crown Prince Moulay Al Hassan **Obv:** Head 3/4 left **Rev:** Crowned arms with supporters above value

| Date | Mintage | F12 | VF20 | XF40 | MS60 | MS63 |
|---|---|---|---|---|---|---|
| ND (2003) | — | PF65 100 | | | | |

**Y# 120 250 DIRHAMS**
25.00 g., 0.925 Silver 0.7435 oz. ASW, 37 mm. **Ruler:** Mohammed VI **Subject:** 50th Anniversary - Kingdom **Obv:** Conjoined heads right **Rev:** Crowned arms with supporters above value

| Date | Mintage | F12 | VF20 | XF40 | MS60 | MS63 |
|---|---|---|---|---|---|---|
| AH1424-2003 | — | PF65 100 | | | | |
| AH1424-2003 | — | — | — | — | 60.00 | 80.00 |

**Y# 151 250 DIRHAMS**
25.00 g., 0.925 Silver 0.7435 oz. ASW, 37 mm. **Ruler:** Mohammed VI **Subject:** International day of People with Disabilities **Rev:** Family on globe

| Date | Mintage | F12 | VF20 | XF40 | MS60 | MS63 |
|---|---|---|---|---|---|---|
| 2003 | — | — | — | — | — | 70.00 |
| 2003 | — | PF65 100 | | | | |

**Y# 121 250 DIRHAMS**
25.00 g., 0.925 Silver 0.7435 oz. ASW, 37 mm. **Ruler:** Mohammed VI **Subject:** Year of Handicapped Persons **Obv:** Head 3/4 left **Rev:** Stylized figures

| Date | Mintage | F12 | VF20 | XF40 | MS60 | MS63 |
|---|---|---|---|---|---|---|
| AH1425-2004 | — | — | — | — | 60.00 | 80.00 |

**Y# 122 250 DIRHAMS**
25.00 g., 0.925 Silver 0.7435 oz. ASW, 37 mm. **Ruler:** Mohammed VI **Subject:** 5th Anniversary of Mohammed VI's Reign **Obv:** Head 3/4 left, national arms **Rev:** Crowned arms with supporters above value **Edge:** Reeded **Note:** Vitually identical to Y-107, 108 and 111.

| Date | Mintage | F12 | VF20 | XF40 | MS60 | MS63 |
|---|---|---|---|---|---|---|
| AH1425-2004 | — | — | — | — | 60.00 | 80.00 |

**Y# 123 250 DIRHAMS**
25.00 g., 0.925 Silver 0.7435 oz. ASW, 37 mm. **Ruler:** Mohammed VI **Subject:** 30th Anniversary - Green March **Obv:** Head 3/4 left **Rev:** Men marching left with flags aloft

| Date | Mintage | F12 | VF20 | XF40 | MS60 | MS63 |
|---|---|---|---|---|---|---|
| AH1426-2005 | — | — | — | — | 60.00 | 80.00 |

**Y# 124 250 DIRHAMS**
25.00 g., 0.925 Silver 0.7435 oz. ASW, 37 mm. **Ruler:** Mohammed VI **Subject:** 6th Anniversary of Mohammed VI's Reign **Obv:** Head 3/4 left **Rev:** Crowned arms with supporters above value **Edge:** Reeded **Note:** Virtually identical to Y-107, 108, 111 and 122

| Date | Mintage | F12 | VF20 | XF40 | MS60 | MS63 |
|---|---|---|---|---|---|---|
| AH1426-2005 | — | — | — | — | 60.00 | 80.00 |

**Y# 125 250 DIRHAMS**
25.00 g., 0.925 Silver 0.7435 oz. ASW, 37 mm. **Ruler:** Mohammed VI **Subject:** 6th Anniversary of Mohammed VI's Reign **Obv:** Head 3/4 left **Rev:** Crowned arms with supporters above value **Edge:** Reeded **Note:** Virtually identical to Y-107, 108, 111 and 122

| Date | Mintage | F12 | VF20 | XF40 | MS60 | MS63 |
|---|---|---|---|---|---|---|
| AH1427-2006 | — | — | — | — | 60.00 | 80.00 |

**Y# 126 250 DIRHAMS**
25.00 g., 0.925 Silver 0.7435 oz. ASW, 37 mm. **Ruler:** Mohammed VI **Subject:** 8th Anniversary of Mohammed VI's reign **Obv:** Head 3/4 left **Rev:** Corwned arms with supporters, value below **Edge:** Reeded

| Date | Mintage | F12 | VF20 | XF40 | MS60 | MS63 |
|---|---|---|---|---|---|---|
| AH1428/2007 | — | — | — | — | 60.00 | 80.00 |

**Y# 153 250 DIRHAMS**
25.00 g., 0.925 Silver 0.7435 oz. ASW **Ruler:** Mohammed VI **Subject:** Birth of Princess Lalla Khaduija **Rev:** National arms

| Date | Mintage | F12 | VF20 | XF40 | MS60 | MS63 |
|---|---|---|---|---|---|---|
| 2007 | — | — | — | — | — | 70.00 |
| 2007 | — | PF65 100 | | | | |

**Y# 127 250 DIRHAMS**
25.00 g., 0.925 Silver 0.7435 oz. ASW, 37 mm. **Ruler:** Mohammed VI **Subject:** 9th Anniversary of Mohammed VI's reign **Obv:** Head 3/4 left **Rev:** Crowned arms with supporters above value **Edge:** Reeded

| Date | Mintage | F12 | VF20 | XF40 | MS60 | MS63 |
|---|---|---|---|---|---|---|
| AH1429-2008 | 1,000 | PF65 125 | | | | |

**Y# 128 250 DIRHAMS**
25.00 g., 0.925 Silver 0.7435 oz. ASW, 37 mm. **Ruler:** Mohammed VI **Subject:** 12 Centuries of Monarchy

| Date | Mintage | F12 | VF20 | XF40 | MS60 | MS63 |
|---|---|---|---|---|---|---|
| AH1429-2008 | 5,000 | PF63 70.00 | PF65 80.00 | | | |

**Y# 133 250 DIRHAMS**
6.45 g., 0.900 Gold 0.1866 oz. AGW, 21 mm. **Ruler:** Mohammed VI **Subject:** 12 Centuries of Monarchy

| Date | Mintage | F12 | VF20 | XF40 | MS60 | MS63 |
|---|---|---|---|---|---|---|
| AH1429-2008 | 3,000 | PF63 325 | PF65 350 | | | |

**Y# 129 250 DIRHAMS**
25.00 g., 0.925 Silver 0.7435 oz. ASW, 37 mm. **Ruler:** Mohammed VI **Subject:** 10th Anniversary of Mohammed VI's reign **Obv:** Head 3/4 left **Rev:** Crowned arms with supporters above value **Edge:** Reeded

| Date | Mintage | F12 | VF20 | XF40 | MS60 | MS63 |
|---|---|---|---|---|---|---|
| AH1430-2009 | 1,500 | PF65 100 | | | | |

**Y# 130 250 DIRHAMS**
25.00 g., 0.925 Silver 0.7435 oz. ASW, 37 mm. **Ruler:** Mohammed VI **Subject:** Bank al Maghrib, 50th Anniversary **Obv:** Head 3/4 left

| Date | Mintage | F12 | VF20 | XF40 | MS60 | MS63 |
|---|---|---|---|---|---|---|
| AH1430-2009 | — | PF65 120 | | | | |

**Y# 131 250 DIRHAMS**
25.00 g., 0.925 Silver 0.7435 oz. ASW, 37 mm. **Ruler:** Mohammed VI **Subject:** 11th Anniversary of Mohammed VI's reign **Obv:** Head 3/4 left **Rev:** Crowned arms with supporters above value **Edge:** Reeded

| Date | Mintage | F12 | VF20 | XF40 | MS60 | MS63 |
|---|---|---|---|---|---|---|
| AH1431-2010 | 1,500 | PF65 100 | | | | |

**Y# 132 250 DIRHAMS**
25.00 g., 0.925 Silver 0.7435 oz. ASW, 37 mm. **Ruler:** Mohammed VI **Subject:** Green March, 35th Anniversary **Edge:** Reeded

| Date | Mintage | F12 | VF20 | XF40 | MS60 | MS63 |
|---|---|---|---|---|---|---|
| AH1431-2010 | 1,000 | PF65 125 | | | | |

**Y# 157 250 DIRHAMS**
28.28 g., 0.925 Silver 0.841 oz. ASW, 38.61 mm. **Ruler:** Mohammed VI **Subject:** Moroccan Phosphate Co., 90th Anniversary **Rev:** Phosphate mining and agriculture

| Date | Mintage | F12 | VF20 | XF40 | MS60 | MS63 |
|---|---|---|---|---|---|---|
| 2010 | 3,000 | PF63 90.00 | PF65 100 | | | |

**Y# 142 250 DIRHAMS**
28.28 g., 0.925 Silver 0.841 oz. ASW, 38.61 mm. **Ruler:** Mohammed VI **Subject:** 12th Anniversary of Enthronement **Obv:** Head left **Rev:** Royal Palace of Rabat

| Date | Mintage | F12 | VF20 | XF40 | MS60 | MS63 |
|---|---|---|---|---|---|---|
| 2012 | — | PF65 150 | | | | |

**Y# 159 250 DIRHAMS**
Silver ASW **Ruler:** Mohammed VI **Subject:** Mohammed VI, Coronation, 12th Anniversary **Rev:** Palace

| Date | Mintage | F12 | VF20 | XF40 | MS60 | MS63 |
|---|---|---|---|---|---|---|
| 2011 | — | PF65 150 | | | | |

**Y# 163 250 DIRHAMS**
28.28 g., 0.925 Silver 0.841 oz. ASW, 38.61 mm. **Ruler:** Mohammed VI **Subject:** Dar As-Sikkah, 25th Anniversary **Edge:** Reeded

| Date | Mintage | F12 | VF20 | XF40 | MS60 | MS63 |
|---|---|---|---|---|---|---|
| AH1433-2012 | 1,000 | PF65 125 | | | | |

**Y# 164 250 DIRHAMS**
28.28 g., 0.925 Silver 0.841 oz. ASW, 38.61 mm. **Ruler:** Mohammed VI **Subject:** Mohammed VI, 13th Anniversary of reign **Edge Lettering:** Reeded

| Date | Mintage | F12 | VF20 | XF40 | MS60 | MS63 |
|---|---|---|---|---|---|---|
| AH1433-2012 | 1,000 | PF65 125 | | | | |

**Y# 165 250 DIRHAMS**
28.28 g., 0.925 Silver 0.841 oz. ASW, 38.61 mm. **Ruler:** Mohammed VI **Subject:** UNESCO sites in Rabat **Edge:** Reeded

| Date | Mintage | F12 | VF20 | XF40 | MS60 | MS63 |
|---|---|---|---|---|---|---|
| AH1433-2012 | 1,000 | PF65 125 | | | | |

**Y# 166 250 DIRHAMS**
28.28 g., 0.925 Silver 0.841 oz. ASW, 38.61 mm. **Ruler:** Mohammed VI **Subject:** Mohammed VI, 50th Birthday **Edge:** Reeded

| Date | Mintage | F12 | VF20 | XF40 | MS60 | MS63 |
|---|---|---|---|---|---|---|
| AH1434-2013 | 1,000 | PF65 125 | | | | |

**Y# 135 500 DIRHAMS**
Bi-Metallic **Ruler:** Mohammed VI **Obv:** Head left **Rev:** Building **Note:** Silver and gold similar to Y#130.

| Date | Mintage | F12 | VF20 | XF40 | MS60 | MS63 |
|---|---|---|---|---|---|---|
| AH1430-2009 | — | PF65 1,650 | | | | |

**Y# 150 1000 DIRHAMS**
25.00 g., 0.9999 Gold 0.8037 oz. AGW, 37 mm. **Ruler:** Mohammed VI **Subject:** Mohammed VI, 40th Birthday **Rev:** National arms

| Date | Mintage | F12 | VF20 | XF40 | MS60 | MS63 |
|---|---|---|---|---|---|---|
| 2003 | — | PF65 1,500 | | | | |

**Y# 152 1000 DIRHAMS**
25.00 g., 0.9999 Gold 0.8037 oz. AGW, 37 mm. **Ruler:** Mohammed VI **Subject:** Mohammed VI, 41st Birthday **Rev:** National arms

| Date | Mintage | F12 | VF20 | XF40 | MS60 | MS63 |
|---|---|---|---|---|---|---|
| 2004 | — | PF65 1,500 | | | | |

**Y# 154 1000 DIRHAMS**
Gold AGW **Ruler:** Mohammed VI **Subject:** Bank al Maghrib, 50th Anniversary **Rev:** Central Bank Building

| Date | Mintage | F12 | VF20 | XF40 | MS60 | MS63 |
|---|---|---|---|---|---|---|
| 2009 | — | PF65 2,600 | | | | |

**Y# 155 1000 DIRHAMS**
Gold AGW **Ruler:** Mohammed VI **Subject:** Mohammed VI, Coronation 10th Anniversary

| Date | Mintage | F12 | VF20 | XF40 | MS60 | MS63 |
|---|---|---|---|---|---|---|
| 2009 | — | PF65 2,600 | | | | |

**Y# 156 1000 DIRHAMS**
Gold AGW **Ruler:** Mohammed VI **Subject:** Mohammed VI, 46th Birthday

| Date | Mintage | F12 | VF20 | XF40 | MS60 | MS63 |
|---|---|---|---|---|---|---|
| 2009 | — | PF65 2,600 | | | | |

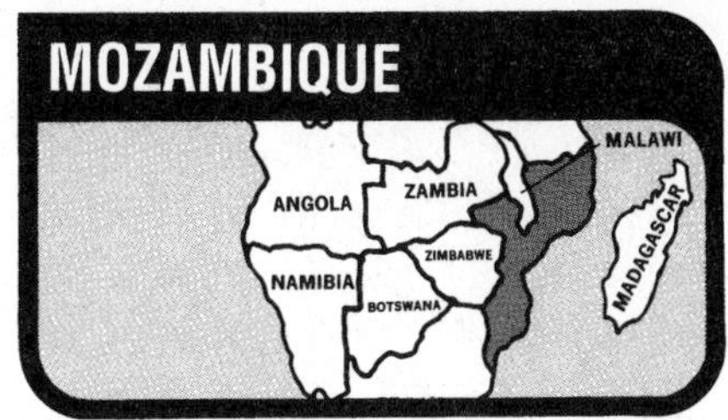


The Republic of Mozambique, a former overseas province of Portugal, stretches for 1,430 miles (2,301 km.) along the southeast coast of Africa, has an area of 302,330 sq. mi. (801,590 sq. km.) and a population of 14.1 million, 99 % of whom are native Africans of the Bantu tribes. Capital: Maputo. Agriculture is the chief industry. Cashew nuts, cotton, sugar, copra and tea are exported.

Mozambique became a member of the Commonwealth of Nations in November 1995. The President is Head of State; the Prime Minister is Head of Government.

# REPUBLIC

## REFORM COINAGE

100 Centavos = 1 Metical

### KM# 130 1000 METICAIS

25.71 g., 0.980 Silver 0.8101 oz. ASW, 38.5 mm. **Subject:** Pedro De Covilha, 1498 **Obv:** National arms within circle **Rev:** Sailing ship within circle **Edge:** Reeded

| Date | Mintage | VF20 | XF40 | MS60 | MS63 | MS65 |
|---|---|---|---|---|---|---|
| 2003 | — | **PF63** 35.00 | **PF65** 45.00 | | | |

### KM# 141 1000 METICAIS

25.71 g., 0.980 Silver 0.8101 oz. ASW, 38.6 mm. **Obv:** National arms **Rev:** Vasco de Gamma

| Date | Mintage | VF20 | XF40 | MS60 | MS63 | MS65 |
|---|---|---|---|---|---|---|
| 2004 | — | **PF63** 35.00 | **PF65** 45.00 | | | |

### KM# 142 1000 METICAIS

25.71 g., 0.980 Silver 0.8101 oz. ASW, 38.6 mm. **Obv:** National arms **Rev:** David Livingstone and map of Africa

| Date | Mintage | VF20 | XF40 | MS60 | MS63 | MS65 |
|---|---|---|---|---|---|---|
| 2004 | — | **PF63** 35.00 | **PF65** 45.00 | | | |

### KM# 131 10000 METICAIS

8.04 g., Bi-Metallic Stainless Steel center in Brass ring, 26.6 mm. **Obv:** National arms within circle **Rev:** Rhino within circle **Edge:** Segmented reeding

| Date | Mintage | VF20 | XF40 | MS60 | MS63 | MS65 |
|---|---|---|---|---|---|---|
| 2003 | — | — | 1.50 | 2.50 | 4.00 | 9.00 |

## REFORM COINAGE

(New) Metical = 1,000 Meticals

### KM# 132 CENTAVO

2.00 g., Copper Plated Steel, 15 mm. **Obv:** Bank logo, date **Obv. Legend:** BANCO DE MOÇAMBIQUE **Rev:** Rhinoceros standing left, value **Edge:** Plain

| Date | Mintage | VF20 | XF40 | MS60 | MS63 | MS65 |
|---|---|---|---|---|---|---|
| 2006 | — | — | — | — | 0.15 | 0.25 |

### KM# 133 5 CENTAVOS

2.30 g., Copper Plated Steel, 19 mm. **Obv:** Bank logo, date **Obv. Legend:** BANCO DE MOÇAMBIQUE **Rev:** Cheetah standing left, value **Edge:** Reeded

| Date | Mintage | VF20 | XF40 | MS60 | MS63 | MS65 |
|---|---|---|---|---|---|---|
| 2006 | — | — | 0.10 | 0.20 | 0.25 | 0.35 |

### KM# 134 10 CENTAVOS

3.06 g., Brass Plated Steel, 17 mm. **Obv:** Bank logo, date **Obv. Legend:** BANCO DE MOÇAMBIQUE **Rev:** Farmer cultivating with tractor, value **Edge:** Reeded

| Date | Mintage | VF20 | XF40 | MS60 | MS63 | MS65 |
|---|---|---|---|---|---|---|
| 2006 | — | — | 0.15 | 0.25 | 0.35 | 0.50 |

### KM# 135 20 CENTAVOS

4.10 g., Brass Plated Steel, 20 mm. **Obv:** Bank logo, date **Obv. Legend:** BANCO DE MOÇAMBIQUE **Rev:** Cotton plant, value **Edge:** Reeded

| Date | Mintage | VF20 | XF40 | MS60 | MS63 | MS65 |
|---|---|---|---|---|---|---|
| 2006 | — | — | 0.20 | 0.35 | 0.50 | 0.75 |

### KM# 136 50 CENTAVOS

5.74 g., Brass Plated Steel, 23 mm. **Obv:** Bank logo, date **Obv. Legend:** BANCO DE MOÇAMBIQUE **Rev:** Giant Kingfisher perched on branch, value **Edge:** Reeded

| Date | Mintage | VF20 | XF40 | MS60 | MS63 | MS65 |
|---|---|---|---|---|---|---|
| 2006 | — | — | 0.50 | 0.75 | 1.25 | 1.75 |

### KM# 137 METICAL

5.30 g., Nickel Plated Steel, 21 mm. **Obv:** Bank logo, date **Obv. Legend:** BANCO DE MOÇAMBIQUE **Rev:** Young woman seated left writing, value **Edge:** Plain **Shape:** 7-sided

| Date | Mintage | VF20 | XF40 | MS60 | MS63 | MS65 |
|---|---|---|---|---|---|---|
| 2006 | — | — | 0.45 | 0.65 | 1.20 | 1.50 |

### KM# 138 2 METICAIS

6.00 g., Nickel Plated Steel, 24 mm. **Obv:** Bank logo, date **Obv. Legend:** BANCO DE MOÇAMBIQUE **Rev:** Coelacanth fish, value **Edge:** Segmented reeding

| Date | Mintage | VF20 | XF40 | MS60 | MS63 | MS65 |
|---|---|---|---|---|---|---|
| 2006 | — | — | 0.75 | 1.25 | 1.75 | 2.50 |

### KM# 139 5 METICAIS

6.50 g., Nickel Plated Steel, 27 mm. **Obv:** Bank logo, date **Obv. Legend:** BANCO DE MOÇAMBIQUE **Rev:** Timbila (similar to a xylophone), value **Edge:** Reeded

| Date | Mintage | VF20 | XF40 | MS60 | MS63 | MS65 |
|---|---|---|---|---|---|---|
| 2006 | — | — | 1.20 | 2.00 | 3.00 | 4.00 |

### KM# 140 10 METICAIS

7.50 g., Bi-Metallic Nickel Clad Steel center in Brass ring., 25 mm. **Obv:** Bank logo **Obv. Legend:** BANCO • DE • MOCAMBIQUE **Rev:** Modern bank building, value below **Edge:** Reeded

| Date | Mintage | VF20 | XF40 | MS60 | MS63 | MS65 |
|---|---|---|---|---|---|---|
| 2006 | — | — | 1.50 | 2.50 | 3.75 | 5.00 |

# NAGORNO-KARABAKH

TURKEY GEORGIA RUSSIA ARMENIA KAZAKHSTAN AZERBAIJAN UZBEKISTAN IRAN Caspian Sea

Nagorno-Karabakh, an ethnically Armenian enclave inside Azerbaijan (pop., 1991 est.: 193,000), SW region. It occupies an area of 1,700 sq mi (4,400 square km) on the NE flank of the Karabakh Mountain Range, with the capital city of Stepanakert.

Russia annexed the area from Persia in 1813, and in 1923 it was established as an autonomous province of the Azerbaijan S.S.R. In 1988 the region's ethnic Armenian majority demonstrated against Azerbaijani rule, and in 1991, after the breakup of the U.S.S.R. brought independence to Armenia and Azerbaijan, war broke out between the two ethnic groups. On January 8, 1992 the leaders of Nagorno-Karabakh declared independence as the Republic of Mountainous Karabakh (RMK). Since 1994, following a cease-fire, ethnic Armenians have held Karabakh, though officially it remains part of Azerbaijan. Karabakh remains sovereign, but the political and military condition is volatile and tensions frequently flare into skirmishes.

Its marvelous nature and geographic situation, have all facilitated Karabakh to be a center of science, poetry and, especially, of the musical culture of Azerbaijan.

**MONETARY SYSTEM**
100 Luma = 1 Dram

## REPUBLIC

### STANDARD COINAGE

**KM# 6 50 LUMA**
0.95 g., Aluminum, 19.8 mm. **Obv:** National arms **Rev:** Horse cantering left **Edge:** Plain

| Date | Mintage | VF20 | XF40 | MS60 | MS63 | MS65 |
|---|---|---|---|---|---|---|
| 2004 | — | — | — | 0.50 | 1.00 | 1.25 |

**KM# 7 50 LUMA**
0.95 g., Aluminum, 19.8 mm. **Obv:** National arms **Rev:** Gazelle **Edge:** Plain

| Date | Mintage | VF20 | XF40 | MS60 | MS63 | MS65 |
|---|---|---|---|---|---|---|
| 2004 | — | — | — | 0.50 | 1.00 | 1.25 |

**KM# 8 DRAM**
1.13 g., Aluminum, 21.7 mm. **Obv:** National arms **Rev:** Pheasant **Edge:** Plain

| Date | Mintage | VF20 | XF40 | MS60 | MS63 | MS65 |
|---|---|---|---|---|---|---|
| 2004 | — | — | — | 0.50 | 1.00 | 1.25 |

**KM# 9 DRAM**
1.12 g., Aluminum, 21.7 mm. **Obv:** National arms **Rev:** 1/2-length Saint facing **Edge:** Plain

| Date | Mintage | VF20 | XF40 | MS60 | MS63 | MS65 |
|---|---|---|---|---|---|---|
| 2004 | — | — | — | 0.65 | 1.25 | 1.50 |

**KM# 10 DRAM**
1.13 g., Aluminum, 21.7 mm. **Obv:** National arms **Rev:** Cheetah facing **Edge:** Plain

| Date | Mintage | VF20 | XF40 | MS60 | MS63 | MS65 |
|---|---|---|---|---|---|---|
| 2004 | — | — | — | 0.50 | 1.00 | 1.25 |

**KM# 11 5 DRAMS**
4.40 g., Brass, 21.8 mm. **Obv:** National arms **Rev:** Church **Edge:** Plain

| Date | Mintage | VF20 | XF40 | MS60 | MS63 | MS65 |
|---|---|---|---|---|---|---|
| 2004 | — | — | — | 0.75 | 1.50 | 2.00 |

**KM# 12 5 DRAMS**
4.50 g., Brass, 21.8 mm. **Obv:** National arms **Rev:** Monument faces **Edge:** Plain

| Date | Mintage | VF20 | XF40 | MS60 | MS63 | MS65 |
|---|---|---|---|---|---|---|
| 2004 | — | — | — | 0.75 | 1.50 | 2.00 |

**KM# 23 1000 DRAMS**
31.43 g., 0.999 Silver 1.0095 oz. ASW, 38.9 mm. **Obv:** National arms **Rev:** Archer **Edge:** Plain

| Date | Mintage | VF20 | XF40 | MS60 | MS63 | MS65 |
|---|---|---|---|---|---|---|
| 2003 | — | PF63 75.00 | PF65 100 | | | |

**KM# 24 1000 DRAMS**
31.33 g., 0.999 Silver 1.0063 oz. ASW, 38.39 mm. **Series:** Armenian architectural sculpture **Obv:** National arms **Rev:** Church of the Holy Cross at Aghthamar, Turkey **Edge:** Plain

| Date | Mintage | VF20 | XF40 | MS60 | MS63 | MS65 |
|---|---|---|---|---|---|---|
| 2003 | — | PF63 75.00 | PF65 100 | | | |

**KM# 19 1000 DRAMS**
31.37 g., 0.999 Silver 1.0076 oz. ASW, 38.9 mm. **Obv:** National arms **Rev:** Leopard head facing **Edge:** Plain

| Date | Mintage | VF20 | XF40 | MS60 | MS63 | MS65 |
|---|---|---|---|---|---|---|
| 2004 | — | PF63 85.00 | PF65 120 | | | |

**KM# 19a 1000 DRAMS**
31.37 g., 0.999 Silver Gilt 1.0076 oz., 38.9 mm. **Obv:** National arms **Rev:** Leopard head facing **Edge:** Plain

| Date | Mintage | VF20 | XF40 | MS60 | MS63 | MS65 |
|---|---|---|---|---|---|---|
| 2004 | — | PF63 75.00 | PF65 100 | | | |

**KM# 20 1000 DRAMS**
31.37 g., 0.999 Silver 1.0076 oz. ASW, 38.9 mm. **Obv:** National arms **Rev:** Standing Brown Bear **Edge:** Plain

| Date | Mintage | VF20 | XF40 | MS60 | MS63 | MS65 |
|---|---|---|---|---|---|---|
| 2004 | — | PF63 85.00 | PF65 120 | | | |

**KM# 20a 1000 DRAMS**
31.37 g., 0.999 Silver Gilt 1.0076 oz., 38.9 mm. **Obv:** National arms **Rev:** Standing Brown Bear **Edge:** Plain

| Date | Mintage | VF20 | XF40 | MS60 | MS63 | MS65 |
|---|---|---|---|---|---|---|
| 2004 | — | PF63 85.00 | PF65 120 | | | |

**KM# 21 1000 DRAMS**
31.37 g., 0.999 Silver 1.0076 oz. ASW, 38.9 mm. **Obv:** National arms **Rev:** Eagle head within circle **Edge:** Plain

| Date | Mintage | VF20 | XF40 | MS60 | MS63 | MS65 |
|---|---|---|---|---|---|---|
| 2004 | — | PF63 75.00 | PF65 100 | | | |

**KM# 21a 1000 DRAMS**
31.37 g., 0.999 Silver Gilt 1.0076 oz., 38.9 mm. **Obv:** National arms **Rev:** Eagle head within circle **Edge:** Plain

| Date | Mintage | VF20 | XF40 | MS60 | MS63 | MS65 |
|---|---|---|---|---|---|---|
| 2004 | — | PF63 85.00 | PF65 120 | | | |

**KM# 22 1000 DRAMS**
31.12 g., 0.999 Silver 0.9995 oz. ASW, 38.9 mm. **Obv:** National arms **Rev:** 1918 Genocide Victims Monument **Edge:** Plain

| Date | Mintage | VF20 | XF40 | MS60 | MS63 | MS65 |
|---|---|---|---|---|---|---|
| 2004 | — | PF63 65.00 | PF65 90.00 | | | |

**KM# 25 1000 DRAMS**
31.30 g., 0.999 Silver 1.0053 oz. ASW, 38.92 mm. **Obv:** National arms **Rev:** Bust of Kevork Chavoush 3/4 left **Edge:** Plain

| Date | Mintage | VF20 | XF40 | MS60 | MS63 | MS65 |
|---|---|---|---|---|---|---|
| 2004 | — | PF63 75.00 | PF65 100 | | | |

# NAMIBIA

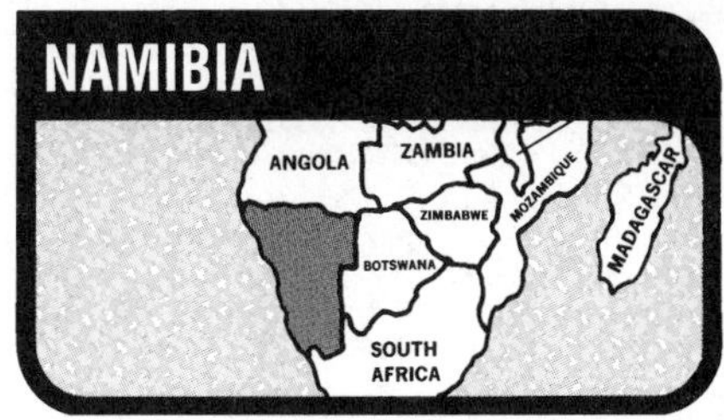


The Republic of Namibia, once the German colonial territory of German South West Africa, and later South West Africa, is situated on the Atlantic coast of southern Africa, bounded on the north by Angola, on the east by Botswana, and on the south by South Africa. It has an area of 318,261 sq. mi. (824,290 sq. km.) and a population of *1.4 million. Capital: Windhoek. Diamonds, copper, lead, zinc, and cattle are exported.

On June 17, 1985 the Transitional Government of National Unity was installed. Negotiations were held in 1988 between Angola, Cuba, and South Africa reaching a peaceful settlement on Aug. 5, 1988. By April 1989 Cuban troops were to withdraw from Angola and South African troops from Namibia. The Transitional Government resigned on Feb. 28, 1988 for the upcoming elections of the constituent assembly in Nov. 1989. Independence was finally achieved on March 12, 1990 within the Commonwealth of Nations. The President is the Head of State; the Prime Minister is Head of Government.

**MONETARY SYSTEM**
100 Cents = 1 Namibia Dollar

## REPUBLIC

### DECIMAL COINAGE

**KM# 1 5 CENTS**
2.20 g., Nickel Plated Steel, 17 mm. **Obv:** National arms **Rev:** Value left, aloe plant within 3/4 sun design

| Date | Mintage | VF20 | XF40 | MS60 | MS63 | MS65 |
|---|---|---|---|---|---|---|
| 2002 | — | — | — | 0.20 | 0.50 | 0.75 |
| 2007 | — | — | — | 0.20 | 0.50 | 0.75 |
| 2009 | — | — | — | 0.20 | 0.50 | 0.75 |
| 2012 | — | — | — | 0.20 | 0.50 | 0.75 |

**KM# 2 10 CENTS**
3.40 g., Nickel Plated Steel, 21.5 mm. **Obv:** National arms **Rev:** Camelthorn tree right, partial sun design left, value below

| Date | Mintage | VF20 | XF40 | MS60 | MS63 | MS65 |
|---|---|---|---|---|---|---|
| 2002 | — | — | — | 0.35 | 1.00 | 1.25 |
| 2009 | — | — | — | 0.35 | 1.00 | 1.25 |
| 2012 | — | — | — | 0.35 | 1.00 | 1.25 |

**KM# 3 50 CENTS**
4.43 g., Nickel Plated Steel, 24 mm. **Obv:** National arms **Rev:** Quiver tree right, partial sun design upper left, value below

| Date | Mintage | VF20 | XF40 | MS60 | MS63 | MS65 |
|---|---|---|---|---|---|---|
| 2008 | — | — | — | 0.75 | 1.75 | 2.00 |
| 2010 | — | — | — | 0.75 | 1.75 | 2.00 |

**KM# 4 DOLLAR**
5.00 g., Brass, 22.4 mm. **Obv:** National arms **Rev:** Value divides Bateleur eagle at right, partial sun design at left

| Date | Mintage | VF20 | XF40 | MS60 | MS63 | MS65 |
|---|---|---|---|---|---|---|
| 2002 | — | — | — | 1.25 | 3.50 | 6.00 |
| 2006 | — | — | — | 1.25 | 3.50 | 6.00 |
| 2008 | — | — | — | 1.25 | 3.50 | 6.00 |
| 2010 | — | — | — | 1.25 | 3.50 | 6.00 |

**KM# 5 5 DOLLARS**
6.22 g., Brass, 24.9 mm. **Obv:** National arms **Rev:** Partial sun design at top, value at center, African fish eagle below

| Date | Mintage | VF20 | XF40 | MS60 | MS63 | MS65 |
|---|---|---|---|---|---|---|
| 2012 | — | — | — | 1.50 | 2.50 | 5.00 |

**KM# 21 10 DOLLARS**
Bi-Metallic Aluminum-Bronze center in Copper-Nickel ring, 30 mm. **Subject:** Bank of Namibia, 20th Anniversary **Obv:** National arms **Rev:** Dr. Sam Nujoma bust facing **Edge:** Segmented reeding

| Date | Mintage | VF20 | XF40 | MS60 | MS63 | MS65 |
|---|---|---|---|---|---|---|
| 2010 | — | — | — | 3.50 | 5.00 | 7.50 |

**KM# 23 10 DOLLARS**
1.13 g., 0.999 Gold 0.0364 oz. AGW, 13.92 mm. **Series:** 20th Anniversary of the Bank of Namibia

| Date | Mintage | VF20 | XF40 | MS60 | MS63 | MS65 |
|---|---|---|---|---|---|---|
| 2010 | — | PF63 75.00 | PF65 90.00 | | | |

**KM# 22 20 DOLLARS**
28.28 g., 0.925 Silver 0.841 oz. ASW, 38.61 mm. **Subject:** 20th Anniversary of the Bank of Namibia

| Date | Mintage | VF20 | XF40 | MS60 | MS63 | MS65 |
|---|---|---|---|---|---|---|
| 2010 | Est. 2000 | PF63 70.00 | PF65 80.00 | | | |

# NAURU

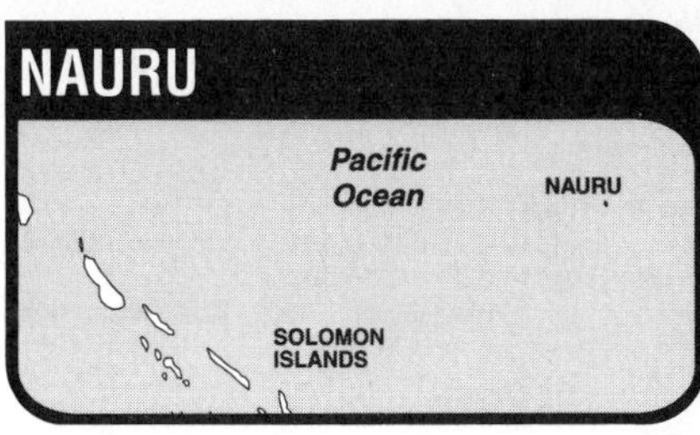


The Republic of Nauru, formerly Pleasant Island, is an island republic in the western Pacific Ocean west of the Gilbert Islands. It has an area of 8-1/2 sq. mi. and a population of 7,254. It is known for its phosphate deposits. Nauru is a special member of the Commonwealth of Nations.

**RULER**
British, until 1968

**MONETARY SYSTEM**
100 Cents = 1 (Australian) Dollar

## REPUBLIC

### DECIMAL COINAGE

**KM# 38 DOLLAR**
27.00 g., Silver Plated Copper, 38.6 mm. **Subject:** Guardian Angel **Obv:** Arms **Rev:** Angel standing, swarovski crystals in hair

| Date | Mintage | VF20 | XF40 | MS60 | MS63 | MS65 |
|---|---|---|---|---|---|---|
| 2009 | 10,000 | PF65 40.00 | | | | |

**KM# 45 5 DOLLARS**
Silver, 39 mm. **Subject:** Elizabeth II and Prince Philip, 60th Wedding Anniversary **Obv:** National arms **Rev:** Wedding portraits

| Date | Mintage | VF20 | XF40 | MS60 | MS63 | MS65 |
|---|---|---|---|---|---|---|
| 2007 | — | PF65 45.00 | | | | |

**KM# 46 5 DOLLARS**
Silver, 39 mm. **Subject:** Elizabeth II and Prince Philip, 60th Wedding anniversary **Obv:** National arms **Rev:** Engagement photo

| Date | Mintage | VF20 | XF40 | MS60 | MS63 | MS65 |
|---|---|---|---|---|---|---|
| 2007 | — | PF65 45.00 | | | | |

**KM# 36 5 DOLLARS**
0.50 g., 0.999 Gold 0.0161 oz. AGW, 11 mm. **Subject:** Kaiser Wilhelm **Obv:** Arms **Rev:** Bust right

| Date | Mintage | VF20 | XF40 | MS60 | MS63 | MS65 |
|---|---|---|---|---|---|---|
| 2008 | — | PF65 65.00 | | | | |

**KM# 37 5 DOLLARS**
0.50 g., 0.999 Gold 0.0161 oz. AGW, 11 mm. **Subject:** Christmas **Obv:** Arms **Rev:** Bells ringing

| Date | Mintage | VF20 | XF40 | MS60 | MS63 | MS65 |
|---|---|---|---|---|---|---|
| 2008 | — | PF65 65.00 | | | | |

**KM# 80 5 DOLLARS**
28.28 g., 0.925 Silver 0.841 oz. ASW, 38.61 mm. **Subject:** Royal Air Force, 90th Anniversary **Rev:** De Havilland Tiger Moth and Avro Anson

| Date | Mintage | VF20 | XF40 | MS60 | MS63 | MS65 |
|---|---|---|---|---|---|---|
| 2008 | — | PF65 35.00 | | | | |

**KM# 39 5 DOLLARS**
0.50 g., 0.999 Gold 0.0161 oz. AGW, 11 mm. **Subject:** Christmas **Obv:** Arms **Rev:** Teddy bear seated

| Date | Mintage | VF20 | XF40 | MS60 | MS63 | MS65 |
|---|---|---|---|---|---|---|
| 2009 | — | PF65 65.00 | | | | |

**KM# 84 5 DOLLARS**
0.50 g., 0.999 Gold 0.0161 oz. AGW, 11 mm. **Subject:** Investor coins of the World - Vreneli

| Date | Mintage | VF20 | XF40 | MS60 | MS63 | MS65 |
|---|---|---|---|---|---|---|
| 2010 | Est. 10000 | PF65 65.00 | | | | |

**KM# 85 5 DOLLARS**
0.50 g., 0.999 Gold 0.0161 oz. AGW, 11 mm. **Subject:** Investor gold coins of the world - Franz Joseph I

| Date | Mintage | VF20 | XF40 | MS60 | MS63 | MS65 |
|---|---|---|---|---|---|---|
| 2010 | Est. 10000 | PF65 65.00 | | | | |

**KM# 86 5 DOLLARS**
0.50 g., 0.999 Gold 0.0161 oz. AGW, 11 mm. **Subject:** Investor coins of the World - French rooster

| Date | Mintage | VF20 | XF40 | MS60 | MS63 | MS65 |
|---|---|---|---|---|---|---|
| 2010 | Est. 5000 | PF65 65.00 | | | | |

**KM# 18 10 DOLLARS**
31.10 g., 0.999 Silver 0.9989 oz. ASW **Subject:** Discontinuation of the German Mark **Obv:** National arms **Obv. Legend:** BANK OF NAURU

| Date | Mintage | VF20 | XF40 | MS60 | MS63 | MS65 |
|---|---|---|---|---|---|---|
| 2001 | — | PF65 75.00 | | | | |

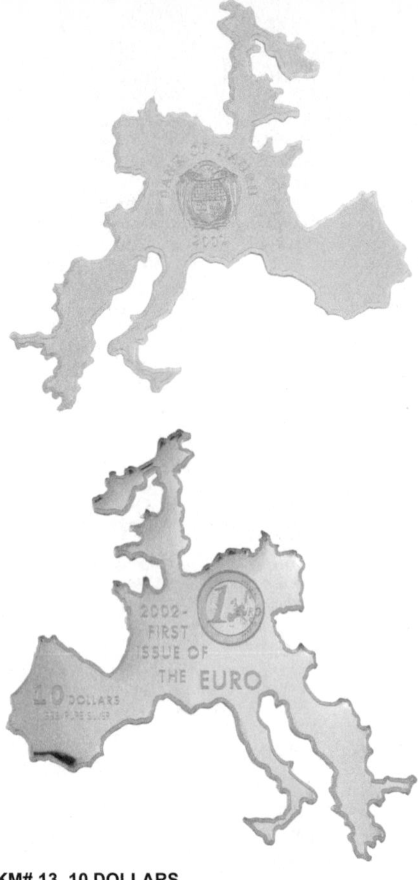


**KM# 13 10 DOLLARS**
31.25 g., 0.999 Silver 1.0037 oz. ASW 71.5 x 72, 72 mm. **Subject:** First Euro Coinage **Obv:** National arms, matte finish **Rev:** Denomination, inscription and partially gold-plated 1 Euro reverse coin design, Proof finish **Edge:** Plain **Shape:** Like a map

| Date | Mintage | VF20 | XF40 | MS60 | MS63 | MS65 |
|---|---|---|---|---|---|---|
| 2002 | — | PF65 75.00 | | | | |

**KM# 14 10 DOLLARS**
34.60 g., 0.925 Silver 1.029 oz. ASW with gold plated or gold attachment, 38.5 mm. **Subject:** Brandenburg Gate **Obv:** National arms **Rev:** Brandenburg Gate **Edge:** Plain **Note:** Gold color 1mm thick

| Date | Mintage | VF20 | XF40 | MS60 | MS63 | MS65 |
|---|---|---|---|---|---|---|
| 2002 Proof/ Matte | — | PF65 90.00 | | | | |

**KM# 15 10 DOLLARS**
31.10 g., 0.999 Silver 0.9989 oz. ASW, 40 mm. **Series:** Save the Whales **Obv:** National arms **Obv. Legend:** BANK OF NAURU **Rev:** Blue Whale on mother-of-pearl insert **Edge:** Plain

| Date | Mintage | VF20 | XF40 | MS60 | MS63 | MS65 |
|---|---|---|---|---|---|---|
| 2002 | 2,000 | PF65 95.00 | | | | |

**KM# 50 10 DOLLARS**
31.11 g., 0.999 Silver 0.999 oz. ASW, 40 mm. **Rev:** Coloseum in color

| Date | Mintage | VF20 | XF40 | MS60 | MS63 | MS65 |
|---|---|---|---|---|---|---|
| 2002 | 2,001 | PF65 60.00 | | | | |

**KM# 51 10 DOLLARS**
22.22 g., 0.999 Silver 0.7137 oz. ASW, 35x45 mm. **Subject:** Indroduction of Euro **Shape:** Irregular

| Date | Mintage | VF20 | XF40 | MS60 | MS63 | MS65 |
|---|---|---|---|---|---|---|
| 2002 | 2,500 | PF65 55.00 | | | | |

**KM# 19 10 DOLLARS**
31.10 g., 0.999 Silver 0.9989 oz. ASW **Subject:** European Union - Mark and Euro **Obv:** National arms **Obv. Legend:** BANK OF NAURU

| Date | Mintage | VF20 | XF40 | MS60 | MS63 | MS65 |
|---|---|---|---|---|---|---|
| 2003 | 5,000 | PF65 95.00 | | | | |

**KM# 20 10 DOLLARS**
1.24 g., 0.999 Gold 0.0398 oz. AGW, 13.92 mm. **Subject:** First Anniversary of the Euro **Obv:** National arms **Obv. Legend:** BANK OF NAURU **Rev:** Euro symbol **Edge:** Reeded

| Date | Mintage | VF20 | XF40 | MS60 | MS63 | MS65 |
|---|---|---|---|---|---|---|
| 2003 | — | PF65 85.00 | | | | |

**KM# 21 10 DOLLARS**
1.24 g., 0.999 Gold 0.0398 oz. AGW **Subject:** Treasure of Priamos in Troja **Obv:** National arms **Obv. Legend:** BANK OF NAURU

| Date | Mintage | VF20 | XF40 | MS60 | MS63 | MS65 |
|---|---|---|---|---|---|---|
| 2003 | — | PF65 95.00 | | | | |

**KM# 22 10 DOLLARS**
1.24 g., 0.999 Gold 0.0398 oz. AGW **Subject:** Treasure of Nibelungen **Obv:** National arms **Obv. Legend:** BANK OF NAURU

| Date | Mintage | VF20 | XF40 | MS60 | MS63 | MS65 |
|---|---|---|---|---|---|---|
| 2003 | — | PF65 95.00 | | | | |

**KM# 23 10 DOLLARS**
30.95 g., Silver With removable gold or gilt 2.6g Reichstag building attachment with 2004/ NAURU 0077 on reverse **Subject:** European Monuments **Obv:** National arms **Obv. Legend:** BANK OF NAURU **Rev. Legend:** GERMANY - DEUTSCHER REICHSTAG **Edge:** Plain

| Date | Mintage | VF20 | XF40 | MS60 | MS63 | MS65 |
|---|---|---|---|---|---|---|
| 2003 Proof/ Matte | — | PF65 120 | | | | |

**KM# 52 10 DOLLARS**
31.10 g., 0.925 Silver 0.9249 oz. ASW, 38.61 mm. **Subject:** Euro, 1st Anniversary **Rev:** Euro currency symbol

| Date | Mintage | VF20 | XF40 | MS60 | MS63 | MS65 |
|---|---|---|---|---|---|---|
| 2003 | 5,000 | PF65 85.00 | | | | |

**KM# 53 10 DOLLARS**
31.10 g., 0.925 Silver 0.9249 oz. ASW, 38.61 mm. **Rev:** St. Peter's Basilica

| Date | Mintage | VF20 | XF40 | MS60 | MS63 | MS65 |
|---|---|---|---|---|---|---|
| 2003 | Est. 7500 | — | — | — | — | 75.00 |

**KM# 54 10 DOLLARS**
31.10 g., 0.925 Silver 0.9249 oz. ASW, 38.61 mm. **Rev:** Church in Dresden

| Date | Mintage | VF20 | XF40 | MS60 | MS63 | MS65 |
|---|---|---|---|---|---|---|
| 2004 | — | — | — | — | — | 75.00 |

**KM# 55 10 DOLLARS**
31.10 g., 0.999 Silver 0.9989 oz. ASW, 38.61 mm. **Rev:** Colesum in Rome

| Date | Mintage | VF20 | XF40 | MS60 | MS63 | MS65 |
|---|---|---|---|---|---|---|
| 2004 | 7,500 | — | — | — | — | 75.00 |

**KM# 56 10 DOLLARS**
31.10 g., 0.925 Silver 0.9249 oz. ASW, 38.61 mm. **Rev:** Royal Palace in Monaco

| Date | Mintage | VF20 | XF40 | MS60 | MS63 | MS65 |
|---|---|---|---|---|---|---|
| 2004 | 7,500 | — | — | — | — | 75.00 |

**KM# 24 10 DOLLARS**
Silver With removable gold or gilt attachment **Series:** European Monuments **Subject:** Palazzo Pubblico in San Marino **Obv:** National arms **Obv. Legend:** BANK OF NAURU **Edge:** Plain

| Date | Mintage | VF20 | XF40 | MS60 | MS63 | MS65 |
|---|---|---|---|---|---|---|
| 2005 Proof/Matte | — | PF65 120 | | | | |

**KM# 25 10 DOLLARS**
1.24 g., 0.999 Gold 0.0398 oz. AGW **Subject:** East Gothic stylized eagle broach from Domagnano, Italy in National Museum in Nuremburg **Obv:** National arms **Obv. Legend:** BANK OF NAURU

| Date | Mintage | VF20 | XF40 | MS60 | MS63 | MS65 |
|---|---|---|---|---|---|---|
| 2005 | 25,000 | PF65 65.00 | | | | |

**KM# 26 10 DOLLARS**
1.24 g., 0.999 Gold 0.0398 oz. AGW **Subject:** Angela Dorothea Merkel, Chancellor of Germany **Obv:** National arms **Obv. Legend:** BANK OF NAURU

| Date | Mintage | VF20 | XF40 | MS60 | MS63 | MS65 |
|---|---|---|---|---|---|---|
| 2005 | — | PF65 75.00 | | | | |

**KM# 35 10 DOLLARS**
31.11 g., 0.999 Silver 0.999 oz. ASW **Subject:** German Railways, 150th Anniversary **Obv:** National Arms **Rev:** Baureihi "01

| Date | Mintage | VF20 | XF40 | MS60 | MS63 | MS65 |
|---|---|---|---|---|---|---|
| 2005 | — | PF65 60.00 | | | | |

**KM# 40 10 DOLLARS**
1.24 g., 0.999 Gold 0.0398 oz. AGW, 13.92 mm. **Obv:** National Arms **Rev:** Ludwig Erhard

| Date | Mintage | VF20 | XF40 | MS60 | MS63 | MS65 |
|---|---|---|---|---|---|---|
| 2005 | — | PF65 75.00 | | | | |

**KM# 41 10 DOLLARS**
31.10 g., 0.999 Silver 0.9989 oz. ASW, 38.61 mm. **Rev:** Tower Bridge, gilt

| Date | Mintage | VF20 | XF40 | MS60 | MS63 | MS65 |
|---|---|---|---|---|---|---|
| 2005 | 2,000 | PF65 150 | | | | |

**KM# 43 10 DOLLARS**
31.11 g., 0.999 Silver 0.999 oz. ASW, 38.6 mm. **Rev:** St. Stephens Church, Vienna partially gilt

| Date | Mintage | VF20 | XF40 | MS60 | MS63 | MS65 |
|---|---|---|---|---|---|---|
| 2005 | 2,000 | PF65 50.00 | | | | |

**KM# 57 10 DOLLARS**
31.10 g., 0.925 Silver 0.9249 oz. ASW, 38.61 mm. **Rev:** St. Basil's Cathedral, Moscow

| Date | Mintage | VF20 | XF40 | MS60 | MS63 | MS65 |
|---|---|---|---|---|---|---|
| 2005 Proof | 7,500 | — | — | — | — | 75.00 |

**KM# 58 10 DOLLARS**
1.24 g., 0.999 Gold 0.0398 oz. AGW, 13.92 mm. **Subject:** Konrad Adenauer

| Date | Mintage | VF20 | XF40 | MS60 | MS63 | MS65 |
|---|---|---|---|---|---|---|
| 2005 | — | PF65 75.00 | | | | |

**KM# 59 10 DOLLARS**
1.24 g., 0.999 Gold 0.0398 oz. AGW, 13.92 mm. **Subject:** Kurt Georg Kiesinger

| Date | Mintage | VF20 | XF40 | MS60 | MS63 | MS65 |
|---|---|---|---|---|---|---|
| 2005 | — | PF65 75.00 | | | | |

**KM# 60 10 DOLLARS**
1.24 g., 0.999 Gold 0.0398 oz. AGW, 13.92 mm. **Subject:** Willy Brandt

| Date | Mintage | VF20 | XF40 | MS60 | MS63 | MS65 |
|---|---|---|---|---|---|---|
| 2005 | — | PF65 75.00 | | | | |

**KM# 61 10 DOLLARS**
1.24 g., 0.999 Gold 0.0398 oz. AGW, 13.92 mm. **Subject:** Helmut Schmidt

| Date | Mintage | VF20 | XF40 | MS60 | MS63 | MS65 |
|---|---|---|---|---|---|---|
| 2005 | — | PF65 75.00 | | | | |

**KM# 62 10 DOLLARS**
1.24 g., 0.999 Gold 0.0398 oz. AGW, 13.92 mm. **Subject:** Helmut Kohl

| Date | Mintage | VF20 | XF40 | MS60 | MS63 | MS65 |
|---|---|---|---|---|---|---|
| 2005 | — | PF65 75.00 | | | | |

**KM# 63 10 DOLLARS**
1.24 g., 0.999 Gold 0.0398 oz. AGW, 13.92 mm. **Subject:** Gerhard Schröder

| Date | Mintage | VF20 | XF40 | MS60 | MS63 | MS65 |
|---|---|---|---|---|---|---|
| 2005 | — | PF65 70.00 | | | | |

**KM# 27 10 DOLLARS**
1.24 g., 0.999 Gold 0.0398 oz. AGW **Subject:** Konrad Adenauer at 1949 demonstration **Obv:** National arms **Obv. Legend:** BANK OF NAURU

| Date | Mintage | VF20 | XF40 | MS60 | MS63 | MS65 |
|---|---|---|---|---|---|---|
| 2006 | 15,000 | PF65 75.00 | | | | |

**KM# 28 10 DOLLARS**
1.24 g., 0.999 Gold 0.0398 oz. AGW **Subject:** Volkswagen **Obv:** National arms **Obv. Legend:** BANK OF NAURU

| Date | Mintage | VF20 | XF40 | MS60 | MS63 | MS65 |
|---|---|---|---|---|---|---|
| 2006 | — | PF65 75.00 | | | | |

**KM# 29 10 DOLLARS**
1.24 g., 0.999 Gold 0.0398 oz. AGW **Subject:** Conrad Schumann in Berlin 1961 **Obv:** National arms **Obv. Legend:** BANK OF NAURU

| Date | Mintage | VF20 | XF40 | MS60 | MS63 | MS65 |
|---|---|---|---|---|---|---|
| 2006 | — | PF65 75.00 | | | | |

**KM# 30 10 DOLLARS**
1.24 g., 0.999 Gold 0.0398 oz. AGW **Subject:** Olympic Stadium in Munich 1972 **Obv:** National arms **Obv. Legend:** BANK OF NAURU

| Date | Mintage | VF20 | XF40 | MS60 | MS63 | MS65 |
|---|---|---|---|---|---|---|
| 2006 | — | PF65 75.00 | | | | |

**KM# 31 10 DOLLARS**
1.24 g., 0.999 Gold 0.0398 oz. AGW **Subject:** Independent Activists 1980 **Obv:** National arms **Obv. Legend:** BANK OF NAURU

| Date | Mintage | VF20 | XF40 | MS60 | MS63 | MS65 |
|---|---|---|---|---|---|---|
| 2006 | — | PF65 75.00 | | | | |

**KM# 32 10 DOLLARS**
1.24 g., 0.999 Gold 0.0398 oz. AGW **Subject:** Brandenburg Gate in Berlin 1990 **Obv. Legend:** BANK OF NAURU

| Date | Mintage | VF20 | XF40 | MS60 | MS63 | MS65 |
|---|---|---|---|---|---|---|
| 2006 | — | PF65 75.00 | | | | |

**KM# 33 10 DOLLARS**
1.24 g., 0.999 Gold 0.0398 oz. AGW **Subject:** European Union 2002 **Obv:** National arms **Obv. Legend:** BANK OF NAURU

| Date | Mintage | VF20 | XF40 | MS60 | MS63 | MS65 |
|---|---|---|---|---|---|---|
| 2006 | — | PF65 75.00 | | | | |

**KM# 34 10 DOLLARS**
1.24 g., 0.999 Gold 0.0398 oz. AGW **Subject:** Johannes Rau, German President, 1999-2004 **Obv:** National arms **Obv. Legend:** BANK OF NAURU

| Date | Mintage | VF20 | XF40 | MS60 | MS63 | MS65 |
|---|---|---|---|---|---|---|
| 2006 | — | PF65 75.00 | | | | |

**KM# 42 10 DOLLARS**
31.10 g., 0.999 Silver 0.9989 oz. ASW, 38.61 mm. **Rev:** Tower of Pisa, gilt

| Date | Mintage | VF20 | XF40 | MS60 | MS63 | MS65 |
|---|---|---|---|---|---|---|
| 2006 | 2,000 | PF65 150 | | | | |

**KM# 64 10 DOLLARS**
1.24 g., 0.999 Gold 0.0398 oz. AGW, 13.92 mm. **Subject:** Theodor Heuss

| Date | Mintage | VF20 | XF40 | MS60 | MS63 | MS65 |
|---|---|---|---|---|---|---|
| 2006 | Est. 10000 | PF65 75.00 | | | | |

**KM# 65 10 DOLLARS**
1.24 g., 0.999 Gold 0.0398 oz. AGW, 13.92 mm. **Subject:** Heinrich Lübke

| Date | Mintage | VF20 | XF40 | MS60 | MS63 | MS65 |
|---|---|---|---|---|---|---|
| 2006 | Est. 10000 | PF65 75.00 | | | | |

**KM# 66 10 DOLLARS**
1.24 g., 0.999 Gold 0.0398 oz. AGW, 13.92 mm. **Subject:** Gustav Heinemann

| Date | Mintage | VF20 | XF40 | MS60 | MS63 | MS65 |
|---|---|---|---|---|---|---|
| 2006 | Est. 10000 | PF65 75.00 | | | | |

**KM# 67 10 DOLLARS**
1.24 g., 0.999 Gold 0.0398 oz. AGW, 13.92 mm. **Subject:** Walter Scheel

| Date | Mintage | VF20 | XF40 | MS60 | MS63 | MS65 |
|---|---|---|---|---|---|---|
| 2006 | Est.1000 | PF65 75.00 | | | | |

**KM# 68 10 DOLLARS**
1.24 g., 0.999 Gold 0.0398 oz. AGW, 13.92 mm. **Subject:** Karl Carstens

| Date | Mintage | VF20 | XF40 | MS60 | MS63 | MS65 |
|---|---|---|---|---|---|---|
| 2006 | Est. 10000 | PF65 75.00 | | | | |

**KM# 69 10 DOLLARS**
1.24 g., 0.999 Gold 0.0398 oz. AGW, 13.92 mm. **Subject:** Richard Freiherr von Weizsäcker

| Date | Mintage | VF20 | XF40 | MS60 | MS63 | MS65 |
|---|---|---|---|---|---|---|
| 2006 | Est. 10000 | PF65 75.00 | | | | |

**KM# 70 10 DOLLARS**
1.24 g., 0.999 Gold 0.0398 oz. AGW, 13.92 mm. **Subject:** Roman Herzog

| Date | Mintage | VF20 | XF40 | MS60 | MS63 | MS65 |
|---|---|---|---|---|---|---|
| 2006 | Est. 10000 | PF65 75.00 | | | | |

**KM# 71 10 DOLLARS**
1.24 g., 0.999 Gold 0.0398 oz. AGW, 13.92 mm. **Subject:** Horst Köhler

| Date | Mintage | VF20 | XF40 | MS60 | MS63 | MS65 |
|---|---|---|---|---|---|---|
| 2006 | Est. 10000 | PF65 75.00 | | | | |

**KM# 72 10 DOLLARS**
31.11 g., 0.925 Silver 0.925 oz. ASW, 38.61 mm. **Rev:** Cathedral Santiago de Compostela

| Date | Mintage | VF20 | XF40 | MS60 | MS63 | MS65 |
|---|---|---|---|---|---|---|
| 2006 | Est. 5000 | — | — | — | — | 65.00 |

**KM# 73 10 DOLLARS**
31.11 g., 0.925 Silver 0.925 oz. ASW, 38.61 mm. **Rev:** Mt. St. Michel

| Date | Mintage | VF20 | XF40 | MS60 | MS63 | MS65 |
|---|---|---|---|---|---|---|
| 2006 | Est. 5000 | — | — | — | — | 65.00 |

**KM# 74 10 DOLLARS**
31.11 g., 0.925 Silver 0.925 oz. ASW, 38.61 mm. **Rev:** Axon in Brussels

| Date | Mintage | VF20 | XF40 | MS60 | MS63 | MS65 |
|---|---|---|---|---|---|---|
| 2006 | Est. 5000 | — | — | — | — | 65.00 |

**KM# 75 10 DOLLARS**
28.28 g., 0.925 Silver 0.841 oz. ASW, 38.61 mm. **Subject:** World Cup Football **Rev:** Brandenburg Gate

| Date | Mintage | VF20 | XF40 | MS60 | MS63 | MS65 |
|---|---|---|---|---|---|---|
| 2007 | — | PF65 55.00 | | | | |

**KM# 76 10 DOLLARS**
1.24 g., 0.999 Gold 0.0398 oz. AGW, 13.92 mm. **Rev:** Micronesia

| Date | Mintage | VF20 | XF40 | MS60 | MS63 | MS65 |
|---|---|---|---|---|---|---|
| 2007 | — | PF65 80.00 | | | | |

**KM# 77 10 DOLLARS**
28.28 g., 0.925 Silver 0.841 oz. ASW, 38.61 mm. **Subject:** Sylt to Hamburg Steam Train

| Date | Mintage | VF20 | XF40 | MS60 | MS63 | MS65 |
|---|---|---|---|---|---|---|
| 2007 | Est. 5000 | PF65 45.00 | | | | |

**KM# 79 10 DOLLARS**
28.28 g., 0.925 Silver 0.841 oz. ASW, 38.61 mm. **Rev:** Suspended subway

| Date | Mintage | VF20 | XF40 | MS60 | MS63 | MS65 |
|---|---|---|---|---|---|---|
| 2008 | — | PF65 50.00 | | | | |

**KM# 81 10 DOLLARS**
31.10 g., 0.999 Silver 0.9989 oz. ASW, 38.61 mm. **Rev:** Santa Claus in color

| Date | Mintage | VF20 | XF40 | MS60 | MS63 | MS65 |
|---|---|---|---|---|---|---|
| 2008 | Est. 15000 | — | — | — | — | 75.00 |

**KM# 82 10 DOLLARS**
0.925 Silver **Subject:** Worldcup Soccer in South Africa

| Date | Mintage | VF20 | XF40 | MS60 | MS63 | MS65 |
|---|---|---|---|---|---|---|
| 2009 | Est. 10000 | PF65 60.00 | | | | |

**KM# 83 10 DOLLARS**
1.00 g., 0.999 Gold 0.0321 oz. AGW, 13.92 mm. **Subject:** World Cup Soccer in South Africa **Rev:** Mascott leopard Zakumi

| Date | Mintage | VF20 | XF40 | MS60 | MS63 | MS65 |
|---|---|---|---|---|---|---|
| 2009 | Est. 5000 | PF65 55.00 | | | | |

**KM# 87 10 DOLLARS**
28.28 g., 0.925 Silver 0.841 oz. ASW, 38.61 mm. **Rev:** German Railways Locomotive 18201

| Date | Mintage | VF20 | XF40 | MS60 | MS63 | MS65 |
|---|---|---|---|---|---|---|
| 2010 | — | PF65 70.00 | | | | |

**KM# 88 10 DOLLARS**
0.925 Silver, 34 mm. **Rev:** Leipzig-Dresden Railway's locomotive Saxonia

| Date | Mintage | VF20 | XF40 | MS60 | MS63 | MS65 |
|---|---|---|---|---|---|---|
| 2010 | Est. 10000 | PF65 30.00 | | | | |

**KM# 47 10 DOLLARS**
Silver, 39 mm. **Subject:** WWII AZNAC troops **Obv:** Head in tiaria right, National arms at right **Rev:** Flag and Bugler

| Date | Mintage | VF20 | XF40 | MS60 | MS63 | MS65 |
|---|---|---|---|---|---|---|
| 2011 | — | PF65 30.00 | | | | |

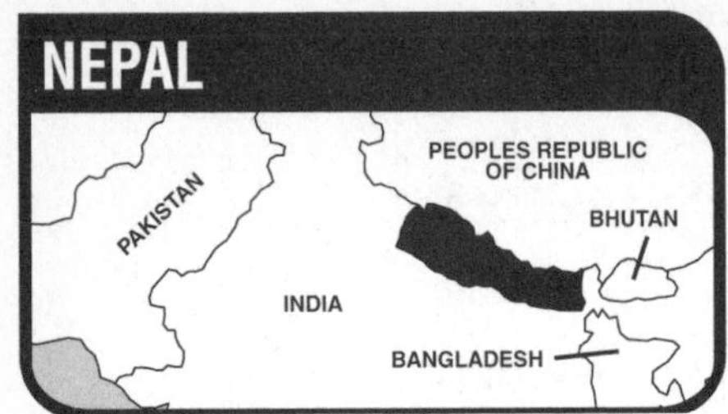


The Kingdom of Nepal, the world's only surviving Hindu kingdom, is a landlocked country occupying the southern slopes of the Himalayas. It has an area of 56,136 sq. mi. (140,800 sq. km.) and a population of 27 million. Capital: Kathmandu. Nepal has deposits of coal, copper, iron and cobalt, but they are largely unexploited. Agriculture is the principal economic activity. Rice, timber and jute are exported, with tourism being the other major foreign exchange earner.

On June 2, 2001 tragedy struck the royal family when Crown Prince Dipendra used an assault rifle to kill his father, mother and other members of the royal family as the result of a dispute over his current lady friend. He died 48 hours later, as King, from self inflicted gunshot wounds. Gyanendra began his second reign as King (his first was a short time as a toddler, 1950-51).

**DATING**

**Bikram Samvat Era (VS)**

From 1888AD most copper coins were dated in the Bikram Samvat (VS) era. To convert take VS date - 57 =AD date. Coins with this era have VS before the year in the listing. With the exception of a few gold coins struck in 1890 & 1892, silver and gold coins only changed to the VS era in 1911AD, but now this era is used for all coins struck in Nepal.

**RULERS**

**SHAH DYNASTY**

ज्ञानेन्द्र वीर विक्रम

Gyanendra Bir Bikram
VS2058-/2001AD

**NUMERALS**

Nepal has used more variations of numerals on their coins than any other nation. The most common are illustrated in the numeral chart in the introduction. The chart below illustrates some variations encompassing the last four centuries.

| 1 | 2 | 3 | 4 | 5 | 6 | 7 | 8 | 9 | 0 |
|---|---|---|---|---|---|---|---|---|---|
| १ | २ | ३ | ४ | ५ | ६ | ७ | ८ | ९ | ० |

**NUMERICS**

| | |
|---|---|
| One | एक |
| Two | दुइ |
| Ten | दसा |
| Twenty-five | पचीसा |
| Fifty | पचासा |
| Hundred | सय |

**DENOMINATIONS**

Rupee — रुपैयाँ

Legend on reverse

श्री श्री श्री गोरषनाथ

Shri Shri Shri Gorakhanatha in 8 petals

# KINGDOM

## Gyanendra Bir Bikram
### VS2058-2064 / 2001- 2007AD

## DECIMAL COINAGE

100 Paisa = 1 Rupee

**KM# 1173 10 PAISA**
Aluminum, 17 mm. **Obv:** Royal crown **Edge:** Plain

| Date | Mintage | F12 | VF20 | XF40 | MS60 | MS63 |
|---|---|---|---|---|---|---|
| VS2058 (2001) | — | — | — | — | 1.00 | 1.50 |

**KM# 1148 25 PAISA**
Aluminum, 20 mm. **Obv:** Royal crown **Edge:** Plain

| Date | Mintage | F12 | VF20 | XF40 | MS60 | MS63 |
|---|---|---|---|---|---|---|
| VS2058 | — | — | — | — | 0.50 | 0.75 |
| VS2059 | — | — | — | — | 0.50 | 0.75 |
| VS2060 | — | — | — | — | 0.50 | 0.75 |

**KM# 1149 50 PAISA**
Aluminum, 22.5 mm. **Obv:** Royal crown **Rev:** Swayambhunath **Edge:** Plain

| Date | Mintage | F12 | VF20 | XF40 | MS60 | MS63 |
|---|---|---|---|---|---|---|
| VS2058 | — | — | — | — | 0.50 | 0.75 |
| VS2059 | — | — | — | — | 0.50 | 0.75 |

**KM# 1179 50 PAISA**
1.41 g., Aluminum, 22.5 mm. **Obv:** Crown above crossed flags **Rev:** Swayambhunath **Edge:** Plain

| Date | Mintage | F12 | VF20 | XF40 | MS60 | MS63 |
|---|---|---|---|---|---|---|
| VS2060 (2003) | — | — | — | — | 0.40 | 0.60 |
| VS2061 (2004) | — | — | — | — | 0.40 | 0.60 |

**KM# 1150.1 RUPEE**
Brass Plated Steel **Rev:** Large (8.5mm) temple, medium '1' (4.5mm) **Edge:** Reeded **Note:** Non-magnetic.

| Date | Mintage | F12 | VF20 | XF40 | MS60 | MS63 |
|---|---|---|---|---|---|---|
| VS2058 | — | — | — | — | 1.00 | 1.50 |

**KM# 1150.2 RUPEE**
Brass Plated Steel **Obv:** Traditional design **Rev:** Small (7mm high) temple, small (4mm) "1 **Edge:** Plain **Note:** Magnetic.

| Date | Mintage | F12 | VF20 | XF40 | MS60 | MS63 |
|---|---|---|---|---|---|---|
| VS2058 | — | — | — | — | 1.00 | 1.50 |
| VS2059 | — | — | — | — | 1.00 | 1.50 |
| VS2060 | — | — | — | — | 1.00 | 1.50 |

**KM# 1150.3 RUPEE**
3.96 g., Brass, 20 mm. **Obv:** Traditional design **Rev:** Small (6.5mm high) temple, small (4mm) "1 **Edge:** Plain

| Date | Mintage | F12 | VF20 | XF40 | MS60 | MS63 |
|---|---|---|---|---|---|---|
| VS2058 | — | — | — | — | 0.50 | 0.75 |

**KM# 1150.4 RUPEE**
3.96 g., Brass Plated Steel, 20 mm. **Obv:** Traditional design **Rev:** Small (7mm high) temple, large (4.5mm) "1 **Note:** Magnetic.

| Date | Mintage | F12 | VF20 | XF40 | MS60 | MS63 |
|---|---|---|---|---|---|---|
| VS2059 | — | — | — | — | 1.00 | 1.50 |
| VS2060 | — | — | — | — | 1.00 | 1.50 |

**KM# 1180 RUPEE**
3.96 g., Brass Plated Steel, 20 mm. **Obv:** Traditional design **Rev:** Wagheshwari Temple **Edge:** Plain **Note:** 1" in denomination of a different style.

| Date | Mintage | F12 | VF20 | XF40 | MS60 | MS63 |
|---|---|---|---|---|---|---|
| VS2061 (2004) | — | — | — | — | 0.75 | 1.25 |

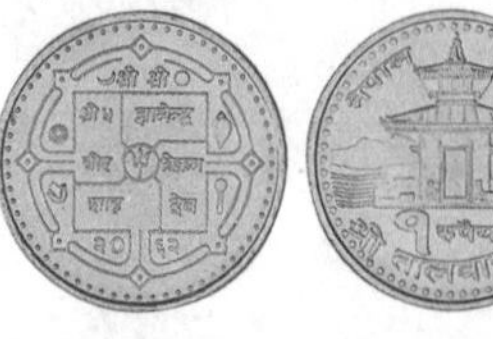

**KM# 1181 RUPEE**
3.94 g., Brass Plated Steel, 19.95 mm. **Obv:** Traditional design **Rev:** Sri Talbarahi Temple with outline mountain scene behind **Edge:** Plain

| Date | Mintage | F12 | VF20 | XF40 | MS60 | MS63 |
|---|---|---|---|---|---|---|
| VS2062(2005) | — | — | — | 0.50 | 1.20 | 1.60 |

**KM# 1151.2 2 RUPEES**
Brass, 25 mm. **Obv:** Traditional design **Rev:** Three domed building **Edge:** Plain

| Date | Mintage | F12 | VF20 | XF40 | MS60 | MS63 |
|---|---|---|---|---|---|---|
| VS2058 | — | — | — | — | 1.50 | 2.00 |
| VS2059 | — | — | — | — | 1.50 | 2.00 |
| VS2060 | — | — | — | — | 1.50 | 2.00 |

**KM# 1170 2 RUPEES**
4.94 g., Brass, 25 mm. **Obv:** Traditional square design **Rev:** People with flag celebrating 50 Years of Democracy **Edge:** Plain

| Date | Mintage | F12 | VF20 | XF40 | MS60 | MS63 |
|---|---|---|---|---|---|---|
| VS2058(2001) | — | — | — | — | 0.50 | 0.75 |

**KM# 1151.1 2 RUPEES**
5.07 g., Brass Plated Steel, 25 mm. **Obv:** Traditional design **Rev:** Three domed building **Edge:** Plain **Note:** Edge varieties exist. Prev. KM#1151. Magnetic.

| Date | Mintage | F12 | VF20 | XF40 | MS60 | MS63 |
|---|---|---|---|---|---|---|
| VS2060 | — | — | — | — | 1.50 | 2.00 |

**KM# 1151.1a 2 RUPEES**
6.70 g., Silver, 25 mm. **Obv:** Traditional design **Rev:** Three domed building **Edge:** Plain

| Date | Mintage | F12 | VF20 | XF40 | MS60 | MS63 |
|---|---|---|---|---|---|---|
| VS2060(2003) | — | — | — | — | 100 | 135 |

**KM# 1159 25 RUPEE**
8.36 g., Copper-Nickel, 29.1 mm. **Obv:** Crowned bust right **Rev:** Traditional design **Edge:** Plain

| Date | Mintage | F12 | VF20 | XF40 | MS60 | MS63 |
|---|---|---|---|---|---|---|
| VS2058 | — | — | — | — | 4.00 | 5.50 |
| VS2059 | — | — | — | — | 4.00 | 5.50 |

**KM# 1164 25 RUPEE**
8.60 g., Copper-Nickel, 29.1 mm. **Subject:** Silver Jubilee **Obv:** Traditional design **Rev:** Stylized face design **Edge:** Plain

| Date | Mintage | F12 | VF20 | XF40 | MS60 | MS63 |
|---|---|---|---|---|---|---|
| VS2060 | — | — | — | — | 4.00 | 5.50 |

**KM# 1183 25 RUPEE**
8.55 g., Copper-Nickel, 29.1 mm. **Subject:** World Hindu Federation **Obv:** Traditional design **Edge:** Plain

| Date | Mintage | F12 | VF20 | XF40 | MS60 | MS63 |
|---|---|---|---|---|---|---|
| VS2062 (2005) | — | — | — | — | 4.00 | 5.50 |

**KM# 1160 50 RUPEE**
20.10 g., Brass, 37.7 mm. **Subject:** 50th Anniversary of Scouting in Nepal **Obv:** Traditional design **Rev:** Scouting emblem within beaded wreath **Edge:** Plain

| Date | Mintage | F12 | VF20 | XF40 | MS60 | MS63 |
|---|---|---|---|---|---|---|
| VS2058 | — | — | — | — | 9.00 | 11.00 |

**KM# 1182 50 RUPEE**
8.60 g., Copper-Nickel, 29 mm. **Subject:** Golden Jubilee of Supreme Court **Obv:** Traditional design **Rev:** Supreme Court building **Edge:** Plain

| Date | Mintage | F12 | VF20 | XF40 | MS60 | MS63 |
|---|---|---|---|---|---|---|
| VS2063 (2006) | — | — | — | — | 6.00 | 9.00 |

**KM# 1157 100 RUPEE**
20.00 g., Brass, 38.7 mm. **Subject:** Buddha **Obv:** Traditional design **Rev:** Seated Buddha teaching five seated monks **Edge:** Reeded

| Date | Mintage | F12 | VF20 | XF40 | MS60 | MS63 |
|---|---|---|---|---|---|---|
| VS2058 | 30,000 | — | — | — | 10.00 | 12.00 |

**KM# 1161 200 RUPEE**
18.10 g., 0.500 Silver 0.291 oz. ASW, 29.6 mm. **Subject:** 50th Anniversary of the Nepal Chamber of Commerce **Obv:** Traditional design **Rev:** Swastika within rotary gear **Edge:** Plain

| Date | Mintage | F12 | VF20 | XF40 | MS60 | MS63 |
|---|---|---|---|---|---|---|
| VS2059 | — | — | — | — | 20.00 | 25.00 |

**KM# 1162 200 RUPEE**
18.10 g., 0.500 Silver 0.291 oz. ASW, 29.6 mm. **Subject:** 50th Anniversary of Civil Service **Obv:** Traditional design **Rev:** Crown above flags and value **Edge:** Plain

| Date | Mintage | F12 | VF20 | XF40 | MS60 | MS63 |
|---|---|---|---|---|---|---|
| VS2059 | — | — | — | — | 20.00 | 25.00 |

**KM# 1171 250 RUPEE**
18.00 g., 0.500 Silver 0.2894 oz. ASW, 29 mm. **Subject:** 2600th Anniversary of Bhagawan Mahavir **Obv:** Traditional design **Rev:** Haloed head above value **Edge:** Plain

| Date | Mintage | F12 | VF20 | XF40 | MS60 | MS63 |
|---|---|---|---|---|---|---|
| VS2058 | — | — | — | — | 25.00 | 30.00 |

**KM# 1176 250 RUPEE**
17.83 g., 0.500 Silver 0.2866 oz. ASW, 31.6 mm. **Subject:** Marwadi, non-profit making organization **Obv:** Traditional design **Rev:** Swastika within circle **Edge:** Reeded

| Date | Mintage | F12 | VF20 | XF40 | MS60 | MS63 |
|---|---|---|---|---|---|---|
| VS2060 (2003) | — | — | — | — | 25.00 | 30.00 |

**KM# 1184 250 RUPEE**
18.00 g., Silver, 32 mm. **Subject:** 400th Anniversary of Guru Granth Sahib **Obv:** Traditional design **Rev:** Holy Book of Sikhs **Edge:** Reeded

| Date | Mintage | F12 | VF20 | XF40 | MS60 | MS63 |
|---|---|---|---|---|---|---|
| VS2061 | — | — | — | — | 25.00 | 30.00 |

**KM# 1174 300 RUPEE**
22.50 g., 0.500 Silver 0.3617 oz. ASW, 31.8 mm. **Subject:** Economic Growth Through Export **Obv:** Traditional design **Rev:** Two joined hands in front of globe **Edge:** Reeded

| Date | Mintage | F12 | VF20 | XF40 | MS60 | MS63 |
|---|---|---|---|---|---|---|
| VS2060 | — | — | — | — | 22.00 | 28.00 |

**KM# 1163 500 RUPEE**
23.34 g., 0.900 Silver 0.6754 oz. ASW, 32 mm. **Subject:** 50th Anniversary of the Conquest of Mt. Everest **Obv:** Traditional design **Rev:** Mountain and map above value **Edge:** Reeded

| Date | Mintage | F12 | VF20 | XF40 | MS60 | MS63 |
|---|---|---|---|---|---|---|
| VS2060 | — | — | — | — | 30.00 | 35.00 |

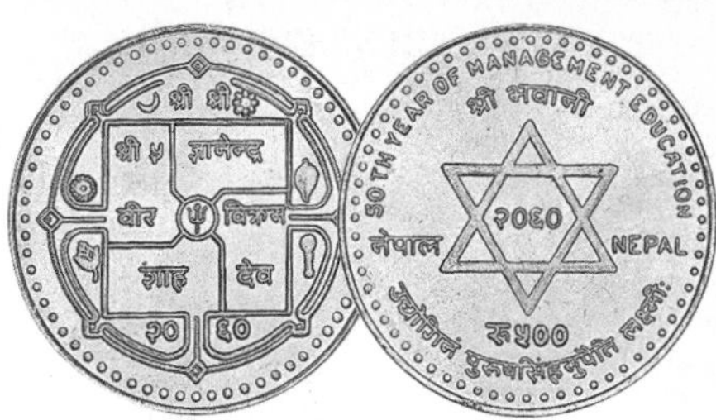

**KM# 1177 500 RUPEE**
23.00 g., 0.900 Silver 0.6655 oz. ASW, 31.7 mm. **Subject:** Management Education 50th Anniversary **Obv:** Traditional design **Rev:** Six point star outline **Edge:** Reeded

| Date | Mintage | F12 | VF20 | XF40 | MS60 | MS63 |
|---|---|---|---|---|---|---|
| VS2060 (2003) | — | — | — | — | 30.00 | 35.00 |

**KM# 1185 500 RUPEE**
20.10 g., Silver, 32 mm. **Subject:** 50th Anniversary of Nepal-United Nations **Obv:** Traditional design **Rev:** Head of the late King Mahendra Bir Birkam **Edge:** Reeded

| Date | Mintage | F12 | VF20 | XF40 | MS60 | MS63 |
|---|---|---|---|---|---|---|
| VS2062 | — | — | — | — | 25.00 | 30.00 |

**KM# 1175 1000 RUPEE**
35.00 g., Silver, 40 mm. **Subject:** 100 Years - Rotary Club **Edge:** Reeded

| Date | Mintage | F12 | VF20 | XF40 | MS60 | MS63 |
|---|---|---|---|---|---|---|
| VS2062 (2005) | — | — | — | — | 45.00 | 50.00 |

**KM# 1178 1000 RUPEE**
35.20 g., 0.500 Silver 0.5659 oz. ASW, 40 mm. **Subject:** Rastriya Bank 50th Anniversary **Obv:** Traditional square design **Rev:** Bank seal above value **Edge:** Reeded

| Date | Mintage | F12 | VF20 | XF40 | MS60 | MS63 |
|---|---|---|---|---|---|---|
| VS2062 (2005) | — | — | — | — | 27.00 | 32.00 |

**KM# 1158 1500 RUPEE**
20.00 g., 0.925 Silver 0.5948 oz. ASW, 38.7 mm. **Subject:** Buddha **Obv:** Traditional design **Rev:** Seated Buddha teaching five seated monks **Edge:** Reeded

| Date | Mintage | F12 | VF20 | XF40 | MS60 | MS63 |
|---|---|---|---|---|---|---|
| VS2058 | 15,000 | PF60 30.00 | PF63 35.00 | | | |

**KM# 1172 2000 RUPEE**
31.20 g., 0.720 Silver 0.7222 oz. ASW, 40 mm. **Subject:** Gyanendra's Accession to the Throne **Obv:** Crowned bust right **Rev:** Upright sword above value in circular design **Edge:** Reeded

| Date | Mintage | F12 | VF20 | XF40 | MS60 | MS63 |
|---|---|---|---|---|---|---|
| VS2058 | — | — | — | — | 40.00 | 45.00 |

**KM# 1201 2000 RUPEE**
31.11 g., 0.999 Silver 0.999 oz. ASW, 40 mm. **Subject:** Conquest of Mt. Everest 50th Anniversary **Rev:** Sir Edmond Hillary and Tenzing Norgay at Summit

| Date | Mintage | F12 | VF20 | XF40 | MS60 | MS63 |
|---|---|---|---|---|---|---|
| VS2060 (2003) | 8,000 | PF60 70.00 | PF63 80.00 | | | |

**KM# 1191 2000 RUPEE**
31.20 g., 0.925 Silver 0.9279 oz. ASW, 38.61 mm. **Subject:** 2006 FIFA World Cup - Germany **Obv:** Traditional design

| Date | Mintage | F12 | VF20 | XF40 | MS60 | MS63 |
|---|---|---|---|---|---|---|
| VS2063 (2006) | — | — | — | — | 45.00 | 50.00 |

## ASARFI GOLD COINAGE

Fractional designations are approximate for this series. Actual Gold Weight (AGW) is used to identify each type.

(Asarphi)

**KM# 1200 ASARPHI**

7.77 g., 0.9999 Gold 0.2498 oz. AGW, 22 mm. **Subject:** Conquest of Mt. Everest **Rev:** Sir Edward Hillary and Tenzing Norgay at Summit

| Date | Mintage | F12 | VF20 | XF40 | MS60 | MS63 |
|---|---|---|---|---|---|---|
| VS2060 (2003) | 2,000 | — | — | — | 750 | 800 |

**KM# 1153 0.3G ASARPHI**

0.30 g., 0.9999 Gold 0.0096 oz. AGW, 7 mm. **Subject:** Buddha **Obv:** Traditional design **Rev:** Seated Buddha **Edge:** Plain

| Date | Mintage | VG8 | F12 | VF20 | XF40 | MS63 |
|---|---|---|---|---|---|---|
| VS2058 (2001) | 30,000 | — | — | — | — | 25.00 |

**KM# 1154 1/25-OZ. ASARFI**

1.24 g., 0.9999 Gold 0.040 oz. AGW, 13.92 mm. **Subject:** Buddha **Obv:** Traditional design **Rev:** Seated Buddha **Edge:** Reeded

| Date | Mintage | VG8 | F12 | VF20 | XF40 | MS63 |
|---|---|---|---|---|---|---|
| VS2058 (2001) | 25,000 | — | — | — | — | 75.00 |

**KM# 1155 1/10-OZ. ASARFI**

3.11 g., 0.9999 Gold 0.100 oz. AGW, 17.95 mm. **Subject:** Buddha **Obv:** Traditional design **Rev:** Seated Buddha **Edge:** Reeded

| Date | Mintage | VG8 | F12 | VF20 | XF40 | MS63 |
|---|---|---|---|---|---|---|
| VS2058 (2001) | 15,000 | — | — | — | — | 185 |

**KM# 1156 1/2-OZ. ASARFI**

15.55 g., 0.9999 Gold 0.500 oz. AGW, 27 mm. **Subject:** Buddha **Obv:** Traditional design **Rev:** Seated Buddha **Edge:** Reeded

| Date | Mintage | VG8 | F12 | VF20 | XF40 | MS63 |
|---|---|---|---|---|---|---|
| VS2058 (2001) | 2,500 | PF63 900 | | | | |

# DEMOCRATIC REPUBLIC

## DECIMAL COINAGE

100 Paisa = 1 Rupee

**KM# 1204 RUPEE**

Brass Plated Steel, 19 mm. **Obv:** Mt. Everest within square **Rev:** Map of Nepal

| Date | Mintage | F12 | VF20 | XF40 | MS60 | MS63 |
|---|---|---|---|---|---|---|
| VS2064 | — | — | — | — | 2.00 | 3.50 |

**KM# 1188 2 RUPEES**

5.00 g., Brass Plated Steel, 24.93 mm. **Obv:** Mount Everest within square **Rev:** Farmer plowing with water buffalos **Edge:** Plain

| Date | Mintage | F12 | VF20 | XF40 | MS60 | MS63 |
|---|---|---|---|---|---|---|
| VS2063(2006) | — | — | — | 1.50 | 2.75 | 4.00 |

**KM# 1186 25 RUPEE**

8.50 g., Copper-Nickel, 29 mm. **Subject:** 125th Anniversary - First Nepal Postal Stamp Issue **Obv:** Features image of legendary 1 Anna stamp **Rev:** Traditional mailman on the reverse

| Date | Mintage | F12 | VF20 | XF40 | MS60 | MS63 |
|---|---|---|---|---|---|---|
| VS2063 | — | — | — | — | 7.00 | 9.00 |
| VS2064 | — | — | — | — | 7.00 | 9.00 |

**KM# 1189 50 RUPEE**

8.60 g., Copper-Nickel, 29 mm. **Subject:** 250th Anniversary Hindu festival "Kimari Jatra **Obv:** Kumari Temple at Durbar Square in Kathmandu **Rev:** Bust of Goddess Kumari facing **Edge:** Plain

| Date | Mintage | F12 | VF20 | XF40 | MS60 | MS63 |
|---|---|---|---|---|---|---|
| VS2064 | — | — | — | — | 8.00 | 10.00 |

**KM# 1208 50 RUPEE**

Silver ASW **Subject:** National Numismatic Museum

| Date | Mintage | F12 | VF20 | XF40 | MS60 | MS63 |
|---|---|---|---|---|---|---|
| 2012 | — | — | — | — | — | 9.00 |

**KM# 1206 50 RUPEE**

8.60 g., Copper-Nickel, 29 mm. **Subject:** International year of Cooperation **Rev:** Stick figures holding large square

| Date | Mintage | F12 | VF20 | XF40 | MS60 | MS63 |
|---|---|---|---|---|---|---|
| VS2069 | — | — | — | — | — | 10.00 |

**KM# 1190 500 RUPEE**

14.19 g., 0.500 Silver 0.2281 oz. ASW, 32 mm. **Subject:** 250th Anniversary Hindu festival "Kimari Jatra **Obv:** Kumari Temple at Durbar Square in Kathmandu **Rev:** Bust of Goddess Kumari facing **Edge:** Reeded

| Date | Mintage | F12 | VF20 | XF40 | MS60 | MS63 |
|---|---|---|---|---|---|---|
| VS2064 | — | — | — | — | 25.00 | 30.00 |

**KM# 1207 1000 RUPEE**

35.20 g., 0.500 Silver 0.5659 oz. ASW, 40 mm. **Subject:** International year of Cooperation **Rev:** Stick figures holding up large square

| Date | Mintage | F12 | VF20 | XF40 | MS60 | MS63 |
|---|---|---|---|---|---|---|
| VS2069 | — | PF63 27.50 | | | | |

## MINT SETS

| KM# | Date | Mintage | Identification | Issue Price | Mkt Val |
|---|---|---|---|---|---|
| MSA19 | 1996, 1995, 2011 (3) | — | KM#709.2 (1996), 711 (1995), 737 (2011) | | 8.00 |

# NETHERLANDS

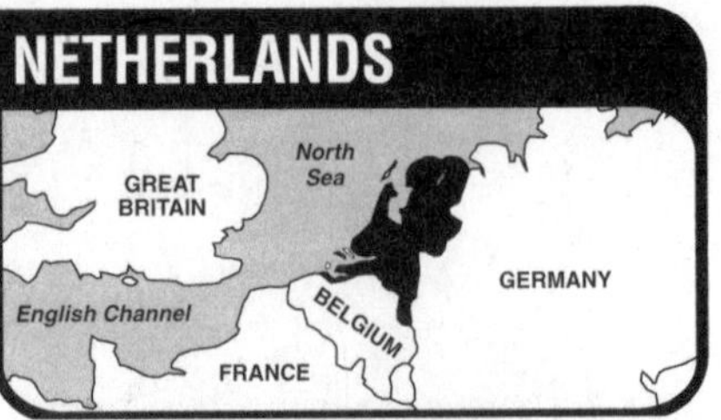


The Kingdom of the Netherlands, a country of Western Europe fronting on the North Sea and bordered by Belgium and Germany, has an area of 15,770 sq. mi. (41,500 sq. km.) and a population of 16.4 million. Capital: Amsterdam, but the seat of government is at The Hague. The economy is based on dairy farming and a variety of industrial activities. Chemicals, yarns and fabrics, and meat products are exported.

**NOTE:** Excepting the World War II issues struck at U.S. mints, all of the modern coins were struck at the Utrecht Mint (or at the annex in the Birmingham Mint, 1980-2000) and bear the caduceus mint mark of that facility. They also bear the mintmasters' marks.

The BES-islands (Bonaire, St. Eustatius and Saba) have been added to the Netherlands as special municipalities on Oct. 10, 2010. On these islands the U.S. dollar has been the official currency.

**RULERS**

**KINGDOM OF THE NETHERLANDS**

Beatrix, 1980-2013

Willam-Alexander 2013-

**MINT PRIVY MARKS**

**Utrecht**

| Date | Privy Mark |
|---|---|
| 1806-present | Caduceus |

**MINTMASTERS' PRIVY MARKS**

**Utrecht Mint**

| Date | Privy Mark |
|---|---|
| 2001 | Wine tendril w/grapes |
| 2002 | Wine tendril w/grapes and star |
| 2003 | Sails of a clipper |

**NOTE:** A star adjoining the privy mark indicates that the piece was struck at the beginning of the term of office of a successor. (The star was used only if the successor had not chosen his own mark yet.)

**NOTE:** Since October 1999, the Dutch Mint has taken the title of Royal Dutch Mint.

**MONETARY SYSTEM**

**Until January 29, 2002**

100 Cents = 1 Gulden

**Since January 1, 2002**

100 Euro Cents = 1 Euro

# KINGDOM

## DECIMAL COINAGE

**KM# 202 5 CENTS**

3.50 g., Bronze, 21 mm. **Ruler:** Beatrix **Obv:** Head left with vertical inscription **Rev:** Value within vertical lines **Edge:** Plain

| Date | Mintage | VF20 | XF40 | MS60 | MS63 | MS65 |
|---|---|---|---|---|---|---|
| 2001 | 15,815,000 | — | — | — | 0.70 | — |
| 2001 | 17,000 | PF65 4.00 | | | | |

**KM# 203 10 CENTS**

1.50 g., Nickel, 15 mm. **Ruler:** Beatrix **Obv:** Head left with vertical inscription **Rev:** Value and vertical lines **Edge:** Reeded

| Date | Mintage | VF20 | XF40 | MS60 | MS63 | MS65 |
|---|---|---|---|---|---|---|
| 2001 | 25,600,000 | — | — | 0.45 | 0.75 | — |
| 2001 | 17,000 | PF65 4.00 | | | | |

### KM# 204 25 CENTS

3.00 g., Nickel, 19 mm. **Ruler:** Beatrix **Obv:** Head left with vertical inscription **Obv. Inscription:** Beatrix/Konincin Der/ Nederlanden **Rev:** Value within vertical and horizontal lines **Edge:** Reeded

| Date | Mintage | VF20 | XF40 | MS60 | MS63 | MS65 |
|---|---|---|---|---|---|---|
| 2001 | 11,515,000 | — | — | 0.30 | 1.00 | — |
| 2001 | 17,000 | PF65 5.00 | | | | |

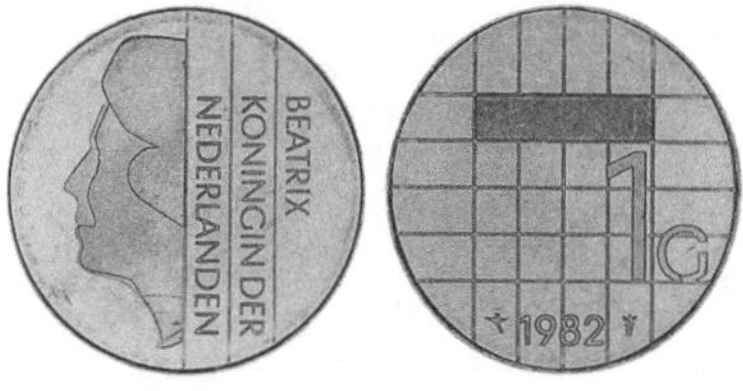

### KM# 205 GULDEN

6.00 g., Nickel, 25 mm. **Ruler:** Beatrix **Obv:** Head left with vertical inscription **Rev:** Value within vertical and horizontal lines **Edge Lettering:** GOD * ZIJ * MET * ONS *

| Date | Mintage | VF20 | XF40 | MS60 | MS63 | MS65 |
|---|---|---|---|---|---|---|
| 2001 | 6,414,500 | — | — | — | 1.25 | — |
| 2001 | 17,000 | PF65 5.00 | | | | |

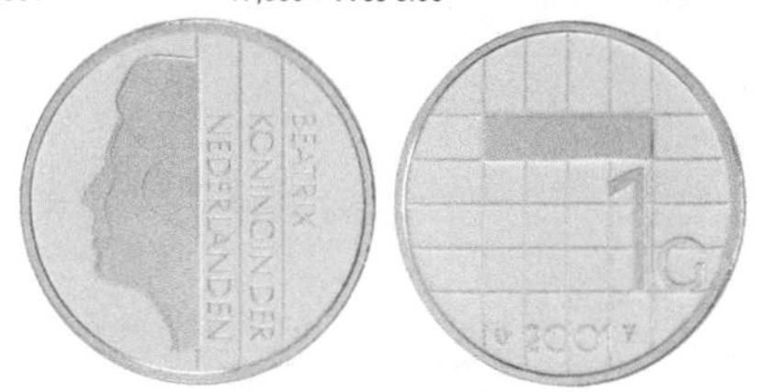

### KM# 205a GULDEN

7.10 g., 0.925 Silver 0.2111 oz. ASW **Ruler:** Beatrix **Obv:** Head left with vertical inscription **Rev:** Value within vertical and horizontal lines **Edge Lettering:** GOD*ZIJ*MET*OMS*

| Date | Mintage | VF20 | XF40 | MS60 | MS63 | MS65 |
|---|---|---|---|---|---|---|
| 2001 Prooflike | 200,000 | — | — | — | 15.00 | — |

### KM# 205b GULDEN

13.20 g., 0.999 Gold 0.424 oz. AGW **Ruler:** Beatrix **Obv:** Head left with vertical inscription **Rev:** Value within vertical and horizontal lines **Edge Lettering:** GOD*ZIJ*MET*ONS* **Note:** Prev. KM#205a.

| Date | Mintage | VF20 | XF40 | MS60 | MS63 | MS65 |
|---|---|---|---|---|---|---|
| 2001 Prooflike | 25,500 | — | — | — | 700 | — |

Note: Mintage includes KM#205c.

### KM# 205c GULDEN

13.20 g., 0.999 Gold 0.424 oz. AGW **Ruler:** Beatrix **Obv:** Head left with vertical inscription **Rev:** Value within vertical and horizontal lines **Edge:** Plain, missing lettering

| Date | Mintage | VF20 | XF40 | MS60 | MS63 | MS65 |
|---|---|---|---|---|---|---|
| 2001 Prooflike | Est. 500 | — | — | — | 1,800 | — |

### KM# 233 GULDEN

6.00 g., Nickel, 25 mm. **Ruler:** Beatrix **Obv:** Head left within inscription **Rev:** Child art design **Edge Lettering:** GOD * ZIJ * MET * ONS *

| Date | Mintage | VF20 | XF40 | MS60 | MS63 | MS65 |
|---|---|---|---|---|---|---|
| 2001 | 16,009,000 | — | — | — | 4.00 | — |
| 2001 Prooflike | 32,000 | — | — | — | 6.00 | — |

### KM# 233a GULDEN

7.10 g., 0.925 Silver 0.2111 oz. ASW, 25 mm. **Ruler:** Beatrix **Obv:** Head left within inscription **Rev:** Child art design **Edge Lettering:** GOD * ZIJ * MET * ONS *

| Date | Mintage | VF20 | XF40 | MS60 | MS63 | MS65 |
|---|---|---|---|---|---|---|
| 2001 Prooflike | 360 | — | — | — | 3,300 | — |

Note: Given as gifts to workers at the mint

### KM# 233b GULDEN

13.20 g., 0.999 Gold 0.424 oz. AGW, 25 mm. **Ruler:** Beatrix **Obv:** Head left within inscription **Rev:** Child art design **Note:** 98 of 100 pieces melted down, with 2 known in museum collections.

| Date | Mintage | VF20 | XF40 | MS60 | MS63 | MS65 |
|---|---|---|---|---|---|---|
| 2001 Prooflike; Rare | 100 | — | — | — | — | — |

### KM# 206 2-1/2 GULDEN

10.00 g., Nickel, 29 mm. **Ruler:** Beatrix **Obv:** Head left with vertical inscription **Rev:** Value within horizontal, vertical and diagonal lines **Edge Lettering:** GOD * ZIJ * MET * ONS *

| Date | Mintage | VF20 | XF40 | MS60 | MS63 | MS65 |
|---|---|---|---|---|---|---|
| 2001 | 315,000 | — | — | 4.00 | 6.00 | — |
| 2001 | 17,000 | PF65 7.50 | | | | |

### KM# 210 5 GULDEN

9.25 g., Bronze Clad Nickel, 23.5 mm. **Ruler:** Beatrix **Obv:** Head left with vertical inscription **Rev:** Value within horizontal, vertical and diagonal lines **Edge:** GOD * ZIJ * MET * ONS *

| Date | Mintage | VF20 | XF40 | MS60 | MS63 | MS65 |
|---|---|---|---|---|---|---|
| 2001 | 115,000 | — | — | 5.00 | 10.00 | — |
| 2001 | 17,000 | PF65 7.00 | | | | |

## EURO COINAGE

European Union Issues

### KM# 234 EURO CENT

2.30 g., Copper Plated Steel, 16.2 mm. **Ruler:** Beatrix **Obv:** Head left among stars **Rev:** Value and globe **Edge:** Plain

| Date | Mintage | VF20 | XF40 | MS60 | MS63 | MS65 |
|---|---|---|---|---|---|---|
| 2001 | 179,800,000 | — | — | 0.35 | 0.50 | 0.75 |
| 2001 Proof | 16,500 | — | — | — | — | — |
| 2002 | 600,000 | — | — | 3.00 | 1.25 | 1.50 |
| 2002 | 16,500 | PF65 5.00 | | | | |
| 2003 | 5,866,000 | — | — | 0.50 | 0.75 | 1.00 |
| 2003 | 13,000 | PF65 4.00 | | | | |
| 2004 | 11,396,000 | — | — | 0.50 | 0.75 | 1.00 |
| 2004 | 5,000 | PF65 4.00 | | | | |
| 2005 | 545,000 | — | — | 1.50 | 2.00 | 2.50 |
| 2005 | 5,000 | PF65 4.00 | | | | |
| 2006 | 378,000 | — | — | 1.50 | 2.00 | 2.50 |
| 2006 | 3,500 | PF65 4.00 | | | | |
| 2007 | 332,000 | — | — | 1.50 | 2.00 | 2.50 |
| 2007 | 10,000 | PF65 3.50 | | | | |
| 2008 | 413,000 | — | — | 1.50 | 2.00 | 2.50 |
| 2008 | 10,000 | PF65 3.50 | | | | |
| 2009 | 335,000 | — | — | 1.50 | 2.00 | 2.50 |
| 2009 | 75,000 | PF65 3.50 | | | | |
| 2010 | 235,000 | — | — | 1.50 | 2.00 | 2.50 |
| 2010 | 5,000 | PF65 3.50 | | | | |
| 2011 | 50,000,000 | — | — | 1.50 | 2.00 | 2.50 |
| 2011 | 330,000 | — | — | 1.50 | 2.00 | 2.50 |
| 2011 | 5,000 | PF65 3.50 | | | | |
| 2012 | — | — | — | 1.50 | 2.00 | 2.50 |
| 2012 | 5,000 | PF65 3.50 | | | | |
| 2013 | — | — | — | 1.50 | 2.00 | 2.50 |
| 2013 | 5,000 | PF65 3.50 | | | | |

### KM# 344 EURO CENT

2.30 g., Copper Plated Steel, 16.3 mm. **Ruler:** Willem-Alexander **Obv:** Head right **Rev:** Value and globe

| Date | Mintage | VF20 | XF40 | MS60 | MS63 | MS65 |
|---|---|---|---|---|---|---|
| 2014 | 5,000 | PF65 4.00 | | | | |
| 2014 | — | — | — | 1.50 | 2.00 | 2.50 |

### KM# 235 2 EURO CENT

3.06 g., Copper Plated Steel, 18.7 mm. **Ruler:** Beatrix **Obv:** Head left among stars **Rev:** Value and globe **Edge:** Grooved

| Date | Mintage | VF20 | XF40 | MS60 | MS63 | MS65 |
|---|---|---|---|---|---|---|
| 2001 | 142,100,000 | — | — | 0.50 | 0.75 | 1.00 |
| 2001 Proof | 16,500 | — | — | — | — | — |
| 2002 | 52,224,000 | — | — | 0.75 | 1.00 | 1.50 |
| 2002 Proof | 16,500 | — | — | — | — | — |
| 2003 | 150,750,000 | — | — | 0.50 | 0.75 | 1.00 |
| 2003 Proof | 13,000 | — | — | — | — | — |
| 2004 | 115,622,000 | — | — | 0.50 | 0.75 | 1.00 |
| 2004 | 5,000 | PF65 4.00 | | | | |
| 2005 | 595,000 | — | — | 1.50 | 2.00 | 2.50 |
| 2005 | 5,000 | PF65 4.00 | | | | |
| 2006 | 378,000 | — | — | 1.50 | 2.00 | 2.50 |
| 2006 | 3,500 | PF65 4.00 | | | | |
| 2007 | 338,000 | — | — | 1.50 | 2.00 | 2.50 |
| 2007 | 10,000 | PF65 3.50 | | | | |
| 2008 | 413,000 | — | — | 1.50 | 2.00 | 2.50 |
| 2008 | 10,000 | PF65 3.50 | | | | |
| 2009 | 335,000 | — | — | 1.50 | 2.00 | 2.50 |
| 2009 | 75,000 | PF65 3.50 | | | | |
| 2010 | 235,000 | — | — | 1.50 | 2.00 | 2.50 |
| 2010 | 5,000 | PF65 3.50 | | | | |
| 2011 | 330,000 | — | — | 1.50 | 2.00 | 2.50 |
| 2011 | 5,000 | PF65 3.50 | | | | |
| 2012 | — | — | — | 1.50 | 2.00 | 2.50 |
| 2012 | 5,000 | PF65 3.50 | | | | |
| 2013 | — | — | — | 1.50 | 2.00 | 2.50 |
| 2013 | 5,000 | PF65 3.50 | | | | |

### KM# 345 2 EURO CENT

3.06 g., Copper Plated Steel, 18.7 mm. **Ruler:** Willem-Alexander **Obv:** Head right **Rev:** Value and globe

| Date | Mintage | VF20 | XF40 | MS60 | MS63 | MS65 |
|---|---|---|---|---|---|---|
| 2014 | 5,000 | PF65 4.00 | | | | |
| 2014 | — | — | — | 1.50 | 2.00 | 2.50 |

### KM# 236 5 EURO CENT

3.92 g., Copper Plated Steel, 21.25 mm. **Ruler:** Beatrix **Obv:** Head left among stars **Rev:** Value and globe **Edge:** Plain

| Date | Mintage | VF20 | XF40 | MS60 | MS63 | MS65 |
|---|---|---|---|---|---|---|
| 2001 | 206,400,000 | — | — | 0.50 | 0.75 | 1.00 |
| 2001 Proof | 16,500 | — | — | — | — | — |
| 2002 | 700,000 | — | — | 1.75 | 3.50 | 5.00 |
| 2002 Proof | 16,500 | — | — | — | — | — |
| 2003 | 874,000 | — | — | 1.50 | 2.00 | 2.50 |
| 2003 Proof | 13,000 | — | — | — | — | — |
| 2004 | 306,000 | — | — | 2.00 | 2.50 | 3.00 |
| 2004 | 5,000 | PF65 4.00 | | | | |
| 2005 | 80,605,000 | — | — | 1.00 | 1.25 | 1.75 |
| 2005 | 5,000 | PF65 4.00 | | | | |
| 2006 | 60,318,000 | — | — | 1.00 | 1.25 | 1.75 |
| 2006 | 3,500 | PF65 4.00 | | | | |
| 2007 | 75,764,000 | — | — | 1.00 | 1.25 | 1.75 |
| 2007 | 10,000 | PF65 3.50 | | | | |
| 2008 | 50,413,000 | — | — | 1.00 | 1.25 | 1.75 |
| 2008 | 10,000 | PF65 3.50 | | | | |
| 2009 | 70,335,000 | — | — | 1.00 | 1.25 | 1.75 |
| 2009 | 75,000 | PF65 3.50 | | | | |
| 2010 | 70,235,000 | — | — | 1.00 | 1.25 | 1.75 |
| 2010 | 5,000 | PF65 3.50 | | | | |
| 2011 | 40,100,000 | — | — | 1.00 | 1.25 | 1.75 |
| 2011 | 5,000 | PF65 3.50 | | | | |
| 2012 | — | — | — | 1.00 | 1.25 | 1.75 |
| 2012 | 5,000 | PF65 3.50 | | | | |
| 2013 | — | — | — | 1.00 | 1.25 | 1.75 |
| 2013 | 5,000 | PF65 3.50 | | | | |

**KM# 346 5 EURO CENT**
Copper Plated Steel, 21.25 mm. **Ruler:** Willem-Alexander **Obv:** Head right **Rev:** Value and globe

| Date | Mintage | VF20 | XF40 | MS60 | MS63 | MS65 |
|---|---|---|---|---|---|---|
| 2014 | 5,000 | PF65 4.00 | | | | |
| 2014 | — | — | — | 1.00 | 1.25 | 1.75 |

**KM# 237 10 EURO CENT**
4.10 g., Brass, 19.7 mm. **Ruler:** Beatrix **Obv:** Head left among stars **Rev:** Value and map

| Date | Mintage | VF20 | XF40 | MS60 | MS63 | MS65 |
|---|---|---|---|---|---|---|
| 2001 | 194,200,000 | — | — | 0.75 | 1.00 | 1.50 |
| 2001 Proof | 16,500 | — | — | — | — | — |
| 2002 | 600,000 | — | — | 1.50 | 2.00 | 2.50 |
| 2002 Proof | 16,500 | — | — | — | — | — |
| 2003 | 818,000 | — | — | 1.50 | 2.00 | 2.50 |
| 2003 Proof | 13,000 | — | — | — | — | — |
| 2004 | 262,000 | — | — | 2.00 | 2.50 | 3.00 |
| 2004 | 5,000 | PF65 6.00 | | | | |
| 2005 | 510,000 | — | — | 1.75 | 2.00 | 2.50 |
| 2005 | 5,000 | PF65 6.00 | | | | |
| 2006 | 393,000 | — | — | 1.75 | 2.50 | 3.00 |
| 2006 | 3,500 | PF65 6.00 | | | | |

**KM# 268 10 EURO CENT**
4.10 g., Brass, 19.7 mm. **Ruler:** Beatrix **Obv:** Head of Queen Beatrix left **Rev:** Relief map of Western Europe, stars, lines and value

| Date | Mintage | VF20 | XF40 | MS60 | MS63 | MS65 |
|---|---|---|---|---|---|---|
| 2007 | 292,000 | — | — | 1.75 | 2.50 | 3.00 |
| 2007 | 10,000 | PF65 5.00 | | | | |
| 2008 | 363,000 | — | — | 1.75 | 2.75 | 3.50 |
| 2008 | 10,000 | PF65 5.00 | | | | |
| 2009 | 285,000 | — | — | 1.75 | 2.50 | 3.00 |
| 2009 | 7,500 | PF65 5.00 | | | | |
| 2010 | 202,000 | — | — | 1.75 | 2.50 | 3.00 |
| 2010 | 5,000 | PF65 5.00 | | | | |
| 2011 | 220,000 | — | — | 1.75 | 2.50 | 3.00 |
| 2011 | 5,000 | PF65 5.00 | | | | |
| 2012 | — | — | — | 1.75 | 2.50 | 3.00 |
| 2012 | 5,000 | PF65 5.00 | | | | |
| 2013 | — | — | — | 1.75 | 2.50 | 3.00 |
| 2013 | 5,000 | PF65 5.00 | | | | |

**KM# 347 10 EURO CENT**
4.10 g., Brass, 19.7 mm. **Ruler:** Willem-Alexander **Obv:** Head right **Rev:** Relief map of Western Europe, stars, lines and value

| Date | Mintage | VF20 | XF40 | MS60 | MS63 | MS65 |
|---|---|---|---|---|---|---|
| 2014 | 5,000 | PF65 6.00 | | | | |
| 2014 | — | — | — | 1.75 | 2.50 | 3.00 |

**KM# 238 20 EURO CENT**
5.74 g., Brass, 22.2 mm. **Ruler:** Beatrix **Obv:** Head left among stars **Rev:** Value and map **Edge:** Notched

| Date | Mintage | VF20 | XF40 | MS60 | MS63 | MS65 |
|---|---|---|---|---|---|---|
| 2001 | 92,300,000 | — | — | 1.00 | 1.25 | 1.75 |
| 2001 Proof | 16,500 | — | — | — | — | — |
| 2002 | 50,691,000 | — | — | 1.00 | 1.25 | 1.75 |
| 2002 Proof | 16,500 | — | — | — | — | — |
| 2003 | 57,821,000 | — | — | 1.00 | 1.25 | 1.75 |
| 2003 Proof | 13,000 | — | — | — | — | — |
| 2004 | 20,430,000 | — | — | 1.00 | 1.50 | 2.00 |
| 2004 | 5,000 | PF65 8.00 | | | | |
| 2005 | 510,000 | — | — | 2.00 | 3.00 | 3.50 |
| 2005 | 5,000 | PF65 8.00 | | | | |
| 2006 | 393,000 | — | — | 2.00 | 3.00 | 3.50 |
| 2006 | 3,500 | PF65 8.00 | | | | |

**KM# 269 20 EURO CENT**
5.70 g., Brass, 22.2 mm. **Ruler:** Beatrix **Obv:** Head of Queen Beatrix left **Rev:** Relief map of Western Europe, stars, lines and value **Edge:** Notched

| Date | Mintage | VF20 | XF40 | MS60 | MS63 | MS65 |
|---|---|---|---|---|---|---|
| 2007 | 510,000 | — | — | 2.00 | 3.00 | 3.50 |
| 2007 | 10,000 | PF65 7.00 | | | | |
| 2008 | 293,000 | — | — | 2.50 | 3.00 | 3.50 |
| 2008 | 10,000 | PF65 7.00 | | | | |
| 2009 | 363,000 | — | — | 2.00 | 3.00 | 3.50 |
| 2009 | 7,500 | PF65 7.00 | | | | |
| 2010 | 285,000 | — | — | 2.50 | 3.00 | 3.50 |
| 2010 | 5,000 | PF65 7.00 | | | | |
| 2011 | 202,000 | — | — | 2.50 | 3.00 | 3.50 |
| 2011 | 5,000 | PF65 7.00 | | | | |
| 2012 | — | — | — | 2.50 | 3.00 | 3.50 |
| 2012 | 5,000 | PF65 7.00 | | | | |
| 2013 | — | — | — | 2.50 | 3.00 | 3.50 |
| 2013 | 5,000 | PF65 7.00 | | | | |

**KM# 348 20 EURO CENT**
5.70 g., Brass, 22.2 mm. **Ruler:** Willem-Alexander **Obv:** Head right **Rev:** Relief map of Western Europe, stars, lines and value

| Date | Mintage | VF20 | XF40 | MS60 | MS63 | MS65 |
|---|---|---|---|---|---|---|
| 2014 | 5,000 | PF65 8.00 | | | | |
| 2014 | — | — | — | 2.50 | 3.00 | 3.50 |

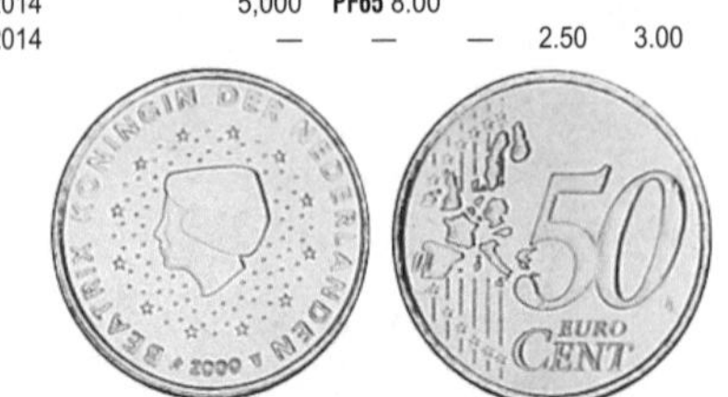

**KM# 239 50 EURO CENT**
7.80 g., Brass, 24.2 mm. **Ruler:** Beatrix **Obv:** Head left among stars **Rev:** Value and map **Edge:** Notched

| Date | Mintage | VF20 | XF40 | MS60 | MS63 | MS65 |
|---|---|---|---|---|---|---|
| 2001 | 87,000,000 | — | — | 1.25 | 1.50 | 2.00 |
| 2001 Proof | 16,500 | — | — | — | — | — |
| 2002 | 80,160,000 | — | — | 1.25 | 1.50 | 2.00 |
| 2002 Proof | 16,500 | — | — | — | — | — |
| 2003 | 810,000 | — | — | 2.00 | 2.50 | 3.00 |
| 2003 Proof | 13,000 | — | — | — | — | — |
| 2004 | 269,000 | — | — | 2.25 | 3.00 | 3.50 |
| 2004 | 5,000 | PF65 10.00 | | | | |
| 2005 | 510,000 | — | — | 2.00 | 2.50 | 3.00 |
| 2005 | 5,964 | PF65 10.00 | | | | |
| 2006 | 363,000 | — | — | 2.00 | 2.50 | 3.00 |
| 2006 | 3,500 | PF65 10.00 | | | | |

**KM# 270 50 EURO CENT**
7.80 g., Brass, 24.2 mm. **Ruler:** Beatrix **Obv:** Head of Quen Beatrix left **Rev:** Relief map of Western Europe, stars, lines and value **Edge:** Notched

| Date | Mintage | VF20 | XF40 | MS60 | MS63 | MS65 |
|---|---|---|---|---|---|---|
| 2006 | — | — | — | 2.00 | 2.75 | 3.50 |
| 2007 | 293,000 | — | — | 2.00 | 2.75 | 3.50 |
| 2007 | 10,000 | PF65 9.00 | | | | |
| 2008 | 263,000 | — | — | 2.00 | 2.75 | 3.50 |
| 2008 | 10,000 | PF65 9.00 | | | | |
| 2009 | 285,000 | — | — | 2.00 | 2.75 | 3.50 |
| 2009 | 7,500 | PF65 9.00 | | | | |
| 2010 | 202,000 | — | — | 2.00 | 2.75 | 3.50 |
| 2010 | 5,000 | PF65 9.00 | | | | |
| 2011 | 220,000 | — | — | 2.00 | 2.75 | 3.50 |
| 2011 | 5,000 | PF65 9.00 | | | | |
| 2012 | — | — | — | 2.00 | 2.75 | 3.50 |
| 2012 | 5,000 | PF65 9.00 | | | | |
| 2013 | — | — | — | 2.00 | 2.75 | 3.50 |
| 2013 | 5,000 | PF65 9.00 | | | | |

**KM# 349 50 EURO CENT**
7.80 g., Brass, 24.2 mm. **Ruler:** Willem-Alexander **Obv:** Head right **Rev:** Relief map of Western Europe, stars, lines and value

| Date | Mintage | VF20 | XF40 | MS60 | MS63 | MS65 |
|---|---|---|---|---|---|---|
| 2014 | 5,000 | PF65 10.00 | | | | |
| 2014 | — | — | — | 2.00 | 2.75 | 3.50 |

**KM# 240 EURO**
7.50 g., Bi-Metallic Copper-Nickel center in Brass ring, 23.2 mm. **Ruler:** Beatrix **Obv:** Half head left within 1/2 circle and star border, name within vertical lines **Rev:** Value and map within circle **Edge:** Segmented reeding

| Date | Mintage | VF20 | XF40 | MS60 | MS63 | MS65 |
|---|---|---|---|---|---|---|
| 2001 | 67,200,000 | — | — | 2.50 | 3.00 | 4.00 |
| 2001 Proof | 16,500 | — | — | — | — | — |
| 2002 | 22,560,000 | — | — | 2.50 | 3.00 | 4.00 |
| 2002 Proof | 16,500 | — | — | — | — | — |
| 2003 | 950,000 | — | — | 3.50 | 4.00 | 4.00 |
| 2003 Proof | 13,000 | — | — | — | — | — |
| 2004 | 235,000 | — | — | 5.00 | 6.00 | 7.00 |
| 2004 | 5,000 | PF65 15.00 | | | | |
| 2005 | 332,000 | — | — | 4.00 | 5.00 | 6.00 |
| 2005 | 5,964 | PF65 15.00 | | | | |
| 2006 | 393,000 | — | — | 4.00 | 5.00 | 6.00 |
| 2006 | 3,500 | PF65 15.00 | | | | |

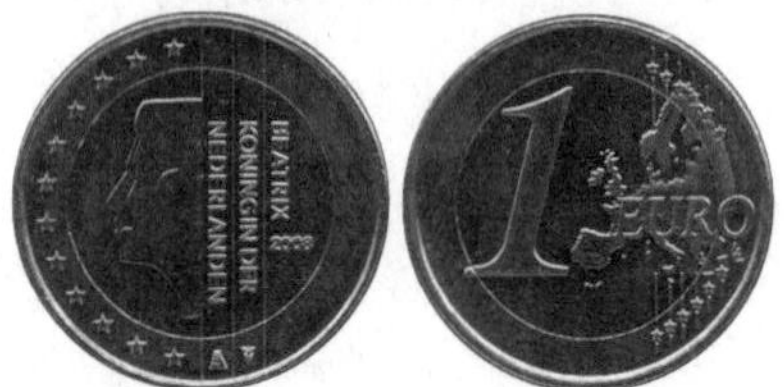

**KM# 271 EURO**
7.50 g., Bi-Metallic Copper-Nickel center in Nickel-Brass ring, 23.25 mm. **Ruler:** Beatrix **Obv:** Queen's profile left **Rev:** Relief map of Western Europe, stars, lines and value **Edge:** Segmented reeding

| Date | Mintage | VF20 | XF40 | MS60 | MS63 | MS65 |
|---|---|---|---|---|---|---|
| 2007 | 224,000 | — | — | 3.50 | 4.00 | 5.00 |
| 2007 | 10,000 | PF65 14.50 | | | | |
| 2008 | 288,000 | — | — | 3.50 | 4.00 | 5.00 |
| 2008 | 10,000 | PF65 14.50 | | | | |
| 2009 | 185,000 | — | — | 3.50 | 4.00 | 5.00 |
| 2009 | 7,500 | PF65 14.50 | | | | |
| 2010 | 166,000 | — | — | 3.50 | 4.00 | 5.00 |
| 2010 | 5,000 | PF65 14.50 | | | | |
| 2011 | 220,000 | — | — | 3.50 | 4.00 | 5.00 |
| 2011 | 5,000 | PF65 14.50 | | | | |
| 2012 | — | — | — | 3.50 | 4.00 | 5.00 |
| 2012 | 5,000 | PF65 14.50 | | | | |
| 2013 | — | — | — | 3.50 | 4.00 | 5.00 |
| 2013 | 5,000 | PF65 14.50 | | | | |

**KM# 350 EURO**
7.50 g., Bi-Metallic Copper-Nickel center in Nickel-Brass ring, 23.25 mm. **Ruler:** Willem-Alexander **Obv:** Head right **Rev:** Relief map of Western Europe, stars, lines and value **Edge:** Segmented reeding

| Date | Mintage | VF20 | XF40 | MS60 | MS63 | MS65 |
|---|---|---|---|---|---|---|
| 2014 | 5,000 | PF65 14.50 | | | | |
| 2014 | — | — | — | 3.50 | 4.00 | 5.00 |

**KM# 241 2 EURO**
8.50 g., Bi-Metallic Nickel-Brass center in Copper-Nickel ring, 25.75 mm. **Ruler:** Beatrix **Obv:** Profile left within 1/2 circle and star border, name within vertical lines **Rev:** Value and map within circle **Edge Lettering:** GOD * ZIJ * MET * ONS *

| Date | Mintage | VF20 | XF40 | MS60 | MS63 | MS65 |
|---|---|---|---|---|---|---|
| 2001 | 116,400,000 | — | — | — | 4.00 | 4.50 |
| 2001 Proof | 16,500 | — | — | — | — | — |
| 2002 | 36,432,000 | — | — | — | 4.50 | 12.00 |
| 2002 Proof | 16,500 | — | — | — | — | — |
| 2003 | 749,000 | — | — | — | 5.50 | 8.00 |
| 2003 Proof | 13,000 | — | — | — | — | — |
| 2004 | 245,000 | — | — | — | 7.00 | 12.00 |
| 2004 | 5,000 | PF65 18.00 | | | | |
| 2005 | 332,000 | — | — | — | 6.00 | 8.00 |
| 2005 | 5,964 | PF65 18.00 | | | | |
| 2006 | 341,000 | — | — | — | 6.00 | 10.00 |
| 2006 | 3,500 | PF65 18.00 | | | | |

**KM# 272 2 EURO**
8.50 g., Bi-Metallic Nickel-Brass center in Copper-Nickel ring, 25.75 mm. **Ruler:** Beatrix **Obv:** Queen's profile left **Rev:** Relief map of Western Europe, stars, lines and value **Edge Lettering:** GOD * ZIJ * MET * ONS *

| Date | Mintage | VF20 | XF40 | MS60 | MS63 | MS65 |
|---|---|---|---|---|---|---|
| 2007 | 345,000 | — | — | — | 6.00 | 8.00 |
| 2007 | 10,000 | PF65 17.50 | | | | |
| 2008 | 288,000 | — | — | — | 6.00 | 8.00 |
| 2008 | 10,000 | PF65 17.50 | | | | |
| 2009 | 225,000 | — | — | — | 6.00 | 8.00 |
| 2009 | 7,500 | PF65 17.50 | | | | |
| 2010 | 166,000 | — | — | — | 6.00 | 8.00 |
| 2010 | 5,000 | PF65 17.50 | | | | |
| 2011 | 220,000 | — | — | — | 6.00 | 8.00 |
| 2011 | 5,000 | PF65 17.50 | | | | |
| 2012 | — | — | — | — | 6.00 | 8.00 |
| 2012 | 5,000 | PF65 17.50 | | | | |
| 2013 | — | — | — | — | 6.00 | 8.00 |
| 2013 | 5,000 | PF65 17.50 | | | | |

**KM# 273 2 EURO**
8.50 g., Bi-Metallic Nickel-Brass center in Copper-Nickel ring, 25.75 mm. **Ruler:** Beatrix **Subject:** 50th Anniversary Treaty of Rome **Obv:** Open treaty book **Rev:** Large value at left, modified outline of Europe at right **Edge Lettering:** GOD * ZU * MET * ONS * **Note:** 15,000 BU coins are in a Benelux set

| Date | Mintage | VF20 | XF40 | MS60 | MS63 | MS65 |
|---|---|---|---|---|---|---|
| 2007 | 6,333,000 | — | — | — | 6.00 | 15.00 |
| 2007 | 10,000 | PF65 22.00 | | | | |

**KM# 282 2 EURO**
8.50 g., Bi-Metallic Nickel-Brass center in Copper-Nickel ring, 25.75 mm. **Ruler:** Beatrix **Subject:** European Monetary Union, 10th Anniversary **Rev:** Stick figure and euro symbol **Edge Lettering:** *GOD *ZIJ *MET *ONS

| Date | Mintage | VF20 | XF40 | MS60 | MS63 | MS65 |
|---|---|---|---|---|---|---|
| 2009 | 5,300,000 | — | — | — | 4.50 | 15.00 |
| 2009 Proof from set | 7,500 | PF65 60.00 | | | | |
| 2009 Proof in box | 2,000 | PF65 160 | | | | |

**KM# 303 2 EURO**
8.50 g., Bi-Metallic Nickel-Brass center in Copper-Nickel ring, 25.75 mm. **Ruler:** Beatrix **Obv:** Beatrix at left, Erasmus writing at right

| Date | Mintage | VF20 | XF40 | MS60 | MS63 | MS65 |
|---|---|---|---|---|---|---|
| 2011 | 4,003,000 | — | — | — | 4.50 | 30.00 |
| 2011 Proof from set | 5,000 | PF65 50.00 | | | | |
| 2011 Proof in box | 2,000 | PF65 140 | | | | |

**KM# 315 2 EURO**
8.50 g., Bi-Metallic Nickel-Brass center in Copper-Nickel ring, 25.75 mm. **Ruler:** Beatrix **Subject:** 10 years of euro-coins **Obv:** Euro symbol on globe, child-like images around

| Date | Mintage | VF20 | XF40 | MS60 | MS63 | MS65 |
|---|---|---|---|---|---|---|
| 2012 | 3,500,000 | — | — | — | 4.50 | — |
| 2012 Special Unc. | 15,000 | — | — | — | — | 15.00 |
| 2012 | — | PF65 25.00 | | | | |

**KM# 324 2 EURO**
8.50 g., Bi-Metallic Nickel-Brass center in Copper-Nickel ring, 25.75 mm. **Ruler:** Willem-Alexander **Subject:** Kingdom, 200th Anniversary **Obv:** Ribbon portrait of seven Dutch rulers **Edge:** Reeded and lettered **Edge Lettering:** GOD * ZIJ * MET * ONS *

| Date | Mintage | VF20 | XF40 | MS60 | MS63 | MS65 |
|---|---|---|---|---|---|---|
| 2013 | 20,000,000 | — | — | — | — | 4.50 |
| 2013 BU card | — | — | — | — | — | 15.00 |
| 2013 | 3,500 | PF65 50.00 | | | | |

**KM# 324a 2 EURO**
8.50 g., Bi-Metallic Nickel-Brass center in Copper-Nickel ring, 25.75 mm. **Ruler:** Willem-Alexander **Subject:** Kingdom, 200th Anniversary **Obv:** Ribbon portrait of seven Dutch rulers, Willem-Alexander's head in orange ribbon; stars in red, white and blue

| Date | Mintage | VF20 | XF40 | MS60 | MS63 | MS65 |
|---|---|---|---|---|---|---|
| 2013 | 1,500 | PF65 75.00 | | | | |

**KM# 332 2 EURO**
8.50 g., Bi-Metallic Nickel-Brass center in Copper-Nickel ring, 25.75 mm. **Ruler:** Willem-Alexander **Subject:** Abdication of Queen Beatrix **Obv:** Beatrix and Willem-Alexander heads left **Edge:** Reeded and lettered **Edge Lettering:** GOD * ZIJ * MET * ONS *

| Date | Mintage | VF20 | XF40 | MS60 | MS63 | MS65 |
|---|---|---|---|---|---|---|
| 2013 | 20,000,000 | — | — | — | — | 4.50 |
| 2013 BU in card | 25,000 | — | — | — | — | 15.00 |
| 2013 | 10,000 | PF65 50.00 | | | | |

**KM# 351 2 EURO**
8.50 g., Bi-Metallic Nickel-Brass center in Copper-Nickel ring, 25.75 mm. **Ruler:** Willem-Alexander **Obv:** Head right **Rev:** Relief map of Western Europe, stars, lines and value **Edge:** Reeded and lettered **Edge Lettering:** GOD * ZUJ * MET * ONS *

| Date | Mintage | VF20 | XF40 | MS60 | MS63 | MS65 |
|---|---|---|---|---|---|---|
| 2014 | 5,000 | PF65 17.50 | | | | |
| 2014 | — | — | — | — | 6.00 | 8.00 |

**KM# 245 5 EURO**
11.90 g., 0.925 Silver 0.3539 oz. ASW, 29 mm. **Ruler:** Beatrix **Subject:** Vincent Van Gogh **Obv:** Head facing **Rev:** Tilted head facing **Edge Lettering:** GOD * ZIJ * MET * ONS *

| Date | Mintage | VF20 | XF40 | MS60 | MS63 | MS65 |
|---|---|---|---|---|---|---|
| ND(2003) | 1,000,000 | — | — | — | 5.00 | 15.00 |
| ND-2003 Prooflike | 100,000 | — | — | — | — | 30.00 |

**KM# 252 5 EURO**
11.90 g., 0.925 Silver 0.3539 oz. ASW **Ruler:** Beatrix **Subject:** New EEC member countries **Obv:** Head left **Rev:** Names of old and new member countries **Edge Lettering:** GOD * ZIJ * MET * ONS *

| Date | Mintage | VF20 | XF40 | MS60 | MS63 | MS65 |
|---|---|---|---|---|---|---|
| 2004 | 600,000 | — | — | — | 5.00 | 17.50 |
| 2004 | 55,000 | PF65 90.00 | | | | |

**KM# 253 5 EURO**
11.90 g., 0.925 Silver 0.3539 oz. ASW **Ruler:** Beatrix **Subject:** 50th Anniversary - End of colonization of Netherlands Antilles **Obv:** Head left **Rev:** Fruit and date within beaded circle **Edge Lettering:** GOD * ZIJ * MET * ONS *

| Date | Mintage | VF20 | XF40 | MS60 | MS63 | MS65 |
|---|---|---|---|---|---|---|
| 2004 | 650,000 | — | — | — | 5.00 | 17.50 |
| 2004 | 26,900 | PF65 45.00 | | | | |

**KM# 254 5 EURO**
11.91 g., 0.925 Silver 0.3542 oz. ASW, 29 mm. **Ruler:** Beatrix **Subject:** 60th Anniversary of Liberation **Obv:** Queen's image **Rev:** Value and dots **Edge Lettering:** GOD * ZIJ * MET * ONS *

| Date | Mintage | VF20 | XF40 | MS60 | MS63 | MS65 |
|---|---|---|---|---|---|---|
| 2005 | 630,000 | — | — | — | 5.00 | 17.50 |
| 2005 | 40,000 | PF65 40.00 | | | | |

**KM# 255 5 EURO**
11.90 g., 0.925 Silver 0.3539 oz. ASW, 29 mm. **Ruler:** Beatrix **Obv:** Queen's silhouette centered on a world globe **Rev:** Value above Australia on a world globe **Edge Lettering:** GOD * ZIJ * MET * ONS *

| Date | Mintage | VF20 | XF40 | MS60 | MS63 | MS65 |
|---|---|---|---|---|---|---|
| 2006 | 500,000 | — | — | — | 5.00 | 17.50 |
| 2006 | 22,500 | PF65 45.00 | | | | |

**KM# 266 5 EURO**
11.90 g., 0.925 Silver 0.3539 oz. ASW, 28.9 mm. **Ruler:** Beatrix **Obv:** Queen Beatrix **Rev:** Rembrandt **Edge Lettering:** GOD * Z IJ * MET * ONS *

| Date | Mintage | VF20 | XF40 | MS60 | MS63 | MS65 |
|---|---|---|---|---|---|---|
| ND(2006) | 655,000 | — | — | — | 5.00 | 17.50 |
| ND-2006 | 35,000 | PF65 35.00 | | | | |

**KM# 267 5 EURO**
11.90 g., 0.925 Silver 0.3539 oz. ASW, 29 mm. **Ruler:** Beatrix **Subject:** Tax Service, 200th Anniversary **Obv:** Queen's portrait **Rev:** Circles with dates 1806-2006 **Edge Lettering:** GOD * ZIJ * MET * ONS *

| Date | Mintage | VF20 | XF40 | MS60 | MS63 | MS65 |
|---|---|---|---|---|---|---|
| 2006 | 359,189 | — | — | — | 5.00 | 17.50 |
| 2006 Prooflike | 40,000 | — | — | — | — | 25.00 |
| 2006 | 15,000 | PF65 60.00 | | | | |

**KM# 277 5 EURO**
11.90 g., 0.925 Silver 0.3539 oz. ASW, 29 mm. **Ruler:** Beatrix **Subject:** Admiral M.A. de Ruyter, 400th Anniversary of Birth **Obv:** Queen's head 1/4 left **Rev:** deRuyter's head 1/4 right **Edge Lettering:** GOD * ZIJ * MET * ONS *

| Date | Mintage | VF20 | XF40 | MS60 | MS63 | MS65 |
|---|---|---|---|---|---|---|
| 2007 | 520,500 | — | — | — | 5.00 | 17.50 |
| 2007 | 17,500 | PF65 40.00 | | | | |

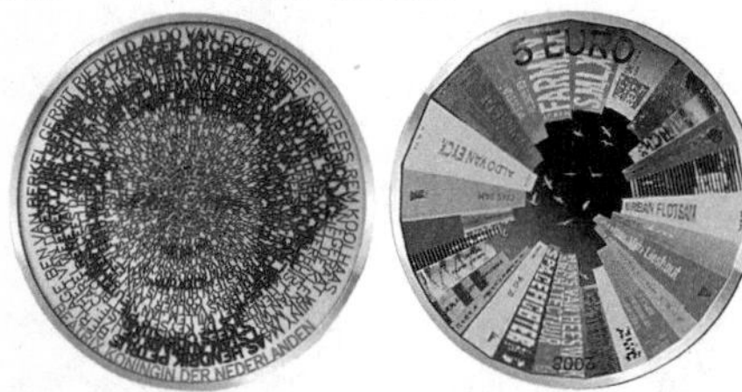

**KM# 279 5 EURO**
10.50 g., Silver Plated Copper, 29 mm. **Ruler:** Beatrix **Subject:** Architecture **Obv:** Portrait facing in names of famous Architects **Rev:** Architecture books around map of the Netherlands

| Date | Mintage | VF20 | XF40 | MS60 | MS63 | MS65 |
|---|---|---|---|---|---|---|
| 2008 | 350,000 | — | — | — | 10.00 | 15.00 |

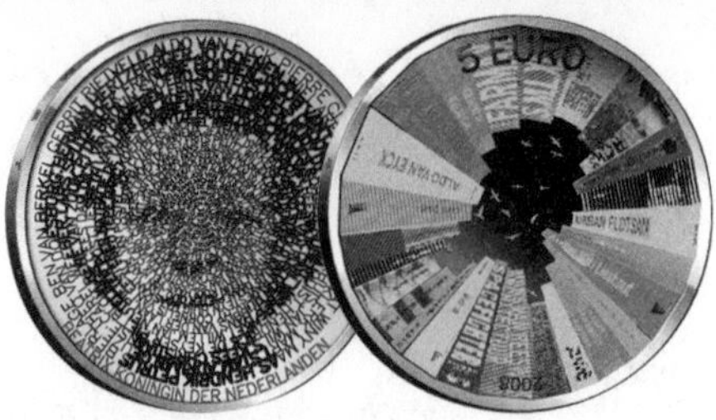

**KM# 280 5 EURO**
15.50 g., 0.925 Silver 0.461 oz. ASW, 33 mm. **Ruler:** Beatrix **Subject:** Architecture **Obv:** Portrait facing in names of famous architects **Rev:** Books around map of the Netherlands **Edge Lettering:** GOD * ZIJ * MET * ONS *

| Date | Mintage | VF20 | XF40 | MS60 | MS63 | MS65 |
|---|---|---|---|---|---|---|
| 2008 | 24,505 | PF65 40.00 | | | | |

**KM# 283 5 EURO**
10.50 g., Silver Plated Copper, 29 mm. **Ruler:** Beatrix **Subject:** Manhattan 400th Anniversary **Obv:** Tip of Manhattan Island today **Rev:** Tip of Manhattan Island in 1609

| Date | Mintage | VF20 | XF40 | MS60 | MS63 | MS65 |
|---|---|---|---|---|---|---|
| 2009 | 303,209 | — | — | — | 10.00 | 15.00 |

**KM# 284 5 EURO**
15.50 g., 0.925 Silver 0.461 oz. ASW, 33 mm. **Ruler:** Beatrix **Subject:** Manhattan 400th Anniversary **Obv:** Bottom tip of Manhattan Island today **Rev:** Bottom tip of Manhattan Island in 1609 **Edge Lettering:** GOD * ZIJ * MET * ONS *

| Date | Mintage | VF20 | XF40 | MS60 | MS63 | MS65 |
|---|---|---|---|---|---|---|
| 2009 | 20,000 | PF65 55.00 | | | | |

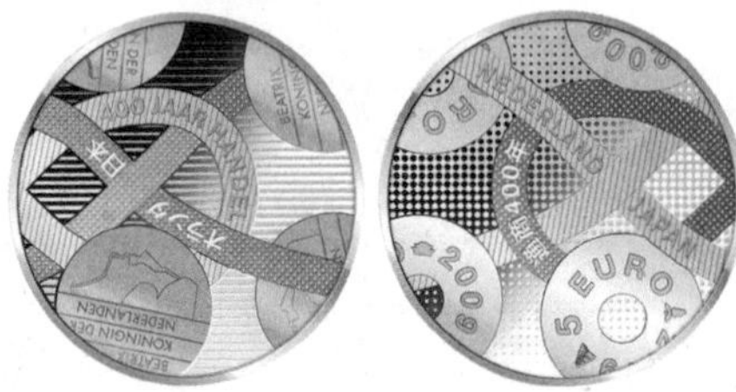

**KM# 289 5 EURO**
10.50 g., Silver Plated Copper, 29 mm. **Ruler:** Beatrix **Subject:** Netherlands-Japanese Friendship **Obv:** Guilder design of 1982 with Queen **Rev:** Value and date

| Date | Mintage | VF20 | XF40 | MS60 | MS63 | MS65 |
|---|---|---|---|---|---|---|
| 2009 | 343,859 | — | — | — | 8.00 | 10.00 |

**KM# 290 5 EURO**
15.50 g., 0.925 Silver 0.461 oz. ASW, 33 mm. **Ruler:** Beatrix **Subject:** Netherlands-Japanese Friendship **Obv:** Guilder design of 1982 with Queen **Rev:** Value and date **Edge Lettering:** GOD * ZIJ * MET * ONS *

| Date | Mintage | VF20 | XF40 | MS60 | MS63 | MS65 |
|---|---|---|---|---|---|---|
| 2009 | 45,000 | PF65 40.00 | | | | |

**KM# 297 5 EURO**
10.50 g., Silver Plated Copper, 29 mm. **Ruler:** Beatrix **Subject:** Max Havelaar, 150th Anniversary of Birth **Obv:** Queen **Rev:** Ink pen, words in spiral, figures walking around edge **Edge Lettering:** GOD * ZIJ * MET * ONS *

| Date | Mintage | VF20 | XF40 | MS60 | MS63 | MS65 |
|---|---|---|---|---|---|---|
| 2010 | 275,010 | — | — | — | 9.00 | 12.00 |

**KM# 298 5 EURO**
11.90 g., 0.925 Silver 0.3539 oz. ASW, 33 mm. **Ruler:** Beatrix **Subject:** Max Havelaar, 150th Anniversary **Obv:** Queen **Rev:** Ink pen, words in spiral, figures walking around edge **Edge Lettering:** GOD * ZIJ * MET * ONS *

| Date | Mintage | VF20 | XF40 | MS60 | MS63 | MS65 |
|---|---|---|---|---|---|---|
| 2010 | 15,000 | PF65 50.00 | | | | |

**KM# 300 5 EURO**
10.50 g., Silver Plated Copper, 29 mm. **Ruler:** Beatrix **Subject:** Waterland **Obv:** Queens bust facing and reflected in water **Rev:** Map of the Netherlands, partily below sea level

| Date | Mintage | VF20 | XF40 | MS60 | MS63 | MS65 |
|---|---|---|---|---|---|---|
| 2010 | 227,500 | — | — | — | — | 10.00 |

**KM# 301 5 EURO**
15.50 g., 0.925 Silver 0.461 oz. ASW, 33 mm. **Ruler:** Beatrix **Subject:** Waterland **Obv:** Queen's bust facing, and reflected in water **Rev:** Map of the Netherlands, partly below sea level

| Date | Mintage | VF20 | XF40 | MS60 | MS63 | MS65 |
|---|---|---|---|---|---|---|
| 2010 | 17,500 | PF65 45.00 | | | | |

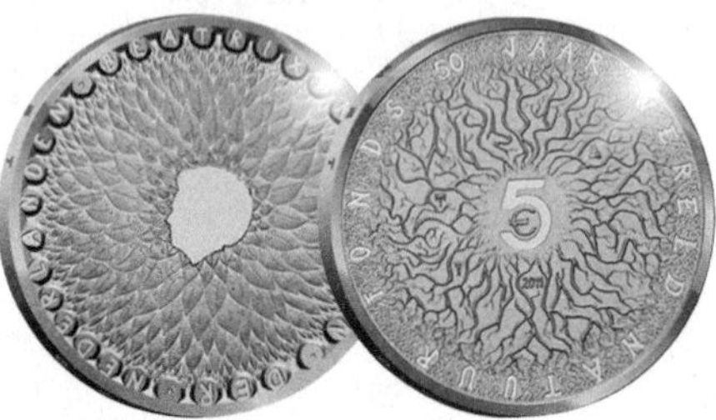

**KM# 304 5 EURO**
15.50 g., 0.925 Silver 0.461 oz. ASW, 33 mm. **Ruler:** Beatrix **Subject:** World Wildlife Fund, 50th Anniversary **Obv:** Profile left at center of tree leaves **Rev:** Value at center of root system **Edge Lettering:** GOD * ZIJ * MET * ONS *

| Date | Mintage | VF20 | XF40 | MS60 | MS63 | MS65 |
|---|---|---|---|---|---|---|
| 2011 | 17,500 | PF65 40.00 | | | | |

**KM# 305 5 EURO**
10.50 g., Silver Plated Copper, 29 mm. **Ruler:** Beatrix **Subject:** World Wildlife Fund, 50th Anniversary **Obv:** Profile head at center of tree leaves **Rev:** Value at center of root system **Edge Lettering:** GOD * ZIJ * MET * ONS *

| Date | Mintage | VF20 | XF40 | MS60 | MS63 | MS65 |
|---|---|---|---|---|---|---|
| 2011 | 250,000 | PF65 10.00 | | | | |

**KM# 307 5 EURO**
10.50 g., Silver Plated Copper, 29 mm. **Ruler:** Beatrix **Subject:** Mint building, 100th Anniversary. **Obv:** Bust facing **Rev:** Screw press and a QR-code which is to scan with a **Edge Lettering:** GOD * ZIJ * MET * ONS *

| Date | Mintage | VF20 | XF40 | MS60 | MS63 | MS65 |
|---|---|---|---|---|---|---|
| 2011 | 71,618 | — | — | — | — | 15.00 |

**KM# 308 5 EURO**
15.50 g., 0.925 Silver 0.461 oz. ASW, 33 mm. **Ruler:** Beatrix **Subject:** Mint building, 100th Anniversary. **Obv:** Bust facing **Rev:** Screw press and a QR-code which is able to be scanned with a mobile telephone **Edge Lettering:** GOD * ZIJ * MET * ONS *

| Date | Mintage | VF20 | XF40 | MS60 | MS63 | MS65 |
|---|---|---|---|---|---|---|
| 2011 | 17,500 | PF65 40.00 | | | | |

**KM# 310 5 EURO**
Silver Plated Copper, 29 mm. **Ruler:** Beatrix **Subject:** Painting **Obv:** Queen looking at city view painting **Rev:** Window **Edge Lettering:** GOD * ZIJ * MET * ONS *

| Date | Mintage | VF20 | XF40 | MS60 | MS63 | MS65 |
|---|---|---|---|---|---|---|
| 2011 | 230,000 | — | — | — | 10.00 | 12.00 |

**KM# 311 5 EURO**
15.50 g., 0.925 Silver 0.461 oz. ASW, 33 mm. **Ruler:** Beatrix **Subject:** Painting **Obv:** Queen looking at city view painting **Rev:** Window **Edge Lettering:** GOD * ZIJ * MET * ONS *

| Date | Mintage | VF20 | XF40 | MS60 | MS63 | MS65 |
|---|---|---|---|---|---|---|
| 2011 | 250,000 | — | — | — | — | 30.00 |
| 2011 | 12,500 | **PF65** 40.00 | | | | |

**KM# 316 5 EURO**
10.50 g., Silver Plated Copper, 29 mm. **Ruler:** Beatrix **Subject:** 400 years of diplomatic relations Netherlands-Turkey **Edge Lettering:** GOD * ZIJ * MET * ONS *

| Date | Mintage | VF20 | XF40 | MS60 | MS63 | MS65 |
|---|---|---|---|---|---|---|
| 2012 | 250,000 | — | — | — | 10.00 | 15.00 |

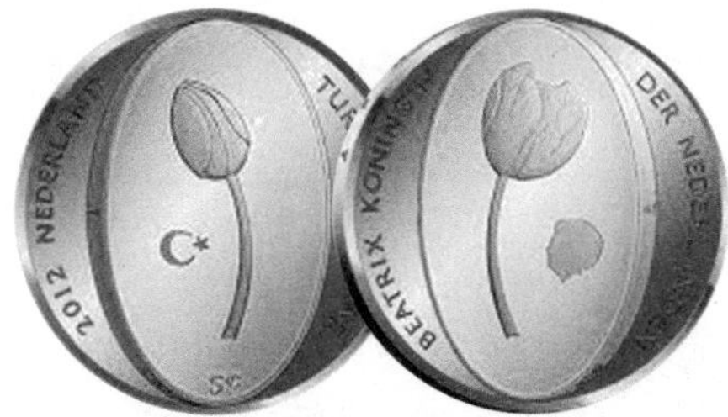

**KM# 317 5 EURO**
15.50 g., 0.925 Silver 0.461 oz. ASW, 33 mm. **Ruler:** Beatrix **Subject:** 400 years of diplomatic relations Netherlands-Turkey **Edge Lettering:** GOD * ZIJ * MET * ONS *

| Date | Mintage | VF20 | XF40 | MS60 | MS63 | MS65 |
|---|---|---|---|---|---|---|
| 2012 | 12,500 | **PF65** 45.00 | | | | |

**KM# 317.1 5 EURO**
15.50 g., 0.925 Silver 0.461 oz. ASW, 33 mm. **Ruler:** Beatrix **Subject:** Netherlands-Turkey diplomatic relations, 400th Anniversary **Rev:** Tulip colored orange

| Date | Mintage | VF20 | XF40 | MS60 | MS63 | MS65 |
|---|---|---|---|---|---|---|
| 2012 | 750 | **PF65** 250 | | | | |

**KM# 317.2 5 EURO**
15.50 g., 0.925 Silver 0.461 oz. ASW, 33 mm. **Ruler:** Beatrix **Rev:** Tulip in red

| Date | Mintage | VF20 | XF40 | MS60 | MS63 | MS65 |
|---|---|---|---|---|---|---|
| 2012 | 750 | **PF65** 250 | | | | |

**KM# 317.3 5 EURO**
15.50 g., 0.925 Silver 0.461 oz. ASW, 33 mm. **Ruler:** Beatrix **Rev:** Tulip in white

| Date | Mintage | VF20 | XF40 | MS60 | MS63 | MS65 |
|---|---|---|---|---|---|---|
| 2012 | 750 | **PF65** 250 | | | | |

**KM# 317.4 5 EURO**
15.50 g., 0.925 Silver 0.461 oz. ASW, 33 mm. **Ruler:** Beatrix **Rev:** Tulip in blue

| Date | Mintage | VF20 | XF40 | MS60 | MS63 | MS65 |
|---|---|---|---|---|---|---|
| 2012 | 750 | **PF65** 250 | | | | |

**KM# 321 5 EURO**
10.50 g., Silver Plated Copper, 29 mm. **Subject:** Amsterdam Canals **Rev:** Hemisphere map with Amsterdam canal map

| Date | Mintage | VF20 | XF40 | MS60 | MS63 | MS65 |
|---|---|---|---|---|---|---|
| 2012 | 218,014 | — | — | — | — | 10.00 |
| 2012 BU in card | 10,000 | — | — | — | — | 25.00 |

**KM# 322 5 EURO**
15.50 g., 0.925 Silver 0.461 oz. ASW, 33 mm. **Subject:** Amsterdam Canal **Rev:** Hemisphere map and map of Amsterdam Canals

| Date | Mintage | VF20 | XF40 | MS60 | MS63 | MS65 |
|---|---|---|---|---|---|---|
| 2012 | 12,500 | **PF65** 60.00 | | | | |

**KM# 327 5 EURO**
10.50 g., Silver Plated Copper, 29 mm. **Ruler:** Beatrix **Subject:** Sculpture

| Date | Mintage | VF20 | XF40 | MS60 | MS63 | MS65 |
|---|---|---|---|---|---|---|
| 2012 | 218,013 | — | — | — | — | 10.00 |
| 2012 BU in card | 10,000 | — | — | — | — | 20.00 |

**KM# 328 5 EURO**
15.50 g., 0.925 Silver 0.461 oz. ASW, 33 mm. **Ruler:** Beatrix **Subject:** Sculpture

| Date | Mintage | VF20 | XF40 | MS60 | MS63 | MS65 |
|---|---|---|---|---|---|---|
| 2012 | 12,500 | **PF65** 50.00 | | | | |

**KM# 325 5 EURO**
10.50 g., Silver Plated Copper, 29 mm. **Ruler:** Willem-Alexander **Subject:** Peace treaty of Utrecht **Obv:** Head of Queen in front of building with 35 feather pens **Rev:** Feathers drawing a globe

| Date | Mintage | VF20 | XF40 | MS60 | MS63 | MS65 |
|---|---|---|---|---|---|---|
| 2013 | 220,000 | — | — | — | — | 10.00 |
| 2013 BU in card | 10,000 | — | — | — | — | 25.00 |

**KM# 326 5 EURO**
15.50 g., 0.925 Silver 0.461 oz. ASW, 33 mm. **Ruler:** Beatrix **Subject:** 1713 Peace Treaty of Utrecht

| Date | Mintage | VF20 | XF40 | MS60 | MS63 | MS65 |
|---|---|---|---|---|---|---|
| 2013 | 6,500 | **PF65** 60.00 | | | | |

**KM# 333 5 EURO**
10.50 g., Silver Plated Copper, 29 mm. **Ruler:** Willem-Alexander **Subject:** Peace Palace in the Hague, 100th Anniversary **Obv:** Head right **Rev:** Two people looking at the Peace Palace

| Date | Mintage | VF20 | XF40 | MS60 | MS63 | MS65 |
|---|---|---|---|---|---|---|
| 2013 | 220,000 | — | — | — | — | 10.00 |
| 2013 BU in card | 10,000 | — | — | — | — | 20.00 |

**KM# 334 5 EURO**
15.50 g., 0.925 Silver 0.461 oz. ASW, 33 mm. **Ruler:** Willem-Alexander **Subject:** Peace Palace at the Hague, 100th Anniversary **Obv:** Head right **Rev:** Two people looking at the Peace Palace

| Date | Mintage | VF20 | XF40 | MS60 | MS63 | MS65 |
|---|---|---|---|---|---|---|
| 2013 | 12,500 | **PF65** 60.00 | | | | |

**KM# 336 5 EURO**
10.50 g., Silver Plated Copper, 29 mm. **Ruler:** Willem-Alexander **Subject:** Rietveld Schroder **Obv:** Head right on Atlantic hemisphere in fingerprint **Rev:** House on Eastern hemisphere fingerprint

| Date | Mintage | VF20 | XF40 | MS60 | MS63 | MS65 |
|---|---|---|---|---|---|---|
| 2013 | 250,000 | — | — | — | — | 10.00 |
| 2013 BU on card | — | — | — | — | — | 25.00 |

**KM# 337 5 EURO**
15.50 g., 0.925 Silver 0.461 oz. ASW, 33 mm. **Ruler:** Willem-Alexander **Subject:** Rietveld Schroder house **Obv:** Head right on Atlantic hemisphere in fingerprint **Rev:** House on Eastern hemisphere in fingerprint

| Date | Mintage | VF20 | XF40 | MS60 | MS63 | MS65 |
|---|---|---|---|---|---|---|
| 2013 | 12,500 | **PF65** 60.00 | | | | |

**KM# 243 10 EURO**
17.80 g., 0.925 Silver 0.5294 oz. ASW, 33 mm. **Ruler:** Beatrix **Subject:** Wedding of Willem-Alexander and Maxima **Obv:** Queen's head left **Rev:** Conjoined busts left **Edge Lettering:** GOD * ZIJ * MET * ONS *

| Date | Mintage | VF20 | XF40 | MS60 | MS63 | MS65 |
|---|---|---|---|---|---|---|
| 2002 | 990,800 | — | — | — | 8.00 | 40.00 |
| 2002 | 80,000 | **PF65** 55.00 | | | | |

**KM# 244 10 EURO**
6.72 g., 0.900 Gold 0.1944 oz. AGW, 22.5 mm. **Ruler:** Beatrix **Subject:** Crown Prince's Wedding **Obv:** Head left **Rev:** Two facing silhouettes **Edge:** Reeded

| Date | Mintage | VF20 | XF40 | MS60 | MS63 | MS65 |
|---|---|---|---|---|---|---|
| 2002 Prooflike | 33,000 | — | — | — | — | 400 |

**KM# 246 10 EURO**
6.72 g., 0.900 Gold 0.1944 oz. AGW, 22.5 mm. **Ruler:** Beatrix **Subject:** Vincent Van Gogh **Obv:** Head facing **Rev:** Tilted head facing **Edge:** Reeded

| Date | Mintage | VF20 | XF40 | MS60 | MS63 | MS65 |
|---|---|---|---|---|---|---|
| ND(2003) Prooflike | 20,000 | — | — | — | — | 400 |

**KM# 247 10 EURO**
6.72 g., 0.900 Gold 0.1944 oz. AGW, 22.5 mm. **Ruler:** Beatrix **Subject:** New EEC members **Obv:** Head left **Rev:** Value and legend **Edge:** Reeded

| Date | Mintage | VF20 | XF40 | MS60 | MS63 | MS65 |
|---|---|---|---|---|---|---|
| 2004 | 6,000 | **PF65** 700 | | | | |

**KM# 248 10 EURO**
17.80 g., 0.925 Silver 0.5294 oz. ASW, 33 mm. **Ruler:** Beatrix **Obv:** Head left **Rev:** Multi-views of Prince Willem-Alexander, Princess Catherina-Amalia and Princess Maxima **Edge Lettering:** GOD * ZIJ * MET * ONS *

| Date | Mintage | VF20 | XF40 | MS60 | MS63 | MS65 |
|---|---|---|---|---|---|---|
| 2004 | 1,000,000 | — | — | — | 8.00 | 25.00 |
| 2004 | 50,000 | **PF65** 40.00 | | | | |

**KM# 251 10 EURO**
6.72 g., 0.900 Gold 0.1944 oz. AGW, 22.5 mm. **Ruler:** Beatrix **Subject:** 50 Years of Domestic Autonomy, 1954-2004 (for Netherlands Antilles) **Obv:** Small head left **Rev:** Fruit and date within beaded circle **Edge:** Reeded

| Date | Mintage | VF20 | XF40 | MS60 | MS63 | MS65 |
|---|---|---|---|---|---|---|
| 2004 | 3,800 | **PF65** 600 | | | | |

**KM# 261 10 EURO**
17.80 g., 0.925 Silver 0.5294 oz. ASW, 33 mm. **Ruler:** Beatrix **Subject:** Silver Jubilee of Reign **Obv:** Queen's photo **Rev:** Queen taking oath photo **Edge Lettering:** GOD * ZIJ * MET * ONS *

| Date | Mintage | VF20 | XF40 | MS60 | MS63 | MS65 |
|---|---|---|---|---|---|---|
| 2005 | 1,000,000 | — | — | — | 8.00 | 25.00 |
| 2005 | 59,754 | PF65 40.00 | | | | |

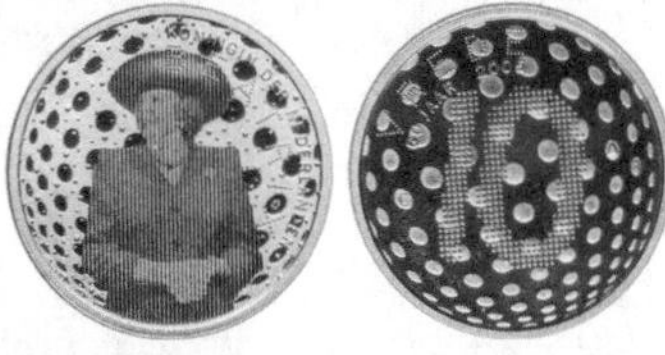

**KM# 264 10 EURO**
6.72 g., 0.900 Gold 0.1944 oz. AGW, 22.5 mm. **Ruler:** Beatrix **Subject:** 60th Anniversary of Liberation **Obv:** Queen and dots **Rev:** Value and dots **Edge:** Reeded

| Date | Mintage | VF20 | XF40 | MS60 | MS63 | MS65 |
|---|---|---|---|---|---|---|
| 2005 | 6,000 | PF65 600 | | | | |

**KM# 292 10 EURO**
6.72 g., 0.900 Gold 0.1944 oz. AGW, 22.5 mm. **Ruler:** Beatrix **Series:** Tax Services, 200th Anniversary **Obv:** Queen's portrait **Rev:** Florin of 1807 **Edge:** Reeded

| Date | Mintage | VF20 | XF40 | MS60 | MS63 | MS65 |
|---|---|---|---|---|---|---|
| 2006 | 5,500 | PF65 600 | | | | |

**KM# 293 10 EURO**
6.72 g., 0.900 Gold 0.1944 oz. AGW, 22.5 mm. **Ruler:** Beatrix **Subject:** Netherlands-Australian Friendship, 400th Anniversary **Obv:** Queens portrait within lines of a globe **Rev:** Australia, value and dates **Edge:** Reeded

| Date | Mintage | VF20 | XF40 | MS60 | MS63 | MS65 |
|---|---|---|---|---|---|---|
| 2006 | 3,500 | PF65 800 | | | | |

**KM# 294 10 EURO**
6.72 g., 0.900 Gold 0.1944 oz. AGW, 22.5 mm. **Ruler:** Beatrix **Subject:** Rembrandt, 400th Anniversary of Birth **Obv:** Queen's portrait **Rev:** Self-portrait **Edge:** Reeded

| Date | Mintage | VF20 | XF40 | MS60 | MS63 | MS65 |
|---|---|---|---|---|---|---|
| 2006 | 8,500 | PF65 400 | | | | |

**KM# 278 10 EURO**
6.72 g., 0.900 Gold 0.1944 oz. AGW, 22.5 mm. **Ruler:** Beatrix **Subject:** Admiral M.A. de Ruyter, 400th Birthday **Obv:** Head 1/4 left **Rev:** Head 1/4 right **Edge:** Reeded

| Date | Mintage | VF20 | XF40 | MS60 | MS63 | MS65 |
|---|---|---|---|---|---|---|
| 2007 | 7,000 | PF65 400 | | | | |

**KM# 281 10 EURO**
6.72 g., 0.900 Gold 0.1944 oz. AGW, 22.5 mm. **Ruler:** Beatrix **Subject:** Architecture **Obv:** Portrait facing in names of famous architects **Rev:** Architecture books around map of the Netherlands **Edge:** Reeded

| Date | Mintage | VF20 | XF40 | MS60 | MS63 | MS65 |
|---|---|---|---|---|---|---|
| 2008 | 8,000 | PF65 400 | | | | |

**KM# 285 10 EURO**
6.72 g., 0.900 Gold 0.1944 oz. AGW, 22.5 mm. **Ruler:** Beatrix **Subject:** Dutch settlement of Manhattan, NY 400th Anniversary **Obv:** Bottom tip of Manhattan Island today **Rev:** Bottom tip of Manhattan Island in 1609 **Edge:** Reeded

| Date | Mintage | VF20 | XF40 | MS60 | MS63 | MS65 |
|---|---|---|---|---|---|---|
| 2009 | 6,500 | PF65 400 | | | | |

**KM# 291 10 EURO**
6.72 g., 0.900 Gold 0.1944 oz. AGW, 22.5 mm. **Ruler:** Beatrix **Subject:** Netherlands-Japanese Friendship **Obv:** Guilder design of 1982 with Queen **Rev:** Value and date **Edge:** Reeded

| Date | Mintage | VF20 | XF40 | MS60 | MS63 | MS65 |
|---|---|---|---|---|---|---|
| 2009 | 5,418 | PF65 400 | | | | |

**KM# 299 10 EURO**
6.72 g., 0.900 Gold 0.1944 oz. AGW, 22.5 mm. **Ruler:** Beatrix **Subject:** Max Havelaar, 150th Anniversary of Birth **Rev:** Ink pen, words in spiral, firgures walking around edge **Edge:** Reeded

| Date | Mintage | VF20 | XF40 | MS60 | MS63 | MS65 |
|---|---|---|---|---|---|---|
| 2010 | 4,699 | PF65 400 | | | | |

**KM# 302 10 EURO**
6.72 g., 0.900 Gold 0.1944 oz. AGW, 22.5 mm. **Ruler:** Beatrix **Subject:** Waterland **Obv:** Bust of Queen facing and reflected in water **Rev:** Map of the Netherlands, partly under sea level

| Date | Mintage | VF20 | XF40 | MS60 | MS63 | MS65 |
|---|---|---|---|---|---|---|
| 2010 | 4,500 | PF65 400 | | | | |

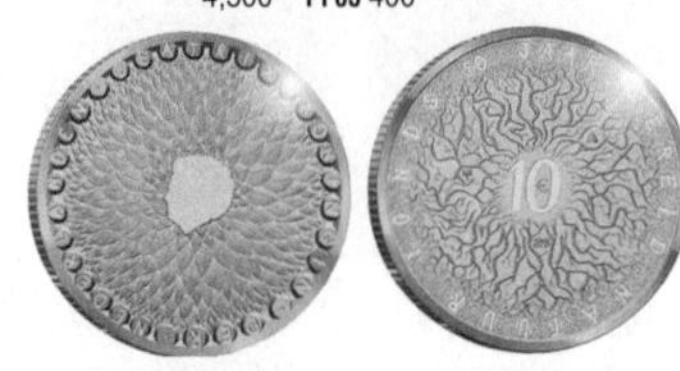

**KM# 306 10 EURO**
6.72 g., 0.900 Gold 0.1944 oz. AGW, 22.5 mm. **Ruler:** Beatrix **Subject:** World Wildlife Fund, 50th Anniversary **Obv:** Profile left at center of tree leaves **Rev:** Value at center of root system **Edge:** Reeded

| Date | Mintage | VF20 | XF40 | MS60 | MS63 | MS65 |
|---|---|---|---|---|---|---|
| 2011 | 4,000 | PF65 400 | | | | |

**KM# 309 10 EURO**
6.75 g., 0.900 Gold 0.1953 oz. AGW, 22.5 mm. **Ruler:** Beatrix **Obv:** Head facing **Rev:** Screw press and a QR-code which is able to be scanned with a mobile telephone **Edge:** Reeded

| Date | Mintage | VF20 | XF40 | MS60 | MS63 | MS65 |
|---|---|---|---|---|---|---|
| 2011 | 4,000 | PF65 400 | | | | |

**KM# 312 10 EURO**
6.72 g., 0.900 Gold 0.1944 oz. AGW, 22.5 mm. **Ruler:** Beatrix **Subject:** Painting **Obv:** Queen looking at city view painting **Rev:** Window **Edge:** Reeded

| Date | Mintage | VF20 | XF40 | MS60 | MS63 | MS65 |
|---|---|---|---|---|---|---|
| 2011 | 3,500 | PF65 400 | | | | |

**KM# 318 10 EURO**
6.72 g., 0.900 Gold 0.1944 oz. AGW, 22.5 mm. **Ruler:** Beatrix **Subject:** 400 years of diplomatic relations Netherlands-Turkey **Edge:** Reeded

| Date | Mintage | VF20 | XF40 | MS60 | MS63 | MS65 |
|---|---|---|---|---|---|---|
| 2012 | — | PF65 400 | | | | |

**KM# 323 10 EURO**
6.72 g., 0.900 Gold 0.1944 oz. AGW, 22.5 mm. **Ruler:** Beatrix **Subject:** Amsterdam Canals **Obv:** Hemisphere map with fingerprint design **Rev:** Hemisphere map and map of Amsterdam canals

| Date | Mintage | VF20 | XF40 | MS60 | MS63 | MS65 |
|---|---|---|---|---|---|---|
| 2012 | 2,000 | PF65 500 | | | | |

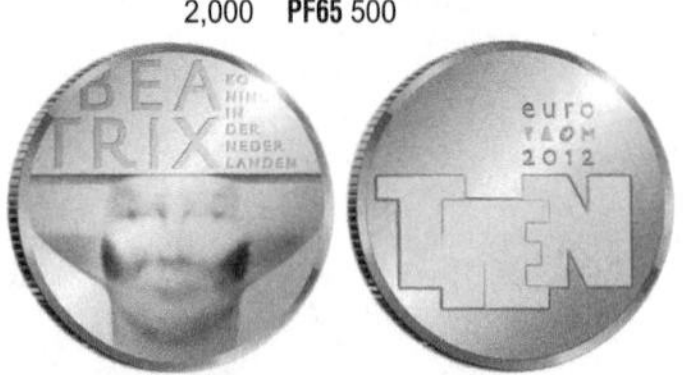


**KM# 329 10 EURO**
6.72 g., 0.900 Gold 0.1944 oz. AGW, 22.5 mm. **Ruler:** Beatrix **Subject:** Sculpture **Obv:** Head facing **Edge:** Reeded

| Date | Mintage | VF20 | XF40 | MS60 | MS63 | MS65 |
|---|---|---|---|---|---|---|
| 2012 | 2,000 | PF65 500 | | | | |

**KM# 330 10 EURO**
6.72 g., 0.900 Gold 0.1944 oz. AGW, 22.5 mm. **Ruler:** Beatrix **Subject:** Peace treaty of Utrecht **Obv:** Head of Queen in front of building with 35 featherpens **Rev:** Feathers drawing a globe and in center, shield of Utrecht **Edge:** Reeded

| Date | Mintage | VF20 | XF40 | MS60 | MS63 | MS65 |
|---|---|---|---|---|---|---|
| 2013 | 2,000 | PF65 500 | | | | |

**KM# 335 10 EURO**
6.72 g., 0.900 Gold 0.1944 oz. AGW, 22.5 mm. **Ruler:** Willem-Alexander **Subject:** Peace Palace in the Hague, 100th Anniversary

| Date | Mintage | VF20 | XF40 | MS60 | MS63 | MS65 |
|---|---|---|---|---|---|---|
| 2013 | 2,000 | PF65 500 | | | | |

**KM# 338 10 EURO**
6.72 g., 0.900 Gold 0.1944 oz. AGW, 22.5 mm. **Ruler:** Willem-Alexander **Subject:** Rietveld Schroder house **Obv:** Head right on Atlantic hemisphere in fingerprint **Rev:** House on Eastern hemisphere in fingerprint

| Date | Mintage | VF20 | XF40 | MS60 | MS63 | MS65 |
|---|---|---|---|---|---|---|
| 2013 | 2,000 | PF65 500 | | | | |

**KM# 339 10 EURO**
15.50 g., Silver Plated Copper, 33 mm. **Ruler:** Willem-Alexander **Rev:** Crowd looking toward King

| Date | Mintage | VF20 | XF40 | MS60 | MS63 | MS65 |
|---|---|---|---|---|---|---|
| 2013 | 400,000 | — | — | — | — | 20.00 |
| 2013 BU in card | 10,000 | — | — | — | — | 35.00 |

**KM# 340 10 EURO**
15.50 g., 0.900 Silver 0.4485 oz. ASW, 38 mm. **Ruler:** Willem-Alexander **Rev:** Crowd looking toward King

| Date | Mintage | VF20 | XF40 | MS60 | MS63 | MS65 |
|---|---|---|---|---|---|---|
| 2013 | 12,500 | PF65 70.00 | | | | |

**KM# 249 20 EURO**
8.50 g., 0.900 Gold 0.246 oz. AGW, 25 mm. **Ruler:** Beatrix **Subject:** Birth of Crown-Princess - Catharina-Amalia - July 12, 2003 **Obv:** Bust left **Rev:** Holographic images: left, Princess Maxima; front, Princess Catharina-Amalia; right, Prince Willem-Alexander **Edge:** Reeded

| Date | Mintage | VF20 | XF40 | MS60 | MS63 | MS65 |
|---|---|---|---|---|---|---|
| 2004 | 5,345 | PF65 530 | | | | |

**KM# 262 20 EURO**
8.50 g., 0.900 Gold 0.246 oz. AGW, 25 mm. **Ruler:** Beatrix **Subject:** Silver Jubilee of Reign **Obv:** Queen's photo **Rev:** Queen taking oath photo **Edge:** Reeded

| Date | Mintage | VF20 | XF40 | MS60 | MS63 | MS65 |
|---|---|---|---|---|---|---|
| 2005 | 5,001 | PF65 530 | | | | |

**KM# 341 20 EURO**
8.50 g., 0.900 Gold 0.246 oz. AGW, 25 mm. **Ruler:** Willem-Alexander **Rev:** Crowd looking toward king

| Date | Mintage | VF20 | XF40 | MS60 | MS63 | MS65 |
|---|---|---|---|---|---|---|
| 2013 | 2,500 | PF65 700 | | | | |

**KM# 250 50 EURO**
13.44 g., 0.900 Gold 0.3889 oz. AGW, 27 mm. **Ruler:** Beatrix **Subject:** Birth of Crown-Princess - Catharina-Amalia - July 12, 2003 **Obv:** Bust left **Rev:** Holographic images: left, Princess Maxima; front, Princess Catharina-Amalia; right, Prince Willem-Alexander **Edge:** Reeded

| Date | Mintage | VF20 | XF40 | MS60 | MS63 | MS65 |
|---|---|---|---|---|---|---|
| 2004 | 3,500 | PF65 775 | | | | |

**KM# 263 50 EURO**
13.44 g., 0.900 Gold 0.3889 oz. AGW, 27 mm. **Ruler:** Beatrix **Subject:** Silver Jubilee of Reign **Obv:** Queen's photo **Rev:** Queen taking oath photo **Edge:** Reeded

| Date | Mintage | VF20 | XF40 | MS60 | MS63 | MS65 |
|---|---|---|---|---|---|---|
| 2005 | 3,500 | PF65 775 | | | | |

**KM# 342 50 EURO**
13.44 g., 0.900 Gold 0.3889 oz. AGW, 27 mm. **Ruler:** Willem-Alexander **Rev:** Crowd looking toward king

| Date | Mintage | VF20 | XF40 | MS60 | MS63 | MS65 |
|---|---|---|---|---|---|---|
| 2013 | 1,000 | PF65 1,000 | | | | |

## TRADE COINAGE

**KM# 190.2 DUCAT**
3.49 g., 0.983 Gold 0.1104 oz. AGW **Ruler:** Beatrix **Obv:** Knight divides date with larger letters in legend **Rev:** Inscription within decorated square

| Date | Mintage | VF20 | XF40 | MS60 | MS63 | MS65 |
|---|---|---|---|---|---|---|
| 2001 | — | PF65 250 | | | | |
| 2002 | — | PF65 250 | | | | |
| 2003 | 3,800 | PF65 250 | | | | |
| 2004 | 2,120 | PF65 450 | | | | |
| 2005 | 2,243 | PF65 200 | | | | |
| 2006 | 2,097 | PF65 300 | | | | |
| 2007 | 2,250 | PF65 250 | | | | |
| 2008 | 3,260 | PF65 250 | | | | |
| 2009 | 2,750 | PF65 250 | | | | |
| 2010 | 1,870 | PF65 250 | | | | |
| 2011 | — | PF65 250 | | | | |
| 2012 | — | PF65 250 | | | | |

**KM# 211 2 DUCAT**
6.99 g., 0.983 Gold 0.2208 oz. AGW, 26 mm. **Ruler:** Beatrix **Obv:** Knight divides date within beaded circle **Rev:** Inscription within decorated square

| Date | Mintage | VF20 | XF40 | MS60 | MS63 | MS65 |
|---|---|---|---|---|---|---|
| 2002 B | 6,650 | PF65 475 | | | | |
| 2003 B | 4,500 | PF65 475 | | | | |
| 2004 B | 2,015 | PF65 475 | | | | |
| 2005 B | 3,500 | PF65 475 | | | | |
| 2006 B | 1,800 | PF65 550 | | | | |
| 2007 B | 2,000 | PF65 475 | | | | |
| 2008 B | 2,100 | PF65 475 | | | | |
| 2009 B | 2,000 | PF65 475 | | | | |
| 2010 B | 2,000 | PF65 475 | | | | |
| 2011 B | 1,640 | PF65 500 | | | | |
| 2012 B | — | PF65 500 | | | | |
| 2013 B | — | PF65 500 | | | | |

## SILVER BULLION COINAGE

**KM# 242 SILVER DUCAT**
28.25 g., 0.873 Silver 0.7929 oz. ASW, 40 mm. **Ruler:** Beatrix **Obv:** Crowned shield **Rev:** Armored knight with sword divides date and circle, shield in front **Edge:** Reeded **Note:** Utrecht coin design circa 1659 based on KM#48.

| Date | Mintage | VF20 | XF40 | MS60 | MS63 | MS65 |
|---|---|---|---|---|---|---|
| 2001 B | 9,000 | PF65 40.00 | | | | |

**KM# 256 SILVER DUCAT**
28.25 g., 0.873 Silver 0.7929 oz. ASW, 40 mm. **Ruler:** Beatrix **Obv:** Crowned shield **Rev:** Armored knight with Gelderland arms **Edge:** Reeded

| Date | Mintage | VF20 | XF40 | MS60 | MS63 | MS65 |
|---|---|---|---|---|---|---|
| 2002 B | 9,400 | PF65 40.00 | | | | |

**KM# 257 SILVER DUCAT**
28.25 g., 0.873 Silver 0.7929 oz. ASW, 40 mm. **Ruler:** Beatrix **Obv:** Crowned shield **Rev:** Armored knight with sword holding arms of Holland **Edge:** Reeded

| Date | Mintage | VF20 | XF40 | MS60 | MS63 | MS65 |
|---|---|---|---|---|---|---|
| 2003 B | 4,100 | PF65 50.00 | | | | |

**KM# 258 SILVER DUCAT**
28.25 g., 0.873 Silver 0.7929 oz. ASW, 40 mm. **Ruler:** Beatrix **Obv:** Crowned shield **Rev:** Armored knight holding sword with Zeeland arms **Edge:** Reeded

| Date | Mintage | VF20 | XF40 | MS60 | MS63 | MS65 |
|---|---|---|---|---|---|---|
| 2004 B | 4,109 | PF65 50.00 | | | | |

**KM# 259 SILVER DUCAT**
28.25 g., 0.873 Silver 0.7929 oz. ASW, 40 mm. **Ruler:** Beatrix **Obv:** Crowned shield **Rev:** Armored knight holding sword with Friesland arms **Edge:** Reeded

| Date | Mintage | VF20 | XF40 | MS60 | MS63 | MS65 |
|---|---|---|---|---|---|---|
| 2005 B | 4,000 | PF65 50.00 | | | | |

**KM# 260 SILVER DUCAT**
28.25 g., 0.873 Silver 0.7929 oz. ASW, 40 mm. **Ruler:** Beatrix **Obv:** Crowned shield **Rev:** Armored knight holding sword with Groningen arms **Edge:** Reeded

| Date | Mintage | VF20 | XF40 | MS60 | MS63 | MS65 |
|---|---|---|---|---|---|---|
| 2006 B | 4,000 | PF65 50.00 | | | | |

**KM# 275 SILVER DUCAT**
28.25 g., 0.873 Silver 0.7929 oz. ASW, 40 mm. **Ruler:** Beatrix **Obv:** Crowned shield **Rev:** Armored knight holding sword with Overyssel arms **Edge:** Reeded

| Date | Mintage | VF20 | XF40 | MS60 | MS63 | MS65 |
|---|---|---|---|---|---|---|
| 2007 | 3,500 | PF65 45.00 | | | | |

**KM# 295 SILVER DUCAT**
28.25 g., 0.873 Silver 0.7929 oz. ASW, 40 mm. **Ruler:** Beatrix **Subject:** Northern Brabant **Obv:** Crowned shield **Rev:** John I, Count of Brabant standing with shield **Edge:** Reeded

| Date | Mintage | VF20 | XF40 | MS60 | MS63 | MS65 |
|---|---|---|---|---|---|---|
| 2008 | 3,000 | PF65 50.00 | | | | |

**KM# 286 SILVER DUCAT**
28.25 g., 0.873 Silver 0.7929 oz. ASW, 40 mm. **Ruler:** Beatrix **Rev:** Jan I standing with sword and Gelderland arms

| Date | Mintage | VF20 | XF40 | MS60 | MS63 | MS65 |
|---|---|---|---|---|---|---|
| 2009 | 3,000 | PF65 50.00 | | | | |

**KM# 296 SILVER DUCAT**
28.25 g., 0.873 Silver 0.7929 oz. ASW, 40 mm. **Ruler:** Beatrix **Subject:** Limburg **Obv:** Crowned shield **Rev:** Philip II of Montmorency, Count of Horne, standing **Edge:** Reeded

| Date | Mintage | VF20 | XF40 | MS60 | MS63 | MS65 |
|---|---|---|---|---|---|---|
| 2009 | 3,500 | PF65 50.00 | | | | |

### KM# 287 SILVER DUCAT

28.25 g., 0.875 Silver 0.7947 oz. ASW, 40 mm. **Ruler:** Beatrix **Obv:** William of Orange standing with Zuid-Holland arms **Edge:** Reeded

| Date | Mintage | VF20 | XF40 | MS60 | MS63 | MS65 |
|---|---|---|---|---|---|---|
| 2010 | 2,850 | PF65 50.00 | | | | |

### KM# 288 SILVER DUCAT

28.25 g., 0.875 Silver 0.7947 oz. ASW, 40 mm. **Ruler:** Beatrix **Obv:** Frederik Hendrik standing with Gelderland arms **Edge:** Reeded

| Date | Mintage | VF20 | XF40 | MS60 | MS63 | MS65 |
|---|---|---|---|---|---|---|
| 2010 | 3,100 | PF65 50.00 | | | | |

### KM# 313 SILVER DUCAT

28.25 g., 0.873 Silver 0.7929 oz. ASW, 40 mm. **Ruler:** Beatrix **Obv:** Crowned shield **Rev:** Floris V **Edge:** Reeded

| Date | Mintage | VF20 | XF40 | MS60 | MS63 | MS65 |
|---|---|---|---|---|---|---|
| 2011 | — | PF65 50.00 | | | | |

### KM# 314 SILVER DUCAT

28.25 g., 0.875 Silver 0.7947 oz. ASW, 40 mm. **Ruler:** Beatrix **Subject:** Zeeland **Obv:** Crowned shield **Rev:** Michiel de Ruyter with shield of Zeeland **Edge:** Reeded

| Date | Mintage | VF20 | XF40 | MS60 | MS63 | MS65 |
|---|---|---|---|---|---|---|
| 2011 | — | PF65 50.00 | | | | |

### KM# 319 SILVER DUCAT

28.25 g., 0.875 Silver 0.7947 oz. ASW, 40 mm. **Ruler:** Beatrix **Subject:** Utrecht **Obv:** Crowned shield **Rev:** Stadtholder Willem III with shield of Utrecht **Edge:** Reeded

| Date | Mintage | VF20 | XF40 | MS60 | MS63 | MS65 |
|---|---|---|---|---|---|---|
| 2012 | — | PF65 60.00 | | | | |

### KM# 320 SILVER DUCAT

28.25 g., 0.875 Silver 0.7947 oz. ASW, 40 mm. **Ruler:** Beatrix **Subject:** Friesland **Obv:** Crowned shield **Rev:** Willem Lodewijk van Nassau - Dillenbrug with shield of Friesland **Edge:** Reeded

| Date | Mintage | VF20 | XF40 | MS60 | MS63 | MS65 |
|---|---|---|---|---|---|---|
| 2012 | — | PF65 60.00 | | | | |

### KM# 331 SILVER DUCAT

28.25 g., 0.875 Silver 0.7947 oz. ASW, 40 mm. **Ruler:** Beatrix **Subject:** Overijssel

| Date | Mintage | VF20 | XF40 | MS60 | MS63 | MS65 |
|---|---|---|---|---|---|---|
| 2013 | — | PF65 60.00 | | | | |

### KM# 343 SILVER DUCAT

28.25 g., 0.875 Silver 0.7947 oz. ASW, 40 mm. **Ruler:** Willem-Alexander **Subject:** Groningen **Edge:** Reeded

| Date | Mintage | VF20 | XF40 | MS60 | MS63 | MS65 |
|---|---|---|---|---|---|---|
| 2013 | — | PF65 60.00 | | | | |

### KM# 352 SILVER DUCAT

28.25 g., 0.875 Silver 0.7947 oz. ASW, 40 mm. **Ruler:** Willem-Alexander **Subject:** Friesland **Edge:** Reeded

| Date | Mintage | F12 | VF20 | XF40 | MS60 | MS63 |
|---|---|---|---|---|---|---|
| 2014 | — | PF65 60.00 | | | | |

## PATTERNS

Including off metal strikes

| KM# | Date | Mintage | Identification | Mkt Val |
|---|---|---|---|---|
| Pn164 | 2001 | — | Gulden Nickel Medal rotation | — |
| Pn165 | 2001 | — | 2 Euro Cent Nickel | 100 |
| Pn166 | 2001 | — | Euro Brass KM240 | 150 |

## MINT SETS

| KM# | Date | Mintage | Identification | Issue Price | Mkt Val |
|---|---|---|---|---|---|
| MS5 | 2001 (6) | 85,000 | KM#202-206, 210 | 12.00 | 25.00 |
| MS6 | 2001 (8) | 68,000 | KM#234-241 Charity set, disabled sport | 15.00 | 17.00 |
| MS7 | 2001 (6) | 120,000 | KM#202-206, 210 Introduction Euro-coins, no medal | 15.00 | 25.00 |
| MS8 | 2001 (6) | 1,000 | KM#202-206, 210 BOLEGO-VOK | — | 60.00 |
| MS9 | 2001 (6) | 1,000 | KM#202-206, 210 De Akerendam II, with a silver 2 stuiver coin from the wreck | 125 | 145 |
| MS10 | 2001 (6) | 1,000 | KM#202-206, 210 United Seven Provinces Groningen | 40.00 | 40.00 |
| MS11 | 2001 (6) | 1,000 | KM#202-206, 210 United Seven Provinces Utrecht | 40.00 | 40.00 |
| MS12 | 2001 (6) | 21,000 | KM#202-206, 210 Baby set + bear medal | 15.50 | 25.00 |
| MS13 | 2001 (6) | 1,015 | KM#202-206, 210 Onderlinge "s-Grdevenhage | — | 70.00 |
| MS14 | 2002 (8) | 105,000 | KM#234-241 Charity set, blind escort dogs fund | 15.00 | 30.00 |
| MS15 | 2002 (8) | 59,500 | KM#234-241 Last FDS-set | 15.00 | 30.00 |
| MS16 | 2002 (8) | 25,000 | KM#234-241 Baby set + bear medal | 15.50 | 30.00 |
| MS17 | 2002 (8) | 10,000 | KM#234-241 Wedding-set + medal | 15.50 | 35.00 |
| MS18 | 2002 (8) | 3,500 | KM#234-241 Queen Beatrix + medal | 20.00 | 110 |
| MS19 | 2002 (8) | 2,002 | KM#234-241 10th day of the Mint + medal | 22.00 | 175 |
| MS20 | 2002 (8) | 10,000 | KM#234-241 VOC set I + medal | 22.00 | 35.00 |
| MS21 | 2002 (8) | 10,000 | KM#234-241 VOC set II + medal | 22.00 | 30.00 |
| MS22 | 2002 (8) | 10,000 | KM#234-241 VOC set III + medal | 22.00 | 30.00 |
| MS23 | 2002 (8) | 10,000 | KM#234-241 VOC set IV + medal | 22.00 | 30.00 |
| MS24 | 2002 (8) | 3,000 | KM#234-241 BVC + medal | 30.00 | 40.00 |
| MS25 | 2002 (8) | 9,200 | KM#234-241 10 Euro + poststamp | 30.00 | 30.00 |
| MS26 | 2002 (8) | 2,500 | KM#234-241VVV-Iris gift set | 20.00 | 40.00 |
| MS27 | 2002 (8) | 1,000 | KM#234-241 Theo Peters (Christmas) + medal | 99.00 | 90.00 |
| MS28 | 2003 (8) | 75,000 | KM#234-241 Charity set, epilepsy fund | 15.50 | 25.00 |
| MS29 | 2003 (8) | 15,000 | KM#234-241 Information set Denmark | 20.00 | 40.00 |
| MS30 | 2003 (8) | 10,000 | KM#234-241 VVV-Iris gift set | 20.00 | 25.00 |
| MS31 | 2003 (8) | 10,000 | KM#234-241 VOC set V + medal | 22.00 | 25.00 |
| MS32 | 2003 (8) | 10,000 | KM#234-241 VOC set VI + medal | 42.00 | 45.00 |
| MS33 | 2003 (8) | 2,003 | KM#234-241 Day of the mint + medal | 25.00 | 140 |
| MS34 | 2003 (8) | 1,000 | KM#234-241 Theo Peters jubilee set + bi-colour medal | — | 30.00 |
| MS35 | 2003 (8) | 100 | KM#234-241 Theo Peters jubilee set + silver medal | 70.00 | 70.00 |
| MS36 | 2003 (8) | 25 | KM#234-241 Theo Peters jubilee set + golden medal | 400 | 410 |
| MS37 | 2003 (8) | 25,000 | KM#234-241 Baby set + bear medal | 20.00 | 25.00 |
| MS38 | 2003 (8) | 15,000 | KM#234-241 Wedding-set + medal | 20.00 | 25.00 |
| MS39 | 2003 (8) | 1,000 | KM#234-241 Theo Peters Christmas set + bi-colour medal | — | 30.00 |
| MS40 | 2003 (8) | 150 | KM#234-241 Theo Peters Christmas set + silver medal | 70.00 | 70.00 |
| MS41 | 2003 (8) | 50 | KM#234-241 Theo Peters Christmas set + golden medal | 400 | 1,000 |
| MS42 | 2003 (8) | 3,500 | KM#234-241 Mint masters I + medal | 20.00 | 60.00 |
| MS43 | 2003 (8) | 1,000 | KM#234-241 World Money Fair Basel | 20.00 | 130 |
| MS44 | 2003 (8) | 15,000 | KM#234-241 Information set Hungaria | 20.00 | 40.00 |
| MS45 | 2003 (8) | 20,000 | KM#234-241 Royal birthset of Princess Catharina-Amalia December 7 + silver medal | 22.00 | 25.00 |
| MS46 | 2003 (8) | 10,000 | KM#234-241 Benelux set, with Belgium (8) KM#224-231 and Luxembourg (8) KM#75-81 | 40.00 | 45.00 |
| MS47 | 2003 (8) | 10,000 | KM#234-241 Charles V set + medal, with Germany (8) KM#207-214, Spain (8) KM#1040-1047, Belgium (8) KM#224-231, and Austria (8) KM#3082-3089 | 85.00 | 85.00 |

| KM# | Date | Mintage | Identification | Issue Price | Mkt Val |
|---|---|---|---|---|---|
| MS48 | 2004 (8) | 3,500 | KM#234-241 Mint-masters II + medal | 20.00 | 60.00 |
| MS49 | 2004 (8) | 10,000 | KM#234-241 Wedding-set + medal | 18.00 | 30.00 |
| MS50 | 2004 (8) | 20,000 | KM#234-241 Baby set + bear medal | 20.00 | 30.00 |
| MS51 | 2004 (8) | 1,000 | KM#234-241 World Money Fair Basel | 20.00 | 110 |
| MS52 | 2004 (8) | 35,000 | KM#234-241 Benelux: Belgium, Netherlands + Luxembourg. With silver medal | 60.00 | 60.00 |
| MS53 | 2004 (8) | 10,000 | KM#234-241 Queen Juliana-set + silver guilder KM#184 and 30mm silver medal | 25.00 | 30.00 |
| MS54 | 2004 (8) | 1,500 | KM#234-241 Theo Peters Christmas set + bi-colour medal | 30.00 | 30.00 |
| MS55 | 2004 (8) | 3,500 | KME234-241 VVV-Iris gift set | 30.00 | 25.00 |
| MS56 | 2004 (8) | 150 | KM#234-241 Theo Peters Christmas set + silver medal | 100 | 100 |
| MS57 | 2004 (8) | 50 | KM#234-241 Theo Peters Christmas set + golden medal | 500 | 500 |
| MS58 | 2004 (8) | 50,000 | KM#234-241 Charity set, Fire-burn Centre | 18.00 | 30.00 |
| MS59 | 2004 (8) | 2,004 | KM#234-241 Day of the Mint + medal | 25.00 | 150 |
| MS60 | 2005 (8) | 3,500 | KM#234-241 Mint-masters III + medal | 20.00 | 60.00 |
| MS61 | 2005 (8) | 2,005 | KM#234-241 Day of the Mint + medal | 25.00 | 150 |
| MS62 | 2005 (8) | 10,000 | KM#234-241 Wedding-set + medal | 18.00 | 27.50 |
| MS63 | 2005 (8) | 20,000 | KM#234-241 Baby set + bear medal | 20.00 | 27.50 |
| MS64 | 2005 (8) | 20,000 | KM#234-241 Nijntje-set (Dick Bruna) + medal | 18.00 | 27.50 |
| MS65 | 2005 (8) | 55,000 | KM#234-241 Charity set: Princess Beatrix Fonds | 18.00 | 27.50 |
| MS66 | 2005 (8) | 20,000 | KM#234-241 Beneluz: Belgium, Netherlands + Luxembourg. With silver medal | 60.00 | 60.00 |
| MS67 | 2005 (8) | 1,000 | KM#234-241 World Money Fair Basel | 25.00 | 110 |
| MS68 | 2005 (8) | 15,000 | KM#234-241 60th Anniversary Libera-tion + Canadian 25 ct | 35.00 | 35.00 |
| MS69 | 2005 (8) | 1,000 | KM#234-241 Theo Peters Christmas set + bi-colour medal | 30.00 | 30.00 |
| MS70 | 2005 (8) | 100 | KM#234-241 Theo Peters Christmas set + silver medal | 120 | 120 |
| MS71 | 2005 (8) | 25 | KM#234-241 Theo Peters Christmas set + golden medal | 550 | 550 |
| MS72 | 2006 (8) | 3,500 | KM#234-241 Mint-masters IV + medal | 20.00 | 40.00 |
| MS73 | 2006 (8) | 4,000 | KM#234-241 5 sets with a Rembrandt silver medal and one set with the Rem-brandt 5 euro coin | 250 | 250 |
| MS74 | 2006 (8) | 500 | KM#234-241 5 sets with a Rembrandt silver medal and one set with the Rem-brandt 10 euro coin | 900 | 900 |
| MS75 | 2006 (8) | 45,000 | KM#234-241 Charity set: (Kika) | 18.00 | 30.00 |
| MS76 | 2006 (8) | 2,750 | KM#234-241 Baby set boy + bear medal | 20.00 | 30.00 |
| MS77 | 2006 (8) | 100 | KM#234-241 Baby set boy + silver medal | — | 95.00 |
| MS78 | 2006 (8) | 25 | KM#234-241 Baby set boy + gold medal | — | 500 |
| MS79 | 2006 (8) | 2,750 | KM#234-241 Baby set girl + bear medal | 20.00 | 30.00 |
| MS80 | 2006 (8) | 100 | KM#234-241 Baby set girl + silver medal | — | 95.00 |
| MS81 | 2006 (8) | 25 | KM#234-241 Baby set girl + gold medal | — | 500 |
| MS82 | 2006 (8) | 15,000 | KM#234-241 Beneluz: Belgium, Netherlands + Luxembourg. With silver medal | 65.00 | 65.00 |
| MS83 | 2006 (8) | 1,050 | KM#234-241 Wedding-set + medal | 22.00 | 30.00 |
| MS84 | 2006 (8) | 1,500 | KM#234-241 Christmas set Royal Dutch Mint | 30.00 | 30.00 |
| MS85 | 2006 (8) | 600 | KM#234-241 Theo Peters Christmas set + bi-colour medal | 35.00 | 40.00 |
| MS86 | 2006 (8) | 100 | KM#234-241 Christmas set + silver medal | 150 | 150 |
| MS87 | 2006 (8) | 25 | KM#234-241 Christ-mas set + golden medal | 650 | 650 |
| MS88 | 2006 (8) | 1,000 | KM#234-241 Berlin Coin Fair | 25.00 | 45.00 |
| MS89 | 2006 (8) | 2,006 | KM#234-241 Day of the Mint + medal | 25.00 | 120 |
| MS90 | 2006 (8) | 10,000 | KM#234-241 200 years coins in King-dom Holland | 25.00 | 30.00 |
| MS91 | 2006 (8) | 3,500 | KM#234-236, 268-272 Mintmasters V + medal | 20.00 | 40.00 |
| MS92 | 2007 (8) | 100 | KM#234-236, 268-272 Mintmasters V + silver medal | — | 600 |
| MS93 | 2007 (8) | 3,500 | KM#234-236, 268-272 5 sets Michiel de Ruyter + silver medal and one set with the Michiel de Ruyter 5 euro coin BU | 250 | 250 |
| MS94 | 2007 (8) | 500 | KM#234-236, 268-272 5 sets Michiel de Ruyter + silver medal and one set with the Michiel de Ruyter 10 euro coin | 900 | 900 |
| MS95 | 2007 (8) | 40,000 | KM#234-236, 268-272 Charity set | 18.00 | 27.50 |
| MS96 | 2007 (8) | 3,000 | KM#234-236, 268-272 Baby set boy + bear medal | 20.00 | 27.50 |
| MS96 | 2007 (8) | 100 | KM#234-236, 268-272 Baby set boy + silver medal | — | 95.00 |
| MS97 | 2007 (8) | 3,000 | KM#234-236, 268-272 Baby set girl + bear medal | 20.00 | 27.50 |
| MS98 | 2007 (8) | 100 | KM#234-236, 268-272 Baby set girl + silver medal | — | 95.00 |
| MS99 | 2007 (8) | 15,000 | KM#234-236, 268-272 Benelux: Belgium, Netherlands + Luxembourg. With silver medal + 3x 2 Euro Rome Treaty | 75.00 | 75.00 |
| MS100 | 2007 (8) | 1,050 | KM#234-236, 268-272 Wedding-set + medal | 22.00 | 27.50 |
| MS101 | 2007 (8) | 1,000 | KM#234-236, 268-272 Christmas set + bi-colour medal | 35.00 | 40.00 |
| MS102 | 2007 (8) | 100 | KM#234-236, 268-272 Christmas set + silver medal | 150 | 150 |
| MS103 | 2007 (8) | 25 | KM#234-236, 268-272 Christmas set + golden medal | 650 | 650 |
| MS104 | 2007 (8) | 500 | KM#234-236, 268-272 Berlin Coin Fair | 25.00 | 90.00 |
| MS105 | 2007 (8) | 2,007 | KM#234-236, 268-272 Day of the Mint + medal | 25.00 | 100 |
| MS106 | 2007 (8) | 5,000 | KM#234-236, 268-272 200 years of Royal predicate | 25.00 | 28.00 |
| MS110 | 2008 (8) | 3,500 | KM#234-236, 268-272 Mintmasters VI + medal | 20.00 | 40.00 |
| MS111 | 2008 (8) | 100 | KM#234-236, 268-272 Mintmasters VI + silver medal | 20.00 | 500 |
| MS112 | 2008 (8) | 40,000 | KM#234-236, 268-272 National set | 20.00 | 27.50 |
| MS113 | 2008 (8) | 2,500 | KM#234-236, 268-272 Baby set boy + bear medal | 25.00 | 27.50 |
| MS114 | 2008 (8) | 100 | KM#234-236, 268-272 Baby set boy + silver medal | 65.00 | 65.00 |
| MS115 | 2008 (8) | 2,500 | KM#234-236, 268-272 Baby set girl + bear medal | 25.00 | 27.50 |
| MS116 | 2008 (8) | 100 | KM#234-236, 268-272 Baby set girl + silver medal | 65.00 | 65.00 |
| MS117 | 2008 (8) | 12,500 | KM#234-236, 268-272 Benelux: Belgium, Netherlands + Luxembourg. With silver medal | 75.00 | 75.00 |
| MS118 | 2008 (8) | 1,250 | KM#234-236, 268-272 Wedding-set + medal | 22.00 | 27.50 |
| MS119 | 2008 (8) | 500 | KM#234-236, 268-272 Christmas set + bi-colour medal | 35.00 | 40.00 |
| MS120 | 2008 (8) | 50 | KM#234-236, 268-272 Christmas set + silver medal | 130 | 135 |
| MS121 | 2008 (8) | 25 | KM#234-236, 268-272 Christmas set + golden medal | 850 | 850 |
| MS122 | 2008 (8) | 500 | KM#234-236, 268-272 Berlin Coin Fair | 25.00 | 75.00 |
| MS123 | 2008 (8) | 2,008 | KM#234-236, 268-272 Day of the Mint + medal | 25.00 | 80.00 |
| MS124 | 2008 (8) | 5,000 | KM#234-236, 268-272 150 year Queen Emma + silver medal | 32.00 | 35.00 |
| MS125 | 2008 (8) | 500 | KM#234-236, 268-272 Theo Peters Jubilation set + bi-colour medal | 35.00 | 40.00 |
| MS126 | 2008 (8) | 50 | KM#234-236, 268-272 Theo Peters Jubilation set + silver medal | 130 | 135 |
| MS127 | 2008 (8) | 25 | KM#234-236, 268-272 Theo Peters Jubilation set + golden medal | 850 | 850 |
| MS128 | 2008 (8) | 500 | KM#234-236, 268-272 5 sets "2 centuries Amsterdam capitol of the Netherlands" + gold plated silver medals and one set with the golden Arctecture 10 euro coin | 900 | 1,000 |
| MS129 | 2009 (8) | 3,500 | KM#234-236, 268-272 Mintmasters VII + medal | 22.00 | 40.00 |
| MS130 | 2009 (8) | 100 | KM#234-236, 268-272 Mintmasters VII + silver medal | 22.00 | 500 |
| MS131 | 2009 (8) | 35,000 | KM#234-236, 268-272 National set | 20.00 | 27.50 |
| MS132 | 2009 (8) | 2,500 | KM#234-236, 268-272 Baby set boy + bear medal | 25.00 | 27.50 |
| MS133 | 2009 (8) | 250 | KM#234-236, 268-272 Baby set boy + silver medal | 65.00 | 65.00 |
| MS134 | 2009 (8) | 2,500 | KM#234-236, 268-272 Baby set girl + bear medal | 25.00 | 27.50 |
| MS135 | 2009 (8) | 250 | KM#234-236, 268-272 Baby set girl + silver medal | 65.00 | 65.00 |
| MS136 | 2009 (8) | 12,500 | KM#234-236, 268-272 Benelux: Belgium, Netherlands + Luxembourg. With silver medal | 75.00 | 75.00 |
| MS137 | 2009 (8) | 1,250 | KM#234-236, 268-272 Wedding-set + medal | 22.00 | 27.50 |
| MS138 | 2009 (8) | 500 | KM#234-236, 268-272 Christmas set + bi-colour medal | 35.00 | 40.00 |
| MS139 | 2009 (8) | 500 | KM#234-236, 268-272 Berlin Coin Fair | 25.00 | 95.00 |
| MS140 | 2009 (8) | 2,009 | KM#234-236, 268-272 | 25.00 | 80.00 |
| MS141 | 2009 (8) | 5,000 | KM#234-236, 268-272 100 year anniv. Queen Juliana + silver medal | 32.00 | 35.00 |
| MS142 | 2009 (8) | 1,000 | KM#234-236, 268-272 Mercedes jubileum (2010) | — | 65.00 |
| MS143 | 2009 (8) | 500 | KM#234-236, 268-272 Tokyo Coin Fair | — | 375 |
| MS144 | 2010 (8) | 3,500 | KM#234-236, 268-272 Museum coin treasures 1 + medal | 22.00 | 40.00 |

| KM# | Date | Mintage | Identification | Issue Price | Mkt Val |
|---|---|---|---|---|---|
| MS145 | 2010 (8) | 100 | KM#234-236, 268-272 Museum coin treasures 1 + silver medal | 22.00 | 500 |
| MS146 | 2010 (8) | 25,000 | KM#234-236, 268-272 National set | 20.00 | 27.50 |
| MS147 | 2010 (8) | 2,000 | KM#234-236, 268-272 Baby set boy + bear medal | 30.00 | 30.00 |
| MS148 | 2010 (8) | 250 | KM#234-236, 268-272 Baby set boy + silver medal | 75.00 | 75.00 |
| MS150 | 2010 (8) | 250 | KM#234-236, 268-272 Baby set girl + silver medal | 75.00 | 75.00 |
| MS151 | 2010 (8) | 12,500 | KM#234-236, 268-262 Benelux: Belgium, Netherlands + Luxembourg. With silver medal | 75.00 | 75.00 |
| MS152 | 2010 (8) | 1,000 | KM#234-236, 268-272 Wedding-set + medal | 22.00 | 27.50 |
| MS153 | 2010 (8) | 500 | KM#234-236, 268-272 Christmas set + bi-colour medal | 40.00 | 40.00 |
| MS154 | 2010 (8) | 500 | KM#234-236, 268-272 Berlin Coin Fair | 25.00 | 95.00 |
| MS155 | 2010 (8) | 2,010 | KM#234-236, 268-272 Day of the Mint + medal | 25.00 | 80.00 |
| MS156 | 2010 (8) | 5,000 | KM#234-236, 268-272 30th anniv. Reign Queen Beatrix + silver medal | 40.00 | 40.00 |
| MS157 | 2011 (8) | 3,500 | KM#234-236, 268-272 Museum coin treasures 2 + medal | 30.00 | 40.00 |
| MS158 | 2011 (8) | 100 | KM#234-236, 268-272 Museum coin treasures 2 + silver medal | 30.00 | 500 |
| MS159 | 2011 (8) | 25,000 | KM#234-236, 268-272 National set | 30.00 | 30.00 |
| MS160 | 2011 (8) | 5,000 | KM#234-236, 268-272 Birth set + bear medal | 30.00 | 30.00 |
| MS161 | 2011 (8) | 1,250 | KM#234-236, 268-272 Baby set boy + bear medal | 30.00 | 30.00 |
| MS162 | 2011 (8) | 100 | KM#234-236, 268-272 Baby set boy + silver medal | 80.00 | 80.00 |
| MS163 | 2011 (8) | 2,000 | KM#234-236, 268-272 Baby set girl + bear medal | 30.00 | 30.00 |
| MS164 | 2011 (8) | 100 | KM#234-236, 268-272 Baby set girl + silver medal | 80.00 | 80.00 |
| MS165 | 2011 (8) | 10,000 | KM#234-236, 268-272 Beneluz: Belgium, Netherlands + Luxembourg. With silver medal | 75.00 | 75.00 |
| MS166 | 2011 (8) | 750 | KM#234-236, 268-272 Wedding set + medal | 30.00 | 30.00 |
| MS167 | 2011 (8) | 400 | KM#234-236, 268-272 Christmas set + bi-colour medal | 45.00 | 45.00 |
| MS168 | 2011 (9) | 400 | KM#234-236, 268-272, 298 Christmas set + bi-colour medal | 65.00 | 65.00 |
| MS169 | 2011 (8) | 500 | KM#234-236, 268-272 Berlin Coin Fair | 25.00 | 95.00 |
| MS170 | 2011 (8) | 2,011 | KM#234-236, 268-272 100th anniv. Bith Prince Bernhard + silver medal | 25.00 | 80.00 |
| MS171 | 2011 (8) | 5,000 | KM#234-236, 268-272 100th anniv. Bith Prince Bernhard + silver medal | 45.00 | 45.00 |
| MS172 | 2012 (8) | — | KM#234-236, 268-272 Museum coin treasures 2 + medal | 30.00 | 40.00 |
| MS173 | 2012 (8) | — | KM#234-236, 268-272 Museum coin treasures 2 + silver medal | 30.00 | 500 |
| MS174 | 2012 (8) | — | KM#234-236, 268-272 National set | 30.00 | 30.00 |
| MS175 | 2012 (8) | — | KM#234-236, 268-272 Birth set + bear medal | 30.00 | 30.00 |
| MS176 | 2012 (8) | — | KM#234-236, 268-272 Baby set boy + bear medal | 30.00 | 30.00 |
| MS177 | 2012 (8) | — | KM#234-236, 268-272 Baby set boy + silver medal | 80.00 | 80.00 |
| MS178 | 2012 (8) | — | KM#234-236, 268-272 Baby set girl + bear medal | 30.00 | 30.00 |
| MS179 | 2012 (8) | — | KM#234-236, 268-272 Baby set girl + silver medal | 80.00 | 80.00 |
| MS180 | 2012 (8) | — | KM#234-236, 268-272 Benelux: Belgium Netherlands + Luxembourg. With silver medal | 75.00 | 75.00 |
| MS181 | 2012 (8) | — | KM#234-236, 268-272 Berlin Coin Fair | 25.00 | 95.00 |

## PROOF SETS

| KM# | Date | Mintage | Identification | Issue Price | Mkt Val |
|---|---|---|---|---|---|
| PS54 | 2001 (7) | 17,000 | KM#202-207, 210 Booklet 5 guilder | 50.00 | 110 |
| PS55 | 2001 (2) | 500 | KM#190.2, 242 Gold + silver ducat | — | 220 |
| PS56 | 2002 (2) | — | KM#190.2, 211 Golden ducats | — | 650 |
| PS58 | 2003 (2) | — | KM#190.2, 211 Golden ducats in wooden box | 230 | 650 |
| PS59 | 2003 (8) | 2,000 | KM#234-241 Frigateship "The Netherland" + silver medal and numbered ingot. "Mintmaster Set" in wooden box | 125 | 125 |
| PS66 | 2002 (3) | — | KM#190.2, 211, 256 Golden ducats + silver ducat | — | 665 |
| PS68 | 2004 (8) | 5,000 | KM#234-241 Proof-set in wooden box | 60.00 | 90.00 |
| PS69 | 2005 (8) | 5,000 | KM#234-241 Proof-set in wooden box | 60.00 | 90.00 |
| PS70 | 2005 (2) | 2,500 | KM#254, 264 60 years of freedom | — | 550 |
| PS71 | 2006 (8) | 3,500 | KM#234-241, Proof-set in wooden box | — | 90.00 |
| PS72 | 2006 (1) | — | 5 Euro KM#255, Australian $5 | 90.00 | 110 |
| PS73 | 2006 (1) | — | 5 Euro KM#255, 10 Euro, Australian $5 and $10 | — | 650 |
| PS74 | 2007 (9) | 10,000 | KM#234-236, 268-272, 273 | — | 90.00 |
| PS75 | 2008 (8) | 10,000 | KM#234-236, 268-272 | — | 65.00 |
| PS77 | 2004 (8) | 1,000 | KM#234-241 Value transport over sea during the eighty year of war + silver medal and numbered ingot. "Mintmaster Set" in wooden box | 125 | 125 |
| PS78 | 2005 (8) | 1,000 | KM#234-241 Value transport over sea 1650-1750 + silver medal and numbered ingot. "Mintmaster Set" in wooden box | 125 | 125 |
| PS79 | 2006 (8) | 1,500 | KM#234-241 Plus silver medal and numbered ingot. "Mintmaster Set" in wooden box | 125 | 125 |
| PS80 | 2009 (1) | 2,000 | KM281 EMU | 25.00 | 150 |
| PS81 | 2009 (9) | 7,500 | KM234-236, 268-272, 281 | — | 65.00 |
| PS82 | 2010 (8) | 5,000 | KM234-236, 268-272 | — | 60.00 |
| PS83 | 2011 (1) | 1,500 | KM298 Erasmus | 30.00 | 140 |
| PS84 | 2011 (9) | 5,000 | KM234-236, 268-272, 298 | — | 100 |
| PS88 | 2004 (8) | 10,000 | KM#234-241 | — | 70.00 |
| PS89 | 2005 (8) | 10,000 | KM#234-241 | — | 70.00 |
| PS89 | 2005 (8) | 10,000 | KM#234-241 | — | 70.00 |
| PS83 | 2011 (1) | 1,500 | KM298 Erasmus | 30.00 | 140 |
| PS84 | 2011 (9) | 5,000 | KM234-236, 268-272, 298 | — | 100 |
| PS85 | 2009 (9) | 7,500 | KM234-236, 268-272, 281 | — | 65.00 |
| PS86 | 2010 (8) | 5,000 | KM234-236, 268-272 | — | 60.00 |
| PS88 | 2004 (8) | 10,000 | KM#234-241 | — | 70.00 |
| PS89 | 2005 (8) | 10,000 | KM#234-241 | — | 70.00 |

## PROOF-LIKE SETS (PL)

| KM# | Date | Mintage | Identification | Issue Price | Mkt Val |
|---|---|---|---|---|---|
| PL3 | 2001 (8) | 16,500 | KM#234-241 | 50.00 | 40.00 |
| PL4 | 2002 (2) | — | KM#243, 244 Wedding set (10 Euro in silver and gold) in plastic box | 145 | 400 |
| PL5 | 2002 (2) | — | KM#243, 244 Wedding set in wooden box | 145 | 400 |
| PL6 | 2002 (8) | 15,500 | KM#234-241 | 50.00 | 40.00 |
| PL7 | 2003 (8) | 10,000 | KM#234-241 | 50.00 | 40.00 |
| PL12 | 2001 (8) | 16,500 | KM#234-241 | 50.00 | 40.00 |
| PL13 | 2002 (2) | — | KM#243-244 Wedding set (10 Euro silver and gold) in plastic box | 145 | 400 |
| PL14 | 2002 (2) | — | KM#243-244 Wedding set in wooden box | 145 | 400 |
| PL15 | 2002 (8) | 16,500 | KM#234-241 | 50.00 | 40.00 |
| PL16 | 2003 (8) | 16,500 | KM#234-241 | 50.00 | 40.00 |

## SELECT SETS (FLEUR DE COIN)

| KM# | Date | Mintage | Identification | Issue Price | Mkt Val |
|---|---|---|---|---|---|
| SS90 | 2001 (6) | 120,000 | KM#202-206, 210 Introduction to Euro Coins | 15.00 | 25.00 |
| SS91 | 2001 (6) | 3,400 | KM#202-206, 210 Queen Julianna Medal | 17.50 | 30.00 |
| SS92 | 2001 (6) | 100 | KM#202-206, 210 Queen Julianna Medal; some coins dated 2000 in error | 17.50 | 150 |
| SS93 | 2001 (6) | 1,000 | KM#202-206, 210 BOLEGO - VOK | — | 120 |
| SS94 | 2001 (6) | 1,000 | KM#202-206, 210, 2 Stuiver coin from the wreck of the De Akerendam II | 125 | 120 |
| SS95 | 2001 (6) | 1,000 | KM#202-206, 210 United Provinces, Groningen Medal | 40.00 | 20.00 |
| SS96 | 2001 (6) | 21,000 | KM#202-206, 210 Baby set plus bear medal | 15.50 | 25.00 |
| SS97 | 2001 (6) | 1,015 | KM#202-206, 210 Onderlinge "'s-Gravenhage" | 70.00 | 250 |

## SPECIMEN FDC SETS (FLEUR DE COIN)

| KM# | Date | Mintage | Identification | Issue Price | Mkt Val |
|---|---|---|---|---|---|
| SS95A | 2001 (6) | 1,000 | KM202-206, 210 United Provinces, Utrecht Medal | 40.00 | 40.00 |

# NETHERLANDS ANTILLES

The Netherlands Antilles, comprises two groups of islands in the West Indies: Aruba (until 1986), Bonaire and Curacao and their dependencies near the Venezuelan coast and St. Eustatius, Saba, and the southern part of St. Martin (St. Maarten) southeast of Puerto Rico. The island group has an area of 371 sq. mi. (960 sq. km.) and a population of 225,000. Capital: Willemstad. Chief industries are the refining of crude oil and tourism. Petroleum products and phosphates are exported.

**RULERS**

Beatrix, 1980-2013
William Alexander, 2013-

**Utrecht Mint**
**(privy marks only)**

| Date | Privy Mark |
|---|---|
| 2001 | Wine tendril with grapes |
| 2002 | Wine tendril with grapes and star |
| 2003 | Sails of a clipper |

**MONETARY SYSTEM**

100 Cents = 1 Gulden

# DUTCH ADMINISTRATION

## DECIMAL COINAGE

### KM# 32 CENT

0.70 g., Aluminum, 14 mm. **Ruler:** Beatrix **Obv:** Orange blossom within circle **Rev:** Value within circle of geometric designed border **Edge:** Reeded

| Date | Mintage | VF20 | XF40 | MS60 | MS63 | MS65 |
|---|---|---|---|---|---|---|
| 2001 (u) | 12,806,500 | — | 0.10 | 0.15 | 0.25 | 0.50 |
| 2002 (u) In sets only | 6,000 | — | — | — | — | 2.00 |
| 2003 (u) | 19,604,000 | — | 0.10 | 0.30 | 0.60 | 1.50 |
| 2004 (u) In sets only | 7,100 | — | — | — | — | 1.50 |
| 2005 (u) | 22,404,000 | — | 0.10 | 0.30 | 0.60 | 1.50 |
| 2006 (u) | 110,000 | — | 0.10 | 0.30 | 0.60 | 1.50 |
| 2007 (u) | 5,000 | — | 0.10 | 0.30 | 0.60 | 1.50 |
| 2008 (u) | 16,742,000 | — | 0.10 | 0.30 | 0.60 | 1.50 |
| 2009 (u) In sets only | 2,000 | — | — | — | — | 1.50 |
| 2010 (u) In sets only | 2,000 | — | — | — | — | 1.50 |
| 2011 (u) In sets only | 2,000 | — | — | — | — | 1.50 |
| 2012 (u) | 8,282,000 | — | 0.10 | 0.30 | 0.60 | 1.50 |

### KM# 33 5 CENTS

1.16 g., Aluminum, 16 mm. **Ruler:** Beatrix **Obv:** Orange blossom within circle **Rev:** Value within circle, geometric designed border **Edge:** Reeded

| Date | Mintage | VF20 | XF40 | MS60 | MS63 | MS65 |
|---|---|---|---|---|---|---|
| 2001 | 2,006,500 | — | 0.20 | 0.30 | 0.60 | 1.25 |
| 2002 In sets only | 6,000 | — | — | — | — | 2.50 |
| 2003 | 3,104,000 | — | 0.30 | 0.40 | 0.60 | 1.25 |
| 2004 | 2,402,100 | — | 0.30 | 0.35 | 0.50 | 1.25 |
| 2005 | 1,609,000 | — | 0.30 | 0.35 | 0.50 | 1.50 |
| 2006 | 1,602,000 | — | 0.30 | 0.35 | 0.50 | 1.50 |
| 2007 In sets only | 2,000 | — | 0.30 | 0.35 | 0.50 | 1.50 |
| 2008 | 3,602,000 | — | 0.30 | 0.35 | 0.50 | 1.50 |
| 2009 | 1,052,000 | — | 0.30 | 0.35 | 0.50 | 1.50 |
| 2010 | 337,000 | — | 0.30 | 0.35 | 0.50 | 1.50 |
| 2011 In sets only | 2,000 | — | — | — | — | 1.50 |
| 2012 | 20,202,000 | — | 0.30 | 0.35 | 0.50 | 1.50 |
| 2013 (u) In sets only | 2,000 | — | — | — | — | 3.00 |

### KM# 34 10 CENTS

3.00 g., Nickel Bonded Steel, 18 mm. **Ruler:** Beatrix **Obv:** Orange blossom within circle **Rev:** Value within circle, geometric designed border **Edge:** Reeded

| Date | Mintage | VF20 | XF40 | MS60 | MS63 | MS65 |
|---|---|---|---|---|---|---|
| 2001 In sets only | 11,500 | — | — | — | — | 3.00 |
| 2002 In sets only | 6,000 | — | — | — | — | 3.00 |
| 2003 | 2,104,000 | — | 0.50 | 0.65 | 1.00 | 1.75 |
| 2004 | 2,202,100 | — | 0.50 | 0.65 | 1.00 | 1.75 |
| 2005 | 1,410,000 | — | 0.50 | 0.65 | 1.00 | 1.75 |
| 2006 | 1,402,000 | — | 0.50 | 0.65 | 1.00 | 1.75 |
| 2007 | 202,000 | — | 0.50 | 0.65 | 1.00 | 1.75 |
| 2008 | 3,872,000 | — | 0.50 | 0.65 | 1.00 | 1.75 |
| 2009 | 1,112,000 | — | 0.50 | 0.65 | 1.00 | 1.75 |
| 2010 | 2,402,000 | — | 0.50 | 0.65 | 1.00 | 1.75 |
| 2011 | 2,000 | — | — | 0.50 | 1.00 | 2.00 |
| 2012 | 2,452,000 | — | — | 0.50 | 1.00 | 2.00 |
| 2013 In sets only | 2,000 | — | — | — | — | 3.00 |

### KM# 35 25 CENTS

3.50 g., Nickel Bonded Steel, 20.2 mm. **Ruler:** Beatrix **Obv:** Orange blossom within circle **Rev:** Value within circle, geometric designed border **Edge:** Reeded

| Date | Mintage | VF20 | XF40 | MS60 | MS63 | MS65 |
|---|---|---|---|---|---|---|
| 2001 In sets only | 11,500 | — | — | — | — | 3.00 |
| 2002 In sets only | 6,000 | — | — | — | — | 3.00 |
| 2003 | 1,404,000 | — | 0.50 | 0.75 | 1.25 | 1.50 |
| 2004 | 1,502,100 | — | 0.50 | 0.75 | 1.25 | 1.50 |
| 2005 | 110,000 | — | 0.50 | 0.75 | 1.25 | 1.50 |
| 2006 | 102,000 | — | 0.50 | 0.75 | 1.25 | 1.50 |
| 2007 In sets only | 2,000 | — | 0.50 | 0.75 | 1.25 | 1.50 |
| 2008 | 992,000 | — | 0.50 | 0.75 | 1.25 | 1.50 |
| 2009 | 2,072,000 | — | 0.50 | 0.75 | 1.25 | 1.50 |
| 2010 | 17,988,100 | — | 0.50 | 0.75 | 1.25 | 1.50 |
| 2011 In sets only | 2,000 | — | — | — | — | 3.00 |
| 2012 | 227,000 | — | — | 0.75 | 1.25 | 2.00 |
| 2013 In sets only | 2,000 | — | — | — | — | 3.00 |

### KM# 36 50 CENTS

5.00 g., Aureate Steel, 24 mm. **Ruler:** Beatrix **Obv:** Orange blossom within circle, designed border **Rev:** Value within circle of pearls and shell border **Edge:** Plain **Shape:** 4-sided

| Date | Mintage | VF20 | XF40 | MS60 | MS63 | MS65 |
|---|---|---|---|---|---|---|
| 2001 In sets only | 11,500 | — | — | — | — | 4.00 |
| 2002 In sets only | 6,000 | — | — | — | — | 6.00 |
| 2003 In sets only | 9,000 | — | — | — | — | 4.00 |
| 2004 In sets only | 7,100 | — | — | — | — | 4.00 |
| 2005 | 15,000 | — | 0.75 | 1.50 | 3.00 | 4.00 |
| 2006 In sets only | 2,000 | — | — | — | — | 6.00 |
| 2007 | 7,000 | — | 0.75 | 1.50 | 3.00 | 4.00 |
| 2008 | 7,000 | — | 0.75 | 1.50 | 3.00 | 4.00 |
| 2009 In sets only | 2,000 | — | — | — | — | 6.00 |
| 2010 In sets only | 2,000 | — | — | — | — | 6.00 |
| 2011 In sets only | 2,000 | — | — | — | — | 6.00 |
| 2012 In sets only | 2,000 | — | — | — | — | 6.00 |
| 2013 In sets only | 2,000 | — | — | — | — | 6.00 |

### KM# 37 GULDEN

6.00 g., Aureate Steel, 24 mm. **Ruler:** Beatrix **Obv:** Head left **Rev:** Crowned shield divides value above date and ribbon **Edge Lettering:** GOD * ZIJ * MET * ONS *

| Date | Mintage | VF20 | XF40 | MS60 | MS63 | MS65 |
|---|---|---|---|---|---|---|
| 2001 In sets only | 11,500 | — | — | — | — | 4.00 |
| 2002 In sets only | 6,000 | — | — | — | — | 6.00 |
| 2003 | 504,000 | — | 0.75 | 1.25 | 2.00 | 4.00 |
| 2004 In sets only | 7,100 | — | — | — | — | 6.00 |
| 2005 | 805,000 | — | 0.75 | 1.25 | 2.00 | 4.00 |
| 2006 In sets only | 2,000 | — | — | — | — | 7.00 |
| 2007 | 7,000 | — | 0.75 | 1.50 | 3.00 | 5.00 |
| 2008 | 1,202,000 | — | 0.75 | 1.25 | 2.00 | 4.00 |
| 2009 | 857,000 | — | 0.75 | 1.25 | 2.00 | 4.00 |
| 2010 | 1,292,000 | — | 0.75 | 1.25 | 2.00 | 4.00 |
| 2011 In sets only | 2,000 | — | — | — | — | 7.00 |
| 2012 In sets only | 2,000 | — | — | — | — | 7.00 |
| 2013 In sets only | 2,000 | — | — | — | — | 7.00 |

### KM# 38 2-1/2 GULDEN

9.00 g., Aureate Steel, 28 mm. **Ruler:** Beatrix **Obv:** Head left **Rev:** Crowned shield divides value above date and ribbon **Edge Lettering:** GOD * ZIJ * MET * ONS *

| Date | Mintage | VF20 | XF40 | MS60 | MS63 | MS65 |
|---|---|---|---|---|---|---|
| 2001 In sets only | 11,500 | — | — | — | — | 6.00 |
| 2002 In sets only | 6,000 | — | — | — | — | 10.00 |
| 2003 In sets only | 9,000 | — | — | — | — | 10.00 |
| 2004 In sets only | 7,100 | — | — | — | — | 10.00 |
| 2005 | 15,000 | — | 1.00 | 3.00 | 5.00 | 10.00 |
| 2006 In sets only | 2,000 | — | — | — | — | 10.00 |
| 2007 | 7,000 | — | 1.00 | 2.50 | 5.00 | 10.00 |
| 2008 | 7,000 | — | 1.00 | 2.50 | 5.00 | 10.00 |
| 2009 In sets only | 2,000 | — | — | — | — | 10.00 |
| 2010 In sets only | 2,000 | — | — | — | — | 10.00 |
| 2011 In sets only | 2,000 | — | — | — | — | 10.00 |
| 2012 In sets only | 2,000 | — | — | — | — | 10.00 |
| 2013 In sets only | 2,000 | — | — | — | — | 10.00 |

### KM# 43 5 GULDEN

14.00 g., Aureate Bonded Steel, 26 mm. **Ruler:** Beatrix **Obv:** Head left **Rev:** Crowned shield divides value above date and ribbon **Edge Lettering:** GOD * ZIJ * MET * ONS *

| Date | Mintage | VF20 | XF40 | MS60 | MS63 | MS65 |
|---|---|---|---|---|---|---|
| 2001 In sets only | 9,500 | — | — | — | — | 10.00 |
| 2002 In sets only | 6,000 | — | — | — | — | 10.00 |
| 2003 In sets only | 7,000 | — | — | — | — | 10.00 |
| 2004 | 102,100 | — | 2.00 | 3.00 | 4.00 | 8.00 |
| 2005 | 11,000 | — | 2.00 | 3.50 | 5.00 | 10.00 |
| 2006 In sets only | 2,000 | — | — | — | — | 10.00 |
| 2007 | 5,000 | — | 2.00 | 3.00 | 4.00 | 10.00 |
| 2008 | 119,000 | — | 2.00 | 3.00 | 4.00 | 10.00 |
| 2009 | 227,000 | — | 2.00 | 3.00 | 4.00 | 10.00 |
| 2010 | 302,000 | — | 2.00 | 3.00 | 4.00 | 10.00 |
| 2011 In sets only | 2,000 | — | — | — | — | 10.00 |
| 2012 In sets only | 2,000 | — | — | — | — | 10.00 |
| 2013 In sets only | 2,000 | — | — | — | — | 10.00 |

### KM# 74.1 5 GULDEN

11.00 g., Aureate Bonded Steel, 26 mm. **Ruler:** Beatrix **Subject:** 50th Anniversary - End To Dutch Colonial Rule **Obv:** Head left **Rev:** Triangular signatures around value **Edge Lettering:** GOD * ZIJ * MET * ONS *

| Date | Mintage | VF20 | XF40 | MS60 | MS63 | MS65 |
|---|---|---|---|---|---|---|
| 2004 | 10,000 | — | 7.00 | 9.00 | 15.00 | 20.00 |

### KM# 74 5 GULDEN

11.90 g., 0.925 Silver 0.3539 oz. ASW, 29 mm. **Ruler:** Beatrix **Subject:** 50th Anniversary - Charter for the Kingdom of Netherlands including Aruba as third party **Obv:** Head left **Rev:** Triangular design with hands writing signatures around value **Edge Lettering:** GOD * ZIJ * MET * ONS *

| Date | Mintage | VF20 | XF40 | MS60 | MS63 | MS65 |
|---|---|---|---|---|---|---|
| 2004 (u) | 4,000 | PF63 25.00 | PF65 35.00 | | | |

### KM# 76 5 GULDEN

11.90 g., 0.925 Silver 0.3539 oz. ASW, 29 mm. **Ruler:** Beatrix **Subject:** Queen's Silver Jubilee **Obv:** Head left **Rev:** Child art and value **Edge Lettering:** GOD * ZIJ * MET * ONS *

| Date | Mintage | VF20 | XF40 | MS60 | MS63 | MS65 |
|---|---|---|---|---|---|---|
| 2005 (u) | 4,000 | PF63 25.00 | PF65 35.00 | | | |

### KM# 76.1 5 GULDEN

11.00 g., Aureate Bonded Steel, 26 mm. **Ruler:** Beatrix **Subject:** Queen's Silver Jubilee **Obv:** Head left **Rev:** Child art and value **Edge Lettering:** GOD * ZIJ * MET * ONS *

| Date | Mintage | VF20 | XF40 | MS60 | MS63 | MS65 |
|---|---|---|---|---|---|---|
| 2005 | 10,000 | — | 7.00 | 9.00 | 15.00 | 20.00 |

### KM# 80 5 GULDEN

11.90 g., 0.925 Silver 0.3539 oz. ASW, 29 mm. **Ruler:** Beatrix **Subject:** 50 Years Brishopric Willemstad **Obv:** Logo Brishopric **Rev:** Cathedral **Edge Lettering:** GOD * Z'J * MET * ONS *

| Date | Mintage | VF20 | XF40 | MS60 | MS63 | MS65 |
|---|---|---|---|---|---|---|
| 2008 | — | PF63 25.00 | PF65 35.00 | | | |

### KM# 79 5 GULDEN

11.90 g., 0.925 Silver 0.3539 oz. ASW, 29 mm. **Ruler:** Beatrix **Obv:** Antoine Maduro **Rev:** Crowned shield divides value **Edge Lettering:** GOD * ZIJ * MET * ONS *

| Date | Mintage | VF20 | XF40 | MS60 | MS63 | MS65 |
|---|---|---|---|---|---|---|
| 2009 | 1,250 | PF63 30.00 | PF65 40.00 | | | |

### KM# 85 5 GULDEN

10.40 g., Aureate Bonded Steel, 26 mm. **Ruler:** Beatrix **Subject:** Abdication of Beatrix **Obv:** Value and national arms **Rev:** Beatrix and Willem-Alexander left above Curacao flag in color

| Date | Mintage | VF20 | XF40 | MS60 | MS63 | MS65 |
|---|---|---|---|---|---|---|
| 2013 | 11,000 | — | — | — | — | 15.00 |

### KM# 86 5 GULDEN

10.40 g., Aureate Bonded Steel, 26 mm. **Ruler:** Beatrix **Obv:** Value and national arms **Rev:** Beatrix and Willem-Alexander left above St. Martin flag in color

| Date | Mintage | VF20 | XF40 | MS60 | MS63 | MS65 |
|---|---|---|---|---|---|---|
| 2013 | 11,000 | — | — | — | — | 15.00 |

### KM# 87 5 GULDEN

11.90 g., 0.925 Silver 0.3539 oz. ASW, 29 mm. **Ruler:** Willem-Alexander **Subject:** Welcome to the King **Obv:** Crown with three shield under value **Rev:** Willem-Alexander right

| Date | Mintage | VF20 | XF40 | MS60 | MS63 | MS65 |
|---|---|---|---|---|---|---|
| 2013 | 2,000 | PF63 55.00 | PF65 65.00 | | | |

### KM# 88 5 GULDEN

11.90 g., 0.925 Silver 0.3539 oz. ASW, 29 mm. **Ruler:** Willem-Alexander **Subject:** End of Slavery, 150th Anniversary **Obv:** Crowned weapon divides 5-G above date **Rev:** Stick figures and one is cutting chain

| Date | Mintage | VF20 | XF40 | MS60 | MS63 | MS65 |
|---|---|---|---|---|---|---|
| 2013 | 3,000 | PF63 25.00 | PF65 35.00 | | | |

### KM# 89 5 GULDEN

26.50 g., Copper-Nickel-Zinc, 39 mm. **Ruler:** Willem-Alexander **Subject:** Curaçao North Sea Jazz Festival **Obv:** Crowned shield above date **Rev:** Sax player in green and yellow

| Date | Mintage | VF20 | XF40 | MS60 | MS63 | MS65 |
|---|---|---|---|---|---|---|
| 2013 | 3,000 | PF63 25.00 | PF65 35.00 | | | |

### KM# 49 10 GULDEN

31.10 g., 0.925 Silver 0.925 oz. ASW, 40 mm. **Ruler:** Beatrix **Subject:** Gold Trade Coins: Sulla Aureus **Obv:** Crowned shield divides value above date and ribbon **Rev:** Bust facing with two gold coins at lower left **Edge:** Plain

| Date | Mintage | VF20 | XF40 | MS60 | MS63 | MS65 |
|---|---|---|---|---|---|---|
| 2001 (u) | 589 | PF65 80.00 | | | | |

### KM# 50 10 GULDEN

31.10 g., 0.925 Silver 0.925 oz. ASW, 40 mm. **Ruler:** Beatrix **Subject:** Gold Trade Coins: Constantin I Solidus **Obv:** Crowned shield divides value above date and ribbon **Rev:** Bust facing with two gold coins at lower right **Edge:** Plain

| Date | Mintage | VF20 | XF40 | MS60 | MS63 | MS65 |
|---|---|---|---|---|---|---|
| 2001 (u) | 578 | PF65 80.00 | | | | |

### KM# 51 10 GULDEN

31.10 g., 0.925 Silver 0.925 oz. ASW, 40 mm. **Ruler:** Beatrix **Subject:** Gold Trade Coins: Clovis I Tremissis fiorino d'oro **Obv:** Crowned shield divides value above date and ribbon **Rev:** Bust facing with two gold coins **Edge:** Plain

| Date | Mintage | VF20 | XF40 | MS60 | MS63 | MS65 |
|---|---|---|---|---|---|---|
| 2001 (u) | 566 | PF65 80.00 | | | | |

### KM# 52 10 GULDEN

31.10 g., 0.925 Silver 0.925 oz. ASW, 40 mm. **Ruler:** Beatrix **Subject:** Gold Trade Coins: Cosimo de'Medici Fiorino d'oro **Obv:** Crowned shield divides value above date and ribbon **Rev:** Bust facing with two gold coins **Edge:** Plain

| Date | Mintage | VF20 | XF40 | MS60 | MS63 | MS65 |
|---|---|---|---|---|---|---|
| 2001 (u) | 575 | PF65 80.00 | | | | |

### KM# 53 10 GULDEN

31.10 g., 0.925 Silver 0.925 oz. ASW, 40 mm. **Ruler:** Beatrix **Subject:** Gold Trade Coins: Dandolo Ducato d'Oro **Obv:** Crowned shield divides value above date and ribbon **Rev:** Bust facing with two gold coins **Edge:** Plain

| Date | Mintage | VF20 | XF40 | MS60 | MS63 | MS65 |
|---|---|---|---|---|---|---|
| 2001 (u) | 490 | PF65 80.00 | | | | |

### KM# 54 10 GULDEN

31.10 g., 0.925 Silver 0.925 oz. ASW, 40 mm. **Ruler:** Beatrix **Subject:** Gold Trade Coins: Philips IV Ecu d'or la chaise **Obv:** Crowned shield divides value above date and ribbon **Rev:** Bust facing with two gold coins **Edge:** Plain

| Date | Mintage | VF20 | XF40 | MS60 | MS63 | MS65 |
|---|---|---|---|---|---|---|
| 2001 (u) | 460 | PF65 80.00 | | | | |

### KM# 55 10 GULDEN

31.10 g., 0.925 Silver 0.925 oz. ASW, 40 mm. **Ruler:** Beatrix **Subject:** Gold Trade Coins: Edward III Nobel **Obv:** Crowned shield divides value above date and ribbon **Rev:** Crowned bust facing with two gold coins **Edge:** Plain

| Date | Mintage | VF20 | XF40 | MS60 | MS63 | MS65 |
|---|---|---|---|---|---|---|
| 2001 (u) | 575 | PF65 80.00 | | | | |

### KM# 56 10 GULDEN

31.10 g., 0.925 Silver 0.925 oz. ASW, 40 mm. **Ruler:** Beatrix **Subject:** Gold Trade Coins: Carolus IV Rhine Gold Guilder **Obv:** Crowned shield divides value above date and ribbon **Rev:** Bust facing with two gold coins **Edge:** Plain

| Date | Mintage | VF20 | XF40 | MS60 | MS63 | MS65 |
|---|---|---|---|---|---|---|
| 2001 (u) | 430 | PF65 80.00 | | | | |

### KM# 57 10 GULDEN

31.10 g., 0.925 Silver 0.925 oz. ASW, 40 mm. **Ruler:** Beatrix **Subject:** Gold Trade Coins: John II Franc d'or a cheval **Obv:** Crowned shield divides value above date and ribbon **Rev:** Bust facing with two gold coins **Edge:** Plain

| Date | Mintage | VF20 | XF40 | MS60 | MS63 | MS65 |
|---|---|---|---|---|---|---|
| 2001 (u) | 464 | PF65 80.00 | | | | |

### KM# 58 10 GULDEN

31.10 g., 0.925 Silver 0.925 oz. ASW, 40 mm. **Ruler:** Beatrix **Subject:** Gold Trade Coins: Philip the Good Adriesguilder **Obv:** Crowned shield divides value above date and ribbon **Rev:** Bust facing with two gold coins **Edge:** Plain

| Date | Mintage | VF20 | XF40 | MS60 | MS63 | MS65 |
|---|---|---|---|---|---|---|
| 2001 (u) | 250 | PF65 120 | | | | |

### KM# 59 10 GULDEN

31.10 g., 0.925 Silver 0.925 oz. ASW, 40 mm. **Ruler:** Beatrix **Subject:** Gold Trade Coins: Louis XI Ecu d'or au soleil **Obv:** Crowned shield divides value above date and ribbon **Rev:** Bust facing with two gold coins **Edge:** Plain

| Date | Mintage | VF20 | XF40 | MS60 | MS63 | MS65 |
|---|---|---|---|---|---|---|
| 2001 (u) | 450 | PF65 80.00 | | | | |

### KM# 60 10 GULDEN

31.10 g., 0.925 Silver 0.925 oz. ASW, 40 mm. **Ruler:** Beatrix **Subject:** Gold Trade Coins: Elisabeth I Sovereign **Obv:** Crowned shield divides value above date and ribbon **Rev:** Bust facing with two gold coins **Edge:** Plain

| Date | Mintage | VF20 | XF40 | MS60 | MS63 | MS65 |
|---|---|---|---|---|---|---|
| 2001 (u) | 450 | PF65 80.00 | | | | |

### KM# 61 10 GULDEN

31.10 g., 0.925 Silver 0.925 oz. ASW, 40 mm. **Ruler:** Beatrix **Subject:** Gold Trade Coins: Carolus V Carolus Guilder **Obv:** Crowned shield divides value above date and ribbon **Rev:** Bust facing with two gold coins **Edge:** Plain

| Date | Mintage | VF20 | XF40 | MS60 | MS63 | MS65 |
|---|---|---|---|---|---|---|
| 2001 (u) | 440 | PF65 80.00 | | | | |

### KM# 62 10 GULDEN

31.10 g., 0.925 Silver 0.925 oz. ASW, 40 mm. **Ruler:** Beatrix **Subject:** Gold Trade Coins: Philips II Real **Obv:** Crowned shield divides value above date and ribbon **Rev:** Bust facing with two gold coins **Edge:** Plain

| Date | Mintage | VF20 | XF40 | MS60 | MS63 | MS65 |
|---|---|---|---|---|---|---|
| 2001 (u) | 440 | PF65 80.00 | | | | |

### KM# 63 10 GULDEN

31.10 g., 0.925 Silver 0.925 oz. ASW, 40 mm. **Ruler:** Beatrix **Subject:** Gold Trade Coins: Maurits Ducat **Obv:** Crowned shield divides value above date and ribbon **Rev:** Bust facing with two gold coins **Edge:** Plain

| Date | Mintage | VF20 | XF40 | MS60 | MS63 | MS65 |
|---|---|---|---|---|---|---|
| 2001 (u) | 443 | PF65 80.00 | | | | |

### KM# 64 10 GULDEN

31.10 g., 0.925 Silver 0.925 oz. ASW, 40 mm. **Ruler:** Beatrix **Subject:** Gold Trade Coins: Isabella and Albrecht Double Albertin **Obv:** Crowned shield divides value above date and ribbon **Rev:** Conjoined busts facing with two gold coins **Edge:** Plain

| Date | Mintage | VF20 | XF40 | MS60 | MS63 | MS65 |
|---|---|---|---|---|---|---|
| 2001 (u) | 490 | PF65 80.00 | | | | |

### KM# 65 10 GULDEN

31.10 g., 0.925 Silver 0.925 oz. ASW, 40 mm. **Ruler:** Beatrix **Subject:** Gold Trade Coins: William III Golden Rider **Obv:** Crowned shield divides value above date and ribbon **Rev:** Bust facing with two gold coins **Edge:** Plain

| Date | Mintage | VF20 | XF40 | MS60 | MS63 | MS65 |
|---|---|---|---|---|---|---|
| 2001 (u) | 440 | PF65 80.00 | | | | |

### KM# 66 10 GULDEN

31.10 g., 0.925 Silver 0.925 oz. ASW, 40 mm. **Ruler:** Beatrix **Subject:** Gold Trade Coins: Louis XIII Louis d'or **Obv:** Crowned shield divides value above date and ribbon **Rev:** Bust facing with two gold coins **Edge:** Plain

| Date | Mintage | VF20 | XF40 | MS60 | MS63 | MS65 |
|---|---|---|---|---|---|---|
| 2001 (u) | 440 | PF65 80.00 | | | | |

### KM# 67 10 GULDEN

31.10 g., 0.925 Silver 0.925 oz. ASW, 40 mm. **Ruler:** Beatrix **Subject:** Gold Trade Coins: Catherine the Great Rubel **Obv:** Crowned shield divides value above date and ribbon **Rev:** Crowned laureate bust facing with two gold coins **Edge:** Plain

| Date | Mintage | VF20 | XF40 | MS60 | MS63 | MS65 |
|---|---|---|---|---|---|---|
| 2001 (u) | 560 | PF65 100 | | | | |

### KM# 68 10 GULDEN

31.10 g., 0.925 Silver 0.925 oz. ASW, 40 mm. **Ruler:** Beatrix **Subject:** Gold Trade Coins: Maria Theresia Double Sovereign **Obv:** Crowned shield divides value above date and ribbon **Rev:** Bust facing with two gold coins **Edge:** Plain

| Date | Mintage | VF20 | XF40 | MS60 | MS63 | MS65 |
|---|---|---|---|---|---|---|
| 2001 (u) | 440 | PF65 80.00 | | | | |

**KM# 69 10 GULDEN**
31.10 g., 0.925 Silver 0.925 oz. ASW, 40 mm. **Ruler:** Beatrix **Subject:** Gold Trade Coins: Napolean Bonaparte 20 Franc **Obv:** Crowned shield divides value above date and ribbon **Rev:** Bust facing with two gold coins **Edge:** Plain

| Date | Mintage | VF20 | XF40 | MS60 | MS63 | MS65 |
|---|---|---|---|---|---|---|
| 2001 (u) | 555 | PF65 80.00 | | | | |

**KM# 70 10 GULDEN**
31.10 g., 0.925 Silver 0.925 oz. ASW, 40 mm. **Ruler:** Beatrix **Series:** Gold Trade Coins: Wilhelmina gold 10 Guilder **Obv:** Crowned shield divides value above date and ribbon **Rev:** Bust facing with two gold coins **Edge:** Plain

| Date | Mintage | VF20 | XF40 | MS60 | MS63 | MS65 |
|---|---|---|---|---|---|---|
| 2001 (u) | 440 | PF65 80.00 | | | | |

**KM# 71 10 GULDEN**
31.10 g., 0.925 Silver 0.925 oz. ASW, 40 mm. **Ruler:** Beatrix **Subject:** Gold Trade Coins: George III Sovereign **Obv:** Crowned shield divides value above date and ribbon **Rev:** Bust facing with two gold coins **Edge:** Plain

| Date | Mintage | VF20 | XF40 | MS60 | MS63 | MS65 |
|---|---|---|---|---|---|---|
| 2001 (u) | 440 | PF65 80.00 | | | | |

**KM# 72 10 GULDEN**
31.10 g., 0.925 Silver 0.925 oz. ASW, 40 mm. **Ruler:** Beatrix **Subject:** Gold Trade Coins: Albert I Belgium 20 Franc **Obv:** Crowned shield divides value above date and ribbon **Rev:** Bust facing with two gold coins **Edge:** Plain

| Date | Mintage | VF20 | XF40 | MS60 | MS63 | MS65 |
|---|---|---|---|---|---|---|
| 2001 (u) | 490 | PF65 80.00 | | | | |

**KM# 84 10 GULDEN**
17.00 g., 0.925 Silver 0.5056 oz. ASW, 33 mm. **Ruler:** Beatrix **Subject:** Mariage of Willem-Alexander and Maxima **Obv:** Queen's head left **Rev:** Conjoined busts left **Edge Lettering:** GOD * ZIJ * MET * ONS *

| Date | Mintage | VF20 | XF40 | MS60 | MS63 | MS65 |
|---|---|---|---|---|---|---|
| 2002 (u) | 1,500 | PF63 40.00 | PF65 50.00 | | | |

**KM# 75 10 GULDEN**
6.72 g., 0.900 Gold 0.1944 oz. AGW **Ruler:** Beatrix **Subject:** 50th Anniversary - End to Dutch Colonial Rule **Obv:** Head left **Rev:** Triangular signatures around value **Edge:** Reeded

| Date | Mintage | VF20 | XF40 | MS60 | MS63 | MS65 |
|---|---|---|---|---|---|---|
| 2004 | 1,000 | PF65 400 | | | | |

**KM# 77 10 GULDEN**
6.72 g., 0.900 Gold 0.1944 oz. AGW, 22.5 mm. **Ruler:** Beatrix **Subject:** Queen's Silver Jubilee **Obv:** Head left **Rev:** Child art and value **Edge:** Reeded

| Date | Mintage | VF20 | XF40 | MS60 | MS63 | MS65 |
|---|---|---|---|---|---|---|
| 2005 (u) | 1,500 | PF65 400 | | | | |

**KM# 78 10 GULDEN**
1.24 g., 0.999 Gold 0.040 oz. AGW, 13.92 mm. **Ruler:** Beatrix **Subject:** Year of the Dolphin **Obv:** Head left **Obv. Legend:** BEATRIX KONINGIN DER NEDERLANDEN **Rev:** Stylized outlines of birds above dolphins at sunset **Rev. Legend:** NEDERLANDSE ANTILLEN - JAAR VAN DE DOLFIJN **Edge:** Reeded

| Date | Mintage | VF20 | XF40 | MS60 | MS63 | MS65 |
|---|---|---|---|---|---|---|
| 2007 (u) | 5,000 | PF65 90.00 | | | | |

**KM# 81 10 GULDEN**
17.80 g., 0.925 Silver 0.5294 oz. ASW, 33 mm. **Ruler:** Beatrix **Subject:** Farewell to the Netherlands Antilles **Obv:** Autonomy monument with five birds **Rev:** Crowned shield divided value **Edge Lettering:** GOD * ZIJ * MET * ONS *

| Date | Mintage | VF20 | XF40 | MS60 | MS63 | MS65 |
|---|---|---|---|---|---|---|
| 2010 (u) | 5,000 | PF63 40.00 | PF65 50.00 | | | |

**KM# 90 10 GULDEN**
3.36 g., 0.900 Gold 0.0974 oz. AGW **Ruler:** Willem-Alexander

| Date | Mintage | VF20 | XF40 | MS60 | MS63 | MS65 |
|---|---|---|---|---|---|---|
| 2013 | 750 | PF65 150 | | | | |

**KM# 82 25 GULDEN**
25.00 g., 0.925 Silver 0.7435 oz. ASW, 38 mm. **Ruler:** Beatrix **Subject:** 175 Year Bank of the Netherlands Antilles **Rev:** Sailing ship

| Date | Mintage | VF20 | XF40 | MS60 | MS63 | MS65 |
|---|---|---|---|---|---|---|
| 2003 Prooflike | 1,500 | — | — | — | — | 50.00 |

**KM# 83 25 GULDEN**
25.00 g., 0.925 Silver 0.7435 oz. ASW, 38 mm. **Ruler:** Beatrix **Subject:** 50 Years of Monument Care **Rev:** Folker FXVIII plane over route map **Edge Lettering:** GOD * ZIJ * MET * ONS *

| Date | Mintage | VF20 | XF40 | MS60 | MS63 | MS65 |
|---|---|---|---|---|---|---|
| 2004 | 5,000 | PF63 45.00 | PF65 55.00 | | | |

## MINT SETS

| KM# | Date | Mintage | Identification | Issue Price | Mkt Val |
|---|---|---|---|---|---|
| MS22 | 2001 (8) | 6,500 | KM#32-38, 43 | 15.00 | 20.00 |
| MS23 | 2002 (8) | 6,000 | KM#32-38, 43 | 15.00 | 25.00 |
| MS24 | 2003 (8) | 4,000 | KM#32-38, 43 | 15.00 | 25.00 |
| MS25 | 2004 (8) | 2,100 | KM32-38, 43 | 15.00 | 30.00 |
| MS26 | 2005 (8) | 3,500 | KM32-38, 43 | 17.00 | 25.00 |
| MS27 | 2006 (8) | 2,000 | KM#32-38, 43 | 20.00 | 30.00 |
| MS28 | 2007 (8) | 2,000 | KM#32-38, 43 | 20.00 | 25.00 |
| MS29 | 2008 (8) | 2,000 | KM#32-38, 43 | 21.00 | 25.00 |
| MS30 | 2009 (8) | 2,000 | KM#32-38, 43 | 27.00 | 27.00 |
| MS31 | 2010 (8) | 2,000 | KM#32-38, 43 | 28.00 | 28.00 |
| MS32 | 2011 (8) | 2,000 | KM#32-38, 43 | 28.00 | 30.00 |
| MS33 | 2012 (8) | 2,000 | KM#32-38, 43 | 28.00 | 30.00 |

# NEW CALEDONIA

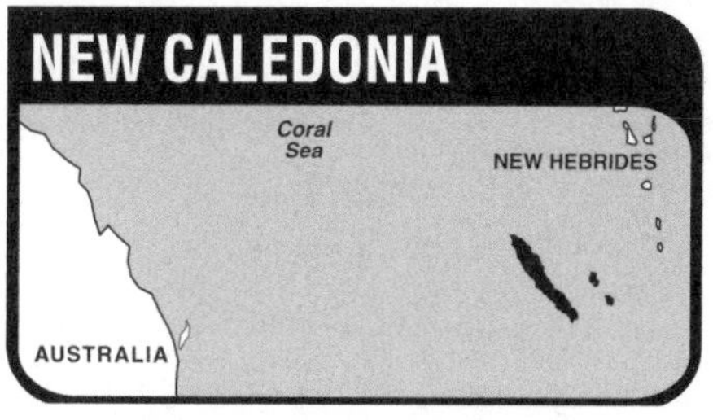


The French Associated State of New Caledonia is a group of about 25 islands in the South Pacific. They are situated about 750 miles (1,207 km.) east of Australia. The territory, which includes the dependencies of Isle des Pins, Loyalty Islands, Isle Huon, Isles Belep, Isles Chesterfield, Isle Walpole, Wallis and Futuna Islands and has a total land area of 7,358 sq. mi.(19,060 sq. km.) and a population of *156,000. Capital: Noumea. The islands are rich in minerals; New Caledonia has some of the world's largest known deposit of nickel. Nickel, nickel castings, coffee and copra are exported.

**MINT MARK**
Paris, privy marks only

**MONETARY SYSTEM**
100 Centimes = 1 Franc

## FRENCH OVERSEAS TERRITORY

1958-1998

## DECIMAL COINAGE

**KM# 10 FRANC**
1.30 g., Aluminum, 23 mm. **Obv:** Seated figure holding torch, legend added **Obv. Legend:** I. E. O. M. **Rev:** Kagu bird within sprigs below value

| Date | Mintage | VF20 | XF40 | MS60 | MS63 | MS65 |
|---|---|---|---|---|---|---|
| 2001 (a) | 100,000 | — | — | 0.45 | 0.65 | 1.25 |
| 2002 (a) | 1,200,000 | — | — | 0.45 | 0.65 | 1.25 |
| 2003 (a) | 2,000,000 | — | — | 0.45 | 0.65 | 1.25 |
| 2004 (a) | 1,200,000 | — | — | 0.45 | 0.65 | 1.25 |
| 2005 (a) | 700,000 | — | — | 0.45 | 0.65 | 1.25 |
| 2006 (a) | 1,600,000 | — | — | 0.45 | 0.65 | 1.25 |
| 2007 (a) | 2,000,000 | — | — | 0.45 | 0.65 | 1.25 |
| 2008 (a) | 2,800,000 | — | — | 0.45 | 0.65 | 1.25 |
| 2009 (a) | — | — | — | 0.45 | 0.65 | 1.25 |
| 2010 (a) | — | — | — | 0.45 | 0.65 | 1.25 |
| 2011 (a) | — | — | — | 0.45 | 0.65 | 1.25 |
| 2012 (a) | — | — | — | 0.45 | 0.65 | 1.25 |

**KM# 14 2 FRANCS**
2.20 g., Aluminum, 27 mm. **Obv:** Seated figure holding torch, legend added **Obv. Legend:** I. E. O. M. **Rev:** Kagu bird and value within sprigs

| Date | Mintage | VF20 | XF40 | MS60 | MS63 | MS65 |
|---|---|---|---|---|---|---|
| 2001 (a) | 800,000 | — | 0.25 | 0.40 | 0.75 | 1.50 |
| 2002 (a) | 1,200,000 | — | 0.25 | 0.40 | 0.75 | 1.50 |
| 2003 (a) | 2,400,000 | — | 0.20 | 0.35 | 0.65 | 1.50 |
| 2004 (a) | 200,000 | — | 0.20 | 0.35 | 0.65 | 1.50 |
| 2005 (a) | 530,000 | — | 0.20 | 0.35 | 0.65 | 1.50 |
| 2006 (a) | 1,200,000 | — | 0.20 | 0.35 | 0.65 | 1.50 |
| 2007 (a) | 600,000 | — | 0.20 | 0.35 | 0.65 | 1.50 |
| 2008 (a) | 2,400,000 | — | 0.20 | 0.35 | 0.65 | 1.50 |
| 2009 (a) | — | — | 0.20 | 0.35 | 0.65 | 1.50 |
| 2011 (a) | — | — | 0.20 | 0.35 | 0.65 | 1.50 |

**KM# 16 5 FRANCS**
3.75 g., Aluminum, 31 mm. **Obv:** Seated figure holding torch, legend added **Obv. Legend:** I. E. O. M. **Rev:** Kagu bird and value within sprigs

| Date | Mintage | VF20 | XF40 | MS60 | MS63 | MS65 |
|---|---|---|---|---|---|---|
| 2001 (a) | 600,000 | — | 0.40 | 0.60 | 1.25 | 2.50 |
| 2002 (a) | 480,000 | — | 0.40 | 0.60 | 1.25 | 2.50 |
| 2003 (a) | 700,000 | — | 0.40 | 0.60 | 1.00 | 2.00 |
| 2004 (a) | 1,000,000 | — | 0.40 | 0.60 | 1.00 | 2.00 |
| 2005 (a) | 360,000 | — | 0.40 | 0.60 | 1.00 | 2.00 |
| 2006 (a) | 480,000 | — | 0.40 | 0.60 | 1.00 | 2.00 |
| 2007 (a) | 960,000 | — | 0.40 | 0.60 | 1.00 | 2.00 |
| 2008 (a) | 1,700,000 | — | 0.40 | 0.60 | 1.00 | 2.00 |
| 2009 (a) | — | — | 0.40 | 0.60 | 1.00 | 2.00 |
| 2010 (a) | — | — | 0.40 | 0.60 | 1.00 | 2.00 |
| 2011 (a) | — | — | 0.40 | 0.60 | 1.00 | 2.00 |

**KM# 11 10 FRANCS**
6.00 g., Nickel, 24 mm. **Obv:** Liberty head left **Obv. Legend:** I. E. O. M. **Rev:** Sailboat above value

| Date | Mintage | VF20 | XF40 | MS60 | MS63 | MS65 |
|---|---|---|---|---|---|---|
| 2001 (a) | 100,000 | — | 0.65 | 1.00 | 1.25 | 2.75 |
| 2002 (a) | 200,000 | — | 0.65 | 1.00 | 1.25 | 2.75 |
| 2003 (a) | 800,000 | — | 0.65 | 1.00 | 1.25 | 2.75 |
| 2004 (a) | 600,000 | — | 0.65 | 1.00 | 1.25 | 2.75 |
| 2005 (a) | 64,000 | — | 0.65 | 1.00 | 1.25 | 2.75 |

**KM# 12 20 FRANCS**
10.00 g., Nickel, 28.5 mm. **Obv:** Liberty head left **Obv. Legend:** I. O. E. M. **Rev:** Three ox heads above value

| Date | Mintage | VF20 | XF40 | MS60 | MS63 | MS65 |
|---|---|---|---|---|---|---|
| 2001 (a) | 150,000 | — | 1.00 | 1.25 | 1.75 | 3.25 |
| 2002 (a) | 250,000 | — | 1.00 | 1.25 | 1.75 | 3.25 |
| 2003 (a) | 250,000 | — | 1.00 | 1.25 | 1.75 | 3.25 |
| 2004 (a) | 500,000 | — | 1.00 | 1.25 | 1.75 | 3.25 |
| 2005 (a) | 300,000 | — | 1.00 | 1.25 | 1.75 | 3.25 |

### KM# 13 50 FRANCS

15.00 g., Nickel, 33 mm. **Obv:** Liberty head left **Obv. Legend:** I. E. O. M. **Rev:** Hut above value in center of palm and pine trees

| Date | Mintage | VF20 | XF40 | MS60 | MS63 | MS65 |
|---|---|---|---|---|---|---|
| 2001 (a) | 100,000 | — | 1.25 | 1.50 | 2.00 | 4.00 |
| 2002 (a) | — | — | 1.25 | 1.50 | 2.00 | 4.00 |
| 2003 (a) | 75,000 | — | 1.25 | 1.50 | 2.00 | 4.00 |
| 2004 (a) | 150,000 | — | 1.25 | 1.50 | 2.00 | 4.00 |
| 2005 (a) | 54,000 | — | 1.25 | 1.50 | 2.00 | 4.00 |

### KM# 15 100 FRANCS

10.00 g., Nickel-Bronze, 30 mm. **Obv:** Liberty head left **Rev:** Hut above value in center of palm and pine trees

| Date | Mintage | VF20 | XF40 | MS60 | MS63 | MS65 |
|---|---|---|---|---|---|---|
| 2001 (a) | 100,000 | — | 1.50 | 2.00 | 3.00 | 5.00 |
| 2002 (a) | 620,000 | — | 1.50 | 2.00 | 3.00 | 6.00 |
| 2003 (a) | 500,000 | — | 1.50 | 2.00 | 3.00 | 5.00 |
| 2004 (a) | 500,000 | — | 1.50 | 2.00 | 3.00 | 5.00 |
| 2005 (a) | 180,000 | — | 1.50 | 2.00 | 3.00 | 5.00 |

## FRENCH ASSOCIATED STATE

1998-

### KM# 11a 10 FRANCS

6.00 g., Copper-Nickel, 24 mm. **Obv:** Liberty head left **Rev:** Sailboat above value **Edge:** Reeded

| Date | Mintage | VF20 | XF40 | MS60 | MS63 | MS65 |
|---|---|---|---|---|---|---|
| 2006 (a) | 60,000 | — | 0.45 | 0.65 | 1.25 | 2.75 |
| 2007 (a) | 1,000,000 | — | 0.45 | 0.65 | 1.25 | 2.75 |
| 2008 (a) | 1,200,000 | — | 0.45 | 0.65 | 1.25 | 2.75 |
| 2009 (a) | — | — | 0.45 | 0.65 | 1.25 | 2.75 |
| 2010 (a) | — | — | 0.45 | 0.65 | 1.25 | 2.75 |
| 2011 (a) | — | — | 0.45 | 0.65 | 1.25 | 2.75 |

### KM# 12a 20 FRANCS

10.00 g., Copper-Nickel, 28.5 mm. **Obv:** Liberty head left **Rev:** Three ox heads above value **Edge:** Reeded

| Date | Mintage | VF20 | XF40 | MS60 | MS63 | MS65 |
|---|---|---|---|---|---|---|
| 2006 (a) | 300,000 | — | 0.60 | 1.00 | 1.75 | 3.25 |
| 2007 (a) | 800,000 | — | 0.60 | 1.00 | 1.75 | 3.25 |
| 2008 (a) | 800,000 | — | 0.60 | 1.00 | 1.75 | 3.25 |
| 2009 (a) | — | — | 0.60 | 1.00 | 1.75 | 3.25 |
| 2010 (a) | — | — | 0.60 | 1.00 | 1.75 | 3.25 |
| 2011 (a) | — | — | 0.60 | 1.00 | 1.75 | 3.25 |

### KM# 13a 50 FRANCS

15.00 g., Copper-Nickel **Obv:** Liberty head left **Rev:** Hut in center of palm and pine trees, value below **Edge:** Reeded

| Date | Mintage | VF20 | XF40 | MS60 | MS63 | MS65 |
|---|---|---|---|---|---|---|
| 2006 (a) | 75,000 | — | 0.70 | 1.25 | 2.00 | 4.00 |
| 2007 (a) | 225,000 | — | 0.70 | 1.25 | 2.00 | 4.00 |
| 2008 (a) | 375,000 | — | 0.70 | 1.25 | 2.00 | 4.00 |
| 2009 (a) | — | — | 0.70 | 1.25 | 2.00 | 4.00 |

### KM# 15a 100 FRANCS

10.00 g., Aluminum-Bronze, 30 mm. **Obv:** Liberty head left **Rev:** Hut above value in center of palm and pine trees **Edge:** Reeded

| Date | Mintage | VF20 | XF40 | MS60 | MS63 | MS65 |
|---|---|---|---|---|---|---|
| 2006 (a) | 300,000 | — | 0.75 | 1.50 | 3.00 | 5.00 |
| 2007 (a) | 800,000 | — | 0.75 | 1.50 | 3.00 | 5.00 |
| 2008 (a) | 1,100,000 | — | 0.75 | 1.50 | 3.00 | 5.00 |
| 2009 (a) | — | — | 0.75 | 1.50 | 3.00 | 5.00 |
| 2010 (a) | — | — | 0.75 | 1.50 | 3.00 | 5.00 |

## MINT SETS

| KM# | Date | Mintage | Identification | Issue Price | Mkt Val |
|---|---|---|---|---|---|
| MS1 | 2001 (7) | 3,000 | KM#10-16 | — | 25.00 |
| MS2 | 2002 (7) | 5,000 | KM#10-16 | — | 25.00 |
| MS3 | 2004 (7) | 3,000 | KM#10-16 | — | 25.00 |

# NEW ZEALAND

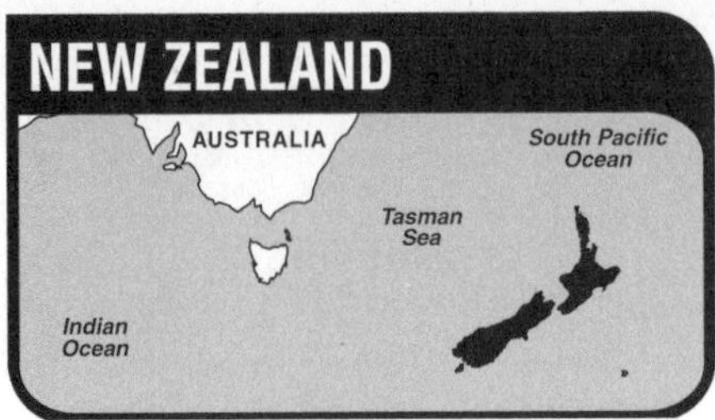


New Zealand, a parliamentary state located in the Southwest Pacific 1,250 miles (2,011 km.) east of Australia, has an area of 103,883 sq. mi. (268,680 sq. km.) and a population of *3.4 million. Capital: Wellington. Wool, meat, dairy products and some manufactured items are exported.

Decimal Currency was introduced in 1967 with special sets commemorating the last issues of pound sterling (1965) and the first of the decimal issues. Since then dollars and sets of coins have been issued nearly every year.

New Zealand is a founding member of the Commonwealth of Nations. Elizabeth II is the Head of State as the Queen of New Zealand; the Prime Minister is the Head of Government.

**RULER**

British

## STATE

1907 - present

## DECIMAL COINAGE

100 Cents = 1 Dollar

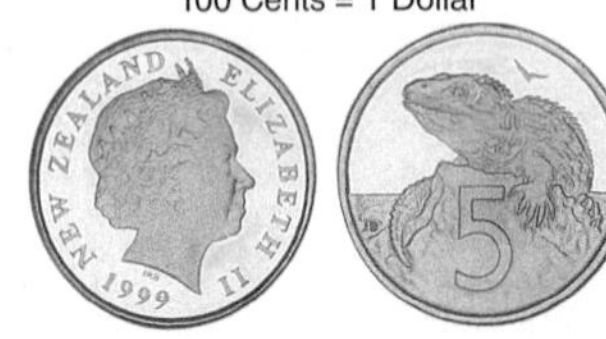


### KM# 116 5 CENTS

2.83 g., Copper-Nickel, 19.43 mm. **Ruler:** Elizabeth II **Obv:** Head with tiara right **Rev:** Value below tuatara **Edge:** Reeded **Note:** Many recalled and melted in 2006.

| Date | Mintage | VF20 | XF40 | MS60 | MS63 | MS65 |
|---|---|---|---|---|---|---|
| 2001 (l) | 20,000,000 | — | 0.10 | 0.25 | 0.50 | 1.00 |
| 2001 (c) Sets only | 2,910 | — | — | — | — | 4.00 |
| 2001 (c) | 1,364 | PF65 3.00 | | | | |
| 2002 (l) | 40,500,000 | — | 0.10 | 0.25 | 0.50 | 1.00 |
| 2002 (c) Sets only | 3,000 | — | — | — | — | 5.00 |
| 2002 (c) | 1,500 | PF65 3.00 | | | | |
| 2003 (l) | 30,000,000 | — | — | 0.25 | 0.50 | 1.00 |
| 2003 (c) Sets only | 1,496 | — | — | — | — | 5.00 |
| 2003 | 3,000 | PF65 3.00 | | | | |
| 2004 (l) | 15,000,000 | — | — | — | 2.00 | 3.00 |
| Note: All but 48,000 melted. Many of these survivors have recently come onto the NZ market in bulk. | | | | | | |
| 2004 (c) Sets only | 2,800 | — | — | — | — | 22.00 |
| 2004 (c) | 1,750 | PF65 3.00 | | | | |
| 2005 (c) Sets only | 3,000 | — | — | — | — | 10.00 |
| 2005 (c) | 2,250 | PF65 3.00 | | | | |
| 2006 (c) Sets only | — | — | — | — | — | 10.00 |
| 2006 (c) | — | PF65 3.00 | | | | |

### KM# 117 10 CENTS

5.66 g., Copper-Nickel, 23.62 mm. **Ruler:** Elizabeth II **Obv:** Head with tiara right **Rev:** Value above koruru **Edge:** Reeded **Note:** Many recalled and melted in 2006.

| Date | Mintage | VF20 | XF40 | MS60 | MS63 | MS65 |
|---|---|---|---|---|---|---|
| 2001 (l) | 10,000,000 | — | 0.10 | 0.20 | 0.30 | 0.50 |
| 2001 (c) Sets only | 2,910 | — | — | — | — | 6.00 |
| 2001 (c) | 1,364 | PF65 4.00 | | | | |
| 2002 (l) | 10,000,000 | — | 0.10 | 0.20 | 0.30 | 0.50 |
| 2002 (c) | 1,500 | PF65 4.00 | | | | |
| 2002 (c) Sets only | 3,000 | — | — | — | — | 5.00 |
| 2003 (l) | 13,000,000 | — | 0.10 | 0.20 | 0.30 | 0.50 |
| 2003 (c) Sets only | 3,000 | — | — | — | — | 5.00 |
| 2003 (l) | 1,496 | PF65 4.00 | | | | |
| 2004 (l) | 6,500,000 | — | — | 0.20 | 0.30 | 0.50 |
| 2004 (c) Sets only | — | — | — | — | — | 5.00 |
| 2004 (c) | 1,750 | PF65 4.00 | | | | |
| 2005 | 2,000,000 | — | — | — | 20.00 | 30.00 |
| Note: All but 28,000 melted | | | | | | |
| 2005 (c) Sets only | 3,000 | — | — | — | — | 20.00 |
| 2005 (c) | 2,250 | PF65 4.00 | | | | |
| 2006 (c) Sets only | 3,000 | — | — | — | — | 10.00 |
| 2006 (c) | 2,100 | PF65 4.00 | | | | |

### KM# 117a 10 CENTS

3.31 g., Copper Plated Steel, 20.5 mm. **Ruler:** Elizabeth II **Obv:** Head with tiara right **Rev:** Value above koruru **Edge:** Plain

| Date | Mintage | VF20 | XF40 | MS60 | MS63 | MS65 |
|---|---|---|---|---|---|---|
| 2006 (o) | 140,200,000 | — | — | — | 0.20 | 0.40 |
| 2007 (o) | 15,000,000 | — | — | — | — | — |
| 2007 (c) Sets only | 5,000 | — | — | — | — | 5.00 |
| 2007 (c) | 3,500 | PF65 4.00 | | | | |
| 2008 (l) Sets only | 4,000 | — | — | — | — | 5.00 |
| 2008 (l) | 3,000 | PF65 4.00 | | | | |
| 2009 (o) | 30,000,000 | — | — | — | 0.20 | 0.40 |
| 2009 (w) Sets only | 2,000 | — | — | — | — | 5.00 |
| 2009 (w) | 1,500 | PF65 4.00 | | | | |
| 2011 (o) | 10,400,000 | — | — | — | 0.20 | 0.40 |

### KM# 117b 10 CENTS

3.73 g., Copper, 20.5 mm. **Ruler:** Elizabeth II **Obv:** Head with tiara right **Rev:** Value above koruru

| Date | Mintage | VF20 | XF40 | MS60 | MS63 | MS65 |
|---|---|---|---|---|---|---|
| 2010 (u) | 2,000 | — | — | — | — | 4.00 |
| 2010 (u) | 1,500 | PF65 5.00 | | | | |
| 2011 (u) | 2,000 | — | — | — | — | 4.00 |
| 2011 (u) | 1,500 | PF65 5.00 | | | | |
| 2012 (u) | 2,000 | — | — | — | — | 4.00 |
| 2012 (u) | 1,500 | PF65 5.00 | | | | |

### KM# 117c 10 CENTS

4.37 g., Silver, 20.5 mm. **Ruler:** Elizabeth II **Obv:** Head with tiara right **Rev:** Value above koruru **Edge:** Plain

| Date | Mintage | VF20 | XF40 | MS60 | MS63 | MS65 |
|---|---|---|---|---|---|---|
| 2011 (u) | 1,200 | PF65 25.00 | | | | |

### KM# 117d 10 CENTS

4.37 g., Silver selectively gold plated, 20.5 mm. **Ruler:** Elizabeth II **Obv:** Head with tiara right **Rev:** Value above koruru **Edge:** Plain

| Date | Mintage | VF20 | XF40 | MS60 | MS63 | MS65 |
|---|---|---|---|---|---|---|
| 2012 (u) | 1,000 | PF65 25.00 | | | | |

### KM# 234 10 CENTS

3.31 g., Copper Plated Steel, 20.5 mm. **Ruler:** Elizabeth II **Obv:** Head with tiara right **Rev:** Tuatara right **Edge:** Plain

| Date | Mintage | VF20 | XF40 | MS60 | MS63 | MS65 |
|---|---|---|---|---|---|---|
| 2007 (c) Sets only | 15,000 | — | — | — | 0.50 | 5.00 |

### KM# 118 20 CENTS

11.31 g., Copper-Nickel, 28.58 mm. **Ruler:** Elizabeth II **Obv:** Head with tiara right **Rev:** Value below Pukaki **Edge:** Reeded **Note:** Many recalled and melted in 2006.

| Date | Mintage | VF20 | XF40 | MS60 | MS63 | MS65 |
|---|---|---|---|---|---|---|
| 2001 (c) | 1,364 | PF65 10.00 | | | | |
| 2001 (c) Sets only | 2,910 | — | — | — | — | 7.00 |
| 2002 (l) | 7,000,000 | — | — | — | 0.40 | 0.65 |
| 2002 (c) Sets only | 3,000 | — | — | — | — | 7.00 |
| 2002 (c) | 1,500 | PF65 10.00 | | | | |
| 2003 (c) Sets only | 3,000 | — | — | — | — | 7.00 |
| 2003 (c) | 3,000 | PF65 10.00 | | | | |
| 2004 (l) | 8,500,000 | — | — | — | 0.40 | 0.65 |
| 2004 (c) Sets only | 2,800 | — | — | — | — | 8.00 |
| 2004 (c) | 1,750 | PF65 10.00 | | | | |
| 2005 (l) | 4,000,000 | — | — | — | — | 12.00 |
| Note: All but 178,000 melted | | | | | | |
| 2005 (c) Sets only | 3,000 | — | — | — | — | 7.00 |
| 2005 (c) | 2,250 | PF65 10.00 | | | | |
| 2006 (c) Sets only | 3,000 | — | — | — | — | 7.00 |
| 2006 (c) | 2,100 | PF65 10.00 | | | | |

### KM# 118a 20 CENTS

4.00 g., Nickel Plated Steel, 21.75 mm. **Ruler:** Elizabeth II **Obv:** Head with tiara right **Rev:** Value below Pukaki **Shape:** Scalloped

| Date | Mintage | VF20 | XF40 | MS60 | MS63 | MS65 |
|---|---|---|---|---|---|---|
| 2006 (o) | 116,600,000 | — | — | — | 0.40 | 0.65 |
| 2007 (c) Sets only | 5,000 | — | — | — | — | 7.00 |
| 2007 (c) | 4,000 | PF65 8.00 | | | | |
| 2008 (o) | 80,000,000 | — | — | — | 0.40 | 0.65 |
| 2008 (l) Sets only | 4,000 | — | — | — | — | 7.00 |
| 2008 (l) | 3,000 | PF65 8.00 | | | | |
| 2009 (w) Sets only | 2,000 | — | — | — | — | 7.00 |
| 2009 (w) | 1,500 | PF65 8.00 | | | | |

### KM# 118b 20 CENTS

4.45 g., Copper-Nickel, 21.75 mm. **Ruler:** Elizabeth II **Obv:** Head with tiara right **Rev:** Value below Pukaki **Edge:** Scalloped

| Date | Mintage | VF20 | XF40 | MS60 | MS63 | MS65 |
|---|---|---|---|---|---|---|
| 2010 (u) | 2,000 | — | — | — | — | 7.00 |
| 2010 (u) | 1,500 | PF65 8.00 | | | | |
| 2011 (u) | 2,000 | — | — | — | — | 7.00 |
| 2011 (u) | 1,500 | PF65 8.00 | | | | |
| 2012 (u) | 2,000 | — | — | — | — | 7.00 |
| 2012 (u) | 1,500 | PF65 8.00 | | | | |

### KM# 118c 20 CENTS

5.30 g., 0.999 Silver 0.1702 oz. ASW, 21.75 mm. **Ruler:** Elizabeth II **Obv:** Head with tiara right **Rev:** Value below Pukaki **Edge:** Plain

| Date | Mintage | VF20 | XF40 | MS60 | MS63 | MS65 |
|---|---|---|---|---|---|---|
| 2011 (u) | 1,200 | PF65 30.00 | | | | |
| 2012 (u) | 1,000 | PF65 30.00 | | | | |

### KM# 119 50 CENTS

13.61 g., Copper-Nickel, 31.75 mm. **Ruler:** Elizabeth II **Obv:** Head with tiara right **Rev:** H.M.S. Endeavour and value **Edge:** Segmented reeding **Note:** Many recalled and melted in 2006.

| Date | Mintage | VF20 | XF40 | MS60 | MS63 | MS65 |
|---|---|---|---|---|---|---|
| 2001 (l) | 5,000,000 | — | 0.50 | 0.75 | 1.00 | 1.50 |
| 2001 (c) Sets only | 2,910 | — | — | — | — | 7.00 |
| 2001 (c) | 1,364 | PF65 9.00 | | | | |
| 2002 (l) | 3,000,000 | — | 0.50 | 0.75 | 1.00 | 1.50 |
| 2002 (c) Sets only | 3,000 | — | — | — | — | 6.00 |
| 2002 (c) | 1,500 | PF65 9.00 | | | | |
| 2003 (l) | 2,500,000 | — | 0.50 | 0.75 | 1.00 | 1.50 |
| 2003 (c) Sets only | 3,000 | — | — | — | — | 6.00 |
| 2003 (c) | 1,496 | PF65 9.00 | | | | |
| 2004 (l) | 2,000,000 | — | 0.50 | 0.75 | 1.00 | 1.50 |
| 2004 (c) Sets only | 2,800 | — | — | — | — | 7.00 |
| 2004 (c) | 1,750 | PF65 9.00 | | | | |
| 2005 (l) | 1,000,000 | — | — | — | — | 6.00 |
| Note: All but 503,800 melted | | | | | | |
| 2005 (c) Sets only | 3,000 | — | — | — | — | 6.00 |
| 2005 (c) | 2,250 | PF65 9.00 | | | | |
| 2006 (c) Sets only | 3,000 | — | — | — | — | 6.00 |
| 2006 (c) | 2,100 | PF65 9.00 | | | | |

### KM# 135 50 CENTS

13.61 g., Copper-Nickel, 31.75 mm. **Ruler:** Elizabeth II **Subject:** Lord of the Rings **Obv:** Head with tiara right **Rev:** Frodo's head facing to left of vine and value **Edge:** Reeded

| Date | Mintage | VF20 | XF40 | MS60 | MS63 | MS65 |
|---|---|---|---|---|---|---|
| 2003 (l) | 41,221 | — | — | — | — | 15.00 |

### KM# 136 50 CENTS

13.61 g., Copper-Nickel, 31.75 mm. **Ruler:** Elizabeth II **Subject:** Lord of the Rings **Obv:** Head with tiara right **Rev:** Head of Gandalf with hat facing and value **Edge:** Reeded

| Date | Mintage | VF20 | XF40 | MS60 | MS63 | MS65 |
|---|---|---|---|---|---|---|
| 2003 (l) | 41,221 | — | — | — | — | 15.00 |

### KM# 137 50 CENTS

13.61 g., Copper-Nickel, 31.75 mm. **Ruler:** Elizabeth II **Subject:** Lord of the Rings **Obv:** Head with tiara right **Rev:** Head of Aragorn facing and value **Edge:** Reeded

| Date | Mintage | VF20 | XF40 | MS60 | MS63 | MS65 |
|---|---|---|---|---|---|---|
| 2003 (l) | 41,221 | — | — | — | — | 15.00 |

### KM# 138 50 CENTS

13.61 g., Copper-Nickel, 31.75 mm. **Ruler:** Elizabeth II **Subject:** Lord of the Rings **Obv:** Head with tiara right **Rev:** Head of Gollum facing and value **Edge:** Reeded

| Date | Mintage | VF20 | XF40 | MS60 | MS63 | MS65 |
|---|---|---|---|---|---|---|
| 2003 (l) | 38,400 | — | — | — | — | 15.00 |

### KM# 139 50 CENTS

13.61 g., Copper-Nickel, 31.75 mm. **Ruler:** Elizabeth II **Subject:** Lord of the Rings **Obv:** Head with tiara right **Rev:** Saruman, value **Edge:** Reeded

| Date | Mintage | VF20 | XF40 | MS60 | MS63 | MS65 |
|---|---|---|---|---|---|---|
| 2003 (l) | 38,400 | — | — | — | — | 15.00 |

### KM# 140 50 CENTS

13.61 g., Copper-Nickel, 31.75 mm. **Ruler:** Elizabeth II **Subject:** Lord of the Rings **Obv:** Head with tiara right **Rev:** Head of Sauron left and value **Edge:** Reeded

| Date | Mintage | VF20 | XF40 | MS60 | MS63 | MS65 |
|---|---|---|---|---|---|---|
| 2003 (l) | 38,400 | — | — | — | — | 15.00 |

### KM# 235 50 CENTS

13.61 g., Copper-Nickel, 31.75 mm. **Ruler:** Elizabeth II **Subject:** Lord of the Rings **Obv:** Head with tiara right **Rev:** Boromir

| Date | Mintage | VF20 | XF40 | MS60 | MS63 | MS65 |
|---|---|---|---|---|---|---|
| 2003 (l) | 6,889 | — | — | — | — | 18.00 |

### KM# 236 50 CENTS

13.61 g., Copper-Nickel, 31.75 mm. **Ruler:** Elizabeth II **Subject:** Lord of the Rings **Obv:** Head with tiara right **Rev:** Gimli

| Date | Mintage | VF20 | XF40 | MS60 | MS63 | MS65 |
|---|---|---|---|---|---|---|
| 2003 (l) | 6,889 | — | — | — | — | 18.00 |

### KM# 237 50 CENTS

13.61 g., Copper-Nickel, 31.75 mm. **Ruler:** Elizabeth II **Subject:** Lord of the Rings **Obv:** Head with tiara right **Rev:** Legolas

| Date | Mintage | VF20 | XF40 | MS60 | MS63 | MS65 |
|---|---|---|---|---|---|---|
| 2003 (l) | 6,889 | — | — | — | — | 18.00 |

### KM# 238 50 CENTS

13.61 g., Copper-Nickel, 31.75 mm. **Ruler:** Elizabeth II **Subject:** Lord of the Rings **Obv:** Head with tiara right **Rev:** Merry

| Date | Mintage | VF20 | XF40 | MS60 | MS63 | MS65 |
|---|---|---|---|---|---|---|
| 2003 (l) | 6,889 | — | — | — | — | 18.00 |

### KM# 239 50 CENTS

13.61 g., Copper-Nickel, 31.75 mm. **Ruler:** Elizabeth II **Subject:** Lord of the Rings **Obv:** Head with tiara right **Rev:** Pippin

| Date | Mintage | VF20 | XF40 | MS60 | MS63 | MS65 |
|---|---|---|---|---|---|---|
| 2003 (l) | 6,889 | — | — | — | — | 18.00 |

### KM# 240 50 CENTS

13.61 g., Copper-Nickel, 31.75 mm. **Ruler:** Elizabeth II **Subject:** Lord of the Rings **Obv:** Head with tiara right **Rev:** Sam

| Date | Mintage | VF20 | XF40 | MS60 | MS63 | MS65 |
|---|---|---|---|---|---|---|
| 2003 (l) | 6,889 | — | — | — | — | 18.00 |

### KM# 241 50 CENTS

13.61 g., Copper-Nickel, 31.75 mm. **Ruler:** Elizabeth II **Subject:** Lord of the Rings **Obv:** Head with tiara right **Rev:** Arwen

| Date | Mintage | VF20 | XF40 | MS60 | MS63 | MS65 |
|---|---|---|---|---|---|---|
| 2003 (l) | 4,068 | — | — | — | — | 20.00 |

### KM# 242 50 CENTS

13.61 g., Copper-Nickel, 31.75 mm. **Ruler:** Elizabeth II **Subject:** Lord of the Rings **Obv:** Head with tiara right **Rev:** Elrond

| Date | Mintage | VF20 | XF40 | MS60 | MS63 | MS65 |
|---|---|---|---|---|---|---|
| 2003 (l) | 4,068 | — | — | — | — | 20.00 |

### KM# 243 50 CENTS

13.61 g., Copper-Nickel, 31.75 mm. **Ruler:** Elizabeth II **Subject:** Lord of the Rings **Obv:** Head with tiara right **Rev:** Eowyn

| Date | Mintage | VF20 | XF40 | MS60 | MS63 | MS65 |
|---|---|---|---|---|---|---|
| 2003 (l) | 4,068 | — | — | — | — | 20.00 |

### KM# 244 50 CENTS

13.61 g., Copper-Nickel, 31.75 mm. **Ruler:** Elizabeth II **Subject:** Lord of the Rings **Obv:** Head with tiara right **Rev:** Galadriel

| Date | Mintage | VF20 | XF40 | MS60 | MS63 | MS65 |
|---|---|---|---|---|---|---|
| 2003 (l) | 4,068 | — | — | — | — | 20.00 |

### KM# 245 50 CENTS

13.61 g., Copper-Nickel, 31.75 mm. **Ruler:** Elizabeth II **Subject:** Lord of the Rings **Obv:** Head with tiara right **Rev:** An Orc

| Date | Mintage | VF20 | XF40 | MS60 | MS63 | MS65 |
|---|---|---|---|---|---|---|
| 2003 (l) | 4,068 | — | — | — | — | 20.00 |

### KM# 246 50 CENTS

13.61 g., Copper-Nickel, 31.75 mm. **Ruler:** Elizabeth II **Subject:** Lord of the Rings **Obv:** Head with tiara right **Rev:** Treebeard

| Date | Mintage | VF20 | XF40 | MS60 | MS63 | MS65 |
|---|---|---|---|---|---|---|
| 2003 (l) | 4,068 | — | — | — | — | 20.00 |

**KM# 119a 50 CENTS**
5.00 g., Nickel Plated Steel, 24.75 mm. **Ruler:** Elizabeth II **Obv:** Head with tiara right **Rev:** Ship, H.M.S. Endeavour

| Date | Mintage | VF20 | XF40 | MS60 | MS63 | MS65 |
|---|---|---|---|---|---|---|
| 2006 (o) | 70,200,000 | — | — | — | 0.75 | 1.00 |
| 2007 (c) Sets only | 5,000 | — | — | — | — | 6.00 |
| 2007 (c) | 3,500 | PF65 8.00 | | | | |
| 2008 (l) Sets only | 4,000 | — | — | — | — | 6.00 |
| 2008 (l) | 3,000 | PF65 8.00 | | | | |
| 2009 (o) | 20,000,000 | — | — | — | 0.75 | 1.00 |
| 2009 (w) Sets only | 2,000 | — | — | — | — | 6.00 |
| 2009 (w) | 1,500 | PF65 9.00 | | | | |

**KM# 279 50 CENTS**
Aluminum-Bronze, 38.74 mm. **Ruler:** Elizabeth II **Subject:** Narnia **Obv:** Head with tiara right **Rev:** Peter

| Date | Mintage | VF20 | XF40 | MS60 | MS63 | MS65 |
|---|---|---|---|---|---|---|
| 2006 (c) | 20,000 | — | — | — | — | 5.00 |

**KM# 280 50 CENTS**
Aluminum-Bronze, 38.74 mm. **Ruler:** Elizabeth II **Subject:** Narnia **Obv:** Head with tiara right **Rev:** Susan

| Date | Mintage | VF20 | XF40 | MS60 | MS63 | MS65 |
|---|---|---|---|---|---|---|
| 2006 (c) | 20,000 | — | — | — | — | 5.00 |

**KM# 281 50 CENTS**
Aluminum-Bronze, 38.74 mm. **Ruler:** Elizabeth II **Subject:** Narnia **Obv:** Head with tiara right **Rev:** Edmund

| Date | Mintage | VF20 | XF40 | MS60 | MS63 | MS65 |
|---|---|---|---|---|---|---|
| 2006 (c) | 20,000 | — | — | — | — | 5.00 |

**KM# 282 50 CENTS**
Aluminum-Bronze, 38.74 mm. **Ruler:** Elizabeth II **Subject:** Narnia **Obv:** Head with tiara right **Rev:** Lucy

| Date | Mintage | VF20 | XF40 | MS60 | MS63 | MS65 |
|---|---|---|---|---|---|---|
| 2006 (c) | 20,000 | — | — | — | — | 5.00 |

**KM# 283 50 CENTS**
Aluminum-Bronze, 38.74 mm. **Ruler:** Elizabeth II **Subject:** Narnia **Obv:** Head with tiara right **Rev:** Mr. Tumnus

| Date | Mintage | VF20 | XF40 | MS60 | MS63 | MS65 |
|---|---|---|---|---|---|---|
| 2006 (c) | 20,000 | — | — | — | — | 5.00 |

**KM# 284 50 CENTS**
Aluminum-Bronze, 38.74 mm. **Ruler:** Elizabeth II **Subject:** Narnia **Obv:** Head with tiara right **Rev:** Ginarrbrik

| Date | Mintage | VF20 | XF40 | MS60 | MS63 | MS65 |
|---|---|---|---|---|---|---|
| 2006 (c) | 20,000 | — | — | — | — | 5.00 |

**KM# 119b 50 CENTS**
5.60 g., Copper-Nickel, 24.75 mm. **Ruler:** Elizabeth II **Obv:** Head with tiara right **Rev:** Ship, H.M.S. Endeavour

| Date | Mintage | VF20 | XF40 | MS60 | MS63 | MS65 |
|---|---|---|---|---|---|---|
| 2010 (u) | 2,000 | — | — | — | — | 6.00 |
| 2010 (u) | 1,500 | PF65 9.00 | | | | |
| 2011 (u) | 2,000 | — | — | — | — | 6.00 |
| 2011 (u) | 1,500 | PF65 9.00 | | | | |
| 2012 (u) | 2,000 | — | — | — | — | 6.00 |
| 2012 (u) | 1,500 | PF65 9.00 | | | | |

**KM# 119c 50 CENTS**
6.59 g., 0.999 Silver 0.2117 oz. ASW, 24.75 mm. **Ruler:** Elizabeth II **Obv:** Head with tiara right **Rev:** Ship, H.M.S. Endeavor **Edge:** Plain

| Date | Mintage | VF20 | XF40 | MS60 | MS63 | MS65 |
|---|---|---|---|---|---|---|
| 2011 (u) | 1,200 | PF65 45.00 | | | | |
| 2012 (u) | 1,000 | PF65 45.00 | | | | |

**KM# 120 DOLLAR**
8.00 g., Aluminum-Bronze, 23 mm. **Ruler:** Elizabeth II **Obv:** Head with tiara right **Rev:** Kiwi bird within sprigs, value below **Edge:** Segmented reeding

| Date | Mintage | VF20 | XF40 | MS60 | MS63 | MS65 |
|---|---|---|---|---|---|---|
| 2001 (c) Sets only | 2,910 | — | — | — | — | 4.00 |
| 2001 (c) | 1,364 | PF65 5.00 | | | | |
| 2002 (l) | 8,000,000 | — | — | 1.00 | 1.50 | 2.50 |
| 2002 (c) Sets only | 4,000 | — | — | — | — | 4.00 |
| 2002 (c) | 1,500 | PF65 5.00 | | | | |
| 2003 (l) | 4,000,000 | — | — | 1.00 | 1.50 | 2.50 |
| 2003 (c) Sets only | 5,000 | — | — | — | — | 4.00 |
| 2003 (c) | 1,750 | PF65 5.00 | | | | |
| 2004 (l) | 2,700,000 | — | — | 1.00 | 1.50 | 2.50 |
| 2004 (c) Sets only | 3,500 | — | — | — | — | 4.00 |
| 2004 (c) | 2,250 | PF65 5.00 | | | | |
| 2005 (l) | 2,000,000 | — | — | 1.00 | 1.50 | 2.50 |
| 2005 (c) Sets only | 4,000 | — | — | — | — | 4.00 |
| 2005 (c) | 2,250 | PF65 5.00 | | | | |
| 2006 (c) Sets only | 3,000 | — | — | — | — | 4.00 |
| 2006 (c) | 2,100 | PF65 5.00 | | | | |
| 2007 (c) | 5,000 | — | — | — | — | 4.00 |
| 2007 (c) | 3,500 | PF65 5.00 | | | | |
| 2008 (l) | 6,000,000 | — | — | 1.00 | 1.50 | 2.50 |
| 2008 (l) Sets only | 4,000 | — | — | — | — | 4.00 |
| 2008 (l) | 3,000 | PF65 5.00 | | | | |
| 2009 (w) Sets only | 2,000 | — | — | — | — | 4.00 |
| 2009 (w) | 1,500 | PF65 5.00 | | | | |
| 2010 (l) | 10,000,000 | — | — | 1.00 | 1.50 | 2.50 |

**KM# 141 DOLLAR**
28.28 g., Aluminum-Bronze, 38.61 mm. **Ruler:** Elizabeth II **Subject:** Lord of the Rings **Obv:** Head with tiara right **Rev:** Inscribed ring around value **Edge:** Reeded

| Date | Mintage | VF20 | XF40 | MS60 | MS63 | MS65 |
|---|---|---|---|---|---|---|
| 2003 (l) | 30,081 | — | — | — | 15.00 | 18.00 |

Note: Mintage includes 10,454 in sets.

**KM# 141a DOLLAR**
28.28 g., 0.925 Silver 0.841 oz. ASW selective gold plating, 38.61 mm. **Ruler:** Elizabeth II **Obv:** Head with tiara right **Rev:** Gold-plated ring and edge **Edge:** Reeded

| Date | Mintage | VF20 | XF40 | MS60 | MS63 | MS65 |
|---|---|---|---|---|---|---|
| 2003 (l) | 39,244 | PF65 70.00 | | | | |

**KM# 142 DOLLAR**
28.28 g., Aluminum-Bronze, 38.61 mm. **Ruler:** Elizabeth II **Subject:** Lord of the Rings **Obv:** Head with tiara right **Rev:** Head of Frodo looking down above inscription **Edge:** Reeded

| Date | Mintage | VF20 | XF40 | MS60 | MS63 | MS65 |
|---|---|---|---|---|---|---|
| 2003 (l) | 10,454 | — | — | — | — | 10.00 |

**KM# 143 DOLLAR**
28.28 g., Aluminum-Bronze, 38.61 mm. **Ruler:** Elizabeth II **Subject:** Lord of the Rings **Obv:** Head with tiara right **Rev:** View of Sauron, value **Edge:** Reeded

| Date | Mintage | VF20 | XF40 | MS60 | MS63 | MS65 |
|---|---|---|---|---|---|---|
| 2003 (l) | 10,454 | — | — | — | — | 10.00 |

**KM# 247 DOLLAR**
28.28 g., 0.925 Silver 0.841 oz. ASW, 38.61 mm. **Ruler:** Elizabeth II **Subject:** Lord of the Rings **Obv:** Head with tiara right **Rev:** Aragorn's Coronation

| Date | Mintage | VF20 | XF40 | MS60 | MS63 | MS65 |
|---|---|---|---|---|---|---|
| 2003 (l) | 3,057 | PF65 70.00 | | | | |

**KM# 248 DOLLAR**
28.28 g., 0.925 Silver 0.841 oz. ASW, 38.61 mm. **Ruler:** Elizabeth II **Subject:** Lord of the Rings **Obv:** Head with tiara right **Rev:** King Theoden

| Date | Mintage | VF20 | XF40 | MS60 | MS63 | MS65 |
|---|---|---|---|---|---|---|
| 2003 (l) | 2,022 | PF65 70.00 | | | | |

**KM# 249 DOLLAR**
28.28 g., 0.925 Silver 0.841 oz. ASW, 38.61 mm. **Ruler:** Elizabeth II **Subject:** Lord of the Rings **Obv:** Head with tiara right **Rev:** Flight to the Ford

| Date | Mintage | VF20 | XF40 | MS60 | MS63 | MS65 |
|---|---|---|---|---|---|---|
| 2003 (l) | 2,020 | **PF65** 70.00 | | | | |

**KM# 250 DOLLAR**
28.28 g., 0.925 Silver 0.841 oz. ASW, 38.61 mm. **Ruler:** Elizabeth II **Subject:** Lord of the Rings **Obv:** Head with tiara right **Rev:** Mirror of Galadriel

| Date | Mintage | VF20 | XF40 | MS60 | MS63 | MS65 |
|---|---|---|---|---|---|---|
| 2003 (l) | 2,036 | **PF65** 70.00 | | | | |

**KM# 251 DOLLAR**
28.28 g., 0.925 Silver 0.841 oz. ASW, 38.61 mm. **Ruler:** Elizabeth II **Subject:** Lord of the Rings **Obv:** Head with tiara right **Rev:** Frodo offering ring to Nazgul

| Date | Mintage | VF20 | XF40 | MS60 | MS63 | MS65 |
|---|---|---|---|---|---|---|
| 2003 (l) | 1,784 | **PF65** 70.00 | | | | |

**KM# 252 DOLLAR**
28.28 g., 0.925 Silver 0.841 oz. ASW, 38.61 mm. **Ruler:** Elizabeth II **Subject:** Lord of the Rings **Obv:** Head with tiara right **Rev:** Bridge of Kazad-Dum

| Date | Mintage | VF20 | XF40 | MS60 | MS63 | MS65 |
|---|---|---|---|---|---|---|
| 2003 (l) | 952 | **PF65** 70.00 | | | | |

**KM# 253 DOLLAR**
28.28 g., 0.925 Silver 0.841 oz. ASW, 38.61 mm. **Ruler:** Elizabeth II **Subject:** Lord of the Rings **Obv:** Head with tiara right **Rev:** Shelob's Lair

| Date | Mintage | VF20 | XF40 | MS60 | MS63 | MS65 |
|---|---|---|---|---|---|---|
| 2003 (l) | 917 | **PF65** 70.00 | | | | |

**KM# 254 DOLLAR**
28.28 g., 0.925 Silver 0.841 oz. ASW, 38.61 mm. **Ruler:** Elizabeth II **Subject:** Lord of the Rings **Obv:** Head with tiara right **Rev:** Taming of Smeagol

| Date | Mintage | VF20 | XF40 | MS60 | MS63 | MS65 |
|---|---|---|---|---|---|---|
| 2003 (l) | 1,017 | **PF65** 70.00 | | | | |

**KM# 255 DOLLAR**
28.28 g., 0.925 Silver 0.841 oz. ASW, 38.61 mm. **Ruler:** Elizabeth II **Subject:** Lord of the Rings **Obv:** Head with tiara right **Rev:** Dark Lord's Tower and the Eye

| Date | Mintage | VF20 | XF40 | MS60 | MS63 | MS65 |
|---|---|---|---|---|---|---|
| 2003 (l) | 1,002 | **PF65** 70.00 | | | | |

**KM# 256 DOLLAR**
28.28 g., 0.925 Silver 0.841 oz. ASW, 38.61 mm. **Ruler:** Elizabeth II **Subject:** Lord of the Rings **Obv:** Head with tiara right **Rev:** Knife in the Dark

| Date | Mintage | VF20 | XF40 | MS60 | MS63 | MS65 |
|---|---|---|---|---|---|---|
| 2003 (l) | 967 | **PF65** 70.00 | | | | |

**KM# 257 DOLLAR**
28.28 g., 0.925 Silver 0.841 oz. ASW, 38.61 mm. **Ruler:** Elizabeth II **Subject:** Lord of the Rings **Obv:** Head with tiara right **Rev:** Gandalf and Saruman

| Date | Mintage | VF20 | XF40 | MS60 | MS63 | MS65 |
|---|---|---|---|---|---|---|
| 2003 (l) | 867 | **PF65** 70.00 | | | | |

**KM# 258 DOLLAR**
28.28 g., 0.925 Silver 0.841 oz. ASW, 38.61 mm. **Ruler:** Elizabeth II **Subject:** Lord of the Rings **Obv:** Head with tiara right **Rev:** Council of Elrond

| Date | Mintage | VF20 | XF40 | MS60 | MS63 | MS65 |
|---|---|---|---|---|---|---|
| 2003 (l) | 1,204 | **PF65** 70.00 | | | | |

**KM# 259 DOLLAR**
28.28 g., 0.925 Silver 0.841 oz. ASW, 38.61 mm. **Ruler:** Elizabeth II **Subject:** Lord of the Rings **Obv:** Head with tiara right **Rev:** Helm's Deep

| Date | Mintage | VF20 | XF40 | MS60 | MS63 | MS65 |
|---|---|---|---|---|---|---|
| 2003 (l) | 967 | **PF65** 70.00 | | | | |

**KM# 260 DOLLAR**
28.28 g., 0.925 Silver 0.841 oz. ASW, 38.61 mm. **Ruler:** Elizabeth II **Subject:** Lord of the Rings **Obv:** Head with tiara right **Rev:** Frodo & Co. at Mt. Doom

| Date | Mintage | VF20 | XF40 | MS60 | MS63 | MS65 |
|---|---|---|---|---|---|---|
| 2003 (l) | 917 | **PF65** 70.00 | | | | |

**KM# 261 DOLLAR**
28.28 g., 0.925 Silver 0.841 oz. ASW, 38.61 mm. **Ruler:** Elizabeth II **Subject:** Lord of the Rings **Obv:** Head with tiara right **Rev:** Departure of Boromir

| Date | Mintage | VF20 | XF40 | MS60 | MS63 | MS65 |
|---|---|---|---|---|---|---|
| 2003 (l) | 917 | PF65 70.00 | | | | |

**KM# 262 DOLLAR**
28.28 g., 0.925 Silver 0.841 oz. ASW, 38.61 mm. **Ruler:** Elizabeth II **Subject:** Lord of the Rings **Obv:** Head with tiara right **Rev:** Meeting of Treebeard

| Date | Mintage | VF20 | XF40 | MS60 | MS63 | MS65 |
|---|---|---|---|---|---|---|
| 2003 (l) | 867 | PF65 70.00 | | | | |

**KM# 263 DOLLAR**
28.28 g., 0.925 Silver 0.841 oz. ASW, 38.61 mm. **Ruler:** Elizabeth II **Subject:** Lord of the Rings **Obv:** Head with tiara right **Rev:** Battle of Minas Tirith / Pelenor Fields

| Date | Mintage | VF20 | XF40 | MS60 | MS63 | MS65 |
|---|---|---|---|---|---|---|
| 2003 (l) | 867 | PF65 70.00 | | | | |

**KM# 264 DOLLAR**
28.28 g., 0.925 Silver 0.841 oz. ASW, 38.61 mm. **Ruler:** Elizabeth II **Subject:** Lord of the Rings **Obv:** Head with tiara right **Rev:** Gandalf Reappears

| Date | Mintage | VF20 | XF40 | MS60 | MS63 | MS65 |
|---|---|---|---|---|---|---|
| 2003 (l) | 967 | PF65 70.00 | | | | |

**KM# 265 DOLLAR**
28.28 g., 0.925 Silver 0.841 oz. ASW, 38.61 mm. **Ruler:** Elizabeth II **Subject:** Lord of the Rings **Obv:** Head with tiara right **Rev:** Army of the Dead

| Date | Mintage | VF20 | XF40 | MS60 | MS63 | MS65 |
|---|---|---|---|---|---|---|
| 2003 (l) | 917 | PF65 70.00 | | | | |

**KM# 266 DOLLAR**
28.28 g., 0.925 Silver 0.841 oz. ASW, 38.61 mm. **Ruler:** Elizabeth II **Subject:** Lord of the Rings **Obv:** Head with tiara right **Rev:** Travel to the Undying Lands

| Date | Mintage | VF20 | XF40 | MS60 | MS63 | MS65 |
|---|---|---|---|---|---|---|
| 2003 (l) | 867 | PF65 70.00 | | | | |

**KM# 267 DOLLAR**
28.28 g., 0.925 Silver 0.841 oz. ASW, 38.61 mm. **Ruler:** Elizabeth II **Subject:** Lord of the Rings **Obv:** Head with tiara right **Rev:** Great River

| Date | Mintage | VF20 | XF40 | MS60 | MS63 | MS65 |
|---|---|---|---|---|---|---|
| 2003 (l) | 867 | PF65 70.00 | | | | |

**KM# 268 DOLLAR**
28.28 g., 0.925 Silver 0.841 oz. ASW, 38.61 mm. **Ruler:** Elizabeth II **Subject:** Lord of the Rings **Obv:** Head with tiara right **Rev:** Death of the Witch King

| Date | Mintage | VF20 | XF40 | MS60 | MS63 | MS65 |
|---|---|---|---|---|---|---|
| 2003 (l) | 867 | PF65 70.00 | | | | |

**KM# 269 DOLLAR**
28.28 g., 0.925 Silver 0.841 oz. ASW, 38.61 mm. **Ruler:** Elizabeth II **Subject:** Lord of the Rings **Obv:** Head with tiara right **Rev:** March of the Oliphants

| Date | Mintage | VF20 | XF40 | MS60 | MS63 | MS65 |
|---|---|---|---|---|---|---|
| 2003 (l) | 867 | PF65 70.00 | | | | |

**KM# 152 DOLLAR**
28.28 g., Copper-Nickel, 38.6 mm. **Ruler:** Elizabeth II **Obv:** Crowned head right **Rev:** Little spotted kiwi **Edge:** Reeded

| Date | Mintage | VF20 | XF40 | MS60 | MS63 | MS65 |
|---|---|---|---|---|---|---|
| 2004 (c) | 2,500 | — | — | — | — | 45.00 |

**KM# 152a DOLLAR**
31.14 g., 0.999 Silver 1.000 oz. ASW, 40 mm. **Ruler:** Elizabeth II **Obv:** Crowned head right **Rev:** Little spotted kiwi **Edge:** Reeded

| Date | Mintage | VF20 | XF40 | MS60 | MS63 | MS65 |
|---|---|---|---|---|---|---|
| 2004 (c) | 2,000 | PF65 50.00 | | | | |

Note: Includes 500 struck in 2008 for sets.

**KM# 153 DOLLAR**
31.64 g., 0.999 Silver 1.0161 oz. ASW, 40 mm. **Ruler:** Elizabeth II **Obv:** Crowned head right **Rev:** Rowi Kiwi **Edge:** Reeded

| Date | Mintage | VF20 | XF40 | MS60 | MS63 | MS65 |
|---|---|---|---|---|---|---|
| 2005 (w) | 4,000 | — | — | — | — | 45.00 |

**KM# 153a DOLLAR**
31.64 g., 0.999 Silver 1.0161 oz. ASW, 38.74 mm. **Ruler:** Elizabeth II **Rev:** Rowi Kiwi

| Date | Mintage | VF20 | XF40 | MS60 | MS63 | MS65 |
|---|---|---|---|---|---|---|
| 2005 (w) | 2,700 | PF65 80.00 | | | | |

Note: Mintage includes 500 struck in 2008 for sets.

**KM# 154 DOLLAR**
31.14 g., 0.999 Silver 1.000 oz. ASW, 40 mm. **Ruler:** Elizabeth II **Subject:** ANZAC **Obv:** Crowned head right **Rev:** Soldiers seated, multicolor flag in background **Edge:** Reeded

| Date | Mintage | VF20 | XF40 | MS60 | MS63 | MS65 |
|---|---|---|---|---|---|---|
| 2005 (w) P | 15,000 | PF65 110 | | | | |

### KM# 156 DOLLAR

28.28 g., Aluminum-Bronze, 38.61 mm. **Ruler:** Elizabeth II **Subject:** Lions Rugby Tour **Obv:** Crowned head right **Rev:** Rugby player, lion's crest and New Zealand map

| Date | Mintage | VF20 | XF40 | MS60 | MS63 | MS65 |
|---|---|---|---|---|---|---|
| 2005 (l) | 15,000 | — | — | — | — | 20.00 |

### KM# 156a DOLLAR

28.28 g., 0.925 Silver 0.841 oz. ASW, 38.61 mm. **Ruler:** Elizabeth II **Series:** Rugby player, Lions crest & New Zealand map **Subject:** Lions Rugby Tour **Obv:** Crowned head right **Edge:** Reeded

| Date | Mintage | VF20 | XF40 | MS60 | MS63 | MS65 |
|---|---|---|---|---|---|---|
| 2005 (l) | 5,000 | PF65 50.00 | | | | |

### KM# 157 DOLLAR

Aluminum-Bronze, 38.74 mm. **Ruler:** Elizabeth II **Subject:** ANZAC **Obv:** Crowned head right **Rev:** Soldiers from Chunuk Bair battle with rifles and bayonets **Edge:** Reeded

| Date | Mintage | VF20 | XF40 | MS60 | MS63 | MS65 |
|---|---|---|---|---|---|---|
| 2005 | 15,000 | PF65 25.00 | | | | |

### KM# 159 DOLLAR

20.00 g., Aluminum-Bronze, 38.74 mm. **Ruler:** Elizabeth II **Subject:** King Kong **Obv:** Crowned head right **Rev:** King Kong **Edge:** Reeded

| Date | Mintage | VF20 | XF40 | MS60 | MS63 | MS65 |
|---|---|---|---|---|---|---|
| 2005 (w) | 7,000 | — | — | — | — | 20.00 |

### KM# 160 DOLLAR

20.00 g., Aluminum-Bronze, 38.74 mm. **Ruler:** Elizabeth II **Subject:** King Kong **Obv:** Crowned head right **Rev:** Multicolored King Kong **Edge:** Reeded

| Date | Mintage | VF20 | XF40 | MS60 | MS63 | MS65 |
|---|---|---|---|---|---|---|
| 2005 (w) | 4,000 | — | — | — | — | 35.00 |

### KM# 161 DOLLAR

20.00 g., Aluminum-Bronze, 38.74 mm. **Ruler:** Elizabeth II **Subject:** King Kong **Obv:** Crowned head right **Rev:** Carl Denham and camera in multicolor **Edge:** Reeded

| Date | Mintage | VF20 | XF40 | MS60 | MS63 | MS65 |
|---|---|---|---|---|---|---|
| 2005 | 4,000 | — | — | — | — | 35.00 |

### KM# 162 DOLLAR

20.00 g., Aluminum-Bronze, 38.74 mm. **Ruler:** Elizabeth II **Subject:** King Kong **Obv:** Crowned head right **Rev:** Ann Darrow and Jack Driscoll multicolored **Edge:** Reeded

| Date | Mintage | VF20 | XF40 | MS60 | MS63 | MS65 |
|---|---|---|---|---|---|---|
| 2005 | 4,000 | — | — | — | — | 35.00 |

### KM# 164 DOLLAR

31.14 g., 0.999 Silver 1.000 oz. ASW partially gold plated, 40.6 mm. **Ruler:** Elizabeth II **Obv:** Crowned head right **Rev:** King Kong partially gold plated

| Date | Mintage | VF20 | XF40 | MS60 | MS63 | MS65 |
|---|---|---|---|---|---|---|
| 2005 (w) | 3,000 | PF65 70.00 | | | | |

### KM# 276 DOLLAR

20.00 g., Aluminum-Bronze, 38.74 mm. **Ruler:** Elizabeth II **Subject:** Emblem **Obv:** Head with tiara right **Rev:** Rowi and chick inside patterned ring **Note:** Part of a pair issued with Australia.

| Date | Mintage | VF20 | XF40 | MS60 | MS63 | MS65 |
|---|---|---|---|---|---|---|
| 2005 (w) | 20,000 | — | — | — | — | 25.00 |

### KM# 158 DOLLAR

28.28 g., 0.999 Silver 0.9083 oz. ASW, 38.61 mm. **Ruler:** Elizabeth II **Subject:** FIFA **Obv:** Crowned head right **Rev:** Soccer player, silver fern and map

| Date | Mintage | VF20 | XF40 | MS60 | MS63 | MS65 |
|---|---|---|---|---|---|---|
| 2006 (v) | 7,500 | PF65 50.00 | | | | |

### KM# 285 DOLLAR

31.10 g., 0.999 Silver 0.9989 oz. ASW with gold highlights, 40 mm. **Ruler:** Elizabeth II **Subject:** Narnia **Obv:** Head with tiara right **Rev:** White Witch

| Date | Mintage | VF20 | XF40 | MS60 | MS63 | MS65 |
|---|---|---|---|---|---|---|
| 2006 (c) | 2,000 | PF65 70.00 | | | | |

### KM# 286 DOLLAR

20.00 g., Aluminum-Bronze, 38.74 mm. **Ruler:** Elizabeth II **Subject:** Narnia **Obv:** Head with tiara right **Rev:** Asian, lion standing right

| Date | Mintage | VF20 | XF40 | MS60 | MS63 | MS65 |
|---|---|---|---|---|---|---|
| 2006 (c) | 8,000 | — | — | — | — | 20.00 |

### KM# 287 DOLLAR

31.14 g., 0.999 Silver 1.000 oz. ASW With Gold highlights, 40 mm. **Ruler:** Elizabeth II **Subject:** Narnia **Obv:** Head with tiara right **Rev:** Asian

| Date | Mintage | VF20 | XF40 | MS60 | MS63 | MS65 |
|---|---|---|---|---|---|---|
| 2006 (c) | 4,320 | PF65 70.00 | | | | |

### KM# 288 DOLLAR

31.14 g., 0.999 Silver 1.000 oz. ASW, 40 mm. **Ruler:** Elizabeth II **Subject:** Narnia **Obv:** Head with tiara right **Rev:** Wardrobe from the Lion, Witch and Wardrobe series

| Date | Mintage | VF20 | XF40 | MS60 | MS63 | MS65 |
|---|---|---|---|---|---|---|
| 2006 (c) | 1,000 | PF65 70.00 | | | | |

### KM# 289 DOLLAR

20.00 g., Aluminum-Bronze, 38.74 mm. **Ruler:** Elizabeth II **Subject:** Queen's 80th Birthday **Obv:** Head with tiara right **Rev:** Heraldic arms

| Date | Mintage | VF20 | XF40 | MS60 | MS63 | MS65 |
|---|---|---|---|---|---|---|
| 2006 | 2,000 | — | — | — | — | 30.00 |

### KM# 290 DOLLAR

31.14 g., 0.999 Silver 1.000 oz. ASW, 38.74 mm. **Ruler:** Elizabeth II **Subject:** Queen's 80th Birthday **Obv:** Head with tiara right **Rev:** Heraldic arms

| Date | Mintage | VF20 | XF40 | MS60 | MS63 | MS65 |
|---|---|---|---|---|---|---|
| 2006 | 1,500 | PF65 85.00 | | | | |

### KM# 291 DOLLAR

31.14 g., 0.999 Silver 1.000 oz. ASW, 40 mm. **Ruler:** Elizabeth II **Obv:** Head with tiara right **Rev:** North Island Brown Kiwi **Edge:** Reeded

| Date | Mintage | VF20 | XF40 | MS60 | MS63 | MS65 |
|---|---|---|---|---|---|---|
| 2006 (w) | 3,000 | — | — | — | — | 50.00 |

### KM# 291a DOLLAR

31.14 g., 0.999 Silver 1.000 oz. ASW, 40 mm. **Ruler:** Elizabeth II **Obv:** Head with tiara right **Rev:** North Island Brown Kiwi **Edge:** Reeded

| Date | Mintage | VF20 | XF40 | MS60 | MS63 | MS65 |
|---|---|---|---|---|---|---|
| 2006 (w) | 2,000 | PF65 80.00 | | | | |

Note: Mintage includes 500 struck in 2008 for sets.

### KM# 293 DOLLAR

20.00 g., Aluminum-Bronze, 38.74 mm. **Ruler:** Elizabeth II **Subject:** NZ Gold Rushes - West Coast **Obv:** Head with tiara right **Rev:** 1860s miners

| Date | Mintage | VF20 | XF40 | MS60 | MS63 | MS65 |
|---|---|---|---|---|---|---|
| 2006 (w) | 1,500 | — | — | — | — | 35.00 |

### KM# 294 DOLLAR

31.14 g., 0.999 Silver 1.000 oz. ASW with gold highlights, 40.60 mm. **Ruler:** Elizabeth II **Subject:** NZ Gold Rushes - Thames/Coromandel **Obv:** Head with tiara right **Rev:** Gold panning

| Date | Mintage | VF20 | XF40 | MS60 | MS63 | MS65 |
|---|---|---|---|---|---|---|
| 2006 (w) | 1,200 | PF65 110 | | | | |

### KM# 232 DOLLAR

31.14 g., 0.999 Silver 1.000 oz. ASW, 40 mm. **Ruler:** Elizabeth II **Subject:** Aoraki - Mount Cook, Japanese Friendship **Obv:** Head with tiara right **Obv. Legend:** NEW ZEALAND - ELIZABETH II **Rev:** Flowers in bloom, Mount Cook in background multicolor **Note:** Also released in a Japanese proof set.

| Date | Mintage | VF20 | XF40 | MS60 | MS63 | MS65 |
|---|---|---|---|---|---|---|
| 2007 (j) | 70,000 | PF65 90.00 | | | | |

### KM# 296 DOLLAR

1.24 g., 0.999 Gold 0.040 oz. AGW, 13.92 mm. **Ruler:** Elizabeth II **Subject:** 50th Anniversary of Scott Base **Obv:** Head with tiara right **Rev:** Scott Base, Antarctica and International Polar Year logo

| Date | Mintage | VF20 | XF40 | MS60 | MS63 | MS65 |
|---|---|---|---|---|---|---|
| 2007 (m) | 10,000 | PF65 100 | | | | |

### KM# 297 DOLLAR

31.14 g., 0.999 Silver 1.000 oz. ASW, 40 mm. **Ruler:** Elizabeth II **Subject:** 50th Anniversary of Scott Base **Obv:** Head with tiara right **Rev:** Scott Base, Antarctica and International Polar Year logo

| Date | Mintage | VF20 | XF40 | MS60 | MS63 | MS65 |
|---|---|---|---|---|---|---|
| 2007 (m) | 10,000 | PF65 80.00 | | | | |

**KM# 298 DOLLAR**
28.28 g., Copper-Nickel, 38.61 mm. **Ruler:** Elizabeth II **Subject:** Scouting Centenary **Obv:** Head with tiara right

| Date | Mintage | VF20 | XF40 | MS60 | MS63 | MS65 |
|---|---|---|---|---|---|---|
| 2007 (l) | 1,900 | — | — | — | — | 50.00 |

**KM# 298a DOLLAR**
28.28 g., 0.925 Silver 0.841 oz. ASW, 38.61 mm. **Ruler:** Elizabeth II **Subject:** Scouting Centenary **Obv:** Head with tiara right

| Date | Mintage | VF20 | XF40 | MS60 | MS63 | MS65 |
|---|---|---|---|---|---|---|
| 2007 (l) | 1,500 | PF65 85.00 | | | | |

**KM# 300 DOLLAR**
31.14 g., 0.999 Silver 1.000 oz. ASW, 40 mm. **Ruler:** Elizabeth II **Obv:** Head with tiara right **Rev:** Great Spotted Kiwi **Edge:** Reeded

| Date | Mintage | VF20 | XF40 | MS60 | MS63 | MS65 |
|---|---|---|---|---|---|---|
| 2007 (m) | 4,000 | — | — | — | — | 50.00 |

**KM# 300a DOLLAR**
31.14 g., 0.999 Silver 1.000 oz. ASW, 40 mm. **Ruler:** Elizabeth II **Obv:** Head with tiara right **Rev:** Great Spotted Kiwi **Edge:** Reeded

| Date | Mintage | VF20 | XF40 | MS60 | MS63 | MS65 |
|---|---|---|---|---|---|---|
| 2007 (m) | 3,000 | PF65 100 | | | | |

Note: Mintage includes 500 struck in 2008 for sets.

**KM# 302 DOLLAR**
31.14 g., Copper-Nickel, 40 mm. **Ruler:** Elizabeth II **Subject:** Elizabeth & Philip Diamond Wedding **Obv:** Head with tiara right **Rev:** Royal crests **Edge:** Reeded

| Date | Mintage | VF20 | XF40 | MS60 | MS63 | MS65 |
|---|---|---|---|---|---|---|
| 2007 (m) | 1,600 | — | — | — | — | 32.00 |

**KM# 302a DOLLAR**
31.11 g., 0.999 Silver 0.999 oz. ASW, 40 mm. **Ruler:** Elizabeth II **Subject:** Elizabeth & Philip Diamond Wedding **Obv:** Head with tiara right **Rev:** Royal crests **Edge:** Reeded

| Date | Mintage | VF20 | XF40 | MS60 | MS63 | MS65 |
|---|---|---|---|---|---|---|
| 2007 (m) | 1,500 | PF65 85.00 | | | | |

**KM# 309 DOLLAR**
31.14 g., 0.999 Silver 1.000 oz. ASW, 40 mm. **Ruler:** Elizabeth II **Obv:** Head with tiara right **Rev:** Haast Tokoeka Kiwi

| Date | Mintage | VF20 | XF40 | MS60 | MS63 | MS65 |
|---|---|---|---|---|---|---|
| 2008 (w) | 8,000 | — | — | — | — | 60.00 |

**KM# 309a DOLLAR**
31.14 g., 0.999 Silver 1.000 oz. ASW, 40 mm. **Ruler:** Elizabeth II **Obv:** Head with tiara right **Rev:** Haast Tokoeka Kiwi

| Date | Mintage | VF20 | XF40 | MS60 | MS63 | MS65 |
|---|---|---|---|---|---|---|
| 2008 (w) | 5,000 | PF65 85.00 | | | | |

Note: Includes 500 for 2004-2008 sets.

**KM# 311 DOLLAR**
31.14 g., 0.999 Silver 1.000 oz. ASW, 40.6 mm. **Ruler:** Elizabeth II **Subject:** Sir Edmund Hillary **Obv:** Head with tiara right **Rev:** Hillary with Mt. Everest in background

| Date | Mintage | VF20 | XF40 | MS60 | MS63 | MS65 |
|---|---|---|---|---|---|---|
| 2008 (w) | 10,000 | PF65 90.00 | | | | |

**KM# 321 DOLLAR**
30.80 g., Brass, 30 mm. **Ruler:** Elizabeth II **Rev:** Sir Edmond Hillary with Mt. Everest **Edge:** Reeded **Note:** Sold in a PNC cover only

| Date | Mintage | VF20 | XF40 | MS60 | MS63 | MS65 |
|---|---|---|---|---|---|---|
| 2008 (w) | 4,000 | — | — | — | — | 20.00 |

**KM# 322 DOLLAR**
28.28 g., Copper-Nickel, 40 mm. **Ruler:** Elizabeth II **Obv:** Head with tiara right **Rev:** Kiwi with map of New Zealand **Edge:** Reeded

| Date | Mintage | VF20 | XF40 | MS60 | MS63 | MS65 |
|---|---|---|---|---|---|---|
| 2009 (m) | 10,000 | — | — | — | — | 50.00 |

**KM# 322a DOLLAR**
31.14 g., 0.999 Silver 1.000 oz. ASW, 40 mm. **Ruler:** Elizabeth II **Subject:** Icons of New Zealand **Rev:** Kiwi with map of New Zealand **Edge:** Reeded

| Date | Mintage | VF20 | XF40 | MS60 | MS63 | MS65 |
|---|---|---|---|---|---|---|
| 2009 (m) | 7,500 | PF65 80.00 | | | | |

**KM# 323 DOLLAR**
31.14 g., 0.999 Silver 1.000 oz. ASW, 40 mm. **Ruler:** Elizabeth II **Obv:** Bust right **Rev:** Southern Right Whale **Edge:** Reeded

| Date | Mintage | VF20 | XF40 | MS60 | MS63 | MS65 |
|---|---|---|---|---|---|---|
| 2009 (m) Prooflike | 11,500 | — | — | — | — | 70.00 |

**KM# 324 DOLLAR**
31.14 g., 0.999 Silver 1.000 oz. ASW, 40 mm. **Ruler:** Elizabeth II **Rev:** Haast's Eagle

| Date | Mintage | VF20 | XF40 | MS60 | MS63 | MS65 |
|---|---|---|---|---|---|---|
| 2009 (m) Prooflike | 11,500 | — | — | — | — | 80.00 |

**KM# 325 DOLLAR**
31.14 g., 0.999 Silver 1.000 oz. ASW, 40 mm. **Ruler:** Elizabeth II **Rev:** Giant Moa

| Date | Mintage | VF20 | XF40 | MS60 | MS63 | MS65 |
|---|---|---|---|---|---|---|
| 2009 (m) Prooflike | 1,500 | — | — | — | — | 85.00 |

**KM# 326 DOLLAR**
31.14 g., 0.999 Silver 1.000 oz. ASW, 40 mm. **Ruler:** Elizabeth II **Rev:** Colossal squid **Edge:** Reeded

| Date | Mintage | VF20 | XF40 | MS60 | MS63 | MS65 |
|---|---|---|---|---|---|---|
| 2009 (m) Prooflike | 1,500 | — | — | — | — | 85.00 |

**KM# 327 DOLLAR**
31.14 g., 0.999 Silver 1.000 oz. ASW, 40 mm. **Ruler:** Elizabeth II **Rev:** Giant Weta **Edge:** Reeded

| Date | Mintage | VF20 | XF40 | MS60 | MS63 | MS65 |
|---|---|---|---|---|---|---|
| 2009 (m) Prooflike | 1,500 | — | — | — | — | 85.00 |

**KM# 328 DOLLAR**
26.45 g., Copper-Nickel-Zinc, 39.19 mm. **Ruler:** Elizabeth II **Subject:** Reserve Bank of New Zealand, 75th Anniversary **Rev:** Tui and Kowhai as on 1940-65 bronze penny

| Date | Mintage | VF20 | XF40 | MS60 | MS63 | MS65 |
|---|---|---|---|---|---|---|
| 2009 (o) | 2,000 | — | — | — | — | 30.00 |

**KM# 120a DOLLAR**
8.60 g., Brass **Ruler:** Elizabeth II **Obv:** Head with tiara right **Rev:** Kiwi bird within sprigs, value below **Edge:** Segmented reeding

| Date | Mintage | VF20 | XF40 | MS60 | MS63 | MS65 |
|---|---|---|---|---|---|---|
| 2010 (u) | 2,000 | — | — | — | — | 4.00 |
| 2010 (u) | 1,500 | PF65 5.00 | | | | |
| 2011 (u) | 2,000 | — | — | — | — | 4.00 |
| 2011 (u) | 1,500 | PF65 5.00 | | | | |
| 2012 (u) | 2,000 | — | — | — | — | 4.00 |
| 2012 (u) | 1,500 | PF65 5.00 | | | | |

**KM# 331 DOLLAR**
31.14 g., 0.999 Silver 1.000 oz. ASW, 40 mm. **Ruler:** Elizabeth II **Subject:** Icons of New Zealand **Rev:** Kiwi and Southern Cross **Edge:** Reeded

| Date | Mintage | VF20 | XF40 | MS60 | MS63 | MS65 |
|---|---|---|---|---|---|---|
| 2010 (m) | Est. 12500 | — | — | — | — | 60.00 |

**KM# 331a DOLLAR**
31.14 g., 0.999 Silver 1.000 oz. ASW, 40 mm. **Ruler:** Elizabeth II **Rev:** Kiwi and Southern Cross **Edge:** Reeded

| Date | Mintage | VF20 | XF40 | MS60 | MS63 | MS65 |
|---|---|---|---|---|---|---|
| 2010 (m) | — | PF65 90.00 | | | | |

**KM# 333 DOLLAR**
31.14 g., 0.999 Silver 1.000 oz. ASW, 40 mm. **Ruler:** Elizabeth II **Subject:** 2010 FIFA World Cup **Rev:** Soccer player with stylized NZ koru **Edge:** Reeded

| Date | Mintage | VF20 | XF40 | MS60 | MS63 | MS65 |
|---|---|---|---|---|---|---|
| 2010 (m) | 10,000 | — | — | — | — | 100 |

Note: Mintage includes 1500 in NZ Post packaging.

**KM# 336 DOLLAR**
31.11 g., 0.999 Silver 0.999 oz. ASW, 40 mm. **Ruler:** Elizabeth II **Obv:** Head with tiara right **Rev:** Allosaurus

| Date | Mintage | VF20 | XF40 | MS60 | MS63 | MS65 |
|---|---|---|---|---|---|---|
| 2010 (m) Prooflike | 1,500 | — | — | — | — | 90.00 |

**KM# 337 DOLLAR**
31.11 g., 0.999 Silver 0.999 oz. ASW, 40 mm. **Ruler:** Elizabeth II **Obv:** Head with tiara right **Rev:** Anhanguera

| Date | Mintage | VF20 | XF40 | MS60 | MS63 | MS65 |
|---|---|---|---|---|---|---|
| 2010 (m) Prooflike | 1,500 | — | — | — | — | 90.00 |

**KM# 338 DOLLAR**
31.11 g., 0.999 Silver 0.999 oz. ASW, 40 mm. **Ruler:** Elizabeth II **Obv:** Head with tiara right **Rev:** Mauisaurus

| Date | Mintage | VF20 | XF40 | MS60 | MS63 | MS65 |
|---|---|---|---|---|---|---|
| 2010 (m) Prooflike | 1,500 | — | — | — | — | 90.00 |

**KM# 339 DOLLAR**
31.11 g., 0.999 Silver 0.999 oz. ASW, 40 mm. **Ruler:** Elizabeth II **Obv:** Head with tiara right **Rev:** Moanasaurus

| Date | Mintage | VF20 | XF40 | MS60 | MS63 | MS65 |
|---|---|---|---|---|---|---|
| 2010 (m) Prooflike | 1,500 | — | — | — | — | 90.00 |

**KM# 340 DOLLAR**
31.11 g., 0.999 Silver 0.999 oz. ASW, 40 mm. **Ruler:** Elizabeth II **Obv:** Head with tiara right **Rev:** Titanosaurus

| Date | Mintage | VF20 | XF40 | MS60 | MS63 | MS65 |
|---|---|---|---|---|---|---|
| 2010 (m) Prooflike | 1,500 | — | — | — | — | 90.00 |

**KM# 341 DOLLAR**
31.11 g., 0.999 Silver 0.999 oz. ASW, 40 mm. **Ruler:** Elizabeth II **Obv:** Head with tiara right **Rev:** Multicolor tiki with huia feathers

| Date | Mintage | VF20 | XF40 | MS60 | MS63 | MS65 |
|---|---|---|---|---|---|---|
| 2010 (m) | 4,000 | PF65 130 | | | | |

**KM# 344 DOLLAR**
31.11 g., 0.999 Silver 0.999 oz. ASW, 40 mm. **Ruler:** Elizabeth II **Obv:** Head with tiara right **Rev:** Black field with repeating fern pattern **Edge:** Reeded

| Date | Mintage | VF20 | XF40 | MS60 | MS63 | MS65 |
|---|---|---|---|---|---|---|
| 2010 (m) | 10,000 | PF65 100 | | | | |

**KM# 120b DOLLAR**
10.73 g., 0.999 Silver 0.3446 oz. ASW, 23 mm. **Ruler:** Elizabeth II **Obv:** Head with tiara right **Rev:** Kiwi bird within sprigs, value below **Edge:** Segmented reeding

| Date | Mintage | VF20 | XF40 | MS60 | MS63 | MS65 |
|---|---|---|---|---|---|---|
| 2011 (u) | 1,200 | PF65 50.00 | | | | |
| 2012 (u) | 1,000 | PF65 50.00 | | | | |

**KM# 335 DOLLAR**
31.14 g., 0.999 Silver 1.000 oz. ASW, 40 mm. **Ruler:** Elizabeth II **Obv:** Head with tiara right **Rev:** Kiwi and silver fern **Edge:** Reeded

| Date | Mintage | VF20 | XF40 | MS60 | MS63 | MS65 |
|---|---|---|---|---|---|---|
| 2011 (m) Prooflike | 10,000 | — | — | — | — | 65.00 |

**KM# 335a DOLLAR**
31.11 g., 0.999 Silver 0.999 oz. ASW, 40 mm. **Ruler:** Elizabeth II **Obv:** Head in tiara right **Rev:** Kiwi and fern

| Date | Mintage | VF20 | XF40 | MS60 | MS63 | MS65 |
|---|---|---|---|---|---|---|
| 2011 | 7,000 | PF65 75.00 | | | | |

**KM# 343 DOLLAR**
Copper-Nickel, 30 mm. **Ruler:** Elizabeth II **Obv:** Head with tiara right **Rev:** All Black logo with repeating fern pattern in background **Edge:** Reeded

| Date | Mintage | VF20 | XF40 | MS60 | MS63 | MS65 |
|---|---|---|---|---|---|---|
| 2011 (m) | 10,000 | — | — | — | — | 30.00 |

**KM# 345 DOLLAR**

31.11 g., 0.999 Silver 0.999 oz. ASW, 40 mm. **Ruler:** Elizabeth II **Obv:** Head with tiara right **Rev:** All Blacks performing the Haka before a rugby match **Edge Lettering:** KA MATE, KA MATE! KA ORA, KA ORA!

| Date | Mintage | VF20 | XF40 | MS60 | MS63 | MS65 |
|---|---|---|---|---|---|---|
| 2011 (m) | 3,000 | PF65 140 | | | | |

**KM# 346 DOLLAR**

31.11 g., 0.999 Silver 0.999 oz. ASW selective gold plating, 40 mm. **Ruler:** Elizabeth II **Obv:** Head with tiara right **Rev:** Webb Ellis Cup selectively gold palted **Edge:** Reeded

| Date | Mintage | VF20 | XF40 | MS60 | MS63 | MS65 |
|---|---|---|---|---|---|---|
| 2011 (m) | 15,000 | PF65 130 | | | | |

**KM# 347 DOLLAR**

31.14 g., 0.999 Silver 1.000 oz. ASW, 38.85 mm. **Ruler:** Elizabeth II **Subject:** 1987 Champions **Obv:** Head with tiara right **Rev:** 1987 All Black player fending off opponent **Edge:** Reeded

| Date | Mintage | VF20 | XF40 | MS60 | MS63 | MS65 |
|---|---|---|---|---|---|---|
| 2011 (w) | 2,011 | PF65 150 | | | | |

**KM# 350 DOLLAR**

31.11 g., 0.999 Silver 0.999 oz. ASW, 40 mm. **Ruler:** Elizabeth II **Obv:** Head with tiara right **Rev:** Kiwi and kowhai flowers **Edge:** Reeded

| Date | Mintage | VF20 | XF40 | MS60 | MS63 | MS65 |
|---|---|---|---|---|---|---|
| 2012 (m) Prooflike | 13,500 | — | — | — | — | 80.00 |
| 2012 (m) | 5,000 | PF65 130 | | | | |
| 2013 (m) | — | — | — | — | — | 80.00 |
| 2013 (m) | — | PF65 130 | | | | |

**KM# 351 DOLLAR**

31.11 g., 0.999 Silver 0.999 oz. ASW, 38.6 mm. **Ruler:** Elizabeth II **Subject:** Maori Art **Obv:** Head with tiara right **Rev:** Hei matau (neck pendant) **Edge:** Notched

| Date | Mintage | VF20 | XF40 | MS60 | MS63 | MS65 |
|---|---|---|---|---|---|---|
| 2012 (u) | 3,000 | PF65 140 | | | | |

**KM# 354 DOLLAR**

31.11 g., 0.999 Silver 0.999 oz. ASW, 40 mm. **Ruler:** Elizabeth II **Subject:** 50th Years of Firendship - New Zealand and Samoa **Rev:** New Zealand and Samoa designs, color background

| Date | Mintage | VF20 | XF40 | MS60 | MS63 | MS65 |
|---|---|---|---|---|---|---|
| 2012 | 1,000 | PF65 75.00 | | | | |

**KM# 356 DOLLAR**

Silver, 40 mm. **Ruler:** Elizabeth II **Subject:** Elizabeth II, 60th Anniversary of Reign **Rev:** Elizabeth II delivering Christmas Message, color flora

| Date | Mintage | VF20 | XF40 | MS60 | MS63 | MS65 |
|---|---|---|---|---|---|---|
| 2012 proof | — | PF65 75.00 | | | | |

**KM# 357 DOLLAR**

Silver, 40 mm. **Ruler:** Elizabeth II **Subject:** New Zealand Air Force, 75th Anniversary **Rev:** Pilot and Skyhawk aircraft, "missing man" formation

| Date | Mintage | VF20 | XF40 | MS60 | MS63 | MS65 |
|---|---|---|---|---|---|---|
| 2012 | — | PF65 75.00 | | | | |

**KM# 358 DOLLAR**

31.11 g., 0.999 Silver 0.999 oz. ASW, 40 mm. **Ruler:** Elizabeth II **Subject:** Bilbo Baggins

| Date | Mintage | VF20 | XF40 | MS60 | MS63 | MS65 |
|---|---|---|---|---|---|---|
| 2012 | 1,000 | PF65 150 | | | | |

**KM# 359 DOLLAR**

31.11 g., 0.999 Silver 0.999 oz. ASW, 40 mm. **Ruler:** Elizabeth II **Subject:** Radagast

| Date | Mintage | VF20 | XF40 | MS60 | MS63 | MS65 |
|---|---|---|---|---|---|---|
| 2012 | 1,000 | PF65 150 | | | | |

**KM# 360 DOLLAR**

31.11 g., 0.999 Silver 0.999 oz. ASW, 40 mm. **Ruler:** Elizabeth II **Subject:** Elrond

| Date | Mintage | VF20 | XF40 | MS60 | MS63 | MS65 |
|---|---|---|---|---|---|---|
| 2012 | 1,000 | PF65 150 | | | | |

**KM# 361 DOLLAR**

31.11 g., 0.999 Silver 0.999 oz. ASW, 40 mm. **Ruler:** Elizabeth II **Subject:** Thorin Oakenshield

| Date | Mintage | VF20 | XF40 | MS60 | MS63 | MS65 |
|---|---|---|---|---|---|---|
| 2012 | 1,000 | PF65 150 | | | | |

**KM# 362 DOLLAR**

31.11 g., 0.999 Silver 0.999 oz. ASW, 40 mm. **Ruler:** Elizabeth II **Subject:** Gandalf

| Date | Mintage | VF20 | XF40 | MS60 | MS63 | MS65 |
|---|---|---|---|---|---|---|
| 2012 | 1,000 | PF65 150 | | | | |

**KM# 363 DOLLAR**

31.11 g., 0.999 Silver 0.999 oz. ASW, 40 mm. **Ruler:** Elizabeth II **Subject:** Gollum

| Date | Mintage | VF20 | XF40 | MS60 | MS63 | MS65 |
|---|---|---|---|---|---|---|
| 2012 | 1,000 | PF65 150 | | | | |

**KM# 364 DOLLAR**

Aluminum-Bronze **Ruler:** Elizabeth II **Rev:** Bilbo Baggins examining contract with Dwarves

| Date | Mintage | VF20 | XF40 | MS60 | MS63 | MS65 |
|---|---|---|---|---|---|---|
| 2012 | — | PF65 15.00 | | | | |

**KM# 365 DOLLAR**
Aluminum-Bronze **Ruler:** Elizabeth II **Subject:** Thorin Oakenshield

| Date | Mintage | VF20 | XF40 | MS60 | MS63 | MS65 |
|---|---|---|---|---|---|---|
| 2012 | — | PF65 15.00 | | | | |

**KM# 366 DOLLAR**
Aluminum-Bronze **Ruler:** Elizabeth II **Subject:** Gandalf and Radagast

| Date | Mintage | VF20 | XF40 | MS60 | MS63 | MS65 |
|---|---|---|---|---|---|---|
| 2012 | — | PF65 15.00 | | | | |

**KM# 367 DOLLAR**
Aluminum-Bronze **Ruler:** Elizabeth II **Subject:** Three Dwarves

| Date | Mintage | VF20 | XF40 | MS60 | MS63 | MS65 |
|---|---|---|---|---|---|---|
| 2012 | — | PF65 15.00 | | | | |

**KM# 372 DOLLAR**
31.11 g., 0.999 Silver 0.999 oz. ASW gilt ring, 40 mm. **Ruler:** Elizabeth II **Rev:** Bilbo Baggins, staff in right hand

| Date | Mintage | VF20 | XF40 | MS60 | MS63 | MS65 |
|---|---|---|---|---|---|---|
| 2012 | 20,000 | PF65 150 | | | | |

**KM# 373 DOLLAR**
31.10 g., 0.999 Silver 0.9989 oz. ASW, 40 mm. **Ruler:** Elizabeth II **Subject:** Maori Art - Koru **Obv:** Portrait of Her Majesty Queen Elizabeth II **Rev:** Koru, ferns and God of the Forest

| Date | Mintage | VF20 | XF40 | MS60 | MS63 | MS65 |
|---|---|---|---|---|---|---|
| 2013 | Est. 2000 | PF65 75.00 | | | | |

**KM# 121 2 DOLLARS**
10.00 g., Aluminum-Bronze, 26.5 mm. **Ruler:** Elizabeth II **Obv:** Head with tiara right **Rev:** White heron (kotuku) above value **Edge:** Reeded with security groove

| Date | Mintage | VF20 | XF40 | MS60 | MS63 | MS65 |
|---|---|---|---|---|---|---|
| 2001 (l) | 3,000,000 | — | — | 2.00 | 3.00 | 5.00 |
| 2001 (c) Sets only | 2,910 | — | — | — | — | 6.00 |
| 2001 (c) | 2,000 | PF65 7.50 | | | | |
| 2002 (l) | 6,000,000 | — | — | 2.00 | 3.00 | 5.00 |
| 2002 (c) Sets only | 3,000 | — | — | — | — | 6.00 |
| 2002 (c) | 2,000 | PF65 7.50 | | | | |
| 2003 (l) | 6,000,000 | — | — | 2.00 | 3.00 | 5.00 |
| 2003 (c) Sets only | 3,000 | — | — | — | — | 6.00 |
| 2003 (c) | 3,000 | PF65 7.50 | | | | |
| 2004 (c) Sets only | 2,800 | — | — | — | — | 5.00 |
| 2004 | 3,500 | PF65 7.50 | | | | |
| 2005 (l) | 5,000,000 | — | — | 2.00 | 3.00 | 5.00 |
| 2005 (c) Sets only | 3,000 | — | — | — | — | 6.00 |
| 2005 (c) | 3,000 | PF65 7.50 | | | | |
| 2006 (c) Sets only | 3,000 | — | — | — | — | 6.00 |
| 2006 (c) | 2,100 | PF65 7.50 | | | | |
| 2007 (c) | 5,000 | — | — | — | — | 6.00 |
| 2007 (c) | 4,000 | PF65 7.50 | | | | |
| 2008 (l) Sets only | 4,000 | — | — | — | — | 6.00 |
| 2008 (l) | 3,000 | PF65 7.50 | | | | |
| 2009 (w) Sets only | 2,000 | — | — | — | — | 6.00 |
| 2009 (w) | 1,500 | PF65 7.50 | | | | |
| 2011 (l) | 8,000,000 | — | — | 2.00 | 3.00 | 5.00 |

**KM# 121a 2 DOLLARS**
11.25 g., Brass, 26.5 mm. **Ruler:** Elizabeth II **Obv:** Head with tiara right **Rev:** White heron (kotuku) above value **Edge:** Reeded with security groove

| Date | Mintage | VF20 | XF40 | MS60 | MS63 | MS65 |
|---|---|---|---|---|---|---|
| 2010 (u) | 2,000 | — | — | — | — | 6.00 |
| 2010 (u) | 1,500 | PF65 7.50 | | | | |
| 2011 (u) | 2,000 | — | — | — | — | 6.00 |
| 2011 (u) | 1,500 | PF65 7.50 | | | | |
| 2012 (u) | 2,000 | — | — | — | — | 6.00 |
| 2012 (u) | 1,500 | PF65 7.50 | | | | |

**KM# 121b 2 DOLLARS**
14.12 g., 0.999 Silver 0.4535 oz. ASW, 26.5 mm. **Ruler:** Elizabeth II **Obv:** Head with tiara right **Rev:** White heron (kotuku) above value **Edge:** Reeded with security groove

| Date | Mintage | VF20 | XF40 | MS60 | MS63 | MS65 |
|---|---|---|---|---|---|---|
| 2011 (u) | 1,200 | PF65 75.00 | | | | |
| 2012 (u) | 1,000 | PF65 75.00 | | | | |

**KM# 128 5 DOLLARS**
28.28 g., Copper-Nickel, 38.6 mm. **Ruler:** Elizabeth II **Subject:** Kereru Bird **Obv:** Head with tiara right **Rev:** Wood Pigeon on branch **Edge:** Reeded

| Date | Mintage | VF20 | XF40 | MS60 | MS63 | MS65 |
|---|---|---|---|---|---|---|
| 2001 (l) | 1,500 | — | — | — | — | 25.00 |

**KM# 128a 5 DOLLARS**
28.28 g., 0.999 Silver 0.9083 oz. ASW **Ruler:** Elizabeth II **Obv:** Head with tiara right **Rev:** Pigeon on branch

| Date | Mintage | VF20 | XF40 | MS60 | MS63 | MS65 |
|---|---|---|---|---|---|---|
| 2001 | 1,000 | PF65 85.00 | | | | |

**KM# 149 5 DOLLARS**
28.28 g., 0.925 Silver 0.841 oz. ASW, 38.6 mm. **Ruler:** Elizabeth II **Subject:** Royal Visit (canceled after coin issue) **Obv:** Head with tiara right **Rev:** Queen with flowers and two girls **Edge:** Reeded

| Date | Mintage | VF20 | XF40 | MS60 | MS63 | MS65 |
|---|---|---|---|---|---|---|
| 2001 | 2,000 | PF65 100 | | | | |

Note: 200 issued in stamp cover

**KM# 131 5 DOLLARS**
28.28 g., Copper-Nickel, 38.6 mm. **Ruler:** Elizabeth II **Subject:** Architectural Heritage **Obv:** Head with tiara right **Rev:** Auckland Sky Tower **Edge:** Reeded

| Date | Mintage | VF20 | XF40 | MS60 | MS63 | MS65 |
|---|---|---|---|---|---|---|
| 2002 (l) | 3,000 | — | — | — | — | 12.50 |

Note: 500 pieces were housed in a stamp cover

**KM# 131a 5 DOLLARS**
28.28 g., 0.925 Silver 0.841 oz. ASW, 38.6 mm. **Ruler:** Elizabeth II **Subject:** Architectural Heritage **Obv:** Head with tiara right **Rev:** Auckland Sky Tower **Edge:** Reeded

| Date | Mintage | VF20 | XF40 | MS60 | MS63 | MS65 |
|---|---|---|---|---|---|---|
| 2002 (l) | 2,000 | PF65 80.00 | | | | |

Note: 500 pieces were housed in a stamp cover

**KM# 145 5 DOLLARS**
27.22 g., Copper-Nickel, 38.74 mm. **Ruler:** Elizabeth II **Obv:** Head with tiara right **Rev:** Hector's Dolphins jumping out of the water **Edge:** Reeded

| Date | Mintage | VF20 | XF40 | MS60 | MS63 | MS65 |
|---|---|---|---|---|---|---|
| 2002 (c) | 4,000 | — | — | — | — | 35.00 |

Note: 500 pieces were housed in a stamp covers

### KM# 145a 5 DOLLARS

27.22 g., 0.999 Silver 0.8743 oz. ASW **Ruler:** Elizabeth II **Obv:** Head with tiara right **Rev:** Two Hector's Dolphins jumping out of the water **Edge:** Reeded

| Date | Mintage | VF20 | XF40 | MS60 | MS63 | MS65 |
|---|---|---|---|---|---|---|
| 2002 (c) | Est. 2000 | — | — | — | — | 100 |

Note: 500 in stamp covers

### KM# 151 5 DOLLARS

28.28 g., 0.925 Silver Gilt 0.841 oz., 38.61 mm. **Ruler:** Elizabeth II **Subject:** Queen's Jubilee **Obv:** Gilt head with tiara right **Rev:** Scepter with "Great Star of Africa' at left of vertical band with crowns and shields **Edge:** Reeded

| Date | Mintage | VF20 | XF40 | MS60 | MS63 | MS65 |
|---|---|---|---|---|---|---|
| 2002 (l) | 25,000 | PF65 80.00 | | | | |

Note: 100 pieces were housed in a stamp cover, value $85

### KM# 272 5 DOLLARS

28.28 g., Copper-Nickel, 38.61 mm. **Ruler:** Elizabeth II **Subject:** America's cup

| Date | Mintage | VF20 | XF40 | MS60 | MS63 | MS65 |
|---|---|---|---|---|---|---|
| 2002 (l) | 6,000 | — | — | — | — | 20.00 |

### KM# 272a 5 DOLLARS

28.28 g., 0.925 Silver 0.841 oz. ASW, 38.61 mm. **Ruler:** Elizabeth II **Subject:** America's Cup **Obv:** Head with tiara right **Rev:** Yachts

| Date | Mintage | VF20 | XF40 | MS60 | MS63 | MS65 |
|---|---|---|---|---|---|---|
| 2002 (l) | 4,000 | PF65 60.00 | | | | |

Note: Includes 500 in stamp cover, value $60.

### KM# 132 5 DOLLARS

26.70 g., Copper-Nickel, 38.6 mm. **Ruler:** Elizabeth II **Obv:** Head with tiara right **Rev:** Giant Kokopu fish divides circle **Edge:** Reeded

| Date | Mintage | VF20 | XF40 | MS60 | MS63 | MS65 |
|---|---|---|---|---|---|---|
| 2003 (c) | 2,400 | — | — | — | 14.00 | 27.00 |

Note: Includes 400 issued in a stamp cover.

### KM# 132a 5 DOLLARS

28.28 g., 0.999 Silver 0.9083 oz. ASW Gold plated, 38.6 mm. **Ruler:** Elizabeth II **Obv:** Head with tiara right **Rev:** Giant Kokopu fish **Edge:** Reeded

| Date | Mintage | VF20 | XF40 | MS60 | MS63 | MS65 |
|---|---|---|---|---|---|---|
| 2003 (c) | 1,700 | PF65 75.00 | | | | |

Note: Includes 200 issued in a stamp cover

### KM# 133 5 DOLLARS

26.72 g., Copper-Nickel, 38.6 mm. **Ruler:** Elizabeth II **Subject:** Chatham Island Taiko **Obv:** Head with tiara right **Rev:** Magenta Petrel **Edge:** Reeded

| Date | Mintage | VF20 | XF40 | MS60 | MS63 | MS65 |
|---|---|---|---|---|---|---|
| 2004(2003) | 1,350 | — | — | — | — | 35.00 |

### KM# 147 5 DOLLARS

28.23 g., 0.925 Silver 0.8395 oz. ASW, 38.6 mm. **Ruler:** Elizabeth II **Subject:** 50th Anniversary of Coronation **Obv:** Gold plated crowned head right **Rev:** Crown above fern and flowers **Edge:** Reeded

| Date | Mintage | VF20 | XF40 | MS60 | MS63 | MS65 |
|---|---|---|---|---|---|---|
| 2003 | 25,000 | PF65 80.00 | | | | |

Note: Includes 100 issued in a stamp cover

### KM# 133a 5 DOLLARS

28.28 g., 0.999 Silver 0.9083 oz. ASW, 38.74 mm. **Ruler:** Elizabeth II **Obv:** Head with tiara right **Rev:** Chatham Island Taiko

| Date | Mintage | VF20 | XF40 | MS60 | MS63 | MS65 |
|---|---|---|---|---|---|---|
| 2004 | 1,300 | PF65 70.00 | | | | |

### KM# 146 5 DOLLARS

27.22 g., Copper-Nickel, 38.74 mm. **Ruler:** Elizabeth II **Obv:** Head with tiara right **Rev:** Fiordland Crested Penguin **Edge:** Reeded

| Date | Mintage | VF20 | XF40 | MS60 | MS63 | MS65 |
|---|---|---|---|---|---|---|
| 2005(2004) | 4,000 | — | — | — | 25.00 | 30.00 |

### KM# 146a 5 DOLLARS

27.22 g., 0.999 Silver 0.8743 oz. ASW, 38.74 mm. **Ruler:** Elizabeth II **Obv:** Head with tiara right **Rev:** Fiordland Crested Penguin **Edge:** Reeded

| Date | Mintage | VF20 | XF40 | MS60 | MS63 | MS65 |
|---|---|---|---|---|---|---|
| 2005 | 3,500 | — | — | — | — | 60.00 |

### KM# 148 5 DOLLARS

27.22 g., Copper-Nickel, 38.74 mm. **Ruler:** Elizabeth II **Obv:** Head with tiara right **Rev:** Falcon on tree stump **Edge:** Reeded

| Date | Mintage | VF20 | XF40 | MS60 | MS63 | MS65 |
|---|---|---|---|---|---|---|
| 2006 | 4,000 | — | — | — | 25.00 | 30.00 |

### KM# 148a 5 DOLLARS

28.28 g., 0.999 Silver 0.9083 oz. ASW, 38.74 mm. **Ruler:** Elizabeth II **Obv:** Head with tiara right **Rev:** New Zealand Falcon on tree stump **Edge:** Reeded

| Date | Mintage | VF20 | XF40 | MS60 | MS63 | MS65 |
|---|---|---|---|---|---|---|
| 2006 | 2,500 | PF65 60.00 | | | | |

### KM# 150 5 DOLLARS

27.22 g., Copper-Nickel, 38.74 mm. **Ruler:** Elizabeth II **Subject:** Tuatara **Obv:** Head with tiara right **Rev:** Tuatara (Sphenodon punctatus), a lizard-like reptile **Edge:** Reeded

| Date | Mintage | VF20 | XF40 | MS60 | MS63 | MS65 |
|---|---|---|---|---|---|---|
| 2007 (c) | 2,200 | — | — | — | 25.00 | 30.00 |

### KM# 150a 5 DOLLARS

28.28 g., 0.999 Silver 0.9083 oz. ASW, 38.74 mm. **Ruler:** Elizabeth II **Subject:** Tuatara **Obv:** Head with tiara right **Rev:** Tuatara right **Edge:** Reeded

| Date | Mintage | VF20 | XF40 | MS60 | MS63 | MS65 |
|---|---|---|---|---|---|---|
| 2007 (c) | 2,700 | PF65 80.00 | | | | |

### KM# 233 5 DOLLARS

28.28 g., Copper-Nickel, 38.6 mm. **Ruler:** Elizabeth II **Subject:** Hamilton's frog **Obv:** Head with tiara right **Obv. Legend:** NEW ZEALAND - ELIZABETH II **Rev:** Frog perched on branch at left center

| Date | Mintage | VF20 | XF40 | MS60 | MS63 | MS65 |
|---|---|---|---|---|---|---|
| 2008 (l) | 4,000 | — | — | — | 35.00 | 40.00 |

### KM# 233a 5 DOLLARS

28.28 g., 0.999 Silver 0.9083 oz. ASW, 38.61 mm. **Ruler:** Elizabeth II **Rev:** Hamilton's frog **Edge:** Reeded

| Date | Mintage | VF20 | XF40 | MS60 | MS63 | MS65 |
|---|---|---|---|---|---|---|
| 2008 (l) | 4,000 | PF65 90.00 | | | | |

Note: Mintage includes 1500 struck in 2009

### KM# 329 5 DOLLARS

22.00 g., Copper-Nickel, 38.60 mm. **Ruler:** Elizabeth II **Rev:** Kakapo **Edge:** Reeded

| Date | Mintage | VF20 | XF40 | MS60 | MS63 | MS65 |
|---|---|---|---|---|---|---|
| 2009 (w) | 2,000 | — | — | — | 25.00 | 30.00 |

### KM# 329a 5 DOLLARS

31.14 g., 0.999 Silver 1.000 oz. ASW, 38.61 mm. **Ruler:** Elizabeth II **Rev:** Kakapo

| Date | Mintage | VF20 | XF40 | MS60 | MS63 | MS65 |
|---|---|---|---|---|---|---|
| 2009 (w) | 4,000 | PF65 90.00 | | | | |

### KM# 334 5 DOLLARS

31.10 g., Copper-Nickel, 38.7 mm. **Ruler:** Elizabeth II **Series:** Maui's Dolphin, subspecies of the Hector Dolphin **Rev:** Dolphin jumping right **Edge:** Reeded

| Date | Mintage | VF20 | XF40 | MS60 | MS63 | MS65 |
|---|---|---|---|---|---|---|
| 2010 | 2,000 | — | — | — | — | 35.00 |

### KM# 334a 5 DOLLARS

31.11 g., 0.999 Silver 0.999 oz. ASW, 38.7 mm. **Ruler:** Elizabeth II **Obv:** Head with tiara right **Rev:** Maui's Dolphin **Edge:** Reeded

| Date | Mintage | VF20 | XF40 | MS60 | MS63 | MS65 |
|---|---|---|---|---|---|---|
| 2010 (u) | 4,000 | PF65 90.00 | | | | |

### KM# 348 5 DOLLARS

31.11 g., Copper-Nickel, 38.7 mm. **Ruler:** Elizabeth II **Obv:** Head with tiara right **Rev:** Yellow-eyed Penguin **Edge:** Reeded

| Date | Mintage | VF20 | XF40 | MS60 | MS63 | MS65 |
|---|---|---|---|---|---|---|
| 2011 (u) | 2,000 | — | — | — | — | 35.00 |

### KM# 348a 5 DOLLARS

31.11 g., 0.999 Silver 0.999 oz. ASW, 38.7 mm. **Ruler:** Elizabeth II **Obv:** Head with tiara right **Rev:** Yellow-eyed Penguin **Edge:** Reeded

| Date | Mintage | VF20 | XF40 | MS60 | MS63 | MS65 |
|---|---|---|---|---|---|---|
| 2011 (u) | 4,000 | PF65 100 | | | | |

### KM# 355 5 DOLLARS

Silver, 40 mm. **Ruler:** Elizabeth II **Rev:** Fairy Tern in flight

| Date | Mintage | VF20 | XF40 | MS60 | MS63 | MS65 |
|---|---|---|---|---|---|---|
| 2012 | — | PF65 65.00 | | | | |

### KM# 129 10 DOLLARS

3.89 g., 0.999 Gold 0.1249 oz. AGW, 18 mm. **Ruler:** Elizabeth II **Obv:** Head with tiara right **Rev:** Salvage ship above value **Edge:** Reeded

| Date | Mintage | VF20 | XF40 | MS60 | MS63 | MS65 |
|---|---|---|---|---|---|---|
| 2001 | 600 | PF65 275 | | | | |

### KM# 130 10 DOLLARS

7.78 g., 0.999 Gold 0.2498 oz. AGW, 22 mm. **Ruler:** Elizabeth II **Obv:** Head with tiara right **Rev:** Ship above value **Edge:** Reeded

| Date | Mintage | VF20 | XF40 | MS60 | MS63 | MS65 |
|---|---|---|---|---|---|---|
| 2001 | 600 | PF65 525 | | | | |

### KM# 273 10 DOLLARS

Nickel-Brass gold plated, 28.4 mm. **Ruler:** Elizabeth II **Subject:** America's Cup **Obv:** Head with tiara right **Rev:** Map, cup and yachts

| Date | Mintage | VF20 | XF40 | MS60 | MS63 | MS65 |
|---|---|---|---|---|---|---|
| 2002 (l) | 5,000 | — | — | — | — | 45.00 |

### KM# 274 10 DOLLARS

15.55 g., 0.999 Gold 0.4995 oz. AGW, 28.4 mm. **Ruler:** Elizabeth II **Subject:** America's Cup **Obv:** Head with tiara right **Rev:** Map, cup and yachts

| Date | Mintage | VF20 | XF40 | MS60 | MS63 | MS65 |
|---|---|---|---|---|---|---|
| 2002 (l) | 900 | PF65 950 | | | | |

### KM# 144 10 DOLLARS

39.94 g., 0.917 Gold 1.1775 oz. AGW, 38.61 mm. **Ruler:** Elizabeth II **Subject:** Lord of the Rings **Obv:** Head with tiara right **Rev:** The One Ring **Edge:** Reeded

| Date | Mintage | VF20 | XF40 | MS60 | MS63 | MS65 |
|---|---|---|---|---|---|---|
| 2003 (l) | 1,198 | PF65 2,300 | | | | |

### KM# 270 10 DOLLARS

39.94 g., 0.917 Gold 1.1775 oz. AGW, 38.61 mm. **Ruler:** Elizabeth II **Subject:** Lord of the Rings **Obv:** Head with tiara right **Rev:** Frodo **Edge:** Reeded

| Date | Mintage | VF20 | XF40 | MS60 | MS63 | MS65 |
|---|---|---|---|---|---|---|
| 2003 (l) | 142 | PF65 2,300 | | | | |

### KM# 271 10 DOLLARS

39.94 g., 0.917 Gold 1.1775 oz. AGW, 38.61 mm. **Ruler:** Elizabeth II **Subject:** Lord of the Rings **Obv:** Head with tiara right **Rev:** Sauron **Edge:** Reeded

| Date | Mintage | VF20 | XF40 | MS60 | MS63 | MS65 |
|---|---|---|---|---|---|---|
| 2003 (l) | 142 | PF65 2,300 | | | | |

### KM# 275 10 DOLLARS

38.50 g., 0.917 Gold 1.1351 oz. AGW, 38.61 mm. **Ruler:** Elizabeth II **Subject:** Pukaki **Obv:** Head with tiara right **Rev:** Statue of Pukaki **Edge:** Reeded

| Date | Mintage | VF20 | XF40 | MS60 | MS63 | MS65 |
|---|---|---|---|---|---|---|
| 2004 (l) | 300 | PF65 5,000 | | | | |
| 2004 (l) NW RB Proof | 2 | — | — | — | — | — |

Note: Initials added for presention to Ngati Whakaue (Maori tribe) and the Reserve Bank.

### KM# 155 10 DOLLARS

7.78 g., 0.999 Gold 0.2498 oz. AGW, 20.1 mm. **Ruler:** Elizabeth II **Subject:** ANZAC **Obv:** Crowned head right **Rev:** New Zealand soldier playing bugle in front of War Memorial **Edge:** Reeded

| Date | Mintage | VF20 | XF40 | MS60 | MS63 | MS65 |
|---|---|---|---|---|---|---|
| 2005 (w) | 1,000 | — | — | — | — | 500 |

### KM# 165 10 DOLLARS

7.99 g., 0.917 Gold 0.2355 oz. AGW, 22.05 mm. **Ruler:** Elizabeth II **Subject:** Lions Rugby Tour **Obv:** Crowned head right **Edge:** Reeded

| Date | Mintage | VF20 | XF40 | MS60 | MS63 | MS65 |
|---|---|---|---|---|---|---|
| 2005 (l) | 1,000 | PF65 475 | | | | |

### KM# 295 10 DOLLARS

31.14 g., 0.999 Gold 1.000 oz. AGW, 34 mm. **Ruler:** Elizabeth II **Subject:** Narnia **Obv:** Head with tiara right **Rev:** Asian

| Date | Mintage | VF20 | XF40 | MS60 | MS63 | MS65 |
|---|---|---|---|---|---|---|
| 2006 | 365 | PF65 2,100 | | | | |

### KM# 307 10 DOLLARS

7.78 g., 0.999 Gold 0.2498 oz. AGW, 20 mm. **Ruler:** Elizabeth II **Subject:** Queen's 80th birthday **Obv:** Head with tiara right **Rev:** Heraldic arms

| Date | Mintage | VF20 | XF40 | MS60 | MS63 | MS65 |
|---|---|---|---|---|---|---|
| 2006 | 500 | PF65 550 | | | | |

### KM# 308 10 DOLLARS

15.55 g., 0.999 Gold 0.4996 oz. AGW, 25.10 mm. **Ruler:** Elizabeth II **Subject:** Gold Rushes - Otago **Obv:** Head with tiara right **Rev:** Picks, shovels and nuggets

| Date | Mintage | VF20 | XF40 | MS60 | MS63 | MS65 |
|---|---|---|---|---|---|---|
| 2006 (w) | 300 | PF65 1,000 | | | | |

### KM# 304 10 DOLLARS

7.78 g., 0.999 Gold 0.2497 oz. AGW, 26 mm. **Ruler:** Elizabeth II **Subject:** Elizabeth & Philip Diamond Wedding Anniversary **Obv:** Head with tiara right **Rev:** Royal crests

| Date | Mintage | VF20 | XF40 | MS60 | MS63 | MS65 |
|---|---|---|---|---|---|---|
| 2007 (m) | 300 | PF65 550 | | | | |

### KM# 305 10 DOLLARS

31.14 g., 0.917 Gold 0.9179 oz. AGW, 38.61 mm. **Ruler:** Elizabeth II **Subject:** Scouting centenary **Obv:** Head with tiara right

| Date | Mintage | VF20 | XF40 | MS60 | MS63 | MS65 |
|---|---|---|---|---|---|---|
| 2007 (l) | 150 | PF65 1,850 | | | | |

### KM# 306 10 DOLLARS

7.79 g., 0.999 Gold 0.2501 oz. AGW, 20.6 mm. **Ruler:** Elizabeth II **Subject:** Sir Edmund Hilary **Obv:** Head with tiara right **Rev:** Ed Hilary with Mt. Everest in background

| Date | Mintage | VF20 | XF40 | MS60 | MS63 | MS65 |
|---|---|---|---|---|---|---|
| 2008 (w) | 1,953 | PF65 525 | | | | |

### KM# 330 10 DOLLARS

7.78 g., 0.999 Gold 0.2497 oz. AGW, 26 mm. **Ruler:** Elizabeth II **Subject:** Icons of New Zealand **Rev:** Kiwi and map of New Zealand **Edge:** Reeded

| Date | Mintage | VF20 | XF40 | MS60 | MS63 | MS65 |
|---|---|---|---|---|---|---|
| 2009 (m) | 1,500 | PF65 575 | | | | |

### KM# 332 10 DOLLARS

7.78 g., 0.999 Gold 0.2497 oz. AGW, 26. mm. **Ruler:** Elizabeth II **Subject:** Icons of New Zealand **Rev:** Kiwi and Southern Cross **Edge:** Reeded

| Date | Mintage | VF20 | XF40 | MS60 | MS63 | MS65 |
|---|---|---|---|---|---|---|
| 2010 (m) | 1,800 | PF65 575 | | | | |

### KM# 342 10 DOLLARS

31.11 g., 0.999 Gold 0.999 oz. AGW, 40 mm. **Ruler:** Elizabeth II **Subject:** Maori Art **Obv:** Head with tiara right **Rev:** Tiki with huia feathers

| Date | Mintage | VF20 | XF40 | MS60 | MS63 | MS65 |
|---|---|---|---|---|---|---|
| 2010 (m) | 500 | PF65 2,650 | | | | |

### KM# 349 10 DOLLARS

7.77 g., 0.999 Gold 0.2496 oz. AGW, 26 mm. **Ruler:** Elizabeth II **Obv:** Head with tiara right **Rev:** Kiwi and silver fern **Edge:** Reeded

| Date | Mintage | VF20 | XF40 | MS60 | MS63 | MS65 |
|---|---|---|---|---|---|---|
| 2011 (m) | 995 | PF65 775 | | | | |

### KM# 352 10 DOLLARS

7.77 g., 0.999 Gold 0.2496 oz. AGW, 26 mm. **Ruler:** Elizabeth II **Obv:** Head with tiara right **Rev:** Kiwi and kowhai flowers **Edge:** Reeded

| Date | Mintage | VF20 | XF40 | MS60 | MS63 | MS65 |
|---|---|---|---|---|---|---|
| 2012 (m) | 950 | PF65 900 | | | | |

### KM# 353 10 DOLLARS

31.11 g., 0.999 Gold 0.999 oz. AGW with insert, 38.6 mm. **Ruler:** Elizabeth II **Subject:** Maori Art **Obv:** Head with tiara right **Rev:** Hei Matau (neck pendant) **Edge:** Notched

| Date | Mintage | VF20 | XF40 | MS60 | MS63 | MS65 |
|---|---|---|---|---|---|---|
| 2012 (u) | 250 | PF65 3,950 | | | | |

### KM# 368 10 DOLLARS

31.11 g., 0.999 Gold 0.999 oz. AGW, 39 mm. **Ruler:** Elizabeth II **Rev:** Bilbo Baggins, staff in his right hand; Hobbit hole door in background

| Date | Mintage | VF20 | XF40 | MS60 | MS63 | MS65 |
|---|---|---|---|---|---|---|
| 2012 | 250 | PF65 3,700 | | | | |

### KM# 369 10 DOLLARS

31.11 g., 0.999 Gold 0.999 oz. AGW, 39 mm. **Ruler:** Elizabeth II **Subject:** Gandalf

| Date | Mintage | VF20 | XF40 | MS60 | MS63 | MS65 |
|---|---|---|---|---|---|---|
| 2012 | 250 | PF65 3,500 | | | | |

**KM# 370 10 DOLLARS**
31.11 g., 0.999 Gold 0.999 oz. AGW, 39 mm. **Ruler:** Elizabeth II **Subject:** Thorin Oakenshield

| Date | Mintage | VF20 | XF40 | MS60 | MS63 | MS65 |
|---|---|---|---|---|---|---|
| 2012 | 250 | **PF65** 3,500 | | | | |

**KM# 371 10 DOLLARS**
31.11 g., 0.999 Gold 0.999 oz. AGW, 39 mm. **Ruler:** Elizabeth II **Rev:** Bilbo Baggins, staff in his left hand

| Date | Mintage | VF20 | XF40 | MS60 | MS63 | MS65 |
|---|---|---|---|---|---|---|
| 2012 | 1,000 | **PF65** 3,500 | | | | |

## MINT SETS

| KM# | Date | Mintage | Identification | Issue Price | Mkt Val |
|---|---|---|---|---|---|
| MS50 | 2001 (7) | 2,910 | KM#116-121, 128 | 18.50 | 60.00 |
| MS51 | 2002 (7) | 3,000 | KM#116-121, 145. Hector's dolphin. | 18.00 | 60.00 |
| MS52 | 2003 (7) | 3,000 | KM#116-121, 132. Giant Kokopu. | 18.00 | 100 |
| MS53 | 2003 (6) | 34,332 | KM#135-140. Lord of the Rings, Light vs. Dark set. | 19.95 | 100 |
| MS55 | 2003 (18) | 4,068 | KM#135-140; 235-246. Lord of the Rings. Character collection. | — | 325 |
| MS56 | 2003 (3) | 10,454 | KM#141, 142, 143. Lord of the Rings. Battle for the Ring set. | 29.95 | 35.00 |
| MS57 | 2004 (7) | 2,800 | KM#116-121, 133. Taiko. | 33.00 | 150 |
| MS58 | 2005 (7) | 3,000 | KM#116-121; 146. Crested Penguin. | 33.00 | 120 |
| MS59 | 2006 (7) | 3,000 | KM#116-121; 148. Falcon. | 33.00 | 120 |
| MS60 | 2003-5-6 (7) | 5,000 | Mixed Set for Change over to smaller size coins. KM#116 (2003); 117-119 (2005); KM#117a-119a (2006). | 7.50 | 70.00 |
| MS61 | 2007 (6) | 5,000 | KM#117a-119a; 120-121; 150. Tuatara. | 33.00 | 50.00 |
| MS62 | 2008 (6) | 4,000 | KM#117a-119a; 120-121; 233. Hamilton's frog. | 37.50 | 50.00 |
| MS63 | 2009 (6) | 2,000 | KM#117a-119a; 120-121; 329. Kakapo. | — | 55.00 |
| MS64 | 2009 (5) | 1,500 | KM#323-327. Giants of New Zealand. | — | 400 |
| MS65 | 2010 (6) | 2,000 | KM#117b, 118b, 119b, 120a, 121a, 334. Maui's dolphin. | 59.00 | 65.00 |
| MS66 | 2010 (5) | 1,500 | KM#336-340. Ancient Reptiles of New Zealand. | — | 450 |
| MS67 | 2011 (6) | 2,000 | KM#117b, 118b, 119b, 120a, 121a, 348. Yellow-eyed Penguin. | — | 65.00 |

## PROOF SETS

| KM# | Date | Mintage | Identification | Issue Price | Mkt Val |
|---|---|---|---|---|---|
| PS45 | 2001 (7) | 1,364 | KM#116-121, 128a | 49.25 | 170 |
| PS46 | 2001 (2) | 600 | KM#129-130 | 400 | 800 |
| PS47 | 2002 (7) | 1,500 | KM#116-121, 145a | 60.00 | 140 |
| PS48 | 2003 (6) | 810 | KM#141a and 5 others. | — | 350 |
| PS49 | 2003 (0) | — | Five coins as per PS48, less 141a | — | — |
| PS50 | 2003 (3) | 133 | KM#144; 270; 271. Lord of the Rings. Gold set. | — | 6,900 |
| PS51 | 2003 (2) | 9 | KM#270; 271. Lord of the Rings. | — | 4,600 |
| PS52 | 2003 (7) | 1,496 | KM#116-121, 132a. | 60.00 | 125 |
| PS53 | 2004 (7) | 1,750 | KM#116-121, 133a. Chatham Islands Taiko | — | 200 |
| PS54 | 2005 (7) | 2,250 | KM#116-121; 146a. Crested Penguin. | 88.00 | 165 |
| PS55 | 2006 (7) | 2,100 | KM#116-121; 148a. Falcon. | 90.00 | 145 |
| PS56 | 2006 (3) | 1,000 | KM#285; 287; 288. | — | 225 |
| PS57 | 2007 (6) | 2,200 | KM#117a-119a; 120-121; 150a. Tuatara. | 88.00 | 115 |
| PS58 | 2007 (7) | 69,000 | KM#232, NZ Aoraki dollar and Japan 95.2; 96.2; 97.2; 98.2; 101.2; 125. | 115 | 110 |
| PS59 | 2008 (6) | 1,441 | KM#117a-119a; 120-121; 233a. Hamilton's frog. | 94.00 | 125 |
| PS61 | 2009 (6) | 1,041 | KM#117a-119a; 120-121; 329a. Kakapo. | — | 125 |
| PS62 | 2010 (6) | 1,500 | KM#117b, 118b, 119b, 120a, 121a, 334a. Maui's dolphin. | 149 | 125 |
| PS63 | 2011 (6) | 500 | KM#117b, 118b, 119b, 120a, 121a, 348a. Yellow-eyed Penguin. | — | 135 |
| PS64 | 2011 (5) | 2,011 | KM346, 347, plus Australian, British and South African coins. | 695 | 700 |
| PS65 | 2011 (5) | 1,200 | KM#117c, 118c, 119c, 120b, 121b. | 275 | 225 |
| PS66 | 2012 (5) | 1,000 | KM#117d, 118c, 119c, 120b, 121b. | 275 | 225 |

# NICARAGUA

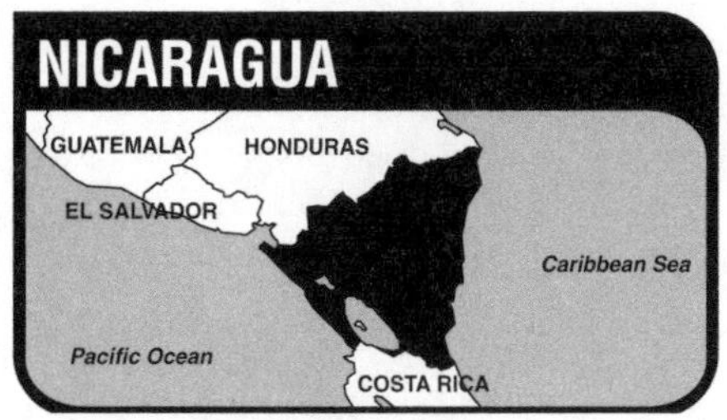


The Republic of Nicaragua, situated in Central America between Honduras and Costa Rica, has an area of 50,193 sq. mi. (129,494 sq. km.) and a population of *3.7 million. Capital: Managua. Agriculture, mining (gold and silver) and hardwood logging are the principal industries. Cotton, meat, coffee and sugar are exported.

**MONETARY SYSTEM**
100 Centavos = 1 Cordoba

## REPUBLIC

## DECIMAL COINAGE

**KM# 97 5 CENTAVOS**
3.00 g., Copper Plated Steel, 18.5 mm. **Obv:** National arms **Rev:** Value within circle **Edge:** Plain

| Date | Mintage | VF20 | XF40 | MS60 | MS63 | MS65 |
|---|---|---|---|---|---|---|
| 2002 | — | — | — | 0.25 | 0.50 | 0.75 |

**KM# 98 10 CENTAVOS**
4.00 g., Brass Plated Steel, 20.5 mm. **Obv:** National arms **Rev:** Value within circle **Edge:** Reeded and plain sections

| Date | Mintage | VF20 | XF40 | MS60 | MS63 | MS65 |
|---|---|---|---|---|---|---|
| 2002 | — | — | — | 0.25 | 0.50 | 0.75 |

**KM# 105 10 CENTAVOS**
Aluminum, 20.5 mm. **Obv:** National arms **Rev:** Value at center

| Date | Mintage | VF20 | XF40 | MS60 | MS63 | MS65 |
|---|---|---|---|---|---|---|
| 2007 | — | — | — | 0.25 | 0.50 | 0.75 |

**KM# 99 25 CENTAVOS**
5.00 g., Brass Plated Steel, 23.25 mm. **Obv:** National arms **Rev:** Value within circle **Edge:** Segmented reeding

| Date | Mintage | VF20 | XF40 | MS60 | MS63 | MS65 |
|---|---|---|---|---|---|---|
| 2002 | — | — | — | 0.25 | 0.50 | 0.75 |
| 2003 | — | — | — | 0.25 | 0.50 | 0.75 |
| 2007 | — | — | — | 0.25 | 0.50 | 0.75 |

**KM# 104 25 CENTAVOS**
Brass **Obv:** Arms **Rev:** Value at center **Rev. Legend:** EN DIOS CONFIAMOS

| Date | Mintage | VF20 | XF40 | MS60 | MS63 | MS65 |
|---|---|---|---|---|---|---|
| 2007 | — | — | — | 0.25 | 0.50 | 0.75 |

**KM# 89 CORDOBA**
6.20 g., Nickel Clad Steel, 25 mm. **Obv:** National emblem **Rev:** Value above sprigs within circle **Edge:** Reeded

| Date | Mintage | VF20 | XF40 | MS60 | MS63 | MS65 |
|---|---|---|---|---|---|---|
| 2002 | — | — | — | 1.00 | 1.50 | 2.00 |

**KM# 101 CORDOBA**
6.25 g., Nickel Clad Steel, 25 mm. **Obv:** National arms **Rev:** Large value "1" **Rev. Legend:** EN DIOS CONFIAMOS **Edge:** Reeded

| Date | Mintage | VF20 | XF40 | MS60 | MS63 | MS65 |
|---|---|---|---|---|---|---|
| 2002 | — | 0.35 | 0.75 | 1.00 | 1.50 | 2.00 |
| 2007 | — | 0.35 | 0.75 | 1.00 | 1.50 | 2.00 |
| 2008 | — | 0.35 | 0.75 | 1.00 | 1.50 | 2.00 |
| 2009 | — | 0.35 | 0.75 | 1.00 | 1.50 | 2.00 |
| 2010 | — | 0.35 | 0.75 | 1.00 | 1.50 | 2.00 |

**KM# 111 5 CORDOBAS**
7.80 g., Nickel Plated Steel, 28 mm. **Obv:** Large value at center **Rev:** Sun over mountains

| Date | Mintage | VF20 | XF40 | MS60 | MS63 | MS65 |
|---|---|---|---|---|---|---|
| 2012 | 10,000,000 | — | — | 1.00 | 1.50 | 2.00 |

**KM# 100 10 CORDOBAS**
27.12 g., 0.925 Silver 0.8065 oz. ASW, 40 mm. **Subject:** Ibero-America **Obv:** National arms in circle of arms **Rev:** Sail boat **Edge:** Reeded

| Date | Mintage | VF20 | XF40 | MS60 | MS63 | MS65 |
|---|---|---|---|---|---|---|
| 2002 | — | PF63 30.00 | PF65 42.00 | | | |

**KM# 106 10 CORDOBAS**
27.00 g., 0.925 Silver 0.803 oz. ASW, 40 mm. **Obv:** National arms within circle of other state arms **Rev:** Leon Cathedral

| Date | Mintage | VF20 | XF40 | MS60 | MS63 | MS65 |
|---|---|---|---|---|---|---|
| 2005 | — | PF63 35.00 | PF65 50.00 | | | |

**KM# 102 10 CORDOBAS**
8.47 g., Brass Plated Steel, 26.5 mm. **Obv:** National arms **Rev:** Value at upper left, circular latent image BCN below, statue of Andrés Castro at right **Edge Lettering:** B C N repeated 4 times

| Date | Mintage | VF20 | XF40 | MS60 | MS63 | MS65 |
|---|---|---|---|---|---|---|
| 2007 | — | — | — | 1.50 | 2.50 | 4.00 |

**KM# 107 10 CORDOBAS**
27.00 g., 0.925 Silver 0.803 oz. ASW, 40 mm. **Obv:** National arms within circle of other national arms **Rev:** Baseball batter on field

| Date | Mintage | VF20 | XF40 | MS60 | MS63 | MS65 |
|---|---|---|---|---|---|---|
| 2007 | — | PF63 35.00 | PF65 50.00 | | | |

**KM# 108 10 CORDOBAS**
27.00 g., 0.925 Silver 0.803 oz. ASW, 40 mm. **Obv:** National arms within circle of other state arms **Rev:** One Cordoba coin of 1912 at center

| Date | Mintage | VF20 | XF40 | MS60 | MS63 | MS65 |
|---|---|---|---|---|---|---|
| ND-2010 | — | PF63 35.00 | PF65 50.00 | | | |

**KM# 109 50 CORDOBAS**
40.00 g., 0.583 Gold 0.7498 oz. AGW, 40 mm. **Subject:** Central Bank, 50th Anniversary **Obv:** National arms **Rev:** Central Bank building on map of Nicaragua

| Date | Mintage | VF20 | XF40 | MS60 | MS63 | MS65 |
|---|---|---|---|---|---|---|
| 2010 | — | PF65 1,100 | | | | |

**KM# 110 50 CORDOBAS**
21.00 g., Copper-Nickel, 35 mm. **Obv:** National arms **Rev:** Bird and flower in color

| Date | Mintage | VF20 | XF40 | MS60 | MS63 | MS65 |
|---|---|---|---|---|---|---|
| 2010 | — | — | — | — | 15.00 | 25.00 |

**KM# 110a 50 CORDOBAS**
31.10 g., 0.999 Silver 0.9989 oz. ASW, 35 mm. **Obv:** National arms **Rev:** Bird and flower in color

| Date | Mintage | VF20 | XF40 | MS60 | MS63 | MS65 |
|---|---|---|---|---|---|---|
| 2010 | — | PF63 45.00 | PF65 60.00 | | | |

**KM# 110b 50 CORDOBAS**
31.10 g., 0.999 Gold 0.9989 oz. AGW, 35 mm. **Obv:** National arms **Rev:** Bird and flower in color

| Date | Mintage | VF20 | XF40 | MS60 | MS63 | MS65 |
|---|---|---|---|---|---|---|
| 2010 | — | PF65 1,750 | | | | |

**KM# 112 100 CORDOBAS**
31.10 g., 0.900 Silver 0.8999 oz. ASW, 35 mm. **Obv:** Large value in center **Rev:** Sun over mountains

| Date | Mintage | VF20 | XF40 | MS60 | MS63 | MS65 |
|---|---|---|---|---|---|---|
| 2012 | 1,000 | — | — | 55.00 | 65.00 | 75.00 |

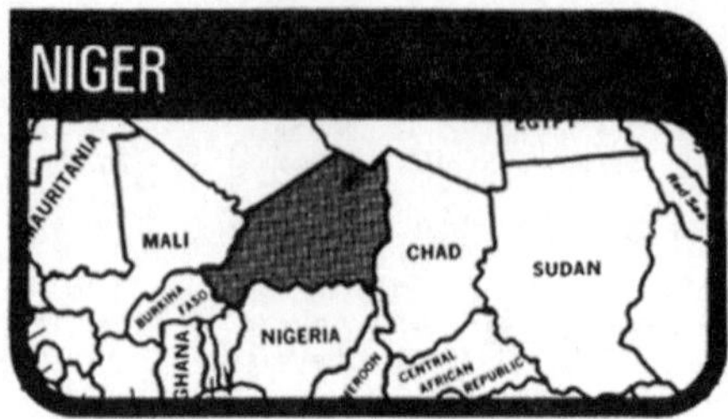


The Republic of Niger, located in West Africa's Sahara region 1,000 miles (1,609 km.) from the Mediterranean shore, has an area of 489,191 sq. mi. (1,267,000 sq. km.) and a population of *7.4 million. Capital: Niamey. The economy is based on subsistence agriculture and raising livestock. Peanuts, peanut oil, and livestock are exported.

## REPUBLIC

### DECIMAL COINAGE

**KM# 17 1000 FRANCS**
20.00 g., 0.925 Silver 0.5948 oz. ASW, 38.61 mm. **Obv:** Shield and flags **Rev:** Mecca pointer and amethyst crystal

| Date | Mintage | VF20 | XF40 | MS60 | MS63 | MS65 |
|---|---|---|---|---|---|---|
| 2012 | 1,000 | PF65 100 | | | | |

**KM# 18 1000 FRANCS**
20.00 g., 0.925 Silver 0.5948 oz. ASW, 38.61 mm. **Subject:** African Hippo **Rev:** Hippo in water with mouth wide open

| Date | Mintage | VF20 | XF40 | MS60 | MS63 | MS65 |
|---|---|---|---|---|---|---|
| 2012 | 500 | PF65 125 | | | | |

**KM# 19 1000 FRANCS**
20.00 g., 0.925 Silver 0.5948 oz. ASW, 38.61 mm. **Obv:** Shield and crossed flags **Rev:** Striped Jackel (Canis adustus) in color

| Date | Mintage | VF20 | XF40 | MS60 | MS63 | MS65 |
|---|---|---|---|---|---|---|
| 2012 | 1,000 | PF65 125 | | | | |

**KM# 21 1000 FRANCS**
20.00 g., 0.925 Silver 0.5948 oz. ASW, 38.61 mm. **Subject:** The Flert by Mucha **Rev:** Couple in Victorian attire in color

| Date | Mintage | VF20 | XF40 | MS60 | MS63 | MS65 |
|---|---|---|---|---|---|---|
| 2012 | — | PF65 100 | | | | |

**KM# 20 1000 FRANCS**
20.00 g., 0.925 Silver 0.5948 oz. ASW, 38.61 mm. **Subject:** Coyote - Canis Latrans

| Date | Mintage | VF20 | XF40 | MS60 | MS63 | MS65 |
|---|---|---|---|---|---|---|
| 2013 | Est. 1000 | PF65 75.00 | | | | |

**KM# 22 1000 FRANCS CFA**
31.11 g., 0.999 Silver 0.999 oz. ASW, 38.61 mm. **Obv:** National arms **Rev:** Fennec (desert fox) facing

| Date | Mintage | VF20 | XF40 | MS60 | MS63 | MS65 |
|---|---|---|---|---|---|---|
| 2013 Antique patina | 1,000 | — | — | — | 40.00 | — |

**KM# 23 1000 FRANCS CFA**
31.11 g., 0.999 Silver 0.999 oz. ASW, 38.61 mm. **Obv:** National arms **Rev:** Fennec (desert fox) with yellow jade insert color

| Date | Mintage | VF20 | XF40 | MS60 | MS63 | MS65 |
|---|---|---|---|---|---|---|
| 2013 Antique patina | 500 | — | — | — | 40.00 | — |

# NIGERIA

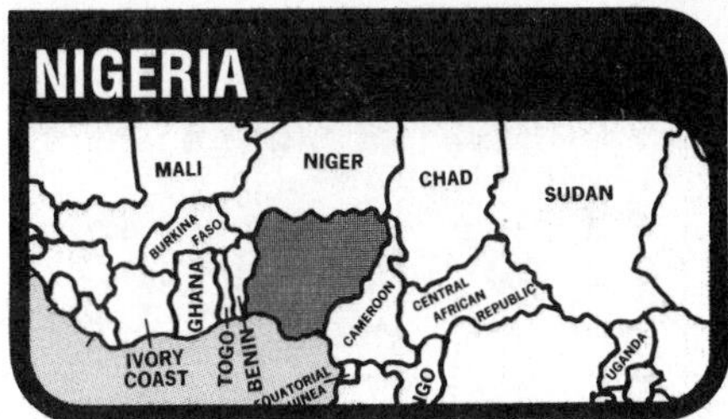


The Federal Republic of Nigeria, situated on the Atlantic coast of West Africa has an area of 356,669 sq. mi. (923,770 sq. km.). Nigeria is a member of the Commonwealth of Nations. The President is the Head of State and the Head of Government.

## FEDERAL REPUBLIC

### DECIMAL COINAGE

100 Kobo = 1 Naira

**KM# 17 KOBO**
4.67 g., Brass, 23.2 mm. **Obv:** Arms with supporters **Rev:** Monkey musicians below value **Edge:** Reeded

| Date | Mintage | VF20 | XF40 | MS60 | MS63 | MS65 |
|---|---|---|---|---|---|---|
| 2003 | — | — | — | — | 15.00 | 20.00 |

**KM# 13.3 50 KOBO**
3.50 g., Nickel Clad Steel, 19.44 mm. **Obv:** Arms with supporters **Obv. Legend:** FEDERAL REPUBLIC OF NIGERIA **Rev:** Value at left, corn cob and stalk at right **Edge:** Plain **Note:** Reduced size.

| Date | Mintage | VF20 | XF40 | MS60 | MS63 | MS65 |
|---|---|---|---|---|---|---|
| 2006 | — | — | — | 0.50 | 1.00 | 1.35 |

**KM# 18 NAIRA**
5.43 g., Bi-Metallic Brass center in Stainless Steel ring, 21.48 mm. **Obv:** National arms **Obv. Legend:** FEDERAL REPUBLIC OF NIGERIA **Rev:** Small bust of Herbert Macaulay above value **Edge:** Plain

| Date | Mintage | VF20 | XF40 | MS60 | MS63 | MS65 |
|---|---|---|---|---|---|---|
| 2006 | — | — | — | 1.25 | 2.00 | 3.00 |

**KM# 19 2 NAIRA**
7.48 g., Bi-Metallic Stainless Steel center in Copper-Brass ring, 25.99 mm. **Obv:** National arms **Obv. Legend:** FEDERAL REPUBLIC OF NIGERIA **Rev:** Large value, National Assembly in background **Edge:** Coarse reeding

| Date | Mintage | VF20 | XF40 | MS60 | MS63 | MS65 |
|---|---|---|---|---|---|---|
| 2006 | — | — | — | 2.00 | 3.00 | 5.00 |

# NIUE

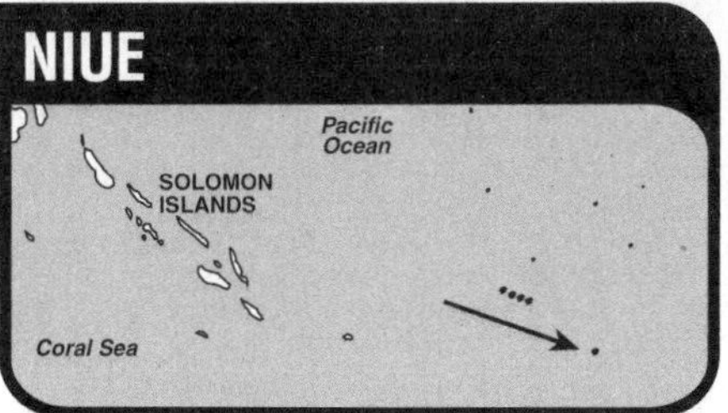


Niue, or Savage Island, a dependent state of New Zealand, ruled by the Queen of England, is located in the Pacific Ocean east of Tonga and southeast of Samoa. The size is 100 sq. mi. (260 sq. km.) with a population of approx. 1,500. Chief village and port is Alofi. Vanilla, noni and taro are exported.

**MINT MARK**
PM - Pobjoy Mint

## NEW ZEALAND DEPENDENT STATE

### DECIMAL COINAGE

**KM# 193 5 CENTS**
4.30 g., Copper Plated Bronze, 19 mm. **Ruler:** Elizabeth II **Obv:** Head right **Rev:** Two whales

| Date | Mintage | VF20 | XF40 | MS60 | MS63 | MS65 |
|---|---|---|---|---|---|---|
| 2009 | — | — | — | 0.50 | 1.00 | 2.00 |
| 2010 | — | — | — | 0.50 | 1.00 | 2.00 |

**KM# 194 10 CENTS**
5.80 g., Copper Plated Bronze, 22 mm. **Ruler:** Elizabeth II **Obv:** Head right **Rev:** Coconut crab **Edge:** Reeded

| Date | Mintage | VF20 | XF40 | MS60 | MS63 | MS65 |
|---|---|---|---|---|---|---|
| 2009 | — | — | — | 0.75 | 1.50 | 2.00 |
| 2010 | — | — | — | 0.75 | 1.50 | 2.00 |

**KM# 195 20 CENTS**
7.30 g., Nickel Plated Bronze, 25 mm. **Ruler:** Elizabeth II **Obv:** Head right **Rev:** Two scuba divers and coral

| Date | Mintage | VF20 | XF40 | MS60 | MS63 | MS65 |
|---|---|---|---|---|---|---|
| 2009 | — | — | — | 1.00 | 2.00 | 3.00 |
| 2010 | — | — | — | 1.00 | 2.00 | 3.00 |

**KM# 606 50 CENTS**
15.55 g., 0.999 Silver 0.4994 oz. ASW, 35 mm. **Ruler:** Elizabeth II **Subject:** Olympics **Rev:** Boxers, ancient and modern

| Date | Mintage | VF20 | XF40 | MS60 | MS63 | MS65 |
|---|---|---|---|---|---|---|
| 2004-2008 | — | PF65 40.00 | | | | |

**KM# 607 50 CENTS**
15.50 g., 0.999 Silver 0.4978 oz. ASW, 35 mm. **Ruler:** Elizabeth II **Subject:** Olympics **Rev:** Long Jumpers - ancient and modern

| Date | Mintage | VF20 | XF40 | MS60 | MS63 | MS65 |
|---|---|---|---|---|---|---|
| 2004-2008 | — | PF65 40.00 | | | | |

**KM# 608 50 CENTS**
15.50 g., 0.999 Silver 0.4978 oz. ASW, 35 mm. **Ruler:** Elizabeth II **Subject:** Olympics **Rev:** Shot Put, ancient and modern

| Date | Mintage | VF20 | XF40 | MS60 | MS63 | MS65 |
|---|---|---|---|---|---|---|
| 2004-2008 | — | PF65 40.00 | | | | |

**KM# 609 50 CENTS**
15.50 g., 0.999 Silver 0.4978 oz. ASW, 35 mm. **Ruler:** Elizabeth II **Subject:** Olympics **Rev:** Archer, ancient and modern

| Date | Mintage | VF20 | XF40 | MS60 | MS63 | MS65 |
|---|---|---|---|---|---|---|
| 2004-2008 | — | PF65 40.00 | | | | |

**KM# 610 50 CENTS**
15.50 g., 0.999 Silver 0.4978 oz. ASW, 35 mm. **Ruler:** Elizabeth II **Subject:** Olympics **Rev:** Equestrian - ancient and modern views

| Date | Mintage | VF20 | XF40 | MS60 | MS63 | MS65 |
|---|---|---|---|---|---|---|
| 2004-2008 | — | PF65 40.00 | | | | |

**KM# 611 50 CENTS**
15.50 g., 0.999 Silver 0.4978 oz. ASW, 35 mm. **Ruler:** Elizabeth II **Subject:** Olympics **Rev:** Discus - ancient and modern views

| Date | Mintage | VF20 | XF40 | MS60 | MS63 | MS65 |
|---|---|---|---|---|---|---|
| 2004-2008 | — | PF65 40.00 | | | | |

**KM# 612 50 CENTS**
15.50 g., 0.999 Silver 0.4978 oz. ASW, 35 mm. **Ruler:** Elizabeth II **Subject:** Olympics **Rev:** Track - ancient and modern views

| Date | Mintage | VF20 | XF40 | MS60 | MS63 | MS65 |
|---|---|---|---|---|---|---|
| 2004-2008 | — | PF65 40.00 | | | | |

**KM# 613 50 CENTS**
15.50 g., 0.999 Silver 0.4978 oz. ASW, 35 mm. **Ruler:** Elizabeth II **Subject:** Olympics **Rev:** Wrestlers - ancient and modern views

| Date | Mintage | VF20 | XF40 | MS60 | MS63 | MS65 |
|---|---|---|---|---|---|---|
| 2004-2008 | — | PF65 40.00 | | | | |

**KM# 614 50 CENTS**
15.50 g., 0.999 Silver 0.4978 oz. ASW, 35 mm. **Ruler:** Elizabeth II **Subject:** Olympics **Rev:** Javelin thrower - ancient and modern views

| Date | Mintage | VF20 | XF40 | MS60 | MS63 | MS65 |
|---|---|---|---|---|---|---|
| 2004-2008 | — | PF65 40.00 | | | | |

**KM# 615 50 CENTS**
15.50 g., 0.999 Silver 0.4978 oz. ASW, 35 mm. **Ruler:** Elizabeth II **Subject:** Olympics **Rev:** Soccer - ancient and modern view

| Date | Mintage | VF20 | XF40 | MS60 | MS63 | MS65 |
|---|---|---|---|---|---|---|
| 2004-2008 | — | PF65 40.00 | | | | |

**KM# 616 50 CENTS**
15.50 g., 0.999 Silver 0.4978 oz. ASW, 35 mm. **Ruler:** Elizabeth II **Subject:** Olympics **Rev:** Field Hockey - ancient and modern views

| Date | Mintage | VF20 | XF40 | MS60 | MS63 | MS65 |
|---|---|---|---|---|---|---|
| 2004-2008 | — | PF65 40.00 | | | | |

**KM# 263 50 CENTS**
15.55 g., 0.999 Silver 0.4994 oz. ASW, 35 mm. **Ruler:** Elizabeth II **Series:** Year of the Rooster **Rev:** Multicolor rooster standing right, sunrise

| Date | Mintage | VF20 | XF40 | MS60 | MS63 | MS65 |
|---|---|---|---|---|---|---|
| 2005 | — | PF65 30.00 | | | | |

**KM# 292 50 CENTS**
15.55 g., 0.999 Silver 0.4994 oz. ASW, 35 mm. **Ruler:** Elizabeth II **Subject:** Year of the Dog **Rev:** Multicolor dog

| Date | Mintage | VF20 | XF40 | MS60 | MS63 | MS65 |
|---|---|---|---|---|---|---|
| 2005 | — | PF65 35.00 | | | | |

**KM# 189 50 CENTS**
15.50 g., 0.999 Silver 0.4978 oz. ASW, 28 mm. **Ruler:** Elizabeth II **Subject:** Year of the Pig **Obv:** Head right **Rev:** Multicolor pig

| Date | Mintage | VF20 | XF40 | MS60 | MS63 | MS65 |
|---|---|---|---|---|---|---|
| 2007 | — | PF65 50.00 | | | | |

**KM# 196 50 CENTS**
9.30 g., Nickel Plated Bronze, 28 mm. **Ruler:** Elizabeth II **Obv:** Head right **Rev:** Outrigger canoe **Edge:** Segmented reeding

| Date | Mintage | VF20 | XF40 | MS60 | MS63 | MS65 |
|---|---|---|---|---|---|---|
| 2009 | — | — | — | 2.50 | 4.00 | 7.50 |
| 2010 | — | — | — | 2.50 | 4.00 | 7.50 |

**KM# 1105 250 CENTS**
3.11 g., 0.999 Gold 0.0999 oz. AGW, 16 mm. **Ruler:** Elizabeth II **Subject:** Family of Rohans: Camille de Rohan

| Date | Mintage | VF20 | XF40 | MS60 | MS63 | MS65 |
|---|---|---|---|---|---|---|
| 2013 | Est. 500 | PF65 200 | | | | |

**KM# 1106 250 CENTS**
3.11 g., 0.999 Gold 0.0999 oz. AGW, 16 mm. **Ruler:** Elizabeth II **Subject:** Family of Rohans: Henri II de Rohan

| Date | Mintage | VF20 | XF40 | MS60 | MS63 | MS65 |
|---|---|---|---|---|---|---|
| 2013 | Est. 500 | PF65 200 | | | | |

**KM# 1107 250 CENTS**
3.11 g., 0.999 Gold 0.0999 oz. AGW, 16 mm. **Ruler:** Elizabeth II **Subject:** Family of Rohans: Louis Rene de Rohan

| Date | Mintage | VF20 | XF40 | MS60 | MS63 | MS65 |
|---|---|---|---|---|---|---|
| 2013 | Est. 500 | PF65 200 | | | | |

**KM# 1108 250 CENTS**
3.11 g., 0.999 Gold 0.0999 oz. AGW, 16 mm. **Ruler:** Elizabeth II **Subject:** Family of Rohans: Marie de Rohan

| Date | Mintage | VF20 | XF40 | MS60 | MS63 | MS65 |
|---|---|---|---|---|---|---|
| 2013 | Est. 500 | PF65 200 | | | | |

**KM# 786 2012 CENTS**
31.10 g., 0.999 Silver 0.9989 oz. ASW, 30.5x5.5 mm. **Ruler:** Elizabeth II **Obv:** Queen's head at left, Titanic sailing left **Rev:** Ship's bell and other items **Shape:** oval

| Date | Mintage | VF20 | XF40 | MS60 | MS63 | MS65 |
|---|---|---|---|---|---|---|
| 2012 | — | PF65 100 | | | | |

**KM# 786a 2012 CENTS**
31.10 g., 0.999 Silver 0.9989 oz. ASW, 31.5x5.5 mm. **Ruler:** Elizabeth II **Obv:** Queen's head at left, Titanic sailing left, sky in color **Rev:** Ship's bell and other items **Shape:** oval

| Date | Mintage | VF20 | XF40 | MS60 | MS63 | MS65 |
|---|---|---|---|---|---|---|
| 2012 | Est. 200 | PF65 100 | | | | |

**KM# 462 1/33 DOLLAR**
42.50 g., 0.999 Silver 1.365 oz. ASW, 41.7x40 mm. **Ruler:** Elizabeth II **Rev:** Sistine Chapel Corner featuring Haman's punishment

| Date | Mintage | VF20 | XF40 | MS60 | MS63 | MS65 |
|---|---|---|---|---|---|---|
| 2010 | 500 | PF65 75.00 | | | | |

**KM# 463 1/33 DOLLAR**
42.50 g., 0.999 Silver 1.365 oz. ASW, 41.7x40 mm. **Ruler:** Elizabeth II **Rev:** Sistine Chapel Arch featuring the Prophet Jonah

| Date | Mintage | VF20 | XF40 | MS60 | MS63 | MS65 |
|---|---|---|---|---|---|---|
| 2010 | 500 | PF65 75.00 | | | | |

**KM# 464 1/33 DOLLAR**
42.50 g., 0.999 Silver 1.365 oz. ASW, 41.7x40 mm. **Ruler:** Elizabeth II **Rev:** Sistine Chapel Corner Spandrel featuring the Brazen Serpent

| Date | Mintage | VF20 | XF40 | MS60 | MS63 | MS65 |
|---|---|---|---|---|---|---|
| 2010 | 500 | PF65 75.00 | | | | |

**KM# 465 1/33 DOLLAR**
26.80 g., 0.999 Silver 0.8608 oz. ASW, 29x36.1 mm. **Ruler:** Elizabeth II **Rev:** Sistine Chapel Arch featuring the Prophet Jeremiah

| Date | Mintage | VF20 | XF40 | MS60 | MS63 | MS65 |
|---|---|---|---|---|---|---|
| 2010 | 500 | PF65 60.00 | | | | |

**KM# 466 1/33 DOLLAR**
26.80 g., 0.999 Silver 0.8608 oz. ASW, 29x36.1 mm. **Ruler:** Elizabeth II **Rev:** Sistine Chapel Arch with Salmon

| Date | Mintage | VF20 | XF40 | MS60 | MS63 | MS65 |
|---|---|---|---|---|---|---|
| 2010 | 500 | PF65 60.00 | | | | |

**KM# 467 1/33 DOLLAR**
26.80 g., 0.999 Silver 0.8608 oz. ASW, 29x36.1 mm. **Ruler:** Elizabeth II **Rev:** Sistine Chapel Arch with Persian Sibyl

| Date | Mintage | VF20 | XF40 | MS60 | MS63 | MS65 |
|---|---|---|---|---|---|---|
| 2010 | 500 | PF65 60.00 | | | | |

**KM# 468 1/33 DOLLAR**
21.00 g., 0.999 Silver 0.6745 oz. ASW, 23x36.1 mm. **Ruler:** Elizabeth II **Rev:** Sistine Chapel Arch with Roboam

| Date | Mintage | VF20 | XF40 | MS60 | MS63 | MS65 |
|---|---|---|---|---|---|---|
| 2010 | 500 | PF65 45.00 | | | | |

**KM# 469 1/33 DOLLAR**
26.80 g., 0.999 Silver 0.8608 oz. ASW, 29x36.1 mm. **Ruler:** Elizabeth II **Rev:** Sistine Chapel Arch with Prophet Ezekiel

| Date | Mintage | VF20 | XF40 | MS60 | MS63 | MS65 |
|---|---|---|---|---|---|---|
| 2010 | 500 | PF65 60.00 | | | | |

### KM# 470 1/33 DOLLAR
26.80 g., 0.999 Silver 0.8608 oz. ASW, 29x36.1 mm. **Ruler:** Elizabeth II **Rev:** Sistine Chapel Arch with Ozias

| Date | Mintage | VF20 | XF40 | MS60 | MS63 | MS65 |
|---|---|---|---|---|---|---|
| 2010 | 500 | PF65 60.00 | | | | |

### KM# 471 1/33 DOLLAR
21.00 g., 0.999 Silver 0.6745 oz. ASW, 23x36.1 mm. **Ruler:** Elizabeth II **Rev:** Sistine Chapel Arch with Erythraean Sibyl

| Date | Mintage | VF20 | XF40 | MS60 | MS63 | MS65 |
|---|---|---|---|---|---|---|
| 2010 | 500 | PF65 45.00 | | | | |

### KM# 472 1/33 DOLLAR
26.80 g., 0.999 Silver 0.8608 oz. ASW, 29x36.1 mm. **Ruler:** Elizabeth II **Rev:** Sistine Chapel Arch with Zorobabel

| Date | Mintage | VF20 | XF40 | MS60 | MS63 | MS65 |
|---|---|---|---|---|---|---|
| 2010 | 500 | PF65 55.00 | | | | |

### KM# 473 1/33 DOLLAR
21.00 g., 0.999 Silver 0.6745 oz. ASW, 23x36.1 mm. **Ruler:** Elizabeth II **Rev:** Sistine Chapel Arch with Prophel Joel

| Date | Mintage | VF20 | XF40 | MS60 | MS63 | MS65 |
|---|---|---|---|---|---|---|
| 2010 | 500 | PF65 45.00 | | | | |

### KM# 474 1/33 DOLLAR
35.50 g., 0.999 Silver 1.1402 oz. ASW, 29x47.8 mm. **Ruler:** Elizabeth II **Rev:** Sistine Chapel vault depicting Genesis creation story of Separation of Light from Darkness

| Date | Mintage | VF20 | XF40 | MS60 | MS63 | MS65 |
|---|---|---|---|---|---|---|
| 2010 | 500 | PF65 75.00 | | | | |

### KM# 475 1/33 DOLLAR
35.50 g., 0.999 Silver 1.1402 oz. ASW, 29x47.8 mm. **Ruler:** Elizabeth II **Rev:** Sistine Chapel vault depecting Genesis story of Creation of Sun and Moon

| Date | Mintage | VF20 | XF40 | MS60 | MS63 | MS65 |
|---|---|---|---|---|---|---|
| 2010 | 500 | PF65 75.00 | | | | |

### KM# 476 1/33 DOLLAR
35.50 g., 0.999 Silver 1.1402 oz. ASW, 29x47.8 mm. **Ruler:** Elizabeth II **Rev:** Sistine Chapel vault depicting Genesis creation story of the Separation of Land and Water

| Date | Mintage | VF20 | XF40 | MS60 | MS63 | MS65 |
|---|---|---|---|---|---|---|
| 2010 | 500 | PF65 75.00 | | | | |

### KM# 477 1/33 DOLLAR
28.00 g., 0.999 Silver 0.8993 oz. ASW, 23x47.8 mm. **Ruler:** Elizabeth II **Rev:** Sistine Chapel vault depicting Genesis story of the Creation of Adam

| Date | Mintage | VF20 | XF40 | MS60 | MS63 | MS65 |
|---|---|---|---|---|---|---|
| 2010 | 500 | PF65 60.00 | | | | |

### KM# 478 1/33 DOLLAR
35.50 g., 0.999 Silver 1.1402 oz. ASW, 29x47.8 mm. **Ruler:** Elizabeth II **Rev:** Sistine Chapel vault depicting the story of the Creation of Eve

| Date | Mintage | VF20 | XF40 | MS60 | MS63 | MS65 |
|---|---|---|---|---|---|---|
| 2010 | 500 | PF65 75.00 | | | | |

### KM# 479 1/33 DOLLAR
28.00 g., 0.999 Silver 0.8993 oz. ASW, 23x47.8 mm. **Ruler:** Elizabeth II **Rev:** Sistine Chapel vault depicting the Genesis story of Original Sin

| Date | Mintage | VF20 | XF40 | MS60 | MS63 | MS65 |
|---|---|---|---|---|---|---|
| 2010 | 500 | PF65 60.00 | | | | |

### KM# 480 1/33 DOLLAR
35.50 g., 0.999 Silver 1.1402 oz. ASW, 29x47.7 mm. **Ruler:** Elizabeth II **Rev:** Sistine Chapel vault depicting the Genesis story of the Sacrifice of Noah

| Date | Mintage | VF20 | XF40 | MS60 | MS63 | MS65 |
|---|---|---|---|---|---|---|
| 2010 | 500 | PF65 75.00 | | | | |

### KM# 481 1/33 DOLLAR
28.00 g., 0.999 Silver 0.8993 oz. ASW, 23x47.8 mm. **Ruler:** Elizabeth II **Rev:** Sistine Chapel vault depicting the Genesis story of the Flood

| Date | Mintage | VF20 | XF40 | MS60 | MS63 | MS65 |
|---|---|---|---|---|---|---|
| 2010 | 500 | PF65 60.00 | | | | |

### KM# 482 1/33 DOLLAR
35.50 g., 0.999 Silver 1.1402 oz. ASW, 29x47.8 mm. **Ruler:** Elizabeth II **Rev:** Sistine Chapel vault depicting the Genesis story of the Drunkenness of Noah

| Date | Mintage | VF20 | XF40 | MS60 | MS63 | MS65 |
|---|---|---|---|---|---|---|
| 2010 | 500 | PF65 75.00 | | | | |

### KM# 483 1/33 DOLLAR
26.80 g., 0.999 Silver 0.8608 oz. ASW, 29x36.1 mm. **Ruler:** Elizabeth II **Rev:** Sistine Chapel Arch depicting the Libyan Sibyl

| Date | Mintage | VF20 | XF40 | MS60 | MS63 | MS65 |
|---|---|---|---|---|---|---|
| 2010 | 500 | PF65 60.00 | | | | |

### KM# 484 1/33 DOLLAR
26.80 g., 0.999 Silver 0.8608 oz. ASW, 29x36.1 mm. **Ruler:** Elizabeth II **Rev:** Sistine Chapel Arch depicting Jesse

| Date | Mintage | VF20 | XF40 | MS60 | MS63 | MS65 |
|---|---|---|---|---|---|---|
| 2010 | 500 | PF65 60.00 | | | | |

### KM# 485 1/33 DOLLAR
26.80 g., 0.999 Silver 0.8608 oz. ASW, 29x36.1 mm. **Ruler:** Elizabeth II **Rev:** Sistine Chapel Arch depicting the Prophet Daniel

| Date | Mintage | VF20 | XF40 | MS60 | MS63 | MS65 |
|---|---|---|---|---|---|---|
| 2010 | 500 | PF65 60.00 | | | | |

### KM# 486 1/33 DOLLAR
21.00 g., 0.999 Silver 0.6745 oz. ASW, 23x36.1 mm. **Ruler:** Elizabeth II **Rev:** Sistine Chapel Arch depicting Asa

| Date | Mintage | VF20 | XF40 | MS60 | MS63 | MS65 |
|---|---|---|---|---|---|---|
| 2010 | 500 | PF65 45.00 | | | | |

### KM# 487 1/33 DOLLAR
26.80 g., 0.999 Silver 0.8608 oz. ASW, 29x36.1 mm. **Ruler:** Elizabeth II **Rev:** Sistine Chapel Arch depicting the Cumaean Sibyl

| Date | Mintage | VF20 | XF40 | MS60 | MS63 | MS65 |
|---|---|---|---|---|---|---|
| 2010 | 500 | PF65 60.00 | | | | |

### KM# 488 1/33 DOLLAR
21.00 g., 0.999 Silver 0.6745 oz. ASW, 23x36.1 mm. **Ruler:** Elizabeth II **Rev:** Sistine Chapel Arch depicting Ezxekias

| Date | Mintage | VF20 | XF40 | MS60 | MS63 | MS65 |
|---|---|---|---|---|---|---|
| 2010 | 500 | PF65 45.00 | | | | |

### KM# 489 1/33 DOLLAR
26.80 g., 0.999 Silver 0.8608 oz. ASW, 29x.36.1 mm. **Ruler:** Elizabeth II **Rev:** Sistine Chapel Arch depicting the Prophet Isiah

| Date | Mintage | VF20 | XF40 | MS60 | MS63 | MS65 |
|---|---|---|---|---|---|---|
| 2010 | 500 | PF65 60.00 | | | | |

### KM# 490 1/33 DOLLAR
26.80 g., 0.999 Silver 0.8608 oz. ASW, 29x36.1 mm. **Ruler:** Elizabeth II **Rev:** Sistine Chapel Arch depicting Josias

| Date | Mintage | VF20 | XF40 | MS60 | MS63 | MS65 |
|---|---|---|---|---|---|---|
| 2010 | 500 | PF65 60.00 | | | | |

### KM# 491 1/33 DOLLAR
21.00 g., 0.999 Silver 0.6745 oz. ASW, 23x36.1 mm. **Ruler:** Elizabeth II **Rev:** Sistine Chapel Arch depicting the Delphic Sibyl

| Date | Mintage | VF20 | XF40 | MS60 | MS63 | MS65 |
|---|---|---|---|---|---|---|
| 2010 | 500 | PF65 45.00 | | | | |

### KM# 492 1/33 DOLLAR
42.50 g., 0.999 Silver 1.365 oz. ASW, 41.7x40 mm. **Ruler:** Elizabeth II **Rev:** Sistine Chapel corner spandrel depicting David & Goliath

| Date | Mintage | VF20 | XF40 | MS60 | MS63 | MS65 |
|---|---|---|---|---|---|---|
| 2010 | 500 | PF65 75.00 | | | | |

### KM# 493 1/33 DOLLAR
42.50 g., 0.999 Silver 1.365 oz. ASW, 41.7x40 mm. **Ruler:** Elizabeth II **Rev:** Sistine Chapel Arch vault depicting the Prophet Zechariah

| Date | Mintage | VF20 | XF40 | MS60 | MS63 | MS65 |
|---|---|---|---|---|---|---|
| 2010 | 500 | PF65 75.00 | | | | |

### KM# 494 1/33 DOLLAR
42.50 g., 0.999 Silver 1.365 oz. ASW, 41.7x40 mm. **Ruler:** Elizabeth II **Rev:** Sistine Chapel corner spandrel depicting Judith & Holofornes

| Date | Mintage | VF20 | XF40 | MS60 | MS63 | MS65 |
|---|---|---|---|---|---|---|
| 2010 | 500 | PF65 75.00 | | | | |

### KM# 526 1/24 DOLLAR
42.50 g., 0.999 Silver 1.365 oz. ASW, 41.7x40 mm. **Ruler:** Elizabeth II **Obv:** Head with tiara right **Rev:** Partial DaVinci drawing

| Date | Mintage | VF20 | XF40 | MS60 | MS63 | MS65 |
|---|---|---|---|---|---|---|
| 2011 | 500 | PF65 75.00 | | | | |

### KM# 527 1/24 DOLLAR
42.50 g., 0.999 Silver 1.365 oz. ASW, 41.7x40 mm. **Ruler:** Elizabeth II **Obv:** Head with tiara right **Rev:** Partial DaVinci drawing

| Date | Mintage | VF20 | XF40 | MS60 | MS63 | MS65 |
|---|---|---|---|---|---|---|
| 2011 | 500 | PF65 75.00 | | | | |

### KM# 528 1/24 DOLLAR
42.50 g., 0.999 Silver 1.365 oz. ASW, 41.7x40 mm. **Ruler:** Elizabeth II **Obv:** Head with tiara right **Rev:** Partial DaVinci drawing

| Date | Mintage | VF20 | XF40 | MS60 | MS63 | MS65 |
|---|---|---|---|---|---|---|
| 2011 | 500 | PF65 75.00 | | | | |

### KM# 529 1/24 DOLLAR
42.50 g., 0.999 Silver 1.365 oz. ASW, 41.7x40 mm. **Ruler:** Elizabeth II **Obv:** Head with tiara right **Rev:** Partial DaVinci drawing

| Date | Mintage | VF20 | XF40 | MS60 | MS63 | MS65 |
|---|---|---|---|---|---|---|
| 2011 | 500 | PF65 75.00 | | | | |

### KM# 530 1/24 DOLLAR
42.50 g., 0.999 Silver 1.365 oz. ASW, 41.7x40 mm. **Ruler:** Elizabeth II **Obv:** Head with tiara right **Rev:** Partial DaVinci drawing

| Date | Mintage | VF20 | XF40 | MS60 | MS63 | MS65 |
|---|---|---|---|---|---|---|
| 2011 | 500 | PF65 75.00 | | | | |

### KM# 531 1/24 DOLLAR
42.50 g., 0.999 Silver 1.365 oz. ASW, 41.7x40 mm. **Ruler:** Elizabeth II **Obv:** Head with tiara right **Rev:** Partial DaVinci drawing

| Date | Mintage | VF20 | XF40 | MS60 | MS63 | MS65 |
|---|---|---|---|---|---|---|
| 2011 | 500 | PF65 75.00 | | | | |

### KM# 532 1/24 DOLLAR
42.50 g., 0.999 Silver 1.365 oz. ASW, 41.7x40 mm. **Ruler:** Elizabeth II **Obv:** Head with tiara right **Rev:** Partial DaVinci drawing

| Date | Mintage | VF20 | XF40 | MS60 | MS63 | MS65 |
|---|---|---|---|---|---|---|
| 2011 | 500 | PF65 75.00 | | | | |

### KM# 533 1/24 DOLLAR
42.50 g., 0.999 Silver 1.365 oz. ASW **Ruler:** Elizabeth II **Obv:** Head in tiara right **Rev:** Partial DaVinci drawing

| Date | Mintage | VF20 | XF40 | MS60 | MS63 | MS65 |
|---|---|---|---|---|---|---|
| 2011 | 500 | PF65 75.00 | | | | |

### KM# 534 1/24 DOLLAR
42.50 g., 0.999 Silver 1.365 oz. ASW, 41.7x40 mm. **Ruler:** Elizabeth II **Obv:** Head with tiara right **Rev:** Partial DaVinci drawing

| Date | Mintage | VF20 | XF40 | MS60 | MS63 | MS65 |
|---|---|---|---|---|---|---|
| 2011 | 500 | PF65 75.00 | | | | |

### KM# 535 1/24 DOLLAR
42.50 g., 0.999 Silver 1.365 oz. ASW, 41.7x40 mm. **Ruler:** Elizabeth II **Obv:** Head with tiara right **Rev:** Partial DaVinci drawing

| Date | Mintage | VF20 | XF40 | MS60 | MS63 | MS65 |
|---|---|---|---|---|---|---|
| 2011 | 500 | PF65 75.00 | | | | |

### KM# 536 1/24 DOLLAR
42.50 g., 0.999 Silver 1.365 oz. ASW, 41.7x40 mm. **Ruler:** Elizabeth II **Obv:** Head in tiara right **Rev:** Partial DaVinci drawing

| Date | Mintage | VF20 | XF40 | MS60 | MS63 | MS65 |
|---|---|---|---|---|---|---|
| 2011 | 500 | PF65 75.00 | | | | |

### KM# 537 1/24 DOLLAR
42.50 g., 0.999 Silver 1.365 oz. ASW, 41.7x40 mm. **Ruler:** Elizabeth II **Obv:** Head with tiara right **Rev:** Partial DaVinci drawing

| Date | Mintage | VF20 | XF40 | MS60 | MS63 | MS65 |
|---|---|---|---|---|---|---|
| 2011 | 500 | PF65 75.00 | | | | |

### KM# 538 1/24 DOLLAR
42.50 g., 0.999 Silver 1.365 oz. ASW, 41.7x40 mm. **Ruler:** Elizabeth II **Obv:** Head with tiara right **Rev:** Partial DaVinci drawing

| Date | Mintage | VF20 | XF40 | MS60 | MS63 | MS65 |
|---|---|---|---|---|---|---|
| 2011 | 500 | PF65 75.00 | | | | |

### KM# 539 1/24 DOLLAR
42.50 g., 0.999 Silver 1.365 oz. ASW, 41.7x40 mm. **Ruler:** Elizabeth II **Obv:** Head with tiara right **Rev:** Partial DaVinci drawing

| Date | Mintage | VF20 | XF40 | MS60 | MS63 | MS65 |
|---|---|---|---|---|---|---|
| 2011 | 500 | PF65 75.00 | | | | |

### KM# 540 1/24 DOLLAR
42.50 g., 0.999 Silver 1.365 oz. ASW, 41.7x40 mm. **Ruler:** Elizabeth II **Obv:** Head with tiara right **Rev:** Partial DaVinci drawing

| Date | Mintage | VF20 | XF40 | MS60 | MS63 | MS65 |
|---|---|---|---|---|---|---|
| 2011 | 500 | PF65 75.00 | | | | |

### KM# 541 1/24 DOLLAR
42.50 g., 0.999 Silver 1.365 oz. ASW, 41.7x40 mm. **Ruler:** Elizabeth II **Obv:** Head with tiara right **Rev:** Partial DaVinci drawing

| Date | Mintage | VF20 | XF40 | MS60 | MS63 | MS65 |
|---|---|---|---|---|---|---|
| 2011 | 500 | PF65 75.00 | | | | |

### KM# 542 1/24 DOLLAR
42.50 g., 0.999 Silver 1.365 oz. ASW, 41.7x40 mm. **Ruler:** Elizabeth II **Obv:** Head with tiara right **Rev:** Partial DaVinci drawing

| Date | Mintage | VF20 | XF40 | MS60 | MS63 | MS65 |
|---|---|---|---|---|---|---|
| 2011 | 500 | PF65 75.00 | | | | |

### KM# 543 1/24 DOLLAR
42.50 g., 0.999 Silver 1.365 oz. ASW, 41.7x40 mm. **Ruler:** Elizabeth II **Obv:** Head with tiara right **Rev:** Partial DaVinci drawing

| Date | Mintage | VF20 | XF40 | MS60 | MS63 | MS65 |
|---|---|---|---|---|---|---|
| 2011 | 500 | PF65 75.00 | | | | |

### KM# 544 1/24 DOLLAR
42.50 g., 0.999 Silver 1.365 oz. ASW, 41.7x40 mm. **Ruler:** Elizabeth II **Obv:** Head with tiara right **Rev:** Partial DaVinci drawing

| Date | Mintage | VF20 | XF40 | MS60 | MS63 | MS65 |
|---|---|---|---|---|---|---|
| 2011 | 500 | PF65 75.00 | | | | |

### KM# 545 1/24 DOLLAR
42.50 g., 0.999 Silver 1.365 oz. ASW, 41.7x40 mm. **Ruler:** Elizabeth II **Obv:** Head with tiara right **Rev:** Partial DaVinci drawing

| Date | Mintage | VF20 | XF40 | MS60 | MS63 | MS65 |
|---|---|---|---|---|---|---|
| 2011 | 500 | PF65 75.00 | | | | |

### KM# 546 1/24 DOLLAR
42.50 g., 0.999 Silver 1.365 oz. ASW, 41.7x40 mm. **Ruler:** Elizabeth II **Obv:** Head with tiara right **Rev:** Partial DaVinci drawing

| Date | Mintage | VF20 | XF40 | MS60 | MS63 | MS65 |
|---|---|---|---|---|---|---|
| 2011 | 500 | PF65 75.00 | | | | |

### KM# 547 1/24 DOLLAR
42.50 g., 0.999 Silver 1.365 oz. ASW, 41.7x40 mm. **Ruler:** Elizabeth II **Obv:** Head with tiara right **Rev:** Partial DaVinci drawing

| Date | Mintage | VF20 | XF40 | MS60 | MS63 | MS65 |
|---|---|---|---|---|---|---|
| 2011 | 500 | PF65 75.00 | | | | |

**KM# 548 1/24 DOLLAR**
42.50 g., 0.999 Silver 1.365 oz. ASW, 41.7x40 mm. **Ruler:** Elizabeth II **Obv:** Head with tiara right **Rev:** Partial DaVinci drawing

| Date | Mintage | VF20 | XF40 | MS60 | MS63 | MS65 |
|---|---|---|---|---|---|---|
| 2011 | 500 | PF65 75.00 | | | | |

**KM# 549 1/24 DOLLAR**
42.50 g., 0.999 Silver 1.365 oz. ASW, 41.7x40 mm. **Ruler:** Elizabeth II **Obv:** Head with tiara right **Rev:** Partial DaVinci drawing

| Date | Mintage | VF20 | XF40 | MS60 | MS63 | MS65 |
|---|---|---|---|---|---|---|
| 2011 | 500 | PF65 75.00 | | | | |

**KM# 624 1/14 DOLLAR**
15.00 g., 0.999 Silver 0.4818 oz. ASW, 29x48 mm. **Ruler:** Elizabeth II **Obv:** Head with tiara right **Rev:** Two scenes from the Passion of Christ **Shape:** Vertical rectangle

| Date | Mintage | VF20 | XF40 | MS60 | MS63 | MS65 |
|---|---|---|---|---|---|---|
| 2001 | 250 | PF65 45.00 | | | | |

**KM# 625 1/14 DOLLAR**
15.00 g., 0.999 Silver 0.4818 oz. ASW, 29x48 mm. **Ruler:** Elizabeth II **Obv:** Head with tiara right **Rev:** Two scenes from the Passion of Christ **Shape:** Vertical rectangle

| Date | Mintage | VF20 | XF40 | MS60 | MS63 | MS65 |
|---|---|---|---|---|---|---|
| 2011 | 250 | PF65 45.00 | | | | |

**KM# 626 1/14 DOLLAR**
15.00 g., 0.999 Silver 0.4818 oz. ASW, 29x48 mm. **Ruler:** Elizabeth II **Obv:** Head in tiara right **Rev:** Two scenes from the Passion of Christ **Shape:** Vertical rectangle

| Date | Mintage | VF20 | XF40 | MS60 | MS63 | MS65 |
|---|---|---|---|---|---|---|
| 2011 | 250 | PF65 45.00 | | | | |

**KM# 627 1/14 DOLLAR**
15.00 g., 0.999 Silver 0.4818 oz. ASW, 36x48 mm. **Ruler:** Elizabeth II **Obv:** Head in tiara right **Rev:** The Cruxifixion of Christ **Shape:** Vertical rectangle

| Date | Mintage | VF20 | XF40 | MS60 | MS63 | MS65 |
|---|---|---|---|---|---|---|
| 2011 | 250 | PF65 50.00 | | | | |

**KM# 628 1/14 DOLLAR**
15.00 g., 0.999 Silver 0.4818 oz. ASW, 29x48 mm. **Ruler:** Elizabeth II **Obv:** Head with tiara right **Rev:** Two scenes form the Passion of Christ **Shape:** Vertical rectangle

| Date | Mintage | VF20 | XF40 | MS60 | MS63 | MS65 |
|---|---|---|---|---|---|---|
| 2011 | 250 | PF65 45.00 | | | | |

**KM# 629 1/14 DOLLAR**
15.00 g., 0.999 Silver 0.4818 oz. ASW, 29x48 mm. **Ruler:** Elizabeth II **Obv:** Head with tiara right **Rev:** Two scenes from the Passion of Christ **Shape:** Vertical rectangle

| Date | Mintage | VF20 | XF40 | MS60 | MS63 | MS65 |
|---|---|---|---|---|---|---|
| 2011 | 250 | PF65 40.00 | | | | |

**KM# 630 1/14 DOLLAR**
15.00 g., 0.999 Silver 0.4818 oz. ASW, 29x48 mm. **Ruler:** Elizabeth II **Obv:** Head with tiara right **Rev:** Two scenes from the Passion of Christ **Shape:** Vertical rectangle

| Date | Mintage | VF20 | XF40 | MS60 | MS63 | MS65 |
|---|---|---|---|---|---|---|
| 2011 | 250 | PF65 45.00 | | | | |

**KM# 631 1/14 DOLLAR**
15.00 g., 0.999 Silver 0.4818 oz. ASW, 29x48 mm. **Ruler:** Elizabeth II **Obv:** Head with tiara right **Rev:** Two scenes from the Passion of Christ **Shape:** Vertical rectangle

| Date | Mintage | VF20 | XF40 | MS60 | MS63 | MS65 |
|---|---|---|---|---|---|---|
| 2011 | 250 | PF65 45.00 | | | | |

**KM# 632 1/14 DOLLAR**
15.00 g., 0.999 Silver 0.4818 oz. ASW, 29x48 mm. **Ruler:** Elizabeth II **Obv:** Head with tiara right **Rev:** Two scenes from the Passion of Christ **Shape:** Vertical rectangle

| Date | Mintage | VF20 | XF40 | MS60 | MS63 | MS65 |
|---|---|---|---|---|---|---|
| 2011 | 250 | PF65 45.00 | | | | |

**KM# 633 1/14 DOLLAR**
15.00 g., 0.999 Silver 0.4818 oz. ASW, 29x48 mm. **Ruler:** Elizabeth II **Obv:** Head with tiara right **Rev:** Two scenes from the Passion of Christ **Shape:** Vertical rectangle

| Date | Mintage | VF20 | XF40 | MS60 | MS63 | MS65 |
|---|---|---|---|---|---|---|
| 2011 | 250 | PF65 45.00 | | | | |

**KM# 634 1/14 DOLLAR**
15.00 g., 0.999 Silver 0.4818 oz. ASW, 36x48 mm. **Ruler:** Elizabeth II **Obv:** Head with tiara right **Rev:** Two scenes from the Passion of Christ **Shape:** Vertical rectangle

| Date | Mintage | VF20 | XF40 | MS60 | MS63 | MS65 |
|---|---|---|---|---|---|---|
| 2011 | 250 | PF65 50.00 | | | | |

**KM# 635 1/14 DOLLAR**
15.00 g., 0.999 Silver 0.4818 oz. ASW, 29x48 mm. **Ruler:** Elizabeth II **Obv:** Head with tiara right **Rev:** Two scenes from the Passion of Christ **Shape:** Vertical rectangle

| Date | Mintage | VF20 | XF40 | MS60 | MS63 | MS65 |
|---|---|---|---|---|---|---|
| 2011 | 250 | PF65 45.00 | | | | |

**KM# 636 1/14 DOLLAR**
15.00 g., 0.999 Silver 0.4818 oz. ASW, 29x48 mm. **Ruler:** Elizabeth II **Obv:** Head with tiara right **Rev:** Two scenes from the Passion of Christ **Shape:** Vertical rectangle

| Date | Mintage | VF20 | XF40 | MS60 | MS63 | MS65 |
|---|---|---|---|---|---|---|
| 2011 | 250 | PF65 45.00 | | | | |

**KM# 637 1/14 DOLLAR**
15.00 g., 0.999 Silver 0.4818 oz. ASW, 29x48 mm. **Ruler:** Elizabeth II **Obv:** Head with tiara right **Rev:** Two scenes from the Passion of Christ **Shape:** Vertical rectangle

| Date | Mintage | VF20 | XF40 | MS60 | MS63 | MS65 |
|---|---|---|---|---|---|---|
| 2011 | 250 | PF65 45.00 | | | | |

**KM# 574 1/9 DOLLAR**
25.40 g., 0.999 Silver 0.8158 oz. ASW, 24x41 mm. **Ruler:** Elizabeth II **Subject:** Fragment of Villa of Mysteries Fresco **Shape:** Vertical rectangle

| Date | Mintage | VF20 | XF40 | MS60 | MS63 | MS65 |
|---|---|---|---|---|---|---|
| 2011 | 250 | PF65 60.00 | | | | |

**KM# 575 1/9 DOLLAR**
25.40 g., 0.999 Silver 0.8158 oz. ASW, 24x41 mm. **Ruler:** Elizabeth II **Subject:** Villa of Mysteries Fresco

| Date | Mintage | VF20 | XF40 | MS60 | MS63 | MS65 |
|---|---|---|---|---|---|---|
| 2011 | 250 | PF65 60.00 | | | | |

**KM# 576 1/9 DOLLAR**
33.80 g., 0.999 Silver 1.0856 oz. ASW, 32x41 mm. **Ruler:** Elizabeth II **Subject:** Villa of Mysteries Fresco

| Date | Mintage | VF20 | XF40 | MS60 | MS63 | MS65 |
|---|---|---|---|---|---|---|
| 2011 | 250 | PF65 60.00 | | | | |

**KM# 577 1/9 DOLLAR**
33.80 g., 0.999 Silver 1.0856 oz. ASW, 32.41 mm. **Ruler:** Elizabeth II **Subject:** Villa of Mysteries Fresco

| Date | Mintage | VF20 | XF40 | MS60 | MS63 | MS65 |
|---|---|---|---|---|---|---|
| 2011 | 250 | PF65 60.00 | | | | |

**KM# 578 1/9 DOLLAR**
50.70 g., 0.999 Silver 1.6284 oz. ASW, 48x41 mm. **Ruler:** Elizabeth II **Subject:** Villa of Mysteries Fresco

| Date | Mintage | VF20 | XF40 | MS60 | MS63 | MS65 |
|---|---|---|---|---|---|---|
| 2011 | 250 | PF65 85.00 | | | | |

**KM# 579 1/9 DOLLAR**
50.70 g., 0.999 Silver 1.6284 oz. ASW, 48x41 mm. **Ruler:** Elizabeth II **Subject:** Villa of Mysteries Fresco

| Date | Mintage | VF20 | XF40 | MS60 | MS63 | MS65 |
|---|---|---|---|---|---|---|
| 2011 | 250 | PF65 85.00 | | | | |

**KM# 580 1/9 DOLLAR**
33.80 g., 0.999 Silver 1.0856 oz. ASW, 32x41 mm. **Ruler:** Elizabeth II **Subject:** Villa of Mysteries Fresco

| Date | Mintage | VF20 | XF40 | MS60 | MS63 | MS65 |
|---|---|---|---|---|---|---|
| 2011 | 250 | PF65 60.00 | | | | |

**KM# 581 1/9 DOLLAR**
50.70 g., 0.999 Silver 1.6284 oz. ASW, 48x41 mm. **Ruler:** Elizabeth II **Subject:** Villa of Mysteries Fresco

| Date | Mintage | VF20 | XF40 | MS60 | MS63 | MS65 |
|---|---|---|---|---|---|---|
| 2011 | 250 | PF65 85.00 | | | | |

**KM# 582 1/9 DOLLAR**
50.70 g., 0.999 Silver 1.6284 oz. ASW, 48x41 mm. **Ruler:** Elizabeth II **Subject:** Villa of Mysteries Fresco

| Date | Mintage | VF20 | XF40 | MS60 | MS63 | MS65 |
|---|---|---|---|---|---|---|
| 2011 | 250 | PF65 85.00 | | | | |

**KM# 123 DOLLAR**
28.28 g., Copper-Nickel, 38.6 mm. **Ruler:** Elizabeth II **Subject:** Snoopy as an Ace **Obv:** Crowned head right **Rev:** Snoopy flying his dog house **Edge:** Reeded

| Date | Mintage | VF20 | XF40 | MS60 | MS63 | MS65 |
|---|---|---|---|---|---|---|
| 2001 | 100,000 | — | — | 1.50 | 2.50 | 4.00 |

**KM# 128 DOLLAR**
28.28 g., Copper-Nickel, 38.6 mm. **Ruler:** Elizabeth II **Series:** Pokemon **Obv:** Crowned shield within sprigs **Rev:** Bulbasaur **Edge:** Reeded

| Date | Mintage | VF20 | XF40 | MS60 | MS63 | MS65 |
|---|---|---|---|---|---|---|
| 2001 | 100,000 | — | — | 7.00 | 10.00 | 12.00 |

**KM# 129 DOLLAR**
7.77 g., 0.999 Silver 0.2496 oz. ASW, 22 mm. **Ruler:** Elizabeth II **Series:** Pokemon **Obv:** Crowned shield within sprigs **Rev:** Bulbasaur **Edge:** Reeded

| Date | Mintage | VF20 | XF40 | MS60 | MS63 | MS65 |
|---|---|---|---|---|---|---|
| 2001 | 20,000 | PF65 16.00 | | | | |

**KM# 131 DOLLAR**
28.28 g., Copper-Nickel, 38.6 mm. **Ruler:** Elizabeth II **Series:** Pokemon **Obv:** Crowned shield within sprigs **Rev:** Charmander **Edge:** Reeded

| Date | Mintage | VF20 | XF40 | MS60 | MS63 | MS65 |
|---|---|---|---|---|---|---|
| 2001 | 100,000 | — | — | 7.00 | 10.00 | 12.00 |

**KM# 132 DOLLAR**
7.77 g., 0.999 Silver 0.2496 oz. ASW, 22 mm. **Ruler:** Elizabeth II **Series:** Pokemon **Obv:** Crowned shield within sprigs **Rev:** Charmander **Edge:** Reeded

| Date | Mintage | VF20 | XF40 | MS60 | MS63 | MS65 |
|---|---|---|---|---|---|---|
| 2001 | 20,000 | PF65 16.00 | | | | |

**KM# 134 DOLLAR**
28.28 g., Copper-Nickel, 38.6 mm. **Ruler:** Elizabeth II **Series:** Pokemon **Obv:** Crowned shield within sprigs **Rev:** Meowth **Edge:** Reeded

| Date | Mintage | VF20 | XF40 | MS60 | MS63 | MS65 |
|---|---|---|---|---|---|---|
| 2001 | 100,000 | — | — | 7.00 | 10.00 | 12.00 |

**KM# 135 DOLLAR**
7.77 g., 0.999 Silver 0.2496 oz. ASW, 22 mm. **Ruler:** Elizabeth II **Series:** Pokemon **Obv:** Crowned shield within sprigs **Rev:** Meowth **Edge:** Reeded

| Date | Mintage | VF20 | XF40 | MS60 | MS63 | MS65 |
|---|---|---|---|---|---|---|
| 2001 | 20,000 | PF65 16.00 | | | | |

### KM# 137 DOLLAR

28.28 g., Copper-Nickel, 38.6 mm. **Ruler:** Elizabeth II **Series:** Pokemon **Obv:** Crowned shield within sprigs **Rev:** Pikachu **Edge:** Reeded

| Date | Mintage | VF20 | XF40 | MS60 | MS63 | MS65 |
|---|---|---|---|---|---|---|
| 2001 | 100,000 | — | — | 7.00 | 10.00 | 12.00 |

### KM# 138 DOLLAR

7.77 g., 0.999 Silver 0.2496 oz. ASW, 22 mm. **Ruler:** Elizabeth II **Series:** Pokemon **Obv:** Crowned shield within sprigs **Rev:** Pikachu **Edge:** Reeded

| Date | Mintage | VF20 | XF40 | MS60 | MS63 | MS65 |
|---|---|---|---|---|---|---|
| 2001 | 20,000 | PF65 16.00 | | | | |

### KM# 140 DOLLAR

28.28 g., Copper-Nickel, 38.6 mm. **Ruler:** Elizabeth II **Series:** Pokemon **Obv:** Crowned shield within sprigs **Rev:** Squirtle **Edge:** Reeded

| Date | Mintage | VF20 | XF40 | MS60 | MS63 | MS65 |
|---|---|---|---|---|---|---|
| 2001 | 100,000 | — | — | 7.00 | 10.00 | 12.00 |

### KM# 141 DOLLAR

7.77 g., 0.999 Silver 0.2496 oz. ASW, 22 mm. **Ruler:** Elizabeth II **Series:** Pokemon **Obv:** Crowned shield within sprigs **Rev:** Squirtle **Edge:** Reeded

| Date | Mintage | VF20 | XF40 | MS60 | MS63 | MS65 |
|---|---|---|---|---|---|---|
| 2001 | 20,000 | PF65 16.00 | | | | |

### KM# 146 DOLLAR

28.28 g., Copper-Nickel, 38.6 mm. **Ruler:** Elizabeth II **Subject:** Pokemon Series **Obv:** Crowned shield within sprigs **Rev:** Pikachu **Edge:** Reeded

| Date | Mintage | VF20 | XF40 | MS60 | MS63 | MS65 |
|---|---|---|---|---|---|---|
| 2002 PM | 100,000 | — | — | 1.50 | 2.50 | 4.00 |

### KM# 151 DOLLAR

28.28 g., Copper-Nickel, 38.6 mm. **Ruler:** Elizabeth II **Subject:** Pokemon Series **Obv:** Crowned shield within sprigs **Rev:** Pichu **Edge:** Reeded

| Date | Mintage | VF20 | XF40 | MS60 | MS63 | MS65 |
|---|---|---|---|---|---|---|
| 2002 PM | 100,000 | — | — | 1.50 | 2.50 | 4.00 |

### KM# 156 DOLLAR

28.28 g., Copper-Nickel, 38.6 mm. **Ruler:** Elizabeth II **Subject:** Pokemon Series **Obv:** Crowned shield within sprigs **Rev:** Mewtwo **Edge:** Reeded

| Date | Mintage | VF20 | XF40 | MS60 | MS63 | MS65 |
|---|---|---|---|---|---|---|
| 2002 PM | 100,000 | — | — | 1.50 | 2.50 | 4.00 |

### KM# 161 DOLLAR

28.28 g., Copper-Nickel, 38.6 mm. **Ruler:** Elizabeth II **Subject:** Pokemon Series **Obv:** Crowned shield within sprigs **Rev:** Entei **Edge:** Reeded

| Date | Mintage | VF20 | XF40 | MS60 | MS63 | MS65 |
|---|---|---|---|---|---|---|
| 2002 PM | 100,000 | — | — | 1.50 | 2.50 | 4.00 |

### KM# 166 DOLLAR

28.28 g., Copper-Nickel, 38.6 mm. **Ruler:** Elizabeth II **Subject:** Pokemon Series **Obv:** Crowned shield within sprigs **Rev:** Celebi **Edge:** Reeded

| Date | Mintage | VF20 | XF40 | MS60 | MS63 | MS65 |
|---|---|---|---|---|---|---|
| 2002 PM | 100,000 | — | — | 1.50 | 2.50 | 4.00 |

### KM# 186 DOLLAR

31.11 g., 0.999 Silver 0.999 oz. ASW **Ruler:** Elizabeth II **Subject:** Marshalls of China's Army, 50th Anniversary **Obv:** Head right **Rev:** Multicolor scene of military men

| Date | Mintage | VF20 | XF40 | MS60 | MS63 | MS65 |
|---|---|---|---|---|---|---|
| 2005 | 1,000 | — | — | — | — | 70.00 |

### KM# 187 DOLLAR

31.11 g., 0.999 Silver 0.999 oz. ASW **Ruler:** Elizabeth II **Subject:** World War II, 60th Anniversary **Obv:** Bust right **Rev:** Multicolor badge

| Date | Mintage | VF20 | XF40 | MS60 | MS63 | MS65 |
|---|---|---|---|---|---|---|
| 2005 | 1,000 | — | — | — | — | 70.00 |

### KM# 188 DOLLAR

31.11 g., 0.999 Silver 0.999 oz. ASW **Ruler:** Elizabeth II **Series:** Bust right **Obv:** Multicolor image of two astronauts, rocket and map of China

| Date | Mintage | VF20 | XF40 | MS60 | MS63 | MS65 |
|---|---|---|---|---|---|---|
| 2005 | — | PF65 75.00 | | | | |

### KM# 262 DOLLAR

Bronze partially silvered, 38.61 mm. **Ruler:** Elizabeth II **Subject:** Thomas Alva Edison **Rev:** Lightbulb

| Date | Mintage | VF20 | XF40 | MS60 | MS63 | MS65 |
|---|---|---|---|---|---|---|
| 2005 | — | — | — | — | — | 30.00 |

### KM# 262a DOLLAR

31.11 g., 0.999 Silver 0.999 oz. ASW partially gilt **Ruler:** Elizabeth II **Subject:** Thomas Alva Edison **Rev:** Lightbulb, partially gilt

| Date | Mintage | VF20 | XF40 | MS60 | MS63 | MS65 |
|---|---|---|---|---|---|---|
| 2005 | Est. 2500 | PF65 100 | | | | |

### KM# 264 DOLLAR

31.10 g., 0.999 Silver 0.9989 oz. ASW, 45 mm. **Ruler:** Elizabeth II **Subject:** Year of the Rooster **Rev:** Multicolor rooster standing right, sunrise

| Date | Mintage | VF20 | XF40 | MS60 | MS63 | MS65 |
|---|---|---|---|---|---|---|
| 2005 | — | PF65 55.00 | | | | |

### KM# 275 DOLLAR

31.11 g., 0.999 Silver 0.999 oz. ASW **Ruler:** Elizabeth II **Subject:** 60th Anniversary, China

| Date | Mintage | VF20 | XF40 | MS60 | MS63 | MS65 |
|---|---|---|---|---|---|---|
| 2005 | Est. 1000 | PF65 120 | | | | |

### KM# 276 DOLLAR

31.11 g., 0.999 Silver 0.999 oz. ASW **Ruler:** Elizabeth II **Subject:** Mao Zedong and the Red Army in Beijing

| Date | Mintage | VF20 | XF40 | MS60 | MS63 | MS65 |
|---|---|---|---|---|---|---|
| 2005 | — | PF65 100 | | | | |

### KM# 277 DOLLAR

31.11 g., 0.999 Silver 0.999 oz. ASW, 45 mm. **Ruler:** Elizabeth II **Subject:** Chinese space achievements **Rev:** Multicolor rocket, flag, map

| Date | Mintage | VF20 | XF40 | MS60 | MS63 | MS65 |
|---|---|---|---|---|---|---|
| 2005 | Est. 5000 | PF65 75.00 | | | | |

### KM# 293 DOLLAR

31.11 g., 0.999 Silver 0.999 oz. ASW, 45 mm. **Ruler:** Elizabeth II **Subject:** Year of the Dog **Rev:** Multicolor dog

| Date | Mintage | VF20 | XF40 | MS60 | MS63 | MS65 |
|---|---|---|---|---|---|---|
| 2005 | — | PF65 60.00 | | | | |

### KM# 300 DOLLAR

31.11 g., 0.999 Silver 0.999 oz. ASW, 45 mm. **Ruler:** Elizabeth II **Subject:** Dogs of the World **Rev:** Multicolor Bichon standing before the Louvre

| Date | Mintage | VF20 | XF40 | MS60 | MS63 | MS65 |
|---|---|---|---|---|---|---|
| 2006 | Est. 3000 | PF65 60.00 | | | | |

### KM# 301 DOLLAR

31.11 g., 0.999 Silver 0.999 oz. ASW, 45 mm. **Ruler:** Elizabeth II **Subject:** Dogs of the World **Rev:** Multicolor Welsh Corgi before Buckingham Palace

| Date | Mintage | VF20 | XF40 | MS60 | MS63 | MS65 |
|---|---|---|---|---|---|---|
| 2006 | Est. 3000 | PF65 60.00 | | | | |

### KM# 302 DOLLAR

31.11 g., 0.999 Silver 0.999 oz. ASW, 45 mm. **Ruler:** Elizabeth II **Subject:** Dogs of the World **Rev:** Poodle before the Palace at Versailles

| Date | Mintage | VF20 | XF40 | MS60 | MS63 | MS65 |
|---|---|---|---|---|---|---|
| 2006 | Est. 3000 | PF65 60.00 | | | | |

### KM# 303 DOLLAR

31.11 g., 0.999 Silver 0.999 oz. ASW, 45 mm. **Ruler:** Elizabeth II **Subject:** Dogs of the World **Rev:** Bare dog before the Potala Plast

| Date | Mintage | VF20 | XF40 | MS60 | MS63 | MS65 |
|---|---|---|---|---|---|---|
| 2006 | Est. 3000 | PF65 60.00 | | | | |

### KM# 304 DOLLAR

31.11 g., 0.999 Silver 0.999 oz. ASW, 45 mm. **Ruler:** Elizabeth II **Subject:** Dogs of the World **Rev:** Pekineese before the Palastmuseum

| Date | Mintage | VF20 | XF40 | MS60 | MS63 | MS65 |
|---|---|---|---|---|---|---|
| 2006 | Est. 3000 | PF65 60.00 | | | | |

### KM# 305 DOLLAR

31.11 g., 0.999 Silver 0.999 oz. ASW, 45 mm. **Ruler:** Elizabeth II **Subject:** Dogs of the World **Rev:** Malteser before the Schonbrunn

| Date | Mintage | VF20 | XF40 | MS60 | MS63 | MS65 |
|---|---|---|---|---|---|---|
| 2006 | Est. 3000 | PF65 60.00 | | | | |

### KM# 306 DOLLAR

31.11 g., 0.999 Silver 0.999 oz. ASW, 45 mm. **Ruler:** Elizabeth II **Subject:** Dogs of the World **Rev:** Japanese Chin before Emperor's palace in Kyoto

| Date | Mintage | VF20 | XF40 | MS60 | MS63 | MS65 |
|---|---|---|---|---|---|---|
| 2006 | Est. 3000 | PF65 60.00 | | | | |

### KM# 307 DOLLAR

31.11 g., 0.999 Silver 0.999 oz. ASW, 45 mm. **Ruler:** Elizabeth II **Subject:** Dogs of the World **Rev:** King Charles Spaniel before Westminster Abbey

| Date | Mintage | VF20 | XF40 | MS60 | MS63 | MS65 |
|---|---|---|---|---|---|---|
| 2006 | — | PF65 60.00 | | | | |

### KM# 308 DOLLAR

31.11 g., 0.999 Silver 0.999 oz. ASW, 45 mm. **Ruler:** Elizabeth II **Subject:** Dogs of the World **Rev:** Butterfly dog before the Kings Palace in Madrid

| Date | Mintage | VF20 | XF40 | MS60 | MS63 | MS65 |
|---|---|---|---|---|---|---|
| 2006 | Est. 3000 | PF65 60.00 | | | | |

### KM# 309 DOLLAR

31.11 g., 0.999 Silver 0.999 oz. ASW, 45 mm. **Ruler:** Elizabeth II **Subject:** Olympics **Rev:** Discus thrower

| Date | Mintage | VF20 | XF40 | MS60 | MS63 | MS65 |
|---|---|---|---|---|---|---|
| ND | Est. 2008 | PF65 70.00 | | | | |

### KM# 310 DOLLAR

31.11 g., 0.999 Silver 0.999 oz. ASW, 45 mm. **Ruler:** Elizabeth II **Subject:** Olympics **Rev:** Sprinter

| Date | Mintage | VF20 | XF40 | MS60 | MS63 | MS65 |
|---|---|---|---|---|---|---|
| ND | Est. 2008 | PF65 70.00 | | | | |

### KM# 311 DOLLAR

31.11 g., 0.999 Silver 0.999 oz. ASW, 45 mm. **Ruler:** Elizabeth II **Subject:** Olympics **Rev:** Long Jump

| Date | Mintage | VF20 | XF40 | MS60 | MS63 | MS65 |
|---|---|---|---|---|---|---|
| ND | — | PF65 70.00 | | | | |

### KM# 312 DOLLAR

31.11 g., 0.999 Silver 0.999 oz. ASW, 45 mm. **Ruler:** Elizabeth II **Subject:** Olympics **Rev:** Javelin Thrower

| Date | Mintage | VF20 | XF40 | MS60 | MS63 | MS65 |
|---|---|---|---|---|---|---|
| ND | Est. 2008 | PF65 70.00 | | | | |

### KM# 313 DOLLAR

31.11 g., 0.999 Silver 0.999 oz. ASW, 45 mm. **Ruler:** Elizabeth II **Subject:** Olympics **Rev:** Weightlifter

| Date | Mintage | VF20 | XF40 | MS60 | MS63 | MS65 |
|---|---|---|---|---|---|---|
| ND | Est. 2008 | PF65 70.00 | | | | |

### KM# 314 DOLLAR

31.11 g., 0.999 Silver 0.999 oz. ASW, 45 mm. **Ruler:** Elizabeth II **Subject:** Olympics **Rev:** Hammer Throw

| Date | Mintage | VF20 | XF40 | MS60 | MS63 | MS65 |
|---|---|---|---|---|---|---|
| ND | Est. 2008 | PF65 70.00 | | | | |

**KM# 315 DOLLAR**

31.11 g., 0.999 Silver 0.999 oz. ASW, 45 mm. **Ruler:** Elizabeth II **Subject:** Olympics **Rev:** Archery

| Date | Mintage | VF20 | XF40 | MS60 | MS63 | MS65 |
|---|---|---|---|---|---|---|
| ND | Est. 2008 | PF65 70.00 | | | | |

**KM# 316 DOLLAR**

31.11 g., 0.999 Silver 0.999 oz. ASW, 45 mm. **Ruler:** Elizabeth II **Subject:** Olympics **Rev:** Lacrosse player

| Date | Mintage | VF20 | XF40 | MS60 | MS63 | MS65 |
|---|---|---|---|---|---|---|
| ND | Est. 2008 | PF65 70.00 | | | | |

**KM# 317 DOLLAR**

31.11 g., 0.999 Silver 0.999 oz. ASW, 45 mm. **Ruler:** Elizabeth II **Subject:** Olympics **Rev:** Soccer player

| Date | Mintage | VF20 | XF40 | MS60 | MS63 | MS65 |
|---|---|---|---|---|---|---|
| ND | Est. 2008 | PF65 70.00 | | | | |

**KM# 318 DOLLAR**

31.11 g., 0.999 Silver 0.999 oz. ASW, 45 mm. **Ruler:** Elizabeth II **Subject:** Olympics **Rev:** Boxer

| Date | Mintage | VF20 | XF40 | MS60 | MS63 | MS65 |
|---|---|---|---|---|---|---|
| ND | Est. 2008 | PF65 70.00 | | | | |

**KM# 319 DOLLAR**

31.11 g., 0.999 Silver 0.999 oz. ASW, 45 mm. **Ruler:** Elizabeth II **Subject:** Olympics **Rev:** Equestrian

| Date | Mintage | VF20 | XF40 | MS60 | MS63 | MS65 |
|---|---|---|---|---|---|---|
| ND | Est. 2008 | PF65 70.00 | | | | |

**KM# 320 DOLLAR**

31.11 g., 0.999 Silver 0.999 oz. ASW, 45 mm. **Ruler:** Elizabeth II **Subject:** Olympics **Rev:** Wrestler

| Date | Mintage | VF20 | XF40 | MS60 | MS63 | MS65 |
|---|---|---|---|---|---|---|
| ND | Est. 2008 | PF65 70.00 | | | | |

**KM# 321 DOLLAR**

31.11 g., 0.999 Silver 0.999 oz. ASW, 35x46 mm. **Ruler:** Elizabeth II **Subject:** Life of Christ **Rev:** Radiant Mary **Shape:** Vertical rectangle

| Date | Mintage | VF20 | XF40 | MS60 | MS63 | MS65 |
|---|---|---|---|---|---|---|
| 2006 | Est. 1000 | PF65 100 | | | | |

**KM# 322 DOLLAR**

31.11 g., 0.999 Silver 0.999 oz. ASW, 35x46 mm. **Ruler:** Elizabeth II **Subject:** Life of Christ **Rev:** Mary and Child (1483) **Shape:** Vertical rectangle

| Date | Mintage | VF20 | XF40 | MS60 | MS63 | MS65 |
|---|---|---|---|---|---|---|
| 2006 | Est. 1000 | PF65 100 | | | | |

**KM# 323 DOLLAR**

31.11 g., 0.999 Silver 0.999 oz. ASW, 35x46 mm. **Ruler:** Elizabeth II **Subject:** Life of Christ **Rev:** Christ in the Jordan (1478) **Shape:** Vertical rectangle

| Date | Mintage | VF20 | XF40 | MS60 | MS63 | MS65 |
|---|---|---|---|---|---|---|
| 2006 | Est. 1000 | PF65 100 | | | | |

**KM# 324 DOLLAR**

31.11 g., 0.999 Silver 0.999 oz. ASW, 35x46 mm. **Ruler:** Elizabeth II **Subject:** Life of Christ **Rev:** Jesus Christ (1481) **Shape:** Vertical rectangle

| Date | Mintage | VF20 | XF40 | MS60 | MS63 | MS65 |
|---|---|---|---|---|---|---|
| 2006 | Est. 1000 | PF65 100 | | | | |

**KM# 325 DOLLAR**

31.11 g., 0.999 Silver 0.999 oz. ASW, 35x46 mm. **Ruler:** Elizabeth II **Subject:** Life of Christ **Rev:** Betrayal of Judas (1303) **Shape:** Vertical rectangle

| Date | Mintage | VF20 | XF40 | MS60 | MS63 | MS65 |
|---|---|---|---|---|---|---|
| 2006 | Est. 1000 | PF65 100 | | | | |

**KM# 326 DOLLAR**

31.11 g., 0.999 Silver 0.999 oz. ASW, 35x46 mm. **Ruler:** Elizabeth II **Subject:** Life of Christ **Rev:** Stations of the Cross (1517) **Shape:** Vertical rectangle

| Date | Mintage | VF20 | XF40 | MS60 | MS63 | MS65 |
|---|---|---|---|---|---|---|
| 2006 | Est. 1000 | PF65 100 | | | | |

**KM# 327 DOLLAR**

31.11 g., 0.999 Silver 0.999 oz. ASW, 35x46 mm. **Ruler:** Elizabeth II **Subject:** Life of Christ **Rev:** Jesus on the Cross (1558) **Shape:** Vertical rectangle

| Date | Mintage | VF20 | XF40 | MS60 | MS63 | MS65 |
|---|---|---|---|---|---|---|
| 2006 | Est. 1000 | PF65 100 | | | | |

**KM# 328 DOLLAR**

31.11 g., 0.999 Silver 0.999 oz. ASW, 35x46 mm. **Ruler:** Elizabeth II **Subject:** Life of Christ **Rev:** Ascension (1520) **Shape:** Vertical rectangle

| Date | Mintage | VF20 | XF40 | MS60 | MS63 | MS65 |
|---|---|---|---|---|---|---|
| 2006 | Est. 1000 | PF65 100 | | | | |

**KM# 329 DOLLAR**

31.11 g., 0.999 Silver 0.999 oz. ASW, 35x45 mm. **Ruler:** Elizabeth II **Subject:** Life of Christ **Rev:** Heaven **Shape:** Vertical rectangle

| Date | Mintage | VF20 | XF40 | MS60 | MS63 | MS65 |
|---|---|---|---|---|---|---|
| 2006 | Est. 1000 | PF65 100 | | | | |

**KM# 331 DOLLAR**

28.28 g., 0.925 Silver 0.841 oz. ASW, 38.61 mm. **Ruler:** Elizabeth II **Subject:** Year of the Pig **Rev:** Pig grazing

| Date | Mintage | VF20 | XF40 | MS60 | MS63 | MS65 |
|---|---|---|---|---|---|---|
| 2006 | Est. 5000 | — | — | — | — | 55.00 |

**KM# 176 DOLLAR**

28.28 g., 0.925 Silver 0.841 oz. ASW **Ruler:** Elizabeth II **Obv:** Tiarra head of Elizabeth II right at left, multicolor Van Gogh's painting "Starry Night" with 3 zircon crystals as stars at center right. **Obv. Inscription:** ELIZABETH II - NIUE ISLAND **Rev:** Van Gogh's painting "Vase with Twelve Sunflowers" at left, self portrait of artist with brush at upper right **Rev. Inscription:** VAN GOGH / Vincent **Edge:** Plain **Shape:** Rectangular, 39.94 x 27.97 mm

| Date | Mintage | VF20 | XF40 | MS60 | MS63 | MS65 |
|---|---|---|---|---|---|---|
| 2007 | 10,000 | PF65 85.00 | | | | |

**KM# 332 DOLLAR**

28.28 g., 0.925 Silver 0.841 oz. ASW **Ruler:** Elizabeth II **Subject:** Year of the Pig **Rev:** Three little pigs dancing, brick house, wolf

| Date | Mintage | VF20 | XF40 | MS60 | MS63 | MS65 |
|---|---|---|---|---|---|---|
| 2007 | — | — | — | — | — | 55.00 |

**KM# 334 DOLLAR**

28.28 g., 0.925 Silver 0.841 oz. ASW, 38.61 mm. **Ruler:** Elizabeth II **Rev:** Female advancing left with long dress **Rev. Legend:** Change Flies to the Moon

| Date | Mintage | VF20 | XF40 | MS60 | MS63 | MS65 |
|---|---|---|---|---|---|---|
| 2007 | Est. 5000 | — | — | — | — | 55.00 |

**KM# 335 DOLLAR**

28.28 g., 0.925 Silver 0.841 oz. ASW, 38.61 mm. **Ruler:** Elizabeth II **Rev:** Man weilding axe against tree **Rev. Legend:** Wu Gang cuts the sweet-scented osmanthus tree

| Date | Mintage | VF20 | XF40 | MS60 | MS63 | MS65 |
|---|---|---|---|---|---|---|
| 2007 | — | — | — | — | — | 55.00 |

**KM# 336 DOLLAR**

28.28 g., 0.925 Silver 0.841 oz. ASW, 38.61 mm. **Ruler:** Elizabeth II **Rev:** Group visiting palace **Rev. Legend:** Emperor Mint of Tang Dynasty visit the Moon Palace at Night

| Date | Mintage | VF20 | XF40 | MS60 | MS63 | MS65 |
|---|---|---|---|---|---|---|
| 2007 | Est. 5000 | — | — | — | — | 65.00 |

**KM# 337 DOLLAR**

28.28 g., 0.925 Silver 0.841 oz. ASW, 38.61 mm. **Ruler:** Elizabeth II **Rev:** Rabbit with mortar and pestile in house yard **Rev. Legend:** The jade rabbit pounds the medicine of immortality

| Date | Mintage | VF20 | XF40 | MS60 | MS63 | MS65 |
|---|---|---|---|---|---|---|
| 2007 Proof | — | — | — | — | — | 55.00 |

**KM# 192 DOLLAR**

31.11 g., 0.999 Silver 0.999 oz. ASW **Ruler:** Elizabeth II **Subject:** Year of the Ox **Obv:** Head right **Rev:** Multicolor ox

| Date | Mintage | VF20 | XF40 | MS60 | MS63 | MS65 |
|---|---|---|---|---|---|---|
| 2008//2009 | 10,000 | PF65 75.00 | | | | |

**KM# 201 DOLLAR**

28.28 g., 0.925 Silver 0.841 oz. ASW, 38.61 mm. **Ruler:** Elizabeth II **Subject:** Amber Road **Obv:** Roman cart and map, Elizabeth II head at lower left **Rev:** Church, goblet, ancient coin, amber insert **Rev. Legend:** ELBLAG SZLAK BURSZTYNOWY

| Date | Mintage | VF20 | XF40 | MS60 | MS63 | MS65 |
|---|---|---|---|---|---|---|
| 2008 Antique finish | 10,000 | — | — | — | — | 100 |

**KM# 202 DOLLAR**

28.28 g., 0.925 Silver 0.841 oz. ASW, 38.61 mm. **Ruler:** Elizabeth II **Subject:** Amber Road **Obv:** Roman cart, map, Elizabeth II head at lower left **Rev:** Antonius Pius coins, Nepture statue, mine shaft, amber insert **Rev. Legend:** GDANSK SZLAK BURSZTYNOWY

| Date | Mintage | VF20 | XF40 | MS60 | MS63 | MS65 |
|---|---|---|---|---|---|---|
| 2008 Antique finish | 10,000 | — | — | — | — | 90.00 |

**KM# 203 DOLLAR**
28.28 g., 0.925 Silver 0.841 oz. ASW, 38.61 mm. **Ruler:** Elizabeth II **Subject:** Amber Road **Obv:** Roman cart, map, Elizabeth II head at lower left **Rev:** Building, statue, amber insert **Rev. Legend:** WROCLAW SZLAK BURSZTYNOWY

| Date | Mintage | VF20 | XF40 | MS60 | MS63 | MS65 |
|---|---|---|---|---|---|---|
| 2008 Antique finish | 10,000 | — | — | — | — | 100 |

**KM# 204 DOLLAR**
28.28 g., 0.999 Silver 0.9083 oz. ASW, 38.61 mm. **Ruler:** Elizabeth II **Subject:** Amber Road **Rev:** Castle, sword, amber insert **Rev. Legend:** SZLAK BURSZTYNOWY KALININGRAD

| Date | Mintage | VF20 | XF40 | MS60 | MS63 | MS65 |
|---|---|---|---|---|---|---|
| 2008 Antique finish | 10,000 | — | — | — | — | 100 |

**KM# 211 DOLLAR**
28.28 g., 0.925 Silver 0.841 oz. ASW, 28x40 mm. **Ruler:** Elizabeth II **Obv:** Head of Elizabeth II at lower left, Portrait of Lautrec at top right **Rev:** Toulouse-Lautrec and can-can girl

| Date | Mintage | VF20 | XF40 | MS60 | MS63 | MS65 |
|---|---|---|---|---|---|---|
| 2008 | 15,000 | PF65 100 | | | | |

**KM# 212 DOLLAR**
Silver **Ruler:** Elizabeth II **Rev:** Ox seated multicolor lotus flower

| Date | Mintage | VF20 | XF40 | MS60 | MS63 | MS65 |
|---|---|---|---|---|---|---|
| 2008 Antique finish | — | — | — | — | — | 55.00 |

**KM# 338 DOLLAR**
31.11 g., 0.999 Silver 0.999 oz. ASW, 45 mm. **Ruler:** Elizabeth II **Subject:** Year of the Rat **Rev:** Rat in field, sun rays above

| Date | Mintage | VF20 | XF40 | MS60 | MS63 | MS65 |
|---|---|---|---|---|---|---|
| 2008 | Est. 8000 | — | — | — | — | 65.00 |

**KM# 339 DOLLAR**
31.11 g., 0.999 Silver 0.999 oz. ASW, 45 mm. **Ruler:** Elizabeth II **Subject:** Year of the Rat **Rev:** Rat left before house

| Date | Mintage | VF20 | XF40 | MS60 | MS63 | MS65 |
|---|---|---|---|---|---|---|
| 2008 | Est. 8000 | — | — | — | — | 65.00 |

**KM# 340 DOLLAR**
31.11 g., 0.999 Silver 0.999 oz. ASW, 45 mm. **Ruler:** Elizabeth II **Subject:** Year of the Rat **Rev:** Rat standing on hind legs sniffing flora

| Date | Mintage | VF20 | XF40 | MS60 | MS63 | MS65 |
|---|---|---|---|---|---|---|
| 2008 | Est. 8000 | — | — | — | — | 70.00 |

**KM# 341 DOLLAR**
31.11 g., 0.999 Silver 0.999 oz. ASW, 45 mm. **Ruler:** Elizabeth II **Rev:** Multicolor Happy mouse

| Date | Mintage | VF20 | XF40 | MS60 | MS63 | MS65 |
|---|---|---|---|---|---|---|
| 2008 | — | PF65 60.00 | | | | |

**KM# 342 DOLLAR**
31.11 g., 0.999 Silver 0.999 oz. ASW, 45 mm. **Ruler:** Elizabeth II **Rev:** Multicolor wealthy rat

| Date | Mintage | VF20 | XF40 | MS60 | MS63 | MS65 |
|---|---|---|---|---|---|---|
| 2008 | — | PF65 60.00 | | | | |

**KM# 343 DOLLAR**
31.11 g., 0.999 Silver 0.999 oz. ASW, 45 mm. **Ruler:** Elizabeth II **Rev:** Multicolor happy rat

| Date | Mintage | VF20 | XF40 | MS60 | MS63 | MS65 |
|---|---|---|---|---|---|---|
| 2008 | — | PF65 60.00 | | | | |

**KM# 344 DOLLAR**
31.11 g., 0.999 Silver 0.999 oz. ASW, 45 mm. **Ruler:** Elizabeth II **Rev:** Multicolor successful rat

| Date | Mintage | VF20 | XF40 | MS60 | MS63 | MS65 |
|---|---|---|---|---|---|---|
| 2008 | — | PF65 60.00 | | | | |

**KM# 345 DOLLAR**
31.11 g., 0.999 Silver 0.999 oz. ASW, 45 mm. **Ruler:** Elizabeth II **Rev:** Multicolor rat holding charm

| Date | Mintage | VF20 | XF40 | MS60 | MS63 | MS65 |
|---|---|---|---|---|---|---|
| 2008 | Est. 10000 | PF65 60.00 | | | | |

**KM# 346 DOLLAR**
3.11 g., 0.999 Gold 0.0999 oz. AGW, 18 mm. **Ruler:** Elizabeth II **Rev:** Rat in garden

| Date | Mintage | VF20 | XF40 | MS60 | MS63 | MS65 |
|---|---|---|---|---|---|---|
| 2008 | Est. 10000 | PF65 185 | | | | |

**KM# 347 DOLLAR**
28.28 g., 0.925 Silver 0.841 oz. ASW, 38.61 mm. **Ruler:** Elizabeth II **Rev:** Rat standing infront of multicolor cut cheese wheel

| Date | Mintage | VF20 | XF40 | MS60 | MS63 | MS65 |
|---|---|---|---|---|---|---|
| 2008 | Est. 10000 | PF65 50.00 | | | | |

**KM# 348 DOLLAR**
28.28 g., 0.925 Silver 0.841 oz. ASW, 38.61 mm. **Ruler:** Elizabeth II **Rev:** Multicolor dancing mice in garland

| Date | Mintage | VF20 | XF40 | MS60 | MS63 | MS65 |
|---|---|---|---|---|---|---|
| 2008 | — | PF65 50.00 | | | | |

**KM# 197 DOLLAR**
17.30 g., Aluminum-Brass, 32 mm. **Ruler:** Elizabeth II **Obv:** Head right **Rev:** Swordfish **Edge:** Reeded

| Date | Mintage | VF20 | XF40 | MS60 | MS63 | MS65 |
|---|---|---|---|---|---|---|
| 2009 | — | — | — | 4.50 | 7.50 | 12.50 |

**KM# 231 DOLLAR**
31.10 g., 0.999 Silver 0.999 oz. ASW, 38.6 mm. **Ruler:** Elizabeth II **Subject:** Year of the Tiger **Rev:** Tiger cub in basket playing with ball

| Date | Mintage | VF20 | XF40 | MS60 | MS63 | MS65 |
|---|---|---|---|---|---|---|
| 2009 | 6,000 | PF65 80.00 | | | | |

**KM# 232 DOLLAR**
31.10 g., 0.999 Silver 0.999 oz. ASW, 38.6 mm. **Ruler:** Elizabeth II **Subject:** Year of the Tiger **Rev:** Tiger advancing left

| Date | Mintage | VF20 | XF40 | MS60 | MS63 | MS65 |
|---|---|---|---|---|---|---|
| 2009 | 6,000 | PF65 80.00 | | | | |

**KM# 551 DOLLAR**
28.28 g., 0.925 Silver 0.841 oz. ASW, 38.61 mm. **Ruler:** Elizabeth II **Subject:** Father Frost **Rev:** Father and Mrs. Frost standing, multicolor

| Date | Mintage | VF20 | XF40 | MS60 | MS63 | MS65 |
|---|---|---|---|---|---|---|
| 2009 | Est. 6000 | PF65 65.00 | | | | |

**KM# 198 DOLLAR**
17.30 g., Copper Plated Bronze, 32 mm. **Ruler:** Elizabeth II **Obv:** Head right **Rev:** Taro leaves **Edge:** Reeded

| Date | Mintage | VF20 | XF40 | MS60 | MS63 | MS65 |
|---|---|---|---|---|---|---|
| 2010 | — | — | — | 4.50 | 7.50 | 12.50 |

**KM# 234 DOLLAR**
28.28 g., 0.925 Silver 0.841 oz. ASW, 40x40 mm. **Ruler:** Elizabeth II **Obv:** Head right, footprints in field **Rev:** Antilocapra Americana, two antelope running right **Shape:** Square

| Date | Mintage | VF20 | XF40 | MS60 | MS63 | MS65 |
|---|---|---|---|---|---|---|
| 2010 | 9,000 | PF65 80.00 | | | | |

**KM# 235 DOLLAR**
28.28 g., 0.925 Silver 0.841 oz. ASW, 38.6 mm. **Ruler:** Elizabeth II **Obv:** Head right **Rev:** Lycaena Virgavreae multicolor butterfly

| Date | Mintage | VF20 | XF40 | MS60 | MS63 | MS65 |
|---|---|---|---|---|---|---|
| 2010 | 8,000 | PF65 80.00 | | | | |

**KM# 236 DOLLAR**
14.14 g., 0.925 Silver 0.4205 oz. ASW, 25x28 mm. **Ruler:** Elizabeth II **Obv:** Head right on musical score **Rev:** Chopin bust at left, score **Shape:** Square

| Date | Mintage | VF20 | XF40 | MS60 | MS63 | MS65 |
|---|---|---|---|---|---|---|
| 2010 | 6,000 | PF65 80.00 | | | | |

### KM# 238 DOLLAR

28.28 g., 0.925 Silver 0.841 oz. ASW, 36.81 mm. **Ruler:** Elizabeth II **Subject:** Fire **Obv:** Head right, images of early man **Rev:** Volcano and men around fire in multicolor

| Date | Mintage | VF20 | XF40 | MS60 | MS63 | MS65 |
|---|---|---|---|---|---|---|
| 2010 | 6,000 | PF65 100 | | | | |

### KM# 239 DOLLAR

28.28 g., 0.925 Silver 0.841 oz. ASW, 40x28 mm. **Ruler:** Elizabeth II **Obv:** Head right, aircraft propeller, wing schematic **Rev:** Greek warrior shield and multicolor Icarus in flight **Shape:** Rectangle

| Date | Mintage | VF20 | XF40 | MS60 | MS63 | MS65 |
|---|---|---|---|---|---|---|
| 2010 | 6,000 | PF65 100 | | | | |

### KM# 240 DOLLAR

28.28 g., 0.925 Silver 0.841 oz. ASW, 28x40 mm. **Ruler:** Elizabeth II **Obv:** Head right, propeller, wing schematic **Rev:** Montgolfier brothers and balloon **Shape:** Rectangle

| Date | Mintage | VF20 | XF40 | MS60 | MS63 | MS65 |
|---|---|---|---|---|---|---|
| 2010 | 6,000 | PF65 75.00 | | | | |

### KM# 241 DOLLAR

28.28 g., 0.925 Silver 0.841 oz. ASW, 40x28 mm. **Ruler:** Elizabeth II **Obv:** Head right, Monet painting **Rev:** Claude Monet portrait and painting **Shape:** Verticle rectangle

| Date | Mintage | VF20 | XF40 | MS60 | MS63 | MS65 |
|---|---|---|---|---|---|---|
| 2010 | 15,000 | PF65 120 | | | | |

### KM# 242 DOLLAR

28.28 g., 0.925 Silver 0.841 oz. ASW, 38.61 mm. **Ruler:** Elizabeth II **Obv:** Elizabeth II head at top left, building **Rev:** Napoleon at left, troops in color at right

| Date | Mintage | VF20 | XF40 | MS60 | MS63 | MS65 |
|---|---|---|---|---|---|---|
| 2010 | 10,000 | PF65 90.00 | | | | |

### KM# 243 DOLLAR

28.28 g., 0.925 Silver 0.841 oz. ASW, 38.6 mm. **Ruler:** Elizabeth II **Subject:** 65th Anniversary - End of World War II **Obv:** Head right at top, three Soviet medals below **Rev:** Soviet flat, rose and eternal light

| Date | Mintage | VF20 | XF40 | MS60 | MS63 | MS65 |
|---|---|---|---|---|---|---|
| 2010 | 7,000 | PF65 95.00 | | | | |

### KM# 244 DOLLAR

28.28 g., 0.925 Silver 0.841 oz. ASW, 38.6 mm. **Ruler:** Elizabeth II **Obv:** Head at left, ship, coins, artifacts **Rev:** Stupsk

| Date | Mintage | VF20 | XF40 | MS60 | MS63 | MS65 |
|---|---|---|---|---|---|---|
| 2010 | 8,000 | PF65 90.00 | | | | |

### KM# 365 DOLLAR

28.28 g., 0.925 Silver 0.841 oz. ASW, 38.61 mm. **Ruler:** Elizabeth II **Subject:** WWII, 65th Anniversary **Obv:** Elizabeth II head, WWI medal and two stars below **Rev:** Russian flag and medal ribbon

| Date | Mintage | VF20 | XF40 | MS60 | MS63 | MS65 |
|---|---|---|---|---|---|---|
| 2010 | 7,000 | PF65 60.00 | | | | |

### KM# 366 DOLLAR

28.28 g., 0.925 Silver 0.841 oz. ASW, 38.61 mm. **Ruler:** Elizabeth II **Obv:** Enlarged butterfly wing **Rev:** Butterfly - Parnassius Apollo

| Date | Mintage | VF20 | XF40 | MS60 | MS63 | MS65 |
|---|---|---|---|---|---|---|
| 2010 | 8,000 | PF65 65.00 | | | | |

### KM# 367 DOLLAR

28.28 g., 0.925 Silver 0.841 oz. ASW, 38.61 mm. **Ruler:** Elizabeth II **Subject:** Amber Route - Stare Hradisko **Rev:** Amber insert, old celtic style coin

| Date | Mintage | VF20 | XF40 | MS60 | MS63 | MS65 |
|---|---|---|---|---|---|---|
| 2010 Antique finish | 10,000 | — | — | — | — | 85.00 |

### KM# 369 DOLLAR

14.14 g., 0.925 Silver 0.4205 oz. ASW, 32 mm. **Ruler:** Elizabeth II **Subject:** Cartoon Characters - Mis Uszatek **Obv:** Elizabeth II head left, movie film **Rev:** Image of rabbits and bear

| Date | Mintage | VF20 | XF40 | MS60 | MS63 | MS65 |
|---|---|---|---|---|---|---|
| 2010 | 8,000 | PF65 40.00 | | | | |

### KM# 370 DOLLAR

28.28 g., 0.925 Silver 0.841 oz. ASW, 38.61 mm. **Ruler:** Elizabeth II **Obv:** Elizabeth II head right, Cupid **Rev:** Romeo and Juliet about to kiss

| Date | Mintage | VF20 | XF40 | MS60 | MS63 | MS65 |
|---|---|---|---|---|---|---|
| 2010 | 9,000 | PF65 60.00 | | | | |

### KM# 392 DOLLAR

14.14 g., 0.925 Silver 0.4205 oz. ASW, 32 mm. **Ruler:** Elizabeth II **Subject:** Cartoon Characters - Wolf and the Hare **Rev:** Wolf and hare characters in multicolor

| Date | Mintage | VF20 | XF40 | MS60 | MS63 | MS65 |
|---|---|---|---|---|---|---|
| 2010 | 8,000 | PF65 50.00 | | | | |

### KM# 393 DOLLAR

28.28 g., 0.925 Silver 0.841 oz. ASW, 40x28 mm. **Ruler:** Elizabeth II **Obv:** Queen's head at top left, three airplane views **Rev:** Otto Lilienthal and the glider **Shape:** Rectangle

| Date | Mintage | VF20 | XF40 | MS60 | MS63 | MS65 |
|---|---|---|---|---|---|---|
| 2010 | 6,000 | PF65 70.00 | | | | |

### KM# 394 DOLLAR

28.28 g., 0.925 Silver 0.841 oz. ASW, 38.8 mm. **Ruler:** Elizabeth II **Obv:** Queen's head right within star pattern **Rev:** Two portraits of Sitting Bull in multicolor

| Date | Mintage | VF20 | XF40 | MS60 | MS63 | MS65 |
|---|---|---|---|---|---|---|
| 2010 | 6,000 | PF65 75.00 | | | | |

### KM# 395 DOLLAR

28.28 g., 0.925 Silver 0.841 oz. ASW, 40x40 mm. **Ruler:** Elizabeth II **Obv:** Head in tiara right within diamond, footprints in background **Rev:** Platypus (Ornithorhynchus anatinus) **Shape:** Square

| Date | Mintage | VF20 | XF40 | MS60 | MS63 | MS65 |
|---|---|---|---|---|---|---|
| 2010 | 9,000 | PF65 65.00 | | | | |

**KM# 396 DOLLAR**

28.28 g., 0.925 Silver 0.841 oz. ASW with amber insert, 38.61 mm. **Ruler:** Elizabeth II **Subject:** Amber Route - Carnuntum **Rev:** Arches, ancient coin and statue

| Date | Mintage | VF20 | XF40 | MS60 | MS63 | MS65 |
|---|---|---|---|---|---|---|
| 2010 Antique patina | 10,000 | PF65 85.00 | | | | |

**KM# 398 DOLLAR**

28.28 g., 0.925 Silver 0.841 oz. ASW with amber insert, 38.61 mm. **Ruler:** Elizabeth II **Subject:** Amber Route - Szombathely **Rev:** Cathedral, ancient coin

| Date | Mintage | VF20 | XF40 | MS60 | MS63 | MS65 |
|---|---|---|---|---|---|---|
| 2010 Antique patina | 10,000 | PF65 85.00 | | | | |

**KM# 400 DOLLAR**

28.28 g., 0.925 Silver 0.841 oz. ASW, 27x45 mm. **Ruler:** Elizabeth II **Subject:** Milan Cathedral **Obv:** Cathedral's flying buttresses, stained glass colored inset **Rev:** Front facade of cathedral, stained glass colored inset **Shape:** Vertical oval

| Date | Mintage | VF20 | XF40 | MS60 | MS63 | MS65 |
|---|---|---|---|---|---|---|
| 2010 | 5,000 | PF65 70.00 | | | | |

**KM# 401 DOLLAR**

28.28 g., 0.925 Silver 0.841 oz. ASW, 27x45 mm. **Ruler:** Elizabeth II **Subject:** Cologne Cathedral **Obv:** Cathedral side exterior, stained glass colored inset **Rev:** Cathedral floor plan and facade, stained glass colored inset **Shape:** Vertical oval

| Date | Mintage | VF20 | XF40 | MS60 | MS63 | MS65 |
|---|---|---|---|---|---|---|
| 2010 | 5,000 | PF65 70.00 | | | | |

**KM# 402 DOLLAR**

28.28 g., 0.925 Silver 0.841 oz. ASW, 27x45 mm. **Ruler:** Elizabeth II **Subject:** Notre Dame Cathedral **Obv:** Cathedral side view, stained glass colored inset **Rev:** Linear cathedral interior view, cathedral facade, stained glass colored inset **Shape:** Vertical oval

| Date | Mintage | VF20 | XF40 | MS60 | MS63 | MS65 |
|---|---|---|---|---|---|---|
| 2010 | 5,000 | PF65 70.00 | | | | |

**KM# 403 DOLLAR**

28.28 g., 0.925 Silver 0.841 oz. ASW, 28x40 mm. **Ruler:** Elizabeth II **Subject:** Alfons Mucha, 150th Anniversary of Birth **Obv:** Standing Female in multicolor **Rev:** Female portrait and Mucha portrait in multicolor **Shape:** Vertical Rectangle

| Date | Mintage | VF20 | XF40 | MS60 | MS63 | MS65 |
|---|---|---|---|---|---|---|
| 2010 | 5,000 | PF65 80.00 | | | | |

**KM# 404 DOLLAR**

28.28 g., 0.925 Silver 0.841 oz. ASW, 28x40 mm. **Ruler:** Elizabeth II **Subject:** Carl Brullov **Obv:** Female on horseback in color **Rev:** Two females with grape wreath above, Brullov portrait, Three nuns singing below; all in color **Shape:** Vertical Rectangle

| Date | Mintage | VF20 | XF40 | MS60 | MS63 | MS65 |
|---|---|---|---|---|---|---|
| 2010 | 5,000 | PF65 75.00 | | | | |

**KM# 406 DOLLAR**

28.28 g., 0.925 Silver 0.841 oz. ASW, 40x40 mm. **Ruler:** Elizabeth II **Obv:** Head with tiara right, in diamond, footprints in background **Rev:** Venus Flytrap in color **Shape:** Square

| Date | Mintage | VF20 | XF40 | MS60 | MS63 | MS65 |
|---|---|---|---|---|---|---|
| 2010 | 9,000 | PF65 75.00 | | | | |

**KM# 407 DOLLAR**

28.28 g., 0.925 Silver 0.841 oz. ASW, 41 mm. **Ruler:** Elizabeth II **Subject:** Good Luck **Obv:** Head with tiara right, horseshoes below **Rev:** Horseshoes and clover

| Date | Mintage | VF20 | XF40 | MS60 | MS63 | MS65 |
|---|---|---|---|---|---|---|
| 2010 | 10,000 | PF65 70.00 | | | | |

**KM# 412 DOLLAR**

28.28 g., 0.925 Silver 0.841 oz. ASW, 38.61 mm. **Ruler:** Elizabeth II **Subject:** Siberia **Obv:** Head with tiara right **Rev:** Khanty-Mansiysk

| Date | Mintage | VF20 | XF40 | MS60 | MS63 | MS65 |
|---|---|---|---|---|---|---|
| 2010 Proof-like | 4,000 | — | — | — | — | 70.00 |

**KM# 413 DOLLAR**

28.28 g., 0.925 Silver 0.841 oz. ASW, 38.61 mm. **Ruler:** Elizabeth II **Subject:** Siberia **Obv:** Head with tiara right **Rev:** Uray

| Date | Mintage | VF20 | XF40 | MS60 | MS63 | MS65 |
|---|---|---|---|---|---|---|
| 2010 Proof-like | 4,000 | — | — | — | — | 70.00 |

**KM# 414 DOLLAR**

28.28 g., 0.925 Silver 0.841 oz. ASW, 38.61 mm. **Ruler:** Elizabeth II **Subject:** Siberia **Obv:** Head with tiara right **Rev:** Surgut

| Date | Mintage | VF20 | XF40 | MS60 | MS63 | MS65 |
|---|---|---|---|---|---|---|
| 2010 Proof-like | 4,000 | — | — | — | — | 70.00 |

**KM# 415 DOLLAR**
28.28 g., 0.925 Silver 0.841 oz. ASW, 38.61 mm. **Ruler:** Elizabeth II **Subject:** Siberia **Obv:** Head with tiara right **Rev:** Nizhnevartovsk

| Date | Mintage | VF20 | XF40 | MS60 | MS63 | MS65 |
|---|---|---|---|---|---|---|
| 2010 Proof-like | 4,000 | — | — | — | — | 70.00 |

**KM# 417 DOLLAR**
28.28 g., 0.925 Silver 0.841 oz. ASW, 38.61 mm. **Ruler:** Elizabeth II **Subject:** Famous Love Stories - Samson and Delilah **Obv:** Head with tiara right, Cupid below **Rev:** Portraits of Samson and Delilah

| Date | Mintage | VF20 | XF40 | MS60 | MS63 | MS65 |
|---|---|---|---|---|---|---|
| 2010 | 9,000 | PF65 70.00 | | | | |

**KM# 418 DOLLAR**
31.10 g., 0.999 Silver 0.9989 oz. ASW, 40 mm. **Ruler:** Elizabeth II **Subject:** Jaroslawl, 100th Anniversary **Obv:** Head with tiara right **Rev:** Banner in color

| Date | Mintage | VF20 | XF40 | MS60 | MS63 | MS65 |
|---|---|---|---|---|---|---|
| 2010 | 2,000 | PF65 75.00 | | | | |

**KM# 419 DOLLAR**
31.10 g., 0.999 Silver 0.9989 oz. ASW, 40 mm. **Ruler:** Elizabeth II **Subject:** Jaroslawl, 1000th Anniversary **Obv:** Head with tiara right **Rev:** Three church towers in color

| Date | Mintage | VF20 | XF40 | MS60 | MS63 | MS65 |
|---|---|---|---|---|---|---|
| 2010 | 9,000 | PF65 75.00 | | | | |

**KM# 420 DOLLAR**
31.10 g., 0.999 Silver 0.9989 oz. ASW, 40 mm. **Ruler:** Elizabeth II **Subject:** Jaroslawl, 1000th Anniversary **Obv:** Head in tiara right **Rev:** Town square in color

| Date | Mintage | VF20 | XF40 | MS60 | MS63 | MS65 |
|---|---|---|---|---|---|---|
| 2010 | 9,000 | PF65 75.00 | | | | |

**KM# 421 DOLLAR**
28.28 g., 0.925 Silver 0.841 oz. ASW, 36.81 mm. **Ruler:** Elizabeth II **Subject:** Cultural Achievements **Obv:** Head with tiara at center **Rev:** Bow and arrows, Bow and firestarting kit

| Date | Mintage | VF20 | XF40 | MS60 | MS63 | MS65 |
|---|---|---|---|---|---|---|
| 2010 | 6,000 | PF65 80.00 | | | | |

**KM# 422 DOLLAR**
28.28 g., 0.925 Silver 0.841 oz. ASW, 44 mm. **Ruler:** Elizabeth II **Subject:** Christmas star **Obv:** Head with tiara right, snowflakes around **Rev:** Children before christmas tree in color **Shape:** 7-pointed star

| Date | Mintage | VF20 | XF40 | MS60 | MS63 | MS65 |
|---|---|---|---|---|---|---|
| 2010 | 15,000 | PF65 95.00 | | | | |

**KM# 426 DOLLAR**
28.28 g., 0.925 Silver 0.841 oz. ASW, 41 mm. **Ruler:** Elizabeth II **Subject:** Four Leaf Clover **Obv:** Head with titara right, clovers **Rev:** four clovers and ripple background

| Date | Mintage | VF20 | XF40 | MS60 | MS63 | MS65 |
|---|---|---|---|---|---|---|
| 2010 | 10,000 | PF65 70.00 | | | | |

**KM# 427 DOLLAR**
28.28 g., 0.925 Silver 0.841 oz. ASW, 38.61 mm. **Ruler:** Elizabeth II **Subject:** Veliky Novgorod **Obv:** Head with tiara right, montage of ship and coins at right **Rev:** Market scene, Church; city arms below

| Date | Mintage | VF20 | XF40 | MS60 | MS63 | MS65 |
|---|---|---|---|---|---|---|
| 2010 | 8,000 | PF65 75.00 | | | | |

**KM# 428 DOLLAR**
28.28 g., 0.925 Silver 0.841 oz. ASW, 38.61 mm. **Ruler:** Elizabeth II **Subject:** Year of the Rabbit **Obv:** Head with tiara right **Rev:** Rabbit seated in field

| Date | Mintage | VF20 | XF40 | MS60 | MS63 | MS65 |
|---|---|---|---|---|---|---|
| 2010 | 3,000 | PF65 75.00 | | | | |

**KM# 429 DOLLAR**
28.28 g., 0.925 Silver 0.841 oz. ASW, 38.61 mm. **Ruler:** Elizabeth II **Subject:** Year of the Rabbit **Obv:** Head with tiara right **Rev:** Two rabbits holding heart at center

| Date | Mintage | VF20 | XF40 | MS60 | MS63 | MS65 |
|---|---|---|---|---|---|---|
| 2010 | 3,000 | PF65 75.00 | | | | |

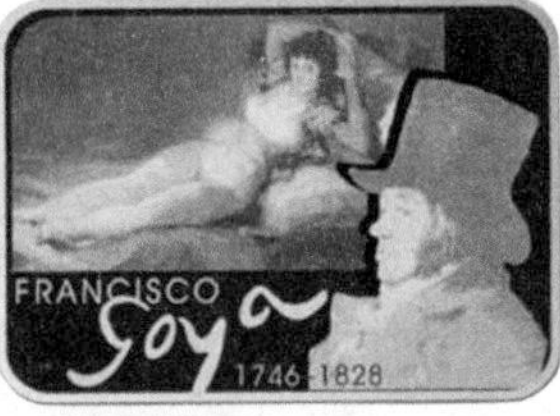


**KM# 432 DOLLAR**
28.28 g., 0.925 Silver 0.841 oz. ASW, 40x28 mm. **Ruler:** Elizabeth II **Subject:** Francisco Goya **Obv:** Head with tiara right at left, painting of man and woman at right **Rev:** Goya and Clothed female reclining **Shape:** Rectangle

| Date | Mintage | VF20 | XF40 | MS60 | MS63 | MS65 |
|---|---|---|---|---|---|---|
| 2010 | 10,000 | PF65 70.00 | | | | |

**KM# 433 DOLLAR**
28.28 g., 0.925 Silver 0.841 oz. ASW, 38.61 mm. **Ruler:** Elizabeth II **Subject:** Peter the Great **Obv:** Head with tiara right above ship and city view **Rev:** Half-length figure holding coins, map in background

| Date | Mintage | VF20 | XF40 | MS60 | MS63 | MS65 |
|---|---|---|---|---|---|---|
| 2010 | 4,000 | **PF65** 75.00 | | | | |

**KM# 434 DOLLAR**
28.28 g., 0.925 Silver 0.841 oz. ASW, 38.61 mm. **Ruler:** Elizabeth II **Subject:** Sea of Love **Obv:** Head in tiara right above sunset at sea with heart at center **Rev:** Two white doves in flight over sea, within heart

| Date | Mintage | VF20 | XF40 | MS60 | MS63 | MS65 |
|---|---|---|---|---|---|---|
| 2010 | 7,000 | **PF65** 80.00 | | | | |

**KM# 440 DOLLAR**
28.28 g., Copper-Nickel, 38.61 mm. **Ruler:** Elizabeth II **Subject:** Lifetime of Service **Obv:** Head in tiara right **Rev:** Conjoined busts of Elizabeth II and Prince Philip

| Date | Mintage | VF20 | XF40 | MS60 | MS63 | MS65 |
|---|---|---|---|---|---|---|
| 2010 | — | — | — | — | — | 20.00 |

**KM# 440a DOLLAR**
28.28 g., 0.925 Silver 0.841 oz. ASW, 38.61 mm. **Ruler:** Elizabeth II **Subject:** Lifetime of Service **Obv:** Head with tiara right **Rev:** Conjoined busts of Elizabeth II and Prince Philip

| Date | Mintage | VF20 | XF40 | MS60 | MS63 | MS65 |
|---|---|---|---|---|---|---|
| 2010 | 19,500 | **PF65** 50.00 | | | | |

**KM# 441 DOLLAR**
31.10 g., 0.999 Silver 0.9989 oz. ASW, 38.61 mm. **Ruler:** Elizabeth II **Subject:** Slovic mythology - Perun **Rev:** Two warriors, tree in background

| Date | Mintage | VF20 | XF40 | MS60 | MS63 | MS65 |
|---|---|---|---|---|---|---|
| 2010 | 1,000 | **PF65** 65.00 | | | | |

**KM# 454 DOLLAR**
Silver **Ruler:** Elizabeth II **Subject:** Polish Stadiums **Rev:** Michail Ktzov stadium

| Date | Mintage | VF20 | XF40 | MS60 | MS63 | MS65 |
|---|---|---|---|---|---|---|
| 2010 | — | **PF65** 75.00 | | | | |

**KM# 455 DOLLAR**
Silver **Ruler:** Elizabeth II **Subject:** Polish Stadiums **Rev:** Gdansk

| Date | Mintage | VF20 | XF40 | MS60 | MS63 | MS65 |
|---|---|---|---|---|---|---|
| 2010 | — | **PF65** 75.00 | | | | |

**KM# 456 DOLLAR**
31.10 g., 0.999 Silver 0.999 oz. ASW, 40 mm. **Ruler:** Elizabeth II **Subject:** Giah Thong - safe conduct pass **Obv:** Head with tiara right **Rev:** Two soldiers below Viet Nam flag

| Date | Mintage | VF20 | XF40 | MS60 | MS63 | MS65 |
|---|---|---|---|---|---|---|
| 2010 Prooflike | — | — | — | — | — | 50.00 |

**KM# 495 DOLLAR**
28.28 g., 0.925 Silver 0.841 oz. ASW, 38.61 mm. **Ruler:** Elizabeth II **Subject:** Zodiac Mucha Paintings **Rev:** Aries

| Date | Mintage | VF20 | XF40 | MS60 | MS63 | MS65 |
|---|---|---|---|---|---|---|
| 2010 | 10,000 | **PF65** 65.00 | | | | |

**KM# 496 DOLLAR**
28.28 g., 0.925 Silver 0.841 oz. ASW, 38.61 mm. **Ruler:** Elizabeth II **Subject:** Zodiac Mucha Paintings **Rev:** Taurus

| Date | Mintage | VF20 | XF40 | MS60 | MS63 | MS65 |
|---|---|---|---|---|---|---|
| 2010 | 10,000 | **PF65** 65.00 | | | | |

**KM# 497 DOLLAR**
28.28 g., 0.925 Silver 0.841 oz. ASW, 38.61 mm. **Ruler:** Elizabeth II **Subject:** Zodiac Mucha Paintings **Rev:** Gemini

| Date | Mintage | VF20 | XF40 | MS60 | MS63 | MS65 |
|---|---|---|---|---|---|---|
| 2010 | 10,000 | **PF65** 65.00 | | | | |

**KM# 498 DOLLAR**
28.28 g., 0.925 Silver 0.841 oz. ASW, 38.61 mm. **Ruler:** Elizabeth II **Subject:** Zodiac Mucha Paintings **Rev:** Cancer

| Date | Mintage | VF20 | XF40 | MS60 | MS63 | MS65 |
|---|---|---|---|---|---|---|
| 2010 | 10,000 | **PF65** 65.00 | | | | |

**KM# 499 DOLLAR**
28.28 g., 0.925 Silver 0.841 oz. ASW **Ruler:** Elizabeth II **Subject:** Zodiac Mucha Paintings **Rev:** Leo

| Date | Mintage | VF20 | XF40 | MS60 | MS63 | MS65 |
|---|---|---|---|---|---|---|
| 2010 | 10,000 | **PF65** 65.00 | | | | |

**KM# 500 DOLLAR**
28.25 g., 0.925 Silver 0.8401 oz. ASW, 38.61 mm. **Ruler:** Elizabeth II **Subject:** Zodiac Mucha Paintings **Rev:** Virgo

| Date | Mintage | VF20 | XF40 | MS60 | MS63 | MS65 |
|---|---|---|---|---|---|---|
| 2010 | 10,000 | **PF65** 65.00 | | | | |

**KM# 501 DOLLAR**
28.28 g., 0.925 Silver 0.841 oz. ASW, 38.61 mm. **Ruler:** Elizabeth II **Subject:** Zodiac Mucha Paintings **Rev:** Libra

| Date | Mintage | VF20 | XF40 | MS60 | MS63 | MS65 |
|---|---|---|---|---|---|---|
| 2010 | 10,000 | **PF65** 65.00 | | | | |

**KM# 502 DOLLAR**
28.28 g., 0.925 Silver 0.841 oz. ASW, 38.61 mm. **Ruler:** Elizabeth II **Subject:** Zodiac Mucha Paintings **Rev:** Scorpio

| Date | Mintage | VF20 | XF40 | MS60 | MS63 | MS65 |
|---|---|---|---|---|---|---|
| 2010 | 10,000 | PF65 65.00 | | | | |

**KM# 503 DOLLAR**
28.28 g., 0.925 Silver 0.841 oz. ASW, 38.61 mm. **Ruler:** Elizabeth II **Subject:** Zodiac Mucha Paintings **Rev:** Sagittarius

| Date | Mintage | VF20 | XF40 | MS60 | MS63 | MS65 |
|---|---|---|---|---|---|---|
| 2010 | 10,000 | PF65 65.00 | | | | |

**KM# 557 DOLLAR**
28.28 g., 0.925 Silver 0.841 oz. ASW, 30x50 mm. **Ruler:** Elizabeth II **Subject:** Westminister Abbey **Obv:** Head with tiara at left, interior view of end windows **Rev:** Exterior view with rose window detail **Shape:** vertical oval

| Date | Mintage | VF20 | XF40 | MS60 | MS63 | MS65 |
|---|---|---|---|---|---|---|
| 2010 | 5,000 | PF65 100 | | | | |

**KM# 558 DOLLAR**
28.28 g., 0.925 Silver 0.841 oz. ASW, 30x50 mm. **Ruler:** Elizabeth II **Subject:** Stephansdom, Wein **Obv:** Head in tiara at left, view of organ screena dn statue detail **Rev:** Exterior rendering and detail **Shape:** Vertical oval

| Date | Mintage | VF20 | XF40 | MS60 | MS63 | MS65 |
|---|---|---|---|---|---|---|
| 2010 | 5,000 | PF65 100 | | | | |

**KM# 943 DOLLAR**
28.28 g., 0.925 Silver 0.841 oz. ASW, 36.81 mm. **Ruler:** Elizabeth II **Subject:** Butterflies - Maculinea Arion **Rev:** Blue butterfly

| Date | Mintage | VF20 | XF40 | MS60 | MS63 | MS65 |
|---|---|---|---|---|---|---|
| 2010 Proof | Est. 8000 | PF65 65.00 | | | | |

**KM# 435 DOLLAR**
15.55 g., 0.925 Silver 0.4624 oz. ASW, 35 mm. **Ruler:** Elizabeth II **Subject:** Prehistoric art - Chauvet cave **Rev:** Two figures of cats

| Date | Mintage | VF20 | XF40 | MS60 | MS63 | MS65 |
|---|---|---|---|---|---|---|
| 2011 | 1,000 | PF65 65.00 | | | | |

**KM# 436 DOLLAR**
15.55 g., 0.925 Silver 0.4624 oz. ASW, 35 mm. **Ruler:** Elizabeth II **Subject:** Prehistoric art - Altamira cave **Rev:** Bison artwork

| Date | Mintage | VF20 | XF40 | MS60 | MS63 | MS65 |
|---|---|---|---|---|---|---|
| 2011 | 1,000 | PF65 65.00 | | | | |

**KM# 437 DOLLAR**
15.55 g., 0.925 Silver 0.4624 oz. ASW, 35 mm. **Ruler:** Elizabeth II **Subject:** Prehistoric art - Lascaux cave **Rev:** Horse art

| Date | Mintage | VF20 | XF40 | MS60 | MS63 | MS65 |
|---|---|---|---|---|---|---|
| 2011 | 1,000 | PF65 65.00 | | | | |

**KM# 438 DOLLAR**
15.55 g., 0.925 Silver 0.4624 oz. ASW, 35 mm. **Ruler:** Elizabeth II **Subject:** Prehistoric art - Jabbaren cave **Rev:** Male figure with bow

| Date | Mintage | VF20 | XF40 | MS60 | MS63 | MS65 |
|---|---|---|---|---|---|---|
| 2011 | 1,000 | PF65 65.00 | | | | |

**KM# 439 DOLLAR**
15.55 g., 0.925 Silver 0.4624 oz. ASW, 35 mm. **Ruler:** Elizabeth II **Subject:** Prehistoric art - Tadrart cave **Rev:** Elephant art

| Date | Mintage | VF20 | XF40 | MS60 | MS63 | MS65 |
|---|---|---|---|---|---|---|
| 2011 | 1,000 | PF65 65.00 | | | | |

**KM# 504 DOLLAR**
28.28 g., 0.925 Silver 0.841 oz. ASW, 38.61 mm. **Ruler:** Elizabeth II **Subject:** Zodiac Mucha Paintings **Rev:** Capricorn

| Date | Mintage | VF20 | XF40 | MS60 | MS63 | MS65 |
|---|---|---|---|---|---|---|
| 2011 | 10,000 | PF65 65.00 | | | | |

**KM# 505 DOLLAR**
28.28 g., 0.925 Silver 0.841 oz. ASW, 38.61 mm. **Ruler:** Elizabeth II **Subject:** Zodiac Mucha Painting **Rev:** Aquarius

| Date | Mintage | VF20 | XF40 | MS60 | MS63 | MS65 |
|---|---|---|---|---|---|---|
| 2011 | 10,000 | PF65 65.00 | | | | |

**KM# 506 DOLLAR**
28.28 g., 0.925 Silver 0.841 oz. ASW, 38.61 mm. **Ruler:** Elizabeth II **Subject:** Zodiac Mucha Paintings **Rev:** Pisces

| Date | Mintage | VF20 | XF40 | MS60 | MS63 | MS65 |
|---|---|---|---|---|---|---|
| 2011 | 10,000 | PF65 65.00 | | | | |

**KM# 508 DOLLAR**
Silver **Ruler:** Elizabeth II **Subject:** Russian Cartoons

| Date | Mintage | VF20 | XF40 | MS60 | MS63 | MS65 |
|---|---|---|---|---|---|---|
| 2011 | — | PF65 70.00 | | | | |

**KM# 509 DOLLAR**
Silver **Ruler:** Elizabeth II **Subject:** Russian Cartoons

| Date | Mintage | VF20 | XF40 | MS60 | MS63 | MS65 |
|---|---|---|---|---|---|---|
| 2011 | — | PF65 70.00 | | | | |

**KM# 510 DOLLAR**
28.28 g., 0.925 Silver 0.841 oz. ASW, 55.6x41.6 mm. **Ruler:** Elizabeth II **Subject:** Year of the Rabbit **Rev:** Rabbit in the snow **Shape:** Horizontal oval

| Date | Mintage | VF20 | XF40 | MS60 | MS63 | MS65 |
|---|---|---|---|---|---|---|
| 2011 | 5,000 | PF65 55.00 | | | | |

**KM# 514 DOLLAR**
31.11 g., Silver Plated Copper-Nickel, 40 mm. **Ruler:** Elizabeth II **Subject:** Royal Engagement **Obv:** Head with tiara right **Rev:** Prince William and Catherine Middleton facing

| Date | Mintage | VF20 | XF40 | MS60 | MS63 | MS65 |
|---|---|---|---|---|---|---|
| 2011 | 10,000 | PF65 25.00 | | | | |

**KM# 515 DOLLAR**
31.10 g., Silver Plated Copper, 40 mm. **Ruler:** Elizabeth II **Subject:** Diana - A wife, Princess, Mother, Legend

| Date | Mintage | VF20 | XF40 | MS60 | MS63 | MS65 |
|---|---|---|---|---|---|---|
| 2011 | 10,000 | PF65 20.00 | | | | |

**KM# 516 DOLLAR**
31.10 g., Silver Plated Copper, 40 mm. **Ruler:** Elizabeth II **Subject:** Diana - Wedding to Charles

| Date | Mintage | VF20 | XF40 | MS60 | MS63 | MS65 |
|---|---|---|---|---|---|---|
| 2011 | 10,000 | PF65 20.00 | | | | |

**KM# 517 DOLLAR**
31.10 g., Silver Plated Copper, 40 mm. **Ruler:** Elizabeth II **Subject:** Diana - Engagement to Prince Charles

| Date | Mintage | VF20 | XF40 | MS60 | MS63 | MS65 |
|---|---|---|---|---|---|---|
| 2011 | 10,000 | PF65 20.00 | | | | |

**KM# 518 DOLLAR**
31.10 g., Silver Plated Copper, 40 mm. **Ruler:** Elizabeth II **Subject:** Diana - Quote

| Date | Mintage | VF20 | XF40 | MS60 | MS63 | MS65 |
|---|---|---|---|---|---|---|
| 2011 | 10,000 | PF65 20.00 | | | | |

**KM# 519 DOLLAR**
31.10 g., Silver Plated Copper, 40 mm. **Ruler:** Elizabeth II **Subject:** Diana - Mother Teresa

| Date | Mintage | VF20 | XF40 | MS60 | MS63 | MS65 |
|---|---|---|---|---|---|---|
| 2011 | 10,000 | PF65 20.00 | | | | |

**KM# 520 DOLLAR**
31.10 g., Silver Plated Copper, 40 mm. **Ruler:** Elizabeth II **Subject:** Diana - We will always remember

| Date | Mintage | VF20 | XF40 | MS60 | MS63 | MS65 |
|---|---|---|---|---|---|---|
| 2011 | 10,000 | PF65 20.00 | | | | |

**KM# 555 DOLLAR**
28.28 g., 0.925 Silver 0.841 oz. ASW, 38.61 mm. **Ruler:** Elizabeth II **Subject:** Hanseatic Towns - Szezecin **Obv:** Head with tiara right at left, map and ship **Rev:** Churches and ship at dock, town shield

| Date | Mintage | VF20 | XF40 | MS60 | MS63 | MS65 |
|---|---|---|---|---|---|---|
| 2011 | Est. 3000 | PF65 75.00 | | | | |

**KM# 559 DOLLAR**
28.28 g., 0.925 Silver 0.841 oz. ASW, 38.61 mm. **Ruler:** Elizabeth II **Subject:** Russian municipalities - Krasnoyarsk **Obv:** Head with tiara right **Rev:** Town view

| Date | Mintage | VF20 | XF40 | MS60 | MS63 | MS65 |
|---|---|---|---|---|---|---|
| 2011 | 2,000 | PF65 85.00 | | | | |

**KM# 560 DOLLAR**
28.28 g., 0.925 Silver 0.841 oz. ASW, 38.61 mm. **Ruler:** Elizabeth II **Subject:** Russian municipalities - Norilsk **Obv:** Head with tiara right **Rev:** Town view, shield above

| Date | Mintage | VF20 | XF40 | MS60 | MS63 | MS65 |
|---|---|---|---|---|---|---|
| 2011 | 2,000 | PF65 85.00 | | | | |

**KM# 561 DOLLAR**
28.28 g., 0.925 Silver 0.841 oz. ASW, 38.61 mm. **Ruler:** Elizabeth II **Subject:** Russian municipalities - Belgorod **Obv:** Head with tiara right **Rev:** Statue at center, shield at left, tower at right

| Date | Mintage | VF20 | XF40 | MS60 | MS63 | MS65 |
|---|---|---|---|---|---|---|
| 2011 | 2,000 | PF65 85.00 | | | | |

**KM# 562 DOLLAR**
28.28 g., 0.925 Silver 0.841 oz. ASW, 30x50 mm. **Ruler:** Elizabeth II **Subject:** Russian municipalities - Irkutsk **Obv:** Head with tiara right **Rev:** Town view **Shape:** Vertical oval

| Date | Mintage | VF20 | XF40 | MS60 | MS63 | MS65 |
|---|---|---|---|---|---|---|
| 2011 | 2,000 | PF65 85.00 | | | | |

**KM# 571 DOLLAR**
28.28 g., 0.925 Silver 0.841 oz. ASW, 40x40 mm. **Ruler:** Elizabeth II **Obv:** Head with diadem right, tracks in background **Rev:** Flying frog, Rhacophorus reinwardti **Shape:** Square

| Date | Mintage | VF20 | XF40 | MS60 | MS63 | MS65 |
|---|---|---|---|---|---|---|
| 2011 | 5,000 | PF65 75.00 | | | | |

**KM# 583 DOLLAR**
14.14 g., 0.925 Silver 0.4205 oz. ASW, 32 mm. **Ruler:** Elizabeth II **Subject:** Russian comics - Bolek i Lolek **Rev:** Two western children on horseback

| Date | Mintage | VF20 | XF40 | MS60 | MS63 | MS65 |
|---|---|---|---|---|---|---|
| 2011 | Est. 4000 | PF65 55.00 | | | | |

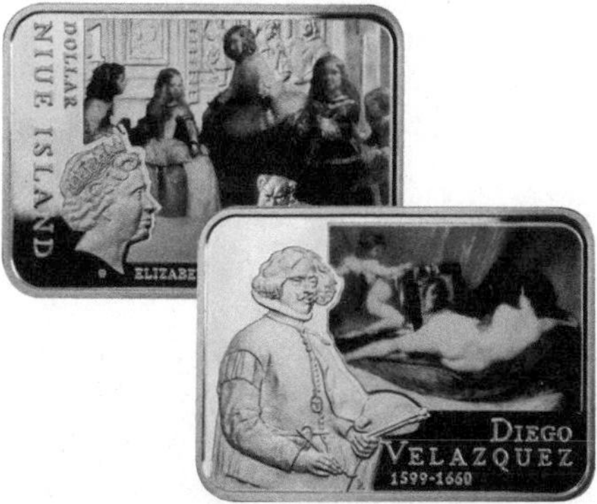


**KM# 585 DOLLAR**
28.28 g., 0.925 Silver 0.841 oz. ASW, 40x28 mm. **Ruler:** Elizabeth II **Obv:** Head with tiara right, five girls in painting **Rev:** Diego Velazquez and painting of female nude

| Date | Mintage | VF20 | XF40 | MS60 | MS63 | MS65 |
|---|---|---|---|---|---|---|
| 2011 | Est. 5000 | PF65 95.00 | | | | |

**KM# 586 DOLLAR**
28.28 g., 0.925 Silver 0.841 oz. ASW, 38.61 mm. **Ruler:** Elizabeth II **Subject:** Amber Route - Aquileia **Rev:** Statue of Romulus and Remus and wolf, amber insert

| Date | Mintage | VF20 | XF40 | MS60 | MS63 | MS65 |
|---|---|---|---|---|---|---|
| 2011 Antique finish | Est. 10000 | — | — | — | — | 85.00 |

**KM# 617 DOLLAR**
28.28 g., 0.925 Silver 0.841 oz. ASW, 38.61 mm. **Ruler:** Elizabeth II **Obv:** Bust with tiara right before sailing ship in ornate frame **Rev:** Yunona and Avos facing each other in color, ship below

| Date | Mintage | VF20 | XF40 | MS60 | MS63 | MS65 |
|---|---|---|---|---|---|---|
| 2011 | Est. 5000 | PF65 75.00 | | | | |

**KM# 618 DOLLAR**
28.28 g., 0.925 Silver 0.841 oz. ASW, 38.61 mm. **Ruler:** Elizabeth II **Obv:** Head with tiara at left, map and sailing ship at right, HANSA on ribbon above **Rev:** Town view of the port of Szczecin

| Date | Mintage | VF20 | XF40 | MS60 | MS63 | MS65 |
|---|---|---|---|---|---|---|
| 2011 | Est. 3000 | PF65 75.00 | | | | |

**KM# 619 DOLLAR**
28.28 g., 0.925 Silver 0.841 oz. ASW, 41 mm. **Ruler:** Elizabeth II **Obv:** Head in tiara at left, elephant in designs **Rev:** Two elephants at tree, elephant in hologram

| Date | Mintage | VF20 | XF40 | MS60 | MS63 | MS65 |
|---|---|---|---|---|---|---|
| 2011 | Est. 10000 | PF65 75.00 | | | | |

**KM# 621 DOLLAR**
16.81 g., 0.925 Silver 0.4999 oz. ASW, 36.81 mm. **Ruler:** Elizabeth II **Obv:** Head with tiara right **Rev:** Chinese dragon prancing right with ball

| Date | Mintage | VF20 | XF40 | MS60 | MS63 | MS65 |
|---|---|---|---|---|---|---|
| 2011 | Est. 6000 | PF65 75.00 | | | | |

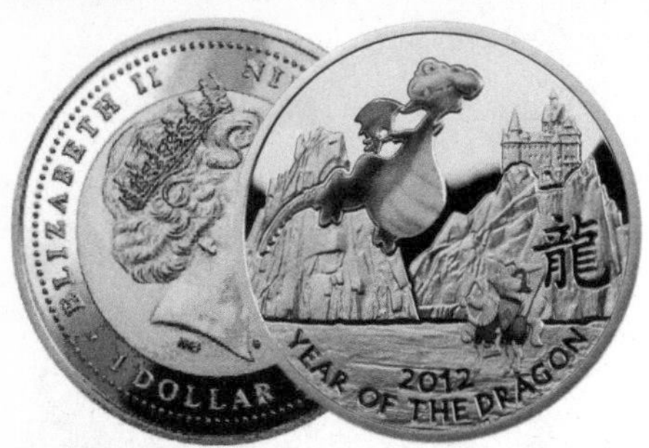


**KM# 622 DOLLAR**
16.81 g., 0.925 Silver 0.4999 oz. ASW, 36.81 mm. **Ruler:** Elizabeth II **Obv:** Head with tiara right **Rev:** Child's fantasy dragon, knight and castle

| Date | Mintage | VF20 | XF40 | MS60 | MS63 | MS65 |
|---|---|---|---|---|---|---|
| 2011 | Est. 6000 | **PF65** 75.00 | | | | |

**KM# 641 DOLLAR**
28.28 g., 0.925 Silver 0.841 oz. ASW, 40x28 mm. **Ruler:** Elizabeth II **Obv:** Portrait at left, painting **Rev:** Portrait at left, painting **Shape:** Horizontal rectangle

| Date | Mintage | VF20 | XF40 | MS60 | MS63 | MS65 |
|---|---|---|---|---|---|---|
| 2011 | 5,000 | **PF65** 100 | | | | |

**KM# 647 DOLLAR**
31.11 g., 0.999 Silver 0.999 oz. ASW, 38.61 mm. **Ruler:** Elizabeth II **Subject:** First European to cross the Simpson Desert **Obv:** Head with tiara right **Rev:** Simpson Desert and Ted Colson in 3-D color **Edge:** Reeded

| Date | Mintage | VF20 | XF40 | MS60 | MS63 | MS65 |
|---|---|---|---|---|---|---|
| 2011 | 2,000 | **PF65** 75.00 | | | | |

**KM# 652 DOLLAR**
28.28 g., 0.925 Silver 0.841 oz. ASW, 38.61 mm. **Ruler:** Elizabeth II **Subject:** Papilio Machaon **Obv:** Head in tiara right, butterfly wing in background **Rev:** Butterfly in color

| Date | Mintage | VF20 | XF40 | MS60 | MS63 | MS65 |
|---|---|---|---|---|---|---|
| 2011 | Est. 5000 | **PF65** 65.00 | | | | |

**KM# 653 DOLLAR**
Silver Plated Copper, 40 mm. **Ruler:** Elizabeth II **Subject:** Star Wars - Obi-Wan Kenobi

| Date | Mintage | VF20 | XF40 | MS60 | MS63 | MS65 |
|---|---|---|---|---|---|---|
| 2011 | — | — | — | — | — | 25.00 |

**KM# 654 DOLLAR**
Silver Plated Copper, 40 mm. **Ruler:** Elizabeth II **Subject:** Star Wars - Yoda

| Date | Mintage | VF20 | XF40 | MS60 | MS63 | MS65 |
|---|---|---|---|---|---|---|
| 2011 | Est. 50000 | — | — | — | — | 25.00 |

**KM# 655 DOLLAR**
Silver Plated Copper, 40 mm. **Ruler:** Elizabeth II **Subject:** Star Wars - Princess Leia

| Date | Mintage | VF20 | XF40 | MS60 | MS63 | MS65 |
|---|---|---|---|---|---|---|
| 2011 | Est. 50000 | — | — | — | — | 25.00 |

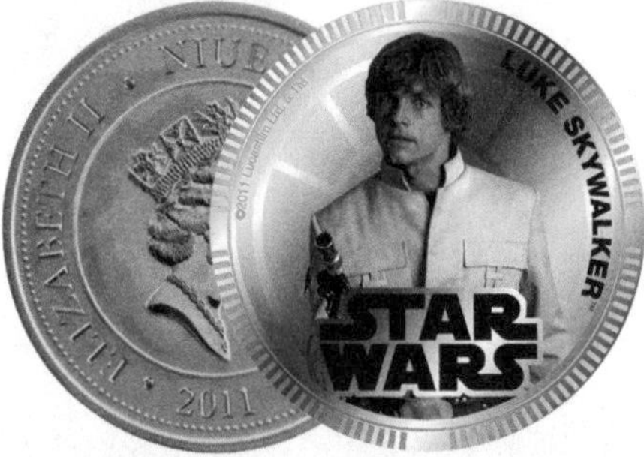


**KM# 656 DOLLAR**
Silver Plated Copper, 40 mm. **Ruler:** Elizabeth II **Subject:** Star Wars - Luke Skywalker

| Date | Mintage | VF20 | XF40 | MS60 | MS63 | MS65 |
|---|---|---|---|---|---|---|
| 2011 | Est. 50000 | — | — | — | — | 25.00 |

**KM# 657 DOLLAR**
Silver Plated Copper, 40 mm. **Ruler:** Elizabeth II **Subject:** Star Wars - C3PO

| Date | Mintage | VF20 | XF40 | MS60 | MS63 | MS65 |
|---|---|---|---|---|---|---|
| 2011 | Est. 50000 | — | — | — | — | 25.00 |

**KM# 658 DOLLAR**
Silver Plated Copper, 40 mm. **Ruler:** Elizabeth II **Subject:** Star Wars - R2-D2

| Date | Mintage | VF20 | XF40 | MS60 | MS63 | MS65 |
|---|---|---|---|---|---|---|
| 2011 | Est. 50000 | — | — | — | — | 25.00 |

**KM# 659 DOLLAR**
Silver Plated Copper, 40 mm. **Ruler:** Elizabeth II **Subject:** Star Wars - Darth Vader

| Date | Mintage | VF20 | XF40 | MS60 | MS63 | MS65 |
|---|---|---|---|---|---|---|
| 2011 | — | — | — | — | — | 25.00 |

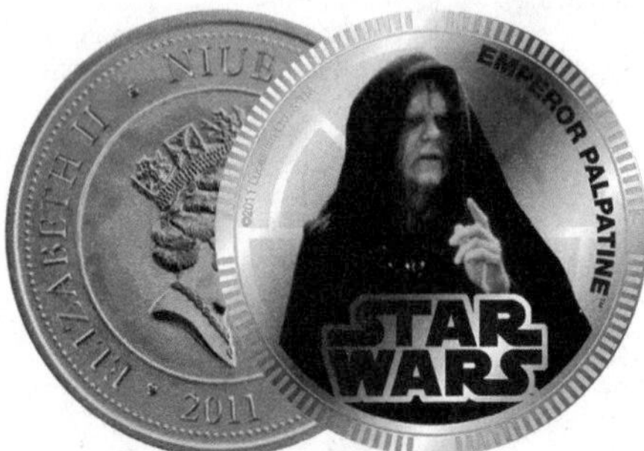


**KM# 660 DOLLAR**
Silver Plated Copper, 40 mm. **Ruler:** Elizabeth II **Subject:** Star Wars - Emperor Palpatine

| Date | Mintage | VF20 | XF40 | MS60 | MS63 | MS65 |
|---|---|---|---|---|---|---|
| 2011 | Est. 50000 | — | — | — | — | 25.00 |

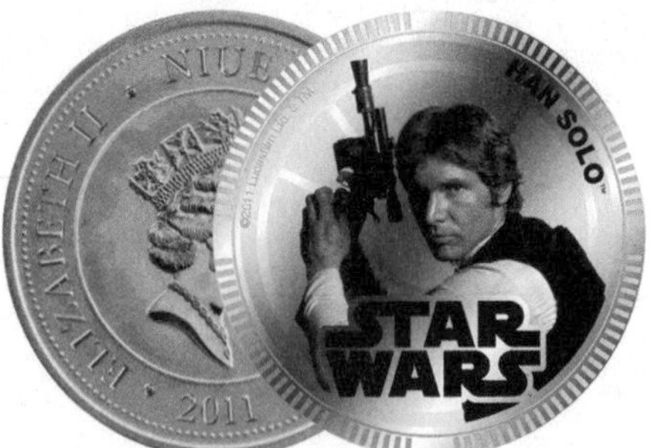


**KM# 661 DOLLAR**
Silver Plated Copper, 40 mm. **Ruler:** Elizabeth II **Subject:** Star Wars - Han Solo

| Date | Mintage | VF20 | XF40 | MS60 | MS63 | MS65 |
|---|---|---|---|---|---|---|
| 2011 | — | — | — | — | — | 25.00 |

## KM# 662 DOLLAR

Silver Plated Copper, 40 mm. **Ruler:** Elizabeth II **Subject:** Star Wars - Chewbacca

| Date | Mintage | VF20 | XF40 | MS60 | MS63 | MS65 |
|---|---|---|---|---|---|---|
| 2011 | Est. 50000 | — | — | — | — | 25.00 |

## KM# 674 DOLLAR

28.28 g., 0.925 Silver 0.841 oz. ASW, 40x28 mm. **Ruler:** Elizabeth II **Rev:** Orville and Wilbur Wright **Shape:** Rectangle

| Date | Mintage | VF20 | XF40 | MS60 | MS63 | MS65 |
|---|---|---|---|---|---|---|
| 2011 | Est. 6000 | PF65 75.00 | | | | |

## KM# 688 DOLLAR

16.81 g., 0.925 Silver 0.4999 oz. ASW gilt, 38.61 mm. **Ruler:** Elizabeth II **Subject:** Amber Route **Rev:** Map of European cities

| Date | Mintage | VF20 | XF40 | MS60 | MS63 | MS65 |
|---|---|---|---|---|---|---|
| 2011 | Est. 15000 | PF65 85.00 | | | | |

## KM# 690 DOLLAR

28.28 g., 0.925 Silver 0.841 oz. ASW, 40.7 mm. **Ruler:** Elizabeth II **Subject:** Lucky-coin - Ladybug **Obv:** Head with tiara right, ladybug and flowers **Rev:** Ladybug and flowers

| Date | Mintage | VF20 | XF40 | MS60 | MS63 | MS65 |
|---|---|---|---|---|---|---|
| 2011 | Est. 10000 | PF65 80.00 | | | | |

## KM# 703 DOLLAR

10.00 g., 0.925 Silver 0.2974 oz. ASW, 13x30 mm. **Ruler:** Elizabeth II **Rev:** Amber insert in gilt floral motif **Shape:** Vertical rectangle

| Date | Mintage | VF20 | XF40 | MS60 | MS63 | MS65 |
|---|---|---|---|---|---|---|
| 2011 | Est. 12000 | — | — | — | — | 50.00 |

## KM# 704 DOLLAR

28.28 g., 0.925 Silver 0.841 oz. ASW, 30x50 mm. **Ruler:** Elizabeth II **Subject:** Barcerlona Cathedral **Obv:** Cross and interior cathedral view **Rev:** Exterior cathedral view **Shape:** Oval

| Date | Mintage | VF20 | XF40 | MS60 | MS63 | MS65 |
|---|---|---|---|---|---|---|
| 2011 | 5,000 | PF65 100 | | | | |

## KM# 705 DOLLAR

28.28 g., 0.925 Silver 0.841 oz. ASW, 30x50 mm. **Ruler:** Elizabeth II **Subject:** Prague's St. Wenceslas Cathedral **Obv:** Cathedral window at top, side exterior view below **Rev:** Cathedral window and ceiling motif **Shape:** Vertical Oval

| Date | Mintage | VF20 | XF40 | MS60 | MS63 | MS65 |
|---|---|---|---|---|---|---|
| 2011 | 5,000 | PF65 100 | | | | |

## KM# 706 DOLLAR

28.28 g., 0.925 Silver 0.841 oz. ASW, 30x50 mm. **Ruler:** Elizabeth II **Subject:** Cracow's St. Mary Cathedral **Obv:** Cathedral window and sculpture scene **Rev:** Cathedral Window, exterior view and ceiling rendering **Shape:** Vertical oval

| Date | Mintage | VF20 | XF40 | MS60 | MS63 | MS65 |
|---|---|---|---|---|---|---|
| 2011 | 1,500 | PF65 100 | | | | |

## KM# 707 DOLLAR

28.28 g., 0.925 Silver 0.841 oz. ASW, 35x45 mm. **Ruler:** Elizabeth II **Subject:** Love Love Love **Obv:** Queens head within open egg design **Rev:** Two cherubs and heart **Shape:** Vertical oval

| Date | Mintage | VF20 | XF40 | MS60 | MS63 | MS65 |
|---|---|---|---|---|---|---|
| 2011 | 7,000 | PF65 100 | | | | |

## KM# 709 DOLLAR

16.81 g., 0.925 Silver 0.4999 oz. ASW, 38.61 mm. **Ruler:** Elizabeth II **Obv:** Ancient horsecart **Obv. Legend:** SZLAK BURSZTYNOWY **Rev:** Neptune statue, ancient coin, mine building, amber insert **Rev. Legend:** GDANSK

| Date | Mintage | VF20 | XF40 | MS60 | MS63 | MS65 |
|---|---|---|---|---|---|---|
| 2011 | Est. 12000 | PF65 90.00 | | | | |

## KM# 711 DOLLAR

14.14 g., 0.925 Silver 0.4205 oz. ASW, 32 mm. **Ruler:** Elizabeth II **Subject:** Russian Cartoon - Reksio **Rev:** Dog, cat and rooster in color

| Date | Mintage | VF20 | XF40 | MS60 | MS63 | MS65 |
|---|---|---|---|---|---|---|
| 2011 | Est. 6000 | PF65 100 | | | | |

## KM# 741 DOLLAR

28.28 g., 0.925 Silver 0.841 oz. ASW **Ruler:** Elizabeth II **Obv:** Head crowned at top, key **Rev:** Cat walking through open door **Shape:** Irregular

| Date | Mintage | VF20 | XF40 | MS60 | MS63 | MS65 |
|---|---|---|---|---|---|---|
| 2011 | 7,000 | PF65 75.00 | | | | |

**KM# 942 DOLLAR**
28.28 g., 0.925 Silver 0.841 oz. ASW, 38.61 mm. **Ruler:** Elizabeth II **Subject:** Hanseatic Towns: Rostock

| Date | Mintage | VF20 | XF40 | MS60 | MS63 | MS65 |
|---|---|---|---|---|---|---|
| 2011 | Est. 8000 | **PF65** 85.00 | | | | |

**KM# 644 DOLLAR**
28.28 g., 0.925 Silver 0.841 oz. ASW, 35.1x45.1 mm. **Ruler:** Elizabeth II **Subject:** Year of the Dragon **Obv:** Head with crown right **Rev:** Multicolor dragon **Shape:** Vertical oval

| Date | Mintage | VF20 | XF40 | MS60 | MS63 | MS65 |
|---|---|---|---|---|---|---|
| 2012 | 5,000 | **PF65** 100 | | | | |

**KM# 645 DOLLAR**
28.28 g., 0.925 Silver 0.841 oz. ASW, 35.1x45.1 mm. **Ruler:** Elizabeth II **Subject:** Year of the Dragon **Obv:** Head with crown right **Rev:** Multicolor juvenile dragon **Shape:** Vertical oval

| Date | Mintage | VF20 | XF40 | MS60 | MS63 | MS65 |
|---|---|---|---|---|---|---|
| 2012 | 5,000 | **PF65** 100 | | | | |

**KM# 646 DOLLAR**
28.28 g., 0.925 Silver 0.841 oz. ASW, 45.1x35.1 mm. **Ruler:** Elizabeth II **Subject:** Year of the Dragon **Obv:** Head with crown right **Rev:** Multicolor Love dragon forming heart **Shape:** Horizontal oval

| Date | Mintage | VF20 | XF40 | MS60 | MS63 | MS65 |
|---|---|---|---|---|---|---|
| 2012 | 5,000 | **PF65** 100 | | | | |

**KM# 687 DOLLAR**
31.11 g., 0.925 Silver 0.925 oz. ASW, 39 mm. **Ruler:** Elizabeth II **Rev:** Crowned fantasy fish **Shape:** 12-sided

| Date | Mintage | VF20 | XF40 | MS60 | MS63 | MS65 |
|---|---|---|---|---|---|---|
| 2012 | 2,000 | **PF65** 80.00 | | | | |

**KM# 725 DOLLAR**
Nickel Plated Copper, 40.7 mm. **Ruler:** Elizabeth II **Subject:** Star Wars - Tusken Raider

| Date | Mintage | VF20 | XF40 | MS60 | MS63 | MS65 |
|---|---|---|---|---|---|---|
| 2012 | 50,000 | — | — | — | — | 25.00 |

**KM# 726 DOLLAR**
Nickel Plated Copper, 40.7 mm. **Ruler:** Elizabeth II **Subject:** Star Wars - Ewok Wicket

| Date | Mintage | VF20 | XF40 | MS60 | MS63 | MS65 |
|---|---|---|---|---|---|---|
| 2012 | 50,000 | — | — | — | — | 25.00 |

**KM# 727 DOLLAR**
Silver, 40.7 mm. **Ruler:** Elizabeth II **Subject:** Star Wars - Nien Nunb

| Date | Mintage | VF20 | XF40 | MS60 | MS63 | MS65 |
|---|---|---|---|---|---|---|
| 2012 | 50,000 | — | — | — | — | 25.00 |

**KM# 728 DOLLAR**
Nickel Plated Copper, 40.7 mm. **Ruler:** Elizabeth II **Subject:** Star Wars - Lando Calrissian

| Date | Mintage | VF20 | XF40 | MS60 | MS63 | MS65 |
|---|---|---|---|---|---|---|
| 2012 | 50,000 | — | — | — | — | 25.00 |

**KM# 729 DOLLAR**
Nickel Plated Copper, 40.7 mm. **Ruler:** Elizabeth II **Subject:** Star Wars - Grand Moff Tarkin

| Date | Mintage | VF20 | XF40 | MS60 | MS63 | MS65 |
|---|---|---|---|---|---|---|
| 2012 | 50,000 | — | — | — | — | 25.00 |

**KM# 730 DOLLAR**
Nickel Plated Copper, 40.7 mm. **Ruler:** Elizabeth II **Subject:** Star Wars - Stormtrooper

| Date | Mintage | VF20 | XF40 | MS60 | MS63 | MS65 |
|---|---|---|---|---|---|---|
| 2012 | 50,000 | — | — | — | — | 25.00 |

**KM# 731 DOLLAR**
Nickel Plated Copper, 40.7 mm. **Ruler:** Elizabeth II **Subject:** Star Wars - Jabba the Hutt

| Date | Mintage | VF20 | XF40 | MS60 | MS63 | MS65 |
|---|---|---|---|---|---|---|
| 2012 | 50,000 | — | — | — | — | 25.00 |

**KM# 732 DOLLAR**
Nickel Plated Copper, 40.7 mm. **Ruler:** Elizabeth II **Subject:** Star Wars - Admiral Ackbar

| Date | Mintage | VF20 | XF40 | MS60 | MS63 | MS65 |
|---|---|---|---|---|---|---|
| 2012 | 50,000 | — | — | — | — | 25.00 |

**KM# 733 DOLLAR**
Nickel Plated Copper, 40.7 mm. **Ruler:** Elizabeth II **Subject:** Star Wars - Jawa

| Date | Mintage | VF20 | XF40 | MS60 | MS63 | MS65 |
|---|---|---|---|---|---|---|
| 2012 | 50,000 | — | — | — | — | 25.00 |

**KM# 734 DOLLAR**
Nickel Plated Copper, 40.7 mm. **Ruler:** Elizabeth II **Subject:** Star Wars - Boba Fett

| Date | Mintage | VF20 | XF40 | MS60 | MS63 | MS65 |
|---|---|---|---|---|---|---|
| 2012 | 50,000 | — | — | — | — | 25.00 |

**KM# 735 DOLLAR**
28.28 g., 0.925 Silver 0.841 oz. ASW, 38.61 mm. **Ruler:** Elizabeth II **Subject:** Hannibal Barkas **Obv:** Two elephant heads facing each other **Rev:** Hannibal's head left above three war elephants

| Date | Mintage | VF20 | XF40 | MS60 | MS63 | MS65 |
|---|---|---|---|---|---|---|
| 2012 | Est. 5000 | PF65 120 | | | | |

**KM# 739 DOLLAR**
15.55 g., 0.999 Silver 0.4994 oz. ASW, 36 mm. **Ruler:** Elizabeth II **Subject:** Viet Nam War, 50th Anniversary of Australia's involvement **Rev:** Two soldiers on patrol, on close, helicopter above

| Date | Mintage | VF20 | XF40 | MS60 | MS63 | MS65 |
|---|---|---|---|---|---|---|
| 2012 | 2,500 | PF65 50.00 | | | | |

**KM# 757 DOLLAR**
25.00 g., 0.925 Silver 0.7435 oz. ASW, 40 mm. **Ruler:** Elizabeth II **Subject:** Battle for Australia - Bombing of Darwin **Rev:** Soldier with machine gun post and Japanese plane in sky, ship in distance

| Date | Mintage | VF20 | XF40 | MS60 | MS63 | MS65 |
|---|---|---|---|---|---|---|
| 2012 | Est. 1942 | PF65 75.00 | | | | |

**KM# 758 DOLLAR**
25.00 g., 0.925 Silver 0.7435 oz. ASW, 40 mm. **Ruler:** Elizabeth II **Subject:** Battle for Australia - Sydney Harbor **Rev:** Sub, ship and pontoon plane with Sydney Harbor bridge

| Date | Mintage | VF20 | XF40 | MS60 | MS63 | MS65 |
|---|---|---|---|---|---|---|
| 2012 | Est. 1942 | PF65 100 | | | | |

**KM# 759 DOLLAR**
25.00 g., 0.925 Silver 0.7435 oz. ASW, 40 mm. **Ruler:** Elizabeth II **Subject:** Battle for Australia - Kokoda Track **Rev:** Two injured soldiers being protected by third

| Date | Mintage | VF20 | XF40 | MS60 | MS63 | MS65 |
|---|---|---|---|---|---|---|
| 2012 | Est. 1942 | PF65 100 | | | | |

**KM# 760 DOLLAR**
25.00 g., 0.925 Silver 0.7435 oz. ASW, 40 mm. **Ruler:** Elizabeth II **Subject:** Battle for Australia - Coral Sea **Rev:** Battle ship and planes

| Date | Mintage | VF20 | XF40 | MS60 | MS63 | MS65 |
|---|---|---|---|---|---|---|
| 2012 | Est. 1942 | PF65 100 | | | | |

**KM# 761 DOLLAR**
25.00 g., 0.925 Silver 0.7435 oz. ASW, 40 mm. **Ruler:** Elizabeth II **Subject:** First car to cross Australia - The Brush **Obv:** Head with crown right **Rev:** Early automobile, color landscape below

| Date | Mintage | VF20 | XF40 | MS60 | MS63 | MS65 |
|---|---|---|---|---|---|---|
| 2012 | Est. 2500 | PF65 100 | | | | |

**KM# 763 DOLLAR**
28.28 g., 0.925 Silver 0.841 oz. ASW, 30x50 mm. **Ruler:** Elizabeth II **Rev:** Fisherman and nice trout **Rev. Legend:** BEGINNER'S LUCK **Shape:** Vertical oval

| Date | Mintage | VF20 | XF40 | MS60 | MS63 | MS65 |
|---|---|---|---|---|---|---|
| 2012 | Est. 7000 | PF65 120 | | | | |

**KM# 764 DOLLAR**
28.28 g., 0.925 Silver 0.841 oz. ASW, 28x40 mm. **Ruler:** Elizabeth II **Subject:** Ksenia of Petersburg **Rev:** Female saint with cane, church at lower left **Shape:** Vertical rectangle

| Date | Mintage | VF20 | XF40 | MS60 | MS63 | MS65 |
|---|---|---|---|---|---|---|
| 2012 | Est. 7000 | PF65 100 | | | | |

**KM# 765 DOLLAR**
28.28 g., 0.925 Silver 0.841 oz. ASW, 38.61 mm. **Ruler:** Elizabeth II **Subject:** Russian Cities - Kuzbas **Rev:** Statue of Worker, gear in background

| Date | Mintage | VF20 | XF40 | MS60 | MS63 | MS65 |
|---|---|---|---|---|---|---|
| 2012 | Est. 4000 | PF65 100 | | | | |

**KM# 766 DOLLAR**
28.28 g., 0.925 Silver 0.841 oz. ASW, 38.61 mm. **Ruler:** Elizabeth II **Subject:** Russian Cities - Novosibirsk **Rev:** Church tower, bridge in distance

| Date | Mintage | VF20 | XF40 | MS60 | MS63 | MS65 |
|---|---|---|---|---|---|---|
| 2012 | Est. 2000 | PF65 100 | | | | |

**KM# 767 DOLLAR**
28.28 g., 0.925 Silver 0.841 oz. ASW, 38.61 mm. **Ruler:** Elizabeth II **Subject:** Stars Flight **Rev:** International Space Station and Russian stamp

| Date | Mintage | VF20 | XF40 | MS60 | MS63 | MS65 |
|---|---|---|---|---|---|---|
| 2012 | Est. 5000 | PF65 100 | | | | |

## KM# 768 DOLLAR

28.28 g., 0.925 Silver 0.841 oz. ASW, 38.61 mm. **Ruler:** Elizabeth II **Subject:** War of 1812 - Artillery **Rev:** Soldier standing beside cannon

| Date | Mintage | VF20 | XF40 | MS60 | MS63 | MS65 |
|---|---|---|---|---|---|---|
| 2012 | Est. 5000 | PF65 100 | | | | |

## KM# 769 DOLLAR

28.28 g., 0.925 Silver 0.841 oz. ASW, 38.61 mm. **Ruler:** Elizabeth II **Subject:** War of 1812 - Cavalry **Rev:** Horseman with sword

| Date | Mintage | VF20 | XF40 | MS60 | MS63 | MS65 |
|---|---|---|---|---|---|---|
| 2012 | — | PF65 100 | | | | |

## KM# 770 DOLLAR

28.28 g., 0.925 Silver 0.841 oz. ASW, 38.61 mm. **Ruler:** Elizabeth II **Subject:** War of 1812 - Infantry **Rev:** Soldier with rifle

| Date | Mintage | VF20 | XF40 | MS60 | MS63 | MS65 |
|---|---|---|---|---|---|---|
| 2012 | Est. 5000 | PF65 100 | | | | |

## KM# 771 DOLLAR

28.28 g., 0.925 Silver 0.841 oz. ASW, 38.61 mm. **Ruler:** Elizabeth II **Subject:** War of 1812 - Generals

| Date | Mintage | VF20 | XF40 | MS60 | MS63 | MS65 |
|---|---|---|---|---|---|---|
| 2012 | — | PF65 100 | | | | |

## KM# 772 DOLLAR

27.50 g., Silver Plated Copper-Nickel, 40 mm. **Ruler:** Elizabeth II **Subject:** Benedict XVI's visit to Brazil, 5th Anniversary **Rev:** Statue of Nossa Senhora, image of Benedict

| Date | Mintage | VF20 | XF40 | MS60 | MS63 | MS65 |
|---|---|---|---|---|---|---|
| 2012 | Est. 1000 | PF65 25.00 | | | | |

## KM# 773 DOLLAR

16.81 g., 0.925 Silver 0.4999 oz. ASW, 38.61 mm. **Ruler:** Elizabeth II **Subject:** Stare Hradisko **Obv:** Queen's head at left, two horse cart at right **Rev:** Celtic coin image and art, amber insert

| Date | Mintage | VF20 | XF40 | MS60 | MS63 | MS65 |
|---|---|---|---|---|---|---|
| 2012 | Est. 12000 | PF65 65.00 | | | | |

## KM# 775 DOLLAR

16.81 g., 0.925 Silver 0.4999 oz. ASW, 29x39 mm. **Ruler:** Elizabeth II **Subject:** Imperial Faberge Eggs - Coronation egg **Rev:** Egg and state coach

| Date | Mintage | VF20 | XF40 | MS60 | MS63 | MS65 |
|---|---|---|---|---|---|---|
| 2012 | Est. 9999 | PF65 95.00 | | | | |

## KM# 779 DOLLAR

16.81 g., 0.925 Silver 0.4999 oz. ASW, 38.61 mm. **Ruler:** Elizabeth II **Subject:** Silk Route - Wroclaw **Obv:** Queen's head at left, two horse cart at right **Rev:** Old building at left, statue at right

| Date | Mintage | VF20 | XF40 | MS60 | MS63 | MS65 |
|---|---|---|---|---|---|---|
| 2012 | Est. 12000 | PF65 85.00 | | | | |

## KM# 781 DOLLAR

28.28 g., 0.925 Silver 0.841 oz. ASW, 38.61 mm. **Ruler:** Elizabeth II **Subject:** March 8th, International Woman's Day **Obv:** Head with tiara right **Rev:** Flowers, date in Russian

| Date | Mintage | VF20 | XF40 | MS60 | MS63 | MS65 |
|---|---|---|---|---|---|---|
| 2012 | Est. 2000 | PF65 75.00 | | | | |

## KM# 787 DOLLAR

0.30 g., 0.999 Gold 0.0096 oz. AGW, 11 mm. **Ruler:** Elizabeth II **Obv:** Head with tiara right **Rev:** Princess Grace of Monaco (Grace Kelly) head left

| Date | Mintage | VF20 | XF40 | MS60 | MS63 | MS65 |
|---|---|---|---|---|---|---|
| 2012 | — | PF65 75.00 | | | | |

## KM# 790 DOLLAR

28.28 g., 0.925 Silver 0.841 oz. ASW, 28x40 mm. **Ruler:** Elizabeth II **Subject:** Art of Hunting, Fox Hunt **Obv:** Pointer, left **Rev:** Fox, hounds and riders **Shape:** Vertical rectangle

| Date | Mintage | VF20 | XF40 | MS60 | MS63 | MS65 |
|---|---|---|---|---|---|---|
| 2012 | 4,000 | PF65 120 | | | | |

## KM# 792 DOLLAR

14.14 g., 0.925 Silver 0.4205 oz. ASW, 49.9x32.8x9.15 mm. **Ruler:** Elizabeth II **Subject:** Swallow's Nest **Obv:** Island view **Rev:** Castle atop cliff **Shape:** Irregular

| Date | Mintage | VF20 | XF40 | MS60 | MS63 | MS65 |
|---|---|---|---|---|---|---|
| 2012 | Est. 3000 | PF65 100 | | | | |

## KM# 794 DOLLAR

16.81 g., 0.925 Silver 0.4999 oz. ASW, 38.61 mm. **Ruler:** Elizabeth II **Subject:** Szlak Bursztynowy - Szombathely **Rev:** Old coin, building, amber insert

| Date | Mintage | VF20 | XF40 | MS60 | MS63 | MS65 |
|---|---|---|---|---|---|---|
| 2012 | Est. 12000 | PF65 75.00 | | | | |

## KM# 800 DOLLAR

28.28 g., 0.925 Silver 0.841 oz. ASW, 38.61 mm. **Ruler:** Elizabeth II **Rev:** Goliath Birdwing butterfly **Rev. Legend:** ORNITHOPTERA GOLIATH

| Date | Mintage | VF20 | XF40 | MS60 | MS63 | MS65 |
|---|---|---|---|---|---|---|
| 2012 | Est. 8000 | PF65 100 | | | | |

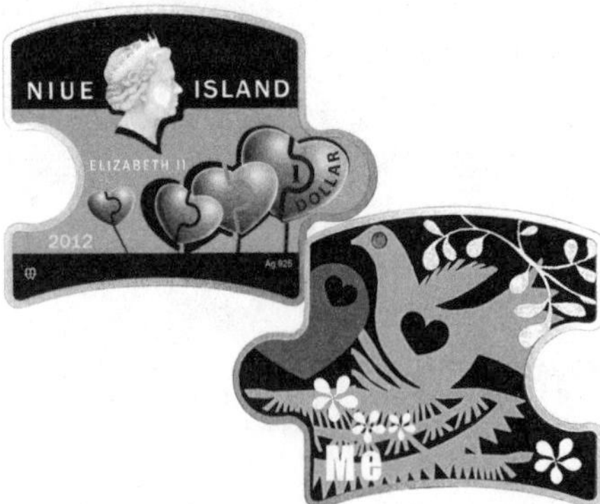


## KM# 804 DOLLAR

14.14 g., 0.925 Silver 0.4205 oz. ASW, 37x30 mm. **Ruler:** Elizabeth II **Subject:** Me **Obv:** Queen's head with tiara right, four baloon hearts **Rev:** Bird facing left **Shape:** Irregular

| Date | Mintage | VF20 | XF40 | MS60 | MS63 | MS65 |
|---|---|---|---|---|---|---|
| 2012 | Est. 10000 | PF65 75.00 | | | | |

**KM# 805 DOLLAR**
14.14 g., 0.925 Silver 0.4205 oz. ASW, 37x30 mm. **Ruler:** Elizabeth II **Subject:** You **Obv:** Queen's head in tiara at right, three heart baloons **Rev:** Bird facing right **Shape:** Irregular

| Date | Mintage | VF20 | XF40 | MS60 | MS63 | MS65 |
|---|---|---|---|---|---|---|
| 2012 | Est. 10000 | PF65 75.00 | | | | |

**KM# 828 DOLLAR**
28.28 g., 0.925 Silver 0.841 oz. ASW, 36.61 mm. **Ruler:** Elizabeth II **Obv:** Crowned ehad right within soccer ball motif **Rev:** Poznan stadium

| Date | Mintage | VF20 | XF40 | MS60 | MS63 | MS65 |
|---|---|---|---|---|---|---|
| 2012 | 1,000 | PF65 90.00 | | | | |

**KM# 829 DOLLAR**
28.28 g., 0.925 Silver 0.841 oz. ASW, 38.61 mm. **Ruler:** Elizabeth II **Obv:** Head in tiara right within soccer ball motif **Rev:** Wroclaw stadium

| Date | Mintage | VF20 | XF40 | MS60 | MS63 | MS65 |
|---|---|---|---|---|---|---|
| 2012 | 1,000 | PF65 90.00 | | | | |

**KM# 830 DOLLAR**
28.28 g., 0.925 Silver 0.841 oz. ASW, 38.61 mm. **Ruler:** Elizabeth II **Obv:** Head with tiara right within soccer ball motif **Rev:** Lviv stadium

| Date | Mintage | VF20 | XF40 | MS60 | MS63 | MS65 |
|---|---|---|---|---|---|---|
| 2012 | 1,000 | PF65 90.00 | | | | |

**KM# 831 DOLLAR**
28.28 g., 0.925 Silver 0.841 oz. ASW, 38.61 mm. **Ruler:** Elizabeth II **Obv:** Head with tiara right within soccer ball motif **Rev:** Kiev stadium

| Date | Mintage | VF20 | XF40 | MS60 | MS63 | MS65 |
|---|---|---|---|---|---|---|
| 2012 | 1,000 | PF65 90.00 | | | | |

**KM# 832 DOLLAR**
28.28 g., 0.925 Silver 0.841 oz. ASW, 38.61 mm. **Ruler:** Elizabeth II **Obv:** Head with tiara right within soccer ball motif **Rev:** Donetsk stadium

| Date | Mintage | VF20 | XF40 | MS60 | MS63 | MS65 |
|---|---|---|---|---|---|---|
| 2012 | 1,000 | PF65 90.00 | | | | |

**KM# 833 DOLLAR**
28.28 g., 0.925 Silver 0.841 oz. ASW, 38.61 mm. **Ruler:** Elizabeth II **Obv:** Head with tiara right within soccer ball motif **Rev:** Kharkiv stadium

| Date | Mintage | VF20 | XF40 | MS60 | MS63 | MS65 |
|---|---|---|---|---|---|---|
| 2012 | 1,000 | PF65 90.00 | | | | |

**KM# 841 DOLLAR**
16.81 g., 0.925 Silver 0.4999 oz. ASW, 38.61 mm. **Ruler:** Elizabeth II **Subject:** Amber Route **Obv:** Head with tiara at left, cart, map **Rev:** Ruins, statue, coin and amber insert **Rev. Legend:** CARNUNTUM

| Date | Mintage | VF20 | XF40 | MS60 | MS63 | MS65 |
|---|---|---|---|---|---|---|
| 2012 | 12,000 | PF65 65.00 | | | | |

**KM# 843 DOLLAR**
16.81 g., 0.925 Silver 0.4999 oz. ASW, 38.61 mm. **Ruler:** Elizabeth II **Subject:** Amber Route **Obv:** Head with tiara at left, cart, map **Rev:** She-wolf statue, mosaic, coin and amber insert **Rev. Legend:** AQUILEIA

| Date | Mintage | VF20 | XF40 | MS60 | MS63 | MS65 |
|---|---|---|---|---|---|---|
| 2012 | 12,000 | PF65 65.00 | | | | |

**KM# 847 DOLLAR**
0.999 Silver **Ruler:** Elizabeth II **Obv:** Crowned head right **Rev:** Statue of Amore and Psyche **Shape:** Irregular

| Date | Mintage | VF20 | XF40 | MS60 | MS63 | MS65 |
|---|---|---|---|---|---|---|
| 2012 | 1,000 | PF65 50.00 | | | | |

**KM# 848 DOLLAR**
0.999 Silver, 38.61 mm. **Ruler:** Elizabeth II **Obv:** Crowned head at left **Rev:** Amor and Psyche statue cut out in center

| Date | Mintage | VF20 | XF40 | MS60 | MS63 | MS65 |
|---|---|---|---|---|---|---|
| 2012 | 1,000 | PF65 50.00 | | | | |

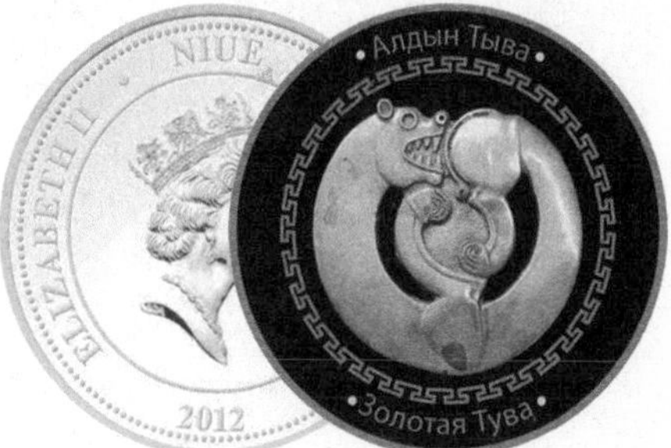


**KM# 852 DOLLAR**
28.28 g., 0.925 Silver 0.841 oz. ASW, 38.61 mm. **Ruler:** Elizabeth II **Subject:** Russian Municipalties - Tyra **Obv:** Crowned head right **Rev:** Ancient carving

| Date | Mintage | VF20 | XF40 | MS60 | MS63 | MS65 |
|---|---|---|---|---|---|---|
| 2012 | 2,000 | PF65 100 | | | | |

**KM# 853 DOLLAR**
20.00 g., 0.999 Silver 0.6424 oz. ASW, 40 mm. **Ruler:** Elizabeth II **Obv:** Crowned head right **Rev:** Vysotsky head at right

| Date | Mintage | VF20 | XF40 | MS60 | MS63 | MS65 |
|---|---|---|---|---|---|---|
| 2012 | 5,000 | PF65 100 | | | | |

**KM# 854 DOLLAR**
28.28 g., 0.925 Silver 0.841 oz. ASW, 38.61 mm. **Ruler:** Elizabeth II **Obv:** Crowned head right **Rev:** Alexander Nevski at right, warriors on horseback at left.

| Date | Mintage | VF20 | XF40 | MS60 | MS63 | MS65 |
|---|---|---|---|---|---|---|
| 2012 | 5,000 | PF65 100 | | | | |

**KM# 855 DOLLAR**
16.81 g., 0.925 Silver 0.4999 oz. ASW, 29x39 mm. **Ruler:** Elizabeth II **Obv:** Head with tiara right above open egg **Rev:** Imperial Faberge Egg - Cockerel Egg

| Date | Mintage | VF20 | XF40 | MS60 | MS63 | MS65 |
|---|---|---|---|---|---|---|
| 2012 | Est. 9999 | PF65 95.00 | | | | |

**KM# 877 DOLLAR**
28.28 g., 0.925 Silver 0.841 oz. ASW, 41 mm. **Ruler:** Elizabeth II **Obv:** Head with tiara right above snake insert **Rev:** Two snakes forming heart shape, snake insert below

| Date | Mintage | VF20 | XF40 | MS60 | MS63 | MS65 |
|---|---|---|---|---|---|---|
| 2012//2013 | Est. 10000 | PF65 85.00 | | | | |

**KM# 878 DOLLAR**
16.81 g., 0.925 Silver 0.4999 oz. ASW, 38.61 mm. **Ruler:** Elizabeth II **Obv:** Head with tiara right **Rev:** Snake coiled around itself

| Date | Mintage | VF20 | XF40 | MS60 | MS63 | MS65 |
|---|---|---|---|---|---|---|
| 2012//2013 | Est. 10000 | PF65 50.00 | | | | |

**KM# 879 DOLLAR**
28.28 g., 0.925 Silver 0.841 oz. ASW, 38.61 mm. **Ruler:** Elizabeth II **Obv:** Head with tiara right **Rev:** Two rabbits holding heart

| Date | Mintage | VF20 | XF40 | MS60 | MS63 | MS65 |
|---|---|---|---|---|---|---|
| 2012 | Est. 15000 | PF65 100 | | | | |

**KM# 892 DOLLAR**
28.28 g., 0.925 Silver 0.841 oz. ASW, 35 x 45 mm. **Ruler:** Elizabeth II **Subject:** Iverskaya Chapel

| Date | Mintage | VF20 | XF40 | MS60 | MS63 | MS65 |
|---|---|---|---|---|---|---|
| 2012 | Est. 7000 | PF65 110 | | | | |

**KM# 893 DOLLAR**
28.28 g., 0.925 Silver 0.841 oz. ASW, 28.61 mm. **Ruler:** Elizabeth II **Subject:** Pskov

| Date | Mintage | VF20 | XF40 | MS60 | MS63 | MS65 |
|---|---|---|---|---|---|---|
| 2012 | Est. 2000 | PF65 120 | | | | |

**KM# 894 DOLLAR**
28.28 g., 0.925 Silver 0.841 oz. ASW, 28 x 40 mm. **Ruler:** Elizabeth II **Subject:** Saints of the Cities: John of Kronshtadt

| Date | Mintage | VF20 | XF40 | MS60 | MS63 | MS65 |
|---|---|---|---|---|---|---|
| 2012 | Est. 7000 | PF65 100 | | | | |

**KM# 895 DOLLAR**
28.28 g., 0.925 Silver 0.841 oz. ASW, 28 x 40 mm. **Ruler:** Elizabeth II **Subject:** Saints of the Cities: St. Matrona

| Date | Mintage | VF20 | XF40 | MS60 | MS63 | MS65 |
|---|---|---|---|---|---|---|
| 2012 | Est. 7000 | PF65 100 | | | | |

**KM# 899 DOLLAR**
31.10 g., 0.999 Silver 0.9989 oz. ASW, 32 mm. **Ruler:** Elizabeth II **Subject:** Merentibus Silver

| Date | Mintage | VF20 | XF40 | MS60 | MS63 | MS65 |
|---|---|---|---|---|---|---|
| 2012 | Est. 5000 | PF65 80.00 | | | | |

**KM# 900 DOLLAR**
0.999 Silver **Ruler:** Elizabeth II **Subject:** Durer Codex: Dürer Coat of Arms

| Date | Mintage | VF20 | XF40 | MS60 | MS63 | MS65 |
|---|---|---|---|---|---|---|
| 2012 | Est. 300 | PF65 170 | | | | |

**KM# 901 DOLLAR**
0.999 Silver **Ruler:** Elizabeth II **Subject:** Durer Codex: Adam & Eve

| Date | Mintage | VF20 | XF40 | MS60 | MS63 | MS65 |
|---|---|---|---|---|---|---|
| 2012 | Est. 300 | PF65 170 | | | | |

**KM# 902 DOLLAR**
0.999 Silver **Ruler:** Elizabeth II **Subject:** Durer Codex: Melencolia I

| Date | Mintage | VF20 | XF40 | MS60 | MS63 | MS65 |
|---|---|---|---|---|---|---|
| 2012 | Est. 300 | PF65 170 | | | | |

**KM# 903 DOLLAR**
0.999 Silver **Ruler:** Elizabeth II **Subject:** Durer Codex: The Southern Hemisphere

| Date | Mintage | VF20 | XF40 | MS60 | MS63 | MS65 |
|---|---|---|---|---|---|---|
| 2012 | Est. 300 | PF65 170 | | | | |

**KM# 904 DOLLAR**
0.999 Silver **Ruler:** Elizabeth II **Subject:** Durer Codex: The Sun of Justice

| Date | Mintage | VF20 | XF40 | MS60 | MS63 | MS65 |
|---|---|---|---|---|---|---|
| 2012 | Est. 300 | PF65 170 | | | | |

**KM# 905 DOLLAR**
0.999 Silver **Ruler:** Elizabeth II **Subject:** Durer Codex: Praying Hands

| Date | Mintage | VF20 | XF40 | MS60 | MS63 | MS65 |
|---|---|---|---|---|---|---|
| 2012 | Est. 300 | PF65 170 | | | | |

**KM# 906 DOLLAR**
0.999 Silver **Ruler:** Elizabeth II **Subject:** Durer Codex: Small Triumpal Car

| Date | Mintage | VF20 | XF40 | MS60 | MS63 | MS65 |
|---|---|---|---|---|---|---|
| 2012 | Est. 300 | PF65 170 | | | | |

**KM# 907 DOLLAR**
0.999 Silver **Ruler:** Elizabeth II **Subject:** Durer Codex: Hercules kills the birds symphalic

| Date | Mintage | VF20 | XF40 | MS60 | MS63 | MS65 |
|---|---|---|---|---|---|---|
| 2012 | Est. 300 | PF65 170 | | | | |

**KM# 908 DOLLAR**
0.999 Silver **Ruler:** Elizabeth II **Subject:** Durer Codex: Apollo with Solar Disc

| Date | Mintage | VF20 | XF40 | MS60 | MS63 | MS65 |
|---|---|---|---|---|---|---|
| 2012 | Est. 300 | PF65 170 | | | | |

**KM# 909 DOLLAR**
0.999 Silver **Ruler:** Elizabeth II **Subject:** Durer Codex: Praying Hands

| Date | Mintage | VF20 | XF40 | MS60 | MS63 | MS65 |
|---|---|---|---|---|---|---|
| 2012 | Est. 300 | PF65 170 | | | | |

**KM# 910 DOLLAR**
0.999 Silver **Ruler:** Elizabeth II **Subject:** Durer Codex: Hands of Christ

| Date | Mintage | VF20 | XF40 | MS60 | MS63 | MS65 |
|---|---|---|---|---|---|---|
| 2012 | Est. 300 | PF65 170 | | | | |

**KM# 911 DOLLAR**
0.999 Silver **Ruler:** Elizabeth II **Subject:** Durer Codex: Madonna with music making Angel

| Date | Mintage | VF20 | XF40 | MS60 | MS63 | MS65 |
|---|---|---|---|---|---|---|
| 2012 | Est. 300 | PF65 170 | | | | |

**KM# 912 DOLLAR**
0.999 Silver **Ruler:** Elizabeth II **Subject:** Durer Codex: Nemesis

| Date | Mintage | VF20 | XF40 | MS60 | MS63 | MS65 |
|---|---|---|---|---|---|---|
| 2012 | Est. 300 | PF65 170 | | | | |

**KM# 913 DOLLAR**
0.999 Silver **Ruler:** Elizabeth II **Subject:** Durer Codex:Praying Hands

| Date | Mintage | VF20 | XF40 | MS60 | MS63 | MS65 |
|---|---|---|---|---|---|---|
| 2012 | Est. 300 | PF65 170 | | | | |

**KM# 914 DOLLAR**
0.999 Silver **Ruler:** Elizabeth II **Subject:** Durer Codex: Madonna on the Crescent

| Date | Mintage | VF20 | XF40 | MS60 | MS63 | MS65 |
|---|---|---|---|---|---|---|
| 2012 | Est. 300 | PF65 170 | | | | |

**KM# 915 DOLLAR**
0.999 Silver **Ruler:** Elizabeth II **Subject:** Durer Codex: Rhinoceros

| Date | Mintage | VF20 | XF40 | MS60 | MS63 | MS65 |
|---|---|---|---|---|---|---|
| 2012 | Est. 300 | PF65 170 | | | | |

**KM# 916 DOLLAR**
0.999 Silver **Ruler:** Elizabeth II **Subject:** Durer Codex: Two Lions

| Date | Mintage | VF20 | XF40 | MS60 | MS63 | MS65 |
|---|---|---|---|---|---|---|
| 2012 | Est. 300 | PF65 170 | | | | |

**KM# 917 DOLLAR**
0.999 Silver **Ruler:** Elizabeth II **Subject:** Durer Codex: Abduction

| Date | Mintage | VF20 | XF40 | MS60 | MS63 | MS65 |
|---|---|---|---|---|---|---|
| 2012 | Est 300 | PF65 170 | | | | |

**KM# 918 DOLLAR**
0.999 Silver **Ruler:** Elizabeth II **Subject:** Durer Codex: Nude Woman with Zodiac

| Date | Mintage | VF20 | XF40 | MS60 | MS63 | MS65 |
|---|---|---|---|---|---|---|
| 2012 | Est. 300 | PF65 170 | | | | |

**KM# 919 DOLLAR**
0.999 Silver **Ruler:** Elizabeth II **Subject:** Durer Codex: Small Horse

| Date | Mintage | VF20 | XF40 | MS60 | MS63 | MS65 |
|---|---|---|---|---|---|---|
| 2012 | Est. 300 | PF65 170 | | | | |

**KM# 920 DOLLAR**
0.999 Silver **Ruler:** Elizabeth II **Subject:** Durer Codex: Agony in the garden

| Date | Mintage | VF20 | XF40 | MS60 | MS63 | MS65 |
|---|---|---|---|---|---|---|
| 2012 | Est. 300 | PF65 170 | | | | |

**KM# 921 DOLLAR**
0.999 Silver **Ruler:** Elizabeth II **Subject:** Durer Codex: Saint George

| Date | Mintage | VF20 | XF40 | MS60 | MS63 | MS65 |
|---|---|---|---|---|---|---|
| 2012 | Est. 300 | PF65 170 | | | | |

**KM# 922 DOLLAR**
0.999 Silver **Ruler:** Elizabeth II **Subject:** Durer Codex: St. Peter

| Date | Mintage | VF20 | XF40 | MS60 | MS63 | MS65 |
|---|---|---|---|---|---|---|
| 2012 | Est. 300 | PF65 170 | | | | |

**KM# 923 DOLLAR**
0.999 Silver **Ruler:** Elizabeth II **Subject:** Durer Codex: St. John healing the Cripple

| Date | Mintage | VF20 | XF40 | MS60 | MS63 | MS65 |
|---|---|---|---|---|---|---|
| 2012 | Est. 300 | PF65 170 | | | | |

**KM# 925 DOLLAR**
31.10 g., 0.925 Gold 0.9249 oz. AGW Colorized and Gold Guilded, 39 mm. **Ruler:** Elizabeth II **Subject:** Team Rubin

| Date | Mintage | VF20 | XF40 | MS60 | MS63 | MS65 |
|---|---|---|---|---|---|---|
| 2012 Proof-like | Est. 1000 | PF65 100 | | | | |

**KM# 926 DOLLAR**
31.10 g., 0.925 Silver 0.9249 oz. ASW Gold guilded, 39 mm. **Ruler:** Elizabeth II **Subject:** Team Rubin

| Date | Mintage | VF20 | XF40 | MS60 | MS63 | MS65 |
|---|---|---|---|---|---|---|
| 2012 Proof-like | Est. 1000 | PF65 100 | | | | |

**KM# 927 DOLLAR**
31.10 g., 0.925 Silver 0.9249 oz. ASW Gold gilded, 39 mm. **Ruler:** Elizabeth II **Subject:** Team Rubin

| Date | Mintage | VF20 | XF40 | MS60 | MS63 | MS65 |
|---|---|---|---|---|---|---|
| 2012 | Est. 1000 | PF65 100 | | | | |

**KM# 933 DOLLAR**
13.00 g., 0.999 Silver 0.4175 oz. ASW, 28 mm. **Ruler:** Elizabeth II **Subject:** Ctyrlistek: Pinda

| Date | Mintage | VF20 | XF40 | MS60 | MS63 | MS65 |
|---|---|---|---|---|---|---|
| 2012 | Est. 400 | PF65 120 | | | | |

**KM# 934 DOLLAR**
13.00 g., 0.999 Silver 0.4175 oz. ASW, 28 mm. **Ruler:** Elizabeth II **Subject:** Ctyrlistek: Myojulin

| Date | Mintage | VF20 | XF40 | MS60 | MS63 | MS65 |
|---|---|---|---|---|---|---|
| 2012 | Est. 400 | PF65 120 | | | | |

**KM# 935 DOLLAR**
13.00 g., 0.999 Silver 0.4175 oz. ASW, 28 mm. **Ruler:** Elizabeth II **Subject:** Ctyrlistek: Bobik

| Date | Mintage | VF20 | XF40 | MS60 | MS63 | MS65 |
|---|---|---|---|---|---|---|
| 2012 | Est. 400 | PF65 120 | | | | |

**KM# 936 DOLLAR**
13.00 g., 0.999 Silver 0.4175 oz. ASW, 28 mm. **Ruler:** Elizabeth II **Subject:** Ctyrlistek: Fifinka

| Date | Mintage | VF20 | XF40 | MS60 | MS63 | MS65 |
|---|---|---|---|---|---|---|
| 2012 | Est. 400 | PF65 120 | | | | |

**KM# 953 DOLLAR**
16.81 g., 0.925 Silver 0.4999 oz. ASW, 39 x 29 mm. **Ruler:** Elizabeth II **Subject:** Imperial Faberge Eggs: Swan Egg

| Date | Mintage | VF20 | XF40 | MS60 | MS63 | MS65 |
|---|---|---|---|---|---|---|
| 2012 | Est. 9999 | PF65 95.00 | | | | |

**KM# 954 DOLLAR**
28.28 g., 0.925 Silver 0.841 oz. ASW, 40 x 40 mm. **Ruler:** Elizabeth II **Subject:** Lady With an Ermine

| Date | Mintage | VF20 | XF40 | MS60 | MS63 | MS65 |
|---|---|---|---|---|---|---|
| 2012 | Est. 3000 | PF65 120 | | | | |

**KM# 956 DOLLAR**
16.81 g., 0.925 Silver 0.4999 oz. ASW, 39 x 29 mm. **Ruler:** Elizabeth II **Subject:** Imperial Faberge Eggs: Moscow Kremlin Egg

| Date | Mintage | VF20 | XF40 | MS60 | MS63 | MS65 |
|---|---|---|---|---|---|---|
| 2012 | Est. 9999 | PF65 95.00 | | | | |

**KM# 981 DOLLAR**
28.28 g., 0.925 Silver 0.841 oz. ASW, 40 mm. **Ruler:** Elizabeth II **Subject:** The Horsemen of the Apocalypse: Center coin

| Date | Mintage | VF20 | XF40 | MS60 | MS63 | MS65 |
|---|---|---|---|---|---|---|
| 2012 | Est. 777 | PF65 150 | | | | |

**KM# 982 DOLLAR**
28.28 g., 0.925 Silver 0.841 oz. ASW, 40 mm. **Ruler:** Elizabeth II **Subject:** Four Horsemen of the Apocalypse: White Horse

| Date | Mintage | VF20 | XF40 | MS60 | MS63 | MS65 |
|---|---|---|---|---|---|---|
| 2012 | Est. 777 | PF65 150 | | | | |

**KM# 983 DOLLAR**
28.28 g., 0.925 Silver 0.841 oz. ASW, 40 mm. **Ruler:** Elizabeth II **Subject:** Four Horsemen of the Apocalypse: Black Horse

| Date | Mintage | VF20 | XF40 | MS60 | MS63 | MS65 |
|---|---|---|---|---|---|---|
| 2012 | Est. 777 | PF65 150 | | | | |

**KM# 984 DOLLAR**
28.28 g., 0.925 Silver 0.841 oz. ASW, 40 mm. **Ruler:** Elizabeth II **Subject:** The Horsemen of the Apocalypse: Pale Horse

| Date | Mintage | VF20 | XF40 | MS60 | MS63 | MS65 |
|---|---|---|---|---|---|---|
| 2012 | Est. 777 | PF65 150 | | | | |

**KM# 985 DOLLAR**
28.28 g., 0.925 Silver 0.841 oz. ASW, 40 mm. **Ruler:** Elizabeth II **Subject:** Four Horsemen of the Apocalypse: Red Horse

| Date | Mintage | VF20 | XF40 | MS60 | MS63 | MS65 |
|---|---|---|---|---|---|---|
| 2012 | Est. 777 | PF65 150 | | | | |

**KM# 1000 DOLLAR**
16.81 g., 0.925 Silver 0.4999 oz. ASW, 39 x 29 mm. **Ruler:** Elizabeth II **Subject:** Imperial Faberge Eggs: Bouquet of Lilies

| Date | Mintage | VF20 | XF40 | MS60 | MS63 | MS65 |
|---|---|---|---|---|---|---|
| 2012 | Est. 9999 | PF65 95.00 | | | | |

**KM# 1190 DOLLAR**
16.81 g., 0.925 Silver 0.4999 oz. ASW, 39 x 29 mm. **Ruler:** Elizabeth II **Subject:** Imperial Faberge Eggs: Rosebud Egg

| Date | Mintage | VF20 | XF40 | MS60 | MS63 | MS65 |
|---|---|---|---|---|---|---|
| 2012 | — | PF65 75.00 | | | | |

**KM# 1247 DOLLAR**
28.28 g., 0.925 Silver 0.841 oz. ASW, 38.61 mm. **Ruler:** Elizabeth II **Subject:** Catherine II

| Date | Mintage | VF20 | XF40 | MS60 | MS63 | MS65 |
|---|---|---|---|---|---|---|
| 2012 | Est. 4000 | PF65 125 | | | | |

**KM# 849 DOLLAR**
20.50 g., 0.999 Silver 0.6584 oz. ASW, 38.61 mm. **Ruler:** Elizabeth II **Obv:** Crowned head at left, coiled snake at center **Rev:** Coiled snake at center, cobra below

| Date | Mintage | VF20 | XF40 | MS60 | MS63 | MS65 |
|---|---|---|---|---|---|---|
| 2013 | 4,000 | PF65 120 | | | | |

**KM# 850 DOLLAR**
15.50 g., 0.999 Silver 0.4978 oz. ASW, 50 mm. **Ruler:** Elizabeth II **Obv:** Head in tiara right, curles in background **Rev:** Colored snake **Shape:** Ying-Yang

| Date | Mintage | VF20 | XF40 | MS60 | MS63 | MS65 |
|---|---|---|---|---|---|---|
| 2013 | 5,000 | PF65 55.00 | | | | |

**KM# 851 DOLLAR**
15.50 g., 0.925 Silver 0.461 oz. ASW, 50 mm. **Ruler:** Elizabeth II **Obv:** Crowned head right and waves in background **Rev:** Colored snake **Shape:** Ying-Yang

| Date | Mintage | VF20 | XF40 | MS60 | MS63 | MS65 |
|---|---|---|---|---|---|---|
| 2013 | 5,000 | PF65 55.00 | | | | |

**KM# 861 DOLLAR**
7.77 g., 0.999 Silver 0.2496 oz. ASW, 22.1x22.1 mm. **Ruler:** Elizabeth II **Obv:** Crowned head right **Rev:** Monopoly board corner square - Go **Shape:** Square

| Date | Mintage | VF20 | XF40 | MS60 | MS63 | MS65 |
|---|---|---|---|---|---|---|
| 2013 | 5,000 | PF65 40.00 | | | | |

**KM# 862 DOLLAR**
7.77 g., 0.999 Silver 0.2496 oz. ASW, 22.1x22.1 mm. **Ruler:** Elizabeth II **Obv:** Crowned head right **Rev:** Monopoly board corner square - Free Parking **Shape:** Square

| Date | Mintage | VF20 | XF40 | MS60 | MS63 | MS65 |
|---|---|---|---|---|---|---|
| 2013 | 5,000 | PF65 40.00 | | | | |

**KM# 863 DOLLAR**
7.77 g., 0.999 Silver 0.2496 oz. ASW, 22.1x22.1 mm. **Ruler:** Elizabeth II **Obv:** Crowned head right **Rev:** Monopoly board corner square - Go to Jail **Shape:** Square

| Date | Mintage | VF20 | XF40 | MS60 | MS63 | MS65 |
|---|---|---|---|---|---|---|
| 2013 | 5,000 | PF65 40.00 | | | | |

**KM# 864 DOLLAR**
7.77 g., 0.999 Silver 0.2496 oz. ASW, 22.1x22.1 mm. **Ruler:** Elizabeth II **Obv:** Crowned head right **Rev:** Monopoly board corner square - Jail **Shape:** Square

| Date | Mintage | VF20 | XF40 | MS60 | MS63 | MS65 |
|---|---|---|---|---|---|---|
| 2013 | 5,000 | PF65 40.00 | | | | |

**KM# 868 DOLLAR**
15.55 g., 0.999 Silver 0.4994 oz. ASW, 36 mm. **Ruler:** Elizabeth II **Obv:** Crowned head right **Rev:** Coral Snake, chinese characters above

| Date | Mintage | VF20 | XF40 | MS60 | MS63 | MS65 |
|---|---|---|---|---|---|---|
| 2013 | 8,000 | PF65 50.00 | | | | |

**KM# 873 DOLLAR**
20.00 g., Silver Plated Copper, 38.61 mm. **Ruler:** Elizabeth II **Obv:** Crowned head right **Rev:** Snake head facing ready to bite

| Date | Mintage | VF20 | XF40 | MS60 | MS63 | MS65 |
|---|---|---|---|---|---|---|
| 2013 Proof-like | 1,500 | — | — | — | — | 25.00 |

**KM# 874 DOLLAR**
28.28 g., 0.925 Silver 0.841 oz. ASW, 35x45 mm. **Ruler:** Elizabeth II **Obv:** Crowned head right **Rev:** Snake in color, coiled and raised up **Shape:** Vertical oval

| Date | Mintage | VF20 | XF40 | MS60 | MS63 | MS65 |
|---|---|---|---|---|---|---|
| 2013 | 3,000 | PF65 100 | | | | |

**KM# 875 DOLLAR**
28.28 g., 0.925 Silver 0.841 oz. ASW, 35x45 mm. **Ruler:** Elizabeth II **Obv:** Crowned head right **Rev:** Humorous baby snake in color **Shape:** Vertical oval

| Date | Mintage | VF20 | XF40 | MS60 | MS63 | MS65 |
|---|---|---|---|---|---|---|
| 2013 | 7,000 | PF65 100 | | | | |

**KM# 876 DOLLAR**
28.28 g., 0.925 Silver 0.841 oz. ASW, 35x45 mm. **Ruler:** Elizabeth II **Obv:** Crowned head right **Rev:** Love snake, coiled up as heart **Shape:** Vertical oval

| Date | Mintage | VF20 | XF40 | MS60 | MS63 | MS65 |
|---|---|---|---|---|---|---|
| 2013 | 7,000 | PF65 100 | | | | |

**KM# 891 DOLLAR**
28.28 g., 0.925 Silver 0.841 oz. ASW, 35 x 45 mm. **Ruler:** Elizabeth II **Subject:** Love Tree

| Date | Mintage | VF20 | XF40 | MS60 | MS63 | MS65 |
|---|---|---|---|---|---|---|
| 2013 | Est. 7000 | PF65 75.00 | | | | |

**KM# 967 DOLLAR**
25.50 g., 0.925 Silver 0.7584 oz. ASW, 30 x 40 mm. **Ruler:** Elizabeth II **Subject:** Russian ABCs - Letter B

| Date | Mintage | VF20 | XF40 | MS60 | MS63 | MS65 |
|---|---|---|---|---|---|---|
| 2013 | Est. 5000 | PF65 100 | | | | |

**KM# 968 DOLLAR**
25.50 g., 0.925 Silver 0.7584 oz. ASW, 30 x 40 mm. **Ruler:** Elizabeth II **Subject:** Russian ABCs: Letter C

| Date | Mintage | VF20 | XF40 | MS60 | MS63 | MS65 |
|---|---|---|---|---|---|---|
| 2013 | — | PF65 100 | | | | |

**KM# 969 DOLLAR**
25.50 g., 0.925 Silver 0.7584 oz. ASW, 30 x 40 mm. **Ruler:** Elizabeth II **Subject:** Russian ABCs: Letter A

| Date | Mintage | VF20 | XF40 | MS60 | MS63 | MS65 |
|---|---|---|---|---|---|---|
| 2013 | Est. 5000 | PF65 100 | | | | |

**KM# 970 DOLLAR**
0.999 Silver, 38.61 mm. **Ruler:** Elizabeth II **Subject:** Pieta - Inside

| Date | Mintage | VF20 | XF40 | MS60 | MS63 | MS65 |
|---|---|---|---|---|---|---|
| 2013 | Est. 1000 | PF65 150 | | | | |

**KM# 971 DOLLAR**
0.999 Silver, 38.61 mm. **Ruler:** Elizabeth II **Subject:** Pieta - Outside

| Date | Mintage | VF20 | XF40 | MS60 | MS63 | MS65 |
|---|---|---|---|---|---|---|
| 2013 | Est. 1000 | PF65 150 | | | | |

**KM# 991 DOLLAR**
28.28 g., 0.925 Silver 0.841 oz. ASW, 38.61 mm. **Ruler:** Elizabeth II **Subject:** Iris Barbata

| Date | Mintage | VF20 | XF40 | MS60 | MS63 | MS65 |
|---|---|---|---|---|---|---|
| 2013 | Est. 7000 | PF65 75.00 | | | | |

**KM# 992 DOLLAR**
28.28 g., 0.925 Silver 0.841 oz. ASW **Ruler:** Elizabeth II **Subject:** Iris Florentina

| Date | Mintage | VF20 | XF40 | MS60 | MS63 | MS65 |
|---|---|---|---|---|---|---|
| 2013 | Est. 7000 | PF65 75.00 | | | | |

**KM# 993 DOLLAR**
28.28 g., 0.925 Silver 0.841 oz. ASW, 38.61 mm. **Ruler:** Elizabeth II **Subject:** Iris Siberica

| Date | Mintage | VF20 | XF40 | MS60 | MS63 | MS65 |
|---|---|---|---|---|---|---|
| 2013 | Est. 7000 | PF65 75.00 | | | | |

**KM# 1001 DOLLAR**
42.50 g., 0.999 Silver 1.365 oz. ASW, 41.7 x 40 mm. **Ruler:** Elizabeth II **Subject:** Divine Comedy - 1 of 24

| Date | Mintage | VF20 | XF40 | MS60 | MS63 | MS65 |
|---|---|---|---|---|---|---|
| 2013 | Est.250 | PF65 175 | | | | |

**KM# 1002 DOLLAR**
42.50 g., 0.999 Silver 1.365 oz. ASW, 41.7 x 40 mm. **Ruler:** Elizabeth II **Subject:** Divine Comedy - 2 of 24

| Date | Mintage | VF20 | XF40 | MS60 | MS63 | MS65 |
|---|---|---|---|---|---|---|
| 2013 | Est. 250 | PF65 175 | | | | |

**KM# 1003 DOLLAR**
42.50 g., 0.999 Silver 1.365 oz. ASW, 41.7 x 40 mm. **Ruler:** Elizabeth II **Subject:** Divine Comedy - 3 of 24

| Date | Mintage | VF20 | XF40 | MS60 | MS63 | MS65 |
|---|---|---|---|---|---|---|
| 2013 | Est. 250 | PF65 175 | | | | |

**KM# 1004 DOLLAR**
42.50 g., 0.999 Silver 1.365 oz. ASW, 41.7 x 40 mm. **Ruler:** Elizabeth II **Subject:** Divine Comedy - 4 of 24

| Date | Mintage | VF20 | XF40 | MS60 | MS63 | MS65 |
|---|---|---|---|---|---|---|
| 2013 | Est. 250 | PF65 175 | | | | |

**KM# 1005 DOLLAR**
42.50 g., 0.999 Silver 1.365 oz. ASW, 41.7 x 40 mm. **Ruler:** Elizabeth II **Subject:** Divine Comedy - 5 of 24

| Date | Mintage | VF20 | XF40 | MS60 | MS63 | MS65 |
|---|---|---|---|---|---|---|
| 2013 | Est. 250 | PF65 175 | | | | |

**KM# 1006 DOLLAR**
42.50 g., 0.999 Silver 1.365 oz. ASW, 41.7 x 40 mm. **Ruler:** Elizabeth II **Subject:** Divine Comedy - 6 of 24

| Date | Mintage | VF20 | XF40 | MS60 | MS63 | MS65 |
|---|---|---|---|---|---|---|
| 2013 | Est. 250 | PF65 175 | | | | |

**KM# 1007 DOLLAR**
42.50 g., 0.999 Silver 1.365 oz. ASW, 41.7 x 40 mm. **Ruler:** Elizabeth II **Subject:** Divine Comedy - 7 of 24

| Date | Mintage | VF20 | XF40 | MS60 | MS63 | MS65 |
|---|---|---|---|---|---|---|
| 2013 | Est. 250 | PF65 175 | | | | |

**KM# 1008 DOLLAR**
42.50 g., 0.999 Silver 1.365 oz. ASW, 41.7 x 40 mm. **Ruler:** Elizabeth II **Subject:** Divine Comedy - 8 of 24

| Date | Mintage | VF20 | XF40 | MS60 | MS63 | MS65 |
|---|---|---|---|---|---|---|
| 2013 | Est. 250 | PF65 175 | | | | |

**KM# 1009 DOLLAR**
42.50 g., 0.999 Silver 1.365 oz. ASW, 41.7 x 40 mm. **Ruler:** Elizabeth II **Subject:** Divine Comedy - 9 of 24

| Date | Mintage | VF20 | XF40 | MS60 | MS63 | MS65 |
|---|---|---|---|---|---|---|
| 2013 | Est. 250 | PF65 175 | | | | |

**KM# 1010 DOLLAR**
42.50 g., 0.999 Silver 1.365 oz. ASW, 41.7 x 40 mm. **Ruler:** Elizabeth II **Subject:** Divine Comedy - 10 of 24

| Date | Mintage | VF20 | XF40 | MS60 | MS63 | MS65 |
|---|---|---|---|---|---|---|
| 2013 | Est. 250 | PF65 175 | | | | |

**KM# 1011 DOLLAR**
42.50 g., 0.999 Silver 1.365 oz. ASW, 41.7 x 40 mm. **Ruler:** Elizabeth II **Subject:** Divine Comedy - 11 of 24

| Date | Mintage | VF20 | XF40 | MS60 | MS63 | MS65 |
|---|---|---|---|---|---|---|
| 2013 | Est. 250 | PF65 175 | | | | |

**KM# 1012 DOLLAR**
42.50 g., 0.999 Silver 1.365 oz. ASW, 41.7 x 40 mm. **Ruler:** Elizabeth II **Subject:** Divine Comedy - 12 of 24

| Date | Mintage | VF20 | XF40 | MS60 | MS63 | MS65 |
|---|---|---|---|---|---|---|
| 2013 | Est. 250 | PF65 175 | | | | |

**KM# 1013 DOLLAR**
42.50 g., 0.999 Silver 1.365 oz. ASW, 41.7 x 40 mm. **Ruler:** Elizabeth II **Subject:** Divine Comedy - 13 of 24

| Date | Mintage | VF20 | XF40 | MS60 | MS63 | MS65 |
|---|---|---|---|---|---|---|
| 2013 | Est. 250 | PF65 175 | | | | |

**KM# 1014 DOLLAR**
42.50 g., 0.999 Silver 1.365 oz. ASW, 41.7 x 40 mm. **Ruler:** Elizabeth II **Subject:** Divine Comedy - 14 of 24

| Date | Mintage | VF20 | XF40 | MS60 | MS63 | MS65 |
|---|---|---|---|---|---|---|
| 2013 | Est. 250 | PF65 175 | | | | |

**KM# 1015 DOLLAR**
42.50 g., 0.999 Silver 1.365 oz. ASW, 41.7 x 40 mm. **Ruler:** Elizabeth II **Subject:** Divine Comedy - 15 of 24

| Date | Mintage | VF20 | XF40 | MS60 | MS63 | MS65 |
|---|---|---|---|---|---|---|
| 2013 | Est. 250 | PF65 175 | | | | |

**KM# 1016 DOLLAR**
42.50 g., 0.999 Silver 1.365 oz. ASW, 41.7 x 40 mm. **Ruler:** Elizabeth II **Subject:** Divine Comedy - 16 of 24

| Date | Mintage | VF20 | XF40 | MS60 | MS63 | MS65 |
|---|---|---|---|---|---|---|
| 2013 | Est. 250 | PF65 175 | | | | |

**KM# 1017 DOLLAR**
42.50 g., 0.999 Silver 1.365 oz. ASW, 41.7 x 40 mm. **Ruler:** Elizabeth II **Subject:** Divine Comedy - 17 of 24

| Date | Mintage | VF20 | XF40 | MS60 | MS63 | MS65 |
|---|---|---|---|---|---|---|
| 2013 | Est. 250 | PF65 175 | | | | |

**KM# 1018 DOLLAR**
42.50 g., 0.999 Silver 1.365 oz. ASW, 41.7 x 40 mm. **Ruler:** Elizabeth II **Subject:** Divine Comedy - 18 of 24

| Date | Mintage | VF20 | XF40 | MS60 | MS63 | MS65 |
|---|---|---|---|---|---|---|
| 2013 | Est. 250 | PF65 175 | | | | |

**KM# 1019 DOLLAR**
42.50 g., 0.999 Silver 1.365 oz. ASW, 41.7 x 40 mm. **Ruler:** Elizabeth II **Subject:** Divine Comedy - 19 of 24

| Date | Mintage | VF20 | XF40 | MS60 | MS63 | MS65 |
|---|---|---|---|---|---|---|
| 2013 | Est. 250 | PF65 175 | | | | |

**KM# 1020 DOLLAR**
42.50 g., 0.999 Silver 1.365 oz. ASW, 41.7 x 40 mm. **Ruler:** Elizabeth II **Subject:** Divine Comedy - 20 of 24

| Date | Mintage | VF20 | XF40 | MS60 | MS63 | MS65 |
|---|---|---|---|---|---|---|
| 2013 | Est. 250 | PF65 175 | | | | |

**KM# 1021 DOLLAR**
42.50 g., 0.999 Silver 1.365 oz. ASW, 41.7 x 40 mm. **Ruler:** Elizabeth II **Subject:** Divine Comedy - 21 of 24

| Date | Mintage | VF20 | XF40 | MS60 | MS63 | MS65 |
|---|---|---|---|---|---|---|
| 2013 | Est. 250 | PF65 175 | | | | |

**KM# 1022 DOLLAR**
42.50 g., 0.999 Silver 1.365 oz. ASW, 41.7 x 40 mm. **Ruler:** Elizabeth II **Subject:** Divine Comedy - 22 of 24

| Date | Mintage | VF20 | XF40 | MS60 | MS63 | MS65 |
|---|---|---|---|---|---|---|
| 2013 | Est. 250 | PF65 175 | | | | |

**KM# 1023 DOLLAR**
42.50 g., 0.999 Silver 1.365 oz. ASW, 41.7 x 40 mm. **Ruler:** Elizabeth II **Subject:** Divine Comedy - 23 of 24

| Date | Mintage | VF20 | XF40 | MS60 | MS63 | MS65 |
|---|---|---|---|---|---|---|
| 2013 | Est. 250 | PF65 175 | | | | |

**KM# 1024 DOLLAR**
42.50 g., 0.999 Silver 1.365 oz. ASW, 41.7 x 40 mm. **Ruler:** Elizabeth II **Subject:** Divine Comedy - 24 of 24

| Date | Mintage | VF20 | XF40 | MS60 | MS63 | MS65 |
|---|---|---|---|---|---|---|
| 2013 | Est. 250 | PF65 175 | | | | |

**KM# 1075 DOLLAR**
15.55 g., 0.999 Silver 0.4994 oz. ASW **Ruler:** Elizabeth II **Subject:** Australian Soldiers

| Date | Mintage | VF20 | XF40 | MS60 | MS63 | MS65 |
|---|---|---|---|---|---|---|
| 2013 | Est. 2000 | PF65 75.00 | | | | |

**KM# 1078 DOLLAR**
14.14 g., 0.925 Silver 0.4205 oz. ASW, 32 mm. **Ruler:** Elizabeth II **Subject:** Cartoon Characters: Tom & Jerry

| Date | Mintage | VF20 | XF40 | MS60 | MS63 | MS65 |
|---|---|---|---|---|---|---|
| 2013 | Est. 6000 | PF65 75.00 | | | | |

**KM# 1081 DOLLAR**
31.10 g., 0.999 Silver 0.9989 oz. ASW, 50 x 27.3 mm. **Ruler:** Elizabeth II **Subject:** In Love - Left

| Date | Mintage | VF20 | XF40 | MS60 | MS63 | MS65 |
|---|---|---|---|---|---|---|
| 2013 | Est. 4444 | PF65 80.00 | | | | |

**KM# 1082 DOLLAR**
31.10 g., 0.999 Silver 0.9989 oz. ASW, 50 x 27.3 mm. **Ruler:** Elizabeth II **Subject:** In Love - Right

| Date | Mintage | VF20 | XF40 | MS60 | MS63 | MS65 |
|---|---|---|---|---|---|---|
| 2013 | Est. 4444 | PF65 80.00 | | | | |

**KM# 1083 DOLLAR**
31.10 g., 0.999 Silver 0.9989 oz. ASW, 45 x 31 mm. **Ruler:** Elizabeth II **Subject:** The Orient Express (Engraved) **Obv:** Steam train advancing left **Rev:** Company Logo **Shape:** Horizontal oval

| Date | Mintage | VF20 | XF40 | MS60 | MS63 | MS65 |
|---|---|---|---|---|---|---|
| 2013 | — | PF65 150 | | | | |

**KM# 1083a DOLLAR**
31.10 g., 0.999 Silver 0.9989 oz. ASW, 45 x 31 mm. **Ruler:** Elizabeth II **Subject:** Orient Express (Colored) **Obv:** Steam train advancing left **Rev:** Company logo **Shape:** Horizontal oval

| Date | Mintage | VF20 | XF40 | MS60 | MS63 | MS65 |
|---|---|---|---|---|---|---|
| 2013 | Est. 400 | PF65 150 | | | | |

**KM# 1084 DOLLAR**
16.00 g., 0.999 Silver 0.5139 oz. ASW, 34 mm. **Ruler:** Elizabeth II **Subject:** Czech Olympian Series: Javelin

| Date | Mintage | VF20 | XF40 | MS60 | MS63 | MS65 |
|---|---|---|---|---|---|---|
| 2013 | Est. 500 | PF65 125 | | | | |

**KM# 1085 DOLLAR**
16.00 g., 0.999 Silver 0.5139 oz. ASW, 34 mm. **Ruler:** Elizabeth II **Subject:** Czech Olympian Series: Running

| Date | Mintage | VF20 | XF40 | MS60 | MS63 | MS65 |
|---|---|---|---|---|---|---|
| 2013 | Est. 500 | PF65 125 | | | | |

**KM# 1086 DOLLAR**
16.00 g., 0.999 Silver 0.5139 oz. ASW, 34 mm. **Ruler:** Elizabeth II **Subject:** Czech Olympians: Rowing

| Date | Mintage | VF20 | XF40 | MS60 | MS63 | MS65 |
|---|---|---|---|---|---|---|
| 2013 | Est. 500 | PF65 125 | | | | |

**KM# 1087 DOLLAR**
16.00 g., 0.999 Silver 0.5139 oz. ASW, 34 mm. **Ruler:** Elizabeth II **Subject:** Czech Olympians: Cycling

| Date | Mintage | VF20 | XF40 | MS60 | MS63 | MS65 |
|---|---|---|---|---|---|---|
| 2013 | Est. 500 | PF65 125 | | | | |

**KM# 1088 DOLLAR**
7.78 g., 0.999 Gold 0.2499 oz. AGW, 22 mm. **Ruler:** Elizabeth II **Subject:** Czech Olympians: Javelin

| Date | Mintage | VF20 | XF40 | MS60 | MS63 | MS65 |
|---|---|---|---|---|---|---|
| 2013 | Est. 200 | PF65 125 | | | | |

**KM# 1089 DOLLAR**
7.78 g., 0.999 Gold 0.2499 oz. AGW, 22 mm. **Ruler:** Elizabeth II **Subject:** Czech Olympians: Running

| Date | Mintage | VF20 | XF40 | MS60 | MS63 | MS65 |
|---|---|---|---|---|---|---|
| 2013 | — | PF65 125 | | | | |

**KM# 1090 DOLLAR**
7.78 g., 0.999 Gold 0.2499 oz. AGW, 22 mm. **Ruler:** Elizabeth II **Subject:** Czech Olympians: Rowing

| Date | Mintage | VF20 | XF40 | MS60 | MS63 | MS65 |
|---|---|---|---|---|---|---|
| 2013 | — | PF65 125 | | | | |

**KM# 1091 DOLLAR**
7.78 g., 0.999 Gold 0.2499 oz. AGW, 22 mm. **Ruler:** Elizabeth II **Subject:** Czech Olympians: Cycling

| Date | Mintage | VF20 | XF40 | MS60 | MS63 | MS65 |
|---|---|---|---|---|---|---|
| 2013 | Est. 200 | PF65 125 | | | | |

**KM# 1092 DOLLAR**
15.55 g., 0.999 Silver 0.4994 oz. ASW, 36 mm. **Ruler:** Elizabeth II **Subject:** Tooth Fairy

| Date | Mintage | VF20 | XF40 | MS60 | MS63 | MS65 |
|---|---|---|---|---|---|---|
| 2013 | Est. 5000 | PF65 45.00 | | | | |

**KM# 1094 DOLLAR**
15.55 g., 0.999 Silver 0.4994 oz. ASW, 36 mm. **Ruler:** Elizabeth II **Subject:** Dr. Who - First Doctor, William Hartnell

| Date | Mintage | VF20 | XF40 | MS60 | MS63 | MS65 |
|---|---|---|---|---|---|---|
| 2013 | Est. 4000 | PF65 75.00 | | | | |

**KM# 1095 DOLLAR**
15.55 g., 0.999 Silver 0.4994 oz. ASW, 36 mm. **Ruler:** Elizabeth II **Subject:** Dr. Who - Second Doctor, Patrick Troughton

| Date | Mintage | VF20 | XF40 | MS60 | MS63 | MS65 |
|---|---|---|---|---|---|---|
| 2013 | Est. 4000 | PF65 75.00 | | | | |

**KM# 1096 DOLLAR**
15.55 g., 0.999 Silver 0.4994 oz. ASW, 36 mm. **Ruler:** Elizabeth II **Subject:** Dr. Who - Third Doctor, Jon Pertwee

| Date | Mintage | VF20 | XF40 | MS60 | MS63 | MS65 |
|---|---|---|---|---|---|---|
| 2013 | Est. 4000 | **PF65** 75.00 | | | | |

**KM# 1097 DOLLAR**
15.55 g., 0.999 Silver 0.4994 oz. ASW, 36 mm. **Ruler:** Elizabeth II **Subject:** Dr. Who - Fourth Doctor, Tom Baker

| Date | Mintage | VF20 | XF40 | MS60 | MS63 | MS65 |
|---|---|---|---|---|---|---|
| 2013 | Est. 4000 | **PF65** 75.00 | | | | |

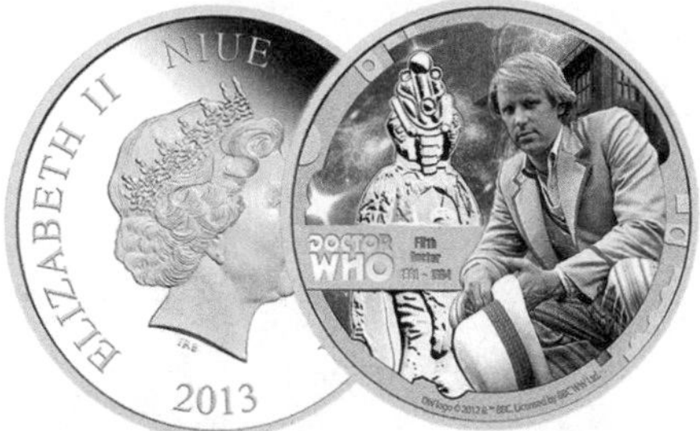


**KM# 1098 DOLLAR**
15.50 g., 0.999 Silver 0.4978 oz. ASW, 36 mm. **Ruler:** Elizabeth II **Subject:** Dr. Who - Fifth Doctor, Peter Davison

| Date | Mintage | VF20 | XF40 | MS60 | MS63 | MS65 |
|---|---|---|---|---|---|---|
| 2013 | Est. 4000 | **PF65** 75.00 | | | | |

**KM# 1099 DOLLAR**
15.50 g., 0.999 Silver 0.4978 oz. ASW, 36 mm. **Ruler:** Elizabeth II **Subject:** Dr. Who - Sixth Doctor, Colin Baker

| Date | Mintage | VF20 | XF40 | MS60 | MS63 | MS65 |
|---|---|---|---|---|---|---|
| 2013 | Est. 4000 | **PF65** 75.00 | | | | |

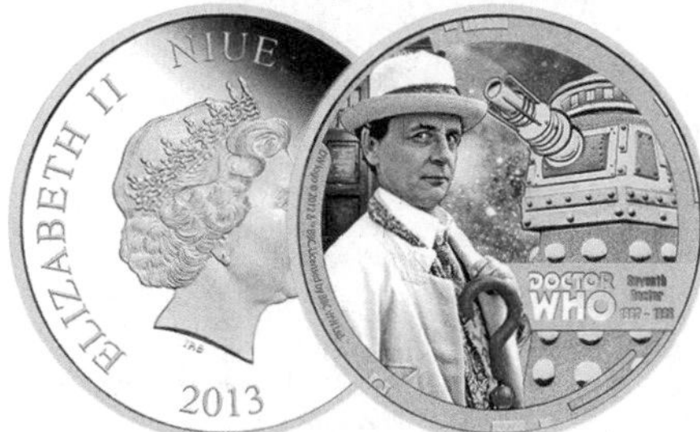


**KM# 1100 DOLLAR**
15.50 g., 0.999 Silver 0.4978 oz. ASW, 36 mm. **Ruler:** Elizabeth II **Subject:** Dr. Who - Seventh Doctor, Sylvester McCoy

| Date | Mintage | VF20 | XF40 | MS60 | MS63 | MS65 |
|---|---|---|---|---|---|---|
| 2013 | Est. 4000 | **PF65** 75.00 | | | | |

**KM# 1101 DOLLAR**
15.50 g., 0.999 Silver 0.4978 oz. ASW, 36 mm. **Ruler:** Elizabeth II **Subject:** Dr. Who - Eighth Doctor, Paul McGann

| Date | Mintage | VF20 | XF40 | MS60 | MS63 | MS65 |
|---|---|---|---|---|---|---|
| 2013 | Est. 4000 | **PF65** 75.00 | | | | |

**KM# 1102 DOLLAR**
15.50 g., 0.999 Silver 0.4978 oz. ASW **Ruler:** Elizabeth II **Subject:** Dr. Who - Ninth Doctor, Christopher Eccleston **Shape:** 36

| Date | Mintage | VF20 | XF40 | MS60 | MS63 | MS65 |
|---|---|---|---|---|---|---|
| 2013 | Est. 4000 | **PF65** 75.00 | | | | |

**KM# 1103 DOLLAR**
15.50 g., 0.999 Silver 0.4978 oz. ASW, 36 mm. **Ruler:** Elizabeth II **Subject:** Dr. Who - Tenth Doctor, David Tennant

| Date | Mintage | VF20 | XF40 | MS60 | MS63 | MS65 |
|---|---|---|---|---|---|---|
| 2013 | Est. 4000 | **PF65** 75.00 | | | | |

**KM# 1104 DOLLAR**
15.50 g., 0.999 Silver 0.4978 oz. ASW, 36 mm. **Ruler:** Elizabeth II **Subject:** Dr. Who - Eleventh Doctor, Matt Smith

| Date | Mintage | VF20 | XF40 | MS60 | MS63 | MS65 |
|---|---|---|---|---|---|---|
| 2013 | Est. 4000 | **PF65** 75.00 | | | | |

**KM# 1109 DOLLAR**
16.00 g., 0.999 Silver 0.5139 oz. ASW, 34 mm. **Ruler:** Elizabeth II **Subject:** Family of Rohans: Camille de Rohan

| Date | Mintage | VF20 | XF40 | MS60 | MS63 | MS65 |
|---|---|---|---|---|---|---|
| 2013 | Est. 800 | **PF65** 50.00 | | | | |

**KM# 1110 DOLLAR**
16.00 g., 0.999 Silver 0.5139 oz. ASW, 34 mm. **Ruler:** Elizabeth II **Subject:** Family of Rohans: Henri de Rohan

| Date | Mintage | VF20 | XF40 | MS60 | MS63 | MS65 |
|---|---|---|---|---|---|---|
| 2013 | Est. 800 | **PF65** 50.00 | | | | |

**KM# 1111 DOLLAR**
16.00 g., 0.999 Silver 0.5139 oz. ASW, 34 mm. **Ruler:** Elizabeth II **Subject:** Family of Rohans: Louis Rene de Rohan

| Date | Mintage | VF20 | XF40 | MS60 | MS63 | MS65 |
|---|---|---|---|---|---|---|
| 2013 | Est. 800 | **PF65** 50.00 | | | | |

**KM# 1112 DOLLAR**
16.00 g., 0.999 Silver 0.5139 oz. ASW, 34 mm. **Ruler:** Elizabeth II **Subject:** Family of Rohans: Marie de Rohan

| Date | Mintage | VF20 | XF40 | MS60 | MS63 | MS65 |
|---|---|---|---|---|---|---|
| 2013 | — | **PF65** 50.00 | | | | |

**KM# 1115 DOLLAR**
28.28 g., 0.925 Silver 0.841 oz. ASW, 35 x 45 mm. **Ruler:** Elizabeth II **Subject:** Jurassic Period: Life on the Ground

| Date | Mintage | VF20 | XF40 | MS60 | MS63 | MS65 |
|---|---|---|---|---|---|---|
| 2013 | Est. 7000 | **PF65** 65.00 | | | | |

**KM# 1116 DOLLAR**
28.28 g., 0.925 Silver 0.841 oz. ASW, 35 x 45 mm. **Ruler:** Elizabeth II **Subject:** Jurassic Period: Life Under Water

| Date | Mintage | VF20 | XF40 | MS60 | MS63 | MS65 |
|---|---|---|---|---|---|---|
| 2013 | Est. 7000 | **PF65** 65.00 | | | | |

**KM# 1119 DOLLAR**
14.14 g., 0.925 Silver 0.4205 oz. ASW, 32 mm. **Ruler:** Elizabeth II **Subject:** Cartoon Characters: Scooby Doo

| Date | Mintage | VF20 | XF40 | MS60 | MS63 | MS65 |
|---|---|---|---|---|---|---|
| 2013 | Est. 6000 | **PF65** 75.00 | | | | |

**KM# 1120 DOLLAR**
28.28 g., 0.925 Silver 0.841 oz. ASW, 40 x 28 mm. **Ruler:** Elizabeth II **Subject:** A Russian Beauty

| Date | Mintage | VF20 | XF40 | MS60 | MS63 | MS65 |
|---|---|---|---|---|---|---|
| 2013 | Est. 8888 | **PF65** 80.00 | | | | |

**KM# 1125 DOLLAR**
10.00 g., 0.925 Silver 0.2974 oz. ASW, 32 mm. **Ruler:** Elizabeth II **Subject:** Magic Calendar of Happiness - April

| Date | Mintage | VF20 | XF40 | MS60 | MS63 | MS65 |
|---|---|---|---|---|---|---|
| 2013 | Est. 5555 | **PF65** 65.00 | | | | |

**KM# 1127 DOLLAR**

28.28 g., 0.925 Silver 0.841 oz. ASW, 40 x 28 mm. **Ruler:** Elizabeth II **Subject:** Tropical Coral Fish

| Date | Mintage | VF20 | XF40 | MS60 | MS63 | MS65 |
|---|---|---|---|---|---|---|
| 2013 | Est. 8000 | PF65 75.00 | | | | |

**KM# 1128 DOLLAR**

28.28 g., 0.925 Silver 0.841 oz. ASW, 40 x 28 mm. **Ruler:** Elizabeth II **Subject:** Royal Gramma

| Date | Mintage | VF20 | XF40 | MS60 | MS63 | MS65 |
|---|---|---|---|---|---|---|
| 2013 | Est. 8000 | PF65 75.00 | | | | |

**KM# 1129 DOLLAR**

28.28 g., 0.925 Silver 0.841 oz. ASW, 40 x 28 mm. **Ruler:** Elizabeth II **Subject:** Royal Blue Tang

| Date | Mintage | VF20 | XF40 | MS60 | MS63 | MS65 |
|---|---|---|---|---|---|---|
| 2013 | Est. 8000 | PF65 75.00 | | | | |

**KM# 1130 DOLLAR**

15.55 g., 0.999 Silver 0.4994 oz. ASW, 36 mm. **Ruler:** Elizabeth II **Series:** Scented Flowers: Kowhai

| Date | Mintage | VF20 | XF40 | MS60 | MS63 | MS65 |
|---|---|---|---|---|---|---|
| 2013 | Est. 8000 | PF65 50.00 | | | | |

**KM# 1131 DOLLAR**

15.55 g., 0.999 Silver 0.4994 oz. ASW, 36 mm. **Ruler:** Elizabeth II **Subject:** Scented Flowers: Rose

| Date | Mintage | VF20 | XF40 | MS60 | MS63 | MS65 |
|---|---|---|---|---|---|---|
| 2013 | Est. 8000 | PF65 50.00 | | | | |

**KM# 1144 DOLLAR**

20.00 g., 0.925 Silver 0.5948 oz. ASW, 38.61 mm. **Ruler:** Elizabeth II **Subject:** Ghost Ships - Mary Celeste

| Date | Mintage | VF20 | XF40 | MS60 | MS63 | MS65 |
|---|---|---|---|---|---|---|
| 2013 | Est. 1000 | PF65 120 | | | | |

**KM# 1148 DOLLAR**

28.28 g., 0.925 Silver 0.841 oz. ASW, 38.61 mm. **Ruler:** Elizabeth II **Subject:** Belgorod

| Date | Mintage | VF20 | XF40 | MS60 | MS63 | MS65 |
|---|---|---|---|---|---|---|
| 2013 | — | PF65 85.00 | | | | |

**KM# 1149 DOLLAR**

28.28 g., 0.925 Silver 0.841 oz. ASW, 38.61 mm. **Ruler:** Elizabeth II **Subject:** Murmansk

| Date | Mintage | VF20 | XF40 | MS60 | MS63 | MS65 |
|---|---|---|---|---|---|---|
| 2013 | Est. 2000 | PF65 85.00 | | | | |

**KM# 1150 DOLLAR**

28.28 g., 0.999 Silver 0.9083 oz. ASW, 28 x 40 mm. **Ruler:** Elizabeth II **Subject:** 10 Kopecks 1860 - First Polish Stamp

| Date | Mintage | VF20 | XF40 | MS60 | MS63 | MS65 |
|---|---|---|---|---|---|---|
| 2013 | — | PF65 150 | | | | |

**KM# 1158 DOLLAR**

33.63 g., 0.925 Silver 1.0001 oz. ASW, 38.61 mm. **Ruler:** Elizabeth II **Subject:** Day of the Capital Astana

| Date | Mintage | VF20 | XF40 | MS60 | MS63 | MS65 |
|---|---|---|---|---|---|---|
| 2013 Proof | Est. 3000 | — | — | — | — | — |

**KM# 1159 DOLLAR**

33.63 g., 0.925 Silver 1.0001 oz. ASW, 38.61 mm. **Ruler:** Elizabeth II **Subject:** Day of the Constitution

| Date | Mintage | VF20 | XF40 | MS60 | MS63 | MS65 |
|---|---|---|---|---|---|---|
| 2013 Proof | Est. 3000 | — | — | — | — | — |

**KM# 1160 DOLLAR**

10.00 g., 0.925 Silver 0.2974 oz. ASW, 32 mm. **Ruler:** Elizabeth II **Subject:** Magic Calendar of Happiness - May

| Date | Mintage | VF20 | XF40 | MS60 | MS63 | MS65 |
|---|---|---|---|---|---|---|
| 2013 | Est. 5555 | PF65 65.00 | | | | |

**KM# 1161 DOLLAR**

10.00 g., 0.925 Silver 0.2974 oz. ASW, 32 mm. **Ruler:** Elizabeth II **Subject:** Magic Calendar of Happiness - June

| Date | Mintage | VF20 | XF40 | MS60 | MS63 | MS65 |
|---|---|---|---|---|---|---|
| 2013 | Est. 5555 | PF65 65.00 | | | | |

**KM# 1162 DOLLAR**

10.00 g., 0.925 Silver 0.2974 oz. ASW, 32 mm. **Ruler:** Elizabeth II **Subject:** Magic Calendar of Happiness - July

| Date | Mintage | VF20 | XF40 | MS60 | MS63 | MS65 |
|---|---|---|---|---|---|---|
| 2013 | — | PF65 65.00 | | | | |

**KM# 1164 DOLLAR**

33.63 g., 0.925 Silver 1.0001 oz. ASW, 38.61 mm. **Ruler:** Elizabeth II **Subject:** Betashar

| Date | Mintage | VF20 | XF40 | MS60 | MS63 | MS65 |
|---|---|---|---|---|---|---|
| 2013 | Est. 3000 | PF65 90.00 | | | | |

**KM# 1170 DOLLAR**

28.28 g., 0.925 Silver 0.841 oz. ASW, 38.61 mm. **Ruler:** Elizabeth II **Subject:** Anna Ioannova - Replicas of the Russian Emperor

| Date | Mintage | VF20 | XF40 | MS60 | MS63 | MS65 |
|---|---|---|---|---|---|---|
| 2013 | Est. 4000 | PF65 75.00 | | | | |

**KM# 1185 DOLLAR**

15.55 g., 0.999 Silver 0.4994 oz. ASW, 25 x 40 mm. **Ruler:** Elizabeth II **Subject:** Humpback Whale

| Date | Mintage | VF20 | XF40 | MS60 | MS63 | MS65 |
|---|---|---|---|---|---|---|
| 2013 Proof | — | — | — | — | — | — |

**KM# 1186 DOLLAR**

20.00 g., 0.999 Silver 0.6424 oz. ASW Painted with inserted printed mineral glass inlay, 54 x 32 mm. **Ruler:** Elizabeth II **Subject:** Superbia

| Date | Mintage | VF20 | XF40 | MS60 | MS63 | MS65 |
|---|---|---|---|---|---|---|
| 2013 | 1,000 | PF65 125 | | | | |

**KM# 1187 DOLLAR**

16.81 g., 0.925 Silver 0.4999 oz. ASW, 38.61 mm. **Ruler:** Elizabeth II **Subject:** Treasures of Traditions

| Date | Mintage | VF20 | XF40 | MS60 | MS63 | MS65 |
|---|---|---|---|---|---|---|
| 2013 Proof | Est. 1000 | — | — | — | — | — |

**KM# 1191 DOLLAR**

31.00 g., Copper-Nickel, 41 mm. **Ruler:** Elizabeth II **Subject:** Paavo Nurmi

| Date | Mintage | VF20 | XF40 | MS60 | MS63 | MS65 |
|---|---|---|---|---|---|---|
| 2013 Proof | Est. 30000 | — | — | — | — | — |

**KM# 1195 DOLLAR**

28.28 g., 0.925 Silver 0.841 oz. ASW, 38.61 mm. **Ruler:** Elizabeth II **Subject:** Orlovsky Trotter

| Date | Mintage | VF20 | XF40 | MS60 | MS63 | MS65 |
|---|---|---|---|---|---|---|
| 2013 | Est. 2000 | PF65 95.00 | | | | |

**KM# 1196 DOLLAR**

25.00 g., 0.925 Silver 0.7435 oz. ASW, 40 mm. **Ruler:** Elizabeth II **Subject:** Oil Discovery 1953

| Date | Mintage | VF20 | XF40 | MS60 | MS63 | MS65 |
|---|---|---|---|---|---|---|
| 2013 | Est. 4000 | PF65 100 | | | | |

**KM# 1197 DOLLAR**

33.63 g., 0.925 Silver 1.0001 oz. ASW, 38.61 mm. **Ruler:** Elizabeth II **Subject:** May 1st

| Date | Mintage | VF20 | XF40 | MS60 | MS63 | MS65 |
|---|---|---|---|---|---|---|
| 2013 Proof | Est. 3000 | — | — | — | — | — |

**KM# 1198 DOLLAR**

28.28 g., 0.925 Silver 0.841 oz. ASW, 40 x 40 mm. **Ruler:** Elizabeth II **Subject:** Madonna Under the Fir Tree

| Date | Mintage | VF20 | XF40 | MS60 | MS63 | MS65 |
|---|---|---|---|---|---|---|
| 2013 | Est. 2000 | PF65 125 | | | | |

**KM# 1202 DOLLAR**

25.00 g., 0.925 Silver 0.7435 oz. ASW, 38.61 mm. **Ruler:** Elizabeth II **Rev:** Oil rigs in color

| Date | Mintage | VF20 | XF40 | MS60 | MS63 | MS65 |
|---|---|---|---|---|---|---|
| 2013 | — | PF65 40.00 | | | | |

**KM# 1230 DOLLAR**

16.81 g., 0.999 Silver 0.5399 oz. ASW, 39.00 x 29.20 mm. **Ruler:** Elizabeth II **Subject:** Iwan Wigowski

| Date | Mintage | VF20 | XF40 | MS60 | MS63 | MS65 |
|---|---|---|---|---|---|---|
| 2013 | Est. 1555 | PF65 40.00 | | | | |

**KM# 1231 DOLLAR**

16.81 g., 0.999 Silver 0.5399 oz. ASW, 39.00 x 29.20 mm. **Ruler:** Elizabeth II **Subject:** Piotr Sagajdaczny

| Date | Mintage | VF20 | XF40 | MS60 | MS63 | MS65 |
|---|---|---|---|---|---|---|
| 2013 | Est. 1555 | PF65 40.00 | | | | |

**KM# 1232 DOLLAR**
16.81 g., 0.999 Silver 0.5399 oz. ASW, 39.00 x 29.20 mm. **Ruler:** Elizabeth II **Subject:** Iwan Mazepa

| Date | Mintage | VF20 | XF40 | MS60 | MS63 | MS65 |
|---|---|---|---|---|---|---|
| 2013 | Est. 1555 | PF65 40.00 | | | | |

**KM# 1233 DOLLAR**
16.81 g., 0.999 Silver 0.5399 oz. ASW, 39.00 x 29.90 mm. **Ruler:** Elizabeth II **Subject:** Dymitr Wisznewecki

| Date | Mintage | VF20 | XF40 | MS60 | MS63 | MS65 |
|---|---|---|---|---|---|---|
| 2013 | Est. 1555 | PF65 40.00 | | | | |

**KM# 1234 DOLLAR**
16.81 g., 0.999 Silver 0.5399 oz. ASW, 39.00 x 29.20 mm. **Ruler:** Elizabeth II **Subject:** Bogdon Chmienicki

| Date | Mintage | VF20 | XF40 | MS60 | MS63 | MS65 |
|---|---|---|---|---|---|---|
| 2013 | Est. 1555 | PF65 40.00 | | | | |

**KM# 1235 DOLLAR**
16.81 g., 0.999 Silver 0.5399 oz. ASW, 39.00 x 29.20 mm. **Ruler:** Elizabeth II **Subject:** Piotr Doroszenko

| Date | Mintage | VF20 | XF40 | MS60 | MS63 | MS65 |
|---|---|---|---|---|---|---|
| 2013 | Est. 1555 | PF65 40.00 | | | | |

**KM# 1236 DOLLAR**
16.81 g., 0.999 Silver 0.5399 oz. ASW, 39.00 x 29.20 mm. **Ruler:** Elizabeth II **Subject:** Filip Orlik

| Date | Mintage | VF20 | XF40 | MS60 | MS63 | MS65 |
|---|---|---|---|---|---|---|
| 2013 | Est. 1555 | PF65 40.00 | | | | |

**KM# 1237 DOLLAR**
15.56 g., 0.9999 Gold 0.5002 oz. AGW, 28 mm. **Ruler:** Elizabeth II **Subject:** Richard Wagner

| Date | Mintage | VF20 | XF40 | MS60 | MS63 | MS65 |
|---|---|---|---|---|---|---|
| 2013 | Est. 150 | PF65 1,250 | | | | |

**KM# 1243 DOLLAR**
28.28 g., 0.925 Silver 0.841 oz. ASW, 38.6 mm. **Ruler:** Elizabeth II **Subject:** 60th Anniversary of the Corronation

| Date | Mintage | VF20 | XF40 | MS60 | MS63 | MS65 |
|---|---|---|---|---|---|---|
| 2013 Proof | Est. 1500 | — | — | — | — | — |

**KM# 1243a DOLLAR**
28.28 g., Copper-Nickel, 38.6 mm. **Ruler:** Elizabeth II **Subject:** 60th Anniversary of the Corronation

| Date | Mintage | VF20 | XF40 | MS60 | MS63 | MS65 |
|---|---|---|---|---|---|---|
| 2013 | — | — | — | — | — | — |

**KM# 1243b DOLLAR**
Brass, 36 mm. **Ruler:** Elizabeth II **Subject:** 60th Anniversary of the Corronation

| Date | Mintage | VF20 | XF40 | MS60 | MS63 | MS65 |
|---|---|---|---|---|---|---|
| 2013 | Est. 3600 | — | — | — | — | — |

**KM# 1245 DOLLAR**
20.00 g., 0.925 Silver 0.5948 oz. ASW, 38.61 mm. **Ruler:** Elizabeth II **Subject:** 2014 FIFA World Cup Brazil

| Date | Mintage | VF20 | XF40 | MS60 | MS63 | MS65 |
|---|---|---|---|---|---|---|
| 2013 Proof | Est. 10000 | — | — | — | — | — |

**KM# 1259 DOLLAR**
Silver ASW, 38.6 mm. **Ruler:** Elizabeth II **Subject:** Fashion Wedding **Rev:** Bride in Wedding gown

| Date | Mintage | VF20 | XF40 | MS60 | MS63 | MS65 |
|---|---|---|---|---|---|---|
| 2013 | Est. 1000 | PF65 75.00 | | | | |

**KM# 1260 DOLLAR**
31.11 g., 0.999 Silver 0.999 oz. ASW, 40 mm. **Ruler:** Elizabeth II **Subject:** Sozunsky Mint, 250th Anniversary

| Date | Mintage | VF20 | XF40 | MS60 | MS63 | MS65 |
|---|---|---|---|---|---|---|
| 2013 | 1,000 | PF65 75.00 | | | | |

**KM# 1263 DOLLAR**
14.14 g., 0.925 Silver 0.4205 oz. ASW, 32 mm. **Ruler:** Elizabeth II **Rev:** Tweetie bird

| Date | Mintage | VF20 | XF40 | MS60 | MS63 | MS65 |
|---|---|---|---|---|---|---|
| 2013 | Est. 6000 | PF65 25.00 | | | | |

**KM# 1264 DOLLAR**
14.14 g., 0.925 Silver 0.4205 oz. ASW, 32 mm. **Ruler:** Elizabeth II **Rev:** Buggs Bunny

| Date | Mintage | VF20 | XF40 | MS60 | MS63 | MS65 |
|---|---|---|---|---|---|---|
| 2013 | Est. 6000 | PF65 40.00 | | | | |

**KM# 1154 DOLLAR**
15.55 g., 0.925 Silver 0.4624 oz. ASW, 38.61 mm. **Ruler:** Elizabeth II **Subject:** Fashion - Art

| Date | Mintage | VF20 | XF40 | MS60 | MS63 | MS65 |
|---|---|---|---|---|---|---|
| 2014 | Est. 1000 | PF65 65.00 | | | | |

**KM# 1166 DOLLAR**
25.00 g., 0.925 Silver 0.7435 oz. ASW, 40 mm. **Ruler:** Elizabeth II **Subject:** Legendary Australian Horses

| Date | Mintage | VF20 | XF40 | MS60 | MS63 | MS65 |
|---|---|---|---|---|---|---|
| 2014 | — | PF65 75.00 | | | | |

**KM# 1167 DOLLAR**
25.00 g., 0.925 Silver 0.7435 oz. ASW, 40 mm. **Ruler:** Elizabeth II **Subject:** Legendary Australian Horses

| Date | Mintage | VF20 | XF40 | MS60 | MS63 | MS65 |
|---|---|---|---|---|---|---|
| 2014 | — | PF65 75.00 | | | | |

**KM# 1168 DOLLAR**
25.00 g., 0.925 Silver 0.7435 oz. ASW, 40 mm. **Ruler:** Elizabeth II **Subject:** Legendary Australian Horses

| Date | Mintage | VF20 | XF40 | MS60 | MS63 | MS65 |
|---|---|---|---|---|---|---|
| 2014 | Est. 2000 | PF65 75.00 | | | | |

**KM# 1169 DOLLAR**
25.00 g., 0.925 Silver 0.7435 oz. ASW, 40 mm. **Ruler:** Elizabeth II **Subject:** Legendary Australian Horses

| Date | Mintage | VF20 | XF40 | MS60 | MS63 | MS65 |
|---|---|---|---|---|---|---|
| 2014 | Est. 2000 | PF65 75.00 | | | | |

**KM# 1268 DOLLAR**
17.55 g., 0.999 Silver 0.5637 oz. ASW, 38.61 mm. **Ruler:** Elizabeth II **Subject:** Endangered species - Panda **Rev:** Panda in color

| Date | Mintage | VF20 | XF40 | MS60 | MS63 | MS65 |
|---|---|---|---|---|---|---|
| 2014 | Est. 2000 | PF65 50.00 | | | | |

**KM# 1269 DOLLAR**
17.55 g., 0.999 Silver 0.5637 oz. ASW, 38.61 mm. **Ruler:** Elizabeth II **Subject:** Endangered species - Hyacinth Macaw **Rev:** Hyacinth Macaw in color

| Date | Mintage | VF20 | XF40 | MS60 | MS63 | MS65 |
|---|---|---|---|---|---|---|
| 2014 | Est. 2000 | PF65 50.00 | | | | |

**KM# 1270 DOLLAR**
17.55 g., 0.999 Silver 0.5637 oz. ASW, 38.61 mm. **Ruler:** Elizabeth II **Subject:** Endangered species - Siberian tiger **Rev:** Siberian tiger in color

| Date | Mintage | VF20 | XF40 | MS60 | MS63 | MS65 |
|---|---|---|---|---|---|---|
| 2014 | Est. 2000 | PF65 50.00 | | | | |

**KM# 1271 DOLLAR**
17.55 g., 0.999 Silver 0.5637 oz. ASW, 38.61 mm. **Ruler:** Elizabeth II **Subject:** Endangered species - Grey's Zebra **Rev:** Grey's Zebra in color

| Date | Mintage | VF20 | XF40 | MS60 | MS63 | MS65 |
|---|---|---|---|---|---|---|
| 2014 | Est. 2000 | PF65 50.00 | | | | |

**KM# 1272 DOLLAR**
14.14 g., 0.999 Silver 0.4542 oz. ASW, 32 mm. **Ruler:** Elizabeth II **Subject:** Good Luck **Rev:** Gilt stork insert

| Date | Mintage | VF20 | XF40 | MS60 | MS63 | MS65 |
|---|---|---|---|---|---|---|
| 1272 | Est. 3333 | PF65 50.00 | | | | |

**KM# 1273 DOLLAR**
14.140 Silver ASW .999, 32 mm. **Ruler:** Elizabeth II **Subject:** Good Luck **Rev:** Gilt angel insert

| Date | Mintage | VF20 | XF40 | MS60 | MS63 | MS65 |
|---|---|---|---|---|---|---|
| 2014 | Est. 3333 | PF65 50.00 | | | | |

**KM# 1274 DOLLAR**
14.14 g., 0.999 Silver 0.4542 oz. ASW, 32 mm. **Ruler:** Elizabeth II **Subject:** Good Luck **Rev:** Gilt pig insert

| Date | Mintage | VF20 | XF40 | MS60 | MS63 | MS65 |
|---|---|---|---|---|---|---|
| 2014 | Est. 3333 | PF65 50.00 | | | | |

**KM# 1275 DOLLAR**
7.50 g., 0.999 Silver 0.2409 oz. ASW, 38.61 mm. **Ruler:** Elizabeth II **Rev:** Bengal cat with crystal eyes

| Date | Mintage | VF20 | XF40 | MS60 | MS63 | MS65 |
|---|---|---|---|---|---|---|
| 2014 | Est. 1500 | PF65 50.00 | | | | |

**KM# 1276 DOLLAR**
78.00 g., 0.999 Silver 2.5052 oz. ASW, 41.5x55.5 mm. **Ruler:** Elizabeth II **Rev:** Kiwi partially gilt **Shape:** Vertical oval

| Date | Mintage | VF20 | XF40 | MS60 | MS63 | MS65 |
|---|---|---|---|---|---|---|
| 2014 | Est. 4444 | PF65 100 | | | | |

**KM# 1277 DOLLAR**
15.55 g., 0.999 Silver 0.4994 oz. ASW, 38.61 mm. **Ruler:** Elizabeth II **Subject:** Always with you, left side of heart **Shape:** Half heart

| Date | Mintage | VF20 | XF40 | MS60 | MS63 | MS65 |
|---|---|---|---|---|---|---|
| 2014 | Est. 5555 | PF65 50.00 | | | | |

**KM# 1278 DOLLAR**
15.55 g., 0.999 Silver 0.4994 oz. ASW, 38.61 mm. **Ruler:** Elizabeth II **Subject:** Always with you **Shape:** Half heart

| Date | Mintage | VF20 | XF40 | MS60 | MS63 | MS65 |
|---|---|---|---|---|---|---|
| 2014 | Est. 5555 | PF65 50.00 | | | | |

**KM# 265 2 DOLLARS**
62.21 g., 0.999 Silver 1.9981 oz. ASW, 55 mm. **Ruler:** Elizabeth II **Subject:** Year of the Rooster **Rev:** Multicolor rooster standing right, sunrise

| Date | Mintage | VF20 | XF40 | MS60 | MS63 | MS65 |
|---|---|---|---|---|---|---|
| 2005 | — | PF65 85.00 | | | | |

**KM# 269 2 DOLLARS**
1.24 g., 0.999 Gold 0.0398 oz. AGW, 14 mm. **Ruler:** Elizabeth II **Subject:** Year of the Rooster

| Date | Mintage | VF20 | XF40 | MS60 | MS63 | MS65 |
|---|---|---|---|---|---|---|
| 2005 | — | PF65 80.00 | | | | |

**KM# 270 2 DOLLARS**
1.56 g., 0.999 Gold 0.0501 oz. AGW, 18 mm. **Ruler:** Elizabeth II **Subject:** Year of the Rooster

| Date | Mintage | VF20 | XF40 | MS60 | MS63 | MS65 |
|---|---|---|---|---|---|---|
| 2005 | — | PF65 110 | | | | |

**KM# 271 2 DOLLARS**
3.11 g., 0.999 Gold 0.0999 oz. AGW, 18 mm. **Ruler:** Elizabeth II **Subject:** Year of the Rooster

| Date | Mintage | VF20 | XF40 | MS60 | MS63 | MS65 |
|---|---|---|---|---|---|---|
| 2005 | — | PF65 185 | | | | |

**KM# 278 2 DOLLARS**
3.11 g., 0.999 Gold 0.0999 oz. AGW, 18 mm. **Ruler:** Elizabeth II **Subject:** Chinese space achievements **Rev:** Multicolor rocket, flag, map

| Date | Mintage | VF20 | XF40 | MS60 | MS63 | MS65 |
|---|---|---|---|---|---|---|
| 2005 | — | PF65 195 | | | | |

**KM# 279 2 DOLLARS**
31.11 g., 0.999 Silver 0.999 oz. ASW, 35x46 mm. **Ruler:** Elizabeth II **Subject:** Impressionist paintings **Rev:** Multicolor painting of a bridge **Shape:** Vertical rectangle

| Date | Mintage | VF20 | XF40 | MS60 | MS63 | MS65 |
|---|---|---|---|---|---|---|
| 2005 | Est. 2005 | PF65 65.00 | | | | |

**KM# 280 2 DOLLARS**
31.11 g., 0.999 Silver 0.999 oz. ASW, 35x46 mm. **Ruler:** Elizabeth II **Subject:** Impressionist paintings **Rev:** Multicolor painting of a female **Shape:** Vertical rectangle

| Date | Mintage | VF20 | XF40 | MS60 | MS63 | MS65 |
|---|---|---|---|---|---|---|
| 2005 | Est. 2005 | PF65 65.00 | | | | |

**KM# 281 2 DOLLARS**
31.11 g., 0.999 Silver 0.999 oz. ASW, 35x46 mm. **Ruler:** Elizabeth II **Subject:** Impressionists paintings **Rev:** Multicolor painting of a village **Shape:** Vertical rectangle

| Date | Mintage | VF20 | XF40 | MS60 | MS63 | MS65 |
|---|---|---|---|---|---|---|
| 2005 | Est. 2005 | PF65 65.00 | | | | |

**KM# 282 2 DOLLARS**
31.11 g., 0.999 Silver 0.999 oz. ASW, 35x46 mm. **Ruler:** Elizabeth II **Subject:** Impressionist paintings **Rev:** Multicolor painting of a seaside **Shape:** Vertical rectangle

| Date | Mintage | VF20 | XF40 | MS60 | MS63 | MS65 |
|---|---|---|---|---|---|---|
| 2005 | Est. 2005 | PF65 65.00 | | | | |

**KM# 283 2 DOLLARS**
31.11 g., 0.999 Silver 0.999 oz. ASW, 35x46 mm. **Ruler:** Elizabeth II **Subject:** Impressionists paintings **Rev:** Multicolor painting of Paris **Shape:** Vertical rectangle

| Date | Mintage | VF20 | XF40 | MS60 | MS63 | MS65 |
|---|---|---|---|---|---|---|
| 2005 | Est. 2005 | PF65 65.00 | | | | |

**KM# 284 2 DOLLARS**
31.11 g., 0.999 Silver 0.999 oz. ASW, 35x46 mm. **Ruler:** Elizabeth II **Subject:** Impressionist paintings **Rev:** Multicolor painting of female **Shape:** Vertical rectangle

| Date | Mintage | VF20 | XF40 | MS60 | MS63 | MS65 |
|---|---|---|---|---|---|---|
| 2005 | Est. 2005 | PF65 65.00 | | | | |

**KM# 285 2 DOLLARS**
31.11 g., 0.999 Silver 0.999 oz. ASW, 35x46 mm. **Ruler:** Elizabeth II **Subject:** Impressionist paintings **Rev:** Multicolor painting of dancers **Shape:** Vertical rectangle

| Date | Mintage | VF20 | XF40 | MS60 | MS63 | MS65 |
|---|---|---|---|---|---|---|
| 2005 | — | PF65 65.00 | | | | |

**KM# 286 2 DOLLARS**
31.11 g., 0.999 Silver 0.999 oz. ASW, 35x46 mm. **Ruler:** Elizabeth II **Subject:** Impressionists paintings **Rev:** Multicolor painting of Fifer **Shape:** Vertical rectangle

| Date | Mintage | VF20 | XF40 | MS60 | MS63 | MS65 |
|---|---|---|---|---|---|---|
| 2005 | Est. 2005 | PF65 65.00 | | | | |

**KM# 287 2 DOLLARS**
31.11 g., 0.999 Silver 0.999 oz. ASW, 35x46 mm. **Ruler:** Elizabeth II **Subject:** Impressionists paintings **Rev:** Multicolor painting of boats **Shape:** Vertical rectangle

| Date | Mintage | VF20 | XF40 | MS60 | MS63 | MS65 |
|---|---|---|---|---|---|---|
| 2005 | Est. 2005 | PF65 65.00 | | | | |

**KM# 288 2 DOLLARS**
31.11 g., 0.999 Silver 0.999 oz. ASW, 35x46 mm. **Ruler:** Elizabeth II **Subject:** Impressionist paintings **Obv:** Multicolor painting of Paris scene **Shape:** Vertical rectangle

| Date | Mintage | VF20 | XF40 | MS60 | MS63 | MS65 |
|---|---|---|---|---|---|---|
| 2005 | Est. 2005 | PF65 65.00 | | | | |

**KM# 289 2 DOLLARS**
31.11 g., 0.999 Silver 0.999 oz. ASW, 35x46 mm. **Ruler:** Elizabeth II **Subject:** Impressionists paintings **Rev:** Multicolor painting of a maiden **Shape:** Vertical rectangle

| Date | Mintage | VF20 | XF40 | MS60 | MS63 | MS65 |
|---|---|---|---|---|---|---|
| 2005 | Est. 2005 | PF65 65.00 | | | | |

**KM# 290 2 DOLLARS**
31.11 g., 0.999 Silver 0.999 oz. ASW, 35x46 mm. **Ruler:** Elizabeth II **Subject:** Impresionists paintings **Rev:** Multicolor painting of an artist **Shape:** Vertical rectangle

| Date | Mintage | VF20 | XF40 | MS60 | MS63 | MS65 |
|---|---|---|---|---|---|---|
| 2005 | Est. 2005 | PF65 65.00 | | | | |

**KM# 291 2 DOLLARS**
31.11 g., 0.999 Silver 0.999 oz. ASW, 35x46 mm. **Ruler:** Elizabeth II **Subject:** Impressionists paintings **Rev:** Multicolor painting of Canada **Shape:** Vertical rectangle

| Date | Mintage | VF20 | XF40 | MS60 | MS63 | MS65 |
|---|---|---|---|---|---|---|
| 2005 | Est. 2005 | PF65 65.00 | | | | |

**KM# 294 2 DOLLARS**
62.20 g., 0.999 Silver 1.9978 oz. ASW, 55 mm. **Ruler:** Elizabeth II **Subject:** Year of the Dog **Rev:** Multicolor dog

| Date | Mintage | VF20 | XF40 | MS60 | MS63 | MS65 |
|---|---|---|---|---|---|---|
| 2005 | — | PF65 95.00 | | | | |

**KM# 298 2 DOLLARS**
1.56 g., 0.999 Gold 0.0501 oz. AGW, 16 mm. **Ruler:** Elizabeth II **Subject:** Year of the Dog **Rev:** Multicolor dog

| Date | Mintage | VF20 | XF40 | MS60 | MS63 | MS65 |
|---|---|---|---|---|---|---|
| 2005 | — | PF65 95.00 | | | | |

**KM# 299 2 DOLLARS**
3.11 g., 0.999 Gold 0.0999 oz. AGW, 18 mm. **Ruler:** Elizabeth II **Subject:** Year of the Dog **Rev:** Multicolor dog

| Date | Mintage | VF20 | XF40 | MS60 | MS63 | MS65 |
|---|---|---|---|---|---|---|
| 2005 | — | PF65 185 | | | | |

**KM# 330 2 DOLLARS**
62.20 g., 0.999 Silver 1.9978 oz. ASW, 30x70 mm. **Ruler:** Elizabeth II **Subject:** Life of Christ **Rev:** Last Supper (1495) **Shape:** Vertical rectangle

| Date | Mintage | VF20 | XF40 | MS60 | MS63 | MS65 |
|---|---|---|---|---|---|---|
| 2006 | Est. 1000 | PF65 175 | | | | |

**KM# 190 2 DOLLARS**
1.50 g., 0.999 Gold 0.0482 oz. AGW **Ruler:** Elizabeth II **Subject:** Year of the Pig **Obv:** Head right **Rev:** Multicolor pig

| Date | Mintage | VF20 | XF40 | MS60 | MS63 | MS65 |
|---|---|---|---|---|---|---|
| 2007 | — | PF65 95.00 | | | | |

**KM# 205 2 DOLLARS**
31.11 g., 0.999 Silver 0.999 oz. ASW, 40.7 mm. **Ruler:** Elizabeth II **Subject:** Peoples Republic of China, 60th Anniversary **Rev:** Dragon and scenes of China in multicolor

| Date | Mintage | VF20 | XF40 | MS60 | MS63 | MS65 |
|---|---|---|---|---|---|---|
| 2008 | 6,888 | PF65 175 | | | | |

**KM# 185 2 DOLLARS**
31.11 g., 0.999 Silver 0.999 oz. ASW Partially gilt, 40 mm. **Ruler:** Elizabeth II **Subject:** Year of the Ox **Rev:** Gilt ox advancing left

| Date | Mintage | VF20 | XF40 | MS60 | MS63 | MS65 |
|---|---|---|---|---|---|---|
| 2009 | 20,000 | PF65 185 | | | | |

**KM# 199 2 DOLLARS**
25.00 g., 0.925 Silver 0.7435 oz. ASW, 38.6 mm. **Ruler:** Elizabeth II **Rev:** Two spinner dolphins leaping, swarovski crystal chip in eye

| Date | Mintage | VF20 | XF40 | MS60 | MS63 | MS65 |
|---|---|---|---|---|---|---|
| 2009 | 2,500 | PF65 50.00 | | | | |

**KM# 200 2 DOLLARS**
0.50 g., 0.999 Gold 0.0161 oz. AGW, 11 mm. **Ruler:** Elizabeth II **Rev:** Two spinner dolphins leaping out of the water

| Date | Mintage | VF20 | XF40 | MS60 | MS63 | MS65 |
|---|---|---|---|---|---|---|
| 2009 | 10,000 | PF65 50.00 | | | | |

**KM# 209 2 DOLLARS**
1.00 g., 0.900 Gold 0.0289 oz. AGW **Ruler:** Elizabeth II **Subject:** Frederic Chopin **Obv:** Elizabeth II head right **Rev:** Chopin bust and autograph

| Date | Mintage | VF20 | XF40 | MS60 | MS63 | MS65 |
|---|---|---|---|---|---|---|
| 2009 | 10,000 | PF65 100 | | | | |

**KM# 210 2 DOLLARS**
31.11 g., 0.999 Silver 0.999 oz. ASW, 40.7 mm. **Ruler:** Elizabeth II **Obv:** Head right **Rev:** Two black swans, multicolor

| Date | Mintage | VF20 | XF40 | MS60 | MS63 | MS65 |
|---|---|---|---|---|---|---|
| 2009 | 10,000 | PF65 80.00 | | | | |

**KM# 215 2 DOLLARS**
31.11 g., 0.999 Silver 0.999 oz. ASW, 40 mm. **Ruler:** Elizabeth II **Subject:** Russian Ballet **Rev:** Anna Pavlova in multicolor

| Date | Mintage | VF20 | XF40 | MS60 | MS63 | MS65 |
|---|---|---|---|---|---|---|
| 2009 Prooflike | 5,000 | — | — | — | — | 120 |

**KM# 216 2 DOLLARS**
31.10 g., 0.999 Silver 0.999 oz. ASW, 40.7 mm. **Ruler:** Elizabeth II **Subject:** Russian Ballet **Rev:** Matilda Kshesinskaya in multicolor

| Date | Mintage | VF20 | XF40 | MS60 | MS63 | MS65 |
|---|---|---|---|---|---|---|
| 2009 Prooflike | 10,000 | — | — | — | — | 100 |

**KM# 217 2 DOLLARS**
31.11 g., 0.999 Silver 0.999 oz. ASW, 40.7 mm. **Ruler:** Elizabeth II **Subject:** Russian Ballet **Rev:** Sergey Lefar in multicolor

| Date | Mintage | VF20 | XF40 | MS60 | MS63 | MS65 |
|---|---|---|---|---|---|---|
| 2009 Prooflike | 10,000 | — | — | — | — | 100 |

**KM# 218 2 DOLLARS**
31.11 g., 0.999 Silver 0.999 oz. ASW, 40.7 mm. **Ruler:** Elizabeth II **Subject:** Russian Ballet **Rev:** Sergi Daighilev in multicolor

| Date | Mintage | VF20 | XF40 | MS60 | MS63 | MS65 |
|---|---|---|---|---|---|---|
| 2009 Prooflike | 10,000 | — | — | — | — | 100 |

**KM# 219 2 DOLLARS**
31.10 g., 0.999 Silver 0.999 oz. ASW, 40.7 mm. **Ruler:** Elizabeth II **Subject:** Russian Ballet **Rev:** Vaslav Fomich Nijinsky

| Date | Mintage | VF20 | XF40 | MS60 | MS63 | MS65 |
|---|---|---|---|---|---|---|
| 2009 Prooflike | 10,000 | — | — | — | — | 100 |

**KM# 220 2 DOLLARS**
31.11 g., 0.999 Silver 0.999 oz. ASW, 40.7 mm. **Ruler:** Elizabeth II **Subject:** Panagyurishte Treasure **Rev:** Vessel in the shape of a female head right

| Date | Mintage | VF20 | XF40 | MS60 | MS63 | MS65 |
|---|---|---|---|---|---|---|
| 2009 | 5,000 | — | — | — | — | 120 |

**KM# 221 2 DOLLARS**
31.11 g., 0.999 Silver 0.999 oz. ASW, 40.7 mm. **Ruler:** Elizabeth II **Subject:** Panagyurishte Treasure **Rev:** Vessel in shape of female head left

| Date | Mintage | VF20 | XF40 | MS60 | MS63 | MS65 |
|---|---|---|---|---|---|---|
| 2009 | 5,000 | — | — | — | — | 120 |

**KM# 222 2 DOLLARS**
31.11 g., 0.999 Silver 0.999 oz. ASW, 40.7 mm. **Ruler:** Elizabeth II **Subject:** Panagyurishte Treasure **Rev:** Vessel in shape of ram's head

| Date | Mintage | VF20 | XF40 | MS60 | MS63 | MS65 |
|---|---|---|---|---|---|---|
| 2009 | 5,000 | — | — | — | — | 120 |

**KM# 223 2 DOLLARS**
31.11 g., 0.999 Silver 0.999 oz. ASW, 40 mm. **Ruler:** Elizabeth II **Subject:** Peoples Republic of China, 60th Anniversary **Rev:** Multicolor background, astronaut, olympic flame and dragon motifs

| Date | Mintage | VF20 | XF40 | MS60 | MS63 | MS65 |
|---|---|---|---|---|---|---|
| 2009 Prooflike | 6,888 | — | — | — | — | 95.00 |

**KM# 224 2 DOLLARS**
31.11 g., 0.999 Silver 0.999 oz. ASW, 40.7 mm. **Ruler:** Elizabeth II **Series:** Soviet Automobiles **Rev:** GAZ 12 ZIM in multicolor

| Date | Mintage | VF20 | XF40 | MS60 | MS63 | MS65 |
|---|---|---|---|---|---|---|
| 2009 Prooflike | 15,000 | — | — | — | — | 80.00 |

**KM# 225 2 DOLLARS**
31.11 g., 0.999 Silver 0.999 oz. ASW, 40.7 mm. **Ruler:** Elizabeth II **Subject:** Soviet Automobiles **Rev:** GAZ M290 Pobeda in multicolor

| Date | Mintage | VF20 | XF40 | MS60 | MS63 | MS65 |
|---|---|---|---|---|---|---|
| 2009 Prooflike | 15,000 | — | — | — | — | 80.00 |

**KM# 226 2 DOLLARS**
31.11 g., 0.999 Silver 0.999 oz. ASW, 40.7 mm. **Ruler:** Elizabeth II **Subject:** Soviet Automobiles **Rev:** GAZ M21 Volga

| Date | Mintage | VF20 | XF40 | MS60 | MS63 | MS65 |
|---|---|---|---|---|---|---|
| 2009 Prooflike | 15,000 | — | — | — | — | 80.00 |

**KM# 227 2 DOLLARS**
31.11 g., 0.999 Silver 0.999 oz. ASW, 40.7 mm. **Ruler:** Elizabeth II **Subject:** Soviet Automobiles **Rev:** Moskvich 400

| Date | Mintage | VF20 | XF40 | MS60 | MS63 | MS65 |
|---|---|---|---|---|---|---|
| 2009 Prooflike | 15,000 | — | — | — | — | 80.00 |

**KM# 229 2 DOLLARS**
31.11 g., 0.999 Silver 0.999 oz. ASW partially gilt, 40 mm. **Ruler:** Elizabeth II **Subject:** Year of the Ox **Rev:** Ox, partially gilt

| Date | Mintage | VF20 | XF40 | MS60 | MS63 | MS65 |
|---|---|---|---|---|---|---|
| 2009 | 2,000 | PF65 100 | | | | |

**KM# 350 2 DOLLARS**
25.00 g., 0.999 Silver 0.803 oz. ASW, 38.61 mm. **Ruler:** Elizabeth II **Rev:** Partridge in a pear tree

| Date | Mintage | VF20 | XF40 | MS60 | MS63 | MS65 |
|---|---|---|---|---|---|---|
| 2009 | 1,500 | PF65 70.00 | | | | |

**KM# 351 2 DOLLARS**
25.00 g., 0.999 Silver 0.803 oz. ASW, 38.61 mm. **Ruler:** Elizabeth II **Rev:** Two turtle doves

| Date | Mintage | VF20 | XF40 | MS60 | MS63 | MS65 |
|---|---|---|---|---|---|---|
| 2009 | 1,500 | PF65 70.00 | | | | |

**KM# 352 2 DOLLARS**
25.00 g., 0.999 Silver 0.803 oz. ASW, 38.61 mm. **Ruler:** Elizabeth II **Rev:** Three French hens

| Date | Mintage | VF20 | XF40 | MS60 | MS63 | MS65 |
|---|---|---|---|---|---|---|
| 2009 | 1,500 | PF65 70.00 | | | | |

**KM# 353 2 DOLLARS**
25.00 g., 0.999 Silver 0.803 oz. ASW, 38.61 mm. **Ruler:** Elizabeth II **Rev:** Four calling birds

| Date | Mintage | VF20 | XF40 | MS60 | MS63 | MS65 |
|---|---|---|---|---|---|---|
| 2009 | 1,500 | PF65 70.00 | | | | |

**KM# 354 2 DOLLARS**
25.00 g., 0.999 Silver 0.803 oz. ASW, 38.61 mm. **Ruler:** Elizabeth II **Rev:** Five golden rings

| Date | Mintage | VF20 | XF40 | MS60 | MS63 | MS65 |
|---|---|---|---|---|---|---|
| 2009 | 1,500 | PF65 70.00 | | | | |

**KM# 355 2 DOLLARS**
25.00 g., 0.999 Silver 0.803 oz. ASW, 38.61 mm. **Ruler:** Elizabeth II **Rev:** Six Geese a-laying

| Date | Mintage | VF20 | XF40 | MS60 | MS63 | MS65 |
|---|---|---|---|---|---|---|
| 2009 | 1,500 | PF65 70.00 | | | | |

**KM# 356 2 DOLLARS**
25.00 g., 0.999 Silver 0.803 oz. ASW, 38.61 mm. **Ruler:** Elizabeth II **Rev:** Seven swans a-swimming

| Date | Mintage | VF20 | XF40 | MS60 | MS63 | MS65 |
|---|---|---|---|---|---|---|
| 2009 | 1,500 | PF65 70.00 | | | | |

**KM# 357 2 DOLLARS**
25.00 g., 0.999 Silver 0.803 oz. ASW, 38.61 mm. **Ruler:** Elizabeth II **Rev:** Eight maids a-milking

| Date | Mintage | VF20 | XF40 | MS60 | MS63 | MS65 |
|---|---|---|---|---|---|---|
| 2009 | 1,500 | PF65 70.00 | | | | |

**KM# 358 2 DOLLARS**
25.00 g., 0.999 Silver 0.803 oz. ASW, 38.61 mm. **Ruler:** Elizabeth II **Rev:** Nine ladies dancing

| Date | Mintage | VF20 | XF40 | MS60 | MS63 | MS65 |
|---|---|---|---|---|---|---|
| 2009 | 1,500 | PF65 70.00 | | | | |

**KM# 359 2 DOLLARS**
25.00 g., 0.999 Silver 0.803 oz. ASW, 38.61 mm. **Ruler:** Elizabeth II **Rev:** Ten Lords a-leaping

| Date | Mintage | VF20 | XF40 | MS60 | MS63 | MS65 |
|---|---|---|---|---|---|---|
| 2009 | 1,500 | PF65 70.00 | | | | |

**KM# 360 2 DOLLARS**
25.00 g., 0.999 Silver 0.803 oz. ASW, 38.61 mm. **Ruler:** Elizabeth II **Rev:** Eleven Pipers Piping

| Date | Mintage | VF20 | XF40 | MS60 | MS63 | MS65 |
|---|---|---|---|---|---|---|
| 2009 | 1,500 | PF65 70.00 | | | | |

**KM# 361 2 DOLLARS**
25.00 g., 0.999 Silver 0.803 oz. ASW, 38.61 mm. **Ruler:** Elizabeth II **Rev:** Twelve drummers drumming

| Date | Mintage | VF20 | XF40 | MS60 | MS63 | MS65 |
|---|---|---|---|---|---|---|
| 2009 | 1,500 | PF65 70.00 | | | | |

**KM# 362 2 DOLLARS**
62.20 g., 0.999 Silver 1.9978 oz. ASW, 63x27 mm. **Ruler:** Elizabeth II **Rev:** Flowers **Shape:** Vertical rectangle

| Date | Mintage | VF20 | XF40 | MS60 | MS63 | MS65 |
|---|---|---|---|---|---|---|
| 2009 | 16,888 | PF65 110 | | | | |

**KM# 552 2 DOLLARS**
Silver **Ruler:** Elizabeth II **Subject:** Russian Cartoons

| Date | Mintage | VF20 | XF40 | MS60 | MS63 | MS65 |
|---|---|---|---|---|---|---|
| 2009 | — | PF65 75.00 | | | | |

**KM# 553 2 DOLLARS**
Silver **Ruler:** Elizabeth II **Subject:** Russian Cartoons

| Date | Mintage | VF20 | XF40 | MS60 | MS63 | MS65 |
|---|---|---|---|---|---|---|
| 2009 | — | PF65 75.00 | | | | |

**KM# 206 2 DOLLARS**
31.11 g., 0.999 Silver 0.999 oz. ASW, 40.7 mm. **Ruler:** Elizabeth II **Rev:** Two white swans, red heart in background

| Date | Mintage | VF20 | XF40 | MS60 | MS63 | MS65 |
|---|---|---|---|---|---|---|
| 2010 | 20,000 | PF65 65.00 | | | | |

**KM# 213 2 DOLLARS**
56.60 g., 0.925 Silver 1.6833 oz. ASW, 55.6x41.6 mm. **Ruler:** Elizabeth II **Subject:** Coronation Egg **Obv:** Open egg - Queen Elizabeth head right **Rev:** Faberge Egg and coach **Shape:** Vertical oval

| Date | Mintage | VF20 | XF40 | MS60 | MS63 | MS65 |
|---|---|---|---|---|---|---|
| 2010 | 5,000 | — | — | — | — | 100 |

**KM# 228 2 DOLLARS**
31.11 g., 0.999 Silver 0.999 oz. ASW, 40 mm. **Ruler:** Elizabeth II **Subject:** Gai Thong Hanh, Safe Conduct Pass **Rev:** Viet Nam flag and soldiers, partially gilt

| Date | Mintage | VF20 | XF40 | MS60 | MS63 | MS65 |
|---|---|---|---|---|---|---|
| 2010 | 5,000 | PF65 140 | | | | |

**KM# 233 2 DOLLARS**
62.21 g., 0.999 Silver 1.9981 oz. ASW partially gilt, 40 mm. **Ruler:** Elizabeth II **Subject:** Year of the Tiger **Rev:** Tiger partially gilt

| Date | Mintage | VF20 | XF40 | MS60 | MS63 | MS65 |
|---|---|---|---|---|---|---|
| 2010 | 20,000 | PF65 120 | | | | |

**KM# 237 2 DOLLARS**
1.00 g., 0.900 Gold 0.0289 oz. AGW, 12 mm. **Ruler:** Elizabeth II **Obv:** Head right **Rev:** Copernicus bust 3/4 left

| Date | Mintage | VF20 | XF40 | MS60 | MS63 | MS65 |
|---|---|---|---|---|---|---|
| 2010 | 5,000 | PF65 75.00 | | | | |

**KM# 245 2 DOLLARS**
31.10 g., 0.999 Silver 0.999 oz. ASW, 40.7 mm. **Ruler:** Elizabeth II **Subject:** Famous express trains - Trans Siberian Express **Rev:** Steam train traveling left, multicolor

| Date | Mintage | VF20 | XF40 | MS60 | MS63 | MS65 |
|---|---|---|---|---|---|---|
| 2010 | 15,000 | PF65 80.00 | | | | |

**KM# 246 2 DOLLARS**
31.10 g., 0.999 Silver 0.999 oz. ASW, 40.7 mm. **Ruler:** Elizabeth II **Subject:** Famous express trains **Rev:** British Railways Flying Scotsman locomotive right, multicolor

| Date | Mintage | VF20 | XF40 | MS60 | MS63 | MS65 |
|---|---|---|---|---|---|---|
| 2010 | 15,000 | PF65 80.00 | | | | |

**KM# 247 2 DOLLARS**
31.10 g., 0.999 Silver 0.999 oz. ASW, 40.7 mm. **Ruler:** Elizabeth II **Subject:** Famous express trains - Orient Express **Rev:** Steam train right, multicolor

| Date | Mintage | VF20 | XF40 | MS60 | MS63 | MS65 |
|---|---|---|---|---|---|---|
| 2010 | 15,000 | PF65 80.00 | | | | |

**KM# 248 2 DOLLARS**
31.10 g., 0.999 Silver 0.999 oz. ASW, 40.7 mm. **Ruler:** Elizabeth II **Subject:** Famous Express trains - 20th Century Limited **Rev:** Streamlined steam train left, multicolored

| Date | Mintage | VF20 | XF40 | MS60 | MS63 | MS65 |
|---|---|---|---|---|---|---|
| 2010 | 15,000 | PF65 80.00 | | | | |

**KM# 251 2 DOLLARS**
31.11 g., 0.999 Silver 0.999 oz. ASW, 38.6 mm. **Ruler:** Elizabeth II **Subject:** Peanuts 60th Anniversary **Rev:** Snoopy as conductor with flowers, Woodstock with red ribbon

| Date | Mintage | VF20 | XF40 | MS60 | MS63 | MS65 |
|---|---|---|---|---|---|---|
| 2010 Prooflike | 3,000 | — | — | — | — | 80.00 |

**KM# 252 2 DOLLARS**
31.11 g., 0.999 Silver 0.999 oz. ASW, 38.6 mm. **Ruler:** Elizabeth II **Subject:** Peanuts 60th Anniversary **Rev:** Charlie Brown with Snoopy and birthday cake

| Date | Mintage | VF20 | XF40 | MS60 | MS63 | MS65 |
|---|---|---|---|---|---|---|
| 2010 Prooflike | 3,000 | — | — | — | — | 80.00 |

**KM# 253 2 DOLLARS**
31.11 g., 0.999 Silver 0.999 oz. ASW, 38.6 mm. **Ruler:** Elizabeth II **Subject:** Peanuts 60th Anniversary **Rev:** Schroeder and Lucy by piano

| Date | Mintage | VF20 | XF40 | MS60 | MS63 | MS65 |
|---|---|---|---|---|---|---|
| 2010 Prooflike | 3,000 | — | — | — | — | 80.00 |

**KM# 371 2 DOLLARS**
56.56 g., 0.925 Silver 1.6821 oz. ASW, 55.6x41.6 mm. **Ruler:** Elizabeth II **Subject:** Faberge egg - Lily of the Valley **Obv:** Elizabeth II head right, open egg **Rev:** Egg on stand **Shape:** Vertical oval

| Date | Mintage | VF20 | XF40 | MS60 | MS63 | MS65 |
|---|---|---|---|---|---|---|
| 2010 | 7,000 | PF65 100 | | | | |

**KM# 372 2 DOLLARS**
31.11 g., 0.999 Silver 0.999 oz. ASW, 37.1x31.9 mm. **Ruler:** Elizabeth II **Subject:** Hello Kitty **Shape:** Heart with ribbon

| Date | Mintage | VF20 | XF40 | MS60 | MS63 | MS65 |
|---|---|---|---|---|---|---|
| 2010 | Est. 3000 | PF65 50.00 | | | | |

**KM# 373 2 DOLLARS**
31.11 g., 0.999 Silver 0.999 oz. ASW, 37.1x31.9 mm. **Ruler:** Elizabeth II **Subject:** Kiki Lala **Shape:** Heart with ribbon

| Date | Mintage | VF20 | XF40 | MS60 | MS63 | MS65 |
|---|---|---|---|---|---|---|
| 2010 | Est. 3000 | PF65 60.00 | | | | |

**KM# 374 2 DOLLARS**
31.11 g., 0.999 Silver 0.999 oz. ASW, 37.1x31.9 mm. **Ruler:** Elizabeth II **Subject:** My Melo **Shape:** Heart with ribbon

| Date | Mintage | VF20 | XF40 | MS60 | MS63 | MS65 |
|---|---|---|---|---|---|---|
| 2010 | Est. 3000 | PF65 60.00 | | | | |

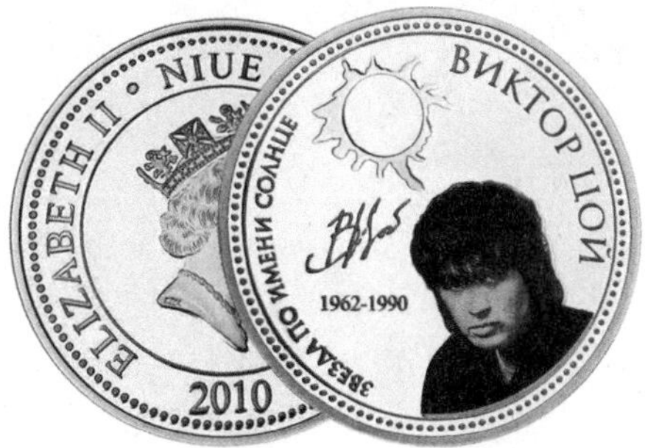


**KM# 381 2 DOLLARS**
31.11 g., 0.999 Silver 0.999 oz. ASW, 40.2 mm. **Ruler:** Elizabeth II **Subject:** Russian Musicians **Rev:** Viktor Tsoy at lower right in multicolor

| Date | Mintage | VF20 | XF40 | MS60 | MS63 | MS65 |
|---|---|---|---|---|---|---|
| 2010 | 2,000 | PF65 65.00 | | | | |

**KM# 382 2 DOLLARS**
31.11 g., 0.999 Silver 0.999 oz. ASW, 40.2 mm. **Ruler:** Elizabeth II **Subject:** Russian Musicians **Rev:** Vladimir Vysotsky at lower right in multicolor

| Date | Mintage | VF20 | XF40 | MS60 | MS63 | MS65 |
|---|---|---|---|---|---|---|
| 2010 | 2,000 | PF65 65.00 | | | | |

**KM# 383 2 DOLLARS**
31.11 g., 0.999 Silver 0.999 oz. ASW, 40.2 mm. **Ruler:** Elizabeth II **Rev:** Portrait in color

| Date | Mintage | VF20 | XF40 | MS60 | MS63 | MS65 |
|---|---|---|---|---|---|---|
| 2010 | Est. 2000 | PF65 65.00 | | | | |

**KM# 384 2 DOLLARS**
31.11 g., 0.999 Silver 0.999 oz. ASW, 38.61 mm. **Ruler:** Elizabeth II **Subject:** Miffy with friends

| Date | Mintage | VF20 | XF40 | MS60 | MS63 | MS65 |
|---|---|---|---|---|---|---|
| 2010 | Est. 3000 | PF65 60.00 | | | | |

**KM# 385 2 DOLLARS**
31.11 g., 0.999 Silver 0.999 oz. ASW, 38.61 mm. **Ruler:** Elizabeth II **Subject:** Miffy on turtle

| Date | Mintage | VF20 | XF40 | MS60 | MS63 | MS65 |
|---|---|---|---|---|---|---|
| 2010 | — | PF65 60.00 | | | | |

**KM# 386 2 DOLLARS**
31.11 g., 0.999 Silver 0.999 oz. ASW, 38.61 mm. **Ruler:** Elizabeth II **Subject:** Miffy celebration

| Date | Mintage | VF20 | XF40 | MS60 | MS63 | MS65 |
|---|---|---|---|---|---|---|
| 2010 | Est. 3000 | PF65 60.00 | | | | |

**KM# 390 2 DOLLARS**
31.10 g., 0.999 Silver 0.999 oz. ASW, 40.7 mm. **Ruler:** Elizabeth II **Subject:** Yamal **Rev:** Child wearing fur coat in multicolor

| Date | Mintage | VF20 | XF40 | MS60 | MS63 | MS65 |
|---|---|---|---|---|---|---|
| 2010 | 5,000 | PF65 55.00 | | | | |

**KM# 391 2 DOLLARS**
31.10 g., 0.999 Silver 0.999 oz. ASW, 40.7 mm. **Ruler:** Elizabeth II **Subject:** Yamal **Rev:** Gas and Oil exploration in multicolor

| Date | Mintage | VF20 | XF40 | MS60 | MS63 | MS65 |
|---|---|---|---|---|---|---|
| 2010 | 5,000 | PF65 55.00 | | | | |

**KM# 408 2 DOLLARS**
31.10 g., 0.999 Silver 0.999 oz. ASW, 40.7 mm. **Ruler:** Elizabeth II **Series:** Russian Transport **Obv:** Head with tiara right **Rev:** Bus in multicolor

| Date | Mintage | VF20 | XF40 | MS60 | MS63 | MS65 |
|---|---|---|---|---|---|---|
| 2010 | 15,000 | PF65 60.00 | | | | |

**KM# 409 2 DOLLARS**

31.10 g., 0.999 Silver 0.999 oz. ASW, 40.7 mm. **Ruler:** Elizabeth II **Subject:** Russian Transport **Obv:** Head with tiara right **Rev:** Trolley Bus in multicolor

| Date | Mintage | VF20 | XF40 | MS60 | MS63 | MS65 |
|---|---|---|---|---|---|---|
| 2010 | 15,000 | PF65 60.00 | | | | |

**KM# 410 2 DOLLARS**

31.10 g., 0.999 Silver 0.999 oz. ASW, 40.7 mm. **Ruler:** Elizabeth II **Subject:** Russian Transport **Obv:** Head with tiara right **Rev:** Metro in color

| Date | Mintage | VF20 | XF40 | MS60 | MS63 | MS65 |
|---|---|---|---|---|---|---|
| 2010 | 15,000 | PF65 60.00 | | | | |

**KM# 411 2 DOLLARS**

31.10 g., 0.999 Silver 0.999 oz. ASW, 40.7 mm. **Ruler:** Elizabeth II **Subject:** Russian Transport **Obv:** Head with tiara right **Rev:** Tram in color

| Date | Mintage | VF20 | XF40 | MS60 | MS63 | MS65 |
|---|---|---|---|---|---|---|
| 2010 | 15,000 | PF65 60.00 | | | | |

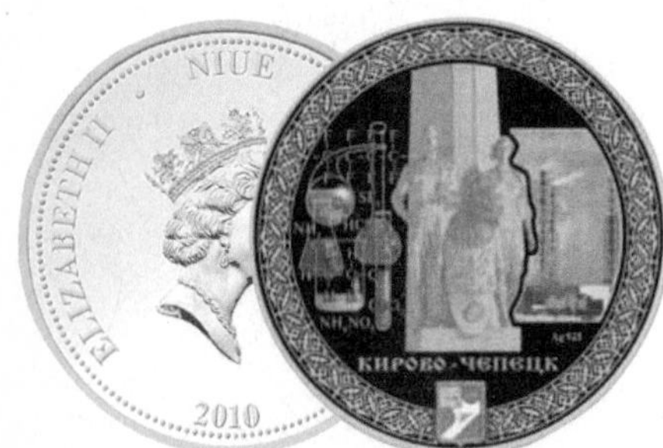


**KM# 416 2 DOLLARS**

28.28 g., 0.925 Silver 0.841 oz. ASW, 38.61 mm. **Ruler:** Elizabeth II **Obv:** Head with tiara right **Rev:** Kirovo Chepetsk

| Date | Mintage | VF20 | XF40 | MS60 | MS63 | MS65 |
|---|---|---|---|---|---|---|
| 2010 | 2,000 | PF65 75.00 | | | | |

**KM# 424 2 DOLLARS**

56.56 g., 0.925 Silver 1.6821 oz. ASW, 41.6x55.6 mm. **Ruler:** Elizabeth II **Subject:** Faberge Imperial Eggs - Clover Leaf **Obv:** Head with tiara right above opened egg **Rev:** Egg on stand in color **Shape:** Vertical oval

| Date | Mintage | VF20 | XF40 | MS60 | MS63 | MS65 |
|---|---|---|---|---|---|---|
| 2010 | 7,000 | PF65 125 | | | | |

**KM# 431 2 DOLLARS**

1.00 g., 0.900 Silver 0.0289 oz. ASW, 12 mm. **Ruler:** Elizabeth II **Subject:** Tadeusz Kosciuszko **Obv:** Head with tiara right **Rev:** Head left, signature below

| Date | Mintage | VF20 | XF40 | MS60 | MS63 | MS65 |
|---|---|---|---|---|---|---|
| 2010 | 5,000 | PF65 50.00 | | | | |

**KM# 442 2 DOLLARS**

25.00 g., 0.925 Silver 0.7435 oz. ASW, 38.61 mm. **Ruler:** Elizabeth II **Subject:** Twelve days of Christmas **Rev:** Partridge in a pear tree

| Date | Mintage | VF20 | XF40 | MS60 | MS63 | MS65 |
|---|---|---|---|---|---|---|
| 2010 | 1,500 | PF65 60.00 | | | | |

**KM# 443 2 DOLLARS**

25.00 g., 0.925 Silver 0.7435 oz. ASW, 38.61 mm. **Ruler:** Elizabeth II **Subject:** Twelve days of Christmas **Rev:** Turtle dove

| Date | Mintage | VF20 | XF40 | MS60 | MS63 | MS65 |
|---|---|---|---|---|---|---|
| 2010 | 1,500 | PF65 60.00 | | | | |

**KM# 444 2 DOLLARS**

25.00 g., 0.925 Silver 0.7435 oz. ASW, 38.61 mm. **Ruler:** Elizabeth II **Subject:** Twelve days of Christmas **Rev:** French hen

| Date | Mintage | VF20 | XF40 | MS60 | MS63 | MS65 |
|---|---|---|---|---|---|---|
| 2010 | 1,500 | PF65 60.00 | | | | |

**KM# 445 2 DOLLARS**

25.00 g., 0.925 Silver 0.7435 oz. ASW **Ruler:** Elizabeth II **Subject:** Twelve days of Christmas **Rev:** Calling bird

| Date | Mintage | VF20 | XF40 | MS60 | MS63 | MS65 |
|---|---|---|---|---|---|---|
| 2010 | 1,500 | PF65 60.00 | | | | |

**KM# 446 2 DOLLARS**

25.00 g., 0.925 Silver 0.7435 oz. ASW, 38.61 mm. **Ruler:** Elizabeth II **Subject:** Twelve days of Christmas **Rev:** Golden rings

| Date | Mintage | VF20 | XF40 | MS60 | MS63 | MS65 |
|---|---|---|---|---|---|---|
| 2010 | 1,500 | PF65 60.00 | | | | |

**KM# 447 2 DOLLARS**

25.00 g., 0.925 Silver 0.7435 oz. ASW, 38.61 mm. **Ruler:** Elizabeth II **Subject:** Twelve days of Christmas **Rev:** Geese a laying

| Date | Mintage | VF20 | XF40 | MS60 | MS63 | MS65 |
|---|---|---|---|---|---|---|
| 2010 | 1,500 | PF65 60.00 | | | | |

**KM# 448 2 DOLLARS**

25.00 g., 0.925 Silver 0.7435 oz. ASW, 38.61 mm. **Ruler:** Elizabeth II **Subject:** Twelve days of Christmas **Rev:** Swans a swimming

| Date | Mintage | VF20 | XF40 | MS60 | MS63 | MS65 |
|---|---|---|---|---|---|---|
| 2010 | 1,500 | PF65 60.00 | | | | |

**KM# 449 2 DOLLARS**

25.00 g., 0.925 Silver 0.7435 oz. ASW, 38.61 mm. **Ruler:** Elizabeth II **Subject:** Twelve days of Christmas **Rev:** Maids a milking

| Date | Mintage | VF20 | XF40 | MS60 | MS63 | MS65 |
|---|---|---|---|---|---|---|
| 2010 | 1,500 | PF65 60.00 | | | | |

**KM# 450 2 DOLLARS**

25.00 g., 0.925 Silver 0.7435 oz. ASW, 38.61 mm. **Ruler:** Elizabeth II **Subject:** Twelve days of Christmas **Rev:** Ladies dancing

| Date | Mintage | VF20 | XF40 | MS60 | MS63 | MS65 |
|---|---|---|---|---|---|---|
| 2010 | 1,500 | PF65 60.00 | | | | |

**KM# 451 2 DOLLARS**

25.00 g., 0.925 Silver 0.7435 oz. ASW, 38.61 mm. **Ruler:** Elizabeth II **Subject:** Twelve days of Christmas **Rev:** Lords a leaping

| Date | Mintage | VF20 | XF40 | MS60 | MS63 | MS65 |
|---|---|---|---|---|---|---|
| 2010 | 1,500 | PF65 60.00 | | | | |

**KM# 452 2 DOLLARS**

25.00 g., 0.925 Silver 0.7435 oz. ASW, 38.61 mm. **Ruler:** Elizabeth II **Subject:** Twelve days of Christmas **Rev:** Pipers piping

| Date | Mintage | VF20 | XF40 | MS60 | MS63 | MS65 |
|---|---|---|---|---|---|---|
| 2010 | 1,500 | PF65 60.00 | | | | |

**KM# 453 2 DOLLARS**

25.00 g., 0.925 Silver 0.7435 oz. ASW, 38.61 mm. **Ruler:** Elizabeth II **Subject:** Twelve days of Christmas **Rev:** Drummers drumming

| Date | Mintage | VF20 | XF40 | MS60 | MS63 | MS65 |
|---|---|---|---|---|---|---|
| 2010 | 1,500 | PF65 60.00 | | | | |

**KM# 457 2 DOLLARS**

31.10 g., 0.999 Silver 0.999 oz. ASW, 38.61 mm. **Ruler:** Elizabeth II **Subject:** Bulgarian theme roses - Survachka **Rev:** Figure-8 floral arangement

| Date | Mintage | VF20 | XF40 | MS60 | MS63 | MS65 |
|---|---|---|---|---|---|---|
| 2010 | 3,000 | PF65 55.00 | | | | |

**KM# 458 2 DOLLARS**

31.10 g., 0.999 Silver 0.999 oz. ASW, 38.61 mm. **Ruler:** Elizabeth II **Subject:** Bulgarian rose **Rev:** Top view into colored pink rose, gilt border

| Date | Mintage | VF20 | XF40 | MS60 | MS63 | MS65 |
|---|---|---|---|---|---|---|
| 2010 | 6,000 | PF65 50.00 | | | | |

**KM# 459 2 DOLLARS**

31.10 g., 0.999 Silver 0.999 oz. ASW, 38.61 mm. **Ruler:** Elizabeth II **Subject:** Bulgarian rose theme - Martenitsa **Rev:** tassle like device

| Date | Mintage | VF20 | XF40 | MS60 | MS63 | MS65 |
|---|---|---|---|---|---|---|
| 2010 | 3,000 | PF65 55.00 | | | | |

**KM# 460 2 DOLLARS**

31.10 g., 0.999 Silver 0.999 oz. ASW, 38.61 mm. **Ruler:** Elizabeth II **Rev:** Saint Peter icon

| Date | Mintage | VF20 | XF40 | MS60 | MS63 | MS65 |
|---|---|---|---|---|---|---|
| 2010 | 2,000 | PF65 60.00 | | | | |

**KM# 461 2 DOLLARS**

31.10 g., 0.999 Silver 0.999 oz. ASW, 38.61 mm. **Ruler:** Elizabeth II **Rev:** Saint Paul icon

| Date | Mintage | VF20 | XF40 | MS60 | MS63 | MS65 |
|---|---|---|---|---|---|---|
| 2010 | 2,000 | PF65 60.00 | | | | |

**KM# 550 2 DOLLARS**

Silver, 40 mm. **Ruler:** Elizabeth II **Subject:** Korean War, 60th Anniversary **Rev:** Soldier in multicolor

| Date | Mintage | VF20 | XF40 | MS60 | MS63 | MS65 |
|---|---|---|---|---|---|---|
| 2010 | 2,000 | PF65 80.00 | | | | |

**KM# 507 2 DOLLARS**

31.10 g., 0.999 Silver 0.9989 oz. ASW, 40.7 mm. **Ruler:** Elizabeth II **Subject:** Love is precious **Rev:** Two pink flamingos within heart

| Date | Mintage | VF20 | XF40 | MS60 | MS63 | MS65 |
|---|---|---|---|---|---|---|
| 2011 | 20,000 | PF65 50.00 | | | | |

**KM# 521 2 DOLLARS**

31.10 g., 0.999 Silver 0.9989 oz. ASW **Ruler:** Elizabeth II **Subject:** The Evangelists - St. Mathew and angel **Rev:** Icon in color

| Date | Mintage | VF20 | XF40 | MS60 | MS63 | MS65 |
|---|---|---|---|---|---|---|
| 2011 | 2,000 | PF65 60.00 | | | | |

**KM# 522 2 DOLLARS**
31.10 g., 0.999 Silver 0.9989 oz. ASW **Ruler:** Elizabeth II **Subject:** The Evangelists - St Mark with lion **Rev:** Icon in color

| Date | Mintage | VF20 | XF40 | MS60 | MS63 | MS65 |
|---|---|---|---|---|---|---|
| 2011 | 2,000 | **PF65** 60.00 | | | | |

**KM# 523 2 DOLLARS**
31.10 g., 0.999 Silver 0.9989 oz. ASW **Ruler:** Elizabeth II **Subject:** The Evangelists - Luke and oxen **Rev:** Icon in color

| Date | Mintage | VF20 | XF40 | MS60 | MS63 | MS65 |
|---|---|---|---|---|---|---|
| 2011 | 2,000 | **PF65** 60.00 | | | | |

**KM# 524 2 DOLLARS**
31.10 g., 0.999 Silver 0.9989 oz. ASW **Ruler:** Elizabeth II **Subject:** The Evangelists - John and eagle **Rev:** Icon in color

| Date | Mintage | VF20 | XF40 | MS60 | MS63 | MS65 |
|---|---|---|---|---|---|---|
| 2011 | 2,000 | **PF65** 60.00 | | | | |

**KM# 525 2 DOLLARS**
31.10 g., 0.999 Silver 0.9989 oz. ASW **Ruler:** Elizabeth II **Subject:** Eternal Love **Rev:** Two white doves within flora and scrolls

| Date | Mintage | VF20 | XF40 | MS60 | MS63 | MS65 |
|---|---|---|---|---|---|---|
| 2011 | 5,000 | **PF65** 50.00 | | | | |

**KM# 563 2 DOLLARS**
31.11 g., 0.999 Silver 0.999 oz. ASW **Ruler:** Elizabeth II **Subject:** Pirates of the Caribbean - Blackbeard **Obv:** Head with crown right **Rev:** Blackbeard in multicolor

| Date | Mintage | VF20 | XF40 | MS60 | MS63 | MS65 |
|---|---|---|---|---|---|---|
| 2011 | 2,000 | **PF65** 70.00 | | | | |

**KM# 564 2 DOLLARS**
31.11 g., 0.999 Silver 0.999 oz. ASW **Ruler:** Elizabeth II **Series:** Pirates of the Caribbean - Bartholomew Roberts **Obv:** Head with crown right **Rev:** Bartholomew Roberts in multicolor

| Date | Mintage | VF20 | XF40 | MS60 | MS63 | MS65 |
|---|---|---|---|---|---|---|
| 2011 | 2,000 | **PF65** 70.00 | | | | |

**KM# 565 2 DOLLARS**
31.11 g., 0.999 Silver 0.999 oz. ASW **Ruler:** Elizabeth II **Subject:** Pirates of the Caribbean - Henry Avery **Obv:** Head with crown right **Rev:** Henry Avery in multicolor

| Date | Mintage | VF20 | XF40 | MS60 | MS63 | MS65 |
|---|---|---|---|---|---|---|
| 2011 | 2,000 | **PF65** 70.00 | | | | |

**KM# 566 2 DOLLARS**
3.11 g., 0.999 Silver 0.0997 oz. ASW **Ruler:** Elizabeth II **Subject:** Pirates of the Caribbean - Calico Jack **Obv:** Head with crown right **Rev:** Calico Jack and two ladies in multicolor

| Date | Mintage | VF20 | XF40 | MS60 | MS63 | MS65 |
|---|---|---|---|---|---|---|
| 2011 | 2,000 | **PF65** 70.00 | | | | |

**KM# 567 2 DOLLARS**
31.11 g., 0.999 Silver 0.999 oz. ASW **Ruler:** Elizabeth II **Subject:** Legends of the Air **Obv:** Head with crown right **Rev:** B-2 Spirit Stealth Bomber in color

| Date | Mintage | VF20 | XF40 | MS60 | MS63 | MS65 |
|---|---|---|---|---|---|---|
| 2011 | 2,000 | **PF65** 60.00 | | | | |

**KM# 568 2 DOLLARS**
31.11 g., 0.999 Silver 0.999 oz. ASW **Ruler:** Elizabeth II **Subject:** Legends of the Air **Obv:** Head with crown right **Rev:** F-16 Fighting Falcon

| Date | Mintage | VF20 | XF40 | MS60 | MS63 | MS65 |
|---|---|---|---|---|---|---|
| 2011 | 2,000 | **PF65** 60.00 | | | | |

**KM# 569 2 DOLLARS**
31.11 g., 0.999 Silver 0.999 oz. ASW **Ruler:** Elizabeth II **Subject:** Legends of the Air **Obv:** Head with crown right **Rev:** AH-64D Apache Longbow in color

| Date | Mintage | VF20 | XF40 | MS60 | MS63 | MS65 |
|---|---|---|---|---|---|---|
| 2011 | 2,000 | **PF65** 60.00 | | | | |

**KM# 570 2 DOLLARS**
31.11 g., 0.999 Silver 0.999 oz. ASW **Ruler:** Elizabeth II **Subject:** Legends of the Air **Obv:** Head with crown right **Rev:** B-52 Stratofortress Bomber

| Date | Mintage | VF20 | XF40 | MS60 | MS63 | MS65 |
|---|---|---|---|---|---|---|
| 2011 | 2,000 | **PF65** 60.00 | | | | |

**KM# 573 2 DOLLARS**
31.11 g., 0.999 Silver 0.999 oz. ASW, 38.61 mm. **Ruler:** Elizabeth II **Subject:** First crossing of the Simpson Desert, 75th Anniversary **Obv:** Head with crown right **Rev:** Ted Colson in color

| Date | Mintage | VF20 | XF40 | MS60 | MS63 | MS65 |
|---|---|---|---|---|---|---|
| 2011 | 2,000 | **PF65** 75.00 | | | | |

**KM# 589 2 DOLLARS**
31.10 g., 0.999 Silver 0.999 oz. ASW, 33x55 mm. **Ruler:** Elizabeth II **Subject:** Kagaya Art Zodiac - Leo

| Date | Mintage | VF20 | XF40 | MS60 | MS63 | MS65 |
|---|---|---|---|---|---|---|
| 2011 | 8,000 | **PF65** 80.00 | | | | |

**KM# 590 2 DOLLARS**
31.10 g., 0.999 Silver 0.999 oz. ASW, 33x55 mm. **Ruler:** Elizabeth II **Subject:** Kagaya Art Zodiac - Virgo

| Date | Mintage | VF20 | XF40 | MS60 | MS63 | MS65 |
|---|---|---|---|---|---|---|
| 2011 | 8,000 | PF65 80.00 | | | | |

**KM# 591 2 DOLLARS**
31.10 g., 0.999 Silver 0.999 oz. ASW, 33x55 mm. **Ruler:** Elizabeth II **Subject:** Kagaya Art Zodiac - Libra **Shape:** Vertical rectangle

| Date | Mintage | VF20 | XF40 | MS60 | MS63 | MS65 |
|---|---|---|---|---|---|---|
| 2011 | 8,000 | PF65 80.00 | | | | |

**KM# 592 2 DOLLARS**
31.10 g., 0.999 Silver 0.999 oz. ASW, 33x55 mm. **Ruler:** Elizabeth II **Subject:** Kagaya Art Zodiac - Scorpio **Shape:** Vertical rectangle

| Date | Mintage | VF20 | XF40 | MS60 | MS63 | MS65 |
|---|---|---|---|---|---|---|
| 2011 | 8,000 | PF65 80.00 | | | | |

**KM# 593 2 DOLLARS**
31.10 g., 0.999 Silver 0.999 oz. ASW, 33x55 mm. **Ruler:** Elizabeth II **Subject:** Kagaya Art Zodiac - Sagittarius **Shape:** Vertical rectangle

| Date | Mintage | VF20 | XF40 | MS60 | MS63 | MS65 |
|---|---|---|---|---|---|---|
| 2011 | 8,000 | PF65 80.00 | | | | |

**KM# 601 2 DOLLARS**
31.10 g., 0.999 Silver 0.999 oz. ASW, 40.7 mm. **Ruler:** Elizabeth II **Subject:** Love Forever **Obv:** Head with crown right **Rev:** Two doves in flight, two golden rings, word Forever in many languages in background

| Date | Mintage | VF20 | XF40 | MS60 | MS63 | MS65 |
|---|---|---|---|---|---|---|
| 2011 | 20,000 | PF65 65.00 | | | | |

**KM# 602 2 DOLLARS**
31.10 g., 0.999 Silver 0.999 oz. ASW, 40.7 mm. **Ruler:** Elizabeth II **Subject:** Supersonic Transport - TU-144 **Rev:** Plane color image

| Date | Mintage | VF20 | XF40 | MS60 | MS63 | MS65 |
|---|---|---|---|---|---|---|
| 2011 | 8,000 | PF65 65.00 | | | | |

**KM# 603 2 DOLLARS**
31.10 g., 0.999 Silver 0.999 oz. ASW, 40.7 mm. **Ruler:** Elizabeth II **Subject:** Supersonic Transport - Concorde **Rev:** Plane color image

| Date | Mintage | VF20 | XF40 | MS60 | MS63 | MS65 |
|---|---|---|---|---|---|---|
| 2011 | 8,000 | PF65 65.00 | | | | |

**KM# 639 2 DOLLARS**
31.14 g., 0.999 Silver 1.000 oz. ASW, 27x47 mm. **Ruler:** Elizabeth II **Subject:** Orthodox shrines, Holy Trinity **Obv:** Head with crown right **Rev:** Five saints seated around table, partially gilt and colored **Edge:** Plain **Shape:** Vertical rectangle, convex

| Date | Mintage | VF20 | XF40 | MS60 | MS63 | MS65 |
|---|---|---|---|---|---|---|
| 2011 | Est. 3000 | PF65 100 | | | | |

**KM# 640 2 DOLLARS**
31.14 g., 0.999 Silver 1.000 oz. ASW, 27x47 mm. **Ruler:** Elizabeth II **Subject:** Orthodox Shrines, Christ Pantokrator **Obv:** Head with crown right **Rev:** Christ facing holding gospels, partially gilt and colored **Edge:** Plain **Shape:** Vertical rectangle, convex

| Date | Mintage | VF20 | XF40 | MS60 | MS63 | MS65 |
|---|---|---|---|---|---|---|
| 2011 | 3,000 | PF65 100 | | | | |

**KM# 642 2 DOLLARS**
31.11 g., 0.999 Silver 0.999 oz. ASW, 55x33 mm. **Ruler:** Elizabeth II **Obv:** Head with crown right **Rev:** First man in space, multicolor **Shape:** rectangle

| Date | Mintage | VF20 | XF40 | MS60 | MS63 | MS65 |
|---|---|---|---|---|---|---|
| 2011 Proof | 5,000 | — | — | — | — | 100 |

**KM# 643 2 DOLLARS**
31.11 g., 0.999 Silver 0.999 oz. ASW, 55x33 mm. **Ruler:** Elizabeth II **Obv:** Head with crown right **Rev:** First space walk

| Date | Mintage | VF20 | XF40 | MS60 | MS63 | MS65 |
|---|---|---|---|---|---|---|
| 2011 | 5,000 | PF65 100 | | | | |

**KM# 663 2 DOLLARS**
31.11 g., 0.999 Silver 0.999 oz. ASW, 40 mm. **Ruler:** Elizabeth II **Subject:** Star Wars - C3PO and R2D2

| Date | Mintage | VF20 | XF40 | MS60 | MS63 | MS65 |
|---|---|---|---|---|---|---|
| 2011 Prooflike | Est. 7500 | — | — | — | — | 120 |

**KM# 664 2 DOLLARS**
31.11 g., 0.999 Silver 0.999 oz. ASW, 40 mm. **Ruler:** Elizabeth II **Subject:** Star Wars - Darth Vader

| Date | Mintage | VF20 | XF40 | MS60 | MS63 | MS65 |
|---|---|---|---|---|---|---|
| 2011 Prooflike | Est. 7500 | — | — | — | — | 120 |

**KM# 665 2 DOLLARS**
31.11 g., 0.999 Silver 0.999 oz. ASW, 40 mm. **Ruler:** Elizabeth II **Subject:** Star Wars - Emperor Palpatine

| Date | Mintage | VF20 | XF40 | MS60 | MS63 | MS65 |
|---|---|---|---|---|---|---|
| 2011 Prooflike | Est. 7500 | — | — | — | — | 120 |

**KM# 666 2 DOLLARS**
31.11 g., 0.999 Silver 0.999 oz. ASW, 40 mm. **Ruler:** Elizabeth II **Subject:** Star Wars - Death Star

| Date | Mintage | VF20 | XF40 | MS60 | MS63 | MS65 |
|---|---|---|---|---|---|---|
| 2011 Prooflike | Est. 7500 | — | — | — | — | 120 |

**KM# 667 2 DOLLARS**
31.11 g., 0.999 Silver 0.999 oz. ASW, 40 mm. **Ruler:** Elizabeth II **Subject:** Star Wars - Han Solo and Chewbacca

| Date | Mintage | VF20 | XF40 | MS60 | MS63 | MS65 |
|---|---|---|---|---|---|---|
| 2011 Prooflike | — | — | — | — | — | 120 |

**KM# 668 2 DOLLARS**
31.11 g., 0.999 Silver 0.999 oz. ASW, 40 mm. **Ruler:** Elizabeth II **Subject:** Star Wars - Luke Skywalker and Princess Leia

| Date | Mintage | VF20 | XF40 | MS60 | MS63 | MS65 |
|---|---|---|---|---|---|---|
| 2011 Prooflike | — | — | — | — | — | 120 |

**KM# 669 2 DOLLARS**
31.11 g., 0.999 Silver 0.999 oz. ASW, 40 mm. **Ruler:** Elizabeth II **Series:** Star Wars - Stormtrooper

| Date | Mintage | VF20 | XF40 | MS60 | MS63 | MS65 |
|---|---|---|---|---|---|---|
| 2011 Prooflike | Est. 7500 | — | — | — | — | 120 |

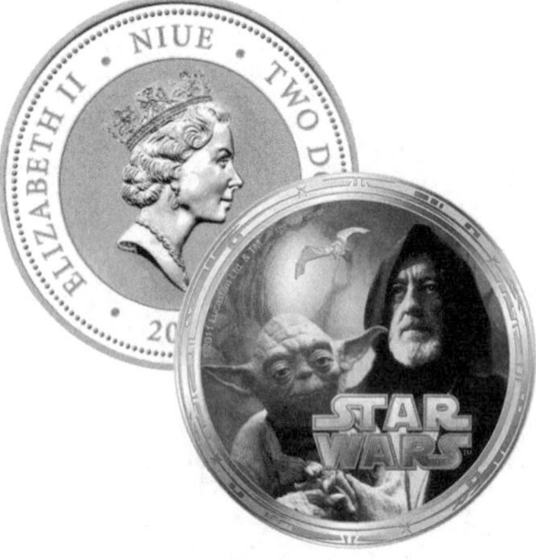


**KM# 670 2 DOLLARS**
31.11 g., 0.999 Silver 0.999 oz. ASW, 40 mm. **Ruler:** Elizabeth II **Subject:** Star Wars - Obi-Wan Kenobi and Yoda

| Date | Mintage | VF20 | XF40 | MS60 | MS63 | MS65 |
|---|---|---|---|---|---|---|
| 2011 Prooflike | Est. 7500 | — | — | — | — | 120 |

**KM# 671 2 DOLLARS**
31.11 g., 0.999 Silver 0.999 oz. ASW, 40 mm. **Ruler:** Elizabeth II **Subject:** Anne Geddes - Boy

| Date | Mintage | VF20 | XF40 | MS60 | MS63 | MS65 |
|---|---|---|---|---|---|---|
| 2011 Prooflike | 3,000 | — | — | — | — | 100 |

**KM# 672 2 DOLLARS**
31.11 g., 0.999 Silver 0.999 oz. ASW, 40 mm. **Ruler:** Elizabeth II **Subject:** Anne Geddes - Girl

| Date | Mintage | VF20 | XF40 | MS60 | MS63 | MS65 |
|---|---|---|---|---|---|---|
| 2011 Prooflike | 3,000 | — | — | — | — | 100 |

**KM# 673 2 DOLLARS**
15.55 g., 0.925 Silver 0.4624 oz. ASW, 35 mm. **Ruler:** Elizabeth II **Rev:** Mexican redknee tarantula in color

| Date | Mintage | VF20 | XF40 | MS60 | MS63 | MS65 |
|---|---|---|---|---|---|---|
| 2011 | 1,250 | — | — | — | — | 125 |

**KM# 692 2 DOLLARS**
31.11 g., 0.999 Silver 0.999 oz. ASW, 38.61 mm. **Ruler:** Elizabeth II **Obv:** Head with crown right **Rev:** Virgin Mary with arms outstretched in color **Edge:** Reeded

| Date | Mintage | VF20 | XF40 | MS60 | MS63 | MS65 |
|---|---|---|---|---|---|---|
| 2011 | 3,000 | **PF65** 100 | | | | |

**KM# 736 2 DOLLARS**
56.56 g., 0.925 Silver 1.6821 oz. ASW, 41.6x55.6 mm. **Ruler:** Elizabeth II **Subject:** Imperial Faberge Egg - Pansy Egg **Obv:** Head right in filigree, open egg below **Rev:** Pansy flowers around closed egg **Shape:** Vertical oval

| Date | Mintage | VF20 | XF40 | MS60 | MS63 | MS65 |
|---|---|---|---|---|---|---|
| 2011 | 7,000 | **PF65** 200 | | | | |

**KM# 802 2 DOLLARS**
31.10 g., 0.999 Silver 0.9989 oz. ASW, 40.7 mm. **Ruler:** Elizabeth II **Rev:** School children playing with globe

| Date | Mintage | VF20 | XF40 | MS60 | MS63 | MS65 |
|---|---|---|---|---|---|---|
| 2011 | Est. 6000 | PF65 100 | | | | |

**KM# 883 2 DOLLARS**
10.00 g., 0.925 Silver 0.2974 oz. ASW, 32 mm. **Ruler:** Elizabeth II **Rev:** Earth in color

| Date | Mintage | VF20 | XF40 | MS60 | MS63 | MS65 |
|---|---|---|---|---|---|---|
| 2011 | — | PF65 75.00 | | | | |

**KM# 884 2 DOLLARS**
12.00 g., 0.925 Silver 0.3569 oz. ASW, 35x35 mm. **Ruler:** Elizabeth II **Subject:** Elements - Air **Shape:** Irregular

| Date | Mintage | VF20 | XF40 | MS60 | MS63 | MS65 |
|---|---|---|---|---|---|---|
| 2011 | — | PF65 75.00 | | | | |

**KM# 885 2 DOLLARS**
12.00 g., 0.925 Silver 0.3569 oz. ASW, 35x35 mm. **Ruler:** Elizabeth II **Subject:** Elements - Water **Shape:** Irregular

| Date | Mintage | VF20 | XF40 | MS60 | MS63 | MS65 |
|---|---|---|---|---|---|---|
| 2011 | — | PF65 85.00 | | | | |

**KM# 886 2 DOLLARS**
12.00 g., 0.925 Silver 0.3569 oz. ASW, 35x35 mm. **Ruler:** Elizabeth II **Subject:** Elements - Land **Shape:** Irregular

| Date | Mintage | VF20 | XF40 | MS60 | MS63 | MS65 |
|---|---|---|---|---|---|---|
| 2011 | — | PF65 85.00 | | | | |

**KM# 887 2 DOLLARS**
12.00 g., 0.925 Silver 0.3569 oz. ASW, 35x35 mm. **Ruler:** Elizabeth II **Subject:** Elements - Fire **Shape:** Irregular

| Date | Mintage | VF20 | XF40 | MS60 | MS63 | MS65 |
|---|---|---|---|---|---|---|
| 2011 | — | PF65 85.00 | | | | |

**KM# 888 2 DOLLARS**
56.56 g., 0.925 Silver 1.6821 oz. ASW, 41.6x56.6 mm. **Ruler:** Elizabeth II **Subject:** Faberge egg - Dutchess of Marlboro egg **Shape:** Vertical oval

| Date | Mintage | VF20 | XF40 | MS60 | MS63 | MS65 |
|---|---|---|---|---|---|---|
| 2011 | — | PF65 100 | | | | |

**KM# 889 2 DOLLARS**
31.11 g., 0.999 Silver 0.999 oz. ASW, 40.7 mm. **Ruler:** Elizabeth II **Obv:** Crowned head right, eternal flame and wreath below **Rev:** WWII Russian Victory celebrations in color

| Date | Mintage | VF20 | XF40 | MS60 | MS63 | MS65 |
|---|---|---|---|---|---|---|
| 2011 | 5,000 | PF65 85.00 | | | | |

**KM# 939 2 DOLLARS**
31.10 g., 0.999 Silver 0.9989 oz. ASW, 45 x 31 mm. **Ruler:** Elizabeth II **Subject:** Family Day

| Date | Mintage | VF20 | XF40 | MS60 | MS63 | MS65 |
|---|---|---|---|---|---|---|
| 2011 Proof | Est. 8000 | — | — | — | — | — |

**KM# 940 2 DOLLARS**
1.00 g., 0.900 Gold 0.0289 oz. AGW, 12 mm. **Ruler:** Elizabeth II **Subject:** Adam Michiewicz

| Date | Mintage | VF20 | XF40 | MS60 | MS63 | MS65 |
|---|---|---|---|---|---|---|
| 2011 Proof | Est. 3000 | — | — | — | — | — |

**KM# 594 2 DOLLARS**
31.10 g., 0.999 Silver 0.999 oz. ASW, 33x55 mm. **Ruler:** Elizabeth II **Subject:** Kagaya Art Zodiac - Capricorn **Shape:** Vertical rectangle

| Date | Mintage | VF20 | XF40 | MS60 | MS63 | MS65 |
|---|---|---|---|---|---|---|
| 2012 | 8,000 | PF65 80.00 | | | | |

**KM# 595 2 DOLLARS**
31.10 g., 0.999 Silver 0.999 oz. ASW, 33x55 mm. **Ruler:** Elizabeth II **Subject:** Kagaya Art Zodiac - Aquarius **Shape:** Vertical rectangle

| Date | Mintage | VF20 | XF40 | MS60 | MS63 | MS65 |
|---|---|---|---|---|---|---|
| 2012 | 8,000 | **PF65** 80.00 | | | | |

**KM# 596 2 DOLLARS**
31.10 g., 0.999 Silver 0.999 oz. ASW, 33x55 mm. **Ruler:** Elizabeth II **Subject:** Kagaya Art Zodiac - Pisces **Shape:** Vertical rectangle

| Date | Mintage | VF20 | XF40 | MS60 | MS63 | MS65 |
|---|---|---|---|---|---|---|
| 2012 | 8,000 | **PF65** 80.00 | | | | |

**KM# 597 2 DOLLARS**
31.10 g., 0.999 Silver 0.999 oz. ASW, 33x55 mm. **Ruler:** Elizabeth II **Subject:** Kagaya Art Zodiac - Aries **Shape:** Vertical rectangle

| Date | Mintage | VF20 | XF40 | MS60 | MS63 | MS65 |
|---|---|---|---|---|---|---|
| 2012 | 8,000 | **PF65** 80.00 | | | | |

**KM# 598 2 DOLLARS**
31.10 g., 0.999 Silver 0.999 oz. ASW, 33x55 mm. **Ruler:** Elizabeth II **Subject:** Kagaya Art Zodiac - Taurus **Shape:** Vertical rectangle

| Date | Mintage | VF20 | XF40 | MS60 | MS63 | MS65 |
|---|---|---|---|---|---|---|
| 2012 | 8,000 | **PF65** 80.00 | | | | |

**KM# 599 2 DOLLARS**
31.10 g., 0.999 Silver 0.999 oz. ASW, 33x55 mm. **Ruler:** Elizabeth II **Subject:** Kagaya Art Zodiac - Gemini **Shape:** Vertical rectangle

| Date | Mintage | VF20 | XF40 | MS60 | MS63 | MS65 |
|---|---|---|---|---|---|---|
| 2012 | 8,000 | **PF65** 80.00 | | | | |

**KM# 600 2 DOLLARS**
31.10 g., 0.999 Silver 0.999 oz. ASW, 33x55 mm. **Ruler:** Elizabeth II **Subject:** Kagaya Art Zodiac - Cancer **Shape:** Vertical rectangle

| Date | Mintage | VF20 | XF40 | MS60 | MS63 | MS65 |
|---|---|---|---|---|---|---|
| 2012 | 8,000 | **PF65** 80.00 | | | | |

**KM# 638 2 DOLLARS**
31.11 g., 0.999 Silver 0.999 oz. ASW, 40.7 mm. **Ruler:** Elizabeth II **Obv:** Head with crown right **Rev:** R.M.S. Titanic sailing right within compass points

| Date | Mintage | VF20 | XF40 | MS60 | MS63 | MS65 |
|---|---|---|---|---|---|---|
| 2012 | 2,229 | **PF65** 225 | | | | |

**KM# 675 2 DOLLARS**
28.28 g., Copper-Nickel, 38.61 mm. **Ruler:** Elizabeth II **Rev:** Crowned state flowers **Edge:** Reeded

| Date | Mintage | VF20 | XF40 | MS60 | MS63 | MS65 |
|---|---|---|---|---|---|---|
| 2012 | — | — | — | — | — | 25.00 |

**KM# 675a 2 DOLLARS**
28.28 g., 0.925 Silver 0.841 oz. ASW, 38.61 mm. **Ruler:** Elizabeth II **Rev:** Crowned state flowers

| Date | Mintage | VF20 | XF40 | MS60 | MS63 | MS65 |
|---|---|---|---|---|---|---|
| 2012 | 19,500 | **PF65** 80.00 | | | | |

**KM# 676 2 DOLLARS**
31.11 g., 0.999 Silver 0.999 oz. ASW, 40.7 mm. **Ruler:** Elizabeth II **Rev:** Florida alligator, gilt **Edge:** Reeded

| Date | Mintage | VF20 | XF40 | MS60 | MS63 | MS65 |
|---|---|---|---|---|---|---|
| 2012 | 2,500 | **PF65** 80.00 | | | | |

**KM# 677 2 DOLLARS**
31.11 g., 0.999 Silver 0.999 oz. ASW, 40.7 mm. **Ruler:** Elizabeth II **Subject:** Year of the Dragon **Rev:** Dragon

| Date | Mintage | VF20 | XF40 | MS60 | MS63 | MS65 |
|---|---|---|---|---|---|---|
| 2012 | 2,500 | **PF65** 80.00 | | | | |

**KM# 691 2 DOLLARS**
31.11 g., 0.999 Silver 0.999 oz. ASW, 27x47 mm. **Ruler:** Elizabeth II **Subject:** Orthodox Shrines **Rev:** Faith, Hope and Charity and their mother, Sofia **Edge:** Plain

| Date | Mintage | VF20 | XF40 | MS60 | MS63 | MS65 |
|---|---|---|---|---|---|---|
| 2012 | 3,000 | PF65 100 | | | | |

**KM# 693 2 DOLLARS**
31.11 g., 0.999 Silver 0.999 oz. ASW partially gilt, 38.61 mm. **Ruler:** Elizabeth II **Rev:** Feng Shui - two Koi Carp gilt

| Date | Mintage | VF20 | XF40 | MS60 | MS63 | MS65 |
|---|---|---|---|---|---|---|
| 2012 | 10,000 | PF65 100 | | | | |

**KM# 694 2 DOLLARS**
31.11 g., 0.999 Silver 0.999 oz. ASW **Ruler:** Elizabeth II **Subject:** Nickelodeon's Sponge Bob **Rev:** Sponge Bob **Shape:** Square

| Date | Mintage | VF20 | XF40 | MS60 | MS63 | MS65 |
|---|---|---|---|---|---|---|
| 2012 | 100,000 | PF65 75.00 | | | | |

**KM# 695 2 DOLLARS**
31.11 g., 0.999 Silver 0.999 oz. ASW **Ruler:** Elizabeth II **Subject:** Nickelodeon's Sponge Bob **Rev:** Patrick Star **Shape:** Square

| Date | Mintage | VF20 | XF40 | MS60 | MS63 | MS65 |
|---|---|---|---|---|---|---|
| 2012 | 100,000 | PF65 75.00 | | | | |

**KM# 696 2 DOLLARS**
31.11 g., 0.999 Silver 0.999 oz. ASW **Ruler:** Elizabeth II **Subject:** Nickelodeon's Sponge Bob **Rev:** Sandy Cheeks **Shape:** Square

| Date | Mintage | VF20 | XF40 | MS60 | MS63 | MS65 |
|---|---|---|---|---|---|---|
| 2012 | 100,000 | PF65 75.00 | | | | |

**KM# 697 2 DOLLARS**
31.11 g., 0.999 Silver 0.999 oz. ASW **Ruler:** Elizabeth II **Subject:** Nickelodeon's Sponge Bob **Rev:** Gary (snail) **Shape:** Square

| Date | Mintage | VF20 | XF40 | MS60 | MS63 | MS65 |
|---|---|---|---|---|---|---|
| 2012 | 100,000 | PF65 75.00 | | | | |

**KM# 712 2 DOLLARS**
31.11 g., 0.999 Silver 0.999 oz. ASW, 40.7 mm. **Ruler:** Elizabeth II **Rev:** Dragon

| Date | Mintage | VF20 | XF40 | MS60 | MS63 | MS65 |
|---|---|---|---|---|---|---|
| 2012 | 50,000 | PF65 50.00 | | | | |

**KM# 717 2 DOLLARS**
31.11 g., 0.9999 Silver 0.9999 oz. ASW, 40.7 mm. **Ruler:** Elizabeth II **Subject:** Star Wars - Battle Droid

| Date | Mintage | VF20 | XF40 | MS60 | MS63 | MS65 |
|---|---|---|---|---|---|---|
| 2012 Prooflike | 10,000 | — | — | — | — | 125 |

**KM# 718 2 DOLLARS**
31.11 g., 0.999 Silver 0.999 oz. ASW, 40.7 mm. **Ruler:** Elizabeth II **Subject:** Star Wars - Darth Maul

| Date | Mintage | VF20 | XF40 | MS60 | MS63 | MS65 |
|---|---|---|---|---|---|---|
| 2012 Prooflike | 10,000 | — | — | — | — | 125 |

**KM# 719 2 DOLLARS**
31.11 g., 0.999 Silver 0.999 oz. ASW, 40.7 mm. **Ruler:** Elizabeth II **Subject:** Star Wars - young Obi Wan Kenobi

| Date | Mintage | VF20 | XF40 | MS60 | MS63 | MS65 |
|---|---|---|---|---|---|---|
| 2012 Prooflike | 10,000 | — | — | — | — | 125 |

**KM# 720 2 DOLLARS**
31.11 g., 0.999 Silver 0.999 oz. ASW, 40.7 mm. **Ruler:** Elizabeth II **Subject:** Star Wars - Mace Windu

| Date | Mintage | VF20 | XF40 | MS60 | MS63 | MS65 |
|---|---|---|---|---|---|---|
| 2012 Prooflike | 10,000 | — | — | — | — | 125 |

**KM# 721 2 DOLLARS**
31.11 g., 0.999 Silver 0.999 oz. ASW, 40.7 mm. **Ruler:** Elizabeth II **Subject:** Star Wars - Yoda

| Date | Mintage | VF20 | XF40 | MS60 | MS63 | MS65 |
|---|---|---|---|---|---|---|
| 2012 Prooflike | 10,000 | — | — | — | — | 125 |

**KM# 722 2 DOLLARS**
31.11 g., 0.999 Silver 0.999 oz. ASW, 40.7 mm. **Ruler:** Elizabeth II **Subject:** Star Wars - Queen Amidala

| Date | Mintage | VF20 | XF40 | MS60 | MS63 | MS65 |
|---|---|---|---|---|---|---|
| 2012 Prooflike | 10,000 | — | — | — | — | 125 |

**KM# 723 2 DOLLARS**
31.11 g., 0.999 Silver 0.999 oz. ASW, 40.7 mm. **Ruler:** Elizabeth II **Subject:** Star Wars - Qui-Gon Jinn

| Date | Mintage | VF20 | XF40 | MS60 | MS63 | MS65 |
|---|---|---|---|---|---|---|
| 2012 Prooflike | 10,000 | — | — | — | — | 125 |

**KM# 724 2 DOLLARS**
31.11 g., 0.999 Silver 0.999 oz. ASW, 40.7 mm. **Ruler:** Elizabeth II **Subject:** Star Wars - young Anakin Skywalker

| Date | Mintage | VF20 | XF40 | MS60 | MS63 | MS65 |
|---|---|---|---|---|---|---|
| 2012 Prooflike | 10,000 | — | — | — | — | 125 |

**KM# 743 2 DOLLARS**
15.55 g., 0.999 Silver 0.4994 oz. ASW, 33 mm. **Ruler:** Elizabeth II **Subject:** Year of the Dragon **Rev:** Dragon with pearl in color

| Date | Mintage | VF20 | XF40 | MS60 | MS63 | MS65 |
|---|---|---|---|---|---|---|
| 2012 | 8,000 | PF65 50.00 | | | | |

**KM# 744 2 DOLLARS**
31.11 g., 0.999 Silver 0.999 oz. ASW, 45x31 mm. **Ruler:** Elizabeth II **Subject:** Year of the Dragon, Lucky Red dragon **Rev:** Red dragon lying down with rays in background **Shape:** Horizontal oval

| Date | Mintage | VF20 | XF40 | MS60 | MS63 | MS65 |
|---|---|---|---|---|---|---|
| 2012 | 4,000 | PF65 100 | | | | |

**KM# 745 2 DOLLARS**
31.11 g., 0.999 Silver 0.999 oz. ASW, 45x31 mm. **Ruler:** Elizabeth II **Subject:** Year of the Dragon - Lucky Blue Dragon **Rev:** Blue dragon lying down, rays in background **Shape:** Horizontal oval

| Date | Mintage | VF20 | XF40 | MS60 | MS63 | MS65 |
|---|---|---|---|---|---|---|
| 2012 | 8,000 | PF65 100 | | | | |

**KM# 746 2 DOLLARS**
31.11 g., 0.999 Silver 0.999 oz. ASW, 40.7 mm. **Ruler:** Elizabeth II **Subject:** Year of the Dragon - Lunar Fan Dragon **Rev:** Dragon seated left, colored lunar hand fan in background

| Date | Mintage | VF20 | XF40 | MS60 | MS63 | MS65 |
|---|---|---|---|---|---|---|
| 2012 | 4,000 | PF65 100 | | | | |

**KM# 756 2 DOLLARS**
56.56 g., 0.925 Silver 1.6821 oz. ASW, 41.6x55.6 mm. **Ruler:** Elizabeth II **Subject:** Imperial Faberge Eggs - Bay Tree **Rev:** Bay tree **Shape:** Vertical oval

| Date | Mintage | VF20 | XF40 | MS60 | MS63 | MS65 |
|---|---|---|---|---|---|---|
| 2012 | Est. 7000 | PF65 125 | | | | |

**KM# 762 2 DOLLARS**
39.60 g., 0.925 Silver 1.1777 oz. ASW, 48.61 mm. **Ruler:** Elizabeth II **Subject:** Love Notes **Rev:** Cupid writing on central tablet

| Date | Mintage | VF20 | XF40 | MS60 | MS63 | MS65 |
|---|---|---|---|---|---|---|
| 2012 | Est. 3000 | PF65 100 | | | | |

**KM# 782 2 DOLLARS**
31.11 g., 0.999 Silver 0.999 oz. ASW, 40.7 mm. **Ruler:** Elizabeth II **Subject:** WWII Nose Art - Yellow Rose

| Date | Mintage | VF20 | XF40 | MS60 | MS63 | MS65 |
|---|---|---|---|---|---|---|
| 2012 | Est. 3000 | — | — | — | — | 80.00 |

**KM# 783 2 DOLLARS**
31.11 g., 0.999 Silver 0.999 oz. ASW, 40.7 mm. **Ruler:** Elizabeth II **Subject:** WWII Nose Art - Briefing Time

| Date | Mintage | VF20 | XF40 | MS60 | MS63 | MS65 |
|---|---|---|---|---|---|---|
| 2012 | — | — | — | — | — | 80.00 |

**KM# 784 2 DOLLARS**
31.11 g., 0.999 Silver 0.999 oz. ASW, 40.7 mm. **Ruler:** Elizabeth II **Subject:** WWII Nose Art - Memphis Belle

| Date | Mintage | VF20 | XF40 | MS60 | MS63 | MS65 |
|---|---|---|---|---|---|---|
| 2012 | — | — | — | — | — | 80.00 |

**KM# 795 2 DOLLARS**
10.00 g., 0.925 Silver 0.2974 oz. ASW, 32 mm. **Ruler:** Elizabeth II **Subject:** Four seasons, central device **Rev:** Flowers, leaves and crystal

| Date | Mintage | VF20 | XF40 | MS60 | MS63 | MS65 |
|---|---|---|---|---|---|---|
| 2012 | — | PF65 70.00 | | | | |

**KM# 796 2 DOLLARS**
12.00 g., 0.925 Silver 0.3569 oz. ASW, 35x35 mm. **Ruler:** Elizabeth II **Subject:** Four seasons - Spring **Rev:** Springtime flora and crystal **Shape:** Irregular

| Date | Mintage | VF20 | XF40 | MS60 | MS63 | MS65 |
|---|---|---|---|---|---|---|
| 2012 | — | PF65 70.00 | | | | |

**KM# 797 2 DOLLARS**
12.00 g., 0.925 Silver 0.3569 oz. ASW, 35x35 mm. **Ruler:** Elizabeth II **Subject:** Four seasons - Summer **Rev:** Summer flora and crystal **Shape:** Irregular

| Date | Mintage | VF20 | XF40 | MS60 | MS63 | MS65 |
|---|---|---|---|---|---|---|
| 2012 | Est. 9999 | PF65 70.00 | | | | |

**KM# 798 2 DOLLARS**
12.00 g., 0.925 Silver 0.3569 oz. ASW, 35x35 mm. **Ruler:** Elizabeth II **Subject:** Four seasons - Autumn **Rev:** Autumn foilage and crystal **Shape:** Irregular

| Date | Mintage | VF20 | XF40 | MS60 | MS63 | MS65 |
|---|---|---|---|---|---|---|
| 2012 | — | PF65 70.00 | | | | |

**KM# 799 2 DOLLARS**
12.00 g., 0.925 Silver 0.3569 oz. ASW, 35x35 mm. **Ruler:** Elizabeth II **Subject:** Four seasons - Winter **Rev:** Winter foilage and crystal **Shape:** Irregular

| Date | Mintage | VF20 | XF40 | MS60 | MS63 | MS65 |
|---|---|---|---|---|---|---|
| 2012 | Est. 9999 | PF65 70.00 | | | | |

**KM# 803 2 DOLLARS**
31.11 g., 0.999 Silver 0.999 oz. ASW, 40.7 mm. **Ruler:** Elizabeth II **Rev:** Great White Shark

| Date | Mintage | VF20 | XF40 | MS60 | MS63 | MS65 |
|---|---|---|---|---|---|---|
| 2012 | 5,000 | PF65 120 | | | | |

**KM# 806 2 DOLLARS**
31.11 g., 0.999 Silver 0.999 oz. ASW, 27x47 mm. **Ruler:** Elizabeth II **Obv:** Crowned head left **Rev:** Katherina icom **Shape:** Vertical rectangle

| Date | Mintage | VF20 | XF40 | MS60 | MS63 | MS65 |
|---|---|---|---|---|---|---|
| 2012 | 2,000 | PF65 100 | | | | |

**KM# 807 2 DOLLARS**
31.11 g., 0.999 Silver 0.999 oz. ASW, 27x47 mm. **Ruler:** Elizabeth II **Obv:** Crowned head right **Rev:** Rublov - Archangel Michael painting **Shape:** Vertical rectangle

| Date | Mintage | VF20 | XF40 | MS60 | MS63 | MS65 |
|---|---|---|---|---|---|---|
| 2012 | 3,000 | PF65 100 | | | | |

**KM# 808 2 DOLLARS**
31.11 g., 0.999 Silver 0.999 oz. ASW, 27x47 mm. **Ruler:** Elizabeth II **Obv:** Crowned head right **Rev:** Rubov - Christ painting **Shape:** Vertical rectangle

| Date | Mintage | VF20 | XF40 | MS60 | MS63 | MS65 |
|---|---|---|---|---|---|---|
| 2012 | 3,000 | PF65 100 | | | | |

**KM# 809 2 DOLLARS**
31.11 g., 0.999 Silver 0.999 oz. ASW, 27x47 mm. **Ruler:** Elizabeth II **Obv:** Crowned head right **Rev:** Rublov - Holy Trinity painting **Shape:** Vertical rectangle

| Date | Mintage | VF20 | XF40 | MS60 | MS63 | MS65 |
|---|---|---|---|---|---|---|
| 2012 | 3,000 | PF65 100 | | | | |

**KM# 810 2 DOLLARS**
31.11 g., 0.999 Silver 0.999 oz. ASW, 27x47 mm. **Ruler:** Elizabeth II **Obv:** Corwned head right **Rev:** Rublov - Apostle Paul painting **Shape:** Vertical rectangle

| Date | Mintage | VF20 | XF40 | MS60 | MS63 | MS65 |
|---|---|---|---|---|---|---|
| 2012 | 3,000 | PF65 100 | | | | |

**KM# 811 2 DOLLARS**
31.11 g., 0.999 Silver 0.999 oz. ASW, 27x47 mm. **Ruler:** Elizabeth II **Obv:** Crowned head right **Rev:** Mary and child **Shape:** Vertical rectangle

| Date | Mintage | VF20 | XF40 | MS60 | MS63 | MS65 |
|---|---|---|---|---|---|---|
| 2012 | 3,000 | PF65 100 | | | | |

**KM# 812 2 DOLLARS**
31.11 g., 0.999 Silver 0.999 oz. ASW, 27x47 mm. **Ruler:** Elizabeth II **Obv:** Crowned head right **Rev:** Christ holding book **Shape:** Vertical rectangle

| Date | Mintage | VF20 | XF40 | MS60 | MS63 | MS65 |
|---|---|---|---|---|---|---|
| 2012 | 3,000 | PF65 100 | | | | |

**KM# 813 2 DOLLARS**
31.11 g., 0.999 Silver 0.999 oz. ASW, 27x47 mm. **Ruler:** Elizabeth II **Obv:** Crowned head right **Rev:** God the father holding book, angels above **Shape:** Vertical rectangle

| Date | Mintage | VF20 | XF40 | MS60 | MS63 | MS65 |
|---|---|---|---|---|---|---|
| 2012 | 3,000 | PF65 100 | | | | |

**KM# 814 2 DOLLARS**
31.11 g., 0.999 Silver 0.999 oz. ASW, 38.61 mm. **Ruler:** Elizabeth II **Obv:** Crowned head right **Rev:** Secret Evening, Christ and deciples around table **Edge:** Reeded

| Date | Mintage | VF20 | XF40 | MS60 | MS63 | MS65 |
|---|---|---|---|---|---|---|
| 2012 | 2,000 | PF65 100 | | | | |

**KM# 818 2 DOLLARS**
0.999 Silver **Ruler:** Elizabeth II **Obv:** Crowned head right **Rev:** Saint facing right

| Date | Mintage | VF20 | XF40 | MS60 | MS63 | MS65 |
|---|---|---|---|---|---|---|
| 2012 | 500 | PF65 100 | | | | |

**KM# 819 2 DOLLARS**
0.999 Silver **Ruler:** Elizabeth II **Obv:** Crowned head right **Rev:** Saint standing right

| Date | Mintage | VF20 | XF40 | MS60 | MS63 | MS65 |
|---|---|---|---|---|---|---|
| 2012 | 500 | PF65 100 | | | | |

**KM# 820 2 DOLLARS**
0.999 Silver **Ruler:** Elizabeth II **Obv:** Crowned head right **Rev:** Saint standing right

| Date | Mintage | VF20 | XF40 | MS60 | MS63 | MS65 |
|---|---|---|---|---|---|---|
| 2012 | 500 | PF65 100 | | | | |

**KM# 821 2 DOLLARS**
0.999 Silver **Ruler:** Elizabeth II **Obv:** Crowned head right **Rev:** Saint standing right

| Date | Mintage | VF20 | XF40 | MS60 | MS63 | MS65 |
|---|---|---|---|---|---|---|
| 2012 | 500 | PF65 100 | | | | |

**KM# 822 2 DOLLARS**
0.999 Silver **Ruler:** Elizabeth II **Obv:** Crowned head right **Rev:** Christ facing

| Date | Mintage | VF20 | XF40 | MS60 | MS63 | MS65 |
|---|---|---|---|---|---|---|
| 2012 | 500 | PF65 150 | | | | |

**KM# 823 2 DOLLARS**
0.999 Silver **Ruler:** Elizabeth II **Obv:** Crowned head right **Rev:** Saint standing left

| Date | Mintage | VF20 | XF40 | MS60 | MS63 | MS65 |
|---|---|---|---|---|---|---|
| 2012 | 500 | PF65 100 | | | | |

**KM# 824 2 DOLLARS**
0.999 Silver **Ruler:** Elizabeth II **Obv:** Crowned head right **Rev:** Saint standing left

| Date | Mintage | VF20 | XF40 | MS60 | MS63 | MS65 |
|---|---|---|---|---|---|---|
| 2012 | 500 | PF65 100 | | | | |

**KM# 825 2 DOLLARS**
0.999 Silver **Ruler:** Elizabeth II **Obv:** Crowned head right **Rev:** Saint standing left

| Date | Mintage | VF20 | XF40 | MS60 | MS63 | MS65 |
|---|---|---|---|---|---|---|
| 2012 | 500 | PF65 100 | | | | |

**KM# 826 2 DOLLARS**
0.999 Silver **Ruler:** Elizabeth II **Obv:** Crowned head right **Rev:** Saint standing left

| Date | Mintage | VF20 | XF40 | MS60 | MS63 | MS65 |
|---|---|---|---|---|---|---|
| 2012 | 500 | PF65 100 | | | | |

**KM# 836 2 DOLLARS**
10.00 g., 0.925 Silver 0.2974 oz. ASW, 32 mm. **Ruler:** Elizabeth II **Obv:** Head with tiara right **Rev:** Palace gate

| Date | Mintage | VF20 | XF40 | MS60 | MS63 | MS65 |
|---|---|---|---|---|---|---|
| 2012 | 6,999 | PF65 70.00 | | | | |

**KM# 837 2 DOLLARS**
12.00 g., 0.925 Silver 0.3569 oz. ASW, 35x35 mm. **Ruler:** Elizabeth II **Obv:** Head with tiara right **Rev:** Palace façade **Shape:** Irregular

| Date | Mintage | VF20 | XF40 | MS60 | MS63 | MS65 |
|---|---|---|---|---|---|---|
| 2012 | 6,999 | PF65 70.00 | | | | |

**KM# 838 2 DOLLARS**
12.00 g., 0.925 Silver 0.3569 oz. ASW, 35x35 mm. **Ruler:** Elizabeth II **Obv:** Head with tiara right **Rev:** Tsar bust **Shape:** Iregular

| Date | Mintage | VF20 | XF40 | MS60 | MS63 | MS65 |
|---|---|---|---|---|---|---|
| 2012 | 6,999 | PF65 70.00 | | | | |

**KM# 839 2 DOLLARS**
12.00 g., 0.925 Silver 0.3569 oz. ASW, 35x35 mm. **Ruler:** Elizabeth II **Obv:** Head with tiara right **Rev:** Building view **Shape:** Irregular

| Date | Mintage | VF20 | XF40 | MS60 | MS63 | MS65 |
|---|---|---|---|---|---|---|
| 2012 | 6,999 | PF65 70.00 | | | | |

**KM# 840 2 DOLLARS**
12.00 g., 0.925 Silver 0.3569 oz. ASW, 35x35 mm. **Ruler:** Elizabeth II **Obv:** Head with tiara right **Rev:** Tsarina bust **Shape:** Irregular

| Date | Mintage | VF20 | XF40 | MS60 | MS63 | MS65 |
|---|---|---|---|---|---|---|
| 2012 | 6,999 | PF65 70.00 | | | | |

**KM# 845 2 DOLLARS**
28.28 g., 0.925 Silver 0.841 oz. ASW, 41 mm. **Ruler:** Elizabeth II **Subject:** Wedding **Obv:** Head with tiara above present, hearts and rings **Rev:** Bridge and groom, rings and bouquet

| Date | Mintage | VF20 | XF40 | MS60 | MS63 | MS65 |
|---|---|---|---|---|---|---|
| 2012 | Est. 15000 | PF65 100 | | | | |

**KM# 866 2 DOLLARS**
31.11 g., 0.999 Silver 0.999 oz. ASW, 40.7 mm. **Ruler:** Elizabeth II **Subject:** Birds of Prey **Obv:** Crowned head right **Rev:** American Bald Eagle

| Date | Mintage | VF20 | XF40 | MS60 | MS63 | MS65 |
|---|---|---|---|---|---|---|
| 2012 | 5,000 | PF65 100 | | | | |

**KM# 867 2 DOLLARS**
31.11 g., 0.999 Silver 0.999 oz. ASW, 40.7 mm. **Ruler:** Elizabeth II **Subject:** Birds of Prey **Obv:** Crowned head right **Rev:** Osprey

| Date | Mintage | VF20 | XF40 | MS60 | MS63 | MS65 |
|---|---|---|---|---|---|---|
| 2012 | 5,000 | PF65 100 | | | | |

**KM# 871 2 DOLLARS**
31.11 g., 0.999 Silver 0.999 oz. ASW, 54x32 mm. **Ruler:** Elizabeth II **Obv:** Crowned head right **Rev:** Blue Iguana head and eye **Shape:** Horizontal oval

| Date | Mintage | VF20 | XF40 | MS60 | MS63 | MS65 |
|---|---|---|---|---|---|---|
| 2012 | 1,000 | PF65 175 | | | | |

**KM# 872 2 DOLLARS**
31.11 g., 0.999 Silver 0.999 oz. ASW, 45 mm. **Ruler:** Elizabeth II **Obv:** Crowned head right **Rev:** Lotto ball mixer

| Date | Mintage | VF20 | XF40 | MS60 | MS63 | MS65 |
|---|---|---|---|---|---|---|
| 2012 | 1,000 | PF65 100 | | | | |

**KM# 882 2 DOLLARS**
56.56 g., 0.925 Silver 1.6821 oz. ASW, 41.6x55.6 mm. **Ruler:** Elizabeth II **Obv:** Head with tiara right above open egg **Rev:** Imperial Faberge Egg - 100th Anniversary of the Patriotic War of 1812 **Shape:** Vertical oval

| Date | Mintage | VF20 | XF40 | MS60 | MS63 | MS65 |
|---|---|---|---|---|---|---|
| 2012 | Est. 7000 | PF65 125 | | | | |

**KM# 896 2 DOLLARS**
28.28 g., 0.925 Silver 0.841 oz. ASW, 44 mm. **Ruler:** Elizabeth II **Subject:** Christmas Star

| Date | Mintage | VF20 | XF40 | MS60 | MS63 | MS65 |
|---|---|---|---|---|---|---|
| 2012 | Est. 7000 | PF65 95.00 | | | | |

**KM# 929 2 DOLLARS**
28.28 g., 0.925 Silver 0.841 oz. ASW, 41 mm. **Ruler:** Elizabeth II **Subject:** Lucky Coin: Horseshoe

| Date | Mintage | VF20 | XF40 | MS60 | MS63 | MS65 |
|---|---|---|---|---|---|---|
| 2012 | Est. 15000 | PF65 65.00 | | | | |

**KM# 930 2 DOLLARS**
28.28 g., 0.925 Silver 0.841 oz. ASW, 41 mm. **Ruler:** Elizabeth II **Subject:** Lucky Coin: Elephant

| Date | Mintage | VF20 | XF40 | MS60 | MS63 | MS65 |
|---|---|---|---|---|---|---|
| 2012 | Est. 15000 | PF65 65.00 | | | | |

**KM# 931 2 DOLLARS**
28.28 g., 0.925 Silver 0.841 oz. ASW, 41 mm. **Ruler:** Elizabeth II **Subject:** Lucky Coins: Four Leaf Clover

| Date | Mintage | VF20 | XF40 | MS60 | MS63 | MS65 |
|---|---|---|---|---|---|---|
| 2012 | Est. 15000 | PF65 65.00 | | | | |

**KM# 932 2 DOLLARS**
28.28 g., 0.925 Silver 0.841 oz. ASW, 41 mm. **Ruler:** Elizabeth II **Subject:** Lucky Coins: Ladybug

| Date | Mintage | VF20 | XF40 | MS60 | MS63 | MS65 |
|---|---|---|---|---|---|---|
| 2012 | Est. 15000 | PF65 65.00 | | | | |

**KM# 949 2 DOLLARS**
62.20 g., 0.925 Silver 1.8498 oz. ASW, 50 mm. **Ruler:** Elizabeth II **Subject:** Amber Room

| Date | Mintage | VF20 | XF40 | MS60 | MS63 | MS65 |
|---|---|---|---|---|---|---|
| 2012 | Est. 2000 | PF65 135 | | | | |

**KM# 957 2 DOLLARS**
31.10 g., 0.999 Silver 0.9989 oz. ASW **Ruler:** Elizabeth II **Subject:** Great Horned Owl

| Date | Mintage | VF20 | XF40 | MS60 | MS63 | MS65 |
|---|---|---|---|---|---|---|
| 2012 | Est. 5000 | PF65 95.00 | | | | |

**KM# 990 2 DOLLARS**
31.10 g., 0.999 Silver 0.9989 oz. ASW, 32 x 45 mm. **Ruler:** Elizabeth II **Subject:** Russian Beauty

| Date | Mintage | VF20 | XF40 | MS60 | MS63 | MS65 |
|---|---|---|---|---|---|---|
| 2012 | Est. 10000 | PF65 85.00 | | | | |

**KM# 1070 2 DOLLARS**
31.10 g., 0.999 Silver 0.9989 oz. ASW, 40 mm. **Ruler:** Elizabeth II **Subject:** Our Friends: Bengal

| Date | Mintage | VF20 | XF40 | MS60 | MS63 | MS65 |
|---|---|---|---|---|---|---|
| 2012 | Est. 8000 | PF65 100 | | | | |

**KM# 1071 2 DOLLARS**
31.10 g., 0.999 Silver 0.9989 oz. ASW, 40 mm. **Ruler:** Elizabeth II **Subject:** Our Friends: Kurilian Bobtail

| Date | Mintage | VF20 | XF40 | MS60 | MS63 | MS65 |
|---|---|---|---|---|---|---|
| 2012 | Est. 8000 | PF65 100 | | | | |

**KM# 1072 2 DOLLARS**
31.10 g., 0.999 Silver 0.9989 oz. ASW, 40 mm. **Ruler:** Elizabeth II **Subject:** Our Friends: Scottish Fold

| Date | Mintage | VF20 | XF40 | MS60 | MS63 | MS65 |
|---|---|---|---|---|---|---|
| 2012 | Est. 8000 | PF65 100 | | | | |

**KM# 1077 2 DOLLARS**
62.20 g., 0.900 Silver 1.7998 oz. ASW With crystal insert, 50 mm. **Ruler:** Elizabeth II **Subject:** Secrets of Lichtenstein

| Date | Mintage | VF20 | XF40 | MS60 | MS63 | MS65 |
|---|---|---|---|---|---|---|
| 2012 | Est. 999 | PF65 225 | | | | |

**KM# 1142 2 DOLLARS**
31.10 g., 0.999 Silver 0.999 oz. ASW, 45.7 x 42.1 mm. **Ruler:** Elizabeth II **Subject:** Christmas Bell **Obv:** Bell - Head with tiara right **Rev:** Three children ice skating with crystal **Shape:** Bell

| Date | Mintage | VF20 | XF40 | MS60 | MS63 | MS65 |
|---|---|---|---|---|---|---|
| 2012 | 3,500 | PF65 75.00 | | | | |

**KM# 1248 2 DOLLARS**

31.11 g., 0.999 Silver 0.999 oz. ASW, 40.7 mm. **Ruler:** Elizabeth II **Subject:** Robert F. Scott **Rev:** Scott portrait and color background

| Date | Mintage | VF20 | XF40 | MS60 | MS63 | MS65 |
|---|---|---|---|---|---|---|
| 2012 | Est. 5000 | PF65 150 | | | | |

**KM# 1249 2 DOLLARS**

31.11 g., 0.999 Silver 0.999 oz. ASW, 40 mm. **Ruler:** Elizabeth II **Subject:** Russian Literature - Lermontov **Obv:** Head with Tiara right

| Date | Mintage | VF20 | XF40 | MS60 | MS63 | MS65 |
|---|---|---|---|---|---|---|
| 2012 | — | PF65 90.00 | | | | |

**KM# 1250 2 DOLLARS**

31.11 g., 0.999 Silver 0.999 oz. ASW, 40 mm. **Ruler:** Elizabeth II **Subject:** Russian Literature - Pushkin **Obv:** Head with tiara right

| Date | Mintage | VF20 | XF40 | MS60 | MS63 | MS65 |
|---|---|---|---|---|---|---|
| 2012 | Est. 8000 | PF65 90.00 | | | | |

**KM# 845a 2 DOLLARS**

28.28 g., 0.925 Gold Plated Silver 0.841 oz., 41 mm. **Ruler:** Elizabeth II **Subject:** Wedding Coin

| Date | Mintage | VF20 | XF40 | MS60 | MS63 | MS65 |
|---|---|---|---|---|---|---|
| 2013 | Est. 22222 | PF65 90.00 | | | | |

**KM# 857 2 DOLLARS**

31.11 g., 0.999 Silver 0.999 oz. ASW, 40.7 mm. **Ruler:** Elizabeth II **Obv:** Crowned head right **Rev:** Transformers - OPTIMUS PRIME

| Date | Mintage | VF20 | XF40 | MS60 | MS63 | MS65 |
|---|---|---|---|---|---|---|
| 2013 | 5,000 | PF65 100 | | | | |

**KM# 858 2 DOLLARS**

31.11 g., 0.999 Silver 0.999 oz. ASW, 40.7 mm. **Ruler:** Elizabeth II **Obv:** Crowned head right **Rev:** Transformers - Megatron

| Date | Mintage | VF20 | XF40 | MS60 | MS63 | MS65 |
|---|---|---|---|---|---|---|
| 2013 | 5,000 | PF65 100 | | | | |

**KM# 859 2 DOLLARS**

31.11 g., 0.999 Silver 0.999 oz. ASW, 30.5x30.5 mm. **Ruler:** Elizabeth II **Obv:** Crowned head right **Rev:** Mr. Monopoly **Shape:** Square

| Date | Mintage | VF20 | XF40 | MS60 | MS63 | MS65 |
|---|---|---|---|---|---|---|
| 2013 | 5,000 | PF65 125 | | | | |

**KM# 860 2 DOLLARS**

31.11 g., 0.999 Silver 0.999 oz. ASW, 30.5x30.5 mm. **Ruler:** Elizabeth II **Obv:** Crowned head right **Rev:** Monopoly Game pieces - car, top hat, thimble, dog, battleship **Shape:** Square

| Date | Mintage | VF20 | XF40 | MS60 | MS63 | MS65 |
|---|---|---|---|---|---|---|
| 2013 | 5,000 | PF65 125 | | | | |

**KM# 870 2 DOLLARS**

31.11 g., 0.999 Silver 0.999 oz. ASW, 45x31 mm. **Ruler:** Elizabeth II **Obv:** Crowned head right **Rev:** Lunar Lucky Snake in color **Shape:** Horizontal oval

| Date | Mintage | VF20 | XF40 | MS60 | MS63 | MS65 |
|---|---|---|---|---|---|---|
| 2013 | 8,000 | PF65 100 | | | | |

**KM# 890 2 DOLLARS**

31.10 g., 0.999 Silver 0.9989 oz. ASW, 29x50 mm. **Ruler:** Elizabeth II **Subject:** Scottsdale Sliver

| Date | Mintage | VF20 | XF40 | MS60 | MS63 | MS65 |
|---|---|---|---|---|---|---|
| 2013 | Est. 350000 | PF65 35.00 | | | | |

**KM# 937 2 DOLLARS**

28.28 g., Copper-Nickel, 38.61 mm. **Ruler:** Elizabeth II **Subject:** Queen's Home - Buckingham Palace

| Date | Mintage | VF20 | XF40 | MS60 | MS63 | MS65 |
|---|---|---|---|---|---|---|
| 2013 | Est. 75000 | PF65 35.00 | | | | |

**KM# 937a 2 DOLLARS**

28.28 g., 0.925 Silver 0.841 oz. ASW, 38.61 mm. **Ruler:** Elizabeth II **Subject:** Queen's Home - Buckingham Palace

| Date | Mintage | VF20 | XF40 | MS60 | MS63 | MS65 |
|---|---|---|---|---|---|---|
| 2013 | Est. 40000 | PF65 65.00 | | | | |

**KM# 938 2 DOLLARS**

28.28 g., Copper-Nickel, 38.61 mm. **Ruler:** Elizabeth II **Subject:** Queen's Home - Westminster Abbey

| Date | Mintage | VF20 | XF40 | MS60 | MS63 | MS65 |
|---|---|---|---|---|---|---|
| 2013 | Est. 75000 | PF65 35.00 | | | | |

**KM# 938a 2 DOLLARS**

28.28 g., 0.925 Silver 0.841 oz. ASW, 38.61 mm. **Ruler:** Elizabeth II **Subject:** Queen's Home - Westminster Abby

| Date | Mintage | VF20 | XF40 | MS60 | MS63 | MS65 |
|---|---|---|---|---|---|---|
| 2013 | Est. 40000 | PF65 65.00 | | | | |

**KM# 951 2 DOLLARS**

31.10 g., 0.999 Silver 0.9989 oz. ASW, 40 mm. **Ruler:** Elizabeth II **Subject:** Love is Precious

| Date | Mintage | VF20 | XF40 | MS60 | MS63 | MS65 |
|---|---|---|---|---|---|---|
| 2013 | — | PF65 85.00 | | | | |

**KM# 958 2 DOLLARS**

31.10 g., 0.999 Silver 0.9989 oz. ASW **Ruler:** Elizabeth II **Subject:** Feng Shui Horses

| Date | Mintage | VF20 | XF40 | MS60 | MS63 | MS65 |
|---|---|---|---|---|---|---|
| 2013 | Est. 8000 | PF65 120 | | | | |

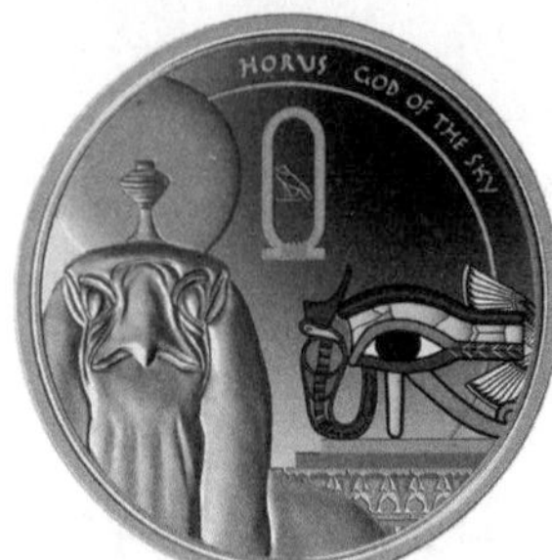


**KM# 962 2 DOLLARS**

25.00 g., 0.999 Silver 0.803 oz. ASW, 38.61 mm. **Ruler:** Elizabeth II **Subject:** Mythologies of the World: The Story of Osiris - Horus

| Date | Mintage | VF20 | XF40 | MS60 | MS63 | MS65 |
|---|---|---|---|---|---|---|
| 2013 | Est. 3000 | PF65 115 | | | | |

**KM# 963 2 DOLLARS**

25.00 g., 0.999 Silver 0.803 oz. ASW, 38.61 mm. **Ruler:** Elizabeth II **Subject:** Mythologies of the World: The Story of Osiris - Isis

| Date | Mintage | VF20 | XF40 | MS60 | MS63 | MS65 |
|---|---|---|---|---|---|---|
| 2013 | — | PF65 115 | | | | |

**KM# 964 2 DOLLARS**
25.00 g., 0.999 Silver 0.803 oz. ASW, 38.61 mm. **Ruler:** Elizabeth II **Subject:** Mythologies of the World: The Story of Osiris - Osiris

| Date | Mintage | VF20 | XF40 | MS60 | MS63 | MS65 |
|---|---|---|---|---|---|---|
| 2013 | Est. 3000 | PF65 115 | | | | |

**KM# 965 2 DOLLARS**
25.00 g., 0.999 Silver 0.803 oz. ASW, 38.61 mm. **Ruler:** Elizabeth II **Subject:** Mythologies of the World: The Story of Osiris - Nephthys

| Date | Mintage | VF20 | XF40 | MS60 | MS63 | MS65 |
|---|---|---|---|---|---|---|
| 2013 | Est. 3000 | PF65 115 | | | | |

**KM# 966 2 DOLLARS**
25.00 g., 0.999 Silver 0.803 oz. ASW, 38.61 mm. **Ruler:** Elizabeth II **Subject:** Mythologies of the World: The Story of Osiris - Set

| Date | Mintage | VF20 | XF40 | MS60 | MS63 | MS65 |
|---|---|---|---|---|---|---|
| 2013 | — | PF65 115 | | | | |

**KM# 986 2 DOLLARS**
31.10 g., 0.999 Silver 0.9989 oz. ASW, 40 mm. **Ruler:** Elizabeth II **Subject:** Caucasian Hostage: Three men and car

| Date | Mintage | VF20 | XF40 | MS60 | MS63 | MS65 |
|---|---|---|---|---|---|---|
| 2013 | Est. 8000 | PF65 60.00 | | | | |

**KM# 989 2 DOLLARS**
31.10 g., 0.999 Silver 0.9989 oz. ASW, 40 mm. **Ruler:** Elizabeth II **Subject:** Love is Precious

| Date | Mintage | VF20 | XF40 | MS60 | MS63 | MS65 |
|---|---|---|---|---|---|---|
| 2013 | — | PF65 60.00 | | | | |

**KM# 994 2 DOLLARS**
31.10 g., 0.999 Silver 0.9989 oz. ASW, 40 mm. **Ruler:** Elizabeth II **Subject:** 50th Anniversary of Dr. Who

| Date | Mintage | VF20 | XF40 | MS60 | MS63 | MS65 |
|---|---|---|---|---|---|---|
| 2013 | Est. 10000 | PF65 125 | | | | |

**KM# 995 2 DOLLARS**
31.10 g., 0.999 Silver 0.9989 oz. ASW, 40 mm. **Ruler:** Elizabeth II **Subject:** Anne Geddes - Protect and Nurture

| Date | Mintage | VF20 | XF40 | MS60 | MS63 | MS65 |
|---|---|---|---|---|---|---|
| 2013 | Est. 5000 | PF65 90.00 | | | | |

**KM# 996 2 DOLLARS**
31.10 g., 0.999 Silver 0.9989 oz. ASW, 27 x 47 mm. **Ruler:** Elizabeth II **Subject:** True Happiness

| Date | Mintage | VF20 | XF40 | MS60 | MS63 | MS65 |
|---|---|---|---|---|---|---|
| 2013 | Est. 9999 | PF65 60.00 | | | | |

**KM# 1093 2 DOLLARS**
31.10 g., 0.999 Silver 0.9989 oz. ASW, 40.7 mm. **Ruler:** Elizabeth II **Subject:** Spiderman

| Date | Mintage | VF20 | XF40 | MS60 | MS63 | MS65 |
|---|---|---|---|---|---|---|
| 2013 | Est. 5000 | PF65 100 | | | | |

**KM# 1113 2 DOLLARS**
31.10 g., 0.999 Silver 0.9989 oz. ASW, 40.7 mm. **Ruler:** Elizabeth II **Series:** Feng Shui Series - Cranes

| Date | Mintage | VF20 | XF40 | MS60 | MS63 | MS65 |
|---|---|---|---|---|---|---|
| 2013 | — | PF65 75.00 | | | | |

**KM# 1117 2 DOLLARS**
33.63 g., 0.925 Silver 1.0001 oz. ASW, 38.61 mm. **Ruler:** Elizabeth II **Subject:** Independence of Kazakhstan

| Date | Mintage | VF20 | XF40 | MS60 | MS63 | MS65 |
|---|---|---|---|---|---|---|
| 2013 Proof | Est. 3000 | — | — | — | — | — |

**KM# 1118 2 DOLLARS**
31.10 g., 0.999 Silver 0.9989 oz. ASW, 54 x 32 mm. **Ruler:** Elizabeth II **Subject:** Critically Endangered Species: Crocodile

| Date | Mintage | VF20 | XF40 | MS60 | MS63 | MS65 |
|---|---|---|---|---|---|---|
| 2013 | Est. 1000 | PF65 150 | | | | |

**KM# 1132 2 DOLLARS**
28.28 g., 0.925 Gold Plated Silver 0.841 oz., 41 mm. **Ruler:** Elizabeth II **Subject:** Lucky Coins - Horseshoe

| Date | Mintage | VF20 | XF40 | MS60 | MS63 | MS65 |
|---|---|---|---|---|---|---|
| 2013 | Est. 22222 | PF65 60.00 | | | | |

**KM# 1133 2 DOLLARS**
28.28 g., 0.925 Gold Plated Silver 0.841 oz., 41 mm. **Ruler:** Elizabeth II **Subject:** Lucky Coins - Four Leaf Clover

| Date | Mintage | VF20 | XF40 | MS60 | MS63 | MS65 |
|---|---|---|---|---|---|---|
| 2013 | Est. 22222 | PF65 60.00 | | | | |

**KM# 1134 2 DOLLARS**
28.28 g., 0.925 Gold Plated Silver 0.841 oz., 41 mm. **Ruler:** Elizabeth II **Subject:** Lucky Coins - Ladybug

| Date | Mintage | VF20 | XF40 | MS60 | MS63 | MS65 |
|---|---|---|---|---|---|---|
| 2013 | Est. 22222 | PF65 60.00 | | | | |

**KM# 1135 2 DOLLARS**
28.28 g., 0.925 Gold Plated Silver 0.841 oz., 41 mm. **Ruler:** Elizabeth II **Subject:** Lucky Coins - Elephant

| Date | Mintage | VF20 | XF40 | MS60 | MS63 | MS65 |
|---|---|---|---|---|---|---|
| 2013 | Est. 22222 | PF65 70.00 | | | | |

**KM# 1136 2 DOLLARS**
31.10 g., 0.925 Silver 0.9249 oz. ASW, 40 mm. **Ruler:** Elizabeth II **Subject:** Caucasian Hostage: Man, woman and donkey

| Date | Mintage | VF20 | XF40 | MS60 | MS63 | MS65 |
|---|---|---|---|---|---|---|
| 2013 | Est. 8000 | PF65 60.00 | | | | |

**KM# 1137 2 DOLLARS**
31.10 g., 0.999 Silver 0.9989 oz. ASW, 40 mm. **Ruler:** Elizabeth II **Subject:** Caucasian Hostage: Butler, man and sheep

| Date | Mintage | VF20 | XF40 | MS60 | MS63 | MS65 |
|---|---|---|---|---|---|---|
| 2013 | Est. 8000 | PF65 60.00 | | | | |

**KM# 1143 2 DOLLARS**
31.10 g., 0.999 Silver 0.999 oz. ASW, 38.61 mm. **Ruler:** Elizabeth II **Subject:** Fennec Fox

| Date | Mintage | VF20 | XF40 | MS60 | MS63 | MS65 |
|---|---|---|---|---|---|---|
| 2013 | — | PF65 75.00 | | | | |

**KM# 1145 2 DOLLARS**
31.10 g., 0.9999 Silver 0.9998 oz. ASW, 40 mm. **Ruler:** Elizabeth II **Subject:** St. Petersburg - Building the Future

| Date | Mintage | VF20 | XF40 | MS60 | MS63 | MS65 |
|---|---|---|---|---|---|---|
| 2013 | — | PF65 120 | | | | |

**KM# 1146 2 DOLLARS**
31.10 g., 0.9999 Silver 0.9998 oz. ASW, 40 mm. **Ruler:** Elizabeth II **Subject:** St. Petersburg - Growing Through the Ages

| Date | Mintage | VF20 | XF40 | MS60 | MS63 | MS65 |
|---|---|---|---|---|---|---|
| 2013 | Est. 4000 | PF65 120 | | | | |

**KM# 1147 2 DOLLARS**
31.10 g., 0.9999 Silver 0.9998 oz. ASW, 40 mm. **Ruler:** Elizabeth II **Subject:** St. Petersburg - White Nights

| Date | Mintage | VF20 | XF40 | MS60 | MS63 | MS65 |
|---|---|---|---|---|---|---|
| 2013 | Est. 4000 | PF65 120 | | | | |

**KM# 1151 2 DOLLARS**
31.10 g., 0.999 Silver 0.9989 oz. ASW, 31x52 mm. **Ruler:** Elizabeth II **Subject:** Pacific Island Birds **Rev:** Pacific Pigeon, Ducula pacifica, or 'Lupe' in Niuean. In color. **Shape:** Vertical rectangle

| Date | Mintage | VF20 | XF40 | MS60 | MS63 | MS65 |
|---|---|---|---|---|---|---|
| 2013 Proof | Est. 3000 | — | — | — | — | — |

**KM# 1152 2 DOLLARS**
31.10 g., 0.999 Silver 0.9989 oz. ASW, 40.7 mm. **Ruler:** Elizabeth II **Subject:** Endangered Species - Venerable Collared Lizard

| Date | Mintage | VF20 | XF40 | MS60 | MS63 | MS65 |
|---|---|---|---|---|---|---|
| 2013 | Est. 5000 | PF65 85.00 | | | | |

**KM# 1153 2 DOLLARS**
31.10 g., 0.999 Silver 0.9989 oz. ASW, 40.7 mm. **Ruler:** Elizabeth II **Subject:** Endangered Species - Grand Cayman Blue Iguana

| Date | Mintage | VF20 | XF40 | MS60 | MS63 | MS65 |
|---|---|---|---|---|---|---|
| 2013 | — | PF65 85.00 | | | | |

**KM# 1157 2 DOLLARS**
56.56 g., 0.999 Silver 1.8166 oz. ASW, 41.6 x 56.56 mm. **Ruler:** Elizabeth II **Subject:** Continents - Europe

| Date | Mintage | VF20 | XF40 | MS60 | MS63 | MS65 |
|---|---|---|---|---|---|---|
| 2013 | Est. 2000 | PF65 200 | | | | |

**KM# 1165 2 DOLLARS**
33.63 g., 0.925 Silver 1.0001 oz. ASW With gold gilding, 38.61 mm. **Ruler:** Elizabeth II **Subject:** Betashar

| Date | Mintage | VF20 | XF40 | MS60 | MS63 | MS65 |
|---|---|---|---|---|---|---|
| 2013 | Est. 3000 | PF65 100 | | | | |

**KM# 1173 2 DOLLARS**
31.10 g., 0.999 Silver 0.9989 oz. ASW, 40.7 mm. **Ruler:** Elizabeth II **Subject:** 50 Years of Spiderman

| Date | Mintage | VF20 | XF40 | MS60 | MS63 | MS65 |
|---|---|---|---|---|---|---|
| 2013 | Est. 1173 | PF65 100 | | | | |

**KM# 1184 2 DOLLARS**
31.10 g., 0.999 Silver 0.9989 oz. ASW, 28 x 51 mm. **Ruler:** Elizabeth II **Subject:** Humpback Whale

| Date | Mintage | VF20 | XF40 | MS60 | MS63 | MS65 |
|---|---|---|---|---|---|---|
| 2013 Proof | — | — | — | — | — | — |

**KM# 1188 2 DOLLARS**
31.10 g., 0.999 Silver 0.9989 oz. ASW, 40.7 mm. **Ruler:** Elizabeth II **Subject:** Real River Monsters - Piranha

| Date | Mintage | VF20 | XF40 | MS60 | MS63 | MS65 |
|---|---|---|---|---|---|---|
| 2013 | Est. 5000 | PF65 75.00 | | | | |

**KM# 1192 2 DOLLARS**
0.50 g., 0.999 Gold 0.0161 oz. AGW, 11 mm. **Ruler:** Elizabeth II **Subject:** Paavo Nurmi

| Date | Mintage | VF20 | XF40 | MS60 | MS63 | MS65 |
|---|---|---|---|---|---|---|
| 2013 Proof | Est. 6000 | — | — | — | — | — |

**KM# 1207 2 DOLLARS**
10.00 g., 0.925 Silver 0.2974 oz. ASW, 32 mm. **Ruler:** Elizabeth II **Subject:** The Monuments of Odessa

| Date | Mintage | VF20 | XF40 | MS60 | MS63 | MS65 |
|---|---|---|---|---|---|---|
| 2013 | Est. 2222 | PF65 60.00 | | | | |

**KM# 1208 2 DOLLARS**
12.00 g., 0.925 Silver 0.3569 oz. ASW, 35 x 35 mm. **Ruler:** Elizabeth II **Subject:** The Monuments of Odessa

| Date | Mintage | VF20 | XF40 | MS60 | MS63 | MS65 |
|---|---|---|---|---|---|---|
| 2013 | Est. 2222 | PF65 60.00 | | | | |

**KM# 1209 2 DOLLARS**
12.00 g., 0.925 Silver 0.3569 oz. ASW, 35 x 35 mm. **Ruler:** Elizabeth II **Subject:** The Monuments of Odessa

| Date | Mintage | VF20 | XF40 | MS60 | MS63 | MS65 |
|---|---|---|---|---|---|---|
| 2013 | Est. 2222 | PF65 60.00 | | | | |

**KM# 1210 2 DOLLARS**
12.00 g., 0.925 Silver 0.3569 oz. ASW, 35 x 35 mm. **Ruler:** Elizabeth II **Subject:** The Monuments of Odessa

| Date | Mintage | VF20 | XF40 | MS60 | MS63 | MS65 |
|---|---|---|---|---|---|---|
| 2013 | — | PF65 60.00 | | | | |

**KM# 1211 2 DOLLARS**
12.00 g., 0.925 Silver 0.3569 oz. ASW, 35 x 35 mm. **Ruler:** Elizabeth II **Subject:** The Monuments of Odessa

| Date | Mintage | VF20 | XF40 | MS60 | MS63 | MS65 |
|---|---|---|---|---|---|---|
| 2013 | — | PF65 60.00 | | | | |

**KM# 1217 2 DOLLARS**
80.00 g., 0.999 Silver 2.5695 oz. ASW, 91.55 x 55 mm. **Ruler:** Elizabeth II **Subject:** Giants of Art - The Creation of Adam (1 of 12)

| Date | Mintage | VF20 | XF40 | MS60 | MS63 | MS65 |
|---|---|---|---|---|---|---|
| 2013 | Est. 750 | PF65 275 | | | | |

**KM# 1229 2 DOLLARS**
31.10 g., 0.999 Silver 0.9989 oz. ASW, 40.7 mm. **Ruler:** Elizabeth II **Subject:** Peregrine Falcon

| Date | Mintage | VF20 | XF40 | MS60 | MS63 | MS65 |
|---|---|---|---|---|---|---|
| 2013 | Est. 5000 | PF65 80.00 | | | | |

**KM# 1240 2 DOLLARS**
28.28 g., 0.925 Silver 0.841 oz. ASW, 41 mm. **Ruler:** Elizabeth II **Subject:** Lucky Coins - Gold Fish

| Date | Mintage | VF20 | XF40 | MS60 | MS63 | MS65 |
|---|---|---|---|---|---|---|
| 2013 | Est. 15000 | PF65 60.00 | | | | |

**KM# 1241 2 DOLLARS**
31.10 g., 0.999 Silver 0.9989 oz. ASW, 40 mm. **Ruler:** Elizabeth II **Subject:** T.E. Lawrence

| Date | Mintage | VF20 | XF40 | MS60 | MS63 | MS65 |
|---|---|---|---|---|---|---|
| 2013 | Est. 1888 | PF65 65.00 | | | | |

**KM# 1242 2 DOLLARS**
56.56 g., 0.925 Silver 1.6821 oz. ASW, 41.6 x 55.6 mm. **Ruler:** Elizabeth II **Subject:** Imperial Faberge Eggs - Kremlin Egg

| Date | Mintage | VF20 | XF40 | MS60 | MS63 | MS65 |
|---|---|---|---|---|---|---|
| 2013 | 7,000 | PF65 145 | | | | |

**KM# 1258 2 DOLLARS**
31.10 g., 0.999 Silver 0.999 oz. ASW, 40.7 mm. **Ruler:** Elizabeth II **Obv:** Head with tiara right **Rev:** Giant Coconut Crab in color

| Date | Mintage | VF20 | XF40 | MS60 | MS63 | MS65 |
|---|---|---|---|---|---|---|
| 2013 | — | PF65 75.00 | | | | |

**KM# 1261 2 DOLLARS**
31.11 g., 0.999 Silver 0.999 oz. ASW, 40 mm. **Ruler:** Elizabeth II **Obv:** Head with tiara right **Rev:** Female representing Ukraine advancing left (from early 20c US lithograph)

| Date | Mintage | VF20 | XF40 | MS60 | MS63 | MS65 |
|---|---|---|---|---|---|---|
| 2013 | Est. 5000 | PF65 175 | | | | |

**KM# 1262 2 DOLLARS**
62.20 g., 0.999 Silver 1.9978 oz. ASW, 50 mm. **Ruler:** Elizabeth II **Subject:** Ark of the Covenant, lapis lusi insert

| Date | Mintage | VF20 | XF40 | MS60 | MS63 | MS65 |
|---|---|---|---|---|---|---|
| 2013 Proof | Est. 1500 | — | — | — | — | 200 |

**KM# 1265 2 DOLLARS**
62.20 g., 0.999 Silver 1.9978 oz. ASW, 50 mm. **Ruler:** Elizabeth II **Rev:** Wawell town view, agate insert

| Date | Mintage | VF20 | XF40 | MS60 | MS63 | MS65 |
|---|---|---|---|---|---|---|
| 2013 Antique patina | Est. 999 | — | — | — | — | 225 |

**KM# 1266 2 DOLLARS**
31.11 g., 0.999 Silver 0.999 oz. ASW, 40 mm. **Ruler:** Elizabeth II **Subject:** Year of the Horse **Rev:** Horse, gilt horse show

| Date | Mintage | VF20 | XF40 | MS60 | MS63 | MS65 |
|---|---|---|---|---|---|---|
| 2014 | Est. 1500 | PF65 100 | | | | |

**KM# 1267 2 DOLLARS**
15.50 g., 0.999 Silver 0.4978 oz. ASW, 32 mm. **Ruler:** Elizabeth II **Subject:** Year of the Horse **Rev:** White horse

| Date | Mintage | VF20 | XF40 | MS60 | MS63 | MS65 |
|---|---|---|---|---|---|---|
| 2014 | Est. 5000 | PF65 100 | | | | |

**KM# 785 3 DOLLARS**
33.30 g., 0.925 Silver 0.9903 oz. ASW, 38.61 mm. **Ruler:** Elizabeth II **Subject:** Polish Radio, station 3 **Obv:** Head with tiara right **Rev:** Radio microphone and sound arcs

| Date | Mintage | VF20 | XF40 | MS60 | MS63 | MS65 |
|---|---|---|---|---|---|---|
| 2012 | — | PF65 75.00 | | | | |

**KM# 1252 3 DOLLARS**
50.00 g., 0.999 Silver 1.6059 oz. ASW, 50 mm. **Ruler:** Elizabeth II **Subject:** Amazing Amazonia **Obv:** Head in tiara right **Rev:** Squirrel Monkey pair in color

| Date | Mintage | VF20 | XF40 | MS60 | MS63 | MS65 |
|---|---|---|---|---|---|---|
| 2012 | — | PF65 300 | | | | |

**KM# 266 5 DOLLARS**
155.50 g., 0.999 Silver 4.9944 oz. ASW, 70 mm. **Ruler:** Elizabeth II **Subject:** Year of the Rooster **Rev:** Multicolor rooster standing right, sunrise

| Date | Mintage | VF20 | XF40 | MS60 | MS63 | MS65 |
|---|---|---|---|---|---|---|
| 2005 | — | PF65 225 | | | | |

**KM# 272 5 DOLLARS**
6.22 g., 0.999 Gold 0.1998 oz. AGW, 25 mm. **Ruler:** Elizabeth II **Subject:** Year of the Rooster

| Date | Mintage | VF20 | XF40 | MS60 | MS63 | MS65 |
|---|---|---|---|---|---|---|
| 2005 | — | PF65 400 | | | | |

**KM# 273 5 DOLLARS**
15.55 g., 0.999 Gold 0.4994 oz. AGW, 33 mm. **Ruler:** Elizabeth II **Subject:** Year of the Rooster

| Date | Mintage | VF20 | XF40 | MS60 | MS63 | MS65 |
|---|---|---|---|---|---|---|
| 2005 | — | PF65 950 | | | | |

**KM# 295 5 DOLLARS**
155.50 g., 0.999 Silver 4.9944 oz. ASW, 70 mm. **Ruler:** Elizabeth II **Subject:** Year of the Dog **Rev:** Multicolor dog

| Date | Mintage | VF20 | XF40 | MS60 | MS63 | MS65 |
|---|---|---|---|---|---|---|
| 2005 | — | PF65 225 | | | | |

**KM# 333 5 DOLLARS**
15.50 g., 0.917 Gold 0.457 oz. AGW, 27 mm. **Ruler:** Elizabeth II **Subject:** Amber Road - Gdansk **Rev:** Nepture statue, castle, amber insert

| Date | Mintage | VF20 | XF40 | MS60 | MS63 | MS65 |
|---|---|---|---|---|---|---|
| 2007 | — | — | — | — | — | 850 |

**KM# 191 5 DOLLARS**
15.50 g., 0.900 Gold 0.4485 oz. AGW, 27 mm. **Ruler:** Elizabeth II **Subject:** Amber road **Obv:** Bust and Roman cart **Rev:** Kaliningrad Castle, Roman coin, Amber insert

| Date | Mintage | VF20 | XF40 | MS60 | MS63 | MS65 |
|---|---|---|---|---|---|---|
| 2008 | 2,000 | PF65 850 | | | | |

**KM# 230 5 DOLLARS**
62.21 g., 0.999 Silver 1.9981 oz. ASW, 50x32 mm. **Ruler:** Elizabeth II **Subject:** Battleship: Tripitz **Shape:** Rectangle

| Date | Mintage | VF20 | XF40 | MS60 | MS63 | MS65 |
|---|---|---|---|---|---|---|
| 2009 | 1,000 | — | — | — | — | 150 |

**KM# 349 5 DOLLARS**
15.50 g., 0.900 Gold 0.4485 oz. AGW, 27 mm. **Ruler:** Elizabeth II **Subject:** Amber Road - Elblag **Rev:** Amber insert

| Date | Mintage | VF20 | XF40 | MS60 | MS63 | MS65 |
|---|---|---|---|---|---|---|
| 2009 | — | PF65 850 | | | | |

**KM# 364 5 DOLLARS**
77.70 g., 0.999 Silver 2.4956 oz. ASW, 50x32 mm. **Ruler:** Elizabeth II **Rev:** Battleship Tirpitz sailing left **Shape:** Wavy rectangle

| Date | Mintage | VF20 | XF40 | MS60 | MS63 | MS65 |
|---|---|---|---|---|---|---|
| 2009 | 1,000 | PF65 175 | | | | |

**KM# 250 5 DOLLARS**
0.50 g., 0.999 Gold 0.0161 oz. AGW, 11 mm. **Ruler:** Elizabeth II **Rev:** Ned Kelly

| Date | Mintage | VF20 | XF40 | MS60 | MS63 | MS65 |
|---|---|---|---|---|---|---|
| 2010 | — | PF65 65.00 | | | | |

**KM# 368 5 DOLLARS**
15.50 g., 0.900 Gold 0.4485 oz. AGW, 27 mm. **Ruler:** Elizabeth II **Subject:** Amber road - Stare Hradisko **Rev:** Amber insert

| Date | Mintage | VF20 | XF40 | MS60 | MS63 | MS65 |
|---|---|---|---|---|---|---|
| 2010 | 2,000 | — | — | — | — | 850 |

**KM# 376 5 DOLLARS**
2.50 g., 0.999 Gold 0.0803 oz. AGW, 14x26.7 mm. **Ruler:** Elizabeth II **Subject:** Kitty **Shape:** Vertical rectangle

| Date | Mintage | VF20 | XF40 | MS60 | MS63 | MS65 |
|---|---|---|---|---|---|---|
| 2010 | — | PF65 175 | | | | |

**KM# 377 5 DOLLARS**
2.50 g., 0.999 Gold 0.0803 oz. AGW, 14x26.7 mm. **Ruler:** Elizabeth II **Subject:** Twin Star characters **Shape:** Vertical rectangle

| Date | Mintage | VF20 | XF40 | MS60 | MS63 | MS65 |
|---|---|---|---|---|---|---|
| 2010 | Est. 2000 | PF65 175 | | | | |

**KM# 378 5 DOLLARS**
2.50 g., 0.999 Gold 0.0803 oz. AGW, 14x26.7 mm. **Ruler:** Elizabeth II **Subject:** Melody **Shape:** Vertical rectangle

| Date | Mintage | VF20 | XF40 | MS60 | MS63 | MS65 |
|---|---|---|---|---|---|---|
| 2010 | Est. 2000 | PF65 175 | | | | |

**KM# 397 5 DOLLARS**
15.50 g., 0.900 Gold 0.4485 oz. AGW, 27 mm. **Ruler:** Elizabeth II **Subject:** Amber Road - Carnuntum **Rev:** Arches, ancient coin, statue

| Date | Mintage | VF20 | XF40 | MS60 | MS63 | MS65 |
|---|---|---|---|---|---|---|
| 2010 | 2,000 | PF65 850 | | | | |

**KM# 399 5 DOLLARS**
15.50 g., 0.900 Gold 0.4485 oz. AGW, 27 mm. **Ruler:** Elizabeth II **Subject:** Amber Route - Szombathely **Rev:** Cathedral, ancient coin

| Date | Mintage | VF20 | XF40 | MS60 | MS63 | MS65 |
|---|---|---|---|---|---|---|
| 2010 Matte finish | 2,000 | PF65 850 | | | | |

**KM# 423 5 DOLLARS**
15.50 g., 0.900 Gold 0.4485 oz. AGW, 27 mm. **Ruler:** Elizabeth II **Subject:** Christmas Star **Obv:** Head with tiara right, snowflakes around **Rev:** Three children and christmas tree, crystal insets

| Date | Mintage | VF20 | XF40 | MS60 | MS63 | MS65 |
|---|---|---|---|---|---|---|
| 2010 | 2,000 | PF65 850 | | | | |

**KM# 430 5 DOLLARS**
15.50 g., 0.900 Gold 0.4485 oz. AGW, 27 mm. **Ruler:** Elizabeth II **Obv:** Head with tiara right, wing enlargement as background **Rev:** Butterfly - Lycaena Virgaureae

| Date | Mintage | VF20 | XF40 | MS60 | MS63 | MS65 |
|---|---|---|---|---|---|---|
| 2010 | 1,000 | PF65 850 | | | | |

**KM# 513 5 DOLLARS**
50.00 g., 0.999 Silver 1.6059 oz. ASW, 35.2x35.2 mm. **Ruler:** Elizabeth II **Subject:** The three kings of 1936 **Obv:** Head with tiara right **Rev:** Busts left of George V, Edward VIII and George VI

| Date | Mintage | VF20 | XF40 | MS60 | MS63 | MS65 |
|---|---|---|---|---|---|---|
| 2011 | 2,500 | PF65 100 | | | | |

**KM# 587 5 DOLLARS**
27.00 g., 0.900 Gold 0.7813 oz. AGW, 27 mm. **Ruler:** Elizabeth II **Subject:** Amber Route - Aquileia **Rev:** Rhomulus and Remus suckling at she-wolf, amber insert

| Date | Mintage | VF20 | XF40 | MS60 | MS63 | MS65 |
|---|---|---|---|---|---|---|
| 2011 | Est. 2000 | — | — | — | — | 1,500 |

**KM# 620 5 DOLLARS**
1.00 g., 0.999 Gold 0.0321 oz. AGW, 12x8 mm. **Ruler:** Elizabeth II **Obv:** Head with crown right **Rev:** Baby tiger, diamond chip and paw print **Shape:** Rectangle

| Date | Mintage | VF20 | XF40 | MS60 | MS63 | MS65 |
|---|---|---|---|---|---|---|
| 2011 | Est. 5000 | PF65 100 | | | | |

**KM# 623 5 DOLLARS**
8.60 g., 0.900 Gold 0.2488 oz. AGW, 22 mm. **Ruler:** Elizabeth II **Obv:** Head with tiara right **Rev:** Dragon rearing upwards, paw to mouth

| Date | Mintage | VF20 | XF40 | MS60 | MS63 | MS65 |
|---|---|---|---|---|---|---|
| 2011 Proof | Est. 1000 | — | — | — | — | 475 |

**KM# 651 5 DOLLARS**
25.00 g., 0.999 Silver 0.803 oz. ASW, 40.6 mm. **Ruler:** Elizabeth II **Obv:** Head with tiara right **Rev:** Tasmanian tiger in lenticular 3-D **Edge:** Reeded

| Date | Mintage | VF20 | XF40 | MS60 | MS63 | MS65 |
|---|---|---|---|---|---|---|
| 2011 | 3,000 | PF65 75.00 | | | | |

**KM# 689 5 DOLLARS**
6.00 g., 0.999 Gold 0.1927 oz. AGW, 21 mm. **Ruler:** Elizabeth II **Subject:** Amber Route **Rev:** Map of European cities

| Date | Mintage | VF20 | XF40 | MS60 | MS63 | MS65 |
|---|---|---|---|---|---|---|
| 2011 | 999 | PF65 400 | | | | |

**KM# 710 5 DOLLARS**
6.00 g., 0.9999 Gold 0.1929 oz. AGW, 21 mm. **Ruler:** Elizabeth II **Obv:** Ancient horsecart **Obv. Legend:** SZLAK BURSZTYNOWY **Rev:** Nepture statue, coin, mine building, amber insert **Rev. Legend:** Gdansk

| Date | Mintage | VF20 | XF40 | MS60 | MS63 | MS65 |
|---|---|---|---|---|---|---|
| 2011 | 999 | PF65 400 | | | | |

**KM# 941 5 DOLLARS**
15.00 g., 0.900 Gold 0.434 oz. AGW, 27 mm. **Ruler:** Elizabeth II **Subject:** Butterflies: Apollo Gold

| Date | Mintage | VF20 | XF40 | MS60 | MS63 | MS65 |
|---|---|---|---|---|---|---|
| 2011 Proof | Est. 1000 | — | — | — | — | — |

**KM# 678 5 DOLLARS**
40.00 g., 0.999 Silver 1.2847 oz. ASW, 29x47 mm. **Ruler:** Elizabeth II **Subject:** Year of the Dragon

| Date | Mintage | VF20 | XF40 | MS60 | MS63 | MS65 |
|---|---|---|---|---|---|---|
| 2012 | — | PF65 100 | | | | |

**KM# 679 5 DOLLARS**
40.00 g., 0.999 Silver 1.2847 oz. ASW, 29x47 mm. **Ruler:** Elizabeth II **Subject:** Year of the Dragon

| Date | Mintage | VF20 | XF40 | MS60 | MS63 | MS65 |
|---|---|---|---|---|---|---|
| 2012 | — | PF65 100 | | | | |

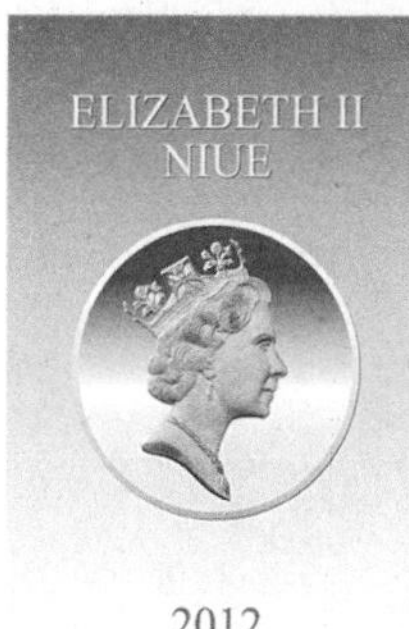

**KM# 680 5 DOLLARS**
40.00 g., 0.999 Silver 1.2847 oz. ASW, 29x47 mm. **Ruler:** Elizabeth II **Subject:** Year of the Dragon

| Date | Mintage | VF20 | XF40 | MS60 | MS63 | MS65 |
|---|---|---|---|---|---|---|
| 2012 | — | PF65 100 | | | | |

**KM# 681 5 DOLLARS**
40.00 g., 0.999 Silver 1.2847 oz. ASW, 29x47 mm. **Ruler:** Elizabeth II **Subject:** Year of the Dragon

| Date | Mintage | VF20 | XF40 | MS60 | MS63 | MS65 |
|---|---|---|---|---|---|---|
| 2012 | — | PF65 100 | | | | |

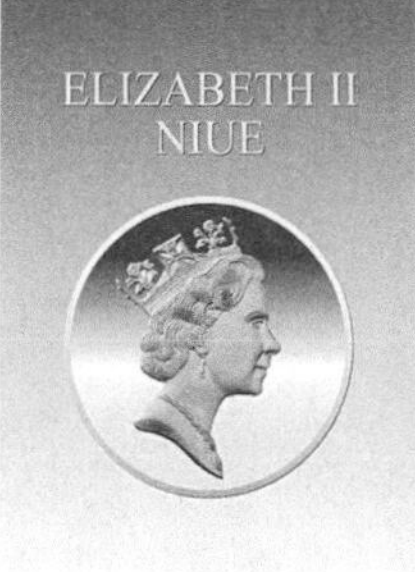

**KM# 682 5 DOLLARS**
40.00 g., 0.999 Silver 1.2847 oz. ASW, 29x47 mm. **Ruler:** Elizabeth II **Subject:** Year of the Dragon

| Date | Mintage | VF20 | XF40 | MS60 | MS63 | MS65 |
|---|---|---|---|---|---|---|
| 2012 | — | PF65 100 | | | | |

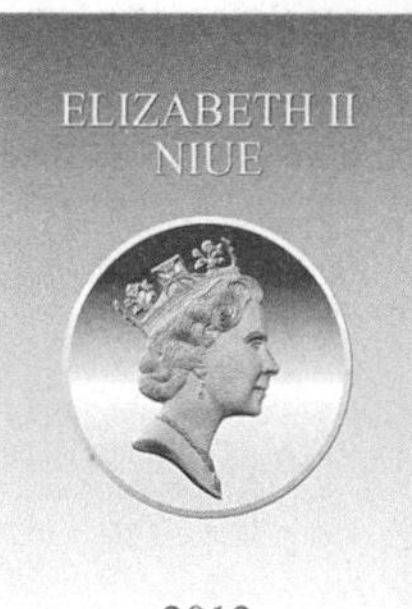

**KM# 683 5 DOLLARS**
40.00 g., 0.999 Silver 1.2847 oz. ASW, 29x47 mm. **Ruler:** Elizabeth II **Subject:** Year of the Dragon

| Date | Mintage | VF20 | XF40 | MS60 | MS63 | MS65 |
|---|---|---|---|---|---|---|
| 2012 | — | PF65 100 | | | | |

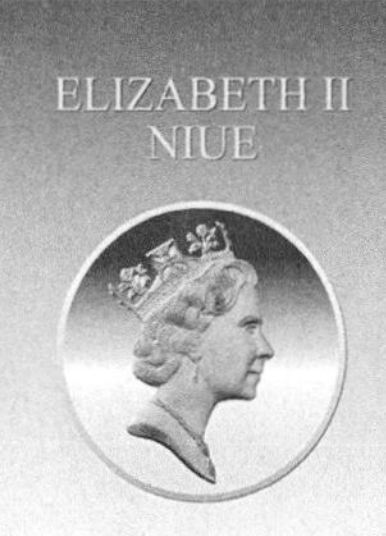

**KM# 684 5 DOLLARS**
40.00 g., 0.999 Silver 1.2847 oz. ASW, 29x47 mm. **Ruler:** Elizabeth II **Subject:** Year of the Dragon

| Date | Mintage | VF20 | XF40 | MS60 | MS63 | MS65 |
|---|---|---|---|---|---|---|
| 2012 | — | PF65 100 | | | | |

**KM# 685 5 DOLLARS**
40.00 g., 0.999 Silver 1.2847 oz. ASW, 29x47 mm. **Ruler:** Elizabeth II **Subject:** Year of the Dragon

| Date | Mintage | VF20 | XF40 | MS60 | MS63 | MS65 |
|---|---|---|---|---|---|---|
| 2012 | — | PF65 100 | | | | |

**KM# 686 5 DOLLARS**
40.00 g., 0.999 Silver 1.2847 oz. ASW, 29x47 mm. **Ruler:** Elizabeth II **Subject:** Year of the Dragon

| Date | Mintage | VF20 | XF40 | MS60 | MS63 | MS65 |
|---|---|---|---|---|---|---|
| 2012 | — | PF65 100 | | | | |

**KM# 698 5 DOLLARS**
0.50 g., 0.999 Gold 0.0161 oz. AGW, 11 mm. **Ruler:** Elizabeth II **Rev:** Ned Kelly standing, name vertically at left **Edge:** Reeded

| Date | Mintage | VF20 | XF40 | MS60 | MS63 | MS65 |
|---|---|---|---|---|---|---|
| 2012 | 5,000 | PF65 75.00 | | | | |

**KM# 716 5 DOLLARS**
1.24 g., 0.9999 Gold 0.0399 oz. AGW, 13.92 mm. **Ruler:** Elizabeth II **Rev:** Dragon

| Date | Mintage | VF20 | XF40 | MS60 | MS63 | MS65 |
|---|---|---|---|---|---|---|
| 2012 | 5,000 | PF65 125 | | | | |

**KM# 738 5 DOLLARS**
155.55 g., 0.999 Silver 4.996 oz. ASW, 65 mm. **Ruler:** Elizabeth II **Subject:** Vietnam War, 50th Anniversary of Australia's involvement **Rev:** Two soldiers with rifles on patrol, helicopter above

| Date | Mintage | VF20 | XF40 | MS60 | MS63 | MS65 |
|---|---|---|---|---|---|---|
| 2012 | 400 | PF65 250 | | | | |

**KM# 748 5 DOLLARS**
100.00 g., 0.999 Silver 3.2119 oz. ASW, 52.5x118 mm. **Ruler:** Elizabeth II **Subject:** DaVinci's Last Supper **Rev:** Bartholomew **Shape:** Vertical rectangle

| Date | Mintage | VF20 | XF40 | MS60 | MS63 | MS65 |
|---|---|---|---|---|---|---|
| 2012 | 750 | PF65 150 | | | | |

**KM# 749 5 DOLLARS**
100.00 g., 0.999 Silver 3.2119 oz. ASW, 52.5x118 mm. **Ruler:** Elizabeth II **Subject:** DaVinci's Last Supper **Rev:** James Minor and Andrew **Shape:** Vertical rectangle

| Date | Mintage | VF20 | XF40 | MS60 | MS63 | MS65 |
|---|---|---|---|---|---|---|
| 2012 | 750 | PF65 150 | | | | |

**KM# 750 5 DOLLARS**
100.00 g., 0.999 Silver 3.2119 oz. ASW, 52.5x118 mm. **Ruler:** Elizabeth II **Subject:** DaVinci's Last Supper **Rev:** Judas Iscariot, Peter and John **Shape:** Vertical rectangle

| Date | Mintage | VF20 | XF40 | MS60 | MS63 | MS65 |
|---|---|---|---|---|---|---|
| 2012 | 750 | PF65 150 | | | | |

**KM# 751 5 DOLLARS**
100.00 g., 0.999 Silver 3.2119 oz. ASW, 52.5x118 mm. **Ruler:** Elizabeth II **Subject:** DaVinci's Last Supper **Rev:** Jesus **Shape:** Vertical rectangle

| Date | Mintage | VF20 | XF40 | MS60 | MS63 | MS65 |
|---|---|---|---|---|---|---|
| 2012 | 750 | PF65 150 | | | | |

**KM# 752 5 DOLLARS**
100.00 g., 0.999 Silver 3.2119 oz. ASW, 52.5x118 mm. **Ruler:** Elizabeth II **Subject:** DaVinci's Last Supper **Rev:** Thomas, James the Greater, Philip **Shape:** Vertical rectangle

| Date | Mintage | VF20 | XF40 | MS60 | MS63 | MS65 |
|---|---|---|---|---|---|---|
| 2012 | 750 | PF65 150 | | | | |

**KM# 753 5 DOLLARS**
100.00 g., 0.999 Silver 3.2119 oz. ASW, 52.5x118 mm. **Ruler:** Elizabeth II **Subject:** DaVinci's Last Supper **Rev:** Matthew **Shape:** Vertical rectangle

| Date | Mintage | VF20 | XF40 | MS60 | MS63 | MS65 |
|---|---|---|---|---|---|---|
| 2012 | 750 | PF65 150 | | | | |

**KM# 754 5 DOLLARS**
100.00 g., 0.999 Silver 3.2119 oz. ASW, 52.5x118 mm. **Ruler:** Elizabeth II **Subject:** DaVinci's Last Supper **Rev:** Jude Thaddeus and Simon the Zealot **Shape:** Vertical rectangle

| Date | Mintage | VF20 | XF40 | MS60 | MS63 | MS65 |
|---|---|---|---|---|---|---|
| 2012 | 750 | PF65 150 | | | | |

**KM# 774 5 DOLLARS**
6.00 g., 0.9999 Gold 0.1929 oz. AGW, 21 mm. **Ruler:** Elizabeth II **Subject:** Stare Hradisko **Obv:** Queen's head at left, two horse cart at right **Rev:** Celtic coin design and art

| Date | Mintage | VF20 | XF40 | MS60 | MS63 | MS65 |
|---|---|---|---|---|---|---|
| 2012 | 999 | PF65 400 | | | | |

**KM# 776 5 DOLLARS**
6.00 g., 0.900 Gold 0.1736 oz. AGW, 16.7x22.3 mm. **Ruler:** Elizabeth II **Subject:** Imperial Faberge Eggs - Coronation egg **Rev:** Egg and state coach

| Date | Mintage | VF20 | XF40 | MS60 | MS63 | MS65 |
|---|---|---|---|---|---|---|
| 2012 | Est. 777 | **PF65** 425 | | | | |

**KM# 780 5 DOLLARS**
6.00 g., 0.9999 Gold 0.1929 oz. AGW, 21 mm. **Ruler:** Elizabeth II **Subject:** Silk Route - Wroclaw **Obv:** Queen's head at left, two horse cart at right **Rev:** Old building at left, statue at right

| Date | Mintage | VF20 | XF40 | MS60 | MS63 | MS65 |
|---|---|---|---|---|---|---|
| 2012 | Est. 999 | **PF65** 400 | | | | |

**KM# 801 5 DOLLARS**
6.00 g., 0.999 Gold 0.1927 oz. AGW, 21 mm. **Ruler:** Elizabeth II **Subject:** Szlak Bursztynowy - Szombathely **Rev:** Building, old coins and amber insert

| Date | Mintage | VF20 | XF40 | MS60 | MS63 | MS65 |
|---|---|---|---|---|---|---|
| 2012 | — | **PF65** 400 | | | | |

**KM# 816 5 DOLLARS**
62.21 g., 0.999 Silver 1.9981 oz. ASW, 50 mm. **Ruler:** Elizabeth II **Subject:** Napoleon and 1812, first design **Obv:** Crowned head right **Rev:** Conjoined busts left of Kutusow and Napoleon, Moscow in flames at left, French troops at right **Edge:** Reeded

| Date | Mintage | VF20 | XF40 | MS60 | MS63 | MS65 |
|---|---|---|---|---|---|---|
| 2012 Antique patina | Est. 500 | **PF65** 150 | | | | |

**KM# 817 5 DOLLARS**
62.21 g., 0.999 Silver 1.9981 oz. ASW, 50 mm. **Ruler:** Elizabeth II **Subject:** Napoleon, 2nd design **Obv:** Crowned head right **Rev:** Conjoined busts left of Napoleon and Kutuzov, French soldiers retreating, Cossacks attacking.

| Date | Mintage | VF20 | XF40 | MS60 | MS63 | MS65 |
|---|---|---|---|---|---|---|
| 2012 Antique patina | Est. 500 | **PF65** 150 | | | | |

**KM# 842 5 DOLLARS**
6.00 g., 0.9999 Gold 0.1929 oz. AGW, 21 mm. **Ruler:** Elizabeth II **Obv:** Head with tiara at left, cart, map **Rev:** Ruins, statue, coin and amber insert **Rev. Legend:** CARNUNTUM

| Date | Mintage | VF20 | XF40 | MS60 | MS63 | MS65 |
|---|---|---|---|---|---|---|
| 2012 | 999 | **PF65** 400 | | | | |

**KM# 844 5 DOLLARS**
6.00 g., 0.9999 Gold 0.1929 oz. AGW, 21 mm. **Ruler:** Elizabeth II **Subject:** Amber Route **Obv:** Head with tiara at left, cart, map **Rev:** She-wold statue, mosaic coin, amber insert **Rev. Legend:** AQUILEIA

| Date | Mintage | VF20 | XF40 | MS60 | MS63 | MS65 |
|---|---|---|---|---|---|---|
| 2012 | 999 | **PF65** 400 | | | | |

**KM# 856 5 DOLLARS**
6.00 g., 0.900 Gold 0.1736 oz. AGW, 16.7x22.3 mm. **Ruler:** Elizabeth II **Obv:** Head with tiara right above open egg **Rev:** Imperial Faberge Eggs - Cockerel **Shape:** Vertical oval

| Date | Mintage | VF20 | XF40 | MS60 | MS63 | MS65 |
|---|---|---|---|---|---|---|
| 2012 | Est. 777 | **PF65** 425 | | | | |

**KM# 897 5 DOLLARS**
20.00 g., 0.999 Silver 0.6424 oz. ASW With Swarovski crystal, 40 mm. **Ruler:** Elizabeth II **Subject:** The Queen's Diamond Jubilee

| Date | Mintage | VF20 | XF40 | MS60 | MS63 | MS65 |
|---|---|---|---|---|---|---|
| 2012 | Est. 2500 | **PF65** 95.00 | | | | |

**KM# 948 5 DOLLARS**
1.00 g., 0.9999 Gold 0.0321 oz. AGW, 12 x 8 mm. **Ruler:** Elizabeth II **Subject:** Brilliant Baby Bear: Polar Bear

| Date | Mintage | VF20 | XF40 | MS60 | MS63 | MS65 |
|---|---|---|---|---|---|---|
| 2012 | Est. 3000 | **PF65** 185 | | | | |

**KM# 952 5 DOLLARS**
6.00 g., 0.900 Gold 0.1736 oz. AGW, 22.3 x 16.7 mm. **Ruler:** Elizabeth II **Subject:** Imperial Faberge Eggs: Swan Egg

| Date | Mintage | VF20 | XF40 | MS60 | MS63 | MS65 |
|---|---|---|---|---|---|---|
| 2012 | Est. 777 | **PF65** 425 | | | | |

**KM# 955 5 DOLLARS**
6.00 g., 0.900 Gold 0.1736 oz. AGW, 22.3 x 16.7 mm. **Ruler:** Elizabeth II **Subject:** Imperial Faberge Eggs: Moscow Kremlin Egg

| Date | Mintage | VF20 | XF40 | MS60 | MS63 | MS65 |
|---|---|---|---|---|---|---|
| 2012 | Est. 777 | **PF65** 425 | | | | |

**KM# 997 5 DOLLARS**
6.00 g., 0.900 Gold 0.1736 oz. AGW, 22.3 x 16.7 mm. **Ruler:** Elizabeth II **Subject:** Imperial Faberge Eggs: Rosebud Egg

| Date | Mintage | VF20 | XF40 | MS60 | MS63 | MS65 |
|---|---|---|---|---|---|---|
| 2012 | Est. 777 | **PF65** 425 | | | | |

**KM# 999 5 DOLLARS**
6.00 g., 0.900 Gold 0.1736 oz. AGW, 22.3 x 16.7 mm. **Ruler:** Elizabeth II **Subject:** Imperial Faberge Eggs: Bouquet of Lilies Egg

| Date | Mintage | VF20 | XF40 | MS60 | MS63 | MS65 |
|---|---|---|---|---|---|---|
| 2012 | Est. 777 | **PF65** 425 | | | | |

**KM# 974 5 DOLLARS**
40.00 g., 0.999 Silver 1.2847 oz. ASW, 36 x 48 mm. **Ruler:** Elizabeth II **Subject:** Vincent Van Gogh Sunflowers 125th Anniversary - 1 of 7

| Date | Mintage | VF20 | XF40 | MS60 | MS63 | MS65 |
|---|---|---|---|---|---|---|
| 2013 | Est. 500 | **PF65** 125 | | | | |

**KM# 975 5 DOLLARS**
40.00 g., 0.999 Silver 1.2847 oz. ASW, 36 x 48 mm. **Ruler:** Elizabeth II **Subject:** Vincent Van Gogh's Sunflowers 125th Anniversary - 2 or 7

| Date | Mintage | VF20 | XF40 | MS60 | MS63 | MS65 |
|---|---|---|---|---|---|---|
| 2013 | Est. 500 | **PF65** 125 | | | | |

**KM# 976 5 DOLLARS**
40.00 g., 0.999 Silver 1.2847 oz. ASW, 36 x 48 mm. **Ruler:** Elizabeth II **Subject:** Vincent Van Gogh's Sunflowers 125th Anniversary - 3 of 7

| Date | Mintage | VF20 | XF40 | MS60 | MS63 | MS65 |
|---|---|---|---|---|---|---|
| 2013 | Est. 500 | **PF65** 125 | | | | |

**KM# 977 5 DOLLARS**
40.00 g., 0.999 Silver 1.2847 oz. ASW, 36 x 48 mm. **Ruler:** Elizabeth II **Subject:** Vincent Van Gogh's Sunflowers 125th Anniversary - 4 of 7

| Date | Mintage | VF20 | XF40 | MS60 | MS63 | MS65 |
|---|---|---|---|---|---|---|
| 2013 | Est. 500 | **PF65** 125 | | | | |

**KM# 978 5 DOLLARS**
40.00 g., 0.999 Silver 1.2847 oz. ASW, 36 x 48 mm. **Ruler:** Elizabeth II **Subject:** Vincent Van Gogh's Sunflowers 125th Anniversary - 5 or 7

| Date | Mintage | VF20 | XF40 | MS60 | MS63 | MS65 |
|---|---|---|---|---|---|---|
| 2013 | Est. 500 | **PF65** 125 | | | | |

**KM# 979 5 DOLLARS**
40.00 g., 0.999 Silver 1.2847 oz. ASW, 36 x 48 mm. **Ruler:** Elizabeth II **Subject:** Vincent Van Gogh's Sunflowers 125th Anniversary - 6 of 7

| Date | Mintage | VF20 | XF40 | MS60 | MS63 | MS65 |
|---|---|---|---|---|---|---|
| 2013 | Est. 500 | **PF65** 125 | | | | |

**KM# 980 5 DOLLARS**
40.00 g., 0.999 Silver 1.2847 oz. ASW, 36 x 48 mm. **Ruler:** Elizabeth II **Subject:** Vincent Van Gogh's Sunflowers 125th Annviersary - 7 of 7

| Date | Mintage | VF20 | XF40 | MS60 | MS63 | MS65 |
|---|---|---|---|---|---|---|
| 2013 | Est. 500 | **PF65** 125 | | | | |

**KM# 1025 5 DOLLARS**
1.00 g., 0.999 Gold 0.0321 oz. AGW, 12 x 8 mm. **Ruler:** Elizabeth II **Subject:** Brilliant Baby Bar - Orangutan

| Date | Mintage | VF20 | XF40 | MS60 | MS63 | MS65 |
|---|---|---|---|---|---|---|
| 2013 | Est. 2000 | **PF65** 185 | | | | |

**KM# 1026 5 DOLLARS**
1.00 g., 0.999 Gold 0.0321 oz. AGW, 12 x 8 mm. **Ruler:** Elizabeth II **Subject:** Brilliant Baby Bar - Tiger

| Date | Mintage | VF20 | XF40 | MS60 | MS63 | MS65 |
|---|---|---|---|---|---|---|
| 2013 | Est. 2000 | PF65 185 | | | | |

**KM# 1073 5 DOLLARS**
5.00 g., 0.999 Gold 0.1606 oz. AGW, 20.7 x 12.25 mm. **Ruler:** Elizabeth II **Subject:** Magic Calendar of Happiness - Spring

| Date | Mintage | VF20 | XF40 | MS60 | MS63 | MS65 |
|---|---|---|---|---|---|---|
| 2013 Proof | Est. 222 | — | — | — | — | — |

**KM# 1114 5 DOLLARS**
62.20 g., 0.999 Silver 1.9978 oz. ASW, 34x70 mm. **Ruler:** Elizabeth II **Subject:** Gods of Ancient Greece - Zeus

| Date | Mintage | VF20 | XF40 | MS60 | MS63 | MS65 |
|---|---|---|---|---|---|---|
| 2013 | Est. 2000 | PF65 135 | | | | |

**KM# 1163 5 DOLLARS**
5.00 g., 0.999 Gold 0.1606 oz. AGW, 20.7 x 12.25 mm. **Ruler:** Elizabeth II **Subject:** Magic Calendar of Happiness - Summer

| Date | Mintage | VF20 | XF40 | MS60 | MS63 | MS65 |
|---|---|---|---|---|---|---|
| 2013 Proof | Est. 222 | — | — | — | — | — |

**KM# 1189 5 DOLLARS**
6.00 g., 0.900 Gold 0.1736 oz. AGW, 22.3 x 16.7 mm. **Ruler:** Elizabeth II **Subject:** Imperial Faberge Eggs: Rosebud Egg

| Date | Mintage | VF20 | XF40 | MS60 | MS63 | MS65 |
|---|---|---|---|---|---|---|
| 2013 | Est. 777 | PF65 425 | | | | |

**KM# 1193 5 DOLLARS**
3.11 g., 0.900 Gold 0.090 oz. AGW, 22.5 mm. **Ruler:** Elizabeth II **Subject:** Paavo Nurmi

| Date | Mintage | VF20 | XF40 | MS60 | MS63 | MS65 |
|---|---|---|---|---|---|---|
| 2013 Proof | Est. 700 | — | — | — | — | — |

**KM# 1205 5 DOLLARS**
6.00 g., 0.900 Gold 0.1736 oz. AGW, 22.3 x 16.7 mm. **Ruler:** Elizabeth II **Subject:** Imperial Faberge Eggs - Bouquet of Lilies Egg

| Date | Mintage | VF20 | XF40 | MS60 | MS63 | MS65 |
|---|---|---|---|---|---|---|
| 2013 | Est. 777 | PF65 425 | | | | |

**KM# 1218 5 DOLLARS**
80.00 g., 0.999 Silver 2.5695 oz. ASW, 91.55 x 55 mm. **Ruler:** Elizabeth II **Subject:** Giants of Art - The Creation of Adam (2 of 12)

| Date | Mintage | VF20 | XF40 | MS60 | MS63 | MS65 |
|---|---|---|---|---|---|---|
| 2013 | Est. 750 | PF65 275 | | | | |

**KM# 1219 5 DOLLARS**
80.00 g., 0.999 Silver 2.5695 oz. ASW, 91.55 x 55 mm. **Ruler:** Elizabeth II **Subject:** Giants of Art - Creation of Adam (3 of 12)

| Date | Mintage | VF20 | XF40 | MS60 | MS63 | MS65 |
|---|---|---|---|---|---|---|
| 2013 | Est. 750 | PF65 275 | | | | |

**KM# 1220 5 DOLLARS**
80.00 g., 0.999 Silver 2.5695 oz. ASW, 91.55 x 55 mm. **Ruler:** Elizabeth II **Subject:** Giants of Art - The Creation of Adam (4 of 12)

| Date | Mintage | VF20 | XF40 | MS60 | MS63 | MS65 |
|---|---|---|---|---|---|---|
| 2013 | Est. 750 | PF65 275 | | | | |

**KM# 1221 5 DOLLARS**
80.00 g., 0.999 Silver 2.5695 oz. ASW, 91.55 x 55 mm. **Ruler:** Elizabeth II **Subject:** Giants of Art - Creation of Adam (5 of 12)

| Date | Mintage | VF20 | XF40 | MS60 | MS63 | MS65 |
|---|---|---|---|---|---|---|
| 2013 | Est. 750 | PF65 275 | | | | |

**KM# 1222 5 DOLLARS**
80.00 g., 0.999 Silver 2.5695 oz. ASW, 91.55 x 55 mm. **Ruler:** Elizabeth II **Subject:** Giants of Art - Creation of Adam (6 of 12)

| Date | Mintage | VF20 | XF40 | MS60 | MS63 | MS65 |
|---|---|---|---|---|---|---|
| 2013 | Est. 750 | PF65 275 | | | | |

**KM# 1223 5 DOLLARS**
80.00 g., 0.999 Silver 2.5695 oz. ASW, 91.55 x 55 mm. **Ruler:** Elizabeth II **Subject:** Giants of Art - Creation of Adam (7 of 12)

| Date | Mintage | VF20 | XF40 | MS60 | MS63 | MS65 |
|---|---|---|---|---|---|---|
| 2013 | Est. 750 | PF65 275 | | | | |

**KM# 1224 5 DOLLARS**
80.00 g., 0.999 Silver 2.5695 oz. ASW, 91.55 x 55 mm. **Ruler:** Elizabeth II **Subject:** Giants of Art - The Creation of Adam (8 of 12)

| Date | Mintage | VF20 | XF40 | MS60 | MS63 | MS65 |
|---|---|---|---|---|---|---|
| 2013 | Est. 750 | PF65 275 | | | | |

**KM# 1225 5 DOLLARS**
80.00 g., 0.999 Silver 2.5695 oz. ASW, 91.55 x 55 mm. **Ruler:** Elizabeth II **Series:** Giants of Art - The Creation of Adam (9 of 12)

| Date | Mintage | VF20 | XF40 | MS60 | MS63 | MS65 |
|---|---|---|---|---|---|---|
| 2013 | Est. 750 | PF65 275 | | | | |

**KM# 1226 5 DOLLARS**
80.00 g., 0.999 Silver 2.5695 oz. ASW, 91.55 x 55 mm. **Ruler:** Elizabeth II **Subject:** Giants of Art - The Creation of Adam

| Date | Mintage | VF20 | XF40 | MS60 | MS63 | MS65 |
|---|---|---|---|---|---|---|
| 2013 | Est. 750 | PF65 275 | | | | |

**KM# 1227 5 DOLLARS**
80.00 g., 0.999 Silver 2.5695 oz. ASW, 91.55 55 mm. **Ruler:** Elizabeth II **Subject:** Giants of Art - Creation of Adam (10 of 12)

| Date | Mintage | VF20 | XF40 | MS60 | MS63 | MS65 |
|---|---|---|---|---|---|---|
| 2013 | Est. 750 | PF65 275 | | | | |

**KM# 1228 5 DOLLARS**
80.00 g., 0.999 Silver 2.5695 oz. ASW, 91.55 x 55 mm. **Ruler:** Elizabeth II **Subject:** Giants of Art - Creation of Adam (12 of 12)

| Date | Mintage | VF20 | XF40 | MS60 | MS63 | MS65 |
|---|---|---|---|---|---|---|
| 2013 | Est. 750 | PF65 275 | | | | |

**KM# 1124 8 DOLLARS**
155.50 g., 0.999 Silver 4.9623 oz. ASW, 65 mm. **Ruler:** Elizabeth II **Subject:** 5 oz. Silver Horse

| Date | Mintage | F12 | VF20 | XF40 | MS60 | MS63 |
|---|---|---|---|---|---|---|
| 2014 | Est. 500 | PF65 1,250 | | | | |

**KM# 124 10 DOLLARS**
28.28 g., 0.925 Silver 0.841 oz. ASW, 38.6 mm. **Ruler:** Elizabeth II **Subject:** Snoopy as an Ace **Obv:** Crowned head right **Rev:** Snoopy flying his dog house **Edge:** Reeded

| Date | Mintage | VF20 | XF40 | MS60 | MS63 | MS65 |
|---|---|---|---|---|---|---|
| 2001 | 10,000 | PF65 35.00 | | | | |

**KM# 130 10 DOLLARS**
28.28 g., 0.925 Silver 0.841 oz. ASW, 38.6 mm. **Ruler:** Elizabeth II **Series:** Pokeman **Obv:** Crowned shield within sprigs **Rev:** Bulbasaur **Edge:** Reeded

| Date | Mintage | VF20 | XF40 | MS60 | MS63 | MS65 |
|---|---|---|---|---|---|---|
| 2001 | 10,000 | PF65 35.00 | | | | |

**KM# 133 10 DOLLARS**
28.28 g., 0.925 Silver 0.841 oz. ASW, 38.6 mm. **Ruler:** Elizabeth II **Series:** Pokeman **Obv:** Crowned shield within sprigs **Rev:** Charmander **Edge:** Reeded

| Date | Mintage | VF20 | XF40 | MS60 | MS63 | MS65 |
|---|---|---|---|---|---|---|
| 2001 | 10,000 | PF65 35.00 | | | | |

**KM# 136 10 DOLLARS**
28.28 g., 0.925 Silver 0.841 oz. ASW, 38.6 mm. **Ruler:** Elizabeth II **Series:** Pokeman **Obv:** Crowned shield within sprigs **Rev:** Meowth **Edge:** Reeded

| Date | Mintage | VF20 | XF40 | MS60 | MS63 | MS65 |
|---|---|---|---|---|---|---|
| 2001 | 10,000 | PF65 35.00 | | | | |

**KM# 139 10 DOLLARS**
28.28 g., 0.925 Silver 0.841 oz. ASW, 38.6 mm. **Ruler:** Elizabeth II **Series:** Pokeman **Obv:** Crowned shield within sprigs **Rev:** Pikachu **Edge:** Reeded

| Date | Mintage | VF20 | XF40 | MS60 | MS63 | MS65 |
|---|---|---|---|---|---|---|
| 2001 | 10,000 | PF65 35.00 | | | | |

**KM# 142 10 DOLLARS**
28.28 g., 0.925 Silver 0.841 oz. ASW, 38.6 mm. **Ruler:** Elizabeth II **Series:** Pokeman **Obv:** Crowned shield within sprigs **Rev:** Squirtle **Edge:** Reeded

| Date | Mintage | VF20 | XF40 | MS60 | MS63 | MS65 |
|---|---|---|---|---|---|---|
| 2001 | 10,000 | PF65 35.00 | | | | |

**KM# 147 10 DOLLARS**
28.28 g., 0.925 Silver 0.841 oz. ASW, 38.6 mm. **Ruler:** Elizabeth II **Subject:** Pokémon Series **Obv:** Crowned shield within sprigs **Rev:** Pikachu **Edge:** Reeded

| Date | Mintage | VF20 | XF40 | MS60 | MS63 | MS65 |
|---|---|---|---|---|---|---|
| 2002 PM | 10,000 | PF65 35.00 | | | | |

**KM# 152 10 DOLLARS**
28.28 g., 0.925 Silver 0.841 oz. ASW, 38.6 mm. **Ruler:** Elizabeth II **Subject:** Pokémon Series **Obv:** Crowned shield within sprigs **Rev:** Pichu **Edge:** Reeded

| Date | Mintage | VF20 | XF40 | MS60 | MS63 | MS65 |
|---|---|---|---|---|---|---|
| 2002 PM | 10,000 | PF65 35.00 | | | | |

**KM# 157 10 DOLLARS**
28.28 g., 0.925 Silver 0.841 oz. ASW, 38.6 mm. **Ruler:** Elizabeth II **Subject:** Pokémon Series **Obv:** Crowned shield within sprigs **Rev:** Mewtwo **Edge:** Reeded

| Date | Mintage | VF20 | XF40 | MS60 | MS63 | MS65 |
|---|---|---|---|---|---|---|
| 2002 PM | 10,000 | PF65 35.00 | | | | |

**KM# 162 10 DOLLARS**
28.28 g., 0.925 Silver 0.841 oz. ASW, 38.6 mm. **Ruler:** Elizabeth II **Subject:** Pokémon Series **Obv:** Crowned shield within sprigs **Rev:** Entei **Edge:** Reeded

| Date | Mintage | VF20 | XF40 | MS60 | MS63 | MS65 |
|---|---|---|---|---|---|---|
| 2002 PM | 10,000 | PF65 35.00 | | | | |

**KM# 167 10 DOLLARS**
28.28 g., 0.925 Silver 0.841 oz. ASW, 38.6 mm. **Ruler:** Elizabeth II **Subject:** Pokémon Series **Obv:** Crowned shield within sprigs **Rev:** Celebi **Edge:** Reeded

| Date | Mintage | VF20 | XF40 | MS60 | MS63 | MS65 |
|---|---|---|---|---|---|---|
| 2002 PM | 10,000 | PF65 35.00 | | | | |

**KM# 274 10 DOLLARS**
31.11 g., 0.999 Gold 0.999 oz. AGW, 38.6 mm. **Ruler:** Elizabeth II **Subject:** Year of the Rooster

| Date | Mintage | VF20 | XF40 | MS60 | MS63 | MS65 |
|---|---|---|---|---|---|---|
| 2005 | — | PF65 2,000 | | | | |

**KM# 254 10 DOLLARS**
155.50 g., 0.999 Silver 4.9944 oz. ASW, 65 mm. **Ruler:** Elizabeth II **Subject:** Peanuts 60th Anniversary **Rev:** Peanut character heads around a central Snoopy

| Date | Mintage | VF20 | XF40 | MS60 | MS63 | MS65 |
|---|---|---|---|---|---|---|
| 2010 Prooflike | 1,000 | — | — | — | — | 225 |

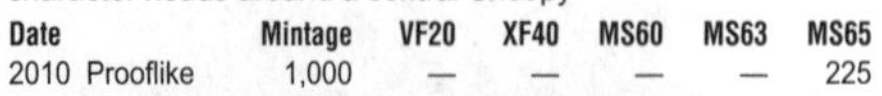

**KM# 375 10 DOLLARS**
100.00 g., 0.999 Silver 3.2119 oz. ASW, 64x54.2 mm. **Ruler:** Elizabeth II **Subject:** Kitty and friends **Shape:** Heart

| Date | Mintage | VF20 | XF40 | MS60 | MS63 | MS65 |
|---|---|---|---|---|---|---|
| 2010 | Est. 1000 | PF65 150 | | | | |

**KM# 387 10 DOLLARS**
155.50 g., 0.999 Silver 4.9944 oz. ASW, 65 mm. **Ruler:** Elizabeth II **Subject:** Miffy with cake

| Date | Mintage | VF20 | XF40 | MS60 | MS63 | MS65 |
|---|---|---|---|---|---|---|
| 2010 | Est. 1500 | PF65 200 | | | | |

**KM# 815 10 DOLLARS**
155.55 g., 0.999 Silver 4.996 oz. ASW, 38.61 mm. **Ruler:** Elizabeth II **Obv:** Crowned head right **Rev:** Secret Evening icon, Christ and deciples around table **Edge:** Reeded

| Date | Mintage | VF20 | XF40 | MS60 | MS63 | MS65 |
|---|---|---|---|---|---|---|
| 2012 | 500 | PF65 375 | | | | |

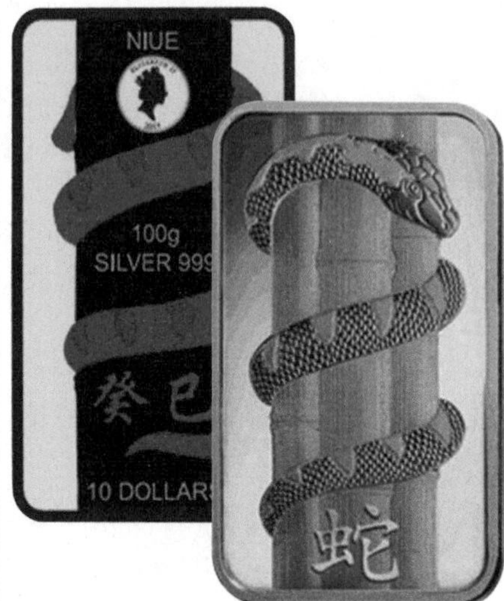


**KM# 1074 10 DOLLARS**
100.00 g., 0.999 Silver 3.2119 oz. ASW, 35x60 mm. **Ruler:** Elizabeth II **Subject:** Year of the Snake

| Date | Mintage | VF20 | XF40 | MS60 | MS63 | MS65 |
|---|---|---|---|---|---|---|
| 2013 | Est. 6000 | PF65 150 | | | | |

**KM# 1181 10 DOLLARS**
1.24 g., 0.9999 Gold 0.0399 oz. AGW, 8.5 x 15 mm. **Ruler:** Elizabeth II **Subject:** Humpback Whale

| Date | Mintage | VF20 | XF40 | MS60 | MS63 | MS65 |
|---|---|---|---|---|---|---|
| 2013 Proof | — | — | — | — | — | — |

**KM# 1183 10 DOLLARS**
155.50 g., 0.999 Silver 4.9944 oz. ASW, 55 x 85 mm. **Ruler:** Elizabeth II **Subject:** Humpback Whale

| Date | Mintage | VF20 | XF40 | MS60 | MS63 | MS65 |
|---|---|---|---|---|---|---|
| 2013 Proof | — | — | — | — | — | — |

**KM# 1194 10 DOLLARS**
10.00 g., 0.900 Gold 0.2894 oz. AGW, 26 mm. **Ruler:** Elizabeth II **Subject:** Paavo Nurmi

| Date | Mintage | VF20 | XF40 | MS60 | MS63 | MS65 |
|---|---|---|---|---|---|---|
| 2013 Proof | Est. 200 | — | — | — | — | — |

**KM# 267 15 DOLLARS**
500.00 g., 0.999 Silver 16.0593 oz. ASW, 100 mm. **Ruler:** Elizabeth II **Subject:** Year of the Rooster **Rev:** Multicolor rooster standing right, sunrise

| Date | Mintage | VF20 | XF40 | MS60 | MS63 | MS65 |
|---|---|---|---|---|---|---|
| 2005 | — | PF65 600 | | | | |

**KM# 296 15 DOLLARS**
500.00 g., 0.999 Silver 16.0593 oz. ASW, 100 mm. **Ruler:** Elizabeth II **Subject:** Year of the Dog **Rev:** Multicolor dog

| Date | Mintage | VF20 | XF40 | MS60 | MS63 | MS65 |
|---|---|---|---|---|---|---|
| 2005 | — | PF65 600 | | | | |

**KM# 898 15 DOLLARS**
7.70 g., 0.9999 Gold 0.2475 oz. AGW, 22 mm. **Ruler:** Elizabeth II **Subject:** Merentibus Gold

| Date | Mintage | VF20 | XF40 | MS60 | MS63 | MS65 |
|---|---|---|---|---|---|---|
| 2012 | Est. 2000 | PF65 500 | | | | |

**KM# 125 20 DOLLARS**
1.24 g., 0.9999 Gold 0.0399 oz. AGW, 13.9 mm. **Ruler:** Elizabeth II **Subject:** Snoopy as an Ace **Obv:** Crowned head right **Rev:** Snoopy flying his dog house **Edge:** Reeded

| Date | Mintage | VF20 | XF40 | MS60 | MS63 | MS65 |
|---|---|---|---|---|---|---|
| 2001 | 10,000 | PF65 80.00 | | | | |

**KM# 148 20 DOLLARS**
1.24 g., 0.9999 Gold 0.0399 oz. AGW, 13.92 mm. **Ruler:** Elizabeth II **Subject:** Pokémon Series **Obv:** Crowned shield within sprigs **Rev:** Pikachu **Edge:** Reeded

| Date | Mintage | VF20 | XF40 | MS60 | MS63 | MS65 |
|---|---|---|---|---|---|---|
| 2002 PM | 10,000 | PF65 80.00 | | | | |

**KM# 153 20 DOLLARS**
1.24 g., 0.9999 Gold 0.0399 oz. AGW, 13.9 mm. **Ruler:** Elizabeth II **Subject:** Pokémon Series **Obv:** Crowned shield within sprigs **Rev:** Pichu **Edge:** Reeded

| Date | Mintage | VF20 | XF40 | MS60 | MS63 | MS65 |
|---|---|---|---|---|---|---|
| 2002 PM | 10,000 | PF65 80.00 | | | | |

**KM# 158 20 DOLLARS**
1.24 g., 0.9999 Gold 0.0399 oz. AGW, 13.92 mm. **Ruler:** Elizabeth II **Subject:** Pokémon Series **Obv:** Crowned shield within sprigs **Rev:** Mewtwo **Edge:** Reeded

| Date | Mintage | VF20 | XF40 | MS60 | MS63 | MS65 |
|---|---|---|---|---|---|---|
| 2002 PM | 10,000 | PF65 80.00 | | | | |

**KM# 163 20 DOLLARS**
1.24 g., 0.9999 Gold 0.0399 oz. AGW, 13.9 mm. **Ruler:** Elizabeth II **Subject:** Pokémon Series **Obv:** Crowned shield within sprigs **Rev:** Entei **Edge:** Reeded

| Date | Mintage | VF20 | XF40 | MS60 | MS63 | MS65 |
|---|---|---|---|---|---|---|
| 2002 PM | 10,000 | PF65 80.00 | | | | |

**KM# 168 20 DOLLARS**
1.24 g., 0.9999 Gold 0.0399 oz. AGW, 13.9 mm. **Ruler:** Elizabeth II **Subject:** Pokémon Series **Obv:** Crowned shield within sprigs **Rev:** Celebi **Edge:** Reeded

| Date | Mintage | VF20 | XF40 | MS60 | MS63 | MS65 |
|---|---|---|---|---|---|---|
| 2002 PM | 10,000 | PF65 80.00 | | | | |

**KM# 379 20 DOLLARS**
0.917 Gold, 13.9x16.7 mm. **Ruler:** Elizabeth II **Subject:** Hello Kitty **Shape:** Face **Note:** Center part to KM#380.

| Date | Mintage | VF20 | XF40 | MS60 | MS63 | MS65 |
|---|---|---|---|---|---|---|
| 2010 | Est. 1000 | PF65 475 | | | | |

**KM# 1180 20 DOLLARS**
3.11 g., 0.9999 Gold 0.100 oz. AGW, 14 x 23 mm. **Ruler:** Elizabeth II **Subject:** Humpback Whale

| Date | Mintage | VF20 | XF40 | MS60 | MS63 | MS65 |
|---|---|---|---|---|---|---|
| 2013 Proof | — | — | — | — | — | — |

**KM# 255 25 DOLLARS**
15.55 g., 0.999 Gold 0.4994 oz. AGW, 22 mm. **Ruler:** Elizabeth II **Subject:** Peanuts 60th Anniversary **Rev:** Snoopy dancing, Charlie Brown's zig-zag shirt pattern in background

| Date | Mintage | VF20 | XF40 | MS60 | MS63 | MS65 |
|---|---|---|---|---|---|---|
| 2010 Prooflike | 1,000 | — | — | — | — | 950 |

**KM# 388 25 DOLLARS**
7.77 g., 0.999 Gold 0.2496 oz. AGW, 22 mm. **Ruler:** Elizabeth II **Subject:** Miffy with key

| Date | Mintage | VF20 | XF40 | MS60 | MS63 | MS65 |
|---|---|---|---|---|---|---|
| 2010 | 1,000 | PF65 475 | | | | |

**KM# 715 25 DOLLARS**
7.78 g., 0.9999 Gold 0.2501 oz. AGW, 22 mm. **Ruler:** Elizabeth II **Rev:** Dragon

| Date | Mintage | VF20 | XF40 | MS60 | MS63 | MS65 |
|---|---|---|---|---|---|---|
| 2012 | 2,000 | PF65 465 | | | | |

**KM# 846 25 DOLLARS**
15.50 g., 0.9999 Gold 0.4983 oz. AGW, 27 mm. **Ruler:** Elizabeth II **Obv:** Head with tiara at left, wreath **Rev:** Stanislaus Augustus head right

| Date | Mintage | VF20 | XF40 | MS60 | MS63 | MS65 |
|---|---|---|---|---|---|---|
| 2012 | 8,000 | PF65 950 | | | | |

**KM# 268 30 DOLLARS**
1000.00 g., 0.999 Silver 32.1186 oz. ASW, 120 mm. **Ruler:** Elizabeth II **Subject:** Year of the Rooster **Rev:** Multicolor rooster standing right, sunrise

| Date | Mintage | VF20 | XF40 | MS60 | MS63 | MS65 |
|---|---|---|---|---|---|---|
| 2005 | — | PF65 1,250 | | | | |

**KM# 297 30 DOLLARS**
1000.00 g., 0.999 Silver 32.1186 oz. ASW, 120 mm. **Ruler:** Elizabeth II **Subject:** Year of the Dog **Rev:** Multicolor dog

| Date | Mintage | VF20 | XF40 | MS60 | MS63 | MS65 |
|---|---|---|---|---|---|---|
| 2005 | — | PF65 1,250 | | | | |

**KM# 380 30 DOLLARS**
0.917 Gold, 30 mm. **Ruler:** Elizabeth II **Subject:** Bears **Note:** Outer ring for KM#379

| Date | Mintage | VF20 | XF40 | MS60 | MS63 | MS65 |
|---|---|---|---|---|---|---|
| 2010 | Est. 1000 | PF65 650 | | | | |

**KM# 742 30 DOLLARS**
1000.00 g., 0.999 Silver 32.1186 oz. ASW, 100 mm. **Ruler:** Elizabeth II **Subject:** Year of the Dragon **Rev:** Dragon with pearl in color

| Date | Mintage | VF20 | XF40 | MS60 | MS63 | MS65 |
|---|---|---|---|---|---|---|
| 2012 | 250 | PF65 1,250 | | | | |

**KM# 788 30 DOLLARS**
1000.00 g., 0.999 Silver 32.1186 oz. ASW, 100 mm. **Ruler:** Elizabeth II **Subject:** Russian municipalities - Belgorod **Obv:** Head with crown right **Rev:** Statue, shield and building

| Date | Mintage | VF20 | XF40 | MS60 | MS63 | MS65 |
|---|---|---|---|---|---|---|
| 2012 | — | PF65 1,300 | | | | |

**KM# 869 30 DOLLARS**
1000.00 g., 0.999 Silver 32.1186 oz. ASW, 100 mm. **Ruler:** Elizabeth II **Obv:** Crowned head right **Rev:** Coral Snake with chinese character above

| Date | Mintage | VF20 | XF40 | MS60 | MS63 | MS65 |
|---|---|---|---|---|---|---|
| 2013 | 300 | PF65 1,000 | | | | |

**KM# 126 50 DOLLARS**
3.11 g., 0.9999 Gold 0.100 oz. AGW, 17.9 mm. **Ruler:** Elizabeth II **Subject:** Snoopy as an Ace **Obv:** Crowned head right **Rev:** Snoopy flying his dog house **Edge:** Reeded

| Date | Mintage | VF20 | XF40 | MS60 | MS63 | MS65 |
|---|---|---|---|---|---|---|
| 2001 | 7,500 | PF65 195 | | | | |

**KM# 149 50 DOLLARS**
3.11 g., 0.9999 Gold 0.100 oz. AGW, 17.9 mm. **Ruler:** Elizabeth II **Subject:** Pokémon Series **Obv:** Crowned shield within sprigs **Rev:** Pikachu **Edge:** Reeded

| Date | Mintage | VF20 | XF40 | MS60 | MS63 | MS65 |
|---|---|---|---|---|---|---|
| 2002 PM | 7,500 | PF65 195 | | | | |

**KM# 154 50 DOLLARS**
3.11 g., 0.9999 Gold 0.100 oz. AGW, 17.9 mm. **Ruler:** Elizabeth II **Subject:** Pokémon Series **Obv:** Crowned shield within sprigs **Rev:** Pichu **Edge:** Reeded

| Date | Mintage | VF20 | XF40 | MS60 | MS63 | MS65 |
|---|---|---|---|---|---|---|
| 2002 PM | 7,500 | PF65 195 | | | | |

**KM# 159 50 DOLLARS**
3.11 g., 0.9999 Gold 0.100 oz. AGW, 17.9 mm. **Ruler:** Elizabeth II **Subject:** Pokémon Series **Obv:** Crowned shield within sprigs **Rev:** Mewtwo **Edge:** Reeded

| Date | Mintage | VF20 | XF40 | MS60 | MS63 | MS65 |
|---|---|---|---|---|---|---|
| 2002 PM | 7,500 | PF65 195 | | | | |

**KM# 164 50 DOLLARS**
3.11 g., 0.9999 Gold 0.100 oz. AGW, 17.9 mm. **Ruler:** Elizabeth II **Subject:** Pokémon Series **Obv:** Crowned shield within sprigs **Rev:** Entei **Edge:** Reeded

| Date | Mintage | VF20 | XF40 | MS60 | MS63 | MS65 |
|---|---|---|---|---|---|---|
| 2002 PM | 7,500 | PF65 195 | | | | |

**KM# 169 50 DOLLARS**
3.11 g., 0.9999 Gold 0.100 oz. AGW, 17.9 mm. **Ruler:** Elizabeth II **Subject:** Pokémon Series **Obv:** Crowned shield within sprigs **Rev:** Celebi **Edge:** Reeded

| Date | Mintage | VF20 | XF40 | MS60 | MS63 | MS65 |
|---|---|---|---|---|---|---|
| 2002 PM | 7,500 | PF65 195 | | | | |

**KM# 256 50 DOLLARS**
15.55 g., 0.9999 Gold 0.4994 oz. AGW, 30 mm. **Ruler:** Elizabeth II **Subject:** Peanuts 60th Anniversary **Rev:** Snoopy as a king

| Date | Mintage | VF20 | XF40 | MS60 | MS63 | MS65 |
|---|---|---|---|---|---|---|
| 2010 Prooflike | 1,000 | — | — | — | — | 1,000 |

**KM# 389 50 DOLLARS**
15.55 g., 0.999 Gold 0.4994 oz. AGW, 30 mm. **Ruler:** Elizabeth II **Subject:** Miffy in flowers

| Date | Mintage | VF20 | XF40 | MS60 | MS63 | MS65 |
|---|---|---|---|---|---|---|
| 2010 | Est. 1000 | PF65 950 | | | | |

**KM# 584 50 DOLLARS**
250.00 g., 0.999 Silver 8.0296 oz. ASW, 67.35x90 mm. **Ruler:** Elizabeth II **Subject:** Russian Royal Family **Obv:** Nicholas II and family standing as Saints in the Othodox Church, head with tiara right below **Rev:** Oval portrait images of the Imperial family **Shape:** Vertical Oval

| Date | Mintage | VF20 | XF40 | MS60 | MS63 | MS65 |
|---|---|---|---|---|---|---|
| 2011 | 400 | PF65 400 | | | | |

**KM# 702 50 DOLLARS**
62.20 g., 0.9999 Gold 1.9996 oz. AGW **Ruler:** Elizabeth II **Rev:** John Wycliff and Jan Hus

| Date | Mintage | VF20 | XF40 | MS60 | MS63 | MS65 |
|---|---|---|---|---|---|---|
| 2011 | Est. 1000 | PF65 3,700 | | | | |

**KM# 714 50 DOLLARS**
31.11 g., 0.9999 Gold 0.9999 oz. AGW, 32 mm. **Ruler:** Elizabeth II **Rev:** Dragon

| Date | Mintage | VF20 | XF40 | MS60 | MS63 | MS65 |
|---|---|---|---|---|---|---|
| 2012 | 2,000 | PF65 1,850 | | | | |

**KM# 777 50 DOLLARS**
31.10 g., 0.9999 Gold 0.9998 oz. AGW, 29.2x39 mm. **Ruler:** Elizabeth II **Subject:** Imperial Faberge Eggs - Corconation Egg **Rev:** Egg and state coach

| Date | Mintage | VF20 | XF40 | MS60 | MS63 | MS65 |
|---|---|---|---|---|---|---|
| 2012 | Est. 333 | PF65 2,000 | | | | |

**KM# 778 50 DOLLARS**
250.00 g., 0.999 Silver 8.0296 oz. ASW, 67.35x90 mm. **Ruler:** Elizabeth II **Subject:** Imperial Faberge Eggs - Coronation Egg **Rev:** Egg and state coach

| Date | Mintage | VF20 | XF40 | MS60 | MS63 | MS65 |
|---|---|---|---|---|---|---|
| 2012 | Est. 333 | PF65 350 | | | | |

**KM# 791 50 DOLLARS**
250.00 g., 0.999 Silver 8.0296 oz. ASW, 67.35x90 mm. **Ruler:** Elizabeth II **Subject:** Great Ukrainian Hetmans **Obv:** Seven shields around central head of Queen Elizabeth **Rev:** Seven busts around central shield **Shape:** Vertical oval

| Date | Mintage | VF20 | XF40 | MS60 | MS63 | MS65 |
|---|---|---|---|---|---|---|
| 2012 | 400 | PF65 400 | | | | |

**KM# 793 50 DOLLARS**
250.00 g., 0.925 Silver 7.4349 oz. ASW, 67.35x90 mm. **Ruler:** Elizabeth II **Subject:** Royal Hunting **Obv:** Saint on horseback **Rev:** Horseman with falcon **Shape:** Vertical oval

| Date | Mintage | VF20 | XF40 | MS60 | MS63 | MS65 |
|---|---|---|---|---|---|---|
| 2012 | Est. 400 | PF65 400 | | | | |

**KM# 827 50 DOLLARS**
31.11 g., 0.9999 Gold 0.9999 oz. AGW, 32 mm. **Ruler:** Elizabeth II **Obv:** Head in tiara at left, branches **Rev:** Head right of Stanislaus Augustus

| Date | Mintage | VF20 | XF40 | MS60 | MS63 | MS65 |
|---|---|---|---|---|---|---|
| 2012 | Est. 16000 | PF65 1,775 | | | | |

**KM# 880 50 DOLLARS**
250.00 g., 0.999 Silver 8.0296 oz. ASW, 90x67.35 mm. **Ruler:** Elizabeth II **Subject:** Russian Royal Charity **Obv:** Head with tiara at top center, four building façades around **Rev:** Oval portraits at left and right, church at center **Shape:** Horizontal oval

| Date | Mintage | VF20 | XF40 | MS60 | MS63 | MS65 |
|---|---|---|---|---|---|---|
| 2012 | Est. 400 | PF65 350 | | | | |

**KM# 972 50 DOLLARS**
15.51 g., 0.9999 Gold 0.4986 oz. AGW, 18 x 30 mm. **Ruler:** Elizabeth II **Subject:** The Last Supper

| Date | Mintage | VF20 | XF40 | MS60 | MS63 | MS65 |
|---|---|---|---|---|---|---|
| 2012 | Est. 500 | PF65 1,000 | | | | |

**KM# 1079 50 DOLLARS**
250.00 g., 0.999 Silver 8.0296 oz. ASW, 67.35x90 mm. **Ruler:** Elizabeth II **Subject:** Russian Royal Road

| Date | Mintage | VF20 | XF40 | MS60 | MS63 | MS65 |
|---|---|---|---|---|---|---|
| 2013 | Est. 400 | PF65 375 | | | | |

**KM# 1179 50 DOLLARS**
7.77 g., 0.999 Gold 0.2496 oz. AGW, 14 x 23 mm. **Ruler:** Elizabeth II **Subject:** Humpback Whale

| Date | Mintage | VF20 | XF40 | MS60 | MS63 | MS65 |
|---|---|---|---|---|---|---|
| 2013 Proof | — | — | — | — | — | — |

**KM# 1076 50 DOLLARS**
186.60 g., 0.999 Silver 5.9933 oz. ASW, 32 x 22.1 mm. **Ruler:** Elizabeth II **Subject:** Fortuna Redux

| Date | Mintage | F12 | VF20 | XF40 | MS60 | MS63 |
|---|---|---|---|---|---|---|
| 2014 | Est. 2500 | PF65 550 | | | | |

**KM# 127 100 DOLLARS**
6.22 g., 0.9999 Gold 0.200 oz. AGW, 22 mm. **Ruler:** Elizabeth II **Subject:** Snoopy as an Ace **Obv:** Crowned head right **Rev:** Snoopy flying his dog house **Edge:** Reeded

| Date | Mintage | VF20 | XF40 | MS60 | MS63 | MS65 |
|---|---|---|---|---|---|---|
| 2001 | 5,000 | PF65 370 | | | | |

**KM# 150 100 DOLLARS**
6.22 g., 0.9999 Gold 0.200 oz. AGW, 22 mm. **Ruler:** Elizabeth II **Subject:** Pokémon Series **Obv:** Crowned shield within sprigs **Rev:** Pikachu **Edge:** Reeded

| Date | Mintage | VF20 | XF40 | MS60 | MS63 | MS65 |
|---|---|---|---|---|---|---|
| 2002 PM | 5,000 | PF65 370 | | | | |

**KM# 155 100 DOLLARS**
6.22 g., 0.9999 Gold 0.200 oz. AGW, 22 mm. **Ruler:** Elizabeth II **Subject:** Pokémon Series **Obv:** Crowned shield within sprigs **Rev:** Pichu **Edge:** Reeded

| Date | Mintage | VF20 | XF40 | MS60 | MS63 | MS65 |
|---|---|---|---|---|---|---|
| 2002 PM | 5,000 | PF65 370 | | | | |

**KM# 160 100 DOLLARS**
6.22 g., 0.9999 Gold 0.200 oz. AGW, 22 mm. **Ruler:** Elizabeth II **Subject:** Pokémon Series **Obv:** Crowned shield within sprigs **Rev:** Mewtwo **Edge:** Reeded

| Date | Mintage | VF20 | XF40 | MS60 | MS63 | MS65 |
|---|---|---|---|---|---|---|
| 2002 PM | 5,000 | PF65 370 | | | | |

**KM# 165 100 DOLLARS**
6.22 g., 0.9999 Gold 0.200 oz. AGW, 22 mm. **Ruler:** Elizabeth II **Subject:** Pokémon Series **Obv:** Crowned shield within sprigs **Rev:** Entei **Edge:** Reeded

| Date | Mintage | VF20 | XF40 | MS60 | MS63 | MS65 |
|---|---|---|---|---|---|---|
| 2002 PM | 5,000 | PF65 370 | | | | |

**KM# 170 100 DOLLARS**
6.22 g., 0.9999 Gold 0.200 oz. AGW, 22 mm. **Ruler:** Elizabeth II **Subject:** Pokémon Series **Obv:** Crowned shield within sprigs **Rev:** Celebi **Edge:** reeded

| Date | Mintage | VF20 | XF40 | MS60 | MS63 | MS65 |
|---|---|---|---|---|---|---|
| 2002 PM | 5,000 | PF65 370 | | | | |

**KM# 425 100 DOLLARS**
93.30 g., 0.900 Gold 2.6997 oz. AGW, 41.6x55.6 mm. **Ruler:** Elizabeth II **Subject:** Imperial Faberge Egg - Coronation Egg **Obv:** Head with tiara right above opened egg **Rev:** Coronation egg and coach **Shape:** Vertical oval

| Date | Mintage | VF20 | XF40 | MS60 | MS63 | MS65 |
|---|---|---|---|---|---|---|
| 2010 | 222 | PF65 5,000 | | | | |

**KM# 511 100 DOLLARS**
31.10 g., 0.999 Gold 0.999 oz. AGW, 38.61 mm. **Ruler:** Elizabeth II **Obv:** Head with tiara right **Rev:** Tasmanian tiger in color

| Date | Mintage | VF20 | XF40 | MS60 | MS63 | MS65 |
|---|---|---|---|---|---|---|
| 2011 | 200 | PF65 2,000 | | | | |

**KM# 572 100 DOLLARS**
93.30 g., 0.900 Gold 2.6997 oz. AGW, 41.6x55.6 mm. **Ruler:** Elizabeth II **Subject:** Imperial Faberge Egg **Obv:** Head with tiara right, open egg below **Rev:** Clover leaf floral egg on stand **Shape:** Vertical oval

| Date | Mintage | VF20 | XF40 | MS60 | MS63 | MS65 |
|---|---|---|---|---|---|---|
| 2011 | 222 | PF65 5,000 | | | | |

**KM# 648 100 DOLLARS**
93.30 g., 0.900 Gold 2.6997 oz. AGW, 41.6x55.6 mm. **Ruler:** Elizabeth II **Subject:** Imperial Easter Egg - Lilly **Obv:** Head with tiara right, open egg below **Rev:** Egg on stand, lillys around

| Date | Mintage | VF20 | XF40 | MS60 | MS63 | MS65 |
|---|---|---|---|---|---|---|
| 2011 | — | PF65 5,000 | | | | |

**KM# 650 100 DOLLARS**
50.00 g., 0.999 Silver 1.6059 oz. ASW partially gilt, 35.2 x 35.2 mm. **Ruler:** Elizabeth II **Obv:** Head with tiara right **Rev:** Three Kings of 1936 - George V, Edward VIII, George VI selectively gilt **Edge:** Reeded **Shape:** Square

| Date | Mintage | VF20 | XF40 | MS60 | MS63 | MS65 |
|---|---|---|---|---|---|---|
| 2011 | 1,500 | PF65 160 | | | | |

**KM# 701 100 DOLLARS**
139.50 g., 0.9999 Gold 4.4846 oz. AGW, 50 mm. **Ruler:** Elizabeth II **Subject:** General Perina, Battle of Britain pilot **Rev:** Perina as pilot

| Date | Mintage | VF20 | XF40 | MS60 | MS63 | MS65 |
|---|---|---|---|---|---|---|
| 2011 | 400 | PF65 8,500 | | | | |

**KM# 747 100 DOLLARS**
400.00 g., 0.9997 Silver 12.8564 oz. ASW gilt, 90 mm. **Ruler:** Elizabeth II **Subject:** Szlak Bursztynowy **Obv:** Queen's head at left, Roman horse cart at right **Rev:** Map of central Europe, amber insert

| Date | Mintage | VF20 | XF40 | MS60 | MS63 | MS65 |
|---|---|---|---|---|---|---|
| 2011 | 245 | PF65 1,250 | | | | |

**KM# 737 100 DOLLARS**
31.11 g., 0.999 Gold 0.999 oz. AGW, 38.61 mm. **Ruler:** Elizabeth II **Rev:** Tasmanian Wedge-Tailed Eagle **Edge:** Reeded and numbered

| Date | Mintage | VF20 | XF40 | MS60 | MS63 | MS65 |
|---|---|---|---|---|---|---|
| 2012 | 150 | PF65 2,000 | | | | |

**KM# 755 100 DOLLARS**
93.30 g., 0.900 Gold 2.6997 oz. AGW, 41.6x55.6 mm. **Ruler:** Elizabeth II **Subject:** Imperial Faberge Eggs - Duchess of Marlborough **Rev:** Serpent at bottom stem of egg **Shape:** Vertical oval

| Date | Mintage | VF20 | XF40 | MS60 | MS63 | MS65 |
|---|---|---|---|---|---|---|
| 2012 | 222 | PF65 5,000 | | | | |

**KM# 834 100 DOLLARS**
93.30 g., 0.900 Gold 2.6997 oz. AGW, 41.6x55.6 mm. **Ruler:** Elizabeth II **Obv:** Head with tiara above opened egg **Rev:** Imperial Faberge Eggs - Pansy Egg **Shape:** Vertical oval

| Date | Mintage | VF20 | XF40 | MS60 | MS63 | MS65 |
|---|---|---|---|---|---|---|
| 2012 | 222 | PF65 4,850 | | | | |

**KM# 835 100 DOLLARS**
93.30 g., 0.900 Gold 2.6997 oz. AGW, 41.6x55.6 mm. **Ruler:** Elizabeth II **Obv:** Head in tiara right above opened egg **Rev:** Imperial Faberge Egg - Bay Tree **Shape:** Vertical oval

| Date | Mintage | VF20 | XF40 | MS60 | MS63 | MS65 |
|---|---|---|---|---|---|---|
| 2012 | 222 | PF65 4,850 | | | | |

**KM# 950 100 DOLLARS**
62.20 g., 0.999 Gold 1.9978 oz. AGW, 40 mm. **Ruler:** Elizabeth II **Subject:** Amber Room

| Date | Mintage | VF20 | XF40 | MS60 | MS63 | MS65 |
|---|---|---|---|---|---|---|
| 2012 | — | PF65 4,500 | | | | |

**KM# 928 100 DOLLARS**
31.10 g., 0.9999 Gold 0.9998 oz. AGW, 38.61 mm. **Ruler:** Elizabeth II **Subject:** Tasmanian Devil

| Date | Mintage | VF20 | XF40 | MS60 | MS63 | MS65 |
|---|---|---|---|---|---|---|
| 2013 | Est. 150 | PF65 1,550 | | | | |

**KM# 1126 100 DOLLARS**
400.00 g., 0.999 Silver 12.8474 oz. ASW, 90 mm. **Ruler:** Elizabeth II **Subject:** Magic Year of Happiness

| Date | Mintage | VF20 | XF40 | MS60 | MS63 | MS65 |
|---|---|---|---|---|---|---|
| 2013 | Est. 222 | PF65 1,150 | | | | |

**KM# 1156 100 DOLLARS**
93.30 g., 0.999 Gold 2.9967 oz. AGW, 41.6 x 55.6 mm. **Ruler:** Elizabeth II **Subject:** Continents - Europe

| Date | Mintage | VF20 | XF40 | MS60 | MS63 | MS65 |
|---|---|---|---|---|---|---|
| 2013 | Est. 100 | PF65 5,000 | | | | |

**KM# 1178 100 DOLLARS**
15.55 g., 0.9999 Gold 0.4999 oz. AGW, 25 x 40 mm. **Ruler:** Elizabeth II **Subject:** Humpback Whale

| Date | Mintage | VF20 | XF40 | MS60 | MS63 | MS65 |
|---|---|---|---|---|---|---|
| 2013 | — | PF65 1,000 | | | | |

**KM# 1182 100 DOLLARS**
1000.00 g., 0.999 Silver 32.1186 oz. ASW, 90 x 135 mm. **Ruler:** Elizabeth II **Subject:** Humpback Whale

| Date | Mintage | VF20 | XF40 | MS60 | MS63 | MS65 |
|---|---|---|---|---|---|---|
| 2013 | — | PF65 750 | | | | |

**KM# 1200 100 DOLLARS**
400.00 g., 0.999 Silver 12.8474 oz. ASW, 90 mm. **Ruler:** Elizabeth II **Subject:** Magic Year of Happiness

| Date | Mintage | VF20 | XF40 | MS60 | MS63 | MS65 |
|---|---|---|---|---|---|---|
| 2013 | — | PF65 350 | | | | |

**KM# 1201 100 DOLLARS**

62.20 g., 0.999 Gold 1.9978 oz. AGW, 40 mm. **Ruler:** Elizabeth II **Subject:** Holy Grail

| Date | Mintage | VF20 | XF40 | MS60 | MS63 | MS65 |
|---|---|---|---|---|---|---|
| 2013 | Est. 150 | PF65 3,750 | | | | |

**KM# 1238 100 DOLLARS**

139.50 g., 0.9999 Gold 4.4846 oz. AGW, 50 mm. **Ruler:** Elizabeth II **Subject:** 40 Ducat of Bolivia

| Date | Mintage | VF20 | XF40 | MS60 | MS63 | MS65 |
|---|---|---|---|---|---|---|
| 2013 | Est. 100 | PF65 8,500 | | | | |

**KM# 1255 100 DOLLARS**

31.11 g., 0.999 Gold 0.999 oz. AGW Colorized, 38.61 mm. **Ruler:** Elizabeth II **Subject:** Tasmanian Devil **Obv:** Head in tiara right

| Date | Mintage | VF20 | XF40 | MS60 | MS63 | MS65 |
|---|---|---|---|---|---|---|
| 2013 | 150 | PF65 3,750 | | | | |

**KM# 1256 100 DOLLARS**

400.00 g., 0.999 Silver 12.8474 oz. ASW, 90 mm. **Ruler:** Elizabeth II **Obv:** Head with tiara right within rays **Rev:** Moon gilt within rays and 12 crystals

| Date | Mintage | VF20 | XF40 | MS60 | MS63 | MS65 |
|---|---|---|---|---|---|---|
| 2013 | — | PF65 800 | | | | |

**KM# 1246 100 DOLLARS**

31.10 g., 0.9999 Gold 0.9934 oz. AGW, 38.61 mm. **Ruler:** Elizabeth II **Subject:** Frilled Neck Lizard

| Date | Mintage | F12 | VF20 | XF40 | MS60 | MS63 |
|---|---|---|---|---|---|---|
| 2014 | Est. 150 | PF65 3,750 | | | | |

**KM# 512 200 DOLLARS**

62.20 g., 0.999 Gold 1.9978 oz. AGW, 35.2x35.2 mm. **Ruler:** Elizabeth II **Subject:** Three kings of 1935 **Obv:** Head with tiara right **Rev:** Head left of George V, Edward VIII and George VI

| Date | Mintage | VF20 | XF40 | MS60 | MS63 | MS65 |
|---|---|---|---|---|---|---|
| 2011 | 75 | PF65 5,000 | | | | |

**KM# 713 200 DOLLARS**

155.55 g., 0.9999 Gold 5.0005 oz. AGW **Ruler:** Elizabeth II **Rev:** Dragon

| Date | Mintage | VF20 | XF40 | MS60 | MS63 | MS65 |
|---|---|---|---|---|---|---|
| 2012 | 100 | PF65 9,500 | | | | |

**KM# 740 200 DOLLARS**

1000.00 g., 0.999 Silver 32.1186 oz. ASW, 118.2x52.7 mm. **Ruler:** Elizabeth II **Obv:** Head with crown at left **Rev:** Two dragons flanking center ball **Shape:** Horizontal rectangle

| Date | Mintage | VF20 | XF40 | MS60 | MS63 | MS65 |
|---|---|---|---|---|---|---|
| 2012 | 1,800 | PF65 1,250 | | | | |

**KM# 1174 200 DOLLARS**

31.10 g., 0.999 Gold 0.9989 oz. AGW, 40 mm. **Ruler:** Elizabeth II **Subject:** Coronation of HM Queen Elizabeth II

| Date | Mintage | VF20 | XF40 | MS60 | MS63 | MS65 |
|---|---|---|---|---|---|---|
| 2013 | Est. 200 | PF65 2,800 | | | | |

**KM# 1177 200 DOLLARS**

31.10 g., 0.999 Gold 0.9989 oz. AGW, 28 x 51 mm. **Ruler:** Elizabeth II **Subject:** Humpback Whale

| Date | Mintage | VF20 | XF40 | MS60 | MS63 | MS65 |
|---|---|---|---|---|---|---|
| 2013 | — | PF65 2,500 | | | | |

**KM# 1244 200 DOLLARS**

31.10 g., 0.9999 Gold 0.9998 oz. AGW, 32.7 mm. **Ruler:** Elizabeth II **Subject:** Doctor Who 50th Anniversary

| Date | Mintage | VF20 | XF40 | MS60 | MS63 | MS65 |
|---|---|---|---|---|---|---|
| 2013 | Est. 500 | PF65 2,450 | | | | |

**KM# 700 250 DOLLARS**

348.50 g., 0.9999 Gold 11.2034 oz. AGW, 65 mm. **Ruler:** Elizabeth II **Rev:** Jan Amos Komensky seated at desk with globe

| Date | Mintage | VF20 | XF40 | MS60 | MS63 | MS65 |
|---|---|---|---|---|---|---|
| 2011 | Est. 250 | PF65 20,000 | | | | |

**KM# 1239 250 DOLLARS**

348.60 g., 0.9999 Gold 11.2066 oz. AGW, 65 mm. **Ruler:** Elizabeth II **Subject:** 100 Ducat of Spytihnev

| Date | Mintage | VF20 | XF40 | MS60 | MS63 | MS65 |
|---|---|---|---|---|---|---|
| 2013 | Est. 50 | PF65 16,500 | | | | |

**KM# 1139 300 DOLLARS**

5000.00 g., 0.999 Silver 160.5929 oz. ASW, 180 mm. **Ruler:** Elizabeth II **Subject:** Chairman Mao

| Date | Mintage | VF20 | XF40 | MS60 | MS63 | MS65 |
|---|---|---|---|---|---|---|
| 2013 | Est. 500 | PF65 3,750 | | | | |

**KM# 973 500 DOLLARS**

750.00 g., 0.999 Silver 24.0889 oz. ASW, 100 mm. **Ruler:** Elizabeth II **Subject:** The Last Supper

| Date | Mintage | VF20 | XF40 | MS60 | MS63 | MS65 |
|---|---|---|---|---|---|---|
| 2012 | Est. 199 | PF65 2,200 | | | | |

**KM# 1176 500 DOLLARS**

155.50 g., 0.9999 Gold 4.9989 oz. AGW, 55 x 85 mm. **Ruler:** Elizabeth II **Subject:** Humpback Whale

| Date | Mintage | VF20 | XF40 | MS60 | MS63 | MS65 |
|---|---|---|---|---|---|---|
| 2013 | — | PF65 9,500 | | | | |

**KM# 1175 1000 DOLLARS**

1000.00 g., 0.9999 Gold 32.1475 oz. AGW, 90 x 135 mm. **Ruler:** Elizabeth II **Subject:** Humpback Whale

| Date | Mintage | VF20 | XF40 | MS60 | MS63 | MS65 |
|---|---|---|---|---|---|---|
| 2013 | — | PF65 47,500 | | | | |

**KM# 405 3000 DOLLARS**

500.00 g., 0.9999 Gold 16.0738 oz. AGW, 67.35x90 mm. **Ruler:** Elizabeth II **Subject:** Russian Royal Family **Obv:** Seven figures as Orthodox Saints, Elizabeth head with tiara below **Rev:** Oval portaits of Nicholas II and his family **Shape:** Vertical Oval

| Date | Mintage | VF20 | XF40 | MS60 | MS63 | MS65 |
|---|---|---|---|---|---|---|
| 2010 | 23 | PF65 29,500 | | | | |

**KM# 588 3000 DOLLARS**

500.00 g., 0.9999 Gold 16.0738 oz. AGW, 67.35x90 mm. **Ruler:** Elizabeth II **Subject:** Royal Hunting **Obv:** Russian saint on horseback, head with tiara right below, multicolor **Rev:** Russian figure on horseback with falcon, multicolor

| Date | Mintage | VF20 | XF40 | MS60 | MS63 | MS65 |
|---|---|---|---|---|---|---|
| 2011 | 40 | PF65 29,500 | | | | |

**KM# 881 3000 DOLLARS**

500.00 g., 0.9999 Gold 16.0738 oz. AGW, 90x67.35 mm. **Ruler:** Elizabeth II **Subject:** Russian Royal Charity **Obv:** Head with tiara at top center, four building façades around **Rev:** Vertical oval portraits flanking church **Shape:** Horizontal oval

| Date | Mintage | VF20 | XF40 | MS60 | MS63 | MS65 |
|---|---|---|---|---|---|---|
| 2012 | Est. 30 | PF65 29,500 | | | | |

### KM# 1080 3000 DOLLARS

500.00 g., 0.9999 Gold 16.0738 oz. AGW, 90 x 67.35 mm. **Ruler:** Elizabeth II **Subject:** RUssian Royal Road

| Date | Mintage | VF20 | XF40 | MS60 | MS63 | MS65 |
|---|---|---|---|---|---|---|
| 2013 | Est. 35 | PF65 29,000 | | | | |

### KM# 699 10000 DOLLARS

1000.00 g., 0.9999 Gold 32.1475 oz. AGW, 85 mm. **Ruler:** Elizabeth II **Rev:** Good Queen Ann seated on throne

| Date | Mintage | VF20 | XF40 | MS60 | MS63 | MS65 |
|---|---|---|---|---|---|---|
| 2011 | Est. 150 | PF65 58,500 | | | | |

### KM# 708 10000 DOLLARS

1000.00 g., 0.9999 Gold 32.1475 oz. AGW, 90 mm. **Ruler:** Elizabeth II **Obv:** Ancient horsecart **Obv. Legend:** SZLAK BURSZTYNOWY **Rev:** European map with cities, amber insert

| Date | Mintage | VF20 | XF40 | MS60 | MS63 | MS65 |
|---|---|---|---|---|---|---|
| 2011 | Est. 12 | PF65 60,000 | | | | |

## MINT SETS

| KM# | Date | Mintage | Identification | Issue Price | Mkt Val |
|---|---|---|---|---|---|
| MS1 | 2009 (5) | 20,000 | KM#193-197 | — | 30.00 |
| MS2 | 2010 (5) | 10,000 | KM#193-196, 198 | — | 30.00 |

# NORWAY

The Kingdom of Norway (Norge, Noreg), a constitutional monarchy located in northwestern Europe, has an area of 150,000sq. mi. (324,220 sq. km.), including the island territories of Spitzbergen (Svalbard) and Jan Mayen, and a population of *4.2 million. Capital: Oslo (Christiania). The diversified economic base of Norway includes shipping, fishing, forestry, agriculture, and manufacturing. Nonferrous metals, paper and paperboard, paper pulp, iron, steel and oil are exported.

**RULER**
Harald V, 1991-

**MINT MARK**
(h) - Crossed hammers – Kongsberg

**MONETARY SYSTEM**
100 Ore = 1 Krone

## KINGDOM

## DECIMAL COINAGE

### KM# 460 50 ØRE

3.60 g., Bronze, 18.5 mm. **Ruler:** Harald V **Obv:** Crown **Rev:** Stylized animal and value **Edge:** Plain

| Date | Mintage | VG8 | F12 | VF20 | XF40 | MS63 |
|---|---|---|---|---|---|---|
| 2001 without star | 16,848,250 | — | — | — | — | 0.50 |
| 2001 with star | 13,291,750 | — | — | — | 1.00 | 3.00 |
| 2001 | 11,500 | PF63 10.00 | | | | |
| 2002 | 28,293,000 | — | — | — | — | 0.40 |
| 2002 | 11,500 | PF63 10.00 | | | | |
| 2003 | 15,522,000 | — | — | — | — | 0.40 |
| 2003 | 10,800 | PF63 10.00 | | | | |
| 2004 | 14,747,500 | — | — | — | — | 0.40 |
| 2004 | 8,550 | PF63 10.00 | | | | |
| 2005 | 4,954,500 | — | — | — | — | 0.40 |
| 2005 | 8,550 | PF63 10.00 | | | | |
| 2006 | 30,218,500 | — | — | — | — | 0.40 |
| 2006 | 8,500 | PF63 10.00 | | | | |
| 2007 | 20,110,500 | — | — | — | — | 0.40 |
| 2007 | 6,582 | PF63 10.00 | | | | |
| 2008 | 19,384,000 | — | — | — | — | 0.40 |
| 2008 | 7,091 | PF63 10.00 | | | | |
| 2009 | 9,897,000 | — | — | — | — | 0.40 |
| 2009 | 6,310 | PF63 10.00 | | | | |
| 2010 | 14,988,000 | — | — | — | — | 0.40 |
| 2010 | 5,119 | PF63 10.00 | | | | |
| 2011 11 in date reversed | 8,300,000 | — | — | — | — | 0.40 |
| 2011 11 in date corrected | 1,666,000 | — | — | — | — | 0.40 |
| 2011 | 4,142 | PF63 10.00 | | | | |

### KM# 462 KRONE

4.35 g., Copper-Nickel, 21 mm. **Ruler:** Harald V **Obv:** Crowned monograms form cross within circle with center hole **Rev:** Bird on vine above center hole date and value below

| Date | Mintage | VG8 | F12 | VF20 | XF40 | MS63 |
|---|---|---|---|---|---|---|
| 2001 without star | 43,128,650 | — | — | — | — | 0.65 |
| 2001 with star | 7,355,350 | — | — | — | 2.00 | 4.00 |
| 2001 | 11,500 | PF63 10.00 | | | | |
| 2002 | 21,313,000 | — | — | — | — | 0.65 |
| 2002 | 11,500 | PF63 10.00 | | | | |
| 2003 | 24,082,000 | — | — | — | — | 0.65 |
| 2003 | 10,800 | PF63 10.00 | | | | |
| 2004 | 25,142,500 | — | — | — | — | 0.65 |
| 2004 | 8,550 | PF63 10.00 | | | | |
| 2005 | 25,639,500 | — | — | — | — | 0.65 |
| 2005 | 8,550 | PF63 10.00 | | | | |
| 2006 | 63,120,500 | — | — | — | — | 0.65 |
| 2006 | 8,500 | PF63 10.00 | | | | |
| 2007 | 47,101,500 | — | — | — | — | 0.65 |
| 2007 | 6,582 | PF63 10.00 | | | | |
| 2008 | 46,040,000 | — | — | — | — | 0.65 |
| 2008 | 7,091 | PF63 10.00 | | | | |
| 2009 | 50,049,000 | — | — | — | — | 0.65 |
| 2009 | 6,310 | PF63 10.00 | | | | |
| 2010 | 40,021,000 | — | — | — | — | 0.65 |
| 2010 | 5,119 | PF63 10.00 | | | | |
| 2011 | 35,042,000 | — | — | — | — | 0.50 |
| 2011 | 4,142 | PF63 10.00 | | | | |
| 2012 | 19,635,000 | — | — | — | — | 0.50 |
| 2012 | 3,437 | PF63 20.00 | | | | |

### KM# 463 5 KRONER

7.85 g., Copper-Nickel, 26 mm. **Ruler:** Harald V **Subject:** Order of St. Olaf **Obv:** Hole at center of order chain **Rev:** Center hole divides sprigs, value above and date below **Edge:** Reeded

| Date | Mintage | VG8 | F12 | VF20 | XF40 | MS63 |
|---|---|---|---|---|---|---|
| 2001 | 480,000 | — | — | — | — | 2.50 |
| 2001 | 11,500 | PF63 13.00 | | | | |
| 2002 | 3,622,000 | — | — | — | — | 1.50 |
| 2002 | 11,500 | PF63 13.00 | | | | |
| 2003 | 816,000 | — | — | — | — | 1.50 |
| 2003 | 10,800 | PF63 13.00 | | | | |
| 2004 | 494,500 | — | — | — | — | 1.50 |
| 2004 | 8,550 | PF63 14.00 | | | | |
| 2005 | 494,500 | — | — | — | — | 2.00 |
| 2005 | 8,550 | PF63 14.00 | | | | |
| 2006 | 500,500 | — | — | — | — | 1.50 |
| 2006 | 8,500 | PF63 14.00 | | | | |
| 2007 | 9,145,000 | — | — | — | — | 1.50 |
| 2007 | 6,582 | PF63 14.00 | | | | |
| 2008 | 5,495,000 | — | — | — | — | 1.50 |
| 2008 | 7,091 | PF63 14.00 | | | | |
| 2009 | 10,014,000 | — | — | — | — | 1.50 |
| 2009 | 6,310 | PF63 14.00 | | | | |
| 2012 | 1,006,000 | — | — | — | — | 1.50 |
| 2012 | 3,437 | PF63 40.00 | | | | |

### KM# 457 10 KRONER

6.80 g., Nickel-Brass, 24 mm. **Ruler:** Harald V **Obv:** Head right **Rev:** Stylized church rooftop, value and date **Edge:** Segmented reeding

| Date | Mintage | VG8 | F12 | VF20 | XF40 | MS63 |
|---|---|---|---|---|---|---|
| 2001 without star | 9,854,000 | — | — | — | — | 3.50 |
| 2001 with star | 10,000 | — | — | — | — | 50.00 |
| 2001 | 11,500 | PF63 10.00 | | | | |
| 2002 | 1,123,000 | — | — | — | — | 3.50 |
| 2002 | 11,500 | PF63 10.00 | | | | |
| 2003 | 946,000 | — | — | — | — | 3.50 |
| 2003 | 10,800 | PF63 10.00 | | | | |
| 2004 | 494,500 | — | — | — | — | 4.50 |
| 2004 | 8,550 | PF63 10.00 | | | | |
| 2005 | 457,500 | — | — | — | — | 4.50 |
| 2005 | 8,550 | PF63 10.00 | | | | |
| 2006 | 488,500 | — | — | — | — | 3.50 |
| 2006 | 8,500 | PF63 10.00 | | | | |
| 2007 | 467,500 | — | — | — | — | 3.50 |
| 2007 | 6,582 | PF63 10.00 | | | | |
| 2008 | 565,508 | — | — | — | — | 3.50 |
| 2009 | 469,000 | — | — | — | — | 3.50 |
| 2009 | 6,310 | PF63 10.00 | | | | |
| 2012 | 1,006,000 | — | — | — | — | 3.00 |
| 2012 | 3,437 | PF63 50.00 | | | | |

### KM# 482 10 KRONER

6.80 g., Nickel-Brass, 24 mm. **Ruler:** Harald V **Subject:** Henrik Vergeland **Obv:** Head right **Rev:** Spectacles and vertical signature

| Date | Mintage | F12 | VF20 | XF40 | MS60 | MS63 |
|---|---|---|---|---|---|---|
| 2008 | 4,620,638 | — | — | — | 3.50 | 10.00 |
| 2008 | 7,091 | PF63 10.00 | | | | |

**KM# 483 10 KRONER**
6.80 g., Nickel-Brass, 24 mm. **Ruler:** Harald V **Subject:** Ole Bull 100th Anniversary of Birth **Obv:** Head right **Rev:** Bust and music score **Edge:** Segmented reeding

| Date | Mintage | F12 | VF20 | XF40 | MS60 | MS63 |
|---|---|---|---|---|---|---|
| 2010 | 974,000 | — | — | — | 3.50 | 10.00 |
| 2010 | 5,119 | **PF63** 10.00 | | | | |

**KM# 484 10 KRONER**
6.80 g., Nickel-Brass, 24 mm. **Ruler:** Harald V **Subject:** Norway's first University, 200th Anniversary **Obv:** Head right **Rev:** Column

| Date | Mintage | F12 | VF20 | XF40 | MS60 | MS63 |
|---|---|---|---|---|---|---|
| 2011 | 2,996,000 | — | — | — | 3.50 | 10.00 |
| 2011 | 4,142 | **PF63** 10.00 | | | | |

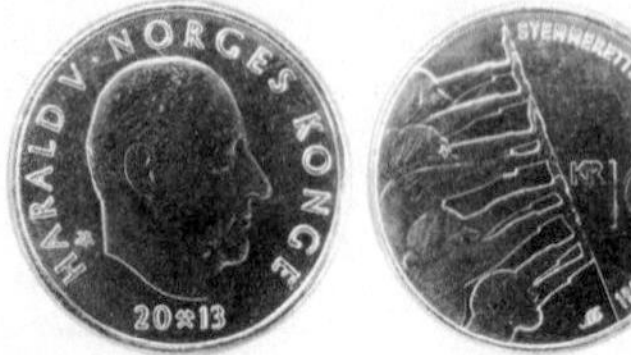


**KM# 488 10 KRONER**
Nickel-Brass **Ruler:** Harald V **Subject:** 100 Years of Women's Sufferage

| Date | Mintage | F12 | VF20 | XF40 | MS60 | MS63 |
|---|---|---|---|---|---|---|
| 2013 | — | — | — | — | — | 3.00 |

**KM# 453 20 KRONER**
9.90 g., Nickel-Brass, 27.5 mm. **Ruler:** Harald V **Obv:** Head right **Rev:** Value above 1/2 ancient boat

| Date | Mintage | VG8 | F12 | VF20 | XF40 | MS63 |
|---|---|---|---|---|---|---|
| 2001 | 4,194,000 | — | — | — | — | 5.00 |
| 2001 with star | 10,000 | — | — | — | — | 200 |
| 2001 | 11,500 | **PF63** 25.00 | | | | |
| 2002 | 18,218,000 | — | — | — | — | 5.00 |
| 2003 | 30,050,000 | — | — | — | — | 5.00 |
| 2003 | 11,100 | **PF63** 25.00 | | | | |
| 2005 | 544,500 | — | — | — | — | 5.00 |
| 2005 | 8,550 | **PF63** 25.00 | | | | |
| 2007 | 486,500 | — | — | — | — | 5.00 |
| 2007 | 6,582 | **PF63** 25.00 | | | | |
| 2008 | 474,000 | — | — | — | — | 5.00 |
| 2008 | 7,091 | **PF63** 25.00 | | | | |
| 2009 | 467,000 | — | — | — | — | 5.00 |
| 2009 | 6,310 | **PF63** 25.00 | | | | |

**KM# 471 20 KRONER**
9.90 g., Nickel-Brass, 27.5 mm. **Ruler:** Harald V **Subject:** Niels Henrik Abel **Obv:** Head right **Rev:** Pair of glasses, dates and value within mathematical graphs **Edge:** Plain

| Date | Mintage | F12 | VF20 | XF40 | MS60 | MS63 |
|---|---|---|---|---|---|---|
| 2002 | 2,230,000 | — | — | — | 5.50 | 12.00 |
| 2002 | 11,500 | **PF63** 25.00 | | | | |

**KM# 478 20 KRONER**
9.90 g., Nickel-Brass, 27.5 mm. **Ruler:** Harald V **Subject:** First Norwegian Railroad **Obv:** Head right **Rev:** Railroad track switch and value **Edge:** Plain

| Date | Mintage | F12 | VF20 | XF40 | MS60 | MS63 |
|---|---|---|---|---|---|---|
| 2004 | 490,500 | — | — | — | 5.50 | 20.00 |
| 2004 | 8,550 | **PF63** 25.00 | | | | |

**KM# 479 20 KRONER**
9.90 g., Nickel-Brass, 27.5 mm. **Ruler:** Harald V **Obv:** Head right **Rev:** Henrik Ibsen caricature walking left, signature **Edge:** Plain

| Date | Mintage | F12 | VF20 | XF40 | MS60 | MS63 |
|---|---|---|---|---|---|---|
| 2006 | 991,500 | — | — | — | 5.50 | 12.00 |
| 2006 | 8,500 | **PF63** 10.00 | | | | |

**KM# 469 100 KRONER**
33.60 g., 0.925 Silver 0.9992 oz. ASW, 39 mm. **Ruler:** Harald V **Subject:** Nobel Peace Prize Centennial **Obv:** Rampant crowned lion left holding axe **Rev:** Head left **Edge:** Plain

| Date | Mintage | F12 | VF20 | XF40 | MS60 | MS63 |
|---|---|---|---|---|---|---|
| 2001 | 50,000 | **PF63** 200 | **PF65** 225 | | | |

**KM# 472 100 KRONER**
33.80 g., 0.925 Silver 1.0052 oz. ASW, 39 mm. **Ruler:** Harald V **Subject:** 1905 Independence from Sweden **Obv:** Three kings **Rev:** Farm field **Edge:** Plain

| Date | Mintage | F12 | VF20 | XF40 | MS60 | MS63 |
|---|---|---|---|---|---|---|
| 2003 | 65,000 | **PF63** 70.00 | **PF65** 80.00 | | | |

**KM# 474 100 KRONER**
33.80 g., 0.925 Silver 1.0052 oz. ASW, 39 mm. **Ruler:** Harald V **Subject:** 1905 Liberation **Obv:** Three kings **Rev:** Off shore ocean oil well **Edge:** Plain

| Date | Mintage | F12 | VF20 | XF40 | MS60 | MS63 |
|---|---|---|---|---|---|---|
| 2004 | 65,000 | **PF63** 70.00 | **PF65** 80.00 | | | |

**KM# 476 100 KRONER**
33.80 g., 0.925 Silver 1.0052 oz. ASW, 39 mm. **Ruler:** Harald V **Obv:** Three kings **Rev:** Circuit board **Edge:** Plain

| Date | Mintage | F12 | VF20 | XF40 | MS60 | MS63 |
|---|---|---|---|---|---|---|
| 2005 | 72,000 | **PF63** 70.00 | **PF65** 80.00 | | | |

**KM# 480 200 KRONER**
16.85 g., 0.925 Silver 0.5011 oz. ASW, 32 mm. **Ruler:** Harald V **Subject:** Henrik Wergeland, 200th Birth Anniversary **Obv:** Head right **Rev:** Spectacles and signature

| Date | Mintage | F12 | VF20 | XF40 | MS60 | MS63 |
|---|---|---|---|---|---|---|
| 2008 | 40,000 | **PF63** 100 | **PF65** 115 | | | |

**KM# 481 200 KRONER**
16.85 g., 0.925 Silver 0.5011 oz. ASW, 32 mm. **Ruler:** Harald V **Subject:** Knut Hamsun 150th Birth Anniversary **Obv:** Crowned shield **Rev:** Strreppled portrait, novel text and signature

| Date | Mintage | F12 | VF20 | XF40 | MS60 | MS63 |
|---|---|---|---|---|---|---|
| 2009 | 40,000 | **PF63** 100 | **PF65** 115 | | | |

**KM# 485 200 KRONER**
16.85 g., 0.925 Silver 0.5011 oz. ASW, 32 mm. **Ruler:** Harald V **Subject:** World Ski Championships, 2011 **Obv:** Head right **Rev:** Different types of skiers

| Date | Mintage | F12 | VF20 | XF40 | MS60 | MS63 |
|---|---|---|---|---|---|---|
| 2011 | 40,000 | **PF63** 100 | **PF65** 115 | | | |

**KM# 486 200 KRONER**
16.85 g., 0.925 Silver 0.5011 oz. ASW, 32 mm. **Ruler:** Harald V **Obv:** Head right **Rev:** Various Athletics, Javelin, track, skating, snowboarding, table tennis.

| Date | Mintage | F12 | VF20 | XF40 | MS60 | MS63 |
|---|---|---|---|---|---|---|
| 2011 | 40,000 | **PF63** 100 | **PF65** 115 | | | |

**KM# 487 200 KRONER**
16.85 g., 0.925 Silver 0.5011 oz. ASW, 32 mm. **Ruler:** Harald V **Subject:** Harold V and Queen Sonia, 75th Birthday **Obv:** Crowned shield **Obv. Legend:** KONGERIKET NORGE **Rev:** Heads 1/4 right of Harold and Sonia **Rev. Legend:** KONG HARALD V DRONNING SONJA 75 AR

| Date | Mintage | F12 | VF20 | XF40 | MS60 | MS63 |
|---|---|---|---|---|---|---|
| 2012 | 40,000 | **PF63** 110 | **PF65** 125 | | | |

**KM# 470 1500 KRONER**
16.96 g., 0.917 Gold 0.500 oz. AGW, 27 mm. **Ruler:** Harald V **Subject:** Nobel Peace Prize Centennial **Obv:** Head right **Rev:** Reverse design of the prize medal **Edge:** Plain

| Date | Mintage | VG8 | F12 | VF20 | XF40 | MS63 |
|---|---|---|---|---|---|---|
| ND-2001 Matte Proof | 7,500 | **PF65** 1,100 | | | | |

**KM# 473 1500 KRONER**
16.96 g., 0.917 Gold 0.500 oz. AGW, 27 mm. **Ruler:** Harald V **Subject:** 1905 Liberation **Obv:** Three kings **Rev:** Various leaf types **Edge:** Plain

| Date | Mintage | F12 | VF20 | XF40 | MS60 | MS63 |
|---|---|---|---|---|---|---|
| 2003 | 10,000 | **PF65** 950 | | | | |

**KM# 475 1500 KRONER**
16.96 g., 0.917 Gold 0.500 oz. AGW, 27 mm. **Ruler:** Harald V **Subject:** 1905 Liberation **Obv:** Three kings **Rev:** Liquid drops on hard surface **Edge:** Plain

| Date | Mintage | F12 | VF20 | XF40 | MS60 | MS63 |
|---|---|---|---|---|---|---|
| 2004 | 10,000 | **PF65** 950 | | | | |

**KM# 477 1500 KRONER**
16.96 g., 0.917 Gold 0.500 oz. AGW, 27 mm. **Ruler:** Harald V **Obv:** Three kings **Rev:** Binary language **Edge:** Plain

| Date | Mintage | F12 | VF20 | XF40 | MS60 | MS63 |
|---|---|---|---|---|---|---|
| 2005 | 10,000 | **PF65** 950 | | | | |

## MINT SETS

| KM# | Date | Mintage | Identification | Issue Price | Mkt Val |
|---|---|---|---|---|---|
| MS66 | 2001 (5) | 17,000 | KM#453, 457, 460, 462, 463. (Uncirculated set, souvenir version, Norwegian text) | 20.00 | 30.00 |
| MS67 | 2001 (5) | — | KM#453, 457, 460, 462, 463 (Uncirculated Set, Souvenir Version, English text). Mintage included with MS66. | — | 30.00 |
| MS68 | 2001 (5) | 30,000 | KM#453, 457, 460, 462, 463. Children's (Baby) Set. | 18.00 | 30.00 |
| MS69 | 2001 (5) | 2,000 | KM#453, 457, 460, 462, 463 plus medal. | 27.00 | 27.00 |
| MS70 | 2001 (5) | — | KM#453, 457, 460, 462, 463. Uncirculated set, classic version (hard plastic case) | — | 30.00 |
| MS71 | 2002 (5) | 55,000 | KM#453, 457, 460, 462, 463, Uncirculated set, classic version (hard plastic case) | — | 32.00 |
| MS72 | 2002 (5) | 9,893 | KM#453, 457, 460, 462, 463 (Uncirculated Set, Souvenir Version, Norwegian text) | — | 30.00 |

| KM# | Date | Mintage | Identification | Issue Price | Mkt Val |
|---|---|---|---|---|---|
| MS73 | 2002 (5) | — | KM#453, 457, 460, 462, 463 (Uncirculated Set, Souvenir Version, English text). Mintage included with MS72. | — | 30.00 |
| MS74 | 2002 (5) | — | KM#453, 457, 460, 462, 463 plus Silver medal Children's (Baby) Set | — | 50.00 |
| MS75 | 2003 (5) | 55,000 | KM#453, 457, 460, 462, 463, Uncirculated set, classic version (hard plastic case) | — | 32.00 |
| MS76 | 2003 (5) | 20,000 | KM#453, 457, 460, 462, 463 (Uncirculated Set, Souvenir Version) | — | 30.00 |
| MS77 | 2003 (5) | 2,000 | KM#453, 457, 460, 462, 463 plus Silver medal Children's (Baby) Set | — | 50.00 |
| MS78 | 2004 (5) | 35,000 | KM#457, 460, 462, 463, 478, (Uncirculated set, classic version (hard plastic case) | — | 28.00 |
| MS79 | 2004 (5) | 6,000 | KM#457, 460, 462, 463, 478 (Uncirculated Set, Souvenir Version) | — | 30.00 |
| MS80 | 2004 (5) | 2,000 | KM#457, 460, 462, 463, 478 plus Silver medal Children's (Baby) Set | — | 50.00 |
| MS81 | 2005 (5) | 32,000 | KM#453, 457, 460, 462, 463, Uncirculated set, classic version (hard plastic case) | — | 25.00 |
| MS82 | 2005 (5) | 6,500 | KM#453, 457, 460, 462, 463 (Uncirculated Set, Souvenir Version) | — | 35.00 |
| MS83 | 2005 (5) | — | KM#453, 457, 460, 462, 463 plus Child in Basket Silver medal (Children's (Baby) Set) | — | 60.00 |
| MS84 | 2005 (5) | 2,005 | KM#453, 457 (proof), 460, 462, 463 plus gilded Silver copy of medal issued for 1905 referendum, all coins minted on June 7, 2005 (Referendum Set) | — | 450 |
| MS85 | 2006 (5) | 27,800 | KM#457, 460, 462, 463, 479 Uncirculated Set, Classic Version (hard plastic case) | — | 28.00 |
| MS86 | 2006 (5) | 5,450 | KM#457, 460, 462, 463, 479 Uncirculated Set, Souvenir Version | — | 30.00 |
| MS87 | 2006 (5) | 800 | KM#457, 460, 462, 463, 479 plus Child in Basket 0.5 oz. 0.999 Silver Medal Children's (Baby) Set | — | 65.00 |
| MS88 | 2006 (5) | 2,006 | KM#457, 460, 462, 463, 479 plus Gold-plated Silver copy of 1906 King Haakon VII Coronation medal, all coins minted on June 22, 2006 (Coronation Set) | — | 375 |
| MS89 | 2007 (5) | 10,000 | KM#453, 457, 460, 462, 463 (Brilliant Uncirculated Set) | — | 58.00 |
| MS90 | 2007 (5) | 26,135 | KM#453, 457, 460, 462, 463 Uncirculated Set, Classic Version (hard plastic case) | — | 30.00 |
| MS91 | 2007 (5) | 5,050 | KM#453, 457, 460, 462, 463 (Uncirculated Set, Souvenir Version) | — | 30.00 |
| MS92 | 2007 (5) | 835 | KM#453, 457, 460, 462, 463 plus Child in Basket 0.5 oz. .999 Silver Medal Children's (Baby) Set | — | 65.00 |
| MS93 | 2007 (5) | 2,007 | KM#453, 457, 460, 462, 463 plus 0.999 Gold-plated 0.925 Silver medal, 32 mm., all coins minted on February 21, 2007 (King Harald V 70th Birthday Set) | — | 700 |
| MS94 | 2008 (5) | 2,924 | KM#453, 460, 462, 463, 482 (Brilliant Uncirculated Set) | — | 58.00 |
| MS95 | 2008 (5) | 26,185 | KM#453, 457, 460, 462, 463 Uncirculated Set, Classic Version (hard plastic case) | — | 40.00 |
| MS96 | 2008 (5) | 5,000 | KM#453, 457, 460, 462, 463 (Un-circulatd Set, Souvenir Version) | — | 30.00 |
| MS97 | 2008 (5) | 600 | KM#453, 457, 460, 462, 463 plus Child in Basket Silver medal Children's (Baby) Set | — | 70.00 |
| MS98 | 2009 (5) | 2,271 | KM#453, 457, 460, 462, 463 (Brilliant Uncirculated Set) | — | 60.00 |
| MS99 | 2009 (5) | 23,400 | KM#453, 457, 460, 462, 463 Uncirculated Set, Classic Version (hard plastic case) | — | 30.00 |
| MS100 | 2009 (5) | 4,251 | KM#453, 457, 460, 462, 463 (Un-circulated Set, Souvenir Version) | — | 30.00 |
| MS101 | 2009 (5) | 675 | KM#453, 457, 460, 462, 463 plus Child in Basket Silver medal Children's (Baby) Set | — | 65.00 |
| MS102 | 2010 (3) | 1,673 | KM#460, 462, 483 (Brilliant Uncirculated Set) | — | 60.00 |
| MS104 | 2010 (3) | 3,823 | KM#460, 462, 483 (Uncirculated Set, Souvenir Version) | — | 35.00 |
| MS105 | 2010 (3) | 460 | KM#460, 462, 483 plus Child in Basket Silver medal (Children's (Baby) Set) | — | 65.00 |
| MS106 | 2011 (3) | 1,073 | KM#460, 462, 484 (Brilliant Uncirculated Set) | — | 58.00 |
| MS107 | 2011 (3) | 18,436 | KM#460, 462, 484 plus 325th Anniversary of the Norwegian Mint bimetallic medal (Uncirculated Set, Classic Version (hard plastic case) | — | 38.00 |
| MS108 | 2011 (3) | 2,454 | KM#460, 462, 484 (Uncirculated Set, Souvenir Version) | — | 38.00 |
| MS109 | 2011 (3) | 466 | KM#460, 462, 484 plus Child in Basket Silver medal (Children's (Baby) Set) | — | 75.00 |
| MS110 | 2012 (3) | 966 | KM#457, 462, 463 (Brilliant Uncirculated Set) | — | 65.00 |
| MS111 | 2012 (3) | 17,407 | KM#457, 462, 463 plus 200th Anniversary of the birth of Peter Christian Asbjornsen medal (Uncirculated Set, classic Version (hard plastic case) | — | 35.00 |
| MS112 | 2012 (3) | 2,208 | KM#457, 462, 463 (Uncirculated Set, Souvenir Version) | — | 35.00 |
| MS113 | 2012 (3) | 274 | KM#457, 462, 463 plus Child in Basket Silver medal (Children's (Baby) Set) | — | 75.00 |

## PROOF SETS

| KM# | Date | Mintage | Identification | Issue Price | Mkt Val |
|---|---|---|---|---|---|
| PS16 | 2001 (5) | 10,000 | KM#453, 457, 460, 462, 463 (Classic Proof Set) | — | 100 |
| PS17 | 2001 (5) | 1,500 | KM#453, 457, 460, 462 463 plus medal (Exclusive Proof Set) | — | 300 |
| PS18 | 2002 (5) | 10,000 | KM#457, 460, 462, 463, 471 (Classic Proof Set) | — | 125 |
| PS19 | 2002 (5) | 1,500 | KM#457, 460, 462, 463, 471 plus medal (Exclusive Proof Set) | — | 450 |
| PS20 | 2003 (5) | 10,000 | KM#453, 457, 460, 462, 463 (Classic Proof Set) | — | 100 |
| PS21 | 2003 (5) | 800 | KM#453, 457, 460, 462, 463 plus 0.5833 Gold 100th Anniversary of the Birth of King Olav V medal (Exclusive Proof Set) | — | 500 |
| PS22 | 2004 (5) | 7,800 | KM#457, 460, 462, 463, 478 (Classic Proof Set) | — | 100 |
| PS23 | 2004 (5) | 750 | KM#457, 460, 462, 463, 478 plus Princess Ingrid Alexandra Gold medal (Exclusive Proof Set) | — | 500 |
| PS24 | 2005 (5) | 7,800 | KM#453, 457, 460, 462, 463 (Classic Proof Set) | — | 100 |
| PS25 | 2005 (5) | 750 | KM#453, 457, 460, 462, 463 plus 0.5833 Gold 7th June-9th June-13th August 1905 medal (Exclusive Proof Set) | — | 500 |
| PS27 | 2006 (5) | 8,000 | KM#457, 460, 462, 463, 479 (Classic Proof Set) | — | 100 |
| PS28 | 2006 (5) | 500 | KM#457, 460, 462, 463, 479 plus 3.295 g., 0.999 Platinum, 14.0 mm. medal (Exclusive Proof Set) | — | 700 |
| PS29 | 2007 (5) | 6,182 | KM#453, 457, 460, 462, 463 (Classic Proof Set) | — | 100 |
| PS30 | 2007 (5) | 400 | KM#453, 457, 460, 462, 463 plus proof 3.00 g., 0.585 Gold-0.265 Silver-0.150 Palladium, 14.0 mm. medal (Exclusive Proof Set) | — | 700 |
| PS31 | 2008 (5) | 6,591 | KM#453, 460, 462, 463, 482 (Classic Proof Set) | — | 100 |
| PS32 | 2008 (5) | 500 | KM#453, 460, 462, 463, 482 plus 3.00 g., 0.585 Gold-0.265 Silver-0.150 Palladium, 14.0 mm. Henrik Wergeland medal (Exclusive Proof Set) | — | 700 |
| PS33 | 2009 (5) | 5,910 | KM#453, 457, 460, 462, 463 (Classic Proof Set) | — | 100 |
| PS34 | 2009 (6) | 400 | KM#453, 457, 460, 462, 463, 481 plus 7.70 g., 0.585 Gold, 22.0 mm. 150th Anniversary of Birth of Knut Hamsun medal (Exclusive Proof Set) | — | 750 |
| PS35 | 2010 (3) | 4,619 | KM#460, 462, 483 plus medal (Classic Proof Set) | — | 130 |
| PS36 | 2010 (3) | 500 | KM#460, 462, 483 plus 7.70 g., 0.585 Gold, 22.0 mm. Liberation of Norway in 1945 medal (Exclusive Proof Set) | — | 750 |
| PS37 | 2011 (3) | 3,642 | KM#460, 462, 484 plus 325th Anniversary of the Norwegian Mint gilded medal (Classic Proof Set) | — | 130 |
| PS38 | 2011 (3) | 500 | KM#460, 462, 484 plus 7.70g., 0.585 Gold, 22.0mm. 100th Anniversary of Roald Amundsen's reaching the South Pole medal (Exclusive Proof Set) | — | 850 |
| PS39 | 2012 (3) | 2,937 | KM#457, 462, 463 (Classic Proof Set) | — | 130 |
| PS40 | 2012 (3) | 500 | KM#457, 462, 463 plus 7.70g. 0.585 Gold, 22.0 mm, 200th Anniversary of Birth of P. Chr.. Aspjørnsen medal (Exclusive Proof Set) | — | 800 |

The Sultanate of Oman (formerly Muscat and Oman), an independent monarchy located in the southeastern part of the Arabian Peninsula, has an area of 82,030 sq. mi. (212,460 sq. km.) and a population of *1.3 million. Capital: Muscat. The economy is based on agriculture, herding and petroleum. Petroleum products, dates, fish and hides are exported.

**RULER:**

Qaboos ibn al-Sa'id, AH1390-/1970AD-

# SULTANATE

## REFORM COINAGE

1972; 1000 Baisa = 1 Omani Rial

**KM# 150 5 BAISA**

2.65 g., Bronze Clad Steel, 19 mm. **Ruler:** Qabus bin Sa'id **Obv:** National arms **Rev:** Value and dates

| Date | Mintage | VF20 | XF40 | MS60 | MS63 | MS65 |
|---|---|---|---|---|---|---|
| AH1429-2008 | — | — | 0.20 | 0.50 | 0.75 | 1.00 |

**KM# 151 10 BAISA**
4.04 g., Bronze Clad Steel, 22.5 mm. **Ruler:** Qabus bin Sa'id **Obv:** National arms **Rev:** Value with both dates

| Date | Mintage | VF20 | XF40 | MS60 | MS63 | MS65 |
|---|---|---|---|---|---|---|
| AH1429-2008 | — | — | 0.30 | 0.75 | 1.00 | 1.25 |

**KM# 152 25 BAISA**
3.03 g., Copper-Nickel, 18 mm. **Ruler:** Qabus bin Sa'id **Obv:** National arms **Rev:** Value and both dates **Edge:** Reeded

| Date | Mintage | VF20 | XF40 | MS60 | MS63 | MS65 |
|---|---|---|---|---|---|---|
| AH1428-2008 | — | 0.15 | 0.35 | 0.90 | 1.35 | 2.25 |
| AH1429-2009 | — | 0.15 | 0.35 | 0.90 | 1.35 | 2.25 |

**KM# 152a 25 BAISA**
2.63 g., Nickel Clad Steel, 17.95 mm. **Ruler:** Qabus bin Sa'id **Obv:** National arms **Rev:** Value with both dates **Edge:** Reeded

| Date | Mintage | VF20 | XF40 | MS60 | MS63 | MS65 |
|---|---|---|---|---|---|---|
| AH1427-2007 | — | — | 0.35 | 0.90 | 1.25 | 2.00 |
| AH1428-2008 | — | — | 0.35 | 0.90 | 1.25 | 2.00 |
| AH1429-2009 | — | — | 0.35 | 0.90 | 1.25 | 2.00 |
| AH1430-2010 | — | — | 0.35 | 0.90 | 1.25 | 2.00 |

**KM# 153 50 BAISA**
6.40 g., Copper-Nickel, 24 mm. **Ruler:** Qabus bin Sa'id **Obv:** National arms **Rev:** Value with both dates **Edge:** Reeded

| Date | Mintage | VF20 | XF40 | MS60 | MS63 | MS65 |
|---|---|---|---|---|---|---|
| AH1429-2008 | — | 0.25 | 0.60 | 1.50 | 2.00 | 3.00 |

**KM# 153a 50 BAISA**
5.57 g., Nickel Clad Steel, 24 mm. **Ruler:** Qabus bin Sa'id **Obv:** National arms **Rev:** Value with both dates **Edge:** Reeded

| Date | Mintage | VF20 | XF40 | MS60 | MS63 | MS65 |
|---|---|---|---|---|---|---|
| AH1427-2007 | — | — | 0.60 | 1.50 | 2.00 | 2.75 |
| AH1428-2008 | — | — | 0.60 | 1.50 | 2.00 | 2.75 |
| AH1429-2009 | — | — | 0.60 | 1.50 | 2.00 | 2.75 |
| AH1430-2010 | — | — | 0.60 | 1.50 | 2.00 | 2.75 |

**KM# 154 OMANI RIAL**
28.28 g., 0.925 Silver 0.841 oz. ASW, 38.6 mm. **Ruler:** Qabus bin Sa'id **Subject:** 31st National Day and Environment Year **Obv:** National arms **Rev:** Multicolor map design **Edge:** Reeded

| Date | Mintage | VF20 | XF40 | MS60 | MS63 | MS65 |
|---|---|---|---|---|---|---|
| 2001 | 500 | — | — | — | 120 | 135 |
| 2001 | 105 | PF63 150 | PF65 170 | | | |

**KM# 154a OMANI RIAL**
37.80 g., 0.916 Gold 1.1132 oz. AGW, 38.6 mm. **Ruler:** Qabus bin Sa'id **Subject:** 31st National Day and Environment Year **Obv:** National arms **Rev:** Multicolor map design **Edge:** Reeded

| Date | Mintage | VF20 | XF40 | MS60 | MS63 | MS65 |
|---|---|---|---|---|---|---|
| 2001 | 105 | PF63 2,200 | PF65 2,300 | | | |
| 2001 | 350 | — | — | — | 2,000 | 2,100 |

**KM# 156 OMANI RIAL**
28.28 g., 0.925 Silver 0.841 oz. ASW, 38.7 mm. **Ruler:** Qabus bin Sa'id **Series:** Environment Collection **Obv:** National arms **Rev:** Hoopoe bird standing right multicolor

| Date | Mintage | VF20 | XF40 | MS60 | MS63 | MS65 |
|---|---|---|---|---|---|---|
| 2002 | 1,000 | PF63 90.00 | PF65 100 | | | |

**KM# 157 OMANI RIAL**
28.28 g., 0.925 Silver 0.841 oz. ASW, 38.7 mm. **Ruler:** Qabus bin Sa'id **Series:** Environment Collection **Obv:** National arms **Rev:** Dolphin right multicolor

| Date | Mintage | VF20 | XF40 | MS60 | MS63 | MS65 |
|---|---|---|---|---|---|---|
| 2002 | 1,000 | PF63 90.00 | PF65 100 | | | |

**KM# 158 OMANI RIAL**
28.28 g., 0.925 Silver 0.841 oz. ASW, 38.7 mm. **Ruler:** Qabus bin Sa'id **Series:** Environment Collection **Obv:** National arms **Rev:** Turtle left multicolor

| Date | Mintage | VF20 | XF40 | MS60 | MS63 | MS65 |
|---|---|---|---|---|---|---|
| 2002 | 1,000 | PF63 90.00 | PF65 100 | | | |

**KM# 159 OMANI RIAL**
28.28 g., 0.925 Silver 0.841 oz. ASW, 38.7 mm. **Ruler:** Qabus bin Sa'id **Series:** Environment Collection **Obv:** National arms **Rev:** Flower multicolor

| Date | Mintage | VF20 | XF40 | MS60 | MS63 | MS65 |
|---|---|---|---|---|---|---|
| 2002 | 1,000 | PF63 90.00 | PF65 100 | | | |

**KM# 160 OMANI RIAL**
28.28 g., 0.925 Silver 0.841 oz. ASW, 38.7 mm. **Ruler:** Qabus bin Sa'id **Series:** Environment Collection **Obv:** National arms **Rev:** Ibex standing left multicolor

| Date | Mintage | VF20 | XF40 | MS60 | MS63 | MS65 |
|---|---|---|---|---|---|---|
| 2002 | 1,000 | PF63 90.00 | PF65 100 | | | |

**KM# 161 OMANI RIAL**
28.28 g., 0.925 Silver 0.841 oz. ASW, 38.7 mm. **Ruler:** Qabus bin Sa'id **Series:** Environment Collection **Obv:** National arms **Rev:** Butterfly multicolor

| Date | Mintage | VF20 | XF40 | MS60 | MS63 | MS65 |
|---|---|---|---|---|---|---|
| 2002 | 1,000 | PF63 90.00 | PF65 100 | | | |

**KM# 155 OMANI RIAL**
28.28 g., 0.925 Silver 0.841 oz. ASW, 38.6 mm. **Ruler:** Qabus bin Sa'id **Subject:** The Sindibad Voyage, 1980/1981 **Obv:** National arms **Rev:** Sailing ship below map within circle **Edge:** Reeded

| Date | Mintage | VF20 | XF40 | MS60 | MS63 | MS65 |
|---|---|---|---|---|---|---|
| 2003 | — | PF63 80.00 | PF65 90.00 | | | |

**KM# 162 OMANI RIAL**
28.28 g., 0.925 Silver 0.841 oz. ASW, 38.7 mm. **Ruler:** Qabus bin Sa'id **Subject:** Population Census - December, 2003

| Date | Mintage | VF20 | XF40 | MS60 | MS63 | MS65 |
|---|---|---|---|---|---|---|
| 2003 Rare | — | — | — | — | — | — |

**KM# 163 OMANI RIAL**
28.28 g., 0.925 Silver 0.841 oz. ASW, 38.7 mm. **Ruler:** Qabus bin Sa'id **Subject:** 35th National Day **Obv:** Oman Map

| Date | Mintage | VF20 | XF40 | MS60 | MS63 | MS65 |
|---|---|---|---|---|---|---|
| AH1427-2005 | — | — | — | 100 | 120 | 135 |

**KM# 164 OMANI RIAL**
28.28 g., 0.925 Silver 0.841 oz. ASW, 38.7 mm. **Ruler:** Qabus bin Sa'id **Subject:** 40th Anniversary of First Oil Export from Oman

| Date | Mintage | VF20 | XF40 | MS60 | MS63 | MS65 |
|---|---|---|---|---|---|---|
| 2007 | — | — | — | 90.00 | 100 | 120 |

**KM# 165 OMANI RIAL**
28.28 g., 0.925 Silver 0.841 oz. ASW, 38.7 mm. **Ruler:** Qabus bin Sa'id **Subject:** 29th GCC Summit held in Muscat in December 2008

| Date | Mintage | VF20 | XF40 | MS60 | MS63 | MS65 |
|---|---|---|---|---|---|---|
| 2008 | — | — | — | 100 | 120 | 135 |

**KM# 166 OMANI RIAL**
28.28 g., 0.925 Silver 0.841 oz. ASW, 38.7 mm. **Ruler:** Qabus bin Sa'id **Subject:** 19th Arabian Gulf Cup

| Date | Mintage | VF20 | XF40 | MS60 | MS63 | MS65 |
|---|---|---|---|---|---|---|
| 2008 | — | — | — | — | 340 | — |

**KM# 168 OMANI RIAL**
28.28 g., 0.999 Silver 0.9083 oz. ASW, 38.61 mm. **Ruler:** Qabus bin Sa'id **Subject:** Royal Opera House **Rev:** Building exterior

| Date | Mintage | VF20 | XF40 | MS60 | MS63 | MS65 |
|---|---|---|---|---|---|---|
| 2011 | 5,500 | **PF63** 75.00 | | **PF65** 85.00 | | |

**KM# 169 OMANI RIAL**
28.28 g., 0.999 Silver 0.9083 oz. ASW, 38.61 mm. **Ruler:** Qabus bin Sa'id **Subject:** Royal Opera House **Rev:** Violin, Tamboreen in color

| Date | Mintage | VF20 | XF40 | MS60 | MS63 | MS65 |
|---|---|---|---|---|---|---|
| 2011 | 5,500 | **PF63** 75.00 | | **PF65** 85.00 | | |

**KM# 170 OMANI RIAL**
28.28 g., 0.999 Silver 0.9083 oz. ASW, 38.61 mm. **Ruler:** Qabus bin Sa'id **Subject:** Royal Opera House **Rev:** Horns, flute and sax in color

| Date | Mintage | VF20 | XF40 | MS60 | MS63 | MS65 |
|---|---|---|---|---|---|---|
| 2011 | 5,500 | **PF63** 75.00 | | **PF65** 85.00 | | |

**KM# 171 OMANI RIAL**
28.28 g., 0.999 Silver 0.9083 oz. ASW, 38.61 mm. **Ruler:** Qabus bin Sa'id **Subject:** Royal Opera House **Rev:** Tamboreen, horns and strings in color

| Date | Mintage | VF20 | XF40 | MS60 | MS63 | MS65 |
|---|---|---|---|---|---|---|
| 2011 | 5,500 | **PF63** 75.00 | | **PF65** 85.00 | | |

**KM# 172 OMANI RIAL**
28.28 g., 0.925 Silver 0.841 oz. ASW, 38.7 mm. **Ruler:** Qabus bin Sa'id **Subject:** Sultan Qaboos University, 25th Anniversary **Obv:** National arms **Rev:** College arms

| Date | Mintage | VF20 | XF40 | MS60 | MS63 | MS65 |
|---|---|---|---|---|---|---|
| 2011 | — | **PF63** 75.00 | | **PF65** 85.00 | | |

**KM# 174 OMANI RIAL**
28.28 g., 0.925 Silver 0.841 oz. ASW, 36.7 mm. **Ruler:** Qabus bin Sa'id **Subject:** Muscat Arab Tourism Capital **Obv:** National arms **Rev:** Logo in color

| Date | Mintage | VF20 | XF40 | MS60 | MS63 | MS65 |
|---|---|---|---|---|---|---|
| 2012 | — | **PF63** 75.00 | | **PF65** 85.00 | | |

**KM# 173 OMANI RIAL**
28.28 g., 0.925 Silver 0.841 oz. ASW, 38.7 mm. **Ruler:** Qabus bin Sa'id **Subject:** National Day, 43th Anniversary **Obv:** Arms **Rev:** Umayyad Dirham

| Date | Mintage | VF20 | XF40 | MS60 | MS63 | MS65 |
|---|---|---|---|---|---|---|
| 2013 | — | **PF63** 75.00 | | **PF65** 85.00 | | |

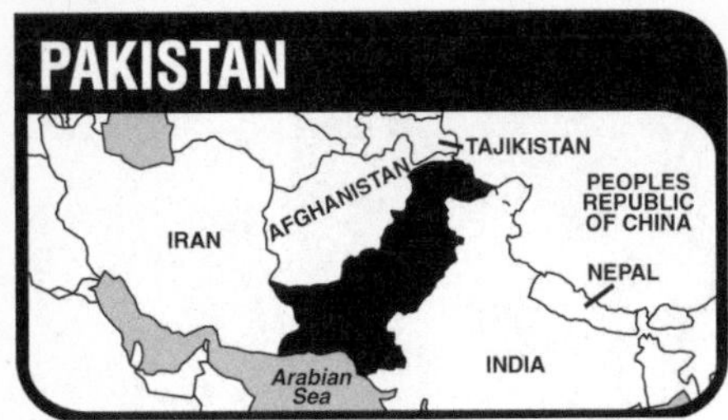


The Islamic Republic of Pakistan, located on the Indian sub-continent between India and Afghanistan, has an area of 310,404 sq. mi. (803,940 sq. km.) and a population of130 million. Capital: Islamabad. Pakistan is mainly an agricultural land although the industrial base is expanding rapidly. Yarn, textiles, cotton, rice, medical instruments, sports equipment and leather are exported.

**TITLE**

Pakistan

# ISLAMIC REPUBLIC

## DECIMAL COINAGE

100 Paisa = 1 Rupee

**KM# 73 25 PAISA**
12.00 g., Copper-Nickel, 30 mm. **Obv:** Star and crescent **Rev:** Submarine surfacing left

| Date | Mintage | VF20 | XF40 | MS60 | MS63 | MS65 |
|---|---|---|---|---|---|---|
| 2014 | — | — | — | 8.00 | 12.00 | 17.50 |

**KM# 62 RUPEE**
4.00 g., Bronze, 20 mm. **Obv:** Head of Jinnah facing left **Rev:** Mosque above value **Edge:** Reeded

| Date | Mintage | VF20 | XF40 | MS60 | MS63 | MS65 |
|---|---|---|---|---|---|---|
| 2001 | 146,996,000 | 0.25 | 0.35 | 0.50 | 0.65 | 0.75 |
| 2002 | 192,252,000 | 0.25 | 0.35 | 0.50 | 0.65 | 0.75 |
| 2003 | 217,996,000 | 0.25 | 0.35 | 0.50 | 0.65 | 0.75 |
| 2004 | 162,210,000 | 0.25 | 0.35 | 0.50 | 0.65 | 0.75 |
| 2005 | 202,330,000 | 0.25 | 0.35 | 0.50 | 0.65 | 0.75 |
| 2006 | 113,135,000 | 0.25 | 0.35 | 0.50 | 0.65 | 0.75 |

**KM# 67 RUPEE**
1.75 g., Aluminum, 20 mm. **Obv:** Head left **Rev:** Mosque

| Date | Mintage | VF20 | XF40 | MS60 | MS63 | MS65 |
|---|---|---|---|---|---|---|
| 2007 | 201,670,000 | — | — | — | — | 2.00 |
| 2008 | 97,953,000 | — | — | — | — | 2.00 |
| 2009 | 80,280,000 | — | — | — | — | 2.00 |
| 2010 | 100,000,000 | — | — | — | — | 2.00 |
| 2011 | — | — | — | — | — | 2.00 |
| 2012 | — | — | — | — | — | 2.00 |
| 2013 | — | — | — | — | — | 2.00 |

**KM# 64 2 RUPEES**
5.00 g., Nickel-Brass, 22.5 mm. **Obv:** Crescent, star and date above sprigs **Rev:** Value below mosque and clouds **Edge:** Reeded

| Date | Mintage | VF20 | XF40 | MS60 | MS63 | MS65 |
|---|---|---|---|---|---|---|
| 2001 | 85,444,000 | 0.30 | 0.45 | 0.65 | 0.85 | 1.00 |
| 2002 | 148,940,000 | 0.30 | 0.45 | 0.65 | 0.85 | 1.00 |
| 2003 | 125,220,000 | 0.30 | 0.45 | 0.65 | 0.85 | 1.00 |
| 2004 | 105,148,000 | 0.30 | 0.45 | 0.65 | 0.85 | 1.00 |
| 2005 | 98,912,000 | 0.30 | 0.45 | 0.65 | 0.85 | 1.00 |
| 2006 | 34,432,000 | 0.30 | 0.45 | 0.65 | 0.85 | 1.00 |

**KM# 68 2 RUPEES**
Aluminum **Obv:** Star and crescent, wheat ears below **Rev:** Mosque

| Date | Mintage | VF20 | XF40 | MS60 | MS63 | MS65 |
|---|---|---|---|---|---|---|
| 2007 | 100,848,000 | — | — | — | — | 2.00 |
| 2008 | — | — | — | — | — | 2.00 |
| 2009 | 100,000,000 | — | — | — | — | 2.00 |
| 2010 | 5,337,000 | — | — | — | — | 2.00 |
| 2011 | — | — | — | — | — | 2.00 |
| 2012 | — | — | — | — | — | 2.00 |
| 2013 | — | — | — | — | — | 2.00 |

**KM# 65 5 RUPEES**
6.50 g., Copper-Nickel, 24 mm. **Obv:** Cresent, star and date above sprays **Rev:** Value within star design and sprigs **Edge:** Reeded

| Date | Mintage | VF20 | XF40 | MS60 | MS63 | MS65 |
|---|---|---|---|---|---|---|
| 2001 | — | 1.00 | 1.50 | 2.00 | 3.00 | 3.25 |
| 2002 | 35,668,000 | 1.00 | 1.50 | 2.00 | 3.00 | 3.25 |
| 2003 | 138,566,000 | 1.00 | 1.50 | 2.00 | 3.00 | 3.25 |
| 2004 | 224,228,000 | 1.00 | 1.50 | 2.00 | 3.00 | 3.25 |
| 2005 | 148,248,000 | 1.00 | 1.50 | 2.00 | 3.00 | 3.25 |
| 2006 | 177,222,000 | 1.00 | 1.50 | 2.00 | 3.00 | 3.25 |

**KM# 66 10 RUPEES**
7.50 g., Copper-Nickel, 27.5 mm. **Obv:** Cresent, star and date above sprays **Rev:** Flowers and inscription **Rev. Inscription:** Year of Fatima Jinnah **Edge:** Reeded

| Date | Mintage | VF20 | XF40 | MS60 | MS63 | MS65 |
|---|---|---|---|---|---|---|
| 2003 | 200,000 | — | — | 3.00 | 4.50 | 6.50 |

**KM# 69 10 RUPEES**
8.25 g., Copper-Nickel, 27.5 mm. **Subject:** Benazir Bhutto **Obv:** Star and crescent, wheat wreath below **Rev:** Bust facing, Urdu script legend above

| Date | Mintage | VF20 | XF40 | MS60 | MS63 | MS65 |
|---|---|---|---|---|---|---|
| 2007 | — | — | — | 4.50 | 7.50 | 10.00 |
| 2008 | 300,000 | — | — | 4.50 | 7.50 | 10.00 |

**KM# 70 10 RUPEES**
8.25 g., Copper-Nickel, 27.5 mm. **Subject:** Pakistan - China Friendship, 60 years of Peoples' Republic of China **Obv:** Crescent and star **Rev:** Pakistan and Chinese flags, clasped hands below

| Date | Mintage | VF20 | XF40 | MS60 | MS63 | MS65 |
|---|---|---|---|---|---|---|
| 2009 | 100,000 | — | — | 3.00 | 4.50 | 6.50 |

**KM# 71 20 RUPEES**
9.50 g., Copper-Nickel, 30 mm. **Subject:** Pakistan-China Friendship, 60th anniversary

| Date | Mintage | VF20 | XF40 | MS60 | MS63 | MS65 |
|---|---|---|---|---|---|---|
| 2011 | — | — | — | 5.00 | 8.00 | 15.00 |

**KM# 72 20 RUPEES**
9.50 g., Copper-Nickel, 30 mm. **Subject:** Lawrence College, 150th Anniversary **Obv:** Star and crescent **Rev:** College arms

| Date | Mintage | VF20 | XF40 | MS60 | MS63 | MS65 |
|---|---|---|---|---|---|---|
| 2011 | — | — | — | 5.00 | 8.00 | 15.00 |

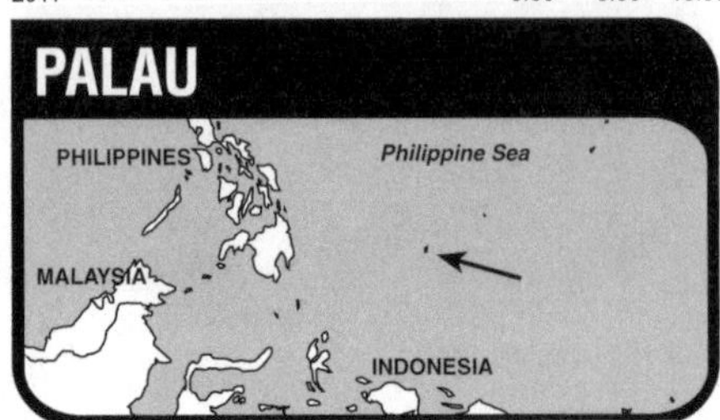


The Republic of Palau, a group of about 100 islands and islets, is generally considered a part of the Caroline Islands. It is located about 1,000 miles southeast of Manila and about the same distance southwest of Saipan and has an area of 179 sq. mi. and a population of 12,116. Capital: Koror.

# REPUBLIC

## MILLED COINAGE

**KM# 52 DOLLAR**
26.86 g., Copper-Nickel, 37.3 mm. **Subject:** Marine Life Protection **Obv:** Mermaid figurehead and value **Rev:** Jellyfish in color **Edge:** Reeded

| Date | Mintage | VF20 | XF40 | MS60 | MS63 | MS65 |
|---|---|---|---|---|---|---|
| 2001 | — | **PF65** 30.00 | | | | |

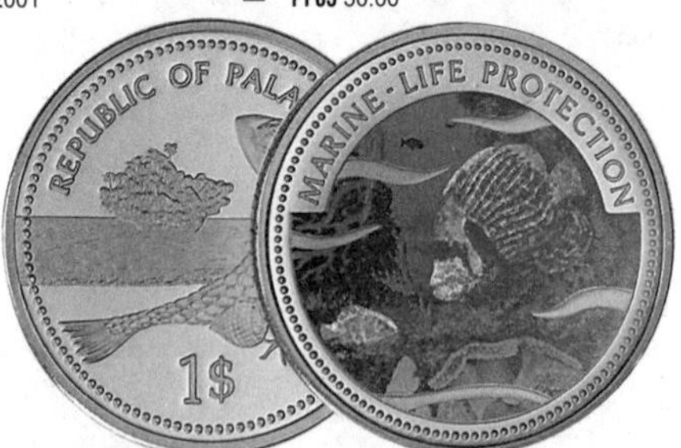

**KM# 60 DOLLAR**
26.80 g., Copper-Nickel, 37.2 mm. **Subject:** Marine Life Protection **Obv:** Seated Mermaid with raised arm above value **Rev:** Two glittering fish **Edge:** Reeded

| Date | Mintage | VF20 | XF40 | MS60 | MS63 | MS65 |
|---|---|---|---|---|---|---|
| 2001 | — | **PF65** 30.00 | | | | |

**KM# 61 DOLLAR**
26.80 g., Copper-Nickel, 37.2 mm. **Subject:** Marine Life Protection **Obv:** Prone Mermaid above value **Rev:** Two glittering fish **Edge:** Reeded

| Date | Mintage | VF20 | XF40 | MS60 | MS63 | MS65 |
|---|---|---|---|---|---|---|
| 2001 | — | PF65 32.50 | | | | |

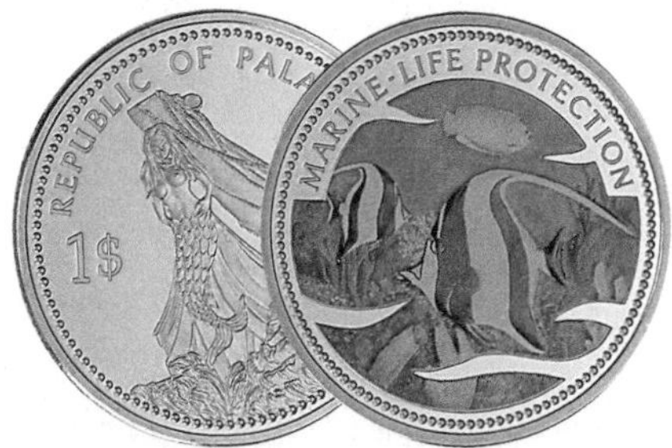


**KM# 62 DOLLAR**
26.80 g., Copper-Nickel, 37.2 mm. **Subject:** Marine Life Protection **Obv:** Figurehead mermaid and value **Rev:** Moorish-Idol fish **Edge:** Reeded

| Date | Mintage | VF20 | XF40 | MS60 | MS63 | MS65 |
|---|---|---|---|---|---|---|
| 2001 | — | PF65 30.00 | | | | |

**KM# 86 DOLLAR**
1.24 g., 0.9999 Gold 0.040 oz. AGW, 13.94 mm. **Subject:** Marine Life Protection **Obv:** Prone Mermaid **Rev:** Two fish

| Date | Mintage | VF20 | XF40 | MS60 | MS63 | MS65 |
|---|---|---|---|---|---|---|
| 2001 | — | PF65 70.00 | | | | |

**KM# 87 DOLLAR**
1.24 g., 0.9999 Gold 0.040 oz. AGW, 13.94 mm. **Subject:** Marine Life Protection **Obv:** Seated Mermaid with raised arm above value **Rev:** Two glittering fish

| Date | Mintage | VF20 | XF40 | MS60 | MS63 | MS65 |
|---|---|---|---|---|---|---|
| 2001 | — | PF65 60.00 | | | | |

**KM# 88 DOLLAR**
1.24 g., 0.9999 Gold 0.040 oz. AGW, 13.94 mm. **Subject:** Marine Life Protection **Obv:** Figurehead Mermaid and value **Rev:** Jellyfish

| Date | Mintage | VF20 | XF40 | MS60 | MS63 | MS65 |
|---|---|---|---|---|---|---|
| 2001 | — | PF65 70.00 | | | | |

**KM# 89 DOLLAR**
1.24 g., 0.9999 Gold 0.040 oz. AGW, 13.94 mm. **Subject:** Marine Life Protection **Obv:** Figurehead Mermaid and value **Rev:** Moorish Idol fish

| Date | Mintage | VF20 | XF40 | MS60 | MS63 | MS65 |
|---|---|---|---|---|---|---|
| 2001 | — | PF65 70.00 | | | | |

**KM# 253 DOLLAR**
1.25 g., 0.999 Gold 0.0401 oz. AGW, 13.9 mm. **Obv:** Mermaid body-surfing wave **Rev:** Blue angelfish

| Date | Mintage | VF20 | XF40 | MS60 | MS63 | MS65 |
|---|---|---|---|---|---|---|
| 2001 | — | PF63 65.00 | PF65 70.00 | | | |

**KM# 254 DOLLAR**
1.24 g., 0.999 Gold 0.0398 oz. AGW, 13.9 mm. **Obv:** Large breasted mermaid on beach **Rev:** Emperor Angelfish

| Date | Mintage | VF20 | XF40 | MS60 | MS63 | MS65 |
|---|---|---|---|---|---|---|
| 2001 | — | PF63 65.00 | PF65 70.00 | | | |

**KM# 287 DOLLAR**
35.00 g., Copper-Nickel, 50 mm. **Obv:** National Arms **Rev:** Cut card corners, Queen of Hearts, Clubs

| Date | Mintage | VF20 | XF40 | MS60 | MS63 | MS65 |
|---|---|---|---|---|---|---|
| ND (2001) Antique finish | — | — | — | — | 10.00 | — |

**KM# 288 DOLLAR**
35.00 g., Copper-Nickel, 50 mm. **Obv:** National arms **Rev:** Cut card corner, Queen of Spades, diamonds

| Date | Mintage | VF20 | XF40 | MS60 | MS63 | MS65 |
|---|---|---|---|---|---|---|
| ND (2001) Antique finish | — | — | — | — | 10.00 | — |

**KM# 56 DOLLAR**
26.80 g., Copper-Nickel, 37.2 mm. **Subject:** Marine Life Protection **Obv:** Mermaid figurehead and value **Rev:** Multicolor fish scene **Edge:** Reeded

| Date | Mintage | VF20 | XF40 | MS60 | MS63 | MS65 |
|---|---|---|---|---|---|---|
| 2002 | — | PF65 30.00 | | | | |

**KM# 57 DOLLAR**
26.80 g., Copper-Nickel, 37.2 mm. **Subject:** Marine Life Protection **Obv:** Mermaid figurehead on approaching ship **Rev:** Multicolor reflective fish scene under an acrylic layer **Edge:** Reeded

| Date | Mintage | VF20 | XF40 | MS60 | MS63 | MS65 |
|---|---|---|---|---|---|---|
| 2002 | — | PF65 35.00 | | | | |

**KM# 63 DOLLAR**
26.80 g., Copper-Nickel, 37.2 mm. **Subject:** Marine Life Protection **Obv:** Figurehead mermaid and value **Rev:** Blue Tang Fish **Edge:** Reeded

| Date | Mintage | VF20 | XF40 | MS60 | MS63 | MS65 |
|---|---|---|---|---|---|---|
| 2002 | — | PF65 35.00 | | | | |

**KM# 64 DOLLAR**
26.80 g., Copper-Nickel, 37.2 mm. **Subject:** Marine Life Protection **Obv:** Figurehead mermaid and value **Rev:** Multicolor whales **Edge:** Reeded

| Date | Mintage | VF20 | XF40 | MS60 | MS63 | MS65 |
|---|---|---|---|---|---|---|
| 2002 | — | PF65 35.00 | | | | |

**KM# 65 DOLLAR**
26.80 g., Copper-Nickel, 37.2 mm. **Subject:** Marine Life Protection **Obv:** Mermaid washing hair and value **Rev:** Multicolor jellyfish **Edge:** Reeded

| Date | Mintage | VF20 | XF40 | MS60 | MS63 | MS65 |
|---|---|---|---|---|---|---|
| 2002 | — | PF65 35.00 | | | | |

**KM# 90 DOLLAR**
1.24 g., 0.9999 Gold 0.040 oz. AGW, 13.94 mm. **Subject:** Marine Life Protection **Obv:** Figurehead Mermaid and value **Rev:** Multicolor whales

| Date | Mintage | VF20 | XF40 | MS60 | MS63 | MS65 |
|---|---|---|---|---|---|---|
| 2002 | — | PF63 65.00 | PF65 70.00 | | | |

**KM# 91 DOLLAR**

1.24 g., 0.9999 Gold 0.040 oz. AGW, 13.94 mm. **Subject:** Marine Life Protection **Obv:** Figurehead Mermaid and value **Rev:** Pufferfish

| Date | Mintage | VF20 | XF40 | MS60 | MS63 | MS65 |
|---|---|---|---|---|---|---|
| 2002 | — | PF63 65.00 | PF65 70.00 | | | |

**KM# 92 DOLLAR**

1.24 g., 0.9999 Gold 0.040 oz. AGW, 13.94 mm. **Subject:** Marine Life Protection **Obv:** Seated Mermaid with both arms raised and value **Rev:** Jellyfish

| Date | Mintage | VF20 | XF40 | MS60 | MS63 | MS65 |
|---|---|---|---|---|---|---|
| 2002 | — | PF63 65.00 | PF65 70.00 | | | |

**KM# 93 DOLLAR**

1.24 g., 0.9999 Gold 0.040 oz. AGW, 13.94 mm. **Subject:** Marine Life Protection **Obv:** Figurehead Mermaid and value **Rev:** Blue Tang Fish

| Date | Mintage | VF20 | XF40 | MS60 | MS63 | MS65 |
|---|---|---|---|---|---|---|
| 2002 | — | PF63 65.00 | PF65 70.00 | | | |

**KM# 94 DOLLAR**

1.24 g., 0.9999 Gold 0.040 oz. AGW, 13.94 mm. **Subject:** Marine Life Protection **Obv:** Figurehead mermaid and value **Rev:** Lionfish

| Date | Mintage | VF20 | XF40 | MS60 | MS63 | MS65 |
|---|---|---|---|---|---|---|
| 2002 | — | PF63 65.00 | PF65 70.00 | | | |

**KM# 66 DOLLAR**

26.80 g., Copper-Nickel, 37.2 mm. **Subject:** Marine Life Protection **Obv:** Mermaid under sun and value **Rev:** Orange crab **Edge:** Reeded

| Date | Mintage | VF20 | XF40 | MS60 | MS63 | MS65 |
|---|---|---|---|---|---|---|
| 2003 | — | PF65 35.00 | | | | |

**KM# 67 DOLLAR**

26.80 g., Copper-Nickel, 37.2 mm. **Subject:** Marine Life Protection **Obv:** Mermaid riding turtle and value **Rev:** Two glittering fish **Edge:** Reeded

| Date | Mintage | VF20 | XF40 | MS60 | MS63 | MS65 |
|---|---|---|---|---|---|---|
| 2003 | — | PF65 35.00 | | | | |

**KM# 68 DOLLAR**

26.80 g., Copper-Nickel, 37.2 mm. **Subject:** Marine Life Protection **Obv:** Seated Mermaid on shell and value **Rev:** Multicolor Orca **Edge:** Reeded

| Date | Mintage | VF20 | XF40 | MS60 | MS63 | MS65 |
|---|---|---|---|---|---|---|
| 2003 | — | PF65 35.00 | | | | |

**KM# 69 DOLLAR**

26.80 g., Copper-Nickel, 37.2 mm. **Subject:** Marine Life Protection **Obv:** Mermaid playing shell guitar and value **Rev:** Green fish **Edge:** Reeded

| Date | Mintage | VF20 | XF40 | MS60 | MS63 | MS65 |
|---|---|---|---|---|---|---|
| 2003 | — | PF65 35.00 | | | | |

**KM# 95 DOLLAR**

1.24 g., 0.9999 Gold 0.040 oz. AGW, 13.94 mm. **Subject:** Marine Life Protection **Obv:** Mermaid riding dolphin and value **Rev:** Starfish

| Date | Mintage | VF20 | XF40 | MS60 | MS63 | MS65 |
|---|---|---|---|---|---|---|
| 2003 | — | PF63 65.00 | PF65 70.00 | | | |

**KM# 96 DOLLAR**

1.24 g., 0.9999 Gold 0.040 oz. AGW, 13.94 mm. **Subject:** Marine Life Protection **Obv:** Seated Mermaid on shell and value **Rev:** Multicolor Orca **Edge:** Reeded

| Date | Mintage | VF20 | XF40 | MS60 | MS63 | MS65 |
|---|---|---|---|---|---|---|
| 2003 Proof | — | PF63 65.00 | PF65 70.00 | | | |

**KM# 97 DOLLAR**

1.24 g., 0.9999 Gold 0.040 oz. AGW, 13.94 mm. **Subject:** Marine Life Protection **Obv:** Mermaid under radiant sun and value **Rev:** Crab

| Date | Mintage | VF20 | XF40 | MS60 | MS63 | MS65 |
|---|---|---|---|---|---|---|
| 2003 | — | PF63 65.00 | PF65 70.00 | | | |

**KM# 98 DOLLAR**

1.24 g., 0.9999 Gold 0.040 oz. AGW, 13.94 mm. **Subject:** Marine Life Protection **Obv:** Mermaid riding turtle and value **Rev:** Two glittering fish

| Date | Mintage | VF20 | XF40 | MS60 | MS63 | MS65 |
|---|---|---|---|---|---|---|
| 2003 | — | PF63 65.00 | PF65 70.00 | | | |

**KM# 256 DOLLAR**

Copper-Nickel, 38.6 mm. **Obv:** Mermaid on dolphin **Rev:** Red starfish - multicolor

| Date | Mintage | VF20 | XF40 | MS60 | MS63 | MS65 |
|---|---|---|---|---|---|---|
| 2003 | — | — | — | — | — | 25.00 |

**KM# 70 DOLLAR**

26.80 g., Copper-Nickel, 37.2 mm. **Subject:** Marine Life Protection **Obv:** Seated Mermaid on rock and value **Rev:** School of blue fish **Edge:** Reeded

| Date | Mintage | VF20 | XF40 | MS60 | MS63 | MS65 |
|---|---|---|---|---|---|---|
| 2004 | — | PF65 35.00 | | | | |

**KM# 71 DOLLAR**

26.80 g., Copper-Nickel, 37.2 mm. **Subject:** Marine Life Protection **Obv:** Side view of Mermaid facing right and value **Rev:** Clownfish **Edge:** Reeded

| Date | Mintage | VF20 | XF40 | MS60 | MS63 | MS65 |
|---|---|---|---|---|---|---|
| 2004 | — | PF65 35.00 | | | | |

**KM# 72 DOLLAR**

26.80 g., Copper-Nickel, 37.2 mm. **Subject:** Marine Life Protection **Obv:** Mermaid flanked by dolphins **Rev:** Multicolor dolphin head **Edge:** Reeded

| Date | Mintage | VF20 | XF40 | MS60 | MS63 | MS65 |
|---|---|---|---|---|---|---|
| 2004 | — | PF65 35.00 | | | | |

**KM# 99 DOLLAR**

1.24 g., 0.9999 Gold 0.040 oz. AGW, 13.94 mm. **Subject:** Marine Life Protection **Obv:** Mermaid under radiant sun and value **Rev:** Clownfish

| Date | Mintage | VF20 | XF40 | MS60 | MS63 | MS65 |
|---|---|---|---|---|---|---|
| 2004 | — | PF63 65.00 | PF65 70.00 | | | |

### KM# 100 DOLLAR

1.24 g., 0.9999 Gold 0.040 oz. AGW, 13.94 mm. **Subject:** Marine Life Protection **Obv:** Mermaid flanked by dolphins **Rev:** Multicolor dolphin head

| Date | Mintage | VF20 | XF40 | MS60 | MS63 | MS65 |
|---|---|---|---|---|---|---|
| 2004 | — | PF63 65.00 | PF65 70.00 | | | |

### KM# 123 DOLLAR

Copper-Nickel, 37.2 mm. **Subject:** Marine Life Protection **Obv:** Mermaid seated inside a giant conch shell **Rev:** Puffer fish **Edge:** Reeded

| Date | Mintage | VF20 | XF40 | MS60 | MS63 | MS65 |
|---|---|---|---|---|---|---|
| 2004 | — | PF65 35.00 | | | | |

### KM# 124 DOLLAR

Copper-Nickel, 37.2 mm. **Subject:** Marine Life Protection **Obv:** Seated Mermaid **Rev:** Sea turtle **Edge:** Reeded

| Date | Mintage | VF20 | XF40 | MS60 | MS63 | MS65 |
|---|---|---|---|---|---|---|
| 2004 | — | PF65 50.00 | | | | |

### KM# 101 DOLLAR

1.24 g., 0.9999 Gold 0.040 oz. AGW, 13.94 mm. **Subject:** Marine Life Protection **Obv:** Mermaid sitting in a shell listening to a conch shell **Rev:** Sea Horse

| Date | Mintage | VF20 | XF40 | MS60 | MS63 | MS65 |
|---|---|---|---|---|---|---|
| 2005 | — | PF63 65.00 | PF65 70.00 | | | |

### KM# 139 DOLLAR

26.80 g., Copper-Nickel, 37.2 mm. **Subject:** Marine Life - Protection **Obv:** Mermaid fixing hair, dolphin jumping **Rev:** School of fish

| Date | Mintage | VF20 | XF40 | MS60 | MS63 | MS65 |
|---|---|---|---|---|---|---|
| 2005 | — | — | — | — | — | 35.00 |

### KM# 140 DOLLAR

26.80 g., Copper-Nickel, 37.2 mm. **Subject:** Marine Life - Protection **Obv:** Mermaid seated in shell, listening to shell **Rev:** Multicolor sea horse

| Date | Mintage | VF20 | XF40 | MS60 | MS63 | MS65 |
|---|---|---|---|---|---|---|
| 2005 | — | — | — | — | — | 35.00 |

### KM# 141 DOLLAR

26.80 g., Copper-Nickel **Subject:** Marine Life - Protection **Obv:** Mermaid and dolphin **Rev:** Multicolor fish scene

| Date | Mintage | VF20 | XF40 | MS60 | MS63 | MS65 |
|---|---|---|---|---|---|---|
| 2005 | — | — | — | — | — | 35.00 |

### KM# 255 DOLLAR

Copper-Nickel, 38.6 mm. **Obv:** Mermaid seated on rock **Rev:** Stingray - multicolor

| Date | Mintage | VF20 | XF40 | MS60 | MS63 | MS65 |
|---|---|---|---|---|---|---|
| 2005 | — | — | — | — | — | 35.00 |

### KM# 125 DOLLAR

Copper-Nickel, 37.2 mm. **Subject:** Marine Life Protection **Obv:** Mermaid with head tilted back **Rev:** Barracuda

| Date | Mintage | VF20 | XF40 | MS60 | MS63 | MS65 |
|---|---|---|---|---|---|---|
| 2006 | — | PF65 35.00 | | | | |

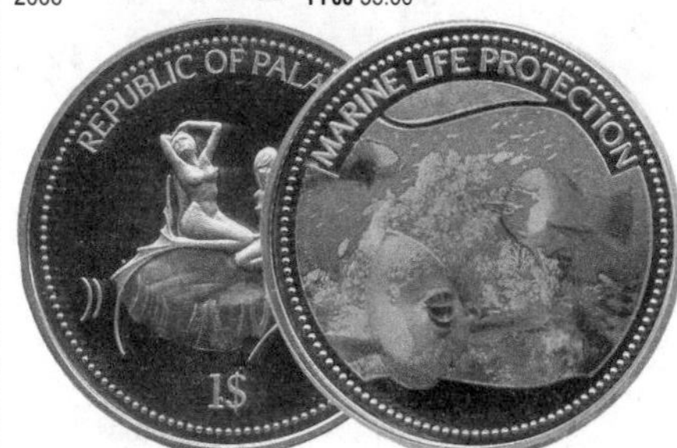


### KM# 126 DOLLAR

Copper-Nickel, 37.2 mm. **Subject:** Marine Life Protection **Obv:** Two mermaids **Rev:** Parrot fish

| Date | Mintage | VF20 | XF40 | MS60 | MS63 | MS65 |
|---|---|---|---|---|---|---|
| 2006 | — | PF65 50.00 | | | | |

### KM# 127 DOLLAR

Copper-Nickel, 37.2 mm. **Subject:** Marine Life Protection **Obv:** Mermaid swimming downward **Rev:** Hog Fish **Edge:** Reeded

| Date | Mintage | VF20 | XF40 | MS60 | MS63 | MS65 |
|---|---|---|---|---|---|---|
| 2006 | — | PF65 30.00 | | | | |

### KM# 128 DOLLAR

Copper-Nickel, 37.2 mm. **Subject:** Marine Life Protection **Obv:** Seated mermaid with bird perched on outstretched hand **Rev:** Mahi Mahi **Edge:** Reeded

| Date | Mintage | VF20 | XF40 | MS60 | MS63 | MS65 |
|---|---|---|---|---|---|---|
| 2006 | — | PF65 45.00 | | | | |

### KM# 129 DOLLAR

Copper-Nickel, 37.2 mm. **Subject:** Marine Life Protection **Obv:** Mermaid, sailing ship and sun **Rev:** Box Fish **Edge:** Reeded

| Date | Mintage | VF20 | XF40 | MS60 | MS63 | MS65 |
|---|---|---|---|---|---|---|
| 2006 | — | PF65 45.00 | | | | |

### KM# 142 DOLLAR

20.00 g., 0.999 Silver 0.6424 oz. ASW **Obv:** Arms **Rev:** Snowflake with blue crystal **Shape:** 38.6

| Date | Mintage | VF20 | XF40 | MS60 | MS63 | MS65 |
|---|---|---|---|---|---|---|
| 2006 | 2,500 | PF65 65.00 | | | | |

### KM# 257 DOLLAR

25.00 g., 0.925 Silver 0.7435 oz. ASW, 38.6 mm. **Obv:** Arms **Rev:** White pearl in shell **Shape:** Heart

| Date | Mintage | VF20 | XF40 | MS60 | MS63 | MS65 |
|---|---|---|---|---|---|---|
| 2006 | 500 | PF65 125 | | | | |

### KM# 322 DOLLAR

0.50 g., 0.999 Gold 0.0161 oz. AGW, 11.8 mm. **Obv:** National arms **Rev:** Elephant shrew

| Date | Mintage | VF20 | XF40 | MS60 | MS63 | MS65 |
|---|---|---|---|---|---|---|
| 2006 | — | PF63 60.00 | PF65 70.00 | | | |

**KM# 323 DOLLAR**

0.50 g., 0.999 Gold 0.0161 oz. AGW, 11.8 mm. **Obv:** National arms **Rev:** Rhino beetle

| Date | Mintage | VF20 | XF40 | MS60 | MS63 | MS65 |
|---|---|---|---|---|---|---|
| 2006 | — | PF63 60.00 PF65 70.00 | | | | |

**KM# 324 DOLLAR**

0.50 g., 0.999 Gold 0.0161 oz. AGW, 11.8 mm. **Obv:** National arms **Rev:** Buffalo Weaver

| Date | Mintage | VF20 | XF40 | MS60 | MS63 | MS65 |
|---|---|---|---|---|---|---|
| 2006 | — | PF63 60.00 PF65 70.00 | | | | |

**KM# 325 DOLLAR**

0.50 g., 0.999 Gold 0.0161 oz. AGW, 11.8 mm. **Obv:** National arms **Rev:** Ant lion

| Date | Mintage | VF20 | XF40 | MS60 | MS63 | MS65 |
|---|---|---|---|---|---|---|
| 2006 | — | PF63 60.00 PF65 70.00 | | | | |

**KM# 326 DOLLAR**

0.50 g., 0.999 Gold 0.0161 oz. AGW, 11.8 mm. **Obv:** National arms **Rev:** Leopard tortoise

| Date | Mintage | VF20 | XF40 | MS60 | MS63 | MS65 |
|---|---|---|---|---|---|---|
| 2006 | — | PF63 60.00 PF65 70.00 | | | | |

**KM# 334 DOLLAR**

27.00 g., Copper-Nickel, 38.61 mm. **Rev:** Eclectus Parrot head right

| Date | Mintage | VF20 | XF40 | MS60 | MS63 | MS65 |
|---|---|---|---|---|---|---|
| 2006 | Est. 5000 | PF65 20.00 | | | | |

**KM# 335 DOLLAR**

27.00 g., Copper-Nickel, 38.61 mm. **Rev:** Fruit dove head right

| Date | Mintage | VF20 | XF40 | MS60 | MS63 | MS65 |
|---|---|---|---|---|---|---|
| 2006 | Est. 5000 | PF65 20.00 | | | | |

**KM# 336 DOLLAR**

27.00 g., Copper-Nickel, 38.61 mm. **Rev:** Rainbow lorikeet head left

| Date | Mintage | VF20 | XF40 | MS60 | MS63 | MS65 |
|---|---|---|---|---|---|---|
| 2006 | Est. 5000 | PF65 20.00 | | | | |

**KM# 116 DOLLAR**

25.73 g., Silver Plated Bronze, 38.6 mm. **Obv:** National arms **Rev:** Multicolor Pope John Paul II with cross **Edge:** Reeded

| Date | Mintage | VF20 | XF40 | MS60 | MS63 | MS65 |
|---|---|---|---|---|---|---|
| 2007 | — | PF65 37.50 | | | | |

**KM# 118 DOLLAR**

27.00 g., Copper-Nickel, 38.61 mm. **Series:** Marine Life Protection **Obv:** Neptune reclining with trident, mermaid at his side **Obv. Legend:** REPUBLIC OF PALAU **Rev:** Multicolor Doctor Fish

| Date | Mintage | VF20 | XF40 | MS60 | MS63 | MS65 |
|---|---|---|---|---|---|---|
| 2007 | 5,000 | PF65 35.00 | | | | |

**KM# 120 DOLLAR**

0.50 g., 0.999 Gold 0.0161 oz. AGW, 11.0 mm. **Obv:** Shield with Neptune holding trident, mermaid reclining at his side, RAINBOW'S / END below **Obv. Legend:** REPUBLIC OF PALAU **Shape:** 4-leaf clover **Note:** Uniface

| Date | Mintage | VF20 | XF40 | MS60 | MS63 | MS65 |
|---|---|---|---|---|---|---|
| 2007 | 25,000 | PF63 40.00 PF65 50.00 | | | | |

**KM# 121 DOLLAR**

27.00 g., Copper-Nickel, 38.61 mm. **Obv:** Shield with Neptune holding trident, mermaid reclining at his side, RAINBOW'S / END below **Obv. Legend:** REPUBLIC OF PALAU **Rev:** Red racing car 3/4 left **Rev. Legend:** FERRARI - 60 YEARS ANNIVERSARY

| Date | Mintage | VF20 | XF40 | MS60 | MS63 | MS65 |
|---|---|---|---|---|---|---|
| ND(2007) | 5,000 | PF65 35.00 | | | | |

**KM# 144 DOLLAR**

27.00 g., 0.925 Silver 0.803 oz. ASW **Obv:** Shield **Rev:** Multicolor John Paul II waving

| Date | Mintage | VF20 | XF40 | MS60 | MS63 | MS65 |
|---|---|---|---|---|---|---|
| 2007 | — | PF65 45.00 | | | | |

**KM# 145 DOLLAR**

1.24 g., 0.999 Gold 0.040 oz. AGW, 13.92 mm. **Subject:** Marine Life - Protection **Obv:** Neptune and mermaid seated on rocks **Rev:** Tropical fish

| Date | Mintage | VF20 | XF40 | MS60 | MS63 | MS65 |
|---|---|---|---|---|---|---|
| 2007 | — | PF63 70.00 PF65 75.00 | | | | |

**KM# 150 DOLLAR**

25.00 g., 0.925 Silver 0.7435 oz. ASW **Subject:** Pacific Wildlife **Obv:** Shield **Rev:** Multicolor seahorse

| Date | Mintage | VF20 | XF40 | MS60 | MS63 | MS65 |
|---|---|---|---|---|---|---|
| 2007 | — | PF65 70.00 | | | | |

**KM# 258 DOLLAR**

25.00 g., 0.999 Silver 0.803 oz. ASW **Subject:** Pacific Wildlife **Rev:** Seahorse - prism

| Date | Mintage | VF20 | XF40 | MS60 | MS63 | MS65 |
|---|---|---|---|---|---|---|
| 2007 | — | PF65 50.00 | | | | |

**KM# 337 DOLLAR**

0.50 g., 0.999 Gold 0.0161 oz. AGW, 11 mm. **Subject:** Christopher Columbus, 500th Anniversary **Rev:** Columbus' flagship, Santa Maria

| Date | Mintage | VF20 | XF40 | MS60 | MS63 | MS65 |
|---|---|---|---|---|---|---|
| 2007 | — | PF63 70.00 PF65 75.00 | | | | |

**KM# 338 DOLLAR**

1.24 g., 0.999 Gold 0.0398 oz. AGW, 13.92 mm. **Subject:** Easter, 2007 **Rev:** Christ's Resurrection

| Date | Mintage | VF20 | XF40 | MS60 | MS63 | MS65 |
|---|---|---|---|---|---|---|
| 2007 | Est. 15000 | PF63 90.00 PF65 100 | | | | |

**KM# 339 DOLLAR**

0.50 g., 0.999 Gold 0.0161 oz. AGW, 11 mm. **Subject:** Deutsche Bundesbank, 50th anniversary **Rev:** Pile of coins

| Date | Mintage | VF20 | XF40 | MS60 | MS63 | MS65 |
|---|---|---|---|---|---|---|
| 2007 | — | PF63 70.00 PF65 75.00 | | | | |

**KM# 154 DOLLAR**

26.80 g., Copper-Nickel silver plated, 38.61 mm. **Subject:** 150th Anniversary of the Appriations **Obv:** Shield **Rev:** Statue of Our Lady of Lourdes and holy water vile

| Date | Mintage | VF20 | XF40 | MS60 | MS63 | MS65 |
|---|---|---|---|---|---|---|
| 2008 | — | PF65 22.50 | | | | |

**KM# 155 DOLLAR**

26.80 g., Copper-Nickel, 37.2 mm. **Subject:** Dealer Button **Obv:** Shield **Rev:** Vegas Chips and cards, Ace of Clubs corner cut

| Date | Mintage | VF20 | XF40 | MS60 | MS63 | MS65 |
|---|---|---|---|---|---|---|
| 2008 | — | — | — | — | — | 15.00 |

**KM# 156 DOLLAR**

26.80 g., Copper-Nickel, 37.2 mm. **Subject:** Dealer Buttons **Obv:** Shield **Rev:** Vegas Chips and cards, Ace of Diamonds corner cut

| Date | Mintage | VF20 | XF40 | MS60 | MS63 | MS65 |
|---|---|---|---|---|---|---|
| 2008 | — | — | — | — | — | 15.00 |

**KM# 157 DOLLAR**

26.80 g., Copper-Nickel, 37.2 mm. **Subject:** Dear Buttons **Obv:** Shield **Rev:** Vegas Chips and cards, Ace of Heats corner cut

| Date | Mintage | VF20 | XF40 | MS60 | MS63 | MS65 |
|---|---|---|---|---|---|---|
| 2008 | — | — | — | — | — | 15.00 |

**KM# 158 DOLLAR**

26.80 g., Copper-Nickel, 37.2 mm. **Obv:** Shield **Rev:** Vegas chips and cards, Ace of Spades corner cut

| Date | Mintage | VF20 | XF40 | MS60 | MS63 | MS65 |
|---|---|---|---|---|---|---|
| 2008 | — | — | — | — | — | 15.00 |

**KM# 159 DOLLAR**

1.24 g., 0.999 Gold 0.0398 oz. AGW, 13.9 mm. **Subject:** St. Francis of Assisi **Obv:** Shield **Rev:** Bust facing

| Date | Mintage | VF20 | XF40 | MS60 | MS63 | MS65 |
|---|---|---|---|---|---|---|
| 2008 | — | PF63 70.00 | PF65 75.00 | | | |

**KM# 160 DOLLAR**

1.24 g., 0.990 Gold 0.0396 oz. AGW, 13.9 mm. **Subject:** St, Francis of Assisi **Obv:** Shield **Rev:** Multicolor bust facing

| Date | Mintage | VF20 | XF40 | MS60 | MS63 | MS65 |
|---|---|---|---|---|---|---|
| 2008 | — | — | — | — | — | 80.00 |

**KM# 161 DOLLAR**

0.50 g., 0.999 Gold 0.0161 oz. AGW, 11 mm. **Obv:** Shield **Rev:** Multicolor poppy **Shape:** Irregular

| Date | Mintage | VF20 | XF40 | MS60 | MS63 | MS65 |
|---|---|---|---|---|---|---|
| 2008 | — | — | — | — | — | 60.00 |

**KM# 162 DOLLAR**

0.50 g., 0.999 Gold 0.0161 oz. AGW, 11 mm. **Subject:** Everlasting love **Obv:** Shield **Rev:** Heart **Shape:** Heart

| Date | Mintage | VF20 | XF40 | MS60 | MS63 | MS65 |
|---|---|---|---|---|---|---|
| 2008 | — | — | — | — | — | 60.00 |

**KM# 163 DOLLAR**

1.24 g., 0.999 Gold 0.040 oz. AGW **Subject:** Marine Life-Protection **Obv:** Neptune and mermaid seated on rock **Rev:** Grey reef shark

| Date | Mintage | VF20 | XF40 | MS60 | MS63 | MS65 |
|---|---|---|---|---|---|---|
| 2008 | 1,500 | PF65 85.00 | | | | |

**KM# 164 DOLLAR**

26.80 g., Copper-Nickel, 37.2 mm. **Subject:** Endangered Wildlife **Obv:** Shield **Rev:** Multicolor Tiger shark

| Date | Mintage | VF20 | XF40 | MS60 | MS63 | MS65 |
|---|---|---|---|---|---|---|
| 2008 | — | — | — | — | — | 35.00 |

**KM# 165 DOLLAR**

26.80 g., Copper-Nickel, 37.2 mm. **Subject:** Endangered Wildlife **Obv:** Shield **Rev:** Multicolor Hawksbill turtle

| Date | Mintage | VF20 | XF40 | MS60 | MS63 | MS65 |
|---|---|---|---|---|---|---|
| 2008 | — | — | — | — | — | 37.50 |

**KM# 166 DOLLAR**

26.80 g., Copper-Nickel, 37.2 mm. **Subject:** Endangered Wildlife **Obv:** Shield **Rev:** Multicolored Regal angelfish swimming right

| Date | Mintage | VF20 | XF40 | MS60 | MS63 | MS65 |
|---|---|---|---|---|---|---|
| 2008 | — | PF65 37.50 | | | | |

**KM# 167 DOLLAR**

26.80 g., Copper-Nickel, 37.2 mm. **Subject:** Endangered Wildlife **Obv:** Shield **Rev:** Multicolor Spiny lobster

| Date | Mintage | VF20 | XF40 | MS60 | MS63 | MS65 |
|---|---|---|---|---|---|---|
| 2008 | — | PF65 30.00 | | | | |

**KM# 259 DOLLAR**

0.50 g., 0.999 Gold 0.0161 oz. AGW, 11 mm. **Subject:** Sitting bull **Obv:** Shield **Rev:** Portrait facing

| Date | Mintage | VF20 | XF40 | MS60 | MS63 | MS65 |
|---|---|---|---|---|---|---|
| 2008 | — | PF63 50.00 | PF65 60.00 | | | |

**KM# 449 DOLLAR**

27.00 g., Copper-Nickel, 38.61 mm. **Obv:** National arms **Rev:** Great white shark in color

| Date | Mintage | VF20 | XF40 | MS60 | MS63 | MS65 |
|---|---|---|---|---|---|---|
| 2008 | — | PF65 35.00 | | | | |

**KM# 450 DOLLAR**

27.00 g., Copper-Nickel, 38.61 mm. **Subject:** Manfred Albrecht von Richtofen (The Red Baron) **Obv:** National arms **Rev:** Bust in oval below red tri-wing plane

| Date | Mintage | VF20 | XF40 | MS60 | MS63 | MS65 |
|---|---|---|---|---|---|---|
| 2008 | — | PF65 75.00 | | | | |

**KM# 451 DOLLAR**

25.00 g., 0.999 Silver 0.803 oz. ASW, 38.61 mm. **Obv:** National arms **Rev:** Butterfly

| Date | Mintage | VF20 | XF40 | MS60 | MS63 | MS65 |
|---|---|---|---|---|---|---|
| 2008 | — | PF65 80.00 | | | | |

**KM# 177 DOLLAR**
1.24 g., 0.999 Gold 0.040 oz. AGW, 13.9 mm. **Obv:** Shield **Rev:** Madonna and child

| Date | Mintage | VF20 | XF40 | MS60 | MS63 | MS65 |
|---|---|---|---|---|---|---|
| ND(2009) | 25,000 | PF63 75.00 | PF65 80.00 | | | |

**KM# 178 DOLLAR**
1.24 g., 0.999 Gold 0.040 oz. AGW, 13.9 mm. **Subject:** FIAA World Cup - South Africa **Obv:** Shield **Rev:** Soccer ball, South African flag and Water Buffalo

| Date | Mintage | VF20 | XF40 | MS60 | MS63 | MS65 |
|---|---|---|---|---|---|---|
| 2009 | — | PF63 70.00 | PF65 75.00 | | | |

**KM# 222 DOLLAR**
27.00 g., Silver Plated Copper, 38.6 mm. **Rev:** Lighthouse of Alexandria, multicolor

| Date | Mintage | VF20 | XF40 | MS60 | MS63 | MS65 |
|---|---|---|---|---|---|---|
| 2009 Prooflike | 5,000 | — | — | — | — | 20.00 |

**KM# 223 DOLLAR**
27.00 g., Silver Plated Copper, 38.6 mm. **Rev:** Zeus statue, multicolor

| Date | Mintage | VF20 | XF40 | MS60 | MS63 | MS65 |
|---|---|---|---|---|---|---|
| 2009 Prooflike | — | — | — | — | — | 20.00 |

**KM# 224 DOLLAR**
27.00 g., Silver Plated Copper, 38.6 mm. **Rev:** Hanging Garden of Babylon, multicolor

| Date | Mintage | VF20 | XF40 | MS60 | MS63 | MS65 |
|---|---|---|---|---|---|---|
| 2009 Prooflike | 5,000 | — | — | — | — | 20.00 |

**KM# 225 DOLLAR**
27.00 g., Silver Plated Copper, 38.6 mm. **Rev:** Mausoleum, multicolor

| Date | Mintage | VF20 | XF40 | MS60 | MS63 | MS65 |
|---|---|---|---|---|---|---|
| 2009 Prooflike | 5,000 | — | — | — | — | 20.00 |

**KM# 226 DOLLAR**
27.00 g., Silver Plated Copper, 38.6 mm. **Rev:** Pyramids, multicolor

| Date | Mintage | VF20 | XF40 | MS60 | MS63 | MS65 |
|---|---|---|---|---|---|---|
| 2009 Prooflike | 5,000 | — | — | — | — | 20.00 |

**KM# 227 DOLLAR**
27.00 g., Silver Plated Copper, 38.6 mm. **Rev:** Artemis temple, multicolor

| Date | Mintage | VF20 | XF40 | MS60 | MS63 | MS65 |
|---|---|---|---|---|---|---|
| 2009 Prooflike | 5,000 | — | — | — | — | 20.00 |

**KM# 228 DOLLAR**
27.00 g., Silver Plated Copper, 38.6 mm. **Rev:** Colossus of Rhodes, multicolor

| Date | Mintage | VF20 | XF40 | MS60 | MS63 | MS65 |
|---|---|---|---|---|---|---|
| 2009 Prooflike | 5,000 | — | — | — | — | 20.00 |

**KM# 229 DOLLAR**
27.00 g., Silver Plated Copper, 38.6 mm. **Subject:** Ducati - Casey Stoner **Rev:** Motorcycle left, multicolor

| Date | Mintage | VF20 | XF40 | MS60 | MS63 | MS65 |
|---|---|---|---|---|---|---|
| 2009 Prooflike | 2,008 | — | — | — | — | 25.00 |

**KM# 230 DOLLAR**
27.00 g., Silver Plated Copper, 38.6 mm. **Subject:** Ducati - Troy Bayliss **Rev:** Motorcycle, multicolor

| Date | Mintage | VF20 | XF40 | MS60 | MS63 | MS65 |
|---|---|---|---|---|---|---|
| 2009 Prooflike | 2,008 | — | — | — | — | 25.00 |

**KM# 233 DOLLAR**
27.00 g., Copper-Nickel, 38.6 mm. **Subject:** Marine Life Protection **Obv:** Neptune standing, two mermaids below **Rev:** Lionfish, multicolor

| Date | Mintage | VF20 | XF40 | MS60 | MS63 | MS65 |
|---|---|---|---|---|---|---|
| 2009 Prooflike | 5,000 | — | — | — | — | 25.00 |

**KM# 234 DOLLAR**
1.00 g., 0.999 Gold 0.0321 oz. AGW, 13.9 mm. **Subject:** Marine Life Protection **Rev:** Lionfish

| Date | Mintage | VF20 | XF40 | MS60 | MS63 | MS65 |
|---|---|---|---|---|---|---|
| 2009 | 25,000 | PF63 60.00 | PF65 70.00 | | | |

**KM# 235 DOLLAR**
0.50 g., 0.999 Gold 0.0161 oz. AGW, 11.8 mm. **Subject:** Augustus Aureus **Rev:** Head laureate right

| Date | Mintage | VF20 | XF40 | MS60 | MS63 | MS65 |
|---|---|---|---|---|---|---|
| MMIX (2009) | 15,000 | — | — | — | — | 40.00 |

**KM# 236 DOLLAR**
0.50 g., 0.999 Gold 0.0161 oz. AGW, 11.8 mm. **Subject:** Germanicus Dupondius **Rev:** General in quadriga right

| Date | Mintage | VF20 | XF40 | MS60 | MS63 | MS65 |
|---|---|---|---|---|---|---|
| MMIX (2009) | 15,000 | — | — | — | — | 40.00 |

**KM# 237 DOLLAR**
0.50 g., 0.999 Gold 0.0161 oz. AGW, 11.8 mm. **Subject:** Julius Caesar Denarius **Rev:** Head laureate right

| Date | Mintage | VF20 | XF40 | MS60 | MS63 | MS65 |
|---|---|---|---|---|---|---|
| MMIX (2009) | 15,000 | — | — | — | — | 40.00 |

**KM# 238 DOLLAR**
0.50 g., 0.999 Gold 0.0161 oz. AGW, 11.8 mm. **Subject:** Brutus Denarius **Rev:** Cap flanked by two daggers

| Date | Mintage | VF20 | XF40 | MS60 | MS63 | MS65 |
|---|---|---|---|---|---|---|
| MMIX (2009) | 15,000 | — | — | — | — | 40.00 |

**KM# 239 DOLLAR**
1.24 g., 0.999 Gold 0.0398 oz. AGW, 13.9 mm. **Subject:** Salesian Order, 150th Anniversary **Rev:** Don Bosco facing

| Date | Mintage | VF20 | XF40 | MS60 | MS63 | MS65 |
|---|---|---|---|---|---|---|
| 2009 | 15,000 | PF63 65.00 | PF65 75.00 | | | |

**KM# 240 DOLLAR**
0.50 g., 0.999 Gold 0.0161 oz. AGW, 11 mm. **Rev:** Pebbled **Shape:** 5-pointed star

| Date | Mintage | VF20 | XF40 | MS60 | MS63 | MS65 |
|---|---|---|---|---|---|---|
| ND (2009) | 25,000 | — | — | — | — | 40.00 |

**KM# 241 DOLLAR**
1.24 g., 0.999 Gold 0.0398 oz. AGW, 13.9 mm. **Subject:** Fontana de Trevi **Rev:** Trevi fountain and building facade

| Date | Mintage | VF20 | XF40 | MS60 | MS63 | MS65 |
|---|---|---|---|---|---|---|
| 2009 Proof | 15,000 | — | — | — | — | 75.00 |

**KM# 244 DOLLAR**
0.50 g., 0.999 Gold 0.0161 oz. AGW, 11.8 mm. **Subject:** First didrachm **Rev:** Twins sucking at she-wolf

| Date | Mintage | VF20 | XF40 | MS60 | MS63 | MS65 |
|---|---|---|---|---|---|---|
| MMIX (2009) | 15,000 | — | — | — | — | 40.00 |

**KM# 245 DOLLAR**
0.50 g., 0.999 Gold 0.0161 oz. AGW, 11.8 mm. **Subject:** Claudius aureus **Rev:** Head laureate right

| Date | Mintage | VF20 | XF40 | MS60 | MS63 | MS65 |
|---|---|---|---|---|---|---|
| MMIX (2009) | 15,000 | — | — | — | — | 40.00 |

**KM# 246 DOLLAR**
0.50 g., 0.999 Gold 0.0161 oz. AGW, 11.8 mm. **Subject:** Tiberius aureus **Rev:** Head laureate right

| Date | Mintage | VF20 | XF40 | MS60 | MS63 | MS65 |
|---|---|---|---|---|---|---|
| MMIX (2009) | 15,000 | — | — | — | — | 40.00 |

**KM# 247 DOLLAR**
0.50 g., 0.999 Gold 0.0161 oz. AGW, 11.8 mm. **Subject:** Caligula aureus **Rev:** Head laureate right

| Date | Mintage | VF20 | XF40 | MS60 | MS63 | MS65 |
|---|---|---|---|---|---|---|
| MMIX (2009) | 15,000 | — | — | — | — | 40.00 |

**KM# 260 DOLLAR**
Silver Plated Copper, 30x30 mm. **Subject:** 2000th Anniversary Teutobury Forest Battle **Obv:** Shield **Rev:** Warrior in forest battle, multicolor **Shape:** Square

| Date | Mintage | VF20 | XF40 | MS60 | MS63 | MS65 |
|---|---|---|---|---|---|---|
| MMIX (2009) | 2,500 | PF65 30.00 | | | | |

**KM# 261 DOLLAR**
25.00 g., 0.999 Silver 0.803 oz. ASW, 38.6 mm. **Subject:** Pacific Wildlife **Obv:** Arms **Rev:** Barn Swallow - prism

| Date | Mintage | VF20 | XF40 | MS60 | MS63 | MS65 |
|---|---|---|---|---|---|---|
| 2009 | 2,500 | PF65 50.00 | | | | |

**KM# 262 DOLLAR**
25.00 g., 0.999 Silver 0.803 oz. ASW, 38.6 mm. **Subject:** Pacific Wildlife **Obv:** Arms **Rev:** Gecko on rock - prism

| Date | Mintage | VF20 | XF40 | MS60 | MS63 | MS65 |
|---|---|---|---|---|---|---|
| 2009 | 2,500 | PF65 50.00 | | | | |

**KM# 263 DOLLAR**
0.50 g., 0.999 Gold 0.0161 oz. AGW, 11 mm. **Rev:** 4-leaf clover, green

| Date | Mintage | VF20 | XF40 | MS60 | MS63 | MS65 |
|---|---|---|---|---|---|---|
| 2009 | — | — | — | — | — | 65.00 |

**KM# 269 DOLLAR**
Copper-Nickel, 37.2 mm. **Subject:** Protect Wildlife - Angelfish **Rev:** Angelfish - Prisim

| Date | Mintage | VF20 | XF40 | MS60 | MS63 | MS65 |
|---|---|---|---|---|---|---|
| 2009 | — | — | — | — | — | 35.00 |

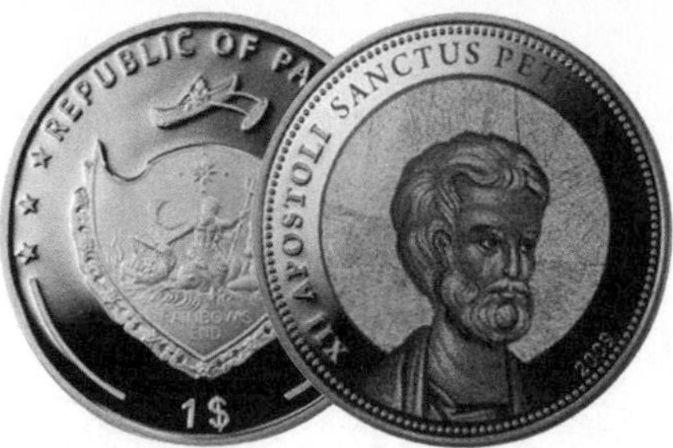


**KM# 270 DOLLAR**
Copper-Nickel, 37.2 mm. **Subject:** Apostles - Peter **Rev:** Multicolor icon image

| Date | Mintage | VF20 | XF40 | MS60 | MS63 | MS65 |
|---|---|---|---|---|---|---|
| 2009 | 1,000 | PF65 25.00 | | | | |

**KM# 271 DOLLAR**
Copper-Nickel, 37.2 mm. **Subject:** Apostles - James Minor **Rev:** Multicolor icon image

| Date | Mintage | VF20 | XF40 | MS60 | MS63 | MS65 |
|---|---|---|---|---|---|---|
| 2009 | 1,000 | PF65 25.00 | | | | |

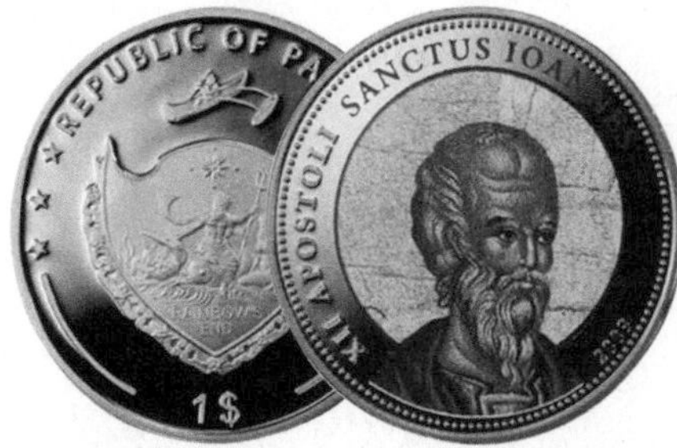


**KM# 272 DOLLAR**
Copper-Nickel, 37.2 mm. **Subject:** Apostles - John **Rev:** Multicolor icon image

| Date | Mintage | VF20 | XF40 | MS60 | MS63 | MS65 |
|---|---|---|---|---|---|---|
| 2009 | 1,000 | PF65 25.00 | | | | |

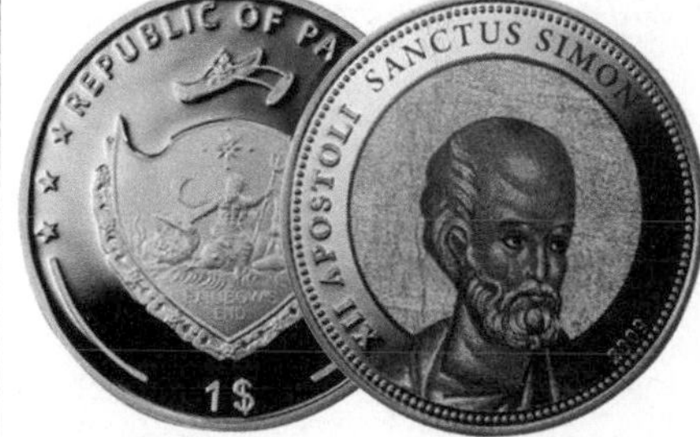


**KM# 273 DOLLAR**
Copper-Nickel, 37.2 mm. **Subject:** Apostle - Simon **Rev:** Multicolor icon image

| Date | Mintage | VF20 | XF40 | MS60 | MS63 | MS65 |
|---|---|---|---|---|---|---|
| 2009 | 1,000 | PF65 25.00 | | | | |

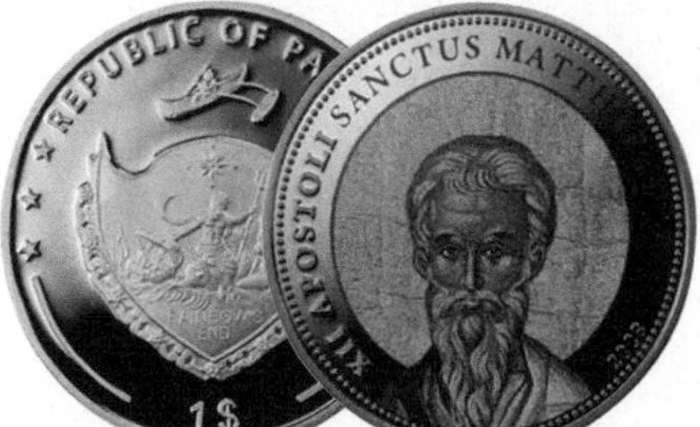


**KM# 274 DOLLAR**
Copper-Nickel, 37.2 mm. **Subject:** Apostles - Matthaeus **Rev:** Multicolor icon image

| Date | Mintage | VF20 | XF40 | MS60 | MS63 | MS65 |
|---|---|---|---|---|---|---|
| 2009 | 1,000 | PF65 25.00 | | | | |

**KM# 275 DOLLAR**
Copper-Nickel, 37.2 mm. **Subject:** Apostles - Thomas **Rev:** Multicolor icon image

| Date | Mintage | VF20 | XF40 | MS60 | MS63 | MS65 |
|---|---|---|---|---|---|---|
| 2009 | 1,000 | PF65 25.00 | | | | |

**KM# 276 DOLLAR**
Copper-Nickel, 37.2 mm. **Subject:** Apostles - Judas Thaddaeus **Rev:** Multicolor icon image

| Date | Mintage | VF20 | XF40 | MS60 | MS63 | MS65 |
|---|---|---|---|---|---|---|
| 2009 | 1,000 | PF65 25.00 | | | | |

**KM# 277 DOLLAR**
Copper-Nickel, 37.2 mm. **Subject:** Apostles - Bartholomew **Rev:** Multicolor icon image

| Date | Mintage | VF20 | XF40 | MS60 | MS63 | MS65 |
|---|---|---|---|---|---|---|
| 2009 | 1,000 | PF65 25.00 | | | | |

**KM# 278 DOLLAR**
Copper-Nickel, 37.2 mm. **Subject:** Apostles - Philip **Rev:** Multicolor icon image

| Date | Mintage | VF20 | XF40 | MS60 | MS63 | MS65 |
|---|---|---|---|---|---|---|
| 2009 | 1,000 | PF65 25.00 | | | | |

**KM# 279 DOLLAR**
Copper-Nickel, 37.2 mm. **Subject:** Apostles - John Major **Rev:** Multicolor icon image

| Date | Mintage | VF20 | XF40 | MS60 | MS63 | MS65 |
|---|---|---|---|---|---|---|
| 2009 | 1,000 | PF65 25.00 | | | | |

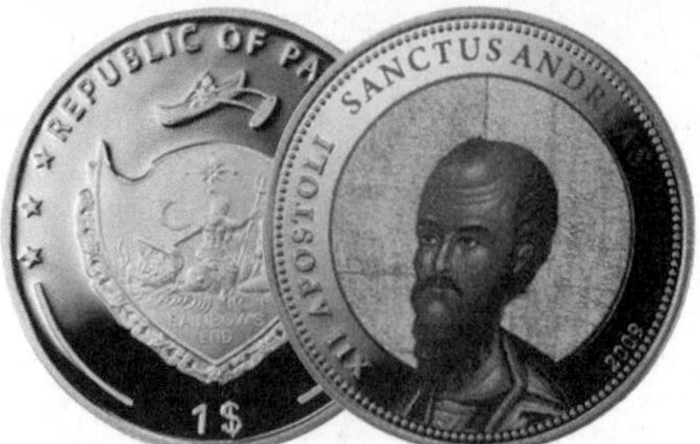

**KM# 280 DOLLAR**
Copper-Nickel, 37.2 mm. **Subject:** Apostles - Andrew **Rev:** Multicolor icon image

| Date | Mintage | VF20 | XF40 | MS60 | MS63 | MS65 |
|---|---|---|---|---|---|---|
| 2009 | 1,000 | PF65 25.00 | | | | |

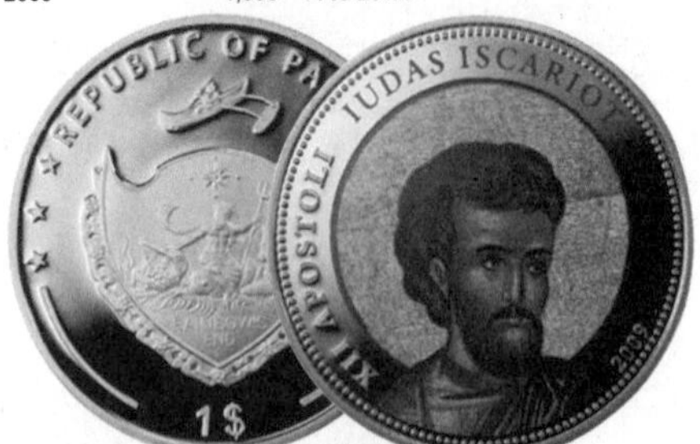

**KM# 281 DOLLAR**
Copper-Nickel, 37.2 mm. **Subject:** Apostles - Judas Iscariot **Rev:** Multicolor icon image

| Date | Mintage | VF20 | XF40 | MS60 | MS63 | MS65 |
|---|---|---|---|---|---|---|
| 2009 | 1,000 | PF65 25.00 | | | | |

**KM# 282 DOLLAR**
26.80 g., Copper-Nickel, 37.2 mm. **Subject:** Endangered Wildlife - Orange Lined Tigerfish **Rev:** Multicolor fish left

| Date | Mintage | VF20 | XF40 | MS60 | MS63 | MS65 |
|---|---|---|---|---|---|---|
| 2009 | — | PF65 35.00 | | | | |

**KM# 283 DOLLAR**
26.80 g., Copper-Nickel, 37.2 mm. **Subject:** Endangered Wildlife - Blue Grilled Angelfish **Rev:** Multicolor fish

| Date | Mintage | VF20 | XF40 | MS60 | MS63 | MS65 |
|---|---|---|---|---|---|---|
| 2009 | — | PF65 35.00 | | | | |

**KM# 284 DOLLAR**
26.80 g., Copper-Nickel, 37.2 mm. **Subject:** Endangered Wildlife - Green Turtle **Rev:** Multicolor turtle

| Date | Mintage | VF20 | XF40 | MS60 | MS63 | MS65 |
|---|---|---|---|---|---|---|
| 2009 | — | PF65 35.00 | | | | |

**KM# 285 DOLLAR**
26.80 g., Copper-Nickel, 37.2 mm. **Subject:** Endangered Wildlife - Sailfin Tang fish **Rev:** Multicolor fish right

| Date | Mintage | VF20 | XF40 | MS60 | MS63 | MS65 |
|---|---|---|---|---|---|---|
| 2009 | — | PF65 35.00 | | | | |

**KM# 286 DOLLAR**
26.80 g., Copper-Nickel, 37.2 mm. **Subject:** Endangered Wildlife - Clown Trigger fish **Rev:** Multicolor fish left

| Date | Mintage | VF20 | XF40 | MS60 | MS63 | MS65 |
|---|---|---|---|---|---|---|
| 2009 | — | PF65 35.00 | | | | |

**KM# 321 DOLLAR**
0.50 g., 0.999 Gold 0.0161 oz. AGW, 11.8 mm. **Obv:** National arms **Rev:** Pamir, sail training vessel

| Date | Mintage | VF20 | XF40 | MS60 | MS63 | MS65 |
|---|---|---|---|---|---|---|
| 2009 | 25,000 | PF63 60.00 | PF65 70.00 | | | |

**KM# 448 DOLLAR**
27.00 g., Copper-Nickel, 38.61 mm. **Obv:** National arms **Rev:** Two spotted fish in color

| Date | Mintage | VF20 | XF40 | MS60 | MS63 | MS65 |
|---|---|---|---|---|---|---|
| 2009 | — | PF65 35.00 | | | | |

**KM# 454 DOLLAR**
Silver Plated Copper, 35 x 35 mm. **Subject:** Battle of Teutoburg Forest **Rev:** Roman Legion in color

| Date | Mintage | VF20 | XF40 | MS60 | MS63 | MS65 |
|---|---|---|---|---|---|---|
| 2009 | — | PF65 60.00 | | | | |

**KM# 455 DOLLAR**
Silver Plated, 30 x 30 mm. **Subject:** Forest Battle **Obv:** Walhalia Arminius

| Date | Mintage | VF20 | XF40 | MS60 | MS63 | MS65 |
|---|---|---|---|---|---|---|
| 2009 | — | PF65 20.00 | | | | |

**KM# 266 DOLLAR**
25.00 g., 0.925 Silver 0.7435 oz. ASW, 30x30 mm. **Subject:** Battle of Grimwald **Rev:** Vyautas and Jagiello busts **Shape:** Square

| Date | Mintage | VF20 | XF40 | MS60 | MS63 | MS65 |
|---|---|---|---|---|---|---|
| 2010 | — | PF65 30.00 | | | | |

**KM# 267 DOLLAR**
25.00 g., 0.999 Silver 0.803 oz. ASW, 30x30 mm. **Subject:** Battle of Grunwald **Rev:** Warrior on horseback in color **Shape:** Square

| Date | Mintage | VF20 | XF40 | MS60 | MS63 | MS65 |
|---|---|---|---|---|---|---|
| 2010 | 2,500 | PF65 35.00 | | | | |

**KM# 268 DOLLAR**
25.00 g., 0.999 Silver 0.803 oz. ASW, 30x30 mm. **Subject:** Battle of Grunwald **Rev:** Knight kneeling in color **Shape:** Square

| Date | Mintage | VF20 | XF40 | MS60 | MS63 | MS65 |
|---|---|---|---|---|---|---|
| 2010 | 2,500 | PF65 35.00 | | | | |

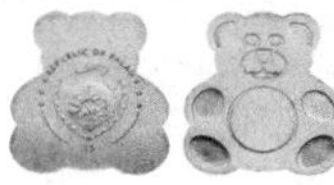

**KM# 303 DOLLAR**
0.50 g., 0.999 Gold 0.0161 oz. AGW, 11mm mm. **Obv:** National arms **Rev:** Teddy bear **Shape:** Irregular

| Date | Mintage | VF20 | XF40 | MS60 | MS63 | MS65 |
|---|---|---|---|---|---|---|
| ND(2010) | 25,000 | — | — | — | — | 75.00 |

**KM# 307 DOLLAR**
35.00 g., Copper-Nickel, 50 mm. **Subject:** Hold Cards **Obv:** National arms **Rev:** King of Hearts and Clubs

| Date | Mintage | VF20 | XF40 | MS60 | MS63 | MS65 |
|---|---|---|---|---|---|---|
| 2010 Antique patina | 5,000 | — | — | — | 25.00 | — |

**KM# 308 DOLLAR**
35.00 g., Copper-Nickel, 50 mm. **Subject:** Hold Cards **Obv:** National arms **Rev:** King of Spades and Diamonds

| Date | Mintage | VF20 | XF40 | MS60 | MS63 | MS65 |
|---|---|---|---|---|---|---|
| 2010 Antique patina | 5,000 | — | — | — | 25.00 | — |

**KM# 309 DOLLAR**
0.50 g., 0.9999 Gold 0.0161 oz. AGW, 11.8 mm. **Obv:** National arms **Rev:** Nero coin

| Date | Mintage | VF20 | XF40 | MS60 | MS63 | MS65 |
|---|---|---|---|---|---|---|
| 2010 | 15,000 | — | — | — | — | 60.00 |

**KM# 310 DOLLAR**
0.50 g., 0.9999 Gold 0.0161 oz. AGW, 11.8 mm. **Obv:** National arms **Rev:** Vespasian coin

| Date | Mintage | VF20 | XF40 | MS60 | MS63 | MS65 |
|---|---|---|---|---|---|---|
| 2010 | 15,000 | — | — | — | — | 60.00 |

**KM# 311 DOLLAR**
0.50 g., 0.999 Silver 0.0161 oz. ASW, 11.8 mm. **Obv:** National arms **Rev:** Titus coin

| Date | Mintage | VF20 | XF40 | MS60 | MS63 | MS65 |
|---|---|---|---|---|---|---|
| 2010 | 15,000 | — | — | — | — | 60.00 |

**KM# 312 DOLLAR**
0.50 g., 0.9999 Gold 0.0161 oz. AGW, 11.8 mm. **Obv:** National arms **Rev:** Domitian coin

| Date | Mintage | VF20 | XF40 | MS60 | MS63 | MS65 |
|---|---|---|---|---|---|---|
| 2010 | 15,000 | — | — | — | — | 60.00 |

**KM# 313 DOLLAR**
27.00 g., Silver Plated Copper, 38.61 mm. **Obv:** Mermaid **Rev:** Hammerhead shark color image

| Date | Mintage | VF20 | XF40 | MS60 | MS63 | MS65 |
|---|---|---|---|---|---|---|
| 2010 Prooflike | 5,000 | — | — | — | — | 28.00 |

**KM# 315 DOLLAR**
1.00 g., 0.9999 Gold 0.0321 oz. AGW, 13.92 mm. **Obv:** Mermaid **Rev:** Hammerhead sharks

| Date | Mintage | VF20 | XF40 | MS60 | MS63 | MS65 |
|---|---|---|---|---|---|---|
| 2010 | 25,000 | PF63 80.00 | PF65 90.00 | | | |

**KM# 316 DOLLAR**
27.00 g., Silver Plated Copper, 35x35 mm. **Obv:** National arms **Rev:** Fernando Alonso and racecar in color

| Date | Mintage | VF20 | XF40 | MS60 | MS63 | MS65 |
|---|---|---|---|---|---|---|
| 2010 Prooflike | 5,000 | — | — | — | — | 35.00 |

**KM# 317 DOLLAR**
0.50 g., 0.9999 Gold 0.0161 oz. AGW, 11 mm. **Obv:** National arms **Rev:** Angel **Shape:** Irregular

| Date | Mintage | VF20 | XF40 | MS60 | MS63 | MS65 |
|---|---|---|---|---|---|---|
| ND(2010) | 15,000 | — | — | — | — | 50.00 |

**KM# 327 DOLLAR**
0.50 g., 0.999 Gold 0.0161 oz. AGW, 11.8 mm. **Obv:** National arms **Rev:** Romulus & Remus

| Date | Mintage | VF20 | XF40 | MS60 | MS63 | MS65 |
|---|---|---|---|---|---|---|
| 2010 | 15,000 | PF63 40.00 | PF65 50.00 | | | |

**KM# 429 DOLLAR**
Copper-Nickel, 38.61 mm. **Obv:** National arms **Rev:** Our Lady of Fatima statue in color at left, Pope benedict XVI at right

| Date | Mintage | VF20 | XF40 | MS60 | MS63 | MS65 |
|---|---|---|---|---|---|---|
| 2010 | — | PF65 25.00 | | | | |

## KM# 445 DOLLAR

1.24 g., 0.999 Gold 0.0398 oz. AGW, 13.92 mm. **Obv:** Naitonal arms **Rev:** Mary, Joseph and Jesus **Rev. Legend:** CHRISTMAS

| Date | Mintage | VF20 | XF40 | MS60 | MS63 | MS65 |
|---|---|---|---|---|---|---|
| 2010 | — | PF63 80.00 | PF65 90.00 | | | |

## KM# 468 DOLLAR

0.50 g., 0.999 Gold 0.0161 oz. AGW, 11 mm. **Obv:** National arms **Shape:** 5-pointed star

| Date | Mintage | VF20 | XF40 | MS60 | MS63 | MS65 |
|---|---|---|---|---|---|---|
| 2010 | — | — | — | — | — | 40.00 |

## KM# 340 DOLLAR

27.00 g., Silver Plated Copper, 38.61 mm. **Subject:** John Paul II **Rev:** Visions at Fatima

| Date | Mintage | VF20 | XF40 | MS60 | MS63 | MS65 |
|---|---|---|---|---|---|---|
| 2011 Prooflike | 2,500 | — | — | — | — | 22.00 |

## KM# 341 DOLLAR

27.00 g., Silver Plated Copper, 38.61 mm. **Subject:** John Paul II **Rev:** Election as pope

| Date | Mintage | VF20 | XF40 | MS60 | MS63 | MS65 |
|---|---|---|---|---|---|---|
| 2011 Prooflike | 2,500 | — | — | — | — | 22.00 |

## KM# 342 DOLLAR

27.00 g., Silver Plated Copper, 38.61 mm. **Subject:** John Paul II **Rev:** Death

| Date | Mintage | VF20 | XF40 | MS60 | MS63 | MS65 |
|---|---|---|---|---|---|---|
| 2011 Prooflike | 2,500 | — | — | — | — | 22.00 |

## KM# 343 DOLLAR

27.00 g., Silver Plated Copper, 38.61 mm. **Subject:** John Paul II **Rev:** Anouncement as Venerable

| Date | Mintage | VF20 | XF40 | MS60 | MS63 | MS65 |
|---|---|---|---|---|---|---|
| 2011 Prooflike | 2,500 | — | — | — | — | 22.00 |

## KM# 344 DOLLAR

27.00 g., Silver Plated Copper, 38.61 mm. **Subject:** John Paul II **Rev:** Miracle healing of a Sister

| Date | Mintage | VF20 | XF40 | MS60 | MS63 | MS65 |
|---|---|---|---|---|---|---|
| 2011 Prooflike | 2,500 | — | — | — | — | 22.00 |

## KM# 345 DOLLAR

27.00 g., Silver Plated Copper, 38.61 mm. **Subject:** John Paul II **Rev:** Benedict VXI's pronouncement

| Date | Mintage | VF20 | XF40 | MS60 | MS63 | MS65 |
|---|---|---|---|---|---|---|
| 2011 Prooflike | 2,500 | — | — | — | — | 22.00 |

## KM# 346 DOLLAR

27.00 g., Silver Plated Copper, 38.61 mm. **Subject:** John Paul II **Rev:** Opening the cause for sainthood

| Date | Mintage | VF20 | XF40 | MS60 | MS63 | MS65 |
|---|---|---|---|---|---|---|
| 2011 Prooflike | 2,500 | — | — | — | — | 22.00 |

## KM# 347 DOLLAR

27.00 g., Silver Plated Copper, 38.61 mm. **Subject:** John Paul II **Rev:** Ceremony of Beautification

| Date | Mintage | VF20 | XF40 | MS60 | MS63 | MS65 |
|---|---|---|---|---|---|---|
| 2011 Prooflike | 2,500 | — | — | — | — | 22.00 |

## KM# 349 DOLLAR

0.50 g., 0.999 Gold 0.0161 oz. AGW, 11.8 mm. **Rev:** Roman Coin - Coliseum

| Date | Mintage | VF20 | XF40 | MS60 | MS63 | MS65 |
|---|---|---|---|---|---|---|
| 2011 | — | PF63 45.00 | PF65 55.00 | | | |

## KM# 350 DOLLAR

0.50 g., 0.999 Gold 0.0161 oz. AGW, 11.8 mm. **Rev:** Roman Coin - Trajain

| Date | Mintage | VF20 | XF40 | MS60 | MS63 | MS65 |
|---|---|---|---|---|---|---|
| 2011 | — | PF63 45.00 | PF65 55.00 | | | |

## KM# 351 DOLLAR

0.50 g., 0.999 Gold 0.0161 oz. AGW, 11.8 mm. **Rev:** Roman Coin - Hadrian

| Date | Mintage | VF20 | XF40 | MS60 | MS63 | MS65 |
|---|---|---|---|---|---|---|
| 2011 | — | PF63 45.00 | PF65 55.00 | | | |

## KM# 352 DOLLAR

0.50 g., 0.999 Gold 0.0161 oz. AGW, 11.8 mm. **Rev:** Roman Coin - Marcus Aurillus

| Date | Mintage | VF20 | XF40 | MS60 | MS63 | MS65 |
|---|---|---|---|---|---|---|
| 2011 | — | PF63 45.00 | PF65 55.00 | | | |

## KM# 370 DOLLAR

0.50 g., 0.999 Gold 0.0161 oz. AGW, 11.8 mm. **Obv:** National arms **Rev:** Diocletian coin

| Date | Mintage | VF20 | XF40 | MS60 | MS63 | MS65 |
|---|---|---|---|---|---|---|
| 2011 | — | — | — | — | — | 60.00 |

## KM# 371 DOLLAR

0.50 g., 0.999 Gold 0.0161 oz. AGW, 11.8 mm. **Obv:** National arms **Rev:** Aurelian coin

| Date | Mintage | VF20 | XF40 | MS60 | MS63 | MS65 |
|---|---|---|---|---|---|---|
| 2011 | — | — | — | — | — | 60.00 |

## KM# 372 DOLLAR

0.50 g., 0.999 Gold 0.0161 oz. AGW, 11.8 mm. **Obv:** National arms **Rev:** Caracalla coin

| Date | Mintage | VF20 | XF40 | MS60 | MS63 | MS65 |
|---|---|---|---|---|---|---|
| 2011 | — | — | — | — | — | 60.00 |

## KM# 373 DOLLAR

0.50 g., 0.999 Gold 0.0161 oz. AGW, 11.8 mm. **Obv:** National arms **Rev:** Septimius Severus coin

| Date | Mintage | VF20 | XF40 | MS60 | MS63 | MS65 |
|---|---|---|---|---|---|---|
| 2011 | — | — | — | — | — | 60.00 |

## KM# 405 DOLLAR

1.24 g., 0.999 Gold 0.0398 oz. AGW, 13.94 mm. **Obv:** Mermaid reclining on rock **Rev:** Anemone fish

| Date | Mintage | VF20 | XF40 | MS60 | MS63 | MS65 |
|---|---|---|---|---|---|---|
| 2011 | — | PF63 80.00 | PF65 90.00 | | | |

## KM# 406 DOLLAR

27.00 g., Silver Plated Copper-Nickel, 38.6 mm. **Obv:** Mermaid reclining on rock **Rev:** Anemone fish (maroon clown fish) in color

| Date | Mintage | VF20 | XF40 | MS60 | MS63 | MS65 |
|---|---|---|---|---|---|---|
| 2011 | — | — | — | — | — | 25.00 |

**KM# 408 DOLLAR**
27.00 g., Copper-Nickel, 38.61 mm. **Obv:** National arms **Rev:** Harry Houdini bust at left, top had and wand at right

| Date | Mintage | VF20 | XF40 | MS60 | MS63 | MS65 |
|---|---|---|---|---|---|---|
| 2011 | — | — | — | — | — | 25.00 |

**KM# 410 DOLLAR**
0.50 g., 0.999 Gold 0.0161 oz. AGW, 11 mm. **Obv:** National arms **Rev:** Golden Butterfly **Shape:** Irregular

| Date | Mintage | VF20 | XF40 | MS60 | MS63 | MS65 |
|---|---|---|---|---|---|---|
| ND(2011) | — | PF65 85.00 | | | | |

**KM# 452 DOLLAR**
25.00 g., 0.999 Silver 0.803 oz. ASW, 38.61 mm. **Obv:** National arms **Rev:** Long nose hawk fish

| Date | Mintage | VF20 | XF40 | MS60 | MS63 | MS65 |
|---|---|---|---|---|---|---|
| 2011 | — | PF65 75.00 | | | | |

**KM# 453 DOLLAR**
25.00 g., 0.999 Silver 0.803 oz. ASW, 38.61 mm. **Obv:** National arms **Rev:** Two striped fish

| Date | Mintage | VF20 | XF40 | MS60 | MS63 | MS65 |
|---|---|---|---|---|---|---|
| 2011 | — | PF65 75.00 | | | | |

**KM# 130 2 DOLLARS**
10.00 g., 0.999 Silver 0.3212 oz. ASW, 30 mm. **Obv:** Shield with Neptune holding trident, mermaid reclining at his side **Obv. Legend:** REPUBLIC OF PALAU **Rev:** Red racing car 3/4 right **Rev. Legend:** FERRARI - 60 YEARS ANNIVERSARY

| Date | Mintage | VF20 | XF40 | MS60 | MS63 | MS65 |
|---|---|---|---|---|---|---|
| ND(2007) | 2,500 | PF65 45.00 | | | | |

**KM# 131 2 DOLLARS**
10.00 g., 0.999 Silver 0.3212 oz. ASW, 30 mm. **Obv:** Shield with Neptune holding trident, mermaid reclining at his side **Obv. Legend:** REPUBLIC OF PALAU **Rev:** Red racing car 3/4 right **Rev. Legend:** FERRARI - 60 YEARS ANNIVERSARY

| Date | Mintage | VF20 | XF40 | MS60 | MS63 | MS65 |
|---|---|---|---|---|---|---|
| ND(2007) | 2,500 | PF65 45.00 | | | | |

**KM# 132 2 DOLLARS**
10.00 g., 0.999 Silver 0.3212 oz. ASW, 30 mm. **Obv:** Shield with Neptune holding trident, mermaid reclining at his side **Obv. Legend:** REPUBLIC OF PALAU **Rev:** Red racing car front view **Rev. Legend:** FERRARI - 60 YEARS ANNIVERSARY

| Date | Mintage | VF20 | XF40 | MS60 | MS63 | MS65 |
|---|---|---|---|---|---|---|
| ND(2007) | 2,500 | PF65 45.00 | | | | |

**KM# 133 2 DOLLARS**
10.00 g., 0.999 Silver 0.3212 oz. ASW, 30 mm. **Obv:** Shield with Neptune holding trident, mermaid reclining at his side **Obv. Legend:** REPUBLIC OF PALAU **Rev:** Looking down on red racing car approaching in turn **Rev. Legend:** FERRARI - 60 YEARS ANNIVERSARY

| Date | Mintage | VF20 | XF40 | MS60 | MS63 | MS65 |
|---|---|---|---|---|---|---|
| ND(2007) | 2,500 | PF65 45.00 | | | | |

**KM# 134 2 DOLLARS**
10.00 g., 0.999 Silver 0.3212 oz. ASW, 30 mm. **Obv:** Shield with Neptune holding trident, reclining mermaid at his side **Obv. Legend:** REPUBLIC OF PALAU **Rev:** Front view of red racing car **Rev. Legend:** FERRARI - 60 YEARS ANNIVERSARY

| Date | Mintage | VF20 | XF40 | MS60 | MS63 | MS65 |
|---|---|---|---|---|---|---|
| ND(2007) | 2,500 | PF65 45.00 | | | | |

**KM# 135 2 DOLLARS**
10.00 g., 0.999 Silver 0.3212 oz. ASW, 30.0 mm. **Obv:** Shield with Neptune holding trident, mermaid reclining at his side **Obv. Legend:** REPUBLIC OF PALAU **Rev:** Red racing car approaching 3/4 right **Rev. Legend:** FERRARI - 60 YEARS ANNIVERSARY

| Date | Mintage | VF20 | XF40 | MS60 | MS63 | MS65 |
|---|---|---|---|---|---|---|
| ND(2007) | 2,500 | PF65 45.00 | | | | |

**KM# 319 2 DOLLARS**
15.50 g., 0.925 Silver 0.461 oz. ASW, 35 mm. **Subject:** World of Insects **Obv:** National arms **Rev:** Large color dragon fly - Blue Eye Hawker

| Date | Mintage | VF20 | XF40 | MS60 | MS63 | MS65 |
|---|---|---|---|---|---|---|
| 2010 | 1,000 | PF65 100 | | | | |

**KM# 375 2 DOLLARS**
15.50 g., 0.925 Silver 0.461 oz. ASW, 35 mm. **Subject:** Grasshopper

| Date | Mintage | VF20 | XF40 | MS60 | MS63 | MS65 |
|---|---|---|---|---|---|---|
| 2010 | — | PF65 100 | | | | |

**KM# 353 2 DOLLARS**
15.50 g., 0.999 Silver 0.4978 oz. ASW, 35 mm. **Subject:** Bible stories - Creation of the World

| Date | Mintage | VF20 | XF40 | MS60 | MS63 | MS65 |
|---|---|---|---|---|---|---|
| 2011 | 1,000 | PF65 65.00 | | | | |

**KM# 354 2 DOLLARS**
15.50 g., 0.999 Silver 0.4978 oz. ASW, 35 mm. **Subject:** Bible stories - Adam and Eve

| Date | Mintage | VF20 | XF40 | MS60 | MS63 | MS65 |
|---|---|---|---|---|---|---|
| 2011 | 1,000 | PF65 65.00 | | | | |

**KM# 355 2 DOLLARS**
15.50 g., 0.999 Silver 0.4978 oz. ASW, 35 mm. **Subject:** Bible stories - Cain and Abel

| Date | Mintage | VF20 | XF40 | MS60 | MS63 | MS65 |
|---|---|---|---|---|---|---|
| 2011 | 1,000 | PF65 65.00 | | | | |

**KM# 356 2 DOLLARS**
15.50 g., 0.999 Silver 0.4978 oz. ASW, 35 mm. **Subject:** Bible stories - 10 Commandments

| Date | Mintage | VF20 | XF40 | MS60 | MS63 | MS65 |
|---|---|---|---|---|---|---|
| 2011 | 1,000 | PF65 65.00 | | | | |

**KM# 357 2 DOLLARS**
15.57 g., 0.925 Silver 0.463 oz. ASW, 35 mm. **Obv:** National arms **Rev:** Atelopus Certus, orange frog in color

| Date | Mintage | VF20 | XF40 | MS60 | MS63 | MS65 |
|---|---|---|---|---|---|---|
| 2011 | 500 | PF65 85.00 | | | | |

**KM# 358 2 DOLLARS**
151.57 g., 0.925 Silver 4.5076 oz. ASW, 35 mm. **Obv:** National arms **Rev:** Green frog in color

| Date | Mintage | VF20 | XF40 | MS60 | MS63 | MS65 |
|---|---|---|---|---|---|---|
| 2011 | 500 | PF65 85.00 | | | | |

**KM# 359 2 DOLLARS**
15.57 g., 0.925 Silver 0.463 oz. ASW, 35 mm. **Obv:** National arms **Rev:** Atelopus Cerus, purple frog in color

| Date | Mintage | VF20 | XF40 | MS60 | MS63 | MS65 |
|---|---|---|---|---|---|---|
| 2011 | 500 | PF65 85.00 | | | | |

## KM# 360 2 DOLLARS

15.50 g., 0.925 Silver 0.461 oz. ASW, 35 mm. **Rev:** Bombus Latreille - Bumble bee in color

| Date | Mintage | VF20 | XF40 | MS60 | MS63 | MS65 |
|---|---|---|---|---|---|---|
| 2011 | 1,000 | **PF65** 100 | | | | |

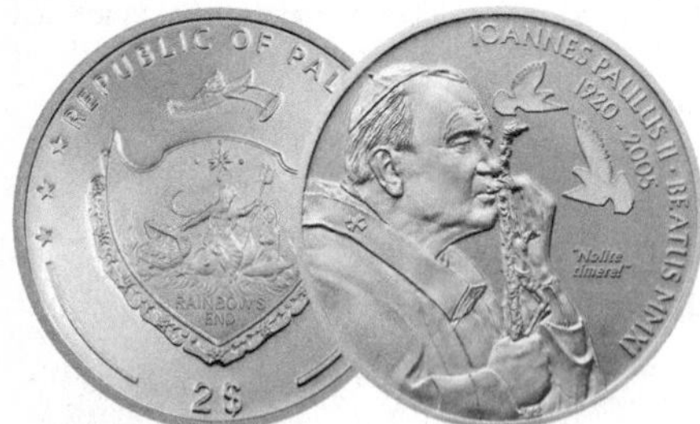


## KM# 361 2 DOLLARS

15.57 g., 0.925 Silver 0.463 oz. ASW, 35 mm. **Rev:** John Paul II with cross croizer, doves

| Date | Mintage | VF20 | XF40 | MS60 | MS63 | MS65 |
|---|---|---|---|---|---|---|
| 2011 | 1,000 | **PF65** 60.00 | | | | |

## KM# 362 2 DOLLARS

25.00 g., 0.925 Silver 0.7435 oz. ASW, 38.61 mm. **Obv:** National Arms **Rev:** Abu Simbel temple entrance with insert

| Date | Mintage | VF20 | XF40 | MS60 | MS63 | MS65 |
|---|---|---|---|---|---|---|
| 2011 | 999 | **PF65** 100 | | | | |

## KM# 363 2 DOLLARS

25.00 g., 0.925 Silver 0.7435 oz. ASW, 41x31 mm. **Subject:** Opera - Carmen **Rev:** Couple kissing in color, two other opera scenes **Shape:** Rectangle

| Date | Mintage | VF20 | XF40 | MS60 | MS63 | MS65 |
|---|---|---|---|---|---|---|
| 2011 | 999 | **PF65** 75.00 | | | | |

## KM# 366 2 DOLLARS

25.00 g., 0.925 Silver 0.7435 oz. ASW, 38.61 mm. **Subject:** Princess of the Sea **Rev:** Apricot pearl and shell

| Date | Mintage | VF20 | XF40 | MS60 | MS63 | MS65 |
|---|---|---|---|---|---|---|
| 2011 | 2,500 | **PF65** 100 | | | | |

## KM# 409 2 DOLLARS

25.00 g., 0.925 Silver 0.7435 oz. ASW, 38.61 mm. **Obv:** National arms **Rev:** Harry Houdini bust at left, top had and wand at right

| Date | Mintage | VF20 | XF40 | MS60 | MS63 | MS65 |
|---|---|---|---|---|---|---|
| 2011 | — | **PF65** 60.00 | | | | |

## KM# 442 2 DOLLARS

Silver, 38.61 mm. **Obv:** National arms **Rev:** Giant Prickly Stick Insect in color on flora

| Date | Mintage | VF20 | XF40 | MS60 | MS63 | MS65 |
|---|---|---|---|---|---|---|
| 2011 | — | **PF65** 100 | | | | |

## KM# 456 2 DOLLARS

15.50 g., 0.925 Silver 0.461 oz. ASW, 35 mm. **Subject:** World of Insects: Bombus Bee

| Date | Mintage | VF20 | XF40 | MS60 | MS63 | MS65 |
|---|---|---|---|---|---|---|
| 2011 Proof | 1,000 | **PF65** 65.00 | | | | |

## KM# 426 2 DOLLARS

15.50 g., Silver partially gilt, 35 mm. **Obv:** National arms **Rev:** Jansa Gora Monastery, Pope John Paul II, and rose

| Date | Mintage | VF20 | XF40 | MS60 | MS63 | MS65 |
|---|---|---|---|---|---|---|
| 2012 | — | **PF65** 50.00 | | | | |

## KM# 433 2 DOLLARS

25.00 g., 0.925 Silver 0.7435 oz. ASW, 45x45 mm. **Obv:** National arms **Rev:** Winged heart **Shape:** Heart

| Date | Mintage | VF20 | XF40 | MS60 | MS63 | MS65 |
|---|---|---|---|---|---|---|
| 2012 | — | **PF65** 55.00 | | | | |

## KM# 467 2 DOLLARS

15.50 g., 0.925 Silver 0.461 oz. ASW, 35 mm. **Subject:** Bible stories - Birth of Jesus

| Date | Mintage | VF20 | XF40 | MS60 | MS63 | MS65 |
|---|---|---|---|---|---|---|
| 2012 | 1,000 | **PF65** 100 | | | | |

## KM# 457 2 DOLLARS

15.55 g., Silver, 35 mm. **Subject:** World of Frogs - Litoria Caerulea

| Date | Mintage | VF20 | XF40 | MS60 | MS63 | MS65 |
|---|---|---|---|---|---|---|
| 2013 | Est. 1000 | **PF65** 55.00 | | | | |

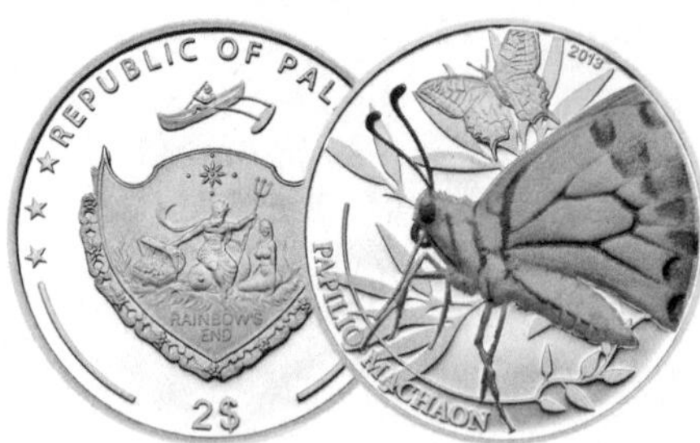


## KM# 459 2 DOLLARS

15.55 g., Silver, 35 mm. **Series:** Butterfly

| Date | Mintage | VF20 | XF40 | MS60 | MS63 | MS65 |
|---|---|---|---|---|---|---|
| 2013 | Est. 1000 | **PF65** 55.00 | | | | |

## KM# 460 2 DOLLARS

15.50 g., Silver, 35 mm. **Subject:** 2nd Commandment

| Date | Mintage | VF20 | XF40 | MS60 | MS63 | MS65 |
|---|---|---|---|---|---|---|
| 2013 | Est. 1000 | **PF65** 65.00 | | | | |

## KM# 465 2 DOLLARS

15.50 g., 0.925 Silver 0.461 oz. ASW, 35 mm. **Subject:** Biblical stories - Noah

| Date | Mintage | VF20 | XF40 | MS60 | MS63 | MS65 |
|---|---|---|---|---|---|---|
| 2013 | 1,000 | **PF65** 85.00 | | | | |

**KM# 472 2 DOLLARS**
15.00 g., Bi-Metallic, 30 mm. **Subject:** 30th Anniversary of Panda coinage

| Date | Mintage | VF20 | XF40 | MS60 | MS63 | MS65 |
|---|---|---|---|---|---|---|
| 2013 | 1,000 | PF65 50.00 | | | | |

**KM# 53 5 DOLLARS**
25.00 g., 0.900 Silver 0.7234 oz. ASW, 37.2 mm. **Series:** Marine Life Protection **Obv:** Neptune **Rev:** Multicolor jellyfish **Edge:** Reeded

| Date | Mintage | VF20 | XF40 | MS60 | MS63 | MS65 |
|---|---|---|---|---|---|---|
| 2001 | — | PF65 70.00 | | | | |

**KM# 75 5 DOLLARS**
25.00 g., 0.900 Silver 0.7234 oz. ASW, 37.2 mm. **Subject:** Marine Life Protection **Obv:** Neptune behind Polynesian ship and value **Rev:** Moorish-Idol fish **Edge:** Reeded

| Date | Mintage | VF20 | XF40 | MS60 | MS63 | MS65 |
|---|---|---|---|---|---|---|
| 2001 | — | PF65 70.00 | | | | |

**KM# 76 5 DOLLARS**
Silver, 37.2 mm. **Subject:** Marine Life Protection **Obv:** Neptune riding seahorse and value **Rev:** Fish **Edge:** Reeded

| Date | Mintage | VF20 | XF40 | MS60 | MS63 | MS65 |
|---|---|---|---|---|---|---|
| 2001 | — | PF65 70.00 | | | | |

**KM# 115 5 DOLLARS**
25.00 g., 0.900 Silver 0.7234 oz. ASW, 37.2 mm. **Subject:** Marine Life Protection **Obv:** Neptune waist deep in water above value with mermaid to the left and behind **Rev:** Multicolor iridescent fish scene **Edge:** Reeded

| Date | Mintage | VF20 | XF40 | MS60 | MS63 | MS65 |
|---|---|---|---|---|---|---|
| 2001 | — | PF65 65.00 | | | | |

**KM# 331 5 DOLLARS**
25.00 g., 0.900 Silver 0.7234 oz. ASW, 38.61 mm. **Rev:** Angelfish

| Date | Mintage | VF20 | XF40 | MS60 | MS63 | MS65 |
|---|---|---|---|---|---|---|
| 2001 | — | PF65 45.00 | | | | |

**KM# 77 5 DOLLARS**
25.00 g., 0.900 Silver 0.7234 oz. ASW, 37.2 mm. **Subject:** Marine Life Protection **Obv:** Neptune in shell boat **Rev:** Blue Tang Fish **Edge:** Reeded

| Date | Mintage | VF20 | XF40 | MS60 | MS63 | MS65 |
|---|---|---|---|---|---|---|
| 2002 | — | PF65 70.00 | | | | |

**KM# 78 5 DOLLARS**
25.00 g., 0.900 Silver 0.7234 oz. ASW, 37.2 mm. **Subject:** Marine Life Protection **Obv:** Neptune in sea chariot **Rev:** Multicolor whales **Edge:** Reeded

| Date | Mintage | VF20 | XF40 | MS60 | MS63 | MS65 |
|---|---|---|---|---|---|---|
| 2002 | — | PF65 70.00 | | | | |

**KM# 79 5 DOLLARS**
25.00 g., 0.900 Silver 0.7234 oz. ASW, 37.2 mm. **Subject:** Marine Life Protection **Obv:** Zeus and value **Rev:** Multicolor puffer fish **Edge:** Reeded

| Date | Mintage | VF20 | XF40 | MS60 | MS63 | MS65 |
|---|---|---|---|---|---|---|
| 2002 | — | PF65 70.00 | | | | |

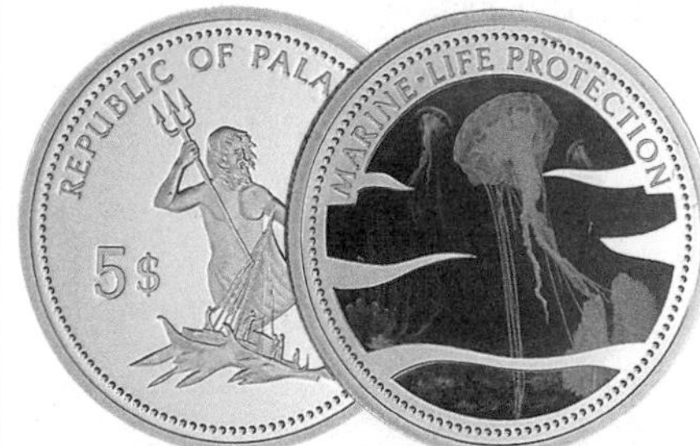


**KM# 80 5 DOLLARS**
25.00 g., 0.900 Silver 0.7234 oz. ASW, 37.2 mm. **Subject:** Marine Life Protection **Obv:** Neptune standing behind Polynesian ship **Rev:** Multicolor Jellyfish **Edge:** Reeded

| Date | Mintage | VF20 | XF40 | MS60 | MS63 | MS65 |
|---|---|---|---|---|---|---|
| 2002 | — | PF65 65.00 | | | | |

**KM# 102 5 DOLLARS**
25.00 g., 0.900 Silver 0.7234 oz. ASW, 32 mm. **Subject:** Marine Life Protection **Obv:** Neptune in sea chariot with two merhorses **Rev:** Two multicolor reflective fish

| Date | Mintage | VF20 | XF40 | MS60 | MS63 | MS65 |
|---|---|---|---|---|---|---|
| 2002 | — | PF65 55.00 | | | | |

**KM# 332 5 DOLLARS**
25.00 g., 0.900 Silver 0.7234 oz. ASW, 38.61 mm. **Rev:** Blowfish

| Date | Mintage | VF20 | XF40 | MS60 | MS63 | MS65 |
|---|---|---|---|---|---|---|
| 2002 | Est. 3000 | PF65 50.00 | | | | |

**KM# 103 5 DOLLARS**
25.00 g., 0.900 Silver 0.7234 oz. ASW, 32 mm. **Subject:** Marine Life Protection **Obv:** Neptune standing in waves **Rev:** Multicolor starfish

| Date | Mintage | VF20 | XF40 | MS60 | MS63 | MS65 |
|---|---|---|---|---|---|---|
| 2003 | — | PF65 55.00 | | | | |

**KM# 104 5 DOLLARS**
25.00 g., 0.900 Silver 0.7234 oz. ASW, 32 mm. **Subject:** Marine Life Protection **Obv:** Neptune standing in sea chariot **Rev:** Two multicolor reflective fish

| Date | Mintage | VF20 | XF40 | MS60 | MS63 | MS65 |
|---|---|---|---|---|---|---|
| 2003 | — | PF65 55.00 | | | | |

**KM# 105 5 DOLLARS**
25.00 g., 0.900 Silver 0.7234 oz. ASW, 32 mm. **Subject:** Marine Life Protection **Rev:** Multicolor Orca

| Date | Mintage | VF20 | XF40 | MS60 | MS63 | MS65 |
|---|---|---|---|---|---|---|
| 2003 | — | PF65 55.00 | | | | |

**KM# 106 5 DOLLARS**
25.00 g., 0.900 Silver 0.7234 oz. ASW, 32 mm. **Subject:** Marine Life Protection **Obv:** Neptune in sea chariot **Rev:** Multicolor Napoleon Fish

| Date | Mintage | VF20 | XF40 | MS60 | MS63 | MS65 |
|---|---|---|---|---|---|---|
| 2003 | — | PF65 55.00 | | | | |

**KM# 333 5 DOLLARS**
25.00 g., 0.900 Silver 0.7234 oz. ASW, 38.61 mm. **Rev:** Crab

| Date | Mintage | VF20 | XF40 | MS60 | MS63 | MS65 |
|---|---|---|---|---|---|---|
| 2003 | Est. 3000 | PF65 50.00 | | | | |

**KM# 81 5 DOLLARS**
25.00 g., 0.900 Silver 0.7234 oz. ASW, 37.2 mm. **Subject:** Marine Life Protection **Obv:** Neptune with treasure chest **Rev:** Clownfish **Edge:** Reeded

| Date | Mintage | VF20 | XF40 | MS60 | MS63 | MS65 |
|---|---|---|---|---|---|---|
| 2004 | — | PF65 70.00 | | | | |

**KM# 107 5 DOLLARS**
25.00 g., 0.900 Silver 0.7234 oz. ASW, 32 mm. **Subject:** Marine Life Protection **Obv:** Neptune seated behind mermaid **Rev:** Multicolor school of sweetlips fish

| Date | Mintage | VF20 | XF40 | MS60 | MS63 | MS65 |
|---|---|---|---|---|---|---|
| 2004 | — | PF65 55.00 | | | | |

**KM# 108 5 DOLLARS**
25.00 g., 0.900 Silver 0.7234 oz. ASW, 32 mm. **Subject:** Marine Life Protection **Obv:** Standing Neptune and ship **Rev:** Multicolor Porcupine fish

| Date | Mintage | VF20 | XF40 | MS60 | MS63 | MS65 |
|---|---|---|---|---|---|---|
| 2004 | — | PF65 70.00 | | | | |

**KM# 109 5 DOLLARS**
25.00 g., 0.900 Silver 0.7234 oz. ASW, 32 mm. **Subject:** Marine Life Protection **Obv:** Neptune in sea chariot **Rev:** Multicolor Loggerhead turtle

| Date | Mintage | VF20 | XF40 | MS60 | MS63 | MS65 |
|---|---|---|---|---|---|---|
| 2004 | — | PF65 70.00 | | | | |

**KM# 110 5 DOLLARS**
25.00 g., 0.900 Silver 0.7234 oz. ASW, 32 mm. **Subject:** Marine Life Protection **Obv:** Neptune and merhorse **Rev:** Multicolor dolphin head

| Date | Mintage | VF20 | XF40 | MS60 | MS63 | MS65 |
|---|---|---|---|---|---|---|
| 2004 | — | PF65 70.00 | | | | |

**KM# 111 5 DOLLARS**
25.00 g., 0.900 Silver 0.7234 oz. ASW, 32 mm. **Subject:** Marine Life Protection **Obv:** Neptune flanked by mermaids **Rev:** Multicolor sea horse

| Date | Mintage | VF20 | XF40 | MS60 | MS63 | MS65 |
|---|---|---|---|---|---|---|
| 2005 | — | PF65 70.00 | | | | |

**KM# 113 5 DOLLARS**
25.00 g., 0.900 Silver 0.7234 oz. ASW, 32 mm. **Subject:** Marine Life Protection **Obv:** Neptune flanked by mermaids **Rev:** Multicolor fish with ring-like stripes **Edge:** Reeded

| Date | Mintage | VF20 | XF40 | MS60 | MS63 | MS65 |
|---|---|---|---|---|---|---|
| 2005 | — | PF65 70.00 | | | | |

**KM# 114 5 DOLLARS**
25.00 g., 0.900 Silver 0.7234 oz. ASW, 32 mm. **Subject:** Marine Life Protection **Obv:** Neptune in shell boat talking to a dolphin **Rev:** Multicolor reef fish scene **Edge:** Reeded

| Date | Mintage | VF20 | XF40 | MS60 | MS63 | MS65 |
|---|---|---|---|---|---|---|
| 2006 | — | PF65 70.00 | | | | |

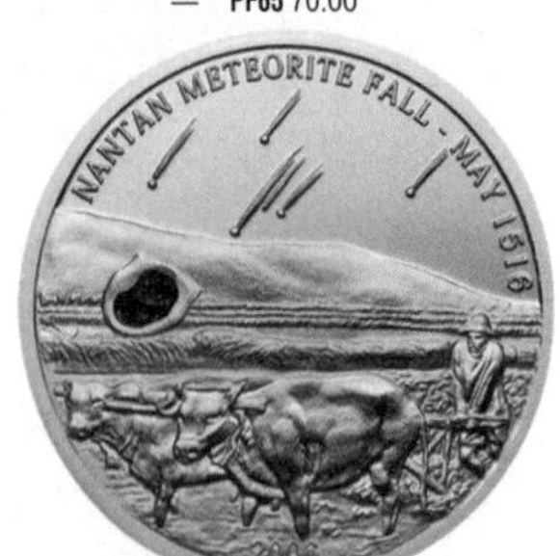


**KM# 143 5 DOLLARS**
25.00 g., 0.925 Silver 0.7435 oz. ASW with meteorite insert. **Subject:** Nantan Meteroite fall, May 1516 **Obv:** Shield **Rev:** Farmer and oxen plowing field, meteorite insert

| Date | Mintage | VF20 | XF40 | MS60 | MS63 | MS65 |
|---|---|---|---|---|---|---|
| 2006 | 2,500 | PF65 100 | | | | |

**KM# 185 5 DOLLARS**
24.85 g., 0.999 Silver 0.7981 oz. ASW, 38.6 mm. **Rev:** Black pearl oyster

| Date | Mintage | VF20 | XF40 | MS60 | MS63 | MS65 |
|---|---|---|---|---|---|---|
| 2006 | 2,500 | PF65 300 | | | | |

**KM# 186 5 DOLLARS**
25.00 g., 0.999 Silver 0.803 oz. ASW, 38.61 mm. **Subject:** Pacific Wildlife **Rev:** Rainbow Lorikeet head left

| Date | Mintage | VF20 | XF40 | MS60 | MS63 | MS65 |
|---|---|---|---|---|---|---|
| 2006 | 5,000 | PF65 50.00 | | | | |

**KM# 187 5 DOLLARS**
25.00 g., 0.999 Silver 0.803 oz. ASW, 38.61 mm. **Subject:** Pacific Wildlife **Rev:** Eclectus Parrot head right

| Date | Mintage | VF20 | XF40 | MS60 | MS63 | MS65 |
|---|---|---|---|---|---|---|
| 2006 | 5,000 | PF65 50.00 | | | | |

**KM# 188 5 DOLLARS**
25.00 g., 0.999 Silver 0.803 oz. ASW, 38.61 mm. **Subject:** Pacific Wildlife **Rev:** Fruit dove head right

| Date | Mintage | VF20 | XF40 | MS60 | MS63 | MS65 |
|---|---|---|---|---|---|---|
| 2006 | 5,000 | PF65 50.00 | | | | |

**KM# 189 5 DOLLARS**
31.11 g., 0.999 Silver 0.999 oz. ASW, 38.61 mm. **Subject:** One ounce of luck **Rev:** Four-leaf clover

| Date | Mintage | VF20 | XF40 | MS60 | MS63 | MS65 |
|---|---|---|---|---|---|---|
| 2006 | 5,000 | PF65 65.00 | | | | |

**KM# 190 5 DOLLARS**
25.00 g., 0.925 Silver 0.7435 oz. ASW, 38.61 mm. **Subject:** Dream Island **Rev:** Pacific island scene - beach, boat and sunset

| Date | Mintage | VF20 | XF40 | MS60 | MS63 | MS65 |
|---|---|---|---|---|---|---|
| 2006 | 5,000 | PF65 45.00 | | | | |

**KM# 443 5 DOLLARS**
25.00 g., 0.925 Silver 0.7435 oz. ASW, 38.61 mm. **Obv:** National arms **Rev:** Volcano, lava in color

| Date | Mintage | VF20 | XF40 | MS60 | MS63 | MS65 |
|---|---|---|---|---|---|---|
| 2006 | — | PF65 100 | | | | |

**KM# 119 5 DOLLARS**
25.00 g., 0.900 Silver 0.7234 oz. ASW, 38.61 mm. **Series:** Marine Life Protection **Obv:** Neptune reclining with trident, mermaid at his side **Obv. Legend:** REPUBLIC OF PALAU **Rev:** Multicolor Doctor Fish

| Date | Mintage | VF20 | XF40 | MS60 | MS63 | MS65 |
|---|---|---|---|---|---|---|
| 2007 | 1,500 | PF65 120 | | | | |

**KM# 122 5 DOLLARS**
25.00 g., 0.500 Silver 0.4019 oz. ASW, 38.61 mm. **Obv:** Shield with Neptune holding trident, mermaid reclining at his side, RAINBOW'S / End below **Obv. Legend:** REPUBLIC OF PALAU **Rev:** Red racing car 3/4 right **Rev. Legend:** FERRARI - 60 YEARS ANNIVERSARY

| Date | Mintage | VF20 | XF40 | MS60 | MS63 | MS65 |
|---|---|---|---|---|---|---|
| ND(2007) | 2,500 | PF65 75.00 | | | | |

**KM# 136 5 DOLLARS**
25.00 g., 0.925 Silver 0.7435 oz. ASW, 38.61 mm. **Series:** Pacific Wildlife **Obv:** National arms **Obv. Legend:** REPUBLIC OF PALAU **Rev:** Saltwater Crocodile with green crystal eye

| Date | Mintage | VF20 | XF40 | MS60 | MS63 | MS65 |
|---|---|---|---|---|---|---|
| 2007 | 2,500 | PF65 65.00 | | | | |

**KM# 138 5 DOLLARS**
24.70 g., Silver, 38.6 mm. **Series:** Marine Life Protection **Obv:** National arms with Neptune and mermaid **Rev:** Pearl in oyster shell - multicolor **Edge:** Reeded

| Date | Mintage | VF20 | XF40 | MS60 | MS63 | MS65 |
|---|---|---|---|---|---|---|
| 2007 | 2,500 | PF65 185 | | | | |

**KM# 151 5 DOLLARS**
25.00 g., 0.925 Silver 0.7435 oz. ASW, 38.6 mm. **Subject:** Pacific Wildlife **Obv:** Shield **Rev:** Multicolor nautilus shell

| Date | Mintage | VF20 | XF40 | MS60 | MS63 | MS65 |
|---|---|---|---|---|---|---|
| 2007 | — | PF65 70.00 | | | | |

**KM# 152 5 DOLLARS**
25.00 g., 0.925 Silver 0.7435 oz. ASW **Subject:** Pacific Wildlife **Obv:** Shield **Rev:** Multicolor starfish

| Date | Mintage | VF20 | XF40 | MS60 | MS63 | MS65 |
|---|---|---|---|---|---|---|
| 2007 | — | PF65 70.00 | | | | |

**KM# 153 5 DOLLARS**
25.00 g., 0.925 Silver 0.7435 oz. ASW **Subject:** Good heavens! **Obv:** Multicolor devil and angel child **Shape:** Heart

| Date | Mintage | VF20 | XF40 | MS60 | MS63 | MS65 |
|---|---|---|---|---|---|---|
| 2007 | 2,500 | PF65 65.00 | | | | |

**KM# 428 5 DOLLARS**
25.00 g., 0.999 Silver 0.803 oz. ASW, 38.61 mm. **Obv:** Water Vial and National arms **Rev:** Statue of Mary at Lourds, Water Vial

| Date | Mintage | VF20 | XF40 | MS60 | MS63 | MS65 |
|---|---|---|---|---|---|---|
| 2007 | 5,000 | PF65 100 | | | | |

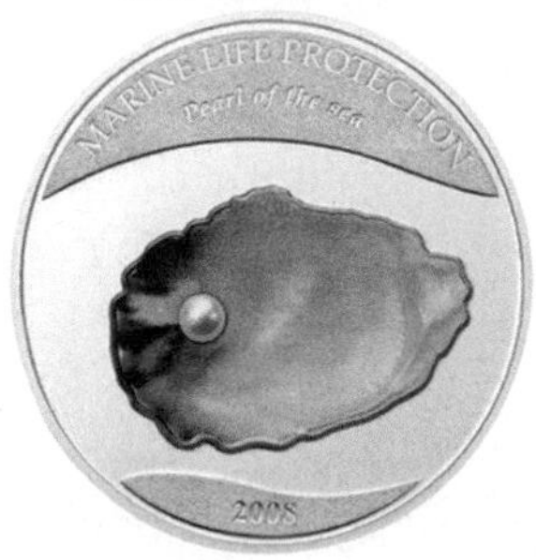


**KM# 137 5 DOLLARS**
24.70 g., 0.925 Silver 0.7346 oz. ASW, 38.5 mm. **Obv:** Outrigger canoe above shield **Obv. Legend:** REPUBLIC OF PALAU **Rev:** Pearl in colorized shell **Rev. Legend:** MARINE LIFE PROTECTION / Pearl of the sea **Edge:** Reeded

| Date | Mintage | VF20 | XF40 | MS60 | MS63 | MS65 |
|---|---|---|---|---|---|---|
| 2008 | 2,500 | PF65 125 | | | | |

**KM# 168 5 DOLLARS**
25.00 g., 0.925 Silver 0.7435 oz. ASW, 30x45 mm. **Obv:** Shield **Rev:** Don Quixote in armor **Shape:** Vertical oval

| Date | Mintage | VF20 | XF40 | MS60 | MS63 | MS65 |
|---|---|---|---|---|---|---|
| 2008 | — | PF65 70.00 | | | | |

**KM# 169 5 DOLLARS**
25.00 g., 0.925 Silver 0.7435 oz. ASW, 37.2 mm. **Subject:** Pacific Wildlife **Obv:** Shield **Rev:** Multicolor hologram, blue butterfly (Papilio Pericles)

| Date | Mintage | VF20 | XF40 | MS60 | MS63 | MS65 |
|---|---|---|---|---|---|---|
| 2008 | 2,500 | PF65 60.00 | | | | |

**KM# 170 5 DOLLARS**
25.00 g., 0.925 Silver 0.7435 oz. ASW, 37.2 mm. **Subject:** Pacific Wildlife **Obv:** Shield **Rev:** Multicolor sulphur butterfly (Hebomoia Leucippe)

| Date | Mintage | VF20 | XF40 | MS60 | MS63 | MS65 |
|---|---|---|---|---|---|---|
| 2008 | 2,500 | PF65 60.00 | | | | |

**KM# 171 5 DOLLARS**
25.00 g., 0.925 Silver 0.7435 oz. ASW, 37.2 mm. **Subject:** Pacific Wildlife **Obv:** Shield **Rev:** Multicolor hologram, butterfly

| Date | Mintage | VF20 | XF40 | MS60 | MS63 | MS65 |
|---|---|---|---|---|---|---|
| 2008 | 2,500 | PF65 60.00 | | | | |

**KM# 172 5 DOLLARS**
25.00 g., 0.925 Silver 0.7435 oz. ASW, 38.6 mm. **Subject:** Telescope, 400th Anniversary **Obv:** Shield **Rev:** Hans Lippersheg, lens insert

| Date | Mintage | VF20 | XF40 | MS60 | MS63 | MS65 |
|---|---|---|---|---|---|---|
| 2008 Matte finish | 1,608 | — | — | — | — | 70.00 |

**KM# 173 5 DOLLARS**
25.00 g., 0.925 Silver 0.7435 oz. ASW, 38.6 mm. **Subject:** Telescope, 400th Anniversary **Obv:** Shield **Rev:** The Hubble Telescope, lens insert

| Date | Mintage | VF20 | XF40 | MS60 | MS63 | MS65 |
|---|---|---|---|---|---|---|
| 2008 Matte finish | 1,608 | — | — | — | — | 70.00 |

**KM# 174 5 DOLLARS**
Copper-Nickel, 38.6 mm. **Subject:** Endangered Wildlife **Obv:** Shield **Rev:** Multicolor yellow fish

| Date | Mintage | VF20 | XF40 | MS60 | MS63 | MS65 |
|---|---|---|---|---|---|---|
| 2008 Proof | — | — | — | — | — | 25.00 |

**KM# 175 5 DOLLARS**
25.00 g., 0.925 Silver 0.7435 oz. ASW, 38.6 mm. **Subject:** Everything for you **Obv:** Shield **Rev:** Multicolor, outstretched hand, ribbon above **Shape:** Heart

| Date | Mintage | VF20 | XF40 | MS60 | MS63 | MS65 |
|---|---|---|---|---|---|---|
| 2008 | 2,500 | PF65 100 | | | | |

**KM# 192 5 DOLLARS**
25.00 g., 0.925 Silver 0.7435 oz. ASW partially gilt, 30x45 mm. **Subject:** Illusion Autum Leaves **Rev:** Gilt leaf **Shape:** Oval

| Date | Mintage | VF20 | XF40 | MS60 | MS63 | MS65 |
|---|---|---|---|---|---|---|
| 2008 | 2,500 | PF65 75.00 | | | | |

**KM# 447 5 DOLLARS**
25.00 g., 0.925 Silver 0.7435 oz. ASW, 38.61 mm. **Subject:** 2008 Summer Olympics **Obv:** National arms **Rev:** Kyacker paddeling right

| Date | Mintage | VF20 | XF40 | MS60 | MS63 | MS65 |
|---|---|---|---|---|---|---|
| 2008 | — | PF65 75.00 | | | | |

**KM# 179 5 DOLLARS**
25.00 g., 0.925 Silver 0.7435 oz. ASW, 38.61 mm. **Subject:** Scent of Paradise **Obv:** Shield **Rev:** Multicolor open coconut, scented

| Date | Mintage | VF20 | XF40 | MS60 | MS63 | MS65 |
|---|---|---|---|---|---|---|
| 2009 | 2,500 | — | — | — | — | 65.00 |

**KM# 180 5 DOLLARS**
25.00 g., 0.925 Silver 0.7435 oz. ASW, 38.5 mm. **Subject:** Jewels of the Sea **Obv:** Shield **Rev:** Multicolor blue oyster with inset pearl

| Date | Mintage | VF20 | XF40 | MS60 | MS63 | MS65 |
|---|---|---|---|---|---|---|
| 2009 | 2,500 | PF65 150 | | | | |

**KM# 181 5 DOLLARS**
25.00 g., 0.925 Silver 0.7435 oz. ASW, 38.5 mm. **Subject:** Louis Braille, 200th Anniversary of Birth **Obv:** Shield **Rev:** Portrait of Braile

| Date | Mintage | VF20 | XF40 | MS60 | MS63 | MS65 |
|---|---|---|---|---|---|---|
| 2009 Matte finish | 2,500 | — | — | — | — | 45.00 |

**KM# 182 5 DOLLARS**
25.00 g., 0.925 Silver 0.7435 oz. ASW **Subject:** Missing you **Obv:** Shield **Rev:** Two angels, multicolor, crystal insert **Shape:** Heart

| Date | Mintage | VF20 | XF40 | MS60 | MS63 | MS65 |
|---|---|---|---|---|---|---|
| 2009 | 2,500 | PF65 55.00 | | | | |

**KM# 196 5 DOLLARS**
25.00 g., 0.925 Silver 0.7435 oz. ASW, 38.61 mm. **Subject:** Pacific Wildlife **Rev:** Angelfish

| Date | Mintage | VF20 | XF40 | MS60 | MS63 | MS65 |
|---|---|---|---|---|---|---|
| 2009 | 2,500 | PF65 60.00 | | | | |

**KM# 197 5 DOLLARS**
25.00 g., 0.925 Silver 0.7435 oz. ASW, 38.61 mm. **Subject:** Pacific Wildlife **Rev:** Barn Swallow

| Date | Mintage | VF20 | XF40 | MS60 | MS63 | MS65 |
|---|---|---|---|---|---|---|
| 2009 | 2,500 | PF65 60.00 | | | | |

**KM# 198 5 DOLLARS**
25.00 g., 0.925 Silver 0.7435 oz. ASW, 38.61 mm. **Subject:** Pacific Wildlife **Rev:** Gecko

| Date | Mintage | VF20 | XF40 | MS60 | MS63 | MS65 |
|---|---|---|---|---|---|---|
| 2009 | 2,500 | PF65 60.00 | | | | |

**KM# 199 5 DOLLARS**
25.00 g., 0.925 Silver 0.7435 oz. ASW, 38.61 mm. **Subject:** Exceptional Animals **Rev:** Bird of Paradise

| Date | Mintage | VF20 | XF40 | MS60 | MS63 | MS65 |
|---|---|---|---|---|---|---|
| 2009 | 2,500 | **PF65** 55.00 | | | | |

**KM# 200 5 DOLLARS**
25.00 g., 0.925 Silver 0.7435 oz. ASW, 38.61 mm. **Subject:** Exceptional Animals **Rev:** Peacock

| Date | Mintage | VF20 | XF40 | MS60 | MS63 | MS65 |
|---|---|---|---|---|---|---|
| 2009 | 2,500 | **PF65** 55.00 | | | | |

**KM# 201 5 DOLLARS**
25.00 g., 0.925 Silver 0.7435 oz. ASW, 38.61 mm. **Subject:** Marine Life Protection **Rev:** Lionfish

| Date | Mintage | VF20 | XF40 | MS60 | MS63 | MS65 |
|---|---|---|---|---|---|---|
| 2009 | 1,500 | **PF65** 65.00 | | | | |

**KM# 202 5 DOLLARS**
25.00 g., 0.999 Silver 0.803 oz. ASW, 38.61 mm. **Subject:** Fall of the Berlin Wall **Rev:** Brandenburg Gate, half with and half without wall

| Date | Mintage | VF20 | XF40 | MS60 | MS63 | MS65 |
|---|---|---|---|---|---|---|
| 2009 | 2,009 | **PF65** 110 | | | | |

**KM# 203 5 DOLLARS**
20.00 g., 0.925 Silver 0.5948 oz. ASW, 38.61 mm. **Rev:** Sail training vessel Pamir

| Date | Mintage | VF20 | XF40 | MS60 | MS63 | MS65 |
|---|---|---|---|---|---|---|
| 2009 | 2,500 | **PF65** 65.00 | | | | |

**KM# 204 5 DOLLARS**
25.00 g., 0.925 Silver 0.7435 oz. ASW, 38.61 mm. **Subject:** Wonders of the Ancient World **Rev:** Lighthouse at Alexandria

| Date | Mintage | VF20 | XF40 | MS60 | MS63 | MS65 |
|---|---|---|---|---|---|---|
| 2009 | 2,500 | **PF65** 80.00 | | | | |

**KM# 205 5 DOLLARS**
25.00 g., 0.925 Silver 0.7435 oz. ASW **Subject:** Wonders of the Ancient World **Rev:** Statue of Zeus

| Date | Mintage | VF20 | XF40 | MS60 | MS63 | MS65 |
|---|---|---|---|---|---|---|
| 2009 | 2,500 | **PF65** 80.00 | | | | |

**KM# 206 5 DOLLARS**
25.00 g., 0.925 Silver 0.7435 oz. ASW, 38.61 mm. **Subject:** Wonders of the Ancient World **Rev:** Hanging Gardens of Babylon

| Date | Mintage | VF20 | XF40 | MS60 | MS63 | MS65 |
|---|---|---|---|---|---|---|
| 2009 | 2,500 | **PF65** 80.00 | | | | |

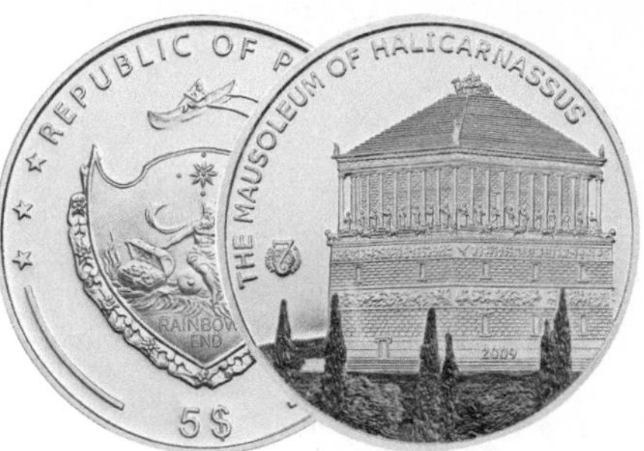


**KM# 207 5 DOLLARS**
25.00 g., 0.925 Silver 0.7435 oz. ASW, 38.61 mm. **Subject:** Wonders of the Ancient World **Rev:** Mausoleum of Halicarnassus

| Date | Mintage | VF20 | XF40 | MS60 | MS63 | MS65 |
|---|---|---|---|---|---|---|
| 2009 | 2,500 | **PF65** 80.00 | | | | |

**KM# 208 5 DOLLARS**
25.00 g., 0.925 Silver 0.7435 oz. ASW, 38.61 mm. **Subject:** Wonders of the Ancient World **Rev:** Pyramids of Giza

| Date | Mintage | VF20 | XF40 | MS60 | MS63 | MS65 |
|---|---|---|---|---|---|---|
| 2009 | 2,500 | **PF65** 80.00 | | | | |

**KM# 209 5 DOLLARS**
25.00 g., 0.925 Silver 0.7435 oz. ASW, 38.61 mm. **Subject:** Wonders of the Ancient World **Rev:** Temple of Artemis

| Date | Mintage | VF20 | XF40 | MS60 | MS63 | MS65 |
|---|---|---|---|---|---|---|
| 2009 | 2,500 | **PF65** 80.00 | | | | |

**KM# 210 5 DOLLARS**
25.00 g., 0.925 Silver 0.7435 oz. ASW, 38.61 mm. **Subject:** Wonders of the Ancient World **Rev:** Colossus of Rhodes

| Date | Mintage | VF20 | XF40 | MS60 | MS63 | MS65 |
|---|---|---|---|---|---|---|
| 2009 | 2,500 | **PF65** 80.00 | | | | |

**KM# 211 5 DOLLARS**
25.00 g., 0.925 Silver 0.7435 oz. ASW, 38.6 mm. **Subject:** Flora and Mountains of the Alps **Rev:** Zugspitze and blue flower

| Date | Mintage | VF20 | XF40 | MS60 | MS63 | MS65 |
|---|---|---|---|---|---|---|
| 2009 | 2,500 | **PF65** 60.00 | | | | |

**KM# 212 5 DOLLARS**
25.00 g., 0.925 Silver 0.7435 oz. ASW, 38.61 mm. **Subject:** Flora and Mountains of the Alps **Rev:** Grossglockner and white flower

| Date | Mintage | VF20 | XF40 | MS60 | MS63 | MS65 |
|---|---|---|---|---|---|---|
| 2009 | 2,500 | **PF65** 60.00 | | | | |

**KM# 213 5 DOLLARS**
25.00 g., 0.925 Silver 0.7435 oz. ASW, 38.61 mm. **Subject:** Flora and Mountains of the Alps **Rev:** Matterhorn and pink flower

| Date | Mintage | VF20 | XF40 | MS60 | MS63 | MS65 |
|---|---|---|---|---|---|---|
| 2009 | 2,500 | **PF65** 60.00 | | | | |

**KM# 214 5 DOLLARS**
25.00 g., 0.925 Silver 0.7435 oz. ASW, 38.61 mm. **Subject:** Flora and Mountains of the Alps **Rev:** Dachstein and purple flower

| Date | Mintage | VF20 | XF40 | MS60 | MS63 | MS65 |
|---|---|---|---|---|---|---|
| 2009 | 2,500 | **PF65** 60.00 | | | | |

**KM# 215 5 DOLLARS**
25.00 g., 0.925 Silver 0.7435 oz. ASW, 38.61 mm. **Subject:** Flora and Mountains of the Alps **Rev:** Mont Blanc and orange flower

| Date | Mintage | VF20 | XF40 | MS60 | MS63 | MS65 |
|---|---|---|---|---|---|---|
| 2009 | 2,500 | **PF65** 60.00 | | | | |

**KM# 216 5 DOLLARS**
25.00 g., 0.925 Silver 0.7435 oz. ASW, 38.61 mm. **Subject:** Flora and Mountains of the Alps **Rev:** Watzmann and purple flower

| Date | Mintage | VF20 | XF40 | MS60 | MS63 | MS65 |
|---|---|---|---|---|---|---|
| 2009 | 2,500 | **PF65** 60.00 | | | | |

**KM# 217 5 DOLLARS**
25.00 g., 0.925 Silver 0.7435 oz. ASW, 38.61 mm. **Subject:** Flora and Mountains of the Alps **Rev:** Oetscher and yellow flower

| Date | Mintage | VF20 | XF40 | MS60 | MS63 | MS65 |
|---|---|---|---|---|---|---|
| 2009 | 2,500 | **PF65** 60.00 | | | | |

**KM# 218 5 DOLLARS**
25.00 g., 0.925 Silver 0.7435 oz. ASW, 38.61 mm. **Subject:** Flora and Mountains of the Alps **Rev:** Piz Buin and pink flower

| Date | Mintage | VF20 | XF40 | MS60 | MS63 | MS65 |
|---|---|---|---|---|---|---|
| 2009 | 2,500 | **PF65** 60.00 | | | | |

**KM# 242 5 DOLLARS**
20.00 g., 0.925 Silver 0.5948 oz. ASW, 38.6 mm. **Subject:** Finnish icebreaker Tarmo **Rev:** Ship left in ice pack

| Date | Mintage | VF20 | XF40 | MS60 | MS63 | MS65 |
|---|---|---|---|---|---|---|
| 2009 | 2,500 | **PF65** 60.00 | | | | |

**KM# 264 5 DOLLARS**
25.00 g., 0.925 Silver 0.7435 oz. ASW, 38.61 mm. **Subject:** Treasures of the World - Emeralds **Rev:** Mule mine cart and emerald insert

| Date | Mintage | VF20 | XF40 | MS60 | MS63 | MS65 |
|---|---|---|---|---|---|---|
| 2009 Antique | 2,000 | **PF65** 85.00 | | | | |

**KM# 265 5 DOLLARS**
25.00 g., 0.925 Silver 0.7435 oz. ASW, 38.6 mm. **Obv:** Arms **Rev:** Our Lady of the Gate of Dawn, partially gilt

| Date | Mintage | VF20 | XF40 | MS60 | MS63 | MS65 |
|---|---|---|---|---|---|---|
| 2009 | 1,000 | **PF65** 75.00 | | | | |

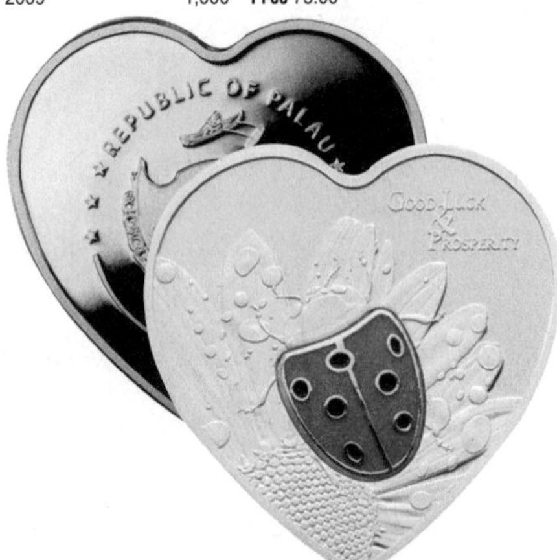

**KM# 432 5 DOLLARS**
25.00 g., 0.925 Silver 0.7435 oz. ASW, 45x45 mm. **Obv:** National arms **Rev:** Ladybug in color on flora **Rev. Legend:** Good Luck & Prosperity **Shape:** Heart

| Date | Mintage | VF20 | XF40 | MS60 | MS63 | MS65 |
|---|---|---|---|---|---|---|
| 2009 | 2,500 | **PF65** 65.00 | | | | |

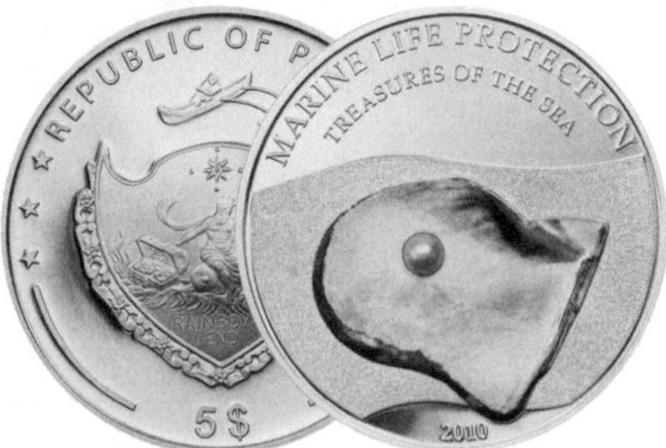

**KM# 248 5 DOLLARS**
25.00 g., 0.925 Silver 0.7435 oz. ASW, 38.6 mm. **Subject:** Marine Life Protection **Rev:** Blue freshwater pearl set within multicolor shell

| Date | Mintage | VF20 | XF40 | MS60 | MS63 | MS65 |
|---|---|---|---|---|---|---|
| 2010 | 2,500 | **PF65** 85.00 | | | | |

**KM# 249 5 DOLLARS**
25.00 g., 0.925 Silver 0.7435 oz. ASW, 38.6 mm. **Subject:** Scent of Paradise - Sea breeze fragrance **Rev:** Female surfboarder in multicolor wave

| Date | Mintage | VF20 | XF40 | MS60 | MS63 | MS65 |
|---|---|---|---|---|---|---|
| 2010 | 2,500 | — | — | — | — | 65.00 |

**KM# 289 5 DOLLARS**
25.00 g., 0.925 Silver 0.7435 oz. ASW, 38.61 mm. **Obv:** National arms **Rev:** St. Basil's Cathedral in color

| Date | Mintage | VF20 | XF40 | MS60 | MS63 | MS65 |
|---|---|---|---|---|---|---|
| 2010 | 2,500 | **PF65** 60.00 | | | | |

**KM# 290 5 DOLLARS**
25.00 g., 0.925 Silver 0.7435 oz. ASW, 38.61 mm. **Obv:** National arms **Rev:** Statue of Liberty in color

| Date | Mintage | VF20 | XF40 | MS60 | MS63 | MS65 |
|---|---|---|---|---|---|---|
| 2010 | 2,500 | **PF65** 60.00 | | | | |

**KM# 291 5 DOLLARS**
25.00 g., 0.925 Silver 0.7435 oz. ASW, 38.61 mm. **Obv:** National arms **Rev:** Kiyomizu Temple in color

| Date | Mintage | VF20 | XF40 | MS60 | MS63 | MS65 |
|---|---|---|---|---|---|---|
| 2010 | 2,500 | **PF65** 60.00 | | | | |

**KM# 292 5 DOLLARS**
25.00 g., 0.925 Silver 0.7435 oz. ASW, 38.61 mm. **Obv:** National arms **Rev:** Neuschwanstein Castle in color

| Date | Mintage | VF20 | XF40 | MS60 | MS63 | MS65 |
|---|---|---|---|---|---|---|
| 2010 | 2,500 | **PF65** 60.00 | | | | |

**KM# 293 5 DOLLARS**
25.00 g., 0.925 Silver 0.7435 oz. ASW, 38.61 mm. **Obv:** National arms **Rev:** Mt. Everest and Meconopsis betonicifolia in color

| Date | Mintage | VF20 | XF40 | MS60 | MS63 | MS65 |
|---|---|---|---|---|---|---|
| 2010 | 250 | **PF65** 60.00 | | | | |

**KM# 294 5 DOLLARS**
25.00 g., 0.925 Silver 0.7435 oz. ASW, 38.61 mm. **Obv:** National arms **Rev:** Mt. Kilimanjaro and Protea kilimandscharica in color

| Date | Mintage | VF20 | XF40 | MS60 | MS63 | MS65 |
|---|---|---|---|---|---|---|
| 2010 | 2,500 | **PF65** 60.00 | | | | |

**KM# 295 5 DOLLARS**
25.00 g., 0.925 Silver 0.7435 oz. ASW, 38.61 mm. **Obv:** National arms **Rev:** Mt. Elbrus and Rhododendron in color

| Date | Mintage | VF20 | XF40 | MS60 | MS63 | MS65 |
|---|---|---|---|---|---|---|
| 2010 | 2,500 | **PF65** 60.00 | | | | |

**KM# 296 5 DOLLARS**
25.00 g., 0.925 Silver 0.7435 oz. ASW, 38.61 mm. **Obv:** National arms **Rev:** Carstensz Pyramid and Orchidacae in color

| Date | Mintage | VF20 | XF40 | MS60 | MS63 | MS65 |
|---|---|---|---|---|---|---|
| 2010 | 2,500 | **PF65** 60.00 | | | | |

**KM# 297 5 DOLLARS**
25.00 g., 0.925 Silver 0.7435 oz. ASW, 38.61 mm. **Obv:** National arms **Rev:** Mount McKinley and Anaphalis margaritacea in color

| Date | Mintage | VF20 | XF40 | MS60 | MS63 | MS65 |
|---|---|---|---|---|---|---|
| 2010 | 2,500 | **PF65** 60.00 | | | | |

**KM# 298 5 DOLLARS**
25.00 g., 0.925 Silver 0.7435 oz. ASW, 38.61 mm. **Obv:** National arms **Rev:** Mt. Aconcagua and Aechmea distichantha in color

| Date | Mintage | VF20 | XF40 | MS60 | MS63 | MS65 |
|---|---|---|---|---|---|---|
| 2010 | 2,500 | **PF65** 60.00 | | | | |

**KM# 299 5 DOLLARS**
25.00 g., 0.925 Silver 0.7435 oz. ASW, 38.61 mm. **Obv:** National arms **Rev:** Mt. Vinson and Colobanthus quitensis in color

| Date | Mintage | VF20 | XF40 | MS60 | MS63 | MS65 |
|---|---|---|---|---|---|---|
| 2010 | 2,500 | **PF65** 60.00 | | | | |

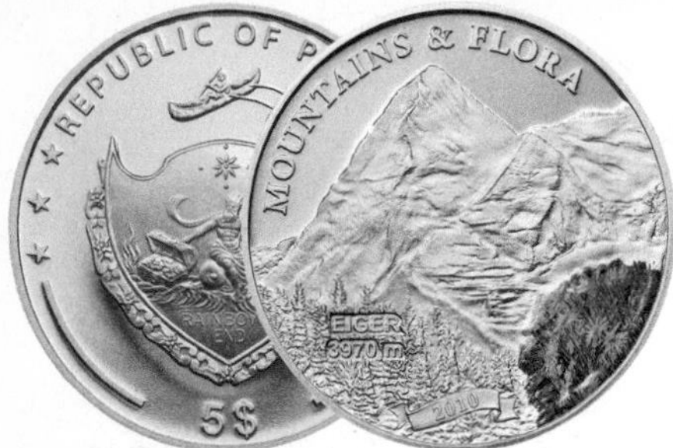


**KM# 300 5 DOLLARS**
25.00 g., 0.925 Silver 0.7435 oz. ASW, 38.61 mm. **Obv:** National arms **Rev:** Mt. Elger and Arnica montana in color

| Date | Mintage | VF20 | XF40 | MS60 | MS63 | MS65 |
|---|---|---|---|---|---|---|
| 2010 | 2,500 | **PF65** 60.00 | | | | |

**KM# 301 5 DOLLARS**
25.00 g., 0.925 Silver 0.7435 oz. ASW, 38.61 mm. **Obv:** National arms **Rev:** Ayers Rock and Calytrix longiflora in color

| Date | Mintage | VF20 | XF40 | MS60 | MS63 | MS65 |
|---|---|---|---|---|---|---|
| 2010 | 2,500 | **PF65** 60.00 | | | | |

**KM# 302 5 DOLLARS**
25.00 g., 0.925 Silver 0.7435 oz. ASW, 38.61 mm. **Obv:** National arms **Rev:** Mt. Alpspitze and Campanula alpina in color

| Date | Mintage | VF20 | XF40 | MS60 | MS63 | MS65 |
|---|---|---|---|---|---|---|
| 2010 | 2,500 | **PF65** 60.00 | | | | |

**KM# 306 5 DOLLARS**
25.00 g., 0.925 Silver 0.7435 oz. ASW, 38.61 mm. **Obv:** Naitonal arms **Rev:** Christmas star above winter home scene in color

| Date | Mintage | VF20 | XF40 | MS60 | MS63 | MS65 |
|---|---|---|---|---|---|---|
| 2010 | 2,500 | **PF65** 60.00 | | | | |

**KM# 314 5 DOLLARS**
25.00 g., 0.925 Silver 0.7435 oz. ASW, 38.61 mm. **Obv:** National arms **Rev:** Hammerhead shark in color image

| Date | Mintage | VF20 | XF40 | MS60 | MS63 | MS65 |
|---|---|---|---|---|---|---|
| 2010 | 1,500 | **PF65** 70.00 | | | | |

**KM# 379 5 DOLLARS**
25.00 g., 0.925 Silver 0.7435 oz. ASW, 38.61 mm. **Obv:** National arms **Rev:** Acropolis in color

| Date | Mintage | VF20 | XF40 | MS60 | MS63 | MS65 |
|---|---|---|---|---|---|---|
| 2010 | 2,500 | **PF65** 50.00 | | | | |

**KM# 388 5 DOLLARS**
25.00 g., 0.925 Silver 0.7435 oz. ASW **Obv:** National arms **Rev:** Angkor Wat in color **Shape:** 38.61

| Date | Mintage | VF20 | XF40 | MS60 | MS63 | MS65 |
|---|---|---|---|---|---|---|
| 2010 | 2,500 | **PF65** 50.00 | | | | |

**KM# 389 5 DOLLARS**
25.00 g., 0.925 Silver 0.7435 oz. ASW, 38.61 mm. **Obv:** National arms **Rev:** Statues of Easter Island in color

| Date | Mintage | VF20 | XF40 | MS60 | MS63 | MS65 |
|---|---|---|---|---|---|---|
| 2010 | 2,500 | **PF65** 50.00 | | | | |

**KM# 390 5 DOLLARS**
25.00 g., 0.925 Silver 0.7435 oz. ASW, 38.61 mm. **Obv:** National arms **Rev:** Eiffel Tower in color

| Date | Mintage | VF20 | XF40 | MS60 | MS63 | MS65 |
|---|---|---|---|---|---|---|
| 2010 | 2,500 | **PF65** 50.00 | | | | |

**KM# 430 5 DOLLARS**
25.00 g., 0.925 Silver 0.7435 oz. ASW, 38.61 mm. **Obv:** National arms **Rev:** Gem engraver cutting saphire on wheel

| Date | Mintage | VF20 | XF40 | MS60 | MS63 | MS65 |
|---|---|---|---|---|---|---|
| 2010 Antique patina | 2,000 | — | — | — | — | 200 |

**KM# 446 5 DOLLARS**
25.00 g., 0.925 Silver 0.7435 oz. ASW, 38.61 mm. **Subject:** Mother Theresa of Calcutta, 100th Anniversary of Birth **Obv:** National arms **Rev:** Mother Theresa at left, blue color design of Sister's of Charity order habbit in field

| Date | Mintage | VF20 | XF40 | MS60 | MS63 | MS65 |
|---|---|---|---|---|---|---|
| 2010 | — | **PF65** 80.00 | | | | |

**KM# 364 5 DOLLARS**
25.00 g., 0.999 Silver 0.803 oz. ASW **Subject:** Treasures of the World **Rev:** Mine scene, ruby insert

| Date | Mintage | VF20 | XF40 | MS60 | MS63 | MS65 |
|---|---|---|---|---|---|---|
| 2011 Antique patina | 2,000 | — | — | — | — | 200 |

**KM# 365 5 DOLLARS**
25.00 g., 0.925 Silver 0.7435 oz. ASW, 38.61 mm. **Subject:** Cuddley Bear **Rev:** Teddy bear patch

| Date | Mintage | VF20 | XF40 | MS60 | MS63 | MS65 |
|---|---|---|---|---|---|---|
| 2011 | — | **PF65** 75.00 | | | | |

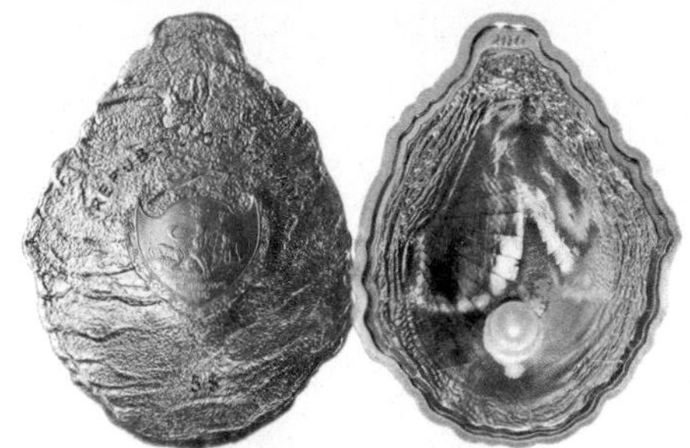

**KM# 374 5 DOLLARS**
25.00 g., 0.999 Silver 0.803 oz. ASW, 30x38 mm. **Subject:** Oyster shell and pearl inset **Shape:** Irregular

| Date | Mintage | VF20 | XF40 | MS60 | MS63 | MS65 |
|---|---|---|---|---|---|---|
| 2011 | 2,000 | — | — | — | — | 450 |

**KM# 376 5 DOLLARS**
25.00 g., 0.925 Silver 0.7435 oz. ASW, 38.61 mm. **Obv:** National arms **Rev:** Potala Palace in color

| Date | Mintage | VF20 | XF40 | MS60 | MS63 | MS65 |
|---|---|---|---|---|---|---|
| 2011 | 2,500 | **PF65** 50.00 | | | | |

**KM# 377 5 DOLLARS**
25.00 g., 0.925 Silver 0.7435 oz. ASW, 38.61 mm. **Obv:** National arms **Rev:** Tower Bridge in color

| Date | Mintage | VF20 | XF40 | MS60 | MS63 | MS65 |
|---|---|---|---|---|---|---|
| 2011 | 2,500 | **PF65** 50.00 | | | | |

**KM# 378 5 DOLLARS**
25.00 g., 0.925 Silver 0.7435 oz. ASW, 38.61 mm. **Obv:** National arms **Rev:** Temple of Heaven in color

| Date | Mintage | VF20 | XF40 | MS60 | MS63 | MS65 |
|---|---|---|---|---|---|---|
| 2011 | 2,500 | **PF65** 50.00 | | | | |

**KM# 380 5 DOLLARS**
25.00 g., 0.925 Silver 0.7435 oz. ASW, 38.61 mm. **Obv:** National arms **Rev:** Stonehenge in color

| Date | Mintage | VF20 | XF40 | MS60 | MS63 | MS65 |
|---|---|---|---|---|---|---|
| 2011 | 2,500 | **PF65** 50.00 | | | | |

**KM# 381 5 DOLLARS**
25.00 g., 0.925 Silver 0.7435 oz. ASW, 38.61 mm. **Obv:** National arms **Rev:** Schonebrunn Palace in color

| Date | Mintage | VF20 | XF40 | MS60 | MS63 | MS65 |
|---|---|---|---|---|---|---|
| 2011 | 2,500 | **PF65** 50.00 | | | | |

**KM# 382 5 DOLLARS**
25.00 g., 0.925 Silver 0.7435 oz. ASW, 38.61 mm. **Obv:** National arms **Rev:** Chapel Bridge in color

| Date | Mintage | VF20 | XF40 | MS60 | MS63 | MS65 |
|---|---|---|---|---|---|---|
| 2011 | 2,500 | **PF65** 50.00 | | | | |

**KM# 383 5 DOLLARS**
25.00 g., 0.925 Silver 0.7435 oz. ASW, 38.61 mm. **Obv:** National arms **Rev:** Florence Cathedral

| Date | Mintage | VF20 | XF40 | MS60 | MS63 | MS65 |
|---|---|---|---|---|---|---|
| 2011 | 2,500 | **PF65** 50.00 | | | | |

**KM# 384 5 DOLLARS**
25.00 g., 0.925 Silver 0.7435 oz. ASW, 38.61 mm. **Obv:** National arms **Rev:** CN Tower in color

| Date | Mintage | VF20 | XF40 | MS60 | MS63 | MS65 |
|---|---|---|---|---|---|---|
| 2011 | 2,500 | **PF65** 50.00 | | | | |

**KM# 385 5 DOLLARS**
25.00 g., 0.925 Silver 0.7435 oz. ASW, 38.61 mm. **Obv:** National arms **Rev:** Timbuktu in color

| Date | Mintage | VF20 | XF40 | MS60 | MS63 | MS65 |
|---|---|---|---|---|---|---|
| 2011 | 2,500 | **PF65** 50.00 | | | | |

**KM# 386 5 DOLLARS**
25.00 g., 0.925 Silver 0.7435 oz. ASW, 38.61 mm. **Obv:** National arms **Rev:** Leaning Tower of Pisa in color

| Date | Mintage | VF20 | XF40 | MS60 | MS63 | MS65 |
|---|---|---|---|---|---|---|
| 2011 | 2,500 | **PF65** 50.00 | | | | |

**KM# 387 5 DOLLARS**
25.00 g., 0.925 Silver 0.7435 oz. ASW, 38.61 mm. **Obv:** National arms **Rev:** Sydney Opera House in color

| Date | Mintage | VF20 | XF40 | MS60 | MS63 | MS65 |
|---|---|---|---|---|---|---|
| 2011 | 2,500 | **PF65** 50.00 | | | | |

**KM# 391 5 DOLLARS**
25.00 g., 0.925 Silver 0.7435 oz. ASW, 38.61 mm. **Obv:** National arms **Rev:** Mount Rushmore in color

| Date | Mintage | VF20 | XF40 | MS60 | MS63 | MS65 |
|---|---|---|---|---|---|---|
| 2011 | 2,500 | **PF65** 50.00 | | | | |

**KM# 392 5 DOLLARS**
25.00 g., 0.925 Silver 0.7435 oz. ASW, 38.61 mm. **Obv:** National arms **Rev:** Persepolis - Shiraz in color

| Date | Mintage | VF20 | XF40 | MS60 | MS63 | MS65 |
|---|---|---|---|---|---|---|
| 2011 | 2,500 | **PF65** 50.00 | | | | |

**KM# 393 5 DOLLARS**
25.00 g., 0.925 Silver 0.7435 oz. ASW, 38.61 mm. **Obv:** National arms **Rev:** Alhambra in color

| Date | Mintage | VF20 | XF40 | MS60 | MS63 | MS65 |
|---|---|---|---|---|---|---|
| 2011 | 2,500 | **PF65** 50.00 | | | | |

**KM# 397 5 DOLLARS**
25.00 g., 0.925 Silver 0.7435 oz. ASW, 38.61 mm. **Obv:** National arms **Rev:** K-2 and flora in color

| Date | Mintage | VF20 | XF40 | MS60 | MS63 | MS65 |
|---|---|---|---|---|---|---|
| 2011 | 2,500 | **PF65** 60.00 | | | | |

**KM# 398 5 DOLLARS**
25.00 g., 0.925 Silver 0.7435 oz. ASW, 38.61 mm. **Obv:** National arms **Rev:** Mount Kenya and flora in color

| Date | Mintage | VF20 | XF40 | MS60 | MS63 | MS65 |
|---|---|---|---|---|---|---|
| 2011 | 2,500 | **PF65** 60.00 | | | | |

**KM# 399 5 DOLLARS**
25.00 g., 0.925 Silver 0.7435 oz. ASW, 38.61 mm. **Obv:** National arms **Rev:** Mount Logan and flora in color

| Date | Mintage | VF20 | XF40 | MS60 | MS63 | MS65 |
|---|---|---|---|---|---|---|
| 2011 | 2,500 | **PF65** 60.00 | | | | |

**KM# 400 5 DOLLARS**
25.00 g., 0.925 Silver 0.7435 oz. ASW, 38.61 mm. **Obv:** National arms **Rev:** Mount Tyree and flora in color

| Date | Mintage | VF20 | XF40 | MS60 | MS63 | MS65 |
|---|---|---|---|---|---|---|
| 2011 | 2,500 | **PF65** 60.00 | | | | |

**KM# 401 5 DOLLARS**
25.00 g., 0.925 Silver 0.7435 oz. ASW, 38.61 mm. **Obv:** National Arms **Rev:** Dyke-Tau and flora in color

| Date | Mintage | VF20 | XF40 | MS60 | MS63 | MS65 |
|---|---|---|---|---|---|---|
| 2011 | 2,500 | **PF65** 60.00 | | | | |

**KM# 402 5 DOLLARS**
25.00 g., 0.925 Silver 0.7435 oz. ASW, 38.61 mm. **Obv:** National arms **Rev:** Ojos del Salado and flora in color

| Date | Mintage | VF20 | XF40 | MS60 | MS63 | MS65 |
|---|---|---|---|---|---|---|
| 2011 | 2,500 | **PF65** 60.00 | | | | |

**KM# 403 5 DOLLARS**
25.00 g., 0.925 Silver 0.7435 oz. ASW, 38.61 mm. **Obv:** National arms **Rev:** Puncak Trikora and flora in color

| Date | Mintage | VF20 | XF40 | MS60 | MS63 | MS65 |
|---|---|---|---|---|---|---|
| 2011 | 2,500 | **PF65** 60.00 | | | | |

**KM# 404 5 DOLLARS**
25.00 g., 0.925 Silver 0.7435 oz. ASW, 38.61 mm. **Subject:** Scent of Paradise **Obv:** National arms **Rev:** Large insence burner in color

| Date | Mintage | VF20 | XF40 | MS60 | MS63 | MS65 |
|---|---|---|---|---|---|---|
| 2011 | — | **PF65** 65.00 | | | | |

**KM# 434 5 DOLLARS**
Silver Plated Copper, 35x35 mm. **Obv:** National arms **Rev:** Ferrari FI 2000 in color

| Date | Mintage | VF20 | XF40 | MS60 | MS63 | MS65 |
|---|---|---|---|---|---|---|
| 2011 | — | **PF65** 40.00 | | | | |

**KM# 435 5 DOLLARS**
Silver Plated Copper, 35x35 mm. **Obv:** National arms **Rev:** Ferrari 500 F-2

| Date | Mintage | VF20 | XF40 | MS60 | MS63 | MS65 |
|---|---|---|---|---|---|---|
| 2011 | — | **PF65** 40.00 | | | | |

**KM# 436 5 DOLLARS**
Silver Plated Copper, 45x45 mm. **Obv:** National arms **Rev:** Ferrari F-2007

| Date | Mintage | VF20 | XF40 | MS60 | MS63 | MS65 |
|---|---|---|---|---|---|---|
| 2011 | — | **PF65** 40.00 | | | | |

**KM# 437 5 DOLLARS**
Silver Plated Copper, 35x35 mm. **Obv:** National arms **Rev:** Ferrari 158 F-1

| Date | Mintage | VF20 | XF40 | MS60 | MS63 | MS65 |
|---|---|---|---|---|---|---|
| 2011 | — | **PF65** 40.00 | | | | |

**KM# 438 5 DOLLARS**
Silver Plated Copper, 35x35 mm. **Obv:** National arms **Rev:** Ferrari 246 F-1

| Date | Mintage | VF20 | XF40 | MS60 | MS63 | MS65 |
|---|---|---|---|---|---|---|
| 2011 | — | **PF65** 40.00 | | | | |

**KM# 439 5 DOLLARS**
Silver Plated Copper, 35x35 mm. **Obv:** National arms **Rev:** Ferrari D-50

| Date | Mintage | VF20 | XF40 | MS60 | MS63 | MS65 |
|---|---|---|---|---|---|---|
| 2011 | — | **PF65** 40.00 | | | | |

**KM# 440 5 DOLLARS**
Silver Plated Copper, 35x35 mm. **Obv:** National arms **Rev:** Ferrari 126 C-2

| Date | Mintage | VF20 | XF40 | MS60 | MS63 | MS65 |
|---|---|---|---|---|---|---|
| 2011 | — | **PF65** 40.00 | | | | |

**KM# 441 5 DOLLARS**
Silver Plated Copper, 35x35 mm. **Obv:** National arms **Rev:** Ferrari 312 T

| Date | Mintage | VF20 | XF40 | MS60 | MS63 | MS65 |
|---|---|---|---|---|---|---|
| 2011 | — | **PF65** 40.00 | | | | |

**KM# 444 5 DOLLARS**
25.00 g., 0.925 Silver 0.7435 oz. ASW, 38.61 mm. **Obv:** National arms **Rev:** Pear in white clam shell

| Date | Mintage | VF20 | XF40 | MS60 | MS63 | MS65 |
|---|---|---|---|---|---|---|
| 2011 | — | **PF65** 125 | | | | |

**KM# 415 5 DOLLARS**
25.00 g., 0.925 Silver 0.7435 oz. ASW, 38.61 mm. **Obv:** National arms **Rev:** Brandenburg Gate in color

| Date | Mintage | VF20 | XF40 | MS60 | MS63 | MS65 |
|---|---|---|---|---|---|---|
| 2012 | 2,500 | **PF65** 80.00 | | | | |

**KM# 416 5 DOLLARS**
25.00 g., 0.925 Silver 0.7435 oz. ASW, 38.61 mm. **Obv:** National arms **Rev:** Itsukushima Shrine in color

| Date | Mintage | VF20 | XF40 | MS60 | MS63 | MS65 |
|---|---|---|---|---|---|---|
| 2012 | 2,500 | **PF65** 80.00 | | | | |

**KM# 417 5 DOLLARS**
25.00 g., 0.925 Silver 0.7435 oz. ASW, 38.61 mm. **Obv:** National arms **Rev:** Palmyra ruins in color

| Date | Mintage | VF20 | XF40 | MS60 | MS63 | MS65 |
|---|---|---|---|---|---|---|
| 2012 | 2,500 | **PF65** 80.00 | | | | |

**KM# 418 5 DOLLARS**
25.00 g., 0.925 Silver 0.7435 oz. ASW, 38.61 mm. **Obv:** National arms **Rev:** St. Patrick's Cathedral, Dublin in color

| Date | Mintage | VF20 | XF40 | MS60 | MS63 | MS65 |
|---|---|---|---|---|---|---|
| 2012 | 2,500 | **PF65** 80.00 | | | | |

**KM# 419 5 DOLLARS**
25.00 g., 0.925 Silver 0.7435 oz. ASW, 38.61 mm. **Obv:** National arms **Rev:** Hagia Sophia in color

| Date | Mintage | VF20 | XF40 | MS60 | MS63 | MS65 |
|---|---|---|---|---|---|---|
| 2012 | 2,500 | **PF65** 80.00 | | | | |

**KM# 420 5 DOLLARS**
25.00 g., 0.925 Silver 0.7435 oz. ASW, 38.61 mm. **Obv:** National arms **Rev:** Vienna Ferris Wheel in color

| Date | Mintage | VF20 | XF40 | MS60 | MS63 | MS65 |
|---|---|---|---|---|---|---|
| 2012 | 2,500 | **PF65** 80.00 | | | | |

**KM# 421 5 DOLLARS**
25.00 g., 0.925 Silver 0.7435 oz. ASW, 38.61 mm. **Obv:** National arms **Rev:** Teotihuacan in color

| Date | Mintage | VF20 | XF40 | MS60 | MS63 | MS65 |
|---|---|---|---|---|---|---|
| 2012 | 2,500 | **PF65** 80.00 | | | | |

### KM# 422 5 DOLLARS

25.00 g., 0.925 Silver 0.7435 oz. ASW, 38.61 mm. **Obv:** National arms **Rev:** Western Wall in color

| Date | Mintage | VF20 | XF40 | MS60 | MS63 | MS65 |
|---|---|---|---|---|---|---|
| 2012 | 2,500 | PF65 80.00 | | | | |

### KM# 425.1 5 DOLLARS

25.00 g., 0.925 Silver 0.7435 oz. ASW, 38.61 mm. **Obv:** National arms **Rev:** Four leaf clover, date at bottom flanked by three small clover on each side

| Date | Mintage | VF20 | XF40 | MS60 | MS63 | MS65 |
|---|---|---|---|---|---|---|
| 2012 | — | PF65 100 | | | | |

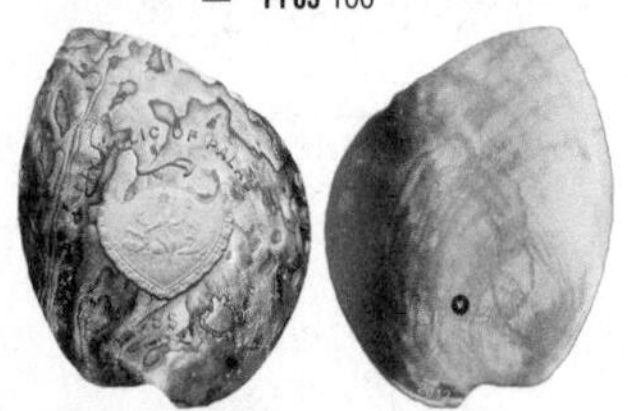

### KM# 427 5 DOLLARS

Silver, 20x30 mm. **Obv:** Haliotis oyster shell, National arms **Rev:** Oyster shell with pearl and multicolors **Shape:** Irregular

| Date | Mintage | VF20 | XF40 | MS60 | MS63 | MS65 |
|---|---|---|---|---|---|---|
| 2012 Matte finish | — | PF65 150 | | | | |

### KM# 466 5 DOLLARS

31.10 g., 0.999 Silver 0.999 oz. ASW, 38.6 mm. **Rev:** Red Squirrel, crystal insert

| Date | Mintage | VF20 | XF40 | MS60 | MS63 | MS65 |
|---|---|---|---|---|---|---|
| 2012 Antique Patina | 1,000 | PF65 100 | | | | |

### KM# 425.2 5 DOLLARS

25.00 g., 0.925 Silver 0.7435 oz. ASW, 38.61 mm. **Obv:** National arms **Rev:** Four leaf clover, date at bottom

| Date | Mintage | VF20 | XF40 | MS60 | MS63 | MS65 |
|---|---|---|---|---|---|---|
| 2013 | — | PF65 100 | | | | |

### KM# 462 5 DOLLARS

20.00 g., Silver, 38.61 mm. **Subject:** Seven Wonders of the World **Rev:** Lighthouse at Alexandria in color

| Date | Mintage | VF20 | XF40 | MS60 | MS63 | MS65 |
|---|---|---|---|---|---|---|
| 2013 | 2,500 | PF65 65.00 | | | | |

### KM# 463 5 DOLLARS

20.00 g., 0.925 Silver 0.5948 oz. ASW, 38.61 mm. **Subject:** Wonders of the World **Obv:** National arms **Rev:** Facade of St. Peter's Basilica in color

| Date | Mintage | VF20 | XF40 | MS60 | MS63 | MS65 |
|---|---|---|---|---|---|---|
| 2013 | Est. 2500 | PF65 75.00 | | | | |

### KM# 464 5 DOLLARS

20.00 g., 0.925 Silver 0.5948 oz. ASW, 38.61 mm. **Subject:** Seven Wonders of the World **Obv:** National arms **Rev:** Big Ben in color

| Date | Mintage | VF20 | XF40 | MS60 | MS63 | MS65 |
|---|---|---|---|---|---|---|
| 2013 | — | PF65 75.00 | | | | |

### KM# 473 5 DOLLARS

25.00 g., 0.925 Silver 0.7435 oz. ASW, 38.61 mm. **Subject:** Marine Life Protection - Pearl insert

| Date | Mintage | VF20 | XF40 | MS60 | MS63 | MS65 |
|---|---|---|---|---|---|---|
| 2014 | 2,500 | PF65 70.00 | | | | |

### KM# 191 10 DOLLARS

62.21 g., 0.999 Silver 1.9979 oz. ASW, 50 mm. **Subject:** Tiffany Art **Rev:** Renaissance doorway

| Date | Mintage | VF20 | XF40 | MS60 | MS63 | MS65 |
|---|---|---|---|---|---|---|
| 2007 Matte Proof | 999 | PF65 1,200 | | | | |

### KM# 193 10 DOLLARS

62.21 g., 0.999 Silver 1.9981 oz. ASW, 50 mm. **Subject:** Tiffany Art **Rev:** Mannerism, staircase design

| Date | Mintage | VF20 | XF40 | MS60 | MS63 | MS65 |
|---|---|---|---|---|---|---|
| 2008 Matte Proof | 999 | PF65 900 | | | | |

### KM# 194 10 DOLLARS

62.21 g., 0.999 Silver 1.9981 oz. ASW, 42x42 mm. **Subject:** WWII Battleships **Rev:** Japan's Yamato

| Date | Mintage | VF20 | XF40 | MS60 | MS63 | MS65 |
|---|---|---|---|---|---|---|
| 2008 | 1,000 | PF65 300 | | | | |

### KM# 195 10 DOLLARS

62.21 g., 0.999 Silver 1.9981 oz. ASW, 42x42 mm. **Subject:** WWII Battleships **Rev:** USS Missouri, gilt eagle above

| Date | Mintage | VF20 | XF40 | MS60 | MS63 | MS65 |
|---|---|---|---|---|---|---|
| 2008 | 1,000 | PF65 175 | | | | |

### KM# 184 10 DOLLARS

62.25 g., 0.999 Silver 1.9994 oz. ASW, 42x42 mm. **Subject:** WWII Battleships **Obv:** Shield **Rev:** Bismarck, gilt Iron Cross above **Shape:** Square

| Date | Mintage | VF20 | XF40 | MS60 | MS63 | MS65 |
|---|---|---|---|---|---|---|
| 2009 | — | PF65 165 | | | | |

**KM# 219 10 DOLLARS**
62.21 g., 0.999 Silver 1.9981 oz. ASW, 50 mm. **Subject:** Tiffany Art **Rev:** Baroque facade

| Date | Mintage | VF20 | XF40 | MS60 | MS63 | MS65 |
|---|---|---|---|---|---|---|
| 2009 Matte Proof | — | **PF65** 600 | | | | |

**KM# 220 10 DOLLARS**
62.21 g., 0.999 Silver 1.9981 oz. ASW, 50 mm. **Rev:** Amber insert

| Date | Mintage | VF20 | XF40 | MS60 | MS63 | MS65 |
|---|---|---|---|---|---|---|
| 2009 Matte Proof | 2,500 | **PF65** 400 | | | | |

**KM# 221 10 DOLLARS**
62.21 g., 0.999 Silver 1.9981 oz. ASW, 42x42 mm. **Subject:** WWII Battleship **Rev:** Britains's HMS Prince of Wales, gilt Union Jack above

| Date | Mintage | VF20 | XF40 | MS60 | MS63 | MS65 |
|---|---|---|---|---|---|---|
| 2009 | 1,000 | **PF65** 145 | | | | |

**KM# 250 10 DOLLARS**
62.20 g., 0.999 Silver 1.9978 oz. ASW, 42x42 mm. **Subject:** Russian Battleship Marat **Rev:** Battleship sailing left

| Date | Mintage | VF20 | XF40 | MS60 | MS63 | MS65 |
|---|---|---|---|---|---|---|
| 2010 | 1,000 | **PF65** 80.00 | | | | |

**KM# 252 10 DOLLARS**
64.21 g., 0.999 Silver 2.0623 oz. ASW, 50 mm. **Subject:** Tiffany Art - Rococo **Obv:** Arms at lower right, glass insert **Rev:** Cherus at left, glass insert

| Date | Mintage | VF20 | XF40 | MS60 | MS63 | MS65 |
|---|---|---|---|---|---|---|
| 2010 Antique | 999 | — | — | — | — | 650 |

**KM# 304 10 DOLLARS**
62.21 g., 0.925 Silver 1.8501 oz. ASW, 42x42 mm. **Obv:** National arms **Rev:** French Battleship Richelieu, gilt flag at top **Shape:** Square

| Date | Mintage | VF20 | XF40 | MS60 | MS63 | MS65 |
|---|---|---|---|---|---|---|
| 2010 | 1,000 | **PF65** 100 | | | | |

**KM# 320 10 DOLLARS**
62.20 g., 0.925 Silver 1.8498 oz. ASW, 55 mm. **Subject:** Sagrada Familia **Obv:** National arms **Rev:** Scenes from the Birth of Jesus, insert

| Date | Mintage | VF20 | XF40 | MS60 | MS63 | MS65 |
|---|---|---|---|---|---|---|
| 2010 | 2,500 | **PF65** 115 | | | | |

**KM# 318 10 DOLLARS**
62.21 g., 0.999 Silver 1.9981 oz. ASW, 50 mm. **Subject:** Tiffany Glass **Obv:** National arms **Rev:** Theater box, red glass insert

| Date | Mintage | VF20 | XF40 | MS60 | MS63 | MS65 |
|---|---|---|---|---|---|---|
| 2011 Antique patina | 999 | — | — | — | 175 | — |

**KM# 367 10 DOLLARS**
62.20 g., 0.999 Silver 1.9978 oz. ASW, 50 mm. **Subject:** Neuschwanstein Castle **Obv:** Exterior of Castle **Rev:** Interior of castle, insert

| Date | Mintage | VF20 | XF40 | MS60 | MS63 | MS65 |
|---|---|---|---|---|---|---|
| 2011 Antique finish | 2,500 | — | — | — | 375 | — |

**KM# 368 10 DOLLARS**
62.20 g., 0.999 Silver 1.9978 oz. ASW, 50 mm. **Subject:** Tiffany Art - Manueline **Rev:** Glass insert

| Date | Mintage | VF20 | XF40 | MS60 | MS63 | MS65 |
|---|---|---|---|---|---|---|
| 2011 Antique finish | 999 | — | — | — | 650 | — |

**KM# 369 10 DOLLARS**
62.20 g., 0.999 Silver 1.9978 oz. ASW partially gilt, 42x42 mm. **Rev:** Battleship H.M.A.S. Australia, gilt flag above **Shape:** Square

| Date | Mintage | VF20 | XF40 | MS60 | MS63 | MS65 |
|---|---|---|---|---|---|---|
| 2011 | — | **PF65** 150 | | | | |

**KM# 395 10 DOLLARS**
62.21 g., 0.999 Silver 1.9981 oz. ASW, 42x42 mm. **Obv:** National arms **Rev:** RN Vittorio Veneto

| Date | Mintage | VF20 | XF40 | MS60 | MS63 | MS65 |
|---|---|---|---|---|---|---|
| 2011 | 1,000 | PF65 110 | | | | |

**KM# 411 10 DOLLARS**
62.21 g., 0.999 Silver 1.9981 oz. ASW, 42x42 mm. **Subject:** Saint Patrick's Cathedral, New York **Obv:** Interior nave view, window of St. Patrick **Rev:** Exterior cathedral spires, window of St. Patrick

| Date | Mintage | VF20 | XF40 | MS60 | MS63 | MS65 |
|---|---|---|---|---|---|---|
| 2011 Antique patina | 1,000 | — | — | — | 250 | — |

**KM# 412 10 DOLLARS**
62.21 g., 0.999 Silver 1.9981 oz. ASW, 42x42 mm. **Obv:** Santiago de Compostela interior statues, window of St. John the Baptist **Rev:** Santiago de Compostela exterior view

| Date | Mintage | VF20 | XF40 | MS60 | MS63 | MS65 |
|---|---|---|---|---|---|---|
| 2011 Antique patina | 1,000 | — | — | — | 275 | — |

**KM# 413 10 DOLLARS**
62.21 g., 0.999 Silver 1.9981 oz. ASW, 42x42 mm. **Obv:** St. Peter's Bascilica, window of the Holy Spirit **Rev:** St. Peter's Bascilica, window of the Holy Spirit

| Date | Mintage | VF20 | XF40 | MS60 | MS63 | MS65 |
|---|---|---|---|---|---|---|
| 2011 Antique patina | 1,000 | — | — | — | 275 | — |

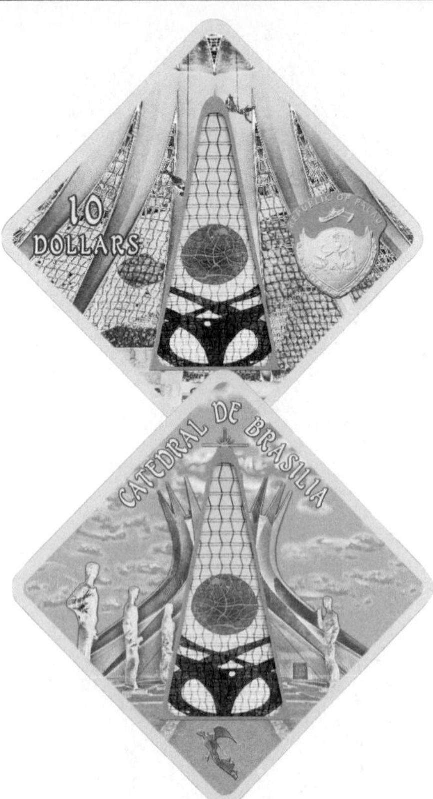

**KM# 414 10 DOLLARS**
62.21 g., 0.999 Silver 1.9981 oz. ASW, 42x42 mm. **Obv:** Brasilia Cathedral, esterior arches, blue window **Rev:** Brasilia Cathedral, figures, blue window

| Date | Mintage | VF20 | XF40 | MS60 | MS63 | MS65 |
|---|---|---|---|---|---|---|
| 2011 Antique patina | 1,000 | — | — | — | 275 | — |

**KM# 423 10 DOLLARS**
62.21 g., 0.999 Silver 1.9981 oz. ASW, 50 mm. **Subject:** Tiffany Glass, Neoclassicism **Obv:** Archway, green glass insert **Rev:** Alcove, green glass insert

| Date | Mintage | VF20 | XF40 | MS60 | MS63 | MS65 |
|---|---|---|---|---|---|---|
| 2012 Antique patina | 999 | — | — | — | 625 | — |

**KM# 424 10 DOLLARS**
62.21 g., 0.999 Silver 1.9981 oz. ASW, 50 mm. **Obv:** Moscow Kremlin interior room, red glass insert **Rev:** Moscow Kremlin exterior, red glass insert

| Date | Mintage | VF20 | XF40 | MS60 | MS63 | MS65 |
|---|---|---|---|---|---|---|
| 2012 Antique patina | 999 | PF65 600 | | | | |

**KM# 458 10 DOLLARS**
50.00 g., Silver, 42 x 42 mm. **Subject:** Votive Church Stained Glass

| Date | Mintage | VF20 | XF40 | MS60 | MS63 | MS65 |
|---|---|---|---|---|---|---|
| 2013 | — | PF65 200 | | | | |

**KM# 469 10 DOLLARS**
50.00 g., 0.925 Silver 1.487 oz. ASW, 42x42 mm. **Obv:** Versailles Hall of Mirrors and National shield **Shape:** Diamond square

| Date | Mintage | VF20 | XF40 | MS60 | MS63 | MS65 |
|---|---|---|---|---|---|---|
| 2013 | 999 | PF65 155 | | | | |

**KM# 471 10 DOLLARS**
62.20 g., 0.999 Silver 1.9978 oz. ASW **Subject:** Tiffany Art - Vatican **Obv:** St. Peter's Basilica

| Date | Mintage | VF20 | XF40 | MS60 | MS63 | MS65 |
|---|---|---|---|---|---|---|
| 2013 Antique patina | 999 | — | — | — | 300 | — |

**KM# 474 10 DOLLARS**
62.20 g., 0.999 Silver 1.9978 oz. ASW, 50 mm. **Subject:** Tiffany Art - Baroque - Dresden

| Date | Mintage | VF20 | XF40 | MS60 | MS63 | MS65 |
|---|---|---|---|---|---|---|
| 2014 Antique patina | 999 | — | — | — | 750 | — |

**KM# 176 20 DOLLARS**
164.00 g., 0.999 Silver 5.2674 oz. ASW, 63 mm. **Obv:** Auto wheel cover **Rev:** Side sillouette of Corvette Z60

| Date | Mintage | VF20 | XF40 | MS60 | MS63 | MS65 |
|---|---|---|---|---|---|---|
| 2008 | — | PF65 275 | | | | |

**KM# 461 50 DOLLARS**
62.20 g., 0.999 Silver 1.9978 oz. ASW partially gilt, 65 mm. **Subject:** Mask of Tut gilt

| Date | Mintage | VF20 | XF40 | MS60 | MS63 | MS65 |
|---|---|---|---|---|---|---|
| 2012 | 300 | PF65 65.00 | | | | |

**KM# 183 500 DOLLARS**
77.70 g., 0.999 Gold 2.4956 oz. AGW, 42x42 mm. **Obv:** Shield **Rev:** Battleship Bismark

| Date | Mintage | VF20 | XF40 | MS60 | MS63 | MS65 |
|---|---|---|---|---|---|---|
| 2009 | 77 | PF65 4,500 | | | | |

**KM# 243 500 DOLLARS**
77.75 g., 0.999 Gold 2.4972 oz. AGW, 42x42 mm. **Subject:** H.M.S. Prince of Wales **Rev:** Battleship right, Royal Navy flag above

| Date | Mintage | VF20 | XF40 | MS60 | MS63 | MS65 |
|---|---|---|---|---|---|---|
| 2009 | 77 | PF65 4,500 | | | | |

**KM# 251 500 DOLLARS**
77.75 g., 0.999 Gold 2.4972 oz. AGW, 42x42 mm. **Subject:** Battleship Marat **Rev:** Battleship sailing left

| Date | Mintage | VF20 | XF40 | MS60 | MS63 | MS65 |
|---|---|---|---|---|---|---|
| 2010 | 77 | PF65 4,500 | | | | |

**KM# 305 500 DOLLARS**
77.75 g., 0.9999 Gold 2.4995 oz. AGW, 42x42 mm. **Obv:** National arms **Rev:** French battleship Richelieu **Shape:** Square

| Date | Mintage | VF20 | XF40 | MS60 | MS63 | MS65 |
|---|---|---|---|---|---|---|
| 2010 | 77 | PF65 4,500 | | | | |

**KM# 394 500 DOLLARS**
77.75 g., 0.999 Gold 2.4972 oz. AGW, 42x42 mm. **Obv:** National arms **Rev:** H.M.A.S. Australia

| Date | Mintage | VF20 | XF40 | MS60 | MS63 | MS65 |
|---|---|---|---|---|---|---|
| 2011 | 77 | PF65 4,500 | | | | |

**KM# 396 500 DOLLARS**
77.70 g., 0.999 Gold 2.4956 oz. AGW, 42x42 mm. **Obv:** National arms **Rev:** RN Vittorio Veneto

| Date | Mintage | VF20 | XF40 | MS60 | MS63 | MS65 |
|---|---|---|---|---|---|---|
| 2011 | 77 | PF65 4,500 | | | | |

## PROOF SETS

| KM# | Date | Mintage | Identification | Issue Price | Mkt Val |
|---|---|---|---|---|---|
| PS4 | 2007 (6) | 2,500 | KM#130-135 | — | 375 |

# PANAMA

The Republic of Panama, a Central American country situated between Costa Rica and Colombia, has an area of 29,762 sq. mi. (78,200 sq. km.) and a population of *2.4 million. Capital: Panama City. The Panama Canal is the country's biggest asset; servicing world related transit trade and international commerce. Bananas, refined petroleum, sugar and shrimp are exported.

**MONETARY SYSTEM**

100 Centesimos = 1 Balboa

## REPUBLIC

### DECIMAL COINAGE

**KM# 125 CENTESIMO**

2.50 g., Copper Plated Zinc, 19.05 mm. **Obv:** Written value **Obv. Legend:** REPUBLICA DE PANAMA **Rev:** Native Urraca bust left **Edge:** Plain

| Date | Mintage | F12 | VF20 | XF40 | MS60 | MS63 |
|---|---|---|---|---|---|---|
| 2001 (c) | 160,000,000 | — | — | — | 0.25 | 0.50 |
| 2008 (c) | — | — | — | — | 0.25 | 0.50 |

**KM# 133 5 CENTESIMOS**

5.00 g., Copper-Nickel, 21.15 mm. **Subject:** Sara Sotillo **Obv:** National coat of arms **Obv. Legend:** REPUBLICA DE PANAMA **Rev:** Head of Sotillo 3/4 right **Edge:** Plain

| Date | Mintage | F12 | VF20 | XF40 | MS60 | MS63 |
|---|---|---|---|---|---|---|
| 2001 (c) | 8,000,000 | — | — | — | 0.25 | 0.75 |
| 2008 (c) | — | — | — | — | 0.25 | 0.75 |

**KM# 127 1/10 BALBOA**

2.27 g., Copper-Nickel Clad Copper, 17.91 mm. **Obv:** National coat of arms **Obv. Legend:** REPUBLICA DE PANAMA **Rev:** Armored bust of Balboa left **Edge:** Reeded

| Date | Mintage | F12 | VF20 | XF40 | MS60 | MS63 |
|---|---|---|---|---|---|---|
| 2001 (c) | 15,000,000 | — | — | 0.50 | 0.75 | 1.00 |
| 2008 (c) | 28,000,000 | — | — | 0.50 | 0.75 | 1.00 |

**KM# 135 25 CENTESIMOS**

5.67 g., Copper-Nickel Clad Copper, 24.26 mm. **Obv:** National coat of arms **Obv. Legend:** REPUBLICA DE PANAMA **Rev:** Tower and Spanish ruins **Edge:** Reeded **Note:** Released in 2004

| Date | Mintage | F12 | VF20 | XF40 | MS60 | MS63 |
|---|---|---|---|---|---|---|
| 2003 (c) | 6,000,000 | — | — | 0.50 | 2.00 | 3.00 |
| 2003 (c) | 2,000 | PF63 25.00 | PF65 30.00 | | | |

**KM# 136 25 CENTESIMOS**

5.67 g., Copper-Nickel Clad Copper, 24.26 mm. **Obv:** National coat of arms **Obv. Legend:** REPUBLICA DE PANAMA **Rev:** King's Bridge **Rev. Legend:** Puente Del Rey **Edge:** Reeded

| Date | Mintage | F12 | VF20 | XF40 | MS60 | MS63 |
|---|---|---|---|---|---|---|
| 2005 (c) | 3,000,000 | — | — | — | 1.00 | 1.50 |
| 2005 (c) | 2,000 | PF63 20.00 | PF65 25.00 | | | |

**KM# 128 1/4 BALBOA**

5.67 g., Copper-Nickel Clad Copper, 24.26 mm. **Obv:** National coat of arms **Obv. Legend:** REPUBLICA DE PANAMA **Rev:** Armored bust of Balboa left **Edge:** Reeded

| Date | Mintage | F12 | VF20 | XF40 | MS60 | MS63 |
|---|---|---|---|---|---|---|
| 2001 (c) | 12,000,000 | — | — | 0.35 | 0.75 | 1.50 |

**KM# 137.1 1/4 BALBOA**

5.67 g., Copper-Nickel Clad Copper, 24.26 mm. **Subject:** Breast Cancer Awareness **Obv:** National coat of arms **Obv. Legend:** REPUBLICA DE PANAMA **Rev:** Ribbon **Rev. Legend:** Protegete Mujer **Edge:** Reeded

| Date | Mintage | F12 | VF20 | XF40 | MS60 | MS63 |
|---|---|---|---|---|---|---|
| 2008 (c) | 14,000,000 | — | — | — | 0.50 | 1.00 |

Note: Also available in a laminated Breast Cancer Awareness pink bookmark

**KM# 137.2 1/4 BALBOA**

5.67 g., Copper-Nickel Clad Copper, 24.26 mm. **Subject:** Breast Cancer Awareness **Obv:** National coat of arms **Obv. Legend:** REPUBLICA DE PANAMA **Rev:** Pink Ribbon **Rev. Legend:** Protegete Mujer **Edge:** Reeded

| Date | Mintage | F12 | VF20 | XF40 | MS60 | MS63 |
|---|---|---|---|---|---|---|
| 2008 (c) Proof, pink colored ribbon | 2,500 | PF63 75.00 | PF65 80.00 | | | |

Note: Pink ribbon proof issued in red plush case with black cardboard sleeve with printed pink ribbon

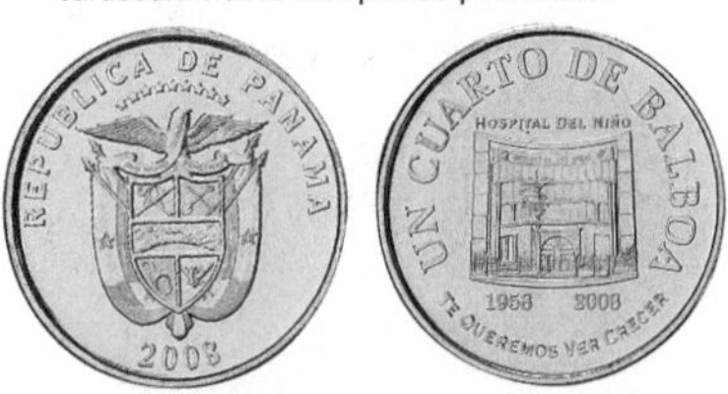

**KM# 138 1/4 BALBOA**

5.67 g., Copper-Nickel Clad Copper, 24.26 mm. **Subject:** 50th Anniversary of the Children's Hospital **Obv:** National coat of arms **Obv. Legend:** REPUBLICA DE PANAMA **Rev:** Children's Hospital **Edge:** Reeded

| Date | Mintage | F12 | VF20 | XF40 | MS60 | MS63 |
|---|---|---|---|---|---|---|
| 2008 (c) | 6,000,000 | — | — | — | 1.00 | 2.00 |
| 2008 (c) | 1,000 | PF63 35.00 | PF65 40.00 | | | |

**KM# 139 50 CENTESIMOS**

11.34 g., Copper-Nickel Clad Copper, 30.6 mm. **Subject:** Centenary of the National Bank of Panama **Obv:** National coat of arms **Obv. Legend:** REPUBLICA DE PANAMA **Rev:** BNP Building - Banco Nacional de Panama **Rev. Legend:** BANCO NACIONAL DE PANAMA CENTENARIO **Edge:** Reeded

| Date | Mintage | F12 | VF20 | XF40 | MS60 | MS63 |
|---|---|---|---|---|---|---|
| 2009 (c) | 4,000,000 | — | — | — | 2.00 | 3.00 |
| 2009 (c) | 2,000 | PF63 40.00 | PF65 45.00 | | | |

**KM# 129 1/2 BALBOA**

11.34 g., Copper-Nickel Clad Copper, 30.61 mm. **Obv:** National coat of arms **Obv. Legend:** REPUBLICA DE PANAMA **Rev:** Armored bust of Balboa left **Edge:** Reeded

| Date | Mintage | F12 | VF20 | XF40 | MS60 | MS63 |
|---|---|---|---|---|---|---|
| 2001 (c) | 600,000 | — | — | 1.00 | 2.25 | 4.00 |
| 2008 (c) | 5,800,000 | — | — | 0.75 | 1.25 | 2.00 |

**KM# 140 1/2 BALBOA**

13.17 g., Copper-Nickel Clad Copper, 30.61 mm. **Subject:** Convent of the Conception **Obv:** National arms **Rev:** Building ruins **Edge:** Reeded

| Date | Mintage | F12 | VF20 | XF40 | MS60 | MS63 |
|---|---|---|---|---|---|---|
| 2010 (c) | 3,000,000 | — | — | — | 2.00 | 3.00 |

**KM# 142 1/2 BALBOA**

13.17 g., Copper-Nickel Clad Copper, 30.61 mm. **Obv:** National arms **Obv. Legend:** REPUBLICA DE PANAMA / MEDIO BALBOA **Rev:** Crowned Hapsburg shield **Rev. Legend:** MONEDA DE 1580 / PANAMA VIEJO

| Date | Mintage | F12 | VF20 | XF40 | MS60 | MS63 |
|---|---|---|---|---|---|---|
| 2011 | 3,000,000 | — | — | — | 2.00 | 3.00 |

**KM# 143 1/2 BALBOA**

11.34 g., Copper-Nickel Clad Copper, 30.61 mm. **Subject:** Casa Reales

| Date | Mintage | F12 | VF20 | XF40 | MS60 | MS63 |
|---|---|---|---|---|---|---|
| 2012 | — | — | — | — | 2.00 | 3.00 |

**KM# 144 1/2 BALBOA**
13.17 g., Copper-Nickel Clad Copper, 30.61 mm. **Obv:** National arms **Rev:** Balboa standing in water

| Date | Mintage | F12 | VF20 | XF40 | MS60 | MS63 |
|---|---|---|---|---|---|---|
| 2013 | 3,000,000 | — | — | — | 2.00 | 3.00 |

**KM# 144a 1/2 BALBOA**
13.17 g., 0.9999 Silver 0.4234 oz. ASW, 30.61 mm. **Subject:** 500th Anniversary of the Discovery of the South Sea **Obv:** National Coat of Arms **Rev:** Vasco Nunez de Balboa

| Date | Mintage | F12 | VF20 | XF40 | MS60 | MS63 |
|---|---|---|---|---|---|---|
| 2013 | 2,000 | **PF65** 75.00 | | | | |

**KM# 145 1/2 BALBOA**
13.17 g., Copper-Nickel Clad Copper, 30.61 mm. **Subject:** 100th Anniversary of Inauguration of the Panama Canal **Obv:** National Coat of Arms **Rev:** King of Spain Carlos V

| Date | Mintage | F12 | VF20 | XF40 | MS60 | MS63 |
|---|---|---|---|---|---|---|
| 2014 | 3,000,000 | — | — | — | 2.00 | 3.00 |

**KM# 145a 1/2 BALBOA**
13.17 g., 0.9999 Silver 0.4234 oz. ASW, 30.61 mm. **Subject:** 100th Anniversary of the Inauguration of the Panama Canal **Obv:** National Coat of Arms **Rev:** King of Spain Carlos V

| Date | Mintage | F12 | VF20 | XF40 | MS60 | MS63 |
|---|---|---|---|---|---|---|
| 2014 | 2,000 | **PF65** 75.00 | | | | |

**KM# 134 BALBOA**
22.68 g., Copper-Nickel Clad Copper, 38.1 mm. **Obv:** Bust of President Mireya Moscoso left, flanked by dates of her presidency **Rev:** Flag and canal scene **Edge:** Reeded

| Date | Mintage | F12 | VF20 | XF40 | MS60 | MS63 |
|---|---|---|---|---|---|---|
| 2004 (c) | 2,000 | **PF63** 50.00 | | **PF65** 55.00 | | |
| 2004 (c) | 348,000 | — | — | 1.50 | 4.50 | 12.00 |

**KM# 141 BALBOA**
7.20 g., Bi-Metallic Brass center in Nickel ring, both plated on Stainless Steel core, 26.5 mm. **Obv:** National arms **Obv. Legend:** REPUBLICA DE PANAMA / date **Rev:** Balboa left **Rev. Legend:** VASCO NUNEZ DE BALBOA / UN BALBOA **Edge Lettering:** PANAMA (reeding) 1 BALBOA (reeding)

| Date | Mintage | F12 | VF20 | XF40 | MS60 | MS63 |
|---|---|---|---|---|---|---|
| 2011 | 40,000,000 | — | — | — | 1.50 | 2.00 |

# PAPUA NEW GUINEA

The Independent State of Papua New Guinea occupies the eastern half of the island of New Guinea. It lies north of Australia near the equator and borders on West Irian. The country, which includes nearby Bismark archipelago, Buka and Bougainville, has an area of 178,260 sq. mi. (461,690 sq. km.) and a population of 3.7 million that is divided into more than 1,000 separate tribes, speaking more than 700 mutually unintelligible languages. Capital: Port Moresby. The economy is agricultural, and exports copra, rubber, cocoa, coffee, tea, gold and copper.

Papua New Guinea is a member of the Commonwealth of Nations. Elizabeth II is Head of State, as Queen of Papua New Guinea.

## CONSTITUTIONAL MONARCHY

Commonwealth of Nations

### STANDARD COINAGE

**KM# 1 TOEA**
2.00 g., Bronze, 17.65 mm. **Obv:** National emblem **Rev:** Butterfly and value **Edge:** Plain

| Date | Mintage | VF20 | XF40 | MS60 | MS63 | MS65 |
|---|---|---|---|---|---|---|
| 2001 | — | — | 0.25 | 0.60 | 1.00 | 1.50 |
| 2002 | — | — | 0.15 | 0.50 | 1.00 | 1.50 |
| 2004 | — | — | 0.10 | 0.50 | 1.00 | 1.50 |

**KM# 2 2 TOEA**
4.10 g., Bronze, 21.6 mm. **Obv:** National emblem **Rev:** Lion fish **Edge:** Plain

| Date | Mintage | VF20 | XF40 | MS60 | MS63 | MS65 |
|---|---|---|---|---|---|---|
| 2001 | — | — | 0.30 | 0.50 | 0.75 | 2.50 |
| 2002 | — | — | 0.25 | 0.40 | 0.60 | 2.00 |
| 2004 | — | — | 0.15 | 0.25 | 0.45 | 1.25 |

**KM# 3a 5 TOEA**
2.55 g., Nickel Plated Steel, 19.53 mm. **Obv:** National emblem **Rev:** Plateless turtle **Edge:** Reeded

| Date | Mintage | VF20 | XF40 | MS60 | MS63 | MS65 |
|---|---|---|---|---|---|---|
| 2002 | — | — | 0.50 | 0.70 | 1.25 | 2.50 |
| 2004 | — | — | 0.50 | 0.70 | 1.25 | 2.50 |
| 2005 | — | — | 0.40 | 0.60 | 1.00 | 2.00 |
| 2010 | — | — | 0.40 | 0.60 | 1.00 | 2.00 |

**KM# 4 10 TOEA**
5.65 g., Copper-Nickel, 23.72 mm. **Obv:** National emblem **Rev:** Cuscus and value **Edge:** Reeded

| Date | Mintage | VF20 | XF40 | MS60 | MS63 | MS65 |
|---|---|---|---|---|---|---|
| 2001 | — | — | — | 0.80 | 1.50 | 2.00 |

**KM# 4a 10 TOEA**
5.16 g., Nickel Plated Steel, 23.72 mm. **Obv:** National emblem **Rev:** Cuscus and value **Edge:** Reeded

| Date | Mintage | VF20 | XF40 | MS60 | MS63 | MS65 |
|---|---|---|---|---|---|---|
| 2002 | — | — | 0.80 | 1.00 | 2.00 | 3.00 |
| 2004 | — | — | 0.80 | 1.00 | 2.00 | 3.00 |
| 2005 | — | — | 0.60 | 0.80 | 1.50 | 3.00 |
| 2006 | — | — | 0.60 | 0.80 | 1.50 | 2.50 |
| 2009 | — | — | 0.60 | 0.80 | 1.50 | 2.50 |
| 2010 | — | — | 0.60 | 0.80 | 1.50 | 2.50 |

**KM# 5a 20 TOEA**
10.13 g., Nickel Plated Steel, 28.65 mm. **Obv:** National emblem **Rev:** Bennett's Cassowary and value **Edge:** Reeded

| Date | Mintage | VF20 | XF40 | MS60 | MS63 | MS65 |
|---|---|---|---|---|---|---|
| 2004 | — | — | 0.80 | 1.00 | 2.00 | 3.00 |
| 2005 | — | — | 0.80 | 1.00 | 2.00 | 3.00 |
| 2006 | — | — | 0.60 | 0.80 | 1.50 | 2.50 |
| 2009 | — | — | 0.60 | 0.80 | 1.50 | 2.50 |
| 2010 | — | — | 0.60 | 0.80 | 1.50 | 2.50 |

**KM# 53 50 TOEA**
12.10 g., Nickel Plated Steel, 30 mm. **Subject:** St. John's Ambulance, 50th Anniversary **Obv:** National emblem **Rev:** Ambulance corps logo **Shape:** 7-sided

| Date | Mintage | VF20 | XF40 | MS60 | MS63 | MS65 |
|---|---|---|---|---|---|---|
| 2007 | — | — | — | 2.50 | 3.50 | 5.00 |

**KM# 54 50 TOEA**
12.10 g., Nickel Plated Steel, 30 mm. **Subject:** Bank of Papua New Guinea, 35th Anniversary **Obv:** National emblem **Rev:** Bank logo in colored central applique

| Date | Mintage | VF20 | XF40 | MS60 | MS63 | MS65 |
|---|---|---|---|---|---|---|
| 2008 | — | — | — | 2.50 | 3.50 | 5.00 |

**KM# 6a KINA**
14.61 g., Nickel Plated Steel, 33.28 mm. **Obv:** Native design **Rev:** Two Salt Water Crocodiles **Edge:** Reeded

| Date | Mintage | VF20 | XF40 | MS60 | MS63 | MS65 |
|---|---|---|---|---|---|---|
| 2002 | — | — | 1.60 | 3.00 | 4.00 | 5.00 |
| 2004 | — | — | 1.40 | 2.50 | 3.50 | 4.50 |

**KM# 6b KINA**
11.13 g., Nickel Plated Steel, 30 mm. **Obv:** Native design **Rev:** Two Salt Water Crocodiles **Edge:** Reeded

| Date | Mintage | VF20 | XF40 | MS60 | MS63 | MS65 |
|---|---|---|---|---|---|---|
| 2005 | — | — | 1.20 | 2.00 | 3.00 | 4.00 |
| 2010 | — | — | 1.20 | 2.00 | 3.00 | 4.00 |

**KM# 59 KINA**
0.50 g., 0.999 Gold 0.0161 oz. AGW, 11 mm. **Subject:** Birdwing Butterfly

| Date | Mintage | VF20 | XF40 | MS60 | MS63 | MS65 |
|---|---|---|---|---|---|---|
| 2011 | Est. 5000 | PF63 35.00 | PF65 45.00 | | | |

**KM# 60 KINA**
0.50 g., 0.585 Gold 0.0094 oz. AGW with 24Kt plating, 11 mm. **Subject:** Bird of Paradise

| Date | Mintage | VF20 | XF40 | MS60 | MS63 | MS65 |
|---|---|---|---|---|---|---|
| 2013 | Est. 5000 | PF63 50.00 | PF65 55.00 | | | |

**KM# 62 KINA**
0.585 Gold AGW with 24Kt plating, 11 mm. **Subject:** Albert Einstein

| Date | Mintage | VF20 | XF40 | MS60 | MS63 | MS65 |
|---|---|---|---|---|---|---|
| 2013 | Est. 7500 | PF63 50.00 | PF65 55.00 | | | |

**KM# 51 2 KINA**
12.20 g., Bi-Metallic Aluminum-Bronze center in Copper-Nickel ring, 33.3 mm. **Subject:** Bank of Papua New Guinea, 35th Anniversary **Obv:** Bird of Paradise **Rev:** Bank logo **Edge:** Reeded

| Date | Mintage | VF20 | XF40 | MS60 | MS63 | MS65 |
|---|---|---|---|---|---|---|
| 2008 | — | — | — | — | — | 5.00 |

**KM# 57 5 KINA**
28.28 g., 0.925 Silver 0.841 oz. ASW, 38.61 mm. **Subject:** Diamond Jubilee of Queen Elizabeth II - Sword of State

| Date | Mintage | VF20 | XF40 | MS60 | MS63 | MS65 |
|---|---|---|---|---|---|---|
| 2011 | Est. 10000 | PF63 65.00 | PF65 70.00 | | | |

**KM# 58 5 KINA**
1.24 g., 0.999 Gold 0.0398 oz. AGW, 13.92 mm. **Subject:** Bird of Paradise

| Date | Mintage | VF20 | XF40 | MS60 | MS63 | MS65 |
|---|---|---|---|---|---|---|
| 2011 | Est. 5000 | PF63 85.00 | PF65 95.00 | | | |

**KM# 56 5 KINA**
Silver, 38.61 mm. **Subject:** Belgrave - Gembrook Railway, Victoria, Australia, 50th Anniversary of re-opening **Obv:** Bird of Paradise **Rev:** Steam train and map of Belgrave-Gembrook route

| Date | Mintage | VF20 | XF40 | MS60 | MS63 | MS65 |
|---|---|---|---|---|---|---|
| 2012 | — | PF63 75.00 | PF65 85.00 | | | |

**KM# 61 5 KINA**
20.00 g., 0.925 Silver 0.5948 oz. ASW with enamel color, 38.61 mm. **Subject:** 2014 FIFA World Cup - Brazil

| Date | Mintage | VF20 | XF40 | MS60 | MS63 | MS65 |
|---|---|---|---|---|---|---|
| 2013 | Est. 10000 | PF63 75.00 | PF65 80.00 | | | |

**KM# 63 5 KINA**
0.50 g., 0.999 Gold 0.0161 oz. AGW, 11 mm. **Subject:** Albert Einstein

| Date | Mintage | VF20 | XF40 | MS60 | MS63 | MS65 |
|---|---|---|---|---|---|---|
| 2013 | Est. 7500 | PF63 50.00 | PF65 55.00 | | | |

**KM# 64 5 KINA**
20.00 g., 0.925 Gold 0.5948 oz. AGW, 38.61 mm. **Subject:** 2014 FIFA World Cup - All in one Rhythm

| Date | Mintage | VF20 | XF40 | MS60 | MS63 | MS65 |
|---|---|---|---|---|---|---|
| 2013 | Est. 10000 | PF63 75.00 | PF65 80.00 | | | |

**KM# 65 5 KINA**
31.11 g., 0.999 Silver 0.999 oz. ASW, 38.61 mm. **Rev:** Tree Kangaroo with Swarovski crystal eyes

| Date | Mintage | VF20 | XF40 | MS60 | MS63 | MS65 |
|---|---|---|---|---|---|---|
| 2013 Antique patina | 1,000 | — | — | — | — | 40.00 |

**KM# 66 5 KINA**
31.11 g., 0.999 Silver 0.999 oz. ASW, 38.61 mm. **Rev:** Green Tree Monitor in color

| Date | Mintage | VF20 | XF40 | MS60 | MS63 | MS65 |
|---|---|---|---|---|---|---|
| 2014 | — | PF65 40.00 | | | | |

# PARAGUAY

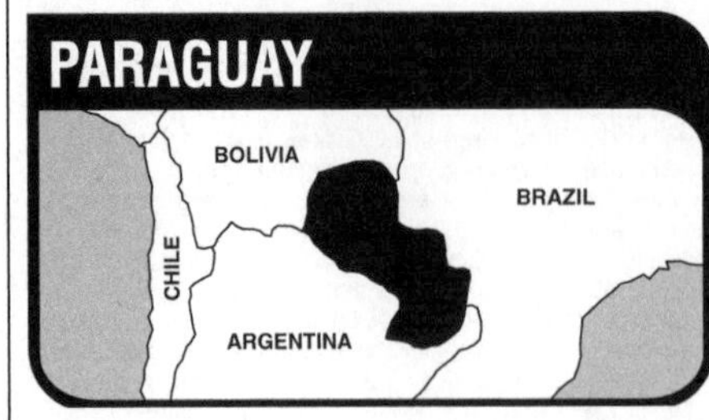


The Republic of Paraguay, a landlocked country in the heart of South America surrounded by Argentina, Bolivia and Brazil, has an area of 157,048 sq. mi. (406,750 sq. km.) and a population of *4.5 million, 95 percent of whom are of mixed Spanish and Indian descent. Capital: Asuncion. The country is predominantly agrarian, with no important mineral deposits or oil reserves. Meat, timber, hides, oilseeds, tobacco and cotton account for 70 per-cent of Paraguay's export revenue.

During the Triple Alliance War (1864-1870) in which Paraguay faced Argentina, Brazil and Uruguay, Asuncion's ladies gathered in an Assembly on Feb. 24, 1867 and decided to give up their jewelry in order to help the national defense. The President of the Republic, Francisco Solano Lopez accepted the offering and ordered one twentieth of it be used to mint the first Paraguayan gold coins according to the Decree of the 11th of Sept.1867.

Two dies were made, one by Bouvet, and another by an American, Leonard Charles, while only the die made by Bouvet was eventually used.

**MINT MARK**
HF – LeLocle (Swiss)

## REPUBLIC

### REFORM COINAGE

100 Centimos = 1 Guarani

**KM# 209 20 CENTIMOS**
27.00 g., 0.925 Silver 0.803 oz. ASW **Subject:** Ibero-American Series **Obv:** National arms in center of other country's arms **Rev:** Ñanduti and value **Edge:** Reeded

| Date | Mintage | VF20 | XF40 | MS60 | MS63 | MS65 |
|---|---|---|---|---|---|---|
| 2012 | — | PF63 100 | PF65 110 | | | |

**KM# 197 GUARANI**
27.00 g., 0.925 Silver 0.803 oz. ASW, 39.7 mm. **Subject:** 50th Anniversary of the Central Bank **Obv:** Naval gunship **Obv. Legend:** REPUBLICA DEL PARAGUAY **Obv. Inscription:** CAÑONERO PARAGUAY **Rev:** Bank building within circle **Rev. Legend:** BANCO CENTRAL DEL PARAGUAY **Edge:** Reeded

| Date | Mintage | VF20 | XF40 | MS60 | MS63 | MS65 |
|---|---|---|---|---|---|---|
| 2002 | 3,000 | PF63 75.00 | PF65 80.00 | | | |

**KM# 199 GUARANI**
26.86 g., 0.925 Silver 0.7988 oz. ASW, 40.03 mm. **Series:** 5th Ibero-America **Subject:** Encounter of the Two Worlds **Obv:** National arms in center with ten national arms in outer circle **Obv. Legend:** REPUBLICA DEL PARAGUAY **Rev:** Native in canoe with outline of South America in background at left, early sailing ship at lower right. **Rev. Legend:** ENCUENTRO DE DOS MUNDOS **Edge:** Reeded

| Date | Mintage | VF20 | XF40 | MS60 | MS63 | MS65 |
|---|---|---|---|---|---|---|
| 2002 | — | PF63 60.00 | PF65 65.00 | | | |

**KM# 200 GUARANI**
27.00 g., 0.925 Silver 0.803 oz. ASW **Subject:** 60th Anniversary of Currency Reform **Obv:** National arms **Obv. Legend:** REPUBLICA DEL PARAGUAY **Rev:** Outline map of Paraguay **Edge:** Reeded

| Date | Mintage | VF20 | XF40 | MS60 | MS63 | MS65 |
|---|---|---|---|---|---|---|
| 2003 | — | PF63 80.00 | PF65 90.00 | | | |

**KM# 201 GUARANI**
26.90 g., 0.925 Silver 0.800 oz. ASW, 40.04 mm. **Subject:** FIFA - XVIII World Football Championship - Germany 2006 **Obv:** National arms **Obv. Legend:** REPUBLICA DEL PARAGUAY **Rev:** Two opponents after ball **Rev. Legend:** COPA MUNDIAL DE LA FIFA - ALEMANIA **Edge:** Reeded

| Date | Mintage | VF20 | XF40 | MS60 | MS63 | MS65 |
|---|---|---|---|---|---|---|
| 2003 | 50,000 | PF63 50.00 | PF65 60.00 | | | |

**KM# 202 GUARANI**
27.00 g., 0.925 Silver 0.803 oz. ASW **Subject:** FIFA - XVIII World Football Championship - Germany 2006 **Obv:** National arms **Obv. Legend:** REPUBLICA DEL PARAGUAY **Rev:** Ball in goal **Edge:** Reeded

| Date | Mintage | VF20 | XF40 | MS60 | MS63 | MS65 |
|---|---|---|---|---|---|---|
| 2004 | 50,000 | PF63 50.00 | PF65 60.00 | | | |

**KM# 204 GUARANI**
27.00 g., 0.925 Silver 0.803 oz. ASW **Series:** 6th Ibero-America **Subject:** Encounter of the Two Worlds **Obv:** National arms in center with ten national arms in outer circle **Obv. Legend:** REPUBLICA DEL PARAGUAY **Rev:** Church of the Most Holy, Trinidad in Yaguarón **Rev. Legend:** ENCUENTRO DE DOS MUNDOS - IGLESIA DE LA SANTISIMA TRINIDAD **Edge:** Reeded

| Date | Mintage | VF20 | XF40 | MS60 | MS63 | MS65 |
|---|---|---|---|---|---|---|
| 2005 | — | PF63 65.00 | PF65 75.00 | | | |

**KM# 205 GUARANI**
27.00 g., 0.925 Silver 0.803 oz. ASW **Subject:** Ibero-American series **Obv:** National arms within circle of other country's arms **Rev:** First coin of Paraguay, 1845 **Edge:** Reeded

| Date | Mintage | VF20 | XF40 | MS60 | MS63 | MS65 |
|---|---|---|---|---|---|---|
| 2010 | — | PF63 100 | PF65 110 | | | |

**KM# 210 GUARANI**
27.00 g., 0.925 Silver 0.803 oz. ASW **Subject:** Currency Reform, 70th Anniversary **Obv:** Guarani Native head 1/4 right **Rev:** Large value within palm and olive leave branch **Edge:** Reeded

| Date | Mintage | VF20 | XF40 | MS60 | MS63 | MS65 |
|---|---|---|---|---|---|---|
| 2013 | 700 | PF63 100 | PF65 110 | | | |

**KM# 211 GUARANI**
6.80 g., 0.999 Gold 0.2184 oz. AGW **Subject:** Currency Reform, 70th Anniversary **Obv:** Guarani Native head 1/4 right **Rev:** Large value within palm and olive leaves wreath **Edge:** Reeded

| Date | Mintage | VF20 | XF40 | MS60 | MS63 | MS65 |
|---|---|---|---|---|---|---|
| 2013 | 70 | PF63 725 | PF65 750 | | | |

**KM# 212 GUARANI**
27.000 Silver ASW .925 **Subject:** 2014 FIFA World Cup - Brazil **Obv:** National emblem **Rev:** Soccer player and fans in stands with flags

| Date | Mintage | VF20 | XF40 | MS60 | MS63 | MS65 |
|---|---|---|---|---|---|---|
| 2013 | — | PF63 100 | PF65 110 | | | |

**KM# 191a 50 GUARANIES**
Brass Plated Steel **Obv:** Uniformed bust facing **Rev:** Value above river dam **Note:** Magnetic

| Date | Mintage | VF20 | XF40 | MS60 | MS63 | MS65 |
|---|---|---|---|---|---|---|
| 2005 | 10,000,000 | — | — | 0.50 | 0.75 | 1.00 |

**KM# 191b 50 GUARANIES**
1.01 g., Aluminum, 18.98 mm. **Obv:** Bust of Major General J.F. Estigarribia facing **Obv. Legend:** REPUBLICA DEL PARAGUAY **Rev:** Acaray River Dam **Rev. Inscription:** REPRESA ACARAY **Edge:** Plain **Note:** Reduced size

| Date | Mintage | VF20 | XF40 | MS60 | MS63 | MS65 |
|---|---|---|---|---|---|---|
| 2006 | 25,000,000 | — | — | 0.60 | 1.00 | 2.00 |
| 2008 | — | — | — | 0.60 | 1.00 | 2.00 |
| 2011 | 25,000,000 | — | — | 0.60 | 1.00 | 2.00 |
| 2012 | 25,000,000 | — | — | 0.60 | 1.00 | 2.00 |

**KM# 177a 100 GUARANIES**
5.45 g., Brass Plated Steel **Obv:** Bust of General Jose E. Dias facing **Obv. Legend:** REPUBLICA DEL PARAGUAY **Rev:** Ruins of Humaita **Rev. Inscription:** RUINAS DE HUMAITA 1865/70 **Note:** Reduced weight and thickness.

| Date | Mintage | VF20 | XF40 | MS60 | MS63 | MS65 |
|---|---|---|---|---|---|---|
| 2004 | 15,000,000 | — | — | 0.80 | 1.50 | 2.00 |
| 2005 | 10,000,000 | — | — | 0.80 | 1.50 | 2.00 |

**KM# 177b 100 GUARANIES**
3.66 g., Nickel-Steel, 20.94 mm. **Obv:** Bust of General Jose E. Dias facing **Obv. Legend:** REPUBLICA DEL PARAGUAY **Rev:** Ruins of Humaita **Rev. Inscription:** RUINAS DE HUMAITA 1865/70 **Edge:** Plain

| Date | Mintage | VF20 | XF40 | MS60 | MS63 | MS65 |
|---|---|---|---|---|---|---|
| 2006 | 30,000,000 | — | — | 0.80 | 1.50 | 2.00 |
| 2007 | 25,000,000 | — | — | 0.80 | 1.50 | 2.00 |
| 2008 | — | — | — | 0.80 | 1.50 | 2.00 |
| 2011 | 20,000,000 | — | — | 0.80 | 1.50 | 2.00 |
| 2012 | 25,000,000 | — | — | 0.80 | 1.50 | 2.00 |

**KM# 206 100 GUARANIES**
14.70 g., Nordic Gold, 33 mm. **Subject:** Independence, 200th Anniversary **Obv:** Rider on horseback with flag in color **Rev:** Independence House

| Date | Mintage | VF20 | XF40 | MS60 | MS63 | MS65 |
|---|---|---|---|---|---|---|
| 2011 | — | PF63 50.00 | PF65 60.00 | | | |

**KM# 207 150 GUARANIES**
27.00 g., 0.925 Silver 0.803 oz. ASW **Subject:** Independence, 200th Anniversary **Obv:** Rider on horseback with flag in color **Rev:** Independence House

| Date | Mintage | VF20 | XF40 | MS60 | MS63 | MS65 |
|---|---|---|---|---|---|---|
| 2011 | 3,000 | PF63 100 | PF65 110 | | | |

**KM# 208 200 GUARANIES**
6.75 g., 0.999 Gold 0.2168 oz. AGW **Subject:** Independence, 200th Anniversary **Obv:** Rider on horseback with flag in color **Rev:** Independence House

| Date | Mintage | VF20 | XF40 | MS60 | MS63 | MS65 |
|---|---|---|---|---|---|---|
| 2011 | 2,000 | PF63 775 | PF65 800 | | | |

**KM# 195 500 GUARANIES**
7.82 g., Brass Plated Steel **Obv:** Head of General Bernardino Caballero facing **Obv. Legend:** REPUBLICA DEL PARAGUAY **Rev:** Bank above value within circle **Rev. Legend:** BANCO CENTRAL DEL PARAGUAY

| Date | Mintage | VF20 | XF40 | MS60 | MS63 | MS65 |
|---|---|---|---|---|---|---|
| 2002 | 15,000,000 | — | — | 1.50 | 2.25 | 3.00 |
| 2005 | 5,000,000 | — | — | 1.50 | 2.25 | 3.00 |

**KM# 195a 500 GUARANIES**
4.80 g., Nickel-Steel, 23 mm. **Obv:** Head of General Bernardino Caballero facing **Obv. Legend:** REPUBLICA DEL PARAGUAY **Rev:** Bank above value in circle **Rev. Legend:** BANCO CENTRAL DEL PARAGUAY **Edge:** Plain

| Date | Mintage | VF20 | XF40 | MS60 | MS63 | MS65 |
|---|---|---|---|---|---|---|
| 2006 | 12,000,000 | — | — | 1.00 | 2.00 | 2.50 |
| 2007 | 25,000,000 | — | — | 1.00 | 2.00 | 2.50 |
| 2008 | — | — | — | 1.00 | 2.00 | 2.50 |
| 2011 | 20,000,000 | — | — | 1.00 | 2.00 | 2.50 |
| 2012 | 20,000,000 | — | — | 1.00 | 2.00 | 2.50 |

**KM# 198 MIL (1000) GUARANIES**
6.07 g., Nickel-Steel, 25 mm. **Obv:** Bust of Major General Francisco Solano Lopez facing **Obv. Legend:** REPUBLICA DEL PARAGUAY **Rev:** National Heroes Pantheon **Rev. Legend:** BANCO CENTRAL DEL PARAGUAY **Rev. Inscription:** PANTEON NACIONAL / DE LOS HEROES **Edge:** Plain

| Date | Mintage | VF20 | XF40 | MS60 | MS63 | MS65 |
|---|---|---|---|---|---|---|
| 2006 | 25,000,000 | — | — | 1.50 | 2.50 | 4.00 |
| 2007 | 35,000,000 | — | — | 1.50 | 2.50 | 4.00 |
| 2008 | — | — | — | 1.50 | 2.50 | 4.00 |

**KM# 203 1500 GUARANIES**
6.70 g., 0.999 Gold 0.2152 oz. AGW **Subject:** XVIII World Football Championship - Germany 2006 **Obv:** National arms **Obv. Legend:** REPUBLICA DEL PARAGUAY **Rev:** Ball in goal

| Date | Mintage | VF20 | XF40 | MS60 | MS63 | MS65 |
|---|---|---|---|---|---|---|
| 2004 | 25,000 | PF63 430 | PF65 450 | | | |

The Republic of Peru, located on the Pacific coast of South America, has an area of 496,225 sq. mi. (1,285,220sq. km.) and a population of *21.4 million. Capital: Lima. The diversified economy includes mining, fishing and agriculture. Fishmeal, copper, sugar, zinc and iron ore are exported.

**MINT MARKS**
L, LIMAE (monogram), Lima
(monogram), LIMA = Lima

# REPUBLIC

## REFORM COINAGE

1991; 1/M Intis = 1 Nuevo Sol;
100 (New) Centimos = 1 Nuevo Sol

**KM# 303.4 CENTIMO**
1.88 g., Brass, 15.9 mm. **Obv:** National arms, accent mark above "u **Rev:** Without Braille dots, no Chavez **Edge:** Plain **Note:** LIMA monogram is mint mark.

| Date | Mintage | VF20 | XF40 | MS60 | MS63 | MS65 |
|---|---|---|---|---|---|---|
| 2002 LIMA | 2,100,000 | — | — | 0.20 | 0.50 | 0.75 |
| 2004 LIMA | 2,000,000 | — | — | 0.20 | 0.50 | 0.75 |
| 2005 LIMA | 22,700,000 | — | — | 0.10 | 0.25 | 0.40 |
| 2006 LIMA | 19,700,000 | — | — | 0.10 | 0.25 | 0.40 |

**KM# 303.4a CENTIMO**
0.82 g., Aluminum, 16 mm. **Obv:** National arms **Rev:** Value flanked by designs **Edge:** Plain **Note:** LIMA monogram is mint mark.

| Date | Mintage | VF20 | XF40 | MS60 | MS63 | MS65 |
|---|---|---|---|---|---|---|
| 2006 LIMA | 19,200,000 | — | — | 0.20 | 0.50 | 0.75 |
| 2007 LIMA | 48,800,000 | — | — | 0.10 | 0.25 | 0.30 |
| 2008 LIMA | 63,800,000 | — | — | 0.10 | 0.25 | 0.30 |
| 2009 LIMA | 62,000,000 | — | — | 0.10 | 0.25 | 0.30 |
| 2010 LIMA | 73,000,000 | — | — | 0.10 | 0.25 | 0.30 |
| 2011 LIMA | 14,700,000 | — | — | 0.10 | 0.25 | 0.30 |

## KM# 304.4 5 CENTIMOS

2.69 g., Brass, 18 mm. **Obv:** National arms, accent above "u" **Rev:** Value flanked by designs. Without Braille dots, with accent above "e" **Edge:** Plain **Note:** LIMA monogram is mint mark.

| Date | Mintage | VF20 | XF40 | MS60 | MS63 | MS65 |
|---|---|---|---|---|---|---|
| 2002 LIMA | 3,940,000 | — | — | 0.15 | 0.35 | 0.50 |
| 2005 LIMA | 8,900,000 | — | — | 0.15 | 0.35 | 0.50 |
| 2006 LIMA | 11,400,000 | — | — | 0.15 | 0.35 | 0.50 |
| 2007 LIMA | 12,800,000 | — | — | 0.15 | 0.35 | 0.50 |

## KM# 304.4a 5 CENTIMOS

1.02 g., Aluminum, 18 mm. **Obv:** National arms **Rev:** Value flanked by native designs **Edge:** Plain **Note:** LIMA monogram is mint mark.

| Date | Mintage | VF20 | XF40 | MS60 | MS63 | MS65 |
|---|---|---|---|---|---|---|
| 2007 LIMA | 12,400,000 | — | — | 0.15 | 0.35 | 0.50 |
| 2008 LIMA | 11,600,000 | — | — | 0.10 | 0.30 | 0.40 |
| 2009 LIMA | 20,000,000 | — | — | 0.10 | 0.30 | 0.40 |
| 2010 LIMA | 24,000,000 | — | — | 0.10 | 0.30 | 0.40 |
| 2011 LIMA | 36,000,000 | — | — | 0.10 | 0.30 | 0.40 |
| 2012 LIMA | 32,700,000 | — | — | 0.10 | 0.30 | 0.40 |
| 2013 LIMA | 24,000,000 | — | — | 0.10 | 0.20 | 0.30 |
| 2014 LIMA | — | — | — | 0.10 | 0.20 | 0.30 |

## KM# 305.4 10 CENTIMOS

3.50 g., Brass, 20.5 mm. **Obv:** National arms, accent above "u" **Rev:** Without braille dots, accent above "e" **Edge:** Plain **Note:** LIMA monogram is mint mark.

| Date | Mintage | VF20 | XF40 | MS60 | MS63 | MS65 |
|---|---|---|---|---|---|---|
| 2001 LIMA | 50,000,000 | — | — | 0.30 | 0.65 | 0.85 |
| 2002 LIMA | 37,420,000 | — | — | 0.30 | 0.65 | 0.85 |
| 2003 LIMA | 56,000,000 | — | — | 0.30 | 0.65 | 0.85 |
| 2004 LIMA | 27,500,000 | — | — | 0.30 | 0.65 | 0.85 |
| 2005 LIMA | 39,500,000 | — | — | 0.20 | 0.40 | 0.50 |
| 2006 LIMA | 54,200,000 | — | — | 0.20 | 0.40 | 0.50 |
| 2007 LIMA | 64,800,000 | — | — | 0.20 | 0.40 | 0.50 |
| 2008 LIMA | 79,400,000 | — | — | 0.20 | 0.40 | 0.50 |
| 2009 LIMA | 63,000,000 | — | — | 0.20 | 0.40 | 0.50 |
| 2010 LIMA | 82,000,000 | — | — | 0.20 | 0.40 | 0.50 |
| 2011 LIMA | 94,000,000 | — | — | 0.20 | 0.40 | 0.50 |
| 2012 LIMA | 112,700,000 | — | — | 0.20 | 0.40 | 0.50 |
| 2013 LIMA | 117,000,000 | — | — | 0.20 | 0.40 | 0.50 |
| 2014 LIMA | — | — | — | 0.15 | 0.30 | 0.40 |

## KM# 306.4 20 CENTIMOS

4.40 g., Brass, 23 mm. **Obv:** National arms, accent above "u" **Rev:** Without braille dots, accent above "e" **Edge:** Plain **Note:** LIMA monogram is mint mark.

| Date | Mintage | VF20 | XF40 | MS60 | MS63 | MS65 |
|---|---|---|---|---|---|---|
| 2001 LIMA | 13,000,000 | — | — | 0.35 | 0.85 | 1.20 |
| 2002 LIMA | 9,000,000 | — | — | 0.35 | 0.85 | 1.20 |
| 2003 LIMA | 2,000,000 | — | — | 0.40 | 1.00 | 1.25 |
| 2004 LIMA | 15,200,000 | — | — | 0.35 | 0.85 | 1.20 |
| 2006 LIMA | 3,700,000 | — | — | 0.30 | 0.75 | 1.00 |
| 2007 LIMA | 18,000,000 | — | — | 0.20 | 0.50 | 0.75 |
| 2008 LIMA | 24,300,000 | — | — | 0.20 | 0.50 | 0.75 |
| 2009 LIMA | 15,500,000 | — | — | 0.20 | 0.50 | 0.75 |
| 2010 LIMA | 25,000,000 | — | — | 0.20 | 0.50 | 0.75 |
| 2011 LIMA | 23,000,000 | — | — | 0.20 | 0.50 | 0.75 |
| 2012 LIMA | 25,800,000 | — | — | 0.20 | 0.50 | 0.75 |
| 2013 LIMA | 29,000,000 | — | — | 0.15 | 0.40 | 0.50 |
| 2014 LIMA | — | — | — | 0.15 | 0.40 | 0.50 |

## KM# 307.4 50 CENTIMOS

5.45 g., Copper-Nickel-Zinc, 22 mm. **Obv:** National arms, accent above "u" **Rev:** Without braille, accent above "e" **Edge:** Reeded **Note:** LIMA monogram is mint mark.

| Date | Mintage | VF20 | XF40 | MS60 | MS63 | MS65 |
|---|---|---|---|---|---|---|
| 2001 LIMA | 11,000,000 | — | — | 0.75 | 1.25 | 1.75 |
| 2002 LIMA | 12,000,000 | — | — | 0.75 | 1.25 | 1.75 |
| 2003 LIMA | 30,000,000 | — | — | 0.75 | 1.25 | 1.75 |
| 2004 LIMA | 6,000,000 | — | — | 0.75 | 1.25 | 1.75 |
| 2005 LIMA | 14,600,000 | — | — | 0.35 | 0.75 | 1.00 |
| 2006 LIMA | 24,200,000 | — | — | 0.35 | 0.75 | 1.00 |
| 2007 LIMA | 31,200,000 | — | — | 0.35 | 0.75 | 1.00 |
| 2008 LIMA | 36,200,000 | — | — | 0.35 | 0.75 | 1.00 |
| 2009 LIMA | 26,700,000 | — | — | 0.35 | 0.75 | 1.00 |
| 2010 LIMA | 5,180,000 | — | — | 0.35 | 0.75 | 1.00 |
| 2011 LIMA | 38,000,000 | — | — | 0.35 | 0.75 | 1.00 |
| 2012 LIMA | 24,900,000 | — | — | 0.35 | 0.75 | 1.00 |
| 2013 LIMA | 34,000,000 | — | — | 0.35 | 0.75 | 1.00 |
| 2014 LIMA | — | — | — | 0.35 | 0.75 | 1.00 |

## KM# 308.4 NUEVO SOL

7.32 g., Copper-Nickel-Zinc, 25.5 mm. **Obv:** National arms, accent above "u **Rev:** Without braille, accent above "e **Edge:** Reeded **Note:** LIMA monogram is mint mark.

| Date | Mintage | VF20 | XF40 | MS60 | MS63 | MS65 |
|---|---|---|---|---|---|---|
| 2001 LIMA | 10,000,000 | — | — | 0.75 | 1.50 | 3.00 |
| 2002 LIMA | 8,000,000 | — | — | 0.75 | 1.50 | 3.00 |
| 2003 LIMA | 5,000,000 | — | — | 0.75 | 1.50 | 3.00 |
| 2004 LIMA | 13,900,000 | — | — | 0.75 | 1.50 | 3.00 |
| 2005 LIMA | 14,600,000 | — | — | 0.65 | 1.25 | 1.75 |
| 2006 LIMA | 19,700,000 | — | — | 0.65 | 1.25 | 1.75 |
| 2007 LIMA | 36,700,000 | — | — | 0.50 | 1.00 | 1.50 |
| 2008 LIMA | 42,800,000 | — | — | 0.50 | 1.00 | 1.50 |
| 2009 LIMA | 34,330,000 | — | — | 0.50 | 1.00 | 1.50 |
| 2010 LIMA | 2,000,000 | — | — | 1.00 | 2.00 | 3.50 |
| 2011 LIMA | 23,000,000 | — | — | 0.50 | 1.00 | 1.50 |

## KM# 329 NUEVO SOL

33.63 g., 0.925 Silver 1.000 oz. ASW, 37 mm. **Subject:** 450th Anniversary - San Marcos University **Obv:** National arms **Rev:** University seal and building **Edge:** Reeded **Note:** LIMA monogram is mint mark.

| Date | Mintage | VF20 | XF40 | MS60 | MS63 | MS65 |
|---|---|---|---|---|---|---|
| 2001 LIMA | Est. 5000 | — | — | — | 60.00 | 65.00 |

## KM# 330 NUEVO SOL

33.63 g., 0.925 Silver 1.000 oz. ASW, 37 mm. **Subject:** 50th Anniversary - Numismatic Society of Peru **Obv:** National arms **Rev:** Stylized design within circle **Edge:** Reeded **Note:** LIMA monogram is mint mark.

| Date | Mintage | VF20 | XF40 | MS60 | MS63 | MS65 |
|---|---|---|---|---|---|---|
| 2001 LIMA | Est. 1000 | — | — | — | 60.00 | 65.00 |

## KM# 331 NUEVO SOL

33.63 g., 0.925 Silver 1.000 oz. ASW, 37 mm. **Subject:** 200th Anniversary - von Humboldt's visit to Peru **Obv:** National arms **Rev:** Seated figure 1/4 left **Edge:** Reeded **Note:** LIMA monogram is mint mark.

| Date | Mintage | VF20 | XF40 | MS60 | MS63 | MS65 |
|---|---|---|---|---|---|---|
| 2002 LIMA | Est. 1000 | — | — | — | 45.00 | 50.00 |

## KM# 334 NUEVO SOL

27.00 g., 0.925 Silver 0.803 oz. ASW, 40 mm. **Series:** Ibero-America **Obv:** National arms in center with ten national arms in outer circle **Obv. Legend:** BANCO CENTRAL DE RESERVA DEL PERÚ **Rev:** Ceramic - Indians in reed boats **Rev. Legend:** PERÚ **Edge:** Reeded

| Date | Mintage | VF20 | XF40 | MS60 | MS63 | MS65 |
|---|---|---|---|---|---|---|
| 2002 (M) | Est. 5000 | **PF63** | 50.00 | **PF65** | 60.00 | |

## KM# 332 NUEVO SOL

33.63 g., 0.925 Silver 1.000 oz. ASW, 37 mm. **Subject:** 125th Anniversary of the Inmaculate Jesuitas - Lima College **Obv:** National arms **Rev:** Statue and 3/4 crowned shield **Edge:** Reeded **Note:** LIMA monogram is mint mark.

| Date | Mintage | VF20 | XF40 | MS60 | MS63 | MS65 |
|---|---|---|---|---|---|---|
| 2003 LIMA | Est. 1000 | — | — | — | 45.00 | 50.00 |

## KM# 333 NUEVO SOL

33.63 g., 0.925 Silver 1.000 oz. ASW, 37 mm. **Subject:** 180th Anniversary of Peru's Congress **Obv:** National arms **Rev:** Statue in front of building **Edge:** Reeded **Note:** LIMA monogram is mint mark.

| Date | Mintage | VF20 | XF40 | MS60 | MS63 | MS65 |
|---|---|---|---|---|---|---|
| 2003 LIMA | Est. 1000 | — | — | — | 60.00 | 65.00 |

## KM# 335 NUEVO SOL

27.00 g., 0.925 Silver 0.803 oz. ASW, 40 mm. **Subject:** FIFA World Cup Soccer **Obv:** Arms within wreath **Rev:** Action scene beneath globe **Edge:** Reeded

| Date | Mintage | VF20 | XF40 | MS60 | MS63 | MS65 |
|---|---|---|---|---|---|---|
| 2004 (M) | Est. 50000 | **PF63** | 60.00 | **PF65** | 70.00 | |

**KM# 339 NUEVO SOL**

27.00 g., 0.925 Silver 0.803 oz. ASW, 40 mm. **Series:** Ibero-American **Subject:** Lost city of the Incas **Obv:** National arms in center with ten national arms in outer ring **Obv. Legend:** BANCO CENTRAL DE RESERVA DEL PERÚ **Rev:** Village ruins **Rev. Legend:** MACHU PICCHU . PERÚ **Edge:** Reeded

| Date | Mintage | VF20 | XF40 | MS60 | MS63 | MS65 |
|---|---|---|---|---|---|---|
| 2005 (M) | Est. 5000 | **PF63** 70.00 | **PF65** 80.00 | | | |

**KM# 356 NUEVO SOL**

33.63 g., 0.925 Silver 1.000 oz. ASW, 37 mm. **Subject:** Lima Regatta Club, 130th Anniversary **Edge:** Reeded

| Date | Mintage | VF20 | XF40 | MS60 | MS63 | MS65 |
|---|---|---|---|---|---|---|
| 2005 LIMA | Est. 1000 | — | — | — | 60.00 | 65.00 |

**KM# 357 NUEVO SOL**

27.00 g., 0.925 Silver 0.803 oz. ASW, 40 mm. **Series:** Ibero-American **Subject:** Volleyball **Rev:** Two volleyball players and net **Edge:** Reeded

| Date | Mintage | VF20 | XF40 | MS60 | MS63 | MS65 |
|---|---|---|---|---|---|---|
| 2007 (M) | Est. 2000 | **PF63** 65.00 | **PF65** 75.00 | | | |

**KM# 358 NUEVO SOL**

33.63 g., 0.925 Silver 1.000 oz. ASW, 37 mm. **Subject:** Lima-Huancayo Railway, 100th Anniversary **Rev:** Deisel and Steam trains in valley **Edge:** Reeded

| Date | Mintage | VF20 | XF40 | MS60 | MS63 | MS65 |
|---|---|---|---|---|---|---|
| 2008 LIMA | Est. 1000 | — | — | — | 45.00 | 50.00 |

**KM# 340 NUEVO SOL**

7.32 g., Copper-Nickel-Zinc, 25.5 mm. **Series:** Wealth and Pride of Peru **Subject:** Tumi de Oro **Obv:** National arms **Rev:** Tumi de Oro **Edge:** Reeded

| Date | Mintage | VF20 | XF40 | MS60 | MS63 | MS65 |
|---|---|---|---|---|---|---|
| 2010 Lima | 10,000,000 | — | — | 0.75 | 1.50 | 3.00 |

**KM# 341 NUEVO SOL**

7.32 g., Copper-Nickel-Zinc, 25.5 mm. **Series:** Wealth and Pride of Peru **Subject:** Sarcophagus of Karajia **Obv:** National arms **Rev:** Sarcophagus of Karajia **Edge:** Reeded

| Date | Mintage | VF20 | XF40 | MS60 | MS63 | MS65 |
|---|---|---|---|---|---|---|
| 2010 LIMA | 10,000,000 | — | — | 0.75 | 1.50 | 3.00 |

**KM# 342 NUEVO SOL**

7.32 g., Copper-Nickel-Zinc, 25.5 mm. **Series:** Wealth and Pride of Peru **Obv:** National Arms **Rev:** Estela de Ramondi **Edge:** Reeded

| Date | Mintage | VF20 | XF40 | MS60 | MS63 | MS65 |
|---|---|---|---|---|---|---|
| 2010 LIMA | 10,000,000 | — | — | 0.75 | 1.50 | 3.00 |

**KM# 359 NUEVO SOL**

27.00 g., 0.925 Silver 0.803 oz. ASW, 40 mm. **Series:** Ibero-American **Subject:** Historical coins of Peru

| Date | Mintage | VF20 | XF40 | MS60 | MS63 | MS65 |
|---|---|---|---|---|---|---|
| 2010 (M) | Est. 2000 | **PF63** 75.00 | **PF65** 85.00 | | | |

**KM# 345 NUEVO SOL**

7.30 g., Copper-Nickel-Zinc, 25.5 mm. **Series:** Wealth and Pride of Peru **Obv:** National arms **Rev:** Chullpas de Sillustani ruins **Edge:** Reeded

| Date | Mintage | VF20 | XF40 | MS60 | MS63 | MS65 |
|---|---|---|---|---|---|---|
| 2011 | 10,000,000 | — | — | 0.75 | 1.50 | 3.00 |

**KM# 346 NUEVO SOL**

7.32 g., Copper-Nickel-Zinc, 25.5 mm. **Series:** Wealth and Pride of Peru **Rev:** Monastery of Santa Catalina and plaza **Edge:** Reeded

| Date | Mintage | VF20 | XF40 | MS60 | MS63 | MS65 |
|---|---|---|---|---|---|---|
| 2011 LIMA | 10,000,000 | — | — | 0.75 | 1.50 | 3.00 |

**KM# 360 NUEVO SOL**

7.32 g., Copper-Nickel-Zinc, 25.5 mm. **Series:** Wealth and Pride of Peru **Obv:** National arms **Rev:** Machu Picchu ruins **Edge:** Reeded

| Date | Mintage | VF20 | XF40 | MS60 | MS63 | MS65 |
|---|---|---|---|---|---|---|
| 2011 | 10,000,000 | — | — | 0.75 | 1.50 | 3.00 |

**KM# 361 NUEVO SOL**

7.32 g., Copper-Nickel-Zinc, 25.5 mm. **Series:** Wealth and Pride of Peru **Obv:** National arms **Rev:** Gran Pajaten site

| Date | Mintage | VF20 | XF40 | MS60 | MS63 | MS65 |
|---|---|---|---|---|---|---|
| 2011 | 10,000,000 | — | — | 0.75 | 1.50 | 3.00 |

**KM# 362 NUEVO SOL**

7.32 g., Copper-Nickel-Zinc, 25.5 mm. **Series:** Wealth and Pride of Peru **Subject:** Piedra de Saywite **Obv:** National arms **Rev:** Monolith and animals and geometric designs **Edge:** Reeded

| Date | Mintage | VF20 | XF40 | MS60 | MS63 | MS65 |
|---|---|---|---|---|---|---|
| 2012 | 10,000,000 | — | — | 0.75 | 1.50 | 3.00 |

**KM# 363 NUEVO SOL**

7.32 g., Copper-Nickel-Zinc, 25.5 mm. **Series:** Wealth and Pride of Peru **Subject:** Fortaleza del Real Felipe **Obv:** National arms **Rev:** Fortress ruins **Edge:** Reeded

| Date | Mintage | VF20 | XF40 | MS60 | MS63 | MS65 |
|---|---|---|---|---|---|---|
| 2012 | 10,000,000 | — | — | 0.75 | 1.50 | 3.00 |

**KM# 364 NUEVO SOL**

7.32 g., Copper-Nickel-Zinc, 25.5 mm. **Series:** Wealth and Pride of Peru **Subject:** Templo del Sol Vilcashuaman **Obv:** National arms **Rev:** Temple ruins

| Date | Mintage | VF20 | XF40 | MS60 | MS63 | MS65 |
|---|---|---|---|---|---|---|
| 2012 | 10,000,000 | — | — | 0.75 | 1.50 | 3.00 |

**KM# 365 NUEVO SOL**

7.32 g., Copper-Nickel-Zinc, 25.5 mm. **Series:** Wealth and Pride of Peru **Obv:** National Arms **Rev:** Monolith of Kuntur Wasi **Edge:** Reeded

| Date | Mintage | VF20 | XF40 | MS60 | MS63 | MS65 |
|---|---|---|---|---|---|---|
| 2012 | 10,000,000 | — | — | 0.75 | 1.50 | 3.00 |

**KM# 366 NUEVO SOL**

7.32 g., Copper-Nickel-Zinc, 25.5 mm. **Obv:** National arms **Rev:** Value within wreath

| Date | Mintage | VF20 | XF40 | MS60 | MS63 | MS65 |
|---|---|---|---|---|---|---|
| 2012 LIMA | 30,200,000 | — | — | 0.50 | 1.00 | 1.50 |
| 2013 LIMA | 23,000,000 | — | — | 0.50 | 1.00 | 1.50 |
| 2014 LIMA | — | — | — | 0.50 | 1.00 | 1.50 |

**KM# 369 NUEVO SOL**

27.00 g., 0.925 Silver 0.803 oz. ASW, 40 mm. **Series:** Ibero-American **Subject:** 20th Anniversary **Obv:** National arms of Peru in center, Ten arms around **Rev:** Design elements of nine previous coins **Edge:** Reeded

| Date | Mintage | VF20 | XF40 | MS60 | MS63 | MS65 |
|---|---|---|---|---|---|---|
| 2012 (M) | Est. 2000 | **PF63** 45.00 | **PF65** 50.00 | | | |

**KM# 368 NUEVO SOL**

7.32 g., Copper-Nickel-Zinc, 25.5 mm. **Series:** Wealth and Pride of Peru **Subject:** Textile Art of Paracas **Obv:** National arms **Rev:** Textile with designs

| Date | Mintage | VF20 | XF40 | MS60 | MS63 | MS65 |
|---|---|---|---|---|---|---|
| 2013 LIMA | 10,000,000 | — | — | 0.65 | 1.25 | 2.25 |

**KM# 370 NUEVO SOL**

33.63 g., 0.925 Silver 1.000 oz. ASW, 37 mm. **Subject:** 150th Anniversary of the Adoption of the Sol Monetary Unit **Obv:** National arms, legends BANCO CENTRAL DE RESERVA DEL PERU **Rev:** Seated liberty and legends FIRME Y FELIZ POR LA UNION, UN SOL and 1863-2013 (Similar to 1 Sol of 1864) **Edge Lettering:** Reeded

| Date | Mintage | VF20 | XF40 | MS60 | MS63 | MS65 |
|---|---|---|---|---|---|---|
| 2013 LIMA | Est. 5000 | — | — | — | 50.00 | 55.00 |

**KM# 371 NUEVO SOL**

7.32 g., Copper-Nickel-Zinc, 25.5 mm. **Series:** Wealth and Pride of Peru **Subject:** Inca Temple of Huaytara **Obv:** National arms **Rev:** Wall and tower **Edge:** Reeded

| Date | Mintage | VF20 | XF40 | MS60 | MS63 | MS65 |
|---|---|---|---|---|---|---|
| 2013 LIMA | 10,000,000 | — | — | 0.65 | 1.25 | 2.25 |

**KM# 372 NUEVO SOL**

7.32 g., Copper-Nickel-Zinc, 25.5 mm. **Series:** Wealth and Pride of Peru **Subject:** Temple of Kotosh **Obv:** National arms **Rev:** Crossed hands and wall of temple

| Date | Mintage | VF20 | XF40 | MS60 | MS63 | MS65 |
|---|---|---|---|---|---|---|
| 2013 LIMA | 10,000,000 | — | — | 0.65 | 1.25 | 2.25 |

**KM# 373 NUEVO SOL**

7.32 g., Copper-Nickel-Zinc, 25.5 mm. **Series:** Wealth and Pride of Peru **Subject:** Archeological complex of Tunanmarca **Obv:** National arms **Rev:** Ruins of Tunanmarca

| Date | Mintage | VF20 | XF40 | MS60 | MS63 | MS65 |
|---|---|---|---|---|---|---|
| 2013 LIMA | 10,000,000 | — | — | 0.65 | 1.25 | 2.25 |

**KM# 374 NUEVO SOL**

7.320 Copper-Nickel-Zinc, 25.5 mm. **Series:** Natural Resources of Peru **Subject:** Anchovy **Obv:** National arms **Rev:** Two anchovies and plant **Edge:** Reeded

| Date | Mintage | VF20 | XF40 | MS60 | MS63 | MS65 |
|---|---|---|---|---|---|---|
| 2013 LIMA | 10,000,000 | — | — | 0.65 | 1.25 | 2.25 |

**KM# 375 NUEVO SOL**

7.32 g., Copper-Nickel-Zinc, 25.5 mm. **Series:** Natural Resources of Peru **Subject:** Cocoa Bean **Obv:** National arms **Rev:** Cocoa tree, cocoa pods

| Date | Mintage | VF20 | XF40 | MS60 | MS63 | MS65 |
|---|---|---|---|---|---|---|
| 2013 LIMA | 10,000,000 | — | — | 0.65 | 1.25 | 2.25 |

**KM# 376 NUEVO SOL**

7.32 g., Copper-Nickel-Zinc, 25.5 mm. **Series:** Natural Resources of Peru **Obv:** National arms **Rev:** Quinoa plant **Edge:** Reeded

| Date | Mintage | VF20 | XF40 | MS60 | MS63 | MS65 |
|---|---|---|---|---|---|---|
| 2013 LIMA | 10,000,000 | — | — | 0.65 | 1.25 | 2.25 |

**KM# 377 NUEVO SOL**

33.63 g., 0.925 Silver 1.0001 oz. ASW, 37 mm. **Obv:** National arms **Rev:** Jose Abelardo Quinones and plane **Edge:** Reeded

| Date | Mintage | F12 | VF20 | XF40 | MS60 | MS63 |
|---|---|---|---|---|---|---|
| 2014 LIMA | — | **PF63** 45.00 | **PF65** 50.00 | | | |

**KM# 378 NUEVO SOL**

33.63 g., 0.925 Silver 1.0001 oz. ASW, 37 mm. **Subject:** El Comerio newspaper, 175th Anniversary **Obv:** National Arms **Rev:** Building **Edge:** Reeded

| Date | Mintage | F12 | VF20 | XF40 | MS60 | MS63 |
|---|---|---|---|---|---|---|
| 2014 LIMA | — | **PF63** 45.00 | **PF65** 50.00 | | | |

**KM# 313 2 NUEVOS SOLES**

5.62 g., Bi-Metallic Nickel-Brass center in Stainless Steel ring, 22.2 mm. **Obv:** National arms within circle **Rev:** Stylized bird in flight to left of value within circle **Edge:** Plain **Note:** LIMA monogram is mint mark.

| Date | Mintage | VF20 | XF40 | MS60 | MS63 | MS65 |
|---|---|---|---|---|---|---|
| 2002 LIMA | 6,000,000 | — | — | 1.50 | 3.00 | 4.50 |
| 2003 LIMA | 5,000,000 | — | — | 1.50 | 3.00 | 4.50 |
| 2004 LIMA | 3,000,000 | — | — | 1.75 | 3.50 | 5.00 |
| 2005 LIMA | 6,000,000 | — | — | 0.65 | 1.25 | 2.50 |
| 2006 LIMA | 5,100,000 | — | — | 0.65 | 1.25 | 2.50 |
| 2007 LIMA | 7,000,000 | — | — | 0.65 | 1.25 | 2.50 |
| 2008 LIMA | 5,800,000 | — | — | 0.65 | 1.25 | 2.50 |
| 2009 LIMA | 7,000,000 | — | — | 0.65 | 1.25 | 2.50 |

**KM# 343 2 NUEVOS SOLES**

5.62 g., Bi-Metallic Brass center in Stainless Steel ring, 22.38 mm. **Obv:** National Arms **Rev:** Hummingbird from the Inca Lines, large value at right

| Date | Mintage | VF20 | XF40 | MS60 | MS63 | MS65 |
|---|---|---|---|---|---|---|
| 2010 LIMA | 6,235,000 | — | — | 0.65 | 1.25 | 2.50 |
| 2011 LIMA | 17,000,000 | — | — | 0.65 | 1.25 | 2.50 |
| 2012 LIMA | 18,730,000 | — | — | 0.65 | 1.25 | 2.50 |
| (2013) LIMA | 6,000,000 | — | — | 0.65 | 1.25 | 2.50 |
| 2014 LIMA | — | — | — | 0.65 | 1.25 | 2.50 |

**KM# 316 5 NUEVOS SOLES**

6.67 g., Bi-Metallic Nickel-Brass center in Stainless Steel ring, 24.32 mm. **Obv:** National arms within circle **Rev:** Stylized bird in flight to left of value within circle **Edge:** Reeded **Note:** LIMA monogram is mint mark.

| Date | Mintage | VF20 | XF40 | MS60 | MS63 | MS65 |
|---|---|---|---|---|---|---|
| 2001 LIMA | 5,000,000 | — | — | 2.00 | 4.00 | 5.50 |
| 2002 LIMA | 2,000,000 | — | — | 2.50 | 4.50 | 6.00 |
| 2005 LIMA | 6,000,000 | — | — | 1.75 | 3.50 | 5.00 |
| 2006 LIMA | 5,500,000 | — | — | 1.75 | 3.50 | 5.00 |
| 2007 LIMA | 6,400,000 | — | — | 1.75 | 3.50 | 5.00 |
| 2008 LIMA | 9,900,000 | — | — | 1.25 | 2.50 | 4.00 |
| 2009 LIMA | 10,000,000 | — | — | 1.00 | 2.00 | 3.50 |

**KM# 344 5 NUEVOS SOLES**

6.67 g., Bi-Metallic Brass center in Stainless Steel ring, 24.38 mm. **Obv:** National Arms **Rev:** Frigate bird from the Nasca lines, large value at right

| Date | Mintage | VF20 | XF40 | MS60 | MS63 | MS65 |
|---|---|---|---|---|---|---|
| 2010 LIMA | 6,000,000 | — | — | 1.50 | 3.00 | 4.50 |
| 2011 LIMA | 15,000,000 | — | — | 1.00 | 2.00 | 3.50 |
| 2012 LIMA | 14,900,000 | — | — | 1.00 | 2.00 | 3.50 |
| 2013 LIMA | 7,000,000 | — | — | 1.00 | 2.00 | 3.50 |
| 2014 LIMA | — | — | — | 1.00 | 2.00 | 3.50 |

# PHILIPPINES

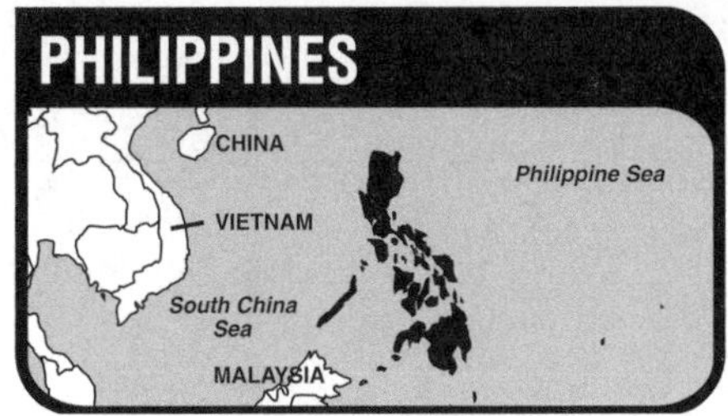


The Republic of the Philippines, an archipelago in the western Pacific 500 miles (805 km.) from the southeast coast of Asia, has an area of 115,830 sq. mi. (300,000 sq. km.) and a population of *64.9 million. Capital: Manila. The economy of the 7,000-island group is based on agriculture, forestry and fishing. Timber, coconut products, sugar and hemp are exported.

**MINT MARKS**

BSP - Bangko Sentral Pilipinas

M, MA - Manila

## REPUBLIC

### REFORM COINAGE

100 Sentimos = 1 Piso

**KM# 273 SENTIMO**

2.00 g., Copper Plated Steel, 15.5 mm. **Obv:** Value and date **Rev:** Central bank seal within circle and gear design, 1993 (date Central Bank was established) below **Rev. Legend:** BANGKO SENTRAL NG PILIPINAS - 1993

| Date | Mintage | VF20 | XF40 | MS60 | MS63 | MS65 |
|---|---|---|---|---|---|---|
| 2001 | — | — | — | 0.10 | 0.15 | 0.20 |
| 2002 | — | — | — | 0.10 | 0.15 | 0.20 |
| 2004 | — | — | — | 0.10 | 0.15 | 0.20 |
| 2005 | — | — | — | 0.10 | 0.15 | 0.20 |
| 2006 | — | — | — | 0.10 | 0.15 | 0.20 |
| 2007 | — | — | — | 0.10 | 0.15 | 0.20 |
| 2008 | — | — | — | 0.10 | 0.15 | 0.20 |
| 2009 | — | — | — | 0.10 | 0.15 | 0.20 |
| 2011 | — | — | — | — | 0.50 | 0.75 |

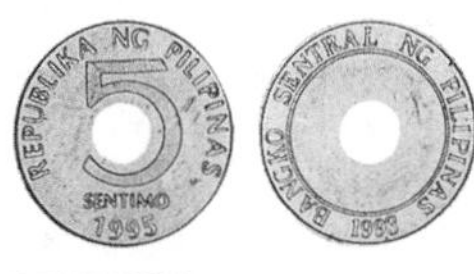

**KM# 268 5 SENTIMOS**

1.90 g., Copper Plated Steel, 15.5 mm. **Obv:** Numeral value around center hole **Rev:** Hole in center with date, bank and name around border, 1993 (date Central Bank was established) below **Rev. Legend:** BANGKO CENTRAL NG PILIPINAS - 1993 **Edge:** Plain

| Date | Mintage | VF20 | XF40 | MS60 | MS63 | MS65 |
|---|---|---|---|---|---|---|
| 2001 | — | — | — | 0.10 | 0.20 | 0.25 |
| 2002 | — | — | — | 0.10 | 0.20 | 0.25 |
| 2003 | — | — | — | 0.20 | 0.20 | 0.25 |
| 2004 | — | — | — | 0.20 | 0.50 | 0.75 |
| 2005 | — | — | — | 0.10 | 0.20 | 0.25 |
| 2006 | — | — | — | 0.10 | 0.20 | 0.25 |
| 2007 | — | — | — | 0.10 | 0.20 | 0.25 |
| 2008 | — | — | — | 0.10 | 0.20 | 0.25 |
| 2009 | — | — | — | 0.10 | 0.20 | 0.25 |
| 2010 | — | — | — | 0.10 | 0.20 | 0.25 |
| 2011 | — | — | — | 0.10 | 0.20 | 0.25 |
| 2012 | — | — | — | 0.10 | 0.20 | 0.25 |

**KM# 270.1 10 SENTIMOS**

2.50 g., Copper Plated Steel, 17 mm. **Obv:** Value and date **Rev:** Central Bank seal within circle and gear design, 1993 (date Central Bank was established) below **Rev. Legend:** BANGKO SENTRAL NG PILIPINAS - 1993 **Edge:** Reeded

| Date | Mintage | VF20 | XF40 | MS60 | MS63 | MS65 |
|---|---|---|---|---|---|---|
| 2001 | — | — | 0.10 | 0.20 | 0.30 | 0.40 |
| 2002 | — | — | 0.10 | 0.20 | 0.30 | 0.40 |
| 2004 | — | — | 0.45 | 0.75 | 1.50 | 2.50 |
| 2005 | — | — | 0.10 | 0.20 | 0.30 | 0.40 |

**KM# 270.2 10 SENTIMOS**

2.50 g., Copper Plated Steel, 17 mm. **Obv:** Value high on coin, different font, date **Rev:** Central Bank seal within circle and gear design **Rev. Legend:** BANGKO SENTRAL NG PILIPINAS - 1993 **Edge:** Reeded

| Date | Mintage | VF20 | XF40 | MS60 | MS63 | MS65 |
|---|---|---|---|---|---|---|
| 2006 | — | — | 0.10 | 0.20 | 0.30 | 0.40 |
| 2007 | — | — | 0.10 | 0.20 | 0.30 | 0.40 |
| 2008 | — | — | 0.10 | 0.20 | 0.30 | 0.40 |
| 2009 | — | — | 0.10 | 0.20 | 0.30 | 0.40 |
| 2010 | — | — | 0.10 | 0.20 | 0.30 | 0.40 |
| 2011 | — | — | 0.10 | 0.20 | 0.30 | 0.40 |
| 2012 | — | — | 0.10 | 0.20 | 0.30 | 0.40 |

**KM# 271 25 SENTIMOS**

3.80 g., Brass, 20 mm. **Obv:** Value and date **Rev:** Central Bank seal within circle and gear design, 1993 (date Central Bank was established) below **Rev. Legend:** BANGKO SENTRAL NG PILIPINAS - 1993 **Edge:** Plain

| Date | Mintage | VF20 | XF40 | MS60 | MS63 | MS65 |
|---|---|---|---|---|---|---|
| 2001 | — | 0.10 | 0.25 | 0.35 | 0.60 | 0.80 |
| 2002 | — | 0.10 | 0.25 | 0.35 | 0.60 | 0.80 |
| 2003 | — | 0.10 | 0.25 | 0.35 | 0.60 | 0.80 |

**KM# 271a 25 SENTIMOS**

3.60 g., Brass Plated Steel, 20 mm. **Obv:** Value and date **Rev:** Central Bank seal within circle and gear design **Rev. Legend:** BANGKO SENTRAL NG PILIPINAS - 1993 **Edge:** Plain

| Date | Mintage | VF20 | XF40 | MS60 | MS63 | MS65 |
|---|---|---|---|---|---|---|
| 2004 | — | — | 0.25 | 1.00 | 2.00 | 2.50 |
| 2005 | — | — | 0.25 | 0.50 | 1.00 | 1.25 |
| 2006 | — | — | 0.25 | 0.50 | 1.00 | 1.25 |
| 2007 | — | — | 0.25 | 0.50 | 1.00 | 1.25 |
| 2008 | — | — | 0.15 | 0.25 | 0.50 | 1.00 |
| 2009 | — | — | 0.15 | 0.25 | 0.50 | 1.00 |
| 2010 | — | — | 0.15 | 0.25 | 0.50 | 1.00 |
| 2011 | — | — | 0.15 | 0.25 | 0.50 | 1.00 |
| 2012 | — | — | 0.15 | 0.25 | 0.50 | 1.00 |
| 2013 | — | — | 0.15 | 0.25 | 0.50 | 1.00 |

**KM# 269 PISO**

6.10 g., Copper-Nickel, 24 mm. **Obv:** Head of Jose Rizal right, value and date **Rev:** Bank seal within circle and gear design, 1993 (date Central Bank was established) below **Rev. Legend:** BANGKO SENTRAL NG PILIPINAS - 1993 **Edge:** Reeded

| Date | Mintage | VF20 | XF40 | MS60 | MS63 | MS65 |
|---|---|---|---|---|---|---|
| 2001 | — | 0.25 | 0.45 | 0.65 | 1.25 | 1.75 |
| 2002 | — | 0.25 | 0.45 | 0.65 | 1.25 | 1.75 |
| 2003 Non Magnetic | — | — | — | — | — | 11.00 |

**KM# 269a PISO**

5.40 g., Nickel Plated Steel, 24 mm. **Obv:** Head of Jose Rizal right, value and date **Rev:** Bank seal within circle and gear design **Rev. Legend:** BANGKO SENTRAL NG PILIPINAS - 1993 **Edge:** Reeded

| Date | Mintage | VF20 | XF40 | MS60 | MS63 | MS65 |
|---|---|---|---|---|---|---|
| 2003 | — | — | — | 1.00 | 2.00 | 3.00 |
| 2004 | — | — | — | 3.00 | 5.00 | 7.00 |
| 2005 | — | — | 0.45 | 0.65 | 1.10 | 1.50 |
| 2006 | — | — | 0.45 | 0.65 | 1.10 | 1.50 |
| 2007 | — | — | 0.45 | 0.65 | 1.10 | 3.00 |
| 2008 | — | — | 0.45 | 0.65 | 1.10 | 3.00 |
| 2009 | — | — | 0.45 | 0.65 | 1.10 | 1.50 |
| 2010 | — | — | 0.45 | 0.65 | 1.10 | 1.50 |
| 2011 | — | — | 0.45 | 0.65 | 1.10 | 1.50 |
| 2012 | — | — | 0.45 | 0.65 | 1.10 | 1.50 |

**KM# 284 PISO**

5.35 g., Nickel Plated Steel, 24 mm. **Subject:** Jose Rizal 150th Birth Anniversary **Edge:** Reeded

| Date | Mintage | VF20 | XF40 | MS60 | MS63 | MS65 |
|---|---|---|---|---|---|---|
| 2011 | 10,000,000 | — | — | 0.50 | 1.00 | 1.50 |

**KM# 272 5 PISO**

7.70 g., Nickel-Brass, 27 mm. **Obv:** Head of Emilio Aguinaldo right, value and date within scalloped border **Rev:** Central Bank seal within circle and gear design within scalloped border, 1993 (date Central Bank was established) below **Rev. Legend:** BANGKO SENTRAL NG PILIPINAS - 1993 **Edge:** Plain

| Date | Mintage | VF20 | XF40 | MS60 | MS63 | MS65 |
|---|---|---|---|---|---|---|
| 2001 BSP | — | 1.00 | 2.00 | 2.50 | 3.00 | 4.50 |
| 2002 | — | 0.35 | 0.70 | 1.00 | 1.75 | 3.00 |
| 2003 | — | 0.35 | 0.70 | 1.00 | 1.75 | 3.00 |
| 2004 | — | 0.50 | 1.00 | 2.50 | 4.50 | 6.00 |
| 2005 | — | 0.35 | 0.70 | 1.00 | 1.75 | 4.00 |
| 2006 | — | 0.35 | 0.70 | 1.00 | 1.75 | 3.00 |
| 2007 | — | 0.35 | 0.70 | 1.00 | 1.75 | 3.00 |
| 2008 | — | 0.35 | 0.70 | 1.00 | 1.75 | 3.00 |
| 2009 | — | 0.35 | 0.70 | 1.00 | 1.75 | 3.00 |
| 2010 | — | 0.35 | 0.70 | 1.00 | 1.75 | 3.00 |
| 2011 | — | 0.35 | 0.70 | 1.00 | 1.75 | 3.00 |
| 2012 | — | 0.35 | 0.70 | 1.00 | 1.75 | 3.00 |

**KM# 278 10 PISO**

8.70 g., Bi-Metallic Aluminum-Bronze center in Copper-Nickel ring, 26.5 mm. **Obv:** Conjoined heads right within circle **Rev:** Bank seal within circle and gear design, 1993 (date Central Bank was established) below **Rev. Legend:** BANGKO SENTRAL NG PILIPINAS - 1993 **Edge:** Segmented reeding

| Date | Mintage | VF20 | XF40 | MS60 | MS63 | MS65 |
|---|---|---|---|---|---|---|
| 2001 | — | 0.70 | 1.40 | 2.00 | 3.50 | 5.50 |
| 2002 | — | 0.60 | 0.80 | 1.00 | 2.00 | 3.00 |
| 2003 | — | 0.60 | 0.80 | 1.50 | 3.00 | 4.00 |
| 2004 | — | 0.80 | 2.00 | 3.50 | 5.00 | 8.00 |
| 2005 | — | 0.75 | 1.50 | 2.25 | 3.75 | 5.00 |
| 2006 | — | 0.60 | 0.80 | 1.50 | 3.00 | 4.00 |
| 2007 | — | 0.75 | 1.50 | 2.25 | 3.75 | 5.00 |
| 2008 | — | 0.75 | 1.50 | 2.25 | 3.75 | 5.00 |
| 2009 | — | 0.75 | 1.50 | 2.25 | 3.75 | 5.00 |
| 2010 | — | 0.75 | 1.50 | 2.25 | 3.75 | 5.00 |
| 2011 | — | — | — | — | 7.50 | 10.00 |
| 2012 | — | 0.75 | 1.50 | 2.50 | 3.75 | 5.00 |

### MINT SETS

| KM# | Date | Mintage | Identification | Issue Price | Mkt Val |
|---|---|---|---|---|---|
| MS39 | 2005 (7) | — | KM#268-273, 278 plus medal | 10.00 | 15.00 |
| MS40 | 2006 (7) | — | KM#268-273, 278 | 10.00 | 15.00 |
| MS41 | 2009 (7) | — | KM#268-273, 278 | 25.00 | 30.00 |
| MS42 | 2011 (7) | — | KM#268-273, 278 plus Rizal Medal | 25.00 | 32.00 |

# PITCAIRN ISLANDS

PERU

South Pacific Ocean

A small volcanic island, along with the uninhabited islands of Oeno, Henderson, and Ducie, constitute the British Colony of Pitcairn Islands. The main island has an area of about 2 sq. mi. (5 sq. km.) and a population of *68. It is located 1350 miles southeast of Tahiti. The islanders subsist on fishing, garden produce and crops. The sale of postage stamps and carved curios to passing ships brings cash income.

New Zealand currency has been used since July 10, 1967.

## BRITISH COLONY

### REGULAR COINAGE

**KM# 54 5 CENTS**
3.40 g., Copper Plated Bronze, 19 mm. **Ruler:** Elizabeth II **Obv:** Head right **Rev:** Anchor from the H.M.A.V. Bounty

| Date | Mintage | VF20 | XF40 | MS60 | MS63 | MS65 |
|---|---|---|---|---|---|---|
| 2009 | 20,000 | — | — | — | 1.25 | 2.00 |
| 2010 | 20,000 | — | — | — | 1.25 | 2.00 |

**KM# 55 10 CENTS**
4.60 g., Copper Plated Bronze, 22 mm. **Ruler:** Elizabeth II **Obv:** Head right **Rev:** Bell from H.M.A.V. Bounty **Edge:** Reeded

| Date | Mintage | VF20 | XF40 | MS60 | MS63 | MS65 |
|---|---|---|---|---|---|---|
| 2009 | 20,000 | — | — | — | 1.50 | 3.00 |
| 2010 | 20,000 | — | — | — | 1.50 | 3.00 |

**KM# 56 20 CENTS**
6.50 g., Nickel Plated Bronze, 25 mm. **Ruler:** Elizabeth II **Obv:** Head right **Rev:** Bible from H.M.A.V. Bounty

| Date | Mintage | VF20 | XF40 | MS60 | MS63 | MS65 |
|---|---|---|---|---|---|---|
| 2009 | 20,000 | — | — | — | 2.50 | 5.00 |
| 2010 | 20,000 | — | — | — | 2.50 | 5.00 |

**KM# 57 50 CENTS**
8.00 g., Copper-Nickel **Ruler:** Elizabeth II **Obv:** Head right **Rev:** Pitcairn Longboat

| Date | Mintage | VF20 | XF40 | MS60 | MS63 | MS65 |
|---|---|---|---|---|---|---|
| 2009 | — | — | — | — | 3.50 | 7.00 |
| 2010 | — | — | — | — | 3.50 | 7.00 |

**KM# 14 DOLLAR**
Copper-Nickel, 38.8 mm. **Ruler:** Elizabeth II **Obv:** Bust facing right **Rev:** Queen Mum, Elizabeth II and Margaret facing **Rev. Legend:** 80th Birthday of H.M. Queen Elizabeth II

| Date | Mintage | VF20 | XF40 | MS60 | MS63 | MS65 |
|---|---|---|---|---|---|---|
| 2006 | — | — | — | — | — | 10.00 |

**KM# 58 DOLLAR**
16.30 g., Aluminum-Brass, 32 mm. **Ruler:** Elizabeth II **Obv:** Head right **Rev:** Cannon from H.A.M.V. Bounty **Edge:** Reeded

| Date | Mintage | VF20 | XF40 | MS60 | MS63 | MS65 |
|---|---|---|---|---|---|---|
| 2009 | 20,000 | — | — | — | — | 10.00 |
| 2010 | 20,000 | — | — | — | — | 10.00 |

**KM# 45 2 DOLLARS**
31.11 g., 0.999 Silver 0.999 oz. ASW, 40.7 mm. **Ruler:** Elizabeth II **Subject:** Year of the Rat **Rev:** Multicolor rat seated right

| Date | Mintage | VF20 | XF40 | MS60 | MS63 | MS65 |
|---|---|---|---|---|---|---|
| 2008 Prooflike | 30,000 | — | — | — | — | 75.00 |

**KM# 46 2 DOLLARS**
31.11 g., 0.999 Silver 0.999 oz. ASW, 40.7 mm. **Ruler:** Elizabeth II **Rev:** Multicolor HMAV Bounty under full sail right

| Date | Mintage | VF20 | XF40 | MS60 | MS63 | MS65 |
|---|---|---|---|---|---|---|
| 2008 Prooflike | 5,000 | — | — | — | — | 65.00 |

**KM# 47 2 DOLLARS**
31.11 g., 0.999 Silver 0.999 oz. ASW Partially gilt, 40.7 mm. **Ruler:** Elizabeth II **Rev:** HMAV Bounty under full sail right

| Date | Mintage | VF20 | XF40 | MS60 | MS63 | MS65 |
|---|---|---|---|---|---|---|
| 2008 | 1,500 | PF65 90.00 | | | | |

**KM# 51 2 DOLLARS**
31.11 g., 0.999 Silver 0.999 oz. ASW partially gilt, 40.7 mm. **Ruler:** Elizabeth II **Rev:** Captain William Bligh partially gilt

| Date | Mintage | VF20 | XF40 | MS60 | MS63 | MS65 |
|---|---|---|---|---|---|---|
| 2009 | 1,500 | PF65 120 | | | | |

**KM# 59 2 DOLLARS**
19.50 g., Aluminum-Brass, 35 mm. **Ruler:** Elizabeth II **Obv:** Head right **Rev:** Helm (wheel) from H.M.A.V. Bounty **Edge:** Seqmented reeding

| Date | Mintage | VF20 | XF40 | MS60 | MS63 | MS65 |
|---|---|---|---|---|---|---|
| 2009 | 20,000 | — | — | — | — | 12.00 |

**KM# 67 2 DOLLARS**
31.11 g., Silver partially gilt, 40.7 mm. **Ruler:** Elizabeth II **Rev:** Ox striding right, gilt

| Date | Mintage | VF20 | XF40 | MS60 | MS63 | MS65 |
|---|---|---|---|---|---|---|
| 2009 | 15,000 | PF65 75.00 | | | | |

**KM# 68 2 DOLLARS**
31.11 g., 0.999 Silver 0.999 oz. ASW, 40.7 mm. **Ruler:** Elizabeth II **Rev:** Ox striding right, color

| Date | Mintage | VF20 | XF40 | MS60 | MS63 | MS65 |
|---|---|---|---|---|---|---|
| 2009 | 15,000 | PF65 75.00 | | | | |

**KM# 60 2 DOLLARS**
Brass, 36 mm. **Ruler:** Elizabeth II **Rev:** H.M.A.V. Bounty at sail **Edge:** Segmented reeding

| Date | Mintage | VF20 | XF40 | MS60 | MS63 | MS65 |
|---|---|---|---|---|---|---|
| 2010 | 20,000 | — | — | — | — | 15.00 |

**KM# 61 2 DOLLARS**
15.50 g., 0.925 Silver 0.461 oz. ASW, 35 mm. **Ruler:** Elizabeth II **Subject:** Deep sea fish **Rev:** Black sea devil (Melanocetus Johnsonii) in color

| Date | Mintage | VF20 | XF40 | MS60 | MS63 | MS65 |
|---|---|---|---|---|---|---|
| 2010 | 1,000 | PF65 95.00 | | | | |

**KM# 62 2 DOLLARS**
15.55 g., 0.925 Silver 0.4624 oz. ASW, 35 mm. **Ruler:** Elizabeth II **Subject:** Deep sea fish **Rev:** White spotted jellyfish in color

| Date | Mintage | VF20 | XF40 | MS60 | MS63 | MS65 |
|---|---|---|---|---|---|---|
| 2010 | — | PF65 95.00 | | | | |

**KM# 63 2 DOLLARS**
15.55 g., 0.925 Silver 0.4624 oz. ASW, 35 mm. **Ruler:** Elizabeth II **Subject:** Deep sea fish **Rev:** Laternfish (Mychtophios) in color

| Date | Mintage | VF20 | XF40 | MS60 | MS63 | MS65 |
|---|---|---|---|---|---|---|
| 2010 | 1,000 | **PF65** 95.00 | | | | |

**KM# 65 2 DOLLARS**
31.11 g., 0.999 Silver 0.999 oz. ASW partially gilt, 40.7 mm. **Ruler:** Elizabeth II **Rev:** H.M.A.V. Bounty at sail, gilt

| Date | Mintage | VF20 | XF40 | MS60 | MS63 | MS65 |
|---|---|---|---|---|---|---|
| 2010 | 3,000 | **PF65** 140 | | | | |

**KM# 66 2 DOLLARS**
31.11 g., 0.999 Silver 0.999 oz. ASW partially gilt, 40.7 mm. **Ruler:** Elizabeth II **Rev:** Fletcher Christian facing, partially gilt

| Date | Mintage | VF20 | XF40 | MS60 | MS63 | MS65 |
|---|---|---|---|---|---|---|
| 2010 | 3,000 | **PF65** 140 | | | | |

**KM# 64 2 DOLLARS**
31.11 g., 0.999 Silver 0.999 oz. ASW, 40.7 mm. **Ruler:** Elizabeth II **Subject:** Alice in Wonderland **Rev:** March Hare within backward clock face

| Date | Mintage | VF20 | XF40 | MS60 | MS63 | MS65 |
|---|---|---|---|---|---|---|
| 2011 | 15,000 | **PF65** 75.00 | | | | |

**KM# 69 2 DOLLARS**
31.11 g., 0.999 Silver 0.999 oz. ASW, 40.7 mm. **Ruler:** Elizabeth II **Rev:** Rabbit in snow, multicolor

| Date | Mintage | VF20 | XF40 | MS60 | MS63 | MS65 |
|---|---|---|---|---|---|---|
| 2011 | 15,000 | **PF65** 125 | | | | |

**KM# 71 2 DOLLARS**
15.50 g., 0.925 Silver 0.461 oz. ASW, 35 mm. **Ruler:** Elizabeth II **Rev:** Cotylorhiza Tuberculata, Jellyfish in color

| Date | Mintage | VF20 | XF40 | MS60 | MS63 | MS65 |
|---|---|---|---|---|---|---|
| 2011 | 1,000 | **PF65** 95.00 | | | | |

**KM# 72 2 DOLLARS**
15.50 g., 0.925 Silver 0.461 oz. ASW, 35 mm. **Ruler:** Elizabeth II **Rev:** Chrysaora Achlyos, black jellyfish in color

| Date | Mintage | VF20 | XF40 | MS60 | MS63 | MS65 |
|---|---|---|---|---|---|---|
| 2011 | 1,000 | **PF65** 95.00 | | | | |

**KM# 73 2 DOLLARS**
15.50 g., 0.925 Silver 0.461 oz. ASW, 35 mm. **Ruler:** Elizabeth II **Rev:** Anoplogaster Cornuta, Fangtooth fish in color

| Date | Mintage | VF20 | XF40 | MS60 | MS63 | MS65 |
|---|---|---|---|---|---|---|
| 2011 | 1,000 | **PF65** 95.00 | | | | |

**KM# 74 2 DOLLARS**
15.50 g., 0.925 Silver 0.461 oz. ASW, 35 mm. **Ruler:** Elizabeth II **Rev:** Melanostomias Biseriatus in color

| Date | Mintage | VF20 | XF40 | MS60 | MS63 | MS65 |
|---|---|---|---|---|---|---|
| 2011 | 1,000 | **PF65** 95.00 | | | | |

**KM# 75 2 DOLLARS**
15.55 g., 0.925 Silver 0.4624 oz. ASW, 35 mm. **Ruler:** Elizabeth II **Subject:** Deep Sea Fish

| Date | Mintage | VF20 | XF40 | MS60 | MS63 | MS65 |
|---|---|---|---|---|---|---|
| 2013 | Est. 1000 | **PF65** 95.00 | | | | |

**KM# 76 2 DOLLARS**
31.11 g., 0.999 Silver 0.999 oz. ASW, 40.7 mm. **Ruler:** Elizabeth II **Obv:** Head crowned right **Rev:** Cunard's Queen Elizabeth II passenger ship sailing right in color

| Date | Mintage | VF20 | XF40 | MS60 | MS63 | MS65 |
|---|---|---|---|---|---|---|
| 2013 | — | **PF65** 150 | | | | |

**KM# 77 2 DOLLARS**
31.11 g., 0.999 Silver 0.999 oz. ASW, 30x51 mm. **Ruler:** Elizabeth II **Rev:** Henderson Island Fruit dove on branch right in color **Shape:** Vertical rectangle

| Date | Mintage | VF20 | XF40 | MS60 | MS63 | MS65 |
|---|---|---|---|---|---|---|
| 2013 | 3,000 | **PF65** 75.00 | | | | |

**KM# 12 5 DOLLARS**
31.10 g., 0.999 Silver 0.9989 oz. ASW with Mother-of-Pearl inset, 40 mm. **Ruler:** Elizabeth II **Series:** Save the Whales **Obv:** Crowned bust right **Obv. Legend:** ELIZABETH II • PITCAIRN ISLANDS **Rev:** Humpback Whale and date on mother-of-pearl inset **Edge:** Plain

| Date | Mintage | VF20 | XF40 | MS60 | MS63 | MS65 |
|---|---|---|---|---|---|---|
| 2002 | 2,000 | **PF65** 95.00 | | | | |

**KM# 50 5 DOLLARS**
1.27 g., 0.9999 Gold 0.0408 oz. AGW, 13.92 mm. **Ruler:** Elizabeth II **Obv:** Crowned bust right **Obv. Legend:** Elizabeth II Pitcairn Islands **Rev:** Bounty Bible and ship

| Date | Mintage | VF20 | XF40 | MS60 | MS63 | MS65 |
|---|---|---|---|---|---|---|
| 2005 | — | PF65 90.00 | | | | |

**KM# 48 10 DOLLARS**
1.24 g., 0.9999 Gold 0.040 oz. AGW, 14 mm. **Ruler:** Elizabeth II **Rev:** HMAV Bounty under full sail right

| Date | Mintage | VF20 | XF40 | MS60 | MS63 | MS65 |
|---|---|---|---|---|---|---|
| 2008 | 10,000 | PF65 165 | | | | |

**KM# 49 25 DOLLARS**
7.77 g., 0.999 Gold 0.2496 oz. AGW, 22 mm. **Ruler:** Elizabeth II **Rev:** HMAV Bounty under full sail right

| Date | Mintage | VF20 | XF40 | MS60 | MS63 | MS65 |
|---|---|---|---|---|---|---|
| 2008 | 1,500 | PF65 750 | | | | |

## MINT SETS

| KM# | Date | Mintage | Identification | Issue Price | Mkt Val |
|---|---|---|---|---|---|
| MS1 | 2009 (6) | 20,000 | KM#54; 55; 56; 57; 58; 59 | — | 45.00 |
| MS2 | 2010 (6) | 20,000 | KM#54; 55; 56; 57; 58; 60 | — | 45.00 |

# POLAND

The Republic of Poland, located in central Europe, has an area of 120,725 sq. mi. (312,680 sq. km.) and a population of *38.2 million. Capital: Warszawa (Warsaw). The economy is essentially agricultural, but industrial activity provides the products for foreign trade. Machinery, coal, coke, iron, steel and transport equipment are exported.

**MINT MARKS**

MV, MW, MW-monogram - Warsaw Mint, 1965-
CHI - Valcambi, Switzerland

Other letters appearing with date denote the Mintmaster at the time the coin was struck.

## REPUBLIC

Democratic

## REFORM COINAGE

As far back as 1990, production was initiated for the new 1 Grosz - 1 Zlotych coins for a forthcoming monetary reform. It wasn't announced until the Act of July 7, 1994 and was enacted on January 1, 1995.

100 Old Zlotych = 1 Grosz; 10,000 Old Zlotych = 1 Zloty

**Y# 276 GROSZ**
1.64 g., Brass, 15.5 mm. **Obv:** National arms **Obv. Legend:** RZECZPOSPOLITA POLSKA **Rev:** Drooping oak leaf over value **Edge:** Reeded

| Date | Mintage | VF20 | XF40 | MS60 | MS63 | MS65 |
|---|---|---|---|---|---|---|
| 2001 MW | 210,000,020 | — | — | 0.10 | 0.20 | 0.40 |
| 2002 MW | 240,000,000 | — | — | 0.10 | 0.20 | 0.40 |
| 2003 MW | 250,000,000 | — | — | 0.10 | 0.20 | 0.40 |
| 2004 MW | 300,000,000 | — | — | 0.10 | 0.20 | 0.40 |
| 2005 MW | 375,000,000 | — | — | 0.10 | 0.20 | 0.40 |
| 2006 MW | 184,000,000 | — | — | 0.10 | 0.20 | 0.40 |
| 2007 MW | 330,000,000 | — | — | 0.10 | 0.20 | 0.40 |
| 2008 MW | — | — | — | 0.10 | 0.20 | 0.40 |
| 2009 MW | — | — | — | 0.10 | 0.20 | 0.40 |
| 2010 MW | — | — | — | 0.10 | 0.20 | 0.40 |
| 2011 MW | — | — | — | 0.10 | 0.20 | 0.40 |
| 2012 MW | — | — | — | 0.10 | 0.20 | 0.40 |

**Y# 277 2 GROSZE**
2.13 g., Brass, 17.5 mm. **Obv:** National arms **Obv. Legend:** RZECZPOSPOLITA POLSKA **Rev:** Drooping oak leaves above value **Edge:** Plain

| Date | Mintage | VF20 | XF40 | MS60 | MS63 | MS65 |
|---|---|---|---|---|---|---|
| 2001 MW | 86,100,000 | — | — | 0.15 | 0.25 | 0.50 |
| 2002 MW | 83,910,000 | — | — | 0.15 | 0.25 | 0.50 |
| 2003 MW | 80,000,000 | — | — | 0.15 | 0.25 | 0.50 |
| 2004 MW | 100,000,000 | — | — | 0.15 | 0.25 | 0.50 |
| 2005 MW | 163,003,250 | — | — | 0.15 | 0.25 | 0.50 |
| 2006 MW | 105,000,000 | — | — | 0.15 | 0.25 | 0.50 |
| 2007 MW | 160,000,000 | — | — | 0.15 | 0.25 | 0.50 |
| 2008 MW | — | — | — | 0.15 | 0.25 | 0.50 |
| 2009 MW | — | — | — | 0.15 | 0.25 | 0.50 |
| 2010 MW | — | — | — | 0.15 | 0.25 | 0.50 |
| 2011 MW | — | — | — | 0.15 | 0.25 | 0.50 |
| 2012 MW | — | — | — | 0.15 | 0.25 | 0.50 |
| 2013 MW | — | — | — | 0.15 | 0.25 | 0.50 |

**Y# 278 5 GROSZY**
2.59 g., Brass, 19.5 mm. **Obv:** National arms **Obv. Legend:** RZECZPOSPOLITA POLSKA **Rev:** Value at upper left of oak leaves **Edge:** Segmented reeding

| Date | Mintage | VF20 | XF40 | MS60 | MS63 | MS65 |
|---|---|---|---|---|---|---|
| 2001 MW | 67,368,000 | — | — | 0.25 | 0.45 | 0.75 |
| 2002 MW | 67,200,000 | — | — | 0.25 | 0.45 | 0.75 |
| 2003 MW | 48,000,000 | — | — | 0.25 | 0.45 | 0.75 |
| 2004 MW | 62,500,000 | — | — | 0.25 | 0.45 | 0.75 |
| 2005 MW | 113,000,000 | — | — | 0.25 | 0.45 | 0.75 |
| 2006 MW | 54,000,000 | — | — | 0.25 | 0.45 | 0.75 |
| 2007 MW | 116,000,000 | — | — | 0.25 | 0.45 | 0.75 |
| 2008 MW | — | — | — | 0.25 | 0.45 | 0.75 |
| 2009 MW | — | — | — | 0.25 | 0.45 | 0.75 |
| 2010 MW | — | — | — | 0.25 | 0.45 | 0.75 |
| 2011 MW | — | — | — | 0.25 | 0.45 | 0.75 |
| 2012 MW | — | — | — | 0.25 | 0.45 | 0.75 |
| 2013 MW | — | — | — | 0.25 | 0.45 | 0.75 |

**Y# 279 10 GROSZY**
2.55 g., Copper-Nickel, 16.5 mm. **Obv:** National arms **Obv. Legend:** RZECZPOSPOLITA POLSKA **Rev:** Value within wreath

| Date | Mintage | VF20 | XF40 | MS60 | MS63 | MS65 |
|---|---|---|---|---|---|---|
| 2001 MW | 62,820,000 | — | — | 0.40 | 0.60 | 1.00 |
| 2002 MW | 10,500,000 | — | — | 0.40 | 0.60 | 1.00 |
| 2003 MW | 31,500,000 | — | — | 0.40 | 0.60 | 1.00 |
| 2004 MW | 70,500,000 | — | — | 0.40 | 0.60 | 1.00 |
| 2005 MW | 94,000,000 | — | — | 0.40 | 0.60 | 1.00 |
| 2006 MW | 40,000,000 | — | — | 0.40 | 0.60 | 1.00 |
| 2007 MW | 100,000,000 | — | — | 0.40 | 0.60 | 1.00 |
| 2008 MW | — | — | — | 0.40 | 0.60 | 1.00 |
| 2009 MW | — | — | — | 0.40 | 0.60 | 1.00 |
| 2010 MW | — | — | — | 0.40 | 0.60 | 1.00 |
| 2011 MW | — | — | — | 0.40 | 0.60 | 1.00 |
| 2012 MW | — | — | — | 0.40 | 0.60 | 1.00 |

**Y# 280 20 GROSZY**
3.22 g., Copper-Nickel, 18.5 mm. **Obv:** National arms **Obv. Legend:** RZECZPOSPOLITA POLSKA **Rev:** Value within artistic design **Edge:** Reeded

| Date | Mintage | VF20 | XF40 | MS60 | MS63 | MS65 |
|---|---|---|---|---|---|---|
| 2001 MW | 41,980,001 | — | — | 0.65 | 0.85 | 1.25 |
| 2002 MW | 10,500,000 | — | — | 0.65 | 0.85 | 1.25 |
| 2003 MW | 20,400,000 | — | — | 0.65 | 0.85 | 1.25 |
| 2004 MW | 40,000,025 | — | — | 0.65 | 0.85 | 1.25 |
| 2005 MW | 37,000,000 | — | — | 0.65 | 0.85 | 1.25 |
| 2006 MW | 35,000,000 | — | — | 0.65 | 0.85 | 1.25 |
| 2007 MW | 68,000,000 | — | — | 0.65 | 0.85 | 1.25 |
| 2008 MW | — | — | — | 0.65 | 0.85 | 1.25 |
| 2009 MW | — | — | — | 0.65 | 0.85 | 1.25 |
| 2010 MW | — | — | — | 0.65 | 0.85 | 1.25 |
| 2011 MW | — | — | — | 0.65 | 0.85 | 1.25 |
| 2012 MW | — | — | — | 0.65 | 0.85 | 1.25 |

**Y# 281 50 GROSZY**
3.94 g., Copper-Nickel, 20.5 mm. **Obv:** National arms **Obv. Legend:** RZECZPOSPOLITA POLSKA **Rev:** Value to right of sprig **Edge:** Reeded

| Date | Mintage | VF20 | XF40 | MS60 | MS63 | MS65 |
|---|---|---|---|---|---|---|
| 2008 MW | — | — | — | 1.00 | 1.25 | 1.75 |
| 2009 MW | — | — | — | 1.00 | 1.25 | 1.75 |
| 2010 MW | — | — | — | 1.00 | 1.25 | 1.75 |
| 2011 MW | — | — | — | 1.00 | 1.25 | 1.75 |
| 2012 MW | — | — | — | 1.00 | 1.25 | 1.75 |
| 2013 MW | — | — | — | 1.00 | 1.25 | 1.75 |

**Y# 282 ZŁOTY**
5.03 g., Copper-Nickel, 23 mm. **Obv:** National arms **Obv. Legend:** RZECZPOSPOLITA POLSKA **Rev:** Value within wreath **Edge:** Segmented reeding

| Date | Mintage | VF20 | XF40 | MS60 | MS63 | MS65 |
|---|---|---|---|---|---|---|
| 2008 MW | — | — | — | 1.75 | 2.00 | 2.75 |
| 2009 MW | — | — | — | 1.75 | 2.00 | 2.75 |
| 2010 MW | — | — | — | 1.75 | 2.00 | 2.75 |
| 2012 MW | — | — | — | 1.75 | 2.00 | 2.75 |
| 2013 MW | — | — | — | 1.75 | 2.00 | 2.75 |

**Y# 283 2 ZŁOTE**
5.21 g., Bi-Metallic Copper-Nickel center in Aluminum-Bronze ring, 21.5 mm. **Obv:** National arms within circle **Obv. Legend:** RZECZPOSPOLITA POLSKA **Rev:** Value flanked by oak leaves **Edge:** Plain

| Date | Mintage | VF20 | XF40 | MS60 | MS63 | MS65 |
|---|---|---|---|---|---|---|
| 2005 MW | 5,000,000 | — | — | 4.00 | 4.50 | 5.50 |
| 2006 MW | 5,000,000 | — | — | 4.00 | 4.50 | 5.50 |
| 2007 MW | 20,000,000 | — | — | 4.00 | 4.50 | 5.50 |

Note: Varieties exist with or without pellets flanking date on obverse.

| Date | Mintage | VF20 | XF40 | MS60 | MS63 | MS65 |
|---|---|---|---|---|---|---|
| 2008 MW | — | — | — | 4.00 | 4.50 | 5.50 |
| 2009 MW | — | — | — | 4.00 | 4.50 | 5.50 |
| 2010 MW | — | — | — | 4.00 | 4.50 | 5.50 |

**Y# 408 2 ZŁOTE**
8.15 g., Brass, 27 mm. **Subject:** Wieliczka Salt Mine **Obv:** Crowned eagle with wings open **Rev:** Ancient salt miners

| Date | Mintage | VF20 | XF40 | MS60 | MS63 | MS65 |
|---|---|---|---|---|---|---|
| 2001 | 500,000 | — | 3.50 | 7.00 | 12.00 | 15.00 |

**Y# 410 2 ZŁOTE**
8.15 g., Brass, 27 mm. **Subject:** Amber Route **Obv:** Crowned eagle with wings open **Rev:** Ancient Roman coin and map with route marked in stars

| Date | Mintage | VF20 | XF40 | MS60 | MS63 | MS65 |
|---|---|---|---|---|---|---|
| 2001 | 500,000 | — | 3.50 | 7.00 | 12.00 | 15.00 |

**Y# 412 2 ZŁOTE**

8.15 g., Brass, 27 mm. **Subject:** 15 Years of the Constitutional Court **Obv:** Crowned eagle with wings open **Rev:** Crowned eagle head and scale **Edge:** * NBP * eight times

| Date | Mintage | VF20 | XF40 | MS60 | MS63 | MS65 |
|---|---|---|---|---|---|---|
| 2001 MW | 500,000 | — | — | 3.00 | 5.00 | 7.00 |

**Y# 414 2 ZŁOTE**

8.15 g., Brass, 27 mm. **Obv:** Crowned eagle with wings open **Rev:** Butterfly **Edge:** * NBP * eight times

| Date | Mintage | VF20 | XF40 | MS60 | MS63 | MS65 |
|---|---|---|---|---|---|---|
| 2001 MW | 600,000 | — | 4.00 | 8.00 | 15.00 | 18.00 |

**Y# 418 2 ZŁOTE**

8.15 g., Brass, 27 mm. **Subject:** Cardinal Stefan Wyszynski **Obv:** Crowned eagle with wings open **Rev:** Bust left wearing mitre **Edge:** NBP" eight times

| Date | Mintage | VF20 | XF40 | MS60 | MS63 | MS65 |
|---|---|---|---|---|---|---|
| 2001 MW | 1,200,000 | — | — | 3.00 | 5.00 | 7.00 |

**Y# 421 2 ZŁOTE**

8.15 g., Brass, 27 mm. **Subject:** Michal Siedlecki **Obv:** Crowned eagle with wings open **Rev:** Bust left and art work **Edge:** NBP eight times

| Date | Mintage | VF20 | XF40 | MS60 | MS63 | MS65 |
|---|---|---|---|---|---|---|
| 2001 MW | 600,000 | — | — | 3.00 | 5.00 | 7.00 |

**Y# 422 2 ZŁOTE**

8.15 g., Brass, 27 mm. **Subject:** Koledicy **Obv:** Crowned eagle with wings open **Rev:** Christmas celebration scene

| Date | Mintage | VF20 | XF40 | MS60 | MS63 | MS65 |
|---|---|---|---|---|---|---|
| 2001 MW | 600,000 | — | — | 3.00 | 5.00 | 7.00 |

**Y# 423 2 ZŁOTE**

8.15 g., Brass, 27 mm. **Subject:** Jan III Sobieski **Obv:** Crowned eagle with wings open **Rev:** Bust facing **Edge Lettering:** * NBP * eight times

| Date | Mintage | VF20 | XF40 | MS60 | MS63 | MS65 |
|---|---|---|---|---|---|---|
| 2001 MW | 500,000 | — | 3.50 | 7.00 | 12.00 | 15.00 |

**Y# 426 2 ZŁOTE**

8.15 g., Brass, 27 mm. **Subject:** Henryk Wieniawski **Obv:** Crowned eagle with wings open **Rev:** Bust left and violin **Edge Lettering:** * NBP * eight times

| Date | Mintage | VF20 | XF40 | MS60 | MS63 | MS65 |
|---|---|---|---|---|---|---|
| 2001 MW | 600,000 | — | — | 3.00 | 5.00 | 7.00 |

**Y# 427 2 ZŁOTE**

8.15 g., Brass, 27 mm. **Obv:** Crowned eagle with wings open **Rev:** European Pond Turtles **Edge Lettering:** * NBP * eight times

| Date | Mintage | VF20 | XF40 | MS60 | MS63 | MS65 |
|---|---|---|---|---|---|---|
| 2002 MW | 750,000 | — | 3.50 | 7.00 | 12.00 | 15.00 |

**Y# 431 2 ZŁOTE**

8.15 g., Brass, 27 mm. **Subject:** Bronislaw Malinowski **Obv:** Crowned eagle with wings open **Rev:** Bust facing and Trobriand Islanders **Edge Lettering:** * NBP * eight times

| Date | Mintage | VF20 | XF40 | MS60 | MS63 | MS65 |
|---|---|---|---|---|---|---|
| 2002 MW | 680,000 | — | — | 3.50 | 5.50 | 7.50 |

**Y# 433 2 ZŁOTE**

8.15 g., Brass, 27 mm. **Subject:** World Cup Soccer **Obv:** National arms **Rev:** Soccer players **Edge Lettering:** * NBP * eight times

| Date | Mintage | VF20 | XF40 | MS60 | MS63 | MS65 |
|---|---|---|---|---|---|---|
| 2002 MW | 1,000,000 | — | — | 3.00 | 5.00 | 7.00 |

**Y# 439 2 ZŁOTE**

8.10 g., Brass, 26.8 mm. **Subject:** August II (1697-1706, 1709-1733) **Obv:** National arms **Rev:** Head facing **Edge Lettering:** * NBP * eight times

| Date | Mintage | VF20 | XF40 | MS60 | MS63 | MS65 |
|---|---|---|---|---|---|---|
| 2002 MW | 620,000 | — | — | 4.00 | 7.00 | 9.00 |

**Y# 440 2 ZŁOTE**

8.15 g., Brass, 27 mm. **Subject:** Gen. Wladyslaw Anders **Obv:** Crowned eagle with wings open **Rev:** Uniformed bust facing and cross **Edge Lettering:** * NBP * eight times

| Date | Mintage | VF20 | XF40 | MS60 | MS63 | MS65 |
|---|---|---|---|---|---|---|
| 2002 MW | 680,000 | — | — | 3.00 | 5.00 | 7.00 |

**Y# 443 2 ZŁOTE**

8.15 g., Brass, 27 mm. **Subject:** Malbork Castle **Obv:** Crowned eagle with wings open **Rev:** Castle **Edge Lettering:** * NBP * eight times

| Date | Mintage | VF20 | XF40 | MS60 | MS63 | MS65 |
|---|---|---|---|---|---|---|
| 2002 MW | 680,000 | — | — | 3.00 | 5.00 | 7.00 |

**Y# 444 2 ZŁOTE**

8.15 g., Brass, 27 mm. **Subject:** Jan Matejko **Obv:** Denomination, crowned eagle and artist's palette **Rev:** Jester behind portrait **Edge Lettering:** * NBP * eight times

| Date | Mintage | VF20 | XF40 | MS60 | MS63 | MS65 |
|---|---|---|---|---|---|---|
| 2002 MW | 700,000 | — | — | 3.00 | 5.00 | 7.00 |

**Y# 445 2 ZŁOTE**

8.15 g., Brass, 27 mm. **Subject:** Eels **Obv:** Crowned eagle with wings open **Rev:** Two European eels **Edge Lettering:** * NBP * eight times

| Date | Mintage | VF20 | XF40 | MS60 | MS63 | MS65 |
|---|---|---|---|---|---|---|
| 2003 MW | 450,000 | — | 6.00 | 12.00 | 20.00 | 25.00 |

**Y# 446 2 ZŁOTE**

7.75 g., Brass, 27 mm. **Subject:** Children **Obv:** Children and square design above crowned eagle, date and value **Rev:** Children on square design **Edge Lettering:** * NBP * eight times **Note:** Center hole.

| Date | Mintage | VF20 | XF40 | MS60 | MS63 | MS65 |
|---|---|---|---|---|---|---|
| 2003 MW | 2,500,000 | — | — | 4.50 | 6.50 | 9.50 |

**Y# 447 2 ZŁOTE**
8.15 g., Brass, 27 mm. **Subject:** City of Poznan (Posen) **Obv:** Crowned eagle with wings open **Rev:** Clock face and tower flanked by goat heads **Edge Lettering:** * NBP * eight times

| Date | Mintage | VF20 | XF40 | MS60 | MS63 | MS65 |
|---|---|---|---|---|---|---|
| 2003 MW | 600,000 | — | — | 5.00 | 8.00 | 10.00 |

**Y# 451 2 ZŁOTE**
8.15 g., Brass, 27 mm. **Subject:** Easter Monday Festival **Obv:** Crowned eagle with wings open **Rev:** Festival scene **Edge Lettering:** * NBP * eight times

| Date | Mintage | VF20 | XF40 | MS60 | MS63 | MS65 |
|---|---|---|---|---|---|---|
| 2003 MW | 600,000 | — | — | 4.00 | 7.00 | 9.00 |

**Y# 455 2 ZŁOTE**
8.15 g., Brass, 27 mm. **Subject:** Petroleum and Gas Industry 150th Anniversary **Obv:** Crowned eagle with wings open **Rev:** Portrait and refinery **Edge Lettering:** * NBP * eight times

| Date | Mintage | VF20 | XF40 | MS60 | MS63 | MS65 |
|---|---|---|---|---|---|---|
| 2003 MW | 600,000 | — | — | 3.50 | 5.50 | 7.50 |

**Y# 456 2 ZŁOTE**
8.15 g., Brass, 27 mm. **Subject:** General B. S. Maczek **Obv:** Crowned eagle with wings open **Rev:** Military uniformed portrait **Edge Lettering:** * NBP * eight times

| Date | Mintage | VF20 | XF40 | MS60 | MS63 | MS65 |
|---|---|---|---|---|---|---|
| 2003 MW | 700,000 | — | — | 3.00 | 5.00 | 7.00 |

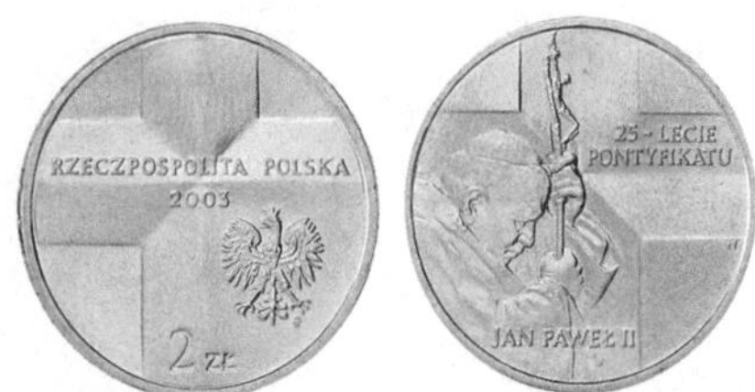

**Y# 465 2 ZŁOTE**
8.15 g., Brass, 27 mm. **Subject:** Pope John Paul II **Obv:** Small national arms at lower right with cross in background **Obv. Legend:** RZECZPOSPOLITA POLSKA **Rev:** Pope in prayer at left, cross in background **Edge Lettering:** * NBP * eight times

| Date | Mintage | VF20 | XF40 | MS60 | MS63 | MS65 |
|---|---|---|---|---|---|---|
| 2003 MW | 2,000,000 | — | — | 3.00 | 5.00 | 7.00 |

**Y# 473 2 ZŁOTE**
8.15 g., Brass, 27 mm. **Obv:** Crowned eagle with wings open **Rev:** Stanislaus Leszcywski **Edge Lettering:** * NBP * eight times

| Date | Mintage | VF20 | XF40 | MS60 | MS63 | MS65 |
|---|---|---|---|---|---|---|
| 2003 MW | 600,000 | — | — | 3.50 | 5.50 | 7.50 |

**Y# 477 2 ZŁOTE**
8.15 g., Brass, 27 mm. **Obv:** Crowned eagle with wings open and artist's palette **Rev:** Self portrait of Jacek Malczewski **Edge Lettering:** * NBP * eight times

| Date | Mintage | VF20 | XF40 | MS60 | MS63 | MS65 |
|---|---|---|---|---|---|---|
| 2003 MW | 600,000 | — | — | 3.50 | 5.50 | 7.50 |

**Y# 464 2 ZŁOTE**
8.15 g., Brass, 27 mm. **Obv:** Crowned eagle with wings open **Rev:** Harbor Porpoises **Edge Lettering:** * NBP * eight times

| Date | Mintage | VF20 | XF40 | MS60 | MS63 | MS65 |
|---|---|---|---|---|---|---|
| 2004 MW | 800,000 | — | 3.50 | 7.00 | 12.00 | 15.00 |

**Y# 479 2 ZŁOTE**
8.15 g., Brass, 27 mm. **Subject:** 80th Anniversary of the Modern Zloty Currency **Obv:** Crowned eagle with wings open above value **Rev:** Bust left **Edge Lettering:** * NBP * eight times

| Date | Mintage | VF20 | XF40 | MS60 | MS63 | MS65 |
|---|---|---|---|---|---|---|
| 2004 MW | 800,000 | — | — | 3.00 | 5.00 | 7.00 |

**Y# 481 2 ZŁOTE**
8.15 g., Brass, 27 mm. **Subject:** Poland Joining the European Union **Obv:** Crowned eagle with wings open above value **Rev:** Map and stars **Edge Lettering:** * NBP * eight times

| Date | Mintage | VF20 | XF40 | MS60 | MS63 | MS65 |
|---|---|---|---|---|---|---|
| 2004 MW | 1,000,000 | — | — | 3.00 | 5.00 | 7.00 |

**Y# 484 2 ZŁOTE**
8.15 g., Brass, 27 mm. **Subject:** Dolnoslaskie (Lower Silesian) District **Obv:** Crowned eagle with wings open on map **Rev:** Silesian eagle on shield **Edge Lettering:** * NBP * eight times

| Date | Mintage | VF20 | XF40 | MS60 | MS63 | MS65 |
|---|---|---|---|---|---|---|
| 2004 MW | 700,000 | — | — | 4.00 | 6.00 | 8.00 |

**Y# 485 2 ZŁOTE**
8.15 g., Brass, 27 mm. **Subject:** Kujawsko-Pomorskie District **Obv:** Crowned eagle with wings open on map **Rev:** Shield with crowned half eagle and griffin **Edge Lettering:** * NBP * eight times

| Date | Mintage | VF20 | XF40 | MS60 | MS63 | MS65 |
|---|---|---|---|---|---|---|
| 2004 MW | 750,000 | — | — | 7.00 | 12.00 | 15.00 |

**Y# 486 2 ZŁOTE**
8.15 g., Brass, 27 mm. **Subject:** Lubuskie District **Obv:** Crowned eagle with wings open on map **Rev:** Shield with stag left **Edge Lettering:** * NBP * eight times

| Date | Mintage | VF20 | XF40 | MS60 | MS63 | MS65 |
|---|---|---|---|---|---|---|
| 2004 MW | 820,000 | — | — | 3.00 | 5.00 | 7.00 |

**Y# 487 2 ZŁOTE**
8.15 g., Brass, 27 mm. **Subject:** Lodzkie District **Obv:** Crowned eagle with wings open on map **Rev:** Shield with two creatures above an eagle **Edge Lettering:** * NBP * eight times

| Date | Mintage | VF20 | XF40 | MS60 | MS63 | MS65 |
|---|---|---|---|---|---|---|
| 2004 MW | 920,000 | — | — | 3.00 | 5.00 | 7.00 |

**Y# 488 2 ZŁOTE**
8.15 g., Brass, 27 mm. **Subject:** Malopolskie District **Obv:** Crowned eagle with wings open on map **Rev:** Shield with crowned eagle **Edge Lettering:** * NBP * eight times

| Date | Mintage | VF20 | XF40 | MS60 | MS63 | MS65 |
|---|---|---|---|---|---|---|
| 2004 MW | 920,000 | — | — | 3.00 | 5.00 | 7.00 |

**Y# 489 2 ZŁOTE**
8.15 g., Brass, 27 mm. **Subject:** Mazowieckie District **Obv:** Crowned eagle with wings open on map **Rev:** Eagle on shield **Edge Lettering:** * NBP * eight times

| Date | Mintage | VF20 | XF40 | MS60 | MS63 | MS65 |
|---|---|---|---|---|---|---|
| 2004 MW | 920,000 | — | — | 3.00 | 5.00 | 7.00 |

**Y# 490 2 ZŁOTE**
8.15 g., Brass, 27 mm. **Subject:** Podkarpackie District **Obv:** Crowned eagle with wings open on map **Rev:** Shield with iron cross above griffin and lion **Edge Lettering:** * NBP * eight times

| Date | Mintage | VF20 | XF40 | MS60 | MS63 | MS65 |
|---|---|---|---|---|---|---|
| 2004 MW | 920,000 | — | — | 3.00 | 5.00 | 7.00 |

### Y# 491 2 ZŁOTE

8.15 g., Brass, 27 mm. **Subject:** Podlaskie District **Obv:** Crowned eagle with wings open on map **Rev:** Shield with Polish eagle above Lithuanian knight **Edge Lettering:** * NBP * eight times

| Date | Mintage | VF20 | XF40 | MS60 | MS63 | MS65 |
|---|---|---|---|---|---|---|
| 2004 MW | 900,000 | — | — | 3.00 | 5.00 | 7.00 |

### Y# 492 2 ZŁOTE

8.15 g., Brass, 27 mm. **Subject:** Pomorskie District **Obv:** Crowned eagle with wings open on map **Rev:** Griffin on shield **Edge Lettering:** * NBP * eight times

| Date | Mintage | VF20 | XF40 | MS60 | MS63 | MS65 |
|---|---|---|---|---|---|---|
| 2004 MW | 900,000 | — | — | 3.00 | 5.00 | 7.00 |

### Y# 493 2 ZŁOTE

8.15 g., Brass, 27 mm. **Subject:** Slaskie (Silesia) District **Obv:** Crowned eagle with wings open on map **Rev:** Eagle on shield **Edge Lettering:** * NBP * eight times

| Date | Mintage | VF20 | XF40 | MS60 | MS63 | MS65 |
|---|---|---|---|---|---|---|
| 2004 MW | 960,000 | — | — | 3.00 | 5.00 | 7.00 |

### Y# 496 2 ZŁOTE

8.15 g., Brass, 27 mm. **Subject:** Warsaw Uprising 60th Anniversary **Obv:** Crowned eagle with wings open **Rev:** Resistance symbol on brick wall **Edge Lettering:** * NBP * eight times

| Date | Mintage | VF20 | XF40 | MS60 | MS63 | MS65 |
|---|---|---|---|---|---|---|
| 2004 MW | 900,000 | — | — | 3.00 | 5.00 | 7.00 |

### Y# 499 2 ZŁOTE

8.15 g., Brass, 27 mm. **Obv:** Crowned eagle with wings open **Rev:** Gen. Stanislaw F. Sosabowski **Edge Lettering:** * NBP * eight times

| Date | Mintage | VF20 | XF40 | MS60 | MS63 | MS65 |
|---|---|---|---|---|---|---|
| 2004 MW | 850,000 | — | — | 3.00 | 5.00 | 7.00 |

### Y# 501 2 ZŁOTE

8.15 g., Brass, 27 mm. **Subject:** Polish Police 85th Anniversary **Obv:** Crowned eagle with wings open **Rev:** Police badge **Edge Lettering:** * NBP * eight times

| Date | Mintage | VF20 | XF40 | MS60 | MS63 | MS65 |
|---|---|---|---|---|---|---|
| 2004 MW | 760,000 | — | — | 3.00 | 5.00 | 7.00 |

### Y# 503 2 ZŁOTE

8.15 g., Brass, 27 mm. **Subject:** Polish Senate **Obv:** Crowned eagle with wings open **Rev:** Senate eagle and speaker's staff **Edge Lettering:** * NBP * eight times

| Date | Mintage | VF20 | XF40 | MS60 | MS63 | MS65 |
|---|---|---|---|---|---|---|
| 2004 MW | 760,000 | — | — | 3.00 | 5.00 | 7.00 |

### Y# 505 2 ZŁOTE

8.15 g., Brass, 27 mm. **Obv:** Crowned eagle with wings open **Rev:** Aleksander Czekanowski (1833-1876) **Edge Lettering:** * NBP * eight times

| Date | Mintage | VF20 | XF40 | MS60 | MS63 | MS65 |
|---|---|---|---|---|---|---|
| 2004 MW | 700,000 | — | — | 3.00 | 5.00 | 7.00 |

### Y# 507 2 ZŁOTE

8.15 g., Brass, 27 mm. **Obv:** National arms **Obv. Legend:** RZECZPOSPOLITA POLSKA **Rev:** Harvest fest couple in folk costume at left, large group in background at right **Rev. Legend:** DOZYNKI **Edge Lettering:** * NBP * eight times

| Date | Mintage | VF20 | XF40 | MS60 | MS63 | MS65 |
|---|---|---|---|---|---|---|
| 2004 MW | 850,000 | — | — | 3.00 | 5.00 | 7.00 |

### Y# 509 2 ZŁOTE

8.15 g., Brass, 27 mm. **Subject:** Warsaw Fine Arts Academy Centennial **Obv:** Crowned eagle with wings open **Rev:** Painter's hands **Edge Lettering:** * NBP * eight times

| Date | Mintage | VF20 | XF40 | MS60 | MS63 | MS65 |
|---|---|---|---|---|---|---|
| 2004 MW | 850,000 | — | — | 3.00 | 5.00 | 7.00 |

### Y# 512 2 ZŁOTE

8.15 g., Brass, 27 mm. **Obv:** Crowned eagle with wings open and artist's palette **Rev:** Stanislaw Wyspianski (1869-1907) **Edge Lettering:** * NBP * eight times

| Date | Mintage | VF20 | XF40 | MS60 | MS63 | MS65 |
|---|---|---|---|---|---|---|
| 2004 MW | 900,000 | — | — | 3.00 | 5.00 | 7.00 |

### Y# 514 2 ZŁOTE

8.15 g., Brass, 27 mm. **Obv:** National arms on outlined map **Rev:** Wojewodztwo-Lubelskie arms with stag on shield **Edge Lettering:** * NBP * eight times

| Date | Mintage | VF20 | XF40 | MS60 | MS63 | MS65 |
|---|---|---|---|---|---|---|
| 2004 MW | 820,000 | — | — | — | 7.50 | 10.00 |

### Y# 516 2 ZŁOTE

8.15 g., Brass, 27 mm. **Subject:** Olympics **Obv:** Crowned eagle with wings open **Rev:** Ancient runners **Edge Lettering:** * NBP * eight times

| Date | Mintage | VF20 | XF40 | MS60 | MS63 | MS65 |
|---|---|---|---|---|---|---|
| 2004 MW | 1,000,000 | — | — | 3.00 | 5.00 | 7.00 |

### Y# 607 2 ZŁOTE

8.15 g., Brass, 27 mm. **Obv:** National arms on outlined map **Obv. Legend:** RZECZPOSPOLITA POLSKA **Rev:** Region arms **Rev. Legend:** WOJEWODZTWO - OPOLSKIE **Edge Lettering:** * NBP * eight times

| Date | Mintage | VF20 | XF40 | MS60 | MS63 | MS65 |
|---|---|---|---|---|---|---|
| 2004 MW | 900,000 | — | — | 3.00 | 5.00 | 7.00 |

### Y# 520 2 ZŁOTE

8.15 g., Brass, 27 mm. **Obv:** National arms **Rev:** Owl perched on nest with owlets **Rev. Legend:** PUCHACZ - Bubo-bubo **Edge Lettering:** * NBP * eight times

| Date | Mintage | VF20 | XF40 | MS60 | MS63 | MS65 |
|---|---|---|---|---|---|---|
| 2005 MW | 990,000 | — | — | 4.00 | 7.00 | 9.00 |

### Y# 521 2 ZŁOTE

8.15 g., Brass, 27 mm. **Obv:** Crowned eagle with wings open **Rev:** Ship within circle **Edge Lettering:** * NBP * eight times

| Date | Mintage | VF20 | XF40 | MS60 | MS63 | MS65 |
|---|---|---|---|---|---|---|
| 2005 MW | 920,000 | — | — | 3.50 | 5.50 | 7.50 |

**Y# 522 2 ZŁOTE**
8.15 g., Brass, 26.8 mm. **Subject:** Japan's Aichi Expo **Obv:** Crowned eagle with wings open **Rev:** Two cranes flying over Mt. Fuji with rising sun background **Edge Lettering:** * NBP * eight times

| Date | Mintage | VF20 | XF40 | MS60 | MS63 | MS65 |
|---|---|---|---|---|---|---|
| 2005 MW | 1,000,000 | — | — | 3.50 | 5.50 | 7.50 |

**Y# 524 2 ZŁOTE**
8.15 g., Brass, 27 mm. **Subject:** Obrony Jasnej Gory **Obv:** Crowned eagle with wings open **Rev:** Half length figure left and bombarded city scene **Edge Lettering:** * NBP * eight times

| Date | Mintage | VF20 | XF40 | MS60 | MS63 | MS65 |
|---|---|---|---|---|---|---|
| 2005 MW | 1,000,000 | — | — | 4.00 | 6.00 | 8.00 |

**Y# 525 2 ZŁOTE**
8.15 g., Brass, 27 mm. **Subject:** Pope John-Paul II **Obv:** National arms **Obv. Legend:** RZECZPOSPOLITA POLSKA **Rev:** Bust right at left, outline of St. Peter's Baslica at center right **Edge Lettering:** * NBP * eight times

| Date | Mintage | VF20 | XF40 | MS60 | MS63 | MS65 |
|---|---|---|---|---|---|---|
| 2005 MW | 4,000,000 | — | — | 4.00 | 6.00 | 8.00 |

**Y# 527 2 ZŁOTE**
8.15 g., Brass, 27 mm. **Obv:** Crowned eagle with wings open **Rev:** Bust 1/4 left with horse head and goose at left **Edge Lettering:** * NBP * eight times

| Date | Mintage | VF20 | XF40 | MS60 | MS63 | MS65 |
|---|---|---|---|---|---|---|
| 2005 MW | 850,000 | — | — | 3.00 | 5.00 | 7.00 |

**Y# 528 2 ZŁOTE**
8.15 g., Brass, 27 mm. **Obv:** Crowned eagle above wall **Rev:** Kolobrzeg Lighthouse **Edge Lettering:** * NBP * eight times

| Date | Mintage | VF20 | XF40 | MS60 | MS63 | MS65 |
|---|---|---|---|---|---|---|
| 2005 MW | 1,100,000 | — | — | 3.00 | 5.00 | 7.00 |

**Y# 529 2 ZŁOTE**
8.15 g., Brass, 27 mm. **Obv:** National arms above gateway **Rev:** Wioclawek Cathedral **Edge Lettering:** * NBP * eight times

| Date | Mintage | VF20 | XF40 | MS60 | MS63 | MS65 |
|---|---|---|---|---|---|---|
| 2005 MW | 1,100,000 | — | — | 3.00 | 5.00 | 7.00 |

**Y# 530 2 ZŁOTE**
8.15 g., Brass, 27 mm. **Obv:** National arms **Rev:** Bust of King Stanislaus Poniatowski right **Edge Lettering:** * NBP * eight times

| Date | Mintage | VF20 | XF40 | MS60 | MS63 | MS65 |
|---|---|---|---|---|---|---|
| 2005 MW | 990,000 | — | — | 3.00 | 5.00 | 7.00 |

**Y# 541 2 ZŁOTE**
8.15 g., Brass, 27 mm. **Obv:** Eagle, value, palette and paint brushes **Rev:** Painter Tadeusz Makowski **Edge Lettering:** * NBP * eight times

| Date | Mintage | VF20 | XF40 | MS60 | MS63 | MS65 |
|---|---|---|---|---|---|---|
| 2005 MW | 900,000 | — | — | 3.00 | 5.00 | 7.00 |

**Y# 558 2 ZŁOTE**
8.15 g., Brass, 27 mm. **Subject:** 60th Anniversary of WWII **Obv:** National arms **Edge Lettering:** * NBP * eight times

| Date | Mintage | VF20 | XF40 | MS60 | MS63 | MS65 |
|---|---|---|---|---|---|---|
| 2005 MW | 1,000,000 | — | — | 3.00 | 5.00 | 7.00 |

**Y# 560 2 ZŁOTE**
8.15 g., Brass, 27 mm. **Obv:** National arms on outline map **Obv. Legend:** RZECZPOSPOLITA POLSKA **Rev:** Region arms **Rev. Legend:** WOJEWOZTWO SWIETOKRZYSKIE **Edge Lettering:** * NBP * eight times

| Date | Mintage | VF20 | XF40 | MS60 | MS63 | MS65 |
|---|---|---|---|---|---|---|
| 2005 MW | 900,000 | — | — | 3.00 | 5.00 | 7.00 |

**Y# 562 2 ZŁOTE**
8.15 g., Brass, 27 mm. **Obv:** National arms **Rev:** Region Wielkopolskie **Edge Lettering:** * NBP * eight times

| Date | Mintage | VF20 | XF40 | MS60 | MS63 | MS65 |
|---|---|---|---|---|---|---|
| 2005 MW | 940,000 | — | — | 3.00 | 5.00 | 7.00 |

**Y# 563 2 ZŁOTE**
8.15 g., Brass, 27 mm. **Obv:** National arms on outlined map **Obv. Legend:** RZECZPOSPOLITA POLSKA **Rev:** Region arms **Rev. Legend:** WOJEWODZTWO ZACHODIOPOMORSKIE **Edge Lettering:** * NBP * eight times

| Date | Mintage | VF20 | XF40 | MS60 | MS63 | MS65 |
|---|---|---|---|---|---|---|
| 2005 | — | — | — | 3.00 | 5.00 | 7.00 |

**Y# 564 2 ZŁOTE**
8.15 g., Brass, 27 mm. **Obv:** National arms **Rev:** City of Gniezno **Edge Lettering:** * NBP * eight times

| Date | Mintage | VF20 | XF40 | MS60 | MS63 | MS65 |
|---|---|---|---|---|---|---|
| 2005 | 1,250,000 | — | — | 3.00 | 5.00 | 7.00 |

**Y# 565 2 ZŁOTE**
8.15 g., Brass, 27 mm. **Obv:** National arms **Rev:** Solidarity **Edge Lettering:** * NBP * eight times

| Date | Mintage | VF20 | XF40 | MS60 | MS63 | MS65 |
|---|---|---|---|---|---|---|
| 2005 MW | 1,000,000 | — | — | 3.00 | 5.00 | 7.00 |

**Y# 608 2 ZŁOTE**
8.15 g., Brass, 27 mm. **Subject:** 500th Anniversary Birth of Nikolaja Reja **Obv:** National arms **Obv. Legend:** RZECZPOSPOLITA POLSKA **Rev:** Bust of Reja facing 3/4 right **Edge Lettering:** NBP eight times

| Date | Mintage | VF20 | XF40 | MS60 | MS63 | MS65 |
|---|---|---|---|---|---|---|
| 2005 | 850,000 | — | — | 3.00 | 5.00 | 7.00 |

**Y# 614 2 ZŁOTE**
8.15 g., Brass, 27 mm. **Obv:** National arms on outlined map **Obv. Legend:** RZECZPOSPOLITA POLSKA **Rev:** Region arms **Rev. Legend:** WOJEWÓDZTWO WARMINSKO - MAZURSKIE **Edge Lettering:** * NBP * eight times

| Date | Mintage | VF20 | XF40 | MS60 | MS63 | MS65 |
|---|---|---|---|---|---|---|
| 2005 MW | 900,000 | — | — | 3.00 | 5.00 | 7.00 |

### Y# 753 2 ZŁOTE

8.15 g., Brass, 27 mm. **Subject:** Cizsyn **Rev:** Round tower

| Date | Mintage | VF20 | XF40 | MS60 | MS63 | MS65 |
|---|---|---|---|---|---|---|
| 2005 MW | — | — | — | 3.00 | 5.00 | 7.00 |

### Y# 532 2 ZŁOTE

8.15 g., Brass, 27 mm. **Obv:** National arms **Rev:** St. John's Night dancer **Edge Lettering:** * NBP * eight times

| Date | Mintage | VF20 | XF40 | MS60 | MS63 | MS65 |
|---|---|---|---|---|---|---|
| 2006 MW | 1,000,000 | — | — | 2.50 | 4.00 | 6.00 |

### Y# 534 2 ZŁOTE

8.15 g., Brass, 27 mm. **Obv:** National arms **Rev:** Alpine Marmot standing **Edge Lettering:** * NBP * eight times

| Date | Mintage | VF20 | XF40 | MS60 | MS63 | MS65 |
|---|---|---|---|---|---|---|
| 2006 MW | 1,400,000 | — | — | 3.00 | 6.00 | 8.00 |

### Y# 543 2 ZŁOTE

8.15 g., Brass, 27 mm. **Obv:** Polish Eagle above castle gate **Rev:** Bochnia church **Edge Lettering:** * NBP * eight times

| Date | Mintage | VF20 | XF40 | MS60 | MS63 | MS65 |
|---|---|---|---|---|---|---|
| 2006 MW | 1,100,000 | — | — | 3.00 | 5.00 | 7.00 |

### Y# 544 2 ZŁOTE

8.15 g., Brass, 27 mm. **Obv:** Polish Eagle above castle gate **Rev:** Chelm church **Edge Lettering:** * NBP * eight times

| Date | Mintage | VF20 | XF40 | MS60 | MS63 | MS65 |
|---|---|---|---|---|---|---|
| 2006 MW | 1,100,000 | — | — | 3.00 | 5.00 | 7.00 |

### Y# 545 2 ZŁOTE

8.15 g., Brass, 27 mm. **Obv:** Polish Eagle above castle gate **Rev:** Chelmno Palace **Edge Lettering:** * NBP * eight times

| Date | Mintage | VF20 | XF40 | MS60 | MS63 | MS65 |
|---|---|---|---|---|---|---|
| 2006 MW | 1,100,000 | — | — | 3.00 | 5.00 | 7.00 |

### Y# 546 2 ZŁOTE

8.15 g., Brass, 27 mm. **Obv:** Polish Eagle above castle gate **Rev:** Elblag tower **Edge Lettering:** * NBP * eight times

| Date | Mintage | VF20 | XF40 | MS60 | MS63 | MS65 |
|---|---|---|---|---|---|---|
| 2006 MW | 1,100,000 | — | — | 3.00 | 5.00 | 7.00 |

### Y# 547 2 ZŁOTE

8.15 g., Brass, 27 mm. **Obv:** Polish Eagle above castle gate **Rev:** Castle **Rev. Legend:** KOSCIOL W. HACZOWIE **Edge Lettering:** * NBP * eight times

| Date | Mintage | VF20 | XF40 | MS60 | MS63 | MS65 |
|---|---|---|---|---|---|---|
| 2006 MW | 1,000,000 | — | — | 3.00 | 5.00 | 7.00 |

### Y# 548 2 ZŁOTE

8.15 g., Brass, 27 mm. **Obv:** National arms above gateway **Rev:** Legnica tower and building **Edge Lettering:** * NBP * eight times

| Date | Mintage | VF20 | XF40 | MS60 | MS63 | MS65 |
|---|---|---|---|---|---|---|
| 2006 MW | 1,100,000 | — | — | 3.00 | 5.00 | 7.00 |

### Y# 549 2 ZŁOTE

8.15 g., Brass, 27 mm. **Obv:** Polish Eagle above castle gate **Rev:** Pszczyna palace **Edge Lettering:** * NBP * eight times

| Date | Mintage | VF20 | XF40 | MS60 | MS63 | MS65 |
|---|---|---|---|---|---|---|
| 2006 MW | 1,100,000 | — | — | 3.00 | 5.00 | 7.00 |

### Y# 550 2 ZŁOTE

8.15 g., Brass, 27 mm. **Obv:** Polish Eagle above castle gate **Rev:** Sandomierz palace **Edge Lettering:** * NBP * eight times

| Date | Mintage | VF20 | XF40 | MS60 | MS63 | MS65 |
|---|---|---|---|---|---|---|
| 2006 MW | 1,100,000 | — | — | 3.00 | 5.00 | 7.00 |

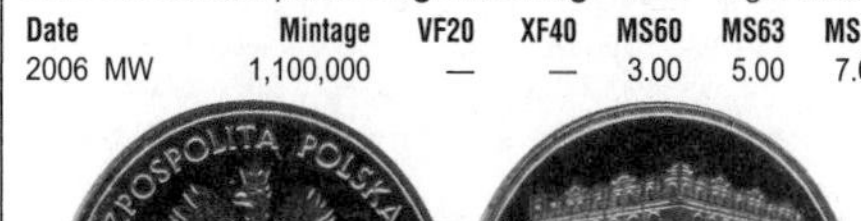

### Y# 566 2 ZŁOTE

8.15 g., Brass, 27 mm. **Obv:** National arms **Rev:** City of Jaroslaw **Edge Lettering:** * NBP * eight times

| Date | Mintage | VF20 | XF40 | MS60 | MS63 | MS65 |
|---|---|---|---|---|---|---|
| 2006 MW | 1,200,000 | — | — | 3.00 | 5.00 | 7.00 |

### Y# 569 2 ZŁOTE

8.15 g., Brass, 27 mm. **Obv:** National arms **Rev:** Castle Zagan **Edge Lettering:** * NBP * eight times

| Date | Mintage | VF20 | XF40 | MS60 | MS63 | MS65 |
|---|---|---|---|---|---|---|
| 2006 MW | 1,100,000 | — | — | 3.00 | 5.00 | 7.00 |

### Y# 570 2 ZŁOTE

815.00 g., Brass, 27 mm. **Obv:** National arms above gateway **Rev:** City of Nysa **Edge Lettering:** * NBP * eight times

| Date | Mintage | VF20 | XF40 | MS60 | MS63 | MS65 |
|---|---|---|---|---|---|---|
| 2006 MW | 1,100,000 | — | — | 3.00 | 5.00 | 7.00 |

### Y# 571 2 ZŁOTE

8.15 g., Brass, 27 mm. **Subject:** 30th Anniversary of June 1976 **Obv:** National arms **Edge Lettering:** * NBP * eight times

| Date | Mintage | VF20 | XF40 | MS60 | MS63 | MS65 |
|---|---|---|---|---|---|---|
| 2006 MW | 1,000,000 | — | — | 3.00 | 5.00 | 7.00 |

### Y# 573 2 ZŁOTE

8.15 g., Brass, 27 mm. **Obv:** Polish eagle above wall **Rev:** Nowy Sacz church **Edge Lettering:** * NBP * eight times

| Date | Mintage | VF20 | XF40 | MS60 | MS63 | MS65 |
|---|---|---|---|---|---|---|
| 2006 MW | 1,100,000 | — | — | 3.00 | 5.00 | 7.00 |

### Y# 574 2 ZŁOTE

8.15 g., Brass, 27 mm. **Subject:** 500th Anniversary of the Publication of the Statute by Laski **Obv:** National arms above value **Rev:** Jan Laski and book **Edge Lettering:** * NBP * eight times

| Date | Mintage | VF20 | XF40 | MS60 | MS63 | MS65 |
|---|---|---|---|---|---|---|
| 2006 MW | 1,000,000 | — | — | 3.00 | 5.00 | 7.00 |

**Y# 575 2 ZŁOTE**

8.15 g., Brass, 27 mm. **Subject:** Aleksander Gierymski (painter) **Obv:** Palette, brushes at left, national arms at right **Obv. Legend:** RZECZPOSPOLITA POLSKA **Rev:** Bust of Gierymski facing at left, coastline village in background **Edge Lettering:** * NBP * eight times

| Date | Mintage | VF20 | XF40 | MS60 | MS63 | MS65 |
|---|---|---|---|---|---|---|
| 2006 MW | 1,000,000 | — | — | 3.00 | 5.00 | 7.00 |

**Y# 576 2 ZŁOTE**

8.15 g., Brass, 27 mm. **Obv:** National arms **Rev:** Knight on horseback **Edge Lettering:** * NBP * eight times

| Date | Mintage | VF20 | XF40 | MS60 | MS63 | MS65 |
|---|---|---|---|---|---|---|
| 2006 MW | 1,000,000 | — | — | 3.00 | 5.00 | 7.00 |

**Y# 580 2 ZŁOTE**

8.15 g., Brass, 27 mm. **Obv:** Polish eagle above wall **Rev:** Kalisz building **Edge Lettering:** * NBP * eight times

| Date | Mintage | VF20 | XF40 | MS60 | MS63 | MS65 |
|---|---|---|---|---|---|---|
| 2006 MW | 1,100,000 | — | — | 3.00 | 5.00 | 7.00 |

**Y# 582 2 ZŁOTE**

8.15 g., Brass, 27 mm. **Obv:** National arms **Obv. Legend:** RZECZPOSPOLITA POLSKA **Rev:** Queen's head left as on KM-20, coin design from 1932 **Edge Lettering:** * NBP * eight times

| Date | Mintage | VF20 | XF40 | MS60 | MS63 | MS65 |
|---|---|---|---|---|---|---|
| 2006 MW | 1,000,000 | — | — | 3.00 | 5.00 | 7.00 |

**Y# 605 2 ZŁOTE**

8.15 g., Brass, 27 mm. **Obv:** National arms **Obv. Legend:** RZECZPOSPOLITA POLSKA **Rev:** Skier and marksman standing **Rev. Legend:** XX ZIMOWE IGAZYSKA OLIMPIJSKIE - TURYN **Edge Lettering:** * NBP * eight times

| Date | Mintage | VF20 | XF40 | MS60 | MS63 | MS65 |
|---|---|---|---|---|---|---|
| 2006 MW | 1,200,000 | — | — | 3.00 | 5.00 | 7.00 |

**Y# 606 2 ZŁOTE**

8.15 g., Brass, 27 mm. **Obv:** National arms **Obv. Legend:** RZECZPOSPOLITA POLSKA **Rev:** Large soccer ball with fancy linked date 2006 **Rev. Legend:** MISTRZOSTWA SWIATA W PItCE NOZNEJ NIEMCY - FIFA **Edge Lettering:** * NBP * eight times

| Date | Mintage | VF20 | XF40 | MS60 | MS63 | MS65 |
|---|---|---|---|---|---|---|
| 2006 MW | 1,200,000 | — | — | 3.00 | 5.00 | 7.00 |

**Y# 609 2 ZŁOTE**

8.15 g., Brass, 27 mm. **Subject:** 100th Anniversary - Warsaw School of Economics **Obv:** National arms **Obv. Legend:** RZECZPOSPOLITA POLSKA **Rev:** School facade **Rev. Legend:** SZKOLA CLOWNA HANDLOWA W WARSZAWIE **Rev. Inscription:** Large SGH **Edge Lettering:** * NBP * eight times

| Date | Mintage | VF20 | XF40 | MS60 | MS63 | MS65 |
|---|---|---|---|---|---|---|
| 2006 MW | 1,000,000 | — | — | 3.00 | 5.00 | 7.00 |

**Y# 577 2 ZŁOTE**

8.15 g., Brass, 27 mm. **Obv:** Crowned eagle **Rev:** Kwidzyn Castle **Edge Lettering:** * NBP * eight times

| Date | Mintage | VF20 | XF40 | MS60 | MS63 | MS65 |
|---|---|---|---|---|---|---|
| 2007 MW | 1,000,000 | — | — | 3.00 | 5.00 | 7.00 |

**Y# 578 2 ZŁOTE**

8.15 g., Brass, 27 mm. **Obv:** Crowned eagle **Rev:** Grey Seal and silhouette **Edge Lettering:** * NBP * eight times

| Date | Mintage | VF20 | XF40 | MS60 | MS63 | MS65 |
|---|---|---|---|---|---|---|
| 2007 MW | 1,000,000 | — | — | 4.00 | 7.00 | 9.00 |

**Y# 586 2 ZŁOTE**

8.15 g., Brass, 27 mm. **Subject:** 75th Anniversary Breaking the Enigma Code **Obv:** National arms **Obv. Legend:** RZECZPOSPOLITA POLSKA **Rev:** Enigma machine wheel **Edge Lettering:** * NBP * eight times

| Date | Mintage | VF20 | XF40 | MS60 | MS63 | MS65 |
|---|---|---|---|---|---|---|
| 2007 MW | 900,000 | — | — | 3.00 | 5.00 | 7.00 |

**Y# 590 2 ZŁOTE**

8.15 g., Brass, 27 mm. **Obv:** National arms **Obv. Legend:** RZECZPOSPOLITA POLSKA **Rev:** Bust of Domeyko facing **Rev. Legend:** IGNACY DOMEYKO 1802 - 1889 **Edge Lettering:** * NBP * eight times

| Date | Mintage | VF20 | XF40 | MS60 | MS63 | MS65 |
|---|---|---|---|---|---|---|
| 2007 MW | 900,000 | — | — | 3.00 | 5.00 | 7.00 |

**Y# 591 2 ZŁOTE**

8.03 g., Brass, 26.77 mm. **Subject:** Konrad Korzeniowski (Joseph Conrad), 100th Anniversary of Death **Obv:** National arms **Obv. Legend:** RZECZPOSPOLITA POLSKA **Rev:** Head of Korzeniowski facing slightly right at left, open book at lower center, sailing ship at right **Edge Lettering:** NBP repeated

| Date | Mintage | VF20 | XF40 | MS60 | MS63 | MS65 |
|---|---|---|---|---|---|---|
| 2007 | — | — | — | 3.00 | 4.00 | 6.00 |

**Y# 592 2 ZŁOTE**

8.15 g., Brass, 27 mm. **Subject:** History of Zloty **Obv:** Nike at left, obverse of 5 Zlotych, Y#18, national arms below **Obv. Legend:** RZECZPOLPOLITA POLSKA **Rev:** Spray at left of reverse of 5 Zlotych, Y# 18 **Edge Lettering:** * NBP * eight times

| Date | Mintage | VF20 | XF40 | MS60 | MS63 | MS65 |
|---|---|---|---|---|---|---|
| 2007 MW | 900,000 | — | — | 3.00 | 5.00 | 7.00 |

**Y# 594 2 ZŁOTE**

8.15 g., Brass, 27 mm. **Subject:** 750th Anniversary Municipality of Krakau **Obv:** National arms **Obv. Legend:** RZECZPOSPOLITA POLSKA **Rev:** Knight standing facing with spear and shield **Edge Lettering:** * NBP * eight times

| Date | Mintage | VF20 | XF40 | MS60 | MS63 | MS65 |
|---|---|---|---|---|---|---|
| 2007 MW | 900,000 | — | — | 3.00 | 5.00 | 7.00 |

**Y# 610 2 ZŁOTE**

8.15 g., Brass, 27 mm. **Subject:** Artic Explorers Antoni B. Dombrowolski and Henryk Arctowski **Obv:** National arms **Obv. Legend:** RZECZPOSPOLITA POLSKA **Rev:** Explorer's bust facing at bottom, sailing ship in background **Edge Lettering:** * NBP * eight times

| Date | Mintage | VF20 | XF40 | MS60 | MS63 | MS65 |
|---|---|---|---|---|---|---|
| 2007 MW | 900,000 | — | — | 3.00 | 5.00 | 7.00 |

**Y# 611 2 ZŁOTE**

8.15 g., Brass, 27 mm. **Obv:** National arms **Obv. Legend:** RZECZPOSPOLITA POLSKA **Rev:** Ciezkozbrojny in armor, horseback left **Rev. Legend:** RYCERZ CIEZKOZBROJNY-XV **Edge Lettering:** * NBP * eight times

| Date | Mintage | VF20 | XF40 | MS60 | MS63 | MS65 |
|---|---|---|---|---|---|---|
| 2007 MW | 900,000 | — | — | 3.00 | 5.00 | 7.00 |

**Y# 612 2 ZŁOTE**

8.15 g., Brass, 27 mm. **Subject:** 70th Anniversary Death of Szymanowski **Obv:** National arms **Obv. Legend:** RZECZPOSPOLITA POLSKA **Rev:** Bust facing 3/4 right at left, music score in background **Rev. Legend:** ROCZNICA URODZIN KAROLA SYMANOWSKIEGO **Edge Lettering:** * NBP * eight times

| Date | Mintage | VF20 | XF40 | MS60 | MS63 | MS65 |
|---|---|---|---|---|---|---|
| 2007 MW | 900,000 | — | — | 3.00 | 5.00 | 7.00 |

**Y# 613 2 ZŁOTE**

8.15 g., Brass, 27 mm. **Obv:** National arms above gateway **Obv. Legend:** RZECZPOSPOLITA POLSKA **Rev:** Buildings **Rev. Legend:** STARGARD - SZCZECINSKI **Edge Lettering:** * NBP * eight times

| Date | Mintage | VF20 | XF40 | MS60 | MS63 | MS65 |
|---|---|---|---|---|---|---|
| 2007 MW | 1,000,000 | — | — | 3.00 | 5.00 | 7.00 |

**Y# 615 2 ZŁOTE**

8.15 g., Brass, 27 mm. **Obv:** National arms above gateway **Obv. Legend:** RZECZPOSPOLITA POLSKA **Rev:** Building with branches at left and right **Rev. Legend:** BRZEG **Edge Lettering:** * NBP * eight times

| Date | Mintage | VF20 | XF40 | MS60 | MS63 | MS65 |
|---|---|---|---|---|---|---|
| 2007 MW | 1,000,000 | — | — | 3.00 | 5.00 | 7.00 |

**Y# 616 2 ZŁOTE**

8.15 g., Brass, 27 mm. **Obv:** National arms above gateway **Obv. Legend:** RZECZPOSPOLITA POLSKA **Rev:** Church **Rev. Legend:** LOMZA **Edge Lettering:** * NBP alternating normal and inverted 4x

| Date | Mintage | VF20 | XF40 | MS60 | MS63 | MS65 |
|---|---|---|---|---|---|---|
| 2007 MW | 1,000,000 | — | — | 3.00 | 5.00 | 7.00 |

**Y# 617 2 ZŁOTE**

8.15 g., Brass, 27 mm. **Obv:** National arms above gateway **Obv. Legend:** RZECZPOSPOLITA POLSKA **Rev:** Church **Rev. Legend:** PLOCK **Edge Lettering:** * NBP * eight times

| Date | Mintage | VF20 | XF40 | MS60 | MS63 | MS65 |
|---|---|---|---|---|---|---|
| 2007 MW | 1,000,000 | — | — | 3.00 | 5.00 | 7.00 |

**Y# 618 2 ZŁOTE**

8.15 g., Brass, 27 mm. **Obv:** National arms above gateway **Obv. Legend:** RZECZPOSPOLITA POLSKA **Rev:** Church **Rev. Legend:** PRZEMYSL **Edge Lettering:** * NBP * eight times

| Date | Mintage | VF20 | XF40 | MS60 | MS63 | MS65 |
|---|---|---|---|---|---|---|
| 2007 MW | 1,000,000 | — | — | 3.00 | 5.00 | 7.00 |

**Y# 619 2 ZŁOTE**

8.15 g., Brass, 27 mm. **Obv:** National arms above gateway **Obv. Legend:** RZECZPOSPOLITA POLSKA **Rev:** Towered gateway **Rev. Legend:** RACIBÓRZ **Edge Lettering:** * NBP * eight times

| Date | Mintage | VF20 | XF40 | MS60 | MS63 | MS65 |
|---|---|---|---|---|---|---|
| 2007 MW | 1,000,000 | — | — | 3.00 | 5.00 | 7.00 |

**Y# 620 2 ZŁOTE**

8.15 g., Brass, 27 mm. **Obv:** National arms above gateway **Obv. Legend:** RZECZPOSPOLITA POLSKA **Rev:** Church **Rev. Legend:** SLUPSK **Edge Lettering:** NBP repeated

| Date | Mintage | VF20 | XF40 | MS60 | MS63 | MS65 |
|---|---|---|---|---|---|---|
| 2007 MW | 1,000,000 | — | — | 3.00 | 5.00 | 7.00 |

**Y# 621 2 ZŁOTE**

8.15 g., Brass, 27 mm. **Obv:** National arms above gateway **Obv. Legend:** RZECZPOSPOLITA POLSKA **Rev:** Church **Rev. Legend:** SWIDNICA **Edge Lettering:** * NBP * eight times

| Date | Mintage | VF20 | XF40 | MS60 | MS63 | MS65 |
|---|---|---|---|---|---|---|
| 2007 MW | 1,000,000 | — | — | 3.00 | 5.00 | 7.00 |

**Y# 622 2 ZŁOTE**

8.15 g., Brass, 27 mm. **Obv:** National arms **Obv. Legend:** RZECZPOSPOLITA POLSKE **Rev:** Town view **Rev. Legend:** MIASTO SREDNIOWIECZNE - W TORUNIU **Edge Lettering:** * NBP * eight times

| Date | Mintage | VF20 | XF40 | MS60 | MS63 | MS65 |
|---|---|---|---|---|---|---|
| 2007 MW | 900,000 | — | — | 3.00 | 5.00 | 7.00 |

**Y# 623 2 ZŁOTE**

8.15 g., Brass, 27 mm. **Obv:** National arms above gateway **Obv. Legend:** RZECZPOSPOLITA POLSKA **Rev:** Church **Rev. Legend:** GORZÓW WIELKOPOLSKI **Edge Lettering:** * NBP * eight times

| Date | Mintage | VF20 | XF40 | MS60 | MS63 | MS65 |
|---|---|---|---|---|---|---|
| 2007 MW | 1,000,000 | — | — | 3.00 | 5.00 | 7.00 |

**Y# 624 2 ZŁOTE**

8.15 g., Brass, 27 mm. **Obv:** National arms above gateway **Obv. Legend:** RZECZPOSPOLITA POLSKA **Rev:** Church at lower right, houses to left, fortress in upper background **Rev. Legend:** KLODZKO **Edge Lettering:** * NBP * eight times

| Date | Mintage | VF20 | XF40 | MS60 | MS63 | MS65 |
|---|---|---|---|---|---|---|
| 2007 MW | 1,000,000 | — | — | 3.00 | 5.00 | 7.00 |

**Y# 625 2 ZŁOTE**

8.15 g., Brass, 27 mm. **Obv:** National arms above gateway **Obv. Legend:** RZECZPOSPOLITA POLSKE **Rev:** Church **Rev. Legend:** TARNOW **Edge Lettering:** * NBP * eight times

| Date | Mintage | VF20 | XF40 | MS60 | MS63 | MS65 |
|---|---|---|---|---|---|---|
| 2007 MW | 1,000,000 | — | — | 3.00 | 5.00 | 7.00 |

**Y# 626 2 ZŁOTE**

8.15 g., Brass, 27 mm. **Subject:** Leon Wyczolkowski **Obv:** Artist's palette, brushes at left, national arms at right **Obv. Legend:** RZECZPOSPOLITA POLSKA **Rev:** Bust facing **Edge Lettering:** * NBP * eight times

| Date | Mintage | VF20 | XF40 | MS60 | MS63 | MS65 |
|---|---|---|---|---|---|---|
| 2007 MW | 900,000 | — | — | 3.00 | 5.00 | 7.00 |

**Y# 627 2 ZŁOTE**
8.15 g., Brass, 27 mm. **Obv:** National arms above flags **Obv. Legend:** RZECZPOSPOLITA POLSKA **Rev:** Peregrine Falcon perched on branch **Rev. Legend:** SOKOL WEDROWNY - Falco peregrinus **Edge Lettering:** * NBP * eight times

| Date | Mintage | VF20 | XF40 | MS60 | MS63 | MS65 |
|---|---|---|---|---|---|---|
| 2008 MW | 1,600,000 | — | — | 3.00 | 4.00 | 6.00 |

**Y# 628 2 ZŁOTE**
8.15 g., Brass, 27 mm. **Obv:** National arms above gateway **Obv. Legend:** RZECZPOSPOLITA POLSKA **Rev:** National arms ar upper left, Piotrków Tribunal building at lower right **Rev. Legend:** PIOTRKÓW - TRYBUNALSKI **Edge Lettering:** * NBP * eight times

| Date | Mintage | VF20 | XF40 | MS60 | MS63 | MS65 |
|---|---|---|---|---|---|---|
| 2008 MW | 1,100,000 | — | 0.90 | 2.25 | 3.00 | 5.00 |

**Y# 629 2 ZŁOTE**
8.15 g., Brass, 27 mm. **Subject:** 40th Anniversary "Rocznica" March **Obv:** National arms above value **Obv. Legend:** RZECZPOSPOLITA POLSKA **Rev:** University of Warsaw coat of arms above political protest marchers **Edge Lettering:** * NBP * eight times

| Date | Mintage | VF20 | XF40 | MS60 | MS63 | MS65 |
|---|---|---|---|---|---|---|
| 2008 MW | 1,400,000 | — | 0.90 | 2.25 | 3.00 | 5.00 |

**Y# 630 2 ZŁOTE**
8.15 g., Brass, 27 mm. **Obv:** National arms above gateway **Obv. Legend:** RZECZPOSPOLITA POLSKA **Rev:** Building **Rev. Legend:** LOWICZ **Edge Lettering:** * NBP * eight times

| Date | Mintage | VF20 | XF40 | MS60 | MS63 | MS65 |
|---|---|---|---|---|---|---|
| 2008 MW | 1,100,000 | — | 0.90 | 2.25 | 3.00 | 5.00 |

**Y# 631 2 ZŁOTE**
8.15 g., Brass, 27 mm. **Obv:** National arms above gateway **Obv. Legend:** RZECZPOSPOLITA POLSKA **Rev:** Monument **Rev. Legend:** KONIN **Edge Lettering:** * NBP * eight times

| Date | Mintage | VF20 | XF40 | MS60 | MS63 | MS65 |
|---|---|---|---|---|---|---|
| 2008 MW | 1,100,000 | — | 0.90 | 2.25 | 3.00 | 5.00 |

**Y# 633 2 ZŁOTE**
8.15 g., Brass, 27 mm. **Subject:** 65th Anniversary Warsaw Uprising **Obv:** National arms **Obv. Legend:** RZECZPOSPOLITA POLSKA **Rev:** Star of David in barbed wire, female freedom fighter at right. **Rev. Legend:** POWSTANIA W GETCIE WARSZAWSKIM 65. ROCZNICA **Edge Lettering:** * NBP * eight times

| Date | Mintage | VF20 | XF40 | MS60 | MS63 | MS65 |
|---|---|---|---|---|---|---|
| 2008 MW | 1,750,000 | — | — | 3.00 | 5.00 | 7.00 |

**Y# 634 2 ZŁOTE**
8.15 g., Brass, 27 mm. **Subject:** Zbigniew Herbert **Obv:** National arms **Obv. Legend:** RZECZPOSPOLITA POLSKA **Rev:** Head of Herbert right **Edge Lettering:** * NBP * eight times

| Date | Mintage | VF20 | XF40 | MS60 | MS63 | MS65 |
|---|---|---|---|---|---|---|
| 2008 MW | 1,510,000 | — | — | 3.00 | 4.00 | 6.00 |

**Y# 638 2 ZŁOTE**
8.15 g., Brass, 27 mm. **Subject:** Siberian Exiles **Obv:** National arms **Obv. Legend:** RZECZPOSPOLITA POLSKA **Rev:** Bleak forest **Rev. Inscription:** SYBIRACY **Edge Lettering:** * NBP * eight times

| Date | Mintage | VF20 | XF40 | MS60 | MS63 | MS65 |
|---|---|---|---|---|---|---|
| 2008 MW | 1,500,000 | — | — | 3.00 | 4.00 | 6.00 |

**Y# 641 2 ZŁOTE**
8.15 g., Brass, 27 mm. **Subject:** Kazimierz Dolny **Obv:** National arms **Obv. Legend:** RZECZPOSPOLITA POLSKA **Rev:** City view **Edge Lettering:** * NBP * eight times

| Date | Mintage | VF20 | XF40 | MS60 | MS63 | MS65 |
|---|---|---|---|---|---|---|
| 2008 MW | 1,380,000 | — | — | 3.00 | 4.00 | 6.00 |

**Y# 644 2 ZŁOTE**
8.15 g., Brass, 27 mm. **Subject:** 29th Olympic Games Beijing 2008 **Obv:** Eagle **Rev:** Two rowers in boat & a square **Edge Lettering:** * NBP * eight times

| Date | Mintage | VF20 | XF40 | MS60 | MS63 | MS65 |
|---|---|---|---|---|---|---|
| 2008 | 2,000,000 | — | — | 3.00 | 4.00 | 6.00 |

**Y# 648 2 ZŁOTE**
8.15 g., Brass, 27 mm. **Subject:** Polish Travellers & Explorers **Obv:** Eagle **Rev:** Bust of Bronislaw Pilsudski **Edge Lettering:** * NBP * eight times

| Date | Mintage | VF20 | XF40 | MS60 | MS63 | MS65 |
|---|---|---|---|---|---|---|
| 2008 | 1,100,000 | — | — | 3.00 | 4.00 | 6.00 |

**Y# 650 2 ZŁOTE**
8.15 g., Brass, 27 mm. **Subject:** 90th Anniversary of Regaining Freedom **Obv:** Eagle **Rev:** Order of Polonia Restituta **Edge Lettering:** * NBP * eight times

| Date | Mintage | VF20 | XF40 | MS60 | MS63 | MS65 |
|---|---|---|---|---|---|---|
| 2008 | 1,200,000 | — | — | 3.00 | 4.00 | 6.00 |

**Y# 656 2 ZŁOTE**
8.15 g., Brass, 27 mm. **Subject:** 450th Anniversary of the Polish Post **Obv:** Eagle **Rev:** Post rider on horse **Edge:** NBP

| Date | Mintage | VF20 | XF40 | MS60 | MS63 | MS65 |
|---|---|---|---|---|---|---|
| 2008 | 1,400,000 | — | — | 3.00 | 4.00 | 6.00 |

**Y# 659 2 ZŁOTE**
8.15 g., Brass, 27 mm. **Subject:** 400th Anniversary of Polish settlement in North America **Obv:** Eagle **Rev:** Man blowing glassware **Edge Lettering:** * NBP * eight times

| Date | Mintage | VF20 | XF40 | MS60 | MS63 | MS65 |
|---|---|---|---|---|---|---|
| 2008 | 1,200,000 | — | — | 3.00 | 4.00 | 6.00 |

**Y# 662 2 ZŁOTE**
8.15 g., Brass, 27 mm. **Subject:** 90th Anniversary of the Greater Poland Uprising **Obv:** Eagle **Rev:** Bust of Igancy Jan Paderewski, soldiers at bottom **Edge Lettering:** * NBP * eight times

| Date | Mintage | VF20 | XF40 | MS60 | MS63 | MS65 |
|---|---|---|---|---|---|---|
| 2008 | 1,100,000 | — | — | 3.00 | 4.00 | 6.00 |

**Y# 663 2 ZŁOTE**
8.15 g., Brass, 27 mm. **Subject:** Belsko - Biala **Obv:** National arms above gateway **Rev:** Building

| Date | Mintage | VF20 | XF40 | MS60 | MS63 | MS65 |
|---|---|---|---|---|---|---|
| 2008 MW | — | — | — | 3.00 | 4.00 | 6.00 |

**Y# 670 2 ZŁOTE**

8.15 g., Brass, 27 mm. **Subject:** Polish Cavalry **Obv:** National arms above value **Rev:** Hussar Knights, XVII Century

| Date | Mintage | VF20 | XF40 | MS60 | MS63 | MS65 |
|---|---|---|---|---|---|---|
| 2009 MW | 1,400,000 | — | — | 3.00 | 4.00 | 6.00 |

**Y# 673 2 ZŁOTE**

8.15 g., Brass, 27 mm. **Subject:** Supreme Chamber of Control, 90th Anniversary **Obv:** National arms above value **Rev:** Building

| Date | Mintage | VF20 | XF40 | MS60 | MS63 | MS65 |
|---|---|---|---|---|---|---|
| 2009 MW | 1,200,000 | — | — | 3.00 | 4.00 | 6.00 |

**Y# 675 2 ZŁOTE**

8.15 g., Brass, 27 mm. **Subject:** Central Banking, 180th Anniversary **Obv:** National arms above value **Rev:** Five coins

| Date | Mintage | VF20 | XF40 | MS60 | MS63 | MS65 |
|---|---|---|---|---|---|---|
| 2009 MW | 1,300,000 | — | — | 3.00 | 4.00 | 6.00 |

**Y# 678 2 ZŁOTE**

8.15 g., Brass, 27 mm. **Subject:** Green Lizards **Obv:** National arms above value **Rev:** Two green lizards on rocks (lacerta viridis) **Rev. Legend:** JASZCZURKA

| Date | Mintage | VF20 | XF40 | MS60 | MS63 | MS65 |
|---|---|---|---|---|---|---|
| 2009 MW | 1,700,000 | — | — | 3.00 | 4.00 | 6.00 |

**Y# 680 2 ZŁOTE**

8.15 g., Brass, 27 mm. **Subject:** General Elections of 1989 **Obv:** National arms above eagle **Rev:** Election notice within wreath

| Date | Mintage | VF20 | XF40 | MS60 | MS63 | MS65 |
|---|---|---|---|---|---|---|
| 2009 MW | 1,300,000 | — | — | 3.00 | 4.00 | 6.00 |

**Y# 684 2 ZŁOTE**

8.15 g., Brass, 27 mm. **Subject:** Czeslaw Niemen **Obv:** National arms above value **Rev:** Two dimensional facing portrait

| Date | Mintage | VF20 | XF40 | MS60 | MS63 | MS65 |
|---|---|---|---|---|---|---|
| 2009 MW | 1,400,000 | — | — | 3.00 | 4.00 | 6.00 |

**Y# 687 2 ZŁOTE**

8.15 g., Brass, 27 mm. **Subject:** Poets of the Warsaw uprising, 65th Anniversary **Obv:** National arms above eagle

| Date | Mintage | VF20 | XF40 | MS60 | MS63 | MS65 |
|---|---|---|---|---|---|---|
| 2009 MW | 1,400,000 | — | — | 3.00 | 4.00 | 6.00 |

**Y# 690 2 ZŁOTE**

8.15 g., Brass, 27 mm. **Subject:** First Cadre March **Obv:** National arms above value **Rev:** Military badge

| Date | Mintage | VF20 | XF40 | MS60 | MS63 | MS65 |
|---|---|---|---|---|---|---|
| 2009 MW | 1,000,000 | — | — | 3.00 | 4.00 | 6.00 |

**Y# 692 2 ZŁOTE**

8.15 g., Brass, 27 mm. **Subject:** Liquidation of Lodz Ghetto **Obv:** National arms above value **Rev:** Silhouette of Ghetto

| Date | Mintage | VF20 | XF40 | MS60 | MS63 | MS65 |
|---|---|---|---|---|---|---|
| 2009 MW | 1,000,000 | — | — | 3.00 | 4.00 | 6.00 |

**Y# 694 2 ZŁOTE**

8.15 g., Brass, 27 mm. **Subject:** Westerplatte **Obv:** National arms above value **Rev:** Three soldiers and map

| Date | Mintage | VF20 | XF40 | MS60 | MS63 | MS65 |
|---|---|---|---|---|---|---|
| 2009 | 1,400,000 | — | — | 3.00 | 4.00 | 6.00 |

**Y# 697 2 ZŁOTE**

8.15 g., Brass, 27 mm. **Subject:** Tatar Mountain Rescue **Obv:** National arms above value **Rev:** Mountain climber

| Date | Mintage | VF20 | XF40 | MS60 | MS63 | MS65 |
|---|---|---|---|---|---|---|
| 2009 MW | 1,400,000 | — | — | 3.00 | 4.00 | 6.00 |

**Y# 700 2 ZŁOTE**

8.15 g., Brass, 27 mm. **Subject:** Fr. Jerzy Popieluszko, 25th Anniversary of Murder **Obv:** National arms above value **Rev:** Portrait and candle memorial

| Date | Mintage | VF20 | XF40 | MS60 | MS63 | MS65 |
|---|---|---|---|---|---|---|
| 2009 MW | 1,500,000 | — | — | 3.00 | 4.00 | 6.00 |

**Y# 703 2 ZŁOTE**

8.15 g., Brass, 27 mm. **Subject:** Poles saving Jews **Obv:** National arms above value **Rev:** Broken brick wall

| Date | Mintage | VF20 | XF40 | MS60 | MS63 | MS65 |
|---|---|---|---|---|---|---|
| 2009 MW | 1,400,000 | — | — | 3.00 | 4.00 | 6.00 |

**Y# 705 2 ZŁOTE**

8.15 g., Brass, 27 mm. **Subject:** Wald Strzeminski **Obv:** Artist palette and National arms **Rev:** Portrait at left

| Date | Mintage | VF20 | XF40 | MS60 | MS63 | MS65 |
|---|---|---|---|---|---|---|
| 2009 MW | 1,300,000 | — | — | 3.00 | 4.00 | 6.00 |

**Y# 707 2 ZŁOTE**

8.15 g., Brass, 27 mm. **Subject:** Polish Underground **Obv:** National arms above value **Rev:** Monogram of resistance and map of Poland

| Date | Mintage | VF20 | XF40 | MS60 | MS63 | MS65 |
|---|---|---|---|---|---|---|
| 2009 MW | 1,000,000 | — | — | 3.00 | 4.00 | 6.00 |

**Y# 709 2 ZŁOTE**

8.15 g., Brass, 27 mm. **Subject:** Czestochowa **Rev:** Church

| Date | Mintage | VF20 | XF40 | MS60 | MS63 | MS65 |
|---|---|---|---|---|---|---|
| 2009 MW | — | — | — | 3.00 | 4.00 | 6.00 |

**Y# 710 2 ZŁOTE**

8.15 g., Brass, 27 mm. **Subject:** Jedrzejow Cistercian Monastery **Rev:** Church

| Date | Mintage | VF20 | XF40 | MS60 | MS63 | MS65 |
|---|---|---|---|---|---|---|
| 2009 MW | — | — | — | 3.00 | 4.00 | 6.00 |

**Y# 711 2 ZŁOTE**

8.15 g., Brass, 27 mm. **Subject:** Trzebnica **Rev:** Building

| Date | Mintage | VF20 | XF40 | MS60 | MS63 | MS65 |
|---|---|---|---|---|---|---|
| 2009 MW | — | — | — | 3.00 | 4.00 | 6.00 |

**Y# 712 2 ZŁOTE**
8.15 g., Brass, 27 mm. **Subject:** Liberation of Auschwitz **Obv:** National arms above value **Rev:** Three prisoners and camp gate sign

| Date | Mintage | VF20 | XF40 | MS60 | MS63 | MS65 |
|---|---|---|---|---|---|---|
| 2010 MW | 1,000,000 | — | — | 3.00 | 4.00 | 6.00 |

**Y# 715 2 ZŁOTE**
8.15 g., Brass, 27 mm. **Subject:** Vancouver Winter Olympics **Obv:** National arms above value **Rev:** Ski jump athlete

| Date | Mintage | VF20 | XF40 | MS60 | MS63 | MS65 |
|---|---|---|---|---|---|---|
| 2010 MW | 1,400,000 | — | — | 3.00 | 4.00 | 6.00 |

**Y# 718 2 ZŁOTE**
8.15 g., Brass, 27 mm. **Subject:** Imperial Guard **Obv:** National arms above value **Rev:** Napoleonic era mounted soldier

| Date | Mintage | VF20 | XF40 | MS60 | MS63 | MS65 |
|---|---|---|---|---|---|---|
| 2010 MW | 1,400,000 | — | — | 3.00 | 4.00 | 6.00 |

**Y# 721 2 ZŁOTE**
8.15 g., Brass, 27 mm. **Subject:** Katyn Crime **Obv:** National arms above value **Rev:** City name above cap

| Date | Mintage | VF20 | XF40 | MS60 | MS63 | MS65 |
|---|---|---|---|---|---|---|
| 2010 MW | 1,000,000 | — | — | 3.00 | 4.00 | 6.00 |

**Y# 723 2 ZŁOTE**
8.15 g., Brass, 27 mm. **Obv:** National arms above value **Rev:** Bat

| Date | Mintage | VF20 | XF40 | MS60 | MS63 | MS65 |
|---|---|---|---|---|---|---|
| 2010 | — | — | — | 3.00 | 4.00 | 6.00 |

**Y# 725 2 ZŁOTE**
8.15 g., Brass, 27 mm. **Subject:** Polish Scouting Centennial

| Date | Mintage | VF20 | XF40 | MS60 | MS63 | MS65 |
|---|---|---|---|---|---|---|
| 2010 MW | 1,100,000 | — | — | 3.00 | 4.00 | 6.00 |

**Y# 727 2 ZŁOTE**
8.15 g., Brass, 27 mm. **Subject:** Popular Music - Krzystof Komeda

| Date | Mintage | VF20 | XF40 | MS60 | MS63 | MS65 |
|---|---|---|---|---|---|---|
| 2010 MW | 1,400,000 | — | — | 3.00 | 4.00 | 6.00 |

**Y# 730 2 ZŁOTE**
8.15 g., Brass, 27 mm. **Subject:** Jan Twardowski

| Date | Mintage | VF20 | XF40 | MS60 | MS63 | MS65 |
|---|---|---|---|---|---|---|
| 2010 MW | 1,000,000 | — | — | 3.00 | 4.00 | 6.00 |

**Y# 732 2 ZŁOTE**
8.15 g., Brass, 27 mm. **Subject:** Battles of Grunwald and Kluszyn

| Date | Mintage | VF20 | XF40 | MS60 | MS63 | MS65 |
|---|---|---|---|---|---|---|
| 2010 MW | 1,400,000 | — | — | 3.00 | 4.00 | 6.00 |

**Y# 735 2 ZŁOTE**
8.15 g., Brass **Subject:** Battle of Warsaw

| Date | Mintage | VF20 | XF40 | MS60 | MS63 | MS65 |
|---|---|---|---|---|---|---|
| 2010 MW | 1,200,000 | — | — | 3.00 | 4.00 | 6.00 |

**Y# 737 2 ZŁOTE**
8.15 g., Brass, 27 mm. **Subject:** August of 1980

| Date | Mintage | VF20 | XF40 | MS60 | MS63 | MS65 |
|---|---|---|---|---|---|---|
| 2010 MW | 1,400,000 | — | — | 3.00 | 4.00 | 6.00 |

**Y# 742 2 ZŁOTE**
8.15 g., Brass, 27 mm. **Subject:** Polish Explorers - Benedykt Dybowski

| Date | Mintage | VF20 | XF40 | MS60 | MS63 | MS65 |
|---|---|---|---|---|---|---|
| 2010 MW Proof | 1,200,000 | — | — | 3.00 | 4.00 | 6.00 |

**Y# 744 2 ZŁOTE**
8.15 g., Brass, 27 mm. **Subject:** City of Krzeszow

| Date | Mintage | VF20 | XF40 | MS60 | MS63 | MS65 |
|---|---|---|---|---|---|---|
| 2010 MW | 1,000,000 | — | — | 3.00 | 4.00 | 6.00 |

**Y# 746 2 ZŁOTE**
8.15 g., Brass, 27 mm. **Subject:** Arthur Grottger, painter

| Date | Mintage | VF20 | XF40 | MS60 | MS63 | MS65 |
|---|---|---|---|---|---|---|
| 2010 MW | 1,300,000 | — | — | 3.00 | 4.00 | 6.00 |

**Y# 749 2 ZŁOTE**
8.15 g., Brass, 27 mm. **Subject:** City of Kalwaria Zebrzydowska **Obv:** National Arms above value **Rev:** Statue of Saint, Church in background

| Date | Mintage | VF20 | XF40 | MS60 | MS63 | MS65 |
|---|---|---|---|---|---|---|
| 2010 MW | — | — | — | 3.00 | 4.00 | 6.00 |

**Y# 751 2 ZŁOTE**
8.15 g., Brass, 27 mm. **Subject:** City of Warsaw

| Date | Mintage | VF20 | XF40 | MS60 | MS63 | MS65 |
|---|---|---|---|---|---|---|
| 2010 MW | — | — | — | 3.00 | 4.00 | 6.00 |

**Y# 752 2 ZŁOTE**
815.00 g., Brass, 27 mm. **Subject:** City of Trzemeszno

| Date | Mintage | VF20 | XF40 | MS60 | MS63 | MS65 |
|---|---|---|---|---|---|---|
| 2010 | — | — | — | 3.00 | 4.00 | 6.00 |

**Y# 759 2 ZŁOTE**
8.15 g., Brass, 27 mm. **Subject:** City of Gorlice **Obv:** National Arms above value **Rev:** City view

| Date | Mintage | VF20 | XF40 | MS60 | MS63 | MS65 |
|---|---|---|---|---|---|---|
| 2010 | 1,000,000 | — | — | 3.00 | 4.00 | 6.00 |

**Y# 760 2 ZŁOTE**
8.15 g., Brass, 27 mm. **Subject:** City of Miechow **Obv:** National Arms above value **Rev:** Building tower

| Date | Mintage | VF20 | XF40 | MS60 | MS63 | MS65 |
|---|---|---|---|---|---|---|
| 2010 | 1,000,000 | — | — | 3.00 | 4.00 | 6.00 |

**Y# 761 2 ZŁOTE**
8.15 g., Brass, 27 mm. **Subject:** City of Katowice **Obv:** National Arms above value **Rev:** Town factory view

| Date | Mintage | VF20 | XF40 | MS60 | MS63 | MS65 |
|---|---|---|---|---|---|---|
| 2010 | 1,000,000 | — | — | 3.00 | 4.00 | 6.00 |

**Y# 762 2 ZŁOTE**
8.15 g., Brass, 27 mm. **Subject:** Borsuk **Obv:** National Arms above value **Rev:** Eurasian Badgers

| Date | Mintage | VF20 | XF40 | MS60 | MS63 | MS65 |
|---|---|---|---|---|---|---|
| 2011 | 1,500,000 | — | — | 3.00 | 4.00 | 6.00 |

**Y# 764 2 ZŁOTE**
8.15 g., Brass, 27 mm. **Subject:** Zofia Stryjenska **Obv:** National arms, value and artist pallet with brushes **Rev:** Portrait facing

| Date | Mintage | VF20 | XF40 | MS60 | MS63 | MS65 |
|---|---|---|---|---|---|---|
| 2011 | 1,000,000 | — | — | 3.00 | 4.00 | 6.00 |

**Y# 767 2 ZŁOTE**
8.15 g., Brass, 27 mm. **Subject:** Independent Student's Union, 30th Anniversary

| Date | Mintage | VF20 | XF40 | MS60 | MS63 | MS65 |
|---|---|---|---|---|---|---|
| 2011 MW | 800,000 | — | — | 3.00 | 4.00 | 6.00 |

**Y# 769 2 ZŁOTE**
8.15 g., Brass, 27 mm. **Subject:** Smolensk plane crash

| Date | Mintage | VF20 | XF40 | MS60 | MS63 | MS65 |
|---|---|---|---|---|---|---|
| 2011 MW | 800,000 | — | — | 3.00 | 4.00 | 6.00 |

**Y# 772 2 ZŁOTE**
8.15 g., Brass, 27 mm. **Subject:** Beatification of Pope John Paul II **Obv:** Eagle **Rev:** Bust within rays

| Date | Mintage | VF20 | XF40 | MS60 | MS63 | MS65 |
|---|---|---|---|---|---|---|
| 2011 MW | 1,000,000 | — | — | 3.00 | 4.00 | 6.00 |

**Y# 777 2 ZŁOTE**
8.15 g., Brass, 27 mm. **Subject:** Poland's presidency of the Council of the European Union

| Date | Mintage | VF20 | XF40 | MS60 | MS63 | MS65 |
|---|---|---|---|---|---|---|
| 2011 MW | 800,000 | — | — | 3.00 | 4.00 | 6.00 |

**Y# 780 2 ZŁOTE**
8.15 g., Brass, 27 mm. **Subject:** History of the Polish Cavalry - Uhlan

| Date | Mintage | VF20 | XF40 | MS60 | MS63 | MS65 |
|---|---|---|---|---|---|---|
| 2011 MW | 1,000,000 | — | — | 3.00 | 4.00 | 6.00 |

**Y# 783 2 ZŁOTE**
8.15 g., Brass, 27 mm. **Subject:** Gdynia

| Date | Mintage | VF20 | XF40 | MS60 | MS63 | MS65 |
|---|---|---|---|---|---|---|
| 2011 MW | 800,000 | — | — | 3.00 | 4.00 | 6.00 |

**Y# 784 2 ZŁOTE**
8.15 g., Brass, 27 mm. **Subject:** Warsaw Pilgrimage to the Marian Shrine of Jasna Gora in Czestochowa, 300th Anniversary

| Date | Mintage | VF20 | XF40 | MS60 | MS63 | MS65 |
|---|---|---|---|---|---|---|
| 2011 MW | 800,000 | — | — | 3.00 | 4.00 | 6.00 |

**Y# 785 2 ZŁOTE**
8.15 g., Brass, 27 mm. **Subject:** Czeslaw Milosz

| Date | Mintage | VF20 | XF40 | MS60 | MS63 | MS65 |
|---|---|---|---|---|---|---|
| 2011 MW | 800,000 | — | — | 3.00 | 4.00 | 6.00 |

**Y# 788 2 ZŁOTE**
8.15 g., Brass, 27 mm. **Subject:** Mlawa

| Date | Mintage | VF20 | XF40 | MS60 | MS63 | MS65 |
|---|---|---|---|---|---|---|
| 2011 MW | 800,000 | — | — | 3.00 | 4.00 | 6.00 |

**Y# 789 2 ZŁOTE**
8.15 g., Brass, 27 mm. **Subject:** Ignacy Jan Paderewski

| Date | Mintage | VF20 | XF40 | MS60 | MS63 | MS65 |
|---|---|---|---|---|---|---|
| 2011 MW | 800,000 | — | — | 3.00 | 4.00 | 6.00 |

**Y# 792 2 ZŁOTE**
8.15 g., Brass, 27 mm. **Subject:** Silesian Uprising

| Date | Mintage | VF20 | XF40 | MS60 | MS63 | MS65 |
|---|---|---|---|---|---|---|
| 2011 MW | 800,000 | — | — | 3.00 | 4.00 | 6.00 |

**Y# 794 2 ZŁOTE**
8.15 g., Brass, 27 mm. **Subject:** Poznan

| Date | Mintage | VF20 | XF40 | MS60 | MS63 | MS65 |
|---|---|---|---|---|---|---|
| 2011 MW | 800,000 | — | — | 3.00 | 4.00 | 6.00 |

**Y# 795 2 ZŁOTE**
8.15 g., Brass, 27 mm. **Subject:** Society for the Protection of the Blind, 100th Anniversary

| Date | Mintage | VF20 | XF40 | MS60 | MS63 | MS65 |
|---|---|---|---|---|---|---|
| 2011 MW | 800,000 | — | — | 3.00 | 4.00 | 6.00 |

**Y# 797 2 ZŁOTE**
8.15 g., Brass, 27 mm. **Subject:** Ferdynand Ossendowski

| Date | Mintage | VF20 | XF40 | MS60 | MS63 | MS65 |
|---|---|---|---|---|---|---|
| 2011 MW | 900,000 | — | — | 3.00 | 4.00 | 6.00 |

**Y# 799 2 ZŁOTE**
8.15 g., Brass, 27 mm. **Subject:** Polonia Warszawa football club

| Date | Mintage | VF20 | XF40 | MS60 | MS63 | MS65 |
|---|---|---|---|---|---|---|
| 2011 MW | 800,000 | — | — | 3.00 | 4.00 | 6.00 |

**Y# 801 2 ZŁOTE**

8.15 g., Brass, 27 mm. **Subject:** Jeremi Przybora and Jerzy Wasowski

| Date | Mintage | VF20 | XF40 | MS60 | MS63 | MS65 |
|---|---|---|---|---|---|---|
| 2011 MW | 800,000 | — | — | 3.00 | 4.00 | 6.00 |

**Y# 804 2 ZŁOTE**

8.15 g., Brass, 27 mm. **Subject:** Lodz **Rev:** Building and architectural detail

| Date | Mintage | VF20 | XF40 | MS60 | MS63 | MS65 |
|---|---|---|---|---|---|---|
| 2011 MW | — | — | — | 3.00 | 4.00 | 6.00 |

**Y# 805 2 ZŁOTE**

8.15 g., Brass, 27 mm. **Subject:** Krakow **Rev:** Church along riverfront

| Date | Mintage | VF20 | XF40 | MS60 | MS63 | MS65 |
|---|---|---|---|---|---|---|
| 2011 MW Proof | — | — | — | 3.00 | 4.00 | 6.00 |

**Y# 806 2 ZŁOTE**

8.15 g., Brass, 27 mm. **Subject:** Kalisz **Rev:** Chruch

| Date | Mintage | VF20 | XF40 | MS60 | MS63 | MS65 |
|---|---|---|---|---|---|---|
| 2011 MW | — | — | — | 3.00 | 4.00 | 6.00 |

**Y# 809 2 ZŁOTE**

8.15 g., Brass, 27 mm. **Subject:** Christmas Charity Orchestra, 20th Anniversary **Rev:** Guitar with love hearts

| Date | Mintage | VF20 | XF40 | MS60 | MS63 | MS65 |
|---|---|---|---|---|---|---|
| 2012 MW | — | — | — | 3.00 | 4.00 | 6.00 |

**Y# 811 2 ZŁOTE**

8.15 g., Brass, 27 mm. **Subject:** Cooperative Banking in Poland, 150th Anniversary **Rev:** Stack of bank notes and coins at left, wheat ear in center, figures of people holding hands at right

| Date | Mintage | VF20 | XF40 | MS60 | MS63 | MS65 |
|---|---|---|---|---|---|---|
| 2012 MW | — | — | — | 3.00 | 4.00 | 6.00 |

**Y# 813 2 ZŁOTE**

8.15 g., Brass, 27 mm. **Subject:** Ulma, Baranek and Kowalski families **Rev:** Mother holding child

| Date | Mintage | VF20 | XF40 | MS60 | MS63 | MS65 |
|---|---|---|---|---|---|---|
| 2012 MW | — | — | — | 3.00 | 4.00 | 6.00 |

**Y# 816 2 ZŁOTE**

8.15 g., Brass, 27 mm. **Subject:** Polish Radio, 50th Anniversary

| Date | Mintage | VF20 | XF40 | MS60 | MS63 | MS65 |
|---|---|---|---|---|---|---|
| 2012 MW | 800,000 | — | — | 3.00 | 4.00 | 6.00 |

**Y# 817 2 ZŁOTE**

8.15 g., Brass, 27 mm. **Subject:** Stefan Banach

| Date | Mintage | VF20 | XF40 | MS60 | MS63 | MS65 |
|---|---|---|---|---|---|---|
| 2012 MW | 800,000 | — | — | 3.00 | 4.00 | 6.00 |

**Y# 820 2 ZŁOTE**

8.15 g., Brass, 27 mm. **Subject:** Blyskawica, destroyer

| Date | Mintage | VF20 | XF40 | MS60 | MS63 | MS65 |
|---|---|---|---|---|---|---|
| 2012 MW | 800,000 | — | — | 3.00 | 4.00 | 6.00 |

**Y# 821 2 ZŁOTE**

8.15 g., Brass, 27 mm. **Subject:** National Museum in Warsaw, 150th Anniversary

| Date | Mintage | VF20 | XF40 | MS60 | MS63 | MS65 |
|---|---|---|---|---|---|---|
| 2012 | 800,000 | — | — | 3.00 | 4.00 | 6.00 |

**Y# 823 2 ZŁOTE**

8.15 g., Brass, 27 mm. **Subject:** European Football Championships

| Date | Mintage | VF20 | XF40 | MS60 | MS63 | MS65 |
|---|---|---|---|---|---|---|
| 2012 MW | 1,000,000 | — | — | 3.00 | 4.00 | 6.00 |

**Y# 832 2 ZŁOTE**

8.15 g., Brass, 27 mm. **Subject:** London Olympics, 2012; Polish Team

| Date | Mintage | VF20 | XF40 | MS60 | MS63 | MS65 |
|---|---|---|---|---|---|---|
| 2012 MW | 1,000,000 | — | — | 3.00 | 4.00 | 6.00 |

**Y# 835 2 ZŁOTE**

8.15 g., Brass **Subject:** Krzemionki Opatowskie **Shape:** 27

| Date | Mintage | VF20 | XF40 | MS60 | MS63 | MS65 |
|---|---|---|---|---|---|---|
| 2012 MW | 800,000 | — | — | 3.00 | 4.00 | 6.00 |

**Y# 837 2 ZŁOTE**

8.15 g., Brass, 27 mm. **Subject:** Orzel, submarine

| Date | Mintage | VF20 | XF40 | MS60 | MS63 | MS65 |
|---|---|---|---|---|---|---|
| 2012 MW | 800,000 | — | — | 3.00 | 4.00 | 6.00 |

**Y# 838 2 ZŁOTE**

8.15 g., Brass, 27 mm. **Subject:** Boleslaw Prus

| Date | Mintage | VF20 | XF40 | MS60 | MS63 | MS65 |
|---|---|---|---|---|---|---|
| 2012 MW | 8,000,000 | — | — | 3.00 | 4.00 | 6.00 |

**Y# 841 2 ZŁOTE**

8.15 g., Brass, 27 mm. **Subject:** Dragon, light cruiser

| Date | Mintage | VF20 | XF40 | MS60 | MS63 | MS65 |
|---|---|---|---|---|---|---|
| 2012 MW | 800,000 | — | — | 3.00 | 4.00 | 6.00 |

**Y# 842 2 ZŁOTE**

8.15 g., Brass, 27 mm. **Subject:** Piotr Michalowski, painter

| Date | Mintage | VF20 | XF40 | MS60 | MS63 | MS65 |
|---|---|---|---|---|---|---|
| 2012 MW | 800,000 | — | — | 3.00 | 4.00 | 6.00 |

**Y# 844 2 ZŁOTYCH**
8.15 g., Brass, 27 mm. **Obv:** Eagle **Rev:** Destroyer Piorun

| Date | Mintage | VF20 | XF40 | MS60 | MS63 | MS65 |
|---|---|---|---|---|---|---|
| 2012 MW | 800,000 | — | — | — | 3.00 | 5.00 |

**Y# 847 2 ZŁOTYCH**
8.15 g., Brass, 27 mm. **Subject:** London Olympics, 2012 **Obv:** Eagle **Rev:** Runner motif

| Date | Mintage | VF20 | XF40 | MS60 | MS63 | MS65 |
|---|---|---|---|---|---|---|
| 2012 MW | 1,000,000 | — | — | — | 3.00 | 5.00 |

**Y# 848 2 ZŁOTYCH**
8.15 g., Brass, 27 mm. **Obv:** Eagle **Rev:** Missile ship - Gdynia

| Date | Mintage | VF20 | XF40 | MS60 | MS63 | MS65 |
|---|---|---|---|---|---|---|
| 2013 MW | 800,000 | — | — | — | 3.00 | 5.00 |

**Y# 852 2 ZŁOTYCH**
8.15 g., Brass, 27 mm. **Subject:** January 1863 Uprising, 150th Anniversary **Obv:** Eagle **Rev:** Female blessing kneeling soldier, flag in backgorund

| Date | Mintage | VF20 | XF40 | MS60 | MS63 | MS65 |
|---|---|---|---|---|---|---|
| 2013 MW | 800,000 | — | — | — | 3.00 | 5.00 |

**Y# 854 2 ZŁOTYCH**
8.15 g., Brass, 27 mm. **Subject:** Polish Theatre, 100th Anniversary **Obv:** Eagle **Rev:** Theatre façade

| Date | Mintage | VF20 | XF40 | MS60 | MS63 | MS65 |
|---|---|---|---|---|---|---|
| 2013 MW | 800,000 | — | — | — | 3.00 | 5.00 |

**Y# 856 2 ZŁOTYCH**
8.15 g., Copper-Aluminum-Nickel, 27 mm. **Subject:** Cyprian Norwid

| Date | Mintage | VF20 | XF40 | MS60 | MS63 | MS65 |
|---|---|---|---|---|---|---|
| 2013 MW | Est. 800000 | — | — | — | 3.00 | 5.00 |

**Y# 859 2 ZŁOTYCH**
8.15 g., Copper-Aluminum-Nickel, 27 mm. **Subject:** Polish Ships - Warszawa Guided-Missle Destroyer

| Date | Mintage | VF20 | XF40 | MS60 | MS63 | MS65 |
|---|---|---|---|---|---|---|
| 2013 MW | Est. 800000 | — | — | — | 3.00 | 5.00 |

**Y# 862 2 ZŁOTYCH**
8.15 g., Copper-Aluminum-Nickel, 27 mm. **Subject:** Polish Ships - Lublin Class Minelayer - Landing Ship

| Date | Mintage | VF20 | XF40 | MS60 | MS63 | MS65 |
|---|---|---|---|---|---|---|
| 2013 MW | — | — | — | — | 3.00 | 5.00 |

**Y# 864 2 ZŁOTYCH**
8.15 g., Copper-Aluminum-Nickel, 27 mm. **Subject:** Polish Football Clubs - Warta Poznan

| Date | Mintage | VF20 | XF40 | MS60 | MS63 | MS65 |
|---|---|---|---|---|---|---|
| 2013 MW | 800,000 | — | — | — | 3.00 | 5.00 |

**Y# 866 2 ZŁOTYCH**
8.15 g., Copper-Aluminum-Nickel, 27 mm. **Subject:** Polish Ships - ORP Gen. K. Pulaski Guided-Missile Frigate

| Date | Mintage | VF20 | XF40 | MS60 | MS63 | MS65 |
|---|---|---|---|---|---|---|
| 2013 MW | Est. 800000 | — | — | — | 3.00 | 5.00 |

**Y# 870 2 ZŁOTYCH**
8.15 g., Copper-Aluminum-Nickel, 27 mm. **Subject:** Witold Lutoslawski

| Date | Mintage | VF20 | XF40 | MS60 | MS63 | MS65 |
|---|---|---|---|---|---|---|
| 2013 MW | — | — | — | — | 3.00 | 5.00 |

**Y# 873 2 ZŁOTYCH**
8.15 g., Copper-Aluminum-Nickel, 27 mm. **Subject:** 200th Anniversary of the Death of Prince Jozef Poinatowski

| Date | Mintage | VF20 | XF40 | MS60 | MS63 | MS65 |
|---|---|---|---|---|---|---|
| 2013 MW | Est. 800000 | — | — | — | 3.00 | 5.00 |

**Y# 876 2 ZŁOTYCH**
8.15 g., Copper-Aluminum-Nickel, 27 mm. **Subject:** 50th Anniversary of the Polish Society for the Mentally Handicapped

| Date | Mintage | VF20 | XF40 | MS60 | MS63 | MS65 |
|---|---|---|---|---|---|---|
| 2013 MW | Est. 800000 | — | — | — | 3.00 | 5.00 |

**Y# 878 2 ZŁOTYCH**
8.15 g., Copper-Aluminum-Nickel, 27 mm. **Subject:** Animals of the World - Europian Bison

| Date | Mintage | VF20 | XF40 | MS60 | MS63 | MS65 |
|---|---|---|---|---|---|---|
| 2013 MW | Est. 10000000 | — | — | — | 3.00 | 5.00 |

**Y# 880 2 ZŁOTYCH**
8.15 g., Copper-Aluminum-Nickel, 27 mm. **Subject:** 200th Anniversary of the Birth of Hipolit Cegielski

| Date | Mintage | VF20 | XF40 | MS60 | MS63 | MS65 |
|---|---|---|---|---|---|---|
| 2013 MW | Est. 800000 | — | — | — | 3.00 | 5.00 |

**Y# 883 2 ZŁOTYCH**
8.15 g., Copper-Aluminum-Nickel, 27 mm. **Subject:** History of Polish Popular Music - Agniezka Osiecka

| Date | Mintage | VF20 | XF40 | MS60 | MS63 | MS65 |
|---|---|---|---|---|---|---|
| 2013 MW | Est. 800000 | — | — | — | 3.00 | 5.00 |

**Y# 893 2 ZŁOTYCH**
8.15 g., Brass, 27 mm. **Subject:** Polish Olympic Team, Sochi 2014

| Date | Mintage | VF20 | XF40 | MS60 | MS63 | MS65 |
|---|---|---|---|---|---|---|
| 2014 | 800,000 | — | — | 3.00 | 4.00 | 6.00 |

**Y# 896 2 ZŁOTYCH**
8.15 g., Brass, 27 mm. **Subject:** Konik Horse

| Date | Mintage | VF20 | XF40 | MS60 | MS63 | MS65 |
|---|---|---|---|---|---|---|
| 2014 | 800,000 | — | — | — | 3.00 | 5.00 |

**Y# 901 2 ZŁOTYCH**
8.15 g., Brass, 27 mm. **Subject:** Jan Karski, 100th Anniversary of Birth

| Date | Mintage | VF20 | XF40 | MS60 | MS63 | MS65 |
|---|---|---|---|---|---|---|
| 2014 | 700,000 | — | — | — | 3.00 | 5.00 |

**Y# 851 10 ZŁOTY**
14.14 g., 0.925 Silver 0.4205 oz. ASW, 32 mm. **Subject:** January 1893 Uprising, 150th Anniversary **Obv:** Anchor logo, pries and eagle **Rev:** Tri-part shield crowned, arms in background

| Date | Mintage | VF20 | XF40 | MS60 | MS63 | MS65 |
|---|---|---|---|---|---|---|
| 2013 MW | 28,000 | PF63 40.00 | PF65 50.00 | | | |

**Y# 853 10 ZŁOTY**
14.00 g., 0.925 Silver 0.4164 oz. ASW, 40x26 mm. **Subject:** Polish Theatre, 100th Anniversary **Obv:** Shield and Eagle **Rev:** Exterior of the theater, open curtian in color **Shape:** Oval

| Date | Mintage | VF20 | XF40 | MS60 | MS63 | MS65 |
|---|---|---|---|---|---|---|
| 2013 MW | 28,000 | PF63 45.00 | PF65 55.00 | | | |

**Y# 284 5 ZŁOTYCH**
6.54 g., Bi-Metallic Aluminum-Bronze center in Copper-Nickel ring, 24 mm. **Obv:** National arms within circle **Obv. Legend:** RZECZPOSPOLITA POLSKA **Rev:** Value within circle flanked by oak leaves

| Date | Mintage | VF20 | XF40 | MS60 | MS63 | MS65 |
|---|---|---|---|---|---|---|
| 2008 MW | — | — | — | 7.00 | 8.00 | 10.00 |
| 2009 MW | — | — | — | 7.00 | 8.00 | 10.00 |
| 2010 MW | — | — | — | 7.00 | 8.00 | 10.00 |

**Y# 800 5 ZŁOTYCH**
7.07 g., 0.925 Silver 0.2103 oz. ASW, 24 mm. **Subject:** Polonia Warszawa football club

| Date | Mintage | VF20 | XF40 | MS60 | MS63 | MS65 |
|---|---|---|---|---|---|---|
| 2011 MW | 50,000 | PF63 15.00 | PF65 20.00 | | | |

**Y# 863 5 ZŁOTYCH**
7.07 g., 0.925 Silver 0.2103 oz. ASW, 24 mm. **Subject:** History of Polish Coin - Denarius of Boleslaw I the Brave

| Date | Mintage | VF20 | XF40 | MS60 | MS63 | MS65 |
|---|---|---|---|---|---|---|
| 2013 MW Proof | — | — | — | 7.00 | 8.00 | 10.00 |

**Y# 865 5 ZŁOTYCH**
7.07 g., 0.925 Silver 0.2103 oz. ASW, 24 mm. **Subject:** Polish Football Club - Warta Poznan

| Date | Mintage | VF20 | XF40 | MS60 | MS63 | MS65 |
|---|---|---|---|---|---|---|
| 2013 MW Proof | Est. 40000 | — | — | 7.00 | 8.00 | 10.00 |

**Y# 869 5 ZŁOTYCH**
7.07 g., 0.925 Silver 0.2103 oz. ASW, 24 mm. **Subject:** History of Polish Coin - Denarius of Boleslaw II the Bold

| Date | Mintage | VF20 | XF40 | MS60 | MS63 | MS65 |
|---|---|---|---|---|---|---|
| 2013 MW Proof | Est. 20000 | — | — | 7.00 | 8.00 | 10.00 |

**Y# 904 5 ZŁOTYCH**
6.54 g., Bi-Metallic Aluminum-Bronze center in Copper-Nickel ring, 24 mm. **Subject:** Discover Poland

| Date | Mintage | VF20 | XF40 | MS60 | MS63 | MS65 |
|---|---|---|---|---|---|---|
| 2014 | 1,200,000 | — | — | 7.00 | 8.00 | 10.00 |

**Y# 913 5 ZŁOTYCH**
6.54 g., Bi-Metallic Aluminum-Bronze center in Copper-Nickel ring, 24 mm. **Subject:** Discover Poland

| Date | Mintage | VF20 | XF40 | MS60 | MS63 | MS65 |
|---|---|---|---|---|---|---|
| 2014 | 1,200,000 | — | — | 7.00 | 8.00 | 10.00 |

**Y# 406 10 ZŁOTYCH**
14.14 g., 0.925 Silver 0.4205 oz. ASW **Subject:** Year 2001 **Obv:** Crowned eagle with wings open **Rev:** Printed circuit board

| Date | Mintage | VF20 | XF40 | MS60 | MS63 | MS65 |
|---|---|---|---|---|---|---|
| 2001 MW | 35,000 | PF63 35.00 | PF65 55.00 | | | |

**Y# 413 10 ZŁOTYCH**
14.14 g., 0.925 Silver 0.4205 oz. ASW, 32 mm. **Subject:** 15 Years of the Constitutional Court **Obv:** Crowned eagle suspended from a judge's neck chain **Rev:** Crowned eagle head and balance scale **Edge Lettering:** TRYBUNAL KONSTYTUCYJNY W SLUZBIE PANSTWA PRAWA

| Date | Mintage | VF20 | XF40 | MS60 | MS63 | MS65 |
|---|---|---|---|---|---|---|
| 2001 MW | 25,000 | PF63 45.00 | PF65 65.00 | | | |

**Y# 419 10 ZŁOTYCH**
14.14 g., 0.925 Silver 0.4205 oz. ASW, 32 mm. **Subject:** Cardinal Stefan Wyszynski **Obv:** Crowned eagle with wings open above ribbon **Rev:** Half length figure facing with raised hands **Edge Lettering:** 100 • ROCZNIA URODZIN

| Date | Mintage | VF20 | XF40 | MS60 | MS63 | MS65 |
|---|---|---|---|---|---|---|
| 2001 MW | 60,000 | PF63 25.00 | PF65 30.00 | | | |

**Y# 425 10 ZŁOTYCH**
14.21 g., 0.925 Silver 0.4226 oz. ASW, 32 mm. **Subject:** Jan III Sobieski **Obv:** Crowned eagle with wings open **Rev:** 3/4 armored bust facing with army in background **Edge:** Plain

| Date | Mintage | VF20 | XF40 | MS60 | MS63 | MS65 |
|---|---|---|---|---|---|---|
| 2001 MW | 24,000 | PF63 40.00 | PF65 50.00 | | | |

**Y# 458 10 ZŁOTYCH**
14.14 g., 0.925 Silver 0.4205 oz. ASW, 32 mm. **Obv:** Crowned eagle with wings open **Rev:** Jan Sobieski, half-length figure in armor standing **Edge:** Plain

| Date | Mintage | VF20 | XF40 | MS60 | MS63 | MS65 |
|---|---|---|---|---|---|---|
| 2001 MW | 17,000 | PF63 65.00 | PF65 85.00 | | | |

**Y# 459 10 ZŁOTYCH**
14.14 g., 0.925 Silver 0.4205 oz. ASW, 32 mm. **Obv:** Three violins **Rev:** Henryk Wieniawski **Edge:** Plain

| Date | Mintage | VF20 | XF40 | MS60 | MS63 | MS65 |
|---|---|---|---|---|---|---|
| 2001 MW | 28,000 | PF63 35.00 | PF65 55.00 | | | |

**Y# 460 10 ZŁOTYCH**
14.14 g., 0.925 Silver 0.4205 oz. ASW, 32 mm. **Obv:** Crowned eagle with wings open above fish **Rev:** Michal Siedlecki **Edge:** Plain

| Date | Mintage | VF20 | XF40 | MS60 | MS63 | MS65 |
|---|---|---|---|---|---|---|
| 2001 MW | 26,000 | PF63 30.00 | PF65 50.00 | | | |

**Y# 432 10 ZŁOTYCH**
14.14 g., 0.925 Silver 0.4205 oz. ASW, 32 mm. **Subject:** Bronislaw Malinowski **Obv:** Small crowned eagle with wings open to right of bust facing **Rev:** Trobriand Islands village scene **Edge Lettering:** etnolog, antropolog kultury

| Date | Mintage | VF20 | XF40 | MS60 | MS63 | MS65 |
|---|---|---|---|---|---|---|
| 2002 MW | — | PF63 25.00 | PF65 35.00 | | | |

**Y# 434 10 ZŁOTYCH**
14.14 g., 0.925 Silver 0.4205 oz. ASW, 32 mm. **Subject:** World Cup Soccer **Obv:** Crowned eagle with wings open **Rev:** Soccer player **Edge Lettering:** etnolog, antropolog kultury

| Date | Mintage | VF20 | XF40 | MS60 | MS63 | MS65 |
|---|---|---|---|---|---|---|
| 2002 MW | — | PF63 22.00 | PF65 27.00 | | | |

**Y# 435 10 ZŁOTYCH**
14.14 g., 0.925 Silver 0.4205 oz. ASW, 32 mm. **Subject:** World Cup Soccer **Obv:** Amber soccer ball inset entering goal net **Rev:** Two soccer players with amber soccer ball inset **Edge Lettering:** etnolog, antropolog kultury

| Date | Mintage | VF20 | XF40 | MS60 | MS63 | MS65 |
|---|---|---|---|---|---|---|
| 2002 MW | — | PF63 35.00 | PF65 55.00 | | | |

**Y# 437 10 ZŁOTYCH**
14.14 g., 0.925 Silver 0.4205 oz. ASW, 32 mm. **Subject:** Pope John Paul II **Obv:** Crowned eagle with wings open within two views of praying Pope **Rev:** Pope facing radiant Holy Door **Edge:** Plain

| Date | Mintage | VF20 | XF40 | MS60 | MS63 | MS65 |
|---|---|---|---|---|---|---|
| 2002 MW | 80,000 | PF63 25.00 | PF65 35.00 | | | |

**Y# 441 10 ZŁOTYCH**
14.20 g., 0.925 Silver 0.4223 oz. ASW, 32 mm. **Subject:** Gen. Wladyslaw Anders **Obv:** Crowned eagle with wings open, cross and multicolor flowers **Rev:** Uniformed bust right **Edge:** Plain

| Date | Mintage | VF20 | XF40 | MS60 | MS63 | MS65 |
|---|---|---|---|---|---|---|
| 2002 MW | 40,000 | PF63 55.00 | PF65 75.00 | | | |

**Y# 450 10 ZŁOTYCH**
14.14 g., 0.925 Silver 0.4205 oz. ASW, 32 mm. **Subject:** August II (1697-1706, 1709-1735) **Obv:** Crowned eagle with wings open **Rev:** Portrait and Order of the White Eagle **Edge:** Plain

| Date | Mintage | VF20 | XF40 | MS60 | MS63 | MS65 |
|---|---|---|---|---|---|---|
| 2002 MW | 30,000 | PF63 35.00 | PF65 55.00 | | | |

**Y# 448 10 ZŁOTYCH**
14.14 g., 0.925 Silver 0.4205 oz. ASW, 32 mm. **Subject:** City of Poznan (Posen) **Obv:** Old coin design and arched door **Rev:** Old coin design and city view **Edge:** Plain

| Date | Mintage | VF20 | XF40 | MS60 | MS63 | MS65 |
|---|---|---|---|---|---|---|
| 2003 MW | 39,000 | PF63 35.00 | PF65 55.00 | | | |

**Y# 453 10 ZŁOTYCH**
14.14 g., 0.925 Silver 0.4205 oz. ASW, 32 mm. **Subject:** Great Orchestra of Christmas Charity **Obv:** Large inscribed heart above crowned eagle with wings open **Rev:** Boy playing flute **Edge:** Plain

| Date | Mintage | VF20 | XF40 | MS60 | MS63 | MS65 |
|---|---|---|---|---|---|---|
| 2003 MW | 47,000 | PF63 35.00 | PF65 55.00 | | | |

**Y# 468 10 ZŁOTYCH**
14.14 g., 0.925 Silver 0.4205 oz. ASW, 32 mm. **Obv:** Tanks on battlefield **Rev:** General Maczek **Edge:** Plain

| Date | Mintage | VF20 | XF40 | MS60 | MS63 | MS65 |
|---|---|---|---|---|---|---|
| 2003 MW | 44,000 | PF63 25.00 | PF65 35.00 | | | |

**Y# 469 10 ZŁOTYCH**
14.14 g., 0.925 Silver 0.4205 oz. ASW, 32 mm. **Subject:** Gas and Oil Industry **Obv:** Crowned eagle and highway leading to city view **Rev:** Portrait and refinery **Edge:** Plain

| Date | Mintage | VF20 | XF40 | MS60 | MS63 | MS65 |
|---|---|---|---|---|---|---|
| 2003 MW | 43,000 | PF63 25.00 | PF65 35.00 | | | |

**Y# 474 10 ZŁOTYCH**
14.14 g., 0.925 Silver 0.4205 oz. ASW, 32 mm. **Obv:** Crowned eagle with wings open **Rev:** Stanislaus I and wife's portrait **Edge:** Plain

| Date | Mintage | VF20 | XF40 | MS60 | MS63 | MS65 |
|---|---|---|---|---|---|---|
| 2003 MW | 45,000 | PF63 25.00 | PF65 35.00 | | | |

**Y# 475 10 ZŁOTYCH**
14.14 g., 0.925 Silver 0.4205 oz. ASW, 32 mm. **Obv:** Crowned eagle with wings open **Rev:** Half-length figure of Stanislaus I with his wife in background **Edge:** Plain

| Date | Mintage | VF20 | XF40 | MS60 | MS63 | MS65 |
|---|---|---|---|---|---|---|
| 2003 MW | 40,000 | PF63 30.00 | PF65 40.00 | | | |

**Y# 480 10 ZŁOTYCH**
14.14 g., 0.925 Silver 0.4205 oz. ASW, 32 mm. **Subject:** 80th Anniversary of the Modern Zloty Currency **Obv:** Man wearing glasses behind crowned eagle with wings open **Rev:** Bust left **Edge:** Plain

| Date | Mintage | VF20 | XF40 | MS60 | MS63 | MS65 |
|---|---|---|---|---|---|---|
| 2004 MW | 55,000 | PF63 22.00 | PF65 32.00 | | | |

**Y# 482 10 ZŁOTYCH**
14.14 g., 0.925 Silver 0.4205 oz. ASW, 32 mm. **Subject:** Poland Joining the European Union **Obv:** Crowned eagle in blue circle with yellow stars **Rev:** Multicolor European Union and Polish flags **Edge:** Plain

| Date | Mintage | VF20 | XF40 | MS60 | MS63 | MS65 |
|---|---|---|---|---|---|---|
| 2004 MW | 78,000 | PF63 25.00 | PF65 35.00 | | | |

**Y# 497 10 ZŁOTYCH**
14.14 g., 0.925 Silver 0.4205 oz. ASW, 32 mm. **Subject:** Warsaw Uprising 60th Anniversary **Obv:** Crowned eagle and value on resistance symbol **Rev:** Polish soldier wearing captured German helmet **Edge:** Plain

| Date | Mintage | VF20 | XF40 | MS60 | MS63 | MS65 |
|---|---|---|---|---|---|---|
| 2004 MW | 92,000 | PF63 18.00 | PF65 25.00 | | | |

**Y# 500 10 ZŁOTYCH**
14.14 g., 0.925 Silver 0.4205 oz. ASW, 32 mm. **Obv:** Polish paratrooper badge **Rev:** Gen. Sosabowski and descending paratrooper **Edge:** Plain

| Date | Mintage | VF20 | XF40 | MS60 | MS63 | MS65 |
|---|---|---|---|---|---|---|
| 2004 MW | 56,000 | PF63 18.00 | PF65 25.00 | | | |

**Y# 502 10 ZŁOTYCH**

14.14 g., 0.925 Silver 0.4205 oz. ASW, 32 mm. **Subject:** Polish Police 85th Anniversary **Obv:** Crowned eagle with wings open **Rev:** Seal partially overlapping police badge **Edge:** Plain

| Date | Mintage | VF20 | XF40 | MS60 | MS63 | MS65 |
|---|---|---|---|---|---|---|
| 2004 MW | 65,000 | PF63 20.00 | PF65 30.00 | | | |

**Y# 506 10 ZŁOTYCH**

14.14 g., 0.925 Silver 0.4205 oz. ASW, 32 mm. **Obv:** Siberian landscape above crowned eagle and value **Rev:** Aleksander Czekanowski (1833-1876) **Edge:** Plain

| Date | Mintage | VF20 | XF40 | MS60 | MS63 | MS65 |
|---|---|---|---|---|---|---|
| 2004 MW | 45,000 | PF63 18.00 | PF65 25.00 | | | |

**Y# 510 10 ZŁOTYCH**

14.14 g., 0.925 Silver 0.4205 oz. ASW, 32 mm. **Subject:** Warsaw Fine Arts Academy Centennial **Obv:** Crowned eagle with wings open within city square **Rev:** Art studio, color painting on stand **Edge:** Plain

| Date | Mintage | VF20 | XF40 | MS60 | MS63 | MS65 |
|---|---|---|---|---|---|---|
| 2004 MW | 75,000 | PF63 20.00 | PF65 30.00 | | | |

Antique patina

**Y# 517 10 ZŁOTYCH**

14.14 g., 0.925 Silver 0.4205 oz. ASW, 32 mm. **Subject:** Olympics **Obv:** Crowned eagle with wings open and woman **Rev:** Fencers in front of Parthenon **Edge:** Plain

| Date | Mintage | VF20 | XF40 | MS60 | MS63 | MS65 |
|---|---|---|---|---|---|---|
| 2004 MW | 70,000 | PF63 18.00 | PF65 25.00 | | | |

**Y# 518 10 ZŁOTYCH**

14.14 g., 0.925 Silver 0.4205 oz. ASW, 32 mm. **Subject:** Olympics **Obv:** Crowned eagle with wings open within gold plated center **Rev:** Ancient athlete within gold plated circle **Edge:** Plain

| Date | Mintage | VF20 | XF40 | MS60 | MS63 | MS65 |
|---|---|---|---|---|---|---|
| 2004 MW | 90,000 | PF63 18.00 | PF65 25.00 | | | |

**Y# 523 10 ZŁOTYCH**

14.23 g., 0.925 Silver 0.4232 oz. ASW, 43.2 x 29.2 mm. **Subject:** Japan's Aichi Expo **Obv:** Monument **Rev:** Two cranes **Edge:** Plain **Shape:** Quarter of circle

| Date | Mintage | VF20 | XF40 | MS60 | MS63 | MS65 |
|---|---|---|---|---|---|---|
| 2005 MW | 80,000 | PF63 25.00 | PF65 35.00 | | | |

**Y# 526 10 ZŁOTYCH**

14.14 g., 0.925 Silver 0.4205 oz. ASW partially gilt, 32.1 mm. **Obv:** Crowned eagle with wings open above date and grasping hands **Rev:** Gold plated bust right and church **Edge:** Plain

| Date | Mintage | VF20 | XF40 | MS60 | MS63 | MS65 |
|---|---|---|---|---|---|---|
| 2005 MW | — | PF63 20.00 | PF65 30.00 | | | |

**Y# 537 10 ZŁOTYCH**

14.14 g., 0.925 Silver 0.4205 oz. ASW, 32 mm. **Obv:** Horse drawn carriage **Rev:** Green duck at left and Konstanty Ildefons Galczynski in top hat at right **Edge:** Plain

| Date | Mintage | VF20 | XF40 | MS60 | MS63 | MS65 |
|---|---|---|---|---|---|---|
| 2005 MW | 62,000 | PF63 18.00 | PF65 25.00 | | | |

**Y# 539 10 ZŁOTYCH**

14.14 g., 0.925 Silver 0.4205 oz. ASW, 32 mm. **Obv:** Baptismal font and Polish eagle **Rev:** Pope John Paul II and St. Peter's Basilica **Edge:** Plain

| Date | Mintage | VF20 | XF40 | MS60 | MS63 | MS65 |
|---|---|---|---|---|---|---|
| 2005 MW | 170,000 | PF63 20.00 | PF65 30.00 | | | |

**Y# 552 10 ZŁOTYCH**

14.14 g., 0.925 Silver 0.4205 oz. ASW, 32 mm. **Obv:** Crowned eagle above value **Rev:** Stanislaw August Poniatowski and shadow **Edge:** Plain

| Date | Mintage | VF20 | XF40 | MS60 | MS63 | MS65 |
|---|---|---|---|---|---|---|
| 2005 MW | 60,000 | PF63 20.00 | PF65 30.00 | | | |

**Y# 553 10 ZŁOTYCH**

14.14 g., 0.925 Silver 0.4205 oz. ASW, 32 mm. **Obv:** Crowned eagle above value **Rev:** Stanislaw August Poniatowski and crowned monogram **Edge:** Plain

| Date | Mintage | VF20 | XF40 | MS60 | MS63 | MS65 |
|---|---|---|---|---|---|---|
| 2005 MW | 60,000 | PF63 20.00 | PF65 30.00 | | | |

**Y# 554 10 ZŁOTYCH**

14.14 g., 0.925 Silver 0.4205 oz. ASW, 32 mm. **Subject:** End of WWII 60th Anniversary **Obv:** Crowned eagle above soldier silhouettes and value **Rev:** City view in ruins above bird with green sprig **Edge:** Plain

| Date | Mintage | VF20 | XF40 | MS60 | MS63 | MS65 |
|---|---|---|---|---|---|---|
| 2005 MW | 70,000 | PF63 22.00 | PF65 32.00 | | | |

**Y# 568 10 ZŁOTYCH**

14.14 g., 0.925 Silver 0.4205 oz. ASW, 32 mm. **Obv:** Sail ship and obverse design of Y-31 **Rev:** Reverse design of Y-31 on radiant design **Edge:** Lettered

| Date | Mintage | VF20 | XF40 | MS60 | MS63 | MS65 |
|---|---|---|---|---|---|---|
| 2005 MW | 61,000 | PF63 25.00 | PF65 35.00 | | | |

**Y# 596 10 ZŁOTYCH**

14.18 g., 0.925 Silver 0.4217 oz. ASW, 32 mm. **Subject:** 500th Anniversary - Birth of M. Reja **Obv:** National arms in oval, value below **Obv. Legend:** RZECZPOSPOLITA POLSKA **Rev:** Bust of Reja 3/4 right **Rev. Legend:** 500. ROCZNICA URODZIN MIKOLAJA REJA **Edge:** Plain

| Date | Mintage | VF20 | XF40 | MS60 | MS63 | MS65 |
|---|---|---|---|---|---|---|
| 2005 MW | 60,000 | PF63 18.00 | PF65 25.00 | | | |

**Y# 555 10 ZŁOTYCH**
14.14 g., 0.925 Silver 0.4205 oz. ASW, 32 mm. **Subject:** 2006 Winter Olympics **Obv:** Snow boarder above crowned eagle **Rev:** Snow boarder **Edge:** Plain

| Date | Mintage | VF20 | XF40 | MS60 | MS63 | MS65 |
|---|---|---|---|---|---|---|
| 2006 MW | 71,400 | PF63 20.00 | PF65 30.00 | | | |

**Y# 556 10 ZŁOTYCH**
14.14 g., 0.925 Silver 0.4205 oz. ASW, 32 mm. **Subject:** 2006 Winter Olympics **Obv:** Small national arms at left, figure skating couple at center **Obv. Legend:** RZECZPOSPOLITA POLSKA **Rev:** Female figure skater **Rev. Legend:** XX ZIMOWE IGRZYSKA OLIMPIJSKIE **Edge:** Plain

| Date | Mintage | VF20 | XF40 | MS60 | MS63 | MS65 |
|---|---|---|---|---|---|---|
| 2006 MW | 72,000 | PF63 20.00 | PF65 30.00 | | | |

**Y# 598 10 ZŁOTYCH**
14.15 g., 0.925 Silver 0.4208 oz. ASW, 32 mm. **Subject:** 30th Anniversary June 1976 **Obv:** National arms divides denomination, split railroad tracks below **Obv. Legend:** RZECZPOSPOLITA POLSKA **Rev:** 3/4 length woman standing with child, outlined row of shielded forces in background **Rev. Legend:** 30. ROCZNICA - CZERWCA 1976 **Edge:** Plain

| Date | Mintage | VF20 | XF40 | MS60 | MS63 | MS65 |
|---|---|---|---|---|---|---|
| 2006 MW | 56,000 | PF63 20.00 | PF65 30.00 | | | |

**Y# 599 10 ZŁOTYCH**
14.18 g., 0.925 Silver 0.4217 oz. ASW, 32 mm. **Series:** History of the Zloty **Obv:** National arms at upper left, 1932 dated 10 Zlotych obverse at lower right, building facade in background **Obv. Legend:** RZECZPOSPOLITA POLSKA **Rev:** Reverse of 1932 dated coin with head of Queen Jadwiga **Rev. Legend:** DZIEJE ZLOTEGO **Edge:** Plain

| Date | Mintage | VF20 | XF40 | MS60 | MS63 | MS65 |
|---|---|---|---|---|---|---|
| 2006 MW | 61,000 | PF63 20.00 | PF65 30.00 | | | |

**Y# 754 10 ZŁOTYCH**
14.14 g., Bi-Metallic, 32 mm. **Subject:** World Cup soccer **Obv:** Eagle within net **Rev:** Player kicking ball, sun

| Date | Mintage | VF20 | XF40 | MS60 | MS63 | MS65 |
|---|---|---|---|---|---|---|
| 2006 | — | PF63 20.00 | PF65 30.00 | | | |

**Y# 890 10 ZŁOTYCH**
14.14 g., 0.925 Silver 0.4205 oz. ASW **Subject:** 500th Anniversary **Rev:** Coronation scene

| Date | Mintage | VF20 | XF40 | MS60 | MS63 | MS65 |
|---|---|---|---|---|---|---|
| 2006 | — | PF63 18.00 | PF65 25.00 | | | |

**Y# 585 10 ZŁOTYCH**
14.14 g., 0.925 Silver 0.4205 oz. ASW, 32 mm. **Obv:** Mountains, Polish Eagle and value **Rev:** Ignacy Domeyko **Edge:** Plain

| Date | Mintage | VF20 | XF40 | MS60 | MS63 | MS65 |
|---|---|---|---|---|---|---|
| 2007 MW | 55,000 | PF63 18.00 | PF65 25.00 | | | |

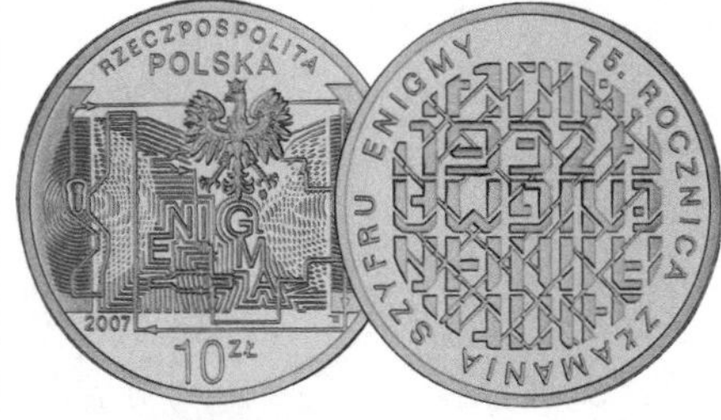

**Y# 587 10 ZŁOTYCH**
14.14 g., 0.925 Silver 0.4205 oz. ASW, 32 mm. **Subject:** 75th Anniversary - Breaking the Enigma Code **Obv:** Polish Eagle on circuit board **Rev:** Segmented letters **Edge:** Lettered

| Date | Mintage | VF20 | XF40 | MS60 | MS63 | MS65 |
|---|---|---|---|---|---|---|
| 2007 MW | 55,000 | PF63 35.00 | PF65 45.00 | | | |

**Y# 589 10 ZŁOTYCH**
14.14 g., 0.925 Silver 0.4205 oz. ASW, 32 mm. **Obv:** Angel, Polish Eagle and obverse coin design of Y-18 **Rev:** Reverse coin design of Y-18 on wheat ears **Edge:** Plain

| Date | Mintage | VF20 | XF40 | MS60 | MS63 | MS65 |
|---|---|---|---|---|---|---|
| 2007 MW | 57,000 | PF63 30.00 | PF65 40.00 | | | |

**Y# 595 10 ZŁOTYCH**
14.14 g., 0.925 Silver 0.4205 oz. ASW, 32 mm. **Subject:** Munincipality of Krakow, 750th Anniversary **Obv:** City gate tower, national arms at lower right **Obv. Legend:** RZECZPOSPOLITA POLSKA **Rev:** Knight with shield standing facing

| Date | Mintage | VF20 | XF40 | MS60 | MS63 | MS65 |
|---|---|---|---|---|---|---|
| 2007 MW | 58,000 | PF63 20.00 | PF65 30.00 | | | |

**Y# 600 10 ZŁOTYCH**
14.10 g., 0.925 Silver 0.4193 oz. ASW, 32 mm. **Subject:** 125th Anniversary - Birth of Szymanowskiego **Obv:** Piano keys at left, national arms on music score at right **Obv. Legend:** RZECZPOSPOLITA POLSKA **Rev:** Bust of Szymanowskiego 3/4 left, music composition at back of head and over upper body, dates as hologram at left **Rev. Legend:** 125. ROCZNICA URODZIN KAROLA SZYMANOWSKIEGO **Edge:** Plain

| Date | Mintage | VF20 | XF40 | MS60 | MS63 | MS65 |
|---|---|---|---|---|---|---|
| 2007 MW | 55,000 | PF63 18.00 | PF65 25.00 | | | |

**Y# 601 10 ZŁOTYCH**
14.30 g., 0.925 Silver 0.4253 oz. ASW, 14 mm. **Subject:** Arctic Explorers **Obv:** Sailing ship at center, national arms at right with denomination below **Obv. Legend:** RZECZPOSPOLITA POLSKA **Rev:** Busts of Henryk Arctowski and Antoni Dobrowolski facing, polar outline map at lower left **Edge:** Plain

| Date | Mintage | VF20 | XF40 | MS60 | MS63 | MS65 |
|---|---|---|---|---|---|---|
| 2007 MW | 60,000 | PF63 20.00 | PF65 30.00 | | | |

**Y# 602 10 ZŁOTYCH**
14.05 g., 0.925 Silver 0.4178 oz. ASW, 31.95 x 22.39 mm. **Obv:** Helmeted national arms, sword and denomination below **Obv. Legend:** RZECZPOSPOLITA - POLSKA **Rev:** Chivalrous knight on horseback jousting right **Rev. Inscription:** RYCERZ - CIEZKOZBROJNY **Edge:** Plain **Shape:** Rectangular

| Date | Mintage | VF20 | XF40 | MS60 | MS63 | MS65 |
|---|---|---|---|---|---|---|
| 2007 MW | 57,000 | PF63 30.00 | PF65 40.00 | | | |

**Y# 632 10 ZŁOTYCH**
14.14 g., 0.925 Silver 0.4205 oz. ASW, 32 mm. **Subject:** 40th Anniversary "Rocznica" March **Obv:** National arms at upper right, manuscript pages fluttering at left **Obv. Legend:** RZECZPOSPOLITA POLSKA **Rev:** Student protesters in front of gates of Warsaw University, military police in silhouette in foreground

| Date | Mintage | VF20 | XF40 | MS60 | MS63 | MS65 |
|---|---|---|---|---|---|---|
| 2008 MW | 118,000 | PF63 20.00 | PF65 30.00 | | | |

**Y# 635 10 ZŁOTYCH**
14.14 g., 0.925 Silver 0.4205 oz. ASW, 32 mm. **Subject:** Zbigniew Herbert **Obv:** Bust of Herbert 3/4 right at left, national arms at lower right **Rev:** Statue of Nike **Edge:** Plain

| Date | Mintage | VF20 | XF40 | MS60 | MS63 | MS65 |
|---|---|---|---|---|---|---|
| 2008 MW | 113,000 | PF63 20.00 | PF65 30.00 | | | |

**Y# 639 10 ZŁOTYCH**
14.14 g., 0.925 Silver 0.4205 oz. ASW, 32 mm. **Subject:** Siberian Exiles **Obv:** Small national arms at left, human outlines at right **Obv. Legend:** RZECZPOSPOLITA POLSKA **Rev:** Tree lines with imbedded triangular crystal below **Rev. Inscription:** SYBIRACY **Edge:** Plain

| Date | Mintage | VF20 | XF40 | MS60 | MS63 | MS65 |
|---|---|---|---|---|---|---|
| 2008 MW | 135,000 | PF63 20.00 | PF65 30.00 | | | |

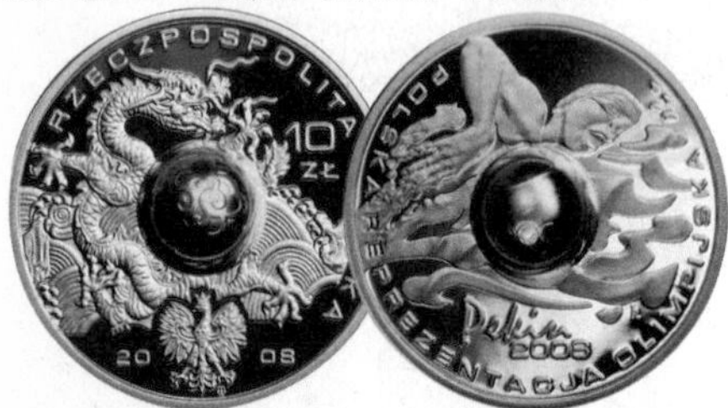

**Y# 645 10 ZŁOTYCH**
14.40 g., 0.925 Silver 0.4282 oz. ASW with gilt center, 32 mm. **Subject:** The 29th Olympic Games Beijing 2008 **Obv:** Chinese ornament & dragon **Rev:** Swimmer

| Date | Mintage | VF20 | XF40 | MS60 | MS63 | MS65 |
|---|---|---|---|---|---|---|
| 2008 | 140,000 | PF63 25.00 | PF65 40.00 | | | |

**Y# 646 10 ZŁOTYCH**
14.14 g., 0.925 Silver 0.4205 oz. ASW, 32 mm. **Subject:** The 29th Olympic Games Beijing 2008 **Obv:** Square hole & an eagle **Rev:** Square hole & a windsurfer

| Date | Mintage | VF20 | XF40 | MS60 | MS63 | MS65 |
|---|---|---|---|---|---|---|
| 2008 | 150,000 | PF63 20.00 | PF65 30.00 | | | |

**Y# 649 10 ZŁOTYCH**
14.14 g., 0.925 Silver 0.4205 oz. ASW, 32 mm. **Subject:** Polish Travellers & Explorers **Obv:** Man & woman holding child **Rev:** Bust of Bronislaw Pilsudski

| Date | Mintage | VF20 | XF40 | MS60 | MS63 | MS65 |
|---|---|---|---|---|---|---|
| 2008 | 99,000 | PF63 22.00 | PF65 32.00 | | | |

**Y# 655 10 ZŁOTYCH**
14.14 g., 0.925 Silver 0.4205 oz. ASW, 32 mm. **Subject:** 450th Anniversary of the Polish Post **Obv:** Eagle on top right, post stamp in center with man on horse **Rev:** Post courier

| Date | Mintage | VF20 | XF40 | MS60 | MS63 | MS65 |
|---|---|---|---|---|---|---|
| 2008 | 135,000 | PF63 25.00 | PF65 35.00 | | | |

**Y# 658 10 ZŁOTYCH**
14.14 g., 0.925 Silver 0.4205 oz. ASW, 32 mm. **Subject:** 400th Anniversary - Polish Settlement in North America **Obv:** Man blowing glassware left **Rev:** Man blowing glassware right

| Date | Mintage | VF20 | XF40 | MS60 | MS63 | MS65 |
|---|---|---|---|---|---|---|
| 2008 | 126,000 | PF63 25.00 | PF65 35.00 | | | |

**Y# 661 10 ZŁOTYCH**
14.14 g., 0.925 Silver 0.4205 oz. ASW, 32 mm. **Subject:** 90th Anniversary of the Greater Poland Uprising **Obv:** Eagle at top, Commander riding horse followed by soldiers **Rev:** Rose at left, Bust of Igancy Jan Paderewski at right

| Date | Mintage | VF20 | XF40 | MS60 | MS63 | MS65 |
|---|---|---|---|---|---|---|
| 2008 | 107,000 | PF63 25.00 | PF65 35.00 | | | |

**Y# 671 10 ZŁOTYCH**
14.40 g., 0.925 Silver 0.4282 oz. ASW, 22x32 mm. **Obv:** Eagle, flag and armor **Rev:** Hussar Knights, XVII Century **Shape:** Vertical rectangle

| Date | Mintage | VF20 | XF40 | MS60 | MS63 | MS65 |
|---|---|---|---|---|---|---|
| 2009 | 100,000 | PF63 20.00 | PF65 30.00 | | | |

**Y# 674 10 ZŁOTYCH**
14.14 g., 0.925 Silver 0.4205 oz. ASW, 32 mm. **Subject:** Supreme Chamber, 90th Anniversary **Obv:** Building **Rev:** Monogram hologram

| Date | Mintage | VF20 | XF40 | MS60 | MS63 | MS65 |
|---|---|---|---|---|---|---|
| 2009 MW | 100,000 | PF63 25.00 | PF65 35.00 | | | |

**Y# 676 10 ZŁOTYCH**
14.14 g., 0.925 Silver 0.4205 oz. ASW, 32 mm. **Subject:** Central Banking, 180th Anniversary **Obv:** National arms above building **Rev:** Portrait above banknote

| Date | Mintage | VF20 | XF40 | MS60 | MS63 | MS65 |
|---|---|---|---|---|---|---|
| 2009 MW | 92,000 | PF63 22.00 | PF65 32.00 | | | |

**Y# 681 10 ZŁOTYCH**
14.14 g., 0.925 Silver 0.4205 oz. ASW, 32 mm. **Subject:** General Elections of 1989 **Obv:** Eagle **Rev:** Pope John Paul II and Solidarity banner in color

| Date | Mintage | VF20 | XF40 | MS60 | MS63 | MS65 |
|---|---|---|---|---|---|---|
| 2009 MW | 100,000 | PF63 25.00 | PF65 35.00 | | | |

**Y# 685 10 ZŁOTYCH**
14.14 g., 0.925 Silver 0.4205 oz. ASW, 29x29 mm. **Subject:** Czeslaw Niemen **Obv:** National arms and large portrait **Rev:** Female crying **Shape:** Square

| Date | Mintage | VF20 | XF40 | MS60 | MS63 | MS65 |
|---|---|---|---|---|---|---|
| 2009 MW | 100,000 | PF63 20.00 | PF65 30.00 | | | |

**Y# 686 10 ZŁOTYCH**
14.14 g., 0.925 Silver 0.4205 oz. ASW, 32 mm. **Subject:** Cezeslaw Neiman **Obv:** National arms and portrait **Rev:** Abstract painting

| Date | Mintage | VF20 | XF40 | MS60 | MS63 | MS65 |
|---|---|---|---|---|---|---|
| 2009 MW | 100,000 | PF63 20.00 | PF65 30.00 | | | |

### Y# 688 10 ZŁOTYCH

14.14 g., 0.925 Silver 0.4205 oz. ASW Gold plated center in silver ring, 27 mm. **Subject:** Poets of the Uprising **Obv:** National arms **Rev:** Tadeusz Gajcy portrait

| Date | Mintage | VF20 | XF40 | MS60 | MS63 | MS65 |
|---|---|---|---|---|---|---|
| 2009 MW | 100,000 | PF63 22.00 | PF65 32.00 | | | |

### Y# 689 10 ZŁOTYCH

14.14 g., 0.925 Silver 0.4205 oz. ASW with gold plated ring, 32 mm. **Subject:** Poets of the uprising **Obv:** National arms **Rev:** Krzystof Baczynski portrait facing

| Date | Mintage | VF20 | XF40 | MS60 | MS63 | MS65 |
|---|---|---|---|---|---|---|
| 2009 MW | 100,000 | PF63 22.00 | PF65 32.00 | | | |

### Y# 691 10 ZŁOTYCH

14.14 g., 0.925 Silver 0.4205 oz. ASW, 32 mm. **Subject:** First Cadre Company March **Obv:** National arms and eagle atop stelle monument **Rev:** Troops marching, song and music

| Date | Mintage | VF20 | XF40 | MS60 | MS63 | MS65 |
|---|---|---|---|---|---|---|
| 2009 MW | 50,000 | PF63 35.00 | PF65 45.00 | | | |

### Y# 695 10 ZŁOTYCH

14.14 g., 0.925 Silver 0.4205 oz. ASW, 32 mm. **Subject:** 70th Anniversary of the start of World War II **Obv:** Eagle and map of Nazi and Soviet invasion **Rev:** Planes dropping bombs on Wielun

| Date | Mintage | VF20 | XF40 | MS60 | MS63 | MS65 |
|---|---|---|---|---|---|---|
| 2009 MW | 100,000 | PF63 25.00 | PF65 35.00 | | | |

### Y# 698 10 ZŁOTYCH

14.14 g., 0.925 Silver 0.4205 oz. ASW, 32 mm. **Series:** Tatar Rescues, 100th Anniversary **Obv:** National arms and logo colorized **Rev:** Mountains and figure of Karlowicz

| Date | Mintage | VF20 | XF40 | MS60 | MS63 | MS65 |
|---|---|---|---|---|---|---|
| 2009 MW | 100,000 | PF63 20.00 | PF65 30.00 | | | |

### Y# 701 10 ZŁOTYCH

14.14 g., 0.925 Silver 0.4205 oz. ASW, 32 mm. **Subject:** Fr. Jerzy Popielosko, 25th Anniversary of Murder **Obv:** Rose on monument **Rev:** Statue and tear drop on map of Poland

| Date | Mintage | VF20 | XF40 | MS60 | MS63 | MS65 |
|---|---|---|---|---|---|---|
| 2009 MW | 100,000 | PF63 22.00 | PF65 32.00 | | | |

### Y# 708 10 ZŁOTYCH

14.14 g., 0.925 Silver 0.4205 oz. ASW, 32 mm. **Subject:** Polish Underground State **Obv:** National arms and monogram and cloth flag **Rev:** Figure and cloth flag

| Date | Mintage | VF20 | XF40 | MS60 | MS63 | MS65 |
|---|---|---|---|---|---|---|
| 2009 MW | 50,000 | PF63 25.00 | PF65 35.00 | | | |

### Y# 713 10 ZŁOTYCH

14.14 g., 0.925 Silver 0.4205 oz. ASW, 32 mm. **Subject:** Auschwitz liberation **Obv:** National arms, camp sign and barbed wire fence **Rev:** Prisoner and barbed wire fence

| Date | Mintage | VF20 | XF40 | MS60 | MS63 | MS65 |
|---|---|---|---|---|---|---|
| 2010 MW | 80,000 | PF63 25.00 | PF65 35.00 | | | |

### Y# 716 10 ZŁOTYCH

14.14 g., 0.925 Silver 0.4205 oz. ASW, 32 mm. **Subject:** Vancouver Winter Olympics **Obv:** Speedskaters **Rev:** Biathlon

| Date | Mintage | VF20 | XF40 | MS60 | MS63 | MS65 |
|---|---|---|---|---|---|---|
| 2010 MW | 80,000 | PF63 18.00 | PF65 25.00 | | | |

### Y# 719 10 ZŁOTYCH

14.14 g., 0.925 Silver 0.4205 oz. ASW, 32x22 mm. **Subject:** Napoleonic Imperial Guard **Obv:** National arms and helmet **Rev:** Mounted Napoleonic Guard member **Shape:** Vertical rectangle

| Date | Mintage | VF20 | XF40 | MS60 | MS63 | MS65 |
|---|---|---|---|---|---|---|
| 2010 MW | 100,000 | PF63 35.00 | PF65 45.00 | | | |

### Y# 722 10 ZŁOTYCH

14.14 g., 0.925 Silver 0.4205 oz. ASW, 32 mm. **Subject:** Katyn Crime **Obv:** National emblem and silhouette of a badge **Rev:** Field of crosses

| Date | Mintage | VF20 | XF40 | MS60 | MS63 | MS65 |
|---|---|---|---|---|---|---|
| 2010 MW Antiqued | 80,000 | — | — | — | 30.00 | — |

### Y# 726 10 ZŁOTYCH

14.14 g., 0.925 Silver 0.4205 oz. ASW, 32 mm. **Subject:** Polish Scouting Centennial

| Date | Mintage | VF20 | XF40 | MS60 | MS63 | MS65 |
|---|---|---|---|---|---|---|
| 2010 MW | 90,000 | PF63 18.00 | PF65 25.00 | | | |

### Y# 728 10 ZŁOTYCH

14.14 g., 0.925 Silver 0.4205 oz. ASW, 32 mm. **Subject:** Krzystof Komeda **Rev:** Komeda and movie film real

| Date | Mintage | VF20 | XF40 | MS60 | MS63 | MS65 |
|---|---|---|---|---|---|---|
| 2010 MW | 60,000 | PF63 20.00 | PF65 30.00 | | | |

### Y# 729 10 ZŁOTYCH

14.14 g., 0.925 Silver 0.4205 oz. ASW, 28.2x28.2 mm. **Subject:** Krzysztof Komeda **Shape:** Square

| Date | Mintage | VF20 | XF40 | MS60 | MS63 | MS65 |
|---|---|---|---|---|---|---|
| 2010 MW | 60,000 | PF63 25.00 | PF65 35.00 | | | |

### Y# 731 10 ZŁOTYCH

14.14 g., 0.925 Silver 0.4205 oz. ASW, 32 mm. **Subject:** Jan Twardowski

| Date | Mintage | VF20 | XF40 | MS60 | MS63 | MS65 |
|---|---|---|---|---|---|---|
| 2010 MW | 80,000 | PF63 18.00 | PF65 25.00 | | | |

**Y# 733 10 ZŁOTYCH**
14.14 g., 0.925 Silver 0.4205 oz. ASW, 40x26 mm. **Subject:** Battles of Grunwald, Kluszyn **Shape:** Oval

| Date | Mintage | VF20 | XF40 | MS60 | MS63 | MS65 |
|---|---|---|---|---|---|---|
| 2010 MW | 100,000 | PF63 25.00 | PF65 35.00 | | | |

**Y# 738 10 ZŁOTYCH**
14.14 g., 0.925 Silver 0.4205 oz. ASW, 32 mm. **Subject:** August of 1980, 30th Anniversary

| Date | Mintage | VF20 | XF40 | MS60 | MS63 | MS65 |
|---|---|---|---|---|---|---|
| 2010 MW | 100,000 | PF63 20.00 | PF65 30.00 | | | |

**Y# 743 10 ZŁOTYCH**
14.14 g., 0.925 Silver 0.4205 oz. ASW, 32 mm. **Subject:** Polish Explorers - Benedykt Dybowski

| Date | Mintage | VF20 | XF40 | MS60 | MS63 | MS65 |
|---|---|---|---|---|---|---|
| 2010 MW | 100,000 | PF63 25.00 | PF65 35.00 | | | |

**Y# 750 10 ZŁOTYCH**
14.14 g., 0.925 Silver 0.4205 oz. ASW, 40x26 mm. **Subject:** Battle of Grunwald **Shape:** Oval

| Date | Mintage | VF20 | XF40 | MS60 | MS63 | MS65 |
|---|---|---|---|---|---|---|
| 2010 MW | 100,000 | PF63 30.00 | PF65 40.00 | | | |

**Y# 758 10 ZŁOTYCH**
14.14 g., 0.925 Silver 0.4205 oz. ASW, 32 mm. **Subject:** Benedykt Dybowski **Obv:** Books **Rev:** Bust facing, map in background

| Date | Mintage | VF20 | XF40 | MS60 | MS63 | MS65 |
|---|---|---|---|---|---|---|
| 2010 | 60,000 | PF63 25.00 | PF65 35.00 | | | |

**Y# 768 10 ZŁOTYCH**
14.14 g., 0.925 Silver 0.4205 oz. ASW, 32 mm. **Subject:** Independent Student's Union, 30th Anniversary

| Date | Mintage | VF20 | XF40 | MS60 | MS63 | MS65 |
|---|---|---|---|---|---|---|
| 2011 MW | 50,000 | PF63 25.00 | PF65 35.00 | | | |

**Y# 770 10 ZŁOTYCH**
14.14 g., 0.925 Silver 0.4205 oz. ASW, 32 mm. **Subject:** Smolensk plane crash

| Date | Mintage | VF20 | XF40 | MS60 | MS63 | MS65 |
|---|---|---|---|---|---|---|
| 2011 MW | 30,000 | PF63 35.00 | PF65 45.00 | | | |

**Y# 778 10 ZŁOTYCH**
14.14 g., 0.925 Silver 0.4205 oz. ASW, 32 mm. **Subject:** Poland's presidency of the Council of the European Union

| Date | Mintage | VF20 | XF40 | MS60 | MS63 | MS65 |
|---|---|---|---|---|---|---|
| 2011 MW | 50,000 | PF63 25.00 | PF65 35.00 | | | |

**Y# 781 10 ZŁOTYCH**
14.14 g., 0.925 Silver 0.4205 oz. ASW, 22.4x32 mm. **Subject:** History of the Polish Cavalry - Ulan of the Second Republic **Obv:** Eagle above military items: saddle, rifle, banners, lances and sword **Rev:** Cavalry officer on horseback **Shape:** Vertical rectangle

| Date | Mintage | VF20 | XF40 | MS60 | MS63 | MS65 |
|---|---|---|---|---|---|---|
| 2011 MW | 50,000 | PF63 25.00 | PF65 35.00 | | | |

**Y# 786 10 ZŁOTYCH**
14.14 g., 0.925 Silver 0.4205 oz. ASW, 32 mm. **Subject:** Czeslaw Milosz

| Date | Mintage | VF20 | XF40 | MS60 | MS63 | MS65 |
|---|---|---|---|---|---|---|
| 2011 MW | 50,000 | PF63 25.00 | PF65 35.00 | | | |

**Y# 790 10 ZŁOTYCH**
14.14 g., 0.925 Silver 0.4205 oz. ASW, 32 mm. **Subject:** Ignacy Jan Paderewski

| Date | Mintage | VF20 | XF40 | MS60 | MS63 | MS65 |
|---|---|---|---|---|---|---|
| 2011 MW | 50,000 | PF63 22.00 | PF65 32.00 | | | |

**Y# 793 10 ZŁOTYCH**
14.14 g., 0.925 Silver 0.4205 oz. ASW, 32 mm. **Subject:** Silesian Uprising

| Date | Mintage | VF20 | XF40 | MS60 | MS63 | MS65 |
|---|---|---|---|---|---|---|
| 2011 MW | 50,000 | PF63 20.00 | PF65 30.00 | | | |

**Y# 796 10 ZŁOTYCH**
14.14 g., 0.925 Silver 0.4205 oz. ASW, 32 mm. **Subject:** Society for the Protection of the Blind, 100th Anniversary

| Date | Mintage | VF20 | XF40 | MS60 | MS63 | MS65 |
|---|---|---|---|---|---|---|
| 2011 MW | 50,000 | PF63 35.00 | PF65 45.00 | | | |

**Y# 798 10 ZŁOTYCH**
14.14 g., 0.925 Silver 0.4205 oz. ASW, 32 mm. **Subject:** Ferdynand Ossendowski

| Date | Mintage | VF20 | XF40 | MS60 | MS63 | MS65 |
|---|---|---|---|---|---|---|
| 2011 MW | 50,000 | PF63 25.00 | PF65 35.00 | | | |

**Y# 802 10 ZŁOTYCH**
14.14 g., 0.925 Silver 0.4205 oz. ASW, 28.2x28.2 mm. **Subject:** Jeremi Przybora and Jerzy Wasowski **Shape:** Square

| Date | Mintage | VF20 | XF40 | MS60 | MS63 | MS65 |
|---|---|---|---|---|---|---|
| 2011 MW | 50,000 | PF63 30.00 | PF65 40.00 | | | |

**Y# 803 10 ZŁOTYCH**
14.14 g., 0.925 Silver 0.4205 oz. ASW, 32 mm. **Subject:** Jeremi Przybora and Jerzy Wasowski

| Date | Mintage | VF20 | XF40 | MS60 | MS63 | MS65 |
|---|---|---|---|---|---|---|
| 2011 MW | 50,000 | PF63 22.00 | PF65 32.00 | | | |

**Y# 810 10 ZŁOTYCH**
14.14 g., 0.925 Silver 0.4205 oz. ASW, 28.7x30 mm. **Subject:** Christmas Charity Orchestra, 20th Anniversary **Obv:** Piano keyboard **Rev:** Guitar with hearts **Shape:** Heart

| Date | Mintage | VF20 | XF40 | MS60 | MS63 | MS65 |
|---|---|---|---|---|---|---|
| 2012 MW | 60,000 | PF63 40.00 | PF65 50.00 | | | |

**Y# 812 10 ZŁOTYCH**
14.14 g., 0.925 Silver 0.4205 oz. ASW, 32 mm. **Subject:** Cooperative Banking in Poland, 150th Anniversary **Obv:** Eagle at left, bank building at right **Rev:** Pile of coin and banknotes at center, semi-circle of stick figures holding hands at right

| Date | Mintage | VF20 | XF40 | MS60 | MS63 | MS65 |
|---|---|---|---|---|---|---|
| 2012 MW | 40,000 | PF63 25.00 | PF65 35.00 | | | |

**Y# 818 10 ZŁOTYCH**
14.14 g., 0.925 Silver 0.4205 oz. ASW, 32 mm. **Subject:** Stefan Banach

| Date | Mintage | VF20 | XF40 | MS60 | MS63 | MS65 |
|---|---|---|---|---|---|---|
| 2012 MW | 45,000 | PF63 25.00 | PF65 35.00 | | | |

**Y# 822 10 ZŁOTYCH**
14.14 g., 0.925 Silver 0.4205 oz. ASW, 32 mm. **Subject:** National Museum in Warsaw, 150th Anniversary

| Date | Mintage | VF20 | XF40 | MS60 | MS63 | MS65 |
|---|---|---|---|---|---|---|
| 2012 MW | 45,000 | PF63 25.00 | PF65 35.00 | | | |

**Y# 824 10 ZŁOTYCH**
33.62 g., 0.925 Silver 0.9998 oz. ASW, 27.3x50 mm. **Subject:** European Football Championship **Shape:** Yin-Yang **Note:** A yin-Yang design, with the other half being a Ukraine 10 Hryvnia coin.

| Date | Mintage | VF20 | XF40 | MS60 | MS63 | MS65 |
|---|---|---|---|---|---|---|
| 2012 MW | 5,000 | PF65 175 | | | | |

**Y# 825 10 ZŁOTYCH**
14.14 g., 0.925 Silver 0.4205 oz. ASW, 28.8x28.8 mm. **Subject:** European Football Championship **Note:** Part of a four coin design.

| Date | Mintage | VF20 | XF40 | MS60 | MS63 | MS65 |
|---|---|---|---|---|---|---|
| 2012 MW | 15,000 | PF65 85.00 | | | | |

**Y# 826 10 ZŁOTYCH**
14.14 g., 0.925 Silver 0.4205 oz. ASW, 28.8x28.8 mm. **Subject:** European Football Championship **Note:** Part of a four coin design.

| Date | Mintage | VF20 | XF40 | MS60 | MS63 | MS65 |
|---|---|---|---|---|---|---|
| 2012 MW | 15,000 | PF65 85.00 | | | | |

**Y# 827 10 ZŁOTYCH**
14.14 g., 0.925 Silver 0.4205 oz. ASW, 28.8x28.8 mm. **Subject:** European Football Championships **Note:** Part of a four coin design.

| Date | Mintage | VF20 | XF40 | MS60 | MS63 | MS65 |
|---|---|---|---|---|---|---|
| 2012 MW | 15,000 | PF65 85.00 | | | | |

**Y# 828 10 ZŁOTYCH**
14.14 g., 0.925 Silver 0.4205 oz. ASW, 28.8x.28.8 mm. **Subject:** European Football Championships **Note:** Part of a four coin design.

| Date | Mintage | VF20 | XF40 | MS60 | MS63 | MS65 |
|---|---|---|---|---|---|---|
| 2012 MW | 15,000 | PF65 85.00 | | | | |

**Y# 833 10 ZŁOTYCH**
14.14 g., 0.925 Silver 0.4205 oz. ASW, 32 mm. **Subject:** London Olympics, 2012, Polish Team

| Date | Mintage | VF20 | XF40 | MS60 | MS63 | MS65 |
|---|---|---|---|---|---|---|
| 2012 MW | 50,000 | PF63 25.00 | PF65 35.00 | | | |

**Y# 839 10 ZŁOTYCH**
14.14 g., 0.925 Silver 0.4205 oz. ASW, 32 mm. **Subject:** Boleslaw Prus

| Date | Mintage | VF20 | XF40 | MS60 | MS63 | MS65 |
|---|---|---|---|---|---|---|
| 2012 MW | 30,000 | PF63 30.00 | PF65 40.00 | | | |

**Y# 857 10 ZŁOTYCH**
14.14 g., 0.925 Silver 0.4205 oz. ASW with 3D Hologram, 32 mm. **Subject:** Cyprian Norwid

| Date | Mintage | VF20 | XF40 | MS60 | MS63 | MS65 |
|---|---|---|---|---|---|---|
| 2013 MW | Est. 28000 | PF63 42.00 | PF65 52.00 | | | |

**Y# 871 10 ZŁOTYCH**
14.14 g., 0.925 Silver 0.4205 oz. ASW, 32 mm. **Subject:** Witold Lutoslawski

| Date | Mintage | VF20 | XF40 | MS60 | MS63 | MS65 |
|---|---|---|---|---|---|---|
| 2013 MW | Est. 28000 | PF63 30.00 | PF65 40.00 | | | |

**Y# 874 10 ZŁOTYCH**
14.14 g., 0.925 Silver 0.4205 oz. ASW, 32 mm. **Subject:** 200th Anniversary of the Death of Prince Jozef Poniatowski

| Date | Mintage | VF20 | XF40 | MS60 | MS63 | MS65 |
|---|---|---|---|---|---|---|
| 2013 MW | Est. 28000 | PF63 30.00 | PF65 40.00 | | | |

**Y# 877 10 ZŁOTYCH**
14.14 g., 0.925 Silver 0.4205 oz. ASW, 32 mm. **Subject:** 50th Anniversary of the Polish Society for the Mentally Handicapped

| Date | Mintage | VF20 | XF40 | MS60 | MS63 | MS65 |
|---|---|---|---|---|---|---|
| 2013 MW | Est. 25000 | PF63 35.00 | PF65 45.00 | | | |

**Y# 881 10 ZŁOTYCH**
14.14 g., 0.925 Silver 0.4205 oz. ASW, 32 mm. **Subject:** 200th Anniversary of the Birth of Hipolit Cegielski

| Date | Mintage | VF20 | XF40 | MS60 | MS63 | MS65 |
|---|---|---|---|---|---|---|
| 2013 MW | Est. 28000 | PF63 30.00 | PF65 40.00 | | | |

**Y# 884 10 ZŁOTYCH**
14.14 g., 0.925 Silver 0.4205 oz. ASW, 28.2 x 28.2 mm. **Subject:** History of Polish Popular Music - Agnieszka Osiecka

| Date | Mintage | VF20 | XF40 | MS60 | MS63 | MS65 |
|---|---|---|---|---|---|---|
| 2013 MW | Est. 28000 | PF63 30.00 | PF65 40.00 | | | |

**Y# 885 10 ZŁOTYCH**
14.14 g., 0.925 Silver 0.4205 oz. ASW, 32 mm. **Subject:** History of Polish Popular Music - Agnieszka Osiecka

| Date | Mintage | VF20 | XF40 | MS60 | MS63 | MS65 |
|---|---|---|---|---|---|---|
| 2013 MW | Est. 28000 | PF63 30.00 | PF65 40.00 | | | |

**Y# 894 10 ZŁOTYCH**
14.14 g., 0.925 Silver 0.4205 oz. ASW, 32 mm. **Subject:** Polish Olympic Team, Sochi 2014

| Date | Mintage | VF20 | XF40 | MS60 | MS63 | MS65 |
|---|---|---|---|---|---|---|
| 2014 | 30,000 | PF63 25.00 | PF65 35.00 | | | |

**Y# 900 10 ZŁOTYCH**
14.14 g., 0.925 Silver 0.4205 oz. ASW, 32 mm. **Subject:** Old Polish Coins - Boleslaw the Wry-Mouthed, denarius

| Date | Mintage | VF20 | XF40 | MS60 | MS63 | MS65 |
|---|---|---|---|---|---|---|
| 2014 | 20,000 | PF63 40.00 | PF65 50.00 | | | |

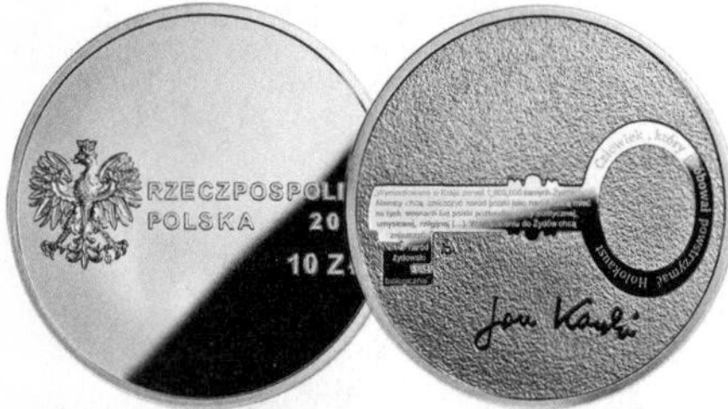


**Y# 902 10 ZŁOTYCH**
14.14 g., 0.925 Silver 0.4205 oz. ASW, 32 mm. **Subject:** Jan Karski, 100th Anniversary of Birth

| Date | Mintage | VF20 | XF40 | MS60 | MS63 | MS65 |
|---|---|---|---|---|---|---|
| 2014 | 30,000 | PF63 25.00 | PF65 35.00 | | | |

**Y# 909 10 ZŁOTYCH**
14.14 g., 0.925 Silver 0.4205 oz. ASW, 32 mm. **Subject:** Polish Coins - Mieszko the Elder, Bracteate

| Date | Mintage | VF20 | XF40 | MS60 | MS63 | MS65 |
|---|---|---|---|---|---|---|
| 2014 | 20,000 | PF63 25.00 | PF65 35.00 | | | |

**Y# 910 10 ZŁOTYCH**
14.14 g., 0.925 Silver 0.4205 oz. ASW, 32 mm. **Subject:** Stefan Zeromski, 150th Anniversary of Birth

| Date | Mintage | VF20 | XF40 | MS60 | MS63 | MS65 |
|---|---|---|---|---|---|---|
| 2014 | 30,000 | PF63 25.00 | PF65 35.00 | | | |

**Y# 916 10 ZŁOTYCH**
28.28 g., 0.925 Silver 0.841 oz. ASW, 32 mm. **Subject:** Historical Polish Coins - Leszek I the White - bracteate

| Date | Mintage | VF20 | XF40 | MS60 | MS63 | MS65 |
|---|---|---|---|---|---|---|
| 2014 | 20,000 | PF63 40.00 | PF65 50.00 | | | |

**Y# 917 10 ZŁOTYCH**
14.14 g., 0.925 Silver 0.4205 oz. ASW, 32 mm. **Subject:** Grezegorz Ciechowski, musician

| Date | Mintage | VF20 | XF40 | MS60 | MS63 | MS65 |
|---|---|---|---|---|---|---|
| 2014 | 30,000 | PF63 30.00 | PF65 40.00 | | | |

**Y# 918 10 ZŁOTYCH**
14.14 g., 0.925 Silver 0.4205 oz. ASW, 28.2x28.2 mm. **Subject:** Grzegorz Ciechowski, musician

| Date | Mintage | VF20 | XF40 | MS60 | MS63 | MS65 |
|---|---|---|---|---|---|---|
| 2014 | 30,000 | PF63 25.00 | PF65 35.00 | | | |

**Y# 920 10 ZŁOTYCH**
14.14 g., 0.925 Silver 0.4205 oz. ASW, 32 mm. **Subject:** Canonization of John Paul II

| Date | Mintage | VF20 | XF40 | MS60 | MS63 | MS65 |
|---|---|---|---|---|---|---|
| 2014 | — | PF63 35.00 | PF65 55.00 | | | |

**Y# 409 20 ZŁOTYCH**
28.28 g., 0.925 Silver 0.841 oz. ASW, 38.6 mm. **Subject:** Wieliezce Salt Mine **Obv:** Crowned eagle with wings open in center of rock **Rev:** Ancient salt miners **Edge:** Plain

| Date | Mintage | VF20 | XF40 | MS60 | MS63 | MS65 |
|---|---|---|---|---|---|---|
| 2001 MW | — | PF65 175 | | | | |

**Y# 411 20 ZŁOTYCH**
28.28 g., 0.925 Silver 0.841 oz. ASW, 38.6 mm. **Subject:** Amber Route **Obv:** Crowned eagle and two ancient Roman silver cups **Rev:** Piece of amber mounted above an ancient Roman coin design and map with the route marked with stars **Edge:** Plain

| Date | Mintage | VF20 | XF40 | MS60 | MS63 | MS65 |
|---|---|---|---|---|---|---|
| 2001 MW Antique finish | 30,000 | — | — | — | 525 | — |

**Y# 415 20 ZŁOTYCH**
28.28 g., 0.925 Silver 0.841 oz. ASW, 38.6 mm. **Obv:** Crowned eagle with wings open flanked by flags **Rev:** European Swallowtail Butterfly **Edge:** Plain

| Date | Mintage | VF20 | XF40 | MS60 | MS63 | MS65 |
|---|---|---|---|---|---|---|
| 2001 MW | 27,000 | PF65 200 | | | | |

**Y# 424 20 ZŁOTYCH**
28.77 g., 0.925 Silver 0.8556 oz. ASW, 38.6 mm. **Subject:** Christmas **Obv:** Ornate city view **Rev:** Celebration scene including an attached zirconia star **Edge:** Plain

| Date | Mintage | VF20 | XF40 | MS60 | MS63 | MS65 |
|---|---|---|---|---|---|---|
| 2001 MW Antique patina | 55,000 | — | — | — | 125 | — |

**Y# 428 20 ZŁOTYCH**
28.28 g., 0.925 Silver 0.841 oz. ASW, 38.6 mm. **Obv:** Crowned eagle with wings open flanked by flags **Rev:** European Pond Turtles **Edge:** Plain

| Date | Mintage | VF20 | XF40 | MS60 | MS63 | MS65 |
|---|---|---|---|---|---|---|
| 2002 | 35,000 | PF65 120 | | | | |

**Y# 442 20 ZŁOTYCH**
28.05 g., 0.925 Silver 0.8342 oz. ASW, 39.94x27.93 mm. **Subject:** Jan Matejko **Obv:** Seated figure with crowned eagle at lower right **Rev:** Head facing with multicolor artist's palette **Edge:** Plain **Shape:** Rectangle

| Date | Mintage | VF20 | XF40 | MS60 | MS63 | MS65 |
|---|---|---|---|---|---|---|
| 2002 MW | 57,000 | PF65 135 | | | | |

**Y# 457 20 ZŁOTYCH**
28.28 g., 0.925 Silver 0.841 oz. ASW, 38.6 mm. **Obv:** National arms at lower left, castle complex in background **Rev:** Malborku castle, reddish-brown ceramic applique, **Rev. Legend:** ZAMEK W MALBORKU **Edge:** Plain

| Date | Mintage | VF20 | XF40 | MS60 | MS63 | MS65 |
|---|---|---|---|---|---|---|
| 2002 MW Antique patina | 51,000 | — | — | — | 70.00 | — |

**Y# 449 20 ZŁOTYCH**
28.47 g., 0.925 Silver 0.8467 oz. ASW, 38.6 mm. **Obv:** Crowned eagle with wings open **Rev:** European Eels and world globe **Edge:** Plain

| Date | Mintage | VF20 | XF40 | MS60 | MS63 | MS65 |
|---|---|---|---|---|---|---|
| 2003 MW | — | PF65 185 | | | | |

**Y# 452 20 ZŁOTYCH**
28.28 g., 0.925 Silver 0.841 oz. ASW, 38.6 mm. **Subject:** Easter Monday Festival **Obv:** Crowned eagle on lace curtain above lamb and multicolor Easter eggs **Rev:** Festival scene **Edge:** Plain

| Date | Mintage | VF20 | XF40 | MS60 | MS63 | MS65 |
|---|---|---|---|---|---|---|
| 2003 MW | 44,000 | PF65 70.00 | | | | |

**Y# 471 20 ZŁOTYCH**
28.28 g., 0.925 Silver 0.841 oz. ASW, 40 x 40 mm. **Obv:** Standing Pope John Paul II **Rev:** Pope"s portrait **Edge:** Plain **Shape:** Square

| Date | Mintage | VF20 | XF40 | MS60 | MS63 | MS65 |
|---|---|---|---|---|---|---|
| 2003 MW | 83,000 | PF65 55.00 | | | | |

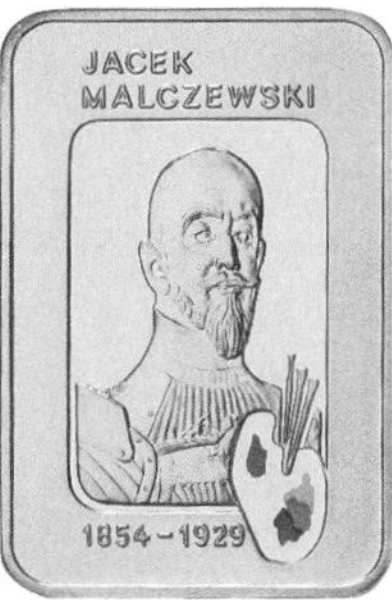

**Y# 478 20 ZŁOTYCH**
28.28 g., 0.925 Silver 0.841 oz. ASW, 27.93x39.94 mm. **Obv:** Death" allegory closing an old man's eyes, national arms at lower right **Rev:** Self portrait of Jacek Malczewski, palette at lower right multicolor **Edge:** Plain **Shape:** Rectangle

| Date | Mintage | VF20 | XF40 | MS60 | MS63 | MS65 |
|---|---|---|---|---|---|---|
| 2003 MW | 64,000 | PF65 45.00 | | | | |

**Y# 498 20 ZŁOTYCH**
28.28 g., 0.925 Silver 0.841 oz. ASW, 38.6 mm. **Subject:** Lodz Ghetto (1940-1944) **Obv:** Silhouette on wall **Rev:** Child with a pot **Edge:** Plain

| Date | Mintage | VF20 | XF40 | MS60 | MS63 | MS65 |
|---|---|---|---|---|---|---|
| 2004 MW Matte | 64,000 | — | — | — | 40.00 | 45.00 |

**Y# 504 20 ZŁOTYCH**
28.28 g., 0.925 Silver 0.841 oz. ASW, 38.6 mm. **Subject:** Polish Senate **Obv:** Crowned eagle above Senate chamber **Rev:** Senate eagle and speaker's staff **Edge:** Plain

| Date | Mintage | VF20 | XF40 | MS60 | MS63 | MS65 |
|---|---|---|---|---|---|---|
| 2004 MW | 67,000 | PF65 55.00 | | | | |

**Y# 508 20 ZŁOTYCH**
28.28 g., 0.925 Silver 0.841 oz. ASW, 38.6 mm. **Obv:** Crowned eagle in harvest wreath **Rev:** Harvest fest parade **Edge:** Plain

| Date | Mintage | VF20 | XF40 | MS60 | MS63 | MS65 |
|---|---|---|---|---|---|---|
| 2004 MW | 74,000 | PF65 40.00 | | | | |

**Y# 513 20 ZŁOTYCH**
28.28 g., 0.925 Silver 0.841 oz. ASW, 40x28 mm. **Obv:** Mother and children **Rev:** Stanislaw Wyspianski (1869-1907) **Edge:** Plain

| Date | Mintage | VF20 | XF40 | MS60 | MS63 | MS65 |
|---|---|---|---|---|---|---|
| 2004 MW | 80,000 | PF65 40.00 | | | | |

**Y# 515 20 ZŁOTYCH**
28.28 g., 0.925 Silver 0.841 oz. ASW, 38.6 mm. **Obv:** National arms **Obv. Legend:** RZECZPOSPOLITA POLSKA **Rev:** 2 Harbor Porpoises **Rev. Legend:** MORSWIN - Phocoena phocoena **Edge:** Plain

| Date | Mintage | VF20 | XF40 | MS60 | MS63 | MS65 |
|---|---|---|---|---|---|---|
| 2004 MW | 56,000 | PF65 120 | | | | |

**Y# 531 20 ZŁOTYCH**
28.84 g., 0.925 Silver 0.8577 oz. ASW, 38.6 mm. **Obv:** Polish eagle above value **Rev:** Eagle Owl with nestlings **Edge:** Plain

| Date | Mintage | VF20 | XF40 | MS60 | MS63 | MS65 |
|---|---|---|---|---|---|---|
| 2005 MW | 61,000 | PF65 100 | | | | |

**Y# 542 20 ZŁOTYCH**
28.28 g., 0.925 Silver 0.841 oz. ASW, 28 x 40 mm. **Obv:** Sneak thief stealing from a miser **Rev:** Painter Tadeusz Makowski **Edge:** Plain **Shape:** Rectangular

| Date | Mintage | VF20 | XF40 | MS60 | MS63 | MS65 |
|---|---|---|---|---|---|---|
| 2005 MW | 70,000 | PF65 45.00 | | | | |

**Y# 597 20 ZŁOTYCH**
28.50 g., 0.925 Silver 0.8476 oz. ASW, 38.5 mm. **Subject:** 350 Years, Defence of Góry **Obv:** National arms to right of outlined Góry **Obv. Legend:** RZECZPOSPOLITA POLSKA **Obv. Inscription:** Tutaj zawsze / bylismy woini / JAN PAWEL II **Rev:** 1/2 length figure of man at lower right, Góry under bombardment in background **Rev. Legend:** 350 - LECIE OBRONY JASNEJ GÓRY **Edge:** Lettered **Edge Lettering:** CZESTOCHOWA 2005 repeated three times

| Date | Mintage | VF20 | XF40 | MS60 | MS63 | MS65 |
|---|---|---|---|---|---|---|
| 2005 MW | 69,000 | PF65 45.00 | | | | |

**Y# 533 20 ZŁOTYCH**
28.84 g., 0.925 Silver 0.8577 oz. ASW, 38.6 mm. **Obv:** Youth enjoying nature, eagle above value at right **Rev:** Multicolor holographic ferns **Edge:** Plain

| Date | Mintage | VF20 | XF40 | MS60 | MS63 | MS65 |
|---|---|---|---|---|---|---|
| 2006 MW | 65,000 | PF65 80.00 | | | | |

**Y# 535 20 ZŁOTYCH**
28.84 g., 0.925 Silver 0.8577 oz. ASW, 38.6 mm. **Obv:** Polish eagle above value **Rev:** Alpine Marmot standing **Edge:** Plain

| Date | Mintage | VF20 | XF40 | MS60 | MS63 | MS65 |
|---|---|---|---|---|---|---|
| 2006 MW | 60,000 | PF65 85.00 | | | | |

**Y# 584 20 ZŁOTYCH**
28.47 g., 0.925 Silver 0.8467 oz. ASW, 38.6 mm. **Obv:** Polish Eagle on old wood **Rev:** Multi-color wood behind Haczowie church **Edge:** Plain

| Date | Mintage | VF20 | XF40 | MS60 | MS63 | MS65 |
|---|---|---|---|---|---|---|
| 2006 MW | — | PF65 45.00 | | | | |

### Y# 604 20 ZŁOTYCH

28.14 g., Silver, 39.95x27.97 mm. **Subject:** Aleksander Gierymski **Obv:** National arms at upper right, painting of elderly woman carrying baskets **Rev:** Bust of Gierymski facing at center, harbor scene at right, painter's palette at lower left multicolor **Edge:** Plain **Shape:** Rectangle

| Date | Mintage | VF20 | XF40 | MS60 | MS63 | MS65 |
|---|---|---|---|---|---|---|
| 2006 MW | 66,000 | PF65 45.00 | | | | |

### Y# 579 20 ZŁOTYCH

28.28 g., 0.925 Silver 0.841 oz. ASW, 38.6 mm. **Obv:** Crowned eagle **Rev:** Two Grey Seal females and pup with two silhouettes in background **Edge:** Plain

| Date | Mintage | VF20 | XF40 | MS60 | MS63 | MS65 |
|---|---|---|---|---|---|---|
| 2007 MW | 58,000 | PF65 85.00 | | | | |

### Y# 603 20 ZŁOTYCH

28.25 g., 0.925 Silver 0.8401 oz. ASW, 38.5 mm. **Subject:** Medieval Principality of Sredniowieczne in Torin **Obv:** City arms at right, national arms below walled city gate in background **Obv. Legend:** RZECZPOSPOLITA POLSKA **Rev:** City view **Rev. Legend:** MIASTO SREDNIOWIECZNE W TORUNIU **Edge:** Plain

| Date | Mintage | VF20 | XF40 | MS60 | MS63 | MS65 |
|---|---|---|---|---|---|---|
| 2007 MW | 58,000 | PF65 50.00 | | | | |

### Y# 891 20 ZŁOTYCH

28.28 g., 0.925 Silver 0.841 oz. ASW **Subject:** Leon Cuyczolkowski **Rev:** Portrait facing - color pallet at left

| Date | Mintage | VF20 | XF40 | MS60 | MS63 | MS65 |
|---|---|---|---|---|---|---|
| 2007 | — | PF65 45.00 | | | | |

### Y# 636 20 ZŁOTYCH

28.28 g., 0.925 Silver 0.841 oz. ASW, 38.6 mm. **Subject:** 65th Anniversary Warsaw Ghetto Uprising **Obv:** Small national arms at left, flames, shattered wall **Obv. Legend:** RZECZPOSPOLITA POLSKA **Rev:** Tree, Star of David, wall in backgound **Rev. Inscription:** 65. ROCZNICA POWSTANIA / W GETCIE WARSZAWSKIM **Edge:** Plain

| Date | Mintage | VF20 | XF40 | MS60 | MS63 | MS65 |
|---|---|---|---|---|---|---|
| 2008 MW | — | PF65 45.00 | | | | |

### Y# 637 20 ZŁOTYCH

28.28 g., 0.925 Silver 0.841 oz. ASW, 38.61 mm. **Obv:** National arms **Obv. Legend:** RZECZPOSPOLITA POLSKA **Rev:** Peregrine Falcon by 2 chicks in nest at right **Rev. Legend:** SOKOL WEDROWNY - Falco peregrinus **Edge:** Plain

| Date | Mintage | VF20 | XF40 | MS60 | MS63 | MS65 |
|---|---|---|---|---|---|---|
| 2008 MW | 107,000 | PF65 55.00 | | | | |

### Y# 642 20 ZŁOTYCH

28.28 g., 0.925 Silver 0.841 oz. ASW, 38.61 mm. **Subject:** Kazimierez Dolny **Obv:** Part of a wall and an eagle **Rev:** Houses and a well

| Date | Mintage | VF20 | XF40 | MS60 | MS63 | MS65 |
|---|---|---|---|---|---|---|
| 2008 | 125,000 | PF65 45.00 | | | | |

### Y# 651 20 ZŁOTYCH

28.28 g., 0.925 Silver 0.841 oz. ASW, 38.61 mm. **Subject:** 90th Anniversary of Regaining Freedom **Obv:** War decoration left side, eagle top right **Rev:** 3 generals

| Date | Mintage | VF20 | XF40 | MS60 | MS63 | MS65 |
|---|---|---|---|---|---|---|
| 2008 | 110,000 | PF65 42.00 | | | | |

### Y# 679 20 ZŁOTYCH

28.28 g., 0.925 Silver 0.841 oz. ASW, 38.6 mm. **Subject:** Green Lizard **Obv:** National arms above value **Rev:** Two green lizards in nature

| Date | Mintage | VF20 | XF40 | MS60 | MS63 | MS65 |
|---|---|---|---|---|---|---|
| 2009 MW | 100,000 | PF65 45.00 | | | | |

### Y# 693 20 ZŁOTYCH

28.28 g., 0.925 Silver 0.841 oz. ASW, 38.6 mm. **Subject:** Liquidation of the Lotz Ghetto **Obv:** New oak sprig amongst broken bricks **Rev:** Oak tree, bare and with leaves, star of David within

| Date | Mintage | VF20 | XF40 | MS60 | MS63 | MS65 |
|---|---|---|---|---|---|---|
| 2009 MW Antiqued | 50,000 | — | — | — | 48.00 | — |

### Y# 704 20 ZŁOTYCH

28.28 g., 0.925 Silver 0.841 oz. ASW, 38.6 mm. **Subject:** Honoring Poles who saved the Jews **Obv:** National arms above broken brick wall **Rev:** Three portraits

| Date | Mintage | VF20 | XF40 | MS60 | MS63 | MS65 |
|---|---|---|---|---|---|---|
| 2009 MW | 100,000 | PF65 40.00 | | | | |

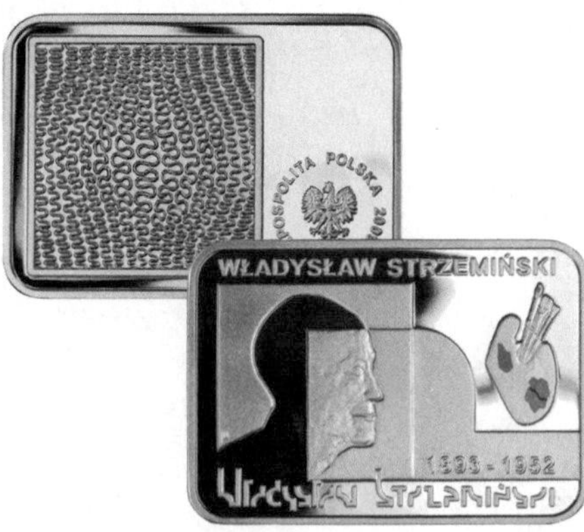


### Y# 706 20 ZŁOTYCH

28.28 g., 0.925 Silver 0.841 oz. ASW, 40x28 mm. **Subject:** Wald Strzeminski **Obv:** Portrait and multicolor palette **Rev:** Artwork **Shape:** Rectangle

| Date | Mintage | VF20 | XF40 | MS60 | MS63 | MS65 |
|---|---|---|---|---|---|---|
| 2009 MW | 100,000 | PF65 45.00 | | | | |

**Y# 724 20 ZŁOTYCH**
28.28 g., 0.925 Silver 0.841 oz. ASW, 38.61 mm. **Subject:** Lesser Horseshoe Bat

| Date | Mintage | VF20 | XF40 | MS60 | MS63 | MS65 |
|---|---|---|---|---|---|---|
| 2010 MW | 100,000 | PF65 40.00 | | | | |

**Y# 736 20 ZŁOTYCH**
28.28 g., 0.925 Silver 0.841 oz. ASW, 38.6 mm. **Subject:** Battle of Warsaw **Rev:** Battle scene in color

| Date | Mintage | VF20 | XF40 | MS60 | MS63 | MS65 |
|---|---|---|---|---|---|---|
| 2010 MW | 100,000 | PF65 42.00 | | | | |

**Y# 745 20 ZŁOTYCH**
28.28 g., 0.925 Silver 0.841 oz. ASW, 38.61 mm. **Subject:** Krzeszow

| Date | Mintage | VF20 | XF40 | MS60 | MS63 | MS65 |
|---|---|---|---|---|---|---|
| 2010 MW | 80,000 | PF65 50.00 | | | | |

**Y# 747 20 ZŁOTYCH**
28.28 g., 0.925 Silver 0.841 oz. ASW, 28x40 mm. **Subject:** Artur Grottger **Shape:** Vertical rectangle

| Date | Mintage | VF20 | XF40 | MS60 | MS63 | MS65 |
|---|---|---|---|---|---|---|
| 2010 MW | 100,000 | PF65 45.00 | | | | |

**Y# 763 20 ZŁOTYCH**
28.28 g., 0.925 Silver 0.841 oz. ASW, 38.6 mm. **Subject:** Borsuk **Obv:** National Arms above value **Rev:** Eurasian Badgers

| Date | Mintage | VF20 | XF40 | MS60 | MS63 | MS65 |
|---|---|---|---|---|---|---|
| 2011 | 80,000 | PF65 50.00 | | | | |

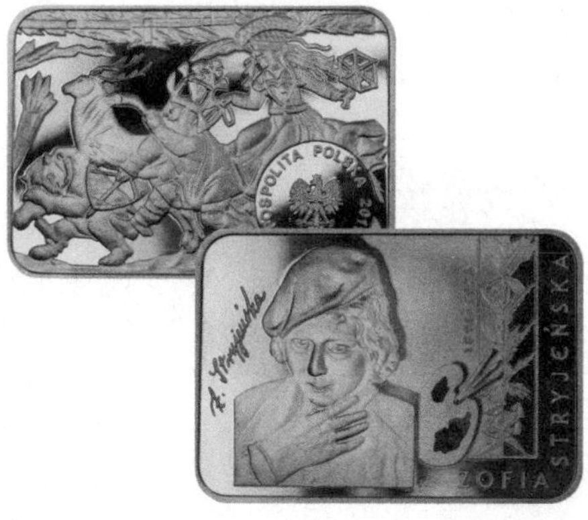


**Y# 765 20 ZŁOTYCH**
28.28 g., 0.925 Silver 0.841 oz. ASW, 40x28 mm. **Subject:** Zofia Stryjenska **Obv:** Horseback scene, National Arms at right **Rev:** Portrait with artist pallet with brushes **Shape:** Rectangle

| Date | Mintage | VF20 | XF40 | MS60 | MS63 | MS65 |
|---|---|---|---|---|---|---|
| 2011 | 50,000 | PF65 50.00 | | | | |

**Y# 771 20 ZŁOTYCH**
28.28 g., 0.925 Silver 0.841 oz. ASW, 38.61 mm. **Subject:** Smolensk plane crash

| Date | Mintage | VF20 | XF40 | MS60 | MS63 | MS65 |
|---|---|---|---|---|---|---|
| 2011 MW | — | PF65 42.00 | | | | |

**Y# 773 20 ZŁOTYCH**
14.14 g., 0.925 Silver 0.4205 oz. ASW, 38.61 mm. **Subject:** John Paul II Beautification **Rev:** Pope waving, earth in background in color

| Date | Mintage | VF20 | XF40 | MS60 | MS63 | MS65 |
|---|---|---|---|---|---|---|
| 2011 MW | 80,000 | PF65 65.00 | | | | |

**Y# 814 20 ZŁOTYCH**
28.28 g., 0.925 Silver 0.841 oz. ASW, 38.61 mm. **Subject:** Ulma, Baranek and Kowalski families **Obv:** Fields and town view **Rev:** Family faces seen thru broken fenceboards

| Date | Mintage | VF20 | XF40 | MS60 | MS63 | MS65 |
|---|---|---|---|---|---|---|
| 2012 MW Antique patina | 40,000 | — | — | — | 60.00 | — |

**Y# 829 20 ZŁOTYCH**
28.28 g., 0.925 Silver 0.841 oz. ASW, 36.2x36.2 mm. **Subject:** European Football Championships

| Date | Mintage | VF20 | XF40 | MS60 | MS63 | MS65 |
|---|---|---|---|---|---|---|
| 2012 MW | 35,000 | PF65 85.00 | | | | |

**Y# 836 20 ZŁOTYCH**
28.28 g., 0.925 Silver 0.841 oz. ASW, 38.61 mm. **Subject:** Krzemionki Opatowskie

| Date | Mintage | VF20 | XF40 | MS60 | MS63 | MS65 |
|---|---|---|---|---|---|---|
| 2012 MW | 45,000 | PF65 65.00 | | | | |

**Y# 843 20 ZŁOTYCH**
28.28 g., 0.925 Silver 0.841 oz. ASW, 40x28 mm. **Subject:** Piotr Michalowski, painter **Shape:** Rectangle

| Date | Mintage | VF20 | XF40 | MS60 | MS63 | MS65 |
|---|---|---|---|---|---|---|
| 2012 MW | 30,000 | PF65 75.00 | | | | |

**Y# 855 20 ZŁOTYCH**
31.11 g., 0.999 Silver 0.999 oz. ASW, 40 mm. **Obv:** Eagle **Rev:** Red-necked Wallaby

| Date | Mintage | VF20 | XF40 | MS60 | MS63 | MS65 |
|---|---|---|---|---|---|---|
| 2013 MW | 10,000 | PF65 250 | | | | |

**Y# 879 20 ZŁOTYCH**
28.28 g., 0.925 Silver 0.841 oz. ASW, 38.61 mm. **Subject:** Animals of the World - European Bison

| Date | Mintage | VF20 | XF40 | MS60 | MS63 | MS65 |
|---|---|---|---|---|---|---|
| 2013 MW | Est. 35000 | PF65 65.00 | | | | |

**Y# 897 20 ZŁOTYCH**
28.28 g., 0.925 Silver 0.8356 oz. ASW, 38.61 mm. **Subject:** Konik horse

| Date | Mintage | F12 | VF20 | XF40 | MS60 | MS63 |
|---|---|---|---|---|---|---|
| 2014 | 45,000 | PF65 75.00 | | | | |

**Y# 905 20 ZŁOTYCH**
31.10 g., 0.925 Silver 0.9249 oz. ASW, 38.61 mm. **Subject:** Turkish-Polish relations, 600th Anniversary

| Date | Mintage | VF20 | XF40 | MS60 | MS63 | MS65 |
|---|---|---|---|---|---|---|
| 2014 | 10,000 | PF65 50.00 | | | | |

**Y# 906 20 ZŁOTYCH**
31.10 g., 0.925 Silver 0.9249 oz. ASW, 38.61 mm. **Subject:** Patriots 1944, Citizens 2014

| Date | Mintage | VF20 | XF40 | MS60 | MS63 | MS65 |
|---|---|---|---|---|---|---|
| 2014 | 35,000 | PF65 50.00 | | | | |

**Y# 912 20 ZŁOTYCH**
28.28 g., 0.925 Silver 0.841 oz. ASW, 40x28 mm. **Subject:** Jozef Chelmonski, painter **Shape:** Rectangle

| Date | Mintage | VF20 | XF40 | MS60 | MS63 | MS65 |
|---|---|---|---|---|---|---|
| 2014 | 30,000 | PF65 55.00 | | | | |

**Y# 682 25 ZŁOTYCH**
1.00 g., 0.900 Gold 0.0289 oz. AGW, 12 mm. **Subject:** General Elections of 1989 **Obv:** National arms above value **Rev:** Solidarity logo

| Date | Mintage | VF20 | XF40 | MS60 | MS63 | MS65 |
|---|---|---|---|---|---|---|
| 2009 MW | 40,000 | PF65 65.00 | | | | |

**Y# 740 25 ZŁOTYCH**
1.00 g., 0.900 Gold 0.0289 oz. AGW, 12 mm. **Subject:** Constitutional Tribunal

| Date | Mintage | VF20 | XF40 | MS60 | MS63 | MS65 |
|---|---|---|---|---|---|---|
| 2010 MW | 10,000 | PF65 75.00 | | | | |

**Y# 774 25 ZŁOTYCH**
1.00 g., 0.900 Gold 0.0289 oz. AGW, 12 mm. **Subject:** John Paul II Beatification

| Date | Mintage | VF20 | XF40 | MS60 | MS63 | MS65 |
|---|---|---|---|---|---|---|
| 2011 MW | 10,000 | PF65 75.00 | | | | |

**Y# 739 30 ZŁOTYCH**
1.70 g., 0.900 Gold 0.0492 oz. AGW, 16 mm. **Subject:** August of 1980

| Date | Mintage | VF20 | XF40 | MS60 | MS63 | MS65 |
|---|---|---|---|---|---|---|
| 2010 MW | 50,000 | PF65 100 | | | | |

**Y# 702 37 ZŁOTYCH**
1.75 g., 0.900 Gold 0.0506 oz. AGW, 16 mm. **Subject:** Fr. Jorzy Popieluszko, 25th Anniversary of Murder **Obv:** National arms above large 37 **Rev:** Many hands holding crosses

| Date | Mintage | VF20 | XF40 | MS60 | MS63 | MS65 |
|---|---|---|---|---|---|---|
| 2009 MW | 60,000 | PF65 100 | | | | |

**Y# 652 50 ZŁOTYCH**
3.13 g., Gold, 18 mm. **Subject:** 90th Annniversary of Regaining Freedom **Obv:** Tomb of the unknown soldier **Rev:** Mounted Commander-In-Chief Jósef Pilsudski

| Date | Mintage | VF20 | XF40 | MS60 | MS63 | MS65 |
|---|---|---|---|---|---|---|
| 2008 | 8,800 | PF65 125 | | | | |

**Y# 892 50 ZŁOTYCH**
3.13 g., Gold, 18 mm. **Subject:** John Paul II Beatification

| Date | Mintage | VF20 | XF40 | MS60 | MS63 | MS65 |
|---|---|---|---|---|---|---|
| 2011 | — | — | — | — | — | — |

**Y# 850 50 ZŁOTYCH**
62.20 g., 0.9999 Silver 1.9996 oz. ASW, 45 mm. **Subject:** King Stanislaw August - Boleslaw I the Brave **Obv:** Long leagend, eagle at bottom **Rev:** Crowned bust right

| Date | Mintage | VF20 | XF40 | MS60 | MS63 | MS65 |
|---|---|---|---|---|---|---|
| 2013 MW | Est. 5000 | — | — | — | 450 | — |

**Y# 860 50 ZŁOTYCH**
62.20 g., 0.999 Silver 1.9978 oz. ASW, 45 mm. **Subject:** Treasures of King Stanislaw August - Venceslaus II of Bohemia

| Date | Mintage | VF20 | XF40 | MS60 | MS63 | MS65 |
|---|---|---|---|---|---|---|
| 2013 MW | Est. 5000 | — | — | — | 400 | — |

**Y# 867 50 ZŁOTYCH**
62.20 g., 0.999 Silver 1.9978 oz. ASW, 45 mm. **Subject:** Treasures of King Stanislaw August - Wladyslaw the Short

| Date | Mintage | VF20 | XF40 | MS60 | MS63 | MS65 |
|---|---|---|---|---|---|---|
| 2013 MW | — | — | — | — | 375 | — |

**Y# 898 50 ZŁOTYCH**
Silver ASW **Subject:** Stanislaw August - Casimir the Great

| Date | Mintage | VF20 | XF40 | MS60 | MS63 | MS65 |
|---|---|---|---|---|---|---|
| 2014 | 5,000 | PF65 150 | | | | |

**Y# 907 50 ZŁOTYCH**
62.20 g., 0.999 Silver 1.9978 oz. ASW, 45 mm. **Subject:** King Stanislaw August - Louis the Great

| Date | Mintage | VF20 | XF40 | MS60 | MS63 | MS65 |
|---|---|---|---|---|---|---|
| 2014 | 5,000 | PF65 150 | | | | |

**Y# 914 50 ZŁOTYCH**
62.20 g., 0.999 Silver 1.9978 oz. ASW, 45 mm. **Subject:** Stanislaw August - Hedwig

| Date | Mintage | VF20 | XF40 | MS60 | MS63 | MS65 |
|---|---|---|---|---|---|---|
| 2014 | 5,000 | PF65 150 | | | | |

**Y# 416 100 ZŁOTYCH**
8.00 g., 0.900 Gold 0.2315 oz. AGW, 21 mm. **Subject:** Wladyslaw I (1320-33) **Obv:** Crowned eagle with wings open **Rev:** Crowned bust facing **Edge:** Plain

| Date | Mintage | VF20 | XF40 | MS60 | MS63 | MS65 |
|---|---|---|---|---|---|---|
| 2001 MW | — | PF65 875 | | | | |

**Y# 417 100 ZŁOTYCH**
8.00 g., 0.900 Gold 0.2315 oz. AGW, 21 mm. **Subject:** Boleslaw III (1102-1138) **Obv:** Crowned eagle with wings open **Rev:** Pointed crowned bust facing **Edge:** Plain

| Date | Mintage | VF20 | XF40 | MS60 | MS63 | MS65 |
|---|---|---|---|---|---|---|
| 2001 MW | 2,000 | PF65 875 | | | | |

**Y# 462 100 ZŁOTYCH**

8.00 g., 0.900 Gold 0.2315 oz. AGW, 21 mm. **Obv:** Crowned eagle with wings open **Rev:** Jan Sobieski III **Edge:** Plain

| Date | Mintage | VF20 | XF40 | MS60 | MS63 | MS65 |
|---|---|---|---|---|---|---|
| 2001 MV | 2,200 | **PF65** 875 | | | | |

**Y# 429 100 ZŁOTYCH**

8.00 g., 0.900 Gold 0.2315 oz. AGW, 21 mm. **Obv:** Crowned eagle with wings open **Rev:** Crowned bust facing **Edge:** Plain

| Date | Mintage | VF20 | XF40 | MS60 | MS63 | MS65 |
|---|---|---|---|---|---|---|
| 2002 MW | 2,400 | **PF65** 875 | | | | |

**Y# 430 100 ZŁOTYCH**

8.00 g., 0.900 Gold 0.2315 oz. AGW, 21 mm. **Obv:** Crowned eagle with wings open **Rev:** Crowned bust 1/4 left **Edge:** Plain

| Date | Mintage | VF20 | XF40 | MS60 | MS63 | MS65 |
|---|---|---|---|---|---|---|
| 2002 MW | 2,200 | **PF65** 875 | | | | |

**Y# 436 100 ZŁOTYCH**

8.00 g., 0.900 Gold 0.2315 oz. AGW, 21 mm. **Subject:** World Cup Soccer **Obv:** Crowned eagle with wings open and world background **Rev:** Soccer player **Edge:** Plain

| Date | Mintage | VF20 | XF40 | MS60 | MS63 | MS65 |
|---|---|---|---|---|---|---|
| 2002 MW | — | **PF65** 450 | | | | |

**Y# 454 100 ZŁOTYCH**

8.00 g., 0.900 Gold 0.2315 oz. AGW, 21 mm. **Obv:** Crowned eagle with wings open **Rev:** Uniformed bust 1/4 left **Edge:** Plain

| Date | Mintage | VF20 | XF40 | MS60 | MS63 | MS65 |
|---|---|---|---|---|---|---|
| 2003 MW | 2,000 | **PF65** 1,000 | | | | |

**Y# 466 100 ZŁOTYCH**

8.00 g., 0.900 Gold 0.2315 oz. AGW, 21 mm. **Subject:** 750th Anniversary - City Charter **Obv:** Door knocker and church **Rev:** Clock face and tower **Edge:** Plain

| Date | Mintage | VF20 | XF40 | MS60 | MS63 | MS65 |
|---|---|---|---|---|---|---|
| 2003 MW | 2,100 | **PF65** 750 | | | | |

**Y# 467 100 ZŁOTYCH**

8.00 g., 0.900 Gold 0.2315 oz. AGW, 21 mm. **Obv:** Crowned eagle with wings open **Rev:** Kazimierz IV (1447-1492) **Edge:** Plain

| Date | Mintage | VF20 | XF40 | MS60 | MS63 | MS65 |
|---|---|---|---|---|---|---|
| 2003 MW | 2,300 | **PF65** 750 | | | | |

**Y# 476 100 ZŁOTYCH**

8.00 g., 0.900 Gold 0.2315 oz. AGW, 21 mm. **Obv:** Crowned eagle with wings open **Rev:** Stanislaus I and eagle **Edge:** Plain

| Date | Mintage | VF20 | XF40 | MS60 | MS63 | MS65 |
|---|---|---|---|---|---|---|
| 2003 MW | 2,500 | **PF65** 750 | | | | |

**Y# 494 100 ZŁOTYCH**

8.00 g., 0.900 Gold 0.2315 oz. AGW, 21 mm. **Obv:** Crowned eagle with wings open **Rev:** King Przemysl II (1295-1296) **Edge:** Plain

| Date | Mintage | VF20 | XF40 | MS60 | MS63 | MS65 |
|---|---|---|---|---|---|---|
| 2004 MW | 3,400 | **PF65** 550 | | | | |

**Y# 495 100 ZŁOTYCH**

8.00 g., 0.900 Gold 0.2315 oz. AGW, 21 mm. **Obv:** Crowned eagle with wings open **Rev:** King Zygmunt I (1506-1548) **Edge:** Plain

| Date | Mintage | VF20 | XF40 | MS60 | MS63 | MS65 |
|---|---|---|---|---|---|---|
| 2004 MW | 3,400 | **PF65** 550 | | | | |

**Y# 540 100 ZŁOTYCH**

8.00 g., 0.900 Gold 0.2315 oz. AGW, 21 mm. **Obv:** St. Peters Basilica dome **Rev:** Pope John Paul II and baptismal font **Edge:** Plain

| Date | Mintage | VF20 | XF40 | MS60 | MS63 | MS65 |
|---|---|---|---|---|---|---|
| 2005 MW | 18,700 | **PF65** 450 | | | | |

**Y# 888 100 ZŁOTYCH**

15.50 g., 0.900 Gold 0.4485 oz. AGW **Obv:** Eagle **Rev:** August II bust

| Date | Mintage | VF20 | XF40 | MS60 | MS63 | MS65 |
|---|---|---|---|---|---|---|
| 2005 | — | **PF65** 800 | | | | |

**Y# 581 100 ZŁOTYCH**

8.00 g., 0.900 Gold 0.2315 oz. AGW, 21 mm. **Obv:** Line of soccer players on soccer ball surface with Polish eagle in one of the sections **Rev:** Two soccer players **Edge:** Plain

| Date | Mintage | VF20 | XF40 | MS60 | MS63 | MS65 |
|---|---|---|---|---|---|---|
| 2006 MW | — | **PF65** 450 | | | | |

**Y# 640 100 ZŁOTYCH**

8.00 g., 0.900 Gold 0.2315 oz. AGW, 21 mm. **Subject:** Siberian Exiles **Obv:** Small national arms at left, bleak forest at right **Obv. Legend:** RZECZPOSPOLITA POLSKA **Rev:** Grieving mother with child by tree at lower right, building in background at left **Rev. Legend:** SYBIRACY

| Date | Mintage | VF20 | XF40 | MS60 | MS63 | MS65 |
|---|---|---|---|---|---|---|
| 2008 MW | 12,000 | **PF65** 450 | | | | |

**Y# 657 100 ZŁOTYCH**

8.00 g., 0.900 Gold 0.2315 oz. AGW, 21 mm. **Subject:** 400th Anniversary of Polish Settlement in North America **Obv:** Eagle in center against compass rose. Outline of Europe & North America. **Rev:** Center compass rose surrounded by 4 men working

| Date | Mintage | VF20 | XF40 | MS60 | MS63 | MS65 |
|---|---|---|---|---|---|---|
| 2008 | 9,500 | **PF65** 450 | | | | |

**Y# 699 100 ZŁOTYCH**

8.00 g., 0.900 Gold 0.2315 oz. AGW, 21 mm. **Subject:** Tatar Rescue, 100th Anniversary **Obv:** Figure of Mariusz Zaruski **Rev:** Mountains and reszue helicopter image

| Date | Mintage | VF20 | XF40 | MS60 | MS63 | MS65 |
|---|---|---|---|---|---|---|
| 2009 MW | 10,000 | **PF65** 450 | | | | |

**Y# 714 100 ZŁOTYCH**

8.00 g., 0.900 Gold 0.2315 oz. AGW, 21 mm. **Subject:** Auschwitz liberation **Obv:** Prisoner and railroad track entrance **Rev:** Buildings

| Date | Mintage | VF20 | XF40 | MS60 | MS63 | MS65 |
|---|---|---|---|---|---|---|
| 2010 MW | 8,000 | **PF65** 450 | | | | |

**Y# 741 100 ZŁOTYCH**

8.00 g., 0.900 Gold 0.2315 oz. AGW, 21 mm. **Subject:** Constitutional Tribunal

| Date | Mintage | VF20 | XF40 | MS60 | MS63 | MS65 |
|---|---|---|---|---|---|---|
| 2010 MW | 5,000 | **PF65** 450 | | | | |

**Y# 766 100 ZŁOTYCH**

8.00 g., 0.900 Gold 0.2315 oz. AGW, 21 mm. **Subject:** Smolensk plane crash **Rev:** President Lech Kaczynski and wife Maria

| Date | Mintage | VF20 | XF40 | MS60 | MS63 | MS65 |
|---|---|---|---|---|---|---|
| 2011 | — | **PF65** 475 | | | | |

**Y# 775 100 ZŁOTYCH**

8.00 g., 0.900 Gold 0.2315 oz. AGW, 21 mm. **Subject:** John Paul II Beatification

| Date | Mintage | VF20 | XF40 | MS60 | MS63 | MS65 |
|---|---|---|---|---|---|---|
| 2011 MW | 8,000 | **PF65** 450 | | | | |

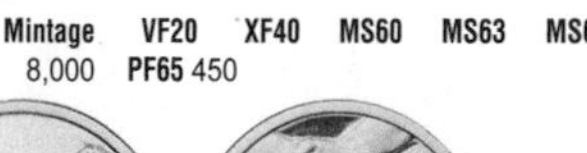

**Y# 779 100 ZŁOTYCH**

8.00 g., 0.900 Gold 0.2315 oz. AGW, 21 mm. **Subject:** Poland's presidency of the Council of the European Union

| Date | Mintage | VF20 | XF40 | MS60 | MS63 | MS65 |
|---|---|---|---|---|---|---|
| 2011 MW | 4,000 | **PF65** 500 | | | | |

**Y# 830 100 ZŁOTYCH**
8.00 g., 0.900 Gold 0.2315 oz. AGW, 21 mm. **Subject:** European Football Championships

| Date | Mintage | VF20 | XF40 | MS60 | MS63 | MS65 |
|---|---|---|---|---|---|---|
| 2012 MW | 4,000 | **PF65** 500 | | | | |

**Y# 407 200 ZŁOTYCH**
15.20 g., 0.900 Tri-Metallic 0.4398 oz. Gold with Palladium center, Gold with Silver ring, Gold with Copper outer limit, 27 mm. **Subject:** Year 2001 **Obv:** Crowned eagle with wings open within a swirl **Rev:** Couple looking into the future **Edge:** Plain

| Date | Mintage | VF20 | XF40 | MS60 | MS63 | MS65 |
|---|---|---|---|---|---|---|
| 2001 MW | — | **PF65** 900 | | | | |

**Y# 420 200 ZŁOTYCH**
15.50 g., 0.900 Gold 0.4485 oz. AGW, 27 mm. **Subject:** Cardinal Stefan Wyszynski **Obv:** Pillar divides arms and eagle **Rev:** Bust left within arch **Edge Lettering:** 100 ROCZNIA URODZIN

| Date | Mintage | VF20 | XF40 | MS60 | MS63 | MS65 |
|---|---|---|---|---|---|---|
| 2001 MW | 4,500 | **PF65** 850 | | | | |

**Y# 463 200 ZŁOTYCH**
15.50 g., 0.900 Gold 0.4485 oz. AGW, 27 mm. **Obv:** Standing violinist **Rev:** Henryk Wieniawski **Edge Lettering:** XII MIEDZYNARODOWY KONKURS SKRZYPCOWY IM HENRYKA WIENIAWSKIEGO

| Date | Mintage | VF20 | XF40 | MS60 | MS63 | MS65 |
|---|---|---|---|---|---|---|
| 2001 MW | 2,000 | **PF65** 1,150 | | | | |

**Y# 438 200 ZŁOTYCH**
15.50 g., 0.900 Gold 0.4485 oz. AGW, 27 mm. **Subject:** Pope John Paul II **Obv:** Bust left and small eagle with wings open **Rev:** Pope facing radiant Holy Door **Edge:** Plain

| Date | Mintage | VF20 | XF40 | MS60 | MS63 | MS65 |
|---|---|---|---|---|---|---|
| 2002 MW | 5,000 | **PF65** 1,200 | | | | |

**Y# 470 200 ZŁOTYCH**
15.50 g., 0.900 Gold 0.4485 oz. AGW, 27 mm. **Subject:** Gas and Oil Industry **Obv:** Crowned eagle, oil wells and refinery **Rev:** Scientist at work **Edge:** Plain

| Date | Mintage | VF20 | XF40 | MS60 | MS63 | MS65 |
|---|---|---|---|---|---|---|
| 2003 MW | 2,100 | **PF65** 1,250 | | | | |

**Y# 472 200 ZŁOTYCH**
15.50 g., 0.900 Gold 0.4485 oz. AGW, 27 mm. **Obv:** Standing Pope John Paul II **Rev:** Seated Pope **Edge:** Plain

| Date | Mintage | VF20 | XF40 | MS60 | MS63 | MS65 |
|---|---|---|---|---|---|---|
| 2003 MW | 4,900 | **PF65** 1,300 | | | | |

**Y# 483 200 ZŁOTYCH**
15.50 g., 0.900 Gold 0.4485 oz. AGW, 27 mm. **Subject:** Poland Joining the European Union **Obv:** Polish euro coin design elements **Rev:** Polish euro coin design elements **Edge:** Plain

| Date | Mintage | VF20 | XF40 | MS60 | MS63 | MS65 |
|---|---|---|---|---|---|---|
| 2004 MW | 4,400 | **PF65** 850 | | | | |

**Y# 511 200 ZŁOTYCH**
15.50 g., 0.900 Gold 0.4485 oz. AGW, 27 mm. **Subject:** Warsaw Fine Arts Academy Centennial **Obv:** Campus view **Rev:** Statue and building **Edge:** Plain

| Date | Mintage | VF20 | XF40 | MS60 | MS63 | MS65 |
|---|---|---|---|---|---|---|
| 2004 MW | 5,000 | **PF65** 850 | | | | |

**Y# 519 200 ZŁOTYCH**
15.50 g., 0.900 Gold 0.4485 oz. AGW, 27 mm. **Subject:** Olympics **Obv:** Woman and crowned eagle **Rev:** Ancient runners painted on pottery **Edge:** Plain

| Date | Mintage | VF20 | XF40 | MS60 | MS63 | MS65 |
|---|---|---|---|---|---|---|
| 2004 MW | 6,000 | **PF65** 850 | | | | |

**Y# 536 200 ZŁOTYCH**
15.50 g., 0.900 Gold 0.4485 oz. AGW, 27 mm. **Obv:** Chopin **Rev:** Nagoya Castle roof tops and Mt. Fuji **Edge:** Plain **Note:** Aichi Expo Japan

| Date | Mintage | VF20 | XF40 | MS60 | MS63 | MS65 |
|---|---|---|---|---|---|---|
| 2005 MW | 4,200 | **PF65** 875 | | | | |

**Y# 538 200 ZŁOTYCH**
15.50 g., 0.900 Gold 0.4485 oz. AGW, 27 mm. **Obv:** Horse drawn carriage **Rev:** Konstanty Ildefons Galczynski in top hat **Edge:** Plain

| Date | Mintage | VF20 | XF40 | MS60 | MS63 | MS65 |
|---|---|---|---|---|---|---|
| 2005 MW | 3,500 | **PF65** 900 | | | | |

**Y# 886 200 ZŁOTYCH**
15.50 g., 0.900 Gold 0.4485 oz. AGW, 27 mm. **Obv:** Solidarity Logo **Rev:** Dove

| Date | Mintage | VF20 | XF40 | MS60 | MS63 | MS65 |
|---|---|---|---|---|---|---|
| 2005 | 4,600 | **PF65** 800 | | | | |

**Y# 887 200 ZŁOTYCH**
15.50 g., 0.900 Gold 0.4485 oz. AGW **Obv:** Eagle **Rev:** Planes in flight

| Date | Mintage | VF20 | XF40 | MS60 | MS63 | MS65 |
|---|---|---|---|---|---|---|
| 2005 | 4,400 | **PF65** 800 | | | | |

**Y# 889 200 ZŁOTYCH**
15.50 g., 0.900 Gold 0.4485 oz. AGW **Subject:** Mikolaja Reja -500th Anniversary **Obv:** Quill pen

| Date | Mintage | VF20 | XF40 | MS60 | MS63 | MS65 |
|---|---|---|---|---|---|---|
| 2005 | 3,600 | **PF65** 800 | | | | |

**Y# 665 200 ZŁOTYCH**
15.50 g., 0.900 Gold 0.4485 oz. AGW. **Subject:** 125 Anniversary of Birth of Symanowski **Obv:** Bar of music **Rev:** Bust right with sheet music behind.

| Date | Mintage | VF20 | XF40 | MS60 | MS63 | MS65 |
|---|---|---|---|---|---|---|
| 2007 | 8,000 | **PF65** 850 | | | | |

**Y# 672 200 ZŁOTYCH**
15.50 g., 0.900 Gold 0.4485 oz. AGW, 27 mm. **Obv:** Helmet and breastplate **Rev:** Knight of the 15th Century

| Date | Mintage | VF20 | XF40 | MS60 | MS63 | MS65 |
|---|---|---|---|---|---|---|
| 2007 | 10,500 | **PF65** 850 | | | | |

**Y# 643 200 ZŁOTYCH**
15.50 g., 0.900 Gold 0.4485 oz. AGW, 27 mm. **Subject:** Zbigniew Herbert **Obv:** Eagle and Zbigniew Herbert **Rev:** Mounted statue of Marcus Aurelius

| Date | Mintage | VF20 | XF40 | MS60 | MS63 | MS65 |
|---|---|---|---|---|---|---|
| 2008 | 11,200 | **PF65** 850 | | | | |

**Y# 647 200 ZŁOTYCH**
15.50 g., 0.900 Gold 0.4485 oz. AGW, 27 mm. **Series:** The 29th Olympic Games Beijing 2008 **Obv:** Two kites and an eagle **Rev:** Female pole vault jumper

| Date | Mintage | VF20 | XF40 | MS60 | MS63 | MS65 |
|---|---|---|---|---|---|---|
| 2008 | — | **PF65** 850 | | | | |

**Y# 653 200 ZŁOTYCH**

15.50 g., 0.900 Gold 0.4485 oz. AGW, 27 mm. **Subject:** 90th Anniversary of Regaining Freedom **Obv:** Tomb of the unknown soldier **Rev:** Mounted Commander-In-Chief Jozef Pilsudski

| Date | Mintage | VF20 | XF40 | MS60 | MS63 | MS65 |
|---|---|---|---|---|---|---|
| 2008 | 10,000 | PF65 850 | | | | |

**Y# 654 200 ZŁOTYCH**

15.50 g., 0.900 Gold 0.4485 oz. AGW, 27 mm. **Subject:** 450 years of the Polish Post **Obv:** Eagle right, bottom against post stamp **Rev:** Horse with rider crossing bridge

| Date | Mintage | VF20 | XF40 | MS60 | MS63 | MS65 |
|---|---|---|---|---|---|---|
| 2008 | 11,000 | PF65 850 | | | | |

**Y# 660 200 ZŁOTYCH**

15.50 g., 0.900 Gold 0.4485 oz. AGW, 27 mm. **Subject:** 90th Anniversary of the Greater Poland Uprising **Obv:** Eagle at left, eagle at right with chain **Rev:** Charging cavalrymen and German soldiers firing at them

| Date | Mintage | VF20 | XF40 | MS60 | MS63 | MS65 |
|---|---|---|---|---|---|---|
| 2008 | 9,400 | PF65 850 | | | | |

**Y# 664 200 ZŁOTYCH**

15.50 g., 0.900 Gold 0.4485 oz. AGW, 27 mm. **Subject:** Warsaw Ghetto **Obv:** Building on fire, Naitonal arms **Rev:** Face looking out from broken brick wall

| Date | Mintage | VF20 | XF40 | MS60 | MS63 | MS65 |
|---|---|---|---|---|---|---|
| 2008 MW | 12,000 | PF65 850 | | | | |

**Y# 677 200 ZŁOTYCH**

15.50 g., 0.900 Gold 0.4485 oz. AGW, 27 mm. **Subject:** Central Banking, 180th Anniversary **Obv:** National arms above crowned shield **Rev:** Building and portrait

| Date | Mintage | VF20 | XF40 | MS60 | MS63 | MS65 |
|---|---|---|---|---|---|---|
| 2009 MW | 8,500 | PF65 850 | | | | |

**Y# 683 200 ZŁOTYCH**

15.50 g., 0.900 Gold 0.4485 oz. AGW, 27 mm. **Subject:** General election of 1989 **Obv:** National arms above shipyard scene **Rev:** Lech Walesa silhouette before crowd

| Date | Mintage | VF20 | XF40 | MS60 | MS63 | MS65 |
|---|---|---|---|---|---|---|
| 2009 MW | 10,000 | PF65 850 | | | | |

**Y# 696 200 ZŁOTYCH**

15.15 g., 0.900 Gold 0.4384 oz. AGW, 27 mm. **Obv:** Eagle and statue, flames in background **Rev:** Stefan Starzonski, Warsaw Mayor; Burning of the Clock Tower

| Date | Mintage | VF20 | XF40 | MS60 | MS63 | MS65 |
|---|---|---|---|---|---|---|
| 2009 | 10,500 | PF65 850 | | | | |

**Y# 717 200 ZŁOTYCH**

15.50 g., 0.900 Gold 0.4485 oz. AGW, 27 mm. **Subject:** Vancouver Winter Olympics **Obv:** Downhill skiing **Rev:** Cross Country skiing

| Date | Mintage | VF20 | XF40 | MS60 | MS63 | MS65 |
|---|---|---|---|---|---|---|
| 2010 MW | 8,000 | PF65 850 | | | | |

**Y# 720 200 ZŁOTYCH**

15.50 g., 0.900 Gold 0.4485 oz. AGW, 27 mm. **Subject:** Napoleonic Imperial Guard **Obv:** Pile of arms **Rev:** Galloping guardsman

| Date | Mintage | VF20 | XF40 | MS60 | MS63 | MS65 |
|---|---|---|---|---|---|---|
| 2010 MW | 10,500 | PF65 850 | | | | |

**Y# 734 200 ZŁOTYCH**

15.50 g., 0.900 Gold 0.4485 oz. AGW, 27 mm. **Subject:** Battles of Grunwald and Kluszyn

| Date | Mintage | VF20 | XF40 | MS60 | MS63 | MS65 |
|---|---|---|---|---|---|---|
| 2010 MW | 10,500 | PF65 850 | | | | |

**Y# 782 200 ZŁOTYCH**

15.50 g., 0.900 Gold 0.4485 oz. AGW, 27 mm. **Subject:** Polish Cavalry - Uhlan **Edge Lettering:** 22.4x32

| Date | Mintage | VF20 | XF40 | MS60 | MS63 | MS65 |
|---|---|---|---|---|---|---|
| 2011 MW | 5,000 | PF65 875 | | | | |

**Y# 787 200 ZŁOTYCH**

15.50 g., 0.900 Gold 0.4485 oz. AGW, 27 mm. **Subject:** Czeslaw Milosz

| Date | Mintage | VF20 | XF40 | MS60 | MS63 | MS65 |
|---|---|---|---|---|---|---|
| 2011 MW | 4,000 | PF65 875 | | | | |

**Y# 791 200 ZŁOTYCH**

15.50 g., 0.900 Gold 0.4485 oz. AGW, 27 mm. **Subject:** Ignacy Jan Paderewski

| Date | Mintage | VF20 | XF40 | MS60 | MS63 | MS65 |
|---|---|---|---|---|---|---|
| 2011 MW | 3,000 | PF65 900 | | | | |

**Y# 819 200 ZŁOTYCH**

15.50 g., 0.900 Gold 0.4485 oz. AGW, 27 mm. **Subject:** Stefan Banach

| Date | Mintage | VF20 | XF40 | MS60 | MS63 | MS65 |
|---|---|---|---|---|---|---|
| 2012 MW | 4,000 | PF65 875 | | | | |

**Y# 834 200 ZŁOTYCH**

15.50 g., 0.900 Gold 0.4485 oz. AGW, 27 mm. **Subject:** London Olympics, 2012, Polish Team

| Date | Mintage | VF20 | XF40 | MS60 | MS63 | MS65 |
|---|---|---|---|---|---|---|
| 2012 MW | 5,000 | PF65 875 | | | | |

**Y# 840 200 ZŁOTYCH**

15.50 g., 0.900 Gold 0.4485 oz. AGW, 27 mm. **Subject:** Boleslaw Prus

| Date | Mintage | VF20 | XF40 | MS60 | MS63 | MS65 |
|---|---|---|---|---|---|---|
| 2012 MW | 3,000 | PF65 900 | | | | |

**Y# 858 200 ZŁOTYCH**

15.50 g., 0.900 Gold 0.4485 oz. AGW, 27 mm. **Subject:** Cyprian Norwid

| Date | Mintage | VF20 | XF40 | MS60 | MS63 | MS65 |
|---|---|---|---|---|---|---|
| 2013 MW | Est. 2500 | PF65 950 | | | | |

**Y# 872 200 ZŁOTYCH**

15.50 g., 0.900 Gold 0.4485 oz. AGW, 27 mm. **Subject:** Witold Lutoslawski

| Date | Mintage | VF20 | XF40 | MS60 | MS63 | MS65 |
|---|---|---|---|---|---|---|
| 2013 MW | Est. 2500 | PF65 850 | | | | |

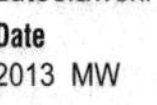

**Y# 875 200 ZŁOTYCH**

15.50 g., 0.900 Gold 0.4485 oz. AGW, 27 mm. **Subject:** 200th Anniversary of the Death of Prince Jozef Poniatowski

| Date | Mintage | VF20 | XF40 | MS60 | MS63 | MS65 |
|---|---|---|---|---|---|---|
| 2013 MW | Est. 3000 | PF65 850 | | | | |

**Y# 882 200 ZŁOTYCH**

15.50 g., 0.900 Gold 0.4485 oz. AGW, 27 mm. **Subject:** 200th Anniversary of the Birth of Hipolit Cegielski

| Date | Mintage | VF20 | XF40 | MS60 | MS63 | MS65 |
|---|---|---|---|---|---|---|
| 2013 MW | Est. 2500 | PF65 850 | | | | |

**Y# 895 200 ZŁOTYCH**

15.50 g., 0.900 Gold 0.4485 oz. AGW, 27 mm. **Subject:** Polish Olympic Team, Sochi 2014

| Date | Mintage | F12 | VF20 | XF40 | MS60 | MS63 |
|---|---|---|---|---|---|---|
| 2014 | 2,500 | PF65 900 | | | | |

**Y# 903 200 ZŁOTYCH**

15.50 g., 0.900 Gold 0.4485 oz. AGW, 27 mm. **Subject:** Jan Karski, 100th Anniversary of Birth

| Date | Mintage | F12 | VF20 | XF40 | MS60 | MS63 |
|---|---|---|---|---|---|---|
| 2014 | 2,500 | PF65 800 | | | | |

**Y# 911 200 ZŁOTYCH**

15.50 g., 0.900 Gold 0.4485 oz. AGW, 27 mm. **Subject:** Stefan Zeromski, 150th Anniversary of Birth

| Date | Mintage | F12 | VF20 | XF40 | MS60 | MS63 |
|---|---|---|---|---|---|---|
| 2014 | 2,500 | PF65 500 | | | | |

**Y# 831 500 ZŁOTYCH**

62.20 g., 0.999 Gold 1.9978 oz. AGW, 40 mm. **Subject:** European Football Championships

| Date | Mintage | VF20 | XF40 | MS60 | MS63 | MS65 |
|---|---|---|---|---|---|---|
| 2012 MW | 1,000 | PF65 3,750 | | | | |

**Y# 849 500 ZŁOTYCH**

62.20 g., 0.9999 Gold 1.9996 oz. AGW, 45 mm. **Subject:** King Stanislaw August - Boleslaw I the Brave **Obv:** Long legend and eagle at bottom **Rev:** Crowned bust right

| Date | Mintage | VF20 | XF40 | MS60 | MS63 | MS65 |
|---|---|---|---|---|---|---|
| 2013 MW | Est. 750 | — | — | — | 5,000 | — |

**Y# 861 500 ZŁOTYCH**

62.20 g., 0.9999 Gold 1.9996 oz. AGW, 45 mm. **Subject:** Treasures of King Stanislaw August - Venceslaus II of Bohemia

| Date | Mintage | VF20 | XF40 | MS60 | MS63 | MS65 |
|---|---|---|---|---|---|---|
| 2013 MW | — | — | — | — | 4,500 | — |

**Y# 868 500 ZŁOTYCH**

62.20 g., 0.9999 Gold 1.9996 oz. AGW, 45 mm. **Subject:** Treasures of King Stanislaw August - Wladyslaw the Short

| Date | Mintage | VF20 | XF40 | MS60 | MS63 | MS65 |
|---|---|---|---|---|---|---|
| 2013 MW | Est. 750 | — | — | — | 4,500 | — |

**Y# 899 500 ZŁOTYCH**

62.20 g., 0.999 Gold 1.9978 oz. AGW, 45 mm. **Subject:** Stanislaw August - Casimir the Great

| Date | Mintage | F12 | VF20 | XF40 | MS60 | MS63 |
|---|---|---|---|---|---|---|
| 2014 | 750 | PF65 275 | | | | |

**Y# 908 500 ZŁOTYCH**

62.20 g., 0.999 Gold 1.9978 oz. AGW, 45 mm. **Subject:** King Stanislaw August - Louis the Great

| Date | Mintage | F12 | VF20 | XF40 | MS60 | MS63 |
|---|---|---|---|---|---|---|
| 2014 | 750 | PF65 2,750 | | | | |

**Y# 915 500 ZŁOTYCH**

62.62 g., 0.999 Gold 2.0113 oz. AGW, 45 mm. **Subject:** Stanislaw August - Hedwig

| Date | Mintage | F12 | VF20 | XF40 | MS60 | MS63 |
|---|---|---|---|---|---|---|
| 2014 | 750 | PF65 2,750 | | | | |

**Y# 776 1000 ZŁOTYCH**

93.30 g., 0.999 Gold 2.9967 oz. AGW, 50 mm. **Subject:** John Paul II Beautification

| Date | Mintage | VF20 | XF40 | MS60 | MS63 | MS65 |
|---|---|---|---|---|---|---|
| 2011 MW | 500 | PF65 5,750 | | | | |

## GOLD BULLION COINAGE

**Y# 292 50 ZŁOTYCH**

3.10 g., 0.9999 Gold 0.0997 oz. AGW, 18 mm. **Obv:** Crowned eagle with wings open, all within circle **Rev:** Golden eagle

| Date | Mintage | VF20 | XF40 | MS60 | MS63 | MS65 |
|---|---|---|---|---|---|---|
| 2002 | 500 | — | — | 115 | 220 | — |
| 2004 | 2,000 | — | — | 115 | 200 | — |
| 2006 | 1,600 | — | — | 115 | 200 | — |
| 2007 | 2,000 | — | — | 115 | 200 | — |
| 2008 | — | — | — | 115 | 200 | — |

**Y# 293 100 ZŁOTYCH**

7.78 g., 0.9999 Gold 0.2501 oz. AGW, 22 mm. **Obv:** Crowned eagle with wings open, all within circle **Rev:** Golden eagle

| Date | Mintage | VF20 | XF40 | MS60 | MS63 | MS65 |
|---|---|---|---|---|---|---|
| 2002 | 800 | — | — | 289 | 475 | — |
| 2004 | 1,000 | — | — | 289 | 475 | — |
| 2006 | 900 | — | — | 289 | 475 | — |
| 2007 | 1,500 | — | — | 289 | 475 | — |
| 2008 | — | — | — | 289 | 475 | — |

### Y# 294 200 ZŁOTYCH

15.50 g., 0.900 Gold 0.4485 oz. AGW, 27 mm. **Obv:** Crowned eagle with wings open within beaded circle **Rev:** Golden eagle

| Date | Mintage | VF20 | XF40 | MS60 | MS63 | MS65 |
|---|---|---|---|---|---|---|
| 2002 | 1,000 | — | — | 518 | 850 | — |
| 2004 | 1,000 | — | — | 518 | 850 | — |
| 2006 | 900 | — | — | 518 | 850 | — |
| 2007 | 1,500 | — | — | 518 | 850 | — |
| 2008 | — | — | — | 518 | 850 | — |

### Y# 295 500 ZŁOTYCH

31.10 g., 0.9999 Gold 0.9999 oz. AGW **Obv:** Crowned eagle with wings open within beaded circle **Rev:** Golden eagle

| Date | Mintage | VF20 | XF40 | MS60 | MS63 | MS65 |
|---|---|---|---|---|---|---|
| 2002 | 1,000 | — | — | 1,155 | 1,850 | — |
| 2004 | 2,500 | — | — | 1,155 | 1,850 | — |
| 2006 | 600 | — | — | 1,155 | 1,850 | — |
| 2007 | 2,500 | — | — | 1,155 | 1,850 | — |
| 2008 | — | — | — | 1,155 | 1,850 | — |

## MINT SETS

| KM# | Date | Mintage | Identification | Issue Price | Mkt Val |
|---|---|---|---|---|---|
| MS5 | 2007 (11) | 2,000 | Y#276-284, 465, 525, mixed date set - 1995-2007 | 39.95 | 37.50 |

# PORTUGAL

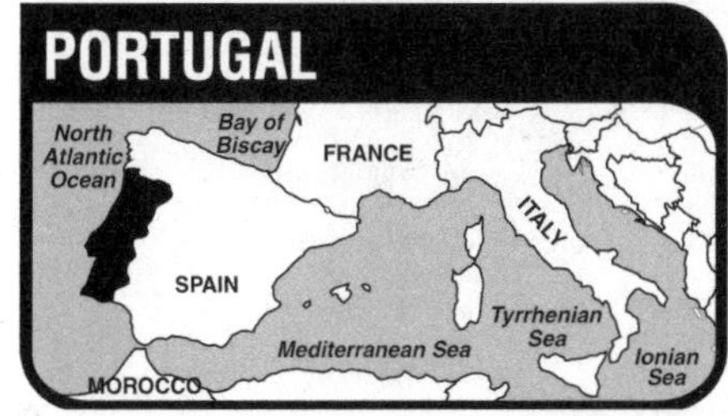


The Portuguese Republic, located in the western part of the Iberian Peninsula in southwestern Europe, has an area of 35,553 sq. mi. (92,080 sq. km.) and a population of *10.5 million. Capital: Lisbon. Portugal's economy is based on agriculture, tourism, minerals, fisheries and a rapidly expanding industrial sector. Textiles account for 33% of the exports and Portuguese wine is world famous. Portugal has become Europe's number one producer of copper and the world's largest producer of cork.

**RULER**

Republic, 1910 to date

**MONETARY SYSTEM**

100 Cents = 1 Euro

# REPUBLIC

## DECIMAL COINAGE

### KM# 631a ESCUDO

4.60 g., 0.9167 Gold 0.1356 oz. AGW, 16 mm. **Subject:** Last Escudo **Obv:** Design above shield with "Au" above top left corner of shield **Rev:** Flower design above value **Edge:** Plain

| Date | Mintage | F12 | VF20 | XF40 | MS60 | MS63 |
|---|---|---|---|---|---|---|
| 2001 INCM | 50,000 | — | — | — | 235 | 250 |
| 2001 INCM | — | PF65 225 | | | | |

### KM# 634.1 20 ESCUDOS

6.90 g., Copper-Nickel, 26.5 mm. **Obv:** Shield divides date with value below **Obv. Legend:** REPUBLICA PORTUGUESA **Rev:** Nautical windrose

| Date | Mintage | VF20 | XF40 | MS60 | MS63 | MS65 |
|---|---|---|---|---|---|---|
| 2001 INCM | Est. 250000 | — | — | 2.75 | 3.50 | — |

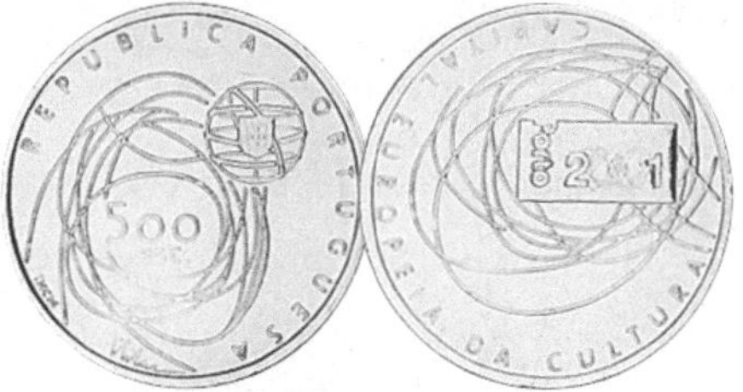

### KM# 733 500 ESCUDOS

13.96 g., 0.500 Silver 0.2244 oz. ASW, 30.1 mm. **Subject:** Porto, European Culture Capital **Obv:** National arms and value **Rev:** Stylized design **Edge:** Reeded

| Date | Mintage | VF20 | XF40 | MS60 | MS63 | MS65 |
|---|---|---|---|---|---|---|
| 2001 INCM | — | — | — | 8.50 | 9.50 | — |
| 2001 INCM | 10,000 | PF65 60.00 | | | | |

### KM# 733a 500 ESCUDOS

Gold **Subject:** Porto, European Culture Capital **Obv:** National arms and value **Rev:** Stylized design **Edge:** Reeded

| Date | Mintage | VF20 | XF40 | MS60 | MS63 | MS65 |
|---|---|---|---|---|---|---|
| 2001 INCM | 5,000 | PF65 550 | | | | |

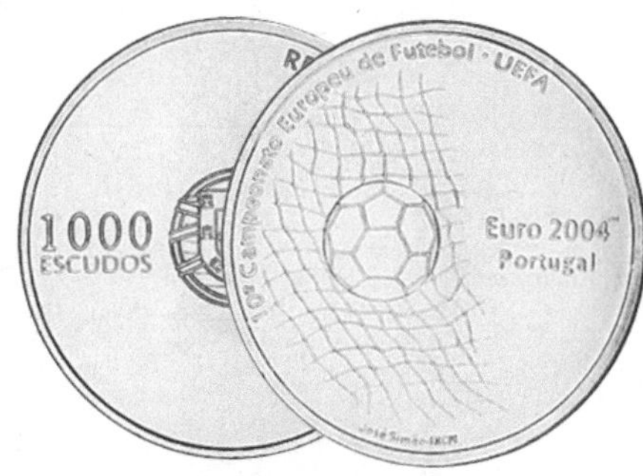

### KM# 734 1000 ESCUDOS

26.95 g., 0.500 Silver 0.4332 oz. ASW, 40 mm. **Obv:** National arms and value **Obv. Legend:** REPUBLICA PORTUGUESA 2001 **Rev:** Soccer ball within net **Rev. Legend:** 10º Campeonato Europeu de Futebol - UEFA Euro 2004 Portugal **Edge:** Reeded

| Date | Mintage | VF20 | XF40 | MS60 | MS63 | MS65 |
|---|---|---|---|---|---|---|
| 2001 INCM | 50,000 | — | — | 17.50 | 18.50 | 22.00 |
| 2001 INCM | — | PF65 75.00 | | | | |

## EURO COINAGE

European Union Issues

### KM# 740 EURO CENT

2.30 g., Copper Plated Steel, 16.25 mm. **Obv:** Royal seal of 1134 with country name and cross **Rev:** Value and globe **Edge:** Plain

| Date | Mintage | VF20 | XF40 | MS60 | MS63 | MS65 |
|---|---|---|---|---|---|---|
| 2002 | 278,106,172 | — | — | 0.35 | 0.50 | 0.65 |
| 2002 | 15,000 | PF65 7.00 | | | | |
| 2003 | 50,000 | — | — | 0.35 | 0.50 | 0.65 |
| 2003 | 15,000 | PF65 7.00 | | | | |
| 2004 | 75,000,000 | — | — | 0.35 | 0.50 | 0.65 |
| 2004 | 15,000 | PF65 7.00 | | | | |
| 2005 | 40,000,000 | — | — | 0.35 | 0.50 | 0.65 |
| 2005 | 10,000 | PF65 7.00 | | | | |
| 2006 | 30,000,000 | — | — | 0.35 | 0.50 | 0.65 |
| 2006 | 3,000 | PF65 7.00 | | | | |
| 2007 | 105,000,000 | — | — | 0.35 | 0.50 | 0.65 |
| 2007 | 2,500 | PF65 7.00 | | | | |
| 2008 | 75,000,000 | — | — | 0.35 | 0.50 | 0.65 |
| 2008 | 3,500 | PF65 7.00 | | | | |
| 2009 | 60,000,000 | — | — | 0.35 | 0.50 | 0.65 |
| 2009 | 4,000 | PF65 7.00 | | | | |
| 2010 | 15,000,000 | — | — | 0.35 | 0.50 | 0.65 |
| 2010 | 4,500 | PF65 7.00 | | | | |
| 2011 | 20,000,000 | — | — | 0.35 | 0.50 | 0.65 |
| 2011 | 4,500 | PF65 7.00 | | | | |
| 2012 | 50,000,000 | — | — | 0.35 | 0.50 | 0.65 |
| 2012 | 4,500 | PF65 7.00 | | | | |
| 2013 | — | — | — | 0.35 | 0.50 | 0.65 |
| 2013 | — | PF65 7.00 | | | | |
| 2014 | — | — | — | 0.35 | 0.50 | 0.65 |
| 2014 | — | PF65 7.00 | | | | |

### KM# 741 2 EURO CENT

3.06 g., Copper Plated Steel, 18.75 mm. **Obv:** Royal seal of 1134 with country name and cross **Rev:** Value and globe **Edge:** Grooved

| Date | Mintage | VF20 | XF40 | MS60 | MS63 | MS65 |
|---|---|---|---|---|---|---|
| 2002 | 324,376,590 | — | — | 0.50 | 0.65 | 0.85 |
| 2002 | 15,000 | PF65 9.00 | | | | |
| 2003 | 50,000 | — | — | — | 2.50 | 3.00 |
| Note: Sets only | | | | | | |
| 2003 | 15,000 | PF65 9.00 | | | | |
| 2004 | 1,000,000 | — | — | 0.50 | 0.65 | 0.85 |
| 2004 | 15,000 | PF65 9.00 | | | | |
| 2005 | 10,000,000 | — | — | 0.50 | 0.65 | 0.85 |
| 2005 | 10,000 | PF65 9.00 | | | | |
| 2006 | 1,000,000 | — | — | 0.50 | 0.65 | 0.85 |
| 2006 | 3,000 | PF65 9.00 | | | | |
| 2007 | 10,000,000 | — | — | 0.50 | 0.65 | 0.85 |
| 2007 | 2,500 | PF65 9.00 | | | | |
| 2008 | 35,000,000 | — | — | 0.50 | 0.65 | 0.85 |
| 2008 | 3,500 | PF65 9.00 | | | | |
| 2009 | 45,000,000 | — | — | 0.50 | 0.65 | 0.85 |
| 2009 | 4,000 | PF65 9.00 | | | | |
| 2010 | 10,000,000 | — | — | 0.50 | 0.65 | 0.85 |
| 2010 | 4,500 | PF65 9.00 | | | | |
| 2011 | 30,000,000 | — | — | 0.50 | 0.65 | 0.85 |
| 2011 | 4,500 | PF65 9.00 | | | | |
| 2012 | 35,000,000 | — | — | 0.50 | 0.65 | 0.85 |
| 2012 | 4,500 | PF65 9.00 | | | | |
| 2013 | — | — | — | 0.50 | 0.65 | 0.85 |
| 2013 | — | PF65 9.00 | | | | |
| 2014 | — | — | — | — | 0.65 | 0.85 |
| 2014 | — | PF65 9.00 | | | | |

### KM# 742 5 EURO CENT

3.92 g., Copper Plated Steel, 21.25 mm. **Obv:** Royal seal of 1134 with country name and cross **Rev:** Value and globe **Edge:** Plain

| Date | Mintage | VF20 | XF40 | MS60 | MS63 | MS65 |
|---|---|---|---|---|---|---|
| 2002 | 234,512,047 | — | — | 0.75 | 1.00 | 1.25 |
| 2002 | 15,000 | PF65 10.00 | | | | |
| 2003 | 50,000 | — | — | — | 4.00 | 5.00 |
| Note: Sets only | | | | | | |
| 2003 | 15,000 | PF65 10.00 | | | | |
| 2004 | 40,000,000 | — | — | 0.75 | 1.00 | 1.25 |
| 2004 | 15,000 | PF65 10.00 | | | | |
| 2005 | 30,000,000 | — | — | 0.75 | 1.00 | 1.25 |
| 2005 | 10,000 | PF65 10.00 | | | | |
| 2006 | 20,000,000 | — | — | 0.75 | 1.00 | 1.25 |
| 2006 | 3,000 | PF65 10.00 | | | | |
| 2007 | 25,000,000 | — | — | 0.75 | 1.00 | 1.25 |
| 2007 | 2,500 | PF65 10.00 | | | | |
| 2008 | 25,000,000 | — | — | 0.75 | 1.00 | 1.25 |
| 2008 | 3,500 | PF65 10.00 | | | | |
| 2009 | 25,000,000 | — | — | 0.75 | 1.00 | 1.25 |
| 2009 | 4,000 | PF65 10.00 | | | | |
| 2010 | 5,000,000 | — | — | 0.75 | 1.00 | 1.25 |
| 2010 | 4,500 | PF65 10.00 | | | | |
| 2011 | 25,000,000 | — | — | 0.75 | 1.00 | 1.25 |
| 2011 | 4,500 | PF65 10.00 | | | | |
| 2012 | 15,000,000 | — | — | 0.75 | 1.00 | 1.25 |
| 2012 | 4,500 | PF65 10.00 | | | | |
| 2013 | — | — | — | 0.75 | 1.00 | 1.25 |
| 2013 | — | PF65 10.00 | | | | |
| 2014 | — | — | — | — | 1.00 | 1.25 |
| 2014 | — | PF65 10.00 | | | | |

### KM# 743 10 EURO CENT

4.10 g., Brass, 19.75 mm. **Obv:** Royal seal of 1142, country name in circular design **Rev:** Value and map **Edge:** Reeded

| Date | Mintage | VF20 | XF40 | MS60 | MS63 | MS65 |
|---|---|---|---|---|---|---|
| 2002 | 220,289,835 | — | — | 0.75 | 1.00 | 1.25 |
| 2002 | 15,000 | PF65 12.00 | | | | |
| 2003 | 6,332,000 | — | — | 1.00 | 1.50 | 2.00 |
| 2003 | 15,000 | PF65 12.00 | | | | |
| 2004 | 1,000,000 | — | — | 1.50 | 2.00 | 2.50 |
| 2004 | 15,000 | PF65 12.00 | | | | |
| 2005 | 1,000,000 | — | — | 1.50 | 2.00 | 2.50 |
| 2005 | 10,000 | PF65 12.00 | | | | |
| 2006 | 1,000,000 | — | — | 1.50 | 2.00 | 2.50 |
| 2006 | 3,000 | PF65 12.00 | | | | |
| 2007 | 21,500 | — | — | 1.50 | 2.00 | 2.50 |
| 2007 | 2,500 | PF65 12.00 | | | | |

### KM# 763 10 EURO CENT

4.10 g., Brass, 19.75 mm. **Obv:** Royal seal of 1142, country name in circular design **Rev:** Relief map of Western Europe, stars, lines and value **Edge:** Reeded

| Date | Mintage | VF20 | XF40 | MS60 | MS63 | MS65 |
|---|---|---|---|---|---|---|
| 2008 | 1,000,000 | — | — | 1.50 | 2.00 | 2.50 |
| 2008 | 3,500 | PF65 12.00 | | | | |
| 2009 | 10,000,000 | — | — | 1.50 | 2.00 | 2.50 |
| 2009 | 4,000 | PF65 12.00 | | | | |
| 2010 | — | — | — | 1.50 | 2.00 | 2.50 |
| 2010 | 4,500 | PF65 12.00 | | | | |
| 2011 | — | — | — | 1.50 | 2.00 | 2.50 |
| 2011 | 4,500 | PF65 12.00 | | | | |
| 2012 | — | — | — | 1.50 | 2.00 | 2.50 |
| 2012 | 4,500 | PF65 12.00 | | | | |
| 2013 | — | — | — | 1.50 | 2.00 | 2.50 |
| 2013 | — | PF65 12.00 | | | | |
| 2014 | — | — | — | 1.00 | 2.00 | 2.50 |
| 2014 | — | PF65 12.00 | | | | |

### KM# 744 20 EURO CENT

5.74 g., Brass, 22.25 mm. **Obv:** Royal seal of 1142, country name in circular design **Rev:** Value and map **Edge:** Notched

| Date | Mintage | VF20 | XF40 | MS60 | MS63 | MS65 |
|---|---|---|---|---|---|---|
| 2002 | 147,411,038 | — | — | 1.00 | 1.25 | 1.50 |
| 2002 | 15,000 | PF65 14.00 | | | | |
| 2003 | 9,493,600 | — | — | 1.25 | 1.50 | 2.00 |
| 2003 | 15,000 | PF65 14.00 | | | | |
| 2004 | 1,000,000 | — | — | 1.50 | 2.00 | 2.50 |
| 2004 | 15,000 | PF65 14.00 | | | | |
| 2005 | 25,000,000 | — | — | 1.50 | 2.00 | 2.50 |
| 2005 | 10,000 | PF65 14.00 | | | | |
| 2006 | 20,000,000 | — | — | 1.50 | 2.00 | 2.50 |
| 2006 | 3,000 | PF65 14.00 | | | | |
| 2007 | 21,500 | — | — | 1.50 | 2.00 | 2.50 |
| 2007 | 2,500 | PF65 14.00 | | | | |

### KM# 764 20 EURO CENT

5.74 g., Brass, 22.25 mm. **Obv:** Royal seal of 1142, country name in circular design **Rev:** Relief map of Western Europe, stars, lines and value **Edge:** Notched

| Date | Mintage | VF20 | XF40 | MS60 | MS63 | MS65 |
|---|---|---|---|---|---|---|
| 2008 | 1,000,000 | — | — | 1.50 | 2.00 | 2.50 |
| 2008 | 3,500 | PF65 14.00 | | | | |
| 2009 | 20,000,000 | — | — | 1.50 | 2.00 | 2.50 |
| 2009 | 4,000 | PF65 14.00 | | | | |
| 2010 | 5,000,000 | — | — | 1.50 | 2.00 | 2.50 |
| 2010 | 4,500 | PF65 14.00 | | | | |
| 2011 | 10,000,000 | — | — | 1.50 | 2.00 | 2.50 |
| 2011 | 4,500 | PF65 14.00 | | | | |
| 2012 | — | — | — | 1.50 | 2.00 | 2.50 |
| 2012 | 4,500 | PF65 14.00 | | | | |
| 2013 | — | — | — | 1.50 | 2.00 | 2.50 |
| 2013 | — | PF65 14.00 | | | | |
| 2014 | — | — | — | 1.50 | 2.00 | 2.50 |
| 2014 | — | PF65 14.00 | | | | |

### KM# 777 1/4 EURO

1.56 g., 0.999 Gold 0.0501 oz. AGW, 14 mm. **Series:** Portugal Universal **Subject:** King Alfons I, the Conqueror **Obv:** National arms, value **Obv. Legend:** REPÚBLICA PORTUGUESA **Rev:** Stylized 3/4 length armored figure standing facing **Rev. Legend:** D. AFONSO HENRIQUES **Edge:** Reeded **Note:** Each coin is numbered.

| Date | Mintage | VF20 | XF40 | MS60 | MS63 | MS65 |
|---|---|---|---|---|---|---|
| 2006 | 30,000 | — | — | — | 145 | 165 |

### KM# 826 1/4 EURO

1.56 g., 0.999 Gold 0.0501 oz. AGW, 14 mm. **Subject:** Anthony of Padua

| Date | Mintage | VF20 | XF40 | MS60 | MS63 | MS65 |
|---|---|---|---|---|---|---|
| 2007 | 30,000 | — | — | — | 125 | 145 |

### KM# 827 1/4 EURO

1.56 g., 0.999 Gold 0.0501 oz. AGW, 14 mm. **Subject:** King Denis

| Date | Mintage | VF20 | XF40 | MS60 | MS63 | MS65 |
|---|---|---|---|---|---|---|
| 2008 | 30,000 | — | — | — | 125 | 145 |

### KM# 787 1/4 EURO

1.56 g., 0.999 Gold 0.0501 oz. AGW, 14 mm. **Subject:** Vasco da Gama

| Date | Mintage | VF20 | XF40 | MS60 | MS63 | MS65 |
|---|---|---|---|---|---|---|
| 2009 | 20,000 | — | — | — | 125 | 145 |

### KM# 794 1/4 EURO

1.56 g., 0.999 Gold 0.0501 oz. AGW, 14 mm. **Subject:** Luis Vaz de Camoes

| Date | Mintage | VF20 | XF40 | MS60 | MS63 | MS65 |
|---|---|---|---|---|---|---|
| 2010 | 15,000 | — | — | — | 145 | 165 |

### KM# 805 1/4 EURO

1.56 g., 0.999 Gold 0.0501 oz. AGW, 14 mm. **Subject:** Fr. António Vieira **Obv:** National arms **Rev:** Linear portrait of Vieira

| Date | Mintage | VF20 | XF40 | MS60 | MS63 | MS65 |
|---|---|---|---|---|---|---|
| 2011 | 10,000 | — | — | — | 125 | 145 |

### KM# 807 1/4 EURO

1.56 g., 0.999 Gold 0.0501 oz. AGW, 14 mm. **Subject:** Spain and Portugal's accession to the European Union, 25th Anniversary

| Date | Mintage | VF20 | XF40 | MS60 | MS63 | MS65 |
|---|---|---|---|---|---|---|
| 2011 | 12,500 | — | — | — | 125 | 145 |

### KM# 814 1/4 EURO

1.56 g., 0.999 Gold 0.0501 oz. AGW, 14 mm. **Subject:** Carlos Seixas, composer **Obv:** National arms **Rev:** Head facing, name at left, dates at right

| Date | Mintage | VF20 | XF40 | MS60 | MS63 | MS65 |
|---|---|---|---|---|---|---|
| 2012 | 15,000 | — | — | — | 145 | 165 |

### KM# 745 50 EURO CENT

7.80 g., Brass, 24.25 mm. **Obv:** Royal seal of 1142, country name in circular design **Rev:** Value and map **Edge:** Reeded

| Date | Mintage | VF20 | XF40 | MS60 | MS63 | MS65 |
|---|---|---|---|---|---|---|
| 2002 | 151,947,133 | — | — | 1.50 | 2.00 | 2.50 |
| 2002 | 15,000 | PF65 16.00 | | | | |
| 2003 | 10,353,000 | — | — | 1.50 | 2.00 | 2.50 |
| 2003 | 15,000 | PF65 16.00 | | | | |
| 2004 | 1,000,000 | — | — | 2.50 | 3.00 | 3.50 |
| 2004 | 15,000 | PF65 16.00 | | | | |
| 2005 | 1,000,000 | — | — | 2.50 | 3.00 | 3.50 |
| 2005 | 10,000 | PF65 16.00 | | | | |
| 2006 | 1,000,000 | — | — | 2.50 | 3.00 | 3.50 |
| 2006 | 3,000 | PF65 16.00 | | | | |
| 2007 | 21,500 | — | — | 2.50 | 3.00 | 3.50 |
| 2007 | 2,500 | PF65 16.00 | | | | |

### KM# 765 50 EURO CENT

7.80 g., Brass, 24.25 mm. **Obv:** Royal seal of 1142, country name in circular design **Rev:** Relief map of Western Europe, stars, lines and value **Edge:** Reeded

| Date | Mintage | VF20 | XF40 | MS60 | MS63 | MS65 |
|---|---|---|---|---|---|---|
| 2008 | 5,000,000 | — | — | 2.50 | 3.00 | 3.50 |
| 2008 | 3,500 | PF65 16.00 | | | | |
| 2009 | 20,000,000 | — | — | 2.50 | 3.00 | 3.50 |
| 2009 | 4,000 | PF65 16.00 | | | | |
| 2010 | 20,000,000 | — | — | 2.50 | 3.00 | 3.50 |
| 2010 | 4,500 | PF65 16.00 | | | | |
| 2011 | — | — | — | 2.50 | 3.00 | 3.50 |
| 2011 | 4,500 | PF65 16.00 | | | | |
| 2012 | — | — | — | 2.50 | 3.00 | 3.50 |
| 2012 | 4,500 | PF65 16.00 | | | | |
| 2013 | — | — | — | 2.50 | 3.00 | 3.50 |
| 2013 | — | PF65 16.00 | | | | |
| 2014 | — | PF65 16.00 | | | | |
| 2014 | — | — | — | 2.50 | 3.00 | 3.50 |

### KM# 746 EURO

7.50 g., Bi-Metallic Copper-Nickel center in Nickel-Brass ring, 23.25 mm. **Obv:** Royal seal of 1144, country name in looped design **Rev:** Value and map **Edge:** Segmented reeding

| Date | Mintage | VF20 | XF40 | MS60 | MS63 | MS65 |
|---|---|---|---|---|---|---|
| 2002 | 100,228,135 | — | — | 2.00 | 2.50 | 3.00 |
| Note: Variety in the edge milling, 28 or 29. | | | | | | |
| 2002 | 15,000 | PF65 18.00 | | | | |
| 2003 | 16,206,875 | — | — | 2.00 | 2.50 | 3.00 |
| 2003 | 15,000 | PF65 18.00 | | | | |
| 2004 | 20,000,000 | — | — | 2.00 | 2.50 | 3.00 |
| 2004 | 15,000 | PF65 18.00 | | | | |
| 2005 | 20,000,000 | — | — | 2.00 | 2.50 | 3.00 |
| 2005 | 10,000 | PF65 18.00 | | | | |
| 2006 | 20,000,000 | — | — | 2.00 | 2.50 | 3.00 |
| 2006 | 3,000 | PF65 18.00 | | | | |
| 2007 | 4,935,400 | — | — | 2.00 | 2.50 | 3.00 |
| 2007 | 2,500 | PF65 18.00 | | | | |

### KM# 766 EURO

7.50 g., Bi-Metallic Copper-Nickel center in Nickel-Brass ring, 23.25 mm. **Obv:** Royal seal of 1144, country name in looped design **Rev:** Relief map of Western Europe, stars, lines and value **Edge:** Segmented reeding

| Date | Mintage | VF20 | XF40 | MS60 | MS63 | MS65 |
|---|---|---|---|---|---|---|
| 2008 | 5,000,000 | — | — | 2.75 | 3.50 | 4.00 |
| 2008 | 3,500 | PF65 18.00 | | | | |
| 2009 | 20,000,000 | — | — | 2.75 | 3.50 | 4.00 |
| 2009 | 4,000 | PF65 18.00 | | | | |
| 2010 | 20,000,000 | — | — | 2.75 | 3.50 | 4.00 |
| 2010 | 4,500 | PF65 18.00 | | | | |
| 2011 | 5,000,000 | — | — | 2.75 | 3.50 | 4.00 |
| 2011 | 4,500 | PF65 18.00 | | | | |
| 2012 | — | — | — | 2.75 | 3.50 | 4.00 |
| 2012 | 4,500 | PF65 18.00 | | | | |
| 2013 | — | — | — | 2.75 | 3.50 | 4.00 |
| 2013 | — | PF65 18.00 | | | | |
| 2014 | — | — | — | 2.75 | 3.50 | 4.00 |
| 2014 | — | PF65 18.00 | | | | |

### KM# 828 1-1/2 EURO

10.00 g., Copper-Nickel, 26.5 mm. **Subject:** Internaitonal Medical Care **Obv:** National Arms **Rev:** AMI logo

| Date | Mintage | VF20 | XF40 | MS60 | MS63 | MS65 |
|---|---|---|---|---|---|---|
| 2008 | 300,000 | — | — | 10.00 | 12.50 | 15.00 |

### KM# 828a 1-1/2 EURO

8.00 g., Copper-Nickel, 26.5 mm. **Subject:** International Medical Assistance **Obv:** National arms **Rev:** AMI logo

| Date | Mintage | VF20 | XF40 | MS60 | MS63 | MS65 |
|---|---|---|---|---|---|---|
| 2008 Special Unc. | 50,000 | — | — | — | 25.00 | 30.00 |

### KM# 828b 1-1/2 EURO

10.00 g., 0.925 Silver 0.2974 oz. ASW, 26.5 mm. **Subject:** International Medical Assistance **Obv:** National arms **Rev:** AMI logo

| Date | Mintage | VF20 | XF40 | MS60 | MS63 | MS65 |
|---|---|---|---|---|---|---|
| 2008 | 5,000 | PF65 60.00 | | | | |

### KM# 788 1-1/2 EURO

10.37 g., 0.999 Gold 0.3331 oz. AGW, 26.5 mm. **Subject:** Numismatics - Marabitino of Sancho II **Obv:** Cross of shields **Rev:** King on horseback

| Date | Mintage | VF20 | XF40 | MS60 | MS63 | MS65 |
|---|---|---|---|---|---|---|
| 2009 | 2,500 | PF65 650 | | | | |

### KM# 789 1-1/2 EURO

Copper-Nickel, 26.5 mm. **Obv:** Numismatics - Marabitino of Sancho II

| Date | Mintage | VF20 | XF40 | MS60 | MS63 | MS65 |
|---|---|---|---|---|---|---|
| 2009 Proof | 150,000 | — | — | 5.00 | 6.00 | 7.00 |

**KM# 795 1-1/2 EURO**
8.00 g., Copper-Nickel, 26.5 mm. **Subject:** Against Famine

| Date | Mintage | VF20 | XF40 | MS60 | MS63 | MS65 |
|---|---|---|---|---|---|---|
| 2010 | 100,000 | — | — | 5.00 | 6.00 | 7.00 |
| 2010 INCM Special Unc. | 100,000 | — | — | — | 10.00 | 12.00 |

**KM# 795a 1-1/2 EURO**
10.00 g., 0.925 Silver 0.2974 oz. ASW, 26.5 mm. **Subject:** Against Famine

| Date | Mintage | VF20 | XF40 | MS60 | MS63 | MS65 |
|---|---|---|---|---|---|---|
| 2010 | 5,000 | PF65 55.00 | | | | |

**KM# 747 2 EURO**
8.50 g., Bi-Metallic Nickel-Brass center in Copper-Nickel ring, 25.75 mm. **Obv:** Royal seal of 1144, country name in looped design **Rev:** Value and map **Edge:** Reeding over castles and shields

| Date | Mintage | VF20 | XF40 | MS60 | MS63 | MS65 |
|---|---|---|---|---|---|---|
| 2002 | 61,930,775 | — | — | 3.50 | 4.00 | 5.00 |
| 2002 | 15,000 | PF65 22.00 | | | | |
| 2003 | 5,979,750 | — | — | 4.25 | 5.00 | 6.00 |
| 2003 | 15,000 | PF65 22.00 | | | | |
| 2004 | 1,000,000 | — | — | 5.50 | 6.00 | 7.00 |
| 2004 | 15,000 | PF65 22.00 | | | | |
| 2005 | 1,000,000 | — | — | 5.50 | 6.00 | 7.00 |
| 2005 | 10,000 | PF65 22.00 | | | | |
| 2006 | 1,000,000 | — | — | 5.50 | 6.00 | 7.00 |
| 2006 | 3,000 | PF65 22.00 | | | | |
| 2007 | 21,500 | — | — | 5.50 | 6.00 | 7.00 |
| 2007 | 2,500 | PF65 22.00 | | | | |

**KM# 771 2 EURO**
8.50 g., Bi-Metallic Nickel-Brass center in Copper-Nickel ring, 25.75 mm. **Subject:** 50th Anniversary Treaty of Rome **Obv:** Open treaty book **Rev:** Large value at left, modified outline of Europe at right **Edge:** Reeded and lettered

| Date | Mintage | VF20 | XF40 | MS60 | MS63 | MS65 |
|---|---|---|---|---|---|---|
| 2007 | 1,500,000 | — | — | 4.50 | 6.00 | 7.00 |
| 2007 Prooflike | 15,000 | — | — | — | 12.50 | 15.00 |
| 2007 | 5,000 | PF65 25.00 | | | | |

**KM# 772 2 EURO**
8.50 g., Bi-Metallic Nickel-Brass center in Copper-Nickel ring, 25.75 mm. **Subject:** European Union President **Obv:** Large tree, small national arms at lower left **Obv. Inscription:** POR / TV / GAL **Rev:** Large value at left, revised map of Europe at right **Edge:** Reeded with repeated symbols

| Date | Mintage | VF20 | XF40 | MS60 | MS63 | MS65 |
|---|---|---|---|---|---|---|
| 2007 | 1,250,000 | — | — | 4.50 | 6.00 | 7.00 |
| 2007 Prooflike | 15,000 | — | — | — | 12.50 | 15.00 |
| 2007 | 5,000 | PF65 25.00 | | | | |

**KM# 767 2 EURO**
8.52 g., Bi-Metallic Nickel-Brass center in Copper-Nickel ring, 25.7 mm. **Obv:** Royal seal of 1144, country name in looped design **Rev:** Relief map of Western Europe, stars, lines and value **Edge:** Reeding over castles and shields

| Date | Mintage | VF20 | XF40 | MS60 | MS63 | MS65 |
|---|---|---|---|---|---|---|
| 2008 Sets only | — | — | — | — | 6.00 | 7.00 |
| 2008 | 3,500 | PF65 22.00 | | | | |
| 2009 Sets only | — | — | — | — | 6.00 | 7.00 |
| 2009 | 4,000 | PF65 22.00 | | | | |
| 2010 | — | — | — | — | 6.00 | 7.00 |
| 2010 | 4,500 | PF65 22.00 | | | | |
| 2011 | — | — | — | — | 6.00 | 7.00 |
| 2011 | 4,500 | PF65 22.00 | | | | |
| 2012 | — | — | — | — | 6.00 | 7.00 |
| 2012 | 4,500 | PF65 22.00 | | | | |
| 2013 | — | — | — | — | 6.00 | 7.00 |
| 2013 | — | PF65 22.00 | | | | |
| 2014 | — | — | — | — | 6.00 | 7.00 |
| 2014 | — | PF65 22.00 | | | | |

**KM# 784 2 EURO**
8.50 g., Bi-Metallic Nickel-Brass center in Copper-Nickel ring, 25.75 mm. **Subject:** Declaration of Human Rights, 60th Anniversary **Obv:** Seal above field

| Date | Mintage | VF20 | XF40 | MS60 | MS63 | MS65 |
|---|---|---|---|---|---|---|
| 2008 | 1,000,000 | — | — | 4.00 | 5.00 | 6.00 |
| 2008 | 10,000 | PF65 25.00 | | | | |

**KM# 785 2 EURO**
8.50 g., Bi-Metallic Nickel-Brass center in Copper-Nickel ring, 25.75 mm. **Subject:** European Monetary Union, 10th Anniversary **Obv:** Stick figure and Euro symbol

| Date | Mintage | VF20 | XF40 | MS60 | MS63 | MS65 |
|---|---|---|---|---|---|---|
| 2009 | 1,250,000 | — | — | 6.00 | 12.00 | 15.00 |
| 2009 | 15,000 | PF65 25.00 | | | | |

**KM# 786 2 EURO**
8.50 g., Bi-Metallic Nickel-Brass center in Copper-Nickel ring, 25.75 mm. **Subject:** Lusofonia Games **Rev:** Figure with long flowing ribbon

| Date | Mintage | VF20 | XF40 | MS60 | MS63 | MS65 |
|---|---|---|---|---|---|---|
| 2009 | 1,275,000 | — | — | — | 5.00 | 6.00 |
| 2009 | 10,000 | PF65 25.00 | | | | |

**KM# 796 2 EURO**
8.50 g., Bi-Metallic Nickel-Brass center in Copper-Nickel ring, 25.75 mm. **Subject:** Portuguese Republic, 100th Anniversary

| Date | Mintage | VF20 | XF40 | MS60 | MS63 | MS65 |
|---|---|---|---|---|---|---|
| 2010 | 10,000 | PF65 20.00 | | | | |
| 2010 | 1,265,000 | — | — | 6.00 | 7.00 | 8.00 |

**KM# 804 2 EURO**
8.50 g., Bi-Metallic Nickel-Brass center in Copper-Nickel ring, 25.75 mm. **Subject:** Fernão Mendes Pinto, 500th Anniversary of Birth **Obv:** Sailing ship right

| Date | Mintage | VF20 | XF40 | MS60 | MS63 | MS65 |
|---|---|---|---|---|---|---|
| 2011 | 500,000 | — | — | 6.00 | 7.00 | 8.00 |
| 2011 Special Unc. | 12,500 | — | — | — | 9.00 | 10.00 |
| 2011 | 7,500 | PF65 25.00 | | | | |

**KM# 812 2 EURO**
8.50 g., Bi-Metallic Nickel-Brass center in Copper-Nickel ring, 25.75 mm. **Subject:** Euro circulation, 10th Anniversary **Obv:** Euro symbol on globe, childlike images around

| Date | Mintage | VF20 | XF40 | MS60 | MS63 | MS65 |
|---|---|---|---|---|---|---|
| 2012 | 500,000 | — | — | 6.00 | 7.00 | 8.00 |
| 2012 Special Unc. | 10,000 | — | — | — | 9.00 | 10.00 |
| 2012 | 10,000 | PF65 25.00 | | | | |

**KM# 813 2 EURO**
8.50 g., Bi-Metallic Nickel-Brass center in Copper-Nickel ring, 25.75 mm. **Subject:** Guimarães, European Cultural Capital **Obv:** Stylized cross and castle

| Date | Mintage | VF20 | XF40 | MS60 | MS63 | MS65 |
|---|---|---|---|---|---|---|
| 2012 | 500,000 | — | — | 6.00 | 7.00 | 8.00 |
| 2012 Special Unc. | 10,000 | — | — | — | 9.00 | 10.00 |
| 2012 | 10,000 | PF65 25.00 | | | | |

**KM# 783 2-1/2 EURO**
9.85 g., Copper-Nickel, 28 mm. **Obv:** Small national arms on stringed instrument at right **Rev:** Fado musician at lower left **Edge:** Coarse reeding

| Date | Mintage | VF20 | XF40 | MS60 | MS63 | MS65 |
|---|---|---|---|---|---|---|
| 2008 | 150,000 | — | — | 6.00 | 9.00 | 10.00 |

**KM# 783a 2-1/2 EURO**
12.00 g., 0.925 Silver 0.3569 oz. ASW, 28 mm. **Obv:** Small national arms on stringed instrument at right **Rev:** Fado musician at lower left

| Date | Mintage | VF20 | XF40 | MS60 | MS63 | MS65 |
|---|---|---|---|---|---|---|
| 2008 | 20,000 | PF65 60.00 | | | | |

**KM# 790 2-1/2 EURO**
10.00 g., Copper-Nickel, 28 mm. **Subject:** Bejing Olympics

| Date | Mintage | VF20 | XF40 | MS60 | MS63 | MS65 |
|---|---|---|---|---|---|---|
| 2008 | 487,500 | — | — | 6.00 | 7.00 | 8.00 |

**KM# 790a 2-1/2 EURO**
12.00 g., 0.925 Silver 0.3569 oz. ASW, 28 mm. **Subject:** Bejing Olympics

| Date | Mintage | VF20 | XF40 | MS60 | MS63 | MS65 |
|---|---|---|---|---|---|---|
| 2008 | 12,500 | PF65 60.00 | | | | |

**KM# 824 2-1/2 EURO**
10.00 g., Copper-Nickel, 28 mm. **Subject:** UNESCO - World Historic Site, Porto **Obv:** National arms **Rev:** Bridge and town view

| Date | Mintage | VF20 | XF40 | MS60 | MS63 | MS65 |
|---|---|---|---|---|---|---|
| 2008 | 80,000 | — | — | 10.00 | 15.00 | 17.00 |

**KM# 824a 2-1/2 EURO**
12.00 g., 0.925 Silver 0.3569 oz. ASW, 28 mm. **Subject:** UNESCO Historic Site - Porto **Obv:** National arms **Rev:** Bridge and town view

| Date | Mintage | VF20 | XF40 | MS60 | MS63 | MS65 |
|---|---|---|---|---|---|---|
| 2008 | 5,000 | PF65 60.00 | | | | |

**KM# 825 2-1/2 EURO**
10.00 g., Copper-Nickel, 28 mm. **Subject:** UNESCO Historic Site - Wine region of Alto Douro **Obv:** National arms and river **Rev:** Terraced fields

| Date | Mintage | VF20 | XF40 | MS60 | MS63 | MS65 |
|---|---|---|---|---|---|---|
| 2008 80000 | — | — | — | 10.00 | 12.50 | 15.00 |

**KM# 825a 2-1/2 EURO**
12.00 g., 0.925 Silver 0.3569 oz. ASW, 28 mm. **Subject:** UNESCO historic sites - Wine region of Alto Douro **Obv:** National arms and river **Rev:** Terraced fields

| Date | Mintage | VF20 | XF40 | MS60 | MS63 | MS65 |
|---|---|---|---|---|---|---|
| 2008 | 5,000 | PF65 60.00 | | | | |

**KM# 791 2-1/2 EURO**
Copper-Nickel, 28 mm. **Subject:** Portugese Literature **Obv:** Portrait of Fernando António Nogueira de Seabra, and text **Rev:** Stylized portrait of Luis Vaz de Camões and lines

| Date | Mintage | VF20 | XF40 | MS60 | MS63 | MS65 |
|---|---|---|---|---|---|---|
| 2009 | 150,000 | — | — | 6.00 | 7.00 | 8.00 |

**KM# 791a 2-1/2 EURO**
12.00 g., 0.925 Silver 0.3569 oz. ASW, 28 mm. **Subject:** Portuguese Literature

| Date | Mintage | VF20 | XF40 | MS60 | MS63 | MS65 |
|---|---|---|---|---|---|---|
| 2009 | 14,000 | PF65 60.00 | | | | |

**KM# 791b 2-1/2 EURO**
15.55 g., 0.999 Gold 0.4994 oz. AGW, 28 mm. **Subject:** Portuguese Literature

| Date | Mintage | VF20 | XF40 | MS60 | MS63 | MS65 |
|---|---|---|---|---|---|---|
| 2009 | 2,500 | PF65 950 | | | | |

**KM# 792 2-1/2 EURO**
Copper-Nickel, 28 mm. **Subject:** UNESCO Heritage Site - Hieronymites Monastery **Obv:** Arched cieling design, National arms **Rev:** Façade detail

| Date | Mintage | VF20 | XF40 | MS60 | MS63 | MS65 |
|---|---|---|---|---|---|---|
| 2009 | 150,000 | — | — | 6.00 | 7.00 | 8.00 |

**KM# 792a 2-1/2 EURO**
12.00 g., 0.925 Silver 0.3569 oz. ASW, 28 mm. **Subject:** UNESCO World Heritage Site - Hieronymites Monastery **Obv:** Arched ceiling design, National arms **Rev:** Façade detail

| Date | Mintage | VF20 | XF40 | MS60 | MS63 | MS65 |
|---|---|---|---|---|---|---|
| 2009 | 5,000 | PF65 60.00 | | | | |

**KM# 793 2-1/2 EURO**
10.00 g., Copper-Nickel, 28 mm. **Obv:** National arms, rope splice below **Rev:** UNESCO World Heritage Site - Belém

| Date | Mintage | VF20 | XF40 | MS60 | MS63 | MS65 |
|---|---|---|---|---|---|---|
| 2009 | 150,000 | — | — | 6.00 | 7.00 | 8.00 |

**KM# 793a 2-1/2 EURO**
12.00 g., 0.925 Silver 0.3569 oz. ASW, 28 mm. **Subject:** UNESCO - World Heritage Site - Belém **Obv:** Naitonal arms, rope splice below **Rev:** Fortress

| Date | Mintage | VF20 | XF40 | MS60 | MS63 | MS65 |
|---|---|---|---|---|---|---|
| 2009 | 5,000 | PF65 60.00 | | | | |

**KM# 797 2-1/2 EURO**
10.00 g., Copper-Nickel, 28 mm. **Subject:** FIFA Soccer - South Africa

| Date | Mintage | VF20 | XF40 | MS60 | MS63 | MS65 |
|---|---|---|---|---|---|---|
| 2010 INCM | 120,000 | — | — | 6.00 | 7.00 | 8.00 |

**KM# 797a 2-1/2 EURO**
12.00 g., 0.925 Silver 0.3569 oz. ASW, 28 mm. **Subject:** FIFA Soccer - South Africa

| Date | Mintage | VF20 | XF40 | MS60 | MS63 | MS65 |
|---|---|---|---|---|---|---|
| 2010 INCM | 12,500 | PF65 55.00 | | | | |

**KM# 798 2-1/2 EURO**
10.00 g., Copper-Nickel, 28 mm. **Subject:** Palace Square, Lisbon

| Date | Mintage | VF20 | XF40 | MS60 | MS63 | MS65 |
|---|---|---|---|---|---|---|
| 2010 INCM | 120,000 | — | — | 6.00 | 7.00 | 8.00 |

**KM# 798a 2-1/2 EURO**
12.00 g., 0.925 Silver 0.3569 oz. ASW, 28 mm. **Subject:** Palace Square, Lisbon

| Date | Mintage | VF20 | XF40 | MS60 | MS63 | MS65 |
|---|---|---|---|---|---|---|
| 2010 INCM | 15,000 | PF65 55.00 | | | | |

**KM# 798b 2-1/2 EURO**
15.55 g., 0.999 Gold 0.4994 oz. AGW, 28 mm. **Subject:** Palace Square, Lisbon

| Date | Mintage | VF20 | XF40 | MS60 | MS63 | MS65 |
|---|---|---|---|---|---|---|
| 2010 INCM | 2,500 | PF65 950 | | | | |

**KM# 800 2-1/2 EURO**
10.00 g., Copper-Nickel, 28 mm. **Subject:** Torres Defence Line, 200th Anniversary

| Date | Mintage | VF20 | XF40 | MS60 | MS63 | MS65 |
|---|---|---|---|---|---|---|
| 2010 INCM | — | — | — | 6.00 | 7.00 | 8.00 |

**KM# 800a 2-1/2 EURO**
12.00 g., 0.925 Silver 0.3569 oz. ASW, 28 mm. **Subject:** Torres Defence Line, 200th Anniversary

| Date | Mintage | VF20 | XF40 | MS60 | MS63 | MS65 |
|---|---|---|---|---|---|---|
| 2010 INCM | — | PF65 55.00 | | | | |

**KM# 801 2-1/2 EURO**
10.00 g., Copper-Nickel, 28 mm. **Subject:** UNESCO World Cultural Heritage site - Coa Valley

| Date | Mintage | VF20 | XF40 | MS60 | MS63 | MS65 |
|---|---|---|---|---|---|---|
| 2010 INCM | 120,000 | — | — | 6.00 | 7.00 | 8.00 |

**KM# 801a 2-1/2 EURO**
12.00 g., 0.925 Silver 0.3569 oz. ASW, 28 mm. **Subject:** UNESCO World Cultural Heritage Site - Coa Valley

| Date | Mintage | VF20 | XF40 | MS60 | MS63 | MS65 |
|---|---|---|---|---|---|---|
| 2010 INCM | 5,000 | PF65 60.00 | | | | |

**KM# 806 2-1/2 EURO**
10.00 g., Copper-Nickel, 28 mm. **Subject:** European explorers **Obv:** National arms, tree branch and Chinese characters **Rev:** Two portraits

| Date | Mintage | VF20 | XF40 | MS60 | MS63 | MS65 |
|---|---|---|---|---|---|---|
| 2011 | 100,000 | — | — | — | 7.00 | 8.00 |

**KM# 806a 2-1/2 EURO**
12.00 g., 0.925 Silver 0.3569 oz. ASW, 28 mm. **Subject:** European explorers **Obv:** National arms, tree branch and Chinese characters **Rev:** Two portraits

| Date | Mintage | VF20 | XF40 | MS60 | MS63 | MS65 |
|---|---|---|---|---|---|---|
| 2011 | — | PF65 55.00 | | | | |

**KM# 806b 2-1/2 EURO**
15.55 g., 0.999 Gold 0.4994 oz. AGW, 28 mm. **Subject:** European explorers **Obv:** National arms, tree branch, Chinese characters **Rev:** Two portraits

| Date | Mintage | VF20 | XF40 | MS60 | MS63 | MS65 |
|---|---|---|---|---|---|---|
| 2011 | — | PF65 950 | | | | |

**KM# 809 2-1/2 EURO**
10.00 g., Copper-Nickel, 28 mm. **Subject:** Army College, 100th Anniversary **Obv:** National arms and sword **Rev:** Sword and cadet cap

| Date | Mintage | VF20 | XF40 | MS60 | MS63 | MS65 |
|---|---|---|---|---|---|---|
| 2011 | 100,000 | — | — | — | 7.00 | 8.00 |

**KM# 809a 2-1/2 EURO**
12.00 g., 0.925 Silver 0.3569 oz. ASW, 28 mm. **Subject:** Army College, 100th Anniversary **Obv:** National arms and sword **Rev:** Sword and cadet cap

| Date | Mintage | VF20 | XF40 | MS60 | MS63 | MS65 |
|---|---|---|---|---|---|---|
| 2011 | — | PF65 55.00 | | | | |

**KM# 810 2-1/2 EURO**
10.00 g., Copper-Nickel, 28 mm. **Subject:** Pico Island, Azores. Wine growing landscape **Obv:** National arms and tree **Rev:** Grape leaf and vine fields

| Date | Mintage | VF20 | XF40 | MS60 | MS63 | MS65 |
|---|---|---|---|---|---|---|
| 2011 | 100,000 | — | — | — | 7.00 | 8.00 |

**KM# 810a 2-1/2 EURO**
12.00 g., 0.925 Silver 0.3569 oz. ASW, 28 mm. **Subject:** Pico Island, Azores, Wine growing landscape **Obv:** National arms and tree **Rev:** Wine leaf, wine fields in background

| Date | Mintage | VF20 | XF40 | MS60 | MS63 | MS65 |
|---|---|---|---|---|---|---|
| 2011 | 3,000 | PF65 55.00 | | | | |

**KM# 815 2-1/2 EURO**
10.00 g., Copper-Nickel, 28 mm. **Subject:** José Malhoa **Obv:** Female model at left, national arms at right **Rev:** Malhoa half-length figure with artist pallet and brushes

| Date | Mintage | VF20 | XF40 | MS60 | MS63 | MS65 |
|---|---|---|---|---|---|---|
| 2012 | 100,000 | — | — | — | 6.00 | 7.00 |

**KM# 815a 2-1/2 EURO**
12.00 g., 0.925 Silver 0.3569 oz. ASW, 28 mm. **Subject:** José Malhoa **Obv:** Female model seated at left, national arms at right **Rev:** Malhoa half-length figure standing with artist pallet and brushes

| Date | Mintage | VF20 | XF40 | MS60 | MS63 | MS65 |
|---|---|---|---|---|---|---|
| 2012 | 10,000 | PF65 55.00 | | | | |

**KM# 815b 2-1/2 EURO**
15.55 g., 0.999 Gold 0.4994 oz. AGW, 28 mm. **Subject:** José Malhoa **Obv:** Female model seated at left, national arms at right **Rev:** Malhoa half-length figure standing wiht artist pallet and brushes

| Date | Mintage | VF20 | XF40 | MS60 | MS63 | MS65 |
|---|---|---|---|---|---|---|
| 2012 | 1,500 | PF65 950 | | | | |

**KM# 816 2-1/2 EURO**
10.00 g., Copper-Nickel, 28 mm. **Subject:** Portugal's participation in 2012 London Olympics **Obv:** National arms and laurel branch **Rev:** Two judo players, geometric pattern

| Date | Mintage | VF20 | XF40 | MS60 | MS63 | MS65 |
|---|---|---|---|---|---|---|
| 2012 | 300,000 | — | — | — | 10.00 | 12.00 |

**KM# 816a 2-1/2 EURO**

12.00 g., 0.925 Silver 0.3569 oz. ASW, 28 mm. **Subject:** Portugal's participation in 2012 London Olympics **Obv:** National arms and laurel branch **Rev:** Judo players, geometric pattern

| Date | Mintage | VF20 | XF40 | MS60 | MS63 | MS65 |
|---|---|---|---|---|---|---|
| 2012 | 5,000 | PF65 55.00 | | | | |

**KM# 816b 2-1/2 EURO**

Bi-Metallic 3.1 g. Gold center in 12 g. Silver ring, 28 mm. **Subject:** Portugal's participation in 2012 London Olympics **Obv:** National arms and laurel branch **Rev:** Judo players and geometric pattern

| Date | Mintage | VF20 | XF40 | MS60 | MS63 | MS65 |
|---|---|---|---|---|---|---|
| 2012 | 2,500 | PF65 600 | | | | |

**KM# 819 2-1/2 EURO**

12.00 g., Copper-Nickel, 28 mm. **Subject:** Guimarães - UNESCO World Heritage site **Obv:** National arms and city plan **Rev:** Linear architectural representations

| Date | Mintage | VF20 | XF40 | MS60 | MS63 | MS65 |
|---|---|---|---|---|---|---|
| 2012 | 100,000 | — | — | — | 25.00 | 28.00 |

**KM# 819a 2-1/2 EURO**

12.00 g., 0.925 Silver 0.3569 oz. ASW, 28 mm. **Subject:** Guimarães - UNESCO World Heritage site **Obv:** National arms, linear city plan **Rev:** Linear architectural renderings

| Date | Mintage | VF20 | XF40 | MS60 | MS63 | MS65 |
|---|---|---|---|---|---|---|
| 2012 | 3,000 | PF65 55.00 | | | | |

**KM# 830 2-1/2 EURO**

12.00 g., Silver, 28 mm. **Subject:** 100th Anniversary of Lisbon University

| Date | Mintage | VF20 | XF40 | MS60 | MS63 | MS65 |
|---|---|---|---|---|---|---|
| 2012 Proof | — | — | — | — | — | — |

**KM# 829 2-1/2 EURO**

12.00 g., Silver, 28 mm. **Subject:** Jose Saramago, nobel winner 1998 **Rev:** Portrait at right

| Date | Mintage | VF20 | XF40 | MS60 | MS63 | MS65 |
|---|---|---|---|---|---|---|
| 2013 Proof | Est. 7500 | — | — | — | — | — |

**KM# 749 5 EURO**

14.00 g., 0.500 Silver 0.2251 oz. ASW, 30 mm. **Subject:** 150th Anniversary - First Portuguese Postage Stamp **Obv:** National arms and value within partial stamp design **Rev:** Partial postal stamp design **Edge:** Reeded

| Date | Mintage | VF20 | XF40 | MS60 | MS63 | MS65 |
|---|---|---|---|---|---|---|
| 2003 INCM | 300,000 | — | — | 22.50 | 30.00 | 32.00 |

**KM# 749a 5 EURO**

14.00 g., 0.925 Silver 0.4164 oz. ASW, 30 mm. **Obv:** National arms and value within partial stamp design **Rev:** Partial postal stamp design

| Date | Mintage | VF20 | XF40 | MS60 | MS63 | MS65 |
|---|---|---|---|---|---|---|
| 2003 INCM | 20,000 | — | — | — | 30.00 | 32.00 |
| 2003 INCM | 20,000 | PF65 55.00 | | | | |

**KM# 749b 5 EURO**

17.50 g., 0.9166 Gold 0.5157 oz. AGW, 30 mm. **Obv:** National arms and value within partial stamp design **Rev:** Partial postal stamp design

| Date | Mintage | VF20 | XF40 | MS60 | MS63 | MS65 |
|---|---|---|---|---|---|---|
| 2003 INCM | 10,000 | PF65 1,000 | | | | |

**KM# 754 5 EURO**

14.00 g., 0.500 Silver 0.2251 oz. ASW, 30 mm. **Subject:** Convent of Christ **Obv:** National arms above value flanked by designs **Rev:** Ornate convent window **Edge:** Reeded

| Date | Mintage | VF20 | XF40 | MS60 | MS63 | MS65 |
|---|---|---|---|---|---|---|
| 2004 INCM | 300,000 | — | — | 30.00 | 32.50 | 35.00 |

**KM# 754a 5 EURO**

14.00 g., 0.925 Silver 0.4164 oz. ASW, 30 mm. **Subject:** Convent of Christ **Obv:** National arms above value flanked by designs **Rev:** Ornate convent window **Edge:** Reeded

| Date | Mintage | VF20 | XF40 | MS60 | MS63 | MS65 |
|---|---|---|---|---|---|---|
| 2004 INCM | 10,000 | PF65 60.00 | | | | |

**KM# 755 5 EURO**

14.00 g., 0.500 Silver 0.2251 oz. ASW, 30 mm. **Subject:** Historic City of Evora **Obv:** National arms and value on city map silhouette **Rev:** Architectural highlights **Edge:** Reeded

| Date | Mintage | VF20 | XF40 | MS60 | MS63 | MS65 |
|---|---|---|---|---|---|---|
| 2004 INCM | 300,000 | — | — | 30.00 | 32.50 | 35.00 |

**KM# 755a 5 EURO**

14.00 g., 0.925 Silver 0.4164 oz. ASW, 30 mm. **Subject:** Historic City of Evora **Obv:** National arms and value on city map silhouette **Rev:** Architectural highlights **Edge:** Reeded

| Date | Mintage | VF20 | XF40 | MS60 | MS63 | MS65 |
|---|---|---|---|---|---|---|
| 2004 INCM | 10,000 | PF65 60.00 | | | | |

**KM# 760 5 EURO**

14.00 g., 0.500 Silver 0.2251 oz. ASW, 30 mm. **Obv:** National arms within circle **Obv. Legend:** REPUBLICA POTUGUESA **Rev:** Angra do Heroismo - Azores Terceira, emblem above **Rev. Legend:** CENTRO HISTÓRICO DE ANGRA DO HEROISMA **Edge:** Reeded

| Date | Mintage | VF20 | XF40 | MS60 | MS63 | MS65 |
|---|---|---|---|---|---|---|
| 2005 | 300,000 | — | — | 30.00 | 32.50 | 35.00 |

**KM# 760a 5 EURO**

14.00 g., 0.925 Silver 0.4164 oz. ASW, 30 mm. **Obv:** National arms within circle **Obv. Legend:** REPUBLICA PORTUGUESA **Rev:** Angra do Heroisma - Azores Terceira, emblem above **Rev. Legend:** CENTRO HISTÓRICO DE ANGRA DO HEROISMA **Edge:** Reeded

| Date | Mintage | VF20 | XF40 | MS60 | MS63 | MS65 |
|---|---|---|---|---|---|---|
| 2005 | 15,000 | PF65 60.00 | | | | |

**KM# 761 5 EURO**

14.00 g., 0.500 Silver 0.2251 oz. ASW, 30 mm. **Obv:** Design divides national arms and value **Obv. Legend:** REPUBLICA PORTUGUESA **Rev:** Batalha monastery and emblem **Rev. Legend:** MONTEIRO DA BATALHA **Edge:** Reeded

| Date | Mintage | VF20 | XF40 | MS60 | MS63 | MS65 |
|---|---|---|---|---|---|---|
| 2005 | 300,000 | — | — | 30.00 | 32.50 | 35.00 |

**KM# 761a 5 EURO**

14.00 g., 0.925 Silver 0.4164 oz. ASW, 30 mm. **Obv:** Design divides national arms and value **Obv. Legend:** REPUBLICA PORTUGUESA **Rev:** Batalha monastery and emblem **Rev. Legend:** MONTEIRO DA BATALHA **Edge:** Reeded

| Date | Mintage | VF20 | XF40 | MS60 | MS63 | MS65 |
|---|---|---|---|---|---|---|
| 2005 | 15,000 | PF65 60.00 | | | | |

**KM# 762 5 EURO**

14.00 g., 0.500 Silver 0.2251 oz. ASW, 30 mm. **Subject:** 800th Anniversary Birth of Pope John XXI **Obv:** National arms at lower right with archways in backgound **Obv. Legend:** REPUBLICA PORTUGUESA **Rev:** 1/2 length figure of Pope facing at right with staff dividing dates, small shield at left **Edge:** Reeded

| Date | Mintage | VF20 | XF40 | MS60 | MS63 | MS65 |
|---|---|---|---|---|---|---|
| 2005 INCM | 300,000 | — | — | 30.00 | 32.50 | 35.00 |

**KM# 762a 5 EURO**

14.00 g., 0.925 Silver 0.4164 oz. ASW, 30 mm. **Subject:** 800th Anniversary Birth of Pope John XXI **Obv:** National arms at lower right with archways in backgound **Obv. Legend:** REPUBLICA PORTUGUESA **Rev:** 1/2 length figure of Pope facing at right with staff dividing dates, small shield at left **Edge:** Reeded

| Date | Mintage | VF20 | XF40 | MS60 | MS63 | MS65 |
|---|---|---|---|---|---|---|
| 2005 INCM | 15,000 | PF65 65.00 | | | | |

**KM# 762b 5 EURO**

17.50 g., 0.9167 Gold 0.5158 oz. AGW, 30 mm. **Subject:** 800th Anniversary Birth of Pope John XXI **Obv:** National arms at lower right, archways in background **Obv. Legend:** REPUBLICA PORTUGUESA **Edge:** Reeded

| Date | Mintage | VF20 | XF40 | MS60 | MS63 | MS65 |
|---|---|---|---|---|---|---|
| 2005 INCM | 7,500 | PF65 1,000 | | | | |

**KM# 769 5 EURO**

14.00 g., 0.500 Silver 0.2251 oz. ASW, 30 mm. **Subject:** UNESCO - Cultural preservation **Obv:** National arms above value **Obv. Legend:** REPUBLICA PORTUGUESA **Rev:** Outlined view **Rev. Legend:** PAISAGEM CULTURAL DE SINTRA **Edge:** Reeded

| Date | Mintage | VF20 | XF40 | MS60 | MS63 | MS65 |
|---|---|---|---|---|---|---|
| 2006 INCM | 82,000 | — | — | 30.00 | 32.50 | 35.00 |

**KM# 769a 5 EURO**

14.00 g., 0.925 Silver 0.4164 oz. ASW, 30 mm. **Subject:** UNESCO - Cultural preservation **Obv:** National arms above value **Obv. Legend:** REPUBLICA PORTUGUESA **Rev:** Outlined view **Rev. Legend:** PAISAGEM CULTURAL DE SINTRA **Edge:** Reeded

| Date | Mintage | VF20 | XF40 | MS60 | MS63 | MS65 |
|---|---|---|---|---|---|---|
| 2006 INCM | 6,000 | PF65 60.00 | | | | |

### KM# 779 5 EURO

14.00 g., 0.500 Silver 0.2251 oz. ASW **Subject:** Alcobaça Monastery **Obv:** National arms **Obv. Legend:** REPÚBLICA PORTUGUESA **Edge:** Reeded

| Date | Mintage | VF20 | XF40 | MS60 | MS63 | MS65 |
|---|---|---|---|---|---|---|
| 2006 INCM | 82,000 | — | — | 25.00 | 27.50 | 30.00 |

### KM# 779a 5 EURO

14.00 g., 0.925 Silver 0.4164 oz. ASW **Subject:** Alcobaça Monestary **Obv:** National arms **Obv. Legend:** REPÚBLICA PORTUGUESA **Edge:** Reeded

| Date | Mintage | VF20 | XF40 | MS60 | MS63 | MS65 |
|---|---|---|---|---|---|---|
| 2006 INCM | 6,000 | PF65 60.00 | | | | |

### KM# 770 5 EURO

14.00 g., 0.500 Silver 0.2251 oz. ASW, 30 mm. **Subject:** World Scouting Centennial **Obv:** Portuguese Arms, World Scouting emblem **Obv. Legend:** REPUBLICA PORTUGUESA 1907-2007 CENTENARIO DO ESCUTISMO MUNDIAL **Rev:** Linear portrait of Lord Robert Baden-Powell **Rev. Legend:** UM MUNDO UMA PROMESA **Edge:** Reeded

| Date | Mintage | VF20 | XF40 | MS60 | MS63 | MS65 |
|---|---|---|---|---|---|---|
| ND(2007) | 70,000 | — | — | 25.00 | 27.50 | 30.00 |

### KM# 770a 5 EURO

14.00 g., 0.925 Silver 0.4164 oz. ASW, 30 mm. **Subject:** World Scouting Centennial **Obv:** National arms, World Scouting emblem **Obv. Legend:** REPUBLICA PORTUGUESA 1907 - 2007 CENTENARIO DO ESCUTISMO MUNDIAL **Rev:** Linear portrait of Lord Robert Baden-Powell **Rev. Legend:** UM MUNDO UMA PROMESA **Edge:** Reeded

| Date | Mintage | VF20 | XF40 | MS60 | MS63 | MS65 |
|---|---|---|---|---|---|---|
| ND-2007 | 10,000 | PF65 60.00 | | | | |

### KM# 781 5 EURO

14.04 g., 0.500 Silver 0.2257 oz. ASW, 30 mm. **Subject:** Equal Opportunities **Obv:** Small national arms above moon shaped arc **Obv. Legend:** República Portuguesa **Rev:** Small 3 persons logo above 12 stars along rim **Rev. Legend:** Ano Europeu da Igualdade de Oportunidades para Todos **Edge:** Reeded

| Date | Mintage | VF20 | XF40 | MS60 | MS63 | MS65 |
|---|---|---|---|---|---|---|
| 2007 INCM | 70,000 | — | — | 25.00 | 27.50 | 30.00 |

### KM# 781a 5 EURO

14.00 g., 0.925 Silver 0.4164 oz. ASW, 30 mm. **Subject:** Equal Opportunities **Obv:** Small national arms above moon shaped arc **Obv. Legend:** República Portuguesa **Rev:** Small 3 persons logo above 12 stars along rim **Rev. Legend:** Ano Europeu da Igualdade de Oportunidades para Todos **Edge:** Reeded

| Date | Mintage | VF20 | XF40 | MS60 | MS63 | MS65 |
|---|---|---|---|---|---|---|
| 2007 INCM | 7,500 | PF65 65.00 | | | | |

### KM# 782 5 EURO

13.95 g., 0.500 Silver 0.2243 oz. ASW, 30 mm. **Series:** UNESCO - World Heritage **Subject:** National Forest Reserve in Madeira Nature Park **Obv:** National arms **Obv. Legend:** REPÚBLICA PORTUGUESA **Rev:** Foliage with small UNESCO World Heritage logo at lower right **Rev. Legend:** FLORESTA LAURISSILVA DA MADEIRA **Edge:** Reeded

| Date | Mintage | VF20 | XF40 | MS60 | MS63 | MS65 |
|---|---|---|---|---|---|---|
| 2007 INCM | 75,000 | — | — | 25.00 | 27.50 | 30.00 |

### KM# 782a 5 EURO

14.00 g., 0.925 Silver 0.4164 oz. ASW, 30 mm. **Series:** UNESCO - World Heritage **Subject:** National Forest Reserve in Madeira Nature Park **Obv:** National arms **Obv. Legend:** REPÚBLICA PORTUGUESA **Rev:** Foliage with small UNESCO World Heritage logo at lower right **Rev. Legend:** FLORESTA LAURISSILVA DA MADEIRA **Edge:** Reeded

| Date | Mintage | VF20 | XF40 | MS60 | MS63 | MS65 |
|---|---|---|---|---|---|---|
| 2007 INCM | 6,000 | PF65 65.00 | | | | |

### KM# 802 5 EURO

14.00 g., Copper-Nickel, 30 mm. **Subject:** Numismatic Treasurers - Justo of John II

| Date | Mintage | VF20 | XF40 | MS60 | MS63 | MS65 |
|---|---|---|---|---|---|---|
| 2010 INCM | 150,000 | — | — | 12.00 | 15.00 | 18.00 |

### KM# 802a 5 EURO

15.55 g., 0.999 Gold 0.4994 oz. AGW, 30 mm. **Subject:** Numismatic Treasurers - Justo of John II

| Date | Mintage | VF20 | XF40 | MS60 | MS63 | MS65 |
|---|---|---|---|---|---|---|
| 2010 INCM | 2,500 | PF65 950 | | | | |

### KM# 817 5 EURO

14.00 g., Copper-Nickel, 30 mm. **Subject:** Numismatic Treasurers - João V **Obv:** Bust right **Rev:** Crowned arms

| Date | Mintage | VF20 | XF40 | MS60 | MS63 | MS65 |
|---|---|---|---|---|---|---|
| 2012 L | 150,000 | — | — | — | 25.00 | 30.00 |

### KM# 817a 5 EURO

15.55 g., 0.999 Gold 0.4994 oz. AGW, 30 mm. **Subject:** Numismatic Treasurers - João V **Obv:** Bust right **Rev:** Crowned shield

| Date | Mintage | VF20 | XF40 | MS60 | MS63 | MS65 |
|---|---|---|---|---|---|---|
| 2012 | — | PF65 950 | | | | |

### KM# 811 7.5 EURO

18.50 g., Copper-Nickel, 33 mm. **Subject:** Numismatic Treasurers - Manuel I **Obv:** Short cross **Rev:** National Arms in center of dourble ring legend

| Date | Mintage | VF20 | XF40 | MS60 | MS63 | MS65 |
|---|---|---|---|---|---|---|
| 2011 | 100,000 | PF65 35.00 | | | | |

### KM# 811a 7.5 EURO

23.33 g., 0.999 Gold 0.7493 oz. AGW, 33 mm. **Subject:** Numismatic Treasurers - Manuel I **Obv:** Short Cross **Rev:** Crowned national shield within double ring legend

| Date | Mintage | VF20 | XF40 | MS60 | MS63 | MS65 |
|---|---|---|---|---|---|---|
| 2011 | — | PF65 1,425 | | | | |

### KM# 750 8 EURO

21.10 g., 0.500 Silver 0.3392 oz. ASW, 36 mm. **Obv:** National arms, value and flag-covered globe **Rev:** Flag-covered globe and "Euro 2004" soccer games logo **Edge:** Reeded

| Date | Mintage | VF20 | XF40 | MS60 | MS63 | MS65 |
|---|---|---|---|---|---|---|
| 2003 INCM | 1,500,000 | — | — | 35.00 | 37.50 | 42.00 |

### KM# 750a 8 EURO

31.10 g., 0.925 Silver 0.9249 oz. ASW, 36 mm. **Obv:** National arms, value and flag-covered globe **Rev:** Flag-covered globe and "Euro 2004" soccer games logo

| Date | Mintage | VF20 | XF40 | MS60 | MS63 | MS65 |
|---|---|---|---|---|---|---|
| 2003 INCM Prooflike | 30,000 | — | — | — | 100 | 120 |
| 2003 INCM | 15,000 | PF65 165 | | | | |

### KM# 750b 8 EURO

31.10 g., 0.9166 Gold 0.9165 oz. AGW, 36 mm. **Obv:** National arms, value and flag-covered globe **Rev:** Flag-covered globe and "Euro 2004" soccer games logo

| Date | Mintage | VF20 | XF40 | MS60 | MS63 | MS65 |
|---|---|---|---|---|---|---|
| 2003 INCM | 10,000 | PF65 1,850 | | | | |

### KM# 751 8 EURO

21.10 g., 0.500 Silver 0.3392 oz. ASW, 36 mm. **Obv:** National arms and value below many bubbles **Rev:** Euro 2004" soccer games logo below many hearts **Edge:** Reeded

| Date | Mintage | VF20 | XF40 | MS60 | MS63 | MS65 |
|---|---|---|---|---|---|---|
| 2003 INCM | 1,500,000 | — | — | 35.00 | 37.50 | 42.00 |

### KM# 751a 8 EURO

31.10 g., 0.925 Silver 0.9249 oz. ASW, 36 mm. **Obv:** National arms and value below many bubbles **Rev:** Euro 2004" soccer games logo below many hearts

| Date | Mintage | VF20 | XF40 | MS60 | MS63 | MS65 |
|---|---|---|---|---|---|---|
| 2003 INCM Prooflike | — | — | — | — | 100 | 120 |
| 2003 INCM | 15,000 | PF65 165 | | | | |

### KM# 751b 8 EURO

31.10 g., 0.9166 Gold 0.9165 oz. AGW, 36 mm. **Obv:** National arms and value below many bubbles **Rev:** Euro 2004" soccer games logo below many hearts

| Date | Mintage | VF20 | XF40 | MS60 | MS63 | MS65 |
|---|---|---|---|---|---|---|
| 2003 INCM | 10,000 | PF65 1,850 | | | | |

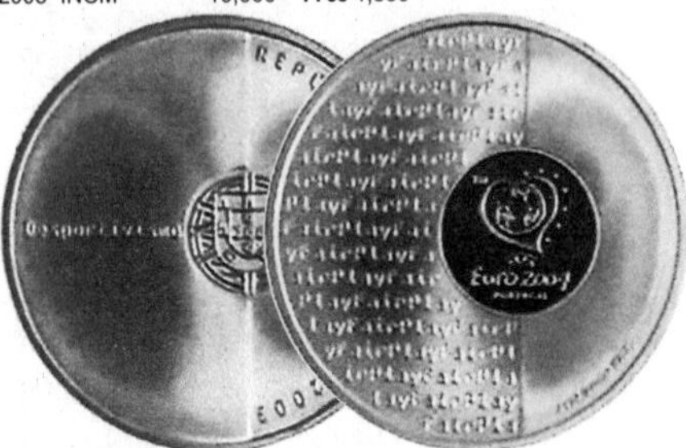

### KM# 752 8 EURO

21.10 g., 0.500 Silver 0.3392 oz. ASW, 36 mm. **Obv:** National arms and value **Rev:** Euro 2004" soccer games logo in center with partial text background **Edge:** Reeded

| Date | Mintage | VF20 | XF40 | MS60 | MS63 | MS65 |
|---|---|---|---|---|---|---|
| 2003 INCM | 1,500,000 | — | — | 35.00 | 37.50 | 42.00 |

### KM# 752a 8 EURO

31.10 g., 0.925 Silver 0.9249 oz. ASW, 36 mm. **Obv:** National arms and value **Rev:** Euro 2004" soccer games logo in center with partial text background

| Date | Mintage | VF20 | XF40 | MS60 | MS63 | MS65 |
|---|---|---|---|---|---|---|
| 2003 INCM Prooflike | — | — | — | — | 100 | 120 |
| 2003 INCM | 15,000 | PF65 165 | | | | |

### KM# 752b 8 EURO

31.10 g., 0.9166 Gold 0.9165 oz. AGW, 36 mm. **Obv:** National arms and value **Rev:** Euro 2004" soccer games logo in center with partial text background

| Date | Mintage | VF20 | XF40 | MS60 | MS63 | MS65 |
|---|---|---|---|---|---|---|
| 2003 INCM | 10,000 | PF65 1,850 | | | | |

### KM# 753 8 EURO

21.22 g., 0.500 Silver 0.3411 oz. ASW, 36 mm. **Subject:** Expansion of the European Union **Obv:** Radiant national arms and value **Rev:** European map **Edge:** Reeded

| Date | Mintage | VF20 | XF40 | MS60 | MS63 | MS65 |
|---|---|---|---|---|---|---|
| 2004 INCM | 300,000 | — | — | 25.00 | 27.50 | 30.00 |

### KM# 753a 8 EURO

31.10 g., 0.925 Silver 0.9249 oz. ASW, 36 mm. **Subject:** Expansion of the European Union **Obv:** Radiant national arms and value **Rev:** European map **Edge:** Reeded

| Date | Mintage | VF20 | XF40 | MS60 | MS63 | MS65 |
|---|---|---|---|---|---|---|
| 2004 INCM | 35,000 | PF63 50.00 | PF65 60.00 | | | |

### KM# 756 8 EURO

21.00 g., 0.500 Silver 0.3376 oz. ASW, 36 mm. **Subject:** Euro 2004 Soccer **Obv:** National arms **Rev:** Stylized goal keeper **Edge:** Reeded

| Date | Mintage | VF20 | XF40 | MS60 | MS63 | MS65 |
|---|---|---|---|---|---|---|
| 2004 INCM | 1,500,000 | — | — | 25.00 | 27.50 | 30.00 |

### KM# 756a 8 EURO

31.10 g., 0.925 Silver 0.9249 oz. ASW, 36 mm. **Subject:** Euro 2004 Soccer **Obv:** National arms **Rev:** Stylized goal keeper **Edge:** Reeded

| Date | Mintage | VF20 | XF40 | MS60 | MS63 | MS65 |
|---|---|---|---|---|---|---|
| 2004 INCM | 30,000 | — | — | — | 80.00 | 85.00 |
| 2004 INCM | 15,000 | PF65 150 | | | | |

### KM# 756b 8 EURO

31.10 g., 0.9166 Gold 0.9165 oz. AGW, 36 mm. **Subject:** Euro 2004 Soccer **Obv:** National arms **Rev:** Stylized goal keeper **Edge:** Reeded

| Date | Mintage | VF20 | XF40 | MS60 | MS63 | MS65 |
|---|---|---|---|---|---|---|
| 2004 INCM | 10,000 | PF65 1,850 | | | | |

### KM# 757 8 EURO

21.00 g., 0.925 Silver 0.6245 oz. ASW, 36 mm. **Subject:** Euro 2004 Soccer **Obv:** National arms **Rev:** Face of player making shot **Edge:** Reeded

| Date | Mintage | VF20 | XF40 | MS60 | MS63 | MS65 |
|---|---|---|---|---|---|---|
| 2004 INCM | 1,500,000 | — | — | 25.00 | 27.50 | 30.00 |

### KM# 757a 8 EURO

31.10 g., 0.925 Silver 0.9249 oz. ASW, 36 mm. **Subject:** Euro 2004 Soccer **Obv:** National arms **Rev:** Face of player making a shot **Edge:** Reeded

| Date | Mintage | VF20 | XF40 | MS60 | MS63 | MS65 |
|---|---|---|---|---|---|---|
| 2004 INCM | 15,000 | PF65 150 | | | | |
| 2004 INCM | 30,000 | — | — | — | 80.00 | 85.00 |

### KM# 757b 8 EURO

31.10 g., 0.9166 Gold 0.9165 oz. AGW, 36 mm. **Subject:** Euro 2004 Soccer **Obv:** National arms **Rev:** Face of player making a shot **Edge:** Reeded

| Date | Mintage | VF20 | XF40 | MS60 | MS63 | MS65 |
|---|---|---|---|---|---|---|
| 2004 INCM | 10,000 | PF65 1,850 | | | | |

### KM# 758 8 EURO

21.00 g., 0.500 Silver 0.3376 oz. ASW, 36 mm. **Subject:** Euro 2004 Soccer **Obv:** National arms **Rev:** Symbolic explosion of a goal **Edge:** Reeded

| Date | Mintage | VF20 | XF40 | MS60 | MS63 | MS65 |
|---|---|---|---|---|---|---|
| 2004 INCM | 1,500,000 | — | — | 25.00 | 27.50 | 30.00 |

### KM# 758a 8 EURO

31.10 g., 0.925 Silver 0.9249 oz. ASW, 36 mm. **Subject:** Euro 2004 Soccer **Obv:** National arms **Rev:** Symbolic explosion of a goal **Edge:** Reeded

| Date | Mintage | VF20 | XF40 | MS60 | MS63 | MS65 |
|---|---|---|---|---|---|---|
| 2004 INCM | 30,000 | — | — | — | 80.00 | 85.00 |
| 2004 INCM | 15,000 | PF65 150 | | | | |

### KM# 758b 8 EURO

31.10 g., 0.9166 Gold 0.9165 oz. AGW, 36 mm. **Subject:** Euro 2004 Soccer **Obv:** National arms **Rev:** Symbolic explosion of a goal **Edge:** Reeded

| Date | Mintage | VF20 | XF40 | MS60 | MS63 | MS65 |
|---|---|---|---|---|---|---|
| 2004 INCM | 10,000 | PF65 1,850 | | | | |

### KM# 773 8 EURO

21.00 g., 0.500 Silver 0.3376 oz. ASW, 36 mm. **Subject:** 60th Anniversary End of WW II **Obv:** Quill pens horizontal at left center, national arms at lower righr **Obv. Inscription:** REPÚBLICA PORTUGUESA **Rev:** Four quill pens upright, outlined map of Europe in background **Rev. Inscription:** FIM DA II GUERRA MUNDIAL **Edge:** Reeded

| Date | Mintage | VF20 | XF40 | MS60 | MS63 | MS65 |
|---|---|---|---|---|---|---|
| 2005 INCM | 300,000 | — | — | 30.00 | 32.50 | 35.00 |

### KM# 773a 8 EURO

31.10 g., 0.925 Silver 0.9249 oz. ASW, 36 mm. **Subject:** 60th Anniversary End of WW II **Obv:** Quill pens horizontal at left center, national arms at lower right **Obv. Inscription:** REPÚBLICA PORTUGUESA **Rev:** Four quill pens upright, outlined map of Europe in background **Rev. Inscription:** FIM DA II GUERRA MUNDIAL **Edge:** Reeded

| Date | Mintage | VF20 | XF40 | MS60 | MS63 | MS65 |
|---|---|---|---|---|---|---|
| 2005 INCM | 35,000 | PF63 60.00 | PF65 70.00 | | | |

### KM# 776 8 EURO

20.80 g., 0.500 Silver 0.3344 oz. ASW, 36 mm. **Series:** Famous Europeans **Subject:** Prince Henry the Navigator **Obv:** Small national arms and shield **Obv. Legend:** REPÚBLICA PORTUGUESA **Rev:** Tiny bust 3/4 right **Edge:** Reeded

| Date | Mintage | VF20 | XF40 | MS60 | MS63 | MS65 |
|---|---|---|---|---|---|---|
| 2006 INCM | 100,000 | — | — | 30.00 | 32.50 | 35.00 |

### KM# 776a 8 EURO

31.10 g., 0.925 Silver 0.9249 oz. ASW, 36 mm. **Series:** Famous Europeans **Subject:** Prince Henry the Navigator **Obv:** Small national arms and shield **Obv. Legend:** REPÚBLICA PORTUGUESA **Rev:** Tiny bust 3/4 right **Edge:** Reeded

| Date | Mintage | VF20 | XF40 | MS60 | MS63 | MS65 |
|---|---|---|---|---|---|---|
| 2006 INCM | 35,000 | PF63 55.00 | PF65 65.00 | | | |

### KM# 778 8 EURO

21.00 g., 0.500 Silver 0.3376 oz. ASW, 36 mm. **Subject:** 150th Anniversary Railroad Lisbon - Carregado **Obv:** National arms on wavy flag **Obv. Legend:** REPÚBLICA PORTUGUESA **Rev:** Vertical railroad track divides two shields **Rev. Legend:** 150 ANOS DA PRIMEIRA LINHA FERREA LISBOA CARREGADO **Edge:** Reeded

| Date | Mintage | VF20 | XF40 | MS60 | MS63 | MS65 |
|---|---|---|---|---|---|---|
| 2006 INCM | 100,000 | — | — | 32.50 | 35.00 | 38.00 |

### KM# 778a 8 EURO

31.10 g., 0.925 Silver 0.9249 oz. ASW, 36 mm. **Subject:** 150th Anniversary Railroad Lisbon - Carregado **Obv:** National srms on wavy flag **Obv. Legend:** REPÚBLICA PORTUGUESA **Rev:** Vertical railroad track divides two shields **Rev. Legend:** 150 ANOSDA PRIMEIRA LINHA FERREA LISBOA CARREGADO **Edge:** Reeded

| Date | Mintage | VF20 | XF40 | MS60 | MS63 | MS65 |
|---|---|---|---|---|---|---|
| 2006 INCM | 35,000 | PF63 65.00 | PF65 75.00 | | | |

### KM# 822 8 EURO

21.00 g., 0.500 Silver 0.3376 oz. ASW, 36 mm. **Subject:** Early flying inventions - the Passarola of Bartolomeu de Gusmão **Obv:** Large value and small national arms **Rev:** Schematic of flying machine

| Date | Mintage | VF20 | XF40 | MS60 | MS63 | MS65 |
|---|---|---|---|---|---|---|
| 2007 | 70,000 | — | — | 20.00 | 25.00 | 28.00 |

### KM# 822a 8 EURO

31.11 g., 0.925 Silver 0.925 oz. ASW, 36 mm. **Subject:** Early flying inventions - the Passarola of Bartolomeu de Gusmão **Obv:** Large value, small national arms **Rev:** Schematic of early flying machine

| Date | Mintage | VF20 | XF40 | MS60 | MS63 | MS65 |
|---|---|---|---|---|---|---|
| 2007 | 25,000 | PF65 65.00 | | | | |

### KM# 748 10 EURO

27.00 g., 0.500 Silver 0.434 oz. ASW, 40 mm. **Subject:** Nautica **Obv:** National arms within circle of assorted shields **Rev:** Sailing ship and sextant **Edge:** Reeded

| Date | Mintage | VF20 | XF40 | MS60 | MS63 | MS65 |
|---|---|---|---|---|---|---|
| 2003 INCM | 350,000 | — | — | 22.50 | 25.00 | 28.00 |

### KM# 748a 10 EURO

27.00 g., 0.925 Silver 0.803 oz. ASW, 40 mm. **Obv:** National arms within circle of assorted shields **Rev:** Sailing ship and sextant **Edge:** Reeded

| Date | Mintage | VF20 | XF40 | MS60 | MS63 | MS65 |
|---|---|---|---|---|---|---|
| 2003 INCM | 10,000 | PF65 70.00 | | | | |

### KM# 759 10 EURO

27.00 g., 0.500 Silver 0.434 oz. ASW, 40 mm. **Subject:** Olympics **Obv:** National arms above stylized value **Rev:** Stylized sail above Olympic rings **Edge:** Reeded

| Date | Mintage | VF20 | XF40 | MS60 | MS63 | MS65 |
|---|---|---|---|---|---|---|
| 2004 INCM | 350,000 | — | — | 25.00 | 27.50 | 30.00 |

### KM# 759a 10 EURO

27.00 g., 0.925 Silver 0.803 oz. ASW, 40 mm. **Subject:** Olympics **Obv:** National arms above stylized value **Rev:** Stylized sail above Olympic rings **Edge:** Reeded

| Date | Mintage | VF20 | XF40 | MS60 | MS63 | MS65 |
|---|---|---|---|---|---|---|
| 2004 INCM | 15,000 | PF65 65.00 | | | | |

### KM# 768 10 EURO

27.00 g., 0.500 Silver 0.434 oz. ASW, 40 mm. **Subject:** Arquitectura e Monumentos - Sé do Porto **Obv:** National arms above value in circle of multi-national coats of arms **Rev:** Church facade **Edge:** Reeded

| Date | Mintage | VF20 | XF40 | MS60 | MS63 | MS65 |
|---|---|---|---|---|---|---|
| 2005 INCM | — | — | — | — | 30.00 | 35.00 |
| 2005 INCM | 300,000 | PF63 75.00 | PF65 85.00 | | | |

### KM# 820 10 EURO

27.00 g., 0.500 Silver 0.434 oz. ASW, 40 mm. **Subject:** Iberoamerican series - Architecture **Rev:** Façade of the Cathedral Sé de Porto

| Date | Mintage | VF20 | XF40 | MS60 | MS63 | MS65 |
|---|---|---|---|---|---|---|
| 2005 | 30,000 | — | — | 30.00 | 35.00 | 38.00 |

### KM# 820a 10 EURO

27.00 g., 0.925 Silver 0.803 oz. ASW, 40 mm. **Subject:** Iberoamerican Series - Architecture **Rev:** Façade of Cathedral of Sé do Porto

| Date | Mintage | VF20 | XF40 | MS60 | MS63 | MS65 |
|---|---|---|---|---|---|---|
| 2005 | 12,000 | PF65 115 | | | | |

### KM# 774 10 EURO

27.00 g., 0.500 Silver 0.434 oz. ASW, 40 mm. **Subject:** XVIII World Championship Football Games - Germany 2006 **Obv:** National arms above stadium **Obv. Legend:** REPÚBLICA PORTUGUESA **Rev:** Circular legend above sticks representing stadium fans **Rev. Legend:** CAMPEONATO DO MUNDO DE FUTEBOL FIFA ALEMANHA 2006 **Edge:** Reeded

| Date | Mintage | VF20 | XF40 | MS60 | MS63 | MS65 |
|---|---|---|---|---|---|---|
| 2006 INCM | 100,000 | — | — | 37.50 | 40.00 | 45.00 |

### KM# 774a 10 EURO

27.00 g., 0.925 Silver 0.803 oz. ASW, 40 mm. **Subject:** XVIII World Championship Football Games - Germany 2006 **Obv:** National arms above stadium **Obv. Inscription:** REPÚBLICA PORTUGUESA **Rev:** Circular legend above sticks representing stadium fans **Edge:** Reeded

| Date | Mintage | VF20 | XF40 | MS60 | MS63 | MS65 |
|---|---|---|---|---|---|---|
| 2006 INCM | 25,000 | PF63 75.00 | PF65 85.00 | | | |

### KM# 775 10 EURO

27.00 g., 0.500 Silver 0.434 oz. ASW, 40 mm. **Subject:** 20th Anniversary of Spain and Portugal's membership in the European Union **Obv:** National arms **Obv. Legend:** REPÚBLICA PORTUGUESA **Rev:** Viaduct, outlined map of Europe above **Rev. Legend:** ADESÃO AS COMUNIDADES EUROPIAS **Edge:** Reeded

| Date | Mintage | VF20 | XF40 | MS60 | MS63 | MS65 |
|---|---|---|---|---|---|---|
| 2006 INCM | 100,000 | — | — | 27.50 | 30.00 | 35.00 |

### KM# 775a 10 EURO

27.00 g., 0.925 Silver 0.803 oz. ASW, 40 mm. **Subject:** 20th Anniversary of Spain and Portugal's membership in European Union **Obv:** National arms **Obv. Legend:** REPÚBLICA PORTUGUESA **Rev:** Viaduct, outlined map of Europe above **Rev. Legend:** ADESÃO AS COMUNIDADES EUROPIAS **Edge:** Reeded

| Date | Mintage | VF20 | XF40 | MS60 | MS63 | MS65 |
|---|---|---|---|---|---|---|
| 2006 INCM | 25,000 | PF63 60.00 | PF65 70.00 | | | |

**KM# 821 10 EURO**
27.00 g., 0.500 Silver 0.434 oz. ASW, 40 mm. **Subject:** Iberoamerican Series - Olympics **Rev:** Warrior running, two modern runners

| Date | Mintage | VF20 | XF40 | MS60 | MS63 | MS65 |
|---|---|---|---|---|---|---|
| 2007 | 100,000 | — | — | 25.00 | 30.00 | 35.00 |

**KM# 821a 10 EURO**
27.00 g., 0.925 Silver 0.803 oz. ASW, 40 mm. **Subject:** Iberoamerican Series - Olympics **Rev:** Ancient warrior running, two modern runners

| Date | Mintage | VF20 | XF40 | MS60 | MS63 | MS65 |
|---|---|---|---|---|---|---|
| 2007 | 12,000 | **PF65** 115 | | | | |

**KM# 823 10 EURO**
27.00 g., 0.500 Silver 0.434 oz. ASW, 40 mm. **Subject:** Sailing World Cup - Cascais **Obv:** National arms and stylized sails and waves **Rev:** Stylized sails and waves

| Date | Mintage | VF20 | XF40 | MS60 | MS63 | MS65 |
|---|---|---|---|---|---|---|
| 2007 | 70,000 | — | — | 25.00 | 30.00 | 35.00 |

**KM# 823a 10 EURO**
27.00 g., 0.925 Silver 0.803 oz. ASW, 40 mm. **Subject:** World Sailing Championships - Cascais **Obv:** National arms and stylized sails and waves **Rev:** Stylized sails and waves

| Date | Mintage | VF20 | XF40 | MS60 | MS63 | MS65 |
|---|---|---|---|---|---|---|
| 2007 | 7,500 | **PF65** 75.00 | | | | |

**KM# 803 10 EURO**
27.00 g., 0.925 Silver 0.803 oz. ASW, 40 mm. **Subject:** The Escudo

| Date | Mintage | VF20 | XF40 | MS60 | MS63 | MS65 |
|---|---|---|---|---|---|---|
| 2010 INCM | 100,000 | — | — | 32.50 | 35.00 | 40.00 |

**KM# 803a 10 EURO**
27.00 g., 0.500 Silver 0.434 oz. ASW, 40 mm. **Subject:** The Escudo

| Date | Mintage | VF20 | XF40 | MS60 | MS63 | MS65 |
|---|---|---|---|---|---|---|
| 2010 INCM | 12,000 | **PF65** 85.00 | | | | |

**KM# 808 10 EURO**
27.00 g., Copper-Nickel, 40 mm. **Subject:** Spain and Portugal's accession to the European Union, 25th Anniversary

| Date | Mintage | VF20 | XF40 | MS60 | MS63 | MS65 |
|---|---|---|---|---|---|---|
| 2011 | 100,000 | — | — | — | 7.00 | 9.00 |

**KM# 808a 10 EURO**
27.00 g., 0.925 Silver 0.803 oz. ASW, 40 mm. **Subject:** Spain and Portugal's accession to the European Union, 25th Anniversary

| Date | Mintage | VF20 | XF40 | MS60 | MS63 | MS65 |
|---|---|---|---|---|---|---|
| 2011 | 6,000 | **PF65** 55.00 | | | | |

**KM# 818 10 EURO**
27.00 g., Copper-Nickel, 40 mm. **Subject:** Ibero-American series, 20th Anniversary **Obv:** National arms in center of other countries arms **Rev:** Stylized sails

| Date | Mintage | VF20 | XF40 | MS60 | MS63 | MS65 |
|---|---|---|---|---|---|---|
| 2012 | 100,000 | — | — | — | 25.00 | 30.00 |

**KM# 818a 10 EURO**
27.00 g., 0.925 Silver 0.803 oz. ASW, 40 mm. **Subject:** Ibero-American series, 20th Anniversary **Obv:** National arms at center of other national arms **Rev:** Stylized sails

| Date | Mintage | VF20 | XF40 | MS60 | MS63 | MS65 |
|---|---|---|---|---|---|---|
| 2012 | 10,000 | **PF65** 55.00 | | | | |

## MINT SETS

| KM# | Date | Mintage | Identification | Issue Price | Mkt Val |
|---|---|---|---|---|---|
| MS32 | 2002 (8) | 50,000 | KM#740-747 | — | 50.00 |
| MS33 | 2003 (8) | 50,000 | KM#740-747 | — | 50.00 |
| MS34 | 2004 (8) | 50,000 | KM#740-747 | — | 45.00 |
| MS35 | 2005 (8) | 30,000 | KM#740-747 | — | 45.00 |
| MS36 | 2006 (8) | 12,500 | KM#740-747 | — | 45.00 |

## PROOF SETS

| KM# | Date | Mintage | Identification | Issue Price | Mkt Val |
|---|---|---|---|---|---|
| PS45 | 2002 (8) | 15,000 | KM#740-747 | — | 100 |
| PS46 | 2003 (8) | 15,000 | kM#740-747 | — | 100 |
| PS47 | 2004 (8) | 15,000 | KM#740-747 | — | 100 |
| PS48 | 2005 (8) | 10,000 | KM#740-747 | — | 100 |
| PS49 | 2006 (8) | 3,000 | KM#740-747 | — | 100 |
| PS50 | 2007 (8) | 2,500 | KM#740-747 | — | 300 |
| PS51 | 2008 (8) | 3,500 | KM#740-742, 763-767 | — | 150 |
| PS52 | 2009 (8) | 4,000 | KM#740-742, 763-767 | — | 150 |
| PS53 | 2010 (8) | 4,500 | KM#740-742, 763-767 | — | 100 |
| PS54 | 2011 (8) | 3,500 | KM#740-742, 763-767 | — | 100 |

# QATAR

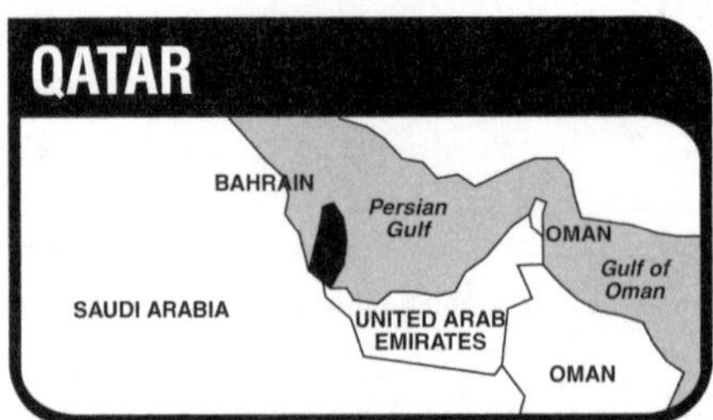


The State of Qatar, an emirate in the Persian Gulf between Bahrain and Trucial Oman, has an area of 4,247 sq. mi. (11,000 sq. km.) and a population of *469,000. Capital: Doha. Oil is the chief industry and export.

**TITLES**

دولة قطر

Daulat Qatar

**RULER**

**Al-Thani Dynasty**

Hamad bin Khalifah, 1995-

**MONETARY SYSTEM**

100 Dirhem = 1 Riyal

## STATE

## STANDARD COINAGE

**KM# 69 DIRHAM**
Copper Plated Steel, 15 mm. **Ruler:** Hamad bin Khalifa **Obv:** National Arms **Rev:** Value

| Date | Mintage | VF20 | XF40 | MS60 | MS63 | MS65 |
|---|---|---|---|---|---|---|
| AH1429-2008 | — | — | — | 5.00 | 7.00 | 9.00 |
| AH1433-2012 | — | — | — | 4.00 | 6.00 | 7.00 |

**KM# 12 5 DIRHAMS**
3.75 g., Bronze, 21.9 mm. **Ruler:** Hamad bin Khalifa **Obv:** National arms **Rev:** Value **Edge:** Plain

| Date | Mintage | VF20 | XF40 | MS60 | MS63 | MS65 |
|---|---|---|---|---|---|---|
| AH1427-2006 | — | — | 0.35 | 0.75 | 1.00 | 1.50 |

**KM# 13 10 DIRHAMS**
7.50 g., Bronze, 27 mm. **Ruler:** Hamad bin Khalifa **Obv:** National arms **Rev:** Value **Edge:** Plain

| Date | Mintage | VF20 | XF40 | MS60 | MS63 | MS65 |
|---|---|---|---|---|---|---|
| AH1427-2006 | — | — | 0.60 | 1.65 | 2.50 | 3.50 |

**KM# 8 25 DIRHAMS**
3.50 g., Copper-Nickel, 20 mm. **Ruler:** Hamad bin Khalifa **Obv:** National arms **Rev:** Value **Rev. Legend:** STATE OF QATAR **Edge:** Reeded

| Date | Mintage | VF20 | XF40 | MS60 | MS63 | MS65 |
|---|---|---|---|---|---|---|
| AH1424-2003 | — | 0.30 | 0.65 | 1.50 | 2.00 | 3.00 |

**KM# 14 25 DIRHAMS**
3.50 g., Copper-Nickel, 20 mm. **Ruler:** Hamad bin Khalifa **Obv:** National arms **Rev:** Value **Edge:** Reeded

| Date | Mintage | VF20 | XF40 | MS60 | MS63 | MS65 |
|---|---|---|---|---|---|---|
| AH1427-2006 | — | — | 0.75 | 1.85 | 2.25 | 3.50 |
| AH1429-2008 | — | — | 0.75 | 1.85 | 2.25 | 3.50 |
| AH1433-2012 | — | — | 0.75 | 1.85 | 2.25 | 3.50 |

**KM# 14a 25 DIRHAMS**
Nickel Plated Steel, 20 mm. **Ruler:** Hamad bin Khalifa **Obv:** National Arms **Rev:** Value

| Date | Mintage | VF20 | XF40 | MS60 | MS63 | MS65 |
|---|---|---|---|---|---|---|
| AH1429-2008 | — | — | — | 1.00 | 1.50 | 3.00 |

**KM# 9 50 DIRHAMS**
6.50 g., Copper-Nickel, 25 mm. **Ruler:** Hamad bin Khalifa **Obv:** National arms **Rev:** Value **Edge:** Reeded

| Date | Mintage | VF20 | XF40 | MS60 | MS63 | MS65 |
|---|---|---|---|---|---|---|
| AH1424-2003 | — | — | — | 2.00 | 3.00 | 5.00 |

**KM# 15 50 DIRHAMS**
6.50 g., Copper-Nickel, 25 mm. **Ruler:** Hamad bin Khalifa **Obv:** National arms **Rev:** Value **Edge:** Reeded

| Date | Mintage | VF20 | XF40 | MS60 | MS63 | MS65 |
|---|---|---|---|---|---|---|
| AH1427-2006 | — | — | 0.80 | 2.00 | 2.75 | 4.00 |
| AH1429-2008 | — | — | 0.80 | 2.00 | 2.75 | 4.00 |
| AH1433-2012 | — | — | 0.80 | 2.00 | 2.75 | 4.00 |

**KM# 15a 50 DIRHAMS**
6.50 g., Nickel Plated Steel, 25 mm. **Ruler:** Hamad bin Khalifa **Obv:** National Arms **Rev:** Value

| Date | Mintage | VF20 | XF40 | MS60 | MS63 | MS65 |
|---|---|---|---|---|---|---|
| AH1429-2008 | — | — | — | 2.25 | 4.50 | 7.00 |

**KM# 16 RIYAL**
Aluminum-Bronze **Ruler:** Hamad bin Khalifa **Subject:** 15th Asian Games **Obv:** Arms above value **Rev:** Multicolor Fox on Bicycle, cartoon character

| Date | Mintage | VF20 | XF40 | MS60 | MS63 | MS65 |
|---|---|---|---|---|---|---|
| 2006 | — | — | — | — | 25.00 | 30.00 |

**KM# 34 RIYAL**
Aluminum-Bronze, 38.74 mm. **Ruler:** Hamad bin Khalifa **Subject:** 15th Asian Games **Obv:** Arms **Rev:** Multicolor mascot with flag

| Date | Mintage | VF20 | XF40 | MS60 | MS63 | MS65 |
|---|---|---|---|---|---|---|
| 2006 | 25,000 | — | — | — | 25.00 | 30.00 |

**KM# 35 RIYAL**
Aluminum-Bronze, 38.74 mm. **Ruler:** Hamad bin Khalifa **Subject:** 15th Asian Games **Obv:** Arms **Rev:** Multicolor mascot kicking soccer ball

| Date | Mintage | VF20 | XF40 | MS60 | MS63 | MS65 |
|---|---|---|---|---|---|---|
| 2006 | 25,000 | — | — | — | 25.00 | 30.00 |

**KM# 36 RIYAL**
Aluminum-Bronze, 38.74 mm. **Ruler:** Hamad bin Khalifa **Subject:** 15th Asian Games **Obv:** Arms **Rev:** Three multicolor torches

| Date | Mintage | VF20 | XF40 | MS60 | MS63 | MS65 |
|---|---|---|---|---|---|---|
| 2006 | 25,000 | — | — | — | 25.00 | 30.00 |

**KM# 37 RIYAL**
Aluminum-Bronze, 38.74 mm. **Ruler:** Hamad bin Khalifa **Subject:** 15th Asian Games **Obv:** Arms **Rev:** Two figures with linked arms

| Date | Mintage | VF20 | XF40 | MS60 | MS63 | MS65 |
|---|---|---|---|---|---|---|
| 2006 | 25,000 | — | — | — | 25.00 | 30.00 |

**KM# 38 RIYAL**
Aluminum-Bronze, 38.74 mm. **Ruler:** Hamad bin Khalifa **Subject:** 15th Asian Games **Obv:** Arms **Rev:** Figure with outstretched arms

| Date | Mintage | VF20 | XF40 | MS60 | MS63 | MS65 |
|---|---|---|---|---|---|---|
| 2006 | 25,000 | — | — | — | 25.00 | 30.00 |

**KM# 25 10 RIYALS**
31.10 g., 0.999 Silver 0.999 oz. ASW, 40.5 mm. **Ruler:** Hamad bin Khalifa **Subject:** 15th Asian Games **Obv:** Arms **Rev:** Runner trailing green color

| Date | Mintage | VF20 | XF40 | MS60 | MS63 | MS65 |
|---|---|---|---|---|---|---|
| 2006 | 25,000 | **PF63** 100 | **PF65** 110 | | | |

**KM# 26 10 RIYALS**
31.10 g., 0.999 Silver 0.999 oz. ASW, 40.5 mm. **Ruler:** Hamad bin Khalifa **Subject:** 15th Asian Games **Obv:** Arms **Rev:** Cyclist trailing red color

| Date | Mintage | VF20 | XF40 | MS60 | MS63 | MS65 |
|---|---|---|---|---|---|---|
| 2006 | 25,000 | **PF63** 100 | **PF65** 110 | | | |

**KM# 27 10 RIYALS**
31.10 g., 0.999 Silver 0.999 oz. ASW, 40.5 mm. **Ruler:** Hamad bin Khalifa **Subject:** 15th Asian Games **Obv:** Arms **Rev:** Soccer player legs on green color

| Date | Mintage | VF20 | XF40 | MS60 | MS63 | MS65 |
|---|---|---|---|---|---|---|
| 2006 | 25,000 | **PF63** 100 | **PF65** 110 | | | |

**KM# 28 10 RIYALS**
31.10 g., 0.999 Silver 0.999 oz. ASW, 40.5 mm. **Ruler:** Hamad bin Khalifa **Subject:** 15th Asian Games **Obv:** Arms **Rev:** Ribbon dancer trailing red color

| Date | Mintage | VF20 | XF40 | MS60 | MS63 | MS65 |
|---|---|---|---|---|---|---|
| 2006 | 25,000 | **PF63** 100 | **PF65** 110 | | | |

**KM# 29 10 RIYALS**
31.10 g., 0.999 Silver 0.999 oz. ASW, 40.5 mm. **Ruler:** Hamad bin Khalifa **Subject:** 15th Asian Games **Obv:** Arms **Rev:** Karate contestants and dark yellow color

| Date | Mintage | VF20 | XF40 | MS60 | MS63 | MS65 |
|---|---|---|---|---|---|---|
| 2006 | 25,000 | **PF63** 100 | **PF65** 110 | | | |

**KM# 30 10 RIYALS**
31.10 g., 0.999 Silver 0.999 oz. ASW, 40.5 mm. **Ruler:** Hamad bin Khalifa **Subject:** 15th Asian Games **Obv:** Arms **Rev:** Swimmer in aqua colored water

| Date | Mintage | VF20 | XF40 | MS60 | MS63 | MS65 |
|---|---|---|---|---|---|---|
| 2006 | 25,000 | **PF63** 100 | **PF65** 110 | | | |

**KM# 31 10 RIYALS**
31.10 g., 0.999 Silver 0.999 oz. ASW, 40.5 mm. **Ruler:** Hamad bin Khalifa **Subject:** 15th Asian Games **Obv:** Arms **Rev:** Table tennis player and orange-brownish color

| Date | Mintage | VF20 | XF40 | MS60 | MS63 | MS65 |
|---|---|---|---|---|---|---|
| 2006 | 25,000 | **PF63** 100 | **PF65** 110 | | | |

**KM# 32 10 RIYALS**
31.10 g., 0.999 Silver 0.999 oz. ASW, 40.5 mm. **Ruler:** Hamad bin Khalifa **Subject:** 15th Asian Games **Obv:** Arms **Rev:** Tennis player and aqua color

| Date | Mintage | VF20 | XF40 | MS60 | MS63 | MS65 |
|---|---|---|---|---|---|---|
| 2006 | 25,000 | **PF63** 100 | **PF65** 110 | | | |

**KM# 33 10 RIYALS**
31.10 g., 0.999 Silver 0.999 oz. ASW, 40.5 mm. **Ruler:** Hamad bin Khalifa **Subject:** 15th Asian Games **Obv:** Arms **Rev:** Volleyball player trailing purple color

| Date | Mintage | VF20 | XF40 | MS60 | MS63 | MS65 |
|---|---|---|---|---|---|---|
| 2006 | 25,000 | **PF63** 100 | **PF65** 110 | | | |

**KM# 40 100 RIYALS**
24.00 g., 0.925 Silver 0.7137 oz. ASW, 37 mm. **Ruler:** Hamad bin Khalifa **Subject:** Yousif al Sharif **Obv:** Wing desing **Rev:** Male bust

| Date | Mintage | VF20 | XF40 | MS60 | MS63 | MS65 |
|---|---|---|---|---|---|---|
| 2002 Proof | — | — | — | — | — | — |

**KM# 42 100 RIYALS**
100.00 g., 0.999 Silver 3.2119 oz. ASW, 80 mm. **Ruler:** Hamad bin Khalifa **Subject:** Doha Cultural festival

| Date | Mintage | VF20 | XF40 | MS60 | MS63 | MS65 |
|---|---|---|---|---|---|---|
| 2003 Proof | — | — | — | — | — | — |

**KM# 17 100 RIYALS**
Gold **Ruler:** Hamad bin Khalifa **Subject:** 15th Asian Games **Obv:** Arms above value **Rev:** Games mascot Fox on Bicycle cartoon character

| Date | Mintage | VF20 | XF40 | MS60 | MS63 | MS65 |
|---|---|---|---|---|---|---|
| 2006 | Est. 10000 | **PF65** 550 | | | | |

**KM# 18 100 RIYALS**
17.00 g., 0.920 Gold 0.5028 oz. AGW, 31 mm. **Ruler:** Hamad bin Khalifa **Obv:** Arms **Rev:** Central Bank building **Edge:** Reeded

| Date | Mintage | VF20 | XF40 | MS60 | MS63 | MS65 |
|---|---|---|---|---|---|---|
| 2006 | 300 | **PF65** 1,500 | | | | |

**KM# 19 100 RIYALS**
10.00 g., 0.9999 Gold 0.3215 oz. AGW, 24.5 mm. **Ruler:** Hamad bin Khalifa **Subject:** 15th Asian Games **Obv:** Arms **Rev:** Khalifa Stadium **Edge:** Reeded

| Date | Mintage | VF20 | XF40 | MS60 | MS63 | MS65 |
|---|---|---|---|---|---|---|
| 2006 | — | **PF65** 650 | | | | |

**KM# 20 100 RIYALS**
10.00 g., 0.9999 Gold 0.3215 oz. AGW, 24.5 mm. **Ruler:** Hamad bin Khalifa **Subject:** 15th Asian Games **Obv:** Arms **Rev:** Two oryxes head-butting **Edge:** Reeded

| Date | Mintage | VF20 | XF40 | MS60 | MS63 | MS65 |
|---|---|---|---|---|---|---|
| 2006 | — | **PF65** 650 | | | | |

**KM# 21 100 RIYALS**
10.00 g., 0.9999 Gold 0.3215 oz. AGW, 24.5 mm. **Ruler:** Hamad bin Khalifa **Subject:** 15th Asian Games **Obv:** Arms **Rev:** Falcon bust **Edge:** Reeded

| Date | Mintage | VF20 | XF40 | MS60 | MS63 | MS65 |
|---|---|---|---|---|---|---|
| 2006 | — | **PF65** 650 | | | | |

### KM# 22 100 RIYALS

10.00 g., 0.9999 Gold 0.3215 oz. AGW, 24.5 mm. **Ruler:** Hamad bin Khalifa **Subject:** 15th Asian Games **Obv:** Arms **Rev:** Coffee pot **Edge:** Reeded

| Date | Mintage | VF20 | XF40 | MS60 | MS63 | MS65 |
|---|---|---|---|---|---|---|
| 2006 | — | PF65 650 | | | | |

### KM# 23 100 RIYALS

10.00 g., 0.9999 Gold 0.3215 oz. AGW, 24.5 mm. **Ruler:** Hamad bin Khalifa **Subject:** 15th Asian Games **Obv:** Arms **Rev:** Radiant sun **Edge:** Reeded

| Date | Mintage | VF20 | XF40 | MS60 | MS63 | MS65 |
|---|---|---|---|---|---|---|
| 2006 | — | PF65 650 | | | | |

### KM# 76 100 RIYALS

22.24 g., 0.925 Silver 0.6614 oz. ASW, 37 mm. **Ruler:** Hamad bin Khalifa **Subject:** 2008 Arab States Stamp Exhibition **Obv:** National Arms **Rev:** Two profiles right

| Date | Mintage | VF20 | XF40 | MS60 | MS63 | MS65 |
|---|---|---|---|---|---|---|
| 2008 | 1,000 | PF65 100 | | | | |

### KM# 77 100 RIYALS

22.24 g., 0.925 Silver 0.6614 oz. ASW, 37 mm. **Ruler:** Hamad bin Khalifa **Subject:** Central Municipal Council, 10th Anniversary **Obv:** National Arms in color **Rev:** Democracy House in color

| Date | Mintage | VF20 | XF40 | MS60 | MS63 | MS65 |
|---|---|---|---|---|---|---|
| 2009 Proof | — | — | — | — | — | — |

### KM# 78 100 RIYALS

122.00 g., 0.920 Silver 3.6086 oz. ASW, 70 mm. **Ruler:** Hamad bin Khalifa **Subject:** 10th Gulf Cooperation Council Banking Conference

| Date | Mintage | VF20 | XF40 | MS60 | MS63 | MS65 |
|---|---|---|---|---|---|---|
| 2011 | 500 | PF65 400 | | | | |

### KM# 47 200 RIYALS

Gold **Ruler:** Hamad bin Khalifa **Subject:** al Wabra Wildlife Preservation, 50th Anniversary **Rev:** Blue headed macaw

| Date | Mintage | VF20 | XF40 | MS60 | MS63 | MS65 |
|---|---|---|---|---|---|---|
| 2003 Proof | 240 | — | — | — | — | — |

### KM# 67 200 RIYALS

0.999 Silver, 40 mm. **Ruler:** Hamad bin Khalifa **Subject:** Doha Cultural Festival **Obv:** Wing emblem **Rev:** Four men seated under archway

| Date | Mintage | VF20 | XF40 | MS60 | MS63 | MS65 |
|---|---|---|---|---|---|---|
| 2004 Proof | — | — | — | — | — | — |

### KM# 79 200 RIYALS

122.00 g., 0.920 Silver 3.6086 oz. ASW gilt, 70 mm. **Ruler:** Hamad bin Khalifa **Subject:** 10th Gulf Cooperation Council Banking Conference

| Date | Mintage | VF20 | XF40 | MS60 | MS63 | MS65 |
|---|---|---|---|---|---|---|
| 2011 | 500 | PF63 325 | PF65 350 | | | |

### KM# 11 250 RIYALS

Silver **Ruler:** Hamad bin Khalifa **Subject:** 4th WTO Conference **Obv:** National arms **Rev:** WTO logo, value, date, and legend in English and Islamic

| Date | Mintage | VF20 | XF40 | MS60 | MS63 | MS65 |
|---|---|---|---|---|---|---|
| AH1422 (2001) | 1,000 | PF63 650 | | | | |

### KM# 41 250 RIYALS

31.00 g., 0.999 Gold 0.9957 oz. AGW, 37 mm. **Ruler:** Hamad bin Khalifa **Subject:** Yousif al Sharif **Obv:** Wing design **Rev:** Male bust

| Date | Mintage | VF20 | XF40 | MS60 | MS63 | MS65 |
|---|---|---|---|---|---|---|
| 2002 Proof | — | — | — | — | — | — |

### KM# 43 250 RIYALS

100.00 g., 0.999 Silver 3.2119 oz. ASW partially gilt, 80 mm. **Ruler:** Hamad bin Khalifa **Subject:** Doha Cultural festival

| Date | Mintage | VF20 | XF40 | MS60 | MS63 | MS65 |
|---|---|---|---|---|---|---|
| 2003 | 1,000 | PF63 250 | PF65 275 | | | |

### KM# 44 250 RIYALS

120.00 g., 0.999 Silver 3.8542 oz. ASW, 60 mm. **Ruler:** Hamad bin Khalifa **Subject:** al Wabra Wildlife Preservation, 50th Anniversary **Rev:** Blue headed macaw in color

| Date | Mintage | VF20 | XF40 | MS60 | MS63 | MS65 |
|---|---|---|---|---|---|---|
| 2003 | 1,800 | PF63 250 | PF65 275 | | | |

### KM# 45 250 RIYALS

120.00 g., 0.999 Silver 3.8542 oz. ASW, 60 mm. **Ruler:** Hamad bin Khalifa **Subject:** al Wabra Wildlife Preservation, 50th Anniversary **Rev:** bird in color

| Date | Mintage | VF20 | XF40 | MS60 | MS63 | MS65 |
|---|---|---|---|---|---|---|
| 2003 | 1,800 | PF63 250 | PF65 275 | | | |

### KM# 46 250 RIYALS

120.00 g., 0.999 Silver 3.8542 oz. ASW, 60 mm. **Ruler:** Hamad bin Khalifa **Subject:** al Wabra Wildlife Preservation, 50th Anniversary **Rev:** Macaw in color

| Date | Mintage | VF20 | XF40 | MS60 | MS63 | MS65 |
|---|---|---|---|---|---|---|
| 2003 | 1,800 | PF63 250 | PF65 275 | | | |

### KM# 53 250 RIYALS

120.00 g., 0.999 Silver 3.8542 oz. ASW, 60 mm. **Ruler:** Hamad bin Khalifa **Subject:** al Wabra Wildlife Preservation, 50th Anniversary **Rev:** Gazelle

| Date | Mintage | VF20 | XF40 | MS60 | MS63 | MS65 |
|---|---|---|---|---|---|---|
| 2003 | 1,800 | PF63 250 | PF65 275 | | | |

### KM# 54 250 RIYALS

120.00 g., 0.999 Silver 3.8542 oz. ASW, 60 mm. **Ruler:** Hamad bin Khalifa **Subject:** al Wabra Wildlife Preservation, 50th Anniversary **Rev:** Sommering gazelle

| Date | Mintage | VF20 | XF40 | MS60 | MS63 | MS65 |
|---|---|---|---|---|---|---|
| 2003 | 1,800 | PF63 250 | PF65 275 | | | |

### KM# 55 250 RIYALS

120.00 g., 0.999 Silver 3.8542 oz. ASW, 60 mm. **Ruler:** Hamad bin Khalifa **Subject:** al Wabra Wildlife Preservation, 50th Anniversary **Rev:** Dama gazelle

| Date | Mintage | VF20 | XF40 | MS60 | MS63 | MS65 |
|---|---|---|---|---|---|---|
| 2003 | 1,800 | PF63 250 | PF65 275 | | | |

### KM# 56 250 RIYALS

120.00 g., 0.999 Silver 3.8542 oz. ASW, 60 mm. **Ruler:** Hamad bin Khalifa **Subject:** al Wabra Wildlife Preservation, 50th Anniversary **Rev:** Stilt gazelle

| Date | Mintage | VF20 | XF40 | MS60 | MS63 | MS65 |
|---|---|---|---|---|---|---|
| 2003 | 1,800 | PF63 250 | PF65 275 | | | |

### KM# 65 250 RIYALS

120.00 g., 0.999 Silver 3.8542 oz. ASW, 60 mm. **Ruler:** Hamad bin Khalifa **Subject:** National Council for Culture, Arts and Heritage, 5th Anniversary **Obv:** Bust 1/4 left **Rev:** Text and emblem

| Date | Mintage | VF20 | XF40 | MS60 | MS63 | MS65 |
|---|---|---|---|---|---|---|
| 2003 | 1,000 | PF63 275 | PF65 300 | | | |

### KM# 70 250 RIYALS

120.00 g., 0.999 Silver 3.8542 oz. ASW, 60 mm. **Ruler:** Hamad bin Khalifa **Subject:** National Council for Culture, Arts and Heritage

| Date | Mintage | VF20 | XF40 | MS60 | MS63 | MS65 |
|---|---|---|---|---|---|---|
| 2006 | — | PF63 225 | PF65 250 | | | |

### KM# 39 300 RIYALS

1000.00 g., 0.999 Silver 32.1186 oz. ASW, 100.0 mm. **Ruler:** Hamad bin Khalifa **Obv:** National arms **Obv. Legend:** STATE OF QATAR **Rev:** Sports montage around game's logo **Rev. Inscription:** 15TH ASIAN GAMES / DOHA 2006 **Edge:** Plain

| Date | Mintage | VF20 | XF40 | MS60 | MS63 | MS65 |
|---|---|---|---|---|---|---|
| 2006 | 5,000 | PF65 1,250 | | | | |

### KM# 68 1000 RIYALS

0.999 Gold, 40 mm. **Ruler:** Hamad bin Khalifa **Subject:** Doha Coultural Festival **Obv:** Wing design **Rev:** Four men seated under archway

| Date | Mintage | VF20 | XF40 | MS60 | MS63 | MS65 |
|---|---|---|---|---|---|---|
| 2004 Proof | — | — | — | — | — | — |

### KM# 48 2000 RIYALS

Gold **Ruler:** Hamad bin Khalifa **Subject:** al Wabra Wildlife Preservation, 50th Anniversary **Rev:** bird

| Date | Mintage | VF20 | XF40 | MS60 | MS63 | MS65 |
|---|---|---|---|---|---|---|
| 2003 Proof | 240 | — | — | — | — | — |

### KM# 72 2000 RIYALS

40.64 g., 0.925 Silver 1.2086 oz. ASW, 50 mm. **Ruler:** Hamad bin Khalifa **Subject:** National Day **Obv:** National Arms in color **Rev:** State of Qatar, National arms in color

| Date | Mintage | VF20 | XF40 | MS60 | MS63 | MS65 |
|---|---|---|---|---|---|---|
| 2007 | 500 | PF65 900 | | | | |

### KM# 73 2000 RIYALS

40.64 g., 0.925 Silver 1.2086 oz. ASW, 50 mm. **Ruler:** Hamad bin Khalifa **Subject:** National Day **Obv:** National Arms in color **Rev:** Qatar Central Bank, National arms in color

| Date | Mintage | VF20 | XF40 | MS60 | MS63 | MS65 |
|---|---|---|---|---|---|---|
| 2007 | 500 | PF65 900 | | | | |

### KM# 49 5000 RIYALS

Gold **Ruler:** Hamad bin Khalifa **Subject:** al Wabra Wildlife Preservation, 50th Anniversary **Rev:** macaw

| Date | Mintage | VF20 | XF40 | MS60 | MS63 | MS65 |
|---|---|---|---|---|---|---|
| 2003 Proof | 240 | — | — | — | — | — |

### KM# 57 5000 RIYALS

Gold **Ruler:** Hamad bin Khalifa **Subject:** al Wabra Wildlife Preservation, 50th Anniversary **Rev:** Gazelle

| Date | Mintage | VF20 | XF40 | MS60 | MS63 | MS65 |
|---|---|---|---|---|---|---|
| 2003 Proof | 240 | — | — | — | — | — |

### KM# 58 5000 RIYALS

Gold **Ruler:** Hamad bin Khalifa **Subject:** al Wabra Wildlife Preservation, 50th Anniversary **Rev:** Sommering Gazelle

| Date | Mintage | VF20 | XF40 | MS60 | MS63 | MS65 |
|---|---|---|---|---|---|---|
| 2003 Proof | 240 | — | — | — | — | — |

### KM# 59 5000 RIYALS

Gold **Ruler:** Hamad bin Khalifa **Subject:** al Wabra Wildlife Preservation, 50th Anniversary **Rev:** Dama Gazelle

| Date | Mintage | VF20 | XF40 | MS60 | MS63 | MS65 |
|---|---|---|---|---|---|---|
| 2003 Proof | 240 | — | — | — | — | — |

### KM# 60 5000 RIYALS

Gold **Ruler:** Hamad bin Khalifa **Subject:** al Wabra Wildlife Preservation, 50th Anniversary **Rev:** Stilt Gazelle

| Date | Mintage | VF20 | XF40 | MS60 | MS63 | MS65 |
|---|---|---|---|---|---|---|
| 2003 Proof | 240 | — | — | — | — | — |

### KM# 66 5000 RIYALS

160.00 g., 0.999 Gold 5.139 oz. AGW, 60 mm. **Ruler:** Hamad bin Khalifa **Subject:** National Council for Culture, Arts and Heritage, 5th Anniversary **Obv:** Bust 1/4 left **Rev:** Text and emblem

| Date | Mintage | VF20 | XF40 | MS60 | MS63 | MS65 |
|---|---|---|---|---|---|---|
| 2003 | 500 | PF65 9,750 | | | | |

### KM# 71 5000 RIYALS

160.00 g., 0.999 Gold 5.139 oz. AGW, 60 mm. **Ruler:** Hamad bin Khalifa **Subject:** National Council for Culture, Arts and Heritage

| Date | Mintage | VF20 | XF40 | MS60 | MS63 | MS65 |
|---|---|---|---|---|---|---|
| 2006 Proof | — | — | — | — | — | — |

### KM# 50 10000 RIYALS

Platinum APW **Ruler:** Hamad bin Khalifa **Subject:** al Wabra Wildlife Preservation, 50th Anniversary **Rev:** Blue headed macaw

| Date | Mintage | VF20 | XF40 | MS60 | MS63 | MS65 |
|---|---|---|---|---|---|---|
| 2003 Proof | 120 | — | — | — | — | — |

### KM# 51 10000 RIYALS

Platinum APW **Ruler:** Hamad bin Khalifa **Subject:** al Wabra Wildlife Preservation, 50th Anniversary **Rev:** bird

| Date | Mintage | VF20 | XF40 | MS60 | MS63 | MS65 |
|---|---|---|---|---|---|---|
| 2003 Proof | 120 | — | — | — | — | — |

### KM# 52 10000 RIYALS

Platinum APW **Ruler:** Hamad bin Khalifa **Subject:** al Wabra Wildlife Preservation, 50th Anniversary **Rev:** Macaw

| Date | Mintage | VF20 | XF40 | MS60 | MS63 | MS65 |
|---|---|---|---|---|---|---|
| 2003 Proof | 120 | — | — | — | — | — |

### KM# 61 10000 RIYALS

Platinum APW **Ruler:** Hamad bin Khalifa **Subject:** al Wabra Wildlife Preservation, 50th Anniversary **Rev:** Gazelle

| Date | Mintage | VF20 | XF40 | MS60 | MS63 | MS65 |
|---|---|---|---|---|---|---|
| 2003 Proof | 120 | — | — | — | — | — |

### KM# 62 10000 RIYALS

Platinum APW **Ruler:** Hamad bin Khalifa **Subject:** al Wabra Wildlife Preservation, 50th Anniversary **Rev:** Sommering gazelle

| Date | Mintage | VF20 | XF40 | MS60 | MS63 | MS65 |
|---|---|---|---|---|---|---|
| 2003 Proof | 120 | — | — | — | — | — |

### KM# 63 10000 RIYALS

Platinum APW **Ruler:** Hamad bin Khalifa **Subject:** al Wabra Wildlife Preservation, 50th Anniversary **Rev:** Dama gazelle

| Date | Mintage | VF20 | XF40 | MS60 | MS63 | MS65 |
|---|---|---|---|---|---|---|
| 2003 Proof | 120 | — | — | — | — | — |

### KM# 64 10000 RIYALS

Platinum APW **Ruler:** Hamad bin Khalifa **Subject:** al Wabra Wildlife Preservation, 50th Anniversary **Rev:** Stilt gazelle

| Date | Mintage | VF20 | XF40 | MS60 | MS63 | MS65 |
|---|---|---|---|---|---|---|
| 2003 Proof | 120 | — | — | — | — | — |

### KM# 24 10000 RIYALS

1000.00 g., 0.9999 Gold 32.1475 oz. AGW, 75.3 mm. **Ruler:** Hamad bin Khalifa **Subject:** 15th Asian Games **Obv:** Arms **Rev:** Radiant sun **Edge:** Reeded **Note:** Illustration reduced.

| Date | Mintage | VF20 | XF40 | MS60 | MS63 | MS65 |
|---|---|---|---|---|---|---|
| 2006 | — | PF65 57,500 | | | | |

### KM# 74 10000 RIYALS

70.16 g., 0.916 Gold 2.0662 oz. AGW, 50 mm. **Ruler:** Hamad bin Khalifa **Subject:** National Day **Obv:** National Arms **Rev:** State of Qatar, National Arms

| Date | Mintage | VF20 | XF40 | MS60 | MS63 | MS65 |
|---|---|---|---|---|---|---|
| 2007 | 500 | PF65 4,500 | | | | |

### KM# 75 10000 RIYALS

70.16 g., 0.916 Gold 2.0662 oz. AGW, 50 mm. **Ruler:** Hamad bin Khalifa **Subject:** National Day **Obv:** National Arms **Rev:** Qatar Central Bank, National Arms

| Date | Mintage | VF20 | XF40 | MS60 | MS63 | MS65 |
|---|---|---|---|---|---|---|
| 2007 | 500 | PF65 4,500 | | | | |

# ROMANIA

Romania (formerly the Socialist Republic of Romania), a country in southeast Europe, has an area of 91,699 sq. mi. (237,500 sq. km.) and a population of 23.2 million. Capital: Bucharest. Machinery, foodstuffs, raw minerals and petroleum products are exported. Heavy industry and oil have become increasingly important to the economy since 1959. Romania joined the European Union in January 2007.

**MONETARY SYSTEM**

100 Bani = 1 Leu

## REPUBLIC

## STANDARD COINAGE

### KM# 115 LEU

2.52 g., Copper Plated Steel, 19 mm. **Obv:** Value flanked by sprigs **Rev:** Shield divides date

| Date | Mintage | VF20 | XF40 | MS60 | MS63 | MS65 |
|---|---|---|---|---|---|---|
| 2002 | 1,500 | PF65 5.00 | | | | |
| 2003 | 2,000 | PF65 5.00 | | | | |
| 2004 | 2,000 | PF65 5.00 | | | | |
| 2005 | — | — | 0.15 | 0.50 | 0.75 | 1.50 |
| 2005 | — | PF65 6.00 | | | | |
| 2006 | 1,000 | PF65 6.00 | | | | |

### KM# 114 5 LEI

3.30 g., Nickel Plated Steel, 21 mm. **Obv:** Value flanked by oak leaves **Rev:** Shield divides date **Edge:** Plain

| Date | Mintage | VF20 | XF40 | MS60 | MS63 | MS65 |
|---|---|---|---|---|---|---|
| 2002 | 1,500 | PF65 5.00 | | | | |
| 2003 | 2,000 | PF65 5.00 | | | | |
| 2004 | — | PF65 5.00 | | | | |
| 2005 | — | PF65 5.00 | | | | |

### KM# 116 10 LEI

4.70 g., Nickel Clad Steel, 23 mm. **Obv:** Value within sprigs **Rev:** Shield divides date **Edge:** Plain

| Date | Mintage | VF20 | XF40 | MS60 | MS63 | MS65 |
|---|---|---|---|---|---|---|
| 2002 | 1,500 | PF65 6.00 | | | | |
| 2003 | 2,000 | PF65 6.00 | | | | |

### KM# 109 20 LEI

5.00 g., Brass Clad Steel, 24 mm. **Obv:** Crowned bust of Prince Stefan Cel Mare facing, flanked by dots **Rev:** Value and date within half sprigs and dots **Edge:** Plain **Note:** Date varieties exist.

| Date | Mintage | VF20 | XF40 | MS60 | MS63 | MS65 |
|---|---|---|---|---|---|---|
| 2002 | 1,500 | PF65 7.50 | | | | |
| 2003 | 2,000 | PF65 7.50 | | | | |

### KM# 110 50 LEI

5.90 g., Brass Clad Steel, 26 mm. **Obv:** Bust left flanked by dots **Rev:** Sprig divides date and value **Edge:** Plain

| Date | Mintage | VF20 | XF40 | MS60 | MS63 | MS65 |
|---|---|---|---|---|---|---|
| 2002 | 1,500 | PF65 8.00 | | | | |
| 2003 | 2,000 | PF65 8.00 | | | | |

### KM# 159 50 LEI

15.55 g., 0.999 Silver 0.4995 oz. ASW, 31.1 mm. **Series:** Romanian Aviation **Obv:** AVIONUL VUIA 1 - 1906 airplane **Rev:** Traian Vuia **Edge:** Plain **Shape:** Octagonal

| Date | Mintage | VF20 | XF40 | MS60 | MS63 | MS65 |
|---|---|---|---|---|---|---|
| 2001 | 500 | PF65 165 | | | | |

### KM# 160 50 LEI

15.55 g., 0.999 Silver 0.4995 oz. ASW, 31.1 mm. **Series:** Romanian Aviation **Obv:** Avionul Coanda 1910, world's first (?) jet airplane **Rev:** Portrait of Henri Coanda **Edge:** Plain **Shape:** Octagonal

| Date | Mintage | VF20 | XF40 | MS60 | MS63 | MS65 |
|---|---|---|---|---|---|---|
| 2001 | 500 | PF65 165 | | | | |

### KM# 161 50 LEI

15.55 g., 0.999 Silver 0.4995 oz. ASW, 27 mm. **Series:** Romanian Aviation **Obv:** IAR CV-11 airplane **Rev:** Elie Carafoli **Edge:** Plain **Shape:** Octagonal

| Date | Mintage | VF20 | XF40 | MS60 | MS63 | MS65 |
|---|---|---|---|---|---|---|
| 2001 | 500 | PF65 165 | | | | |

### KM# 167 50 LEI

15.55 g., 0.999 Silver 0.4995 oz. ASW, 29.5 mm. **Subject:** National Parks: Retezat **Obv:** National arms in triangular design **Rev:** Chamois **Edge:** Plain **Shape:** Rounded triangle

| Date | Mintage | VF20 | XF40 | MS60 | MS63 | MS65 |
|---|---|---|---|---|---|---|
| 2002 | 500 | PF65 200 | | | | |

### KM# 168 50 LEI

15.55 g., 0.999 Silver 0.4995 oz. ASW, 29.5 mm. **Subject:** National Parks: Pietrosul Mare **Obv:** National arms in triangular design **Rev:** Eagle **Edge:** Plain **Shape:** Rounded triangle

| Date | Mintage | VF20 | XF40 | MS60 | MS63 | MS65 |
|---|---|---|---|---|---|---|
| 2002 | 500 | PF65 200 | | | | |

### KM# 169 50 LEI

15.55 g., 0.999 Silver 0.4995 oz. ASW, 29.5 mm. **Subject:** National Parks: Piatra Craiului **Obv:** National arms in triangular design **Rev:** Lynx **Edge:** Plain **Shape:** Rounded triangle

| Date | Mintage | VF20 | XF40 | MS60 | MS63 | MS65 |
|---|---|---|---|---|---|---|
| 2002 | 500 | PF65 200 | | | | |

### KM# 186 50 LEI

15.55 g., 0.999 Silver 0.4995 oz. ASW, 27 mm. **Subject:** Birds **Obv:** Stylized water drop **Rev:** Dalmatian Pelicans within circle **Edge:** Plain

| Date | Mintage | VF20 | XF40 | MS60 | MS63 | MS65 |
|---|---|---|---|---|---|---|
| 2003 | 500 | PF65 100 | | | | |

### KM# 187 50 LEI

15.55 g., 0.999 Silver 0.4995 oz. ASW, 27 mm. **Subject:** Birds **Obv:** Stylized water drop **Rev:** Great Egret within circle **Edge:** Plain

| Date | Mintage | VF20 | XF40 | MS60 | MS63 | MS65 |
|---|---|---|---|---|---|---|
| 2003 | 500 | PF65 100 | | | | |

### KM# 188 50 LEI

15.55 g., 0.999 Silver 0.4995 oz. ASW, 27 mm. **Subject:** Birds **Obv:** Stylized water drop **Rev:** Common Kingfisher within circle **Edge:** Plain

| Date | Mintage | VF20 | XF40 | MS60 | MS63 | MS65 |
|---|---|---|---|---|---|---|
| 2003 | 500 | PF65 100 | | | | |

### KM# 111 100 LEI

8.75 g., Nickel Plated Steel, 29 mm. **Obv:** Bust with headdress 1/4 right **Rev:** Value within sprigs **Edge Lettering:** ROMANIA

| Date | Mintage | VF20 | XF40 | MS60 | MS63 | MS65 |
|---|---|---|---|---|---|---|
| 2002 | 1,500 | PF65 8.00 | | | | |
| 2003 | 2,000 | PF65 8.00 | | | | |
| 2004 | 2,000 | PF65 8.00 | | | | |
| 2005 | — | — | 0.45 | 0.65 | 1.25 | 2.50 |
| 2005 | 2,000 | PF65 9.00 | | | | |
| 2006 | 1,000 | PF65 9.00 | | | | |

### KM# 165 100 LEI

1.22 g., 0.999 Gold 0.0393 oz. AGW, 13.9 mm. **Subject:** History of Gold - "The Apahida Eagle **Obv:** National arms in ornamental circle above value **Edge:** Plain

| Date | Mintage | VF20 | XF40 | MS60 | MS63 | MS65 |
|---|---|---|---|---|---|---|
| 2003 | 2,000 | PF65 125 | | | | |

### KM# 198 100 LEI

1.24 g., 0.999 Gold 0.040 oz. AGW, 13.93 mm. **Obv:** National arms in wreath **Obv. Legend:** ROMANIA **Rev:** Medieval helmet **Edge:** Reeded

| Date | Mintage | VF20 | XF40 | MS60 | MS63 | MS65 |
|---|---|---|---|---|---|---|
| 2003 | — | PF65 100 | | | | |

**KM# 166 100 LEI**

1.22 g., 0.999 Gold 0.0393 oz. AGW, 14 mm. **Subject:** History of Gold - Engolpion **Obv:** National arms and country name above two stylized birds and value **Rev:** Jeweled double headed eagle pendant

| Date | Mintage | VF20 | XF40 | MS60 | MS63 | MS65 |
|---|---|---|---|---|---|---|
| 2004 | 1,000 | PF65 165 | | | | |

**KM# 145 500 LEI**

3.70 g., Aluminum, 25 mm. **Obv:** Shield within sprigs **Rev:** Value within 3/4 wreath **Edge:** Lettered **Edge Lettering:** ROMANIA (three times)

| Date | Mintage | VF20 | XF40 | MS60 | MS63 | MS65 |
|---|---|---|---|---|---|---|
| 2001 | — | — | 0.45 | 0.65 | 1.25 | 2.00 |
| 2002 | 1,500 | PF65 7.00 | | | | |
| 2003 | 2,000 | PF65 7.00 | | | | |
| 2004 | 2,000 | PF65 7.00 | | | | |
| 2005 | — | — | 0.50 | 0.75 | 1.50 | 3.00 |
| 2005 | 1,000 | PF65 8.00 | | | | |
| 2006 | — | — | 0.50 | 0.75 | 1.50 | 3.00 |
| 2006 | — | PF65 8.00 | | | | |

**KM# 170 500 LEI**

6.22 g., 0.999 Gold 0.1998 oz. AGW, 11.75 mm. **Subject:** History of Gold - Treasure of Pietroasa **Rev:** "Big Clip" of Pietroasa

| Date | Mintage | VF20 | XF40 | MS60 | MS63 | MS65 |
|---|---|---|---|---|---|---|
| (2001) | 250 | — | — | — | — | 700 |

**KM# 171 500 LEI**

6.22 g., 0.999 Gold 0.1998 oz. AGW, 11.75 mm. **Subject:** History of Gold - Treasure of Pietroasa **Rev:** "Medium Clip" of Pietroasa

| Date | Mintage | VF20 | XF40 | MS60 | MS63 | MS65 |
|---|---|---|---|---|---|---|
| 2001 | 250 | — | — | — | — | 700 |

**KM# 172 500 LEI**

6.22 g., 0.999 Gold 0.1998 oz. AGW, 11.75 mm. **Subject:** History of Gold - Treasure of Pietroasa **Rev:** 12-sided golden bowl

| Date | Mintage | VF20 | XF40 | MS60 | MS63 | MS65 |
|---|---|---|---|---|---|---|
| 2001 | 250 | — | — | — | — | 700 |

**KM# 173 500 LEI**

6.22 g., 0.999 Gold 0.1998 oz. AGW, 11.75 mm. **Subject:** History of Gold - Treasure of Pietroasa **Rev:** Pitcher

| Date | Mintage | VF20 | XF40 | MS60 | MS63 | MS65 |
|---|---|---|---|---|---|---|
| 2001 | 250 | — | — | — | — | 700 |

**KM# 176 500 LEI**

6.22 g., 0.999 Gold 0.1998 oz. AGW, 23.2 mm. **Subject:** Christian Monuments **Rev:** Mogoşoaia Palace **Shape:** Square

| Date | Mintage | VF20 | XF40 | MS60 | MS63 | MS65 |
|---|---|---|---|---|---|---|
| 2001 | 250 | — | — | — | — | 550 |

**KM# 174 500 LEI**

6.22 g., 0.999 Gold 0.1998 oz. AGW, 23.2 mm. **Subject:** Christian Monuments **Rev:** Bistritza Monastery

| Date | Mintage | VF20 | XF40 | MS60 | MS63 | MS65 |
|---|---|---|---|---|---|---|
| 2002 | 250 | — | — | — | — | 550 |

**KM# 175 500 LEI**

6.22 g., 0.999 Gold 0.1998 oz. AGW, 23.2 mm. **Subject:** Christian Monuments **Rev:** Colţa Church

| Date | Mintage | VF20 | XF40 | MS60 | MS63 | MS65 |
|---|---|---|---|---|---|---|
| 2002 | 250 | — | — | — | — | 550 |

**KM# 177 500 LEI**

31.10 g., 0.999 Silver 0.999 oz. ASW, 37 mm. **Subject:** 150th Anniversary - Birth of Ciprian Porumbescu, Composer **Obv:** Partial piano and violin left of National arms and value **Rev:** Portrait and musical score **Edge:** Plain

| Date | Mintage | VF20 | XF40 | MS60 | MS63 | MS65 |
|---|---|---|---|---|---|---|
| 2003 | 500 | PF65 160 | | | | |

**KM# 178 500 LEI**

31.10 g., 0.999 Silver 0.999 oz. ASW, 37 mm. **Subject:** 500th Anniversary - Establishment of Bishopric of Ramnic **Obv:** National arms and value above inscription **Rev:** Bishopric's coat-of-arms **Edge:** Plain

| Date | Mintage | VF20 | XF40 | MS60 | MS63 | MS65 |
|---|---|---|---|---|---|---|
| 2003 | 500 | PF65 160 | | | | |

**KM# 179 500 LEI**

31.10 g., 0.999 Silver 0.999 oz. ASW, 37 mm. **Subject:** Romanian Numismatic Society Centennial **Obv:** Cornucopia pouring forth coins, value below **Rev:** Minerva and torch **Rev. Legend:** CENTENARUL SOCIETATII NUMISMATICE ROMANE, 1903-2003 **Edge:** Plain

| Date | Mintage | VF20 | XF40 | MS60 | MS63 | MS65 |
|---|---|---|---|---|---|---|
| 2003 | 1,000 | PF65 150 | | | | |

**KM# 163 500 LEI**

31.10 g., 0.999 Silver 0.999 oz. ASW, 37 mm. **Subject:** Christian Feudal Art Monuments **Obv:** National arms, date and value at left, belfry tower of church at right **Rev:** Cotroceni Monastery church **Edge:** Plain **Shape:** 10-sided

| Date | Mintage | VF20 | XF40 | MS60 | MS63 | MS65 |
|---|---|---|---|---|---|---|
| 2004 | 500 | PF65 150 | | | | |

**KM# 164 500 LEI**

31.10 g., 0.999 Silver 0.999 oz. ASW, 37 mm. **Subject:** Christian Feudal Art Monuments **Obv:** National arms, bell and value **Rev:** St. Trei Ierarhi church in Iasi **Edge:** Plain **Shape:** 10-sided

| Date | Mintage | VF20 | XF40 | MS60 | MS63 | MS65 |
|---|---|---|---|---|---|---|
| 2004 | 500 | PF65 150 | | | | |

**KM# 180 500 LEI**

31.10 g., 0.999 Silver 0.999 oz. ASW, 37 mm. **Subject:** 140th Anniversary - University of Bucharest **Obv:** Vertical inscription divides National arms, value and date at left. University emblem at right **Obv. Inscription:** ROMANIA **Rev:** Cameo at right and crowned arms at left above University Building **Rev. Inscription:** Upper: UNIVERSITATEA DIN BUCURESTI / 140 DE ANI; Lower: INTEMEIATA LA 1864 DE / AL IOAN CUZA **Edge:** Plain

| Date | Mintage | VF20 | XF40 | MS60 | MS63 | MS65 |
|---|---|---|---|---|---|---|
| 2004 | 500 | PF65 180 | | | | |

**KM# 193 500 LEI**

31.10 g., 0.999 Silver 0.999 oz. ASW, 37 mm. **Subject:** 150th Anniversary - Birth of Anghel Saligny **Obv:** Arms at left above Cernavoda bridge, inscription, date, and value below **Obv. Inscription:** PODUL DE LA CERNAVODA **Rev:** Bust of bridge builder Anghel Saligny half right, life dates at right, his signature below at left **Edge:** Plain

| Date | Mintage | VF20 | XF40 | MS60 | MS63 | MS65 |
|---|---|---|---|---|---|---|
| 2004 | 500 | PF65 350 | | | | |

**KM# 218 500 LEI**

31.11 g., 0.999 Gold 0.999 oz. AGW, 35 mm. **Subject:** Union of the Principalities of Moldavia and Wallachia, 150th Anniversary

| Date | Mintage | VF20 | XF40 | MS60 | MS63 | MS65 |
|---|---|---|---|---|---|---|
| 2009 | 250 | PF65 1,900 | | | | |

**KM# 153 1000 LEI**

2.00 g., Aluminum, 22 mm. **Subject:** Constantin Brancoveanu **Obv:** Value above shield within lined circle **Rev:** Bust with headdress facing **Edge:** Plain with serrated sections

| Date | Mintage | VF20 | XF40 | MS60 | MS63 | MS65 |
|---|---|---|---|---|---|---|
| 2001 | — | — | 0.25 | 0.65 | 1.25 | 2.50 |
| 2002 | — | — | 0.25 | 0.65 | 1.25 | 2.50 |
| 2002 | 1,500 | PF65 12.00 | | | | |
| 2003 | — | — | 0.25 | 0.65 | 1.25 | 2.50 |
| 2003 | 2,000 | PF65 12.00 | | | | |
| 2004 | — | — | 0.25 | 0.65 | 1.25 | 2.50 |
| 2004 | 2,000 | PF65 12.00 | | | | |
| 2005 | — | — | 0.25 | 0.65 | 1.25 | 2.50 |
| 2005 | — | PF65 13.00 | | | | |
| 2006 | 1,000 | PF65 13.00 | | | | |

**KM# 156 1000 LEI**

15.55 g., 0.999 Gold 0.4995 oz. AGW, 27 mm. **Subject:** 1900th Anniversary of the First Roman-Dacian War **Obv:** Traian's column and shield **Rev:** Monument divides cameos **Edge:** Plain

| Date | Mintage | VF20 | XF40 | MS60 | MS63 | MS65 |
|---|---|---|---|---|---|---|
| 2001 | 500 | PF65 950 | | | | |

**KM# 181 2000 LEI**

25.00 g., Bi-Metallic .999 Silver, 10g center in .999 Gold, 15g ring, 35 mm. **Subject:** Ion Heliade Radulescu (1802-1872) **Obv:** Lyre at left, national arms at right in divided circle design **Rev:** Ion Heliade Radulescu above signature **Edge:** Reeded

| Date | Mintage | VF20 | XF40 | MS60 | MS63 | MS65 |
|---|---|---|---|---|---|---|
| 2002 | 500 | PF65 1,000 | | | | |

**KM# 158 5000 LEI**

2.50 g., Aluminum, 24 mm. **Obv:** Value and country name **Rev:** Sprig divides date and shield **Edge:** Plain **Shape:** 12-sided

| Date | Mintage | VF20 | XF40 | MS60 | MS63 | MS65 |
|---|---|---|---|---|---|---|
| 2001 | — | — | — | 0.50 | 0.75 | 1.00 |
| 2002 | 1,500 | PF65 15.00 | | | | |
| 2002 | — | — | — | 0.50 | 0.75 | 1.00 |
| 2003 | — | — | — | 0.25 | 0.50 | 0.75 |
| 2003 | 2,000 | PF65 15.00 | | | | |
| 2004 | 2,000 | PF65 16.00 | | | | |
| 2004 | — | — | — | 0.25 | 0.50 | 0.75 |
| 2005 | — | — | — | 0.25 | 0.50 | 0.75 |
| 2005 | 2,000 | PF65 17.00 | | | | |
| 2006 | 1,000 | PF65 17.00 | | | | |

**KM# 162 5000 LEI**
31.10 g., 0.999 Gold 0.999 oz. AGW, 35 mm. **Subject:** Constantin Brancusi 125th Anniversary of Birth **Obv:** National arms, value and sculpture **Rev:** Bearded portrait and signature **Edge:** Plain

| Date | Mintage | VF20 | XF40 | MS60 | MS63 | MS65 |
|---|---|---|---|---|---|---|
| 2001 | 500 | PF65 2,250 | | | | |

**KM# 183 5000 LEI**
31.10 g., 0.999 Gold 0.999 oz. AGW, 35 mm. **Subject:** Ion Luca Caragiale, playright (1852-1912) **Obv:** National arms, value and masks of Comedy and Tragedy **Rev:** Portrait **Edge:** Plain

| Date | Mintage | VF20 | XF40 | MS60 | MS63 | MS65 |
|---|---|---|---|---|---|---|
| 2002 | 250 | PF65 2,500 | | | | |

**KM# 184 5000 LEI**
31.10 g., 0.999 Gold 0.999 oz. AGW, 35 mm. **Subject:** Bran Castle (1378-2003) **Obv:** Two coats of arms on shield above value **Rev:** Castle view **Edge:** Plain

| Date | Mintage | VF20 | XF40 | MS60 | MS63 | MS65 |
|---|---|---|---|---|---|---|
| 2003 | 250 | PF65 2,000 | | | | |

**KM# 185 5000 LEI**
31.10 g., 0.999 Gold 0.999 oz. AGW, 35 mm. **Subject:** Stephen the Great **Obv:** National arms, value above coin design in wall **Rev:** Portrait of Stephan and Putna Monastery

| Date | Mintage | VF20 | XF40 | MS60 | MS63 | MS65 |
|---|---|---|---|---|---|---|
| 2004 | 250 | PF65 2,000 | | | | |

## REFORM COINAGE - 2005

10,000 Old Leu = 1 New Leu

**KM# 189 BAN**
2.40 g., Brass Plated Steel, 16.8 mm. **Subject:** Monetary Reform of 2005 **Obv:** National arms flanked by stars **Rev:** Value **Edge:** Plain

| Date | Mintage | VF20 | XF40 | MS60 | MS63 | MS65 |
|---|---|---|---|---|---|---|
| 2005 | — | — | — | 0.30 | 0.50 | 0.75 |
| 2005 | — | PF65 2.50 | | | | |
| 2006 | — | — | — | 0.30 | 0.50 | 0.75 |
| 2006 | — | PF65 2.50 | | | | |
| 2007 | — | — | — | 0.30 | 0.50 | 0.75 |
| 2007 | — | PF65 2.50 | | | | |
| 2008 | — | — | — | 0.30 | 0.50 | 0.75 |
| 2008 | — | PF65 2.50 | | | | |
| 2009 | — | — | — | 0.30 | 0.50 | 0.75 |
| 2009 | — | PF65 2.50 | | | | |
| 2010 | — | — | — | 0.30 | 0.50 | 0.75 |
| 2010 | — | PF65 2.50 | | | | |
| 2011 | — | — | — | 0.30 | 0.50 | 0.75 |
| 2011 | — | PF65 2.50 | | | | |
| 2012 | — | — | — | 0.30 | 0.50 | 0.75 |
| 2013 | — | — | — | 0.30 | 0.50 | 0.75 |

**KM# 190 5 BANI**
2.80 g., Copper Plated Steel, 18.25 mm. **Subject:** Monetary Reform of 2005 **Obv:** National arms flanked by stars **Obv. Legend:** ROMANIA **Rev:** Value **Edge:** Reeded

| Date | Mintage | VF20 | XF40 | MS60 | MS63 | MS65 |
|---|---|---|---|---|---|---|
| 2005 | — | — | — | 0.50 | 0.75 | 1.00 |
| 2005 | — | PF65 5.00 | | | | |
| 2006 | — | — | — | 0.50 | 0.75 | 1.00 |
| 2006 | — | PF65 5.00 | | | | |
| 2007 | — | — | — | 0.50 | 0.75 | 1.00 |
| 2007 | — | PF65 5.00 | | | | |
| 2008 | — | — | — | 0.50 | 0.75 | 1.00 |
| 2008 | — | PF65 5.00 | | | | |
| 2009 | — | — | — | 0.50 | 0.75 | 1.00 |
| 2009 | — | PF65 5.00 | | | | |
| 2010 | — | — | — | 0.50 | 0.75 | 1.00 |
| 2010 | — | PF65 5.00 | | | | |
| 2011 | — | — | — | 0.50 | 0.75 | 1.00 |
| 2011 | — | PF65 5.00 | | | | |
| 2012 | — | — | — | 0.50 | 0.75 | 1.00 |

**KM# 191 10 BANI**
4.00 g., Nickel Plated Steel, 20.4 mm. **Subject:** Monetary Reform of 2005 **Obv:** National arms flanked by stars **Obv. Legend:** ROMANIA **Rev:** Value **Edge:** Segmented reeding

| Date | Mintage | VF20 | XF40 | MS60 | MS63 | MS65 |
|---|---|---|---|---|---|---|
| 2005 | — | — | — | 0.65 | 0.85 | 1.25 |
| 2005 | — | PF65 7.00 | | | | |
| 2006 | — | — | — | 0.60 | 0.80 | 1.20 |
| 2006 | — | PF65 7.00 | | | | |
| 2007 | — | — | — | 0.50 | 0.75 | 1.00 |
| 2007 | — | PF65 7.00 | | | | |
| 2008 | — | — | — | 0.50 | 0.70 | 0.90 |
| 2008 | — | PF65 7.00 | | | | |
| 2009 | — | — | — | 0.50 | 0.70 | 0.90 |
| 2009 | — | PF65 7.00 | | | | |
| 2010 | — | — | — | 0.50 | 0.70 | 0.90 |
| 2010 | — | PF65 7.00 | | | | |
| 2011 | — | — | — | 0.50 | 0.70 | 0.90 |
| 2011 | — | PF65 7.00 | | | | |
| 2012 | — | — | — | 0.50 | 0.70 | 0.90 |

**KM# 192 50 BANI**
6.10 g., Nickel-Brass, 23.75 mm. **Subject:** Monetary Reform of 2005 **Obv:** National arms flanked by stars **Obv. Legend:** ROMANIA **Rev:** Value **Edge:** Lettered **Edge Lettering:** ROMANIA twice **Note:** Orientation of edge lettering varies.

| Date | Mintage | VF20 | XF40 | MS60 | MS63 | MS65 |
|---|---|---|---|---|---|---|
| 2005 | — | — | — | 0.85 | 1.00 | 1.50 |
| 2005 | — | PF65 10.00 | | | | |
| 2006 | — | — | — | 0.75 | 0.85 | 1.25 |
| 2006 | — | PF65 10.00 | | | | |
| 2007 | — | — | — | 0.65 | 0.75 | 1.00 |
| 2007 | — | PF65 10.00 | | | | |
| 2008 | — | — | — | 0.65 | 0.75 | 1.00 |
| 2008 | — | PF65 10.00 | | | | |
| 2009 | — | — | — | 0.65 | 0.75 | 1.00 |
| 2009 | — | PF65 10.00 | | | | |
| 2010 | — | — | — | 0.65 | 0.75 | 1.00 |
| 2010 | — | PF65 10.00 | | | | |
| 2011 | — | — | — | 0.65 | 0.75 | 1.00 |
| 2011 | — | PF65 10.00 | | | | |
| 2012 | — | — | — | 0.65 | 0.75 | 1.00 |

**KM# 259 50 BANI**
6.10 g., Nickel-Brass, 23.75 mm. **Subject:** Aurel Vlaicu

| Date | Mintage | VF20 | XF40 | MS60 | MS63 | MS65 |
|---|---|---|---|---|---|---|
| 2010 | 5,000,000 | — | — | 0.65 | 1.00 | 1.50 |
| Note: Medal rotation | | | | | | |
| 2010 | 1,000 | PF65 150 | | | | |
| Note: Medal rotation | | | | | | |
| 2010 | 5,000 | PF65 25.00 | | | | |
| Note: Coin rotation | | | | | | |
| 2011 Proof | 1,000 | — | — | — | — | — |
| Note: Medal rotation | | | | | | |

**KM# 260 50 BANI**
6.10 g., Nickel-Brass, 23.75 mm. **Subject:** Mircea the old

| Date | Mintage | VF20 | XF40 | MS60 | MS63 | MS65 |
|---|---|---|---|---|---|---|
| 2011 | — | — | — | 0.65 | 0.75 | 1.00 |

**KM# 287 50 BANI**
6.05 g., Nickel-Brass, 23.75 mm. **Subject:** Neagoe Basarab **Obv:** Large 50 above National shield, cathedral façade in background **Rev:** Crowned bust at left, cathedral at right

| Date | Mintage | VF20 | XF40 | MS60 | MS63 | MS65 |
|---|---|---|---|---|---|---|
| 2012 | — | — | — | 1.00 | 1.50 | 2.00 |

**KM# 209 LEU**
23.50 g., Copper Plated Tombac, 37 mm. **Subject:** 140th Anniversary Founding Romanian Academy **Edge:** Plain

| Date | Mintage | VF20 | XF40 | MS60 | MS63 | MS65 |
|---|---|---|---|---|---|---|
| 2006 | 35 | PF65 750 | | | | |

**KM# 199 LEU**
23.50 g., Copper Plated Tombac, 37 mm. **Subject:** 130th Anniversary of Proclamation of Independence **Obv:** Shield and "The Smardan Assault" painting by Nicolae Grigorescu **Rev:** Meeting of the Parliament

| Date | Mintage | VF20 | XF40 | MS60 | MS63 | MS65 |
|---|---|---|---|---|---|---|
| 2007 | 130 | PF65 250 | | | | |

**KM# 220 LEU**
23.50 g., Copper Plated Tombac, 37 mm. **Subject:** Centennial - Birth of Mircea Eliade **Obv:** Shield and value **Rev:** Portrait facing **Edge:** Reeded

| Date | Mintage | VF20 | XF40 | MS60 | MS63 | MS65 |
|---|---|---|---|---|---|---|
| 2007 | 250 | PF65 150 | | | | |

**KM# 223 LEU**
23.50 g., Copper Plated Tombac, 37 mm. **Subject:** Dimitrie Cantemir, (Prince of Moldavia 1673-1723), Scientist **Edge:** Reeded

| Date | Mintage | VF20 | XF40 | MS60 | MS63 | MS65 |
|---|---|---|---|---|---|---|
| 2007 | 250 | PF65 150 | | | | |

**KM# 226 LEU**
23.50 g., Copper Plated Tombac, 37 mm. **Subject:** Stephan the Great **Edge:** Reeded

| Date | Mintage | VF20 | XF40 | MS60 | MS63 | MS65 |
|---|---|---|---|---|---|---|
| 2007 | 250 | PF65 150 | | | | |

**KM# 289 LEU**
23.50 g., Copper Plated Tombac, 37 mm. **Subject:** Ovid, 2000th Anniversary of Banishment **Obv:** Large value above national shield **Rev:** Bust right in thought

| Date | Mintage | VF20 | XF40 | MS60 | MS63 | MS65 |
|---|---|---|---|---|---|---|
| 2008 | 1,000 | PF65 50.00 | | | | |

**KM# 291 LEU**
23.50 g., Copper Plated Tombac, 37 mm. **Subject:** NATO meeting in Bucharest **Obv:** National shield and NATO logo **Rev:** NATO country map and building

| Date | Mintage | VF20 | XF40 | MS60 | MS63 | MS65 |
|---|---|---|---|---|---|---|
| 2008 | 1,000 | PF65 50.00 | | | | |

**KM# 234 LEU**
23.50 g., Copper Plated Tombac, 37 mm. **Subject:** Nicolae Balcescu, 190th Anniversary of Birth

| Date | Mintage | VF20 | XF40 | MS60 | MS63 | MS65 |
|---|---|---|---|---|---|---|
| 2009 | 1,000 | PF65 75.00 | | | | |

**KM# 258 LEU**
23.50 g., Copper Plated Tombac, 37 mm. **Subject:** Bucharest, 550th Anniversary **Obv:** Vlad Ţepeş **Rev:** Buildings

| Date | Mintage | VF20 | XF40 | MS60 | MS63 | MS65 |
|---|---|---|---|---|---|---|
| 2009 | 250 | PF65 150 | | | | |

**KM# 261 LEU**
23.50 g., Copper Plated Tombac, 37 mm. **Subject:** Central Bank, 130th Anniversary

| Date | Mintage | VF20 | XF40 | MS60 | MS63 | MS65 |
|---|---|---|---|---|---|---|
| 2010 | 1,500 | PF65 65.00 | | | | |

**KM# 208 5 LEI**
31.10 g., 0.999 Silver 0.9989 oz. ASW, 37 mm. **Subject:** 100th Anniversary - Birth of Grigore Vasiliu-Birlic **Edge:** Plain

| Date | Mintage | VF20 | XF40 | MS60 | MS63 | MS65 |
|---|---|---|---|---|---|---|
| 2005 | 150 | PF65 1,200 | | | | |

**KM# 210 5 LEI**
31.10 g., 0.999 Silver 0.9989 oz. ASW, 37 mm. **Subject:** 140th Anniversary Founding Romanian Academy **Edge:** Plain

| Date | Mintage | VF20 | XF40 | MS60 | MS63 | MS65 |
|---|---|---|---|---|---|---|
| 2006 | 500 | PF65 300 | | | | |

**KM# 212 5 LEI**
31.10 g., 0.999 Silver 0.9989 oz. ASW, 37 mm. **Subject:** Christian Feudal Art - "Wooden Church from Ieud-Deal **Obv:** Fragment of mural in Ieud Church depicting Isaac, Abraham and Jacob at top, inscription, value and date in lower half **Obv. Inscription:** ROMANIA **Rev:** Front view of Ieud Church against frosted background **Rev. Inscription:** BISERICA DE LEMN IEUD DEAL **Edge:** Plain

| Date | Mintage | VF20 | XF40 | MS60 | MS63 | MS65 |
|---|---|---|---|---|---|---|
| 2006 | 500 | PF65 170 | | | | |

**KM# 213 5 LEI**
31.10 g., 0.999 Silver 0.999 oz. ASW, 37 mm. **Subject:** 150th Anniversary - Establishment of the European Commission of the Danube **Edge:** Plain

| Date | Mintage | VF20 | XF40 | MS60 | MS63 | MS65 |
|---|---|---|---|---|---|---|
| 2006 | 500 | PF65 170 | | | | |

**KM# 216 5 LEI**
31.10 g., 0.999 Silver 0.999 oz. ASW, 37 mm. **Subject:** Church fron Densus **Obv:** Christ icon on pillar at left, national shield at right **Rev:** Church at left, arch at right

| Date | Mintage | VF20 | XF40 | MS60 | MS63 | MS65 |
|---|---|---|---|---|---|---|
| 2006 | 500 | PF65 160 | | | | |

**KM# 200 5 LEI**
15.55 g., 0.999 Silver 0.4994 oz. ASW, 30 mm. **Subject:** 130th Anniversary of Proclamation of Independence **Obv:** Shield and "The Smardan Assault" painting by Nicolae Grigorescu **Rev:** Meeting of the Parliament

| Date | Mintage | VF20 | XF40 | MS60 | MS63 | MS65 |
|---|---|---|---|---|---|---|
| 2007 | 130 | PF65 500 | | | | |

**KM# 217 5 LEI**
31.10 g., 0.999 Silver 0.999 oz. ASW, 37 mm. **Subject:** Sibiu - European Capital of Culture **Obv:** 2 city towers in Sibiu at left, fortress wall connecting them, Potter's Tower in background, coat of arms at right **Obv. Inscription:** ROMANIA **Rev:** City of Sibiu's logo at bottom, 2 line inscription at left, 3 line inscription at right, 4 famous edifices at center **Rev. Inscription:** SIBIU / 2007 and CAPITALA / CULTURALA / EUROPEANA **Edge:** Plain

| Date | Mintage | VF20 | XF40 | MS60 | MS63 | MS65 |
|---|---|---|---|---|---|---|
| 2007 | 500 | PF65 400 | | | | |

**KM# 221 5 LEI**
15.55 g., 0.999 Silver 0.4994 oz. ASW, 30 mm. **Subject:** Centennial - Birth of Mircea Eliade **Obv:** Shield and value **Rev:** Portrait facing **Edge:** Reeded

| Date | Mintage | VF20 | XF40 | MS60 | MS63 | MS65 |
|---|---|---|---|---|---|---|
| 2007 | 250 | PF65 300 | | | | |

**KM# 224 5 LEI**
15.55 g., 0.999 Silver 0.4994 oz. ASW, 30 mm. **Subject:** Dimitrie Cantemir, (Prince of Moldavia 1673-1723), Scientist **Edge:** Reeded

| Date | Mintage | VF20 | XF40 | MS60 | MS63 | MS65 |
|---|---|---|---|---|---|---|
| 2007 | 250 | PF65 300 | | | | |

**KM# 227 5 LEI**
15.50 g., 0.999 Silver 0.4978 oz. ASW, 30 mm. **Subject:** Stephan the Great **Edge:** Reeded

| Date | Mintage | VF20 | XF40 | MS60 | MS63 | MS65 |
|---|---|---|---|---|---|---|
| 2007 | 250 | PF65 300 | | | | |

**KM# 242 5 LEI**
15.55 g., 0.999 Silver 0.4994 oz. ASW, 30 mm. **Subject:** Ovidivs Naso **Rev:** Half-length figure

| Date | Mintage | VF20 | XF40 | MS60 | MS63 | MS65 |
|---|---|---|---|---|---|---|
| 2008 | 500 | PF65 170 | | | | |

**KM# 292 5 LEI**
15.55 g., 0.999 Silver 0.4994 oz. ASW, 30 mm. **Subject:** NATO meeting in Bucharest **Obv:** National shield **Rev:** NATO country map and building

| Date | Mintage | VF20 | XF40 | MS60 | MS63 | MS65 |
|---|---|---|---|---|---|---|
| 2008 | 500 | PF65 125 | | | | |

**KM# 207 10 LEI**
1.22 g., 0.999 Gold 0.0393 oz. AGW, 13.92 mm. **Subject:** History of Gold - The Persinari Hoard **Edge:** Reeded

| Date | Mintage | VF20 | XF40 | MS60 | MS63 | MS65 |
|---|---|---|---|---|---|---|
| 2005 | 1,000 | PF65 200 | | | | |

**KM# 203 10 LEI**
1.22 g., 0.999 Gold 0.0393 oz. AGW, 13.92 mm. **Subject:** Histoy of Gold - The Cucuteni Báiceni Hoard **Obv:** Romania's Coat of Arms with denomination **Rev:** Cheekpiece of the gold helmet in the Cucuteni-Baiceni hoard **Edge:** Reeded

| Date | Mintage | VF20 | XF40 | MS60 | MS63 | MS65 |
|---|---|---|---|---|---|---|
| 2006 | 500 | PF65 250 | | | | |

**KM# 229 10 LEI**
31.10 g., 0.999 Silver 0.999 oz. ASW, 37 mm. **Subject:** 50th Anniversary - Treaty of Rome **Edge:** Reeded

| Date | Mintage | VF20 | XF40 | MS60 | MS63 | MS65 |
|---|---|---|---|---|---|---|
| 2007 | 500 | PF65 400 | | | | |

**KM# 240 10 LEI**
31.11 g., 0.999 Silver 0.999 oz. ASW, 37 mm. **Subject:** Petroleum Industry, 150th Anniversary **Rev:** Oil derrick and pump

| Date | Mintage | VF20 | XF40 | MS60 | MS63 | MS65 |
|---|---|---|---|---|---|---|
| 2007 | 500 | PF65 150 | | | | |

**KM# 241 10 LEI**
31.11 g., 0.999 Silver 0.999 oz. ASW, 37 mm. **Subject:** Snagov Monastery **Rev:** Building and bust

| Date | Mintage | VF20 | XF40 | MS60 | MS63 | MS65 |
|---|---|---|---|---|---|---|
| 2007 | 500 | PF65 170 | | | | |

**KM# 288 10 LEI**
1.24 g., 0.999 Gold 0.0398 oz. AGW, 13.92 mm. **Rev:** Drinking horn from Poroina

| Date | Mintage | VF20 | XF40 | MS60 | MS63 | MS65 |
|---|---|---|---|---|---|---|
| 2007 | 500 | PF65 100 | | | | |

**KM# 230 10 LEI**
31.10 g., 0.999 Silver 0.9989 oz. ASW, 37 mm. **Subject:** 150th Anniversary of First Postage Stamp **Rev:** Cap de Bour" (bull's head) stamp **Edge:** Reeded

| Date | Mintage | VF20 | XF40 | MS60 | MS63 | MS65 |
|---|---|---|---|---|---|---|
| 2008 | 1,000 | PF65 175 | | | | |

**KM# 231 10 LEI**
31.10 g., 0.999 Silver 0.999 oz. ASW, 37 mm. **Subject:** 80th Anniversary Romanian Broadcasting Co. **Obv:** Radio Romania, years 1928 and 2008, coat of arms **Rev:** Radio set from 30's, logo of Radio Romania, headphones **Edge:** Reeded

| Date | Mintage | VF20 | XF40 | MS60 | MS63 | MS65 |
|---|---|---|---|---|---|---|
| 2008 | 500 | PF65 300 | | | | |

**KM# 232 10 LEI**
1.24 g., 0.999 Gold 0.040 oz. AGW, 13.92 mm. **Subject:** Hoard of Hinova **Obv:** Romanian Coat of Arms, necklace parts **Rev:** Necklace parts, four bell shaped necklace parts, muff **Edge:** Reeded

| Date | Mintage | VF20 | XF40 | MS60 | MS63 | MS65 |
|---|---|---|---|---|---|---|
| 2008 | 500 | PF65 135 | | | | |

**KM# 244 10 LEI**
31.11 g., 0.999 Silver 0.999 oz. ASW, 37 mm. **Subject:** Costin Kirțiescu **Rev:** Bust facing

| Date | Mintage | VF20 | XF40 | MS60 | MS63 | MS65 |
|---|---|---|---|---|---|---|
| 2008 | 500 | PF65 170 | | | | |

**KM# 245 10 LEI**
31.11 g., 0.999 Silver 0.999 oz. ASW, 37 mm. **Subject:** First printed book in Walachia, 500th Anniversary **Rev:** Building and printers at press

| Date | Mintage | VF20 | XF40 | MS60 | MS63 | MS65 |
|---|---|---|---|---|---|---|
| 2008 | 500 | PF65 170 | | | | |

**KM# 246 10 LEI**
31.11 g., 0.999 Silver 0.999 oz. ASW, 37 mm. **Subject:** Simon Barnutiu **Rev:** Bust facing

| Date | Mintage | VF20 | XF40 | MS60 | MS63 | MS65 |
|---|---|---|---|---|---|---|
| 2008 | 500 | PF65 150 | | | | |

**KM# 247 10 LEI**
31.11 g., 0.999 Silver 0.999 oz. ASW, 37 mm. **Subject:** Cozia Monastery **Rev:** Church building

| Date | Mintage | VF20 | XF40 | MS60 | MS63 | MS65 |
|---|---|---|---|---|---|---|
| 2008 | 500 | PF65 165 | | | | |

**KM# 248 10 LEI**
31.11 g., 0.999 Silver 0.999 oz. ASW, 37 mm. **Subject:** Sambata des Sus Monastery **Rev:** Church building

| Date | Mintage | VF20 | XF40 | MS60 | MS63 | MS65 |
|---|---|---|---|---|---|---|
| 2008 | 500 | PF65 165 | | | | |

**KM# 249 10 LEI**
31.11 g., 0.999 Silver 0.999 oz. ASW, 37 mm. **Subject:** Voroneţ Monastery **Rev:** Church building

| Date | Mintage | VF20 | XF40 | MS60 | MS63 | MS65 |
|---|---|---|---|---|---|---|
| 2008 | 500 | PF65 165 | | | | |

**KM# 236 10 LEI**
31.11 g., 0.999 Silver 0.999 oz. ASW, 37 mm. **Subject:** Nicolae Balcescu, 190th Anniversary of Birth

| Date | Mintage | VF20 | XF40 | MS60 | MS63 | MS65 |
|---|---|---|---|---|---|---|
| 2009 | 1,000 | PF65 85.00 | | | | |

**KM# 250 10 LEI**
31.11 g., 0.999 Silver 0.999 oz. ASW, 37 mm. **Subject:** European Monitary Union, 10th Anniversary **Rev:** Stick figure and Euro symbol

| Date | Mintage | VF20 | XF40 | MS60 | MS63 | MS65 |
|---|---|---|---|---|---|---|
| 2009 | 1,000 | PF65 150 | | | | |

**KM# 251 10 LEI**
31.11 g., 0.999 Silver 0.999 oz. ASW, 37 mm. **Subject:** Alexander Macedonski **Rev:** Bust left

| Date | Mintage | VF20 | XF40 | MS60 | MS63 | MS65 |
|---|---|---|---|---|---|---|
| 2009 | 500 | PF65 150 | | | | |

**KM# 252 10 LEI**
31.11 g., 0.999 Silver 0.999 oz. ASW, 37 mm. **Subject:** Walachia's establishment as an Archdiocese, 650th Anniversary **Rev:** Archbishop and Cathedral

| Date | Mintage | VF20 | XF40 | MS60 | MS63 | MS65 |
|---|---|---|---|---|---|---|
| 2009 | 500 | PF65 170 | | | | |

**KM# 253 10 LEI**
31.11 g., 0.999 Silver 0.999 oz. ASW, 37 mm. **Subject:** Statistical Office, 150th Anniversary **Rev:** Two busts and document

| Date | Mintage | VF20 | XF40 | MS60 | MS63 | MS65 |
|---|---|---|---|---|---|---|
| 2009 | 500 | PF65 150 | | | | |

**KM# 254 10 LEI**
31.11 g., 0.999 Silver 0.999 oz. ASW, 37 mm. **Subject:** Bucharest - Giurgiu Railway, 150th Anniversary **Rev:** Steam train

| Date | Mintage | VF20 | XF40 | MS60 | MS63 | MS65 |
|---|---|---|---|---|---|---|
| 2009 | 500 | PF65 170 | | | | |

**KM# 255 10 LEI**
31.11 g., 0.999 Silver 0.999 oz. ASW, 37 mm. **Subject:** Bucharest, 550th Anniversary **Rev:** Architectural elements

| Date | Mintage | VF20 | XF40 | MS60 | MS63 | MS65 |
|---|---|---|---|---|---|---|
| 2009 | 500 | PF65 160 | | | | |

**KM# 256 10 LEI**
31.11 g., 0.999 Silver 0.999 oz. ASW, 37 mm. **Subject:** Constanta Harbor, 100th Anniversary **Rev:** Ship and buildings

| Date | Mintage | VF20 | XF40 | MS60 | MS63 | MS65 |
|---|---|---|---|---|---|---|
| 2009 | 500 | PF65 160 | | | | |

**KM# 257 10 LEI**
31.11 g., 0.999 Silver 0.999 oz. ASW, 37 mm. **Subject:** Tropaeum Traiani, 1900th Anniversary **Rev:** Ancient Roman building, Emperor Trajan

| Date | Mintage | VF20 | XF40 | MS60 | MS63 | MS65 |
|---|---|---|---|---|---|---|
| 2009 | 500 | PF65 150 | | | | |

**KM# 238 10 LEI**
1.24 g., 0.999 Gold 0.0398 oz. AGW, 13.92 mm. **Subject:** History of Gold **Rev:** Gold collar from the Gepids hoard

| Date | Mintage | VF20 | XF40 | MS60 | MS63 | MS65 |
|---|---|---|---|---|---|---|
| 2010 | 500 | PF65 90.00 | | | | |

**KM# 262 10 LEI**
31.11 g., 0.999 Silver 0.999 oz. ASW **Subject:** Central Bank, 130th Anniversary **Shape:** 37

| Date | Mintage | VF20 | XF40 | MS60 | MS63 | MS65 |
|---|---|---|---|---|---|---|
| 2010 | 3,000 | PF65 75.00 | | | | |

**KM# 266 10 LEI**
31.11 g., 0.999 Silver 0.999 oz. ASW, 37 mm. **Subject:** Romanian Orthodox Church Patriarchs **Rev:** Miron Cristea

| Date | Mintage | VF20 | XF40 | MS60 | MS63 | MS65 |
|---|---|---|---|---|---|---|
| 2010 | 1,000 | PF65 75.00 | | | | |

**KM# 267 10 LEI**
31.11 g., 0.999 Silver 0.999 oz. ASW, 37 mm. **Subject:** Romanian Orthodox Church Patriarchs **Rev:** Nicodim Munteanu

| Date | Mintage | VF20 | XF40 | MS60 | MS63 | MS65 |
|---|---|---|---|---|---|---|
| 2010 | 1,000 | PF65 75.00 | | | | |

**KM# 268 10 LEI**
31.11 g., 0.999 Silver 0.999 oz. ASW, 37 mm. **Subject:** Romanian Orthodox Church Patriarchs **Rev:** Justinian Marina

| Date | Mintage | VF20 | XF40 | MS60 | MS63 | MS65 |
|---|---|---|---|---|---|---|
| 2010 | 1,000 | PF65 75.00 | | | | |

**KM# 269 10 LEI**
31.11 g., 0.999 Silver 0.999 oz. ASW, 37 mm. **Subject:** Romanian Orthodox Church Patriarchs **Rev:** Justin Moisescu

| Date | Mintage | VF20 | XF40 | MS60 | MS63 | MS65 |
|---|---|---|---|---|---|---|
| 2010 | 1,000 | PF65 75.00 | | | | |

**KM# 270 10 LEI**
31.11 g., 0.999 Silver 0.999 oz. ASW, 37 mm. **Subject:** Romanian Orthodox Church Patriarchs **Rev:** Teoctist Arapasu

| Date | Mintage | VF20 | XF40 | MS60 | MS63 | MS65 |
|---|---|---|---|---|---|---|
| 2010 | 1,000 | PF65 75.00 | | | | |

**KM# 271 10 LEI**
31.11 g., 0.999 Silver 0.999 oz. ASW, 37 mm. **Subject:** Hariclea Darclee **Obv:** Opera House

| Date | Mintage | VF20 | XF40 | MS60 | MS63 | MS65 |
|---|---|---|---|---|---|---|
| 2010 | 1,000 | PF65 75.00 | | | | |

**KM# 272 10 LEI**
31.11 g., 0.999 Silver 0.999 oz. ASW, 37 mm. **Subject:** August Treboniu Laurian, 200th Anniversary of Birth **Obv:** She-wolf and twins

| Date | Mintage | VF20 | XF40 | MS60 | MS63 | MS65 |
|---|---|---|---|---|---|---|
| 2010 | 1,000 | PF65 75.00 | | | | |

**KM# 273 10 LEI**
31.11 g., 0.999 Silver 0.999 oz. ASW, 37 mm. **Subject:** Stefan Ciobotaraşu, 100th Anniversary of Birth **Obv:** Movie Theater

| Date | Mintage | VF20 | XF40 | MS60 | MS63 | MS65 |
|---|---|---|---|---|---|---|
| 2010 | 1,000 | PF65 75.00 | | | | |

**KM# 274 10 LEI**
31.11 g., 0.999 Silver 0.999 oz. ASW, 37 mm. **Obv:** Turboprop aircraft, 1910 **Rev:** Henri Coanda

| Date | Mintage | VF20 | XF40 | MS60 | MS63 | MS65 |
|---|---|---|---|---|---|---|
| 2010 | 1,000 | PF65 75.00 | | | | |

**KM# 276 10 LEI**
31.11 g., 0.999 Silver 0.999 oz. ASW, 37 mm. **Subject:** Grigore Alexandrescu, 200th Anniversary of Birth

| Date | Mintage | VF20 | XF40 | MS60 | MS63 | MS65 |
|---|---|---|---|---|---|---|
| 2010 | 1,000 | PF65 75.00 | | | | |

**KM# 277 10 LEI**
1.24 g., 0.999 Gold 0.0398 oz. AGW, 13.92 mm. **Subject:** History of Gold - Church of Sfantul Nicolae

| Date | Mintage | VF20 | XF40 | MS60 | MS63 | MS65 |
|---|---|---|---|---|---|---|
| 2011 | 500 | PF65 90.00 | | | | |

**KM# 279 10 LEI**
31.11 g., 0.999 Silver 0.999 oz. ASW, 37 mm. **Subject:** Letterpress printing in Romanian language, 450th Anniversary

| Date | Mintage | VF20 | XF40 | MS60 | MS63 | MS65 |
|---|---|---|---|---|---|---|
| 2011 | 500 | PF65 140 | | | | |

**KM# 280 10 LEI**
31.11 g., 0.999 Silver 0.999 oz. ASW, 37 mm. **Subject:** George Bacovia, 130th Anniversary of Birth

| Date | Mintage | VF20 | XF40 | MS60 | MS63 | MS65 |
|---|---|---|---|---|---|---|
| 2011 | 500 | PF65 140 | | | | |

**KM# 281 10 LEI**
31.11 g., 0.999 Silver 0.999 oz. ASW, 37 mm. **Subject:** Nicolae Milescu, 375th Anniversary of Birth

| Date | Mintage | VF20 | XF40 | MS60 | MS63 | MS65 |
|---|---|---|---|---|---|---|
| 2011 | 500 | PF65 140 | | | | |

**KM# 282 10 LEI**
31.11 g., 0.999 Silver 0.999 oz. ASW, 37 mm. **Subject:** ASTRA, 150th Anniversary **Obv:** Andrei Saguna **Rev:** Timotei Cipariu, George Baritiu, Ioan Puscariu

| Date | Mintage | VF20 | XF40 | MS60 | MS63 | MS65 |
|---|---|---|---|---|---|---|
| 2011 | 500 | PF65 140 | | | | |

**KM# 283 10 LEI**
31.11 g., 0.999 Silver 0.999 oz. ASW, 37 mm. **Subject:** Romanian Military, 150th Anniversary **Obv:** Alexandru Ioan Cuza **Rev:** Mounted officer before infantry

| Date | Mintage | VF20 | XF40 | MS60 | MS63 | MS65 |
|---|---|---|---|---|---|---|
| 2011 | 500 | PF65 140 | | | | |

**KM# 285 10 LEI**
1.24 g., 0.999 Gold 0.0398 oz. AGW, 13.92 mm. **Subject:** History of Gold - Chain with cross

| Date | Mintage | VF20 | XF40 | MS60 | MS63 | MS65 |
|---|---|---|---|---|---|---|
| 2011 | 500 | PF65 90.00 | | | | |

**KM# 286 10 LEI**
31.11 g., 0.999 Silver 0.999 oz. ASW, 37 mm. **Subject:** Euro, 10th Anniversary **Obv:** Building and map of Romania **Rev:** Euro as world currency

| Date | Mintage | VF20 | XF40 | MS60 | MS63 | MS65 |
|---|---|---|---|---|---|---|
| 2012 | 500 | PF65 150 | | | | |

**KM# 211 50 LEI**
6.45 g., 0.900 Gold 0.1866 oz. AGW, 21 mm. **Subject:** 140th Anniversary Founding Romanian Academy **Edge:** Plain

| Date | Mintage | VF20 | XF40 | MS60 | MS63 | MS65 |
|---|---|---|---|---|---|---|
| 2006 | 35 | PF65 3,000 | | | | |

**KM# 201 100 LEI**
6.45 g., 0.900 Gold 0.1867 oz. AGW, 21 mm. **Subject:** 130th Anniversary of Proclamation of Independence **Obv:** Shield and "The Smardan Assault" painting by Nicole Grigorescu **Rev:** Meeting of the Parliament

| Date | Mintage | VF20 | XF40 | MS60 | MS63 | MS65 |
|---|---|---|---|---|---|---|
| 2007 | 130 | PF65 1,500 | | | | |

**KM# 222 100 LEI**
6.45 g., 0.900 Gold 0.1866 oz. AGW, 21 mm. **Subject:** Centennial - Birth of Mircea Eliade **Obv:** Shield and value **Rev:** Portrait facing **Edge:** Reeded

| Date | Mintage | VF20 | XF40 | MS60 | MS63 | MS65 |
|---|---|---|---|---|---|---|
| 2007 | 250 | PF65 900 | | | | |

**KM# 225 100 LEI**
6.45 g., 0.900 Gold 0.1866 oz. AGW, 21 mm. **Subject:** Dimitrie Cantemir, (Prince of Moldavia 1710-1711), Scientist **Edge:** Reeded

| Date | Mintage | VF20 | XF40 | MS60 | MS63 | MS65 |
|---|---|---|---|---|---|---|
| 2007 | 250 | PF65 900 | | | | |

**KM# 228 100 LEI**
6.45 g., 0.900 Gold 0.1867 oz. AGW, 21 mm. **Subject:** 550th Anniversary - Ascension Prince Stephan the Great into Moldavia **Edge:** Reeded

| Date | Mintage | VF20 | XF40 | MS60 | MS63 | MS65 |
|---|---|---|---|---|---|---|
| 2007 | 250 | PF65 900 | | | | |

**KM# 235 100 LEI**
6.45 g., 0.999 Gold 0.2072 oz. AGW, 21 mm. **Subject:** Battles of Marasti, Marasesti, Oituz 90th Anniversary **Obv:** Mausoleum of Marasesti **Rev:** Group of soldiers at Battle of Marasti

| Date | Mintage | VF20 | XF40 | MS60 | MS63 | MS65 |
|---|---|---|---|---|---|---|
| 2007 | 250 | PF65 550 | | | | |

**KM# 290 100 LEI**
6.45 g., 0.900 Gold 0.1866 oz. AGW, 21 mm. **Subject:** Ovid, 2000th Anniversary of Banishment **Obv:** Large value above National shield **Rev:** Bust right in thought

| Date | Mintage | VF20 | XF40 | MS60 | MS63 | MS65 |
|---|---|---|---|---|---|---|
| 2008 | 250 | PF65 400 | | | | |

**KM# 293 100 LEI**
6.45 g., 0.900 Gold 0.1866 oz. AGW, 21 mm. **Subject:** NATO meeting in Bucharest **Obv:** National shield **Rev:** NATO country map and building

| Date | Mintage | VF20 | XF40 | MS60 | MS63 | MS65 |
|---|---|---|---|---|---|---|
| 2008 | 500 | PF65 450 | | | | |

**KM# 264 100 LEI**
6.45 g., 0.900 Gold 0.1866 oz. AGW, 21 mm. **Subject:** Eugeniu Carada, 100th Anniversary of Death

| Date | Mintage | VF20 | XF40 | MS60 | MS63 | MS65 |
|---|---|---|---|---|---|---|
| 2010 | 500 | PF65 450 | | | | |

**KM# 275 100 LEI**
6.45 g., 0.999 Gold 0.2072 oz. AGW, 21 mm. **Subject:** Maria Alexandria Victoria, 135th Anniversary of Birth

| Date | Mintage | VF20 | XF40 | MS60 | MS63 | MS65 |
|---|---|---|---|---|---|---|
| 2010 | 1,000 | PF65 500 | | | | |

**KM# 284 100 LEI**
6.45 g., 0.999 Gold 0.2072 oz. AGW, 21 mm. **Subject:** Wallachian uprising, 190th Anniversary **Rev:** Tudor Vladimirescu

| Date | Mintage | VF20 | XF40 | MS60 | MS63 | MS65 |
|---|---|---|---|---|---|---|
| 2011 | 500 | PF65 500 | | | | |

**KM# 263 200 LEI**
15.55 g., 0.999 Gold 0.4994 oz. AGW, 27 mm. **Subject:** Central Bank, 130th Anniversary

| Date | Mintage | VF20 | XF40 | MS60 | MS63 | MS65 |
|---|---|---|---|---|---|---|
| 2010 | 1,500 | PF65 950 | | | | |

**KM# 265 200 LEI**
15.55 g., 0.999 Gold 0.4994 oz. AGW, 27 mm. **Subject:** Romanian Orthodox Church

| Date | Mintage | VF20 | XF40 | MS60 | MS63 | MS65 |
|---|---|---|---|---|---|---|
| 2010 | 1,000 | PF65 1,000 | | | | |

**KM# 278 200 LEI**
15.55 g., 0.999 Gold 0.4994 oz. AGW, 27 mm. **Subject:** Cozia Monastery

| Date | Mintage | VF20 | XF40 | MS60 | MS63 | MS65 |
|---|---|---|---|---|---|---|
| 2011 | 250 | PF65 1,300 | | | | |

**KM# 194 500 LEI**
31.10 g., 0.999 Silver 0.999 oz. ASW, 37 mm. **Subject:** 125th Anniversary - National Bank **Obv:** National arms and coin design of 5 Lei dated 1880 **Rev:** Bank building **Edge:** Plain

| Date | Mintage | VF20 | XF40 | MS60 | MS63 | MS65 |
|---|---|---|---|---|---|---|
| 2005 | — | PF65 1,000 | | | | |

**KM# 206 500 LEI**
31.10 g., 0.999 Gold 0.9989 oz. AGW, 35 mm. **Subject:** 50th Anniversary - Death of George Enescu **Edge:** Plain

| Date | Mintage | VF20 | XF40 | MS60 | MS63 | MS65 |
|---|---|---|---|---|---|---|
| 2005 | 250 | PF65 2,250 | | | | |

**KM# 214 500 LEI**
31.10 g., 0.999 Gold 0.999 oz. AGW, 35 mm. **Subject:** 350th Anniversary - Establishment of the Patriarchal Cathedral **Edge:** Plain

| Date | Mintage | VF20 | XF40 | MS60 | MS63 | MS65 |
|---|---|---|---|---|---|---|
| 2006 | 250 | PF65 3,000 | | | | |

**KM# 204 500 LEI**
31.10 g., 0.999 Gold 0.999 oz. AGW, 35 mm. **Subject:** Romania's Accession to European Union, January 1 2007 **Obv:** Romania's Coat of Arms surrounded by 12 stars of European Union **Rev:** Map of the European Union including Romania **Edge:** Plain

| Date | Mintage | VF20 | XF40 | MS60 | MS63 | MS65 |
|---|---|---|---|---|---|---|
| 2007 | 250 | PF65 3,000 | | | | |

**KM# 205 500 LEI**
31.10 g., 0.999 Gold 0.999 oz. AGW, 35 mm. **Subject:** Nicolae Balcescu (1819-1852) **Obv:** Romania's Coat of Arms and **Obv. Inscription:** Justice and Brotherhood **Rev:** Portrait of Nicolae Balcescu **Edge:** Plain

| Date | Mintage | VF20 | XF40 | MS60 | MS63 | MS65 |
|---|---|---|---|---|---|---|
| 2007 | 250 | PF65 2,250 | | | | |

**KM# 215 500 LEI**
31.11 g., 0.999 Gold 0.999 oz. AGW, 35 mm. **Subject:** Statehood, 90th Anniversary **Obv:** Shield **Rev:** Crown

| Date | Mintage | VF20 | XF40 | MS60 | MS63 | MS65 |
|---|---|---|---|---|---|---|
| 2008 | 3,000 | PF65 1,850 | | | | |

**KM# 219 500 LEI**
31.11 g., 0.999 Gold 0.999 oz. AGW, 35 mm. **Subject:** Carol I, 170th Anniversary of Birth

| Date | Mintage | VF20 | XF40 | MS60 | MS63 | MS65 |
|---|---|---|---|---|---|---|
| 2009 | 250 | PF65 1,850 | | | | |

**KM# 233 500 LEI**
31.11 g., 0.999 Gold 0.999 oz. AGW, 35 mm. **Subject:** Bucharest, 550th Anniversary

| Date | Mintage | VF20 | XF40 | MS60 | MS63 | MS65 |
|---|---|---|---|---|---|---|
| 2009 | — | PF65 1,850 | | | | |

**KM# 237 500 LEI**
31.11 g., 0.999 Gold 0.999 oz. AGW, 35 mm. **Subject:** Nicolae Balcescu, 190th Anniversary of Birth

| Date | Mintage | VF20 | XF40 | MS60 | MS63 | MS65 |
|---|---|---|---|---|---|---|
| 2009 | — | PF65 1,850 | | | | |

**KM# 239 500 LEI**
31.11 g., 0.999 Gold 0.999 oz. AGW, 35 mm. **Subject:** Mihai Eminescu, 160th Anniversary of Birth

| Date | Mintage | VF20 | XF40 | MS60 | MS63 | MS65 |
|---|---|---|---|---|---|---|
| 2010 | — | PF65 1,850 | | | | |

## MINT SETS

| KM# | Date | Mintage | Identification | Issue Price | Mkt Val |
|---|---|---|---|---|---|
| MS4 | 2006 (4) | — | KM189-192, plus medal | — | 75.00 |
| MS5 | 2007 (4) | 1,000 | KM189-192, plus medal | — | 60.00 |
| MS6 | 2005 (4) | — | KM#189-192 | — | 50.00 |

## PROOF SETS

| KM# | Date | Mintage | Identification | Issue Price | Mkt Val |
|---|---|---|---|---|---|
| PS4 | 2001 (3) | 500 | KM#159, 160, 161 | 80.00 | 525 |
| PS5 | 2002 (9) | 1,500 | KM#109-111, 114-116, 145, 153, 158 | 20.00 | 75.00 |
| PS6 | 2003 (9) | 2,000 | KM#109-111, 114-116, 145, 153, 158 | 20.00 | 75.00 |
| PS7 | 2003 (3) | 500 | KM#186, 187, 188 | — | 325 |
| PSA8 | 2004 (5) | — | KM#111, 115, 145, 153, 158 | — | 50.00 |
| PS8 | 2004 (2) | 500 | KM#163, 164 | — | 325 |
| PS9 | 2005 (10) | — | KM#111, 115, 145, 153, 158, 189-192 plus medal | — | 80.00 |
| PS10 | 2006 (10) | — | KM#111, 115, 145, 153, 158, 189-192 | — | 80.00 |
| PS11 | 2006 (3) | — | KM#209, 210, 211 | — | 4,050 |
| PS12 | 2007 (3) | — | KM#220, 221, 222 | — | 1,350 |
| PS13 | 2007 (3) | — | KM#223, 224, 225 | — | 1,350 |
| PS14 | 2007 (3) | — | KM#226, 227, 228 | — | 1,350 |
| PS15 | 2007 (5) | — | KM#189-192 plus Silver 75th Anniversary of Rodna Mountains National Park medal | — | 50.00 |
| PS17 | 2008 (4) | — | KM#189-192 plus silver medal Antipa Museum | — | 50.00 |

The Russia Federation, formerly the central power of the Union of Soviet Socialist Republics and now of the Commonwealth of Independent States occupies the northern part of Asia and the eastern part of Europe, has an area of 17,075,400 sq. km. Capital: Moscow. Exports include iron and steel, crude oil, timber, and nonferrous metals.

In the fall of 1991, events moved swiftly in the Soviet Union. Estonia, Latvia and Lithuania won their independence and were recognized by Moscow, Sept. 6. The Commonwealth of Independent States was formed Dec. 8, 1991 in Mensk by Belarus, Russia and Ukraine. It was expanded at a summit Dec. 21, 1991 to include 11 of the 12 remaining republics (excluding Georgia) of the old U.S.S.R. -

# RUSSIAN FEDERATION

Issued by the БАНК РОССИИ (Bank of Russia)

## REFORM COINAGE

1,000 Old Roubles = 1 New Rouble
January 1, 1998

**Y# 600 KOPEK**
1.50 g., Copper-Nickel Plated Steel, 15.5 mm. **Obv:** St. George **Obv. Legend:** БАНК РОССИИ **Rev:** Value above vine sprig **Edge:** Plain

| Date | Mintage | VF20 | XF40 | MS60 | MS63 | MS65 |
|---|---|---|---|---|---|---|
| 2001 M | — | — | — | 0.30 | 0.40 | 0.60 |
| 2001 СП | — | — | — | 0.30 | 0.40 | 0.60 |
| 2002 M | — | — | — | 0.30 | 0.40 | 0.60 |
| 2002 СП | — | — | — | 0.30 | 0.40 | 0.60 |
| 2003 M | — | — | — | 0.30 | 0.40 | 0.60 |
| 2003 СП | — | — | — | 0.30 | 0.40 | 0.60 |
| 2004 M | — | — | — | 0.30 | 0.40 | 0.60 |
| 2004 СП | — | — | — | 0.30 | 0.40 | 0.60 |
| 2005 M | — | — | — | 0.30 | 0.40 | 0.60 |
| 2005 СП | — | — | — | 0.30 | 0.40 | 0.60 |
| 2006 M | — | — | — | 0.30 | 0.40 | 0.60 |
| 2006 СП | — | — | — | 0.30 | 0.40 | 0.60 |
| 2007 M | — | — | — | 0.30 | 0.40 | 0.60 |
| 2007 СП | — | — | — | 0.30 | 0.40 | 0.60 |
| 2008 M | — | — | — | 0.30 | 0.40 | 0.60 |
| 2008 СП | — | — | — | 0.30 | 0.40 | 0.60 |
| 2009 M | — | — | — | 1.00 | 2.00 | 3.50 |
| 2009 СП | — | — | — | 1.00 | 2.00 | 3.50 |

**Y# 601 5 KOPEKS**

2.60 g., Copper-Nickel Clad Steel, 18.5 mm. **Obv:** St. George **Obv. Legend:** БАНК РОССИИ **Rev:** Value above vine sprig **Edge:** Plain

| Date | Mintage | VF20 | XF40 | MS60 | MS63 | MS65 |
|---|---|---|---|---|---|---|
| 2001 M | — | — | — | 0.40 | 0.60 | 0.85 |
| 2001 СП | — | — | — | 0.40 | 0.60 | 0.85 |
| 2002 | — | 80.00 | 95.00 | 120 | — | — |
| 2002 M | — | — | — | 0.40 | 0.60 | 0.90 |
| 2002 СП | — | — | — | 0.40 | 0.60 | 0.90 |
| 2003 | — | 10.00 | 15.00 | 25.00 | — | — |
| 2003 M | — | — | — | 0.35 | 0.50 | 0.75 |
| 2003 СП | — | — | — | 0.35 | 0.50 | 0.75 |
| 2004 M | — | — | — | 0.35 | 0.50 | 0.75 |
| 2004 СП | — | — | — | 0.35 | 0.50 | 0.75 |
| 2005 M | — | — | — | 0.35 | 0.50 | 0.75 |
| 2005 СП | — | — | — | 0.35 | 0.50 | 0.75 |
| 2006 M | — | — | — | 0.35 | 0.50 | 0.75 |
| 2006 СП | — | — | — | 0.35 | 0.50 | 0.75 |
| 2007 M | — | — | — | 0.35 | 0.50 | 0.75 |
| 2007 СП | — | — | — | 0.35 | 0.50 | 0.75 |
| 2008 M | — | — | — | 0.35 | 0.50 | 0.75 |
| 2008 СП | — | — | — | 0.35 | 0.50 | 0.75 |
| 2009 M | — | — | — | 1.00 | 2.00 | 3.50 |
| 2009 СП | — | — | — | 1.00 | 2.00 | 3.50 |

**Y# 602 10 KOPEKS**

1.95 g., Brass, 17.5 mm. **Obv:** St. George horseback right slaying dragon **Rev:** Value above vine sprig **Edge:** Reeded

| Date | Mintage | VF20 | XF40 | MS60 | MS63 | MS65 |
|---|---|---|---|---|---|---|
| 2001 M | — | — | — | 0.50 | 0.80 | 1.10 |
| 2001 СП | — | — | — | 0.50 | 0.80 | 1.10 |
| 2002 M | — | — | — | 0.50 | 0.80 | 1.10 |
| 2002 СП | — | — | — | 0.50 | 0.80 | 1.10 |
| 2003 M | — | — | — | 0.50 | 0.80 | 1.10 |
| 2003 СП | — | — | — | 0.50 | 0.80 | 1.10 |
| 2004 M | — | — | — | 0.50 | 0.80 | 1.10 |
| 2004 СП | — | — | — | 0.50 | 0.80 | 1.10 |
| 2005 M | — | — | — | 0.50 | 0.80 | 1.10 |
| 2005 СП | — | — | — | 0.50 | 0.80 | 1.10 |
| 2006 M | — | — | — | 0.50 | 0.80 | 1.10 |
| 2006 СП | — | — | — | 0.50 | 0.80 | 1.10 |

**Y# 602a 10 KOPEKS**

1.85 g., Tombac Plated Steel, 17.5 mm. **Obv:** St. George on horseback slaying dragon to right **Obv. Legend:** БАНК РОССИИ **Rev:** Denomination above vine sprig **Edge:** Plain

| Date | Mintage | VF20 | XF40 | MS60 | MS63 | MS65 |
|---|---|---|---|---|---|---|
| 2006 M | — | — | — | 0.50 | 0.80 | 1.10 |
| 2006 СП | — | — | — | 0.50 | 0.80 | 1.10 |
| 2007 M | — | — | — | 0.50 | 0.80 | 1.10 |
| 2007 СП | — | — | — | 0.50 | 0.80 | 1.10 |
| 2008 M | — | — | — | 0.50 | 0.80 | 1.10 |
| 2008 СП | — | — | — | 0.50 | 0.80 | 1.10 |
| 2009 M | — | — | — | 0.50 | 0.80 | 1.10 |
| 2009 СП | — | — | — | 0.50 | 0.80 | 1.10 |
| 2010 M | — | — | — | 0.50 | 0.80 | 1.10 |
| 2010 СП | — | — | — | 0.50 | 0.80 | 1.10 |
| 2011 M | — | — | — | 0.50 | 0.80 | 1.10 |
| 2012 M | — | — | — | 0.50 | 0.80 | 1.10 |

**Y# 603 50 KOPEKS**

2.90 g., Brass, 19.5 mm. **Obv:** St. George on horseback slaying dragon right **Rev:** Value above vine sprig **Edge:** Reeded

| Date | Mintage | VF20 | XF40 | MS60 | MS63 | MS65 |
|---|---|---|---|---|---|---|
| 2001 M Rare | — | — | 5,000 | — | — | — |
| 2002 M | — | — | — | 1.50 | 3.00 | 5.00 |
| 2002 СП | — | — | — | 1.50 | 3.00 | 5.00 |
| 2003 M | — | — | — | 0.80 | 1.00 | 1.25 |
| 2003 СП | — | — | — | 0.80 | 1.00 | 1.25 |
| 2004 M | — | — | — | 0.80 | 1.00 | 1.25 |
| 2004 СП | — | — | — | 0.80 | 1.00 | 1.25 |
| 2005 M | — | — | — | 0.80 | 1.00 | 1.25 |
| 2005 СП | — | — | — | 0.80 | 1.00 | 1.25 |
| 2006 M | — | — | — | 0.80 | 1.00 | 1.25 |
| 2006 СП | — | — | — | 0.80 | 1.00 | 1.25 |

**Y# 603a 50 KOPEKS**

2.75 g., Brass Clad Steel, 19.5 mm. **Obv:** St. George on horseback slaying dragon right **Rev:** Value above vine sprig **Edge:** Plain

| Date | Mintage | VF20 | XF40 | MS60 | MS63 | MS65 |
|---|---|---|---|---|---|---|
| 2006 M | — | — | — | 0.80 | 1.00 | 1.25 |
| 2006 СП | — | — | — | 0.80 | 1.00 | 1.25 |
| 2007 M | — | — | — | 0.80 | 1.00 | 1.25 |
| 2007 СП | — | — | — | 0.80 | 1.00 | 1.25 |
| 2008 M | — | — | — | 0.80 | 1.00 | 1.25 |
| 2008 СП | — | — | — | 0.80 | 1.00 | 1.25 |
| 2009 M | — | — | — | 0.80 | 1.00 | 1.25 |
| 2009 СП | — | — | — | 0.80 | 1.00 | 1.25 |
| 2010 M | — | — | — | 0.80 | 1.00 | 1.25 |
| 2010 СП | — | — | — | 0.80 | 1.00 | 1.25 |
| 2011 M | — | — | — | 0.80 | 1.00 | 1.25 |
| 2012 M | — | — | — | 0.80 | 1.00 | 1.25 |

**Y# 604 ROUBLE**

3.25 g., Copper-Nickel-Zinc, 20.5 mm. **Obv:** Double-headed eagle **Rev:** Value **Edge:** Reeded

| Date | Mintage | VF20 | XF40 | MS60 | MS63 | MS65 |
|---|---|---|---|---|---|---|
| 2001 M Rare | — | — | — | — | — | — |

**Y# 731 ROUBLE**

3.21 g., Copper-Nickel, 20.7 mm. **Obv:** Double-headed eagle **Rev:** Stylized design above hologram **Edge:** Reeded

| Date | Mintage | VF20 | XF40 | MS60 | MS63 | MS65 |
|---|---|---|---|---|---|---|
| 2001 СПМД | 100,000,000 | — | — | 1.50 | 2.00 | 3.50 |

**Y# 732 ROUBLE**

17.43 g., 0.900 Silver 0.5043 oz. ASW, 32.8 mm. **Subject:** Sturgeon **Obv:** Double-headed eagle within beaded circle **Rev:** Sakhalin sturgeon and other fish **Edge:** Reeded

| Date | Mintage | VF20 | XF40 | MS60 | MS63 | MS65 |
|---|---|---|---|---|---|---|
| 2001 | 7,500 | PF65 60.00 | | | | |

**Y# 745 ROUBLE**

17.40 g., 0.900 Silver 0.5035 oz. ASW, 32.8 mm. **Obv:** Double-headed eagle within beaded circle **Rev:** Altai argalia sheep **Edge:** Reeded

| Date | Mintage | VF20 | XF40 | MS60 | MS63 | MS65 |
|---|---|---|---|---|---|---|
| 2001 (sp) | 7,500 | PF65 65.00 | | | | |

**Y# 746 ROUBLE**

17.40 g., 0.900 Silver 0.5035 oz. ASW, 32.8 mm. **Obv:** Double-headed eagle within beaded circle **Rev:** Beavers **Edge:** Reeded

| Date | Mintage | VF20 | XF40 | MS60 | MS63 | MS65 |
|---|---|---|---|---|---|---|
| 2001 (sp) | 7,500 | PF65 65.00 | | | | |

**Y# 758 ROUBLE**

17.44 g., 0.900 Silver 0.5046 oz. ASW, 33 mm. **Obv:** Double-headed eagle within beaded circle **Rev:** Chinese Goral **Edge:** Reeded

| Date | Mintage | VF20 | XF40 | MS60 | MS63 | MS65 |
|---|---|---|---|---|---|---|
| 2002 (sp) | 10,000 | PF65 50.00 | | | | |

**Y# 759 ROUBLE**

17.44 g., 0.900 Silver 0.5046 oz. ASW, 33 mm. **Obv:** Double-headed eagle within beaded circle **Rev:** Sei Whale **Edge:** Reeded

| Date | Mintage | VF20 | XF40 | MS60 | MS63 | MS65 |
|---|---|---|---|---|---|---|
| 2002 (sp) | 10,000 | PF65 50.00 | | | | |

**Y# 760 ROUBLE**

17.44 g., 0.900 Silver 0.5046 oz. ASW, 33 mm. **Subject:** Golden Eagle **Obv:** Double-headed eagle within beaded circle **Rev:** Golden Eagle with nestling **Edge:** Reeded

| Date | Mintage | VF20 | XF40 | MS60 | MS63 | MS65 |
|---|---|---|---|---|---|---|
| 2002 (sp) | 10,000 | PF65 50.00 | | | | |

**Y# 770 ROUBLE**

8.53 g., 0.925 Silver 0.2537 oz. ASW, 25 mm. **Subject:** Ministry of Education **Obv:** Double-headed eagle within beaded circle **Rev:** Seedling within open book **Edge:** Reeded

| Date | Mintage | VF20 | XF40 | MS60 | MS63 | MS65 |
|---|---|---|---|---|---|---|
| 2002 (m) | 3,000 | PF65 50.00 | | | | |

**Y# 771 ROUBLE**
8.53 g., 0.925 Silver 0.2537 oz. ASW, 25 mm. **Subject:** Ministry of Finances **Obv:** Double-headed eagle within beaded circle **Rev:** Caduceus in monogram **Edge:** Reeded

| Date | Mintage | VF20 | XF40 | MS60 | MS63 | MS65 |
|---|---|---|---|---|---|---|
| 2002 (sp) | 3,000 | **PF65** 50.00 | | | | |

**Y# 772 ROUBLE**
8.53 g., 0.925 Silver 0.2537 oz. ASW, 25 mm. **Subject:** Ministry of Economic Development **Obv:** Double-headed eagle within beaded circle **Rev:** Crowned double-headed eagle with cornucopia and caduceus **Edge:** Reeded

| Date | Mintage | VF20 | XF40 | MS60 | MS63 | MS65 |
|---|---|---|---|---|---|---|
| 2002 (sp) | 3,000 | **PF65** 50.00 | | | | |

**Y# 773 ROUBLE**
8.53 g., 0.925 Silver 0.2537 oz. ASW, 25 mm. **Subject:** Ministry of Foreign Affairs **Obv:** Double-headed eagle within beaded circle **Rev:** Crowned two-headed eagle above crossed sprigs **Edge:** Reeded

| Date | Mintage | VF20 | XF40 | MS60 | MS63 | MS65 |
|---|---|---|---|---|---|---|
| 2002 (sp) | 3,000 | **PF65** 50.00 | | | | |

**Y# 774 ROUBLE**
8.53 g., 0.925 Silver 0.2537 oz. ASW, 25 mm. **Subject:** Ministry of Internal Affairs **Obv:** Double-headed eagle within beaded circle **Rev:** Crowned two-headed eagle with round breast **Edge:** Reeded

| Date | Mintage | VF20 | XF40 | MS60 | MS63 | MS65 |
|---|---|---|---|---|---|---|
| 2002 (sp) | 3,000 | **PF65** 50.00 | | | | |

**Y# 775 ROUBLE**
8.53 g., 0.925 Silver 0.2537 oz. ASW, 25 mm. **Subject:** Ministry of Justice **Obv:** Double-headed eagle within beaded circle **Rev:** Crowned double-headed eagle with column on breast shield **Edge:** Reeded

| Date | Mintage | VF20 | XF40 | MS60 | MS63 | MS65 |
|---|---|---|---|---|---|---|
| 2002 (sp) | 3,000 | **PF65** 50.00 | | | | |

**Y# 776 ROUBLE**
8.53 g., 0.925 Silver 0.2537 oz. ASW, 25 mm. **Subject:** Russian Armed Forces **Obv:** Double-headed eagle within beaded circle **Rev:** Double-headed eagle with crowned top pointed breast shield **Edge:** Reeded

| Date | Mintage | VF20 | XF40 | MS60 | MS63 | MS65 |
|---|---|---|---|---|---|---|
| 2002 (m) | 3,000 | **PF65** 50.00 | | | | |

**Y# 833 ROUBLE**
3.25 g., Copper-Nickel-Zinc, 20.5 mm. **Obv:** Two headed eagle above curved bank name and date, denomination above **Rev:** Value and flower **Edge:** Reeded

| Date | Mintage | VF20 | XF40 | MS60 | MS63 | MS65 |
|---|---|---|---|---|---|---|
| 2002 (m) Mint sets only | 15,000 | — | — | — | — | — |
| 2002 (sp) Mint sets only | 15,000 | — | — | — | — | — |
| 2003 (sp) | 15,000 | — | 300 | 400 | 500 | — |
| 2005 (m) | — | — | — | 2.00 | 3.00 | 5.00 |
| 2005 (sp) | — | — | — | 2.00 | 3.00 | 5.00 |
| 2006 (m) | — | — | — | 2.00 | 3.00 | 5.00 |
| 2006 (sp) | — | — | — | 2.00 | 3.00 | 5.00 |
| 2007 (m) | — | — | — | 2.00 | 3.00 | 5.00 |
| 2007 (sp) | — | — | — | 2.00 | 3.00 | 5.00 |
| 2008 (m) | — | — | — | 2.00 | 3.00 | 5.00 |
| 2008 (sp) | — | — | — | 2.00 | 3.00 | 5.00 |
| 2009 (m) | — | — | — | 2.00 | 3.00 | 5.00 |
| 2009 (sp) | — | — | — | 2.00 | 3.00 | 5.00 |

**Y# A834 ROUBLE**
7.78 g., 0.925 Silver 0.2314 oz. ASW, 25 mm. **Subject:** St. Petersburg **Obv:** Double-headed eagle within beaded circle **Rev:** Angel on steeple of Cathedral in fortress

| Date | Mintage | VF20 | XF40 | MS60 | MS63 | MS65 |
|---|---|---|---|---|---|---|
| 2002 | 5,000 | **PF65** 25.00 | | | | |

**Y# 835 ROUBLE**
7.78 g., 0.925 Silver 0.2314 oz. ASW, 25 mm. **Subject:** St. Petersburg **Obv:** Double-headed eagle within beaded circle **Rev:** Sphinx

| Date | Mintage | VF20 | XF40 | MS60 | MS63 | MS65 |
|---|---|---|---|---|---|---|
| 2002 | 5,000 | **PF65** 25.00 | | | | |

**Y# 836 ROUBLE**
7.78 g., 0.925 Silver 0.2314 oz. ASW, 25 mm. **Subject:** St. Petersburg **Obv:** Double-headed eagle within beaded circle **Rev:** Small ship

| Date | Mintage | VF20 | XF40 | MS60 | MS63 | MS65 |
|---|---|---|---|---|---|---|
| 2002 | 5,000 | **PF65** 25.00 | | | | |

**Y# 837 ROUBLE**
7.78 g., 0.925 Silver 0.2314 oz. ASW, 25 mm. **Subject:** St. Petersburg **Obv:** Double-headed eagle within beaded circle **Rev:** Lion

| Date | Mintage | VF20 | XF40 | MS60 | MS63 | MS65 |
|---|---|---|---|---|---|---|
| 2002 | 5,000 | **PF65** 25.00 | | | | |

**Y# 838 ROUBLE**
7.78 g., 0.925 Silver 0.2314 oz. ASW, 25 mm. **Subject:** St. Petersburg **Obv:** Double-headed eagle within beaded circle **Rev:** Horse sculpture

| Date | Mintage | VF20 | XF40 | MS60 | MS63 | MS65 |
|---|---|---|---|---|---|---|
| 2002 | 5,000 | **PF65** 25.00 | | | | |

**Y# 839 ROUBLE**
7.78 g., 0.925 Silver 0.2314 oz. ASW, 25 mm. **Subject:** St. Petersburg **Obv:** Double-headed eagle within beaded circle **Rev:** Griffin

| Date | Mintage | VF20 | XF40 | MS60 | MS63 | MS65 |
|---|---|---|---|---|---|---|
| 2002 | 5,000 | **PF65** 25.00 | | | | |

**Y# 814 ROUBLE**
17.40 g., 0.900 Silver 0.5035 oz. ASW, 32.8 mm. **Obv:** Double-headed eagle within beaded circle **Rev:** Arctic foxes **Edge:** Reeded

| Date | Mintage | VF20 | XF40 | MS60 | MS63 | MS65 |
|---|---|---|---|---|---|---|
| 2003 (sp) | 10,000 | **PF65** 35.00 | | | | |

**Y# 815 ROUBLE**
17.40 g., 0.900 Silver 0.5035 oz. ASW, 32.8 mm. **Obv:** Double-headed eagle within beaded circle **Rev:** Chinese Softshell turtle **Edge:** Reeded

| Date | Mintage | VF20 | XF40 | MS60 | MS63 | MS65 |
|---|---|---|---|---|---|---|
| 2003 (sp) | 10,000 | **PF65** 40.00 | | | | |

**Y# 816 ROUBLE**
17.40 g., 0.900 Silver 0.5035 oz. ASW, 32.8 mm. **Obv:** Double-headed eagle within beaded circle **Rev:** Pygmy Cormorant drying its wings **Edge:** Reeded

| Date | Mintage | VF20 | XF40 | MS60 | MS63 | MS65 |
|---|---|---|---|---|---|---|
| 2003 (sp) | 10,000 | **PF65** 35.00 | | | | |

**Y# 828 ROUBLE**

17.28 g., 0.900 Silver 0.500 oz. ASW, 33 mm. **Obv:** Two headed eagle within beaded circle **Rev:** Amur Forest Cat on branch **Edge:** Reeded

| Date | Mintage | VF20 | XF40 | MS60 | MS63 | MS65 |
|---|---|---|---|---|---|---|
| 2004 (sp) | 10,000 | PF65 35.00 | | | | |

**Y# 881 ROUBLE**

17.40 g., 0.900 Silver 0.5035 oz. ASW, 32.8 mm. **Obv:** Double-headed eagle within beaded circle **Rev:** Rush Toad **Edge:** Reeded

| Date | Mintage | VF20 | XF40 | MS60 | MS63 | MS65 |
|---|---|---|---|---|---|---|
| 2004 | — | PF65 60.00 | | | | |

**Y# 1029 ROUBLE**

16.80 g., 0.925 Silver 0.4996 oz. ASW, 32.8 mm. **Subject:** The Great Bustard

| Date | Mintage | VF20 | XF40 | MS60 | MS63 | MS65 |
|---|---|---|---|---|---|---|
| 2004 | — | PF65 35.00 | | | | |

**Y# 882 ROUBLE**

17.40 g., 0.925 Silver 0.5175 oz. ASW, 32.8 mm. **Obv:** Double-headed eagle within beaded circle **Rev:** Two Marbled Murrelet sea birds **Edge:** Reeded

| Date | Mintage | VF20 | XF40 | MS60 | MS63 | MS65 |
|---|---|---|---|---|---|---|
| 2005 | — | PF65 35.00 | | | | |

**Y# 883 ROUBLE**

17.40 g., 0.925 Silver 0.5175 oz. ASW, 32.8 mm. **Obv:** Double-headed eagle within beaded circle **Rev:** Asiatic Wild Dog **Edge:** Reeded

| Date | Mintage | VF20 | XF40 | MS60 | MS63 | MS65 |
|---|---|---|---|---|---|---|
| 2005 | — | PF65 35.00 | | | | |

**Y# 884 ROUBLE**

17.40 g., 0.925 Silver 0.5175 oz. ASW, 32.8 mm. **Obv:** Double-headed eagle within beaded circle **Rev:** Volkhov Whitefish **Edge:** Reeded

| Date | Mintage | VF20 | XF40 | MS60 | MS63 | MS65 |
|---|---|---|---|---|---|---|
| 2005 | — | PF65 35.00 | | | | |

**Y# 916 ROUBLE**

8.53 g., 0.925 Silver 0.2537 oz. ASW, 25 mm. **Obv:** Double-headed eagle **Rev:** Russian Navy Emblem **Edge:** Reeded

| Date | Mintage | VF20 | XF40 | MS60 | MS63 | MS65 |
|---|---|---|---|---|---|---|
| 2005 | 10,000 | PF65 25.00 | | | | |

**Y# 917 ROUBLE**

8.53 g., 0.925 Silver 0.2537 oz. ASW, 25 mm. **Obv:** Double-headed eagle **Rev:** Russian Marine circa 1705 **Edge:** Reeded

| Date | Mintage | VF20 | XF40 | MS60 | MS63 | MS65 |
|---|---|---|---|---|---|---|
| 2005 | 10,000 | PF65 25.00 | | | | |

**Y# 918 ROUBLE**

8.53 g., 0.925 Silver 0.2537 oz. ASW, 25 mm. **Obv:** Double-headed eagle **Rev:** Russian Marine circa 2005 **Edge:** Reeded

| Date | Mintage | VF20 | XF40 | MS60 | MS63 | MS65 |
|---|---|---|---|---|---|---|
| 2005 | 10,000 | PF65 25.00 | | | | |

**Y# 981 ROUBLE**

17.40 g., 0.925 Silver 0.5175 oz. ASW, 33 mm. **Obv:** Double headed eagle **Rev:** Mongolian Gazelle **Edge:** Reeded

| Date | Mintage | VF20 | XF40 | MS60 | MS63 | MS65 |
|---|---|---|---|---|---|---|
| 2006 | — | PF65 65.00 | | | | |

**Y# 1058 ROUBLE**

33.90 g., 0.925 Silver 1.0082 oz. ASW, 39 mm. **Subject:** Swan Goose

| Date | Mintage | VF20 | XF40 | MS60 | MS63 | MS65 |
|---|---|---|---|---|---|---|
| 2006 | — | PF65 45.00 | | | | |

**Y# 1059 ROUBLE**

33.90 g., 0.925 Silver 1.0082 oz. ASW, 39 mm. **Subject:** Ussury Clawed Newt

| Date | Mintage | VF20 | XF40 | MS60 | MS63 | MS65 |
|---|---|---|---|---|---|---|
| 2006 | — | PF65 45.00 | | | | |

**Y# 1069 ROUBLE**

8.53 g., 0.925 Silver 0.2537 oz. ASW, 25 mm. **Subject:** Airborne Troops

| Date | Mintage | VF20 | XF40 | MS60 | MS63 | MS65 |
|---|---|---|---|---|---|---|
| 2006 | — | PF65 25.00 | | | | |

**Y# 1070 ROUBLE**

8.53 g., 0.925 Silver 0.2537 oz. ASW, 25 mm. **Subject:** Airborne Troops

| Date | Mintage | VF20 | XF40 | MS60 | MS63 | MS65 |
|---|---|---|---|---|---|---|
| 2006 | — | PF65 25.00 | | | | |

**Y# 1071 ROUBLE**

8.53 g., 0.925 Silver 0.2537 oz. ASW, 25 mm. **Subject:** Airborne Troops

| Date | Mintage | VF20 | XF40 | MS60 | MS63 | MS65 |
|---|---|---|---|---|---|---|
| 2006 | — | PF65 25.00 | | | | |

**Y# 1072 ROUBLE**

8.53 g., 0.925 Silver 0.2537 oz. ASW, 25 mm. **Subject:** Submarine Forces

| Date | Mintage | VF20 | XF40 | MS60 | MS63 | MS65 |
|---|---|---|---|---|---|---|
| 2006 | — | PF65 25.00 | | | | |

**Y# 1073 ROUBLE**
8.53 g., 0.925 Silver 0.2537 oz. ASW, 25 mm. **Subject:** Submarine Forces

| Date | Mintage | VF20 | XF40 | MS60 | MS63 | MS65 |
|---|---|---|---|---|---|---|
| 2006 | — | PF65 25.00 | | | | |

**Y# 1074 ROUBLE**
8.53 g., 0.925 Silver 0.2537 oz. ASW, 25 mm. **Subject:** Submarine Forces

| Date | Mintage | VF20 | XF40 | MS60 | MS63 | MS65 |
|---|---|---|---|---|---|---|
| 2006 | — | PF65 25.00 | | | | |

**Y# 961 ROUBLE**
17.40 g., 0.925 Silver 0.5175 oz. ASW, 33 mm. **Obv:** Double headed eagle **Rev:** Red banded snake **Edge:** Reeded

| Date | Mintage | VF20 | XF40 | MS60 | MS63 | MS65 |
|---|---|---|---|---|---|---|
| 2007 | — | PF65 35.00 | | | | |

**Y# 962 ROUBLE**
17.40 g., 0.925 Silver 0.5175 oz. ASW, 33 mm. **Obv:** Double headed eagle **Rev:** Pallid Harrier in flight

| Date | Mintage | VF20 | XF40 | MS60 | MS63 | MS65 |
|---|---|---|---|---|---|---|
| 2007 | — | PF65 65.00 | | | | |

**Y# 1109 ROUBLE**
33.90 g., 0.925 Silver 1.0082 oz. ASW, 39 mm. **Subject:** Ringed seal

| Date | Mintage | VF20 | XF40 | MS60 | MS63 | MS65 |
|---|---|---|---|---|---|---|
| 2007 | — | PF65 45.00 | | | | |

**Y# 1110 ROUBLE**
8.53 g., 0.925 Silver 0.2537 oz. ASW, 25 mm. **Subject:** Space Force

| Date | Mintage | VF20 | XF40 | MS60 | MS63 | MS65 |
|---|---|---|---|---|---|---|
| 2007 | — | PF65 30.00 | | | | |

**Y# 1111 ROUBLE**
8.53 g., 0.925 Silver 0.2537 oz. ASW, 25 mm. **Subject:** Space Force

| Date | Mintage | VF20 | XF40 | MS60 | MS63 | MS65 |
|---|---|---|---|---|---|---|
| 2007 | — | PF65 30.00 | | | | |

**Y# 1112 ROUBLE**
8.53 g., 0.925 Silver 0.2537 oz. ASW, 25 mm. **Subject:** Space Force

| Date | Mintage | VF20 | XF40 | MS60 | MS63 | MS65 |
|---|---|---|---|---|---|---|
| 2007 | — | PF65 40.00 | | | | |

**Y# 833a ROUBLE**
3.00 g., Nickel Plated Steel, 20.5 mm. **Obv:** Two headed eagle above curved bank name and date, denomination above **Rev:** Value and flower

| Date | Mintage | VF20 | XF40 | MS60 | MS63 | MS65 |
|---|---|---|---|---|---|---|
| 2009 ММД | — | — | — | 0.75 | 1.50 | 2.50 |
| 2009 СПМД | — | — | — | 0.75 | 1.50 | 2.50 |
| 2010 ММД | — | — | — | 0.75 | 1.50 | 2.50 |
| 2010 СПМД | — | — | — | 2.00 | 3.00 | 5.00 |
| 2011 ММД | — | — | — | 0.75 | 1.50 | 2.50 |
| 2012 ММД | — | — | — | 0.75 | 1.50 | 2.50 |

**Y# 1204 ROUBLE**
8.53 g., 0.925 Silver 0.2537 oz. ASW, 25 mm. **Subject:** Air Force

| Date | Mintage | VF20 | XF40 | MS60 | MS63 | MS65 |
|---|---|---|---|---|---|---|
| 2009 | — | PF65 30.00 | | | | |

**Y# 1205 ROUBLE**
8.53 g., 0.925 Silver 0.2537 oz. ASW, 25 mm. **Subject:** Air Force

| Date | Mintage | VF20 | XF40 | MS60 | MS63 | MS65 |
|---|---|---|---|---|---|---|
| 2009 | — | PF65 30.00 | | | | |

**Y# 1206 ROUBLE**
8.53 g., 0.925 Silver 0.2537 oz. ASW, 25 mm. **Subject:** Air Force

| Date | Mintage | VF20 | XF40 | MS60 | MS63 | MS65 |
|---|---|---|---|---|---|---|
| 2009 | — | PF65 30.00 | | | | |

**Y# 1244 ROUBLE**
8.53 g., 0.925 Silver 0.2537 oz. ASW, 25 mm. **Subject:** Armored Forces **Rev:** Crowned eagle emblem

| Date | Mintage | VF20 | XF40 | MS60 | MS63 | MS65 |
|---|---|---|---|---|---|---|
| 2010 | — | PF65 30.00 | | | | |

**Y# 1245 ROUBLE**
8.53 g., 0.925 Silver 0.2537 oz. ASW, 25 mm. **Subject:** Armored Force **Rev:** Tank advancing left

| Date | Mintage | VF20 | XF40 | MS60 | MS63 | MS65 |
|---|---|---|---|---|---|---|
| 2010 | — | PF65 30.00 | | | | |

**Y# 1246 ROUBLE**
8.53 g., 0.925 Silver 0.2537 oz. ASW, 25 mm. **Subject:** Armored Force **Rev:** Tank advancing right

| Date | Mintage | VF20 | XF40 | MS60 | MS63 | MS65 |
|---|---|---|---|---|---|---|
| 2010 | — | PF65 30.00 | | | | |

**Y# 1253 ROUBLE**
8.53 g., 0.925 Silver 0.2537 oz. ASW, 25 mm. **Subject:** Russian Aviation

| Date | Mintage | VF20 | XF40 | MS60 | MS63 | MS65 |
|---|---|---|---|---|---|---|
| 2010 | — | PF65 30.00 | | | | |

**Y# 1254 ROUBLE**
8.53 g., 0.925 Silver 0.2537 oz. ASW, 25 mm. **Subject:** Russian Aviation

| Date | Mintage | VF20 | XF40 | MS60 | MS63 | MS65 |
|---|---|---|---|---|---|---|
| 2010 | — | PF65 30.00 | | | | |

**Y# 1302 ROUBLE**
8.53 g., 0.925 Silver 0.2537 oz. ASW, 25 mm. **Subject:** Russian Aviation **Rev:** TU-144 flying right, color tracer

| Date | Mintage | VF20 | XF40 | MS60 | MS63 | MS65 |
|---|---|---|---|---|---|---|
| 2011 | 5,000 | PF65 30.00 | | | | |

**Y# 1303 ROUBLE**
8.53 g., 0.925 Silver 0.2537 oz. ASW, 25 mm. **Subject:** Russian Aviation **Rev:** U-2 biplane in flight left, color tracer

| Date | Mintage | VF20 | XF40 | MS60 | MS63 | MS65 |
|---|---|---|---|---|---|---|
| 2011 | 5,000 | **PF65** 30.00 | | | | |

**Y# 1310 ROUBLE**
8.53 g., 0.925 Silver 0.2537 oz. ASW, 25 mm. **Subject:** Strategis Missile Forces **Rev:** Emblem with crowned double ehaded eagle

| Date | Mintage | VF20 | XF40 | MS60 | MS63 | MS65 |
|---|---|---|---|---|---|---|
| 2011 | 5,000 | **PF65** 30.00 | | | | |

**Y# 1311 ROUBLE**
8.53 g., 0.925 Silver 0.2537 oz. ASW, 25 mm. **Subject:** Strategic Missile Forces **Rev:** Mobile missile system

| Date | Mintage | VF20 | XF40 | MS60 | MS63 | MS65 |
|---|---|---|---|---|---|---|
| 2011 | 5,000 | **PF65** 30.00 | | | | |

**Y# 1312 ROUBLE**
8.53 g., 0.925 Silver 0.2537 oz. ASW, 25 mm. **Subject:** Strategic Missile Forces **Rev:** Missile system against mountian background

| Date | Mintage | VF20 | XF40 | MS60 | MS63 | MS65 |
|---|---|---|---|---|---|---|
| 2011 | 5,000 | **PF65** 30.00 | | | | |

**Y# 1355 ROUBLE**
8.53 g., 0.925 Silver 0.2537 oz. ASW, 25 mm. **Subject:** Russian Aviation, I-16

| Date | Mintage | VF20 | XF40 | MS60 | MS63 | MS65 |
|---|---|---|---|---|---|---|
| 2012 | 5,000 | **PF65** 30.00 | | | | |

**Y# 1356 ROUBLE**
8.53 g., 0.925 Silver 0.2537 oz. ASW, 25 mm. **Subject:** Russian Aviation, IL-76

| Date | Mintage | VF20 | XF40 | MS60 | MS63 | MS65 |
|---|---|---|---|---|---|---|
| 2012 | 5,000 | **PF65** 30.00 | | | | |

**Y# 1375 ROUBLE**
8.53 g., 0.925 Silver 0.2537 oz. ASW, 25 mm. **Subject:** Court of Arbitration

| Date | Mintage | VF20 | XF40 | MS60 | MS63 | MS65 |
|---|---|---|---|---|---|---|
| 2012 | 3,000 | **PF65** 35.00 | | | | |

**Y# 1428 ROUBLE**
8.53 g., 0.925 Silver 0.2537 oz. ASW, 25 mm. **Subject:** Russian Aviation **Rev:** Tu-160 in flight right

| Date | Mintage | VF20 | XF40 | MS60 | MS63 | MS65 |
|---|---|---|---|---|---|---|
| 2013 СПМД | 5,000 | **PF65** 30.00 | | | | |

**Y# 1429 ROUBLE**
8.53 g., 0.925 Silver 0.2537 oz. ASW, 25 mm. **Subject:** Russian aviation **Rev:** AHT-25 plane in flight

| Date | Mintage | VF20 | XF40 | MS60 | MS63 | MS65 |
|---|---|---|---|---|---|---|
| 2013 СПМД | 5,000 | **PF65** 40.00 | | | | |

**Y# 1512 ROUBLE**
3.00 g., Nickel Plated Steel, 20.5 mm. **Rev:** New rouble symbol at left

| Date | Mintage | F12 | VF20 | XF40 | MS60 | MS63 |
|---|---|---|---|---|---|---|
| 2014 | 100,000,000 | — | — | — | 2.00 | 3.00 |

**Y# 1564 ROUBLE**
8.53 g., 0.925 Silver 0.2537 oz. ASW, 25 mm. **Rev:** YAK-3 flying left, color field

| Date | Mintage | F12 | VF20 | XF40 | MS60 | MS63 |
|---|---|---|---|---|---|---|
| 2014 | 5,000 | **PF65** 65.00 | | | | |

**Y# 1565 ROUBLE**
8.53 g., 0.925 Silver 0.2537 oz. ASW, 25 mm. **Rev:** BE-200 flying right, color field

| Date | Mintage | F12 | VF20 | XF40 | MS60 | MS63 |
|---|---|---|---|---|---|---|
| 2014 | 5,000 | **PF65** 65.00 | | | | |

**Y# 605 2 ROUBLES**
5.10 g., Copper-Nickel-Zinc, 23 mm. **Obv:** Double-headed eagle **Rev:** Value and vine sprig **Edge:** Segmented reeding

| Date | Mintage | VF20 | XF40 | MS60 | MS63 | MS65 |
|---|---|---|---|---|---|---|
| 2001 M Rare | — | — | — | — | — | — |

**Y# 675 2 ROUBLES**
5.10 g., Copper-Nickel, 23 mm. **Subject:** Yuri Gagarin **Obv:** Value and date to left of vine sprig **Rev:** Uniformed bust facing **Edge:** Segmented reeding

| Date | Mintage | VF20 | XF40 | MS60 | MS63 | MS65 |
|---|---|---|---|---|---|---|
| 2001 | — | 100 | 125 | 175 | — | — |
| 2001 ММД | 10,000,000 | — | — | 2.00 | 4.00 | 6.00 |
| 2001 СПМД | 10,000,000 | — | — | 2.00 | 4.00 | 6.00 |

**Y# 730 2 ROUBLES**
17.00 g., 0.925 Silver 0.5056 oz. ASW, 33 mm. **Subject:** V.I. Dal **Obv:** Double-headed eagle **Rev:** Portrait, book, signature, figures **Edge:** Reeded

| Date | Mintage | VF20 | XF40 | MS60 | MS63 | MS65 |
|---|---|---|---|---|---|---|
| 2001 (m) | 7,500 | **PF65** 80.00 | | | | |

**Y# 742 2 ROUBLES**
17.00 g., 0.925 Silver 0.5056 oz. ASW, 33 mm. **Subject:** Zodiac Signs **Obv:** Double-headed eagle within beaded circle **Rev:** Leo **Edge:** Reeded

| Date | Mintage | VF20 | XF40 | MS60 | MS63 | MS65 |
|---|---|---|---|---|---|---|
| 2002 (m) | — | **PF63** 45.00 | **PF65** 55.00 | | | |

**Y# 747 2 ROUBLES**
17.00 g., 0.925 Silver 0.5056 oz. ASW, 33 mm. **Subject:** Zodiac Signs **Obv:** Double-headed eagle within beaded circle **Rev:** Virgo and stars **Edge:** Reeded

| Date | Mintage | VF20 | XF40 | MS60 | MS63 | MS65 |
|---|---|---|---|---|---|---|
| 2002 (m) | 20,000 | **PF63** 45.00 | **PF65** 55.00 | | | |

**Y# 761 2 ROUBLES**
17.00 g., 0.925 Silver 0.5056 oz. ASW, 33 mm. **Subject:** Zodiac Signs **Obv:** Double-headed eagle within beaded circle **Rev:** Capricorn **Edge:** Reeded

| Date | Mintage | VF20 | XF40 | MS60 | MS63 | MS65 |
|---|---|---|---|---|---|---|
| 2002 (sp) | 20,000 | **PF63** 45.00 | **PF65** 55.00 | | | |

**Y# 762 2 ROUBLES**
17.00 g., 0.925 Silver 0.5056 oz. ASW, 33 mm. **Subject:** Zodiac Signs **Obv:** Double-headed eagle within beaded circle **Rev:** Sagittarius **Edge:** Reeded

| Date | Mintage | VF20 | XF40 | MS60 | MS63 | MS65 |
|---|---|---|---|---|---|---|
| 2002 (sp) | 20,000 | **PF63** 45.00 | **PF65** 55.00 | | | |

**Y# 766 2 ROUBLES**
17.00 g., 0.925 Silver 0.5056 oz. ASW, 33 mm. **Subject:** Zodiac Signs **Obv:** Double-headed eagle within beaded circle **Rev:** Scorpion **Edge:** Reeded

| Date | Mintage | VF20 | XF40 | MS60 | MS63 | MS65 |
|---|---|---|---|---|---|---|
| 2002 (m) | 20,000 | **PF63** 45.00 | **PF65** 55.00 | | | |

**Y# 768 2 ROUBLES**
17.00 g., 0.925 Silver 0.5056 oz. ASW, 33 mm. **Subject:** Zodiac Signs **Obv:** Double-headed eagle **Rev:** Balance scale **Edge:** Reeded

| Date | Mintage | VF20 | XF40 | MS60 | MS63 | MS65 |
|---|---|---|---|---|---|---|
| 2002 (sp) | 20,000 | **PF63** 45.00 | **PF65** 55.00 | | | |

**Y# 793 2 ROUBLES**
17.00 g., 0.925 Silver 0.5056 oz. ASW, 33 mm. **Subject:** L.P. Orlova **Obv:** Double-headed eagle **Rev:** Head facing **Edge:** Reeded

| Date | Mintage | VF20 | XF40 | MS60 | MS63 | MS65 |
|---|---|---|---|---|---|---|
| 2002 (m) | 10,000 | **PF65** 40.00 | | | | |

**Y# 834 2 ROUBLES**
5.10 g., Copper-Nickel-Zinc, 23 mm. **Obv:** Two headed eagle above curved bank name and date, denomination above **Rev:** Value and flower **Edge:** Segmented reeding

| Date | Mintage | VF20 | XF40 | MS60 | MS63 | MS65 |
|---|---|---|---|---|---|---|
| 2002 ММД Mint sets only | 15,000 | — | — | — | — | — |
| 2002 СПМД Mint sets only | 15,000 | — | — | — | — | — |
| 2003 ММД | 15,000 | — | 300 | 400 | 500 | — |
| 2006 ММД | — | — | — | 4.00 | 5.00 | 7.00 |
| 2006 СПМД | — | — | — | 4.00 | 5.00 | 7.00 |
| 2007 ММД | — | — | — | 4.00 | 5.00 | 7.00 |
| 2007 СПМД | — | — | — | 4.00 | 5.00 | 7.00 |
| 2008 ММД | — | — | — | 4.00 | 5.00 | 7.00 |
| 2008 СПМД | — | — | — | 4.00 | 5.00 | 7.00 |
| 2009 ММД | — | — | — | 4.00 | 5.00 | 7.00 |
| 2009 СПМД | — | — | — | 4.00 | 5.00 | 7.00 |

**Y# 803 2 ROUBLES**
17.10 g., 0.925 Silver 0.5085 oz. ASW, 32.8 mm. **Subject:** Zodiac signs **Obv:** Double-headed eagle within beaded circle **Rev:** Pisces **Edge:** Reeded

| Date | Mintage | VF20 | XF40 | MS60 | MS63 | MS65 |
|---|---|---|---|---|---|---|
| 2003 (sp) | 20,000 | **PF63** 45.00 | **PF65** 55.00 | | | |

**Y# 804 2 ROUBLES**
17.10 g., 0.925 Silver 0.5085 oz. ASW, 32.8 mm. **Subject:** Zodiac signs **Obv:** Double-headed eagle within beaded circle **Rev:** Aquarius **Edge:** Reeded

| Date | Mintage | VF20 | XF40 | MS60 | MS63 | MS65 |
|---|---|---|---|---|---|---|
| 2003 (m) | 20,000 | **PF63** 45.00 | **PF65** 55.00 | | | |

**Y# 820 2 ROUBLES**
17.00 g., 0.925 Silver 0.5056 oz. ASW, 33 mm. **Subject:** Zodiac signs **Obv:** Double-headed eagle within beaded circle **Rev:** Cancer Crayfish **Edge:** Reeded

| Date | Mintage | VF20 | XF40 | MS60 | MS63 | MS65 |
|---|---|---|---|---|---|---|
| 2003 (sp) | 20,000 | **PF63** 45.00 | **PF65** 55.00 | | | |

**Y# 840 2 ROUBLES**
16.81 g., 0.925 Silver 0.4999 oz. ASW, 33 mm. **Rev:** Guil Yarovsky

| Date | Mintage | VF20 | XF40 | MS60 | MS63 | MS65 |
|---|---|---|---|---|---|---|
| 2003 (m) | 10,000 | **PF65** 40.00 | | | | |

**Y# 841 2 ROUBLES**
16.81 g., 0.925 Silver 0.4999 oz. ASW, 33 mm. **Rev:** Fedor Tyutchev

| Date | Mintage | VF20 | XF40 | MS60 | MS63 | MS65 |
|---|---|---|---|---|---|---|
| 2003 (sp) | 10,000 | **PF65** 40.00 | | | | |

**Y# 844 2 ROUBLES**
17.00 g., 0.925 Silver 0.5056 oz. ASW, 33 mm. **Subject:** Zodiac Signs **Obv:** Double-headed eagle within beaded circle **Rev:** Aries

| Date | Mintage | VF20 | XF40 | MS60 | MS63 | MS65 |
|---|---|---|---|---|---|---|
| 2003 | 20,000 | **PF63** 45.00 | **PF65** 55.00 | | | |

**Y# 845 2 ROUBLES**
17.00 g., 0.925 Silver 0.5056 oz. ASW, 33 mm. **Subject:** Zodiac Signs **Obv:** Double-headed eagle within beaded circle **Rev:** Taurus

| Date | Mintage | VF20 | XF40 | MS60 | MS63 | MS65 |
|---|---|---|---|---|---|---|
| 2003 | 20,000 | **PF63** 45.00 | **PF65** 55.00 | | | |

**Y# 846 2 ROUBLES**
17.00 g., 0.925 Silver 0.5056 oz. ASW, 33 mm. **Subject:** Zodiac Signs **Obv:** Double-headed eagle within beaded circle **Rev:** Gemini

| Date | Mintage | VF20 | XF40 | MS60 | MS63 | MS65 |
|---|---|---|---|---|---|---|
| 2003 | 20,000 | **PF63** 45.00 | **PF65** 55.00 | | | |

**Y# 842 2 ROUBLES**
16.81 g., 0.925 Silver 0.4999 oz. ASW, 33 mm. **Rev:** V. P. Tchkalov

| Date | Mintage | VF20 | XF40 | MS60 | MS63 | MS65 |
|---|---|---|---|---|---|---|
| 2004 (m) | 7,000 | **PF65** 50.00 | | | | |

**Y# 843 2 ROUBLES**
16.81 g., 0.925 Silver 0.4999 oz. ASW, 33 mm. **Rev:** Mikhail Glinka

| Date | Mintage | VF20 | XF40 | MS60 | MS63 | MS65 |
|---|---|---|---|---|---|---|
| 2004 (m) | 7,000 | **PF65** 50.00 | | | | |

**Y# 1021 2 ROUBLES**
16.80 g., 0.925 Silver 0.4996 oz. ASW, 33 mm. **Subject:** Sini Rerikh, 100th Anniversary of Birth

| Date | Mintage | VF20 | XF40 | MS60 | MS63 | MS65 |
|---|---|---|---|---|---|---|
| 2004 | — | **PF65** 60.00 | | | | |

**Y# 897 2 ROUBLES**
17.00 g., 0.925 Silver 0.5056 oz. ASW, 33 mm. **Obv:** Double-headed eagle **Rev:** Gemini twins **Edge:** Reeded

| Date | Mintage | VF20 | XF40 | MS60 | MS63 | MS65 |
|---|---|---|---|---|---|---|
| 2005 | 20,000 | **PF63** 45.00 | **PF65** 55.00 | | | |

**Y# 899 2 ROUBLES**
17.00 g., 0.925 Silver 0.5056 oz. ASW, 33 mm. **Obv:** Double-headed eagle **Rev:** Cancer Crayfish **Edge:** Reeded

| Date | Mintage | VF20 | XF40 | MS60 | MS63 | MS65 |
|---|---|---|---|---|---|---|
| 2005 | 20,000 | **PF63** 45.00 | **PF65** 55.00 | | | |

**Y# 901 2 ROUBLES**
17.00 g., 0.925 Silver 0.5056 oz. ASW, 33 mm. **Obv:** Double-headed eagle **Rev:** Leo lion **Edge:** Reeded

| Date | Mintage | VF20 | XF40 | MS60 | MS63 | MS65 |
|---|---|---|---|---|---|---|
| 2005 | 20,000 | **PF63** 45.00 | **PF65** 55.00 | | | |

**Y# 905 2 ROUBLES**
17.00 g., 0.925 Silver 0.5056 oz. ASW, 33 mm. **Obv:** Double-headed eagle **Rev:** Mikhail Sholokhov with pen in hand **Edge:** Reeded

| Date | Mintage | VF20 | XF40 | MS60 | MS63 | MS65 |
|---|---|---|---|---|---|---|
| 2005 | 10,000 | **PF65** 40.00 | | | | |

**Y# 909 2 ROUBLES**
17.00 g., 0.925 Silver 0.5056 oz. ASW, 33 mm. **Obv:** Double-headed eagle **Rev:** Peter Klodt viewing man and horse statue **Edge:** Reeded

| Date | Mintage | VF20 | XF40 | MS60 | MS63 | MS65 |
|---|---|---|---|---|---|---|
| 2005 | 10,000 | **PF65** 40.00 | | | | |

**Y# 914 2 ROUBLES**
17.00 g., 0.925 Silver 0.5056 oz. ASW, 33 mm. **Obv:** Double-headed eagle **Rev:** Virgo standing lady **Edge:** Reeded

| Date | Mintage | VF20 | XF40 | MS60 | MS63 | MS65 |
|---|---|---|---|---|---|---|
| 2005 | 20,000 | **PF63** 45.00 | **PF65** 55.00 | | | |

**Y# 919 2 ROUBLES**
17.00 g., 0.925 Silver 0.5056 oz. ASW, 33 mm. **Obv:** Double-headed eagle **Rev:** Libra - 2 stylized birds forming a balance scale **Edge:** Reeded

| Date | Mintage | VF20 | XF40 | MS60 | MS63 | MS65 |
|---|---|---|---|---|---|---|
| 2005 | 20,000 | **PF63** 45.00 | **PF65** 55.00 | | | |

**Y# 921 2 ROUBLES**
17.00 g., 0.925 Silver 0.5056 oz. ASW, 33 mm. **Obv:** Double-headed eagle **Rev:** Scorpio scorpion **Edge:** Reeded

| Date | Mintage | VF20 | XF40 | MS60 | MS63 | MS65 |
|---|---|---|---|---|---|---|
| 2005 | 20,000 | **PF63** 45.00 | **PF65** 55.00 | | | |

**Y# 926 2 ROUBLES**
17.00 g., 0.925 Silver 0.5056 oz. ASW, 33 mm. **Obv:** Double-headed eagle **Rev:** Sagittarius the archer **Edge:** Reeded

| Date | Mintage | VF20 | XF40 | MS60 | MS63 | MS65 |
|---|---|---|---|---|---|---|
| 2005 | 20,000 | **PF63** 45.00 | **PF65** 55.00 | | | |

**Y# 928 2 ROUBLES**
17.00 g., 0.925 Silver 0.5056 oz. ASW, 33 mm. **Obv:** Double-headed eagle **Rev:** Capricorn as half goat and fish **Edge:** Reeded

| Date | Mintage | VF20 | XF40 | MS60 | MS63 | MS65 |
|---|---|---|---|---|---|---|
| 2005 | 20,000 | **PF63** 45.00 | **PF65** 55.00 | | | |

**Y# 930 2 ROUBLES**
17.00 g., 0.925 Silver 0.5056 oz. ASW, 33 mm. **Obv:** Double-headed eagle **Rev:** Pisces as catfish and sturgeon **Edge:** Reeded

| Date | Mintage | VF20 | XF40 | MS60 | MS63 | MS65 |
|---|---|---|---|---|---|---|
| 2005 | 20,000 | **PF63** 45.00 | **PF65** 55.00 | | | |

**Y# 932 2 ROUBLES**
17.00 g., 0.925 Silver 0.5056 oz. ASW, 33 mm. **Obv:** Double-headed eagle **Rev:** Aries ram **Edge:** Reeded

| Date | Mintage | VF20 | XF40 | MS60 | MS63 | MS65 |
|---|---|---|---|---|---|---|
| 2005 | 20,000 | **PF63** 45.00 | **PF65** 55.00 | | | |

**Y# 934 2 ROUBLES**
17.00 g., 0.925 Silver 0.5056 oz. ASW, 33 mm. **Obv:** Double-headed eagle **Rev:** Taurus bull **Edge:** Reeded

| Date | Mintage | VF20 | XF40 | MS60 | MS63 | MS65 |
|---|---|---|---|---|---|---|
| 2005 | 20,000 | **PF63** 45.00 **PF65** 55.00 | | | | |

**Y# 936 2 ROUBLES**
17.00 g., 0.925 Silver 0.5056 oz. ASW, 33 mm. **Obv:** Double-headed eagle **Rev:** Aquarius water carrier **Edge:** Reeded

| Date | Mintage | VF20 | XF40 | MS60 | MS63 | MS65 |
|---|---|---|---|---|---|---|
| 2005 | 20,000 | **PF63** 45.00 **PF65** 55.00 | | | | |

**Y# 1054 2 ROUBLES**
16.80 g., 0.925 Silver 0.4996 oz. ASW, 33 mm. **Subject:** O. K. Antonov, 100th Anniversary of Birth

| Date | Mintage | VF20 | XF40 | MS60 | MS63 | MS65 |
|---|---|---|---|---|---|---|
| 2006 | — | **PF65** 50.00 | | | | |

**Y# 1055 2 ROUBLES**
16.80 g., 0.925 Silver 0.4996 oz. ASW, 33 mm. **Subject:** M. A. Vrubel, 150th Anniversary of Birth

| Date | Mintage | VF20 | XF40 | MS60 | MS63 | MS65 |
|---|---|---|---|---|---|---|
| 2006 | — | **PF65** 50.00 | | | | |

**Y# 1056 2 ROUBLES**
16.80 g., 0.925 Silver 0.4996 oz. ASW, 33 mm. **Subject:** A. A. Ivanov, 200th Anniversary of Birth

| Date | Mintage | VF20 | XF40 | MS60 | MS63 | MS65 |
|---|---|---|---|---|---|---|
| 2006 | — | **PF65** 50.00 | | | | |

**Y# 1057 2 ROUBLES**
16.80 g., 0.925 Silver 0.4996 oz. ASW, 33 mm. **Subject:** D. D. Shostakovich, 100th Anniversary of Birth

| Date | Mintage | VF20 | XF40 | MS60 | MS63 | MS65 |
|---|---|---|---|---|---|---|
| 2006 | — | **PF65** 50.00 | | | | |

**Y# 967 2 ROUBLES**
17.00 g., 0.925 Silver 0.5056 oz. ASW, 33.0 mm. **Subject:** 100th Anniversary Birth of Gerasimov **Obv:** Two-headed eagle **Rev:** Gerasimov recreating a man's face **Rev. Legend:** M. M. ГЕРАСИМОВ

| Date | Mintage | VF20 | XF40 | MS60 | MS63 | MS65 |
|---|---|---|---|---|---|---|
| 2007 (m) | 10,000 | **PF65** 45.00 | | | | |

**Y# 968 2 ROUBLES**
17.00 g., 0.925 Silver 0.5056 oz. ASW, 33.0 mm. **Subject:** 150th Anniversary Birth of Tsiolkovsky **Rev:** Bust of Tsiolkovsky 3/4 right at left, scheme of two flight vehicles with earth in background at upper right **Rev. Legend:** К. Э. ЦИОЛКОВСКИЈ **Edge:** Reeded

| Date | Mintage | VF20 | XF40 | MS60 | MS63 | MS65 |
|---|---|---|---|---|---|---|
| 2007 (m) | 10,000 | **PF65** 45.00 | | | | |

**Y# 1104 2 ROUBLES**
16.80 g., 0.925 Silver 0.4996 oz. ASW, 33 mm. **Subject:** S.P. Korolyov, 100th Anniversary of Birth

| Date | Mintage | VF20 | XF40 | MS60 | MS63 | MS65 |
|---|---|---|---|---|---|---|
| 2007 | — | **PF65** 50.00 | | | | |

**Y# 1105 2 ROUBLES**
16.80 g., 0.925 Silver 0.4996 oz. ASW, 33 mm. **Subject:** V.M. Bekhterev, 150th Anniversary of Birth

| Date | Mintage | VF20 | XF40 | MS60 | MS63 | MS65 |
|---|---|---|---|---|---|---|
| 2007 | — | **PF65** 50.00 | | | | |

**Y# 1106 2 ROUBLES**
16.80 g., 0.925 Silver 0.4996 oz. ASW, 33 mm. **Subject:** L. Euler, 300th Anniversary of Birth

| Date | Mintage | VF20 | XF40 | MS60 | MS63 | MS65 |
|---|---|---|---|---|---|---|
| 2007 | — | **PF65** 50.00 | | | | |

**Y# 1107 2 ROUBLES**
16.80 g., 0.925 Silver 0.4996 oz. ASW, 33 mm. **Subject:** V. P. Soloviev - Sedoy, 100th Anniversary of Birth

| Date | Mintage | VF20 | XF40 | MS60 | MS63 | MS65 |
|---|---|---|---|---|---|---|
| 2007 | — | **PF65** 50.00 | | | | |

**Y# 979 2 ROUBLES**
15.55 g., 0.925 Silver 0.4624 oz. ASW, 33 mm. **Obv:** Double headed eagle **Rev:** Black caped marmot **Edge:** Reeded

| Date | Mintage | VF20 | XF40 | MS60 | MS63 | MS65 |
|---|---|---|---|---|---|---|
| 2008 | — | **PF65** 45.00 | | | | |

**Y# 980 2 ROUBLES**
15.55 g., 0.925 Silver 0.4624 oz. ASW, 33 mm. **Obv:** Double headed eagle **Rev:** Shemaya fish **Edge:** Reeded

| Date | Mintage | VF20 | XF40 | MS60 | MS63 | MS65 |
|---|---|---|---|---|---|---|
| 2008 | — | **PF65** 50.00 | | | | |

**Y# 1131 2 ROUBLES**
16.80 g., 0.925 Silver 0.4996 oz. ASW, 33 mm. **Subject:** L. D. Landau, 100th Anniversary of Birth

| Date | Mintage | VF20 | XF40 | MS60 | MS63 | MS65 |
|---|---|---|---|---|---|---|
| 2008 | — | **PF65** 70.00 | | | | |

**Y# 1132 2 ROUBLES**
16.80 g., 0.925 Silver 0.4996 oz. ASW, 33 mm. **Subject:** V. P. Glushko, 100th Anniversary of Birth

| Date | Mintage | VF20 | XF40 | MS60 | MS63 | MS65 |
|---|---|---|---|---|---|---|
| 2008 | — | **PF65** 55.00 | | | | |

**Y# 1133 2 ROUBLES**
16.80 g., 0.925 Silver 0.4996 oz. ASW, 33 mm. **Subject:** D. F. Oistrakh, 100th Anniversary of Birth

| Date | Mintage | VF20 | XF40 | MS60 | MS63 | MS65 |
|---|---|---|---|---|---|---|
| 2008 | — | **PF65** 55.00 | | | | |

**Y# 1134 2 ROUBLES**
16.80 g., 0.925 Silver 0.4996 oz. ASW, 33 mm. **Subject:** I. M. Frank. 100th Anniversary of Birth

| Date | Mintage | VF20 | XF40 | MS60 | MS63 | MS65 |
|---|---|---|---|---|---|---|
| 2008 | — | **PF65** 55.00 | | | | |

**Y# 1135 2 ROUBLES**
16.80 g., 0.925 Silver 0.4996 oz. ASW, 33 mm. **Subject:** N. N. Nosoc, 100th Anniversary of Birth

| Date | Mintage | VF20 | XF40 | MS60 | MS63 | MS65 |
|---|---|---|---|---|---|---|
| 2008 | — | **PF65** 55.00 | | | | |

**Y# 1136 2 ROUBLES**
16.80 g., 0.925 Silver 0.4996 oz. ASW, 33 mm. **Subject:** V. I. Nemirovich, 100th Anniversary of Birth

| Date | Mintage | VF20 | XF40 | MS60 | MS63 | MS65 |
|---|---|---|---|---|---|---|
| 2008 | — | **PF65** 50.00 | | | | |

**Y# 1137 2 ROUBLES**
16.80 g., 0.925 Silver 0.4996 oz. ASW, 33 mm. **Subject:** E. V. Vuchetich, 100th Anniversary of Birth

| Date | Mintage | VF20 | XF40 | MS60 | MS63 | MS65 |
|---|---|---|---|---|---|---|
| 2008 | — | **PF65** 50.00 | | | | |

**Y# 1146 2 ROUBLES**
16.80 g., 0.925 Silver 0.4996 oz. ASW, 33 mm. **Subject:** Emperor Dragon Fly

| Date | Mintage | VF20 | XF40 | MS60 | MS63 | MS65 |
|---|---|---|---|---|---|---|
| 2008 | — | **PF65** 45.00 | | | | |

**Y# 834a 2 ROUBLES**
5.00 g., Nickel Plated Steel, 23 mm. **Obv:** Two headed eagle above curved bank name and date, denomination above **Rev:** Value and flower **Edge:** Segmented reeding

| Date | Mintage | VF20 | XF40 | MS60 | MS63 | MS65 |
|---|---|---|---|---|---|---|
| 2009 ММД | — | — | — | 0.50 | 1.00 | 1.50 |
| 2009 СПМД | — | — | — | 0.50 | 1.00 | 1.50 |
| 2010 ММД | — | — | — | 0.50 | 1.00 | 1.50 |
| 2010 СПМД | — | — | — | 0.50 | 1.00 | 1.50 |
| 2011 ММД | — | — | — | 0.50 | 1.00 | 1.50 |
| 2012 ММД | — | — | — | 0.50 | 1.00 | 1.50 |

**Y# 1158 2 ROUBLES**
16.80 g., 0.925 Silver 0.4996 oz. ASW, 33 mm. **Subject:** D. I. Mendeleyev, 175th Anniversary of Birth

| Date | Mintage | VF20 | XF40 | MS60 | MS63 | MS65 |
|---|---|---|---|---|---|---|
| 2009 | — | **PF65** 50.00 | | | | |

**Y# 1190 2 ROUBLES**
16.80 g., 0.925 Silver 0.4996 oz. ASW, 33 mm. **Subject:** A. V. Koltsov, 200th Anniversary of Birth

| Date | Mintage | VF20 | XF40 | MS60 | MS63 | MS65 |
|---|---|---|---|---|---|---|
| 2009 | — | **PF65** 50.00 | | | | |

**Y# 1191 2 ROUBLES**
16.80 g., 0.925 Silver 0.4996 oz. ASW, 33 mm. **Subject:** A. N. Voronikhin, 250th Anniversary of Birth

| Date | Mintage | VF20 | XF40 | MS60 | MS63 | MS65 |
|---|---|---|---|---|---|---|
| 2009 | — | **PF65** 60.00 | | | | |

**Y# 1192 2 ROUBLES**
16.80 g., 0.925 Silver 0.4996 oz. ASW, 33 mm. **Subject:** G. S. Ulanova, 100th Anniversary of Birth

| Date | Mintage | VF20 | XF40 | MS60 | MS63 | MS65 |
|---|---|---|---|---|---|---|
| 2009 | — | **PF65** 60.00 | | | | |

**Y# 1193 2 ROUBLES**
16.80 g., 0.925 Silver 0.4996 oz. ASW, 33 mm. **Subject:** L. I. Yashin, Soccer player

| Date | Mintage | VF20 | XF40 | MS60 | MS63 | MS65 |
|---|---|---|---|---|---|---|
| 2009 | — | **PF65** 100 | | | | |

**Y# 1194 2 ROUBLES**
16.80 g., 0.925 Silver 0.4996 oz. ASW, 33 mm. **Subject:** E. I. Beskov, Soccer player

| Date | Mintage | VF20 | XF40 | MS60 | MS63 | MS65 |
|---|---|---|---|---|---|---|
| 2009 | — | **PF65** 100 | | | | |

**Y# 1195 2 ROUBLES**
16.80 g., 0.925 Silver 0.4996 oz. ASW, 33 mm. **Subject:** E. A. Stresov, Soccer player

| Date | Mintage | VF20 | XF40 | MS60 | MS63 | MS65 |
|---|---|---|---|---|---|---|
| 2009 | — | **PF65** 100 | | | | |

**Y# 1196 2 ROUBLES**
16.80 g., 0.925 Silver 0.4996 oz. ASW, 33 mm. **Subject:** V. M. Bobrov, Hockey player

| Date | Mintage | VF20 | XF40 | MS60 | MS63 | MS65 |
|---|---|---|---|---|---|---|
| 2009 | — | PF65 125 | | | | |

**Y# 1197 2 ROUBLES**
16.80 g., 0.925 Silver 0.4996 oz. ASW, 33 mm. **Subject:** A. N. Maltzev, Hockey player

| Date | Mintage | VF20 | XF40 | MS60 | MS63 | MS65 |
|---|---|---|---|---|---|---|
| 2009 | — | PF65 125 | | | | |

**Y# 1198 2 ROUBLES**
16.80 g., 0.925 Silver 0.4996 oz. ASW, 33 mm. **Subject:** V. B. Kharlamov, Hockey player

| Date | Mintage | VF20 | XF40 | MS60 | MS63 | MS65 |
|---|---|---|---|---|---|---|
| 2009 | — | PF65 125 | | | | |

**Y# 1216 2 ROUBLES**
16.80 g., 0.925 Silver 0.4996 oz. ASW, 33 mm. **Subject:** N. I. Pirogov, 200th Anniversary of Birth

| Date | Mintage | VF20 | XF40 | MS60 | MS63 | MS65 |
|---|---|---|---|---|---|---|
| 2010 | — | PF65 65.00 | | | | |

**Y# 1217 2 ROUBLES**
16.80 g., 0.925 Silver 0.4996 oz. ASW, 33 mm. **Subject:** I. I. Levitan, 150th Anniversary of Birth

| Date | Mintage | VF20 | XF40 | MS60 | MS63 | MS65 |
|---|---|---|---|---|---|---|
| 2010 | — | PF65 100 | | | | |

**Y# 1218 2 ROUBLES**
16.80 g., 0.925 Silver 0.4996 oz. ASW, 33 mm. **Subject:** G. S. Ulanova, 100th Anniversary of Birth

| Date | Mintage | VF20 | XF40 | MS60 | MS63 | MS65 |
|---|---|---|---|---|---|---|
| 2010 | — | PF65 55.00 | | | | |

**Y# 1248 2 ROUBLES**
16.80 g., 0.925 Silver 0.4996 oz. ASW, 33 mm. **Subject:** Sika Deer

| Date | Mintage | VF20 | XF40 | MS60 | MS63 | MS65 |
|---|---|---|---|---|---|---|
| 2010 | — | PF65 45.00 | | | | |

**Y# 1249 2 ROUBLES**
16.80 g., 0.925 Silver 0.4996 oz. ASW, 33 mm. **Subject:** Short tailed albatross

| Date | Mintage | VF20 | XF40 | MS60 | MS63 | MS65 |
|---|---|---|---|---|---|---|
| 2010 | — | PF65 45.00 | | | | |

**Y# 1250 2 ROUBLES**
16.80 g., 0.925 Silver 0.4996 oz. ASW, 33 mm. **Subject:** Gjursa

| Date | Mintage | VF20 | XF40 | MS60 | MS63 | MS65 |
|---|---|---|---|---|---|---|
| 2010 | — | PF65 45.00 | | | | |

**Y# 1307 2 ROUBLES**
22.26 g., 0.925 Silver 0.662 oz. ASW, 34 mm. **Subject:** Year of Russian Culture and Language in Italy **Obv:** St. George slaying dragon **Rev:** St. Nicholas church in Bari

| Date | Mintage | VF20 | XF40 | MS60 | MS63 | MS65 |
|---|---|---|---|---|---|---|
| 2011 | 10,000 | PF65 60.00 | | | | |

**Y# 1319 2 ROUBLES**
17.00 g., 0.925 Silver 0.5056 oz. ASW, 33 mm. **Subject:** M.M. Botvinnik **Rev:** Chess player and board

| Date | Mintage | VF20 | XF40 | MS60 | MS63 | MS65 |
|---|---|---|---|---|---|---|
| 2011 | 3,000 | PF65 100 | | | | |

**Y# 1320 2 ROUBLES**
17.00 g., 0.925 Silver 0.5056 oz. ASW, 33 mm. **Subject:** A.I. Raykin **Rev:** Portrait left **Edge:** Reeded

| Date | Mintage | VF20 | XF40 | MS60 | MS63 | MS65 |
|---|---|---|---|---|---|---|
| 2011 | 3,000 | PF65 125 | | | | |

**Y# 1325 2 ROUBLES**
16.81 g., 0.925 Silver 0.4999 oz. ASW, 33 mm. **Subject:** I.A. Goncharov, 200th Anniversary of Birth **Rev:** Half-length figure seated reading

| Date | Mintage | VF20 | XF40 | MS60 | MS63 | MS65 |
|---|---|---|---|---|---|---|
| 2012 | 5,000 | PF65 60.00 | | | | |

**Y# 1326 2 ROUBLES**
16.81 g., 0.925 Silver 0.4999 oz. ASW, 33 mm. **Subject:** P.A. Stolypin, 150th Anniversary of Birth **Rev:** Half-length figure standing in cap and with hands behind back

| Date | Mintage | VF20 | XF40 | MS60 | MS63 | MS65 |
|---|---|---|---|---|---|---|
| 2012 | 5,000 | PF65 60.00 | | | | |

**Y# 1327 2 ROUBLES**
16.81 g., 0.999 Silver 0.5399 oz. ASW, 33 mm. **Subject:** M.V. Nesterov, 150th Anniversary of Birth

| Date | Mintage | VF20 | XF40 | MS60 | MS63 | MS65 |
|---|---|---|---|---|---|---|
| 2012 | 3,000 | PF65 60.00 | | | | |

**Y# 1328 2 ROUBLES**

16.81 g., 0.925 Silver 0.4999 oz. ASW, 33 mm. **Subject:** I.N. Kramskoy, 175th Anniversary of Birth **Rev:** Portrait painting in color

| Date | Mintage | VF20 | XF40 | MS60 | MS63 | MS65 |
|---|---|---|---|---|---|---|
| 2012 | 5,000 | PF65 60.00 | | | | |

**Y# 1329 2 ROUBLES**

16.81 g., 0.925 Silver 0.4999 oz. ASW, 33 mm. **Subject:** A.I. Vasilyev, 270th Anniversary of Birth

| Date | Mintage | VF20 | XF40 | MS60 | MS63 | MS65 |
|---|---|---|---|---|---|---|
| 2012 | 5,000 | PF65 60.00 | | | | |

**Y# 1357 2 ROUBLES**

16.80 g., 0.925 Silver 0.4996 oz. ASW, 33 mm. **Subject:** Alpine Weasel

| Date | Mintage | VF20 | XF40 | MS60 | MS63 | MS65 |
|---|---|---|---|---|---|---|
| 2012 | 5,000 | PF65 55.00 | | | | |

**Y# 1358 2 ROUBLES**

16.80 g., 0.925 Silver 0.4996 oz. ASW, 33 mm. **Subject:** Yellow-billed Loon

| Date | Mintage | VF20 | XF40 | MS60 | MS63 | MS65 |
|---|---|---|---|---|---|---|
| 2012 | 5,000 | PF65 55.00 | | | | |

**Y# 1359 2 ROUBLES**

16.80 g., 0.925 Silver 0.4996 oz. ASW, 33 mm. **Subject:** Emerald Rosalia Beetle

| Date | Mintage | VF20 | XF40 | MS60 | MS63 | MS65 |
|---|---|---|---|---|---|---|
| 2012 | 5,000 | PF65 55.00 | | | | |

**Y# 1361 2 ROUBLES**

16.80 g., 0.925 Silver 0.4996 oz. ASW, 33 mm. **Subject:** M.G. Isakova, skater

| Date | Mintage | VF20 | XF40 | MS60 | MS63 | MS65 |
|---|---|---|---|---|---|---|
| 2012 | 3,000 | PF65 60.00 | | | | |

**Y# 1362 2 ROUBLES**

16.80 g., 0.925 Silver 0.4996 oz. ASW, 33 mm. **Subject:** L.P. Skoblikova, skater

| Date | Mintage | VF20 | XF40 | MS60 | MS63 | MS65 |
|---|---|---|---|---|---|---|
| 2012 | 3,000 | PF65 60.00 | | | | |

**Y# 1363 2 ROUBLES**

16.80 g., 0.925 Silver 0.4996 oz. ASW, 33 mm. **Subject:** E.R. Grishin, skater

| Date | Mintage | VF20 | XF40 | MS60 | MS63 | MS65 |
|---|---|---|---|---|---|---|
| 2012 | 3,000 | PF65 60.00 | | | | |

**Y# 1391 2 ROUBLES**

5.00 g., Nickel Plated Steel, 23 mm. **Subject:** War of 1812, 200th Anniversary

| Date | Mintage | VF20 | XF40 | MS60 | MS63 | MS65 |
|---|---|---|---|---|---|---|
| 2012 | 5,000,000 | — | — | 1.00 | 2.00 | 3.50 |

**Y# 1392 2 ROUBLES**

5.00 g., Nickel Plated Steel, 23 mm. **Subject:** General Field-Marshal M.I. Kutuzov

| Date | Mintage | VF20 | XF40 | MS60 | MS63 | MS65 |
|---|---|---|---|---|---|---|
| 2012 ММД | 5,000,000 | — | — | 1.00 | 2.00 | 3.50 |

**Y# 1393 2 ROUBLES**

5.00 g., Nickel Plated Steel, 23 mm. **Subject:** General Field Marshal M.B. Barklay de Tolly

| Date | Mintage | VF20 | XF40 | MS60 | MS63 | MS65 |
|---|---|---|---|---|---|---|
| 2012 ММД | 5,000,000 | — | — | 1.00 | 2.00 | 3.50 |

**Y# 1394 2 ROUBLES**

5.00 g., Nickel Plated Steel, 23 mm. **Subject:** Infantry General P.I. Bagration

| Date | Mintage | VF20 | XF40 | MS60 | MS63 | MS65 |
|---|---|---|---|---|---|---|
| 2012 ММД | 5,000,000 | — | — | 1.00 | 2.00 | 3.50 |

**Y# 1395 2 ROUBLES**

5.00 g., Nickel Plated Steel, 23 mm. **Subject:** Calvary General L.L. Benningsen

| Date | Mintage | VF20 | XF40 | MS60 | MS63 | MS65 |
|---|---|---|---|---|---|---|
| 2012 ММД | 5,000,000 | — | — | 1.00 | 2.00 | 3.50 |

**Y# 1396 2 ROUBLES**

5.00 g., Nickel Plated Steel, 23 mm. **Subject:** General Field-Marshal P.H. Witgenstein

| Date | Mintage | VF20 | XF40 | MS60 | MS63 | MS65 |
|---|---|---|---|---|---|---|
| 2012 ММД | 5,000,000 | — | — | 1.00 | 2.00 | 3.50 |

**Y# 1397 2 ROUBLES**

5.00 g., Nickel Plated Steel, 23 mm. **Subject:** Lieutenant General D.V. Davidov

| Date | Mintage | VF20 | XF40 | MS60 | MS63 | MS65 |
|---|---|---|---|---|---|---|
| 2012 ММД | 5,000,000 | — | — | 1.00 | 2.00 | 3.50 |

**Y# 1398 2 ROUBLES**

5.00 g., Nickel Plated Steel, 23 mm. **Subject:** Infantry General, D.S. Dohkturov

| Date | Mintage | VF20 | XF40 | MS60 | MS63 | MS65 |
|---|---|---|---|---|---|---|
| 2012 ММД | 5,000,000 | — | — | 1.00 | 2.00 | 3.50 |

**Y# 1399 2 ROUBLES**

5.00 g., Nickel Plated Steel, 23 mm. **Subject:** Staff Captain N.A. Durova

| Date | Mintage | VF20 | XF40 | MS60 | MS63 | MS65 |
|---|---|---|---|---|---|---|
| 2012 ММД | 5,000,000 | — | — | 1.00 | 2.00 | 3.50 |

**Y# 1400 2 ROUBLES**

5.00 g., Nickel Plated Steel, 23 mm. **Subject:** Infantry General A.P. Yermolov

| Date | Mintage | VF20 | XF40 | MS60 | MS63 | MS65 |
|---|---|---|---|---|---|---|
| 2012 ММД | 5,000,000 | — | — | 1.00 | 2.00 | 3.50 |

**Y# 1401 2 ROUBLES**
5.00 g., Nickel Plated Steel, 23 mm. **Subject:** Kozhina Vasilisa, organizer of the partisan movement

| Date | Mintage | VF20 | XF40 | MS60 | MS63 | MS65 |
|---|---|---|---|---|---|---|
| 2012 ММД | 5,000,000 | — | — | 1.00 | 2.00 | 3.50 |

**Y# 1402 2 ROUBLES**
5.00 g., Nickel Plated Steel, 23 mm. **Subject:** Major General A.I. Kutaisov

| Date | Mintage | VF20 | XF40 | MS60 | MS63 | MS65 |
|---|---|---|---|---|---|---|
| 2012 ММД | 5,000,000 | — | — | 1.00 | 2.00 | 3.50 |

**Y# 1403 2 ROUBLES**
5.00 g., Nickel Plated Steel, 23 mm. **Subject:** Infantry General M.A. Miloradovich

| Date | Mintage | VF20 | XF40 | MS60 | MS63 | MS65 |
|---|---|---|---|---|---|---|
| 2012 ММД | 5,000,000 | — | — | 1.00 | 2.00 | 3.50 |

**Y# 1404 2 ROUBLES**
5.00 g., Nickel Plated Steel, 23 mm. **Subject:** Infantry General A.I. Osterman-Tolstoi

| Date | Mintage | VF20 | XF40 | MS60 | MS63 | MS65 |
|---|---|---|---|---|---|---|
| 2012 ММД | 5,000,000 | — | — | 1.00 | 2.00 | 3.50 |

**Y# 1405 2 ROUBLES**
5.00 g., Nickel Plated Steel, 23 mm. **Subject:** Calvary General N.N. Rayevsky

| Date | Mintage | VF20 | XF40 | MS60 | MS63 | MS65 |
|---|---|---|---|---|---|---|
| 2012 ММД | 5,000,000 | — | — | 1.00 | 2.00 | 3.50 |

**Y# 1406 2 ROUBLES**
5.00 g., Nickel Plated Steel, 23 mm. **Subject:** Calvary General M.I. Platov

| Date | Mintage | VF20 | XF40 | MS60 | MS63 | MS65 |
|---|---|---|---|---|---|---|
| 2012 ММД | 5,000,000 | — | — | 1.00 | 2.00 | 3.50 |

**Y# 1407 2 ROUBLES**
5.00 g., Nickel Plated Steel, 23 mm. **Subject:** Tsar Alexander I

| Date | Mintage | VF20 | XF40 | MS60 | MS63 | MS65 |
|---|---|---|---|---|---|---|
| 2012 ММД | 5,000,000 | — | — | 1.00 | 2.00 | 3.50 |

**Y# 1419 2 ROUBLES**
17.00 g., 0.925 Silver 0.5056 oz. ASW, 33 mm. **Subject:** A.S. Dargomyzhsky, 200th Anniversary of Birth **Rev:** Water nymph and water-mill at left, Dargomyzhsky portrait at right **Edge:** Reeded

| Date | Mintage | VF20 | XF40 | MS60 | MS63 | MS65 |
|---|---|---|---|---|---|---|
| 2013 ММД | 5,000 | PF65 50.00 | | | | |

**Y# 1426 2 ROUBLES**
17.00 g., 0.925 Silver 0.5056 oz. ASW, 33 mm. **Subject:** V.I. Vernadsky, 150th Anniversary of Birth **Rev:** Bust at center, lattice sphere and stars in background **Edge:** Reeded

| Date | Mintage | VF20 | XF40 | MS60 | MS63 | MS65 |
|---|---|---|---|---|---|---|
| 2013 СПМД | 5,000 | PF65 50.00 | | | | |

**Y# 1427 2 ROUBLES**
17.00 g., 0.925 Silver 0.5056 oz. ASW, 33 mm. **Subject:** V.S.Chernomyrdin, 75th Anniversary of Birth **Rev:** Bust left **Edge:** Reeded

| Date | Mintage | VF20 | XF40 | MS60 | MS63 | MS65 |
|---|---|---|---|---|---|---|
| 2013 ММД | 5,000 | PF65 50.00 | | | | |

**Y# 1431 2 ROUBLES**
17.00 g., 0.925 Silver 0.5056 oz. ASW, 33 mm. **Subject:** A.I. Pokryshkin, 100th Anniversary of Birth **Rev:** Bust at left, plane at right **Edge:** Reeded

| Date | Mintage | VF20 | XF40 | MS60 | MS63 | MS65 |
|---|---|---|---|---|---|---|
| 2013 ММД | 5,000 | PF65 50.00 | | | | |

**Y# 1553 2 ROUBLES**
17.00 g., 0.925 Silver 0.5056 oz. ASW, 33 mm. **Rev:** Soldatov sheatfish

| Date | Mintage | F12 | VF20 | XF40 | MS60 | MS63 |
|---|---|---|---|---|---|---|
| 2014 | 5,000 | PF65 50.00 | | | | |

**Y# 1550 2 ROUBLES**
17.00 g., 0.925 Silver 0.5056 oz. ASW, 33 mm. **Subject:** V.N. Chelomey, 100th Anniversary of Birth **Rev:** Bust facing right, orbital space station at right

| Date | Mintage | F12 | VF20 | XF40 | MS60 | MS63 |
|---|---|---|---|---|---|---|
| 2014 | 3,000 | PF65 50.00 | | | | |

**Y# 1551 2 ROUBLES**
17.00 g., 0.925 Silver 0.5056 oz. ASW, 33 mm. **Rev:** Asiatic wild donkey galloping left

| Date | Mintage | F12 | VF20 | XF40 | MS60 | MS63 |
|---|---|---|---|---|---|---|
| 2014 | 5,000 | PF65 50.00 | | | | |

**Y# 1552 2 ROUBLES**
17.00 g., 0.925 Silver 0.5056 oz. ASW, 33 mm. **Rev:** Glossy ibis

| Date | Mintage | F12 | VF20 | XF40 | MS60 | MS63 |
|---|---|---|---|---|---|---|
| 2014 | 5,000 | PF65 50.00 | | | | |

**Y# 677 3 ROUBLES**
34.88 g., 0.900 Silver 1.0093 oz. ASW, 39 mm. **Subject:** 225 Years - Bolshoi Theater **Obv:** Double-headed eagle **Rev:** Standing figures facing **Edge:** Reeded

| Date | Mintage | VF20 | XF40 | MS60 | MS63 | MS65 |
|---|---|---|---|---|---|---|
| 2001 | 7,500 | PF65 75.00 | | | | |

**Y# 680 3 ROUBLES**
34.88 g., 0.900 Silver 1.0093 oz. ASW, 39 mm. **Subject:** 40th Anniversary of Manned Space Flight - Yuri Gagarin **Obv:** Double-headed eagle **Rev:** Uniformed bust holding dove **Edge:** Reeded

| Date | Mintage | VF20 | XF40 | MS60 | MS63 | MS65 |
|---|---|---|---|---|---|---|
| 2001 | 7,500 | PF65 125 | | | | |

**Y# 682 3 ROUBLES**
34.88 g., 0.900 Silver 1.0093 oz. ASW, 39 mm. **Subject:** Siberian Exploration **Obv:** Double-headed eagle **Rev:** Men riding horses, deer and sleds **Edge:** Reeded

| Date | Mintage | VF20 | XF40 | MS60 | MS63 | MS65 |
|---|---|---|---|---|---|---|
| 2001 | 5,000 | PF65 100 | | | | |

**Y# 733 3 ROUBLES**
34.88 g., 0.900 Silver 1.0093 oz. ASW, 39 mm. **Subject:** 200th Anniversary of Navigation School **Obv:** Double-headed eagle **Rev:** Navigational tools and building **Edge:** Reeded

| Date | Mintage | VF20 | XF40 | MS60 | MS63 | MS65 |
|---|---|---|---|---|---|---|
| 2001 | 5,000 | PF65 80.00 | | | | |

**Y# 734 3 ROUBLES**
34.88 g., 0.900 Silver 1.0093 oz. ASW, 39 mm. **Subject:** First Moscow Savings Bank **Obv:** Double-headed eagle **Rev:** Beehive above building within circle **Edge:** Reeded

| Date | Mintage | VF20 | XF40 | MS60 | MS63 | MS65 |
|---|---|---|---|---|---|---|
| 2001 | 17,500 | PF63 50.00 | PF65 60.00 | | | |

**Y# 735 3 ROUBLES**
34.88 g., 0.900 Silver 1.0093 oz. ASW, 39 mm. **Subject:** State Labor Savings Bank **Obv:** Double-headed eagle **Rev:** Dam, passbook and tractor **Edge:** Reeded

| Date | Mintage | VF20 | XF40 | MS60 | MS63 | MS65 |
|---|---|---|---|---|---|---|
| 2001 | 17,500 | PF63 50.00 | PF65 60.00 | | | |

**Y# 736 3 ROUBLES**
34.88 g., 0.900 Silver 1.0093 oz. ASW, 39 mm. **Subject:** Savings Bank of the Russian Federation **Obv:** Double-headed eagle **Rev:** Chevrons above building **Edge:** Reeded

| Date | Mintage | VF20 | XF40 | MS60 | MS63 | MS65 |
|---|---|---|---|---|---|---|
| 2001 | 17,500 | PF63 50.00 | PF65 60.00 | | | |

**Y# 737 3 ROUBLES**
34.88 g., 0.900 Silver 1.0093 oz. ASW, 39 mm. **Subject:** 10th Anniversary - Commonwealth of Independent States **Obv:** Double-headed eagle **Rev:** Hologram below logo **Edge:** Reeded

| Date | Mintage | VF20 | XF40 | MS60 | MS63 | MS65 |
|---|---|---|---|---|---|---|
| 2001 | 7,500 | PF63 55.00 | PF65 65.00 | | | |

**Y# 738 3 ROUBLES**
34.88 g., 0.900 Silver 1.0093 oz. ASW, 39 mm. **Subject:** Olympics **Obv:** Double-headed eagle **Rev:** Cross-country skiers **Edge:** Reeded

| Date | Mintage | VF20 | XF40 | MS60 | MS63 | MS65 |
|---|---|---|---|---|---|---|
| 2002 | 25,000 | PF63 45.00 | PF65 55.00 | | | |

**Y# 744 3 ROUBLES**
34.88 g., 0.900 Silver 1.0093 oz. ASW, 39 mm. **Subject:** St. John's Nunnery, St. Petersburg **Obv:** Double-headed eagle **Rev:** Nunnery and cameo **Edge:** Reeded

| Date | Mintage | VF20 | XF40 | MS60 | MS63 | MS65 |
|---|---|---|---|---|---|---|
| 2002 | — | PF63 225 | PF65 250 | | | |

**Y# 755 3 ROUBLES**
34.88 g., 0.900 Silver 1.0093 oz. ASW, 39 mm. **Subject:** Admiral Nakhimov **Obv:** Double-headed eagle **Rev:** Monument, Admiral with cannon and naval battle scene **Edge:** Reeded

| Date | Mintage | VF20 | XF40 | MS60 | MS63 | MS65 |
|---|---|---|---|---|---|---|
| 2002 (sp) | 10,000 | PF65 80.00 | | | | |

**Y# 756 3 ROUBLES**
34.88 g., 0.900 Silver 1.0093 oz. ASW, 39 mm. **Subject:** Hermitage **Obv:** Double-headed eagle **Rev:** Statues and arch **Edge:** Reeded

| Date | Mintage | VF20 | XF40 | MS60 | MS63 | MS65 |
|---|---|---|---|---|---|---|
| 2002 (sp) | 10,000 | PF65 75.00 | | | | |

**Y# 778 3 ROUBLES**
34.88 g., 0.900 Silver 1.0093 oz. ASW, 39 mm. **Subject:** Kideksha **Obv:** Double-headed eagle **Rev:** Three churches on river bank **Edge:** Reeded

| Date | Mintage | VF20 | XF40 | MS60 | MS63 | MS65 |
|---|---|---|---|---|---|---|
| 2002 (sp) | 10,000 | PF63 85.00 | PF65 100 | | | |

**Y# 779 3 ROUBLES**
34.88 g., 0.900 Silver 1.0093 oz. ASW, 39 mm. **Subject:** Iversky Monastery, Valdaiy **Obv:** Double-headed eagle **Rev:** Building complex on an island in Lake Valdaiy **Edge:** Reeded

| Date | Mintage | VF20 | XF40 | MS60 | MS63 | MS65 |
|---|---|---|---|---|---|---|
| 2002 (sp) | 10,000 | PF63 85.00 | PF65 100 | | | |

**Y# 780 3 ROUBLES**
34.88 g., 0.900 Silver 1.0093 oz. ASW, 39 mm. **Subject:** Miraculous Savior Church **Obv:** Double-headed eagle **Rev:** Church with separate bell tower **Edge:** Reeded

| Date | Mintage | VF20 | XF40 | MS60 | MS63 | MS65 |
|---|---|---|---|---|---|---|
| 2002 (m) | 5,000 | **PF63** 120 | **PF65** 135 | | | |

**Y# 781 3 ROUBLES**
34.88 g., 0.900 Silver 1.0093 oz. ASW, 39 mm. **Subject:** Works of Dionissy **Obv:** Double-headed eagle **Rev:** The Crucifix **Edge:** Reeded

| Date | Mintage | VF20 | XF40 | MS60 | MS63 | MS65 |
|---|---|---|---|---|---|---|
| 2002 (sp) | 10,000 | **PF63** 115 | **PF65** 135 | | | |

**Y# 787 3 ROUBLES**
34.88 g., 0.900 Silver 1.0093 oz. ASW, 39 mm. **Subject:** World Cup Soccer **Obv:** Double-headed eagle **Rev:** Soccer ball within circle of players **Edge:** Reeded

| Date | Mintage | VF20 | XF40 | MS60 | MS63 | MS65 |
|---|---|---|---|---|---|---|
| 2002 (sp) | 25,000 | **PF65** 60.00 | | | | |

**Y# 801 3 ROUBLES**
34.80 g., 0.900 Silver 1.007 oz. ASW, 38.7 mm. **Subject:** Veborg **Obv:** Double-headed eagle **Rev:** Sailing ships and buildings **Edge:** Reeded

| Date | Mintage | VF20 | XF40 | MS60 | MS63 | MS65 |
|---|---|---|---|---|---|---|
| 2003 (sp) | 10,000 | **PF63** 55.00 | **PF65** 65.00 | | | |

**Y# 802 3 ROUBLES**
34.75 g., 0.900 Silver 1.0055 oz. ASW, 38.7 mm. **Subject:** Lunar Calendar **Obv:** National emblem **Rev:** Mountain goat in crescent **Edge:** Reeded

| Date | Mintage | VF20 | XF40 | MS60 | MS63 | MS65 |
|---|---|---|---|---|---|---|
| 2003 (m) | 15,000 | **PF63** 60.00 | **PF65** 75.00 | | | |

**Y# 805 3 ROUBLES**
34.84 g., 0.900 Silver 1.0081 oz. ASW, 38.8 mm. **Subject:** Zodiac signs **Obv:** Double-headed eagle within beaded circle **Rev:** Leo **Edge:** Reeded

| Date | Mintage | VF20 | XF40 | MS60 | MS63 | MS65 |
|---|---|---|---|---|---|---|
| 2003 (m) | 30,000 | **PF63** 60.00 | **PF65** 75.00 | | | |

**Y# 806 3 ROUBLES**
34.74 g., 0.900 Silver 1.0052 oz. ASW, 38.8 mm. **Subject:** St. Daniel's Monastery **Obv:** Double-headed eagle **Rev:** Statue and monastery **Edge:** Reeded

| Date | Mintage | VF20 | XF40 | MS60 | MS63 | MS65 |
|---|---|---|---|---|---|---|
| 2003 (m) | 10,000 | **PF65** 50.00 | | | | |

**Y# 807 3 ROUBLES**
34.74 g., 0.900 Silver 1.0052 oz. ASW, 38.8 mm. **Subject:** World Biathlon Championships **Obv:** Double-headed eagle **Rev:** Rifleman and archer on skis **Edge:** Reeded

| Date | Mintage | VF20 | XF40 | MS60 | MS63 | MS65 |
|---|---|---|---|---|---|---|
| 2003 (m) | 7,500 | **PF65** 60.00 | | | | |

**Y# 808 3 ROUBLES**
34.74 g., 0.900 Silver 1.0052 oz. ASW, 38.8 mm. **Obv:** Double-headed eagle **Rev:** Monastery **Edge:** Reeded

| Date | Mintage | VF20 | XF40 | MS60 | MS63 | MS65 |
|---|---|---|---|---|---|---|
| 2003 (m) | 10,000 | **PF65** 50.00 | | | | |

**Y# 809 3 ROUBLES**
34.74 g., 0.900 Silver 1.0052 oz. ASW, 38.8 mm. **Subject:** First Kamchatka Expedition **Obv:** Double-headed eagle **Rev:** Natives, fish and ship **Edge:** Reeded

| Date | Mintage | VF20 | XF40 | MS60 | MS63 | MS65 |
|---|---|---|---|---|---|---|
| 2003 (sp) | 10,000 | **PF65** 80.00 | | | | |

**Y# 810 3 ROUBLES**
34.74 g., 0.900 Silver 1.0052 oz. ASW, 38.8 mm. **Subject:** Zodiac signs **Obv:** Double-headed eagle within beaded circle **Rev:** Virgo **Edge:** Reeded

| Date | Mintage | VF20 | XF40 | MS60 | MS63 | MS65 |
|---|---|---|---|---|---|---|
| 2003 (sp) | 30,000 | **PF63** 60.00 | **PF65** 75.00 | | | |

**Y# 811 3 ROUBLES**
34.74 g., 0.900 Silver 1.0052 oz. ASW, 38.8 mm. **Subject:** Zodiac signs **Obv:** Double-headed eagle within beaded circle **Rev:** Libra **Edge:** Reeded

| Date | Mintage | VF20 | XF40 | MS60 | MS63 | MS65 |
|---|---|---|---|---|---|---|
| 2003 (m) | 30,000 | **PF63** 60.00 | **PF65** 75.00 | | | |

**Y# 812 3 ROUBLES**
34.74 g., 0.900 Silver 1.0052 oz. ASW, 38.8 mm. **Subject:** Diveyevsky Monastery **Obv:** Double-headed eagle **Rev:** Cameo above churches **Edge:** Reeded

| Date | Mintage | VF20 | XF40 | MS60 | MS63 | MS65 |
|---|---|---|---|---|---|---|
| 2003 (sp) | 10,000 | **PF63** 120 | **PF65** 135 | | | |

**Y# 813 3 ROUBLES**
34.74 g., 0.900 Silver 1.0052 oz. ASW, 38.8 mm. **Subject:** Zodiac Signs **Obv:** Double-headed eagle within beaded circle **Rev:** Scorpio **Edge:** Reeded

| Date | Mintage | VF20 | XF40 | MS60 | MS63 | MS65 |
|---|---|---|---|---|---|---|
| 2003 (m) | 30,000 | **PF65** 75.00 | | | | |

**Y# 848 3 ROUBLES**
34.56 g., 0.900 Silver 1.000 oz. ASW, 39 mm. **Subject:** Zodiac Signs **Obv:** Double-headed eagle within beaded circle **Rev:** Sagittarius

| Date | Mintage | VF20 | XF40 | MS60 | MS63 | MS65 |
|---|---|---|---|---|---|---|
| 2003 (sp) | 30,000 | **PF63** 60.00 | **PF65** 75.00 | | | |

**Y# 849 3 ROUBLES**
34.56 g., 0.900 Silver 1.000 oz. ASW, 39 mm. **Subject:** Zodiac Signs **Obv:** Double-headed eagle within beaded circle **Rev:** Capricorn

| Date | Mintage | VF20 | XF40 | MS60 | MS63 | MS65 |
|---|---|---|---|---|---|---|
| 2003 (m) | 30,000 | **PF63** 60.00 | **PF65** 75.00 | | | |

**Y# 885 3 ROUBLES**
34.80 g., 0.900 Silver 1.007 oz. ASW, 38.7 mm. **Subject:** City of Pskov 1100th Anniversary **Obv:** Double-headed eagle **Rev:** Walled city view **Edge:** Reeded

| Date | Mintage | VF20 | XF40 | MS60 | MS63 | MS65 |
|---|---|---|---|---|---|---|
| 2003 (sp) | — | **PF63** 85.00 | **PF65** 100 | | | |

**Y# 1012 3 ROUBLES**
33.90 g., 0.925 Silver 1.0082 oz. ASW, 39 mm. **Subject:** Year of the Goat

| Date | Mintage | VF20 | XF40 | MS60 | MS63 | MS65 |
|---|---|---|---|---|---|---|
| 2003 | — | **PF65** 50.00 | | | | |

**Y# 850 3 ROUBLES**
34.56 g., 0.900 Silver 1.000 oz. ASW, 39 mm. **Subject:** Lunar Calendar **Rev:** Monkey

| Date | Mintage | VF20 | XF40 | MS60 | MS63 | MS65 |
|---|---|---|---|---|---|---|
| 2004 (m) | 15,000 | **PF63** 60.00 | **PF65** 75.00 | | | |

**Y# 851 3 ROUBLES**
34.56 g., 0.900 Silver 1.000 oz. ASW, 39 mm. **Subject:** Zodiac Signs **Obv:** Double-headed eagle within beaded circle **Rev:** Aquarius

| Date | Mintage | VF20 | XF40 | MS60 | MS63 | MS65 |
|---|---|---|---|---|---|---|
| 2004 (sp) | 30,000 | **PF63** 60.00 | **PF65** 75.00 | | | |

**Y# 852 3 ROUBLES**
34.56 g., 0.900 Silver 1.000 oz. ASW, 39 mm. **Rev:** Tomsk

| Date | Mintage | VF20 | XF40 | MS60 | MS63 | MS65 |
|---|---|---|---|---|---|---|
| 2004 (m) | 8,000 | **PF65** 115 | | | | |

**Y# 853 3 ROUBLES**
34.56 g., 0.900 Silver 1.000 oz. ASW, 39 mm. **Subject:** Zodiac Signs **Obv:** Double-headed eagle within beaded circle **Rev:** Pisces

| Date | Mintage | VF20 | XF40 | MS60 | MS63 | MS65 |
|---|---|---|---|---|---|---|
| 2004 (m) | 30,000 | **PF63** 60.00 | **PF65** 75.00 | | | |

**Y# 854 3 ROUBLES**
34.56 g., 0.900 Silver 1.000 oz. ASW, 39 mm. **Rev:** Epiphany Cathedral, Moscow

| Date | Mintage | VF20 | XF40 | MS60 | MS63 | MS65 |
|---|---|---|---|---|---|---|
| 2004 (m) | 8,000 | **PF65** 115 | | | | |

**Y# 855 3 ROUBLES**
34.56 g., 0.900 Silver 1.000 oz. ASW, 39 mm. **Subject:** Zodiac Signs **Obv:** Double-headed eagle within beaded circle **Rev:** Aries

| Date | Mintage | VF20 | XF40 | MS60 | MS63 | MS65 |
|---|---|---|---|---|---|---|
| 2004 (sp) | 30,000 | **PF63** 60.00 | **PF65** 75.00 | | | |

**Y# 856 3 ROUBLES**
34.56 g., 0.900 Silver 1.000 oz. ASW, 39 mm. **Rev:** Soccer

| Date | Mintage | VF20 | XF40 | MS60 | MS63 | MS65 |
|---|---|---|---|---|---|---|
| 2004 (sp) | 10,000 | **PF63** 60.00 | **PF65** 75.00 | | | |

**Y# 857 3 ROUBLES**
34.56 g., 0.900 Silver 1.000 oz. ASW, 39 mm. **Subject:** Zodiac Signs **Obv:** Double-headed eagle within beaded circle **Rev:** Taurus

| Date | Mintage | VF20 | XF40 | MS60 | MS63 | MS65 |
|---|---|---|---|---|---|---|
| 2004 (sp) | 30,000 | PF63 60.00 | PF65 75.00 | | | |

**Y# 858 3 ROUBLES**
34.56 g., 0.900 Silver 1.000 oz. ASW, 39 mm. **Rev:** Olympic torch

| Date | Mintage | VF20 | XF40 | MS60 | MS63 | MS65 |
|---|---|---|---|---|---|---|
| 2004 (m) | 20,000 | PF63 55.00 | PF65 65.00 | | | |

**Y# 859 3 ROUBLES**
34.56 g., 0.900 Silver 1.000 oz. ASW, 39 mm. **Subject:** Zodiac Signs **Obv:** Double-headed eagle within beaded circle **Rev:** Gemini

| Date | Mintage | VF20 | XF40 | MS60 | MS63 | MS65 |
|---|---|---|---|---|---|---|
| 2004 (m) | 30,000 | PF63 65.00 | PF65 75.00 | | | |

**Y# 860 3 ROUBLES**
34.56 g., 0.900 Silver 1.000 oz. ASW, 39 mm. **Subject:** Zodiac Signs **Obv:** Double-headed eagle within beaded circle **Rev:** Cancer

| Date | Mintage | VF20 | XF40 | MS60 | MS63 | MS65 |
|---|---|---|---|---|---|---|
| 2004 (sp) | 30,000 | PF63 60.00 | PF65 75.00 | | | |

**Y# 861 3 ROUBLES**
34.56 g., 0.900 Silver 1.000 oz. ASW, 39 mm. **Rev:** Church of the Sign of the Holy Mother of God

| Date | Mintage | VF20 | XF40 | MS60 | MS63 | MS65 |
|---|---|---|---|---|---|---|
| 2004 (m) | 8,000 | PF63 110 | PF65 125 | | | |

**Y# 863 3 ROUBLES**
34.56 g., 0.900 Silver 1.000 oz. ASW, 39 mm. **Rev:** Peter I's monetary reform

| Date | Mintage | VF20 | XF40 | MS60 | MS63 | MS65 |
|---|---|---|---|---|---|---|
| 2004 (sp) | 8,000 | PF63 325 | PF65 375 | | | |

**Y# 1013 3 ROUBLES**
33.90 g., 0.925 Silver 1.0082 oz. ASW, 39 mm. **Subject:** 2nd Kamchatka Expedition, 1733-43

| Date | Mintage | VF20 | XF40 | MS60 | MS63 | MS65 |
|---|---|---|---|---|---|---|
| 2004 | — | PF63 65.00 | PF65 75.00 | | | |

**Y# 862 3 ROUBLES**
33.90 g., 0.925 Silver 1.0082 oz. ASW, 39 mm. **Subject:** Theophanes the Greek **Rev:** Transfiguration icon

| Date | Mintage | VF20 | XF40 | MS60 | MS63 | MS65 |
|---|---|---|---|---|---|---|
| 2004 | — | PF63 110 | PF65 125 | | | |

**Y# 1020 3 ROUBLES**
33.90 g., 0.925 Silver 1.0082 oz. ASW, 39 mm. **Subject:** Church of the Virgin Nativity in Gordniya

| Date | Mintage | VF20 | XF40 | MS60 | MS63 | MS65 |
|---|---|---|---|---|---|---|
| 2004 | — | PF63 110 | PF65 125 | | | |

**Y# 1022 3 ROUBLES**
33.90 g., 0.925 Silver 1.0082 oz. ASW, 39 mm. **Subject:** Reindeer

| Date | Mintage | VF20 | XF40 | MS60 | MS63 | MS65 |
|---|---|---|---|---|---|---|
| 2004 | — | PF63 65.00 | PF65 75.00 | | | |

**Y# 892 3 ROUBLES**
33.94 g., 0.925 Silver 1.0094 oz. ASW, 39 mm. **Obv:** Double-headed eagle **Rev:** Rooster and crescent moon **Edge:** Reeded

| Date | Mintage | VF20 | XF40 | MS60 | MS63 | MS65 |
|---|---|---|---|---|---|---|
| 2005 | 15,000 | PF63 60.00 | PF65 75.00 | | | |

**Y# 893 3 ROUBLES**
33.94 g., 0.925 Silver 1.0094 oz. ASW, 39 mm. **Subject:** 60th Anniversary - Victory Over Germany **Obv:** Double-headed eagle **Rev:** Soldier and wife circa 1945 **Edge:** Reeded

| Date | Mintage | VF20 | XF40 | MS60 | MS63 | MS65 |
|---|---|---|---|---|---|---|
| 2005 | 35,000 | PF63 45.00 | PF65 60.00 | | | |

**Y# 903 3 ROUBLES**
33.94 g., 0.925 Silver 1.0094 oz. ASW, 39 mm. **Obv:** Double-headed eagle **Rev:** St. Nicholas Cathedral in Kaliningrad **Edge:** Reeded

| Date | Mintage | VF20 | XF40 | MS60 | MS63 | MS65 |
|---|---|---|---|---|---|---|
| 2005 | 10,000 | PF63 60.00 | PF65 75.00 | | | |

**Y# 904 3 ROUBLES**

33.94 g., 0.925 Silver 1.0094 oz. ASW, 39 mm. **Obv:** Double-headed eagle **Rev:** Kropotkin Metro Station in Moscow **Edge:** Reeded

| Date | Mintage | VF20 | XF40 | MS60 | MS63 | MS65 |
|---|---|---|---|---|---|---|
| 2005 | 10,000 | **PF63** 60.00 | **PF65** 75.00 | | | |

**Y# 906 3 ROUBLES**

33.94 g., 0.925 Silver 1.0094 oz. ASW, 39 mm. **Subject:** Helsinki Games **Obv:** Double-headed eagle **Rev:** Stylized track and field athletes **Edge:** Reeded

| Date | Mintage | VF20 | XF40 | MS60 | MS63 | MS65 |
|---|---|---|---|---|---|---|
| 2005 | 10,000 | **PF63** 60.00 | **PF65** 75.00 | | | |

**Y# 908 3 ROUBLES**

33.94 g., 0.925 Silver 1.0094 oz. ASW, 39 mm. **Obv:** Double-headed eagle **Rev:** Virgin Monastery in Raifa, Tatarstan **Edge:** Reeded

| Date | Mintage | VF20 | XF40 | MS60 | MS63 | MS65 |
|---|---|---|---|---|---|---|
| 2005 | 10,000 | **PF63** 50.00 | **PF65** 65.00 | | | |

**Y# 910 3 ROUBLES**

33.94 g., 0.925 Silver 1.0094 oz. ASW, 39 mm. **Obv:** Double-headed eagle **Rev:** Kazan Theater Building **Edge:** Reeded

| Date | Mintage | VF20 | XF40 | MS60 | MS63 | MS65 |
|---|---|---|---|---|---|---|
| 2005 | 10,000 | **PF63** 60.00 | **PF65** 75.00 | | | |

**Y# 923 3 ROUBLES**

33.94 g., 0.925 Silver 1.0094 oz. ASW, 39 mm. **Subject:** 625th Anniversary - Battle of Kulikovo **Obv:** Double-headed eagle **Rev:** Carved Lion and Griffin between opposing armies **Edge:** Reeded

| Date | Mintage | VF20 | XF40 | MS60 | MS63 | MS65 |
|---|---|---|---|---|---|---|
| 2005 | 10,000 | **PF63** 60.00 | **PF65** 75.00 | | | |

**Y# 955 3 ROUBLES**

33.94 g., 0.925 Silver 1.0094 oz. ASW, 39 mm. **Subject:** Moscow's Lomonosov University **Obv:** Two headed eagle **Rev:** Lomonosov statue before university building and Moscow skyline **Edge:** Reeded

| Date | Mintage | VF20 | XF40 | MS60 | MS63 | MS65 |
|---|---|---|---|---|---|---|
| 2005 (m) | 10,000 | **PF63** 50.00 | **PF65** 65.00 | | | |

**Y# 1038 3 ROUBLES**

33.90 g., 0.925 Silver 1.0082 oz. ASW, 39 mm. **Subject:** I. V. Russakov, House of Culture

| Date | Mintage | VF20 | XF40 | MS60 | MS63 | MS65 |
|---|---|---|---|---|---|---|
| 2005 | — | **PF63** 50.00 | **PF65** 65.00 | | | |

**Y# 1039 3 ROUBLES**

33.90 g., 0.925 Silver 1.0082 oz. ASW, 39 mm. **Subject:** Novosibirsk State Academic Opera & Ballet

| Date | Mintage | VF20 | XF40 | MS60 | MS63 | MS65 |
|---|---|---|---|---|---|---|
| 2005 | — | **PF63** 60.00 | **PF65** 75.00 | | | |

**Y# 1040 3 ROUBLES**

33.90 g., 0.925 Silver 1.0082 oz. ASW, 39 mm. **Subject:** Year of the dog

| Date | Mintage | VF20 | XF40 | MS60 | MS63 | MS65 |
|---|---|---|---|---|---|---|
| 2006 | — | **PF63** 60.00 | **PF65** 75.00 | | | |

**Y# 1041 3 ROUBLES**

33.90 g., 0.925 Silver 1.0082 oz. ASW, 39 mm. **Subject:** Parliament, 100th Anniversary

| Date | Mintage | VF20 | XF40 | MS60 | MS63 | MS65 |
|---|---|---|---|---|---|---|
| 2006 | — | **PF63** 50.00 | **PF65** 65.00 | | | |

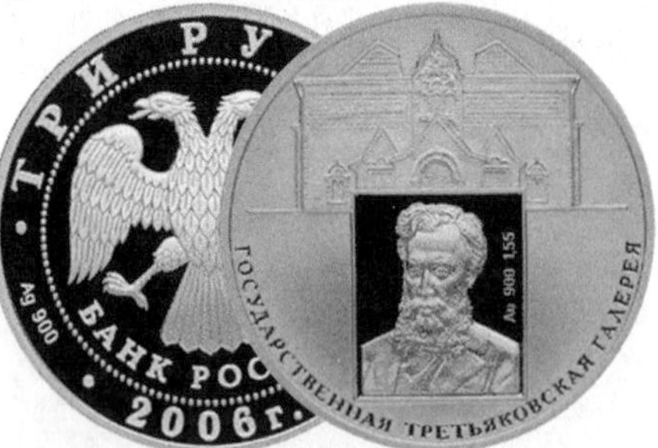


**Y# 1046 3 ROUBLES**

33.90 g., 0.925 Silver 1.0082 oz. ASW, 39 mm. **Subject:** Tretyakov State Gallery, 150th Anniversary

| Date | Mintage | VF20 | XF40 | MS60 | MS63 | MS65 |
|---|---|---|---|---|---|---|
| 2006 | — | **PF63** 200 | **PF65** 250 | | | |

**Y# 1048 3 ROUBLES**

33.90 g., 0.925 Silver 1.0082 oz. ASW, 39 mm. **Subject:** Russia Savings

| Date | Mintage | VF20 | XF40 | MS60 | MS63 | MS65 |
|---|---|---|---|---|---|---|
| 2006 | — | **PF63** 50.00 | **PF65** 65.00 | | | |

**Y# 1052 3 ROUBLES**

33.90 g., 0.925 Silver 1.0082 oz. ASW, 39 mm. **Subject:** State Bank Building, Nizhny Novgorod

| Date | Mintage | VF20 | XF40 | MS60 | MS63 | MS65 |
|---|---|---|---|---|---|---|
| 2006 | — | PF63 50.00 | PF65 65.00 | | | |

**Y# 1060 3 ROUBLES**
33.90 g., 0.925 Silver 1.0082 oz. ASW, 39 mm. **Subject:** Moscow's Kremlin and Red Square

| Date | Mintage | VF20 | XF40 | MS60 | MS63 | MS65 |
|---|---|---|---|---|---|---|
| 2006 | — | PF63 60.00 | PF65 70.00 | | | |

**Y# 1065 3 ROUBLES**
33.90 g., 0.925 Silver 1.0082 oz. ASW, 39 mm. **Subject:** XX Winter Olympics, Torino

| Date | Mintage | VF20 | XF40 | MS60 | MS63 | MS65 |
|---|---|---|---|---|---|---|
| 2006 | 12,500 | PF63 75.00 | PF65 95.00 | | | |

**Y# 1066 3 ROUBLES**
33.90 g., 0.925 Silver 1.0082 oz. ASW, 39 mm. **Subject:** FIFA World Cup, Germany

| Date | Mintage | VF20 | XF40 | MS60 | MS63 | MS65 |
|---|---|---|---|---|---|---|
| 2006 | — | PF63 65.00 | PF65 75.00 | | | |

**Y# 1079 3 ROUBLES**
33.90 g., 0.925 Silver 1.0082 oz. ASW, 39 mm. **Subject:** Year of the Dog

| Date | Mintage | VF20 | XF40 | MS60 | MS63 | MS65 |
|---|---|---|---|---|---|---|
| 2006 | — | PF65 60.00 | | | | |

**Y# 966 3 ROUBLES**
33.94 g., 0.925 Silver 1.0094 oz. ASW, 39 mm. **Subject:** 250th Anniversary Academy of the Arts **Obv:** Two-headed eagle **Rev:** Relief image of Minerva group **Rev. Legend:** РОССИЈСКАЯ - АКАДЕМИЯ ХУДОЖЕСТВ **Edge:** Reeded

| Date | Mintage | VF20 | XF40 | MS60 | MS63 | MS65 |
|---|---|---|---|---|---|---|
| 2007 (m) | 10,000 | PF63 50.00 | PF65 65.00 | | | |

**Y# 992 3 ROUBLES**
33.90 g., 0.925 Silver 1.0082 oz. ASW, 39 mm. **Subject:** Year of the Pig **Obv:** Double headed eagle **Rev:** Stylized pig

| Date | Mintage | VF20 | XF40 | MS60 | MS63 | MS65 |
|---|---|---|---|---|---|---|
| 2009 | 15,000 | PF63 70.00 | PF65 80.00 | | | |

**Y# 1080 3 ROUBLES**
33.90 g., 0.925 Silver 1.0082 oz. ASW, 39 mm. **Subject:** International Arctic Year

| Date | Mintage | VF20 | XF40 | MS60 | MS63 | MS65 |
|---|---|---|---|---|---|---|
| 2007 | — | PF63 60.00 | PF65 75.00 | | | |

**Y# 1087 3 ROUBLES**
33.90 g., 0.925 Silver 1.0082 oz. ASW **Subject:** First Artificial Earth Satellite, 50th Anniversary

| Date | Mintage | VF20 | XF40 | MS60 | MS63 | MS65 |
|---|---|---|---|---|---|---|
| 2007 | — | PF63 55.00 | PF65 65.00 | | | |

**Y# 1088 3 ROUBLES**
33.90 g., 0.925 Silver 1.0082 oz. ASW, 39 mm. **Subject:** Andrew Rublyov

| Date | Mintage | VF20 | XF40 | MS60 | MS63 | MS65 |
|---|---|---|---|---|---|---|
| 2007 | — | PF63 55.00 | PF65 65.00 | | | |

**Y# 1092 3 ROUBLES**
33.90 g., 0.925 Silver 1.0082 oz. ASW, 39 mm. **Subject:** Bashkira, 450th Anniversary of annexation by Russia

| Date | Mintage | VF20 | XF40 | MS60 | MS63 | MS65 |
|---|---|---|---|---|---|---|
| 2007 | — | PF63 55.00 | PF65 65.00 | | | |

**Y# 1100 3 ROUBLES**
33.90 g., 0.925 Silver 1.0082 oz. ASW, 39 mm. **Subject:** Nevyansk inclined tower, Sverdlorsk Region

| Date | Mintage | VF20 | XF40 | MS60 | MS63 | MS65 |
|---|---|---|---|---|---|---|
| 2007 | — | PF63 55.00 | PF65 65.00 | | | |

**Y# 1103 3 ROUBLES**
33.90 g., 0.925 Silver 1.0082 oz. ASW, 39 mm. **Subject:** Kazan Railway Station, Moscow

| Date | Mintage | VF20 | XF40 | MS60 | MS63 | MS65 |
|---|---|---|---|---|---|---|
| 2007 | — | PF63 55.00 | PF65 65.00 | | | |

**Y# 1114 3 ROUBLES**
33.90 g., 0.925 Silver 1.0082 oz. ASW, 39 mm. **Subject:** Year of the Rat

| Date | Mintage | VF20 | XF40 | MS60 | MS63 | MS65 |
|---|---|---|---|---|---|---|
| 2007 | 20,000 | PF63 70.00 | PF65 80.00 | | | |

**Y# 1113 3 ROUBLES**
33.90 g., 0.925 Silver 1.0082 oz. ASW, 39 mm. **Subject:** Year of the Bull

| Date | Mintage | VF20 | XF40 | MS60 | MS63 | MS65 |
|---|---|---|---|---|---|---|
| 2008 | 20,000 | PF63 70.00 | PF65 80.00 | | | |

**Y# 1115 3 ROUBLES**
33.90 g., 0.925 Silver 1.0082 oz. ASW, 39 mm. **Subject:** Russian Postage Stamp - 150th Anniversary of Introduction

| Date | Mintage | VF20 | XF40 | MS60 | MS63 | MS65 |
|---|---|---|---|---|---|---|
| 2008 | 8,000 | PF65 650 | | | | |

**Y# 1118 3 ROUBLES**
33.90 g., 0.925 Silver 1.0082 oz. ASW, 39 mm. **Subject:** I. M. Schenov Medical Academy, 250th Anniversary

| Date | Mintage | VF20 | XF40 | MS60 | MS63 | MS65 |
|---|---|---|---|---|---|---|
| 2008 | 3,000 | PF65 250 | | | | |

**Y# 1119 3 ROUBLES**
33.90 g., 0.925 Silver 1.0082 oz. ASW, 39 mm. **Subject:** Udmurtiya, 450th Anniversary of annexation into Russia

| Date | Mintage | VF20 | XF40 | MS60 | MS63 | MS65 |
|---|---|---|---|---|---|---|
| 2008 | 10,000 | PF63 70.00 | PF65 80.00 | | | |

**Y# 1124 3 ROUBLES**
33.90 g., 0.925 Silver 1.0082 oz. ASW, 39 mm. **Subject:** Cathedral of St. Demetrius, Vladimir

| Date | Mintage | VF20 | XF40 | MS60 | MS63 | MS65 |
|---|---|---|---|---|---|---|
| 2008 | 10,000 | PF63 70.00 | PF65 80.00 | | | |

**Y# 1126 3 ROUBLES**
33.90 g., 0.925 Silver 1.0082 oz. ASW, 39 mm. **Subject:** N. I. Sevastyanov, House of Trade Unions

| Date | Mintage | VF20 | XF40 | MS60 | MS63 | MS65 |
|---|---|---|---|---|---|---|
| 2008 | 7,500 | PF63 70.00 | PF65 80.00 | | | |

**Y# 1127 3 ROUBLES**
33.90 g., 0.925 Silver 1.0082 oz. ASW, 39 mm. **Subject:** Cathedral of the Nativity of our Lady, Snetogorsk

| Date | Mintage | VF20 | XF40 | MS60 | MS63 | MS65 |
|---|---|---|---|---|---|---|
| 2008 | 10,000 | PF63 70.00 | PF65 80.00 | | | |

**Y# 1128 3 ROUBLES**
33.90 g., 0.925 Silver 1.0082 oz. ASW, 39 mm. **Subject:** Assumption Church (Admiralty's)

| Date | Mintage | VF20 | XF40 | MS60 | MS63 | MS65 |
|---|---|---|---|---|---|---|
| 2008 | 10,000 | PF63 70.00 | PF65 80.00 | | | |

**Y# 1129 3 ROUBLES**
33.90 g., 0.925 Silver 1.0082 oz. ASW, 39 mm. **Subject:** St. Nicholas Cathedral, Yakutsk

| Date | Mintage | VF20 | XF40 | MS60 | MS63 | MS65 |
|---|---|---|---|---|---|---|
| 2008 | 10,000 | PF63 70.00 | PF65 80.00 | | | |

**Y# 1130 3 ROUBLES**
33.90 g., 0.925 Silver 1.0082 oz. ASW, 39 mm. **Subject:** St. Vladimir Cathedral, Zadonsk

| Date | Mintage | VF20 | XF40 | MS60 | MS63 | MS65 |
|---|---|---|---|---|---|---|
| 2008 | 10,000 | PF63 70.00 | PF65 80.00 | | | |

**Y# 1138 3 ROUBLES**
33.90 g., 0.925 Silver 1.0082 oz. ASW, 39 mm. **Subject:** European Beaver

| Date | Mintage | VF20 | XF40 | MS60 | MS63 | MS65 |
|---|---|---|---|---|---|---|
| 2008 | 10,000 | PF63 70.00 | PF65 80.00 | | | |

**Y# 1147 3 ROUBLES**
33.90 g., 0.925 Silver 1.0082 oz. ASW, 39 mm. **Subject:** Kamchatka Volcano

| Date | Mintage | VF20 | XF40 | MS60 | MS63 | MS65 |
|---|---|---|---|---|---|---|
| 2008 | 10,000 | PF63 70.00 | PF65 80.00 | | | |

**Y# 1150 3 ROUBLES**
33.90 g., 0.925 Silver 1.0082 oz. ASW, 39 mm. **Subject:** World walking Race Cup, Cheboksary

| Date | Mintage | VF20 | XF40 | MS60 | MS63 | MS65 |
|---|---|---|---|---|---|---|
| 2008 | 5,000 | PF63 70.00 | PF65 80.00 | | | |

**Y# 1151 3 ROUBLES**
33.90 g., 0.925 Silver 1.0082 oz. ASW, 39 mm. **Subject:** City of Moscow

| Date | Mintage | VF20 | XF40 | MS60 | MS63 | MS65 |
|---|---|---|---|---|---|---|
| 2008 | 5,000 | PF63 70.00 | PF65 80.00 | | | |

**Y# 1152 3 ROUBLES**
33.90 g., 0.925 Silver 1.0082 oz. ASW, 39 mm. **Subject:** 29th Summer Olympics Bejing

| Date | Mintage | VF20 | XF40 | MS60 | MS63 | MS65 |
|---|---|---|---|---|---|---|
| 2008 | 10,000 | PF63 70.00 | PF65 80.00 | | | |

**Y# 1159 3 ROUBLES**
33.90 g., 0.925 Silver 1.0082 oz. ASW, 39 mm. **Subject:** Moon research, 50th Anniversary

| Date | Mintage | VF20 | XF40 | MS60 | MS63 | MS65 |
|---|---|---|---|---|---|---|
| 2009 | 5,000 | PF63 115 | PF65 135 | | | |

**Y# 1161 3 ROUBLES**
33.90 g., 0.925 Silver 1.0082 oz. ASW, 39 mm. **Subject:** Russian Currency

| Date | Mintage | VF20 | XF40 | MS60 | MS63 | MS65 |
|---|---|---|---|---|---|---|
| 2009 | 5,000 | PF63 85.00 | PF65 100 | | | |

**Y# 1166 3 ROUBLES**
33.90 g., 0.925 Silver 1.0082 oz. ASW, 39 mm. **Subject:** A. P. Chekhov, 150th Anniversary of Birth

| Date | Mintage | VF20 | XF40 | MS60 | MS63 | MS65 |
|---|---|---|---|---|---|---|
| 2009 | 5,000 | PF63 70.00 | PF65 80.00 | | | |

**Y# 1170 3 ROUBLES**
33.90 g., 0.925 Silver 1.0082 oz. ASW, 39 mm. **Subject:** Kalmyk Peoples, 400th Anniversary of annexation into Russia

| Date | Mintage | VF20 | XF40 | MS60 | MS63 | MS65 |
|---|---|---|---|---|---|---|
| 2009 | 5,000 | PF63 70.00 | PF65 80.00 | | | |

**Y# 1173 3 ROUBLES**
33.90 g., 0.925 Silver 1.0082 oz. ASW, 39 mm. **Subject:** N. V. Gogol, 200th Anniversary of Birth

| Date | Mintage | VF20 | XF40 | MS60 | MS63 | MS65 |
|---|---|---|---|---|---|---|
| 2009 | 5,000 | PF63 70.00 | PF65 80.00 | | | |

**Y# 1177 3 ROUBLES**
33.90 g., 0.925 Silver 1.0082 oz. ASW, 39 mm. **Subject:** Poltava Battle, 300th Anniversary

| Date | Mintage | VF20 | XF40 | MS60 | MS63 | MS65 |
|---|---|---|---|---|---|---|
| 2009 | 10,000 | PF63 55.00 | PF65 65.00 | | | |

**Y# 1180 3 ROUBLES**
33.90 g., 0.925 Silver 1.0082 oz. ASW, 39 mm. **Subject:** St. George the Victorious

| Date | Mintage | VF20 | XF40 | MS60 | MS63 | MS65 |
|---|---|---|---|---|---|---|
| 2009 ММД | 280,000 | — | — | — | 55.00 | 60.00 |
| 2009 СПМД | Inc. above | — | — | — | 60.00 | 65.00 |
| 2010 ММД | 500,000 | — | — | — | 55.00 | 60.00 |
| 2010 СПМД | Inc. above | — | — | — | 60.00 | 65.00 |

**Y# 1182 3 ROUBLES**
33.90 g., 0.925 Silver 1.0082 oz. ASW, 39 mm. **Subject:** Vitebsky Railway Station, St. Petersburg

| Date | Mintage | VF20 | XF40 | MS60 | MS63 | MS65 |
|---|---|---|---|---|---|---|
| 2009 | 7,500 | PF63 70.00 | PF65 80.00 | | | |

**Y# 1183 3 ROUBLES**
33.90 g., 0.925 Silver 1.0082 oz. ASW, 39 mm. **Subject:** Tula Kremlin

| Date | Mintage | VF20 | XF40 | MS60 | MS63 | MS65 |
|---|---|---|---|---|---|---|
| 2009 | 10,000 | PF63 70.00 | PF65 80.00 | | | |

**Y# 1185 3 ROUBLES**
33.90 g., 0.925 Silver 1.0082 oz. ASW, 39 mm. **Subject:** Odygitriya Church

| Date | Mintage | VF20 | XF40 | MS60 | MS63 | MS65 |
|---|---|---|---|---|---|---|
| 2009 | 10,000 | PF63 55.00 | PF65 65.00 | | | |

**Y# 1188 3 ROUBLES**
33.90 g., 0.925 Silver 1.0082 oz. ASW, 39 mm. **Subject:** Intercession Cathedral, Voronezsh

| Date | Mintage | VF20 | XF40 | MS60 | MS63 | MS65 |
|---|---|---|---|---|---|---|
| 2009 | 5,000 | PF63 300 | PF65 325 | | | |

**Y# 1189 3 ROUBLES**
33.90 g., 0.925 Silver 1.0082 oz. ASW, 39 mm. **Subject:** Tales of the Russian People

| Date | Mintage | VF20 | XF40 | MS60 | MS63 | MS65 |
|---|---|---|---|---|---|---|
| 2009 | 5,000 | PF63 90.00 | PF65 100 | | | |

**Y# 1199 3 ROUBLES**
33.90 g., 0.925 Silver 1.0082 oz. ASW, 39 mm. **Subject:** Velikly Novgorod

| Date | Mintage | VF20 | XF40 | MS60 | MS63 | MS65 |
|---|---|---|---|---|---|---|
| 2009 | 10,000 | PF63 70.00 | PF65 80.00 | | | |

**Y# 1207 3 ROUBLES**
33.90 g., 0.925 Silver 1.0082 oz. ASW, 39 mm. **Subject:** Fauna - Bear

| Date | Mintage | VF20 | XF40 | MS60 | MS63 | MS65 |
|---|---|---|---|---|---|---|
| 2009 | 5,000 | PF63 90.00 | PF65 100 | | | |

**Y# 1208 3 ROUBLES**
33.90 g., 0.925 Silver 1.0082 oz. ASW, 39 mm. **Series:** Year of the Tiger

| Date | Mintage | VF20 | XF40 | MS60 | MS63 | MS65 |
|---|---|---|---|---|---|---|
| 2009 | 15,000 | PF63 70.00 | PF65 80.00 | | | |

**Y# 1219 3 ROUBLES**
33.90 g., 0.925 Silver 1.0082 oz. ASW, 39 mm. **Subject:** Savior's Transfiguration Cathedral, Bolkhov

| Date | Mintage | VF20 | XF40 | MS60 | MS63 | MS65 |
|---|---|---|---|---|---|---|
| 2010 | 10,000 | PF63 75.00 | PF65 90.00 | | | |

**Y# 1220 3 ROUBLES**
33.90 g., 0.925 Silver 1.0082 oz. ASW, 39 mm. **Subject:** Vovnushki Battle tower

| Date | Mintage | VF20 | XF40 | MS60 | MS63 | MS65 |
|---|---|---|---|---|---|---|
| 2010 | 10,000 | PF63 75.00 | PF65 90.00 | | | |

**Y# 1221 3 ROUBLES**
33.90 g., 0.925 Silver 1.0082 oz. ASW, 39 mm. **Subject:** Holy Trinity Church, St. Petersburg

| Date | Mintage | VF20 | XF40 | MS60 | MS63 | MS65 |
|---|---|---|---|---|---|---|
| 2010 | 10,000 | PF63 70.00 | PF65 85.00 | | | |

**Y# 1222 3 ROUBLES**
33.90 g., 0.925 Silver 1.0082 oz. ASW, 39 mm. **Subject:** Round Square, Petrozavodsk

| Date | Mintage | VF20 | XF40 | MS60 | MS63 | MS65 |
|---|---|---|---|---|---|---|
| 2010 | 5,000 | PF63 70.00 | PF65 85.00 | | | |

**Y# 1228 3 ROUBLES**
33.90 g., 0.925 Silver 1.0082 oz. ASW, 39 mm. **Subject:** Bank of Russia, 150th Anniversary

| Date | Mintage | VF20 | XF40 | MS60 | MS63 | MS65 |
|---|---|---|---|---|---|---|
| 2010 | 10,000 | PF63 70.00 | PF65 80.00 | | | |

**Y# 1232 3 ROUBLES**
33.90 g., 0.925 Silver 1.0082 oz. ASW, 39 mm. **Subject:** UNESCO Heritage Site - Yaroslav

| Date | Mintage | VF20 | XF40 | MS60 | MS63 | MS65 |
|---|---|---|---|---|---|---|
| 2010 | 10,000 | PF63 70.00 | PF65 80.00 | | | |

**Y# 1241 3 ROUBLES**
33.90 g., 0.925 Silver 1.0082 oz. ASW, 39 mm. **Subject:** Great Patriotic War, 65th Anniversary

| Date | Mintage | VF20 | XF40 | MS60 | MS63 | MS65 |
|---|---|---|---|---|---|---|
| 2010 | 7,500 | PF63 85.00 | PF65 95.00 | | | |

**Y# 1242 3 ROUBLES**
33.90 g., 0.925 Silver 1.0082 oz. ASW, 39 mm. **Subject:** Great Patriotic War, 65th Anniversary

| Date | Mintage | VF20 | XF40 | MS60 | MS63 | MS65 |
|---|---|---|---|---|---|---|
| 2010 | 7,500 | PF63 85.00 | PF65 95.00 | | | |

**Y# 1243 3 ROUBLES**
33.90 g., 0.925 Silver 1.0082 oz. ASW, 39 mm. **Subject:** Great Patriotic War, 65th Anniversary

| Date | Mintage | VF20 | XF40 | MS60 | MS63 | MS65 |
|---|---|---|---|---|---|---|
| 2010 | 7,500 | PF63 85.00 | PF65 95.00 | | | |

**Y# 1247 3 ROUBLES**
33.90 g., 0.925 Silver 1.0082 oz. ASW, 39 mm. **Subject:** Year of the Rabbit

| Date | Mintage | VF20 | XF40 | MS60 | MS63 | MS65 |
|---|---|---|---|---|---|---|
| 2010 | 20,000 | **PF63** 70.00 | **PF65** 80.00 | | | |

**Y# 1251 3 ROUBLES**
33.90 g., 0.925 Silver 1.0082 oz. ASW, 39 mm. **Subject:** EAEC, 10th Anniversary

| Date | Mintage | VF20 | XF40 | MS60 | MS63 | MS65 |
|---|---|---|---|---|---|---|
| 2010 | 5,000 | **PF63** 80.00 | **PF65** 95.00 | | | |

**Y# 1252 3 ROUBLES**
33.90 g., 0.925 Silver 1.0082 oz. ASW, 39 mm. **Subject:** EAEC, National Costumes

| Date | Mintage | VF20 | XF40 | MS60 | MS63 | MS65 |
|---|---|---|---|---|---|---|
| 2010 | 5,000 | **PF63** 75.00 | **PF65** 85.00 | | | |

**Y# 1265 3 ROUBLES**
33.90 g., 0.925 Silver 1.0082 oz. ASW **Subject:** Russian Census

| Date | Mintage | VF20 | XF40 | MS60 | MS63 | MS65 |
|---|---|---|---|---|---|---|
| 2010 | 7,500 | **PF63** 80.00 | **PF65** 95.00 | | | |

**Y# 1269 3 ROUBLES**
33.90 g., 0.925 Silver 1.0082 oz. ASW, 33 mm. **Subject:** I. K. Rodnina and A.G. Zaitsev, Figure skater

| Date | Mintage | VF20 | XF40 | MS60 | MS63 | MS65 |
|---|---|---|---|---|---|---|
| 2010 | 3,000 | **PF65** 135 | | | | |

**Y# 1271 3 ROUBLES**
33.90 g., 0.925 Silver 1.0082 oz. ASW, 33 mm. **Subject:** L. A. Pakhomova and A. G. Gorshkov, Figure skaters

| Date | Mintage | VF20 | XF40 | MS60 | MS63 | MS65 |
|---|---|---|---|---|---|---|
| 2010 | 3,000 | **PF65** 135 | | | | |

**Y# 1273 3 ROUBLES**
33.90 g., 0.925 Silver 1.0082 oz. ASW, 39 mm. **Subject:** 39th World Chess Olympics

| Date | Mintage | VF20 | XF40 | MS60 | MS63 | MS65 |
|---|---|---|---|---|---|---|
| 2010 | 5,000 | **PF63** 80.00 | **PF65** 95.00 | | | |

**Y# 1282 3 ROUBLES**
33.90 g., 0.999 Silver 1.0888 oz. ASW, 39 mm. **Subject:** Cathedral of the Virgin of Kazan and St. Sergiy of Radonezh, City of Kursk **Rev:** St. Sergius Kazansky Cathedral in Kursk **Edge:** Reeded

| Date | Mintage | VF20 | XF40 | MS60 | MS63 | MS65 |
|---|---|---|---|---|---|---|
| 2011 СПМД | 7,500 | **PF63** 80.00 | **PF65** 90.00 | | | |

**Y# 1285 3 ROUBLES**
33.90 g., 0.925 Silver 1.0082 oz. ASW, 39 mm. **Rev:** Flag above five soldiers

| Date | Mintage | VF20 | XF40 | MS60 | MS63 | MS65 |
|---|---|---|---|---|---|---|
| 2011 | 3,000 | **PF65** 325 | | | | |

**Y# 1287 3 ROUBLES**
33.90 g., 0.999 Silver 1.0888 oz. ASW, 39 mm. **Rev:** U.A. Gagarian agains background of stars and earth in color **Edge:** Reeded

| Date | Mintage | VF20 | XF40 | MS60 | MS63 | MS65 |
|---|---|---|---|---|---|---|
| 2011 | 7,500 | **PF63** 90.00 | **PF65** 100 | | | |

**Y# 1289 3 ROUBLES**
33.90 g., 0.999 Silver 1.0888 oz. ASW, 39 mm. **Rev:** Female in national costume and wildlife native to Buryat flanking

| Date | Mintage | VF20 | XF40 | MS60 | MS63 | MS65 |
|---|---|---|---|---|---|---|
| 2011 | 3,000 | **PF63** 150 | **PF65** 175 | | | |

**Y# 1293 3 ROUBLES**
33.90 g., 0.925 Silver 1.0082 oz. ASW, 39 mm. **Subject:** 2014 Winter Olympics - Sochi - Biathlon **Rev:** Athlethe on skies with rifle, pitsunda pinecone in color at lower right

| Date | Mintage | VF20 | XF40 | MS60 | MS63 | MS65 |
|---|---|---|---|---|---|---|
| 2014 | 35,000 | **PF65** 125 | | | | |

**Y# 1294 3 ROUBLES**
1294.00 g., 0.925 Silver 38.4828 oz. ASW, 39 mm. **Subject:** 2014 Winter Olympics - Sochi - Alpine Skiing **Rev:** Mountain skier and magnolia in color at lower right

| Date | Mintage | VF20 | XF40 | MS60 | MS63 | MS65 |
|---|---|---|---|---|---|---|
| 2014 | 35,000 | **PF65** 125 | | | | |

**Y# 1295 3 ROUBLES**
33.90 g., 0.925 Silver 1.0082 oz. ASW, 39 mm. **Subject:** 2014 Winter Olympics - Sochi - Figure Skater **Rev:** Figure skater and Voronov snowdrop in color at lower right

| Date | Mintage | VF20 | XF40 | MS60 | MS63 | MS65 |
|---|---|---|---|---|---|---|
| 2014 | 35,000 | PF65 125 | | | | |

**Y# 1296 3 ROUBLES**
33.90 g., 0.925 Silver 1.0082 oz. ASW, 39 mm. **Subject:** 2014 Winter Olympics - Sochi - Hockey **Rev:** Hockey player and branch of cork oak in color at lower left

| Date | Mintage | VF20 | XF40 | MS60 | MS63 | MS65 |
|---|---|---|---|---|---|---|
| 2014 | 35,000 | PF65 125 | | | | |

**Y# 1315 3 ROUBLES**
33.90 g., 0.925 Silver 1.0082 oz. ASW, 39 mm. **Rev:** Three children picking flowers and drawing

| Date | Mintage | VF20 | XF40 | MS60 | MS63 | MS65 |
|---|---|---|---|---|---|---|
| 2011 | 5,000 | PF63 100 | PF65 115 | | | |

**Y# 1316 3 ROUBLES**
33.90 g., 0.925 Silver 1.0082 oz. ASW, 39 mm. **Subject:** The Great Silk Way **Rev:** Camel rider against a background of desert ruins

| Date | Mintage | VF20 | XF40 | MS60 | MS63 | MS65 |
|---|---|---|---|---|---|---|
| 2011 | 5,000 | PF63 75.00 | PF65 90.00 | | | |

**Y# 1330 3 ROUBLES**
33.90 g., 0.925 Silver 1.0082 oz. ASW, 39 mm. **Subject:** Temple of the Sanctifier Martin the Confessor in Moscow

| Date | Mintage | VF20 | XF40 | MS60 | MS63 | MS65 |
|---|---|---|---|---|---|---|
| 2012 | 5,000 | PF63 75.00 | PF65 90.00 | | | |

**Y# 1331 3 ROUBLES**
33.90 g., 0.925 Silver 1.0082 oz. ASW, 39 mm. **Subject:** Kolotsky Assumption Monastery, Mozhaisk District of Moscow Region

| Date | Mintage | VF20 | XF40 | MS60 | MS63 | MS65 |
|---|---|---|---|---|---|---|
| 2012 | 5,000 | PF63 75.00 | PF65 90.00 | | | |

**Y# 1332 3 ROUBLES**
33.90 g., 0.925 Silver 1.0082 oz. ASW, 39 mm. **Subject:** Luzhetsky Ferapontov Monastery, Mozhaisk, Moscow region

| Date | Mintage | VF20 | XF40 | MS60 | MS63 | MS65 |
|---|---|---|---|---|---|---|
| 2012 | 5,000 | PF63 75.00 | PF65 90.00 | | | |

**Y# 1333 3 ROUBLES**
33.90 g., 0.925 Silver 1.0082 oz. ASW, 39 mm. **Subject:** Transfiguration Cathedral, Belozersk, Vologda region

| Date | Mintage | VF20 | XF40 | MS60 | MS63 | MS65 |
|---|---|---|---|---|---|---|
| 2012 | 5,000 | PF63 75.00 | PF65 90.00 | | | |

**Y# 1334 3 ROUBLES**
33.90 g., 0.925 Silver 1.0082 oz. ASW, 39 mm. **Subject:** Cathedral of the Saint Virgin's Nativity, Vladimir region

| Date | Mintage | VF20 | XF40 | MS60 | MS63 | MS65 |
|---|---|---|---|---|---|---|
| 2012 | 5,000 | PF63 75.00 | PF65 90.00 | | | |

**Y# 1339 3 ROUBLES**
33.90 g., 0.925 Silver 1.0082 oz. ASW, 39 mm. **Subject:** Millennium of the Unity of the Mordovian people within the Peoples of the Russian State

| Date | Mintage | VF20 | XF40 | MS60 | MS63 | MS65 |
|---|---|---|---|---|---|---|
| 2012 | 3,000 | PF63 185 | PF65 200 | | | |

**Y# 1342 3 ROUBLES**
33.90 g., 0.925 Silver 1.0082 oz. ASW, 39 mm. **Subject:** People's Volunteer Corps, 400th Anniversary

| Date | Mintage | VF20 | XF40 | MS60 | MS63 | MS65 |
|---|---|---|---|---|---|---|
| 2012 | 5,000 | PF63 75.00 | PF65 90.00 | | | |

**Y# 1345 3 ROUBLES**
33.90 g., 0.925 Silver 1.0082 oz. ASW, 39 mm. **Subject:** Russia's victory in the War of 1812

| Date | Mintage | VF20 | XF40 | MS60 | MS63 | MS65 |
|---|---|---|---|---|---|---|
| 2012 | 5,000 | PF63 75.00 | PF65 90.00 | | | |

**Y# 1351 3 ROUBLES**
33.90 g., 0.925 Silver 1.0082 oz. ASW, 39 mm. **Subject:** Pushkin State Museum of Fine Arts, Moscow, 100th Anniversary

| Date | Mintage | VF20 | XF40 | MS60 | MS63 | MS65 |
|---|---|---|---|---|---|---|
| 2012 | 5,000 | PF63 125 | PF65 150 | | | |

**Y# 1353 3 ROUBLES**
33.90 g., 0.925 Silver 1.0082 oz. ASW, 39 mm. **Subject:** UNESCO World Heritage Site - Vrangel Island **Rev:** Walrus and Polar Awl in flight

| Date | Mintage | VF20 | XF40 | MS60 | MS63 | MS65 |
|---|---|---|---|---|---|---|
| 2012 | 5,000 | PF63 75.00 | PF65 90.00 | | | |

**Y# 1354 3 ROUBLES**
33.90 g., 0.925 Silver 1.0082 oz. ASW, 39 mm. **Subject:** UNESCO World Heritage Site - Church of the Ascension in Kolomenskoye **Rev:** Church building with tall central tower

| Date | Mintage | VF20 | XF40 | MS60 | MS63 | MS65 |
|---|---|---|---|---|---|---|
| 2012 | 5,000 | PF63 75.00 | PF65 90.00 | | | |

**Y# 1364 3 ROUBLES**
33.90 g., 0.925 Silver 1.0082 oz. ASW, 39 mm. **Subject:** European Judo Championship, Chelyabinsk

| Date | Mintage | VF20 | XF40 | MS60 | MS63 | MS65 |
|---|---|---|---|---|---|---|
| 2012 | 3,000 | PF63 140 | PF65 160 | | | |

**Y# 1366 3 ROUBLES**
33.90 g., 0.925 Silver 1.0082 oz. ASW, 39 mm. **Subject:** Year of the Dragon

| Date | Mintage | VF20 | XF40 | MS60 | MS63 | MS65 |
|---|---|---|---|---|---|---|
| 2012 | 15,000 | PF63 70.00 | PF65 80.00 | | | |

**Y# 1367 3 ROUBLES**
33.90 g., 0.925 Silver 1.0082 oz. ASW, 39 mm. **Subject:** Origin of Russian Statehood, 1150th Anniversary

| Date | Mintage | VF20 | XF40 | MS60 | MS63 | MS65 |
|---|---|---|---|---|---|---|
| 2012 | 5,000 | PF63 90.00 | PF65 100 | | | |

**Y# 1374 3 ROUBLES**
33.90 g., 0.925 Silver 1.0082 oz. ASW, 39 mm. **Subject:** Russian language and literature in the French Republic and the French language and literature in the Russian Federation

| Date | Mintage | VF20 | XF40 | MS60 | MS63 | MS65 |
|---|---|---|---|---|---|---|
| 2012 | 5,000 | PF65 65.00 | | | | |

**Y# 1377 3 ROUBLES**
33.90 g., 0.925 Silver 1.0082 oz. ASW, 39 mm. **Subject:** Arms production in Tula, 300th Anniversary

| Date | Mintage | VF20 | XF40 | MS60 | MS63 | MS65 |
|---|---|---|---|---|---|---|
| 2012 | 5,000 | PF63 75.00 | PF65 90.00 | | | |

**Y# 1379 3 ROUBLES**
33.90 g., 0.925 Silver 1.0082 oz. ASW, 39 mm. **Subject:** Air Force, 100th Anniversary

| Date | Mintage | VF20 | XF40 | MS60 | MS63 | MS65 |
|---|---|---|---|---|---|---|
| 2012 | 3,000 | PF63 375 | PF65 400 | | | |

**Y# 1505 3 ROUBLES**
31.50 g., 0.999 Silver 1.0117 oz. ASW, 23x35 mm. **Subject:** 2014 Winter Olympics, Sochi **Rev:** Bear Mascot **Shape:** Vertical rectangle

| Date | Mintage | VF20 | XF40 | MS60 | MS63 | MS65 |
|---|---|---|---|---|---|---|
| 2012 | 300,000 | — | — | — | 35.00 | 40.00 |

**Y# 1422 3 ROUBLES**
33.94 g., 0.925 Silver 1.0094 oz. ASW, 39 mm. **Rev:** Female athlete holding Kazan Universiade banner above city skyline

| Date | Mintage | VF20 | XF40 | MS60 | MS63 | MS65 |
|---|---|---|---|---|---|---|
| 2013 СПМД | 7,500 | PF63 70.00 | PF65 80.00 | | | |

**Y# 1430 3 ROUBLES**
33.94 g., 0.925 Silver 1.0094 oz. ASW, 39 mm. **Subject:** City of Penza, 350th Anniversary of founding **Rev:** Monument to first settlers in center, town view around

| Date | Mintage | VF20 | XF40 | MS60 | MS63 | MS65 |
|---|---|---|---|---|---|---|
| 2013 | 5,000 | PF63 75.00 | PF65 90.00 | | | |

**Y# 1434 3 ROUBLES**
33.94 g., 0.925 Silver 1.0094 oz. ASW, 39 mm. **Subject:** A.S. Shein **Rev:** Half-length Shein at left with saber, fortress and sailing ship at right **Edge:** Reeded

| Date | Mintage | VF20 | XF40 | MS60 | MS63 | MS65 |
|---|---|---|---|---|---|---|
| 2013 ММД | 7,500 | PF63 70.00 | PF65 80.00 | | | |

**Y# 1446 3 ROUBLES**

33.94 g., 0.925 Silver 1.0094 oz. ASW, 39 mm. **Subject:** City of Smolensk, 1150th Anniversary of founding **Rev:** Saints Peter and Paul Church and St. Varvara Martyr Chruch

| Date | Mintage | VF20 | XF40 | MS60 | MS63 | MS65 |
|---|---|---|---|---|---|---|
| 2013 ММД | 5,000 | PF63 75.00 | PF65 90.00 | | | |

**Y# 1449 3 ROUBLES**

33.94 g., 0.925 Silver 1.0094 oz. ASW, 39 mm. **Subject:** Russian victory over Germany at battle of Stalingrad, 70th Anniversary **Rev:** Battle Monument in Volgograd **Edge:** Reeded

| Date | Mintage | VF20 | XF40 | MS60 | MS63 | MS65 |
|---|---|---|---|---|---|---|
| 2013 ММД | 5,000 | PF63 75.00 | PF65 90.00 | | | |

**Y# 1452 3 ROUBLES**

33.94 g., 0.925 Silver 1.0094 oz. ASW, 39 mm. **Subject:** Year of Russa in Germany, and Germany in Russia **Rev:** Gothic Cathedral at left, Orthodox Cathedral at right, ribbon of flags vertical thru center **Edge:** Reeded

| Date | Mintage | VF20 | XF40 | MS60 | MS63 | MS65 |
|---|---|---|---|---|---|---|
| 2013 СПМД | 5,000 | PF63 75.00 | PF65 90.00 | | | |

**Y# 1455 3 ROUBLES**

33.94 g., 0.924 Silver 1.0083 oz. ASW, 39 mm. **Subject:** Architectural Monuments - Assumption Cathedral on Gorodok in Zvenigorod **Rev:** Cathedral view **Edge:** Reeded

| Date | Mintage | VF20 | XF40 | MS60 | MS63 | MS65 |
|---|---|---|---|---|---|---|
| 2013 ММД | 7,500 | PF63 70.00 | PF65 80.00 | | | |

**Y# 1456 3 ROUBLES**

33.94 g., 0.925 Silver 1.0094 oz. ASW, 39 mm. **Subject:** Architectural Monuments - Cathedral of Virgin's Saint Entrance Presentation in Cheboksary **Rev:** Cathedral view **Edge:** Reeded

| Date | Mintage | VF20 | XF40 | MS60 | MS63 | MS65 |
|---|---|---|---|---|---|---|
| 2013 СПМД | 7,500 | PF63 70.00 | PF65 80.00 | | | |

**Y# 1458 3 ROUBLES**

33.94 g., 0.925 Silver 1.0094 oz. ASW, 39 mm. **Subject:** World Track and Field Championships - Moscow **Rev:** Sprinter right, track around **Edge:** Reeded

| Date | Mintage | VF20 | XF40 | MS60 | MS63 | MS65 |
|---|---|---|---|---|---|---|
| 2013 ММД | 5,000 | PF63 75.00 | PF65 90.00 | | | |

**Y# 1459 3 ROUBLES**

33.94 g., 0.925 Silver 1.0094 oz. ASW, 39 mm. **Subject:** Architectural Monuments - Trinity Cathedral, Verkhoturye **Rev:** Cathedral view **Edge:** Reeded

| Date | Mintage | VF20 | XF40 | MS60 | MS63 | MS65 |
|---|---|---|---|---|---|---|
| 2013 ММД | 7,500 | PF63 70.00 | PF65 80.00 | | | |

**Y# 1463 3 ROUBLES**

33.94 g., 0.925 Silver 1.0094 oz. ASW, 39 mm. **Subject:** Architectural Monuments - Saint Nikolas the Miracle Man Marine Cathedral, Kronstadt **Rev:** Cathedral view **Edge:** Reeded

| Date | Mintage | VF20 | XF40 | MS60 | MS63 | MS65 |
|---|---|---|---|---|---|---|
| 2013 СПМД | 7,500 | PF63 70.00 | PF65 80.00 | | | |

**Y# 1502 3 ROUBLES**

31.50 g., 0.999 Silver 1.0117 oz. ASW, 23x35 mm. **Subject:** 2014 Winter Paralympics, Sochi **Rev:** Paralympic mascot - Hare **Shape:** Vertical rectangle

| Date | Mintage | VF20 | XF40 | MS60 | MS63 | MS65 |
|---|---|---|---|---|---|---|
| 2013 | 300,000 | — | — | — | 30.00 | 35.00 |

**Y# 1475 3 ROUBLES**

33.94 g., 0.925 Silver 1.0094 oz. ASW, 39 mm. **Subject:** 2014 Winter Paralympics, Sochi **Rev:** Skeleton

| Date | Mintage | VF20 | XF40 | MS60 | MS63 | MS65 |
|---|---|---|---|---|---|---|
| 2014 | 35,000 | PF65 100 | | | | |

**Y# 1476 3 ROUBLES**

33.94 g., 0.925 Silver 1.0094 oz. ASW, 39 mm. **Subject:** 2014 Winter Olympics, Sochi **Rev:** Snowboard

| Date | Mintage | VF20 | XF40 | MS60 | MS63 | MS65 |
|---|---|---|---|---|---|---|
| 2014 | 35,000 | PF65 125 | | | | |

**Y# 1477 3 ROUBLES**

33.94 g., 0.925 Silver 1.0094 oz. ASW, 39 mm. **Subject:** 2014 Winter Olympics, Sochi **Rev:** Ski Jumping

| Date | Mintage | VF20 | XF40 | MS60 | MS63 | MS65 |
|---|---|---|---|---|---|---|
| 2014 | 35,000 | PF65 125 | | | | |

**Y# 1478 3 ROUBLES**
33.94 g., 0.925 Silver 1.0094 oz. ASW, 39 mm. **Subject:** 2014 Winter Olympics, Sochi **Rev:** Freestyle Skiing

| Date | Mintage | VF20 | XF40 | MS60 | MS63 | MS65 |
|---|---|---|---|---|---|---|
| 2014 | 35,000 | **PF65** 125 | | | | |

**Y# 1483 3 ROUBLES**
33.94 g., 0.925 Silver 1.0094 oz. ASW, 39 mm. **Subject:** 2014 Winter Olympics, Sochi **Rev:** Curling

| Date | Mintage | VF20 | XF40 | MS60 | MS63 | MS65 |
|---|---|---|---|---|---|---|
| 2014 | 35,000 | **PF65** 125 | | | | |

**Y# 1484 3 ROUBLES**
33.94 g., 0.925 Silver 1.0094 oz. ASW, 39 mm. **Subject:** 2014 Winter Olympics, Sochi **Rev:** Nordic Combined - Skier and Ski Jumper

| Date | Mintage | VF20 | XF40 | MS60 | MS63 | MS65 |
|---|---|---|---|---|---|---|
| 2014 | 35,000 | **PF65** 125 | | | | |

**Y# 1485 3 ROUBLES**
33.94 g., 0.925 Silver 1.0094 oz. ASW, 39 mm. **Subject:** 2014 Winter Olympics, Sochi **Rev:** Speed Skating

| Date | Mintage | VF20 | XF40 | MS60 | MS63 | MS65 |
|---|---|---|---|---|---|---|
| 2014 | 35,000 | **PF65** 125 | | | | |

**Y# 1486 3 ROUBLES**
33.94 g., 0.925 Silver 1.0094 oz. ASW, 39 mm. **Subject:** 2014 Winter Olympics, Sochi **Rev:** Luge

| Date | Mintage | VF20 | XF40 | MS60 | MS63 | MS65 |
|---|---|---|---|---|---|---|
| 2014 | 35,000 | **PF65** 125 | | | | |

**Y# 1491 3 ROUBLES**
33.94 g., 0.925 Silver 1.0094 oz. ASW, 39 mm. **Subject:** 2014 Winter Olympics, Sochi **Rev:** Two-man Bobsleigh

| Date | Mintage | VF20 | XF40 | MS60 | MS63 | MS65 |
|---|---|---|---|---|---|---|
| 2014 | 35,000 | **PF65** 125 | | | | |

**Y# 1492 3 ROUBLES**
33.94 g., 0.925 Silver 1.0094 oz. ASW, 39 mm. **Subject:** 2014 Winter Olympics, Sochi **Rev:** Cross-country skiing

| Date | Mintage | VF20 | XF40 | MS60 | MS63 | MS65 |
|---|---|---|---|---|---|---|
| 35000 | — | **PF65** 125 | | | | |

**Y# 1493 3 ROUBLES**
33.94 g., 0.925 Silver 1.0094 oz. ASW, 39 mm. **Subject:** 2014 Winter Paralympics, Sochi **Rev:** Ice-sledge Hockey

| Date | Mintage | VF20 | XF40 | MS60 | MS63 | MS65 |
|---|---|---|---|---|---|---|
| 2014 | 35,000 | **PF65** 125 | | | | |

**Y# 1494 3 ROUBLES**
33.94 g., 0.925 Silver 1.0094 oz. ASW, 39 mm. **Subject:** 2014 Winter Olympics, Sochi **Rev:** Short track speed skating

| Date | Mintage | VF20 | XF40 | MS60 | MS63 | MS65 |
|---|---|---|---|---|---|---|
| 2014 | 35,000 | **PF65** 125 | | | | |

**Y# 1510 3 ROUBLES**
33.94 g., 0.925 Silver 1.0094 oz. ASW, 39 mm. **Subject:** Moscow Zoo, 150th Anniversary **Rev:** Pallas' cat and tower, animals and birds around

| Date | Mintage | F12 | VF20 | XF40 | MS60 | MS63 |
|---|---|---|---|---|---|---|
| 2014 | 3,000 | **PF65** 75.00 | | | | |

**Y# 1511 3 ROUBLES**
33.94 g., 0.925 Silver 1.0094 oz. ASW, 39 mm. **Subject:** Agency for Deposits Insurance **Rev:** Coins, banknotes and logo

| Date | Mintage | F12 | VF20 | XF40 | MS60 | MS63 |
|---|---|---|---|---|---|---|
| 2014 | 3,000 | **PF65** 75.00 | | | | |

**Y# 1513 3 ROUBLES**
33.94 g., 0.925 Silver 1.0094 oz. ASW, 39 mm. **Rev:** New Rouble symbol

| Date | Mintage | F12 | VF20 | XF40 | MS60 | MS63 |
|---|---|---|---|---|---|---|
| 2014 Antique Patina | 1,000 | **PF65** 75.00 | | | | |
| 2014 | 500 | **PF65** 75.00 | | | | |

**Y# 1520 3 ROUBLES**
33.94 g., 0.925 Silver 1.0094 oz. ASW, 39 mm. **Subject:** World Judo Championship, Chelyabinsk **Rev:** Judo players

| Date | Mintage | F12 | VF20 | XF40 | MS60 | MS63 |
|---|---|---|---|---|---|---|
| 2014 | 3,000 | PF65 100 | | | | |

**Y# 1525 3 ROUBLES**
33.94 g., 0.925 Silver 1.0094 oz. ASW, 39 mm. **Subject:** Mikhail Yuryevich Lermontov, 200th Anniversary of Birth **Rev:** Uniformed officer at right, Two soldiers talking at left, mounted troops in background - scene from "Borodino

| Date | Mintage | F12 | VF20 | XF40 | MS60 | MS63 |
|---|---|---|---|---|---|---|
| 2014 | 3,000 | PF65 75.00 | | | | |

**Y# 1528 3 ROUBLES**
33.94 g., 0.925 Silver 1.0094 oz. ASW, 39 mm. **Subject:** Rev. Sergius Radonezhsky, 700th Anniversary of Birth **Rev:** Scene from painting by V.A. Chelyshev of Radonezhsky blessing Dmitry Donskoy before the march for the Kulikovo field

| Date | Mintage | F12 | VF20 | XF40 | MS60 | MS63 |
|---|---|---|---|---|---|---|
| 2014 | 7,500 | PF65 100 | | | | |

**Y# 1532 3 ROUBLES**
33.94 g., 0.925 Silver 1.0094 oz. ASW, 39 mm. **Obv:** Unity of Russia and Tuva and Kyzyl City founding **Edge Lettering:** Arat Square with Music and Drama Theatre, Buddhist temple and parliament

| Date | Mintage | F12 | VF20 | XF40 | MS60 | MS63 |
|---|---|---|---|---|---|---|
| 2014 | 300 | PF65 100 | | | | |

**Y# 1538 3 ROUBLES**
33.940 Silver 0.925, 39 mm. **Rev:** Church of St. Nikolas, Moscow

| Date | Mintage | F12 | VF20 | XF40 | MS60 | MS63 |
|---|---|---|---|---|---|---|
| 2014 | 3,000 | PF65 100 | | | | |

**Y# 1539 3 ROUBLES**
33.94 g., 0.925 Silver 1.0094 oz. ASW, 39 mm. **Rev:** Chruch of Tkhaba-Yerdy in Republic of Ingushetia

| Date | Mintage | F12 | VF20 | XF40 | MS60 | MS63 |
|---|---|---|---|---|---|---|
| 2014 | 5,000 | PF65 100 | | | | |

**Y# 1540 3 ROUBLES**
33.94 g., 0.925 Silver 1.0094 oz. ASW, 39 mm. **Rev:** Museum house of I.S. Turgenev in the Oral Region

| Date | Mintage | F12 | VF20 | XF40 | MS60 | MS63 |
|---|---|---|---|---|---|---|
| 2014 | 5,000 | PF65 100 | | | | |

**Y# 1541 3 ROUBLES**
33.94 g., 0.925 Silver 1.0094 oz. ASW, 39 mm. **Rev:** Church of St. George, Dzivgis Village, Republic of Northern Ossetia-Alania

| Date | Mintage | F12 | VF20 | XF40 | MS60 | MS63 |
|---|---|---|---|---|---|---|
| 2014 | 5,000 | PF65 100 | | | | |

**Y# 1545 3 ROUBLES**
33.94 g., 0.925 Silver 1.0094 oz. ASW, 39 mm. **Rev:** Gostiny Dvor, Orenburg

| Date | Mintage | F12 | VF20 | XF40 | MS60 | MS63 |
|---|---|---|---|---|---|---|
| 2014 | 5,000 | PF65 100 | | | | |

**Y# 799 5 ROUBLES**
6.45 g., Copper-Nickel Clad Copper, 25 mm. **Obv:** Two headed eagle above curved bank name and denomination **Rev:** Value and flower **Edge:** Segmented reeding

| Date | Mintage | VF20 | XF40 | MS60 | MS63 | MS65 |
|---|---|---|---|---|---|---|
| 2002 ММД In sets only | 15,000 | — | — | — | — | — |
| 2002 СПМД In sets only | 15,000 | — | — | — | — | — |
| 2003 ММД | 15,000 | — | 150 | 200 | 250 | — |
| 2008 ММД | — | — | — | 3.00 | 4.00 | 6.00 |
| 2008 СПМД | — | — | — | 3.00 | 4.00 | 6.00 |
| 2009 СПМД | — | — | — | 4.00 | 5.00 | 7.00 |
| 2009 ММД | — | — | — | 3.00 | 4.00 | 6.00 |

**Y# 829 5 ROUBLES**
47.24 g., Bi-Metallic .900 Silver 21.34g center in .900 Gold 25.9g ring, 39.5 mm. **Obv:** Double-headed eagle **Rev:** Uglich city view **Edge:** Reeded

| Date | Mintage | VF20 | XF40 | MS60 | MS63 | MS65 |
|---|---|---|---|---|---|---|
| 2004 (sp) | 5,000 | PF65 1,350 | | | | |

**Y# 1075 5 ROUBLES**
47.50 g., Bi-Metallic .900 Silver 21.34g center in .900 Gold 25.9g ring **Subject:** Bogolyvbovo Township

| Date | Mintage | VF20 | XF40 | MS60 | MS63 | MS65 |
|---|---|---|---|---|---|---|
| 2006 | 1,000 | PF63 1,250 | PF65 1,750 | | | |

**Y# 1076 5 ROUBLES**
47.24 g., Bi-Metallic .900 Silver 21.34g center in .900 Gold 25.9g ring, 39.5 mm. **Subject:** City of Turyev-Polsky

| Date | Mintage | VF20 | XF40 | MS60 | MS63 | MS65 |
|---|---|---|---|---|---|---|
| 2006 | 1,000 | PF63 1,250 | PF65 1,750 | | | |

**Y# 1154 5 ROUBLES**
47.50 g., Bi-Metallic .925 Silver 21.34g center in .900 Gold 25.9g ring, 39.5 mm. **Subject:** Pereslavl Zalessky

| Date | Mintage | VF20 | XF40 | MS60 | MS63 | MS65 |
|---|---|---|---|---|---|---|
| 2008 | 1,000 | PF63 1,250 | PF65 1,750 | | | |

**Y# 1155 5 ROUBLES**
47.50 g., Bi-Metallic .925 Silver 21.34g center in .900 Gold 25.9g ring, 39.5 mm. **Subject:** Alexandrov

| Date | Mintage | VF20 | XF40 | MS60 | MS63 | MS65 |
|---|---|---|---|---|---|---|
| 2008 | 1,000 | PF63 1,250 | PF65 1,750 | | | |

**Y# 799a 5 ROUBLES**
6.00 g., Nickel Plated Steel, 25 mm. **Obv:** Two headed eagle above curved bank name and denomination **Rev:** Value and flower **Edge:** Segmented reeding

| Date | Mintage | VF20 | XF40 | MS60 | MS63 | MS65 |
|---|---|---|---|---|---|---|
| 2009 ММД | — | — | — | 2.00 | 3.00 | 5.00 |
| 2009 СПМД | — | — | — | 2.00 | 3.00 | 5.00 |
| 2010 ММД | — | — | — | 2.00 | 3.00 | 5.00 |
| 2010 СПМД | — | — | — | 4.00 | 5.00 | 7.00 |
| 2011 ММД | — | — | — | 2.00 | 3.00 | 5.00 |
| 2012 ММД | — | — | — | 2.00 | 3.00 | 5.00 |

**Y# 1408 5 ROUBLES**
6.00 g., Nickel Plated Steel, 25 mm. **Subject:** Battle of Smolensk, War of 1812

| Date | Mintage | VF20 | XF40 | MS60 | MS63 | MS65 |
|---|---|---|---|---|---|---|
| 2012 ММД | 5,000,000 | — | — | 2.00 | 3.00 | 5.00 |

**Y# 1409 5 ROUBLES**
6.00 g., Nickel Plated Steel, 25 mm. **Subject:** Battle of Borodino, War of 1812

| Date | Mintage | VF20 | XF40 | MS60 | MS63 | MS65 |
|---|---|---|---|---|---|---|
| 2012 ММД | 5,000,000 | — | — | 2.00 | 3.00 | 5.00 |

**Y# 1410 5 ROUBLES**
6.00 g., Nickel Plated Steel, 25 mm. **Subject:** Battle of Tarutino, War of 1812

| Date | Mintage | VF20 | XF40 | MS60 | MS63 | MS65 |
|---|---|---|---|---|---|---|
| 2012 ММД | 5,000,000 | — | — | 2.00 | 3.00 | 5.00 |

**Y# 1411 5 ROUBLES**
6.00 g., Nickel Plated Steel, 25 mm. **Subject:** Battle of Maloyaroslavets, War of 1812

| Date | Mintage | VF20 | XF40 | MS60 | MS63 | MS65 |
|---|---|---|---|---|---|---|
| 2012 | 5,000,000 | — | — | 2.00 | 3.00 | 5.00 |

**Y# 1412 5 ROUBLES**
6.00 g., Nickel Plated Steel, 25 mm. **Subject:** Battle of Vyazma, War of 1812

| Date | Mintage | VF20 | XF40 | MS60 | MS63 | MS65 |
|---|---|---|---|---|---|---|
| 2012 ММД | 5,000,000 | — | — | 2.00 | 3.00 | 5.00 |

**Y# 1413 5 ROUBLES**
6.00 g., Nickel Plated Steel, 25 mm. **Subject:** Battle of Krasnoye, War of 1812

| Date | Mintage | VF20 | XF40 | MS60 | MS63 | MS65 |
|---|---|---|---|---|---|---|
| 2012 ММД | 5,000,000 | — | — | 2.00 | 3.00 | 5.00 |

**Y# 1414 5 ROUBLES**
6.00 g., Nickel Plated Steel, 25 mm. **Subject:** Battle of Berezina, War of 1812

| Date | Mintage | VF20 | XF40 | MS60 | MS63 | MS65 |
|---|---|---|---|---|---|---|
| 2012 ММД | 5,000,000 | — | — | 2.00 | 3.00 | 5.00 |

**Y# 1415 5 ROUBLES**
6.00 g., Nickel Plated Steel, 25 mm. **Subject:** Battle of Kulm, War of 1812

| Date | Mintage | VF20 | XF40 | MS60 | MS63 | MS65 |
|---|---|---|---|---|---|---|
| 2012 ММД | 5,000,000 | — | — | 2.00 | 3.00 | 5.00 |

**Y# 1416 5 ROUBLES**
6.00 g., Nickel Plated Steel, 25 mm. **Subject:** Battle of Leipzig, War of 1812

| Date | Mintage | VF20 | XF40 | MS60 | MS63 | MS65 |
|---|---|---|---|---|---|---|
| 2012 ММД | 5,000,000 | — | — | 2.00 | 3.00 | 5.00 |

**Y# 1417 5 ROUBLES**
6.00 g., Nickel Plated Steel, 25 mm. **Subject:** Capture of Paris, War of 1812

| Date | Mintage | VF20 | XF40 | MS60 | MS63 | MS65 |
|---|---|---|---|---|---|---|
| 2012 ММД | 5,000,000 | — | — | 2.00 | 3.00 | 5.00 |

**Y# 1554 5 ROUBLES**
6.00 g., Nickel Plated Steel, 25 mm. **Subject:** Battle of Moscow, WWII **Obv:** Value at left **Rev:** Monument to the defenders of Moscow

| Date | Mintage | VF20 | XF40 | MS60 | MS63 | MS65 |
|---|---|---|---|---|---|---|
| 2014 | 2,000,000 | — | — | 2.00 | 3.00 | 5.00 |

**Y# 1555 5 ROUBLES**
6.00 g., Nickel Plated Steel, 25 mm. **Subject:** Battle of Stalingrad, WWII **Obv:** Value at left **Rev:** Statue to the heroes of the Stalingrad battle

| Date | Mintage | VF20 | XF40 | MS60 | MS63 | MS65 |
|---|---|---|---|---|---|---|
| 2014 | 2,000,000 | — | — | 2.00 | 3.00 | 5.00 |

**Y# 1556 5 ROUBLES**
6.00 g., Nickel Plated Steel, 25 mm. **Subject:** Battle of the Caucasus, WWII **Obv:** Value at left **Rev:** Monument to the defenders of the Elkhotova Gates

| Date | Mintage | VF20 | XF40 | MS60 | MS63 | MS65 |
|---|---|---|---|---|---|---|
| 2014 | 2,000,000 | — | — | 2.00 | 3.00 | 5.00 |

**Y# 1557 5 ROUBLES**
6.00 g., Nickel Plated Steel, 25 mm. **Subject:** Battle of Kursk, WWII **Obv:** Value at left **Rev:** Monument of two tanks

| Date | Mintage | VF20 | XF40 | MS60 | MS63 | MS65 |
|---|---|---|---|---|---|---|
| 2014 | 2,000,000 | — | — | 2.00 | 3.00 | 5.00 |

**Y# 1558 5 ROUBLES**
6.00 g., Nickel Plated Steel, 25 mm. **Subject:** Battle of Dnieper, WWII **Obv:** Value at left **Rev:** Monument group

| Date | Mintage | VF20 | XF40 | MS60 | MS63 | MS65 |
|---|---|---|---|---|---|---|
| 2014 | 2,000,000 | — | — | 2.00 | 3.00 | 5.00 |

**Y# 1559 5 ROUBLES**
6.00 g., Nickel Plated Steel, 25 mm. **Subject:** Dnieper-Carpathian Operation, WWII **Obv:** Value at left **Rev:** Victory statue in Krvvoy Rog

| Date | Mintage | VF20 | XF40 | MS60 | MS63 | MS65 |
|---|---|---|---|---|---|---|
| 2014 | 2,000,000 | — | — | 2.00 | 3.00 | 5.00 |

**Y# 1560 5 ROUBLES**
6.00 g., Nickel Plated Steel, 25 mm. **Subject:** Battle of Leningrad, WWII **Obv:** Value at left **Rev:** Motherland statue at Piskaryev Cemetery

| Date | Mintage | VF20 | XF40 | MS60 | MS63 | MS65 |
|---|---|---|---|---|---|---|
| 2014 | 2,000,000 | — | — | 2.00 | 3.00 | 5.00 |

**Y# 1561 5 ROUBLES**
6.00 g., Nickel Plated Steel, 25 mm. **Subject:** Byelorussian Operation, WWII **Obv:** Value at left **Rev:** Segment from the Mound of Glory monument in the Smolyevichi District of the Minsk Region

| Date | Mintage | VF20 | XF40 | MS60 | MS63 | MS65 |
|---|---|---|---|---|---|---|
| 2014 | 2,000,000 | — | — | 2.00 | 3.00 | 5.00 |

**Y# 1562 5 ROUBLES**
6.00 g., Nickel Plated Steel, 25 mm. **Subject:** Lvov-Sandomierz Operation, WWII **Obv:** Value at left **Rev:** Segment of the Monument of Glory in Lvov

| Date | Mintage | VF20 | XF40 | MS60 | MS63 | MS65 |
|---|---|---|---|---|---|---|
| 2014 | 2,000,000 | — | — | 2.00 | 3.00 | 5.00 |

**Y# 1563 5 ROUBLES**
6.00 g., Nickel Plated Steel, 25 mm. **Subject:** Iasi-Kishinev Operation, WWII **Obv:** Value at left **Rev:** Monument to the Liberators of Kishinev

| Date | Mintage | VF20 | XF40 | MS60 | MS63 | MS65 |
|---|---|---|---|---|---|---|
| 2014 | 2,000,000 | — | — | 2.00 | 3.00 | 5.00 |

**Y# 676 10 ROUBLES**
8.22 g., Bi-Metallic Copper-Nickel center in Brass ring, 27 mm. **Subject:** Yuri Gagarin **Obv:** Value with latent image in zero within circle and sprigs **Rev:** Helmeted bust 1/4 right **Edge:** Reeding over denomination

| Date | Mintage | VF20 | XF40 | MS60 | MS63 | MS65 |
|---|---|---|---|---|---|---|
| 2001 ММД | 10,000,000 | — | — | 4.00 | 5.00 | 7.00 |
| 2001 СПМД | 10,000,000 | — | — | 4.00 | 5.00 | 7.00 |

**Y# 686 10 ROUBLES**
1.61 g., 0.999 Gold 0.0517 oz. AGW, 12 mm. **Subject:** Bolshoi Theater 225 Years **Obv:** Double-headed eagle within circle **Rev:** Building above number 225 **Edge:** Reeded

| Date | Mintage | VF20 | XF40 | MS60 | MS63 | MS65 |
|---|---|---|---|---|---|---|
| 2001 | 3,000 | **PF65** 110 | | | | |

**Y# 739 10 ROUBLES**
8.22 g., Bi-Metallic Copper-Nickel center in Brass ring, 27 mm. **Subject:** Ancient Towns - Derbent **Obv:** Value with latent image in zero within circle and sprigs **Rev:** Shield above walled city view **Edge:** Reeding over denomination

| Date | Mintage | VF20 | XF40 | MS60 | MS63 | MS65 |
|---|---|---|---|---|---|---|
| 2002 ММД | 5,000,000 | — | — | 4.00 | 5.00 | 7.00 |

**Y# 740 10 ROUBLES**
8.22 g., Bi-Metallic Copper-Nickel center in Brass ring, 27 mm. **Subject:** Ancient Towns - Kostroma **Obv:** Value with latent image in zero within circle and sprigs **Rev:** Cupola, shield and river view **Edge:** Reeding over denomination

| Date | Mintage | VF20 | XF40 | MS60 | MS63 | MS65 |
|---|---|---|---|---|---|---|
| 2002 СПМД | 5,000,000 | — | — | 4.00 | 6.00 | 8.00 |

**Y# 741 10 ROUBLES**
8.22 g., Bi-Metallic Copper-Nickel center in Brass ring, 27 mm. **Subject:** Ancient Towns - Staraya Russa **Obv:** Value with latent image in zero within circle and sprigs **Rev:** Shield and cathedral **Edge:** Reeding over denomination

| Date | Mintage | VF20 | XF40 | MS60 | MS63 | MS65 |
|---|---|---|---|---|---|---|
| 2002 СПМД | 5,000,000 | — | — | 4.00 | 6.00 | 8.00 |

**Y# 748 10 ROUBLES**
8.22 g., Bi-Metallic Copper-Nickel center in Brass ring, 27 mm. **Subject:** Ministry of Education **Obv:** Value with latent image in zero within circle and sprigs **Rev:** Seedling within open book **Edge:** Reeding over denomination

| Date | Mintage | VF20 | XF40 | MS60 | MS63 | MS65 |
|---|---|---|---|---|---|---|
| 2002 ММД | 5,000,000 | — | — | 4.00 | 6.00 | 8.00 |

**Y# 749 10 ROUBLES**
8.22 g., Bi-Metallic Copper-Nickel center in Brass ring, 27 mm. **Subject:** Ministry of Finance **Obv:** Value with latent image in zero within circle and sprigs **Rev:** Caduceus within monogram **Edge:** Reeding over denomination

| Date | Mintage | VF20 | XF40 | MS60 | MS63 | MS65 |
|---|---|---|---|---|---|---|
| 2002 СПМД | 5,000,000 | — | — | 4.00 | 6.00 | 8.00 |

**Y# 750 10 ROUBLES**
8.22 g., Bi-Metallic Copper-Nickel center in Brass ring, 27 mm. **Subject:** Ministry of Economic Development and Trade **Obv:** Value with latent image in zero within circle and sprigs **Rev:** Crowned double-headed eagle with cornucopia and caduceus **Edge:** Reeding over denomination

| Date | Mintage | VF20 | XF40 | MS60 | MS63 | MS65 |
|---|---|---|---|---|---|---|
| 2002 СПМД | 5,000,000 | — | — | 4.00 | 6.00 | 8.00 |

**Y# 751 10 ROUBLES**
8.22 g., Bi-Metallic Copper-Nickel center in Brass ring, 27 mm. **Subject:** Ministry of Foreign Affairs **Obv:** Value with latent image in zero within circle and sprigs **Rev:** Crowned double-headed eagle above crossed sprigs **Edge:** Reeding over denomination

| Date | Mintage | VF20 | XF40 | MS60 | MS63 | MS65 |
|---|---|---|---|---|---|---|
| 2002 СПМД | 5,000,000 | — | — | 5.00 | 7.00 | 9.00 |

**Y# 752 10 ROUBLES**
8.22 g., Bi-Metallic Copper-Nickel center in Brass ring, 27 mm. **Subject:** Ministry of Internal Affairs **Obv:** Value with latent image in zero within circle and sprigs **Rev:** Crowned double-headed eagle with round breast shield **Edge:** Reeding over denomination

| Date | Mintage | VF20 | XF40 | MS60 | MS63 | MS65 |
|---|---|---|---|---|---|---|
| 2002 ММД | 5,000,000 | — | — | 5.00 | 7.00 | 9.00 |

**Y# 753 10 ROUBLES**
8.22 g., Bi-Metallic Copper-Nickel center in Brass ring, 27 mm. **Subject:** Ministry of Justice **Obv:** Value with latent image in zero within circle and sprigs **Rev:** Crowned double-headed eagle with column on breast shield **Edge:** Reeding over denomination

| Date | Mintage | VF20 | XF40 | MS60 | MS63 | MS65 |
|---|---|---|---|---|---|---|
| 2002 СПМД | 5,000,000 | — | — | 4.00 | 6.00 | 8.00 |

**Y# 754 10 ROUBLES**
8.22 g., Bi-Metallic Copper-Nickel center in Brass ring, 27 mm. **Subject:** Russian Armed Forces **Obv:** Value with latent image in zero within circle and sprigs **Rev:** Crowned double-headed eagle with crowned pointed top shield **Edge:** Reeding over denomination

| Date | Mintage | VF20 | XF40 | MS60 | MS63 | MS65 |
|---|---|---|---|---|---|---|
| 2002 ММД | 5,000,000 | — | — | 5.00 | 7.00 | 9.00 |

**Y# 800 10 ROUBLES**
8.44 g., Bi-Metallic Copper-Nickel center in Brass ring, 27.1 mm. **Subject:** Pskov **Obv:** Value with latent image in zero within circle and sprigs **Rev:** Shield above walled city **Edge:** Reeding over lettering

| Date | Mintage | VF20 | XF40 | MS60 | MS63 | MS65 |
|---|---|---|---|---|---|---|
| 2003 СПМД | 5,000,000 | — | — | 5.00 | 7.00 | 9.00 |

**Y# 817 10 ROUBLES**
8.34 g., Bi-Metallic Copper-Nickel center in Brass ring, 27 mm. **Obv:** Value with latent image in zero within circle and sprigs **Rev:** Murom city view and tilted oval shields within circle **Edge:** Reeded and lettered

| Date | Mintage | VF20 | XF40 | MS60 | MS63 | MS65 |
|---|---|---|---|---|---|---|
| 2003 (sp) | 5,000,000 | — | — | 5.00 | 7.00 | 9.00 |

**Y# 818 10 ROUBLES**
8.34 g., Bi-Metallic Copper-Nickel center in Brass ring, 27 mm. **Obv:** Value with latent image in zero within circle and sprigs **Rev:** Kasimov city view and shield within circle **Edge:** Reeded and lettered

| Date | Mintage | VF20 | XF40 | MS60 | MS63 | MS65 |
|---|---|---|---|---|---|---|
| 2003 СПМД | 5,000,000 | — | — | 5.00 | 7.00 | 9.00 |

**Y# 819 10 ROUBLES**
8.34 g., Bi-Metallic Copper-Nickel center in Brass ring, 27 mm. **Subject:** Dorogobuzh **Obv:** Value with latent image in zero within circle and sprigs **Rev:** Monument, city view and shield within circle **Edge:** Reeded and lettered

| Date | Mintage | VF20 | XF40 | MS60 | MS63 | MS65 |
|---|---|---|---|---|---|---|
| 2003 ММД | 5,000,000 | — | — | 5.00 | 7.00 | 9.00 |

**Y# 824 10 ROUBLES**
8.46 g., Bi-Metallic Copper-Nickel center in Brass ring, 27.1 mm. **Subject:** Town of Ryazhsk **Obv:** Value with latent image in zero within circle and sprigs **Obv. Legend:** БАНК РОССИИ **Rev:** City view and crowned shield within circle **Edge:** Reeded and lettered

| Date | Mintage | VF20 | XF40 | MS60 | MS63 | MS65 |
|---|---|---|---|---|---|---|
| 2004 ММД | — | — | — | 5.00 | 7.00 | 9.00 |

**Y# 825 10 ROUBLES**
8.46 g., Bi-Metallic Copper-Nickel center in Brass ring, 27.1 mm. **Subject:** Town of Dmitrov **Obv:** Value with latent image in zero within circle and sprigs **Obv. Legend:** БАНК РОССИИ **Rev:** City view and crowned shield within circle **Edge:** Reeded and lettered

| Date | Mintage | VF20 | XF40 | MS60 | MS63 | MS65 |
|---|---|---|---|---|---|---|
| 2004 ММД | 5,000,000 | — | — | 5.00 | 7.00 | 9.00 |

**Y# 826 10 ROUBLES**
8.46 g., Bi-Metallic Copper-Nickel center in Brass ring, 27.1 mm. **Subject:** Town of Kem **Obv:** Value with latent image in zero within circle and sprigs **Obv. Legend:** БАНК РОССИИ **Rev:** City view and crowned shield within circle **Edge:** Reeded and lettered

| Date | Mintage | VF20 | XF40 | MS60 | MS63 | MS65 |
|---|---|---|---|---|---|---|
| 2004 СПМД | 5,000,000 | — | — | 5.00 | 7.00 | 9.00 |

**Y# 827 10 ROUBLES**
8.40 g., Bi-Metallic Copper-Nickel center in Brass ring, 27 mm. **Subject:** Great Victory, 60th Anniversary **Obv:** Value with latent image in zero within circle and sprigs **Rev:** WWII eternal flame monument above date and sprig within circle **Edge:** Reeded and lettered

| Date | Mintage | VF20 | XF40 | MS60 | MS63 | MS65 |
|---|---|---|---|---|---|---|
| 2005 ММД | 30,000,000 | — | — | 5.00 | 7.00 | 9.00 |
| 2005 СПМД | 30,000,000 | — | — | 5.00 | 7.00 | 9.00 |

**Y# 886 10 ROUBLES**
8.23 g., Bi-Metallic Copper-Nickel center in Brass ring, 27 mm. **Obv:** Value with latent image in zero within circle and sprigs **Rev:** Moscow coat of arms within circle **Edge:** Reeded and lettered

| Date | Mintage | VF20 | XF40 | MS60 | MS63 | MS65 |
|---|---|---|---|---|---|---|
| 2005 ММД | 10,000,000 | — | — | 5.00 | 7.00 | 9.00 |

**Y# 887 10 ROUBLES**
8.23 g., Bi-Metallic Copper-Nickel center in Brass ring, 27 mm. **Obv:** Value with latent image in zero within circle and sprigs **Rev:** Leningrad Oblast coat of arms within circle **Edge:** Reeded and lettered

| Date | Mintage | VF20 | XF40 | MS60 | MS63 | MS65 |
|---|---|---|---|---|---|---|
| 2005 СПМД | 10,000,000 | — | — | 5.00 | 7.00 | 9.00 |

**Y# 888 10 ROUBLES**
8.23 g., Bi-Metallic Copper-Nickel center in Brass ring, 27 mm. **Obv:** Value with latent image in zero within circle and sprigs **Rev:** Tverskaya arms within circle **Edge:** Reeded and lettered

| Date | Mintage | VF20 | XF40 | MS60 | MS63 | MS65 |
|---|---|---|---|---|---|---|
| 2005 ММД | 10,000,000 | — | — | 5.00 | 7.00 | 9.00 |

**Y# 889 10 ROUBLES**
8.23 g., Bi-Metallic Copper-Nickel center in Brass ring, 27 mm. **Obv:** Value with latent image in zero within circle and sprigs **Rev:** Krasnodarskiy Kray coat of arms **Edge:** Reeded and lettered

| Date | Mintage | VF20 | XF40 | MS60 | MS63 | MS65 |
|---|---|---|---|---|---|---|
| 2005 (m) | 10,000,000 | — | — | 5.00 | 7.00 | 9.00 |

**Y# 890 10 ROUBLES**
8.23 g., Bi-Metallic Copper-Nickel center in Brass ring, 27 mm. **Obv:** Value with latent image in zero within circle and sprigs **Rev:** Orlovskaya Oblast coat of arms within circle **Edge:** Reeded and lettered

| Date | Mintage | VF20 | XF40 | MS60 | MS63 | MS65 |
|---|---|---|---|---|---|---|
| 2005 (m) | 10,000,000 | — | — | 5.00 | 7.00 | 9.00 |

**Y# 891 10 ROUBLES**
8.23 g., Bi-Metallic Copper-Nickel center in Brass ring, 27 mm. **Obv:** Value with latent image in zero within circle and sprigs **Rev:** Tatarstan Republic coat of arms within circle **Edge:** Reeded and lettered

| Date | Mintage | VF20 | XF40 | MS60 | MS63 | MS65 |
|---|---|---|---|---|---|---|
| 2005 СПМД | 10,000,000 | — | — | 5.00 | 7.00 | 9.00 |

**Y# 943 10 ROUBLES**
8.23 g., Bi-Metallic Copper-Nickel center in Brass ring, 27.1 mm. **Obv:** Large value **Rev:** City of Kazan and arms

| Date | Mintage | VF20 | XF40 | MS60 | MS63 | MS65 |
|---|---|---|---|---|---|---|
| 2005 СПМД | 5,000,000 | — | — | 5.00 | 7.00 | 9.00 |

**Y# 944 10 ROUBLES**
8.23 g., Bi-Metallic Copper-Nickel center in Brass ring, 27.1 mm. **Obv:** Large value **Rev:** City of Borovsk and arms

| Date | Mintage | VF20 | XF40 | MS60 | MS63 | MS65 |
|---|---|---|---|---|---|---|
| 2005 СПМД | 5,000,000 | — | — | 5.00 | 7.00 | 9.00 |

**Y# 945 10 ROUBLES**
8.23 g., Bi-Metallic Copper-Nickel center in Brass ring, 27.1 mm. **Obv:** Large value **Rev:** City of Mzensk and shield

| Date | Mintage | VF20 | XF40 | MS60 | MS63 | MS65 |
|---|---|---|---|---|---|---|
| 2005 ММД | 5,000,000 | — | — | 5.00 | 7.00 | 9.00 |

**Y# 946 10 ROUBLES**
8.23 g., Bi-Metallic Copper-Nickel center in Brass ring, 27.1 mm. **Obv:** Large value **Rev:** City of Kaliningrad and shield

| Date | Mintage | VF20 | XF40 | MS60 | MS63 | MS65 |
|---|---|---|---|---|---|---|
| 2005 ММД | 5,000,000 | — | — | 5.00 | 7.00 | 9.00 |

**Y# 938 10 ROUBLES**
8.23 g., Bi-Metallic Copper-Nickel center in Brass ring, 27 mm. **Obv:** Value with latent image in zero within circle and sprigs **Rev:** Republic of Altai arms **Edge:** Lettered and reeded

| Date | Mintage | VF20 | XF40 | MS60 | MS63 | MS65 |
|---|---|---|---|---|---|---|
| 2006 СПМД | 10,000,000 | — | — | 5.00 | 7.00 | 9.00 |

**Y# 939 10 ROUBLES**
8.23 g., Bi-Metallic Copper-Nickel center in Brass ring, 27 mm. **Obv:** Value with latent image in zero within circle and sprigs **Rev:** Chita Region arms **Edge:** Lettered and reeded

| Date | Mintage | VF20 | XF40 | MS60 | MS63 | MS65 |
|---|---|---|---|---|---|---|
| 2006 СПМД | 10,000,000 | — | — | 5.00 | 7.00 | 9.00 |

**Y# 940 10 ROUBLES**
8.23 g., Bi-Metallic Copper-Nickel center in Brass ring, 27 mm. **Obv:** Value with latent image in zero within circle and sprigs **Rev:** Primorskij Kraj Maritime Territory coat of arms **Edge:** Lettered and reeded

| Date | Mintage | VF20 | XF40 | MS60 | MS63 | MS65 |
|---|---|---|---|---|---|---|
| 2006 ММД | 10,000,000 | — | — | 5.00 | 7.00 | 9.00 |

**Y# 941 10 ROUBLES**
8.23 g., Bi-Metallic Copper-Nickel center in Brass ring, 27 mm. **Obv:** Value with latent image in zero within circle and sprigs **Rev:** Sakha (Yakutiya) Republic coat of arms **Edge:** Lettered and reeded

| Date | Mintage | VF20 | XF40 | MS60 | MS63 | MS65 |
|---|---|---|---|---|---|---|
| 2006 СПМД | 10,000,000 | — | — | 5.00 | 7.00 | 9.00 |

**Y# 942 10 ROUBLES**
8.23 g., Bi-Metallic Copper-Nickel center in Brass ring, 27 mm. **Obv:** Value with latent image in zero within circle and sprigs **Rev:** Sakhalinskaya Oblast coat of arms **Edge:** Lettered and reeded

| Date | Mintage | VF20 | XF40 | MS60 | MS63 | MS65 |
|---|---|---|---|---|---|---|
| 2006 ММД | 10,000,000 | — | — | 5.00 | 7.00 | 9.00 |

**Y# 947 10 ROUBLES**
8.23 g., Bi-Metallic Copper-Nickel center in Brass ring, 27.1 mm. **Obv:** Large value **Rev:** City of Belgorod and shield

| Date | Mintage | VF20 | XF40 | MS60 | MS63 | MS65 |
|---|---|---|---|---|---|---|
| 2006 ММД | 5,000,000 | — | — | 5.00 | 7.00 | 9.00 |

**Y# 948 10 ROUBLES**
8.23 g., Bi-Metallic Copper-Nickel center in Brass ring, 27.1 mm. **Obv:** Large value **Rev:** City of Kargopol and shield

| Date | Mintage | VF20 | XF40 | MS60 | MS63 | MS65 |
|---|---|---|---|---|---|---|
| 2006 ММД | 5,000,000 | — | — | 5.00 | 7.00 | 9.00 |

**Y# 949 10 ROUBLES**
8.23 g., Bi-Metallic Copper-Nickel center in Brass ring, 27.1 mm. **Obv:** Large value **Rev:** City of Turzhok and shield

| Date | Mintage | VF20 | XF40 | MS60 | MS63 | MS65 |
|---|---|---|---|---|---|---|
| 2006 СПМД | 5,000,000 | — | — | 5.00 | 7.00 | 9.00 |

**Y# 963 10 ROUBLES**
8.30 g., Bi-Metallic Copper-Nickel center in Brass ring, 27 mm. **Obv:** Value with latent image in zero within circle and sprays **Rev:** Vologda church **Edge:** Reeded and lettered **Edge Lettering:** Denomination repeated

| Date | Mintage | VF20 | XF40 | MS60 | MS63 | MS65 |
|---|---|---|---|---|---|---|
| 2007 ММД | 2,500,000 | — | — | 5.00 | 7.00 | 9.00 |
| 2007 СПМД | 2,500,000 | — | — | 5.00 | 7.00 | 9.00 |

**Y# 964 10 ROUBLES**
8.30 g., Bi-Metallic Copper-Nickel center in Brass ring, 27 mm. **Obv:** Value with latent image in zero within circle and sprays **Rev:** Veliky Ustyug city view **Edge:** Reeded and lettered **Edge Lettering:** Denomination repeated

| Date | Mintage | VF20 | XF40 | MS60 | MS63 | MS65 |
|---|---|---|---|---|---|---|
| 2007 ММД | 2,500,000 | — | — | 5.00 | 7.00 | 9.00 |
| 2007 СПМД | 2,500,000 | — | — | 5.00 | 7.00 | 9.00 |

**Y# 965 10 ROUBLES**
8.30 g., Bi-Metallic Copper-Nickel center in Brass ring, 27 mm. **Obv:** Value with latent image in zero within circle and sprays **Rev:** Gdov church **Edge:** Reeded and lettered **Edge Lettering:** Denomination repeated

| Date | Mintage | VF20 | XF40 | MS60 | MS63 | MS65 |
|---|---|---|---|---|---|---|
| 2007 ММД | 2,500,000 | — | — | 5.00 | 7.00 | 9.00 |
| 2007 СПМД | 2,500,000 | — | — | 5.00 | 7.00 | 9.00 |

**Y# 970 10 ROUBLES**
8.57 g., Bi-Metallic Copper-Nickel center in Brass ring, 27.08 mm. **Obv:** Value with latent image in zero within circle and sprays **Obv. Legend:** БАНК РОССИИ **Rev:** Rostovskaya Oblast arms **Edge:** Reeded and lettered **Edge Lettering:** Denomination repeated

| Date | Mintage | VF20 | XF40 | MS60 | MS63 | MS65 |
|---|---|---|---|---|---|---|
| 2007 СПМД | 10,000,000 | — | — | 4.00 | 6.00 | 8.00 |

**Y# 971 10 ROUBLES**
8.57 g., Bi-Metallic Copper-Nickel center in Brass ring, 27.08 mm. **Obv:** Value with latent image in zero within circle and sprays **Obv. Legend:** БАНК РОССИИ **Rev:** Khakassia Republic arms **Edge:** Reeded and lettered **Edge Lettering:** Denomination repeated

| Date | Mintage | VF20 | XF40 | MS60 | MS63 | MS65 |
|---|---|---|---|---|---|---|
| 2007 СПМД | 10,000,000 | — | — | 5.00 | 7.00 | 9.00 |

**Y# 972 10 ROUBLES**
8.57 g., Bi-Metallic Copper-Nickel center in Brass ring, 27.08 mm. **Obv:** Value with latent image in zero within circle and sprays **Obv. Legend:** БАНК РОССИИ **Rev:** Bashkortostan Republic arms **Edge:** Reeded and lettered **Edge Lettering:** Denomination repeated

| Date | Mintage | VF20 | XF40 | MS60 | MS63 | MS65 |
|---|---|---|---|---|---|---|
| 2007 ММД | 10,000,000 | — | — | 5.00 | 7.00 | 9.00 |

**Y# 973 10 ROUBLES**
8.57 g., Bi-Metallic Copper-Nickel center in Brass ring, 27.08 mm. **Obv:** Value with latent image in zero within circle and sprays **Obv. Legend:** БАНК РОССИИ **Rev:** Archangelskaya Oblast arms **Edge:** Reeded and lettered **Edge Lettering:** Denomination repeated

| Date | Mintage | VF20 | XF40 | MS60 | MS63 | MS65 |
|---|---|---|---|---|---|---|
| 2007 СПМД | 10,000,000 | — | — | 5.00 | 7.00 | 9.00 |

**Y# 974 10 ROUBLES**
8.57 g., Bi-Metallic Copper-Nickel center in brass ring., 27.08 mm. **Obv:** Value with latent image in zero within circle and sprays **Obv. Legend:** БАНК РОССИИ **Rev:** Novosibirskaya Oblast arms **Edge:** Reeded and lettered **Edge Lettering:** Denomination repeated

| Date | Mintage | VF20 | XF40 | MS60 | MS63 | MS65 |
|---|---|---|---|---|---|---|
| 2007 ММД | 10,000,000 | — | — | 5.00 | 7.00 | 9.00 |

**Y# 993 10 ROUBLES**
8.23 g., Bi-Metallic Copper-Nickel center in Brass ring **Subject:** Lipetskaya Oblast

| Date | Mintage | VF20 | XF40 | MS60 | MS63 | MS65 |
|---|---|---|---|---|---|---|
| 2007 ММД | 10,000,000 | — | — | 2.00 | 3.00 | 5.00 |

**Y# 975 10 ROUBLES**
8.20 g., Bi-Metallic Copper-Nickel center in Brass ring, 27.1 mm. **Obv:** Value with latent image in zero within circle and sprays **Obv. Legend:** БАНК РОССИИ **Rev:** Udmurtia Republic arms **Rev. Legend:** УДМУРТСКАЯ РЕСПУБЛИКА **Edge:** Reeded and lettered **Edge Lettering:** Denomination repeated

| Date | Mintage | VF20 | XF40 | MS60 | MS63 | MS65 |
|---|---|---|---|---|---|---|
| 2008 ММД | 5,000,000 | — | 1.00 | 2.00 | 3.00 | 5.00 |
| 2008 СПМД | 5,000,000 | — | 1.00 | 2.00 | 3.00 | 5.00 |

**Y# 976 10 ROUBLES**
8.28 g., Bi-Metallic Copper-Nickel center in brass ring., 27.1 mm. **Series:** Ancient cities **Subject:** Vladimir **Obv:** Value with latent image in zero within circle and sprays **Obv. Legend:** БАНК РОССИИ **Rev:** Small shield at upper left above city view **Rev. Legend:** ВЛАДИМИР **Edge:** Reeded and lettered **Edge Lettering:** Denomination repeated

| Date | Mintage | VF20 | XF40 | MS60 | MS63 | MS65 |
|---|---|---|---|---|---|---|
| 2008 ММД | 2,500,000 | — | 1.00 | 2.00 | 3.00 | 5.00 |
| 2008 СПМД | 2,500,000 | — | 1.00 | 2.00 | 3.00 | 5.00 |

**Y# 977 10 ROUBLES**
8.23 g., Bi-Metallic Copper-Nickel center in Brass ring, 27 mm. **Obv:** Value with latent image in zero within circle and sprays **Obv. Legend:** БАНК РОССИИ **Rev:** Astrakhanskaya Oblast arms **Edge:** Reeded and lettered **Edge Lettering:** Denomination repeated

| Date | Mintage | VF20 | XF40 | MS60 | MS63 | MS65 |
|---|---|---|---|---|---|---|
| 2008 ММД | 5,000,000 | — | 1.00 | 2.00 | 3.00 | 5.00 |
| 2008 СПМД | 5,000,000 | — | 1.00 | 2.00 | 3.00 | 5.00 |

**Y# 978 10 ROUBLES**
8.16 g., Bi-Metallic Copper-Nickel center in brass ring, 27 mm. **Obv:** Value with latent image in zero within circle and sprays **Obv. Legend:** БАНК РОССИИ **Rev:** Sverdlovskaya Oblast arms **Edge:** Reeded and lettered **Edge Lettering:** Denomination repeated

| Date | Mintage | VF20 | XF40 | MS60 | MS63 | MS65 |
|---|---|---|---|---|---|---|
| 2008 ММД | 5,000,000 | — | 1.00 | 2.00 | 3.00 | 5.00 |
| 2008 СПМД | 5,000,000 | — | 1.00 | 2.00 | 3.00 | 5.00 |

**Y# 986 10 ROUBLES**
8.08 g., Bi-Metallic Copper-Nickel center in Brass ring, 27 mm. **Rev:** Azov town view

| Date | Mintage | VF20 | XF40 | MS60 | MS63 | MS65 |
|---|---|---|---|---|---|---|
| 2008 ММД | 2,500,000 | — | — | 2.00 | 3.50 | 5.50 |
| 2008 СПМД | 2,500,000 | — | — | 2.00 | 3.50 | 5.50 |

**Y# 991 10 ROUBLES**
8.08 g., Bi-Metallic Copper-Nickel center in Brass ring, 27 mm. **Rev:** Kabardino-Balkaria Republic Arms

| Date | Mintage | VF20 | XF40 | MS60 | MS63 | MS65 |
|---|---|---|---|---|---|---|
| 2008 ММД | 5,000,000 | — | — | 2.00 | 3.50 | 5.50 |
| 2008 СПМД | 5,000,000 | — | — | 2.00 | 3.50 | 5.50 |

**Y# 994 10 ROUBLES**
8.23 g., Bi-Metallic Copper-Nickel center in Brass ring **Subject:** Priozersk

| Date | Mintage | VF20 | XF40 | MS60 | MS63 | MS65 |
|---|---|---|---|---|---|---|
| 2008 ММД | 2,500,000 | — | — | 2.00 | 3.50 | 5.50 |
| 2008 СПМД | 2,500,000 | — | — | 2.00 | 3.50 | 5.50 |

**Y# 995 10 ROUBLES**
8.23 g., Bi-Metallic Copper-Nickel center in Brass ring **Subject:** Smolensk

| Date | Mintage | VF20 | XF40 | MS60 | MS63 | MS65 |
|---|---|---|---|---|---|---|
| 2008 ММД | 2,500,000 | — | — | 2.00 | 3.50 | 5.50 |
| 2008 СПМД | 2,500,000 | — | — | 2.00 | 3.50 | 5.50 |

**Y# 982 10 ROUBLES**
8.08 g., Bi-Metallic Copper-Nickel center in Brass ring, 27 mm. **Rev:** Kaluga town view

| Date | Mintage | VF20 | XF40 | MS60 | MS63 | MS65 |
|---|---|---|---|---|---|---|
| 2009 ММД | 2,500,000 | — | — | 2.00 | 3.50 | 5.50 |
| 2009 СПМД | 2,500,000 | — | — | 2.00 | 3.50 | 5.50 |

**Y# 983 10 ROUBLES**
8.08 g., Bi-Metallic Copper-Nickel center in Brass ring, 27 mm. **Rev:** Vyborg town view

| Date | Mintage | VF20 | XF40 | MS60 | MS63 | MS65 |
|---|---|---|---|---|---|---|
| 2009 ММД | 2,500,000 | — | — | 2.00 | 3.50 | 5.50 |
| 2009 СПМД | 2,500,000 | — | — | 2.00 | 3.50 | 5.50 |

### Y# 984 10 ROUBLES

8.08 g., Bi-Metallic Copper-Nickel center in Brass ring, 27 mm. **Rev:** Galich town view

| Date | Mintage | VF20 | XF40 | MS60 | MS63 | MS65 |
|---|---|---|---|---|---|---|
| 2009 ММД | 2,500,000 | — | — | 2.00 | 3.50 | 5.50 |
| 2009 СПМД | 2,500,000 | — | — | 2.00 | 3.50 | 5.50 |

### Y# 985 10 ROUBLES

8.08 g., Bi-Metallic Copper-Nickel center in Brass ring, 27 mm. **Rev:** Kalmykiya Republic arms

| Date | Mintage | VF20 | XF40 | MS60 | MS63 | MS65 |
|---|---|---|---|---|---|---|
| 2009 ММД | 5,000,000 | — | — | 2.00 | 3.50 | 5.50 |
| 2009 СПМД | 5,000,000 | — | — | 2.00 | 3.50 | 5.50 |

### Y# 987 10 ROUBLES

8.08 g., Bi-Metallic Copper-Nickel center in Brass ring, 27 mm. **Rev:** Adygeya Republic arms

| Date | Mintage | VF20 | XF40 | MS60 | MS63 | MS65 |
|---|---|---|---|---|---|---|
| 2009 ММД | 5,000,000 | — | — | 2.00 | 3.50 | 5.50 |
| 2009 СПМД | 5,000,000 | — | — | 2.00 | 3.50 | 5.50 |

### Y# 988 10 ROUBLES

8.08 g., Bi-Metallic Copper-Nickel center in Brass ring, 27 mm. **Rev:** Veliky Novgorod arms

| Date | Mintage | VF20 | XF40 | MS60 | MS63 | MS65 |
|---|---|---|---|---|---|---|
| 2009 ММД | 2,500,000 | — | — | 2.00 | 3.50 | 5.50 |
| 2009 СПМД | 2,500,000 | — | — | 2.00 | 3.50 | 5.50 |

### Y# 989 10 ROUBLES

8.08 g., Bi-Metallic Copper-Nickel center in Brass ring, 27 mm. **Rev:** Jewish Autonomous Oblast Arms

| Date | Mintage | VF20 | XF40 | MS60 | MS63 | MS65 |
|---|---|---|---|---|---|---|
| 2009 ММД | 5,000,000 | — | — | 2.00 | 3.50 | 5.50 |
| 2009 СПМД | 5,000,000 | — | — | 2.00 | 3.50 | 5.50 |

### Y# 996 10 ROUBLES

8.08 g., Bi-Metallic Copper-Nickel center in Brass ring **Subject:** Komi Republic

| Date | Mintage | VF20 | XF40 | MS60 | MS63 | MS65 |
|---|---|---|---|---|---|---|
| 2009 СПМД | 10,000,000 | — | — | 2.00 | 3.50 | 5.50 |

### Y# 997 10 ROUBLES

8.08 g., Bi-Metallic Copper-Nickel center in Brass ring **Subject:** Kirovskaya Oblast

| Date | Mintage | VF20 | XF40 | MS60 | MS63 | MS65 |
|---|---|---|---|---|---|---|
| 2009 СПМД | 10,000,000 | — | — | 2.00 | 3.50 | 5.50 |

### Y# 998 10 ROUBLES

5.63 g., Brass Plated Steel, 22 mm. **Obv:** Double headed eagle **Rev:** Value

| Date | Mintage | VF20 | XF40 | MS60 | MS63 | MS65 |
|---|---|---|---|---|---|---|
| 2009 ММД | — | — | — | 2.50 | 4.00 | 6.00 |
| 2010 ММД | — | — | — | 2.50 | 4.00 | 6.00 |
| 2010 СПМД | — | — | — | 2.50 | 4.00 | 6.00 |
| 2011 ММД | — | — | — | 2.50 | 4.00 | 6.00 |
| 2012 ММД | — | — | — | 2.50 | 4.00 | 6.00 |

### Y# 1274 10 ROUBLES

8.08 g., Bi-Metallic Copper-Nickel center in Brass ring, 27 mm. **Subject:** Russian Census

| Date | Mintage | VF20 | XF40 | MS60 | MS63 | MS65 |
|---|---|---|---|---|---|---|
| 2010 | 2,300,000 | — | — | 4.00 | 6.00 | 8.00 |

### Y# 1275 10 ROUBLES

8.08 g., Bi-Metallic Copper-Nickel center in Brass ring, 27 mm. **Subject:** Bryansk

| Date | Mintage | VF20 | XF40 | MS60 | MS63 | MS65 |
|---|---|---|---|---|---|---|
| 2010 | 10,000,000 | — | — | 4.00 | 6.00 | 8.00 |

### Y# 1276 10 ROUBLES

8.08 g., Bi-Metallic Copper-Nickel center in Brass ring, 27 mm. **Subject:** Yurevets, Ivanovo Region

| Date | Mintage | VF20 | XF40 | MS60 | MS63 | MS65 |
|---|---|---|---|---|---|---|
| 2010 | 10,000,000 | — | — | 4.00 | 6.00 | 8.00 |

### Y# 1277 10 ROUBLES

8.08 g., Bi-Metallic Copper-Nickel center in Brass ring, 27 mm. **Series:** Permskiy Krai

| Date | Mintage | VF20 | XF40 | MS60 | MS63 | MS65 |
|---|---|---|---|---|---|---|
| 2010 | 200,000 | — | — | 45.00 | 65.00 | 75.00 |

### Y# 1278 10 ROUBLES

8.08 g., Bi-Metallic Copper-Nickel center in Brass ring, 27 mm. **Subject:** Nenets Autonomous Region

| Date | Mintage | VF20 | XF40 | MS60 | MS63 | MS65 |
|---|---|---|---|---|---|---|
| 2010 | 1,950,000 | — | — | 4.00 | 6.00 | 8.00 |

### Y# 1279 10 ROUBLES

8.08 g., Bi-Metallic Copper-Nickel center in Brass ring, 27 mm. **Subject:** Chechen Republic

| Date | Mintage | VF20 | XF40 | MS60 | MS63 | MS65 |
|---|---|---|---|---|---|---|
| 2010 | 100,000 | — | — | 100 | 150 | — |

### Y# 1280 10 ROUBLES

8.08 g., Bi-Metallic Copper-Nickel center in Brass ring, 27 mm. **Subject:** Yamalo-Nenetskiy Autonomous Area

| Date | Mintage | VF20 | XF40 | MS60 | MS63 | MS65 |
|---|---|---|---|---|---|---|
| 2010 | 100,000 | — | — | 250 | 300 | — |

### Y# 1466 10 ROUBLES

5.63 g., Brass Plated Steel, 22 mm. **Subject:** Great Patriotic War, 65th Anniversary **Edge:** Segmented reeding

| Date | Mintage | VF20 | XF40 | MS60 | MS63 | MS65 |
|---|---|---|---|---|---|---|
| 2010 ММД | — | — | — | 3.00 | 4.00 | 6.00 |

### Y# 1283 10 ROUBLES

8.08 g., Bi-Metallic Copper-Nickel center in Brass ring, 27 mm. **Rev:** Solikamsk town view

| Date | Mintage | VF20 | XF40 | MS60 | MS63 | MS65 |
|---|---|---|---|---|---|---|
| 2011 СПМД | — | — | — | 3.00 | 4.00 | 6.00 |

**Y# 1284 10 ROUBLES**
8.08 g., Bi-Metallic Copper-Nickel center in Brass ring, 27 mm. **Rev:** Yelets city view

| Date | Mintage | VF20 | XF40 | MS60 | MS63 | MS65 |
|---|---|---|---|---|---|---|
| 2011 СПМД | — | — | — | 3.00 | 4.00 | 6.00 |

**Y# 1292 10 ROUBLES**
8.08 g., Bi-Metallic Copper-Nickel center in Brass ring, 27 mm. **Rev:** Shield of the Republic of Buryatia

| Date | Mintage | VF20 | XF40 | MS60 | MS63 | MS65 |
|---|---|---|---|---|---|---|
| 2011 СПМД | — | — | — | 3.00 | 4.00 | 6.00 |

**Y# 1305 10 ROUBLES**
5.63 g., Brass Plated Steel, 22 mm. **Subject:** Belgorod **Edge:** Segmented reeding

| Date | Mintage | VF20 | XF40 | MS60 | MS63 | MS65 |
|---|---|---|---|---|---|---|
| 2011 СПМД | 10,000,000 | — | — | 3.00 | 4.00 | 6.00 |

**Y# 1308 10 ROUBLES**
5.63 g., Brass Plated Steel, 22 mm. **Subject:** Kursk city arms **Edge:** Segmented reeding

| Date | Mintage | VF20 | XF40 | MS60 | MS63 | MS65 |
|---|---|---|---|---|---|---|
| 2011 СПМД | 10,000,000 | — | — | 3.00 | 4.00 | 6.00 |

**Y# 1309 10 ROUBLES**
5.63 g., Brass Plated Steel, 22 mm. **Subject:** Orel city arms

| Date | Mintage | VF20 | XF40 | MS60 | MS63 | MS65 |
|---|---|---|---|---|---|---|
| 2011 | 10,000,000 | — | — | 3.00 | 4.00 | 6.00 |

**Y# 1313 10 ROUBLES**
8.08 g., Bi-Metallic Copper-Nickel center in Brass ring, 27 mm. **Rev:** Voronezh Region arms

| Date | Mintage | VF20 | XF40 | MS60 | MS63 | MS65 |
|---|---|---|---|---|---|---|
| 2011 | 10,000,000 | — | — | 3.00 | 4.00 | 6.00 |

**Y# 1314 10 ROUBLES**
5.63 g., Brass Plated Steel, 22 mm. **Rev:** Vladikavkaz city arms **Edge:** Segmented reeding

| Date | Mintage | VF20 | XF40 | MS60 | MS63 | MS65 |
|---|---|---|---|---|---|---|
| 2011 СПМД | 10,000,000 | — | — | 3.00 | 4.00 | 6.00 |

**Y# 1318 10 ROUBLES**
5.63 g., Brass Plated Steel, 22 mm. **Rev:** Malgobek city arms **Edge:** Segmented reeding

| Date | Mintage | VF20 | XF40 | MS60 | MS63 | MS65 |
|---|---|---|---|---|---|---|
| 2011 СПМД | 10,000,000 | — | — | 3.00 | 4.00 | 6.00 |

**Y# 1323 10 ROUBLES**
5.63 g., Brass Plated Steel, 22 mm. **Rev:** Rzhev city arms **Edge:** Segmented reeding

| Date | Mintage | VF20 | XF40 | MS60 | MS63 | MS65 |
|---|---|---|---|---|---|---|
| 2011 СПМД | 10,000,000 | — | — | 3.00 | 4.00 | 6.00 |

**Y# 1467 10 ROUBLES**
5.63 g., Brass Plated Steel, 22 mm. **Rev:** Elnya city arms **Edge:** Segmented reeding

| Date | Mintage | VF20 | XF40 | MS60 | MS63 | MS65 |
|---|---|---|---|---|---|---|
| 2011 СПМД | — | — | — | 2.50 | 4.00 | 6.00 |

**Y# 1468 10 ROUBLES**
5.63 g., Brass Plated Steel, 22 mm. **Subject:** First orbital flight, 50th anniversary **Rev:** Rocket on launch pad **Edge:** Segmented reeding

| Date | Mintage | VF20 | XF40 | MS60 | MS63 | MS65 |
|---|---|---|---|---|---|---|
| 2011 (SP) | — | — | — | 3.00 | 4.00 | 6.00 |

**Y# 1380 10 ROUBLES**
8.08 g., Bi-Metallic Copper-Nickel center in Brass ring, 27 mm. **Subject:** Belozersk, Vologda region

| Date | Mintage | VF20 | XF40 | MS60 | MS63 | MS65 |
|---|---|---|---|---|---|---|
| 2012 | 5,000,000 | — | — | 2.50 | 4.00 | 6.00 |

**Y# 1381 10 ROUBLES**
5.63 g., Brass Plated Steel, 22 mm. **Rev:** Voronezh city arms **Edge:** Segmented reeding

| Date | Mintage | VF20 | XF40 | MS60 | MS63 | MS65 |
|---|---|---|---|---|---|---|
| 2012 СПМД | 10,000,000 | — | — | 2.50 | 4.00 | 6.00 |

**Y# 1382 10 ROUBLES**
5.63 g., Brass Plated Steel, 22 mm. **Rev:** Luga city arms **Edge:** Segmented reeding

| Date | Mintage | VF20 | XF40 | MS60 | MS63 | MS65 |
|---|---|---|---|---|---|---|
| 2012 СПМД | 10,000,000 | — | — | 2.50 | 4.00 | 6.00 |

**Y# 1383 10 ROUBLES**
5.63 g., Brass Plated Steel, 22 mm. **Rev:** Polyarny city arms **Edge:** Segmented reeding

| Date | Mintage | VF20 | XF40 | MS60 | MS63 | MS65 |
|---|---|---|---|---|---|---|
| 2012 СПМД | 10,000,000 | — | — | 2.50 | 4.00 | 6.00 |

**Y# 1384 10 ROUBLES**
5.63 g., Brass Plated Steel, 22 mm. **Rev:** Rostov-on-Don city arms **Edge:** Segmented reeding

| Date | Mintage | VF20 | XF40 | MS60 | MS63 | MS65 |
|---|---|---|---|---|---|---|
| 2012 СПМД | 10,000,000 | — | — | 2.50 | 4.00 | 6.00 |

**Y# 1385 10 ROUBLES**
5.63 g., Brass Plated Steel, 22 mm. **Rev:** Tuapse city arms **Edge:** Segmented reeding

| Date | Mintage | VF20 | XF40 | MS60 | MS63 | MS65 |
|---|---|---|---|---|---|---|
| 2012 СПМД | 10,000,000 | — | — | 2.50 | 4.00 | 6.00 |

**Y# 1386 10 ROUBLES**
5.63 g., Brass Plated Steel, 22 mm. **Rev:** Velikiye Luki city arms **Edge:** Segmented reeding

| Date | Mintage | VF20 | XF40 | MS60 | MS63 | MS65 |
|---|---|---|---|---|---|---|
| 2012 СПМД | 10,000,000 | — | — | 2.50 | 4.00 | 6.00 |

**Y# 1387 10 ROUBLES**
5.63 g., Brass Plated Steel, 22 mm. **Subject:** Veliky Novgorod city arms

| Date | Mintage | VF20 | XF40 | MS60 | MS63 | MS65 |
|---|---|---|---|---|---|---|
| 2012 | 10,000,000 | — | — | 2.50 | 4.00 | 6.00 |

### Y# 1388 10 ROUBLES

5.63 g., Brass Plated Steel, 22 mm. **Rev:** Dmitrov city arms

| Date | Mintage | VF20 | XF40 | MS60 | MS63 | MS65 |
|---|---|---|---|---|---|---|
| 2012 | 10,000,000 | — | — | 2.50 | 4.00 | 6.00 |

### Y# 1389 10 ROUBLES

5.63 g., Brass Plated Steel, 22 mm. **Subject:** Origin of Russian Statehood, 1150th Anniversary

| Date | Mintage | VF20 | XF40 | MS60 | MS63 | MS65 |
|---|---|---|---|---|---|---|
| 2012 | 10,000,000 | — | — | 2.50 | 4.00 | 6.00 |

### Y# 1390 10 ROUBLES

5.63 g., Brass Plated Steel, 22 mm. **Subject:** War of 1812, 200th Anniversary

| Date | Mintage | VF20 | XF40 | MS60 | MS63 | MS65 |
|---|---|---|---|---|---|---|
| 2012 | 10,000,000 | — | — | 2.50 | 4.00 | 6.00 |

### Y# 1420 10 ROUBLES

5.63 g., Brass Plated Steel, 22 mm. **Rev:** Logo of the Kazan Universiade **Edge:** Segmented reeding

| Date | Mintage | VF20 | XF40 | MS60 | MS63 | MS65 |
|---|---|---|---|---|---|---|
| 2013 СПМД | 100,000,000 | — | — | 3.00 | 4.00 | 6.00 |

### Y# 1421 10 ROUBLES

5.63 g., Brass Plated Steel, 22 mm. **Rev:** Snow Leopard mascott of the Kazan Universiade running on stadium track with torch **Edge:** Segmented reeding

| Date | Mintage | VF20 | XF40 | MS60 | MS63 | MS65 |
|---|---|---|---|---|---|---|
| 2013 СПМД | 10,000,000 | — | — | 3.00 | 4.00 | 6.00 |

### Y# 1433 10 ROUBLES

5.63 g., Brass Plated Steel, 22 mm. **Subject:** Town of Vyazma **Rev:** Shield **Edge:** Segmented reeding

| Date | Mintage | VF20 | XF40 | MS60 | MS63 | MS65 |
|---|---|---|---|---|---|---|
| 2013 СПМД | 10,000,000 | — | — | 3.00 | 4.00 | 6.00 |

### Y# 1445 10 ROUBLES

5.63 g., Brass Plated Steel, 22 mm. **Subject:** Town of Kronstadt **Rev:** Shield

| Date | Mintage | VF20 | XF40 | MS60 | MS63 | MS65 |
|---|---|---|---|---|---|---|
| 2013 СПМД | 10,000,000 | — | — | 3.00 | 4.00 | 6.00 |

### Y# 1450 10 ROUBLES

5.63 g., Brass Plated Steel, 22 mm. **Subject:** Russian victory over Germany at Battle of Stalingrad, 70th Anniversary **Rev:** Monument in Volgograd

| Date | Mintage | VF20 | XF40 | MS60 | MS63 | MS65 |
|---|---|---|---|---|---|---|
| 2013 ММД | 10,000,000 | — | — | 3.00 | 4.00 | 6.00 |

### Y# 1453 10 ROUBLES

5.63 g., Brass Plated Steel, 22 mm. **Subject:** Town of Naro-Fominsk **Rev:** City Shield

| Date | Mintage | VF20 | XF40 | MS60 | MS63 | MS65 |
|---|---|---|---|---|---|---|
| 2013 СПМД | 10,000,000 | — | — | 3.00 | 4.00 | 6.00 |

### Y# 1461 10 ROUBLES

5.63 g., Brass Plated Steel, 22 mm. **Subject:** Town of Pskov **Rev:** Town Shield **Edge:** Segmented reeding

| Date | Mintage | VF20 | XF40 | MS60 | MS63 | MS65 |
|---|---|---|---|---|---|---|
| 2013 СПМД | 10,000,000 | — | — | 3.00 | 4.00 | 6.00 |

### Y# 1462 10 ROUBLES

5.63 g., Brass Plated Steel, 22 mm. **Subject:** Town of Kozelsk **Rev:** Town shield **Edge:** Segmented reeding

| Date | Mintage | VF20 | XF40 | MS60 | MS63 | MS65 |
|---|---|---|---|---|---|---|
| 2013 СПМД | 10,000,000 | — | — | 3.00 | 4.00 | 6.00 |

### Y# 1465 10 ROUBLES

5.63 g., Brass Plated Steel, 22 mm. **Subject:** Towns - Arkhangelsk **Rev:** Town Shield **Edge:** Segmented reeding

| Date | Mintage | VF20 | XF40 | MS60 | MS63 | MS65 |
|---|---|---|---|---|---|---|
| 2013 СПМД | 10,000,000 | — | — | 3.00 | 4.00 | 6.00 |

### Y# 1469 10 ROUBLES

5.63 g., Brass Plated Steel, 22 mm. **Rev:** Volokolarusk city arms **Edge:** Segmented reeding

| Date | Mintage | VF20 | XF40 | MS60 | MS63 | MS65 |
|---|---|---|---|---|---|---|
| 2013 | — | — | — | 2.50 | 4.00 | 6.00 |

### Y# 1470 10 ROUBLES

8.08 g., Bi-Metallic Copper-Nickel center in Brass ring, 27 mm. **Subject:** Osetia-Alareia Area

| Date | Mintage | VF20 | XF40 | MS60 | MS63 | MS65 |
|---|---|---|---|---|---|---|
| 2013 СПБ | — | — | — | 3.00 | 4.00 | 6.00 |

### Y# 1471 10 ROUBLES

8.08 g., Bi-Metallic Copper-Nickel center in Brass ring, 27 mm. **Subject:** Dagestan Region

| Date | Mintage | VF20 | XF40 | MS60 | MS63 | MS65 |
|---|---|---|---|---|---|---|
| 2013 | — | — | — | 15.00 | 17.50 | 20.00 |

### Y# 1514 10 ROUBLES

292.00 g., Brass, 75 mm. **Subject:** Honoring the Russian winners at the 2012 Summer Olympics, London **Obv:** Names of the 2012 Olympic medalists **Rev:** Palm, sports figures and QR-code

| Date | Mintage | VF20 | XF40 | MS60 | MS63 | MS65 |
|---|---|---|---|---|---|---|
| 2014 | 500 | **PF65** 250 | | | | |

### Y# 1523 10 ROUBLES

5.63 g., Brass Plated Steel, 22 mm. **Subject:** Crimea's entry into the Russian Federation **Obv:** Value **Rev:** Map of Crimea and Swallow's nest tower near Gaspra

| Date | Mintage | VF20 | XF40 | MS60 | MS63 | MS65 |
|---|---|---|---|---|---|---|
| 2014 | 10,000,000 | — | — | 2.50 | 4.00 | 6.00 |

### Y# 1524 10 ROUBLES

5.63 g., Brass Plated Steel, 22 mm. **Subject:** Crimea's entry into the Russian Federation **Obv:** Value **Rev:** Map of Crimea and Monument to the Scuttled Ships in Sevastopol Bay

| Date | Mintage | VF20 | XF40 | MS60 | MS63 | MS65 |
|---|---|---|---|---|---|---|
| 2014 | 10,000,000 | — | — | 2.50 | 4.00 | 6.00 |

**Y# 1535 10 ROUBLES**
8.40 g., Bi-Metallic Copper-Nickel center in Brass ring, 27 mm. **Obv:** Value **Rev:** Nerekhta town view and shield

| Date | Mintage | VF20 | XF40 | MS60 | MS63 | MS65 |
|---|---|---|---|---|---|---|
| 2014 | 5,000,000 | — | — | 2.50 | 4.00 | 6.00 |

**Y# 1566 10 ROUBLES**
8.40 g., Bi-Metallic Brass center in Copper-Nickel ring, 27 mm. **Obv:** Value at center **Rev:** Penza Region Arms

| Date | Mintage | VF20 | XF40 | MS60 | MS63 | MS65 |
|---|---|---|---|---|---|---|
| 2014 | 10,000,000 | — | — | 2.50 | 4.00 | 5.50 |

**Y# 1567 10 ROUBLES**
8.40 g., Bi-Metallic Brass center in Copper-Nickel ring, 27 mm. **Obv:** Value at center **Rev:** Saratov Regions Arms

| Date | Mintage | F12 | VF20 | XF40 | MS60 | MS63 |
|---|---|---|---|---|---|---|
| 2014 | 10,000,000 | — | — | 2.50 | 4.00 | 5.50 |

**Y# 1568 10 ROUBLES**
8.40 g., Bi-Metallic Brass center in Copper-Nickel ring, 27 mm. **Rev:** Republic of Ingushetia Arms

| Date | Mintage | VF20 | XF40 | MS60 | MS63 | MS65 |
|---|---|---|---|---|---|---|
| 2014 | 10,000,000 | — | — | 2.50 | 4.00 | 5.50 |

**Y# 1569 10 ROUBLES**
8.40 g., Bi-Metallic Brass center in Copper-Nickel ring, 27 mm. **Rev:** Tyumen Region Arms

| Date | Mintage | VF20 | XF40 | MS60 | MS63 | MS65 |
|---|---|---|---|---|---|---|
| 2014 | 10,000,000 | — | — | 2.50 | 4.00 | 5.50 |

**Y# 1570 10 ROUBLES**
8.40 g., Bi-Metallic Brass center in Copper-Nickel ring, 27 mm. **Obv:** Value at center **Rev:** Chelyabinsk Regions Arms

| Date | Mintage | VF20 | XF40 | MS60 | MS63 | MS65 |
|---|---|---|---|---|---|---|
| 2014 | 10,000,000 | — | — | 2.50 | 4.00 | 5.50 |

**Y# 1571 10 ROUBLES**
5.63 g., Brass Plated Steel, 22 mm. **Obv:** Value at center **Rev:** Nalchik Arms

| Date | Mintage | VF20 | XF40 | MS60 | MS63 | MS65 |
|---|---|---|---|---|---|---|
| 2014 | 10,000,000 | — | — | 2.50 | 4.00 | 6.00 |

**Y# 1572 10 ROUBLES**
5.63 g., Brass Plated Steel, 22 mm. **Obv:** Value at center **Rev:** Vyborg Arms

| CM Date | Host Date | VF20 | XF40 | MS60 | MS63 | MS65 |
|---|---|---|---|---|---|---|
| | 2014 | — | — | 2.50 | 4.00 | 5.00 |

**Y# 1573 10 ROUBLES**
5.63 g., Bronze Plated Steel, 5.63 mm. **Obv:** Value at center **Rev:** Stary Oskol Arms

| Date | Mintage | VF20 | XF40 | MS60 | MS63 | MS65 |
|---|---|---|---|---|---|---|
| 2014 | 10,000,000 | — | — | 2.50 | 4.00 | 5.00 |

**Y# 1574 10 ROUBLES**
5.63 g., Bronze Plated Steel, 22 mm. **Obv:** Value at center **Rev:** Vadivostok Arms

| Date | Mintage | VF20 | XF40 | MS60 | MS63 | MS65 |
|---|---|---|---|---|---|---|
| 2014 | 10,000,000 | — | — | 2.50 | 4.00 | 5.00 |

**Y# 1575 10 ROUBLES**
5.63 g., Bronze Plated Steel, 22 mm. **Rev:** Tikhvin Arms

| Date | Mintage | VF20 | XF40 | MS60 | MS63 | MS65 |
|---|---|---|---|---|---|---|
| 2014 | 10,000,000 | — | — | 2.50 | 4.00 | 5.00 |

**Y# 1576 10 ROUBLES**
5.63 g., Brass Plated Steel, 22 mm. **Obv:** Value at center **Rev:** Tver Arms

| Date | Mintage | VF20 | XF40 | MS60 | MS63 | MS65 |
|---|---|---|---|---|---|---|
| 2014 | 10,000,000 | — | — | 2.50 | 4.00 | 5.00 |

**Y# 1577 10 ROUBLES**
5.63 g., Bronze Plated Steel, 22 mm. **Rev:** Anapa Arms

| Date | Mintage | VF20 | XF40 | MS60 | MS63 | MS65 |
|---|---|---|---|---|---|---|
| 2014 | 10,000,000 | — | — | 2.50 | 4.00 | 5.00 |

**Y# 678 25 ROUBLES**
173.29 g., 0.900 Silver 5.0143 oz. ASW, 60 mm. **Subject:** Bolshoi Theater 225 Years **Obv:** Double-headed eagle **Rev:** Dancing couple scene **Edge:** Reeded **Note:** Illustration reduced.

| Date | Mintage | VF20 | XF40 | MS60 | MS63 | MS65 |
|---|---|---|---|---|---|---|
| 2001 | 2,000 | PF65 350 | | | | |

**Y# 683 25 ROUBLES**
173.29 g., 0.900 Silver 5.0143 oz. ASW, 60 mm. **Subject:** Siberian Exploration **Obv:** Double-headed eagle **Rev:** Standing king and river boats **Edge:** Reeded **Note:** Illustration reduced.

| Date | Mintage | VF20 | XF40 | MS60 | MS63 | MS65 |
|---|---|---|---|---|---|---|
| 2001 | 1,000 | PF65 650 | | | | |

**Y# 687 25 ROUBLES**
3.20 g., 0.999 Gold 0.1028 oz. AGW, 16 mm. **Subject:** Bolshoi Theater **Obv:** Double-headed eagle **Rev:** Ballerina **Edge:** Reeded

| Date | Mintage | VF20 | XF40 | MS60 | MS63 | MS65 |
|---|---|---|---|---|---|---|
| 2001 | 2,500 | PF65 200 | | | | |

**Y# 794 25 ROUBLES**
173.13 g., 0.900 Silver 5.0096 oz. ASW, 60.2 mm. **Subject:** Foundation of Russian Savings Banks **Obv:** Double-headed eagle **Rev:** Czar Nicholas I and document **Edge:** Reeded

| Date | Mintage | VF20 | XF40 | MS60 | MS63 | MS65 |
|---|---|---|---|---|---|---|
| 2001 (m) | 10,500 | PF65 275 | | | | |

**Y# 999 25 ROUBLES**
173.29 g., 0.900 Silver 5.0143 oz. ASW, 60 mm. **Subject:** Bolshoi Theater, 225th Anniversary

| Date | Mintage | VF20 | XF40 | MS60 | MS63 | MS65 |
|---|---|---|---|---|---|---|
| 2001 | — | PF65 350 | | | | |

**Y# 1001 25 ROUBLES**
173.29 g., 0.900 Silver 5.0143 oz. ASW, 60 mm. **Subject:** Siberia - Development and Exploration

| Date | Mintage | VF20 | XF40 | MS60 | MS63 | MS65 |
|---|---|---|---|---|---|---|
| 2001 | — | PF65 350 | | | | |

**Y# 743 25 ROUBLES**
3.20 g., 0.999 Gold 0.1028 oz. AGW, 16 mm. **Subject:** Zodiac Signs: **Obv:** Double-headed eagle within beaded circle **Rev:** Leo **Edge:** Reeded

| Date | Mintage | VF20 | XF40 | MS60 | MS63 | MS65 |
|---|---|---|---|---|---|---|
| 2002 | 10,000 | PF65 200 | | | | |

**Y# 763 25 ROUBLES**
3.20 g., 0.999 Gold 0.1028 oz. AGW, 16 mm. **Subject:** Zodiac Signs **Obv:** Double-headed eagle within beaded circle **Rev:** Capricorn **Edge:** Reeded

| Date | Mintage | VF20 | XF40 | MS60 | MS63 | MS65 |
|---|---|---|---|---|---|---|
| 2002 (m) | 10,000 | — | — | — | 200 | 225 |

**Y# 764 25 ROUBLES**
3.20 g., 0.999 Gold 0.1028 oz. AGW, 16 mm. **Subject:** Zodiac Signs **Obv:** Double-headed eagle within beaded circle **Rev:** Virgo **Edge:** Reeded

| Date | Mintage | VF20 | XF40 | MS60 | MS63 | MS65 |
|---|---|---|---|---|---|---|
| 2002 (sp) | 10,000 | — | — | — | 200 | 225 |

**Y# 765 25 ROUBLES**
3.20 g., 0.999 Gold 0.1028 oz. AGW, 16 mm. **Subject:** Zodiac Signs **Obv:** Double-headed eagle within beaded circle **Rev:** Sagittarius **Edge:** Reeded

| Date | Mintage | VF20 | XF40 | MS60 | MS63 | MS65 |
|---|---|---|---|---|---|---|
| 2002 (SP) | 10,000 | — | — | — | 200 | 225 |

**Y# 767 25 ROUBLES**
3.20 g., 0.999 Gold 0.1028 oz. AGW, 16 mm. **Subject:** Zodiac signs **Obv:** Double-headed eagle within beaded circle **Rev:** Scorpio **Edge:** Reeded

| Date | Mintage | VF20 | XF40 | MS60 | MS63 | MS65 |
|---|---|---|---|---|---|---|
| 2002 (m) | 10,000 | — | — | — | 200 | 225 |

**Y# 769 25 ROUBLES**
3.20 g., 0.999 Gold 0.1028 oz. AGW **Subject:** Zodiac Signs **Obv:** Double-headed eagle within beaded circle **Rev:** Libra **Edge:** Reeded

| Date | Mintage | VF20 | XF40 | MS60 | MS63 | MS65 |
|---|---|---|---|---|---|---|
| 2002 (sp) | 10,000 | — | — | — | 200 | 225 |

**Y# 777 25 ROUBLES**
173.29 g., 0.900 Silver 5.0143 oz. ASW, 60 mm. **Subject:** Czar Alexander I **Obv:** Double-headed eagle **Rev:** Head right and crowned double-headed eagle above document text **Edge:** Reeded **Note:** Illustration reduced.

| Date | Mintage | VF20 | XF40 | MS60 | MS63 | MS65 |
|---|---|---|---|---|---|---|
| 2002 (m) | 1,500 | PF65 400 | | | | |

**Y# 785 25 ROUBLES**
173.29 g., 0.900 Silver 5.0143 oz. ASW, 60 mm. **Subject:** Admiral Nakhimov **Obv:** Double-headed eagle **Rev:** Admiral watching naval battle **Edge:** Reeded **Note:** Illustration reduced.

| Date | Mintage | VF20 | XF40 | MS60 | MS63 | MS65 |
|---|---|---|---|---|---|---|
| 2002 (sp) | 2,000 | PF65 350 | | | | |

**Y# 790 25 ROUBLES**
173.29 g., 0.900 Silver 5.0143 oz. ASW, 60 mm. **Subject:** Hermitage **Obv:** Double-headed eagle **Rev:** Staircase viewed through doorway **Edge:** Reeded **Note:** Illustration reduced.

| Date | Mintage | VF20 | XF40 | MS60 | MS63 | MS65 |
|---|---|---|---|---|---|---|
| 2002 (sp) | 2,000 | PF65 350 | | | | |

**Y# 821 25 ROUBLES**
3.20 g., 0.999 Gold 0.1028 oz. AGW, 16 mm. **Subject:** Zodiac signs **Obv:** Double-headed eagle within beaded circle **Rev:** Cancer **Edge:** Reeded

| Date | Mintage | VF20 | XF40 | MS60 | MS63 | MS65 |
|---|---|---|---|---|---|---|
| 2003 (sp) | 50,000 | — | — | — | 200 | 225 |

**Y# 864 25 ROUBLES**
172.80 g., 0.900 Silver 5.0001 oz. ASW, 60 mm. **Rev:** St. Sercius Monastery

| Date | Mintage | VF20 | XF40 | MS60 | MS63 | MS65 |
|---|---|---|---|---|---|---|
| 2003 | 2,000 | PF65 350 | | | | |

**Y# 865 25 ROUBLES**
172.80 g., 0.900 Silver 5.0001 oz. ASW, 60 mm. **Rev:** Shlisselburg

| Date | Mintage | VF20 | XF40 | MS60 | MS63 | MS65 |
|---|---|---|---|---|---|---|
| 2003 (m) | 2,000 | PF65 350 | | | | |

**Y# 866 25 ROUBLES**
172.80 g., 0.900 Silver 5.0001 oz. ASW, 60 mm. **Rev:** Kamchatka

| Date | Mintage | VF20 | XF40 | MS60 | MS63 | MS65 |
|---|---|---|---|---|---|---|
| 2003 | 2,000 | PF65 350 | | | | |

### Y# 1003 25 ROUBLES

3.20 g., 0.999 Gold 0.1028 oz. AGW, 16 mm. **Subject:** Aquarius

| Date | Mintage | VF20 | XF40 | MS60 | MS63 | MS65 |
|---|---|---|---|---|---|---|
| 2003 | — | PF65 350 | | | | |

### Y# 1004 25 ROUBLES

3.20 g., 0.999 Silver 0.1028 oz. ASW, 16 mm. **Subject:** Pisces

| Date | Mintage | VF20 | XF40 | MS60 | MS63 | MS65 |
|---|---|---|---|---|---|---|
| 2003 | — | PF65 350 | | | | |

### Y# 1005 25 ROUBLES

3.20 g., 0.999 Silver 0.1028 oz. ASW, 16 mm. **Subject:** Aries

| Date | Mintage | VF20 | XF40 | MS60 | MS63 | MS65 |
|---|---|---|---|---|---|---|
| 2003 | — | PF65 350 | | | | |

### Y# 1006 25 ROUBLES

3.20 g., 0.999 Silver 0.1028 oz. ASW, 16 mm. **Subject:** Taurus

| Date | Mintage | VF20 | XF40 | MS60 | MS63 | MS65 |
|---|---|---|---|---|---|---|
| 2003 | — | PF65 350 | | | | |

### Y# 830 25 ROUBLES

177.96 g., 0.900 Bi-Metallic 5.1494 oz. .900 Silver 172.78g planchet with .900 Gold 5.18g insert, 60 mm. **Subject:** Monetary reform of Peter the Great **Obv:** Double-headed eagle **Rev:** Gold insert replicating the obverse and reverse designs of a 1704 one rouble coin **Edge:** Reeded **Note:** Illustration reduced.

| Date | Mintage | VF20 | XF40 | MS60 | MS63 | MS65 |
|---|---|---|---|---|---|---|
| 2004 (sp) | 1,000 | PF65 1,000 | | | | |

### Y# 867 25 ROUBLES

172.80 g., 0.900 Silver 5.0001 oz. ASW, 60 mm. **Rev:** Valaam Church

| Date | Mintage | VF20 | XF40 | MS60 | MS63 | MS65 |
|---|---|---|---|---|---|---|
| 2004 | 1,500 | PF65 375 | | | | |

### Y# 1014 25 ROUBLES

173.29 g., 0.900 Silver 5.0143 oz. ASW, 60 mm. **Subject:** 2nd Kamchatka Expedition, 1733-43

| Date | Mintage | VF20 | XF40 | MS60 | MS63 | MS65 |
|---|---|---|---|---|---|---|
| 2004 | — | PF65 350 | | | | |

### Y# 1019 25 ROUBLES

173.29 g., 0.900 Silver 5.0143 oz. ASW, 60 mm. **Subject:** Holy Trinity - St. Sergius Lavra in Sergiev Posad

| Date | Mintage | VF20 | XF40 | MS60 | MS63 | MS65 |
|---|---|---|---|---|---|---|
| 2004 | — | PF65 350 | | | | |

### Y# 1023 25 ROUBLES

173.29 g., 0.900 Silver 5.0143 oz. ASW, 60 mm. **Subject:** Reindeer

| Date | Mintage | VF20 | XF40 | MS60 | MS63 | MS65 |
|---|---|---|---|---|---|---|
| 2004 | — | PF65 350 | | | | |

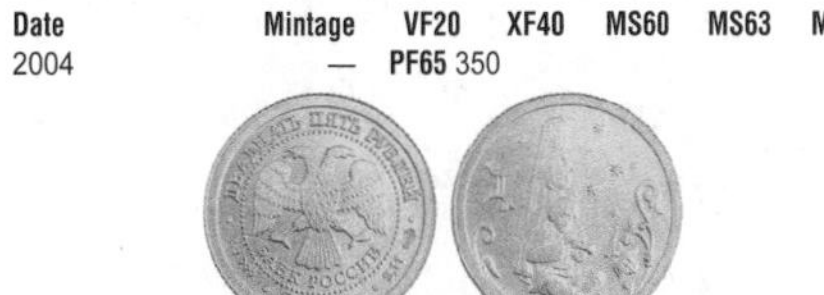

### Y# 898 25 ROUBLES

3.20 g., 0.999 Gold 0.1028 oz. AGW, 16 mm. **Obv:** Double-headed eagle **Rev:** Gemini twins **Edge:** Reeded

| Date | Mintage | VF20 | XF40 | MS60 | MS63 | MS65 |
|---|---|---|---|---|---|---|
| 2005 | 10,000 | — | — | — | 200 | 225 |

### Y# 900 25 ROUBLES

3.20 g., 0.999 Gold 0.1028 oz. AGW, 16 mm. **Obv:** Double-headed eagle **Rev:** Cancer crawfish **Edge:** Reeded

| Date | Mintage | VF20 | XF40 | MS60 | MS63 | MS65 |
|---|---|---|---|---|---|---|
| 2005 | 10,000 | PF65 200 | | | | |

### Y# 902 25 ROUBLES

3.20 g., 0.999 Gold 0.1028 oz. AGW, 16 mm. **Obv:** Double-headed eagle **Rev:** Leo lion **Edge:** Reeded

| Date | Mintage | VF20 | XF40 | MS60 | MS63 | MS65 |
|---|---|---|---|---|---|---|
| 2005 | 10,000 | — | — | — | 220 | 245 |

### Y# 915 25 ROUBLES

3.20 g., 0.999 Gold 0.1028 oz. AGW, 16 mm. **Obv:** Double-headed eagle **Rev:** Virgos standing lady **Edge:** Reeded

| Date | Mintage | VF20 | XF40 | MS60 | MS63 | MS65 |
|---|---|---|---|---|---|---|
| 2005 | 10,000 | PF65 200 | | | | |

### Y# 920 25 ROUBLES

3.20 g., 0.999 Gold 0.1028 oz. AGW, 16 mm. **Obv:** Double-headed eagle **Rev:** Two stylized birds forming balance scale **Edge:** Reeded

| Date | Mintage | VF20 | XF40 | MS60 | MS63 | MS65 |
|---|---|---|---|---|---|---|
| 2005 | 10,000 | — | — | — | 220 | 245 |

### Y# 922 25 ROUBLES

3.20 g., 0.999 Gold 0.1028 oz. AGW, 16 mm. **Obv:** Double-headed eagle **Rev:** Scorpio scorpion **Edge:** Reeded

| Date | Mintage | VF20 | XF40 | MS60 | MS63 | MS65 |
|---|---|---|---|---|---|---|
| 2005 | 10,000 | — | — | — | 220 | 245 |

### Y# 924 25 ROUBLES

169.00 g., 0.925 Silver 5.026 oz. ASW, 60 mm. **Subject:** 625th Anniversary - Battle of Kulikovo **Obv:** Double-headed eagle **Rev:** Mounted warriors above and below crossed swords **Edge:** Reeded **Note:** Illustration reduced.

| Date | Mintage | VF20 | XF40 | MS60 | MS63 | MS65 |
|---|---|---|---|---|---|---|
| 2005 | 1,500 | PF65 375 | | | | |

### Y# 927 25 ROUBLES

3.20 g., 0.999 Gold 0.1028 oz. AGW, 16 mm. **Obv:** Double-headed eagle **Rev:** Sagittarius the archer **Edge:** Reeded

| Date | Mintage | VF20 | XF40 | MS60 | MS63 | MS65 |
|---|---|---|---|---|---|---|
| 2005 | 10,000 | — | — | — | 220 | 245 |

**Y# 929 25 ROUBLES**
3.20 g., 0.999 Gold 0.1028 oz. AGW, 16 mm. **Obv:** Double-headed eagle **Rev:** Capricorn as half goat and fish **Edge:** Reeded

| Date | Mintage | VF20 | XF40 | MS60 | MS63 | MS65 |
|---|---|---|---|---|---|---|
| 2005 | 10,000 | — | — | — | 220 | 245 |

**Y# 931 25 ROUBLES**
3.20 g., 0.999 Gold 0.1028 oz. AGW, 16 mm. **Obv:** Double-headed eagle **Rev:** Pisces as catfish and sturgeon **Edge:** Reeded

| Date | Mintage | VF20 | XF40 | MS60 | MS63 | MS65 |
|---|---|---|---|---|---|---|
| 2005 | 10,000 | — | — | — | 220 | 245 |

**Y# 933 25 ROUBLES**
3.20 g., 0.999 Gold 0.1028 oz. AGW, 16 mm. **Obv:** Double-headed eagle **Rev:** Aries ram **Edge:** Reeded

| Date | Mintage | VF20 | XF40 | MS60 | MS63 | MS65 |
|---|---|---|---|---|---|---|
| 2005 | 10,000 | — | — | — | 220 | 245 |

**Y# 935 25 ROUBLES**
3.20 g., 0.999 Gold 0.1028 oz. AGW, 16 mm. **Obv:** Double-headed eagle **Rev:** Taurus bull **Edge:** Reeded

| Date | Mintage | VF20 | XF40 | MS60 | MS63 | MS65 |
|---|---|---|---|---|---|---|
| 2005 | 10,000 | — | — | — | 220 | 245 |

**Y# 937 25 ROUBLES**
3.20 g., 0.999 Gold 0.1028 oz. AGW, 16 mm. **Obv:** Double-headed eagle **Rev:** Aquarius water carrier **Edge:** Reeded

| Date | Mintage | VF20 | XF40 | MS60 | MS63 | MS65 |
|---|---|---|---|---|---|---|
| 2005 | 10,000 | — | — | — | 220 | 245 |

**Y# 1047 25 ROUBLES**
169.00 g., 0.925 Silver 5.026 oz. ASW, 60 mm. **Subject:** Tretyakov State Galler, 150th Anniversary

| Date | Mintage | VF20 | XF40 | MS60 | MS63 | MS65 |
|---|---|---|---|---|---|---|
| 2006 | 1,000 | **PF65** 1,000 | | | | |

**Y# 1050 25 ROUBLES**
169.00 g., 0.925 Silver 5.026 oz. ASW, 60 mm. **Subject:** Malye Korely

| Date | Mintage | VF20 | XF40 | MS60 | MS63 | MS65 |
|---|---|---|---|---|---|---|
| 2006 | 1,000 | **PF65** 350 | | | | |

**Y# 1051 25 ROUBLES**
169.00 g., 0.925 Silver 5.026 oz. ASW, 60 mm. **Subject:** Tikhvin Monastery, Dome of the Mother of God

| Date | Mintage | VF20 | XF40 | MS60 | MS63 | MS65 |
|---|---|---|---|---|---|---|
| 2006 | 1,000 | **PF65** 350 | | | | |

**Y# 1053 25 ROUBLES**
169.00 g., 0.925 Silver 5.026 oz. ASW, 60 mm. **Subject:** Konevsky Monastery of St. Virgin's Nativity

| Date | Mintage | VF20 | XF40 | MS60 | MS63 | MS65 |
|---|---|---|---|---|---|---|
| 2006 | 1,000 | **PF65** 350 | | | | |

**Y# 969 25 ROUBLES**
169.00 g., 0.925 Silver 5.026 oz. ASW, 60 mm. **Obv:** Two-headed eagle **Rev:** Vyatka St. Trifon Monastery of the Assumption, Kirov **Edge:** Reeded **Note:** Illustration reduced

| Date | Mintage | VF20 | XF40 | MS60 | MS63 | MS65 |
|---|---|---|---|---|---|---|
| 2007 (sp) | 2,000 | **PF65** 350 | | | | |

**Y# 1083 25 ROUBLES**
169.00 g., 0.925 Silver 5.026 oz. ASW, 60 mm. **Subject:** Russian Railways, 150th Anniversary

| Date | Mintage | VF20 | XF40 | MS60 | MS63 | MS65 |
|---|---|---|---|---|---|---|
| 2007 | 1,000 | **PF65** 500 | | | | |

**Y# 1084 25 ROUBLES**
169.00 g., 0.925 Silver 5.026 oz. ASW, 60 mm. **Subject:** F. A. Golovin, first Order of St. Andrew awardee

| Date | Mintage | VF20 | XF40 | MS60 | MS63 | MS65 |
|---|---|---|---|---|---|---|
| 2007 | — | **PF65** 350 | | | | |

**Y# 1101 25 ROUBLES**
169.00 g., 0.925 Silver 5.026 oz. ASW, 60 mm. **Subject:** St. Artemy Verkolsky Monastery, Arkhamgelsk

| Date | Mintage | VF20 | XF40 | MS60 | MS63 | MS65 |
|---|---|---|---|---|---|---|
| 2007 | — | **PF65** 350 | | | | |

**Y# 1102 25 ROUBLES**
169.00 g., 0.925 Silver 5.026 oz. ASW, 60 mm. **Subject:** Pskov-Pechersky Holy Monastery of the Assumption

| Date | Mintage | VF20 | XF40 | MS60 | MS63 | MS65 |
|---|---|---|---|---|---|---|
| 2007 | 2,000 | **PF65** 350 | | | | |

**Y# 1116 25 ROUBLES**
169.00 g., 0.925 Silver 5.026 oz. ASW, 60 mm. **Subject:** Goznak, 190th Anniversary

| Date | Mintage | VF20 | XF40 | MS60 | MS63 | MS65 |
|---|---|---|---|---|---|---|
| 2008 | 1,500 | **PF65** 1,000 | | | | |

**Y# 1125 25 ROUBLES**
169.00 g., 0.925 Silver 5.026 oz. ASW, 60 mm. **Subject:** Astrakhan Kremlin

| Date | Mintage | VF20 | XF40 | MS60 | MS63 | MS65 |
|---|---|---|---|---|---|---|
| 2008 | 2,000 | **PF65** 400 | | | | |

**Y# 1139 25 ROUBLES**
169.00 g., 0.925 Silver 5.026 oz. ASW, 60 mm. **Subject:** European Beaver

| Date | Mintage | VF20 | XF40 | MS60 | MS63 | MS65 |
|---|---|---|---|---|---|---|
| 2008 | 1,500 | **PF65** 400 | | | | |

**Y# 1160 25 ROUBLES**
168.00 g., 0.925 Silver 4.9962 oz. ASW, 60 mm. **Subject:** Alexander I Monument, 175th Anniversary

| Date | Mintage | VF20 | XF40 | MS60 | MS63 | MS65 |
|---|---|---|---|---|---|---|
| 2009 | 1,000 | **PF65** 525 | | | | |

**Y# 1178 25 ROUBLES**
168.00 g., 0.925 Silver 4.9962 oz. ASW, 60 mm. **Subject:** Poltava Battle, 300th Anniversary

| Date | Mintage | VF20 | XF40 | MS60 | MS63 | MS65 |
|---|---|---|---|---|---|---|
| 2009 | 1,500 | **PF65** 350 | | | | |

**Y# 1184 25 ROUBLES**
168.00 g., 0.925 Silver 4.9962 oz. ASW, 60 mm. **Subject:** Arkhangelskoye Museum

| Date | Mintage | VF20 | XF40 | MS60 | MS63 | MS65 |
|---|---|---|---|---|---|---|
| 2009 | 1,500 | **PF65** 350 | | | | |

**Y# 1186 25 ROUBLES**
168.00 g., 0.925 Silver 4.9962 oz. ASW, 60 mm. **Subject:** St. Trinity Monastery, Pensu Region

| Date | Mintage | VF20 | XF40 | MS60 | MS63 | MS65 |
|---|---|---|---|---|---|---|
| 2009 | 1,500 | **PF65** 350 | | | | |

**Y# 1187 25 ROUBLES**
168.00 g., 0.925 Silver 4.9962 oz. ASW, 60 mm. **Subject:** St. Nikolas Monastary, Staraya Ladoga

| Date | Mintage | VF20 | XF40 | MS60 | MS63 | MS65 |
|---|---|---|---|---|---|---|
| 2009 | 1,500 | **PF65** 350 | | | | |

**Y# 1200 25 ROUBLES**
168.00 g., 0.925 Silver 4.9962 oz. ASW, 60 mm. **Subject:** Velikly Novgorod

| Date | Mintage | VF20 | XF40 | MS60 | MS63 | MS65 |
|---|---|---|---|---|---|---|
| 2009 | 1,500 | **PF65** 350 | | | | |

**Y# 1223 25 ROUBLES**
168.00 g., 0.925 Silver 4.9962 oz. ASW, 60 mm. **Subject:** Khmelita, Griboyedov family estate

| Date | Mintage | VF20 | XF40 | MS60 | MS63 | MS65 |
|---|---|---|---|---|---|---|
| 2010 | 1,500 | **PF65** 350 | | | | |

**Y# 1224 25 ROUBLES**
168.00 g., 0.925 Silver 4.9962 oz. ASW, 60 mm. **Subject:** Kirillo Belosersk Monastery

| Date | Mintage | VF20 | XF40 | MS60 | MS63 | MS65 |
|---|---|---|---|---|---|---|
| 2010 | 2,000 | **PF65** 400 | | | | |

**Y# 1225 25 ROUBLES**
168.00 g., 0.925 Silver 4.9962 oz. ASW, 60 mm. **Subject:** Alezxandro - Svirsky Monestary

| Date | Mintage | VF20 | XF40 | MS60 | MS63 | MS65 |
|---|---|---|---|---|---|---|
| 2010 | 1,500 | **PF65** 350 | | | | |

**Y# 1226 25 ROUBLES**
168.00 g., 0.925 Silver 4.9962 oz. ASW, 60 mm. **Subject:** Sanaksarsky Monestary

| Date | Mintage | VF20 | XF40 | MS60 | MS63 | MS65 |
|---|---|---|---|---|---|---|
| 2010 | 1,500 | **PF65** 350 | | | | |

**Y# 1229 25 ROUBLES**
168.00 g., 0.925 Silver 4.9962 oz. ASW, 60 mm. **Subject:** Bank of Russia, 150th Anniversary

| Date | Mintage | VF20 | XF40 | MS60 | MS63 | MS65 |
|---|---|---|---|---|---|---|
| 2010 | 1,000 | **PF65** 350 | | | | |

**Y# 1233 25 ROUBLES**
169.00 g., 0.925 Silver 5.026 oz. ASW, 60 mm. **Subject:** UNESCO Heritage Site - Yaroslav

| Date | Mintage | VF20 | XF40 | MS60 | MS63 | MS65 |
|---|---|---|---|---|---|---|
| 2010 | 1,500 | **PF65** 350 | | | | |

**Y# 1298 25 ROUBLES**
10.00 g., Copper-Nickel, 27 mm. **Subject:** 2014 Winter Olympics - Sochi **Obv:** Double-headed eagle, value below **Rev:** Mountain **Edge:** Reeded

| Date | Mintage | VF20 | XF40 | MS60 | MS63 | MS65 |
|---|---|---|---|---|---|---|
| 2011 | 10,000,000 | — | — | — | 8.00 | 10.00 |
| Note: Value in card packaging is $40. | | | | | | |
| 2014 | 10,000,000 | — | — | — | 8.00 | 10.00 |

**Y# 1298a 25 ROUBLES**
10.00 g., Copper-Nickel, 27 mm. **Subject:** 2014 Winter Olympics - Sochi **Rev:** Color features

| Date | Mintage | VF20 | XF40 | MS60 | MS63 | MS65 |
|---|---|---|---|---|---|---|
| 2011 | — | — | — | — | 35.00 | 40.00 |

**Y# 1304 25 ROUBLES**
168.00 g., 0.925 Silver 4.9962 oz. ASW, 60 mm. **Subject:** Virgin Mary Monastery, Kazan **Rev:** Icon in color and building complex

| Date | Mintage | VF20 | XF40 | MS60 | MS63 | MS65 |
|---|---|---|---|---|---|---|
| 2011 | 2,000 | **PF65** 400 | | | | |

**Y# 1306 25 ROUBLES**
168.00 g., 0.925 Silver 4.9962 oz. ASW, 60 mm. **Subject:** Pavlovsky Palace and park **Rev:** Hilltop building, bridge in forefront, female statues flankings **Edge:** Reeded

| Date | Mintage | VF20 | XF40 | MS60 | MS63 | MS65 |
|---|---|---|---|---|---|---|
| 2011 | 1,500 | **PF65** 350 | | | | |

**Y# 1317 25 ROUBLES**
168.00 g., 0.925 Silver 4.9962 oz. ASW, 60 mm. **Subject:** Virgin's Saint Entrance Presentation Monastery, Optin **Rev:** Monastery buildings

| Date | Mintage | VF20 | XF40 | MS60 | MS63 | MS65 |
|---|---|---|---|---|---|---|
| 2011 | 2,000 | **PF65** 350 | | | | |

**Y# 1321 25 ROUBLES**
168.00 g., 0.925 Silver 4.9962 oz. ASW, 60 mm. **Subject:** Year of Italian Culture and Language in Russia **Rev:** Town vies of Sergiev Posad and Bari, Icon at center, Russian and Italian flags below in color

| Date | Mintage | VF20 | XF40 | MS60 | MS63 | MS65 |
|---|---|---|---|---|---|---|
| 2011 | 1,000 | **PF65** 1,000 | | | | |

**Y# 1322 25 ROUBLES**
168.00 g., 0.925 Silver 4.9962 oz. ASW, 60 mm. **Subject:** Kazan Cathedral, St. Petersburg **Rev:** Ariel view of Cathedral and plaza **Edge:** Reeded

| Date | Mintage | VF20 | XF40 | MS60 | MS63 | MS65 |
|---|---|---|---|---|---|---|
| 2011 | 1,500 | **PF65** 400 | | | | |

**Y# 1335 25 ROUBLES**
169.00 g., 0.925 Silver 5.026 oz. ASW, 60 mm. **Subject:** Museum-Estate of V.D. Polenov, Tula region

| Date | Mintage | VF20 | XF40 | MS60 | MS63 | MS65 |
|---|---|---|---|---|---|---|
| 2012 | 2,000 | **PF65** 400 | | | | |

**Y# 1336 25 ROUBLES**
169.00 g., 0.925 Silver 5.026 oz. ASW, 60 mm. **Subject:** Voskresensky New Jerusalem Monastery, Istra, Moscow region

| Date | Mintage | VF20 | XF40 | MS60 | MS63 | MS65 |
|---|---|---|---|---|---|---|
| 2012 | 2,000 | **PF65** 400 | | | | |

**Y# 1337 25 ROUBLES**
169.00 g., 0.925 Silver 5.026 oz. ASW, 60 mm. **Subject:** Spaso-Borodinsky Monastery, Moscow region

| Date | Mintage | VF20 | XF40 | MS60 | MS63 | MS65 |
|---|---|---|---|---|---|---|
| 2012 | 2,000 | **PF65** 400 | | | | |

**Y# 1338 25 ROUBLES**
169.00 g., 0.925 Silver 5.026 oz. ASW, 60 mm. **Subject:** Alexeevo-Akatov Monastery, Voronezh

| Date | Mintage | VF20 | XF40 | MS60 | MS63 | MS65 |
|---|---|---|---|---|---|---|
| 2012 | 1,500 | **PF65** 525 | | | | |

**Y# 1343 25 ROUBLES**
169.00 g., 0.925 Silver 5.026 oz. ASW, 60 mm. **Subject:** People's Volunteer Corps, 400th Anniversary

| Date | Mintage | VF20 | XF40 | MS60 | MS63 | MS65 |
|---|---|---|---|---|---|---|
| 2012 | 1,000 | **PF65** 525 | | | | |

**Y# 1346 25 ROUBLES**
169.00 g., 0.925 Silver 5.026 oz. ASW, 100 mm. **Subject:** Russia's victory in the War of 1812

| Date | Mintage | VF20 | XF40 | MS60 | MS63 | MS65 |
|---|---|---|---|---|---|---|
| 2012 | 2,000 | **PF65** 400 | | | | |

**Y# 1347 25 ROUBLES**
169.00 g., 0.925 Silver 5.026 oz. ASW, 60 mm. **Subject:** Russia's victory in the War of 1812

| Date | Mintage | VF20 | XF40 | MS60 | MS63 | MS65 |
|---|---|---|---|---|---|---|
| 2012 | 2,000 | **PF65** 400 | | | | |

**Y# 1352 25 ROUBLES**
169.00 g., 0.925 Silver 5.026 oz. ASW, 60 mm. **Subject:** Pushkin State Museum of Fine Arts, Moscow, 100th Anniversary

| Date | Mintage | VF20 | XF40 | MS60 | MS63 | MS65 |
|---|---|---|---|---|---|---|
| 2012 | 1,000 | **PF65** 525 | | | | |

**Y# 1360 25 ROUBLES**
169.00 g., 0.925 Silver 5.026 oz. ASW, 60 mm. **Subject:** Asia-Pacific Economic Cooperation summit, Vladivostok **Rev:** APEC logo in color

| Date | Mintage | VF20 | XF40 | MS60 | MS63 | MS65 |
|---|---|---|---|---|---|---|
| 2012 | 1,000 | **PF65** 650 | | | | |

**Y# 1368 25 ROUBLES**
10.00 g., Copper-Nickel, 27 mm. **Subject:** 2014 Winter Olympics - Sochi **Rev:** Olympics Mascott

| Date | Mintage | VF20 | XF40 | MS60 | MS63 | MS65 |
|---|---|---|---|---|---|---|
| 2014 | — | — | — | — | 25.00 | 30.00 |
| 2014 | 10,000,000 | — | — | — | 8.00 | 10.00 |

**Y# 1368a 25 ROUBLES**
10.00 g., Copper-Nickel, 27 mm. **Subject:** 2014 Winter Olympics, Sochi **Rev:** Three mascots in color

| Date | Mintage | VF20 | XF40 | MS60 | MS63 | MS65 |
|---|---|---|---|---|---|---|
| 2012 | — | — | — | — | 35.00 | 40.00 |

**Y# 1372 25 ROUBLES**

169.00 g., 0.925 Silver 5.026 oz. ASW, 60 mm. **Subject:** Architecture

| Date | Mintage | VF20 | XF40 | MS60 | MS63 | MS65 |
|---|---|---|---|---|---|---|
| 2012 | 1,500 | **PF65** 400 | | | | |

**Y# 1373 25 ROUBLES**

169.00 g., 0.925 Silver 5.026 oz. ASW, 60 mm. **Subject:** Architecture

| Date | Mintage | VF20 | XF40 | MS60 | MS63 | MS65 |
|---|---|---|---|---|---|---|
| 2012 | 1,500 | **PF65** 400 | | | | |

**Y# 1378 25 ROUBLES**

169.00 g., 0.925 Silver 5.026 oz. ASW, 60 mm. **Subject:** Winter Palace in St. Petersburg, 250th Anniversary

| Date | Mintage | VF20 | XF40 | MS60 | MS63 | MS65 |
|---|---|---|---|---|---|---|
| 2012 | 1,500 | **PF65** 285 | | | | |

**Y# 1423 25 ROUBLES**

169.00 g., 0.925 Silver 5.026 oz. ASW, 60 mm. **Rev:** Two wrestlers, Kazan Universiade logo and city skyline

| Date | Mintage | VF20 | XF40 | MS60 | MS63 | MS65 |
|---|---|---|---|---|---|---|
| 2013 СПМД | 1,500 | **PF65** 300 | | | | |

**Y# 1432 25 ROUBLES**

169.00 g., 0.925 Silver 5.026 oz. ASW, 60 mm. **Rev:** Kazan Kremlin, national flag of Russia and Italy, and Verona sports arena **Edge:** Reeded

| Date | Mintage | VF20 | XF40 | MS60 | MS63 | MS65 |
|---|---|---|---|---|---|---|
| 2013 СПМД | 1,000 | **PF65** 300 | | | | |

**Y# 1435 25 ROUBLES**

169.00 g., 0.925 Silver 5.026 oz. ASW, 60 mm. **Subject:** A.S. Shein **Rev:** Half-length Shein at right **Edge:** Reeded

| Date | Mintage | VF20 | XF40 | MS60 | MS63 | MS65 |
|---|---|---|---|---|---|---|
| 2013 ММД | 1,500 | **PF65** 300 | | | | |

**Y# 1437 25 ROUBLES**

169.00 g., 0.925 Silver 5.026 oz. ASW, 60 mm. **Subject:** Dynamo Soccer Club, 90th Anniversary **Rev:** Three soccer players around ball **Edge:** Reeded

| Date | Mintage | VF20 | XF40 | MS60 | MS63 | MS65 |
|---|---|---|---|---|---|---|
| 2013 СПМД | 2,000 | **PF65** 300 | | | | |

**Y# 1438 25 ROUBLES**

169.00 g., 0.925 Silver 5.026 oz. ASW, 60 mm. **Subject:** Dynamo Hockey club, 90th Anniversary **Rev:** Three hockey players at puck **Edge:** Reeded

| Date | Mintage | VF20 | XF40 | MS60 | MS63 | MS65 |
|---|---|---|---|---|---|---|
| 2013 СПМД | 2,000 | **PF65** 300 | | | | |

**Y# 1439 25 ROUBLES**

169.00 g., 0.925 Silver 5.026 oz. ASW, 60 mm. **Subject:** Dynamo Sports Club, 90th Anniversary **Rev:** Biathlon view, skier and two shooters **Edge:** Reeded

| Date | Mintage | VF20 | XF40 | MS60 | MS63 | MS65 |
|---|---|---|---|---|---|---|
| 2013 ММД | 2,000 | **PF65** 300 | | | | |

**Y# 1447 25 ROUBLES**
169.00 g., 0.925 Silver 5.026 oz. ASW, 60 mm. **Subject:** City of Smolensk, 1150th Anniversary of founding **Rev:** Assumption Cathedral and building montage **Edge:** Reeded

| Date | Mintage | VF20 | XF40 | MS60 | MS63 | MS65 |
|---|---|---|---|---|---|---|
| 2013 ММД | 1,500 | PF65 300 | | | | |

**Y# 1454 25 ROUBLES**
169.00 g., 0.925 Silver 5.026 oz. ASW, 60 mm. **Subject:** Architectural Monuments - Ostankino estate **Rev:** Estate building **Edge:** Reeded

| Date | Mintage | VF20 | XF40 | MS60 | MS63 | MS65 |
|---|---|---|---|---|---|---|
| 2013 ММД | 1,500 | PF65 300 | | | | |

**Y# 1457 25 ROUBLES**
169.00 g., 0.925 Silver 5.026 oz. ASW, 60 mm. **Subject:** Architectural Masterpieces - Architect Rossi-Street in St. Petersburg **Rev:** Rossi at left, street view at right **Edge:** Reeded

| Date | Mintage | VF20 | XF40 | MS60 | MS63 | MS65 |
|---|---|---|---|---|---|---|
| 2013 СПМД | 1,500 | PF65 300 | | | | |

**Y# 1460 25 ROUBLES**
169.00 g., 0.925 Silver 5.026 oz. ASW, 60 mm. **Subject:** Architectural Monuments - Saint Assumption Monastery, Staritsa **Rev:** Cathedral view **Edge:** Reeded

| Date | Mintage | VF20 | XF40 | MS60 | MS63 | MS65 |
|---|---|---|---|---|---|---|
| 2013 СПМД | 1,500 | PF65 300 | | | | |

**Y# 1464 25 ROUBLES**
169.00 g., 0.925 Silver 5.026 oz. ASW, 60 mm. **Subject:** Architectural Monuments - Saint Joseph Volotsky Monastery, Teryaevo **Rev:** View of walled monastery

| Date | Mintage | VF20 | XF40 | MS60 | MS63 | MS65 |
|---|---|---|---|---|---|---|
| 2013 ММД | 1,500 | PF65 300 | | | | |

**Y# 1472 25 ROUBLES**
10.00 g., Copper-Nickel, 27 mm. **Subject:** 2014 Winter Paralympics, Sochi **Rev:** Two mascots

| Date | Mintage | VF20 | XF40 | MS60 | MS63 | MS65 |
|---|---|---|---|---|---|---|
| 2014 | — | — | — | — | 25.00 | 30.00 |
| 2014 | 10,000,000 | — | — | — | 8.00 | 10.00 |

**Y# 1472a 25 ROUBLES**
10.00 g., Copper-Nickel, 27 mm. **Subject:** 2014 Winter Paralympics - Sochi **Rev:** Two mascots in color

| Date | Mintage | VF20 | XF40 | MS60 | MS63 | MS65 |
|---|---|---|---|---|---|---|
| 2013 | — | — | — | — | 40.00 | 45.00 |

**Y# 1501 25 ROUBLES**
10.00 g., Copper-Nickel, 27 mm. **Subject:** 2014 Winter Olympics, Sochi **Rev:** Map of Russia and route of torch relay

| Date | Mintage | VF20 | XF40 | MS60 | MS63 | MS65 |
|---|---|---|---|---|---|---|
| 2014 | 19,750,000 | — | — | — | 8.00 | 10.00 |

**KM# 1501a 25 ROUBLES**
10.00 g., Copper-Nickel, 27 mm. **Subject:** 2014 Winter Olympics, Sochi **Rev:** Map of Russia and route of torch relay, Torch and legend in color

| Date | Mintage | VF20 | XF40 | MS60 | MS63 | MS65 |
|---|---|---|---|---|---|---|
| 2014 | — | — | — | — | 40.00 | 45.00 |

**Y# 1517 25 ROUBLES**
169.00 g., 0.925 Silver 5.026 oz. ASW, 60 mm. **Subject:** Baikal-Amur Railway Main Line, 40th Anniversary of construction **Rev:** Crew laying track, route map and logo below

| Date | Mintage | F12 | VF20 | XF40 | MS60 | MS63 |
|---|---|---|---|---|---|---|
| 2014 | 1,000 | PF65 250 | | | | |

**Y# 1522.1 25 ROUBLES**
169.00 g., 0.925 Silver 5.026 oz. ASW, 60 mm. **Subject:** Galileo Galilei, 450th Anniversary of Birth **Rev:** Galileo with globe, telescope and starry sky

| Date | Mintage | F12 | VF20 | XF40 | MS60 | MS63 |
|---|---|---|---|---|---|---|
| 2014 | 850 | PF65 250 | | | | |

**Y# 1522.2 25 ROUBLES**
169.00 g., 0.925 Silver 5.026 oz. ASW, 60 mm. **Subject:** Galileo Galilei, 450th Anniversary of Birth **Rev:** Galileo with telescope, globe and starry sky in color

| Date | Mintage | F12 | VF20 | XF40 | MS60 | MS63 |
|---|---|---|---|---|---|---|
| 2014 | 150 | PF65 475 | | | | |

**Y# 1526 25 ROUBLES**
169.00 g., 0.925 Silver 5.026 oz. ASW, 60 mm. **Subject:** Mikhail Yurevich Lermontov, 200th Anniversary of Birth **Rev:** Bust at lower right, manuscript page and characters from "Masquerade

| Date | Mintage | F12 | VF20 | XF40 | MS60 | MS63 |
|---|---|---|---|---|---|---|
| 2014 | 1,000 | PF65 400 | | | | |

**Y# 1536 25 ROUBLES**
169.00 g., 0.925 Silver 5.026 oz. ASW, 60 mm. **Rev:** M.F. Kazakov bust at top center, Senate Palace of the Moscow Kremlin

| Date | Mintage | F12 | VF20 | XF40 | MS60 | MS63 |
|---|---|---|---|---|---|---|
| 2014 | 1,500 | PF65 350 | | | | |

**Y# 1537 25 ROUBLES**
169.00 g., 0.925 Silver 5.026 oz. ASW, 60 mm. **Rev:** August Montferrand at left, St. Isaac Cathedral in St. Petersburg at right

| Date | Mintage | F12 | VF20 | XF40 | MS60 | MS63 |
|---|---|---|---|---|---|---|
| 2014 | 1,500 | PF65 350 | | | | |

**Y# 1542 25 ROUBLES**
169.00 g., 0.925 Silver 5.026 oz. ASW, 60 mm. **Rev:** Golutvin Monastery, Kolomna, Moscow Region

| Date | Mintage | F12 | VF20 | XF40 | MS60 | MS63 |
|---|---|---|---|---|---|---|
| 2014 | 1,500 | PF65 350 | | | | |

**Y# 1543 25 ROUBLES**
169.00 g., 0.925 Silver 5.026 oz. ASW, 60 mm. **Rev:** Spaso-Eleasarovsky Monastery, Pskov Region

| Date | Mintage | F12 | VF20 | XF40 | MS60 | MS63 |
|---|---|---|---|---|---|---|
| 2014 | 1,500 | PF65 350 | | | | |

**Y# 1544 25 ROUBLES**
169.00 g., 0.925 Silver 5.026 oz. ASW, 60 mm. **Rev:** Historical Museum, Moscow

| Date | Mintage | F12 | VF20 | XF40 | MS60 | MS63 |
|---|---|---|---|---|---|---|
| 2014 | 1,500 | PF65 350 | | | | |

**Y# 679 50 ROUBLES**
8.75 g., 0.999 Gold 0.281 oz. AGW, 22.6 mm. **Subject:** Bolshoi Theater **Obv:** Double-headed eagle within beaded circle **Rev:** Dueling figures **Edge:** Reeded

| Date | Mintage | VF20 | XF40 | MS60 | MS63 | MS65 |
|---|---|---|---|---|---|---|
| 2001 | 2,000 | PF65 550 | | | | |

**Y# 684 50 ROUBLES**
8.75 g., 0.900 Gold 0.2532 oz. AGW, 22.6 mm. **Subject:** Siberian Exploration **Obv:** Double-headed eagle within beaded circle **Rev:** Head with hat 1/4 right and boat **Edge:** Reeded

| Date | Mintage | VF20 | XF40 | MS60 | MS63 | MS65 |
|---|---|---|---|---|---|---|
| 2001 | 1,500 | PF65 600 | | | | |

**Y# 757 50 ROUBLES**
8.64 g., 0.900 Gold 0.2501 oz. AGW, 22.6 mm. **Subject:** Olympics **Obv:** Double-headed eagle within beaded circle **Rev:** Figure skater and flying eagle **Edge:** Reeded

| Date | Mintage | VF20 | XF40 | MS60 | MS63 | MS65 |
|---|---|---|---|---|---|---|
| 2002 | 3,000 | PF65 575 | | | | |

**Y# 782 50 ROUBLES**
7.89 g., 0.999 Gold 0.2534 oz. AGW, 22.6 mm. **Subject:** Works of Dionissy **Obv:** Double-headed eagle within beaded circle **Rev:** Half-length figure holding child flanked by double headed eagle and church **Edge:** Reeded

| Date | Mintage | VF20 | XF40 | MS60 | MS63 | MS65 |
|---|---|---|---|---|---|---|
| 2002 (m) | 1,500 | PF65 600 | | | | |

**Y# 786 50 ROUBLES**
8.75 g., 0.900 Gold 0.2532 oz. AGW, 22.6 mm. **Subject:** Admiral Nakhimov **Obv:** Double-headed eagle within beaded circle **Rev:** Bust facing within circle above flags and anchor **Edge:** Reeded

| Date | Mintage | VF20 | XF40 | MS60 | MS63 | MS65 |
|---|---|---|---|---|---|---|
| 2002 (sp) | 1,500 | PF65 600 | | | | |

**Y# 788 50 ROUBLES**
8.75 g., 0.900 Gold 0.2532 oz. AGW, 22.6 mm. **Subject:** World Cup Soccer **Obv:** Double-headed eagle within beaded circle **Rev:** Stylized player kicking soccer ball **Edge:** Reeded

| Date | Mintage | VF20 | XF40 | MS60 | MS63 | MS65 |
|---|---|---|---|---|---|---|
| 2002 (m) | 3,000 | PF65 575 | | | | |

**Y# 822 50 ROUBLES**
7.89 g., 0.999 Gold 0.2534 oz. AGW, 22.6 mm. **Subject:** Zodiac Signs **Obv:** Double-headed eagle within beaded circle **Rev:** Virgo **Edge:** Reeded

| Date | Mintage | VF20 | XF40 | MS60 | MS63 | MS65 |
|---|---|---|---|---|---|---|
| 2003 (sp) | 30,000 | — | — | — | 475 | 500 |

**Y# 823 50 ROUBLES**
7.89 g., 0.999 Gold 0.2534 oz. AGW, 22.6 mm. **Subject:** Zodiac signs **Obv:** Double-headed eagle within beaded circle **Rev:** Libra **Edge:** Reeded

| Date | Mintage | VF20 | XF40 | MS60 | MS63 | MS65 |
|---|---|---|---|---|---|---|
| 2003 (m) | 30,000 | — | — | — | 475 | 500 |

**Y# 868 50 ROUBLES**
8.64 g., 0.900 Gold 0.250 oz. AGW, 23 mm. **Rev:** Peter I monetary reform

| Date | Mintage | VF20 | XF40 | MS60 | MS63 | MS65 |
|---|---|---|---|---|---|---|
| 2003 (m) | 1,500 | **PF65** 600 | | | | |

**Y# 869 50 ROUBLES**
8.64 g., 0.900 Gold 0.250 oz. AGW, 23 mm. **Rev:** Ski race

| Date | Mintage | VF20 | XF40 | MS60 | MS63 | MS65 |
|---|---|---|---|---|---|---|
| 2003 (m) | 1,500 | **PF65** 600 | | | | |

**Y# 1007 50 ROUBLES**
8.64 g., 0.925 Gold 0.2569 oz. AGW, 22.6 mm. **Subject:** Leo

| Date | Mintage | VF20 | XF40 | MS60 | MS63 | MS65 |
|---|---|---|---|---|---|---|
| 2003 | — | **PF65** 475 | | | | |

**Y# 1009 50 ROUBLES**
7.79 g., 0.999 Gold 0.2502 oz. AGW, 22.6 mm. **Subject:** Scorpion

| Date | Mintage | VF20 | XF40 | MS60 | MS63 | MS65 |
|---|---|---|---|---|---|---|
| 2003 | — | **PF65** 475 | | | | |

**Y# 1010 50 ROUBLES**
7.78 g., 0.999 Gold 0.2499 oz. AGW, 22.6 mm. **Subject:** Sagatarius

| Date | Mintage | VF20 | XF40 | MS60 | MS63 | MS65 |
|---|---|---|---|---|---|---|
| 2003 | — | **PF65** 475 | | | | |

**Y# 1011 50 ROUBLES**
7.78 g., 0.999 Gold 0.2499 oz. AGW, 22.6 mm. **Subject:** Capricorn

| Date | Mintage | VF20 | XF40 | MS60 | MS63 | MS65 |
|---|---|---|---|---|---|---|
| 2003 | — | **PF65** 475 | | | | |

**Y# 870 50 ROUBLES**
8.64 g., 0.900 Gold 0.250 oz. AGW, 23 mm. **Rev:** Soccer player

| Date | Mintage | VF20 | XF40 | MS60 | MS63 | MS65 |
|---|---|---|---|---|---|---|
| 2004 (sp) | 1,000 | **PF65** 650 | | | | |

**Y# 871 50 ROUBLES**
8.64 g., 0.900 Gold 0.250 oz. AGW, 23 mm. **Rev:** Olympic athletes

| Date | Mintage | VF20 | XF40 | MS60 | MS63 | MS65 |
|---|---|---|---|---|---|---|
| 2004 (m) | 2,000 | **PF65** 550 | | | | |

**Y# 872 50 ROUBLES**
8.64 g., 0.900 Gold 0.250 oz. AGW, 23 mm. **Subject:** Theophanes the Greek **Rev:** Virgin of the Son Icon

| Date | Mintage | VF20 | XF40 | MS60 | MS63 | MS65 |
|---|---|---|---|---|---|---|
| 2004 (m) | 1,500 | **PF65** 575 | | | | |

**Y# 1025 50 ROUBLES**
7.78 g., 0.999 Gold 0.2499 oz. AGW, 22.6 mm. **Subject:** Reindeer

| Date | Mintage | VF20 | XF40 | MS60 | MS63 | MS65 |
|---|---|---|---|---|---|---|
| 2004 | — | **PF65** 475 | | | | |

**Y# 1030 50 ROUBLES**
7.78 g., 0.999 Gold 0.2499 oz. AGW, 22.6 mm. **Subject:** Aquarius

| Date | Mintage | VF20 | XF40 | MS60 | MS63 | MS65 |
|---|---|---|---|---|---|---|
| 2004 | — | **PF65** 475 | | | | |

**Y# 1031 50 ROUBLES**
7.78 g., 0.999 Gold 0.2499 oz. AGW, 22.6 mm. **Rev:** Pisces

| Date | Mintage | VF20 | XF40 | MS60 | MS63 | MS65 |
|---|---|---|---|---|---|---|
| 2004 | — | **PF65** 475 | | | | |

**Y# 1032 50 ROUBLES**
7.78 g., 0.999 Gold 0.2499 oz. AGW, 22.6 mm. **Subject:** Aries

| Date | Mintage | VF20 | XF40 | MS60 | MS63 | MS65 |
|---|---|---|---|---|---|---|
| 2004 | — | **PF65** 475 | | | | |

**Y# 1033 50 ROUBLES**
7.78 g., 0.999 Gold 0.2499 oz. AGW, 22.6 mm. **Subject:** Taurus

| Date | Mintage | VF20 | XF40 | MS60 | MS63 | MS65 |
|---|---|---|---|---|---|---|
| 2004 | — | **PF65** 475 | | | | |

**Y# 1034 50 ROUBLES**
7.78 g., 0.999 Gold 0.2499 oz. AGW, 22.6 mm. **Subject:** Gemni

| Date | Mintage | VF20 | XF40 | MS60 | MS63 | MS65 |
|---|---|---|---|---|---|---|
| 2004 | — | **PF65** 475 | | | | |

**Y# 1035 50 ROUBLES**
7.78 g., 0.999 Gold 0.2499 oz. AGW, 22.6 mm. **Subject:** Cancer

| Date | Mintage | VF20 | XF40 | MS60 | MS63 | MS65 |
|---|---|---|---|---|---|---|
| 2004 | — | **PF65** 475 | | | | |

**Y# 894 50 ROUBLES**
7.89 g., 0.999 Gold 0.2534 oz. AGW, 22.6 mm. **Subject:** 60th Anniversary - Victory Over Germany **Obv:** Double-headed eagle **Rev:** 60th Anniversary - Victory Over Germany medal **Edge:** Reeded

| Date | Mintage | VF20 | XF40 | MS60 | MS63 | MS65 |
|---|---|---|---|---|---|---|
| 2005 | 7,000 | **PF65** 500 | | | | |

**Y# 907 50 ROUBLES**
7.89 g., 0.999 Gold 0.2534 oz. AGW, 22.6 mm. **Subject:** Helsinki Games **Obv:** Double-headed eagle **Rev:** Stylized track and field athletes **Edge:** Reeded

| Date | Mintage | VF20 | XF40 | MS60 | MS63 | MS65 |
|---|---|---|---|---|---|---|
| 2005 | 1,500 | **PF65** 575 | | | | |

**Y# 911 50 ROUBLES**
7.89 g., 0.999 Gold 0.2534 oz. AGW, 22.6 mm. **Obv:** Double-headed eagle **Rev:** Kazan University Building **Edge:** Reeded

| Date | Mintage | VF20 | XF40 | MS60 | MS63 | MS65 |
|---|---|---|---|---|---|---|
| 2005 | 1,500 | PF65 475 | | | | |

**Y# 1049 50 ROUBLES**
7.78 g., 0.999 Gold 0.2499 oz. AGW, 22.6 mm. **Rev:** St. George the Victorious

| Date | Mintage | VF20 | XF40 | MS60 | MS63 | MS65 |
|---|---|---|---|---|---|---|
| 2006 | 150,000 | — | — | — | 475 | 500 |
| 2007 | 500,000 | — | — | — | 475 | 500 |
| 2008 | 630,000 | — | — | — | 475 | 500 |
| 2009 | 1,500,000 | — | — | — | 475 | 500 |
| 2010 | 640,000 | — | — | — | 475 | 500 |
| 2012 | 500,000 | — | — | — | 475 | 500 |
| 2012 | 10,000 | PF65 500 | | | | |

**Y# 1063 50 ROUBLES**
7.78 g., 0.999 Gold 0.2499 oz. AGW, 22.6 mm. **Subject:** Moscow's Kremlin and Red Square

| Date | Mintage | VF20 | XF40 | MS60 | MS63 | MS65 |
|---|---|---|---|---|---|---|
| 2006 | — | PF65 600 | | | | |

**Y# 1067 50 ROUBLES**
7.78 g., 0.999 Gold 0.2499 oz. AGW, 22.6 mm. **Subject:** XX Winter Olympics, Torino

| Date | Mintage | VF20 | XF40 | MS60 | MS63 | MS65 |
|---|---|---|---|---|---|---|
| 2006 | — | PF65 550 | | | | |

**Y# 1068 50 ROUBLES**
7.78 g., 0.999 Gold 0.2499 oz. AGW, 22.6 mm. **Subject:** FIFA World Cup, Germany

| Date | Mintage | VF20 | XF40 | MS60 | MS63 | MS65 |
|---|---|---|---|---|---|---|
| 2006 | — | PF65 550 | | | | |

**Y# 1090 50 ROUBLES**
7.78 g., 0.999 Gold 0.2499 oz. AGW, 22.6 mm. **Subject:** Andrew Rublyov

| Date | Mintage | VF20 | XF40 | MS60 | MS63 | MS65 |
|---|---|---|---|---|---|---|
| 2007 | — | PF65 550 | | | | |

**Y# 1094 50 ROUBLES**
7.78 g., 0.925 Gold 0.2314 oz. AGW, 22.6 mm. **Subject:** Bashkiria, 450th Anniversary of of annexation by Russia

| Date | Mintage | VF20 | XF40 | MS60 | MS63 | MS65 |
|---|---|---|---|---|---|---|
| 2007 | — | PF65 550 | | | | |

**Y# 1097 50 ROUBLES**
7.78 g., 0.999 Gold 0.2499 oz. AGW, 22.6 mm. **Subject:** Khakassia, 300th Anniversary of of annexation by Russia

| Date | Mintage | VF20 | XF40 | MS60 | MS63 | MS65 |
|---|---|---|---|---|---|---|
| 2007 | — | PF65 550 | | | | |

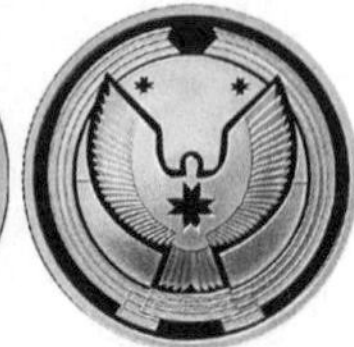

**Y# 1121 50 ROUBLES**
7.78 g., 0.999 Gold 0.2499 oz. AGW, 22.6 mm. **Subject:** Udmurtiya, 450th Anniversary of annexation into Russia

| Date | Mintage | VF20 | XF40 | MS60 | MS63 | MS65 |
|---|---|---|---|---|---|---|
| 2008 | — | PF65 550 | | | | |

**Y# 1141 50 ROUBLES**
7.78 g., 0.999 Gold 0.2499 oz. AGW, 22.6 mm. **Subject:** European Beaver

| Date | Mintage | VF20 | XF40 | MS60 | MS63 | MS65 |
|---|---|---|---|---|---|---|
| 2008 | — | PF65 750 | | | | |

**Y# 1153 50 ROUBLES**
7.78 g., 0.999 Gold 0.2499 oz. AGW, 22.6 mm. **Subject:** 29th Summer Olympics, Bejing

| Date | Mintage | VF20 | XF40 | MS60 | MS63 | MS65 |
|---|---|---|---|---|---|---|
| 2008 | — | PF65 550 | | | | |

**Y# 1168 50 ROUBLES**
7.78 g., 0.999 Gold 0.2499 oz. AGW, 22.6 mm. **Subject:** A. P. Chekhov, 150th Anniversary of Birth

| Date | Mintage | VF20 | XF40 | MS60 | MS63 | MS65 |
|---|---|---|---|---|---|---|
| 2009 | — | PF65 550 | | | | |

**Y# 1172 50 ROUBLES**
7.78 g., 0.999 Gold 0.2499 oz. AGW, 22.6 mm. **Subject:** Kalmyk Peoples, 400th Anniversary of annexation into Russia

| Date | Mintage | VF20 | XF40 | MS60 | MS63 | MS65 |
|---|---|---|---|---|---|---|
| 2009 | — | PF65 550 | | | | |

**Y# 1175 50 ROUBLES**
7.78 g., 0.999 Gold 0.2499 oz. AGW, 22.6 mm. **Subject:** N. V. Gogol, 200th Anniversary of Birth

| Date | Mintage | VF20 | XF40 | MS60 | MS63 | MS65 |
|---|---|---|---|---|---|---|
| 2009 | — | PF65 550 | | | | |

**Y# 1202 50 ROUBLES**
7.78 g., 0.999 Gold 0.2499 oz. AGW, 22.6 mm. **Subject:** Velikly Novgorod

| Date | Mintage | VF20 | XF40 | MS60 | MS63 | MS65 |
|---|---|---|---|---|---|---|
| 2009 | — | PF65 550 | | | | |

**Y# 1230 50 ROUBLES**
7.78 g., 0.999 Gold 0.2499 oz. AGW, 22.6 mm. **Subject:** Bank of Russia, 150th Anniversary

| Date | Mintage | VF20 | XF40 | MS60 | MS63 | MS65 |
|---|---|---|---|---|---|---|
| 2010 | — | PF65 600 | | | | |

**Y# 1235 50 ROUBLES**
7.78 g., 0.999 Gold 0.2499 oz. AGW, 22.6 mm. **Subject:** UNESCO Heritage Site - Yaroslav

| Date | Mintage | VF20 | XF40 | MS60 | MS63 | MS65 |
|---|---|---|---|---|---|---|
| 2010 | — | PF65 550 | | | | |

**Y# 1239 50 ROUBLES**
7.78 g., 0.999 Gold 0.2499 oz. AGW, 22.6 mm. **Subject:** A. P. Chekhov, 200th Anniversary of birth

| Date | Mintage | VF20 | XF40 | MS60 | MS63 | MS65 |
|---|---|---|---|---|---|---|
| 2010 | — | PF65 600 | | | | |

**Y# 1286 50 ROUBLES**
7.78 g., 0.999 Gold 0.2499 oz. AGW, 22.6 mm. **Rev:** Griffin with sword and shield above garland **Edge:** Reeded

| Date | Mintage | VF20 | XF40 | MS60 | MS63 | MS65 |
|---|---|---|---|---|---|---|
| 2011 | 750 | PF65 600 | | | | |

**Y# 1291 50 ROUBLES**
7.78 g., 0.999 Gold 0.2499 oz. AGW, 22.6 mm. **Rev:** Emblem of the Republic of Buryatia

| Date | Mintage | VF20 | XF40 | MS60 | MS63 | MS65 |
|---|---|---|---|---|---|---|
| 2011 | 1,000 | PF65 650 | | | | |

### Y# 1300 50 ROUBLES

7.78 g., 0.999 Gold 0.2499 oz. AGW, 22.6 mm. **Subject:** 2014 Winter Olympics - Sochi **Rev:** Four-man Bobsled **Edge:** Reeded

| Date | Mintage | VF20 | XF40 | MS60 | MS63 | MS65 |
|---|---|---|---|---|---|---|
| 2014 (2011) | 20,000 | **PF65** 500 | | | | |

### Y# 1301 50 ROUBLES

7.78 g., 0.999 Gold 0.2499 oz. AGW, 22.6 mm. **Subject:** 2014 Winter Olympics - Sochi - Curling **Rev:** Skip and sweeper with stones in play

| Date | Mintage | VF20 | XF40 | MS60 | MS63 | MS65 |
|---|---|---|---|---|---|---|
| 2014 (2011) | 20,000 | **PF65** 500 | | | | |

### Y# 1341 50 ROUBLES

7.78 g., 0.999 Gold 0.2499 oz. AGW, 22.6 mm. **Subject:** Millennium of the Unity of the Mordovian people within the Peoples of the Russian State

| Date | Mintage | VF20 | XF40 | MS60 | MS63 | MS65 |
|---|---|---|---|---|---|---|
| 2012 | 100 | **PF65** 750 | | | | |

### Y# 1349 50 ROUBLES

7.78 g., 0.999 Gold 0.2499 oz. AGW, 22.6 mm. **Subject:** Russia's victory in the War of 1812 **Rev:** Bust left

| Date | Mintage | VF20 | XF40 | MS60 | MS63 | MS65 |
|---|---|---|---|---|---|---|
| 2012 | 1,000 | **PF65** 650 | | | | |

### Y# 1365 50 ROUBLES

7.78 g., 0.999 Gold 0.2499 oz. AGW, 22.6 mm. **Subject:** European Judo Championship, Chelyabinsk

| Date | Mintage | VF20 | XF40 | MS60 | MS63 | MS65 |
|---|---|---|---|---|---|---|
| 2012 | 750 | **PF65** 675 | | | | |

### Y# 1369 50 ROUBLES

7.78 g., 0.999 Gold 0.2499 oz. AGW, 22.6 mm. **Subject:** Origin of Russian Statehood, 1150th Anniversary

| Date | Mintage | VF20 | XF40 | MS60 | MS63 | MS65 |
|---|---|---|---|---|---|---|
| 2012 | 1,500 | **PF65** 575 | | | | |

### Y# 1376 50 ROUBLES

7.78 g., 0.999 Gold 0.2499 oz. AGW, 22.6 mm. **Subject:** Court of Arbitration

| Date | Mintage | VF20 | XF40 | MS60 | MS63 | MS65 |
|---|---|---|---|---|---|---|
| 2012 | 750 | **PF65** 675 | | | | |

### Y# 1506 50 ROUBLES

7.95 g., 0.999 Gold 0.2553 oz. AGW, 14x20 mm. **Subject:** 2014 Winter Olympics, Sochi **Rev:** Bear Mascot **Shape:** Vertical rectangle

| Date | Mintage | VF20 | XF40 | MS60 | MS63 | MS65 |
|---|---|---|---|---|---|---|
| 2012 | 300,000 | — | — | — | 300 | 350 |

### Y# 1424 50 ROUBLES

7.89 g., 0.999 Gold 0.2534 oz. AGW, 22.6 mm. **Rev:** Logo and track of Kazan Universiade, city skyline **Edge:** Reeded

| Date | Mintage | VF20 | XF40 | MS60 | MS63 | MS65 |
|---|---|---|---|---|---|---|
| 2013 СПМД | 1,500 | **PF65** 500 | | | | |

### Y# 1436 50 ROUBLES

7.89 g., 0.925 Gold 0.2346 oz. AGW, 22.6 mm. **Subject:** A.S. Shein **Rev:** Bust facing

| Date | Mintage | VF20 | XF40 | MS60 | MS63 | MS65 |
|---|---|---|---|---|---|---|
| 2013 ММД | 1,500 | **PF65** 500 | | | | |

### Y# 1448 50 ROUBLES

7.89 g., 0.999 Gold 0.2534 oz. AGW, 22.6 mm. **Subject:** City of Smolensk, 1150th Anniversary of founding **Rev:** City shield

| Date | Mintage | VF20 | XF40 | MS60 | MS63 | MS65 |
|---|---|---|---|---|---|---|
| 2013 ММД | 1,500 | **PF65** 500 | | | | |

### Y# 1503 50 ROUBLES

7.95 g., 0.999 Gold 0.2553 oz. AGW, 14x20 mm. **Subject:** 2014 Winter Paralympics, Sochi **Rev:** Paralympic mascot - Hare **Shape:** Vertical rectangle

| Date | Mintage | VF20 | XF40 | MS60 | MS63 | MS65 |
|---|---|---|---|---|---|---|
| 2013 | 300,000 | — | — | — | 450 | 500 |

### Y# 1479 50 ROUBLES

7.89 g., 0.999 Gold 0.2534 oz. AGW, 22.6 mm. **Subject:** 2014 Winter Olympics, Sochi **Rev:** Skating

| Date | Mintage | VF20 | XF40 | MS60 | MS63 | MS65 |
|---|---|---|---|---|---|---|
| 2014 | 20,000 | **PF65** 400 | | | | |

### Y# 1480 50 ROUBLES

7.89 g., 0.999 Gold 0.2534 oz. AGW, 22.6 mm. **Subject:** 2014 Winter Olympics, Sochi **Rev:** Cross Country Skiing

| Date | Mintage | VF20 | XF40 | MS60 | MS63 | MS65 |
|---|---|---|---|---|---|---|
| 2014 | 20,000 | **PF65** 450 | | | | |

### Y# 1487 50 ROUBLES

7.89 g., 0.999 Gold 0.2534 oz. AGW, 22.6 mm. **Subject:** 2014 Winter Olympics, Sochi **Rev:** Historic view of Hockey player and goalie

| Date | Mintage | VF20 | XF40 | MS60 | MS63 | MS65 |
|---|---|---|---|---|---|---|
| 2014 | 40,000 | **PF65** 450 | | | | |

### Y# 1488 50 ROUBLES

7.89 g., 0.999 Gold 0.2534 oz. AGW **Subject:** 2014 Winter Olympics, Sochi **Rev:** Historic view of Ski jumper

| Date | Mintage | VF20 | XF40 | MS60 | MS63 | MS65 |
|---|---|---|---|---|---|---|
| 2014 | 20,000 | **PF65** 450 | | | | |

### Y# 1495 50 ROUBLES

7.89 g., 0.999 Gold 0.2534 oz. AGW, 22.6 mm. **Subject:** 2014 Winter Olympics, Sochi **Rev:** Historic view of Biathlon participant

| Date | Mintage | VF20 | XF40 | MS60 | MS63 | MS65 |
|---|---|---|---|---|---|---|
| 2014 | 20,000 | **PF65** 450 | | | | |

### Y# 1496 50 ROUBLES

7.89 g., 0.999 Gold 0.2534 oz. AGW, 22.6 mm. **Subject:** 2014 Winter Olympics, Sochi **Rev:** Historic view of male figure skater

| Date | Mintage | VF20 | XF40 | MS60 | MS63 | MS65 |
|---|---|---|---|---|---|---|
| 2014 | 20,000 | **PF65** 450 | | | | |

**Y# 1515 50 ROUBLES**
337.30 g., 0.925 Silver 10.0311 oz. ASW, 75 mm. **Obv:** Names of the 2012 Olympics winners **Rev:** Laurel branch, athletes, QR-code below

| Date | Mintage | F12 | VF20 | XF40 | MS60 | MS63 |
|---|---|---|---|---|---|---|
| 2014 | 500 | PF65 650 | | | | |

**Y# 1518 50 ROUBLES**
7.78 g., 0.999 Gold 0.2499 oz. AGW, 22.6 mm. **Subject:** Baikal-Amur Railway main line, 40th Anniversary of construction **Rev:** Bridge at left, male and female workers in profile at right

| Date | Mintage | F12 | VF20 | XF40 | MS60 | MS63 |
|---|---|---|---|---|---|---|
| 2014 | 750 | PF65 450 | | | | |

**Y# 1521 50 ROUBLES**
7.89 g., 0.999 Gold 0.2534 oz. AGW, 22.6 mm. **Subject:** World Judo Championship, Chelyabinsk **Rev:** Two Judo players

| Date | Mintage | F12 | VF20 | XF40 | MS60 | MS63 |
|---|---|---|---|---|---|---|
| 2014 | 750 | PF65 450 | | | | |

**Y# 1527 50 ROUBLES**
Gold, 22.6 mm. **Subject:** Mikhail Yurevich Lermontov, 200th Anniversary of Birth **Rev:** Portrait at right, small sailing boat at left, signature above

| Date | Mintage | F12 | VF20 | XF40 | MS60 | MS63 |
|---|---|---|---|---|---|---|
| 2014 | 1,500 | PF65 450 | | | | |

**Y# 1529 50 ROUBLES**
7.89 g., 0.999 Gold 0.2534 oz. AGW, 22.6 mm. **Subject:** Rev. Sergius Radonezhsky, 700th Anniversary of Birth **Rev:** Trinity Cathedral

| Date | Mintage | F12 | VF20 | XF40 | MS60 | MS63 |
|---|---|---|---|---|---|---|
| 2014 | 1,500 | PF65 450 | | | | |

**Y# 1533 50 ROUBLES**
7.89 g., 0.999 Gold 0.2534 oz. AGW, 22.6 mm. **Subject:** Unity of Russia and Tuva, founding of Kyzyl city **Rev:** Horseman and sun, arms of the Republic of Tyva

| Date | Mintage | F12 | VF20 | XF40 | MS60 | MS63 |
|---|---|---|---|---|---|---|
| 2014 | 1,000 | PF65 450 | | | | |

**Y# 681 100 ROUBLES**
1111.10 g., 0.900 Silver 32.1504 oz. ASW, 100 mm. **Subject:** 40th Anniversary of Manned Space Flight - Yuri Gagarin **Obv:** Double-headed eagle **Rev:** Astronaut and rocket in space **Edge:** Reeded

| Date | Mintage | VF20 | XF40 | MS60 | MS63 | MS65 |
|---|---|---|---|---|---|---|
| 2001 | 750 | PF65 2,000 | | | | |

**Y# 685 100 ROUBLES**
17.45 g., 0.900 Gold 0.5049 oz. AGW, 30 mm. **Subject:** Siberian Exploration **Obv:** Double-headed eagle within beaded circle **Rev:** Head and silhouette left, sailboat and other designs **Edge:** Reeded

| Date | Mintage | VF20 | XF40 | MS60 | MS63 | MS65 |
|---|---|---|---|---|---|---|
| 2001 | 1,000 | PF65 1,150 | | | | |

**Y# 688 100 ROUBLES**
15.72 g., 0.999 Gold 0.5049 oz. AGW, 30 mm. **Subject:** Bolshoi Theater 225 Years **Obv:** Double-headed eagle within beaded circle **Rev:** Three dancers with swords **Edge:** Reeded

| Date | Mintage | VF20 | XF40 | MS60 | MS63 | MS65 |
|---|---|---|---|---|---|---|
| 2001 | 1,500 | PF65 1,100 | | | | |

**Y# 689 100 ROUBLES**
1111.10 g., 0.900 Silver 32.1504 oz. ASW, 100 mm. **Subject:** Bolshoi Theater 225 Years **Obv:** Double-headed eagle **Rev:** Casino gambling scene **Edge:** Reeded

| Date | Mintage | VF20 | XF40 | MS60 | MS63 | MS65 |
|---|---|---|---|---|---|---|
| 2001 | 500 | PF65 2,150 | | | | |

**Y# 795 100 ROUBLES**
1111.12 g., 0.900 Silver 32.151 oz. ASW, 100 mm. **Subject:** The Bark Sedov **Obv:** Double-headed eagle **Rev:** Ship flanked by compass and cameo **Edge:** Reeded **Note:** Illustration reduced.

| Date | Mintage | VF20 | XF40 | MS60 | MS63 | MS65 |
|---|---|---|---|---|---|---|
| 2001 (m) | 500 | PF65 2,200 | | | | |

**Y# 783 100 ROUBLES**
1111.12 g., 0.900 Silver 32.151 oz. ASW, 100 mm. **Subject:** Works of Dionissy **Obv:** Double-headed eagle **Rev:** St. Ferapont Monastery in the center of a fresco covered cross **Edge:** Reeded

| Date | Mintage | VF20 | XF40 | MS60 | MS63 | MS65 |
|---|---|---|---|---|---|---|
| 2002 (sp) Prooflike | 500 | — | — | — | — | 2,750 |

**Y# 789 100 ROUBLES**
1111.12 g., 0.900 Silver 32.151 oz. ASW, 100 mm. **Subject:** World Cup Soccer **Obv:** Double-headed eagle **Rev:** Soccer ball design with map and players **Edge:** Reeded

| Date | Mintage | VF20 | XF40 | MS60 | MS63 | MS65 |
|---|---|---|---|---|---|---|
| 2002 (sp) | 500 | PF65 2,200 | | | | |

**Y# 791 100 ROUBLES**
1111.12 g., 0.900 Silver 32.151 oz. ASW, 100 mm. **Subject:** Hermitage **Obv:** Double-headed eagle **Rev:** Statues and arches **Edge:** Reeded

| Date | Mintage | VF20 | XF40 | MS60 | MS63 | MS65 |
|---|---|---|---|---|---|---|
| 2002 (sp) | 1,000 | PF65 1,800 | | | | |

**Y# 792 100 ROUBLES**
17.45 g., 0.900 Gold 0.5049 oz. AGW, 30 mm. **Subject:** Hermitage **Obv:** Double-headed eagle within beaded circle **Rev:** Ancient battle scene sculpted on comb **Edge:** Reeded

| Date | Mintage | VF20 | XF40 | MS60 | MS63 | MS65 |
|---|---|---|---|---|---|---|
| 2002 (sp) | 1,000 | PF65 1,250 | | | | |

**Y# 873 100 ROUBLES**
1111.12 g., 0.900 Silver 32.151 oz. ASW, 100 mm. **Rev:** St. Petersburg

| Date | Mintage | VF20 | XF40 | MS60 | MS63 | MS65 |
|---|---|---|---|---|---|---|
| 2003 (m) | 1,000 | PF65 2,000 | | | | |

**Y# 874 100 ROUBLES**
17.45 g., 0.900 Gold 0.5049 oz. AGW, 30 mm. **Rev:** Petrozavodsk

| Date | Mintage | VF20 | XF40 | MS60 | MS63 | MS65 |
|---|---|---|---|---|---|---|
| 2003 (m) | 1,000 | PF65 1,250 | | | | |

**Y# 875 100 ROUBLES**
17.45 g., 0.900 Gold 0.5049 oz. AGW, 30 mm. **Rev:** Kamchatka

| Date | Mintage | VF20 | XF40 | MS60 | MS63 | MS65 |
|---|---|---|---|---|---|---|
| 2003 (sp) | 1,500 | PF65 1,100 | | | | |

**Y# 831 100 ROUBLES**
1111.12 g., 0.900 Silver 32.151 oz. ASW, 100 mm. **Obv:** Double-headed eagle **Rev:** Panel of icons painted by Theophanes the Greek **Edge:** Reeded

| Date | Mintage | VF20 | XF40 | MS60 | MS63 | MS65 |
|---|---|---|---|---|---|---|
| 2004 (sp) | 500 | PF65 2,300 | | | | |

**Y# 832 100 ROUBLES**
17.28 g., 0.900 Gold 0.500 oz. AGW, 30 mm. **Subject:** 2nd Kamchatka Expedition **Obv:** Double-headed eagle **Rev:** Shaman and two seated men **Edge:** Reeded

| Date | Mintage | VF20 | XF40 | MS60 | MS63 | MS65 |
|---|---|---|---|---|---|---|
| 2004 (sp) | 1,500 | PF65 1,100 | | | | |

**Y# 1024 100 ROUBLES**
1111.12 g., 0.900 Silver 32.151 oz. ASW, 100 mm. **Subject:** Reindeer

| Date | Mintage | VF20 | XF40 | MS60 | MS63 | MS65 |
|---|---|---|---|---|---|---|
| 2004 | — | PF65 1,850 | | | | |

**Y# 1026 100 ROUBLES**
17.55 g., 0.900 Gold 0.5078 oz. AGW, 30 mm. **Subject:** Reindeer

| Date | Mintage | VF20 | XF40 | MS60 | MS63 | MS65 |
|---|---|---|---|---|---|---|
| 2004 | — | PF65 2,000 | | | | |

**Y# 1036 100 ROUBLES**
1111.72 g., 0.900 Silver 32.1683 oz. ASW, 100 mm. **Subject:** Rostov

| Date | Mintage | VF20 | XF40 | MS60 | MS63 | MS65 |
|---|---|---|---|---|---|---|
| 2004 | — | PF65 1,850 | | | | |

**Y# 895 100 ROUBLES**
1083.74 g., 0.925 Silver 32.2298 oz. ASW, 100 mm. **Subject:** 60th Anniversary Victory Over Germany **Obv:** Double-headed eagle **Rev:** Decorated locomotive returning soldiers circa 1945 **Edge:** Reeded

| Date | Mintage | VF20 | XF40 | MS60 | MS63 | MS65 |
|---|---|---|---|---|---|---|
| 2005 | 2,000 | **PF65** 1,850 | | | | |

**Y# 912 100 ROUBLES**
1083.74 g., 0.925 Silver 32.2298 oz. ASW, 100 mm. **Obv:** Double-headed eagle **Rev:** Kazan city view with mausoleums **Edge:** Reeded

| Date | Mintage | VF20 | XF40 | MS60 | MS63 | MS65 |
|---|---|---|---|---|---|---|
| 2005 | 500 | **PF65** 2,000 | | | | |

**Y# 925 100 ROUBLES**
1083.74 g., 0.925 Silver 32.2298 oz. ASW, 100 mm. **Subject:** 625th Anniversary - Battle of Kulikovo **Obv:** Double-headed eagle **Rev:** Battle of Kulikovo beginning scene **Edge:** Reeded

| Date | Mintage | VF20 | XF40 | MS60 | MS63 | MS65 |
|---|---|---|---|---|---|---|
| 2005 | 500 | **PF65** 2,000 | | | | |

**Y# 1044 100 ROUBLES**
1083.74 g., 0.925 Silver 32.2298 oz. ASW, 100 mm. **Subject:** Frigate Myr

| Date | Mintage | VF20 | XF40 | MS60 | MS63 | MS65 |
|---|---|---|---|---|---|---|
| 2006 | — | **PF65** 1,750 | | | | |

**Y# 1061 100 ROUBLES**
1083.74 g., 0.925 Silver 32.2298 oz. ASW, 100 mm. **Subject:** Moscow's Kremlin and Red Square

| Date | Mintage | VF20 | XF40 | MS60 | MS63 | MS65 |
|---|---|---|---|---|---|---|
| 2006 | — | **PF65** 1,750 | | | | |

**Y# 1077 100 ROUBLES**
1083.74 g., 0.925 Silver 32.2298 oz. ASW, 100 mm. **Subject:** Bogolyubovo Township

| Date | Mintage | VF20 | XF40 | MS60 | MS63 | MS65 |
|---|---|---|---|---|---|---|
| 2006 | — | **PF65** 1,850 | | | | |

**Y# 1078 100 ROUBLES**
1083.74 g., 0.925 Silver 32.2298 oz. ASW, 100 mm. **Subject:** Yuryev Polsky

| Date | Mintage | VF20 | XF40 | MS60 | MS63 | MS65 |
|---|---|---|---|---|---|---|
| 2006 | — | **PF65** 1,850 | | | | |

**Y# 1081 100 ROUBLES**
1083.74 g., 0.925 Silver 32.2298 oz. ASW, 100 mm. **Subject:** International Artic Year

| Date | Mintage | VF20 | XF40 | MS60 | MS63 | MS65 |
|---|---|---|---|---|---|---|
| 2007 | — | **PF65** 1,850 | | | | |

**Y# 1085 100 ROUBLES**
1083.74 g., 0.925 Silver 32.2298 oz. ASW, 100 mm. **Subject:** Russian railways, 175th Anniversary

| Date | Mintage | VF20 | XF40 | MS60 | MS63 | MS65 |
|---|---|---|---|---|---|---|
| 2007 | — | **PF65** 1,850 | | | | |

**Y# 1089 100 ROUBLES**
1083.74 g., 0.925 Silver 32.2298 oz. ASW, 100 mm. **Subject:** Andrew Rublyov

| Date | Mintage | VF20 | XF40 | MS60 | MS63 | MS65 |
|---|---|---|---|---|---|---|
| 2007 | — | **PF65** 1,850 | | | | |

**Y# 1093 100 ROUBLES**
1083.74 g., 0.925 Silver 32.2298 oz. ASW, 100 mm. **Subject:** Bashkiria, 450th Anniversary of Annexation by Russia

| Date | Mintage | VF20 | XF40 | MS60 | MS63 | MS65 |
|---|---|---|---|---|---|---|
| 2007 | — | **PF65** 400 | | | | |

**Y# 1096 100 ROUBLES**
1083.74 g., 0.925 Silver 32.2298 oz. ASW, 100 mm. **Subject:** Khakassia, 300th Anniversary of Annexation by Russia

| Date | Mintage | VF20 | XF40 | MS60 | MS63 | MS65 |
|---|---|---|---|---|---|---|
| 2007 | — | **PF65** 1,850 | | | | |

**Y# 1120 100 ROUBLES**
1083.74 g., 0.925 Silver 32.2298 oz. ASW, 100 mm. **Subject:** Udmurtiya, 450th Anniversary of Annexation into Russia

| Date | Mintage | VF20 | XF40 | MS60 | MS63 | MS65 |
|---|---|---|---|---|---|---|
| 2008 | — | **PF65** 1,850 | | | | |

**Y# 1140 100 ROUBLES**
1083.74 g., 0.925 Silver 32.2298 oz. ASW, 100 mm. **Subject:** European Beaver

| Date | Mintage | VF20 | XF40 | MS60 | MS63 | MS65 |
|---|---|---|---|---|---|---|
| 2008 | — | **PF65** 1,850 | | | | |

**Y# 1142 100 ROUBLES**
17.45 g., 0.900 Gold 0.5049 oz. AGW, 30 mm. **Subject:** European Beaver

| Date | Mintage | VF20 | XF40 | MS60 | MS63 | MS65 |
|---|---|---|---|---|---|---|
| 2008 | — | **PF65** 1,100 | | | | |

**Y# 1143 100 ROUBLES**
1046.00 g., 0.925 Silver 31.1074 oz. ASW, 100 mm. **Subject:** European Beaver

| Date | Mintage | VF20 | XF40 | MS60 | MS63 | MS65 |
|---|---|---|---|---|---|---|
| 2008 | — | **PF65** 1,750 | | | | |

**Y# 1148 100 ROUBLES**
1083.74 g., 0.925 Silver 32.2298 oz. ASW, 100 mm. **Subject:** Kamchatka Volcano

| Date | Mintage | VF20 | XF40 | MS60 | MS63 | MS65 |
|---|---|---|---|---|---|---|
| 2008 | — | **PF65** 1,850 | | | | |

**Y# 1156 100 ROUBLES**
1083.74 g., 0.925 Silver 32.2298 oz. ASW, 100 mm. **Subject:** Pereslaval Zalessky

| Date | Mintage | VF20 | XF40 | MS60 | MS63 | MS65 |
|---|---|---|---|---|---|---|
| 2008 | — | **PF65** 1,850 | | | | |

**Y# 1157 100 ROUBLES**
1046.00 g., 0.999 Silver 33.596 oz. ASW, 100 mm. **Subject:** Alexandrov

| Date | Mintage | VF20 | XF40 | MS60 | MS63 | MS65 |
|---|---|---|---|---|---|---|
| 2008 | — | **PF65** 2,000 | | | | |

**Y# 1162 100 ROUBLES**
1083.74 g., 0.925 Silver 32.2298 oz. ASW, 100 mm. **Subject:** Russian Currency

| Date | Mintage | VF20 | XF40 | MS60 | MS63 | MS65 |
|---|---|---|---|---|---|---|
| 2009 | 250 | **PF65** 2,750 | | | | |

**Y# 1163 100 ROUBLES**
17.45 g., 0.900 Gold 0.5049 oz. AGW, 30 mm. **Subject:** Russian Currency

| Date | Mintage | VF20 | XF40 | MS60 | MS63 | MS65 |
|---|---|---|---|---|---|---|
| 2009 | 27,000 | **PF65** 1,000 | | | | |

**Y# 1167 100 ROUBLES**
168.00 g., 0.925 Silver 4.9962 oz. ASW, 60 mm. **Subject:** A. P. Chekhov, 150th Anniversary of Birth

| Date | Mintage | VF20 | XF40 | MS60 | MS63 | MS65 |
|---|---|---|---|---|---|---|
| 2009 | — | **PF65** 400 | | | | |

**Y# 1171 100 ROUBLES**
1083.74 g., 0.925 Silver 32.2298 oz. ASW, 100 mm. **Subject:** Kalmyk Peoples, 400th Anniversary of annexation into Russia

| Date | Mintage | VF20 | XF40 | MS60 | MS63 | MS65 |
|---|---|---|---|---|---|---|
| 2009 | — | PF65 2,000 | | | | |

**Y# 1174 100 ROUBLES**
1083.74 g., 0.925 Silver 32.2298 oz. ASW, 100 mm. **Subject:** N. V. Gogol, 200th Anniversary of Birth

| Date | Mintage | VF20 | XF40 | MS60 | MS63 | MS65 |
|---|---|---|---|---|---|---|
| 2009 | 500 | PF65 1,850 | | | | |

**Y# 1179 100 ROUBLES**
1083.74 g., 0.925 Silver 32.2298 oz. ASW, 100 mm. **Subject:** Poltava Battle, 300th Anniversary

| Date | Mintage | VF20 | XF40 | MS60 | MS63 | MS65 |
|---|---|---|---|---|---|---|
| 2009 | 500 | PF65 1,850 | | | | |

**Y# 1238 100 ROUBLES**
1083.74 g., 0.925 Silver 32.2298 oz. ASW, 100 mm. **Subject:** A. P. Chekhov, 200th Anniversary of Birth

| Date | Mintage | VF20 | XF40 | MS60 | MS63 | MS65 |
|---|---|---|---|---|---|---|
| 2010 Prooflike | 500 | — | — | — | — | 1,850 |

**Y# 1290 100 ROUBLES**
1083.74 g., 0.925 Silver 32.2298 oz. ASW, 100 mm. **Rev:** Man playing stringed instrument, others in backbround **Edge:** Reeded

| Date | Mintage | VF20 | XF40 | MS60 | MS63 | MS65 |
|---|---|---|---|---|---|---|
| 2011 | 300 | PF65 2,000 | | | | |

**Y# 1299 100 ROUBLES**
1083.74 g., 0.925 Silver 32.2298 oz. ASW, 100 mm. **Subject:** 2014 Winter Olympics - Sochi **Rev:** Montage of Russian winter sports

| Date | Mintage | VF20 | XF40 | MS60 | MS63 | MS65 |
|---|---|---|---|---|---|---|
| 2014 | 1,200 | PF65 1,700 | | | | |

**Y# 1324 100 ROUBLES**
15.55 g., 0.999 Gold 0.4994 oz. AGW, 30 mm. **Rev:** St. George the Victorious

| Date | Mintage | VF20 | XF40 | MS60 | MS63 | MS65 |
|---|---|---|---|---|---|---|
| 2012 | 10,000 | PF65 1,000 | | | | |

**Y# 1340 100 ROUBLES**
1083.74 g., 0.925 Silver 32.2298 oz. ASW, 100 mm. **Subject:** Millennium of the Unity of the Mordovian people within the Peoples of the Russian State

| Date | Mintage | VF20 | XF40 | MS60 | MS63 | MS65 |
|---|---|---|---|---|---|---|
| 2012 | 300 | PF65 2,000 | | | | |

**Y# 1344 100 ROUBLES**
1083.74 g., 0.925 Silver 32.2298 oz. ASW, 100 mm. **Subject:** People's Volunteer Corps, 400th Anniversary

| Date | Mintage | VF20 | XF40 | MS60 | MS63 | MS65 |
|---|---|---|---|---|---|---|
| 2012 | 500 | PF65 2,000 | | | | |

**Y# A1368 100 ROUBLES**
1111.12 g., 0.925 Silver 33.0441 oz. ASW, 60 mm. **Subject:** Origin of the Russian Statehood, 1150th Anniversary

| Date | Mintage | VF20 | XF40 | MS60 | MS63 | MS65 |
|---|---|---|---|---|---|---|
| 2012 Prooflike | 300 | — | — | — | — | 2,000 |

**Y# 1516 100 ROUBLES**
339.32 g., 0.925 Silver 10.0912 oz. ASW Gilt, 75 mm. **Obv:** Names of 2012 Olympic winners **Rev:** Laurel branch, athletes, QR-code below

| Date | Mintage | VF20 | XF40 | MS60 | MS63 | MS65 |
|---|---|---|---|---|---|---|
| 2014 | 500 | PF65 650 | | | | |

**Y# 1440 100 ROUBLES**
1083.00 g., 0.925 Silver 32.2078 oz. ASW, 100 mm. **Subject:** Dynamo Sports Club, 90th Anniversary **Rev:** Sport views in eleven discs surrounding central D-in-diamond logo **Edge:** Reeded

| Date | Mintage | VF20 | XF40 | MS60 | MS63 | MS65 |
|---|---|---|---|---|---|---|
| 2013 СПМД | 750 | PF65 1,000 | | | | |

**Y# 1451 100 ROUBLES**
15.72 g., 0.999 Gold 0.5049 oz. AGW, 30 mm. **Subject:** Russian victory over Germany at Battle of Stalingrad, 70th Anniversary **Rev:** Motherland monument at top, soldiers from Volgograd monument below

| Date | Mintage | VF20 | XF40 | MS60 | MS63 | MS65 |
|---|---|---|---|---|---|---|
| 2013 ММД | 500 | PF65 850 | | | | |

**Y# 1504 100 ROUBLES**
15.82 g., 0.999 Gold 0.5081 oz. AGW, 17x28 mm. **Subject:** 2014 Winter Paralympics, Sochi **Rev:** Paralympic mascot - Hare **Shape:** Vertical rectangle

| Date | Mintage | VF20 | XF40 | MS60 | MS63 | MS65 |
|---|---|---|---|---|---|---|
| 2013 | — | — | — | — | — | 750 |

**Y# 1481 100 ROUBLES**
1083.74 g., 0.925 Silver 32.2298 oz. ASW, 100 mm. **Subject:** 2014 Winter Olympics, Sochi **Rev:** Russian winter folk game scenes

| Date | Mintage | VF20 | XF40 | MS60 | MS63 | MS65 |
|---|---|---|---|---|---|---|
| 2014 | 1,200 | PF65 1,500 | | | | |

**Y# 1489 100 ROUBLES**
1083.74 g., 0.925 Silver 32.2298 oz. ASW, 100 mm. **Subject:** 2014 Winter Olympics, Sochi **Rev:** Winter folk scene - sleding

| Date | Mintage | VF20 | XF40 | MS60 | MS63 | MS65 |
|---|---|---|---|---|---|---|
| 2014 | 1,200 | PF65 1,200 | | | | |

**Y# 1497 100 ROUBLES**
1083.74 g., 0.925 Silver 32.2298 oz. ASW, 100 mm. **Subject:** 2014 Winter Olympics, Sochi **Rev:** Winter folk scenes - Snow forts

| Date | Mintage | VF20 | XF40 | MS60 | MS63 | MS65 |
|---|---|---|---|---|---|---|
| 2014 | 1,200 | PF65 1,200 | | | | |

**Y# 1507 100 ROUBLES**
15.82 g., 0.999 Gold 0.5081 oz. AGW, 17x28 mm. **Subject:** 2014 Winter Olympics, Sochi **Rev:** Bear Mascot **Shape:** Vertical rectangle

| Date | Mintage | VF20 | XF40 | MS60 | MS63 | MS65 |
|---|---|---|---|---|---|---|
| 2012 | 100,000 | — | — | — | — | 700 |

**Y# 1530 100 ROUBLES**
1083.74 g., 0.925 Silver 32.2298 oz. ASW, 100 mm. **Subject:** Rev. Sergius Radonezhsky, 700th Anniversary of Birth **Rev:** Scene from M.V. Nesterov painting "Vision of young Bartholomew" Youth with cloaked man

| Date | Mintage | F12 | VF20 | XF40 | MS60 | MS63 |
|---|---|---|---|---|---|---|
| 2014 Prooflike | 300 | — | — | — | — | 1,250 |

**Y# 1534 100 ROUBLES**
1083.74 g., 0.925 Silver 32.2298 oz. ASW, 100 mm. **Subject:** Unity of Russia and Tuva, founding of Kyzyl City **Rev:** Yurta interior with woman and child, scenes above

| Date | Mintage | F12 | VF20 | XF40 | MS60 | MS63 |
|---|---|---|---|---|---|---|
| 2014 Prooflike | 200 | — | — | — | — | 1,250 |

**Y# 1546 100 ROUBLES**
1083.74 g., 0.925 Silver 32.2298 oz. ASW, 100 mm. **Rev:** Three scenes of Judo players, Japanese Cherry blossoms in background

| Date | Mintage | F12 | VF20 | XF40 | MS60 | MS63 |
|---|---|---|---|---|---|---|
| 2014 Prooflike | 500 | — | — | — | — | — |

**Y# 877 200 ROUBLES**
3342.39 g., 0.900 Silver 96.7142 oz. ASW, 130 mm. **Rev:** Peter I monetary reform

| Date | Mintage | VF20 | XF40 | MS60 | MS63 | MS65 |
|---|---|---|---|---|---|---|
| 2003 (sp) | 300 | PF65 5,250 | | | | |

**Y# 1027 200 ROUBLES**
31.11 g., 0.999 Gold 0.999 oz. AGW, 30 mm. **Subject:** Reindeer

| Date | Mintage | VF20 | XF40 | MS60 | MS63 | MS65 |
|---|---|---|---|---|---|---|
| 2004 | 500 | PF65 3,250 | | | | |

**Y# 1042 200 ROUBLES**
31.10 g., 0.999 Gold 0.9989 oz. AGW, 30 mm. **Subject:** Parliament, 100th Anniversary

| Date | Mintage | VF20 | XF40 | MS60 | MS63 | MS65 |
|---|---|---|---|---|---|---|
| 2006 | 750 | PF65 2,000 | | | | |

**Y# 1062 200 ROUBLES**
3138.00 g., 0.925 Silver 93.3223 oz. ASW, 100 mm. **Subject:** Moscow's Kremlin and Red Square

| Date | Mintage | VF20 | XF40 | MS60 | MS63 | MS65 |
|---|---|---|---|---|---|---|
| 2006 | 200 | PF65 6,500 | | | | |

**Y# 1144 200 ROUBLES**
31.11 g., 0.999 Gold 0.999 oz. AGW **Subject:** European Beaver

| Date | Mintage | VF20 | XF40 | MS60 | MS63 | MS65 |
|---|---|---|---|---|---|---|
| 2008 | 500 | PF65 3,250 | | | | |

**Y# 1169 200 ROUBLES**
31.11 g., 0.999 Gold 0.999 oz. AGW, 30 mm. **Subject:** A. P. Chekhov, 150th Anniversary of Birth

| Date | Mintage | VF20 | XF40 | MS60 | MS63 | MS65 |
|---|---|---|---|---|---|---|
| 2009 | 500 | PF65 2,000 | | | | |

**Y# 1176 200 ROUBLES**
3120.00 g., 0.925 Silver 92.787 oz. ASW, 100 mm. **Subject:** N. V. Gogol, 200th Anniversary of Birth

| Date | Mintage | VF20 | XF40 | MS60 | MS63 | MS65 |
|---|---|---|---|---|---|---|
| 2009 | — | PF65 6,500 | | | | |

**Y# 1201 200 ROUBLES**
31.11 g., 0.999 Gold 0.999 oz. AGW, 30 mm. **Subject:** Velikly Novgorod

| Date | Mintage | VF20 | XF40 | MS60 | MS63 | MS65 |
|---|---|---|---|---|---|---|
| 2009 | 200 | PF65 7,500 | | | | |

**Y# 1209 200 ROUBLES**
31.11 g., 0.999 Gold 0.999 oz. AGW **Series:** Speed Skating

| Date | Mintage | VF20 | XF40 | MS60 | MS63 | MS65 |
|---|---|---|---|---|---|---|
| 2009 | 500 | PF65 2,000 | | | | |

**Y# 1210 200 ROUBLES**
31.10 g., 0.999 Gold 0.9989 oz. AGW **Subject:** Ski Jumping

| Date | Mintage | VF20 | XF40 | MS60 | MS63 | MS65 |
|---|---|---|---|---|---|---|
| 2009 | 500 | PF65 2,000 | | | | |

**Y# 1211 200 ROUBLES**
31.10 g., 0.999 Gold 0.9989 oz. AGW, 33 mm. **Subject:** Luge

| Date | Mintage | VF20 | XF40 | MS60 | MS63 | MS65 |
|---|---|---|---|---|---|---|
| 2009 | 500 | PF65 2,000 | | | | |

**Y# 1212 200 ROUBLES**
31.11 g., 0.999 Gold 0.999 oz. AGW, 33 mm. **Subject:** Biathlon

| Date | Mintage | VF20 | XF40 | MS60 | MS63 | MS65 |
|---|---|---|---|---|---|---|
| 2009 | 500 | PF65 2,000 | | | | |

**Y# 1213 200 ROUBLES**
31.11 g., 0.999 Gold 0.999 oz. AGW **Subject:** Figure Skating

| Date | Mintage | VF20 | XF40 | MS60 | MS63 | MS65 |
|---|---|---|---|---|---|---|
| 2009 | 500 | PF65 2,000 | | | | |

**Y# 1234 200 ROUBLES**
3130.00 g., 0.925 Silver 93.0844 oz. ASW **Subject:** UNESCO Heritage Site - Yaroslav

| Date | Mintage | VF20 | XF40 | MS60 | MS63 | MS65 |
|---|---|---|---|---|---|---|
| 2010 | 200 | PF65 6,000 | | | | |

**Y# 1240 200 ROUBLES**
31.10 g., 0.999 Gold 0.9989 oz. AGW **Subject:** A. P. Chekhov, 200th Anniversary of Birth

| Date | Mintage | VF20 | XF40 | MS60 | MS63 | MS65 |
|---|---|---|---|---|---|---|
| 2010 | 500 | PF65 2,500 | | | | |

**Y# 1255 200 ROUBLES**
31.10 g., 0.999 Gold 0.9989 oz. AGW **Subject:** Hockey

| Date | Mintage | VF20 | XF40 | MS60 | MS63 | MS65 |
|---|---|---|---|---|---|---|
| 2010 | — | PF65 2,500 | | | | |

**Y# 1256 200 ROUBLES**
31.10 g., 0.999 Gold 0.9989 oz. AGW **Subject:** Ski Race

| Date | Mintage | VF20 | XF40 | MS60 | MS63 | MS65 |
|---|---|---|---|---|---|---|
| 2010 | 500 | PF65 2,500 | | | | |

**Y# 1257 200 ROUBLES**
31.10 g., 0.999 Gold 0.9989 oz. AGW **Subject:** Nordic Combined

| Date | Mintage | VF20 | XF40 | MS60 | MS63 | MS65 |
|---|---|---|---|---|---|---|
| 2010 | 500 | PF65 2,500 | | | | |

**Y# 1258 200 ROUBLES**
31.10 g., 0.999 Gold 0.9989 oz. AGW **Subject:** Freestyle Skiing

| Date | Mintage | VF20 | XF40 | MS60 | MS63 | MS65 |
|---|---|---|---|---|---|---|
| 2010 | 500 | PF65 2,500 | | | | |

**Y# 1259 200 ROUBLES**
31.10 g., 0.999 Gold 0.9989 oz. AGW **Subject:** Short Track Speed Skating

| Date | Mintage | VF20 | XF40 | MS60 | MS63 | MS65 |
|---|---|---|---|---|---|---|
| 2010 | 500 | PF65 2,500 | | | | |

**Y# 1260 200 ROUBLES**
31.10 g., 0.999 Gold 0.9989 oz. AGW **Subject:** Curling

| Date | Mintage | VF20 | XF40 | MS60 | MS63 | MS65 |
|---|---|---|---|---|---|---|
| 2010 | 500 | PF65 2,500 | | | | |

**Y# 1261 200 ROUBLES**
31.10 g., 0.999 Gold 0.9989 oz. AGW **Subject:** Snowboarding

| Date | Mintage | VF20 | XF40 | MS60 | MS63 | MS65 |
|---|---|---|---|---|---|---|
| 2010 | 500 | PF65 2,500 | | | | |

**Y# 1262 200 ROUBLES**
31.10 g., 0.999 Gold 0.9989 oz. AGW **Subject:** Skeleton

| Date | Mintage | VF20 | XF40 | MS60 | MS63 | MS65 |
|---|---|---|---|---|---|---|
| 2010 | 500 | PF65 2,500 | | | | |

**Y# 1263 200 ROUBLES**
31.10 g., 0.999 Gold 0.9989 oz. AGW **Subject:** Bobsled

| Date | Mintage | VF20 | XF40 | MS60 | MS63 | MS65 |
|---|---|---|---|---|---|---|
| 2010 | 500 | PF65 2,500 | | | | |

**Y# 1264 200 ROUBLES**
31.10 g., 0.999 Gold 0.9989 oz. AGW **Subject:** Mountain Skiing

| Date | Mintage | VF20 | XF40 | MS60 | MS63 | MS65 |
|---|---|---|---|---|---|---|
| 2010 | 500 | PF65 2,500 | | | | |

**Y# 1441 200 ROUBLES**
31.37 g., 0.999 Gold 1.0076 oz. AGW, 33 mm. **Subject:** Dynamo Sports Club, 90th Anniversary **Rev:** Three soccer players **Edge:** Reeded

| Date | Mintage | VF20 | XF40 | MS60 | MS63 | MS65 |
|---|---|---|---|---|---|---|
| 2013 СПМД | 500 | PF65 1,700 | | | | |

**Y# 1442 200 ROUBLES**
31.37 g., 0.999 Gold 1.0076 oz. AGW, 33 mm. **Subject:** Dynamo Sports Club, 90th Anniversary **Rev:** Three hockey players **Edge:** Reeded

| Date | Mintage | VF20 | XF40 | MS60 | MS63 | MS65 |
|---|---|---|---|---|---|---|
| 2013 СПМД | 500 | PF65 1,700 | | | | |

**Y# 1443 200 ROUBLES**
31.37 g., 0.999 Gold 1.0076 oz. AGW, 33 mm. **Subject:** Dynamo Sports Club, 90th Anniversary **Rev:** Cross-country skier **Edge:** Reeded

| Date | Mintage | VF20 | XF40 | MS60 | MS63 | MS65 |
|---|---|---|---|---|---|---|
| 2013 ММД | 500 | PF65 1,700 | | | | |

**Y# 1498 200 ROUBLES**
3252.30 g., 925.000 Silver 96721.5104 oz. ASW, 130 mm. **Subject:** 2014 Winter Olympics, Sochi **Rev:** Athletic facilities at Sochi

| Date | Mintage | VF20 | XF40 | MS60 | MS63 | MS65 |
|---|---|---|---|---|---|---|
| 2014 Prooflike | 500 | — | — | — | — | 4,000 |

**Y# 1547 200 ROUBLES**
31.37 g., 0.999 Gold 1.0076 oz. AGW, 33 mm. **Rev:** Judo School emblem and Japanese cherry tree

| Date | Mintage | F12 | VF20 | XF40 | MS60 | MS63 |
|---|---|---|---|---|---|---|
| 2014 | 500 | PF65 1,400 | | | | |

**Y# 1348 500 ROUBLES**
5555.60 g., 0.925 Silver 165.2203 oz. ASW, 150 mm. **Subject:** Russia's victory in the War of 1812

| Date | Mintage | VF20 | XF40 | MS60 | MS63 | MS65 |
|---|---|---|---|---|---|---|
| 2012 | 50 | PF65 6,000 | | | | |

**Y# 796 1000 ROUBLES**
156.40 g., 0.999 Gold 5.0233 oz. AGW, 50 mm. **Subject:** The Bark Sedov **Obv:** Double-headed eagle **Rev:** Four-masted sailing ship **Edge:** Reeded

| Date | Mintage | VF20 | XF40 | MS60 | MS63 | MS65 |
|---|---|---|---|---|---|---|
| 2001 (m) | 250 | PF65 10,000 | | | | |

**Y# 878 1000 ROUBLES**
156.40 g., 0.999 Gold 5.0233 oz. AGW, 50 mm. **Rev:** Cronstadt

| Date | Mintage | VF20 | XF40 | MS60 | MS63 | MS65 |
|---|---|---|---|---|---|---|
| 2003 (m) | 250 | PF65 10,000 | | | | |

**Y# 1037 1000 ROUBLES**
1046.00 g., 0.925 Silver 31.1074 oz. ASW, 100 mm. **Subject:** Uglich

| Date | Mintage | VF20 | XF40 | MS60 | MS63 | MS65 |
|---|---|---|---|---|---|---|
| 2004 | — | PF65 1,750 | | | | |

**Y# 1045 1000 ROUBLES**
1000.00 g., 0.999 Gold 32.1186 oz. AGW, 100 mm. **Subject:** Frigate Myr

| Date | Mintage | VF20 | XF40 | MS60 | MS63 | MS65 |
|---|---|---|---|---|---|---|
| 2006 | — | PF65 60,000 | | | | |

**Y# 1082 1000 ROUBLES**
156.00 g., 0.999 Gold 5.0105 oz. AGW, 100 mm. **Subject:** International Artic Year

| Date | Mintage | VF20 | XF40 | MS60 | MS63 | MS65 |
|---|---|---|---|---|---|---|
| 2007 | — | PF65 10,000 | | | | |

**Y# 1164 1000 ROUBLES**
156.00 g., 0.999 Gold 5.0105 oz. AGW, 100 mm. **Subject:** Russian Currency

| Date | Mintage | VF20 | XF40 | MS60 | MS63 | MS65 |
|---|---|---|---|---|---|---|
| 2009 | — | PF65 10,000 | | | | |

**Y# 1227 1000 ROUBLES**
155.50 g., 0.999 Gold 4.9944 oz. AGW, 100 mm. **Subject:** Warship - Goto Predestination

| Date | Mintage | VF20 | XF40 | MS60 | MS63 | MS65 |
|---|---|---|---|---|---|---|
| 2010 | — | PF65 10,000 | | | | |

**Y# 1281 1000 ROUBLES**
155.50 g., 0.999 Gold 4.9944 oz. AGW, 50 mm. **Subject:** Beginning of Great Reforms - Abolition of Serfdom **Rev:** Man plowing, quill pen and signature on document

| Date | Mintage | VF20 | XF40 | MS60 | MS63 | MS65 |
|---|---|---|---|---|---|---|
| 2011 ММД | 250 | PF65 10,000 | | | | |

**Y# 1288 1000 ROUBLES**
155.50 g., 0.999 Gold 4.9944 oz. AGW, 50 mm. **Rev:** U.A. Gagarin in spacesuit waving

| Date | Mintage | VF20 | XF40 | MS60 | MS63 | MS65 |
|---|---|---|---|---|---|---|
| 2011 | 500 | PF65 10,000 | | | | |

**Y# 1297 1000 ROUBLES**
155.50 g., 0.999 Gold 4.9944 oz. AGW, 50 mm. **Subject:** 2014 Winter Olympics - Sochi - Flora of Sochi **Rev:** Goddess Flora who's hair has plants of the Sochi region, female figure skater to right

| Date | Mintage | VF20 | XF40 | MS60 | MS63 | MS65 |
|---|---|---|---|---|---|---|
| 2014 | 600 | PF65 10,000 | | | | |

**Y# 1418 1000 ROUBLES**
155.50 g., 0.999 Gold 4.9944 oz. AGW, 100 mm. **Subject:** Battleship Ingermanland

| Date | Mintage | VF20 | XF40 | MS60 | MS63 | MS65 |
|---|---|---|---|---|---|---|
| 2012 | 500 | **PF65** 10,000 | | | | |

**Y# 1444 1000 ROUBLES**
156.40 g., 0.999 Gold 5.0233 oz. AGW, 50 mm. **Subject:** Dynamo Sports Club, 90th Anniversary **Rev:** Six sports in discs, D-in-diamond logo **Edge:** Reeded

| Date | Mintage | VF20 | XF40 | MS60 | MS63 | MS65 |
|---|---|---|---|---|---|---|
| 2013 ММД | 500 | **PF65** 7,500 | | | | |

**Y# 1482 1000 ROUBLES**
156.40 g., 0.999 Gold 5.0233 oz. AGW, 50 mm. **Subject:** 2014 Winter Olympics, Sochi **Rev:** Hockey player at left, antelope, buffalo, cat, Female at right

| Date | Mintage | VF20 | XF40 | MS60 | MS63 | MS65 |
|---|---|---|---|---|---|---|
| 2014 | 600 | **PF65** 7,500 | | | | |

**Y# 1519 1000 ROUBLES**
156.40 g., 0.999 Gold 5.0233 oz. AGW, 50 mm. **Subject:** Russian Navy's victory at the Battle of Gangut, 1714

| Date | Mintage | F12 | VF20 | XF40 | MS60 | MS63 |
|---|---|---|---|---|---|---|
| 2014 | 250 | **PF65** 9,000 | | | | |

**Y# 1548 1000 ROUBLES**
156.40 g., 0.999 Gold 5.0233 oz. AGW, 50 mm. **Rev:** Judo hold by a policeman at bottom center, V.S. Oschepkov portrait at top left

| Date | Mintage | F12 | VF20 | XF40 | MS60 | MS63 |
|---|---|---|---|---|---|---|
| 2014 | 300 | **PF65** 8,000 | | | | |

**Y# 1578 1000 ROUBLES**
156.40 g., 0.999 Gold 5.0233 oz. AGW, 50 mm. **Subject:** Statue of the Provincial and District Zemstvo Agencies, 150th Anniversary **Rev:** Document with scenes around

| Date | Mintage | F12 | VF20 | XF40 | MS60 | MS63 |
|---|---|---|---|---|---|---|
| 2014 | 250 | **PF65** 8,000 | | | | |

**Y# 1579 1000 ROUBLES**
156.40 g., 0.999 Gold 5.0233 oz. AGW, 50 mm. **Subject:** Establishment of Judicial Regulations, 150th Anniversary **Rev:** Documents and Judicial scenes around

| Date | Mintage | F12 | VF20 | XF40 | MS60 | MS63 |
|---|---|---|---|---|---|---|
| 2014 | 250 | **PF65** 8,000 | | | | |

**Y# 784 10000 ROUBLES**
1001.10 g., 0.999 Gold 32.1539 oz. AGW, 100 mm. **Subject:** Works of Dionissy **Obv:** Double-headed eagle **Rev:** Interior view of the carved portal of the Virgin of the Nativity Church **Edge:** Reeded

| Date | Mintage | VF20 | XF40 | MS60 | MS63 | MS65 |
|---|---|---|---|---|---|---|
| 2002 (sp) | 100 | **PF65** 60,000 | | | | |

**Y# 879 10000 ROUBLES**
1001.10 g., 0.999 Gold 32.1539 oz. AGW, 100 mm. **Rev:** St. Petersburg area map

| Date | Mintage | VF20 | XF40 | MS60 | MS63 | MS65 |
|---|---|---|---|---|---|---|
| 2003 | 200 | **PF65** 57,500 | | | | |

**Y# 1017 10000 ROUBLES**
1000.00 g., 0.999 Gold 32.1186 oz. AGW, 100 mm. **Subject:** Theophanes the Greek

| Date | Mintage | VF20 | XF40 | MS60 | MS63 | MS65 |
|---|---|---|---|---|---|---|
| 2004 | — | PF65 60,000 | | | | |

**Y# 1028 10000 ROUBLES**
1000.00 g., 0.999 Gold 32.1186 oz. AGW, 100 mm. **Subject:** Reindeer

| Date | Mintage | VF20 | XF40 | MS60 | MS63 | MS65 |
|---|---|---|---|---|---|---|
| 2004 | 100 | PF65 60,000 | | | | |

**Y# 896 10000 ROUBLES**
1001.10 g., 0.999 Gold 32.1539 oz. AGW, 100 mm. **Subject:** 60th Anniversary - Victory Over Germany **Obv:** Double-headed eagle **Rev:** Soldiers dishonoring captured Nazi flags and standards **Edge:** Reeded

| Date | Mintage | VF20 | XF40 | MS60 | MS63 | MS65 |
|---|---|---|---|---|---|---|
| 2005 | 250 | PF65 57,500 | | | | |

**Y# 913 10000 ROUBLES**
1001.10 g., 0.999 Gold 32.1539 oz. AGW, 100 mm. **Obv:** Two headed eagle **Rev:** Kazan Kremlin view **Edge:** Reeded

| Date | Mintage | VF20 | XF40 | MS60 | MS63 | MS65 |
|---|---|---|---|---|---|---|
| 2005 | 150 | PF65 58,000 | | | | |

**Y# 1043 10000 ROUBLES**
1083.74 g., 0.925 Gold 32.2298 oz. AGW, 100 mm. **Subject:** Parliament, 100th Anniversary

| Date | Mintage | VF20 | XF40 | MS60 | MS63 | MS65 |
|---|---|---|---|---|---|---|
| 2006 | 100 | PF65 60,000 | | | | |

**Y# 1064 10000 ROUBLES**
1000.00 g., 0.999 Gold 32.1186 oz. AGW, 100 mm. **Subject:** Moscow's Kremlin and Red Square

| Date | Mintage | VF20 | XF40 | MS60 | MS63 | MS65 |
|---|---|---|---|---|---|---|
| 2006 | — | PF65 60,000 | | | | |

**Y# 1091 10000 ROUBLES**
1000.00 g., 0.999 Gold 32.1186 oz. AGW, 100 mm. **Subject:** Andrew Rublyov

| Date | Mintage | VF20 | XF40 | MS60 | MS63 | MS65 |
|---|---|---|---|---|---|---|
| 2007 | — | PF65 60,000 | | | | |

**Y# 1095 10000 ROUBLES**
1000.00 g., 0.999 Gold 32.1186 oz. AGW, 100 mm. **Subject:** Bashkiria, 450th Anniversary of Annexation by Russia

| Date | Mintage | VF20 | XF40 | MS60 | MS63 | MS65 |
|---|---|---|---|---|---|---|
| 2007 | — | PF65 60,000 | | | | |

**Y# 1098 10000 ROUBLES**
1000.00 g., 0.999 Gold 32.1186 oz. AGW, 100 mm. **Subject:** Khakassia, 300th Anniversary of Annexation by Russia

| Date | Mintage | VF20 | XF40 | MS60 | MS63 | MS65 |
|---|---|---|---|---|---|---|
| 2007 | — | PF65 60,000 | | | | |

**Y# 1122 10000 ROUBLES**
1000.00 g., 0.999 Gold 32.1186 oz. AGW, 100 mm. **Subject:** Udmurtiya, 450th Anniversary of Annexation into Russia

| Date | Mintage | VF20 | XF40 | MS60 | MS63 | MS65 |
|---|---|---|---|---|---|---|
| 2008 | — | PF65 58,000 | | | | |

**Y# 1145 10000 ROUBLES**
1000.00 g., 0.999 Gold 32.1186 oz. AGW, 100 mm. **Subject:** European Beaver

| Date | Mintage | VF20 | XF40 | MS60 | MS63 | MS65 |
|---|---|---|---|---|---|---|
| 2008 | — | PF65 58,000 | | | | |

**Y# 1149 10000 ROUBLES**
1000.00 g., 0.999 Gold 32.1186 oz. AGW, 100 mm. **Subject:** Kamchatka Volcano

| Date | Mintage | VF20 | XF40 | MS60 | MS63 | MS65 |
|---|---|---|---|---|---|---|
| 2008 | — | PF65 58,000 | | | | |

**Y# 1203 10000 ROUBLES**
1000.00 g., 0.999 Gold 32.1186 oz. AGW, 100 mm. **Subject:** Velikly Novgorod

| Date | Mintage | VF20 | XF40 | MS60 | MS63 | MS65 |
|---|---|---|---|---|---|---|
| 2009 | — | PF65 58,000 | | | | |

**Y# 1236 10000 ROUBLES**
1000.00 g., 0.999 Gold 32.1186 oz. AGW, 100 mm. **Subject:** UNESCO Heritage Site - Yaroslav

| Date | Mintage | VF20 | XF40 | MS60 | MS63 | MS65 |
|---|---|---|---|---|---|---|
| 2010 Prooflike | — | — | — | — | — | 58,000 |

**Y# 1370 10000 ROUBLES**
1000.00 g., 0.999 Gold 32.1186 oz. AGW, 100 mm. **Subject:** Origin of Russian Statehood, 1150th Anniversary

| Date | Mintage | VF20 | XF40 | MS60 | MS63 | MS65 |
|---|---|---|---|---|---|---|
| 2012 Prooflike | 75 | — | — | — | — | 60,000 |

**Y# 1371 10000 ROUBLES**
1000.00 g., 0.999 Gold 32.1186 oz. AGW, 100 mm. **Subject:** Sberbank, 170 Years

| Date | Mintage | VF20 | XF40 | MS60 | MS63 | MS65 |
|---|---|---|---|---|---|---|
| 2012 Prooflike | 75 | — | — | — | — | 60,000 |

**Y# 1425 10000 ROUBLES**
1003.00 g., 0.999 Gold 32.2149 oz. AGW, 100 mm. **Rev:** Nine sport scenes, Kazan Universiade logo and city skyline **Edge:** Reeded

| Date | Mintage | VF20 | XF40 | MS60 | MS63 | MS65 |
|---|---|---|---|---|---|---|
| 2013 СПМД | 100 | PF65 43,000 | | | | |

**Y# 1490 10000 ROUBLES**
1004.40 g., 0.999 Gold 32.2599 oz. AGW, 100 mm. **Subject:** 2014 Winter Olympics, Sochi **Rev:** Prometheus with torch at center, seven sport views around

| Date | Mintage | VF20 | XF40 | MS60 | MS63 | MS65 |
|---|---|---|---|---|---|---|
| 2014 | 250 | PF65 40,000 | | | | |

**Y# 1499 10000 ROUBLES**
1004.40 g., 0.999 Gold 32.2599 oz. AGW, 100 mm. **Subject:** 2014 Winter Olympics, Sochi **Rev:** Allegory of Matseta pouring water from jug, seven sport scenes around

| Date | Mintage | VF20 | XF40 | MS60 | MS63 | MS65 |
|---|---|---|---|---|---|---|
| 2014 | 250 | PF65 45,000 | | | | |

**Y# 1531 10000 ROUBLES**
1004.40 g., 0.999 Gold 32.2599 oz. AGW, 100 mm. **Subject:** Rev. Sergius Radonezhsky, 700th Anniversary of Birth **Rev:** V.A. Chukharkin's sculpture of Radonezhsky and Trinity Cathedral complex in backgorund

| Date | Mintage | F12 | VF20 | XF40 | MS60 | MS63 |
|---|---|---|---|---|---|---|
| 2014 Proof-like | Est. 100 | — | — | — | — | 58,000 |

**Y# 1549 10000 ROUBLES**
1004.40 g., 0.999 Gold 32.2599 oz. AGW, 100 mm. **Rev:** Judo scenes around

| Date | Mintage | F12 | VF20 | XF40 | MS60 | MS63 |
|---|---|---|---|---|---|---|
| 2014 Prooflike | 75 | — | — | — | — | — |

**Y# 1117 25000 ROUBLES**
1000.00 g., 0.999 Gold 32.1186 oz. AGW, 100 mm. **Subject:** Goznak, 190th Anniversary

| Date | Mintage | VF20 | XF40 | MS60 | MS63 | MS65 |
|---|---|---|---|---|---|---|
| 2008 | — | PF65 58,000 | | | | |

**Y# 1165 25000 ROUBLES**
1000.00 g., 0.999 Gold 32.1186 oz. AGW, 100 mm. **Subject:** Russian Currency

| Date | Mintage | VF20 | XF40 | MS60 | MS63 | MS65 |
|---|---|---|---|---|---|---|
| 2009 | — | PF65 58,000 | | | | |

**Y# 1350 25000 ROUBLES**
3000.00 g., 0.999 Gold 96.3557 oz. AGW, 120 mm. **Subject:** Russia's victory in the War of 1812

| Date | Mintage | VF20 | XF40 | MS60 | MS63 | MS65 |
|---|---|---|---|---|---|---|
| 2012 | 50 | PF65 175,000 | | | | |

**Y# 1500 25000 ROUBLES**
3013.46 g., 0.999 Gold 96.788 oz. AGW, 120 mm. **Subject:** 2014 Winter Olympics, Sochi - Olympic Movement in Russia **Rev:** Winter and Summer Olympic sports

| Date | Mintage | VF20 | XF40 | MS60 | MS63 | MS65 |
|---|---|---|---|---|---|---|
| 2014 Prooflike | 100 | — | — | — | — | 120,000 |

**Y# 1231 50000 ROUBLES**
5000.00 g., 0.999 Gold 160.5929 oz. AGW **Subject:** Bank of Russia, 150th Anniversary

| Date | Mintage | VF20 | XF40 | MS60 | MS63 | MS65 |
|---|---|---|---|---|---|---|
| 2010 Prooflike | — | — | — | — | — | 285,000 |

## MINT SETS

| KM# | Date | Mintage | Identification | Issue Price | Mkt Val |
|---|---|---|---|---|---|
| MS44 | 2002 (7) | — | Y#600-603, 797-799, plus mint medal | 7.50 | 15.00 |

# RWANDA

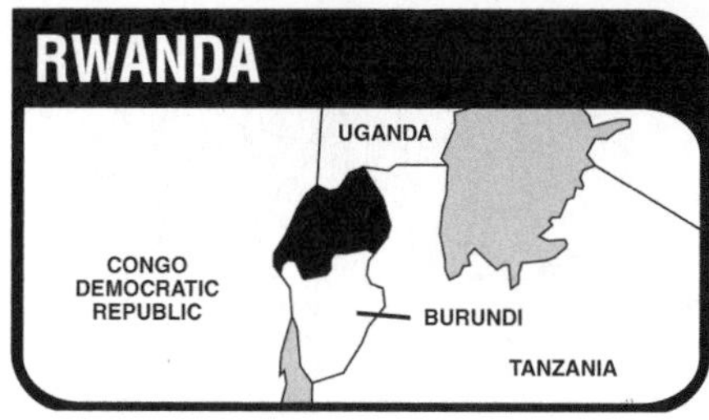


The Republic of Rwanda, located in central Africa between the Republic of the Congo and Tanzania, has an area of 10,169 sq. mi. (26,340 sq. km.) and a population of 7.3 million. Capital: Kigali. The economy is based on agriculture and mining. Coffee and tin are exported.

For earlier coinage see Belgian Congo, and Rwanda and Burundi.

**MINT MARKS**

(a) - Paris, privy marks only
(b) - Brussels, privy marks only

**MONETARY SYSTEM**

100 Centimes = 1 Franc

## REPUBLIC

### STANDARD COINAGE

**KM# 22 FRANC**

0.07 g., Aluminum, 16 mm. **Obv:** National arms **Rev:** Sorghum plant **Edge:** Plain

| Date | Mintage | VF20 | XF40 | MS60 | MS63 | MS65 |
|---|---|---|---|---|---|---|
| 2003 | — | — | 0.25 | 0.65 | 1.00 | 1.50 |

**KM# 23 5 FRANCS**

2.96 g., Brass Plated Steel, 20 mm. **Obv:** National arms **Rev:** Coffee plant **Edge:** Plain

| Date | Mintage | VF20 | XF40 | MS60 | MS63 | MS65 |
|---|---|---|---|---|---|---|
| 2003 | — | — | 0.25 | 0.65 | 1.00 | 1.50 |

**KM# 33 5 FRANCS**

2.96 g., Brass Plated Steel, 20 mm. **Obv:** National arms **Rev:** Coffee plant **Rev. Legend:** BANKI NKURU YU RWANDA

| Date | Mintage | VF20 | XF40 | MS60 | MS63 | MS65 |
|---|---|---|---|---|---|---|
| 2009 | — | — | 0.25 | 0.65 | 1.00 | 1.50 |

**KM# 24 10 FRANCS**

5.00 g., Brass Plated Steel, 23.9 mm. **Obv:** National arms **Rev:** Banana tree **Edge:** Plain

| Date | Mintage | VF20 | XF40 | MS60 | MS63 | MS65 |
|---|---|---|---|---|---|---|
| 2003 | — | — | 0.45 | 1.00 | 1.50 | 2.00 |
| 2009 | — | — | 0.45 | 1.00 | 1.50 | 2.00 |

**KM# 34 10 FRANCS**

5.00 g., Brass Plated Steel, 23.9 mm. **Obv:** National arms **Rev:** Banana tree **Rev. Legend:** BANKI NKURU YU RWANDA

| Date | Mintage | VF20 | XF40 | MS60 | MS63 | MS65 |
|---|---|---|---|---|---|---|
| 2009 | — | — | 0.25 | 0.65 | 1.00 | 1.50 |

**KM# 25 20 FRANCS**

3.50 g., Nickel Plated Steel, 20 mm. **Obv:** National arms **Rev:** Coffee plant seedling **Edge:** Reeded

| Date | Mintage | VF20 | XF40 | MS60 | MS63 | MS65 |
|---|---|---|---|---|---|---|
| 2003 | — | — | — | 1.75 | 2.00 | 2.50 |
| 2009 | — | — | — | 1.75 | 2.00 | 2.50 |

**KM# 35 20 FRANCS**

Nickel Plated Steel, 20 mm. **Obv:** National arms **Rev:** Coffee plant seedling **Rev. Legend:** BANKI NKURU YU RWANDA **Edge:** Reeded

| Date | Mintage | VF20 | XF40 | MS60 | MS63 | MS65 |
|---|---|---|---|---|---|---|
| 2009 | — | — | — | 1.75 | 2.00 | 2.50 |

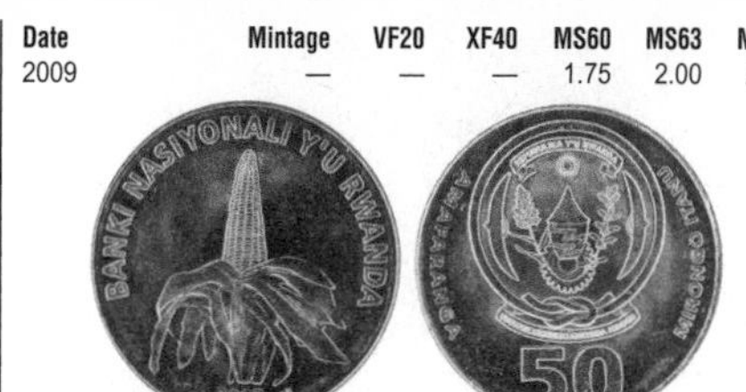

**KM# 26 50 FRANCS**

5.80 g., Nickel Plated Steel, 24 mm. **Obv:** National arms **Rev:** Ear of corn within husks **Edge:** Reeded

| Date | Mintage | VF20 | XF40 | MS60 | MS63 | MS65 |
|---|---|---|---|---|---|---|
| 2003 (a) | — | — | — | 2.50 | 3.50 | 5.00 |

**KM# 36 50 FRANCS**

5.80 g., Nickel Plated Steel, 24 mm. **Obv:** National arms **Rev:** Ear of corn within husks **Rev. Legend:** BANKI NKURU YU RWANDA **Edge:** Reeded

| Date | Mintage | VF20 | XF40 | MS60 | MS63 | MS65 |
|---|---|---|---|---|---|---|
| 2009 | — | — | — | 2.50 | 3.50 | 5.00 |
| 2011 | — | — | — | 2.50 | 3.50 | 5.00 |

**KM# 39 50 FRANCS**

31.05 g., 0.999 Silver 0.9973 oz. ASW, 38.61 mm. **Rev:** Map of Africa, Zebra

| Date | Mintage | VF20 | XF40 | MS60 | MS63 | MS65 |
|---|---|---|---|---|---|---|
| 2011 | — | PF63 75.00 | PF65 85.00 | | | |

**KM# 37 50 FRANCS**

31.11 g., 0.999 Silver 0.999 oz. ASW, 38.61 mm. **Rev:** Map of Africa, Two Rhinos at lower left

| Date | Mintage | VF20 | XF40 | MS60 | MS63 | MS65 |
|---|---|---|---|---|---|---|
| 2012 | Est. 5000 | PF63 75.00 | PF65 85.00 | | | |

**KM# 38 50 FRANCS**

31.11 g., 0.999 Silver 0.999 oz. ASW, 38.61 mm. **Rev:** Map of Africa, Two cheetahs at lower left

| Date | Mintage | VF20 | XF40 | MS60 | MS63 | MS65 |
|---|---|---|---|---|---|---|
| 2013 | Est. 5000 | PF63 75.00 | PF65 85.00 | | | |

**KM# 43 50 FRANCS**

31.11 g., 0.999 Silver 0.999 oz. ASW **Obv:** National arms **Rev:** Map of Africa, two impala at left

| Date | Mintage | VF20 | XF40 | MS60 | MS63 | MS65 |
|---|---|---|---|---|---|---|
| 2014 | Est. 10000 | — | — | — | 35.00 | 40.00 |

**KM# 32 100 FRANCS**

Bi-Metallic Copper center in Copper-Nickel ring, 27 mm. **Obv:** National arms **Rev:** Value **Rev. Legend:** BANKI NKURU YU RWANDA

| Date | Mintage | VF20 | XF40 | MS60 | MS63 | MS65 |
|---|---|---|---|---|---|---|
| 2007 | — | — | — | 3.50 | 5.00 | 7.50 |

**KM# 28 200 FRANCS**

1.00 g., 0.999 Gold 0.0321 oz. AGW, 13.9 mm. **Subject:** 75th Birthday Dian Fossey **Obv:** National arms **Obv. Legend:** BANKI NASIYONALI Y'U RWANDA **Rev:** Fossey facing holding monkey **Edge:** Plain

| Date | Mintage | VF20 | XF40 | MS60 | MS63 | MS65 |
|---|---|---|---|---|---|---|
| 2007 | 15,000 | PF63 70.00 | PF65 80.00 | | | |

**KM# 30 500 FRANCS**

22.20 g., 0.900 Silver 0.6424 oz. ASW **Obv:** National arms **Obv. Legend:** BANQUE NATIONALE DU RWANDA **Rev:** Stalk of bananas on leaves

| Date | Mintage | VF20 | XF40 | MS60 | MS63 | MS65 |
|---|---|---|---|---|---|---|
| 2002 (a) | 500 | PF65 110 | | | | |

**KM# 31 500 FRANCS**

22.20 g., 0.900 Silver 0.6424 oz. ASW **Subject:** Euro Parity **Obv:** Arms **Rev:** Plant

| Date | Mintage | VF20 | XF40 | MS60 | MS63 | MS65 |
|---|---|---|---|---|---|---|
| 2002 | 500 | PF65 110 | | | | |

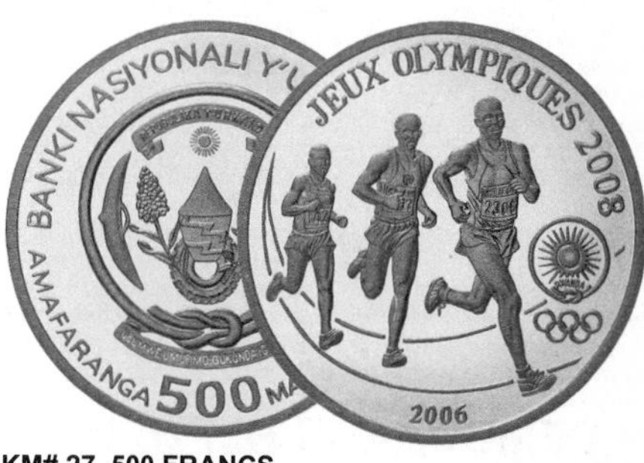


**KM# 27 500 FRANCS**

20.00 g., 0.999 Silver 0.6424 oz. ASW, 38 mm. **Subject:** Olympic Games 2008 - Peking, marathon races **Obv:** National arms **Obv. Legend:** BANKI NASIYONALI Y'U RWANDA **Rev:** Three male marathon runners, Rwanda Olympic logo at right **Rev. Legend:** JEUX OLYMPIQUES **Edge:** Plain

| Date | Mintage | VF20 | XF40 | MS60 | MS63 | MS65 |
|---|---|---|---|---|---|---|
| 2006 | — | PF65 95.00 | | | | |

**KM# 44 500 FRANCS**

20.00 g., 0.999 Silver 0.6424 oz. ASW, 40 mm. **Subject:** Year of the Snake **Rev:** Snake with green crystal inserts

| Date | Mintage | VF20 | XF40 | MS60 | MS63 | MS65 |
|---|---|---|---|---|---|---|
| 2013 | — | PF65 95.00 | | | | |

**KM# 29 1000 FRANCS**

93.30 g., 0.999 Silver and Gold 2.9967 oz., 65 mm. **Obv:** National arms **Obv. Legend:** BANKI NASIYONALI Y'U RWANDA **Rev:** Gilt elephant family of four with diamonds inset in eyes **Rev. Legend:** AFRICAN ELEPHANT **Edge:** Plain

| Date | Mintage | VF20 | XF40 | MS60 | MS63 | MS65 |
|---|---|---|---|---|---|---|
| 2007 | 1,500 | — | — | — | — | 5,000 |
| 2007 | 500 | PF65 5,500 | | | | |

**KM# 45 1000 FRANCS**

96.30 g., 0.925 Silver 2.8639 oz. ASW, 38.61 mm. **Subject:** Year of the Horse **Rev:** Horse in agate

| Date | Mintage | VF20 | XF40 | MS60 | MS63 | MS65 |
|---|---|---|---|---|---|---|
| 2014 | 888 | PF65 700 | | | | |

# SAHARAWI ARAB D.R.

The Saharawi Arab Democratic Republic, located in northwest Africa has an area of 102,703 sq. mi. and a population (census taken 1974) of 76,425. Formerly known as Spanish Sahara, the area is bounded on the north by Morocco, on the east and southeast by Mauritania, on the northeast by Algeria, and on the west by the Atlantic Ocean. Capital: El Aaium. Agriculture, fishing and mining are the three main industries. Exports are barley, livestock and phosphates. The SADR is a "government in exile". It currently controls about 20% of its claimed **territory**, the former **Spanish colony** of **Western Sahara; Morocco** controls and administers the majority of the territory as its **Southern Provinces**. SADR claims control over a zone largely bordering Mauritania, described as "the **Free Zone**," although characterized by Morocco as a buffer zone.

## DEMOCRATIC REPUBLIC

### STANDARD COINAGE

**KM# 54 1000 PESETAS**
19.94 g., 0.999 Silver 0.6404 oz. ASW, 38.1 mm. **Obv:** National arms **Rev:** Soccer player and stadium **Edge:** Plain

| Date | Mintage | VF20 | XF40 | MS60 | MS63 | MS65 |
|---|---|---|---|---|---|---|
| 2002 | — | PF63 40.00 | | PF65 50.00 | | |

# SAINT HELENA & ASCENSION

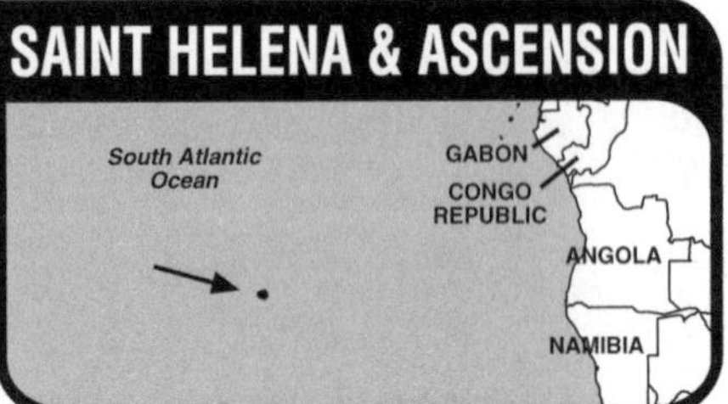


## BRITISH OVERSEAS TERRITORY

### STANDARD COINAGE

100 Pence = 1 Pound

**KM# 13a PENNY**
3.50 g., Copper Plated Steel, 20.28 mm. **Ruler:** Elizabeth II **Obv:** Crowned head right **Rev:** Tuna above value **Edge:** Plain

| Date | Mintage | VF20 | XF40 | MS60 | MS63 | MS65 |
|---|---|---|---|---|---|---|
| 2003 | — | — | 0.15 | 0.25 | 0.35 | 0.75 |

**KM# 12a 2 PENCE**
Copper Plated Steel, 25.9 mm. **Ruler:** Elizabeth II **Obv:** Crowned head right **Rev:** Value below donkey

| Date | Mintage | VF20 | XF40 | MS60 | MS63 | MS65 |
|---|---|---|---|---|---|---|
| 2003 | — | — | 0.20 | 0.40 | 0.60 | 1.25 |
| 2006 | — | — | 0.20 | 0.40 | 0.60 | 1.25 |

**KM# 22 5 PENCE**
3.25 g., Copper-Nickel, 18 mm. **Ruler:** Elizabeth II **Obv:** Crowned head right **Rev:** Giant tortoise

| Date | Mintage | VF20 | XF40 | MS60 | MS63 | MS65 |
|---|---|---|---|---|---|---|
| 2003 | — | — | 1.00 | 1.50 | 2.50 | 5.00 |
| 2006 | — | — | 1.00 | 1.50 | 2.50 | 5.00 |

**KM# 23 10 PENCE**
6.50 g., Copper-Nickel, 24.5 mm. **Ruler:** Elizabeth II **Obv:** Crowned head right **Rev:** Dolphins

| Date | Mintage | VF20 | XF40 | MS60 | MS63 | MS65 |
|---|---|---|---|---|---|---|
| 2003 | — | — | 1.25 | 2.00 | 3.00 | 5.00 |
| 2006 | — | — | 1.25 | 2.00 | 3.00 | 5.00 |

**KM# 55 10 PENCE**
15.55 g., 0.999 Silver 0.4994 oz. ASW, 27 mm. **Ruler:** Elizabeth II **Obv:** Head with crown right **Rev:** Peacock displayed

| Date | Mintage | VF20 | XF40 | MS60 | MS63 | MS65 |
|---|---|---|---|---|---|---|
| 2012 | Est. 20000 | PF65 32.50 | | | | |

**KM# 21 20 PENCE**
5.00 g., Copper-Nickel, 21.4 mm. **Ruler:** Elizabeth II **Obv:** Crowned head right **Rev:** Ebony flower **Shape:** 7-sided

| Date | Mintage | VF20 | XF40 | MS60 | MS63 | MS65 |
|---|---|---|---|---|---|---|
| 2003 | — | — | 0.65 | 1.25 | 1.50 | 2.50 |

**KM# 56 20 PENCE**
31.11 g., 0.999 Silver 0.999 oz. ASW, 38.61 mm. **Ruler:** Elizabeth II **Obv:** Head with crown right **Rev:** Peacock displayed

| Date | Mintage | VF20 | XF40 | MS60 | MS63 | MS65 |
|---|---|---|---|---|---|---|
| 2012 | Est. 20000 | PF65 55.00 | | | | |

**KM# 27 50 PENCE**
8.00 g., Copper-Nickel, 27.3 mm. **Ruler:** Elizabeth II **Obv:** Head with crown right **Rev:** Green Sea Turtle **Shape:** 7-sided

| Date | Mintage | VF20 | XF40 | MS60 | MS63 | MS65 |
|---|---|---|---|---|---|---|
| 2003 | — | — | — | — | 3.00 | 5.00 |
| 2006 | — | — | — | — | 3.00 | 5.00 |

**KM# 57 50 PENCE**
5.83 g., 0.999 Gold 0.1873 oz. AGW, 20 mm. **Ruler:** Elizabeth II **Obv:** Head with crown right **Rev:** Lion walking left, palm tree in background

| Date | Mintage | VF20 | XF40 | MS60 | MS63 | MS65 |
|---|---|---|---|---|---|---|
| 2012 | Est. 3250 | PF65 400 | | | | |

**KM# 17 POUND**
9.50 g., Nickel-Brass, 22.5 mm. **Ruler:** Elizabeth II **Obv:** Crowned head right **Rev:** Sooty terns (Wideawake birds)

| Date | Mintage | VF20 | XF40 | MS60 | MS63 | MS65 |
|---|---|---|---|---|---|---|
| 2003 | — | — | — | 3.00 | 5.00 | 7.00 |
| 2006 | — | — | — | 3.00 | 5.00 | 7.00 |

**KM# 58 POUND**
11.66 g., 0.9999 Gold 0.3748 oz. AGW, 26 mm. **Ruler:** Elizabeth II **Obv:** Head with crown right **Rev:** Lion advancing left, palm tree in background

| Date | Mintage | VF20 | XF40 | MS60 | MS63 | MS65 |
|---|---|---|---|---|---|---|
| 2012 | 3,250 | PF65 725 | | | | |

**KM# 26 2 POUNDS**
11.81 g., Nickel-Brass, 28.3 mm. **Ruler:** Elizabeth II **Obv:** Crowned bust right **Rev:** National arms above value **Edge:** Reeded and lettered **Edge Lettering:** 500TH ANNIVERSARY

| Date | Mintage | VF20 | XF40 | MS60 | MS63 | MS65 |
|---|---|---|---|---|---|---|
| 2002 | — | — | 6.00 | — | 10.00 | 12.00 |

**KM# 25 2 POUNDS**
12.00 g., Bi-Metallic Copper-Nickel center in Brass ring, 28.4 mm. **Ruler:** Elizabeth II **Obv:** Crowned bust right **Rev:** National Arms **Edge:** Reeded and lettered **Edge Lettering:** LOYAL AND FAITHFUL

| Date | Mintage | VF20 | XF40 | MS60 | MS63 | MS65 |
|---|---|---|---|---|---|---|
| 2003 | — | — | 9.00 | — | 15.00 | 17.00 |
| 2006 | — | — | 9.00 | — | 15.00 | 17.00 |

**KM# 60 5 POUNDS**
28.28 g., 0.925 Silver 0.841 oz. ASW, 38.61 mm. **Ruler:** Elizabeth II **Subject:** Queen Elizabeth II 60th Wedding Anniversary **Shape:** 7-Sided

| Date | Mintage | VF20 | XF40 | MS60 | MS63 | MS65 |
|---|---|---|---|---|---|---|
| 2007 | Est. 30000 | PF63 35.00 | PF65 40.00 | | | |

**KM# 61 5 POUNDS**
28.28 g., 0.925 Silver 0.841 oz. ASW, 38.61 mm. **Ruler:** Elizabeth II **Subject:** Buckingham Palace **Shape:** 7-Sided

| Date | Mintage | VF20 | XF40 | MS60 | MS63 | MS65 |
|---|---|---|---|---|---|---|
| 2007 | Est. 30000 | PF63 35.00 | PF65 40.00 | | | |

### KM# 62 5 POUNDS

28.28 g., 0.925 Silver 0.841 oz. ASW, 38.61 mm. **Ruler:** Elizabeth II **Subject:** Armed Services **Shape:** 7-Sided

| Date | Mintage | VF20 | XF40 | MS60 | MS63 | MS65 |
|---|---|---|---|---|---|---|
| 2007 | Est. 30000 | PF63 35.00 | PF65 40.00 | | | |

### KM# 28 5 POUNDS

28.28 g., 0.925 Silver 0.841 oz. ASW, 38.61 mm. **Ruler:** Elizabeth II **Obv:** Head with crown right **Rev:** Hawker Hurricane, emblem in color

| Date | Mintage | VF20 | XF40 | MS60 | MS63 | MS65 |
|---|---|---|---|---|---|---|
| 2008 | 20,000 | PF63 47.00 | PF65 55.00 | | | |

### KM# 29 5 POUNDS

28.28 g., 0.925 Silver 0.841 oz. ASW, 38.61 mm. **Ruler:** Elizabeth II **Obv:** Head with crown right **Rev:** Sir Douglas Bader

| Date | Mintage | VF20 | XF40 | MS60 | MS63 | MS65 |
|---|---|---|---|---|---|---|
| 2008 | 20,000 | PF63 47.00 | PF65 55.00 | | | |

### KM# 30 5 POUNDS

28.28 g., 0.925 Silver 0.841 oz. ASW, 38.61 mm. **Ruler:** Elizabeth II **Obv:** Head with crown right **Rev:** Spitfire, emblem in color

| Date | Mintage | VF20 | XF40 | MS60 | MS63 | MS65 |
|---|---|---|---|---|---|---|
| 2008 | 20,000 | PF63 47.00 | PF65 55.00 | | | |

### KM# 31 5 POUNDS

28.28 g., 0.925 Silver 0.841 oz. ASW, 38.61 mm. **Ruler:** Elizabeth II **Obv:** Head with crown right **Rev:** Johnnie Johnson, emblem in color

| Date | Mintage | VF20 | XF40 | MS60 | MS63 | MS65 |
|---|---|---|---|---|---|---|
| 2008 | 20,000 | PF63 47.00 | PF65 55.00 | | | |

### KM# 32 5 POUNDS

28.28 g., 0.925 Silver 0.841 oz. ASW, 38.61 mm. **Ruler:** Elizabeth II **Obv:** Head with crown right **Rev:** Mosquito, emblem in color

| Date | Mintage | VF20 | XF40 | MS60 | MS63 | MS65 |
|---|---|---|---|---|---|---|
| 2008 | 20,000 | PF63 47.00 | PF65 55.00 | | | |

### KM# 33 5 POUNDS

28.28 g., 0.925 Silver 0.841 oz. ASW, 38.61 mm. **Ruler:** Elizabeth II **Obv:** Head with crown right **Rev:** John Braham, emblem in color

| Date | Mintage | VF20 | XF40 | MS60 | MS63 | MS65 |
|---|---|---|---|---|---|---|
| 2008 | 20,000 | PF63 47.00 | PF65 55.00 | | | |

### KM# 34 5 POUNDS

28.28 g., 0.925 Silver 0.841 oz. ASW, 38.61 mm. **Ruler:** Elizabeth II **Obv:** Head with crown right **Rev:** Bomber Avro 698 Vulcan, emblem in color

| Date | Mintage | VF20 | XF40 | MS60 | MS63 | MS65 |
|---|---|---|---|---|---|---|
| 2008 | 20,000 | PF63 47.00 | PF65 55.00 | | | |

### KM# 35 5 POUNDS

28.28 g., 0.925 Silver 0.841 oz. ASW, 38.61 mm. **Ruler:** Elizabeth II **Obv:** Head with crown right **Rev:** Leonard Cheshire, emblem in color

| Date | Mintage | VF20 | XF40 | MS60 | MS63 | MS65 |
|---|---|---|---|---|---|---|
| 2008 | 20,000 | PF63 47.00 | PF65 55.00 | | | |

### KM# 36 5 POUNDS

28.28 g., 0.925 Silver 0.841 oz. ASW, 38.61 mm. **Ruler:** Elizabeth II **Obv:** Head with crown right **Rev:** Lancaster, emblem in color

| Date | Mintage | VF20 | XF40 | MS60 | MS63 | MS65 |
|---|---|---|---|---|---|---|
| 2008 | 20,000 | PF63 47.00 | PF65 55.00 | | | |

### KM# 37 5 POUNDS

28.28 g., 0.925 Silver 0.841 oz. ASW, 38.61 mm. **Ruler:** Elizabeth II **Obv:** Head with crown right **Rev:** Guy Penrose Gibson, emblem in color

| Date | Mintage | VF20 | XF40 | MS60 | MS63 | MS65 |
|---|---|---|---|---|---|---|
| 2008 | 20,000 | PF63 47.00 | PF65 55.00 | | | |

### KM# 38 5 POUNDS

28.28 g., 0.925 Silver 0.841 oz. ASW, 38.61 mm. **Ruler:** Elizabeth II **Obv:** Head with crown right **Rev:** Harrier, emblem in color

| Date | Mintage | VF20 | XF40 | MS60 | MS63 | MS65 |
|---|---|---|---|---|---|---|
| 2008 | 20,000 | PF63 47.00 | PF65 55.00 | | | |

### KM# 39 5 POUNDS

28.28 g., 0.925 Silver 0.841 oz. ASW, 38.61 mm. **Ruler:** Elizabeth II **Obv:** Head with crown right **Rev:** David Lord, emblem in color

| Date | Mintage | VF20 | XF40 | MS60 | MS63 | MS65 |
|---|---|---|---|---|---|---|
| 2008 | 20,000 | PF63 47.00 | PF65 55.00 | | | |

### KM# 40 5 POUNDS

28.28 g., 0.925 Silver 0.841 oz. ASW, 38.61 mm. **Ruler:** Elizabeth II **Obv:** Head with crown right **Rev:** The Gnat, emblem in color

| Date | Mintage | VF20 | XF40 | MS60 | MS63 | MS65 |
|---|---|---|---|---|---|---|
| 2008 | 20,000 | PF63 47.00 | PF65 55.00 | | | |

### KM# 41 5 POUNDS

28.28 g., 0.925 Silver 0.841 oz. ASW, 38.61 mm. **Ruler:** Elizabeth II **Obv:** Head with crown right **Rev:** Ray Hanna, emblem in color

| Date | Mintage | VF20 | XF40 | MS60 | MS63 | MS65 |
|---|---|---|---|---|---|---|
| 2008 | 20,000 | PF63 47.00 | PF65 55.00 | | | |

### KM# 42 5 POUNDS

28.28 g., 0.925 Silver 0.841 oz. ASW, 38.61 mm. **Ruler:** Elizabeth II **Obv:** Head with crown right **Rev:** SESA, emblem in color

| Date | Mintage | VF20 | XF40 | MS60 | MS63 | MS65 |
|---|---|---|---|---|---|---|
| 2008 | 20,000 | PF63 47.00 | PF65 55.00 | | | |

### KM# 43 5 POUNDS

28.28 g., 0.925 Silver 0.841 oz. ASW, 38.61 mm. **Ruler:** Elizabeth II **Obv:** Head with crown right **Rev:** Mick Mannock, emblem in color

| Date | Mintage | VF20 | XF40 | MS60 | MS63 | MS65 |
|---|---|---|---|---|---|---|
| 2008 | — | PF63 47.00 | PF65 55.00 | | | |

### KM# 44 5 POUNDS

28.28 g., 0.925 Silver 0.841 oz. ASW, 38.61 mm. **Ruler:** Elizabeth II **Obv:** Head with crown right **Rev:** Typhoon, emblem in color

| Date | Mintage | VF20 | XF40 | MS60 | MS63 | MS65 |
|---|---|---|---|---|---|---|
| 2008 | 20,000 | PF63 47.00 | PF65 55.00 | | | |

### KM# 45 5 POUNDS

28.28 g., 0.925 Silver 0.841 oz. ASW, 38.61 mm. **Ruler:** Elizabeth II **Obv:** Head with crown right **Rev:** Sir Hugh Trenchard, emblem in color

| Date | Mintage | VF20 | XF40 | MS60 | MS63 | MS65 |
|---|---|---|---|---|---|---|
| 2008 | 20,000 | PF63 47.00 | PF65 55.00 | | | |

### KM# 59 5 POUNDS

28.28 g., 0.925 Silver 0.841 oz. ASW, 38.61 mm. **Ruler:** Elizabeth II **Obv:** Head with tiara right **Rev:** Flags of Commonwealth nations on globe

| Date | Mintage | VF20 | XF40 | MS60 | MS63 | MS65 |
|---|---|---|---|---|---|---|
| 2012 | — | PF63 45.00 | PF65 55.00 | | | |

### KM# 46 25 POUNDS

7.98 g., 0.9167 Gold 0.2352 oz. AGW, 22 mm. **Ruler:** Elizabeth II **Obv:** Head with crown right **Rev:** Hurricane

| Date | Mintage | VF20 | XF40 | MS60 | MS63 | MS65 |
|---|---|---|---|---|---|---|
| 2008 | 500 | PF65 500 | | | | |

### KM# 47 25 POUNDS

7.98 g., 0.9167 Gold 0.2352 oz. AGW, 22 mm. **Ruler:** Elizabeth II **Obv:** Head with crown right **Rev:** Spitfire

| Date | Mintage | VF20 | XF40 | MS60 | MS63 | MS65 |
|---|---|---|---|---|---|---|
| 2008 | 500 | PF65 500 | | | | |

### KM# 48 25 POUNDS

7.98 g., 0.9167 Gold 0.2352 oz. AGW, 22 mm. **Ruler:** Elizabeth II **Obv:** Head with crown right **Rev:** Mosquito

| Date | Mintage | VF20 | XF40 | MS60 | MS63 | MS65 |
|---|---|---|---|---|---|---|
| 2008 | 500 | PF65 500 | | | | |

### KM# 49 25 POUNDS

7.98 g., 0.9167 Gold 0.2352 oz. AGW, 22 mm. **Ruler:** Elizabeth II **Obv:** Head with crown right **Rev:** Bomber Avro 698 Vulcan

| Date | Mintage | VF20 | XF40 | MS60 | MS63 | MS65 |
|---|---|---|---|---|---|---|
| 2008 | 500 | PF65 500 | | | | |

### KM# 50 25 POUNDS

7.98 g., 0.9167 Gold 0.2352 oz. AGW, 22 mm. **Ruler:** Elizabeth II **Obv:** Head with crown right **Rev:** Lancaster

| Date | Mintage | VF20 | XF40 | MS60 | MS63 | MS65 |
|---|---|---|---|---|---|---|
| 2008 | 500 | PF65 500 | | | | |

### KM# 51 25 POUNDS

7.98 g., 0.9167 Gold 0.2352 oz. AGW, 22 mm. **Ruler:** Elizabeth II **Obv:** Head with crown right **Rev:** Harrier

| Date | Mintage | VF20 | XF40 | MS60 | MS63 | MS65 |
|---|---|---|---|---|---|---|
| 2008 | 500 | PF65 500 | | | | |

### KM# 52 25 POUNDS

7.98 g., 0.9167 Gold 0.2352 oz. AGW, 22 mm. **Ruler:** Elizabeth II **Obv:** Head with crown right **Rev:** The Gnat

| Date | Mintage | VF20 | XF40 | MS60 | MS63 | MS65 |
|---|---|---|---|---|---|---|
| 2008 | 500 | PF65 500 | | | | |

### KM# 53 25 POUNDS

7.98 g., 0.9167 Gold 0.2352 oz. AGW, 22 mm. **Ruler:** Elizabeth II **Obv:** Head with crown right **Rev:** SESA

| Date | Mintage | VF20 | XF40 | MS60 | MS63 | MS65 |
|---|---|---|---|---|---|---|
| 2008 | 500 | PF65 500 | | | | |

### KM# 54 25 POUNDS

7.98 g., 0.9167 Gold 0.2352 oz. AGW, 22 mm. **Ruler:** Elizabeth II **Obv:** Head with crown right **Rev:** Typhoon

| Date | Mintage | VF20 | XF40 | MS60 | MS63 | MS65 |
|---|---|---|---|---|---|---|
| 2008 | 500 | PF65 500 | | | | |

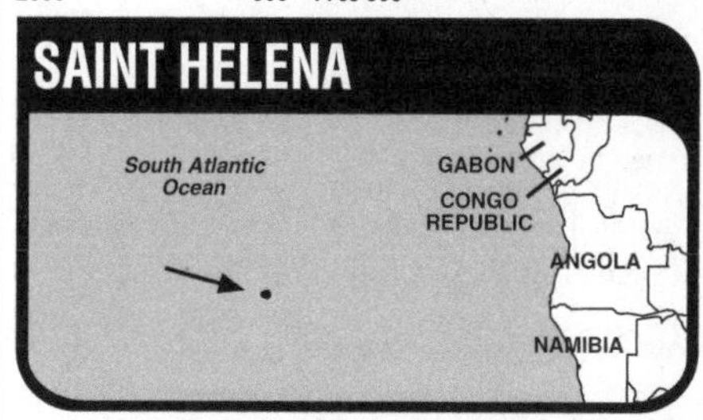


Saint Helena, a British colony located about 1,150 miles (1,850 km.) from the west coast of Africa, has an area of 47 sq. mi. (410 sq. km.) and a population of *7,000. Capital: Jamestown. Flax, lace, and rope are produced for export. Ascension and Tristan da Cunha are dependencies of Saint Helena.

**MONETARY SYSTEM**

100 Pence = 1 Pound

## BRITISH COLONY

## STANDARD COINAGE

### KM# 19 50 PENCE

38.60 g., Copper-Nickel, 38.6 mm. **Ruler:** Elizabeth II **Subject:** 75th Birthday of Queen Elizabeth II **Obv:** Crowned bust right **Rev:** Bust facing within circle and rose sprigs **Edge:** Reeded

| Date | Mintage | VF20 | XF40 | MS60 | MS63 | MS65 |
|---|---|---|---|---|---|---|
| 2001 | — | — | — | — | 6.00 | 9.00 |

### KM# 19a 50 PENCE

28.28 g., 0.925 Silver 0.841 oz. ASW, 38.6 mm. **Ruler:** Elizabeth II **Subject:** 75th Birthday of Queen Elizabeth II **Obv:** Crowned bust right **Rev:** Bust facing within circle and rose sprigs **Edge:** Reeded

| Date | Mintage | VF20 | XF40 | MS60 | MS63 | MS65 |
|---|---|---|---|---|---|---|
| 2001 | 10,000 | PF63 40.00 | PF65 45.00 | | | |

### KM# 19b 50 PENCE

47.54 g., 0.9166 Gold 1.401 oz. AGW, 38.6 mm. **Ruler:** Elizabeth II **Subject:** 75th Birthday of Queen Elizabeth II **Obv:** Crowned bust right **Rev:** Bust facing within circle and rose sprigs **Edge:** Reeded

| Date | Mintage | VF20 | XF40 | MS60 | MS63 | MS65 |
|---|---|---|---|---|---|---|
| 2001 | 75 | PF65 2,750 | | | | |

### KM# 20 50 PENCE

28.55 g., Copper-Nickel, 38.6 mm. **Ruler:** Elizabeth II **Subject:** Queen Victoria's Death **Obv:** Crowned bust right **Rev:** Half-length figure facing and ship within circle **Edge:** Reeded

| Date | Mintage | VF20 | XF40 | MS60 | MS63 | MS65 |
|---|---|---|---|---|---|---|
| 2001 | — | — | — | — | 6.00 | 9.00 |

### KM# 20a 50 PENCE

28.28 g., 0.925 Silver 0.841 oz. ASW, 38.6 mm. **Ruler:** Elizabeth II **Subject:** Centennial - Death of Queen Victoria **Obv:** Crowned bust right **Rev:** Half-length figure facing and ship within circle **Edge:** Reeded

| Date | Mintage | VF20 | XF40 | MS60 | MS63 | MS65 |
|---|---|---|---|---|---|---|
| 2001 | 10,000 | PF63 40.00 | PF65 45.00 | | | |

**KM# 20b 50 PENCE**

47.54 g., 0.9166 Gold 1.401 oz. AGW, 38.6 mm. **Ruler:** Elizabeth II **Subject:** Centennial - Death of Queen Victoria **Obv:** Crowned bust right **Rev:** Half-length figure facing and ship within circle **Edge:** Reeded

| Date | Mintage | VF20 | XF40 | MS60 | MS63 | MS65 |
|---|---|---|---|---|---|---|
| 2001 | 100 | PF65 2,700 | | | | |

**KM# 23 50 PENCE**

28.28 g., Copper-Nickel, 38.6 mm. **Ruler:** Elizabeth II **Subject:** 50th Anniversary - Queen Elizabeth II's Accession **Obv:** Crowned bust right **Rev:** Crown on pillow within circle **Edge:** Reeded

| Date | Mintage | VF20 | XF40 | MS60 | MS63 | MS65 |
|---|---|---|---|---|---|---|
| ND(2002) | — | — | — | — | 6.00 | 9.00 |

**KM# 23a 50 PENCE**

28.28 g., 0.925 Silver 0.841 oz. ASW, 38.6 mm. **Ruler:** Elizabeth II **Subject:** 50th Anniversary - Queen Elizabeth's Accession **Obv:** Crowned bust right **Rev:** Crown on pillow within circle **Edge:** Reeded

| Date | Mintage | VF20 | XF40 | MS60 | MS63 | MS65 |
|---|---|---|---|---|---|---|
| ND(2002) | 10,000 | PF63 38.00 | PF65 42.00 | | | |

**KM# 24 50 PENCE**

28.28 g., Copper-Nickel, 38.6 mm. **Ruler:** Elizabeth II **Subject:** To Celebrate a Life of Duty, Dignity and Love, 1900-2002 **Obv:** Crowned bust right **Rev:** Conjoined busts right **Edge:** Reeded

| Date | Mintage | VF20 | XF40 | MS60 | MS63 | MS65 |
|---|---|---|---|---|---|---|
| ND(2002) | — | — | — | — | 6.00 | 9.00 |

**KM# 24a 50 PENCE**

28.28 g., 0.925 Silver 0.841 oz. ASW, 38.6 mm. **Ruler:** Elizabeth II **Subject:** To Celebrate a Life of Duty, Dignity and Love, 1900-2002 **Obv:** Crowned bust right **Rev:** Conjoined busts right **Edge:** Reeded

| Date | Mintage | VF20 | XF40 | MS60 | MS63 | MS65 |
|---|---|---|---|---|---|---|
| ND(2002) | 10,000 | PF63 38.00 | PF65 42.00 | | | |

**KM# 25 50 PENCE**

28.28 g., Copper-Nickel, 38.6 mm. **Ruler:** Elizabeth II **Subject:** 500th Anniversary - Discovery of St. Helena **Obv:** Crowned bust right **Rev:** Half length figure right and ship above 1502 date **Edge:** Reeded

| Date | Mintage | VF20 | XF40 | MS60 | MS63 | MS65 |
|---|---|---|---|---|---|---|
| ND(2002) | — | — | — | — | 9.00 | 12.00 |

**KM# 25a 50 PENCE**

28.28 g., 0.925 Silver 0.841 oz. ASW, 38.6 mm. **Ruler:** Elizabeth II **Subject:** 500th Anniversary - Discovery of St. Helena **Obv:** Crowned bust right **Rev:** Half length figure right and ship above 1502 date **Edge:** Reeded

| Date | Mintage | VF20 | XF40 | MS60 | MS63 | MS65 |
|---|---|---|---|---|---|---|
| ND(2002) | 5,000 | PF63 45.00 | PF65 50.00 | | | |

**KM# 26 50 PENCE**

28.28 g., Copper-Nickel, 38.6 mm. **Ruler:** Elizabeth II **Obv:** Crowned bust right **Rev:** Bust 1/4 left, ship HMS Paramour and a comet **Edge:** Reeded

| Date | Mintage | VF20 | XF40 | MS60 | MS63 | MS65 |
|---|---|---|---|---|---|---|
| ND(2002) | — | — | — | — | 9.00 | 12.00 |

**KM# 26a 50 PENCE**

28.28 g., 0.925 Silver 0.841 oz. ASW, 38.6 mm. **Ruler:** Elizabeth II **Obv:** Crowned bust right **Rev:** Bust 1/4 left, ship HMS Paramour and a comet **Edge:** Reeded

| Date | Mintage | VF20 | XF40 | MS60 | MS63 | MS65 |
|---|---|---|---|---|---|---|
| ND(2002) | 5,000 | PF63 45.00 | PF65 50.00 | | | |

**KM# 27 50 PENCE**

28.28 g., Copper-Nickel, 38.6 mm. **Ruler:** Elizabeth II **Obv:** Crowned bust right **Rev:** Bust 1/4 right and the HMS Resolution **Edge:** Reeded

| Date | Mintage | VF20 | XF40 | MS60 | MS63 | MS65 |
|---|---|---|---|---|---|---|
| ND(2002) | — | — | — | — | 9.00 | 12.00 |

**KM# 27a 50 PENCE**

28.28 g., 0.925 Silver 0.841 oz. ASW, 38.6 mm. **Ruler:** Elizabeth II **Obv:** Crowned bust right **Rev:** Bust 1/4 right and the HMS Resolution **Edge:** Reeded

| Date | Mintage | VF20 | XF40 | MS60 | MS63 | MS65 |
|---|---|---|---|---|---|---|
| ND(2002) | 5,000 | PF63 45.00 | PF65 50.00 | | | |

**KM# 28 50 PENCE**

28.28 g., Copper-Nickel, 38.6 mm. **Ruler:** Elizabeth II **Obv:** Crowned bust right **Rev:** Half length figure facing and the ship HMS Northumberland **Edge:** Reeded

| Date | Mintage | VF20 | XF40 | MS60 | MS63 | MS65 |
|---|---|---|---|---|---|---|
| ND(2002) | — | — | — | — | 9.00 | 12.00 |

**KM# 28a 50 PENCE**

28.28 g., 0.925 Silver 0.841 oz. ASW, 38.6 mm. **Ruler:** Elizabeth II **Obv:** Queen Elizabeth II **Rev:** Napoleon and the ship HMS Northumberland **Edge:** Reeded

| Date | Mintage | VF20 | XF40 | MS60 | MS63 | MS65 |
|---|---|---|---|---|---|---|
| ND(2002) | 5,000 | PF63 45.00 | PF65 50.00 | | | |

**KM# 29 50 PENCE**

28.28 g., Copper-Nickel, 38.6 mm. **Ruler:** Elizabeth II **Obv:** Crowned bust right **Rev:** Four conjoined busts left plus the HMS Vanguard **Edge:** Reeded

| Date | Mintage | VF20 | XF40 | MS60 | MS63 | MS65 |
|---|---|---|---|---|---|---|
| ND(2002) | — | — | — | — | 6.00 | 9.00 |

**KM# 29a 50 PENCE**

28.28 g., 0.925 Silver 0.841 oz. ASW, 38.6 mm. **Ruler:** Elizabeth II **Obv:** Crowned bust right **Rev:** Four conjoined busts left plus the HMS Vanguard **Edge:** Reeded

| Date | Mintage | VF20 | XF40 | MS60 | MS63 | MS65 |
|---|---|---|---|---|---|---|
| ND(2002) | 5,000 | PF63 40.00 | PF65 45.00 | | | |

**KM# 30 50 PENCE**

28.28 g., Copper-Nickel, 38.6 mm. **Ruler:** Elizabeth II **Subject:** 50th Anniversary of Queen Elizabeth's Coronation **Obv:** Crowned bust right **Rev:** Crowned Queen facing with scepter and orb **Edge:** Reeded

| Date | Mintage | VF20 | XF40 | MS60 | MS63 | MS65 |
|---|---|---|---|---|---|---|
| ND(2003) | — | — | — | — | 9.00 | 12.00 |

**KM# 30a 50 PENCE**

28.28 g., 0.925 Silver 0.841 oz. ASW, 38.6 mm. **Ruler:** Elizabeth II **Subject:** 50th Anniversary - Queen Elizabeth's Coronation **Obv:** Crowned bust right **Rev:** Crowned Queen facing with scepter and orb **Edge:** Reeded

| Date | Mintage | VF20 | XF40 | MS60 | MS63 | MS65 |
|---|---|---|---|---|---|---|
| ND(2003) | 5,000 | PF63 45.00 | PF65 50.00 | | | |

**KM# 30b 50 PENCE**

39.94 g., 0.9166 Gold 1.177 oz. AGW, 38.6 mm. **Ruler:** Elizabeth II **Subject:** 50th Anniversary of Queen's Coronation **Obv:** Crowned bust right **Rev:** Crowned Queen facing with scepter and orb **Edge:** Reeded

| Date | Mintage | VF20 | XF40 | MS60 | MS63 | MS65 |
|---|---|---|---|---|---|---|
| ND(2003) | 50 | PF65 2,500 | | | | |

**KM# 31 50 PENCE**
28.28 g., Copper-Nickel, 38.6 mm. **Ruler:** Elizabeth II **Subject:** 50th Anniversary of Coronation **Obv:** Crowned bust right **Rev:** Coronation implements **Edge:** Reeded

| Date | Mintage | VF20 | XF40 | MS60 | MS63 | MS65 |
|---|---|---|---|---|---|---|
| ND(2003) | — | — | — | — | 9.00 | 12.00 |

**KM# 31a 50 PENCE**
28.28 g., 0.925 Silver 0.841 oz. ASW, 38.6 mm. **Ruler:** Elizabeth II **Subject:** 50th Anniversary - Queen Elizabeth II's Coronation **Obv:** Crowned bust right **Rev:** Coronation implements **Edge:** Reeded

| Date | Mintage | VF20 | XF40 | MS60 | MS63 | MS65 |
|---|---|---|---|---|---|---|
| ND(2003) | 5,000 | PF63 45.00 | PF65 50.00 | | | |

**KM# 31b 50 PENCE**
39.94 g., 0.9166 Gold 1.177 oz. AGW, 38.6 mm. **Ruler:** Elizabeth II **Subject:** 50th Anniversary of Coronation **Obv:** Crowned bust right **Rev:** Coronation implements **Edge:** Reeded

| Date | Mintage | VF20 | XF40 | MS60 | MS63 | MS65 |
|---|---|---|---|---|---|---|
| ND(2003) | 50 | PF65 2,500 | | | | |

## PIEDFORT

| KM# | Date | Mintage | Identification | Mkt Val |
|---|---|---|---|---|
| P3 | ND(2002) | 500 | 50 Pence 0.925 Silver Proof. | 125 |

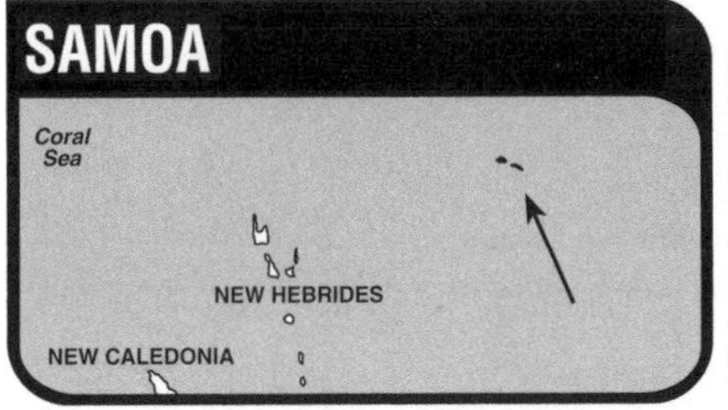


The Independent State of Samoa (formerly Western Samoa), located in the Pacific Ocean 1,600 miles (2,574 km.) northeast of New Zealand, has an area of 1,097 sq. mi. (2,860 sq. km.) and a population of *182,000. Capital: Apia. The economy is based on agriculture, fishing and tourism. Copra, cocoa and bananas are exported.

Samoa is a member of the Commonwealth of Nations. The Chief Executive is Chief of State. The prime minister is the Head of Government. The present Head of State, Malietoa Tanumafili II, holds his position for life. The Legislative Assembly will elect future Heads of State for 5-year terms.

Samoa, which had used New Zealand coinage, converted to a decimal coinage in 1967.

**RULER**
Malietoa Tanumafili II, 1962-2007
Tuiatua Tupua Tamasese Efi, 2007-

**MONETARY SYSTEM**
100 Sene = 1 Tala

# CONSTITUTIONAL MONARCHY

### Commonwealth of Nations

## STANDARD COINAGE

**KM# 131 5 SENE**
2.84 g., Copper-Nickel, 19.5 mm. **Obv:** Head left **Rev:** Pineapple and value **Edge:** Reeded **Note:** Western" dropped from country name

| Date | Mintage | VF20 | XF40 | MS60 | MS63 | MS65 |
|---|---|---|---|---|---|---|
| 2002 | — | — | 0.30 | 0.40 | 0.50 | 1.00 |
| 2006 | — | — | 0.30 | 0.40 | 0.50 | 1.00 |
| 2010 | — | — | 0.30 | 0.40 | 0.50 | 1.00 |

**KM# 167 5 SENE**
Nickel Plated Steel

| Date | Mintage | VF20 | XF40 | MS60 | MS63 | MS65 |
|---|---|---|---|---|---|---|
| 2010 | — | — | — | 0.40 | 0.50 | 1.00 |

**KM# 132 10 SENE**
5.65 g., Copper-Nickel, 23.6 mm. **Obv:** Head left **Rev:** Taro leaves and value **Edge:** Reeded **Note:** Western" dropped from country name

| Date | Mintage | VF20 | XF40 | MS60 | MS63 | MS65 |
|---|---|---|---|---|---|---|
| 2002 | — | — | 0.35 | 0.50 | 0.75 | 1.50 |
| 2006 | — | — | 0.35 | 0.50 | 0.75 | 1.50 |
| 2010 | — | — | 0.35 | 0.50 | 0.75 | 1.50 |

**KM# 168 10 SENE**
2.79 g., Nickel Plated Steel, 18.5 mm. **Obv:** President Efi bust 3/4 left **Rev:** Fautasi, boat race

| Date | Mintage | VF20 | XF40 | MS60 | MS63 | MS65 |
|---|---|---|---|---|---|---|
| 2010 | — | — | 0.35 | 0.50 | 0.75 | 1.50 |
| 2011 | — | — | 0.35 | 0.50 | 0.75 | 1.50 |

**KM# 168a 10 SENE**
3.52 g., 0.999 Silver 0.1131 oz. ASW, 19 mm. **Obv:** Efi portrait **Rev:** Fautasi

| Date | Mintage | VF20 | XF40 | MS60 | MS63 | MS65 |
|---|---|---|---|---|---|---|
| 2011 | 2,500 | PF65 5.00 | | | | |

**KM# 133 20 SENE**
11.40 g., Copper-Nickel, 28.45 mm. **Obv:** Head left **Rev:** Breadfruits and value **Edge:** Reeded **Note:** Western" dropped from country name

| Date | Mintage | VF20 | XF40 | MS60 | MS63 | MS65 |
|---|---|---|---|---|---|---|
| 2002 | — | — | 0.40 | 0.60 | 1.00 | 2.00 |
| 2006 | — | — | 0.40 | 0.60 | 1.00 | 2.00 |

**KM# 169 20 SENE**
3.64 g., Nickel Plated Steel, 22 mm. **Obv:** Efi portrait 3/4 left **Rev:** Teuila flower (Alpina Purpurata)

| Date | Mintage | VF20 | XF40 | MS60 | MS63 | MS65 |
|---|---|---|---|---|---|---|
| 2010 | — | — | 0.40 | 0.60 | 1.00 | 2.00 |
| 2011 | — | — | 0.40 | 0.60 | 1.00 | 2.00 |

**KM# 169a 20 SENE**
4.64 g., 0.999 Silver 0.149 oz. ASW, 21 mm. **Obv:** Efi portrait **Rev:** Alpinia purpurata

| Date | Mintage | VF20 | XF40 | MS60 | MS63 | MS65 |
|---|---|---|---|---|---|---|
| 2011 | 2,500 | PF65 7.00 | | | | |

**KM# 134 50 SENE**
14.13 g., Copper-Nickel, 32.3 mm. **Obv:** Head left **Rev:** Banana tree and value **Edge:** Reeded **Note:** Western" dropped from country name

| Date | Mintage | VF20 | XF40 | MS60 | MS63 | MS65 |
|---|---|---|---|---|---|---|
| 2002 | — | — | 0.75 | 1.25 | 2.00 | 3.50 |
| 2006 | — | — | 0.75 | 1.25 | 2.00 | 3.50 |
| 2010 | — | — | 0.75 | 1.25 | 2.00 | 3.50 |

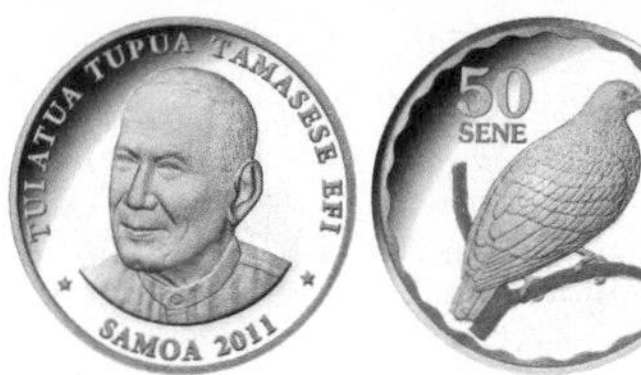

**KM# 170 50 SENE**
5.47 g., Nickel Plated Steel, 23.5 mm. **Obv:** Efi portrait 3/4 left **Rev:** Manumea bird (Didunculus strigiostris) right

| Date | Mintage | VF20 | XF40 | MS60 | MS63 | MS65 |
|---|---|---|---|---|---|---|
| 2010 | — | — | 0.75 | 1.25 | 2.00 | 3.50 |
| 2011 | — | — | 0.75 | 1.25 | 2.00 | 3.50 |

**KM# 170a 50 SENE**
6.95 g., 0.999 Silver 0.2232 oz. ASW, 24.2 mm. **Obv:** Efi portrait **Rev:** Columbidae right

| Date | Mintage | VF20 | XF40 | MS60 | MS63 | MS65 |
|---|---|---|---|---|---|---|
| 2011 | 2,500 | PF65 9.50 | | | | |

**KM# 135 TALA**
9.50 g., Brass, 30 mm. **Obv:** Head left **Rev:** National arms above value and banner flanked by sprigs **Edge:** Reeded **Note:** Western" dropped from country name

| Date | Mintage | VF20 | XF40 | MS60 | MS63 | MS65 |
|---|---|---|---|---|---|---|
| 2002 | — | — | — | 1.50 | 2.50 | 3.50 |
| 2006 | — | — | — | 1.50 | 2.50 | 3.50 |

**KM# 180 TALA**
0.80 g., 0.9999 Gold 0.0257 oz. AGW, 11 mm. **Obv:** National arms **Rev:** Maya Calendar

| Date | Mintage | VF20 | XF40 | MS60 | MS63 | MS65 |
|---|---|---|---|---|---|---|
| 2008 | 10,000 | PF65 51.00 | | | | |

**KM# 150 TALA**
Goldine Plated Metal **Subject:** Thomas Mann **Obv:** Arms **Rev:** Bust facing

| Date | Mintage | VF20 | XF40 | MS60 | MS63 | MS65 |
|---|---|---|---|---|---|---|
| 2009 | — | — | — | — | — | 30.00 |

**KM# 151 TALA**
Goldine Plated Metal **Subject:** Hercules & Hydra

| Date | Mintage | VF20 | XF40 | MS60 | MS63 | MS65 |
|---|---|---|---|---|---|---|
| 2009 | — | — | — | — | — | 25.00 |

**KM# 152 TALA**
Goldine Plated Metal **Subject:** Alhambra

| Date | Mintage | VF20 | XF40 | MS60 | MS63 | MS65 |
|---|---|---|---|---|---|---|
| 2009 | — | — | — | — | — | 25.00 |

**KM# 153 TALA**
Goldine Plated Metal **Rev:** Golden horn

| Date | Mintage | VF20 | XF40 | MS60 | MS63 | MS65 |
|---|---|---|---|---|---|---|
| 2009 | — | — | — | — | — | 25.00 |

**KM# 154 TALA**
Goldine Plated Metal **Rev:** Sphinx

| Date | Mintage | VF20 | XF40 | MS60 | MS63 | MS65 |
|---|---|---|---|---|---|---|
| 2009 | — | — | — | — | — | 25.00 |

**KM# 155 TALA**
Goldine Plated Metal **Rev:** Kaiser Wilhelm II

| Date | Mintage | VF20 | XF40 | MS60 | MS63 | MS65 |
|---|---|---|---|---|---|---|
| 2009 | — | — | — | — | — | 25.00 |

**KM# 156 TALA**
Goldine Plated Metal **Rev:** Hagia Sophia

| Date | Mintage | VF20 | XF40 | MS60 | MS63 | MS65 |
|---|---|---|---|---|---|---|
| 2009 | — | — | — | — | — | 25.00 |

**KM# 185 TALA**
0.50 g., 0.999 Gold 0.0161 oz. AGW, 11 mm. **Obv:** National arms **Rev:** Barbarossa bust

| Date | Mintage | VF20 | XF40 | MS60 | MS63 | MS65 |
|---|---|---|---|---|---|---|
| 2009 | 10,000 | PF65 36.00 | | | | |

**KM# 186 TALA**
0.50 g., 0.999 Gold 0.0161 oz. AGW, 11 mm. **Obv:** National arms **Rev:** Marcus Tullius Cicero bust facing

| Date | Mintage | VF20 | XF40 | MS60 | MS63 | MS65 |
|---|---|---|---|---|---|---|
| 2009 | 10,000 | PF65 36.00 | | | | |

**KM# 187 TALA**
0.50 g., 0.999 Gold 0.0161 oz. AGW, 11 mm. **Obv:** National arms **Rev:** Marie Curie and atom design

| Date | Mintage | VF20 | XF40 | MS60 | MS63 | MS65 |
|---|---|---|---|---|---|---|
| 2009 | 10,000 | PF65 36.00 | | | | |

**KM# 188 TALA**
26.03 g., Copper-Nickel plated silver, 38.61 mm. **Subject:** London Olympics, 2012 **Obv:** National arms **Rev:** White water kyacker

| Date | Mintage | VF20 | XF40 | MS60 | MS63 | MS65 |
|---|---|---|---|---|---|---|
| 2009 | 30,000 | PF65 15.00 | | | | |

**KM# 189 TALA**
0.50 g., 0.999 Gold 0.0161 oz. AGW, 11 mm. **Obv:** National arms **Rev:** Pallas Athene bust right

| Date | Mintage | VF20 | XF40 | MS60 | MS63 | MS65 |
|---|---|---|---|---|---|---|
| 2009 | 10,000 | PF65 36.00 | | | | |

**KM# 190 TALA**
0.50 g., 0.999 Gold 0.0161 oz. AGW, 11 mm. **Obv:** National arms **Rev:** Basilica of San Marco, Venice

| Date | Mintage | VF20 | XF40 | MS60 | MS63 | MS65 |
|---|---|---|---|---|---|---|
| 2009 | 10,000 | PF65 36.00 | | | | |

**KM# 191 TALA**
0.50 g., 0.9999 Gold 0.0161 oz. AGW, 11 mm. **Obv:** National arms **Rev:** Thomas Mann bust facing

| Date | Mintage | VF20 | XF40 | MS60 | MS63 | MS65 |
|---|---|---|---|---|---|---|
| 2009 | 10,000 | PF65 36.00 | | | | |

**KM# 171 TALA**
6.00 g., Aluminum-Bronze, 21.5 mm. **Rev:** Kava bowl **Shape:** 7-sides

| Date | Mintage | VF20 | XF40 | MS60 | MS63 | MS65 |
|---|---|---|---|---|---|---|
| 2010 | — | — | — | 1.50 | 2.50 | 3.50 |
| 2011 | — | — | — | 1.50 | 2.50 | 3.50 |

**KM# 174 TALA**
0.50 g., 0.999 Gold 0.0161 oz. AGW, 11 mm. **Obv:** National arms **Rev:** Samoan Flying Fox (bat) in flight

| Date | Mintage | VF20 | XF40 | MS60 | MS63 | MS65 |
|---|---|---|---|---|---|---|
| 2010 | 10,000 | PF65 39.00 | | | | |

**KM# 214 TALA**
0.50 g., 0.999 Gold 0.0161 oz. AGW, 11 mm. **Obv:** National arms **Rev:** Nicolaus Copernicus bust at left, solar system

| Date | Mintage | VF20 | XF40 | MS60 | MS63 | MS65 |
|---|---|---|---|---|---|---|
| 2010 | 10,000 | PF65 36.00 | | | | |

**KM# 215 TALA**
0.50 g., 0.999 Gold 0.0161 oz. AGW, 11 mm. **Subject:** German Railways, 175th Anniversary **Obv:** National arms **Rev:** Early steam locomotive and modern high speed train

| Date | Mintage | VF20 | XF40 | MS60 | MS63 | MS65 |
|---|---|---|---|---|---|---|
| 2010 | 5,000 | PF65 36.00 | | | | |

**KM# 216 TALA**
0.50 g., 0.999 Gold 0.0161 oz. AGW, 11 mm. **Obv:** National arms **Rev:** Johannes Hevelius bust at right

| Date | Mintage | VF20 | XF40 | MS60 | MS63 | MS65 |
|---|---|---|---|---|---|---|
| 2010 | 10,000 | PF65 36.00 | | | | |

**KM# 171a TALA**
7.77 g., 0.999 Silver 0.2496 oz. ASW, 21.5 mm. **Obv:** Efi portrait **Rev:** Kava

| Date | Mintage | VF20 | XF40 | MS60 | MS63 | MS65 |
|---|---|---|---|---|---|---|
| 2011 | 2,500 | PF65 12.00 | | | | |

**KM# 219 TALA**
0.50 g., 0.999 Gold 0.0161 oz. AGW, 11 mm. **Obv:** National arms **Rev:** Pope John Paul II lat left holding cross croizer

| Date | Mintage | VF20 | XF40 | MS60 | MS63 | MS65 |
|---|---|---|---|---|---|---|
| 2011 | 10,000 | PF65 36.00 | | | | |

**KM# 230 TALA**
0.999 Silver **Subject:** 50th Anniversary of Independance **Obv:** Kings head 3/4 left **Rev:** Native sailing boat and sunset

| Date | Mintage | VF20 | XF40 | MS60 | MS63 | MS65 |
|---|---|---|---|---|---|---|
| 2012 | Est. 1500 | PF65 75.00 | | | | |

**KM# 257 TALA**
0.50 g., 0.999 Gold 0.0161 oz. AGW, 11 mm. **Subject:** The Brothers Grimm **Obv:** National arms **Rev:** Two portraits left

| Date | Mintage | VF20 | XF40 | MS60 | MS63 | MS65 |
|---|---|---|---|---|---|---|
| 2012 | Est. 5000 | PF65 36.00 | | | | |

**KM# 234 TALA**
0.50 g., 0.585 Gold 0.0094 oz. AGW with 24Kt plating, 11 mm. **Subject:** Copernicus

| Date | Mintage | VF20 | XF40 | MS60 | MS63 | MS65 |
|---|---|---|---|---|---|---|
| 2013 | Est. 5000 | PF65 25.00 | | | | |

**KM# 240 TALA**
0.50 g., 0.585 Gold 0.0094 oz. AGW with 24Kt plating, 11 mm. **Subject:** Moonlanding

| Date | Mintage | VF20 | XF40 | MS60 | MS63 | MS65 |
|---|---|---|---|---|---|---|
| 2013 | Est. 5000 | PF65 25.00 | | | | |

**KM# 178 2 TALA**
8.00 g., Aluminum-Bronze, 25.6 mm. **Obv:** Efi portrait 3/4 right **Rev:** National arms **Shape:** Scalloped

| Date | Mintage | VF20 | XF40 | MS60 | MS63 | MS65 |
|---|---|---|---|---|---|---|
| 2011 | — | — | — | 3.00 | 5.00 | 8.00 |

**KM# 193 2 TALA**
Aluminum-Bronze, 25.6 mm. **Rev:** National arms **Shape:** Scalloped

| Date | Mintage | VF20 | XF40 | MS60 | MS63 | MS65 |
|---|---|---|---|---|---|---|
| 2011 | — | — | — | — | — | 9.00 |

**KM# 193a 2 TALA**
10.37 g., 0.999 Silver 0.3331 oz. ASW, 25.6 mm. **Obv:** Efi portrait **Rev:** National arms

| Date | Mintage | VF20 | XF40 | MS60 | MS63 | MS65 |
|---|---|---|---|---|---|---|
| 2011 | 2,500 | PF65 18.00 | | | | |

**KM# 249 2 TALA**
6.80 g., 0.333 Silver 0.0728 oz. ASW, 30 mm. **Subject:** Porsche 911, 50th Anniversary

| Date | Mintage | VF20 | XF40 | MS60 | MS63 | MS65 |
|---|---|---|---|---|---|---|
| 2013 | Est. 5000 | PF65 40.00 | | | | |

**KM# 250 2 TALA**
6.80 g., 0.333 Silver 0.0728 oz. ASW, 30 mm. **Subject:** Volkswagon Beetle, 75th Anniversary

| Date | Mintage | VF20 | XF40 | MS60 | MS63 | MS65 |
|---|---|---|---|---|---|---|
| 2013 | Est. 5000 | PF65 40.00 | | | | |

**KM# 165 5 TALA**
28.28 g., 0.925 Silver 0.841 oz. ASW, 38.61 mm. **Obv:** National Arms **Rev:** Steam Locomotive centennial

| Date | Mintage | VF20 | XF40 | MS60 | MS63 | MS65 |
|---|---|---|---|---|---|---|
| 2007 | Est. 5000 | PF63 65.00 | PF65 75.00 | | | |

**KM# 181 5 TALA**
28.28 g., 0.925 Silver 0.841 oz. ASW, 38.61 mm. **Obv:** National arms **Rev:** S.M.S. Bismark sailing right

| Date | Mintage | VF20 | XF40 | MS60 | MS63 | MS65 |
|---|---|---|---|---|---|---|
| 2008 | 5,000 | PF65 75.00 | | | | |

**KM# 182 5 TALA**
28.28 g., 0.925 Silver 0.841 oz. ASW, 38.61 mm. **Subject:** Bejing Olympics, 2008 **Obv:** National arms **Rev:** Track runner

| Date | Mintage | VF20 | XF40 | MS60 | MS63 | MS65 |
|---|---|---|---|---|---|---|
| 2008 | 10,000 | PF63 55.00 | PF65 65.00 | | | |

**KM# 166 5 TALA**
31.11 g., 0.999 Silver 0.999 oz. ASW, 38.6 mm. **Obv:** National arms **Rev:** John Paul II at right and as figure in flames

| Date | Mintage | VF20 | XF40 | MS60 | MS63 | MS65 |
|---|---|---|---|---|---|---|
| 2009 | Est. 2000 | PF63 75.00 | PF65 85.00 | | | |

**KM# 179 5 TALA**
31.11 g., 0.999 Silver 0.999 oz. ASW, 38.61 mm. **Subject:** First pacific class locomotive **Obv:** National arms **Rev:** Badische IVf locomotive

| Date | Mintage | VF20 | XF40 | MS60 | MS63 | MS65 |
|---|---|---|---|---|---|---|
| 2009 | 5,000 | PF63 65.00 | PF65 75.00 | | | |

**KM# 192 5 TALA**
28.28 g., 0.925 Silver 0.841 oz. ASW, 38.61 mm. **Subject:** German Railways, 175th Anniversary **Obv:** National arms **Rev:** BR-23 locomotive and V-80 locomotive

| Date | Mintage | VF20 | XF40 | MS60 | MS63 | MS65 |
|---|---|---|---|---|---|---|
| 2009 | 5,000 | **PF63** 65.00 | **PF65** 75.00 | | | |

**KM# 194 5 TALA**
28.28 g., 0.925 Silver 0.841 oz. ASW, 38.61 mm. **Subject:** London Olympics, 2012 **Obv:** National arms **Rev:** White water kyacker

| Date | Mintage | VF20 | XF40 | MS60 | MS63 | MS65 |
|---|---|---|---|---|---|---|
| 2009 Proof | 10,000 | — | — | — | — | 75.00 |

**KM# 217 5 TALA**
28.28 g., 0.925 Silver 0.841 oz. ASW, 38.61 mm. **Subject:** German Railways, 175th Anniversary **Obv:** National arms **Rev:** Montage of locomotive and stations

| Date | Mintage | VF20 | XF40 | MS60 | MS63 | MS65 |
|---|---|---|---|---|---|---|
| 2010 | 5,000 | **PF63** 65.00 | **PF65** 75.00 | | | |

**KM# 218 5 TALA**
28.28 g., 0.925 Silver 0.841 oz. ASW, 38.61 mm. **Obv:** National arms **Rev:** Lilienthal Glider

| Date | Mintage | VF20 | XF40 | MS60 | MS63 | MS65 |
|---|---|---|---|---|---|---|
| 2010 | Est. 5000 | **PF63** 65.00 | **PF65** 75.00 | | | |

**KM# 258 5 TALA**
12.00 g., 0.925 Silver 0.3569 oz. ASW, 38.61 mm. **Subject:** First Commandment **Obv:** National arms

| Date | Mintage | VF20 | XF40 | MS60 | MS63 | MS65 |
|---|---|---|---|---|---|---|
| 2012 | 5,000 | **PF65** 40.00 | | | | |

**KM# 259 5 TALA**
12.00 g., 0.925 Silver 0.3569 oz. ASW, 38.61 mm. **Subject:** Second Commandment **Obv:** National arms

| Date | Mintage | VF20 | XF40 | MS60 | MS63 | MS65 |
|---|---|---|---|---|---|---|
| 2012 | 5,000 | **PF65** 40.00 | | | | |

**KM# 260 5 TALA**
12.00 g., 0.925 Silver 0.3569 oz. ASW, 38.61 mm. **Subject:** Third Commandment **Obv:** National arms

| Date | Mintage | VF20 | XF40 | MS60 | MS63 | MS65 |
|---|---|---|---|---|---|---|
| 2012 | 5,000 | **PF65** 40.00 | | | | |

**KM# 261 5 TALA**
12.00 g., 0.925 Silver 0.3569 oz. ASW, 38.61 mm. **Subject:** Fourth Commandment **Obv:** National arms

| Date | Mintage | VF20 | XF40 | MS60 | MS63 | MS65 |
|---|---|---|---|---|---|---|
| 2012 | 5,000 | **PF65** 40.00 | | | | |

**KM# 262 5 TALA**
12.00 g., 0.925 Silver 0.3569 oz. ASW, 38.61 mm. **Subject:** Fifth Commandment **Obv:** National arms

| Date | Mintage | VF20 | XF40 | MS60 | MS63 | MS65 |
|---|---|---|---|---|---|---|
| 2012 | 5,000 | **PF65** 40.00 | | | | |

**KM# 263 5 TALA**
12.00 g., 0.925 Silver 0.3569 oz. ASW, 38.61 mm. **Subject:** Sixth Commandment **Obv:** National arms

| Date | Mintage | VF20 | XF40 | MS60 | MS63 | MS65 |
|---|---|---|---|---|---|---|
| 2012 | 5,000 | **PF65** 40.00 | | | | |

**KM# 264 5 TALA**
12.00 g., 0.925 Silver 0.3569 oz. ASW, 38.61 mm. **Subject:** Seventh Commandment **Obv:** National arms

| Date | Mintage | VF20 | XF40 | MS60 | MS63 | MS65 |
|---|---|---|---|---|---|---|
| 2012 | 5,000 | **PF65** 40.00 | | | | |

**KM# 265 5 TALA**
12.00 g., 0.925 Silver 0.3569 oz. ASW, 38.61 mm. **Subject:** Eighth Commandment **Obv:** National arms

| Date | Mintage | VF20 | XF40 | MS60 | MS63 | MS65 |
|---|---|---|---|---|---|---|
| 2012 | 5,000 | **PF65** 40.00 | | | | |

**KM# 266 5 TALA**
12.00 g., 0.925 Silver 0.3569 oz. ASW, 38.61 mm. **Subject:** Ninth Commandment **Obv:** National arms

| Date | Mintage | VF20 | XF40 | MS60 | MS63 | MS65 |
|---|---|---|---|---|---|---|
| 2012 | 5,000 | **PF65** 40.00 | | | | |

### KM# 267 5 TALA

12.00 g., 0.925 Silver 0.3569 oz. ASW, 38.61 mm. **Subject:** Tenth Commandment **Obv:** National arms

| Date | Mintage | VF20 | XF40 | MS60 | MS63 | MS65 |
|---|---|---|---|---|---|---|
| 2012 | 5,000 | PF65 12.00 | | | | |

### KM# 268 5 TALA

20.00 g., 0.925 Silver 0.5948 oz. ASW **Subject:** World Champion Train, 1954 **Obv:** National Arms **Rev:** Train

| Date | Mintage | VF20 | XF40 | MS60 | MS63 | MS65 |
|---|---|---|---|---|---|---|
| 2012 | 5,000 | PF65 55.00 | | | | |

### KM# 269 5 TALA

15.00 g., 0.925 Silver 0.4461 oz. ASW, 34 mm. **Subject:** Frederick II, 300th Anniversary **Obv:** National arms **Rev:** Portrait at center of five designs

| Date | Mintage | VF20 | XF40 | MS60 | MS63 | MS65 |
|---|---|---|---|---|---|---|
| 2012 | 5,000 | PF65 60.00 | | | | |

### KM# 226 5 TALA

20.00 g., 0.999 Silver 0.6424 oz. ASW, 38.61 mm. **Subject:** Martin Luther King Jr. - I Have a Dream Speech, 50th Anniversary **Obv:** National Arms **Rev:** MLK portrait with 24kt. gold

| Date | Mintage | VF20 | XF40 | MS60 | MS63 | MS65 |
|---|---|---|---|---|---|---|
| 2013 | Est. 2500 | PF65 50.00 | | | | |

### KM# 227 5 TALA

20.00 g., 0.999 Silver 0.6424 oz. ASW, 38.61 mm. **Subject:** Martin Luther King's I Have a Dream Speech, 50th Anniversary **Obv:** National Arms **Rev:** MLK portrait at left - text at right

| Date | Mintage | VF20 | XF40 | MS60 | MS63 | MS65 |
|---|---|---|---|---|---|---|
| 2013 | Est. 2500 | PF65 50.00 | | | | |

### KM# 232 5 TALA

20.00 g., 0.925 Silver 0.5948 oz. ASW, 38.61 mm. **Subject:** 2016 Olympics - Cycling

| Date | Mintage | VF20 | XF40 | MS60 | MS63 | MS65 |
|---|---|---|---|---|---|---|
| 2013 | Est. 10000 | PF65 50.00 | | | | |

### KM# 233 5 TALA

20.00 g., 0.925 Silver 0.5948 oz. ASW, 38.61 mm. **Subject:** 2014 FIFA World Cup - Brazil

| Date | Mintage | VF20 | XF40 | MS60 | MS63 | MS65 |
|---|---|---|---|---|---|---|
| 2013 | Est. 10000 | PF65 50.00 | | | | |

### KM# 235 5 TALA

28.28 g., 0.925 Silver 0.841 oz. ASW, 38.61 mm. **Subject:** Nicolaus Copernicus

| Date | Mintage | VF20 | XF40 | MS60 | MS63 | MS65 |
|---|---|---|---|---|---|---|
| 2013 | Est. 7500 | PF63 65.00 | PF65 75.00 | | | |

### KM# 236 5 TALA

0.50 g., 0.999 Gold 0.0161 oz. AGW, 11 mm. **Subject:** Magna Mater Austriae

| Date | Mintage | VF20 | XF40 | MS60 | MS63 | MS65 |
|---|---|---|---|---|---|---|
| 2013 | Est. 5000 | PF65 36.00 | | | | |

### KM# 237 5 TALA

0.50 g., 0.999 Gold AGW, 11 mm. **Subject:** Wilhelmina

| Date | Mintage | F12 | VF20 | XF40 | MS60 | MS63 |
|---|---|---|---|---|---|---|
| 2013 | Est. 5000 | PF65 50.00 | | | | |

### KM# 238 5 TALA

0.50 g., 0.999 Gold 0.0161 oz. AGW, 11 mm. **Subject:** Umberto I

| Date | Mintage | VF20 | XF40 | MS60 | MS63 | MS65 |
|---|---|---|---|---|---|---|
| 2013 | Est. 5000 | PF65 36.00 | | | | |

### KM# 239 5 TALA

0.50 g., 0.999 Gold 0.0161 oz. AGW, 11 mm. **Subject:** Moonlanding

| Date | Mintage | VF20 | XF40 | MS60 | MS63 | MS65 |
|---|---|---|---|---|---|---|
| 2013 | 7,500 | PF65 75.00 | | | | |

### KM# 241 5 TALA

0.50 g., 0.999 Gold 0.0161 oz. AGW, 11 mm. **Subject:** John F. Kennedy

| Date | Mintage | VF20 | XF40 | MS60 | MS63 | MS65 |
|---|---|---|---|---|---|---|
| 2013 | Est. 10000 | PF65 36.00 | | | | |

### KM# 242 5 TALA

20.00 g., 0.925 Silver 0.5948 oz. ASW with color, 38.61 mm. **Series:** John F. Kennedy

| Date | Mintage | VF20 | XF40 | MS60 | MS63 | MS65 |
|---|---|---|---|---|---|---|
| 2013 | Est. 2500 | PF65 23.00 | | | | |

### KM# 244 5 TALA

15.00 g., 0.925 Silver 0.4461 oz. ASW, 34 mm. **Subject:** Saxonia, 175th Anniversary

| Date | Mintage | VF20 | XF40 | MS60 | MS63 | MS65 |
|---|---|---|---|---|---|---|
| 2013 | Est. 10000 | PF65 75.00 | | | | |

### KM# 245 5 TALA

20.00 g., 0.925 Silver 0.5948 oz. ASW **Subject:** 2014 FIFA World Cup - Brazil **Rev:** Soccer player and skyline of Rio

| Date | Mintage | VF20 | XF40 | MS60 | MS63 | MS65 |
|---|---|---|---|---|---|---|
| 2013 | Est. 10000 | PF65 50.00 | | | | |

### KM# 246 5 TALA

0.50 g., 0.999 Gold 0.0161 oz. AGW, 11 mm. **Subject:** L'Hercule

| Date | Mintage | VF20 | XF40 | MS60 | MS63 | MS65 |
|---|---|---|---|---|---|---|
| 2013 | Est. 5000 | PF65 36.00 | | | | |

### KM# 248 5 TALA

20.00 g., 0.925 Silver 0.5948 oz. ASW, 38.61 mm. **Subject:** Vogelfugline

| Date | Mintage | VF20 | XF40 | MS60 | MS63 | MS65 |
|---|---|---|---|---|---|---|
| 2013 | Est. 3000 | PF65 75.00 | | | | |

### KM# 137 10 TALA

31.10 g., 0.999 Silver 0.9989 oz. ASW with Mother-of-Pearl insert, 40 mm. **Series:** Save the Whales **Obv:** National arms above value and banner flanked by sprigs **Obv. Legend:** SAMOA I SISIFO **Rev:** Bowhead Whale on mother-of-pearl insert **Edge:** Plain

| Date | Mintage | VF20 | XF40 | MS60 | MS63 | MS65 |
|---|---|---|---|---|---|---|
| 2002 | 2,000 | PF65 95.00 | | | | |

### KM# 139 10 TALA

31.47 g., 0.925 Silver 0.9359 oz. ASW **Subject:** XXVIII Summer Olympics - Athens **Obv:** National arms **Obv. Legend:** SAMOA I SISIFO **Rev:** Swimming - two divers

| Date | Mintage | VF20 | XF40 | MS60 | MS63 | MS65 |
|---|---|---|---|---|---|---|
| 2003 | — | PF63 50.00 | PF65 60.00 | | | |

### KM# 140 10 TALA

1.24 g., 0.999 Gold 0.0398 oz. AGW **Series:** World Statesmen **Subject:** Mahatma Gandhi **Obv:** National arms **Obv. Legend:** SAMOA I SISIFO

| Date | Mintage | VF20 | XF40 | MS60 | MS63 | MS65 |
|---|---|---|---|---|---|---|
| 2003 | — | PF65 68.00 | | | | |

### KM# 141 10 TALA

1.24 g., 0.999 Gold 0.0398 oz. AGW **Series:** World Statesmen **Subject:** Konrad Adenauer **Obv:** National arms **Obv. Legend:** SAMOA I SISIFO

| Date | Mintage | VF20 | XF40 | MS60 | MS63 | MS65 |
|---|---|---|---|---|---|---|
| 2003 | — | PF65 68.00 | | | | |

### KM# 146 10 TALA

1.23 g., .999 Gold 0.03980oz. AGW, 13.89 mm. **Obv:** National arms **Obv. Legend:** SAMOA SISIFO **Rev:** Bust of Fletcher Christian 3/4 left at left, sailing ship "H. M. S. Bounty" at right **Edge:** Reeded

| Date | Mintage | VF20 | XF40 | MS60 | MS63 | MS65 |
|---|---|---|---|---|---|---|
| 2003 | — | PF65 68.00 | | | | |

### KM# 159 10 TALA

1.24 g., 0.999 Gold 0.0398 oz. AGW, 13.92 mm. **Obv:** National arms **Rev:** Theodore Roosevelt

| Date | Mintage | VF20 | XF40 | MS60 | MS63 | MS65 |
|---|---|---|---|---|---|---|
| 2003 | Est. 2000 | PF65 68.00 | | | | |

### KM# 160 10 TALA

1.24 g., 0.999 Gold 0.0398 oz. AGW, 13.92 mm. **Obv:** National arms **Rev:** Winston Churchill

| Date | Mintage | VF20 | XF40 | MS60 | MS63 | MS65 |
|---|---|---|---|---|---|---|
| 2003 | Est. 2000 | PF65 68.00 | | | | |

### KM# 161 10 TALA

1.24 g., 0.999 Gold 0.0398 oz. AGW, 13.92 mm. **Obv:** National arms **Rev:** Charles de Gaulle

| Date | Mintage | VF20 | XF40 | MS60 | MS63 | MS65 |
|---|---|---|---|---|---|---|
| 2003 | Est. 2000 | PF65 68.00 | | | | |

### KM# 162 10 TALA

1.24 g., 0.999 Gold 0.0398 oz. AGW, 13.92 mm. **Obv:** National arms **Rev:** John F. Kennedy

| Date | Mintage | VF20 | XF40 | MS60 | MS63 | MS65 |
|---|---|---|---|---|---|---|
| 2003 | Est. 2000 | PF65 68.00 | | | | |

### KM# 143 10 TALA

28.58 g., Silver, 38.61 mm. **Obv:** National arms **Obv. Legend:** SAMOA I SISIFO **Rev:** Sailing ship "La Récherche **Rev. Legend:** JEAN FRANCOIS GALAUP - COMTE DE LA PEROUSE **Edge:** Reeded

| Date | Mintage | VF20 | XF40 | MS60 | MS63 | MS65 |
|---|---|---|---|---|---|---|
| 2004 | — | PF63 45.00 | PF65 55.00 | | | |

### KM# 142 10 TALA

1.24 g., 0.999 Gold 0.0398 oz. AGW **Subject:** Death of Pope John-Paul II **Obv:** National arms

| Date | Mintage | VF20 | XF40 | MS60 | MS63 | MS65 |
|---|---|---|---|---|---|---|
| 2005 | 15,000 | — | — | — | — | 75.00 |
| 2005 | 3,300 | PF65 68.00 | | | | |

### KM# 163 10 TALA

1.24 g., 0.999 Gold 0.0398 oz. AGW, 13.92 mm. **Obv:** National arms **Rev:** 2006 FIFA World Cup Germany logo

| Date | Mintage | VF20 | XF40 | MS60 | MS63 | MS65 |
|---|---|---|---|---|---|---|
| 2005 | Est. 25000 | PF65 68.00 | | | | |

### KM# 164 10 TALA

1.24 g., 0.999 Gold 0.0398 oz. AGW, 13.92 mm. **Obv:** National arms **Rev:** Pope Benedict XVI in robes and mitre giving blessing

| Date | Mintage | VF20 | XF40 | MS60 | MS63 | MS65 |
|---|---|---|---|---|---|---|
| 2006 | — | PF65 68.00 | | | | |

### KM# 183 10 TALA

1.00 g., 0.9999 Gold 0.0321 oz. AGW, 13.92 mm. **Obv:** National arms **Rev:** S.M.S. Bismark siling right

| Date | Mintage | VF20 | XF40 | MS60 | MS63 | MS65 |
|---|---|---|---|---|---|---|
| 2008 | 15,000 | PF65 56.00 | | | | |

### KM# 184 10 TALA

1.24 g., 0.9999 Gold 0.0399 oz. AGW, 13.92 mm. **Obv:** National arms **Rev:** Hans Christian Andersen bust right

| Date | Mintage | VF20 | XF40 | MS60 | MS63 | MS65 |
|---|---|---|---|---|---|---|
| 2008 | 10,000 | PF65 68.00 | | | | |

## KM# 195 10 TALA

28.28 g., 0.999 Silver 0.9083 oz. ASW partially gilt, 38.61 mm. **Subject:** 10 Commandments - 1st Commandment **Obv:** National arms **Rev:** Two men worshiping a calf at an altar

| Date | Mintage | VF20 | XF40 | MS60 | MS63 | MS65 |
|---|---|---|---|---|---|---|
| 2009 | 5,000 | PF63 65.00 | PF65 75.00 | | | |

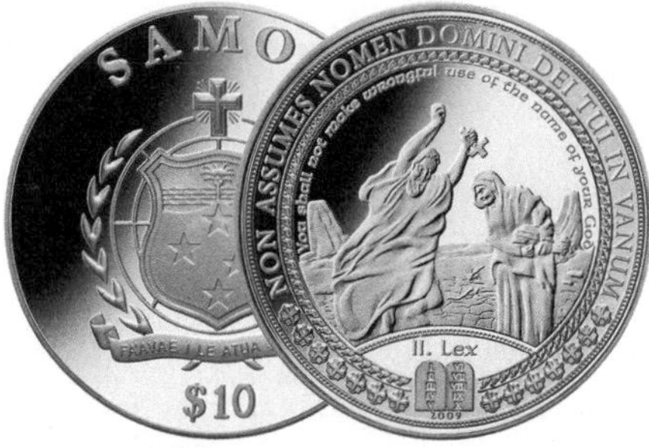


## KM# 196 10 TALA

28.28 g., 0.925 Silver 0.841 oz. ASW partially gilt, 38.61 mm. **Subject:** 10 Commandments - 2nd Commandment **Obv:** National arms **Rev:** Two men standing in the desert

| Date | Mintage | VF20 | XF40 | MS60 | MS63 | MS65 |
|---|---|---|---|---|---|---|
| 2009 | 5,000 | PF63 65.00 | PF65 75.00 | | | |

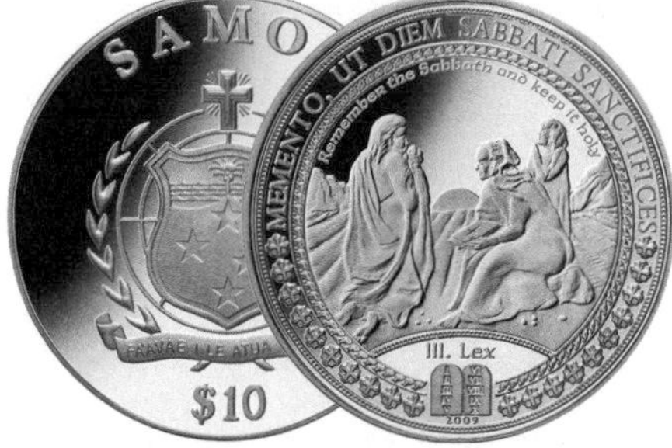


## KM# 197 10 TALA

28.28 g., 0.925 Silver 0.841 oz. ASW partially gilt, 38.61 mm. **Subject:** 10 Commandments - 3rd Commandment **Obv:** National arms **Rev:** Parents and child on a field

| Date | Mintage | VF20 | XF40 | MS60 | MS63 | MS65 |
|---|---|---|---|---|---|---|
| 2009 | 5,000 | PF63 65.00 | PF65 75.00 | | | |

## KM# 198 10 TALA

28.28 g., 0.925 Silver 0.841 oz. ASW partially gilt, 38.61 mm. **Subject:** 10 Commandments - 4th Commandment **Obv:** National arms **Rev:** Mother seated with child, father standing

| Date | Mintage | VF20 | XF40 | MS60 | MS63 | MS65 |
|---|---|---|---|---|---|---|
| 2009 | 5,000 | PF63 65.00 | PF65 75.00 | | | |

## KM# 199 10 TALA

28.28 g., 0.925 Silver 0.841 oz. ASW partially gilt, 38.61 mm. **Subject:** 10 Commandments - 5th Commandment **Obv:** National arms **Rev:** Man holding sword over kneeling man

| Date | Mintage | VF20 | XF40 | MS60 | MS63 | MS65 |
|---|---|---|---|---|---|---|
| 2009 | 5,000 | PF63 65.00 | PF65 75.00 | | | |

## KM# 205 10 TALA

28.28 g., 0.925 Silver 0.841 oz. ASW partially gilt, 38.61 mm. **Subject:** Charles Darwin, 200th Anniversary of Birth **Obv:** National arms **Rev:** Galapagos Island Finches

| Date | Mintage | VF20 | XF40 | MS60 | MS63 | MS65 |
|---|---|---|---|---|---|---|
| 2009 | 2,009 | PF63 65.00 | PF65 75.00 | | | |

## KM# 206 10 TALA

28.28 g., 0.925 Silver 0.841 oz. ASW partially gilt, 38.61 mm. **Subject:** Charles Darwin, 200th Anniversary of Birth **Obv:** National arms **Rev:** Galapagos Iguana

| Date | Mintage | VF20 | XF40 | MS60 | MS63 | MS65 |
|---|---|---|---|---|---|---|
| 2009 | 2,009 | PF63 65.00 | PF65 75.00 | | | |

## KM# 207 10 TALA

28.28 g., 0.925 Silver 0.841 oz. ASW partially gilt, 38.61 mm. **Subject:** Charles Darwin, 200th Anniversary of Birth **Obv:** National arms **Rev:** The H.M.R.S. Beagle and voyage map

| Date | Mintage | VF20 | XF40 | MS60 | MS63 | MS65 |
|---|---|---|---|---|---|---|
| 2009 | 2,009 | PF63 65.00 | PF65 75.00 | | | |

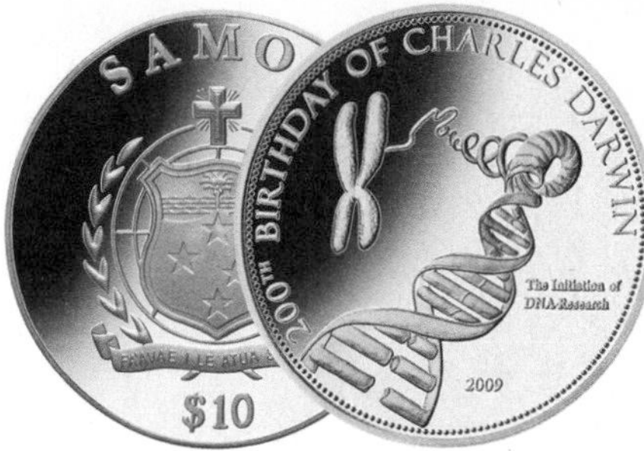


## KM# 208 10 TALA

28.28 g., 0.925 Silver 0.841 oz. ASW partially gilt, 38.61 mm. **Subject:** Charles Darwin, 200th Anniversary of Birth **Obv:** National arms **Rev:** DNA-Double helix and a chromosome

| Date | Mintage | VF20 | XF40 | MS60 | MS63 | MS65 |
|---|---|---|---|---|---|---|
| 2009 | 2,009 | PF63 65.00 | PF65 75.00 | | | |

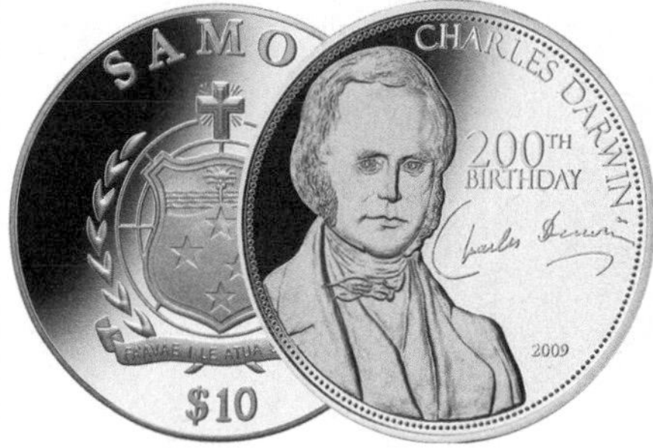


## KM# 209 10 TALA

28.28 g., 0.925 Silver 0.841 oz. ASW partially gilt, 38.61 mm. **Subject:** Charles Darwin, 200th Anniversary of Birth **Obv:** National arms **Rev:** Galapagos Oldest Tortoise

| Date | Mintage | VF20 | XF40 | MS60 | MS63 | MS65 |
|---|---|---|---|---|---|---|
| 2009 | 2,009 | PF63 65.00 | PF65 75.00 | | | |

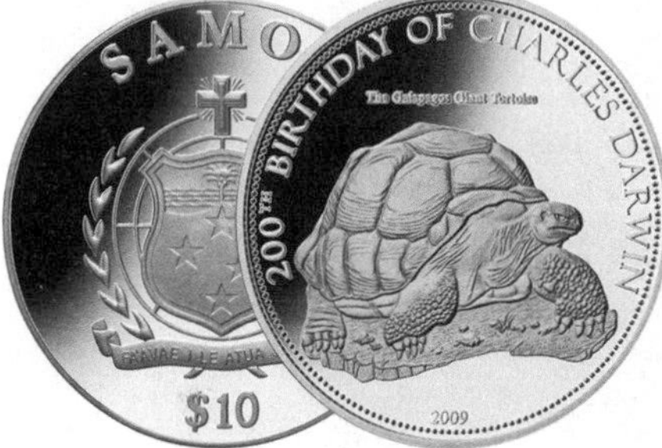


## KM# 210 10 TALA

28.28 g., 0.925 Silver 0.841 oz. ASW partially gilt, 38.61 mm. **Subject:** Charles Darwin, 200th Anniversary of Birth **Obv:** National arms **Rev:** Darwin portrait at left

| Date | Mintage | VF20 | XF40 | MS60 | MS63 | MS65 |
|---|---|---|---|---|---|---|
| 2009 | 2,009 | PF63 65.00 | PF65 75.00 | | | |

## KM# 211 10 TALA

1.24 g., 0.9999 Gold 0.0399 oz. AGW, 13.92 mm. **Obv:** National arms **Rev:** Nicolaus Copernicus bust and solar system

| Date | Mintage | VF20 | XF40 | MS60 | MS63 | MS65 |
|---|---|---|---|---|---|---|
| 2009 | 10,000 | PF65 68.00 | | | | |

## KM# 212 10 TALA

1.24 g., 0.9999 Gold 0.0399 oz. AGW, 13.92 mm. **Obv:** National arms **Rev:** Johannes Hevelius bust at right

| Date | Mintage | VF20 | XF40 | MS60 | MS63 | MS65 |
|---|---|---|---|---|---|---|
| 2009 | 5,000 | PF65 68.00 | | | | |

## KM# 213 10 TALA

1.24 g., 0.999 Gold 0.0398 oz. AGW, 13.92 mm. **Obv:** National arms **Rev:** Marie Curie and atom symbol

| Date | Mintage | VF20 | XF40 | MS60 | MS63 | MS65 |
|---|---|---|---|---|---|---|
| 2009 | 5,000 | PF65 68.00 | | | | |

**KM# 172 10 TALA**
20.00 g., 0.925 Silver 0.5948 oz. ASW, 38.61 mm. **Obv:** National arms **Rev:** Sailing ship Preussen

| Date | Mintage | VF20 | XF40 | MS60 | MS63 | MS65 |
|---|---|---|---|---|---|---|
| 2010 | 2,500 | PF63 65.00 | PF65 75.00 | | | |

**KM# 173 10 TALA**
25.00 g., 0.925 Silver 0.7435 oz. ASW, 38.61 mm. **Obv:** National arms **Rev:** Samoan Flying Fox (bat) hanging, with colored eyes

| Date | Mintage | VF20 | XF40 | MS60 | MS63 | MS65 |
|---|---|---|---|---|---|---|
| 2010 | 2,500 | PF63 65.00 | PF65 75.00 | | | |

**KM# 200 10 TALA**
28.28 g., 0.999 Silver 0.9083 oz. ASW partially gilt, 38.61 mm. **Subject:** 10 Commandments - 6th Commandment **Obv:** National arms **Rev:** Man seated near half-naked reclining female

| Date | Mintage | VF20 | XF40 | MS60 | MS63 | MS65 |
|---|---|---|---|---|---|---|
| 2010 | 5,000 | PF63 65.00 | PF65 75.00 | | | |

**KM# 201 10 TALA**
28.28 g., 0.925 Silver 0.841 oz. ASW partially gilt, 38.61 mm. **Subject:** 10 Commandments - 7th Commandment **Obv:** National arms **Rev:** Three men walking

| Date | Mintage | VF20 | XF40 | MS60 | MS63 | MS65 |
|---|---|---|---|---|---|---|
| 2010 | 5,000 | PF63 65.00 | PF65 75.00 | | | |

**KM# 202 10 TALA**
28.28 g., 0.999 Silver 0.9083 oz. ASW partially gilt, 38.61 mm. **Subject:** 10 Commandments - 8th Commandment **Obv:** National arms **Rev:** One man talking to another

| Date | Mintage | VF20 | XF40 | MS60 | MS63 | MS65 |
|---|---|---|---|---|---|---|
| 2010 | 5,000 | PF63 65.00 | PF65 75.00 | | | |

**KM# 203 10 TALA**
28.28 g., 0.999 Silver 0.9083 oz. ASW partially gilt, 38.61 mm. **Subject:** 10 Commandment - 9th Commandment **Obv:** National arms **Rev:** Female entering river to bathe, male watching from behind tree

| Date | Mintage | VF20 | XF40 | MS60 | MS63 | MS65 |
|---|---|---|---|---|---|---|
| 2010 | 5,000 | PF63 65.00 | PF65 75.00 | | | |

**KM# 204 10 TALA**
28.28 g., 0.925 Silver 0.841 oz. ASW partially gilt, 38.61 mm. **Subject:** 10 Commandments - 10th Commandment **Obv:** National arms **Rev:** Temple building and man standing at right

| Date | Mintage | VF20 | XF40 | MS60 | MS63 | MS65 |
|---|---|---|---|---|---|---|
| 2010 | 5,000 | PF63 65.00 | PF65 75.00 | | | |

**KM# 225 10 TALA**
28.28 g., 0.999 Silver 0.9083 oz. ASW, 38.61 mm. **Subject:** Mother Teresa, 10th Anniversary of Beatification **Obv:** National arms **Rev:** Mother Teresa holding globe and rosary **Edge Lettering:** BEATI MISERICORDES

| Date | Mintage | VF20 | XF40 | MS60 | MS63 | MS65 |
|---|---|---|---|---|---|---|
| 2013 | Est. 2003 | PF65 60.00 | | | | |

**KM# 228 10 TALA**
28.80 g., 0.999 Silver 0.925 oz. ASW, 38.61 mm. **Subject:** JFK's "Ich Bin Ein Berliner" speech, 50th Anniversary **Obv:** National arms **Rev:** JFK portrait in pop art colors

| Date | Mintage | VF20 | XF40 | MS60 | MS63 | MS65 |
|---|---|---|---|---|---|---|
| 2013 | — | PF65 50.00 | | | | |

**KM# 229 10 TALA**
28.80 g., 0.999 Silver 0.925 oz. ASW, 38.61 mm. **Subject:** JFK's "Ich Bein Ein Berliner" speech, 50th Anniversary **Obv:** National arms **Rev:** JFK portrait, speech in micro text

| Date | Mintage | VF20 | XF40 | MS60 | MS63 | MS65 |
|---|---|---|---|---|---|---|
| 2013 | Est. 2500 | PF65 50.00 | | | | |

**KM# 243 10 TALA**
31.11 g., 0.999 Silver 0.999 oz. ASW with color, 38.61 mm. **Subject:** Neil Armstrong

| Date | Mintage | VF20 | XF40 | MS60 | MS63 | MS65 |
|---|---|---|---|---|---|---|
| 2013 | Est. 999 | PF65 75.00 | | | | |

**KM# 220 100 TALA**
5.00 g., 0.9999 Gold 0.1607 oz. AGW, 23.3x14 mm. **Obv:** Value and national arms **Rev:** Battlehsip Bismarck **Shape:** Rectangle

| Date | Mintage | VF20 | XF40 | MS60 | MS63 | MS65 |
|---|---|---|---|---|---|---|
| 2011 | 1,000 | PF65 350 | | | | |

**KM# 221 100 TALA**
5.00 g., 0.999 Gold 0.1606 oz. AGW, 23.3x14 mm. **Obv:** Value and national arms **Rev:** Battleship H.M.S. Hood **Shape:** Rectangle

| Date | Mintage | VF20 | XF40 | MS60 | MS63 | MS65 |
|---|---|---|---|---|---|---|
| 2011 | 1,000 | PF65 350 | | | | |

**KM# 222 100 TALA**
5.00 g., 0.999 Gold 0.1606 oz. AGW, 23.3x14 mm. **Obv:** Value and national arms **Rev:** Battleship U.S.S. Missouri **Shape:** Rectangle

| Date | Mintage | VF20 | XF40 | MS60 | MS63 | MS65 |
|---|---|---|---|---|---|---|
| 2011 | 1,000 | PF65 350 | | | | |

**KM# 223 100 TALA**
5.00 g., 0.9999 Gold 0.1607 oz. AGW, 23.3x14 mm. **Obv:** Value and national arms **Rev:** Battleship S.M.S. Friedrich der Grosse **Shape:** Rectangle

| Date | Mintage | VF20 | XF40 | MS60 | MS63 | MS65 |
|---|---|---|---|---|---|---|
| 2011 | 1,000 | PF65 350 | | | | |

**KM# 224 100 TALA**
5.00 g., 0.9999 Gold 0.1607 oz. AGW, 23.3x14 mm. **Obv:** Value and national arms **Rev:** Battleship Yamato **Shape:** Rectangle

| Date | Mintage | VF20 | XF40 | MS60 | MS63 | MS65 |
|---|---|---|---|---|---|---|
| 2011 | 1,000 | PF65 350 | | | | |

**KM# 252 100 TALA**
5.00 g., 0.9999 Gold 0.1607 oz. AGW, 23.3x14 mm. **Obv:** National arms at right **Rev:** Battleship Tirpitz **Shape:** Rectangle

| Date | Mintage | VF20 | XF40 | MS60 | MS63 | MS65 |
|---|---|---|---|---|---|---|
| 2012 | 1,000 | PF65 350 | | | | |

**KM# 253 100 TALA**
5.00 g., 0.9999 Gold 0.1607 oz. AGW, 23.3x14 mm. **Obv:** National arms at right **Rev:** Battleship Richelieu **Shape:** Rectangle

| Date | Mintage | VF20 | XF40 | MS60 | MS63 | MS65 |
|---|---|---|---|---|---|---|
| 2012 | 1,000 | PF65 350 | | | | |

**KM# 254 100 TALA**
5.00 g., 0.9999 Gold 0.1607 oz. AGW, 23.3x14 mm. **Obv:** National arms at right **Rev:** Battleship Nassau **Shape:** Rectangle

| Date | Mintage | VF20 | XF40 | MS60 | MS63 | MS65 |
|---|---|---|---|---|---|---|
| 2012 | 1,000 | PF65 350 | | | | |

**KM# 255 100 TALA**

5.00 g., 0.9999 Gold 0.1607 oz. AGW, 23.3x14 mm. **Obv:** National arms at right **Rev:** Battleship HMS Dradnought **Shape:** Rectangle

| Date | Mintage | VF20 | XF40 | MS60 | MS63 | MS65 |
|---|---|---|---|---|---|---|
| 2012 | — | PF65 350 | | | | |

**KM# 256 100 TALA**

5.00 g., 0.9999 Gold 0.1607 oz. AGW, 23.3x14 mm. **Obv:** National arms at right **Rev:** Battleship Szent István **Shape:** Rectangle

| Date | Mintage | VF20 | XF40 | MS60 | MS63 | MS65 |
|---|---|---|---|---|---|---|
| 2012 | 1,000 | PF65 350 | | | | |

# SAN MARINO

The Republic of San Marino, the oldest and smallest republic in the world is located in north central Italy entirely surrounded by the Province of Emilia-Romagna. It has an area of 24 sq. mi. (60 sq. km.) and a population of *23,000. Capital: San Marino. The principal economic activities are farming, livestock raising, cheese making, tourism and light manufacturing. Building stone, lime, wheat, hides and baked goods are exported. The government derives most of its revenue from the sale of postage stamps for philatelic purposes.

San Marino has its own coinage, but Italian and Vatican City coins and currency are also in circulation.

**MINT MARKS**

R - Rome

**MONETARY SYSTEM**

100 Centesimi = 1 Lira

## REPUBLIC

### STANDARD COINAGE

**KM# 424 10 LIRE**

1.60 g., Aluminum, 23.3 mm. **Obv:** Three towers within circle **Rev:** Wheat stalks and value **Edge:** Plain

| Date | Mintage | VF20 | XF40 | MS60 | MS63 | MS65 |
|---|---|---|---|---|---|---|
| 2001 R | — | — | — | — | 0.35 | 0.50 |

**KM# 425 20 LIRE**

3.60 g., Aluminum-Bronze, 21.8 mm. **Obv:** Three towers within circle **Rev:** Two dolphins and value **Edge:** Plain

| Date | Mintage | VF20 | XF40 | MS60 | MS63 | MS65 |
|---|---|---|---|---|---|---|
| 2001 R | — | — | — | — | 1.00 | 2.00 |

**KM# 426 50 LIRE**

4.50 g., Copper-Nickel, 19 mm. **Obv:** Three towers within circle **Rev:** Tree and value **Edge:** Plain

| Date | Mintage | VF20 | XF40 | MS60 | MS63 | MS65 |
|---|---|---|---|---|---|---|
| 2001 R | — | — | — | — | 0.85 | 1.50 |

**KM# 427 100 LIRE**

4.50 g., Copper-Nickel, 22 mm. **Obv:** Three towers within circle **Rev:** Grasping hands and value **Edge:** Plain and reeded sections

| Date | Mintage | VF20 | XF40 | MS60 | MS63 | MS65 |
|---|---|---|---|---|---|---|
| 2001 R | — | — | — | — | 1.25 | 2.00 |

**KM# 428 200 LIRE**

5.00 g., Aluminum-Bronze, 24 mm. **Obv:** Three towers within circle **Rev:** Broken chain, leaves, vines and value **Edge:** Reeded

| Date | Mintage | VF20 | XF40 | MS60 | MS63 | MS65 |
|---|---|---|---|---|---|---|
| 2001 R | — | — | — | — | 1.50 | 2.50 |

**KM# 429 500 LIRE**

Bi-Metallic Aluminum-Bronze center in Stainless Steel ring, 25.8 mm. **Obv:** Three towers within circle **Rev:** Three different plant stalks and value **Edge:** Segmented reeding **Note:** 6.8 grams.

| Date | Mintage | VF20 | XF40 | MS60 | MS63 | MS65 |
|---|---|---|---|---|---|---|
| 2001 R | — | — | — | — | 3.00 | 5.00 |

**KM# 430 1000 LIRE**

8.80 g., Bi-Metallic Stainless-Steel center in Aluminum-Bronze ring, 27 mm. **Obv:** Three towers within circle **Rev:** Value within circle of birds **Edge:** Segmented reeding

| Date | Mintage | VF20 | XF40 | MS60 | MS63 | MS65 |
|---|---|---|---|---|---|---|
| 2001 R | — | — | — | — | 7.00 | 9.00 |

**KM# 431 5000 LIRE**

18.00 g., 0.835 Silver 0.4832 oz. ASW, 32 mm. **Obv:** Three towers within circle **Rev:** Dove on laurel branch above value **Edge:** Reeded and plain sections

| Date | Mintage | VF20 | XF40 | MS60 | MS63 | MS65 |
|---|---|---|---|---|---|---|
| 2001 R | — | — | — | — | 22.50 | 27.50 |

**KM# 436 5000 LIRE**

18.00 g., 0.835 Silver 0.4832 oz. ASW, 32 mm. **Subject:** Last Lire Coinage **Obv:** Crowned arms within sprigs **Rev:** Feather above six old coin designs with value below, all within beaded border **Edge:** Lettered

| Date | Mintage | VF20 | XF40 | MS60 | MS63 | MS65 |
|---|---|---|---|---|---|---|
| 2001 R | 20,000 | PF65 25.00 | | | | |

**KM# 432 10000 LIRE**

22.00 g., 0.835 Silver 0.5906 oz. ASW, 34 mm. **Subject:** Ferrari **Obv:** Crowned arms within sprigs **Rev:** Race car with "FERRARI" background **Edge:** Reeded and plain sections

| Date | Mintage | VF20 | XF40 | MS60 | MS63 | MS65 |
|---|---|---|---|---|---|---|
| 2001 R | 20,000 | PF65 45.00 | | | | |

**KM# 437 10000 LIRE**

22.00 g., 0.835 Silver 0.5906 oz. ASW, 34 mm. **Subject:** Last Lire Coinage **Obv:** Crowned arms within sprigs **Rev:** Feather above six old coin designs with value below, all within star border **Edge:** Reeded and plain sections

| Date | Mintage | VF20 | XF40 | MS60 | MS63 | MS65 |
|---|---|---|---|---|---|---|
| 2001 R | 20,000 | PF65 42.00 | | | | |

**KM# 438 10000 LIRE**

22.00 g., 0.835 Silver 0.5906 oz. ASW, 34 mm. **Subject:** 2nd International Chambers of Commerce Convention **Obv:** Crowned arms within sprigs **Rev:** Mercury running by a computer **Edge:** Segmented reeding

| Date | Mintage | VF20 | XF40 | MS60 | MS63 | MS65 |
|---|---|---|---|---|---|---|
| 2001 R | 19,987 | PF65 42.00 | | | | |

**KM# 433 1/2 SCUDO**

1.61 g., 0.900 Gold 0.0466 oz. AGW, 13.8 mm. **Subject:** Cavaliere **Obv:** Crowned arms within sprigs **Rev:** Horse and rider **Edge:** Reeded

| Date | Mintage | VF20 | XF40 | MS60 | MS63 | MS65 |
|---|---|---|---|---|---|---|
| 2001 R | 4,500 | PF65 90.00 | | | | |

**KM# 434 SCUDO**

3.22 g., 0.900 Gold 0.0932 oz. AGW, 16 mm. **Subject:** Tiziano **Obv:** Crowned arms within sprigs **Rev:** Bearded bust left **Edge:** Reeded

| Date | Mintage | VF20 | XF40 | MS60 | MS63 | MS65 |
|---|---|---|---|---|---|---|
| 2001 R | 4,500 | PF65 180 | | | | |

**KM# 435 2 SCUDI**

6.44 g., 0.900 Gold 0.1863 oz. AGW, 21 mm. **Subject:** Flora **Obv:** Crowned arms within sprigs **Rev:** Bust 1/4 left and value **Edge:** Reeded

| Date | Mintage | VF20 | XF40 | MS60 | MS63 | MS65 |
|---|---|---|---|---|---|---|
| 2001 R | 4,500 | PF65 345 | | | | |

**KM# 457 2 SCUDI**

6.45 g., 0.900 Gold 0.1867 oz. AGW, 21 mm. **Obv:** Crowned arms within sprigs **Rev:** Madonna and Child **Edge:** Reeded

| Date | Mintage | VF20 | XF40 | MS60 | MS63 | MS65 |
|---|---|---|---|---|---|---|
| 2002 R | 2,950 | PF65 345 | | | | |

**KM# 459 2 SCUDI**

6.45 g., 0.900 Gold 0.1867 oz. AGW, 21 mm. **Obv:** Crowned arms within sprigs **Rev:** Nostradamus above value **Edge:** Reeded

| Date | Mintage | VF20 | XF40 | MS60 | MS63 | MS65 |
|---|---|---|---|---|---|---|
| 2003 R | 7,500 | PF65 345 | | | | |

### KM# 464 2 SCUDI

6.45 g., 0.900 Gold 0.1867 oz. AGW, 21 mm. **Subject:** The Domagnano Treasure **Obv:** Crowned arms within sprigs **Rev:** Gothic Eagle Brooch, 5 Mark coin of 1952 **Edge:** Reeded

| Date | Mintage | VF20 | XF40 | MS60 | MS63 | MS65 |
|---|---|---|---|---|---|---|
| 2004 R | 6,494 | PF65 345 | | | | |

### KM# 345 2 SCUDI

6.45 g., 0.900 Gold 0.1866 oz. AGW, 21 mm. **Subject:** Rotary International, 100th Anniversary **Rev:** Rotary emblem

| Date | Mintage | VF20 | XF40 | MS60 | MS63 | MS65 |
|---|---|---|---|---|---|---|
| 2005 R | 4,249 | PF65 395 | | | | |

### KM# 346 2 SCUDI

6.45 g., 0.900 Gold 0.1866 oz. AGW, 21 mm. **Subject:** General meeting of the heads of families, 100th Anniversary **Rev:** Three females with the fruits of democracy

| Date | Mintage | VF20 | XF40 | MS60 | MS63 | MS65 |
|---|---|---|---|---|---|---|
| 2006 R | 2,821 | PF65 395 | | | | |

### KM# 347 2 SCUDI

6.45 g., 0.900 Gold 0.1866 oz. AGW, 21 mm. **Subject:** Diplomatic relations with Japan, 50th Anniversary **Rev:** Shrine of Jinmu Tenno (1889) in Kashihara

| Date | Mintage | VF20 | XF40 | MS60 | MS63 | MS65 |
|---|---|---|---|---|---|---|
| 2007 R | 7,536 | PF65 395 | | | | |

### KM# 493 2 SCUDI

6.41 g., 0.900 Gold 0.1855 oz. AGW, 21 mm. **Subject:** Pompeo Batoni, 300th Anniversary of Brith **Obv:** Arms **Rev:** Batoni's statue group "San Marino Risolleva la Republica

| Date | Mintage | VF20 | XF40 | MS60 | MS63 | MS65 |
|---|---|---|---|---|---|---|
| 2008 R | 2,100 | PF65 395 | | | | |

### KM# 450 2 SCUDI

6.45 g., 0.900 Gold 0.1866 oz. AGW, 21 mm. **Subject:** Art treasures of San Marino **Rev:** Ceres Bronze Statue by Albert E. Carrier Belleuse

| Date | Mintage | VF20 | XF40 | MS60 | MS63 | MS65 |
|---|---|---|---|---|---|---|
| 2009 R | 2,100 | PF65 395 | | | | |

### KM# 451 2 SCUDI

6.45 g., 0.900 Gold 0.1866 oz. AGW, 21 mm. **Subject:** Art treasures of San Marino **Rev:** Justice with scales by Bernardino Mei

| Date | Mintage | VF20 | XF40 | MS60 | MS63 | MS65 |
|---|---|---|---|---|---|---|
| 2010 R | 2,100 | PF65 395 | | | | |

### KM# 517 2 SCUDI

6.45 g., 0.900 Gold 0.1866 oz. AGW, 21 mm. **Subject:** Christmas **Rev:** Nativity scene

| Date | Mintage | VF20 | XF40 | MS60 | MS63 | MS65 |
|---|---|---|---|---|---|---|
| 2011 R | 1,600 | PF65 445 | | | | |

### KM# 439 5 SCUDI

16.97 g., 0.9166 Gold 0.500 oz. AGW, 28 mm. **Subject:** San Marino's World Bank Membership **Obv:** Crowned arms within sprigs **Rev:** Orchid and bee within globe **Edge:** Reeded

| Date | Mintage | VF20 | XF40 | MS60 | MS63 | MS65 |
|---|---|---|---|---|---|---|
| 2001 R | 4,000 | PF65 900 | | | | |

### KM# 348 5 SCUDI

16.13 g., 0.900 Gold 0.4667 oz. AGW, 28 mm. **Subject:** Diplomatic relations with Japan, 50th Anniversary **Rev:** Jinmu Tenno

| Date | Mintage | VF20 | XF40 | MS60 | MS63 | MS65 |
|---|---|---|---|---|---|---|
| 2007 R | 7,130 | PF65 850 | | | | |

## EURO COINAGE

### KM# 440 EURO CENT

2.27 g., Copper Plated Steel, 16.2 mm. **Obv:** Il Montale **Rev:** Value and globe **Edge:** Plain

| Date | Mintage | VF20 | XF40 | MS60 | MS63 | MS65 |
|---|---|---|---|---|---|---|
| 2002 R | 125,000 | — | — | — | — | 40.00 |
| 2003 R Sets only | 70,000 | — | — | — | — | 42.00 |
| 2004 R | 1,500,000 | — | — | — | — | 20.00 |
| 2005 R Sets only | 70,000 | — | — | — | — | 20.00 |
| 2006 R | 2,730,000 | — | — | — | 8.00 | 12.00 |
| 2007 R | — | — | — | — | 8.00 | 12.00 |
| 2008 R | — | — | — | — | 8.00 | 12.00 |
| 2008 R | 13,000 | PF65 10.00 | | | | |
| 2009 R | — | — | — | — | 8.00 | 12.00 |
| 2009 R | 13,500 | PF65 10.00 | | | | |
| 2010 R | — | — | — | — | 8.00 | 12.00 |
| 2010 R | 8,600 | PF65 10.00 | | | | |
| 2011 R | — | — | — | — | 8.00 | 12.00 |
| 2011 R | 8,600 | PF65 10.00 | | | | |
| 2012 R | — | — | — | — | 8.00 | 12.00 |
| 2013 R | — | — | — | — | 8.00 | 12.00 |

### KM# 441 2 EURO CENT

3.03 g., Copper Plated Steel, 18.7 mm. **Obv:** Stefano Gallietti, Liberty fighter **Rev:** Value and globe **Edge:** Grooved

| Date | Mintage | VF20 | XF40 | MS60 | MS63 | MS65 |
|---|---|---|---|---|---|---|
| 2002 R | 125,000 | — | — | — | — | 40.00 |
| 2003 R Sets only | 70,000 | — | — | — | — | 42.00 |
| 2004 R | 1,395,000 | — | — | — | — | 20.00 |
| 2005 R Sets only | 150,000 | — | — | — | — | 20.00 |
| 2006 R | 2,730,000 | — | — | — | 8.00 | 12.00 |
| 2007 R | — | — | — | — | 8.00 | 12.00 |
| 2008 R | — | — | — | — | 8.00 | 12.00 |
| 2008 R | 13,000 | PF65 10.00 | | | | |
| 2009 R | — | — | — | — | 8.00 | 12.00 |
| 2009 R | 13,500 | PF65 10.00 | | | | |
| 2010 R | — | — | — | — | 8.00 | 12.00 |
| 2010 R | 8,600 | PF65 10.00 | | | | |
| 2011 R | — | — | — | — | 8.00 | 12.00 |
| 2011 R | 8,600 | PF65 10.00 | | | | |
| 2012 R | — | — | — | — | 8.00 | 12.00 |
| 2013 R | — | — | — | — | 8.00 | 12.00 |

### KM# 442 5 EURO CENT

3.86 g., Copper Plated Steel, 21.2 mm. **Obv:** Guaita tower **Rev:** Value and globe **Edge:** Plain

| Date | Mintage | VF20 | XF40 | MS60 | MS63 | MS65 |
|---|---|---|---|---|---|---|
| 2002 R | 125,000 | — | — | — | — | 40.00 |
| 2003 R Sets only | 70,000 | — | — | — | — | 42.00 |
| 2004 R | 1,000,000 | — | — | — | — | 20.00 |
| 2005 R Sets only | 70,000 | — | — | — | — | 20.00 |
| 2006 R | 2,880,000 | — | — | — | 8.00 | 12.00 |
| 2007 R | — | — | — | — | 8.00 | 12.00 |
| 2008 R | — | — | — | — | 8.00 | 12.00 |
| 2008 R | 13,000 | PF65 10.00 | | | | |
| 2009 R | — | — | — | — | 8.00 | 12.00 |
| 2009 R | 13,500 | PF65 10.00 | | | | |
| 2010 R | — | — | — | — | 8.00 | 12.00 |
| 2010 R | 8,600 | PF65 10.00 | | | | |
| 2011 R | — | — | — | — | 8.00 | 12.00 |
| 2011 R | 8,600 | PF65 10.00 | | | | |
| 2012 R | — | — | — | — | 8.00 | 12.00 |
| 2013 R | — | — | — | — | 8.00 | 12.00 |

### KM# 443 10 EURO CENT

4.07 g., Brass, 19.7 mm. **Obv:** Building Basilica del Santo Marinus **Rev:** Map and value **Edge:** Reeded

| Date | Mintage | VF20 | XF40 | MS60 | MS63 | MS65 |
|---|---|---|---|---|---|---|
| 2002 R | 125,000 | — | — | — | — | 40.00 |
| 2003 R Sets only | 70,000 | — | — | — | — | 42.00 |
| 2004 R | 180,000 | — | — | — | — | 22.00 |
| 2005 R Sets only | 70,000 | — | — | — | — | 22.00 |
| 2006 R Sets only | 65,000 | — | — | — | — | 20.00 |
| 2007 R | — | — | — | — | — | 18.00 |

### KM# 482 10 EURO CENT

4.07 g., Brass, 19.7 mm. **Obv:** Basilica de Santo Marinus facade **Rev:** Relief maps of Western Europe, value and stars

| Date | Mintage | VF20 | XF40 | MS60 | MS63 | MS65 |
|---|---|---|---|---|---|---|
| 2008 R | — | — | — | — | 8.00 | 12.00 |
| 2008 R | 13,000 | PF65 12.00 | | | | |
| 2009 R | — | — | — | — | 8.00 | 12.00 |
| 2009 R | 13,500 | PF65 12.00 | | | | |
| 2010 R | — | — | — | — | 8.00 | 12.00 |
| 2010 R | 8,600 | PF65 12.00 | | | | |
| 2011 R | — | — | — | — | 8.00 | 12.00 |
| 2011 R | 8,600 | PF65 12.00 | | | | |
| 2012 R | — | — | — | — | 8.00 | 12.00 |
| 2013 R | — | — | — | — | 8.00 | 12.00 |

### KM# 444 20 EURO CENT

5.73 g., Brass, 22.1 mm. **Obv:** St. Marinus from a portrait by van Guercino **Rev:** Map and value **Edge:** Notched

| Date | Mintage | VF20 | XF40 | MS60 | MS63 | MS65 |
|---|---|---|---|---|---|---|
| 2002 R | 267,400 | — | — | — | 18.00 | 20.00 |
| 2003 R | 430,000 | — | — | — | 15.00 | 18.00 |
| 2004 R Sets only | 70,000 | — | — | — | 15.00 | 18.00 |
| 2005 R | 310,000 | — | — | — | 15.00 | 18.00 |
| 2006 R Sets only | 70,000 | — | — | — | 15.00 | 18.00 |
| 2007 R | — | — | — | — | 14.00 | 16.00 |

### KM# 483 20 EURO CENT

5.73 g., Brass **Obv:** Saint holding Monte Titano **Rev:** Relief map of Western Europe, value and stars

| Date | Mintage | VF20 | XF40 | MS60 | MS63 | MS65 |
|---|---|---|---|---|---|---|
| 2008 R | — | — | — | — | 8.00 | 12.00 |
| 2008 R | 13,000 | PF65 15.00 | | | | |
| 2009 R | — | — | — | — | 8.00 | 12.00 |
| 2009 R | 13,500 | PF65 15.00 | | | | |
| 2010 R | — | — | — | — | 8.00 | 12.00 |
| 2010 R | 8,600 | PF65 15.00 | | | | |
| 2011 R | — | — | — | — | 8.00 | 12.00 |
| 2011 R | 8,600 | PF65 15.00 | | | | |
| 2012 R | — | — | — | — | 8.00 | 12.00 |
| 2013 R | — | — | — | — | 8.00 | 12.00 |

### KM# 445 50 EURO CENT

7.81 g., Brass, 24.2 mm. **Obv:** Fortress of San Marino **Rev:** Map and value **Edge:** Reeded

| Date | Mintage | VF20 | XF40 | MS60 | MS63 | MS65 |
|---|---|---|---|---|---|---|
| 2002 R | 230,400 | — | — | — | 20.00 | 22.50 |
| 2003 R | 415,000 | — | — | — | 17.50 | 20.00 |
| 2004 R Sets only | 70,000 | — | — | — | 17.50 | 20.00 |
| 2005 R | 179,000 | — | — | — | 17.50 | 20.00 |
| 2006 R | 343,880 | — | — | — | 15.00 | 18.00 |
| 2007 R | — | — | — | — | 14.00 | 16.00 |

### KM# 484 50 EURO CENT

7.80 g., Brass, 24.2 mm. **Obv:** Buildings on hill top **Rev:** Relief map of Western Europe, value and stars

| Date | Mintage | VF20 | XF40 | MS60 | MS63 | MS65 |
|---|---|---|---|---|---|---|
| 2008 R | — | — | — | — | 10.00 | 12.00 |
| 2008 R | 13,000 | PF65 13.00 | | | | |
| 2009 R | — | — | — | — | 10.00 | 12.00 |
| 2009 R | 13,500 | PF65 13.00 | | | | |
| 2010 R | — | — | — | — | 10.00 | 12.00 |
| 2010 R | 8,600 | PF65 13.00 | | | | |
| 2011 R | — | — | — | — | 10.00 | 12.00 |
| 2011 R | 8,600 | PF65 13.00 | | | | |
| 2012 R | 36,000 | — | — | — | 10.00 | 12.00 |
| 2013 R | — | — | — | — | 10.00 | 12.00 |

### KM# 446 EURO

7.50 g., Bi-Metallic Copper-Nickel center in Nickel-Brass ring, 23.25 mm. **Obv:** Crowned arms within sprigs and circle within star border **Rev:** Value and map **Edge:** Segmented reeding

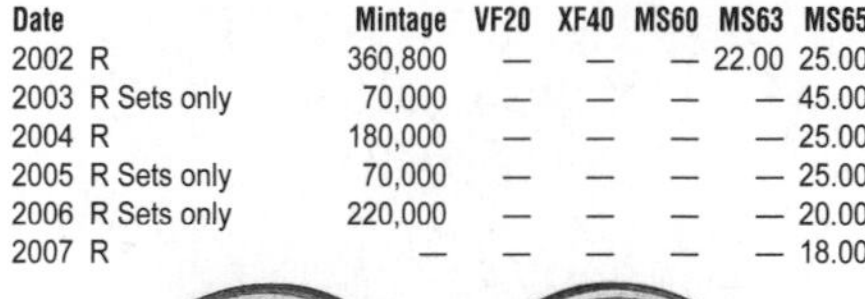

| Date | Mintage | VF20 | XF40 | MS60 | MS63 | MS65 |
|---|---|---|---|---|---|---|
| 2002 R | 360,800 | — | — | — | 22.00 | 25.00 |
| 2003 R Sets only | 70,000 | — | — | — | — | 45.00 |
| 2004 R | 180,000 | — | — | — | — | 25.00 |
| 2005 R Sets only | 70,000 | — | — | — | — | 25.00 |
| 2006 R Sets only | 220,000 | — | — | — | — | 20.00 |
| 2007 R | — | — | — | — | — | 18.00 |

**KM# 485 EURO**
7.50 g., Bi-Metallic Copper-Nickel center in Nickel-Brass ring, 23.25 mm. **Obv:** Covered arms within wreath and stars **Rev:** Relief map of Western Europe, value and stars **Edge:** Segmented reeding

| Date | Mintage | VF20 | XF40 | MS60 | MS63 | MS65 |
|---|---|---|---|---|---|---|
| 2008 R | — | — | — | — | 12.00 | 15.00 |
| 2008 R | 13,000 | PF65 15.00 | | | | |
| 2009 R | 1,096,672 | — | — | — | 12.00 | 15.00 |
| 2009 R | 13,500 | PF65 15.00 | | | | |
| 2010 R | 996,134 | — | — | — | 12.00 | 15.00 |
| 2010 R | 8,600 | PF65 15.00 | | | | |
| 2011 R | — | — | — | — | 12.00 | 15.00 |
| 2011 R | 8,600 | PF65 15.00 | | | | |
| 2012 R | 10,000 | — | — | — | 12.00 | 15.00 |
| 2012 R | — | PF65 15.00 | | | | |
| 2013 R | — | — | — | — | 12.00 | 15.00 |

**KM# 447 2 EURO**
8.50 g., Bi-Metallic Nickel-Brass center in Copper-Nickel ring, 25.75 mm. **Obv:** Government building **Rev:** Value and map **Edge:** Reeded with 2's and stars

| Date | Mintage | VF20 | XF40 | MS60 | MS63 | MS65 |
|---|---|---|---|---|---|---|
| 2002 R | 255,760 | — | — | — | 25.00 | 28.00 |
| 2003 R Sets only | 70,000 | — | — | — | — | 45.00 |
| 2004 R Sets only | 70,000 | — | — | — | — | 28.00 |
| 2005 R Sets only | 210,000 | — | — | — | — | 28.00 |
| 2006 R Sets only | 190,000 | — | — | — | — | 22.00 |
| 2007 R | — | — | — | — | — | 20.00 |

**KM# 467 2 EURO**
8.50 g., Bi-Metallic Nickel-Brass center in Copper-Nickel ring, 25.75 mm. **Obv:** Crowned arms within sprigs **Rev:** Bartolomeo Borghesi **Edge:** Alternating stars and 2's

| Date | Mintage | VF20 | XF40 | MS60 | MS63 | MS65 |
|---|---|---|---|---|---|---|
| 2004 R | 110,000 | — | — | — | 135 | 150 |

**KM# 469 2 EURO**
8.50 g., Bi-Metallic Nickel-Brass center in Copper-Nickel ring, 25.75 mm. **Obv:** Galileo Galilei at telescope

| Date | Mintage | VF20 | XF40 | MS60 | MS63 | MS65 |
|---|---|---|---|---|---|---|
| 2005 R | 130,000 | — | — | — | 135 | 150 |

**KM# 478 2 EURO**
8.50 g., Bi-Metallic Nickel-Brass center in Copper-Nickel ring, 25.75 mm. **Subject:** Christopher Columbus, 500th Anniversary of Death **Obv:** Head of Columbus within border of stars **Rev:** Map and value

| Date | Mintage | VF20 | XF40 | MS60 | MS63 | MS65 |
|---|---|---|---|---|---|---|
| 2006 R | 120,000 | — | — | — | 100 | 125 |

**KM# 481 2 EURO**
8.50 g., Bi-Metallic Nickel-Brass center in Copper-Nickel ring, 25.75 mm. **Subject:** Giuseppe Garibaldi, 200th Anniversary of Birth **Obv:** Half length bust facing **Rev:** Relief map of Western Europe, value and stars

| Date | Mintage | VF20 | XF40 | MS60 | MS63 | MS65 |
|---|---|---|---|---|---|---|
| 2007 R | 130,000 | — | — | — | 60.00 | 75.00 |

**KM# 486 2 EURO**
8.50 g., Bi-Metallic Nickel-Brass center in Copper-Nickel ring, 25.75 mm. **Obv:** Palace **Rev:** Relief map of Western Europe, value and stars

| Date | Mintage | VF20 | XF40 | MS60 | MS63 | MS65 |
|---|---|---|---|---|---|---|
| 2008 R | — | — | — | — | 24.00 | 28.00 |
| 2008 R | 13,000 | PF65 20.00 | | | | |
| 2009 R | — | — | — | — | 24.00 | 28.00 |
| 2009 R | 13,500 | PF65 20.00 | | | | |
| 2010 R | — | — | — | — | 24.00 | 28.00 |
| 2010 R | 8,600 | PF65 20.00 | | | | |
| 2011 R | 631,831 | — | — | — | 24.00 | 28.00 |
| 2011 R | 8,600 | PF65 20.00 | | | | |
| 2012 R | 627,249 | — | — | — | 24.00 | 28.00 |
| 2013 R | — | — | — | — | 24.00 | 28.00 |

**KM# 487 2 EURO**
8.50 g., Bi-Metallic Nickel-Brass center in Copper-Nickel ring, 25.75 mm. **Subject:** European Year of Intercultural Dialogue **Obv:** Five figures with arms outstretched, books below **Rev:** Relief map of Western Europe, value and stars

| Date | Mintage | VF20 | XF40 | MS60 | MS63 | MS65 |
|---|---|---|---|---|---|---|
| 2008 R | 130,000 | — | — | — | 70.00 | 90.00 |

**KM# 490 2 EURO**
8.50 g., Bi-Metallic Nickel-Brass center in Copper-Nickel ring, 25.75 mm. **Subject:** Creativity and Innovation **Obv:** Chemical flasks and book

| Date | Mintage | VF20 | XF40 | MS60 | MS63 | MS65 |
|---|---|---|---|---|---|---|
| 2009 R | — | — | — | — | 45.00 | 55.00 |

**KM# 494 2 EURO**
8.50 g., Bi-Metallic Nickel-Brass center in Copper-Nickel ring, 25.75 mm. **Subject:** Sandra Botticeli, 500th Anniversary of Death

| Date | Mintage | VF20 | XF40 | MS60 | MS63 | MS65 |
|---|---|---|---|---|---|---|
| 2010 R | 130,000 | — | — | — | 45.00 | 55.00 |

**KM# 500 2 EURO**
8.50 g., Bi-Metallic Nickel-Brass center in Copper-Nickel ring, 25.75 mm. **Subject:** Hgiorgio Vasari, 500th Anniversary of Birth

| Date | Mintage | VF20 | XF40 | MS60 | MS63 | MS65 |
|---|---|---|---|---|---|---|
| 2011 R | 130,000 | — | — | — | 35.00 | 45.00 |

**KM# 519 2 EURO**
8.50 g., Bi-Metallic Nickel-Brass center in Copper-Nickel ring, 25.75 mm. **Obv:** Euro symbol

| Date | Mintage | VF20 | XF40 | MS60 | MS63 | MS65 |
|---|---|---|---|---|---|---|
| 2012 R | 125,000 | — | — | — | 35.00 | 45.00 |
| 2012 R | 5,000 | PF65 55.00 | | | | |

**KM# 294 2 EURO**
8.50 g., Bi-Metallic Nickel-Brass center in Copper-Nickel ring, 25.75 mm. **Obv:** Building

| Date | Mintage | VF20 | XF40 | MS60 | MS63 | MS65 |
|---|---|---|---|---|---|---|
| 2013 | — | — | — | — | 35.00 | 45.00 |

**KM# 295 2 EURO**
8.50 g., Bi-Metallic Nickel-Brass center in Copper-Nickel ring, 25.75 mm. **Obv:** Giacomo Puccini

| Date | Mintage | VF20 | XF40 | MS60 | MS63 | MS65 |
|---|---|---|---|---|---|---|
| 2014 | — | — | — | — | 35.00 | 45.00 |

**KM# 296 2 EURO**
8.50 g., Bi-Metallic Nickel-Brass center in Copper-Nickel ring, 25.75 mm. **Obv:** Donato Bramante

| Date | Mintage | VF20 | XF40 | MS60 | MS63 | MS65 |
|---|---|---|---|---|---|---|
| 2014 | — | — | — | — | 35.00 | 45.00 |

**KM# 448 5 EURO**
18.00 g., 0.925 Silver 0.5353 oz. ASW, 32 mm. **Subject:** Welcome Euro **Obv:** Three ostrich feathers and towers **Rev:** Circle of roses

| Date | Mintage | VF20 | XF40 | MS60 | MS63 | MS65 |
|---|---|---|---|---|---|---|
| 2002 R | 37,000 | PF63 65.00 | PF65 75.00 | | | |

**KM# 452 5 EURO**
18.00 g., 0.925 Silver 0.5353 oz. ASW, 32 mm. **Obv:** National arms **Rev:** Allegorical depiction of Independence, Tolerance and Liberty

| Date | Mintage | VF20 | XF40 | MS60 | MS63 | MS65 |
|---|---|---|---|---|---|---|
| 2003 R | 70,000 | — | — | — | 35.00 | 40.00 |

**KM# 453 5 EURO**
18.00 g., 0.925 Silver 0.5353 oz. ASW, 32 mm. **Subject:** 2004 Olympics **Obv:** Stylized three towers **Rev:** Ancient Olympians **Edge:** Reeded

| Date | Mintage | VF20 | XF40 | MS60 | MS63 | MS65 |
|---|---|---|---|---|---|---|
| 2003 R | 37,742 | PF63 45.00 | PF65 50.00 | | | |

**KM# 458 5 EURO**
18.00 g., 0.925 Silver 0.5353 oz. ASW, 32 mm. **Obv:** National arms **Rev:** Value behind Bartolomeo Borghesi

| Date | Mintage | VF20 | XF40 | MS60 | MS63 | MS65 |
|---|---|---|---|---|---|---|
| 2004 R | 70,000 | — | — | — | 30.00 | 35.00 |

**KM# 462 5 EURO**
18.00 g., 0.925 Silver 0.5353 oz. ASW, 32 mm. **Obv:** Three stylized ostrich feathers and towers **Rev:** Two soccer players

| Date | Mintage | VF20 | XF40 | MS60 | MS63 | MS65 |
|---|---|---|---|---|---|---|
| 2004 R | 29,673 | PF63 40.00 | PF65 45.00 | | | |

**KM# 468 5 EURO**
18.00 g., 0.925 Silver 0.5353 oz. ASW, 32 mm. **Obv:** Three towers **Rev:** Antonio Onofri and value

| Date | Mintage | VF20 | XF40 | MS60 | MS63 | MS65 |
|---|---|---|---|---|---|---|
| 2005 R | 70,000 | — | — | — | 30.00 | 35.00 |

**KM# 511 5 EURO**
18.00 g., 0.925 Silver 0.5353 oz. ASW, 32 mm. **Subject:** Winter Olympics, Turin **Rev:** Large snowflake, snowman on skies

| Date | Mintage | VF20 | XF40 | MS60 | MS63 | MS65 |
|---|---|---|---|---|---|---|
| 2005 R | 26,786 | PF63 45.00 | PF65 50.00 | | | |

**KM# 525 5 EURO**
22.00 g., 0.925 Silver 0.6543 oz. ASW **Obv:** National arms **Rev:** Soldier with flag

| Date | Mintage | VF20 | XF40 | MS60 | MS63 | MS65 |
|---|---|---|---|---|---|---|
| 2005 | 969 | PF65 45.00 | | | | |

**KM# 472 5 EURO**
18.00 g., 0.925 Silver 0.5353 oz. ASW, 32 mm. **Obv:** Portrait of Melchiorie Delfico

| Date | Mintage | VF20 | XF40 | MS60 | MS63 | MS65 |
|---|---|---|---|---|---|---|
| 2006 R | 65,000 | — | — | — | 30.00 | 35.00 |

**KM# 476 5 EURO**
18.00 g., 0.925 Silver 0.5353 oz. ASW, 32 mm. **Subject:** Andrea Mantegna, 500th Anniversary of Death **Obv:** Three towers **Rev:** Statue of soldier and naked female

| Date | Mintage | VF20 | XF40 | MS60 | MS63 | MS65 |
|---|---|---|---|---|---|---|
| 2006 R | 18,986 | PF63 35.00 | PF65 40.00 | | | |

**KM# 473 5 EURO**
18.00 g., 0.925 Silver 0.5353 oz. ASW, 32 mm. **Subject:** Equal Opportunity between the sexes **Obv:** Three ostrich feathers and towers **Obv. Legend:** REPUBLICA DI SAN MARINO **Rev:** Nude female at left, nude male at right, ribbon across symbols within circle above, value below **Rev. Inscription:** PARI OPPORTITA **Edge:** Reeded

| Date | Mintage | VF20 | XF40 | MS60 | MS63 | MS65 |
|---|---|---|---|---|---|---|
| 2007 R | 70,000 | — | — | — | 30.00 | 35.00 |

**KM# 474 5 EURO**
18.00 g., 0.925 Silver 0.5353 oz. ASW, 32 mm. **Subject:** 50th Anniversary Death of Toscanini **Obv:** Stylized national arms **Obv. Legend:** REPUBBLICA DI SAN MARINO **Rev:** Head of Toscanini left **Edge:** Reeded

| Date | Mintage | VF20 | XF40 | MS60 | MS63 | MS65 |
|---|---|---|---|---|---|---|
| ND-2007 R | 17,736 | PF63 35.00 | PF65 40.00 | | | |

**KM# 512 5 EURO**
18.00 g., 0.925 Silver 0.5353 oz. ASW, 32 mm. **Rev:** Winds, land and sea

| Date | Mintage | VF20 | XF40 | MS60 | MS63 | MS65 |
|---|---|---|---|---|---|---|
| 2008 R | 50,000 | — | — | — | 30.00 | 35.00 |

**KM# 513 5 EURO**
18.00 g., 0.925 Silver 0.5353 oz. ASW, 32 mm. **Subject:** Summer Olympics, Peking **Rev:** Ribbon Dancer

| Date | Mintage | VF20 | XF40 | MS60 | MS63 | MS65 |
|---|---|---|---|---|---|---|
| 2008 R | 21,000 | PF63 40.00 | PF65 45.00 | | | |

**KM# 506 5 EURO**
18.00 g., 0.925 Silver 0.5353 oz. ASW, 32 mm. **Subject:** Kepler **Obv:** Kepler bust and globe **Rev:** Planets orbit around central sun

| Date | Mintage | VF20 | XF40 | MS60 | MS63 | MS65 |
|---|---|---|---|---|---|---|
| 2009 R | 13,400 | PF63 45.00 | PF65 50.00 | | | |

**KM# 515 5 EURO**
18.00 g., 0.925 Silver 0.5353 oz. ASW, 32 mm. **Subject:** Year of Astronomy **Obv:** Planets in orbit **Rev:** Planets in orbit, Astrolab

| Date | Mintage | VF20 | XF40 | MS60 | MS63 | MS65 |
|---|---|---|---|---|---|---|
| 2009 R | 50,000 | — | — | — | 30.00 | 35.00 |

**KM# 495 5 EURO**
18.00 g., 0.925 Silver 0.5353 oz. ASW, 32 mm. **Subject:** Shanghai Expo

| Date | Mintage | VF20 | XF40 | MS60 | MS63 | MS65 |
|---|---|---|---|---|---|---|
| 2010 R | 10,000 | PF63 60.00 | PF65 65.00 | | | |

**KM# 496 5 EURO**
18.00 g., 0.925 Silver 0.5353 oz. ASW, 32 mm. **Subject:** Michelangelo Caravaggio, 500th Anniverdary of Death

| Date | Mintage | VF20 | XF40 | MS60 | MS63 | MS65 |
|---|---|---|---|---|---|---|
| 2010 R | 48,000 | — | — | — | 30.00 | 35.00 |

**KM# 501 5 EURO**
18.00 g., 0.925 Silver 0.5353 oz. ASW, 32 mm. **Subject:** European Discoveries **Obv:** Crowned coat of arms **Rev:** Busts of Antonio & Roberto Pazzaglia, Mt. Everest in background

| Date | Mintage | VF20 | XF40 | MS60 | MS63 | MS65 |
|---|---|---|---|---|---|---|
| 2011 R | 10,000 | PF63 45.00 | PF65 50.00 | | | |

**KM# 502 5 EURO**
18.00 g., 0.925 Silver 0.5353 oz. ASW, 32 mm. **Subject:** 50th Anniversary of man in space **Rev:** Gagarin and Shepard, Vostok I and Freedom 7 spacecraft

| Date | Mintage | VF20 | XF40 | MS60 | MS63 | MS65 |
|---|---|---|---|---|---|---|
| 2011 R | 48,000 | — | — | — | 30.00 | 35.00 |

**KM# 520 5 EURO**
18.00 g., 0.925 Silver 0.5353 oz. ASW, 32 mm. **Subject:** Giovanni Pascoli, 100th Anniversary of Death **Obv:** National arms **Rev:** Bust at right

| Date | Mintage | VF20 | XF40 | MS60 | MS63 | MS65 |
|---|---|---|---|---|---|---|
| 2012 R | 40,000 | PF63 35.00 | PF65 40.00 | | | |

**KM# 521 5 EURO**
18.00 g., 0.925 Silver 0.5353 oz. ASW, 32 mm. **Subject:** Amerigo Vespucci, 500th Anniversary of Death **Obv:** National arms **Rev:** Vespucci standing holding astrolobe to the stars

| Date | Mintage | VF20 | XF40 | MS60 | MS63 | MS65 |
|---|---|---|---|---|---|---|
| 2012 R | 12,000 | PF63 50.00 | PF65 55.00 | | | |

**KM# 524 5 EURO**
18.00 g., 0.925 Silver 0.5353 oz. ASW, 32 mm. **Subject:** Federico Fellini, 20th Anniversary of Death **Obv:** Head left **Rev:** Character and name on banner

| Date | Mintage | VF20 | XF40 | MS60 | MS63 | MS65 |
|---|---|---|---|---|---|---|
| 2013 | 30,000 | — | — | — | — | 50.00 |

**KM# 529 5 EURO**
18.00 g., 0.925 Silver 0.5353 oz. ASW, 32 mm. **Obv:** Crowned shield **Rev:** J.F. Kennedy and flag

| Date | Mintage | VF20 | XF40 | MS60 | MS63 | MS65 |
|---|---|---|---|---|---|---|
| 2013 | 8,000 | PF65 75.00 | | | | |

**KM# 528 5 EURO**
18.00 g., 0.925 Silver 0.5353 oz. ASW, 32 mm. **Subject:** Verona's staging of Aida

| Date | Mintage | VF20 | XF40 | MS60 | MS63 | MS65 |
|---|---|---|---|---|---|---|
| 2013 | — | PF65 35.00 | | | | |

**KM# 531 20 LIRE**
6.45 g., 0.900 Gold 0.1867 oz. AGW, 21 mm. **Obv:** Crowned shield **Rev:** Serravalle town gate

| Date | Mintage | VF20 | XF40 | MS60 | MS63 | MS65 |
|---|---|---|---|---|---|---|
| 2013 | — | PF65 450 | | | | |

**KM# 449 10 EURO**
22.00 g., 0.925 Silver 0.6543 oz. ASW, 34 mm. **Subject:** Welcome Euro **Obv:** Three ostrich feathers and towers **Rev:** Infant sleeping in flower

| Date | Mintage | VF20 | XF40 | MS60 | MS63 | MS65 |
|---|---|---|---|---|---|---|
| 2002 R | 36,995 | PF63 90.00 | PF65 100 | | | |

**KM# 454 10 EURO**
22.00 g., 0.925 Silver 0.6543 oz. ASW, 34 mm. **Subject:** 2004 Olympics **Obv:** Three stylized towers **Rev:** Modern Olympians **Edge:** Segmented reeding

| Date | Mintage | VF20 | XF40 | MS60 | MS63 | MS65 |
|---|---|---|---|---|---|---|
| 2003 R | 37,741 | PF63 65.00 | PF65 75.00 | | | |

**KM# 463 10 EURO**
22.00 g., 0.925 Silver 0.6543 oz. ASW, 34 mm. **Obv:** Three stylized ostrich feathers and towers **Rev:** Two soccer players

| Date | Mintage | VF20 | XF40 | MS60 | MS63 | MS65 |
|---|---|---|---|---|---|---|
| 2004 R | 29,617 | PF63 60.00 | PF65 70.00 | | | |

**KM# 344 10 EURO**
22.00 g., 0.925 Silver 0.6543 oz. ASW **Subject:** Uniformed National Military, 500th Anniversary **Obv:** National arms **Rev:** Soldier with flag

| Date | Mintage | VF20 | XF40 | MS60 | MS63 | MS65 |
|---|---|---|---|---|---|---|
| 2005 R | 21,969 | PF63 45.00 | PF65 50.00 | | | |

**KM# 477 10 EURO**
22.00 g., 0.925 Silver 0.6543 oz. ASW, 34 mm. **Subject:** Antonio Canova **Obv:** Three towers **Rev:** The Three Graces

| Date | Mintage | VF20 | XF40 | MS60 | MS63 | MS65 |
|---|---|---|---|---|---|---|
| 2006 R | 17,859 | PF63 60.00 | PF65 65.00 | | | |

**KM# 475 10 EURO**
22.00 g., 0.925 Silver 0.6543 oz. ASW, 34 mm. **Subject:** 100th Anniversary - Birthday of Giosuè Carducci **Obv:** Stylized national arms **Obv. Legend:** REPUBBLICA DI SAN MARINO **Rev:** 1/2 length figure of Carducci facing with quill pen in hand at table **Rev. Legend:** CARDUCCI **Edge:** Segmented reeding

| Date | Mintage | VF20 | XF40 | MS60 | MS63 | MS65 |
|---|---|---|---|---|---|---|
| ND-2007 R | 14,615 | PF63 50.00 | PF65 55.00 | | | |

### KM# 514 10 EURO

22.00 g., 0.925 Silver 0.6543 oz. ASW, 34 mm. **Subject:** Andrea Palladio, 500th Anniversary of Birth **Rev:** Building façade

| Date | Mintage | VF20 | XF40 | MS60 | MS63 | MS65 |
|---|---|---|---|---|---|---|
| 2008 R | 17,000 | PF63 60.00 | | PF65 65.00 | | |

### KM# 516 10 EURO

22.00 g., 0.925 Silver 0.6543 oz. ASW, 34 mm. **Subject:** Euro, 10th Anniversary

| Date | Mintage | VF20 | XF40 | MS60 | MS63 | MS65 |
|---|---|---|---|---|---|---|
| 2009 R | 12,500 | PF63 55.00 | | PF65 60.00 | | |

### KM# 497 10 EURO

22.00 g., 0.925 Silver 0.6543 oz. ASW, 34 mm. **Subject:** Robert Schumann, 200th Anniversary of Birth

| Date | Mintage | VF20 | XF40 | MS60 | MS63 | MS65 |
|---|---|---|---|---|---|---|
| 2010 R | 10,000 | PF63 50.00 | | PF65 55.00 | | |

### KM# 503 10 EURO

22.00 g., 0.925 Silver 0.6543 oz. ASW, 34 mm. **Subject:** Euro, 10th Anniversary **Obv:** Montage of partial coin designs

| Date | Mintage | VF20 | XF40 | MS60 | MS63 | MS65 |
|---|---|---|---|---|---|---|
| 2011 R | 10,000 | PF63 55.00 | | PF65 60.00 | | |

### KM# 523 10 EURO

Silver, 34 mm. **Subject:** Aligi Sassu, sculptor

| Date | Mintage | VF20 | XF40 | MS60 | MS63 | MS65 |
|---|---|---|---|---|---|---|
| 2012 | — | PF65 75.00 | | | | |

### KM# 522 10 EURO

22.00 g., 0.925 Silver 0.6543 oz. ASW, 34 mm. **Subject:** Machiavelli's "The Prince"

| Date | Mintage | VF20 | XF40 | MS60 | MS63 | MS65 |
|---|---|---|---|---|---|---|
| 2013 | — | PF63 45.00 | | PF65 50.00 | | |

### KM# 530 10 EURO

22.00 g., 0.925 Silver 0.6543 oz. ASW, 34 mm. **Subject:** Emilio Greco, 100th Anniversary of Birth **Obv:** Crowned shield **Rev:** Female figure skater left

| Date | Mintage | VF20 | XF40 | MS60 | MS63 | MS65 |
|---|---|---|---|---|---|---|
| 2013 | — | PF65 75.00 | | | | |

### KM# 460 20 EURO

6.45 g., 0.900 Gold 0.1867 oz. AGW, 21 mm. **Subject:** Ravenna, 1600th Anniversary **Obv:** National arms **Rev:** Female figure from bas-relief wall design **Edge:** Reeded

| Date | Mintage | VF20 | XF40 | MS60 | MS63 | MS65 |
|---|---|---|---|---|---|---|
| 2002 R | 4,510 | PF65 375 | | | | |

### KM# 455 20 EURO

6.45 g., 0.900 Gold 0.1867 oz. AGW, 21 mm. **Obv:** Three ostrich feathers **Rev:** Giotto's "Presentation of Jesus at the Temple **Edge:** Reeded

| Date | Mintage | VF20 | XF40 | MS60 | MS63 | MS65 |
|---|---|---|---|---|---|---|
| 2003 R | 7,281 | PF65 375 | | | | |

### KM# 465 20 EURO

6.45 g., 0.900 Gold 0.1867 oz. AGW, 21 mm. **Obv:** Three plumes **Rev:** Marco Polo meeting Kublai Khan **Edge:** Reeded

| Date | Mintage | VF20 | XF40 | MS60 | MS63 | MS65 |
|---|---|---|---|---|---|---|
| 2004 R | 5,885 | PF65 375 | | | | |

### KM# 470 20 EURO

6.45 g., 0.900 Gold 0.1867 oz. AGW, 21 mm. **Subject:** International Day of Peace **Obv:** Stylized faces and leaves

| Date | Mintage | VF20 | XF40 | MS60 | MS63 | MS65 |
|---|---|---|---|---|---|---|
| 2005 R | 3,914 | PF65 375 | | | | |

### KM# 479 20 EURO

6.45 g., 0.900 Gold 0.1866 oz. AGW, 21 mm. **Subject:** Giovan Battista Belluzzi, 500th Birthday **Obv:** Crowned shield **Rev:** Fortification plan

| Date | Mintage | VF20 | XF40 | MS60 | MS63 | MS65 |
|---|---|---|---|---|---|---|
| 2006 R | 2,684 | PF65 375 | | | | |

### KM# 507 20 EURO

6.45 g., 0.900 Gold 0.1867 oz. AGW

| Date | Mintage | VF20 | XF40 | MS60 | MS63 | MS65 |
|---|---|---|---|---|---|---|
| 2007 R | 2,105 | PF65 350 | | | | |

### KM# 491 20 EURO

6.45 g., 0.900 Gold 0.1866 oz. AGW **Subject:** Roman Antiquities **Obv:** Arms **Rev:** Small statue of Mercury

| Date | Mintage | VF20 | XF40 | MS60 | MS63 | MS65 |
|---|---|---|---|---|---|---|
| 2008 R | 2,100 | PF65 375 | | | | |

### KM# 509 20 EURO

6.45 g., 0.900 Gold 0.1867 oz. AGW, 21 mm.

| Date | Mintage | VF20 | XF40 | MS60 | MS63 | MS65 |
|---|---|---|---|---|---|---|
| 2009 R | 2,000 | PF65 350 | | | | |

### KM# 498 20 EURO

6.45 g., 0.900 Gold 0.1867 oz. AGW, 21 mm. **Subject:** Treasurers from San Marino - Wooden bust of St. Agata

| Date | Mintage | VF20 | XF40 | MS60 | MS63 | MS65 |
|---|---|---|---|---|---|---|
| 2010 R | 2,000 | PF65 375 | | | | |

### KM# 504 20 EURO

6.45 g., 0.900 Gold 0.1867 oz. AGW, 21 mm. **Subject:** Treasures from San Marino

| Date | Mintage | VF20 | XF40 | MS60 | MS63 | MS65 |
|---|---|---|---|---|---|---|
| 2011 R | 1,600 | PF65 375 | | | | |

### KM# 526 20 EURO

6.45 g., 0.900 Gold 0.1866 oz. AGW, 21 mm. **Subject:** San Marino Architecture **Obv:** Crowned shield **Rev:** Borgo Maggiore

| Date | Mintage | VF20 | XF40 | MS60 | MS63 | MS65 |
|---|---|---|---|---|---|---|
| 2012 | 1,600 | PF65 450 | | | | |

### KM# 461 50 EURO

16.13 g., 0.900 Gold 0.4667 oz. AGW, 28 mm. **Subject:** 1600th Anniversary of Ravenna **Obv:** National arms **Rev:** Wall painting **Edge:** Reeded

| Date | Mintage | VF20 | XF40 | MS60 | MS63 | MS65 |
|---|---|---|---|---|---|---|
| 2002 R | 4,510 | PF65 900 | | | | |

### KM# 456 50 EURO

16.13 g., 0.900 Gold 0.4667 oz. AGW, 28 mm. **Obv:** Three ostrich feathers **Rev:** Giotto's "The Pentecost **Edge:** Reeded

| Date | Mintage | VF20 | XF40 | MS60 | MS63 | MS65 |
|---|---|---|---|---|---|---|
| 2003 R | 7,281 | PF65 900 | | | | |

### KM# 466 50 EURO

16.13 g., 0.900 Gold 0.4667 oz. AGW, 28 mm. **Obv:** Three plumes **Rev:** Marco Polo **Edge:** Reeded

| Date | Mintage | VF20 | XF40 | MS60 | MS63 | MS65 |
|---|---|---|---|---|---|---|
| 2004 R | 5,885 | PF65 900 | | | | |

### KM# 471 50 EURO

16.13 g., 0.900 Gold 0.4667 oz. AGW, 28 mm. **Subject:** International Day of Peace **Obv:** Group of people gathering

| Date | Mintage | VF20 | XF40 | MS60 | MS63 | MS65 |
|---|---|---|---|---|---|---|
| 2005 R | 3,914 | PF65 900 | | | | |

### KM# 480 50 EURO

16.13 g., 0.900 Gold 0.4667 oz. AGW, 28 mm. **Subject:** Giovan Batista Belluzzi **Obv:** Crowned shield **Rev:** Bust right

| Date | Mintage | VF20 | XF40 | MS60 | MS63 | MS65 |
|---|---|---|---|---|---|---|
| 2006 R | 2,684 | PF65 900 | | | | |

### KM# 508 50 EURO

16.13 g., 0.900 Gold 0.4667 oz. AGW, 28 mm.

| Date | Mintage | VF20 | XF40 | MS60 | MS63 | MS65 |
|---|---|---|---|---|---|---|
| 2007 R | 2,105 | PF65 900 | | | | |

### KM# 492 50 EURO

16.13 g., 0.900 Gold 0.4667 oz. AGW, 28 mm. **Subject:** Antiquities **Obv:** Arms **Rev:** Two bronze fibulae

| Date | Mintage | VF20 | XF40 | MS60 | MS63 | MS65 |
|---|---|---|---|---|---|---|
| 2008 R | 2,100 | PF65 900 | | | | |

### KM# 510 50 EURO

16.13 g., 0.900 Gold 0.4667 oz. AGW, 28 mm.

| Date | Mintage | VF20 | XF40 | MS60 | MS63 | MS65 |
|---|---|---|---|---|---|---|
| 2009 R | 2,000 | PF65 900 | | | | |

### KM# 499 50 EURO

16.13 g., 0.900 Gold 0.4667 oz. AGW, 28 mm. **Subject:** Treasurers from San Marino - Saint Marinus

| Date | Mintage | VF20 | XF40 | MS60 | MS63 | MS65 |
|---|---|---|---|---|---|---|
| 2010 R | 2,000 | PF65 900 | | | | |

### KM# 505 50 EURO

16.13 g., 0.900 Gold 0.4667 oz. AGW, 28 mm. **Subject:** Treasures from San Marino

| Date | Mintage | VF20 | XF40 | MS60 | MS63 | MS65 |
|---|---|---|---|---|---|---|
| 2011 R | 1,600 | PF65 900 | | | | |

### KM# 527 50 EURO

16.13 g., 0.900 Gold 0.4667 oz. AGW, 28 mm. **Subject:** San Marino Architecture **Obv:** Crowned shield **Rev:** Borgo Maggiore

| Date | Mintage | VF20 | XF40 | MS60 | MS63 | MS65 |
|---|---|---|---|---|---|---|
| 2012 | 1,600 | PF65 850 | | | | |

### KM# 532 50 EURO

16.13 g., 0.900 Gold 0.4667 oz. AGW, 28 mm. **Obv:** Crowned shield **Rev:** Serravalle city square

| Date | Mintage | VF20 | XF40 | MS60 | MS63 | MS65 |
|---|---|---|---|---|---|---|
| 2013 | — | PF65 800 | | | | |

## MINT SETS

| KM# | Date | Mintage | Identification | Issue Price | Mkt Val |
|---|---|---|---|---|---|
| MS61 | 2001 (8) | 2,000 | KM424-431 | 18.00 | 50.00 |
| MS62 | 2002 (8) | 120,000 | KM440 - 447 | — | 275 |
| MS63 | 2003 (9) | — | KM#440-447, 452 | 55.00 | 350 |
| MS64 | 2004 (9) | — | KM#440-447, 458 | 55.00 | 220 |
| MS65 | 2005 (9) | — | KM#440-447, 468 | 55.00 | 225 |
| MS66 | 2006 (9) | 65,000 | KM#440-447, 472 | — | 185 |
| MS67 | 2007 (3) | — | KM#443, 444, 447 | 27.50 | 55.00 |
| MS68 | 2007 (9) | — | KM#440-447, 473 | 120 | 160 |

## PROOF SETS

| KM# | Date | Mintage | Identification | Issue Price | Mkt Val |
|---|---|---|---|---|---|
| PS14 | 2001 (3) | 4,500 | KM433-435 | 178 | 500 |
| PSA15 | 2001 (2) | — | KM#436, 437 | — | 70.00 |
| PS15 | 2002 (2) | 37,000 | KM#448-449 | — | 175 |
| PS16 | 2002 (2) | 4,550 | KM#460-461 | — | 1,150 |
| PS17 | 2003 (2) | 7,300 | KM#455-456 | — | 975 |
| PS18 | 2004 (2) | 7,300 | KM#465-466 | — | 975 |
| PS19 | 2005 (2) | 5,300 | KM#470-471 | — | 1,050 |
| PS20 | 2008 (8) | 13,000 | KM#440-442, 482-486 | — | 135 |
| PS21 | 2009 (8) | 13,500 | KM#440-443, 482-486 | — | 135 |
| PS22 | 2010 (8) | 8,600 | KM#440-442, 482-486 | — | 135 |
| PS23 | 2011 (8) | 8,600 | KM#440-442, 482-486 | — | 135 |

# SAUDI ARABIA

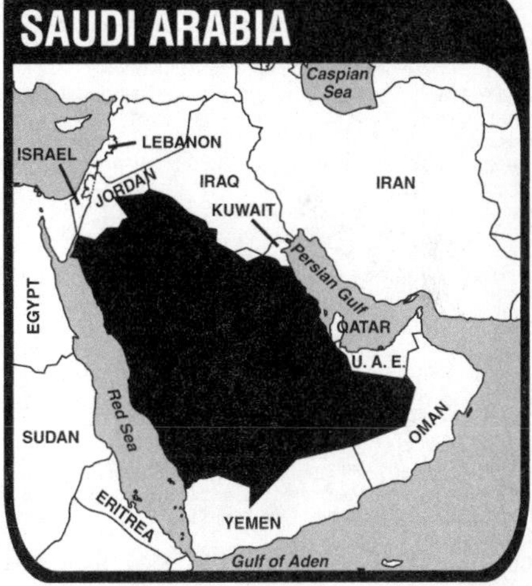


The Kingdom of Saudi Arabia, an independent and absolute hereditary monarchy comprising the former sultanate of Nejd, the old kingdom of Hejaz, Asir and Al Hasa, occupies four-fifths of the Arabian peninsula. The kingdom has an area of 830,000 sq. mi. (2,149,690 sq. km.) and a population of *16.1 million. Capital: Riyadh. The economy is based on oil, which provides 85 percent of Saudi Arabia's revenue.

**TITLES**

العربية السعودية

Al-Arabiya(t) as-Sa'udiya(t)

المملكة العربية السعودية

Al-Mamlaka(t) al-'Arabiya(t) as-Sa'udiya(t)

**RULERS**

**al Sa'ud Dynasty**

Fahad bin Abd Al-Aziz, AH1403-1426/1982-2005AD

Abdullah bin Abdul Aziz, AH1426-/2005AD

# KINGDOM

## REFORM COINAGE

5 Halala = 1 Ghirsh; 100 Halala = 1 Riyal

### KM# 69 5 HALALA (Ghirsh)

Copper-Nickel **Ruler:** Abdullah bin Abdul Aziz **Obv:** National emblem at center **Rev:** Legend above inscription in circle, dividing value, date below

| Date | Mintage | VF20 | XF40 | MS60 | MS63 | MS65 |
|---|---|---|---|---|---|---|
| AH1430(2009) | — | 0.30 | 0.60 | 0.80 | 1.50 | 2.00 |

### KM# 62 10 HALALA (2 Ghirsh)

4.00 g., Copper-Nickel, 21 mm. **Ruler:** Fahad Bin Abd Al-Aziz **Obv:** National emblem at center, legend above and below **Rev:** Legend above inscription in circle dividing value, date below **Edge:** Reeded

| Date | Mintage | VF20 | XF40 | MS60 | MS63 | MS65 |
|---|---|---|---|---|---|---|
| AH1423 | — | 0.15 | 0.35 | 0.50 | 0.75 | 1.50 |

### KM# 70 10 HALALA (2 Ghirsh)

Copper-Nickel **Ruler:** Abdullah bin Abdul Aziz **Obv:** National emblem at center **Rev:** Legend above inscription in circle, dividing value, date below

| Date | Mintage | VF20 | XF40 | MS60 | MS63 | MS65 |
|---|---|---|---|---|---|---|
| AH1430(2009) | — | 0.30 | 0.60 | 0.80 | 1.50 | 2.50 |

### KM# 63 25 HALALA (1/4 Riyal)

5.00 g., Copper-Nickel, 23 mm. **Ruler:** Fahad Bin Abd Al-Aziz **Obv:** National emblem at center, legend above and below **Rev:** Legend above inscription in circle dividing value, date below **Edge:** Reeded

| Date | Mintage | VF20 | XF40 | MS60 | MS63 | MS65 |
|---|---|---|---|---|---|---|
| AH1423 | — | 0.20 | 0.45 | 0.75 | 1.25 | 1.75 |

### KM# 71 25 HALALA (1/4 Riyal)

Bi-Metallic Copper-Nickel center in Brass ring **Ruler:** Abdullah bin Abdul Aziz **Obv:** National emblem at center **Rev:** Legend above inscription in circle, divides value, date below

| Date | Mintage | VF20 | XF40 | MS60 | MS63 | MS65 |
|---|---|---|---|---|---|---|
| AH1427 (2006) | — | 0.20 | 0.45 | 0.75 | 1.25 | 1.75 |
| AH1430 (2009) | — | 0.20 | 0.45 | 0.75 | 1.25 | 1.75 |
| AH1433 (2012) | — | 0.20 | 0.45 | 0.75 | 1.25 | 1.75 |

### KM# 64 50 HALALA (1/2 Riyal)

6.50 g., Copper-Nickel, 26 mm. **Ruler:** Fahad Bin Abd Al-Aziz **Obv:** National emblem at center, legend above and below **Rev:** Legend above inscription in circle dividing value, date below **Edge:** Reeded

| Date | Mintage | VF20 | XF40 | MS60 | MS63 | MS65 |
|---|---|---|---|---|---|---|
| AH1423 | — | 0.75 | 1.00 | 1.50 | 2.50 | 4.00 |

### KM# 68 50 HALALA (1/2 Riyal)

6.50 g., Copper-Nickel, 26 mm. **Ruler:** Abdullah bin Abdul Aziz **Obv:** National emblem at center **Rev:** Legend above inscription in circle, dividing value, date below **Edge:** Reeded

| Date | Mintage | VF20 | XF40 | MS60 | MS63 | MS65 |
|---|---|---|---|---|---|---|
| AH1427 (2006) | — | 0.30 | 0.60 | 1.00 | 1.50 | 2.50 |
| AH1428 (2007) | — | 0.30 | 0.60 | 1.00 | 1.50 | 2.50 |
| AH1431 (2010) | — | 0.30 | 0.60 | 1.00 | 1.50 | 2.00 |

### KM# 72 100 HALALA (1 Riyal)

Bi-Metallic Brass center in Copper-Nickel ring, 23 mm. **Ruler:** Abdullah bin Abdul Aziz **Obv:** National emblem at center **Rev:** Legend above inscription, divides value, date below **Edge:** Reeded

| Date | Mintage | VF20 | XF40 | MS60 | MS63 | MS65 |
|---|---|---|---|---|---|---|
| AH1427(2006) | — | 1.50 | 2.50 | 3.50 | 4.50 | 6.00 |
| AH1429(2008) | — | 1.50 | 2.50 | 3.50 | 4.50 | 6.00 |

# SERBIA

The Republic of Serbia, a former inland Balkan kingdom has an area of 34,116 sq. mi. (88,361 sq. km.). Capital: Belgrade.

**MINT MARKS**

A - Paris
(a) - Paris, privy mark only
H - Birmingham
V - Vienna
ÁÏ - (BP) Budapest

**MONETARY SYSTEM**

100 Para = 1 Dinara
DENOMINATIONS
ÏÀÐÀ = Para
ÏÀÐÅ = Pare
ÄÈÍÀÐ = Dinar
ÄÈÍÀÐÀ = Dinara

# REPUBLIC

## STANDARD COINAGE

### KM# 34 DINAR

4.34 g., Copper-Nickel-Zinc, 20 mm. **Obv:** National Bank emblem within circle **Rev:** Bank building and value **Edge:** Reeded

| Date | Mintage | VF20 | XF40 | MS60 | MS63 | MS65 |
|---|---|---|---|---|---|---|
| 2003 | 10,326,000 | — | 0.25 | 0.50 | 0.75 | 1.00 |
| 2004 | 25,038,000 | — | 0.25 | 0.50 | 0.75 | 1.00 |

### KM# 39 DINAR

4.26 g., Nickel-Brass, 20 mm. **Obv:** Crowned and mantled arms **Rev:** National Bank and value **Edge:** Segmented reeding

| Date | Mintage | VF20 | XF40 | MS60 | MS63 | MS65 |
|---|---|---|---|---|---|---|
| 2005 | 32,452,000 | — | 0.25 | 0.50 | 0.75 | 1.00 |
| 2006 | 39,550,000 | — | 0.25 | 0.50 | 0.75 | 1.00 |
| 2007 | 20,000,000 | — | 0.25 | 0.50 | 0.75 | 1.00 |
| 2008 | 10,093,000 | — | 0.25 | 0.50 | 0.75 | 1.00 |
| 2009 | 10,008,000 | — | 0.25 | 0.50 | 0.75 | 1.00 |

### KM# 48 DINAR

4.20 g., Copper Plated Steel, 20 mm. **Obv:** Arms **Rev:** National Bank and value

| Date | Mintage | VF20 | XF40 | MS60 | MS63 | MS65 |
|---|---|---|---|---|---|---|
| 2009 | 35,750,000 | — | 0.25 | 0.50 | 0.75 | 1.00 |
| 2010 | 30,600,000 | — | 0.25 | 0.50 | 0.75 | 1.00 |
| 2011 | 24,785,000 | — | 0.25 | 0.50 | 0.75 | 1.00 |

### KM# 54 DINAR

4.20 g., Copper Plated Steel, 20 mm. **Obv:** Arms, flat bottom crown above shield **Rev:** National Bank building and value

| Date | Mintage | VF20 | XF40 | MS60 | MS63 | MS65 |
|---|---|---|---|---|---|---|
| 2011 | — | — | 0.25 | 0.50 | 0.75 | 1.00 |
| 2012 | — | — | 0.25 | 0.50 | 0.75 | 1.00 |

### KM# 35 2 DINARA

5.24 g., Copper-Nickel-Zinc, 22 mm. **Obv:** National Bank emblem within circle **Rev:** Gracanica Monastery and value **Edge:** Reeded

| Date | Mintage | VF20 | XF40 | MS60 | MS63 | MS65 |
|---|---|---|---|---|---|---|
| 2003 | 15,216,000 | — | 0.25 | 0.50 | 0.75 | 1.00 |

### KM# 46 2 DINARA

5.15 g., Nickel-Brass, 22 mm. **Obv:** Crowned and mantled arms **Rev:** Gracanica Monastery and value **Edge:** Segmented reeding

| Date | Mintage | VF20 | XF40 | MS60 | MS63 | MS65 |
|---|---|---|---|---|---|---|
| 2006 | 15,385,500 | — | 0.25 | 0.50 | 0.75 | 1.00 |
| 2007 | 15,002,500 | — | 0.25 | 0.50 | 0.75 | 1.00 |
| 2008 | 10,093,000 | — | 0.25 | 0.50 | 0.75 | 1.00 |
| 2009 | 10,008,000 | — | 0.25 | 0.50 | 0.75 | 1.00 |

### KM# 49 2 DINARA

5.05 g., Copper Plated Steel, 22 mm. **Obv:** Arms **Rev:** Gracanica Monastery and value

| Date | Mintage | VF20 | XF40 | MS60 | MS63 | MS65 |
|---|---|---|---|---|---|---|
| 2009 | 27,845,000 | — | 0.25 | 0.50 | 0.75 | 1.00 |
| 2010 | 9,600,000 | — | 0.25 | 0.50 | 0.75 | 1.00 |
| 2011 | 12,400,000 | — | 0.25 | 0.50 | 0.75 | 1.00 |

### KM# 55 2 DINARA

5.05 g., Copper Plated Steel, 22 mm. **Obv:** Arms, flat bottom crown above shield **Rev:** Gracanica Monastery and value

| Date | Mintage | VF20 | XF40 | MS60 | MS63 | MS65 |
|---|---|---|---|---|---|---|
| 2011 | — | — | 0.25 | 0.50 | 0.75 | 1.00 |
| 2012 | — | — | 0.25 | 0.50 | 0.75 | 1.00 |

### KM# 36 5 DINARA

6.23 g., Copper-Nickel-Zinc, 22 mm. **Obv:** National Bank emblem within circle **Rev:** Krusedol Monastery and value **Edge:** Reeded

| Date | Mintage | VF20 | XF40 | MS60 | MS63 | MS65 |
|---|---|---|---|---|---|---|
| 2003 | 15,184,000 | — | 0.35 | 1.00 | 1.25 | 1.50 |

**KM# 40 5 DINARA**
6.13 g., Nickel-Brass, 24 mm. **Obv:** Crowned and mantled arms **Rev:** Krusedol Monastery and value **Edge:** Segmented reeding

| Date | Mintage | VF20 | XF40 | MS60 | MS63 | MS65 |
|---|---|---|---|---|---|---|
| 2005 | 5,099,500 | — | 0.35 | 1.00 | 1.25 | 1.50 |
| 2006 | 10,372,500 | — | 0.35 | 1.00 | 1.25 | 1.50 |
| 2007 | 14,998,500 | — | 0.35 | 1.00 | 1.25 | 1.50 |
| 2008 | 15,093,500 | — | 0.35 | 1.00 | 1.25 | 1.50 |
| 2009 | 9,998,500 | — | 0.35 | 1.00 | 1.25 | 1.50 |
| 2010 | 15,005,000 | — | 0.35 | 1.00 | 1.25 | 1.50 |
| 2011 | 13,626,500 | — | 0.35 | 1.00 | 1.25 | 1.50 |

**KM# 56 5 DINARA**
Nickel-Brass, 24 mm. **Obv:** Arms, flat bottom crown above shield **Rev:** Krusedol Monastery

| Date | Mintage | VF20 | XF40 | MS60 | MS63 | MS65 |
|---|---|---|---|---|---|---|
| 2011 | — | — | 0.35 | 1.00 | 1.25 | 1.50 |
| 2012 | — | — | 0.35 | 1.00 | 1.25 | 1.50 |
| 2013 | — | — | 0.35 | 1.00 | 1.25 | 1.50 |

**KM# 37 10 DINARA**
7.77 g., Copper-Nickel-Zinc, 26 mm. **Obv:** National Bank emblem within circle **Rev:** Studenica Monastery and value **Edge:** Reeded

| Date | Mintage | VF20 | XF40 | MS60 | MS63 | MS65 |
|---|---|---|---|---|---|---|
| 2003 | 15,166,500 | — | 0.35 | 1.00 | 1.25 | 1.50 |

**KM# 41 10 DINARA**
7.77 g., Copper-Nickel-Zinc, 26 mm. **Obv:** Crowned and mantled arms **Rev:** Studenica Monastery and value **Edge:** Segmented reeding

| Date | Mintage | VF20 | XF40 | MS60 | MS63 | MS65 |
|---|---|---|---|---|---|---|
| 2005 | 5,099,500 | — | 0.35 | 1.00 | 1.25 | 1.50 |
| 2006 | 1,019,500 | — | 0.35 | 1.00 | 1.25 | 1.50 |
| 2007 | 1,050,500 | — | 0.35 | 1.00 | 1.25 | 1.50 |
| 2010 | 500,250 | — | 0.35 | 1.00 | 1.25 | 1.50 |
| 2011 | 500,250 | — | 0.35 | 1.00 | 1.25 | 1.50 |

**KM# 51 10 DINARA**
7.77 g., Copper-Nickel-Zinc, 26 mm. **Subject:** 25th Summer Universiade, Belgrade **Obv:** Arms **Rev:** Logo

| Date | Mintage | VF20 | XF40 | MS60 | MS63 | MS65 |
|---|---|---|---|---|---|---|
| 2009 | 500,000 | — | 0.50 | 1.00 | 1.25 | 1.50 |

**KM# 57 10 DINARA**
7.77 g., Copper-Nickel-Zinc, 26 mm. **Obv:** Arms, flat bottom crown above shield **Rev:** Studenica Monastery and value

| Date | Mintage | VF20 | XF40 | MS60 | MS63 | MS65 |
|---|---|---|---|---|---|---|
| 2011 | — | — | 0.50 | 1.00 | 1.25 | 1.50 |
| 2012 | — | — | 0.50 | 1.00 | 1.25 | 1.50 |

**KM# 38 20 DINARA**
9.00 g., Copper-Nickel-Zinc, 28 mm. **Obv:** National Bank emblem within circle **Rev:** Temple of St. Sava and value **Edge:** Reeded

| Date | Mintage | VF20 | XF40 | MS60 | MS63 | MS65 |
|---|---|---|---|---|---|---|
| 2003 | 25,497,500 | — | 0.50 | 1.00 | 1.25 | 1.50 |

**KM# 42 20 DINARA**
9.00 g., Copper-Nickel-Zinc, 28 mm. **Obv:** Crowned and mantled Serbian royal arms **Rev:** Nikola Tesla **Edge:** Segmented reeding

| Date | Mintage | VF20 | XF40 | MS60 | MS63 | MS65 |
|---|---|---|---|---|---|---|
| 2006 | 992,500 | — | 0.50 | 1.00 | 1.25 | 1.50 |

**KM# 47 20 DINARA**
9.00 g., Copper-Nickel-Zinc, 28 mm. **Subject:** Dositej Obradovic, 1742-1811 **Obv:** National arms **Obv. Legend:** РЕПУБЛИКА СРБИЈА - REPUBLIKA SRBIJA **Rev:** Bust facing slightly left **Edge:** Segmented reeding

| Date | Mintage | VF20 | XF40 | MS60 | MS63 | MS65 |
|---|---|---|---|---|---|---|
| 2007 | 1,020,000 | — | 0.50 | 1.00 | 1.25 | 1.50 |

**KM# 52 20 DINARA**
9.00 g., Copper-Nickel-Zinc, 28 mm. **Obv:** National arms **Rev:** Milutin Milankovic profile 3/4 left

| Date | Mintage | VF20 | XF40 | MS60 | MS63 | MS65 |
|---|---|---|---|---|---|---|
| 2009 | 494,500 | — | 0.50 | 1.00 | 1.25 | 1.50 |

**KM# 61 20 DINARA**
9.00 g., Copper-Nickel-Zinc, 28 mm. **Obv:** Crowned arms **Rev:** Georg Weifert

| Date | Mintage | VF20 | XF40 | MS60 | MS63 | MS65 |
|---|---|---|---|---|---|---|
| 2010 | 500,000 | — | 0.50 | 1.00 | 1.25 | 1.50 |

**KM# 53 20 DINARA**
9.00 g., Copper-Nickel-Zinc, 28 mm. **Obv:** National arms **Rev:** Ivo Andric

| Date | Mintage | VF20 | XF40 | MS60 | MS63 | MS65 |
|---|---|---|---|---|---|---|
| 2011 | 500,000 | — | 0.50 | 1.00 | 1.25 | 1.50 |

**KM# 62 20 DINARA**
9.00 g., Copper-Nickel-Zinc, 28 mm. **Obv:** Crowned shield **Rev:** Mihajlo Pupin

| Date | Mintage | VF20 | XF40 | MS60 | MS63 | MS65 |
|---|---|---|---|---|---|---|
| 2012 | — | — | 0.50 | 1.00 | 1.25 | 1.50 |

**KM# 43 1000 DINARA**
13.00 g., 0.925 Silver 0.3866 oz. ASW, 30 mm. **Obv:** Crowned and mantled Serbian royal arms **Rev:** Nikola Tesla **Edge:** Segmented reeding

| Date | Mintage | VF20 | XF40 | MS60 | MS63 | MS65 |
|---|---|---|---|---|---|---|
| 2006 | 2,000 | **PF63** 25.00 | **PF65** 30.00 | | | |

**KM# 59 1000 DINARA**
13.00 g., 0.925 Silver 0.3866 oz. ASW, 30 mm. **Obv:** Crowned arms **Rev:** Dimitrije Obradovic

| Date | Mintage | VF20 | XF40 | MS60 | MS63 | MS65 |
|---|---|---|---|---|---|---|
| 2007 | Est. 1000 | **PF65** 35.00 | | | | |

**KM# 44 5000 DINARA**
3.46 g., 0.900 Gold 0.100 oz. AGW, 20 mm. **Obv:** Crowned and mantled Serbian royal arms **Rev:** Nikola Tesla

| Date | Mintage | VF20 | XF40 | MS60 | MS63 | MS65 |
|---|---|---|---|---|---|---|
| 2006 | 2,000 | **PF63** 175 | **PF65** 200 | | | |

**KM# 60 5000 DINARA**
3.46 g., 0.900 Gold 0.1001 oz. AGW, 20 mm. **Obv:** Crowned shield **Rev:** Dimitrije Obradovic

| Date | Mintage | VF20 | XF40 | MS60 | MS63 | MS65 |
|---|---|---|---|---|---|---|
| 2007 | 500 | **PF65** 175 | | | | |

**KM# 45 10000 DINARA**
8.64 g., 0.900 Gold 0.250 oz. AGW, 25 mm. **Obv:** Crowned and mantled Serbian royal arms **Rev:** Nikola Tesla

| Date | Mintage | VF20 | XF40 | MS60 | MS63 | MS65 |
|---|---|---|---|---|---|---|
| 2006 | 1,000 | PF63 425 | PF65 475 | | | |

## MINT SETS

| KM# | Date | Mintage | Identification | Issue Price | Mkt Val |
|---|---|---|---|---|---|
| MS1 | 2003 (5) | — | KM34-38 | — | 15.00 |
| MS2 | 2005 (3) | — | KM39-41 | — | 10.00 |
| MS3 | 2006 (5) | — | KM#39-42, 46 | — | 16.00 |
| MS4 | 2007 (5) | — | KM#39-42, 47 | — | 16.00 |

## PROOF SETS

| KM# | Date | Mintage | Identification | Issue Price | Mkt Val |
|---|---|---|---|---|---|
| PS1 | 2006 (3) | — | KM#43-45 | — | 710 |

# SEYCHELLES

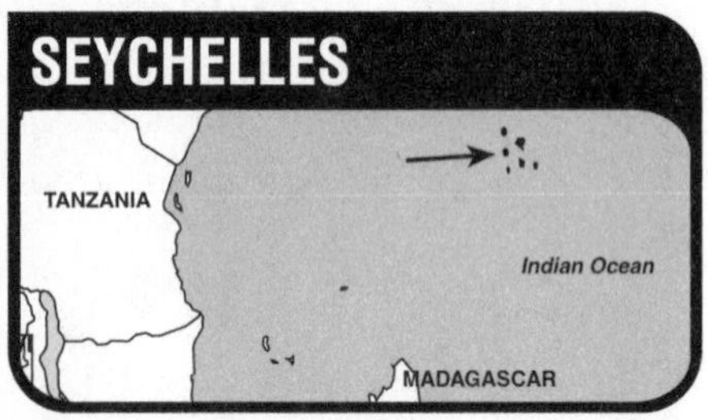


The Republic of Seychelles, an archipelago of 85 granite and coral islands situated in the Indian Ocean 600 miles (965 km.) northeast of Madagascar, has an area of 156 sq. mi. (455 sq. km.) and a population of *70,000. Among these islands are the Aldabra Islands, the Farquhar Group, and Ile Desroches, which the United Kingdom ceded to the Seychelles upon its independence. Capital: Victoria, on Mahe. The economy is based on fishing, a plantation system of agriculture, and tourism. Copra, cinnamon and vanilla are exported.

Seychelles is a member of the Commonwealth of Nations. The president is the Head of State and of the Government.

**MINT MARKS**
(sa) - M in oval – South African Mint Co. (starting in 2000, not PM)
None - British Royal Mint

**MONETARY SYSTEM**
100 Cents = 1 Rupee

## REPUBLIC

### STANDARD COINAGE

**KM# 46.2 CENT**
1.43 g., Brass, 16.03 mm. **Obv:** Altered coat of arms **Rev:** Mud Crab **Edge:** Plain

| Date | Mintage | VF20 | XF40 | MS60 | MS63 | MS65 |
|---|---|---|---|---|---|---|
| 2004 | — | — | 0.15 | 0.20 | 0.35 | 0.65 |

**KM# 47.2 5 CENTS**
2.00 g., Brass, 18 mm. **Obv:** Altered coat of arms **Rev:** Tapioca plant

| Date | Mintage | VF20 | XF40 | MS60 | MS63 | MS65 |
|---|---|---|---|---|---|---|
| 2003 | — | — | 0.10 | 0.20 | 0.30 | 0.50 |

**KM# 47a 5 CENTS**
1.97 g., Brass Plated Steel, 17.97 mm. **Obv:** National arms **Rev:** Tapioca plant **Edge:** Plain

| Date | Mintage | VF20 | XF40 | MS60 | MS63 | MS65 |
|---|---|---|---|---|---|---|
| 2007 PM | — | — | 0.10 | 0.20 | 0.30 | 0.50 |
| 2010 PM | — | — | 0.10 | 0.20 | 0.30 | 0.50 |

**KM# 48.2 10 CENTS**
3.34 g., Brass, 21 mm. **Obv:** Altered coat of arms **Rev:** Yellowfin tuna **Edge:** Plain

| Date | Mintage | VF20 | XF40 | MS60 | MS63 | MS65 |
|---|---|---|---|---|---|---|
| 2003 | — | 0.10 | 0.25 | 0.50 | 1.00 | 1.50 |

**KM# 48a 10 CENTS**
3.37 g., Brass Plated Steel, 21 mm. **Obv:** National arms **Rev:** Black parrot, value **Edge:** Plain

| Date | Mintage | VF20 | XF40 | MS60 | MS63 | MS65 |
|---|---|---|---|---|---|---|
| 2007 PM | — | 0.15 | 0.30 | 0.50 | 0.75 | 1.00 |

**KM# 49a 25 CENTS**
2.97 g., Nickel Clad Steel, 18.9 mm. **Obv:** National arms **Rev:** Black Parrot and value **Edge:** Plain

| Date | Mintage | VF20 | XF40 | MS60 | MS63 | MS65 |
|---|---|---|---|---|---|---|
| 2003 PM | — | — | 0.40 | 0.60 | 1.00 | 1.25 |
| 2007 PM | — | — | 0.40 | 0.60 | 1.00 | 1.25 |
| 2010 PM | — | — | 0.40 | 0.60 | 1.00 | 1.25 |
| 2012 PM | — | — | 0.40 | 0.60 | 1.00 | 1.25 |

**KM# 50.2 RUPEE**
6.18 g., Copper-Nickel, 25.46 mm. **Obv:** Altered coat of arms **Rev:** Triton Conch Shell **Edge:** Reeded

| Date | Mintage | VF20 | XF40 | MS60 | MS63 | MS65 |
|---|---|---|---|---|---|---|
| 2007 | — | — | 0.25 | 0.50 | 0.75 | 1.00 |
| 2010 PM | — | — | 0.25 | 0.50 | 0.75 | 1.00 |

**KM# 51.2 5 RUPEES**
9.00 g., Copper-Nickel, 29 mm. **Obv:** Altered arms **Rev:** Fruit tree divides value **Edge:** Reeded

| Date | Mintage | VF20 | XF40 | MS60 | MS63 | MS65 |
|---|---|---|---|---|---|---|
| 2007 | — | — | 0.50 | 0.75 | 1.00 | 1.50 |
| 2010 | — | — | 0.50 | 0.75 | 1.00 | 1.50 |

**KM# 118 5 RUPEES**
28.28 g., Copper-Nickel, 38.6 mm. **Subject:** John Paul II memorial **Obv:** National Arms **Rev:** John Paul II in mitre waving

| Date | Mintage | VF20 | XF40 | MS60 | MS63 | MS65 |
|---|---|---|---|---|---|---|
| 2005 | — | — | — | 3.00 | 5.00 | 7.00 |

**KM# 119 5 RUPEES**
28.28 g., Copper-Nickel, 38.6 mm. **Obv:** National Arms **Rev:** Benedict XVI blessing crowd at St. Peter's Square

| Date | Mintage | VF20 | XF40 | MS60 | MS63 | MS65 |
|---|---|---|---|---|---|---|
| 2005 | — | — | — | 4.00 | 6.00 | 8.00 |

**KM# 127 5 RUPEES**
28.28 g., Copper-Nickel, 38.61 mm. **Subject:** 80th Birthday of Queen Elizabeth II

| Date | Mintage | VF20 | XF40 | MS60 | MS63 | MS65 |
|---|---|---|---|---|---|---|
| 2006 Proof | — | — | — | 9.00 | 12.00 | 16.00 |

**KM# 142 5 RUPEES**
28.28 g., Copper-Nickel, 38.6 mm. **Obv:** National arms **Rev:** Pope Francis head left at center of stations of the cross

| Date | Mintage | VF20 | XF40 | MS60 | MS63 | MS65 |
|---|---|---|---|---|---|---|
| 2013 | Est. 50000 | — | — | — | — | 12.50 |

**KM# 144 5 RUPEES**
28.28 g., Copper-Nickel, 38.6 mm. **Subject:** Canonization **Obv:** National arms **Rev:** Pope John Paul II and Mary statue

| Date | Mintage | VF20 | XF40 | MS60 | MS63 | MS65 |
|---|---|---|---|---|---|---|
| 2014 | — | — | — | — | — | 12.50 |

**KM# 126 10 RUPEES**
0.50 g., 0.585 Gold 0.0094 oz. AGW, 11 mm. **Subject:** Pitcher Plant

| Date | Mintage | VF20 | XF40 | MS60 | MS63 | MS65 |
|---|---|---|---|---|---|---|
| 2012 | Est. 5000 | PF63 28.00 | PF65 35.00 | | | |

**KM# 138 10 RUPEES**
0.50 g., 0.585 Gold 0.0094 oz. AGW with 24Kt plating, 11 mm. **Subject:** Gandhi

| Date | Mintage | VF20 | XF40 | MS60 | MS63 | MS65 |
|---|---|---|---|---|---|---|
| 2013 | Est. 7500 | PF65 40.00 | | | | |

**KM# 141 10 RUPEES**
12.00 g., 0.925 Silver 0.3569 oz. ASW, 38.6 mm. **Obv:** National arms **Rev:** Pope Francis profile left at center of circle of the stations of the cross

| Date | Mintage | VF20 | XF40 | MS60 | MS63 | MS65 |
|---|---|---|---|---|---|---|
| 2013 | Est. 10000 | PF65 30.00 | | | | |

**KM# 120 25 RUPEES**
28.28 g., 0.925 Silver 0.841 oz. ASW, 38.6 mm. **Obv:** National arms **Rev:** Description John Paul II in mitre waving **Edge:** Reeded

| Date | Mintage | VF20 | XF40 | MS60 | MS63 | MS65 |
|---|---|---|---|---|---|---|
| 2005 | — | PF60 22.00 | PF63 32.00 | PF65 42.00 | | |

**KM# 121 25 RUPEES**
28.28 g., 0.925 Silver 0.841 oz. ASW, 38.6 mm. **Obv:** National arms **Rev:** Benedict XVI blessing crowd at St. Peter's Square **Edge:** Reeded

| Date | Mintage | VF20 | XF40 | MS60 | MS63 | MS65 |
|---|---|---|---|---|---|---|
| 2005 | — | PF60 22.00 | PF63 32.00 | PF65 42.00 | | |

**KM# 128 25 RUPEES**
28.28 g., 0.925 Silver 0.841 oz. ASW, 38.61 mm. **Subject:** 80th Birthday of Queen Elizabeth II

| Date | Mintage | VF20 | XF40 | MS60 | MS63 | MS65 |
|---|---|---|---|---|---|---|
| 2006 | — | PF60 22.00 | PF63 32.00 | PF65 42.00 | | |

**KM# 129 25 RUPEES**
28.28 g., 0.925 Silver 0.841 oz. ASW, 38.61 mm. **Subject:** 2006 World Cup - Germany

| Date | Mintage | VF20 | XF40 | MS60 | MS63 | MS65 |
|---|---|---|---|---|---|---|
| 2006 | — | PF60 22.00 | PF63 32.00 | PF65 42.00 | | |

**KM# 130 25 RUPEES**
28.28 g., 0.925 Silver 0.841 oz. ASW, 38.61 mm. **Subject:** 35th Anniversary of Independence

| Date | Mintage | VF20 | XF40 | MS60 | MS63 | MS65 |
|---|---|---|---|---|---|---|
| 2011 | — | PF60 22.00 | PF63 27.00 | PF65 32.00 | | |

**KM# 131 25 RUPEES**
1.24 g., 0.999 Gold 0.0398 oz. AGW, 14 mm. **Subject:** 35 Years of Independence

| Date | Mintage | VF20 | XF40 | MS60 | MS63 | MS65 |
|---|---|---|---|---|---|---|
| 2011 | 2,500 | PF65 75.00 | | | | |

**KM# 132 25 RUPEES**
1.24 g., 0.999 Gold 0.0398 oz. AGW, 14 mm. **Subject:** Independence, 39th Anniversary **Obv:** National arms **Rev:** Island view

| Date | Mintage | VF20 | XF40 | MS60 | MS63 | MS65 |
|---|---|---|---|---|---|---|
| 2011 | 2,500 | PF65 100 | | | | |

**KM# 133 25 RUPEES**
28.28 g., 0.925 Silver 0.841 oz. ASW, 38.61 mm. **Obv:** Arms **Rev:** Island View

| Date | Mintage | VF20 | XF40 | MS60 | MS63 | MS65 |
|---|---|---|---|---|---|---|
| 2011 | 2,500 | PF65 100 | | | | |

**KM# 139 25 RUPEES**
0.925 Silver ASW, 38.61 mm. **Obv:** Head right and arms **Rev:** Elizabeth II and family

| Date | Mintage | VF20 | XF40 | MS60 | MS63 | MS65 |
|---|---|---|---|---|---|---|
| 2011 | — | PF65 75.00 | | | | |

**KM# 125 25 RUPEES**
20.00 g., 0.925 Silver 0.5948 oz. ASW, 38.61 mm. **Subject:** 2014 FIFA World Cup - Brazil

| Date | Mintage | VF20 | XF40 | MS60 | MS63 | MS65 |
|---|---|---|---|---|---|---|
| 2012 | Est. 10000 | PF63 45.00 | PF65 55.00 | | | |

**KM# 134 25 RUPEES**
0.50 g., 0.999 Gold 0.0161 oz. AGW, 11 mm. **Subject:** Birth of Prince George **Obv:** National arms **Rev:** W+K monogram, crown & baby's feet

| Date | Mintage | VF20 | XF40 | MS60 | MS63 | MS65 |
|---|---|---|---|---|---|---|
| 2013 | 5,000 | PF65 55.00 | | | | |

**KM# 136 25 RUPEES**
20.00 g., 0.925 Silver 0.5948 oz. ASW, 38.61 mm. **Subject:** 2016 Olympics - Kayak

| Date | Mintage | VF20 | XF40 | MS60 | MS63 | MS65 |
|---|---|---|---|---|---|---|
| 2013 | Est. 10000 | PF65 75.00 | | | | |

**KM# 137 25 RUPEES**
0.50 g., 0.999 Gold 0.0161 oz. AGW, 11 mm. **Subject:** Ghandi

| Date | Mintage | VF20 | XF40 | MS60 | MS63 | MS65 |
|---|---|---|---|---|---|---|
| 2013 | Est. 7500 | PF65 75.00 | | | | |

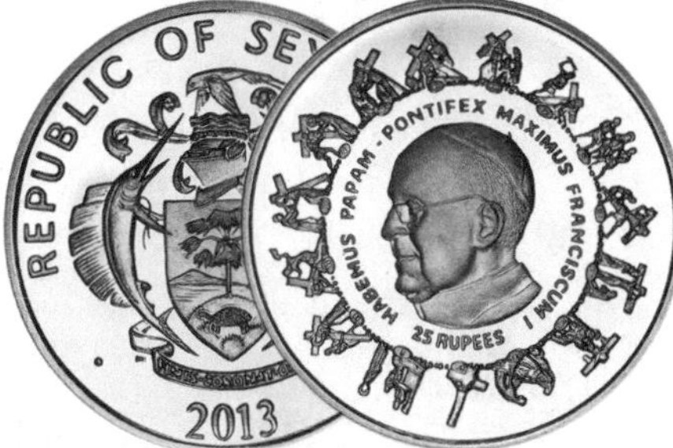


**KM# 140 25 RUPEES**
28.28 g., 0.925 Silver 0.841 oz. ASW, 38.61 mm. **Obv:** National arms **Rev:** Pope Francis head left at center of stations of the cross

| Date | Mintage | VF20 | XF40 | MS60 | MS63 | MS65 |
|---|---|---|---|---|---|---|
| 2013 | Est. 10000 | PF65 65.00 | | | | |

**KM# 143 25 RUPEES**
28.28 g., 0.925 Silver 0.841 oz. ASW, 38.6 mm. **Subject:** Canonization **Obv:** National arms **Rev:** Pope John Paul II and Mary statue

| Date | Mintage | F12 | VF20 | XF40 | MS60 | MS63 |
|---|---|---|---|---|---|---|
| 2014 | Est. 10000 | PF65 60.00 | | | | |

**KM# 135 50 RUPEES**
93.30 g., 0.925 Silver 2.7747 oz. ASW, 50 mm. **Obv:** National arms **Rev:** W+K monogram, crown and baby's feet, blue crystal nisert

| Date | Mintage | VF20 | XF40 | MS60 | MS63 | MS65 |
|---|---|---|---|---|---|---|
| 2013 | 999 | PF65 175 | | | | |

**KM# 122 250 RUPEES**
6.22 g., 0.9999 Gold 0.200 oz. AGW, 22 mm. **Obv:** National arms **Rev:** Description John Paul II in mitre waving **Edge:** Reeded

| Date | Mintage | VF20 | XF40 | MS60 | MS63 | MS65 |
|---|---|---|---|---|---|---|
| 2005 | — | PF63 350 | PF65 400 | | | |

**KM# 123 250 RUPEES**
6.22 g., 0.9999 Gold 0.200 oz. AGW, 22 mm. **Obv:** National arms **Rev:** Benedict XVI blessing crowd at St. Peter's Square **Edge:** Reeded

| Date | Mintage | VF20 | XF40 | MS60 | MS63 | MS65 |
|---|---|---|---|---|---|---|
| 2005 | — | PF63 350 | PF65 400 | | | |

# SHAWNEE TRIBAL NATION

## SOVEREIGN NATION

### MILLED COINAGE

**KM# 1 DOLLAR**
31.20 g., 0.9999 Silver 1.003 oz. ASW, 39 mm. **Obv:** Tribal seal **Obv. Legend:** THE SOVEREIGN NATION OF THE SHAWNEE TRIBE **Rev:** Bust of Chief Chief "Shooting Star" Tecumseh right **Edge:** Reeded

| Date | Mintage | VF20 | XF40 | MS60 | MS63 | MS65 |
|---|---|---|---|---|---|---|
| 2002 | 50,000 | — | — | — | 35.00 | 45.00 |
| 2002 | — | PF65 75.00 | | | | |

**KM# 3 DOLLAR**
31.20 g., 0.9999 Silver 1.003 oz. ASW, 39 mm. **Obv:** Tribal seal **Obv. Legend:** THE SOVEREIGN NATION OF THE SHAWNEE TRIBE **Rev:** Lewis, Clark and Drouillard scouting **Edge:** Reeded

| Date | Mintage | VF20 | XF40 | MS60 | MS63 | MS65 |
|---|---|---|---|---|---|---|
| 2003 | 50,000 | — | — | — | 40.00 | 50.00 |
| 2003 | — | PF65 75.00 | | | | |

**KM# 10 DOLLAR**
124.41 g., 0.999 Silver 3.9959 oz. ASW

| Date | Mintage | VF20 | XF40 | MS60 | MS63 | MS65 |
|---|---|---|---|---|---|---|
| 2003 | 10,000 | PF65 185 | | | | |

**KM# 5 DOLLAR**
31.20 g., 0.9999 Silver 1.003 oz. ASW, 39 mm. **Obv:** Tribal seal **Obv. Legend:** THE SOVEREIGN NATION OF THE SHAWNEE TRIBE **Rev:** Flag behing Indian Chief and Thomas Jefferson standing, eagle on shield at their feet **Edge:** Reeded

| Date | Mintage | VF20 | XF40 | MS60 | MS63 | MS65 |
|---|---|---|---|---|---|---|
| 2004 | 50,000 | — | — | — | 40.00 | 50.00 |
| 2004 | — | PF65 75.00 | | | | |

**KM# 15 DOLLAR**
31.31 g., 0.999 Silver 1.0056 oz. ASW, 40.6 mm. **Obv:** Tribal seal **Obv. Legend:** THE SOVEREIGN NATION OF THE SHAWNEE TRIBE **Rev:** Lewis, Clark, Dromillard and Sacagawea in a canoe **Rev. Legend:** EXPEDITION OF DISCOVERY **Edge:** Reeded

| Date | Mintage | VF20 | XF40 | MS60 | MS63 | MS65 |
|---|---|---|---|---|---|---|
| 2005 | 50,000 | — | — | — | 40.00 | 50.00 |
| 2005 | 20,000 | PF65 75.00 | | | | |

**KM# 20 DOLLAR**
31.21 g., 0.9999 Silver 1.0033 oz. ASW, 40.6 mm. **Obv:** Tribal seal **Obv. Legend:** THE SOVEREIGN NATION OF THE SHAWNEE TRIBE **Rev:** 1/2 length figure of Tenskwatawa "the prophet" 3/4 left **Rev. Legend:** PROPHET TENSKWATAWA **Edge:** Reeded

| Date | Mintage | VF20 | XF40 | MS60 | MS63 | MS65 |
|---|---|---|---|---|---|---|
| 2006 | 20,000 | PF65 75.00 | | | | |
| 2006 | 50,000 | — | — | — | 40.00 | 50.00 |

**KM# 24 DOLLAR**
31.11 g., 0.999 Silver 0.999 oz. ASW, 39 mm. **Subject:** Battle of the Wabash **Rev:** Indian warrior on horseback **Edge:** Reeded

| Date | Mintage | VF20 | XF40 | MS60 | MS63 | MS65 |
|---|---|---|---|---|---|---|
| 2007 | 20,000 | PF65 75.00 | | | | |
| 2007 | 50,000 | — | — | — | 45.00 | 55.00 |

**KM# 26 DOLLAR**
31.11 g., 0.999 Silver 0.999 oz. ASW, 39 mm. **Subject:** Battle of Point Pleasant **Rev:** Indian warrior on horseback **Edge:** Reeded

| Date | Mintage | VF20 | XF40 | MS60 | MS63 | MS65 |
|---|---|---|---|---|---|---|
| 2008 | 50,000 | — | — | — | 45.00 | 55.00 |
| 2008 | 20,000 | PF65 80.00 | | | | |

**KM# 28 DOLLAR**
31.11 g., 0.999 Silver 0.999 oz. ASW **Rev:** Battle of Fallen Timber

| Date | Mintage | VF20 | XF40 | MS60 | MS63 | MS65 |
|---|---|---|---|---|---|---|
| 2009 | 20,000 | PF65 80.00 | | | | |
| 2009 | 50,000 | — | — | — | 45.00 | 55.00 |

**KM# 30 DOLLAR**
31.31 g., 0.999 Silver 1.0056 oz. ASW, 39 mm. **Subject:** Comet of 1811 **Rev:** Indian seated looking at comet in sky **Edge:** Reeded

| Date | Mintage | VF20 | XF40 | MS60 | MS63 | MS65 |
|---|---|---|---|---|---|---|
| 2011 | — | PF65 80.00 | | | | |

**KM# 2 5 DOLLARS**
6.22 g., 0.9999 Gold 0.200 oz. AGW, 20 mm. **Obv:** Arms **Obv. Legend:** THE SOVEREIGN NATION OF THE SHAWNEE TRIBE **Rev:** Bust of Tecumseh "Shooting Star" 3/4 left **Edge:** Reeded

| Date | Mintage | VF20 | XF40 | MS60 | MS63 | MS65 |
|---|---|---|---|---|---|---|
| 2002 | — | PF65 450 | | | | |

**KM# 4 5 DOLLARS**
6.22 g., 0.9999 Gold 0.200 oz. AGW, 22.5 mm. **Obv:** Arms **Obv. Legend:** THE SOVEREIGN NATION OF THE SHAWNEE TRIBE **Rev:** Bust of George Drouillard 3/4 right **Rev. Legend:** GEORGE DROUILLARD SIGN TALKER

| Date | Mintage | VF20 | XF40 | MS60 | MS63 | MS65 |
|---|---|---|---|---|---|---|
| 2003 | — | PF65 450 | | | | |

**KM# 6 5 DOLLARS**
6.22 g., 0.999 Gold 0.1998 oz. AGW, 22 mm. **Obv:** Arms **Obv. Legend:** THE SOVEREIGN NATION OF THE SHAWNEE TRIBE **Rev:** Sacagawea with child and horse **Edge:** Reeded

| Date | Mintage | VF20 | XF40 | MS60 | MS63 | MS65 |
|---|---|---|---|---|---|---|
| 2004 | — | PF65 450 | | | | |

**KM# 16 5 DOLLARS**
6.30 g., 0.9999 Gold 0.2025 oz. AGW, 22.5 mm. **Obv:** Tribal seal **Obv. Legend:** THE SOVEREIGN NATION OF THE SHAWNEE TRIBE **Rev:** Sacagawea with papoose on horseback right **Rev. Legend:** EXPEDITION OF DISCOVERY **Edge:** Reeded

| Date | Mintage | VF20 | XF40 | MS60 | MS63 | MS65 |
|---|---|---|---|---|---|---|
| 2005 | 5,000 | PF65 450 | | | | |

**KM# 21 5 DOLLARS**
6.25 g., 0.9999 Gold 0.2009 oz. AGW, 22.5 mm. **Obv:** Tribal seal **Obv. Legend:** THE SOVEREIGN NATION OF THE SHAWNEE TRIBE **Rev:** Bust of Chief Tecumseh 3/4 right **Rev. Legend:** TECVMSEH **Edge:** Reeded

| Date | Mintage | VF20 | XF40 | MS60 | MS63 | MS65 |
|---|---|---|---|---|---|---|
| 2006 | 5,000 | PF65 450 | | | | |

**KM# 25 5 DOLLARS**
6.25 g., 0.999 Gold 0.2007 oz. AGW **Rev:** Chief Blue Jacket

| Date | Mintage | VF20 | XF40 | MS60 | MS63 | MS65 |
|---|---|---|---|---|---|---|
| 2007 | 5,000 | PF65 450 | | | | |

**KM# 27 5 DOLLARS**
6.25 g., 0.999 Gold 0.2007 oz. AGW **Rev:** Chief Cornstalk

| Date | Mintage | VF20 | XF40 | MS60 | MS63 | MS65 |
|---|---|---|---|---|---|---|
| 2008 | 5,000 | PF65 450 | | | | |

**KM# 29 5 DOLLARS**
6.25 g., 0.999 Gold 0.2007 oz. AGW **Rev:** Chief Black-Hoof

| Date | Mintage | VF20 | XF40 | MS60 | MS63 | MS65 |
|---|---|---|---|---|---|---|
| 2009 | 5,000 | PF65 450 | | | | |

**KM# 7 50 DOLLARS**
15.55 g., 0.999 Gold 0.4994 oz. AGW, 30.1 mm. **Rev:** George Drouillard

| Date | Mintage | VF20 | XF40 | MS60 | MS63 | MS65 |
|---|---|---|---|---|---|---|
| 2003 | 999 | PF65 900 | | | | |

**KM# 11 50 DOLLARS**
15.55 g., 0.999 Gold 0.4994 oz. AGW, 30.1 mm. **Rev:** Sacagawea with child and horse

| Date | Mintage | VF20 | XF40 | MS60 | MS63 | MS65 |
|---|---|---|---|---|---|---|
| 2004 | — | PF65 900 | | | | |

**KM# 17 50 DOLLARS**
15.55 g., 0.9999 Gold 0.4999 oz. AGW, 30.1 mm. **Obv:** Tribal seal **Obv. Legend:** THE SOVEREIGN NATION OF THE SHAWNEE TRIBE **Rev:** Sacagawea with papoose on horseback right **Rev. Legend:** EXPEDITION OF DISCOVERY **Edge:** Reeded

| Date | Mintage | VF20 | XF40 | MS60 | MS63 | MS65 |
|---|---|---|---|---|---|---|
| 2005 | 999 | PF65 900 | | | | |

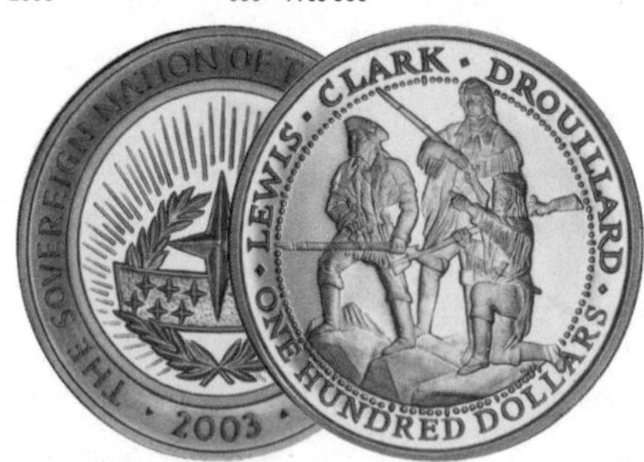

**KM# 8 100 DOLLARS**
30.91 g., 0.9999 Gold 0.9937 oz. AGW, 38.9 mm. **Obv:** Tribal seal **Obv. Legend:** THE SOVEREIGN NATION OF THE SHAWNEE TRIBE **Rev:** Bust of "Sign Talker" 3/4 right **Rev. Legend:** GEORGE DROILLARD "SIGN TALKER **Edge:** Milled

| Date | Mintage | VF20 | XF40 | MS60 | MS63 | MS65 |
|---|---|---|---|---|---|---|
| 2003 | 999 | PF65 1,850 | | | | |

**KM# 12 100 DOLLARS**
31.11 g., 0.999 Gold 0.999 oz. AGW **Rev:** Sacagawea and child

| Date | Mintage | VF20 | XF40 | MS60 | MS63 | MS65 |
|---|---|---|---|---|---|---|
| 2004 | — | PF65 1,850 | | | | |

**KM# 18 100 DOLLARS**
31.11 g., 0.999 Gold 0.999 oz. AGW **Rev:** Sacagawea and child on horseback

| Date | Mintage | VF20 | XF40 | MS60 | MS63 | MS65 |
|---|---|---|---|---|---|---|
| 2005 | 999 | PF65 1,850 | | | | |

**KM# 23 100 DOLLARS**
62.21 g., 0.999 Bi-Metallic 1.9981 oz. 1 oz. gold and 1 oz. silver **Rev:** Lewis and Clark

| Date | Mintage | VF20 | XF40 | MS60 | MS63 | MS65 |
|---|---|---|---|---|---|---|
| 2005 | 500 | PF65 2,000 | | | | |

**KM# 9 500 DOLLARS**
93.50 g., 0.9999 Gold 3.0058 oz. AGW **Obv:** Tribal seal **Obv. Legend:** THE SOVEREIGN NATION OF THE SHAWNEE TRIBE **Rev:** Lewis, Clark and Drouillard scouting **Rev. Legend:** LEWIS • CLARK • DROUILLARD **Edge:** Reeded

| Date | Mintage | VF20 | XF40 | MS60 | MS63 | MS65 |
|---|---|---|---|---|---|---|
| 2003 | 300 | PF65 5,800 | | | | |

**KM# 13 500 DOLLARS**
15.54 g., 0.999 Platinum 0.4991 oz. APW, 30 mm. **Obv:** Tribal seal **Obv. Legend:** THE SOVEREIGN NATION OF THE SHAWNEE TRIBE **Rev:** Flag and shield between standing Chief and Thomas Jefferson **Rev. Legend:** EXPEDITION OF DISCOVERY **Edge:** Reeded

| Date | Mintage | VF20 | XF40 | MS60 | MS63 | MS65 |
|---|---|---|---|---|---|---|
| 2004 | 999 | PF65 1,150 | | | | |

**KM# 23A 500 DOLLARS**
15.55 g., 0.999 Platinum 0.4994 oz. APW **Rev:** Shawnee Chief and Thomas Jefferson standing

| Date | Mintage | VF20 | XF40 | MS60 | MS63 | MS65 |
|---|---|---|---|---|---|---|
| 2005 | 999 | PF65 1,150 | | | | |

**KM# 14 1000 DOLLARS**
31.00 g., 0.9999 Platinum 0.9966 oz. APW, 38.7 mm. **Obv:** Tribal seal **Obv. Legend:** THE SOVEREIGN NATION OF THE SHAWNEE TRIBE **Rev:** Flag and shield between standing Chief and Thomas Jefferson **Rev. Legend:** EXPEDITION OF DISCOVERY **Edge:** Reeded

| Date | Mintage | VF20 | XF40 | MS60 | MS63 | MS65 |
|---|---|---|---|---|---|---|
| 2004 | 300 | PF65 2,750 | | | | |

**KM# 22 1000 DOLLARS**
31.11 g., 0.999 Platinum 0.999 oz. APW **Rev:** Shawnee Chief and Thomas Jefferson standing

| Date | Mintage | VF20 | XF40 | MS60 | MS63 | MS65 |
|---|---|---|---|---|---|---|
| 2005 | 300 | PF65 2,750 | | | | |

# SIERRA LEONE

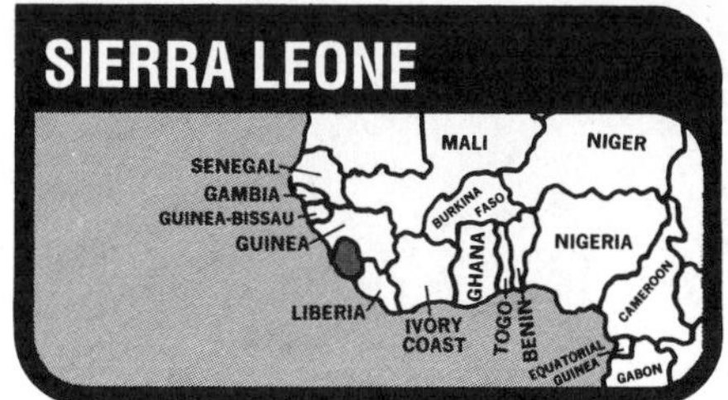


The Republic of Sierra Leone is located in western Africa between Guinea and Liberia, has an area of 27,699 sq. mi. (71,740 sq. km.) and a population of *4.1 million. Capital: Freetown. The economy is predominantly agricultural but mining contributes significantly to export revenues. Diamonds, iron ore, palm kernels, cocoa, and coffee are exported.

Sierra Leone is a member of the Commonwealth of Nations. The president is Chief of State and Head of Government.

**MONETARY SYSTEM**

Beginning 1964

100 Cents = 1 Leone

## REPUBLIC

### STANDARD COINAGE

**KM# 295 20 LEONES**

3.92 g., Copper-Nickel, 21.7 mm. **Obv:** Value within fish and beaded circle **Rev:** Chimpanzee facing **Edge:** Plain

| Date | Mintage | VF20 | XF40 | MS60 | MS63 | MS65 |
|---|---|---|---|---|---|---|
| 2003 | — | — | — | 0.35 | 0.65 | 1.25 |

**KM# 302 100 LEONES**

28.28 g., Copper-Nickel, 38.6 mm. **Subject:** 40th Anniversary - Bank of Sierra Leone **Obv:** Bank President Kabbah **Rev:** Lion **Edge:** Reeded

| Date | Mintage | VF20 | XF40 | MS60 | MS63 | MS65 |
|---|---|---|---|---|---|---|
| ND (2004) PM | 5,000 | — | — | — | 15.00 | 18.00 |

**KM# 296 500 LEONES**

7.20 g., Bi-Metallic Stainless Steel center in Brass ring, 24 mm. **Obv:** Building within circle **Rev:** Bust with hat facing within circle **Edge:** Plain **Shape:** 10-sided

| Date | Mintage | VF20 | XF40 | MS60 | MS63 | MS65 |
|---|---|---|---|---|---|---|
| 2004 | — | — | — | — | 7.50 | 9.00 |

**KM# 346 500 LEONES**

28.28 g., Bronze, 38.6 mm. **Subject:** 40th Anniversary - Bank of Sierra Leone **Obv:** Bank President Kabbah **Rev:** Lion, denomination as "Le 500 **Edge:** Reeded

| Date | Mintage | VF20 | XF40 | MS60 | MS63 | MS65 |
|---|---|---|---|---|---|---|
| ND-2004 PM | 10,000 | — | — | — | 15.00 | 18.00 |

### DOLLAR DENOMINATED COINAGE

**KM# 198 DOLLAR**

28.28 g., Copper-Nickel, 38.6 mm. **Subject:** Year of the Snake **Obv:** National arms **Rev:** Snake **Edge:** Reeded

| Date | Mintage | VF20 | XF40 | MS60 | MS63 | MS65 |
|---|---|---|---|---|---|---|
| 2001 | — | — | — | — | 7.50 | 10.00 |

**KM# 206 DOLLAR**

Copper-Nickel, 38.6 mm. **Subject:** P'an Ku **Obv:** National arms **Rev:** Dragon

| Date | Mintage | VF20 | XF40 | MS60 | MS63 | MS65 |
|---|---|---|---|---|---|---|
| 2001 | — | — | — | — | 7.50 | 10.00 |

**KM# 214 DOLLAR**

Copper-Nickel, 38.6 mm. **Subject:** P'an Ku **Obv:** National arms **Rev:** Dragon and three animals

| Date | Mintage | VF20 | XF40 | MS60 | MS63 | MS65 |
|---|---|---|---|---|---|---|
| 2001 | — | — | — | — | 7.50 | 10.00 |

**KM# 222 DOLLAR**

28.49 g., Copper-Nickel, 38.5 mm. **Series:** The Big Five **Obv:** National arms **Rev:** Rhino **Edge:** Reeded

| Date | Mintage | VF20 | XF40 | MS60 | MS63 | MS65 |
|---|---|---|---|---|---|---|
| 2001 PM | — | — | — | — | 9.00 | 12.00 |

**KM# 225 DOLLAR**

28.49 g., Copper-Nickel, 38.6 mm. **Series:** The Big Five **Obv:** National arms **Rev:** Lion **Edge:** Reeded

| Date | Mintage | VF20 | XF40 | MS60 | MS63 | MS65 |
|---|---|---|---|---|---|---|
| 2001 PM | — | — | — | — | 7.50 | 10.00 |

**KM# 228 DOLLAR**

28.49 g., Copper-Nickel, 38.6 mm. **Series:** The Big Five **Obv:** National arms **Rev:** Leopard **Edge:** Reeded

| Date | Mintage | VF20 | XF40 | MS60 | MS63 | MS65 |
|---|---|---|---|---|---|---|
| 2001 PM | — | — | — | — | 7.50 | 10.00 |

**KM# 231 DOLLAR**

28.49 g., Copper-Nickel, 38.6 mm. **Series:** The Big Five **Obv:** National arms **Rev:** Elephants **Edge:** Reeded

| Date | Mintage | VF20 | XF40 | MS60 | MS63 | MS65 |
|---|---|---|---|---|---|---|
| 2001 PM | — | — | — | — | 7.50 | 10.00 |

**KM# 234 DOLLAR**

28.49 g., Copper-Nickel, 38.6 mm. **Series:** The Big Five **Obv:** National arms **Rev:** Buffalo **Edge:** Reeded

| Date | Mintage | VF20 | XF40 | MS60 | MS63 | MS65 |
|---|---|---|---|---|---|---|
| 2001 PM | — | — | — | — | 7.50 | 10.00 |

**KM# 237 DOLLAR**

28.49 g., Copper-Nickel, 38.5 mm. **Series:** The Big Five **Obv:** National arms **Rev:** All five animals **Edge:** Reeded

| Date | Mintage | VF20 | XF40 | MS60 | MS63 | MS65 |
|---|---|---|---|---|---|---|
| 2001 PM | — | — | — | — | 7.50 | 10.00 |

**KM# 241.1 DOLLAR**

28.54 g., Copper-Nickel, 38.65 mm. **Series:** Big Cats **Obv:** National arms **Rev:** Male and female lions **Edge:** Reeded

| Date | Mintage | VF20 | XF40 | MS60 | MS63 | MS65 |
|---|---|---|---|---|---|---|
| 2001 PM | — | — | — | — | 9.00 | 12.00 |

**KM# 241.2 DOLLAR**

28.54 g., Copper-Nickel, 38.65 mm. **Series:** Big Cats **Obv:** National arms **Rev:** Multi-colored male and female lions **Edge:** Reeded

| Date | Mintage | VF20 | XF40 | MS60 | MS63 | MS65 |
|---|---|---|---|---|---|---|
| 2001 PM | — | — | — | — | 12.00 | 14.00 |

**KM# 242.1 DOLLAR**

28.54 g., Copper-Nickel, 38.65 mm. **Series:** Big Cats **Obv:** National arms **Rev:** Tiger **Edge:** Reeded

| Date | Mintage | VF20 | XF40 | MS60 | MS63 | MS65 |
|---|---|---|---|---|---|---|
| 2001 PM | — | — | — | — | 7.50 | 10.00 |

**KM# 242.2 DOLLAR**

28.54 g., Copper-Nickel, 38.65 mm. **Series:** Big Cats **Obv:** National arms **Rev:** Multi-colored Tiger **Edge:** Reeded

| Date | Mintage | VF20 | XF40 | MS60 | MS63 | MS65 |
|---|---|---|---|---|---|---|
| 2001 PM | — | — | — | — | 12.00 | 14.00 |

**KM# 243.1 DOLLAR**

28.54 g., Copper-Nickel, 38.65 mm. **Series:** Big Cats **Obv:** National arms **Rev:** Cheetah **Edge:** Reeded

| Date | Mintage | VF20 | XF40 | MS60 | MS63 | MS65 |
|---|---|---|---|---|---|---|
| 2001 PM | — | — | — | — | 9.50 | 12.00 |

**KM# 243.2 DOLLAR**

28.54 g., Copper-Nickel, 38.65 mm. **Series:** Big Cats **Obv:** National arms **Rev:** Multi-colored Cheetah **Edge:** Reeded

| Date | Mintage | VF20 | XF40 | MS60 | MS63 | MS65 |
|---|---|---|---|---|---|---|
| 2001 PM | — | — | — | — | 12.00 | 14.00 |

**KM# 244.1 DOLLAR**

28.54 g., Copper-Nickel, 38.65 mm. **Series:** Big Cats **Obv:** National arms **Rev:** Cougar **Edge:** Reeded

| Date | Mintage | VF20 | XF40 | MS60 | MS63 | MS65 |
|---|---|---|---|---|---|---|
| 2001 PM | — | — | — | — | 7.50 | 10.00 |

**KM# 244.2 DOLLAR**

28.54 g., Copper-Nickel, 38.65 mm. **Series:** Big Cats **Obv:** National arms **Rev:** Multi-colored Cougar **Edge:** Reeded

| Date | Mintage | VF20 | XF40 | MS60 | MS63 | MS65 |
|---|---|---|---|---|---|---|
| 2001 PM | — | — | — | — | 12.00 | 14.00 |

**KM# 245.1 DOLLAR**

28.54 g., Copper-Nickel, 38.65 mm. **Series:** Big Cats **Obv:** National arms **Rev:** Black panther **Edge:** Reeded

| Date | Mintage | VF20 | XF40 | MS60 | MS63 | MS65 |
|---|---|---|---|---|---|---|
| 2001 PM | — | — | — | — | 7.50 | 10.00 |

**KM# 245.2 DOLLAR**

28.54 g., Copper-Nickel, 38.65 mm. **Series:** Big Cats **Obv:** National arms **Rev:** Multi-colored Black Panther **Edge:** Reeded

| Date | Mintage | VF20 | XF40 | MS60 | MS63 | MS65 |
|---|---|---|---|---|---|---|
| 2001 PM | — | — | — | — | 12.00 | 14.00 |

**KM# 256 DOLLAR**
28.28 g., Copper-Nickel, 38.6 mm. **Subject:** Year of the Horse **Obv:** National arms **Rev:** Horse **Edge:** Reeded

| Date | Mintage | VF20 | XF40 | MS60 | MS63 | MS65 |
|---|---|---|---|---|---|---|
| 2002 | — | — | — | — | 12.00 | 14.00 |

**KM# 264 DOLLAR**
28.28 g., Copper-Nickel, 38.6 mm. **Subject:** RMS Titanic **Obv:** National arms **Rev:** Titanic at dock **Edge:** Reeded

| Date | Mintage | VF20 | XF40 | MS60 | MS63 | MS65 |
|---|---|---|---|---|---|---|
| 2002 | — | — | — | — | 7.00 | 9.00 |

**KM# 268 DOLLAR**
28.28 g., Copper-Nickel, 38.6 mm. **Subject:** Queen's Golden Jubilee **Obv:** National arms **Rev:** Queen Elizabeth II and Prince Philip visiting blacksmiths in Sierra Leone **Edge:** Reeded

| Date | Mintage | VF20 | XF40 | MS60 | MS63 | MS65 |
|---|---|---|---|---|---|---|
| 2002 | — | — | — | — | 7.00 | 9.00 |

**KM# 269 DOLLAR**
28.28 g., Copper-Nickel, 38.6 mm. **Subject:** Queen's Golden Jubilee **Obv:** National arms **Rev:** Queen, Prince Charles and Princess Anne **Edge:** Reeded

| Date | Mintage | VF20 | XF40 | MS60 | MS63 | MS65 |
|---|---|---|---|---|---|---|
| 2002 | — | — | — | — | 7.00 | 9.00 |

**KM# 276 DOLLAR**
28.28 g., Copper-Nickel, 38.6 mm. **Subject:** British Queen Mother **Obv:** National arms **Rev:** Queen Mother with dog in garden **Edge:** Reeded

| Date | Mintage | VF20 | XF40 | MS60 | MS63 | MS65 |
|---|---|---|---|---|---|---|
| 2002 | — | — | — | — | 7.00 | 9.00 |

**KM# 279 DOLLAR**
28.28 g., Copper-Nickel, 38.6 mm. **Subject:** Queen Mother **Obv:** National arms **Rev:** Queen Mother with daughters **Edge:** Reeded

| Date | Mintage | VF20 | XF40 | MS60 | MS63 | MS65 |
|---|---|---|---|---|---|---|
| 2002 | — | — | — | — | 7.00 | 9.00 |

**KM# 282 DOLLAR**
28.28 g., Copper-Nickel, 38.6 mm. **Subject:** Queen's Golden Jubilee **Obv:** National arms **Rev:** Queen Elizabeth and a young Prince Charles **Edge:** Reeded

| Date | Mintage | VF20 | XF40 | MS60 | MS63 | MS65 |
|---|---|---|---|---|---|---|
| 2002 | — | — | — | — | 7.00 | 9.00 |

**KM# 285 DOLLAR**
28.28 g., Copper-Nickel, 38.6 mm. **Subject:** Queen's Golden Jubilee **Obv:** National arms **Rev:** Queen Elizabeth and Prince Philip **Edge:** Reeded

| Date | Mintage | VF20 | XF40 | MS60 | MS63 | MS65 |
|---|---|---|---|---|---|---|
| 2002 | — | — | — | — | 7.00 | 9.00 |

**KM# 288 DOLLAR**
28.28 g., Copper-Nickel, 38.6 mm. **Subject:** Olympics **Obv:** National arms **Rev:** Victory goddess Nike **Edge:** Reeded

| Date | Mintage | VF20 | XF40 | MS60 | MS63 | MS65 |
|---|---|---|---|---|---|---|
| 2003 | — | — | — | — | 7.00 | 9.00 |
| 2004 | — | — | — | — | 7.00 | 9.00 |

**KM# 291 DOLLAR**
28.28 g., Copper-Nickel, 38.6 mm. **Subject:** Olympics **Obv:** National arms **Rev:** Ancient archer **Edge:** Reeded

| Date | Mintage | VF20 | XF40 | MS60 | MS63 | MS65 |
|---|---|---|---|---|---|---|
| 2003 | — | — | — | — | 7.00 | 9.00 |
| 2004 | — | — | — | — | 7.00 | 9.00 |

**KM# 297 DOLLAR**
28.28 g., Copper-Nickel, 38.6 mm. **Obv:** National arms **Rev:** Nelson Mandela **Edge:** Reeded

| Date | Mintage | VF20 | XF40 | MS60 | MS63 | MS65 |
|---|---|---|---|---|---|---|
| 2004 | — | — | — | — | 12.00 | 14.00 |

**KM# 300 DOLLAR**
28.28 g., Copper-Nickel, 38.6 mm. **Obv:** National arms **Rev:** Ronald Reagan **Edge:** Reeded

| Date | Mintage | VF20 | XF40 | MS60 | MS63 | MS65 |
|---|---|---|---|---|---|---|
| 2004 | — | — | — | — | 12.00 | 14.00 |

**KM# 304 DOLLAR**
28.42 g., Copper-Nickel, 38.6 mm. **Obv:** National arms **Rev:** Giraffe **Edge:** Reeded

| Date | Mintage | VF20 | XF40 | MS60 | MS63 | MS65 |
|---|---|---|---|---|---|---|
| 2005 | — | — | — | — | 9.00 | 12.00 |

**KM# 305 DOLLAR**
28.42 g., Copper-Nickel, 38.6 mm. **Obv:** National arms **Rev:** Crocodile **Edge:** Reeded

| Date | Mintage | VF20 | XF40 | MS60 | MS63 | MS65 |
|---|---|---|---|---|---|---|
| 2005 | — | — | — | — | 9.00 | 12.00 |

**KM# 306 DOLLAR**
28.42 g., Copper-Nickel, 38.6 mm. **Obv:** National arms **Rev:** Hippo in water **Edge:** Reeded

| Date | Mintage | VF20 | XF40 | MS60 | MS63 | MS65 |
|---|---|---|---|---|---|---|
| 2005 | — | — | — | — | 9.00 | 12.00 |

**KM# 315 DOLLAR**
Copper-Nickel **Series:** 60th Anniversary End of WW II **Subject:** Battle of Britian **Obv:** National arms **Obv. Legend:** REPUBLIC OF SIERRA LEONE **Rev:** Planes in flight

| Date | Mintage | VF20 | XF40 | MS60 | MS63 | MS65 |
|---|---|---|---|---|---|---|
| 2005 | — | — | — | — | 7.00 | 9.00 |

**KM# 316 DOLLAR**
Copper-Nickel **Series:** 60th Anniversary End of WW II **Subject:** The Battle of the Atlantic **Obv:** National arms **Obv. Legend:** REPUBLIC OF SIERRA LEONE **Rev:** Plane and ship convoy

| Date | Mintage | VF20 | XF40 | MS60 | MS63 | MS65 |
|---|---|---|---|---|---|---|
| 2005 | — | — | — | — | 7.00 | 9.00 |

**KM# 317 DOLLAR**
Copper-Nickel **Series:** 60th Anniversary End of WW II **Subject:** Battle of El Alamein **Obv:** National arms **Obv. Legend:** REPUBLIC OF SIERRA LEONE **Rev:** Tank, plane and ground troops

| Date | Mintage | VF20 | XF40 | MS60 | MS63 | MS65 |
|---|---|---|---|---|---|---|
| 2005 | — | — | — | — | 7.00 | 9.00 |

**KM# 318 DOLLAR**
Copper-Nickel **Series:** 60th Anniversay End of WW II **Subject:** Battle of the Bulge **Obv:** National arms **Obv. Legend:** REPUBLIC OF SIERRA LEONE **Rev:** Forest battle scene

| Date | Mintage | VF20 | XF40 | MS60 | MS63 | MS65 |
|---|---|---|---|---|---|---|
| 2005 | — | — | — | — | 7.00 | 9.00 |

**KM# 319 DOLLAR**
Copper-Nickel **Series:** 60th Anniversary End of WW II **Subject:** The Battle of Berlin **Obv:** National arms **Obv. Legend:** REPUBLIC OF SIERRA LEONE **Rev:** Berlin city view, tank

| Date | Mintage | VF20 | XF40 | MS60 | MS63 | MS65 |
|---|---|---|---|---|---|---|
| 2005 | — | — | — | — | 7.00 | 9.00 |

**KM# 320 DOLLAR**
Copper-Nickel **Series:** 60th Anniversary End of WW II **Subject:** The Heavy Water Raids **Obv:** National arms **Obv. Legend:** REPUBLIC OF SIERRA LEONE **Rev:** Troops on skies, factory in ruins

| Date | Mintage | VF20 | XF40 | MS60 | MS63 | MS65 |
|---|---|---|---|---|---|---|
| 2005 | — | — | — | — | 7.00 | 9.00 |

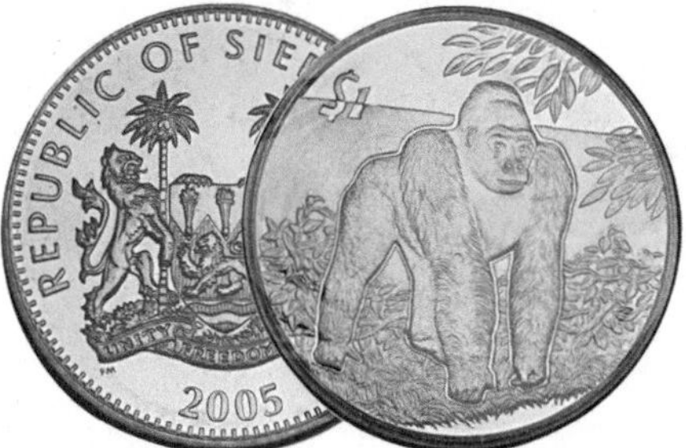

**KM# 321 DOLLAR**
Copper-Nickel **Obv:** National Arms **Rev:** Mountain Gorillia

| Date | Mintage | VF20 | XF40 | MS60 | MS63 | MS65 |
|---|---|---|---|---|---|---|
| 2005 | — | — | — | — | 9.00 | 12.00 |

**KM# 322 DOLLAR**
Copper-Nickel **Rev:** John Paul II head left, within ring of the Stations of the Cross

| Date | Mintage | VF20 | XF40 | MS60 | MS63 | MS65 |
|---|---|---|---|---|---|---|
| 2005 | — | — | — | — | 7.00 | 9.00 |

**KM# 323 DOLLAR**
Copper-Nickel **Rev:** Benedict XVI and St. Peter's

| Date | Mintage | VF20 | XF40 | MS60 | MS63 | MS65 |
|---|---|---|---|---|---|---|
| 2005 | — | — | — | — | 7.00 | 9.00 |

**KM# 345 DOLLAR**
28.50 g., Copper-Nickel, 38.58 mm. **Subject:** Death of Prince Rainier III **Obv:** National arms **Rev:** Bust left, small knight horseback right on neck **Edge:** Reeded

| Date | Mintage | VF20 | XF40 | MS60 | MS63 | MS65 |
|---|---|---|---|---|---|---|
| 2005 | — | — | — | — | 4.00 | 6.00 |

**KM# 308 DOLLAR**
28.37 g., Copper-Nickel, 38.5 mm. **Obv:** National arms **Rev:** Stegosaurus **Edge:** Reeded

| Date | Mintage | VF20 | XF40 | MS60 | MS63 | MS65 |
|---|---|---|---|---|---|---|
| 2006 | — | — | — | — | 11.00 | 13.00 |

**KM# 309 DOLLAR**
28.37 g., Copper-Nickel, 38.5 mm. **Obv:** National arms **Rev:** Tyrannosaurus Rex **Edge:** Reeded

| Date | Mintage | VF20 | XF40 | MS60 | MS63 | MS65 |
|---|---|---|---|---|---|---|
| 2006 | — | — | — | — | 11.00 | 13.00 |

**KM# 310 DOLLAR**
28.37 g., Copper-Nickel, 38.5 mm. **Obv:** National arms **Rev:** Triceratops **Edge:** Reeded

| Date | Mintage | VF20 | XF40 | MS60 | MS63 | MS65 |
|---|---|---|---|---|---|---|
| 2006 | — | — | — | — | 11.00 | 13.00 |

**KM# 311 DOLLAR**
28.37 g., Copper-Nickel, 38.5 mm. **Obv:** National arms **Rev:** Lion **Edge:** Reeded

| Date | Mintage | VF20 | XF40 | MS60 | MS63 | MS65 |
|---|---|---|---|---|---|---|
| 2006 | — | — | — | — | 9.00 | 12.00 |

**KM# 312 DOLLAR**
28.37 g., Copper-Nickel, 38.5 mm. **Obv:** National arms **Rev:** Dromedary Camel **Edge:** Reeded

| Date | Mintage | VF20 | XF40 | MS60 | MS63 | MS65 |
|---|---|---|---|---|---|---|
| 2006 | — | — | — | — | 9.00 | 12.00 |

**KM# 313 DOLLAR**
28.37 g., Copper-Nickel, 38.63 mm. **Obv:** National arms **Rev:** Chimpanzee **Edge:** Reeded

| Date | Mintage | VF20 | XF40 | MS60 | MS63 | MS65 |
|---|---|---|---|---|---|---|
| 2006 | — | — | — | — | 9.00 | 12.00 |

**KM# 314 DOLLAR**
28.37 g., Copper-Nickel, 38.5 mm. **Obv:** National arms **Rev:** Impala **Edge:** Reeded

| Date | Mintage | VF20 | XF40 | MS60 | MS63 | MS65 |
|---|---|---|---|---|---|---|
| 2006 | — | — | — | — | 9.00 | 12.00 |

**KM# 324 DOLLAR**
Copper-Nickel **Obv:** National Arms **Rev:** Brontosaurus

| Date | Mintage | VF20 | XF40 | MS60 | MS63 | MS65 |
|---|---|---|---|---|---|---|
| 2006 | — | — | — | — | 11.00 | 13.00 |

**KM# 326 DOLLAR**
28.37 g., Copper-Nickel, 38.5 mm. **Rev:** Cheetah

| Date | Mintage | VF20 | XF40 | MS60 | MS63 | MS65 |
|---|---|---|---|---|---|---|
| 2007 | — | — | — | — | 11.00 | 13.00 |

**KM# 327 DOLLAR**
28.37 g., Copper-Nickel, 38.5 mm. **Rev:** Zebra

| Date | Mintage | VF20 | XF40 | MS60 | MS63 | MS65 |
|---|---|---|---|---|---|---|
| 2007 | — | — | — | — | 11.00 | 13.00 |

**KM# 328 DOLLAR**
28.37 g., Copper-Nickel, 38.5 mm. **Rev:** Rhino

| Date | Mintage | VF20 | XF40 | MS60 | MS63 | MS65 |
|---|---|---|---|---|---|---|
| 2007 | — | — | — | — | 11.00 | 13.00 |

**KM# 329 DOLLAR**
28.37 g., Copper-Nickel, 38.5 mm. **Obv:** Arms **Rev:** African elephant

| Date | Mintage | VF20 | XF40 | MS60 | MS63 | MS65 |
|---|---|---|---|---|---|---|
| 2007 | — | — | — | — | 12.00 | 14.00 |

### KM# 347 DOLLAR

28.37 g., Copper-Nickel, 38.6 mm. **Series:** Nocturnal Creatures of Africa **Obv:** National arms **Rev:** Duiker Antelope standing left, facing **Edge:** Reeded **Note:** Blackened finish.

| Date | Mintage | VF20 | XF40 | MS60 | MS63 | MS65 |
|---|---|---|---|---|---|---|
| 2008 | — | — | — | — | 14.00 | 17.00 |

### KM# 348 DOLLAR

28.37 g., Copper-Nickel, 38.6 mm. **Series:** Nocturnal Creatures of Africa **Obv:** National arms **Rev:** Bush Baby on tree limb **Edge:** Reeded **Note:** Blackened finish.

| Date | Mintage | VF20 | XF40 | MS60 | MS63 | MS65 |
|---|---|---|---|---|---|---|
| 2008 | — | — | — | — | 14.00 | 17.00 |

### KM# 349 DOLLAR

28.37 g., Copper-Nickel, 38.6 mm. **Series:** Nocturnal Creatures of Africa **Obv:** National arms **Rev:** Honey Badger **Edge:** Reeded **Note:** Blackened finish

| Date | Mintage | VF20 | XF40 | MS60 | MS63 | MS65 |
|---|---|---|---|---|---|---|
| 2008 | — | — | — | — | 14.00 | 17.00 |

### KM# 350 DOLLAR

28.37 g., Copper-Nickel, 38.6 mm. **Series:** Nocturnal Creatures of Africa **Obv:** National arms. **Rev:** Pygmy Hippopotamus in water facing **Edge:** Reeded **Note:** Blackened finish.

| Date | Mintage | VF20 | XF40 | MS60 | MS63 | MS65 |
|---|---|---|---|---|---|---|
| 2008 | — | — | — | — | 14.00 | 17.00 |

### KM# 358 DOLLAR (100 Cents)

28.28 g., Copper-Nickel, 38.61 mm. **Subject:** Michael Jackson, Death **Rev:** Portrait facing

| Date | Mintage | VF20 | XF40 | MS60 | MS63 | MS65 |
|---|---|---|---|---|---|---|
| 2009 | — | — | — | — | 4.00 | 6.00 |

### KM# 364 DOLLAR (100 Cents)

28.28 g., Copper-Nickel, 38.61 mm. **Obv:** National arms **Rev:** Diana Monkey

| Date | Mintage | VF20 | XF40 | MS60 | MS63 | MS65 |
|---|---|---|---|---|---|---|
| 2009 | — | — | — | — | 4.00 | 6.00 |

### KM# 365 DOLLAR (100 Cents)

28.28 g., Copper-Nickel, 38.61 mm. **Obv:** National arms **Rev:** Capuchin Monkey

| Date | Mintage | VF20 | XF40 | MS60 | MS63 | MS65 |
|---|---|---|---|---|---|---|
| 2009 | — | — | — | — | 4.00 | 6.00 |

### KM# 360 DOLLAR (100 Cents)

28.28 g., Copper-Nickel, 38.61 mm. **Subject:** Winter Olympics, Vancouver, 2010 **Rev:** Totem pole at center, Canadian animals around

| Date | Mintage | VF20 | XF40 | MS60 | MS63 | MS65 |
|---|---|---|---|---|---|---|
| 2010 | — | — | — | — | 4.00 | 6.00 |

### KM# 361 DOLLAR (100 Cents)

28.28 g., Copper-Nickel, 38.61 mm. **Subject:** Winter Olympics, Vancouver, 2010 **Rev:** Totem pole at center, Skier and skater flanking

| Date | Mintage | VF20 | XF40 | MS60 | MS63 | MS65 |
|---|---|---|---|---|---|---|
| 2010 | — | — | — | — | 4.00 | 6.00 |

### KM# 366 DOLLAR (100 Cents)

28.28 g., Copper-Nickel, 38.61 mm. **Obv:** National arms **Rev:** Chipanzee

| Date | Mintage | VF20 | XF40 | MS60 | MS63 | MS65 |
|---|---|---|---|---|---|---|
| 2010 | — | — | — | — | 4.00 | 6.00 |

### KM# 367 DOLLAR (100 Cents)

28.28 g., Copper-Nickel, 38.61 mm. **Obv:** National arms **Rev:** Orangutan

| Date | Mintage | VF20 | XF40 | MS60 | MS63 | MS65 |
|---|---|---|---|---|---|---|
| 2010 | — | — | — | — | 4.00 | 6.00 |

### KM# 376 DOLLAR (100 Cents)

28.28 g., Copper-Nickel, 38.61 mm. **Subject:** Summer Olympics - London **Obv:** National Arms **Rev:** Pole vaulter

| Date | Mintage | VF20 | XF40 | MS60 | MS63 | MS65 |
|---|---|---|---|---|---|---|
| 2010 | — | — | — | — | 4.00 | 6.00 |

### KM# 377 DOLLAR (100 Cents)

28.28 g., Copper-Nickel, 38.61 mm. **Subject:** Summer Olympics - London **Obv:** National arms **Rev:** Archery

| Date | Mintage | VF20 | XF40 | MS60 | MS63 | MS65 |
|---|---|---|---|---|---|---|
| 2010 | — | — | — | — | 4.00 | 6.00 |

### KM# 379 DOLLAR (100 Cents)

28.28 g., Copper-Nickel, 38.61 mm. **Subject:** Summer Olympics - London **Obv:** National arms **Rev:** Track

| Date | Mintage | VF20 | XF40 | MS60 | MS63 | MS65 |
|---|---|---|---|---|---|---|
| 2010 | — | — | — | — | 4.00 | 6.00 |

### KM# 368 DOLLAR (100 Cents)

28.28 g., Copper-Nickel, 38.61 mm. **Obv:** National arms **Rev:** Mountain Gorilla

| Date | Mintage | VF20 | XF40 | MS60 | MS63 | MS65 |
|---|---|---|---|---|---|---|
| 2011 | — | — | — | — | 4.00 | 6.00 |

### KM# 369 DOLLAR (100 Cents)

28.28 g., Copper-Nickel, 38.61 mm. **Obv:** National arms **Rev:** Agile Gibon

| Date | Mintage | VF20 | XF40 | MS60 | MS63 | MS65 |
|---|---|---|---|---|---|---|
| 2011 | — | — | — | — | 4.00 | 6.00 |

### KM# 199 10 DOLLARS

28.28 g., 0.925 Silver 0.841 oz. ASW, 38.6 mm. **Subject:** Year of the Snake **Obv:** National arms **Rev:** Snake on bamboo **Edge:** Reeded

| Date | Mintage | VF20 | XF40 | MS60 | MS63 | MS65 |
|---|---|---|---|---|---|---|
| 2001 | — | PF65 50.00 | | | | |

### KM# 207 10 DOLLARS

28.28 g., 0.925 Silver 0.841 oz. ASW, 38.6 mm. **Subject:** P'an Ku **Obv:** National arms **Rev:** Dragon

| Date | Mintage | VF20 | XF40 | MS60 | MS63 | MS65 |
|---|---|---|---|---|---|---|
| 2001 | Est. 5000 | PF65 50.00 | | | | |

### KM# 215 10 DOLLARS

28.28 g., 0.925 Silver 0.841 oz. ASW, 38.6 mm. **Subject:** P'an Ku **Obv:** National arms **Rev:** Dragon and three animals

| Date | Mintage | VF20 | XF40 | MS60 | MS63 | MS65 |
|---|---|---|---|---|---|---|
| 2001 | Est. 5000 | PF65 50.00 | | | | |

### KM# 223 10 DOLLARS

28.28 g., 0.925 Silver 0.841 oz. ASW, 38.6 mm. **Series:** The Big Five **Obv:** National arms **Rev:** Rhino and value within circle **Edge:** Reeded

| Date | Mintage | VF20 | XF40 | MS60 | MS63 | MS65 |
|---|---|---|---|---|---|---|
| 2001 | — | PF63 40.00 | PF65 50.00 | | | |

### KM# 226 10 DOLLARS

28.28 g., 0.925 Silver 0.841 oz. ASW, 38.6 mm. **Series:** The Big Five **Obv:** National arms **Rev:** Lion head and value within circle

| Date | Mintage | VF20 | XF40 | MS60 | MS63 | MS65 |
|---|---|---|---|---|---|---|
| 2001 | Est. 10000 | PF63 40.00 | PF65 50.00 | | | |

### KM# 229 10 DOLLARS

28.28 g., 0.925 Silver 0.841 oz. ASW, 38.6 mm. **Series:** The Big Five **Obv:** National arms **Rev:** Leopard and value within circle

| Date | Mintage | VF20 | XF40 | MS60 | MS63 | MS65 |
|---|---|---|---|---|---|---|
| 2001 | Est. 10000 | PF63 40.00 | PF65 50.00 | | | |

### KM# 232 10 DOLLARS

28.28 g., 0.925 Silver 0.841 oz. ASW, 38.6 mm. **Series:** The Big Five **Obv:** National arms **Rev:** Elephants and value within circle

| Date | Mintage | VF20 | XF40 | MS60 | MS63 | MS65 |
|---|---|---|---|---|---|---|
| 2001 | Est. 10000 | PF63 40.00 | PF65 50.00 | | | |

### KM# 235 10 DOLLARS

28.28 g., 0.925 Silver 0.841 oz. ASW, 38.6 mm. **Series:** The Big Five **Obv:** National arms **Rev:** Buffalo and value within circle

| Date | Mintage | VF20 | XF40 | MS60 | MS63 | MS65 |
|---|---|---|---|---|---|---|
| 2001 | Est. 10000 | PF63 40.00 | PF65 50.00 | | | |

### KM# 238 10 DOLLARS

28.28 g., 0.925 Silver 0.841 oz. ASW, 38.6 mm. **Series:** The Big Five **Obv:** National arms **Rev:** All five animals within circle

| Date | Mintage | VF20 | XF40 | MS60 | MS63 | MS65 |
|---|---|---|---|---|---|---|
| 2001 | Est. 10000 | PF63 40.00 | PF65 50.00 | | | |

### KM# 246.1 10 DOLLARS

28.28 g., 0.925 Silver 0.841 oz. ASW, 38.6 mm. **Series:** Big Cats **Obv:** National arms **Rev:** Male and female lions **Edge:** Reeded

| Date | Mintage | VF20 | XF40 | MS60 | MS63 | MS65 |
|---|---|---|---|---|---|---|
| 2001 | 10,000 | PF63 40.00 | PF65 45.00 | | | |

### KM# 246.2 10 DOLLARS

28.28 g., 0.925 Silver 0.841 oz. ASW, 38.6 mm. **Series:** Big Cats **Obv:** National arms **Rev:** Multi-colored male and female lions **Edge:** Reeded

| Date | Mintage | VF20 | XF40 | MS60 | MS63 | MS65 |
|---|---|---|---|---|---|---|
| 2001 | — | PF63 50.00 | PF65 55.00 | | | |

### KM# 247.1 10 DOLLARS

28.28 g., 0.925 Silver 0.841 oz. ASW, 38.6 mm. **Series:** Big Cats **Obv:** National arms **Rev:** Tiger **Edge:** Reeded

| Date | Mintage | VF20 | XF40 | MS60 | MS63 | MS65 |
|---|---|---|---|---|---|---|
| 2001 | — | PF63 40.00 | PF65 45.00 | | | |

### KM# 247.2 10 DOLLARS

28.28 g., 0.925 Silver 0.841 oz. ASW, 38.6 mm. **Series:** Big Cats **Obv:** National arms **Rev:** Multi-colored Tiger **Edge:** Reeded

| Date | Mintage | VF20 | XF40 | MS60 | MS63 | MS65 |
|---|---|---|---|---|---|---|
| 2001 | — | PF63 50.00 | PF65 55.00 | | | |

**KM# 248.1 10 DOLLARS**
28.28 g., 0.925 Silver 0.841 oz. ASW, 38.6 mm. **Series:** Big Cats **Obv:** National arms **Rev:** Cheetah head facing **Edge:** Reeded

| Date | Mintage | VF20 | XF40 | MS60 | MS63 | MS65 |
|---|---|---|---|---|---|---|
| 2001 | 10,000 | PF63 40.00 | PF65 40.00 | | | |

**KM# 248.2 10 DOLLARS**
28.28 g., 0.925 Silver 0.841 oz. ASW, 38.6 mm. **Series:** Big Cats **Obv:** National arms **Rev:** Multi-colored Cheetah head facing **Edge:** Reeded

| Date | Mintage | VF20 | XF40 | MS60 | MS63 | MS65 |
|---|---|---|---|---|---|---|
| 2001 | — | PF63 45.00 | PF65 50.00 | | | |

**KM# 249.1 10 DOLLARS**
28.28 g., 0.925 Silver 0.841 oz. ASW, 38.6 mm. **Series:** Big Cats **Obv:** National arms **Rev:** Cougar **Edge:** Reeded

| Date | Mintage | VF20 | XF40 | MS60 | MS63 | MS65 |
|---|---|---|---|---|---|---|
| 2001 | 10,000 | PF63 40.00 | PF65 45.00 | | | |

**KM# 249.2 10 DOLLARS**
28.28 g., 0.925 Silver 0.841 oz. ASW, 38.6 mm. **Series:** Big Cats **Obv:** National arms **Rev:** Multi-colored Cougar **Edge:** Reeded

| Date | Mintage | VF20 | XF40 | MS60 | MS63 | MS65 |
|---|---|---|---|---|---|---|
| 2001 | — | PF63 50.00 | PF65 55.00 | | | |

**KM# 250.1 10 DOLLARS**
28.28 g., 0.925 Silver 0.841 oz. ASW, 38.6 mm. **Series:** Big Cats **Obv:** National arms **Rev:** Leopard **Edge:** Reeded

| Date | Mintage | VF20 | XF40 | MS60 | MS63 | MS65 |
|---|---|---|---|---|---|---|
| 2001 | 10,000 | PF63 40.00 | PF65 45.00 | | | |

**KM# 250.2 10 DOLLARS**
28.28 g., 0.925 Silver 0.841 oz. ASW, 38.6 mm. **Series:** Big Cats **Obv:** National arms **Rev:** Multi-colored Leopard **Edge:** Reeded

| Date | Mintage | VF20 | XF40 | MS60 | MS63 | MS65 |
|---|---|---|---|---|---|---|
| 2001 | — | PF63 50.00 | PF65 55.00 | | | |

**KM# 257 10 DOLLARS**
28.28 g., 0.925 Silver 0.841 oz. ASW, 38.6 mm. **Subject:** Year of the Horse **Obv:** National arms **Rev:** Horse divides circle **Edge:** Reeded

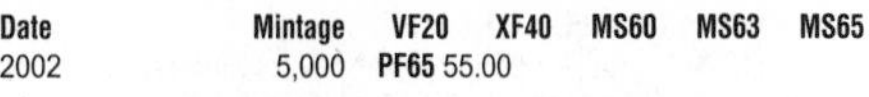

| Date | Mintage | VF20 | XF40 | MS60 | MS63 | MS65 |
|---|---|---|---|---|---|---|
| 2002 | 5,000 | PF65 55.00 | | | | |

**KM# 265 10 DOLLARS**
28.28 g., 0.925 Silver 0.841 oz. ASW, 38.6 mm. **Subject:** RMS Titanic **Obv:** National arms **Rev:** Titanic at dock **Edge:** Reeded

| Date | Mintage | VF20 | XF40 | MS60 | MS63 | MS65 |
|---|---|---|---|---|---|---|
| 2002 | 10,000 | PF63 50.00 | PF65 55.00 | | | |

**KM# 270 10 DOLLARS**
28.28 g., 0.925 Silver 0.841 oz. ASW Gold clad, 38.6 mm. **Subject:** Queen's Golden Jubilee **Obv:** National arms **Rev:** Queen Elizabeth II and Prince Philip visiting blacksmiths in Sierra Leone **Edge:** Reeded

| Date | Mintage | VF20 | XF40 | MS60 | MS63 | MS65 |
|---|---|---|---|---|---|---|
| 2002 | 10,000 | PF63 50.00 | PF65 55.00 | | | |

**KM# 271 10 DOLLARS**
28.28 g., 0.925 Silver 0.841 oz. ASW Gold clad, 38.6 mm. **Subject:** Queen's Golden Jubilee **Obv:** National arms **Rev:** Queen Elizabeth II, Prince Charles and Princess Anne **Edge:** Reeded

| Date | Mintage | VF20 | XF40 | MS60 | MS63 | MS65 |
|---|---|---|---|---|---|---|
| 2002 | 10,000 | PF63 45.00 | PF65 50.00 | | | |

**KM# 277 10 DOLLARS**
28.28 g., 0.925 Silver 0.841 oz. ASW Gold clad, 38.6 mm. **Subject:** British Queen Mother **Obv:** National arms **Rev:** Bust facing in garden with dog within sprigs **Edge:** Reeded

| Date | Mintage | VF20 | XF40 | MS60 | MS63 | MS65 |
|---|---|---|---|---|---|---|
| 2002 | 10,000 | PF63 50.00 | PF65 55.00 | | | |

**KM# 280 10 DOLLARS**
28.28 g., 0.925 Silver 0.841 oz. ASW Gold clad, 38.6 mm. **Subject:** British Queen Mother **Obv:** National arms **Rev:** Conjoined busts facing within sprigs **Edge:** Reeded

| Date | Mintage | VF20 | XF40 | MS60 | MS63 | MS65 |
|---|---|---|---|---|---|---|
| 2002 | 10,000 | PF63 50.00 | PF65 55.00 | | | |

**KM# 283 10 DOLLARS**
28.28 g., 0.925 Silver 0.841 oz. ASW Gold clad, 38.6 mm. **Subject:** Queen Elizabeth's Golden Jubilee **Obv:** National arms **Rev:** Queen and young Prince Charles **Edge:** Reeded

| Date | Mintage | VF20 | XF40 | MS60 | MS63 | MS65 |
|---|---|---|---|---|---|---|
| 2002 | 10,000 | PF63 45.00 | PF65 50.00 | | | |

**KM# 286 10 DOLLARS**
28.28 g., 0.925 Silver 0.841 oz. ASW Gold clad, 38.6 mm. **Subject:** Queen Elizabeth's Golden Jubilee **Obv:** National arms **Rev:** Queen and Prince Philip **Edge:** Reeded

| Date | Mintage | VF20 | XF40 | MS60 | MS63 | MS65 |
|---|---|---|---|---|---|---|
| 2002 | 10,000 | PF63 45.00 | PF65 50.00 | | | |

**KM# 289 10 DOLLARS**
28.28 g., 0.925 Silver 0.841 oz. ASW, 38.6 mm. **Subject:** Olympics **Obv:** National arms **Rev:** Victory goddess Nike **Edge:** Reeded **Note:** The leone is the official currency of Sierra Leone

| Date | Mintage | VF20 | XF40 | MS60 | MS63 | MS65 |
|---|---|---|---|---|---|---|
| 2003 | 10,000 | PF63 45.00 | PF65 50.00 | | | |
| 2004 | 10,000 | PF63 45.00 | PF65 50.00 | | | |

**KM# 292 10 DOLLARS**
28.28 g., 0.925 Silver 0.841 oz. ASW, 38.6 mm. **Subject:** Olympics **Obv:** National arms **Rev:** Ancient archer **Edge:** Reeded

| Date | Mintage | VF20 | XF40 | MS60 | MS63 | MS65 |
|---|---|---|---|---|---|---|
| 2003 | 10,000 | PF63 45.00 | PF65 50.00 | | | |
| 2004 | 10,000 | PF63 45.00 | PF65 50.00 | | | |

**KM# 298 10 DOLLARS**
28.28 g., 0.925 Silver 0.841 oz. ASW, 38.6 mm. **Obv:** National arms **Rev:** Nelson Mandela **Edge:** Reeded

| Date | Mintage | VF20 | XF40 | MS60 | MS63 | MS65 |
|---|---|---|---|---|---|---|
| 2004 | 10,000 | PF63 50.00 | PF65 55.00 | | | |

**KM# 301 10 DOLLARS**
28.28 g., 0.925 Silver 0.841 oz. ASW, 38.6 mm. **Obv:** National arms **Rev:** Ronald Reagan **Edge:** Reeded

| Date | Mintage | VF20 | XF40 | MS60 | MS63 | MS65 |
|---|---|---|---|---|---|---|
| 2004 | 10,000 | PF63 50.00 | PF65 55.00 | | | |

**KM# 307 10 DOLLARS**
28.62 g., 0.925 Silver 0.8511 oz. ASW, 38.5 mm. **Obv:** National arms **Rev:** Giraffe **Edge:** Reeded

| Date | Mintage | VF20 | XF40 | MS60 | MS63 | MS65 |
|---|---|---|---|---|---|---|
| 2005 | — | PF63 45.00 | PF65 50.00 | | | |

**KM# 339 10 DOLLARS**
28.28 g., 0.925 Silver 0.841 oz. ASW **Series:** 60th Anniversary of WW II **Subject:** Battle of Britain **Obv:** National arms **Obv. Legend:** REPUBLIC OF SIERRA LEONE **Rev:** Planes in flight

| Date | Mintage | VF20 | XF40 | MS60 | MS63 | MS65 |
|---|---|---|---|---|---|---|
| 2005 | — | PF63 40.00 | PF65 45.00 | | | |

**KM# 340 10 DOLLARS**
28.28 g., 0.925 Silver 0.841 oz. ASW **Series:** 60th Anniversary End of WW II **Subject:** The Battle of the Atlantic **Obv:** National arms **Obv. Legend:** REPUBLIC OF SIERRA LEONE **Rev:** Plane and ship convoy

| Date | Mintage | VF20 | XF40 | MS60 | MS63 | MS65 |
|---|---|---|---|---|---|---|
| 2005 | — | PF63 40.00 | PF65 45.00 | | | |

**KM# 341 10 DOLLARS**
28.28 g., 0.925 Silver 0.841 oz. ASW **Series:** 60th Anniversary End of WW II **Subject:** Battle of El Alamein **Obv:** National arms **Obv. Legend:** REPUBLIC OF SIERRA LEONE **Rev:** Tank, plane and ground troops

| Date | Mintage | VF20 | XF40 | MS60 | MS63 | MS65 |
|---|---|---|---|---|---|---|
| 2005 | — | PF63 40.00 | PF65 45.00 | | | |

**KM# 342 10 DOLLARS**
28.28 g., 0.925 Silver 0.841 oz. ASW **Series:** 60th Anniversary End of WW II **Subject:** Battle of the Bulge **Obv:** National arms **Obv. Legend:** REPUBLIC OF SIERRA LEONE **Rev:** Forest battle scene

| Date | Mintage | VF20 | XF40 | MS60 | MS63 | MS65 |
|---|---|---|---|---|---|---|
| 2005 | — | PF63 40.00 | PF65 45.00 | | | |

**KM# 343 10 DOLLARS**
28.28 g., 0.925 Silver 0.841 oz. ASW **Series:** 60th Anniversary End of WW II **Subject:** Battle of Berlin **Obv:** National arms **Obv. Legend:** REPUBLIC OF SIERRA LEONE **Rev:** Berlin city view, tank

| Date | Mintage | VF20 | XF40 | MS60 | MS63 | MS65 |
|---|---|---|---|---|---|---|
| 2005 | — | PF63 40.00 | PF65 45.00 | | | |

**KM# 344 10 DOLLARS**
28.28 g., 0.925 Silver 0.841 oz. ASW **Series:** 60th Anniversary End of WW II **Subject:** The Heavy Water Raids **Obv:** National arms **Obv. Legend:** REPUBLIC OF SIERRA LEONE **Rev:** Troops on skies, factory in ruins

| Date | Mintage | VF20 | XF40 | MS60 | MS63 | MS65 |
|---|---|---|---|---|---|---|
| 2005 | — | PF63 40.00 | PF65 45.00 | | | |

**KM# 330 10 DOLLARS**
28.28 g., 0.925 Silver 0.841 oz. ASW **Series:** Crown Jewels **Obv:** Arms **Obv. Legend:** REPUBLIC OF SIERRA LEONE **Rev:** Imperial State crown with ruby setting **Rev. Legend:** CROWN JEWELS **Edge:** Reeded

| Date | Mintage | VF20 | XF40 | MS60 | MS63 | MS65 |
|---|---|---|---|---|---|---|
| 2006 | — | PF65 120 | | | | |

**KM# 331 10 DOLLARS**
28.28 g., 0.925 Silver 0.841 oz. ASW **Series:** Crown Jewels **Obv:** Arms **Obv. Legend:** REPUBLIC OF SIERRA LEONE **Rev:** Sword of State with sapphire setting **Rev. Legend:** CROWN JEWELS **Edge:** Reeded

| Date | Mintage | VF20 | XF40 | MS60 | MS63 | MS65 |
|---|---|---|---|---|---|---|
| 2006 | — | PF65 120 | | | | |

**KM# 332 10 DOLLARS**
28.28 g., 0.925 Silver 0.841 oz. ASW **Series:** Crown Jewels **Obv:** Arms **Obv. Legend:** REPUBLIC OF SIERRA LEONE **Rev:** St. Edward's Crown with emerald setting **Rev. Legend:** CROWN JEWELS **Edge:** Reeded

| Date | Mintage | VF20 | XF40 | MS60 | MS63 | MS65 |
|---|---|---|---|---|---|---|
| 2006 | — | PF65 120 | | | | |

**KM# 333 10 DOLLARS**
28.28 g., 0.925 Silver 0.841 oz. ASW **Series:** Crown Jewels **Obv:** Arms **Obv. Legend:** REPUBLIC OF SIERRA LEONE **Rev:** Orb and Sceptre with the cross with diamond setting **Rev. Legend:** CROWN JEWELS **Edge:** Reeded

| Date | Mintage | VF20 | XF40 | MS60 | MS63 | MS65 |
|---|---|---|---|---|---|---|
| 2006 | — | PF65 120 | | | | |

**KM# 334 10 DOLLARS**
Copper-Nickel **Subject:** 80th Birthday of Queen Elizabeth II **Obv:** Arms **Obv. Legend:** REPUBLIC OF SIERRA LEONE **Rev:** Elizabeth II seated giving Christmas message **Edge:** Reeded

| Date | Mintage | VF20 | XF40 | MS60 | MS63 | MS65 |
|---|---|---|---|---|---|---|
| 2006 | — | — | — | — | 16.50 | 18.50 |

**KM# 334a 10 DOLLARS**
28.28 g., 0.925 Silver 0.841 oz. ASW **Subject:** 80th Birthday of Queen Elizabeth II **Obv:** Arms **Obv. Legend:** REPUBLIC OF SIERRA LEONE **Rev:** Elizabeth II seated giving Christmas Message **Edge:** Reeded

| Date | Mintage | VF20 | XF40 | MS60 | MS63 | MS65 |
|---|---|---|---|---|---|---|
| 2006 | — | PF63 65.00 | PF65 75.00 | | | |

**KM# 335 10 DOLLARS**
Copper-Nickel **Subject:** 80th Bithday of Queen Elizabeth II **Obv:** Arms **Obv. Legend:** REPUBLIC OF SIERRA LEONE **Rev:** Elizabeth II at 2002 Golden Jubilee celebrations in London, Concorde and Red Arrows doing flypass over Buckingham Palace **Edge:** Reeded

| Date | Mintage | VF20 | XF40 | MS60 | MS63 | MS65 |
|---|---|---|---|---|---|---|
| 2006 | — | — | — | — | 16.50 | 18.50 |

**KM# 335a 10 DOLLARS**
28.28 g., 0.925 Silver 0.841 oz. ASW **Subject:** 80th Birthday of Queen Elizabeth Ii **Obv:** Arms **Obv. Legend:** REPUBLIC OF SIERRA LEONE **Rev:** Elizabeth II at 2002 Golden Jubilee celebrations in London, Concorde and Red Arrows doing flypass over Buckingham Palace **Edge:** Reeded

| Date | Mintage | VF20 | XF40 | MS60 | MS63 | MS65 |
|---|---|---|---|---|---|---|
| 2006 | — | PF63 65.00 | PF65 75.00 | | | |

**KM# 336 10 DOLLARS**
Copper-Nickel **Subject:** 80th Birthday of Queen Elizabeth II **Obv:** Arms **Obv. Legend:** REPUBLIC OF SIERRA LEONE **Rev:** Elizabeth II presenting 1966 Football World Cup to English team **Edge:** Reeded

| Date | Mintage | VF20 | XF40 | MS60 | MS63 | MS65 |
|---|---|---|---|---|---|---|
| 2006 | — | — | — | — | 16.50 | 18.50 |

**KM# 336a 10 DOLLARS**
28.28 g., 0.925 Silver 0.841 oz. ASW **Subject:** 80th Birthday of Queen Elizabeth II **Obv:** Arms **Obv. Legend:** REPUBLIC OF SIERRA LEONE **Rev:** Elizabeth II presenting 1966 Football World Cup to English team **Edge:** Reeded

| Date | Mintage | VF20 | XF40 | MS60 | MS63 | MS65 |
|---|---|---|---|---|---|---|
| 2006 | — | PF63 65.00 | PF65 75.00 | | | |

**KM# 337 10 DOLLARS**
Copper-Nickel **Subject:** 80th Birthday of Queen Elizabeth II **Obv:** Arms **Obv. Legend:** REPUBLIC OF SIERRA LEONE **Rev:** Investiture of Charles as Prince of Wales in 1969 **Edge:** Reeded

| Date | Mintage | VF20 | XF40 | MS60 | MS63 | MS65 |
|---|---|---|---|---|---|---|
| 2006 | — | — | — | — | 16.50 | 18.50 |

**KM# 337a 10 DOLLARS**
0.9167 Silver **Subject:** 80th Birthday of Queen Elizabeth II **Obv:** Arms **Obv. Legend:** REPUBLIC OF SIERRA LEONE **Rev:** Investiture of Charles as Prince of Wales in 1969 **Edge:** Reeded

| Date | Mintage | VF20 | XF40 | MS60 | MS63 | MS65 |
|---|---|---|---|---|---|---|
| 2006 | — | PF63 65.00 | PF65 75.00 | | | |

**KM# 338 10 DOLLARS**
Copper-Nickel **Subject:** 10th Anniversary Death of Princess Diana **Obv:** Arms **Obv. Legend:** REPUBLIC OF SIERRA LEONE **Rev:** Diana with sons, Prince William and Prince Harry facing **Rev. Legend:** DIANA — PRINCESS OF WALES **Edge:** Reeded

| Date | Mintage | VF20 | XF40 | MS60 | MS63 | MS65 |
|---|---|---|---|---|---|---|
| 2007 | — | — | — | — | 16.50 | 18.50 |

**KM# 338a 10 DOLLARS**
28.28 g., 0.925 Silver 0.841 oz. ASW **Subject:** 10th Anniversary Death of Princess Diana **Obv:** Arms **Obv. Legend:** REPUBLIC OF SIERRA LEONE **Rev:** Diana with sons, Prince William and Prince Harry facing **Rev. Legend:** DIANA — PRINCESS OF WALES **Edge:** Reeded

| Date | Mintage | VF20 | XF40 | MS60 | MS63 | MS65 |
|---|---|---|---|---|---|---|
| 2007 | — | PF63 65.00 | PF65 75.00 | | | |

**KM# 352 10 DOLLARS**
31.11 g., 0.999 Silver 0.999 oz. ASW, 38.61 mm. **Subject:** Marian Shrines **Rev:** Fatima with Holy Water insert

| Date | Mintage | VF20 | XF40 | MS60 | MS63 | MS65 |
|---|---|---|---|---|---|---|
| 2009 | — | PF65 30.00 | | | | |

**KM# 353 10 DOLLARS**
31.11 g., 0.999 Silver 0.999 oz. ASW, 38.61 mm. **Subject:** Marian Shrines **Rev:** Lourdes with Holy Water insert

| Date | Mintage | VF20 | XF40 | MS60 | MS63 | MS65 |
|---|---|---|---|---|---|---|
| 2009 | — | PF65 30.00 | | | | |

**KM# 354 10 DOLLARS**
31.11 g., 0.999 Silver 0.999 oz. ASW, 38.61 mm. **Subject:** Marian Shrines **Rev:** Laredo with Holy Water insert

| Date | Mintage | VF20 | XF40 | MS60 | MS63 | MS65 |
|---|---|---|---|---|---|---|
| 2009 | — | PF65 30.00 | | | | |

**KM# 359 10 DOLLARS**
31.11 g., 0.999 Silver 0.999 oz. ASW, 38.61 mm. **Subject:** Michael Jackson, Death **Rev:** Portrait facing

| Date | Mintage | VF20 | XF40 | MS60 | MS63 | MS65 |
|---|---|---|---|---|---|---|
| 2009 | — | PF65 30.00 | | | | |

**KM# 370 10 DOLLARS**
28.28 g., 0.925 Silver 0.841 oz. ASW, 38.61 mm. **Obv:** National arms **Rev:** Diana Monkey

| Date | Mintage | VF20 | XF40 | MS60 | MS63 | MS65 |
|---|---|---|---|---|---|---|
| 2009 | — | PF65 30.00 | | | | |

**KM# 371 10 DOLLARS**
28.28 g., 0.925 Silver 0.841 oz. ASW, 38.61 mm. **Obv:** National arms **Rev:** Capuchin Monkey

| Date | Mintage | VF20 | XF40 | MS60 | MS63 | MS65 |
|---|---|---|---|---|---|---|
| 2009 | — | PF65 30.00 | | | | |

**KM# 362 10 DOLLARS**
28.28 g., 0.925 Silver 0.841 oz. ASW, 38.61 mm. **Subject:** Winter Olympics, Vancouver, 2010 **Rev:** Totem pole at center, Canadian animals around

| Date | Mintage | VF20 | XF40 | MS60 | MS63 | MS65 |
|---|---|---|---|---|---|---|
| 2010 | — | PF65 30.00 | | | | |

**KM# 363 10 DOLLARS**
28.28 g., 0.925 Silver 0.841 oz. ASW, 38.61 mm. **Subject:** Totem pole at center, skier and skater flanking

| Date | Mintage | VF20 | XF40 | MS60 | MS63 | MS65 |
|---|---|---|---|---|---|---|
| 2010 | — | PF65 30.00 | | | | |

**KM# 372 10 DOLLARS**
28.28 g., 0.925 Silver 0.841 oz. ASW, 38.61 mm. **Obv:** National arms **Rev:** Orangutan

| Date | Mintage | VF20 | XF40 | MS60 | MS63 | MS65 |
|---|---|---|---|---|---|---|
| 2010 | — | PF65 30.00 | | | | |

**KM# 373 10 DOLLARS**
28.28 g., 0.925 Silver 0.841 oz. ASW, 38.61 mm. **Obv:** National arms **Rev:** Chipanzee

| Date | Mintage | VF20 | XF40 | MS60 | MS63 | MS65 |
|---|---|---|---|---|---|---|
| 2010 | — | PF65 30.00 | | | | |

**KM# 375 10 DOLLARS**
28.28 g., Copper-Nickel, 38.61 mm. **Subject:** World Cup Soccer **Rev:** Soccer field and players

| Date | Mintage | VF20 | XF40 | MS60 | MS63 | MS65 |
|---|---|---|---|---|---|---|
| 2010 | — | — | — | — | — | 10.00 |

**KM# 378 10 DOLLARS**
28.28 g., Copper-Nickel, 38.61 mm. **Subject:** Summer Olympics - London **Obv:** National arms **Rev:** Basketball

| Date | Mintage | VF20 | XF40 | MS60 | MS63 | MS65 |
|---|---|---|---|---|---|---|
| 2010 | — | — | — | — | — | 10.00 |

**KM# 380 10 DOLLARS**
28.28 g., 0.925 Silver 0.841 oz. ASW, 38.61 mm. **Subject:** Summer Olympics, London **Obv:** National arms **Rev:** Pole Vaulter

| Date | Mintage | VF20 | XF40 | MS60 | MS63 | MS65 |
|---|---|---|---|---|---|---|
| 2010 | — | PF65 30.00 | | | | |
| 2012 | — | PF65 30.00 | | | | |

**KM# 381 10 DOLLARS**
28.28 g., 0.925 Silver 0.841 oz. ASW, 38.61 mm. **Subject:** Summer Olympics - London **Obv:** National arms **Rev:** Archery

| Date | Mintage | VF20 | XF40 | MS60 | MS63 | MS65 |
|---|---|---|---|---|---|---|
| 2010 | — | PF65 30.00 | | | | |
| 2012 | — | PF65 30.00 | | | | |

**KM# 382 10 DOLLARS**
28.28 g., 0.925 Silver 0.841 oz. ASW, 38.61 mm. **Subject:** Summer Olympics, London **Obv:** National arms **Rev:** Basketball

| Date | Mintage | VF20 | XF40 | MS60 | MS63 | MS65 |
|---|---|---|---|---|---|---|
| 2010 | — | PF65 30.00 | | | | |
| 2012 | — | PF65 30.00 | | | | |

**KM# 383 10 DOLLARS**
28.28 g., 0.925 Silver 0.841 oz. ASW, 38.61 mm. **Subject:** Summer Olympics - London **Obv:** National arms **Rev:** Hurdles

| Date | Mintage | VF20 | XF40 | MS60 | MS63 | MS65 |
|---|---|---|---|---|---|---|
| 2010 | — | PF65 30.00 | | | | |
| 2012 | — | PF65 30.00 | | | | |

**KM# 351 10 DOLLARS**
28.28 g., 0.925 Silver 0.841 oz. ASW, 38.61 mm. **Obv:** National arms **Rev:** Mountain Gorilla

| Date | Mintage | VF20 | XF40 | MS60 | MS63 | MS65 |
|---|---|---|---|---|---|---|
| 2011 PM | — | PF63 65.00 | PF65 75.00 | | | |

**KM# 374 10 DOLLARS**
28.28 g., 0.925 Silver 0.841 oz. ASW, 38.61 mm. **Obv:** National arms **Rev:** Agile Gibon

| Date | Mintage | VF20 | XF40 | MS60 | MS63 | MS65 |
|---|---|---|---|---|---|---|
| 2011 | — | PF65 30.00 | | | | |

**KM# 200 20 DOLLARS**
1.24 g., 0.999 Gold 0.040 oz. AGW, 13.9 mm. **Subject:** Year of the Snake **Obv:** National arms **Rev:** Snake **Edge:** Reeded

| Date | Mintage | VF20 | XF40 | MS60 | MS63 | MS65 |
|---|---|---|---|---|---|---|
| 2001 | — | PF65 75.00 | | | | |

**KM# 208 20 DOLLARS**
1.24 g., 0.999 Gold 0.040 oz. AGW, 13.9 mm. **Subject:** P'an Ku **Obv:** National arms **Rev:** Dragon

| Date | Mintage | VF20 | XF40 | MS60 | MS63 | MS65 |
|---|---|---|---|---|---|---|
| 2001 | Est. 5000 | PF65 75.00 | | | | |

**KM# 216 20 DOLLARS**
1.24 g., 0.999 Gold 0.040 oz. AGW, 13.9 mm. **Subject:** P'an Ku **Obv:** National arms **Rev:** Dragon and three animals

| Date | Mintage | VF20 | XF40 | MS60 | MS63 | MS65 |
|---|---|---|---|---|---|---|
| 2001 | — | PF65 75.00 | | | | |

**KM# 258 20 DOLLARS**
1.24 g., 0.999 Gold 0.0398 oz. AGW, 13.92 mm. **Subject:** Year of the Horse **Obv:** National arms **Rev:** Horse **Edge:** Reeded

| Date | Mintage | VF20 | XF40 | MS60 | MS63 | MS65 |
|---|---|---|---|---|---|---|
| 2002 | 5,000 | PF65 75.00 | | | | |

**KM# 272 30 DOLLARS**
6.22 g., 0.375 Gold 0.075 oz. AGW, 22 mm. **Subject:** Queen's Golden Jubilee **Obv:** National arms **Rev:** Queen Elizabeth II and Prince Philip **Edge:** Reeded

| Date | Mintage | VF20 | XF40 | MS60 | MS63 | MS65 |
|---|---|---|---|---|---|---|
| 2002 | — | PF65 150 | | | | |

**KM# 273 30 DOLLARS**
6.22 g., 0.375 Gold 0.075 oz. AGW, 22 mm. **Subject:** Queen's Golden Jubilee **Obv:** National arms **Rev:** Queen Elizabeth II, Prince Charles and Princess Anne **Edge:** Reeded

| Date | Mintage | VF20 | XF40 | MS60 | MS63 | MS65 |
|---|---|---|---|---|---|---|
| 2002 | — | PF65 150 | | | | |

**KM# 201 50 DOLLARS**
3.11 g., 0.999 Gold 0.0999 oz. AGW, 18 mm. **Subject:** Year of the Snake **Obv:** National arms **Rev:** Snake **Edge:** Reeded

| Date | Mintage | VF20 | XF40 | MS60 | MS63 | MS65 |
|---|---|---|---|---|---|---|
| 2001 | Est. 10000 | PF65 185 | | | | |

**KM# 209 50 DOLLARS**
3.11 g., 0.999 Gold 0.0999 oz. AGW, 18 mm. **Subject:** P'an Ku **Obv:** National arms **Rev:** Dragon

| Date | Mintage | VF20 | XF40 | MS60 | MS63 | MS65 |
|---|---|---|---|---|---|---|
| 2001 | Est. 5000 | PF65 185 | | | | |

**KM# 217 50 DOLLARS**
3.11 g., 0.999 Gold 0.0999 oz. AGW, 18 mm. **Subject:** P'an Ku **Obv:** National arms **Rev:** Dragon and three animals

| Date | Mintage | VF20 | XF40 | MS60 | MS63 | MS65 |
|---|---|---|---|---|---|---|
| 2001 | Est. 5000 | PF65 185 | | | | |

**KM# 259 50 DOLLARS**
3.11 g., 0.999 Gold 0.0999 oz. AGW, 18 mm. **Subject:** Year of the Horse **Obv:** National arms **Rev:** Horse **Edge:** Reeded

| Date | Mintage | VF20 | XF40 | MS60 | MS63 | MS65 |
|---|---|---|---|---|---|---|
| 2002 | 5,000 | PF65 185 | | | | |

**KM# 266 50 DOLLARS**
155.55 g., 0.9999 Silver 5.0005 oz. ASW, 65 mm. **Subject:** RMS Titanic **Obv:** National arms **Rev:** Titanic at dock **Edge:** Reeded

| Date | Mintage | VF20 | XF40 | MS60 | MS63 | MS65 |
|---|---|---|---|---|---|---|
| 2002 | — | PF65 210 | | | | |

**KM# 202 100 DOLLARS**
6.22 g., 0.999 Gold 0.1998 oz. AGW, 22 mm. **Subject:** Year of the Snake **Obv:** National arms **Rev:** Snake **Edge:** Reeded

| Date | Mintage | VF20 | XF40 | MS60 | MS63 | MS65 |
|---|---|---|---|---|---|---|
| 2001 | — | PF65 360 | | | | |

**KM# 210 100 DOLLARS**
6.22 g., 0.999 Gold 0.1998 oz. AGW, 22 mm. **Subject:** P'an Ku **Obv:** National arms **Rev:** Dragon

| Date | Mintage | VF20 | XF40 | MS60 | MS63 | MS65 |
|---|---|---|---|---|---|---|
| 2001 | Est. 10000 | PF65 360 | | | | |

**KM# 218 100 DOLLARS**
6.22 g., 0.999 Gold 0.1998 oz. AGW, 22 mm. **Subject:** P'an Ku **Obv:** National arms **Rev:** Dragon and three animals

| Date | Mintage | VF20 | XF40 | MS60 | MS63 | MS65 |
|---|---|---|---|---|---|---|
| 2001 | Est. 10000 | PF65 360 | | | | |

**KM# 224 100 DOLLARS**
6.22 g., 0.999 Gold 0.1998 oz. AGW, 22 mm. **Series:** The Big Five **Obv:** National arms **Rev:** Rhino **Edge:** Reeded

| Date | Mintage | VF20 | XF40 | MS60 | MS63 | MS65 |
|---|---|---|---|---|---|---|
| 2001 | Est. 5000 | PF65 360 | | | | |

**KM# 227 100 DOLLARS**
6.22 g., 0.999 Gold 0.1998 oz. AGW, 22 mm. **Series:** The Big Five **Obv:** National arms **Rev:** Lion

| Date | Mintage | VF20 | XF40 | MS60 | MS63 | MS65 |
|---|---|---|---|---|---|---|
| 2001 | — | PF65 360 | | | | |

**KM# 230 100 DOLLARS**
6.22 g., 0.999 Gold 0.1998 oz. AGW, 22 mm. **Series:** The Big Five **Obv:** National arms **Rev:** Leopard

| Date | Mintage | VF20 | XF40 | MS60 | MS63 | MS65 |
|---|---|---|---|---|---|---|
| 2001 | Est. 5000 | PF65 360 | | | | |

**KM# 233 100 DOLLARS**
6.22 g., 0.999 Gold 0.1998 oz. AGW, 22 mm. **Series:** The Big Five **Obv:** National arms **Rev:** Elephants

| Date | Mintage | VF20 | XF40 | MS60 | MS63 | MS65 |
|---|---|---|---|---|---|---|
| 2001 | Est. 5000 | PF65 360 | | | | |

**KM# 236 100 DOLLARS**
6.22 g., 0.999 Gold 0.1998 oz. AGW, 22 mm. **Series:** The Big Five **Obv:** National arms **Rev:** Buffalo

| Date | Mintage | VF20 | XF40 | MS60 | MS63 | MS65 |
|---|---|---|---|---|---|---|
| 2001 | Est. 5000 | PF65 360 | | | | |

**KM# 239 100 DOLLARS**
6.22 g., 0.999 Gold 0.1998 oz. AGW, 22 mm. **Series:** The Big Five **Obv:** National arms **Rev:** All five animals

| Date | Mintage | VF20 | XF40 | MS60 | MS63 | MS65 |
|---|---|---|---|---|---|---|
| 2001 | — | PF65 360 | | | | |

**KM# 251 100 DOLLARS**
6.22 g., 0.999 Gold 0.1998 oz. AGW, 22 mm. **Series:** Big Cats **Obv:** National arms **Rev:** Male and female lions **Edge:** Reeded

| Date | Mintage | VF20 | XF40 | MS60 | MS63 | MS65 |
|---|---|---|---|---|---|---|
| 2001 | 5,000 | PF65 360 | | | | |

**KM# 252 100 DOLLARS**
6.22 g., 0.999 Gold 0.1998 oz. AGW, 22 mm. **Series:** Big Cats **Rev:** Tiger **Edge:** Reeded

| Date | Mintage | VF20 | XF40 | MS60 | MS63 | MS65 |
|---|---|---|---|---|---|---|
| 2001 | 5,000 | PF65 360 | | | | |

**KM# 253 100 DOLLARS**
6.22 g., 0.999 Gold 0.1998 oz. AGW, 22 mm. **Series:** Big Cats **Rev:** Cheetah **Edge:** Reeded

| Date | Mintage | VF20 | XF40 | MS60 | MS63 | MS65 |
|---|---|---|---|---|---|---|
| 2001 | 5,000 | PF65 360 | | | | |

**KM# 254 100 DOLLARS**
6.22 g., 0.999 Gold 0.1998 oz. AGW, 22 mm. **Series:** Big Cats **Rev:** Cougar **Edge:** Reeded

| Date | Mintage | VF20 | XF40 | MS60 | MS63 | MS65 |
|---|---|---|---|---|---|---|
| 2001 | 5,000 | PF65 360 | | | | |

### KM# 255 100 DOLLARS
6.22 g., 0.999 Gold 0.1998 oz. AGW, 22 mm. **Series:** Big Cats **Rev:** Black panther **Edge:** Reeded

| Date | Mintage | VF20 | XF40 | MS60 | MS63 | MS65 |
|---|---|---|---|---|---|---|
| 2001 | 5,000 | PF65 360 | | | | |

### KM# 260 100 DOLLARS
6.22 g., 0.999 Gold 0.1998 oz. AGW, 22 mm. **Subject:** Year of the Horse **Obv:** National arms **Rev:** Horse **Edge:** Reeded

| Date | Mintage | VF20 | XF40 | MS60 | MS63 | MS65 |
|---|---|---|---|---|---|---|
| 2002 | 2,000 | PF65 360 | | | | |

### KM# 274 100 DOLLARS
6.22 g., 0.9999 Gold 0.200 oz. AGW, 22 mm. **Subject:** Queen's Golden Jubilee **Obv:** National arms **Rev:** Queen Elizabeth II and Prince Philip **Edge:** Reeded

| Date | Mintage | VF20 | XF40 | MS60 | MS63 | MS65 |
|---|---|---|---|---|---|---|
| 2002 | — | PF65 360 | | | | |

### KM# 275 100 DOLLARS
6.22 g., 0.9999 Gold 0.200 oz. AGW, 22 mm. **Subject:** Queen's Golden Jubilee **Obv:** National arms **Rev:** Queen Elizabeth II, Prince Charles and Princess Anne **Edge:** Reeded

| Date | Mintage | VF20 | XF40 | MS60 | MS63 | MS65 |
|---|---|---|---|---|---|---|
| 2002 | — | PF65 360 | | | | |

### KM# 278 100 DOLLARS
6.22 g., 0.9999 Gold 0.200 oz. AGW, 22 mm. **Subject:** British Queen Mother **Obv:** National arms **Rev:** Queen Mother in garden with dog **Edge:** Reeded

| Date | Mintage | VF20 | XF40 | MS60 | MS63 | MS65 |
|---|---|---|---|---|---|---|
| 2002 | 2,000 | PF65 360 | | | | |

### KM# 281 100 DOLLARS
6.22 g., 0.9999 Gold 0.200 oz. AGW, 22 mm. **Subject:** British Queen Mother **Obv:** National arms **Rev:** Queen Mother with daughters **Edge:** Reeded

| Date | Mintage | VF20 | XF40 | MS60 | MS63 | MS65 |
|---|---|---|---|---|---|---|
| 2002 | 2,000 | PF65 360 | | | | |

### KM# 284 100 DOLLARS
6.22 g., 0.9999 Gold 0.200 oz. AGW, 22 mm. **Subject:** Queen Elizabeth's Golden Jubilee **Obv:** National arms **Rev:** Queen and young Prince Charles **Edge:** Reeded

| Date | Mintage | VF20 | XF40 | MS60 | MS63 | MS65 |
|---|---|---|---|---|---|---|
| 2002 | 2,002 | PF65 360 | | | | |

### KM# 287 100 DOLLARS
6.22 g., 0.9999 Gold 0.200 oz. AGW, 22 mm. **Subject:** Queen Elizabeth's Golden Jubilee **Obv:** National arms **Rev:** Queen and Prince Philip **Edge:** Reeded

| Date | Mintage | VF20 | XF40 | MS60 | MS63 | MS65 |
|---|---|---|---|---|---|---|
| 2002 | 2,002 | PF65 360 | | | | |

### KM# 290 100 DOLLARS
6.22 g., 0.9999 Gold 0.200 oz. AGW, 22 mm. **Subject:** Olympics **Obv:** National arms **Rev:** Victory goddess Nike **Edge:** Reeded

| Date | Mintage | VF20 | XF40 | MS60 | MS63 | MS65 |
|---|---|---|---|---|---|---|
| 2003 | 5,000 | PF65 360 | | | | |
| 2004 | 5,000 | PF65 360 | | | | |

### KM# 293 100 DOLLARS
6.22 g., 0.9999 Gold 0.200 oz. AGW, 22 mm. **Subject:** Olympics **Obv:** National arms **Rev:** Ancient archer **Edge:** Reeded

| Date | Mintage | VF20 | XF40 | MS60 | MS63 | MS65 |
|---|---|---|---|---|---|---|
| 2003 | 5,000 | PF65 360 | | | | |
| 2004 | 5,000 | PF65 360 | | | | |

### KM# 267 150 DOLLARS
1000.00 g., 0.9999 Silver 32.1475 oz. ASW, 85 mm. **Subject:** RMS Titanic **Obv:** National arms **Rev:** Titanic at dock **Edge:** Reeded

| Date | Mintage | VF20 | XF40 | MS60 | MS63 | MS65 |
|---|---|---|---|---|---|---|
| 2002 | — | PF65 1,350 | | | | |

### KM# 203 250 DOLLARS
15.51 g., 0.999 Gold 0.4982 oz. AGW, 30 mm. **Subject:** Year of the Snake **Obv:** National arms **Rev:** Snake **Edge:** Reeded

| Date | Mintage | VF20 | XF40 | MS60 | MS63 | MS65 |
|---|---|---|---|---|---|---|
| 2001 | Est. 5000 | PF65 900 | | | | |

### KM# 211 250 DOLLARS
15.55 g., 0.999 Gold 0.4995 oz. AGW, 30 mm. **Subject:** P'an Ku **Obv:** National arms **Rev:** Dragon

| Date | Mintage | VF20 | XF40 | MS60 | MS63 | MS65 |
|---|---|---|---|---|---|---|
| 2001 | Est. 2000 | PF65 900 | | | | |

### KM# 219 250 DOLLARS
15.55 g., 0.999 Gold 0.4995 oz. AGW, 30 mm. **Subject:** P'an Ku **Obv:** National arms **Rev:** Dragon and three animals

| Date | Mintage | VF20 | XF40 | MS60 | MS63 | MS65 |
|---|---|---|---|---|---|---|
| 2001 | Est. 2000 | PF65 900 | | | | |

### KM# 261 250 DOLLARS
15.55 g., 0.999 Gold 0.4994 oz. AGW, 30 mm. **Subject:** Year of the Horse **Obv:** National arms **Rev:** Horse **Edge:** Reeded

| Date | Mintage | VF20 | XF40 | MS60 | MS63 | MS65 |
|---|---|---|---|---|---|---|
| 2002 | 2,000 | PF65 900 | | | | |

### KM# 204 500 DOLLARS
31.10 g., 0.999 Gold 0.999 oz. AGW, 32.7 mm. **Subject:** Year of the Snake **Obv:** National arms **Rev:** Snake **Edge:** Reeded

| Date | Mintage | VF20 | XF40 | MS60 | MS63 | MS65 |
|---|---|---|---|---|---|---|
| 2001 | Est. 1000 | PF65 1,750 | | | | |

### KM# 212 500 DOLLARS
31.10 g., 0.999 Gold 0.999 oz. AGW, 32.7 mm. **Subject:** P'an Ku **Obv:** National arms **Rev:** Dragon

| Date | Mintage | VF20 | XF40 | MS60 | MS63 | MS65 |
|---|---|---|---|---|---|---|
| 2001 | Est. 1000 | PF65 1,750 | | | | |

### KM# 220 500 DOLLARS
31.10 g., 0.999 Gold 0.999 oz. AGW, 32.7 mm. **Subject:** P'an Ku **Obv:** National arms **Rev:** Dragon and three animals

| Date | Mintage | VF20 | XF40 | MS60 | MS63 | MS65 |
|---|---|---|---|---|---|---|
| 2001 | Est. 1000 | PF65 1,750 | | | | |

### KM# 262 500 DOLLARS
31.10 g., 0.999 Gold 0.9989 oz. AGW, 32.7 mm. **Subject:** Year of the Horse **Obv:** National arms **Rev:** Horse **Edge:** Reeded

| Date | Mintage | VF20 | XF40 | MS60 | MS63 | MS65 |
|---|---|---|---|---|---|---|
| 2002 | 1,000 | PF65 1,750 | | | | |

### KM# 294 500 DOLLARS
31.10 g., 0.9999 Gold 0.9998 oz. AGW, 32.7 mm. **Obv:** National arms **Rev:** Multicolor Astro Boy cartoon **Edge:** Reeded

| Date | Mintage | VF20 | XF40 | MS60 | MS63 | MS65 |
|---|---|---|---|---|---|---|
| 2003 | 2,003 | PF65 1,750 | | | | |

### KM# 299 500 DOLLARS
31.10 g., 0.9999 Gold 0.9999 oz. AGW, 32.7 mm. **Obv:** National arms **Rev:** Nelson Mandela **Edge:** Reeded

| Date | Mintage | VF20 | XF40 | MS60 | MS63 | MS65 |
|---|---|---|---|---|---|---|
| 2004 | — | PF65 1,750 | | | | |

### KM# 205 2500 DOLLARS
155.52 g., 0.999 Gold 4.995 oz. AGW, 50 mm. **Subject:** Year of the Snake **Obv:** National arms **Rev:** Snake **Edge:** Reeded

| Date | Mintage | VF20 | XF40 | MS60 | MS63 | MS65 |
|---|---|---|---|---|---|---|
| 2001 | Est. 250 | PF65 9,000 | | | | |

### KM# 213 2500 DOLLARS
155.52 g., 0.999 Gold 4.995 oz. AGW, 50 mm. **Subject:** P'an Ku **Obv:** National arms **Rev:** Dragon

| Date | Mintage | VF20 | XF40 | MS60 | MS63 | MS65 |
|---|---|---|---|---|---|---|
| 2001 | Est. 250 | PF65 9,000 | | | | |

### KM# 263 2500 DOLLARS
155.51 g., 0.999 Gold 4.9948 oz. AGW, 50 mm. **Subject:** Year of the Horse **Obv:** National arms **Rev:** Horse **Edge:** Reeded

| Date | Mintage | VF20 | XF40 | MS60 | MS63 | MS65 |
|---|---|---|---|---|---|---|
| 2002 | 250 | PF65 9,000 | | | | |

## MINT SETS

| KM# | Date | Mintage | Identification | Issue Price | Mkt Val |
|---|---|---|---|---|---|
| MS2 | 2006 (4) | — | KM# 334-337 | 65.00 | 75.00 |

## PROOF SETS

| KM# | Date | Mintage | Identification | Issue Price | Mkt Val |
|---|---|---|---|---|---|
| PS7 | 2006 (4) | — | KM# 330-333 | 450 | 480 |
| PS8 | 2006 (4) | — | KM# 334a-337a | 300 | 300 |

# SINGAPORE

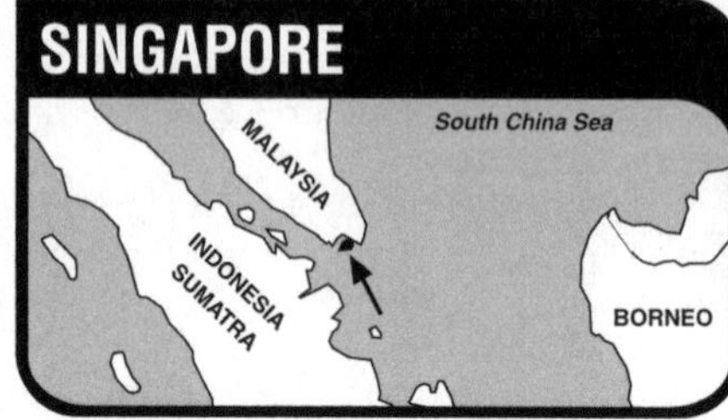


The Republic of Singapore, a member of the Commonwealth of Nations situated off the southern tip of the Malay peninsula, has an area of 224 sq. mi. (633 sq. km.) and a population of *2.7 million. Capital: Singapore. The economy is based on entrepôt trade, manufacturing and oil. Rubber, petroleum products, machinery and spices are exported.

The President is Chief of State. The prime minister is Head of Government.

**MINT MARK**

sm = *"sm"* - Singapore Mint monogram

**MONETARY SYSTEM**

100 Cents = 1 Dollar

## REPUBLIC

### STANDARD COINAGE

100 Cents = 1 Dollar

### KM# 98 CENT
1.24 g., Copper Plated Zinc, 15.9 mm. **Obv:** National arms **Rev:** Value divides plants **Edge:** Plain **Note:** Similar to KM#49 but motto ribbon on arms curves down at center.

| Date | Mintage | VF20 | XF40 | MS60 | MS63 | MS65 |
|---|---|---|---|---|---|---|
| 2001 | 40,101,738 | — | — | 0.10 | 0.15 | 0.25 |
| 2002 Sets only | 84,577 | — | — | — | 0.15 | 0.25 |

### KM# 98a CENT
1.81 g., 0.925 Silver 0.0538 oz. ASW, 15.9 mm. **Obv:** National arms **Rev:** Value divides plants

| Date | Mintage | VF20 | XF40 | MS60 | MS63 | MS65 |
|---|---|---|---|---|---|---|
| 2001 sm | 6,000 | PF65 2.50 | | | | |
| 2002 sm | 6,300 | PF65 2.50 | | | | |

### KM# 99 5 CENTS
1.56 g., Aluminum-Bronze, 16.75 mm. **Obv:** National arms **Rev:** Fruit salad plant **Edge:** Reeded **Note:** Similar to KM#50 but motto ribbon on arms curves down at center.

| Date | Mintage | VF20 | XF40 | MS60 | MS63 | MS65 |
|---|---|---|---|---|---|---|
| 2001 | 13,101,738 | — | — | 0.20 | 0.30 | 0.45 |
| 2002 | 33,556,000 | — | — | 0.20 | 0.30 | 0.45 |
| 2003 | 16,508,980 | — | — | 0.20 | 0.30 | 0.45 |
| 2003 | 4,550 | PF65 3.00 | | | | |
| 2004 | 20,070,000 | — | — | 0.20 | 0.30 | 0.45 |
| 2004 | 3,500 | PF65 3.00 | | | | |
| 2005 | 70,061,981 | — | — | 0.20 | 0.30 | 0.45 |
| 2006 Sets only | 53,214 | — | — | — | — | 0.50 |
| 2007 | 22,884,889 | — | — | 0.20 | 0.30 | 0.45 |
| 2008 Sets only | 55,000 | — | — | — | — | 0.50 |
| 2009 | 19,850,000 | — | — | 0.20 | 0.30 | 0.45 |
| 2010 | Est. 5160000 | — | — | 0.20 | 0.30 | 0.45 |
| 2011 | — | — | — | 0.20 | 0.30 | 0.45 |
| 2012 | — | — | — | 0.20 | 0.30 | 0.45 |
| 2013 Sets only | Est. 160000 | — | — | — | — | 0.50 |

### KM# 99a 5 CENTS
2.00 g., 0.925 Silver 0.0595 oz. ASW, 16.75 mm. **Obv:** National arms **Rev:** Fruit salad plant

| Date | Mintage | VF20 | XF40 | MS60 | MS63 | MS65 |
|---|---|---|---|---|---|---|
| 2001 sm | 6,000 | PF65 2.75 | | | | |
| 2002 sm | 6,300 | PF65 2.75 | | | | |
| 2003 sm | 4,900 | PF65 2.75 | | | | |
| 2004 sm | 4,000 | PF65 2.75 | | | | |
| 2005 sm | 3,250 | PF65 2.75 | | | | |

### KM# 100 10 CENTS
2.60 g., Copper-Nickel, 18.5 mm. **Obv:** National arms **Rev:** Star Jasmine plant **Edge:** Reeded **Note:** Similar to KM#51 but motto ribbon on arms curves down at center.

| Date | Mintage | VF20 | XF40 | MS60 | MS63 | MS65 |
|---|---|---|---|---|---|---|
| 2001 Sets only | 101,738 | — | — | — | — | 0.50 |
| 2002 Sets only | 84,577 | — | — | — | — | 0.50 |
| 2003 | 21,578,980 | — | — | 0.20 | 0.30 | 0.45 |
| 2003 | 4,550 | PF65 4.00 | | | | |
| 2004 Sets only | 70,000 | — | — | — | — | 0.50 |
| 2004 | 3,500 | PF65 4.00 | | | | |
| 2005 | 50,021,981 | — | — | 0.20 | 0.30 | 0.45 |
| 2006 Sets only | 53,214 | — | — | — | — | 0.50 |
| 2007 | 50,054,889 | — | — | 0.20 | 0.30 | 0.45 |
| 2008 Sets only | 55,000 | — | — | — | — | 0.50 |
| 2009 | 38,790,000 | — | — | 0.20 | 0.30 | 0.45 |
| 2010 Sets only | — | — | — | — | — | 0.50 |
| 2011 | — | — | — | 0.20 | 0.30 | 0.45 |
| 2012 | — | — | — | 0.20 | 0.30 | 0.45 |
| 2013 Sets only | Est. 160000 | — | — | — | — | 0.50 |

### KM# 100a 10 CENTS
3.05 g., 0.925 Silver 0.0907 oz. ASW, 18.5 mm. **Obv:** National arms **Rev:** Star Jasmine plant **Edge:** Reeded

| Date | Mintage | VF20 | XF40 | MS60 | MS63 | MS65 |
|---|---|---|---|---|---|---|
| 2001 sm | 6,000 | PF65 4.00 | | | | |
| 2002 sm | 6,300 | PF65 4.00 | | | | |
| 2003 sm | 4,900 | PF65 4.00 | | | | |
| 2004 sm | 4,000 | PF65 4.00 | | | | |
| 2005 sm | 3,250 | PF65 4.00 | | | | |

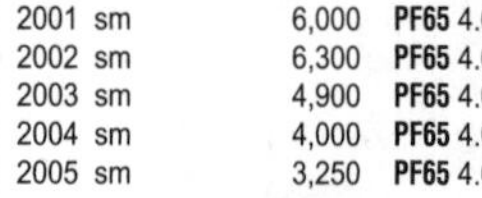

### KM# 101 20 CENTS
4.50 g., Copper-Nickel, 21.36 mm. **Obv:** National arms **Rev:** Powder-puff plant above value **Edge:** Reeded **Note:** Similar to KM#52 but motto ribbon on arms curves down at center.

| Date | Mintage | VF20 | XF40 | MS60 | MS63 | MS65 |
|---|---|---|---|---|---|---|
| 2001 Sets only | 101,738 | — | — | — | — | 1.25 |
| 2002 Sets only | 84,577 | — | — | — | — | 1.50 |
| 2003 Sets only | 68,980 | — | — | — | — | 1.50 |
| 2003 | 4,550 | PF65 5.00 | | | | |
| 2004 Sets only | 70,000 | — | — | — | — | 1.50 |
| 2004 | 3,500 | PF65 5.00 | | | | |

| Date | Mintage | VF20 | XF40 | MS60 | MS63 | MS65 |
|---|---|---|---|---|---|---|
| 2005 Sets only | 61,981 | — | — | — | — | 1.50 |
| 2006 | 40,143,214 | — | — | 0.60 | 0.75 | 1.00 |
| 2007 | 30,144,889 | — | — | 0.60 | 0.75 | 1.00 |
| 2008 Sets only | 55,000 | — | — | — | — | 1.50 |
| 2009 | 30,160,000 | — | — | 0.60 | 0.75 | 1.00 |
| 2010 | Est. 10030000 | — | — | 0.60 | 0.75 | 1.00 |
| 2011 | — | — | — | 0.60 | 0.75 | 1.00 |
| 2012 | — | — | — | 0.60 | 0.75 | 1.00 |
| 2013 Sets only | Est. 160000 | — | — | — | — | 1.25 |

### KM# 101a 20 CENTS

5.24 g., 0.925 Silver 0.1558 oz. ASW, 21.36 mm. **Obv:** National arms **Rev:** Powder puff plant above value **Edge:** Reeded

| Date | Mintage | VF20 | XF40 | MS60 | MS63 | MS65 |
|---|---|---|---|---|---|---|
| 2001 sm | 6,000 | PF65 7.00 | | | | |
| 2002 sm | 6,300 | PF65 7.00 | | | | |
| 2003 sm | 4,900 | PF65 7.00 | | | | |
| 2004 sm | 4,000 | PF65 7.00 | | | | |
| 2005 sm | 3,250 | PF65 7.00 | | | | |

### KM# 102 50 CENTS

7.29 g., Copper-Nickel, 24.66 mm. **Obv:** National arms **Rev:** Yellow Allamanda plant above value **Edge Lettering:** REPUBLIC OF SINGAPORE (lion's head) **Note:** Similar to KM#53 but motto ribbon on arms curves down at center.

| Date | Mintage | VF20 | XF40 | MS60 | MS63 | MS65 |
|---|---|---|---|---|---|---|
| 2001 Sets only | 101,738 | — | — | — | — | 1.50 |
| 2002 Sets only | 84,577 | — | — | — | — | 1.50 |
| 2003 Sets only | 69,980 | — | — | — | — | 1.50 |
| 2003 | 4,550 | PF65 6.00 | | | | |
| 2004 Sets only | 70,000 | — | — | — | — | 1.50 |
| 2004 | 3,500 | PF65 6.00 | | | | |
| 2005 | 25,057,981 | — | — | 0.75 | 1.00 | 1.25 |
| 2006 Sets only | 53,214 | — | — | — | — | 1.50 |
| 2007 | 28,764,889 | — | — | 0.75 | 1.00 | 1.25 |
| 2008 Sets only | 55,000 | — | — | — | — | 1.50 |
| 2009 | 12,390,000 | — | — | 0.75 | 1.00 | 1.25 |
| 2010 | Est. 8270000 | — | — | 0.75 | 1.00 | 1.25 |
| 2011 | — | — | — | 0.75 | 1.00 | 1.25 |
| 2012 | — | — | — | 0.75 | 1.00 | 1.25 |
| 2013 Sets only | Est. 160000 | — | — | — | — | 1.50 |

### KM# 102a 50 CENTS

8.56 g., 0.925 Silver 0.2546 oz. ASW, 24.66 mm. **Obv:** National arms **Rev:** Yellow Allamanda plant above value

| Date | Mintage | VF20 | XF40 | MS60 | MS63 | MS65 |
|---|---|---|---|---|---|---|
| 2001 sm | 6,000 | PF65 12.00 | | | | |
| 2002 sm | 6,300 | PF65 12.00 | | | | |
| 2003 sm | 4,900 | PF65 12.00 | | | | |
| 2004 sm | 1,900 | PF65 12.00 | | | | |
| 2005 sm | 3,250 | PF65 12.00 | | | | |

### KM# 103 DOLLAR

6.30 g., Aluminum-Bronze, 22.4 mm. **Obv:** National arms **Rev:** Periwinkle flower **Edge:** Reeded **Note:** Similar to KM#54 but motto ribbon on arms curves down at center.

| Date | Mintage | VF20 | XF40 | MS60 | MS63 | MS65 |
|---|---|---|---|---|---|---|
| 2001 | 40,941,738 | — | — | 1.50 | 2.25 | 3.00 |
| 2002 | 35,744,577 | — | — | 1.50 | 2.25 | 3.00 |
| 2003 | 31,968,980 | — | — | 1.50 | 2.25 | 3.00 |
| 2003 | 4,550 | PF65 10.00 | | | | |
| 2004 | 34,450,000 | — | — | 1.50 | 2.25 | 3.00 |
| 2004 | 3,500 | PF65 10.00 | | | | |
| 2005 Sets only | 61,891 | — | — | — | — | 3.50 |
| 2006 | 63,053,214 | — | — | 1.50 | 2.25 | 3.00 |
| 2007 Sets only | 54,889 | — | — | — | — | 3.50 |
| 2008 | 10,375,000 | — | — | 1.50 | 2.25 | 3.00 |
| 2009 | 21,750,000 | — | — | 1.50 | 2.25 | 3.00 |
| 2010 | — | — | — | 1.50 | 2.75 | 3.00 |
| 2011 | — | — | — | 1.50 | 2.75 | 3.00 |
| 2012 | — | — | — | 1.50 | 2.75 | 3.00 |
| 2013 Sets only | Est. 160000 | — | — | — | — | 3.50 |

### KM# 103a DOLLAR

8.05 g., 0.925 Silver 0.2394 oz. ASW, 22.4 mm. **Obv:** National arms **Rev:** Periwinkle flower

| Date | Mintage | VF20 | XF40 | MS60 | MS63 | MS65 |
|---|---|---|---|---|---|---|
| 2001 sm | 6,000 | PF65 15.00 | | | | |
| 2002 sm | 6,300 | PF65 15.00 | | | | |
| 2003 sm | 4,900 | PF65 15.00 | | | | |
| 2004 sm | 4,000 | PF65 15.00 | | | | |
| 2005 sm | 3,250 | PF65 15.00 | | | | |

### KM# 212 DOLLAR

1.56 g., 0.9999 Gold 0.050 oz. AGW, 13.9 mm. **Series:** Lunar **Subject:** Year of the Snake **Obv:** National arms **Rev:** Stylized lion's head right, snake privy mark at lower left

| Date | Mintage | VF20 | XF40 | MS60 | MS63 | MS65 |
|---|---|---|---|---|---|---|
| 2001 | 339 | — | — | — | — | 78.00 |
| 2001 sm | 240 | PF65 75.00 | | | | |

### KM# 217 DOLLAR

1.56 g., 0.9999 Gold 0.050 oz. AGW, 13.9 mm. **Series:** Lunar **Subject:** Year of the Horse **Obv:** National arms **Rev:** Stylized lion's head right, horse privy mark at lower left

| Date | Mintage | VF20 | XF40 | MS60 | MS63 | MS65 |
|---|---|---|---|---|---|---|
| 2002 | 160 | — | — | — | — | 78.00 |
| 2002 sm | 215 | PF65 75.00 | | | | |

### KM# 222 DOLLAR

0.30 g., 0.9999 Gold 0.0096 oz. AGW, 7 mm. **Series:** Lunar **Subject:** Year of the Goat **Obv:** National arms **Rev:** Stylized goat standing right facing left

| Date | Mintage | VF20 | XF40 | MS60 | MS63 | MS65 |
|---|---|---|---|---|---|---|
| 2003 sm Prooflike | 5,362 | — | — | — | — | 32.50 |

### KM# 184 DOLLAR

7.29 g., Copper-Nickel, 24.7 mm. **Subject:** Old World Charm - Balestier **Obv:** Arms with supporters **Rev:** Old buildings **Edge:** Reeded

| Date | Mintage | VF20 | XF40 | MS60 | MS63 | MS65 |
|---|---|---|---|---|---|---|
| 2004 sm Prooflike | 3,486 | — | — | — | — | 10.00 |

### KM# 184a DOLLAR

8.56 g., 0.999 Silver 0.2749 oz. ASW, 24.7 mm. **Subject:** Old World Charm - Balestier **Obv:** Arms with supporters **Rev:** Old buildings **Note:** Colorized

| Date | Mintage | VF20 | XF40 | MS60 | MS63 | MS65 |
|---|---|---|---|---|---|---|
| 2004 sm | 2,009 | PF65 27.50 | | | | |

### KM# 186 DOLLAR

0.30 g., 0.9999 Gold 0.0096 oz. AGW, 7 mm. **Series:** Lunar **Subject:** Year of the Monkey **Obv:** National arms **Rev:** Stylized monkey sitting left **Edge:** Plain

| Date | Mintage | VF20 | XF40 | MS60 | MS63 | MS65 |
|---|---|---|---|---|---|---|
| 2004 Prooflike | 3,200 | — | — | — | — | 32.50 |

### KM# 190 DOLLAR

7.29 g., Copper-Nickel, 24.7 mm. **Subject:** Old World Charm - Jalan Besar

| Date | Mintage | VF20 | XF40 | MS60 | MS63 | MS65 |
|---|---|---|---|---|---|---|
| 2004 sm Prooflike | 3,470 | — | — | — | — | 10.00 |

### KM# 190a DOLLAR

8.56 g., 0.999 Silver 0.2749 oz. ASW, 24.7 mm. **Subject:** Old World Charm - Jalan Besar **Note:** Colorized

| Date | Mintage | VF20 | XF40 | MS60 | MS63 | MS65 |
|---|---|---|---|---|---|---|
| 2004 sm | 2,844 | PF65 27.50 | | | | |

### KM# 191 DOLLAR

7.29 g., Copper-Nickel, 24.7 mm. **Subject:** Old World Charm - Joo Chiat

| Date | Mintage | VF20 | XF40 | MS60 | MS63 | MS65 |
|---|---|---|---|---|---|---|
| 2004 sm Prooflike | 3,551 | — | — | — | — | 10.00 |

### KM# 191a DOLLAR

8.56 g., 0.999 Silver 0.2749 oz. ASW, 24.7 mm. **Subject:** Old World Charm - Joo Chiat **Note:** Colorized

| Date | Mintage | VF20 | XF40 | MS60 | MS63 | MS65 |
|---|---|---|---|---|---|---|
| 2004 sm | 2,863 | PF65 27.50 | | | | |

### KM# 192 DOLLAR

7.29 g., Copper-Nickel, 24.7 mm. **Subject:** Old World Charm - Tanjong Katong

| Date | Mintage | VF20 | XF40 | MS60 | MS63 | MS65 |
|---|---|---|---|---|---|---|
| 2004 sm Prooflike | 3,555 | — | — | — | — | 10.00 |

### KM# 192a DOLLAR

8.56 g., 0.999 Silver 0.2749 oz. ASW, 24.7 mm. **Subject:** Old World Charm - Tanjong Katong

| Date | Mintage | VF20 | XF40 | MS60 | MS63 | MS65 |
|---|---|---|---|---|---|---|
| 2004 sm | 2,263 | PF65 27.50 | | | | |

### KM# 233 DOLLAR

0.30 g., 0.9999 Gold 0.0096 oz. AGW, 7 mm. **Series:** Lunar **Subject:** Year of the Rooster **Obv:** National arms **Rev:** Stylized rooster standing right

| Date | Mintage | VF20 | XF40 | MS60 | MS63 | MS65 |
|---|---|---|---|---|---|---|
| 2005 sm Prooflike | 2,817 | — | — | — | — | 32.50 |

### KM# 244 DOLLAR

18.00 g., Copper-Nickel, 33 mm. **Series:** Urban Redevelopment **Obv:** National arms **Rev:** Anak Bukit

| Date | Mintage | VF20 | XF40 | MS60 | MS63 | MS65 |
|---|---|---|---|---|---|---|
| 2005 sm Prooflike | 2,620 | PF65 12.00 | | | | |

### KM# 244a DOLLAR

17.30 g., 0.9999 Silver 0.5562 oz. ASW, 33 mm. **Series:** Urban Redevelopment **Obv:** National arms **Rev:** Anak Bukit - multicolor

| Date | Mintage | VF20 | XF40 | MS60 | MS63 | MS65 |
|---|---|---|---|---|---|---|
| 2005 sm | 2,450 | PF65 45.00 | | | | |

### KM# 245 DOLLAR

18.00 g., Copper-Nickel, 33 mm. **Series:** Singapore Identity Plan **Obv:** National arms **Rev:** Coronation

| Date | Mintage | VF20 | XF40 | MS60 | MS63 | MS65 |
|---|---|---|---|---|---|---|
| 2005 sm Prooflike | 2,620 | PF65 12.00 | | | | |

### KM# 245a DOLLAR

17.30 g., 0.9999 Silver 0.5562 oz. ASW, 33 mm. **Series:** Singapore Identity Plan **Obv:** National arms **Rev:** Coronation - multicolor

| Date | Mintage | VF20 | XF40 | MS60 | MS63 | MS65 |
|---|---|---|---|---|---|---|
| 2005 sm | 790 | PF65 45.00 | | | | |

### KM# 246 DOLLAR

18.00 g., Copper-Nickel, 33 mm. **Series:** Singapore Identity Plan **Obv:** National arms **Rev:** Jalan Leban and Casuarina Road

| Date | Mintage | VF20 | XF40 | MS60 | MS63 | MS65 |
|---|---|---|---|---|---|---|
| 2005 sm Prooflike | 2,620 | PF65 12.00 | | | | |

### KM# 246a DOLLAR

17.00 g., 0.9999 Silver 0.5465 oz. ASW, 33 mm. **Series:** Singapore Identity Plan **Obv:** National arms **Rev:** Jalan Leban and Casuarina Road - multicolor

| Date | Mintage | VF20 | XF40 | MS60 | MS63 | MS65 |
|---|---|---|---|---|---|---|
| 2005 sm | 790 | PF65 45.00 | | | | |

### KM# 247 DOLLAR

18.00 g., Copper-Nickel, 33 mm. **Series:** Singapore Identity Plan **Obv:** National arms **Rev:** Springleaf

| Date | Mintage | VF20 | XF40 | MS60 | MS63 | MS65 |
|---|---|---|---|---|---|---|
| 2005 sm Prooflike | 2,620 | — | — | — | — | 15.00 |

### KM# 247a DOLLAR

17.30 g., 0.9999 Silver 0.5562 oz. ASW, 33 mm. **Series:** Singapore Identity Plan **Obv:** National arms **Rev:** Springleaf - multicolor

| Date | Mintage | VF20 | XF40 | MS60 | MS63 | MS65 |
|---|---|---|---|---|---|---|
| 2005 sm | 2,450 | PF65 45.00 | | | | |

### KM# 248 DOLLAR

18.00 g., Copper-Nickel, 33 mm. **Series:** Singapore Identity Plan **Obv:** National arms **Rev:** Thomson Village

| Date | Mintage | VF20 | XF40 | MS60 | MS63 | MS65 |
|---|---|---|---|---|---|---|
| 2005 sm Prooflike | 2,620 | — | — | — | — | 15.00 |

### KM# 248a DOLLAR

17.30 g., 0.9999 Silver 0.5562 oz. ASW, 33 mm. **Series:** Singapore Identity Plan **Obv:** National arms **Rev:** Thomson Village - multicolor

| Date | Mintage | VF20 | XF40 | MS60 | MS63 | MS65 |
|---|---|---|---|---|---|---|
| 2005 sm | 800 | PF65 45.00 | | | | |

### KM# 249 DOLLAR

0.30 g., 0.9999 Gold 0.0096 oz. AGW **Series:** Lunar **Subject:** Year of the Dog **Obv:** National arms **Rev:** Stylized dog standing left

| Date | Mintage | VF20 | XF40 | MS60 | MS63 | MS65 |
|---|---|---|---|---|---|---|
| 2006 sm Prooflike | 2,004 | — | — | — | — | 32.50 |

### KM# 259 DOLLAR

18.00 g., Copper-Nickel, 33 mm. **Series:** Singapore Identity Plan **Obv:** National arms **Rev:** Changi Village - multicolor

| Date | Mintage | VF20 | XF40 | MS60 | MS63 | MS65 |
|---|---|---|---|---|---|---|
| 2007 sm Prooflike | 2,568 | — | — | — | — | 15.00 |

### KM# 259a DOLLAR

17.30 g., 0.999 Silver 0.5557 oz. ASW, 33 mm. **Series:** Singapore Identity Plan **Obv:** National arms **Rev:** Changi Village - multicolor

| Date | Mintage | VF20 | XF40 | MS60 | MS63 | MS65 |
|---|---|---|---|---|---|---|
| 2007 sm | 976 | PF65 37.50 | | | | |

### KM# 260 DOLLAR

18.00 g., Copper-Nickel, 33 mm. **Series:** Singapore Identity Plan **Obv:** National arms **Rev:** Pasir Ris Park - multicolor

| Date | Mintage | VF20 | XF40 | MS60 | MS63 | MS65 |
|---|---|---|---|---|---|---|
| 2007 sm Prooflike | 2,430 | — | — | — | — | 15.00 |

### KM# 260a DOLLAR

17.30 g., 0.999 Silver 0.5557 oz. ASW, 33 mm. **Series:** Urban Redevelopment **Obv:** National arms **Rev:** Pasir Ris Park - multicolor

| Date | Mintage | VF20 | XF40 | MS60 | MS63 | MS65 |
|---|---|---|---|---|---|---|
| 2007 sm | 936 | PF65 37.50 | | | | |

### KM# 261 DOLLAR

Copper-Nickel **Series:** Urban Redevelopment **Obv:** National arms **Rev:** Pulau Ubin - multicolor

| Date | Mintage | VF20 | XF40 | MS60 | MS63 | MS65 |
|---|---|---|---|---|---|---|
| 2007 sm Prooflike | 2,408 | — | — | — | — | 12.50 |

### KM# 261a DOLLAR

17.30 g., 0.999 Silver 0.5557 oz. ASW, 33 mm. **Series:** Urban Redevelopment **Obv:** National arms **Rev:** Pulau Ubin - multicolor

| Date | Mintage | VF20 | XF40 | MS60 | MS63 | MS65 |
|---|---|---|---|---|---|---|
| 2007 sm | 2,327 | PF65 32.50 | | | | |

### KM# 262 DOLLAR

Copper-Nickel **Series:** Urban Redevelopment **Obv:** National arms **Rev:** Punggoi Point and Coney Island - multicolor

| Date | Mintage | VF20 | XF40 | MS60 | MS63 | MS65 |
|---|---|---|---|---|---|---|
| 2007 sm Prooflike | 2,387 | — | — | — | — | 12.50 |

### KM# 262a DOLLAR

17.30 g., 0.999 Silver 0.5557 oz. ASW, 33 mm. **Series:** Singapore Identity Plan **Obv:** National arms **Rev:** Punggoi Point and Coney Island - multicolor

| Date | Mintage | VF20 | XF40 | MS60 | MS63 | MS65 |
|---|---|---|---|---|---|---|
| 2007 sm | 2,289 | PF65 32.50 | | | | |

### KM# 263 DOLLAR

0.30 g., 0.9999 Gold 0.0096 oz. AGW **Series:** Lunar **Subject:** Year of the Boar **Obv:** National arms **Rev:** Stylized boar running right

| Date | Mintage | VF20 | XF40 | MS60 | MS63 | MS65 |
|---|---|---|---|---|---|---|
| 2007 sm Prooflike | 2,500 | — | — | — | — | 32.50 |

### KM# 269 DOLLAR

0.30 g., 0.9999 Gold 0.0096 oz. AGW **Series:** Lunar **Subject:** Year of the Rat **Obv:** National arms **Rev:** Stylized rat lying left

| Date | Mintage | VF20 | XF40 | MS60 | MS63 | MS65 |
|---|---|---|---|---|---|---|
| 2008 sm | 2,434 | — | — | — | — | 32.50 |

### KM# 290 DOLLAR

Copper-Nickel **Obv:** Supported arms **Rev:** Multicolor Kent Ridge Park

| Date | Mintage | VF20 | XF40 | MS60 | MS63 | MS65 |
|---|---|---|---|---|---|---|
| 2008 Prooflike | 2,250 | PF65 10.00 | | | | |

### KM# 290a DOLLAR

17.30 g., 0.999 Silver 0.5557 oz. ASW **Obv:** Supported arms **Rev:** Multicolor Kent Ridge Park

| Date | Mintage | VF20 | XF40 | MS60 | MS63 | MS65 |
|---|---|---|---|---|---|---|
| 2008 | 850 | PF65 37.50 | | | | |

### KM# 291 DOLLAR

Copper-Nickel **Obv:** Supported arms **Rev:** Multicolor Labrador Nature Reserve

| Date | Mintage | VF20 | XF40 | MS60 | MS63 | MS65 |
|---|---|---|---|---|---|---|
| 2008 Prooflike | 2,250 | PF65 10.00 | | | | |

### KM# 291a DOLLAR

17.30 g., 0.999 Silver 0.5557 oz. ASW **Obv:** Supported arms **Rev:** Multicolor Labrador Nature Reserve

| Date | Mintage | VF20 | XF40 | MS60 | MS63 | MS65 |
|---|---|---|---|---|---|---|
| 2008 | 850 | PF65 37.50 | | | | |

### KM# 292 DOLLAR

Copper-Nickel **Obv:** Supported arms **Rev:** Multicolor Mount Faber Building

| Date | Mintage | VF20 | XF40 | MS60 | MS63 | MS65 |
|---|---|---|---|---|---|---|
| 2008 Prooflike | 2,800 | — | — | — | — | 10.00 |

### KM# 292a DOLLAR

17.30 g., 0.999 Silver 0.5557 oz. ASW **Obv:** Supported arms **Rev:** Multicolor Mount Faber Building

| Date | Mintage | VF20 | XF40 | MS60 | MS63 | MS65 |
|---|---|---|---|---|---|---|
| 2008 | 2,300 | PF65 37.50 | | | | |

### KM# 293 DOLLAR

Copper-Nickel **Obv:** Supported arms **Rev:** Multicolor Telok Blangah Hill Park

| Date | Mintage | VF20 | XF40 | MS60 | MS63 | MS65 |
|---|---|---|---|---|---|---|
| 2008 Prooflike | 2,300 | — | — | — | — | 10.00 |

### KM# 293a DOLLAR

17.30 g., 0.999 Silver 0.5557 oz. ASW **Obv:** Supported arms **Rev:** Multicolor Telok Blangah Hill Park

| Date | Mintage | VF20 | XF40 | MS60 | MS63 | MS65 |
|---|---|---|---|---|---|---|
| 2008 | 2,200 | PF65 37.50 | | | | |

### KM# 294 DOLLAR

0.30 g., 0.999 Gold 0.0096 oz. AGW, 7 mm. **Subject:** Year of the Ox **Obv:** Supported arms **Rev:** Ox

| Date | Mintage | VF20 | XF40 | MS60 | MS63 | MS65 |
|---|---|---|---|---|---|---|
| 2009 | 3,000 | — | — | — | 30.00 | 35.00 |

### KM# 308 DOLLAR

0.30 g., 0.9999 Gold 0.0096 oz. AGW, 7 mm. **Subject:** Year of the Snake **Rev:** Snake

| Date | Mintage | VF20 | XF40 | MS60 | MS63 | MS65 |
|---|---|---|---|---|---|---|
| 2013 | Est. 10000 | — | — | — | — | 45.00 |

### KM# 314 DOLLAR

7.62 g., Bi-Metallic Copper-Nickel center in Aluminum-Bronze ring, 24.65 mm. **Obv:** National arms **Rev:** Value at left, lion at right, color flora at center **Edge:** Reeded

| Date | Mintage | VF20 | XF40 | MS60 | MS63 | MS65 |
|---|---|---|---|---|---|---|
| 2013 | — | — | — | — | 6.00 | 8.00 |

### KM# 196 2 DOLLARS

Copper-Nickel **Subject:** Tribute to Healthcare Givers **Obv:** National arms **Rev:** Five 3/4 length people standing facing, clinic in background

| Date | Mintage | VF20 | XF40 | MS60 | MS63 | MS65 |
|---|---|---|---|---|---|---|
| 2003 sm 32021 Prooflike | | — | — | — | — | 15.00 |

### KM# 196a 2 DOLLARS

0.999 Silver **Subject:** Tribute to Healthcare Givers **Obv:** National arms **Rev:** Five 3/4 length people standing facing, clinic in background

| Date | Mintage | VF20 | XF40 | MS60 | MS63 | MS65 |
|---|---|---|---|---|---|---|
| 2003 sm | 5,200 | PF65 60.00 | | | | |

### KM# 223 2 DOLLARS

20.00 g., 0.999 Silver 0.6424 oz. ASW, 38.70 mm. **Series:** Lunar **Subject:** Year of the Goat **Obv:** National arms **Rev:** Stylized goat standing right facing left

| Date | Mintage | VF20 | XF40 | MS60 | MS63 | MS65 |
|---|---|---|---|---|---|---|
| 2003 sm | 2,000 | PF65 60.00 | | | | |

### KM# 229 2 DOLLARS

20.00 g., 0.999 Silver 0.6424 oz. ASW, 38.7 mm. **Series:** Lunar **Subject:** Year of the Monkey **Obv:** National arms **Rev:** Stylized monkey sitting left

| Date | Mintage | VF20 | XF40 | MS60 | MS63 | MS65 |
|---|---|---|---|---|---|---|
| 2004 sm | 2,180 | PF65 60.00 | | | | |

### KM# 234 2 DOLLARS

20.00 g., Copper-Nickel, 38.7 mm. **Series:** Lunar **Subject:** Year of the Rooster **Obv:** National arms **Rev:** Rooster standing right

| Date | Mintage | VF20 | XF40 | MS60 | MS63 | MS65 |
|---|---|---|---|---|---|---|
| 2005 sm Prooflike | 79,115 | — | — | — | — | 15.00 |

### KM# 234a 2 DOLLARS

20.00 g., 0.9999 Silver 0.643 oz. ASW, 38.7 mm. **Series:** Lunar **Subject:** Year of the Rooster **Obv:** National arms **Rev:** Stylized rooster standing right

| Date | Mintage | VF20 | XF40 | MS60 | MS63 | MS65 |
|---|---|---|---|---|---|---|
| 2005 sm | 4,879 | PF65 42.50 | | | | |

### KM# 242 2 DOLLARS

Copper-Nickel **Subject:** 40th National Day Parade **Obv:** National arms **Rev:** Fireworks, parade in government plaza, multicolor

| Date | Mintage | VF20 | XF40 | MS60 | MS63 | MS65 |
|---|---|---|---|---|---|---|
| 2005 sm Prooflike | 5,443 | PF65 15.00 | | | | |

### KM# 242a 2 DOLLARS

20.00 g., 0.9999 Silver 0.643 oz. ASW **Subject:** 40th National Day Parade **Obv:** National arms **Rev:** Fireworks, parade in government plaza

| Date | Mintage | VF20 | XF40 | MS60 | MS63 | MS65 |
|---|---|---|---|---|---|---|
| 2005 sm | 4,204 | PF65 60.00 | | | | |

### KM# 250 2 DOLLARS
20.00 g., Copper-Nickel **Series:** Lunar **Subject:** Year of the Dog **Obv:** National arms **Rev:** Stylized dog standing left

| Date | Mintage | VF20 | XF40 | MS60 | MS63 | MS65 |
|---|---|---|---|---|---|---|
| 2006 sm Prooflike | 69,552 | PF65 15.00 | | | | |

### KM# 250a 2 DOLLARS
20.00 g., 0.9999 Silver 0.643 oz. ASW **Series:** Lunar **Subject:** Year of the Dog **Obv:** National arms **Rev:** Stylized dog standing left

| Date | Mintage | VF20 | XF40 | MS60 | MS63 | MS65 |
|---|---|---|---|---|---|---|
| 2006 sm | 4,500 | PF65 60.00 | | | | |

### KM# 258 2 DOLLARS
Copper-Nickel **Subject:** 41st National Day **Obv:** National arms **Rev:** People in stadium, emblem - multicolor

| Date | Mintage | VF20 | XF40 | MS60 | MS63 | MS65 |
|---|---|---|---|---|---|---|
| 2006 sm Prooflike | 4,300 | PF65 15.00 | | | | |

### KM# 258a 2 DOLLARS
20.00 g., 0.999 Silver 0.6424 oz. ASW **Subject:** 41st National Day **Obv:** National arms **Rev:** People in stadium, emblem - multicolor

| Date | Mintage | VF20 | XF40 | MS60 | MS63 | MS65 |
|---|---|---|---|---|---|---|
| 2006 sm | 4,100 | PF65 60.00 | | | | |

### KM# 193 2 DOLLARS
20.00 g., Copper-Nickel, 38.70 mm. **Subject:** 42nd National Day Parade **Obv:** Arms with supporters **Obv. Legend:** SINGAPURA - SINGAPORE **Rev:** Colored overlay with four children above Marina Bay floating platform **Edge:** Reeded

| Date | Mintage | VF20 | XF40 | MS60 | MS63 | MS65 |
|---|---|---|---|---|---|---|
| 2007 Prooflike | 6,400 | — | — | — | — | 13.50 |

### KM# 193a 2 DOLLARS
20.00 g., 0.999 Silver 0.6424 oz. ASW, 38.70 mm. **Subject:** 42nd National Day Parade **Obv:** Arms with supporters **Obv. Legend:** SINGAPURA - SINGAPORE **Rev:** Colored overlay with four children above Marina Bay floating platform **Edge:** Reeded

| Date | Mintage | VF20 | XF40 | MS60 | MS63 | MS65 |
|---|---|---|---|---|---|---|
| 2007 | 6,150 | PF65 42.50 | | | | |

### KM# 264 2 DOLLARS
Copper-Nickel **Series:** Lunar **Subject:** Year of the Boar **Obv:** National arms **Rev:** Stylized boar running right

| Date | Mintage | VF20 | XF40 | MS60 | MS63 | MS65 |
|---|---|---|---|---|---|---|
| 2007 sm Prooflike | 63,930 | — | — | — | — | 12.00 |

### KM# 264a 2 DOLLARS
20.00 g., 0.999 Silver 0.6424 oz. ASW **Series:** Lunar **Subject:** Year of the Boar **Obv:** National arms **Rev:** Stylized boar running right

| Date | Mintage | VF20 | XF40 | MS60 | MS63 | MS65 |
|---|---|---|---|---|---|---|
| 2007 sm | 6,000 | PF65 45.00 | | | | |

### KM# 270 2 DOLLARS
20.00 g., Copper-Nickel **Series:** Lunar **Subject:** Year of the Rat **Obv:** National arms **Rev:** Stylized rat lying left

| Date | Mintage | VF20 | XF40 | MS60 | MS63 | MS65 |
|---|---|---|---|---|---|---|
| 2008 sm Prooflike | 58,637 | — | — | — | — | 12.50 |

### KM# 270a 2 DOLLARS
20.00 g., 0.999 Silver 0.6424 oz. ASW **Series:** Lunar **Subject:** Year of the Rat **Obv:** National arms **Rev:** Stylized rat lying left

| Date | Mintage | VF20 | XF40 | MS60 | MS63 | MS65 |
|---|---|---|---|---|---|---|
| 2008 sm | 5,789 | PF65 45.00 | | | | |

### KM# 287 2 DOLLARS
Copper-Nickel, 38.7 mm. **Subject:** Formula 1 - Singapore Grand Prix **Obv:** Supported arms **Rev:** Formula 1 racecar and skyline

| Date | Mintage | VF20 | XF40 | MS60 | MS63 | MS65 |
|---|---|---|---|---|---|---|
| 2008 | 7,000 | PF65 10.00 | | | | |

### KM# 295 2 DOLLARS
Copper-Nickel **Subject:** Year of the Ox **Obv:** Supported arms

| Date | Mintage | VF20 | XF40 | MS60 | MS63 | MS65 |
|---|---|---|---|---|---|---|
| 2009 Prooflike | 80,000 | — | — | — | — | 10.00 |

### KM# 296 2 DOLLARS
20.00 g., 0.999 Silver 0.6424 oz. ASW **Subject:** Year of the Ox **Obv:** Supported arms **Rev:** Ox

| Date | Mintage | VF20 | XF40 | MS60 | MS63 | MS65 |
|---|---|---|---|---|---|---|
| 2009 | 6,000 | PF65 37.50 | | | | |

### KM# 303 2 DOLLARS
Copper-Nickel, 38.7 mm. **Subject:** Independence, 44th Anniversary **Note:** Partially colorized

| Date | Mintage | VF20 | XF40 | MS60 | MS63 | MS65 |
|---|---|---|---|---|---|---|
| 2009 Prooflike | 6,000 | — | — | — | — | 15.00 |

### KM# 303a 2 DOLLARS
20.00 g., 0.999 Silver 0.6424 oz. ASW, 38.7 mm. **Series:** Indpendence, 44th Anniversary **Note:** Colorized

| Date | Mintage | VF20 | XF40 | MS60 | MS63 | MS65 |
|---|---|---|---|---|---|---|
| 2009 | 5,000 | PF65 40.00 | | | | |

### KM# 312 2 DOLLARS
20.00 g., 0.999 Silver 0.6424 oz. ASW, 38.07 mm. **Subject:** Year of the Snake **Rev:** Snake

| Date | Mintage | VF20 | XF40 | MS60 | MS63 | MS65 |
|---|---|---|---|---|---|---|
| 2013 | Est. 10000 | PF65 55.00 | | | | |

### KM# 313 2 DOLLARS
20.00 g., Copper-Nickel, 38.07 mm. **Subject:** Year of the Snake **Rev:** Snake

| Date | Mintage | VF20 | XF40 | MS60 | MS63 | MS65 |
|---|---|---|---|---|---|---|
| 2013 Proof-like | Est. 80000 | PF65 15.00 | | | | |

### KM# 104.1a 5 DOLLARS
8.25 g., 0.925 Silver 0.2454 oz. ASW, 23.3 mm. **Obv:** National arms **Rev:** Vanda Miss Joaquim flower and value within beaded circle

| Date | Mintage | VF20 | XF40 | MS60 | MS63 | MS65 |
|---|---|---|---|---|---|---|
| 1999 sm | 9,200 | PF65 25.00 | | | | |
| 2001 sm | 6,000 | PF65 25.00 | | | | |
| 2002 sm | 6,300 | PF65 25.00 | | | | |
| 2000 sm | 8,900 | PF65 25.00 | | | | |

### KM# 104.2 5 DOLLARS
6.70 g., Bi-Metallic Aluminumn-Bronze center in Copper-Nickel ring, 23.3 mm. **Obv:** National arms, date and BCCS logo **Rev:** Canda Miss Joaquim flower above value **Edge:** Plain **Note:** Date in hologram

| Date | Mintage | VF20 | XF40 | MS60 | MS63 | MS65 |
|---|---|---|---|---|---|---|
| 2001 Sets only | 101,738 | — | — | — | — | 12.00 |
| 2002 Sets only | 84,577 | — | — | — | — | 12.00 |
| 2003 | — | — | — | — | — | 12.00 |
| 2004 | — | — | — | — | — | 12.00 |
| 2005 | — | — | — | — | — | 12.00 |
| 2006 | — | — | — | — | — | 12.00 |

### KM# 104.2a 5 DOLLARS
8.25 g., 0.925 Silver 0.2454 oz. ASW, 23.3 mm. **Obv:** National arms, date and BCCS logo **Rev:** Vanda Miss Joaquim flower above value **Edge:** Plain

| Date | Mintage | VF20 | XF40 | MS60 | MS63 | MS65 |
|---|---|---|---|---|---|---|
| 2001 sm | 6,000 | PF65 25.00 | | | | |
| 2002 sm | 6,300 | PF65 25.00 | | | | |
| 2003 sm | 4,900 | PF65 25.00 | | | | |
| 2004 sm | 4,000 | PF65 25.00 | | | | |
| 2005 sm | 3,250 | PF65 25.00 | | | | |
| 2006 sm | — | PF65 25.00 | | | | |

### KM# 177 5 DOLLARS
20.00 g., Copper-Nickel, 38.6 mm. **Subject:** Productivity Movement **Obv:** Arms with supporters **Rev:** Spiral design **Edge:** Reeded

| Date | Mintage | VF20 | XF40 | MS60 | MS63 | MS65 |
|---|---|---|---|---|---|---|
| 2001 sm | 5,300 | — | — | — | 12.50 | 15.00 |

### KM# 177a 5 DOLLARS
20.00 g., 0.925 Silver 0.5948 oz. ASW, 38.6 mm. **Subject:** Productivity Movement **Obv:** Arms with supporters **Rev:** Spiral design **Edge:** Reeded

| Date | Mintage | VF20 | XF40 | MS60 | MS63 | MS65 |
|---|---|---|---|---|---|---|
| 2001 sm | 5,650 | PF65 50.00 | | | | |

### KM# 213 5 DOLLARS
3.11 g., 0.9999 Gold 0.100 oz. AGW, 17.9 mm. **Series:** Lunar **Subject:** Year of the Snake **Obv:** National arms **Rev:** Stylized lion's head right, snake privy mark at lower left

| Date | Mintage | VF20 | XF40 | MS60 | MS63 | MS65 |
|---|---|---|---|---|---|---|
| 2001 | 275 | — | — | — | — | 151 |
| 2001 sm | 240 | PF65 145 | | | | |

### KM# 104.3 5 DOLLARS
6.70 g., Bi-Metallic Aluminum-Bronze center in Copper-Nickel ring, 23.3 mm. **Obv:** National arms above latent image "MAS" or "date" **Rev:** Flower and value **Shape:** Scalloped

| Date | Mintage | VF20 | XF40 | MS60 | MS63 | MS65 |
|---|---|---|---|---|---|---|
| 2002 sm | — | — | — | — | — | 10.00 |
| 2003 sm | — | — | — | — | — | 10.00 |
| 2003 sm | 4,550 | PF65 15.00 | | | | |
| 2004 sm | — | — | — | — | — | 10.00 |
| 2004 sm | 3,500 | PF65 15.00 | | | | |
| 2005 sm | — | — | — | — | — | 10.00 |
| 2006 sm | — | — | — | — | — | 10.00 |
| 2007 sm | — | — | — | — | — | 10.00 |
| 2008 sm | — | — | — | — | — | 10.00 |
| 2009 sm | — | — | — | — | — | 10.00 |
| 2010 sm | — | — | — | — | — | 10.00 |
| 2011 sm | — | — | — | — | — | 10.00 |
| 2012 sm | — | — | — | — | — | 10.00 |
| 2013 | — | — | — | — | — | 10.00 |

### KM# 181 5 DOLLARS
20.00 g., Copper-Nickel, 38.7 mm. **Subject:** Esplanade Theaters on the Bay **Obv:** Arms with supporters **Rev:** Stylized symbolic design **Edge:** Reeded

| Date | Mintage | VF20 | XF40 | MS60 | MS63 | MS65 |
|---|---|---|---|---|---|---|
| 2002 sm | 7,430 | — | — | — | 13.50 | 16.50 |

### KM# 181a 5 DOLLARS
20.00 g., 0.999 Silver 0.6424 oz. ASW, 38.7 mm. **Subject:** Esplanade Theaters on the Bay **Obv:** Arms with supporters **Rev:** Stylized symbolic design **Edge:** Reeded

| Date | Mintage | VF20 | XF40 | MS60 | MS63 | MS65 |
|---|---|---|---|---|---|---|
| 2002 sm | 6,540 | PF65 45.00 | | | | |

### KM# 218 5 DOLLARS
3.11 g., 0.999 Gold 0.0999 oz. AGW, 17.9 mm. **Series:** Lunar **Subject:** Year of the Horse **Obv:** National arms **Rev:** Stylized lion's head right, horse privy mark at lower left

| Date | Mintage | VF20 | XF40 | MS60 | MS63 | MS65 |
|---|---|---|---|---|---|---|
| 2002 | 200 | — | — | — | — | 151 |
| 2002 sm | 215 | PF65 145 | | | | |

### KM# 104.3a 5 DOLLARS
8.25 g., 0.925 Silver 0.2454 oz. ASW **Obv:** National arms above latent image "MAS" or date **Rev:** Flower and value **Shape:** Scalloped

| Date | Mintage | VF20 | XF40 | MS60 | MS63 | MS65 |
|---|---|---|---|---|---|---|
| 2003 sm | 4,900 | PF65 25.00 | | | | |
| 2004 sm | 4,000 | PF65 25.00 | | | | |
| 2005 sm | 3,250 | PF65 25.00 | | | | |

### KM# 224 5 DOLLARS
7.78 g., 0.9999 Gold 0.250 oz. AGW, 21.9 mm. **Series:** Lunar **Subject:** Year of the Goat **Obv:** National arms **Rev:** Stylized goat standing right facing left

| Date | Mintage | VF20 | XF40 | MS60 | MS63 | MS65 |
|---|---|---|---|---|---|---|
| 2003 sm | 1,000 | PF65 500 | | | | |

### KM# 230 5 DOLLARS
7.78 g., 0.9999 Gold 0.250 oz. AGW, 21.9 mm. **Series:** Lunar **Subject:** Year of the Monkey **Obv:** National arms **Rev:** Stylized monkey sitting left

| Date | Mintage | VF20 | XF40 | MS60 | MS63 | MS65 |
|---|---|---|---|---|---|---|
| 2004 sm | 1,426 | PF65 500 | | | | |

### KM# 235 5 DOLLARS
7.78 g., 0.9999 Gold 0.250 oz. AGW, 21.9 mm. **Series:** Lunar **Subject:** Year of the Rooster **Obv:** National arms **Rev:** Stylized rooster standing right

| Date | Mintage | VF20 | XF40 | MS60 | MS63 | MS65 |
|---|---|---|---|---|---|---|
| 2005 sm | 1,419 | PF65 500 | | | | |

### KM# 194 5 DOLLARS
20.00 g., 0.999 Silver 0.6424 oz. ASW, 38.7 mm. **Obv:** Arms with supporters **Obv. Legend:** SINGAPURA - SINGAPORE **Rev:** Multicolor Singapore's skyline above world map, golden lion symbol below pointing to location of Singapore **Rev. Legend:** BOARD OF GOVERNORS ANNUAL MEETINGS • SINGAPORE 2006 • INTERNATIONAL MONETARY FUND • WORLD BANK GROUP •

| Date | Mintage | VF20 | XF40 | MS60 | MS63 | MS65 |
|---|---|---|---|---|---|---|
| 2006 sm | 5,450 | PF65 60.00 | | | | |

### KM# 251 5 DOLLARS
7.78 g., 0.9999 Gold 0.2499 oz. AGW **Series:** Lunar **Subject:** Year of the Dog **Obv:** National arms **Rev:** Stylized dog standing left

| Date | Mintage | VF20 | XF40 | MS60 | MS63 | MS65 |
|---|---|---|---|---|---|---|
| 2006 sm | 1,015 | PF65 500 | | | | |

### KM# 256 5 DOLLARS
20.00 g., 0.999 Silver 0.6424 oz. ASW **Series:** Heritage Orchids **Obv:** National arms **Rev:** Vanda Tan Chay Yan - multicolor

| Date | Mintage | VF20 | XF40 | MS60 | MS63 | MS65 |
|---|---|---|---|---|---|---|
| 2006 sm | 8,000 | PF65 60.00 | | | | |

### KM# 257 5 DOLLARS
20.00 g., 0.999 Silver 0.6424 oz. ASW **Series:** Heritage Orchids **Obv:** National arms **Rev:** Aranda Majula - multicolor

| Date | Mintage | VF20 | XF40 | MS60 | MS63 | MS65 |
|---|---|---|---|---|---|---|
| 2006 sm | 8,000 | PF65 60.00 | | | | |

**KM# 265 5 DOLLARS**
7.78 g., 0.9999 Gold 0.2499 oz. AGW **Series:** Lunar **Subject:** Year of the Boar **Obv:** National arms **Rev:** Stylized boar running right

| Date | Mintage | VF20 | XF40 | MS60 | MS63 | MS65 |
|---|---|---|---|---|---|---|
| 2007 sm | 1,060 | PF65 500 | | | | |

**KM# 275 5 DOLLARS**
20.00 g., 0.999 Silver 0.6424 oz. ASW, 38.7 mm. **Series:** Heritage Orchids **Obv:** National arms **Rev:** Dendrobium Singa Mas - multicolor

| Date | Mintage | VF20 | XF40 | MS60 | MS63 | MS65 |
|---|---|---|---|---|---|---|
| 2007 sm | 8,000 | PF65 45.00 | | | | |

**KM# 276 5 DOLLARS**
20.00 g., 0.999 Silver 0.6424 oz. ASW, 38.7 mm. **Series:** Heritage Orchids **Obv:** National arms **Rev:** Vanda Mimi Palmar - multicolor

| Date | Mintage | VF20 | XF40 | MS60 | MS63 | MS65 |
|---|---|---|---|---|---|---|
| 2007 sm | 8,000 | PF65 45.00 | | | | |

**KM# 271 5 DOLLARS**
7.78 g., 0.9999 Gold 0.2499 oz. AGW **Series:** Lunar **Subject:** Year of the Rat **Obv:** National arms **Rev:** Stylized rat lying left

| Date | Mintage | VF20 | XF40 | MS60 | MS63 | MS65 |
|---|---|---|---|---|---|---|
| 2008 sm | 1,200 | PF65 500 | | | | |

**KM# 285 5 DOLLARS**
20.00 g., 0.999 Silver 0.6424 oz. ASW, 38.6 mm. **Subject:** Heritage orchids **Obv:** Supported arms **Rev:** Multicolor yellow orchid - Oncidum Goldiana

| Date | Mintage | VF20 | XF40 | MS60 | MS63 | MS65 |
|---|---|---|---|---|---|---|
| 2008 | 8,000 | PF65 45.00 | | | | |

**KM# 286 5 DOLLARS**
20.00 g., 0.999 Silver 0.6424 oz. ASW, 38.6 mm. **Subject:** Heritage orchids **Obv:** Supported arms **Rev:** Multicolor pink orchid - Aranda Tay Swee Eng

| Date | Mintage | VF20 | XF40 | MS60 | MS63 | MS65 |
|---|---|---|---|---|---|---|
| 2008 | 8,000 | PF65 45.00 | | | | |

**KM# 301 5 DOLLARS**
20.00 g., 0.999 Silver 0.6424 oz. ASW **Subject:** Orchids of Singapore **Obv:** Arms **Rev:** Yellow flower - Spathoglottis Primrose

| Date | Mintage | VF20 | XF40 | MS60 | MS63 | MS65 |
|---|---|---|---|---|---|---|
| 2009 | 8,000 | PF65 45.00 | | | | |

**KM# 302 5 DOLLARS**
20.00 g., 0.999 Silver 0.6424 oz. ASW, 38.7 mm. **Subject:** Orchids of Singapore **Obv:** Arms **Rev:** Pink flower - Vanda Amy

| Date | Mintage | VF20 | XF40 | MS60 | MS63 | MS65 |
|---|---|---|---|---|---|---|
| 2009 | 8,000 | PF65 45.00 | | | | |

**KM# 315 5 DOLLARS**
31.11 g., 0.999 Silver 0.999 oz. ASW, 42.9x39.5 mm. **Subject:** 47th Anniversary of Independence **Obv:** National arms **Rev:** Four children playing, color **Shape:** Heart

| Date | Mintage | VF20 | XF40 | MS60 | MS63 | MS65 |
|---|---|---|---|---|---|---|
| 2012 | — | PF65 125 | | | | |

**KM# 307 5 DOLLARS**
7.77 g., 0.9999 Gold 0.2498 oz. AGW, 21.96 mm. **Subject:** Year of the Snake **Rev:** Snake

| Date | Mintage | VF20 | XF40 | MS60 | MS63 | MS65 |
|---|---|---|---|---|---|---|
| 2013 | — | PF65 600 | | | | |

**KM# 179 10 DOLLARS**
28.00 g., Copper-Nickel, 40.7 mm. **Series:** Lunar **Subject:** Year of the Snake **Obv:** National arms **Rev:** Stylized snake **Edge:** Reeded

| Date | Mintage | VF20 | XF40 | MS60 | MS63 | MS65 |
|---|---|---|---|---|---|---|
| 2001 sm Prooflike | 152,330 | — | — | — | — | 20.00 |

**KM# 179a 10 DOLLARS**
62.21 g., 0.999 Silver 1.998 oz. ASW, 40.7 mm. **Series:** Lunar **Subject:** Year of the Snake **Obv:** National arms **Rev:** Stylized snake **Edge:** Reeded

| Date | Mintage | VF20 | XF40 | MS60 | MS63 | MS65 |
|---|---|---|---|---|---|---|
| 2001 sm | 35,000 | PF63 90.00 | PF65 100 | | | |

**KM# 214 10 DOLLARS**
7.78 g., 0.9999 Gold 0.2499 oz. AGW, 21.9 mm. **Series:** Lunar **Subject:** Year of the Snake **Obv:** National arms **Rev:** Stylized lion's head right, snake privy mark at lower left

| Date | Mintage | VF20 | XF40 | MS60 | MS63 | MS65 |
|---|---|---|---|---|---|---|
| 2001 | 240 | — | — | — | — | 347 |
| 2001 sm | 240 | PF65 332 | | | | |

**KM# 182 10 DOLLARS**
28.00 g., Copper-Nickel, 40.7 mm. **Series:** Lunar **Subject:** Year of the Horse **Obv:** National arms **Rev:** Stylized horse standing left **Edge:** Reeded

| Date | Mintage | VF20 | XF40 | MS60 | MS63 | MS65 |
|---|---|---|---|---|---|---|
| 2002 sm Prooflike | 128,666 | — | — | — | — | 20.00 |

**KM# 182a 10 DOLLARS**
62.21 g., 0.999 Silver 1.998 oz. ASW, 40.7 mm. **Series:** Lunar **Subject:** Year of the Horse **Obv:** National arms **Rev:** Stylized horse standing left **Edge:** Reeded

| Date | Mintage | VF20 | XF40 | MS60 | MS63 | MS65 |
|---|---|---|---|---|---|---|
| 2002 sm | 35,000 | PF63 90.00 | PF65 100 | | | |

**KM# 219 10 DOLLARS**
7.78 g., 0.9999 Gold 0.2499 oz. AGW, 21.9 mm. **Series:** Lunar **Subject:** Year of the Horse **Obv:** National arms **Rev:** Stylized lion's head right, horse privy mark at lower left

| Date | Mintage | VF20 | XF40 | MS60 | MS63 | MS65 |
|---|---|---|---|---|---|---|
| 2002 | 180 | — | — | — | — | 525 |
| 2002 sm | 215 | PF65 475 | | | | |

**KM# 225 10 DOLLARS**
28.00 g., Copper-Nickel, 40.7 mm. **Series:** Lunar **Subject:** Year of the Goat **Obv:** National arms **Rev:** Stylized goat standing right facing left

| Date | Mintage | VF20 | XF40 | MS60 | MS63 | MS65 |
|---|---|---|---|---|---|---|
| 2003 sm Prooflike | 103,047 | — | — | — | — | 20.00 |

**KM# 225a 10 DOLLARS**
62.21 g., 0.999 Silver 1.998 oz. ASW, 40.7 mm. **Series:** Lunar **Subject:** Year of the Goat **Obv:** National arms **Rev:** Stylized goat standing right facing left

| Date | Mintage | VF20 | XF40 | MS60 | MS63 | MS65 |
|---|---|---|---|---|---|---|
| 2003 sm | 35,000 | PF63 90.00 | PF65 100 | | | |

**KM# 185 10 DOLLARS**
31.10 g., 0.9999 Gold 0.9999 oz. AGW, 32.1 mm. **Subject:** 10th Anniversary China-Singapore Suzhou Industrial Park **Obv:** National arms **Rev:** Harmony" Sculpture **Edge:** Lettered edge

| Date | Mintage | VF20 | XF40 | MS60 | MS63 | MS65 |
|---|---|---|---|---|---|---|
| 2004 sm | 500 | PF65 1,850 | | | | |

**KM# 187 10 DOLLARS**
28.00 g., Copper-Nickel, 40.7 mm. **Series:** Lunar **Subject:** Year of the Monkey **Obv:** National arms **Rev:** Stylized monkey sitting left **Edge:** Reeded

| Date | Mintage | VF20 | XF40 | MS60 | MS63 | MS65 |
|---|---|---|---|---|---|---|
| 2004 sm Prooflike | 100,000 | — | — | — | — | 20.00 |

**KM# 187a 10 DOLLARS**
62.21 g., 0.999 Silver 1.998 oz. ASW, 40.7 mm. **Series:** Lunar **Subject:** Year of the Monkey **Obv:** National arms **Rev:** Stylized monkey sitting left **Edge:** Reeded

| Date | Mintage | VF20 | XF40 | MS60 | MS63 | MS65 |
|---|---|---|---|---|---|---|
| 2004 sm | 35,000 | PF63 90.00 | PF65 100 | | | |

**KM# 189 10 DOLLARS**
28.00 g., Copper-Nickel, 40.7 mm. **Subject:** 10th Anniversary China-Singapore Suzhou Industrial Park **Obv:** National arms **Rev:** Harmony" Sculpture **Edge:** Reeded

| Date | Mintage | VF20 | XF40 | MS60 | MS63 | MS65 |
|---|---|---|---|---|---|---|
| 2004 sm Prooflike | 3,511 | — | — | — | — | 20.00 |

**KM# 189a 10 DOLLARS**
20.00 g., 0.999 Silver 0.6424 oz. ASW, 40.7 mm. **Subject:** 10th Anniversary China-Singapore Suzhou Industrial Park **Obv:** National arms **Rev:** Harmony" sculpture **Edge:** Reeded

| Date | Mintage | VF20 | XF40 | MS60 | MS63 | MS65 |
|---|---|---|---|---|---|---|
| 2004 sm | 3,197 | PF65 55.00 | | | | |

**KM# 236 10 DOLLARS**
62.21 g., 0.9999 Silver 1.9998 oz. ASW, 45 mm. **Series:** Lunar **Subject:** Year of the Rooster **Obv:** National arms **Rev:** Stylized rooster standing right

| Date | Mintage | VF20 | XF40 | MS60 | MS63 | MS65 |
|---|---|---|---|---|---|---|
| 2005 sm | 30,000 | PF63 90.00 | PF65 100 | | | |

**KM# 240 10 DOLLARS**
20.00 g., Copper-Nickel, 40.7 mm. **Subject:** National University of Singapore **Obv:** National arms **Rev:** Person, globe and emblem

| Date | Mintage | VF20 | XF40 | MS60 | MS63 | MS65 |
|---|---|---|---|---|---|---|
| 2005 sm Prooflike | 12,264 | — | — | — | — | 22.50 |

**KM# 240a 10 DOLLARS**
20.00 g., 0.9999 Silver 0.643 oz. ASW, 38.7 mm. **Subject:** National University of Singapore **Obv:** National arms **Rev:** Person, globe and emblem

| Date | Mintage | VF20 | XF40 | MS60 | MS63 | MS65 |
|---|---|---|---|---|---|---|
| 2005 sm | 5,293 | PF65 60.00 | | | | |

**KM# 243 10 DOLLARS**
31.10 g., 0.9999 Silver 0.9999 oz. ASW with Gold 2.3g inlay **Subject:** 40th National Day parade **Obv:** National arms **Rev:** Fireworks, parade in government plaza

| Date | Mintage | VF20 | XF40 | MS60 | MS63 | MS65 |
|---|---|---|---|---|---|---|
| 2005 sm | 756 | PF65 245 | | | | |

**KM# 252 10 DOLLARS**
62.20 g., 0.999 Silver 1.9979 oz. ASW **Series:** Lunar **Subject:** Year of the Dog **Obv:** National arms **Rev:** Stylized dog standing left

| Date | Mintage | VF20 | XF40 | MS60 | MS63 | MS65 |
|---|---|---|---|---|---|---|
| 2006 sm | 30,000 | PF63 95.00 | PF65 110 | | | |

**KM# 266 10 DOLLARS**
62.21 g., 0.999 Silver 1.998 oz. ASW, 45 mm. **Series:** Lunar **Subject:** Year of the Boar **Obv:** National arms **Rev:** Stylized pig running right - multicolor

| Date | Mintage | VF20 | XF40 | MS60 | MS63 | MS65 |
|---|---|---|---|---|---|---|
| 2007 sm | 30,000 | PF63 100 | PF65 115 | | | |

**KM# 272 10 DOLLARS**
62.21 g., 0.999 Silver 1.998 oz. ASW **Series:** Lunar **Subject:** Year of the Rat **Obv:** National arms **Rev:** Stylized rat lying left - multicolor

| Date | Mintage | VF20 | XF40 | MS60 | MS63 | MS65 |
|---|---|---|---|---|---|---|
| 2008 sm | 20,000 | PF63 110 | PF65 120 | | | |

**KM# 297 10 DOLLARS**
62.20 g., 0.999 Silver 1.9978 oz. ASW **Subject:** Year of the Ox **Obv:** Supported arms **Rev:** Multicolor Ox

| Date | Mintage | VF20 | XF40 | MS60 | MS63 | MS65 |
|---|---|---|---|---|---|---|
| 2009 | — | PF63 90.00 | PF65 100 | | | |

### KM# 311 10 DOLLARS

62.21 g., 0.999 Silver 1.998 oz. ASW, 45 mm. **Subject:** Year of the Snake **Rev:** Snake in color

| Date | Mintage | VF20 | XF40 | MS60 | MS63 | MS65 |
|---|---|---|---|---|---|---|
| 2013 | — | PF65 140 | | | | |

### KM# 316 10 DOLLARS

62.20 g., 0.999 Silver 1.9979 oz. ASW, 40.7 mm. **Subject:** Year of the Horse **Rev:** Horse right, in color

| Date | Mintage | VF20 | XF40 | MS60 | MS63 | MS65 |
|---|---|---|---|---|---|---|
| 2014 | — | PF65 95.00 | | | | |

### KM# 215 20 DOLLARS

15.55 g., 0.9999 Gold 0.500 oz. AGW, 27 mm. **Series:** Lunar **Subject:** Year of the Snake **Obv:** National arms **Rev:** Stylized lion's head right, snake privy mark at lower left

| Date | Mintage | VF20 | XF40 | MS60 | MS63 | MS65 |
|---|---|---|---|---|---|---|
| 2001 169 | 169 | — | — | — | — | 676 |
| 2001 sm 240 | 240 | PF65 676 | | | | |

### KM# 220 20 DOLLARS

15.55 g., 0.9999 Gold 0.500 oz. AGW, 27 mm. **Series:** Lunar **Subject:** Year of the Horse **Obv:** National arms **Rev:** Stylized lion's head right, horse privy mark at lower left

| Date | Mintage | VF20 | XF40 | MS60 | MS63 | MS65 |
|---|---|---|---|---|---|---|
| 2002 | 165 | — | — | — | — | 676 |
| 2002 sm | 215 | PF65 676 | | | | |

### KM# 226 25 DOLLARS

155.52 g., 0.999 Silver 4.9951 oz. ASW, 65 mm. **Series:** Lunar **Subject:** Year of the Goat **Obv:** National arms **Rev:** Stylized goat standing right facing left

| Date | Mintage | VF20 | XF40 | MS60 | MS63 | MS65 |
|---|---|---|---|---|---|---|
| 2003 sm | 250 | PF65 300 | | | | |

### KM# 231 25 DOLLARS

155.52 g., 0.999 Silver 4.9951 oz. ASW, 65 mm. **Series:** Lunar **Subject:** Year of the Monkey **Obv:** National arms **Rev:** Stylized monkey sitting left

| Date | Mintage | VF20 | XF40 | MS60 | MS63 | MS65 |
|---|---|---|---|---|---|---|
| 2004 sm | 250 | PF65 300 | | | | |

### KM# 237 25 DOLLARS

155.52 g., 0.9999 Silver 4.9996 oz. ASW, 65 mm. **Series:** Lunar **Subject:** Year of the Rooster **Obv:** National arms **Rev:** Stylized rooster standing right

| Date | Mintage | VF20 | XF40 | MS60 | MS63 | MS65 |
|---|---|---|---|---|---|---|
| 2005 sm | 250 | PF65 300 | | | | |

### KM# 253 25 DOLLARS

155.52 g., 0.999 Silver 4.9949 oz. ASW **Series:** Lunar **Subject:** Year of the Dog **Obv:** National arms **Rev:** Stylized dog standing right

| Date | Mintage | VF20 | XF40 | MS60 | MS63 | MS65 |
|---|---|---|---|---|---|---|
| 2006 sm | 250 | PF65 300 | | | | |

### KM# 267 25 DOLLARS

155.52 g., 0.999 Silver 4.9949 oz. ASW **Series:** Lunar **Subject:** Year of the Boar **Obv:** National arms **Rev:** Stylized boar running right

| Date | Mintage | VF20 | XF40 | MS60 | MS63 | MS65 |
|---|---|---|---|---|---|---|
| 2007 sm | 250 | PF65 300 | | | | |

### KM# 273 25 DOLLARS

155.52 g., 0.999 Silver 4.9949 oz. ASW **Series:** Lunar **Subject:** Year of the Rat **Obv:** National arms **Rev:** Stylized rat lying left

| Date | Mintage | VF20 | XF40 | MS60 | MS63 | MS65 |
|---|---|---|---|---|---|---|
| 2008 sm | 250 | PF65 300 | | | | |

### KM# 298 25 DOLLARS

155.50 g., 0.999 Silver 4.9944 oz. ASW **Subject:** Year of the Ox **Obv:** Supported arms **Rev:** Ox

| Date | Mintage | VF20 | XF40 | MS60 | MS63 | MS65 |
|---|---|---|---|---|---|---|
| 2009 | — | PF65 300 | | | | |

### KM# 310 25 DOLLARS

155.52 g., 0.999 Silver 4.9951 oz. ASW, 62 mm. **Subject:** Year of the Snake **Rev:** Snake

| Date | Mintage | VF20 | XF40 | MS60 | MS63 | MS65 |
|---|---|---|---|---|---|---|
| 2013 | — | PF65 565 | | | | |

### KM# 216 50 DOLLARS

31.10 g., 0.9999 Gold 0.9999 oz. AGW, 32.1 mm. **Series:** Lunar **Subject:** Year of the Snake **Obv:** National arms **Rev:** Stylized lion's head right, snake privy mark at lower left

| Date | Mintage | VF20 | XF40 | MS60 | MS63 | MS65 |
|---|---|---|---|---|---|---|
| 2001 | 187 | — | — | — | — | 1,315 |
| 2001 sm | 179 | PF65 1,315 | | | | |

### KM# 221 50 DOLLARS

31.10 g., 0.9999 Gold 0.9999 oz. AGW, 32.1 mm. **Series:** Lunar **Subject:** Year of the Horse **Obv:** National arms **Rev:** Stylized lion's head right, horse privy mark at lower left

| Date | Mintage | VF20 | XF40 | MS60 | MS63 | MS65 |
|---|---|---|---|---|---|---|
| 2002 | 165 | — | — | — | — | 1,315 |
| 2002 sm | 160 | PF65 1,315 | | | | |

### KM# 288 50 DOLLARS

20.00 g., 0.999 Silver 0.6424 oz. ASW **Subject:** Formula 1 - Singapore Grand Prix **Obv:** Supported arms **Rev:** Multicolor race car and skyline

| Date | Mintage | VF20 | XF40 | MS60 | MS63 | MS65 |
|---|---|---|---|---|---|---|
| 2008 | 5,000 | PF65 40.00 | | | | |

### KM# 309 80 DOLLARS

1000.00 g., 0.999 Silver 32.1186 oz. ASW, 100 mm. **Subject:** Year of the Snake **Rev:** Snake

| Date | Mintage | VF20 | XF40 | MS60 | MS63 | MS65 |
|---|---|---|---|---|---|---|
| 2013 Proof-like | — | — | — | — | — | 1,675 |

### KM# 238 100 DOLLARS

31.10 g., 0.9999 Gold 0.9999 oz. AGW, 33 mm. **Series:** Lunar **Subject:** Year of the Rooster **Obv:** National arms **Rev:** Stylized rooster standing right

| Date | Mintage | VF20 | XF40 | MS60 | MS63 | MS65 |
|---|---|---|---|---|---|---|
| 2005 sm | 1,699 | PF65 1,328 | | | | |

### KM# 241 100 DOLLARS

31.10 g., 0.9999 Gold 0.9999 oz. AGW, 33 mm. **Subject:** National University of Singapore **Obv:** National arms **Rev:** Person, globe and emblem

| Date | Mintage | VF20 | XF40 | MS60 | MS63 | MS65 |
|---|---|---|---|---|---|---|
| 2005 sm | 244 | PF65 1,850 | | | | |

### KM# 254 100 DOLLARS

31.10 g., 0.9999 Gold 0.9999 oz. AGW **Series:** Lunar **Subject:** Year of the Dog **Obv:** National arms **Rev:** Stylized dog standing left

| Date | Mintage | VF20 | XF40 | MS60 | MS63 | MS65 |
|---|---|---|---|---|---|---|
| 2006 sm | 1,319 | PF65 1,328 | | | | |

### KM# 268 100 DOLLARS

31.10 g., 0.9999 Gold 0.9999 oz. AGW, 33 mm. **Series:** Lunar **Subject:** Year of the Boar **Obv:** National arms **Rev:** Stylized pig running right

| Date | Mintage | VF20 | XF40 | MS60 | MS63 | MS65 |
|---|---|---|---|---|---|---|
| 2007 sm | 1,220 | PF65 1,328 | | | | |

### KM# 274 100 DOLLARS

31.10 g., 0.9999 Gold 0.9999 oz. AGW **Series:** Lunar **Subject:** Year of the Rat **Obv:** National arms **Rev:** Stylized rat lying left

| Date | Mintage | VF20 | XF40 | MS60 | MS63 | MS65 |
|---|---|---|---|---|---|---|
| 2008 sm | 1,153 | PF65 1,328 | | | | |

### KM# 289 100 DOLLARS

31.00 g., 0.250 Gold 0.2492 oz. AGW, 38.7 mm. **Subject:** Formula 1 - Singapore Grand Prix **Obv:** Supported arms **Rev:** Formula 1 racecar and skyline

| Date | Mintage | VF20 | XF40 | MS60 | MS63 | MS65 |
|---|---|---|---|---|---|---|
| 2008 | 300 | PF65 500 | | | | |

### KM# 299 100 DOLLARS

31.11 g., 0.999 Gold 0.999 oz. AGW **Subject:** Year of the Ox **Obv:** Supported arms **Rev:** Ox

| Date | Mintage | VF20 | XF40 | MS60 | MS63 | MS65 |
|---|---|---|---|---|---|---|
| 2009 | 2,000 | PF65 1,326 | | | | |

### KM# 306 100 DOLLARS

31.10 g., 0.999 Gold 0.999 oz. AGW, 33 mm. **Subject:** Year of the Snake **Rev:** Snake

| Date | Mintage | VF20 | XF40 | MS60 | MS63 | MS65 |
|---|---|---|---|---|---|---|
| 2013 | — | PF65 2,160 | | | | |

### KM# 239 200 DOLLARS

155.52 g., 0.9999 Gold 4.9996 oz. AGW, 60 mm. **Series:** Lunar **Subject:** Year of the Rooster **Obv:** National arms **Rev:** Stylized rooster standing right

| Date | Mintage | VF20 | XF40 | MS60 | MS63 | MS65 |
|---|---|---|---|---|---|---|
| 2005 sm | 84 | PF65 9,750 | | | | |

### KM# 255 200 DOLLARS

155.15 g., 0.9999 Gold 4.9877 oz. AGW **Series:** Lunar **Subject:** Year of the Dog **Obv:** National arms **Rev:** Stylized dog standing left

| Date | Mintage | VF20 | XF40 | MS60 | MS63 | MS65 |
|---|---|---|---|---|---|---|
| 2006 sm | 50 | PF65 9,750 | | | | |

### KM# 300 200 DOLLARS

155.50 g., 0.999 Gold 4.9944 oz. AGW, 60 mm. **Subject:** Year of the Ox **Obv:** Supported arms **Rev:** Ox

| Date | Mintage | VF20 | XF40 | MS60 | MS63 | MS65 |
|---|---|---|---|---|---|---|
| 2009 | 200 | PF65 9,500 | | | | |

### KM# 305 200 DOLLARS

155.52 g., 0.9999 Gold 4.9996 oz. AGW, 60 mm. **Subject:** Year of the Snake **Rev:** Snake

| Date | Mintage | VF20 | XF40 | MS60 | MS63 | MS65 |
|---|---|---|---|---|---|---|
| 2013 | Est. 200 | PF65 9,800 | | | | |

### KM# 318 200 DOLLARS

155.15 g., 0.999 Gold 4.9832 oz. AGW, 60 mm. **Subject:** Year of the Horse **Obv:** National arms **Rev:** Horse right

| Date | Mintage | VF20 | XF40 | MS60 | MS63 | MS65 |
|---|---|---|---|---|---|---|
| 2014 | — | PF65 9,500 | | | | |

### KM# 178 250 DOLLARS

31.10 g., 0.999 Gold 0.999 oz. AGW, 32.1 mm. **Subject:** Year of the Snake **Obv:** National arms **Rev:** Stylized snake **Edge:** Reeded

| Date | Mintage | VF20 | XF40 | MS60 | MS63 | MS65 |
|---|---|---|---|---|---|---|
| 2001 sm | 3,775 | PF65 1,326 | | | | |

### KM# 183 250 DOLLARS

31.10 g., 0.9999 Gold 0.9999 oz. AGW, 32.1 mm. **Subject:** Year of the Horse **Obv:** National arms **Rev:** Horse **Edge:** Reeded

| Date | Mintage | VF20 | XF40 | MS60 | MS63 | MS65 |
|---|---|---|---|---|---|---|
| 2002 sm | 3,199 | PF65 1,328 | | | | |

### KM# 227 250 DOLLARS

31.10 g., 0.9999 Gold 0.9999 oz. AGW, 32.1 mm. **Series:** Lunar **Subject:** Year of the Goat **Obv:** National arms **Rev:** Stylized goat standing right facing left

| Date | Mintage | VF20 | XF40 | MS60 | MS63 | MS65 |
|---|---|---|---|---|---|---|
| 2003 sm | 2,390 | **PF65** 1,328 | | | | |

### KM# 188 250 DOLLARS

31.10 g., 0.9999 Gold 0.9999 oz. AGW, 32.1 mm. **Series:** Lunar **Subject:** Year of the Monkey **Obv:** National arms **Rev:** Stylized monkey sitting left **Edge:** Reeded

| Date | Mintage | VF20 | XF40 | MS60 | MS63 | MS65 |
|---|---|---|---|---|---|---|
| 2004 sm | 2,535 | **PF65** 1,328 | | | | |

### KM# 228 500 DOLLARS

155.52 g., 0.9999 Gold 4.9996 oz. AGW, 55 mm. **Series:** Lunar **Subject:** Year of the Goat **Obv:** National arms **Rev:** Stylized goat standing right facing left

| Date | Mintage | VF20 | XF40 | MS60 | MS63 | MS65 |
|---|---|---|---|---|---|---|
| 2003 sm | 62 | **PF65** 9,750 | | | | |

### KM# 232 500 DOLLARS

155.52 g., 0.9999 Gold 4.9996 oz. AGW, 55 mm. **Series:** Lunar **Subject:** Year of the Monkey **Obv:** National arms **Rev:** Stylized monkey sitting left

| Date | Mintage | VF20 | XF40 | MS60 | MS63 | MS65 |
|---|---|---|---|---|---|---|
| 2004 sm | 76 | **PF65** 9,750 | | | | |

## MINT SETS

| KM# | Date | Mintage | Identification | Issue Price | Mkt Val |
|---|---|---|---|---|---|
| MS38A | 2001 (7) | 101,738 | KM#98-103, 104.2 | — | — |
| MS39 | 2002 (7) | 84,577 | KM#98-103, 104.3 Hongbao | — | 15.00 |
| MS40 | 2003 (6) | 68,980 | KM#99-103, 104.3 Hongbao | — | 15.00 |
| MS41 | 2004 (6) | 70,000 | KM#99-103, 104.3 Hongbao | — | 15.00 |
| MS42 | 2005 (6) | 61,981 | KM#99-103, 104.3 Hongbao | — | 15.00 |
| MS43 | 2006 (7) | 53,214 | KM#99-103, 104.3 Hongbao | — | 15.00 |
| MS44 | 2007 (6) | 54,889 | KM99-103, 104.3 Hongbao | 10.78 | 15.00 |
| MS45 | 2008 (6) | 55,000 | KM#99-103, 104.3 | — | 15.00 |
| MS46 | 2009 (6) | 60,000 | KM#99-103, 104.3 | — | 15.00 |

## PROOF SETS

| KM# | Date | Mintage | Identification | Issue Price | Mkt Val |
|---|---|---|---|---|---|
| PS61 | 2001 (2) | 3,000 | KM#179-180 plus copper-nickel ingot | — | 115 |
| PS62 | 2001 (3) | 2,000 | KM#178-180 plus copper-nickel ingot | — | 2,000 |
| PS63 | 2001 (4) | — | KM#212-215 | — | 1,750 |
| PS64 | 2001 (6) | — | KM#212-216, plus ingot | — | 3,200 |
| PS65 | 2001 (2) | 2,001 | KM#177, 177a | — | 70.00 |
| PS66 | 2001 (7) | 6,000 | KM#98a-103a, 104.2a | — | 70.00 |
| PS67 | 2002 (2) | 3,000 | KM#182, 182a | — | 115 |
| PS68 | 2002 (3) | 2,000 | KM#182, 182a, 183 | — | 2,000 |
| PS69 | 2002 (2) | 2,001 | KM#181, 181a | — | 65.00 |
| PS70 | 2002 (3) | 2,001 | KM#181, 181a, 217 | — | 160 |
| PS71 | 2002 (4) | — | KM#217-220 | — | 1,750 |
| PS72 | 2002 (6) | — | KM#217-221 plus ingot | — | 3,250 |
| PS73 | 2002 (7) | 6,300 | KM#98a-103a, 104.2a | — | 70.00 |
| PS74 | 2003 (2) | 2,003 | KM#196, 196a | — | 75.00 |
| PS75 | 2003 (6) | 4,900 | KM#99a-103a, 104.3a | — | 70.00 |
| PS77 | 2003 (2) | 88 | KM#226, 228 | — | 10,050 |
| PS78 | 2003 (2) | 3,000 | KM#225, 225a | — | 115 |
| PS79 | 2003 (3) | 2,000 | KM#225, 225a, 227 | — | 2,000 |
| PS80 | 2004 (2) | 1,000 | KM#189, 189a | — | 85.00 |
| PS81 | 2004 (3) | 88 | KM#185, 189, 189a | — | 1,950 |
| PS82 | 2004 (6) | 10,000 | KM#98a-103a, 104.3a | — | 70.00 |
| PS83 | 2004 (2) | 1,000 | KM#184, 184a | — | 40.00 |
| PS84 | 2004 (2) | 1,000 | KM#190, 190a | — | 40.00 |
| PS85 | 2004 (2) | 1,000 | KM#191, 191a | — | 40.00 |
| PS86 | 2004 (2) | 1,000 | KM#192, 192a | — | 40.00 |
| PS87 | 2004 (4) | 800 | KM#184a, 190a-192a | — | 110 |
| PS88 | 2004 (8) | 88 | KM#184, 184a, 190, 190a, 191, 191a, 192, 192a | — | 150 |
| PS89 | 2004 (2) | 80 | KM#231, 232 | — | 10,050 |
| PS90 | 2004 (2) | 3,000 | KM#187, 187a | — | 110 |
| PS91 | 2004 (3) | 2,000 | KM#187, 187a, 188 | — | 2,000 |
| PS92 | 2005 (6) | 3,250 | KM#99a-103a, 104.3a | — | 70.00 |
| PS93 | 2005 (2) | 3,000 | KM#234, 236 | — | 110 |
| PS94 | 2005 (2) | 88 | KM#237, 239 | — | 10,050 |
| PS95 | 2005 (3) | 2,000 | KM#234, 236, 238 | — | 2,000 |
| PS97 | 2006 (2) | 8,000 | KM#256, 257 | — | 120 |
| PS99 | 2007 (4) | 800 | KM#259a-262a | — | 130 |
| PS100 | 2007 (2) | 8,000 | KM#275, 276 | 90.00 | 90.00 |
| PS101 | 2007 (2) | 3,000 | KM#193, 193a | 65.00 | 65.00 |

## PROOF-LIKE SETS (PL)

| KM# | Date | Mintage | Identification | Issue Price | Mkt Val |
|---|---|---|---|---|---|
| PL1 | 2004 (4) | 800 | KM#184, 190, 191, 192 | — | 40.00 |
| PL2 | 2007 (4) | 800 | KM#259-262 | — | 50.00 |

# SLOVAKIA

The Republic of Slovakia has an area of 18,923 sq. mi. (49,035 sq. km.) and a population of 4.9 million. Capital: Bratislava. Textiles, steel, and wood products are exported.

**MINT MARK**

Kremnica Mint

## REPUBLIC

## STANDARD COINAGE

100 Halierov = 1 Slovak Koruna (Sk)

### KM# 17 10 HALIEROV

0.72 g., Aluminum, 17 mm. **Obv:** Double cross on shield above inscription **Rev:** Church steeple **Edge:** Plain

| Date | Mintage | VF20 | XF40 | MS60 | MS63 | MS65 |
|---|---|---|---|---|---|---|
| 2001 | 20,330,000 | — | — | 0.25 | 0.35 | 0.50 |
| 2001 | 12,500 | **PF65** 2.50 | | | | |
| 2002 | 37,640,000 | — | — | 0.25 | 0.35 | 0.50 |
| 2002 | 16,100 | **PF65** 1.50 | | | | |
| 2003 Sets only | 3,000 | — | — | — | — | 2.50 |

### KM# 17a 10 HALIEROV

2.85 g., 0.925 Silver 0.0848 oz. ASW, 17 mm.

| Date | Mintage | VF20 | XF40 | MS60 | MS63 | MS65 |
|---|---|---|---|---|---|---|
| 2004 | 4,000 | — | — | — | — | 10.00 |
| 2004 | 2,000 | **PF65** 15.00 | | | | |

### KM# 18 20 HALIEROV

0.95 g., Aluminum, 19.5 mm. **Obv:** Double cross on shield above inscription **Rev:** Krivan Mountain and value **Edge:** Reeded

| Date | Mintage | VF20 | XF40 | MS60 | MS63 | MS65 |
|---|---|---|---|---|---|---|
| 2001 | 21,920,000 | — | — | 0.35 | 0.45 | 0.60 |
| 2001 | 12,500 | **PF65** 2.50 | | | | |
| 2002 | 36,300,000 | — | — | 0.35 | 0.45 | 0.60 |
| 2002 | 16,100 | **PF65** 1.50 | | | | |
| 2003 Sets only | 3,000 | — | — | — | — | 2.50 |

### KM# 18a 20 HALIEROV

3.87 g., 0.925 Silver 0.1151 oz. ASW, 19.5 mm.

| Date | Mintage | VF20 | XF40 | MS60 | MS63 | MS65 |
|---|---|---|---|---|---|---|
| 2004 | 4,000 | — | — | — | — | 15.00 |
| 2004 | 2,000 | **PF65** 20.00 | | | | |

### KM# 35 50 HALIEROV

2.80 g., Copper Plated Steel, 18.75 mm. **Obv:** Double cross on shield above inscription **Rev:** Devin watch tower and value **Edge:** Segmented reeding

| Date | Mintage | VF20 | XF40 | MS60 | MS63 | MS65 |
|---|---|---|---|---|---|---|
| 2001 | 10,400,000 | — | — | 0.45 | 0.60 | 0.75 |
| 2001 | 12,500 | **PF65** 2.50 | | | | |
| 2002 | 11,000,000 | — | — | 0.45 | 0.60 | 0.75 |
| 2002 | 16,100 | **PF65** 1.50 | | | | |
| 2003 | 11,000,000 | — | — | 0.45 | 0.60 | 0.75 |
| 2004 | 16,500,000 | — | — | 0.45 | 0.60 | 0.75 |
| 2004 | — | **PF65** 1.50 | | | | |
| 2005 | 17,000,000 | — | — | 0.45 | 0.60 | 0.75 |
| 2006 | 22,050,000 | — | — | 0.45 | 0.60 | 0.75 |
| 2006 | — | **PF65** 1.50 | | | | |
| 2007 | — | — | — | 0.45 | 0.60 | 0.75 |
| 2008 | — | — | — | 0.45 | 0.60 | 0.75 |
| 2008 | — | **PF65** 1.50 | | | | |

### KM# 12 KORUNA

3.85 g., Bronze Plated Steel, 21 mm. **Subject:** 15th Century of Madonna and Child **Obv:** Double cross on shield above inscription **Rev:** Madonna holding child and value **Edge:** Milled

| Date | Mintage | VF20 | XF40 | MS60 | MS63 | MS65 |
|---|---|---|---|---|---|---|
| 2001 Sets only | 12,500 | — | — | — | — | 1.50 |
| 2001 | — | **PF65** 3.00 | | | | |
| 2002 | 11,000,000 | — | — | 0.50 | 0.75 | 0.90 |
| 2002 | 16,100 | **PF65** 2.50 | | | | |
| 2003 Sets only | 14,000 | — | — | — | — | 1.50 |
| 2004 Sets only | — | — | — | — | — | 1.50 |
| 2004 | — | **PF65** 2.50 | | | | |
| 2005 | 10,000,000 | — | — | 0.50 | 0.75 | 0.90 |
| 2005 | — | **PF65** 2.50 | | | | |
| 2006 | 9,605,000 | — | — | 0.50 | 0.75 | 0.90 |
| 2006 | — | **PF65** 2.50 | | | | |
| 2007 | — | — | — | 0.50 | 0.75 | 0.90 |
| 2008 | — | — | — | 0.50 | 0.75 | 0.90 |
| 2008 | — | **PF65** 2.50 | | | | |

### KM# 13 2 KORUNA

4.40 g., Nickel Plated Steel, 22.5 mm. **Obv:** Double cross on shield above inscription **Rev:** Venus statue and value

| Date | Mintage | VF20 | XF40 | MS60 | MS63 | MS65 |
|---|---|---|---|---|---|---|
| 2001 | 10,668,000 | — | — | 0.60 | 0.85 | 1.00 |
| 2001 | 12,500 | **PF65** 5.00 | | | | |
| 2002 | 11,000,000 | — | — | 0.60 | 0.85 | 1.00 |
| 2002 | 16,100 | **PF65** 2.50 | | | | |
| 2003 | 11,000,000 | — | — | 0.60 | 0.85 | 1.00 |
| 2004 Sets only | — | — | — | — | — | 2.00 |
| 2004 | — | **PF65** 2.50 | | | | |
| 2005 Sets only | — | — | — | — | — | 2.00 |
| 2006 Sets only | — | — | — | — | — | 2.00 |
| 2006 | — | **PF65** 2.50 | | | | |
| 2007 Sets only | — | — | — | — | — | 2.00 |
| 2008 Sets only | — | — | — | — | — | 2.00 |
| 2008 | — | **PF65** 2.50 | | | | |

### KM# 14 5 KORUNA

5.40 g., Nickel Plated Steel, 24.75 mm. **Obv:** Double cross on shield above inscription **Rev:** Celtic coin of BIATEC at upper left of value **Edge:** Milled

| Date | Mintage | VF20 | XF40 | MS60 | MS63 | MS65 |
|---|---|---|---|---|---|---|
| 2001 Sets only | — | — | — | — | — | 2.00 |
| 2001 | 12,500 | **PF65** 6.00 | | | | |
| 2002 | 16,100 | **PF65** 5.00 | | | | |
| 2003 Sets only | 14,000 | — | — | — | — | 2.00 |
| 2004 Sets only | — | — | — | — | — | 2.00 |
| 2004 | — | **PF65** 5.00 | | | | |
| 2005 Sets only | — | — | — | — | — | 2.00 |
| 2006 Sets only | — | — | — | — | — | 2.00 |
| 2006 | — | **PF65** 5.00 | | | | |
| 2007 | — | — | — | 1.00 | 1.25 | 1.50 |
| 2008 Sets only | — | — | — | — | — | 2.00 |
| 2008 | — | **PF65** 5.00 | | | | |

### KM# 11 10 KORUNA

6.60 g., Aluminum-Bronze, 26.5 mm. **Obv:** Double cross on shield above inscription **Rev:** Bronze cross and value

| Date | Mintage | VF20 | XF40 | MS60 | MS63 | MS65 |
|---|---|---|---|---|---|---|
| 2001 Sets only | — | — | — | — | — | 4.00 |
| 2001 | 12,500 | **PF65** 12.50 | | | | |
| 2002 | 16,100 | **PF65** 10.00 | | | | |
| 2003 | 10,923,000 | — | — | 2.00 | 2.50 | 3.00 |

| Date | Mintage | VF20 | XF40 | MS60 | MS63 | MS65 |
|---|---|---|---|---|---|---|
| 2004 Sets only | — | — | — | — | — | 4.00 |
| 2004 | — | PF65 10.00 | | | | |
| 2005 Sets only | — | — | — | — | — | 4.00 |
| 2006 Sets only | — | — | — | — | — | 4.00 |
| 2006 | — | PF65 10.00 | | | | |
| 2007 Sets only | — | — | — | — | — | 4.00 |
| 2008 Sets only | — | — | — | — | — | 4.00 |
| 2008 | — | PF65 10.00 | | | | |

**KM# 11b 10 KORUNA**
15.55 g., 0.999 Gold 0.4994 oz. AGW, 26.5 mm.

| Date | Mintage | VF20 | XF40 | MS60 | MS63 | MS65 |
|---|---|---|---|---|---|---|
| 2008 | — | PF65 1,000 | | | | |

**KM# 67 20 KORUN**
24.48 g., 0.925 Silver 0.728 oz. ASW, 27.1 x 50.6 mm. **Series:** Banknotes **Obv:** Prince Pribina (800-861) **Rev:** Nitra Castle **Edge:** Plain

| Date | Mintage | VF20 | XF40 | MS60 | MS63 | MS65 |
|---|---|---|---|---|---|---|
| 2003 | 6,000 | PF65 60.00 | | | | |

**KM# 68 50 KORUN**
26.63 g., 0.925 Silver 0.792 oz. ASW, 28.2 x 52.8 mm. **Series:** Banknotes **Obv:** Saints Cyril and Methodius (814-885) **Rev:** Two hands **Edge:** Plain

| Date | Mintage | VF20 | XF40 | MS60 | MS63 | MS65 |
|---|---|---|---|---|---|---|
| 2003 | 6,000 | PF65 65.00 | | | | |

**KM# 69 100 KORUN**
28.87 g., 0.925 Silver 0.8586 oz. ASW, 29.3 x 55 mm. **Series:** Banknotes **Obv:** The Levoca Madonna **Rev:** St. James Church in Levoca **Edge:** Plain

| Date | Mintage | VF20 | XF40 | MS60 | MS63 | MS65 |
|---|---|---|---|---|---|---|
| 2003 | — | PF65 75.00 | | | | |

**KM# 59 200 KORUN**
20.00 g., 0.750 Silver 0.4823 oz. ASW, 34 mm. **Subject:** Alexander Dubcek **Obv:** Double cross on shield and tree **Rev:** Head left **Edge Lettering:** LUDSKOST SLOBODA DEMOKRACIA

| Date | Mintage | VF20 | XF40 | MS60 | MS63 | MS65 |
|---|---|---|---|---|---|---|
| 2001 | 12,800 | — | — | — | — | 25.00 |
| 2001 | 3,000 | PF65 70.00 | | | | |

Note: Unc. examples without edge lettering exist. Value $850.

**KM# 60 200 KORUN**
20.00 g., 0.750 Silver 0.4823 oz. ASW, 34 mm. **Subject:** Ludovit Fulla **Obv:** Modern art **Rev:** Head facing in national costume, value and dates **Edge:** Lettered **Note:** 1,800 pieces melted.

| Date | Mintage | VF20 | XF40 | MS60 | MS63 | MS65 |
|---|---|---|---|---|---|---|
| 2002 | 11,300 | — | — | — | — | 25.00 |
| 2002 | 2,400 | PF65 55.00 | | | | |

**KM# 62 200 KORUN**
20.35 g., 0.750 Silver 0.4907 oz. ASW, 34 mm. **Subject:** UNESCO World Heritage site - Vlkolínec **Obv:** Log building and double cross on shield **Rev:** Wooden tower and value **Edge Lettering:** WORLD HERITAGE PATRIMONE MONDIAL **Note:** 900 pieces melted.

| Date | Mintage | VF20 | XF40 | MS60 | MS63 | MS65 |
|---|---|---|---|---|---|---|
| 2002 | 11,500 | — | — | — | — | 25.00 |
| 2002 | — | PF65 55.00 | | | | |

**KM# 65 200 KORUN**
20.00 g., 0.750 Silver 0.4823 oz. ASW, 34 mm. **Subject:** Imrich Karvas **Obv:** Building, national arms and value **Rev:** Portrait **Edge:** Lettered **Edge Lettering:** NARODOHOSPODAR HUMANISTA EUROPAN **Note:** 500 pieces uncirculated melted.

| Date | Mintage | VF20 | XF40 | MS60 | MS63 | MS65 |
|---|---|---|---|---|---|---|
| 2003 | 9,800 | — | — | — | — | 25.00 |
| 2003 | 3,000 | PF65 50.00 | | | | |

**KM# 66 200 KORUN**
20.00 g., 0.750 Silver 0.4823 oz. ASW, 34 mm. **Subject:** Jozef Skultety, Slovak linguist and historian **Obv:** Building below double cross within shield **Rev:** Head facing and value **Edge Lettering:** VYTRVALOST A VERNOST NARODNEMU IDEALU **Note:** 500 pieces uncirculated melted.

| Date | Mintage | VF20 | XF40 | MS60 | MS63 | MS65 |
|---|---|---|---|---|---|---|
| 2003 | 8,800 | — | — | — | — | 30.00 |
| 2003 | 2,700 | PF65 55.00 | | | | |

**KM# 70 200 KORUN**
31.21 g., 0.925 Silver 0.9282 oz. ASW, 30.4 x 57.2 mm. **Series:** Banknotes **Obv:** Head facing and value **Rev:** 18th Century city view and value **Edge:** Plain

| Date | Mintage | VF20 | XF40 | MS60 | MS63 | MS65 |
|---|---|---|---|---|---|---|
| 2003 | 6,000 | PF65 90.00 | | | | |

**KM# 75 200 KORUN**
20.00 g., 0.750 Silver 0.4823 oz. ASW, 34 mm. **Obv:** Kempelen's Chess Machine (1770) **Rev:** Inventor Wolfgang Kemelen (1734-1804) above Bratislava city view **Edge Lettering:** VYNALEZCA - TECHNIK - KONSTRUKTER

| Date | Mintage | VF20 | XF40 | MS60 | MS63 | MS65 |
|---|---|---|---|---|---|---|
| 2004 | 8,000 | — | — | — | — | 25.00 |
| 2004 | 3,200 | PF65 50.00 | | | | |

**KM# 76 200 KORUN**
20.00 g., 0.750 Silver 0.4823 oz. ASW, 34 mm. **Obv:** Church and town hall below double cross within shield **Rev:** Aerial view of Bardejov circa 1768 **Edge Lettering:** WORLD HERITAGE - PATRIMOINE MONDIAL

| Date | Mintage | VF20 | XF40 | MS60 | MS63 | MS65 |
|---|---|---|---|---|---|---|
| 2004 | 8,400 | — | — | — | — | 25.00 |
| 2004 | 3,600 | PF65 50.00 | | | | |

**KM# 77 200 KORUN**
18.00 g., 0.900 Silver 0.5208 oz. ASW, 34 mm. **Obv:** "The Segner Wheel" model **Rev:** Bust with fur hat facing within circle of designs **Edge Lettering:** VYNALEZCA - FYZIK - MATEMATIK - PEDAGOG

| Date | Mintage | VF20 | XF40 | MS60 | MS63 | MS65 |
|---|---|---|---|---|---|---|
| 2004 | 10,500 | — | — | — | — | 25.00 |
| 2004 | 4,700 | PF65 45.00 | | | | |

**KM# 78 200 KORUN**
20.00 g., 0.750 Silver 0.4823 oz. ASW, 34 mm. **Subject:** Slovakian entry into the European Union **Obv:** Circle of stars in arch above national arms **Rev:** Map in arch above value **Edge Lettering:** ROZSIRENIE EUROPSKEJ UNIE O DESAT KRAJIN

| Date | Mintage | VF20 | XF40 | MS60 | MS63 | MS65 |
|---|---|---|---|---|---|---|
| 2004 | 10,100 | — | — | — | — | 25.00 |
| 2004 | 4,700 | PF65 45.00 | | | | |

**KM# 81 200 KORUN**
18.00 g., 0.900 Silver 0.5208 oz. ASW, 34 mm. **Subject:** Leopold I Coronation 350th Anniversary **Obv:** Value and partial castle view **Rev:** Coin design of Leopold I in large size legend **Edge Lettering:** BRATISLAVSKE KORUNOVACIE

| Date | Mintage | VF20 | XF40 | MS60 | MS63 | MS65 |
|---|---|---|---|---|---|---|
| 2005 | 8,900 | — | — | — | — | 25.00 |
| 2005 | 4,800 | PF65 45.00 | | | | |

**KM# 82 200 KORUN**
18.00 g., 0.900 Silver 0.5208 oz. ASW, 34 mm. **Subject:** Treaty of Pressburg **Obv:** Primate's Palace behind French military standard **Rev:** Napoleon and Francis I of Austria **Edge Lettering:** 26 DECEMBER. 5 MIVOSE AN 14

| Date | Mintage | VF20 | XF40 | MS60 | MS63 | MS65 |
|---|---|---|---|---|---|---|
| 2005 | 5,100 | — | — | — | — | 25.00 |
| 2005 | 3,400 | PF65 45.00 | | | | |

**KM# 87 200 KORUN**
18.00 g., 0.900 Silver 0.5208 oz. ASW, 34 mm. **Subject:** 200th Anniversary Birth of Karol Kuzmány **Obv:** Small national arms at upper left, denomination at center **Obv. Inscription:** SLOVENSKÁ / REPUBLIKA **Rev:** Partial medallic head of Kuzmány facing

| Date | Mintage | VF20 | XF40 | MS60 | MS63 | MS65 |
|---|---|---|---|---|---|---|
| 2006 | — | — | — | — | — | 25.00 |
| 2006 | — | PF65 55.00 | | | | |

**KM# 105 200 KORUN**
18.00 g., 0.900 Silver 0.5208 oz. ASW, 34 mm. **Subject:** Josef M. Petzval, Physicist **Obv:** Lens **Rev:** Bust at left

| Date | Mintage | VF20 | XF40 | MS60 | MS63 | MS65 |
|---|---|---|---|---|---|---|
| 2007 | 4,700 | — | — | — | — | 25.00 |
| 2007 | 2,500 | PF65 70.00 | | | | |

**KM# 88 200 KORUN**
18.00 g., 0.900 Silver 0.5208 oz. ASW, 34 mm. **Subject:** 100th Anniversary Birth of Andrej Kmet **Obv:** Small national arms above stylized M-shaped memorial representing the Slovak Museum. **Obv. Legend:** SLOVENSKÁ REPUBLIKA **Rev:** Head of Kmet 3/4 left **Edge:** Lettered **Edge Lettering:** POZNÁVAJME KRAJE SVOJE A POZNÁME SAMYCH SEBA

| Date | Mintage | VF20 | XF40 | MS60 | MS63 | MS65 |
|---|---|---|---|---|---|---|
| 2008 | 8,500 | — | — | — | — | 25.00 |
| 2008 | 3,400 | PF65 75.00 | | | | |

**KM# 56 500 KORUN**
33.63 g., 0.925 Silver 1.0001 oz. ASW, 40 mm. **Subject:** Mala Fatra National Park **Obv:** National arms center of cross formed by beetles (Alpine Salyers) **Rev:** Orchid with mountain background **Edge Lettering:** OCHRANA PRIRODY A KRAJINY **Note:** 400 pieces uncirculated melted.

| Date | Mintage | VF20 | XF40 | MS60 | MS63 | MS65 |
|---|---|---|---|---|---|---|
| 2001 | 10,200 | — | — | — | — | 90.00 |
| 2001 | 1,800 | PF65 250 | | | | |

**KM# 57 500 KORUN**
31.10 g., 0.999 Silver 0.999 oz. ASW, 45 mm. **Subject:** Third Millennium **Obv:** The Universe **Rev:** Three hands **Edge:** Plain **Shape:** 3-sided **Note:** 400 pieces uncirculated melted.

| Date | Mintage | VF20 | XF40 | MS60 | MS63 | MS65 |
|---|---|---|---|---|---|---|
| 2001 | 13,000 | — | — | — | — | 90.00 |
| 2001 | 4,000 | PF65 185 | | | | |

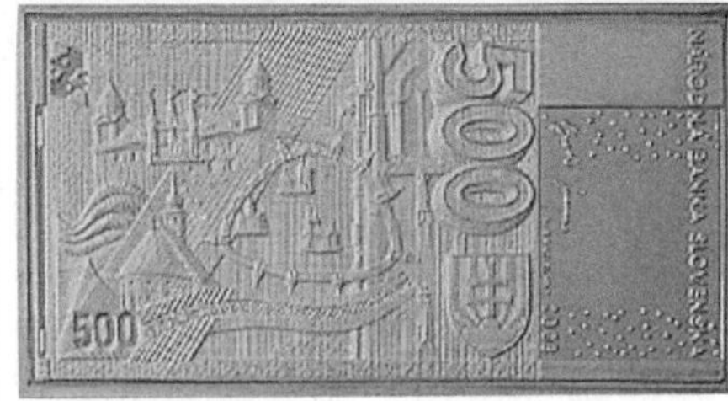

**KM# 71 500 KORUN**
33.63 g., 0.925 Silver 1.0001 oz. ASW, 31.5 x 59.4 mm. **Series:** Banknotes **Obv:** Head facing and value **Rev:** Bratislava Castle view and value **Edge:** Plain

| Date | Mintage | VF20 | XF40 | MS60 | MS63 | MS65 |
|---|---|---|---|---|---|---|
| 2003 | 6,000 | PF65 100 | | | | |

**KM# 85 500 KORUN**
33.63 g., 0.925 Silver 1.0001 oz. ASW, 40 mm. **Subject:** Slovensky Kras National Park **Obv:** 2 Rock buntings above value **Rev:** Dogs Tooth violet flowers in front of Karst cave interior view **Edge Lettering:** OCHRANA PRIRODY A KRAJINY

| Date | Mintage | VF20 | XF40 | MS60 | MS63 | MS65 |
|---|---|---|---|---|---|---|
| 2005 | 8,500 | — | — | — | — | 55.00 |
| 2005 | 3,600 | PF65 90.00 | | | | |

**KM# 84 500 KORUN**
33.63 g., 0.925 Silver 1.0001 oz. ASW, 40 mm. **Subject:** Muranska Planina National Park **Obv:** Wildflowers and Muran castle ruins **Rev:** Two wild horses **Edge Lettering:** OCHRANA PRIRODY A KRAJINY [flower]

| Date | Mintage | VF20 | XF40 | MS60 | MS63 | MS65 |
|---|---|---|---|---|---|---|
| 2006 | 2,800 | PF65 200 | | | | |
| 2006 | 4,300 | — | — | — | — | 95.00 |

**KM# 86 500 KORUN**
33.63 g., 0.925 Silver 1.0001 oz. ASW, 40 mm. **Subject:** 450th Anniversary - Construction Fortress at Komárno **Obv:** Early ships, fortress in background, national arms at lower right **Obv. Legend:** SLOVENSKÁ REPUBLIKA **Rev:** Layout of fortress, horses in battle against Turks below **Rev. Legend:** PEVNOST - KOMÁRNO **Edge Lettering:** NEC ARTE NEC MARTE - COMORRA in relief

| Date | Mintage | VF20 | XF40 | MS60 | MS63 | MS65 |
|---|---|---|---|---|---|---|
| 2007 | 4,600 | — | — | — | — | 80.00 |
| 2007 | 2,600 | PF65 250 | | | | |

**KM# 106 500 KORUN**
33.63 g., 0.925 Silver 1.0001 oz. ASW, 40 mm. **Subject:** National Park - Low Tatra Mountains **Obv:** Mountains, flower and shield **Rev:** Bear in pine tree

| Date | Mintage | VF20 | XF40 | MS60 | MS63 | MS65 |
|---|---|---|---|---|---|---|
| 2008 | 4,300 | — | — | — | — | 75.00 |
| 2008 | 4,800 | PF65 150 | | | | |

**KM# 63 1000 KORUN**
62.21 g., 0.999 Silver 1.998 oz. ASW, 43.6 x 43.6 mm. **Subject:** 10th Anniversary of Republic **Obv:** National arms between hands **Rev:** Value above map **Edge:** Segmented reeding **Shape:** Square

| Date | Mintage | VF20 | XF40 | MS60 | MS63 | MS65 |
|---|---|---|---|---|---|---|
| 2003 | 10,000 | PF65 150 | | | | |

**KM# 72 1000 KORUN**
43.91 g., 0.925 Bi-Metallic 1.3059 oz. .925 Silver 43.91g planchet with .999 Gold .28g insert, 32.6 x 61.6 mm. **Series:** Banknotes **Obv:** Head facing and value **Rev:** The Madonna Protector facing and church of Liptovske Sliace **Edge:** Plain **Note:** Illustration reduced.

| Date | Mintage | VF20 | XF40 | MS60 | MS63 | MS65 |
|---|---|---|---|---|---|---|
| 2003 | 6,000 | PF65 175 | | | | |

**KM# 58 5000 KORUN**
Tri-Metallic 31.1035, .999 Silver, 1.00 oz ASW with 6.22, .999 Gold, .20 oz AGW and .31, .999 Platinum, .10 oz. APW, 50 mm. **Series:** Third Millennium **Obv:** The Universe **Rev:** Three hands **Edge:** Plain **Shape:** Triangular

| Date | Mintage | VF20 | XF40 | MS60 | MS63 | MS65 |
|---|---|---|---|---|---|---|
| 2001 | 8,000 | PF65 500 | | | | |

**KM# 61 5000 KORUN**
9.50 g., 0.900 Gold 0.2749 oz. AGW, 26 mm. **Subject:** Vlkolinec village - UNESCO historic site **Obv:** Enclosed communal well **Rev:** Window and fence **Edge:** Reeded

| Date | Mintage | VF20 | XF40 | MS60 | MS63 | MS65 |
|---|---|---|---|---|---|---|
| 2002 | — | PF65 575 | | | | |

**KM# 73 5000 KORUN**
47.63 g., 0.925 Bi-Metallic 1.4166 oz. .925 Silver 46.65g planchet with two .9999 Gold inserts .964g in total, 33.4 x 63.8 mm. **Series:** Banknotes **Obv:** Head facing and value **Rev:** Stefanik's grave monument **Edge:** Plain **Note:** Illustration reduced.

| Date | Mintage | VF20 | XF40 | MS60 | MS63 | MS65 |
|---|---|---|---|---|---|---|
| 2003 | 6,000 | PF65 275 | | | | |

**KM# 80 5000 KORUN**
9.50 g., 0.900 Gold 0.2749 oz. AGW, 26 mm. **Subject:** Bardejov - UNESCO historic site **Obv:** National arms and value left of Town Hall **Rev:** Zachariah in window frame left of St. Aegidius Church, Bardejov **Edge:** Reeded

| Date | Mintage | VF20 | XF40 | MS60 | MS63 | MS65 |
|---|---|---|---|---|---|---|
| 2004 | 9,000 | PF65 575 | | | | |

**KM# 83 5000 KORUN**
9.50 g., 0.900 Gold 0.2749 oz. AGW, 26 mm. **Subject:** Leopold I Coronation **Obv:** Mounted Herald with Bratislava Castile in background **Rev:** Leopold I and Crown of St. Stephan **Edge:** Reeded

| Date | Mintage | VF20 | XF40 | MS60 | MS63 | MS65 |
|---|---|---|---|---|---|---|
| 2005 | 7,500 | PF65 575 | | | | |

**KM# 89 5000 KORUN**
9.50 g., 0.900 Gold 0.2749 oz. AGW, 26 mm. **Subject:** 400th Anniversary Coronation of King Matthias II **Obv:** Cathedral and Bratislava castle **Obv. Legend:** SLOVENSKÁ - REPUBLIKA **Rev:** 1/2 length figure of Matthias II left, crown in lower foreground, towers of the St. Michael's Gate and franciscan Church in Bratislava in background **Rev. Legend:** KORUNOVÁCIA MATEJA II. / BRATISLAVA **Edge:** Reeded

| Date | Mintage | VF20 | XF40 | MS60 | MS63 | MS65 |
|---|---|---|---|---|---|---|
| 2008 | 4,050 | PF65 575 | | | | |

## KM# 64 10000 KORUN

18.84 g., Bi-Metallic 1.555g, .999 Palladium round center in a 15.55g, .900 Gold square, 29.5 x 29.5 mm. **Subject:** 10th Anniversary of the Republic **Obv:** Young head left within circular inscription above double cross within shield **Rev:** Bratislava castle above value **Edge:** Segmented reeding **Shape:** Square

| Date | Mintage | VF20 | XF40 | MS60 | MS63 | MS65 |
|---|---|---|---|---|---|---|
| 2003 | 6,000 | PF65 1,250 | | | | |

## KM# 79 10000 KORUN

24.88 g., Bi-Metallic .999 Gold 12.4414g 23mm round center in .999 Palladium 12.4414g pentagon, 40 mm. **Subject:** Slovakian entry into the European Union **Obv:** National arms above date in center **Rev:** European map with entry date **Edge:** Plain

| Date | Mintage | VF20 | XF40 | MS60 | MS63 | MS65 |
|---|---|---|---|---|---|---|
| 2004 | 7,200 | PF65 1,200 | | | | |

# EURO COINAGE

European Union Issues

## KM# 95 EURO CENT

2.30 g., Copper Plated Steel, 16.25 mm. **Obv:** Krivan Peak in the Tatras, state emblem **Rev:** Denomination and globe

| Date | Mintage | VF20 | XF40 | MS60 | MS63 | MS65 |
|---|---|---|---|---|---|---|
| 2009 | 90,828,000 | — | — | 0.25 | 0.35 | 0.50 |
| 2009 | 13,300 | PF65 15.00 | | | | |
| 2010 | 30,070,000 | — | — | 0.25 | 0.35 | 0.50 |
| 2010 Prooflike | 5,000 | — | — | — | — | 3.00 |
| 2010 | 5,000 | PF65 8.00 | | | | |
| 2011 | 20,455,000 | — | — | 0.25 | 0.35 | 0.50 |
| 2011 Prooflike | 5,000 | — | — | — | — | 3.00 |
| 2011 | 1,000 | PF65 6.00 | | | | |
| 2012 | 10,545,000 | — | — | 0.25 | 0.35 | 0.50 |
| 2012 Prooflike | 5,000 | — | — | — | — | 3.00 |
| 2012 | 1,000 | PF65 6.00 | | | | |
| 2013 | 25,028,000 | — | — | 0.25 | 0.35 | 0.50 |
| 2013 Prooflike | 3,500 | — | — | — | — | 3.00 |
| 2013 | 1,500 | PF65 6.00 | | | | |
| 2014 Prooflike | — | — | — | — | — | 3.00 |
| 2014 | 3,500 | PF65 6.00 | | | | |

## KM# 96 2 EURO CENT

3.06 g., Copper Plated Steel, 18.75 mm. **Obv:** Krivan Peak in the Tatras, state emblem **Rev:** Denomination and globe **Edge:** Grooved

| Date | Mintage | VF20 | XF40 | MS60 | MS63 | MS65 |
|---|---|---|---|---|---|---|
| 2009 | 80,905,000 | — | — | 0.30 | 0.50 | 0.65 |
| 2009 | 13,300 | PF65 15.00 | | | | |
| 2010 | 50,070,000 | — | — | 0.30 | 0.50 | 0.65 |
| 2010 Prooflike | 5,000 | — | — | — | — | 3.00 |
| 2010 | 5,000 | PF65 8.00 | | | | |
| 2011 | 15,055,000 | — | — | 0.30 | 0.50 | 0.65 |
| 2011 Prooflike | 5,000 | — | — | — | — | 3.00 |
| 2011 | 1,000 | PF65 6.00 | | | | |
| 2012 Sets only | 45,000 | — | — | — | — | 0.75 |
| 2012 Prooflike | 5,000 | — | — | — | — | 3.00 |
| 2012 | 1,000 | PF65 6.00 | | | | |
| 2013 Sets only | 28,000 | — | — | — | — | 0.75 |
| 2013 Prooflike | 3,500 | — | — | — | — | 3.00 |
| 2013 | 1,500 | PF65 6.00 | | | | |
| 2014 Prooflike | — | — | — | — | — | 3.00 |
| 2014 | 3,500 | PF65 6.00 | | | | |

## KM# 97 5 EURO CENT

3.92 g., Copper Plated Steel, 21.25 mm. **Obv:** Krivan Peak in the Tatras - state emblem **Rev:** Denomination and globe

| Date | Mintage | VF20 | XF40 | MS60 | MS63 | MS65 |
|---|---|---|---|---|---|---|
| 2009 | 84,957,000 | — | — | 0.50 | 0.75 | 1.00 |
| 2009 | 13,300 | PF65 15.00 | | | | |
| 2010 Sets only | 70,000 | — | — | — | — | 1.25 |
| 2010 Prooflike | 5,000 | — | — | — | — | 3.00 |
| 2010 | 5,000 | PF65 8.00 | | | | |
| 2011 Sets only | 55,000 | — | — | — | — | 1.25 |
| 2011 Prooflike | 5,000 | — | — | — | — | 3.00 |
| 2011 | 1,000 | PF65 6.00 | | | | |
| 2012 Sets only | 45,000 | — | — | — | — | 1.25 |
| 2012 Prooflike | 5,000 | — | — | — | — | 3.00 |
| 2012 | 1,000 | PF65 6.00 | | | | |
| 2013 Sets only | 28,000 | — | — | — | — | 1.25 |
| 2013 Prooflike | 3,500 | — | — | — | — | 3.00 |
| 2013 | 1,500 | PF65 6.00 | | | | |
| 2014 Prooflike | — | — | — | — | — | 3.00 |
| 2014 | 3,500 | PF65 6.00 | | | | |

## KM# 98 10 EURO CENT

4.10 g., Brass, 19.75 mm. **Obv:** Bratislava Castle and state emblem **Rev:** Expanded relief map of European Union at left, denomination at right **Edge:** Reeded

| Date | Mintage | VF20 | XF40 | MS60 | MS63 | MS65 |
|---|---|---|---|---|---|---|
| 2009 | 74,800,000 | — | — | 0.50 | 0.75 | 1.00 |
| 2009 | 13,300 | PF65 15.00 | | | | |
| 2010 Sets only | 70,000 | — | — | — | — | 1.25 |
| 2010 Prooflike | 5,000 | — | — | — | — | 3.00 |
| 2010 | 5,000 | PF65 8.00 | | | | |
| 2011 Sets only | 55,000 | — | — | — | — | 1.25 |
| 2011 Prooflike | 5,000 | — | — | — | — | 3.00 |
| 2011 | 1,000 | PF65 6.00 | | | | |
| 2012 Sets only | 45,000 | — | — | — | — | 1.25 |
| 2012 Prooflike | 5,000 | — | — | — | — | 3.00 |
| 2012 | 1,000 | PF65 6.00 | | | | |
| 2013 Sets only | 45,000 | — | — | — | — | 1.25 |
| 2013 Prooflike | 3,500 | — | — | — | — | 3.00 |
| 2013 | 1,500 | PF65 6.00 | | | | |
| 2014 Prooflike | — | — | — | — | — | 3.00 |
| 2014 | 3,500 | PF65 6.00 | | | | |

## KM# 99 20 EURO CENT

5.74 g., Brass, 22.25 mm. **Obv:** Bratislava Castle and state emblem **Rev:** Expanded relief map of European Union at left, denomination at right **Edge:** Notched

| Date | Mintage | VF20 | XF40 | MS60 | MS63 | MS65 |
|---|---|---|---|---|---|---|
| 2009 | 66,602,000 | — | — | 0.75 | 1.00 | 1.25 |
| 2009 | 13,300 | PF65 16.00 | | | | |
| 2010 Sets only | 70,000 | — | — | — | — | 1.50 |
| 2010 Prooflike | 5,000 | — | — | — | — | 3.50 |
| 2010 | 5,000 | PF65 10.00 | | | | |
| 2011 Sets only | 55,000 | — | — | — | — | 1.50 |
| 2011 Prooflike | 5,000 | — | — | — | — | 3.50 |
| 2011 | 1,000 | PF65 7.00 | | | | |
| 2012 Sets only | 45,000 | — | — | — | — | 1.50 |
| 2012 Prooflike | 5,000 | — | — | — | — | 3.50 |
| 2012 | 1,000 | PF65 7.00 | | | | |
| 2013 Sets only | 28,000 | — | — | — | — | 1.50 |
| 2013 Prooflike | 3,500 | — | — | — | — | 3.50 |
| 2013 | 1,500 | PF65 7.00 | | | | |
| 2014 Prooflike | — | — | — | — | — | 3.50 |
| 2014 | 3,500 | PF65 7.00 | | | | |

## KM# 100 50 EURO CENT

7.80 g., Brass, 24.25 mm. **Obv:** Bratislava Castle and state shield **Rev:** Expanded relief map of European Union at left, denomination at right **Edge:** Reeded

| Date | Mintage | VF20 | XF40 | MS60 | MS63 | MS65 |
|---|---|---|---|---|---|---|
| 2009 | 59,400,000 | — | — | 1.00 | 1.25 | 1.50 |
| 2009 | 13,300 | PF65 16.00 | | | | |
| 2010 Sets only | 70,000 | — | — | — | — | 1.75 |
| 2010 Prooflike | 5,000 | — | — | — | — | 3.50 |
| 2010 | 5,000 | PF65 10.00 | | | | |
| 2011 Sets only | 55,000 | — | — | — | — | 1.75 |
| 2011 Prooflike | 5,000 | — | — | — | — | 3.50 |
| 2011 | 1,000 | PF65 7.00 | | | | |
| 2012 Sets only | 45,000 | — | — | — | — | 1.75 |
| 2012 Prooflike | 5,000 | — | — | — | — | 3.50 |
| 2012 | 1,000 | PF65 7.00 | | | | |
| 2013 Sets only | 28,000 | — | — | — | — | 1.75 |
| 2013 Prooflike | 3,500 | — | — | — | — | 3.50 |
| 2013 | 1,500 | PF65 7.00 | | | | |
| 2014 Prooflike | — | — | — | — | — | 3.50 |
| 2014 | 3,500 | PF65 7.00 | | | | |

## KM# 101 EURO

7.50 g., Bi-Metallic Copper-Nickel center in Nickel-Brass ring, 23.25 mm. **Obv:** Double cross in middle of three hills **Rev:** Value at left, expanded relief map of European Union at right **Edge:** Segmented reeding

| Date | Mintage | VF20 | XF40 | MS60 | MS63 | MS65 |
|---|---|---|---|---|---|---|
| 2009 | 46,777,000 | — | — | 2.25 | 2.50 | 2.75 |
| 2009 | 13,300 | PF65 20.00 | | | | |
| 2010 Sets only | 70,000 | — | — | — | — | 3.00 |
| 2010 Prooflike | 5,000 | — | — | — | — | 6.00 |
| 2010 | 5,000 | PF65 15.00 | | | | |
| 2011 Sets only | 55,000 | — | — | — | — | 3.00 |
| 2011 Prooflike | 5,000 | — | — | — | — | 6.00 |
| 2011 | 1,000 | PF65 12.00 | | | | |
| 2012 Sets only | 45,000 | — | — | — | — | 3.00 |
| 2012 Prooflike | 5,000 | — | — | — | — | 6.00 |
| 2012 | 1,000 | PF65 12.00 | | | | |
| 2013 Sets only | 28,000 | — | — | — | — | 3.00 |
| 2013 Prooflike | 3,500 | — | — | — | — | 6.00 |
| 2013 | 1,500 | PF65 12.00 | | | | |
| 2014 Prooflike | — | — | — | — | — | 6.00 |
| 2014 | 3,500 | PF65 12.00 | | | | |

## KM# 102 2 EURO

8.50 g., Bi-Metallic Nickel-Brass center in Copper-Nickel ring, 25.75 mm. **Obv:** Double cross on middle of three hills **Rev:** Value at left, expanded map of European Union at left

| Date | Mintage | VF20 | XF40 | MS60 | MS63 | MS65 |
|---|---|---|---|---|---|---|
| 2009 | 39,250,000 | — | — | 4.00 | 5.00 | 6.00 |
| 2009 | 13,300 | PF65 25.00 | | | | |
| 2010 Sets only | 70,000 | — | — | — | — | 6.50 |
| 2010 Prooflike | 5,000 | — | — | — | — | 7.50 |
| 2010 | 5,000 | PF65 20.00 | | | | |
| 2011 | 5,049,000 | — | — | 4.00 | 5.00 | 6.00 |
| 2011 Prooflike | 5,000 | — | — | — | — | 7.50 |
| 2011 | 1,000 | PF65 15.00 | | | | |
| 2012 Sets only | 45,000 | — | — | — | — | 6.50 |
| 2012 Prooflike | 5,000 | — | — | — | — | 7.50 |
| 2012 | 1,000 | PF65 15.00 | | | | |
| 2013 Sets only | 28,000 | — | — | — | — | 6.50 |
| 2013 Prooflike | 3,500 | — | — | — | — | 7.50 |
| 2013 | 1,500 | PF65 15.00 | | | | |
| 2014 Prooflike | — | — | — | — | — | 7.50 |
| 2014 | 3,500 | PF65 15.00 | | | | |

**KM# 103 2 EURO**
8.50 g., Bi-Metallic Nickel-Brass center in Copper-Nickel ring, 25.75 mm. **Subject:** EMU 10th Anniversary **Obv:** Stick figure and large E symbol **Rev:** Expanded relief map of European Union at left, denomination at right

| Date | Mintage | VF20 | XF40 | MS60 | MS63 | MS65 |
|---|---|---|---|---|---|---|
| 2009 Special Unc. | 7,000 | — | — | — | — | 20.00 |
| 2009 | 2,493,000 | — | — | — | 6.00 | 7.50 |

**KM# 107 2 EURO**
8.50 g., Bi-Metallic Nickel-Brass center in Copper-Nickel ring, 25.75 mm. **Subject:** Freedom, 17 November 1989, 20th Anniversary **Obv:** Ringing Freedom bell

| Date | Mintage | VF20 | XF40 | MS60 | MS63 | MS65 |
|---|---|---|---|---|---|---|
| 2009 Special Unc. | 7,000 | — | — | — | — | 20.00 |
| 2009 | 1,000,000 | — | — | — | 6.00 | 7.50 |
| 2009 Prooflike | 1,000 | — | — | — | — | 175 |

**KM# 114 2 EURO**
8.50 g., Bi-Metallic Nickel-Brass center in Copper-Nickel ring, 25.75 mm. **Subject:** Visegrad Group, 20th Anniversary

| Date | Mintage | VF20 | XF40 | MS60 | MS63 | MS65 |
|---|---|---|---|---|---|---|
| 2011 Special Unc. | 7,000 | — | — | — | — | 20.00 |
| 2011 | 981,000 | — | — | — | 5.00 | 6.00 |

**KM# 120 2 EURO**
8.50 g., Bi-Metallic Nickel-Brass center in Copper-Nickel ring, 25.75 mm. **Subject:** Euro coinage, 10th Anniversary **Obv:** Euro symbol on globe at center, child-like rendering around

| Date | Mintage | VF20 | XF40 | MS60 | MS63 | MS65 |
|---|---|---|---|---|---|---|
| 2012 | 1,000,000 | — | — | — | 6.00 | 8.00 |
| 2012 Special Unc. | 7,000 | — | — | — | — | 20.00 |

**KM# 128 2 EURO**
8.50 g., Bi-Metallic Nickel-Brass center in Copper-Nickel ring, 25.75 mm. **Obv:** Saints Cyril and Methodius

| Date | Mintage | VF20 | XF40 | MS60 | MS63 | MS65 |
|---|---|---|---|---|---|---|
| 2013 | 1,000,000 | — | — | — | 6.00 | 8.00 |
| 2013 Special Unc. | 7,000 | — | — | — | — | 20.00 |
| 2013 | 10,300 | PF65 15.00 | | | | |

**KM# 134 2 EURO**
8.50 g., Bi-Metallic Nickel-Brass center in Copper-Nickel ring, 25.75 mm. **Subject:** Slovakia's entry into the European Union, 10th Anniversary

| Date | Mintage | VF20 | XF40 | MS60 | MS63 | MS65 |
|---|---|---|---|---|---|---|
| 2014 | 1,000,000 | — | — | — | 5.00 | 6.00 |
| 2014 Special Unc. | — | — | — | — | — | 20.00 |

**KM# 108 10 EURO**
18.00 g., 0.900 Silver 0.5208 oz. ASW, 34 mm. **Subject:** Aurel Stodola, 150th Anniversary of birth **Obv:** Turbo generator, national shield **Rev:** Portrait **Edge Lettering:** KONSTRUKTER - VYNALEZCA - PEDAGOG

| Date | Mintage | VF20 | XF40 | MS60 | MS63 | MS65 |
|---|---|---|---|---|---|---|
| 2009 | 10,100 | — | — | — | — | 50.00 |
| 2009 | 13,300 | PF65 65.00 | | | | |

**KM# 110 10 EURO**
18.00 g., 0.900 Silver 0.5208 oz. ASW, 34 mm. **Subject:** Wooden Churches of Carpathian Slovakia - UNESCO World Heritage site

| Date | Mintage | VF20 | XF40 | MS60 | MS63 | MS65 |
|---|---|---|---|---|---|---|
| 2010 | — | — | — | — | — | 50.00 |
| 2010 | — | PF65 65.00 | | | | |

**KM# 111 10 EURO**
18.00 g., 0.900 Silver 0.5208 oz. ASW, 34 mm. **Subject:** Martin Kukucin, 150th Anniversary of birth **Obv:** Landscape scene from Brac, "House on the hillside **Rev:** Fortrait facing, cuckoo, signature **Edge Lettering:** PROZAIK - DRAMATIK - PUBLICISTA

| Date | Mintage | VF20 | XF40 | MS60 | MS63 | MS65 |
|---|---|---|---|---|---|---|
| 2010 | 9,900 | — | — | — | — | 50.00 |
| 2010 | 17,325 | PF65 65.00 | | | | |

**KM# 115 10 EURO**
18.00 g., 0.900 Silver 0.5208 oz. ASW, 34 mm. **Subject:** Zobor Documents, 900th Anniversary **Obv:** Two scribes **Rev:** Seal and partial document text

| Date | Mintage | VF20 | XF40 | MS60 | MS63 | MS65 |
|---|---|---|---|---|---|---|
| 2011 | — | PF65 65.00 | | | | |
| 2011 | — | — | — | — | — | 50.00 |

**KM# 116 10 EURO**
18.00 g., 0.900 Silver 0.5208 oz. ASW, 34 mm. **Subject:** Adoption of the memorandum of the Slovak Nation, 150th Anniversary

| Date | Mintage | VF20 | XF40 | MS60 | MS63 | MS65 |
|---|---|---|---|---|---|---|
| 2011 | 9,100 | PF65 65.00 | | | | |
| 2011 | 9,500 | — | — | — | — | 50.00 |

**KM# 117 10 EURO**
18.00 g., 0.900 Silver 0.5208 oz. ASW, 34 mm. **Subject:** Jan Cikker, 100th Anniversary of Birth

| Date | Mintage | VF20 | XF40 | MS60 | MS63 | MS65 |
|---|---|---|---|---|---|---|
| 2011 | 8,900 | PF65 65.00 | | | | |
| 2011 | 7,900 | — | — | — | — | 50.00 |

**KM# 122 10 EURO**
18.00 g., 0.900 Silver 0.5208 oz. ASW, 34 mm. **Subject:** Master Pavol of Levoca **Obv:** Female and shield **Rev:** Bearded male

| Date | Mintage | VF20 | XF40 | MS60 | MS63 | MS65 |
|---|---|---|---|---|---|---|
| 2012 | 7,400 | — | — | — | — | 50.00 |
| 2012 | 11,870 | PF65 65.00 | | | | |

**KM# 123 10 EURO**
18.00 g., 0.900 Silver 0.5208 oz. ASW, 34 mm. **Subject:** Chatam Sofer, 250th Anniversary of Birth **Obv:** City view of Bratislava **Rev:** Chatam Sofer, torah, menorah

| Date | Mintage | VF20 | XF40 | MS60 | MS63 | MS65 |
|---|---|---|---|---|---|---|
| 2012 | 5,800 | — | — | — | — | 50.00 |
| 2012 | 7,900 | PF65 150 | | | | |

**KM# 124 10 EURO**
18.00 g., 0.900 Silver 0.5208 oz. ASW, 34 mm. **Subject:** Anton Bernolak, 250th Anniversary of Birth **Obv:** Quill pen **Rev:** Bust facing

| Date | Mintage | VF20 | XF40 | MS60 | MS63 | MS65 |
|---|---|---|---|---|---|---|
| 2012 | 5,200 | — | — | — | — | 50.00 |
| 2012 | 6,950 | PF65 65.00 | | | | |

**KM# 127 10 EURO**
Silver **Subject:** 20th Anniversary of the National Bank of Slovakia

| Date | Mintage | VF20 | XF40 | MS60 | MS63 | MS65 |
|---|---|---|---|---|---|---|
| 2013 | — | PF65 65.00 | | | | |
| 2013 | — | — | — | — | — | 50.00 |

**KM# 130 10 EURO**
18.00 g., 0.900 Silver 0.5208 oz. ASW, 34 mm. **Subject:** Jozef Karol Hell, 300th Anniversary of Birth

| Date | Mintage | VF20 | XF40 | MS60 | MS63 | MS65 |
|---|---|---|---|---|---|---|
| 2013 | 3,100 | — | — | — | — | 50.00 |
| 2013 | 5,750 | PF65 65.00 | | | | |

**KM# 131 10 EURO**
18.00 g., 0.900 Silver 0.5208 oz. ASW, 34 mm. **Subject:** Matica slovenska Cultural Association, 150th Anniversary

| Date | Mintage | VF20 | XF40 | MS60 | MS63 | MS65 |
|---|---|---|---|---|---|---|
| 2013 | — | — | — | — | — | 50.00 |
| 2013 | — | PF65 65.00 | | | | |

**KM# 133 10 EURO**
18.00 g., 0.900 Silver 0.5208 oz. ASW, 34 mm. **Subject:** Jozef Murgaš, 150th Anniversary of Birth

| Date | Mintage | VF20 | XF40 | MS60 | MS63 | MS65 |
|---|---|---|---|---|---|---|
| 2014 | 3,400 | — | — | — | — | 50.00 |
| 2014 | 6,300 | PF65 65.00 | | | | |

**KM# 109 20 EURO**
33.63 g., 0.925 Silver 1.0001 oz. ASW, 40 mm. **Subject:** National Park - Vel'ká Fatra **Obv:** Fora and national shield **Rev:** Falcon in flight over mountain peak **Edge Lettering:** OCHRANA PRÍRODY A KRAJINY

| Date | Mintage | VF20 | XF40 | MS60 | MS63 | MS65 |
|---|---|---|---|---|---|---|
| 2009 | 9,900 | — | — | — | — | 55.00 |
| 2009 | 12,600 | PF65 65.00 | | | | |

**KM# 112 20 EURO**
33.63 g., 0.925 Silver 1.0001 oz. ASW, 40 mm. **Subject:** Poloniny National Park **Obv:** Mountainside and flowers **Rev:** Two wolves

| Date | Mintage | VF20 | XF40 | MS60 | MS63 | MS65 |
|---|---|---|---|---|---|---|
| 2010 | — | — | — | — | — | 55.00 |
| 2010 | — | PF65 75.00 | | | | |

**KM# 118 20 EURO**
33.63 g., 0.925 Silver 1.0001 oz. ASW, 40 mm. **Subject:** Historical Sites - Trnava

| Date | Mintage | VF20 | XF40 | MS60 | MS63 | MS65 |
|---|---|---|---|---|---|---|
| 2011 | 9,950 | PF65 75.00 | | | | |
| 2011 | 8,150 | — | — | — | — | 60.00 |

**KM# 121 20 EURO**
33.63 g., 0.925 Silver 1.0001 oz. ASW, 40 mm. **Subject:** Historical towns - Trencin **Obv:** Castle, historical Roman inscription and National arms below **Rev:** Rendering of the Trencin historical preservation area

| Date | Mintage | VF20 | XF40 | MS60 | MS63 | MS65 |
|---|---|---|---|---|---|---|
| 2012 | 7,500 | PF65 80.00 | | | | |
| 2012 | 5,900 | — | — | — | — | 65.00 |

**KM# 129 20 EURO**
33.63 g., 0.925 Silver 1.0001 oz. ASW, 40 mm. **Rev:** Montage of Kosice historic sights

| Date | Mintage | VF20 | XF40 | MS60 | MS63 | MS65 |
|---|---|---|---|---|---|---|
| 2013 | — | — | — | — | — | 85.00 |

**KM# 135 20 EURO**
33.63 g., 0.925 Silver 1.0001 oz. ASW, 40 mm. **Subject:** Dubnik Opal Mines **Obv:** Jewelry pendant and bat **Rev:** Bat, mine entrance and mine interior

| Date | Mintage | VF20 | XF40 | MS60 | MS63 | MS65 |
|---|---|---|---|---|---|---|
| 2014 | 2,700 | — | — | — | — | 60.00 |
| 2014 | 5,300 | PF65 80.00 | | | | |

**KM# 113 100 EURO**
9.50 g., 0.900 Gold 0.2749 oz. AGW, 26 mm. **Subject:** Wooden Churches of Carpathian Slovakia - UNESCO Heritage Site **Obv:** Church of St. Francis of Assisi in Hervartov, belfry of the church in Hronsek and Church of St. Nicholas in Brodrzal **Rev:** Baroque altar of All Saints Church in Tvrdosin **Edge:** Reeded

| Date | Mintage | VF20 | XF40 | MS60 | MS63 | MS65 |
|---|---|---|---|---|---|---|
| 2010 | Est. 7000 | PF65 575 | | | | |

**KM# 119 100 EURO**
9.50 g., 0.900 Gold 0.2749 oz. AGW, 26 mm. **Subject:** Prince Pribina Nitra, 1150th Anniversary of Death

| Date | Mintage | VF20 | XF40 | MS60 | MS63 | MS65 |
|---|---|---|---|---|---|---|
| 2011 | 6,800 | PF65 575 | | | | |

**KM# 125 100 EURO**
9.50 g., 0.900 Gold 0.2749 oz. AGW, 26 mm. **Subject:** Charles III, 300th Anniversary of Coronation **Obv:** City View **Rev:** Bust, crown of St. Stephen, Bratislava castle

| Date | Mintage | VF20 | XF40 | MS60 | MS63 | MS65 |
|---|---|---|---|---|---|---|
| 2012 | — | PF65 575 | | | | |

**KM# 132 100 EURO**
9.50 g., 0.900 Gold 0.2749 oz. AGW, 26 mm. **Subject:** Maximilian, 450th Anniversary of Coronation in Bratislava

| Date | Mintage | VF20 | XF40 | MS60 | MS63 | MS65 |
|---|---|---|---|---|---|---|
| 2013 | 4,300 | PF65 575 | | | | |

**KM# 136 100 EURO**
9.50 g., 0.900 Gold 0.2749 oz. AGW, 26 mm. **Subject:** Rastislav, Ruler of Great Moravia

| Date | Mintage | VF20 | XF40 | MS60 | MS63 | MS65 |
|---|---|---|---|---|---|---|
| 2014 | — | PF65 575 | | | | |

## MINT SETS

| KM# | Date | Mintage | Identification | Issue Price | Mkt Val |
|---|---|---|---|---|---|
| MS9 | 2001 (7) | — | KM#11.1-14, 17-18, 35, plus medal | — | 20.00 |
| MS10 | 2002 (7) | — | KM#11-1-14, 17-18, 35, plus medal | — | 17.50 |
| MS11 | 2003 (7) | — | KM#11.1-14, 17-18, 35, plus medal | — | 15.00 |
| MS12 | 2004 (7) | — | KM#11.1-14, 17, 18, 35 plus medal | — | 12.00 |
| MS13 | 2005 (7) | — | KM#11.1-14, 17, 18, 35 plus medal | — | 12.00 |
| MS14 | 2005 (6) | — | KM#11.1, 12-14, 35, Austrian 2005 KM#3088 | — | 10.00 |
| MS15 | 2006 (7) | — | KM#11.1-14, 17, 18, 35 plus medal | — | 12.00 |
| MS16 | 2007 (7) | — | KM#11.1-14, 17, 18, 35 plus medal | — | 12.00 |
| MS17 | 2007 (5) | — | KM11.2, 12-14, 35. National parks | — | 15.00 |
| MS18 | 2007 (5) | — | KM#11.1, 12-14, 35 | — | 12.00 |
| MS19 | 2007 (5) | — | KM#11.1, 12-14, 35. National parks packaging | — | 15.00 |
| MS20 | 2007 (5) | — | KM#11.1, 12-14, 35 and a bimetallic medal and cd. Set to commemorate musician Gejza Dusik | — | 20.00 |
| MS21 | 2009 (8) | 87,100 | KM#95-102. | — | 25.00 |
| MS22 | 2010 (8) | 45,000 | kM#95-102. | — | 25.00 |
| MS23 | 2011 (8) | 25,000 | KM#95-102. | — | 25.00 |
| MS24 | 2012 (8) | 23,000 | KM#95-102. | — | 25.00 |

## PROOF SETS

| KM# | Date | Mintage | Identification | Issue Price | Mkt Val |
|---|---|---|---|---|---|
| PS2 | 2001 (7) | 12,500 | KM#11.1-14, 17-18, 35 | — | 35.00 |
| PS3 | 2002 (7) | 16,500 | KM#11.1-14, 17-18, 35 | — | 25.00 |
| PS4 | 2004 (7) | — | KM#11.1, 12-14, 35, silver strikes of 1993, KM#17-18 | — | 40.00 |
| PS5 | 2006 (6) | — | KM#11.1, 12-14, 35 plus medal. 2006 Torino Winter Olympics | — | 45.00 |
| PS6 | 2008 (6) | — | KM#11.1, 12-14, 35 plus medal. 2008 Peking Olympics | — | 45.00 |
| PS7 | 2009 (9) | 13,300 | KM#95-102 plus medal | — | 125 |
| PS8 | 2010 (9) | 5,000 | KM#95-102 plus medal | — | 80.00 |
| PS9 | 2011 (9) | 5,000 | KM#95-102 plus CN medal | — | 65.00 |
| PS10 | 2011 (9) | 1,000 | KM#95-102 plus CN medal, wood box | — | 350 |
| PS11 | 2012 (9) | 5,000 | KM#95-102 plus medal. | — | 65.00 |

The Republic of Slovenia is located northwest of Yugoslavia in the valleys of the Danube River. It has an area of 7,819 sq. mi. and a population of *1.9 million. Capital: Ljubljana. Agriculture is the main industry with large amounts of hops and fodder crops grown as well as many varieties of fruit trees. Sheep raising, timber production and the mining of mercury from one of the country's oldest mines are also very important to the economy. Slovenia joined the European Union in May 2004.

**MINT MARKS**

Based on last digit in date.
(K) - Kremnitz (Slovakia): open 4, upturned 5
(BP) - Budapest (Hungary): closed 4, down-turned 5

**MONETARY SYSTEM**

100 Stotinov = 1 Tolar
100 Euro Cents = 1 Euro

# REPUBLIC

## STANDARD COINAGE

100 Stotinow = 1 Tolar

### KM# 7 10 STOTINOV

0.55 g., Aluminum, 16 mm. **Obv:** Value within square **Rev:** Olm salamander **Edge:** Plain **Note:** Varieties exist.

| Date | Mintage | VF20 | XF40 | MS60 | MS63 | MS65 |
|---|---|---|---|---|---|---|
| 2001 Sets only | 1,000 | — | — | — | — | 3.00 |
| 2001 | 800 | PF65 5.00 | | | | |
| 2002 Sets only | 1,000 | — | — | — | — | 3.00 |
| 2002 | 800 | PF65 5.00 | | | | |
| 2003 Sets only | 1,000 | — | — | — | — | 3.00 |
| 2003 | 800 | PF65 5.00 | | | | |
| 2004 Sets only | 1,000 | — | — | — | — | 3.00 |
| 2004 | 800 | PF65 5.00 | | | | |
| 2005 Sets only | 3,000 | — | — | — | — | 2.00 |
| 2005 | 1,000 | PF65 5.00 | | | | |
| 2006 Sets only | 4,000 | — | — | — | — | 2.00 |
| 2006 | 1,000 | PF65 5.00 | | | | |

### KM# 8 20 STOTINOV

0.70 g., Aluminum, 18 mm. **Obv:** Value within square **Rev:** Barn owl and value **Edge:** Plain

| Date | Mintage | VF20 | XF40 | MS60 | MS63 | MS65 |
|---|---|---|---|---|---|---|
| 2001 Sets only | 1,000 | — | — | — | — | 4.00 |
| 2001 | 800 | PF65 6.00 | | | | |
| 2002 Sets only | 1,000 | — | — | — | — | 4.00 |
| 2002 | 800 | PF65 6.00 | | | | |
| 2003 Sets only | 1,000 | — | — | — | — | 4.00 |
| 2003 | 800 | PF65 6.00 | | | | |
| 2004 Sets only | 1,000 | — | — | — | — | 4.00 |
| 2004 | 500 | PF65 6.00 | | | | |
| 2005 Sets only | 3,000 | — | — | — | — | 3.00 |
| 2005 | 1,000 | PF65 6.00 | | | | |
| 2006 Sets only | 4,000 | — | — | — | — | 3.00 |
| 2006 | 1,000 | PF65 6.00 | | | | |

### KM# 3 50 STOTINOV

0.85 g., Aluminum, 20 mm. **Obv:** Value within square **Rev:** Bee and value **Edge:** Plain

| Date | Mintage | VF20 | XF40 | MS60 | MS63 | MS65 |
|---|---|---|---|---|---|---|
| 2001 Sets only | 1,000 | — | — | — | — | 6.00 |
| 2001 | 800 | PF65 7.50 | | | | |
| 2002 Sets only | 1,000 | — | — | — | — | 6.00 |
| 2002 | 800 | PF65 7.50 | | | | |
| 2003 Sets only | 1,000 | — | — | — | — | 6.00 |
| 2003 | 800 | PF65 7.50 | | | | |
| 2004 Sets only | 1,000 | — | — | — | — | 6.00 |
| 2004 | 500 | PF65 12.00 | | | | |
| 2005 Sets only | 3,000 | — | — | — | — | 4.00 |
| 2005 | 1,000 | PF65 7.00 | | | | |
| 2006 Sets only | 4,000 | — | — | — | — | 4.00 |
| 2006 | 1,000 | PF65 7.00 | | | | |

### KM# 4 TOLAR

4.50 g., Nickel-Brass, 22 mm. **Obv:** Value within circle **Rev:** Three brown trout **Rev. Legend:** SALMO TRUTTA FARIO **Edge:** Reeded **Note:** Date varieties exist: 1994 = closed or open "4"; 1995 = serif up and serif down in "5".

| Date | Mintage | VF20 | XF40 | MS60 | MS63 | MS65 |
|---|---|---|---|---|---|---|
| 2001 | 10,001,000 | — | — | 0.50 | 0.75 | 1.25 |
| 2001 | 800 | PF65 7.50 | | | | |
| 2002 Sets only | 1,000 | — | — | — | — | 5.00 |
| 2002 | 800 | PF65 7.50 | | | | |
| 2003 Sets only | 1,000 | — | — | — | — | 5.00 |
| 2003 | 800 | PF65 7.50 | | | | |
| 2004 | 10,001,000 | — | — | 0.50 | 0.75 | 1.25 |
| 2004 (K) Sets only | 1,000 | — | — | — | — | 5.00 |
| Note: 4 open to right | | | | | | |
| 2004 | 500 | PF65 8.50 | | | | |
| 2005 Sets only | 3,000 | — | — | — | — | 4.00 |
| 2005 | 1,000 | PF65 7.50 | | | | |
| 2006 Sets only | 4,000 | — | — | — | — | 4.00 |
| 2006 | 1,000 | PF65 7.50 | | | | |

### KM# 5 2 TOLARJA

5.40 g., Nickel-Brass, 24 mm. **Obv:** Value within circle **Rev:** Barn swallow in flight **Rev. Legend:** HIRUNDO RUSTICA **Edge:** Reeded **Note:** Date varieties exist: 1994 = closed or open "4"; 1995 = serif up and serif down in "5".

| Date | Mintage | VF20 | XF40 | MS60 | MS63 | MS65 |
|---|---|---|---|---|---|---|
| 2001 | 10,001,000 | — | — | 0.45 | 0.75 | 1.75 |
| 2001 | 800 | PF65 8.50 | | | | |
| 2002 Sets only | 1,000 | — | — | — | — | 7.00 |
| 2002 | 800 | PF65 8.50 | | | | |
| 2003 Sets only | 1,000 | — | — | — | — | 7.00 |
| 2003 | 800 | PF65 8.50 | | | | |
| 2004 | 10,001,000 | — | — | 0.45 | 0.75 | 1.50 |
| 2004 | 500 | PF65 8.50 | | | | |
| 2005 Sets only | 3,000 | — | — | — | — | 7.00 |
| 2005 | 1,000 | PF65 8.50 | | | | |
| 2006 Sets only | 4,000 | — | — | — | — | 7.00 |
| 2006 | 1,000 | PF65 8.50 | | | | |

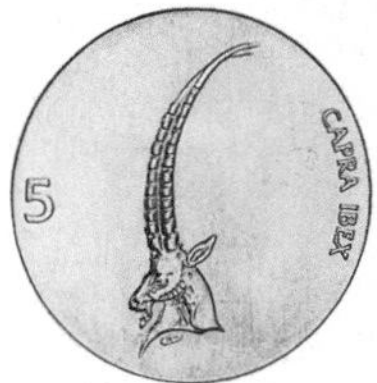


### KM# 6 5 TOLARJEV

6.44 g., Nickel-Brass, 26 mm. **Obv:** Value within circle **Rev:** Head and horns of ibex **Edge:** Reeded **Note:** Date varieties exist: 1994 = closed or open "4"; 1995 = serif up and serif down in "5".

| Date | Mintage | VF20 | XF40 | MS60 | MS63 | MS65 |
|---|---|---|---|---|---|---|
| 2001 Sets only | 1,000 | — | — | — | — | 8.00 |
| 2001 | 800 | PF65 10.00 | | | | |
| 2002 Sets only | 1,000 | — | — | — | — | 8.00 |
| 2002 | 800 | PF65 10.00 | | | | |
| 2003 Sets only | 1,000 | — | — | — | — | 8.00 |
| 2003 | 800 | PF65 10.00 | | | | |
| 2004 Sets only | 1,000 | — | — | — | — | 8.00 |
| 2004 | 500 | PF65 15.00 | | | | |
| 2005 Sets only | 3,000 | — | — | — | — | 7.00 |
| 2005 | 1,000 | PF65 10.00 | | | | |
| 2006 Sets only | 4,000 | — | — | — | — | 7.00 |
| 2006 | 1,000 | PF65 10.00 | | | | |

### KM# 41 10 TOLARJEV

5.75 g., Copper-Nickel, 24 mm. **Obv:** Value within circle **Rev:** Stylized rearing horse **Rev. Legend:** EQUUS **Edge:** Reeded

| Date | Mintage | VF20 | XF40 | MS60 | MS63 | MS65 |
|---|---|---|---|---|---|---|
| 2001 | 29,441,000 | — | — | 1.50 | 2.00 | 3.50 |
| 2001 | 800 | PF65 12.00 | | | | |
| 2002 | 10,037,000 | — | — | 1.50 | 2.00 | 3.50 |
| 2002 | 800 | PF65 12.00 | | | | |
| 2003 Sets only | 1,000 | — | — | — | — | 5.00 |
| 2003 | 800 | PF65 12.00 | | | | |
| 2004 | 10,001,000 | — | — | 1.50 | 2.00 | 3.50 |
| 2004 | 500 | PF65 12.00 | | | | |
| 2005 | 6,003,000 | — | — | 1.50 | 2.00 | 3.50 |
| 2005 | 1,000 | PF65 12.00 | | | | |
| 2006 | 6,001,000 | — | — | 1.50 | 2.00 | 3.50 |
| 2006 | 1,000 | PF65 12.00 | | | | |

### KM# 51 20 TOLARJEV

6.85 g., Copper-Nickel, 24 mm. **Obv:** Value within circle **Rev:** White Stork **Rev. Legend:** CICONIA CICONIA **Edge:** Reeded

| Date | Mintage | VF20 | XF40 | MS60 | MS63 | MS65 |
|---|---|---|---|---|---|---|
| 2003 | 10,001,000 | — | — | 2.50 | 3.50 | 5.00 |
| 2003 | 800 | PF65 15.00 | | | | |
| 2004 | 10,001,000 | — | — | 2.00 | 3.00 | 5.00 |
| 2004 | 500 | PF65 15.00 | | | | |
| 2005 | 12,003,000 | — | — | 2.50 | 3.50 | 5.00 |
| 2005 | 1,000 | PF65 15.00 | | | | |

| Date | Mintage | VF20 | XF40 | MS60 | MS63 | MS65 |
|---|---|---|---|---|---|---|
| 2006 | 4,004,000 | — | — | 2.50 | 3.50 | 5.00 |
| 2006 | 1,000 | PF65 15.00 | | | | |

**KM# 52 50 TOLARJEV**
8.00 g., Copper-Nickel, 26 mm. **Obv:** Value within circle **Rev:** Stylized bull **Rev. Legend:** TAURUS TAURUS **Edge:** Segmented reeding

| Date | Mintage | VF20 | XF40 | MS60 | MS63 | MS65 |
|---|---|---|---|---|---|---|
| 2003 | 10,001,000 | — | — | 1.75 | 2.50 | 4.50 |
| 2003 | 800 | PF65 12.00 | | | | |
| 2004 | 5,001,000 | — | — | 1.75 | 2.50 | 4.50 |
| 2004 | 500 | PF65 15.00 | | | | |
| 2005 | 8,003,000 | — | — | 1.75 | 2.50 | 4.50 |
| 2005 | 1,000 | PF65 12.00 | | | | |
| 2006 Sets only | 4,000 | — | — | — | — | 6.50 |
| 2006 | 1,000 | PF65 12.00 | | | | |

**KM# 42 100 TOLARJEV**
9.10 g., Copper-Nickel, 28 mm. **Subject:** 10th Anniversary of Slovenia and the Tolar **Obv:** Value **Rev:** Tree rings and inscription **Edge:** Reeded

| Date | Mintage | VF20 | XF40 | MS60 | MS63 | MS65 |
|---|---|---|---|---|---|---|
| 2001 | 500,000 | — | — | 2.00 | 3.00 | 4.00 |
| 2001 | 800 | PF65 10.00 | | | | |

**KM# 45 500 TOLARJEV**
8.54 g., Bi-Metallic Copper-Nickel center in Brass ring, 28.1 mm. **Subject:** Soccer **Obv:** Value **Rev:** Soccer player and radiant sun **Edge:** Reeded

| Date | Mintage | VF20 | XF40 | MS60 | MS63 | MS65 |
|---|---|---|---|---|---|---|
| 2002 | 500,000 | — | — | 3.50 | 5.50 | 7.50 |
| 2002 | 800 | PF65 12.50 | | | | |

**KM# 50 500 TOLARJEV**
8.72 g., Bi-Metallic Copper-Nickel center in Brass ring, 27.9 mm. **Subject:** European Year of the Disabled **Obv:** Stylized wheelchair **Rev:** Value **Edge:** Reeded

| Date | Mintage | VF20 | XF40 | MS60 | MS63 | MS65 |
|---|---|---|---|---|---|---|
| 2003 | 200,000 | — | — | 4.00 | 6.00 | 8.00 |
| 2003 | 800 | PF65 13.50 | | | | |

**KM# 57 500 TOLARJEV**
8.60 g., Bi-Metallic Copper-Nickel center in Brass ring, 28 mm. **Obv:** Value **Rev:** Profile left looking down within mathematical graph **Edge:** Reeded

| Date | Mintage | VF20 | XF40 | MS60 | MS63 | MS65 |
|---|---|---|---|---|---|---|
| 2004 | 200,000 | — | — | 4.00 | 6.00 | 8.00 |

| Date | Mintage | VF20 | XF40 | MS60 | MS63 | MS65 |
|---|---|---|---|---|---|---|
| 2004 | 500 | PF65 20.00 | | | | |

**KM# 63 500 TOLARJEV**
8.65 g., Bi-Metallic Copper-Nickel center in Brass ring, 27.9 mm. **Obv:** Perched falcon and value **Rev:** Horizontal line in center divides partial suns **Edge:** Reeded

| Date | Mintage | VF20 | XF40 | MS60 | MS63 | MS65 |
|---|---|---|---|---|---|---|
| 2005 | 103,000 | — | — | 4.00 | 6.25 | 8.50 |
| 2005 | 1,000 | PF65 12.00 | | | | |

**KM# 65 500 TOLARJEV**
8.60 g., Bi-Metallic Copper-Nickel center in Brass ring, 28 mm. **Obv:** Value **Rev:** Anton Tomaz Linhart's silhouette above life dates **Edge:** Reeded

| Date | Mintage | VF20 | XF40 | MS60 | MS63 | MS65 |
|---|---|---|---|---|---|---|
| 2006 | 104,000 | — | — | 4.00 | 6.00 | 8.00 |
| 2006 | 1,000 | PF65 12.00 | | | | |

**KM# 43 2000 TOLARJEV**
15.00 g., 0.925 Silver 0.4461 oz. ASW, 32 mm. **Subject:** 10th Anniversary of Slovenia and the Tolar **Obv:** Value **Rev:** Tree rings and inscription **Edge:** Reeded

| Date | Mintage | VF20 | XF40 | MS60 | MS63 | MS65 |
|---|---|---|---|---|---|---|
| 2001 | 3,000 | PF65 35.00 | | | | |

**KM# 46 2500 TOLARJEV**
15.00 g., 0.925 Silver 0.4461 oz. ASW, 32 mm. **Subject:** Soccer **Obv:** Value **Rev:** Soccer player and radiant sun **Edge:** Reeded

| Date | Mintage | VF20 | XF40 | MS60 | MS63 | MS65 |
|---|---|---|---|---|---|---|
| 2002 | 2,500 | PF65 35.00 | | | | |

**KM# 48 2500 TOLARJEV**
15.00 g., 0.925 Silver 0.4461 oz. ASW, 32 mm. **Subject:** 35th Chess Olympiad **Obv:** Rearing horse and reflection **Rev:** Chess pieces in starting positions and reflection **Edge:** Reeded

| Date | Mintage | VF20 | XF40 | MS60 | MS63 | MS65 |
|---|---|---|---|---|---|---|
| 2002 | 1,000 | PF65 45.00 | | | | |

**KM# 53 2500 TOLARJEV**
15.00 g., 0.925 Silver 0.4461 oz. ASW, 32 mm. **Subject:** European Year of the Disabled **Obv:** Value **Rev:** Stylized wheel chair **Edge:** Reeded

| Date | Mintage | VF20 | XF40 | MS60 | MS63 | MS65 |
|---|---|---|---|---|---|---|
| 2003 | 1,500 | PF65 42.00 | | | | |

**KM# 55 5000 TOLARJEV**
15.00 g., 0.925 Silver 0.4461 oz. ASW, 32 mm. **Subject:** 60th Anniversary of the Slovenian Assembly **Obv:** Value in partial star design **Rev:** Dates in partial star design **Edge:** Reeded

| Date | Mintage | VF20 | XF40 | MS60 | MS63 | MS65 |
|---|---|---|---|---|---|---|
| 2003 | 1,500 | PF65 42.00 | | | | |

**KM# 58 5000 TOLARJEV**
15.00 g., 0.925 Silver 0.4461 oz. ASW, 32 mm. **Obv:** Value **Rev:** Facial profile left looking down within mathematical graph **Edge:** Reeded

| Date | Mintage | VF20 | XF40 | MS60 | MS63 | MS65 |
|---|---|---|---|---|---|---|
| 2004 | 1,500 | PF65 50.00 | | | | |

**KM# 60 5000 TOLARJEV**
15.00 g., 0.925 Silver 0.4461 oz. ASW, 32 mm. **Subject:** 1000th Anniversary Town of Bled **Obv:** Value **Rev:** Castle and towers silhouette **Edge:** Reeded

| Date | Mintage | VF20 | XF40 | MS60 | MS63 | MS65 |
|---|---|---|---|---|---|---|
| 2004 | 1,500 | PF65 50.00 | | | | |

**KM# 62 5000 TOLARJEV**
15.10 g., 0.925 Silver 0.4491 oz. ASW, 32 mm. **Subject:** Slovenian Film Centennial **Obv:** Value above a director's clapboard **Rev:** Film segment **Edge:** Reeded

| Date | Mintage | VF20 | XF40 | MS60 | MS63 | MS65 |
|---|---|---|---|---|---|---|
| 2005 | — | PF65 47.50 | | | | |

**KM# 64 5000 TOLARJEV**
15.10 g., 0.925 Silver 0.4491 oz. ASW, 32 mm. **Obv:** Perched falcon above value **Rev:** Diagonal center line divides partial suns **Edge:** Reeded

| Date | Mintage | VF20 | XF40 | MS60 | MS63 | MS65 |
|---|---|---|---|---|---|---|
| 2005 | — | PF65 47.50 | | | | |

**KM# 91 5000 TOLARJEV**
15.00 g., 0.925 Silver 0.4461 oz. ASW, 32 mm. **Subject:** 1000th Anniversary, mention of town of Bled, 2nd issue

| Date | Mintage | VF20 | XF40 | MS60 | MS63 | MS65 |
|---|---|---|---|---|---|---|
| 2006 | 1,000 | PF65 55.00 | | | | |

**KM# 92 5000 TOLARJEV**
15.00 g., 0.900 Silver 0.434 oz. ASW, 32 mm. **Subject:** Anton Tomaz Linhart, 250th Anniversary of Birth **Rev:** Bust left

| Date | Mintage | VF20 | XF40 | MS60 | MS63 | MS65 |
|---|---|---|---|---|---|---|
| 2006 | 5,000 | PF65 45.00 | | | | |

**KM# 93 5000 TOLARJEV**
15.00 g., 0.925 Silver 0.4461 oz. ASW, 32 mm. **Subject:** Anton Askerc, 150th Anniversary of birth **Rev:** Bust left

| Date | Mintage | VF20 | XF40 | MS60 | MS63 | MS65 |
|---|---|---|---|---|---|---|
| 2006 | 5,000 | PF65 45.00 | | | | |

**KM# 44 20000 TOLARJEV**
7.00 g., 0.900 Gold 0.2025 oz. AGW, 24 mm. **Subject:** 10th Anniversary of Slovenia and the Tolar **Obv:** Value **Rev:** Tree rings and inscription **Edge:** Reeded

| Date | Mintage | VF20 | XF40 | MS60 | MS63 | MS65 |
|---|---|---|---|---|---|---|
| 2001 | 1,000 | PF65 520 | | | | |

**KM# 47 20000 TOLARJEV**
7.00 g., 0.900 Gold 0.2025 oz. AGW, 24 mm. **Subject:** World Cup Soccer **Obv:** Value **Rev:** Soccer player and rising sun **Edge:** Reeded

| Date | Mintage | VF20 | XF40 | MS60 | MS63 | MS65 |
|---|---|---|---|---|---|---|
| 2002 | 500 | PF65 550 | | | | |

**KM# 49 20000 TOLARJEV**
7.00 g., 0.900 Gold 0.2025 oz. AGW, 24 mm. **Subject:** 35th Chess Olympiad **Obv:** Rearing horse and reflection **Rev:** Chess pieces in starting positions and reflection **Edge:** Reeded

| Date | Mintage | VF20 | XF40 | MS60 | MS63 | MS65 |
|---|---|---|---|---|---|---|
| 2002 | 500 | PF65 550 | | | | |

**KM# 54 25000 TOLARJEV**
7.00 g., 0.900 Gold 0.2025 oz. AGW, 24 mm. **Subject:** European Year of the Disabled **Obv:** Value **Rev:** Stylized wheel chair **Edge:** Reeded

| Date | Mintage | VF20 | XF40 | MS60 | MS63 | MS65 |
|---|---|---|---|---|---|---|
| 2003 | 300 | PF65 575 | | | | |

**KM# 56 25000 TOLARJEV**
7.00 g., 0.900 Gold 0.2025 oz. AGW, 24 mm. **Subject:** 60th Anniversary of the Slovenian Assembly **Obv:** Value in partial star design **Rev:** Dates in partial star design **Edge:** Reeded

| Date | Mintage | VF20 | XF40 | MS60 | MS63 | MS65 |
|---|---|---|---|---|---|---|
| 2003 | 300 | PF65 575 | | | | |

**KM# 59 25000 TOLARJEV**
7.00 g., 0.900 Gold 0.2025 oz. AGW, 24 mm. **Subject:** 250th Anniversary of Jurij Vega's Birth **Obv:** Value **Rev:** Facial profile left looking down within mathematical graph **Edge:** Reeded

| Date | Mintage | VF20 | XF40 | MS60 | MS63 | MS65 |
|---|---|---|---|---|---|---|
| 2004 | 300 | PF65 575 | | | | |

**KM# 61 25000 TOLARJEV**
7.00 g., 0.900 Gold 0.2025 oz. AGW, 24 mm. **Subject:** 1000th Anniversary Town of Bled **Obv:** Value **Rev:** Castle and towers silhouette **Edge:** Reeded

| Date | Mintage | VF20 | XF40 | MS60 | MS63 | MS65 |
|---|---|---|---|---|---|---|
| 2004 | 300 | PF65 575 | | | | |

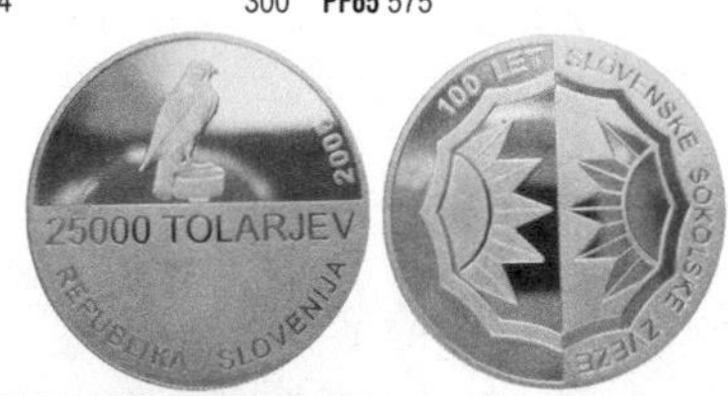


**KM# 66 25000 TOLARJEV**
7.00 g., 0.900 Gold 0.2025 oz. AGW, 24 mm. **Subject:** Centennial of Slovene Sokol Association **Obv:** Perched falcon above value **Rev:** Rising sun and reflection **Edge:** Reeded

| Date | Mintage | VF20 | XF40 | MS60 | MS63 | MS65 |
|---|---|---|---|---|---|---|
| 2005 | 1,000 | PF65 520 | | | | |

**KM# 67 25000 TOLARJEV**
7.00 g., 0.900 Gold 0.2025 oz. AGW, 24 mm. **Subject:** Centennial of Slovene Film **Obv:** Value above clapboard **Rev:** Film segment **Edge:** Reeded

| Date | Mintage | VF20 | XF40 | MS60 | MS63 | MS65 |
|---|---|---|---|---|---|---|
| 2005 | 1,000 | PF65 520 | | | | |

**KM# 83 25000 TOLARJEV**
7.00 g., 0.900 Gold 0.2025 oz. AGW, 24 mm. **Subject:** Anton Askerc **Edge:** Reeded

| Date | Mintage | VF20 | XF40 | MS60 | MS63 | MS65 |
|---|---|---|---|---|---|---|
| 2006 | — | PF65 525 | | | | |

**KM# 84 25000 TOLARJEV**
7.00 g., 0.900 Gold 0.2025 oz. AGW, 24 mm. **Subject:** Anton Tomaz Linhart **Edge:** Reeded

| Date | Mintage | VF20 | XF40 | MS60 | MS63 | MS65 |
|---|---|---|---|---|---|---|
| 2006 | — | PF65 525 | | | | |

**KM# 90 25000 TOLARJEV**
7.00 g., 0.900 Gold 0.2025 oz. AGW, 24 mm. **Subject:** 1000th Anniversary, Town of Bled mention, 2nd issue

| Date | Mintage | VF20 | XF40 | MS60 | MS63 | MS65 |
|---|---|---|---|---|---|---|
| 2006 | 500 | PF65 525 | | | | |

## EURO COINAGE

**KM# 68 EURO CENT**
2.30 g., Copper Plated Steel, 16.25 mm. **Obv:** White Stork **Obv. Legend:** SLOVENIJA, star between each letter **Rev:** Value and globe **Edge:** Plain

| Date | Mintage | VF20 | XF40 | MS60 | MS63 | MS65 |
|---|---|---|---|---|---|---|
| 2007 | 44,800,000 | — | — | 0.15 | 0.25 | 0.35 |
| 2008 | 148,000 | — | — | 0.15 | 0.25 | 0.35 |
| 2008 | 2,000 | PF65 22.00 | | | | |
| 2009 | 17,900,000 | — | — | 0.15 | 0.25 | 0.35 |
| 2010 | 70,000 | — | — | 0.15 | 0.25 | 0.35 |
| 2010 | 5,000 | PF65 5.00 | | | | |
| 2011 | 15,000 | — | — | 1.00 | 1.25 | 1.35 |
| 2011 | 2,000 | PF65 15.00 | | | | |
| 2012 | — | — | — | 0.15 | 0.25 | 0.35 |
| 2012 | 2,000 | PF65 15.00 | | | | |
| 2013 | — | — | — | 0.15 | 0.25 | 0.35 |
| 2013 | — | PF65 15.00 | | | | |
| 2014 | — | — | — | 0.15 | 0.25 | 0.35 |
| 2014 | — | PF65 15.00 | | | | |

**KM# 69 2 EURO CENT**
3.06 g., Copper Plated Steel, 18.75 mm. **Obv:** Princely stone of power in consciousness **Obv. Legend:** SLOVENIJA, star between each letter **Rev:** Value and globe **Edge:** Grooved

| Date | Mintage | VF20 | XF40 | MS60 | MS63 | MS65 |
|---|---|---|---|---|---|---|
| 2007 | 44,250,000 | — | — | 0.25 | 0.50 | 0.65 |
| 2008 | 148,000 | — | — | 0.25 | 0.50 | 0.65 |
| 2008 | 2,000 | PF65 22.00 | | | | |
| 2009 | 12,300,000 | — | — | 0.25 | 0.50 | 0.65 |
| 2010 | 70,000 | — | — | 0.25 | 0.50 | 0.65 |
| 2010 | 5,000 | PF65 5.00 | | | | |
| 2011 | 15,000 | — | — | 1.25 | 1.50 | 1.65 |
| 2011 | 2,000 | PF65 15.00 | | | | |
| 2012 | — | — | — | 0.25 | 0.50 | 0.65 |
| 2012 | 2,000 | PF65 15.00 | | | | |
| 2013 | — | — | — | 0.25 | 0.50 | 0.65 |
| 2013 | — | PF65 15.00 | | | | |
| 2014 | — | — | — | 0.25 | 0.50 | 0.65 |
| 2014 | — | PF65 15.00 | | | | |

**KM# 70 5 EURO CENT**
3.92 g., Copper Plated Steel, 21.25 mm. **Obv:** Sower of Seeds - and stars **Obv. Legend:** SLOVENIJA, star between each letter **Rev:** Value and globe **Edge:** Plain

| Date | Mintage | VF20 | XF40 | MS60 | MS63 | MS65 |
|---|---|---|---|---|---|---|
| 2007 | 43,800,000 | — | — | 0.50 | 0.75 | 1.00 |
| 2008 | 148,000 | — | — | 0.50 | 0.75 | 1.00 |
| 2008 | 2,000 | PF65 22.00 | | | | |
| 2009 | 100,000 | — | — | 0.50 | 0.75 | 1.00 |
| 2010 | 70,000 | — | — | 0.50 | 0.75 | 1.00 |
| 2010 | 5,000 | PF65 5.00 | | | | |
| 2011 | 15,000 | — | — | 1.25 | 1.50 | 2.00 |
| 2011 | 2,000 | PF65 15.00 | | | | |
| 2012 | — | — | — | 0.50 | 0.75 | 1.00 |
| 2012 | 2,000 | PF65 15.00 | | | | |
| 2013 | — | — | — | 0.50 | 0.75 | 1.00 |
| 2013 | — | PF65 15.00 | | | | |
| 2014 | — | — | — | 0.50 | 0.75 | 1.00 |
| 2014 | — | PF65 15.00 | | | | |

**KM# 71 10 EURO CENT**
4.10 g., Brass, 19.75 mm. **Obv:** Plecnik's unrealised plans for Parliament building **Obv. Legend:** SLOVENIJA, star between each letter **Rev:** Value and map **Edge:** Reeded

| Date | Mintage | VF20 | XF40 | MS60 | MS63 | MS65 |
|---|---|---|---|---|---|---|
| 2007 | 42,800,000 | — | — | 0.75 | 1.00 | 1.25 |
| 2008 | 148,000 | — | — | 0.75 | 1.00 | 1.25 |
| 2008 | 2,000 | PF65 22.00 | | | | |
| 2009 | 100,000 | — | — | 0.75 | 1.00 | 1.25 |
| 2010 | 70,000 | — | — | 0.75 | 1.00 | 1.25 |
| 2010 | 5,000 | PF65 5.00 | | | | |
| 2011 | 15,000 | — | — | 1.50 | 2.00 | 2.25 |
| 2011 | 2,000 | PF65 15.00 | | | | |
| 2012 | — | — | — | 0.75 | 1.00 | 1.25 |
| 2012 | 2,000 | PF65 15.00 | | | | |
| 2013 | — | — | — | 0.75 | 1.00 | 1.25 |
| 2013 | — | PF65 15.00 | | | | |
| 2014 | — | — | — | 0.75 | 1.00 | 1.25 |
| 2014 | — | PF65 15.00 | | | | |

**KM# 72 20 EURO CENT**
5.74 g., Brass, 22.25 mm. **Obv:** Two Lipizzaner horses prancing left **Obv. Legend:** SLOVENIJA, star between each letter **Rev:** Value and map **Edge:** Notched

| Date | Mintage | VF20 | XF40 | MS60 | MS63 | MS65 |
|---|---|---|---|---|---|---|
| 2007 | 37,250,000 | — | — | 1.00 | 1.25 | 1.50 |
| 2008 | 148,000 | — | — | 1.00 | 1.25 | 1.50 |
| 2008 | 2,000 | PF65 8.00 | | | | |
| 2009 | 100,000 | — | — | 1.00 | 1.25 | 1.50 |
| 2010 | 70,000 | — | — | 1.00 | 1.25 | 1.50 |
| 2010 | 5,000 | PF65 28.00 | | | | |
| 2011 | 15,000 | — | — | 2.00 | 2.25 | 2.50 |
| 2011 | 2,000 | PF65 18.00 | | | | |
| 2012 | — | — | — | 1.00 | 1.25 | 1.50 |
| 2012 | 2,000 | PF65 18.00 | | | | |
| 2013 | — | — | — | 1.00 | 1.25 | 1.50 |
| 2013 | — | PF65 18.00 | | | | |
| 2014 | — | — | — | 1.00 | 1.25 | 1.50 |
| 2014 | — | PF65 18.00 | | | | |

**KM# 73 50 EURO CENT**
7.80 g., Brass, 24.25 mm. **Obv:** Triglav Mountain (highest peak in Slovenia) and stars **Rev:** Value and map **Edge:** Reeded

| Date | Mintage | VF20 | XF40 | MS60 | MS63 | MS65 |
|---|---|---|---|---|---|---|
| 2007 | 32,400,000 | — | — | 1.25 | 1.50 | 2.00 |
| 2008 | 148,000 | — | — | 1.25 | 1.50 | 2.00 |
| 2008 | 2,000 | PF65 8.00 | | | | |
| 2009 | 100,000 | — | — | 1.25 | 1.50 | 2.00 |
| 2010 | 70,000 | — | — | 1.25 | 1.50 | 2.00 |
| 2010 | 5,000 | PF65 28.00 | | | | |
| 2011 | 15,000 | — | — | 2.00 | 2.50 | 3.00 |
| 2011 | 2,000 | PF65 18.00 | | | | |
| 2012 | — | — | — | 1.25 | 1.50 | 2.00 |
| 2012 | 2,000 | PF65 18.00 | | | | |
| 2013 | — | — | — | 1.25 | 1.50 | 2.00 |
| 2013 | — | PF65 18.00 | | | | |
| 2014 | — | PF65 18.00 | | | | |
| 2014 | — | — | — | 1.25 | 1.50 | 2.00 |

**KM# 74 EURO**
7.50 g., Bi-Metallic Copper-Nickel center in Nickel-Brass ring, 23.25 mm. **Obv:** Bearded Primoz Trubar **Rev:** Value and map **Edge:** Segmented reeding

| Date | Mintage | VF20 | XF40 | MS60 | MS63 | MS65 |
|---|---|---|---|---|---|---|
| 2007 | 29,750,000 | — | — | 2.00 | 2.50 | 3.50 |
| 2008 | 148,000 | — | — | 2.00 | 2.50 | 3.50 |
| 2008 | 2,000 | PF65 35.00 | | | | |
| 2009 | 100,000 | — | — | 2.00 | 2.50 | 3.50 |
| 2010 | 70,000 | — | — | 2.00 | 2.50 | 3.50 |
| 2010 | 5,000 | PF65 15.00 | | | | |
| 2011 | 15,000 | — | — | 2.50 | 3.50 | 4.50 |
| 2011 | 2,000 | PF65 22.00 | | | | |
| 2012 | — | — | — | 2.00 | 2.50 | 3.50 |
| 2012 | 2,000 | PF65 22.00 | | | | |
| 2013 | — | — | — | 2.00 | 2.50 | 3.50 |
| 2013 | — | PF65 22.00 | | | | |
| 2014 | — | — | — | 2.00 | 2.50 | 3.50 |
| 2014 | — | PF65 22.00 | | | | |

**KM# 75 2 EURO**
8.50 g., Bi-Metallic Nickel-Brass center in Copper-Nickel ring, 25.75 mm. **Obv:** France Preseren silhouette and signature **Rev:** Value and map **Edge:** Reeded and lettered

| Date | Mintage | VF20 | XF40 | MS60 | MS63 | MS65 |
|---|---|---|---|---|---|---|
| 2007 | 21,350,000 | — | — | 3.00 | 4.00 | 5.00 |
| 2008 | 148,000 | — | — | 3.00 | 4.00 | 5.00 |
| 2008 | 2,000 | PF65 40.00 | | | | |
| 2009 | 100,000 | — | — | 3.00 | 4.00 | 5.00 |
| 2010 | 70,000 | — | — | 3.00 | 4.00 | 5.00 |
| 2010 | 5,000 | PF65 20.00 | | | | |
| 2011 | 15,000 | — | — | 3.50 | 5.00 | 6.00 |
| 2011 | 2,000 | PF65 28.00 | | | | |
| 2012 | — | — | — | 3.00 | 4.00 | 5.00 |
| 2012 | 2,000 | PF65 28.00 | | | | |
| 2013 | — | — | — | 3.00 | 4.00 | 5.00 |
| 2013 | — | PF65 28.00 | | | | |
| 2014 | — | PF65 28.00 | | | | |

**KM# 106 2 EURO**
8.50 g., Bi-Metallic Nickel-Brass center in Copper-Nickel ring, 25.75 mm. **Subject:** Treaty of Rome, 50th Anniversary

| Date | Mintage | VF20 | XF40 | MS60 | MS63 | MS65 |
|---|---|---|---|---|---|---|
| 2007 Encased in a lucite block | 990 | — | — | — | — | 10.00 |
| 2007 | 399,100 | — | — | 5.00 | 6.50 | 7.50 |

**KM# 80 2 EURO**
8.50 g., Bi-Metallic Nickel-Brass center in Copper-Nickel ring, 25.75 mm. **Subject:** 500th Anniversary Birth of Primoz Tubar **Obv:** Bust of Trubar left at right **Rev:** Large "2" at left, modified map of Europe at right **Edge:** Reeded

| Date | Mintage | VF20 | XF40 | MS60 | MS63 | MS65 |
|---|---|---|---|---|---|---|
| 2008 | 950,000 | — | — | 4.00 | 6.00 | 8.00 |
| 2008 Special Unc. | 10,000 | — | — | — | — | 32.50 |
| 2008 | 40,000 | PF65 45.00 | | | | |

**KM# 82 2 EURO**
8.50 g., Bi-Metallic Nickel-Brass center in Copper-Nickel ring., 25.75 mm. **Subject:** European Monetary Union, 10th Anniversary **Obv:** Stick figure and large E symbol **Rev:** Value at left, modified map of Europe at left

| Date | Mintage | VF20 | XF40 | MS60 | MS63 | MS65 |
|---|---|---|---|---|---|---|
| 2009 | 1,000,000 | — | — | 3.50 | 5.00 | 6.00 |
| 2009 Special Unc. | — | — | — | — | — | 32.50 |
| 2009 | — | PF65 40.00 | | | | |

**KM# 94 2 EURO**
8.50 g., Bi-Metallic Nickel-Brass center in Copper-Nickel ring, 25.75 mm. **Subject:** Ljubljana Botanical Gardens, 200th Anniversary

| Date | Mintage | VF20 | XF40 | MS60 | MS63 | MS65 |
|---|---|---|---|---|---|---|
| 2010 | 20,000 | PF65 50.00 | | | | |
| 2010 | 980,000 | — | — | 6.00 | 8.00 | 10.00 |

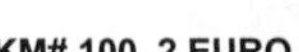

**KM# 100 2 EURO**
8.50 g., Bi-Metallic Nickel-Brass center in Copper-Nickel ring, 25.75 mm. **Subject:** Franc Razman, 100th Anniversary of Birth

| Date | Mintage | VF20 | XF40 | MS60 | MS63 | MS65 |
|---|---|---|---|---|---|---|
| 2011 | 14,000 | PF65 50.00 | | | | |
| 2011 | 486,000 | — | — | 4.00 | 6.00 | 8.00 |

**KM# 107 2 EURO**
8.50 g., Bi-Metallic Nickel-Brass center in Copper-Nickel ring, 25.75 mm. **Subject:** Euro Coinage, 10th Anniversary **Obv:** Euro symbol on globe, child-like renderings around

| Date | Mintage | VF20 | XF40 | MS60 | MS63 | MS65 |
|---|---|---|---|---|---|---|
| 2012 | 1,000 | PF65 25.00 | | | | |
| 2012 | 1,000,000 | — | — | 5.00 | 7.00 | 8.00 |

**KM# 112 2 EURO**
8.50 g., Bi-Metallic Nickel-Brass center in Copper-Nickel ring, 25.75 mm. **Subject:** 800th Anniversary of Postojna Cave Discovery **Rev:** Stylized spiral ending in 2 speleothems

| Date | Mintage | VF20 | XF40 | MS60 | MS63 | MS65 |
|---|---|---|---|---|---|---|
| 2013 | — | — | — | 5.00 | 7.00 | 8.00 |
| 2013 | 8,000 | PF65 15.00 | | | | |

**KM# 117 2 EURO**
8.50 g., Bi-Metallic Nickel-Brass center in Copper-Nickel ring, 25.75 mm. **Obv:** Barbara von Celje

| Date | Mintage | F12 | VF20 | XF40 | MS60 | MS63 |
|---|---|---|---|---|---|---|
| 2014 | — | — | — | — | 5.00 | 7.00 |

**KM# 81 3 EURO**
15.00 g., Bi-Metallic Copper-Nickel center in Aluminum-Bronze ring, 32 mm. **Subject:** Six Month Term as President of the EU 2008 **Obv:** Field of stars representing EU membership **Rev:** Pinwheel

| Date | Mintage | VF20 | XF40 | MS60 | MS63 | MS65 |
|---|---|---|---|---|---|---|
| 2008 | 348,000 | — | — | 6.00 | 8.00 | 10.00 |
| 2008 Special Unc. | 148,000 | — | — | — | — | 20.00 |
| 2008 | 4,000 | PF63 165 | PF65 185 | | | |

**KM# 85 3 EURO**
15.00 g., Bi-Metallic Copper-Nickel center in Aluminum-Bronze ring, 32 mm. **Subject:** First Airplane flight in Slovenia by Edvard Rusjan, 100th Anniversary

| Date | Mintage | VF20 | XF40 | MS60 | MS63 | MS65 |
|---|---|---|---|---|---|---|
| 2009 | 300,000 | — | — | 6.00 | 8.00 | 10.00 |

**KM# 95 3 EURO**
15.00 g., Bi-Metallic Copper-Nickel center in Aluminum-Bronze ring, 32 mm. **Subject:** UNESCO - World Book Capital, Ljubljana

| Date | Mintage | VF20 | XF40 | MS60 | MS63 | MS65 |
|---|---|---|---|---|---|---|
| 2010 | 5,000 | PF65 50.00 | | | | |
| 2010 | — | — | — | 6.00 | 8.00 | 10.00 |

**KM# 101 3 EURO**
7.50 g., Bi-Metallic Copper-Nickel center in Aluminum-Bronze ring, 32 mm. **Subject:** Independence, 20th Anniversary

| Date | Mintage | VF20 | XF40 | MS60 | MS63 | MS65 |
|---|---|---|---|---|---|---|
| 2011 | 4,000 | PF65 110 | | | | |
| 2011 | 5,000 | — | — | — | — | 15.00 |

**KM# 109 3 EURO**
Bi-Metallic, 32 mm. **Subject:** Rudolf Cvetko, 100th Anniversary of Olympic medal win **Obv:** Stylized fencing **Rev:** 7 fencing swords pointed downward

| Date | Mintage | VF20 | XF40 | MS60 | MS63 | MS65 |
|---|---|---|---|---|---|---|
| 2012 | — | — | — | 6.00 | 8.00 | 10.00 |

**KM# 108 3 EURO**
Bi-Metallic **Subject:** 300th Anniversary of 1713 Tolmin Peasant Revolt **Rev:** Scythe and farm implements, large 1713

| Date | Mintage | VF20 | XF40 | MS60 | MS63 | MS65 |
|---|---|---|---|---|---|---|
| 2013 | — | — | — | — | — | — |

**KM# 118 3 EURO**
15.00 g., Bi-Metallic Copper-Nickel center in Nickel-Brass ring, 32 mm. **Subject:** Janez Puhar, 200th Anniversary of Birth

| Date | Mintage | F12 | VF20 | XF40 | MS60 | MS63 |
|---|---|---|---|---|---|---|
| 2014 | 145,000 | — | — | — | 5.00 | 7.00 |
| 2014 | 5,000 | PF65 15.00 | | | | |

**KM# 76 30 EURO**
15.00 g., 0.925 Silver 0.4461 oz. ASW, 32 mm. **Subject:** 250th Anniversary Birth of Valentin Vodnik **Obv:** Value **Obv. Legend:** SLOVENIJA **Rev:** Large bust of Vodnik left

| Date | Mintage | VF20 | XF40 | MS60 | MS63 | MS65 |
|---|---|---|---|---|---|---|
| 2008 | 8,000 | PF63 90.00 | | PF65 100 | | |

**KM# 78 30 EURO**
15.00 g., 0.925 Silver 0.4461 oz. ASW, 32 mm. **Subject:** EU President **Obv:** EU membership stars **Obv. Legend:** SLOVENIJA **Rev:** Pinwheel 5-pointed star

| Date | Mintage | VF20 | XF40 | MS60 | MS63 | MS65 |
|---|---|---|---|---|---|---|
| 2008 | 8,000 | PF63 125 | | PF65 150 | | |

**KM# 86 30 EURO**
15.00 g., 0.925 Silver 0.4461 oz. ASW, 32 mm. **Subject:** First Airplane, 100th Anniversary

| Date | Mintage | VF20 | XF40 | MS60 | MS63 | MS65 |
|---|---|---|---|---|---|---|
| 2009 | 8,000 | PF63 65.00 | | PF65 75.00 | | |

**KM# 88 30 EURO**
15.00 g., 0.925 Silver 0.4461 oz. ASW, 32 mm. **Subject:** Zoran Music, painter

| Date | Mintage | VF20 | XF40 | MS60 | MS63 | MS65 |
|---|---|---|---|---|---|---|
| 2009 | — | PF63 70.00 | | PF65 80.00 | | |

**KM# 96 30 EURO**
15.00 g., 0.925 Silver 0.4461 oz. ASW, 32 mm. **Subject:** UNESCO - World Book Capital, Ljubljana

| Date | Mintage | VF20 | XF40 | MS60 | MS63 | MS65 |
|---|---|---|---|---|---|---|
| 2010 | — | PF63 65.00 | | PF65 75.00 | | |

**KM# 98 30 EURO**
15.00 g., 0.925 Silver 0.4461 oz. ASW, 32 mm. **Subject:** World Ski Jumping Championships, Planica

| Date | Mintage | VF20 | XF40 | MS60 | MS63 | MS65 |
|---|---|---|---|---|---|---|
| 2010 | — | PF63 70.00 | | PF65 80.00 | | |

**KM# 102 30 EURO**
15.00 g., 0.925 Silver 0.4461 oz. ASW, 32 mm. **Subject:** Independence, 20th Anniversary

| Date | Mintage | VF20 | XF40 | MS60 | MS63 | MS65 |
|---|---|---|---|---|---|---|
| 2011 | — | PF63 65.00 | | PF65 75.00 | | |

**KM# 104 30 EURO**
15.00 g., 0.925 Silver 0.4461 oz. ASW, 32 mm. **Series:** World Rowing Championships

| Date | Mintage | VF20 | XF40 | MS60 | MS63 | MS65 |
|---|---|---|---|---|---|---|
| 2011 | — | PF63 65.00 | | PF65 75.00 | | |

**KM# 110 30 EURO**
15.00 g., 0.925 Silver 0.4461 oz. ASW, 32 mm. **Subject:** Rudolf Cvetko - 100th Anniversary of 1st Olympic Medal

| Date | Mintage | VF20 | XF40 | MS60 | MS63 | MS65 |
|---|---|---|---|---|---|---|
| 2012 Proof | Est. 3500 | — | — | — | — | — |

**KM# 115 30 EURO**
15.00 g., 0.925 Silver 0.4461 oz. ASW, 32 mm. **Subject:** European Culture Capital, Maribor

| Date | Mintage | VF20 | XF40 | MS60 | MS63 | MS65 |
|---|---|---|---|---|---|---|
| 2012 | 3,500 | PF65 75.00 | | | | |

**KM# 113 30 EURO**
15.00 g., 0.900 Silver 0.434 oz. ASW, 24 mm. **Subject:** 1713 Tolmin Peasant revolt, 300th Anniversary **Obv:** Value **Rev:** Scythe and farm implements, large 1713

| Date | Mintage | VF20 | XF40 | MS60 | MS63 | MS65 |
|---|---|---|---|---|---|---|
| 2013 | 2,000 | PF65 75.00 | | | | |

**KM# 119 30 EURO**
15.00 g., 0.925 Silver 0.4461 oz. ASW, 32 mm. **Subject:** Janez Puhar, 200th Anniversary of Birth

| Date | Mintage | F12 | VF20 | XF40 | MS60 | MS63 |
|---|---|---|---|---|---|---|
| 2014 | 2,000 | PF65 75.00 | | | | |

**KM# 77 100 EURO**
7.00 g., 0.900 Gold 0.2025 oz. AGW, 24 mm. **Subject:** 250th Anniversary Birth of Valentin Vodnik **Obv:** Value **Obv. Legend:** SLOVENIJA **Rev:** Large bust of Vodnik left

| Date | Mintage | VF20 | XF40 | MS60 | MS63 | MS65 |
|---|---|---|---|---|---|---|
| 2008 | 5,000 | PF65 425 | | | | |

**KM# 79 100 EURO**
7.00 g., 0.900 Gold 0.2025 oz. AGW, 24 mm. **Subject:** EU President **Obv:** EU membership stars **Obv. Legend:** SLOVENIJA **Rev:** Pinwheel 5-pointed star

| Date | Mintage | VF20 | XF40 | MS60 | MS63 | MS65 |
|---|---|---|---|---|---|---|
| 2008 | 5,000 | PF65 625 | | | | |

**KM# 87 100 EURO**
7.00 g., 0.900 Gold 0.2025 oz. AGW, 24 mm. **Subject:** First Airplane, 100th Anniversary

| Date | Mintage | VF20 | XF40 | MS60 | MS63 | MS65 |
|---|---|---|---|---|---|---|
| 2009 | 6,000 | PF65 425 | | | | |

**KM# 89 100 EURO**
7.00 g., 0.900 Gold 0.2025 oz. AGW, 24 mm. **Subject:** Zoran Music, painter

| Date | Mintage | VF20 | XF40 | MS60 | MS63 | MS65 |
|---|---|---|---|---|---|---|
| 2009 | — | PF65 425 | | | | |

**KM# 97 100 EURO**
7.00 g., 0.900 Gold 0.2025 oz. AGW, 24 mm. **Subject:** UNESCO - World Book Capital, Ljubljana

| Date | Mintage | VF20 | XF40 | MS60 | MS63 | MS65 |
|---|---|---|---|---|---|---|
| 2010 | — | PF65 425 | | | | |

**KM# 99 100 EURO**
7.00 g., 0.900 Gold 0.2025 oz. AGW, 24 mm. **Subject:** World Ski Jumping Championships, Planica

| Date | Mintage | VF20 | XF40 | MS60 | MS63 | MS65 |
|---|---|---|---|---|---|---|
| 2010 | — | PF65 425 | | | | |

**KM# 103 100 EURO**
7.00 g., 0.900 Gold 0.2025 oz. AGW, 24 mm. **Subject:** Independence, 20th Anniversary

| Date | Mintage | VF20 | XF40 | MS60 | MS63 | MS65 |
|---|---|---|---|---|---|---|
| 2011 | — | PF65 425 | | | | |

**KM# 105 100 EURO**
7.00 g., 0.900 Gold 0.2025 oz. AGW, 24 mm. **Subject:** World Rowing Championships

| Date | Mintage | VF20 | XF40 | MS60 | MS63 | MS65 |
|---|---|---|---|---|---|---|
| 2011 | — | PF65 425 | | | | |

**KM# 111 100 EURO**
7.00 g., 0.900 Gold 0.2025 oz. AGW, 24 mm. **Subject:** Rudolf Cvetko - 100th Anniversary of 1st Olympic medal

| Date | Mintage | VF20 | XF40 | MS60 | MS63 | MS65 |
|---|---|---|---|---|---|---|
| 2012 | 2,500 | PF65 450 | | | | |

**KM# 116 100 EURO**
7.00 g., 0.900 Gold 0.2025 oz. AGW, 24 mm. **Subject:** European Culture Capital, Maribor

| Date | Mintage | VF20 | XF40 | MS60 | MS63 | MS65 |
|---|---|---|---|---|---|---|
| 2012 | 2,500 | PF65 425 | | | | |

**KM# 114 100 EURO**
7.00 g., 0.900 Gold 0.2025 oz. AGW, 24 mm. **Subject:** 1713 Tolmin Peasant Revolt, 300th Anniversary **Obv:** Large value **Rev:** Scythe and farm implements, large 1713

| Date | Mintage | VF20 | XF40 | MS60 | MS63 | MS65 |
|---|---|---|---|---|---|---|
| 2014 | 1,500 | PF65 450 | | | | |

**KM# 120 100 EURO**
7.00 g., 0.900 Gold 0.2025 oz. AGW, 24 mm. **Subject:** Janez Puhar, 200th Anniversary of Birth

| Date | Mintage | F12 | VF20 | XF40 | MS60 | MS63 |
|---|---|---|---|---|---|---|
| 2014 | 1,500 | PF65 425 | | | | |

## MINT SETS

| KM# | Date | Mintage | Identification | Issue Price | Mkt Val |
|---|---|---|---|---|---|
| MS10 | 2001 (7) | 1,000 | KM#3-8, 41 | 20.00 | 40.00 |
| MS11 | 2002 (8) | 1,000 | KM#3-8, 41, 45 | — | 45.00 |
| MS12 | 2003 (10) | 1,000 | KM#3-8, 41, 50-52 | — | 55.00 |
| MS13 | 2004 (10) | 1,000 | KM#3-8, 41, 51, 52, 57 | — | 45.00 |
| MS14 | 2005 (9) | 3,000 | KM#3-8, 41, 51, 52 | 25.00 | 45.00 |
| MS15 | 2006 (10) | 4,000 | KM#3-8, 41, 51, 52, 65 | 25.00 | 50.00 |
| MS16 | 2007 (8) | 100,000 | KM#68-75 | — | 50.00 |
| MS17 | 2008 (9) | 148,000 | KM#68-75, 81 | — | 50.00 |
| MS18 | 2009 (9) | 100,000 | KM#68-75, 85 | — | 50.00 |
| MS19 | 2010 (10) | 70,000 | KM#68-75, 94, 95 | — | 75.00 |
| MS20 | 2011 (10) | 150,000 | KM#68-75, 100, 101 | — | 100 |

## PROOF SETS

| KM# | Date | Mintage | Identification | Issue Price | Mkt Val |
|---|---|---|---|---|---|
| PS13 | 2001 (8) | 800 | KM#3-8, 41, 42 | — | 70.00 |
| PS14 | 2002 (8) | 800 | KM#3-8, 41, 45 | — | 70.00 |
| PS15 | 2003 (10) | 800 | KM#3-8, 41, 50-52 | 22.50 | 100 |
| PS16 | 2004 (10) | 500 | KM#3-8, 41, 51-52, 57 | — | 120 |
| PS17 | 2005 (10) | 1,000 | KM#3-8, 41, 51-52, 63 | — | 95.00 |
| PS18 | 2006 (10) | 1,000 | KM#3-8, 41, 51-52, 65 | — | 95.00 |
| PS19 | 2008 (9) | 2,000 | KM#68-75, 81 | — | 350 |
| PS20 | 2010 (10) | 5,000 | KM#68-75, 94, 95 | — | 215 |
| PS21 | 2011 (10) | 2,000 | KM#68-75, 100, 101 | — | 315 |

The Solomon Islands are made up of about 200 islands. They are located in the southwest Pacific east of Papua New Guinea, have an area of 10,983 sq. mi. (28,450 sq. km.) and a population of *552,000. Capital: Honiara. The most important islands of the Solomon chain are Guadalcanal (scene of some of the fiercest fighting of World War II), Malaitia, New Georgia, Florida, Vella Lavella, Choiseul, Rendova, San Cristobal, the Lord Howe group, the Santa Cruz islands, and the Duff group. Copra is the only important cash crop but it is hoped that timber will become an economic factor.

Solomon Islands is a member of the Commonwealth of Nations. Queen Elizabeth II is Head of State, as Queen of the Solomon Islands.

**RULER**
British

**MONETARY SYSTEM**
100 Cents = 1 Dollar

# COMMONWEALTH NATION

## STANDARD COINAGE

**KM# 24 CENT**
2.30 g., Bronze Plated Steel, 17.53 mm. **Ruler:** Elizabeth II **Obv:** Crowned head right **Obv. Legend:** ELIZABETH II - SOLOMON ISLANDS **Rev:** Food bowl divides value **Edge:** Plain

| Date | Mintage | VF20 | XF40 | MS60 | MS63 | MS65 |
|---|---|---|---|---|---|---|
| 2005 | — | — | — | 0.35 | 0.50 | 0.75 |
| 2010 | — | — | — | 0.35 | 0.50 | 0.75 |

**KM# 25 2 CENTS**
Bronze Plated Steel, 21.6 mm. **Ruler:** Elizabeth II **Obv:** Crowned head right **Obv. Legend:** ELIZABETH II - SOLOMON ISLANDS **Rev:** Eagle spirit below value **Edge:** Plain

| Date | Mintage | VF20 | XF40 | MS60 | MS63 | MS65 |
|---|---|---|---|---|---|---|
| 2005 | — | — | — | 0.35 | 0.50 | 0.75 |
| 2006 | — | — | — | 0.35 | 0.50 | 0.75 |

**KM# 26a 5 CENTS**
Nickel Plated Steel, 18.4 mm. **Ruler:** Elizabeth II **Obv:** Crowned bust right **Obv. Legend:** ELIZABETH II - SOLOMON ISLANDS **Rev:** Value at left, native mask at center right

| Date | Mintage | VF20 | XF40 | MS60 | MS63 | MS65 |
|---|---|---|---|---|---|---|
| 2005 | — | — | — | 0.50 | 0.75 | 1.00 |

**KM# 27a 10 CENTS**
Nickel Plated Steel, 23.6 mm. **Ruler:** Elizabeth II **Subject:** Ngorieru **Obv:** Crowned head right **Obv. Legend:** ELIZABETH II - SOLOMON ISLANDS **Rev:** Sea spirit divides value **Edge:** Reeded

| Date | Mintage | VF20 | XF40 | MS60 | MS63 | MS65 |
|---|---|---|---|---|---|---|
| 2005 | — | — | — | 0.65 | 0.80 | 1.00 |

**KM# 235 10 CENTS**
2.29 g., Nickel Plated Steel, 17 mm. **Ruler:** Elizabeth II **Obv:** Head with tiara right **Rev:** Sea Spirit Ngoreru from Temotu province

| Date | Mintage | VF20 | XF40 | MS60 | MS63 | MS65 |
|---|---|---|---|---|---|---|
| 2012 | — | — | — | 0.35 | 0.50 | 0.75 |

**KM# 235a 10 CENTS**
2.90 g., Silver, 17 mm. **Ruler:** Elizabeth II **Obv:** Head with tiara right **Rev:** Sea Spirit

| Date | Mintage | VF20 | XF40 | MS60 | MS63 | MS65 |
|---|---|---|---|---|---|---|
| 2012 | 1,500 | PF65 40.00 | | | | |

**KM# 28 20 CENTS**
11.25 g., Nickel Plated Steel, 28.5 mm. **Ruler:** Elizabeth II **Obv:** Crowned head right **Obv. Legend:** ELIZABETH II - SOLOMON ISLANDS **Rev:** Malaita pendant design within circle, denomination appears twice in legend **Edge:** Reeded

| Date | Mintage | VF20 | XF40 | MS60 | MS63 | MS65 |
|---|---|---|---|---|---|---|
| 2005 | — | — | — | 0.85 | 1.00 | 1.25 |

**KM# 236 20 CENTS**
2.84 g., Nickel Plated Steel, 19 mm. **Ruler:** Elizabeth II **Rev:** Malaita pendant design with circle

| Date | Mintage | VF20 | XF40 | MS60 | MS63 | MS65 |
|---|---|---|---|---|---|---|
| 2012 | — | — | — | 0.85 | 1.00 | 1.25 |

**KM# 236a 20 CENTS**
3.52 g., 0.999 Silver 0.1131 oz. ASW, 19 mm. **Ruler:** Elizabeth II **Obv:** Head with tiara right **Rev:** Pendant design

| Date | Mintage | VF20 | XF40 | MS60 | MS63 | MS65 |
|---|---|---|---|---|---|---|
| 2012 | 1,500 | PF65 50.00 | | | | |

**KM# 29 50 CENTS**
10.00 g., Copper-Nickel, 29.5 mm. **Ruler:** Elizabeth II **Obv:** Crowned head right **Obv. Legend:** ELIZABETH II - SOLOMON ISLANDS **Rev:** Arms with supporters **Edge:** Plain **Shape:** 12-sided **Note:** Circulation type.

| Date | Mintage | VF20 | XF40 | MS60 | MS63 | MS65 |
|---|---|---|---|---|---|---|
| 2005 | — | — | — | 2.00 | 2.50 | 3.00 |

**KM# 29a 50 CENTS**
Nickel Plated Steel, 29.5 mm. **Ruler:** Elizabeth II **Shape:** 12-sided

| Date | Mintage | VF20 | XF40 | MS60 | MS63 | MS65 |
|---|---|---|---|---|---|---|
| 2008 | — | — | — | 2.00 | 2.50 | 3.00 |

**KM# 237 50 CENTS**
Nickel Plated Steel, 21 mm. **Ruler:** Elizabeth II **Rev:** Eagle Spirit

| Date | Mintage | VF20 | XF40 | MS60 | MS63 | MS65 |
|---|---|---|---|---|---|---|
| 2012 | — | — | — | 2.00 | 2.50 | 3.00 |

**KM# 237a 50 CENTS**
4.64 g., 0.999 Silver 0.149 oz. ASW, 21 mm. **Ruler:** Elizabeth II **Obv:** Head with tiara right **Rev:** Eagle

| Date | Mintage | VF20 | XF40 | MS60 | MS63 | MS65 |
|---|---|---|---|---|---|---|
| 2012 | 1,500 | PF65 50.00 | | | | |

**KM# 72 DOLLAR**
13.45 g., Copper-Nickel, 30 mm. **Ruler:** Elizabeth II **Obv:** Crowned head right **Obv. Legend:** ELIZABETH II - SOLOMON ISLANDS **Rev:** Sea spirit statue divides value **Edge:** Plain **Shape:** 7-sided

| Date | Mintage | VF20 | XF40 | MS60 | MS63 | MS65 |
|---|---|---|---|---|---|---|
| 2005 | — | — | — | 1.50 | 2.00 | 3.00 |

**KM# 72a DOLLAR**
Nickel Plated Steel, 30 mm. **Ruler:** Elizabeth II **Shape:** 7-sided

| Date | Mintage | VF20 | XF40 | MS60 | MS63 | MS65 |
|---|---|---|---|---|---|---|
| 2008 | — | — | — | 2.00 | 3.00 | 4.00 |

**KM# 159 DOLLAR**
26.00 g., Bronze, 38.61 mm. **Ruler:** Elizabeth II **Rev:** Archangel Michael in color

| Date | Mintage | VF20 | XF40 | MS60 | MS63 | MS65 |
|---|---|---|---|---|---|---|
| 2009 | — | PF65 17.50 | | | | |

**KM# 160 DOLLAR**
26.00 g., Bronze, 38.61 mm. **Ruler:** Elizabeth II **Rev:** Archangel Raphael in color

| Date | Mintage | VF20 | XF40 | MS60 | MS63 | MS65 |
|---|---|---|---|---|---|---|
| 2009 | — | PF65 17.50 | | | | |

**KM# 161 DOLLAR**
26.00 g., Bronze, 38.61 mm. **Ruler:** Elizabeth II **Rev:** Archangel Gabriel in color

| Date | Mintage | VF20 | XF40 | MS60 | MS63 | MS65 |
|---|---|---|---|---|---|---|
| 2009 | — | PF65 17.50 | | | | |

**KM# 182 DOLLAR**
6.23 g., 0.999 Silver 0.2001 oz. ASW, 35 mm. **Ruler:** Elizabeth II **Subject:** Ships and Explorers - HMS Beagle - Charles Darwin

| Date | Mintage | VF20 | XF40 | MS60 | MS63 | MS65 |
|---|---|---|---|---|---|---|
| 2009 | Est. 5000 | PF65 15.00 | | | | |

**KM# 183 DOLLAR**
6.23 g., 0.999 Silver 0.2001 oz. ASW, 35 mm. **Ruler:** Elizabeth II **Subject:** Ships and Explorers - HMS Warrior

| Date | Mintage | VF20 | XF40 | MS60 | MS63 | MS65 |
|---|---|---|---|---|---|---|
| 2009 | — | PF65 15.00 | | | | |

**KM# 184 DOLLAR**
6.23 g., 0.999 Silver 0.2001 oz. ASW, 35 mm. **Ruler:** Elizabeth II **Subject:** Ships and Explorers - Golden Hind - Sir Francis Drake

| Date | Mintage | VF20 | XF40 | MS60 | MS63 | MS65 |
|---|---|---|---|---|---|---|
| 2009 | Est. 5000 | PF65 15.00 | | | | |

**KM# 214 DOLLAR**
31.10 g., Silver Plated Copper Copper Silver Plated with Color, 40 mm. **Ruler:** Elizabeth II **Subject:** Archangels - Gabriel, Colorized

| Date | Mintage | VF20 | XF40 | MS60 | MS63 | MS65 |
|---|---|---|---|---|---|---|
| 2009 | Est. 5000 | PF65 65.00 | | | | |

**KM# 215 DOLLAR**
31.10 g., Silver Plated Copper Copper Silver Plated With Color, 40 mm. **Ruler:** Elizabeth II **Subject:** Archangels - Michael, Colorized

| Date | Mintage | VF20 | XF40 | MS60 | MS63 | MS65 |
|---|---|---|---|---|---|---|
| 2009 | — | PF65 65.00 | | | | |

**KM# 216 DOLLAR**
31.10 g., Silver Plated Copper Copper Silver Plated with Color, 40 mm. **Ruler:** Elizabeth II **Subject:** Archangels - Raphael, Colorized

| Date | Mintage | VF20 | XF40 | MS60 | MS63 | MS65 |
|---|---|---|---|---|---|---|
| 2009 | Est. 5000 | **PF65** 65.00 | | | | |

**KM# 209 DOLLAR**
26.00 g., Silver Plated Copper Cu Silver Plated and Gold Plated with 3 Crystals, 40 mm. **Ruler:** Elizabeth II **Subject:** Royal Dynasties - Royal Wedding, Prince William

| Date | Mintage | VF20 | XF40 | MS60 | MS63 | MS65 |
|---|---|---|---|---|---|---|
| 2011 | Est. 15000 | **PF63** 25.00 | **PF65** 30.00 | | | |

**KM# 210 DOLLAR**
26.00 g., Silver Plated Copper Copper Silver Plated and Gold Plated with 3 Crystals, 40 mm. **Ruler:** Elizabeth II **Subject:** Royal Dynasties - Albert of Monaco

| Date | Mintage | VF20 | XF40 | MS60 | MS63 | MS65 |
|---|---|---|---|---|---|---|
| 2011 | Est. 10000 | **PF63** 25.00 | **PF65** 30.00 | | | |

**KM# 211 DOLLAR**
26.00 g., Silver Plated Copper Copper Silver Plated and Gold Plated with 3 Crystals, 40 mm. **Ruler:** Elizabeth II **Subject:** Royal Dynasties - 50th Birthday of Lady Diana

| Date | Mintage | VF20 | XF40 | MS60 | MS63 | MS65 |
|---|---|---|---|---|---|---|
| 2011 | Est. 10000 | **PF63** 25.00 | **PF65** 30.00 | | | |

**KM# 212 DOLLAR**
26.00 g., Silver Plated Copper Copper Silver Plated and Gold Plated with 3 Crystals, 40 mm. **Ruler:** Elizabeth II **Subject:** Royal Dynasties - 40th Birthday of Maxima of the Netherlands

| Date | Mintage | VF20 | XF40 | MS60 | MS63 | MS65 |
|---|---|---|---|---|---|---|
| 2011 | Est. 10000 | **PF63** 25.00 | **PF65** 30.00 | | | |

**KM# 213 DOLLAR**
26.00 g., Silver Plated Copper Copper Silver Plated and Gold Plated with 3 Crystals, 40 mm. **Ruler:** Elizabeth II **Subject:** Royal Dynasties - 85th Anniversary of HM Queen Elizabeth II

| Date | Mintage | VF20 | XF40 | MS60 | MS63 | MS65 |
|---|---|---|---|---|---|---|
| 2011 | Est. 10000 | **PF63** 25.00 | **PF65** 30.00 | | | |

**KM# 232 DOLLAR**
0.50 g., 0.585 Gold 0.0094 oz. AGW, 11 mm. **Ruler:** Elizabeth II **Series:** Smallest Gold Coins **Subject:** Maya Calendar

| Date | Mintage | VF20 | XF40 | MS60 | MS63 | MS65 |
|---|---|---|---|---|---|---|
| 2012 | Est. 5000 | **PF65** 35.00 | | | | |

**KM# 238 DOLLAR**
Aluminum-Bronze, 21.1 mm. **Ruler:** Elizabeth II **Rev:** Nguzu Nguz

| Date | Mintage | VF20 | XF40 | MS60 | MS63 | MS65 |
|---|---|---|---|---|---|---|
| 2012 | — | — | — | 3.00 | 4.00 | 4.50 |

**KM# 238a DOLLAR**
7.70 g., 0.999 Silver 0.2473 oz. ASW, 21.14 mm. **Ruler:** Elizabeth II **Obv:** Head with tiara right **Rev:** Nguzu Nguzu

| Date | Mintage | VF20 | XF40 | MS60 | MS63 | MS65 |
|---|---|---|---|---|---|---|
| 2012 | 1,500 | **PF65** 50.00 | | | | |

**KM# 263 DOLLAR**
0.50 g., 0.585 Gold 0.0094 oz. AGW with 24Kt plating, 11 mm. **Ruler:** Elizabeth II **Subject:** Hanging gardens of Babylon

| Date | Mintage | VF20 | XF40 | MS60 | MS63 | MS65 |
|---|---|---|---|---|---|---|
| 2013 | 7,000 | **PF65** 65.00 | | | | |

**KM# 264 DOLLAR**
0.50 g., 0.585 Gold 0.0094 oz. AGW with 24Kt plating, 11 mm. **Ruler:** Elizabeth II **Subject:** Statue of Zeus at Olympia

| Date | Mintage | VF20 | XF40 | MS60 | MS63 | MS65 |
|---|---|---|---|---|---|---|
| 2013 | 7,000 | **PF65** 65.00 | | | | |

**KM# 265 DOLLAR**
0.50 g., 0.585 Gold 0.0094 oz. AGW with 24Kt plating, 11 mm. **Ruler:** Elizabeth II **Subject:** Temple of Artemis at Ephesus

| Date | Mintage | VF20 | XF40 | MS60 | MS63 | MS65 |
|---|---|---|---|---|---|---|
| 2013 | 7,000 | **PF65** 65.00 | | | | |

**KM# 266 DOLLAR**
0.50 g., 0.585 Gold 0.0094 oz. AGW with 24Kt plating, 11 mm. **Ruler:** Elizabeth II **Subject:** Mausoleum of Mausollos

| Date | Mintage | VF20 | XF40 | MS60 | MS63 | MS65 |
|---|---|---|---|---|---|---|
| 2013 | 7,000 | **PF65** 65.00 | | | | |

**KM# 267 DOLLAR**
0.50 g., 0.585 Gold 0.0094 oz. AGW with 24Kt plating, 11 mm. **Ruler:** Elizabeth II **Subject:** Colossus of Rhodes

| Date | Mintage | VF20 | XF40 | MS60 | MS63 | MS65 |
|---|---|---|---|---|---|---|
| 2013 | 7,000 | **PF65** 65.00 | | | | |

**KM# 268 DOLLAR**
0.50 g., 0.585 Gold 0.0094 oz. AGW with 24Kt plating, 11 mm. **Ruler:** Elizabeth II **Subject:** Lighthouse at Alexandria

| Date | Mintage | VF20 | XF40 | MS60 | MS63 | MS65 |
|---|---|---|---|---|---|---|
| 2013 | 7,000 | **PF65** 65.00 | | | | |

**KM# 269 DOLLAR**
0.50 g., 0.585 Gold 0.0094 oz. AGW with 24Kt plating, 11 mm. **Ruler:** Elizabeth II **Subject:** Chichen Itza

| Date | Mintage | VF20 | XF40 | MS60 | MS63 | MS65 |
|---|---|---|---|---|---|---|
| 2013 | 7,000 | **PF65** 65.00 | | | | |

**KM# 270 DOLLAR**
0.50 g., 0.585 Gold 0.0094 oz. AGW with 24Kt plating, 11 mm. **Ruler:** Elizabeth II **Subject:** Great Wall of China

| Date | Mintage | VF20 | XF40 | MS60 | MS63 | MS65 |
|---|---|---|---|---|---|---|
| 2013 | 7,000 | **PF65** 65.00 | | | | |

**KM# 271 DOLLAR**
0.50 g., 0.585 Gold 0.0094 oz. AGW with 24Kt plating, 11 mm. **Ruler:** Elizabeth II **Subject:** Christ the Redeemer statue

| Date | Mintage | VF20 | XF40 | MS60 | MS63 | MS65 |
|---|---|---|---|---|---|---|
| 2013 | 7,000 | **PF65** 65.00 | | | | |

**KM# 273 DOLLAR**
0.50 g., 0.585 Gold 0.0094 oz. AGW with 24Kt plating, 11 mm. **Ruler:** Elizabeth II **Subject:** Machu Pichu

| Date | Mintage | VF20 | XF40 | MS60 | MS63 | MS65 |
|---|---|---|---|---|---|---|
| 2013 | 7,000 | **PF65** 65.00 | | | | |

**KM# 274 DOLLAR**
0.50 g., 0.585 Gold 0.0094 oz. AGW with 24Kt plating, 11 mm. **Ruler:** Elizabeth II **Subject:** Petra

| Date | Mintage | VF20 | XF40 | MS60 | MS63 | MS65 |
|---|---|---|---|---|---|---|
| 2013 | 7,000 | **PF65** 65.00 | | | | |

**KM# 275 DOLLAR**
0.50 g., 0.585 Gold 0.0094 oz. AGW with 24Kt plating, 11 mm. **Ruler:** Elizabeth II **Rev:** Taj Mahal

| Date | Mintage | VF20 | XF40 | MS60 | MS63 | MS65 |
|---|---|---|---|---|---|---|
| 2013 | 7,000 | **PF65** 65.00 | | | | |

**KM# 276 DOLLAR**
0.50 g., 0.999 Gold 0.0161 oz. AGW, 11 mm. **Ruler:** Elizabeth II **Subject:** Statue of Liberty

| Date | Mintage | VF20 | XF40 | MS60 | MS63 | MS65 |
|---|---|---|---|---|---|---|
| 2013 | 5,000 | **PF65** 65.00 | | | | |

**KM# 277 DOLLAR**
0.50 g., 0.999 Gold 0.0161 oz. AGW, 11 mm. **Ruler:** Elizabeth II **Subject:** Nefertiti

| Date | Mintage | VF20 | XF40 | MS60 | MS63 | MS65 |
|---|---|---|---|---|---|---|
| 2013 | 7,500 | **PF65** 65.00 | | | | |

**KM# 278 DOLLAR**
0.50 g., 0.585 Gold 0.0094 oz. AGW with 24 Kt. plating, 11 mm. **Ruler:** Elizabeth II **Subject:** Neferititi

| Date | Mintage | VF20 | XF40 | MS60 | MS63 | MS65 |
|---|---|---|---|---|---|---|
| 2013 | 7,500 | **PF65** 65.00 | | | | |

**KM# 83 2 DOLLARS**
62.27 g., 0.999 Silver 2.000 oz. ASW, 50.3 mm. **Subject:** Regional Assistance Mission to Solomon Islands **Obv:** Crowned head right **Rev:** Dove outline over multicolor islands in a sea of country names **Edge:** Reeded

| Date | Mintage | VF20 | XF40 | MS60 | MS63 | MS65 |
|---|---|---|---|---|---|---|
| 2005 | 2,500 | **PF65** 95.00 | | | | |

**KM# 176 2 DOLLARS**
Silver, 38.61 mm. **Ruler:** Elizabeth II **Subject:** Royal visit to the Solomon Islands **Obv:** Heas with tiara right **Rev:** Portraits of Prince Willam and Kate Middleton in color

| Date | Mintage | VF20 | XF40 | MS60 | MS63 | MS65 |
|---|---|---|---|---|---|---|
| 2012 | — | **PF65** 75.00 | | | | |

**KM# 239 2 DOLLARS**
Aluminum-Bronze, 26.3 mm. **Ruler:** Elizabeth II **Rev:** Fossilized clam shells from Western and Choiseul provinces

| Date | Mintage | VF20 | XF40 | MS60 | MS63 | MS65 |
|---|---|---|---|---|---|---|
| 2012 | — | — | — | 4.00 | 5.00 | 6.00 |

**KM# 239a 2 DOLLARS**
24.70 g., 0.999 Silver 0.7933 oz. ASW, 10.3 mm. **Ruler:** Elizabeth II **Obv:** Head with tiara right **Rev:** Bokolo

| Date | Mintage | VF20 | XF40 | MS60 | MS63 | MS65 |
|---|---|---|---|---|---|---|
| 2012 | 1,500 | **PF65** 60.00 | | | | |

**KM# 262 2 DOLLARS**
0.50 g., 0.585 Gold 0.0094 oz. AGW with 24Kt plating, 11 mm. **Ruler:** Elizabeth II **Subject:** Great Pyramids of Giza

| Date | Mintage | VF20 | XF40 | MS60 | MS63 | MS65 |
|---|---|---|---|---|---|---|
| 2013 | 7,000 | **PF65** 65.00 | | | | |

**KM# 130 5 DOLLARS**
25.00 g., 0.900 Silver 0.7234 oz. ASW **Ruler:** Elizabeth II **Rev:** Butterfly fish in color

| Date | Mintage | VF20 | XF40 | MS60 | MS63 | MS65 |
|---|---|---|---|---|---|---|
| 2001 | — | PF65 65.00 | | | | |

**KM# 113 5 DOLLARS**
Copper-Nickel **Ruler:** Elizabeth II **Rev:** Orb

| Date | Mintage | VF20 | XF40 | MS60 | MS63 | MS65 |
|---|---|---|---|---|---|---|
| 2002 | — | — | — | — | — | 15.00 |

**KM# 113a 5 DOLLARS**
28.28 g., 0.925 Silver 0.841 oz. ASW partially gilt, 38.6 mm. **Ruler:** Elizabeth II **Obv:** Bust right gilt **Rev:** Orb

| Date | Mintage | VF20 | XF40 | MS60 | MS63 | MS65 |
|---|---|---|---|---|---|---|
| 2002 | 20,000 | PF63 38.00 | PF65 42.00 | | | |

**KM# 125 5 DOLLARS**
Silver partially gilt, 38.6 mm. **Ruler:** Elizabeth II **Obv:** Head crowned right **Rev:** Mace and coronation scene

| Date | Mintage | VF20 | XF40 | MS60 | MS63 | MS65 |
|---|---|---|---|---|---|---|
| 2002 | — | PF65 50.00 | | | | |

**KM# 75 5 DOLLARS**
28.28 g., Copper-Nickel, 38.6 mm. **Obv:** Crowned head right **Rev:** F-117A Nighthawk Stealth fighter plane **Edge:** Reeded

| Date | Mintage | VF20 | XF40 | MS60 | MS63 | MS65 |
|---|---|---|---|---|---|---|
| 2003 | — | — | — | 5.00 | 7.00 | 9.00 |

**KM# 76 5 DOLLARS**
28.28 g., Copper-Nickel, 38.6 mm. **Obv:** Crowned head right **Rev:** Concorde supersonic airliner **Edge:** Reeded

| Date | Mintage | VF20 | XF40 | MS60 | MS63 | MS65 |
|---|---|---|---|---|---|---|
| 2003 | — | — | — | 5.00 | 7.00 | 9.00 |

**KM# 84 5 DOLLARS**
31.10 g., 0.999 Silver 0.999 oz. ASW, 38.6 mm. **Ruler:** Elizabeth II **Obv:** Maklouf's portrait of Elizabeth II **Rev:** Gold plated pig **Edge:** Reeded **Note:** Year of the Pig

| Date | Mintage | VF20 | XF40 | MS60 | MS63 | MS65 |
|---|---|---|---|---|---|---|
| 2007 | 10,000 | — | — | — | — | 50.00 |

**KM# 85 5 DOLLARS**
31.10 g., 0.999 Silver 0.999 oz. ASW, 38.6 mm. **Ruler:** Elizabeth II **Obv:** Maklouf's portrait of Elizabeth II **Rev:** Dark red pig and piglet **Edge:** Reeded **Note:** Year of the Pig

| Date | Mintage | VF20 | XF40 | MS60 | MS63 | MS65 |
|---|---|---|---|---|---|---|
| 2007 | 10,000 | — | — | — | — | 50.00 |

**KM# 179 5 DOLLARS**
26.03 g., Silver Plated Copper-Nickel, 38.61 mm. **Ruler:** Elizabeth II **Subject:** 2012 London Olympic Games - Discus Thrower

| Date | Mintage | VF20 | XF40 | MS60 | MS63 | MS65 |
|---|---|---|---|---|---|---|
| 2008 | — | PF65 18.00 | | | | |

**KM# 203 5 DOLLARS**
0.50 g., 1.000 Gold 0.0161 oz. AGW, 11 mm. **Ruler:** Elizabeth II **Subject:** Daedalus

| Date | Mintage | VF20 | XF40 | MS60 | MS63 | MS65 |
|---|---|---|---|---|---|---|
| 2008 | Est. 15000 | PF63 40.00 | PF65 45.00 | | | |

**KM# 204 5 DOLLARS**
0.50 g., 1.000 Gold 0.0161 oz. AGW **Ruler:** Elizabeth II **Subject:** Icarus **Issuer:** 11

| Date | Mintage | VF20 | XF40 | MS60 | MS63 | MS65 |
|---|---|---|---|---|---|---|
| 2008 | Est. 15000 | PF63 40.00 | PF65 45.00 | | | |

**KM# 110 5 DOLLARS**
1.22 g., 0.999 Gold 0.0392 oz. AGW, 14 mm. **Ruler:** Elizabeth II **Subject:** Alexander von Humboldt **Obv:** Head right

| Date | Mintage | VF20 | XF40 | MS60 | MS63 | MS65 |
|---|---|---|---|---|---|---|
| 2010 | — | PF65 45.00 | | | | |

**KM# 119 5 DOLLARS**
0.50 g., 0.999 Gold 0.0161 oz. AGW, 11 mm. **Ruler:** Elizabeth II **Subject:** For World Peace **Rev:** John Paul II and Mother Theresa

| Date | Mintage | VF20 | XF40 | MS60 | MS63 | MS65 |
|---|---|---|---|---|---|---|
| 2010 | 10,000 | PF63 60.00 | PF65 70.00 | | | |

**KM# 123 5 DOLLARS**
0.50 g., 0.999 Gold 0.0161 oz. AGW, 11 mm. **Ruler:** Elizabeth II **Rev:** Spotted Cuscus in tree

| Date | Mintage | VF20 | XF40 | MS60 | MS63 | MS65 |
|---|---|---|---|---|---|---|
| 2010 | 15,000 | PF63 60.00 | PF65 70.00 | | | |

**KM# 205 5 DOLLARS**
0.50 g., 0.999 Gold 0.0161 oz. AGW, 11 mm. **Ruler:** Elizabeth II **Subject:** Immanuel Kant

| Date | Mintage | VF20 | XF40 | MS60 | MS63 | MS65 |
|---|---|---|---|---|---|---|
| 2010 | Est. 10000 | PF63 40.00 | PF65 45.00 | | | |

**KM# 206 5 DOLLARS**
0.50 g., 0.999 Gold 0.0161 oz. AGW, 11 mm. **Ruler:** Elizabeth II **Subject:** Alexander Humboldt

| Date | Mintage | VF20 | XF40 | MS60 | MS63 | MS65 |
|---|---|---|---|---|---|---|
| 2010 | Est. 10000 | PF63 40.00 | PF65 45.00 | | | |

**KM# 207 5 DOLLARS**
0.50 g., 0.999 Gold 0.0161 oz. AGW, 11 mm. **Ruler:** Elizabeth II **Subject:** Saint Sophia Cathedral Kiev

| Date | Mintage | VF20 | XF40 | MS60 | MS63 | MS65 |
|---|---|---|---|---|---|---|
| 2010 | Est. 10000 | PF63 40.00 | PF65 45.00 | | | |

**KM# 126 5 DOLLARS**
15.55 g., 0.999 Silver 0.4994 oz. ASW, 35 mm. **Ruler:** Elizabeth II **Rev:** Archangel Gabriel in color

| Date | Mintage | VF20 | XF40 | MS60 | MS63 | MS65 |
|---|---|---|---|---|---|---|
| 2011 | 2,000 | PF65 70.00 | | | | |

**KM# 127 5 DOLLARS**
15.55 g., 0.999 Silver 0.4994 oz. ASW, 35 mm. **Ruler:** Elizabeth II **Rev:** Auchangel Michael

| Date | Mintage | VF20 | XF40 | MS60 | MS63 | MS65 |
|---|---|---|---|---|---|---|
| 2011 | — | PF65 70.00 | | | | |

**KM# 163 5 DOLLARS**
0.50 g., 0.999 Gold 0.0161 oz. AGW, 11 mm. **Ruler:** Elizabeth II **Rev:** Manatee

| Date | Mintage | VF20 | XF40 | MS60 | MS63 | MS65 |
|---|---|---|---|---|---|---|
| 2011 | 10,000 | PF63 45.00 | PF65 55.00 | | | |

**KM# 164 5 DOLLARS**
0.50 g., 0.999 Gold 0.0161 oz. AGW, 11 mm. **Ruler:** Elizabeth II **Rev:** Great Wall of China

| Date | Mintage | VF20 | XF40 | MS60 | MS63 | MS65 |
|---|---|---|---|---|---|---|
| 2011 | Est. 7000 | PF63 40.00 | PF65 45.00 | | | |

**KM# 165 5 DOLLARS**
0.50 g., 0.999 Gold 0.0161 oz. AGW, 11 mm. **Ruler:** Elizabeth II **Rev:** Storehouse at Petra

| Date | Mintage | VF20 | XF40 | MS60 | MS63 | MS65 |
|---|---|---|---|---|---|---|
| 2011 | Est. 7000 | PF63 40.00 | PF65 45.00 | | | |

**KM# 166 5 DOLLARS**
0.50 g., 0.999 Gold 0.0161 oz. AGW, 11 mm. **Ruler:** Elizabeth II **Rev:** Christ statue in Rio de Janeiro

| Date | Mintage | VF20 | XF40 | MS60 | MS63 | MS65 |
|---|---|---|---|---|---|---|
| 2011 | Est. 7000 | PF63 40.00 | PF65 45.00 | | | |

**KM# 167 5 DOLLARS**
0.50 g., 0.999 Gold 0.0161 oz. AGW, 11 mm. **Ruler:** Elizabeth II **Rev:** Machu Picchu

| Date | Mintage | VF20 | XF40 | MS60 | MS63 | MS65 |
|---|---|---|---|---|---|---|
| 2011 | — | PF63 40.00 | PF65 45.00 | | | |

**KM# 168 5 DOLLARS**
0.50 g., 0.999 Gold 0.0161 oz. AGW, 11 mm. **Ruler:** Elizabeth II **Rev:** Stepped pyramid at Chichen Itza

| Date | Mintage | VF20 | XF40 | MS60 | MS63 | MS65 |
|---|---|---|---|---|---|---|
| 2011 | Est. 7000 | PF63 40.00 | PF65 45.00 | | | |

**KM# 169 5 DOLLARS**
0.50 g., 0.999 Gold 0.0161 oz. AGW, 11 mm. **Ruler:** Elizabeth II **Rev:** Colusem in Rome

| Date | Mintage | VF20 | XF40 | MS60 | MS63 | MS65 |
|---|---|---|---|---|---|---|
| 2011 | Est. 7000 | PF63 40.00 | PF65 45.00 | | | |

**KM# 170 5 DOLLARS**
0.50 g., 0.999 Gold 0.0161 oz. AGW, 11 mm. **Ruler:** Elizabeth II **Rev:** Taj Mahal

| Date | Mintage | VF20 | XF40 | MS60 | MS63 | MS65 |
|---|---|---|---|---|---|---|
| 2011 | — | PF63 40.00 | PF65 45.00 | | | |

**KM# 188 5 DOLLARS**
0.50 g., 0.585 Gold 0.0094 oz. AGW 24K Goldplated, 11 mm. **Ruler:** Elizabeth II **Subject:** Ancient Sevens Wonders: Great Pyramids of Giza

| Date | Mintage | VF20 | XF40 | MS60 | MS63 | MS65 |
|---|---|---|---|---|---|---|
| 2011 | Est. 5000 | PF65 35.00 | | | | |

**KM# 189 5 DOLLARS**
0.50 g., 0.585 Gold 0.0094 oz. AGW 24K Gold plated, 11 mm. **Ruler:** Elizabeth II **Subject:** Ancient Seven World Wonders: Hanging Gardens of Babylon

| Date | Mintage | VF20 | XF40 | MS60 | MS63 | MS65 |
|---|---|---|---|---|---|---|
| 2011 | — | PF65 35.00 | | | | |

**KM# 190 5 DOLLARS**
0.50 g., 0.585 Gold 0.0094 oz. AGW 24K Gold Plating, 11 mm. **Ruler:** Elizabeth II **Subject:** Ancient Seven Wonders: Statue of Zeus at Olympia

| Date | Mintage | VF20 | XF40 | MS60 | MS63 | MS65 |
|---|---|---|---|---|---|---|
| 2011 | Est. 5000 | PF65 35.00 | | | | |

**KM# 191 5 DOLLARS**
0.50 g., 0.585 Gold 0.0094 oz. AGW 24K Gold Plated, 11 mm. **Ruler:** Elizabeth II **Subject:** Ancient Seven World Wonders: Temple of Artemis at Ephesus

| Date | Mintage | VF20 | XF40 | MS60 | MS63 | MS65 |
|---|---|---|---|---|---|---|
| 2011 | Est. 5000 | PF65 35.00 | | | | |

**KM# 192 5 DOLLARS**
0.50 g., 0.585 Gold 0.0094 oz. AGW 24K Gold Plating, 11 mm. **Ruler:** Elizabeth II **Subject:** Ancient Seven World Wonders: Mausoleum of Mausollos

| Date | Mintage | VF20 | XF40 | MS60 | MS63 | MS65 |
|---|---|---|---|---|---|---|
| 2011 | Est. 5000 | PF65 35.00 | | | | |

**KM# 193 5 DOLLARS**
0.50 g., 0.585 Gold 0.0094 oz. AGW 24K Gold Plating, 11 mm. **Ruler:** Elizabeth II **Subject:** Ancient Seven World Wonders: The Colossos of Rhodos

| Date | Mintage | VF20 | XF40 | MS60 | MS63 | MS65 |
|---|---|---|---|---|---|---|
| 2011 | Est. 5000 | PF65 35.00 | | | | |

**KM# 194 5 DOLLARS**
0.50 g., 0.585 Gold 0.0094 oz. AGW 24K Gold Plating, 11 mm. **Ruler:** Elizabeth II **Subject:** Ancient Seven World Wonders: Lighthouse of Alexandria

| Date | Mintage | VF20 | XF40 | MS60 | MS63 | MS65 |
|---|---|---|---|---|---|---|
| 2011 | Est. 5000 | PF65 35.00 | | | | |

**KM# 195 5 DOLLARS**
0.50 g., 0.585 Gold 0.0094 oz. AGW 24K Gold Plating, 11 mm. **Ruler:** Elizabeth II **Subject:** New Seven World Wonders: Mexico Chichen Itza

| Date | Mintage | VF20 | XF40 | MS60 | MS63 | MS65 |
|---|---|---|---|---|---|---|
| 2011 | Est. 5000 | PF65 35.00 | | | | |

**KM# 196 5 DOLLARS**
0.50 g., 0.585 Gold 0.0094 oz. AGW 24K Gold Plating, 11 mm. **Ruler:** Elizabeth II **Subject:** New Seven World Wonders: China Great Wall

| Date | Mintage | VF20 | XF40 | MS60 | MS63 | MS65 |
|---|---|---|---|---|---|---|
| 2011 | Est. 5000 | PF65 35.00 | | | | |

**KM# 197 5 DOLLARS**
0.50 g., 0.585 Gold 0.0094 oz. AGW 24K Gold Plating, 11 mm. **Ruler:** Elizabeth II **Subject:** New Seven World Wonders: Brazil Christ Redeemer

| Date | Mintage | VF20 | XF40 | MS60 | MS63 | MS65 |
|---|---|---|---|---|---|---|
| 2011 | — | PF65 35.00 | | | | |

**KM# 198 5 DOLLARS**
0.50 g., 0.585 Gold 0.0094 oz. AGW 24K Gold Plated, 11 mm. **Ruler:** Elizabeth II **Subject:** New Seven World Wonders: Italy Roman Colosseum

| Date | Mintage | VF20 | XF40 | MS60 | MS63 | MS65 |
|---|---|---|---|---|---|---|
| 2011 | Est. 5000 | PF65 35.00 | | | | |

**KM# 199 5 DOLLARS**
0.50 g., 0.585 Gold 0.0094 oz. AGW 24K Gold Plating, 11 mm. **Ruler:** Elizabeth II **Series:** New Seven World Wonders: Inca's Machu Picchu

| Date | Mintage | VF20 | XF40 | MS60 | MS63 | MS65 |
|---|---|---|---|---|---|---|
| 2011 | Est. 5000 | PF65 35.00 | | | | |

**KM# 200 5 DOLLARS**
0.50 g., 0.585 Gold 0.0094 oz. AGW 24K Gold Plated, 11 mm. **Ruler:** Elizabeth II **Subject:** New Seven World Wonders: Jordan Petra

| Date | Mintage | VF20 | XF40 | MS60 | MS63 | MS65 |
|---|---|---|---|---|---|---|
| 2011 | Est. 5000 | PF65 35.00 | | | | |

**KM# 201 5 DOLLARS**
0.50 g., 0.585 Gold 0.0094 oz. AGW 24K Gold Plating, 11 mm. **Ruler:** Elizabeth II **Subject:** New Seven World Wonders: India Taj Mahal

| Date | Mintage | VF20 | XF40 | MS60 | MS63 | MS65 |
|---|---|---|---|---|---|---|
| 2011 | — | PF65 35.00 | | | | |

**KM# 217 5 DOLLARS**
14.18 g., 0.999 Silver 0.4553 oz. ASW, 35 mm. **Ruler:** Elizabeth II **Subject:** Archangels - Gabriel, Colorized

| Date | Mintage | VF20 | XF40 | MS60 | MS63 | MS65 |
|---|---|---|---|---|---|---|
| 2011 | Est. 2500 | PF65 75.00 | | | | |

**KM# 218 5 DOLLARS**
14.18 g., 0.999 Silver 0.4553 oz. ASW, 35 mm. **Ruler:** Elizabeth II **Subject:** Archangels - Michael, Colorized

| Date | Mintage | VF20 | XF40 | MS60 | MS63 | MS65 |
|---|---|---|---|---|---|---|
| 2011 | Est. 2500 | PF65 75.00 | | | | |

**KM# 220 5 DOLLARS**
0.50 g., 0.999 Gold 0.0161 oz. AGW, 11 mm. **Ruler:** Elizabeth II **Subject:** 2014 FIFA World Cup Brazil - 11 Friends: Africa

| Date | Mintage | VF20 | XF40 | MS60 | MS63 | MS65 |
|---|---|---|---|---|---|---|
| 2012 | Est. 7500 | PF65 35.00 | | | | |

**KM# 221 5 DOLLARS**
0.50 g., 0.999 Gold 0.0161 oz. AGW, 11 mm. **Ruler:** Elizabeth II **Subject:** 2014 FIFA World Cup Brazil -11 Friends: Asia

| Date | Mintage | VF20 | XF40 | MS60 | MS63 | MS65 |
|---|---|---|---|---|---|---|
| 2012 | Est. 7500 | PF65 35.00 | | | | |

**KM# 222 5 DOLLARS**
0.50 g., 0.999 Gold 0.0161 oz. AGW, 11 mm. **Ruler:** Elizabeth II **Series:** 2014 FIFA World Cup Brazil - 11 Friends: Brazil

| Date | Mintage | VF20 | XF40 | MS60 | MS63 | MS65 |
|---|---|---|---|---|---|---|
| 2012 | Est. 7500 | PF65 35.00 | | | | |

**KM# 223 5 DOLLARS**
0.50 g., 0.999 Gold 0.0161 oz. AGW, 11 mm. **Ruler:** Elizabeth II **Subject:** 2014 FIFA World Cup Brazil - 11 Friends: Germany

| Date | Mintage | VF20 | XF40 | MS60 | MS63 | MS65 |
|---|---|---|---|---|---|---|
| 2012 | Est. 7500 | PF65 35.00 | | | | |

**KM# 224 5 DOLLARS**
0.50 g., 0.999 Gold 0.0161 oz. AGW, 11 mm. **Ruler:** Elizabeth II **Subject:** 2014 FIFA World Cup Brazil - 11 Friends: Europe

| Date | Mintage | VF20 | XF40 | MS60 | MS63 | MS65 |
|---|---|---|---|---|---|---|
| 2012 | Est. 7500 | PF65 35.00 | | | | |

**KM# 225 5 DOLLARS**
0.50 g., 0.999 Gold 0.0161 oz. AGW, 11 mm. **Ruler:** Elizabeth II **Subject:** 2014 FIFA World Cup Brazil - 11 Friends: North America

| Date | Mintage | VF20 | XF40 | MS60 | MS63 | MS65 |
|---|---|---|---|---|---|---|
| 2012 | Est. 7500 | PF65 35.00 | | | | |

**KM# 226 5 DOLLARS**
0.50 g., 0.999 Gold 0.0161 oz. AGW, 11 mm. **Ruler:** Elizabeth II **Subject:** 2014 FIFA World Cup - 11 Friends: Spain

| Date | Mintage | VF20 | XF40 | MS60 | MS63 | MS65 |
|---|---|---|---|---|---|---|
| 2012 | Est. 7500 | PF65 35.00 | | | | |

**KM# 227 5 DOLLARS**
0.50 g., 0.999 Gold 0.0161 oz. AGW, 11 mm. **Ruler:** Elizabeth II **Series:** 2014 FIFA World Cup Brazil - 11 Friends: South Africa

| Date | Mintage | VF20 | XF40 | MS60 | MS63 | MS65 |
|---|---|---|---|---|---|---|
| 2012 | Est. 7500 | PF65 35.00 | | | | |

**KM# 228 5 DOLLARS**
0.50 g., 0.999 Gold 0.0161 oz. AGW, 11 mm. **Ruler:** Elizabeth II **Subject:** 2014 FIFA World Cup Brazil - 11 Friends: South America

| Date | Mintage | VF20 | XF40 | MS60 | MS63 | MS65 |
|---|---|---|---|---|---|---|
| 2012 | Est. 7500 | PF65 35.00 | | | | |

**KM# 229 5 DOLLARS**
0.50 g., 0.999 Gold 0.0161 oz. AGW, 11 mm. **Ruler:** Elizabeth II **Subject:** 2014 FIFA World Cup Brazil - 11 Friends: Globe

| Date | Mintage | VF20 | XF40 | MS60 | MS63 | MS65 |
|---|---|---|---|---|---|---|
| 2012 | Est. 7500 | PF65 35.00 | | | | |

**KM# 230 5 DOLLARS**
0.50 g., 0.585 Gold 0.0094 oz. AGW 24K Gold Plated, 11 mm. **Ruler:** Elizabeth II **Subject:** Greek Mythology: Ulysses

| Date | Mintage | VF20 | XF40 | MS60 | MS63 | MS65 |
|---|---|---|---|---|---|---|
| 2012 | Est. 10000 | PF65 35.00 | | | | |

**KM# 231 5 DOLLARS**
0.50 g., 0.999 Gold 0.0161 oz. AGW **Ruler:** Elizabeth II **Series:** Smalles Gold Coins **Subject:** Maya Calndar

| Date | Mintage | VF20 | XF40 | MS60 | MS63 | MS65 |
|---|---|---|---|---|---|---|
| 2012 | Est. 5000 | PF65 50.00 | | | | |

### KM# 233 5 DOLLARS

20.00 g., 0.925 Silver 0.5948 oz. ASW, 38.61 mm. **Ruler:** Elizabeth II **Subject:** Great Rulers: Catherine the Great

| Date | Mintage | VF20 | XF40 | MS60 | MS63 | MS65 |
|---|---|---|---|---|---|---|
| 2012 | — | **PF65** 45.00 | | | | |

### KM# 234 5 DOLLARS

20.00 g., 0.925 Silver 0.5948 oz. ASW, 38.61 mm. **Ruler:** Elizabeth II **Subject:** Great Rulers - Peter the Great

| Date | Mintage | VF20 | XF40 | MS60 | MS63 | MS65 |
|---|---|---|---|---|---|---|
| 2012 | Est. 5000 | **PF65** 45.00 | | | | |

### KM# 281 5 DOLLARS

12.00 g., 0.925 Silver 0.3569 oz. ASW, 38.61 mm. **Ruler:** Elizabeth II **Subject:** Giuseppe Verdi

| Date | Mintage | VF20 | XF40 | MS60 | MS63 | MS65 |
|---|---|---|---|---|---|---|
| 2013 | 5,000 | **PF65** 75.00 | | | | |

### KM# 131 10 DOLLARS

1.24 g., 0.999 Gold 0.0398 oz. AGW, 13.92 mm. **Ruler:** Elizabeth II **Rev:** Butterfly fish

| Date | Mintage | VF20 | XF40 | MS60 | MS63 | MS65 |
|---|---|---|---|---|---|---|
| 2001 | — | **PF65** 90.00 | | | | |

### KM# 86 10 DOLLARS

28.36 g., 0.925 Silver 0.8434 oz. ASW, 38.6 mm. **Obv:** Crowned bust right **Obv. Legend:** ELIZABETH II - SOLOMON ISLANDS **Rev:** Bust of Mendana facing at left, early sailing ship at center - right **Rev. Legend:** ALVARO DE MENDANA **Edge:** Reeded

| Date | Mintage | VF20 | XF40 | MS60 | MS63 | MS65 |
|---|---|---|---|---|---|---|
| 2004 | — | **PF65** 50.00 | | | | |

### KM# 124 10 DOLLARS

28.36 g., 0.925 Silver 0.8434 oz. ASW, 38.6 mm. **Ruler:** Elizabeth II **Subject:** Olumpics 2004 **Rev:** Runner, Sydney Opera House and Parthenon

| Date | Mintage | VF20 | XF40 | MS60 | MS63 | MS65 |
|---|---|---|---|---|---|---|
| 2004 | — | **PF65** 50.00 | | | | |

### KM# 140 10 DOLLARS

31.64 g., 0.999 Silver 1.0161 oz. ASW, 40 mm. **Ruler:** Elizabeth II **Subject:** 2006 FIFA World Cup, Germany **Obv:** Head with crown right **Rev:** Two players in color

| Date | Mintage | VF20 | XF40 | MS60 | MS63 | MS65 |
|---|---|---|---|---|---|---|
| 2005 | Est. 5000 | **PF65** 65.00 | | | | |

### KM# 141 10 DOLLARS

1.24 g., 0.999 Gold 0.0398 oz. AGW, 13.92 mm. **Ruler:** Elizabeth II **Rev:** Prospector panning for gold

| Date | Mintage | VF20 | XF40 | MS60 | MS63 | MS65 |
|---|---|---|---|---|---|---|
| 2005 | — | **PF65** 90.00 | | | | |

### KM# 142 10 DOLLARS

1.24 g., 0.999 Gold 0.0398 oz. AGW, 13.92 mm. **Ruler:** Elizabeth II **Subject:** John Lennon, 25th Anniversary of Death **Obv:** Head with crown right **Rev:** Lennon's head facing

| Date | Mintage | VF20 | XF40 | MS60 | MS63 | MS65 |
|---|---|---|---|---|---|---|
| 2005 | — | **PF65** 90.00 | | | | |

### KM# 153 10 DOLLARS

7.78 g., 0.585 Gold 0.1463 oz. AGW, 25 mm. **Ruler:** Elizabeth II **Subject:** 2006 World Cup, Germany

| Date | Mintage | VF20 | XF40 | MS60 | MS63 | MS65 |
|---|---|---|---|---|---|---|
| 2006 | — | **PF65** 325 | | | | |

### KM# 96 10 DOLLARS

1.22 g., 0.999 Gold 0.0392 oz. AGW, 14 mm. **Ruler:** Elizabeth II **Subject:** Wonders of the Ancient World **Obv:** Head right **Rev:** Mausoleum of Mausollos

| Date | Mintage | VF20 | XF40 | MS60 | MS63 | MS65 |
|---|---|---|---|---|---|---|
| 2007 | 7,000 | **PF63** 65.00 | **PF65** 75.00 | | | |

### KM# 97 10 DOLLARS

1.22 g., 0.999 Gold 0.0392 oz. AGW, 14 mm. **Ruler:** Elizabeth II **Subject:** Wonders of the Ancient World **Obv:** Head right **Rev:** Taj Mahal

| Date | Mintage | VF20 | XF40 | MS60 | MS63 | MS65 |
|---|---|---|---|---|---|---|
| 2007 | 7,000 | **PF63** 65.00 | **PF65** 75.00 | | | |

### KM# 98 10 DOLLARS

1.00 g., 0.999 Gold 0.0321 oz. AGW, 13.92 mm. **Ruler:** Elizabeth II **Subject:** New 7 Wonders of the World **Obv:** Head right **Rev:** Treasury at Petra

| Date | Mintage | VF20 | XF40 | MS60 | MS63 | MS65 |
|---|---|---|---|---|---|---|
| 2007 | Est. 7000 | **PF63** 65.00 | **PF65** 75.00 | | | |
| 2009 | Est. 7000 | **PF63** 65.00 | **PF65** 75.00 | | | |

### KM# 99 10 DOLLARS

1.00 g., 0.999 Gold 0.0321 oz. AGW, 13.92 mm. **Ruler:** Elizabeth II **Subject:** New 7 Wonders of the World **Obv:** Head right **Rev:** Colosseum in Rome

| Date | Mintage | VF20 | XF40 | MS60 | MS63 | MS65 |
|---|---|---|---|---|---|---|
| 2007 | Est. 7000 | **PF63** 65.00 | **PF65** 75.00 | | | |
| 2009 | Est. 7000 | **PF63** 65.00 | **PF65** 75.00 | | | |

### KM# 100 10 DOLLARS

1.00 g., 0.999 Gold 0.0321 oz. AGW, 13.92 mm. **Ruler:** Elizabeth II **Subject:** New 7 Wonders of the World **Obv:** Head right **Rev:** Inca's Machu Picchu

| Date | Mintage | VF20 | XF40 | MS60 | MS63 | MS65 |
|---|---|---|---|---|---|---|
| 2007 | Est. 7000 | **PF63** 65.00 | **PF65** 75.00 | | | |
| 2009 | Est. 7000 | **PF63** 65.00 | **PF65** 75.00 | | | |

### KM# 101 10 DOLLARS

1.00 g., 0.999 Gold 0.0321 oz. AGW, 13.92 mm. **Ruler:** Elizabeth II **Subject:** New 7 Wonders of the World **Obv:** Head right **Rev:** Chichen Itza

| Date | Mintage | VF20 | XF40 | MS60 | MS63 | MS65 |
|---|---|---|---|---|---|---|
| 2007 | — | **PF63** 65.00 | **PF65** 75.00 | | | |
| 2009 | Est. 7000 | **PF63** 65.00 | **PF65** 75.00 | | | |

### KM# 102 10 DOLLARS

1.00 g., 0.999 Gold 0.0321 oz. AGW, 13.92 mm. **Ruler:** Elizabeth II **Subject:** New 7 Wonders of the World **Obv:** Head right **Rev:** Great wall of China

| Date | Mintage | VF20 | XF40 | MS60 | MS63 | MS65 |
|---|---|---|---|---|---|---|
| 2007 | Est. 7000 | **PF63** 65.00 | **PF65** 75.00 | | | |
| 2009 | Est. 7000 | **PF63** 65.00 | **PF65** 75.00 | | | |

### KM# 103 10 DOLLARS

1.00 g., 0.999 Gold 0.0321 oz. AGW, 13.92 mm. **Ruler:** Elizabeth II **Subject:** New 7 Wonders of the World **Rev:** Christ Statue in Rio

| Date | Mintage | VF20 | XF40 | MS60 | MS63 | MS65 |
|---|---|---|---|---|---|---|
| 2007 | Est. 7000 | **PF63** 65.00 | **PF65** 75.00 | | | |
| 2009 | — | **PF63** 65.00 | **PF65** 75.00 | | | |

### KM# 105 10 DOLLARS

1.00 g., 0.999 Gold 0.0321 oz. AGW, 13.92 mm. **Ruler:** Elizabeth II **Subject:** Ancient Seven Wonders of the World **Obv:** Head right **Rev:** Colossus of Rhodes

| Date | Mintage | VF20 | XF40 | MS60 | MS63 | MS65 |
|---|---|---|---|---|---|---|
| 2009 | Est. 7000 | **PF63** 65.00 | **PF65** 75.00 | | | |

### KM# 106 10 DOLLARS

1.00 g., 0.999 Gold 0.0321 oz. AGW, 13.92 mm. **Ruler:** Elizabeth II **Subject:** Seven Ancient World Wonders **Obv:** Head right **Rev:** Statue of Zeus at Olympia

| Date | Mintage | VF20 | XF40 | MS60 | MS63 | MS65 |
|---|---|---|---|---|---|---|
| 2009 | 7,000 | **PF63** 65.00 | **PF65** 75.00 | | | |

### KM# 186 10 DOLLARS

1.00 g., 0.999 Gold 0.0321 oz. AGW, 13.92 mm. **Ruler:** Elizabeth II **Subject:** New 7 World Wonders: India Taj Mahal

| Date | Mintage | VF20 | XF40 | MS60 | MS63 | MS65 |
|---|---|---|---|---|---|---|
| 2007 | — | **PF63** 65.00 | **PF65** 75.00 | | | |
| 2009 | Est. 7000 | **PF63** 65.00 | **PF65** 75.00 | | | |

### KM# 240 10 DOLLARS

28.28 g., 0.925 Silver 0.841 oz. ASW, 38.61 mm. **Ruler:** Elizabeth II **Subject:** Royal Train **Shape:** 7-Sided

| Date | Mintage | VF20 | XF40 | MS60 | MS63 | MS65 |
|---|---|---|---|---|---|---|
| 2007 | Est. 30000 | **PF63** 35.00 | **PF65** 40.00 | | | |

### KM# 241 10 DOLLARS

28.28 g., 0.925 Silver 0.841 oz. ASW, 38.61 mm. **Ruler:** Elizabeth II **Subject:** Queen Elizabeth II **Shape:** 7-Sided

| Date | Mintage | VF20 | XF40 | MS60 | MS63 | MS65 |
|---|---|---|---|---|---|---|
| 2007 | Est. 30000 | **PF63** 35.00 | **PF65** 40.00 | | | |

**KM# 250 10 DOLLARS**
28.28 g., 0.925 Silver 0.841 oz. ASW, 38.61 mm. **Ruler:** Elizabeth II **Subject:** Queen Elizabeth II 60th Wedding Anniversary **Shape:** 7-Sided

| Date | Mintage | VF20 | XF40 | MS60 | MS63 | MS65 |
|---|---|---|---|---|---|---|
| 2007 | — | PF63 35.00 | PF65 40.00 | | | |

**KM# 154 10 DOLLARS**
1.24 g., 0.999 Gold 0.0398 oz. AGW, 13.92 mm. **Ruler:** Elizabeth II **Rev:** Legendary chief of El Dorado sprinking water

| Date | Mintage | VF20 | XF40 | MS60 | MS63 | MS65 |
|---|---|---|---|---|---|---|
| 2008 | — | PF65 90.00 | | | | |

**KM# 177 10 DOLLARS**
28.28 g., 0.925 Silver 0.841 oz. ASW, 38.61 mm. **Ruler:** Elizabeth II **Subject:** 2008 Beijing Olympic Games - Handball

| Date | Mintage | VF20 | XF40 | MS60 | MS63 | MS65 |
|---|---|---|---|---|---|---|
| 2008 | Est. 15000 | PF63 45.00 | PF65 50.00 | | | |

**KM# 178 10 DOLLARS**
20.00 g., 0.925 Silver 0.5948 oz. ASW, 38.61 mm. **Ruler:** Elizabeth II **Subject:** 2012 London Olympic Games - Discus Thrower

| Date | Mintage | VF20 | XF40 | MS60 | MS63 | MS65 |
|---|---|---|---|---|---|---|
| 2008 | Est. 10000 | PF63 40.00 | PF65 45.00 | | | |

**KM# 180 10 DOLLARS**
7.77 g., Gold Plated 14K Gold with 24K Goldplating, 25 mm. **Ruler:** Elizabeth II **Subject:** 2012 London Olympic Games - Discus Thrower

| Date | Mintage | VF20 | XF40 | MS60 | MS63 | MS65 |
|---|---|---|---|---|---|---|
| 2008 | Est. 1000 | PF65 500 | | | | |

**KM# 181 10 DOLLARS**
28.28 g., 0.925 Silver 0.841 oz. ASW, 38.61 mm. **Ruler:** Elizabeth II **Subject:** Ships and Explorers - Concord

| Date | Mintage | VF20 | XF40 | MS60 | MS63 | MS65 |
|---|---|---|---|---|---|---|
| 2008 | — | PF65 50.00 | | | | |

**KM# 185 10 DOLLARS**
28.28 g., 0.925 Silver 0.841 oz. ASW, 38.61 mm. **Ruler:** Elizabeth II **Subject:** Railways - ICE

| Date | Mintage | VF20 | XF40 | MS60 | MS63 | MS65 |
|---|---|---|---|---|---|---|
| 2008 | Est. 5000 | PF65 50.00 | | | | |

**KM# 202 10 DOLLARS**
1.24 g., 0.999 Gold 0.0398 oz. AGW, 13.92 mm. **Ruler:** Elizabeth II **Subject:** Eldorado

| Date | Mintage | VF20 | XF40 | MS60 | MS63 | MS65 |
|---|---|---|---|---|---|---|
| 2008 | Est. 15000 | PF63 65.00 | PF65 75.00 | | | |

**KM# 104 10 DOLLARS**
1.00 g., 0.999 Gold 0.0321 oz. AGW, 13.92 mm. **Ruler:** Elizabeth II **Subject:** Ancient Seven World Wonders **Obv:** Head right **Rev:** Giza Pyramids

| Date | Mintage | VF20 | XF40 | MS60 | MS63 | MS65 |
|---|---|---|---|---|---|---|
| 2009 | Est. 7000 | PF63 65.00 | PF65 75.00 | | | |

**KM# 107 10 DOLLARS**
1.00 g., 0.999 Gold 0.0321 oz. AGW, 13.92 mm. **Ruler:** Elizabeth II **Subject:** Ancient Seven Wonders of the World **Obv:** Head right **Rev:** Temple of Artemis at Ephesus

| Date | Mintage | VF20 | XF40 | MS60 | MS63 | MS65 |
|---|---|---|---|---|---|---|
| 2009 | Est. 7000 | PF63 65.00 | PF65 75.00 | | | |

**KM# 108 10 DOLLARS**
1.00 g., 0.999 Gold 0.0321 oz. AGW, 13.92 mm. **Ruler:** Elizabeth II **Subject:** Ancient Seven World Wonders **Obv:** Head right **Rev:** Hanging Gardens of Bablyon

| Date | Mintage | VF20 | XF40 | MS60 | MS63 | MS65 |
|---|---|---|---|---|---|---|
| 2009 | 7,500 | PF63 65.00 | PF65 75.00 | | | |

**KM# 109 10 DOLLARS**
1.00 g., 0.999 Gold 0.0321 oz. AGW, 13.92 mm. **Ruler:** Elizabeth II **Subject:** Ancient Seven Wonders of the World **Obv:** Head right **Rev:** Lighthouse at Alexandria

| Date | Mintage | VF20 | XF40 | MS60 | MS63 | MS65 |
|---|---|---|---|---|---|---|
| 2009 | Est. 7000 | PF63 65.00 | PF65 75.00 | | | |

**KM# 187 10 DOLLARS**
1.00 g., 0.999 Gold 0.0321 oz. AGW, 13.92 mm. **Ruler:** Elizabeth II **Subject:** Ancient 7 World Wonders: Mausoleum of Mausollos

| Date | Mintage | VF20 | XF40 | MS60 | MS63 | MS65 |
|---|---|---|---|---|---|---|
| 2009 | Est. 7000 | PF63 65.00 | PF65 75.00 | | | |

**KM# 120 10 DOLLARS**
20.00 g., 0.925 Silver 0.5948 oz. ASW, 38.61 mm. **Ruler:** Elizabeth II **Subject:** For World Peace **Rev:** John Paul II and Mother Theresa

| Date | Mintage | VF20 | XF40 | MS60 | MS63 | MS65 |
|---|---|---|---|---|---|---|
| 2010 | 2,500 | PF65 75.00 | | | | |

**KM# 121 10 DOLLARS**
20.00 g., 0.925 Silver 0.5948 oz. ASW, 38.61 mm. **Ruler:** Elizabeth II **Rev:** S.M.S. Gneisenau under full sail

| Date | Mintage | VF20 | XF40 | MS60 | MS63 | MS65 |
|---|---|---|---|---|---|---|
| 2010 | 2,500 | PF65 75.00 | | | | |

**KM# 122 10 DOLLARS**
25.00 g., 0.925 Silver 0.7435 oz. ASW, 38.61 mm. **Ruler:** Elizabeth II **Rev:** Spotted Cuscus in color with Swarovsky crystal eyes

| Date | Mintage | VF20 | XF40 | MS60 | MS63 | MS65 |
|---|---|---|---|---|---|---|
| 2010 | 2,500 | PF65 65.00 | | | | |

**KM# 162 10 DOLLARS**
20.00 g., Silver, 38.61 mm. **Ruler:** Elizabeth II **Rev:** Manatee in color

| Date | Mintage | VF20 | XF40 | MS60 | MS63 | MS65 |
|---|---|---|---|---|---|---|
| 2011 | 2,500 | PF65 55.00 | | | | |

**KM# 208 10 DOLLARS**
31.10 g., 0.999 Silver 0.9989 oz. ASW selective gold plating, 40.6 mm. **Ruler:** Elizabeth II **Subject:** Diamond Jubilee of Queen Elizabeth II - Coronation

| Date | Mintage | VF20 | XF40 | MS60 | MS63 | MS65 |
|---|---|---|---|---|---|---|
| 2011 | Est. 10000 | PF63 55.00 | PF65 60.00 | | | |

**KM# 219 10 DOLLARS**
20.00 g., 0.925 Silver 0.5948 oz. ASW, 38.61 mm. **Ruler:** Elizabeth II **Subject:** 2014 FiFA World Cup Brazil

| Date | Mintage | VF20 | XF40 | MS60 | MS63 | MS65 |
|---|---|---|---|---|---|---|
| 2012 | Est. 10000 | PF63 30.00 | PF65 35.00 | | | |

**KM# 260 10 DOLLARS**
28.28 g., 0.925 Silver 0.841 oz. ASW, 38.61 mm. **Ruler:** Elizabeth II **Subject:** 2014 Olympics - Lighting the flame

| Date | Mintage | VF20 | XF40 | MS60 | MS63 | MS65 |
|---|---|---|---|---|---|---|
| 2013 | 5,000 | PF65 75.00 | | | | |

**KM# 261 10 DOLLARS**
20.00 g., 0.925 Silver 0.5948 oz. ASW, 38.61 mm. **Ruler:** Elizabeth II **Subject:** Steeplechase

| Date | Mintage | VF20 | XF40 | MS60 | MS63 | MS65 |
|---|---|---|---|---|---|---|
| 2013 | 7,500 | PF65 75.00 | | | | |

**KM# 279 10 DOLLARS**
31.11 g., 0.999 Silver 0.999 oz. ASW with plating of Rhodium, Ruthenium, Palladium, Platinum and Gold, 66x32 mm. **Ruler:** Elizabeth II **Subject:** Precious 6 in 1 Bar

| Date | Mintage | VF20 | XF40 | MS60 | MS63 | MS65 |
|---|---|---|---|---|---|---|
| 2013 | 10,000 | PF65 100 | | | | |

**KM# 90 25 DOLLARS**
31.11 g., 0.999 Silver 0.999 oz. ASW, 38.61 mm. **Ruler:** Elizabeth II **Obv:** Head right **Rev:** Wright Brother's 1903 Flyer

| Date | Mintage | VF20 | XF40 | MS60 | MS63 | MS65 |
|---|---|---|---|---|---|---|
| 2003 | — | PF65 45.00 | | | | |

**KM# 91 25 DOLLARS**
31.11 g., 0.999 Silver 0.999 oz. ASW, 38.6 mm. **Ruler:** Elizabeth II **Subject:** Don Everhart II **Obv:** Head right **Rev:** AN-225 Mriya

| Date | Mintage | VF20 | XF40 | MS60 | MS63 | MS65 |
|---|---|---|---|---|---|---|
| 2003 | — | PF65 45.00 | | | | |

**KM# 92 25 DOLLARS**
31.11 g., 0.999 Silver 0.999 oz. ASW, 38.61 mm. **Ruler:** Elizabeth II **Obv:** Head right **Rev:** Spitfire

| Date | Mintage | VF20 | XF40 | MS60 | MS63 | MS65 |
|---|---|---|---|---|---|---|
| 2003 | — | PF65 45.00 | | | | |

**KM# 114 25 DOLLARS**
31.11 g., 0.999 Silver 0.999 oz. ASW, 38.61 mm. **Ruler:** Elizabeth II **Rev:** NC 14716 China Clipper

| Date | Mintage | VF20 | XF40 | MS60 | MS63 | MS65 |
|---|---|---|---|---|---|---|
| 2003 | — | PF65 65.00 | | | | |

**KM# 115 25 DOLLARS**
31.10 g., 0.999 Silver 0.9989 oz. ASW, 38.6 mm. **Ruler:** Elizabeth II **Rev:** Messerschmitt ME 262

| Date | Mintage | VF20 | XF40 | MS60 | MS63 | MS65 |
|---|---|---|---|---|---|---|
| 2003 | — | PF65 45.00 | | | | |

**KM# 132 25 DOLLARS**
31.11 g., 0.999 Silver 0.999 oz. ASW, 38.61 mm. **Ruler:** Elizabeth II **Rev:** Sikorsky VS 30

| Date | Mintage | VF20 | XF40 | MS60 | MS63 | MS65 |
|---|---|---|---|---|---|---|
| 2003 | — | PF65 42.50 | | | | |

**KM# 133 25 DOLLARS**
31.11 g., 0.999 Silver 0.999 oz. ASW, 38.61 mm. **Ruler:** Elizabeth II **Rev:** Concorde

| Date | Mintage | VF20 | XF40 | MS60 | MS63 | MS65 |
|---|---|---|---|---|---|---|
| 2003 | — | PF65 42.50 | | | | |

**KM# 134 25 DOLLARS**
31.11 g., 0.999 Silver 0.999 oz. ASW, 38.61 mm. **Ruler:** Elizabeth II **Rev:** Lockheed Martin F-117 Nighthawk

| Date | Mintage | VF20 | XF40 | MS60 | MS63 | MS65 |
|---|---|---|---|---|---|---|
| 2003 | — | PF65 42.50 | | | | |

**KM# 135 25 DOLLARS**
31.11 g., 0.999 Silver 0.999 oz. ASW, 38.61 mm. **Ruler:** Elizabeth II **Rev:** Bell X 1

| Date | Mintage | VF20 | XF40 | MS60 | MS63 | MS65 |
|---|---|---|---|---|---|---|
| 2003 | — | PF65 42.50 | | | | |

**KM# 136 25 DOLLARS**
31.11 g., 0.999 Silver 0.999 oz. ASW, 38.61 mm. **Ruler:** Elizabeth II **Rev:** De Havilland Comet

| Date | Mintage | VF20 | XF40 | MS60 | MS63 | MS65 |
|---|---|---|---|---|---|---|
| 2003 | — | PF65 42.50 | | | | |

**KM# 137 25 DOLLARS**
31.11 g., 0.999 Silver 0.999 oz. ASW, 38.61 mm. **Ruler:** Elizabeth II **Rev:** AV 8B Harrier II

| Date | Mintage | VF20 | XF40 | MS60 | MS63 | MS65 |
|---|---|---|---|---|---|---|
| 2003 | — | PF65 42.50 | | | | |

**KM# 138 25 DOLLARS**
31.11 g., 0.999 Silver 0.999 oz. ASW, 38.61 mm. **Ruler:** Elizabeth II **Rev:** Curtiss Jenny

| Date | Mintage | VF20 | XF40 | MS60 | MS63 | MS65 |
|---|---|---|---|---|---|---|
| 2003 | — | PF65 42.50 | | | | |

**KM# 139 25 DOLLARS**
31.11 g., 0.999 Silver 0.999 oz. ASW, 38.61 mm. **Ruler:** Elizabeth II **Rev:** Douglas DC 3

| Date | Mintage | VF20 | XF40 | MS60 | MS63 | MS65 |
|---|---|---|---|---|---|---|
| 2003 | — | PF65 42.50 | | | | |

**KM# 90a 25 DOLLARS**
31.11 g., 0.999 Silver 0.999 oz. ASW partially plated, 38.61 mm. **Ruler:** Elizabeth II **Rev:** Antonov AN-225 Mrija

| Date | Mintage | VF20 | XF40 | MS60 | MS63 | MS65 |
|---|---|---|---|---|---|---|
| 2005 | — | PF65 55.00 | | | | |

**KM# 90a 25 DOLLARS**
31.10 g., 0.999 Silver 0.9989 oz. ASW partially gilt, 38.61 mm. **Ruler:** Elizabeth II **Rev:** Wright flier of 1903

| Date | Mintage | VF20 | XF40 | MS60 | MS63 | MS65 |
|---|---|---|---|---|---|---|
| 2005 | — | PF65 75.00 | | | | |

**KM# 92a 25 DOLLARS**
31.11 g., 0.999 Silver 0.999 oz. ASW partially gilt, 38.61 mm. **Ruler:** Elizabeth II **Rev:** Spitfire

| Date | Mintage | VF20 | XF40 | MS60 | MS63 | MS65 |
|---|---|---|---|---|---|---|
| 2005 | — | PF65 55.00 | | | | |

**KM# 93 25 DOLLARS**
31.11 g., 0.999 Silver 0.999 oz. ASW **Ruler:** Elizabeth II **Subject:** Trafalgar **Obv:** Head right **Rev:** H.M.S. Victory

| Date | Mintage | VF20 | XF40 | MS60 | MS63 | MS65 |
|---|---|---|---|---|---|---|
| 2005 | — | PF65 45.00 | | | | |

**KM# 114a 25 DOLLARS**
31.11 g., 0.999 Silver 0.999 oz. ASW partially gilt, 38.61 mm. **Ruler:** Elizabeth II **Rev:** NC 14716 China Clipper

| Date | Mintage | VF20 | XF40 | MS60 | MS63 | MS65 |
|---|---|---|---|---|---|---|
| 2005 | — | PF65 55.00 | | | | |

**KM# 115a 25 DOLLARS**
31.11 g., 0.999 Silver 0.999 oz. ASW partially gilt, 38.61 mm. **Ruler:** Elizabeth II **Rev:** Messerschmitt ME 262

| Date | Mintage | VF20 | XF40 | MS60 | MS63 | MS65 |
|---|---|---|---|---|---|---|
| 2005 | — | PF65 55.00 | | | | |

**KM# 132a 25 DOLLARS**
31.11 g., 0.999 Silver 0.999 oz. ASW partially gilt, 38.61 mm. **Ruler:** Elizabeth II **Rev:** Sikorsky VS 300

| Date | Mintage | VF20 | XF40 | MS60 | MS63 | MS65 |
|---|---|---|---|---|---|---|
| 2005 | — | PF65 55.00 | | | | |

**KM# 133a 25 DOLLARS**
31.11 g., 0.999 Silver 0.999 oz. ASW partially gilt, 38.61 mm. **Ruler:** Elizabeth II **Rev:** Concorde

| Date | Mintage | VF20 | XF40 | MS60 | MS63 | MS65 |
|---|---|---|---|---|---|---|
| 2005 | — | PF65 55.00 | | | | |

**KM# 134a 25 DOLLARS**
31.11 g., 0.999 Silver 0.999 oz. ASW partially gilt, 38.61 mm. **Ruler:** Elizabeth II **Rev:** Lockheed Martin F-117 Nighthawk

| Date | Mintage | VF20 | XF40 | MS60 | MS63 | MS65 |
|---|---|---|---|---|---|---|
| 2005 | — | PF65 55.00 | | | | |

**KM# 135a 25 DOLLARS**
31.11 g., 0.999 Silver 0.999 oz. ASW Partially gilt, 38.61 mm. **Ruler:** Elizabeth II **Rev:** Bell X1

| Date | Mintage | VF20 | XF40 | MS60 | MS63 | MS65 |
|---|---|---|---|---|---|---|
| 2005 | — | PF65 55.00 | | | | |

**KM# 136a 25 DOLLARS**
31.11 g., 0.999 Silver 0.999 oz. ASW partially gilt, 38.61 mm. **Ruler:** Elizabeth II **Rev:** De Havilland Comet

| Date | Mintage | VF20 | XF40 | MS60 | MS63 | MS65 |
|---|---|---|---|---|---|---|
| 2005 | — | PF65 55.00 | | | | |

**KM# 137a 25 DOLLARS**
31.11 g., 0.999 Silver 0.999 oz. ASW partially gilt, 38.61 mm. **Ruler:** Elizabeth II **Rev:** AV 8B Harrier II

| Date | Mintage | VF20 | XF40 | MS60 | MS63 | MS65 |
|---|---|---|---|---|---|---|
| 2005 | — | PF65 55.00 | | | | |

**KM# 138a 25 DOLLARS**
31.11 g., 0.999 Silver 0.999 oz. ASW partially gilt, 38.61 mm. **Ruler:** Elizabeth II **Rev:** Curtiss Jenny

| Date | Mintage | VF20 | XF40 | MS60 | MS63 | MS65 |
|---|---|---|---|---|---|---|
| 2005 | — | PF65 55.00 | | | | |

**KM# 139a 25 DOLLARS**
31.11 g., 0.999 Silver 0.999 oz. ASW partially gilt, 38.61 mm. **Ruler:** Elizabeth II **Rev:** Douglas DC 3

| Date | Mintage | VF20 | XF40 | MS60 | MS63 | MS65 |
|---|---|---|---|---|---|---|
| 2005 | — | PF65 55.00 | | | | |

**KM# 143 25 DOLLARS**
31.11 g., 0.999 Silver 0.999 oz. ASW, 38.61 mm. **Ruler:** Elizabeth II **Subject:** Triere

| Date | Mintage | VF20 | XF40 | MS60 | MS63 | MS65 |
|---|---|---|---|---|---|---|
| 2005 | — | PF65 55.00 | | | | |

**KM# 144 25 DOLLARS**
31.11 g., 0.999 Silver 0.999 oz. ASW, 38.61 mm. **Ruler:** Elizabeth II **Subject:** H.M.S. Mary Rose

| Date | Mintage | VF20 | XF40 | MS60 | MS63 | MS65 |
|---|---|---|---|---|---|---|
| 2005 | — | PF65 55.00 | | | | |

**KM# 145 25 DOLLARS**
31.11 g., 0.999 Silver 0.999 oz. ASW, 38.61 mm. **Ruler:** Elizabeth II **Subject:** U.S.S. Bonhomme Richard

| Date | Mintage | VF20 | XF40 | MS60 | MS63 | MS65 |
|---|---|---|---|---|---|---|
| 2005 | — | PF65 55.00 | | | | |

**KM# 146 25 DOLLARS**
31.11 g., 0.999 Silver 0.999 oz. ASW, 38.61 mm. **Ruler:** Elizabeth II **Subject:** H.M.S. Dorsetshire

| Date | Mintage | VF20 | XF40 | MS60 | MS63 | MS65 |
|---|---|---|---|---|---|---|
| 2005 | — | PF65 55.00 | | | | |

**KM# 87 25 DOLLARS**
0.925 Silver **Ruler:** Elizabeth II **Obv:** Crowned bust right **Obv. Legend:** ELIZABETH II - SOLOMON ISLANDS **Rev:** 3/4 length figures of Elizabeth and Prince Philip facing

| Date | Mintage | VF20 | XF40 | MS60 | MS63 | MS65 |
|---|---|---|---|---|---|---|
| 2006 | — | PF65 50.00 | | | | |

**KM# 87a 25 DOLLARS**
31.11 g., 0.999 Silver 0.999 oz. ASW partially gilt **Ruler:** Elizabeth II **Obv:** Head right, partially gilt **Rev:** Wedding of Elizabeth II and Philip. Gothic window behind, gilt 80 above.

| Date | Mintage | VF20 | XF40 | MS60 | MS63 | MS65 |
|---|---|---|---|---|---|---|
| 2006 | — | PF65 50.00 | | | | |

**KM# 95 25 DOLLARS**
31.11 g., 0.999 Silver 0.999 oz. ASW partially gilt, 38.6 mm. **Ruler:** Elizabeth II **Obv:** Head right, partially gilt **Rev:** Queen Elizabeth II and WWII Red Cross Nurse, gilt 80 above.

| Date | Mintage | VF20 | XF40 | MS60 | MS63 | MS65 |
|---|---|---|---|---|---|---|
| 2006 | — | PF65 50.00 | | | | |

**KM# 147 25 DOLLARS**
31.11 g., 0.999 Silver 0.999 oz. ASW, 38.61 mm. **Ruler:** Elizabeth II **Subject:** Turtle boat

| Date | Mintage | VF20 | XF40 | MS60 | MS63 | MS65 |
|---|---|---|---|---|---|---|
| 2006 | — | PF65 55.00 | | | | |

**KM# 148 25 DOLLARS**
31.11 g., 0.999 Silver 0.999 oz. ASW, 38.61 mm. **Ruler:** Elizabeth II **Subject:** Ville de Paris

| Date | Mintage | VF20 | XF40 | MS60 | MS63 | MS65 |
|---|---|---|---|---|---|---|
| 2006 | — | PF65 55.00 | | | | |

**KM# 149 25 DOLLARS**
31.11 g., 0.999 Silver 0.999 oz. ASW, 38.61 mm. **Ruler:** Elizabeth II **Subject:** Admiral Graf Spee

| Date | Mintage | VF20 | XF40 | MS60 | MS63 | MS65 |
|---|---|---|---|---|---|---|
| 2006 | — | PF65 55.00 | | | | |

**KM# 150 25 DOLLARS**
31.11 g., 0.999 Silver 0.999 oz. ASW, 38.61 mm. **Ruler:** Elizabeth II **Subject:** H.M.S. Dreadnought

| Date | Mintage | VF20 | XF40 | MS60 | MS63 | MS65 |
|---|---|---|---|---|---|---|
| 2006 | — | PF65 55.00 | | | | |

**KM# 151 25 DOLLARS**
31.11 g., 0.999 Silver 0.999 oz. ASW, 38.61 mm. **Ruler:** Elizabeth II **Subject:** U.S.S. Hornet

| Date | Mintage | VF20 | XF40 | MS60 | MS63 | MS65 |
|---|---|---|---|---|---|---|
| 2006 | — | PF65 55.00 | | | | |

**KM# 152 25 DOLLARS**
31.11 g., 0.999 Silver 0.999 oz. ASW, 38.61 mm. **Ruler:** Elizabeth II **Subject:** Yamato

| Date | Mintage | VF20 | XF40 | MS60 | MS63 | MS65 |
|---|---|---|---|---|---|---|
| 2006 | — | PF65 55.00 | | | | |

**KM# 251 25 DOLLARS**
31.11 g., 0.999 Silver 0.999 oz. ASW **Ruler:** Elizabeth II **Obv:** Crowned head right **Rev:** Brederode sailing right

| Date | Mintage | VF20 | XF40 | MS60 | MS63 | MS65 |
|---|---|---|---|---|---|---|
| 2007 | — | PF65 100 | | | | |

**KM# 252 25 DOLLARS**
31.11 g., 0.999 Silver 0.999 oz. ASW, 38.61 mm. **Ruler:** Elizabeth II **Obv:** Crowned head right **Rev:** The Mary Rose sailing left

| Date | Mintage | VF20 | XF40 | MS60 | MS63 | MS65 |
|---|---|---|---|---|---|---|
| 2007 | — | PF65 100 | | | | |

**KM# 253 25 DOLLARS**
31.11 g., 0.999 Silver 0.999 oz. ASW, 38.61 mm. **Ruler:** Elizabeth II **Obv:** Crowned head right **Rev:** Roman Trireme sailing ship

| Date | Mintage | VF20 | XF40 | MS60 | MS63 | MS65 |
|---|---|---|---|---|---|---|
| 2007 | — | PF65 100 | | | | |

**KM# 254 25 DOLLARS**
31.11 g., 0.999 Silver 0.999 oz. ASW, 38.61 mm. **Ruler:** Elizabeth II **Obv:** Crowned head right **Rev:** Ming Treasure Ship sailing left

| Date | Mintage | VF20 | XF40 | MS60 | MS63 | MS65 |
|---|---|---|---|---|---|---|
| 2007 | — | PF65 100 | | | | |

**KM# 255 25 DOLLARS**
31.11 g., 0.999 Silver 0.999 oz. ASW, 38.61 mm. **Ruler:** Elizabeth II **Obv:** Crowned head right **Rev:** USS Hartford sailing right

| Date | Mintage | VF20 | XF40 | MS60 | MS63 | MS65 |
|---|---|---|---|---|---|---|
| 2007 | — | PF65 100 | | | | |

**KM# 256 25 DOLLARS**
31.11 g., 0.999 Silver 0.999 oz. ASW, 38.61 mm. **Ruler:** Elizabeth II **Obv:** Crowned head right **Rev:** Nuestra Rosario sailing right

| Date | Mintage | VF20 | XF40 | MS60 | MS63 | MS65 |
|---|---|---|---|---|---|---|
| 2007 | — | PF65 100 | | | | |

**KM# 257 25 DOLLARS**
31.11 g., 0.999 Silver 0.999 oz. ASW, 38.61 mm. **Ruler:** Elizabeth II **Obv:** Crowned head right **Rev:** Fijian Ndrua sailing left

| Date | Mintage | VF20 | XF40 | MS60 | MS63 | MS65 |
|---|---|---|---|---|---|---|
| 2007 | — | PF65 100 | | | | |

**KM# 258 25 DOLLARS**
31.11 g., 0.999 Silver 0.999 oz. ASW, 38.61 mm. **Ruler:** Elizabeth II **Obv:** Crowned head right **Rev:** USS Tautog sailing left

| Date | Mintage | VF20 | XF40 | MS60 | MS63 | MS65 |
|---|---|---|---|---|---|---|
| 2007 | — | PF65 100 | | | | |

**KM# 259 25 DOLLARS**
31.11 g., 0.999 Silver 0.999 oz. ASW, 38.61 mm. **Ruler:** Elizabeth II **Obv:** Crowned head right **Rev:** Venice Galley sailing right

| Date | Mintage | VF20 | XF40 | MS60 | MS63 | MS65 |
|---|---|---|---|---|---|---|
| 2007 | — | PF65 100 | | | | |

**KM# 116 25 DOLLARS**
28.28 g., 0.925 Silver 0.841 oz. ASW, 38.6 mm. **Ruler:** Elizabeth II **Rev:** Press clippings, soldier standing over field cross

| Date | Mintage | VF20 | XF40 | MS60 | MS63 | MS65 |
|---|---|---|---|---|---|---|
| 2008 | — | PF65 50.00 | | | | |

**KM# 117 25 DOLLARS**
28.28 g., 0.925 Silver 0.841 oz. ASW, 38.6 mm. **Ruler:** Elizabeth II **Rev:** Battlefield

| Date | Mintage | VF20 | XF40 | MS60 | MS63 | MS65 |
|---|---|---|---|---|---|---|
| 2008 | — | PF65 50.00 | | | | |

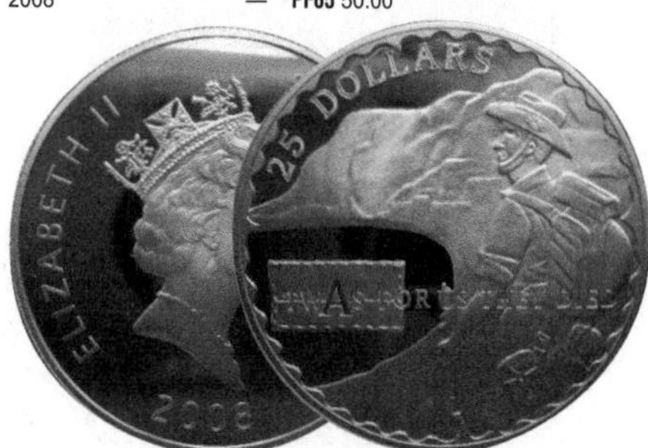

**KM# 118 25 DOLLARS**
28.28 g., 0.925 Silver 0.841 oz. ASW, 38.6 mm. **Ruler:** Elizabeth II **Rev:** Soldier overlooking beach

| Date | Mintage | VF20 | XF40 | MS60 | MS63 | MS65 |
|---|---|---|---|---|---|---|
| 2008 | — | PF65 50.00 | | | | |

**KM# 155 25 DOLLARS**
28.28 g., 0.925 Silver 0.841 oz. ASW, 38.61 mm. **Ruler:** Elizabeth II **Subject:** Cannons

| Date | Mintage | VF20 | XF40 | MS60 | MS63 | MS65 |
|---|---|---|---|---|---|---|
| 2008 | — | PF65 55.00 | | | | |

**KM# 156 25 DOLLARS**
28.28 g., 0.925 Silver 0.841 oz. ASW, 38.61 mm. **Ruler:** Elizabeth II **Subject:** Eastern Front

| Date | Mintage | VF20 | XF40 | MS60 | MS63 | MS65 |
|---|---|---|---|---|---|---|
| 2008 | — | PF65 55.00 | | | | |

**KM# 157 25 DOLLARS**
28.28 g., 0.925 Silver 0.841 oz. ASW, 38.61 mm. **Ruler:** Elizabeth II **Subject:** Truce

| Date | Mintage | VF20 | XF40 | MS60 | MS63 | MS65 |
|---|---|---|---|---|---|---|
| 2008 | — | PF65 55.00 | | | | |

**KM# 280 25 DOLLARS**
93.30 g., 0.999 Silver 2.9967 oz. ASW with color and selective plating, 110x52 mm. **Ruler:** Elizabeth II **Subject:** Nefertiti

| Date | Mintage | VF20 | XF40 | MS60 | MS63 | MS65 |
|---|---|---|---|---|---|---|
| 2013 | 1,000 | PF65 400 | | | | |

**KM# 158 50 DOLLARS**
155.50 g., 0.925 Silver 4.6245 oz. ASW, 65 mm. **Ruler:** Elizabeth II **Rev:** Poppy on war novel

| Date | Mintage | VF20 | XF40 | MS60 | MS63 | MS65 |
|---|---|---|---|---|---|---|
| 2008 | Est. 150 | PF65 225 | | | | |

## PROOF SETS

| KM# | Date | Mintage | Identification | Issue Price | Mkt Val |
|---|---|---|---|---|---|
| PS13 | 2012 (5) | 1,500 | KM#171a-175a | — | — |

# SOMALIA

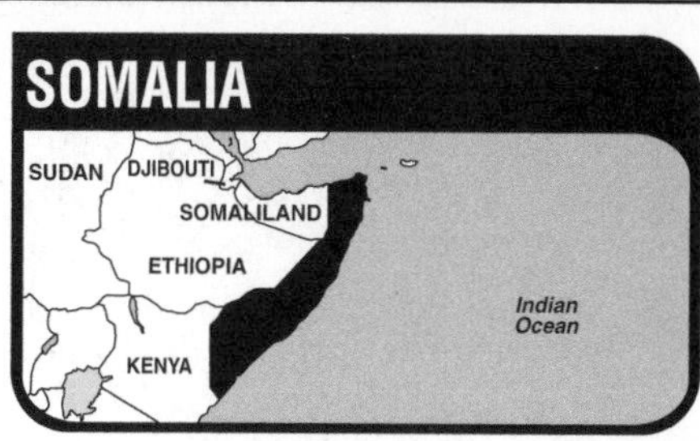


The Somali Republic consists of the former Italian Somaliland and is located on the coast of the eastern projection of the African continent commonly referred to as the "Horn". It has an area of 178,201 sq. mi. (461,657 sq. km.) and a population of *8.2 million. Capital: Mogadishu. The economy is pastoral and agricultural. Livestock, bananas and hides are exported.

The Northern Somali National Movement (SNM) declared a secession of the northwestern Somaliland Republic on May 17, 1991, which is not recognized by the Somali Democratic Republic.

**TITLE**
Al-Jumhuriya(t)as - Somaliya(t)

## REPUBLIC OF SOMALIA

### STANDARD COINAGE

**KM# 45 5 SHILLING / SCELLINI**
1.29 g., Aluminum, 21 mm. **Series:** F.A.O. **Obv:** Crowned arms with supporters **Rev:** Elephant **Edge:** Plain

| Date | Mintage | VF20 | XF40 | MS60 | MS63 | MS65 |
|---|---|---|---|---|---|---|
| 2002 | — | — | — | 0.75 | 1.50 | 1.75 |

**KM# 159 10 SHILLINGS**
25.15 g., Copper-Nickel, 38.66 mm. **Series:** Marine Life Protection **Obv:** National arms **Rev:** Two fish multicolor **Edge:** Reeded

| Date | Mintage | VF20 | XF40 | MS60 | MS63 | MS65 |
|---|---|---|---|---|---|---|
| 2003 | — | PF65 10.00 | | | | |

**KM# 46 10 SHILLINGS / SCELLINI**
1.29 g., Aluminum, 21.9 mm. **Series:** F.A.O. **Obv:** Crowned arms with supporters **Rev:** Camel **Edge:** Plain

| Date | Mintage | VF20 | XF40 | MS60 | MS63 | MS65 |
|---|---|---|---|---|---|---|
| 2002 | — | — | — | 1.00 | 2.00 | 2.25 |

**KM# 175 20 SHILLINGS**
0.62 g., 0.999 Gold 0.0199 oz. AGW **Obv:** Arms **Rev:** Mom and baby elephant

| Date | Mintage | VF20 | XF40 | MS60 | MS63 | MS65 |
|---|---|---|---|---|---|---|
| 2007 | — | PF65 50.00 | | | | |

### KM# 166 25 SHILLINGS

Silver **Obv:** Arms **Rev:** Mozart, multicolor

| Date | Mintage | VF20 | XF40 | MS60 | MS63 | MS65 |
|---|---|---|---|---|---|---|
| 2001 | — | — | — | — | — | 40.00 |

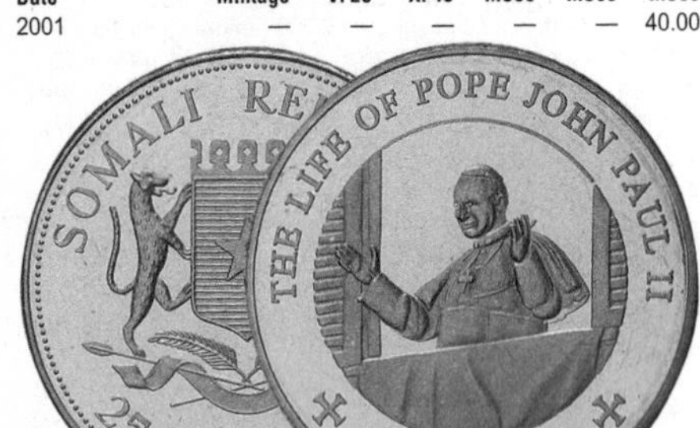

### KM# 155 25 SHILLINGS

28.10 g., Copper-Nickel, 38.73 mm. **Subject:** The Life of Pope John-Paul II **Obv:** National arms **Obv. Legend:** SOMALI REPUBLIC **Rev:** Pope John-Paul II in window at the Vatican **Edge:** Plain

| Date | Mintage | VF20 | XF40 | MS60 | MS63 | MS65 |
|---|---|---|---|---|---|---|
| 2004 | — | — | — | — | 6.00 | 7.00 |

### KM# 156 25 SHILLINGS

28.10 g., Copper-Nickel, 38.73 mm. **Subject:** Life of Pope John Paul II **Obv:** National arms **Obv. Legend:** SOMALI REPUBLIC **Rev:** Pope traveling in special vehicle **Edge:** Plain

| Date | Mintage | VF20 | XF40 | MS60 | MS63 | MS65 |
|---|---|---|---|---|---|---|
| 2004 | — | — | — | — | 6.00 | 7.00 |

### KM# 157 25 SHILLINGS

28.10 g., Copper-Nickel, 38.73 mm. **Subject:** The Life of Pope John-Paul II **Obv:** National arms **Obv. Legend:** SOMALI REPUBLIC **Rev:** Pope blessing Mother Teresa **Edge:** Plain

| Date | Mintage | VF20 | XF40 | MS60 | MS63 | MS65 |
|---|---|---|---|---|---|---|
| 2004 | — | — | — | — | 6.00 | 7.00 |

### KM# 164 25 SHILLINGS

25.80 g., Copper-Nickel, 38.77 mm. **Obv:** National arms **Obv. Legend:** SOMALI REPUBLIC **Rev:** Black rhinoceros walking left **Edge:** Reeded

| Date | Mintage | VF20 | XF40 | MS60 | MS63 | MS65 |
|---|---|---|---|---|---|---|
| 2006 | — | — | — | — | 12.00 | 14.00 |

### KM# 165 25 SHILLINGS

25.80 g., Copper-Nickel, 38.77 mm. **Obv:** National arms **Rev:** Red Kite perched on branch **Edge:** Reeded

| Date | Mintage | VF20 | XF40 | MS60 | MS63 | MS65 |
|---|---|---|---|---|---|---|
| 2006 | — | — | — | — | 12.00 | 14.00 |

### KM# 103 25 SHILLINGS / SCELLINI

4.37 g., Brass, 21.8 mm. **Subject:** Soccer **Obv:** Crowned arms with supporters **Rev:** Soccer player **Edge:** Plain

| Date | Mintage | VF20 | XF40 | MS60 | MS63 | MS65 |
|---|---|---|---|---|---|---|
| 2001 | — | — | — | — | 1.25 | 1.50 |

### KM# 111 50 SHILLINGS

3.90 g., Nickel Clad Steel, 21.9 mm. **Obv:** Crowned arms with supporters **Rev:** Mandrill **Edge:** Plain

| Date | Mintage | VF20 | XF40 | MS60 | MS63 | MS65 |
|---|---|---|---|---|---|---|
| 2002 | — | — | — | — | 0.85 | 1.25 |

### KM# 161 50 SHILLINGS

1.20 g., 0.999 Gold 0.0385 oz. AGW, 13.88 mm. **Subject:** Gold of the Pharaohs **Obv:** National arms **Obv. Legend:** SOMALI REPUBLIC **Rev:** King Tutankhaman's death mask **Edge:** Reeded

| Date | Mintage | VF20 | XF40 | MS60 | MS63 | MS65 |
|---|---|---|---|---|---|---|
| 2002 | — | PF65 80.00 | | | | |

### KM# 109 100 SHILLINGS

10.50 g., 0.999 Silver 0.3372 oz. ASW, 30.1 mm. **Subject:** Soccer **Obv:** Crowned arms with supporters **Rev:** Multicolor soccer player and Brandenburg Gate **Edge:** Reeded

| Date | Mintage | VF20 | XF40 | MS60 | MS63 | MS65 |
|---|---|---|---|---|---|---|
| 2001 | — | PF65 25.00 | | | | |

### KM# 112 100 SHILLINGS

3.54 g., Brass, 18.8 mm. **Obv:** Crowned arms with supporters above value **Rev:** Bust with headdress facing **Edge:** Plain

| Date | Mintage | VF20 | XF40 | MS60 | MS63 | MS65 |
|---|---|---|---|---|---|---|
| 2002 | — | — | — | — | 1.50 | 2.50 |

### KM# 176 200 SHILLINGS

0.62 g., 0.999 Gold 0.0199 oz. AGW, 13.90 mm. **Obv:** Arms **Rev:** Elephant head left

| Date | Mintage | VF20 | XF40 | MS60 | MS63 | MS65 |
|---|---|---|---|---|---|---|
| 2005 | — | PF65 50.00 | | | | |

### KM# 168 250 SHILLINGS

23.00 g., 0.925 Silver 0.684 oz. ASW **Obv:** Arms **Rev:** Victoria, gothic crown

| Date | Mintage | VF20 | XF40 | MS60 | MS63 | MS65 |
|---|---|---|---|---|---|---|
| 2001 | — | PF65 35.00 | | | | |

### KM# 110 250 SHILLINGS

31.11 g., 0.999 Silver 0.999 oz. ASW, 40 mm. **Subject:** Queen of Sheba **Obv:** Crowned arms with supporters **Rev:** Crowned bust 1/4 right **Edge:** Reeded

| Date | Mintage | VF20 | XF40 | MS60 | MS63 | MS65 |
|---|---|---|---|---|---|---|
| 2002 | — | — | — | — | 35.00 | 40.00 |

### KM# 158 250 SHILLINGS

20.05 g., Silver, 38.59 mm. **Obv:** National arms **Obv. Legend:** SOMALI REPUBLIC **Rev:** Laureate bust of Julius Caesar 3/4 left **Edge:** Reeded

| Date | Mintage | VF20 | XF40 | MS60 | MS63 | MS65 |
|---|---|---|---|---|---|---|
| 2002 | — | PF65 32.00 | | | | |

### KM# 162 250 SHILLINGS

1.27 g., 0.999 Gold 0.0408 oz. AGW, 13.90 mm. **Obv:** National arms **Obv. Legend:** SOMALI REPUBLIC **Rev:** Bust of Hans Rühmann facing **Edge:** Reeded

| Date | Mintage | VF20 | XF40 | MS60 | MS63 | MS65 |
|---|---|---|---|---|---|---|
| 2002 | — | PF65 85.00 | | | | |

### KM# 169 250 SHILLINGS

23.00 g., 0.925 Silver 0.684 oz. ASW **Obv:** Arms **Rev:** Soccer player, Brazil

| Date | Mintage | VF20 | XF40 | MS60 | MS63 | MS65 |
|---|---|---|---|---|---|---|
| 2002 | — | — | — | — | — | 45.00 |

### KM# 160 250 SHILLINGS

20.50 g., Silver, 38.56 mm. **Subject:** Wembley Goal - England 1966 **Obv:** National arms **Obv. Legend:** SOMALI REPUBLIC **Rev:** 3 soccer players at goal **Edge:** Reeded

| Date | Mintage | VF20 | XF40 | MS60 | MS63 | MS65 |
|---|---|---|---|---|---|---|
| 2003 | — | PF65 28.00 | | | | |

**KM# 121 250 SHILLINGS**
20.12 g., Silver Plated Base Metal, 38.5 mm. **Obv:** Crowned arms with supporters **Rev:** Multicolor Pope John Paul II and mountains **Edge:** Reeded

| Date | Mintage | VF20 | XF40 | MS60 | MS63 | MS65 |
|---|---|---|---|---|---|---|
| 2005 | — | PF65 16.50 | | | | |

**KM# 123 250 SHILLINGS**
20.12 g., Silver Plated Base Metal, 38.5 mm. **Obv:** Crowned arms with supporters **Rev:** Multicolor Pope John Paul II kissing bible **Edge:** Reeded

| Date | Mintage | VF20 | XF40 | MS60 | MS63 | MS65 |
|---|---|---|---|---|---|---|
| 2005 | — | PF65 16.50 | | | | |

**KM# 125 250 SHILLINGS**
20.12 g., Silver Plated Base Metal, 38.5 mm. **Obv:** Crowned arms with supporters **Rev:** Multicolor Pope John Paul II with flowers **Edge:** Reeded

| Date | Mintage | VF20 | XF40 | MS60 | MS63 | MS65 |
|---|---|---|---|---|---|---|
| 2005 | — | PF65 16.50 | | | | |

**KM# 127 250 SHILLINGS**
20.12 g., Silver Plated Base Metal, 38.5 mm. **Obv:** Crowned arms with supporters **Rev:** Multicolor Pope John Paul II saying mass **Edge:** Reeded

| Date | Mintage | VF20 | XF40 | MS60 | MS63 | MS65 |
|---|---|---|---|---|---|---|
| 2005 | — | PF65 16.50 | | | | |

**KM# 129 250 SHILLINGS**
20.12 g., Silver Plated Base Metal, 38.5 mm. **Obv:** Crowned arms with supporters **Rev:** Multicolor Pope John Paul II with cardinals **Edge:** Reeded

| Date | Mintage | VF20 | XF40 | MS60 | MS63 | MS65 |
|---|---|---|---|---|---|---|
| 2005 | — | PF65 16.50 | | | | |

**KM# 131 250 SHILLINGS**
20.12 g., Silver Plated Base Metal, 38.5 mm. **Obv:** Crowned arms with supporters **Rev:** Pope John Paul II with red vestments **Edge:** Reeded

| Date | Mintage | VF20 | XF40 | MS60 | MS63 | MS65 |
|---|---|---|---|---|---|---|
| 2005 | — | PF65 16.50 | | | | |

**KM# 133 250 SHILLINGS**
20.12 g., Silver Plated Base Metal, 38.5 mm. **Obv:** Crowned arms with supporters **Rev:** Pope John Paul II in white with skull cap **Edge:** Reeded

| Date | Mintage | VF20 | XF40 | MS60 | MS63 | MS65 |
|---|---|---|---|---|---|---|
| 2005 | — | PF65 16.50 | | | | |

**KM# 135 250 SHILLINGS**
20.12 g., Silver Plated Base Metal, 38.5 mm. **Obv:** Crowned arms with supporters **Rev:** Multicolor Pope John Paul II leaning head on staff **Edge:** Reeded

| Date | Mintage | VF20 | XF40 | MS60 | MS63 | MS65 |
|---|---|---|---|---|---|---|
| 2005 | — | PF65 16.50 | | | | |

**KM# 137 250 SHILLINGS**
20.12 g., Silver Plated Base Metal, 38.5 mm. **Obv:** Crowned arms with supporters **Rev:** Multicolor Pope John Paul II with staff facing left **Edge:** Reeded

| Date | Mintage | VF20 | XF40 | MS60 | MS63 | MS65 |
|---|---|---|---|---|---|---|
| 2005 | — | PF65 16.50 | | | | |

**KM# 139 250 SHILLINGS**
20.12 g., Silver Plated Base Metal, 38.5 mm. **Obv:** Crowned arms with supporters **Rev:** Multicolor Pope John Paul II with staff facing half right **Edge:** Reeded

| Date | Mintage | VF20 | XF40 | MS60 | MS63 | MS65 |
|---|---|---|---|---|---|---|
| 2005 | — | PF65 16.50 | | | | |

**KM# 143 250 SHILLINGS**
Copper-Nickel **Obv:** Crowned shield **Obv. Legend:** SOMALI REPUBLIC / 250 SHILLINGS **Rev:** Color applique, German Shephard **Rev. Legend:** YEAR OF THE DOG / 2006 **Edge:** Reeded

| Date | Mintage | VF20 | XF40 | MS60 | MS63 | MS65 |
|---|---|---|---|---|---|---|
| 2006 | — | — | — | — | — | 14.50 |

**KM# 144 250 SHILLINGS**
Copper-Nickel **Obv:** Crowned shield **Obv. Legend:** SOMALI REPUBLIC / 250 SHILLINGS **Rev:** Color applique, Dachsund **Rev. Legend:** YEAR OF THE DOG / 2006 **Edge:** Reeded

| Date | Mintage | VF20 | XF40 | MS60 | MS63 | MS65 |
|---|---|---|---|---|---|---|
| 2006 | — | — | — | — | — | 14.50 |

**KM# 145 250 SHILLINGS**
Copper-Nickel **Obv:** Crowned shield **Obv. Legend:** SOMALI REPUBLIC / 250 SHILLINGS **Rev:** Color applique, Yorkshire Terrier **Rev. Legend:** YEAR OF THE DOG / 2006 **Edge:** Reeded

| Date | Mintage | VF20 | XF40 | MS60 | MS63 | MS65 |
|---|---|---|---|---|---|---|
| 2006 | — | — | — | — | — | 14.50 |

**KM# 146 250 SHILLINGS**
Copper-Nickel **Obv:** Crowned shield **Obv. Legend:** SOMALI REPUBLIC / 250 SHILLINGS **Rev:** Color applique, Scottie (small white) **Rev. Legend:** YEAR OF THE DOG / 2006 **Edge:** Reeded

| Date | Mintage | VF20 | XF40 | MS60 | MS63 | MS65 |
|---|---|---|---|---|---|---|
| 2006 | — | — | — | — | — | 14.50 |

**KM# 147 250 SHILLINGS**
Copper-Nickel **Obv:** Crowned shield **Obv. Legend:** SOMALI REPUBLIC / 250 SHILLINGS **Rev:** Color applique, Wire-haired Terrier **Rev. Legend:** YEAR OF THE DOG / 2006 **Edge:** Reeded

| Date | Mintage | VF20 | XF40 | MS60 | MS63 | MS65 |
|---|---|---|---|---|---|---|
| 2006 | — | — | — | — | — | 14.50 |

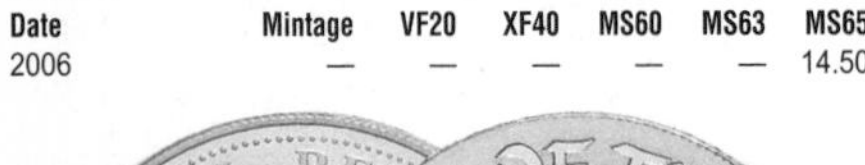

**KM# 148 250 SHILLINGS**
Copper-Nickel **Obv:** Crowned shield **Obv. Legend:** SOMALI REPUBLIC / 250 SHILLINGS **Rev:** Color applique, Bulldog **Rev. Legend:** YEAR OF THE DOG / 2006 **Edge:** Reeded

| Date | Mintage | VF20 | XF40 | MS60 | MS63 | MS65 |
|---|---|---|---|---|---|---|
| 2006 | — | — | — | — | — | 14.50 |

**KM# 149 250 SHILLINGS**
Copper-Nickel **Obv:** Crowned shield **Obv. Legend:** SOMALI REPUBLIC / 250 SHILLINGS **Rev:** Color applique, Golden Retriever **Rev. Legend:** YEAR OF THE DOG **Edge:** Reeded

| Date | Mintage | VF20 | XF40 | MS60 | MS63 | MS65 |
|---|---|---|---|---|---|---|
| 2006 | — | — | — | — | — | 14.50 |

**KM# 150 250 SHILLINGS**
Copper-Nickel **Obv:** Crowned shield **Obv. Legend:** SOMALI REPUBLIC / 250 SHILLINGS **Rev:** Color applique, St. Bernard **Rev. Legend:** YEAR OF THE DOG / 2006 **Edge:** Reeded

| Date | Mintage | VF20 | XF40 | MS60 | MS63 | MS65 |
|---|---|---|---|---|---|---|
| 2006 | — | — | — | — | — | 14.50 |

**KM# 151 250 SHILLINGS**
Copper-Nickel **Obv:** Crowned shield **Obv. Legend:** SOMALI REPUBLIC / 250 SHILLINGS **Rev:** Color applique, Rottweiler **Rev. Legend:** YEAR OF THE DOG / 2006 **Edge:** Reeded

| Date | Mintage | VF20 | XF40 | MS60 | MS63 | MS65 |
|---|---|---|---|---|---|---|
| 2006 | — | — | — | — | — | 14.50 |

**KM# 152 250 SHILLINGS**
Copper-Nickel **Obv:** Crowned shield **Obv. Legend:** SOMALI REPUBLIC / 250 SHILLINGS **Rev:** Color applique, Basset Hound **Rev. Legend:** YEAR OF THE DOG / 2006 **Edge:** Reeded

| Date | Mintage | VF20 | XF40 | MS60 | MS63 | MS65 |
|---|---|---|---|---|---|---|
| 2006 | — | — | — | — | — | 14.50 |

**KM# 153 250 SHILLINGS**
Copper-Nickel **Obv:** Crowned shield **Obv. Legend:** SOMALI REPUBLIC / 250 SHILLINGS **Rev:** Color applique, Sheep Dog **Rev. Legend:** YEAR OF THE DOG / 2006 **Edge:** Reeded

| Date | Mintage | VF20 | XF40 | MS60 | MS63 | MS65 |
|---|---|---|---|---|---|---|
| 2006 | — | — | — | — | — | 14.50 |

**KM# 154 250 SHILLINGS**
Copper-Nickel **Obv:** Crowned shield **Obv. Legend:** SOMALI REPUBLIC / 250 SHILLINGS **Rev:** Color applique, Cocker Spaniel **Rev. Legend:** YEAR OF THE DOG / 2006 **Edge:** Reeded

| Date | Mintage | VF20 | XF40 | MS60 | MS63 | MS65 |
|---|---|---|---|---|---|---|
| 2006 | — | — | — | — | — | 14.50 |

**KM# 170 250 SHILLINGS**
Copper-Nickel Gilt, 38 mm. **Obv:** Arms in cartouche **Rev:** Gold mask of Tutankahamun, enameled

| Date | Mintage | VF20 | XF40 | MS60 | MS63 | MS65 |
|---|---|---|---|---|---|---|
| 2008 | — | — | — | — | — | 17.50 |

**KM# 171 250 SHILLINGS**
Copper-Nickel Gilt, 38 mm. **Obv:** Arms within cartouche **Rev:** Udjat eye, enameled

| Date | Mintage | VF20 | XF40 | MS60 | MS63 | MS65 |
|---|---|---|---|---|---|---|
| 2008 | — | — | — | — | — | 40.00 |

**KM# 172 250 SHILLINGS**
Copper-Nickel **Obv:** Arms within cartouche **Rev:** Statue of Ptah, enameled

| Date | Mintage | VF20 | XF40 | MS60 | MS63 | MS65 |
|---|---|---|---|---|---|---|
| 2008 | — | — | — | — | — | 20.00 |

**KM# 173 250 SHILLINGS**
Copper-Nickel Gilt, 38 mm. **Obv:** Arms in cartouche **Rev:** Scarab Pectoral necklace, enameled

| Date | Mintage | VF20 | XF40 | MS60 | MS63 | MS65 |
|---|---|---|---|---|---|---|
| 2008 | — | — | — | — | — | 20.00 |

**KM# 174 250 SHILLINGS**
Copper-Nickel Gilt, 38 mm. **Obv:** Arms within cartouche **Rev:** Statue of Horus the Elder

| Date | Mintage | VF20 | XF40 | MS60 | MS63 | MS65 |
|---|---|---|---|---|---|---|
| 2008 | — | — | — | — | — | 20.00 |

**KM# 122 500 SHILLINGS**
18.84 g., Silver Plated Base Metal, 34.1 mm. **Obv:** Crowned arms with supporters **Rev:** Multicolor Pope John Paul II and mountains **Edge:** Plain **Shape:** Square with round corners

| Date | Mintage | VF20 | XF40 | MS60 | MS63 | MS65 |
|---|---|---|---|---|---|---|
| 2005 | — | **PF65** 16.50 | | | | |

**KM# 124 500 SHILLINGS**
18.84 g., Silver Plated Base Metal, 34.1 mm. **Obv:** Crowned arms with supporters **Rev:** Multicolor Pope John Paul II kissing bible **Edge:** Plain **Shape:** Square with round corners

| Date | Mintage | VF20 | XF40 | MS60 | MS63 | MS65 |
|---|---|---|---|---|---|---|
| 2005 | — | PF65 16.50 | | | | |

**KM# 126 500 SHILLINGS**
18.84 g., Silver Plated Base Metal, 34.1 mm. **Obv:** Crowned arms with supporters **Rev:** Multicolor Pope John Paul II with flowers **Edge:** Plain **Shape:** Square with round corners

| Date | Mintage | VF20 | XF40 | MS60 | MS63 | MS65 |
|---|---|---|---|---|---|---|
| 2005 | — | PF65 20.00 | | | | |

**KM# 128 500 SHILLINGS**
18.14 g., Silver Plated Base Metal, 34.1 mm. **Obv:** Crowned arms with supporters **Rev:** Multicolor Pope John Paul II saying mass **Edge:** Plain **Shape:** Square with round corners

| Date | Mintage | VF20 | XF40 | MS60 | MS63 | MS65 |
|---|---|---|---|---|---|---|
| 2005 | — | PF65 16.50 | | | | |

**KM# 130 500 SHILLINGS**
18.84 g., Silver Plated Base Metal, 34.1 mm. **Obv:** Crowned arms with supporters **Rev:** Multicolor Pope John Paul II with cardinals **Edge:** Plain **Shape:** Square with round corners

| Date | Mintage | VF20 | XF40 | MS60 | MS63 | MS65 |
|---|---|---|---|---|---|---|
| 2005 | — | PF65 16.50 | | | | |

**KM# 132 500 SHILLINGS**
18.84 g., Silver Plated Base Metal, 34.1 mm. **Obv:** Crowned arms with supporters **Rev:** Pope John Paul II with red vestments **Edge:** Plain **Shape:** Square with round corners

| Date | Mintage | VF20 | XF40 | MS60 | MS63 | MS65 |
|---|---|---|---|---|---|---|
| 2005 | — | PF65 16.50 | | | | |

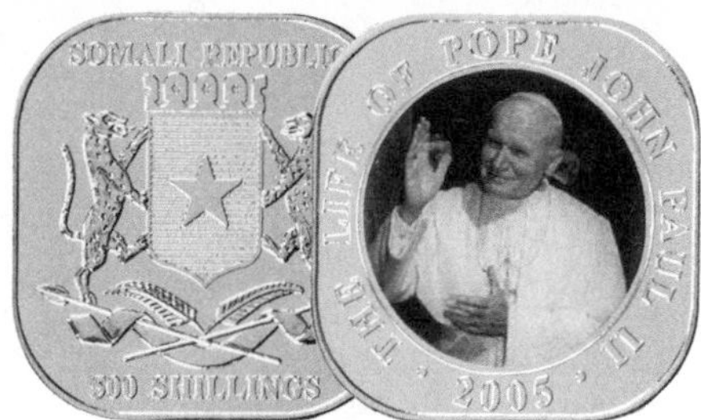


**KM# 134 500 SHILLINGS**
18.84 g., Silver Plated Base Metal, 34.1 mm. **Obv:** Crowned arms with supporters **Rev:** Pope John Paul II in white with skull cap **Edge:** Plain **Shape:** Square with round corners

| Date | Mintage | VF20 | XF40 | MS60 | MS63 | MS65 |
|---|---|---|---|---|---|---|
| 2005 | — | PF65 16.50 | | | | |

**KM# 136 500 SHILLINGS**
18.84 g., Silver Plated Base Metal, 34.1 mm. **Obv:** Crowned arms with supporters **Rev:** Multicolor Pope John Paul II leaning head on staff **Edge:** Plain **Shape:** Square with round corners

| Date | Mintage | VF20 | XF40 | MS60 | MS63 | MS65 |
|---|---|---|---|---|---|---|
| 2005 | — | PF65 16.50 | | | | |

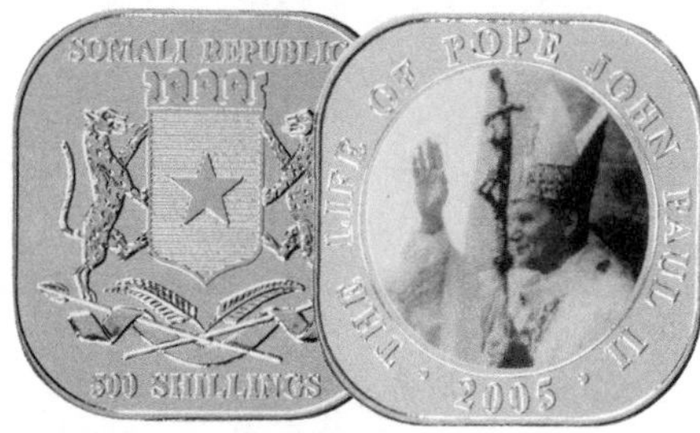


**KM# 138 500 SHILLINGS**
18.84 g., Silver Plated Base Metal, 34.1 mm. **Obv:** Crowned arms with supporters **Rev:** Multicolor Pope John Paul II with staff facing left **Edge:** Plain **Shape:** Square with round corners

| Date | Mintage | VF20 | XF40 | MS60 | MS63 | MS65 |
|---|---|---|---|---|---|---|
| 2005 | — | PF65 16.50 | | | | |

**KM# 140 500 SHILLINGS**
18.84 g., Silver Plated Base Metal, 34.1 mm. **Obv:** Crowned arms with supporters **Rev:** Multicolor Pope John Paul II with staff facing half right **Edge:** Plain **Shape:** Square with round corners

| Date | Mintage | VF20 | XF40 | MS60 | MS63 | MS65 |
|---|---|---|---|---|---|---|
| 2005 | — | PF65 16.50 | | | | |

## BULLION COINAGE

**KM# 200 20 SHILLINGS**
0.62 g., 0.999 Gold 0.0199 oz. AGW, 11 mm. **Rev:** Mother and baby elephant

| Date | Mintage | VF20 | XF40 | MS60 | MS63 | MS65 |
|---|---|---|---|---|---|---|
| 2007 | 20,000 | PF65 50.00 | | | | |

**KM# 208 20 SHILLINGS**
0.62 g., 0.999 Gold 0.0199 oz. AGW

| Date | Mintage | VF20 | XF40 | MS60 | MS63 | MS65 |
|---|---|---|---|---|---|---|
| 2008 | 20,000 | PF65 50.00 | | | | |

**KM# 217 20 SHILLINGS**
0.62 g., 0.999 Gold 0.0199 oz. AGW, 11 mm. **Rev:** Elephant advancing right, sunrise

| Date | Mintage | VF20 | XF40 | MS60 | MS63 | MS65 |
|---|---|---|---|---|---|---|
| 2009 | 20,000 | PF65 50.00 | | | | |

**KM# 226 20 SHILLINGS**
0.62 g., 0.999 Gold 0.0199 oz. AGW, 11 mm. **Rev:** Elephant advacning left, sunrise

| Date | Mintage | VF20 | XF40 | MS60 | MS63 | MS65 |
|---|---|---|---|---|---|---|
| 2010 | 20,000 | PF65 50.00 | | | | |

**KM# 236 20 SHILLINGS**
0.62 g., 0.999 Gold 0.0199 oz. AGW, 11 mm. **Rev:** Mother and baby elephant walking left, sun high up

| Date | Mintage | VF20 | XF40 | MS60 | MS63 | MS65 |
|---|---|---|---|---|---|---|
| 2011 | 20,000 | PF65 50.00 | | | | |

**KM# 177 25 SHILLINGS**
7.78 g., 0.999 Silver 0.2499 oz. ASW

| Date | Mintage | VF20 | XF40 | MS60 | MS63 | MS65 |
|---|---|---|---|---|---|---|
| 2007 | 2,000 | PF65 15.00 | | | | |

**KM# 205 25 SHILLINGS**
7.78 g., 0.999 Silver 0.2499 oz. ASW, 26 mm. **Rev:** Heard of six elephants

| Date | Mintage | VF20 | XF40 | MS60 | MS63 | MS65 |
|---|---|---|---|---|---|---|
| 2008 | 2,000 | PF65 15.00 | | | | |

**KM# 214 25 SHILLINGS**
7.78 g., 0.999 Silver 0.2499 oz. ASW, 26 mm. **Rev:** Elephant advancing right, sunrise

| Date | Mintage | VF20 | XF40 | MS60 | MS63 | MS65 |
|---|---|---|---|---|---|---|
| 2009 | 2,000 | PF65 15.00 | | | | |

**KM# 223 25 SHILLINGS**
7.78 g., 0.999 Silver 0.2499 oz. ASW, 26 mm. **Rev:** Elephant advacning left, sunrise

| Date | Mintage | VF20 | XF40 | MS60 | MS63 | MS65 |
|---|---|---|---|---|---|---|
| 2010 | 2,000 | PF65 15.00 | | | | |

**KM# 232 25 SHILLINGS**
7.78 g., 0.999 Silver 0.2499 oz. ASW, 26 mm. **Rev:** Mother and baby elephant walking left, sun high up

| Date | Mintage | VF20 | XF40 | MS60 | MS63 | MS65 |
|---|---|---|---|---|---|---|
| 2011 | 2,000 | PF65 15.00 | | | | |

**KM# 178 50 SHILLINGS**
15.55 g., 0.999 Silver 0.4994 oz. ASW, 32 mm.

| Date | Mintage | VF20 | XF40 | MS60 | MS63 | MS65 |
|---|---|---|---|---|---|---|
| 2007 | 2,000 | PF65 30.00 | | | | |

**KM# 206 50 SHILLINGS**
15.55 g., 0.999 Silver 0.4994 oz. ASW, 32 mm. **Rev:** Heard of six elephants

| Date | Mintage | VF20 | XF40 | MS60 | MS63 | MS65 |
|---|---|---|---|---|---|---|
| 2008 | — | PF65 30.00 | | | | |

**KM# 209 50 SHILLINGS**
1.24 g., 0.999 Gold 0.0398 oz. AGW, 13.92 mm. **Rev:** Heard of six elephants

| Date | Mintage | VF20 | XF40 | MS60 | MS63 | MS65 |
|---|---|---|---|---|---|---|
| 2008 | 10,000 | PF65 100 | | | | |

**KM# 215 50 SHILLINGS**
15.55 g., 0.999 Silver 0.4994 oz. ASW, 32 mm. **Rev:** Elephant advancing right, sunrise

| Date | Mintage | VF20 | XF40 | MS60 | MS63 | MS65 |
|---|---|---|---|---|---|---|
| 2009 | 2,000 | PF65 30.00 | | | | |

**KM# 218 50 SHILLINGS**
1.24 g., 0.999 Gold 0.0398 oz. AGW, 13.92 mm. **Rev:** Elephant advancing right, sunrise

| Date | Mintage | VF20 | XF40 | MS60 | MS63 | MS65 |
|---|---|---|---|---|---|---|
| 2009 | 10,000 | PF65 100 | | | | |

**KM# 224 50 SHILLINGS**
15.55 g., 0.999 Silver 0.4994 oz. ASW, 32 mm. **Rev:** Elephant advacning left, sunrise

| Date | Mintage | VF20 | XF40 | MS60 | MS63 | MS65 |
|---|---|---|---|---|---|---|
| 2010 | 2,000 | PF65 30.00 | | | | |

**KM# 227 50 SHILLINGS**
1.24 g., 0.999 Gold 0.0398 oz. AGW, 13.92 mm. **Rev:** Elephant advacning left, sunrise

| Date | Mintage | VF20 | XF40 | MS60 | MS63 | MS65 |
|---|---|---|---|---|---|---|
| 2010 | 10,000 | PF65 100 | | | | |

**KM# 233 50 SHILLINGS**
15.55 g., 0.999 Silver 0.4994 oz. ASW, 32 mm. **Rev:** Mother and baby elephant walking left, sun high up

| Date | Mintage | VF20 | XF40 | MS60 | MS63 | MS65 |
|---|---|---|---|---|---|---|
| 2011 | 2,000 | PF65 30.00 | | | | |

**KM# 237 50 SHILLINGS**
1.24 g., 0.999 Gold 0.0398 oz. AGW, 13.92 mm. **Rev:** Mother and baby elephant walking left, sun high up

| Date | Mintage | VF20 | XF40 | MS60 | MS63 | MS65 |
|---|---|---|---|---|---|---|
| 2011 | 10,000 | PF65 100 | | | | |

**KM# 180 100 SHILLINGS**
31.11 g., 0.999 Silver 0.999 oz. ASW, 39 mm. **Rev:** Mother and baby elephant, colored

| Date | Mintage | VF20 | XF40 | MS60 | MS63 | MS65 |
|---|---|---|---|---|---|---|
| 2007 | 5,000 | — | — | — | — | 50.00 |

**KM# 182 100 SHILLINGS**
31.11 g., 0.999 Silver 0.999 oz. ASW, 39 mm. **Obv:** Arms **Rev:** Mom and baby elephant

| Date | Mintage | VF20 | XF40 | MS60 | MS63 | MS65 |
|---|---|---|---|---|---|---|
| 2007 | 20,000 | — | — | — | — | 45.00 |
| 2007 | 5,000 | PF65 55.00 | | | | |

**KM# 182a 100 SHILLINGS**
31.11 g., 0.999 Silver 0.999 oz. ASW partially gilt, 39 mm. **Rev:** Mother and baby elephant, partially gilt

| Date | Mintage | VF20 | XF40 | MS60 | MS63 | MS65 |
|---|---|---|---|---|---|---|
| 2007 | 3,000 | — | — | — | — | 50.00 |

**KM# 203 100 SHILLINGS**
31.11 g., 0.999 Silver 0.999 oz. ASW, 39 mm. **Rev:** Heard of six elephants

| Date | Mintage | VF20 | XF40 | MS60 | MS63 | MS65 |
|---|---|---|---|---|---|---|
| 2008 | 5,000 | PF65 55.00 | | | | |
| 2008 | 20,000 | — | — | — | — | 35.00 |

**KM# 203a 100 SHILLINGS**
31.11 g., 0.999 Silver 0.999 oz. ASW partially gilt, 39 mm. **Obv:** Arms **Rev:** Heard of six elephants

| Date | Mintage | VF20 | XF40 | MS60 | MS63 | MS65 |
|---|---|---|---|---|---|---|
| 2008 | 5,000 | — | — | — | — | 35.00 |

**KM# 204 100 SHILLINGS**
31.11 g., 0.999 Silver 0.999 oz. ASW, 39 mm. **Rev:** Heard of six elephants, multicolored

| Date | Mintage | VF20 | XF40 | MS60 | MS63 | MS65 |
|---|---|---|---|---|---|---|
| 2008 | 5,000 | — | — | — | — | 50.00 |

**KM# 212 100 SHILLINGS**
31.11 g., 0.999 Silver 0.999 oz. ASW, 39 mm. **Rev:** Elephant advancing right, sunrise

| Date | Mintage | VF20 | XF40 | MS60 | MS63 | MS65 |
|---|---|---|---|---|---|---|
| 2009 | 5,000 | PF65 55.00 | | | | |
| 2009 | — | — | — | — | — | 50.00 |

**KM# 212a 100 SHILLINGS**
31.11 g., 0.999 Silver 0.999 oz. ASW partially gilt

| Date | Mintage | VF20 | XF40 | MS60 | MS63 | MS65 |
|---|---|---|---|---|---|---|
| 2009 | 5,000 | — | — | — | — | 55.00 |

**KM# 213 100 SHILLINGS**
31.11 g., 0.999 Silver 0.999 oz. ASW, 39 mm. **Rev:** Elephant advancing right, sunrise, multicolor

| Date | Mintage | VF20 | XF40 | MS60 | MS63 | MS65 |
|---|---|---|---|---|---|---|
| 2009 | 5,000 | — | — | — | — | 55.00 |

**KM# 221 100 SHILLINGS**
31.11 g., 0.999 Silver 0.999 oz. ASW, 39 mm. **Rev:** Elephant advacning left, sunrise

| Date | Mintage | VF20 | XF40 | MS60 | MS63 | MS65 |
|---|---|---|---|---|---|---|
| 2010 | 5,000 | PF65 55.00 | | | | |
| 2010 | — | — | — | — | — | 50.00 |

**KM# 221a 100 SHILLINGS**
31.11 g., 0.999 Silver 0.999 oz. ASW partially gilt

| Date | Mintage | VF20 | XF40 | MS60 | MS63 | MS65 |
|---|---|---|---|---|---|---|
| 2010 | 5,000 | — | — | — | — | 55.00 |

**KM# 222 100 SHILLINGS**
31.11 g., 0.999 Silver 0.999 oz. ASW, 39 mm. **Rev:** Elephant advacning left, sunrise, multicolor

| Date | Mintage | VF20 | XF40 | MS60 | MS63 | MS65 |
|---|---|---|---|---|---|---|
| 2010 | 5,000 | — | — | — | — | 55.00 |

**KM# 230 100 SHILLINGS**
31.11 g., 0.999 Silver 0.999 oz. ASW, 39 mm. **Rev:** Mother and baby elephant walking left, sun high up

| Date | Mintage | VF20 | XF40 | MS60 | MS63 | MS65 |
|---|---|---|---|---|---|---|
| 2011 | — | — | — | — | — | 50.00 |
| 2011 | 5,000 | PF65 55.00 | | | | |

**KM# 230a 100 SHILLINGS**
31.11 g., 0.999 Silver 0.999 oz. ASW partially gilt

| Date | Mintage | VF20 | XF40 | MS60 | MS63 | MS65 |
|---|---|---|---|---|---|---|
| 2011 | 5,000 | — | — | — | — | 55.00 |

**KM# 231 100 SHILLINGS**
31.11 g., 0.999 Silver 0.999 oz. ASW, 39 mm. **Rev:** Mother and baby elephant walking left, sun high up, multicolor

| Date | Mintage | VF20 | XF40 | MS60 | MS63 | MS65 |
|---|---|---|---|---|---|---|
| 2011 | 5,000 | — | — | — | — | 55.00 |

**KM# 188 200 SHILLINGS**
0.62 g., 0.999 Gold 0.0199 oz. AGW

| Date | Mintage | VF20 | XF40 | MS60 | MS63 | MS65 |
|---|---|---|---|---|---|---|
| 2004 | — | PF65 45.00 | | | | |

**KM# 194 200 SHILLINGS**
0.62 g., 0.999 Gold 0.0199 oz. AGW

| Date | Mintage | VF20 | XF40 | MS60 | MS63 | MS65 |
|---|---|---|---|---|---|---|
| 2005 | 20,000 | PF65 45.00 | | | | |

**KM# 179 200 SHILLINGS**
62.20 g., 0.999 Silver 1.9978 oz. ASW, 50 mm.

| Date | Mintage | VF20 | XF40 | MS60 | MS63 | MS65 |
|---|---|---|---|---|---|---|
| 2007 | — | PF65 100 | | | | |

**KM# 207 200 SHILLINGS**
62.20 g., 0.999 Silver 1.9978 oz. ASW, 50 mm. **Rev:** Heard of six elephants

| Date | Mintage | VF20 | XF40 | MS60 | MS63 | MS65 |
|---|---|---|---|---|---|---|
| 2008 | 2,000 | PF65 100 | | | | |

**KM# 216 200 SHILLINGS**
62.20 g., 0.999 Silver 1.9978 oz. ASW, 50 mm. **Rev:** Elephant advancing right, sunrise

| Date | Mintage | VF20 | XF40 | MS60 | MS63 | MS65 |
|---|---|---|---|---|---|---|
| 2009 | 2,000 | PF65 100 | | | | |

**KM# 225 200 SHILLINGS**
62.20 g., 0.999 Silver 1.9978 oz. ASW, 50 mm. **Rev:** Elephant advacning left, sunrise

| Date | Mintage | VF20 | XF40 | MS60 | MS63 | MS65 |
|---|---|---|---|---|---|---|
| 2010 | 2,000 | PF65 100 | | | | |

**KM# 234 200 SHILLINGS**
62.20 g., 0.999 Silver 1.9978 oz. ASW, 50 mm. **Rev:** Mother and baby elephant walking left, sun high up

| Date | Mintage | VF20 | XF40 | MS60 | MS63 | MS65 |
|---|---|---|---|---|---|---|
| 2011 | 2,000 | PF65 100 | | | | |

**KM# 185 250 SHILLINGS**
7.78 g., 0.999 Silver 0.2499 oz. ASW

| Date | Mintage | VF20 | XF40 | MS60 | MS63 | MS65 |
|---|---|---|---|---|---|---|
| 2004 | 2,000 | PF65 15.00 | | | | |

**KM# 191 250 SHILLINGS**
7.78 g., 0.999 Silver 0.2499 oz. ASW

| Date | Mintage | VF20 | XF40 | MS60 | MS63 | MS65 |
|---|---|---|---|---|---|---|
| 2005 | 2,000 | PF65 15.00 | | | | |

**KM# 197 250 SHILLINGS**
7.78 g., 0.999 Silver 0.2499 oz. ASW

| Date | Mintage | VF20 | XF40 | MS60 | MS63 | MS65 |
|---|---|---|---|---|---|---|
| 2006 | 2,000 | PF65 15.00 | | | | |

**KM# 186 500 SHILLINGS**
15.55 g., 0.999 Silver 0.4994 oz. ASW, 32 mm. **Rev:** Elefant facing forward

| Date | Mintage | VF20 | XF40 | MS60 | MS63 | MS65 |
|---|---|---|---|---|---|---|
| 2004 | 2,000 | PF65 30.00 | | | | |

**KM# 192 500 SHILLINGS**
15.55 g., 0.999 Silver 0.4994 oz. ASW

| Date | Mintage | VF20 | XF40 | MS60 | MS63 | MS65 |
|---|---|---|---|---|---|---|
| 2005 | — | PF65 30.00 | | | | |

**KM# 198 500 SHILLINGS**
15.55 g., 0.999 Silver 0.4994 oz. ASW

| Date | Mintage | VF20 | XF40 | MS60 | MS63 | MS65 |
|---|---|---|---|---|---|---|
| 2006 | 2,000 | PF65 30.00 | | | | |

**KM# 183 1000 SHILLINGS**
31.11 g., 0.999 Silver 0.999 oz. ASW

| Date | Mintage | VF20 | XF40 | MS60 | MS63 | MS65 |
|---|---|---|---|---|---|---|
| 2004 | 5,000 | PF65 55.00 | | | | |
| 2004 | 20,000 | — | — | — | — | 50.00 |

**KM# 183a 1000 SHILLINGS**
31.27 g., 0.999 Silver 1.0043 oz. ASW partially gilt, 38.54 mm. **Series:** African Wildlife **Obv:** National arms **Obv. Legend:** SOMALI REPUBLIC **Rev:** Elephant standing facing - gilt **Edge:** Reeded

| Date | Mintage | VF20 | XF40 | MS60 | MS63 | MS65 |
|---|---|---|---|---|---|---|
| 2004 | — | — | — | — | — | 55.00 |

**KM# 184 1000 SHILLINGS**
31.11 g., 0.999 Silver 0.999 oz. ASW multicolored, 39 mm. **Rev:** Elephant facing forward, colored

| Date | Mintage | VF20 | XF40 | MS60 | MS63 | MS65 |
|---|---|---|---|---|---|---|
| 2004 | 5,000 | — | — | — | — | 55.00 |

**KM# 189 1000 SHILLINGS**
31.11 g., 0.999 Silver 0.999 oz. ASW, 39 mm. **Rev:** Elephant profile left thrumpanting

| Date | Mintage | VF20 | XF40 | MS60 | MS63 | MS65 |
|---|---|---|---|---|---|---|
| 2005 | 5,000 | PF65 55.00 | | | | |
| 2005 | 20,000 | — | — | — | — | 50.00 |

**KM# 189a 1000 SHILLINGS**
31.11 g., 0.999 Silver 0.999 oz. ASW partially gilt, 39 mm. **Rev:** Elephant profile left thrumpanting, partially gilt

| Date | Mintage | VF20 | XF40 | MS60 | MS63 | MS65 |
|---|---|---|---|---|---|---|
| 2005 | 3,000 | — | — | — | — | 55.00 |

**KM# 190 1000 SHILLINGS**
31.11 g., 0.999 Silver 0.999 oz. ASW, 39 mm. **Obv:** Arms **Rev:** Elephant profile left thrumpanting, multicolor

| Date | Mintage | VF20 | XF40 | MS60 | MS63 | MS65 |
|---|---|---|---|---|---|---|
| 2005 | 5,000 | — | — | — | — | 45.00 |

**KM# 195 1000 SHILLINGS**
31.11 g., 0.999 Silver 0.999 oz. ASW, 38 mm. **Obv:** Arms **Rev:** Elephant and mountain

| Date | Mintage | VF20 | XF40 | MS60 | MS63 | MS65 |
|---|---|---|---|---|---|---|
| 2006 | 5,000 | PF65 55.00 | | | | |
| 2006 | 20,000 | — | — | — | — | 45.00 |

**KM# 195a 1000 SHILLINGS**
31.11 g., 0.999 Silver 0.999 oz. ASW partially gilt, 39 mm. **Rev:** Elephant, mountain, partially gilt

| Date | Mintage | VF20 | XF40 | MS60 | MS63 | MS65 |
|---|---|---|---|---|---|---|
| 2006 | 3,000 | — | — | — | — | 55.00 |

**KM# 196 1000 SHILLINGS**
31.11 g., 0.999 Silver 0.999 oz. ASW, 39 mm. **Obv:** Arms **Rev:** Elephant, mountian in background. Multicolor

| Date | Mintage | VF20 | XF40 | MS60 | MS63 | MS65 |
|---|---|---|---|---|---|---|
| 2006 | 5,000 | — | — | — | — | 45.00 |

**KM# 181 1000 SHILLINGS**
31.11 g., 0.999 Silver 0.999 oz. ASW, 39 mm. **Obv:** Arms **Rev:** Heard of six elephants, multicolor

| Date | Mintage | VF20 | XF40 | MS60 | MS63 | MS65 |
|---|---|---|---|---|---|---|
| 2008 | — | — | — | — | — | 45.00 |

**KM# 228 1000 SHILLINGS**
31.11 g., 0.999 Gold 0.999 oz. AGW, 38.6 mm. **Rev:** Elephant advacning left, sunrise

| Date | Mintage | VF20 | XF40 | MS60 | MS63 | MS65 |
|---|---|---|---|---|---|---|
| 2010 | — | — | — | — | — | 1,850 |

**KM# 238 1000 SHILLINGS**
31.11 g., 0.999 Gold 0.999 oz. AGW, 38.6 mm. **Rev:** Mother and baby elephant walking left, sun high up

| Date | Mintage | VF20 | XF40 | MS60 | MS63 | MS65 |
|---|---|---|---|---|---|---|
| 2011 | — | — | — | — | — | 1,850 |

**KM# 201 1500 SHILLINGS**
155.50 g., 0.999 Gold 4.9944 oz. AGW, 65 mm. **Rev:** Mother and baby elephant

| Date | Mintage | VF20 | XF40 | MS60 | MS63 | MS65 |
|---|---|---|---|---|---|---|
| 2007 | 99 | PF65 9,250 | | | | |

**KM# 210 1500 SHILLINGS**
155.50 g., 0.999 Gold 4.9944 oz. AGW, 65 mm. **Rev:** Heard of six elephants

| Date | Mintage | VF20 | XF40 | MS60 | MS63 | MS65 |
|---|---|---|---|---|---|---|
| 2008 | 99 | PF65 9,250 | | | | |

**KM# 219 1500 SHILLINGS**
155.50 g., 0.999 Gold 4.9944 oz. AGW, 65 mm. **Rev:** Elephant advancing right, sunrise

| Date | Mintage | VF20 | XF40 | MS60 | MS63 | MS65 |
|---|---|---|---|---|---|---|
| 2009 | 99 | PF65 9,250 | | | | |

**KM# 229 1500 SHILLINGS**
155.50 g., 0.999 Gold 4.9944 oz. AGW, 65 mm. **Rev:** Elephant advacning left, sunrise

| Date | Mintage | VF20 | XF40 | MS60 | MS63 | MS65 |
|---|---|---|---|---|---|---|
| 2010 | 99 | **PF65** 9,250 | | | | |

**KM# 239 1500 SHILLINGS**
155.50 g., 0.999 Gold 4.9944 oz. AGW, 65 mm. **Rev:** Mother and baby elephant walking left, sun high up

| Date | Mintage | VF20 | XF40 | MS60 | MS63 | MS65 |
|---|---|---|---|---|---|---|
| 2011 | 99 | **PF65** 9,250 | | | | |

**KM# 187 2000 SHILLINGS**
62.20 g., 0.999 Silver 1.9978 oz. ASW, 50 mm. **Rev:** Elephant facing forward

| Date | Mintage | VF20 | XF40 | MS60 | MS63 | MS65 |
|---|---|---|---|---|---|---|
| 2004 | 2,000 | **PF63** 100 | **PF65** 120 | | | |

**KM# 193 2000 SHILLINGS**
62.20 g., 0.999 Silver 1.9978 oz. ASW

| Date | Mintage | VF20 | XF40 | MS60 | MS63 | MS65 |
|---|---|---|---|---|---|---|
| 2005 | 2,000 | **PF63** 100 | **PF65** 120 | | | |

**KM# 199 2000 SHILLINGS**
62.20 g., 0.999 Silver 1.9978 oz. ASW

| Date | Mintage | VF20 | XF40 | MS60 | MS63 | MS65 |
|---|---|---|---|---|---|---|
| 2006 | 2,000 | **PF63** 100 | **PF65** 120 | | | |

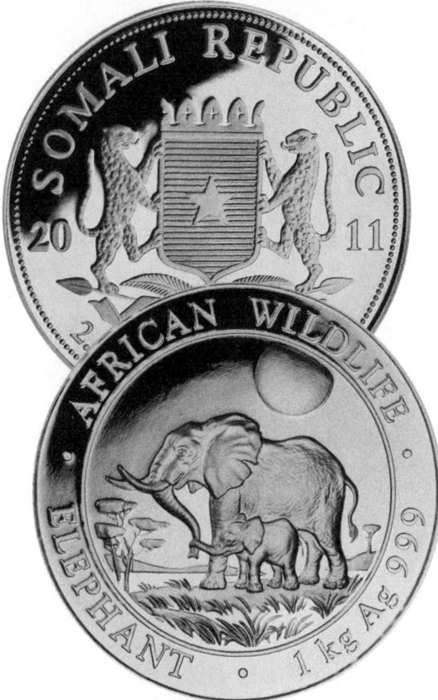


**KM# 235 2000 SHILLINGS**
1000.00 g., 0.999 Silver 32.1186 oz. ASW, 100 mm. **Rev:** Mother and baby elephant walking left, sun high up

| Date | Mintage | VF20 | XF40 | MS60 | MS63 | MS65 |
|---|---|---|---|---|---|---|
| 2011 | — | — | — | — | — | 1,700 |

**KM# 202 5000 SHILLINGS**
1000.00 g., 0.999 Gold 32.1186 oz. AGW

| Date | Mintage | VF20 | XF40 | MS60 | MS63 | MS65 |
|---|---|---|---|---|---|---|
| 2007 | 50 | **PF65** 57,000 | | | | |

**KM# 211 5000 SHILLINGS**
1000.00 g., 0.999 Gold 32.1186 oz. AGW

| Date | Mintage | VF20 | XF40 | MS60 | MS63 | MS65 |
|---|---|---|---|---|---|---|
| 2008 | 50 | **PF65** 57,000 | | | | |

**KM# 220 5000 SHILLINGS**
1000.00 g., 0.999 Gold 32.1186 oz. AGW **Rev:** Elephant advancing right, sunrise

| Date | Mintage | VF20 | XF40 | MS60 | MS63 | MS65 |
|---|---|---|---|---|---|---|
| 2009 | 50 | **PF65** 57,000 | | | | |

# SOMALILAND

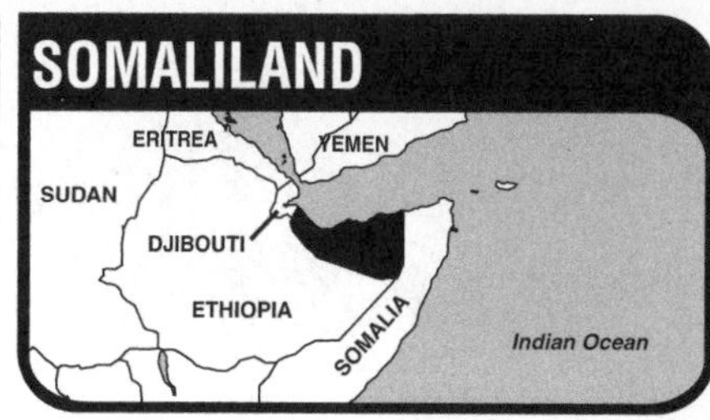


The Somaliland Republic consists of the former British Somaliland Protectorate and is located on the coast of the northeastern projection of the African continent commonly referred to as the "Horn" on the southwestern end of the Gulf of Aden. Bordered by Ethiopia to the west and south and Somalia to the east. It has an area of 68,000* sq. mi. (176,000* sq. km). Capital: Hargeysa. It is mostly arid and mountainous except for the gulf shoreline.

The northern Somali National Movement (SNM) declared a secession of the Somaliland Republic on May 17, 1991, which is not recognized by the Somali Democratic Republic.

## REPUBLIC

### SHILLING COINAGE

**KM# 4 5 SHILLINGS**
1.45 g., Aluminum, 21.9 mm. **Obv:** Value **Rev:** Bust of Sir Richard F. Burton - explorer, divides dates **Edge:** Plain

| Date | Mintage | VF20 | XF40 | MS60 | MS63 | MS65 |
|---|---|---|---|---|---|---|
| 2002 | — | — | — | 0.65 | 1.25 | 1.50 |

**KM# 5 5 SHILLINGS**
1.45 g., Aluminum, 21.9 mm. **Obv:** Value **Rev:** Rooster **Edge:** Plain

| Date | Mintage | VF20 | XF40 | MS60 | MS63 | MS65 |
|---|---|---|---|---|---|---|
| 2002 | — | — | — | 0.50 | 1.00 | 1.25 |

**KM# 19 5 SHILLINGS**
1.24 g., Aluminum, 22 mm. **Obv:** Elephant with calf walking right **Obv. Legend:** REPUBLIC OF SOMALILAND **Rev:** Value **Rev. Legend:** BAANKA SOMALILAND **Edge:** Plain

| Date | Mintage | VF20 | XF40 | MS60 | MS63 | MS65 |
|---|---|---|---|---|---|---|
| 2005 | — | — | — | 0.65 | 1.25 | 1.50 |

**KM# 3 10 SHILLINGS**
3.51 g., Brass, 17.7 mm. **Obv:** Vervet Monkey **Rev:** Value **Edge:** Plain

| Date | Mintage | VF20 | XF40 | MS60 | MS63 | MS65 |
|---|---|---|---|---|---|---|
| 2002 | — | — | — | 0.45 | 0.65 | 1.25 |

**KM# 7 10 SHILLINGS**
4.80 g., Stainless Steel, 24.9 mm. **Obv:** Value **Rev:** Aquarius the water carrier **Edge:** Plain

| Date | Mintage | VF20 | XF40 | MS60 | MS63 | MS65 |
|---|---|---|---|---|---|---|
| 2006 | — | — | — | — | 1.00 | 1.25 |

**KM# 8 10 SHILLINGS**
4.80 g., Stainless Steel, 24.9 mm. **Obv:** Value **Rev:** Pisces the two fish **Edge:** Plain

| Date | Mintage | VF20 | XF40 | MS60 | MS63 | MS65 |
|---|---|---|---|---|---|---|
| 2006 | — | — | — | — | 1.00 | 1.25 |

**KM# 9 10 SHILLINGS**
4.80 g., Stainless Steel, 24.9 mm. **Obv:** Value **Rev:** Aries the ram **Edge:** Plain

| Date | Mintage | VF20 | XF40 | MS60 | MS63 | MS65 |
|---|---|---|---|---|---|---|
| 2006 | — | — | — | — | 1.00 | 1.25 |

**KM# 10 10 SHILLINGS**
4.80 g., Stainless Steel, 24.9 mm. **Obv:** Value **Rev:** Taurus the bull **Edge:** Plain

| Date | Mintage | VF20 | XF40 | MS60 | MS63 | MS65 |
|---|---|---|---|---|---|---|
| 2006 | — | — | — | — | 1.00 | 1.25 |

**KM# 11 10 SHILLINGS**
4.80 g., Stainless Steel, 24.9 mm. **Obv:** Value **Rev:** Gemini twins **Edge:** Plain

| Date | Mintage | VF20 | XF40 | MS60 | MS63 | MS65 |
|---|---|---|---|---|---|---|
| 2006 | — | — | — | — | 1.00 | 1.25 |

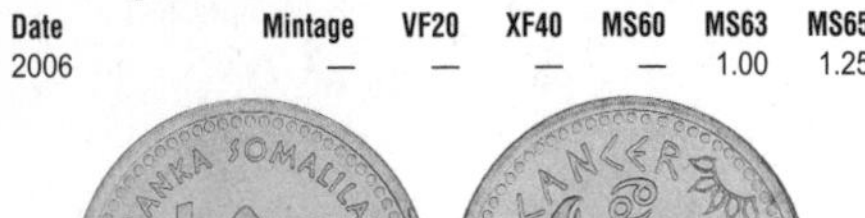

**KM# 12 10 SHILLINGS**
4.80 g., Stainless Steel, 24.9 mm. **Obv:** Value **Rev:** Cancer the crab **Edge:** Plain

| Date | Mintage | VF20 | XF40 | MS60 | MS63 | MS65 |
|---|---|---|---|---|---|---|
| 2006 | — | — | — | — | 1.00 | 1.25 |

**KM# 13 10 SHILLINGS**
4.80 g., Stainless Steel, 24.9 mm. **Obv:** Value **Rev:** Leo the lion **Edge:** Plain

| Date | Mintage | VF20 | XF40 | MS60 | MS63 | MS65 |
|---|---|---|---|---|---|---|
| 2006 | — | — | — | — | 1.00 | 1.25 |

**KM# 14 10 SHILLINGS**
4.80 g., Stainless Steel, 24.9 mm. **Obv:** Value **Rev:** Virgo as a winged woman **Edge:** Plain

| Date | Mintage | VF20 | XF40 | MS60 | MS63 | MS65 |
|---|---|---|---|---|---|---|
| 2006 | — | — | — | — | 1.00 | 1.25 |

**KM# 15 10 SHILLINGS**
4.80 g., Stainless Steel, 24.9 mm. **Obv:** Value **Rev:** Libra balance scale **Edge:** Plain

| Date | Mintage | VF20 | XF40 | MS60 | MS63 | MS65 |
|---|---|---|---|---|---|---|
| 2006 | — | — | — | — | 1.00 | 1.25 |

**KM# 16 10 SHILLINGS**
4.80 g., Stainless Steel, 24.9 mm. **Obv:** Value **Rev:** Scorpio the scorpion **Edge:** Plain

| Date | Mintage | VF20 | XF40 | MS60 | MS63 | MS65 |
|---|---|---|---|---|---|---|
| 2006 | — | — | — | — | 1.00 | 1.25 |

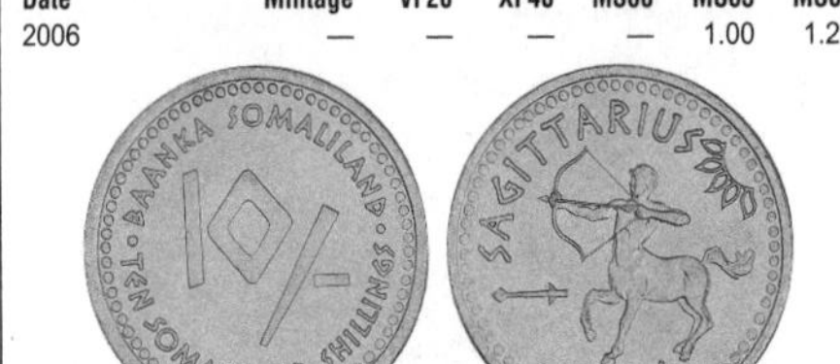

**KM# 17 10 SHILLINGS**
4.80 g., Stainless Steel, 24.9 mm. **Obv:** Value **Rev:** Sagittarius the archer **Edge:** Plain

| Date | Mintage | VF20 | XF40 | MS60 | MS63 | MS65 |
|---|---|---|---|---|---|---|
| 2006 | — | — | — | — | 1.00 | 1.25 |

**KM# 18 10 SHILLINGS**
4.80 g., Stainless Steel, 24.9 mm. **Obv:** Value **Rev:** Capricorn the goat **Edge:** Plain

| Date | Mintage | VF20 | XF40 | MS60 | MS63 | MS65 |
|---|---|---|---|---|---|---|
| 2006 | — | — | — | — | 1.00 | 1.25 |

**KM# 6 20 SHILLINGS**
3.87 g., Stainless Steel, 21.8 mm. **Obv:** Value **Rev:** Greyhound dog **Edge:** Plain

| Date | Mintage | VF20 | XF40 | MS60 | MS63 | MS65 |
|---|---|---|---|---|---|---|
| 2002 | — | — | — | — | 1.00 | 1.50 |

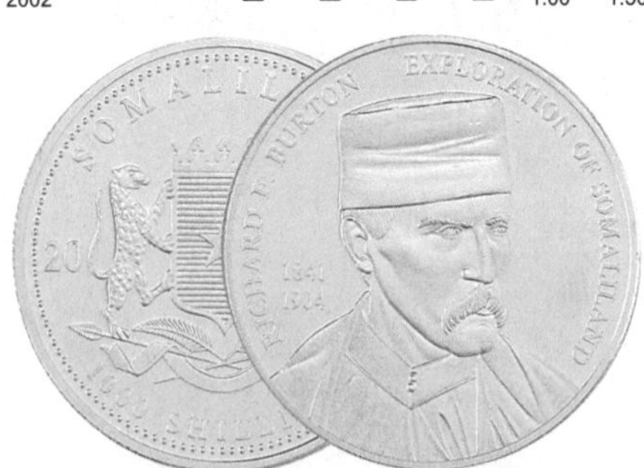

**KM# 2 1000 SHILLINGS**
31.27 g., 0.999 Silver 1.0043 oz. ASW, 38.8 mm. **Obv:** Crowned arms with supporters **Rev:** Bust with hat 3/4 right **Edge:** Reeded

| Date | Mintage | VF20 | XF40 | MS60 | MS63 | MS65 |
|---|---|---|---|---|---|---|
| 2002 | — | — | — | — | 45.00 | 55.00 |

# SOUTH AFRICA

The Republic of South Africa, located at the southern tip of Africa, has an area of 471,445 sq. mi. (1,221,043 sq. km.) and a population of *30.2 million. Capitals: Administrative, Pretoria; Legislative, Cape Town; Judicial, Bloemfontein. Manufacturing, mining and agriculture are the principal industries. Exports include wool, diamonds, gold, and metallic ores.

The apartheid era ended April 27, 1994 with the first democratic election for all people of South Africa. Nelson Mandela was inaugurated President May 10, 1994, and South Africa was readmitted into the Commonwealth of Nations.

South African coins and currency bear inscriptions in tribal languages, Afrikaans and English.

**MONETARY SYSTEM**
100 Cents = 1 Rand

**MINT MARKS**
GRC + paw print = Gold Reef City Mint

## REPUBLIC

### STANDARD COINAGE

100 Cents = 1 Rand

**KM# 221 CENT**
1.50 g., Copper Plated Steel, 15 mm. **Obv:** New national arms **Obv. Legend:** ISEWULA AFRIKA **Rev:** Value divides two sparrows **Edge:** Plain

| Date | Mintage | VF20 | XF40 | MS60 | MS63 | MS65 |
|---|---|---|---|---|---|---|
| 2001 | — | — | 0.15 | 0.25 | 0.35 | 0.50 |
| 2001 | 3,678 | PF65 5.00 | | | | |

**KM# 222 2 CENTS**
3.00 g., Copper Plated Steel, 18 mm. **Obv:** New national arms **Obv. Legend:** AFURIKA TSHIPEMBE **Rev:** Eagle with fish in talons divides value **Edge:** Plain

| Date | Mintage | VF20 | XF40 | MS60 | MS63 | MS65 |
|---|---|---|---|---|---|---|
| 2001 | — | — | — | 0.25 | 0.50 | 0.75 |
| 2001 | 3,678 | PF65 6.00 | | | | |

**KM# 223 5 CENTS**
4.42 g., Copper Plated Steel, 21 mm. **Obv:** New national arms **Obv. Legend:** AFRIKA DZONGA **Rev:** Value and Blue crane **Edge:** Plain

| Date | Mintage | VF20 | XF40 | MS60 | MS63 | MS65 |
|---|---|---|---|---|---|---|
| 2001 | — | 0.10 | 0.25 | 0.40 | 0.65 | 1.00 |
| 2001 | — | PF65 5.00 | | | | |

**KM# 268 5 CENTS**
4.50 g., Copper Plated Steel, 21 mm. **Obv:** New national arms **Obv. Legend:** Ningizimu Afrika **Rev:** Value and Blue crane **Edge:** Plain

| Date | Mintage | VF20 | XF40 | MS60 | MS63 | MS65 |
|---|---|---|---|---|---|---|
| 2002 | — | — | 0.25 | 0.40 | 0.75 | 1.00 |
| 2002 | 3,250 | PF65 5.00 | | | | |

**KM# 324 5 CENTS**
4.50 g., Copper Plated Steel, 21 mm. **Obv:** New national arms **Obv. Legend:** Afrika Dzonga **Rev:** Blue crane and denomination **Edge:** Plain

| Date | Mintage | VF20 | XF40 | MS60 | MS63 | MS65 |
|---|---|---|---|---|---|---|
| 2003 | — | — | 0.25 | 0.40 | 0.75 | 1.00 |
| 2003 | 2,909 | PF65 5.00 | | | | |

**KM# 325 5 CENTS**
4.50 g., Copper Plated Steel, 21 mm. **Obv:** New national arms **Obv. Legend:** South Africa **Rev:** Value and Blue crane **Edge:** Plain

| Date | Mintage | VF20 | XF40 | MS60 | MS63 | MS65 |
|---|---|---|---|---|---|---|
| 2004 | — | — | 0.20 | 0.30 | 0.50 | 0.75 |
| 2004 | 1,935 | PF65 5.00 | | | | |

**KM# 291 5 CENTS**
4.50 g., Copper Plated Steel, 21 mm. **Obv:** New national arms **Obv. Legend:** Aforika Borwa **Rev:** Value and Blue crane **Edge:** Plain

| Date | Mintage | VF20 | XF40 | MS60 | MS63 | MS65 |
|---|---|---|---|---|---|---|
| 2005 | — | — | 0.20 | 0.30 | 0.50 | 0.75 |
| 2005 | — | PF65 5.00 | | | | |

**KM# 486 5 CENTS**
4.50 g., Copper Plated Steel, 21 mm. **Obv:** New National arms **Obv. Legend:** Afrika Borwa **Rev:** Blue crane and value

| Date | Mintage | VF20 | XF40 | MS60 | MS63 | MS65 |
|---|---|---|---|---|---|---|
| 2006 | — | — | — | 0.30 | 0.50 | 0.75 |
| 2006 | — | PF65 5.00 | | | | |

**KM# 340 5 CENTS**
4.51 g., Copper Plated Steel, 21 mm. **Obv:** New national arms **Obv. Legend:** Suid- Afrika **Rev:** Value at left, Blue Crane at right **Edge:** Plain

| Date | Mintage | VF20 | XF40 | MS60 | MS63 | MS65 |
|---|---|---|---|---|---|---|
| 2007 | — | — | 0.20 | 0.30 | 0.50 | 0.75 |
| 2007 | — | PF65 5.00 | | | | |

**KM# 440 5 CENTS**
4.50 g., Copper Plated Steel, 21 mm. **Obv:** New National arms **Obv. Legend:** uMzantsi Afrika **Rev:** Blue crane and value

| Date | Mintage | VF20 | XF40 | MS60 | MS63 | MS65 |
|---|---|---|---|---|---|---|
| 2008 | — | — | — | 0.35 | 0.75 | 1.00 |
| 2008 | — | PF65 5.00 | | | | |

**KM# 464 5 CENTS**
4.50 g., Copper Plated Steel, 21 mm. **Obv:** National arms **Rev:** Value and Blue crane

| Date | Mintage | VF20 | XF40 | MS60 | MS63 | MS65 |
|---|---|---|---|---|---|---|
| 2009 | — | — | — | 0.30 | 0.50 | 0.75 |
| 2009 | — | PF65 5.00 | | | | |

**KM# 493 5 CENTS**
4.50 g., Copper Plated Steel, 21 mm. **Obv:** National arms **Rev:** Value and Blue crane

| Date | Mintage | VF20 | XF40 | MS60 | MS63 | MS65 |
|---|---|---|---|---|---|---|
| 2010 | — | — | — | 0.35 | 0.75 | 1.00 |
| 2010 | — | PF65 5.00 | | | | |

**KM# 500 5 CENTS**
4.50 g., Copper Plated Steel, 21 mm. **Obv:** National arms **Rev:** Blue crane and value

| Date | Mintage | VF20 | XF40 | MS60 | MS63 | MS65 |
|---|---|---|---|---|---|---|
| 2011 | — | — | — | 0.35 | 0.75 | 1.00 |
| 2011 | — | PF65 5.00 | | | | |

**KM# 224 10 CENTS**
2.00 g., Bronze Plated Steel, 16 mm. **Obv:** New national arms **Obv. Legend:** AFRIKA DZONGA **Rev:** Arum Lily and value **Edge:** Reeded

| Date | Mintage | VF20 | XF40 | MS60 | MS63 | MS65 |
|---|---|---|---|---|---|---|
| 2001 | — | — | 0.30 | 0.40 | 0.60 | 1.00 |
| 2001 | 3,678 | PF65 6.00 | | | | |

**KM# 269 10 CENTS**
2.00 g., Bronze Plated Steel, 16 mm. **Obv:** New national arms **Obv. Legend:** Afrika Dzonga **Rev:** Arum Lily and value **Edge:** Reeded

| Date | Mintage | VF20 | XF40 | MS60 | MS63 | MS65 |
|---|---|---|---|---|---|---|
| 2002 | — | — | 0.30 | 0.50 | 0.75 | 1.00 |
| 2002 | 3,250 | PF65 6.00 | | | | |

**KM# 347 10 CENTS**
2.00 g., Bronze Plated Steel, 16 mm. **Obv:** New national arms **Obv. Legend:** South Africa **Rev:** Arum lily and value **Edge:** Reeded

| Date | Mintage | VF20 | XF40 | MS60 | MS63 | MS65 |
|---|---|---|---|---|---|---|
| 2003 | — | — | 0.30 | 0.50 | 0.75 | 1.00 |
| 2003 | 2,909 | PF65 6.00 | | | | |

**KM# 326 10 CENTS**
2.00 g., Bronze Plated Steel, 16 mm. **Obv:** New national arms **Obv. Legend:** Aforika Borwa **Rev:** Arum lily and value **Edge:** Reeded

| Date | Mintage | VF20 | XF40 | MS60 | MS63 | MS65 |
|---|---|---|---|---|---|---|
| 2004 | — | — | 0.30 | 0.50 | 0.75 | 1.00 |
| 2004 | 1,935 | PF65 6.00 | | | | |

**KM# 292 10 CENTS**
2.00 g., Bronze Plated Steel, 16 mm. **Obv:** New national arms **Obv. Legend:** Afrika Borwa **Rev:** Arum Lily and value **Edge:** Reeded

| Date | Mintage | VF20 | XF40 | MS60 | MS63 | MS65 |
|---|---|---|---|---|---|---|
| 2005 | — | — | 0.30 | 0.50 | 0.75 | 1.00 |
| 2005 | — | PF65 6.00 | | | | |

**KM# 487 10 CENTS**
2.00 g., Bronze Plated Steel, 16 mm. **Obv:** National arms **Obv. Legend:** Suid-Afrika **Rev:** Arum lily and value **Edge:** Reeded

| Date | Mintage | VF20 | XF40 | MS60 | MS63 | MS65 |
|---|---|---|---|---|---|---|
| 2006 | — | — | — | 0.50 | 0.75 | 1.00 |
| 2006 | — | PF65 6.00 | | | | |

**KM# 341 10 CENTS**
2.00 g., Bronze Plated Steel, 16 mm. **Obv:** New national arms **Obv. Legend:** uMzantsi - Afrika **Rev:** Alum lily and value **Edge:** Reeded

| Date | Mintage | VF20 | XF40 | MS60 | MS63 | MS65 |
|---|---|---|---|---|---|---|
| 2007 | — | — | 0.30 | 0.50 | 0.75 | 1.00 |
| 2007 | — | PF65 6.00 | | | | |

**KM# 441 10 CENTS**
2.00 g., Bronze Plated Steel, 16 mm. **Obv:** National arms **Obv. Legend:** iNingizimu Afrika **Rev:** Arum lily and value **Edge:** Reeded

| Date | Mintage | VF20 | XF40 | MS60 | MS63 | MS65 |
|---|---|---|---|---|---|---|
| 2008 | — | — | — | 0.50 | 0.75 | 1.00 |
| 2008 | — | PF65 8.00 | | | | |

**KM# 465 10 CENTS**
2.00 g., Copper Plated Steel, 16 mm. **Obv:** National arms **Rev:** Arum lily and value

| Date | Mintage | VF20 | XF40 | MS60 | MS63 | MS65 |
|---|---|---|---|---|---|---|
| 2009 | — | — | — | 0.50 | 0.75 | 1.00 |
| 2009 | — | PF65 8.00 | | | | |

**KM# 494 10 CENTS**
2.00 g., Bronze Plated Steel, 16 mm. **Obv:** National arms **Rev:** Arum Lily and value

| Date | Mintage | VF20 | XF40 | MS60 | MS63 | MS65 |
|---|---|---|---|---|---|---|
| 2010 | — | — | — | 0.60 | 0.90 | 1.20 |
| 2010 | — | PF65 7.00 | | | | |

**KM# 501 10 CENTS**
2.00 g., Bronze Plated Steel, 16 mm. **Obv:** National arms **Rev:** Arum lily and value

| Date | Mintage | VF20 | XF40 | MS60 | MS63 | MS65 |
|---|---|---|---|---|---|---|
| 2011 | — | — | — | 0.50 | 0.75 | 1.00 |
| 2011 | — | PF65 6.00 | | | | |

**KM# 225 20 CENTS**
3.50 g., Bronze Plated Steel, 19 mm. **Obv:** New national arms **Obv. Legend:** AFERIKA BORWA **Rev:** Protea flower and value **Edge:** Reeded

| Date | Mintage | VF20 | XF40 | MS60 | MS63 | MS65 |
|---|---|---|---|---|---|---|
| 2001 | — | — | 0.35 | 0.50 | 0.90 | 1.20 |
| 2001 | 3,678 | PF65 7.00 | | | | |

**KM# 270 20 CENTS**
3.50 g., Bronze Plated Steel, 19 mm. **Obv:** New national arms **Obv. Legend:** South Africa **Rev:** Protea flower and value **Edge:** Reeded

| Date | Mintage | VF20 | XF40 | MS60 | MS63 | MS65 |
|---|---|---|---|---|---|---|
| 2002 | — | — | 0.35 | 0.50 | 0.90 | 1.20 |
| 2002 | 3,250 | PF65 7.00 | | | | |

**KM# 327 20 CENTS**
3.50 g., Bronze Plated Steel, 19 mm. **Obv:** New national arms **Obv. Legend:** Aforika Borwa **Rev:** Protea flower and value **Edge:** Reeded

| Date | Mintage | VF20 | XF40 | MS60 | MS63 | MS65 |
|---|---|---|---|---|---|---|
| 2003 | — | — | 0.35 | 0.50 | 0.90 | 1.20 |
| 2003 | 2,909 | PF65 7.00 | | | | |

**KM# 328 20 CENTS**
3.50 g., Bronze Plated Steel, 19 mm. **Obv:** New national arms **Obv. Legend:** Afrika Borwa **Rev:** Protea flower and value **Edge:** Reeded

| Date | Mintage | VF20 | XF40 | MS60 | MS63 | MS65 |
|---|---|---|---|---|---|---|
| 2004 | — | — | 0.35 | 0.50 | 0.90 | 1.20 |
| 2004 | 1,935 | PF65 7.00 | | | | |

**KM# 293 20 CENTS**
3.50 g., Bronze Plated Steel, 19 mm. **Obv:** New national arms **Obv. Legend:** Suid-Afrika **Rev:** Protea flower and value **Edge:** Reeded **Shape:** Round

| Date | Mintage | VF20 | XF40 | MS60 | MS63 | MS65 |
|---|---|---|---|---|---|---|
| 2005 | — | — | 0.35 | 0.50 | 0.90 | 1.20 |
| 2005 | — | PF65 7.00 | | | | |

**KM# 488 20 CENTS**
3.50 g., Bronze Plated Steel, 19 mm. **Obv:** National arms **Obv. Legend:** uMzantsi Afrika **Rev:** Protea flower and value **Edge:** Reeded

| Date | Mintage | VF20 | XF40 | MS60 | MS63 | MS65 |
|---|---|---|---|---|---|---|
| 2006 | — | — | — | 0.50 | 0.90 | 1.20 |
| 2006 | — | PF65 7.00 | | | | |

**KM# 342 20 CENTS**
3.50 g., Bronze Plated Steel, 19 mm. **Obv:** New national arms **Obv. Legend:** iNingizimu Afrika **Rev:** Protea flower and value **Edge:** Reeded

| Date | Mintage | VF20 | XF40 | MS60 | MS63 | MS65 |
|---|---|---|---|---|---|---|
| 2007 | — | — | 0.35 | 0.50 | 0.90 | 1.20 |
| 2007 | — | PF65 7.00 | | | | |

**KM# 442 20 CENTS**
3.50 g., Bronze Plated Steel, 19 mm. **Obv:** National arms **Rev:** Protea flower and value **Edge:** Reeded

| Date | Mintage | VF20 | XF40 | MS60 | MS63 | MS65 |
|---|---|---|---|---|---|---|
| 2008 | — | — | — | 0.50 | 0.90 | 1.20 |
| 2008 | — | PF65 7.00 | | | | |

**KM# 466 20 CENTS**
3.50 g., Bronze Plated Steel, 19 mm. **Obv:** National arms **Rev:** Protea flower and value

| Date | Mintage | VF20 | XF40 | MS60 | MS63 | MS65 |
|---|---|---|---|---|---|---|
| 2009 | — | — | — | 0.50 | 0.90 | 1.20 |
| 2009 | — | PF65 7.00 | | | | |

**KM# 495 20 CENTS**
3.50 g., Bronze Plated Steel, 19 mm. **Obv:** National arms **Rev:** Protea flower and vlaue

| Date | Mintage | VF20 | XF40 | MS60 | MS63 | MS65 |
|---|---|---|---|---|---|---|
| 2010 | — | PF65 7.00 | | | | |
| 2010 | — | — | — | 0.60 | 1.00 | 1.50 |

**KM# 502 20 CENTS**
3.50 g., Bronze Plated Steel, 19 mm. **Obv:** National arms **Rev:** Protea flower and value

| Date | Mintage | VF20 | XF40 | MS60 | MS63 | MS65 |
|---|---|---|---|---|---|---|
| 2011 | — | — | — | 0.50 | 0.90 | 1.20 |
| 2011 | — | PF65 7.00 | | | | |

**KM# 226 50 CENTS**
5.00 g., Bronze Plated Steel, 22 mm. **Obv:** New national arms **Obv. Legend:** AFERIKA BORWA **Rev:** Strelitzia plant, value **Edge:** Reeded

| Date | Mintage | VF20 | XF40 | MS60 | MS63 | MS65 |
|---|---|---|---|---|---|---|
| 2001 | 1,152,000 | — | 0.50 | 0.75 | 1.20 | 1.60 |
| 2001 | 3,678 | PF65 8.00 | | | | |

**KM# 271 50 CENTS**
5.00 g., Bronze Plated Steel, 22 mm. **Obv:** New national arms **Obv. Legend:** Aforika Borwa **Rev:** Strelitzia plant **Edge:** Reeded

| Date | Mintage | VF20 | XF40 | MS60 | MS63 | MS65 |
|---|---|---|---|---|---|---|
| 2002 | 3,250 | PF65 8.00 | | | | |
| 2002 | 16,000,000 | — | 0.50 | 0.75 | 1.20 | 1.60 |

**KM# 287 50 CENTS**
5.00 g., Bronze Plated Steel, 22 mm. **Obv:** New national arms **Obv. Legend:** Aforika - Borwa **Rev:** Soccer player and value **Edge:** Reeded

| Date | Mintage | VF20 | XF40 | MS60 | MS63 | MS65 |
|---|---|---|---|---|---|---|
| 2002 | — | — | — | 5.00 | 9.00 | 12.00 |

**KM# 276 50 CENTS**
5.00 g., Bronze Plated Steel, 22 mm. **Obv:** New national arms **Obv. Legend:** Aforika Borwa **Rev:** Cricket player diving towards the wicket **Edge:** Reeded

| Date | Mintage | VF20 | XF40 | MS60 | MS63 | MS65 |
|---|---|---|---|---|---|---|
| 2003 | 11,749 | — | — | 5.00 | 9.00 | 12.00 |
| 2003 | — | PF65 15.00 | | | | |

**KM# 330 50 CENTS**
5.00 g., Bronze Plated Steel, 22 mm. **Obv:** New national arms **Obv. Legend:** Afrika Borwa **Rev:** Strelitzia plant, value **Edge:** Reeded

| Date | Mintage | VF20 | XF40 | MS60 | MS63 | MS65 |
|---|---|---|---|---|---|---|
| 2003 | — | — | 0.50 | 0.75 | 1.20 | 1.60 |
| 2003 | 2,909 | PF65 8.00 | | | | |

**KM# 331 50 CENTS**
5.00 g., Bronze Plated Steel, 22 mm. **Obv:** New national arms **Obv. Legend:** Suid Afrika **Rev:** Strelitzia plant, value **Edge:** Reeded

| Date | Mintage | VF20 | XF40 | MS60 | MS63 | MS65 |
|---|---|---|---|---|---|---|
| 2004 | — | — | 0.50 | 0.75 | 1.20 | 1.60 |
| 2004 | 1,935 | PF65 8.00 | | | | |

**KM# 294 50 CENTS**
5.00 g., Bronze Plated Steel, 22 mm. **Obv:** New national arms **Obv. Legend:** uMzantsi Afrika **Rev:** Strelitzia plant, value **Edge:** Reeded

| Date | Mintage | VF20 | XF40 | MS60 | MS63 | MS65 |
|---|---|---|---|---|---|---|
| 2005 | — | — | 0.50 | 0.75 | 1.20 | 1.60 |
| 2005 | — | PF65 8.00 | | | | |

**KM# 489 50 CENTS**
5.00 g., Bronze Plated Steel, 22 mm. **Obv:** National arms **Obv. Legend:** iNingizimu Afrika **Rev:** Strelitzia plant and value **Edge:** Reeded

| Date | Mintage | VF20 | XF40 | MS60 | MS63 | MS65 |
|---|---|---|---|---|---|---|
| 2006 | — | — | — | 0.75 | 1.20 | 1.60 |
| 2006 | — | PF65 8.00 | | | | |

**KM# 343 50 CENTS**
5.00 g., Bronze Plated Steel, 22 mm. **Obv:** National arms **Obv. Legend:** iSewula Afrika **Rev:** Strelitzia plant and value **Edge:** Reeded

| Date | Mintage | VF20 | XF40 | MS60 | MS63 | MS65 |
|---|---|---|---|---|---|---|
| 2007 | — | — | — | 0.75 | 1.20 | 1.60 |
| 2007 | — | PF65 8.00 | | | | |

**KM# 443 50 CENTS**
5.00 g., Bronze Plated Steel, 22 mm. **Obv:** National arms **Obv. Legend:** Afurika Tshipembe **Rev:** Strelitzia plant and value **Edge:** Reeded

| Date | Mintage | VF20 | XF40 | MS60 | MS63 | MS65 |
|---|---|---|---|---|---|---|
| 2008 | — | — | — | 0.75 | 1.20 | 1.60 |
| 2008 | — | PF65 8.00 | | | | |

**KM# 467 50 CENTS**
5.00 g., Bronze Plated Steel, 22 mm. **Obv:** National arms **Rev:** Strelitzia plant

| Date | Mintage | VF20 | XF40 | MS60 | MS63 | MS65 |
|---|---|---|---|---|---|---|
| 2009 | — | — | — | 0.75 | 1.20 | 1.60 |
| 2009 | — | PF65 8.00 | | | | |

**KM# 496 50 CENTS**
5.00 g., Bronze Plated Steel, 22 mm. **Obv:** National arms **Rev:** Strelitzia plant

| Date | Mintage | VF20 | XF40 | MS60 | MS63 | MS65 |
|---|---|---|---|---|---|---|
| 2010 | — | — | — | 0.75 | 1.20 | 1.60 |
| 2010 | — | PF65 8.00 | | | | |

**KM# 503 50 CENTS**
5.00 g., Bronze Plated Steel, 22 mm. **Obv:** National arms **Rev:** Strelitzia plant and value

| Date | Mintage | VF20 | XF40 | MS60 | MS63 | MS65 |
|---|---|---|---|---|---|---|
| 2011 | — | — | — | 0.75 | 1.20 | 1.60 |
| 2011 | — | PF65 10.00 | | | | |

**KM# 554 50 CENTS**
5.00 g., Bronze Plated Steel, 22 mm. **Obv:** National arms **Obv. Legend:** Afrika Dzonga Ningizimu Afrika **Rev:** Bird of Paradise flower

| Date | Mintage | VF20 | XF40 | MS60 | MS63 | MS65 |
|---|---|---|---|---|---|---|
| 2012 | — | — | — | 0.75 | 1.20 | 1.60 |

**KM# 227 RAND**
4.00 g., Nickel Plated Copper, 20 mm. **Obv:** New national arms **Obv. Legend:** SUID-AFRIKA **Rev:** Springbok, value **Edge:** Segmented reeding

| Date | Mintage | VF20 | XF40 | MS60 | MS63 | MS65 |
|---|---|---|---|---|---|---|
| 2001 | — | — | 0.60 | 1.50 | 2.00 | — |
| 2001 | 3,678 | PF63 10.00 | | | | |

**KM# 272 RAND**
4.00 g., Nickel Plated Copper, 20 mm. **Obv:** New national arms **Obv. Legend:** Suid-Afrika Afrika Borwa **Rev:** Springbok, value **Edge:** Segmented reeding

| Date | Mintage | VF20 | XF40 | MS60 | MS63 | MS65 |
|---|---|---|---|---|---|---|
| 2002 | — | — | 0.60 | 1.50 | 2.00 | — |
| 2002 | 3,250 | PF63 10.00 | | | | |

**KM# 275 RAND**
4.00 g., Nickel Plated Copper, 20 mm. **Subject:** Johannesburg World Summit on Sustainable Development **Obv:** New national arms **Obv. Legend:** Suid-Afrika - Afrika Borwa **Rev:** World globe and logo **Edge:** Segmented reeding

| Date | Mintage | VF20 | XF40 | MS60 | MS63 | MS65 |
|---|---|---|---|---|---|---|
| 2002 | — | — | — | 12.00 | 18.00 | — |

**KM# 332 RAND**
4.00 g., Nickel Plated Copper, 20 mm. **Obv:** New national arms **Obv. Legend:** uMzantsi Afrika Suid-Afrika **Rev:** Springbok, value **Edge:** Segmented reeding

| Date | Mintage | VF20 | XF40 | MS60 | MS63 | MS65 |
|---|---|---|---|---|---|---|
| 2003 | — | — | 0.60 | 1.50 | 2.00 | — |
| 2003 | 2,909 | PF63 10.00 | | | | |

**KM# 333 RAND**
4.00 g., Nickel Plated Copper, 20 mm. **Obv:** New national arms **Obv. Legend:** iNingizimu Afrika - uMzantsi Afrika **Rev:** Springbok, value **Edge:** Segmented reeding

| Date | Mintage | VF20 | XF40 | MS60 | MS63 | MS65 |
|---|---|---|---|---|---|---|
| 2004 | — | — | 0.60 | 1.50 | 2.00 | — |
| 2004 | 1,935 | PF63 10.00 | | | | |

**KM# 295 RAND**
4.00 g., Nickel Plated Copper, 20 mm. **Obv:** new national arms **Obv. Legend:** iSewula Afrika - iNingizimu Afrika **Rev:** Springbok, value **Edge:** Segmented reeding **Shape:** Round

| Date | Mintage | VF20 | XF40 | MS60 | MS63 | MS65 |
|---|---|---|---|---|---|---|
| 2005 | — | — | 0.60 | 1.50 | 2.00 | — |
| 2005 | — | PF63 10.00 | | | | |

**KM# 490 RAND**
4.00 g., Nickel Plated Copper, 20 mm. **Obv:** National arms **Obv. Legend:** Afurika Tshipembe - iSewula Afrika **Rev:** Springbok and value

| Date | Mintage | VF20 | XF40 | MS60 | MS63 | MS65 |
|---|---|---|---|---|---|---|
| 2006 | — | — | — | 1.50 | 2.00 | — |
| 2006 | — | PF63 10.00 | | | | |

**KM# 344 RAND**
3.93 g., Nickel Plated Copper, 19.94 mm. **Obv:** Natinal arms **Obv. Legend:** Ningizimu Afrika - Afurika Tshipemba **Rev:** Springbok leaping right **Edge:** segmented reeding

| Date | Mintage | VF20 | XF40 | MS60 | MS63 | MS65 |
|---|---|---|---|---|---|---|
| 2007 | — | — | 0.60 | 1.50 | 2.00 | — |
| 2007 | — | PF63 10.00 | | | | |

**KM# 444 RAND**
4.00 g., Nickel Plated Copper, 20 mm. **Obv:** National arms **Obv. Legend:** Afrika-Dzonga - Ningizimu Afrika **Rev:** Springbok and value

| Date | Mintage | VF20 | XF40 | MS60 | MS63 | MS65 |
|---|---|---|---|---|---|---|
| 2008 | — | — | — | 2.00 | 2.75 | — |
| 2008 | — | PF63 12.00 | | | | |

**KM# 468 RAND**
4.00 g., Nickel Plated Copper, 20 mm. **Obv:** National arms **Rev:** Spingbok

| Date | Mintage | VF20 | XF40 | MS60 | MS63 | MS65 |
|---|---|---|---|---|---|---|
| 2009 | — | — | — | 1.50 | 2.00 | — |
| 2009 | — | PF63 10.00 | | | | |

**KM# 497 RAND**
4.00 g., Nickel Plated Copper, 20 mm. **Obv:** National arms **Rev:** Springbok right

| Date | Mintage | VF20 | XF40 | MS60 | MS63 | MS65 |
|---|---|---|---|---|---|---|
| 2010 | — | — | — | 1.50 | 2.00 | — |
| 2010 | — | PF63 10.00 | | | | |

**KM# 508 RAND**
3.11 g., 0.9999 Gold 0.100 oz. AGW, 16.5 mm. **Subject:** World Cup Soccer

| Date | Mintage | VF20 | XF40 | MS60 | MS63 | MS65 |
|---|---|---|---|---|---|---|
| 2010 | — | PF65 200 | | | | |

**KM# 504 RAND**
20.00 g., Nickel Plated Copper, 20 mm. **Obv:** National arms **Rev:** Springbok and value

| Date | Mintage | VF20 | XF40 | MS60 | MS63 | MS65 |
|---|---|---|---|---|---|---|
| 2011 | — | — | — | 1.50 | 2.00 | — |
| 2011 | — | PF63 10.00 | | | | |

**KM# 228 2 RAND**
5.50 g., Nickel Plated Copper, 23 mm. **Obv:** New national arms **Obv. Legend:** UMZANSTI AFRIKA **Rev:** Greater Kudu, value **Edge:** Segmented reeding

| Date | Mintage | VF20 | XF40 | MS60 | MS63 | MS65 |
|---|---|---|---|---|---|---|
| 2001 | 3,600,000 | — | 0.80 | 2.00 | 3.00 | — |
| 2001 | 3,678 | PF63 12.00 | | | | |

**KM# 273 2 RAND**
5.50 g., Nickel Plated Copper, 23 mm. **Obv:** New national arms **Obv. Legend:** iNingizimu Afrika - uMzantsi Afrika **Rev:** Greater Kudu, value **Edge:** Segmented reeding

| Date | Mintage | VF20 | XF40 | MS60 | MS63 | MS65 |
|---|---|---|---|---|---|---|
| 2002 | 3,250 | PF63 12.00 | | | | |
| 2002 | 12,000,000 | — | 0.80 | 2.00 | 3.50 | — |

**KM# 335 2 RAND**
5.50 g., Nickel Plated Copper, 23 mm. **Obv:** New national arms **Obv. Legend:** iNingizimu Afrika - iSewula Afrika **Rev:** Greater Kudu, value **Edge:** Segmented reeding

| Date | Mintage | VF20 | XF40 | MS60 | MS63 | MS65 |
|---|---|---|---|---|---|---|
| 2003 | 5,000,000 | — | 0.80 | 2.00 | 3.50 | — |
| 2003 | 2,909 | PF63 12.00 | | | | |

**KM# 334 2 RAND**
5.50 g., Nickel Plated Copper, 23 mm. **Subject:** 10 Years of Freedom - 1994-2004 **Obv:** New national arms **Obv. Legend:** SOUTH / AFRICA **Rev:** Value, flag logo, people **Edge:** Segmented reeding **Note:** 5,885 issued in souveneir card.

| Date | Mintage | VF20 | XF40 | MS60 | MS63 | MS65 |
|---|---|---|---|---|---|---|
| 2004 | — | — | 0.80 | 2.00 | 2.75 | — |

**KM# 336 2 RAND**
5.50 g., Nickel Plated Copper, 23 mm. **Obv:** New national arms **Obv. Legend:** Afurika Tshipembe / iSewula Afrika **Rev:** Greater Kudu, value **Edge:** Segmented reeding

| Date | Mintage | VF20 | XF40 | MS60 | MS63 | MS65 |
|---|---|---|---|---|---|---|
| 2004 | — | — | 0.80 | 2.00 | 3.50 | — |
| 2004 | 1,935 | PF63 12.00 | | | | |

**KM# 296 2 RAND**
5.50 g., Nickel Plated Copper, 23 mm. **Obv:** New national arms **Obv. Legend:** Ningizimu Afrika - Afurika Tshipembe **Rev:** Greater Kudu, value **Edge:** Segmented reeding

| Date | Mintage | VF20 | XF40 | MS60 | MS63 | MS65 |
|---|---|---|---|---|---|---|
| 2005 | — | — | 0.80 | 2.00 | 2.75 | — |
| 2005 | — | PF63 12.00 | | | | |

**KM# 491 2 RAND**
5.50 g., Nickel Plated Copper, 23 mm. **Obv:** National arms **Obv. Legend:** Afrika-Dzonga - Ningizimo Afrika **Rev:** Greater kudu and value

| Date | Mintage | VF20 | XF40 | MS60 | MS63 | MS65 |
|---|---|---|---|---|---|---|
| 2006 | — | — | — | 2.00 | 2.75 | — |
| 2006 | — | PF63 12.00 | | | | |

**KM# 345 2 RAND**
5.50 g., Nickel Plated Copper, 23 mm. **Obv:** National arms **Rev:** Greater Kudu

| Date | Mintage | VF20 | XF40 | MS60 | MS63 | MS65 |
|---|---|---|---|---|---|---|
| 2007 | — | — | 0.80 | 2.00 | 3.00 | — |
| 2007 | — | PF63 15.00 | | | | |

**KM# 445 2 RAND**
5.50 g., Nickel Plated Copper, 23 mm. **Obv:** National arms **Obv. Legend:** Afrika-Dzonga - South Africa **Rev:** Kudu at center left, value at right **Edge:** Segmented reeding

| Date | Mintage | VF20 | XF40 | MS60 | MS63 | MS65 |
|---|---|---|---|---|---|---|
| 2008 | — | — | 0.80 | 2.00 | 2.75 | — |
| 2008 | — | PF63 12.00 | | | | |

**KM# 469 2 RAND**
5.50 g., Nickel Plated Copper, 22 mm. **Obv:** National arms **Rev:** Greater Kudu

| Date | Mintage | VF20 | XF40 | MS60 | MS63 | MS65 |
|---|---|---|---|---|---|---|
| 2009 | — | — | — | 2.00 | 2.75 | — |
| 2009 | — | PF63 12.00 | | | | |

**KM# 498 2 RAND**
5.50 g., Nickel Plated Copper, 23 mm. **Obv:** National arms **Rev:** Greater Kudu

| Date | Mintage | VF20 | XF40 | MS60 | MS63 | MS65 |
|---|---|---|---|---|---|---|
| 2010 | — | — | — | 2.00 | 2.75 | — |
| 2010 | — | PF63 12.00 | | | | |

**KM# 505 2 RAND**
5.50 g., Nickel Plated Copper, 23 mm. **Obv:** Naitonal arms **Rev:** Kudo at center

| Date | Mintage | VF20 | XF40 | MS60 | MS63 | MS65 |
|---|---|---|---|---|---|---|
| 2011 | — | — | — | 2.00 | 2.75 | — |
| 2011 | — | PF63 12.00 | | | | |

**KM# 229 5 RAND**
7.00 g., Nickel Plated Copper, 26 mm. **Obv:** New national arms **Obv. Legend:** ININGIZIMU AFRIKA **Rev:** Wildebeest, value **Edge:** Segmented reeding

| Date | Mintage | VF20 | XF40 | MS60 | MS63 | MS65 |
|---|---|---|---|---|---|---|
| 2001 | 2,000,000 | — | 1.20 | 4.50 | 6.00 | — |
| 2001 CW | 779 | — | — | 67.50 | 90.00 | — |
| 2001 | 3,678 | PF63 15.00 | | | | |

**KM# 274 5 RAND**
7.00 g., Nickel Plated Copper, 26 mm. **Obv:** New national arms **Obv. Legend:** Afurika Tshipembe - Isewula Afrika **Rev:** Wildebeest, value **Edge:** Segmented reeding

| Date | Mintage | VF20 | XF40 | MS60 | MS63 | MS65 |
|---|---|---|---|---|---|---|
| 2002 | — | — | 1.20 | 4.50 | 6.00 | — |
| 2002 CW | 106 | — | — | — | 150 | — |
| 2002 | 3,250 | PF63 15.00 | | | | |

**KM# 337 5 RAND**
7.00 g., Nickel Plated Copper, 26 mm. **Obv:** New national arms **Obv. Legend:** Afurika Tshipembe - Ningizimu Afrika **Rev:** Wildebeest, value **Edge:** Segmented reeding

| Date | Mintage | VF20 | XF40 | MS60 | MS63 | MS65 |
|---|---|---|---|---|---|---|
| 2003 | — | — | 1.20 | 4.50 | 6.00 | — |
| 2003 | 2,909 | PF63 15.00 | | | | |

**KM# 281 5 RAND**
9.50 g., Bi-Metallic Brass center in Copper-Nickel ring, 26 mm. **Obv:** New national arms **Obv. Legend:** Afrika-Dzonga - Ningizimu Afrika **Rev:** Wildebeest, value **Edge:** Security type with lettering **Edge Lettering:** SARB R5" repeated ten times

| Date | Mintage | VF20 | XF40 | MS60 | MS63 | MS65 |
|---|---|---|---|---|---|---|
| 2004 | — | — | 1.20 | 5.00 | 6.50 | — |
| 2004 CW | 3,243 | — | — | — | 22.50 | — |
| 2004 | 1,935 | PF65 15.00 | | | | |

**KM# 297 5 RAND**
9.50 g., Bi-Metallic Brass center in Copper-Nickel ring, 26 mm. **Obv:** New national arms **Obv. Legend:** Afrika Dzonga - South Africa **Rev:** Wildebeest, value **Edge:** Security type with lettering **Edge Lettering:** SARB R5" repeated ten times

| Date | Mintage | VF20 | XF40 | MS60 | MS63 | MS65 |
|---|---|---|---|---|---|---|
| 2005 | — | — | 1.20 | 3.75 | 5.00 | — |
| 2005 CW | 997 | — | — | — | 50.00 | — |
| 2005 | — | PF63 15.00 | | | | |

**KM# 492 5 RAND**
5.50 g., Bi-Metallic Brass center in Copper-Nickel ring., 26 mm. **Obv:** National arms **Obv. Legend:** Aforika Borwa - South Africa **Rev:** Wildebeest and value

| Date | Mintage | VF20 | XF40 | MS60 | MS63 | MS65 |
|---|---|---|---|---|---|---|
| 2006 | — | — | — | 4.50 | 6.00 | — |
| 2006 | — | PF63 12.00 | | | | |

**KM# 346 5 RAND**
9.50 g., Bi-Metallic Brass center in Copper-Nickel ring, 26 mm. **Obv:** National arms **Obv. Legend:** Aforika Borwa - Afrika Borwa **Rev:** Wildebeest and value **Edge:** Security type and lettered **Edge Lettering:** SARB R5" repeated ten times

| Date | Mintage | VF20 | XF40 | MS60 | MS63 | MS65 |
|---|---|---|---|---|---|---|
| 2007 | — | — | 1.20 | 3.00 | 4.00 | — |
| 2007 CW | — | — | — | — | 22.50 | — |
| 2007 | — | PF63 15.00 | | | | |

**KM# 439 5 RAND**
9.50 g., Bi-Metallic Brass center in Copper-Nickel ring, 26 mm. **Subject:** Nelson Mandella, 90th Birthday **Obv:** National arms **Rev:** Bust facing

| Date | Mintage | VF20 | XF40 | MS60 | MS63 | MS65 |
|---|---|---|---|---|---|---|
| 2008 | — | — | 1.20 | 3.75 | 5.00 | — |
| 2008 | — | PF63 15.00 | | | | |

**KM# 446 5 RAND**
9.50 g., Bi-Metallic Brass center in Copper-Nickel ring, 26 mm. **Obv:** National arms **Rev:** Wildebeest rearing left

| Date | Mintage | VF20 | XF40 | MS60 | MS63 | MS65 |
|---|---|---|---|---|---|---|
| 2008 | — | — | — | 3.00 | 4.00 | — |
| 2008 CW | — | — | — | — | 22.50 | — |
| 2008 | — | PF63 12.00 | | | | |

**KM# 470 5 RAND**
9.50 g., Bi-Metallic Brass center in Copper-Nickel ring, 26 mm. **Obv:** National arms **Rev:** Wildebeest rearing left

| Date | Mintage | VF20 | XF40 | MS60 | MS63 | MS65 |
|---|---|---|---|---|---|---|
| 2009 CW | — | — | — | — | 22.50 | — |
| 2009 | — | — | — | 3.00 | 4.00 | — |
| 2009 | — | PF63 15.00 | | | | |

**KM# 499 5 RAND**
9.50 g., Bi-Metallic Brass center in Copper-Nickel ring, 26 mm. **Obv:** National arms **Rev:** Wildebeest rearing left

| Date | Mintage | VF20 | XF40 | MS60 | MS63 | MS65 |
|---|---|---|---|---|---|---|
| 2010 | — | — | — | 4.50 | 6.00 | — |
| 2010 CW | — | — | — | — | 22.50 | — |
| 2010 | — | PF63 15.00 | | | | |

**KM# 506 5 RAND**
9.50 g., Bi-Metallic Brass center in Copper-Nickel ring, 26 mm. **Obv:** National arms **Rev:** Wildebeest and value

| Date | Mintage | VF20 | XF40 | MS60 | MS63 | MS65 |
|---|---|---|---|---|---|---|
| 2011 | — | — | — | 4.50 | 6.00 | — |
| 2011 | — | PF63 15.00 | | | | |

**KM# 507 5 RAND**
9.50 g., Bi-Metallic Brass center in Copper-Nickel ring, 26 mm. **Subject:** 90th Anniversary of the Rand **Obv:** National arms **Rev:** Old coin and bank note designs

| Date | Mintage | VF20 | XF40 | MS60 | MS63 | MS65 |
|---|---|---|---|---|---|---|
| 2011 | — | — | — | 4.50 | 7.00 | — |
| 2011 | — | PF63 12.00 | | | | |

**KM# 518 5 RAND**
33.00 g., 0.925 Silver 0.9814 oz. ASW partially gilt, 38.7 mm. **Subject:** South African Reserve Bank, 90th Anniversary **Obv:** National arms **Rev:** Coins and banknotes

| Date | Mintage | VF20 | XF40 | MS60 | MS63 | MS65 |
|---|---|---|---|---|---|---|
| 2011 | Est. 10500 | PF65 55.00 | | | | |

**KM# 555 5 RAND**
9.50 g., Copper-Nickel Plated Nickel, 26 mm. **Obv:** National arms **Obv. Legend:** uMazantsi Afrika iNingizimu Afrika **Rev:** Black wildebeest

| Date | Mintage | VF20 | XF40 | MS60 | MS63 | MS65 |
|---|---|---|---|---|---|---|
| 2012 | — | — | — | 2.00 | 4.00 | — |

## GOLD BULLION COINAGE

**KM# 105 1/10 KRUGERRAND**
3.39 g., 0.917 Gold 0.100 oz. AGW, 16.50 mm. **Obv:** Bust of Paul Kruger left **Obv. Legend:** SUID-AFRIKA - SOUTH AFRICA **Rev:** Springbok walking right divides date **Edge:** Reeded **Note:** 180 edge serrations for uncirculated, 220 serrations for proof

| Date | Mintage | VF20 | XF40 | MS60 | MS63 | MS65 |
|---|---|---|---|---|---|---|
| 2001 | 17,936 | — | — | — | 139 | — |
| 2001 | 4,058 | PF63 200 | | | | |
| 2002 | 12,890 | — | — | — | 139 | — |
| 2002 | 3,110 | PF63 200 | | | | |

| Date | Mintage | VF20 | XF40 | MS60 | MS63 | MS65 |
|---|---|---|---|---|---|---|
| 2003 | 15,893 | — | — | — | 139 | — |
| 2003 | 1,893 | PF63 200 | | | | |
| 2004 | — | — | — | — | 139 | — |
| 2004 | 3,811 | PF63 200 | | | | |
| 2005 | — | — | — | — | 139 | — |
| 2005 | — | PF63 200 | | | | |
| 2006 | — | — | — | — | 139 | — |
| 2006 | — | PF63 200 | | | | |
| 2007 | — | — | — | — | 139 | — |
| 2007 | 4,400 | PF63 200 | | | | |
| 2008 | — | — | — | — | 139 | — |
| 2008 | 4,800 | PF63 200 | | | | |
| 2009 | — | — | — | — | 139 | — |
| 2009 | 6,000 | PF63 200 | | | | |
| 2010 | — | — | — | — | 139 | — |
| 2010 | 6,000 | PF63 200 | | | | |
| 2011 | — | — | — | — | 139 | — |
| 2011 | — | PF63 200 | | | | |
| 2012 | — | — | — | — | 139 | — |
| 2012 | — | PF63 200 | | | | |

**KM# 106 1/4 KRUGERRAND**
8.48 g., 0.917 Gold 0.2501 oz. AGW, 22 mm. **Obv:** Bust of Paul Kruger left **Obv. Legend:** SUID-AFRIKA - SOUTH AFRICA **Rev:** Springbok bounding right divides date **Edge:** Reeded **Note:** 180 edge serrations for uncirculated, 220 serrations for proof

| Date | Mintage | VF20 | XF40 | MS60 | MS63 | MS65 |
|---|---|---|---|---|---|---|
| 2001 | 10,607 | — | — | — | 332 | — |
| 2001 | 3,841 | PF63 475 | | | | |
| 2002 | 10,558 | — | — | — | 332 | — |
| 2002 | 2,442 | PF63 475 | | | | |
| 2003 | 11,468 | — | — | — | 332 | — |
| 2003 | 2,450 | PF63 475 | | | | |
| 2004 | — | — | — | — | 332 | — |
| 2004 | 4,570 | PF63 475 | | | | |
| 2005 | — | — | — | — | 332 | — |
| 2005 | — | PF63 475 | | | | |
| 2006 | — | — | — | — | 332 | — |
| 2006 | — | PF63 475 | | | | |
| 2007 | — | — | — | — | 332 | — |
| 2007 | 4,400 | PF63 475 | | | | |
| 2008 | — | — | — | — | 332 | — |
| 2008 | 4,800 | PF63 475 | | | | |
| 2009 | — | — | — | — | 332 | — |
| 2009 | 6,000 | PF63 475 | | | | |
| 2010 | — | — | — | — | 332 | — |
| 2010 | 6,000 | PF63 475 | | | | |
| 2011 | — | — | — | — | 332 | — |
| 2011 | — | PF63 475 | | | | |
| 2012 | — | — | — | — | 332 | — |
| 2012 | — | PF63 475 | | | | |

**KM# 107 1/2 KRUGERRAND**
16.97 g., 0.917 Gold 0.5002 oz. AGW, 27 mm. **Obv:** Bust of Paul Kruger left **Obv. Legend:** SUID-AFRIKA • SOUTH AFRICA **Rev:** Springbok walking right divides date **Edge:** Reeded **Note:** 180 edge serrations for uncirculated, 220 serrations for proof

| Date | Mintage | VF20 | XF40 | MS60 | MS63 | MS65 |
|---|---|---|---|---|---|---|
| 2001 | 6,429 | — | — | — | 652 | — |
| 2001 | 3,696 | PF63 950 | | | | |
| 2002 | — | — | — | — | 652 | — |
| 2002 | 2,295 | PF63 950 | | | | |
| 2003 | 11,588 | — | — | — | 652 | — |
| 2003 | 1,285 | PF63 950 | | | | |
| 2004 | — | — | — | — | 652 | — |
| 2004 | 3,288 | PF63 950 | | | | |
| 2005 | — | — | — | — | 652 | — |
| 2005 | — | PF63 950 | | | | |
| 2006 | — | — | — | — | 652 | — |
| 2006 | — | PF63 950 | | | | |
| 2007 | — | — | — | — | 652 | — |
| 2007 | 3,400 | PF63 950 | | | | |
| 2008 | — | — | — | — | 652 | — |
| 2008 | 3,300 | PF63 950 | | | | |
| 2009 | — | — | — | — | 652 | — |
| 2009 | 2,500 | PF63 950 | | | | |
| 2010 | — | — | — | — | 652 | — |
| 2010 | 2,500 | PF63 950 | | | | |
| 2011 | — | — | — | — | 652 | — |

| Date | Mintage | VF20 | XF40 | MS60 | MS63 | MS65 |
|---|---|---|---|---|---|---|
| 2011 | — | PF63 950 | | | | |
| 2012 | — | — | — | — | 652 | — |
| 2012 | — | PF63 950 | | | | |

**KM# 73 KRUGERRAND**
33.93 g., 0.917 Gold 1.0003 oz. AGW, 32.7 mm. **Obv:** Bust of Paul Kruger left **Obv. Legend:** SUID — AFRIKA • SOUTH AFRICA **Rev:** Springbok walking right divides date **Edge:** Reeded **Note:** 180 edge serrations for uncirculated, 220 serrations for proof

| Date | Mintage | VF20 | XF40 | MS60 | MS63 | MS65 |
|---|---|---|---|---|---|---|
| 2001 | 5,889 | — | — | — | 1,268 | — |
| 2001 | 5,563 | PF63 1,850 | | | | |
| 2002 | 16,469 | — | — | — | 1,268 | — |
| 2002 | 3,531 | PF63 1,850 | | | | |
| 2003 | 47,789 | — | — | — | 1,268 | — |
| 2003 | 2,136 | PF63 1,850 | | | | |
| 2004 | 71,269 | — | — | — | 1,268 | — |
| 2004 | 3,492 | PF63 1,850 | | | | |
| 2004 W/MM | 500 | PF63 1,850 | | | | |
| 2005 | — | — | — | — | 1,268 | — |
| 2005 | — | PF63 1,850 | | | | |
| 2006 | — | — | — | — | 1,268 | — |
| 2006 | — | PF63 1,850 | | | | |
| 2007 | — | — | — | — | 1,268 | — |
| 2007 | 3,400 | PF63 1,850 | | | | |
| 2008 | — | — | — | — | 1,268 | — |
| 2008 | 3,300 | PF63 1,850 | | | | |
| 2009 | — | — | — | — | 1,268 | — |
| 2009 | 2,500 | PF63 1,850 | | | | |
| 2010 | — | — | — | — | 1,268 | — |
| 2010 | 2,500 | PF63 1,850 | | | | |
| 2011 | — | — | — | — | 1,268 | — |
| 2011 | — | PF63 1,850 | | | | |
| 2012 | — | — | — | — | 1,268 | — |
| 2012 | — | PF63 1,850 | | | | |

## SILVER BULLION NATURA COINAGE

**KM# 242 2-1/2 CENTS**
1.41 g., 0.925 Silver 0.0421 oz. ASW, 16.3 mm. **Obv:** Crowned arms **Rev:** Dolphin **Edge:** Reeded

| Date | Mintage | VF20 | XF40 | MS60 | MS63 | MS65 |
|---|---|---|---|---|---|---|
| 2001 | — | PF65 27.50 | | | | |

**KM# 480 2-1/2 CENTS**
1.41 g., 0.925 Silver 0.0421 oz. ASW, 16.3 mm. **Obv:** Flower **Rev:** Vasco de Gama's ship "Sao Gabriel

| Date | Mintage | VF20 | XF40 | MS60 | MS63 | MS65 |
|---|---|---|---|---|---|---|
| 2009 | 3,500 | PF65 15.00 | | | | |

**KM# 243 5 CENTS**
8.46 g., 0.925 Silver 0.2515 oz. ASW, 26.7 mm. **Series:** Wildlife - Power **Obv:** Cape Buffalo head **Rev:** Two Cape Buffalo heads within circle below value **Edge:** Reeded

| Date | Mintage | VF20 | XF40 | MS60 | MS63 | MS65 |
|---|---|---|---|---|---|---|
| 2001 | 1,853 | PF65 40.00 | | | | |

**KM# 351 5 CENTS**
8.46 g., 0.925 Silver 0.2515 oz. ASW, 26.7 mm. **Series:** Wildlife - Strength **Obv:** Elephant walking, facing **Rev:** Elephant 3/4 left bathing **Edge:** Reeded

| Date | Mintage | VF20 | XF40 | MS60 | MS63 | MS65 |
|---|---|---|---|---|---|---|
| 2002 | 2,425 | PF65 30.00 | | | | |

**KM# 355 5 CENTS**
8.46 g., 0.925 Silver 0.2515 oz. ASW, 26.7 mm. **Series:** Wildlife - Survivor **Obv:** New national arms **Rev:** 2 White Rhinoceros drinking at stream **Edge:** Reeded

| Date | Mintage | VF20 | XF40 | MS60 | MS63 | MS65 |
|---|---|---|---|---|---|---|
| 2003 | 1,870 | PF65 40.00 | | | | |

**KM# 359 5 CENTS**
8.46 g., 0.925 Silver 0.2515 oz. ASW, 26.7 mm. **Series:** Wildlife - The Legend **Obv:** New national arms **Rev:** Head of Leopard right drinking **Edge:** Reeded

| Date | Mintage | VF20 | XF40 | MS60 | MS63 | MS65 |
|---|---|---|---|---|---|---|
| 2004 | — | PF65 40.00 | | | | |

**KM# 320 5 CENTS**
8.46 g., 0.925 Silver 0.2515 oz. ASW, 27.12 mm. **Series:** Wildlife - African Wild Dog **Obv:** New national arms **Rev:** Painted Dog's head facing slightly left **Edge:** Reeded

| Date | Mintage | VF20 | XF40 | MS60 | MS63 | MS65 |
|---|---|---|---|---|---|---|
| 2005 | 1,500 | PF65 40.00 | | | | |

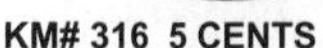

**KM# 316 5 CENTS**
8.46 g., 0.925 Silver 0.2515 oz. ASW, 27 mm. **Series:** Wildlife - Black-backed Jackal **Obv:** New national arms **Rev:** Black-backed jackal drinking **Edge:** Reeded

| Date | Mintage | VF20 | XF40 | MS60 | MS63 | MS65 |
|---|---|---|---|---|---|---|
| 2006 | 1,500 | PF65 40.00 | | | | |

**KM# 363 5 CENTS**
8.46 g., 0.925 Silver 0.2515 oz. ASW, 26.7 mm. **Series:** Wildlife - Kgalagadi Transfrontier Peace Park **Obv:** New national arms **Rev:** Local desert melons, value **Edge:** Reeded

| Date | Mintage | VF20 | XF40 | MS60 | MS63 | MS65 |
|---|---|---|---|---|---|---|
| 2007 | — | PF65 40.00 | | | | |

**KM# 458 5 CENTS**
8.41 g., 0.925 Silver 0.250 oz. ASW, 27 mm. **Subject:** Richtersveld Transfrontier Park **Obv:** Arms **Rev:** Orbea Namaquensis succulant flower

| Date | Mintage | VF20 | XF40 | MS60 | MS63 | MS65 |
|---|---|---|---|---|---|---|
| 2008 | 2,200 | PF65 30.00 | | | | |

**KM# 482 5 CENTS**
8.41 g., 0.925 Silver 0.250 oz. ASW, 27 mm. **Subject:** Maloti Drakensberg Transfrontier Project **Obv:** Arms **Rev:** Spiral Aloe Tree (aloe polyphylla)

| Date | Mintage | VF20 | XF40 | MS60 | MS63 | MS65 |
|---|---|---|---|---|---|---|
| 2009 | 3,700 | PF65 25.00 | | | | |

**KM# 539 5 CENTS**
8.46 g., 0.925 Silver 0.2515 oz. ASW, 27 mm. **Obv:** National arms **Rev:** Flower - Gloriosa superba - Colchicacceae

| Date | Mintage | VF20 | XF40 | MS60 | MS63 | MS65 |
|---|---|---|---|---|---|---|
| 2010 | Est. 2700 | PF65 45.00 | | | | |

**KM# 513 5 CENTS**
8.41 g., 0.925 Silver 0.250 oz. ASW, 27 mm.

| Date | Mintage | VF20 | XF40 | MS60 | MS63 | MS65 |
|---|---|---|---|---|---|---|
| 2011 | — | PF65 40.00 | | | | |

**KM# 529 5 CENTS**
8.45 g., 0.925 Silver 0.2513 oz. ASW, 27 mm. **Subject:** Great Mapungubwe Transfrontier Conservation Area **Obv:** National arms **Rev:** Baobab tree seed pod, sandstone landscape in background

| Date | Mintage | VF20 | XF40 | MS60 | MS63 | MS65 |
|---|---|---|---|---|---|---|
| 2012 | — | PF65 25.00 | | | | |

**KM# 244 10 CENTS**
16.86 g., 0.925 Silver 0.5015 oz. ASW, 32.7 mm. **Series:** Wildlife - Power **Obv:** Cape Buffalo head **Rev:** Two Cape Buffalo bulls fighting **Edge:** Reeded

| Date | Mintage | VF20 | XF40 | MS60 | MS63 | MS65 |
|---|---|---|---|---|---|---|
| 2001 | 1,989 | PF65 65.00 | | | | |

**KM# 352 10 CENTS**
16.81 g., 0.925 Silver 0.500 oz. ASW, 38.3 mm. **Series:** Wildlife - Strength **Obv:** Elephant walking, facing **Rev:** 2 elephant heads facing each other **Edge:** Reeded

| Date | Mintage | VF20 | XF40 | MS60 | MS63 | MS65 |
|---|---|---|---|---|---|---|
| 2002 | 2,395 | PF65 55.00 | | | | |

**KM# 356 10 CENTS**
16.81 g., 0.925 Silver 0.500 oz. ASW, 32.7 mm. **Series:** Wildlife - Survivor **Obv:** New national arms **Rev:** 2 Black Rhinoceros standing, facing **Edge:** Reeded

| Date | Mintage | VF20 | XF40 | MS60 | MS63 | MS65 |
|---|---|---|---|---|---|---|
| 2003 | 1,815 | PF65 65.00 | | | | |

**KM# 360 10 CENTS**
16.81 g., 0.925 Silver 0.500 oz. ASW, 32.7 mm. **Series:** Wildlife - The Legend **Obv:** New national arms **Rev:** Leopard and impala above two leopard cubs playing **Edge:** Reeded

| Date | Mintage | VF20 | XF40 | MS60 | MS63 | MS65 |
|---|---|---|---|---|---|---|
| 2004 | — | PF65 65.00 | | | | |

**KM# 321 10 CENTS**
16.81 g., 0.925 Silver 0.500 oz. ASW, 32.7 mm. **Series:** Wildlife - African Wild Dog **Obv:** New national arms **Rev:** Two Painted Dogs walking right **Edge:** Reeded

| Date | Mintage | VF20 | XF40 | MS60 | MS63 | MS65 |
|---|---|---|---|---|---|---|
| 2005 | 1,500 | PF65 65.00 | | | | |

**KM# 317 10 CENTS**
16.86 g., 0.925 Silver 0.5015 oz. ASW, 32.7 mm. **Series:** Wildlife - Black-backed Jackel **Obv:** New national arms **Rev:** Black-backed jackal chasing birds **Edge:** Reeded

| Date | Mintage | VF20 | XF40 | MS60 | MS63 | MS65 |
|---|---|---|---|---|---|---|
| 2006 | 1,500 | PF65 65.00 | | | | |

**KM# 364 10 CENTS**
16.81 g., 0.925 Silver 0.500 oz. ASW, 32.7 mm. **Series:** Wildlife - Kgaladadi Transfrontier Peace Park **Obv:** New national arms **Rev:** Local tribe, value **Edge:** Reeded

| Date | Mintage | VF20 | XF40 | MS60 | MS63 | MS65 |
|---|---|---|---|---|---|---|
| 2007 | — | PF65 65.00 | | | | |

**KM# 459 10 CENTS**
16.81 g., 0.925 Silver 0.500 oz. ASW, 32.7 mm. **Subject:** Richtersveld Transfrontier Park **Obv:** Arms **Rev:** Local Nama native and livestock

| Date | Mintage | VF20 | XF40 | MS60 | MS63 | MS65 |
|---|---|---|---|---|---|---|
| 2008 | 2,200 | PF65 55.00 | | | | |

**KM# 483 10 CENTS**
16.81 g., 0.925 Silver 0.500 oz. ASW, 32.7 mm. **Subject:** Maloti Drakensberg Transfrontier Project **Obv:** Arms **Rev:** Native Basotho riding pony

| Date | Mintage | VF20 | XF40 | MS60 | MS63 | MS65 |
|---|---|---|---|---|---|---|
| 2009 | 3,700 | PF65 45.00 | | | | |

**KM# 540 10 CENTS**
16.86 g., 0.925 Silver 0.5015 oz. ASW, 32.7 mm. **Obv:** National arms **Rev:** uMhlanga female in Swasiland

| Date | Mintage | VF20 | XF40 | MS60 | MS63 | MS65 |
|---|---|---|---|---|---|---|
| 2010 | Est. 2700 | PF65 55.00 | | | | |

**KM# 514 10 CENTS**
16.81 g., 0.925 Silver 0.500 oz. ASW, 32.7 mm.

| Date | Mintage | VF20 | XF40 | MS60 | MS63 | MS65 |
|---|---|---|---|---|---|---|
| 2011 | — | PF65 65.00 | | | | |

**KM# 530 10 CENTS**
16.86 g., 0.925 Silver 0.5015 oz. ASW, 32.82 mm. **Subject:** Great Mapungubwe Transfrontier Conservation Area **Obv:** National arms **Rev:** Golden Rhino and sandstone rock formations in background

| Date | Mintage | VF20 | XF40 | MS60 | MS63 | MS65 |
|---|---|---|---|---|---|---|
| 2012 | — | PF65 65.00 | | | | |

**KM# 245 20 CENTS**
33.73 g., 0.925 Silver 1.003 oz. ASW, 38.3 mm. **Series:** Wildlife - Power **Obv:** Cape Buffalo head **Rev:** Two Cape Buffalo heads facing **Edge:** Reeded

| Date | Mintage | VF20 | XF40 | MS60 | MS63 | MS65 |
|---|---|---|---|---|---|---|
| 2001 | 1,902 | PF65 85.00 | | | | |

**KM# 353 20 CENTS**
33.73 g., 0.925 Silver 1.003 oz. ASW, 38.3 mm. **Series:** Wildlife - Strength **Obv:** Elephant walking, facing **Rev:** Family of four elephants **Edge:** Reeded

| Date | Mintage | VF20 | XF40 | MS60 | MS63 | MS65 |
|---|---|---|---|---|---|---|
| 2002 | 2,435 | PF65 75.00 | | | | |

**KM# 357 20 CENTS**
33.73 g., 0.925 Silver 1.003 oz. ASW, 38.3 mm. **Series:** Wildlife - Survivor **Obv:** New national arms **Rev:** White Rhinoceros mother with an offspring **Edge:** Reeded

| Date | Mintage | VF20 | XF40 | MS60 | MS63 | MS65 |
|---|---|---|---|---|---|---|
| 2003 | 1,930 | PF65 85.00 | | | | |

**KM# 361 20 CENTS**
33.73 g., 0.925 Silver 1.003 oz. ASW, 38.3 mm. **Series:** Wildlife - The legend **Obv:** New national arms **Rev:** Leopard looking left, cub on branch behind her **Edge:** Reeded

| Date | Mintage | VF20 | XF40 | MS60 | MS63 | MS65 |
|---|---|---|---|---|---|---|
| 2004 | — | PF65 85.00 | | | | |

**KM# 322 20 CENTS**
33.75 g., 0.925 Silver 1.0037 oz. ASW, 38.67 mm. **Series:** Wildlife - African Wild Dog **Obv:** New National arms **Rev:** Three Painted Dogs **Edge:** Reeded

| Date | Mintage | VF20 | XF40 | MS60 | MS63 | MS65 |
|---|---|---|---|---|---|---|
| 2005 | 1,500 | PF65 85.00 | | | | |

**KM# 318 20 CENTS**
33.73 g., 0.925 Silver 1.003 oz. ASW, 38.7 mm. **Series:** Wildlife - Black-backed Jackal **Obv:** National arms **Rev:** Two Black-backed jackals **Edge:** Reeded

| Date | Mintage | VF20 | XF40 | MS60 | MS63 | MS65 |
|---|---|---|---|---|---|---|
| 2006 | 1,500 | PF65 85.00 | | | | |

**KM# 365 20 CENTS**
33.73 g., 0.925 Silver 1.003 oz. ASW, 38.3 mm. **Series:** Wildlife - Kgalagadi Transfrontier Peace Park **Obv:** New national arms **Rev:** Lion's head 3/4 right at left, meerkat standing with offspring at right, value **Edge:** Reeded

| Date | Mintage | VF20 | XF40 | MS60 | MS63 | MS65 |
|---|---|---|---|---|---|---|
| 2007 | — | PF65 85.00 | | | | |

**KM# 460 20 CENTS**
33.73 g., 0.925 Silver 1.003 oz. ASW, 38.7 mm. **Subject:** Richtersveld Transfrontier Park **Obv:** Arms **Rev:** Two shy Kipspringer (Oreotragus oreotragos)

| Date | Mintage | VF20 | XF40 | MS60 | MS63 | MS65 |
|---|---|---|---|---|---|---|
| 2008 | 2,200 | PF65 75.00 | | | | |

**KM# 484 20 CENTS**
33.62 g., 0.925 Silver 0.9998 oz. ASW, 38.72 mm. **Subject:** Maloti Drakensberg Transfrontier Project **Obv:** Arms **Rev:** Cape griffon vulture

| Date | Mintage | VF20 | XF40 | MS60 | MS63 | MS65 |
|---|---|---|---|---|---|---|
| 2009 | 3,700 | PF65 75.00 | | | | |

**KM# 541 20 CENTS**
33.73 g., 0.925 Silver 1.003 oz. ASW, 38.72 mm. **Obv:** National arms **Rev:** Three flamingos and crocodile

| Date | Mintage | VF20 | XF40 | MS60 | MS63 | MS65 |
|---|---|---|---|---|---|---|
| 2010 | Est. 2700 | PF65 65.00 | | | | |

**KM# 515 20 CENTS**
33.73 g., 0.925 Silver 1.003 oz. ASW, 38.72 mm.

| Date | Mintage | VF20 | XF40 | MS60 | MS63 | MS65 |
|---|---|---|---|---|---|---|
| 2011 | — | PF65 85.00 | | | | |

**KM# 531 20 CENTS**
33.73 g., 0.925 Silver 1.003 oz. ASW, 38.3 mm. **Subject:** Great Mapungubwe Transfrontier Conservation Area **Obv:** National arms **Rev:** Pel's Fishing Owl (scotopelia peli) and standstone rock formations in background

| Date | Mintage | VF20 | XF40 | MS60 | MS63 | MS65 |
|---|---|---|---|---|---|---|
| 2012 | — | PF65 85.00 | | | | |

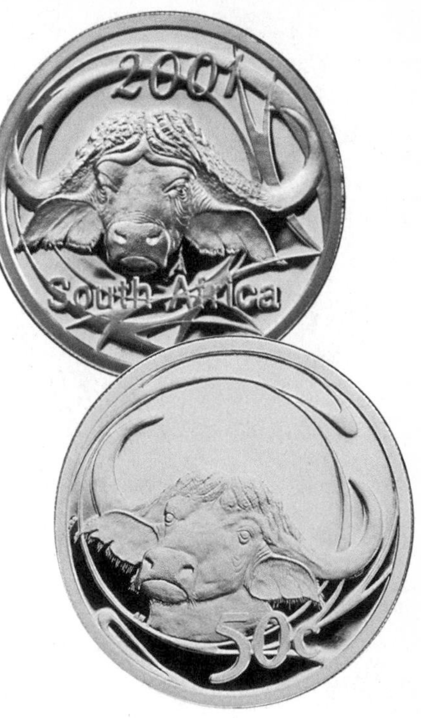

**KM# 246 50 CENTS**
76.40 g., 0.925 Silver 2.2722 oz. ASW, 50 mm. **Series:** Wildlife - Power **Obv:** Cape Buffalo head **Rev:** Cape Buffalo head, value **Edge:** Reeded

| Date | Mintage | VF20 | XF40 | MS60 | MS63 | MS65 |
|---|---|---|---|---|---|---|
| 2001 | 1,866 | PF65 110 | | | | |

**KM# 354 50 CENTS**
76.40 g., 0.925 Silver 2.2722 oz. ASW, 50 mm. **Series:** Wildlife - Strength **Obv:** Elephant walking, facing **Rev:** Elephant right with head raised **Edge:** Reeded

| Date | Mintage | VF20 | XF40 | MS60 | MS63 | MS65 |
|---|---|---|---|---|---|---|
| 2002 | 2,318 | PF65 110 | | | | |

**KM# 358 50 CENTS**
76.40 g., 0.925 Silver 2.2722 oz. ASW, 50 mm. **Series:** Wildlife - Survivor **Obv:** New national arms **Rev:** White Rhinoceros' head 3/4 right, value **Edge:** Reeded

| Date | Mintage | VF20 | XF40 | MS60 | MS63 | MS65 |
|---|---|---|---|---|---|---|
| 2003 | 1,918 | PF65 110 | | | | |

### KM# 362 50 CENTS

76.46 g., 0.925 Silver 2.2739 oz. ASW, 50 mm. **Series:** Wildlife - The Legend **Obv:** New national arms **Rev:** Leopard facing snarling, two leopards at lower left **Edge:** Reeded

| Date | Mintage | VF20 | XF40 | MS60 | MS63 | MS65 |
|---|---|---|---|---|---|---|
| 2004 | — | PF65 110 | | | | |

### KM# 323 50 CENTS

76.86 g., 0.925 Silver 2.2858 oz. ASW, 50.48 mm. **Series:** Wildlife - African Wild Dog **Obv:** New national arms **Rev:** Two painted Dog's heads facing **Edge:** Reeded

| Date | Mintage | VF20 | XF40 | MS60 | MS63 | MS65 |
|---|---|---|---|---|---|---|
| 2005 | 1,500 | PF65 110 | | | | |

### KM# 319 50 CENTS

76.25 g., 0.925 Silver 2.2677 oz. ASW, 50 mm. **Series:** Wildlife - Black-backed Jackal **Obv:** New national arms **Rev:** Two black-backed jackals fighting over a carcass **Edge:** Reeded

| Date | Mintage | VF20 | XF40 | MS60 | MS63 | MS65 |
|---|---|---|---|---|---|---|
| 2006 | 1,500 | PF65 110 | | | | |

### KM# 366 50 CENTS

76.40 g., 0.925 Silver 2.2722 oz. ASW, 50 mm. **Series:** Wildlife - Kgalagadi Transfrontier Peace Park **Obv:** New national arms **Rev:** Antelope running right **Edge:** Reeded

| Date | Mintage | VF20 | XF40 | MS60 | MS63 | MS65 |
|---|---|---|---|---|---|---|
| 2007 | — | PF65 110 | | | | |

### KM# 461 50 CENTS

76.25 g., 0.925 Silver 2.2677 oz. ASW, 50 mm. **Subject:** Richtersveld Transfrontier Park **Obv:** Arms **Rev:** Giant aloe pillansii tree

| Date | Mintage | VF20 | XF40 | MS60 | MS63 | MS65 |
|---|---|---|---|---|---|---|
| 2008 | 2,200 | PF65 110 | | | | |

### KM# 485 50 CENTS

76.25 g., 0.925 Silver 2.2677 oz. ASW, 50 mm. **Subject:** Maloti Drakensberg Transfrontier Project **Obv:** Arms **Rev:** Amphitheatre and Trukela River

| Date | Mintage | VF20 | XF40 | MS60 | MS63 | MS65 |
|---|---|---|---|---|---|---|
| 2009 | 3,700 | PF65 100 | | | | |

### KM# 542 50 CENTS

67.40 g., 0.925 Silver 2.0045 oz. ASW, 50 mm. **Obv:** National arms **Rev:** Sea turtles

| Date | Mintage | VF20 | XF40 | MS60 | MS63 | MS65 |
|---|---|---|---|---|---|---|
| 2010 | Est. 2700 | PF65 115 | | | | |

### KM# 516 50 CENTS

76.40 g., 0.925 Silver 2.2722 oz. ASW, 50 mm.

| Date | Mintage | VF20 | XF40 | MS60 | MS63 | MS65 |
|---|---|---|---|---|---|---|
| 2011 | — | PF65 110 | | | | |

### KM# 532 50 CENTS

76.40 g., 0.925 Silver 2.2722 oz. ASW, 50 mm. **Subject:** Great Mapungubwe Transfrontier Conservation Area **Obv:** National Arms **Rev:** Baobab Tree and sandstone landscape in background

| Date | Mintage | VF20 | XF40 | MS60 | MS63 | MS65 |
|---|---|---|---|---|---|---|
| 2012 | — | PF65 110 | | | | |

### KM# 248 2 RAND

33.63 g., 0.925 Silver 1.000 oz. ASW, 38.7 mm. **Obv:** New national arms **Rev:** Dolphins **Edge:** Reeded

| Date | Mintage | VF20 | XF40 | MS60 | MS63 | MS65 |
|---|---|---|---|---|---|---|
| 2001 | 2,987 | PF65 80.00 | | | | |

### KM# 280 2 RAND

33.63 g., 0.925 Silver 1.000 oz. ASW, 38.7 mm. **Obv:** New national arms **Rev:** Southern Right Whale **Edge:** Reeded

| Date | Mintage | VF20 | XF40 | MS60 | MS63 | MS65 |
|---|---|---|---|---|---|---|
| 2002 | 1,808 | PF65 85.00 | | | | |

### KM# 286 2 RAND

33.63 g., 0.925 Silver 1.000 oz. ASW, 38.7 mm. **Obv:** New national arms **Rev:** Martial and Bateleur Eagles **Edge:** Reeded

| Date | Mintage | VF20 | XF40 | MS60 | MS63 | MS65 |
|---|---|---|---|---|---|---|
| 2003 | 2,166 | PF65 75.00 | | | | |

**KM# 284 2 RAND**
33.63 g., 0.925 Silver 1.000 oz. ASW, 38.7 mm. **Obv:** New national arms **Rev:** Verreaux's Eagle Owl face and value **Edge:** Reeded

| Date | Mintage | VF20 | XF40 | MS60 | MS63 | MS65 |
|---|---|---|---|---|---|---|
| 2004 | — | — | — | — | 50.00 | 55.00 |
| 2004 | 1,752 | PF65 85.00 | | | | |

**KM# 372 2 RAND**
33.63 g., 0.925 Silver 1.000 oz. ASW, 38.7 mm. **Obv:** New national arms **Rev:** Three vultures **Edge:** Reeded

| Date | Mintage | VF20 | XF40 | MS60 | MS63 | MS65 |
|---|---|---|---|---|---|---|
| 2005 | 4,000 | PF65 70.00 | | | | |

**KM# 374 2 RAND**
33.63 g., 0.925 Silver 1.000 oz. ASW, 38.7 mm. **Series:** Bird of Prey **Obv:** New national arms **Rev:** Two Secretary birds **Edge:** Reeded

| Date | Mintage | VF20 | XF40 | MS60 | MS63 | MS65 |
|---|---|---|---|---|---|---|
| 2006 | 4,000 | PF65 75.00 | | | | |

**KM# 481 2 RAND**
33.63 g., 0.925 Silver 1.000 oz. ASW, 38.7 mm. **Obv:** Arms and country name **Rev:** Jan van Riebeeck's ship "Drommedaries

| Date | Mintage | VF20 | XF40 | MS60 | MS63 | MS65 |
|---|---|---|---|---|---|---|
| 2009 | 3,500 | PF65 55.00 | | | | |

## SILVER BULLION PROTEA COINAGE

**KM# 282 2-1/2 CENTS**
1.41 g., 0.925 Silver 0.0421 oz. ASW, 16.3 mm. **Obv:** Protea flower **Rev:** Southern Right Whale **Edge:** Plain

| Date | Mintage | VF20 | XF40 | MS60 | MS63 | MS65 |
|---|---|---|---|---|---|---|
| 2002 | 3,000 | PF65 27.50 | | | | |

**KM# 285 2-1/2 CENTS**
1.41 g., 0.925 Silver 0.0421 oz. ASW, 16.3 mm. **Obv:** Protea flower **Rev:** Martial and Bateleur Eagles **Edge:** Plain

| Date | Mintage | VF20 | XF40 | MS60 | MS63 | MS65 |
|---|---|---|---|---|---|---|
| 2003 | — | PF65 25.00 | | | | |

**KM# 283 2-1/2 CENTS**
1.41 g., 0.925 Silver 0.0421 oz. ASW, 16.3 mm. **Series:** Birds of Prey **Obv:** Protea flower **Rev:** Pearl Spotted Owlet **Edge:** Plain

| Date | Mintage | VF20 | XF40 | MS60 | MS63 | MS65 |
|---|---|---|---|---|---|---|
| 2004 | 2,000 | PF65 25.00 | | | | |

**KM# 348 2-1/2 CENTS**
1.41 g., 0.925 Silver 0.0421 oz. ASW, 16.3 mm. **Obv:** Protea flower **Obv. Legend:** SOUTH AFRICA **Rev:** Vulture alighting **Edge:** Plain

| Date | Mintage | VF20 | XF40 | MS60 | MS63 | MS65 |
|---|---|---|---|---|---|---|
| 2005 | — | PF65 25.00 | | | | |

**KM# 349 2-1/2 CENTS**
1.41 g., 0.925 Silver 0.0421 oz. ASW, 16.3 mm. **Obv:** Protea flower **Obv. Legend:** SOUTH AFRICA **Rev:** Head of Secretary bird **Edge:** Plain

| Date | Mintage | VF20 | XF40 | MS60 | MS63 | MS65 |
|---|---|---|---|---|---|---|
| 2006 | — | PF65 25.00 | | | | |

**KM# 350 2-1/2 CENTS**
1.41 g., 0.925 Silver 0.0421 oz. ASW, 16.3 mm. **Subject:** International Polar Year **Obv:** Protea flower **Obv. Legend:** SOUTH AFRICA **Rev:** Globe displaying South Pole **Edge:** Plain

| Date | Mintage | VF20 | XF40 | MS60 | MS63 | MS65 |
|---|---|---|---|---|---|---|
| 2007 | — | PF65 25.00 | | | | |

**KM# 456 2-1/2 CENTS**
1.41 g., 0.925 Silver 0.0421 oz. ASW, 16.3 mm. **Obv:** Flower **Rev:** Map of Antarctica

| Date | Mintage | VF20 | XF40 | MS60 | MS63 | MS65 |
|---|---|---|---|---|---|---|
| 2008 | 3,000 | PF65 15.00 | | | | |

**KM# 537 2-1/2 CENTS**
1.41 g., 0.925 Silver 0.0421 oz. ASW, 16.3 mm. **Obv:** Protea flower **Rev:** R.M.S. Scot right

| Date | Mintage | VF20 | XF40 | MS60 | MS63 | MS65 |
|---|---|---|---|---|---|---|
| 2010 | Est. 1700 | PF65 30.00 | | | | |

**KM# 519 2-1/2 CENTS**
1.41 g., 0.925 Silver 0.0421 oz. ASW, 16.3 mm. **Obv:** Protea flower **Rev:** Van der Stel ship

| Date | Mintage | VF20 | XF40 | MS60 | MS63 | MS65 |
|---|---|---|---|---|---|---|
| 2011 | Est. 1700 | PF65 35.00 | | | | |

**KM# 556 2-1/2 CENTS**
1.41 g., 0.925 Silver 0.0421 oz. ASW, 16.3 mm. **Obv:** Protea flower **Rev:** Railway train facing

| Date | Mintage | VF20 | XF40 | MS60 | MS63 | MS65 |
|---|---|---|---|---|---|---|
| 2012 | Est. 1700 | PF65 30.00 | | | | |

**KM# 231 RAND**
15.00 g., 0.925 Silver 0.4461 oz. ASW, 32.7 mm. **Subject:** Tourism **Obv:** Protea flower **Rev:** Steam locomotive and flower **Edge:** Reeded

| Date | Mintage | VF20 | XF40 | MS60 | MS63 | MS65 |
|---|---|---|---|---|---|---|
| 2001 | 2,400 | — | — | — | 40.00 | 45.00 |
| 2001 | 1,784 | PF65 65.00 | | | | |

**KM# 277 RAND**
15.00 g., 0.925 Silver 0.4461 oz. ASW, 32.7 mm. **Subject:** Soccer **Obv:** Protea flower **Rev:** Goalkeeper in action **Edge:** Reeded

| Date | Mintage | VF20 | XF40 | MS60 | MS63 | MS65 |
|---|---|---|---|---|---|---|
| 2002 | 1,777 | — | — | — | 40.00 | 45.00 |
| 2002 | 1,250 | PF65 65.00 | | | | |

**KM# 367 RAND**
15.55 g., 0.925 Silver 0.4624 oz. ASW **Subject:** World Summit - Johannesburg **Obv:** Protea flower **Rev:** Globe **Edge:** Reeded

| Date | Mintage | VF20 | XF40 | MS60 | MS63 | MS65 |
|---|---|---|---|---|---|---|
| 2002 | 1,531 | — | — | — | 55.00 | 60.00 |
| 2002 | 1,413 | PF65 75.00 | | | | |

**KM# 298 RAND**
15.05 g., 0.925 Silver 0.4476 oz. ASW, 32.7 mm. **Obv:** Protea flower **Rev:** Cricket player **Edge:** Reeded

| Date | Mintage | VF20 | XF40 | MS60 | MS63 | MS65 |
|---|---|---|---|---|---|---|
| 2003 | 1,697 | — | — | — | 55.00 | 60.00 |
| 2003 | 1,250 | PF65 75.00 | | | | |

**KM# 288 RAND**
15.00 g., 0.925 Silver 0.4461 oz. ASW, 32.7 mm. **Subject:** 10th Anniversary of South African Democracy **Obv:** Protea flower **Rev:** Flora and fauna **Edge:** Reeded

| Date | Mintage | VF20 | XF40 | MS60 | MS63 | MS65 |
|---|---|---|---|---|---|---|
| 2004 | 3,427 | — | — | — | 35.00 | 40.00 |
| 2004 | 2,930 | PF65 50.00 | | | | |

**KM# 368 RAND**
15.00 g., 0.925 Silver 0.4461 oz. ASW, 32.7 mm. **Series:** Nobel Peace Prize Winners **Obv:** Protea flower **Rev:** Bust of Chief A. J. Luthuli facing at center, Luthuli seated at desk left at lower right **Edge:** Reeded

| Date | Mintage | VF20 | XF40 | MS60 | MS63 | MS65 |
|---|---|---|---|---|---|---|
| 2005 | — | — | — | — | 50.00 | 55.00 |
| 2005 | — | PF65 65.00 | | | | |

**KM# 369 RAND**
15.00 g., 0.925 Silver 0.4461 oz. ASW, 32.7 mm. **Series:** Nobel Peace prize Winners **Obv:** Protea flower **Rev:** 1/3 length figure of Archbishop Desmond Mpilo Tutu facing at right **Edge:** Reeded

| Date | Mintage | VF20 | XF40 | MS60 | MS63 | MS65 |
|---|---|---|---|---|---|---|
| 2006 | — | — | — | — | 60.00 | 65.00 |
| 2006 | — | PF65 75.00 | | | | |

**KM# 370 RAND**
15.00 g., 0.925 Silver 0.4461 oz. ASW, 32.7 mm. **Series:** Nobel Peace Prize Winners **Obv:** Protea flower **Rev:** Bust of De Klerk facing **Edge:** Reeded

| Date | Mintage | VF20 | XF40 | MS60 | MS63 | MS65 |
|---|---|---|---|---|---|---|
| 2007 | — | — | — | — | 55.00 | 60.00 |
| 2007 | — | PF65 70.00 | | | | |

**KM# 371 RAND**
15.55 g., 0.925 Silver 0.4624 oz. ASW, 32.7 mm. **Series:** Nobel Peace Prize Winners **Obv:** Protea flower **Rev:** Bust of Mandela facing **Edge:** Reeded

| Date | Mintage | VF20 | XF40 | MS60 | MS63 | MS65 |
|---|---|---|---|---|---|---|
| 2007 | — | — | — | — | 65.00 | 75.00 |
| 2007 | — | PF65 95.00 | | | | |

**KM# 451 RAND**
15.55 g., 0.925 Silver 0.4624 oz. ASW, 32.7 mm. **Obv:** Protea flower **Rev:** Ghandi portrait

| Date | Mintage | VF20 | XF40 | MS60 | MS63 | MS65 |
|---|---|---|---|---|---|---|
| 2008 | — | — | — | — | — | 25.00 |
| 2008 | 11,000 | PF65 30.00 | | | | |

**KM# 475 RAND**
15.55 g., 0.925 Silver 0.4624 oz. ASW, 32.7 mm. **Obv:** Protea flower **Rev:** Portraits of C. J. Langenhoven and N. L. de Villiers with musical score

| Date | Mintage | VF20 | XF40 | MS60 | MS63 | MS65 |
|---|---|---|---|---|---|---|
| 2009 | — | — | — | — | — | 25.00 |
| 2009 | 11,000 | PF65 30.00 | | | | |

### KM# 543 RAND

15.00 g., 0.925 Silver 0.4461 oz. ASW, 32.69 mm. **Obv:** Protea flower **Rev:** Nadine Gordimer

| Date | Mintage | VF20 | XF40 | MS60 | MS63 | MS65 |
|---|---|---|---|---|---|---|
| 2010 | Est. 4000 | — | — | — | 55.00 | 60.00 |

### KM# 521 RAND

15.00 g., 0.925 Silver 0.4461 oz. ASW, 32.7 mm. **Obv:** Protea flower **Rev:** John Maxwell Coetzee

| Date | Mintage | VF20 | XF40 | MS60 | MS63 | MS65 |
|---|---|---|---|---|---|---|
| 2011 | — | — | — | — | 55.00 | 65.00 |
| 2011 Privy Mark A | 600 | — | — | — | 75.00 | — |
| Note: A for Adelaide | | | | | | |

### KM# 538 2 RAND

33.63 g., 0.925 Silver 1.000 oz. ASW, 38.72 mm. **Obv:** Protea flower **Rev:** R.M.S. Windsor Castle III

| Date | Mintage | VF20 | XF40 | MS60 | MS63 | MS65 |
|---|---|---|---|---|---|---|
| 2010 | Est. 1700 | PF65 55.00 | | | | |

### KM# 520 2 RAND

33.63 g., 0.925 Silver 1.000 oz. ASW, 38.7 mm. **Obv:** Protea flower **Rev:** R.M.S. Queen Mary II

| Date | Mintage | VF20 | XF40 | MS60 | MS63 | MS65 |
|---|---|---|---|---|---|---|
| 2011 | Est. 1700 | PF65 55.00 | | | | |

### KM# 557 2 RAND

33.63 g., 0.925 Silver 1.000 oz. ASW, 38.7 mm. **Obv:** Protea flower **Rev:** Railway train

| Date | Mintage | VF20 | XF40 | MS60 | MS63 | MS65 |
|---|---|---|---|---|---|---|
| 2012 | Est. 1700 | PF65 55.00 | | | | |

## SILVER BULLION CULTURE COINAGE

### KM# 558 RAND

15.00 g., 0.925 Silver 0.4461 oz. ASW, 32.7 mm. **Obv:** National arms **Rev:** Walter and Albertina Sisulu

| Date | Mintage | VF20 | XF40 | MS60 | MS63 | MS65 |
|---|---|---|---|---|---|---|
| 2012 | — | — | — | — | 50.00 | 60.00 |

### KM# 373 2 RAND

33.63 g., 0.925 Silver 1.000 oz. ASW, 38.7 mm. **Subject:** 2006 FIFA World Cup Soccer - Germany **Obv:** New national arms **Rev:** Soccer ball above globe **Edge:** Reeded

| Date | Mintage | VF20 | XF40 | MS60 | MS63 | MS65 |
|---|---|---|---|---|---|---|
| 2005 | 50,000 | PF65 60.00 | | | | |

### KM# 435 2 RAND

33.63 g., 0.925 Silver 1.000 oz. ASW, 38.7 mm. **Subject:** 2010 World Cup

| Date | Mintage | VF20 | XF40 | MS60 | MS63 | MS65 |
|---|---|---|---|---|---|---|
| 2006 | 25,000 | — | — | — | — | 50.00 |

### KM# 376 2 RAND

33.63 g., 0.925 Silver 1.000 oz. ASW, 38.7 mm. **Subject:** International Polar Year **Obv:** New national arms **Rev:** Logo above globe **Edge:** Reeded

| Date | Mintage | VF20 | XF40 | MS60 | MS63 | MS65 |
|---|---|---|---|---|---|---|
| 2007 | 6,000 | PF65 75.00 | | | | |

### KM# 377 2 RAND

33.63 g., 0.925 Silver 1.000 oz. ASW, 38.7 mm. **Subject:** 2010 FIFA World Cup Soccer - South Africa **Obv:** New national arms **Rev:** Tower at left, animal heads at top. animal at right, soccer ball ar bottom **Edge:** Reeded

| Date | Mintage | VF20 | XF40 | MS60 | MS63 | MS65 |
|---|---|---|---|---|---|---|
| 2007 | 20,000 | PF65 65.00 | | | | |

### KM# 437 2 RAND

33.63 g., 0.925 Silver 1.000 oz. ASW, 38.7 mm. **Subject:** 2010 World Cup

| Date | Mintage | VF20 | XF40 | MS60 | MS63 | MS65 |
|---|---|---|---|---|---|---|
| 2008 | — | PF65 60.00 | | | | |

### KM# 457 2 RAND

33.63 g., 0.925 Silver 1.000 oz. ASW, 38.7 mm. **Obv:** Arms **Rev:** Polar ship "SA Sgulhas

| Date | Mintage | VF20 | XF40 | MS60 | MS63 | MS65 |
|---|---|---|---|---|---|---|
| 2008 | 3,000 | PF65 80.00 | | | | |

### KM# 546 2 RAND

33.63 g., 0.925 Silver 1.000 oz. ASW, 38.7 mm. **Obv:** National arms **Rev:** FIFA World Cup trophy

| Date | Mintage | VF20 | XF40 | MS60 | MS63 | MS65 |
|---|---|---|---|---|---|---|
| 2010 | Est. 20000 | PF65 65.00 | | | | |

### KM# 524 2 RAND

33.63 g., 0.925 Silver 1.000 oz. ASW, 38.72 mm. **Subject:** World Wildlife Fund, 50th Anniversary **Obv:** National arms **Rev:** Paradise Crane

| Date | Mintage | VF20 | XF40 | MS60 | MS63 | MS65 |
|---|---|---|---|---|---|---|
| 2011 | — | PF65 75.00 | | | | |
| 2011 Proof, Table Mountain privy mark | 300 | — | — | — | — | — |

### KM# 552 2 RAND

33.63 g., 0.925 Silver 1.000 oz. ASW, 38.7 mm. **Obv:** National arms **Rev:** Rugby player advancing left

| Date | Mintage | VF20 | XF40 | MS60 | MS63 | MS65 |
|---|---|---|---|---|---|---|
| 2011 | Est. 2011 | PF65 95.00 | | | | |

### KM# 561 2 RAND

33.63 g., 0.925 Silver 1.000 oz. ASW, 38.7 mm. **Obv:** National arms **Rev:** Map of Antarctica

| Date | Mintage | VF20 | XF40 | MS60 | MS63 | MS65 |
|---|---|---|---|---|---|---|
| 2012 | — | PF65 65.00 | | | | |
| 2012 Proof, 90° S privy mark | — | — | — | — | — | — |

## GOLD BULLION NATURA COINAGE

### KM# 553 RAND

3.11 g., 0.999 Gold 0.0999 oz. AGW, 16.5 mm. **Obv:** National arms **Rev:** Bee

| Date | Mintage | VF20 | XF40 | MS60 | MS63 | MS65 |
|---|---|---|---|---|---|---|
| 2011 | Est. 2000 | PF65 175 | | | | |

### KM# 562 RAND

3.11 g., 0.9999 Gold 0.100 oz. AGW, 16.5 mm. **Obv:** National arms **Rev:** African Monarch butterfly

| Date | Mintage | VF20 | XF40 | MS60 | MS63 | MS65 |
|---|---|---|---|---|---|---|
| 2012 | Est. 2000 | PF65 175 | | | | |

### KM# 517 2 RAND

7.77 g., 0.9999 Gold 0.2498 oz. AGW, 22 mm.

| Date | Mintage | VF20 | XF40 | MS60 | MS63 | MS65 |
|---|---|---|---|---|---|---|
| 2011 | — | PF65 475 | | | | |

### KM# 533 2 RAND

7.77 g., 0.9999 Gold 0.2498 oz. AGW, 22 mm. **Subject:** Khoisan Heritage **Obv:** National Arms **Rev:** Incuse stone carving of an eland

| Date | Mintage | VF20 | XF40 | MS60 | MS63 | MS65 |
|---|---|---|---|---|---|---|
| 2012 | — | PF65 475 | | | | |

### KM# 410 10 RAND

3.11 g., 0.9999 Gold 0.100 oz. AGW, 16.5 mm. **Series:** Natura **Obv:** Cheetah's head **Rev:** Cheetah drinking water **Edge:** Reeded

| Date | Mintage | VF20 | XF40 | MS60 | MS63 | MS65 |
|---|---|---|---|---|---|---|
| 2002 | 3,156 | PF65 200 | | | | |

### KM# 414 10 RAND

3.11 g., 0.9999 Gold 0.100 oz. AGW, 16.5 mm. **Series:** Natura **Obv:** Male and female lion's heads **Rev:** Two lioness drinking water **Edge:** Reeded

| Date | Mintage | VF20 | XF40 | MS60 | MS63 | MS65 |
|---|---|---|---|---|---|---|
| 2003 | 4,233 | PF65 200 | | | | |

### KM# 418 10 RAND

3.11 g., 0.9999 Gold 0.100 oz. AGW, 16.5 mm. **Series:** Natura **Obv:** Caracal's head and shoulders **Rev:** Caracal drinking water **Edge:** Reeded

| Date | Mintage | VF20 | XF40 | MS60 | MS63 | MS65 |
|---|---|---|---|---|---|---|
| 2004 | 1,809 | PF65 210 | | | | |

### KM# 422 10 RAND

3.11 g., 0.9999 Gold 0.100 oz. AGW, 16.5 mm. **Series:** Natura **Obv:** Hippopotamus 1/2 way in water **Rev:** Hippopotamus deeply in water **Edge:** Reeded

| Date | Mintage | VF20 | XF40 | MS60 | MS63 | MS65 |
|---|---|---|---|---|---|---|
| 2005 | — | PF65 210 | | | | |

### KM# 426 10 RAND

3.11 g., 0.9999 Gold 0.100 oz. AGW, 16.5 mm. **Series:** Natura **Obv:** Giraffe's head and neck **Rev:** Giraffe drinking water **Edge:** Reeded

| Date | Mintage | VF20 | XF40 | MS60 | MS63 | MS65 |
|---|---|---|---|---|---|---|
| 2006 | — | PF65 200 | | | | |

### KM# 430 10 RAND

3.11 g., 0.9999 Gold 0.100 oz. AGW, 16.5 mm. **Series:** Natura **Obv:** Forepart of Eland left **Rev:** Eland drinking water right **Edge:** Reeded

| Date | Mintage | VF20 | XF40 | MS60 | MS63 | MS65 |
|---|---|---|---|---|---|---|
| 2007 | — | PF65 200 | | | | |

### KM# 447 10 RAND

3.11 g., 0.999 Gold 0.0999 oz. AGW, 16.5 mm. **Obv:** Large elephant head and elephant family below **Rev:** One elephant eating, three elephants below

| Date | Mintage | VF20 | XF40 | MS60 | MS63 | MS65 |
|---|---|---|---|---|---|---|
| 2008 | 3,300 | PF65 200 | | | | |

### KM# 471 10 RAND

3.11 g., 0.999 Gold 0.0999 oz. AGW, 16.5 mm. **Obv:** White rhino, silouette and forepart **Rev:** Two rhino foreparts facing left within large silouette

| Date | Mintage | VF20 | XF40 | MS60 | MS63 | MS65 |
|---|---|---|---|---|---|---|
| 2009 | 2,500 | PF65 200 | | | | |

**KM# 549 10 RAND**
3.11 g., 0.9999 Gold 0.100 oz. AGW, 16.5 mm. **Obv:** National arms **Rev:** Rhino

| Date | Mintage | VF20 | XF40 | MS60 | MS63 | MS65 |
|---|---|---|---|---|---|---|
| 2010 | Est. 4000 | **PF65** 250 | | | | |

**KM# 509 10 RAND**
3.11 g., 0.9999 Gold 0.100 oz. AGW, 16.5 mm.

| Date | Mintage | VF20 | XF40 | MS60 | MS63 | MS65 |
|---|---|---|---|---|---|---|
| 2011 | — | **PF65** 210 | | | | |

**KM# 525 10 RAND**
3.12 g., 0.9999 Gold 0.1002 oz. AGW, 16.5 mm. **Subject:** Great Mapungubwe Transfrontier Conservation Area

| Date | Mintage | VF20 | XF40 | MS60 | MS63 | MS65 |
|---|---|---|---|---|---|---|
| 2012 | — | **PF65** 210 | | | | |

**KM# 411 20 RAND**
7.78 g., 0.9999 Gold 0.250 oz. AGW, 22 mm. **Series:** Natura **Obv:** Cheetah's head **Rev:** Cheetah family resting **Edge:** Reeded

| Date | Mintage | VF20 | XF40 | MS60 | MS63 | MS65 |
|---|---|---|---|---|---|---|
| 2002 | 2,548 | **PF65** 510 | | | | |

**KM# 415 20 RAND**
7.78 g., 0.9999 Gold 0.250 oz. AGW, 22 mm. **Series:** Natura **Obv:** Male and female lion's heads **Rev:** Lion family resting **Edge:** Reeded

| Date | Mintage | VF20 | XF40 | MS60 | MS63 | MS65 |
|---|---|---|---|---|---|---|
| 2003 | 2,799 | **PF65** 510 | | | | |

**KM# 419 20 RAND**
7.78 g., 0.9999 Gold 0.250 oz. AGW, 22 mm. **Series:** Natura **Obv:** Caracal's head and shoulders **Rev:** Caracal with cub standing right **Edge:** Reeded

| Date | Mintage | VF20 | XF40 | MS60 | MS63 | MS65 |
|---|---|---|---|---|---|---|
| 2004 | 1,407 | **PF65** 520 | | | | |

**KM# 389 20 RAND**
7.78 g., 0.9999 Gold 0.250 oz. AGW, 22 mm. **Series:** World Heritage Site **Subject:** Mapungubwe **Obv:** New national arms **Rev:** Rhinoceros standing right **Edge:** Reeded

| Date | Mintage | VF20 | XF40 | MS60 | MS63 | MS65 |
|---|---|---|---|---|---|---|
| 2005 | 1,000 | **PF65** 520 | | | | |

**KM# 423 20 RAND**
7.78 g., 0.9999 Gold 0.250 oz. AGW, 22 mm. **Series:** Natura **Obv:** Hippopotamus 1/2 way in water **Rev:** Mother and baby Hippopotamus grazing **Edge:** Reeded

| Date | Mintage | VF20 | XF40 | MS60 | MS63 | MS65 |
|---|---|---|---|---|---|---|
| 2005 | — | **PF65** 520 | | | | |

**KM# 427 20 RAND**
7.78 g., 0.9999 Gold 0.250 oz. AGW, 22 mm. **Series:** Natura **Obv:** Giraffe's head and neck **Rev:** Mother and baby giraffes grazing **Edge:** Reeded

| Date | Mintage | VF20 | XF40 | MS60 | MS63 | MS65 |
|---|---|---|---|---|---|---|
| 2006 | — | **PF65** 520 | | | | |

**KM# 431 20 RAND**
7.78 g., 0.9999 Gold 0.250 oz. AGW, 22 mm. **Series:** Natura **Obv:** Forepart of Eland left **Rev:** Mother Eland and calf grazing **Edge:** Reeded

| Date | Mintage | VF20 | XF40 | MS60 | MS63 | MS65 |
|---|---|---|---|---|---|---|
| 2007 | — | **PF65** 520 | | | | |

**KM# 448 20 RAND**
7.78 g., 0.999 Gold 0.2498 oz. AGW, 22 mm. **Obv:** Large elephant head and elephant family below **Rev:** Two elephants fighting, three elephants below

| Date | Mintage | VF20 | XF40 | MS60 | MS63 | MS65 |
|---|---|---|---|---|---|---|
| 2008 | 3,300 | **PF65** 510 | | | | |

**KM# 455 20 RAND**
7.77 g., 0.999 Gold 0.2496 oz. AGW, 22 mm. **Subject:** Vredefort Dome **Obv:** Arms **Rev:** Meteorite

| Date | Mintage | VF20 | XF40 | MS60 | MS63 | MS65 |
|---|---|---|---|---|---|---|
| 2008 | 2,000 | **PF65** 510 | | | | |

**KM# 472 20 RAND**
7.78 g., 0.999 Gold 0.2498 oz. AGW, 22 mm. **Obv:** White rhino silouette and forepart **Rev:** Two rhinos walking forward within silhouette

| Date | Mintage | VF20 | XF40 | MS60 | MS63 | MS65 |
|---|---|---|---|---|---|---|
| 2009 | 2,500 | **PF65** 510 | | | | |

**KM# 550 20 RAND**
7.78 g., 0.9999 Gold 0.2501 oz. AGW, 22 mm. **Obv:** National arms **Rev:** Rhino

| Date | Mintage | VF20 | XF40 | MS60 | MS63 | MS65 |
|---|---|---|---|---|---|---|
| 2010 | Est. 4000 | **PF65** 525 | | | | |

**KM# 510 20 RAND**
7.77 g., 0.9999 Gold 0.2498 oz. AGW, 22 mm.

| Date | Mintage | VF20 | XF40 | MS60 | MS63 | MS65 |
|---|---|---|---|---|---|---|
| 2011 | — | **PF65** 510 | | | | |

**KM# 526 20 RAND**
7.77 g., 0.9999 Gold 0.2498 oz. AGW, 22 mm.

| Date | Mintage | VF20 | XF40 | MS60 | MS63 | MS65 |
|---|---|---|---|---|---|---|
| 2012 | — | **PF65** 510 | | | | |

**KM# 412 50 RAND**
15.55 g., 0.9999 Gold 0.500 oz. AGW, 27 mm. **Series:** Natura **Obv:** Cheetah's head **Rev:** Cheetah attacking Impala **Edge:** Reeded

| Date | Mintage | VF20 | XF40 | MS60 | MS63 | MS65 |
|---|---|---|---|---|---|---|
| 2002 | 2,295 | **PF65** 975 | | | | |

**KM# 416 50 RAND**
15.55 g., 0.9999 Gold 0.500 oz. AGW, 27 mm. **Series:** Natura **Obv:** Male and female lion's heads **Rev:** Female and male lions playing **Edge:** Reeded

| Date | Mintage | VF20 | XF40 | MS60 | MS63 | MS65 |
|---|---|---|---|---|---|---|
| 2003 | 2,600 | **PF65** 975 | | | | |

**KM# 420 50 RAND**
15.55 g., 0.9999 Gold 0.500 oz. AGW, 27 mm. **Series:** Natura **Obv:** Caracal's head and shoulders **Rev:** Caracal eating prey **Edge:** Reeded

| Date | Mintage | VF20 | XF40 | MS60 | MS63 | MS65 |
|---|---|---|---|---|---|---|
| 2004 | 1,327 | **PF65** 1,000 | | | | |

**KM# 424 50 RAND**
15.55 g., 0.9999 Gold 0.500 oz. AGW, 27 mm. **Series:** Natura **Obv:** Hippopotamus 1/2 way in water **Rev:** Hippopotamus submerged in water with head raised above, mouth wide open **Edge:** Reeded

| Date | Mintage | VF20 | XF40 | MS60 | MS63 | MS65 |
|---|---|---|---|---|---|---|
| 2005 | — | **PF65** 1,000 | | | | |

**KM# 428 50 RAND**
15.55 g., 0.9999 Gold 0.500 oz. AGW, 27 mm. **Series:** Natura **Obv:** Giraffe's head and neck **Rev:** Giraffe family walking left **Edge:** Reeded

| Date | Mintage | VF20 | XF40 | MS60 | MS63 | MS65 |
|---|---|---|---|---|---|---|
| 2006 | — | **PF65** 1,000 | | | | |

**KM# 432 50 RAND**
15.55 g., 0.9999 Gold 0.500 oz. AGW, 27 mm. **Series:** Natura **Obv:** Forepart of eland left **Rev:** Three eland running right **Edge:** Reeded

| Date | Mintage | VF20 | XF40 | MS60 | MS63 | MS65 |
|---|---|---|---|---|---|---|
| 2007 | — | **PF65** 1,000 | | | | |

**KM# 449 50 RAND**
15.55 g., 0.9999 Gold 0.500 oz. AGW, 27 mm. **Obv:** Large elephant and elephant family below **Rev:** Three elephants, one trumpeting, three elephants below

| Date | Mintage | VF20 | XF40 | MS60 | MS63 | MS65 |
|---|---|---|---|---|---|---|
| 2008 | 4,800 | **PF65** 975 | | | | |

**KM# 473 50 RAND**
15.55 g., 0.9999 Gold 0.4999 oz. AGW, 27 mm. **Obv:** White rhino silhouette and forpart **Rev:** Two rhinos facing off within large silouette

| Date | Mintage | VF20 | XF40 | MS60 | MS63 | MS65 |
|---|---|---|---|---|---|---|
| 2009 | 4,000 | **PF65** 975 | | | | |

**KM# 551 50 RAND**
15.55 g., 0.9999 Gold 0.4999 oz. AGW, 27 mm. **Obv:** National arms **Rev:** Rhino

| Date | Mintage | VF20 | XF40 | MS60 | MS63 | MS65 |
|---|---|---|---|---|---|---|
| 2010 | Est. 2500 | **PF65** 900 | | | | |

**KM# 511 50 RAND**
15.55 g., 0.9999 Gold 0.500 oz. AGW, 27 mm.

| Date | Mintage | VF20 | XF40 | MS60 | MS63 | MS65 |
|---|---|---|---|---|---|---|
| 2011 | — | **PF65** 975 | | | | |

**KM# 527 50 RAND**
15.55 g., 0.9999 Gold 0.500 oz. AGW, 27 mm.

| Date | Mintage | VF20 | XF40 | MS60 | MS63 | MS65 |
|---|---|---|---|---|---|---|
| 2012 | — | **PF65** 975 | | | | |

**KM# 413 100 RAND**
31.11 g., 0.9999 Gold 1.000 oz. AGW, 32.69 mm. **Series:** Natura **Obv:** Cheetah's head **Rev:** Cheetah posing **Edge:** Reeded

| Date | Mintage | VF20 | XF40 | MS60 | MS63 | MS65 |
|---|---|---|---|---|---|---|
| 2002 | 2,550 | **PF65** 1,900 | | | | |
| 2002 RSA logo | 496 | **PF65** 2,000 | | | | |

**KM# 417 100 RAND**
31.11 g., 0.9999 Gold 1.000 oz. AGW, 32.69 mm. **Series:** Natura **Obv:** Male and female lion's heads **Rev:** Snarling male and female lion's heads **Edge:** Reeded **Note:** L P RSA - LION PARK RSA.

| Date | Mintage | VF20 | XF40 | MS60 | MS63 | MS65 |
|---|---|---|---|---|---|---|
| 2003 | 2,758 | **PF65** 1,900 | | | | |
| 2003 L P RSA | 498 | **PF65** 2,000 | | | | |

**KM# 421 100 RAND**
31.11 g., 0.9999 Gold 1.000 oz. AGW, 32.69 mm. **Series:** Natura **Obv:** Caracal's head and shoulders **Rev:** Caracal crouching on branch left **Edge:** Reeded **Note:** C/C - CARACAL / CARACAL

| Date | Mintage | VF20 | XF40 | MS60 | MS63 | MS65 |
|---|---|---|---|---|---|---|
| 2004 | 1,405 | **PF65** 1,900 | | | | |
| 2004 C/C | 500 | **PF65** 2,000 | | | | |

**KM# 425 100 RAND**
31.11 g., 0.9999 Gold 1.000 oz. AGW, 32.69 mm. **Series:** Natura **Obv:** Hippopotamus 1/2 way in water **Rev:** Two hippopotami submerged in water, heads raised, mouths open faced in combat **Edge:** Reeded **Note:** MAPU - MAPUNGUBWE.

| Date | Mintage | VF20 | XF40 | MS60 | MS63 | MS65 |
|---|---|---|---|---|---|---|
| 2005 | — | **PF65** 1,900 | | | | |
| 2005 MAPU | — | **PF65** 2,000 | | | | |

**KM# 429 100 RAND**
31.11 g., 0.9999 Gold 1.000 oz. AGW, 32.69 mm. **Series:** Natura **Obv:** Giraffe's head and neck **Rev:** Head and neck view of giraffe eating tree leaves **Edge:** Reeded **Note:** lpp/EWT - lion's paw print / EWT.

| Date | Mintage | VF20 | XF40 | MS60 | MS63 | MS65 |
|---|---|---|---|---|---|---|
| 2006 | — | **PF65** 1,900 | | | | |
| 2006 lpp/EWT | — | **PF65** 2,000 | | | | |

**KM# 433 100 RAND**
31.11 g., 0.9999 Gold 1.000 oz. AGW, 32.7 mm. **Series:** Natura **Obv:** Forepart of eland left **Rev:** Eland grazing left **Edge:** Reeded

| Date | Mintage | VF20 | XF40 | MS60 | MS63 | MS65 |
|---|---|---|---|---|---|---|
| 2007 | — | PF65 1,900 | | | | |

**KM# 450 100 RAND**
31.11 g., 0.999 Gold 0.9991 oz. AGW, 32.69 mm. **Obv:** Large elephant head and elephant family below **Rev:** Large elephant facing, three elephants below

| Date | Mintage | VF20 | XF40 | MS60 | MS63 | MS65 |
|---|---|---|---|---|---|---|
| 2008 | 4,800 | PF65 1,900 | | | | |

**KM# 474 100 RAND**
31.11 g., 0.999 Gold 0.9991 oz. AGW, 32.7 mm. **Obv:** White rhino silouette and forepart **Rev:** Rhino standing facing within large silhouette

| Date | Mintage | VF20 | XF40 | MS60 | MS63 | MS65 |
|---|---|---|---|---|---|---|
| 2009 | 4,000 | PF65 1,900 | | | | |

**KM# 552 100 RAND**
31.10 g., 0.9999 Gold 0.9998 oz. AGW, 32.7 mm. **Obv:** National arms **Rev:** Rhino

| Date | Mintage | VF20 | XF40 | MS60 | MS63 | MS65 |
|---|---|---|---|---|---|---|
| 2010 | Est. 2500 | PF65 1,750 | | | | |
| 2010 Proof, Paw and EWT privy mark | Est. 500 | PF65 2,500 | | | | |

Note: For Endangered Wildlife Trust

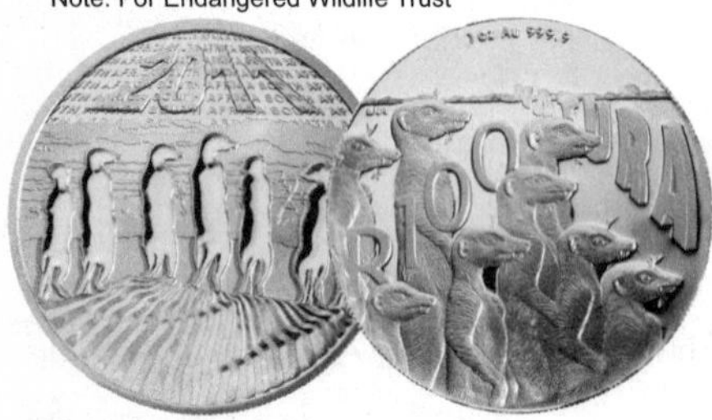

**KM# 512 100 RAND**
31.11 g., 0.9999 Gold 1.000 oz. AGW, 32.7 mm.

| Date | Mintage | VF20 | XF40 | MS60 | MS63 | MS65 |
|---|---|---|---|---|---|---|
| 2011 | — | PF65 1,900 | | | | |

**KM# 528 100 RAND**
31.11 g., 0.9999 Gold 1.000 oz. AGW, 32.7 mm.

| Date | Mintage | VF20 | XF40 | MS60 | MS63 | MS65 |
|---|---|---|---|---|---|---|
| 2012 | — | PF65 1,900 | | | | |

**KM# 264 1/10 OUNCE**
3.11 g., 0.9999 Gold 0.100 oz. AGW, 16.5 mm. **Series:** Natura **Obv:** Gemsbok's upper body **Rev:** Gemsbok drinking **Edge:** Reeded

| Date | Mintage | VF20 | XF40 | MS60 | MS63 | MS65 |
|---|---|---|---|---|---|---|
| 2001 | 3,498 | PF65 210 | | | | |

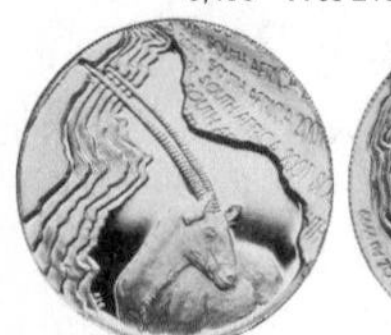

**KM# 265 1/4 OUNCE**
7.78 g., 0.9999 Gold 0.250 oz. AGW, 22 mm. **Series:** Natura **Obv:** Gemsbok's upper body **Rev:** Two Gemsbok bulls facing off **Edge:** Reeded

| Date | Mintage | VF20 | XF40 | MS60 | MS63 | MS65 |
|---|---|---|---|---|---|---|
| 2001 | 2,904 | PF65 510 | | | | |

**KM# 266 1/2 OUNCE**
15.55 g., 0.9999 Gold 0.500 oz. AGW, 27 mm. **Series:** Natura **Obv:** Gemsbok's upper body **Rev:** Gemsbok family grazing **Edge:** Reeded

| Date | Mintage | VF20 | XF40 | MS60 | MS63 | MS65 |
|---|---|---|---|---|---|---|
| 2001 | 2,754 | PF65 975 | | | | |

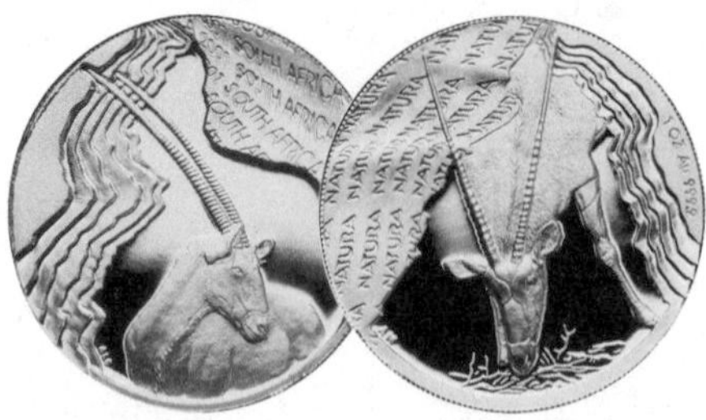

**KM# 267 OUNCE**
31.11 g., 0.9999 Gold 1.000 oz. AGW, 32.69 mm. **Series:** Natura **Obv:** Gemsbok's upper body **Rev:** Gemsbok grazing **Edge:** Reeded **Note:** ghCW - Gemsbok's head CW

| Date | Mintage | VF20 | XF40 | MS60 | MS63 | MS65 |
|---|---|---|---|---|---|---|
| 2001 | 3,104 | PF65 1,900 | | | | |
| 2001 | 491 | PF65 2,000 | | | | |

## GOLD BULLION CULTURE COINAGE

**KM# 378 RAND**
3.11 g., 0.9999 Gold 0.100 oz. AGW, 16.5 mm. **Series:** Cultural **Obv:** New national arms **Obv. Legend:** UMZANTSI AFRIKA - SOUTH AFRICA **Rev:** Three Xhosa tribe members **Edge:** Reeded

| Date | Mintage | VF20 | XF40 | MS60 | MS63 | MS65 |
|---|---|---|---|---|---|---|
| 2001 | — | PF65 675 | | | | |

**KM# 247 RAND**
3.11 g., 0.9999 Gold 0.100 oz. AGW, 16.5 mm. **Series:** Cultural **Obv:** New national arms **Obv. Legend:** UMZANTSI AFRIKA - SOUTH AFRICA **Rev:** Seated Sotho figure with headdress **Edge:** Reeded

| Date | Mintage | VF20 | XF40 | MS60 | MS63 | MS65 |
|---|---|---|---|---|---|---|
| 2001 | 236 | PF65 275 | | | | |

**KM# 379 RAND**
3.11 g., 0.9999 Gold 0.100 oz. AGW, 16.5 mm. **Series:** Cultural **Subject:** Tswana Nation **Obv:** New national arms **Obv. Legend:** Aforika Borwa - South Africa **Rev:** Four tribe people standing **Edge:** Reeded

| Date | Mintage | VF20 | XF40 | MS60 | MS63 | MS65 |
|---|---|---|---|---|---|---|
| 2002 | 300 | PF65 350 | | | | |

**KM# 380 RAND**
3.11 g., 0.9999 Gold 0.100 oz. AGW, 16.5 mm. **Series:** Cultural **Obv:** New national arms **Obv. Legend:** Afrika-Dzonga - South Africa **Rev:** Tsonga tribe dancer and drummer **Edge:** Reeded

| Date | Mintage | VF20 | XF40 | MS60 | MS63 | MS65 |
|---|---|---|---|---|---|---|
| 2003 | 348 | PF65 350 | | | | |

**KM# 381 RAND**
3.11 g., 0.9999 Gold 0.100 oz. AGW, 16.5 mm. **Series:** Cultural **Obv:** New national arms **Obv. Legend:** Afurika Tshipembe - South Africa **Rev:** Six Venda tribe members crossing bridge **Edge:** Reeded

| Date | Mintage | VF20 | XF40 | MS60 | MS63 | MS65 |
|---|---|---|---|---|---|---|
| 2004 | 380 | PF65 350 | | | | |

**KM# 382 RAND**
3.11 g., 0.9999 Gold 0.100 oz. AGW, 16.5 mm. **Series:** Cultural **Obv:** New national arms **Obv. Legend:** iSewula Afrika - South Africa **Rev:** Ndebele woman standing, native print in background **Edge:** Reeded

| Date | Mintage | VF20 | XF40 | MS60 | MS63 | MS65 |
|---|---|---|---|---|---|---|
| 2005 | 1,000 | PF65 210 | | | | |

**KM# 383 RAND**
3.11 g., 0.9999 Gold 0.100 oz. AGW, 16.5 mm. **Series:** Cultural **Obv:** New national arms **Obv. Legend:** Ningizimu Afrika - South Africa **Rev:** 1/2 length figure of Ema-Swati Chief left at right **Edge:** Reeded

| Date | Mintage | VF20 | XF40 | MS60 | MS63 | MS65 |
|---|---|---|---|---|---|---|
| 2006 | 1,000 | PF65 210 | | | | |

**KM# 384 RAND**
3.11 g., 0.9999 Gold 0.100 oz. AGW, 16.5 mm. **Subject:** The Afrikaner Nation **Obv:** New national arms **Obv. Legend:** SOUTH AFRIKA **Rev:** Ox drawn wagon up hillside **Edge:** Reeded

| Date | Mintage | VF20 | XF40 | MS60 | MS63 | MS65 |
|---|---|---|---|---|---|---|
| 2007 | — | PF65 210 | | | | |

**KM# 385 RAND**
3.11 g., 0.9999 Gold 0.100 oz. AGW, 16.5 mm. **Subject:** 2010 FIFA World Cup Soccer - South Africa **Obv:** New national arms **Obv. Legend:** SOUTH AFRICA **Rev:** Bird head at left facing animal at right, soccer ball at bottom **Edge:** Reeded

| Date | Mintage | VF20 | XF40 | MS60 | MS63 | MS65 |
|---|---|---|---|---|---|---|
| 2007 | 10,000 | PF65 200 | | | | |

**KM# 454 RAND**
3.11 g., 0.999 Gold 0.0999 oz. AGW, 16.5 mm. **Obv:** Arms

| Date | Mintage | VF20 | XF40 | MS60 | MS63 | MS65 |
|---|---|---|---|---|---|---|
| 2008 | 1,000 | PF65 210 | | | | |

**KM# 478 RAND**
3.11 g., 0.999 Gold 0.0999 oz. AGW, 16.5 mm. **Subject:** Northern Sotho (Bapedi) peoples **Obv:** Arms **Rev:** Woman seated, cooking

| Date | Mintage | VF20 | XF40 | MS60 | MS63 | MS65 |
|---|---|---|---|---|---|---|
| 2009 | 1,000 | PF65 210 | | | | |

**KM# 535 RAND**
3.11 g., 0.9999 Gold 0.100 oz. AGW, 16.5 mm. **Subject:** FIFA World Cup, 2010 **Obv:** National arms **Rev:** Zakumi mascot

| Date | Mintage | VF20 | XF40 | MS60 | MS63 | MS65 |
|---|---|---|---|---|---|---|
| 2009 | Est. 10000 | PF65 225 | | | | |

**KM# 249 2 RAND**
7.78 g., 0.9999 Gold 0.250 oz. AGW, 22 mm. **Obv:** New national arms **Rev:** Gondwana theoretical landmass and dinosaur **Edge:** Reeded

| Date | Mintage | VF20 | XF40 | MS60 | MS63 | MS65 |
|---|---|---|---|---|---|---|
| 2001 | 558 | PF65 550 | | | | |

**KM# 386 2 RAND**
7.78 g., 0.9999 Gold 0.250 oz. AGW, 22 mm. **Series:** World Heritage Site **Subject:** Robben Island **Obv:** New national arms **Rev:** Carved stone, island in background **Edge:** Reeded

| Date | Mintage | VF20 | XF40 | MS60 | MS63 | MS65 |
|---|---|---|---|---|---|---|
| 2002 | 999 | PF65 550 | | | | |

**KM# 387 2 RAND**
7.78 g., 0.9999 Gold 0.250 oz. AGW, 22 mm. **Series:** World heritage Site **Subject:** Greater St. Lucia Wetland Park **Obv:** New national arms **Rev:** Various birds **Edge:** Reeded

| Date | Mintage | VF20 | XF40 | MS60 | MS63 | MS65 |
|---|---|---|---|---|---|---|
| 2003 | 637 | PF65 550 | | | | |

**KM# 388 2 RAND**
7.78 g., 0.9999 Gold 0.250 oz. AGW, 22 mm. **Series:** World Heritage Park **Subject:** Ukhahlamba" Drakensberg Park **Obv:** New national arms **Rev:** Early painting of animal and hunters **Edge:** Reeded

| Date | Mintage | VF20 | XF40 | MS60 | MS63 | MS65 |
|---|---|---|---|---|---|---|
| 2004 | 750 | PF65 550 | | | | |

**KM# 390 2 RAND**
7.78 g., 0.9999 Gold 0.250 oz. AGW, 22 mm. **Subject:** 2006 FIFA World Cup Soccer - Germany **Obv:** New national arms **Rev:** Soccer ball at center above partial globe within ornate border art **Edge:** Reeded

| Date | Mintage | VF20 | XF40 | MS60 | MS63 | MS65 |
|---|---|---|---|---|---|---|
| 2005 | — | PF65 550 | | | | |

**KM# 391 2 RAND**
7.78 g., 0.9999 Gold 0.250 oz. AGW, 22 mm. **Series:** World Heritage Site **Subject:** Cradle of Mankind **Obv:** New national arms **Rev:** Early man standing at upper left, ape's head at upper right, skull at lower left, value at lower right **Edge:** Reeded

| Date | Mintage | VF20 | XF40 | MS60 | MS63 | MS65 |
|---|---|---|---|---|---|---|
| 2006 | 1,000 | PF65 520 | | | | |

**KM# 392 2 RAND**
7.78 g., 0.9999 Gold 0.250 oz. AGW, 22 mm. **Subject:** 2006 FIFA World Cup Soccer - Germany **Obv:** New national arms **Rev:** Logo in ornate frame **Edge:** Reeded

| Date | Mintage | VF20 | XF40 | MS60 | MS63 | MS65 |
|---|---|---|---|---|---|---|
| 2006 | 15,000 | **PF65** 510 | | | | |

**KM# 393 2 RAND**
7.78 g., 0.9999 Gold 0.250 oz. AGW, 22 mm. **Series:** World Heritage Site **Subject:** Cape Floral **Obv:** New national arms **Rev:** Bird perched on branch at left, plant at center, land in distance **Edge:** Reeded

| Date | Mintage | VF20 | XF40 | MS60 | MS63 | MS65 |
|---|---|---|---|---|---|---|
| 2007 | — | **PF65** 510 | | | | |

**KM# 394 2 RAND**
7.78 g., 0.9999 Gold 0.250 oz. AGW, 22 mm. **Subject:** 2010 FIFA World Cup Soccer - South Africa **Obv:** New national arms **Rev:** Animal in ornate frame at left and right, small soccer ball at bottom below value **Edge:** Reeded

| Date | Mintage | VF20 | XF40 | MS60 | MS63 | MS65 |
|---|---|---|---|---|---|---|
| 2007 | 10,000 | **PF65** 510 | | | | |

**KM# 534 2 RAND**
7.78 g., 0.9999 Gold 0.2501 oz. AGW, 22 mm. **Subject:** FIFA World Cup 2010 **Obv:** National arms **Rev:** Two hands on soccerball

| Date | Mintage | VF20 | XF40 | MS60 | MS63 | MS65 |
|---|---|---|---|---|---|---|
| 2008 | Est. 10000 | **PF65** 450 | | | | |

**KM# 479 2 RAND**
7.77 g., 0.999 Gold 0.2496 oz. AGW, 22 mm. **Subject:** Richtersveld Cultural and Botanical Landscape **Obv:** Arms **Rev:** Native "haru on" hut and aloe pilansil tree

| Date | Mintage | VF20 | XF40 | MS60 | MS63 | MS65 |
|---|---|---|---|---|---|---|
| 2009 | 2,000 | **PF65** 520 | | | | |

**KM# 536 2 RAND**
7.780 Gold AGW, 22 mm. **Subject:** FIFA World Cup, 2010 **Obv:** National arms **Rev:** Zakumi mascot

| Date | Mintage | VF20 | XF40 | MS60 | MS63 | MS65 |
|---|---|---|---|---|---|---|
| 2009 | Est. 10000 | **PF65** 450 | | | | |

**KM# 547 2 RAND**
7.78 g., 0.9999 Gold 0.2501 oz. AGW, 22 mm. **Obv:** National arms **Rev:** FIFA World Cup trophy

| Date | Mintage | VF20 | XF40 | MS60 | MS63 | MS65 |
|---|---|---|---|---|---|---|
| 2010 | Est. 10000 | **PF65** 450 | | | | |

**KM# 559 5 RAND**
3.11 g., 0.999 Gold 0.0999 oz. AGW, 16.5 mm. **Obv:** National arms **Rev:** Walter and Albertina Sisulu

| Date | Mintage | VF20 | XF40 | MS60 | MS63 | MS65 |
|---|---|---|---|---|---|---|
| 2012 | — | **PF65** 200 | | | | |

**KM# 560 25 RAND**
31.10 g., 0.9999 Gold 0.9998 oz. AGW, 32.7 mm. **Obv:** National arms **Rev:** Walter and Albertina Sisulu

| Date | Mintage | VF20 | XF40 | MS60 | MS63 | MS65 |
|---|---|---|---|---|---|---|
| 2012 | — | **PF65** 2,000 | | | | |

**KM# 548 200 RAND**
31.10 g., 0.9999 Gold 0.9998 oz. AGW, 32.7 mm. **Obv:** National arms **Rev:** FIFA World Cup trophy

| Date | Mintage | VF20 | XF40 | MS60 | MS63 | MS65 |
|---|---|---|---|---|---|---|
| 2010 | Est. 10000 | **PF65** 1,750 | | | | |

## GOLD BULLION PROTEA COINAGE

**KM# 278 5 RAND**
3.11 g., 0.9999 Gold 0.100 oz. AGW, 16.5 mm. **Obv:** Protea flower **Rev:** Soccer player heading the ball **Edge:** Reeded

| Date | Mintage | VF20 | XF40 | MS60 | MS63 | MS65 |
|---|---|---|---|---|---|---|
| 2002 | — | **PF65** 210 | | | | |

**KM# 395 5 RAND**
3.11 g., 0.9999 Gold 0.100 oz. AGW, 16.5 mm. **Subject:** 10th Anniversary Soccer "Bafana Bafana **Obv:** Protea flower **Rev:** Two players running right **Edge:** Reeded

| Date | Mintage | VF20 | XF40 | MS60 | MS63 | MS65 |
|---|---|---|---|---|---|---|
| 2002 | 386 | **PF65** 275 | | | | |

**KM# 397 5 RAND**
3.11 g., 0.9999 Gold 0.100 oz. AGW, 16.5 mm. **Subject:** World Summit on Sustainable Development **Obv:** Protea flower **Rev:** Globe featuring Africa **Rev. Inscription:** prosperity **Edge:** Reeded

| Date | Mintage | VF20 | XF40 | MS60 | MS63 | MS65 |
|---|---|---|---|---|---|---|
| 2002 | 511 | **PF65** 225 | | | | |

**KM# 399 5 RAND**
3.11 g., 0.9999 Gold 0.100 oz. AGW, 16.5 mm. **Subject:** Cricket World Cup **Obv:** Protea flower **Rev:** Cricket ball striking stumps **Rev. Inscription:** Protea **Edge:** Reeded

| Date | Mintage | VF20 | XF40 | MS60 | MS63 | MS65 |
|---|---|---|---|---|---|---|
| 2003 | 925 | **PF65** 210 | | | | |

**KM# 289 5 RAND**
3.11 g., 0.9999 Gold 0.100 oz. AGW, 16.5 mm. **Subject:** 10th Anniversary of South African Democracy **Obv:** Protea flower **Rev:** Inscription covered flag **Edge:** Reeded

| Date | Mintage | VF20 | XF40 | MS60 | MS63 | MS65 |
|---|---|---|---|---|---|---|
| 2004 | 1,000 | **PF65** 210 | | | | |

**KM# 401 5 RAND**
3.11 g., 0.9999 Gold 0.100 oz. AGW, 16.5 mm. **Subject:** 10th Anniversay Democracy **Obv:** Protea flower **Rev:** Flag made of constitution **Edge:** Reeded **Note:** 10YF - circular 10 YEARS FREEDOM

| Date | Mintage | VF20 | XF40 | MS60 | MS63 | MS65 |
|---|---|---|---|---|---|---|
| 2004 | 2,089 | **PF65** 375 | | | | |
| 2004 10YF | 492 | **PF65** 600 | | | | |

**KM# 403 5 RAND**
3.11 g., 0.9999 Gold 0.100 oz. AGW, 16.5 mm. **Subject:** Nobel Prize Winners **Obv:** Protea flower **Rev:** Freedom Charter, Luthuli seated left at desk at lower right **Edge:** Reeded **Note:** FR - FREEDOM

| Date | Mintage | VF20 | XF40 | MS60 | MS63 | MS65 |
|---|---|---|---|---|---|---|
| 2005 | 2,000 | **PF65** 210 | | | | |
| 2005 FR | — | **PF65** 600 | | | | |

**KM# 405 5 RAND**
3.11 g., 0.9999 Gold 0.100 oz. AGW, 16.5 mm. **Subject:** Nobel Prize Winners **Obv:** Protea flower **Rev:** Cross, inscription **Edge:** Reeded

| Date | Mintage | VF20 | XF40 | MS60 | MS63 | MS65 |
|---|---|---|---|---|---|---|
| 2006 | 5,600 | **PF65** 210 | | | | |
| 2006 logo | 400 | **PF65** 500 | | | | |

**KM# 407 5 RAND**
3.11 g., 0.9999 Gold 0.100 oz. AGW, 16.5 mm. **Subject:** Nobel Prize winners **Obv:** Protea flower **Rev:** Extract from de Klerk's acceptance speech **Edge:** Reeded

| Date | Mintage | VF20 | XF40 | MS60 | MS63 | MS65 |
|---|---|---|---|---|---|---|
| 2007 | 8,000 | **PF65** 210 | | | | |
| 2007 dove | — | **PF65** 700 | | | | |

**KM# 408 5 RAND**
3.11 g., 0.9999 Gold 0.100 oz. AGW, 16.5 mm. **Subject:** Nobel Prize Winners **Obv:** Protea flower **Rev:** Extract from Mandela's acceptance speech **Edge:** Reeded

| Date | Mintage | VF20 | XF40 | MS60 | MS63 | MS65 |
|---|---|---|---|---|---|---|
| 2007 | — | **PF65** 210 | | | | |
| 2007 dove | — | **PF65** 700 | | | | |

**KM# 452 5 RAND**
3.11 g., 0.999 Gold 0.0999 oz. AGW, 16.5 mm. **Obv:** Protea flower **Rev:** Ghandi figure at prayer

| Date | Mintage | VF20 | XF40 | MS60 | MS63 | MS65 |
|---|---|---|---|---|---|---|
| 2008 | 8,000 | **PF65** 210 | | | | |

**KM# 476 5 RAND**
3.11 g., 0.999 Gold 0.0999 oz. AGW, 16.5 mm. **Obv:** Protea flower **Rev:** Portraits of C. J. Langenhoven and M. L. de Villiers with musical score

| Date | Mintage | VF20 | XF40 | MS60 | MS63 | MS65 |
|---|---|---|---|---|---|---|
| 2009 | 8,000 | **PF65** 200 | | | | |

**KM# 544 5 RAND**
3.11 g., 0.9999 Gold 0.100 oz. AGW, 16.5 mm. **Obv:** Protea plant **Rev:** Nadine Gordimer

| Date | Mintage | VF20 | XF40 | MS60 | MS63 | MS65 |
|---|---|---|---|---|---|---|
| 2010 | Est. 4000 | **PF65** 250 | | | | |

**KM# 522 5 RAND**
3.11 g., 0.9999 Gold 0.100 oz. AGW, 16.5 mm. **Obv:** Protea flower **Rev:** John Maxwell Coetzee

| Date | Mintage | VF20 | XF40 | MS60 | MS63 | MS65 |
|---|---|---|---|---|---|---|
| 2011 | — | **PF65** 250 | | | | |

**KM# 279 25 RAND**
31.10 g., 0.9999 Gold 0.9999 oz. AGW, 32.7 mm. **Obv:** Protea flower **Rev:** Soccer player kicking ball **Edge:** Reeded

| Date | Mintage | VF20 | XF40 | MS60 | MS63 | MS65 |
|---|---|---|---|---|---|---|
| 2002 | 492 | **PF65** 1,900 | | | | |

**KM# 396 25 RAND**
31.11 g., 0.9999 Gold 1.000 oz. AGW, 32.69 mm. **Subject:** 10th Anniversary Soccer "Bafana Bafana **Obv:** Protea flower **Rev:** Two players running left **Edge:** Reeded

| Date | Mintage | VF20 | XF40 | MS60 | MS63 | MS65 |
|---|---|---|---|---|---|---|
| 2002 | 137 | **PF65** 1,950 | | | | |
| 2002 flag/CW | 84 | **PF65** 2,250 | | | | |

**KM# 398 25 RAND**
31.11 g., 0.9999 Gold 1.000 oz. AGW, 32.69 mm. **Subject:** World Summit on Sustainable Development **Obv:** Protea flower **Rev:** Globe featuring Africa **Edge:** Reeded

| Date | Mintage | VF20 | XF40 | MS60 | MS63 | MS65 |
|---|---|---|---|---|---|---|
| 2002 | 421 | **PF65** 1,900 | | | | |

**KM# 400 25 RAND**
31.11 g., 0.9999 Gold 1.000 oz. AGW, 32.69 mm. **Subject:** Cricket World Cup **Obv:** Protea flower **Rev:** Batsman on one knee about to sweep the ball **Rev. Legend:** PROTEA **Edge:** Reeded

| Date | Mintage | VF20 | XF40 | MS60 | MS63 | MS65 |
|---|---|---|---|---|---|---|
| 2003 | 210 | **PF65** 1,950 | | | | |
| 2003 ball/RSA | 208 | **PF65** 1,950 | | | | |

**KM# 402 25 RAND**
31.11 g., 0.9999 Gold 1.000 oz. AGW, 32.69 mm. **Subject:** 10th Anniversary Democracy **Obv:** Protea flower **Rev:** Two heads of Mandela, one left, one facing, Union building in background **Edge:** Reeded **Note:** 10FP - 10/flag, people

| Date | Mintage | VF20 | XF40 | MS60 | MS63 | MS65 |
|---|---|---|---|---|---|---|
| 2004 | 6,000 | **PF65** 3,000 | | | | |
| 2004 10FP | 492 | **PF65** 5,400 | | | | |

**KM# 404 25 RAND**
31.11 g., 0.9999 Gold 1.000 oz. AGW, 32.69 mm. **Subject:** Nobel Prize Winners **Obv:** Protea flower **Rev:** Bust of Chief Albert Luthuli facing **Edge:** Reeded **Note:** FC - FREEDOM / CHARTER / 26 JUNE 1955

| Date | Mintage | VF20 | XF40 | MS60 | MS63 | MS65 |
|---|---|---|---|---|---|---|
| 2005 | 6,000 | **PF65** 1,900 | | | | |
| 2005 FC | — | **PF65** 3,750 | | | | |

**KM# 406 25 RAND**
31.11 g., 0.9999 Gold 1.000 oz. AGW, 32.69 mm. **Subject:** Nobel Prize Winners **Obv:** Protea flower **Rev:** Cross, bust of Archbishop Desmond Tutu right **Edge:** Reeded

| Date | Mintage | VF20 | XF40 | MS60 | MS63 | MS65 |
|---|---|---|---|---|---|---|
| 2006 | 7,600 | **PF65** 1,900 | | | | |
| 2006 logo | 400 | **PF65** 2,600 | | | | |

**KM# 409 25 RAND**
31.11 g., 0.9999 Gold 1.000 oz. AGW, 32.69 mm. **Subject:** Nobel Prize Winners **Obv:** Protea flower **Rev:** Busts of Mandela, de Klerk right **Edge:** Reeded **Note:** d-P - dove Peace

| Date | Mintage | VF20 | XF40 | MS60 | MS63 | MS65 |
|---|---|---|---|---|---|---|
| 2007 | 12,000 | **PF65** 1,900 | | | | |
| 2007 d-P | — | **PF65** 2,750 | | | | |

**KM# 453 25 RAND**
31.11 g., 0.999 Gold 0.9991 oz. AGW, 32.7 mm. **Obv:** Protea flower **Rev:** Ghandi profile at right

| Date | Mintage | VF20 | XF40 | MS60 | MS63 | MS65 |
|---|---|---|---|---|---|---|
| 2008 | 600 | **PF65** 2,000 | | | | |
| 2008 | 12,000 | **PF65** 1,900 | | | | |

**KM# 477 25 RAND**
31.11 g., 0.999 Gold 0.9991 oz. AGW, 32.7 mm. **Obv:** Protea flower **Rev:** Portraits of C. J. Langenhoven and M. L. de Villiers and musical score

| Date | Mintage | VF20 | XF40 | MS60 | MS63 | MS65 |
|---|---|---|---|---|---|---|
| 2009 | 11,000 | **PF65** 1,900 | | | | |

**KM# 545 25 RAND**
31.10 g., 0.9999 Gold 0.9998 oz. AGW, 32.69 mm. **Obv:** Protea flower **Rev:** Nadine Gordimer

| Date | Mintage | VF20 | XF40 | MS60 | MS63 | MS65 |
|---|---|---|---|---|---|---|
| 2010 | Est. 3000 | **PF65** 1,750 | | | | |

**KM# 523 25 RAND**
31.10 g., 0.9999 Gold 0.9998 oz. AGW, 32.7 mm. **Obv:** Protea flower **Rev:** John Maxwell Coetzee

| Date | Mintage | VF20 | XF40 | MS60 | MS63 | MS65 |
|---|---|---|---|---|---|---|
| 2011 | — | **PF65** 1,750 | | | | |
| 2011 Proof, JMC privy mark | — | **PF65** 2,000 | | | | |

**KM# 262 1/10 PROTEA**
3.11 g., 0.9999 Gold 0.100 oz. AGW, 16.5 mm. **Subject:** Tourism **Obv:** Protea flower **Rev:** Lion's head facing, partial shield **Rev. Inscription:** PROTEA **Edge:** Reeded

| Date | Mintage | VF20 | XF40 | MS60 | MS63 | MS65 |
|---|---|---|---|---|---|---|
| 2001 | 1,076 | **PF65** 210 | | | | |

**KM# 263 PROTEA**
31.11 g., 0.9999 Gold 1.000 oz. AGW, 32.6 mm. **Subject:** Tourism **Obv:** Protea flower **Rev:** Child on sandy beach, Table Mountain in background, partial star at right **Rev. Inscription:** PROTEA **Edge:** Reeded

| Date | Mintage | VF20 | XF40 | MS60 | MS63 | MS65 |
|---|---|---|---|---|---|---|
| 2001 | 972 | **PF65** 2,000 | | | | |
| 2001 GRC(pp) | 196 | **PF65** 2,500 | | | | |

## MINT SETS

| KM# | Date | Mintage | Identification | Issue Price | Mkt Val |
|---|---|---|---|---|---|
| MS39 | 2001 (9) | 5,577 | KM#221-229 | — | 60.00 |
| MS38 | 2002 (7) | — | KM#268-274 plus 1- and 2-cent medals | 30.00 | 32.50 |
| MS40 | 2002 (7) | 3,886 | KM#268-274 | — | 52.50 |
| MS41 | 2002 (7) | 1,640 | KM#268-274, circulated coins | — | 17.50 |
| MS42 | 2003 (7) | 2,602 | KM#324, 327, 330, 332, 335, 337, 347 | — | 45.00 |
| MS43 | 2003 (7) | 1,380 | KM#324, 327, 330, 332, 335, 337, 347, circulted coins | — | 10.00 |
| MS44 | 2004 (7) | 1,948 | KM#281, 325, 326, 328, 331, 333, 336 | — | 37.50 |
| MS45 | 2004 (7) | 1,131 | KM#281, 325, 325, 328, 331, 333, 336, circulated coins | — | 17.50 |
| MS46 | 2004 (7) | 325 | KM#281, 325, 326, 328, 331, 333, 336, Baby | — | 22.50 |
| MS47 | 2004 (7) | 23 | KM#281, 325, 326, 328, 331, 333, 336, Wedding | — | 22.50 |
| MS48 | 2005 (7) | — | KM#291-297 | — | 30.00 |
| MS49 | 2005 (7) | — | KM#291-297, circulated coins | — | 15.00 |
| MS50 | 2005 (7) | — | KM#291-297, Baby | — | 23.00 |
| MS51 | 2005 (7) | — | KM#291-297, Wedding | — | 22.50 |
| MS52 | 2006 (7) | — | KM#291-297 | — | 22.50 |
| MS53 | 2006 (7) | — | KM#291-297, circulated coins | — | 15.00 |
| MS54 | 2006 (7) | — | KM#291-297, Baby | — | 15.00 |
| MS55 | 2006 (7) | — | KM#291-297, Wedding | — | 15.00 |
| MS56 | 2007 (7) | — | KM#340-346 | — | 22.50 |
| MS57 | 2007 (7) | — | KM#340-346, circulated coins | — | 15.00 |
| MS58 | 2007 (7) | — | KM#340-346, baby | — | 15.00 |
| MS59 | 2007 (7) | — | KM#340-346, wedding | — | 15.00 |

## PIEFORT PROOF SETS (PPS)

| KM# | Date | Mintage | Identification | Issue Price | Mkt Val |
|---|---|---|---|---|---|
| PS242 | 2007 (4) | — | KM#430-433, leatherette | — | 3,000 |

## PROOF SETS

| KM# | Date | Mintage | Identification | Issue Price | Mkt Val |
|---|---|---|---|---|---|
| PS170 | 2002 (7) | — | KM#268-274 plus 1- and 2-cent medals | 40.00 | 65.00 |
| PS171 | 2005 (4) | 1,500 | KM#320-323 | — | 300 |
| PS172 | 2001 (9) | 3,678 | KM#221-229 | — | 75.00 |
| PS173 | 2001 (9) | — | KM#221-229 wedding | — | 75.00 |
| PS174 | 2002 (7) | — | KM#268-274 | — | 75.00 |
| PS175 | 2002 (7) | 330 | KM#268-274, baby | — | 75.00 |
| PS176 | 2003 (7) | 2,356 | KM#324, 327, 330, 332, 335, 337, 347 | — | 65.00 |
| PS177 | 2003 (7) | 500 | KM#324, 327, 330, 332, 335, 337, 347, baby | — | 65.00 |
| PS178 | 2003 (7) | 53 | KM#324, 327, 330, 332, 335, 337, 347, wedding | — | 65.00 |
| PS179 | 2004 (7) | 1,935 | KM#281, 325, 326, 328, 331, 333, 336 | — | 65.00 |
| PS180 | 2004 (7) | 326 | KM#281, 325, 326, 328, 331, 333, 336, baby | — | 65.00 |
| PS181 | 2004 (7) | 23 | KM#281, 325, 326, 328, 331, 333, 336, wedding | — | 65.00 |
| PS182 | 2005 (7) | — | KM#291-297 | — | 65.00 |
| PS183 | 2005 (7) | — | KM#291-297, baby | — | 65.00 |
| PS184 | 2005 (7) | — | KM#291-297, wedding | — | 65.00 |
| PS185 | 2006 (7) | — | KM#291-297 | — | 65.00 |
| PS186 | 2006 (7) | — | KM#291-297, baby | — | 65.00 |
| PS187 | 2006 (7) | — | KM#291-297, wedding | — | 65.00 |
| PS188 | 2007 (7) | — | KM#340-346 | — | 65.00 |
| PS189 | 2007 (7) | — | KM#340-346, baby | — | 65.00 |
| PS190 | 2007 (7) | — | KM#340-346, wedding | — | 65.00 |
| PS193 | 2001 (4) | 411 | KM#243-246, wooden case | — | 375 |
| PS194 | 2001 (4) | 746 | KM#243-246, velvet (med case) | — | 300 |
| PS195 | 2002 (3) | 81 | KM#234, 243, 351 (mixed dates) | — | 110 |
| PS196 | 2002 (3) | 95 | KM#235, 244, 352 (mixed dates) | — | 185 |
| PS197 | 2002 (3) | 81 | KM#236, 245, 353 (mixed dates) | — | 250 |
| PS198 | 2002 (3) | 92 | KM#237, 246, 354 (mixed dates) | — | 335 |
| PS199 | 2002 (4) | 411 | KM#351-354, wooden case | — | 375 |
| PS200 | 2002 (4) | 746 | KM#351-354, velvet lined case | — | 275 |
| PS201 | 2003 (4) | 59 | KM#234, 243, 351, 355 (mixed dates) | — | 150 |
| PS202 | 2003 (4) | 47 | KM#235, 244, 352, 356 (mixed dates) | — | 250 |
| PS203 | 2003 (4) | 75 | KM#236, 245, 353, 357 (mixed dates) | — | 330 |
| PS204 | 2003 (4) | 62 | KM#237, 246, 354, 358 (mixed dates) | — | 450 |
| PS205 | 2003 (4) | 532 | KM#355-358, wooden case | — | 375 |
| PS206 | 2003 (4) | 1,029 | KM#355-358, velvet lined case | — | 300 |
| PS207 | 2004 (5) | 132 | KM#234, 243, 351, 355, 359 (mixed dates) | — | 200 |
| PS208 | 2004 (5) | 133 | KM#235, 244, 352, 356, 360 (mixed dates) | — | 325 |
| PS209 | 2004 (5) | 181 | KM#236, 245, 353, 357, 361 (mixed dates) | — | 450 |
| PS210 | 2004 (5) | 158 | KM#237, 246, 354, 358, 362 (mixed dates) | — | 555 |
| PS211 | 2004 (4) | 645 | KM#359-362, wooden case | — | 375 |
| PS212 | 2004 (4) | 454 | KM#359-362, velvet lined case | — | 300 |
| PS213 | 2004 (4) | 299 | KM#359-362, plus 1/4 oz. medal | — | 300 |
| PS214 | 2005 (4) | — | KM#320-323, wooden case | — | 300 |
| PS215 | 2005 (4) | — | KM#320-323, velvet lined case | — | 300 |
| PS216 | 2006 (4) | — | KM#316-319, wooden case | — | 300 |
| PS217 | 2006 (4) | — | KM#316-319, velvet lined case | — | 300 |
| PS218 | 2007 (2) | — | KM#363-364, wooden case | — | 150 |
| PS219 | 2007 (2) | — | KM#363-364 | — | 105 |
| PS225 | 2001 (4) | 691 | KM#264-267 | — | 3,500 |
| PS226 | 2001 (4) | 985 | KM#264-267, leatherette | — | 3,500 |
| PS227 | 2001 (4) | 310 | KM#264-267, special export | — | 3,500 |
| PS228 | 2002 (4) | 698 | KM#410-413, prestige | — | 3,500 |
| PS229 | 2002 (4) | 529 | KM#410-413, leatherette | — | 3,500 |
| PS230 | 2002 (4) | 682 | KM#410-413, special | — | 3,500 |
| PS231 | 2003 (4) | 698 | KM#414-417, prestige | — | 3,500 |
| PS232 | 2003 (4) | 908 | KM#414-417, leatherette | — | 3,500 |
| PS233 | 2003 (4) | 722 | KM#414-417, anniversary | — | 3,500 |
| PS234 | 2004 (4) | 700 | KM#418-421, prestige | — | 3,525 |
| PS235 | 2004 (4) | 440 | KM#418-421, leatherette | — | 3,525 |
| PS236 | 2004 (4) | 125 | KM#418-421, special export with silver African Continent | — | 3,525 |
| PS237 | 2005 (4) | — | KM#422-425, prestige | — | 3,525 |
| PS238 | 2005 (4) | — | KM#422-425, leatherette | — | 3,525 |
| PS239 | 2006 (4) | — | KM#426-429, prestige | — | 3,500 |
| PS240 | 2006 (4) | — | KM#426-429, leatherette | — | 3,500 |
| PS241 | 2007 (4) | — | KM#430-433, prestige | — | 3,500 |

# S. GEORGIA & THE S. SANDWICH IS.

ARGENTINA
SOUTH GEORGIA ISLAND
SOUTH SANDWICH ISLANDS
Scotia Sea

South Georgia and the South Sandwich Islands are a dependency of the Falkland Islands, and located about 800 miles east of them. South Georgia is 1,450 sq. mi. (1,770 sq. km.), and the South Sandwich Islands are 120 sq. mi. (311 sq. km.) Fishing and Antarctic research are the main industries. The islands were claimed for Great Britain in 1775 by Captain James Cook.

**RULER**
British since 1775

## BRITISH OVERSEAS TERRITORY

### STANDARD COINAGE

**KM# 55 POUND**
28.28 g., Copper-Nickel, 38.6 mm. **Ruler:** Elizabeth II **Subject:** Kon Tiki Expedition 65th Anniversary **Rev:** Kon Tiki Ship **Mint:** Pobjoy Mint

| Date | Mintage | VF20 | XF40 | MS60 | MS63 | MS65 |
|---|---|---|---|---|---|---|
| 2012 PM | — | **PF65** 9.00 | | | | |

**KM# 55a POUND**
12.00 g., 0.999 Silver 0.3854 oz. ASW, 38.6 mm. **Ruler:** Elizabeth II **Subject:** Kon Tiki Expedition 65th Anniversary **Rev:** Kon Tiki Ship **Mint:** Pobjoy Mint

| Date | Mintage | VF20 | XF40 | MS60 | MS63 | MS65 |
|---|---|---|---|---|---|---|
| 2012 PM | Est. 10000 | **PF63** 40.00 | **PF65** 50.00 | | | |

**KM# 56 POUND**
28.28 g., Copper-Nickel **Ruler:** Elizabeth II **Subject:** Kon Tiki Expedition **Obv:** Portraits right **Rev:** Kon Tiki Mask **Mint:** Pobjoy Mint

| Date | Mintage | VF20 | XF40 | MS60 | MS63 | MS65 |
|---|---|---|---|---|---|---|
| 2012 PM | — | **PF65** 9.00 | | | | |

**KM# 56a POUND**
12.00 g., 0.999 Silver 0.3854 oz. ASW **Ruler:** Elizabeth II **Subject:** Kon Tiki Expedition **Obv:** Portraits right **Rev:** Kon Tiki mask **Mint:** Pobjoy Mint

| Date | Mintage | VF20 | XF40 | MS60 | MS63 | MS65 |
|---|---|---|---|---|---|---|
| 2012 PM | — | **PF63** 40.00 | **PF65** 50.00 | | | |

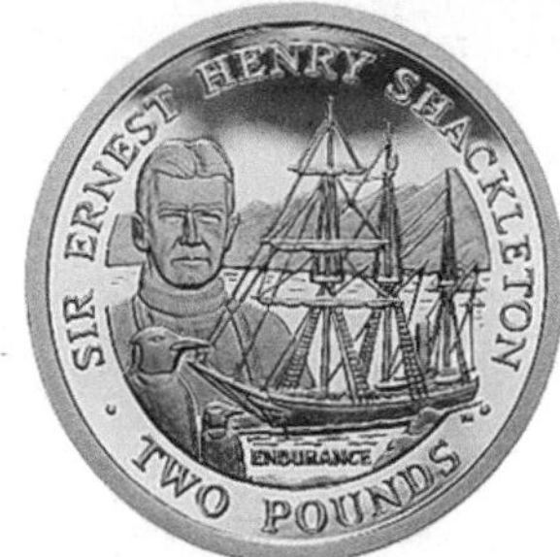


**KM# 7 2 POUNDS**
28.28 g., Copper-Nickel, 38.61 mm. **Ruler:** Elizabeth II **Subject:** Sir Ernest H. Shackleton **Obv:** Crowned bust right **Rev:** Bust facing and ship "Endurance **Edge:** Reeded **Mint:** Pobjoy Mint

| Date | Mintage | VF20 | XF40 | MS60 | MS63 | MS65 |
|---|---|---|---|---|---|---|
| 2001 PM | — | — | — | — | 9.00 | 12.00 |

**KM# 7a 2 POUNDS**
28.28 g., 0.925 Silver 0.841 oz. ASW, 38.61 mm. **Ruler:** Elizabeth II **Obv:** Crowned bust right **Rev:** Bust facing and ship "Endurance **Mint:** Pobjoy Mint

| Date | Mintage | VF20 | XF40 | MS60 | MS63 | MS65 |
|---|---|---|---|---|---|---|
| 2001 PM | Est. 10000 | **PF63** 40.00 | **PF65** 50.00 | | | |

**KM# 9 2 POUNDS**
28.28 g., Copper-Nickel, 38.61 mm. **Ruler:** Elizabeth II **Subject:** Sir Joseph Banks **Obv:** Crowned bust right **Rev:** Cameo and ship **Mint:** Pobjoy Mint

| Date | Mintage | VF20 | XF40 | MS60 | MS63 | MS65 |
|---|---|---|---|---|---|---|
| 2001 PM | — | — | — | — | 9.00 | 12.00 |

**KM# 9a 2 POUNDS**
28.28 g., 0.925 Silver 0.841 oz. ASW, 38.61 mm. **Ruler:** Elizabeth II **Obv:** Crowned bust right **Rev:** Ship and cameo **Mint:** Pobjoy Mint

| Date | Mintage | VF20 | XF40 | MS60 | MS63 | MS65 |
|---|---|---|---|---|---|---|
| 2001 PM | Est. 10000 | **PF63** 40.00 | **PF65** 50.00 | | | |

**KM# 11 2 POUNDS**
28.28 g., Copper-Nickel, 38.6 mm. **Ruler:** Elizabeth II **Subject:** Queen Elizabeth II's Golden Jubilee **Obv:** Crowned bust right **Rev:** Young crowned bust right **Edge:** Reeded **Mint:** Pobjoy Mint

| Date | Mintage | VF20 | XF40 | MS60 | MS63 | MS65 |
|---|---|---|---|---|---|---|
| 2002 PM | — | — | — | — | 9.00 | 12.00 |

**KM# 11a 2 POUNDS**
28.28 g., 0.925 Gold Plated Silver 0.841 oz., 38.6 mm. **Ruler:** Elizabeth II **Subject:** Queen Elizabeth II's Golden Jubilee **Obv:** Crowned bust right **Rev:** Young crowned bust right **Edge:** Reeded **Mint:** Pobjoy Mint

| Date | Mintage | VF20 | XF40 | MS60 | MS63 | MS65 |
|---|---|---|---|---|---|---|
| 2002 PM | 10,000 | **PF63** 40.00 | **PF65** 50.00 | | | |

**KM# 13 2 POUNDS**
28.28 g., Copper-Nickel, 38.6 mm. **Ruler:** Elizabeth II **Subject:** Queen Elizabeth II's Golden Jubilee **Obv:** Crowned bust right **Rev:** Small crown above shield flanked by flower sprigs **Edge:** Reeded **Mint:** Pobjoy Mint

| Date | Mintage | VF20 | XF40 | MS60 | MS63 | MS65 |
|---|---|---|---|---|---|---|
| 2002 PM | — | — | — | — | 9.00 | 12.00 |

**KM# 13a 2 POUNDS**
28.28 g., 0.925 Gold Plated Silver 0.841 oz., 38.6 mm. **Ruler:** Elizabeth II **Subject:** Queen Elizabeth II's Golden Jubilee **Obv:** Crowned bust right **Rev:** Small crown above shield flanked by flower sprigs **Edge:** Reeded **Mint:** Pobjoy Mint

| Date | Mintage | VF20 | XF40 | MS60 | MS63 | MS65 |
|---|---|---|---|---|---|---|
| 2002 PM | 10,000 | **PF63** 40.00 | **PF65** 50.00 | | | |

**KM# 15 2 POUNDS**
28.28 g., Copper-Nickel, 38.6 mm. **Ruler:** Elizabeth II **Subject:** Diana, Princess of Wales - The Work Continues **Obv:** Crowned bust right **Rev:** Head 1/4 left **Edge:** Reeded **Mint:** Pobjoy Mint

| Date | Mintage | VF20 | XF40 | MS60 | MS63 | MS65 |
|---|---|---|---|---|---|---|
| 2002 PM | — | — | — | — | 9.00 | 12.00 |

**KM# 15a 2 POUNDS**
28.28 g., 0.925 Silver 0.841 oz. ASW, 38.6 mm. **Ruler:** Elizabeth II **Subject:** Princess Diana **Obv:** Queen's portrait **Rev:** Diana's portrait **Edge:** reeded **Mint:** Pobjoy Mint

| Date | Mintage | VF20 | XF40 | MS60 | MS63 | MS65 |
|---|---|---|---|---|---|---|
| 2002 PM | 10,000 | **PF63** 40.00 | **PF65** 50.00 | | | |

**KM# 17 2 POUNDS**
28.28 g., Copper-Nickel, 38.6 mm. **Ruler:** Elizabeth II **Subject:** Prince William's 21st Birthday **Obv:** Crowned bust right **Rev:** Arms of Prince William of Wales **Edge:** Reeded **Mint:** Pobjoy Mint

| Date | Mintage | VF20 | XF40 | MS60 | MS63 | MS65 |
|---|---|---|---|---|---|---|
| 2003 PM | — | — | — | — | 9.00 | 12.00 |

**KM# 17a 2 POUNDS**
28.28 g., 0.925 Silver 0.841 oz. ASW, 38.6 mm. **Ruler:** Elizabeth II **Subject:** Prince William's 21st Birthday **Obv:** Crowned bust right **Rev:** Arms of Prince William of Wales **Edge:** Reeded **Mint:** Pobjoy Mint

| Date | Mintage | VF20 | XF40 | MS60 | MS63 | MS65 |
|---|---|---|---|---|---|---|
| 2003 PM | — | **PF63** 40.00 | **PF65** 50.00 | | | |

**KM# 18 2 POUNDS**
28.28 g., Copper-Nickel, 38.6 mm. **Ruler:** Elizabeth II **Obv:** Crowned bust right **Rev:** Capt. Cook, ship and map **Edge:** Reeded **Mint:** Pobjoy Mint

| Date | Mintage | VF20 | XF40 | MS60 | MS63 | MS65 |
|---|---|---|---|---|---|---|
| 2003 PM | — | — | — | — | 9.00 | 12.00 |

**KM# 18a 2 POUNDS**
28.28 g., 0.925 Silver 0.841 oz. ASW, 38.6 mm. **Ruler:** Elizabeth II **Obv:** Crowned bust right **Rev:** Capt. Cook, ship and map **Edge:** Reeded **Mint:** Pobjoy Mint

| Date | Mintage | VF20 | XF40 | MS60 | MS63 | MS65 |
|---|---|---|---|---|---|---|
| 2003 PM | — | **PF63** 40.00 | **PF65** 50.00 | | | |

**KM# 20 2 POUNDS**
28.28 g., Copper-Nickel, 38.6 mm. **Ruler:** Elizabeth II **Obv:** Crowned bust right **Rev:** Sir Ernest Shackleton and icebound ship **Edge:** Reeded **Mint:** Pobjoy Mint

| Date | Mintage | VF20 | XF40 | MS60 | MS63 | MS65 |
|---|---|---|---|---|---|---|
| 2004 PM | — | — | — | — | 12.00 | 15.00 |

**KM# 20a 2 POUNDS**
28.28 g., 0.925 Silver 0.841 oz. ASW, 38.6 mm. **Ruler:** Elizabeth II **Obv:** Crowned bust right **Rev:** Sir Ernest Shackleton and icebound ship **Edge:** Reeded **Mint:** Pobjoy Mint

| Date | Mintage | VF20 | XF40 | MS60 | MS63 | MS65 |
|---|---|---|---|---|---|---|
| 2004 PM | 10,000 | **PF63** 40.00 | **PF65** 50.00 | | | |

**KM# 21 2 POUNDS**
28.28 g., Copper-Nickel, 38.6 mm. **Ruler:** Elizabeth II **Subject:** Centennial of Grytviken **Obv:** Crowned bust right **Rev:** Portrait above ship in harbor **Edge:** Reeded **Mint:** Pobjoy Mint

| Date | Mintage | VF20 | XF40 | MS60 | MS63 | MS65 |
|---|---|---|---|---|---|---|
| 2004 PM | — | — | — | — | 12.00 | 15.00 |

**KM# 21a 2 POUNDS**
28.28 g., 0.925 Silver 0.841 oz. ASW, 38.6 mm. **Ruler:** Elizabeth II **Subject:** Centennial of Grytviken **Obv:** Crowned bust right **Rev:** Portrait above ship in harbor **Edge:** Reeded **Mint:** Pobjoy Mint

| Date | Mintage | VF20 | XF40 | MS60 | MS63 | MS65 |
|---|---|---|---|---|---|---|
| 2004 PM | — | **PF63** 40.00 | **PF65** 50.00 | | | |

**KM# 25 2 POUNDS**
28.28 g., Copper-Nickel, 38.61 mm. **Ruler:** Elizabeth II **Subject:** Marriage of Charles to Parker Bowles **Rev:** Arms of Prince of Wales **Mint:** Pobjoy Mint

| Date | Mintage | VF20 | XF40 | MS60 | MS63 | MS65 |
|---|---|---|---|---|---|---|
| 2005 PM | — | — | — | — | 8.00 | 10.00 |

**KM# 25a 2 POUNDS**
28.28 g., 0.925 Silver 0.841 oz. ASW, 38.61 mm. **Ruler:** Elizabeth II **Subject:** Marriage of Prince Charles to Camilla Parker-Bowles **Mint:** Pobjoy Mint

| Date | Mintage | VF20 | XF40 | MS60 | MS63 | MS65 |
|---|---|---|---|---|---|---|
| 2005 PM | Est. 10000 | **PF63** 45.00 | **PF65** 55.00 | | | |

**KM# 22 2 POUNDS**
28.28 g., Copper-Nickel, 38.61 mm. **Ruler:** Elizabeth II **Obv:** Elizabeth II **Rev:** Rockhopper Penguin and chick **Edge:** Reeded **Mint:** Pobjoy Mint

| Date | Mintage | VF20 | XF40 | MS60 | MS63 | MS65 |
|---|---|---|---|---|---|---|
| 2006 PM | — | — | — | — | 10.00 | 13.00 |

**KM# 22a 2 POUNDS**
28.28 g., 0.925 Silver 0.841 oz. ASW, 38.61 mm. **Ruler:** Elizabeth II **Subject:** Rockhopper Penguin **Mint:** Pobjoy Mint

| Date | Mintage | VF20 | XF40 | MS60 | MS63 | MS65 |
|---|---|---|---|---|---|---|
| 2006 PM | Est. 10000 | **PF63** 45.00 | **PF65** 55.00 | | | |

**KM# 23 2 POUNDS**
28.28 g., Copper-Nickel, 38.61 mm. **Ruler:** Elizabeth II **Obv:** Elizabeth II **Rev:** Elephant Seal and cub **Edge:** Reeded **Mint:** Pobjoy Mint

| Date | Mintage | VF20 | XF40 | MS60 | MS63 | MS65 |
|---|---|---|---|---|---|---|
| 2006 PM | — | — | — | — | 10.00 | 13.00 |

**KM# 23a 2 POUNDS**
28.28 g., 0.925 Silver 0.841 oz. ASW, 38.61 mm. **Ruler:** Elizabeth II **Subject:** Elephant Seal **Mint:** Pobjoy Mint

| Date | Mintage | VF20 | XF40 | MS60 | MS63 | MS65 |
|---|---|---|---|---|---|---|
| 2006 PM | Est. 10000 | **PF63** 45.00 | **PF65** 55.00 | | | |

**KM# 24 2 POUNDS**
28.28 g., Copper-Nickel, 38.61 mm. **Ruler:** Elizabeth II **Obv:** Elizabeth II **Rev:** Humpback Whale and calf **Edge:** Reeded **Mint:** Pobjoy Mint

| Date | Mintage | VF20 | XF40 | MS60 | MS63 | MS65 |
|---|---|---|---|---|---|---|
| 2006 PM | — | — | — | — | 9.00 | 12.00 |

**KM# 24a 2 POUNDS**
28.28 g., 0.925 Silver 0.841 oz. ASW, 38.61 mm. **Ruler:** Elizabeth II **Subject:** Humpback Whale **Mint:** Pobjoy Mint

| Date | Mintage | VF20 | XF40 | MS60 | MS63 | MS65 |
|---|---|---|---|---|---|---|
| 2006 PM | Est. 10000 | **PF63** 45.00 | **PF65** 55.00 | | | |

**KM# 26 2 POUNDS**
28.28 g., Copper-Nickel, 38.61 mm. **Ruler:** Elizabeth II **Subject:** Queen Elizabeth II's 80th Birthday **Rev:** Queen on horseback taking part in Trouping of the Color ceremony **Mint:** Pobjoy Mint

| Date | Mintage | VF20 | XF40 | MS60 | MS63 | MS65 |
|---|---|---|---|---|---|---|
| 2006 PM | — | — | — | — | 8.00 | 10.00 |

**KM# 26a 2 POUNDS**
28.28 g., 0.925 Silver 0.841 oz. ASW, 38.61 mm. **Ruler:** Elizabeth II **Subject:** Queen Elizabeth II's 80th Birthday **Rev:** Queen on horseback taking part in Trouping of the Color ceremony **Mint:** Pobjoy Mint

| Date | Mintage | VF20 | XF40 | MS60 | MS63 | MS65 |
|---|---|---|---|---|---|---|
| 2006 | 25,000 | **PF63** 60.00 | **PF65** 75.00 | | | |

**KM# 27 2 POUNDS**
28.28 g., Copper-Nickel, 38.61 mm. **Ruler:** Elizabeth II **Rev:** Pair of Grey-headed Albatros **Mint:** Pobjoy Mint

| Date | Mintage | VF20 | XF40 | MS60 | MS63 | MS65 |
|---|---|---|---|---|---|---|
| 2006 PM | — | — | — | — | 9.00 | 12.00 |

**KM# 27a 2 POUNDS**
28.28 g., 0.925 Silver 0.841 oz. ASW, 38.61 mm. **Ruler:** Elizabeth II **Subject:** Grey-Headed Albatross **Mint:** Pobjoy Mint

| Date | Mintage | VF20 | XF40 | MS60 | MS63 | MS65 |
|---|---|---|---|---|---|---|
| 2006 PM | Est. 10000 | **PF63** 45.00 | **PF65** 55.00 | | | |

**KM# 28 2 POUNDS**
28.28 g., Copper-Nickel, 38.61 mm. **Ruler:** Elizabeth II **Subject:** Queen Elizabeth II's 80th Birthday **Rev:** 1953 Royal family **Mint:** Pobjoy Mint

| Date | Mintage | VF20 | XF40 | MS60 | MS63 | MS65 |
|---|---|---|---|---|---|---|
| 2006 PM | — | — | — | — | 8.00 | 10.00 |

**KM# 28a 2 POUNDS**
28.28 g., 0.925 Silver 0.841 oz. ASW, 38.61 mm. **Ruler:** Elizabeth II **Subject:** Queen Elizabeth II's 80th Birthday **Rev:** 1953 Royal family **Mint:** Pobjoy Mint

| Date | Mintage | VF20 | XF40 | MS60 | MS63 | MS65 |
|---|---|---|---|---|---|---|
| 2006 | 25,000 | **PF63** 60.00 | **PF65** 75.00 | | | |

**KM# 29 2 POUNDS**
28.28 g., Copper-Nickel, 38.61 mm. **Ruler:** Elizabeth II **Subject:** Queen Elizabeth's II 80th Birthday **Rev:** Wedding of Queen Elizabeth II and Prince Philip **Mint:** Pobjoy Mint

| Date | Mintage | VF20 | XF40 | MS60 | MS63 | MS65 |
|---|---|---|---|---|---|---|
| 2006 PM | — | — | — | — | 8.00 | 10.00 |

**KM# 29a 2 POUNDS**
28.28 g., 0.925 Silver 0.841 oz. ASW, 38.61 mm. **Ruler:** Elizabeth II **Subject:** Queen Elizabeth's II 80th Birthday **Rev:** Wedding of Queen Elizabeth II and Prince Philip **Mint:** Pobjoy Mint

| Date | Mintage | VF20 | XF40 | MS60 | MS63 | MS65 |
|---|---|---|---|---|---|---|
| 2006 | 25,000 | **PF63** 60.00 | **PF65** 75.00 | | | |

**KM# 30 2 POUNDS**
28.28 g., Copper-Nickel, 38.61 mm. **Ruler:** Elizabeth II **Subject:** Queen Elizabeth II's 80th Birthday **Rev:** Queen in Garter robes **Mint:** Pobjoy Mint

| Date | Mintage | VF20 | XF40 | MS60 | MS63 | MS65 |
|---|---|---|---|---|---|---|
| 2006 PM | — | — | — | — | 8.00 | 10.00 |

**KM# 30a 2 POUNDS**
28.28 g., 0.925 Silver 0.841 oz. ASW, 38.61 mm. **Ruler:** Elizabeth II **Subject:** Queen Elizabeth II's 80th Birthday **Rev:** Queen in Garter robes **Mint:** Pobjoy Mint

| Date | Mintage | VF20 | XF40 | MS60 | MS63 | MS65 |
|---|---|---|---|---|---|---|
| 2006 | 25,000 | **PF63** 60.00 | **PF65** 75.00 | | | |

**KM# 31 2 POUNDS**
28.28 g., Copper-Nickel, 38.61 mm. **Ruler:** Elizabeth II **Rev:** Queen Elizabeth II 1926 (1953 portrait) **Mint:** Pobjoy Mint

| Date | Mintage | VF20 | XF40 | MS60 | MS63 | MS65 |
|---|---|---|---|---|---|---|
| 2007 PM | — | — | — | — | 8.00 | 10.00 |

**KM# 32 2 POUNDS**
28.28 g., Copper-Nickel, 38.61 mm. **Ruler:** Elizabeth II **Subject:** 25th Anniversary of Liberation **Rev:** Warship and helicopters **Mint:** Pobjoy Mint

| Date | Mintage | VF20 | XF40 | MS60 | MS63 | MS65 |
|---|---|---|---|---|---|---|
| 2007 PM | — | — | — | — | 8.00 | 10.00 |

**KM# 32a 2 POUNDS**
28.28 g., 0.925 Silver 0.841 oz. ASW, 38.61 mm. **Ruler:** Elizabeth II **Subject:** 25 Years of the Liberation of South Georgia **Mint:** Pobjoy Mint

| Date | Mintage | VF20 | XF40 | MS60 | MS63 | MS65 |
|---|---|---|---|---|---|---|
| 2007 PM | Est. 10000 | **PF63** 45.00 | **PF65** 55.00 | | | |

**KM# 33 2 POUNDS**
28.28 g., Copper-Nickel, 38.61 mm. **Ruler:** Elizabeth II **Rev:** Trans Artic Expedition **Mint:** Pobjoy Mint

| Date | Mintage | VF20 | XF40 | MS60 | MS63 | MS65 |
|---|---|---|---|---|---|---|
| 2007 PM | — | — | — | — | 8.00 | 10.00 |

**KM# 33a 2 POUNDS**
28.28 g., 0.925 Silver 0.841 oz. ASW, 38.61 mm. **Ruler:** Elizabeth II **Subject:** Trans-arctic Expediton **Mint:** Pobjoy Mint

| Date | Mintage | VF20 | XF40 | MS60 | MS63 | MS65 |
|---|---|---|---|---|---|---|
| 2007 PM | Est. 25000 | **PF63** 45.00 | **PF65** 55.00 | | | |

**KM# 34 2 POUNDS**
28.28 g., Copper-Nickel, 38.61 mm. **Ruler:** Elizabeth II **Subject:** International Polar Year **Rev:** Shackelton Expedition **Mint:** Pobjoy Mint

| Date | Mintage | VF20 | XF40 | MS60 | MS63 | MS65 |
|---|---|---|---|---|---|---|
| 2007 PM | — | — | — | — | 8.00 | 10.00 |

**KM# 34a 2 POUNDS**
28.28 g., 0.925 Silver 0.841 oz. ASW, 38.61 mm. **Ruler:** Elizabeth II **Subject:** International Polar Year **Rev:** Sir Ernest Henry Shackleton with dogs in Antarctica **Mint:** Pobjoy Mint

| Date | Mintage | VF20 | XF40 | MS60 | MS63 | MS65 |
|---|---|---|---|---|---|---|
| 2007 PM | Est. 25000 | **PF63** 45.00 | **PF65** 55.00 | | | |

**KM# 35 2 POUNDS**
28.28 g., Copper-Nickel, 38.61 mm. **Ruler:** Elizabeth II **Rev:** Ernest Shacketon **Mint:** Pobjoy Mint

| Date | Mintage | VF20 | XF40 | MS60 | MS63 | MS65 |
|---|---|---|---|---|---|---|
| 2007 PM | — | — | — | — | 8.00 | 10.00 |

**KM# 35a 2 POUNDS**
28.28 g., 0.925 Silver 0.841 oz. ASW, 38.61 mm. **Ruler:** Elizabeth II **Subject:** Sir Ernest Henry Shackleton **Mint:** Pobjoy Mint

| Date | Mintage | VF20 | XF40 | MS60 | MS63 | MS65 |
|---|---|---|---|---|---|---|
| 2007 PM | Est. 10000 | **PF63** 45.00 | **PF65** 55.00 | | | |

**KM# 36 2 POUNDS**
28.28 g., Copper-Nickel, 38.61 mm. **Ruler:** Elizabeth II **Rev:** James Cook **Mint:** Pobjoy Mint

| Date | Mintage | VF20 | XF40 | MS60 | MS63 | MS65 |
|---|---|---|---|---|---|---|
| 2007 PM | — | — | — | — | 8.00 | 10.00 |

**KM# 36a 2 POUNDS**
28.28 g., 0.925 Silver 0.841 oz. ASW, 38.61 mm. **Ruler:** Elizabeth II **Subject:** James Cook **Mint:** Pobjoy Mint

| Date | Mintage | VF20 | XF40 | MS60 | MS63 | MS65 |
|---|---|---|---|---|---|---|
| 2007 PM | Est. 10000 | **PF63** 45.00 | **PF65** 55.00 | | | |

**KM# 37 2 POUNDS**
28.28 g., Copper-Nickel, 38.6 mm. **Ruler:** Elizabeth II **Subject:** Diamond Wedding Anniversary **Obv:** Conjoined busts with Prince Philip right **Obv. Legend:** SOUTH GEORGIA & SOUTH SANDWICH ISLANDS **Rev:** Bust of Princess Elizabeth facing **Rev. Legend:** Diamond Wedding of H.M. Queen Elizabeth II & H.R.H. Prince Philip **Rev. Inscription:** THE BRIDE **Edge:** Reeded **Mint:** Pobjoy Mint

| Date | Mintage | VF20 | XF40 | MS60 | MS63 | MS65 |
|---|---|---|---|---|---|---|
| 2007 | — | — | — | — | 12.00 | 15.00 |

**KM# 37a 2 POUNDS**
28.28 g., 0.925 Silver 0.841 oz. ASW, 38.6 mm. **Ruler:** Elizabeth II **Subject:** Diamond Wedding Anniversary **Obv:** Conjoined busts with Prince Philip right **Obv. Legend:** SOUTH GEORGIA & SOUTH SANDWICH ISLANDS **Rev:** Bust of Princess Elizabeth facing **Rev. Legend:** Diamond Wedding of H.M. Queen Elizabeth II & H.R.H. Prince Philip **Rev. Inscription:** THE BRIDE **Edge:** Reeded **Mint:** Pobjoy Mint

| Date | Mintage | VF20 | XF40 | MS60 | MS63 | MS65 |
|---|---|---|---|---|---|---|
| 2007 | 25,000 | **PF63** 60.00 | **PF65** 75.00 | | | |

**KM# 38 2 POUNDS**
28.28 g., Copper-Nickel, 38.6 mm. **Ruler:** Elizabeth II **Subject:** Diamond Wedding Anniversary **Obv:** Conjoined busts with Prince Philip right **Obv. Legend:** SOUTH GEORGIA & SOUTH SANDWICH ISLANDS **Rev:** Bust of the bridegroom facing **Rev. Legend:** Diamond Wedding of H.M. Queen Elizabeth II & H.R.H. Prince Philip **Rev. Inscription:** THE BRIDEGROOM **Edge:** Reeded **Mint:** Pobjoy Mint

| Date | Mintage | VF20 | XF40 | MS60 | MS63 | MS65 |
|---|---|---|---|---|---|---|
| 2007 | — | — | — | — | 12.00 | 15.00 |

**KM# 38a 2 POUNDS**
28.28 g., 0.925 Silver 0.841 oz. ASW, 38.6 mm. **Ruler:** Elizabeth II **Subject:** Diamond Wedding Anniversary **Obv:** Conjoined busts with Prince Philip right **Obv. Legend:** SOUTH GEORGIA & SOUTH SANDWICH ISLANDS **Rev:** Bust of the bridegroom facing **Rev. Legend:** Diamond Wedding of H.M. Queen Elizabeth II & H.R.H. Prince Philip **Rev. Inscription:** THE BRIDEGROOM **Edge:** Reeded **Mint:** Pobjoy Mint

| Date | Mintage | VF20 | XF40 | MS60 | MS63 | MS65 |
|---|---|---|---|---|---|---|
| 2007 | 25,000 | **PF63** 60.00 | **PF65** 75.00 | | | |

**KM# 39 2 POUNDS**
28.28 g., Copper-Nickel, 38.6 mm. **Ruler:** Elizabeth II **Subject:** Diamond Wedding Anniversary **Obv:** Conjoined busts with Prince Philip right **Obv. Legend:** SOUTH GEORGIA & SOUTH SANDWICH ISLANDS **Rev:** 1/2 length figures of royal engaged couple looking at each other **Rev. Legend:** Diamond Wedding of H.M. Queen Elizabeth II & H.R.H. Prince Philip **Rev. Inscription:** ROYAL ENGAGEMENT • JULY • 10 • 1947 **Edge:** Reeded **Mint:** Pobjoy Mint

| Date | Mintage | VF20 | XF40 | MS60 | MS63 | MS65 |
|---|---|---|---|---|---|---|
| 2007 | — | — | — | — | 12.00 | 15.00 |

**KM# 39a 2 POUNDS**
28.28 g., 0.925 Silver 0.841 oz. ASW, 38.6 mm. **Ruler:** Elizabeth II **Subject:** Diamond Wedding Anniversary **Obv:** Conjoined busts with Prince Philip right **Obv. Legend:** SOUTH GEORGIA & SOUTH SANDWICH ISLANDS **Rev:** 1/2 length figures of royal engaged couple looking at each other **Rev. Legend:** Diamond Wedding of H.M. Queen Elizabeth II & H.R.H. Prince Philip **Rev. Inscription:** ROYAL ENGAGEMENT • JULY • 10 • 1947 **Edge:** Reeded **Mint:** Pobjoy Mint

| Date | Mintage | VF20 | XF40 | MS60 | MS63 | MS65 |
|---|---|---|---|---|---|---|
| 2007 | 25,000 | **PF63** 60.00 | **PF65** 75.00 | | | |

**KM# 40 2 POUNDS**
28.28 g., Copper-Nickel, 38.6 mm. **Ruler:** Elizabeth II **Subject:** Diamond Wedding Anniversary **Obv:** Conjoined busts with Prince Philip right **Obv. Legend:** SOUTH GEORGIA & SOUTH SANDWICH ISLANDS **Rev:** Marriage license, jubilant crowd scene **Rev. Legend:** Diamond Wedding of H.M. Queen Elizabeth II & H.R.H. Prince Philip **Rev. Inscription:** THE MARRIAGE LICENSE **Edge:** Reeded **Mint:** Pobjoy Mint

| Date | Mintage | VF20 | XF40 | MS60 | MS63 | MS65 |
|---|---|---|---|---|---|---|
| 2007 | — | — | — | — | 12.00 | 15.00 |

### KM# 40a 2 POUNDS

28.28 g., 0.925 Silver 0.841 oz. ASW, 38.6 mm. **Ruler:** Elizabeth II **Subject:** Diamond Wedding Anniversary **Obv:** Conjoined busts with Prince Philip right **Obv. Legend:** SOUTH GEORGIA & SOUTH SANDWICH ISLANDS **Rev:** Marriage license, jubilant crowd scene **Rev. Legend:** Diamond Wedding of H.M. Queen Elizabeth II & H.R.H. Prince Philip **Rev. Inscription:** THE MARRIAGE LICENSE **Edge:** Reeded **Mint:** Pobjoy Mint

| Date | Mintage | VF20 | XF40 | MS60 | MS63 | MS65 |
|---|---|---|---|---|---|---|
| 2007 | 25,000 | PF63 60.00 | PF65 75.00 | | | |

### KM# 48 2 POUNDS

28.28 g., 0.925 Silver 0.841 oz. ASW **Ruler:** Elizabeth II **Rev:** King Penguin in color **Shape:** 38.61 **Mint:** Pobjoy Mint

| Date | Mintage | VF20 | XF40 | MS60 | MS63 | MS65 |
|---|---|---|---|---|---|---|
| 2007 PM | Est. 5000 | PF65 75.00 | | | | |

### KM# 42 2 POUNDS

28.28 g., Copper-Nickel, 38.61 mm. **Ruler:** Elizabeth II **Rev:** Four coinage portraits of Elizabeth II **Mint:** Pobjoy Mint

| Date | Mintage | VF20 | XF40 | MS60 | MS63 | MS65 |
|---|---|---|---|---|---|---|
| 2008 PM Proof | — | — | — | — | — | 15.00 |

### KM# 42a 2 POUNDS

28.28 g., 0.925 Silver 0.841 oz. ASW, 38.61 mm. **Ruler:** Elizabeth II **Subject:** Queen Elizabeth II in the Age of Queen Victoria **Mint:** Pobjoy Mint

| Date | Mintage | VF20 | XF40 | MS60 | MS63 | MS65 |
|---|---|---|---|---|---|---|
| 2008 PM | Est. 10000 | PF63 45.00 | PF65 55.00 | | | |

### KM# 49 2 POUNDS

28.28 g., Copper-Nickel, 38.61 mm. **Ruler:** Elizabeth II **Subject:** Royal Air Force, 90th Anniversary **Rev:** C 180 Hercules **Mint:** Pobjoy Mint

| Date | Mintage | VF20 | XF40 | MS60 | MS63 | MS65 |
|---|---|---|---|---|---|---|
| 2008 PM | — | — | — | — | — | 15.00 |

### KM# 49a 2 POUNDS

28.28 g., 0.925 Silver 0.841 oz. ASW, 38.61 mm. **Ruler:** Elizabeth II **Subject:** 90th Anniversary of the British Royal Air Force **Mint:** Pobjoy Mint

| Date | Mintage | VF20 | XF40 | MS60 | MS63 | MS65 |
|---|---|---|---|---|---|---|
| 2008 PM | Est. 10000 | PF63 45.00 | PF65 55.00 | | | |

### KM# 41 2 POUNDS

28.28 g., Copper-Nickel, 38.61 mm. **Ruler:** Elizabeth II **Subject:** The Nimrod Expedition **Rev:** Sailing ship stuck in ice **Mint:** Pobjoy Mint

| Date | Mintage | VF20 | XF40 | MS60 | MS63 | MS65 |
|---|---|---|---|---|---|---|
| 2009 PM | — | — | — | — | — | 15.00 |

### KM# 41a 2 POUNDS

28.28 g., 0.925 Silver 0.841 oz. ASW, 38.61 mm. **Ruler:** Elizabeth II **Subject:** 100th Anniversary of the British Antarctic Expedition **Mint:** Pobjoy Mint

| Date | Mintage | VF20 | XF40 | MS60 | MS63 | MS65 |
|---|---|---|---|---|---|---|
| 2009 PM | Est. 10000 | PF63 45.00 | PF65 55.00 | | | |

### KM# 50 2 POUNDS

28.28 g., Copper-Nickel, 38.61 mm. **Ruler:** Elizabeth II **Rev:** View of icebound sailing ship Terra Nova **Rev. Legend:** CENTENARY OF THE RACE TO THE SOUTH POLE **Mint:** Pobjoy Mint

| Date | Mintage | VF20 | XF40 | MS60 | MS63 | MS65 |
|---|---|---|---|---|---|---|
| 2010 PM | — | — | — | — | — | 15.00 |

### KM# 50a 2 POUNDS

28.28 g., 0.925 Silver 0.841 oz. ASW, 38.61 mm. **Ruler:** Elizabeth II **Subject:** 100th Anniversary of the Antarctic Expedition of Roald Amundesn and Robert Falcon Scott **Mint:** Pobjoy Mint

| Date | Mintage | VF20 | XF40 | MS60 | MS63 | MS65 |
|---|---|---|---|---|---|---|
| 2010 PM | Est. 10000 | PF63 45.00 | PF65 55.00 | | | |

### KM# 43 2 POUNDS

28.28 g., Copper-Nickel, 38.61 mm. **Ruler:** Elizabeth II **Subject:** Frozen Planet **Obv:** Bust with tiara right **Rev:** King Pengiun and young **Mint:** Pobjoy Mint

| Date | Mintage | VF20 | XF40 | MS60 | MS63 | MS65 |
|---|---|---|---|---|---|---|
| 2011 PM | — | — | — | — | 12.00 | 15.00 |

### KM# 43a 2 POUNDS

28.28 g., 0.925 Silver 0.841 oz. ASW, 38.61 mm. **Ruler:** Elizabeth II **Subject:** Frozen Planet **Rev:** King Penguin and young **Mint:** Pobjoy Mint

| Date | Mintage | VF20 | XF40 | MS60 | MS63 | MS65 |
|---|---|---|---|---|---|---|
| 2011 PM | — | PF63 65.00 | PF65 75.00 | | | |

### KM# 44 2 POUNDS

28.28 g., Copper-Nickel, 38.6 mm. **Ruler:** Elizabeth II **Obv:** Bust with tiara right **Rev:** Prince Philip and Elizabeth II, half-length facing above diamond, rays at side **Mint:** Pobjoy Mint

| Date | Mintage | VF20 | XF40 | MS60 | MS63 | MS65 |
|---|---|---|---|---|---|---|
| 2011 PM | — | — | — | — | 9.00 | 12.00 |

### KM# 44a 2 POUNDS

28.28 g., 0.925 Silver 0.841 oz. ASW, 38.6 mm. **Ruler:** Elizabeth II **Obv:** Bust with tiara right **Rev:** Prince Philip and Elizabeth II, half-lenght facing above diamond, rays at side **Mint:** Pobjoy Mint

| Date | Mintage | VF20 | XF40 | MS60 | MS63 | MS65 |
|---|---|---|---|---|---|---|
| 2011 PM | — | PF63 65.00 | PF65 75.00 | | | |

### KM# 51 2 POUNDS

28.28 g., Copper-Nickel, 38.61 mm. **Ruler:** Elizabeth II **Subject:** Royal Wedding **Rev:** Royal Arms of Prince William **Mint:** Pobjoy Mint

| Date | Mintage | VF20 | XF40 | MS60 | MS63 | MS65 |
|---|---|---|---|---|---|---|
| 2011 PM | — | — | — | — | — | 15.00 |

### KM# 51a 2 POUNDS

28.28 g., 0.925 Silver 0.841 oz. ASW, 38.61 mm. **Ruler:** Elizabeth II **Subject:** Marriage of Prince William and Catherine Middleton **Mint:** Pobjoy Mint

| Date | Mintage | VF20 | XF40 | MS60 | MS63 | MS65 |
|---|---|---|---|---|---|---|
| 2011 PM | Est. 10000 | PF63 45.00 | PF65 55.00 | | | |

### KM# 52 2 POUNDS

28.28 g., Copper-Nickel, 38.61 mm. **Ruler:** Elizabeth II **Subject:** Elizabeth II, 60th Anniversary of reign **Rev:** Queen Mother and Princess Elizabeth **Mint:** Pobjoy Mint

| Date | Mintage | VF20 | XF40 | MS60 | MS63 | MS65 |
|---|---|---|---|---|---|---|
| 2012 PM | — | — | — | — | — | 15.00 |

### KM# 52a 2 POUNDS

28.28 g., 0.925 Silver 0.841 oz. ASW, 38.61 mm. **Ruler:** Elizabeth II **Subject:** 60th Anniversary of the Coronation of Queen Elizabeth II **Mint:** Pobjoy Mint

| Date | Mintage | VF20 | XF40 | MS60 | MS63 | MS65 |
|---|---|---|---|---|---|---|
| 2012 PM | Est. 10000 | PF63 45.00 | PF65 55.00 | | | |

### KM# 53 2 POUNDS

28.28 g., Copper-Nickel, 38.61 mm. **Ruler:** Elizabeth II **Rev:** Elizabeth II in hat **Mint:** Pobjoy Mint

| Date | Mintage | VF20 | XF40 | MS60 | MS63 | MS65 |
|---|---|---|---|---|---|---|
| 2012 PM | — | — | — | — | — | 15.00 |

### KM# 53a 2 POUNDS

28.28 g., 0.925 Silver 0.841 oz. ASW, 38.61 mm. **Ruler:** Elizabeth II **Subject:** Queen Elizabeth II - Christmas Speech **Mint:** Pobjoy Mint

| Date | Mintage | VF20 | XF40 | MS60 | MS63 | MS65 |
|---|---|---|---|---|---|---|
| 2012 PM | Est. 10000 | PF63 45.00 | PF65 55.00 | | | |

### KM# 54 2 POUNDS

28.28 g., Copper-Nickel, 38.61 mm. **Ruler:** Elizabeth II **Subject:** Prince William and Kate Middleton, 1st Wedding Anniversary **Rev:** First Kiss on Buckingham Palace Balcony **Mint:** Pobjoy Mint

| Date | Mintage | VF20 | XF40 | MS60 | MS63 | MS65 |
|---|---|---|---|---|---|---|
| 2012 PM | — | — | — | — | — | 15.00 |

### KM# 54a 2 POUNDS

28.28 g., 0.925 Silver 0.841 oz. ASW, 38.61 mm. **Ruler:** Elizabeth II **Subject:** Marriage of Prince William and Catherine Middleton **Mint:** Pobjoy Mint

| Date | Mintage | VF20 | XF40 | MS60 | MS63 | MS65 |
|---|---|---|---|---|---|---|
| 2012 PM | Est. 10000 | PF63 45.00 | PF65 55.00 | | | |

### KM# 31a 2 POUNDS

28.28 g., 0.925 Silver 0.841 oz. ASW, 38.61 mm. **Ruler:** Elizabeth II **Subject:** Queen Elizabeth II **Mint:** Pobjoy Mint

| Date | Mintage | VF20 | XF40 | MS60 | MS63 | MS65 |
|---|---|---|---|---|---|---|
| 2013 PM | Est. 10000 | PF63 45.00 | PF65 55.00 | | | |

### KM# 59 2 POUNDS

10.00 g., 0.990 Titanium 0.3183 oz., 36.1 mm. **Ruler:** Elizabeth II **Subject:** Blue Whale **Mint:** Pobjoy Mint **Note:** Blue in color.

| Date | Mintage | VF20 | XF40 | MS60 | MS63 | MS65 |
|---|---|---|---|---|---|---|
| 2013 PM | Est. 5000 | PF63 45.00 | PF65 55.00 | | | |

### KM# 60 2 POUNDS

28.28 g., Copper-Nickel, 38.6 mm. **Ruler:** Elizabeth II **Subject:** Blue Whale **Mint:** Pobjoy Mint

| Date | Mintage | VF20 | XF40 | MS60 | MS63 | MS65 |
|---|---|---|---|---|---|---|
| 2013 PM | — | — | — | — | — | 75.00 |

### KM# 60a 2 POUNDS

28.28 g., Silver, 38.6 mm. **Ruler:** Elizabeth II **Subject:** Blue Whale **Mint:** Pobjoy Mint

| Date | Mintage | VF20 | XF40 | MS60 | MS63 | MS65 |
|---|---|---|---|---|---|---|
| 2013 PM | Est. 10000 | PF63 50.00 | PF65 60.00 | | | |

### KM# 61 2 POUNDS

28.28 g., Copper-Nickel, 38.6 mm. **Ruler:** Elizabeth II **Subject:** Weddell Seal Pup **Mint:** Pobjoy Mint

| Date | Mintage | VF20 | XF40 | MS60 | MS63 | MS65 |
|---|---|---|---|---|---|---|
| 2013 PM Uncirculated | — | — | — | — | — | 15.00 |

### KM# 61a 2 POUNDS

28.28 g., Silver, 38.6 mm. **Ruler:** Elizabeth II **Subject:** Weddell Seal Pup **Mint:** Pobjoy Mint

| Date | Mintage | VF20 | XF40 | MS60 | MS63 | MS65 |
|---|---|---|---|---|---|---|
| 2013 PM | Est. 10000 | PF63 50.00 | PF65 60.00 | | | |

### KM# 62 2 POUNDS

28.28 g., Copper-Nickel, 38.61 mm. **Ruler:** Elizabeth II **Subject:** Birth of Prince George **Rev:** William and Catherine kissing, blue stork above **Mint:** Pobjoy Mint

| Date | Mintage | VF20 | XF40 | MS60 | MS63 | MS65 |
|---|---|---|---|---|---|---|
| 2013 PM | — | — | — | — | — | 15.00 |

### KM# 62a 2 POUNDS

28.28 g., 0.925 Silver 0.841 oz. ASW, 38.61 mm. **Ruler:** Elizabeth II **Subject:** Birth of Prince George **Rev:** William and Catherine kissing, blue stork above **Mint:** Pobjoy Mint

| Date | Mintage | VF20 | XF40 | MS60 | MS63 | MS65 |
|---|---|---|---|---|---|---|
| 2013 PM | 10,000 | PF63 50.00 | PF65 60.00 | | | |

### KM# 45 4 POUNDS

1.24 g., 0.999 Gold 0.0398 oz. AGW, 13.92 mm. **Ruler:** Elizabeth II **Rev:** Rockhopper Penguin **Mint:** Pobjoy Mint

| Date | Mintage | VF20 | XF40 | MS60 | MS63 | MS65 |
|---|---|---|---|---|---|---|
| 2006 PM | Est. 5000 | PF65 90.00 | | | | |

### KM# 46 4 POUNDS

1.24 g., 0.999 Gold 0.0398 oz. AGW, 13.92 mm. **Ruler:** Elizabeth II **Subject:** Henrik Johan Ibsen, 100th Anniversary of Death **Rev:** Bust facing **Mint:** Pobjoy Mint

| Date | Mintage | VF20 | XF40 | MS60 | MS63 | MS65 |
|---|---|---|---|---|---|---|
| 2006 PM | Est. 7500 | PF65 90.00 | | | | |

### KM# 19 10 POUNDS

155.51 g., 0.999 Silver 4.9948 oz. ASW, 65 mm. **Ruler:** Elizabeth II **Obv:** Crowned bust right **Rev:** Capt. Cook, ship and map **Edge:** Reeded **Mint:** Pobjoy Mint

| Date | Mintage | VF20 | XF40 | MS60 | MS63 | MS65 |
|---|---|---|---|---|---|---|
| 2003 PM | 2,003 | PF65 225 | | | | |

### KM# 8 20 POUNDS

6.22 g., 0.9999 Gold 0.200 oz. AGW, 22 mm. **Ruler:** Elizabeth II **Obv:** Crowned bust right **Rev:** Sir Ernest H. Shackleton and ship **Edge:** Reeded **Mint:** Pobjoy Mint

| Date | Mintage | VF20 | XF40 | MS60 | MS63 | MS65 |
|---|---|---|---|---|---|---|
| 2001 PM | — | PF65 400 | | | | |

### KM# 10 20 POUNDS

6.22 g., 0.9999 Gold 0.200 oz. AGW, 22 mm. **Ruler:** Elizabeth II **Obv:** Crowned bust right **Rev:** Sir Joseph Banks cameo and ship **Mint:** Pobjoy Mint

| Date | Mintage | VF20 | XF40 | MS60 | MS63 | MS65 |
|---|---|---|---|---|---|---|
| 2001 PM | Est. 2000 | PF65 375 | | | | |

### KM# 12 20 POUNDS

6.22 g., 0.999 Gold 0.1998 oz. AGW, 22 mm. **Ruler:** Elizabeth II **Subject:** Queen Elizabeth II's Golden Jubilee **Obv:** Crowned bust right **Rev:** Young crowned bust right **Edge:** Reeded **Mint:** Pobjoy Mint

| Date | Mintage | VF20 | XF40 | MS60 | MS63 | MS65 |
|---|---|---|---|---|---|---|
| 2002 PM | 2,002 | PF65 375 | | | | |

### KM# 14 20 POUNDS

6.22 g., 0.999 Gold 0.1998 oz. AGW, 22 mm. **Ruler:** Elizabeth II **Subject:** Queen Elizabeth II's Golden Jubilee **Obv:** Crowned bust right **Rev:** National arms **Edge:** Reeded **Mint:** Pobjoy Mint

| Date | Mintage | VF20 | XF40 | MS60 | MS63 | MS65 |
|---|---|---|---|---|---|---|
| 2002 PM | 2,002 | PF65 375 | | | | |

### KM# 16 20 POUNDS

6.22 g., 0.9999 Gold 0.200 oz. AGW, 22 mm. **Ruler:** Elizabeth II **Subject:** Princess Diana **Obv:** Crowned bust right **Rev:** Diana's portrait **Edge:** reeded **Mint:** Pobjoy Mint

| Date | Mintage | VF20 | XF40 | MS60 | MS63 | MS65 |
|---|---|---|---|---|---|---|
| 2002 PM | — | PF65 400 | | | | |

### KM# 47 20 POUNDS

6.22 g., 0.999 Gold 0.1998 oz. AGW, 22 mm. **Ruler:** Elizabeth II **Subject:** Henrik Johan Ibsen, 100th Anniversary of Death **Rev:** Bust facing **Mint:** Pobjoy Mint

| Date | Mintage | VF20 | XF40 | MS60 | MS63 | MS65 |
|---|---|---|---|---|---|---|
| 2006 PM | Est. 2000 | PF65 375 | | | | |

### KM# 57 20 POUNDS

6.22 g., 0.999 Gold 0.1998 oz. AGW, 22 mm. **Ruler:** Elizabeth II **Subject:** Kon Tiki Expedition 65th Anniversary **Rev:** Kon Tiki Ship **Mint:** Pobjoy Mint

| Date | Mintage | VF20 | XF40 | MS60 | MS63 | MS65 |
|---|---|---|---|---|---|---|
| 2012 PM | — | PF65 400 | | | | |

### KM# 58 20 POUNDS

6.22 g., 0.999 Gold 0.1998 oz. AGW **Ruler:** Elizabeth II **Subject:** Kon Tiki Expedition **Obv:** Portraits right **Rev:** Kon Tiki Mask **Mint:** Pobjoy Mint

| Date | Mintage | VF20 | XF40 | MS60 | MS63 | MS65 |
|---|---|---|---|---|---|---|
| 2012 PM | — | PF65 400 | | | | |

# SPAIN

The Kingdom of Spain, forming the greater part of the Iberian Peninsula of southwest Europe, has an area of 195,988 sq. mi. (504,714 sq. km.) and a population of 39.4 million including the Balearic and the Canary Islands. Capital: Madrid. The economy is based on agriculture, industry and tourism. Machinery, fruit, vegetables and chemicals are exported.

**RULER**

Juan Carlos I, 1975-2014
Felipe VI, 2014-

**MINT MARK**

After 1982
(M) - Crowned "M" – Madrid

## KINGDOM

## DECIMAL COINAGE

100 Centimos = 1 Peseta

### KM# 832 PESETA

0.55 g., Aluminum, 14 mm. **Ruler:** Juan Carlos I **Obv:** Vertical line divides head left from value **Rev:** Crowned shield flanked by pillars with banner **Edge:** Plain

| Date | Mintage | VF20 | XF40 | MS60 | MS63 | MS65 |
|---|---|---|---|---|---|---|
| 2001 | 62,300,000 | — | 0.10 | 0.30 | 0.50 | — |

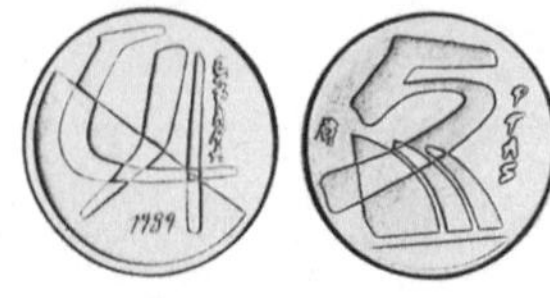

### KM# 833 5 PESETAS

3.00 g., Aluminum-Bronze, 17.5 mm. **Ruler:** Juan Carlos I **Obv:** Stylized JC I and date **Rev:** Value above stylized sailboats **Edge:** Plain

| Date | Mintage | VF20 | XF40 | MS60 | MS63 | MS65 |
|---|---|---|---|---|---|---|
| 2001 | 294,000,000 | — | 0.10 | 0.25 | 0.35 | — |

### KM# 1013 25 PESETAS

4.25 g., Aluminum-Bronze, 19.5 mm. **Ruler:** Juan Carlos I **Obv:** Center hole divides bust left and vertical letters **Rev:** Crowned above center hole, order collar at right, value at left **Edge:** Plain

| Date | Mintage | VF20 | XF40 | MS60 | MS63 | MS65 |
|---|---|---|---|---|---|---|
| 2001 | 91,200,000 | — | — | 2.00 | 2.50 | — |

### KM# 1016 100 PESETAS

9.25 g., Aluminum-Bronze, 24.5 mm. **Ruler:** Juan Carlos I **Subject:** 132nd Anniversary of the Peseta **Obv:** Head left **Rev:** Seated allegorical figure from an old coin design **Edge:** Fleur-de-lis repeated

| Date | Mintage | VF20 | XF40 | MS60 | MS63 | MS65 |
|---|---|---|---|---|---|---|
| 2001 | 142,800,000 | — | — | 2.25 | 2.75 | — |

### KM# 924 500 PESETAS

12.00 g., Aluminum-Bronze, 28 mm. **Ruler:** Juan Carlos I **Obv:** Conjoined heads of Juan Carlos and Sofia left **Rev:** Crowned shield flanked by pillars with banner, vertical value at right

| Date | Mintage | VF20 | XF40 | MS60 | MS63 | MS65 |
|---|---|---|---|---|---|---|
| 2001 | 3,300,000 | — | — | 7.00 | 9.00 | — |

### KM# 1131 500 PESETAS

6.73 g., Silver, 26.96 mm. **Ruler:** Juan Carlos I **Obv:** Minting equipment **Obv. Legend:** ESPAÑA **Rev:** Copy of Charles II silver Reales coin **Rev. Legend:** CASA DE LA MONEDA DE SEGOVIA **Edge:** Reeded **Note:** Aqueduct and crowned M mintmarks appear on obverse

| Date | Mintage | VF20 | XF40 | MS60 | MS63 | MS65 |
|---|---|---|---|---|---|---|
| 2001 | 20,000 | PF63 21.00 | | | | |

### KM# 1017 2000 PESETAS

18.00 g., 0.925 Silver 0.5353 oz. ASW, 32.9 mm. **Ruler:** Juan Carlos I **Subject:** 132nd Anniversary of the Peseta **Obv:** Conjoined heads left **Rev:** Seated allegorical design from the 1869 Spanish coin series **Edge:** Plain

| Date | Mintage | VF20 | XF40 | MS60 | MS63 | MS65 |
|---|---|---|---|---|---|---|
| 2001 | 1,942,835 | — | — | — | 24.00 | 28.00 |

### KM# 1038 2000 PESETAS

27.00 g., 0.925 Silver 0.803 oz. ASW, 40 mm. **Ruler:** Juan Carlos I **Subject:** Segovia Mint's 500th Anniversary **Obv:** Hammer coining scene within beaded circle **Rev:** Segovia Mint 8 reales coin design of 1588 **Edge:** Reeded

| Date | Mintage | VF20 | XF40 | MS60 | MS63 | MS65 |
|---|---|---|---|---|---|---|
| 2001 | 15,000 | PF65 55.00 | | | | |

## EURO COINAGE

European Union Issues

### KM# 1040 EURO CENT

2.30 g., Copper Plated Steel, 16.25 mm. **Ruler:** Juan Carlos I **Obv:** Cathedral of Santiago de Compostela **Rev:** Value and globe **Edge:** Plain

| Date | Mintage | VF20 | XF40 | MS60 | MS63 | MS65 |
|---|---|---|---|---|---|---|
| 2001 (M) | 130,900,000 | — | — | 0.15 | 0.25 | 0.30 |

| Date | Mintage | VF20 | XF40 | MS60 | MS63 | MS65 |
|---|---|---|---|---|---|---|
| 2002 (M) | 141,100,000 | — | — | 0.15 | 0.25 | 0.30 |
| 2002 (M) | 35,000 | PF65 10.00 | | | | |
| 2003 (M) | 670,500,000 | — | — | 0.15 | 0.25 | 0.30 |
| 2003 (M) | 20,000 | PF65 10.00 | | | | |
| 2004 (M) | 206,700,000 | — | — | 0.15 | 0.25 | 0.30 |
| 2005 (M) | 444,200,000 | — | — | 0.15 | 0.25 | 0.30 |
| 2005 (M) | 3,000 | PF65 10.00 | | | | |
| 2006 (M) | 383,900,000 | — | — | 0.15 | 0.25 | 0.35 |
| 2007 (M) | 383,958,434 | — | — | 0.15 | 0.25 | 0.35 |
| 2007 (M) | 5,000 | PF65 10.00 | | | | |
| 2008 (M) | 374,556,940 | — | — | 0.15 | 0.25 | 0.35 |
| 2008 (M) | 5,000 | PF65 10.00 | | | | |
| 2009 (M) | 131,427,500 | — | — | 0.15 | 0.25 | 0.35 |
| 2009 (M) | 5,000 | PF65 10.00 | | | | |

### KM# 1144 EURO CENT

2.30 g., Copper Plated Steel, 16.25 mm. **Ruler:** Juan Carlos I **Obv:** Cathedral of Santiago de Compostela **Rev:** Value and globe

| Date | Mintage | VF20 | XF40 | MS60 | MS63 | MS65 |
|---|---|---|---|---|---|---|
| 2010 | 227,330,000 | — | — | 0.15 | 0.25 | 0.35 |
| 2010 | — | PF65 10.00 | | | | |
| 2011 | 339,340,200 | — | — | 0.15 | 0.25 | 0.35 |
| 2011 | — | PF65 10.00 | | | | |
| 2012 | 400,572,000 | — | — | 0.15 | 0.25 | 0.35 |
| 2012 | — | PF65 10.00 | | | | |
| 2013 | — | — | — | 0.15 | 0.25 | 0.35 |
| 2013 | — | PF65 10.00 | | | | |
| 2014 | — | — | — | 0.15 | 0.25 | 0.35 |
| 2014 | — | PF65 10.00 | | | | |

### KM# 1041 2 EURO CENT

3.06 g., Copper Plated Steel, 18.75 mm. **Ruler:** Juan Carlos I **Obv:** Cathedral of Santiago de Compostela **Rev:** Value and globe **Edge:** Grooved

| Date | Mintage | VF20 | XF40 | MS60 | MS63 | MS65 |
|---|---|---|---|---|---|---|
| 2001 (M) | 463,100,000 | — | — | 0.15 | 0.25 | 0.35 |
| 2002 (M) | 4,100,000 | — | — | 0.65 | 1.25 | 1.50 |
| 2002 (M) | 35,000 | PF65 10.00 | | | | |
| 2003 (M) | 31,600,000 | — | — | 0.50 | 1.00 | 1.25 |
| 2003 (M) | 20,000 | PF65 10.00 | | | | |
| 2004 (M) | 206,700,000 | — | — | 0.15 | 0.25 | 0.30 |
| 2005 (M) | 275,100,000 | — | — | 0.15 | 0.25 | 0.30 |
| 2005 (M) | 3,000 | PF65 10.00 | | | | |
| 2006 (M) | 262,200,000 | — | — | 0.15 | 0.25 | 0.30 |
| 2007 (M) | 185,258,434 | — | — | 0.15 | 0.25 | 0.30 |
| 2007 (M) | 5,000 | PF65 10.00 | | | | |
| 2008 (M) | 191,256,940 | — | — | 0.15 | 0.25 | 0.30 |
| 2008 (M) | 5,000 | PF65 10.00 | | | | |
| 2009 (M) | 164,027,500 | — | — | 0.15 | 0.25 | 0.30 |
| 2009 (M) | 5,000 | PF65 10.00 | | | | |

### KM# 1145 2 EURO CENT

3.06 g., Copper Plated Steel, 18.75 mm. **Ruler:** Juan Carlos I **Obv:** Cathedral of Santiago de Compostela **Rev:** Value and globe **Edge:** Grooved

| Date | Mintage | VF20 | XF40 | MS60 | MS63 | MS65 |
|---|---|---|---|---|---|---|
| 2010 | 153,130,000 | — | — | 0.15 | 0.25 | 0.30 |
| 2010 | — | PF65 10.00 | | | | |
| 2011 | 96,450,200 | — | — | 0.15 | 0.25 | 0.30 |
| 2011 | — | PF65 10.00 | | | | |
| 2012 | 99,572,000 | — | — | 0.15 | 0.25 | 0.30 |
| 2012 | — | PF65 10.00 | | | | |
| 2013 | — | — | — | 0.15 | 0.25 | 0.30 |
| 2013 | — | PF65 10.00 | | | | |
| 2014 | — | — | — | — | — | 0.30 |
| 2014 | — | PF65 10.00 | | | | |

### KM# 1042 5 EURO CENT

3.92 g., Copper Plated Steel, 21.25 mm. **Ruler:** Juan Carlos I **Obv:** Cathedral of Santiago de Compostela **Rev:** Value and globe **Edge:** Plain

| Date | Mintage | VF20 | XF40 | MS60 | MS63 | MS65 |
|---|---|---|---|---|---|---|
| 2001 (M) | 216,100,000 | — | — | 0.25 | 0.50 | 0.60 |
| 2002 (M) | 8,300,000 | — | — | 0.50 | 1.00 | 1.50 |
| 2002 (M) | 35,000 | PF65 10.00 | | | | |
| 2003 (M) | 327,600,000 | — | — | 0.25 | 0.50 | 0.60 |
| 2003 (M) | 8,904 | PF65 10.00 | | | | |
| 2004 (M) | 258,700,000 | — | — | 0.20 | 0.40 | 0.50 |
| 2005 (M) | 411,400,000 | — | — | 0.20 | 0.40 | 0.50 |
| 2005 (M) | 3,000 | PF65 10.00 | | | | |
| 2006 (M) | 142,800,000 | — | — | 0.20 | 0.40 | 0.50 |
| 2007 (M) | 247,058,434 | — | — | 0.20 | 0.40 | 0.50 |
| 2007 (M) | 5,000 | PF65 10.00 | | | | |
| 2008 (M) | 239,056,940 | — | — | 0.20 | 0.40 | 0.50 |
| 2008 (M) | 2,000 | PF65 10.00 | | | | |
| 2009 (M) | 219,737,500 | — | — | 0.20 | 0.40 | 0.50 |
| 2009 (M) | 5,000 | PF65 10.00 | | | | |

### KM# 1146 5 EURO CENT

3.92 g., Copper Plated Steel, 21.25 mm. **Ruler:** Juan Carlos I **Obv:** Cathedral of Santiago de Compostela **Rev:** Value and globe

| Date | Mintage | VF20 | XF40 | MS60 | MS63 | MS65 |
|---|---|---|---|---|---|---|
| 2010 | 203,130,000 | — | — | 0.20 | 0.40 | 0.50 |
| 2010 | — | PF65 10.00 | | | | |
| 2011 | 97,140,200 | — | — | 0.20 | 0.40 | 0.50 |
| 2011 | — | PF65 10.00 | | | | |
| 2012 | 49,772,000 | — | — | 0.20 | 0.40 | 0.50 |
| 2012 | — | PF65 10.00 | | | | |
| 2013 | — | — | — | 0.20 | 0.40 | 0.50 |
| 2013 | — | PF65 10.00 | | | | |
| 2014 | — | — | — | — | — | 0.50 |
| 2014 | — | PF65 10.00 | | | | |

### KM# 1043 10 EURO CENT

4.10 g., Brass, 19.75 mm. **Ruler:** Juan Carlos I **Obv:** Head of Cervantes with ruffed collar 1/4 left within star border **Rev:** Value and map **Edge:** Reeded

| Date | Mintage | VF20 | XF40 | MS60 | MS63 | MS65 |
|---|---|---|---|---|---|---|
| 2001 (M) | 160,100,000 | — | — | 0.30 | 0.60 | 0.75 |
| 2002 (M) | 113,100,000 | — | — | 0.30 | 0.60 | 0.75 |
| 2002 (M) | 35,000 | PF65 10.00 | | | | |
| 2003 (M) | 292,500,000 | — | — | 0.35 | 0.70 | 0.90 |
| 2003 (M) | 20,000 | PF65 10.00 | | | | |
| 2004 (M) | 121,900,000 | — | — | 0.20 | 0.40 | 0.50 |
| 2005 (M) | 321,300,000 | — | — | 0.20 | 0.40 | 0.50 |
| 2005 (M) | 3,000 | PF65 10.00 | | | | |
| 2006 (M) | 91,800,000 | — | — | 0.20 | 0.40 | 0.50 |

### KM# 1070 10 EURO CENT

4.10 g., Brass, 19.75 mm. **Ruler:** Juan Carlos I **Obv:** Cervantes **Rev:** Relief map of Western Europe, stars, lines and value **Edge:** Reeded

| Date | Mintage | VF20 | XF40 | MS60 | MS63 | MS65 |
|---|---|---|---|---|---|---|
| 2007 (M) | 132,058,000 | — | — | 0.40 | 0.75 | 1.00 |
| 2007 (M) | 5,000 | PF65 12.00 | | | | |
| 2008 (M) | 142,256,940 | — | — | 0.40 | 0.75 | 1.00 |
| 2008 (M) | 5,000 | PF65 12.00 | | | | |
| 2009 (M) | 151,327,500 | — | — | 0.40 | 0.75 | 1.00 |
| 2009 (M) | 5,000 | PF65 12.00 | | | | |

### KM# 1147 10 EURO CENT

4.10 g., Brass, 19.75 mm. **Ruler:** Juan Carlos I **Obv:** Cervantes bust at right **Rev:** Relief map of Western Europe, stars, lines and value **Edge:** Reeded

| Date | Mintage | VF20 | XF40 | MS60 | MS63 | MS65 |
|---|---|---|---|---|---|---|
| 2010 | 104,930,000 | — | — | 0.40 | 0.75 | 1.00 |
| 2010 | — | PF65 12.00 | | | | |
| 2011 | 4,440,200 | — | — | 0.40 | 0.75 | 1.00 |
| 2011 | — | PF65 12.00 | | | | |
| 2012 | 3,672,000 | — | — | 0.40 | 0.75 | 1.00 |
| 2012 | — | PF65 12.00 | | | | |
| 2013 | — | — | — | 0.40 | 0.75 | 1.00 |
| 2013 | — | PF65 12.00 | | | | |
| 2014 | — | — | — | — | — | 1.00 |
| 2014 | — | PF65 12.00 | | | | |

### KM# 1044 20 EURO CENT

5.74 g., Brass, 22.25 mm. **Ruler:** Juan Carlos I **Obv:** Head of Cervantes with ruffed collar 1/4 left within star border **Rev:** Value and map **Edge:** Notched

| Date | Mintage | VF20 | XF40 | MS60 | MS63 | MS65 |
|---|---|---|---|---|---|---|
| 2001 (M) | 146,600,000 | — | — | 0.50 | 1.00 | 1.25 |
| 2002 (M) | 91,500,000 | — | — | 0.30 | 0.60 | 0.75 |
| 2002 (M) | 35,000 | PF65 12.00 | | | | |
| 2003 (M) | 4,100,000 | — | — | 0.65 | 1.25 | 1.50 |
| 2003 (M) | 20,000 | PF65 12.00 | | | | |
| 2004 (M) | 3,900,000 | — | — | 0.30 | 0.60 | 0.75 |
| 2005 (M) | 4,000,000 | — | — | 0.30 | 0.60 | 0.75 |
| 2005 (M) | 3,000 | PF65 12.00 | | | | |
| 2006 (M) | 102,000,000 | — | — | 0.30 | 0.60 | 0.75 |

### KM# 1071 20 EURO CENT

5.74 g., Brass, 22.25 mm. **Ruler:** Juan Carlos I **Obv:** Cervantes **Rev:** Relief map of Western Europe, stars, lines and value **Edge:** Notched

| Date | Mintage | VF20 | XF40 | MS60 | MS63 | MS65 |
|---|---|---|---|---|---|---|
| 2007 (M) | 46,458,000 | — | — | 0.50 | 1.00 | 1.25 |
| 2007 (M) | 5,000 | PF65 12.00 | | | | |
| 2008 (M) | 102,256,940 | — | — | 0.50 | 1.00 | 1.25 |
| 2008 (M) | 2,000 | PF65 12.00 | | | | |
| 2009 (M) | 75,327,500 | — | — | 0.50 | 1.00 | 1.25 |
| 2009 (M) | 5,000 | PF65 12.00 | | | | |

### KM# 1148 20 EURO CENT

5.74 g., Brass, 22.25 mm. **Ruler:** Juan Carlos I **Obv:** Cervantes bust at right **Rev:** Relief map of Western Europe, stars, lines and value **Edge:** Notched

| Date | Mintage | VF20 | XF40 | MS60 | MS63 | MS65 |
|---|---|---|---|---|---|---|
| 2010 | 3,830,000 | — | — | 0.50 | 1.00 | 1.25 |
| 2010 | — | PF65 12.00 | | | | |
| 2011 | 3,940,200 | — | — | 0.50 | 1.00 | 1.25 |
| 2011 | — | PF65 12.00 | | | | |
| 2012 | 26,272,000 | — | — | 0.50 | 1.00 | 1.25 |
| 2012 | — | PF65 12.00 | | | | |
| 2013 | — | — | — | 0.50 | 1.00 | 1.25 |
| 2013 | — | PF65 12.00 | | | | |
| 2014 | — | — | — | 0.50 | 1.00 | 1.25 |
| 2014 | — | PF65 12.00 | | | | |

### KM# 1045 50 EURO CENT

7.80 g., Brass, 24.25 mm. **Ruler:** Juan Carlos I **Obv:** Head of Cervantes with ruffed collar 1/4 left within star border **Rev:** Value and map **Edge:** Reeded

| Date | Mintage | VF20 | XF40 | MS60 | MS63 | MS65 |
|---|---|---|---|---|---|---|
| 2001 (M) | 351,100,000 | — | — | 0.50 | 1.00 | 1.25 |
| 2002 (M) | 9,800,000 | — | — | 1.50 | 3.00 | 3.50 |
| 2002 (M) | 35,000 | PF65 12.00 | | | | |
| 2003 (M) | 6,000,000 | — | — | 1.50 | 3.00 | 3.50 |
| 2003 (M) | 20,000 | PF65 12.00 | | | | |
| 2004 (M) | 4,400,000 | — | — | 0.75 | 1.50 | 2.00 |
| 2005 (M) | 3,900,000 | — | — | 0.65 | 1.25 | 1.50 |
| 2005 (M) | 3,000 | PF65 12.00 | | | | |
| 2006 (M) | 4,000,000 | — | — | 0.65 | 1.25 | 1.50 |

### KM# 1072 50 EURO CENT

7.80 g., Brass, 24.25 mm. **Ruler:** Juan Carlos I **Obv:** Cervantes **Rev:** Relief map of Western Europe, stars, lines and value **Edge:** Reeded

| Date | Mintage | VF20 | XF40 | MS60 | MS63 | MS65 |
|---|---|---|---|---|---|---|
| 2007 (M) | 3,958,000 | — | — | 0.65 | 1.25 | 1.50 |
| 2007 (M) | 5,000 | PF65 12.00 | | | | |

| Date | Mintage | VF20 | XF40 | MS60 | MS63 | MS65 |
|---|---|---|---|---|---|---|
| 2008 (M) | 3,956,940 | — | — | 0.65 | 1.25 | 1.50 |
| 2008 (M) | 5,000 | PF65 12.00 | | | | |
| 2009 (M) | 3,927,500 | — | — | 0.65 | 1.25 | 1.50 |
| 2009 (M) | 5,000 | PF65 12.00 | | | | |

**KM# 1149 50 EURO CENT**
7.80 g., Brass, 24.25 mm. **Ruler:** Juan Carlos I **Obv:** Cervantes bust at right **Rev:** Relief map of Western Europe, stars, lines and value **Edge:** Reeded

| Date | Mintage | VF20 | XF40 | MS60 | MS63 | MS65 |
|---|---|---|---|---|---|---|
| 2010 | 3,930,000 | — | — | 0.65 | 1.25 | 1.50 |
| 2010 | — | PF65 12.00 | | | | |
| 2011 | — | — | — | 0.65 | 1.25 | 1.50 |
| 2011 | — | PF65 12.00 | | | | |
| 2012 | 4,072,000 | — | — | 0.65 | 1.25 | 1.50 |
| 2012 | — | PF65 12.00 | | | | |
| 2013 | — | — | — | 0.65 | 1.25 | 1.50 |
| 2013 | — | PF65 12.00 | | | | |

**KM# 1046 EURO**
7.50 g., Bi-Metallic Copper-Nickel center in Nickel-Brass ring, 23.25 mm. **Ruler:** Juan Carlos I **Obv:** Head 1/4 left within circle and star border **Rev:** Value and map within circle **Edge:** Segmented reeding

| Date | Mintage | VF20 | XF40 | MS60 | MS63 | MS65 |
|---|---|---|---|---|---|---|
| 2001 (M) | 259,100,000 | — | — | 1.50 | 3.00 | 4.00 |
| 2002 (M) | 335,600,000 | — | — | 1.00 | 2.00 | 2.50 |
| 2002 (M) | 23,000 | PF65 15.00 | | | | |
| 2003 (M) | 297,400,000 | — | — | 1.00 | 2.00 | 2.50 |
| 2003 (M) | 20,000 | PF65 15.00 | | | | |
| 2004 (M) | 9,870,000 | — | — | 1.00 | 2.00 | 2.50 |
| 2005 (M) | 77,800,000 | — | — | 1.00 | 2.00 | 2.50 |
| 2005 (M) | 3,000 | PF65 15.00 | | | | |
| 2006 (M) | 101,600,000 | — | — | 1.00 | 2.00 | 2.50 |

**KM# 1073 EURO**
7.50 g., Bi-Metallic Copper-Nickel center in Nickel-Brass ring, 23.25 mm. **Ruler:** Juan Carlos I **Obv:** King's portrait **Rev:** Relief map of Western Europe, stars, lines and value **Edge:** Segmented reeding

| Date | Mintage | VF20 | XF40 | MS60 | MS63 | MS65 |
|---|---|---|---|---|---|---|
| 2007 (M) | 150,558,000 | — | — | 1.50 | 3.00 | 3.50 |
| 2007 (M) | 5,000 | PF65 15.00 | | | | |
| 2008 (M) | 154,356,940 | — | — | 1.50 | 3.00 | 3.50 |
| 2008 (M) | 5,000 | PF65 15.00 | | | | |
| 2009 (M) | 60,527,500 | — | — | 1.50 | 3.00 | 3.50 |
| 2009 (M) | 5,000 | PF65 15.00 | | | | |

**KM# 1150 EURO**
7.50 g., Bi-Metallic Copper-Nickel center in Nickel-Brass ring, 23.25 mm. **Ruler:** Juan Carlos I **Obv:** King's portrait at right **Rev:** Relief map of Western Europe, stars, lines and value **Edge:** Segmented reeding

| Date | Mintage | VF20 | XF40 | MS60 | MS63 | MS65 |
|---|---|---|---|---|---|---|
| 2010 | 40,030,000 | — | — | 1.50 | 3.00 | 3.50 |
| 2010 | — | PF65 15.00 | | | | |
| 2011 | 100,540,200 | — | — | 1.50 | 3.00 | 3.50 |
| 2011 | — | PF65 15.00 | | | | |
| 2012 | 3,372,000 | — | — | 1.50 | 3.00 | 3.50 |
| 2012 | — | PF65 15.00 | | | | |
| 2013 | — | — | — | 1.50 | 3.00 | 3.50 |
| 2013 | — | PF65 15.00 | | | | |
| 2014 | — | — | — | 1.50 | 3.00 | 3.50 |
| 2014 | — | PF65 15.00 | | | | |

**KM# 1327 EURO**
7.50 g., Bi-Metallic, 23.25 mm. **Ruler:** Felipe VI **Obv:** Head left **Rev:** Relief map of Western Europe, stars, lines and value

| Date | Mintage | VF20 | XF40 | MS60 | MS63 | MS65 |
|---|---|---|---|---|---|---|
| 2015 | — | — | — | 1.50 | 3.00 | 3.50 |
| 2015 Proof | — | — | — | — | — | — |

**KM# 1047 2 EURO**
8.50 g., Bi-Metallic Nickel-Brass center in Copper-Nickel ring, 25.75 mm. **Ruler:** Juan Carlos I **Obv:** Head 1/4 left within circle and star border **Rev:** Value and map within circle **Edge:** Reeding over stars and 2's

| Date | Mintage | VF20 | XF40 | MS60 | MS63 | MS65 |
|---|---|---|---|---|---|---|
| 2001 (M) | 140,200,000 | — | — | 3.25 | 4.50 | 5.00 |
| 2002 (M) | 164,000,000 | — | — | 3.00 | 3.50 | 4.00 |
| 2002 (M) | 35,000 | PF65 20.00 | | | | |
| 2003 (M) | 44,500,000 | — | — | 3.25 | 4.50 | 5.00 |
| 2003 (M) | 20,000 | PF65 20.00 | | | | |
| 2004 (M) | 4,100,000 | — | — | 3.25 | 4.50 | 5.00 |
| 2005 (M) | 4,000,000 | — | — | 3.25 | 4.50 | 5.00 |
| 2005 (M) | 3,000 | PF65 20.00 | | | | |
| 2006 (M) | 4,000,000 | — | — | 3.25 | 4.50 | 5.00 |

**KM# 1063 2 EURO**
8.50 g., Bi-Metallic Nickel-Brass center in Copper-Nickel ring, 25.75 mm. **Ruler:** Juan Carlos I **Obv:** Stylized half length figure of Don Quixote holding spear within circle and star border **Rev:** Value and map within circle **Edge:** Reeding over stars and 2's **Note:** Mint mark: Crowned M.

| Date | Mintage | VF20 | XF40 | MS60 | MS63 | MS65 |
|---|---|---|---|---|---|---|
| 2005 | 8,000,000 | — | — | 3.50 | 5.00 | 6.00 |
| 2005 | 3,000 | PF65 25.00 | | | | |

**KM# 1074 2 EURO**
8.50 g., Bi-Metallic Nickel-Brass center in Copper-Nickel ring, 25.75 mm. **Ruler:** Juan Carlos I **Obv:** King's portrait **Rev:** Relief map of Western Europe, stars, lines and value **Edge:** Reeding over stars and 2's

| Date | Mintage | VF20 | XF40 | MS60 | MS63 | MS65 |
|---|---|---|---|---|---|---|
| 2007 (M) | 3,958,000 | — | — | 3.50 | 4.75 | 5.00 |
| 2007 (M) | 5,000 | PF65 20.00 | | | | |
| 2008 (M) | 19,456,940 | — | — | 3.50 | 4.75 | 5.00 |
| 2008 (M) | 5,000 | PF65 20.00 | | | | |
| 2009 (M) | 17,427,500 | — | — | 3.50 | 4.75 | 5.00 |
| 2009 (M) | 5,000 | PF65 20.00 | | | | |

**KM# 1130 2 EURO**
8.50 g., Bi-Metallic Nickel-Brass center in Copper-Nickel ring, 25.75 mm. **Ruler:** Juan Carlos I **Subject:** 50th Anniversary Treaty of Rome **Obv:** Open treaty book **Obv. Legend:** ESPAÑA **Rev:** Large value at left, modified outline of Europe at right **Edge:** Reeded with 2's and stars

| Date | Mintage | VF20 | XF40 | MS60 | MS63 | MS65 |
|---|---|---|---|---|---|---|
| 2007 | 7,935,000 | — | — | 5.00 | 7.00 | 9.00 |
| 2007 (M) Special Unc. | 60,000 | — | — | — | — | 20.00 |
| 2007 (M) | 5,000 | PF65 35.00 | | | | |

**KM# 1142.1 2 EURO**
8.50 g., Bi-Metallic Nickel-Brass center in Copper-Nickel ring, 25.75 mm. **Ruler:** Juan Carlos I **Subject:** European Monetary Unit, 10th Anniversary **Obv:** Stick figure and large E symbol **Rev:** Large value at left, modified map of Europe at right **Edge:** Reeded with 2's and stars

| Date | Mintage | VF20 | XF40 | MS60 | MS63 | MS65 |
|---|---|---|---|---|---|---|
| 2009 Small Stars | — | — | — | 3.50 | 5.00 | 6.00 |
| 2009 Special Unc. | — | — | — | — | — | 20.00 |
| 2009 | — | PF65 35.00 | | | | |

**KM# 1142.2 2 EURO**
8.50 g., Bi-Metallic Nickel-Brass center in Copper-Nickel ring, 25.75 mm. **Ruler:** Juan Carlos I **Subject:** European Monetary Unit, 10th Anniversary **Obv:** Stick figure and large E symbol **Edge:** Reeded with 2's and stars

| Date | Mintage | VF20 | XF40 | MS60 | MS63 | MS65 |
|---|---|---|---|---|---|---|
| 2009 Large Stars | — | — | — | — | 40.00 | 45.00 |

**KM# 1151 2 EURO**
8.50 g., Bi-Metallic Nickel-Brass center in Copper-Nickel ring, 25.75 mm. **Ruler:** Juan Carlos I **Obv:** King's portrait at right **Rev:** Relief map of Western Europe, stars, lines and value **Edge:** Reeded with 2's and stars

| Date | Mintage | VF20 | XF40 | MS60 | MS63 | MS65 |
|---|---|---|---|---|---|---|
| 2010 | 3,930,000 | — | — | 3.50 | 4.75 | 5.00 |
| 2010 | — | PF65 20.00 | | | | |
| 2011 | 4,040,200 | — | — | 3.50 | 4.75 | 5.00 |
| 2011 | — | PF65 20.00 | | | | |
| 2012 | 4,072,000 | — | — | 3.50 | 4.75 | 5.00 |
| 2012 | — | PF65 20.00 | | | | |
| 2013 | — | — | — | 3.50 | 4.75 | 5.00 |
| 2013 | — | PF65 20.00 | | | | |
| 2014 | — | — | — | 35.00 | 4.75 | 5.00 |
| 2014 | — | PF65 20.00 | | | | |

**KM# 1152 2 EURO**
8.50 g., Bi-Metallic Nickel-Brass center in Copper-Nickel ring, 25.75 mm. **Ruler:** Juan Carlos I **Subject:** Cordoba - UNESCO Heritage site **Edge:** Reeded with 2's and stars

| Date | Mintage | VF20 | XF40 | MS60 | MS63 | MS65 |
|---|---|---|---|---|---|---|
| 2010 | 5,000 | PF65 25.00 | | | | |
| 2010 | — | — | — | 3.50 | 5.00 | 7.00 |

**KM# 1184 2 EURO**
8.50 g., Bi-Metallic Nickel-Brass center in Copper-Nickel ring, 25.75 mm. **Ruler:** Juan Carlos I **Subject:** UNESCO Heritage Site - Granada **Obv:** The Alhambra **Edge:** Reeded with 2's and stars

| Date | Mintage | VF20 | XF40 | MS60 | MS63 | MS65 |
|---|---|---|---|---|---|---|
| 2011 | 5,000 | PF65 25.00 | | | | |
| 2011 | 8,000,000 | — | — | 3.50 | 5.00 | 7.00 |

**KM# 1252 2 EURO**
8.50 g., Bi-Metallic Nickel-Brass center in Copper-Nickel ring, 25.75 mm. **Ruler:** Juan Carlos I **Subject:** Euro coinage, 10th Anniversary **Obv:** Euro symbol on globe at center, child-like rendering around

| Date | Mintage | VF20 | XF40 | MS60 | MS63 | MS65 |
|---|---|---|---|---|---|---|
| 2012 | — | PF65 25.00 | | | | |
| 2012 | 8,000,000 | — | — | 3.50 | 5.00 | 7.00 |

**KM# 1254 2 EURO**
8.50 g., Bi-Metallic Nickel-Brass center in Copper-Nickel ring, 25.75 mm. **Ruler:** Juan Carlos I **Subject:** Burgos Cathedral

| Date | Mintage | VF20 | XF40 | MS60 | MS63 | MS65 |
|---|---|---|---|---|---|---|
| 2012 | — | — | — | 3.50 | 5.00 | 7.00 |

**KM# 1305 2 EURO**
8.50 g., Bi-Metallic Nickel-Brass center in Copper-Nickel ring, 25.75 mm. **Ruler:** Juan Carlos I **Obv:** Royal Palace of St. Lorenzo de el Escorial

| Date | Mintage | VF20 | XF40 | MS60 | MS63 | MS65 |
|---|---|---|---|---|---|---|
| 2013 | — | — | — | 3.50 | 5.00 | 7.00 |

**KM# 1306 2 EURO**
8.50 g., Bi-Metallic Nickel-Brass center in Copper-Nickel ring, 25.75 mm. **Ruler:** Juan Carlos I **Obv:** Works of Antoni Gaudi

| Date | Mintage | VF20 | XF40 | MS60 | MS63 | MS65 |
|---|---|---|---|---|---|---|
| 2014 | — | — | — | 3.50 | 5.00 | 7.00 |

**KM# 1326 2 EURO**
8.50 g., Bi-Metallic Nickel-Brass center in Copper-Nickel ring, 25.75 mm. **Ruler:** Juan Carlos I **Obv:** Conjoined heads of Juan Carlos and Felipe

| Date | Mintage | VF20 | XF40 | MS60 | MS63 | MS65 |
|---|---|---|---|---|---|---|
| 2014 | 12,000,000 | — | — | 5.00 | 7.00 | 10.00 |

**KM# 1328 2 EURO**
8.50 g., Bi-Metallic, 25.75 mm. **Ruler:** Felipe VI **Obv:** Head left

| Date | Mintage | VF20 | XF40 | MS60 | MS63 | MS65 |
|---|---|---|---|---|---|---|
| 2015 | — | — | — | 3.50 | 5.00 | 7.00 |
| 2015 | — | **PF65** 20.00 | | | | |

**KM# 1153 5 EURO**
13.50 g., 0.925 Silver 0.4015 oz. ASW, 33 mm. **Ruler:** Juan Carlos I **Subject:** Almeria

| Date | Mintage | VF20 | XF40 | MS60 | MS63 | MS65 |
|---|---|---|---|---|---|---|
| 2010 | Est. 15000 | **PF63** 50.00 | **PF65** 55.00 | | | |

**KM# 1154 5 EURO**
13.50 g., 0.925 Silver 0.4015 oz. ASW, 33 mm. **Ruler:** Juan Carlos I **Subject:** Huesca

| Date | Mintage | VF20 | XF40 | MS60 | MS63 | MS65 |
|---|---|---|---|---|---|---|
| 2010 | Est. 15000 | **PF63** 50.00 | **PF65** 55.00 | | | |

**KM# 1155 5 EURO**
13.50 g., 0.925 Silver 0.4015 oz. ASW, 33 mm. **Ruler:** Juan Carlos I **Subject:** Las Palmas G.C.

| Date | Mintage | VF20 | XF40 | MS60 | MS63 | MS65 |
|---|---|---|---|---|---|---|
| 2010 | Est. 20000 | **PF63** 50.00 | **PF65** 55.00 | | | |

**KM# 1156 5 EURO**
13.50 g., 0.925 Silver 0.4015 oz. ASW, 33 mm. **Ruler:** Juan Carlos I **Subject:** Santander

| Date | Mintage | VF20 | XF40 | MS60 | MS63 | MS65 |
|---|---|---|---|---|---|---|
| 2010 | Est. 15000 | **PF63** 50.00 | **PF65** 55.00 | | | |

**KM# 1157 5 EURO**
13.50 g., 0.925 Silver 0.4015 oz. ASW, 33 mm. **Ruler:** Juan Carlos I **Subject:** Avila

| Date | Mintage | VF20 | XF40 | MS60 | MS63 | MS65 |
|---|---|---|---|---|---|---|
| 2010 | Est. 15000 | **PF63** 50.00 | **PF65** 55.00 | | | |

**KM# 1158 5 EURO**
13.50 g., 0.925 Silver 0.4015 oz. ASW, 33 mm. **Ruler:** Juan Carlos I **Subject:** Albacete

| Date | Mintage | VF20 | XF40 | MS60 | MS63 | MS65 |
|---|---|---|---|---|---|---|
| 2010 | Est. 15000 | **PF63** 50.00 | **PF65** 55.00 | | | |

**KM# 1159 5 EURO**
13.50 g., 0.925 Silver 0.4015 oz. ASW, 33 mm. **Ruler:** Juan Carlos I **Subject:** Barcelona

| Date | Mintage | VF20 | XF40 | MS60 | MS63 | MS65 |
|---|---|---|---|---|---|---|
| 2010 | Est. 25000 | **PF63** 50.00 | **PF65** 55.00 | | | |

**KM# 1160 5 EURO**
13.50 g., 0.925 Silver 0.4015 oz. ASW, 33 mm. **Ruler:** Juan Carlos I **Subject:** Ceuta

| Date | Mintage | VF20 | XF40 | MS60 | MS63 | MS65 |
|---|---|---|---|---|---|---|
| 2010 | Est. 15000 | **PF63** 50.00 | **PF65** 55.00 | | | |

**KM# 1161 5 EURO**
13.50 g., 0.925 Silver 0.4015 oz. ASW, 33 mm. **Ruler:** Juan Carlos I **Subject:** Melilla

| Date | Mintage | VF20 | XF40 | MS60 | MS63 | MS65 |
|---|---|---|---|---|---|---|
| 2010 | Est. 15000 | **PF63** 50.00 | **PF65** 55.00 | | | |

**KM# 1162 5 EURO**
13.50 g., 0.925 Silver 0.4015 oz. ASW, 33 mm. **Ruler:** Juan Carlos I **Subject:** Madrid

| Date | Mintage | VF20 | XF40 | MS60 | MS63 | MS65 |
|---|---|---|---|---|---|---|
| 2010 | Est.2500 | **PF63** 45.00 | **PF65** 50.00 | | | |

**KM# 1163 5 EURO**
13.50 g., 0.925 Silver 0.4015 oz. ASW, 33 mm. **Ruler:** Juan Carlos I **Subject:** Pamplona

| Date | Mintage | VF20 | XF40 | MS60 | MS63 | MS65 |
|---|---|---|---|---|---|---|
| 2010 | Est. 15000 | **PF63** 50.00 | **PF65** 55.00 | | | |

**KM# 1164 5 EURO**
13.50 g., 0.925 Silver 0.4015 oz. ASW, 33 mm. **Ruler:** Juan Carlos I **Subject:** Alicante

| Date | Mintage | VF20 | XF40 | MS60 | MS63 | MS65 |
|---|---|---|---|---|---|---|
| 2010 | Est. 20000 | **PF63** 45.00 | **PF65** 50.00 | | | |

**KM# 1226 5 EURO**
13.50 g., 0.925 Silver 0.4015 oz. ASW, 33 mm. **Ruler:** Juan Carlos I **Subject:** Oviedo

| Date | Mintage | VF20 | XF40 | MS60 | MS63 | MS65 |
|---|---|---|---|---|---|---|
| 2011 | Est. 20000 | **PF63** 45.00 | | **PF65** 50.00 | | |

**KM# 1227 5 EURO**
13.50 g., 0.925 Silver 0.4015 oz. ASW **Ruler:** Juan Carlos I **Subject:** Palma de Mallorca

| Date | Mintage | VF20 | XF40 | MS60 | MS63 | MS65 |
|---|---|---|---|---|---|---|
| 2011 | Est. 20000 | **PF63** 45.00 | | **PF65** 50.00 | | |

**KM# 1228 5 EURO**
13.50 g., 0.925 Silver 0.4015 oz. ASW, 33 mm. **Ruler:** Juan Carlos I **Subject:** Santa Cruz de Tenerife

| Date | Mintage | VF20 | XF40 | MS60 | MS63 | MS65 |
|---|---|---|---|---|---|---|
| 2011 | Est. 20000 | **PF63** 45.00 | | **PF65** 50.00 | | |

**KM# 1229 5 EURO**
13.50 g., 0.925 Silver 0.4015 oz. ASW, 33 mm. **Ruler:** Juan Carlos I **Subject:** Teruel

| Date | Mintage | VF20 | XF40 | MS60 | MS63 | MS65 |
|---|---|---|---|---|---|---|
| 2011 | Est. 15000 | **PF63** 45.00 | | **PF65** 50.00 | | |

**KM# 1230 5 EURO**
13.50 g., 0.925 Silver 0.4015 oz. ASW, 33 mm. **Ruler:** Juan Carlos I **Subject:** Bilbao

| Date | Mintage | VF20 | XF40 | MS60 | MS63 | MS65 |
|---|---|---|---|---|---|---|
| 2011 | Est. 20000 | **PF63** 45.00 | | **PF65** 50.00 | | |

**KM# 1231 5 EURO**
13.50 g., 0.925 Silver 0.4015 oz. ASW, 33 mm. **Ruler:** Juan Carlos I **Subject:** Cadiz

| Date | Mintage | VF20 | XF40 | MS60 | MS63 | MS65 |
|---|---|---|---|---|---|---|
| 2011 | — | **PF63** 45.00 | | **PF65** 50.00 | | |

**KM# 1232 5 EURO**
13.50 g., 0.925 Silver 0.4015 oz. ASW, 33 mm. **Ruler:** Juan Carlos I **Subject:** Logrono

| Date | Mintage | VF20 | XF40 | MS60 | MS63 | MS65 |
|---|---|---|---|---|---|---|
| 2011 | Est. 15000 | **PF63** 45.00 | | **PF65** 50.00 | | |

**KM# 1233 5 EURO**
13.50 g., 0.925 Silver 0.4015 oz. ASW, 33 mm. **Ruler:** Juan Carlos I **Subject:** Murcia

| Date | Mintage | VF20 | XF40 | MS60 | MS63 | MS65 |
|---|---|---|---|---|---|---|
| 2011 | Est. 15000 | **PF63** 45.00 | | **PF65** 50.00 | | |

**KM# 1234 5 EURO**
13.50 g., 0.925 Silver 0.4015 oz. ASW, 33 mm. **Ruler:** Juan Carlos I **Subject:** Donostia - San Sebastian

| Date | Mintage | VF20 | XF40 | MS60 | MS63 | MS65 |
|---|---|---|---|---|---|---|
| 2011 | — | **PF63** 45.00 | | **PF65** 50.00 | | |

**KM# 1235 5 EURO**
13.50 g., 0.925 Silver 0.4015 oz. ASW, 33 mm. **Ruler:** Juan Carlos I **Subject:** Zaragoza

| Date | Mintage | VF20 | XF40 | MS60 | MS63 | MS65 |
|---|---|---|---|---|---|---|
| 2011 | — | **PF63** 45.00 | | **PF65** 50.00 | | |

**KM# 1236 5 EURO**
13.50 g., 0.925 Silver 0.4015 oz. ASW, 33 mm. **Ruler:** Juan Carlos I **Subject:** A Coruna

| Date | Mintage | VF20 | XF40 | MS60 | MS63 | MS65 |
|---|---|---|---|---|---|---|
| 2011 | Est. 20000 | **PF63** 45.00 | | **PF65** 50.00 | | |

**KM# 1237 5 EURO**
13.50 g., 0.925 Silver 0.4015 oz. ASW, 33 mm. **Ruler:** Juan Carlos I **Subject:** Badajoz

| Date | Mintage | VF20 | XF40 | MS60 | MS63 | MS65 |
|---|---|---|---|---|---|---|
| 2011 | Est. 15000 | **PF63** 45.00 | | **PF65** 50.00 | | |

**KM# 1238 5 EURO**
13.50 g., 0.925 Silver 0.4015 oz. ASW, 33 mm. **Ruler:** Juan Carlos I **Subject:** Cordoba

| Date | Mintage | VF20 | XF40 | MS60 | MS63 | MS65 |
|---|---|---|---|---|---|---|
| 2011 | Est. 15000 | **PF63** 45.00 | | **PF65** 50.00 | | |

**KM# 1239 5 EURO**
13.50 g., 0.925 Silver 0.4015 oz. ASW, 33 mm. **Ruler:** Juan Carlos I **Subject:** Girona

| Date | Mintage | VF20 | XF40 | MS60 | MS63 | MS65 |
|---|---|---|---|---|---|---|
| 2011 | Est. 15000 | **PF63** 45.00 | | **PF65** 50.00 | | |

**KM# 1240 5 EURO**
13.50 g., 0.925 Silver 0.4015 oz. ASW, 33 mm. **Ruler:** Juan Carlos I **Subject:** Leon

| Date | Mintage | VF20 | XF40 | MS60 | MS63 | MS65 |
|---|---|---|---|---|---|---|
| 2011 | — | **PF63** 45.00 | | **PF65** 50.00 | | |

**KM# 1241 5 EURO**
13.50 g., 0.925 Silver 0.4015 oz. ASW, 33 mm. **Ruler:** Juan Carlos I **Subject:** Lugo

| Date | Mintage | VF20 | XF40 | MS60 | MS63 | MS65 |
|---|---|---|---|---|---|---|
| 2011 | Est. 15000 | **PF63** 45.00 | **PF65** 50.00 | | | |

**KM# 1242 5 EURO**
13.50 g., 0.925 Silver 0.4015 oz. ASW, 33 mm. **Ruler:** Juan Carlos I **Subject:** Burgos

| Date | Mintage | VF20 | XF40 | MS60 | MS63 | MS65 |
|---|---|---|---|---|---|---|
| 2011 | Est. 15000 | **PF63** 45.00 | **PF65** 50.00 | | | |

**KM# 1243 5 EURO**
13.50 g., 0.925 Silver 0.4015 oz. ASW, 33 mm. **Ruler:** Juan Carlos I **Subject:** Caceres

| Date | Mintage | VF20 | XF40 | MS60 | MS63 | MS65 |
|---|---|---|---|---|---|---|
| 2011 | Est. 15000 | **PF63** 45.00 | **PF65** 50.00 | | | |

**KM# 1244 5 EURO**
13.50 g., 0.925 Silver 0.4015 oz. ASW, 33 mm. **Ruler:** Juan Carlos I **Subject:** Castellon de la Plana

| Date | Mintage | VF20 | XF40 | MS60 | MS63 | MS65 |
|---|---|---|---|---|---|---|
| 2011 | Est. 15000 | **PF63** 45.00 | **PF65** 50.00 | | | |

**KM# 1245 5 EURO**
13.50 g., 0.925 Silver 0.4015 oz. ASW, 33 mm. **Ruler:** Juan Carlos I **Subject:** Ciudad Real

| Date | Mintage | VF20 | XF40 | MS60 | MS63 | MS65 |
|---|---|---|---|---|---|---|
| 2011 | Est. 15000 | **PF63** 45.00 | **PF65** 50.00 | | | |

**KM# 1260 5 EURO**
13.50 g., 0.925 Silver 0.4015 oz. ASW, 33 mm. **Ruler:** Juan Carlos I **Subject:** Cuenca

| Date | Mintage | VF20 | XF40 | MS60 | MS63 | MS65 |
|---|---|---|---|---|---|---|
| 2012 | Est. 15000 | **PF63** 45.00 | **PF65** 50.00 | | | |

**KM# 1261 5 EURO**
13.50 g., 0.925 Silver 0.4015 oz. ASW, 33 mm. **Ruler:** Juan Carlos I **Subject:** Granada

| Date | Mintage | VF20 | XF40 | MS60 | MS63 | MS65 |
|---|---|---|---|---|---|---|
| 2012 | Est. 15000 | **PF63** 45.00 | **PF65** 50.00 | | | |

**KM# 1262 5 EURO**
13.50 g., 0.925 Silver 0.4015 oz. ASW, 33 mm. **Ruler:** Juan Carlos I **Subject:** Guadalajara

| Date | Mintage | VF20 | XF40 | MS60 | MS63 | MS65 |
|---|---|---|---|---|---|---|
| 2012 | Est. 15000 | **PF63** 45.00 | **PF65** 50.00 | | | |

**KM# 1263 5 EURO**
13.50 g., 0.925 Silver 0.4015 oz. ASW, 33 mm. **Ruler:** Juan Carlos I **Subject:** Huelva

| Date | Mintage | VF20 | XF40 | MS60 | MS63 | MS65 |
|---|---|---|---|---|---|---|
| 2012 | Est. 15000 | **PF63** 45.00 | **PF65** 50.00 | | | |

**KM# 1264 5 EURO**
13.50 g., 0.925 Silver 0.4015 oz. ASW, 33 mm. **Ruler:** Juan Carlos I **Subject:** Jaen

| Date | Mintage | VF20 | XF40 | MS60 | MS63 | MS65 |
|---|---|---|---|---|---|---|
| 2012 | Est. 15000 | **PF63** 45.00 | **PF65** 50.00 | | | |

**KM# 1265 5 EURO**
13.50 g., 0.925 Silver 0.4015 oz. ASW, 33 mm. **Ruler:** Juan Carlos I **Subject:** Lerida

| Date | Mintage | VF20 | XF40 | MS60 | MS63 | MS65 |
|---|---|---|---|---|---|---|
| 2012 | Est. 15000 | **PF63** 45.00 | **PF65** 50.00 | | | |

**KM# 1266 5 EURO**
13.50 g., 0.925 Silver 0.4015 oz. ASW, 33 mm. **Ruler:** Juan Carlos I **Subject:** Malaga

| Date | Mintage | VF20 | XF40 | MS60 | MS63 | MS65 |
|---|---|---|---|---|---|---|
| 2012 | Est. 15000 | **PF63** 45.00 | **PF65** 50.00 | | | |

**KM# 1267 5 EURO**
13.50 g., 0.925 Silver 0.4015 oz. ASW, 33 mm. **Ruler:** Juan Carlos I **Subject:** Orense

| Date | Mintage | VF20 | XF40 | MS60 | MS63 | MS65 |
|---|---|---|---|---|---|---|
| 2012 | Est. 15000 | **PF63** 45.00 | **PF65** 50.00 | | | |

**KM# 1268 5 EURO**
13.50 g., 0.925 Silver 0.4015 oz. ASW, 33 mm. **Ruler:** Juan Carlos I **Subject:** Palencia

| Date | Mintage | VF20 | XF40 | MS60 | MS63 | MS65 |
|---|---|---|---|---|---|---|
| 2012 | Est. 15000 | **PF63** 45.00 | **PF65** 50.00 | | | |

**KM# 1269 5 EURO**
13.50 g., 0.925 Silver 0.4015 oz. ASW, 33 mm. **Ruler:** Juan Carlos I **Subject:** Pontevedra

| Date | Mintage | VF20 | XF40 | MS60 | MS63 | MS65 |
|---|---|---|---|---|---|---|
| 2012 | Est. 15000 | **PF63** 45.00 | **PF65** 50.00 | | | |

**KM# 1270 5 EURO**
13.50 g., 0.925 Silver 0.4015 oz. ASW, 33 mm. **Ruler:** Juan Carlos I **Subject:** Salamanca

| Date | Mintage | VF20 | XF40 | MS60 | MS63 | MS65 |
|---|---|---|---|---|---|---|
| 2012 | Est. 15000 | PF63 45.00 | PF65 50.00 | | | |

**KM# 1271 5 EURO**
13.50 g., 0.925 Silver 0.4015 oz. ASW, 33 mm. **Ruler:** Juan Carlos I **Subject:** Segovia

| Date | Mintage | VF20 | XF40 | MS60 | MS63 | MS65 |
|---|---|---|---|---|---|---|
| 2012 | Est. 15000 | PF63 45.00 | PF65 50.00 | | | |

**KM# 1272 5 EURO**
13.50 g., 0.925 Silver 0.4015 oz. ASW, 33 mm. **Ruler:** Juan Carlos I **Subject:** Sevilla

| Date | Mintage | VF20 | XF40 | MS60 | MS63 | MS65 |
|---|---|---|---|---|---|---|
| 2012 | Est. 15000 | PF63 45.00 | PF65 50.00 | | | |

**KM# 1273 5 EURO**
13.50 g., 0.925 Silver 0.4015 oz. ASW, 33 mm. **Ruler:** Juan Carlos I **Subject:** Soria

| Date | Mintage | VF20 | XF40 | MS60 | MS63 | MS65 |
|---|---|---|---|---|---|---|
| 2012 | Est. 15000 | PF63 45.00 | PF65 50.00 | | | |

**KM# 1274 5 EURO**
13.50 g., 0.925 Silver 0.4015 oz. ASW, 33 mm. **Ruler:** Juan Carlos I **Subject:** Tarragona

| Date | Mintage | VF20 | XF40 | MS60 | MS63 | MS65 |
|---|---|---|---|---|---|---|
| 2012 | Est. 15000 | PF63 45.00 | PF65 50.00 | | | |

**KM# 1275 5 EURO**
13.50 g., 0.925 Silver 0.4015 oz. ASW, 33 mm. **Ruler:** Juan Carlos I **Subject:** Toledo

| Date | Mintage | VF20 | XF40 | MS60 | MS63 | MS65 |
|---|---|---|---|---|---|---|
| 2012 | Est. 15000 | PF63 45.00 | PF65 50.00 | | | |

**KM# 1276 5 EURO**
13.50 g., 0.925 Silver 0.4015 oz. ASW, 33 mm. **Ruler:** Juan Carlos I **Subject:** Valencia

| Date | Mintage | VF20 | XF40 | MS60 | MS63 | MS65 |
|---|---|---|---|---|---|---|
| 2012 | Est. 15000 | PF63 45.00 | PF65 50.00 | | | |

**KM# 1277 5 EURO**
13.50 g., 0.925 Silver 0.4015 oz. ASW, 33 mm. **Ruler:** Juan Carlos I **Subject:** Valladolid

| Date | Mintage | VF20 | XF40 | MS60 | MS63 | MS65 |
|---|---|---|---|---|---|---|
| 2012 | Est. 15000 | PF63 45.00 | PF65 50.00 | | | |

**KM# 1278 5 EURO**
13.50 g., 0.925 Silver 0.4015 oz. ASW, 33 mm. **Ruler:** Juan Carlos I **Subject:** Vitoria

| Date | Mintage | VF20 | XF40 | MS60 | MS63 | MS65 |
|---|---|---|---|---|---|---|
| 2012 | Est. 15000 | PF63 45.00 | PF65 50.00 | | | |

**KM# 1279 5 EURO**
13.50 g., 0.925 Silver 0.4015 oz. ASW, 33 mm. **Ruler:** Juan Carlos I **Subject:** Zamora

| Date | Mintage | VF20 | XF40 | MS60 | MS63 | MS65 |
|---|---|---|---|---|---|---|
| 2012 | Est. 15000 | PF63 45.00 | PF65 50.00 | | | |

**KM# 1282 5 EURO**
13.00 g., 0.925 Silver 0.3866 oz. ASW Gold plated **Ruler:** Juan Carlos I **Subject:** Juan Carlos, 75th Anniversary of Birth

| Date | Mintage | VF20 | XF40 | MS60 | MS63 | MS65 |
|---|---|---|---|---|---|---|
| 2013 | 7,000 | PF63 100 | | | | |

**KM# 1294 5 EURO**
13.50 g., 0.925 Silver 0.4015 oz. ASW, 33 mm. **Ruler:** Juan Carlos I **Subject:** Royal Palace of La Almudaina

| Date | Mintage | VF20 | XF40 | MS60 | MS63 | MS65 |
|---|---|---|---|---|---|---|
| 2013 | 7,000 | PF63 50.00 | PF65 55.00 | | | |

**KM# 1295 5 EURO**
13.50 g., 0.925 Silver 0.4015 oz. ASW, 33 mm. **Ruler:** Juan Carlos I **Subject:** Abbey of Santa Maria la Real de Huelgas

| Date | Mintage | VF20 | XF40 | MS60 | MS63 | MS65 |
|---|---|---|---|---|---|---|
| 2013 | 7,000 | PF63 50.00 | PF65 55.00 | | | |

**KM# 1296 5 EURO**
13.50 g., 0.925 Silver 0.4015 oz. ASW, 33 mm. **Ruler:** Juan Carlos I **Subject:** Royal Palace of La Granja de San Ildefonso

| Date | Mintage | VF20 | XF40 | MS60 | MS63 | MS65 |
|---|---|---|---|---|---|---|
| 2013 | 7,000 | PF63 50.00 | PF65 55.00 | | | |

**KM# 1297 5 EURO**
13.50 g., 0.925 Silver 0.4015 oz. ASW, 33 mm. **Ruler:** Juan Carlos I **Subject:** Royal Convent of La Encarnación

| Date | Mintage | VF20 | XF40 | MS60 | MS63 | MS65 |
|---|---|---|---|---|---|---|
| 2013 | 7,000 | PF63 50.00 | PF65 55.00 | | | |

**KM# 1298 5 EURO**
13.50 g., 0.925 Silver 0.4015 oz. ASW, 33 mm. **Ruler:** Juan Carlos I **Subject:** Convent of Las Descalzas Reales

| Date | Mintage | VF20 | XF40 | MS60 | MS63 | MS65 |
|---|---|---|---|---|---|---|
| 2013 | 7,000 | PF63 50.00 | PF65 55.00 | | | |

**KM# 1299 5 EURO**
13.50 g., 0.925 Silver 0.4015 oz. ASW, 33 mm. **Ruler:** Juan Carlos I **Subject:** Royal Seat of San Lorenzo de El Escorial

| Date | Mintage | VF20 | XF40 | MS60 | MS63 | MS65 |
|---|---|---|---|---|---|---|
| 2013 | 7,000 | PF63 50.00 | PF65 55.00 | | | |

**KM# 1320 5 EURO**
13.50 g., 0.925 Silver 0.4015 oz. ASW, 33 mm. **Ruler:** Juan Carlos I **Rev:** Royal Palace in Madrid

| Date | Mintage | VF20 | XF40 | MS60 | MS63 | MS65 |
|---|---|---|---|---|---|---|
| 2014 | 7,000 | PF65 45.00 | | | | |

**KM# 1321 5 EURO**
13.50 g., 0.925 Silver 0.4015 oz. ASW, 33 mm. **Ruler:** Juan Carlos I **Rev:** Royal Palace of El Pardo

| Date | Mintage | VF20 | XF40 | MS60 | MS63 | MS65 |
|---|---|---|---|---|---|---|
| 2014 | 7,000 | PF65 45.00 | | | | |

**KM# 1322 5 EURO**
13.50 g., 0.925 Silver 0.4015 oz. ASW, 33 mm. **Ruler:** Juan Carlos I **Rev:** Royal Palace of Aranjuez

| Date | Mintage | VF20 | XF40 | MS60 | MS63 | MS65 |
|---|---|---|---|---|---|---|
| 2014 | 7,000 | PF65 45.00 | | | | |

**KM# 1323 5 EURO**
13.50 g., 0.925 Silver 0.4015 oz. ASW, 33 mm. **Ruler:** Juan Carlos I **Rev:** Royal Palace in Riofrio

| Date | Mintage | VF20 | XF40 | MS60 | MS63 | MS65 |
|---|---|---|---|---|---|---|
| 2014 | 7,000 | PF65 45.00 | | | | |

**KM# 1324 5 EURO**
13.50 g., .
.925 Silver ASW, 33 mm. **Ruler:** Juan Carlos I **Rev:** Cloister of San Jeronimo

| Date | Mintage | VF20 | XF40 | MS60 | MS63 | MS65 |
|---|---|---|---|---|---|---|
| 2014 | 7,000 | PF65 45.00 | | | | |

**KM# 1325 5 EURO**
13.50 g., 0.925 Silver 0.4015 oz. ASW, 33 mm. **Ruler:** Juan Carlos I **Rev:** Convent of Santa Clara

| Date | Mintage | VF20 | XF40 | MS60 | MS63 | MS65 |
|---|---|---|---|---|---|---|
| 2014 | 7,000 | PF65 45.00 | | | | |

**KM# 1048 10 EURO**
27.00 g., 0.925 Silver 0.803 oz. ASW, 40 mm. **Ruler:** Juan Carlos I **Subject:** Spanish Presidency of the European Union **Obv:** Head left **Rev:** Map of Europe **Edge:** Reeded

| Date | Mintage | VF20 | XF40 | MS60 | MS63 | MS65 |
|---|---|---|---|---|---|---|
| 2002 | 29,997 | PF63 60.00 | | | | |

**KM# 1050 10 EURO**
27.00 g., 0.925 Silver 0.803 oz. ASW, 40 mm. **Ruler:** Juan Carlos I **Subject:** Annexation of Minorca **Obv:** Conjoined heads left **Rev:** Uniformed equestrians shaking hands flanked by ships **Edge:** Reeded **Note:** Mint mark: Crowned M.

| Date | Mintage | VF20 | XF40 | MS60 | MS63 | MS65 |
|---|---|---|---|---|---|---|
| 2002 | 8,693 | PF63 85.00 | PF65 100 | | | |

**KM# 1078 10 EURO**
27.00 g., 0.925 Silver 0.803 oz. ASW, 40 mm. **Ruler:** Juan Carlos I **Subject:** XIX Winter Olympics - Salt Lake City **Obv:** Head left **Obv. Legend:** JUAN CARLOS I REY DE ESPAÑA **Rev:** Cross country skier right, stylized snowflake at right **Rev. Legend:** JUEGOS OLIMPICOS DE - INVERNO 2002

| Date | Mintage | VF20 | XF40 | MS60 | MS63 | MS65 |
|---|---|---|---|---|---|---|
| 2002 (M) | 17,703 | PF63 50.00 | PF65 60.00 | | | |

**KM# 1079 10 EURO**
27.00 g., 0.925 Silver 0.803 oz. ASW, 40 mm. **Ruler:** Juan Carlos I **Subject:** XVII Football World Games 2002 - South Korea and Japan **Obv. Legend:** MUNDIAL DE FUTBOL/2002 - ESPAÑA **Rev:** Football against net

| Date | Mintage | VF20 | XF40 | MS60 | MS63 | MS65 |
|---|---|---|---|---|---|---|
| 2002 (M) | 17,126 | PF63 50.00 | PF65 60.00 | | | |

**KM# 1080 10 EURO**
27.00 g., 0.925 Silver 0.803 oz. ASW, 40 mm. **Ruler:** Juan Carlos I **Subject:** XVII Football World Games 2002 - South Korea and Japan **Obv. Legend:** MUNDIAL DE FUTBOL/2002 - ESPAÑA **Rev:** Glove

| Date | Mintage | VF20 | XF40 | MS60 | MS63 | MS65 |
|---|---|---|---|---|---|---|
| 2002 (M) | 7,424 | PF63 50.00 | PF65 60.00 | | | |

**KM# 1082 10 EURO**
27.00 g., 0.925 Silver 0.803 oz. ASW, 40 mm. **Ruler:** Juan Carlos I **Subject:** 150th Anniversary Birth of Antonio Gaudí **Obv:** Bust of Gaudií at right **Obv. Legend:** Año Internacional **Rev:** Casa Milà

| Date | Mintage | VF20 | XF40 | MS60 | MS63 | MS65 |
|---|---|---|---|---|---|---|
| 2002 (M) | 25,000 | PF63 45.00 | PF65 55.00 | | | |

**KM# 1083 10 EURO**
27.00 g., 0.925 Silver 0.803 oz. ASW, 40 mm. **Ruler:** Juan Carlos I **Subject:** 150th Anniversary Birth of Antonio Gaudí **Obv:** Bust of Gaudí at right **Obv. Legend:** Año Internacional **Rev:** El Capricho

| Date | Mintage | VF20 | XF40 | MS60 | MS63 | MS65 |
|---|---|---|---|---|---|---|
| 2002 (M) | 9,183 | PF63 45.00 | PF65 55.00 | | | |

**KM# 1084 10 EURO**
27.00 g., 0.925 Silver 0.803 oz. ASW, 40 mm. **Ruler:** Juan Carlos I **Subject:** 150th Anniversary - Birth of Antonio Gaudí **Obv:** Bust of Gaudí at right **Obv. Legend:** Año Internacional **Rev:** Parque Güell

| Date | Mintage | VF20 | XF40 | MS60 | MS63 | MS65 |
|---|---|---|---|---|---|---|
| 2002 (M) | 14,111 | PF63 45.00 | PF65 55.00 | | | |

**KM# 1087 10 EURO**
27.00 g., 0.925 Silver 0.803 oz. ASW, 40 mm. **Ruler:** Juan Carlos I **Subject:** 100th Anniversary - Birth of Luis Cernuda **Obv:** Head left

| Date | Mintage | VF20 | XF40 | MS60 | MS63 | MS65 |
|---|---|---|---|---|---|---|
| 2002 (M) | 25,000 | PF63 50.00 | PF65 60.00 | | | |

**KM# 1088 10 EURO**
27.00 g., 0.925 Silver 0.803 oz. ASW, 40 mm. **Ruler:** Juan Carlos I **Subject:** 100th Anniversary - Birth of Rafael Alberti **Obv:** Head left **Obv. Legend:** JUAN CARLOS I REY DE ESPAÑA **Rev:** Bust of Alberti facing 3/4 right

| Date | Mintage | VF20 | XF40 | MS60 | MS63 | MS65 |
|---|---|---|---|---|---|---|
| 2002 (M) | 25,000 | PF63 50.00 | PF65 60.00 | | | |

**KM# 1089 10 EURO**
27.00 g., 0.925 Silver 0.803 oz. ASW, 40 mm. **Ruler:** Juan Carlos I **Series:** Ibero-America V - ships **Obv:** Crowned arms in center circle, 10 participating country arms in outer circle **Obv. Legend:** JUAN CARLOS I REY DE ESPAÑA **Rev:** Galleon of the Spanish Armada **Rev. Legend:** ENCUENTRO DE DOS MUNDOS **Note:** Issued in 2003.

| Date | Mintage | VF20 | XF40 | MS60 | MS63 | MS65 |
|---|---|---|---|---|---|---|
| 2002 (M) | 8,000 | PF63 115 | PF65 135 | | | |

**KM# 1052 10 EURO**
27.00 g., 0.925 Silver 0.803 oz. ASW, 40 mm. **Ruler:** Juan Carlos I **Obv:** Head left **Rev:** Sailing ship - De Elcano **Edge:** Reeded

| Date | Mintage | VF20 | XF40 | MS60 | MS63 | MS65 |
|---|---|---|---|---|---|---|
| 2003 | 12,486 | PF63 75.00 | PF65 90.00 | | | |

**KM# 1053 10 EURO**
27.00 g., 0.925 Silver 0.803 oz. ASW, 40 mm. **Ruler:** Juan Carlos I **Obv:** Juan Carlos I **Rev:** Miguel Lopez de Legazpi **Edge:** Reeded

| Date | Mintage | VF20 | XF40 | MS60 | MS63 | MS65 |
|---|---|---|---|---|---|---|
| 2003 | 5,724 | PF63 95.00 | PF65 110 | | | |

**KM# 1054 10 EURO**
27.00 g., 0.925 Silver 0.803 oz. ASW, 40 mm. **Ruler:** Juan Carlos I **Obv:** Head facing **Rev:** Seated female figure and Swan **Edge:** Reeded

| Date | Mintage | VF20 | XF40 | MS60 | MS63 | MS65 |
|---|---|---|---|---|---|---|
| 2004 | 17,597 | PF63 75.00 | PF65 90.00 | | | |

**KM# 1055 10 EURO**
27.00 g., 0.925 Silver 0.803 oz. ASW, 40 mm. **Ruler:** Juan Carlos I **Obv:** Head facing **Rev:** Dali's painting "El gran masturbador" of 1929 **Edge:** Reeded

| Date | Mintage | VF20 | XF40 | MS60 | MS63 | MS65 |
|---|---|---|---|---|---|---|
| 2004 | 15,647 | PF63 75.00 | PF65 90.00 | | | |

**KM# 1056 10 EURO**
27.00 g., 0.925 Silver 0.803 oz. ASW, 40 mm. **Ruler:** Juan Carlos I **Obv:** Head facing **Rev:** Dali's self portrait with bacon strip **Edge:** Reeded

| Date | Mintage | VF20 | XF40 | MS60 | MS63 | MS65 |
|---|---|---|---|---|---|---|
| 2004 | 18,290 | PF63 75.00 | PF65 90.00 | | | |

**KM# 1076 10 EURO**
27.00 g., 0.925 Silver 0.803 oz. ASW, 40 mm. **Ruler:** Juan Carlos I **Subject:** FIFA World Cup **Obv:** Kings head left **Rev:** Goalie jumping for ball by net **Edge:** Reeded **Note:** Issued in 2004.

| Date | Mintage | VF20 | XF40 | MS60 | MS63 | MS65 |
|---|---|---|---|---|---|---|
| 2003 (M) | 25,883 | PF63 70.00 | PF65 80.00 | | | |

**KM# 1090 10 EURO**
27.00 g., 0.925 Silver 0.803 oz. ASW, 40 mm. **Ruler:** Juan Carlos I **Obv:** Conjoined heads left **Obv. Legend:** JUAN CARLOS I Y SOFIA **Rev:** Ediface of Parliament building in Madrid **Rev. Legend:** CONSTITUCION ESPAÑOLA

| Date | Mintage | VF20 | XF40 | MS60 | MS63 | MS65 |
|---|---|---|---|---|---|---|
| 2003 (M) | 7,995 | PF63 85.00 | PF65 100 | | | |

**KM# 1092 10 EURO**
27.00 g., 0.925 Silver 0.803 oz. ASW, 40 mm. **Ruler:** Juan Carlos I **Subject:** 1st Anniversary of Euro **Obv:** Conjoined heads left **Obv. Legend:** PRIMER ANIVERSARIO EURO / JUAN CARLOS I Y SOFIA **Rev:** Europa riding steer left

| Date | Mintage | VF20 | XF40 | MS60 | MS63 | MS65 |
|---|---|---|---|---|---|---|
| 2003 (M) | 50,000 | PF63 70.00 | PF65 80.00 | | | |

**KM# 1094 10 EURO**
27.00 g., 0.925 Silver 0.803 oz. ASW, 40 mm. **Ruler:** Juan Carlos I **Subject:** World Swimming Championship Games - Barcelona 2003 **Obv:** Head left **Obv. Legend:** JUAN CARLOS I REY DE ESPAÑA **Rev:** Swimmer doing the crawl right **Rev. Legend:** X FINA CAMPEONATOS DEL MUNDO DE NATACION

| Date | Mintage | VF20 | XF40 | MS60 | MS63 | MS65 |
|---|---|---|---|---|---|---|
| 2003 (M) | 5,470 | PF63 75.00 | PF65 90.00 | | | |

**KM# 1059 10 EURO**
27.00 g., 0.925 Silver 0.803 oz. ASW, 40 mm. **Ruler:** Juan Carlos I **Obv:** Conjoined heads left **Rev:** Bust of St. James facing **Edge:** Reeded

| Date | Mintage | VF20 | XF40 | MS60 | MS63 | MS65 |
|---|---|---|---|---|---|---|
| 2004 | 12,214 | PF63 75.00 | PF65 90.00 | | | |

**KM# 1060 10 EURO**
27.00 g., 0.925 Silver 0.803 oz. ASW, 40 mm. **Ruler:** Juan Carlos I **Obv:** Conjoined heads left within beaded circle **Rev:** Bust of Isabel I 1/4 left within beaded circle (1451-1504) **Edge:** Reeded

| Date | Mintage | VF20 | XF40 | MS60 | MS63 | MS65 |
|---|---|---|---|---|---|---|
| 2004 | 12,000 | PF63 75.00 | PF65 90.00 | | | |

**KM# 1097 10 EURO**
27.00 g., 0.925 Silver 0.803 oz. ASW, 40 mm. **Ruler:** Juan Carlos I **Subject:** Wedding of Prince Philip and Letizia Ortiz Rocasolano **Obv:** Conjoined heads left **Obv. Legend:** JUAN CARLOS I T SOFÍA **Rev:** Busts of wedding couple facing 3/4 right, crowned shield below **Rev. Legend:** FELIPE Y LETIZIA - 22.V.2004

| Date | Mintage | VF20 | XF40 | MS60 | MS63 | MS65 |
|---|---|---|---|---|---|---|
| 2004 (M) | 40,367 | PF63 45.00 | PF65 55.00 | | | |

**KM# 1099 10 EURO**
27.00 g., 0.925 Silver 0.803 oz. ASW, 40 mm. **Ruler:** Juan Carlos I **Subject:** Expansion of the European Union **Obv:** Head left **Obv. Legend:** JUAN CARLOS I Y SOFIA **Rev:** Outlined map of European Union

| Date | Mintage | VF20 | XF40 | MS60 | MS63 | MS65 |
|---|---|---|---|---|---|---|
| 2004 (M) | 41,448 | PF63 70.00 | PF65 80.00 | | | |

**KM# 1101 10 EURO**
27.00 g., 0.925 Silver 0.803 oz. ASW, 40 mm. **Ruler:** Juan Carlos I **Subject:** XXVIII Summer Olympics - Athens 2004 **Obv:** Conjoined heads left **Obv. Legend:** JUAN CARLOS I Y SOFIA **Rev:** Broad jumper, outlined world map in backgound **Rev. Legend:** JUEGOS OLIMPICOS

| Date | Mintage | VF20 | XF40 | MS60 | MS63 | MS65 |
|---|---|---|---|---|---|---|
| 2004 (M) | 18,790 | PF63 75.00 | PF65 90.00 | | | |

**KM# 1102 10 EURO**
27.00 g., 0.925 Silver 0.803 oz. ASW, 40 mm. **Ruler:** Juan Carlos I **Subject:** XVIII World Football games - Germany 2006 **Obv:** Head left **Obv. Legend:** JUAN CARLOS I REY DE ESPAÑA **Rev:** Goalie deflecting ball at net

| Date | Mintage | VF20 | XF40 | MS60 | MS63 | MS65 |
|---|---|---|---|---|---|---|
| 2004 (M) | 50,000 | PF63 65.00 | PF65 75.00 | | | |

**KM# 1064 10 EURO**
27.00 g., 0.925 Silver 0.803 oz. ASW, 40 mm. **Ruler:** Juan Carlos I **Subject:** 2006 Winter Olympics **Obv:** Juan Carlos **Rev:** Skier **Edge:** Reeded

| Date | Mintage | VF20 | XF40 | MS60 | MS63 | MS65 |
|---|---|---|---|---|---|---|
| 2005 | 25,000 | PF63 70.00 | PF65 80.00 | | | |

**KM# 1065 10 EURO**
27.00 g., 0.925 Silver 0.803 oz. ASW, 40 mm. **Ruler:** Juan Carlos I **Subject:** European Peace and Freedom **Obv:** Juan Carlos **Rev:** European map on clasped hands **Edge:** Reeded

| Date | Mintage | VF20 | XF40 | MS60 | MS63 | MS65 |
|---|---|---|---|---|---|---|
| 2005 | 29,231 | PF63 75.00 | PF65 90.00 | | | |

**KM# 1104 10 EURO**
27.00 g., 0.925 Silver 0.803 oz. ASW, 40 mm. **Ruler:** Juan Carlos I **Obv:** Quixote seated reading a large book **Obv. Legend:** ESPAÑA - IV CENTENARIO DE LA PRIMERA EDICIÓN DE " EL QUIJOTE **Rev:** Quixote being knocked off his horse by windmill blade **Rev. Legend:** LA AVENTURA - DE LOS - MOLINOS DE VIENTO

| Date | Mintage | VF20 | XF40 | MS60 | MS63 | MS65 |
|---|---|---|---|---|---|---|
| 2005 (M) | 11,670 | PF63 75.00 | PF65 85.00 | | | |

**KM# 1105 10 EURO**
27.00 g., 0.925 Silver 0.803 oz. ASW, 40 mm. **Ruler:** Juan Carlos I **Obv:** Quixote seated reading a large book **Obv. Legend:** ESPAÑA - IV CENTENARIO DE LA PREMERA EDICIÓN DE LA "EL QUIJOTE" **Rev:** Quixote thrusting his sword into an animal skin wine sack **Rev. Legend:** BATALLA - CON UNOS CUEROS DE VINO

| Date | Mintage | VF20 | XF40 | MS60 | MS63 | MS65 |
|---|---|---|---|---|---|---|
| 2005 (M) | 7,902 | PF63 75.00 | PF65 85.00 | | | |

**KM# 1106 10 EURO**
27.00 g., 0.925 Silver 0.803 oz. ASW, 40 mm. **Ruler:** Juan Carlos I **Obv:** Quixote seated reading a large book **Obv. Legend:** ESPAÑA - IV CENTENARIO DE LA PRIMERA EDICIÓN DE "EL QUIJOTE **Rev:** Boy mounting a hobby horse with Quixote on it **Rev. Legend:** LA VENIDA DE CLAVAILEÑO CON EL FIN DESTA DILATADA AVENTURA

| Date | Mintage | VF20 | XF40 | MS60 | MS63 | MS65 |
|---|---|---|---|---|---|---|
| 2005 (M) | 7,968 | PF63 75.00 | PF65 85.00 | | | |

**KM# 1109 10 EURO**
27.00 g., 0.925 Silver 0.803 oz. ASW, 40 mm. **Ruler:** Juan Carlos I **Series:** Ibero-America VI - Architecture **Obv:** Crowned arms in center circle, 10 participating country arms in outer circle **Obv. Legend:** JUAN CARLOS I REY DE ESPAÑA **Rev:** General Archives building of West Indes in Seville **Rev. Legend:** ENCUENTRO DE DOS MUNDOS

| Date | Mintage | VF20 | XF40 | MS60 | MS63 | MS65 |
|---|---|---|---|---|---|---|
| 2005 (M) | 3,000 | PF63 100 | PF65 120 | | | |

**KM# 1110 10 EURO**
27.00 g., 0.925 Silver 0.803 oz. ASW, 40 mm. **Ruler:** Juan Carlos I **Rev:** Crowned shield at left, head of Prince Philip at right **Rev. Legend:** XXV ANIVERSARIO - PREMIOS PRÍNCIPE DE ASTURIAS

| Date | Mintage | VF20 | XF40 | MS60 | MS63 | MS65 |
|---|---|---|---|---|---|---|
| 2005 (M) | 12,845 | PF63 75.00 | PF65 90.00 | | | |

**KM# 1114 10 EURO**
27.00 g., 0.925 Silver 0.803 oz. ASW, 40 mm. **Ruler:** Juan Carlos I **Subject:** 500th Anniversary Death of Columbus **Obv:** Bust of Columbus facing at right, astrolabe at lower left **Obv. Legend:** ESPAÑA **Rev:** Sailing ship "Santa Maria **Rev. Legend:** CRISTOBAL COLON **Edge:** Reeded

| Date | Mintage | VF20 | XF40 | MS60 | MS63 | MS65 |
|---|---|---|---|---|---|---|
| 2006 (M) | 9,960 | PF63 85.00 | PF65 100 | | | |

**KM# 1115 10 EURO**
27.00 g., 0.925 Silver 0.803 oz. ASW, 40 mm. **Ruler:** Juan Carlos I **Subject:** 500th Anniversary - Death of Columbus **Obv:** Bust of Columbus facing at left, astrolabe at lower right **Obv. Legend:** ESPAÑA **Rev:** Sailing ship "Pinta **Rev. Legend:** CRISTOBAL COLON **Edge:** Reeded

| Date | Mintage | VF20 | XF40 | MS60 | MS63 | MS65 |
|---|---|---|---|---|---|---|
| 2006 (M) | 6,188 | PF63 85.00 | PF65 100 | | | |

**KM# 1116 10 EURO**
27.00 g., 0.925 Silver 0.803 oz. ASW, 40 mm. **Ruler:** Juan Carlos I **Subject:** 500th Anniversary - Death of Columbus **Obv:** Bust of Columbus facing at right, astrolabe at lower left **Obv. Legend:** ESPAÑA **Rev:** Sailing ship "Niña **Rev. Legend:** CRISTOBAL COLON **Edge:** Reeded

| Date | Mintage | VF20 | XF40 | MS60 | MS63 | MS65 |
|---|---|---|---|---|---|---|
| 2006 (M) | 6,187 | PF63 85.00 | PF65 100 | | | |

**KM# 1119 10 EURO**
27.00 g., 0.925 Silver 0.803 oz. ASW, 40 mm. **Ruler:** Juan Carlos I **Subject:** 20th Anniversay of Spain and Portugal membership in European Union **Obv:** Juan Carlos I **Rev:** Outlined map of Europe, bridge below **Rev. Legend:** ADHESIÓN A LAS COMUNIDADES EUROPEAS **Rev. Inscription:** ESPAÑA - PORTUGAL

| Date | Mintage | VF20 | XF40 | MS60 | MS63 | MS65 |
|---|---|---|---|---|---|---|
| 2006 (M) | 11,100 | PF63 60.00 | PF65 70.00 | | | |

**KM# 1120 10 EURO**
27.00 g., 0.925 Silver 0.803 oz. ASW, 40 mm. **Ruler:** Juan Carlos I **Rev:** Basketball player scoring in front of defender **Rev. Legend:** CAMPEONES DEL MUNDO - JAPÓN 2006

| Date | Mintage | VF20 | XF40 | MS60 | MS63 | MS65 |
|---|---|---|---|---|---|---|
| 2006 (M) | 4,991 | PF63 60.00 | PF65 70.00 | | | |

**KM# 1122 10 EURO**
27.00 g., 0.925 Silver 0.803 oz. ASW, 40 mm. **Ruler:** Juan Carlos I **Obv:** Head left **Obv. Legend:** JUAN CARLOS I REY DE ESPAÑA **Rev:** Charles I (V) standing facing 3/4 right in front of portal **Rev. Legend:** CAROLVS IMPERATOR

| Date | Mintage | VF20 | XF40 | MS60 | MS63 | MS65 |
|---|---|---|---|---|---|---|
| 2006 (M) | 23,799 | PF63 80.00 | PF65 95.00 | | | |

**KM# 1124 10 EURO**
27.00 g., 0.925 Silver 0.803 oz. ASW, 40 mm. **Ruler:** Juan Carlos I **Rev:** Two ornate portals **Rev. Legend:** V ANIVERSARIO DEL EURO

| Date | Mintage | VF20 | XF40 | MS60 | MS63 | MS65 |
|---|---|---|---|---|---|---|
| 2007 | 12,000 | PF63 55.00 | PF65 65.00 | | | |

**KM# 1125 10 EURO**
27.00 g., 0.925 Silver 0.803 oz. ASW, 40 mm. **Ruler:** Juan Carlos I **Rev:** Stone arch bridge **Rev. Legend:** V ANIVERSARIO DEL EURO

| Date | Mintage | VF20 | XF40 | MS60 | MS63 | MS65 |
|---|---|---|---|---|---|---|
| 2007 | 12,000 | PF63 55.00 | PF65 65.00 | | | |

**KM# 1126 10 EURO**
27.00 g., 0.925 Silver 0.803 oz. ASW, 40 mm. **Ruler:** Juan Carlos I **Rev:** Stone archway **Rev. Legend:** V ANIVERSARIO DEL EURO

| Date | Mintage | VF20 | XF40 | MS60 | MS63 | MS65 |
|---|---|---|---|---|---|---|
| 2007 | 12,000 | PF63 55.00 | PF65 65.00 | | | |

**KM# 1132 10 EURO**
27.00 g., 0.925 Silver 0.803 oz. ASW, 40 mm. **Ruler:** Juan Carlos I **Obv:** Conjoined heads left **Obv. Legend:** JUAN CARLOS I Y SOFÍA - AÑO DE ESPAÑA EN CHINA **Rev:** Early silver "Pillar" reales coin with Chinese characters to left and right of pillars **Rev. Legend:** VTRAQUE VNVM

| Date | Mintage | VF20 | XF40 | MS60 | MS63 | MS65 |
|---|---|---|---|---|---|---|
| 2007 | 20,000 | PF63 50.00 | PF65 60.00 | | | |

**KM# 1134 10 EURO**
27.00 g., 0.925 Silver 0.803 oz. ASW, 40 mm. **Ruler:** Juan Carlos I **Obv:** Head left **Obv. Legend:** JUAN CARLOS I REY DE ESPAÑA **Rev:** Basketball player shooting basket **Rev. Legend:** EUROBASKET 2007

| Date | Mintage | VF20 | XF40 | MS60 | MS63 | MS65 |
|---|---|---|---|---|---|---|
| 2007 | 12,000 | PF63 70.00 | PF65 80.00 | | | |

**KM# 1135 10 EURO**
27.00 g., 0.925 Silver 0.803 oz. ASW, 40 mm. **Ruler:** Juan Carlos I **Subject:** Treaty of Rome, 50th Anniversary **Obv:** Head left **Rev:** Map of Western Europe

| Date | Mintage | VF20 | XF40 | MS60 | MS63 | MS65 |
|---|---|---|---|---|---|---|
| 2007 | 15,000 | PF63 50.00 | PF65 60.00 | | | |

**KM# 1137 10 EURO**
27.00 g., 0.925 Silver 0.803 oz. ASW, 40 mm. **Ruler:** Juan Carlos I **Subject:** El Cid 700th Anniversary **Obv:** Female standing before arches **Rev:** Monk writing

| Date | Mintage | VF20 | XF40 | MS60 | MS63 | MS65 |
|---|---|---|---|---|---|---|
| 2007 | 12,000 | PF63 70.00 | PF65 80.00 | | | |

**KM# 1140 10 EURO**

27.00 g., 0.925 Silver 0.803 oz. ASW, 40 mm. **Ruler:** Juan Carlos I **Subject:** International Polar Year **Rev:** Ship left, outline map of Antartica in background

| Date | Mintage | VF20 | XF40 | MS60 | MS63 | MS65 |
|---|---|---|---|---|---|---|
| 2007 | 20,000 | PF63 55.00 | PF65 65.00 | | | |

**KM# 1141 10 EURO**

27.00 g., 0.925 Silver 0.803 oz. ASW, 40 mm. **Ruler:** Juan Carlos I **Subject:** Zaragoza Expo 2008

| Date | Mintage | VF20 | XF40 | MS60 | MS63 | MS65 |
|---|---|---|---|---|---|---|
| 2007 | 25,000 | PF63 50.00 | PF65 60.00 | | | |

**KM# 1187 10 EURO**

27.00 g., 0.925 Silver 0.803 oz. ASW, 40 mm. **Ruler:** Juan Carlos I **Subject:** Expo Zaragoza **Rev:** Bridge

| Date | Mintage | VF20 | XF40 | MS60 | MS63 | MS65 |
|---|---|---|---|---|---|---|
| 2007 | 25,000 | PF63 55.00 | PF65 65.00 | | | |

**KM# 1190 10 EURO**

27.00 g., 0.925 Silver 0.803 oz. ASW, 40 mm. **Ruler:** Juan Carlos I **Subject:** Velazquez

| Date | Mintage | VF20 | XF40 | MS60 | MS63 | MS65 |
|---|---|---|---|---|---|---|
| 2008 | 12,000 | PF63 60.00 | PF65 70.00 | | | |

**KM# 1192 10 EURO**

27.00 g., 0.925 Silver 0.803 oz. ASW, 40 mm. **Ruler:** Juan Carlos I **Subject:** Soccer, European Champions

| Date | Mintage | VF20 | XF40 | MS60 | MS63 | MS65 |
|---|---|---|---|---|---|---|
| 2008 | 20,000 | PF63 60.00 | PF65 70.00 | | | |

**KM# 1194 10 EURO**

27.00 g., 0.925 Silver 0.803 oz. ASW, 40 mm. **Ruler:** Juan Carlos I **Subject:** Numismatic Treasures - Hispano-Greek Pegasus

| Date | Mintage | VF20 | XF40 | MS60 | MS63 | MS65 |
|---|---|---|---|---|---|---|
| 2008 | 12,000 | PF63 60.00 | PF65 70.00 | | | |

**KM# 1196 10 EURO**

27.00 g., 0.925 Silver 0.803 oz. ASW, 40 mm. **Ruler:** Juan Carlos I **Subject:** Olympic Sports - Sailing

| Date | Mintage | VF20 | XF40 | MS60 | MS63 | MS65 |
|---|---|---|---|---|---|---|
| 2008 | — | PF63 50.00 | PF65 60.00 | | | |

**KM# 1199 10 EURO**

27.00 g., 0.925 Silver 0.803 oz. ASW, 40 mm. **Ruler:** Juan Carlos I **Subject:** War of Independence, Manuela Malasana, 200th Anniversary

| Date | Mintage | VF20 | XF40 | MS60 | MS63 | MS65 |
|---|---|---|---|---|---|---|
| 2008 | 12,000 | PF63 55.00 | PF65 65.00 | | | |

**KM# 1200 10 EURO**

27.00 g., 0.925 Silver 0.803 oz. ASW, 40 mm. **Ruler:** Juan Carlos I **Subject:** War of Independence, 200th Anniversary General Castanos

| Date | Mintage | VF20 | XF40 | MS60 | MS63 | MS65 |
|---|---|---|---|---|---|---|
| 2008 | 12,000 | PF63 55.00 | PF65 65.00 | | | |

**KM# 1201 10 EURO**

27.00 g., 0.925 Silver 0.803 oz. ASW, 40 mm. **Ruler:** Juan Carlos I **Subject:** War of Independence, 200th Anniversary El Tambor del Bruc

| Date | Mintage | VF20 | XF40 | MS60 | MS63 | MS65 |
|---|---|---|---|---|---|---|
| 2008 | 20,000 | PF63 70.00 | PF65 80.00 | | | |

**KM# 1203 10 EURO**

27.00 g., 0.925 Silver 0.803 oz. ASW, 40 mm. **Ruler:** Juan Carlos I **Subject:** Alphonse the wise

| Date | Mintage | VF20 | XF40 | MS60 | MS63 | MS65 |
|---|---|---|---|---|---|---|
| 2008 | — | PF63 50.00 | PF65 60.00 | | | |

**KM# 1143 10 EURO**

27.00 g., 0.925 Silver 0.803 oz. ASW, 40 mm. **Ruler:** Juan Carlos I **Obv:** Head left **Rev:** Soccer player, ball and net

| Date | Mintage | VF20 | XF40 | MS60 | MS63 | MS65 |
|---|---|---|---|---|---|---|
| 2009 | 12,000 | PF63 60.00 | PF65 70.00 | | | |

### KM# 1209 10 EURO

27.00 g., 0.925 Silver 0.803 oz. ASW, 40 mm. **Ruler:** Juan Carlos I **Subject:** Dali Busto de mujer retraspectivo

| Date | Mintage | VF20 | XF40 | MS60 | MS63 | MS65 |
|---|---|---|---|---|---|---|
| 2009 | 10,000 | **PF63** 65.00 | **PF65** 75.00 | | | |

### KM# 1210 10 EURO

27.00 g., 0.925 Silver 0.803 oz. ASW, 40 mm. **Ruler:** Juan Carlos I **Subject:** Dali Retrato de Pablo Picasso and S. XXI

| Date | Mintage | VF20 | XF40 | MS60 | MS63 | MS65 |
|---|---|---|---|---|---|---|
| 2009 | 10,000 | **PF63** 65.00 | **PF65** 75.00 | | | |

### KM# 1211 10 EURO

27.00 g., 0.925 Silver 0.803 oz. ASW, 40 mm. **Ruler:** Juan Carlos I **Subject:** Dali Retrato de Gala

| Date | Mintage | VF20 | XF40 | MS60 | MS63 | MS65 |
|---|---|---|---|---|---|---|
| 2009 | 10,000 | **PF63** 65.00 | **PF65** 75.00 | | | |

### KM# 1214 10 EURO

27.00 g., 0.925 Silver 0.803 oz. ASW, 40 mm. **Ruler:** Juan Carlos I **Subject:** Philip II

| Date | Mintage | VF20 | XF40 | MS60 | MS63 | MS65 |
|---|---|---|---|---|---|---|
| 2009 | 18,000 | **PF63** 70.00 | **PF65** 80.00 | | | |

### KM# 1216 10 EURO

27.00 g., 0.925 Silver 0.803 oz. ASW, 40 mm. **Ruler:** Juan Carlos I **Subject:** World Cup Soccer, South Africa

| Date | Mintage | VF20 | XF40 | MS60 | MS63 | MS65 |
|---|---|---|---|---|---|---|
| 2009 | 12,000 | **PF63** 55.00 | **PF65** 65.00 | | | |

### KM# 1169 10 EURO

27.00 g., 0.925 Silver 0.803 oz. ASW, 40 mm. **Ruler:** Juan Carlos I **Subject:** Antoni Gaudi

| Date | Mintage | VF20 | XF40 | MS60 | MS63 | MS65 |
|---|---|---|---|---|---|---|
| 2010 | 10,000 | **PF63** 75.00 | **PF65** 85.00 | | | |

### KM# 1171 10 EURO

27.00 g., 0.925 Silver 0.803 oz. ASW, 40 mm. **Ruler:** Juan Carlos I **Subject:** EU Council Presidency

| Date | Mintage | VF20 | XF40 | MS60 | MS63 | MS65 |
|---|---|---|---|---|---|---|
| 2010 | — | **PF63** 70.00 | **PF65** 80.00 | | | |

### KM# 1173 10 EURO

27.00 g., 0.925 Silver 0.803 oz. ASW, 40 mm. **Ruler:** Juan Carlos I **Subject:** Holy Year 2010 - St. James the Elder

| Date | Mintage | VF20 | XF40 | MS60 | MS63 | MS65 |
|---|---|---|---|---|---|---|
| 2010 | 10,000 | **PF63** 70.00 | **PF65** 80.00 | | | |

### KM# 1174 10 EURO

27.00 g., 0.925 Silver 0.803 oz. ASW, 40 mm. **Ruler:** Juan Carlos I **Subject:** Shanghai Expo

| Date | Mintage | VF20 | XF40 | MS60 | MS63 | MS65 |
|---|---|---|---|---|---|---|
| 2010 | 10,000 | **PF63** 70.00 | **PF65** 80.00 | | | |

### KM# 1175 10 EURO

27.00 g., 0.925 Silver 0.803 oz. ASW, 40 mm. **Ruler:** Juan Carlos I **Subject:** Ibero-American Series - Historical Coins

| Date | Mintage | VF20 | XF40 | MS60 | MS63 | MS65 |
|---|---|---|---|---|---|---|
| 2010 | 12,000 | **PF63** 70.00 | **PF65** 80.00 | | | |

### KM# 1176 10 EURO

27.00 g., 0.925 Silver 0.803 oz. ASW, 40 mm. **Ruler:** Juan Carlos I **Subject:** FIFA World Cup - South Africa 2010

| Date | Mintage | VF20 | XF40 | MS60 | MS63 | MS65 |
|---|---|---|---|---|---|---|
| 2010 | 20,000 | **PF63** 65.00 | **PF65** 75.00 | | | |

### KM# 1178 10 EURO

27.00 g., 0.925 Silver 0.803 oz. ASW, 40 mm. **Ruler:** Juan Carlos I **Subject:** Francisco de Goya - The Clothed Maja

| Date | Mintage | VF20 | XF40 | MS60 | MS63 | MS65 |
|---|---|---|---|---|---|---|
| 2010 | 10,000 | **PF63** 85.00 | **PF65** 95.00 | | | |

### KM# 1179 10 EURO

27.00 g., 0.925 Silver 0.803 oz. ASW, 40 mm. **Ruler:** Juan Carlos I **Subject:** Francisco de Goya - The Grape Harvest

| Date | Mintage | VF20 | XF40 | MS60 | MS63 | MS65 |
|---|---|---|---|---|---|---|
| 2010 | 10,000 | **PF63** 85.00 | **PF65** 95.00 | | | |

### KM# 1180 10 EURO

27.00 g., 0.925 Silver 0.803 oz. ASW, 40 mm. **Ruler:** Juan Carlos I **Subject:** Francisco de Goya - Duel with Clubs

| Date | Mintage | VF20 | XF40 | MS60 | MS63 | MS65 |
|---|---|---|---|---|---|---|
| 2010 | 12,000 | **PF63** 85.00 | **PF65** 95.00 | | | |

### KM# 1165 10 EURO

27.00 g., 0.925 Silver 0.803 oz. ASW, 40 mm. **Ruler:** Juan Carlos I **Subject:** Numismatic Treasurers - Silver Shekel of Carthage

| Date | Mintage | VF20 | XF40 | MS60 | MS63 | MS65 |
|---|---|---|---|---|---|---|
| 2011 | 10,000 | **PF63** 65.00 | **PF65** 75.00 | | | |

### KM# 1185 10 EURO

27.00 g., 0.925 Silver 0.803 oz. ASW, 40 mm. **Ruler:** Juan Carlos I **Subject:** International Year of Chemistry **Rev:** Marie Curie

| Date | Mintage | VF20 | XF40 | MS60 | MS63 | MS65 |
|---|---|---|---|---|---|---|
| 2011 | 10,000 | **PF63** 100 | **PF65** 110 | | | |

### KM# 1219 10 EURO

27.00 g., 0.925 Silver 0.803 oz. ASW, 40 mm. **Ruler:** Juan Carlos I **Subject:** Spain-Portugal

| Date | Mintage | VF20 | XF40 | MS60 | MS63 | MS65 |
|---|---|---|---|---|---|---|
| 2011 | 10,000 | **PF63** 70.00 | **PF65** 80.00 | | | |

**KM# 1220 10 EURO**
27.00 g., 0.925 Silver 0.803 oz. ASW, 40 mm. **Ruler:** Juan Carlos I **Subject:** Historic Spanish Coin, Ibero American series

| Date | Mintage | VF20 | XF40 | MS60 | MS63 | MS65 |
|---|---|---|---|---|---|---|
| 2011 | — | PF63 75.00 | PF65 85.00 | | | |

**KM# 1223 10 EURO**
27.00 g., 0.925 Silver 0.803 oz. ASW, 40 mm. **Ruler:** Juan Carlos I **Subject:** Zurbaran - Hercules

| Date | Mintage | VF20 | XF40 | MS60 | MS63 | MS65 |
|---|---|---|---|---|---|---|
| 2011 | 10,000 | PF63 90.00 | PF65 100 | | | |

**KM# 1224 10 EURO**
27.00 g., 0.925 Silver 0.803 oz. ASW, 40 mm. **Ruler:** Juan Carlos I **Subject:** Ribera-Jacdo

| Date | Mintage | VF20 | XF40 | MS60 | MS63 | MS65 |
|---|---|---|---|---|---|---|
| 2011 | 10,000 | PF63 90.00 | PF65 100 | | | |

**KM# 1225 10 EURO**
27.00 g., 0.925 Silver 0.803 oz. ASW, 40 mm. **Ruler:** Juan Carlos I **Subject:** Musillo - Bren Pastar

| Date | Mintage | VF20 | XF40 | MS60 | MS63 | MS65 |
|---|---|---|---|---|---|---|
| 2011 | 10,000 | PF63 90.00 | PF65 100 | | | |

**KM# 1248 10 EURO**
27.00 g., 0.925 Silver 0.803 oz. ASW, 40 mm. **Ruler:** Juan Carlos I **Subject:** Orellana

| Date | Mintage | VF20 | XF40 | MS60 | MS63 | MS65 |
|---|---|---|---|---|---|---|
| 2011 | 12,000 | PF63 65.00 | PF65 75.00 | | | |

**KM# 1217 10 EURO**
27.00 g., 0.925 Silver 0.803 oz. ASW, 40 mm. **Ruler:** Juan Carlos I **Subject:** Spain-Russia **Note:** The reverse design is the same as a Russian 3 Rouble

| Date | Mintage | VF20 | XF40 | MS60 | MS63 | MS65 |
|---|---|---|---|---|---|---|
| 2012 | 7,500 | PF63 80.00 | PF65 90.00 | | | |

**KM# 1255 10 EURO**
**Ruler:** Juan Carlos I **Subject:** Juan Gris

| Date | Mintage | VF20 | XF40 | MS60 | MS63 | MS65 |
|---|---|---|---|---|---|---|
| 2012 | — | PF63 75.00 | PF65 95.00 | | | |

**KM# 1256 10 EURO**
27.00 g., Silver, 40 mm. **Ruler:** Juan Carlos I **Subject:** 200th Anniversary of Constitution

| Date | Mintage | VF20 | XF40 | MS60 | MS63 | MS65 |
|---|---|---|---|---|---|---|
| 2012 | Est. 10000 | PF63 85.00 | PF65 95.00 | | | |

**KM# 1257 10 EURO**
27.00 g., 0.925 Silver 0.803 oz. ASW, 40 mm. **Ruler:** Juan Carlos I **Subject:** Brasil World Cup 2014 **Rev:** Map and Trophy - Partially gilt

| Date | Mintage | VF20 | XF40 | MS60 | MS63 | MS65 |
|---|---|---|---|---|---|---|
| 2012 | 15,000 | PF63 65.00 | PF65 75.00 | | | |

**KM# 1258 10 EURO**
27.00 g., 0.925 Silver 0.803 oz. ASW, 40 mm. **Ruler:** Juan Carlos I **Subject:** Spain-Japan relations, 400th Anniversary **Obv:** Head left **Rev:** Priest at cross, latent image switches from Spanish to Japanese flag

| Date | Mintage | VF20 | XF40 | MS60 | MS63 | MS65 |
|---|---|---|---|---|---|---|
| 2013 | 30,000 | PF63 85.00 | PF65 95.00 | | | |

**KM# 1259 10 EURO**
27.00 g., 0.925 Silver 0.803 oz. ASW, 40 mm. **Ruler:** Juan Carlos I **Obv:** Head left **Rev:** Cervantes writing at right, Don Quixote and Sanchez at left

| Date | Mintage | VF20 | XF40 | MS60 | MS63 | MS65 |
|---|---|---|---|---|---|---|
| 2013 | 10,000 | PF63 80.00 | PF65 90.00 | | | |

**KM# 1280 10 EURO**
27.00 g., 0.925 Silver 0.803 oz. ASW, 40 mm. **Ruler:** Juan Carlos I **Subject:** Juan Carlos, 75th Anniversary of Birth

| Date | Mintage | VF20 | XF40 | MS60 | MS63 | MS65 |
|---|---|---|---|---|---|---|
| 2013 | 10,000 | PF63 75.00 | PF65 85.00 | | | |

**KM# 1284 10 EURO**
27.00 g., 0.925 Silver 0.803 oz. ASW, 40 mm. **Ruler:** Juan Carlos I **Subject:** Isaac Peral and his submarine, 125th Anniversary

| Date | Mintage | VF20 | XF40 | MS60 | MS63 | MS65 |
|---|---|---|---|---|---|---|
| 2013 | 10,000 | PF63 75.00 | PF65 85.00 | | | |

**KM# 1285 10 EURO**
27.00 g., 0.925 Silver 0.803 oz. ASW, 40 mm. **Ruler:** Juan Carlos I **Subject:** Holey Dollar and Dump, 200th Anniversary

| Date | Mintage | VF20 | XF40 | MS60 | MS63 | MS65 |
|---|---|---|---|---|---|---|
| 2013 | 5,000 | PF63 75.00 | PF65 85.00 | | | |

**KM# 1286 10 EURO**
27.00 g., 0.925 Silver 0.803 oz. ASW, 40 mm. **Ruler:** Juan Carlos I **Subject:** Balboa and the Pacific Ocean, 500th Anniversary

| Date | Mintage | VF20 | XF40 | MS60 | MS63 | MS65 |
|---|---|---|---|---|---|---|
| 2013 | 10,000 | PF63 75.00 | PF65 85.00 | | | |

**KM# 1290 10 EURO**
27.00 g., 0.925 Silver 0.803 oz. ASW, 40 mm. **Ruler:** Juan Carlos I **Subject:** World Cup Brazil, 2014

| Date | Mintage | VF20 | XF40 | MS60 | MS63 | MS65 |
|---|---|---|---|---|---|---|
| 2013 | 10,000 | PF63 75.00 | PF65 85.00 | | | |

**KM# 1292 10 EURO**
27.00 g., 0.925 Silver 0.803 oz. ASW, 40 mm. **Ruler:** Juan Carlos I **Subject:** Granada, 1000th Anniversary **Rev:** Court of Lions in the Alhambra

| Date | Mintage | VF20 | XF40 | MS60 | MS63 | MS65 |
|---|---|---|---|---|---|---|
| 2013 | 10,000 | PF63 75.00 | PF65 85.00 | | | |

**KM# 1300 10 EURO**
27.00 g., 0.925 Silver 0.803 oz. ASW, 40 mm. **Ruler:** Juan Carlos I **Subject:** Titian painting

| Date | Mintage | VF20 | XF40 | MS60 | MS63 | MS65 |
|---|---|---|---|---|---|---|
| 2013 | 10,000 | PF63 85.00 | PF65 95.00 | | | |

**KM# 1301 10 EURO**
27.00 g., 0.925 Silver 0.803 oz. ASW, 40 mm. **Ruler:** Juan Carlos I **Subject:** Rafael paintings

| Date | Mintage | VF20 | XF40 | MS60 | MS63 | MS65 |
|---|---|---|---|---|---|---|
| 2013 | 10,000 | PF63 75.00 | PF65 85.00 | | | |

**KM# 1302 10 EURO**
27.00 g., 0.925 Silver 0.803 oz. ASW, 40 mm. **Ruler:** Juan Carlos I **Subject:** Vicente Lopez paintings

| Date | Mintage | VF20 | XF40 | MS60 | MS63 | MS65 |
|---|---|---|---|---|---|---|
| 2013 | 10,000 | PF63 85.00 | PF65 95.00 | | | |

**KM# 1308 10 EURO**
27.00 g., 0.925 Silver 0.803 oz. ASW, 40 mm. **Ruler:** Juan Carlos I **Subject:** Royal Spanish Academy, 300th Anniversary **Obv:** Head left **Rev:** Columned building entrance

| Date | Mintage | VF20 | XF40 | MS60 | MS63 | MS65 |
|---|---|---|---|---|---|---|
| 2014 | 10,000 | PF65 75.00 | | | | |

**KM# 1309 10 EURO**
27.00 g., 0.925 Silver 0.803 oz. ASW, 40 mm. **Ruler:** Juan Carlos I **Subject:** Manuel de Falla, composer **Rev:** Head facing

| Date | Mintage | VF20 | XF40 | MS60 | MS63 | MS65 |
|---|---|---|---|---|---|---|
| 2014 | 7,500 | PF65 75.00 | | | | |

**KM# 1311 10 EURO**
27.00 g., 0.925 Silver 0.803 oz. ASW, 40 mm. **Ruler:** Juan Carlos I **Subject:** 1 real of Ferdinand and Isabella **Obv:** Old coin **Rev:** Old coin

| Date | Mintage | VF20 | XF40 | MS60 | MS63 | MS65 |
|---|---|---|---|---|---|---|
| 2014 | 7,500 | PF65 75.00 | | | | |

**KM# 1314 10 EURO**
27.00 g., 0.925 Silver 0.803 oz. ASW partially gilt, 40 mm. **Ruler:** Juan Carlos I **Subject:** FIFA World Cup - Brazil **Obv:** Playing field, partially gilt **Rev:** Trophy and two players, partially gilt

| Date | Mintage | VF20 | XF40 | MS60 | MS63 | MS65 |
|---|---|---|---|---|---|---|
| 2014 | 8,000 | PF65 75.00 | | | | |

**KM# 1315 10 EURO**
27.00 g., 0.925 Silver 0.803 oz. ASW, 40 mm. **Ruler:** Juan Carlos I **Subject:** Peter Paul Rubens art in the Prada **Obv:** Three Graces **Rev:** Philip II on horseback

| Date | Mintage | VF20 | XF40 | MS60 | MS63 | MS65 |
|---|---|---|---|---|---|---|
| 2014 | 7,000 | PF65 75.00 | | | | |

**KM# 1316 10 EURO**
27.00 g., 0.925 Silver 0.803 oz. ASW, 40 mm. **Ruler:** Juan Carlos I **Subject:** Paintings of van Dyck in the Prada **Obv:** Two men **Rev:** Group

| Date | Mintage | VF20 | XF40 | MS60 | MS63 | MS65 |
|---|---|---|---|---|---|---|
| 2014 | 7,000 | PF65 75.00 | | | | |

**KM# 1317 10 EURO**
27.00 g., 0.925 Silver 0.803 oz. ASW, 40 mm. **Ruler:** Juan Carlos I **Subject:** El Greco paintings in the Prada **Obv:** Jesus and apostles **Rev:** Jesus off the cross

| Date | Mintage | VF20 | XF40 | MS60 | MS63 | MS65 |
|---|---|---|---|---|---|---|
| 2014 | 7,000 | PF65 70.00 | | | | |

**KM# 1049 12 EURO**
18.00 g., 0.925 Silver 0.5353 oz. ASW, 33 mm. **Ruler:** Juan Carlos I **Subject:** Spanish European Union Presidency **Obv:** Conjoined heads left **Rev:** Distorted star design **Edge:** Reeded

| Date | Mintage | VF20 | XF40 | MS60 | MS63 | MS65 |
|---|---|---|---|---|---|---|
| 2002 | 1,608,400 | — | — | — | 20.00 | 22.00 |
| 2002 Special select | — | — | — | — | — | 25.00 |
| 2002 | Est. 30000 | PF65 42.00 | | | | |

**KM# 1051 12 EURO**
18.00 g., 0.925 Silver 0.5353 oz. ASW, 33 mm. **Ruler:** Juan Carlos I **Subject:** 25th Anniversary of Constitution **Obv:** Conjoined heads left **Rev:** National arms above denomination **Edge:** Plain

| Date | Mintage | VF20 | XF40 | MS60 | MS63 | MS65 |
|---|---|---|---|---|---|---|
| 2003 | 1,468,800 | — | — | — | 23.00 | 25.00 |
| 2003 | 19,346 | PF65 35.00 | | | | |

**KM# 1069 12 EURO**
18.00 g., 0.925 Silver 0.5353 oz. ASW, 33 mm. **Ruler:** Juan Carlos I **Obv:** Juan Carlos and Sofia **Rev:** Felipe and Letizia

| Date | Mintage | VF20 | XF40 | MS60 | MS63 | MS65 |
|---|---|---|---|---|---|---|
| 2004 M | 2,505,700 | — | — | — | 22.00 | 24.00 |

**KM# 1095 12 EURO**
18.00 g., 0.925 Silver 0.5353 oz. ASW, 32.93 mm. **Ruler:** Juan Carlos I **Subject:** 500th Anniversary - Death of Isabel **Obv:** Conjoined heads left **Obv. Legend:** JUAN CARLOS I Y SOFIA **Rev:** Bust of Isabella I left **Rev. Legend:** ISABEL I DE CASTILLA / 1481-1504 **Edge:** Plain

| Date | Mintage | VF20 | XF40 | MS60 | MS63 | MS65 |
|---|---|---|---|---|---|---|
| 2004 (M) | 1,496,100 | — | — | — | 23.00 | 25.00 |
| 2004 (M) | 12,420 | PF65 38.00 | | | | |

**KM# 1096 12 EURO**
18.00 g., 0.925 Silver 0.5353 oz. ASW, 32.94 mm. **Ruler:** Juan Carlos I **Subject:** Wedding of Prince Philip and Letizia Ortiz Rocasolano **Obv:** Conjoined heads left **Obv. Legend:** JUAN CARLOS I Y SOFIA **Rev:** Busts of wedding couple facing 3/4 right **Rev. Legend:** FELIPE Y LETIZIA - 22.V.2004 **Edge:** Plain

| Date | Mintage | VF20 | XF40 | MS60 | MS63 | MS65 |
|---|---|---|---|---|---|---|
| 2004 (M) | 2,505,700 | — | — | — | 22.00 | 24.00 |
| 2004 (M) | 27,655 | PF65 22.00 | | | | |

**KM# 1067 12 EURO**
18.00 g., 0.925 Silver 0.5353 oz. ASW, 33 mm. **Ruler:** Juan Carlos I **Subject:** Don Quixote **Obv:** Conjoined heads left **Rev:** Man seated on books **Edge:** Reeded

| Date | Mintage | VF20 | XF40 | MS60 | MS63 | MS65 |
|---|---|---|---|---|---|---|
| 2005 | 1,880,900 | — | — | — | 22.00 | 24.00 |

**KM# 1113 12 EURO**
18.00 g., 0.925 Silver 0.5353 oz. ASW, 32.95 mm. **Ruler:** Juan Carlos I **Subject:** 500th Anniversary - Death of Columbus **Obv:** Conjoined heads left **Obv. Legend:** JUAN CARLOS I Y SOFIA **Rev:** Bust of Columbus facing 3/4 right, latitude and longitude lines with three small sailing ships in background **Edge:** Plain

| Date | Mintage | VF20 | XF40 | MS60 | MS63 | MS65 |
|---|---|---|---|---|---|---|
| 2006 (M) | 1,379,600 | — | — | — | 22.00 | 24.00 |

**KM# 1129 12 EURO**
18.00 g., 0.925 Silver 0.5353 oz. ASW, 32 mm. **Ruler:** Juan Carlos I **Rev:** Hand with pen **Rev. Legend:** 50 ANIVERSARIO • TRATADO DE ROMA **Rev. Inscription:** EUROPA

| Date | Mintage | VF20 | XF40 | MS60 | MS63 | MS65 |
|---|---|---|---|---|---|---|
| 2007 (M) | 1,002,500 | — | — | — | 22.00 | 24.00 |
| 2007 | 20,000 | PF65 30.00 | | | | |

**KM# 1195 12 EURO**
18.00 g., 0.925 Silver 0.5353 oz. ASW, 33 mm. **Ruler:** Juan Carlos I **Subject:** International Year of Planet Earth

| Date | Mintage | VF20 | XF40 | MS60 | MS63 | MS65 |
|---|---|---|---|---|---|---|
| 2008 | 45,000 | PF65 25.00 | | | | |

**KM# 1212 12 EURO**
18.00 g., 0.925 Silver 0.5353 oz. ASW, 33 mm. **Ruler:** Juan Carlos I **Subject:** European Monetary Union, 10th Anniversary

| Date | Mintage | VF20 | XF40 | MS60 | MS63 | MS65 |
|---|---|---|---|---|---|---|
| 2009 | 20,000 | PF65 25.00 | | | | |

**KM# 1172 12 EURO**
18.00 g., 0.925 Silver 0.5353 oz. ASW, 33 mm. **Ruler:** Juan Carlos I **Subject:** EU Council Presidency

| Date | Mintage | VF20 | XF40 | MS60 | MS63 | MS65 |
|---|---|---|---|---|---|---|
| 2010 | — | PF65 28.00 | | | | |

**KM# 1133 20 EURO**
1.24 g., 0.999 Gold 0.0398 oz. AGW, 13.92 mm. **Ruler:** Juan Carlos I **Obv:** National arms **Obv. Legend:** JUAN CARLOS I REY DE ESPAÑA - AÑO DE ESPAÑA EN CHINA **Rev:** Early silver "Pillar" reales coin with Chinese chopmarks

| Date | Mintage | VF20 | XF40 | MS60 | MS63 | MS65 |
|---|---|---|---|---|---|---|
| 2007 | 15,000 | PF63 100 | PF65 110 | | | |

**KM# 1193 20 EURO**
1.24 g., 0.999 Gold 0.0398 oz. AGW, 13.92 mm. **Ruler:** Juan Carlos I **Subject:** Numismatic Treasures - Roman Aureaus

| Date | Mintage | VF20 | XF40 | MS60 | MS63 | MS65 |
|---|---|---|---|---|---|---|
| 2008 | 12,000 | PF63 100 | PF65 115 | | | |

**KM# 1206 20 EURO**
1.24 g., 0.999 Gold 0.0398 oz. AGW, 13.92 mm. **Ruler:** Juan Carlos I **Subject:** Numismatic Treasures - Spanish coin **Obv:** Obverse of 1609 gold coin **Rev:** Reverse of 1609 gold coin

| Date | Mintage | VF20 | XF40 | MS60 | MS63 | MS65 |
|---|---|---|---|---|---|---|
| 2009 | 12,000 | PF63 100 | PF65 115 | | | |

**KM# 1177 20 EURO**
1.24 g., 0.999 Gold 0.0398 oz. AGW, 13.92 mm. **Ruler:** Juan Carlos I **Subject:** FIFA World Cup - South Africa

| Date | Mintage | VF20 | XF40 | MS60 | MS63 | MS65 |
|---|---|---|---|---|---|---|
| 2010 | 20,000 | PF63 100 | PF65 110 | | | |

**KM# 1183 20 EURO**
18.00 g., 0.925 Silver 0.5353 oz. ASW, 33 mm. **Ruler:** Juan Carlos I **Subject:** FIFA World Cup Winners

| Date | Mintage | VF20 | XF40 | MS60 | MS63 | MS65 |
|---|---|---|---|---|---|---|
| 2010 | 12,000 | PF63 60.00 | | | | |

**KM# 1166 20 EURO**
1.24 g., 0.999 Gold 0.0398 oz. AGW, 13.92 mm. **Ruler:** Juan Carlos I **Subject:** Numismatic Treasures - Leovigild Gold

| Date | Mintage | VF20 | XF40 | MS60 | MS63 | MS65 |
|---|---|---|---|---|---|---|
| 2011 | 12,000 | PF63 100 | PF65 110 | | | |

**KM# 1218 20 EURO**
1.24 g., 0.999 Gold 0.0398 oz. AGW **Ruler:** Juan Carlos I **Subject:** Span & Portugal **Shape:** 13.92

| Date | Mintage | VF20 | XF40 | MS60 | MS63 | MS65 |
|---|---|---|---|---|---|---|
| 2011 | 12,000 | PF63 100 | PF65 110 | | | |

**KM# 1246 20 EURO**
18.00 g., 0.925 Silver 0.5353 oz. ASW, 33 mm. **Ruler:** Juan Carlos I **Subject:** International Women's Day, 100th Anniversary

| Date | Mintage | VF20 | XF40 | MS60 | MS63 | MS65 |
|---|---|---|---|---|---|---|
| 2011 | 12,000 | PF63 50.00 | PF65 60.00 | | | |

**KM# 1281 20 EURO**
1.24 g., 0.999 Gold 0.0398 oz. AGW, 13.92 mm. **Ruler:** Juan Carlos I **Subject:** Juan Carlos, 75th Anniversary of Birth

| Date | Mintage | VF20 | XF40 | MS60 | MS63 | MS65 |
|---|---|---|---|---|---|---|
| 2013 | 12,000 | PF63 75.00 | PF65 85.00 | | | |

**KM# 1312 20 EURO**
1.24 g., 0.999 Gold 0.0398 oz. AGW, 13.92 mm. **Ruler:** Juan Carlos I **Subject:** 1/2 Excelente of Seville **Obv:** Old Coin **Rev:** Old Coin

| Date | Mintage | VF20 | XF40 | MS60 | MS63 | MS65 |
|---|---|---|---|---|---|---|
| 2014 | 10,000 | PF65 100 | | | | |

**KM# 1253 30 EURO**
18.00 g., 0.925 Silver 0.5353 oz. ASW, 33 mm. **Ruler:** Juan Carlos I **Subject:** Juan Carlos, 75th Anniversary of Birth **Obv:** Head left **Rev:** Crowned arms in fleece collar

| Date | Mintage | VF20 | XF40 | MS60 | MS63 | MS65 |
|---|---|---|---|---|---|---|
| 2013 | — | PF65 40.00 | | | | |

**KM# 1307 30 EURO**
18.00 g., 0.925 Silver 0.5353 oz. ASW, 33 mm. **Ruler:** Juan Carlos I **Subject:** El Greco - Dominikos Theotokopoulos, 400th Anniversary of Death **Obv:** Conjoined heads left **Rev:** Half-length bust facing

| Date | Mintage | VF20 | XF40 | MS60 | MS63 | MS65 |
|---|---|---|---|---|---|---|
| 2014 | 2,000,000 | — | — | — | — | 45.00 |

**KM# 1085 50 EURO**
168.75 g., 0.925 Silver 5.0185 oz. ASW, 73 mm. **Ruler:** Juan Carlos I **Subject:** 150th Anniversary - Birth of Antonio Gaudí **Obv:** Bust of Gaudií at right **Obv. Legend:** Año Internacional **Rev:** Sagrada Familia

| Date | Mintage | VF20 | XF40 | MS60 | MS63 | MS65 |
|---|---|---|---|---|---|---|
| 2002 (M) | 7,594 | PF65 450 | | | | |

**KM# 1057 50 EURO**
168.75 g., 0.925 Silver 5.0185 oz. ASW with removeable gold plated silver insert, 73 mm. **Ruler:** Juan Carlos I **Obv:** Dali's "Dream State" painting **Rev:** Dali's "Rhinocerotic Disintegration..." painting **Edge:** Reeded

| Date | Mintage | VF20 | XF40 | MS60 | MS63 | MS65 |
|---|---|---|---|---|---|---|
| 2004 | 10,455 | PF63 550 | PF65 600 | | | |

**KM# 1093 50 EURO**
168.75 g., 0.925 Silver 5.0185 oz. ASW, 73 mm. **Ruler:** Juan Carlos I **Subject:** 1st Anniversary of Euro **Obv:** Conjoined heads left **Obv. Legend:** PREMIER ANIVERSARIO EURO • JUAN CARLOS I Y SOFÍA **Rev:** National arms at center surrounded by various items of architecture

| Date | Mintage | VF20 | XF40 | MS60 | MS63 | MS65 |
|---|---|---|---|---|---|---|
| 2003 | 5,554 | **PF65** 500 | | | | |

**KM# 1061 50 EURO**
168.73 g., 0.925 Silver 5.0179 oz. ASW, 73 mm. **Ruler:** Juan Carlos I **Obv:** Crowned bust left(1451-1504) and castle within beaded circle **Rev:** Surrender of Grenada scene within beaded circle **Edge:** Reeded

| Date | Mintage | VF20 | XF40 | MS60 | MS63 | MS65 |
|---|---|---|---|---|---|---|
| 2004 | 3,158 | **PF65** 500 | | | | |

**KM# 1107 50 EURO**
168.75 g., 0.925 Silver 5.0185 oz. ASW, 73 mm. **Ruler:** Juan Carlos I **Obv:** 1/2 length figure of Miguel de Cervantes Saavedra facing writing in manuscript with quill pen **Obv. Legend:** ESPAÑA - IV CENTENARIO DE LA PRIMERA EDICIÓn DE "EL QUIJOTE **Rev:** Quixote

| Date | Mintage | VF20 | XF40 | MS60 | MS63 | MS65 |
|---|---|---|---|---|---|---|
| 2005 (M) | 5,795 | **PF65** 450 | | | | |

**KM# 1117 50 EURO**
168.75 g., 0.925 Silver 5.0185 oz. ASW, 73 mm. **Ruler:** Juan Carlos I **Subject:** 500th Anniversary - Death of Columbus **Obv:** Landing party at Guanahani **Obv. Legend:** ESPAÑA **Rev:** Columbus standing facing 3/4 left with right arm outstretched standing on outline of the northern part of South America **Rev. Legend:** CRISTOBAL COLON **Edge:** Plain

| Date | Mintage | VF20 | XF40 | MS60 | MS63 | MS65 |
|---|---|---|---|---|---|---|
| 2006 (M) | 4,265 | **PF65** 450 | | | | |

**KM# 1127 50 EURO**
168.75 g., 0.925 Silver 5.0185 oz. ASW, 73 mm. **Ruler:** Juan Carlos I **Rev:** Euro seated on resting bull left **Rev. Legend:** V ANIVERSARIO DEL EURO

| Date | Mintage | VF20 | XF40 | MS60 | MS63 | MS65 |
|---|---|---|---|---|---|---|
| 2007 | 5,000 | **PF63** 400 | **PF65** 425 | | | |

**KM# 1138 50 EURO**
168.75 g., 0.925 Silver 5.0185 oz. ASW, 73 mm. **Ruler:** Juan Carlos I **Subject:** El Cid 700th Anniversary **Obv:** Statue of Rodrigo Diaz de Vivar in Burgos **Rev:** Two seated trumpeters

| Date | Mintage | VF20 | XF40 | MS60 | MS63 | MS65 |
|---|---|---|---|---|---|---|
| 2007 | 6,000 | **PF63** 400 | **PF65** 425 | | | |

**KM# 1189 50 EURO**
168.75 g., 0.925 Silver 5.0185 oz. ASW, 73 mm. **Ruler:** Juan Carlos I **Subject:** Velazquez

| Date | Mintage | VF20 | XF40 | MS60 | MS63 | MS65 |
|---|---|---|---|---|---|---|
| 2008 | 5,000 | **PF63** 400 | **PF65** 425 | | | |

**KM# 1198 50 EURO**
168.75 g., 0.925 Silver 5.0185 oz. ASW, 73 mm. **Ruler:** Juan Carlos I **Subject:** War of Independence, 200th Anniversary

| Date | Mintage | VF20 | XF40 | MS60 | MS63 | MS65 |
|---|---|---|---|---|---|---|
| 2008 | 5,000 | PF63 400 | PF65 425 | | | |

**KM# 1205 50 EURO**
168.75 g., 0.925 Silver 5.0185 oz. ASW, 73 mm. **Ruler:** Juan Carlos I **Subject:** Numismatic Treasurers - Spanish cincuentin

| Date | Mintage | VF20 | XF40 | MS60 | MS63 | MS65 |
|---|---|---|---|---|---|---|
| 2009 | 6,000 | PF63 400 | PF65 425 | | | |

**KM# 1208 50 EURO**
168.75 g., 0.925 Silver 5.0185 oz. ASW, 73 mm. **Ruler:** Juan Carlos I **Subject:** Dali

| Date | Mintage | VF20 | XF40 | MS60 | MS63 | MS65 |
|---|---|---|---|---|---|---|
| 2009 | 5,000 | PF63 425 | PF65 450 | | | |

**KM# 1181 50 EURO**
168.75 g., 0.925 Silver 5.0185 oz. ASW, 73 mm. **Ruler:** Juan Carlos I **Subject:** Francisco de Goya - Witches' Sabbath

| Date | Mintage | VF20 | XF40 | MS60 | MS63 | MS65 |
|---|---|---|---|---|---|---|
| 2010 | 6,000 | PF63 475 | PF65 500 | | | |

**KM# 1222 50 EURO**
168.75 g., 0.999 Silver 5.420 oz. ASW, 73 mm. **Ruler:** Juan Carlos I **Subject:** El Greco

| Date | Mintage | VF20 | XF40 | MS60 | MS63 | MS65 |
|---|---|---|---|---|---|---|
| 2011 | 5,000 | PF63 400 | PF65 425 | | | |

**KM# 1283 50 EURO**
168.75 g., 0.925 Silver 5.0185 oz. ASW, 75 mm. **Ruler:** Juan Carlos I **Subject:** Juan Carlos, 75th Anniversary of Birth

| Date | Mintage | VF20 | XF40 | MS60 | MS63 | MS65 |
|---|---|---|---|---|---|---|
| 2013 | 5,000 | PF65 250 | | | | |

**KM# 1287 50 EURO**
168.75 g., 0.925 Silver 5.0185 oz. ASW, 73 mm. **Ruler:** Juan Carlos I **Subject:** Balboa and the discovery of the Pacific Ocean, 500th Anniversary

| Date | Mintage | VF20 | XF40 | MS60 | MS63 | MS65 |
|---|---|---|---|---|---|---|
| 2013 | 5,000 | PF65 250 | | | | |

**KM# 1303 50 EURO**
168.75 g., 0.925 Silver 5.0185 oz. ASW, 73 mm. **Ruler:** Juan Carlos I **Subject:** Velazquez paintings

| Date | Mintage | VF20 | XF40 | MS60 | MS63 | MS65 |
|---|---|---|---|---|---|---|
| 2013 | 5,000 | PF65 250 | | | | |

**KM# 1318 50 EURO**
168.75 g., 0.925 Silver 5.0185 oz. ASW, 73 mm. **Ruler:** Juan Carlos I **Subject:** Goya paintings in the Prada **Obv:** Man flying kite in group **Rev:** Winter scene

| Date | Mintage | VF20 | XF40 | MS60 | MS63 | MS65 |
|---|---|---|---|---|---|---|
| 2014 | 3,500 | PF65 325 | | | | |

**KM# 1077 100 EURO**
6.75 g., 0.999 Gold 0.2168 oz. AGW, 23 mm. **Ruler:** Juan Carlos I **Obv:** Head left **Obv. Legend:** JUAN CARLOS I REY DE ESPAÑA **Rev:** Player running right kicking ball **Rev. Legend:** ALEMANIA 2006 at bottom **Note:** Issued in 2004.

| Date | Mintage | VF20 | XF40 | MS60 | MS63 | MS65 |
|---|---|---|---|---|---|---|
| 2003 (M) | 8,230 | PF65 600 | | | | |

**KM# 1103 100 EURO**
6.75 g., 0.999 Gold 0.2168 oz. AGW, 23 mm. **Ruler:** Juan Carlos I **Subject:** XVIII World Football Games - Germany 2006 **Obv:** Head left **Obv. Legend:** JUAN CARLOS I REY DE ESPAÑA **Rev:** Goalie deflecting ball at net **Rev. Inscription:** COPA MUNDIAL DE LA FIFA

| Date | Mintage | VF20 | XF40 | MS60 | MS63 | MS65 |
|---|---|---|---|---|---|---|
| 2004 (M) | 25,000 | PF63 500 | PF65 550 | | | |

**KM# 1167 100 EURO**
168.88 g., 0.925 Silver 5.0224 oz. ASW with gold plating, 73 mm. **Ruler:** Juan Carlos I **Subject:** Numismatic treasurers - The Centen, 100 Escudos, 1609

| Date | Mintage | VF20 | XF40 | MS60 | MS63 | MS65 |
|---|---|---|---|---|---|---|
| 2009 | 6,000 | PF63 450 | PF65 475 | | | |

**KM# 1204 100 EURO**
6.75 g., 0.999 Gold 0.2168 oz. AGW, 23 mm. **Ruler:** Juan Carlos I **Subject:** Numismatic Treasures - Spanish Escudo

| Date | Mintage | VF20 | XF40 | MS60 | MS63 | MS65 |
|---|---|---|---|---|---|---|
| 2009 | — | PF63 400 | PF65 425 | | | |

**KM# 1215 100 EURO**
6.75 g., 0.999 Gold 0.2168 oz. AGW, 23 mm. **Ruler:** Juan Carlos I **Subject:** World Cup Soccer, Africa

| Date | Mintage | VF20 | XF40 | MS60 | MS63 | MS65 |
|---|---|---|---|---|---|---|
| 2009 | 6,000 | PF65 550 | | | | |

**KM# 1168 100 EURO**
6.75 g., 0.999 Gold 0.2168 oz. AGW, 23 mm. **Ruler:** Juan Carlos I **Subject:** Numismatic Treasures - Swinthila Gold

| Date | Mintage | VF20 | XF40 | MS60 | MS63 | MS65 |
|---|---|---|---|---|---|---|
| 2011 | 6,000 | PF63 525 | PF65 550 | | | |

**KM# 1289 100 EURO**
6.75 g., 0.999 Gold 0.2168 oz. AGW, 23 mm. **Ruler:** Juan Carlos I **Subject:** Cervantes

| Date | Mintage | VF20 | XF40 | MS60 | MS63 | MS65 |
|---|---|---|---|---|---|---|
| 2013 | 5,000 | PF65 450 | | | | |

**KM# 1291 100 EURO**
6.75 g., 0.999 Gold 0.2168 oz. AGW, 23 mm. **Ruler:** Juan Carlos I **Subject:** World Cup, Brazil, 2014

| Date | Mintage | VF20 | XF40 | MS60 | MS63 | MS65 |
|---|---|---|---|---|---|---|
| 2013 | 4,000 | PF65 450 | | | | |

**KM# 1293 100 EURO**
6.75 g., 0.999 Gold 0.2168 oz. AGW, 23 mm. **Ruler:** Juan Carlos I **Subject:** Granada, 1000th Anniversary **Rev:** Central fountain from the Alhambra

| Date | Mintage | VF20 | XF40 | MS60 | MS63 | MS65 |
|---|---|---|---|---|---|---|
| 2013 | 5,000 | PF65 450 | | | | |

**KM# 1313 100 EURO**
6.75 g., 0.999 Gold 0.2168 oz. AGW, 23 mm. **Ruler:** Juan Carlos I **Subject:** 2 Excelentes of Granada **Obv:** Old coin **Rev:** Old Coin

| Date | Mintage | VF20 | XF40 | MS60 | MS63 | MS65 |
|---|---|---|---|---|---|---|
| 2014 | 8,000 | PF65 375.00 | | | | |

**KM# 1081 200 EURO**
13.50 g., 0.999 Gold 0.4336 oz. AGW, 30 mm. **Ruler:** Juan Carlos I **Subject:** XVII Football World Games 2002 - South Korea and Japan **Obv. Legend:** MUNDIAL DE FUTBOL/2002 - ESPAÑA **Rev:** Ball hitting net

| Date | Mintage | VF20 | XF40 | MS60 | MS63 | MS65 |
|---|---|---|---|---|---|---|
| 2002 (M) | 4,000 | PF65 1,050 | | | | |

**KM# 1075 200 EURO**
13.50 g., 0.999 Gold 0.4336 oz. AGW, 30 mm. **Ruler:** Juan Carlos I **Subject:** Birth of the Euro **Obv:** Spanish King and Queen left **Rev:** Mythological Europa riding on the back of a bull

| Date | Mintage | VF20 | XF40 | MS60 | MS63 | MS65 |
|---|---|---|---|---|---|---|
| 2003 | 20,000 | PF65 1,050 | | | | |

**KM# 1091 200 EURO**
13.50 g., 0.999 Gold 0.4336 oz. AGW **Ruler:** Juan Carlos I **Obv:** Conjoined heads left **Obv. Legend:** JUAN CARLOS I Y SOFIA **Rev:** Ediface of Parliament Building in Madrid **Rev. Legend:** CONSTITUCION ESPANOLA

| Date | Mintage | VF20 | XF40 | MS60 | MS63 | MS65 |
|---|---|---|---|---|---|---|
| 2003 (M) | 4,000 | PF63 800 | PF65 825 | | | |

**KM# 1062 200 EURO**
13.50 g., 0.999 Gold 0.4336 oz. AGW, 30 mm. **Ruler:** Juan Carlos I **Obv:** Seated crowned figures on shield flanked by date and value **Rev:** Crowned busts facing each other on coin design **Edge:** Reeded

| Date | Mintage | VF20 | XF40 | MS60 | MS63 | MS65 |
|---|---|---|---|---|---|---|
| 2004 | 1,936 | PF65 1,200 | | | | |

**KM# 1098 200 EURO**
13.50 g., 0.999 Gold 0.4336 oz. AGW, 30 mm. **Ruler:** Juan Carlos I **Subject:** Wedding of Prince Philip and Letizia Ortiz Rocasolano **Obv:** Conjoined heads left **Obv. Legend:** JUAN CARLOS I Y SOFIA **Rev:** Busts of wedding couple facing 3/4 right at center left, crowned shield at right **Rev. Legend:** FELIPE Y LETIZIA - 22.V.2004

| Date | Mintage | VF20 | XF40 | MS60 | MS63 | MS65 |
|---|---|---|---|---|---|---|
| 2004 (M) | 6,303 | PF65 1,200 | | | | |

**KM# 1100 200 EURO**
13.50 g., 0.999 Gold 0.4336 oz. AGW, 30 mm. **Ruler:** Juan Carlos I **Subject:** Expansion of the European Union **Obv:** Head left **Obv. Legend:** JUAN CARLOS I Y SOFIA **Rev:** Outlined map of the European Union

| Date | Mintage | VF20 | XF40 | MS60 | MS63 | MS65 |
|---|---|---|---|---|---|---|
| 2004 (M) | 5,000 | PF65 1,000 | | | | |

**KM# 1066 200 EURO**
13.50 g., 0.999 Gold 0.4336 oz. AGW, 30 mm. **Ruler:** Juan Carlos I **Subject:** European Peace and Freedom **Obv:** Juan Carlos **Rev:** European map on clasped hands **Edge:** Reeded

| Date | Mintage | VF20 | XF40 | MS60 | MS63 | MS65 |
|---|---|---|---|---|---|---|
| 2005 | 2,350 | PF65 1,100 | | | | |

**KM# 1111 200 EURO**
13.50 g., 0.999 Gold 0.4336 oz. AGW, 30 mm. **Ruler:** Juan Carlos I **Rev:** Crowned shield at left, head of Prince Philip left at right **Rev. Legend:** XXV ANIVERSAIO - PREMIOS PRÍNCIPE DE ASTURIAS

| Date | Mintage | VF20 | XF40 | MS60 | MS63 | MS65 |
|---|---|---|---|---|---|---|
| 2005 (M) | 1,690 | PF65 1,300 | | | | |

**KM# 1123 200 EURO**
13.50 g., 0.999 Gold 0.4336 oz. AGW, 30 mm. **Ruler:** Juan Carlos I **Obv:** Head left **Obv. Legend:** JUAN CARLOS I REY DE ESPAÑA **Rev:** Charles I (V) standing facing 3/4 right in front of portal **Rev. Legend:** CAROLVS IMPERATOR

| Date | Mintage | VF20 | XF40 | MS60 | MS63 | MS65 |
|---|---|---|---|---|---|---|
| 2006 (M) | 3,500 | PF65 1,050 | | | | |

**KM# 1136 200 EURO**
13.50 g., 0.999 Gold 0.4336 oz. AGW, 30 mm. **Ruler:** Juan Carlos I **Subject:** Treaty of Rome, 50th Anniversary **Obv:** Head left **Rev:** Map of Western Europe

| Date | Mintage | VF20 | XF40 | MS60 | MS63 | MS65 |
|---|---|---|---|---|---|---|
| 2007 | 3,500 | PF65 1,050 | | | | |

**KM# 1139 200 EURO**
13.50 g., 0.999 Gold 0.4336 oz. AGW, 30 mm. **Ruler:** Juan Carlos I **Subject:** El Cid, 700th Anniversary **Obv:** Rodrigo Diaz de Vivar bust facing **Rev:** Knight on horseback within rectangle

| Date | Mintage | VF20 | XF40 | MS60 | MS63 | MS65 |
|---|---|---|---|---|---|---|
| 2007 | 3,500 | PF65 1,050 | | | | |

**KM# 1188 200 EURO**
13.50 g., 0.999 Gold 0.4336 oz. AGW, 30 mm. **Ruler:** Juan Carlos I **Subject:** Velazquez

| Date | Mintage | VF20 | XF40 | MS60 | MS63 | MS65 |
|---|---|---|---|---|---|---|
| 2008 | 3,500 | PF65 1,050 | | | | |

**KM# 1191 200 EURO**
13.50 g., 0.999 Gold 0.4336 oz. AGW, 30 mm. **Ruler:** Juan Carlos I **Subject:** Soccer, European Champions

| Date | Mintage | VF20 | XF40 | MS60 | MS63 | MS65 |
|---|---|---|---|---|---|---|
| 2008 | 4,000 | PF65 1,050 | | | | |

**KM# 1202 200 EURO**
13.50 g., 0.999 Gold 0.4336 oz. AGW, 30 mm. **Ruler:** Juan Carlos I **Subject:** Alphonse the Wise

| Date | Mintage | VF20 | XF40 | MS60 | MS63 | MS65 |
|---|---|---|---|---|---|---|
| 2008 | 3,500 | PF65 1,050 | | | | |

**KM# 1213 200 EURO**
13.50 g., 0.999 Gold 0.4336 oz. AGW, 30 mm. **Ruler:** Juan Carlos I **Subject:** Philip II

| Date | Mintage | VF20 | XF40 | MS60 | MS63 | MS65 |
|---|---|---|---|---|---|---|
| 2009 | 3,000 | PF65 1,050 | | | | |

**KM# 1170 200 EURO**
13.50 g., 0.999 Gold 0.4336 oz. AGW, 30 mm. **Ruler:** Juan Carlos I **Subject:** Antoni Gaudi

| Date | Mintage | VF20 | XF40 | MS60 | MS63 | MS65 |
|---|---|---|---|---|---|---|
| 2010 | 3,000 | PF65 1,050 | | | | |

**KM# 1247 200 EURO**
13.50 g., 0.999 Gold 0.4336 oz. AGW, 30 mm. **Ruler:** Juan Carlos I **Subject:** Orellana

| Date | Mintage | VF20 | XF40 | MS60 | MS63 | MS65 |
|---|---|---|---|---|---|---|
| 2011 | 3,000 | PF65 1,050 | | | | |

**KM# 1288 200 EURO**
13.50 g., 0.999 Gold 0.4336 oz. AGW, 30 mm. **Ruler:** Juan Carlos I **Subject:** Balboa and the Pacific Ocean, 500th Anniversary

| Date | Mintage | VF20 | XF40 | MS60 | MS63 | MS65 |
|---|---|---|---|---|---|---|
| 2013 | 3,000 | PF65 1,050 | | | | |

**KM# 1310 200 EURO**
13.50 g., 0.999 Gold 0.4336 oz. AGW, 30 mm. **Ruler:** Juan Carlos I **Subject:** Manuel de Falla, composer **Rev:** Head facing

| Date | Mintage | VF20 | XF40 | MS60 | MS63 | MS65 |
|---|---|---|---|---|---|---|
| 2014 | 2,500 | PF65 1,050 | | | | |

**KM# 1112 300 EURO**
Bi-Metallic .554 AGW Gold center in .343 ASW Silver ring, 40 mm. **Ruler:** Juan Carlos I **Subject:** XVIII World Championship Football Games - Germany 2006 **Obv:** Football player facing kicking ball **Obv. Legend:** ESPAÑA **Rev:** Football player kicking ball into net at foreground **Rev. Legend:** COPA MUNDIAL DE LA FIFA - ALEMANIA **Shape:** 12-sided

| Date | Mintage | VF20 | XF40 | MS60 | MS63 | MS65 |
|---|---|---|---|---|---|---|
| 2005 (M) | 8,000 | PF65 1,350 | | | | |

**KM# 1121 300 EURO**
Bi-Metallic .554 AGW Gold center in .343 ASW Silver ring, 40 mm. **Ruler:** Juan Carlos I **Rev:** Basketball player facing tossing ball **Rev. Legend:** CAMPEONES DEL MUNDO - JAPÓN 2006 **Shape:** 12-sided

| Date | Mintage | VF20 | XF40 | MS60 | MS63 | MS65 |
|---|---|---|---|---|---|---|
| 2006 (M) | 866 | PF65 1,600 | | | | |

**KM# 1086 400 EURO**
27.00 g., 0.999 Gold 0.8672 oz. AGW, 38 mm. **Ruler:** Juan Carlos I **Subject:** 150th Anniversary - Birth of Antonio Gaudí **Obv:** Bust of Gaudí at right **Obv. Legend:** Año Internacional **Rev:** Casa Batlló

| Date | Mintage | VF20 | XF40 | MS60 | MS63 | MS65 |
|---|---|---|---|---|---|---|
| 2002 (M) | 3,000 | PF63 1,700 | | PF65 1,800 | | |

**KM# 1058 400 EURO**
27.00 g., 0.999 Gold 0.8672 oz. AGW, 38 mm. **Ruler:** Juan Carlos I **Obv:** Bust facing **Rev:** Dali's painting "Girl at the Window **Edge:** Reeded

| Date | Mintage | VF20 | XF40 | MS60 | MS63 | MS65 |
|---|---|---|---|---|---|---|
| 2004 | 4,477 | PF63 1,700 | | PF65 1,800 | | |

**KM# 1108 400 EURO**
27.00 g., 0.999 Gold 0.8672 oz. AGW, 38 mm. **Ruler:** Juan Carlos I **Obv:** Quixote seated reading a large book **Obv. Legend:** ESPAÑA - IV CENTENARIO DE LA PRIMERA EDICIÓN DE "EL QUIJOTE **Rev:** Quixote on horseback 3/4 right followed by his friend on a burro **Rev. Legend:** DON QUIJOTE DE LA MANCHA SANCHO PANZA

| Date | Mintage | VF20 | XF40 | MS60 | MS63 | MS65 |
|---|---|---|---|---|---|---|
| 2005 (M) | 2,019 | PF63 1,700 | | PF65 1,800 | | |

**KM# 1118 400 EURO**
27.00 g., 0.999 Gold 0.8672 oz. AGW, 38 mm. **Ruler:** Juan Carlos I **Subject:** 500th Anniversary - Death of Columbus **Obv:** Columbus **Rev:** Audience with Ferdinand and Isabella

| Date | Mintage | VF20 | XF40 | MS60 | MS63 | MS65 |
|---|---|---|---|---|---|---|
| 2006 (M) | 1,850 | PF63 1,700 | | PF65 1,800 | | |

**KM# 1128 400 EURO**
27.00 g., 0.999 Gold 0.8672 oz. AGW, 38 mm. **Ruler:** Juan Carlos I **Rev:** Large ring of stars around globe **Rev. Legend:** V ANIVERSARIO DEL EURO

| Date | Mintage | VF20 | XF40 | MS60 | MS63 | MS65 |
|---|---|---|---|---|---|---|
| 2007 | 3,000 | PF63 1,700 | PF65 1,800 | | | |

**KM# 1197 400 EURO**
27.00 g., 0.999 Gold 0.8672 oz. AGW, 38 mm. **Ruler:** Juan Carlos I **Subject:** War of Independence, 200th Anniversary

| Date | Mintage | VF20 | XF40 | MS60 | MS63 | MS65 |
|---|---|---|---|---|---|---|
| 2008 | 3,500 | PF63 1,700 | PF65 1,800 | | | |

**KM# 1207 400 EURO**
27.00 g., 0.999 Gold 0.8672 oz. AGW, 38 mm. **Ruler:** Juan Carlos I **Subject:** Dali

| Date | Mintage | VF20 | XF40 | MS60 | MS63 | MS65 |
|---|---|---|---|---|---|---|
| 2009 | 3,000 | PF63 1,700 | PF65 1,800 | | | |

**KM# 1182 400 EURO**
27.00 g., 0.999 Gold 0.8672 oz. AGW, 38 mm. **Ruler:** Juan Carlos I **Subject:** Francisco de Goya - Volaverunt

| Date | Mintage | VF20 | XF40 | MS60 | MS63 | MS65 |
|---|---|---|---|---|---|---|
| 2010 | 3,000 | PF63 1,700 | PF65 1,800 | | | |

**KM# 1221 400 EURO**
27.00 g., 0.999 Gold 0.8672 oz. AGW, 38 mm. **Ruler:** Juan Carlos I **Subject:** El Greco

| Date | Mintage | VF20 | XF40 | MS60 | MS63 | MS65 |
|---|---|---|---|---|---|---|
| 2011 | 3,000 | PF63 1,700 | PF65 1,800 | | | |

**KM# 1304 400 EURO**
27.00 g., 0.999 Gold 0.8672 oz. AGW, 38 mm. **Ruler:** Juan Carlos I **Subject:** Albrecht Durer paintings

| Date | Mintage | VF20 | XF40 | MS60 | MS63 | MS65 |
|---|---|---|---|---|---|---|
| 2013 | 3,000 | PF65 1,700 | | | | |

**KM# 1319 400 EURO**
27.00 g., 0.999 Gold 0.8672 oz. AGW, 38 mm. **Ruler:** Juan Carlos I **Subject:** El Greco paintings in the Prado **Obv:** Man's portrait **Rev:** Youth's portrait

| Date | Mintage | VF20 | XF40 | MS60 | MS63 | MS65 |
|---|---|---|---|---|---|---|
| 2014 | 2,000 | PF65 1,750 | | | | |

## MINT SETS

| KM# | Date | Mintage | Identification | Issue Price | Mkt Val |
|---|---|---|---|---|---|
| MS27 | 2000-2001 (8) | 46,426 | KM#832-833, 924, 991-992 (both dated 2000), 1012-1013, 1016 | 15.50 | 35.00 |
| MS28 | 2002 (8) | 99,301 | KM#1040-1047 | — | 15.00 |
| MS29 | 2003 (8) | 149 | KM#1040-1047 | — | 15.00 |
| MS30 | 2004 (8) | 43,000 | KM#1040-1047 | — | 55.00 |
| MS31 | 2005 (8) | 49,923 | KM#1040-1047 | — | 35.00 |
| MS32 | 2006 (8) | 49,996 | KM#1040-1047 | — | 12.50 |
| MS33 | 2007 (8) | — | KM#1040-1042, 1070-1074 | — | 30.00 |

## PROOF SETS

| KM# | Date | Mintage | Identification | Issue Price | Mkt Val |
|---|---|---|---|---|---|
| PS34 | 2002 (9) | 23,000 | KM#1040-1047, 1049 | 125 | 150 |
| PS35 | 2003 (9) | 8,904 | KM#1040-1047, 1051 | — | 320 |
| PS36 | 2005 (9) | 3,000 | KM#1040-1047, 1063 | — | 175 |
| PS38 | 2007 (9) | 1,800 | KM#1040-1042, 1070-1074, 1130 | — | 150 |
| PS39 | 2008 (8) | 2,000 | KM#1040-1042, 1070-1074 | — | 150 |
| PS40 | 2009 (9) | 5,000 | KM#1040-1042, 1070-1074, 1142.1 | — | 150 |
| PS41 | 2010 (9) | 5,000 | KM#1144-1150, 1152 | — | 150 |
| PS42 | 2011 (9) | 5,000 | KM#1144-1151, 1184 | — | 150 |

# SRI (SHRI) LANKA

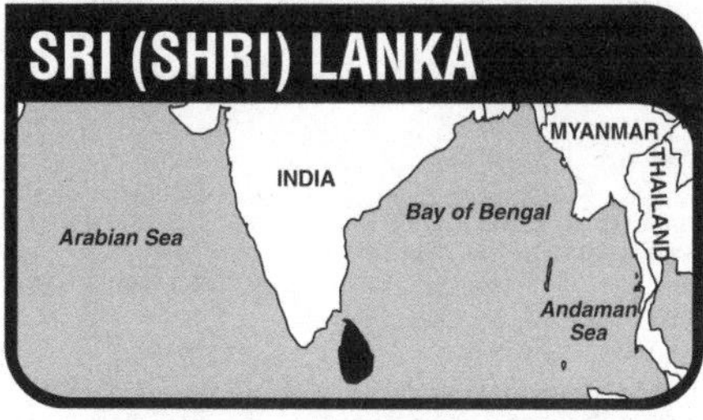


The Democratic Socialist Republic of Sri Lanka (formerly Ceylon) situated in the Indian Ocean 18 miles (29 km.) southeast of India, has an area of 25,332 sq. mi. (65,610 sq. km.) and a population of *16.9 million. Capital: Colombo. The economy is chiefly agricultural. Tea, coconut products and rubber are exported.

Sri Lanka is a member of the Commonwealth of Nations. The president is Chief of State. The prime minister is Head of Government. The present leaders of the country have reverted the country name back to Sri Lanka.

## DEMOCRATIC SOCIALIST REPUBLIC

### DECIMAL COINAGE

100 Cents = 1 Rupee

**KM# 141a 25 CENTS**
Nickel Clad Steel **Obv:** National arms **Rev:** Denomination **Edge:** Reeded

| Date | Mintage | VF20 | XF40 | MS60 | MS63 | MS65 |
|---|---|---|---|---|---|---|
| 2001 | 10,000,000 | — | 0.10 | 0.15 | 0.25 | 0.45 |
| 2002 | 10,000,000 | — | 0.10 | 0.15 | 0.25 | 0.45 |
| 2004 | — | — | 0.10 | 0.15 | 0.25 | 0.45 |

**KM# 141.2b 25 CENTS**
1.17 g., Copper Plated Steel, 16 mm. **Obv:** National arms **Rev:** Denomination

| Date | Mintage | VF20 | XF40 | MS60 | MS63 | MS65 |
|---|---|---|---|---|---|---|
| 2005 | 10,000,000 | — | 0.10 | 0.15 | 0.25 | 0.45 |
| 2006 | 5,000,000 | — | 3.00 | 5.00 | 7.00 | 10.00 |

**KM# 135.2a 50 CENTS**
Nickel Plated Steel, 21.5 mm. **Obv:** National arms **Rev:** Value above designs within wreath **Edge:** Reeded

| Date | Mintage | VF20 | XF40 | MS60 | MS63 | MS65 |
|---|---|---|---|---|---|---|
| 2001 | 30,000,000 | 0.10 | 0.25 | 0.40 | 0.65 | 1.00 |
| 2002 | 10,000,000 | 0.10 | 0.25 | 0.40 | 0.65 | 1.00 |
| 2004 | 1,000,000 | 0.10 | 0.25 | 0.40 | 0.65 | 1.00 |

**KM# 135.2b 50 CENTS**
2.49 g., Copper Plated Steel, 17.92 mm. **Obv:** National arms **Rev:** Value above designs within wreath **Edge:** Reeded

| Date | Mintage | VF20 | XF40 | MS60 | MS63 | MS65 |
|---|---|---|---|---|---|---|
| 2005 | 20,000,000 | — | 0.25 | 0.40 | 0.65 | 1.00 |
| 2006 | 10,000,000 | — | 0.25 | 0.40 | 0.65 | 1.00 |
| 2009 | 5,000,000 | — | 1.00 | 2.00 | 3.00 | 5.00 |

**KM# 136a RUPEE**
Nickel Clad Steel **Obv:** National arms **Rev:** Inscription below designs within wreath **Edge:** Reeded

| Date | Mintage | VF20 | XF40 | MS60 | MS63 | MS65 |
|---|---|---|---|---|---|---|
| 2002 | 50,000,000 | — | 0.50 | 0.70 | 1.00 | 1.50 |
| 2004 | 52,000,000 | — | 0.50 | 0.70 | 1.00 | 1.50 |

**KM# 166 RUPEE**
7.13 g., Copper-Nickel, 25.4 mm. **Subject:** Air Force's 50th Anniversary **Obv:** Badge of the Sri Lanka Air Force **Rev:** Two jets above propeller plane within circle **Edge:** Reeded

| Date | Mintage | VF20 | XF40 | MS60 | MS63 | MS65 |
|---|---|---|---|---|---|---|
| 2001 | 2,000 | PF65 120 | | | | |

**KM# 136.3 RUPEE**
3.62 g., Brass Plated Steel, 20 mm. **Obv:** National emblem **Rev:** Inscription below designs within wreath **Edge:** Segmented reeding

| Date | Mintage | VF20 | XF40 | MS60 | MS63 | MS65 |
|---|---|---|---|---|---|---|
| 2005 | 65,000,000 | — | — | — | 0.75 | 1.00 |
| 2006 | 50,000,000 | — | — | — | 0.75 | 1.00 |
| 2008 | 40,000,000 | — | — | — | 0.75 | 1.00 |
| 2009 | — | — | — | — | 0.75 | 1.00 |
| 2011 | — | — | — | — | 0.75 | 1.00 |

### KM# 147 2 RUPEES

8.25 g., Copper-Nickel, 28.5 mm. **Obv:** National arms **Rev:** Value

| Date | Mintage | VF20 | XF40 | MS60 | MS63 | MS65 |
|---|---|---|---|---|---|---|
| 2001 | 10,000,000 | 0.30 | 0.60 | 0.85 | 1.35 | 1.75 |
| 2002 | 40,000,000 | 0.30 | 0.60 | 0.85 | 1.35 | 1.75 |
| 2004 | — | 0.30 | 0.60 | 0.85 | 1.35 | 1.75 |

### KM# 167 2 RUPEES

8.25 g., Copper-Nickel, 28.5 mm. **Subject:** Colombo Plan's 50th Anniversary **Obv:** Value within inscription above date **Rev:** Gear wheel **Edge:** Reeded

| Date | Mintage | VF20 | XF40 | MS60 | MS63 | MS65 |
|---|---|---|---|---|---|---|
| 2001 | 10,000,000 | — | — | 2.00 | 3.00 | 5.00 |

### KM# 147a 2 RUPEES

7.08 g., Nickel Clad Steel, 28.5 mm. **Obv:** National arms **Rev:** Value **Edge:** Reeded

| Date | Mintage | VF20 | XF40 | MS60 | MS63 | MS65 |
|---|---|---|---|---|---|---|
| 2005 | 50,000,000 | — | 0.45 | 0.65 | 1.10 | 1.50 |
| 2006 | 80,000,000 | — | 0.45 | 0.65 | 1.10 | 1.50 |
| 2007 | 18,000,000 | — | 0.45 | 0.65 | 1.10 | 1.50 |
| 2008 | — | — | 0.45 | 0.65 | 1.10 | 1.50 |
| 2009 | — | — | 0.45 | 0.65 | 1.10 | 1.50 |
| 2011 | — | — | 0.45 | 0.65 | 1.10 | 1.50 |
| 2012 | — | — | 0.45 | 0.65 | 1.10 | 1.50 |
| 2013 | — | — | 0.45 | 0.65 | 1.10 | 1.50 |

### KM# 178 2 RUPEES

7.00 g., Nickel Plated Steel, 28.4 mm. **Subject:** Employees Provident Fund, 50th Anniversary **Obv:** Large 2 **Rev:** Open hands with image of tea pluckers, garment workers and office worker

| Date | Mintage | VF20 | XF40 | MS60 | MS63 | MS65 |
|---|---|---|---|---|---|---|
| 2008 | 2,000,000 | — | — | 1.50 | 2.50 | 3.50 |

### KM# 184 2 RUPEES

7.00 g., Nickel Plated Steel, 28.5 mm. **Obv:** Large value **Rev:** Large 60, Air Force emblem and historic aircraft circling

| Date | Mintage | VF20 | XF40 | MS60 | MS63 | MS65 |
|---|---|---|---|---|---|---|
| 2011 Special Unc | 500 | — | — | — | — | 15.00 |
| 2011 | 3,000,000 | — | — | — | 3.00 | 4.00 |

### KM# 189 2 RUPEES

7.38 g., Nickel Plated Steel, 28.5 mm. **Subject:** Centenary of Scouting **Rev:** Scouting emblem

| Date | Mintage | VF20 | XF40 | MS60 | MS63 | MS65 |
|---|---|---|---|---|---|---|
| 2012 | — | — | — | 2.00 | 3.00 | 5.00 |

### KM# 148.2 5 RUPEES

9.50 g., Nickel-Brass, 23.5 mm. **Obv:** National arms **Rev:** Value **Edge Lettering:** C.B.S.L.

| Date | Mintage | VF20 | XF40 | MS60 | MS63 | MS65 |
|---|---|---|---|---|---|---|
| 2002 | 30,000,000 | 0.35 | 0.65 | 1.00 | 2.00 | 2.75 |
| 2004 | — | 0.35 | 0.65 | 1.00 | 2.00 | 2.75 |

### KM# 168 5 RUPEES

9.52 g., Aluminum-Bronze, 23.4 mm. **Subject:** 250th Annniversary of the "Upasampada" Rite **Obv:** Value **Rev:** 1/2-length figure facing divides dates

| Date | Mintage | VF20 | XF40 | MS60 | MS63 | MS65 |
|---|---|---|---|---|---|---|
| 2003 | 4,000,000 | — | — | — | 2.50 | 4.50 |

### KM# 169 5 RUPEES

9.52 g., Aluminum-Bronze, 23.4 mm. **Subject:** 250th Anniversary - Upasampada **Obv:** Value **Rev:** Bust facing standing behind shield **Edge:** Reeded and lettered

| Date | Mintage | VF20 | XF40 | MS60 | MS63 | MS65 |
|---|---|---|---|---|---|---|
| 2003 | 4,000,000 | — | — | — | 2.50 | 4.50 |

### KM# 148.2a 5 RUPEES

7.67 g., Brass Plated Steel, 23.49 mm. **Obv:** National arms **Rev:** Value **Edge:** Reeded and Lettered **Edge Lettering:** CBSL repeated in various languages

| Date | Mintage | VF20 | XF40 | MS60 | MS63 | MS65 |
|---|---|---|---|---|---|---|
| 2005 | 30,000,000 | — | 0.75 | 1.25 | 1.85 | 2.50 |
| 2006 | 75,000,000 | — | 0.75 | 1.25 | 1.85 | 2.50 |
| 2008 | 20,000,000 | — | 0.75 | 1.25 | 1.85 | 2.50 |
| 2009 | — | — | 0.75 | 1.25 | 1.85 | 2.50 |
| 2011 | — | — | 0.75 | 1.25 | 1.85 | 2.50 |

### KM# 170 5 RUPEES

7.65 g., Brass Plated Steel, 23.5 mm. **Subject:** 2550th Anniversary of Buddha **Obv:** Value **Rev:** Buddha Jayanthi", wheel above mountain **Edge:** Reeded and lettered

| Date | Mintage | VF20 | XF40 | MS60 | MS63 | MS65 |
|---|---|---|---|---|---|---|
| 2006 | 20,000,000 | — | — | — | 3.00 | 4.00 |

### KM# 173 5 RUPEES

7.65 g., Brass Plated Steel, 23.5 mm. **Subject:** Cricket World Cup

| Date | Mintage | VF20 | XF40 | MS60 | MS63 | MS65 |
|---|---|---|---|---|---|---|
| 2007 | 7,860,000 | — | — | — | 3.00 | 4.00 |

### KM# 181 10 RUPEES

8.36 g., Nickel Plated Steel, 26.4 mm. **Obv:** Sri Lanka ensign **Rev:** Large value **Shape:** 11-sided

| Date | Mintage | VF20 | XF40 | MS60 | MS63 | MS65 |
|---|---|---|---|---|---|---|
| 2009 | — | — | — | — | 1.50 | 2.50 |
| 2010 | — | — | — | — | 1.50 | 2.50 |
| 2011 | — | — | — | — | 1.50 | 2.50 |

### KM# 186 10 RUPEES

8.36 g., Nickel Plated Steel, 26.4 mm. **Subject:** Sambuddhatva Jayanti 2600 **Obv:** Large value **Rev:** 24 prong DharmaChakra (wheel of dochrine) **Shape:** 11-sided

| Date | Mintage | VF20 | XF40 | MS60 | MS63 | MS65 |
|---|---|---|---|---|---|---|
| 2011 | 1,500,000 | — | — | — | 1.50 | 2.50 |

### KM# 180 200 RUPEES

11.90 g., 0.925 Silver 0.3539 oz. ASW, 28.4 mm. **Subject:** Customs Service, 200th Anniversary **Obv:** Proposed new Customs Building **Rev:** Customs Logo

| Date | Mintage | VF20 | XF40 | MS60 | MS63 | MS65 |
|---|---|---|---|---|---|---|
| 2009 | 3,000 | PF60 45.00 | PF63 50.00 | PF65 55.00 | | |

### KM# 174 1000 RUPEES

12.00 g., Nickel Plated Steel, 32 mm. **Subject:** Cricket World Cup

| Date | Mintage | VF20 | XF40 | MS60 | MS63 | MS65 |
|---|---|---|---|---|---|---|
| 2007 | 10,000 | — | — | 10.00 | 12.00 | 15.00 |

### KM# 179 1000 RUPEES

Nickel Plated Steel, 28.5 mm. **Subject:** Employees Provident Fund, 50th Anniversary **Obv:** Large 1000 **Rev:** Open hands with image of tea pluckers, garment workers and office worker

| Date | Mintage | VF20 | XF40 | MS60 | MS63 | MS65 |
|---|---|---|---|---|---|---|
| 2008 | 1,200 | PF60 110 | PF63 130 | PF65 150 | | |

**KM# 182 1000 RUPEES**
Copper-Nickel, 27 mm. **Subject:** Sri Lanka Army - 60th Anniversay **Obv:** Army badge above value **Rev:** Soldier standing with flag, map of Sri Lanka in background, two smaller solders at right

| Date | Mintage | VF20 | XF40 | MS60 | MS63 | MS65 |
|---|---|---|---|---|---|---|
| 2009 | 200,000 | — | — | 30.00 | 35.00 | 40.00 |

**KM# 182a 1000 RUPEES**
0.925 Silver, 27 mm. **Subject:** Sri Lanka Army - 60th Anniversary **Obv:** Army badge above value **Rev:** Soldier standing with flag, map of Sri Lanka in background, two smaller solders at right

| Date | Mintage | VF20 | XF40 | MS60 | MS63 | MS65 |
|---|---|---|---|---|---|---|
| 2009 | 10,000 | PF60 40.00 | | PF63 45.00 | PF65 50.00 | |

**KM# 185 1000 RUPEES**
28.28 g., 0.925 Silver 0.841 oz. ASW, 38.61 mm. **Subject:** Sambuddhatva Jayanti 2600 **Obv:** 24 prong Dharma Chakra (wheel of doctrine) **Rev:** Sri Maha Bo-Sapling bowl on a large pedistal

| Date | Mintage | VF20 | XF40 | MS60 | MS63 | MS65 |
|---|---|---|---|---|---|---|
| 2011 | 2,000 | PF60 60.00 | | PF63 65.00 | PF65 70.00 | |

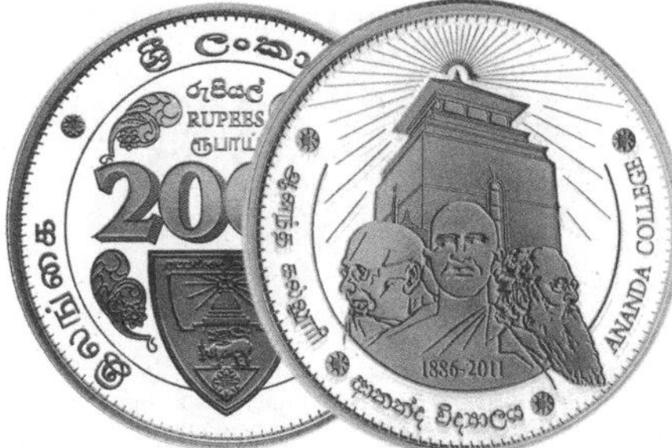


**KM# 188 1000 RUPEES**
28.21 g., Silver, 38.61 mm. **Subject:** 50th Anniversary of the People's Bank **Obv:** Crest at center **Rev:** Gear logo, selective gilt

| Date | Mintage | VF20 | XF40 | MS60 | MS63 | MS65 |
|---|---|---|---|---|---|---|
| 2011 | Est. 2300 | PF60 50.00 | | PF63 55.00 | PF65 60.00 | |

**KM# 190 1000 RUPEES**
20.00 g., 0.925 Silver 0.5948 oz. ASW, 35 mm. **Subject:** Sri Lanka & Japan, 60th Years of Diplomatic Relations **Obv:** National flags above large 60 **Rev:** Color printed images of Hydro dam

| Date | Mintage | VF20 | XF40 | MS60 | MS63 | MS65 |
|---|---|---|---|---|---|---|
| 2012 | 20,000 | PF63 140 | PF65 150 | | | |

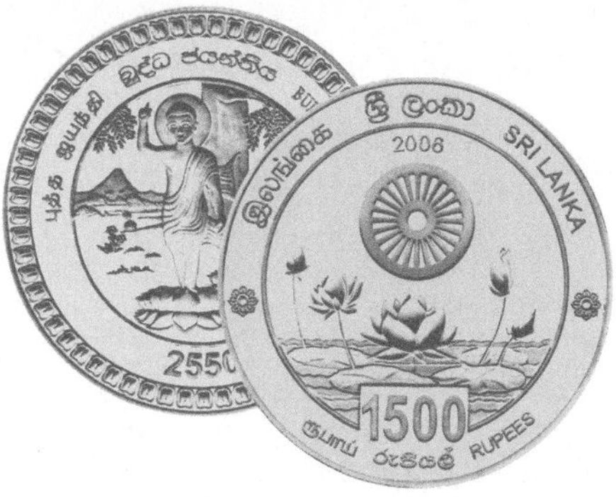


**KM# 171 1500 RUPEES**
28.28 g., 0.925 Silver 0.841 oz. ASW, 38.61 mm. **Subject:** 2550 Anniversary of Buddha

| Date | Mintage | VF20 | XF40 | MS60 | MS63 | MS65 |
|---|---|---|---|---|---|---|
| 2006 | 20,000 | PF60 60.00 | | PF63 75.00 | PF65 85.00 | |

**KM# 172 2000 RUPEE**
28.28 g., 0.925 Silver 0.841 oz. ASW partially gilt **Subject:** 2550 Anniversary of Buddha **Shape:** 38.61

| Date | Mintage | VF20 | XF40 | MS60 | MS63 | MS65 |
|---|---|---|---|---|---|---|
| 2006 | 10,000 | PF60 100 | | PF63 115 | PF65 125 | |

**KM# 187 2000 RUPEE**
28.28 g., 0.925 Silver 0.841 oz. ASW, 38.61 mm. **Subject:** 125th Anniversary of Ananda College **Obv:** Shield **Rev:** Three portraits below building tower (Ananda Viharaya)

| Date | Mintage | VF20 | XF40 | MS60 | MS63 | MS65 |
|---|---|---|---|---|---|---|
| 2011 | Est. 1500 | PF60 45.00 | | PF63 50.00 | PF65 55.00 | |

**KM# 183 5000 RUPEES**
28.28 g., 0.925 Silver 0.841 oz. ASW, 38.61 mm. **Subject:** Central Bank of Sri Lanka, 60th Anniversary **Obv:** Multicolor Central Bank crest at center **Rev:** Banyan tree **Edge:** Reeded

| Date | Mintage | VF20 | XF40 | MS60 | MS63 | MS65 |
|---|---|---|---|---|---|---|
| 2010 | 5,000 | PF60 75.00 | | PF63 85.00 | PF65 95.00 | |

# SUDAN

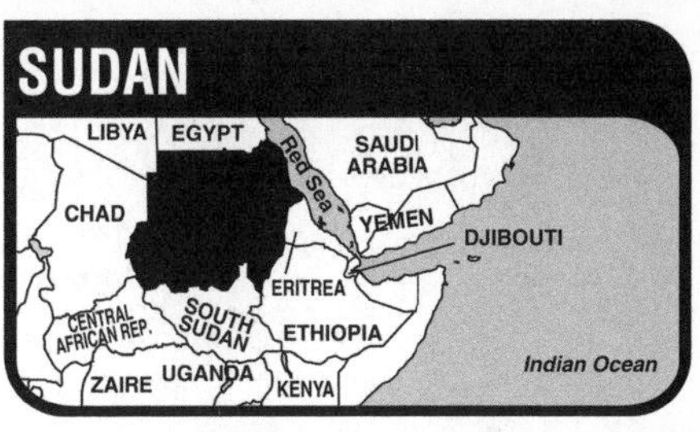


The Republic of the Sudan, located in northeast Africa on the Red Sea between Egypt and Ethiopia, has an area of 967,500 sq. mi. (2,505,810 sq. km.) and a population of *24.5 million. Capital: Khartoum. Agriculture and livestock raising are the chief occupations. Cotton, gum arabic and peanuts are exported.

## REPUBLIC

### REFORM COINAGE

100 Qurush (Piastres) = 1 Dinar
10 Pounds = 1 Dinar

**KM# 119 5 DINARS**
3.35 g., Brass, 19 mm. **Obv:** Value **Rev:** Central Bank building

| Date | Mintage | VF20 | XF40 | MS60 | MS63 | MS65 |
|---|---|---|---|---|---|---|
| AH1424-2003 | — | 0.75 | 1.50 | 3.00 | 5.00 | — |

**KM# 120.1 10 DINARS**
4.68 g., Brass, 22 mm. **Rev:** Central Bank building, "a" above "n" at the left end of the Arabic inscription, 64 border beads

| Date | Mintage | VF20 | XF40 | MS60 | MS63 | MS65 |
|---|---|---|---|---|---|---|
| AH1424-2003 | — | 1.00 | 1.50 | 2.50 | 4.00 | — |

**KM# 120.2 10 DINARS**
4.56 g., Brass, 22 mm. **Obv:** Value **Rev:** Larger Central Bank building, "a" to right of "n" at the left end of the Arabic inscription, 72 border beads

| Date | Mintage | VF20 | XF40 | MS60 | MS63 | MS65 |
|---|---|---|---|---|---|---|
| AH1424-2003 | — | 1.00 | 1.50 | 2.50 | 4.00 | — |

**KM# 121 50 DINARS**
Copper-Nickel, 24 mm. **Rev:** Central Bank building

| Date | Mintage | VF20 | XF40 | MS60 | MS63 | MS65 |
|---|---|---|---|---|---|---|
| AH1423-2002 | — | 2.00 | 3.50 | 6.00 | 9.00 | — |

### REFORM COINAGE

2005
100 Piastres = 1 Pound

**KM# 126 PIASTRE (Ghirsh)**
2.25 g., Aluminum-Bronze, 16 mm. **Obv:** Clay pot **Obv. Legend:** CENTRAL BANK OF SUDAN **Rev:** Value

| Date | Mintage | VF20 | XF40 | MS60 | MS63 | MS65 |
|---|---|---|---|---|---|---|
| 2006 | — | — | 0.90 | 2.25 | 3.00 | — |

**KM# 125 5 PIASTRES**
2.84 g., Brass, 18 mm. **Obv:** National arms **Rev:** Large value **Edge:** Reeded

| Date | Mintage | VF20 | XF40 | MS60 | MS63 | MS65 |
|---|---|---|---|---|---|---|
| 2006 | — | — | 1.20 | 3.00 | 4.00 | — |

**KM# 122 10 PIASTRES**
3.70 g., Nickel, 20 mm. **Obv:** Pyramid **Obv. Legend:** CENTRAL BANK OF SUDAN **Rev:** Large value **Edge:** Reeded

| Date | Mintage | VF20 | XF40 | MS60 | MS63 | MS65 |
|---|---|---|---|---|---|---|
| 2006 | — | — | 1.25 | 3.00 | 4.00 | — |

**KM# 124 20 PIASTRES**
5.00 g., Bi-Metallic Copper-Nickel center in Brass ring, 22 mm. **Obv:** Ankole Bull in right profile **Obv. Legend:** CENTRAL BANK OF SUDAN **Rev:** large value **Edge:** Reeded

| Date | Mintage | VF20 | XF40 | MS60 | MS63 | MS65 |
|---|---|---|---|---|---|---|
| 2006 | — | — | 1.20 | 3.00 | 4.00 | — |

**KM# 123 50 PIASTRES**
5.82 g., Bi-Metallic Brass center in Copper-Nickel ring, 24 mm. **Obv:** Dove in flight **Obv. Legend:** CENTRAL BANK OF SUDAN **Rev:** Value **Edge:** Reeded

| Date | Mintage | VF20 | XF40 | MS60 | MS63 | MS65 |
|---|---|---|---|---|---|---|
| 2006 | — | — | 0.90 | 2.25 | 3.00 | — |

**KM# 127 POUND**
Nickel Plated Steel, 27 mm. **Obv:** Value **Rev:** Central Bank building

| Date | Mintage | VF20 | XF40 | MS60 | MS63 | MS65 |
|---|---|---|---|---|---|---|
| 2011 | — | — | 2.50 | 5.00 | 7.00 | — |

# SURINAME

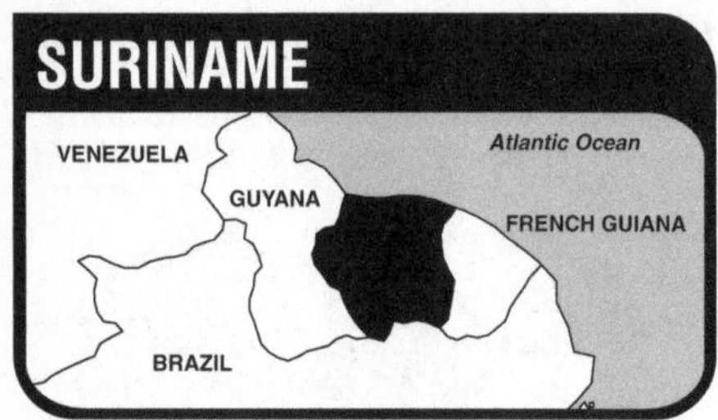


The Republic of Suriname also known as Dutch Guiana, located on the north central coast of South America between Guyana and French Guiana has an area of 63,037 sq. mi. (163,270 sq. km.) and a population of *433,000. Capital: Paramaribo. The country is rich in minerals and forests, and self-sufficient in rice, the staple food crop. The mining, processing and exporting of bauxite is the principal economic activity.

Lieutenants of Amerigo Vespucci sighted the Guiana coast in 1499. Spanish explorers of the 16th century, disappointed at finding no gold, departed leaving the area to be settled by the British in 1652. The colony prospered and the Netherlands acquired it in 1667 in exchange for the Dutch rights in Nieuw Nederland (state of New York). During the European wars of the 18th and 19th centuries, which were fought in part in the new world, Suriname was occupied by the British from 1781-1784 and 1796-1814. Suriname became an autonomous part of the Kingdom of the Netherlands on Dec. 15, 1954. Full independence was achieved on Nov. 25, 1975. In 1980, a coup installed a military government, which has since been dissolved.

**MINT MARKS**
(u) - Utrecht (privy marks only)

**MONETARY SYSTEM**
After January, 2004
1 Dollar = 100 Cents

## REPUBLIC
### MODERN COINAGE

**KM# 11b CENT**
2.50 g., Copper Plated Steel, 18 mm. **Obv:** Arms with supporters within wreath **Rev:** Value divides date within circle **Edge:** Plain

| Date | Mintage | VF20 | XF40 | MS60 | MS63 | MS65 |
|---|---|---|---|---|---|---|
| 2004 (u) Sets only | 4,000 | — | — | — | 6.00 | — |
| 2005 (u) Sets only | 1,500 | — | — | — | 7.00 | — |
| 2006 (u) Sets only | 1,500 | — | — | — | 7.00 | — |
| 2007 (u) Sets only | 1,000 | — | — | — | 7.00 | — |
| 2008 (u) Sets only | 1,000 | — | — | — | 7.00 | — |
| 2009 (u) Sets only | 1,000 | — | — | — | 7.00 | — |
| 2010 (u) Sets only | 1,000 | — | — | — | 7.00 | — |
| 2011 (u) Sets only | 1,000 | — | — | — | 7.00 | — |

**KM# 12.1b 5 CENTS**
3.00 g., Copper Plated Steel, 18 mm. **Obv:** Arms with supporters within circle **Rev:** Value divides date within circle **Edge:** Plain **Shape:** Square

| Date | Mintage | VF20 | XF40 | MS60 | MS63 | MS65 |
|---|---|---|---|---|---|---|
| 2004 (u) Sets only | 4,000 | — | — | — | 6.00 | — |
| 2005 (u) Sets only | 1,500 | — | — | — | 7.00 | — |
| 2006 (u) Sets only | 1,500 | — | — | — | 7.00 | — |
| 2007 (u) Sets only | 1,000 | — | — | — | 7.00 | — |
| 2008 (u) Sets only | 1,000 | — | — | — | 7.00 | — |
| 2009 (u) Sets only | 1,000 | — | — | — | 7.00 | — |
| 2010 (u) Sets only | 1,000 | — | — | — | 7.00 | — |
| 2011 (u) Sets only | 1,000 | — | — | — | 7.00 | — |

**KM# 13a 10 CENTS**
2.00 g., Nickel Plated Steel, 16 mm. **Obv:** Arms with supporters within wreath **Rev:** Value and date within circle **Edge:** Reeded

| Date | Mintage | VF20 | XF40 | MS60 | MS63 | MS65 |
|---|---|---|---|---|---|---|
| 2004 (u) Sets only | 4,000 | — | — | — | 4.50 | — |
| 2005 (u) Sets only | 1,500 | — | — | — | 4.50 | — |
| 2006 (u) Sets only | 1,500 | — | — | — | 4.50 | — |
| 2007 (u) Sets only | 1,000 | — | — | — | 4.50 | — |
| 2008 (u) Sets only | 1,000 | — | — | — | 4.50 | — |
| 2009 | — | — | 0.50 | 1.00 | 2.00 | — |
| 2009 (u) Sets only | 1,000 | — | — | — | 4.50 | — |
| 2010 (u) Sets only | 1,000 | — | — | — | 4.50 | — |
| 2011 (u) Sets only | 1,000 | — | — | — | 4.50 | — |
| 2012 | — | — | 0.50 | 1.00 | 2.00 | — |

**KM# 14a 25 CENTS**
3.50 g., Nickel Plated Steel, 20 mm. **Obv:** Arms with supporters within wreath **Rev:** Value and date within circle **Edge:** Reeded

| Date | Mintage | VF20 | XF40 | MS60 | MS63 | MS65 |
|---|---|---|---|---|---|---|
| 2004 (u) Sets only | 4,000 | — | — | — | 7.00 | — |
| 2005 (u) Sets only | 1,500 | — | — | — | 8.00 | — |
| 2006 (u) Sets only | 1,500 | — | — | — | 8.00 | — |
| 2007 (u) Sets only | 1,000 | — | — | — | 8.00 | — |
| 2008 (u) Sets only | 1,000 | — | — | — | 8.00 | — |
| 2009 (u) Sets only | 1,000 | — | — | — | 8.00 | — |
| 2010 (u) Sets only | 1,000 | — | — | — | 8.00 | — |
| 2011 (u) Sets only | 1,000 | — | — | — | 8.00 | — |

**KM# 23 100 CENTS**
5.65 g., Copper-Nickel, 23 mm. **Obv:** Arms with supporters within wreath **Rev:** Value and date within circle **Edge:** Reeded

| Date | Mintage | VF20 | XF40 | MS60 | MS63 | MS65 |
|---|---|---|---|---|---|---|
| 2004 (u) Sets only | 4,000 | — | — | — | 7.00 | — |
| 2005 (u) Sets only | 1,250 | — | — | — | 8.00 | — |
| 2006 (u) Sets only | 1,500 | — | — | — | 8.00 | — |
| 2007 (u) Sets only | 1,000 | — | — | — | 8.00 | — |
| 2008 (u) Sets only | 1,000 | — | — | — | 8.00 | — |
| 2009 (u) Sets only | 1,000 | — | — | — | 8.00 | — |
| 2010 (u) Sets only | 1,000 | — | — | — | 8.00 | — |
| 2011 (u) Sets only | 1,000 | — | — | — | 8.00 | — |
| 2012 | — | — | — | 1.75 | 3.00 | — |

**KM# 24 250 CENTS**
9.57 g., Copper-Nickel, 28 mm. **Obv:** Arms with supporters within wreath **Rev:** Value and date within circle

| Date | Mintage | VF20 | XF40 | MS60 | MS63 | MS65 |
|---|---|---|---|---|---|---|
| 2004 (u) Sets only | 4,000 | — | — | — | 8.00 | — |
| 2005 (u) Sets only | 1,250 | — | — | — | 10.00 | — |
| 2006 (u) Sets only | 1,500 | — | — | — | 10.00 | — |
| 2007 (u) Sets only | 1,000 | — | — | — | 10.00 | — |
| 2008 (u) Sets only | 1,000 | — | — | — | 10.00 | — |
| 2009 (u) Sets only | 1,000 | — | — | — | 10.00 | — |
| 2010 (u) Sets only | 1,000 | — | — | — | 10.00 | — |
| 2011 (u) Sets only | 1,000 | — | — | — | 10.00 | — |

**KM# 65 20 DOLLARS**
1.24 g., 0.999 Gold 0.040 oz. AGW, 13.92 mm. **Subject:** Antony Nesty's 1988 Gold Medal win at Seoul Olympics, 20th Anniversary **Obv:** Arms with supporters **Rev:** Nesty swimming

| Date | Mintage | VF20 | XF40 | MS60 | MS63 | MS65 |
|---|---|---|---|---|---|---|
| 2008 | 5,000 | **PF63** 75.00 | **PF65** 85.00 | | | |

**KM# 64 400 DOLLARS**
7.98 g., 0.916 Gold 0.235 oz. AGW, 22 mm. **Subject:** 30 Years of Independence **Obv:** Arms with supporters **Rev:** Man kissing flag **Edge:** Reeded

| Date | Mintage | VF20 | XF40 | MS60 | MS63 | MS65 |
|---|---|---|---|---|---|---|
| 2005 | 1,000 | **PF63** 475 | **PF65** 500 | | | |

**KM# 66 500 DOLLARS**
7.98 g., 0.916 Gold 0.235 oz. AGW, 22 mm. **Subject:** Central Bank, 50th Anniversary **Obv:** Arms with supporters **Rev:** 50 jaar Central Bank van Suriname 1957-2007

| Date | Mintage | VF20 | XF40 | MS60 | MS63 | MS65 |
|---|---|---|---|---|---|---|
| 2007 | 1,000 | **PF63** 475 | **PF65** 500 | | | |

## MINT SETS

| KM# | Date | Mintage | Identification | Issue Price | Mkt Val |
|---|---|---|---|---|---|
| MS1 | 2004 (6) | 4,000 | KM#11b, 12.1b, 13a, 14a, 23, 24 | 25.00 | 40.00 |
| MS2 | 2005 (6) | 1,500 | KM#11b, 12.1b, 13a-14a, 23-24 | 25.00 | 45.00 |
| MS3 | 2006 (6) | 1,500 | KM#11b, 12.1b, 13a-14a, 23-24 | 25.00 | 45.00 |
| MS4 | 2007 (6) | 1,000 | KM#11b, 12.1b, 13a-14a, 23-24 | 27.00 | 45.00 |
| MS5 | 2008 (6) | 1,000 | KM#11b, 12.1b, 13a-14a, 23-24 | 27.00 | 45.00 |
| MS6 | 2009 (6) | 1,000 | KM#11b, 12.1b, 13a, 14a, 23, 24 | 27.00 | 40.00 |
| MS7 | 2010 (6) | 1,000 | KM#11b, 12.1b, 13a, 14a, 23, 24 | 27.00 | 45.00 |
| MS8 | 2011 (6) | 1,000 | KM#11b, 12.1b, 13a, 14a, 23, 24 | — | 45.00 |

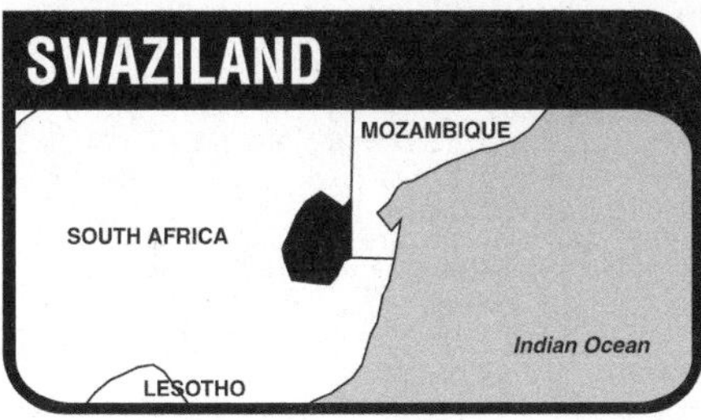


The Kingdom of Swaziland, located in southeastern Africa, has an area of 6,704 sq. mi. (17,360 sq. km.) and a population of *756,000. Capital: Mbabane (administrative); Lobamba (legislative). The diversified economy includes mining, agriculture, and light industry. Asbestos, iron ore, wood pulp, and sugar are exported.

The Kingdom is a member of the Commonwealth of Nations. King Mswati III is Head of State. The prime minister is Head of Government.

**RULER**

King Msawati III, 1986-

**MONETARY SYSTEM**

100 Cents = 1 Luhlanga
25 Luhlanga = 1 Lilangeni
(plural - Emalangeni)

# KINGDOM

## DECIMAL COINAGE

100 Cents = 1 Lilangeni (plural emelangeni)

### KM# 48 5 CENTS

2.10 g., Copper-Nickel, 18.5 mm. **Ruler:** Mswati III **Obv:** Bust 3/4 right **Rev:** Arum lily and value **Edge:** Plain **Shape:** Scalloped

| Date | Mintage | VF20 | XF40 | MS60 | MS63 | MS65 |
|---|---|---|---|---|---|---|
| 2001 | — | — | — | 0.30 | 0.50 | 0.75 |
| 2002 | — | — | — | 0.30 | 0.50 | 0.75 |
| 2003 | — | — | — | 0.30 | 0.50 | 0.75 |
| 2005 | — | — | — | 0.30 | 0.50 | 0.75 |
| 2006 | — | — | — | 0.30 | 0.50 | 0.75 |
| 2007 | — | — | — | 0.30 | 0.50 | 0.75 |
| 2008 | — | — | — | 0.30 | 0.50 | 0.75 |
| 2009 | — | — | — | 0.30 | 0.50 | 0.75 |
| 2010 | — | — | — | 0.30 | 0.50 | 0.75 |

### KM# 56 5 CENTS

Copper Plated Steel **Ruler:** Mswati III

| Date | Mintage | VF20 | XF40 | MS60 | MS63 | MS65 |
|---|---|---|---|---|---|---|
| 2011 | — | — | — | 0.30 | 0.50 | 0.75 |

### KM# 49 10 CENTS

3.60 g., Copper-Nickel, 22 mm. **Ruler:** Mswati III **Obv:** Bust 3/4 right **Rev:** Sugar cane and value **Edge:** Plain **Shape:** Scalloped

| Date | Mintage | VF20 | XF40 | MS60 | MS63 | MS65 |
|---|---|---|---|---|---|---|
| 2001 | — | — | 0.30 | 0.50 | 0.75 | 1.00 |
| 2002 | — | — | 0.30 | 0.50 | 0.75 | 1.00 |
| 2003 | — | — | 0.30 | 0.50 | 0.75 | 1.00 |
| 2005 | — | — | 0.30 | 0.50 | 0.75 | 1.00 |
| 2006 | — | — | 0.30 | 0.50 | 0.75 | 1.00 |
| 2007 | — | — | 0.30 | 0.50 | 0.75 | 1.00 |

### KM# 57 10 CENTS

Copper Plated Steel **Ruler:** Mswati III

| Date | Mintage | VF20 | XF40 | MS60 | MS63 | MS65 |
|---|---|---|---|---|---|---|
| 2011 | — | — | 0.30 | 0.50 | 0.75 | 1.00 |

### KM# 50.2 20 CENTS

5.52 g., Copper-Nickel, 25.2 mm. **Ruler:** Mswati III **Obv:** Small bust 3/4 right **Rev:** Elephant head, value **Edge:** Plain **Shape:** Scalloped

| Date | Mintage | VF20 | XF40 | MS60 | MS63 | MS65 |
|---|---|---|---|---|---|---|
| 2001 | — | — | 0.35 | 0.50 | 0.90 | 2.25 |
| 2002 | — | — | 0.35 | 0.50 | 0.90 | 2.25 |
| 2003 | — | — | 0.35 | 0.50 | 0.90 | 2.25 |
| 2005 | — | — | 0.35 | 0.50 | 0.90 | 2.25 |

### KM# 58 20 CENTS

Copper-Nickel **Ruler:** Mswati III

| Date | Mintage | VF20 | XF40 | MS60 | MS63 | MS65 |
|---|---|---|---|---|---|---|
| 2011 | — | — | 0.35 | 0.50 | 0.90 | 2.25 |

### KM# 52 50 CENTS

8.90 g., Copper-Nickel, 29.45 mm. **Ruler:** Mswati III **Obv:** Head 1/4 right **Rev:** Arms with supporters

| Date | Mintage | VF20 | XF40 | MS60 | MS63 | MS65 |
|---|---|---|---|---|---|---|
| 2001 | — | — | — | 2.25 | 3.75 | 4.50 |
| 2003 | — | — | — | 2.25 | 3.75 | 4.50 |
| 2005 | — | — | — | 2.25 | 3.75 | 4.50 |
| 2007 | — | — | — | 2.25 | 3.75 | 4.50 |

### KM# 59 50 CENTS

Copper-Nickel **Ruler:** Mswati III

| Date | Mintage | VF20 | XF40 | MS60 | MS63 | MS65 |
|---|---|---|---|---|---|---|
| 2011 | — | — | — | 2.25 | 3.75 | 4.50 |

### KM# 45 LILANGENI

9.50 g., Brass, 22.5 mm. **Ruler:** Mswati III **Obv:** Head 1/4 right **Rev:** Bust facing

| Date | Mintage | VF20 | XF40 | MS60 | MS63 | MS65 |
|---|---|---|---|---|---|---|
| 2002 | — | 1.00 | 1.50 | 2.00 | 2.75 | 3.50 |
| 2003 | — | 1.00 | 1.50 | 2.00 | 2.75 | 3.50 |
| 2005 | — | 1.00 | 1.50 | 2.00 | 2.75 | 3.50 |
| 2008 | — | 1.00 | 1.50 | 2.00 | 2.75 | 3.50 |

### KM# 60 LILANGENI

Brass **Ruler:** Mswati III

| Date | Mintage | VF20 | XF40 | MS60 | MS63 | MS65 |
|---|---|---|---|---|---|---|
| 2011 | — | — | — | 2.50 | 3.75 | 4.50 |

### KM# 46 2 EMALANGENI

5.00 g., Brass **Ruler:** Mswati III **Obv:** Head 1/4 right **Rev:** Lilies and value

| Date | Mintage | VF20 | XF40 | MS60 | MS63 | MS65 |
|---|---|---|---|---|---|---|
| 2003 sm. bust | — | — | — | 2.50 | 3.75 | 4.25 |
| 2005 | — | — | — | 2.50 | 3.75 | 4.25 |
| 2008 | — | — | — | 2.50 | 3.75 | 4.25 |
| 2009 | — | — | — | 2.50 | 3.75 | 4.25 |

### KM# 47 5 EMALANGENI

7.60 g., Brass **Ruler:** Mswati III **Obv:** Head 1/4 right **Rev:** Arms with supporters above value that divides date

| Date | Mintage | VF20 | XF40 | MS60 | MS63 | MS65 |
|---|---|---|---|---|---|---|
| 2003 sm. bust | — | — | — | 3.00 | 5.00 | 7.00 |

### KM# 54 5 EMALANGENI

7.60 g., Brass, 27 mm. **Ruler:** Mswati III **Subject:** 40th Anniversary of Independence **Obv:** Head 1/4 right **Rev:** National arms at center

| Date | Mintage | VF20 | XF40 | MS60 | MS63 | MS65 |
|---|---|---|---|---|---|---|
| 2008 | — | — | — | 3.00 | 5.00 | 7.00 |

### KM# 54a 5 EMALANGENI

Gold **Ruler:** Mswati III **Subject:** 40th Anniversary of Independence **Obv:** Head 1/4 right **Rev:** National arms at center

| Date | Mintage | VF20 | XF40 | MS60 | MS63 | MS65 |
|---|---|---|---|---|---|---|
| 2008 Proof, rare | 100 | — | — | — | — | — |

### KM# 55 5 EMALANGENI

7.60 g., Brass, 27 mm. **Ruler:** Mswati III **Subject:** 40th Birthday of King **Obv:** Head 1/4 right **Rev:** National arms at center

| Date | Mintage | VF20 | XF40 | MS60 | MS63 | MS65 |
|---|---|---|---|---|---|---|
| 2008 | — | — | — | 3.00 | 5.00 | 7.00 |

### KM# 55a 5 EMALANGENI

Gold **Ruler:** Mswati III **Subject:** 40th Anniversary of Independence **Obv:** Head 1/4 right **Rev:** National arms at center

| Date | Mintage | VF20 | XF40 | MS60 | MS63 | MS65 |
|---|---|---|---|---|---|---|
| 2008 Proof, rare | 100 | — | — | — | — | — |

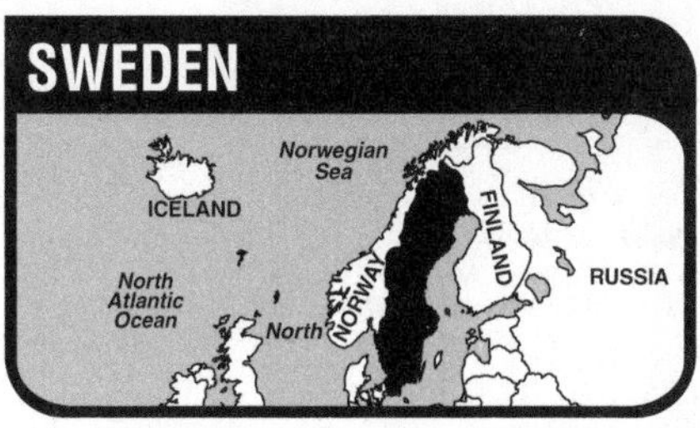


The Kingdom of Sweden, a limited constitutional monarchy located in northern Europe between Norway and Finland, has an area of 173,732 sq. mi. (449,960 sq. km.) and a population of *8.5 million. Capital: Stockholm. Mining, lumbering and a specialized machine industry dominate the economy. Machinery, paper, iron and steel, motor vehicles and wood pulp are exported.

**RULER**

Carl XVI Gustaf, 1973-

**MINT OFFICIALS' INITIALS**

| Letter | Date | Name |
|---|---|---|
| B | 1992-2005 | Stefan Ingves |
| D | 1986-2005 | Bengt Dennis |
| SI | 2006- | Stefan Ingves |

**MONETARY SYSTEM**

100 Ore = 1 Krona

# KINGDOM

## REFORM COINAGE

1873 - present

### KM# 878 50 ÖRE

3.70 g., Bronze, 18.7 mm. **Ruler:** Carl XVI Gustaf **Obv:** Value **Rev:** Three crowns and date **Edge:** Reeded

| Date | Mintage | VF20 | XF40 | MS60 | MS63 | MS65 |
|---|---|---|---|---|---|---|
| 2001 B | 30,120,532 | — | — | 0.15 | 0.25 | 0.35 |
| 2002 B | 32,019,578 | — | — | 0.15 | 0.25 | 0.35 |
| 2003 H | 32,074,768 | — | — | 0.15 | 0.25 | 0.35 |
| 2004 H | 25,958,649 | — | — | 0.15 | 0.25 | 0.35 |
| 2005 H | 25,024,203 | — | — | 0.15 | 0.25 | 0.35 |
| 2006 SI | 30,000,000 | — | — | 0.15 | 0.25 | 0.35 |
| 2007 SI | 50,000,000 | — | — | 0.15 | 0.25 | 0.35 |
| 2008 SI | 35,000,000 | — | — | 0.15 | 0.25 | 0.35 |
| 2009 SI | 20,000,000 | — | — | 0.15 | 0.25 | 0.35 |

### KM# 894 KRONA

7.00 g., Copper-Nickel, 25 mm. **Ruler:** Carl XVI Gustaf **Obv:** Head left **Rev:** Crown and value **Edge:** Reeded

| Date | Mintage | VF20 | XF40 | MS60 | MS63 | MS65 |
|---|---|---|---|---|---|---|
| 2001 B | 23,905,454 | — | — | 0.25 | 0.35 | 0.50 |
| 2002 B | 62,436,783 | — | — | 0.25 | 0.35 | 0.50 |

| Date | Mintage | VF20 | XF40 | MS60 | MS63 | MS65 |
|---|---|---|---|---|---|---|
| 2003 H | 54,178,242 | — | — | 0.25 | 0.35 | 0.50 |
| 2004 H | 42,060,252 | — | — | 0.25 | 0.35 | 0.50 |
| 2005 H | 21,469,169 | — | — | 0.25 | 0.35 | 0.50 |
| 2007 SI | 30,751,250 | — | — | 0.25 | 0.35 | 0.50 |
| 2008 SI | 60,510,000 | — | — | 0.25 | 0.35 | 0.50 |
| 2012 SI | 20,000,000 | — | — | 0.25 | 0.35 | 0.50 |

## KM# 916 KRONA

7.00 g., Copper-Nickel, 25 mm. **Ruler:** Carl XVI Gustaf **Subject:** Separation from Finland, 200 Anniversary **Obv:** Head left **Rev:** Horizontal sea waves **Edge:** Reeded

| Date | Mintage | VF20 | XF40 | MS60 | MS63 | MS65 |
|---|---|---|---|---|---|---|
| 2009 SIS | 40,020,000 | — | — | 0.25 | 0.50 | 0.65 |

## KM# 927 KRONA

7.00 g., Copper-Nickel, 25 mm. **Ruler:** Carl XVI Gustaf **Subject:** 40th Anniversary of reign

| Date | Mintage | VF20 | XF40 | MS60 | MS63 | MS65 |
|---|---|---|---|---|---|---|
| 2013 | 5,000,000 | — | — | 0.65 | 1.00 | 1.25 |

## KM# 853a 5 KRONOR

9.60 g., Copper-Nickel Clad Nickel, 28.5 mm. **Ruler:** Carl XVI Gustaf **Obv:** Crowned monogram **Rev:** Value

| Date | Mintage | VF20 | XF40 | MS60 | MS63 | MS65 |
|---|---|---|---|---|---|---|
| 2001 B | 6,001,481 | — | — | 1.00 | 1.25 | 1.50 |
| 2002 B | 13,054,800 | — | — | 1.00 | 1.25 | 1.50 |
| 2003 H | 11,063,204 | — | — | 1.00 | 1.25 | 1.50 |
| 2004 H | 6,732,730 | — | — | 1.00 | 1.25 | 1.50 |
| 2005 H | 4,372,783 | — | — | 1.00 | 1.25 | 1.50 |
| 2007 H | 628,000 | — | 1.00 | 1.50 | 2.00 | 2.50 |
| 2008 H | 12,000,000 | — | — | 1.00 | 1.25 | 1.50 |
| 2009 H | 10,000,000 | — | — | 1.00 | 1.25 | 1.50 |

## KM# 895 10 KRONOR

6.60 g., Copper-Aluminum-Zinc, 20.5 mm. **Ruler:** Carl XVI Gustaf **Obv:** Head left **Rev:** Three crowns and value **Edge:** Segmented reeding

| Date | Mintage | VF20 | XF40 | MS60 | MS63 | MS65 |
|---|---|---|---|---|---|---|
| 2001 B | 4,171,757 | — | — | 2.00 | 2.50 | 3.00 |
| 2002 B | 12,025,624 | — | — | 2.00 | 2.50 | 3.00 |
| 2003 H | 13,824,632 | — | — | 2.00 | 2.50 | 3.00 |
| 2004 H | 9,045,581 | — | — | 2.00 | 2.50 | 3.00 |
| 2005 H | 13,205,261 | — | — | 2.00 | 2.50 | 3.00 |
| 2006 SI | 4,531,150 | — | — | 2.00 | 2.50 | 3.00 |
| 2007 SI | 15,200,000 | — | — | 2.00 | 2.50 | 3.00 |
| 2008 SI | 12,000,000 | — | — | 2.00 | 2.50 | 3.00 |
| 2009 SI | 3,400,000 | — | — | 2.00 | 2.50 | 3.00 |

## KM# 910 50 KRONOR

22.00 g., Copper-Aluminum-Zinc-Tin, 36 mm. **Ruler:** Carl XVI Gustaf **Subject:** 95th Anniversary - Birth of Astrid Lindgren **Obv:** Playful young girl **Rev:** Astrid Lindgren **Edge:** Plain

| Date | Mintage | VF20 | XF40 | MS60 | MS63 | MS65 |
|---|---|---|---|---|---|---|
| ND (2002) | 100,000 | — | 8.00 | 9.00 | 10.00 | 12.00 |

## KM# 915 50 KRONOR

22.00 g., Copper-Aluminum-Zinc-Tin, 36 mm. **Ruler:** Carl XVI Gustaf **Subject:** 150th Anniversary of Sweden's first postage stamp **Obv:** Winged letter flying over landscape **Rev:** Sweden's first postage stamp design **Edge:** Plain

| Date | Mintage | VF20 | XF40 | MS60 | MS63 | MS65 |
|---|---|---|---|---|---|---|
| ND (2005) | 22,000 | — | — | — | 11.00 | 13.00 |

## KM# 896 200 KRONOR

27.03 g., 0.925 Silver 0.8039 oz. ASW, 36 mm. **Ruler:** Carl XVI Gustaf **Subject:** 25th Wedding Anniversary **Obv:** Conjoined busts left **Rev:** Crowned arms with supporters **Edge:** Plain

| Date | Mintage | VF20 | XF40 | MS60 | MS63 | MS65 |
|---|---|---|---|---|---|---|
| ND-2001 B-E | 40,473 | — | — | 16.00 | 32.00 | 35.00 |

## KM# 900 200 KRONOR

27.00 g., 0.925 Silver 0.803 oz. ASW, 36 mm. **Ruler:** Carl XVI Gustaf **Subject:** Nobel Prize Centennial **Obv:** Seated allegorical figure **Rev:** Nobel's portrait **Edge:** Plain

| Date | Mintage | VF20 | XF40 | MS60 | MS63 | MS65 |
|---|---|---|---|---|---|---|
| 2001 | — | — | — | 17.00 | 35.00 | 40.00 |

## KM# 919 200 KRONOR

27.03 g., 0.925 Silver 0.8039 oz. ASW, 36 mm. **Ruler:** Carl XVI Gustaf **Subject:** Nobel Prize, 100th Anniversary **Edge:** Plain

| Date | Mintage | VF20 | XF40 | MS60 | MS63 | MS65 |
|---|---|---|---|---|---|---|
| 2001 B-E | 29,856 | — | — | 17.00 | 35.00 | 40.00 |

## KM# 908 200 KRONOR

27.03 g., 0.925 Silver 0.8039 oz. ASW, 36 mm. **Ruler:** Carl XVI Gustaf **Subject:** 750th Anniversary of Stockholm **Obv:** City seal with three towers and gate **Rev:** Three towers of city hall **Edge:** Plain

| Date | Mintage | VF20 | XF40 | MS60 | MS63 | MS65 |
|---|---|---|---|---|---|---|
| ND (2002) | 25,000 | — | — | 16.00 | 32.00 | 35.00 |

## KM# 902 200 KRONOR

27.03 g., 0.925 Silver 0.8039 oz. ASW, 36 mm. **Ruler:** Carl XVI Gustaf **Subject:** 30th Anniversary of Reign

| Date | Mintage | VF20 | XF40 | MS60 | MS63 | MS65 |
|---|---|---|---|---|---|---|
| 2003 | 16,500 | — | — | 16.00 | 32.00 | 35.00 |

## KM# 904 200 KRONOR

27.03 g., 0.925 Silver 0.8039 oz. ASW, 36 mm. **Ruler:** Carl XVI Gustaf **Subject:** 700th Anniversary, St. Birgitta **Obv:** Cross in circle above value **Rev:** St. Birgitta **Edge:** Plain

| Date | Mintage | VF20 | XF40 | MS60 | MS63 | MS65 |
|---|---|---|---|---|---|---|
| ND2003 H-E | 39,300 | — | — | 16.00 | 32.00 | 35.00 |

## KM# 911 200 KRONOR

27.03 g., 0.925 Silver 0.8039 oz. ASW, 36 mm. **Ruler:** Carl XVI Gustaf **Subject:** Royal Palace in Stockholm 250th Anniversary **Obv:** Two antique keys over map **Rev:** Royal Palace in Stockholm **Edge:** Plain

| Date | Mintage | VF20 | XF40 | MS60 | MS63 | MS65 |
|---|---|---|---|---|---|---|
| ND2004 H-E | 30,580 | — | — | 16.00 | 32.00 | 35.00 |

## KM# 906 200 KRONOR

27.03 g., 0.925 Silver 0.8039 oz. ASW, 36 mm. **Ruler:** Carl XVI Gustaf **Subject:** Centennial of the end of the Union between Norway and Sweden **Obv:** Split disc **Rev:** Flag on pole and two clouds

| Date | Mintage | VF20 | XF40 | MS60 | MS63 | MS65 |
|---|---|---|---|---|---|---|
| 2005 H-E | 19,494 | — | — | 16.00 | 32.00 | 35.00 |

## KM# 913 200 KRONOR

27.03 g., 0.925 Silver 0.8039 oz. ASW, 36 mm. **Ruler:** Carl XVI Gustaf **Subject:** Dag Hammarskjöld, 100th Anniversary of Birth **Obv:** Stylized flames **Rev:** Dag Hammarskjöld **Edge:** Plain

| Date | Mintage | VF20 | XF40 | MS60 | MS63 | MS65 |
|---|---|---|---|---|---|---|
| ND2005 H-E Prooflike | 18,234 | — | — | 16.00 | 32.00 | 35.00 |

## KM# 921 200 KRONOR

27.03 g., 0.925 Silver 0.8039 oz. ASW, 36 mm. **Ruler:** Carl XVI Gustaf **Subject:** Swedish Railroads, 150th Anniversary

| Date | Mintage | VF20 | XF40 | MS60 | MS63 | MS65 |
|---|---|---|---|---|---|---|
| ND2006 SI-E | 9,995 | — | — | 17.00 | 35.00 | 40.00 |

## KM# 923 200 KRONOR

27.03 g., 0.925 Silver 0.8039 oz. ASW, 36 mm. **Ruler:** Carl XVI Gustaf **Subject:** Carl Linnaeus, 300th Anniversary of Birth **Edge:** Plain

| Date | Mintage | VF20 | XF40 | MS60 | MS63 | MS65 |
|---|---|---|---|---|---|---|
| ND2007 SI-E | 10,600 | — | — | 17.00 | 35.00 | 40.00 |

## KM# 925 200 KRONOR

27.03 g., 0.925 Silver 0.8039 oz. ASW, 36 mm. **Ruler:** Carl XVI Gustaf **Subject:** Selma Lagerlöf, 150th Anniversary of Birth

| Date | Mintage | VF20 | XF40 | MS60 | MS63 | MS65 |
|---|---|---|---|---|---|---|
| 2008 SI-E | 10,200 | — | — | 17.00 | 35.00 | 40.00 |

## KM# 917 300 KRONOR

27.03 g., 0.925 Silver 0.8039 oz. ASW, 36 mm. **Ruler:** Carl XVI Gustaf **Subject:** Wedding of Princess Victoria and Daniel

| Date | Mintage | VF20 | XF40 | MS60 | MS63 | MS65 |
|---|---|---|---|---|---|---|
| 2010 SI-S Prooflike | 12,020 | — | — | 17.00 | 45.00 | 50.00 |

## KM# 901 2000 KRONOR

12.00 g., 0.900 Gold 0.3472 oz. AGW, 26 mm. **Ruler:** Carl XVI Gustaf **Subject:** Nobel Prize Centennial **Obv:** Seated allegorical figure **Rev:** Nobel's portrait **Edge:** Plain

| Date | Mintage | VF20 | XF40 | MS60 | MS63 | MS65 |
|---|---|---|---|---|---|---|
| 2001 | — | — | — | 525 | 625 | 650 |

## KM# 909 2000 KRONOR

12.00 g., 0.900 Gold 0.3472 oz. AGW, 26 mm. **Ruler:** Carl XVI Gustaf **Subject:** 750th Anniversary of Stockholm **Obv:** City seal with three towers and gate **Rev:** Three towers of city hall **Edge:** Plain

| Date | Mintage | VF20 | XF40 | MS60 | MS63 | MS65 |
|---|---|---|---|---|---|---|
| ND2002 Prooflike | 3,596 | — | — | 525 | 625 | 650 |

## KM# 903 2000 KRONOR

12.00 g., 0.900 Gold 0.3472 oz. AGW **Ruler:** Carl XVI Gustaf **Subject:** 30th Anniversary of Reign

| Date | Mintage | VF20 | XF40 | MS60 | MS63 | MS65 |
|---|---|---|---|---|---|---|
| 2003 | 2,000 | — | — | 550 | 650 | 675 |

## KM# 905 2000 KRONOR

12.00 g., 0.900 Gold 0.3472 oz. AGW, 26 mm. **Ruler:** Carl XVI Gustaf **Subject:** St. Birgitta's 700th Anniversary of birth **Obv:** Gothic letter B above value **Rev:** St. Birgitta **Edge:** Plain

| Date | Mintage | VF20 | XF40 | MS60 | MS63 | MS65 |
|---|---|---|---|---|---|---|
| ND2003 | 3,640 | — | — | 525 | 625 | 650 |

## KM# 912 2000 KRONOR

12.00 g., 0.900 Gold 0.3472 oz. AGW, 26 mm. **Ruler:** Carl XVI Gustaf **Subject:** Royal Palace in Stockholm 250th Anniversary **Obv:** Two antique keys over map

| Date | Mintage | VF20 | XF40 | MS60 | MS63 | MS65 |
|---|---|---|---|---|---|---|
| ND2004 Prooflike | 5,734 | — | — | 525 | 625 | 650 |

## KM# 907 2000 KRONOR

12.00 g., 0.900 Gold 0.3472 oz. AGW, 26 mm. **Ruler:** Carl XVI Gustaf **Subject:** Centennial of the end of the Union between Norway and Sweden **Obv:** Split disc **Rev:** Flag pole dividing two clouds

| Date | Mintage | VF20 | XF40 | MS60 | MS63 | MS65 |
|---|---|---|---|---|---|---|
| 2005 H-E | 3,590 | — | — | 525 | 625 | 650 |

## KM# 914 2000 KRONOR

12.00 g., 0.900 Gold 0.3472 oz. AGW, 26 mm. **Ruler:** Carl XVI Gustaf **Subject:** Dag Hammarskjöld, 100th Anniversary of Birth **Obv:** Stylized flames **Rev:** Dag Hammarskjöld **Edge:** Plain

| Date | Mintage | VF20 | XF40 | MS60 | MS63 | MS65 |
|---|---|---|---|---|---|---|
| ND2005 H-E Prooflike | 2,563 | — | — | 550 | 625 | 650 |

## KM# 922 2000 KRONOR

12.00 g., 0.900 Gold 0.3472 oz. AGW, 26 mm. **Ruler:** Carl XVI Gustaf **Subject:** Swedish Railroads, 150th Anniversary

| Date | Mintage | VF20 | XF40 | MS60 | MS63 | MS65 |
|---|---|---|---|---|---|---|
| ND2006 SI-E | 1,395 | — | — | 525 | 625 | 650 |

### KM# 924 2000 KRONOR

12.00 g., 0.900 Gold 0.3472 oz. AGW, 26 mm. **Ruler:** Carl XVI Gustaf **Subject:** Carl Linnaeus, 300th Anniversary of Birth

| Date | Mintage | VF20 | XF40 | MS60 | MS63 | MS65 |
|---|---|---|---|---|---|---|
| ND2007 SI-E | 1,700 | — | — | 525 | 625 | 650 |

### KM# 926 2000 KRONOR

12.00 g., 0.900 Gold 0.3472 oz. AGW, 26 mm. **Ruler:** Carl XVI Gustaf **Subject:** Selma Lagerlof, 150th Anniversary of Birth **Edge:** Plain

| Date | Mintage | VF20 | XF40 | MS60 | MS63 | MS65 |
|---|---|---|---|---|---|---|
| 2008 SI-G | 2,495 | — | — | 500 | 575 | 600 |

### KM# 918 4000 KRONOR

12.00 g., 0.900 Gold 0.3472 oz. AGW, 26 mm. **Ruler:** Carl XVI Gustaf **Subject:** Wedding of Princess Victoria and Daniel Westling **Obv:** Coat of Arms of Princess Victoria **Rev:** Portraits of Bridal couple **Edge:** Plain

| Date | Mintage | VF20 | XF40 | MS60 | MS63 | MS65 |
|---|---|---|---|---|---|---|
| 2010 SI-S Prooflike | 4,370 | — | — | 600 | 650 | 675 |

## MINT SETS

| KM# | Date | Mintage | Identification | Issue Price | Mkt Val |
|---|---|---|---|---|---|
| MS107 | 2002 (4) | — | KM#853a, 878, 894, 895 plus medal (hard plastic case) | — | 10.00 |
| MS108 | 2001 (4) | — | KM#853a, 878, 894, 895 plus medal (hard plastic case) | 30.00 | |
| MS109 | 2001 (4) | — | KM#853a, 878, 894, 895 plus medal (folder) | 30.00 | |
| MS110 | 2002 (4) | — | KM#853a, 878, 894, 895 plus medal (folder) | 30.00 | |
| MS111 | 2003 (4) | — | KM#853a, 878, 894, 895 plus medal (hard plastic case) | 30.00 | |
| MS112 | 2003 (4) | — | KM#853a, 878, 894, 895 plus medal (folder) | 30.00 | |
| MS113 | 2004 (4) | — | KM#853a, 878, 894, 895 plus medal (hard plastic case) | 30.00 | |
| MS114 | 2004 (4) | Est. 8,000 | KM#853a, 878, 894, 895 plus medal (folder) | — | 30.00 |
| MS115 | 2005 (4) | — | KM#853, 878, 894, 895 plus medal (hard plastic case) | 30.00 | |
| MS116 | 2005 (4) | Est. 8,000 | KM#853a, 878, 894, 895 plus medal (folder) | — | 30.00 |
| MS117 | 2006 (2) | — | KM#878, 895 plus medal (hard plastic case) | 30.00 | |
| MS118 | 2007 (4) | Est. 20,000 | KM#853a, 878, 894, 895 plus medal (hard plastic case) | — | 30.00 |
| MS119 | 2008 (4) | — | KM#853a, 878, 894, 895 plus medal (hard plastic case) | 30.00 | |
| MS120 | 2009 (4) | Est. 30,000 | KM#853a, 878, 895, 916 plus medal (hard plastic case) | — | 28.00 |

## PROOF SETS

| KM# | Date | Mintage | Identification | Issue Price | Mkt Val |
|---|---|---|---|---|---|
| PS1 | 2004 (4) | 1,200 | KM#853a, 878, 894, 895 plus 8.64g., 0.900 Gold, 0.25 oz. AGW, 22mm 100th Aniversary of the birth of Greta Garbo medal. | — | 500 |
| PS2 | 2005 (4) | 550 | KM#853a, 878, 894, 895 plus 8.64g., 0.900 Gold, 0.25 oz. AGW, 22 mm medal | — | 600 |

# SWITZERLAND

The Swiss Confederation, located in central Europe north of Italy and south of Germany, has an area of 15,941 sq. mi. (41,290 sq. km.) and a population of *6.6 million. Capital: Bern. The economy centers about a well-developed manufacturing industry. Machinery, chemicals, watches and clocks, and textiles are exported.

The Swiss Constitutions of 1848 and 1874 established a union modeled upon that of the United States.

**MINT MARK**

B – Bern

**MONETARY SYSTEM**

100 Rappen (Centimes) = 1 Franc

## CONFEDERATION

## DECIMAL COINAGE

### KM# 46 RAPPEN

1.50 g., Bronze, 16 mm. **Obv:** Cross **Rev:** Value and oat sprig **Edge:** Plain

| Date | Mintage | VF20 | XF40 | MS60 | MS63 | MS65 |
|---|---|---|---|---|---|---|
| 2001 B | 1,522,000 | — | — | 0.25 | 0.50 | 1.00 |
| 2001 B | 5,184 | **PF65** 2.00 | | | | |
| 2002 B | 2,024,000 | — | — | 0.25 | 0.50 | 1.00 |
| 2002 B | 4,518 | **PF65** 3.00 | | | | |
| 2003 B | 1,522,000 | — | — | 0.25 | 0.50 | 1.00 |
| 2003 B | 4,520 | **PF65** 2.00 | | | | |
| 2004 B | 1,526,000 | — | — | 0.25 | 0.50 | 1.00 |
| 2004 B | 4,168 | **PF65** 2.00 | | | | |
| 2005 B | 1,524,000 | — | — | 0.25 | 0.50 | 1.00 |
| 2005 B | 3,783 | **PF65** 2.00 | | | | |
| 2006 B | 26,000 | — | — | 110 | 145 | 185 |
| Note: In sets only, circulation strikes not released | | | | | | |
| 2006 B | 4,000 | **PF63** 225 | **PF65** 285 | | | |

### KM# 26c 5 RAPPEN

1.80 g., Aluminum-Bronze, 17.15 mm. **Obv:** Crowned head right **Rev:** Value within wreath **Edge:** Plain

| Date | Mintage | VF20 | XF40 | MS60 | MS63 | MS65 |
|---|---|---|---|---|---|---|
| 2001 B | 5,022,000 | — | — | 0.25 | 0.50 | 1.00 |
| 2001 B | 5,184 | **PF65** 2.00 | | | | |
| 2002 B | 12,024,000 | — | — | 0.25 | 0.50 | 1.00 |
| 2002 B | 4,518 | **PF65** 2.00 | | | | |
| 2003 B | 10,022,000 | — | — | 0.25 | 0.50 | 1.00 |
| 2003 B | 4,520 | **PF65** 2.00 | | | | |
| 2004 B | 10,026,000 | — | — | 0.25 | 0.50 | 1.00 |
| 2004 B | 4,168 | **PF65** 2.00 | | | | |
| 2005 B | 13,024,000 | — | — | 0.25 | 0.50 | 1.00 |
| 2005 B | 3,783 | **PF65** 2.00 | | | | |
| 2006 B | 12,026,000 | — | — | 0.25 | 0.50 | 1.00 |
| 2006 B | 4,000 | **PF65** 2.00 | | | | |
| 2007 B | 13,024,000 | — | — | 0.25 | 0.50 | 1.00 |
| 2007 B | 3,415 | **PF65** 2.00 | | | | |
| 2008 B | 40,022,000 | — | — | 0.25 | 0.50 | 1.00 |
| 2008 B | 3,286 | **PF65** 2.00 | | | | |
| 2009 B | 45,022,000 | — | — | 0.25 | 0.50 | 1.00 |
| 2009 B | 3,115 | **PF65** 2.00 | | | | |
| 2010 B | Est. 41022000 | — | — | 0.25 | 0.50 | 1.00 |
| 2010 B | Est. 4000 | **PF65** 2.00 | | | | |
| 2011 B | Est. 50022000 | — | — | 0.25 | 0.50 | 1.00 |
| 2011 B | Est. 4000 | **PF65** 2.00 | | | | |
| 2012 B | Est. 35022000 | — | — | 0.25 | 0.50 | 1.00 |
| 2012 B | Est. 4000 | **PF65** 2.00 | | | | |
| 2013 B | Est. 37020000 | — | — | 0.25 | 0.50 | 1.00 |
| 2013 B | Est. 3500 | **PF65** 2.00 | | | | |
| 2014 | — | — | — | 0.30 | 1.00 | — |
| 2014 | — | **PF60** 2.00 | | | | |
| 2013 B | — | — | — | 0.30 | 1.00 | — |
| 2015 B | — | **PF60** 2.00 | | | | |

### KM# 27 10 RAPPEN

3.00 g., Copper-Nickel, 19.15 mm. **Obv:** Crowned head right **Obv. Legend:** CONFOEDERATIO HELVETICA **Rev:** Value within wreath **Edge:** Plain

| Date | Mintage | VF20 | XF40 | MS60 | MS63 | MS65 |
|---|---|---|---|---|---|---|
| 2001 B | 7,022,000 | — | — | 0.25 | 0.50 | 1.00 |
| 2001 B | 5,184 | **PF65** 3.00 | | | | |
| 2002 B | 15,024,000 | — | — | 0.25 | 0.50 | 1.00 |
| 2002 B | 4,518 | **PF65** 3.00 | | | | |
| 2003 B | 12,022,000 | — | — | 0.25 | 0.50 | 1.00 |
| 2003 B | 4,520 | **PF65** 3.00 | | | | |
| 2004 B | 5,026,000 | — | — | 0.25 | 0.50 | 1.00 |
| 2004 B | 4,168 | **PF65** 3.00 | | | | |
| 2005 B | 7,024,000 | — | — | 0.25 | 0.50 | 1.00 |
| 2005 B | 3,783 | **PF65** 3.00 | | | | |
| 2006 B | 2,026,000 | — | — | 0.25 | 0.50 | 1.00 |
| 2006 B | 4,000 | **PF65** 3.00 | | | | |
| 2007 B | 18,024,000 | — | — | 0.25 | 0.50 | 1.00 |
| 2007 B | 3,415 | **PF65** 3.00 | | | | |
| 2008 B | 35,022,000 | — | — | 0.25 | 0.50 | 1.00 |
| 2008 B | 3,286 | **PF65** 3.00 | | | | |
| 2009 B | 35,022,000 | — | — | 0.25 | 0.50 | 1.00 |
| 2009 B | 3,115 | **PF65** 3.00 | | | | |
| 2010 B | Est. 42022000 | — | — | 0.25 | 0.50 | 1.00 |
| 2010 B | Est. 4000 | **PF65** 3.00 | | | | |
| 2011 B | Est. 35022000 | — | — | 0.25 | 0.50 | 1.00 |
| 2011 B | Est. 4000 | **PF65** 3.00 | | | | |
| 2012 B | Est. 30022000 | — | — | 0.25 | 0.50 | 1.00 |
| 2012 B | Est. 4000 | **PF65** 3.00 | | | | |
| 2013 B | Est. 28020000 | — | — | 0.25 | 0.50 | 1.00 |
| 2013 B | Est. 3500 | **PF65** 3.00 | | | | |
| 2014 | — | — | — | 0.50 | 1.00 | — |
| 2014 | — | **PF60** 2.00 | | | | |
| 2015 B | — | — | — | 0.40 | 1.00 | — |
| 2015 B | — | **PF60** 2.00 | | | | |

### KM# 29a 20 RAPPEN

4.00 g., Copper-Nickel, 21.05 mm. **Obv:** Crowned head right **Rev:** Value within wreath **Edge:** Plain

| Date | Mintage | VF20 | XF40 | MS60 | MS63 | MS65 |
|---|---|---|---|---|---|---|
| 2001 B | 7,022,000 | — | — | 0.50 | 1.00 | 2.00 |
| 2001 B | 5,184 | **PF65** 4.00 | | | | |
| 2002 B | 12,024,000 | — | — | 0.50 | 1.00 | 2.00 |
| 2002 B | 4,518 | **PF65** 4.00 | | | | |
| 2003 B | 10,022,000 | — | — | 0.50 | 1.00 | 2.00 |
| 2003 B | 4,520 | **PF65** 4.00 | | | | |
| 2004 B | 10,026,000 | — | — | 0.50 | 1.00 | 2.00 |
| 2004 B | 4,168 | **PF65** 4.00 | | | | |
| 2005 B | 6,024,000 | — | — | 0.50 | 1.00 | 2.00 |
| 2005 B | 3,783 | **PF65** 4.00 | | | | |
| 2006 B | 5,026,000 | — | — | 0.50 | 1.00 | 2.00 |
| 2006 B | 4,000 | **PF65** 4.00 | | | | |
| 2007 B | 22,024,000 | — | — | 0.50 | 1.00 | 2.00 |
| 2007 B | 3,415 | **PF65** 4.00 | | | | |
| 2008 B | 41,022,000 | — | — | 0.50 | 1.00 | 2.00 |
| 2008 B | 3,286 | **PF65** 4.00 | | | | |
| 2009 B | 32,022,000 | — | — | 0.50 | 1.00 | 2.00 |
| 2009 B | 3,115 | **PF65** 4.00 | | | | |
| 2010 B | Est. 18022000 | — | — | 0.50 | 1.00 | 2.00 |
| 2010 B | Est. 4000 | **PF65** 4.00 | | | | |
| 2011 B | Est. 20022000 | — | — | 0.50 | 1.00 | 2.00 |
| 2011 B | Est. 4000 | **PF65** 4.00 | | | | |
| 2012 B | Est. 32022000 | — | — | 0.50 | 1.00 | 2.00 |
| 2012 B | Est. 4000 | **PF65** 4.00 | | | | |
| 2013 B | Est. 32020000 | — | — | 0.50 | 1.00 | 2.00 |
| 2013 B | Est. 3500 | **PF65** 4.00 | | | | |
| 2014 | — | — | — | 0.75 | 2.00 | — |
| 2014 | — | **PF60** 3.00 | | | | |
| 2015 B | — | — | — | 0.75 | 2.00 | — |
| 2015 B | — | **PF60** 3.00 | | | | |

### KM# 23a.3 1/2 FRANC

2.20 g., Copper-Nickel, 18.2 mm. **Obv:** 23 Stars around figure **Rev:** Value within wreath **Edge:** Reeded

| Date | Mintage | VF20 | XF40 | MS60 | MS63 | MS65 |
|---|---|---|---|---|---|---|
| 2001 B | 6,022,000 | — | — | 1.00 | 2.50 | 3.50 |
| 2001 B | 5,184 | **PF65** 8.00 | | | | |
| 2002 B | 2,024,000 | — | — | 1.00 | 2.50 | 3.50 |
| 2002 B | 4,518 | **PF65** 8.00 | | | | |
| 2003 B | 2,022,000 | — | — | 1.00 | 2.50 | 3.50 |
| 2003 B | 4,520 | **PF65** 8.00 | | | | |
| 2004 B | 2,026,000 | — | — | 1.00 | 2.50 | 3.50 |
| 2004 B | 4,168 | **PF65** 8.00 | | | | |
| 2005 B | 1,024,000 | — | — | 1.00 | 2.50 | 3.50 |
| 2005 B | 3,783 | **PF65** 8.00 | | | | |
| 2006 B | 2,025,000 | — | — | 1.00 | 2.50 | 3.50 |
| 2006 B | 4,000 | **PF65** 8.00 | | | | |
| 2007 B | 18,024,000 | — | — | 1.00 | 2.50 | 3.50 |
| 2007 B | 3,415 | **PF65** 7.00 | | | | |
| 2008 B | 25,022,000 | — | — | 1.00 | 2.00 | 3.00 |
| 2008 B | 3,286 | **PF65** 7.00 | | | | |
| 2009 B | 27,022,000 | — | — | 1.00 | 2.00 | 3.00 |
| 2009 B | 3,115 | **PF65** 7.00 | | | | |
| 2010 B | Est. 27022000 | — | — | 1.00 | 2.00 | 3.00 |
| 2010 B | Est. 4000 | **PF65** 7.00 | | | | |
| 2011 B | Est. 15022000 | — | — | 1.00 | 2.00 | 3.00 |
| 2011 B | Est. 4000 | **PF65** 7.00 | | | | |
| 2012 B | Est. 20022000 | — | — | 1.00 | 2.00 | 3.00 |
| 2012 B | Est. 4000 | **PF65** 7.00 | | | | |
| 2013 B | Est. 23020000 | — | — | 1.00 | 2.00 | 3.00 |
| 2013 B | Est. 3500 | **PF65** 7.00 | | | | |
| 2014 | — | — | — | 1.00 | 3.00 | — |
| 2014 | — | **PF60** 5.00 | | | | |
| 2015 | — | — | — | 1.50 | 3.00 | — |
| 2015 B | — | **PF60** 5.00 | | | | |

**KM# 24a.3 FRANC**
4.40 g., Copper-Nickel, 23.2 mm. **Obv:** 23 Stars around figure **Rev:** Value and date within wreath **Edge:** Reeded

| Date | Mintage | VF20 | XF40 | MS60 | MS63 | MS65 |
|---|---|---|---|---|---|---|
| 2001 B | 3,022,000 | — | — | 1.50 | 2.50 | 4.00 |
| 2001 B | 5,184 | PF65 8.00 | | | | |
| 2002 B | 1,024,000 | — | — | 1.50 | 2.50 | 4.00 |
| 2002 B | 4,518 | PF65 8.00 | | | | |
| 2003 B | 2,022,000 | — | — | 1.50 | 2.50 | 4.00 |
| 2003 B | 4,520 | PF65 8.00 | | | | |
| 2004 B | 2,026,000 | — | — | 1.50 | 2.50 | 4.00 |
| 2004 B | 4,168 | PF65 8.00 | | | | |
| 2005 B | 1,024,000 | — | — | 1.50 | 2.50 | 4.00 |
| 2005 B | 3,783 | PF65 8.00 | | | | |
| 2006 B | 2,026,000 | — | — | 1.50 | 2.50 | 4.00 |
| 2006 B | 4,000 | PF65 8.00 | | | | |
| 2007 B | 3,024,000 | — | — | 1.50 | 2.50 | 4.00 |
| 2007 B | 3,415 | PF65 8.00 | | | | |
| 2008 B | 7,022,000 | — | — | 1.50 | 2.50 | 4.00 |
| 2008 B | 3,286 | PF65 8.00 | | | | |
| 2009 B | 11,022,000 | — | — | 1.50 | 2.50 | 4.00 |
| 2009 B | 3,115 | PF65 8.00 | | | | |
| 2010 B | Est. 15022000 | — | — | 1.50 | 2.50 | 4.00 |
| 2010 B | Est. 4000 | PF65 8.00 | | | | |
| 2011 B | Est. 15022000 | — | — | 1.50 | 2.50 | 4.00 |
| 2011 B | Est. 4000 | PF65 8.00 | | | | |
| 2012 B | Est. 12022000 | — | — | 1.50 | 2.50 | 4.00 |
| 2012 B | Est. 4000 | PF65 8.00 | | | | |
| 2013 B | Est. 12020000 | — | — | 1.50 | 2.50 | 4.00 |
| 2013 B | Est. 3500 | PF65 8.00 | | | | |
| 2014 | — | — | — | 3.00 | 5.00 | — |
| 2014 | — | PF65 7.00 | | | | |
| 2015 B | — | — | — | 3.00 | 5.00 | — |
| 2015 B | — | PF65 7.00 | | | | |

**KM# 21a.3 2 FRANCS**
8.80 g., Copper-Nickel, 27.4 mm. **Obv:** 23 Stars around figure **Rev:** Value within wreath **Edge:** Reeded

| Date | Mintage | VF20 | XF40 | MS60 | MS63 | MS65 |
|---|---|---|---|---|---|---|
| 2001 B | 4,022,000 | — | — | 3.00 | 5.00 | 7.00 |
| 2001 B | 5,184 | PF65 12.00 | | | | |
| 2002 B | 1,024,000 | — | — | 3.00 | 5.00 | 7.00 |
| 2002 B | 4,518 | PF65 12.00 | | | | |
| 2003 B | 1,022,000 | — | 2.50 | 2.00 | 5.00 | 7.00 |
| 2003 B | 4,520 | PF65 12.00 | | | | |
| 2004 B | 1,026,000 | — | 2.50 | 3.00 | 5.00 | 7.00 |
| 2004 B | 4,168 | PF65 12.00 | | | | |
| 2005 B | 2,024,000 | — | — | 3.00 | 5.00 | 7.00 |
| 2005 B | 3,783 | PF65 12.00 | | | | |
| 2006 B | 7,026,000 | — | — | 3.00 | 5.00 | 7.00 |
| 2006 B | 4,000 | PF65 12.00 | | | | |
| 2007 B | 16,024,000 | — | — | 3.00 | 5.00 | 7.00 |
| 2007 B | 3,415 | PF65 12.00 | | | | |
| 2008 B | 6,022,000 | — | — | 3.00 | 5.00 | 7.00 |
| 2008 B | 3,286 | PF65 12.00 | | | | |
| 2009 B | 8,022,000 | — | — | 3.00 | 5.00 | 7.00 |
| 2009 B | 3,115 | PF65 12.00 | | | | |
| 2010 B | Est. 9022000 | — | — | 3.00 | 5.00 | 7.00 |
| 2010 B | Est. 4000 | PF65 12.00 | | | | |
| 2011 B | Est. 7022000 | — | — | 3.00 | 5.00 | 7.00 |
| 2011 B | Est. 4000 | PF65 12.00 | | | | |
| 2012 B | Est. 11022000 | — | — | 3.00 | 5.00 | 7.00 |
| 2012 B | Est. 4000 | PF65 12.00 | | | | |
| 2013 B | Est. 12020000 | — | — | 3.00 | 5.00 | 7.00 |
| 2013 B | Est. 3500 | PF65 12.00 | | | | |
| 2014 | — | — | — | 4.00 | 7.50 | — |
| 2014 | — | PF60 10.00 | | | | |
| 2015 B | — | — | — | 4.50 | 7.50 | — |
| 2015 B | — | PF60 10.00 | | | | |

**KM# 40a.4 5 FRANCS**
13.20 g., Copper-Nickel, 31.45 mm. **Obv:** William Tell right **Rev:** Shield flanked by sprigs **Edge:** DOMINUS PROVIDEBIT and 13 stars raised

| Date | Mintage | VF20 | XF40 | MS60 | MS63 | MS65 |
|---|---|---|---|---|---|---|
| 2001 B | 1,022,000 | — | — | 7.50 | 9.00 | 12.00 |
| 2001 B | 5,184 | PF65 18.00 | | | | |
| 2002 B | 1,024,000 | — | — | 7.50 | 9.00 | 12.00 |
| 2002 B | 4,518 | PF65 18.00 | | | | |
| 2003 B | 1,022,000 | — | — | 7.50 | 9.00 | 12.00 |
| 2003 B | 4,520 | PF65 16.00 | | | | |
| 2004 B | 524,000 | — | — | 7.50 | 9.00 | 12.00 |
| 2004 B | 4,166 | PF65 17.00 | | | | |
| 2005 B | 524,000 | — | — | 7.50 | 9.00 | 12.00 |
| 2005 B | 3,783 | PF65 17.00 | | | | |
| 2006 B | 526,000 | — | — | 7.50 | — | 12.00 |
| 2006 B | 4,000 | PF65 18.00 | | | | |
| 2007 B | 524,000 | — | — | 7.50 | 9.00 | 12.00 |
| 2007 B | 3,415 | PF65 18.00 | | | | |
| 2008 B | 522,000 | — | — | 7.50 | 9.00 | 12.00 |
| 2008 B | 3,286 | PF65 18.00 | | | | |
| 2009 B | 2,022,000 | — | — | 7.50 | 9.00 | 12.00 |
| 2009 B | 3,115 | PF65 18.00 | | | | |
| 2010 B | Est. 5022000 | — | — | 7.50 | 9.00 | 12.00 |
| 2010 B | Est. 4000 | PF65 18.00 | | | | |
| 2011 B | Est. 3022000 | — | — | 7.50 | 9.00 | 12.00 |
| 2011 B | Est. 4000 | PF65 18.00 | | | | |
| 2012 B | Est. 8022000 | — | — | 7.50 | 9.00 | 12.00 |
| 2012 B | Est. 4000 | PF65 18.00 | | | | |
| 2013 B | Est. 8020000 | — | — | 7.50 | 9.00 | 12.00 |
| 2013 B | Est. 3500 | PF65 18.00 | | | | |
| 2014 | Est. 7019000 | — | — | 7.50 | 11.00 | — |
| 2014 | Est. 3000 | PF60 15.00 | PF65 20.00 | | | |
| 2015 | Est. 5010000 | — | — | 7.50 | 11.00 | — |
| 2015 | Est. 3000 | PF60 20.00 | | | | |

## COMMEMORATIVE COINAGE

**KM# 92 5 FRANCS**
15.00 g., Bi-Metallic Nordic gold center in Copper-Nickel ring, 32.85 mm. **Subject:** Zurcher Sechselauten **Obv:** Value within circle **Rev:** Burning strawman within circle **Edge:** Reeded **Edge Lettering:** DOMINUS PROVIDEBIT (13 stars)

| Date | Mintage | VF20 | XF40 | MS60 | MS63 | MS65 |
|---|---|---|---|---|---|---|
| 2001 B | 170,000 | — | — | 7.00 | 9.00 | 12.00 |
| 2001 B | 20,000 | PF65 30.00 | | | | |

**KM# 98 5 FRANCS**
15.00 g., Bi-Metallic Nordic gold center in Copper-Nickel ring, 32.85 mm. **Subject:** Escalade 1602-2002 **Obv:** Value within circle **Rev:** Swirling ladders design within circle **Edge:** Reeded **Edge Lettering:** DOMINUS PROVIDEBIT (13 stars)

| Date | Mintage | VF20 | XF40 | MS60 | MS63 | MS65 |
|---|---|---|---|---|---|---|
| 2002 B | 130,000 | — | — | 7.00 | 9.00 | 12.00 |
| 2002 B | 15,000 | PF65 30.00 | | | | |

**KM# 103 5 FRANCS**
15.00 g., Bi-Metallic Nordic gold center in Copper-Nickel ring, 32.85 mm. **Subject:** Chalandamarz **Obv:** Value within circular inscription and designed wreath **Rev:** Boys shaking bells within 3/4 designed wreath **Edge:** Reeded **Edge Lettering:** DOMINUS PROVIDEBIT (13 stars)

| Date | Mintage | VF20 | XF40 | MS60 | MS63 | MS65 |
|---|---|---|---|---|---|---|
| 2003 B | 96,000 | — | — | 7.00 | 9.00 | 12.00 |
| 2003 B | 12,000 | PF65 30.00 | | | | |

**KM# 107 10 FRANCS**
15.00 g., Bi-Metallic Copper-Nickel center in Aluminum-Bronze ring, 32.85 mm. **Obv:** Value **Rev:** Matterhorn Mountain **Edge:** Segmented reeding

| Date | Mintage | VF20 | XF40 | MS60 | MS63 | MS65 |
|---|---|---|---|---|---|---|
| 2004 B | 91,870 | — | — | 14.00 | 18.00 | 22.00 |
| 2004 B | 12,168 | PF65 45.00 | | | | |

**KM# 111 10 FRANCS**
15.00 g., Bi-Metallic Copper-Nickel center in Aluminum-Bronze ring, 32.85 mm. **Obv:** Value **Rev:** Jungfrau mountain **Edge:** Segmented reeding

| Date | Mintage | VF20 | XF40 | MS60 | MS63 | MS65 |
|---|---|---|---|---|---|---|
| 2005 B | 73,164 | — | — | 14.00 | 16.00 | 20.00 |
| 2005 B | 9,442 | PF65 40.00 | | | | |

**KM# 114 10 FRANCS**
15.00 g., Bi-Metallic Copper-Nickel center in Aluminum-Bronze ring, 32.85 mm. **Obv:** Value **Rev:** Piz Bernina mountain **Edge:** Segmented reeding

| Date | Mintage | VF20 | XF40 | MS60 | MS63 | MS65 |
|---|---|---|---|---|---|---|
| 2006 B | 56,426 | — | — | 14.00 | 16.00 | 20.00 |
| 2006 B | 8,996 | PF65 40.00 | | | | |

**KM# 118 10 FRANCS**
15.00 g., Bi-Metallic Copper-Nickel center in Aluminum-Bronze ring, 32.85 mm. **Subject:** Swiss National Park **Obv:** Value **Rev:** Ibex **Edge:** Segmented reeding

| Date | Mintage | VF20 | XF40 | MS60 | MS63 | MS65 |
|---|---|---|---|---|---|---|
| 2007 B | 75,602 | — | — | 14.00 | 16.00 | 20.00 |
| 2007 B | 10,297 | PF65 40.00 | | | | |

**KM# 126 10 FRANCS**
15.00 g., Bi-Metallic Copper-Nickel center in Aluminum-Bronze ring, 32.85 mm. **Obv:** Small national arms **Obv. Legend:** CONFEDERATIO - HELVETICA **Rev:** Golden Eagle alighting **Rev. Legend:** PARK NATIONAL SUISSE **Edge:** Segmented reeding

| Date | Mintage | VF20 | XF40 | MS60 | MS63 | MS65 |
|---|---|---|---|---|---|---|
| 2008 B | 63,320 | — | — | 14.00 | 16.00 | 20.00 |
| 2008 B | 10,299 | PF65 40.00 | | | | |

**KM# 130 10 FRANCS**
15.00 g., Bi-Metallic Copper-Nickel center in Aluminum-Bronze ring, 32.85 mm. **Subject:** Swiss National Park **Obv:** Value **Rev:** Red deer

| Date | Mintage | VF20 | XF40 | MS60 | MS63 | MS65 |
|---|---|---|---|---|---|---|
| 2009 B | 62,500 | — | — | 14.00 | 16.00 | 20.00 |
| 2009 B | 9,300 | PF65 40.00 | | | | |

**KM# 134 10 FRANCS**
15.00 g., Bi-Metallic Copper-Nickel center in Aluminum-Bronze ring, 32.85 mm. **Subject:** Swiss National Park - Alpine Marmot **Obv:** Value **Rev:** Marmot

| Date | Mintage | VF20 | XF40 | MS60 | MS63 | MS65 |
|---|---|---|---|---|---|---|
| 2010 B | 9,000 | PF65 40.00 | | | | |
| 2010 B | 62,500 | — | — | 14.00 | 16.00 | 20.00 |

**KM# 138 10 FRANCS**
15.00 g., Bi-Metallic Copper-Nickel center in Aluminum-Bronze ring, 33 mm. **Subject:** Bern Onion Market **Obv:** Value **Rev:** Bear of Bern at left, woven plaits of onions at right **Edge:** Segmented reeding

| Date | Mintage | VF20 | XF40 | MS60 | MS63 | MS65 |
|---|---|---|---|---|---|---|
| 2011 B | Est. 12000 | PF65 50.00 | | | | |
| 2011 B | Est. 94000 | — | — | 14.00 | 16.00 | 20.00 |

**KM# 142 10 FRANCS**
15.00 g., Bi-Metallic Copper-Nickel center in Aluminum-Bronze ring, 33 mm. **Subject:** Bull fighting **Rev:** Two bull's heads butting

| Date | Mintage | VF20 | XF40 | MS60 | MS63 | MS65 |
|---|---|---|---|---|---|---|
| 2012 B | Est. 12000 | PF65 60.00 | | | | |
| 2012 B | Est. 94000 | — | — | 14.00 | 18.00 | 24.00 |

**KM# 146 10 FRANCS**
15.00 g., Bi-Metallic Copper-Nickel center in Aluminum-Bronze ring, 33 mm. **Subject:** Silvesterchlausen **Obv:** Swiss cross and value **Rev:** Folk costumes with New Year bell ringers

| Date | Mintage | VF20 | XF40 | MS60 | MS63 | MS65 |
|---|---|---|---|---|---|---|
| 2013 B | Est. 11500 | PF65 60.00 | | | | |
| 2013 B | Est. 92000 | — | — | 14.00 | 18.00 | 24.00 |

**KM# 150 10 FRANCS**
15.00 g., Bi-Metallic Copper-Nickel center in Aluminum-Bronze ring, 32.85 mm. **Subject:** Gansabhauet Sursee **Rev:** Costumed man holding sword, about to behead goose

| Date | Mintage | VF20 | XF40 | MS60 | MS63 | MS65 |
|---|---|---|---|---|---|---|
| 2014 B | Est. 90000 | — | — | 14.00 | 18.00 | 25.00 |
| 2014 B | Est. 11000 | PF65 60.00 | | | | |

**KM# 93 20 FRANCS**
20.00 g., 0.835 Silver 0.5369 oz. ASW, 32.8 mm. **Subject:** Mustair Cloister **Obv:** Church floor plan **Rev:** Cloister of Müstair **Edge Lettering:** DOMINUS PROVIDEBIT and 13 stars

| Date | Mintage | VF20 | XF40 | MS60 | MS63 | MS65 |
|---|---|---|---|---|---|---|
| 2001 B | 48,311 | — | — | 26.00 | 30.00 | 35.00 |
| 2001 B | 14,000 | PF65 55.00 | | | | |

**KM# 94 20 FRANCS**
20.00 g., 0.835 Silver 0.5369 oz. ASW, 32.8 mm. **Subject:** Johanna Spyri **Obv:** Value within handwritten background **Rev:** Bust facing **Edge Lettering:** DOMINUS PROVIDEBIT (13 stars)

| Date | Mintage | VF20 | XF40 | MS60 | MS63 | MS65 |
|---|---|---|---|---|---|---|
| 2001 B | 59,006 | — | — | 26.00 | 30.00 | 35.00 |
| 2001 B | 6,799 | PF65 55.00 | | | | |

**KM# 99 20 FRANCS**
20.00 g., 0.835 Silver 0.5369 oz. ASW, 32.8 mm. **Obv:** St. Gall and bear cub **Rev:** St. Gall Cloister **Edge Lettering:** DOMINUS PROVIDEBIT (13 stars)

| Date | Mintage | VF20 | XF40 | MS60 | MS63 | MS65 |
|---|---|---|---|---|---|---|
| 2002 B | 34,737 | — | — | 26.00 | 30.00 | 35.00 |
| 2002 B | 6,250 | PF65 60.00 | | | | |

**KM# 100 20 FRANCS**
20.00 g., 0.835 Silver 0.5369 oz. ASW, 32.8 mm. **Subject:** REGA **Obv:** Value, inscription and raised cross above rotating propeller **Rev:** Rescue helicopter in flight **Edge Lettering:** DOMINUS PROVIDEBIT (13 stars)

| Date | Mintage | VF20 | XF40 | MS60 | MS63 | MS65 |
|---|---|---|---|---|---|---|
| 2002 B | 36,172 | — | — | 26.00 | 30.00 | 35.00 |
| 2002 B | 6,453 | PF65 60.00 | | | | |

**KM# 101 20 FRANCS**
20.00 g., 0.835 Silver 0.5369 oz. ASW, 32.8 mm. **Subject:** Expo '02 **Obv:** Value and date within circle **Rev:** Child at water's edge within beaded circle **Edge Lettering:** DOMINUS PROVIDEBIT (13 stars)

| Date | Mintage | VF20 | XF40 | MS60 | MS63 | MS65 |
|---|---|---|---|---|---|---|
| 2002 B | 50,045 | — | — | 26.00 | 30.00 | 35.00 |
| 2002 B | 7,691 | PF65 60.00 | | | | |

**KM# 104 20 FRANCS**
19.97 g., 0.835 Silver 0.5361 oz. ASW, 32.8 mm. **Subject:** St. Moritz Ski Championships **Obv:** Value in snow storm **Rev:** Skier in snow storm **Edge Lettering:** DOMINUS PROVIDEBIT (13 stars)

| Date | Mintage | VF20 | XF40 | MS60 | MS63 | MS65 |
|---|---|---|---|---|---|---|
| 2003 B | 38,052 | — | — | 26.00 | 30.00 | 35.00 |
| 2003 B | 6,471 | PF65 60.00 | | | | |

**KM# 106 20 FRANCS**
20.00 g., 0.835 Silver 0.5369 oz. ASW, 32.8 mm. **Subject:** Bern, Old Town **Obv:** Stylized clock tower and buildings **Rev:** Stylized aerial view of Berner Altstadt **Edge Lettering:** DOMINUS PROVIDEBIT

| Date | Mintage | VF20 | XF40 | MS60 | MS63 | MS65 |
|---|---|---|---|---|---|---|
| 2003 B | 37,361 | — | — | 26.00 | 30.00 | 35.00 |
| 2003 B | 5,909 | PF65 60.00 | | | | |

**KM# 108 20 FRANCS**
20.00 g., 0.835 Silver 0.5369 oz. ASW, 32.8 mm. **Obv:** Value **Rev:** The Three Castles of Bellinzona **Edge Lettering:** DOMINUS PROVIDEBIT

| Date | Mintage | VF20 | XF40 | MS60 | MS63 | MS65 |
|---|---|---|---|---|---|---|
| 2004 B | 28,762 | — | — | 26.00 | 30.00 | 35.00 |
| 2004 B | 5,190 | PF65 60.00 | | | | |

**KM# 109 20 FRANCS**
20.00 g., 0.835 Silver 0.5369 oz. ASW, 32.8 mm. **Obv:** Value **Rev:** Chillon Castle and reflection **Edge Lettering:** DOMINUS PROVIDEBIT

| Date | Mintage | VF20 | XF40 | MS60 | MS63 | MS65 |
|---|---|---|---|---|---|---|
| 2004 B | 33,999 | — | — | 26.00 | 30.00 | 35.00 |
| 2004 B | 5,670 | PF65 60.00 | | | | |

**KM# 121 20 FRANCS**

20.00 g., 0.835 Silver 0.5369 oz. ASW, 32.8 mm. **Subject:** FIFA Centennial **Obv:** Soccer ball with value at left **Rev:** Flower in center of cross

| Date | Mintage | VF20 | XF40 | MS60 | MS63 | MS65 |
|---|---|---|---|---|---|---|
| 2004 B Proof only | 13,997 | PF65 200 | | | | |

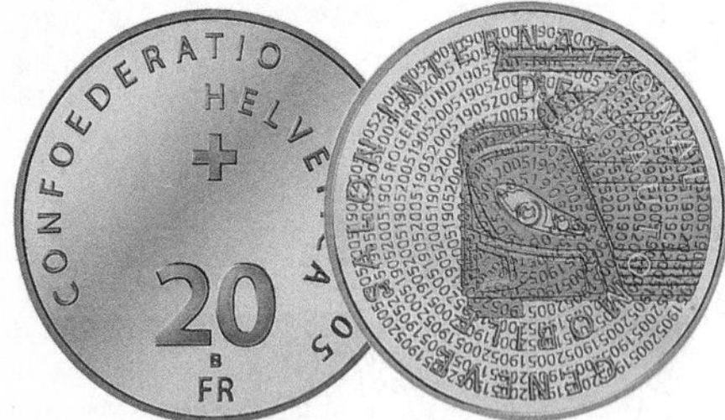


**KM# 112 20 FRANCS**

20.00 g., 0.835 Silver 0.5369 oz. ASW, 32.8 mm. **Subject:** Geneva Motor Show **Obv:** Value **Rev:** Partial view of prototype car **Edge Lettering:** DOMINUS PROVIDEBIT

| Date | Mintage | VF20 | XF40 | MS60 | MS63 | MS65 |
|---|---|---|---|---|---|---|
| 2005 B | 30,792 | — | — | 26.00 | 30.00 | 35.00 |
| 2005 B | 5,996 | PF65 60.00 | | | | |

**KM# 122 20 FRANCS**

20.00 g., 0.835 Silver 0.5369 oz. ASW, 32.8 mm. **Subject:** Chapel Bridge Lucerne **Obv:** Value **Rev:** View of Chapel Bridge **Edge Lettering:** DOMINUS PROVIDEBIT

| Date | Mintage | VF20 | XF40 | MS60 | MS63 | MS65 |
|---|---|---|---|---|---|---|
| 2005 B | 33,471 | — | — | 26.00 | 30.00 | 35.00 |
| 2005 B | 5,246 | PF65 60.00 | | | | |

**KM# 115 20 FRANCS**

20.00 g., 0.835 Silver 0.5369 oz. ASW, 32.8 mm. **Obv:** Value **Rev:** 1906 Post Bus **Edge Lettering:** DOMINUS PROVIDEBIT

| Date | Mintage | VF20 | XF40 | MS60 | MS63 | MS65 |
|---|---|---|---|---|---|---|
| 2006 B | 37,181 | — | — | 26.00 | 30.00 | 35.00 |
| 2006 B | 5,920 | PF65 60.00 | | | | |

**KM# 117 20 FRANCS**

20.00 g., 0.835 Silver 0.5369 oz. ASW, 32.8 mm. **Obv:** Value and legend **Rev:** Swiss Parliament Building **Edge Lettering:** DOMINUS PROVIDEBIT (13 stars)

| Date | Mintage | VF20 | XF40 | MS60 | MS63 | MS65 |
|---|---|---|---|---|---|---|
| 2006 B | 32,304 | — | — | 26.00 | 30.00 | 35.00 |
| 2006 B | 5,068 | PF65 60.00 | | | | |

**KM# 119 20 FRANCS**

20.00 g., 0.835 Silver 0.5369 oz. ASW, 32.8 mm. **Subject:** National Bank Centennial **Obv:** Value **Rev:** Partial face of Arthur Honegger (Composer) **Edge Lettering:** DOMINUS PROVIDEBIT

| Date | Mintage | VF20 | XF40 | MS60 | MS63 | MS65 |
|---|---|---|---|---|---|---|
| 2007 B | 37,125 | — | — | 26.00 | 30.00 | 35.00 |
| 2007 B | 10,251 | PF65 65.00 | | | | |

**KM# 124 20 FRANCS**

20.00 g., 0.835 Silver 0.5369 oz. ASW, 32.8 mm. **Series:** Famous buildings **Subject:** Munot castle of Schaffhausen **Obv. Legend:** CONFEDERATIO - HELVETICA **Rev:** Two views of castle **Rev. Legend:** MUNOT

| Date | Mintage | VF20 | XF40 | MS60 | MS63 | MS65 |
|---|---|---|---|---|---|---|
| 2007 B | 37,150 | — | — | 26.00 | 30.00 | 35.00 |
| 2007 B | 4,946 | PF65 65.00 | | | | |

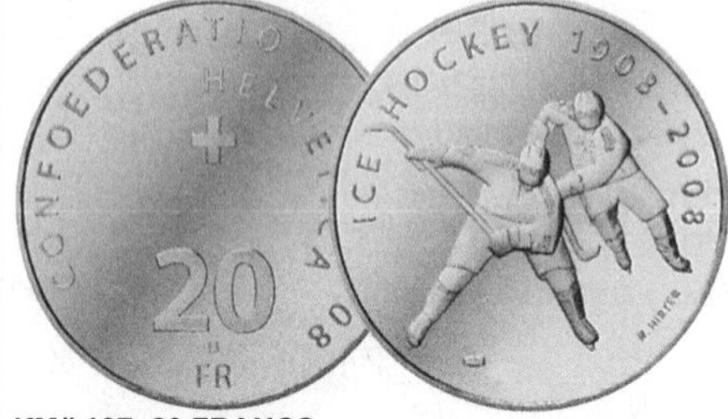


**KM# 127 20 FRANCS**

20.00 g., 0.835 Silver 0.5369 oz. ASW, 32.8 mm. **Subject:** 100th Anniversary Hockey **Obv:** Small national arms **Obv. Legend:** CONFEDERATIO - HELVETICA **Rev:** Two players, one about to swing at puck **Rev. Legend:** ICE HOCKEY 1908-2008

| Date | Mintage | VF20 | XF40 | MS60 | MS63 | MS65 |
|---|---|---|---|---|---|---|
| 2008 B | 43,761 | — | — | 26.00 | 30.00 | 35.00 |
| 2008 B | 4,866 | PF65 65.00 | | | | |

**KM# 128 20 FRANCS**

20.00 g., 0.835 Silver 0.5369 oz. ASW, 32.8 mm. **Subject:** Vitznau-Rigi Cog Railway **Obv:** Value **Rev:** Modern locomotive descending, early locomotive ascending (inverted)

| Date | Mintage | VF20 | XF40 | MS60 | MS63 | MS65 |
|---|---|---|---|---|---|---|
| 2008 B | 47,622 | — | — | 26.00 | 30.00 | 35.00 |
| 2008 B | 7,000 | PF65 65.00 | | | | |

**KM# 131 20 FRANCS**

20.00 g., 0.835 Silver 0.5369 oz. ASW, 32.8 mm. **Subject:** Swiss Museum of Transport, 50th Anniversary **Obv:** National arms and value **Rev:** Spiral of transport vehicles **Edge:** DOMINUS PROVIDEBIT

| Date | Mintage | VF20 | XF40 | MS60 | MS63 | MS65 |
|---|---|---|---|---|---|---|
| 2009 B | 49,017 | — | — | 26.00 | 30.00 | 35.00 |
| 2009 B | 7,000 | PF65 65.00 | | | | |

**KM# 132 20 FRANCS**

20.00 g., 0.835 Silver 0.5369 oz. ASW, 32.8 mm. **Subject:** Brienz-Rothorn Railway **Obv:** Value **Rev:** Locomotive and rail-car

| Date | Mintage | VF20 | XF40 | MS60 | MS63 | MS65 |
|---|---|---|---|---|---|---|
| 2009 B | 48,318 | — | — | 26.00 | 30.00 | 35.00 |
| 2009 B | 7,000 | PF63 50.00 | PF65 58.00 | | | |

**KM# 135 20 FRANCS**

20.00 g., 0.835 Silver 0.5369 oz. ASW, 32.8 mm. **Subject:** 100 Years Bernina Railway **Rev:** Steam train on viaduct

| Date | Mintage | VF20 | XF40 | MS60 | MS63 | MS65 |
|---|---|---|---|---|---|---|
| 2010 B | 49,343 | — | — | 26.00 | 30.00 | 35.00 |
| 2010 B | 7,000 | PF65 70.00 | | | | |

**KM# 136 20 FRANCS**

20.00 g., 0.835 Silver 0.5369 oz. ASW, 32.8 mm. **Subject:** 100 Anniversary Death of Henry Dunant (Red Cross founder) **Rev:** Bust at left, flag

| Date | Mintage | VF20 | XF40 | MS60 | MS63 | MS65 |
|---|---|---|---|---|---|---|
| 2010 B | 49,306 | — | — | 26.00 | 30.00 | 35.00 |
| 2010 B | 7,000 | PF65 70.00 | | | | |

**KM# 139 20 FRANCS**

20.00 g., 0.835 Silver 0.5369 oz. ASW, 33 mm. **Subject:** Max Frisch, 100th Anniversary of Birth **Obv:** Value **Rev:** Facing portrait with pipe

| Date | Mintage | VF20 | XF40 | MS60 | MS63 | MS65 |
|---|---|---|---|---|---|---|
| 2011 B | 7,000 | PF65 70.00 | | | | |
| 2011 B | 49,657 | — | — | 26.00 | 30.00 | 35.00 |

**KM# 140 20 FRANCS**

20.00 g., 0.835 Silver 0.5369 oz. ASW, 33 mm. **Subject:** Pilatus Railway **Obv:** Value, date and inscription "CONFOEDERATIO HELVETICA **Rev:** Electric railway car climbing mountain and inscription "PILATUSBAHN **Edge:** DOMINUS PROVIDEBIT (13 stars)

| Date | Mintage | VF20 | XF40 | MS60 | MS63 | MS65 |
|---|---|---|---|---|---|---|
| 2011 B | Est. 7000 | PF65 80.00 | | | | |
| 2011 B | 49,452 | — | — | 26.00 | 30.00 | 35.00 |

**KM# 143 20 FRANCS**
20.00 g., 0.835 Silver 0.5369 oz. ASW, 33 mm. **Subject:** Jungfrau Railway

| Date | Mintage | VF20 | XF40 | MS60 | MS63 | MS65 |
|---|---|---|---|---|---|---|
| 2012 B | 7,000 | **PF65** 80.00 | | | | |
| 2012 B | 50,000 | — | — | 32.00 | 40.00 | 55.00 |

**KM# 144 20 FRANCS**
20.00 g., 0.835 Silver 0.5369 oz. ASW, 33 mm. **Obv:** Swiss cross, legend, denomination & date **Obv. Legend:** CONFOEDERATIO HELVETICA **Rev:** Comic character Globi carying a cake with candles **Rev. Legend:** GLOBI

| Date | Mintage | VF20 | XF40 | MS60 | MS63 | MS65 |
|---|---|---|---|---|---|---|
| 2012 B | 50,000 | — | — | 30.00 | 36.00 | 50.00 |
| 2012 B | 7,000 | **PF65** 80.00 | | | | |

**KM# 147 20 FRANCS**
20.00 g., 0.835 Silver 0.5369 oz. ASW, 33 mm. **Subject:** First Complete flight over the Alps, 100th Anniversary **Obv:** Swiss cross and value **Rev:** Bi-plane over Alps

| Date | Mintage | VF20 | XF40 | MS60 | MS63 | MS65 |
|---|---|---|---|---|---|---|
| 2013 B | Est. 7000 | **PF65** 80.00 | | | | |
| 2013 B | Est. 50000 | — | — | 30.00 | 35.00 | 40.00 |

**KM# 148 20 FRANCS**
20.00 g., 0.835 Silver 0.5369 oz. ASW, 33 mm. **Subject:** Swiss Wrestling **Obv:** Swiss cross and value **Rev:** Two wrestlers

| Date | Mintage | VF20 | XF40 | MS60 | MS63 | MS65 |
|---|---|---|---|---|---|---|
| 2013 B | Est. 50000 | — | — | 30.00 | 35.00 | 40.00 |
| 2013 B | Est. 7000 | **PF65** 80.00 | | | | |

**KM# 151 20 FRANCS**
20.00 g., 0.835 Silver 0.5369 oz. ASW, 33 mm. **Subject:** Swiss acrobatic air show **Rev:** Planes in formation

| Date | Mintage | VF20 | XF40 | MS60 | MS63 | MS65 |
|---|---|---|---|---|---|---|
| 2014 B | Est. 50000 | — | — | 30.00 | 35.00 | 40.00 |
| 2014 B | Est. 7000 | **PF65** 85.00 | | | | |

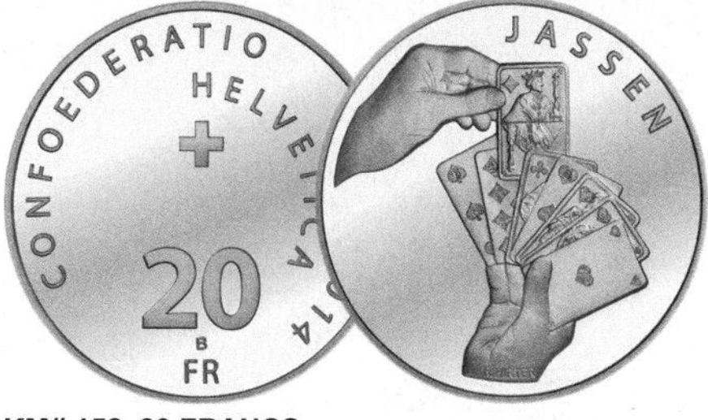

**KM# 152 20 FRANCS**
20.00 g., 0.835 Silver 0.5369 oz. ASW, 33 mm. **Subject:** Jassen card game **Rev:** Hand holding cards

| Date | Mintage | VF20 | XF40 | MS60 | MS63 | MS65 |
|---|---|---|---|---|---|---|
| 2014 B | Est. 50000 | — | — | 30.00 | 35.00 | 40.00 |
| 2014 B | Est. 7000 | **PF65** 85.00 | | | | |

**KM# 95 50 FRANCS**
11.29 g., 0.900 Gold 0.3267 oz. AGW, 25.1 mm. **Obv:** Landscape and value **Rev:** Heidi and goat running **Edge:** Lettered **Edge Lettering:** DOMINUS PROVIDEBIT (13 stars)

| Date | Mintage | VF20 | XF40 | MS60 | MS63 | MS65 |
|---|---|---|---|---|---|---|
| 2001 B | 3,967 | **PF65** 825 | | | | |

**KM# 102 50 FRANCS**
11.29 g., 0.900 Gold 0.3267 oz. AGW, 25.1 mm. **Subject:** Expo '02 **Obv:** Value **Rev:** Aerial view of 3 lakes landscape **Edge:** Lettered **Edge Lettering:** DOMINUS PROVIDEBIT (13 stars)

| Date | Mintage | VF20 | XF40 | MS60 | MS63 | MS65 |
|---|---|---|---|---|---|---|
| 2002 B | 4,856 | **PF65** 675 | | | | |

**KM# 105 50 FRANCS**
11.29 g., 0.900 Gold 0.3267 oz. AGW, 25.1 mm. **Obv:** Skier and value **Rev:** St. Moritz city view **Edge Lettering:** DOMINUS PROVIDEBIT (13 stars)

| Date | Mintage | VF20 | XF40 | MS60 | MS63 | MS65 |
|---|---|---|---|---|---|---|
| 2003 B | 4,000 | **PF65** 675 | | | | |

**KM# 110 50 FRANCS**
11.29 g., 0.900 Gold 0.3267 oz. AGW, 25.1 mm. **Obv:** Value **Rev:** Matterhorn Mountain **Edge Lettering:** DOMINUS PROVIDEBIT (13 stars)

| Date | Mintage | VF20 | XF40 | MS60 | MS63 | MS65 |
|---|---|---|---|---|---|---|
| 2004 B | 7,000 | **PF65** 825 | | | | |

**KM# 123 50 FRANCS**
11.29 g., 0.900 Gold 0.3267 oz. AGW, 25.1 mm. **Subject:** FIFA Centennial **Obv:** FIFA depicting Wilhelm Tell **Rev:** Soccer ball on left value on right

| Date | Mintage | VF20 | XF40 | MS60 | MS63 | MS65 |
|---|---|---|---|---|---|---|
| 2004 B | 10,000 | **PF65** 1,300 | | | | |

**KM# 113 50 FRANCS**
11.29 g., 0.900 Gold 0.3267 oz. AGW, 25.1 mm. **Subject:** Geneva Motor Show **Obv:** Value **Rev:** Partial view of an antique car **Edge Lettering:** DOMINUS PROVIDEBIT

| Date | Mintage | VF20 | XF40 | MS60 | MS63 | MS65 |
|---|---|---|---|---|---|---|
| 2005 B | 6,000 | **PF65** 675 | | | | |

**KM# 116 50 FRANCS**
11.29 g., 0.900 Gold 0.3267 oz. AGW, 25.1 mm. **Obv:** Value **Rev:** Swiss Guardsman **Edge Lettering:** DOMINUS PROVIDEBIT

| Date | Mintage | VF20 | XF40 | MS60 | MS63 | MS65 |
|---|---|---|---|---|---|---|
| 2006 B | 6,000 | **PF65** 750 | | | | |

**KM# 120 50 FRANCS**
11.29 g., 0.900 Gold 0.3267 oz. AGW, 25.1 mm. **Subject:** National Bank Centennial **Obv:** Value **Obv. Legend:** CONFEDERATIO - HELVETICA **Rev:** Lumberjack" from painting by Ferdinand Hodler **Rev. Inscription:** SNB BNS + **Edge Lettering:** DOMINUS PROVIDEBIT

| Date | Mintage | VF20 | XF40 | MS60 | MS63 | MS65 |
|---|---|---|---|---|---|---|
| 2007 B | 6,000 | **PF65** 675 | | | | |

**KM# 129 50 FRANCS**
11.29 g., 0.900 Gold 0.3267 oz. AGW, 25.1 mm. **Subject:** International Year of Planet Earth **Obv:** Value **Rev:** Dancing child with 3 globes above head, in hands and standing on one globe **Rev. Inscription:** DE LA PLANETE TERRE ANNEE INTERNATIONALE **Edge:** DOMINUS PROVIDEBIT

| Date | Mintage | VF20 | XF40 | MS60 | MS63 | MS65 |
|---|---|---|---|---|---|---|
| 2008 B | 6,000 | **PF65** 675 | | | | |

**KM# 133 50 FRANCS**
11.29 g., 0.900 Gold 0.3267 oz. AGW, 25.1 mm. **Subject:** Pro Patria, 100th Anniversary **Obv:** Value **Edge:** DOMINUS PROVIDEBIT

| Date | Mintage | VF20 | XF40 | MS60 | MS63 | MS65 |
|---|---|---|---|---|---|---|
| 2009 B | 6,000 | **PF65** 675 | | | | |

**KM# 137 50 FRANCS**
11.29 g., 0.900 Gold 0.3267 oz. AGW, 25.1 mm. **Subject:** 100th Anniversary Death of Alber Anker (Painter)

| Date | Mintage | VF20 | XF40 | MS60 | MS63 | MS65 |
|---|---|---|---|---|---|---|
| 2010 B | 6,000 | **PF65** 675 | | | | |

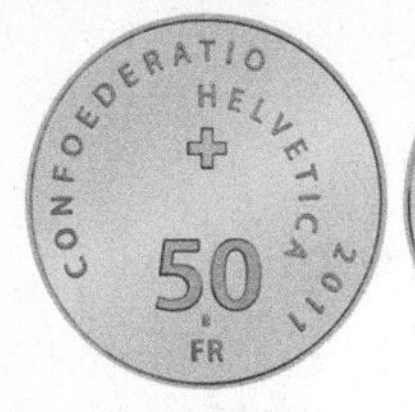

**KM# 141 50 FRANCS**

11.29 g., 0.900 Gold 0.3267 oz. AGW, 25.1 mm. **Subject:** Bell for Ursli **Obv:** Value, date and inscription "CONFOEDERATIO HELVETICA **Rev:** Boy holding bell and inscription "Schellen-Ursli **Edge:** DOMINUS PROVIDEBIT

| Date | Mintage | VF20 | XF40 | MS60 | MS63 | MS65 |
|---|---|---|---|---|---|---|
| 2011 B | 6,000 | PF65 675 | | | | |

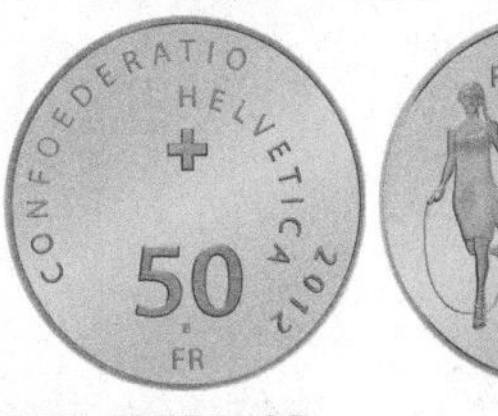

**KM# 145 50 FRANCS**

11.29 g., 0.900 Gold 0.3267 oz. AGW, 25 mm. **Subject:** Pro Juventute 100th Anniversary **Obv:** Swiss cross, legend, denomination and date **Obv. Legend:** CONFOEDERATIO HELVETICA **Rev:** Girl jumping rope, head of boy wearing cap **Rev. Legend:** PRO JUVENTUTE 1912-2012

| Date | Mintage | VF20 | XF40 | MS60 | MS63 | MS65 |
|---|---|---|---|---|---|---|
| 2012 B | 6,000 | PF65 675 | | | | |

**KM# 149 50 FRANCS**

11.29 g., 0.900 Gold 0.3267 oz. AGW, 25 mm. **Subject:** Gotthard mail coach **Obv:** Swiss cross and value **Rev:** Horse drawn mail coach

| Date | Mintage | VF20 | XF40 | MS60 | MS63 | MS65 |
|---|---|---|---|---|---|---|
| 2013 B | Est. 6000 | PF65 650 | | | | |

**KM# 153 50 FRANCS**

11.29 g., 0.900 Gold 0.3267 oz. AGW, 25 mm. **Subject:** National Parks, 100th Anniversary **Rev:** Park valley

| Date | Mintage | VF20 | XF40 | MS60 | MS63 | MS65 |
|---|---|---|---|---|---|---|
| 2014 B | Est. 6000 | PF65 700 | | | | |

## ESSAIS

| KM# | Date | Mintage | Identification | Mkt Val |
|---|---|---|---|---|
| E13 | 2001B | 600 | 20 Francs 0.835 Silver KM#93 | 300 |
| E14 | 2002 | 700 | 5 Francs Bi-Metallic KM#98 | 185 |
| E15 | 2003B | 700 | 5 Francs Bi-Metallic KM#103 | 200 |
| E16 | 2004B | 700 | 10 Francs Bi-Metallic KM#107. | 300 |
| E19 | 2005B | 500 | 20 Francs 0.832 Silver KM#112. | 250 |
| E19 | 2005B | 500 | 20 Francs 0.832 Silver KM#112. | 420 |
| E20 | 2006B | 500 | 20 Francs 0.835 Silver KM#117. | 320 |
| E21 | 2007B | 500 | 20 Francs Silver 33 mm. KM#119. | 250 |
| E22 | 2008B | 700 | 10 Francs Bi-Metallic KM#126 | 225 |
| E23 | 2009B | 500 | 20 Francs 0.835 Silver 33mm KM#132 | 250 |
| E24 | 2010B | 700 | 10 Francs Bi-Metallic KM#134 | 200 |
| E25 | 2011B | 500 | 20 Francs 0.835 Silver KM#139 | 275 |
| E26 | 2012B | 500 | 20 Francs 0.835 Silver KM#144 | 275 |
| E27 | 2013B | 500 | 10 Francs Bi-Metallic KM#146 | 225 |
| E28 | 2014B | 400 | 20 Francs 0.835 Silver KM#151 | 275 |
| E29 | 2015B | 400 | 20 Francs 0.835 Silver Solar Impulse (see above) | 275 |

## BABY MINT SETS

| KM# | Date | Mintage | Identification | Issue Price | Mkt Val |
|---|---|---|---|---|---|
| MS69 | 2013 (7) | Est. 8,000 | KM#21a.3, 23a.3, 24a.3, 26c, 27, 29a, 40a.4 plus medal | — | 42.00 |
| MS71 | 2014 | Est. 8,500 | KM#21a.3, 23a.3, 24a.3, 26, 27, 29a, 40a.4 plus medal | — | 41.00 |
| MS74 | 2015 (7) | — | KM#21a.3, 23a.3, 24a.3, 26c, 27, 29a, 40a.4 plus medal | 42.00 | |

## MINT SETS

| KM# | Date | Mintage | Identification | Issue Price | Mkt Val |
|---|---|---|---|---|---|
| MS35 | 2001 (9) | 21,532 | KM#21a.3, 23a.3, 24a.3, 26c, 27, 29a, 40a.4, 46, 92 Zurich Sechselauten | — | 40.00 |
| MS36 | 2002 (9) | 17,920 | KM#21a.3, 23a.3, 24a.3, 26c, 27, 29a, 40a.4, 46, 98 Escalade | — | 45.00 |
| MS37 | 2002 (9) | 1,974 | KM#21a.3, 23a.3, 24a.3, 26c, 27, 29a, 40a.4, 46, 98, plus a medal. Baby mint set | — | 220 |
| MS38 | 2003 (9) | 17,200 | KM#21a.3, 23a.3, 24a.3, 26c, 27, 29a, 40a.4, 46, 103 Chalandamarz | — | 50.00 |
| MS39 | 2003 (8) | 4,800 | KM#21a.3, 23a.3, 24a.3, 26c, 27, 29a, 40a.2, 46 plus medal; Baby Mint Set | — | 80.00 |
| MS40 | 2004 (9) | 16,000 | KM#21a.3, 23a.3, 24a.3, 26c, 27, 29a, 40a.4, 46, 107 Matterhorn | — | 80.00 |
| MS41 | 2004 (8) | 8,400 | KM#21a.3, 23a.3, 24a.3, 26c, 27, 29a, 40a.2, 46 plus medal; Baby Mint Set | — | 65.00 |
| MS42 | 2005 (9) | 15,279 | KM#21a.3, 23a.3, 24a.3, 26c, 27, 29a, 40a.4, 46, 111 Jung Frau | — | 40.00 |
| MS43 | 2005 (8) | 7,500 | KM#21a.3, 23a.3, 24a.3, 26c, 27, 29a, 40a.2, 46 plus medal; Baby Mint Set | — | 40.00 |
| MS45 | 2006 (8) | 2,000 | KM#21a.3, 23a.3, 24a.3, 26c, 27, 29a, 40a.2, 46 plus medal; Jubilee Mint Set | — | 450 |
| MS46 | 2006 (8) | 8,000 | KM#21a.3, 23a.3, 24a.3, 26c, 27, 29a, 40a.2, 46 plus medal; Baby Mint Set | — | 175 |
| MS47 | 2007 (8) | 14,586 | KM#21a.3, 23a.3, 24a.3, 26c, 27, 29a, 40a.4, 118 | — | 45.00 |
| MS48 | 2007 (7) | 7,500 | KM#21a.3, 23a.3, 24a.3, 26c, 27, 29a, 40a.2, plus medal; Baby Mint Set | — | 45.00 |
| MS49 | 2008 (8) | 13,815 | KM#21a.3, 23a.3, 24a.3, 26c, 27, 29a, 40a.4, 126 | — | 45.00 |
| MS50 | 2008 (7) | 6,996 | KM#21a.3, 23a.3, 24a.3, 26c, 27, 29a, 40a.2, plus medal; Baby Mint Set | — | 40.00 |
| MS51 | 2009 (8) | 12,254 | KM#21a.3, 23a.3, 24a.3, 26c, 27, 29a, 40a4, 130. | — | 50.00 |
| MS52 | 2009 (7) | 7,499 | KM#21a.3, 23a.3, 24a.3, 26c, 27, 29a, 40a.2, plus medal; Baby Mint Set | — | 40.00 |
| MS53 | 2010 (8) | 11,310 | KM#21a.3, 23a.3, 24a.3, 26c, 27, 29a, 40a.2, 134 | — | 50.00 |
| MS54 | 2010 (7) | 8,000 | KM#21a.3, 23a.3, 24a.3, 26c, 27, 29a, 40a.2, plus medal; Baby Mint Set | — | 40.00 |
| MS55 | 2011 (8) | Est. 14000 | KM#21a.3, 23a.3, 24a.3, 26c, 27, 29a, 40a.2, 138 | — | 50.00 |
| MS56 | 2011 (7) | Est. 8000 | KM#21a.3, 23a.3, 24a.3, 26c, 27, 29a, 40a.2, plus medal; Baby Mint Set | — | 40.00 |
| MS58 | 2012 (7) | Est. 8000 | KM#21a.3, 23a.3, 24a.3, 26c, 27, 29a, 40a.4 plus medal. Baby Mint Set | — | 40.00 |
| MS67 | 2012 (8) | Est. 14000 | KM#21a.3, 23a.3, 24a.3, 26c, 27, 29a, 40a.4, 142 | — | 40.00 |
| MS68 | 2013 (8) | Est. 12,000 | KM#21a.3, 23a.3, 24a.3, 26c, 27, 29a, 40a.4, 146 | 42.00 | |
| MS70 | 2014 (8) | Est. 8,500 | KM#21a.3, 23a.3, 24a.3, 26, 27, 29a, 40a.4, 150 | — | 42.00 |
| MS72 | 2014 (7) | Est. 2,000 | KM#21a.3, 23a.3, 24a.3, 26c, 27, 29a, 40a.4 plus medal (Christmas Mint Set) | — | 42.00 |
| MS73 | 2014 (8) | Est. 10,000 | KM#21a.3, 23a.3, 24a.3, 26c, 27, 29a, 40a.4, 10 Fr. Descent of Cattle from Alpine Pastures | — | 42.00 |
| MS75 | 2015 (7) | — | KM#21a.3, 23a.3, 24a.3, 26, 27, 29a, 40a.4 plus medal (Christmas Mint Set) | 42.00 | |

## PROOF SETS

| KM# | Date | Mintage | Identification | Issue Price | Mkt Val |
|---|---|---|---|---|---|
| PS30 | 2001 (9) | 5,184 | KM#21a.3, 23a.3, 24a.3, 26c, 27, 29a, 40a.4, 46, 92 Zurich Sechselauten | — | 75.00 |
| PS31 | 2002 (9) | 4,518 | KM#21a.3, 23a.3, 24a.3, 26c, 27, 29a, 40a.4, 46, 98 Escalade | — | 80.00 |
| PS32 | 2003 (9) | 4,520 | KM#21a.3, 23a.3, 24a.3, 26c, 27, 29a, 40a.4, 46, 103 Chatandamarz | — | 80.00 |
| PS33 | 2004 (9) | 4,168 | KM#21a.3, 23a.3, 24a.3, 26c, 27, 29a, 40a.4, 46, 107 Matterhorn | 68.00 | 95.00 |
| PS34 | 2005 (9) | 3,783 | KM#21a.3, 23a.3, 24a.3, 26c, 27, 29a, 40a.4, 46, 111 | 68.00 | 90.00 |
| PS35 | 2006 (9) | 4,000 | KM#21a.3, 23a.3, 24a.3, 26c, 27, 29a, 40a.4, 46, 114 | 68.00 | 300 |
| PS36 | 2007 (8) | 3,415 | KM#21a.3, 23a.3, 24a.3, 26c, 27, 29a, 40a.4, 118 | 68.00 | 85.00 |
| PS37 | 2008 (8) | 3,286 | KM#21a.3, 23a.3, 24a.3, 26c, 27, 29a, 40a.4, 126 | 72.00 | 90.00 |
| PS38 | 2009 (8) | 3,115 | KM#21a.3, 23a.3, 24a.3, 26c, 27, 29a, 40a.4, 130 | 75.00 | 90.00 |
| PS39 | 2010 (8) | Est. 4000 | KM#21a.3, 23a.3, 24a.3, 26c, 27, 29a, 40a.4, 134 | 75.00 | 90.00 |
| PS40 | 2011 (8) | Est. 4000 | KM#21a.3, 23a.3, 24a.3, 26c, 27, 29a, 40a.2, 138 | — | 90.00 |
| PS41 | 2012 (8) | Est. 4000 | KM#21a.3, 23a.3, 24a.3, 26c, 27, 29a, 40a.4, 142 | — | 90.00 |
| PS42 | 2013 (8) | Est. 3,500 | KM#21a.3, 23a.3, 24a.3, 26c, 27, 29a, 40a.4, 146 | — | 100 |
| PS42 | 2014 (8) | Est. 3,000 | KM#21a.3, 23a.3, 24a.3, 26c, 27, 29a, 40a.4, 150 | — | 100 |
| PS44 | 2015 (8) | Est. 3,000 | KM#21a.3, 23a.3, 24a.3, 26c, 27, 29a, 40a.4, 10 Fr. Descent of Cattle from Alpine Pastures | — | 100 |

**SHOOTING THALER LISTINGS ARE NOW PRESENTED IN *UNUSUAL WORLD COINS***

# SYRIA

The Syrian Arab Republic, located in the Near East at the eastern end of the Mediterranean Sea, has an area of 71,498 sq. mi. (185,180 sq. km.) and a population of *12 million. Capital: Greater Damascus. Agriculture and animal breeding are the chief industries. Cotton, crude oil and livestock are exported.

**TITLES**

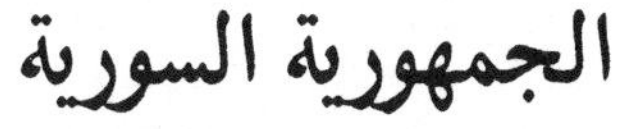


al-Jumhuriya(t) al-Suriya(t)

الجمهورية لعربية السورية

al-Jumhuriya(t) al-Arabiya(t) as-Suriya(t)

## SYRIAN ARAB REPUBLIC

### STANDARD COINAGE

**KM# 129 5 POUNDS**
7.53 g., Nickel Clad Steel, 24.5 mm. **Obv:** National arms within design and beaded border **Rev:** Old fort and latent image above value within design and beaded border **Edge:** Reeded and lettered **Edge Lettering:** CENTRAL BANK 5 SYP

| Date | Mintage | VF20 | XF40 | MS60 | MS63 | MS65 |
|---|---|---|---|---|---|---|
| AH1424-2003 | — | — | — | 1.00 | 1.25 | 1.75 |

**KM# 130 10 POUNDS**
9.53 g., Copper-Nickel-Zinc, 27.4 mm. **Obv:** National arms within beaded border **Rev:** Ancient ruins with latent image within beaded border **Edge Lettering:** 10 SYRIAN POUNDS

| Date | Mintage | VF20 | XF40 | MS60 | MS63 | MS65 |
|---|---|---|---|---|---|---|
| AH1424-2003 | — | — | — | 2.00 | 2.50 | 3.50 |

**KM# 131 25 POUNDS**
8.40 g., Bi-Metallic Copper-Nickel center in Nickel-Brass ring, 25 mm. **Obv:** National arms within beaded border **Rev:** Building and latent image within beaded border **Edge Lettering:** CENTRAL BANK OF SYRIA 25

| Date | Mintage | VF20 | XF40 | MS60 | MS63 | MS65 |
|---|---|---|---|---|---|---|
| AH1424-2003 | — | — | 1.50 | 2.75 | 3.75 | 5.00 |

# TAJIKISTAN

The Republic of Tajikistan (Tadjiquistan), was formed from those regions of Bukhara and Turkestan where the population consisted mainly of Tajiks. It is bordered in the north and west by Uzbekistan and Kyrgyzstan, in the east by China and in the south by Afghanistan. It has an area of 55,240 sq. miles (143,100 sq. km.) and a population of 5.95 million. It includes 2 provinces of Khudzand and Khatlon together with the Gorno-Badakhshan Autonomous Region with a population of 5,092,603. Capital: Dushanbe. Tajikistan was admitted as a constituent republic of the Soviet Union on Dec. 5, 1929. In August 1990 the Tajik Supreme Soviet adopted a declaration of republican sovereignty, and in Dec. 1991 the republic became a member of the CIS.

After demonstrations and fighting, the Communist government was replaced by a Revolutionary Coalition Council on May 7, 1992. Following further demonstrations President Nabiev was ousted on Sept. 7, 1992. Civil war broke out, and the government resigned on Nov. 10, 1992. On Nov. 30, 1992 it was announced that a CIS peacekeeping force would be sent to Tajikistan. A state of emergency was imposed in Jan. 1993. A ceasefire was signed in 1996 and a peace agreement signed in June 1997.

**MONETARY SYSTEM**
100 Drams = 1 Somoni

## REPUBLIC

### DECIMAL COINAGE

**KM# 35 DIRAM**
1.30 g., Brass Plated Copper, 14.5 mm. **Obv:** National arms **Rev:** Value

| Date | Mintage | VF20 | XF40 | MS60 | MS63 | MS65 |
|---|---|---|---|---|---|---|
| 2011 | — | — | — | — | 0.50 | 0.75 |

**KM# 36 2 DIRAMS**
1.60 g., Brass Plated Copper, 16 mm. **Obv:** National arms **Rev:** Value

| Date | Mintage | VF20 | XF40 | MS60 | MS63 | MS65 |
|---|---|---|---|---|---|---|
| 2011 | — | — | — | 0.50 | 0.75 | 1.00 |

**KM# 2.1 5 DIRAMS**
2.00 g., Brass Clad Steel, 16.5 mm. **Obv:** Crown within 1/2 star border **Rev:** Small value within design **Edge:** Plain

| Date | Mintage | VF20 | XF40 | MS60 | MS63 | MS65 |
|---|---|---|---|---|---|---|
| 2001 (sp) | — | — | — | 0.50 | 0.75 | 1.00 |
| 2001 (sp) | — | PF65 2.50 | | | | |

**KM# 2.2 5 DIRAMS**
2.00 g., Brass Clad Steel, 16.5 mm. **Obv:** Crown with 1/2 star border **Rev:** Large value within design

| Date | Mintage | VF20 | XF40 | MS60 | MS63 | MS65 |
|---|---|---|---|---|---|---|
| 2006 (sp) | — | — | — | 0.75 | 1.25 | 1.50 |

**KM# 23 5 DIRAMS**
2.00 g., Brass Plated Steel, 18 mm. **Obv:** Coat of arms **Rev:** Large value with design

| Date | Mintage | VF20 | XF40 | MS60 | MS63 | MS65 |
|---|---|---|---|---|---|---|
| 2011 | — | — | — | 0.50 | 0.75 | 1.00 |

**KM# 3.1 10 DIRAMS**
2.40 g., Brass Clad Steel, 17.5 mm. **Obv:** Crown within 1/2 star border **Rev:** Small value within design **Edge:** Plain

| Date | Mintage | VF20 | XF40 | MS60 | MS63 | MS65 |
|---|---|---|---|---|---|---|
| 2001 (sp) | — | — | — | 0.75 | 1.00 | 1.25 |
| 2001 (sp) | — | PF65 3.00 | | | | |

**KM# 3.2 10 DIRAMS**
2.40 g., Brass Clad Steel, 17.5 mm. **Obv:** Crown within 1/2 star border **Rev:** Large value within design

| Date | Mintage | VF20 | XF40 | MS60 | MS63 | MS65 |
|---|---|---|---|---|---|---|
| 2006 (sp) | — | — | — | 1.00 | 1.50 | 2.00 |

**KM# 24 10 DIRAMS**
3.00 g., Brass Plated Steel, 20.5 mm. **Obv:** Coat of arms **Rev:** Large value with design

| Date | Mintage | VF20 | XF40 | MS60 | MS63 | MS65 |
|---|---|---|---|---|---|---|
| 2011 | — | — | — | 1.00 | 1.50 | 2.00 |

**KM# 4.1 20 DIRAMS**
2.70 g., Brass Clad Steel, 18.5 mm. **Obv:** Crown within 1/2 star border **Rev:** Small value within design **Edge:** Plain

| Date | Mintage | VF20 | XF40 | MS60 | MS63 | MS65 |
|---|---|---|---|---|---|---|
| 2001 (sp) | — | — | — | 1.00 | 1.25 | 1.50 |
| 2001 (sp) | — | PF65 3.75 | | | | |

**KM# 4.2 20 DIRAMS**
2.70 g., Brass Clad Steel, 18.5 mm. **Obv:** Crown within 1/2 star border **Rev:** Large value within design

| Date | Mintage | VF20 | XF40 | MS60 | MS63 | MS65 |
|---|---|---|---|---|---|---|
| 2006 (sp) | — | — | — | 1.50 | 2.00 | 2.50 |

**KM# 25 20 DIRAMS**
4.50 g., Brass Plated Steel, 23.5 mm. **Obv:** Coat of arms **Rev:** Large value with design **Edge:** Reeded

| Date | Mintage | VF20 | XF40 | MS60 | MS63 | MS65 |
|---|---|---|---|---|---|---|
| 2011 | — | — | — | 1.50 | 2.00 | 2.50 |

**KM# 5.1 25 DIRAMS**
2.80 g., Brass, 19.1 mm. **Obv:** Crown within 1/2 star border **Rev:** Small value within design **Edge:** Plain

| Date | Mintage | VF20 | XF40 | MS60 | MS63 | MS65 |
|---|---|---|---|---|---|---|
| 2001 (sp) | — | — | — | 1.50 | 1.75 | 2.00 |
| 2001 (sp) | — | PF65 5.00 | | | | |

### KM# 5.2 25 DIRAMS
2.80 g., Brass, 19.1 mm. **Obv:** Crown within 1/2 star border **Rev:** Large value within design

| Date | Mintage | VF20 | XF40 | MS60 | MS63 | MS65 |
|---|---|---|---|---|---|---|
| 2006 (sp) | — | — | — | 1.75 | 2.50 | 3.00 |

### KM# 5.2a 25 DIRAMS
2.80 g., Brass Plated Steel, 19.1 mm. **Obv:** Crown within 1/2 star border **Rev:** Large value within design **Edge:** Reeded

| Date | Mintage | VF20 | XF40 | MS60 | MS63 | MS65 |
|---|---|---|---|---|---|---|
| 2006 | — | — | — | 2.00 | 3.00 | 3.50 |

### KM# 6.1 50 DIRAMS
3.55 g., Brass, 21 mm. **Obv:** Crown within 1/2 star border **Rev:** Value within design **Edge:** Plain

| Date | Mintage | VF20 | XF40 | MS60 | MS63 | MS65 |
|---|---|---|---|---|---|---|
| 2001 (sp) | — | — | — | 2.00 | 3.00 | 3.50 |
| 2001 (sp) | — | PF65 7.00 | | | | |

### KM# 6.2 50 DIRAMS
3.55 g., Brass, 21 mm. **Obv:** Crown within 1/2 star border **Rev:** Large value within design

| Date | Mintage | VF20 | XF40 | MS60 | MS63 | MS65 |
|---|---|---|---|---|---|---|
| 2006 (sp) | — | — | — | 2.00 | 3.00 | 3.50 |

### KM# 6.2a 50 DIRAMS
3.55 g., Brass Plated Steel, 21 mm. **Obv:** Crown within 1/2 star border **Rev:** Large value within design **Edge:** Reeded

| Date | Mintage | VF20 | XF40 | MS60 | MS63 | MS65 |
|---|---|---|---|---|---|---|
| 2006 | — | — | — | 2.00 | 3.00 | 3.50 |

### KM# 26 50 DIRAMS
5.50 g., Brass Plated Steel, 26 mm. **Obv:** Coat of arms **Rev:** Large value with design **Edge:** Reeded

| Date | Mintage | VF20 | XF40 | MS60 | MS63 | MS65 |
|---|---|---|---|---|---|---|
| 2011 | — | — | — | 2.00 | 3.00 | 3.50 |

### KM# 7 SOMONI
5.15 g., Copper-Nickel-Zinc, 23.9 mm. **Obv:** King's bust 1/2 right **Rev:** Value **Edge:** Segmented reeding

| Date | Mintage | VF20 | XF40 | MS60 | MS63 | MS65 |
|---|---|---|---|---|---|---|
| 2001 (sp) | — | — | — | 3.50 | 5.00 | 6.00 |
| 2001 (sp) | — | PF65 12.00 | | | | |

### KM# 12 SOMONI
5.21 g., Copper-Nickel-Zinc, 24 mm. **Subject:** Year of Aryan Civilization **Obv:** National arms above value **Rev:** Ancient archer in war chariot **Edge:** Segmented reeding

| Date | Mintage | VF20 | XF40 | MS60 | MS63 | MS65 |
|---|---|---|---|---|---|---|
| 2006 (sp) | 100,000 | — | — | 3.50 | 5.00 | 6.00 |

### KM# 13 SOMONI
5.21 g., Copper-Nickel-Zinc, 24 mm. **Subject:** Year of Aryan Civilization **Obv:** National arms above value **Rev:** Two busts left **Edge:** Segmented reeding

| Date | Mintage | VF20 | XF40 | MS60 | MS63 | MS65 |
|---|---|---|---|---|---|---|
| 2006 (sp) | 100,000 | — | — | 3.50 | 5.00 | 6.00 |

### KM# 18 SOMONI
20.00 g., 0.925 Silver 0.5948 oz. ASW, 35 mm. **Subject:** Year of Aryan Civilization **Obv:** National arms above value **Rev:** Two busts left **Edge:** Segmented reeding

| Date | Mintage | VF20 | XF40 | MS60 | MS63 | MS65 |
|---|---|---|---|---|---|---|
| 2006 | 1,500 | PF65 60.00 | | | | |

### KM# 19 SOMONI
20.00 g., 0.925 Silver 0.5948 oz. ASW, 35 mm. **Subject:** Year of Aryan Civilization **Obv:** National arms above value **Rev:** Ancient archer in war chariot **Edge:** Segmented reeding

| Date | Mintage | VF20 | XF40 | MS60 | MS63 | MS65 |
|---|---|---|---|---|---|---|
| 2006 (sp) | 1,500 | PF65 60.00 | | | | |

### KM# 16 SOMONI
5.24 g., Copper-Nickel-Zinc, 24 mm. **Subject:** Jaloliddini Rumi, 800th Anniversary of Birth **Obv:** Small arms above value in cartouche **Rev:** 1/2 length figure facing **Edge:** Segmented reeding

| Date | Mintage | VF20 | XF40 | MS60 | MS63 | MS65 |
|---|---|---|---|---|---|---|
| 2007 | — | — | — | 3.50 | 5.00 | 6.00 |

### KM# 33 SOMONI
20.00 g., 0.925 Silver 0.5948 oz. ASW, 35 mm. **Subject:** Abu Abdullah al Rudaki

| Date | Mintage | VF20 | XF40 | MS60 | MS63 | MS65 |
|---|---|---|---|---|---|---|
| 2007 | 1,000 | PF65 65.00 | | | | |

### KM# 27 SOMONI
5.20 g., Copper-Nickel Plated Steel, 27 mm. **Obv:** Coat of arms **Rev:** Large value with design

| Date | Mintage | VF20 | XF40 | MS60 | MS63 | MS65 |
|---|---|---|---|---|---|---|
| 2011 | — | — | — | 3.50 | 5.00 | 6.00 |

### KM# 8 3 SOMONI
6.30 g., Copper-Nickel-Zinc, 25.5 mm. **Obv:** National arms **Rev:** Crown above value within design **Edge:** Lettered

| Date | Mintage | VF20 | XF40 | MS60 | MS63 | MS65 |
|---|---|---|---|---|---|---|
| 2001 (sp) | — | — | — | 5.00 | 7.00 | 9.00 |
| 2001 (sp) | — | PF65 18.00 | | | | |

### KM# 10 3 SOMONI
6.30 g., Bi-Metallic Copper-Nickel center in Brass ring, 25.5 mm. **Subject:** 80th Year - Dushanbe City **Obv:** Value below arms within circle **Rev:** Statue in arch within circle

| Date | Mintage | VF20 | XF40 | MS60 | MS63 | MS65 |
|---|---|---|---|---|---|---|
| 2004 (sp) | — | — | — | 6.50 | 10.00 | 12.00 |

### KM# 10a 3 SOMONI
6.98 g., 0.925 Silver 0.2076 oz. ASW, 25.5 mm. **Subject:** 80th Anniversary of Republic **Obv:** Value below arms within circle **Rev:** Statue in arch within circle

| Date | Mintage | VF20 | XF40 | MS60 | MS63 | MS65 |
|---|---|---|---|---|---|---|
| 2004 | 1,000 | PF65 75.00 | | | | |

### KM# 14 3 SOMONI
6.30 g., Bi-Metallic Copper-Nickel center in Brass ring, 25.5 mm. **Subject:** 2700th Anniversary of Kulyab **Obv:** National arms above value **Rev:** Kulyab city arms **Edge:** Lettered

| Date | Mintage | VF20 | XF40 | MS60 | MS63 | MS65 |
|---|---|---|---|---|---|---|
| 2006 (sp) | 100,000 | — | — | 6.00 | 7.50 | 10.00 |

### KM# 20 3 SOMONI
26.00 g., 0.925 Silver 0.7732 oz. ASW, 39 mm. **Subject:** 2700th Anniversary of Kulyab **Obv:** National arms above value **Rev:** Kulyab city arms

| Date | Mintage | VF20 | XF40 | MS60 | MS63 | MS65 |
|---|---|---|---|---|---|---|
| 2006 (sp) | 2,000 | PF65 70.00 | | | | |

### KM# 9 5 SOMONI
7.10 g., Copper-Nickel-Zinc, 26.5 mm. **Obv:** Turbaned head right **Rev:** Crown above value within design **Edge:** Segmented reeding with a star

| Date | Mintage | VF20 | XF40 | MS60 | MS63 | MS65 |
|---|---|---|---|---|---|---|
| 2001 (sp) | — | — | — | 7.50 | 10.00 | 12.00 |
| 2001 (sp) | — | PF65 25.00 | | | | |

**KM# 11 5 SOMONI**
6.95 g., Bi-Metallic Copper-Nickel center in Brass ring, 26.5 mm. **Subject:** Constitution, 10th Anniversary **Obv:** Arms above value within circle **Rev:** Flag and book within circle **Edge:** Lettered

| Date | Mintage | VF20 | XF40 | MS60 | MS63 | MS65 |
|---|---|---|---|---|---|---|
| 2004 (sp) | — | — | — | 7.50 | 10.00 | 12.00 |

**KM# 11a 5 SOMONI**
8.55 g., 0.925 Silver 0.2543 oz. ASW, 26.5 mm. **Subject:** 10th Anniversary - Constitution **Obv:** Arms above value within circle **Rev:** Flag and book within circle

| Date | Mintage | VF20 | XF40 | MS60 | MS63 | MS65 |
|---|---|---|---|---|---|---|
| 2004 | 2,000 | PF65 65.00 | | | | |

**KM# 15 5 SOMONI**
7.00 g., Bi-Metallic Copper-Nickel center in Brass ring, 26.5 mm. **Subject:** 15th Anniversary of Independence **Obv:** National arms above value **Rev:** Government building **Edge:** Lettered

| Date | Mintage | VF20 | XF40 | MS60 | MS63 | MS65 |
|---|---|---|---|---|---|---|
| 2006 (sp) | 100,000 | — | — | 7.50 | 10.00 | 12.00 |

**KM# 21 5 SOMONI**
34.00 g., 0.925 Silver 1.0111 oz. ASW, 42 mm. **Subject:** 15th Anniversary of Independence **Obv:** National arms above value **Rev:** Government building

| Date | Mintage | VF20 | XF40 | MS60 | MS63 | MS65 |
|---|---|---|---|---|---|---|
| 2006 (sp) | 2,000 | PF65 75.00 | | | | |

**KM# 17 5 SOMONI**
7.00 g., Bi-Metallic Copper-Nickel center in Brass ring, 26.5 mm. **Subject:** 1150th Anniversary founding of Persian (Tajik) literature by Abuabdullo Rudaki **Obv:** National arms above value **Rev:** Bust of Rudaki left, scroll, feather pen

| Date | Mintage | VF20 | XF40 | MS60 | MS63 | MS65 |
|---|---|---|---|---|---|---|
| 2008 | — | — | — | 7.50 | 10.00 | 12.00 |

**KM# 22 5 SOMONI**
34.00 g., 0.925 Silver 1.0111 oz. ASW, 42 mm. **Subject:** 1150 Anniversary founding of Persian Literature by Abuabdullo Rudaki **Obv:** National arms above value **Rev:** Bust of Rudaki left, scroll, feather pen

| Date | Mintage | VF20 | XF40 | MS60 | MS63 | MS65 |
|---|---|---|---|---|---|---|
| 2008 (sp) | 1,000 | PF65 115 | | | | |

**KM# 34 5 SOMONI**
31.10 g., 0.925 Silver 0.9249 oz. ASW, 38.61 mm. **Subject:** Eurasian Economic Community Capital **Obv:** National arms in color **Rev:** Ismoil Somonj

| Date | Mintage | VF20 | XF40 | MS60 | MS63 | MS65 |
|---|---|---|---|---|---|---|
| 2010 | 2,000 | PF65 135 | | | | |

**KM# 30 50 SOMONI**
10.00 g., 0.900 Gold 0.2894 oz. AGW, 24 mm. **Obv:** State Coat of arms **Rev:** Parliament building

| Date | Mintage | VF20 | XF40 | MS60 | MS63 | MS65 |
|---|---|---|---|---|---|---|
| 2006 | 2,000 | PF65 800 | | | | |

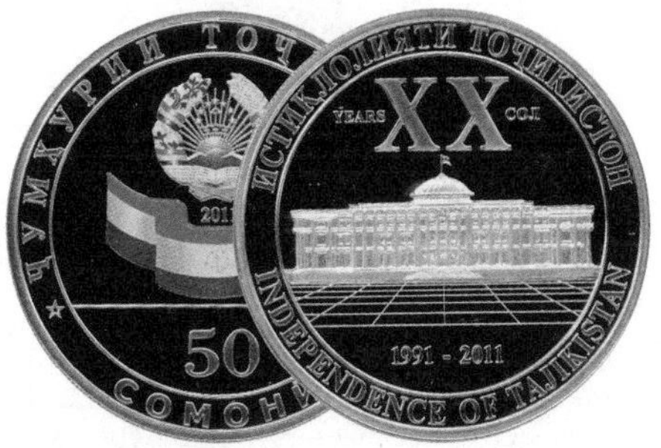

**KM# 28 50 SOMONI**
28.28 g., 0.925 Silver 0.841 oz. ASW, 38.61 mm. **Subject:** 20 Years of Independence **Obv:** Colorized flag and arms **Rev:** Building

| Date | Mintage | VF20 | XF40 | MS60 | MS63 | MS65 |
|---|---|---|---|---|---|---|
| 2011 | — | PF65 125 | | | | |

**KM# 31 100 SOMONI**
15.00 g., 0.900 Gold 0.434 oz. AGW, 28 mm. **Obv:** National arms **Rev:** Parliament building

| Date | Mintage | VF20 | XF40 | MS60 | MS63 | MS65 |
|---|---|---|---|---|---|---|
| 2006 | 2,000 | PF65 1,000 | | | | |

**KM# 29 100 SOMONI**
31.10 g., 0.925 Silver 0.9249 oz. ASW, 38.61 mm. **Subject:** 20th Anniversary of the C.I.S. **Obv:** Emblem, colored dot **Rev:** Map and colored flag

| Date | Mintage | VF20 | XF40 | MS60 | MS63 | MS65 |
|---|---|---|---|---|---|---|
| 2011 | Est. 1000 | PF65 225 | | | | |

**KM# 32 200 SOMONI**
25.00 g., 0.900 Gold 0.7234 oz. AGW, 32 mm. **Obv:** National arms **Rev:** Parliament building

| Date | Mintage | VF20 | XF40 | MS60 | MS63 | MS65 |
|---|---|---|---|---|---|---|
| 2006 | 2,000 | PF65 1,600 | | | | |

## MINT SETS

| KM# | Date | Mintage | Identification | Issue Price | Mkt Val |
|---|---|---|---|---|---|
| MS1 | 2001 (8) | — | KM#2.1-6.1, 7-9 | — | 30.00 |

## PROOF SETS

| KM# | Date | Mintage | Identification | Issue Price | Mkt Val |
|---|---|---|---|---|---|
| PS1 | 2001 (8) | — | KM#2.1-6.1, 7-9 | — | 80.00 |

# TANZANIA

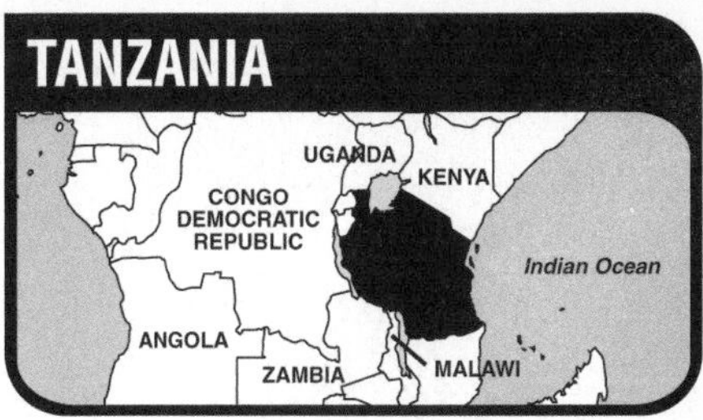


The United Republic of Tanzania, located on the east coast of Africa between Kenya and Mozambique, consists of Tanganyika and the islands of Zanzibar and Pemba. It has an area of 364,900 sq. mi. (945,090 sq. km.) and a population of *25.2 million. Capital: Dodoma. The chief exports are cotton, coffee, diamonds, sisal, cloves, petroleum products, and cashew nuts.

Tanzania is a member of the Commonwealth of Nations. The President is Chief of State.

## REPUBLIC

### STANDARD COINAGE

100 Senti = 1 Shilingi

**KM# 33 50 SHILINGI**
7.91 g., Brass Plated Steel, 22 mm. **Subject:** Conservation **Obv:** Head of Ali Nassan Mwinyi right within circle **Rev:** Mother rhinoceros and calf **Shape:** 7-sided

| Date | Mintage | VF20 | XF40 | MS60 | MS63 | MS65 |
|---|---|---|---|---|---|---|
| 2012 | — | — | — | 1.00 | 2.00 | 3.00 |

**KM# 32 100 SHILINGI**
9.00 g., Brass Plated Steel, 24.5 mm. **Subject:** Conservation **Obv:** Bust of President J.K. Nyerere left **Rev:** Four Impalas running right **Edge:** Reeded

| Date | Mintage | VF20 | XF40 | MS60 | MS63 | MS65 |
|---|---|---|---|---|---|---|
| 2012 | — | — | — | 1.50 | 2.50 | 4.00 |

**KM# 34 200 SHILINGI**
8.00 g., Copper-Nickel-Zinc **Obv:** Head of Sheikh Karume 1/4 left within circle **Rev:** Two lions **Edge:** Segmented reeding

| Date | Mintage | VF20 | XF40 | MS60 | MS63 | MS65 |
|---|---|---|---|---|---|---|
| 2008 | — | — | — | 3.00 | 5.00 | 7.00 |

**KM# 56 500 SHILLINGS**
31.46 g., 0.925 Silver 0.9356 oz. ASW, 38.6 mm. **Obv:** Arms with supporters above value **Rev:** African dhow **Edge:** Reeded

| Date | Mintage | VF20 | XF40 | MS60 | MS63 | MS65 |
|---|---|---|---|---|---|---|
| 2001 | — | PF63 50.00 | | PF65 65.00 | | |

The Kingdom of Thailand (formerly Siam), a constitutional monarchy located in the center of mainland Southeast Asia between Burma and Laos, has an area of 198,457 sq. mi. (514,000 sq. km.) and a population of *55.5 million. Capital: Bangkok. The economy is based on agriculture and mining. Rubber, rice, teakwood, tin and tungsten are exported.

The history of The Kingdom of Siam, the only country in south and Southeast Asia that was never colonized by a European power, dates from the 6th century A.D. when Thai people started to migrate into the area, a process that accelerated with the Mongol invasion of China in the 13th century. After 400 years of sporadic warfare with the neighboring Burmese, King Taskin won the last battle in 1767. He founded a new capital, Dhonburi, on the west bank of the Chao Praya River. King Rama I moved the capital to Bangkok in 1782, thus initiating the so-called Bangkok Period of Siamese coinage characterized by Pot Duang money (bullet coins) stamped with regal symbols.

The Portuguese, who were followed by the Dutch, British and French, introduced the Thai to the Western world. Rama III of the present ruling dynasty negotiated a treaty of friendship and commerce with Britain in 1826, and in 1896 the independence of the kingdom was guaranteed by an Anglo-French accord.

In 1909 Siam ceded to Great Britain its suzerain rights over the dependencies of Kedah, Kelantan, Trengganu and Perlis, Malay states situated in southern Siam just north of British Malaya, which eliminated any British jurisdiction in Siam proper.

The absolute monarchy was changed into a constitutional monarchy in 1932.

On Dec. 8, 1941, after five hours of fighting, Thailand agreed to permit Japanese troops passage through the country to invade Northern British Malaysia. This eventually led to increased Japanese intervention and finally occupation of the country. On Jan. 25, 1942, Thailand declared war on Great Britain and the United States. A free Thai guerilla movement was soon organized to counteract the Japanese. In July 1943 Japan transferred the four northern Malay States back to Thailand. These were returned to Great Britain after peace treaties were signed in 1946.

DATING

Typical BE Dating

1238 1244

Typical CS Dating

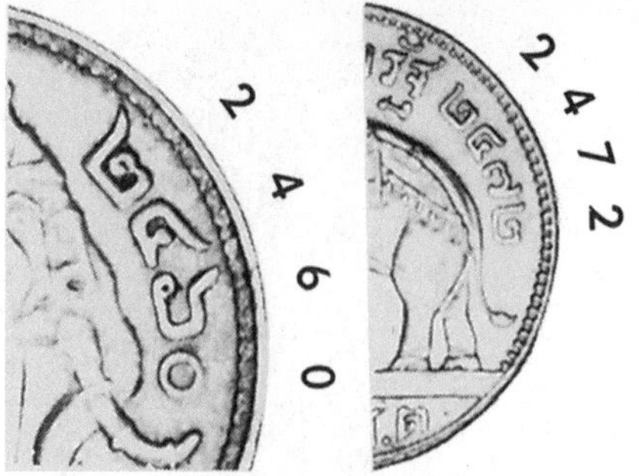


**NOTE**: Sometimes the era designator or *CS* will actually appear on the coin itself.

DENOMINATION

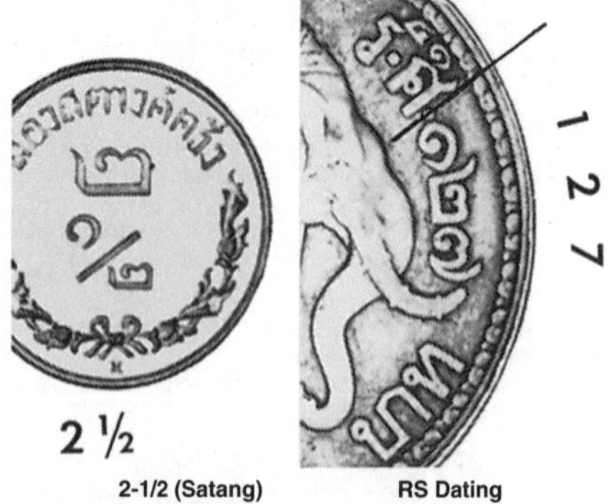


2-1/2 (Satang) RS Dating

**DATE CONVERSION TABLES**

B.E. date - 543 = A.D. date
Ex: 2516 - 543 = 1973
R.S. date + 1781 = A.D. date
Ex: 127 + 1781 = 1908
C.S. date + 638 = A.D. date
Ex 1238 + 638 = 1876

Primary denominations used were 1 Baht, 1/4 and 1/8 Baht up to the reign of Rama IV. Other denominations are much scarcer.

# KINGDOM OF THAILAND

1939-

## DECIMAL COINAGE

25 Satang = 1 Salung; 100 Satang = 1 Baht

### Y# 186 SATANG

0.50 g., Aluminum, 14.58 mm. **Ruler:** Rama IX **Obv:** Head left **Rev:** Haripunchai Temple, Lumpoon province **Edge:** Plain

| Date | Mintage | F12 | VF20 | XF40 | MS60 | MS63 |
|---|---|---|---|---|---|---|
| BE2544 | 50,000 | — | — | — | 0.75 | 1.00 |
| BE2545 | — | — | — | — | 1.50 | 2.00 |
| BE2546 | 10,000 | — | — | — | 1.50 | 2.00 |
| BE2547 | 20,000 | — | — | — | 1.25 | 1.75 |
| BE2548 | 10,000 | — | — | — | 1.50 | 2.00 |
| BE2549 | 3,000 | — | — | — | 3.00 | 4.00 |
| BE2550 | 10,000 | — | — | — | 1.50 | 2.00 |

### Y# 456 SATANG

0.50 g., Aluminum, 15 mm. **Ruler:** Rama IX **Obv:** Bust left **Rev:** Haripunchai Temple, Lumpoon province

| Date | Mintage | F12 | VF20 | XF40 | MS60 | MS63 |
|---|---|---|---|---|---|---|
| BE2551 (2008) | — | — | — | — | 1.50 | 2.00 |
| BE2552 (2009) | 10,000 | — | — | — | 1.50 | 2.00 |
| BE2553 (2010) | 10,000 | — | — | — | 1.50 | 2.00 |

### Y# 208 5 SATANG

0.60 g., Aluminum, 16 mm. **Ruler:** Rama IX **Obv:** Bust left **Rev:** Phra Patom Temple, Nakhon Pathom province **Edge:** Plain

| Date | Mintage | F12 | VF20 | XF40 | MS60 | MS63 |
|---|---|---|---|---|---|---|
| BE2544 | 50,000 | — | — | — | 1.00 | 1.25 |
| BE2546 | 10,000 | — | — | — | 2.00 | 2.50 |
| BE2547 | 10,000 | — | — | — | 2.00 | 2.50 |
| BE2548 | 20,000 | — | — | — | 1.25 | 1.50 |
| BE2549 | 3,000 | — | — | — | 3.00 | 4.00 |
| BE2550 | 10,000 | — | — | — | 2.00 | 2.50 |

### Y# 457 5 SATANG

0.60 g., Aluminum, 16.5 mm. **Ruler:** Rama IX **Obv:** Bust left **Rev:** Phra Patom Temple, Nakhon Pathom province

| Date | Mintage | F12 | VF20 | XF40 | MS60 | MS63 |
|---|---|---|---|---|---|---|
| BE2551 (2008) | 10,000 | — | — | — | 2.00 | 2.50 |
| BE2552 (2009) | 10,000 | — | — | — | 2.00 | 2.50 |
| BE2553 (2010) | 10,000 | — | — | — | 2.00 | 2.50 |

### Y# 209 10 SATANG

0.80 g., Aluminum, 17.5 mm. **Ruler:** Rama IX **Obv:** Young bust left **Rev:** Phra Tat Chungchum Temple, Sakon Nakhon province **Edge:** Plain

| Date | Mintage | F12 | VF20 | XF40 | MS60 | MS63 |
|---|---|---|---|---|---|---|
| BE2544 | 50,000 | — | — | — | 1.00 | 1.50 |
| BE2545 | — | — | — | — | 2.00 | 2.50 |
| BE2546 | 10,000 | — | — | 1.00 | 2.00 | 2.50 |
| BE2547 | 20,000 | — | — | — | 0.75 | 1.75 |
| BE2548 | 10,000 | — | — | 1.00 | 2.00 | 2.50 |
| BE2549 | 3,000 | — | — | 2.00 | 4.00 | 5.00 |
| BE2550 | 10,000 | — | — | 1.00 | 2.00 | 2.50 |

### Y# 458 10 SATANG

0.80 g., Aluminum, 17.5 mm. **Ruler:** Rama IX **Obv:** Bust left **Rev:** Phra Tat Chungchum Temple, Sakon Nakhon province

| Date | Mintage | F12 | VF20 | XF40 | MS60 | MS63 |
|---|---|---|---|---|---|---|
| BE2551 (2008) | — | — | — | 1.00 | 2.00 | 2.50 |
| BE2552 (2009) | 10,000 | — | — | 1.00 | 2.00 | 2.50 |
| BE2553 (2010) | 10,000 | — | — | 1.00 | 2.00 | 2.50 |

### Y# 187 25 SATANG = 1/4 BAHT

1.90 g., Aluminum-Bronze, 16 mm. **Ruler:** Rama IX **Obv:** Head left **Rev:** Mahathat Temple, Nakhon Si Thammarat province **Edge:** Reeded

| Date | Mintage | F12 | VF20 | XF40 | MS60 | MS63 |
|---|---|---|---|---|---|---|
| BE2544 | 10,000 | 1.00 | 2.00 | 3.00 | 5.00 | 6.00 |
| BE2545 | 141,562,000 | 1.00 | 2.00 | 3.00 | 5.00 | 6.00 |
| BE2546 | 82,668,000 | — | — | — | 0.10 | 0.15 |
| BE2547 | 104,830,000 | — | — | — | 0.10 | 0.15 |
| BE2548 | 95,362,000 | — | — | — | 0.10 | 0.15 |
| BE2549 | 120,003,000 | — | — | — | 0.10 | 0.15 |
| BE2550 r | 180,000,000 | — | — | — | 0.10 | 0.15 |
| BE2551 r | 255,600 | — | 0.50 | 0.75 | 1.00 | 1.50 |
| BE2552 | 30,000 | 1.00 | 2.00 | 3.00 | 5.00 | 6.00 |

### Y# 441 25 SATANG = 1/4 BAHT

1.90 g., Copper Plated Steel, 16 mm. **Ruler:** Rama IX **Obv:** King's portrait **Rev:** Mahathat Temple, Nakhon Si Thammarat province

| Date | Mintage | F12 | VF20 | XF40 | MS60 | MS63 |
|---|---|---|---|---|---|---|
| BE2552 (2009) v | 289,995,600 | — | — | — | 0.10 | 0.15 |
| BE2553 (2010) v | 220,000,000 | — | — | — | 0.10 | 0.15 |
| BE2554 (2011) v | — | — | — | — | 0.10 | 0.15 |
| BE2555 (2012) v | — | — | — | — | 0.10 | 0.15 |

### Y# 203 50 SATANG = 1/2 BAHT

2.40 g., Aluminum-Bronze, 18 mm. **Ruler:** Rama IX **Obv:** Head left **Rev:** Soi Suthep Temple, Chiang Mai province

| Date | Mintage | F12 | VF20 | XF40 | MS60 | MS63 |
|---|---|---|---|---|---|---|
| BE2544 | 52,738,000 | — | — | — | 0.10 | 0.15 |
| BE2545 | 102,804,000 | — | — | — | 0.10 | 0.15 |
| BE2546 | 101,200,000 | — | — | — | 0.10 | 0.15 |
| BE2547 | 79,596,000 | — | — | — | 0.10 | 0.15 |
| BE2548 | 99,920,000 | — | — | — | 0.10 | 0.15 |
| BE2549 | 130,803,000 | — | — | — | 0.10 | 0.15 |
| BE2550 | 24,905,000 | — | — | — | 0.10 | 0.15 |
| BE2551 | 27,163,509 | — | — | — | 0.10 | 0.15 |

### Y# 442 50 SATANG = 1/2 BAHT

2.40 g., Copper Plated Steel, 18 mm. **Ruler:** Rama IX **Obv:** King's portrait **Rev:** Doi Suthep Temple, Chiang Mai province

| Date | Mintage | F12 | VF20 | XF40 | MS60 | MS63 |
|---|---|---|---|---|---|---|
| BE2552 (2009) v | 225,000,000 | — | — | — | 0.10 | 0.15 |
| BE2553 (2010) v | 118,536,000 | — | — | — | 0.10 | 0.15 |
| BE2554 (2011) v | — | — | — | — | 0.10 | 0.15 |
| BE2555 (2012) | — | — | — | — | 0.10 | 0.15 |

### Y# 183 BAHT

3.45 g., Copper-Nickel, 20 mm. **Ruler:** Rama IX **Obv:** Head left **Rev:** Phra Kaew Temple, Bangkok **Edge:** Reeded **Note:** Varieties exist.

| Date | Mintage | F12 | VF20 | XF40 | MS60 | MS63 |
|---|---|---|---|---|---|---|
| BE2544 | 385,140,000 | — | — | — | 0.10 | 0.15 |
| BE2545 | 266,025,000 | — | — | — | 0.10 | 0.15 |
| BE2546 | 236,533,000 | — | — | — | 0.10 | 0.15 |
| BE2547 | 903,964,000 | — | — | — | 0.10 | 0.15 |
| BE2548 wg | 1,137,820,000 | — | — | — | 0.10 | 0.15 |
| BE2549 v | 778,061,000 | — | — | — | 0.10 | 0.15 |
| BE2550 wg | 614,866,877 | — | — | — | 0.10 | 0.15 |
| BE2551 | 660,307,123 | — | — | — | 0.10 | 0.15 |

### Y# 443 BAHT

3.00 g., Nickel Plated Steel, 20 mm. **Ruler:** Rama IX **Obv:** King's portrait **Rev:** Phra Kaew Temple, Bangkok **Edge:** Reeded

| Date | Mintage | F12 | VF20 | XF40 | MS60 | MS63 |
|---|---|---|---|---|---|---|
| BE2552 (2009) v | 507,250,000 | — | — | — | 0.10 | 0.15 |
| BE2553 (2010) v | 551,853,000 | — | — | — | 0.10 | 0.15 |
| BE2554 (2011) v | — | — | — | — | 0.10 | 0.15 |
| BE2555 (2012) v | — | — | — | — | 0.10 | 0.15 |
| BE2556-2013 | — | — | — | — | 0.10 | 0.15 |

### Y# 444 2 BAHT

4.40 g., Nickel Plated Steel, 21.75 mm. **Ruler:** Rama IX **Obv:** King's portrait **Rev:** Saket Temple, Bangkok

| Date | Mintage | F12 | VF20 | XF40 | MS60 | MS63 |
|---|---|---|---|---|---|---|
| BE2548 (2005) wg | 60,000 | — | — | — | 0.20 | 0.25 |
| BE2549 (2006) wg | 107,872,500 | — | — | — | 0.20 | 0.25 |
| BE2550 (2007) wg | 232,105,100 | — | — | — | 0.20 | 0.25 |
| BE2552 (2009) | 50,370 | — | — | 2.00 | 4.00 | 6.00 |

### Y# 445 2 BAHT

4.00 g., Aluminum-Bronze, 21.75 mm. **Ruler:** Rama IX **Obv:** King's portrait **Rev:** Saket Temple, Bangkok

| Date | Mintage | F12 | VF20 | XF40 | MS60 | MS63 |
|---|---|---|---|---|---|---|
| BE2551 (2008) | 10,004,000 | — | — | 0.15 | 0.30 | 0.40 |
| BE2552 (2009) | 244,741,000 | — | — | — | 0.20 | 0.25 |
| BE2553 (2010) | 137,228,000 | — | — | — | 0.20 | 0.25 |
| BE2554 (2011) | — | — | — | — | 0.20 | 0.25 |
| BE2555 (2012) | — | — | — | — | 0.20 | 0.25 |
| BE2556-2013 | — | — | — | — | 0.20 | 0.25 |

### Y# 219 5 BAHT

7.50 g., Copper-Nickel Clad Copper, 24 mm. **Ruler:** Rama IX **Obv:** Head left **Rev:** Benchamabophit Temple, Bangkok **Edge:** Coarse reeding

| Date | Mintage | F12 | VF20 | XF40 | MS60 | MS63 |
|---|---|---|---|---|---|---|
| BE2544 | 76,566,000 | — | — | — | 0.50 | 0.75 |
| BE2545 | 29,601,500 | — | — | — | 0.75 | 1.00 |
| BE2546 | 182,000 | 3.00 | 5.00 | 8.00 | 15.00 | 20.00 |
| BE2547 | 120,187,000 | — | — | — | 0.50 | 0.75 |
| BE2548 | 91,079,000 | — | — | — | 0.50 | 0.75 |
| BE2549 | 254,403,000 | — | — | — | 0.50 | 0.75 |
| BE2550 dj | 131,126,000 | — | — | — | 0.50 | 0.75 |
| BE2551 | 220,463,200 | — | — | — | 0.50 | 0.75 |

### Y# 446 5 BAHT

6.00 g., Copper-Nickel Clad Copper, 24 mm. **Ruler:** Rama IX **Obv:** King's portrait **Rev:** Benchamabophit Temp, Bangkok, Temple top does not break legend **Edge:** Coarse Reeding

| Date | Mintage | F12 | VF20 | XF40 | MS60 | MS63 |
|---|---|---|---|---|---|---|
| BE2551 (2008) | 6,225,000 | — | — | — | 0.75 | 1.00 |
| BE2552 (2009) | 308,283,000 | — | — | — | 0.50 | 0.75 |
| BE2553 (2010) | 2,903,000 | — | — | — | 1.00 | 1.25 |
| BE2554 (2011) | — | — | — | — | 0.50 | 0.75 |
| BE2555 (2012) | — | — | — | — | 0.50 | 0.75 |

### Y# 227 10 BAHT

8.50 g., Bi-Metallic Aluminum-Bronze center in Copper-Nickel ring, 26 mm. **Ruler:** Rama IX **Obv:** Head left within circle **Rev:** Arun Temple (Temple of the Dawn), Bankok **Edge:** Segmented reeding **Note:** Varieties exist.

| Date | Mintage | F12 | VF20 | XF40 | MS60 | MS63 |
|---|---|---|---|---|---|---|
| BE2544 | 2,060,000 | — | 0.75 | 2.00 | 5.00 | 6.00 |
| BE2545 | 61,333,000 | — | — | — | 2.25 | 2.75 |
| BE2546 | 49,292,000 | — | — | — | 2.25 | 2.75 |
| BE2547 | 62,689,000 | — | — | — | 2.25 | 2.50 |
| BE2548 | 111,491,000 | — | — | — | 2.00 | 2.50 |
| BE2549 v | 128,903,000 | — | — | — | 2.00 | 2.50 |
| BE2550 v | 130,202,000 | — | — | — | 2.00 | 2.50 |
| BE2551 | 179,165,360 | — | — | — | 2.00 | 2.50 |

### Y# 373 10 BAHT

8.50 g., Bi-Metallic Aluminum-Bronze center in Copper-Nickel ring, 26 mm. **Ruler:** Rama IX **Subject:** Department of Lands, 100th Anniversary, February 17 **Obv:** Conjoined busts facing divides circle **Rev:** Department seal within circle **Edge:** Segmented reeding

| Date | Mintage | F12 | VF20 | XF40 | MS60 | MS63 |
|---|---|---|---|---|---|---|
| BE2544 (2001) | 3,000,000 | — | — | 1.00 | 2.50 | 3.00 |

### Y# 381 10 BAHT

8.50 g., Bi-Metallic Aluminum-Bronze center in Copper-Nickel ring, 26 mm. **Ruler:** Rama IX **Subject:** Irrigation Department, 100th Anniversary, June 13 **Obv:** Conjoined busts facing divides circle **Rev:** Department logo **Edge:** Segmented reeding

| Date | Mintage | F12 | VF20 | XF40 | MS60 | MS63 |
|---|---|---|---|---|---|---|
| BE2545 (2002) | 3,000,000 | — | — | 1.00 | 2.00 | 2.75 |

### Y# 382 10 BAHT

8.50 g., Bi-Metallic Aluminum-Bronze center in Copper-Nickel ring, 26 mm. **Ruler:** Rama IX **Subject:** Department of Internal Trade, 60th Anniversary May 5 **Obv:** Head left **Rev:** Department logo **Edge:** Segmented reeding

| Date | Mintage | F12 | VF20 | XF40 | MS60 | MS63 |
|---|---|---|---|---|---|---|
| BE2545 (2002) | 3,000,000 | — | — | 1.00 | 2.00 | 2.75 |

### Y# 383 10 BAHT

8.50 g., Bi-Metallic Aluminum-Bronze center in Copper-Nickel ring, 26 mm. **Ruler:** Rama IX **Subject:** Highway Department, 90th Anniversary, April 1 **Obv:** Conjoined busts facing divides circle **Rev:** Highway Department logo **Edge:** Segmented reeding

| Date | Mintage | F12 | VF20 | XF40 | MS60 | MS63 |
|---|---|---|---|---|---|---|
| BE2545 (2002) | 3,000,000 | — | — | 1.00 | 2.00 | 2.75 |

### Y# 384 10 BAHT

8.50 g., Bi-Metallic Aluminum-Bronze center in Copper-Nickel ring, 26 mm. **Ruler:** Rama IX **Subject:** Vajira Medical Center, 90th Anniversary, January 2 **Obv:** Conjoined busts facing divides circle **Rev:** Hospital logo **Edge:** Segmented reeding

| Date | Mintage | F12 | VF20 | XF40 | MS60 | MS63 |
|---|---|---|---|---|---|---|
| BE2545 (2002) | 3,500,000 | — | — | 1.00 | 2.00 | 2.75 |

**Y# 387 10 BAHT**

8.50 g., Bi-Metallic Aluminum-Bronze center in Copper-Nickel ring, 26 mm. **Ruler:** Rama IX **Subject:** King's 75th Birthday, December 5 **Obv:** Head left **Rev:** Royal crown in radiant oval **Edge:** Segmented reeding

| Date | Mintage | F12 | VF20 | XF40 | MS60 | MS63 |
|---|---|---|---|---|---|---|
| BE2545 (2002) | 7,500,000 | — | — | 1.00 | 2.00 | 2.75 |

**Y# 385 10 BAHT**

8.50 g., Bi-Metallic Aluminum-Bronze center in Copper-Nickel ring, 26 mm. **Ruler:** Rama IX **Subject:** 20th World Scouting Jamboree **Obv:** Rama IX wearing a scouting uniform **Rev:** Jamboree log **Edge:** Segmented reeding

| Date | Mintage | F12 | VF20 | XF40 | MS60 | MS63 |
|---|---|---|---|---|---|---|
| BE2546 (2003) | 3,000,000 | — | — | 1.00 | 2.00 | 2.75 |

**Y# 391 10 BAHT**

8.50 g., Bi-Metallic Aluminum-Bronze center in Copper-Nickel ring, 26 mm. **Ruler:** Rama IX **Subject:** Inspector General's Department, 100th Anniversary, May 6 **Obv:** Head left within circle **Rev:** Department seal within circle and design **Edge:** Segmented reeding

| Date | Mintage | F12 | VF20 | XF40 | MS60 | MS63 |
|---|---|---|---|---|---|---|
| BE2546 (2003) | 3,000,000 | — | — | 1.00 | 1.75 | 2.50 |

**Y# 392 10 BAHT**

8.50 g., Bi-Metallic Aluminum-Bronze center in Copper-Nickel ring, 26 mm. **Ruler:** Rama IX **Subject:** Princess Galaniwattana, 80th Birthday, May 6 **Obv:** Bust 1/4 right **Rev:** Crowned emblem and value **Edge:** Alternating reeded and plain **Note:** This is the king's sister.

| Date | Mintage | F12 | VF20 | XF40 | MS60 | MS63 |
|---|---|---|---|---|---|---|
| BE2546 (2003) | 2,000,000 | — | — | 1.00 | 1.75 | 2.50 |

**Y# 396 10 BAHT**

8.50 g., Bi-Metallic Aluminum-Bronze center in Copper-Nickel ring, 26 mm. **Ruler:** Rama IX **Subject:** Government Savings Bank, 90th Anniversary, April 1 **Obv:** Uniformed bust facing within circle **Rev:** Bank emblem **Edge:** Segmented reeding

| Date | Mintage | F12 | VF20 | XF40 | MS60 | MS63 |
|---|---|---|---|---|---|---|
| BE2546 (2003) | 2,000,000 | — | — | 1.00 | 2.00 | 2.75 |

**Y# 400 10 BAHT**

8.50 g., Bi-Metallic Aluminum-Bronze center in Copper-Nickel ring, 26 mm. **Ruler:** Rama IX **Subject:** APEC 2003 Summit **Obv:** Head left **Rev:** APEC logo **Edge:** Segmented reeding

| Date | Mintage | F12 | VF20 | XF40 | MS60 | MS63 |
|---|---|---|---|---|---|---|
| BE2546-2003 | 1,000,000 | — | — | 1.00 | 2.25 | 3.00 |

**Y# 405 10 BAHT**

8.50 g., Bi-Metallic Aluminum-Bronze center in Copper-Nickel ring, 26 mm. **Ruler:** Rama IX **Subject:** CITES World Meeting **Obv:** Bust 3/4 left within circle **Rev:** CITES logo **Edge:** Segmented reeding

| Date | Mintage | F12 | VF20 | XF40 | MS60 | MS63 |
|---|---|---|---|---|---|---|
| ND (2003) | — | — | — | 1.00 | 2.00 | 2.75 |

**Y# 409 10 BAHT**

8.50 g., Bi-Metallic Aluminum-Bronze center in Copper-Nickel ring, 26 mm. **Ruler:** Rama IX **Subject:** King Rama V, 150th Anniversary **Obv:** Bust of Rama V left **Rev:** Royal crown **Edge:** Segmented reeding

| Date | Mintage | F12 | VF20 | XF40 | MS60 | MS63 |
|---|---|---|---|---|---|---|
| BE2546 (2003) | 3,600,000 | — | — | 1.00 | 1.80 | 2.50 |

**Y# 414 10 BAHT**

8.50 g., Bi-Metallic Aluminum-Bronze center in Copper-Nickel ring, 26 mm. **Ruler:** Rama IX **Subject:** Anti Drug Campaign **Obv:** Civilian bust left **Rev:** Tear drop shaped logo **Edge:** Segmented reeding

| Date | Mintage | F12 | VF20 | XF40 | MS60 | MS63 |
|---|---|---|---|---|---|---|
| BE2546 (2003) | 3,000,000 | — | — | — | 1.80 | 2.50 |

**Y# 410 10 BAHT**

8.50 g., Bi-Metallic Aluminum-Bronze center in Copper-Nickel ring, 26 mm. **Subject:** Thammasat University, 70th Anniversary **Obv:** Civilian bust 3/4 left **Rev:** Thammasat University seal **Edge:** Segmented reeding

| Date | Mintage | F12 | VF20 | XF40 | MS60 | MS63 |
|---|---|---|---|---|---|---|
| BE2547 (2004) | 3,000,000 | — | — | 1.00 | 1.80 | 2.50 |

**Y# 411 10 BAHT**

8.50 g., Bi-Metallic Aluminum-Bronze center in Copper-Nickel ring, 26 mm. **Ruler:** Rama IX **Subject:** Royal Institute Board, 70th Anniversary **Obv:** 1/2 length civilian busts of 2 kings facing **Rev:** Royal Scholar Institute seal **Edge:** Segmented reeding

| Date | Mintage | F12 | VF20 | XF40 | MS60 | MS63 |
|---|---|---|---|---|---|---|
| BE2547 (2004) | 2,000,000 | — | — | 1.00 | 1.80 | 2.50 |

**Y# 412 10 BAHT**

8.50 g., Bi-Metallic Aluminum-Bronze center in Copper-Nickel ring, 26 mm. **Ruler:** Rama IX **Subject:** Queen's 72nd Birthday **Obv:** Bust of queen facing 3/4 left **Rev:** Royal seal **Edge:** Segmented reeding

| Date | Mintage | F12 | VF20 | XF40 | MS60 | MS63 |
|---|---|---|---|---|---|---|
| BE2547 (2004) | 6,000,000 | — | — | 1.00 | 1.80 | 2.50 |

**Y# 413 10 BAHT**

8.50 g., Bi-Metallic Aluminum-Bronze center in Copper-Nickel ring, 26 mm. **Ruler:** Rama IX **Subject:** IUCN World Conservation Congress **Obv:** Civilian bust 3/4 right **Rev:** IUCN logo **Edge:** Segmented reeding

| Date | Mintage | F12 | VF20 | XF40 | MS60 | MS63 |
|---|---|---|---|---|---|---|
| BE2547 (2004) | — | — | — | 1.00 | 1.80 | 2.50 |

**Y# 415 10 BAHT**

8.50 g., Bi-Metallic Aluminum-Bronze center in Copper-Nickel ring, 26 mm. **Ruler:** Rama IX **Subject:** King Rama IV, 200th Anniversary **Obv:** Bust of Rama IV 3/4 right **Rev:** Royal seal **Edge:** Segmented reeding

| Date | Mintage | F12 | VF20 | XF40 | MS60 | MS63 |
|---|---|---|---|---|---|---|
| BE2547 (2004) | 3,500,000 | — | — | 1.00 | 1.80 | 2.50 |

**Y# 402 10 BAHT**

8.50 g., Bi-Metallic Aluminum-Bronze center in Copper-Nickel ring, 26 mm. **Ruler:** Rama IX **Subject:** Department of the Treasury, 72nd Anniversary **Obv:** Bust 1/4 left within circle **Rev:** Treasury Department seal within circle **Edge:** Segmented reeding

| Date | Mintage | F12 | VF20 | XF40 | MS60 | MS63 |
|---|---|---|---|---|---|---|
| BE2548 (2005) | 3,000,000 | — | — | 1.00 | 2.50 | 3.25 |

**Y# 416 10 BAHT**

8.50 g., Bi-Metallic Aluminum-Bronze center in Copper-Nickel ring, 26 mm. **Ruler:** Rama IX **Subject:** Army Transportation Corp, 100th Anniversary **Obv:** 2 King's military busts left **Rev:** Steering wheel, badge at center **Edge:** Segmented reeding

| Date | Mintage | F12 | VF20 | XF40 | MS60 | MS63 |
|---|---|---|---|---|---|---|
| BE2548 (2005) | 3,000,000 | — | — | 1.00 | 1.80 | 2.50 |

**Y# 418 10 BAHT**

8.50 g., Bi-Metallic Aluminum-Bronze center in Copper-Nickel ring, 26 mm. **Ruler:** Rama IX **Subject:** 25th Asia-Pacific Scout Jamboree **Obv:** Rama IX in scout uniform 3/4 left **Rev:** Logo **Edge:** Segmented reeding

| Date | Mintage | F12 | VF20 | XF40 | MS60 | MS63 |
|---|---|---|---|---|---|---|
| BE2548 (2005) | 3,000,000 | — | — | 1.00 | 1.80 | 2.50 |

**Y# 406 10 BAHT**

8.50 g., Bi-Metallic Aluminum-Bronze center in Copper-Nickel ring, 26 mm. **Ruler:** Rama IX **Subject:** 60th Anniversary of Reign **Obv:** Bust 1/4 left within circle **Rev:** Royal Crown on display **Edge:** Segmented reeding

| Date | Mintage | F12 | VF20 | XF40 | MS60 | MS63 |
|---|---|---|---|---|---|---|
| BE2549 (2006) | 16,000,000 | — | — | 1.00 | 2.50 | 3.25 |

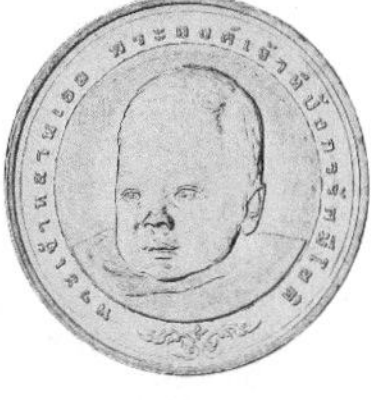

**Y# 417 10 BAHT**

8.50 g., Bi-Metallic Aluminum-Bronze center in Copper-Nickel ring, 26 mm. **Ruler:** Rama IX **Subject:** Princess's Royal Cradle Ceremony **Obv:** Princess's baby head 3/4 left **Rev:** 4-line inscription **Edge:** Segmented reeding

| Date | Mintage | F12 | VF20 | XF40 | MS60 | MS63 |
|---|---|---|---|---|---|---|
| BE2548 (2006) | 3,000,000 | — | — | 1.00 | 1.80 | 2.50 |

**Y# 424 10 BAHT**

8.50 g., Bi-Metallic Aluminum-Bronze center in Copper-Nickel ring, 26 mm. **Ruler:** Rama IX **Subject:** Prince Jaturon Ratsamee, 150th Anniversary of Birth **Obv:** Bust of Prince facing 3/4 right **Rev:** Radiant badge **Edge:** Segmented reeding

| Date | Mintage | F12 | VF20 | XF40 | MS60 | MS63 |
|---|---|---|---|---|---|---|
| BE2549(2006) | — | — | — | 1.00 | 2.50 | 3.25 |

**Y# 428 10 BAHT**

8.50 g., Bi-Metallic Aluminum-Bronze center in Copper-Nickel ring, 26 mm. **Ruler:** Rama IX **Subject:** Secretariat of the Cabinet, 72nd Anniversary **Obv:** Military bust 3/4 right **Rev:** Royal Cabinet seal **Edge:** Segmented reeding **Note:** Minted in 2005 but released in 2006.

| Date | Mintage | F12 | VF20 | XF40 | MS60 | MS63 |
|---|---|---|---|---|---|---|
| BE2547 (2004) | — | — | — | 1.00 | 1.80 | 2.50 |

**Y# 429 10 BAHT**

8.50 g., Bi-Metallic Aluminum-Bronze center in Copper-Nickel ring, 26 mm. **Ruler:** Rama IX **Subject:** Princess Petcharat, 80th Birthday **Obv:** Bust of Princess facing **Rev:** Royal seal of Princess **Edge:** Segmented reeding

| Date | Mintage | F12 | VF20 | XF40 | MS60 | MS63 |
|---|---|---|---|---|---|---|
| BE2548 (2006) | 1,000,000 | — | — | 1.25 | 2.25 | 2.75 |

**Y# 430 10 BAHT**

8.50 g., Bi-Metallic Aluminum-Bronze center in Copper-Nickel ring, 26 mm. **Ruler:** Rama IX **Subject:** Budget Inspection Department, 130th Anniversary **Obv:** Conjoined kings' busts left **Rev:** Ornate scale **Edge:** Segmented reeding

| Date | Mintage | F12 | VF20 | XF40 | MS60 | MS63 |
|---|---|---|---|---|---|---|
| BE2548 (2006) | Est. 3000000 | — | — | 1.00 | 1.80 | 2.50 |

**Y# 431 10 BAHT**

8.50 g., Bi-Metallic Aluminum-Bronze center in Copper-Nickel ring, 26 mm. **Ruler:** Rama IX **Subject:** 60th Anniversary of Reign **Obv:** Bust 3/4 right **Rev:** Royal throne **Edge:** Segmented reeding

| Date | Mintage | F12 | VF20 | XF40 | MS60 | MS63 |
|---|---|---|---|---|---|---|
| BE2549 (2006) | 16,000,000 | — | — | 1.00 | 1.80 | 2.50 |

**Y# 432 10 BAHT**

8.50 g., Bi-Metallic Aluminum-Bronze center in Copper-Nickel ring, 26 mm. **Ruler:** Rama IX **Subject:** Department of Judge Advocate General, 100th Anniversary **Obv:** Conjoined kings' busts left **Rev:** Military emblem with scales of justice in background **Edge:** Segmented reeding

| Date | Mintage | F12 | VF20 | XF40 | MS60 | MS63 |
|---|---|---|---|---|---|---|
| BE2549 (2006) | 3,000,000 | — | — | 1.00 | 1.80 | 2.50 |

**Y# 425 10 BAHT**

8.50 g., Bi-Metallic Aluminum-Bronze center in Copper-Nickel ring, 26 mm. **Ruler:** Rama IX **Subject:** Royal Calvary Division, 100th Anniversary **Obv:** Conjoined kings' busts left **Rev:** Royal crown above emblem **Edge:** Segmented reeding

| Date | Mintage | F12 | VF20 | XF40 | MS60 | MS63 |
|---|---|---|---|---|---|---|
| BE2550 (2007) | 3,000,000 | — | — | 1.00 | 1.75 | 2.50 |

**Y# 426 10 BAHT**

8.50 g., Bi-Metallic Aluminum-Bronze center in Copper-Nickel ring, 26 mm. **Ruler:** Rama IX **Subject:** 1st Thai Commercial Bank, 100th Anniversary **Obv:** Conjoined kings' busts left **Rev:** Garuda Bird **Edge:** Segmented reeding

| Date | Mintage | F12 | VF20 | XF40 | MS60 | MS63 |
|---|---|---|---|---|---|---|
| BE2550 (2007) | 5,000,000 | — | — | 1.00 | 1.75 | 2.50 |

**Y# 433 10 BAHT**

8.50 g., Bi-Metallic Aluminum-Bronze center in Copper-Nickel ring, 26 mm. **Ruler:** Rama IX **Subject:** Queen's WHO Food Safety Award **Obv:** Queen's bust 3/4 right **Rev:** WHO emblem at upper left of inscription in sprays **Edge:** Segmented reeding

| Date | Mintage | F12 | VF20 | XF40 | MS60 | MS63 |
|---|---|---|---|---|---|---|
| BE2550 (2007) | 5,000,000 | — | — | 1.00 | 1.75 | 2.50 |

**Y# 434 10 BAHT**

8.50 g., Bi-Metallic Aluminum-Bronze center in Copper-Nickel ring, 26 mm. **Ruler:** Rama IX **Subject:** Medical Technology Department, 50th Anniversary **Obv:** Robed bust 3/4 right **Rev:** Oval medical seal **Edge:** Segmented reeding

| Date | Mintage | F12 | VF20 | XF40 | MS60 | MS63 |
|---|---|---|---|---|---|---|
| BE2550 (2007) | 3,000,000 | — | — | 1.00 | 1.75 | 2.50 |

**Y# 435 10 BAHT**

8.50 g., Bi-Metallic Aluminum-Bronze center in Copper-Nickel ring, 26 mm. **Ruler:** Rama IX **Subject:** UNIVERSIADE 2007 - World University Games **Obv:** Civilian bust 3/4 right **Rev:** Games logo **Edge:** Segmented reeding

| Date | Mintage | F12 | VF20 | XF40 | MS60 | MS63 |
|---|---|---|---|---|---|---|
| BE2550 (2007) | 5,000,000 | — | — | 1.00 | 1.75 | 2.50 |

**Y# 436 10 BAHT**

8.50 g., Bi-Metallic Aluminum-Bronze center in Copper-Nickel ring, 26 mm. **Ruler:** Rama IX **Subject:** Queen's 75th birthday **Obv:** Bust of Queen wearing tiara 3/4 left **Rev:** Queen's Royal seal **Edge:** Segmented reeding

| Date | Mintage | F12 | VF20 | XF40 | MS60 | MS63 |
|---|---|---|---|---|---|---|
| BE2550 (2007) | 7,500,000 | — | — | 1.00 | 1.75 | 2.50 |

**Y# 437 10 BAHT**

8.50 g., Bi-Metallic Aluminum-Bronze center in Copper-Nickel ring, 26 mm. **Ruler:** Rama IX **Subject:** IAAJS Conference - Bangkok **Obv:** Civilian bust 3/4 left **Rev:** Oval seal with scale above conference logo **Edge:** Segmented reeding

| Date | Mintage | F12 | VF20 | XF40 | MS60 | MS63 |
|---|---|---|---|---|---|---|
| BE2550 (2007) | 3,000,000 | — | — | 1.00 | 1.75 | 2.50 |

**Y# 438 10 BAHT**

8.50 g., Bi-Metallic Aluminum-Bronze center in Copper-Nickel ring, 26 mm. **Ruler:** Rama IX **Subject:** King's 80th birthday **Obv:** Royal bust 3/4 left **Rev:** Royal seal **Edge:** Segmented reeding

| Date | Mintage | F12 | VF20 | XF40 | MS60 | MS63 |
|---|---|---|---|---|---|---|
| BE2550 (2007) | 18,000,000 | — | — | 1.00 | 1.75 | 2.50 |

**Y# 439 10 BAHT**

8.50 g., Bi-Metallic Aluminum-Bronze center in Copper-Nickel ring, 26 mm. **Ruler:** Rama IX **Subject:** 24th SEA Games **Obv:** Civilian bust 3/4 left **Rev:** Games logo above inscription **Edge:** Segmented reeding

| Date | Mintage | F12 | VF20 | XF40 | MS60 | MS63 |
|---|---|---|---|---|---|---|
| BE2550 (2007) | 3,000,000 | — | — | 1.00 | 1.75 | 2.50 |

**Y# 440 10 BAHT**

8.50 g., Bi-Metallic Aluminum-Bronze center in Copper-Nickel ring, 26 mm. **Ruler:** Rama IX **Subject:** Siriraj Hospital, 120th Anniversary **Obv:** Conjoined kings' busts right **Rev:** Royal hospital's seal **Edge:** Segmented reeding

| Date | Mintage | F12 | VF20 | XF40 | MS60 | MS63 |
|---|---|---|---|---|---|---|
| BE2550 (2007) | 3,000,000 | — | — | 1.00 | 1.75 | 2.50 |

**Y# 459 10 BAHT**

8.50 g., Bi-Metallic Aluminum-Bronze center in Copper-Nickel ring, 26 mm. **Ruler:** Rama IX **Obv:** Head left **Rev:** Arun Temple (Temple of the Dawn), Bangkok

| Date | Mintage | F12 | VF20 | XF40 | MS60 | MS63 |
|---|---|---|---|---|---|---|
| BE2551 (2008) | 18,450,000 | — | — | — | 2.00 | 2.75 |
| BE2552 (2009) | 59,107,733 | — | — | — | 2.00 | 2.75 |
| BE2553 (2010) | 1,953,000 | — | — | — | 2.00 | 2.75 |
| BE2554 (2011) | — | — | — | — | 2.00 | 2.75 |
| BE2555 (2012) | — | — | — | — | 2.00 | 2.75 |
| BE2556-2013 | — | — | — | — | 2.00 | 2.75 |

**Y# 460 10 BAHT**

8.50 g., Bi-Metallic Aluminum-Bronze center in Copper-Nickel ring, 26 mm. **Ruler:** Rama IX **Subject:** Thai Postal Service, 125th Anniversary **Obv:** Conjoined busts left **Rev:** Scroll with legend **Edge:** Segmented Reeding

| Date | Mintage | F12 | VF20 | XF40 | MS60 | MS63 |
|---|---|---|---|---|---|---|
| BE2551 (2008) | 3,000,000 | — | — | 1.00 | 2.00 | 2.75 |

**Y# 461 10 BAHT**

8.50 g., Bi-Metallic Aluminum-Bronze center in Copper-Nickel ring, 26 mm. **Ruler:** Rama IX **Subject:** National Research Council, 50th Anniversary **Obv:** Bust left **Rev:** Nucleus surrounded by electrons **Edge:** Segmented Reeding

| Date | Mintage | F12 | VF20 | XF40 | MS60 | MS63 |
|---|---|---|---|---|---|---|
| BE2552 (2009) | 3,000,000 | — | — | — | 2.00 | 2.75 |

**Y# 486 10 BAHT**

8.50 g., Bi-Metallic Aluminum-Bronze center in Copper-Nickel ring, 26 mm. **Ruler:** Rama IX **Subject:** Thailand Army School, 100th Anniversary

| Date | Mintage | F12 | VF20 | XF40 | MS60 | MS63 |
|---|---|---|---|---|---|---|
| RS2552 | — | — | — | — | 3.50 | 5.00 |

**Y# 488 10 BAHT**

8.50 g., Bi-Metallic Aluminum-Bronze center in Copper-Nickel ring, 26 mm. **Ruler:** Rama IX **Subject:** Princess Bejaratana, 84th Birthday

| Date | Mintage | F12 | VF20 | XF40 | MS60 | MS63 |
|---|---|---|---|---|---|---|
| RS2552 | 1,000,000 | — | — | — | 3.50 | 5.00 |

**Y# 497 10 BAHT**

Bi-Metallic Aluminum-bronze center in Copper-nickel ring, 26 mm. **Ruler:** Rama IX **Subject:** 120th Anniversary of the Department of Finance **Obv:** Conjoined heads facing left **Rev:** Seal of the Department of Finance (bird), inscription, value and date **Edge:** Segmented reeding

| Date | Mintage | F12 | VF20 | XF40 | MS60 | MS63 |
|---|---|---|---|---|---|---|
| BE2553 (2010) | 1,000,000 | — | — | — | 2.00 | 2.50 |

**Y# 498 10 BAHT**

Bi-Metallic Aluminum bronze center in copper-nickel ring, 26 mm. **Ruler:** Rama IX **Subject:** 60th Anniversary of the Office of National Economic and Social Development **Obv:** Head of King Rama IX facing 1/4 right and inscriptions **Rev:** Seal of the Office of National Economic and Social Development (statue of three people), inscription, value and date

| Date | Mintage | F12 | VF20 | XF40 | MS60 | MS63 |
|---|---|---|---|---|---|---|
| BE2553 (2010) | — | — | — | — | 2.00 | 2.50 |

**Y# 504 10 BAHT**

8.50 g., Bi-Metallic Aluminum-Bronze center in Copper-Nickel ring, 26 mm. **Ruler:** Rama IX **Subject:** Princess Bejaratana, 84th Birthday **Rev:** Emblem

| Date | Mintage | F12 | VF20 | XF40 | MS60 | MS63 |
|---|---|---|---|---|---|---|
| BE2553 (2010) | — | — | — | — | 2.00 | 2.75 |

**Y# 516 10 BAHT**

8.50 g., Bi-Metallic Aluminum-Bronze center in Copper-Nickel ring, 26 mm. **Ruler:** Rama IX **Subject:** Prince Bhanurangsi Savangwongse, 150th Anniversary of Birth

| Date | Mintage | F12 | VF20 | XF40 | MS60 | MS63 |
|---|---|---|---|---|---|---|
| RS2553 | — | — | — | — | 3.50 | 5.00 |

**Y# 518 10 BAHT**

8.50 g., Bi-Metallic Aluminum-Bronze center in Copper-Nickel ring, 26 mm. **Ruler:** Rama IX **Subject:** National Economic and Social Development Board, 60th Anniversary

| Date | Mintage | F12 | VF20 | XF40 | MS60 | MS63 |
|---|---|---|---|---|---|---|
| RS2553 | 1,000,000 | — | — | — | 3.00 | 5.00 |

**Y# 519 10 BAHT**

8.50 g., Bi-Metallic Aluminum-Bronze center in Copper-Nickel ring, 26 mm. **Ruler:** Rama IX **Subject:** Court of Auditors, 120th Anniversary

| Date | Mintage | F12 | VF20 | XF40 | MS60 | MS63 |
|---|---|---|---|---|---|---|
| RS2553 | 1,000,000 | — | — | — | 3.00 | 5.00 |

**Y# 508 10 BAHT**

8.50 g., Bi-Metallic Copper nickel in brass ring, 26 mm. **Ruler:** Rama IX **Subject:** 100th Anniversary of the Fine Art Department **Obv:** King Rama VI **Rev:** Ganesha

| Date | Mintage | F12 | VF20 | XF40 | MS60 | MS63 |
|---|---|---|---|---|---|---|
| 2012 | — | — | — | — | — | — |

**Y# 510 10 BAHT**

Bi-Metallic Aluminum-Bronze center in Copper-Nickel ring, 26 mm. **Ruler:** Rama IX **Subject:** 100th Anniversary of the Command and General Staff College, Royal National Army

| Date | Mintage | F12 | VF20 | XF40 | MS60 | MS63 |
|---|---|---|---|---|---|---|
| 2012 | Est. 3000000 | — | — | — | — | — |

**Y# 374 20 BAHT**

15.00 g., Copper-Nickel, 32 mm. **Ruler:** Rama IX **Subject:** Chulalongkorn University 84th Anniversary March 26 **Obv:** Three conjoined busts right **Rev:** University emblem divides value **Edge:** Reeded

| Date | Mintage | F12 | VF20 | XF40 | MS60 | MS63 |
|---|---|---|---|---|---|---|
| BE2544 (2001) | 800,040 | — | — | 2.00 | 3.50 | 5.00 |
| BE2544 (2001) | 5,340 | PF63 22.00 | PF65 27.00 | | | |

**Y# 375 20 BAHT**

15.00 g., Copper-Nickel, 32 mm. **Ruler:** Rama IX **Subject:** Civil Service Comission 72nd Anniversary April 1 **Obv:** Conjoined busts left **Rev:** Civil service emblem divides value **Edge:** Reeded

| Date | Mintage | F12 | VF20 | XF40 | MS60 | MS63 |
|---|---|---|---|---|---|---|
| BE2544 (2001) | 500,000 | — | — | 2.00 | 3.50 | 5.00 |
| BE2544 (2001) | 3,340 | PF63 25.00 | PF65 30.00 | | | |

**Y# 386 20 BAHT**

15.00 g., Copper-Nickel, 32 mm. **Ruler:** Rama IX **Subject:** Centennial of Thai Banknotes 2445-2545 **Obv:** Conjoined busts left **Rev:** Coat of arms in center of seal **Edge:** Reeded

| Date | Mintage | F12 | VF20 | XF40 | MS60 | MS63 |
|---|---|---|---|---|---|---|
| BE2545 (2002) | 1,000,000 | — | — | 2.00 | 3.50 | 5.00 |
| BE2545 (2002) | 40,000 | PF63 17.50 | PF65 22.00 | | | |

**Y# 388 20 BAHT**

15.00 g., Copper-Nickel, 32 mm. **Ruler:** Rama IX **Subject:** King's 75th Birthday December 5 **Obv:** Head left **Rev:** Royal crown in radiant oval **Edge:** Reeded **Note:** Minted and released in 2003.

| Date | Mintage | F12 | VF20 | XF40 | MS60 | MS63 |
|---|---|---|---|---|---|---|
| BE2545(2002) | 1,200,000 | — | — | 2.00 | 3.50 | 5.00 |
| BE2545(2002) | 16,000 | PF63 17.50 | PF65 22.00 | | | |

**Y# 393 20 BAHT**

15.00 g., Copper-Nickel, 32 mm. **Ruler:** Rama IX **Subject:** 80th Birthday of Princess Calyani Vadhani **Obv:** Bust 1/4 right **Rev:** Crowned emblem and value **Edge:** Reeded

| Date | Mintage | F12 | VF20 | XF40 | MS60 | MS63 |
|---|---|---|---|---|---|---|
| BE2546 (2003) | 350,000 | — | — | 2.00 | 3.50 | 5.00 |
| BE2546 (2003) | 3,200 | PF63 17.50 | PF65 22.00 | | | |

**Y# 397 20 BAHT**
15.00 g., Copper-Nickel, 32 mm. **Ruler:** Rama IX **Subject:** Centennial of the National Police April 19 **Obv:** Conjoined busts left **Rev:** National Police emblem above banner **Edge:** Reeded

| Date | Mintage | F12 | VF20 | XF40 | MS60 | MS63 |
|---|---|---|---|---|---|---|
| BE2545 (2002) | 600,000 | — | — | 2.00 | 3.50 | 5.00 |
| BE2545 (2002) | 5,000 | PF63 17.50 | PF65 22.00 | | | |

**Y# 398 20 BAHT**
15.00 g., Copper-Nickel, 32 mm. **Ruler:** Rama IX **Subject:** 50th Birthday of the Crown Prince July 28 **Obv:** Bust facing **Rev:** Crowned monogram **Edge:** Reeded

| Date | Mintage | F12 | VF20 | XF40 | MS60 | MS63 |
|---|---|---|---|---|---|---|
| BE2545 (2002) | 300,000 | — | — | 2.00 | 3.50 | 5.00 |
| BE2545 (2002) | 5,000 | PF63 40.00 | PF65 50.00 | | | |

**Y# 419 20 BAHT**
15.00 g., Copper-Nickel, 32 mm. **Ruler:** Rama IX **Subject:** 50th Anniversary of Audit Department of Cooperatives **Edge:** Reeded

| Date | Mintage | F12 | VF20 | XF40 | MS60 | MS63 |
|---|---|---|---|---|---|---|
| BE2545 (2002) | 300,000 | — | — | 2.00 | 3.50 | 5.00 |
| BE2545 (2002) | 3,000 | PF63 17.50 | PF65 22.00 | | | |

**Y# 420 20 BAHT**
15.00 g., Copper-Nickel, 32 mm. **Ruler:** Rama IX **Subject:** 150th Anniversary, Birth of Rama V **Edge:** Reeded

| Date | Mintage | F12 | VF20 | XF40 | MS60 | MS63 |
|---|---|---|---|---|---|---|
| BE2546 (2003) | 1,000,000 | — | — | 2.00 | 3.50 | 5.00 |
| BE2546 (2003) | 26,000 | PF63 18.00 | PF65 24.00 | | | |

**Y# 421 20 BAHT**
15.00 g., Copper-Nickel, 32 mm. **Ruler:** Rama IX **Subject:** Rama IV, 200th Anniversary of Birth **Obv:** King Rama IV **Edge:** Reeded

| Date | Mintage | F12 | VF20 | XF40 | MS60 | MS63 |
|---|---|---|---|---|---|---|
| BE2547 (2004) | 500,000 | — | — | 2.00 | 3.50 | 5.00 |
| BE2547 (2004) | 10,500 | PF63 20.00 | PF65 25.00 | | | |

**Y# 422 20 BAHT**
15.00 g., Copper-Nickel, 32 mm. **Ruler:** Rama IX **Subject:** 72nd Anniversary of Queen's Birthday **Obv:** Head of Queen facing left **Edge:** Reeded

| Date | Mintage | F12 | VF20 | XF40 | MS60 | MS63 |
|---|---|---|---|---|---|---|
| BE2547 (2004) | 600,000 | — | — | 2.00 | 3.50 | 5.00 |
| BE2547 (2004) | 10,000 | PF63 20.00 | PF65 25.00 | | | |

**Y# 462 20 BAHT**
15.00 g., Copper-Nickel, 32 mm. **Ruler:** Rama IX **Subject:** Rama IV, 200th Anniversary of Birth **Obv:** Bust 3/4 right **Rev:** Horizontal oval Royal seal **Edge:** Reeded

| Date | Mintage | F12 | VF20 | XF40 | MS60 | MS63 |
|---|---|---|---|---|---|---|
| BE2547 (2004) | 500,000 | — | — | 2.00 | 4.00 | 6.00 |
| BE2547 (2004) | 10,500 | PF63 15.00 | PF65 18.00 | | | |

**Y# 403 20 BAHT**
15.00 g., Copper-Nickel, 32 mm. **Ruler:** Rama IX **Subject:** Department of the Treasury, 72nd Anniversary **Obv:** Bust 1/4 left **Rev:** Treasury Department seal **Edge:** Reeded

| Date | Mintage | F12 | VF20 | XF40 | MS60 | MS63 |
|---|---|---|---|---|---|---|
| BE2548 (2005) | 300,000 | — | — | 2.00 | 4.00 | 6.00 |
| BE2548 (2005) | 3,000 | PF63 25.00 | PF65 30.00 | | | |

**Y# 423 20 BAHT**
15.00 g., Copper-Nickel, 32 mm. **Ruler:** Rama IX **Subject:** 50th Birthday of Princess Sirinahorn **Obv:** Head of Princess facing right **Edge:** Reeded

| Date | Mintage | F12 | VF20 | XF40 | MS60 | MS63 |
|---|---|---|---|---|---|---|
| BE2548 (2005) | 650,000 | — | — | 2.00 | 4.00 | 6.00 |
| BE2548 (2005) | 12,000 | PF63 20.00 | PF65 25.00 | | | |

**Y# 471 20 BAHT**
15.00 g., Copper-Nickel, 32 mm. **Ruler:** Rama IX **Subject:** Centennial of the National Library **Obv:** Two busts, one facing left, one right **Rev:** Circle with inscription **Edge:** Reeded

| Date | Mintage | F12 | VF20 | XF40 | MS60 | MS63 |
|---|---|---|---|---|---|---|
| BE2548 (2005) Est. 200000 | | — | — | 2.00 | 3.50 | 5.00 |

**Y# 472 20 BAHT**
15.00 g., Copper-Nickel, 32 mm. **Ruler:** Rama IX **Subject:** Princess Rattana, 80th birthday **Obv:** Front facing portrait **Edge:** Reeded **Note:** Minted and released in 2006.

| Date | Mintage | F12 | VF20 | XF40 | MS60 | MS63 |
|---|---|---|---|---|---|---|
| BE2548 (2005) | 200,000 | — | — | 2.00 | 3.50 | 5.00 |

**Y# 407 20 BAHT**
15.00 g., Copper-Nickel, 32 mm. **Ruler:** Rama IX **Subject:** 60th Anniversary of Reign **Obv:** Head left **Rev:** Royal Crown on display **Edge:** Reeded

| Date | Mintage | F12 | VF20 | XF40 | MS60 | MS63 |
|---|---|---|---|---|---|---|
| BE2549 (2006) | 5,600,000 | — | — | 2.00 | 4.00 | 6.00 |
| BE2549 (2006) | 96,000 | PF63 18.50 | PF65 24.00 | | | |

**Y# 473 20 BAHT**
15.00 g., Copper-Nickel, 32 mm. **Ruler:** Rama IX **Subject:** Royal Artificial Rain, 50th Anniversary **Obv:** Statue of King holding book and pencil **Rev:** Artificial rain wing symbol surrounded by rays and legend **Edge:** Reeded

| Date | Mintage | F12 | VF20 | XF40 | MS60 | MS63 |
|---|---|---|---|---|---|---|
| BE2549 (2006) | 3,000,000 | — | — | 2.00 | 3.50 | 5.00 |

**Y# 474 20 BAHT**
15.00 g., Copper-Nickel, 32 mm. **Ruler:** Rama IX **Subject:** UN Development Program Award **Obv:** Head right **Rev:** Chalice on stand with legends **Edge:** Reeded

| Date | Mintage | F12 | VF20 | XF40 | MS60 | MS63 |
|---|---|---|---|---|---|---|
| BE2549 (2006) | 2,200,000 | — | — | 2.00 | 3.50 | 5.00 |

**Y# 450 20 BAHT**
15.00 g., Copper-Nickel, 32 mm. **Ruler:** Rama IX **Subject:** King's 80th Birthday **Obv:** Bust left **Edge:** Reeded

| Date | Mintage | F12 | VF20 | XF40 | MS60 | MS63 |
|---|---|---|---|---|---|---|
| BE 2550 (2007) | 5,800,000 | — | — | 2.00 | 3.50 | 5.00 |
| BE 2550 (2007) | 95,000 | PF63 15.00 | PF65 18.00 | | | |

**Y# 453 20 BAHT**
15.00 g., Copper-Nickel **Ruler:** Rama IX **Subject:** Queen's 75th Birthday **Obv:** Bust left **Edge:** Reeded **Shape:** 32

| Date | Mintage | F12 | VF20 | XF40 | MS60 | MS63 |
|---|---|---|---|---|---|---|
| BE 2550 (2007) | 600,000 | — | — | 2.00 | 3.50 | 5.00 |
| BE 2550 (2007) | 12,000 | PF63 18.00 | PF65 24.00 | | | |

**Y# 475 20 BAHT**
15.00 g., Copper-Nickel, 32 mm. **Ruler:** Rama IX **Subject:** Princess Galyana Vadhana, 84th birthday **Obv:** Head left **Edge:** Reeded

| Date | Mintage | F12 | VF20 | XF40 | MS60 | MS63 |
|---|---|---|---|---|---|---|
| BE2550 (2007) | 700,000 | — | — | 2.00 | 3.50 | 5.00 |
| BE2550 (2007) | 8,400 | PF63 18.00 | PF65 24.00 | | | |

**Y# 476 20 BAHT**
15.00 g., Copper-Nickel, 32 mm. **Ruler:** Rama IX **Subject:** Father of Thai heritage conservation **Obv:** Head left **Edge:** Reeded **Note:** Minted and released in 2008.

| Date | Mintage | F12 | VF20 | XF40 | MS60 | MS63 |
|---|---|---|---|---|---|---|
| BE2550 (2007) | 500,000 | — | — | 2.00 | 3.50 | 5.00 |

**Y# 464 20 BAHT**
15.00 g., Copper-Nickel, 32 mm. **Ruler:** Rama IX **Subject:** Princess Mother, 9th Cycle (108th Anniversary of Birth) **Obv:** Portrait facing left **Rev:** Emblem of Princess Mother Srinakarindra **Edge:** Reeded

| Date | Mintage | F12 | VF20 | XF40 | MS60 | MS63 |
|---|---|---|---|---|---|---|
| BE2551 (2008) | 450,000 | — | — | 2.00 | 3.50 | 5.00 |
| BE2551 (2008) | 5,500 | PF63 20.00 | PF65 25.00 | | | |

**Y# 470 20 BAHT**
15.00 g., Copper-Nickel, 32 mm. **Ruler:** Rama IX **Subject:** King Jessadabodindra

| Date | Mintage | F12 | VF20 | XF40 | MS60 | MS63 |
|---|---|---|---|---|---|---|
| RS2551 | — | — | — | — | 3.50 | 5.00 |

**Y# 477 20 BAHT**
15.00 g., Copper-Nickel, 32 mm. **Ruler:** Rama IX **Subject:** WIPO Award **Obv:** Head left **Rev:** Award medal and legend **Edge:** Reeded **Note:** Minted and released in 2010

| Date | Mintage | F12 | VF20 | XF40 | MS60 | MS63 |
|---|---|---|---|---|---|---|
| BE2551 (2008) | 500,000 | — | — | 2.00 | 3.50 | 5.00 |

**Y# 495 20 BAHT**
15.00 g., Copper-Nickel, 32 mm. **Ruler:** Rama IX **Subject:** King Rama I, Father of Thai Trade **Obv:** Bust facing front and inscription **Rev:** Symbol, inscription, value and date **Edge:** Reeded **Note:** Minted and issued in BE2553

| Date | Mintage | F12 | VF20 | XF40 | MS60 | MS63 |
|---|---|---|---|---|---|---|
| BE2553 (2008) | 500,000 | — | — | — | 3.50 | 4.00 |

**Y# 514 20 BAHT**
15.00 g., Copper-Nickel, 32 mm. **Ruler:** Rama IX **Subject:** Princess Bejaratana, 84th Birthday

| Date | Mintage | F12 | VF20 | XF40 | MS60 | MS63 |
|---|---|---|---|---|---|---|
| RS2552 | 400,000 | — | — | — | 5.00 | — |

**Y# 499 20 BAHT**
15.00 g., Copper-Nickel, 32 mm. **Ruler:** Rama IX **Subject:** 100th Anniversary of Indra College **Obv:** Conjoined busts facing left **Rev:** Symbol, inscription, value and date **Edge:** Reeded **Note:** Minted and issued in BE2553

| Date | Mintage | F12 | VF20 | XF40 | MS60 | MS63 |
|---|---|---|---|---|---|---|
| BE2553 (2010) | 500,000 | — | — | — | 3.50 | 4.00 |

**Y# 506 20 BAHT**
15.00 g., Copper-Nickel, 32 mm. **Ruler:** Rama IX **Subject:** Princess Bejaratana, 84th Birthday **Edge:** Reeded

| Date | Mintage | F12 | VF20 | XF40 | MS60 | MS63 |
|---|---|---|---|---|---|---|
| RS2553 (2010) | — | — | — | — | 3.50 | 5.00 |

**Y# 520 20 BAHT**
15.00 g., Copper-Nickel, 32 mm. **Ruler:** Rama IX **Subject:** Vajiravudh College, 100th Anniversary

| Date | Mintage | F12 | VF20 | XF40 | MS60 | MS63 |
|---|---|---|---|---|---|---|
| RS2553 | 500,000 | — | — | — | 5.00 | 6.00 |

**Y# 511 20 BAHT**
15.00 g., Copper-Nickel, 32 mm. **Ruler:** Rama IX **Subject:** 150th Anniversary of the birth of Prince Ditsawarakuman

| Date | Mintage | F12 | VF20 | XF40 | MS60 | MS63 |
|---|---|---|---|---|---|---|
| 2012 | Est. 1000000 | — | — | — | — | — |

**Y# 512 20 BAHT**
15.00 g., Copper-Nickel, 32 mm. **Ruler:** Rama IX **Subject:** Queen Sirikit 80th Birthday Anniversary

| Date | Mintage | F12 | VF20 | XF40 | MS60 | MS63 |
|---|---|---|---|---|---|---|
| 2012 | 1,500,000 | — | — | — | — | — |

**Y# 513 20 BAHT**
Silver, 32 mm. **Ruler:** Rama IX **Subject:** Department of Alternative Energy 60th Anniversary

| Date | Mintage | F12 | VF20 | XF40 | MS60 | MS63 |
|---|---|---|---|---|---|---|
| 2012 | — | — | — | — | — | — |
| 2012 Proof | — | — | — | — | — | — |

**Y# 524 20 BAHT**
15.00 g., Copper-Nickel, 32 mm. **Ruler:** Rama IX **Subject:** Prince Damrong Rajanubhab, 150th Anniversary of Birth

| Date | Mintage | F12 | VF20 | XF40 | MS60 | MS63 |
|---|---|---|---|---|---|---|
| RS2555 | 1,000,000 | — | — | — | 6.00 | 7.50 |

**Y# 404 50 BAHT**
21.00 g., Copper-Nickel, 36 mm. **Ruler:** Rama IX **Subject:** Air Force 50th Anniversary May 7 **Obv:** Uniformed bust facing **Rev:** Crowned wings within 3/4 wreath **Edge:** Reeded

| Date | Mintage | F12 | VF20 | XF40 | MS60 | MS63 |
|---|---|---|---|---|---|---|
| BE2546 (2003) | 250,000 | — | — | 4.00 | 12.50 | 15.00 |

**Y# 478 50 BAHT**
21.00 g., Copper-Nickel, 36 mm. **Ruler:** Rama IX **Subject:** National Intelligence Agency, 50th Anniversary **Obv:** Head right **Rev:** Emblem of the National Intelligence Agency **Edge:** Reeded **Note:** Minted and released in 2003.

| Date | Mintage | F12 | VF20 | XF40 | MS60 | MS63 |
|---|---|---|---|---|---|---|
| BE2547 (2004) | 200,000 | — | — | 3.50 | 4.50 | 6.00 |

**Y# 479 50 BAHT**
21.00 g., Copper-Nickel, 36 mm. **Ruler:** Rama IX **Subject:** Technological Research **Obv:** Child's head right **Rev:** Small chicken at left, legends **Edge:** Reeded

| Date | Mintage | F12 | VF20 | XF40 | MS60 | MS63 |
|---|---|---|---|---|---|---|
| BE2549 (2006) | 450,000 | — | — | 3.50 | 4.50 | 6.00 |

**Y# 480 50 BAHT**
21.00 g., Copper-Nickel, 36 mm. **Ruler:** Rama IX **Subject:** Naval Academy, 100th Anniversary **Obv:** Conjoined heads left **Rev:** Symbol, inscriptions, value and date **Edge:** Reeded

| Date | Mintage | F12 | VF20 | XF40 | MS60 | MS63 |
|---|---|---|---|---|---|---|
| BE2549 (2006) | 200,000 | — | — | 3.50 | 4.50 | 6.00 |

**Y# 493 50 BAHT**
Copper-Nickel, 36 mm. **Ruler:** Rama IX **Obv:** Head of infant facing right **Rev:** Design including chick, inscription, value and date **Edge:** Reeded

| Date | Mintage | F12 | VF20 | XF40 | MS60 | MS63 |
|---|---|---|---|---|---|---|
| BE2549 (2006) | 450,000 | — | — | — | 4.50 | 6.00 |

**Y# 500 50 BAHT**
21.00 g., Copper-Nickel, 36 mm. **Ruler:** Rama IX **Subject:** 150th Anniversary of Thai Mint **Obv:** Conjoined busts facing 1/2 right and inscription **Rev:** Complex design, inscription, value and date **Edge:** Reeded

| Date | Mintage | F12 | VF20 | XF40 | MS60 | MS63 |
|---|---|---|---|---|---|---|
| BE2553 (2010) | 150,000 | — | — | — | 4.50 | 6.00 |

**Y# 517 50 BAHT**
21.00 g., Copper-Nickel, 36 mm. **Ruler:** Rama IX **Subject:** Royal Thai Mint, 150th Annviersary

| Date | Mintage | F12 | VF20 | XF40 | MS60 | MS63 |
|---|---|---|---|---|---|---|
| RS2553 | — | — | — | — | 6.00 | 7.50 |

**Y# 501 50 BAHT**
21.00 g., Copper-Nickel, 36 mm. **Ruler:** Rama IX **Subject:** King's Seventh Cycle Ceremony **Obv:** Head of King facing 1/2 left **Rev:** Symbol, inscription, value and date **Edge:** Reeded

| Date | Mintage | F12 | VF20 | XF40 | MS60 | MS63 |
|---|---|---|---|---|---|---|
| BE2554 (2011) | Est. 3000000 | — | — | — | 4.50 | 6.00 |

**Y# 509 50 BAHT**
21.00 g., Copper-Nickel, 36 mm. **Ruler:** Rama IX **Obv:** Bust **Rev:** Emblem

| Date | Mintage | F12 | VF20 | XF40 | MS60 | MS63 |
|---|---|---|---|---|---|---|
| 2011 | — | — | — | — | — | — |

**Y# 521 50 BAHT**
21.00 g., Copper-Nickel, 36 mm. **Ruler:** Rama IX **Subject:** King Bhumibol, 84th Birthday

| Date | Mintage | F12 | VF20 | XF40 | MS60 | MS63 |
|---|---|---|---|---|---|---|
| RS2554 | — | — | — | — | 6.00 | 7.50 |

**Y# 389 600 BAHT**
22.00 g., 0.925 Silver 0.6543 oz. ASW, 35 mm. **Ruler:** Rama IX **Subject:** King's 75th Birthday **Obv:** King's portrait **Rev:** Royal crown in radiant oval **Edge:** Reeded

| Date | Mintage | F12 | VF20 | XF40 | MS60 | MS63 |
|---|---|---|---|---|---|---|
| BE2545 (2002) | 14,000 | — | — | 25.00 | 30.00 | 35.00 |
| BE2545 (2002) | 3,000 | PF63 70.00 | PF65 80.00 | | | |

**Y# 481 600 BAHT**
22.00 g., 0.925 Silver 0.6543 oz. ASW, 35 mm. **Ruler:** Rama IX **Subject:** Crown Prince, 50th Birthday **Obv:** Crown Prince bust 1/4 facing left **Rev:** Crowned monogram **Edge:** Reeded

| Date | Mintage | F12 | VF20 | XF40 | MS60 | MS63 |
|---|---|---|---|---|---|---|
| BE2545 (2002) | 5,000 | — | — | 40.00 | 50.00 | 55.00 |
| BE2545 (2002) | 1,000 | PF63 95.00 | PF65 110 | | | |

**Y# 394 600 BAHT**
22.00 g., 0.925 Silver 0.6543 oz. ASW, 35 mm. **Ruler:** Rama IX **Subject:** 80th Birthday of Princess Calgani Vedhana **Obv:** Bust half right **Rev:** Crowned emblem and value **Edge:** Reeded

| Date | Mintage | F12 | VF20 | XF40 | MS60 | MS63 |
|---|---|---|---|---|---|---|
| BE2546 (2003) | 1,000 | PF63 95.00 | PF65 110 | | | |
| BE2546 (2003) | 4,500 | — | — | 35.00 | 45.00 | 50.00 |

**Y# 482 600 BAHT**
22.00 g., 0.925 Silver 0.6543 oz. ASW, 35 mm. **Ruler:** Rama IX **Subject:** Rama V. 150th Anniversary of Birth **Obv:** Rama V bust left **Rev:** Royal Crown **Edge:** Reeded

| Date | Mintage | F12 | VF20 | XF40 | MS60 | MS63 |
|---|---|---|---|---|---|---|
| BE2546 (2003) | 15,000 | — | — | 30.00 | 35.00 | 40.00 |
| BE2546 (2003) | 4,600 | PF63 85.00 | PF65 95.00 | | | |

**Y# 401 600 BAHT**
22.15 g., 0.925 Silver 0.6587 oz. ASW, 35 mm. **Ruler:** Rama IX **Subject:** Queen's 72nd Birthday **Obv:** Crowned monogram **Rev:** Crowned bust of Queen 3/4 right **Edge:** Reeded

| Date | Mintage | F12 | VF20 | XF40 | MS60 | MS63 |
|---|---|---|---|---|---|---|
| BE2547 (2004) | 12,000 | — | — | 30.00 | 35.00 | 40.00 |
| BE2547 (2004) | 3,700 | PF63 85.00 | PF65 95.00 | | | |

**Y# 463 600 BAHT**
22.00 g., 0.925 Silver 0.6543 oz. ASW, 35 mm. **Ruler:** Rama IX **Subject:** King Rama IV, 200th Anniversary of Birth **Obv:** Bust right **Rev:** Horizontal oval **Edge:** Reeded

| Date | Mintage | F12 | VF20 | XF40 | MS60 | MS63 |
|---|---|---|---|---|---|---|
| BE2547 (2004) | 12,000 | — | — | 40.00 | 45.00 | 60.00 |
| BE2547 (2004) | 3,000 | PF63 95.00 | PF65 110 | | | |

**Y# 427 600 BAHT**
22.15 g., 0.925 Silver 0.6587 oz. ASW, 35 mm. **Ruler:** Rama IX **Subject:** Princess Maha Chakri Sirindhorn's 50th Birthday **Obv:** Bust right **Rev:** Oval **Edge:** Reeded

| Date | Mintage | F12 | VF20 | XF40 | MS60 | MS63 |
|---|---|---|---|---|---|---|
| BE2548 (2005) | 15,000 | — | — | 35.00 | 45.00 | 40.00 |
| BE2548 (2005) | 4,000 | PF63 85.00 | PF65 95.00 | | | |

**Y# 467 600 BAHT**
22.15 g., 0.925 Silver 0.6587 oz. ASW, 35 mm. **Ruler:** Rama IX **Subject:** Princess Petcharat, 80th Birthday **Obv:** Bust facing **Rev:** Princess' emblem **Edge:** Reeded

| Date | Mintage | F12 | VF20 | XF40 | MS60 | MS63 |
|---|---|---|---|---|---|---|
| BE2548 (2005) | — | — | — | 40.00 | 55.00 | 60.00 |
| BE2548 (2005) | — | PF63 120 | PF65 135 | | | |

**Y# 484 600 BAHT**
22.00 g., 0.925 Silver 0.6543 oz. ASW, 35 mm. **Ruler:** Rama IX **Subject:** Princess Rattana, 80th birthday **Obv:** Bust facing of Princess **Edge:** Reeded **Note:** Minted and released in 2006.

| Date | Mintage | F12 | VF20 | XF40 | MS60 | MS63 |
|---|---|---|---|---|---|---|
| BE2548 (2005) | 3,500 | — | — | 40.00 | 55.00 | 60.00 |

**Y# 408 600 BAHT**
22.15 g., 0.925 Silver 0.6587 oz. ASW, 35 mm. **Ruler:** Rama IX **Subject:** 60th Anniversary of Reign **Obv:** Rama IX **Rev:** Royal cypher **Edge:** Reeded

| Date | Mintage | F12 | VF20 | XF40 | MS60 | MS63 |
|---|---|---|---|---|---|---|
| BE2549 (2006) | 66,000 | — | — | 30.00 | 35.00 | 40.00 |
| BE2549 (2006) Proof with colored hologram | 16,000 | PF63 90.00 | PF65 100 | | | |

**Y# 485 600 BAHT**
22.00 g., 0.925 Silver 0.6543 oz. ASW **Ruler:** Rama IX **Subject:** Prince Royal Cradle Ceremony **Obv:** Prince's baby head left **Rev:** Four line legend **Edge:** Reeded

| Date | Mintage | F12 | VF20 | XF40 | MS60 | MS63 |
|---|---|---|---|---|---|---|
| BE2549 (2006) | 10,000 | — | — | 40.00 | 45.00 | 50.00 |
| BE2549 (2006) | 3,700 | PF63 85.00 | PF65 95.00 | | | |

**Y# 502 800 BAHT**
22.00 g., 0.925 Silver 0.6543 oz. ASW, 35 mm. **Ruler:** Rama IX **Subject:** King's 84th Birthday **Obv:** Head facing 1/4 left and inscription **Rev:** Symbol, value, date and inscription **Edge:** Reeded

| Date | Mintage | F12 | VF20 | XF40 | MS60 | MS63 |
|---|---|---|---|---|---|---|
| BE2554 (2003) | 100,000 | PF63 55.00 | PF65 60.00 | | | |

**Y# 447 800 BAHT**
22.00 g., 0.990 Silver 0.7002 oz. ASW, 35 mm. **Ruler:** Rama IX **Obv:** Bust left **Rev:** WHO logo and legend

| Date | Mintage | F12 | VF20 | XF40 | MS60 | MS63 |
|---|---|---|---|---|---|---|
| BE2548 | 6,500 | — | — | — | 40.00 | 45.00 |
| BE2548 | Inc. above | PF63 100 | PF65 115 | | | |

**Y# 451 800 BAHT**
22.00 g., 0.990 Silver 0.7002 oz. ASW, 35 mm. **Ruler:** Rama IX **Subject:** King's 80th Birthday **Obv:** Bust left **Edge:** Reeded

| Date | Mintage | F12 | VF20 | XF40 | MS60 | MS63 |
|---|---|---|---|---|---|---|
| BE 2550 (2007) | 80,000 | — | — | — | 35.00 | 40.00 |
| BE 2550 (2007) | 28,000 | PF63 75.00 | PF65 85.00 | | | |

**Y# 454 800 BAHT**
22.00 g., 0.925 Silver 0.6543 oz. ASW, 35 mm. **Ruler:** Rama IX **Subject:** Queen's 75th Birthday **Obv:** Queen's bust left **Rev:** Queen's Royal Seal **Edge:** Reeded

| Date | Mintage | F12 | VF20 | XF40 | MS60 | MS63 |
|---|---|---|---|---|---|---|
| BE 2550 (2007) | 12,000 | — | — | — | 35.00 | 40.00 |
| BE 2550 (2007) | 4,000 | PF63 75.00 | PF65 85.00 | | | |

**Y# 466 800 BAHT**
22.00 g., 0.925 Silver 0.6543 oz. ASW, 35 mm. **Ruler:** Rama IX **Subject:** Princess Galyani Vadhana, 84th Birthday **Obv:** Bust facing right **Rev:** Princess' emblem **Edge:** Reeded

| Date | Mintage | F12 | VF20 | XF40 | MS60 | MS63 |
|---|---|---|---|---|---|---|
| BE2550 (2007) | 11,500 | — | — | — | 35.00 | 40.00 |
| BE2550 (2007) | 1,500 | PF63 95.00 | PF65 110 | | | |

**Y# 465 800 BAHT**
22.00 g., 0.925 Silver 0.6543 oz. ASW, 35 mm. **Ruler:** Rama IX **Subject:** Princess Mother, 9th Cycle (108th Birthday) **Obv:** Bust facing **Rev:** Princess Mother's emblem **Edge:** Reeded

| Date | Mintage | F12 | VF20 | XF40 | MS60 | MS63 |
|---|---|---|---|---|---|---|
| BE2551 (2008) | 11,200 | — | — | — | 35.00 | 40.00 |
| BE2551 (2008) | 1,500 | PF63 95.00 | PF65 110 | | | |

**Y# 468 800 BAHT**
22.00 g., 0.990 Silver 0.7002 oz. ASW, 35 mm. **Ruler:** Rama IX **Subject:** King's WIPO leader award **Obv:** Bust left **Rev:** Award medal and legned **Edge:** Reeded **Note:** Minted and released in 2010.

| Date | Mintage | F12 | VF20 | XF40 | MS60 | MS63 |
|---|---|---|---|---|---|---|
| BE2551 (2008) | 15,000 | PF63 75.00 | PF65 85.00 | | | |

**Y# 515 800 BAHT**
22.00 g., 0.925 Silver 0.6543 oz. ASW, 35 mm. **Ruler:** Rama IX **Subject:** Princess Bejaratana, 84th Birthday

| Date | Mintage | F12 | VF20 | XF40 | MS60 | MS63 |
|---|---|---|---|---|---|---|
| RS2552 | 5,000 | — | — | — | 35.00 | 40.00 |

**Y# 507 800 BAHT**
22.00 g., 0.925 Silver 0.6543 oz. ASW, 35 mm. **Ruler:** Rama IX **Subject:** Princess Bejaratana, 84th Birthday **Edge:** Reeded

| Date | Mintage | F12 | VF20 | XF40 | MS60 | MS63 |
|---|---|---|---|---|---|---|
| BE2553 (2010) | — | — | — | — | 30.00 | 40.00 |

**Y# 522 800 BAHT**
22.00 g., 0.925 Silver 0.6543 oz. ASW, 35 mm. **Ruler:** Rama IX **Subject:** King Bhumibol, 84th Birthday

| Date | Mintage | F12 | VF20 | XF40 | MS60 | MS63 |
|---|---|---|---|---|---|---|
| RS2554 | — | PF63 75.00 | PF65 85.00 | | | |

**Y# 469 900 BAHT**
31.11 g., 0.999 Silver 0.999 oz. ASW, 40.6 mm. **Ruler:** Rama IX **Subject:** UNDP Human Development Lifetime Achievement Award **Obv:** King facing in multicolor applique **Rev:** Award bowl **Edge:** Reeded

| Date | Mintage | F12 | VF20 | XF40 | MS60 | MS63 |
|---|---|---|---|---|---|---|
| BE2549 (2006) | 200,000 | PF63 75.00 | PF65 85.00 | | | |

**Y# 390 7500 BAHT**
15.00 g., 0.900 Gold 0.434 oz. AGW, 26 mm. **Ruler:** Rama IX **Subject:** King's 75th Birthday **Obv:** King's portrait **Rev:** Royal crown in radiant oval **Edge:** Reeded

| Date | Mintage | F12 | VF20 | XF40 | MS60 | MS63 |
|---|---|---|---|---|---|---|
| BE2545(2002) | 6,000 | — | — | — | 800 | 825 |
| BE2545(2002) | 1,200 | PF63 850 | PF65 875 | | | |

**Y# 395 9000 BAHT**
15.00 g., 0.900 Gold 0.434 oz. AGW, 26 mm. **Ruler:** Rama IX **Subject:** 72nd Birthday of Queen **Obv:** Bust half right **Rev:** Crowned emblem and value **Edge:** Reeded

| Date | Mintage | F12 | VF20 | XF40 | MS60 | MS63 |
|---|---|---|---|---|---|---|
| BE2546 (2004) | 6,000 | — | — | — | 800 | 825 |
| BE2546 (2004) | 1,600 | PF63 850 | PF65 875 | | | |

### Y# 490 9000 BAHT

15.00 g., 0.434 Gold 0.2093 oz. AGW, 26 mm. **Ruler:** Rama IX **Subject:** 150th Anniversary of the Birth of Rama V **Obv:** Bust of Rama V facing left and inscription **Rev:** Three symbols, inscription, value and date **Edge:** Reeded

| Date | Mintage | F12 | VF20 | XF40 | MS60 | MS63 |
|---|---|---|---|---|---|---|
| BE2546 (2003) | 5,000 | — | — | — | 800 | 825 |
| BE2546 (2003) | 1,500 | PF63 900 | PF65 925 | | | |

### Y# 491 9000 BAHT

15.00 g., 0.900 Gold 0.434 oz. AGW, 26 mm. **Ruler:** Rama IX **Subject:** Queen Sirikit's 72nd Birthday **Obv:** Bust of Queen facing 1/4 left and inscription **Rev:** Symbol honoring Queen Sirikit, inscription, value and date **Edge:** Reeded

| Date | Mintage | F12 | VF20 | XF40 | MS60 | MS63 |
|---|---|---|---|---|---|---|
| BE2547 (2004) | 6,000 | — | — | — | 800 | 825 |
| BE2547 (2004) | 1,600 | PF63 900 | PF65 925 | | | |

### Y# 492 9000 BAHT

15.00 g., 0.900 Gold 0.434 oz. AGW, 26 mm. **Ruler:** Rama IX **Subject:** 200th Anniversary of the Birth of King Rama IV **Obv:** Bust of King Rama IV facing 3/4 right and inscription **Rev:** Horizontal oval royal seal, inscription, value and date **Edge:** Reeded

| Date | Mintage | F12 | VF20 | XF40 | MS60 | MS63 |
|---|---|---|---|---|---|---|
| BE2547 (2004) | 3,000 | — | — | — | 800 | 825 |
| BE2547 (2004) | 1,000 | PF63 900 | PF65 925 | | | |

### Y# 494 12,000 BAHT

15.00 g., 0.900 Gold 0.434 oz. AGW, 26 mm. **Ruler:** Rama IX **Subject:** 60th Anniversary of Reign **Obv:** Framed head facing 1/4 right **Rev:** Symbol of 60th Anniversary of Reign, value and date **Edge:** Reeded

| Date | Mintage | F12 | VF20 | XF40 | MS60 | MS63 |
|---|---|---|---|---|---|---|
| BE2551 (2008) | 16,000 | — | — | — | 800 | 825 |
| BE2551 (2008) | 9,600 | PF63 900 | PF65 925 | | | |

### Y# 448 16,000 BAHT

15.00 g., 0.900 Gold 0.434 oz. AGW, 26 mm. **Ruler:** Rama IX **Obv:** Bust of Queen Sirikit, right **Rev:** WHO logo and legend **Note:** Minted and issued in BE2550

| Date | Mintage | F12 | VF20 | XF40 | MS60 | MS63 |
|---|---|---|---|---|---|---|
| BE2005 | Est. 3000 | — | — | — | 800 | 825 |
| 2005 | Inc. above | PF63 850 | PF65 875 | | | |

### Y# 452 16,000 BAHT

15.00 g., 0.990 Gold 0.4774 oz. AGW, 26 mm. **Ruler:** Rama IX **Subject:** King's 80th Birthday **Obv:** Bust left **Rev:** Symbols, inscription, value and date **Edge:** Reeded

| Date | Mintage | F12 | VF20 | XF40 | MS60 | MS63 |
|---|---|---|---|---|---|---|
| BE2550 (2007) | 16,800 | — | — | — | 870 | 900 |
| BE2550 (2007) | 12,800 | PF63 925 | PF65 950 | | | |

### Y# 455 16,000 BAHT

15.00 g., 0.900 Gold 0.434 oz. AGW, 26 mm. **Ruler:** Rama IX **Subject:** Queen's 75th Birthday **Obv:** Bust left and inscription **Rev:** Symbol, inscription, value and date **Edge:** Reeded

| Date | Mintage | F12 | VF20 | XF40 | MS60 | MS63 |
|---|---|---|---|---|---|---|
| BE2550 (2007) | 5,000 | — | — | — | 800 | 825 |
| 2550 (2007) | 2,000 | PF63 850 | PF65 875 | | | |

### Y# 489 16,000 BAHT

15.00 g., 0.990 Gold 0.4774 oz. AGW, 26 mm. **Ruler:** Rama IX **Subject:** World Interlectural Propery Organization Award **Obv:** Head left **Rev:** Award Medal and legend **Edge:** Reeded **Note:** Minted and released in 2010.

| Date | Mintage | F12 | VF20 | XF40 | MS60 | MS63 |
|---|---|---|---|---|---|---|
| BE2551 (2008) | 2,000 | PF63 875 | PF65 900 | | | |

### Y# 496 16,000 BAHT

15.00 g., 0.900 Gold 0.434 oz. AGW, 26 mm. **Ruler:** Rama IX **Subject:** 108th Anniversary of the Birth of the Princess Mother **Obv:** Head of Princess Mother facing 1/4 left **Rev:** Symbol, inscription, value and date **Edge:** Reeded

| Date | Mintage | F12 | VF20 | XF40 | MS60 | MS63 |
|---|---|---|---|---|---|---|
| BE2551 (2008) | 400 | PF65 1,000 | | | | |
| BE2551 (2008) | 1,200 | — | — | — | 800 | 825 |

### Y# 503 16,000 BAHT

15.00 g., 0.965 Gold 0.4654 oz. AGW, 26 mm. **Ruler:** Rama IX **Subject:** King's Seventh Cycle Ceremony **Obv:** Head of King facing 1/2 left **Rev:** Synmbol, inscription, value and date **Edge:** Reeded

| Date | Mintage | F12 | VF20 | XF40 | MS60 | MS63 |
|---|---|---|---|---|---|---|
| BE2554 (2011) | Est. 25000 | PF63 1,000 | PF65 1,100 | | | |

### Y# 523 16,000 BAHT

15.00 g., 0.900 Gold 0.434 oz. AGW, 26 mm. **Ruler:** Rama IX **Subject:** King Bhumibol, 84th Birthday

| Date | Mintage | F12 | VF20 | XF40 | MS60 | MS63 |
|---|---|---|---|---|---|---|
| RS2554 | — | PF63 950 | PF65 975 | | | |

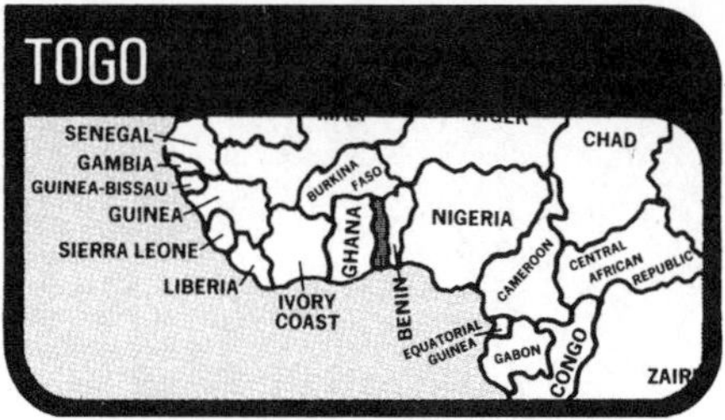


The Togolese Republic (formerly part of German Togoland), situated on the Gulf of Guinea in West Africa between Ghana and Benin, has an area of 21,622 sq. mi. (56,790 sq. km.) and a population of *3.4 million. Capital: Lome. Agriculture and herding, the production of dyewoods, and the mining of phosphates and iron ore are the chief industries. Copra, phosphates and coffee are exported.

**MINT MARK**

(a) - Paris, privy marks only

**MONETARY SYSTEM**

100 Centimes = 1 Franc

## REPUBLIC

## STANDARD COINAGE

100 Centimes = 1 Franc

### KM# 51 100 FRANCS

26.00 g., Copper-Nickel, 38.6 mm. **Rev:** Blue sunbird, prism technology

| Date | Mintage | VF20 | XF40 | MS60 | MS63 | MS65 |
|---|---|---|---|---|---|---|
| 2010 Prooflike | 2,500 | — | — | — | — | 25.00 |

### KM# 52 100 FRANCS

26.00 g., Copper-Nickel, 38.6 mm. **Rev:** Green bird, prism technology

| Date | Mintage | VF20 | XF40 | MS60 | MS63 | MS65 |
|---|---|---|---|---|---|---|
| 2010 Prooflike | 2,500 | — | — | — | — | 25.00 |

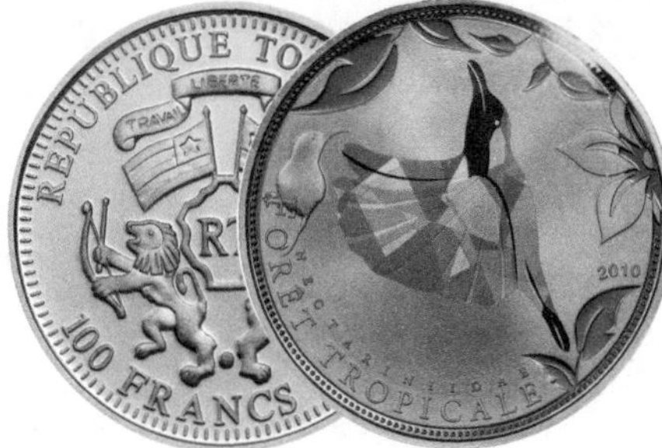


### KM# 53 100 FRANCS

26.00 g., Copper-Nickel, 38.6 mm. **Rev:** Yellow bird, prism technology

| Date | Mintage | VF20 | XF40 | MS60 | MS63 | MS65 |
|---|---|---|---|---|---|---|
| 2010 Prooflike | 2,500 | — | — | — | — | 25.00 |

### KM# 62 100 FRANCS

Silver Plated Base Metal **Rev:** Prism lion standing left

| Date | Mintage | VF20 | XF40 | MS60 | MS63 | MS65 |
|---|---|---|---|---|---|---|
| 2011 | 5,000 | PF65 30.00 | | | | |

### KM# 43 250 FRANCS

5.00 g., 0.999 Silver 0.1606 oz. ASW **Subject:** German President Horst Kohler **Obv:** National arms **Obv. Legend:** REPUBLIQUE TOGOLAISE **Rev:** Gilt figure

| Date | Mintage | VF20 | XF40 | MS60 | MS63 | MS65 |
|---|---|---|---|---|---|---|
| 2004 | — | PF65 15.00 | | | | |

### KM# 29 500 FRANCS

7.05 g., 0.999 Silver 0.2264 oz. ASW, 30 mm. **Obv:** National arms above value **Rev:** Multicolor big cat **Edge:** Plain

| Date | Mintage | VF20 | XF40 | MS60 | MS63 | MS65 |
|---|---|---|---|---|---|---|
| 2001 | — | PF65 25.00 | | | | |

### KM# 41 500 FRANCS

10.00 g., 0.999 Silver 0.3212 oz. ASW **Subject:** XVIII World Football Championship - Germany 2006 **Obv:** National arms **Obv. Legend:** REPUBLIQUE TOGOLAISE **Rev:** Two players, map of Germany in background

| Date | Mintage | VF20 | XF40 | MS60 | MS63 | MS65 |
|---|---|---|---|---|---|---|
| 2001 | — | PF65 22.50 | | | | |

### KM# 60 500 FRANCS

15.00 g., 0.925 Silver 0.4461 oz. ASW, 30 mm. **Obv:** National arms **Rev:** Albrecht Durer portrait

| Date | Mintage | VF20 | XF40 | MS60 | MS63 | MS65 |
|---|---|---|---|---|---|---|
| 2003 | — | PF65 25.00 | | | | |

### KM# 44 500 FRANCS

7.00 g., 0.999 Silver 0.2248 oz. ASW **Subject:** German Chancellor Helmut Schmidt **Obv:** National arms **Obv. Legend:** REPUBLIQUE TOGOLAISE **Rev:** Gilt figure

| Date | Mintage | VF20 | XF40 | MS60 | MS63 | MS65 |
|---|---|---|---|---|---|---|
| ND-2004 | — | PF65 22.50 | | | | |

### KM# 47 500 FRANCS

14.97 g., 0.925 Silver 0.4452 oz. ASW, 30 mm. **Obv:** Arms with supporters **Rev:** Full figures of Johann Wolfgang von Goethe and Friedrich von Schiller on pedestal facing

| Date | Mintage | VF20 | XF40 | MS60 | MS63 | MS65 |
|---|---|---|---|---|---|---|
| 2004 | — | PF65 22.50 | | | | |

### KM# 65 500 FRANCS

15.55 g., 0.925 Silver 0.4624 oz. ASW, 35 mm. **Subject:** Greatest She-Warrior **Rev:** Zenobia standing, color ruins at left

| Date | Mintage | VF20 | XF40 | MS60 | MS63 | MS65 |
|---|---|---|---|---|---|---|
| 2011 | 1,000 | PF65 35.00 | | | | |

**KM# 66 500 FRANCS**
15.50 g., 0.925 Silver 0.461 oz. ASW, 35 mm. **Rev:** St. Olga

| Date | Mintage | VF20 | XF40 | MS60 | MS63 | MS65 |
|---|---|---|---|---|---|---|
| 2011 | Est. 1000 | PF65 35.00 | | | | |

**KM# 17 1000 FRANCS**
14.95 g., 0.999 Silver 0.4802 oz. ASW, 35 mm. **Obv:** National arms **Obv. Legend:** REPUBLIQUE TOGOLAISE **Rev:** German sailing ship **Rev. Legend:** Adler von Lübeck **Edge:** Plain

| Date | Mintage | VF20 | XF40 | MS60 | MS63 | MS65 |
|---|---|---|---|---|---|---|
| 2001 | — | PF65 50.00 | | | | |

**KM# 35 1000 FRANCS**
14.70 g., 0.999 Silver 0.4721 oz. ASW, 36 mm. **Subject:** World Cup Soccer - Bern 1954 **Obv:** National arms **Rev:** Bust facing and tower **Edge:** Plain

| Date | Mintage | VF20 | XF40 | MS60 | MS63 | MS65 |
|---|---|---|---|---|---|---|
| 2001 | — | PF63 40.00 | PF65 50.00 | | | |

**KM# 36 1000 FRANCS**
19.91 g., 0.999 Silver 0.6395 oz. ASW, 38.1 mm. **Subject:** World Cup Soccer - France 1938 **Obv:** National arms **Rev:** Eiffel Tower behind soccer player kicking ball **Edge:** Reeded

| Date | Mintage | VF20 | XF40 | MS60 | MS63 | MS65 |
|---|---|---|---|---|---|---|
| 2001 | — | PF63 40.00 | PF65 50.00 | | | |

**KM# 40 1000 FRANCS**
14.97 g., Silver, 35 mm. **Obv:** National arms **Obv. Legend:** REPUBLIQUE TOGOLAISE **Rev:** Imperial German sailing ship **Rev. Legend:** PREUSSEN **Edge:** Plain

| Date | Mintage | VF20 | XF40 | MS60 | MS63 | MS65 |
|---|---|---|---|---|---|---|
| 2001 | — | PF65 40.00 | | | | |

**KM# 54 1000 FRANCS**
15.00 g., 0.999 Silver 0.4818 oz. ASW, 36 mm. **Rev:** Multicolor Airbus 319 right

| Date | Mintage | VF20 | XF40 | MS60 | MS63 | MS65 |
|---|---|---|---|---|---|---|
| 2001 | — | PF65 35.00 | | | | |

**KM# 37 1000 FRANCS**
19.97 g., 0.999 Silver 0.6414 oz. ASW, 40 mm. **Subject:** World Cup Soccer - USA 1994 **Obv:** National arms **Obv. Legend:** REPUBLIQUE TOGOLAISE **Rev:** Soccer player kicking ball **Rev. Legend:** COUPE MONDIALE DE FOOTBALL **Edge:** Reeded

| Date | Mintage | VF20 | XF40 | MS60 | MS63 | MS65 |
|---|---|---|---|---|---|---|
| 2002 | — | PF63 40.00 | PF65 50.00 | | | |

**KM# 55 1000 FRANCS**
15.00 g., 0.999 Silver 0.4818 oz. ASW, 36 mm. **Rev:** Multicolor Douglas DC-4 and NY skyline

| Date | Mintage | VF20 | XF40 | MS60 | MS63 | MS65 |
|---|---|---|---|---|---|---|
| 2002 | — | PF65 35.00 | | | | |

**KM# 56 1000 FRANCS**
15.00 g., 0.999 Silver 0.4818 oz. ASW **Rev:** Multicolor Caravelle SE-210 before London skyline **Shape:** 36

| Date | Mintage | VF20 | XF40 | MS60 | MS63 | MS65 |
|---|---|---|---|---|---|---|
| 2002 | — | PF65 35.00 | | | | |

**KM# 68 1000 FRANCS**
15.00 g., 0.999 Silver 0.4818 oz. ASW, 35 mm. **Rev:** Doubledecker 170 in color

| Date | Mintage | VF20 | XF40 | MS60 | MS63 | MS65 |
|---|---|---|---|---|---|---|
| 2002 | 5,000 | PF63 50.00 | PF65 60.00 | | | |

**KM# 69 1000 FRANCS**
15.00 g., 0.999 Silver 0.4818 oz. ASW, 35 mm. **Rev:** Douglas DC 2 and Statue of Liberty in color

| Date | Mintage | VF20 | XF40 | MS60 | MS63 | MS65 |
|---|---|---|---|---|---|---|
| 2002 | 5,000 | PF63 50.00 | PF65 60.00 | | | |

**KM# 70 1000 FRANCS**
15.00 g., 0.999 Silver 0.4818 oz. ASW, 35 mm. **Rev:** South Aviation SE 210 Caravelle, London in color

| Date | Mintage | VF20 | XF40 | MS60 | MS63 | MS65 |
|---|---|---|---|---|---|---|
| 2002 | 5,000 | PF63 50.00 | PF65 60.00 | | | |

**KM# 57 1000 FRANCS**
15.00 g., 0.999 Silver 0.4818 oz. ASW, 36 mm. **Rev:** Multicolor Convair 440 at airport

| Date | Mintage | VF20 | XF40 | MS60 | MS63 | MS65 |
|---|---|---|---|---|---|---|
| 2003 | — | PF65 35.00 | | | | |

**KM# 58 1000 FRANCS**
15.00 g., 0.999 Silver 0.4818 oz. ASW, 36 mm. **Rev:** Multicolor McDonnell-Douglas MD-81 right

| Date | Mintage | VF20 | XF40 | MS60 | MS63 | MS65 |
|---|---|---|---|---|---|---|
| 2003 | — | PF65 35.00 | | | | |

**KM# 24 1000 FRANCS**
31.10 g., 0.999 Silver 0.999 oz. ASW, 40 mm. **Obv:** National arms **Obv. Legend:** REPUBLIQUE TOGOLAISE **Rev:** Incuse rendering of statue of Princess Kyninska of Sparta horseback left **Rev. Legend:** SPORTS - ANTIQUES **Edge:** Plain

| Date | Mintage | VF20 | XF40 | MS60 | MS63 | MS65 |
|---|---|---|---|---|---|---|
| 2004 | 2,500 | — | — | — | 65.00 | — |

**KM# 25 1000 FRANCS**
31.10 g., 0.999 Silver 0.999 oz. ASW, 40 mm. **Obv:** National arms **Obv. Legend:** REPUBLIQUE TOGOLAISE **Rev:** Relief rendering of statue of Princess Kyninska of Sparta horseback right **Rev. Legend:** SPORTS - ANTIQUES **Edge:** Plain

| Date | Mintage | VF20 | XF40 | MS60 | MS63 | MS65 |
|---|---|---|---|---|---|---|
| 2004 | 2,500 | — | — | — | 65.00 | — |

**KM# 26 1000 FRANCS**
1.24 g., 0.9999 Gold 0.040 oz. AGW, 13.92 mm. **Obv:** National arms **Obv. Legend:** REPUBLIQUE TOGOLAISE **Rev:** Convex statue of Nike **Edge:** Plain

| Date | Mintage | VF20 | XF40 | MS60 | MS63 | MS65 |
|---|---|---|---|---|---|---|
| 2004 | 5,000 | PF65 80.00 | | | | |

**KM# 27 1000 FRANCS**
1.24 g., 0.9999 Gold 0.040 oz. AGW, 13.92 mm. **Obv:** National arms **Obv. Legend:** REPUBLIQUE TOGOLAISE **Rev:** Concave statue of Nike **Edge:** Plain

| Date | Mintage | VF20 | XF40 | MS60 | MS63 | MS65 |
|---|---|---|---|---|---|---|
| 2004 | 5,000 | PF65 80.00 | | | | |

**KM# 34 1000 FRANCS**
30.92 g., 0.999 Silver 0.9931 oz. ASW, 39 mm. **Obv:** Bust with headdress left within circle **Rev:** Gold plated baboon within circle **Edge:** Reeded **Note:** Date in Chinese numerals.

| Date | Mintage | VF20 | XF40 | MS60 | MS63 | MS65 |
|---|---|---|---|---|---|---|
| 2004 | — | PF65 75.00 | | | | |

**KM# 38 1000 FRANCS**
30.73 g., 0.999 Silver 0.987 oz. ASW, 39 mm. **Subject:** Year of the Monkey **Obv:** Head with headdress 1/4 right within circle **Rev:** Gold plated baboon within circle **Edge:** Reeded **Note:** Note: Date in Chinese numerals.

| Date | Mintage | VF20 | XF40 | MS60 | MS63 | MS65 |
|---|---|---|---|---|---|---|
| 2004 | — | PF65 75.00 | | | | |

**KM# 59 1000 FRANCS**
15.00 g., 0.999 Silver 0.4818 oz. ASW, 36 mm. **Rev:** Multicolor DeHaviland DH-89 biplane

| Date | Mintage | VF20 | XF40 | MS60 | MS63 | MS65 |
|---|---|---|---|---|---|---|
| 2004 | — | PF65 35.00 | | | | |

**KM# 71 1000 FRANCS**
15.00 g., 0.999 Silver 0.4818 oz. ASW, 35 mm. **Rev:** Theodor Heuss, gilt

| Date | Mintage | VF20 | XF40 | MS60 | MS63 | MS65 |
|---|---|---|---|---|---|---|
| 2004 | — | PF63 30.00 | PF65 35.00 | | | |

**KM# 72 1000 FRANCS**
15.00 g., 0.999 Silver 0.4818 oz. ASW, 35 mm. **Rev:** Richard Freiherr von Weizsacker

| Date | Mintage | VF20 | XF40 | MS60 | MS63 | MS65 |
|---|---|---|---|---|---|---|
| 2004 | — | PF63 30.00 | PF65 35.00 | | | |

**KM# 45 1000 FRANCS**
Silver **Subject:** 170th Anniversary German Railroad, Nürnberg - Fürth **Obv:** National arms **Obv. Legend:** REPUBLIQUE TOGOLAISE **Rev:** Early steam locomotive "Adler

| Date | Mintage | VF20 | XF40 | MS60 | MS63 | MS65 |
|---|---|---|---|---|---|---|
| 2005 | — | PF65 55.00 | | | | |

**KM# 73 1000 FRANCS**
15.00 g., 0.999 Silver 0.4818 oz. ASW, 35 mm. **Rev:** Flying "P" liner - Passat

| Date | Mintage | VF20 | XF40 | MS60 | MS63 | MS65 |
|---|---|---|---|---|---|---|
| 2005 | — | PF63 40.00 | PF65 45.00 | | | |

**KM# 74 1000 FRANCS**
1.24 g., 0.9999 Gold 0.0399 oz. AGW, 13.92 mm. **Subject:** Semperoper in Dresden, 20th Anniversary of re-opening

| Date | Mintage | VF20 | XF40 | MS60 | MS63 | MS65 |
|---|---|---|---|---|---|---|
| 2005 | 2,000 | PF65 90.00 | | | | |

**KM# 46 1000 FRANCS**
1.24 g., 0.9999 Gold 0.0399 oz. AGW **Subject:** 250th Anniversary Birth of Wolfgang Amadeus Mozart **Obv:** National arms **Obv. Legend:** REPUBLIQUE TOGOLAISE

| Date | Mintage | VF20 | XF40 | MS60 | MS63 | MS65 |
|---|---|---|---|---|---|---|
| 2006 | — | PF65 85.00 | | | | |

**KM# 48 1000 FRANCS**
25.00 g., 0.925 Silver 0.7435 oz. ASW, 38.6 mm. **Rev:** Blue hummingbird, prism technology

| Date | Mintage | VF20 | XF40 | MS60 | MS63 | MS65 |
|---|---|---|---|---|---|---|
| 2010 | 2,500 | PF65 60.00 | | | | |

**KM# 49 1000 FRANCS**
25.00 g., 0.925 Silver 0.7435 oz. ASW, 38.6 mm. **Rev:** Green hummingbird, prism technology

| Date | Mintage | VF20 | XF40 | MS60 | MS63 | MS65 |
|---|---|---|---|---|---|---|
| 2010 | 2,500 | PF65 65.00 | | | | |

**KM# 50 1000 FRANCS**
25.00 g., 0.925 Silver 0.7435 oz. ASW, 38.6 mm. **Rev:** Prange hummingbird, prism technology

| Date | Mintage | VF20 | XF40 | MS60 | MS63 | MS65 |
|---|---|---|---|---|---|---|
| 2010 | 2,500 | PF65 55.00 | | | | |

**KM# 61 1000 FRANCS**
25.00 g., 0.925 Silver 0.7435 oz. ASW partially plated, 38.61 mm. **Subject:** Year of the Tiger **Obv:** National arms **Rev:** Tiger, gilt

| Date | Mintage | VF20 | XF40 | MS60 | MS63 | MS65 |
|---|---|---|---|---|---|---|
| 2010 | 1,000 | PF65 75.00 | | | | |

**KM# 97 1000 FRANCS**
25.00 g., 0.925 Silver 0.7435 oz. ASW, 38.61 mm. **Subject:** Year of the Tiger **Rev:** Tiger family gilt

| Date | Mintage | VF20 | XF40 | MS60 | MS63 | MS65 |
|---|---|---|---|---|---|---|
| 2010 | 1,000 | PF65 80.00 | | | | |

**KM# 88 1000 FRANCS**
31.10 g., 0.999 Silver 0.9989 oz. ASW, 47x27 mm. **Rev:** Two impalas **Shape:** Rectangle

| Date | Mintage | VF20 | XF40 | MS60 | MS63 | MS65 |
|---|---|---|---|---|---|---|
| 2010 | 250 | PF65 85.00 | | | | |

**KM# 63 1000 FRANCS**
25.00 g., 0.925 Silver 0.7435 oz. ASW **Rev:** Prism Elephant

| Date | Mintage | VF20 | XF40 | MS60 | MS63 | MS65 |
|---|---|---|---|---|---|---|
| 2011 | 2,500 | PF65 65.00 | | | | |

**KM# 64 1000 FRANCS**
25.00 g., 0.925 Silver 0.7435 oz. ASW **Rev:** Prism Zebra

| Date | Mintage | VF20 | XF40 | MS60 | MS63 | MS65 |
|---|---|---|---|---|---|---|
| 2011 | 2,500 | PF65 70.00 | | | | |

**KM# 75 1500 FRANCS**
1.24 g., 0.9999 Gold 0.0399 oz. AGW, 13.92 mm. **Rev:** St. Basil Cathedral in Moscow

| Date | Mintage | VF20 | XF40 | MS60 | MS63 | MS65 |
|---|---|---|---|---|---|---|
| 2005 | 2,000 | PF65 90.00 | | | | |

**KM# 76 1500 FRANCS**
1.24 g., 0.9999 Gold 0.0399 oz. AGW, 13.92 mm. **Rev:** Johann Wolfgang von Goethe

| Date | Mintage | VF20 | XF40 | MS60 | MS63 | MS65 |
|---|---|---|---|---|---|---|
| 2005 | — | PF65 90.00 | | | | |

**KM# 77 1500 FRANCS**
1.24 g., 0.9999 Gold 0.0399 oz. AGW, 13.92 mm. **Rev:** Friedrich von Schiller

| Date | Mintage | VF20 | XF40 | MS60 | MS63 | MS65 |
|---|---|---|---|---|---|---|
| 2005 | — | PF65 90.00 | | | | |

**KM# 78 1500 FRANCS**
1.24 g., 0.9999 Gold 0.0399 oz. AGW, 13.92 mm. **Subject:** Albert Einstein, 50th Anniversary of death

| Date | Mintage | VF20 | XF40 | MS60 | MS63 | MS65 |
|---|---|---|---|---|---|---|
| 2005 | — | PF65 90.00 | | | | |

**KM# 79 1500 FRANCS**
1.24 g., 0.9999 Gold 0.0399 oz. AGW, 13.92 mm. **Rev:** Gotthold Ephraim Lessing

| Date | Mintage | VF20 | XF40 | MS60 | MS63 | MS65 |
|---|---|---|---|---|---|---|
| 2006 | — | PF65 90.00 | | | | |

**KM# 83 1500 FRANCS**
1.00 g., 0.999 Gold 0.0321 oz. AGW, 13.92 mm. **Rev:** Zeus statue

| Date | Mintage | VF20 | XF40 | MS60 | MS63 | MS65 |
|---|---|---|---|---|---|---|
| 2007 | — | PF65 80.00 | | | | |

**KM# 84 1500 FRANCS**
1.00 g., 0.999 Gilt and Multicolored Litho Flan 0.0321 oz., 13.92 mm. **Rev:** Aphrodite statue

| Date | Mintage | VF20 | XF40 | MS60 | MS63 | MS65 |
|---|---|---|---|---|---|---|
| 2007 | — | PF65 80.00 | | | | |

**KM# 85 1500 FRANCS**
1.00 g., 0.999 Gold 0.0321 oz. AGW, 13.92 mm. **Rev:** Dionysus statue

| Date | Mintage | VF20 | XF40 | MS60 | MS63 | MS65 |
|---|---|---|---|---|---|---|
| 2007 | — | PF65 80.00 | | | | |

**KM# 86 1500 FRANCS**
0.50 g., 0.999 Gold 0.0161 oz. AGW, 11 mm. **Rev:** Nefroite between hyrogryphlics

| Date | Mintage | VF20 | XF40 | MS60 | MS63 | MS65 |
|---|---|---|---|---|---|---|
| 2007 | 2,007 | PF63 40.00 | PF65 50.00 | | | |

**KM# 87 1500 FRANCS**
0.50 g., 0.999 Gold 0.0161 oz. AGW, 11 mm. **Subject:** Max Planck, 150th Anniversary of Birth

| Date | Mintage | VF20 | XF40 | MS60 | MS63 | MS65 |
|---|---|---|---|---|---|---|
| 2008 Proof | — | — | — | — | — | 40.00 |

**KM# 93 1500 FRANCS**
0.52 g., 0.999 Gold 0.0167 oz. AGW, 11 mm. **Obv:** National arms **Rev:** Max Planck

| Date | Mintage | VF20 | XF40 | MS60 | MS63 | MS65 |
|---|---|---|---|---|---|---|
| 2008 | 10,000 | PF65 100 | | | | |

**KM# 89 1500 FRANCS**
0.62 g., 0.9999 Gold 0.0199 oz. AGW, 11 mm. **Rev:** Two impalas

| Date | Mintage | VF20 | XF40 | MS60 | MS63 | MS65 |
|---|---|---|---|---|---|---|
| 2010 | 250 | PF65 125 | | | | |

**KM# 94 1500 FRANCS**
62.20 g., 0.999 Silver 1.9978 oz. ASW, 50 mm. **Subject:** Year of the Dragon **Rev:** Dragon with amber insert

| Date | Mintage | VF20 | XF40 | MS60 | MS63 | MS65 |
|---|---|---|---|---|---|---|
| 2012 Antique patina | 999 | — | — | — | 500 | — |

**KM# 95 1500 FRANCS**
62.20 g., 0.999 Silver 1.9978 oz. ASW, 50 mm. **Rev:** Bison head facing with crystal inserts

| Date | Mintage | VF20 | XF40 | MS60 | MS63 | MS65 |
|---|---|---|---|---|---|---|
| 2012 | 999 | PF65 300 | | | | |

**KM# 96 1500 FRANCS**
Silver ASW **Subject:** Year of the Dragon **Rev:** Dragon and egg with young dragon

| Date | Mintage | VF20 | XF40 | MS60 | MS63 | MS65 |
|---|---|---|---|---|---|---|
| 2012 | — | PF65 300 | | | | |

**KM# 39 2000 FRANCS**
62.24 g., 0.9999 Silver 2.0009 oz. ASW, 50 mm. **Subject:** Year of the Monkey **Obv:** Gold plated world globe **Rev:** Gold plated center with radiant holographic monkey within circle **Edge:** Reeded and lettered sections **Edge Lettering:** PAN ASIA BANK TAIWAN in English and Chinese **Note:** Date in Chinese numerals.

| Date | Mintage | VF20 | XF40 | MS60 | MS63 | MS65 |
|---|---|---|---|---|---|---|
| 2004 | — | PF65 125 | | | | |

**KM# 90 2000 FRANCS**
3.11 g., 0.9999 Gold 0.100 oz. AGW, 18 mm. **Rev:** Two impalas

| Date | Mintage | VF20 | XF40 | MS60 | MS63 | MS65 |
|---|---|---|---|---|---|---|
| 2010 | 250 | PF65 125 | | | | |

**KM# 92 5000 FRANCS**
15.55 g., 0.9999 Gold 0.4999 oz. AGW, 30 mm. **Rev:** Two impalas

| Date | Mintage | VF20 | XF40 | MS60 | MS63 | MS65 |
|---|---|---|---|---|---|---|
| 2010 | 250 | PF65 750 | | | | |

**KM# 91 2000 FRANCS**
7.78 g., 0.9999 Gold 0.2501 oz. AGW, 25 mm. **Rev:** Two impalas

| Date | Mintage | VF20 | XF40 | MS60 | MS63 | MS65 |
|---|---|---|---|---|---|---|
| 2010 Proof | 250 | — | — | — | — | 400 |

**KM# 80 1500 FRANCS**
1.24 g., 0.9999 Gold 0.0399 oz. AGW, 13.92 mm. **Subject:** Wilhelm Busch, 175th Anniversary of birth

| Date | Mintage | VF20 | XF40 | MS60 | MS63 | MS65 |
|---|---|---|---|---|---|---|
| 2007 | Est. 15000 | PF65 90.00 | | | | |

# TOKELAU

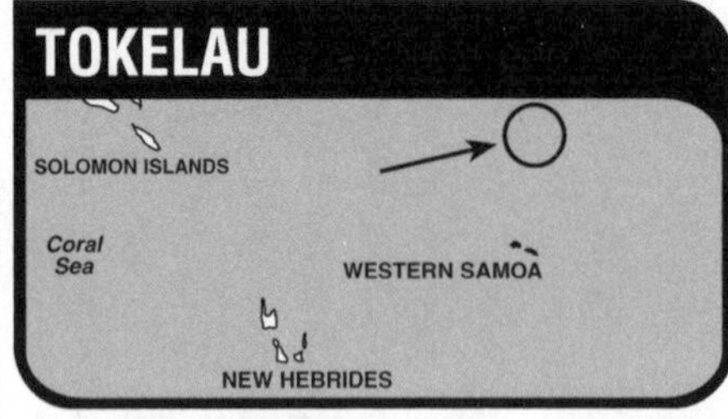


Tokelau or Union Islands, a New Zealand Territory located in the South Pacific 2,100 miles (3,379 km.) northeast of New Zealand and 300 miles (483 km.) north of Samoa, has an area of 4 sq. mi. (10 sq. km.) and a population of *2,000. Geographically, the group consists of four atolls - Atafu, Nukunono, Fakaofo and Swains – but the last belongs to American Samoa (and the United States claims the other three). The people are of Polynesian origin; Samoan is the official language. The New Zealand Minister for Foreign Affairs governs the islands; councils of family elders handle local government at the village level. The chief settlement is Fenuafala, on Fakaofo. It is connected by wireless technology with the offices of the New Zealand Administrative Center, located at Apia, Samoa. Subsistence farming and the production of copra for export are the main occupations. Revenue is also derived from the sale of postage stamps and, since 1978, coins.

Tokelau Islands issued its first coin in 1978, a "$1 Tahi Tala," Tokelauan for "One Dollar."

**RULER**
British

**MINT MARK**
PM - Pobjoy

## NEW ZEALAND TERRITORY
### STANDARD COINAGE

**KM# 54 TALA**
28.28 g., 0.925 Silver 0.841 oz. ASW **Ruler:** Elizabeth II **Subject:** Man from Snowy River **Rev:** Horseman in color

| Date | Mintage | VF20 | XF40 | MS60 | MS63 | MS65 |
|---|---|---|---|---|---|---|
| 2013 | — | PF65 40.00 | | | | |

**KM# 55 TALA**
28.28 g., 0.925 Silver 0.841 oz. ASW, 38.61 mm. **Ruler:** Elizabeth II **Subject:** Australia's First Fleet - Life at Sea **Rev:** Sailors on deck in color

| Date | Mintage | VF20 | XF40 | MS60 | MS63 | MS65 |
|---|---|---|---|---|---|---|
| 2013 | — | PF65 40.00 | | | | |

**KM# 56 TALA**
28.28 g., 0.925 Silver 0.841 oz. ASW, 38.61 mm. **Ruler:** Elizabeth II **Subject:** Australia's First Fleet - The Journey **Rev:** Ships at sea, route map

| Date | Mintage | VF20 | XF40 | MS60 | MS63 | MS65 |
|---|---|---|---|---|---|---|
| 2013 | — | PF65 40.00 | | | | |

**KM# 51 DOLLAR**
31.11 g., 0.999 Silver 0.999 oz. ASW, 38.61 mm. **Ruler:** Elizabeth II **Obv:** Head with tiara right within patterned border **Rev:** Asian tiger head right

| Date | Mintage | VF20 | XF40 | MS60 | MS63 | MS65 |
|---|---|---|---|---|---|---|
| 2013 Antique patina | 2,000 | — | — | — | 40.00 | — |

**KM# 30 5 TALA**
31.10 g., 0.999 Silver 0.9989 oz. ASW with Mother-of-Pearl inlay, 40 mm. **Series:** Save the Whales **Obv:** Crowned head right **Obv. Legend:** TOKELAU **Rev:** Fin Whale on mother of pearl insert **Edge:** Plain

| Date | Mintage | VF20 | XF40 | MS60 | MS63 | MS65 |
|---|---|---|---|---|---|---|
| 2002 | 2,000 | PF65 95.00 | | | | |

**KM# 32 5 TALA**
31.10 g., 0.999 Silver 0.9989 oz. ASW, 40 mm. **Ruler:** Elizabeth II **Obv:** Elizabeth II **Rev:** Capt. Smith and ship General Jackson **Edge:** Reeded

| Date | Mintage | VF20 | XF40 | MS60 | MS63 | MS65 |
|---|---|---|---|---|---|---|
| 2003 | — | PF63 45.00 | PF65 48.00 | | | |

**KM# 47 5 TALA**
Silver, 38.6 mm. **Ruler:** Elizabeth II **Subject:** Endangered Wildlife **Obv:** Head crowned right **Rev:** Pacific Boa around atree branch **Edge:** Reeded

| Date | Mintage | VF20 | XF40 | MS60 | MS63 | MS65 |
|---|---|---|---|---|---|---|
| 2003 | — | PF65 50.00 | | | | |

### KM# 48 5 TALA

Silver, 38.6 mm. **Ruler:** Elizabeth II **Subject:** Olympics, 2004 **Obv:** Head crowned right **Rev:** Runner, swimmer and bicyalist **Edge:** Reeded

| Date | Mintage | VF20 | XF40 | MS60 | MS63 | MS65 |
|---|---|---|---|---|---|---|
| 2004 | — | PF63 47.00 | PF65 50.00 | | | |

### KM# 33 5 TALA

28.65 g., Silver, 38.60 mm. **Ruler:** Elizabeth II **Obv:** Crowned head right **Obv. Legend:** TOKELAU **Rev:** Sailing ship **Rev. Legend:** CUTTY SARK 1869 **Edge:** Reeded

| Date | Mintage | VF20 | XF40 | MS60 | MS63 | MS65 |
|---|---|---|---|---|---|---|
| 2005 | — | PF63 42.00 | PF65 45.00 | | | |

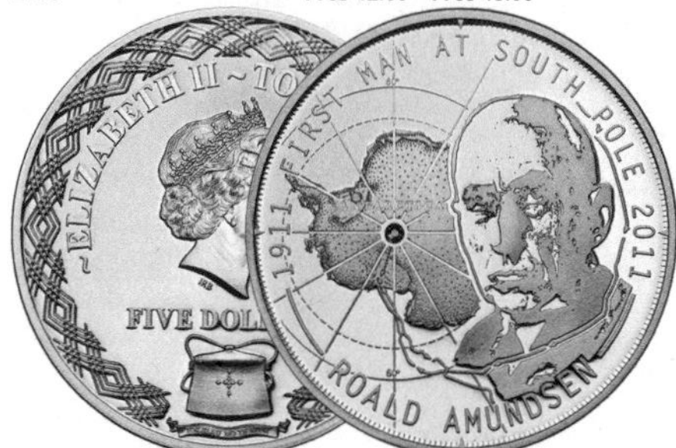


### KM# 49 5 TALA

25.00 g., 0.925 Silver 0.7435 oz. ASW, 38.61 mm. **Ruler:** Elizabeth II **Rev:** Roald Amundsen and jewel inset at South Pole

| Date | Mintage | VF20 | XF40 | MS60 | MS63 | MS65 |
|---|---|---|---|---|---|---|
| 2011 | 2,500 | PF65 65.00 | | | | |

### KM# 53 5 TALA

0.50 g., 0.999 Gold 0.0161 oz. AGW, 13.92 mm. **Ruler:** Elizabeth II **Subject:** Explorers of Australia - William Dampier

| Date | Mintage | VF20 | XF40 | MS60 | MS63 | MS65 |
|---|---|---|---|---|---|---|
| 2013 | — | PF63 225 | | | | |

### KM# 50 5 DOLLARS

Silver, 38.6 mm. **Ruler:** Elizabeth II **Subject:** Dragonfly with crystal eye

| Date | Mintage | VF20 | XF40 | MS60 | MS63 | MS65 |
|---|---|---|---|---|---|---|
| 2012 | — | PF65 75.00 | | | | |

### KM# 52 5 DOLLARS

155.55 g., 0.999 Silver 4.996 oz. ASW, 60.15 mm. **Ruler:** Elizabeth II **Obv:** Head with tiara right within patterned border **Rev:** Asian tiger head right

| Date | Mintage | VF20 | XF40 | MS60 | MS63 | MS65 |
|---|---|---|---|---|---|---|
| 2013 Antique patina | 500 | — | — | — | 250 | — |

### KM# 46 10 TALA

1.24 g., 0.999 Gold 0.0398 oz. AGW, 13.92 mm. **Ruler:** Elizabeth II **Obv:** Crowned head right **Obv. Legend:** TOKELAU **Rev:** Two whales **Rev. Legend:** ENDANGERED WILDLIFE **Edge:** Reeded

| Date | Mintage | VF20 | XF40 | MS60 | MS63 | MS65 |
|---|---|---|---|---|---|---|
| 2003 | — | PF65 85.00 | | | | |

# TONGA

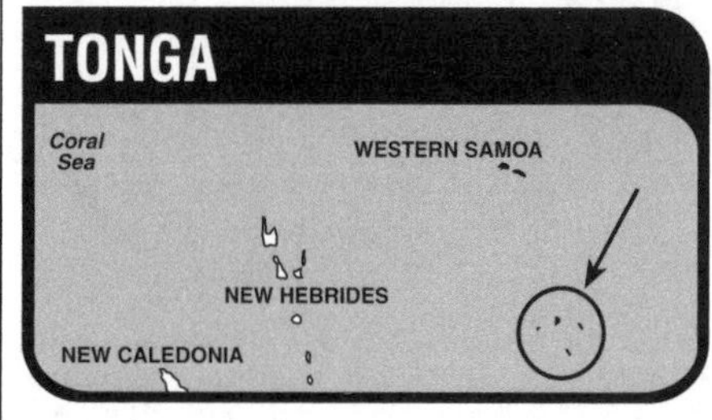


The Kingdom of Tonga (or Friendly Islands) is an archipelago situated in the southern Pacific Ocean south of Western Samoa and east of Fiji comprised of 150 islands. Tonga has an area of 270 sq. mi. (748 sq. km.) and a population of *100,000. Capital: Nuku'alofa. Primarily agricultural, the kingdom exports bananas and copra.

The monarchy is a member of the Commonwealth of Nations. King Siosa Tupou V is Head of State and Government.

**RULER**

King Taufa'ahau IV, 1965-2006
King Siosa Tupou V, 2006-2012

## KINGDOM

## DECIMAL COINAGE

100 Senti = 1 Pa'anga; 100 Pa'anga = 1 Hau

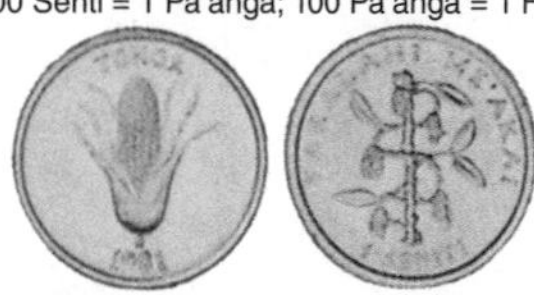

### KM# 66 SENITI

1.80 g., Bronze, 16.51 mm. **Ruler:** Taufa'ahau Tupou IV **Series:** World Food Day **Obv:** Ear of corn **Rev:** Vanilla plant **Edge:** Plain

| Date | Mintage | VF20 | XF40 | MS60 | MS63 | MS65 |
|---|---|---|---|---|---|---|
| 2005 | — | — | 0.10 | 0.20 | 0.35 | 0.75 |
| 2006 | — | — | 0.10 | 0.20 | 0.35 | 0.75 |

### KM# 66a SENITI

Copper Plated Steel, 17.5 mm. **Ruler:** Taufa'ahau Tupou IV **Series:** World Food Day **Obv:** Ear of corn **Obv. Legend:** TONGA **Rev:** Vanilla plant **Rev. Legend:** FAKALAHI ME'AKAI **Edge:** Plain

| Date | Mintage | VF20 | XF40 | MS60 | MS63 | MS65 |
|---|---|---|---|---|---|---|
| 2002 | — | — | 0.10 | 0.20 | 0.35 | 0.75 |
| 2003 | — | — | 0.10 | 0.20 | 0.35 | 0.75 |
| 2004 | — | — | 0.10 | 0.20 | 0.35 | 0.75 |

### KM# 67a 2 SENITI

Copper Plated Steel, 21 mm. **Ruler:** Taufa'ahau Tupou IV **Series:** World Food Day **Obv:** Taro plants **Obv. Legend:** TONGA **Rev:** Paper doll cutouts form design in center circle of sprays **Rev. Legend:** PLANNED FAMILIES • FOOD FOR ALL

| Date | Mintage | VF20 | XF40 | MS60 | MS63 | MS65 |
|---|---|---|---|---|---|---|
| 2002 | — | — | 0.15 | 0.30 | 0.65 | 1.25 |
| 2003 | — | — | 0.15 | 0.30 | 0.65 | 1.25 |
| 2004 | — | — | 0.15 | 0.30 | 0.65 | 1.25 |

### KM# 68 5 SENITI

2.80 g., Copper-Nickel, 19.5 mm. **Ruler:** Taufa'ahau Tupou IV **Series:** World Food Day **Obv:** Hen with chicks **Rev:** Coconuts above sprig **Edge:** Reeded

| Date | Mintage | VF20 | XF40 | MS60 | MS63 | MS65 |
|---|---|---|---|---|---|---|
| 2005 | — | 0.10 | 0.25 | 0.35 | 0.75 | 1.25 |

### KM# 68a 5 SENITI

2.79 g., Nickel Plated Steel, 19.39 mm. **Ruler:** Taufa'ahau Tupou IV **Series:** World Food Day **Obv:** Hen with chicks **Obv. Legend:** TONGA **Rev:** Coconuts **Rev. Legend:** FAKALAHI ME'AKAI **Edge:** Reeded

| Date | Mintage | VF20 | XF40 | MS60 | MS63 | MS65 |
|---|---|---|---|---|---|---|
| 2002 | — | — | 0.25 | 0.35 | 0.75 | 1.35 |
| 2003 | — | — | 0.25 | 0.35 | 0.75 | 1.35 |
| 2004 | — | — | 0.25 | 0.35 | 0.75 | 1.35 |
| 2005 | — | — | 0.25 | 0.35 | 0.75 | 1.35 |

### KM# 69a 10 SENITI

Nickel Plated Steel, 23.5 mm. **Ruler:** Taufa'ahau Tupou IV **Series:** World Food Day **Obv:** Uniformed bust facing **Obv. Legend:** F • A • O - TONGA **Rev:** Banana tree **Rev. Legend:** FAKALAHI ME'AKAI

| Date | Mintage | VF20 | XF40 | MS60 | MS63 | MS65 |
|---|---|---|---|---|---|---|
| 2002 | — | — | 0.30 | 0.50 | 1.00 | 1.75 |
| 2003 | — | — | 0.30 | 0.50 | 1.00 | 1.75 |
| 2004 | — | — | 0.30 | 0.50 | 1.00 | 1.75 |
| 2005 | — | — | 0.30 | 0.50 | 1.00 | 1.75 |

### KM# 70.1 20 SENITI

11.30 g., Nickel Plated Steel, 28.5 mm. **Ruler:** Taufa'ahau Tupou IV **Subject:** FAO - World Food Day **Obv:** Uniformed bust facing **Rev:** Yams

| Date | Mintage | VF20 | XF40 | MS60 | MS63 | MS65 |
|---|---|---|---|---|---|---|
| 2002 | — | 0.25 | 0.50 | 0.65 | 1.25 | 2.00 |
| 2003 | — | 0.25 | 0.50 | 0.65 | 1.25 | 2.00 |
| 2004 | — | 0.25 | 0.50 | 0.65 | 1.25 | 2.00 |

### KM# 70a 50 SENITI

14.60 g., Nickel Plated Steel, 32.5 mm. **Ruler:** Taufa'ahau Tupou IV **Subject:** FAO - World Food Day **Obv:** Uniformed bust facing **Rev:** Tomato plants **Shape:** 12-sided

| Date | Mintage | VF20 | XF40 | MS60 | MS63 | MS65 |
|---|---|---|---|---|---|---|
| 2002 | — | — | 0.45 | 0.75 | 1.50 | 2.50 |
| 2003 | — | — | 0.45 | 0.75 | 1.50 | 2.50 |
| 2004 | — | — | 0.45 | 0.75 | 1.50 | 2.50 |

### KM# 212 PA'ANGA

31.47 g., 0.925 Silver 0.9359 oz. ASW, 38.61 mm. **Ruler:** Siaosi Tupou V **Subject:** History of Seafaring - HMS Descubierta

| Date | Mintage | VF20 | XF40 | MS60 | MS63 | MS65 |
|---|---|---|---|---|---|---|
| 2001 | Est. 5000 | PF65 55.00 | | | | |

### KM# 178 PA'ANGA

31.10 g., 0.999 Silver 0.9989 oz. ASW with Mother-of-Pearl inlay, 40 mm. **Ruler:** Taufa'ahau Tupou IV **Series:** Save the Whales **Obv:** Crown within wreath above national arms within circle **Obv. Legend:** KINGDOM OF TONGA **Rev:** Right Whale on mother of pearl insert **Edge:** Plain

| Date | Mintage | VF20 | XF40 | MS60 | MS63 | MS65 |
|---|---|---|---|---|---|---|
| 2002 | 2,000 | PF65 95.00 | | | | |

### KM# 213 PA'ANGA

31.00 g., 0.925 Silver 0.9219 oz. ASW, 40 mm. **Ruler:** Siaosi Tupou V **Subject:** Farewell to the Luxembourg Franc

| Date | Mintage | VF20 | XF40 | MS60 | MS63 | MS65 |
|---|---|---|---|---|---|---|
| 2002 | Est. 2001 | PF65 80.00 | | | | |

### KM# 182 PA'ANGA

31.47 g., 0.925 Silver 0.9359 oz. ASW **Ruler:** Taufa'ahau Tupou IV **Subject:** 2004 Olympics **Obv:** National arms **Rev:** Kayak crew seen from above

| Date | Mintage | VF20 | XF40 | MS60 | MS63 | MS65 |
|---|---|---|---|---|---|---|
| 2003 | — | PF65 65.00 | | | | |

### KM# 215 PA'ANGA

31.47 g., 0.925 Silver 0.9359 oz. ASW, 38.61 mm. **Ruler:** Siaosi Tupou V **Subject:** History of Seafaring - HMS Adventure & James Cook

| Date | Mintage | VF20 | XF40 | MS60 | MS63 | MS65 |
|---|---|---|---|---|---|---|
| 2003 | — | PF65 55.00 | | | | |

### KM# 217 PA'ANGA

31.47 g., 0.925 Silver 0.9359 oz. ASW, 38.61 mm. **Ruler:** Siaosi Tupou V **Subject:** 2006 Soccer World Cup, Germany

| Date | Mintage | VF20 | XF40 | MS60 | MS63 | MS65 |
|---|---|---|---|---|---|---|
| 2004 | Est. 50000 | PF63 25.00 | PF65 35.00 | | | |

**KM# 218 PA'ANGA**
31.47 g., 0.925 Silver 0.9359 oz. ASW, 38.61 mm. **Ruler:** Siaosi Tupou V **Subject:** History of Seafaring - HMS Beagle & Charles Darwin

| Date | Mintage | VF20 | XF40 | MS60 | MS63 | MS65 |
|---|---|---|---|---|---|---|
| 2005 | — | PF65 55.00 | | | | |

**KM# 219 PA'ANGA**
28.28 g., 0.925 Silver 0.841 oz. ASW, 38.61 mm. **Ruler:** Siaosi Tupou V **Subject:** History of Seafaring - Sailing Ship Heemskerck

| Date | Mintage | VF20 | XF40 | MS60 | MS63 | MS65 |
|---|---|---|---|---|---|---|
| 2005 | — | PF65 55.00 | | | | |

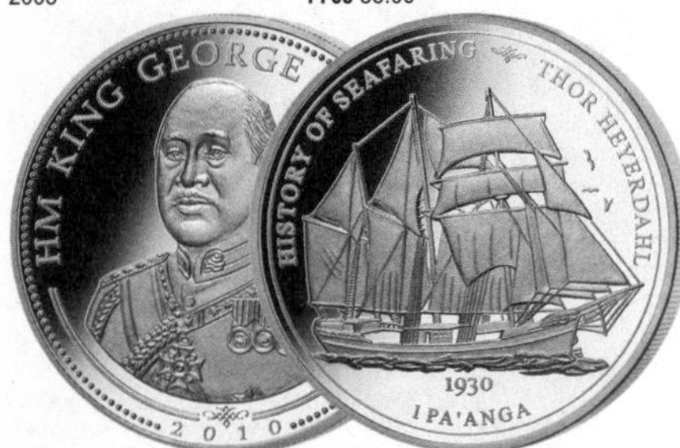

**KM# 187 PA'ANGA**
31.47 g., 0.925 Silver 0.9359 oz. ASW, 38.61 mm. **Ruler:** Siaosi Tupou V **Subject:** Ships and Explorers - Thor Heyerdahl

| Date | Mintage | VF20 | XF40 | MS60 | MS63 | MS65 |
|---|---|---|---|---|---|---|
| 2010 | Est. 5000 | PF65 70.00 | | | | |

**KM# 190 PA'ANGA**
28.28 g., 0.925 Silver 0.841 oz. ASW, 38.61 mm. **Ruler:** Siaosi Tupou V **Subject:** Railways - DB CLass V 200

| Date | Mintage | VF20 | XF40 | MS60 | MS63 | MS65 |
|---|---|---|---|---|---|---|
| 2010 | Est. 5000 | PF65 70.00 | | | | |

**KM# 222 PA'ANGA**
31.47 g., 0.925 Silver 0.9359 oz. ASW, 38.61 mm. **Ruler:** Siaosi Tupou V **Subject:** Railroads of the World - Diesel Locomotives of the German Railway

| Date | Mintage | VF20 | XF40 | MS60 | MS63 | MS65 |
|---|---|---|---|---|---|---|
| 2010 | Est. 10000 | PF63 55.00 | PF65 65.00 | | | |

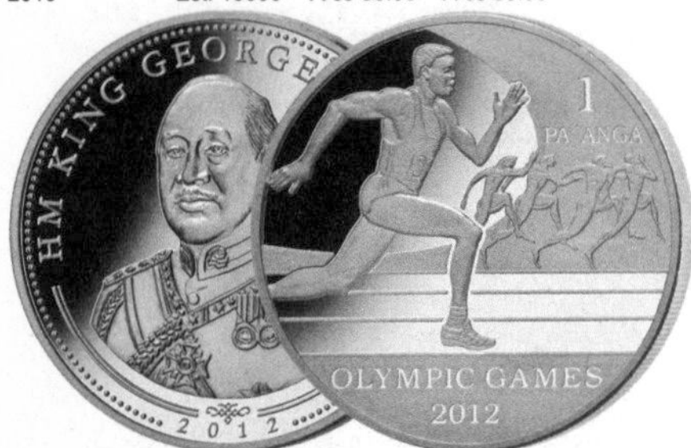

**KM# 183 PA'ANGA**
28.28 g., 0.925 Silver 0.841 oz. ASW, 38.61 mm. **Ruler:** Siaosi Tupou V **Subject:** 2012 London Olympic Games - Runner

| Date | Mintage | VF20 | XF40 | MS60 | MS63 | MS65 |
|---|---|---|---|---|---|---|
| 2012 | Est. 10000 | PF63 65.00 | PF65 75.00 | | | |

**KM# 184 PA'ANGA**
28.28 g., 0.925 Silver 0.841 oz. ASW, 38.61 mm. **Ruler:** Siaosi Tupou V **Subject:** Diamond Jubilee of Queen Elizabeth II - Buckingham Palace

| Date | Mintage | VF20 | XF40 | MS60 | MS63 | MS65 |
|---|---|---|---|---|---|---|
| 2012 | Est. 10000 | PF63 65.00 | PF65 75.00 | | | |

**KM# 186 PA'ANGA**
26.03 g., Silver Plated Copper, 38.61 mm. **Ruler:** Siaosi Tupou V **Subject:** London Olympic Games - Runner

| Date | Mintage | VF20 | XF40 | MS60 | MS63 | MS65 |
|---|---|---|---|---|---|---|
| 2012 | Est. 30000 | PF63 18.00 | PF65 20.00 | | | |

**KM# 179 2 PA'ANGA**
28.28 g., 0.925 Silver 0.841 oz. ASW, 38.61 mm. **Ruler:** Taufa'ahau Tupou IV **Subject:** King's 85th Birthday **Obv:** National arms

| Date | Mintage | VF20 | XF40 | MS60 | MS63 | MS65 |
|---|---|---|---|---|---|---|
| 2003 | — | PF63 125 | PF65 150 | | | |

**KM# 224 5 PA'ANGA**
20.00 g., 0.925 Silver 0.5948 oz. ASW, 38.61 mm. **Subject:** 2014 FIFA World Cup - Brazil

| Date | Mintage | VF20 | XF40 | MS60 | MS63 | MS65 |
|---|---|---|---|---|---|---|
| 2013 | Est. 10000 | PF63 65.00 | PF65 75.00 | | | |

**KM# 188 10 PA'ANGA**
1.24 g., 0.9999 Gold 0.0399 oz. AGW, 13.92 mm. **Ruler:** Siaosi Tupou V **Subject:** Smallest Gold Coins - Hidddensee Treasure **Rev:** Viking ship

| Date | Mintage | VF20 | XF40 | MS60 | MS63 | MS65 |
|---|---|---|---|---|---|---|
| 2003 | Est. 20000 | PF63 70.00 | PF65 80.00 | | | |

**KM# 216 10 PA'ANGA**
1.24 g., 0.999 Gold 0.0398 oz. AGW, 13.92 mm. **Ruler:** Siaosi Tupou V **Subject:** History of Seafaring - HMS Adventure & James Cook

| Date | Mintage | VF20 | XF40 | MS60 | MS63 | MS65 |
|---|---|---|---|---|---|---|
| 2003 | Est. 25000 | PF63 65.00 | PF65 75.00 | | | |

**KM# 220 10 PA'ANGA**
1.24 g., 0.999 Gold 0.0398 oz. AGW, 13.92 mm. **Ruler:** Siaosi Tupou V **Subject:** Coronation of King George Tupov V

| Date | Mintage | VF20 | XF40 | MS60 | MS63 | MS65 |
|---|---|---|---|---|---|---|
| 2008 | — | PF65 75.00 | | | | |

**KM# 189 10 PA'ANGA**
0.50 g., 0.999 Gold 0.0161 oz. AGW, 11 mm. **Ruler:** Siaosi Tupou V **Subject:** Smallest Gold Coins - Trilithon

| Date | Mintage | VF20 | XF40 | MS60 | MS63 | MS65 |
|---|---|---|---|---|---|---|
| 2011 | Est. 10000 | PF63 35.00 | PF65 40.00 | | | |

**KM# 191 10 PA'ANGA**
1.24 g., 0.999 Gold 0.0398 oz. AGW, 13.92 mm. **Ruler:** Siaosi Tupou V **Subject:** Coronation of HM King Siaosi Tupou V

| Date | Mintage | VF20 | XF40 | MS60 | MS63 | MS65 |
|---|---|---|---|---|---|---|
| 2012 | Est. 10000 | PF63 70.00 | PF65 80.00 | | | |

**KM# 225 10 PA'ANGA**
0.50 g., 0.585 Gold 0.0094 oz. AGW with 24Kt plating, 11 mm. **Subject:** Heilala Festival

| Date | Mintage | VF20 | XF40 | MS60 | MS63 | MS65 |
|---|---|---|---|---|---|---|
| 2013 | Est. 10000 | PF63 35.00 | PF65 45.00 | | | |

**KM# 221 50 PA'ANGA**
Gold **Ruler:** Siaosi Tupou V **Subject:** Coronation of King George Tupov V

| Date | Mintage | VF20 | XF40 | MS60 | MS63 | MS65 |
|---|---|---|---|---|---|---|
| 2008 | — | — | — | — | — | — |

**KM# 185 100 PA'ANGA**
7.77 g., 0.585 Gold 0.1461 oz. AGW 24K Gold Plated, 25 mm. **Ruler:** Siaosi Tupou V **Subject:** 2012 London Olympic Games - Runner

| Date | Mintage | VF20 | XF40 | MS60 | MS63 | MS65 |
|---|---|---|---|---|---|---|
| 2012 | Est. 30000 | PF65 325 | | | | |

# TRANSNISTRIA

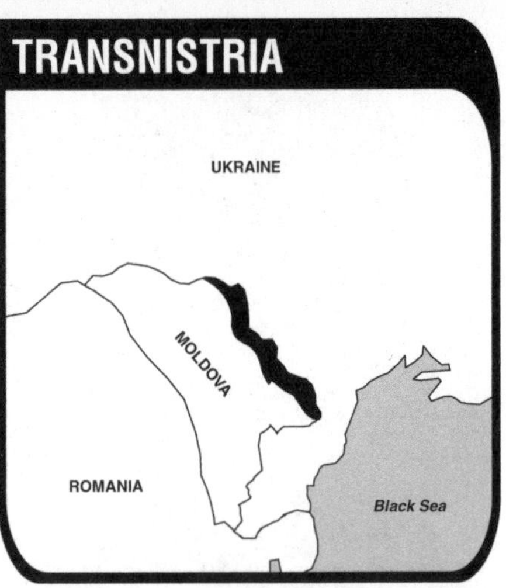


The Pridnestrovskaia Moldavskaia Respublica was formed in 1990, even before the separation of Moldavia from Russia. It has an area of 11,544 sq. mi. (29,900 sq. km.) and a population of 555,000. Capital: Tiraspol.

Transnistria (or Transdniestra) has a president, parliament, army and police forces, but as yet it is lacking international recognition.

## MOLDAVIAN REPUBLIC

### STANDARD COINAGE

1 Rublei = 100 Kopeek

**KM# 172 20 RUBLEI**
62.70 g., 0.999 Gold 2.0138 oz. AGW, 39 mm. **Subject:** 20th Anniversary of the Republic of Moldova

| Date | Mintage | VF20 | XF40 | MS60 | MS63 | MS65 |
|---|---|---|---|---|---|---|
| 2010 | 30 | PF65 4,250 | | | | |

**KM# 173 20 RUBLEI**
125.25 g., 0.999 Gold 4.0229 oz. AGW, 50 mm. **Subject:** 20th Anniversary of the Republic of Moldova

| Date | Mintage | VF20 | XF40 | MS60 | MS63 | MS65 |
|---|---|---|---|---|---|---|
| 2010 | 20 | PF65 8,250 | | | | |

**KM# 142 20 RUBLEI**
33.50 g., 0.925 Silver 0.9963 oz. ASW, 39 mm. **Subject:** 20th Anniversary of the Ministry of Internal Affairs **Obv:** State Arms

| Date | Mintage | VF20 | XF40 | MS60 | MS63 | MS65 |
|---|---|---|---|---|---|---|
| 2011 Proof-like | Est. 200 | PF65 115 | | | | |

**KM# 175 20 RUBLEI**
74.30 g., 0.925 Silver 2.2096 oz. ASW, 52 mm. **Subject:** 20th Anniversary of Banking in Transnistria

| Date | Mintage | VF20 | XF40 | MS60 | MS63 | MS65 |
|---|---|---|---|---|---|---|
| 2011 | 200 | PF65 200 | | | | |

**KM# 50 5 KOPEEK**
0.70 g., Aluminum, 17.9 mm. **Obv:** Modified national arms **Obv. Legend:** ПРИДНЕСТРОВСКАЯ МОЛДАВСКАЯ РЕСПУБЛИКА **Rev:** Value flanked by wheat stalks. **Edge:** Plain **Note:** Prev. KM#2, 16.

| Date | Mintage | VF20 | XF40 | MS60 | MS63 | MS65 |
|---|---|---|---|---|---|---|
| 2005 | — | — | 0.20 | 0.50 | 0.65 | 1.25 |

**KM# 51 10 KOPEEK**
1.00 g., Aluminum, 20 mm. **Obv:** Modified national arms **Obv. Legend:** ПРИДНЕСТРОВСКАЯ МОЛДАВСКАЯ РЕСПУБЛИКА **Rev:** Value flanked by wheat stalks **Edge:** Plain **Note:** Prev. KM#3, 17.

| Date | Mintage | VF20 | XF40 | MS60 | MS63 | MS65 |
|---|---|---|---|---|---|---|
| 2005 | — | — | 0.25 | 0.65 | 0.85 | 1.50 |

**KM# 5 25 KOPEEK**
2.15 g., Aluminum-Bronze, 16.88 mm. **Obv:** National arms **Rev:** Value within sprays **Edge:** Plain

| Date | Mintage | VF20 | XF40 | MS60 | MS63 | MS65 |
|---|---|---|---|---|---|---|
| 2002 | — | 0.15 | 0.35 | 0.75 | 1.25 | 1.75 |

**KM# 52 25 KOPEEK**
Aluminum-Bronze, 16.9 mm. **Obv:** Modified national arms **Obv. Legend:** ПРИДНЕСТРОВСКАЯ МОЛДАВСКАЯ РЕСПУБЛИКА **Rev:** Value within sprays **Edge:** Plain **Note:** Prev. KM#18.

| Date | Mintage | VF20 | XF40 | MS60 | MS63 | MS65 |
|---|---|---|---|---|---|---|
| 2005 | — | 0.15 | 0.35 | 0.75 | 1.25 | 1.75 |

**KM# 52a 25 KOPEEK**
2.10 g., Bronze Plated Steel, 16.9 mm. **Obv:** Modified national arms **Obv. Legend:** ПРИДНЕСТРОВСКАЯ МОЛДАВСКАЯ РЕСПУБЛИКА **Rev:** Value within sprays **Edge:** Plain **Note:** Prev. KM#5a; 18a.

| Date | Mintage | VF20 | XF40 | MS60 | MS63 | MS65 |
|---|---|---|---|---|---|---|
| 2005 | — | 0.15 | 0.35 | 0.75 | 1.25 | 1.75 |

**KM# 53 50 KOPEEK**
2.80 g., Aluminum-Bronze, 19 mm. **Obv:** Modified national arms **Obv. Legend:** ПРИДНЕСТРОВСКАЯ МОЛДАВСКАЯ РЕСПУБЛИКА **Rev:** Value within sprays **Edge:** Plain **Note:** Prev. KM#4a; 19.

| Date | Mintage | VF20 | XF40 | MS60 | MS63 | MS65 |
|---|---|---|---|---|---|---|
| 2005 | — | 0.15 | 0.45 | 1.10 | 1.50 | 2.00 |

**KM# 53a 50 KOPEEK**
Bronze Plated Steel, 19 mm. **Obv:** Modified national arms **Obv. Legend:** ПРИДНЕСТРОВСКАЯ МОЛДАВСКАЯ РЕСПУБЛИКА **Rev:** Value within sprays **Edge:** Plain **Note:** Prev. KM#19a.

| Date | Mintage | VF20 | XF40 | MS60 | MS63 | MS65 |
|---|---|---|---|---|---|---|
| 2005 | — | 0.15 | 0.45 | 1.10 | 1.50 | 2.00 |

**KM# 55 RUBLE**
14.14 g., 0.925 Silver 0.4205 oz. ASW, 32 mm. **Obv:** National Arms **Rev:** Building with dome

| Date | Mintage | VF20 | XF40 | MS60 | MS63 | MS65 |
|---|---|---|---|---|---|---|
| 2005 | 500 | PF65 175 | | | | |

**KM# 77 RUBLE**
14.14 g., 0.925 Silver 0.4205 oz. ASW, 32 mm. **Obv:** National Arms **Rev:** Moth and caterpillar

| Date | Mintage | VF20 | XF40 | MS60 | MS63 | MS65 |
|---|---|---|---|---|---|---|
| 2006 | 1,000 | PF65 145 | | | | |

**KM# 79 RUBLE**
14.14 g., 0.925 Silver 0.4205 oz. ASW, 32 mm. **Obv:** Olympics - Turin **Rev:** Slalom

| Date | Mintage | VF20 | XF40 | MS60 | MS63 | MS65 |
|---|---|---|---|---|---|---|
| 2006 | 500 | PF65 175 | | | | |

**KM# 95 3 RUBLYA**
8.00 g., 0.900 Gold 0.2315 oz. AGW, 21 mm. **Obv:** National Arms **Rev:** Shield **Rev. Legend:** РЫЪНИЦА

| Date | Mintage | VF20 | XF40 | MS60 | MS63 | MS65 |
|---|---|---|---|---|---|---|
| 2007 | 100 | PF63 525 | PF65 550 | | | |

**KM# 97 3 RUBLYA**
8.00 g., 0.900 Gold 0.2315 oz. AGW, 21 mm. **Obv:** National Arms **Rev:** Shield **Rev. Legend:** ТНРАСПОЛЪ

| Date | Mintage | VF20 | XF40 | MS60 | MS63 | MS65 |
|---|---|---|---|---|---|---|
| 2007 | 100 | PF63 525 | PF65 550 | | | |

**KM# 110 3 RUBLYA**
14.14 g., 0.925 Silver 0.4205 oz. ASW, 32 mm. **Obv:** National Arms **Rev:** Aquarius within zodiac emblems

| Date | Mintage | VF20 | XF40 | MS60 | MS63 | MS65 |
|---|---|---|---|---|---|---|
| 2007 | 100 | PF63 95.00 | PF65 125 | | | |

**KM# 145 3 RUBLYA**
8.00 g., 0.900 Gold 0.2315 oz. AGW, 21 mm. **Subject:** Coat of arms of the city of Bendery

| Date | Mintage | VF20 | XF40 | MS60 | MS63 | MS65 |
|---|---|---|---|---|---|---|
| 2008 | 100 | PF63 525 | PF65 550 | | | |

**KM# 155 3 RUBLYA**
8.00 g., 0.900 Gold 0.2315 oz. AGW, 21 mm. **Subject:** Moldovan Metal Works

| Date | Mintage | VF20 | XF40 | MS60 | MS63 | MS65 |
|---|---|---|---|---|---|---|
| 2008 | 100 | PF63 525 | PF65 550 | | | |

**KM# 161 3 RUBLYA**
101.50 g., 0.925 Silver 3.0186 oz. ASW, 50 mm. **Subject:** Endangered Plants and Animals **Rev:** Dog head

| Date | Mintage | VF20 | XF40 | MS60 | MS63 | MS65 |
|---|---|---|---|---|---|---|
| 2008 Proof | 5 | — | — | — | — | — |

**KM# 163 3 RUBLYA**
8.00 g., 0.900 Gold 0.2315 oz. AGW, 21 mm. **Series:** Tribute to 5 Kopek of Moldavia & Wallachea with double headed eagle

| Date | Mintage | VF20 | XF40 | MS60 | MS63 | MS65 |
|---|---|---|---|---|---|---|
| 2009 | 250 | PF63 535 | PF65 550 | | | |

**KM# 100 5 RUBLES**
33.85 g., 0.925 Silver 1.0067 oz. ASW, 39 mm. **Obv:** National Arms **Rev:** Wooley mammoth

| Date | Mintage | VF20 | XF40 | MS60 | MS63 | MS65 |
|---|---|---|---|---|---|---|
| 2007 | 500 | PF63 125 | PF65 145 | | | |

**KM# 101 5 RUBLES**
33.85 g., 0.925 Silver 1.0067 oz. ASW, 39 mm. **Obv:** National Arms **Rev:** Moose

| Date | Mintage | VF20 | XF40 | MS60 | MS63 | MS65 |
|---|---|---|---|---|---|---|
| 2007 | 500 | PF63 125 | PF65 145 | | | |

**KM# 134 5 RUBLES**
33.80 g., 0.925 Silver 1.0052 oz. ASW, 39 mm. **Obv:** National Arms **Rev:** Woolly Mammoth (Archidiskodon Trogrnterii)

| Date | Mintage | VF20 | XF40 | MS60 | MS63 | MS65 |
|---|---|---|---|---|---|---|
| 2007 | 500 | PF63 125 | PF65 145 | | | |

**KM# 156 5 RUBLES**
33.85 g., 0.925 Silver 1.0067 oz. ASW, 39 mm. **Subject:** Prehistoric Finds - Panthera Leo Spelaea Felidae

| Date | Mintage | VF20 | XF40 | MS60 | MS63 | MS65 |
|---|---|---|---|---|---|---|
| 2008 | 500 | PF63 135 | PF65 150 | | | |

**KM# 158 5 RUBLES**
33.85 g., 0.925 Silver 1.0067 oz. ASW, 39 mm. **Subject:** Moldovan Republic Anthem

| Date | Mintage | VF20 | XF40 | MS60 | MS63 | MS65 |
|---|---|---|---|---|---|---|
| 2008 | 1,000 | PF63 120 | PF65 135 | | | |

**KM# 159 5 RUBLES**
33.85 g., 0.925 Silver 1.0067 oz. ASW, 39 mm. **Subject:** 55 Infantry Regiments of Podolskij

| Date | Mintage | VF20 | XF40 | MS60 | MS63 | MS65 |
|---|---|---|---|---|---|---|
| 2008 | 1,000 | PF63 120 | PF65 135 | | | |

**KM# 160 5 RUBLES**
33.85 g., 0.925 Silver 1.0067 oz. ASW, 39 mm. **Subject:** Year of the Familie

| Date | Mintage | VF20 | XF40 | MS60 | MS63 | MS65 |
|---|---|---|---|---|---|---|
| 2008 | 1,000 | PF63 120 | PF65 135 | | | |

**KM# 162 5 RUBLES**
8.00 g., 0.900 Gold 0.2315 oz. AGW, 21 mm. **Subject:** Russian History of Transnistria - Sophie Auguste Friederike von Anhalt-Zerbst also known as Catherine II

| Date | Mintage | VF20 | XF40 | MS60 | MS63 | MS65 |
|---|---|---|---|---|---|---|
| 2009 | 250 | PF63 525 | PF65 535 | | | |

**KM# 170 5 RUBLES**
33.85 g., 39.000 Silver 42.4438 oz. ASW, 39 mm. **Subject:** 65th Anniversary of Victory in Second World War

| Date | Mintage | VF20 | XF40 | MS60 | MS63 | MS65 |
|---|---|---|---|---|---|---|
| 2010 | 250 | PF63 95.00 | PF65 110 | | | |

**KM# 171 5 RUBLES**
33.85 g., 0.925 Silver 1.0067 oz. ASW, 39 mm. **Subject:** 20th Anniversary of the Republic of Moldova

| Date | Mintage | VF20 | XF40 | MS60 | MS63 | MS65 |
|---|---|---|---|---|---|---|
| 2010 | 250 | PF63 95.00 | PF65 110 | | | |

**KM# 141 5 RUBLES**
33.50 g., 0.925 Silver 0.9963 oz. ASW, 39 mm. **Obv:** Yuri Gagarin with color

| Date | Mintage | VF20 | XF40 | MS60 | MS63 | MS65 |
|---|---|---|---|---|---|---|
| 2011 | — | PF63 135 | PF65 150 | | | |

**KM# 176 5 RUBLES**
29.70 g., 0.925 Silver 0.8833 oz. ASW, 37 x 37 mm. **Subject:** Four Seasons - Spring in Color

| Date | Mintage | VF20 | XF40 | MS60 | MS63 | MS65 |
|---|---|---|---|---|---|---|
| 2011 | 250 | PF63 100 | PF65 120 | | | |

**KM# 177 5 RUBLES**
29.70 g., 0.925 Silver 0.8833 oz. ASW, 37 x 37 mm. **Subject:** Four Seasons - Summer in Color

| Date | Mintage | VF20 | XF40 | MS60 | MS63 | MS65 |
|---|---|---|---|---|---|---|
| 2011 | 250 | PF63 100 | PF65 120 | | | |

**KM# 178 5 RUBLES**
29.70 g., 0.925 Silver 0.8833 oz. ASW, 37 x 37 mm. **Subject:** Four Seasons - Fall in Color

| Date | Mintage | VF20 | XF40 | MS60 | MS63 | MS65 |
|---|---|---|---|---|---|---|
| 2011 | 250 | PF63 100 | PF65 120 | | | |

**KM# 179 5 RUBLES**
29.70 g., 0.925 Silver 0.8833 oz. ASW, 37 x 37 mm. **Subject:** Four Seasons - Winter in Color

| Date | Mintage | VF20 | XF40 | MS60 | MS63 | MS65 |
|---|---|---|---|---|---|---|
| 2011 | 250 | PF63 100 | PF65 120 | | | |

**KM# 102 10 RUBLEI**
14.14 g., 0.925 Silver 0.4205 oz. ASW, 32 mm. **Obv:** National Arms **Rev:** Multicolor sprinter

| Date | Mintage | VF20 | XF40 | MS60 | MS63 | MS65 |
|---|---|---|---|---|---|---|
| 2007 | 500 | PF63 80.00 | PF65 100 | | | |

**KM# 103 10 RUBLEI**
14.14 g., 0.925 Silver 0.4205 oz. ASW, 32 mm. **Obv:** National Arms **Rev:** Multicolor female gymnast

| Date | Mintage | VF20 | XF40 | MS60 | MS63 | MS65 |
|---|---|---|---|---|---|---|
| 2007 | 500 | PF63 80.00 | PF65 100 | | | |

**KM# 104 10 RUBLEI**
14.14 g., 0.925 Silver 0.4205 oz. ASW, 32 mm. **Obv:** National Arms **Rev:** Multicolor runner, sports designs

| Date | Mintage | VF20 | XF40 | MS60 | MS63 | MS65 |
|---|---|---|---|---|---|---|
| 2007 | 500 | PF63 80.00 | PF65 100 | | | |

**KM# 105 10 RUBLEI**
14.14 g., 0.925 Silver 0.4205 oz. ASW, 32 mm. **Obv:** National Arms **Rev:** Multicolor javlin thrower

| Date | Mintage | VF20 | XF40 | MS60 | MS63 | MS65 |
|---|---|---|---|---|---|---|
| 2007 | 500 | PF63 80.00 | PF65 100 | | | |

**KM# 106 10 RUBLEI**
14.14 g., 0.925 Silver 0.4205 oz. ASW, 32 mm. **Obv:** National Arms **Rev:** Multicolor runner breaking tape at finish line

| Date | Mintage | VF20 | XF40 | MS60 | MS63 | MS65 |
|---|---|---|---|---|---|---|
| 2007 | 500 | PF63 80.00 | PF65 100 | | | |

**KM# 107 10 RUBLEI**
14.14 g., 0.925 Silver 0.4205 oz. ASW, 32 mm. **Obv:** National Arms **Rev:** Multicolor soccer player

| Date | Mintage | VF20 | XF40 | MS60 | MS63 | MS65 |
|---|---|---|---|---|---|---|
| 2007 | 500 | PF63 80.00 | PF65 100 | | | |

**KM# 111 10 RUBLEI**
14.14 g., 0.925 Silver 0.4205 oz. ASW, 32 mm. **Obv:** National Arms **Rev:** Constellation ophiuchus (man grasping serpant)

| Date | Mintage | VF20 | XF40 | MS60 | MS63 | MS65 |
|---|---|---|---|---|---|---|
| 2007 | 500 | PF63 80.00 | PF65 100 | | | |

**KM# 112 10 RUBLEI**
14.14 g., 0.925 Silver 0.4205 oz. ASW, 32 mm. **Obv:** National Arms **Rev:** Aquarius within circle of zodiac symbols

| Date | Mintage | VF20 | XF40 | MS60 | MS63 | MS65 |
|---|---|---|---|---|---|---|
| 2007 | 500 | PF63 80.00 | PF65 100 | | | |

**KM# 125 10 RUBLEI**
14.14 g., 0.925 Silver 0.4205 oz. ASW, 32 mm. **Obv:** National Arms **Rev:** Sturgeon fish

| Date | Mintage | VF20 | XF40 | MS60 | MS63 | MS65 |
|---|---|---|---|---|---|---|
| 2008 | 500 | PF63 95.00 | PF65 125 | | | |

**KM# 126 10 RUBLEI**
14.14 g., 0.925 Silver 0.4205 oz. ASW, 32 mm. **Obv:** National Arms **Rev:** Owl

| Date | Mintage | VF20 | XF40 | MS60 | MS63 | MS65 |
|---|---|---|---|---|---|---|
| 2008 | 500 | PF63 95.00 | PF65 125 | | | |

**KM# 127 10 RUBLEI**
14.14 g., 0.925 Silver 0.4205 oz. ASW, 32 mm. **Obv:** National Arms **Rev:** Flower

| Date | Mintage | VF20 | XF40 | MS60 | MS63 | MS65 |
|---|---|---|---|---|---|---|
| 2008 | 500 | PF63 95.00 | PF65 125 | | | |

**KM# 128 10 RUBLEI**
14.14 g., 0.925 Silver 0.4205 oz. ASW, 32 mm. **Obv:** National Arms **Rev:** Otter

| Date | Mintage | VF20 | XF40 | MS60 | MS63 | MS65 |
|---|---|---|---|---|---|---|
| 2008 | 500 | PF63 80.00 | PF65 100 | | | |

**KM# 135 10 RUBLEI**
14.14 g., 0.925 Silver 0.4205 oz. ASW, 32 mm. **Obv:** National Arms **Rev:** Lutra otter

| Date | Mintage | VF20 | XF40 | MS60 | MS63 | MS65 |
|---|---|---|---|---|---|---|
| 2008 | 5,000 | PF63 85.00 | PF65 100 | | | |

**KM# 148 10 RUBLEI**
14.14 g., 0.925 Silver 0.4205 oz. ASW, 32 mm. **Subject:** 2008 Summer Olympics - Beijing

| Date | Mintage | VF20 | XF40 | MS60 | MS63 | MS65 |
|---|---|---|---|---|---|---|
| 2008 | 500 | PF63 80.00 | PF65 90.00 | | | |

**KM# 149 10 RUBLEI**
14.14 g., 0.925 Silver 0.4205 oz. ASW, 32 mm. **Subject:** 2008 Summer Olympics, Beijing - Wrestling

| Date | Mintage | VF20 | XF40 | MS60 | MS63 | MS65 |
|---|---|---|---|---|---|---|
| 2008 | 500 | PF63 80.00 | PF65 90.00 | | | |

**KM# 150 10 RUBLEI**
14.14 g., 0.925 Silver 0.4205 oz. ASW, 32 mm. **Subject:** 2008 Summer Olympics, Beijing

| Date | Mintage | VF20 | XF40 | MS60 | MS63 | MS65 |
|---|---|---|---|---|---|---|
| 2008 | 500 | PF63 80.00 | PF65 90.00 | | | |

**KM# 151 10 RUBLEI**
14.14 g., 0.925 Silver 0.4205 oz. ASW, 32 mm. **Series:** 2008 Summer Olympics, Beijing - Rowing

| Date | Mintage | VF20 | XF40 | MS60 | MS63 | MS65 |
|---|---|---|---|---|---|---|
| 2008 | 500 | PF63 80.00 | PF65 90.00 | | | |

**KM# 152 10 RUBLEI**
14.14 g., 0.925 Silver 0.4205 oz. ASW, 32 mm. **Subject:** 2008 Summer Olympics, Beijing - Archery

| Date | Mintage | VF20 | XF40 | MS60 | MS63 | MS65 |
|---|---|---|---|---|---|---|
| 2008 | 500 | PF63 80.00 | PF65 90.00 | | | |

**KM# 153 10 RUBLEI**
14.14 g., 0.925 Silver 0.4205 oz. ASW, 32 mm. **Subject:** 2008 Summer Olympics, Beijing - Table Tennis

| Date | Mintage | VF20 | XF40 | MS60 | MS63 | MS65 |
|---|---|---|---|---|---|---|
| 2008 | 500 | PF63 80.00 | PF65 90.00 | | | |

**KM# 154 10 RUBLEI**
14.14 g., 0.925 Silver 0.4205 oz. ASW, 32 mm. **Subject:** Moldovan Metal Works

| Date | Mintage | VF20 | XF40 | MS60 | MS63 | MS65 |
|---|---|---|---|---|---|---|
| 2008 | 800 | PF63 75.00 | PF65 85.00 | | | |

**KM# 164 10 RUBLEI**
14.14 g., 0.925 Silver 0.4205 oz. ASW, 32 mm. **Subject:** Endangered Plants and Animals - Swan

| Date | Mintage | VF20 | XF40 | MS60 | MS63 | MS65 |
|---|---|---|---|---|---|---|
| 2009 | 500 | PF63 75.00 | PF65 85.00 | | | |

**KM# 165 10 RUBLEI**
14.14 g., 0.925 Silver 0.4205 oz. ASW, 32 mm. **Subject:** Endangered Plants and Animals - Snowdrop Flower

| Date | Mintage | VF20 | XF40 | MS60 | MS63 | MS65 |
|---|---|---|---|---|---|---|
| 2009 | 50 | PF63 75.00 | PF65 85.00 | | | |

### KM# 137 10 RUBLEI
7.89 g., 0.925 Silver 0.2346 oz. ASW, 21 mm. **Obv:** State emblem **Rev:** Death's Head Hawkmoth in color

| Date | Mintage | VF20 | XF40 | MS60 | MS63 | MS65 |
|---|---|---|---|---|---|---|
| 2011 Prooflike | Est. 250 | PF65 100 | | | | |

### KM# 138 10 RUBLEI
13.07 g., Silver, 32 mm. **Rev:** Death's Head Hawkmoth

| Date | Mintage | VF20 | XF40 | MS60 | MS63 | MS65 |
|---|---|---|---|---|---|---|
| 2011 Prooflike | — | PF65 95.00 | | | | |

### KM# 180 10 RUBLEI
7.89 g., 0.925 Silver 0.2346 oz. ASW, 21 mm. **Subject:** Endangered Plants and Animals - Skull Owl in color

| Date | Mintage | VF20 | XF40 | MS60 | MS63 | MS65 |
|---|---|---|---|---|---|---|
| 2011 | 250 | PF65 100 | | | | |

### KM# 181 10 RUBLEI
13.87 g., 0.925 Silver 0.4125 oz. ASW, 32 mm. **Subject:** Endangered Plants and Animals - Skull Owl

| Date | Mintage | VF20 | XF40 | MS60 | MS63 | MS65 |
|---|---|---|---|---|---|---|
| 2011 | 250 | PF65 95.00 | | | | |

### KM# 54 15 RUBLEI
156.40 g., 0.999 Gold 5.0233 oz. AGW, 50 mm. **Obv:** National Arms **Rev:** Building with dome

| Date | Mintage | VF20 | XF40 | MS60 | MS63 | MS65 |
|---|---|---|---|---|---|---|
| 2005 Proof, Rare | 15 | — | — | — | — | — |

### KM# 75 15 RUBLEI
156.40 g., 0.999 Gold 5.0233 oz. AGW, 15 mm. **Obv:** National Arms **Rev:** Building with tower

| Date | Mintage | VF20 | XF40 | MS60 | MS63 | MS65 |
|---|---|---|---|---|---|---|
| 2006 Proof, Rare | 15 | — | — | — | — | — |

### KM# 157 15 RUBLEI
155.50 g., 0.999 Gold 4.9944 oz. AGW, 65 mm. **Subject:** Prehistoric Finds - Mammoth

| Date | Mintage | VF20 | XF40 | MS60 | MS63 | MS65 |
|---|---|---|---|---|---|---|
| 2008 | 10 | PF65 11,500 | | | | |

### KM# 167 15 RUBLEI
31.00 g., 0.925 Silver 0.9219 oz. ASW, 37 x 21 mm. **Subject:** 15th Anniversary of National Custody

| Date | Mintage | VF20 | XF40 | MS60 | MS63 | MS65 |
|---|---|---|---|---|---|---|
| 2009 | 250 | PF63 90.00 | PF65 100 | | | |

### KM# 168 15 RUBLEI
6.10 g., 0.999 Gold 0.1959 oz. AGW, 22 x 13 mm. **Subject:** 15th Anniversary of National Custody

| Date | Mintage | VF20 | XF40 | MS60 | MS63 | MS65 |
|---|---|---|---|---|---|---|
| 2009 | 250 | PF63 525 | PF65 550 | | | |

### KM# 10 100 RUBLEI
14.14 g., 0.925 Silver 0.4205 oz. ASW, 32 mm. **Obv:** National Arms **Rev:** D. Zielinskieg, chemist

| Date | Mintage | VF20 | XF40 | MS60 | MS63 | MS65 |
|---|---|---|---|---|---|---|
| 2001 | 1,000 | PF63 65.00 | PF65 75.00 | | | |

### KM# 11 100 RUBLEI
14.14 g., 0.925 Silver 0.4205 oz. ASW, 32 mm. **Obv:** National Arms **Rev:** S. Berg, fish

| Date | Mintage | VF20 | XF40 | MS60 | MS63 | MS65 |
|---|---|---|---|---|---|---|
| 2001 | 1,000 | PF63 65.00 | PF65 75.00 | | | |

### KM# 12 100 RUBLEI
14.14 g., 0.925 Silver 0.4205 oz. ASW, 32 mm. **Obv:** National Arms **Rev:** N.F. Skilfosowskieg, portrait at right

| Date | Mintage | VF20 | XF40 | MS60 | MS63 | MS65 |
|---|---|---|---|---|---|---|
| 2001 | 1,000 | PF63 65.00 | PF65 75.00 | | | |

### KM# 13 100 RUBLEI
14.14 g., 0.925 Silver 0.4205 oz. ASW, 32 mm. **Obv:** National Arms **Rev:** M.F. Larionowa, bust, painter

| Date | Mintage | VF20 | XF40 | MS60 | MS63 | MS65 |
|---|---|---|---|---|---|---|
| 2001 | 1,000 | PF63 65.00 | PF65 75.00 | | | |

### KM# 14 100 RUBLEI
14.14 g., 0.925 Silver 0.4205 oz. ASW, 32 mm. **Obv:** National Arms **Rev:** Cathedral in Tyraspol

| Date | Mintage | VF20 | XF40 | MS60 | MS63 | MS65 |
|---|---|---|---|---|---|---|
| 2001 | 1,000 | PF63 70.00 | PF65 80.00 | | | |

### KM# 15 100 RUBLEI
14.14 g., 0.925 Silver 0.4205 oz. ASW, 32 mm. **Obv:** National Arms **Rev:** Cathedral XVII

| Date | Mintage | VF20 | XF40 | MS60 | MS63 | MS65 |
|---|---|---|---|---|---|---|
| 2001 | 1,000 | PF63 60.00 | PF65 70.00 | | | |

### KM# 16 100 RUBLEI
14.14 g., 0.925 Silver 0.4205 oz. ASW, 32 mm. **Obv:** National Arms **Rev:** Cathedral 1800

| Date | Mintage | VF20 | XF40 | MS60 | MS63 | MS65 |
|---|---|---|---|---|---|---|
| 2001 | 1,000 | PF63 60.00 | PF65 70.00 | | | |

### KM# 17 100 RUBLEI
14.14 g., 0.925 Silver 0.4205 oz. ASW, 32 mm. **Obv:** National Arms **Rev:** Cathedral of Ascension, Kitskany 1864

| Date | Mintage | VF20 | XF40 | MS60 | MS63 | MS65 |
|---|---|---|---|---|---|---|
| 2001 | 1,000 | PF63 60.00 | PF65 70.00 | | | |

### KM# 18 100 RUBLEI
14.14 g., 0.925 Silver 0.4205 oz. ASW, 32 mm. **Obv:** National Arms **Rev:** Cathedral 1825

| Date | Mintage | VF20 | XF40 | MS60 | MS63 | MS65 |
|---|---|---|---|---|---|---|
| 2001 | 1,000 | PF63 60.00 | PF65 70.00 | | | |

### KM# 19 100 RUBLEI
14.14 g., 0.925 Silver 0.4205 oz. ASW, 32 mm. **Obv:** National Arms **Rev:** Church of St. Trinity, Rashkov 1778

| Date | Mintage | VF20 | XF40 | MS60 | MS63 | MS65 |
|---|---|---|---|---|---|---|
| 2001 | 1,000 | PF63 60.00 | PF65 70.00 | | | |

### KM# 20 100 RUBLEI
14.14 g., 0.925 Silver 0.4205 oz. ASW, 32 mm. **Obv:** National Arms **Rev:** Cathedral XIX

| Date | Mintage | VF20 | XF40 | MS60 | MS63 | MS65 |
|---|---|---|---|---|---|---|
| 2001 | 1,000 | PF63 60.00 | PF65 70.00 | | | |

### KM# 21 100 RUBLEI
14.14 g., 0.925 Silver 0.4205 oz. ASW, 32 mm. **Obv:** National Arms **Rev:** Cathedral 1784

| Date | Mintage | VF20 | XF40 | MS60 | MS63 | MS65 |
|---|---|---|---|---|---|---|
| 2001 | 1,000 | PF63 60.00 | PF65 70.00 | | | |

### KM# 22 100 RUBLEI
14.14 g., 0.925 Silver 0.4205 oz. ASW, 32 mm. **Obv:** National Arms **Rev:** Cathedral 1854

| Date | Mintage | VF20 | XF40 | MS60 | MS63 | MS65 |
|---|---|---|---|---|---|---|
| 2001 | 1,000 | PF63 60.00 | PF65 70.00 | | | |

### KM# 35 100 RUBLEI
14.14 g., 0.925 Silver 0.4205 oz. ASW, 32 mm. **Subject:** City of Tiraspol **Obv:** National arms **Rev:** Statue and buildings **Edge:** Plain **Note:** Prev. KM#7.

| Date | Mintage | VF20 | XF40 | MS60 | MS63 | MS65 |
|---|---|---|---|---|---|---|
| 2002 | — | PF63 70.00 | PF65 80.00 | | | |

### KM# 36 100 RUBLEI
14.14 g., 0.925 Silver 0.4205 oz. ASW, 32 mm. **Subject:** City of Tiraspol **Obv:** National arms **Rev:** Cameo above fortress **Edge:** Plain **Note:** Prev. KM#8.

| Date | Mintage | VF20 | XF40 | MS60 | MS63 | MS65 |
|---|---|---|---|---|---|---|
| 2002 | — | PF63 70.00 | PF65 80.00 | | | |

### KM# 37 100 RUBLEI
14.14 g., 0.925 Silver 0.4205 oz. ASW, 32 mm. **Subject:** 10th Anniversary - Trans-Dniester Republican Bank **Obv:** National arms **Rev:** Colorized monogram within 3/4 wreath with "1992" at top **Edge:** Plain **Note:** Prev. KM#10.

| Date | Mintage | VF20 | XF40 | MS60 | MS63 | MS65 |
|---|---|---|---|---|---|---|
| 2002 | 500 | PF63 75.00 | PF65 85.00 | | | |

### KM# 38 100 RUBLEI
14.16 g., 0.925 Silver 0.4211 oz. ASW, 32 mm. **Subject:** K. K. Gedroets **Obv:** National arms **Rev:** Bust facing flanked by sprigs, beaker and book **Edge:** Plain **Note:** Prev. KM#9.

| Date | Mintage | VF20 | XF40 | MS60 | MS63 | MS65 |
|---|---|---|---|---|---|---|
| 2002 | 500 | PF63 70.00 | PF65 80.00 | | | |

### KM# 40 100 RUBLEI
14.14 g., 0.925 Silver 0.4205 oz. ASW, 32 mm. **Obv:** National Arms **Rev:** Shield **Rev. Legend:** ТИРАСЛОЛБ

| Date | Mintage | VF20 | XF40 | MS60 | MS63 | MS65 |
|---|---|---|---|---|---|---|
| 2002 | 500 | PF63 75.00 | PF65 85.00 | | | |

### KM# 41 100 RUBLEI
14.14 g., 0.925 Silver 0.4205 oz. ASW, 32 mm. **Obv:** National Arms **Rev:** Shield **Rev. Legend:** ГРНГОРКОПОЛL

| Date | Mintage | VF20 | XF40 | MS60 | MS63 | MS65 |
|---|---|---|---|---|---|---|
| 2002 | 500 | PF63 75.00 | PF65 85.00 | | | |

### KM# 42 100 RUBLEI
14.14 g., 0.925 Silver 0.4205 oz. ASW, 32 mm. **Obv:** National arms **Rev:** Shield flanked by sprigs **Edge:** Plain **Note:** Prev. KM#12.

| Date | Mintage | VF20 | XF40 | MS60 | MS63 | MS65 |
|---|---|---|---|---|---|---|
| 2003 | 500 | PF63 70.00 | PF65 80.00 | | | |

### KM# 43 100 RUBLEI
14.14 g., 0.925 Silver 0.4205 oz. ASW, 32 mm. **Obv:** National arms **Rev:** Hoopoe (Upupa Epops) bird on branch **Edge:** Plain **Note:** Prev. KM#11.

| Date | Mintage | VF20 | XF40 | MS60 | MS63 | MS65 |
|---|---|---|---|---|---|---|
| 2003 | 500 | PF63 90.00 | PF65 100 | | | |

### KM# 45 100 RUBLEI
14.14 g., 0.925 Silver 0.4205 oz. ASW, 32 mm. **Obv:** National Army **Rev:** Soccer Player

| Date | Mintage | VF20 | XF40 | MS60 | MS63 | MS65 |
|---|---|---|---|---|---|---|
| 2003 | 500 | PF63 160 | PF65 175 | | | |

### KM# 44 100 RUBLEI
14.14 g., 0.925 Silver 0.4205 oz. ASW, 32 mm. **Obv:** National arms **Rev:** Doe and fawn flanked by trees **Edge:** Plain **Note:** Prev. KM#14.

| Date | Mintage | VF20 | XF40 | MS60 | MS63 | MS65 |
|---|---|---|---|---|---|---|
| 2004 | 1,000 | PF63 100 | PF65 125 | | | |

### KM# 46 100 RUBLEI
14.14 g., 0.925 Silver 0.4205 oz. ASW, 32 mm. **Obv:** National Arms **Rev:** A.G. Rubinstein and music score

| Date | Mintage | VF20 | XF40 | MS60 | MS63 | MS65 |
|---|---|---|---|---|---|---|
| 2004 | 1,000 | PF63 60.00 | PF65 75.00 | | | |

### KM# 47 100 RUBLEI
14.14 g., 0.925 Silver 0.4205 oz. ASW, 32 mm. **Obv:** National Arms **Rev:** JS Grousul

| Date | Mintage | VF20 | XF40 | MS60 | MS63 | MS65 |
|---|---|---|---|---|---|---|
| 2004 | 1,000 | PF63 60.00 | PF65 75.00 | | | |

### KM# 48 100 RUBLEI
14.14 g., 0.925 Silver 0.4205 oz. ASW, 32 mm. **Subject:** 80th Anniversary of Nationhood **Obv:** National arms **Rev:** Map and multicolor flag **Edge:** Plain **Note:** Prev. KM#13.

| Date | Mintage | VF20 | XF40 | MS60 | MS63 | MS65 |
|---|---|---|---|---|---|---|
| 2004 | 500 | PF63 100 | PF65 125 | | | |

### KM# 56 100 RUBLEI
14.14 g., 0.925 Silver 0.4205 oz. ASW, 32 mm. **Obv:** National Arms **Rev:** Building with tower

| Date | Mintage | VF20 | XF40 | MS60 | MS63 | MS65 |
|---|---|---|---|---|---|---|
| 2005 | 500 | PF63 85.00 | PF65 100 | | | |

**KM# 57 100 RUBLEI**
14.14 g., 0.925 Silver 0.4205 oz. ASW, 32 mm. **Obv:** National Arms **Rev:** Zodiac - Capricorn

| Date | Mintage | VF20 | XF40 | MS60 | MS63 | MS65 |
|---|---|---|---|---|---|---|
| 2005 | 1,000 | PF63 70.00 | PF65 80.00 | | | |

**KM# 58 100 RUBLEI**
14.14 g., 0.925 Silver 0.4205 oz. ASW, 32 mm. **Obv:** National Arms **Rev:** Statue and long building

| Date | Mintage | VF20 | XF40 | MS60 | MS63 | MS65 |
|---|---|---|---|---|---|---|
| 2005 | 500 | PF63 85.00 | PF65 100 | | | |

**KM# 59 100 RUBLEI**
14.14 g., 0.925 Silver 0.4205 oz. ASW, 32 mm. **Obv:** National Arms **Rev:** Flag as book

| Date | Mintage | VF20 | XF40 | MS60 | MS63 | MS65 |
|---|---|---|---|---|---|---|
| 2005 | 500 | PF63 95.00 | PF65 110 | | | |

**KM# 60 100 RUBLEI**
14.14 g., 0.925 Silver 0.4205 oz. ASW, 32 mm. **Obv:** National arms **Rev:** Eurasian Griffin bird on rock **Edge:** Plain **Note:** Prev. KM#15.

| Date | Mintage | VF20 | XF40 | MS60 | MS63 | MS65 |
|---|---|---|---|---|---|---|
| 2005 | 1,000 | PF63 100 | PF65 120 | | | |

**KM# 61 100 RUBLEI**
14.14 g., 0.925 Silver 0.4205 oz. ASW, 32 mm. **Obv:** National Arms **Rev:** PP Werszygora

| Date | Mintage | VF20 | XF40 | MS60 | MS63 | MS65 |
|---|---|---|---|---|---|---|
| 2005 | 500 | PF63 80.00 | PF65 90.00 | | | |

**KM# 62 100 RUBLEI**
14.14 g., 0.925 Silver 0.4205 oz. ASW, 32 mm. **Obv:** National Arms **Rev:** Zodiac - Aquarius

| Date | Mintage | VF20 | XF40 | MS60 | MS63 | MS65 |
|---|---|---|---|---|---|---|
| 2005 | 500 | PF63 80.00 | PF65 90.00 | | | |

**KM# 63 100 RUBLEI**
14.14 g., 0.925 Silver 0.4205 oz. ASW, 32 mm. **Obv:** National Arms **Rev:** Zodiac - Pisces

| Date | Mintage | VF20 | XF40 | MS60 | MS63 | MS65 |
|---|---|---|---|---|---|---|
| 2005 | 500 | PF63 80.00 | PF65 90.00 | | | |

**KM# 64 100 RUBLEI**
14.14 g., 0.925 Silver 0.4205 oz. ASW, 32 mm. **Obv:** National Arms **Rev:** Zodiac - Aries

| Date | Mintage | VF20 | XF40 | MS60 | MS63 | MS65 |
|---|---|---|---|---|---|---|
| 2005 | 500 | PF63 80.00 | PF65 90.00 | | | |

**KM# 65 100 RUBLEI**
14.14 g., 0.925 Silver 0.4205 oz. ASW, 32 mm. **Obv:** National Arms **Rev:** Zodiac - Taurus

| Date | Mintage | VF20 | XF40 | MS60 | MS63 | MS65 |
|---|---|---|---|---|---|---|
| 2005 | 500 | PF63 80.00 | PF65 90.00 | | | |

**KM# 66 100 RUBLEI**
14.14 g., 0.925 Silver 0.4205 oz. ASW, 32 mm. **Obv:** National Arms **Rev:** Zodiac - Gemini

| Date | Mintage | VF20 | XF40 | MS60 | MS63 | MS65 |
|---|---|---|---|---|---|---|
| 2005 | 500 | PF63 80.00 | PF65 90.00 | | | |

**KM# 67 100 RUBLEI**
14.14 g., 0.925 Silver 0.4205 oz. ASW, 32 mm. **Obv:** National Arms **Rev:** Zodiac - Cancer

| Date | Mintage | VF20 | XF40 | MS60 | MS63 | MS65 |
|---|---|---|---|---|---|---|
| 2005 | 500 | PF63 80.00 | PF65 90.00 | | | |

**KM# 68 100 RUBLEI**
14.14 g., 0.925 Silver 0.4205 oz. ASW, 32 mm. **Obv:** National Arms **Rev:** Zodiac - Leo

| Date | Mintage | VF20 | XF40 | MS60 | MS63 | MS65 |
|---|---|---|---|---|---|---|
| 2005 | 500 | PF63 80.00 | PF65 90.00 | | | |

**KM# 69 100 RUBLEI**
14.14 g., 0.925 Silver 0.4205 oz. ASW, 32 mm. **Obv:** National Arms **Rev:** Zodiac - Virgo

| Date | Mintage | VF20 | XF40 | MS60 | MS63 | MS65 |
|---|---|---|---|---|---|---|
| 2005 | 500 | PF63 80.00 | PF65 90.00 | | | |

**KM# 70 100 RUBLEI**
14.14 g., 0.925 Silver 0.4205 oz. ASW, 32 mm. **Obv:** National Arms **Rev:** Zodiac - Libra

| Date | Mintage | VF20 | XF40 | MS60 | MS63 | MS65 |
|---|---|---|---|---|---|---|
| 2005 | 500 | PF63 80.00 | PF65 90.00 | | | |

**KM# 71 100 RUBLEI**
14.14 g., 0.925 Silver 0.4205 oz. ASW, 32 mm. **Obv:** National Arms **Rev:** Zodiac - Scorpio

| Date | Mintage | VF20 | XF40 | MS60 | MS63 | MS65 |
|---|---|---|---|---|---|---|
| 2005 | 500 | PF63 80.00 | PF65 90.00 | | | |

**KM# 72 100 RUBLEI**
14.14 g., 0.925 Silver 0.4205 oz. ASW, 32 mm. **Obv:** National Arms **Rev:** Zodiac - Sagittarius

| Date | Mintage | VF20 | XF40 | MS60 | MS63 | MS65 |
|---|---|---|---|---|---|---|
| 2005 | 500 | PF63 80.00 | PF65 90.00 | | | |

**KM# 76 100 RUBLEI**
14.14 g., 0.925 Silver 0.4205 oz. ASW, 32 mm. **Obv:** National Arms **Rev:** Lunar Year of the (fire) Dog

| Date | Mintage | VF20 | XF40 | MS60 | MS63 | MS65 |
|---|---|---|---|---|---|---|
| 2006 | 1,000 | PF63 80.00 | PF65 90.00 | | | |

**KM# 78 100 RUBLEI**
14.14 g., 0.925 Silver 0.4205 oz. ASW, 32 mm. **Obv:** National Arms **Rev:** Stag Beetle

| Date | Mintage | VF20 | XF40 | MS60 | MS63 | MS65 |
|---|---|---|---|---|---|---|
| 2006 | 500 | PF63 100 | PF65 125 | | | |

**KM# 80 100 RUBLEI**
14.14 g., 0.925 Silver 0.4205 oz. ASW, 32 mm. **Obv:** National Arms **Rev:** Biathlon

| Date | Mintage | VF20 | XF40 | MS60 | MS63 | MS65 |
|---|---|---|---|---|---|---|
| 2006 | 300 | PF63 135 | PF65 150 | | | |

**KM# 81 100 RUBLEI**
14.14 g., 0.925 Silver 0.4205 oz. ASW, 32 mm. **Subject:** Turin Olympics **Obv:** National Arms **Rev:** Ski Jump

| Date | Mintage | VF20 | XF40 | MS60 | MS63 | MS65 |
|---|---|---|---|---|---|---|
| 2006 | 200 | PF63 200 | PF65 225 | | | |

**KM# 82 100 RUBLEI**
14.14 g., 0.925 Silver 0.4205 oz. ASW, 32 mm. **Obv:** National Arms **Rev:** Town View - Tyraspol

| Date | Mintage | VF20 | XF40 | MS60 | MS63 | MS65 |
|---|---|---|---|---|---|---|
| 2006 | 500 | PF63 80.00 | PF65 90.00 | | | |

**KM# 83 100 RUBLEI**
14.14 g., 0.925 Silver 0.4205 oz. ASW, 32 mm. **Obv:** National Arms **Rev:** Town view Bendery

| Date | Mintage | VF20 | XF40 | MS60 | MS63 | MS65 |
|---|---|---|---|---|---|---|
| 2006 | 500 | PF63 80.00 | PF65 90.00 | | | |

**KM# 84 100 RUBLEI**
14.14 g., 0.925 Silver 0.4205 oz. ASW, 32 mm. **Obv:** Naational Arms **Rev:** Man in forest legend

| Date | Mintage | VF20 | XF40 | MS60 | MS63 | MS65 |
|---|---|---|---|---|---|---|
| 2006 | 1,000 | PF63 75.00 | PF65 85.00 | | | |

**KM# 85 100 RUBLEI**
14.14 g., 0.925 Silver 0.4205 oz. ASW, 32 mm. **Obv:** National Arms **Rev:** Legend - Fisherman in rowboat

| Date | Mintage | VF20 | XF40 | MS60 | MS63 | MS65 |
|---|---|---|---|---|---|---|
| 2006 | 1,000 | PF63 75.00 | PF65 85.00 | | | |

**KM# 86 100 RUBLEI**
14.14 g., 0.925 Silver 0.4205 oz. ASW, 32 mm. **Obv:** National Arms **Rev:** Legend dragon slayer

| Date | Mintage | VF20 | XF40 | MS60 | MS63 | MS65 |
|---|---|---|---|---|---|---|
| 2006 | 1,000 | PF63 75.00 | PF65 85.00 | | | |

**KM# 87 100 RUBLEI**
14.14 g., 0.925 Silver 0.4205 oz. ASW, 32 mm. **Obv:** National Arms **Rev:** Kossak

| Date | Mintage | VF20 | XF40 | MS60 | MS63 | MS65 |
|---|---|---|---|---|---|---|
| 2006 | 500 | PF63 90.00 | PF65 100 | | | |

**KM# 88 100 RUBLEI**
14.14 g., 0.925 Silver 0.4205 oz. ASW, 32 mm. **Obv:** National Arms **Rev:** General Bursak

| Date | Mintage | VF20 | XF40 | MS60 | MS63 | MS65 |
|---|---|---|---|---|---|---|
| 2006 | 500 | PF63 80.00 | PF65 90.00 | | | |

**KM# 89 100 RUBLEI**
14.14 g., 0.925 Silver 0.4205 oz. ASW, 32 mm. **Obv:** National Arms **Rev:** Multicolor baseball player hitting ball

| Date | Mintage | VF20 | XF40 | MS60 | MS63 | MS65 |
|---|---|---|---|---|---|---|
| 2006 | 500 | PF63 90.00 | PF65 100 | | | |

**KM# 90 100 RUBLEI**
14.14 g., 0.925 Silver 0.4205 oz. ASW, 32 mm. **Obv:** National Arms **Rev:** Cathedral of the Arch Angel Michael

| Date | Mintage | VF20 | XF40 | MS60 | MS63 | MS65 |
|---|---|---|---|---|---|---|
| 2006 | 500 | PF63 80.00 | PF65 90.00 | | | |

**KM# 91 100 RUBLEI**
14.14 g., 0.925 Silver 0.4205 oz. ASW, 32 mm. **Obv:** National Arms **Rev:** Sidor Bialy bust at right

| Date | Mintage | VF20 | XF40 | MS60 | MS63 | MS65 |
|---|---|---|---|---|---|---|
| 2006 | 300 | PF63 100 | PF65 125 | | | |

**KM# 92 100 RUBLEI**
14.14 g., 0.925 Silver 0.4205 oz. ASW, 32 mm. **Obv:** National Arms **Rev:** Seal impression, partially plated

| Date | Mintage | VF20 | XF40 | MS60 | MS63 | MS65 |
|---|---|---|---|---|---|---|
| 2006 | 300 | PF63 100 | PF65 125 | | | |

**KM# 136 100 RUBLEI**
14.14 g., 0.925 Silver 0.4205 oz. ASW, 32 mm. **Obv:** National Arms **Rev:** Monarch butterfly

| Date | Mintage | VF20 | XF40 | MS60 | MS63 | MS65 |
|---|---|---|---|---|---|---|
| 2006 | 1,000 | PF63 90.00 | PF65 100 | | | |

**KM# 96 100 RUBLEI**
14.14 g., 0.925 Silver 0.4205 oz. ASW, 32 mm. **Obv:** National Arms **Rev:** Rybnitsa Shield **Rev. Legend:** РЫЪЦИUА

| Date | Mintage | VF20 | XF40 | MS60 | MS63 | MS65 |
|---|---|---|---|---|---|---|
| 2007 | 500 | PF63 95.00 | PF65 115 | | | |

**KM# 113 100 RUBLEI**
14.14 g., 0.925 Silver 0.4205 oz. ASW, 32 mm. **Obv:** National Arms **Rev:** Lunar year of the pig

| Date | Mintage | VF20 | XF40 | MS60 | MS63 | MS65 |
|---|---|---|---|---|---|---|
| 2007 | 300 | PF63 100 | PF65 125 | | | |

**KM# 114 100 RUBLEI**
14.14 g., 0.925 Silver 0.4205 oz. ASW, 32 mm. **Obv:** National Arms **Rev:** Castle view, 4 towers

| Date | Mintage | VF20 | XF40 | MS60 | MS63 | MS65 |
|---|---|---|---|---|---|---|
| 2007 | 500 | PF63 80.00 | PF65 90.00 | | | |

**KM# 115 100 RUBLEI**
14.14 g., 0.925 Silver 0.4205 oz. ASW, 32 mm. **Subject:** Soroky Fortress **Obv:** National Arms **Rev:** Castle view central tower and gate

| Date | Mintage | VF20 | XF40 | MS60 | MS63 | MS65 |
|---|---|---|---|---|---|---|
| 2007 | 500 | PF63 80.00 | PF65 90.00 | | | |

**KM# 116 100 RUBLEI**
14.14 g., 0.925 Silver 0.4205 oz. ASW, 32 mm. **Obv:** National Arms **Rev:** Zachary Czerega Kulis, ship at left

| Date | Mintage | VF20 | XF40 | MS60 | MS63 | MS65 |
|---|---|---|---|---|---|---|
| 2007 | 300 | PF63 100 | PF65 125 | | | |

**KM# 117 100 RUBLEI**
14.14 g., 0.925 Silver 0.4205 oz. ASW, 32 mm. **Subject:** Anton Goloway **Obv:** National Arms **Rev:** Bust facing

| Date | Mintage | VF20 | XF40 | MS60 | MS63 | MS65 |
|---|---|---|---|---|---|---|
| 2007 | 300 | PF63 100 | PF65 125 | | | |

**KM# 118 100 RUBLEI**
14.14 g., 0.925 Silver 0.4205 oz. ASW, 32 mm. **Obv:** National Arms **Rev:** Alexander Kuszer

| Date | Mintage | VF20 | XF40 | MS60 | MS63 | MS65 |
|---|---|---|---|---|---|---|
| 2007 | 500 | PF63 80.00 | PF65 90.00 | | | |

**KM# 119 100 RUBLEI**
14.14 g., 0.925 Silver 0.4205 oz. ASW, 32 mm. **Obv:** National Arms **Rev:** Field Marshal - Rumiancew-Zadunajski

| Date | Mintage | VF20 | XF40 | MS60 | MS63 | MS65 |
|---|---|---|---|---|---|---|
| 2007 | 300 | PF63 100 | PF65 125 | | | |

**KM# 120 100 RUBLEI**
14.14 g., 0.925 Silver 0.4205 oz. ASW, 32 mm. **Obv:** National Arms **Rev:** General Potiomkin

| Date | Mintage | VF20 | XF40 | MS60 | MS63 | MS65 |
|---|---|---|---|---|---|---|
| 2007 | 300 | PF63 100 | PF65 125 | | | |

**KM# 121 100 RUBLEI**
14.14 g., 0.925 Silver 0.4205 oz. ASW, 32 mm. **Obv:** National Arms **Rev:** General Panin

| Date | Mintage | VF20 | XF40 | MS60 | MS63 | MS65 |
|---|---|---|---|---|---|---|
| 2007 | 300 | PF63 100 | PF65 125 | | | |

**KM# 130 100 RUBLEI**
14.14 g., 0.925 Silver 0.4205 oz. ASW, 32 mm. **Obv:** Naitonal Arms **Rev:** Tulip (Tulipa Biebersteiniana)

| Date | Mintage | VF20 | XF40 | MS60 | MS63 | MS65 |
|---|---|---|---|---|---|---|
| 2008 | — | PF63 100 | PF65 125 | | | |

**KM# 131 100 RUBLEI**
14.14 g., 0.925 Silver 0.4205 oz. ASW, 32 mm. **Obv:** National Arms **Rev:** Moldavian Metal Works shield

| Date | Mintage | VF20 | XF40 | MS60 | MS63 | MS65 |
|---|---|---|---|---|---|---|
| 2008 | 500 | PF63 80.00 | PF65 90.00 | | | |

**KM# 132 100 RUBLEI**
14.14 g., 0.925 Silver 0.4205 oz. ASW, 32 mm. **Obv:** National Arms **Rev:** Field Marshal Piotr Vitgenshtain

| Date | Mintage | VF20 | XF40 | MS60 | MS63 | MS65 |
|---|---|---|---|---|---|---|
| 2008 | 500 | PF63 80.00 | PF65 90.00 | | | |

**KM# 133 100 RUBLEI**
14.14 g., 0.925 Silver 0.4205 oz. ASW, 32 mm. **Obv:** National Arms **Rev:** Belgorod Dnestrovskaya Fortress

| Date | Mintage | VF20 | XF40 | MS60 | MS63 | MS65 |
|---|---|---|---|---|---|---|
| 2008 | 500 | PF63 80.00 | PF65 90.00 | | | |

**KM# 144 100 RUBLEI**
14.14 g., Silver **Subject:** Year of the Rat

| Date | Mintage | VF20 | XF40 | MS60 | MS63 | MS65 |
|---|---|---|---|---|---|---|
| 2008 | 500 | PF63 90.00 | PF65 100 | | | |

**KM# 146 100 RUBLEI**
14.14 g., 0.925 Silver 0.4205 oz. ASW **Subject:** Ancient Fortresses on the Dniester

| Date | Mintage | VF20 | XF40 | MS60 | MS63 | MS65 |
|---|---|---|---|---|---|---|
| 2008 | 500 | PF63 80.00 | PF65 90.00 | | | |

**KM# 147 100 RUBLEI**
14.14 g., 0.925 Silver 0.4205 oz. ASW **Subject:** 90th Birthday of Valentina Soloveva

| Date | Mintage | VF20 | XF40 | MS60 | MS63 | MS65 |
|---|---|---|---|---|---|---|
| 2008 | 500 | PF63 80.00 | PF65 90.00 | | | |

**KM# 129 100 RUBLEI**
14.14 g., 0.925 Silver 0.4205 oz. ASW, 32 mm. **Subject:** Year of the Bull

| Date | Mintage | VF20 | XF40 | MS60 | MS63 | MS65 |
|---|---|---|---|---|---|---|
| 2009 | 500 | PF63 95.00 | PF65 115 | | | |

**KM# 166 100 RUBLEI**
33.85 g., 0.925 Silver 1.0067 oz. ASW, 39 mm. **Subject:** 10th Anniversary of the Transnistria Telephone Company

| Date | Mintage | VF20 | XF40 | MS60 | MS63 | MS65 |
|---|---|---|---|---|---|---|
| 2009 | 570 | PF63 85.00 | PF65 95.00 | | | |

**KM# 169 100 RUBLEI**
14.14 g., 0.925 Silver 0.4205 oz. ASW, 32 mm. **Subject:** Year of the Tiger

| Date | Mintage | VF20 | XF40 | MS60 | MS63 | MS65 |
|---|---|---|---|---|---|---|
| 2010 | 250 | PF63 95.00 | PF65 110 | | | |

**KM# 143 100 RUBLEI**
15.50 g., 0.925 Silver 0.461 oz. ASW, 32 mm. **Subject:** Garry Faif - Architect and Sculptor

| Date | Mintage | VF20 | XF40 | MS60 | MS63 | MS65 |
|---|---|---|---|---|---|---|
| 2011 | Est. 250 | PF63 90.00 | PF65 100 | | | |

**KM# 174 100 RUBLEI**
13.87 g., 0.925 Silver 0.4125 oz. ASW, 32 mm. **Subject:** Chinese Lunar Year of the Rabbit

| Date | Mintage | VF20 | XF40 | MS60 | MS63 | MS65 |
|---|---|---|---|---|---|---|
| 2011 | 300 | PF63 95.00 | PF65 110 | | | |

**KM# 139 100 RUBLEI**
Silver **Obv:** Khotyn Fortress

| Date | Mintage | VF20 | XF40 | MS60 | MS63 | MS65 |
|---|---|---|---|---|---|---|
| 2012 Prooflike | — | PF63 100 | PF65 125 | | | |

**KM# 140 100 RUBLEI**
14.14 g., 0.925 Silver 0.4205 oz. ASW, 32 mm. **Obv:** Arms **Rev:** Year of the Dragon

| Date | Mintage | VF20 | XF40 | MS60 | MS63 | MS65 |
|---|---|---|---|---|---|---|
| 2012 Prooflike | Est. 250 | PF63 100 | PF65 125 | | | |

### KM# 23 1000 RUBLEI

8.00 g., 0.900 Gold 0.2315 oz. AGW, 21 mm. **Obv:** National Arms **Rev:** Church of the Blessed Virgins

| Date | Mintage | VF20 | XF40 | MS60 | MS63 | MS65 |
|---|---|---|---|---|---|---|
| 2001 | 50 | PF65 700 | | | | |

### KM# 24 1000 RUBLEI

8.00 g., 0.900 Gold 0.2315 oz. AGW, 21 mm. **Obv:** National Arms **Rev:** Orthodox Church of the Virgin's Assumption

| Date | Mintage | VF20 | XF40 | MS60 | MS63 | MS65 |
|---|---|---|---|---|---|---|
| 2001 | 50 | PF65 700 | | | | |

### KM# 25 1000 RUBLEI

8.00 g., 0.900 Gold 0.2315 oz. AGW, 21 mm. **Obv:** National Arms **Rev:** 1800 Cathedral of God's Ascension

| Date | Mintage | VF20 | XF40 | MS60 | MS63 | MS65 |
|---|---|---|---|---|---|---|
| 2001 | 50 | PF65 700 | | | | |

### KM# 26 1000 RUBLEI

8.00 g., 0.900 Gold 0.2315 oz. AGW, 21 mm. **Obv:** National Arms **Rev:** Cathedral of the Birth of Christ

| Date | Mintage | VF20 | XF40 | MS60 | MS63 | MS65 |
|---|---|---|---|---|---|---|
| 2001 | 50 | PF65 700 | | | | |

### KM# 27 1000 RUBLEI

8.00 g., 0.900 Gold 0.2315 oz. AGW, 21 mm. **Rev:** Cathedral of the Transfiguration

| Date | Mintage | VF20 | XF40 | MS60 | MS63 | MS65 |
|---|---|---|---|---|---|---|
| 2001 | 50 | PF65 700 | | | | |

### KM# 28 1000 RUBLEI

8.00 g., 0.900 Gold 0.2315 oz. AGW, 21 mm. **Obv:** National Arms **Rev:** Church of the Blessed Virgin's Birth

| Date | Mintage | VF20 | XF40 | MS60 | MS63 | MS65 |
|---|---|---|---|---|---|---|
| 2001 | 50 | PF65 700 | | | | |

### KM# 29 1000 RUBLEI

8.00 g., 0.900 Gold 0.2315 oz. AGW, 21 mm. **Obv:** National Arms **Rev:** Church of the Transfiguration

| Date | Mintage | VF20 | XF40 | MS60 | MS63 | MS65 |
|---|---|---|---|---|---|---|
| 2001 | 50 | PF65 700 | | | | |

### KM# 30 1000 RUBLEI

8.00 g., 0.900 Gold 0.2315 oz. AGW, 21 mm. **Obv:** National Arms **Rev:** Church of the Lifegiving Trinity

| Date | Mintage | VF20 | XF40 | MS60 | MS63 | MS65 |
|---|---|---|---|---|---|---|
| 2001 | 50 | PF65 700 | | | | |

### KM# 31 1000 RUBLEI

8.00 g., 0.900 Gold 0.2315 oz. AGW, 21 mm. **Obv:** National Arms **Rev:** Orthodox Church to the Serbian Paraskeva (1854)

| Date | Mintage | VF20 | XF40 | MS60 | MS63 | MS65 |
|---|---|---|---|---|---|---|
| 2001 | 50 | PF65 700 | | | | |

### KM# 32 1000 RUBLEI

8.00 g., 0.900 Gold 0.2315 oz. AGW, 21 mm. **Obv:** National Arms **Rev:** Church of Michael the Arch Angel in Stoiesti

| Date | Mintage | VF20 | XF40 | MS60 | MS63 | MS65 |
|---|---|---|---|---|---|---|
| 2001 | 50 | PF65 700 | | | | |

## MINT SETS

| KM# | Date | Mintage | Identification | Issue Price | Mkt Val |
|---|---|---|---|---|---|
| MS1 | 2005 (4) | — | KM#50, 51, 52a, 53. | — | 20.00 |

# TRINIDAD & TOBAGO

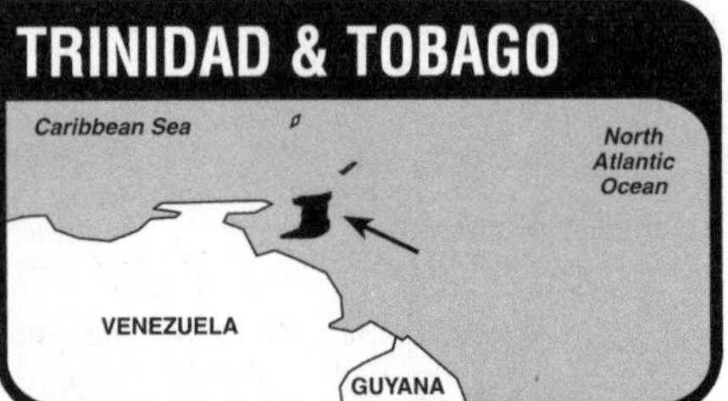


The Republic of Trinidad and Tobago is situated 7 miles (11 km.) off the coast of Venezuela, has an area of 1,981 sq. mi. (5,130 sq. km.) and a population of *1.2 million. Capital: Port-of-Spain. The island of Trinidad contains the world's largest natural asphalt bog. Birds of Paradise live on little Tobago, the only place outside of their native New Guinea where they can be found in a wild state. Petroleum and petroleum products are the mainstay of the economy. Petroleum products, crude oil and sugar are exported.

Trinidad and Tobago is a member of the Commonwealth of Nations. The President is Chief of State. The Prime Minister is Head of Government.

**MONETARY SYSTEM**

100 Cents = 1 Dollar

## REPUBLIC

## STANDARD COINAGE

### KM# 29 CENT

1.95 g., Bronze, 17.76 mm. **Obv:** National arms **Rev:** Hummingbird and value **Edge:** Plain

| Date | Mintage | VF20 | XF40 | MS60 | MS63 | MS65 |
|---|---|---|---|---|---|---|
| 2001 | — | — | 0.10 | 0.20 | 0.30 | 0.40 |
| 2002 | — | — | 0.10 | 0.20 | 0.30 | 0.40 |
| 2003 | — | — | 0.10 | 0.20 | 0.30 | 0.40 |
| 2005 | — | — | 0.10 | 0.20 | 0.30 | 0.40 |
| 2006 | — | — | 0.10 | 0.20 | 0.30 | 0.40 |
| 2007 | — | — | 0.10 | 0.20 | 0.30 | 0.40 |
| 2008 | — | — | 0.10 | 0.20 | 0.30 | 0.40 |
| 2009 | — | — | 0.10 | 0.20 | 0.30 | 0.40 |
| 2010 | — | — | 0.10 | 0.20 | 0.30 | 0.40 |
| 2011 | — | — | 0.10 | 0.20 | 0.30 | 0.40 |

### KM# 30 5 CENTS

3.31 g., Bronze, 21.2 mm. **Obv:** National arms **Rev:** Bird of paradise and value **Edge:** Plain

| Date | Mintage | VF20 | XF40 | MS60 | MS63 | MS65 |
|---|---|---|---|---|---|---|
| 2001 | — | — | 0.15 | 0.25 | 0.45 | 0.60 |
| 2002 | — | — | 0.15 | 0.25 | 0.45 | 0.60 |
| 2003 | — | — | 0.15 | 0.25 | 0.45 | 0.60 |
| 2004 | — | — | 0.15 | 0.25 | 0.45 | 0.60 |
| 2005 | — | — | 0.15 | 0.25 | 0.45 | 0.60 |
| 2006 | — | — | 0.15 | 0.25 | 0.45 | 0.60 |
| 2007 | — | — | 0.15 | 0.25 | 0.45 | 0.60 |
| 2008 | — | — | 0.15 | 0.25 | 0.45 | 0.60 |
| 2009 | — | — | 0.15 | 0.25 | 0.45 | 0.60 |
| 2010 | — | — | 0.15 | 0.25 | 0.45 | 0.60 |

### KM# 31 10 CENTS

1.40 g., Copper-Nickel, 16.2 mm. **Obv:** National arms **Rev:** Hibiscus and value **Edge:** Reeded

| Date | Mintage | VF20 | XF40 | MS60 | MS63 | MS65 |
|---|---|---|---|---|---|---|
| 2001 | — | — | 0.25 | 0.60 | 0.75 | 1.00 |
| 2002 | — | — | 0.25 | 0.60 | 0.75 | 1.00 |
| 2003 | — | — | 0.25 | 0.60 | 0.75 | 1.00 |
| 2004 | — | — | 0.25 | 0.60 | 0.75 | 1.00 |
| 2005 | — | — | 0.25 | 0.60 | 0.75 | 1.00 |
| 2006 | — | — | 0.25 | 0.60 | 0.75 | 1.00 |
| 2007 | — | — | 0.25 | 0.60 | 0.75 | 1.00 |
| 2008 | — | — | 0.25 | 0.60 | 0.75 | 1.00 |

### KM# 32 25 CENTS

3.50 g., Copper-Nickel, 20 mm. **Obv:** National arms **Rev:** Chaconia and value **Edge:** Reeded

| Date | Mintage | VF20 | XF40 | MS60 | MS63 | MS65 |
|---|---|---|---|---|---|---|
| 2001 | — | — | 0.30 | 0.50 | 0.75 | 1.00 |
| 2002 | — | — | 0.30 | 0.50 | 0.75 | 1.00 |
| 2003 | — | — | 0.30 | 0.50 | 0.75 | 1.00 |
| 2004 | — | — | 0.30 | 0.50 | 0.75 | 1.00 |
| 2005 | — | — | 0.30 | 0.50 | 0.75 | 1.00 |
| 2006 | — | — | 0.30 | 0.50 | 0.75 | 1.00 |
| 2007 | — | — | 0.30 | 0.50 | 0.75 | 1.00 |
| 2008 | — | — | 0.30 | 0.50 | 0.75 | 1.00 |

### KM# 33 50 CENTS

7.00 g., Copper-Nickel, 26 mm. **Obv:** National arms **Rev:** Kettle drums and value **Edge:** Reeded

| Date | Mintage | VF20 | XF40 | MS60 | MS63 | MS65 |
|---|---|---|---|---|---|---|
| 2003 | — | — | 1.00 | 2.00 | 3.00 | 4.00 |

### KM# 63 10 DOLLARS

Copper-Nickel **Subject:** FIFA - XVIII World Football Championship - Soca Warriors - Germany 2006 **Obv:** Native hands playing steel drum, gilt **Rev:** Logo

| Date | Mintage | VF20 | XF40 | MS60 | MS63 | MS65 |
|---|---|---|---|---|---|---|
| 2006 | — | — | — | — | 20.00 | 35.00 |

### KM# 64 100 DOLLARS

28.28 g., 0.925 Silver 0.841 oz. ASW **Subject:** FIFA - XVIII World Football Championship - Soca Warriors - Germany 2006 **Obv:** Native hands playing steel drum, gilt **Rev:** Logo

| Date | Mintage | VF20 | XF40 | MS60 | MS63 | MS65 |
|---|---|---|---|---|---|---|
| 2006 | — | PF63 75.00 | PF65 90.00 | | | |

# TRISTAN DA CUNHA

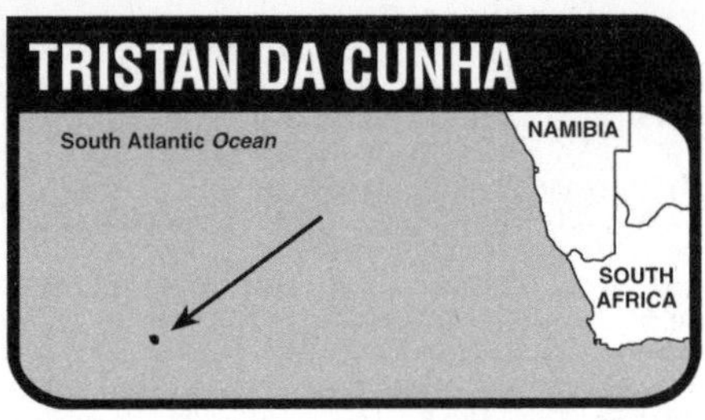


Tristan da Cunha is the principal island and group name of a small cluster of volcanic islands located in the South Atlantic midway between the Cape of Good Hope and South America, and 1,500 miles (2,414 km.) south-southwest of the British colony of St. Helena. The other islands are inaccessible, Gough, and the three Nightingale Islands. The group, which comprises a dependency of St. Helena, has a total area of 40 sq. mi. (104 sq. km.) and a population of less than 300. There is a village of 60 houses called Edinburgh. Potatoes are the staple subsistence crop.

**MONETARY SYSTEM**

100 Pence = 1 Pound

## ST. HELENA DEPENDENCY

## STANDARD COINAGE

### KM# 27 1/2 PENNY

3.83 g., Copper, 16.91 mm. **Ruler:** Elizabeth II **Obv:** Head with tiara right **Rev:** Snipe Eel **Edge:** Plain

| Date | Mintage | VF20 | XF40 | MS60 | MS63 | MS65 |
|---|---|---|---|---|---|---|
| 2008 | — | — | — | 0.40 | 0.75 | 1.00 |

### KM# 28 PENNY

4.63 g., Copper, 18.66 mm. **Ruler:** Elizabeth II **Obv:** Head with tiara right **Rev:** Crayfish **Edge:** Plain

| Date | Mintage | VF20 | XF40 | MS60 | MS63 | MS65 |
|---|---|---|---|---|---|---|
| 2008 | — | — | — | 0.60 | 1.20 | 1.60 |

### KM# 29 2 PENCE

6.60 g., Copper, 22.02 mm. **Ruler:** Elizabeth II **Obv:** Head with tiara right **Rev:** Violet Seasnail **Edge:** Plain

| Date | Mintage | VF20 | XF40 | MS60 | MS63 | MS65 |
|---|---|---|---|---|---|---|
| 2008 | — | — | — | 0.75 | 1.50 | 2.00 |

### KM# 30 5 PENCE

3.74 g., Copper-Nickel, 16.90 mm. **Ruler:** Elizabeth II **Obv:** Head with tiara right **Rev:** Sea Turtle **Edge:** Plain

| Date | Mintage | VF20 | XF40 | MS60 | MS63 | MS65 |
|---|---|---|---|---|---|---|
| 2008 | — | — | — | 1.00 | 2.00 | 2.50 |

### KM# 31 10 PENCE

6.49 g., Copper-Nickel, 22.03 mm. **Ruler:** Elizabeth II **Obv:** Head with tiara right **Rev:** Crab **Edge:** Plain

| Date | Mintage | VF20 | XF40 | MS60 | MS63 | MS65 |
|---|---|---|---|---|---|---|
| 2008 | — | — | — | 1.25 | 2.25 | 3.00 |

**KM# 32 20 PENCE**
6.10 g., Aluminum-Bronze, 22.02 mm. **Ruler:** Elizabeth II **Obv:** Head with tiara right **Rev:** Orcha - Killer Whale **Edge:** Plain

| Date | Mintage | VF20 | XF40 | MS60 | MS63 | MS65 |
|---|---|---|---|---|---|---|
| 2008 | — | — | — | 1.50 | 3.00 | 4.00 |

**KM# 33 25 PENCE**
Bi-Metallic Aluminum-Bronze center in Copper-Nickel ring., 25.76 mm. **Ruler:** Elizabeth II **Obv:** Head with tiara right **Rev:** 2 Bottlenose Dolphins **Edge:** Plain

| Date | Mintage | VF20 | XF40 | MS60 | MS63 | MS65 |
|---|---|---|---|---|---|---|
| 2008 | — | — | — | 4.00 | 6.00 | 8.00 |

**KM# 12 50 PENCE**
29.10 g., Copper-Nickel, 38.6 mm. **Ruler:** Elizabeth II **Subject:** Queen Elizabeth's 75th Birthday **Obv:** Crowned bust right **Rev:** Crowned bust facing **Edge:** Reeded

| Date | Mintage | VF20 | XF40 | MS60 | MS63 | MS65 |
|---|---|---|---|---|---|---|
| 2001 | — | — | — | 4.00 | 6.00 | 9.00 |

**KM# 12a 50 PENCE**
28.28 g., 0.925 Silver 0.841 oz. ASW, 38.6 mm. **Ruler:** Elizabeth II **Subject:** Queen's 75th Birthday **Obv:** Crowned bust right **Rev:** Crowned bust facing **Edge:** Reeded

| Date | Mintage | VF20 | XF40 | MS60 | MS63 | MS65 |
|---|---|---|---|---|---|---|
| 2001 | 10,000 | PF63 40.00 | PF65 45.00 | | | |

**KM# 12b 50 PENCE**
47.54 g., 0.9166 Gold 1.401 oz. AGW, 38.6 mm. **Ruler:** Elizabeth II **Obv:** Crowned bust right **Rev:** Crowned bust facing

| Date | Mintage | VF20 | XF40 | MS60 | MS63 | MS65 |
|---|---|---|---|---|---|---|
| 2001 | 75 | PF65 2,700 | | | | |

**KM# 13 50 PENCE**
29.60 g., Copper-Nickel, 38.7 mm. **Ruler:** Elizabeth II **Subject:** Centennial of Queen Victoria's Death **Obv:** Crowned bust right **Rev:** Crown and veil on half-length figure of Queen Victoria facing left within oval circle **Edge:** Reeded

| Date | Mintage | VF20 | XF40 | MS60 | MS63 | MS65 |
|---|---|---|---|---|---|---|
| 2001 | — | — | — | 6.00 | 8.00 | 10.00 |

**KM# 13a 50 PENCE**
28.28 g., 0.925 Silver 0.841 oz. ASW, 38.6 mm. **Ruler:** Elizabeth II **Subject:** Centennial of Queen Victoria's Death **Obv:** Crowned bust right **Rev:** Crown and veil on half-length figure of Queen Victoria facing left within oval circle **Edge:** Reeded

| Date | Mintage | VF20 | XF40 | MS60 | MS63 | MS65 |
|---|---|---|---|---|---|---|
| 2001 | 10,000 | PF63 50.00 | PF65 55.00 | | | |

**KM# 13b 50 PENCE**
47.54 g., 0.9166 Gold 1.401 oz. AGW, 38.6 mm. **Ruler:** Elizabeth II **Subject:** Centennial of Queen Victoria's Death **Obv:** Crowned bust right **Rev:** Crown and veil on half-length figure of Queen Victoria facing left within oval circle **Edge:** Reeded

| Date | Mintage | VF20 | XF40 | MS60 | MS63 | MS65 |
|---|---|---|---|---|---|---|
| 2001 | 100 | PF65 2,700 | | | | |

**KM# 14 CROWN**
Copper-Nickel, 38.5 mm. **Ruler:** Elizabeth II **Obv:** Crowned bust right **Rev:** Pope John Paul II **Edge:** Reeded

| Date | Mintage | VF20 | XF40 | MS60 | MS63 | MS65 |
|---|---|---|---|---|---|---|
| 2005 | — | — | — | — | 8.50 | 12.00 |

**KM# 14a CROWN**
24.12 g., 0.925 Silver 0.7173 oz. ASW, 38.5 mm. **Ruler:** Elizabeth II **Obv:** Crowned bust right **Rev:** Pope John Paul II **Edge:** Reeded

| Date | Mintage | VF20 | XF40 | MS60 | MS63 | MS65 |
|---|---|---|---|---|---|---|
| 2005 | — | PF63 45.00 | PF65 50.00 | | | |

**KM# 41 CROWN**
Copper-Nickel, 38.6 mm. **Ruler:** Elizabeth II **Obv:** Bust crowned right **Rev:** Conjoined busts left

| Date | Mintage | VF20 | XF40 | MS60 | MS63 | MS65 |
|---|---|---|---|---|---|---|
| 2005 | — | — | — | — | — | 20.00 |

**KM# 43 CROWN**
Copper-Nickel, 38.6 mm. **Ruler:** Elizabeth II **Obv:** Bust in tiara right **Rev:** Lord Nelson's bust 1/4 left

| Date | Mintage | VF20 | XF40 | MS60 | MS63 | MS65 |
|---|---|---|---|---|---|---|
| 2005 | — | — | — | — | — | 15.00 |

**KM# 44 CROWN**
Copper-Nickel, 38.6 mm. **Ruler:** Elizabeth II **Subject:** VE-Day, 60th Anniversary **Obv:** Bust in tiara right **Rev:** Ship, tank, two panes

| Date | Mintage | VF20 | XF40 | MS60 | MS63 | MS65 |
|---|---|---|---|---|---|---|
| 2005 | — | — | — | — | — | 15.00 |

**KM# 15 CROWN**
25.00 g., Copper-Nickel, 38.83 mm. **Ruler:** Elizabeth II **Series:** Privateering ships of the South Atlantic **Obv:** Crowned bust right **Obv. Legend:** ELIZABETH II — TRISTAN DA CUNHA **Rev:** Sailing ship "Tybalt **Edge:** Reeded

| Date | Mintage | VF20 | XF40 | MS60 | MS63 | MS65 |
|---|---|---|---|---|---|---|
| 2006 | — | — | — | — | 8.50 | 12.00 |

**KM# 16 CROWN**
25.00 g., Copper-Nickel, 38.83 mm. **Ruler:** Elizabeth II **Series:** Privateering ships of the South Atlantic **Obv:** Crowned bust right **Obv. Legend:** ELIZABETH II — TRISTAN DA CUNHA **Rev:** Sailing ship "Syren **Edge:** Reeded

| Date | Mintage | VF20 | XF40 | MS60 | MS63 | MS65 |
|---|---|---|---|---|---|---|
| 2006 | — | — | — | — | 8.50 | 12.00 |

**KM# 17 CROWN**
25.00 g., Copper-Nickel, 38.83 mm. **Ruler:** Elizabeth II **Series:** Privateering ships of the South Atlantic **Obv:** Crowned bust right **Obv. Legend:** ELIZABETH II — TRISTAN DA CUNHA **Rev:** Sailing ship "Pride of Baltimore **Edge:** Reeded

| Date | Mintage | VF20 | XF40 | MS60 | MS63 | MS65 |
|---|---|---|---|---|---|---|
| 2006 | — | — | — | — | 8.50 | 12.00 |

**KM# 18 CROWN**
25.00 g., Copper-Nickel, 38.83 mm. **Ruler:** Elizabeth II **Series:** Privateering ships of the South Atlantic **Obv:** Crowned bust right **Obv. Legend:** ELIZABETH II — TRISTAN DA CUNHA **Rev:** Sailing ship "Hornet **Edge:** Reeded

| Date | Mintage | VF20 | XF40 | MS60 | MS63 | MS65 |
|---|---|---|---|---|---|---|
| 2006 | — | — | — | — | 8.50 | 12.00 |

**KM# 19 CROWN**
25.00 g., Copper-Nickel, 38.83 mm. **Ruler:** Elizabeth II **Series:** Privateering ships of the South Atlantic **Obv:** Crowned bust right **Obv. Legend:** ELIZABETH II — TRISTAN DA CUNHA **Rev:** Sailing ship "Griffin **Edge:** Reeded

| Date | Mintage | VF20 | XF40 | MS60 | MS63 | MS65 |
|---|---|---|---|---|---|---|
| 2006 | — | — | — | — | 8.50 | 12.00 |

**KM# 20 CROWN**
25.00 g., Copper-Nickel, 38.83 mm. **Ruler:** Elizabeth II **Series:** Privateering ships of the South Atlantic **Obv:** Crowned bust right **Obv. Legend:** ELIZABETH II — TRISTAN DA CUNHA **Rev:** Sailing ship "Enterprise **Edge:** Reeded

| Date | Mintage | VF20 | XF40 | MS60 | MS63 | MS65 |
|---|---|---|---|---|---|---|
| 2006 | — | — | — | — | 8.50 | 12.00 |

**KM# 21 CROWN**
25.00 g., Copper-Nickel, 38.83 mm. **Ruler:** Elizabeth II **Series:** Privateering ships of the South Atlantic **Obv:** Crowned bust right **Obv. Legend:** ELIZABETH II — TRISTAN DA CUNHA **Rev:** Sailing ship "Columbus **Edge:** Reeded

| Date | Mintage | VF20 | XF40 | MS60 | MS63 | MS65 |
|---|---|---|---|---|---|---|
| 2006 | — | — | — | — | 8.50 | 12.00 |

**KM# 22 CROWN**
25.00 g., Copper-Nickel, 38.8 mm. **Ruler:** Elizabeth II **Series:** Privateering ships of the South Atlantic **Obv:** Crowned bust right **Obv. Legend:** ELIZABETH II — TRISTAN DA CUNHA **Rev:** Sailing ship "Chausseur **Edge:** Reeded

| Date | Mintage | VF20 | XF40 | MS60 | MS63 | MS65 |
|---|---|---|---|---|---|---|
| 2006 | — | — | — | — | 8.50 | 12.00 |

**KM# 23 CROWN**
25.00 g., Copper-Nickel, 38.8 mm. **Ruler:** Elizabeth II **Series:** Privateering ships of the South Atlantic **Obv:** Crowned bust right **Obv. Legend:** ELIZABETH II — TRISTAN DA CUNHA **Rev:** Sailing ship "Cabot **Edge:** Reeded

| Date | Mintage | VF20 | XF40 | MS60 | MS63 | MS65 |
|---|---|---|---|---|---|---|
| 2006 | — | — | — | — | 8.50 | 12.00 |

**KM# 24 CROWN**
25.00 g., Copper-Nickel, 38.8 mm. **Ruler:** Elizabeth II **Series:** Privateering ships of the South Atlantic **Obv:** Crowned bust right **Obv. Legend:** ELIZABETH II — TRISTAN DA CUNHA **Rev:** Sailing ship "Black Prince **Edge:** Reeded

| Date | Mintage | VF20 | XF40 | MS60 | MS63 | MS65 |
|---|---|---|---|---|---|---|
| 2006 | — | — | — | — | 8.50 | 12.00 |

**KM# 25 CROWN**
25.00 g., Copper-Nickel, 38.8 mm. **Ruler:** Elizabeth II **Series:** Privateering ships of the South Atlantic **Obv:** Crowned bust right **Obv. Legend:** ELIZABETH II — TRISTAN DA CUNHA **Rev:** Sailing ship "Argus **Edge:** Reeded

| Date | Mintage | VF20 | XF40 | MS60 | MS63 | MS65 |
|---|---|---|---|---|---|---|
| 2006 | — | — | — | — | 8.50 | 12.00 |

**KM# 26 CROWN**
25.00 g., Copper-Nickel, 38.8 mm. **Ruler:** Elizabeth II **Series:** Privateering ships of the South Atlantic **Obv:** Crowned bust right **Obv. Legend:** ELIZABETH II — TRISTAN DA CUNHA **Rev:** Sailing ship "True Blooded Yankee **Edge:** Reeded

| Date | Mintage | VF20 | XF40 | MS60 | MS63 | MS65 |
|---|---|---|---|---|---|---|
| 2006 | — | — | — | — | 8.50 | 12.00 |

**KM# 34 CROWN**
Copper-Nickel, 39 mm. **Ruler:** Elizabeth II **Obv:** Bust right **Rev:** Two whales

| Date | Mintage | VF20 | XF40 | MS60 | MS63 | MS65 |
|---|---|---|---|---|---|---|
| 2008 | — | — | — | — | — | 15.00 |

**KM# 34a CROWN**
Copper-Nickel, 38 mm. **Ruler:** Elizabeth II **Obv:** Head with tiara right **Rev:** 2 whales, multicolor

| Date | Mintage | VF20 | XF40 | MS60 | MS63 | MS65 |
|---|---|---|---|---|---|---|
| 2008 | — | — | — | — | 8.00 | 15.00 |

**KM# 35 CROWN**
Copper-Nickel, 38.75 mm. **Ruler:** Elizabeth II **Rev:** HMS Victory

| Date | Mintage | VF20 | XF40 | MS60 | MS63 | MS65 |
|---|---|---|---|---|---|---|
| 2008 | — | — | — | — | — | 15.00 |

**KM# 36 CROWN**
25.18 g., Copper-Nickel **Ruler:** Elizabeth II **Obv:** HMS Belfast

| Date | Mintage | VF20 | XF40 | MS60 | MS63 | MS65 |
|---|---|---|---|---|---|---|
| 2008 | — | — | — | — | — | 15.00 |

**KM# 37 CROWN**
25.18 g., Copper-Nickel, 38.75 mm. **Ruler:** Elizabeth II **Obv:** HMS Sceptre

| Date | Mintage | VF20 | XF40 | MS60 | MS63 | MS65 |
|---|---|---|---|---|---|---|
| 2008 | — | — | — | — | — | 15.00 |

**KM# 38 CROWN**
25.18 g., Copper-Nickel, 38.75 mm. **Ruler:** Elizabeth II **Obv:** HMS Beagle

| Date | Mintage | VF20 | XF40 | MS60 | MS63 | MS65 |
|---|---|---|---|---|---|---|
| 2008 | — | — | — | — | — | 15.00 |

**KM# 39 CROWN**
28.15 g., Copper-Nickel, 38.75 mm. **Ruler:** Elizabeth II **Obv:** HMS Dreadnought

| Date | Mintage | VF20 | XF40 | MS60 | MS63 | MS65 |
|---|---|---|---|---|---|---|
| 2008 | — | — | — | — | — | 15.00 |

**KM# 40 CROWN**
28.15 g., Copper-Nickel, 38.75 mm. **Ruler:** Elizabeth II **Rev:** H.M.S. Ark Royal

| Date | Mintage | VF20 | XF40 | MS60 | MS63 | MS65 |
|---|---|---|---|---|---|---|
| 2008 | — | — | — | — | — | 15.00 |

**KM# 46 CROWN**
28.85 g., Copper-Nickel, 38.8 mm. **Ruler:** Elizabeth II **Subject:** H.M.S. Invincible

| Date | Mintage | VF20 | XF40 | MS60 | MS63 | MS65 |
|---|---|---|---|---|---|---|
| 2008 | — | — | — | — | — | 11.00 |

**KM# 47 CROWN**
25.20 g., Copper-Nickel, 38.8 mm. **Ruler:** Elizabeth II **Subject:** H.M.S. Illustrious

| Date | Mintage | VF20 | XF40 | MS60 | MS63 | MS65 |
|---|---|---|---|---|---|---|
| 2008 | — | — | — | — | — | 11.00 |

**KM# 48 CROWN**
25.00 g., Copper-Nickel, 38.8 mm. **Ruler:** Elizabeth II **Subject:** H.M.S. Vanuard

| Date | Mintage | VF20 | XF40 | MS60 | MS63 | MS65 |
|---|---|---|---|---|---|---|
| 2008 | — | — | — | — | — | 11.00 |

**KM# 49 CROWN**
24.79 g., Copper-Nickel, 38.8 mm. **Ruler:** Elizabeth II **Subject:** H.M.S. Victoria

| Date | Mintage | VF20 | XF40 | MS60 | MS63 | MS65 |
|---|---|---|---|---|---|---|
| 2008 | — | — | — | — | — | 11.00 |

**KM# 42 5 POUNDS**
Silver **Ruler:** Elizabeth II **Rev:** St. George slaying dragon

| Date | Mintage | VF20 | XF40 | MS60 | MS63 | MS65 |
|---|---|---|---|---|---|---|
| 2008 | — | — | — | — | 45.00 | 50.00 |

**KM# 45 5 POUNDS**
Silver, 38.6 mm. **Ruler:** Elizabeth II **Obv:** Bust in tiara right **Rev:** Titles of the Queen

| Date | Mintage | VF20 | XF40 | MS60 | MS63 | MS65 |
|---|---|---|---|---|---|---|
| 2008 | — | PF63 50.00 | PF65 55.00 | | | |

## PIEDFORT

| KM# | Date | Mintage | Identification | Mkt Val |
|---|---|---|---|---|
| P1 | 2001 | 500 | 50 Pence 0.925 Silver | 100 |
| P2 | 2001 | 500 | 50 Pence 0.925 Silver Proof KM-13a. | 100 |

# GOUGH ISLAND

## DEPENDANCY

### DECIMAL COINAGE

**KM# 1 HALFPENNY**
Copper Plated Steel, 17 mm. **Ruler:** Elizabeth II **Obv:** Bust right **Obv. Legend:** GOUGH ISLAND Tristan da Cunha **Rev:** Gough moorhen **Edge:** Plain

| Date | Mintage | VF20 | XF40 | MS60 | MS63 | MS65 |
|---|---|---|---|---|---|---|
| 2009 | — | — | — | 0.45 | 0.75 | 1.00 |

**KM# 2 PENNY**
Copper Plated Steel, 18.5 mm. **Ruler:** Elizabeth II **Obv:** Bust right **Obv. Legend:** GOUGH ISLAND Tristan da Cunha **Rev:** Pair of Sooty Albatross **Edge:** Plain

| Date | Mintage | VF20 | XF40 | MS60 | MS63 | MS65 |
|---|---|---|---|---|---|---|
| 2009 | — | — | — | 0.65 | 1.00 | 1.50 |

**KM# 3 2 PENCE**
Copper Plated Steel, 22 mm. **Ruler:** Elizabeth II **Obv:** Bust right **Obv. Legend:** GOUGH ISLAND Tristan da Cunha **Rev:** Pair of Antarctic Tern **Edge:** Plain

| Date | Mintage | VF20 | XF40 | MS60 | MS63 | MS65 |
|---|---|---|---|---|---|---|
| 2009 | — | — | — | 1.00 | 1.50 | 2.00 |

**KM# 4 5 PENCE**
Copper-Nickel Plated Steel, 17 mm. **Ruler:** Elizabeth II **Obv:** Bust right **Obv. Legend:** GOUGH ISLAND Tristan da Cunha **Rev:** Northern Rock Hopper Penguins **Edge:** Plain

| Date | Mintage | VF20 | XF40 | MS60 | MS63 | MS65 |
|---|---|---|---|---|---|---|
| 2009 | — | — | — | 1.25 | 2.00 | 2.50 |

**KM# 5 10 PENCE**
Copper-Nickel Plated Steel, 22 mm. **Ruler:** Elizabeth II **Obv:** Bust right **Obv. Legend:** GOUGH ISLAND Tristan da Cunha **Rev:** Giant Petrel on water **Edge:** Plain

| Date | Mintage | VF20 | XF40 | MS60 | MS63 | MS65 |
|---|---|---|---|---|---|---|
| 2009 | — | — | — | 2.00 | 3.00 | 3.50 |

**KM# 6 20 PENCE**
Brass, 22 mm. **Ruler:** Elizabeth II **Obv:** Bust right **Obv. Legend:** GOUGH ISLAND Tristan da Cunha **Rev:** Antarctic Skua **Edge:** Plain

| Date | Mintage | VF20 | XF40 | MS60 | MS63 | MS65 |
|---|---|---|---|---|---|---|
| 2009 | — | — | — | 3.00 | 4.50 | 5.00 |

**KM# 7 25 PENCE**
Bi-Metallic Brass center in Copper-Nickel ring, 25.8 mm. **Ruler:** Elizabeth II **Obv:** Bust right **Obv. Legend:** GOUGH ISLAND Tristan da Cunha **Rev:** Barn Owl **Edge:** Plain

| Date | Mintage | VF20 | XF40 | MS60 | MS63 | MS65 |
|---|---|---|---|---|---|---|
| 2009 | — | — | — | 5.00 | 8.00 | 9.00 |

**KM# 8 CROWN**
Copper-Nickel, 38.8 mm. **Ruler:** Elizabeth II **Obv:** Bust right **Obv. Legend:** GOUGH ISLAND Tristan da Cunha **Rev:** Peregrine Falcon **Edge:** Plain

| Date | Mintage | VF20 | XF40 | MS60 | MS63 | MS65 |
|---|---|---|---|---|---|---|
| 2009 | — | — | — | 8.00 | 12.00 | 14.00 |

# STOLTENHOFF ISLAND

## DEPENCENCY

### DECIMAL COINAGE

**KM# 1 HALFPENNY**
Copper Plated Steel, 17 mm. **Ruler:** Elizabeth II **Obv:** Bust right **Rev:** Small sailboat - West Riding Tragedy Longboat

| Date | Mintage | VF20 | XF40 | MS60 | MS63 | MS65 |
|---|---|---|---|---|---|---|
| 2008 | — | — | — | 0.45 | 0.75 | 1.00 |

**KM# 2 PENNY**
Copper Plated Steel **Ruler:** Elizabeth II **Obv:** Bust right **Rev:** 18th century sailing ship - Portuguese Carrack type

| Date | Mintage | VF20 | XF40 | MS60 | MS63 | MS65 |
|---|---|---|---|---|---|---|
| 2008 | — | — | — | 0.65 | 1.00 | 1.50 |

**KM# 3 2 PENCE**
Copper Plated Steel, 21.5 mm. **Ruler:** Elizabeth II **Obv:** Bust right **Rev:** Three masted sailing ship - HMS Julia

| Date | Mintage | VF20 | XF40 | MS60 | MS63 | MS65 |
|---|---|---|---|---|---|---|
| 2008 | — | — | — | 1.00 | 1.50 | 2.00 |

**KM# 4 5 PENCE**
Copper-Nickel Plated Steel, 16 mm. **Ruler:** Elizabeth II **Obv:** Bust right **Rev:** Two masted sailing ship - HMS Beagle

| Date | Mintage | VF20 | XF40 | MS60 | MS63 | MS65 |
|---|---|---|---|---|---|---|
| 2008 | — | — | — | 1.25 | 2.00 | 2.50 |

**KM# 5 10 PENCE**
Copper-Nickel Plated Steel, 21.5 mm. **Ruler:** Elizabeth II **Obv:** Bust right **Rev:** Three masted sailing ship - Blenden Hall

| Date | Mintage | VF20 | XF40 | MS60 | MS63 | MS65 |
|---|---|---|---|---|---|---|
| 2008 | — | — | — | 2.00 | 3.00 | 3.50 |

**KM# 6 20 PENCE**
Brass, 21.5 mm. **Ruler:** Elizabeth II **Obv:** Bust right **Rev:** Two masted sailing ship - HMS Satellite

| Date | Mintage | VF20 | XF40 | MS60 | MS63 | MS65 |
|---|---|---|---|---|---|---|
| 2008 | — | — | — | 3.00 | 4.50 | 5.00 |

**KM# 7 25 PENCE**
Bi-Metallic Brass center in Copper-Nickel ring, 25 mm. **Ruler:** Elizabeth II **Obv:** Bust right **Rev:** Sailing ship - Iron Barque West Riding

| Date | Mintage | VF20 | XF40 | MS60 | MS63 | MS65 |
|---|---|---|---|---|---|---|
| 2008 | — | — | — | 4.00 | 7.00 | 8.00 |

**KM# 8 CROWN**
Copper-Nickel, 39 mm. **Ruler:** Elizabeth II **Obv:** Bust right **Rev:** Sailing ship L'Heure du Berger

| Date | Mintage | VF20 | XF40 | MS60 | MS63 | MS65 |
|---|---|---|---|---|---|---|
| 2008 | — | — | — | 6.00 | 10.00 | 12.00 |

# TUNISIA

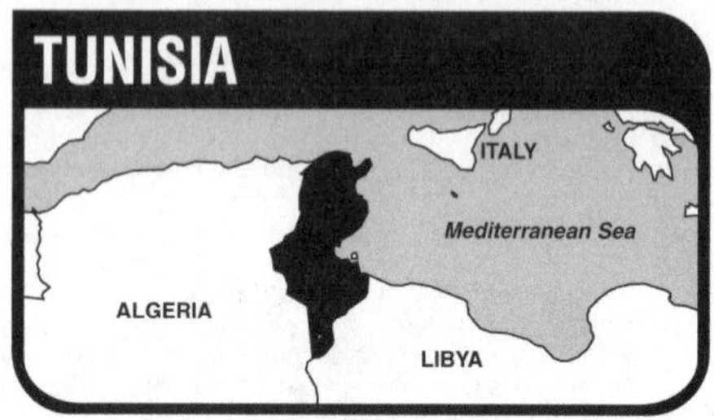


The Republic of Tunisia, located on the northern coast of Africa between Algeria and Libya, has an area of 63,170 sq. mi. (163,610 sq. km.) and a population of *7.9 million. Capital: Tunis. Agriculture is the backbone of the economy. Crude oil, phosphates, olive oil, and wine are exported.

**TITLES**

المملكة التونسية

al-Mamlaka al-Tunisiya

الجمهورية العراقية

al-Jumhuriya al-Tunisiya

al-Amala al-Tunisiya
(Tunisian Protectorate)

## REPUBLIC

### DECIMAL COINAGE

1000 Millim = 1 Dinar

**KM# 348 5 MILLIM**
1.49 g., Aluminum, 24 mm. **Obv:** Oak tree and dates **Rev:** Value within sprigs

| Date | Mintage | VF20 | XF40 | MS60 | MS63 | MS65 |
|---|---|---|---|---|---|---|
| AH1425-2004 | — | — | — | — | 0.50 | 1.00 |
| AH1426-2005 | — | — | — | — | 0.50 | 1.00 |

**KM# 306 10 MILLIM**
3.50 g., Brass, 19 mm. **Obv:** Inscription and dates within inner circle of design **Rev:** Value in center of design **Edge:** Reeded

| Date | Mintage | VF20 | XF40 | MS60 | MS63 | MS65 |
|---|---|---|---|---|---|---|
| AH1425-2004 | — | — | 0.15 | 0.25 | 0.50 | 1.00 |
| AH1426-2005 | — | — | 0.15 | 0.25 | 0.50 | 1.00 |
| AH1429-2008 | — | — | 0.15 | 0.25 | 0.50 | 1.00 |
| AH1432-2011 | — | — | 0.15 | 0.25 | 0.50 | 1.00 |

**KM# 306.1 10 MILLIM**
3.50 g., Brass Plated Steel, 19 mm. **Obv:** Inscription and dates within inner circle of design **Rev:** Value in center of design **Edge:** Reeded

| Date | Mintage | VF20 | XF40 | MS60 | MS63 | MS65 |
|---|---|---|---|---|---|---|
| AHAH1430-2009 | — | — | 0.15 | 0.25 | 0.50 | 1.00 |

**KM# 307 20 MILLIM**
4.50 g., Brass, 22 mm. **Obv:** Inscription and dates within center circle of design **Rev:** Value within center of design

| Date | Mintage | VF20 | XF40 | MS60 | MS63 | MS65 |
|---|---|---|---|---|---|---|
| AH1425-2004 | — | — | — | 0.50 | 0.80 | 1.00 |
| AH1426-2005 | — | — | — | 0.50 | 0.80 | 1.00 |
| AH1432-2011 | — | — | — | 0.50 | 0.80 | 1.00 |

**KM# 307a 20 MILLIM**
Brass Plated Steel

| Date | Mintage | VF20 | XF40 | MS60 | MS63 | MS65 |
|---|---|---|---|---|---|---|
| AH1428-2007 | — | — | — | — | 0.50 | 1.00 |
| AH1430-2009 | — | — | — | — | 0.50 | 1.00 |

**KM# 308 50 MILLIM**
6.00 g., Brass, 25 mm. **Obv:** Inscription and dates within center circle of design **Rev:** Value in center of design

| Date | Mintage | VF20 | XF40 | MS60 | MS63 | MS65 |
|---|---|---|---|---|---|---|
| AH1425-2004 | — | — | 0.65 | 0.85 | 1.25 | 1.50 |
| AH1426-2005 | — | — | 0.65 | 0.85 | 1.25 | 1.50 |
| AH1428-2007 | — | — | 0.65 | 0.85 | 1.25 | 1.50 |
| AH1430-2009 | — | — | 0.65 | 0.85 | 1.25 | 1.50 |

**KM# 309 100 MILLIM**
7.50 g., Brass, 27 mm. **Obv:** Inscription and dates within center circle of design **Rev:** Value in center of design

| Date | Mintage | VF20 | XF40 | MS60 | MS63 | MS65 |
|---|---|---|---|---|---|---|
| AH1425-2004 | — | — | — | 1.25 | 1.50 | 2.00 |
| AH1426-2005 | — | — | — | 1.25 | 1.50 | 2.00 |
| AH1427-2006 | — | — | — | 1.25 | 1.50 | 2.00 |
| AH1429-2008 | — | — | — | 1.25 | 1.50 | 2.00 |
| AH1432-2011 | — | — | — | 1.25 | 1.50 | 2.00 |
| AH1434-2013 | — | — | — | 1.25 | 1.50 | 2.00 |

**KM# 346 1/2 DINAR**
Copper-Nickel **Obv:** Shield within circle **Rev:** 2 hands with fruit and wheat sprig **Note:** Rim width varieties exist.

| Date | Mintage | VF20 | XF40 | MS60 | MS63 | MS65 |
|---|---|---|---|---|---|---|
| AH1426-2005 | — | — | — | 0.50 | 1.50 | 3.00 |
| AH1428-2007 | — | — | — | 0.50 | 1.50 | 3.00 |
| AH1430-2009 | — | — | — | 0.50 | 1.50 | 3.00 |
| AH1432-2011 | — | — | — | 0.50 | 1.50 | 3.00 |

**KM# 347 DINAR**
10.10 g., Copper-Nickel, 28 mm. **Series:** F.A.O. **Obv:** Shield within circle **Rev:** Female half figure right

| Date | Mintage | VF20 | XF40 | MS60 | MS63 | MS65 |
|---|---|---|---|---|---|---|
| AH1428-2007 | — | — | 1.00 | 2.00 | 3.00 | 5.00 |
| AH1430-2009 | — | — | 1.00 | 2.00 | 3.00 | 5.00 |
| AH1432-2011 | — | — | 1.00 | 2.00 | 3.00 | 5.00 |

**KM# 329 5 DINARS**
9.41 g., 0.900 Gold 0.2722 oz. AGW **Subject:** Anniversary of 7 Nov 1987 **Obv:** Shield **Rev:** Upstretched hand, flag **Note:** French legends vary by year.

| Date | Mintage | VF20 | XF40 | MS60 | MS63 | MS65 |
|---|---|---|---|---|---|---|
| 2001-1422 | 40 | — | — | — | 650 | 700 |

**KM# 330 5 DINARS**
9.41 g., 0.900 Gold 0.2722 oz. AGW **Subject:** Anniversary of 7 Nov 1987 **Obv:** Shield **Rev:** Upstretched hand, flag **Note:** Arabic legends vary by year.

| Date | Mintage | VF20 | XF40 | MS60 | MS63 | MS65 |
|---|---|---|---|---|---|---|
| 2001-1421 | 40 | — | — | — | 650 | 700 |

**KM# 350 5 DINARS**
10.00 g., Bi-Metallic Copper-Nickel center in Aluminum-Bronze ring, 29 mm. **Obv:** National arms **Rev:** Former President Habib Bourguiba **Edge:** Segmented reeding **Shape:** 12-sided

| Date | Mintage | VF20 | XF40 | MS60 | MS63 | MS65 |
|---|---|---|---|---|---|---|
| AH1423-2002 | — | — | — | 3.00 | 5.00 | 8.00 |

**KM# 350a 5 DINARS**
Bi-Metallic .925 Silver center in .900 gold ring, 29 mm. **Obv:** National arms **Rev:** Former President Habib Bourguiba **Edge:** 6 reeded and 6 plain sections **Shape:** 12-sided

| Date | Mintage | VF20 | XF40 | MS60 | MS63 | MS65 |
|---|---|---|---|---|---|---|
| AH1423-2002 | — | **PF65** 450 | | | | |

**KM# 435 5 DINARS**
9.48 g., 0.900 Gold 0.2743 oz. AGW, 22 mm. **Subject:** 7 November 1987, 15th Anniversary **Obv:** Shield **Rev:** Stylized dove **Note:** Arabic legends

| Date | Mintage | VF20 | XF40 | MS60 | MS63 | MS65 |
|---|---|---|---|---|---|---|
| AH1423-2002 | 40 | **PF65** 750 | | | | |

**KM# 436 5 DINARS**
9.48 g., 0.900 Gold 0.2743 oz. AGW, 22 mm. **Subject:** 7 November 1987, 15th Anniversary **Obv:** Shield **Rev:** Stylized dove **Note:** French legends

| Date | Mintage | VF20 | XF40 | MS60 | MS63 | MS65 |
|---|---|---|---|---|---|---|
| AH1423-2002 | 40 | **PF65** 750 | | | | |

**KM# 443 5 DINARS**
Bi-Metallic Silver center in Gold ring, 29 mm. **Subject:** 2nd Anniversary of Death **Obv:** Shield **Rev:** Head left

| Date | Mintage | VF20 | XF40 | MS60 | MS63 | MS65 |
|---|---|---|---|---|---|---|
| AH1423-2002 | 750 | **PF65** 375 | | | | |

**KM# 444 5 DINARS**
10.00 g., Bi-Metallic Copper-Nickel center in Copper ring, 29 mm. **Obv:** Shield **Rev:** Head left

| Date | Mintage | VF20 | XF40 | MS60 | MS63 | MS65 |
|---|---|---|---|---|---|---|
| AH1423-2002 | 20,275,000 | — | — | 3.50 | 5.50 | 9.00 |

**KM# 445 5 DINARS**
9.48 g., 0.900 Gold 0.2743 oz. AGW, 22 mm. **Subject:** 7 November 1987, 16th Anniversary **Obv:** Shield **Rev:** Hand with UN logo **Note:** Arabic legends

| Date | Mintage | VF20 | XF40 | MS60 | MS63 | MS65 |
|---|---|---|---|---|---|---|
| AH1424-2003 | 40 | **PF65** 750 | | | | |

**KM# 446 5 DINARS**
9.48 g., 0.900 Gold 0.2743 oz. AGW, 22 mm. **Subject:** 7 November 1987, 16th Anniversary **Obv:** Shield **Rev:** Hand with UN logo **Note:** French legend

| Date | Mintage | VF20 | XF40 | MS60 | MS63 | MS65 |
|---|---|---|---|---|---|---|
| AH1424-2003 | 40 | **PF65** 750 | | | | |

**KM# 455 5 DINARS**
9.40 g., 0.900 Gold 0.272 oz. AGW, 22 mm. **Subject:** 7 November 1987, 17th Anniversary - Elections **Obv:** Shield **Rev:** Star and crescent and stylized flame **Note:** Arabic legend

| Date | Mintage | VF20 | XF40 | MS60 | MS63 | MS65 |
|---|---|---|---|---|---|---|
| AH1425-2004 | 40 | **PF65** 750 | | | | |

**KM# 456 5 DINARS**
9.40 g., 0.900 Gold 0.272 oz. AGW, 22 mm. **Subject:** 7 November 1987, 17th Anniversary - Elections **Obv:** Shield **Rev:** Star and crescent and stylized flame **Note:** French legend

| Date | Mintage | VF20 | XF40 | MS60 | MS63 | MS65 |
|---|---|---|---|---|---|---|
| AH1425-2004 | 40 | **PF65** 750 | | | | |

**KM# 465 5 DINARS**
9.40 g., 0.900 Gold 0.272 oz. AGW, 22 mm. **Subject:** 7 November 1987, 18th Anniversary **Obv:** Shield **Rev:** Globe in stylized ship **Note:** Arabic legend

| Date | Mintage | VF20 | XF40 | MS60 | MS63 | MS65 |
|---|---|---|---|---|---|---|
| AH1426-2005 | 40 | **PF65** 750 | | | | |

**KM# 466 5 DINARS**
9.40 g., 0.900 Gold 0.272 oz. AGW, 22 mm. **Subject:** 7 November 1987, 18th Anniversary **Obv:** Shield **Rev:** Globe in stylized ship **Note:** French legend

| Date | Mintage | VF20 | XF40 | MS60 | MS63 | MS65 |
|---|---|---|---|---|---|---|
| AH1426-2005 Prook | 40 | **PF65** 750 | | | | |

**KM# 472 5 DINARS**
24.00 g., 0.900 Silver 0.6945 oz. ASW, 35 mm. **Subject:** 50th Anniversary **Obv:** Shield **Rev:** Logo **Note:** Arabic legend

| Date | Mintage | VF20 | XF40 | MS60 | MS63 | MS65 |
|---|---|---|---|---|---|---|
| AH1427-2006 | 900 | **PF65** 125 | | | | |

**KM# 473 5 DINARS**
24.00 g., 0.900 Silver 0.6945 oz. ASW, 35 mm. **Subject:** 50th Anniversary **Obv:** Shield **Rev:** Logo **Note:** French legends

| Date | Mintage | VF20 | XF40 | MS60 | MS63 | MS65 |
|---|---|---|---|---|---|---|
| AH1427-2006 | 100 | **PF65** 225 | | | | |

**KM# 478 5 DINARS**
9.40 g., 0.900 Gold 0.272 oz. AGW, 22 mm. **Subject:** 7 November 1987, 19th Anniversary **Obv:** Shield **Rev:** Dove and atom **Note:** Arabic legends

| Date | Mintage | VF20 | XF40 | MS60 | MS63 | MS65 |
|---|---|---|---|---|---|---|
| AH1427-2006 | 40 | **PF65** 750 | | | | |

**KM# 479 5 DINARS**
9.40 g., 0.900 Gold 0.272 oz. AGW, 22 mm. **Subject:** 7 November 1987, 19th Anniversary **Obv:** Shield **Rev:** Dove and atom **Note:** French legend

| Date | Mintage | VF20 | XF40 | MS60 | MS63 | MS65 |
|---|---|---|---|---|---|---|
| AH1427-2006 | 40 | **PF65** 750 | | | | |

**KM# 486 5 DINARS**
24.00 g., 0.900 Silver 0.6945 oz. ASW, 35 mm. **Subject:** 50th Anniversary **Obv:** Shield **Rev:** Ship, scales of Justice **Note:** Arabic legend

| Date | Mintage | VF20 | XF40 | MS60 | MS63 | MS65 |
|---|---|---|---|---|---|---|
| AH1428-2007 | 900 | **PF65** 125 | | | | |

**KM# 487 5 DINARS**
24.00 g., 0.900 Silver 0.6945 oz. ASW, 35 mm. **Subject:** 50th Anniversary **Obv:** Shield **Rev:** Ship, scales of Justice **Note:** French legend

| Date | Mintage | VF20 | XF40 | MS60 | MS63 | MS65 |
|---|---|---|---|---|---|---|
| AH1428-2007 | 100 | PF65 225 | | | | |

**KM# 490 5 DINARS**
9.40 g., 0.900 Gold 0.272 oz. AGW, 22 mm. **Subject:** 7 November 1987, 20th Anniversary **Obv:** Head of Zine el Abidne Ben Ali right **Rev:** Two profiles, keyboard, satellite receiver **Note:** Arabic legend

| Date | Mintage | VF20 | XF40 | MS60 | MS63 | MS65 |
|---|---|---|---|---|---|---|
| AH1428-2007 | 43 | PF65 750 | | | | |

**KM# 491 5 DINARS**
9.40 g., 0.900 Gold 0.272 oz. AGW, 22 mm. **Subject:** 7 November 1987, 20th Anniversary **Obv:** Head of Zine el Abidine Ben Ali right **Rev:** Two profiles, keyboard, satellite receiver **Note:** French legends

| Date | Mintage | VF20 | XF40 | MS60 | MS63 | MS65 |
|---|---|---|---|---|---|---|
| AH1428-2007 | 40 | PF65 750 | | | | |

**KM# 340 10 DINARS**
18.77 g., 0.900 Gold 0.5431 oz. AGW **Subject:** Anniversary - 7 Nov 1987 **Obv:** Shield **Rev:** Upstretched hand, flag **Note:** French legends vary by year.

| Date | Mintage | VF20 | XF40 | MS60 | MS63 | MS65 |
|---|---|---|---|---|---|---|
| 2001-1422 | 40 | — | — | — | 1,050 | 1,150 |

**KM# 341 10 DINARS**
18.77 g., 0.900 Gold 0.5431 oz. AGW **Subject:** Anniversary - 7 Nov 1987 **Obv:** Shield **Rev:** Upstretched hand, flag **Note:** Arabic legends vary by year.

| Date | Mintage | VF20 | XF40 | MS60 | MS63 | MS65 |
|---|---|---|---|---|---|---|
| 2001-1422 | 40 | — | — | — | 1,050 | 1,150 |

**KM# 378 10 DINARS**
38.00 g., 0.900 Silver 1.0996 oz. ASW **Subject:** 14th Anniversary 7 Nov and 19th Mediterranean Games **Edge:** Reeded

| Date | Mintage | VF20 | XF40 | MS60 | MS63 | MS65 |
|---|---|---|---|---|---|---|
| AH1422-2001 | — | — | — | — | — | 275 |

**KM# 430 10 DINARS**
38.00 g., 0.900 Silver 1.0996 oz. ASW, 40 mm. **Subject:** 7 November 1987, 14th Anniversary **Obv:** Shield **Rev:** Open door **Note:** French legend

| Date | Mintage | VF20 | XF40 | MS60 | MS63 | MS65 |
|---|---|---|---|---|---|---|
| AH1422-2001 | 400 | PF65 150 | | | | |

**KM# 379 10 DINARS**
38.00 g., 0.900 Silver 1.0996 oz. ASW **Subject:** 15th Anniversary 7 Nov 1987 **Obv:** National arms **Edge:** Reeded

| Date | Mintage | VF20 | XF40 | MS60 | MS63 | MS65 |
|---|---|---|---|---|---|---|
| AH1423-2002 | — | — | — | — | — | 275 |

**KM# 433 10 DINARS**
38.00 g., 0.900 Silver 1.0996 oz. ASW, 40 mm. **Subject:** 7 November 1987, 15th Anniversary **Obv:** Shield **Rev:** Stylized dove **Note:** Arabic legends

| Date | Mintage | VF20 | XF40 | MS60 | MS63 | MS65 |
|---|---|---|---|---|---|---|
| AH1423-2002 | 490 | PF65 150 | | | | |

**KM# 437 10 DINARS**
18.80 g., 0.900 Gold 0.544 oz. AGW, 28 mm. **Subject:** 7 November 1987, 15th Anniversary **Obv:** Shield **Rev:** Stylized dove **Note:** Arabic legends

| Date | Mintage | VF20 | XF40 | MS60 | MS63 | MS65 |
|---|---|---|---|---|---|---|
| AH1423-2002 | 40 | PF65 1,000 | | | | |

**KM# 438 10 DINARS**
18.80 g., 0.900 Gold 0.544 oz. AGW, 28 mm. **Subject:** 7 November 1987, 15th Anniversary **Obv:** Shield **Rev:** Stylized dove **Note:** French legends

| Date | Mintage | VF20 | XF40 | MS60 | MS63 | MS65 |
|---|---|---|---|---|---|---|
| AH1423-2002 | 40 | PF65 1,000 | | | | |

**KM# 380 10 DINARS**
38.00 g., 0.900 Silver 1.0996 oz. ASW **Subject:** 16th Anniversary 7 Nov 1987 plus International Solidarity Fund **Obv:** National arms **Rev:** Large 16 with hands holding globe within the 6, banner which says International Solidarity Fund **Edge:** Reeded

| Date | Mintage | VF20 | XF40 | MS60 | MS63 | MS65 |
|---|---|---|---|---|---|---|
| AH1424-2003 | — | PF65 300 | | | | |
| AH1424-2003 | — | — | — | — | — | 250 |

**KM# 447 10 DINARS**
18.18 g., 0.900 Gold 0.5261 oz. AGW, 28 mm. **Subject:** 7 November 1987, 16th Anniversary **Obv:** Shield **Rev:** Hand with UN logo **Note:** Arabic legend

| Date | Mintage | VF20 | XF40 | MS60 | MS63 | MS65 |
|---|---|---|---|---|---|---|
| AH1424-2003 | 40 | PF65 1,000 | | | | |

**KM# 448 10 DINARS**
18.18 g., 0.900 Gold 0.5261 oz. AGW, 28 mm. **Subject:** 7 November 1987, 16th Anniversary **Obv:** Shield **Rev:** Hand with UN logo **Note:** French legends

| Date | Mintage | VF20 | XF40 | MS60 | MS63 | MS65 |
|---|---|---|---|---|---|---|
| AH1424-2003 | 40 | PF65 1,000 | | | | |

**KM# 452 10 DINARS**
38.00 g., 0.900 Silver 1.0996 oz. ASW, 40 mm. **Subject:** 7 November 1987, 16th Anniversary **Obv:** Shield **Rev:** Large 16 and globe

| Date | Mintage | VF20 | XF40 | MS60 | MS63 | MS65 |
|---|---|---|---|---|---|---|
| AH1423-2003 | 24 | PF65 225 | | | | |

**KM# 381 10 DINARS**
38.00 g., 0.900 Silver 1.0996 oz. ASW **Subject:** 17th Anniversary of 7 Nov 1987 plus Elections of President and Parliament **Obv:** National arms **Edge:** Reeded

| Date | Mintage | VF20 | XF40 | MS60 | MS63 | MS65 |
|---|---|---|---|---|---|---|
| AH1425-2004 | — | — | — | — | — | 275 |

**KM# 453 10 DINARS**
38.00 g., 0.900 Silver 1.0996 oz. ASW, 40 mm. **Subject:** 7 November 1987, 17th Anniversary - Elections **Obv:** Shield **Rev:** Star and crescent and stylized flame **Note:** Arabic legends

| Date | Mintage | VF20 | XF40 | MS60 | MS63 | MS65 |
|---|---|---|---|---|---|---|
| AH1425-2004 | 375 | PF65 150 | | | | |

**KM# 454 10 DINARS**
38.00 g., 0.900 Silver 1.0996 oz. ASW, 40 mm. **Subject:** 7 November 1987, 17th Anniversary - Elections **Obv:** Shield **Rev:** Star and crescent and stylized flame **Note:** French legends

| Date | Mintage | VF20 | XF40 | MS60 | MS63 | MS65 |
|---|---|---|---|---|---|---|
| AH1425-2004 | 24 | PF65 225 | | | | |

**KM# 457 10 DINARS**
18.80 g., 0.900 Gold 0.544 oz. AGW, 28 mm. **Subject:** 7 November 1987, 17th Anniversary - Elections **Obv:** Shield **Rev:** Star and crescent and stylized flame **Note:** Arabic legend

| Date | Mintage | VF20 | XF40 | MS60 | MS63 | MS65 |
|---|---|---|---|---|---|---|
| AH1425-2004 | 40 | PF65 1,000 | | | | |

**KM# 458 10 DINARS**
18.80 g., 0.900 Gold 0.544 oz. AGW, 28 mm. **Subject:** 7 November 1987, 17th Anniversary - Elections **Obv:** Shield **Rev:** Star and crescent adn stylized flame **Note:** French legend

| Date | Mintage | VF20 | XF40 | MS60 | MS63 | MS65 |
|---|---|---|---|---|---|---|
| AH1425-2004 | 40 | PF65 1,000 | | | | |

**KM# 382 10 DINARS**
38.00 g., 0.900 Silver 1.0996 oz. ASW **Subject:** 18th Anniversary of 7 Nov 1987 and Conference on Information in Tunis 2005 **Edge:** Reeded

| Date | Mintage | VF20 | XF40 | MS60 | MS63 | MS65 |
|---|---|---|---|---|---|---|
| AH1426-2005 | — | — | — | — | — | 275 |

**KM# 463 10 DINARS**
38.00 g., 0.900 Silver 1.0996 oz. ASW, 40 mm. **Subject:** 7 November 1987, 18th Anniversary **Obv:** Shield **Rev:** Globe in stylized ship **Note:** French legends

| Date | Mintage | VF20 | XF40 | MS60 | MS63 | MS65 |
|---|---|---|---|---|---|---|
| AH1426-2005 | 50 | PF65 175 | | | | |

**KM# 464 10 DINARS**
38.00 g., 0.900 Silver 1.0996 oz. ASW, 40 mm. **Subject:** 7 November 1987, 18th Anniversary **Obv:** Shield **Rev:** Globe in stylized ship **Note:** Arabic legend

| Date | Mintage | VF20 | XF40 | MS60 | MS63 | MS65 |
|---|---|---|---|---|---|---|
| AH1426-2005 | 431 | PF65 150 | | | | |

**KM# 467 10 DINARS**
18.80 g., 0.900 Gold 0.544 oz. AGW **Subject:** 7 November 1987, 18th Anniversary **Obv:** Shield **Rev:** Globe in stylized ship **Shape:** 28 **Note:** Arabic legends

| Date | Mintage | VF20 | XF40 | MS60 | MS63 | MS65 |
|---|---|---|---|---|---|---|
| AH1426-2005 | 40 | PF65 1,000 | | | | |

**KM# 468 10 DINARS**
18.80 g., 0.900 Gold 0.544 oz. AGW, 28 mm. **Subject:** 7 November 1987, 18th Anniversary **Obv:** Shield **Rev:** Globe in stylized ship **Note:** French legend

| Date | Mintage | VF20 | XF40 | MS60 | MS63 | MS65 |
|---|---|---|---|---|---|---|
| AH1426-2005 | 40 | PF65 1,000 | | | | |

**KM# 383 10 DINARS**
38.00 g., 0.900 Silver 1.0996 oz. ASW **Subject:** 50th Anniversary of Independence (12.3.1956) **Obv:** National arms **Rev:** Stylized bird, "50", crescent moon with stars

| Date | Mintage | VF20 | XF40 | MS60 | MS63 | MS65 |
|---|---|---|---|---|---|---|
| AH1427-2006 | — | — | — | — | — | 275 |

**KM# 383a 10 DINARS**
19.00 g., 0.900 Gold 0.5498 oz. AGW **Subject:** 50th Anniversary of Independence

| Date | Mintage | VF20 | XF40 | MS60 | MS63 | MS65 |
|---|---|---|---|---|---|---|
| AH1427-2006 | 600 | PF65 1,000 | | | | |

**KM# 474 10 DINARS**
18.80 g., 0.900 Gold 0.544 oz. AGW, 28 mm. **Subject:** 50th Anniversary **Obv:** Shield **Rev:** Logo **Note:** Arabic legends

| Date | Mintage | VF20 | XF40 | MS60 | MS63 | MS65 |
|---|---|---|---|---|---|---|
| AH1427-2006 | 1,800 | PF65 950 | | | | |

**KM# 475 10 DINARS**
18.80 g., 0.900 Gold 0.544 oz. AGW, 28 mm. **Subject:** 50th Anniversary **Obv:** Shield **Rev:** Logo **Note:** French legends

| Date | Mintage | VF20 | XF40 | MS60 | MS63 | MS65 |
|---|---|---|---|---|---|---|
| AH1427-2006 | 200 | PF65 1,000 | | | | |

**KM# 476 10 DINARS**
38.00 g., 0.900 Silver 1.0996 oz. ASW, 40 mm. **Subject:** 7 November 1987, 19th Anniversary **Obv:** Shield **Rev:** Dove and atom **Note:** Arabic legend

| Date | Mintage | VF20 | XF40 | MS60 | MS63 | MS65 |
|---|---|---|---|---|---|---|
| AH1427-2006 | 300 | PF65 150 | | | | |

**KM# 477 10 DINARS**
38.00 g., 0.900 Silver 1.0996 oz. ASW, 40 mm. **Subject:** 7 November 1987, 19th Anniversary **Obv:** Shield **Rev:** Dove and atom **Note:** French legend

| Date | Mintage | VF20 | XF40 | MS60 | MS63 | MS65 |
|---|---|---|---|---|---|---|
| AH1427-2006 Profo | 30 | PF65 225 | | | | |

**KM# 480 10 DINARS**
18.80 g., 0.900 Gold 0.544 oz. AGW, 28 mm. **Subject:** 7 November 1987, 19th Anniversary **Obv:** Shield **Rev:** Dove and atom **Note:** Arabic legend

| Date | Mintage | VF20 | XF40 | MS60 | MS63 | MS65 |
|---|---|---|---|---|---|---|
| AH1427-2006 | 40 | PF65 1,000 | | | | |

**KM# 481 10 DINARS**
18.80 g., 0.900 Gold 0.544 oz. AGW, 28 mm. **Subject:** 7 November 1987, 19th Anniversary **Obv:** Shield **Rev:** Dove and atom **Note:** French legend

| Date | Mintage | VF20 | XF40 | MS60 | MS63 | MS65 |
|---|---|---|---|---|---|---|
| AH1427-2006 | 40 | PF65 1,000 | | | | |

**KM# 488 10 DINARS**
18.80 g., 0.900 Gold 0.544 oz. AGW, 28 mm. **Subject:** 50th Anniversary **Obv:** Shield **Rev:** Ship, scales of Justice **Note:** Arabic legend

| Date | Mintage | VF20 | XF40 | MS60 | MS63 | MS65 |
|---|---|---|---|---|---|---|
| AH1428-2007 | 450 | PF65 975 | | | | |

**KM# 489 10 DINARS**
18.80 g., 0.900 Gold 0.544 oz. AGW, 28 mm. **Subject:** 50th Anniversary **Obv:** Shield **Rev:** Ship, scales of Justice **Note:** French legend

| Date | Mintage | VF20 | XF40 | MS60 | MS63 | MS65 |
|---|---|---|---|---|---|---|
| AH1428-2007 | 50 | PF65 1,000 | | | | |

**KM# 492 10 DINARS**
18.80 g., 0.900 Gold 0.544 oz. AGW, 28 mm. **Subject:** 7 November 1987, 20th Anniversary **Obv:** Head of Zine El abidine Ben Ali right **Rev:** Two profiles, keyboard, satellite receiver **Note:** Arabic legend

| Date | Mintage | VF20 | XF40 | MS60 | MS63 | MS65 |
|---|---|---|---|---|---|---|
| AH1428-2007 | 42 | PF65 1,000 | | | | |

**KM# 493 10 DINARS**
18.80 g., 0.900 Gold 0.544 oz. AGW, 28 mm. **Subject:** 7 November 1987, 20th Anniversary **Obv:** Head of Zine El Abidine Ben Ali right **Rev:** Two profiles, keyboard, satellite receiver **Note:** French legends

| Date | Mintage | VF20 | XF40 | MS60 | MS63 | MS65 |
|---|---|---|---|---|---|---|
| AH1428-2007 | 40 | PF65 1,000 | | | | |

**KM# 396 50 DINARS**
21.00 g., 0.900 Gold 0.6076 oz. AGW, 34 mm. **Subject:** 14th Anniversary 7 Nov 1987 and 19th Mediterranean Games **Edge:** Reeded **Note:** Arabic legends.

| Date | Mintage | VF20 | XF40 | MS60 | MS63 | MS65 |
|---|---|---|---|---|---|---|
| AH1422-2001 | — | PF65 1,200 | | | | |

**KM# 431 50 DINARS**
21.00 g., 0.900 Gold 0.6076 oz. AGW, 34 mm. **Subject:** 7 November 1987, 14th Anniversary **Obv:** Shield **Rev:** Open door **Note:** French legends

| Date | Mintage | VF20 | XF40 | MS60 | MS63 | MS65 |
|---|---|---|---|---|---|---|
| AH1422-2001 | 150 | PF65 1,150 | | | | |

**KM# 397 50 DINARS**
21.00 g., 0.900 Gold 0.6076 oz. AGW, 34 mm. **Subject:** 15th Anniversary of 7 Nov 1987 **Edge:** Reeded

| Date | Mintage | VF20 | XF40 | MS60 | MS63 | MS65 |
|---|---|---|---|---|---|---|
| AH1423-2002 | — | PF65 1,200 | | | | |

**KM# 439 50 DINARS**
21.00 g., 0.900 Gold 0.6076 oz. AGW, 34 mm. **Subject:** 7 November 1987, 15th Anniversary **Obv:** Shield **Rev:** Stylized dove **Note:** Arabic legend

| Date | Mintage | VF20 | XF40 | MS60 | MS63 | MS65 |
|---|---|---|---|---|---|---|
| AH1423-2002 | 580 | PF65 1,100 | | | | |

**KM# 440 50 DINARS**
21.00 g., 0.900 Gold 0.6076 oz. AGW, 21 mm. **Subject:** 7 November 1987, 15th Anniversary **Obv:** Shieeld **Rev:** Stylized dove

| Date | Mintage | VF20 | XF40 | MS60 | MS63 | MS65 |
|---|---|---|---|---|---|---|
| AH1423-2002 | 80 | **PF65** 1,250 | | | | |

**KM# 449 50 DINARS**
21.00 g., 0.900 Gold 0.6076 oz. AGW, 34 mm. **Subject:** 7 November 1987, 16th Anniversary **Obv:** Shield **Rev:** Hand with UN logo **Note:** Arabic legends

| Date | Mintage | VF20 | XF40 | MS60 | MS63 | MS65 |
|---|---|---|---|---|---|---|
| AH1424-2003 | 545 | **PF65** 1,100 | | | | |

**KM# 450 50 DINARS**
21.00 g., 0.900 Gold 0.6076 oz. AGW, 34 mm. **Subject:** 7 November 1987, 16th Anniversary **Obv:** Shield **Rev:** Hand with UN logo **Note:** French legends

| Date | Mintage | VF20 | XF40 | MS60 | MS63 | MS65 |
|---|---|---|---|---|---|---|
| AH1424-2003 | 55 | **PF65** 1,250 | | | | |

**KM# 398 50 DINARS**
21.00 g., 0.900 Gold 0.6076 oz. AGW, 34 mm. **Subject:** 17th Anniversary of 7 Nov 1987 plus Elections of President and Parliament **Edge:** Reeded

| Date | Mintage | VF20 | XF40 | MS60 | MS63 | MS65 |
|---|---|---|---|---|---|---|
| AH1425-2004 | — | **PF65** 1,250 | | | | |

**KM# 459 50 DINARS**
21.00 g., 0.900 Gold 0.6076 oz. AGW, 34 mm. **Subject:** 7 November 1987, 17th Anniversary - Elections **Obv:** Shield **Rev:** Star and crescent and stylized flame **Note:** Arabic legend

| Date | Mintage | VF20 | XF40 | MS60 | MS63 | MS65 |
|---|---|---|---|---|---|---|
| AH1425-2004 | 379 | **PF65** 1,100 | | | | |

**KM# 460 50 DINARS**
21.00 g., 0.900 Gold 0.6076 oz. AGW, 34 mm. **Subject:** 7 November 1987, 17th Anniversary - Elections **Obv:** Shield **Rev:** Star and crescent and stylized flame **Note:** French legend

| Date | Mintage | VF20 | XF40 | MS60 | MS63 | MS65 |
|---|---|---|---|---|---|---|
| AH1425-2004 | 28 | **PF65** 1,250 | | | | |

**KM# 470 50 DINARS**
21.00 g., 0.900 Gold 0.6076 oz. AGW, 34 mm. **Subject:** 7 November 1987, 18th Anniversary **Obv:** Shield **Rev:** Globe and stylized ship **Note:** French legend

| Date | Mintage | VF20 | XF40 | MS60 | MS63 | MS65 |
|---|---|---|---|---|---|---|
| AH1426-2005 | 45 | **PF65** 1,250 | | | | |

**KM# 482 50 DINARS**
21.00 g., 0.900 Gold 0.6076 oz. AGW, 34 mm. **Subject:** 7 November 1987, 19th Anniversary **Obv:** Shield **Rev:** Dove and atom **Note:** Arabic legend

| Date | Mintage | VF20 | XF40 | MS60 | MS63 | MS65 |
|---|---|---|---|---|---|---|
| AH1427-2006 | 183 | **PF65** 1,200 | | | | |

**KM# 483 50 DINARS**
21.00 g., 0.900 Gold 0.6076 oz. AGW, 34 mm. **Subject:** 7 November 1987, 19th Anniversary **Obv:** Shield **Rev:** Dove and atom **Note:** French legends

| Date | Mintage | VF20 | XF40 | MS60 | MS63 | MS65 |
|---|---|---|---|---|---|---|
| AH1427-2006 | 23 | **PF65** 1,250 | | | | |

**KM# 412 100 DINARS**
38.00 g., 0.900 Gold 1.0996 oz. AGW, 40 mm. **Subject:** 14th Anniversary of 7 Nov 1987 and 19th Mediterranean Games **Obv:** National arms **Rev:** Olympic rings divide 2 portals **Edge:** Reeded

| Date | Mintage | VF20 | XF40 | MS60 | MS63 | MS65 |
|---|---|---|---|---|---|---|
| AH1422-2001 | — | **PF65** 2,100 | | | | |

**KM# 432 100 DINARS**
38.00 g., 0.900 Gold 1.0996 oz. AGW, 43 mm. **Subject:** 7 November 1987, 14th Anniversary **Obv:** Shield **Rev:** Open door **Note:** Arabic legend

| Date | Mintage | VF20 | XF40 | MS60 | MS63 | MS65 |
|---|---|---|---|---|---|---|
| AH1422-2001 | 375 | **PF65** 1,950 | | | | |

**KM# 441 100 DINARS**
38.00 g., 0.900 Gold 1.0996 oz. AGW, 43 mm. **Subject:** 7 November 1987, 15th Anniversary **Obv:** Shield **Rev:** Stylized dove **Note:** Arabic legends

| Date | Mintage | VF20 | XF40 | MS60 | MS63 | MS65 |
|---|---|---|---|---|---|---|
| AH1423-2002 | 380 | **PF65** 1,950 | | | | |

**KM# 442 100 DINARS**
38.00 g., 0.900 Gold 1.0996 oz. AGW, 43 mm. **Subject:** 7 November 1987, 15th Anniversary **Obv:** Sheild **Rev:** Stylized dove **Note:** French legend

| Date | Mintage | VF20 | XF40 | MS60 | MS63 | MS65 |
|---|---|---|---|---|---|---|
| AH1423-2002 | 110 | **PF65** 2,000 | | | | |

**KM# 352 100 DINARS**
38.00 g., 0.900 Gold 1.0996 oz. AGW, 40 mm. **Subject:** United Nations **Obv:** National arms above value **Rev:** UN logo on stylized hand **Edge:** Reeded

| Date | Mintage | VF20 | XF40 | MS60 | MS63 | MS65 |
|---|---|---|---|---|---|---|
| AH1424-2003 | — | **PF65** 2,100 | | | | |

**KM# 451 100 DINARS**
38.00 g., 0.900 Gold 1.0996 oz. AGW, 43 mm. **Subject:** 7 November 1987, 16th Anniversary **Obv:** Shield **Rev:** Hand with UN logo **Note:** French text

| Date | Mintage | VF20 | XF40 | MS60 | MS63 | MS65 |
|---|---|---|---|---|---|---|
| AH1424-2003 | 53 | **PF65** 2,100 | | | | |

**KM# 461 100 DINARS**
38.00 g., 0.900 Gold 1.0996 oz. AGW, 43 mm. **Subject:** 7 November 1987, 17th Anniversary - Elections **Obv:** Shield **Rev:** Star and crescent and stylized flame **Note:** Arabic legend

| Date | Mintage | VF20 | XF40 | MS60 | MS63 | MS65 |
|---|---|---|---|---|---|---|
| AH1425-2004 | 385 | **PF65** 1,950 | | | | |

**KM# 462 100 DINARS**
38.00 g., 0.900 Gold 1.0996 oz. AGW, 43 mm. **Subject:** 7 November 1987, 17th Anniversary - Elections **Obv:** Shield **Rev:** Star and crescent and stylized flame **Note:** French legends

| Date | Mintage | VF20 | XF40 | MS60 | MS63 | MS65 |
|---|---|---|---|---|---|---|
| AH1425-2004 | 44 | **PF65** 2,100 | | | | |

**KM# 413 100 DINARS**
38.00 g., 0.900 Gold 1.0996 oz. AGW **Subject:** 18th Anniversary of 7 Nov 1987 and Conference on Information in Tunis 2005 **Edge:** Reeded

| Date | Mintage | VF20 | XF40 | MS60 | MS63 | MS65 |
|---|---|---|---|---|---|---|
| AH1426-2005 | — | **PF65** 2,100 | | | | |

**KM# 469 100 DINARS**
21.00 g., 0.900 Gold 0.6076 oz. AGW, 34 mm. **Subject:** 7 November 1987, 18th Anniversary **Obv:** Shield **Rev:** Globe in stylized ship **Note:** Arabic legend

| Date | Mintage | VF20 | XF40 | MS60 | MS63 | MS65 |
|---|---|---|---|---|---|---|
| AH1426-2005 | 390 | **PF65** 1,100 | | | | |

**KM# 471 100 DINARS**
38.00 g., 0.900 Gold 1.0996 oz. AGW, 43 mm. **Subject:** 7 November 1987, 18th Anniversary **Obv:** Shield **Rev:** Globe in stylized ship **Note:** French legends

| Date | Mintage | VF20 | XF40 | MS60 | MS63 | MS65 |
|---|---|---|---|---|---|---|
| AH1426-2005 | 45 | **PF65** 2,100 | | | | |

**KM# 484 100 DINARS**
38.00 g., 0.900 Gold 1.0996 oz. AGW, 43 mm. **Subject:** 7 November 1987, 19th Anniversary **Obv:** Shield **Rev:** Dove and atom **Note:** Arabic legend

| Date | Mintage | VF20 | XF40 | MS60 | MS63 | MS65 |
|---|---|---|---|---|---|---|
| AH1427-2006 | 212 | **PF65** 2,000 | | | | |

**KM# 485 100 DINARS**
38.00 g., 0.900 Gold 1.0996 oz. AGW, 43 mm. **Subject:** 7 November 1987, 19th Anniversary **Obv:** Shield **Rev:** Dove and atom **Note:** French legend

| Date | Mintage | VF20 | XF40 | MS60 | MS63 | MS65 |
|---|---|---|---|---|---|---|
| AH1427-2006 | 23 | **PF65** 2,200 | | | | |

## TURKEY

The Republic of Turkey, a parliamentary democracy of the Near East located partially in Europe and partially in Asia between the Black and the Mediterranean Seas, has an area of 301,382 sq. mi. (780,580 sq. km.) and a population of *55.4 million. Capital: Ankara. Turkey exports cotton, hazelnuts, and tobacco, and enjoys a virtual monopoly in meerschaum.

# REPUBLIC

## DECIMAL COINAGE

40 Para = 1 Kurus; 100 Kurus = 1 Lira

**KM# 1104 25000 LIRA (25 Bin Lira)**
2.70 g., Brass, 17 mm. **Obv:** Head left **Rev:** Value **Edge:** Plain **Mint:** Istanbul

| Date | Mintage | VF20 | XF40 | MS60 | MS63 | MS65 |
|---|---|---|---|---|---|---|
| 2001 | — | — | — | — | 2.00 | — |
| 2002 | — | — | — | — | 2.00 | — |
| 2003 | — | — | — | — | 2.00 | — |

**KM# 1105 50000 LIRA (50 Bin Lira)**
3.20 g., Copper-Nickel-Zinc, 17.75 mm. **Obv:** Head left within circle **Rev:** Value **Edge:** Plain **Mint:** Istanbul

| Date | Mintage | VF20 | XF40 | MS60 | MS63 | MS65 |
|---|---|---|---|---|---|---|
| 2001 | — | — | — | — | 0.50 | — |
| 2002 | — | — | — | — | 0.50 | — |
| 2003 | — | — | — | — | 0.50 | — |
| 2004 | — | — | — | — | 0.50 | — |

**KM# 1106 100000 LIRA (100 Bin Lira)**
4.60 g., Copper-Nickel-Zinc, 21 mm. **Obv:** Head with hat right within circle **Rev:** Value **Edge:** Plain **Mint:** Istanbul

| Date | Mintage | VF20 | XF40 | MS60 | MS63 | MS65 |
|---|---|---|---|---|---|---|
| 2001 | — | — | — | — | 0.75 | 1.25 |
| 2002 | — | — | — | — | 0.75 | 1.25 |
| 2003 | — | — | — | — | 0.75 | 1.25 |
| 2004 | — | — | — | — | 0.75 | 1.25 |

**KM# 1137 250000 LIRA**
6.42 g., Copper-Nickel-Zinc, 23.4 mm. **Obv:** Bust facing within circle **Rev:** Value **Edge Lettering:** T.C." six times dividing reeded sections **Mint:** Istanbul

| Date | Mintage | VF20 | XF40 | MS60 | MS63 | MS65 |
|---|---|---|---|---|---|---|
| 2002 | — | — | — | — | 1.00 | 1.50 |
| 2003 | — | — | — | — | 1.00 | 1.50 |
| 2004 | — | — | — | — | 1.00 | 1.50 |

**KM# 1161 500000 LIRA**
4.60 g., Copper-Nickel, 21 mm. **Obv:** Value and date within sprigs **Rev:** One sheep **Edge:** Plain **Mint:** Istanbul

| Date | Mintage | VF20 | XF40 | MS60 | MS63 | MS65 |
|---|---|---|---|---|---|---|
| 2002 | — | — | — | — | 2.00 | 3.00 |

**KM# 1162 750000 LIRA**
6.40 g., Copper-Nickel, 23.5 mm. **Obv:** Value and date within sprigs **Rev:** Angora Ram **Edge:** Plain **Mint:** Istanbul

| Date | Mintage | VF20 | XF40 | MS60 | MS63 | MS65 |
|---|---|---|---|---|---|---|
| 2002 | — | — | — | — | 3.00 | 4.00 |

**KM# 1139.1 1000000 LIRA**
11.87 g., Bi-Metallic Brass center in Copper-Nickel ring, 32.1 mm. **Subject:** Foundation of the Mint **Obv:** Building and value within circle **Rev:** Legend and date inscription **Edge:** Plain **Mint:** Istanbul **Note:** This coin type is produced by a machine outside the money museum at the Istanbul Mint. Visitors pay 1 mio lira, press a button and strike a coin with the actual date of their visit. Many other dates exist in unknown and unregistered quantities. Only Turkish months are on struck coins.

| Date | Mintage | VF20 | XF40 | MS60 | MS63 | MS65 |
|---|---|---|---|---|---|---|
| Mayis 2002 | — | — | — | — | 5.00 | 6.00 |
| Haziran 2002 | — | — | — | — | 5.00 | 6.00 |
| Temmuz 2002 | — | — | — | — | 5.00 | 6.00 |
| Agostos 2002 | — | — | — | — | 5.00 | 6.00 |
| Eylul 2002 | — | — | — | — | 5.00 | 6.00 |
| Ekim 2002 | — | — | — | — | 5.00 | 6.00 |
| Kasim 2002 | — | — | — | — | 5.00 | 6.00 |
| Aralik 2002 | — | — | — | — | 5.00 | 6.00 |

**KM# 1163 1000000 LIRA**
12.00 g., Copper-Nickel, 31.9 mm. **Obv:** Value and date within sprigs **Rev:** Turbaned bust 1/4 left divides dates **Edge:** Reeded **Mint:** Istanbul

| Date | Mintage | VF20 | XF40 | MS60 | MS63 | MS65 |
|---|---|---|---|---|---|---|
| 2002 | — | — | — | — | 5.00 | 6.00 |

**KM# 1170 1000000 LIRA**
31.42 g., 0.925 Silver 0.9344 oz. ASW, 38.6 mm. **Subject:** Mevlana Celaleddin-I Rumi **Obv:** Value and date in wreath **Rev:** Turbaned bust **Edge:** Reeded **Mint:** Istanbul

| Date | Mintage | VF20 | XF40 | MS60 | MS63 | MS65 |
|---|---|---|---|---|---|---|
| 2002 | — | **PF65** 40.00 | | | | |

**KM# 1139.2 1000000 LIRA**
Bi-Metallic Brass center in Copper-Nickel ring., 32.1 mm. **Subject:** Foundation of the Mint **Obv:** Building and value within circle **Rev:** Legend and date inscription **Edge:** Plain **Mint:** Istanbul **Note:** This coin type is produced by a machine outside the money museum at the Istanbul Mint. Visitors pay 1 mio lira, press a button and strike a coin with the actual date of their visit. Many other dates exist in unknown and unregistered quantities. The months are listed in both Turkish and English on struck coins.

| Date | Mintage | VF20 | XF40 | MS60 | MS63 | MS65 |
|---|---|---|---|---|---|---|
| Ocak/January 2003 | — | — | — | — | 5.00 | 6.00 |
| Subat/February 2003 | — | — | — | — | 5.00 | 6.00 |
| Mart/March 2003 | — | — | — | — | 5.00 | 6.00 |
| Nisan/April 2003 | — | — | — | — | 5.00 | 6.00 |
| Mayis/May 2003 | — | — | — | — | 5.00 | 6.00 |
| Haziran/June 2003 | — | — | — | — | 5.00 | 6.00 |
| Temmuz/July 2003 | — | — | — | — | 5.00 | 6.00 |
| Agostos/August 2003 | — | — | — | — | 5.00 | 6.00 |
| Eylul/September 2003 | — | — | — | — | 5.00 | 6.00 |
| Ekim/October 2003 | — | — | — | — | 5.00 | 6.00 |
| Kasim/November 2003 | — | — | — | — | 5.00 | 6.00 |
| Aralik/December 2003 | — | — | — | — | 5.00 | 6.00 |

**KM# 1107 3000000 LIRA**
31.47 g., 0.925 Silver 0.9359 oz. ASW, 38.6 mm. **Series:** Olympics **Obv:** Value and date within wreath **Rev:** Long jumper and logo **Edge:** Reeded **Mint:** Istanbul

| Date | Mintage | VF20 | XF40 | MS60 | MS63 | MS65 |
|---|---|---|---|---|---|---|
| 2002 | — | **PF65** 25.00 | | | | |

**KM# 1110 5000000 LIRA**

67.00 g., Bronze, 50 mm. **Subject:** Children's Day **Obv:** Legend and inscription **Rev:** Dancing children **Edge:** Plain **Mint:** Istanbul

| Date | Mintage | VF20 | XF40 | MS60 | MS63 | MS65 |
|---|---|---|---|---|---|---|
| 2001 Matte | 1,583 | — | — | — | 35.00 | — |

**KM# 1117 7500000 LIRA**

31.47 g., 0.925 Silver 0.9359 oz. ASW **Subject:** Iznik Tabak **Obv:** Two peacocks within circle **Rev:** Iznik Tabak (Nicean pottery) 1570; Circle of flowers at center

| Date | Mintage | VF20 | XF40 | MS60 | MS63 | MS65 |
|---|---|---|---|---|---|---|
| 2001 | 1,349 | PF65 50.00 | | | | |

**KM# 1120 7500000 LIRA**

15.40 g., 0.925 Silver 0.458 oz. ASW **Subject:** Bird Series - Saz Horozu **Obv:** Value and date within sprigs **Rev:** Purple swamphen on ground **Edge:** Plain **Shape:** 4-sided **Mint:** Istanbul **Note:** 28.1 x 28.1mm

| Date | Mintage | VF20 | XF40 | MS60 | MS63 | MS65 |
|---|---|---|---|---|---|---|
| 2001 | — | PF65 35.00 | | | | |

**KM# 1121 7500000 LIRA**

15.40 g., 0.925 Silver 0.458 oz. ASW **Subject:** Bird Series - Toy **Obv:** Value and date within sprigs **Rev:** Greater Bustard on ground **Edge:** Plain **Shape:** 4-sided **Mint:** Istanbul **Note:** 28.1 x 28.1mm

| Date | Mintage | VF20 | XF40 | MS60 | MS63 | MS65 |
|---|---|---|---|---|---|---|
| 2001 | — | PF65 35.00 | | | | |

**KM# 1122 7500000 LIRA**

15.40 g., 0.925 Silver 0.458 oz. ASW **Subject:** Bird Series - Yaz Ordegi **Obv:** Value and date within sprigs **Rev:** White-headed Duck on ground **Edge:** Plain **Shape:** 4-sided **Mint:** Istanbul **Note:** 28.1 x 28.1mm

| Date | Mintage | VF20 | XF40 | MS60 | MS63 | MS65 |
|---|---|---|---|---|---|---|
| 2001 | — | PF65 35.00 | | | | |

**KM# 1123 7500000 LIRA**

15.40 g., 0.925 Silver 0.458 oz. ASW **Subject:** Bird Series - Dikkuyruk **Obv:** Value and date within sprigs **Rev:** Marbled teal on water **Edge:** Plain **Shape:** 4-sided **Mint:** Istanbul **Note:** 28.1 x 28.1mm

| Date | Mintage | VF20 | XF40 | MS60 | MS63 | MS65 |
|---|---|---|---|---|---|---|
| 2001 | — | PF65 35.00 | | | | |

**KM# 1124 7500000 LIRA**

15.40 g., 0.925 Silver 0.458 oz. ASW **Subject:** Bird Series - Yesil Arikusu **Obv:** Value and date within sprigs **Rev:** Bee-eater on branch **Edge:** Plain **Shape:** 4-sided **Mint:** Istanbul **Note:** 28.1 x 28.1mm

| Date | Mintage | VF20 | XF40 | MS60 | MS63 | MS65 |
|---|---|---|---|---|---|---|
| 2001 | — | PF65 35.00 | | | | |

**KM# 1125 7500000 LIRA**

15.40 g., 0.925 Silver 0.458 oz. ASW **Subject:** Bird Series - Kucuk Karabatak **Obv:** Value and date within sprigs **Rev:** Three pygmy cormorants **Edge:** Plain **Shape:** 4-sided **Mint:** Istanbul **Note:** 28.1 x 28.1mm

| Date | Mintage | VF20 | XF40 | MS60 | MS63 | MS65 |
|---|---|---|---|---|---|---|
| 2001 | — | PF65 35.00 | | | | |

**KM# 1126 7500000 LIRA**

15.40 g., 0.925 Silver 0.458 oz. ASW **Subject:** Bird Series - Kizil Akbaba **Obv:** Value and date within sprigs **Rev:** Eurasian griffon **Edge:** Plain **Shape:** 4-sided **Mint:** Istanbul **Note:** 28.1 x 28.1mm

| Date | Mintage | VF20 | XF40 | MS60 | MS63 | MS65 |
|---|---|---|---|---|---|---|
| 2001 | — | PF65 35.00 | | | | |

**KM# 1127 7500000 LIRA**

15.40 g., 0.925 Silver 0.458 oz. ASW **Subject:** Bird Series - Sah Kartal **Obv:** Value and date within sprigs **Rev:** Eagles **Edge:** Plain **Shape:** 4-sided **Mint:** Istanbul **Note:** 28.1 x 28.1mm

| Date | Mintage | VF20 | XF40 | MS60 | MS63 | MS65 |
|---|---|---|---|---|---|---|
| 2001 | — | PF65 35.00 | | | | |

**KM# 1128 7500000 LIRA**

15.40 g., 0.925 Silver 0.458 oz. ASW **Subject:** Bird Series - Ala Sigireik **Obv:** Value and date within sprigs **Rev:** Rosy starling on ground **Edge:** Plain **Shape:** 4-sided **Mint:** Istanbul **Note:** 28.1 x 28.1mm

| Date | Mintage | VF20 | XF40 | MS60 | MS63 | MS65 |
|---|---|---|---|---|---|---|
| 2001 | — | PF65 35.00 | | | | |

**KM# 1129 7500000 LIRA**

15.40 g., 0.925 Silver 0.458 oz. ASW **Subject:** Bird Series - Izmir Yalicapkini **Obv:** Value and date within sprigs **Rev:** White-throated kingfisher on stump **Edge:** Plain **Shape:** 4-sided **Mint:** Istanbul **Note:** 28.1 x 28.1mm

| Date | Mintage | VF20 | XF40 | MS60 | MS63 | MS65 |
|---|---|---|---|---|---|---|
| 2001 | — | PF65 35.00 | | | | |

**KM# 1130 7500000 LIRA**

15.40 g., 0.925 Silver 0.458 oz. ASW **Subject:** Bird Series - Turac **Obv:** Value and date within sprigs **Rev:** Black francolin birds on the ground **Edge:** Plain **Shape:** 4-sided **Mint:** Istanbul **Note:** 28.1 x 28.1mm

| Date | Mintage | VF20 | XF40 | MS60 | MS63 | MS65 |
|---|---|---|---|---|---|---|
| 2001 | — | PF65 35.00 | | | | |

**KM# 1131 7500000 LIRA**

15.40 g., 0.925 Silver 0.458 oz. ASW **Subject:** Bird Series - Kelaynak **Obv:** Value and date within sprigs **Rev:** Two Bald Ibis birds on ground **Edge:** Plain **Shape:** 4-sided **Mint:** Istanbul **Note:** 28.1 x 28.1mm

| Date | Mintage | VF20 | XF40 | MS60 | MS63 | MS65 |
|---|---|---|---|---|---|---|
| 2001 | — | PF65 35.00 | | | | |

**KM# 1132 7500000 LIRA**

15.40 g., 0.925 Silver 0.458 oz. ASW **Subject:** Bird Series - Sakalli Akbaba **Obv:** Value and date within sprigs **Rev:** Bearded vulture **Edge:** Plain **Shape:** 4-sided **Mint:** Istanbul **Note:** 28.1 x 28.1mm

| Date | Mintage | VF20 | XF40 | MS60 | MS63 | MS65 |
|---|---|---|---|---|---|---|
| 2001 | — | PF65 35.00 | | | | |

**KM# 1133 7500000 LIRA**
15.40 g., 0.925 Silver 0.458 oz. ASW **Subject:** Bird Series - Tepeli Pelikan **Obv:** Value and date within sprigs **Rev:** Dalmatian pelican on rock **Edge:** Plain **Shape:** Square **Mint:** Istanbul **Note:** 28.1 x 28.1mm

| Date | Mintage | VF20 | XF40 | MS60 | MS63 | MS65 |
|---|---|---|---|---|---|---|
| 2001 | — | PF65 35.00 | | | | |

**KM# 1134 7500000 LIRA**
15.40 g., 0.925 Silver 0.458 oz. ASW **Subject:** Bird Series - Ishakkusu **Obv:** Value and date within sprigs **Rev:** European scops owl on branch **Edge:** Plain **Shape:** Square **Mint:** Istanbul **Note:** 28.1 x 28.1mm

| Date | Mintage | VF20 | XF40 | MS60 | MS63 | MS65 |
|---|---|---|---|---|---|---|
| 2001 | — | PF65 35.00 | | | | |

**KM# 1135 7500000 LIRA**
31.03 g., 0.925 Silver 0.9228 oz. ASW, 38.5 mm. **Subject:** Mevlana Celaleddin-i Rumi **Obv:** Dancer within circle **Rev:** Turbaned bust 3/4 right above dates **Edge:** Reeded **Mint:** Istanbul

| Date | Mintage | VF20 | XF40 | MS60 | MS63 | MS65 |
|---|---|---|---|---|---|---|
| 2001 | — | PF65 45.00 | | | | |

**KM# 1142 7500000 LIRA**
31.25 g., 0.925 Silver 0.9294 oz. ASW, 38.5 mm. **Subject:** Cahit Arf, Turkish mathematician (1910-1997) **Obv:** Mathematical formula within circle **Rev:** 1/2-length figure facing **Edge:** Reeded **Mint:** Istanbul

| Date | Mintage | VF20 | XF40 | MS60 | MS63 | MS65 |
|---|---|---|---|---|---|---|
| 2001 | — | PF65 45.00 | | | | |

**KM# 1143 7500000 LIRA**
31.25 g., 0.925 Silver 0.9294 oz. ASW, 38.5 mm. **Obv:** Ornamented circle design **Rev:** 1/2-length bust facing **Edge:** Reeded **Mint:** Istanbul

| Date | Mintage | VF20 | XF40 | MS60 | MS63 | MS65 |
|---|---|---|---|---|---|---|
| 2001 | — | PF65 45.00 | | | | |

**KM# 1144 7500000 LIRA**
31.25 g., 0.925 Silver 0.9294 oz. ASW, 38.5 mm. **Subject:** Koca Yusuf Baspehlivan **Obv:** Two figures wrestling **Rev:** Portrait on circular background **Edge:** Reeded **Mint:** Istanbul

| Date | Mintage | VF20 | XF40 | MS60 | MS63 | MS65 |
|---|---|---|---|---|---|---|
| 2001 | — | PF65 42.00 | | | | |

**KM# 1145 7500000 LIRA**
15.61 g., 0.925 Silver 0.4642 oz. ASW, 27.9 x 38.6 mm. **Series:** Flowers **Obv:** Value and date within sprigs **Rev:** Paeonia turcica **Edge:** Reeded **Shape:** Oval **Mint:** Istanbul

| Date | Mintage | VF20 | XF40 | MS60 | MS63 | MS65 |
|---|---|---|---|---|---|---|
| 2002 | — | PF65 28.00 | | | | |

**KM# 1146 7500000 LIRA**
15.61 g., 0.925 Silver 0.4642 oz. ASW, 27.9 x 38.6 mm. **Series:** Flowers **Obv:** Value and date within sprigs **Rev:** Orchis anatolica **Edge:** Reeded **Shape:** Oval **Mint:** Istanbul

| Date | Mintage | VF20 | XF40 | MS60 | MS63 | MS65 |
|---|---|---|---|---|---|---|
| 2002 | — | PF65 28.00 | | | | |

**KM# 1147 7500000 LIRA**
15.61 g., 0.925 Silver 0.4642 oz. ASW, 27.9 x 38.6 mm. **Series:** Flowers **Obv:** Value and date within sprigs **Rev:** Iris pamphylica **Edge:** Reeded **Shape:** Oval **Mint:** Istanbul

| Date | Mintage | VF20 | XF40 | MS60 | MS63 | MS65 |
|---|---|---|---|---|---|---|
| 2002 | — | PF65 28.00 | | | | |

**KM# 1148 7500000 LIRA**
15.61 g., 0.925 Silver 0.4642 oz. ASW, 27.9 x 38.6 mm. **Series:** Flowers **Obv:** Value and date within sprigs **Rev:** Gladiolus anatolicus **Edge:** Reeded **Shape:** Oval **Mint:** Istanbul

| Date | Mintage | VF20 | XF40 | MS60 | MS63 | MS65 |
|---|---|---|---|---|---|---|
| 2002 | — | PF65 28.00 | | | | |

**KM# 1149 7500000 LIRA**
15.61 g., 0.925 Silver 0.4642 oz. ASW, 27.9 x 38.6 mm. **Series:** Flowers **Obv:** Value and date within sprigs **Rev:** Crocus sativus **Edge:** Reeded **Shape:** Oval **Mint:** Istanbul

| Date | Mintage | VF20 | XF40 | MS60 | MS63 | MS65 |
|---|---|---|---|---|---|---|
| 2002 | — | PF65 28.00 | | | | |

**KM# 1150 7500000 LIRA**
15.61 g., 0.925 Silver 0.4642 oz. ASW, 27.9 x 38.6 mm. **Series:** Flowers **Obv:** Value and date within sprigs **Rev:** Campanula betulifolia **Edge:** Reeded **Shape:** Oval **Mint:** Istanbul

| Date | Mintage | VF20 | XF40 | MS60 | MS63 | MS65 |
|---|---|---|---|---|---|---|
| 2002 | — | PF65 28.00 | | | | |

**KM# 1151 7500000 LIRA**
15.61 g., 0.925 Silver 0.4642 oz. ASW, 27.9 x 38.6 mm. **Series:** Flowers **Obv:** Value and date within sprigs **Rev:** Centaurea tchihatcheffii **Edge:** Reeded **Shape:** Oval **Mint:** Istanbul

| Date | Mintage | VF20 | XF40 | MS60 | MS63 | MS65 |
|---|---|---|---|---|---|---|
| 2002 | — | PF65 28.00 | | | | |

**KM# 1152 7500000 LIRA**
15.61 g., 0.925 Silver 0.4642 oz. ASW, 27.9 x 38.6 mm. **Series:** Flowers **Obv:** Value and date within sprigs **Rev:** Tchihatchewia isatidea **Edge:** Reeded **Shape:** Oval **Mint:** Istanbul

| Date | Mintage | VF20 | XF40 | MS60 | MS63 | MS65 |
|---|---|---|---|---|---|---|
| 2002 | — | PF65 28.00 | | | | |

**KM# 1153 7500000 LIRA**
15.61 g., 0.925 Silver 0.4642 oz. ASW, 27.9 x 38.6 mm. **Series:** Flowers **Obv:** Value and date within sprigs **Rev:** Linum anatolicum **Edge:** Reeded **Shape:** Oval **Mint:** Istanbul

| Date | Mintage | VF20 | XF40 | MS60 | MS63 | MS65 |
|---|---|---|---|---|---|---|
| 2002 | — | PF65 28.00 | | | | |

**KM# 1154 7500000 LIRA**
15.61 g., 0.925 Silver 0.4642 oz. ASW, 27.9 x 38.6 mm. **Series:** Flowers **Obv:** Value and date within sprigs **Rev:** Cyclamen trochopteranthum **Edge:** Reeded **Shape:** Oval **Mint:** Istanbul

| Date | Mintage | VF20 | XF40 | MS60 | MS63 | MS65 |
|---|---|---|---|---|---|---|
| 2002 | — | PF65 28.00 | | | | |

**KM# 1155 7500000 LIRA**
15.61 g., 0.925 Silver 0.4642 oz. ASW, 27.9 x 38.6 mm. **Series:** Flowers **Obv:** Value and date within sprigs **Rev:** Tulipa orphanidea **Edge:** Reeded **Shape:** Oval **Mint:** Istanbul

| Date | Mintage | VF20 | XF40 | MS60 | MS63 | MS65 |
|---|---|---|---|---|---|---|
| 2002 | — | PF65 28.00 | | | | |

**KM# 1156 7500000 LIRA**
15.61 g., 0.925 Silver 0.4642 oz. ASW, 27.9 x 38.6 mm. **Obv:** Value and date within sprigs **Rev:** Stenbergia candida **Edge:** Reeded **Shape:** Oval **Mint:** Istanbul

| Date | Mintage | VF20 | XF40 | MS60 | MS63 | MS65 |
|---|---|---|---|---|---|---|
| 2002 | — | PF65 28.00 | | | | |

**KM# 1157 7500000 LIRA**
15.61 g., 0.925 Silver 0.4642 oz. ASW, 27.9 x 38.6 mm. **Series:** Flowers **Obv:** Value and date within sprigs **Rev:** Arum maculatum **Edge:** Reeded **Shape:** Oval **Mint:** Istanbul

| Date | Mintage | VF20 | XF40 | MS60 | MS63 | MS65 |
|---|---|---|---|---|---|---|
| 2002 | — | PF65 28.00 | | | | |

**KM# 1118 10000000 LIRA**
31.47 g., 0.925 Silver 0.9359 oz. ASW, 38.6 mm. **Subject:** Divrigi Ulu Camii **Obv:** Artwork within circle **Rev:** Ornate door at the Divrigi ulu Camii (Divrigi Great Mosque) built 1228 in Sivas Province **Edge:** Reeded **Mint:** Istanbul

| Date | Mintage | VF20 | XF40 | MS60 | MS63 | MS65 |
|---|---|---|---|---|---|---|
| 2001 Matte | 15,000 | — | — | — | 40.00 | — |

**KM# 1159 10000000 LIRA**
31.42 g., 0.925 Silver 0.9344 oz. ASW, 38.6 mm. **Subject:** Bogazici'nde Yalilar **Obv:** Value and date within sprigs **Rev:** Waterfront buildings **Edge:** Reeded **Mint:** Istanbul

| Date | Mintage | VF20 | XF40 | MS60 | MS63 | MS65 |
|---|---|---|---|---|---|---|
| 2001 | 4,458 | PF65 40.00 | | | | |

**KM# 1140 10000000 LIRA**
31.46 g., 0.925 Silver 0.9356 oz. ASW, 38.6 mm. **Subject:** 75th Anniversary of TRT (Türkiye Radyo Televizyon) **Obv:** Large mint mark and design within circle **Rev:** Radio microphone **Edge:** Reeded **Mint:** Istanbul

| Date | Mintage | VF20 | XF40 | MS60 | MS63 | MS65 |
|---|---|---|---|---|---|---|
| 2002 | — | PF65 45.00 | | | | |

**KM# 1160 10000000 LIRA**
31.42 g., 0.925 Silver 0.9344 oz. ASW, 38.6 mm. **Obv:** Turkish mint symbol within circle **Rev:** Mosque within surrounding buildings **Edge:** Reeded **Mint:** Istanbul

| Date | Mintage | VF20 | XF40 | MS60 | MS63 | MS65 |
|---|---|---|---|---|---|---|
| 2002 | 2,106 | PF65 45.00 | | | | |

**KM# 1265 150000000 LIRA**
31.49 g., 0.925 Silver 0.9365 oz. ASW, 38.61 mm. **Subject:** 2006 FIFA World Cup **Obv:** Value within wreath **Rev:** Two scoccer players and globe **Edge:** Reeded

| Date | Mintage | VF20 | XF40 | MS60 | MS63 | MS65 |
|---|---|---|---|---|---|---|
| 2003 | Est. 5000 | PF65 50.00 | | | | |

## REFORM DECIMAL COINAGE

2005

100,000 Old Lira = 1 New Lira

**KM# 1164 NEW KURUS**
2.72 g., Aluminum-Bronze, 17 mm. **Obv:** Head of Atatürk left within circle **Rev:** Value **Edge:** Plain **Mint:** Istanbul

| Date | Mintage | VF20 | XF40 | MS60 | MS63 | MS65 |
|---|---|---|---|---|---|---|
| 2005 | 148,419,560 | — | — | — | 0.15 | 0.20 |
| 2006 | 9,002,010 | — | — | — | 0.15 | 0.20 |
| 2007 | 5,357,000 | — | — | — | 0.15 | 0.20 |
| 2008 | — | — | — | — | 0.15 | 0.20 |

**KM# 1165 5 NEW KURUS**
2.95 g., Copper-Nickel-Zinc, 17.1 mm. **Obv:** Head of Atatürk left within circle **Rev:** Value **Edge:** Plain **Mint:** Istanbul

| Date | Mintage | VF20 | XF40 | MS60 | MS63 | MS65 |
|---|---|---|---|---|---|---|
| 2005 | 203,339,160 | — | 0.10 | 0.15 | 0.25 | 0.35 |
| 2006 | 202,253,310 | — | 0.10 | 0.15 | 0.25 | 0.35 |
| 2007 | 122,090,000 | — | 0.10 | 0.15 | 0.25 | 0.35 |
| 2008 | — | — | 0.10 | 0.15 | 0.25 | 0.35 |

**KM# 1166 10 NEW KURUS**
3.83 g., Copper-Nickel-Zinc, 19.4 mm. **Obv:** Head of Atatürk with hat right within circle **Rev:** Value **Edge:** Plain **Mint:** Istanbul

| Date | Mintage | VF20 | XF40 | MS60 | MS63 | MS65 |
|---|---|---|---|---|---|---|
| 2005 | 261,538,050 | — | 0.20 | 0.30 | 0.45 | 0.60 |
| 2006 | 196,717,510 | — | 0.20 | 0.30 | 0.45 | 0.60 |
| 2007 | 134,104,000 | — | 0.20 | 0.30 | 0.45 | 0.60 |
| 2008 | — | — | 0.20 | 0.30 | 0.45 | 0.60 |

**KM# 1167 25 NEW KURUS**
5.30 g., Copper-Nickel-Zinc, 21.5 mm. **Obv:** Bust of Atatürk facing within circle **Rev:** Value **Edge:** Reeded **Mint:** Istanbul

| Date | Mintage | VF20 | XF40 | MS60 | MS63 | MS65 |
|---|---|---|---|---|---|---|
| 2005 | 173,705,760 | — | 0.25 | 0.45 | 0.60 | 0.80 |
| 2006 | 67,803,010 | — | 0.30 | 0.50 | 0.75 | 1.00 |
| 2007 | 33,463,500 | — | 0.25 | 0.45 | 0.60 | 0.80 |
| 2008 | — | — | 0.25 | 0.45 | 0.60 | 0.80 |

**KM# 1168 50 NEW KURUS**
7.00 g., Bi-Metallic Copper-Nickel center in Nickel-Brass ring, 23.8 mm. **Obv:** Head of Atatürk right within circle **Rev:** Value within circle **Edge:** Reeded **Mint:** Istanbul

| Date | Mintage | VF20 | XF40 | MS60 | MS63 | MS65 |
|---|---|---|---|---|---|---|
| 2005 | 203,749,569 | — | 0.60 | 0.75 | 1.50 | 2.00 |
| 2006 | 45,089,010 | — | 0.60 | 0.75 | 1.50 | 2.00 |
| 2007 | 21,946,500 | — | 0.50 | 0.65 | 1.20 | 1.60 |
| 2008 | — | — | 0.50 | 0.65 | 1.20 | 1.60 |

**KM# 1169 NEW LIRA**
8.50 g., Bi-Metallic Nickel-Bronze center in Copper-Nickel-Zinc ring, 26 mm. **Obv:** Bust of Atatürk 3/4 left within circle **Rev:** Value within circle **Edge:** Segmented reeding **Mint:** Istanbul

| Date | Mintage | VF20 | XF40 | MS60 | MS63 | MS65 |
|---|---|---|---|---|---|---|
| 2005 | 305,235,560 | — | — | 1.50 | 2.25 | 3.00 |
| 2006 | 69,247,010 | — | — | 1.50 | 2.25 | 3.00 |
| 2007 | 56,498,200 | — | — | 1.50 | 2.25 | 3.00 |
| 2008 | — | — | — | 1.50 | 2.25 | 3.00 |

**KM# 1171 5 NEW LIRA**
12.00 g., Bi-Metallic Brass center in Copper-Nickel ring, 32 mm. **Subject:** 23rd Universiade in red holder **Obv:** Stylized bird within circle **Rev:** Logo within circle **Mint:** Istanbul

| Date | Mintage | VF20 | XF40 | MS60 | MS63 | MS65 |
|---|---|---|---|---|---|---|
| ND (2005) | 2,957 | — | — | — | 22.00 | 25.00 |

**KM# 1172 5 NEW LIRA**
12.00 g., Bi-Metallic Copper-Nickel center in Brass ring, 32 mm. **Subject:** 23rd Universiade in blue holder **Obv:** Stylized bird within circle **Rev:** Logo within circle **Mint:** Istanbul

| Date | Mintage | VF20 | XF40 | MS60 | MS63 | MS65 |
|---|---|---|---|---|---|---|
| ND (2005) | 2,900 | — | — | — | 22.00 | 25.00 |

**KM# 1195 15 NEW LIRA**
1.24 g., 0.999 Gold 0.0398 oz. AGW, 13.92 mm. **Subject:** Nemrud **Obv:** Value within wreath **Rev:** Two large statue heads **Note:** Dated 2003 but released in 2005

| Date | Mintage | VF20 | XF40 | MS60 | MS63 | MS65 |
|---|---|---|---|---|---|---|
| 2003 | 1,820 | PF63 75.00 | | | | |

**KM# 1193 15 NEW LIRA**
15.55 g., 0.925 Silver 0.4624 oz. ASW, 32 mm. **Obv:** Bird **Rev:** Logo

| Date | Mintage | VF20 | XF40 | MS60 | MS63 | MS65 |
|---|---|---|---|---|---|---|
| 2005 | 1,237 | PF63 40.00 | | | | |

**KM# 1203 15 NEW LIRA**
31.47 g., 0.925 Silver 0.9359 oz. ASW, 38.6 mm. **Subject:** Scouting in Turkey, 100th Anniversary **Obv:** Scout emblem, multicolor **Rev:** Flag, Scouts saluting, camp scene

| Date | Mintage | VF20 | XF40 | MS60 | MS63 | MS65 |
|---|---|---|---|---|---|---|
| 2007 | 1,414 | PF63 50.00 | | | | |

**KM# 1173 20 NEW LIRA**
31.36 g., 0.925 Silver 0.9326 oz. ASW, 38.6 mm. **Obv:** Value within sprigs and circle **Rev:** Aegean Carpet **Edge:** Reeded **Mint:** Istanbul

| Date | Mintage | VF20 | XF40 | MS60 | MS63 | MS65 |
|---|---|---|---|---|---|---|
| 2005 | 1,195 | PF63 70.00 | | | | |

**KM# 1174 20 NEW LIRA**
31.43 g., 0.925 Silver 0.9347 oz. ASW, 38.6 mm. **Obv:** Value within sprigs and circle **Rev:** Mostar Bridge **Edge:** Reeded **Mint:** Istanbul

| Date | Mintage | VF20 | XF40 | MS60 | MS63 | MS65 |
|---|---|---|---|---|---|---|
| 2005 | 1,592 | PF65 75.00 | | | | |

**KM# 1175 20 NEW LIRA**
23.45 g., 0.925 Silver 0.6974 oz. ASW, 38.6 mm. **Obv:** Value within sprigs and circle **Rev:** Angora Goat **Edge:** Reeded **Mint:** Istanbul

| Date | Mintage | VF20 | XF40 | MS60 | MS63 | MS65 |
|---|---|---|---|---|---|---|
| 2005 | 898 | PF63 60.00 | PF65 65.00 | | | |

**KM# 1176 20 NEW LIRA**
23.46 g., 0.925 Silver 0.6977 oz. ASW, 38.6 mm. **Obv:** Value within sprigs and circle **Rev:** Long-eared Desert Hedgehog **Edge:** Reeded **Mint:** Istanbul

| Date | Mintage | VF20 | XF40 | MS60 | MS63 | MS65 |
|---|---|---|---|---|---|---|
| 2005 | 744 | PF63 60.00 | PF65 65.00 | | | |

**KM# 1177 20 NEW LIRA**
23.41 g., 0.925 Silver 0.6962 oz. ASW, 38.6 mm. **Obv:** Value within sprigs and circle **Rev:** Anatolian Mouflon **Edge:** Reeded **Mint:** Istanbul

| Date | Mintage | VF20 | XF40 | MS60 | MS63 | MS65 |
|---|---|---|---|---|---|---|
| 2005 | 779 | PF63 60.00 | PF65 65.00 | | | |

**KM# 1178 20 NEW LIRA**
23.43 g., 0.925 Silver 0.6968 oz. ASW, 38.6 mm. **Obv:** Value within sprigs and circle **Rev:** Striped Hyena **Edge:** Reeded **Mint:** Istanbul

| Date | Mintage | VF20 | XF40 | MS60 | MS63 | MS65 |
|---|---|---|---|---|---|---|
| 2005 | 778 | PF63 60.00 | PF65 65.00 | | | |

**KM# 1179 20 NEW LIRA**
23.43 g., 0.925 Silver 0.6968 oz. ASW, 38.6 mm. **Obv:** Value within sprigs and circle **Rev:** Hazel Dormouse **Edge:** Reeded **Mint:** Istanbul

| Date | Mintage | VF20 | XF40 | MS60 | MS63 | MS65 |
|---|---|---|---|---|---|---|
| 2005 | 744 | PF63 60.00 | PF65 65.00 | | | |

**KM# 1180.1 20 NEW LIRA**
23.50 g., 0.925 Silver 0.6989 oz. ASW, 38.6 mm. **Obv:** Value within sprigs and circle **Rev:** Angora Cat with plain eyes **Edge:** Reeded **Mint:** Istanbul

| Date | Mintage | VF20 | XF40 | MS60 | MS63 | MS65 |
|---|---|---|---|---|---|---|
| 2005 | 5,000 | PF65 60.00 | | | | |

**KM# 1180.2 20 NEW LIRA**
23.50 g., 0.925 Silver 0.6989 oz. ASW, 38.6 mm. **Obv:** Value within sprigs and circle **Rev:** Angora cat with mismatched colored eyes **Edge:** Reeded **Mint:** Istanbul

| Date | Mintage | VF20 | XF40 | MS60 | MS63 | MS65 |
|---|---|---|---|---|---|---|
| 2005 | — | PF65 65.00 | | | | |

### KM# 1181 20 NEW LIRA

23.37 g., 0.999 Silver 0.7506 oz. ASW, 38.6 mm. **Obv:** Value within sprigs and circle **Rev:** Anatolian Leopard **Edge:** Reeded **Mint:** Istanbul

| Date | Mintage | VF20 | XF40 | MS60 | MS63 | MS65 |
|---|---|---|---|---|---|---|
| 2005 | 855 | PF63 60.00 | PF65 65.00 | | | |

### KM# 1182 20 NEW LIRA

23.25 g., 0.925 Silver 0.6914 oz. ASW, 38.6 mm. **Obv:** Value within sprigs and circle **Rev:** Turkish Kangal Dog **Edge:** Reeded **Mint:** Istanbul

| Date | Mintage | VF20 | XF40 | MS60 | MS63 | MS65 |
|---|---|---|---|---|---|---|
| 2005 | 1,128 | PF63 60.00 | PF65 65.00 | | | |

### KM# 1183 20 NEW LIRA

23.46 g., 0.925 Silver 0.6977 oz. ASW, 38.6 mm. **Obv:** Value within sprigs and circle **Rev:** Five-toed Jerboa **Edge:** Reeded **Mint:** Istanbul

| Date | Mintage | VF20 | XF40 | MS60 | MS63 | MS65 |
|---|---|---|---|---|---|---|
| 2005 | 746 | PF63 60.00 | PF65 65.00 | | | |

### KM# 1184 20 NEW LIRA

23.26 g., 0.925 Silver 0.6917 oz. ASW, 38.6 mm. **Obv:** Value within sprigs and circle **Rev:** Brown Bear **Edge:** Reeded **Mint:** Istanbul

| Date | Mintage | VF20 | XF40 | MS60 | MS63 | MS65 |
|---|---|---|---|---|---|---|
| 2005 | 802 | PF63 60.00 | PF65 65.00 | | | |

### KM# 1185 20 NEW LIRA

23.53 g., 0.925 Silver 0.6998 oz. ASW, 38.6 mm. **Obv:** Value within sprigs and circle **Rev:** Desert Monitor **Edge:** Reeded **Mint:** Istanbul

| Date | Mintage | VF20 | XF40 | MS60 | MS63 | MS65 |
|---|---|---|---|---|---|---|
| 2005 | 753 | PF63 60.00 | PF65 65.00 | | | |

### KM# 1188 20 NEW LIRA

31.47 g., 0.925 Silver 0.9359 oz. ASW, 38.6 mm. **Subject:** Edirne Selimiye Mosque **Obv:** Value within wreath **Rev:** Mosque

| Date | Mintage | VF20 | XF40 | MS60 | MS63 | MS65 |
|---|---|---|---|---|---|---|
| 2005 | 1,660 | PF63 55.00 | PF65 60.00 | | | |

### KM# 1189 20 NEW LIRA

31.47 g., 0.925 Silver 0.9359 oz. ASW, 38.6 mm. **Obv:** Crescent and star **Rev:** Large 85 above building

| Date | Mintage | VF20 | XF40 | MS60 | MS63 | MS65 |
|---|---|---|---|---|---|---|
| 2005 | 1,216 | PF63 55.00 | PF65 60.00 | | | |

### KM# 1190 20 NEW LIRA

31.47 g., 0.925 Silver 0.9359 oz. ASW, 38.6 mm. **Subject:** Galatasaray Spor **Obv:** 100 above team mascot **Rev:** GS monogram

| Date | Mintage | VF20 | XF40 | MS60 | MS63 | MS65 |
|---|---|---|---|---|---|---|
| 2005 | 2,828 | PF63 55.00 | PF65 60.00 | | | |

### KM# 1194 20 NEW LIRA

31.47 g., 0.925 Silver 0.9359 oz. ASW, 38.6 mm. **Subject:** Belt Maglova Cultural Heritage site **Obv:** Value within wreath **Rev:** Aqueduct

| Date | Mintage | VF20 | XF40 | MS60 | MS63 | MS65 |
|---|---|---|---|---|---|---|
| 2005 | 1,250 | PF63 55.00 | PF65 60.00 | | | |

### KM# 1191 25 NEW LIRA

31.47 g., 0.925 Silver 0.9359 oz. ASW, 38.6 mm. **Subject:** Galatasaray Spor **Obv:** 100 above team mascot **Rev:** GS monogram, colored

| Date | Mintage | VF20 | XF40 | MS60 | MS63 | MS65 |
|---|---|---|---|---|---|---|
| 2005 | 1,250 | PF63 75.00 | PF65 85.00 | | | |

### KM# 1196 25 NEW LIRA

31.47 g., 0.925 Silver 0.9359 oz. ASW, 38.6 mm. **Subject:** 800 year of Medical Education in Turkey **Obv:** Two snakes **Rev:** Figure

| Date | Mintage | VF20 | XF40 | MS60 | MS63 | MS65 |
|---|---|---|---|---|---|---|
| 2006 | 1,650 | PF63 60.00 | PF65 65.00 | | | |

### KM# 1198 25 NEW LIRA

31.47 g., 0.925 Silver 0.9359 oz. ASW, 38.6 mm. **Subject:** Nevruz of Hatira **Obv:** Flower and rays **Rev:** Statue holding flames

| Date | Mintage | VF20 | XF40 | MS60 | MS63 | MS65 |
|---|---|---|---|---|---|---|
| 2006 | 1,300 | PF63 75.00 | PF65 85.00 | | | |

### KM# 1199 25 NEW LIRA

31.47 g., 0.925 Silver 0.9359 oz. ASW, 38.6 mm. **Subject:** Hattat Hamid Aytac **Obv:** Design **Rev:** Bust facing

| Date | Mintage | VF20 | XF40 | MS60 | MS63 | MS65 |
|---|---|---|---|---|---|---|
| 2006 | 1,301 | PF63 75.00 | PF65 85.00 | | | |

### KM# 1200 25 NEW LIRA

31.47 g., 0.925 Silver 0.9359 oz. ASW, 38.6 mm. **Subject:** T.C. Devlet Demiryollari, 150th Anniversary **Obv:** 150 above laural **Rev:** Building

| Date | Mintage | VF20 | XF40 | MS60 | MS63 | MS65 |
|---|---|---|---|---|---|---|
| 2006 | 1,950 | PF63 55.00 | PF65 60.00 | | | |

### KM# 1201 25 NEW LIRA

31.47 g., 0.925 Silver 0.9359 oz. ASW, 38.6 mm. **Subject:** Mehmet Ersoy Akif, 70th Anniversary of death **Obv:** Scroll **Rev:** Linear portrait facing

| Date | Mintage | VF20 | XF40 | MS60 | MS63 | MS65 |
|---|---|---|---|---|---|---|
| 2006 Antiqued | 1,500 | — | — | — | 55.00 | — |

### KM# 1211 25 NEW LIRA

15.55 g., 0.925 Silver 0.4624 oz. ASW, 38.6x28 mm. **Obv:** Legend **Rev:** Zodiac - Pisces **Shape:** Oval

| Date | Mintage | VF20 | XF40 | MS60 | MS63 | MS65 |
|---|---|---|---|---|---|---|
| 2008 | — | PF63 45.00 | PF65 50.00 | | | |

### KM# 1212 25 NEW LIRA

15.55 g., 0.925 Silver 0.4624 oz. ASW, 38.6x28 mm. **Obv:** Text **Rev:** Zodiac - Aquarius **Shape:** Oval

| Date | Mintage | VF20 | XF40 | MS60 | MS63 | MS65 |
|---|---|---|---|---|---|---|
| 2008 | — | PF63 45.00 | PF65 50.00 | | | |

### KM# 1213 25 NEW LIRA

15.55 g., 0.925 Silver 0.4624 oz. ASW, 38.6x28 mm. **Obv:** Text **Rev:** Zodiac - Capricorn **Shape:** Oval

| Date | Mintage | VF20 | XF40 | MS60 | MS63 | MS65 |
|---|---|---|---|---|---|---|
| 2008 | — | PF63 45.00 | PF65 50.00 | | | |

### KM# 1214 25 NEW LIRA

15.55 g., 0.925 Silver 0.4624 oz. ASW, 38.6x28 mm. **Obv:** Text **Rev:** Zodiac - Sagittarius **Shape:** Oval

| Date | Mintage | VF20 | XF40 | MS60 | MS63 | MS65 |
|---|---|---|---|---|---|---|
| 2008 | — | PF63 45.00 | PF65 50.00 | | | |

### KM# 1215 25 NEW LIRA

15.55 g., 0.925 Silver 0.4624 oz. ASW, 38.6x28 mm. **Obv:** Text **Rev:** Zodiac - Libra **Shape:** Oval

| Date | Mintage | VF20 | XF40 | MS60 | MS63 | MS65 |
|---|---|---|---|---|---|---|
| 2008 | — | PF63 45.00 | PF65 50.00 | | | |

### KM# 1216 25 NEW LIRA

15.55 g., 0.925 Silver 0.4624 oz. ASW, 38.6x28 mm. **Obv:** Text **Rev:** Zodiac - figure **Shape:** Oval

| Date | Mintage | VF20 | XF40 | MS60 | MS63 | MS65 |
|---|---|---|---|---|---|---|
| 2008 | — | PF63 45.00 | PF65 50.00 | | | |

### KM# 1217 25 NEW LIRA

15.55 g., 0.925 Silver 0.4624 oz. ASW, 38.6x28 mm. **Obv:** Text **Rev:** Zodiac - Leo **Shape:** Oval

| Date | Mintage | VF20 | XF40 | MS60 | MS63 | MS65 |
|---|---|---|---|---|---|---|
| 2008 | — | PF63 45.00 | PF65 50.00 | | | |

### KM# 1218 25 NEW LIRA

15.55 g., 0.925 Silver 0.4624 oz. ASW, 38.6x28 mm. **Obv:** Text **Rev:** Zodiac - Virgo **Shape:** Oval

| Date | Mintage | VF20 | XF40 | MS60 | MS63 | MS65 |
|---|---|---|---|---|---|---|
| 2008 | — | PF63 45.00 | PF65 50.00 | | | |

### KM# 1219 25 NEW LIRA

15.55 g., 0.925 Silver 0.4624 oz. ASW, 38.6x28 mm. **Obv:** Text **Rev:** Zodiac - Gemeni **Shape:** Oval

| Date | Mintage | VF20 | XF40 | MS60 | MS63 | MS65 |
|---|---|---|---|---|---|---|
| 2008 | — | PF63 45.00 | PF65 50.00 | | | |

### KM# 1220 25 NEW LIRA

15.55 g., 0.925 Silver 0.4624 oz. ASW, 38.6x28 mm. **Obv:** Text **Rev:** Zodiac - Taurus **Shape:** Oval

| Date | Mintage | VF20 | XF40 | MS60 | MS63 | MS65 |
|---|---|---|---|---|---|---|
| 2008 | — | PF63 45.00 | PF65 50.00 | | | |

### KM# 1221 25 NEW LIRA

15.55 g., 0.925 Silver 0.4624 oz. ASW, 38.6x28 mm. **Obv:** Text **Rev:** Zodiac sign **Shape:** Oval

| Date | Mintage | VF20 | XF40 | MS60 | MS63 | MS65 |
|---|---|---|---|---|---|---|
| 2008 | — | PF63 45.00 | PF65 50.00 | | | |

### KM# 1192 30 NEW LIRA

31.47 g., 0.925 Silver 0.9359 oz. ASW, 38.6 mm. **Subject:** Galatasaray Spor **Obv:** 100 above team mascot **Rev:** GS monogram colored and selective gold plating

| Date | Mintage | VF20 | XF40 | MS60 | MS63 | MS65 |
|---|---|---|---|---|---|---|
| 2005 | 1,106 | PF63 55.00 | PF65 60.00 | | | |

### KM# 1197 30 NEW LIRA

23.33 g., 0.925 Silver 0.6938 oz. ASW partially gold plated, 38.61 mm. **Subject:** Solar Eclipse **Obv:** Turkey map with route of the eclipse **Rev:** Sun, gilt

| Date | Mintage | VF20 | XF40 | MS60 | MS63 | MS65 |
|---|---|---|---|---|---|---|
| 2006 | 2,475 | PF63 90.00 | PF65 100 | | | |

### KM# 1204 30 NEW LIRA

31.47 g., 0.925 Silver 0.9359 oz. ASW, 38.6 mm. **Subject:** Bank of Sarfanbolu **Obv:** Building **Rev:** Landscape

| Date | Mintage | VF20 | XF40 | MS60 | MS63 | MS65 |
|---|---|---|---|---|---|---|
| 2007 | 1,312 | PF63 70.00 | PF65 75.00 | | | |

### KM# 1205 30 NEW LIRA

31.47 g., 0.925 Silver 0.9359 oz. ASW, 38.6 mm. **Obv:** Crescent and star at center of four objects **Rev:** Knotted fabric pattern

| Date | Mintage | VF20 | XF40 | MS60 | MS63 | MS65 |
|---|---|---|---|---|---|---|
| 2007 | 1,210 | PF63 55.00 | PF65 60.00 | | | |

### KM# 1206 30 NEW LIRA

31.47 g., 0.925 Silver 0.9359 oz. ASW, 38.6 mm. **Obv:** Crescent and star within four objects **Rev:** Twirling Dirvishes

| Date | Mintage | VF20 | XF40 | MS60 | MS63 | MS65 |
|---|---|---|---|---|---|---|
| 2007 | 1,224 | PF63 55.00 | PF65 60.00 | | | |

### KM# 1207 30 NEW LIRA

31.47 g., 0.925 Silver 0.9359 oz. ASW, 38.6 mm. **Obv:** Crescent and star within four designs **Rev:** Twirling Dirvish and town facades around

| Date | Mintage | VF20 | XF40 | MS60 | MS63 | MS65 |
|---|---|---|---|---|---|---|
| 2007 | 1,179 | PF63 55.00 | PF65 60.00 | | | |

### KM# 1208 30 NEW LIRA

31.47 g., 0.925 Silver 0.9359 oz. ASW, 38.6 mm. **Obv:** Mosque **Rev:** Entranceway arch

| Date | Mintage | VF20 | XF40 | MS60 | MS63 | MS65 |
|---|---|---|---|---|---|---|
| 2007 | 1,222 | PF63 70.00 | PF65 75.00 | | | |

**KM# 1222 30 NEW LIRA**
10.00 g., 0.925 Silver 0.2974 oz. ASW, 22 mm. **Obv:** Seal within border **Rev:** Large seal rendering

| Date | Mintage | VF20 | XF40 | MS60 | MS63 | MS65 |
|---|---|---|---|---|---|---|
| 2008 | — | PF63 30.00 | PF65 35.00 | | | |

**KM# 1210 35 NEW LIRA**
23.23 g., 0.925 Silver 0.6908 oz. ASW, 38.6 mm. **Subject:** Antikabir, 70th Anniversary **Obv:** Value within wreath **Rev:** Antikabir building

| Date | Mintage | VF20 | XF40 | MS60 | MS63 | MS65 |
|---|---|---|---|---|---|---|
| 2008 | 3,000 | PF63 40.00 | PF65 45.00 | | | |

**KM# 1232 35 NEW LIRA**
23.33 g., 0.925 Silver 0.6938 oz. ASW, 38.6 mm. **Obv:** Value within wreath **Rev:** Bust at left

| Date | Mintage | VF20 | XF40 | MS60 | MS63 | MS65 |
|---|---|---|---|---|---|---|
| 2008 | — | PF63 40.00 | PF65 45.00 | | | |

**KM# 1233 35 NEW LIRA**
23.33 g., 0.925 Silver 0.6938 oz. ASW, 38.6 mm. **Obv:** Classical design **Rev:** Mahmud of Kashgar at right

| Date | Mintage | VF20 | XF40 | MS60 | MS63 | MS65 |
|---|---|---|---|---|---|---|
| 2008 | — | PF63 40.00 | PF65 45.00 | | | |

**KM# 1238 35 NEW LIRA**
23.33 g., 0.925 Silver 0.6938 oz. ASW, 38.6 mm. **Obv:** Value within wreath **Rev:** Sultan on horseback

| Date | Mintage | VF20 | XF40 | MS60 | MS63 | MS65 |
|---|---|---|---|---|---|---|
| 2008 | — | PF63 45.00 | PF65 50.00 | | | |

**KM# 1202 40 NEW LIRA**
31.47 g., 0.925 Silver 0.9359 oz. ASW, 38.6 mm. **Subject:** Troy **Obv:** Linear design **Rev:** Stylized Trojan Horse

| Date | Mintage | VF20 | XF40 | MS60 | MS63 | MS65 |
|---|---|---|---|---|---|---|
| 2007 | 1,500 | PF63 50.00 | PF65 55.00 | | | |

**KM# 1224 40 NEW LIRA**
31.47 g., 0.999 Silver 1.0108 oz. ASW, 38.6 mm. **Obv:** Historic map **Rev:** Kyrgyzstan building

| Date | Mintage | VF20 | XF40 | MS60 | MS63 | MS65 |
|---|---|---|---|---|---|---|
| 2008 Antiqued | — | — | — | — | 80.00 | — |

**KM# 1225 40 NEW LIRA**
31.47 g., 0.925 Silver 0.9359 oz. ASW, 38.6 mm. **Obv:** Village scene **Rev:** Large classical figure

| Date | Mintage | VF20 | XF40 | MS60 | MS63 | MS65 |
|---|---|---|---|---|---|---|
| 2008 | — | PF63 75.00 | PF65 80.00 | | | |

**KM# 1227 40 NEW LIRA**
31.47 g., 0.925 Silver 0.9359 oz. ASW, 38.6 mm. **Obv:** Building **Rev:** Seated figure

| Date | Mintage | VF20 | XF40 | MS60 | MS63 | MS65 |
|---|---|---|---|---|---|---|
| 2008 | — | PF63 45.00 | PF65 50.00 | | | |

**KM# 1228 40 NEW LIRA**
31.47 g., 0.925 Silver 0.9359 oz. ASW, 38.6 mm. **Obv:** Classical intricate design **Rev:** Mosque

| Date | Mintage | VF20 | XF40 | MS60 | MS63 | MS65 |
|---|---|---|---|---|---|---|
| 2008 | — | PF63 45.00 | PF65 50.00 | | | |

**KM# 1229 40 NEW LIRA**
31.47 g., 0.925 Silver 0.9359 oz. ASW, 38.6 mm. **Obv:** Head left above school building **Rev:** Monogram at center

| Date | Mintage | VF20 | XF40 | MS60 | MS63 | MS65 |
|---|---|---|---|---|---|---|
| 2008 | — | PF63 45.00 | PF65 50.00 | | | |

**KM# 1230 40 NEW LIRA**
31.47 g., 0.925 Silver 0.9359 oz. ASW, 38.6 mm. **Obv:** Large tower and acqueduct **Rev:** Classical scene

| Date | Mintage | VF20 | XF40 | MS60 | MS63 | MS65 |
|---|---|---|---|---|---|---|
| 2008 | — | PF63 45.00 | PF65 50.00 | | | |

**KM# 1231 40 NEW LIRA**
31.47 g., 0.925 Silver 0.9359 oz. ASW, 38.6 mm. **Obv:** Tortoise, seal and lighthouse in distance **Rev:** Lighthouse

| Date | Mintage | VF20 | XF40 | MS60 | MS63 | MS65 |
|---|---|---|---|---|---|---|
| 2008 | — | PF63 45.00 | PF65 50.00 | | | |

**KM# 1234 40 NEW LIRA**
23.33 g., 0.925 Silver 0.6938 oz. ASW, 38.6 mm. **Subject:** Vefs Sports Club, 100th Anniversary **Obv:** Club seal multicolor **Rev:** Large 100 and logo

| Date | Mintage | VF20 | XF40 | MS60 | MS63 | MS65 |
|---|---|---|---|---|---|---|
| 2008 | — | PF63 45.00 | PF65 50.00 | | | |

**KM# 1235 40 NEW LIRA**
31.47 g., 0.925 Silver 0.9359 oz. ASW, 38.6 mm. **Obv:** Ancient craft items **Rev:** Cave paintings

| Date | Mintage | VF20 | XF40 | MS60 | MS63 | MS65 |
|---|---|---|---|---|---|---|
| 2008 | — | PF63 45.00 | PF65 50.00 | | | |

**KM# 1236 40 NEW LIRA**
31.47 g., 0.925 Silver 0.9359 oz. ASW, 38.6 mm. **Obv:** Ancient map **Rev:** Uzbekistan mosque

| Date | Mintage | VF20 | XF40 | MS60 | MS63 | MS65 |
|---|---|---|---|---|---|---|
| 2008 Antiqued | — | — | — | 40.00 | 45.00 | — |

**KM# 1237 40 NEW LIRA**
31.47 g., 0.925 Silver 0.9359 oz. ASW, 38.6 mm. **Obv:** Tower **Rev:** Tower

| Date | Mintage | VF20 | XF40 | MS60 | MS63 | MS65 |
|---|---|---|---|---|---|---|
| 2008 | — | PF63 45.00 | PF65 50.00 | | | |

**KM# 1255 50 LIRA**
36.08 g., 0.925 Silver 1.073 oz. ASW, 38.6 mm. **Subject:** Sunlight **Obv:** Eastern Hemisphere logo **Rev:** Eastern Hemisphere in Sun

| Date | Mintage | VF20 | XF40 | MS60 | MS63 | MS65 |
|---|---|---|---|---|---|---|
| 2008 | — | PF63 55.00 | PF65 65.00 | | | |

**KM# 1209 60 NEW LIRA**
1.50 g., 0.916 Gold 0.0442 oz. AGW, 13.95 mm. **Obv:** Text **Rev:** Ancient pottery

| Date | Mintage | VF20 | XF40 | MS60 | MS63 | MS65 |
|---|---|---|---|---|---|---|
| 2007 | 1,925 | PF63 75.00 | PF65 85.00 | | | |

**KM# 1223 100 NEW LIRA**
7.22 g., 0.916 Gold 0.2125 oz. AGW, 22 mm. **Obv:** Seal within border **Rev:** Large seal

| Date | Mintage | VF20 | XF40 | MS60 | MS63 | MS65 |
|---|---|---|---|---|---|---|
| 2008 | — | PF65 425 | | | | |

**KM# 1226 100 NEW LIRA**
7.22 g., 0.916 Gold 0.2125 oz. AGW, 22 mm. **Obv:** Village scene **Rev:** Large classical figure

| Date | Mintage | VF20 | XF40 | MS60 | MS63 | MS65 |
|---|---|---|---|---|---|---|
| 2008 | — | PF65 425 | | | | |

## REFORM DECIMAL COINAGE

2009

**KM# 1239 KURUS**
Copper-Nickel Plated Steel **Obv:** Head of Ataturk left **Rev:** Plant and value

| Date | Mintage | VF20 | XF40 | MS60 | MS63 | MS65 |
|---|---|---|---|---|---|---|
| 2009 | — | — | — | 0.15 | 0.30 | 0.50 |
| 2010 | — | — | — | 0.15 | 0.30 | 0.50 |
| 2011 | — | — | — | 0.15 | 0.30 | 0.50 |
| 2012 | — | — | — | 0.15 | 0.30 | 0.50 |
| 2013 | — | — | — | 0.15 | 0.30 | 0.50 |

**KM# 1240 5 KURUS**
Brass **Obv:** Head of Ataturk left **Rev:** Value and traditional embroidery pattern

| Date | Mintage | VF20 | XF40 | MS60 | MS63 | MS65 |
|---|---|---|---|---|---|---|
| 2009 | — | — | — | 0.15 | 0.30 | 0.50 |
| 2010 | — | — | — | 0.15 | 0.30 | 0.50 |
| 2011 | — | — | — | 0.15 | 0.30 | 0.50 |
| 2012 | — | — | — | 0.15 | 0.30 | 0.50 |
| 2013 | — | — | — | 0.15 | 0.30 | 0.50 |

**KM# 1241 10 KURUS**
Brass **Obv:** Head of Ataturk left **Rev:** Value

| Date | Mintage | VF20 | XF40 | MS60 | MS63 | MS65 |
|---|---|---|---|---|---|---|
| 2009 | — | — | — | 0.15 | 0.30 | 0.50 |
| 2010 | — | — | — | 0.15 | 0.30 | 0.50 |
| 2011 | — | — | — | 0.15 | 0.30 | 0.50 |
| 2012 | — | — | — | 0.15 | 0.30 | 0.50 |
| 2013 | — | — | — | 0.15 | 0.30 | 0.50 |

**KM# 1242 25 KURUS**
Copper-Nickel **Obv:** Head of Ataturk left **Rev:** Value

| Date | Mintage | VF20 | XF40 | MS60 | MS63 | MS65 |
|---|---|---|---|---|---|---|
| 2009 | — | — | — | 0.25 | 0.50 | 0.75 |
| 2010 | — | — | — | 0.25 | 0.50 | 0.75 |
| 2011 | — | — | — | 0.25 | 0.50 | 0.75 |
| 2012 | — | — | — | 0.25 | 0.50 | 0.75 |
| 2013 | — | — | — | 0.25 | 0.50 | 0.75 |

**KM# 1243 50 KURUS**
Bi-Metallic Brass center in Copper-Nickel ring **Obv:** Head of Atatürk left **Rev:** Value above suspension bridge **Edge:** Reeded

| Date | Mintage | VF20 | XF40 | MS60 | MS63 | MS65 |
|---|---|---|---|---|---|---|
| 2009 | — | — | — | 0.35 | 0.75 | 1.00 |
| 2010 | — | — | — | 0.35 | 0.75 | 1.00 |
| 2011 | — | — | — | 0.35 | 0.75 | 1.00 |
| 2012 | — | — | — | 0.35 | 0.75 | 1.00 |
| 2013 | — | — | — | 0.35 | 0.75 | 1.00 |

**KM# 1244 LIRA**
Bi-Metallic Copper-Nickel center in Brass ring **Obv:** Head of Atatürk left **Rev:** Value

| Date | Mintage | VF20 | XF40 | MS60 | MS63 | MS65 |
|---|---|---|---|---|---|---|
| 2009 | — | — | — | 2.00 | 3.00 | 5.00 |
| 2010 | — | — | — | 2.00 | 3.00 | 5.00 |
| 2011 | — | — | — | 2.00 | 3.00 | 5.00 |
| 2012 | — | — | — | 2.00 | 3.00 | 5.00 |
| 2013 | — | — | — | 2.00 | 3.00 | 5.00 |

**KM# 1249 LIRA**
6.40 g., Copper-Nickel, 23.5 mm. **Obv:** Lammergeier standing on rock **Rev:** Two eagles

| Date | Mintage | VF20 | XF40 | MS60 | MS63 | MS65 |
|---|---|---|---|---|---|---|
| 2009 | 120,000 | — | — | 2.50 | 4.50 | 6.00 |

**KM# 1263 LIRA**
8.30 g., Bi-Metallic Copper-Nickel center in Brass ring, 26.15 mm. **Obv:** Value within wreath **Rev:** Elephant and calf

| Date | Mintage | VF20 | XF40 | MS60 | MS63 | MS65 |
|---|---|---|---|---|---|---|
| 2009 | 5,000 | — | — | 4.00 | 7.50 | 10.00 |

**KM# 1264 LIRA**
8.30 g., Bi-Metallic Copper-Nickel center in Brass ring, 26.15 mm. **Obv:** Value within wreath **Rev:** Sea tortoise

| Date | Mintage | VF20 | XF40 | MS60 | MS63 | MS65 |
|---|---|---|---|---|---|---|
| 2009 | 5,000 | — | — | 4.00 | 7.50 | 10.00 |

**KM# 1279 LIRA**
Bi-Metallic Copper-nickel center in Brass ring, 26.15 mm. **Obv:** Value within wreath **Rev:** Cat's bust

| Date | Mintage | VF20 | XF40 | MS60 | MS63 | MS65 |
|---|---|---|---|---|---|---|
| 2010 | — | — | — | 4.00 | 7.50 | 10.00 |

**KM# 1280 LIRA**
Bi-Metallic Nickel center in Brass ring, 26.15 mm. **Obv:** Value within wreath **Rev:** Dog standing facing right

| Date | Mintage | VF20 | XF40 | MS60 | MS63 | MS65 |
|---|---|---|---|---|---|---|
| 2010 | — | — | — | 4.00 | 7.50 | 10.00 |

**KM# 1275 LIRA**
8.30 g., Bi-Metallic Brass center in Copper-Nickel ring, 26.15 mm. **Obv:** Value within wreath **Rev:** Lion advancing - Pathera leo persica

| Date | Mintage | VF20 | XF40 | MS60 | MS63 | MS65 |
|---|---|---|---|---|---|---|
| 2011 | — | — | — | 3.00 | 5.00 | 7.50 |

**KM# 1276 LIRA**
8.30 g., Bi-Metallic Brass center in Copper-Nickel ring, 26.15 mm. **Obv:** Value within wreath **Rev:** Brown bear - Ursus arctos

| Date | Mintage | VF20 | XF40 | MS60 | MS63 | MS65 |
|---|---|---|---|---|---|---|
| 2011 | 4,000 | PF63 15.00 | | | | |
| 2011 | 11,000 | — | — | 3.00 | 5.00 | 7.50 |

**KM# 1281 LIRA**
8.30 g., Bi-Metallic Brass center in Copper-Nickel ring, 26.15 mm. **Obv:** Value within wreath **Rev:** 10th International Turkish Language Olympics

| Date | Mintage | VF20 | XF40 | MS60 | MS63 | MS65 |
|---|---|---|---|---|---|---|
| 2012 | — | — | — | 3.00 | 5.00 | 7.50 |

**KM# 1282 LIRA**
8.30 g., Bi-Metallic Brass center in Copper-Nickel ring, 26.15 mm. **Obv:** Value within wreath **Rev:** 150 Years of the Court

| Date | Mintage | VF20 | XF40 | MS60 | MS63 | MS65 |
|---|---|---|---|---|---|---|
| 2012 | — | — | — | 3.00 | 5.00 | 7.50 |

**KM# 1283 LIRA**
8.30 g., Bi-Metallic Brass Center in Copper-Nickel ring, 26.15 mm. **Obv:** Value within wreath **Rev:** Deer

| Date | Mintage | VF20 | XF40 | MS60 | MS63 | MS65 |
|---|---|---|---|---|---|---|
| 2012 | — | — | — | 3.00 | 5.00 | 7.50 |

**KM# 1284 LIRA**
8.30 g., Bi-Metallic Brass center in Copper-Nickel ring, 26.15 mm. **Obv:** Value within wreath **Rev:** Leopard

| Date | Mintage | VF20 | XF40 | MS60 | MS63 | MS65 |
|---|---|---|---|---|---|---|
| 2012 | — | — | — | 3.00 | 5.00 | 7.50 |

**KM# 1288 LIRA**
8.30 g., Bi-Metallic Brass center in Copper-Nickel ring, 26.15 mm. **Subject:** 10th International Turkish Language Olympics

| Date | Mintage | VF20 | XF40 | MS60 | MS63 | MS65 |
|---|---|---|---|---|---|---|
| 2012 | Est. 1000000 | — | — | 3.00 | 5.00 | 7.50 |

**KM# 1289 LIRA**
8.20 g., Bi-Metallic Brass center in Copper-Nickel ring, 26.15 mm. **Subject:** 150th Anniversary of the Court

| Date | Mintage | VF20 | XF40 | MS60 | MS63 | MS65 |
|---|---|---|---|---|---|---|
| 2012 | Est. 1000000 | — | — | 3.00 | 5.00 | 7.50 |

**KM# 1250 10 LIRA**
23.33 g., Bronze, 38.6 mm. **Obv:** Scroll and inkwell **Rev:** Child's story **Edge:** Reeded

| Date | Mintage | VF20 | XF40 | MS60 | MS63 | MS65 |
|---|---|---|---|---|---|---|
| 2009 Antiqued | — | — | — | — | 15.00 | — |

**KM# 1258 20 LIRA**
27.50 g., Copper-Nickel, 38.6 mm. **Subject:** Year 1430 **Obv:** Inscription within rose wreath **Rev:** Interior of the Grand Mosque in Mecca

| Date | Mintage | VF20 | XF40 | MS60 | MS63 | MS65 |
|---|---|---|---|---|---|---|
| 2009 Antiqued | — | — | — | — | 35.00 | — |

**KM# 1266 20 LIRA**
23.33 g., Bronze, 38.61 mm. **Subject:** 25th Winter Sports Games - Hockey

| Date | Mintage | VF20 | XF40 | MS60 | MS63 | MS65 |
|---|---|---|---|---|---|---|
| 2011 Antique finish | 3,000 | — | — | — | 20.00 | — |

**KM# 1267 20 LIRA**
23.33 g., Brass, 38.61 mm. **Subject:** 25th Winter Sports Games - Hockey

| Date | Mintage | VF20 | XF40 | MS60 | MS63 | MS65 |
|---|---|---|---|---|---|---|
| 2011 Antique patina | 3,000 | — | — | — | 20.00 | — |

**KM# 1269 20 LIRA**
23.33 g., Bronze, 38.61 mm. **Subject:** 25th Winter Sports Games - Skiing

| Date | Mintage | VF20 | XF40 | MS60 | MS63 | MS65 |
|---|---|---|---|---|---|---|
| 2011 Antique patina | 3,000 | — | — | — | 20.00 | — |

**KM# 1270 20 LIRA**
23.33 g., Brass, 38.61 mm. **Subject:** 25th Winter Sports Games - Skiing

| Date | Mintage | VF20 | XF40 | MS60 | MS63 | MS65 |
|---|---|---|---|---|---|---|
| 2011 Antique patina | 3,000 | — | — | — | 20.00 | — |

**KM# 1272 20 LIRA**
23.33 g., Bronze, 38.61 mm. **Subject:** European Youth Games, Trabzon

| Date | Mintage | VF20 | XF40 | MS60 | MS63 | MS65 |
|---|---|---|---|---|---|---|
| 2011 Antique patina | 2,000 | — | — | — | 20.00 | — |

**KM# 1278 20 LIRA**
15.55 g., 0.925 Silver 0.4624 oz. ASW, 28x38.61 mm. **Subject:** Dolmabahce Clock Tower **Shape:** Vertical oval

| Date | Mintage | VF20 | XF40 | MS60 | MS63 | MS65 |
|---|---|---|---|---|---|---|
| 2011 | — | PF63 50.00 | PF65 55.00 | | | |

**KM# 1286 20 LIRA**
23.33 g., Bronze, 38.61 mm. **Subject:** 150th Anniversary of the Court

| Date | Mintage | VF20 | XF40 | MS60 | MS63 | MS65 |
|---|---|---|---|---|---|---|
| 2012 | Est. 3000 | — | — | — | 20.00 | — |

**KM# 1291 20 LIRA**
36.08 g., 0.925 Silver 1.073 oz. ASW, 38.6 mm. **Subject:** Mediterranean Games at Mersin

| Date | Mintage | VF20 | XF40 | MS60 | MS63 | MS65 |
|---|---|---|---|---|---|---|
| 2013 | — | PF63 40.00 | PF65 45.00 | | | |

**KM# 1245 50 LIRA**
36.08 g., 0.925 Silver 1.073 oz. ASW, 38.6 mm. **Obv:** US and Turkish flags **Rev:** Barack Obama portrait facing

| Date | Mintage | VF20 | XF40 | MS60 | MS63 | MS65 |
|---|---|---|---|---|---|---|
| 2009 | 3,000 | PF63 55.00 | PF65 60.00 | | | |

**KM# 1247 50 LIRA**
36.00 g., 0.925 Silver 1.0706 oz. ASW, 38.6 mm. **Obv:** Value within wreath **Rev:** Samsun 90th Anniversary

| Date | Mintage | VF20 | XF40 | MS60 | MS63 | MS65 |
|---|---|---|---|---|---|---|
| 2009 | 3,000 | PF63 55.00 | PF65 60.00 | | | |

**KM# 1251 50 LIRA**
36.08 g., 0.925 Silver 1.073 oz. ASW, 38.6 mm. **Obv:** Scroll and inkwell **Rev:** Children's story character

| Date | Mintage | VF20 | XF40 | MS60 | MS63 | MS65 |
|---|---|---|---|---|---|---|
| 2009 | — | PF63 40.00 | PF65 45.00 | | | |

**KM# 1252 50 LIRA**

36.08 g., 0.925 Silver 1.073 oz. ASW, 38.6 mm. **Subject:** Frederic Chopin, 200th Anniversary **Obv:** Piano and map of Europe **Rev:** Chopin's bust at left, piano at right, score in background

| Date | Mintage | VF20 | XF40 | MS60 | MS63 | MS65 |
|---|---|---|---|---|---|---|
| 2009 | — | PF63 70.00 | PF65 75.00 | | | |

**KM# 1253 50 LIRA**

36.08 g., 0.925 Silver 1.073 oz. ASW, 38.6 mm. **Subject:** IMF Meeting, Istanbul **Obv:** Istanbul Skyline **Rev:** World Bank Group logo, multicolor

| Date | Mintage | VF20 | XF40 | MS60 | MS63 | MS65 |
|---|---|---|---|---|---|---|
| 2009 | — | PF63 60.00 | PF65 65.00 | | | |

**KM# 1254 50 LIRA**

36.08 g., 0.925 Silver 1.073 oz. ASW, 38.6 mm. **Subject:** Water, source of life **Obv:** Eastern Hemisphere logo **Rev:** Clock hands, small amount of water, cracked and dried earth in rest of area

| Date | Mintage | VF20 | XF40 | MS60 | MS63 | MS65 |
|---|---|---|---|---|---|---|
| 2009 | — | PF63 55.00 | PF65 60.00 | | | |

**KM# 1256 50 LIRA**

36.08 g., 0.925 Silver 1.073 oz. ASW, 38.6 mm. **Obv:** Eastern Hemisphere logo **Rev:** Small seedling within light blue colored water droplet, dried earth background

| Date | Mintage | VF20 | XF40 | MS60 | MS63 | MS65 |
|---|---|---|---|---|---|---|
| 2009 Antiqued | — | — | — | 55.00 | — | — |

**KM# 1257 50 LIRA**

36.08 g., 0.925 Silver 1.073 oz. ASW, 38.6 mm. **Obv:** Eastern Hemisphere logo **Rev:** Female face with hair forming waves and vine

| Date | Mintage | VF20 | XF40 | MS60 | MS63 | MS65 |
|---|---|---|---|---|---|---|
| 2009 | — | PF63 55.00 | PF65 60.00 | | | |

**KM# 1259 50 LIRA**

36.00 g., 0.925 Silver 1.0706 oz. ASW, 38.6 mm. **Subject:** Year 1430 **Obv:** Inscription within rose wreath **Rev:** Interior courtyard of Grand Mosque in Mecca

| Date | Mintage | VF20 | XF40 | MS60 | MS63 | MS65 |
|---|---|---|---|---|---|---|
| 2009 | 2,500 | PF63 70.00 | PF65 80.00 | | | |

**KM# 1261 50 LIRA**

36.00 g., 0.925 Silver 1.0706 oz. ASW, 38.6 mm. **Subject:** 150th Anniversary **Obv:** Multicolor shield and text **Rev:** Building facade

| Date | Mintage | VF20 | XF40 | MS60 | MS63 | MS65 |
|---|---|---|---|---|---|---|
| 2009 | 5,000 | PF63 45.00 | PF65 55.00 | | | |

**KM# 1262 50 LIRA**

36.00 g., 0.925 Silver 1.0706 oz. ASW, 38.6 mm. **Subject:** Chalabi clerks **Obv:** Symbol **Rev:** Classical figure seated

| Date | Mintage | VF20 | XF40 | MS60 | MS63 | MS65 |
|---|---|---|---|---|---|---|
| 2009 | 3,000 | PF63 55.00 | PF65 60.00 | | | |

**KM# 1294 50 LIRA**

31.43 g., 0.925 Silver 0.9347 oz. ASW, 38.61 mm. **Rev:** Ahirkapi Lighthouse

| Date | Mintage | VF20 | XF40 | MS60 | MS63 | MS65 |
|---|---|---|---|---|---|---|
| 2010 | — | PF63 70.00 | PF65 75.00 | | | |

**KM# 1295 50 LIRA**

23.23 g., 0.925 Silver 0.6908 oz. ASW, 38.61 mm. **Subject:** Osman Hamdi, 100th Anniversary, Istanbul Archaeological Museum

| Date | Mintage | VF20 | XF40 | MS60 | MS63 | MS65 |
|---|---|---|---|---|---|---|
| 2010 | — | PF63 60.00 | PF65 65.00 | | | |

**KM# 1296 50 LIRA**

Silver, 38.61 mm. **Subject:** FIBA Championship

| Date | Mintage | VF20 | XF40 | MS60 | MS63 | MS65 |
|---|---|---|---|---|---|---|
| 2010 | — | PF63 60.00 | PF65 65.00 | | | |

**KM# 1297 50 LIRA**

36.00 g., 0.925 Silver 1.0706 oz. ASW, 38.61 mm. **Subject:** Republic, 90th Anniversary **Obv:** Arms in color **Rev:** Large 90

| Date | Mintage | VF20 | XF40 | MS60 | MS63 | MS65 |
|---|---|---|---|---|---|---|
| 2010 | — | PF63 55.00 | PF65 60.00 | | | |

**KM# 1298 50 LIRA**

31.47 g., 0.925 Silver 0.9359 oz. ASW, 38.61 mm. **Subject:** Amasya Evleri **Rev:** Houses of Amasya

| Date | Mintage | VF20 | XF40 | MS60 | MS63 | MS65 |
|---|---|---|---|---|---|---|
| 2010 | — | PF63 55.00 | PF65 60.00 | | | |

**KM# 1268 50 LIRA**
31.47 g., Silver, 38.61 mm. **Subject:** 25th Winter Sports Games - Hockey

| Date | Mintage | VF20 | XF40 | MS60 | MS63 | MS65 |
|---|---|---|---|---|---|---|
| 2011 | 3,000 | PF63 50.00 | PF65 60.00 | | | |

**KM# 1271 50 LIRA**
31.47 g., 0.925 Silver 0.9359 oz. ASW, 38.61 mm. **Subject:** 25th Winter Sports Games - Skiing

| Date | Mintage | VF20 | XF40 | MS60 | MS63 | MS65 |
|---|---|---|---|---|---|---|
| 2011 | 3,000 | PF63 50.00 | PF65 60.00 | | | |

**KM# 1273 50 LIRA**
31.47 g., 0.925 Silver 0.9359 oz. ASW, 38.61 mm. **Subject:** European Youth Games, Trabzon

| Date | Mintage | VF20 | XF40 | MS60 | MS63 | MS65 |
|---|---|---|---|---|---|---|
| 2011 | 2,000 | PF63 50.00 | PF65 60.00 | | | |

**KM# 1274 50 LIRA**
31.47 g., 0.925 Silver 0.9359 oz. ASW, 38.61 mm. **Subject:** Hejaz Railway **Obv:** Railway route map from Turkey to Saudi Arabia **Rev:** Railway Station at Medina **Edge:** Reeded

| Date | Mintage | VF20 | XF40 | MS60 | MS63 | MS65 |
|---|---|---|---|---|---|---|
| 2011 | 3,000 | PF63 75.00 | PF65 85.00 | | | |

**KM# 1277 50 LIRA**
31.10 g., 0.925 Silver 0.9249 oz. ASW, 38.61 mm. **Subject:** Pergamon **Rev:** Ruins **Edge:** Reeded

| Date | Mintage | VF20 | XF40 | MS60 | MS63 | MS65 |
|---|---|---|---|---|---|---|
| 2012 | 2,000 | PF63 75.00 | PF65 85.00 | | | |

**KM# 1285 50 LIRA**
31.47 g., Silver, 38.61 mm. **Subject:** 150 Years of the Court

| Date | Mintage | VF20 | XF40 | MS60 | MS63 | MS65 |
|---|---|---|---|---|---|---|
| 2012 | — | PF63 60.00 | PF65 65.00 | | | |

**KM# 1287 50 LIRA**
31.10 g., 0.925 Silver 0.9249 oz. ASW, 38.61 mm. **Subject:** 10th Anniversary of the Olympics

| Date | Mintage | VF20 | XF40 | MS60 | MS63 | MS65 |
|---|---|---|---|---|---|---|
| 2012 | Est. 2000 | PF63 75.00 | PF65 85.00 | | | |

**KM# 1290 50 LIRA**
31.10 g., 0.925 Silver 0.9249 oz. ASW, 38.61 mm. **Obv:** Legend and value **Rev:** Sile Lighthouse

| Date | Mintage | VF20 | XF40 | MS60 | MS63 | MS65 |
|---|---|---|---|---|---|---|
| 2012 | — | PF63 60.00 | PF65 65.00 | | | |

**KM# 1292 50 LIRA**
31.47 g., 0.925 Silver 0.9359 oz. ASW, 38.6 mm. **Subject:** Mediterranean Games at Mersin

| Date | Mintage | VF20 | XF40 | MS60 | MS63 | MS65 |
|---|---|---|---|---|---|---|
| 2013 | — | PF63 55.00 | PF65 60.00 | | | |

**KM# 1293 50 LIRA**
31.47 g., 0.925 Silver 0.9359 oz. ASW, 38.6 mm. **Subject:** Turkey statehood, 90th Anniversary

| Date | Mintage | VF20 | XF40 | MS60 | MS63 | MS65 |
|---|---|---|---|---|---|---|
| 2013 | — | PF63 65.00 | PF65 75.00 | | | |

**KM# 1248 100 LIRA**
1.50 g., 0.916 Gold 0.0442 oz. AGW, 13.95 mm. **Obv:** Classical orniament **Rev:** Hittite artifacts

| Date | Mintage | VF20 | XF40 | MS60 | MS63 | MS65 |
|---|---|---|---|---|---|---|
| 2009 | — | PF63 95.00 | PF65 100 | | | |

**KM# 1246 200 LIRA**
36.08 g., 0.916 Gold 1.0626 oz. AGW, 38.6 mm. **Obv:** US and Turkish flags **Rev:** Barack Obama portrait facing

| Date | Mintage | VF20 | XF40 | MS60 | MS63 | MS65 |
|---|---|---|---|---|---|---|
| 2009 | 1,000 | PF65 1,850 | | | | |

**KM# 1260 200 LIRA**
36.00 g., 0.916 Gold 1.0602 oz. AGW, 38.6 mm. **Obv:** Inscription within rose wreath **Rev:** Central courtyard of the Grand Mosque in Mecca

| Date | Mintage | VF20 | XF40 | MS60 | MS63 | MS65 |
|---|---|---|---|---|---|---|
| 2009 | 1,500 | PF65 1,850 | | | | |

## GOLD BULLION COINAGE

Since 1943, the Turkish government has issued regular and deluxe gold coins in five denominations corresponding to the old traditional 25, 50, 100, 250, and 500 Kurus of the Ottoman period. The regular coins are all dated 1923, plus the year of the republic (e.g. 1923/40 = 1963), de Luxe coins bear actual AD dates. For a few years, 1944-1950, the bust of Ismet Inonu replaced that of Kemal Ataturk.

**KM# 851 25 KURUSH**
1.80 g., 0.917 Gold 0.0532 oz. AGW **Obv:** Head of Atatürk left **Rev:** Legend and date within wreath

| Date | Mintage | VF20 | XF40 | MS60 | MS63 | MS65 |
|---|---|---|---|---|---|---|
| 1923/78 | — | — | 71.00 | 105 | 120 | — |
| 1923/79 | — | — | 71.00 | 105 | 120 | — |
| 1923/70 | — | — | 71.00 | 105 | 120 | — |
| 1923/71 | — | — | 71.00 | 105 | 120 | — |
| 1923/72 | — | — | 71.00 | 105 | 120 | — |
| 1923/73 | — | — | 71.00 | 105 | 120 | — |
| 1923/74 | — | — | 71.00 | 105 | 120 | — |
| 1923/75 | — | — | 71.00 | 105 | 120 | — |
| 1923/76 | — | — | 71.00 | 105 | 120 | — |
| 1923/77 | — | — | 71.00 | 105 | 120 | — |

**KM# 870 25 KURUSH**
1.75 g., 0.917 Gold 0.0517 oz. AGW **Series:** Monnaie de Luxe **Obv:** Head of Atatürk left **Rev:** Country name and date in ornate monogram within circle of stars, floral border surrounds

| Date | Mintage | VF20 | XF40 | MS60 | MS63 | MS65 |
|---|---|---|---|---|---|---|
| 2001 | — | — | 70.00 | 105 | 120 | — |
| 2002 | — | — | 70.00 | 105 | 120 | — |
| 2003 | — | — | 70.00 | 105 | 120 | — |
| 2004 | — | — | 70.00 | 105 | 120 | — |
| 2005 | — | — | 70.00 | 105 | 120 | — |
| 2006 | — | — | 70.00 | 105 | 120 | — |
| 2007 | — | — | 70.00 | 105 | 120 | — |
| 2008 | — | — | 70.00 | 105 | 120 | — |
| 2009 | — | — | 70.00 | 105 | 120 | — |
| 2010 | — | — | 70.00 | 105 | 120 | — |

**KM# 853 50 KURUSH**
3.61 g., 0.917 Gold 0.1064 oz. AGW **Obv:** Head of Atatürk left **Rev:** Legend and date within wreath

| Date | Mintage | VF20 | XF40 | MS60 | MS63 | MS65 |
|---|---|---|---|---|---|---|
| 1923/78 | — | — | 143 | 200 | 225 | — |
| 1923/79 | — | — | 143 | 200 | 225 | — |
| 1923/80 | — | — | 143 | 200 | 225 | — |
| 1923/81 | — | — | 143 | 200 | 225 | — |
| 1923/82 | — | — | 143 | 200 | 225 | — |
| 1923/83 | — | — | 143 | 200 | 225 | — |
| 1923/84 | — | — | 143 | 200 | 225 | — |
| 1923/85 | — | — | 143 | 200 | 225 | — |
| 1923/86 | — | — | 143 | 200 | 225 | — |
| 1923/87 | — | — | 143 | 200 | 225 | — |

**KM# 871 50 KURUSH**
3.51 g., 0.917 Gold 0.1034 oz. AGW **Series:** Monnaie de Luxe **Obv:** Head of Kemal Atatürk left within circle of stars, wreath surrounds **Rev:** Country name and date in ornate monogram within circle of stars, floral border surrounds

| Date | Mintage | VF20 | XF40 | MS60 | MS63 | MS65 |
|---|---|---|---|---|---|---|
| 2001 | — | — | 139 | 200 | 225 | — |
| 2002 | — | — | 139 | 200 | 225 | — |
| 2003 | — | — | 139 | 200 | 225 | — |
| 2004 | — | — | 139 | 200 | 225 | — |
| 2005 | — | — | 139 | 200 | 225 | — |
| 2006 | — | — | 139 | 200 | 225 | — |
| 2007 | — | — | 139 | 200 | 225 | — |
| 2008 | — | — | 139 | 200 | 225 | — |
| 2009 | — | — | 139 | 200 | 225 | — |
| 2010 | — | — | 139 | 200 | 225 | — |

**KM# 872 100 KURUSH**
7.02 g., 0.917 Gold 0.2068 oz. AGW **Series:** Monnaie de Luxe **Obv:** Head of Atatürk left within circle of stars, wreath surrounds **Rev:** Country name and date in ornate monogram within circle of stars, floral border surrounds

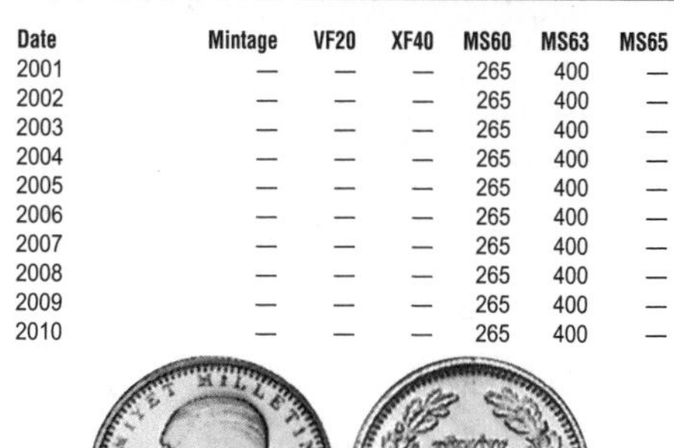

| Date | Mintage | VF20 | XF40 | MS60 | MS63 | MS65 |
|---|---|---|---|---|---|---|
| 2001 | — | — | — | 265 | 400 | — |
| 2002 | — | — | — | 265 | 400 | — |
| 2003 | — | — | — | 265 | 400 | — |
| 2004 | — | — | — | 265 | 400 | — |
| 2005 | — | — | — | 265 | 400 | — |
| 2006 | — | — | — | 265 | 400 | — |
| 2007 | — | — | — | 265 | 400 | — |
| 2008 | — | — | — | 265 | 400 | — |
| 2009 | — | — | — | 265 | 400 | — |
| 2010 | — | — | — | 265 | 400 | — |

**KM# 855 100 KURUSH**
7.22 g., 0.917 Gold 0.2127 oz. AGW **Obv:** Head of Atatürk left **Rev:** Legend and date within wreath

| Date | Mintage | VF20 | XF40 | MS60 | MS63 | MS65 |
|---|---|---|---|---|---|---|
| 1923/78 | — | — | 273 | 400 | 425 | — |
| 1923/79 | — | — | 273 | 400 | 425 | — |
| 1923/80 | — | — | 273 | 400 | 425 | — |
| 1923/81 | — | — | 273 | 400 | 425 | — |
| 1923/82 | — | — | 273 | 400 | 425 | — |
| 1923/83 | — | — | 273 | 400 | 425 | — |
| 1923/84 | — | — | 273 | 400 | 425 | — |
| 1923/85 | — | — | 273 | 400 | 425 | — |
| 1923/86 | — | — | 273 | 400 | 425 | — |
| 1923/87 | — | — | 273 | 400 | 425 | — |

**KM# 873 250 KURUSH**
17.54 g., 0.917 Gold 0.5171 oz. AGW **Series:** Monnaie de Luxe **Obv:** Head of Atatürk left within circle of stars, wreath surrounds **Rev:** Country name and date in ornate monogram within circle of stars, floral border surrounds

| Date | Mintage | VF20 | XF40 | MS60 | MS63 | MS65 |
|---|---|---|---|---|---|---|
| 2001 | — | — | 651 | 1,000 | 1,050 | — |
| 2002 | — | — | 651 | 1,000 | 1,050 | — |
| 2003 | — | — | 651 | 1,000 | 1,050 | — |
| 2004 | — | — | 651 | 1,000 | 1,050 | — |
| 2005 | — | — | 651 | 1,000 | 1,050 | — |
| 2006 | — | — | 651 | 1,000 | 1,050 | — |
| 2007 | — | — | 651 | 1,000 | 1,050 | — |
| 2008 | — | — | 651 | 1,000 | 1,050 | — |
| 2009 | — | — | 651 | 1,000 | 1,050 | — |
| 2010 | — | — | 651 | 1,000 | 1,050 | — |

**KM# 857 250 KURUSH**
18.04 g., 0.917 Gold 0.5319 oz. AGW **Obv:** Head of Atatürk left **Rev:** Legend and date within wreath

| Date | Mintage | VF20 | XF40 | MS60 | MS63 | MS65 |
|---|---|---|---|---|---|---|
| 1923/78 | — | — | 669 | 1,025 | 1,075 | — |
| 1923/79 | — | — | 669 | 1,025 | 1,075 | — |
| 1923/80 | — | — | 669 | 1,025 | 1,075 | — |
| 1923/81 | — | — | 669 | 1,025 | 1,075 | — |
| 1923/82 | — | — | 669 | 1,025 | 1,075 | — |
| 1923/83 | — | — | 669 | 1,025 | 1,075 | — |
| 1923/84 | — | — | 669 | 1,025 | 1,075 | — |
| 1923/85 | — | — | 669 | 1,025 | 1,075 | — |
| 1923/86 | — | — | 669 | 1,025 | 1,075 | — |
| 1923/87 | — | — | 669 | 1,025 | 1,075 | — |

**KM# 859 500 KURUSH**
36.08 g., 0.917 Gold 1.0637 oz. AGW **Obv:** Head of Atatürk left **Rev:** Legend and date within wreath

| Date | Mintage | VF20 | XF40 | MS60 | MS63 | MS65 |
|---|---|---|---|---|---|---|
| 1923/78 | — | — | 1,326 | 1,950 | 2,000 | — |
| 1923/79 | — | — | 1,326 | 1,950 | 2,000 | — |
| 1923/80 | — | — | 1,326 | 1,950 | 2,000 | — |
| 1923/81 | — | — | 1,326 | 1,950 | 2,000 | — |
| 1923/82 | — | — | 1,326 | 1,950 | 2,000 | — |
| 1923/83 | — | — | 1,326 | 1,950 | 2,000 | — |
| 1923/84 | — | — | 1,326 | 1,950 | 2,000 | — |
| 1923/85 | — | — | 1,326 | 1,950 | 2,000 | — |
| 1923/86 | — | — | 1,326 | 1,950 | 2,000 | — |
| 1923/87 | — | — | 1,326 | 1,950 | 2,000 | — |

**KM# 874 500 KURUSH**
35.08 g., 0.917 Gold 1.0342 oz. AGW **Series:** Monnaie de Luxe **Obv:** Head of Atatürk left within circle of stars, wreath surrounds **Rev:** Country name and date in ornate monogram within circle of stars, floral border surrounds

| Date | Mintage | VF20 | XF40 | MS60 | MS63 | MS65 |
|---|---|---|---|---|---|---|
| 2001 | — | — | 1,289 | 1,950 | 2,000 | — |
| 2002 | — | — | 1,289 | 1,950 | 2,000 | — |
| 2003 | — | — | 1,289 | 1,950 | 2,000 | — |
| 2004 | — | — | 1,289 | 1,950 | 2,000 | — |
| 2005 | — | — | 1,289 | 1,950 | 2,000 | — |
| 2006 | — | — | 1,289 | 1,950 | 2,000 | — |
| 2007 | — | — | 1,289 | 1,950 | 2,000 | — |
| 2008 | — | — | 1,289 | 1,950 | 2,000 | — |
| 2009 | — | — | 1,289 | 1,950 | 2,000 | — |
| 2010 | — | — | 1,289 | 1,950 | 2,000 | — |

# TURKMENISTAN

Turkmenistan, (formerly the Turkmen Soviet Socialist Republic) covers the territory of the Trans-Caspian Region of Turkestan, the Charjiui Vilayet of Bukhara and the part of Khiva located on the right bank of the Oxus. Bordered on the north by the Autonomous Kara-Kalpak Republic (a constituent of Uzbekistan), by Iran and Afghanistan on the south, by the Usbek Republic on the east and the Caspian Sea on the west. It has an area of 186,400 sq. mi. (488,100 sq. km.) and a population of 3.5 million. Capital: Ashkhabad (formerly Poltoratsk). Main occupation is agricultural products including cotton and maize. It is rich in minerals, oil, coal, sulphur and salt and is also famous for its carpets, Turkoman horses and Karakui sheep.

The Turkomans arrived in Trancaspia as nomadic Seluk Turks in the 11th century. It often became subjected to one of the neighboring states. Late in the 19th century the Czarist Russians invaded with their first victory at Kyzyl Arvat in 1877, arriving in Ashkhabad in 1882 resulting in submission of the Turkmen tribes. By March 18,1884 the Transcaspian province of Russian Turkestan was formed. During WW I the Czarist government tried to conscript the Turkmen; this led to a revolt in Oct. 1916 under the leadership of Aziz Chapykov. In 1918 the Turks captured Baku from the Red army and the British sent a contingent to Merv to prevent a German-Turkish offensive toward Afghanistan and India. In mid-1919 a Bureau of Turkestan Moslem Communist Organization was formed in Moscow hoping to develop one large republic including all surrounding Turkic areas within a Soviet federation. A Turkestan Autonomous Soviet Socialist Republic was formed and plans to partition Turkestan into five republics according to the principle of nationalities was quickly implemented by Joseph Stalin. On Oct. 27, 1924 Turkmenistan became a Soviet Socialist Republic and was accepted as a member of the U.S.S.R. on Jan. 29, 1925. The Bureau of T.M.C.O. was disbanded in 1934. In Aug. 1990 the Turkmen Supreme Soviet adopted a declaration of sovereignty followed by a declaration of independence in Oct. 1991 joining the Commonwealth of Independent States in Dec. A new constitution was adopted in 1992 providing for an executive presidency.

## REPUBLIC

### STANDARD COINAGE

100 Tenge = 1 Manat

**KM# 106 20 MANAT**
28.28 g., 0.925 Silver 0.841 oz. ASW **Subject:** Census **Obv:** National emblem **Rev:** Map and family

| Date | Mintage | VF20 | XF40 | MS60 | MS63 | MS65 |
|---|---|---|---|---|---|---|
| 2012 | — | — | — | — | — | — |

**KM# 105 50 MANAT**
0.916 Gold **Subject:** Census **Obv:** National emblem **Rev:** Map and family

| Date | Mintage | VF20 | XF40 | MS60 | MS63 | MS65 |
|---|---|---|---|---|---|---|
| 2012 | — | — | — | — | — | — |

**KM# 25 500 MANAT**
28.28 g., 0.925 Silver 0.841 oz. ASW, 38.5 mm. **Subject:** 10th Anniversary of Independence **Obv:** Head of President Saparmyrat Nyyazow left within circle **Rev:** Monument divides dates within circle **Edge:** Reeded

| Date | Mintage | VF20 | XF40 | MS60 | MS63 | MS65 |
|---|---|---|---|---|---|---|
| ND(2001) | 5,000 | PF63 45.00 | PF65 50.00 | | | |

**KM# 41 500 MANAT**
28.28 g., 0.925 Silver 0.841 oz. ASW **Subject:** President's 61st Birthday **Obv:** National Flag

| Date | Mintage | VF20 | XF40 | MS60 | MS63 | MS65 |
|---|---|---|---|---|---|---|
| 2001 | 2,000 | — | — | — | 55.00 | 60.00 |

**KM# 42 500 MANAT**
28.28 g., 0.925 Silver 0.841 oz. ASW **Subject:** President's 61st Birthday **Rev:** State arms

| Date | Mintage | VF20 | XF40 | MS60 | MS63 | MS65 |
|---|---|---|---|---|---|---|
| 2001 | 2,000 | — | — | — | 55.00 | 60.00 |

**KM# 43 500 MANAT**
28.28 g., 0.925 Silver 0.841 oz. ASW **Subject:** Historical leaders **Rev:** Artogrul Grazy Turkmen (1191-1281)

| Date | Mintage | VF20 | XF40 | MS60 | MS63 | MS65 |
|---|---|---|---|---|---|---|
| 2001 | 1,000 | — | — | — | 55.00 | 60.00 |

**KM# 44 500 MANAT**
28.28 g., 0.925 Silver 0.841 oz. ASW **Subject:** Historical leaders **Rev:** Oguz Khan Turkmen

| Date | Mintage | VF20 | XF40 | MS60 | MS63 | MS65 |
|---|---|---|---|---|---|---|
| 2001 | 1,000 | — | — | — | 55.00 | 60.00 |

**KM# 45 500 MANAT**
28.28 g., 0.925 Silver 0.841 oz. ASW **Subject:** Historical leaders **Rev:** Gara Yusup Beg Turkmen

| Date | Mintage | VF20 | XF40 | MS60 | MS63 | MS65 |
|---|---|---|---|---|---|---|
| 2001 | 1,000 | — | — | — | 55.00 | 60.00 |

**KM# 46 500 MANAT**
28.28 g., 0.925 Silver 0.841 oz. ASW **Subject:** Historical leaders **Rev:** Keymir Kor Turkmen

| Date | Mintage | VF20 | XF40 | MS60 | MS63 | MS65 |
|---|---|---|---|---|---|---|
| 2001 | — | — | — | — | 65.00 | 70.00 |

**KM# 47 500 MANAT**
28.28 g., 0.925 Silver 0.841 oz. ASW **Subject:** Historical leaders **Rev:** Uzun Khasan Beg Turkmen

| Date | Mintage | VF20 | XF40 | MS60 | MS63 | MS65 |
|---|---|---|---|---|---|---|
| 2001 | 1,000 | — | — | — | 55.00 | 60.00 |

**KM# 48 500 MANAT**
28.28 g., 0.925 Silver 0.841 oz. ASW **Subject:** Historical leaders **Rev:** Gorogly Beg Turkmen

| Date | Mintage | VF20 | XF40 | MS60 | MS63 | MS65 |
|---|---|---|---|---|---|---|
| 2001 | 1,000 | — | — | — | 55.00 | 60.00 |

**KM# 49 500 MANAT**
28.28 g., 0.925 Silver 0.841 oz. ASW **Subject:** Historical leader **Rev:** Gorkut Ata Turkmen

| Date | Mintage | VF20 | XF40 | MS60 | MS63 | MS65 |
|---|---|---|---|---|---|---|
| 2001 | 1,000 | — | — | — | 55.00 | 60.00 |

**KM# 50 500 MANAT**
28.28 g., 0.925 Silver 0.841 oz. ASW **Subject:** Historical leaders **Rev:** Muhammet Togrul Beg Turkmen

| Date | Mintage | VF20 | XF40 | MS60 | MS63 | MS65 |
|---|---|---|---|---|---|---|
| 2001 | 1,000 | — | — | — | 55.00 | 60.00 |

**KM# 51 500 MANAT**
Silver **Subject:** Historical leaders **Rev:** Muhammet Bayram Khan Turkmen

| Date | Mintage | VF20 | XF40 | MS60 | MS63 | MS65 |
|---|---|---|---|---|---|---|
| 2001 | 1,000 | — | — | — | 55.00 | 60.00 |

**KM# 52 500 MANAT**
28.28 g., 0.925 Silver 0.841 oz. ASW **Subject:** Historical leaders **Rev:** Soltan Sawjar Turkmen

| Date | Mintage | VF20 | XF40 | MS60 | MS63 | MS65 |
|---|---|---|---|---|---|---|
| 2001 | 1,000 | — | — | — | 55.00 | 60.00 |

**KM# 53 500 MANAT**
28.28 g., 0.925 Silver 0.841 oz. ASW, 46 mm. **Subject:** Historical writers **Obv:** State emblem **Rev:** Bust and Laurel branch **Rev. Legend:** Seyitnazar Seydi (1760-1830)

| Date | Mintage | VF20 | XF40 | MS60 | MS63 | MS65 |
|---|---|---|---|---|---|---|
| 2003 | — | — | — | — | 65.00 | 70.00 |

**KM# 54 500 MANAT**
28.28 g., 0.925 Silver 0.841 oz. ASW **Subject:** Historical authors **Obv:** State emblem **Rev:** Bust and Laurel branch **Rev. Legend:** Mammetweli Kemine (1770-1840)

| Date | Mintage | VF20 | XF40 | MS60 | MS63 | MS65 |
|---|---|---|---|---|---|---|
| 2003 | — | — | — | — | 65.00 | 70.00 |

**KM# 55 500 MANAT**
28.28 g., 0.500 Silver 0.4546 oz. ASW, 46 mm. **Subject:** State emblem **Rev:** Bust and Laurel branch **Rev. Legend:** Mollanepes (1810-1862)

| Date | Mintage | VF20 | XF40 | MS60 | MS63 | MS65 |
|---|---|---|---|---|---|---|
| 2003 | — | — | — | — | 50.00 | 55.00 |

**KM# 56 500 MANAT**
28.28 g., 0.925 Silver 0.841 oz. ASW, 46 mm. **Subject:** Historical authors **Obv:** State emblem **Rev:** Bust and Laurel branch **Rev. Legend:** Annagylyc Mataji (1824-1882)

| Date | Mintage | VF20 | XF40 | MS60 | MS63 | MS65 |
|---|---|---|---|---|---|---|
| 2003 | — | — | — | — | 65.00 | 70.00 |

**KM# 62 500 MANAT**
28.28 g., 0.925 Silver 0.841 oz. ASW **Obv:** Bust left **Rev:** Wheat ears as rays

| Date | Mintage | VF20 | XF40 | MS60 | MS63 | MS65 |
|---|---|---|---|---|---|---|
| 2004 | — | — | — | — | 65.00 | 70.00 |

**KM# 64 500 MANAT**
28.28 g., 0.925 Silver 0.841 oz. ASW **Obv:** Bust left **Rev:** Wheat ears forming rays

| Date | Mintage | VF20 | XF40 | MS60 | MS63 | MS65 |
|---|---|---|---|---|---|---|
| 2004 | 1,000 | — | — | — | 55.00 | 60.00 |

**KM# 66 500 MANAT**
28.28 g., 0.925 Silver 0.841 oz. ASW **Subject:** 60th Anniversary of WWII **Obv:** State emblem **Rev:** Soldier standing, rays behind

| Date | Mintage | VF20 | XF40 | MS60 | MS63 | MS65 |
|---|---|---|---|---|---|---|
| 2005 | 1,000 | — | — | — | 65.00 | 70.00 |

**KM# 68 500 MANAT**
28.28 g., 0.925 Silver 0.841 oz. ASW, 75 mm. **Subject:** President Nijazov, 60th Birthday **Obv:** State emblem **Rev:** Head left above tree design

| Date | Mintage | VF20 | XF40 | MS60 | MS63 | MS65 |
|---|---|---|---|---|---|---|
| 2005 | — | — | — | — | 65.00 | 70.00 |

**KM# 40 1000 MANAT**
7.98 g., 0.916 Gold 0.235 oz. AGW, 28.28 mm. **Obv:** President Nyyazow **Rev:** Monument

| Date | Mintage | VF20 | XF40 | MS60 | MS63 | MS65 |
|---|---|---|---|---|---|---|
| 2001 | 1,000 | — | — | — | — | 2,150 |

**KM# 57 1000 MANAT**
47.64 g., 0.916 Gold 1.403 oz. AGW, 46 mm. **Subject:** Historical authors **Obv:** State emblem **Rev:** Bust and Laurel branch **Rev. Legend:** Seyitnazar Seydi (1760-1830)

| Date | Mintage | VF20 | XF40 | MS60 | MS63 | MS65 |
|---|---|---|---|---|---|---|
| 2003 | — | — | — | — | 2,500 | 2,750 |

**KM# 58 1000 MANAT**
47.64 g., 0.916 Gold 1.403 oz. AGW, 46 mm. **Subject:** Historical authors **Obv:** State arms **Rev:** Bust and laurel branch **Rev. Legend:** Mammetweli Kemine

| Date | Mintage | VF20 | XF40 | MS60 | MS63 | MS65 |
|---|---|---|---|---|---|---|
| 2003 | — | — | — | — | 2,500 | 2,750 |

**KM# 59 1000 MANAT**
47.64 g., 0.9167 Gold 1.4041 oz. AGW, 46 mm. **Subject:** Historical authors **Obv:** State emblem **Rev:** Bust and laurel branch **Rev. Legend:** Mollanepes (1810-1862)

| Date | Mintage | VF20 | XF40 | MS60 | MS63 | MS65 |
|---|---|---|---|---|---|---|
| 2003 | — | — | — | — | 2,500 | 2,750 |

**KM# 60 1000 MANAT**
47.64 g., 0.916 Gold 1.403 oz. AGW, 46 mm. **Subject:** Historical authors **Obv:** State emblem **Rev:** Bust and laurel branch **Rev. Legend:** Annagylyc Mataji (1824-1882)

| Date | Mintage | VF20 | XF40 | MS60 | MS63 | MS65 |
|---|---|---|---|---|---|---|
| 2003 | — | — | — | — | 2,500 | 2,750 |

**KM# 61 1000 MANAT**
28.28 g., 0.925 Silver 0.841 oz. ASW **Subject:** 10th Anniversary of Reform

| Date | Mintage | VF20 | XF40 | MS60 | MS63 | MS65 |
|---|---|---|---|---|---|---|
| 2003 | — | — | — | — | 85.00 | 90.00 |

**KM# 63 1000 MANAT**
7.98 g., 0.916 Gold 0.235 oz. AGW **Subject:** 100th Anniversary **Obv:** Bust left **Rev:** Wheat ears forming rays above

| Date | Mintage | VF20 | XF40 | MS60 | MS63 | MS65 |
|---|---|---|---|---|---|---|
| 2004 | — | — | — | — | 1,550 | 1,750 |

**KM# 65 1000 MANAT**
7.98 g., 0.916 Gold 0.235 oz. AGW **Obv:** Bust left **Rev:** Wheat ears forming rays

| Date | Mintage | VF20 | XF40 | MS60 | MS63 | MS65 |
|---|---|---|---|---|---|---|
| 2004 | 250 | — | — | — | 1,550 | 1,750 |

**KM# 67 1000 MANAT**
47.54 g., 0.916 Gold 1.4001 oz. AGW **Subject:** 60th Anniversary of WWII **Obv:** State arms **Rev:** Soldier standing, rays behind

| Date | Mintage | VF20 | XF40 | MS60 | MS63 | MS65 |
|---|---|---|---|---|---|---|
| 2005 | — | — | — | — | 2,500 | 2,750 |

**KM# 69 1000 MANAT**
155.50 g., 0.999 Gold 4.9944 oz. AGW, 75 mm. **Subject:** President Nijazov Goth **Obv:** State emblem **Rev:** Head left above tree

| Date | Mintage | VF20 | XF40 | MS60 | MS63 | MS65 |
|---|---|---|---|---|---|---|
| 2005 | — | — | — | — | 9,000 | 9,500 |

**KM# 70 1000 MANAT**
28.28 g., 0.925 Silver 0.841 oz. ASW **Subject:** Writings of President Nijazov

| Date | Mintage | VF20 | XF40 | MS60 | MS63 | MS65 |
|---|---|---|---|---|---|---|
| 2006 | — | — | — | — | 85.00 | 90.00 |

**KM# 71 1000 MANAT**
28.28 g., 0.925 Silver 0.841 oz. ASW **Subject:** Writings of President Nijazov

| Date | Mintage | VF20 | XF40 | MS60 | MS63 | MS65 |
|---|---|---|---|---|---|---|
| 2006 | — | — | — | — | 85.00 | 90.00 |

**KM# 72 1000 MANAT**
28.28 g., 0.925 Silver 0.841 oz. ASW **Subject:** Writings of President Nijazov

| Date | Mintage | VF20 | XF40 | MS60 | MS63 | MS65 |
|---|---|---|---|---|---|---|
| 2006 | — | — | — | — | 85.00 | 90.00 |

**KM# 73 1000 MANAT**
28.28 g., 0.925 Silver 0.841 oz. ASW **Subject:** Writings of President Nijazov

| Date | Mintage | VF20 | XF40 | MS60 | MS63 | MS65 |
|---|---|---|---|---|---|---|
| 2006 | — | — | — | — | 85.00 | 90.00 |

**KM# 74 1000 MANAT**
28.28 g., 0.925 Silver 0.841 oz. ASW **Subject:** Writings of President Nijazov

| Date | Mintage | VF20 | XF40 | MS60 | MS63 | MS65 |
|---|---|---|---|---|---|---|
| 2006 | — | — | — | — | 85.00 | 90.00 |

**KM# 75 1000 MANAT**
28.28 g., 0.925 Silver 0.841 oz. ASW **Subject:** Writings of President Nijazov

| Date | Mintage | VF20 | XF40 | MS60 | MS63 | MS65 |
|---|---|---|---|---|---|---|
| 2006 | — | — | — | — | 85.00 | 90.00 |

## REFORM COINAGE

January 1, 2009
5000 Old Manat = 1 New Manat
100 Tenge = 1 Manat

**KM# 95 TENGE**
Nickel Plated Steel, 16 mm. **Obv:** Spire over country map **Rev:** Denomination and date

| Date | Mintage | VF20 | XF40 | MS60 | MS63 | MS65 |
|---|---|---|---|---|---|---|
| 2009 | — | — | — | 0.25 | 0.50 | 0.75 |

**KM# 96 2 TENGE**
3.00 g., Nickel Plated Steel, 18 mm. **Obv:** Spire over country map **Rev:** Denomination and date **Edge:** Reeded

| Date | Mintage | VF20 | XF40 | MS60 | MS63 | MS65 |
|---|---|---|---|---|---|---|
| 2009 | — | — | — | 0.35 | 0.75 | 1.00 |

**KM# 97 5 TENGE**
Nickel Plated Steel, 20 mm. **Obv:** Spire over country map **Rev:** Denomination and date

| Date | Mintage | VF20 | XF40 | MS60 | MS63 | MS65 |
|---|---|---|---|---|---|---|
| 2009 | — | — | — | 0.50 | 1.00 | 1.25 |

**KM# 98 10 TENGE**
Brass, 22 mm. **Obv:** Spire over country map **Rev:** Denomination and date

| Date | Mintage | VF20 | XF40 | MS60 | MS63 | MS65 |
|---|---|---|---|---|---|---|
| 2009 | — | — | — | 0.75 | 1.50 | 1.75 |

**KM# 99 20 TENGE**
Brass, 23 mm. **Obv:** Spire over country map **Rev:** Denomination and date

| Date | Mintage | VF20 | XF40 | MS60 | MS63 | MS65 |
|---|---|---|---|---|---|---|
| 2009 | — | — | — | 1.25 | 2.50 | 3.00 |

**KM# 100 50 TENGE**
Brass, 26 mm. **Obv:** Spire over country map **Rev:** Denomination and date

| Date | Mintage | VF20 | XF40 | MS60 | MS63 | MS65 |
|---|---|---|---|---|---|---|
| 2009 | — | — | — | 1.50 | 3.00 | 3.50 |

**KM# 103 MANAT**
9.30 g., Bi-Metallic Stainless-steel center in Brass ring, 27 mm. **Obv:** Spire over country map **Rev:** Denomination and date

| Date | Mintage | VF20 | XF40 | MS60 | MS63 | MS65 |
|---|---|---|---|---|---|---|
| 2010 | — | — | — | 2.00 | 4.00 | 5.00 |

**KM# 104 2 MANAT**
10.40 g., Bi-Metallic Brass center in copper-nickel ring **Obv:** Spire over country map **Rev:** Value and date

| Date | Mintage | VF20 | XF40 | MS60 | MS63 | MS65 |
|---|---|---|---|---|---|---|
| 2010 | — | — | — | 3.00 | 6.00 | 8.00 |

# TURKS & CAICOS ISLANDS

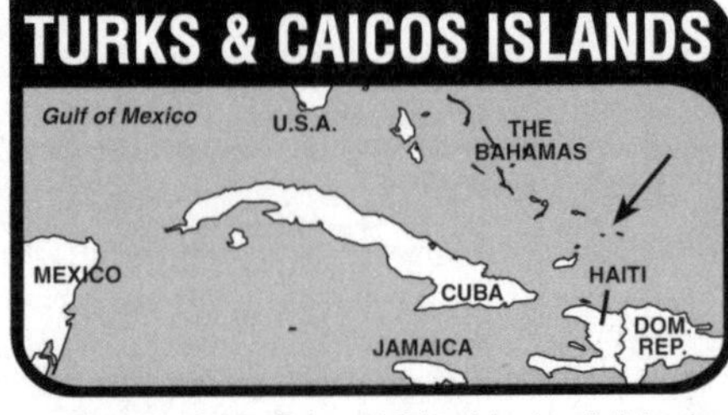


The Colony of the Turks and Caicos Islands, a British colony situated in the West Indies at the eastern end of the Bahama Islands, has an area of 166 sq. mi. (430 sq.km.) and a population of *10,000. Capital: Cockburn Town, on Grand Turk. The principal industry of the colony is the production of salt, which is gathered by raking. Salt, crayfish, and conch shells are exported.

**RULER**
British

**MONETARY SYSTEM**
1 Crown = 1 Dollar U.S.A.

## BRITISH COLONY

### STANDARD COINAGE

**KM# 233 5 CROWNS**
26.43 g., Copper-Nickel, 39.2 mm. **Ruler:** Elizabeth II **Subject:** Royal Navy Submarines **Obv:** Head with tiara right **Rev:** Old and modern submarines **Edge:** Reeded

| Date | Mintage | VF20 | XF40 | MS60 | MS63 | MS65 |
|---|---|---|---|---|---|---|
| 2001 | — | — | — | 6.00 | 10.00 | 12.00 |

**KM# 274 5 CROWNS**
26.50 g., Copper-Nickel, 39 mm. **Ruler:** Elizabeth II **Subject:** 100th Anniversary of the Death of Queen Victoria

| Date | Mintage | VF20 | XF40 | MS60 | MS63 | MS65 |
|---|---|---|---|---|---|---|
| 2001 | — | — | — | — | — | 16.00 |

**KM# 275 5 CROWNS**
Copper-Nickel, 39 mm. **Ruler:** Elizabeth II **Subject:** 100th Anniversary of the Death of Queen Victoria

| Date | Mintage | VF20 | XF40 | MS60 | MS63 | MS65 |
|---|---|---|---|---|---|---|
| 2001 | — | — | — | — | — | 15.00 |

**KM# 279 5 CROWNS**
26.50 g., Copper-Nickel, 39 mm. **Ruler:** Elizabeth II **Subject:** 75th Birthday of Queen Elizabeth II

| Date | Mintage | VF20 | XF40 | MS60 | MS63 | MS65 |
|---|---|---|---|---|---|---|
| 2001 | — | — | — | — | — | 16.00 |

**KM# 281 5 CROWNS**
10.00 g., 0.999 Silver 0.3212 oz. ASW, 31 mm. **Ruler:** Elizabeth II **Subject:** 101st Birthday of Queen Mother Elizabeth

| Date | Mintage | VF20 | XF40 | MS60 | MS63 | MS65 |
|---|---|---|---|---|---|---|
| 2001 | — | PF63 25.00 | PF65 27.00 | | | |

**KM# 282 5 CROWNS**
26.50 g., Copper-Nickel, 39 mm. **Ruler:** Elizabeth II **Subject:** 50th Anniversary of the Coronation of Queen Elizabeth II

| Date | Mintage | VF20 | XF40 | MS60 | MS63 | MS65 |
|---|---|---|---|---|---|---|
| 2002 Proof | — | — | — | — | — | 16.00 |

**KM# 283 5 CROWNS**
26.50 g., Copper-Nickel, 39 mm. **Ruler:** Elizabeth II **Subject:** 50th Anniversary of the Coronation of Queen Elizabeth II

| Date | Mintage | VF20 | XF40 | MS60 | MS63 | MS65 |
|---|---|---|---|---|---|---|
| 2002 | — | — | — | — | — | 16.00 |

**KM# 288 5 CROWNS**
28.28 g., Copper-Nickel, 39 mm. **Ruler:** Elizabeth II **Subject:** Crown Jewels **Rev:** Edward's Crown

| Date | Mintage | VF20 | XF40 | MS60 | MS63 | MS65 |
|---|---|---|---|---|---|---|
| 2004 | — | — | — | — | — | 20.00 |

**KM# 289 5 CROWNS**
28.28 g., Copper-Nickel, 39 mm. **Subject:** Crown Jewels **Rev:** Scepter

| Date | Mintage | VF20 | XF40 | MS60 | MS63 | MS65 |
|---|---|---|---|---|---|---|
| 2004 | — | — | — | — | — | 20.00 |

**KM# 290 5 CROWNS**
28.28 g., Copper-Nickel, 39 mm. **Ruler:** Elizabeth II **Subject:** Crown Jewels **Rev:** Sword

| Date | Mintage | VF20 | XF40 | MS60 | MS63 | MS65 |
|---|---|---|---|---|---|---|
| 2004 | — | — | — | — | — | 20.00 |

**KM# 291 5 CROWNS**
28.28 g., Copper-Nickel **Ruler:** Elizabeth II **Subject:** Crown Jewels **Rev:** Orb

| Date | Mintage | VF20 | XF40 | MS60 | MS63 | MS65 |
|---|---|---|---|---|---|---|
| 2004 | — | — | — | — | — | 20.00 |

**KM# 292 5 CROWNS**
28.28 g., Copper-Nickel, 39 mm. **Ruler:** Elizabeth II **Subject:** Crown Jewels **Rev:** Gold Spoon

| Date | Mintage | VF20 | XF40 | MS60 | MS63 | MS65 |
|---|---|---|---|---|---|---|
| 2004 | — | — | — | — | — | 20.00 |

**KM# 293 5 CROWNS**
28.28 g., Copper-Nickel, 39 mm. **Ruler:** Elizabeth II **Subject:** Crown Jewels **Rev:** Ampulla

| Date | Mintage | VF20 | XF40 | MS60 | MS63 | MS65 |
|---|---|---|---|---|---|---|
| 2004 | — | — | — | — | — | 20.00 |

**KM# 294 5 CROWNS**
28.28 g., Copper-Nickel, 39 mm. **Ruler:** Elizabeth II **Subject:** Crown Jewels **Rev:** Scottish King's Crown

| Date | Mintage | VF20 | XF40 | MS60 | MS63 | MS65 |
|---|---|---|---|---|---|---|
| 2004 | — | — | — | — | — | 20.00 |

**KM# 295 5 CROWNS**
28.28 g., Copper-Nickel, 39 mm. **Ruler:** Elizabeth II **Subject:** Crown Jewels **Rev:** Crown of Queen Victoria

| Date | Mintage | VF20 | XF40 | MS60 | MS63 | MS65 |
|---|---|---|---|---|---|---|
| 2004 | — | — | — | — | — | 20.00 |

**KM# 296 5 CROWNS**
28.28 g., Copper-Nickel, 39 mm. **Ruler:** Elizabeth II **Subject:** Crown Jewels **Rev:** Indian Emperor's Crown

| Date | Mintage | VF20 | XF40 | MS60 | MS63 | MS65 |
|---|---|---|---|---|---|---|
| 2004 | — | — | — | — | — | 20.00 |

**KM# 297 5 CROWNS**
28.28 g., Copper-Nickel, 39 mm. **Subject:** Crown Jewels **Rev:** Crown of Queen Elizabeth

| Date | Mintage | VF20 | XF40 | MS60 | MS63 | MS65 |
|---|---|---|---|---|---|---|
| 2004 | — | — | — | — | — | 20.00 |

**KM# 298 5 CROWNS**
28.28 g., Copper-Nickel, 39 mm. **Ruler:** Elizabeth II **Subject:** Crown Jewels **Rev:** Scepter of the Queen

| Date | Mintage | VF20 | XF40 | MS60 | MS63 | MS65 |
|---|---|---|---|---|---|---|
| 2004 | — | — | — | — | — | 20.00 |

**KM# 299 5 CROWNS**
28.28 g., Copper-Nickel, 39 mm. **Ruler:** Elizabeth II **Subject:** Crown Jewels **Rev:** Rings and Bracelets

| Date | Mintage | VF20 | XF40 | MS60 | MS63 | MS65 |
|---|---|---|---|---|---|---|
| 2004 | — | — | — | — | — | 20.00 |

**KM# 236 20 CROWNS**
31.20 g., 0.999 Silver 1.0021 oz. ASW, 38.9 mm. **Obv:** Crowned head right **Rev:** Bust right facing divides dates **Edge:** Reeded

| Date | Mintage | VF20 | XF40 | MS60 | MS63 | MS65 |
|---|---|---|---|---|---|---|
| 2001 | — | PF63 50.00 | PF65 55.00 | | | |

**KM# 276 20 CROWNS**
Silver **Ruler:** Elizabeth II **Subject:** 100th Anniversary of the Death of Queen Victoria

| Date | Mintage | VF20 | XF40 | MS60 | MS63 | MS65 |
|---|---|---|---|---|---|---|
| 2001 | — | PF63 50.00 | PF65 55.00 | | | |

**KM# 280 20 CROWNS**
31.10 g., 0.999 Silver 0.9989 oz. ASW, 39 mm. **Ruler:** Elizabeth II **Subject:** 75th Birthday of Queen Elizabeth II

| Date | Mintage | VF20 | XF40 | MS60 | MS63 | MS65 |
|---|---|---|---|---|---|---|
| 2001 | — | PF63 50.00 | PF65 55.00 | | | |

**KM# 245 20 CROWNS**
31.16 g., 0.999 Silver 1.0008 oz. ASW, 39 mm. **Ruler:** Elizabeth II **Obv:** Crowned head right **Rev:** Richard II (1377-1399) **Edge:** Reeded

| Date | Mintage | VF20 | XF40 | MS60 | MS63 | MS65 |
|---|---|---|---|---|---|---|
| 2002 | — | PF63 50.00 | PF65 55.00 | | | |

**KM# 246 20 CROWNS**
Hafnium, 38.6 mm. **Ruler:** Elizabeth II **Subject:** H.M. Queen Elizabeth, The Queen Mother **Obv:** Crowned head right **Rev:** Crowned bust right within circle **Edge:** Reeded

| Date | Mintage | VF20 | XF40 | MS60 | MS63 | MS65 |
|---|---|---|---|---|---|---|
| 2002 | — | PF65 145 | | | | |

**KM# 284 20 CROWNS**
31.10 g., 0.999 Silver 0.9989 oz. ASW, 39 mm. **Ruler:** Elizabeth II **Subject:** 50th Anniversary of the Coronation of Queen Elizabeth II

| Date | Mintage | VF20 | XF40 | MS60 | MS63 | MS65 |
|---|---|---|---|---|---|---|
| 2002 | — | PF63 50.00 | PF65 55.00 | | | |

**KM# 285 20 CROWNS**
Silver **Ruler:** Elizabeth II **Subject:** 50th Anniversary of the Coronation of Queen Elizabeth II

| Date | Mintage | VF20 | XF40 | MS60 | MS63 | MS65 |
|---|---|---|---|---|---|---|
| 2002 | — | PF63 50.00 | PF65 55.00 | | | |

**KM# 277 100 CROWNS**
31.10 g., 0.999 Gold 0.9989 oz. AGW, 39 mm. **Ruler:** Elizabeth II **Subject:** 100th Anniversary of the Death of Queen Victoria

| Date | Mintage | VF20 | XF40 | MS60 | MS63 | MS65 |
|---|---|---|---|---|---|---|
| 2001 | Est. 100 | PF65 2,000 | | | | |

**KM# 278 100 CROWNS**
31.10 g., 0.999 Gold 0.9989 oz. AGW, 39 mm. **Ruler:** Elizabeth II **Subject:** 100th Anniversary of the Death of Queen Victoria

| Date | Mintage | VF20 | XF40 | MS60 | MS63 | MS65 |
|---|---|---|---|---|---|---|
| 2001 | — | PF65 2,000 | | | | |

**KM# 286 100 CROWNS**
31.10 g., 0.999 Gold 0.9989 oz. AGW, 39 mm. **Ruler:** Elizabeth II **Subject:** 50th Anniversary of the Coronation of Queen Elizabeth II

| Date | Mintage | VF20 | XF40 | MS60 | MS63 | MS65 |
|---|---|---|---|---|---|---|
| 2002 | — | PF65 2,000 | | | | |

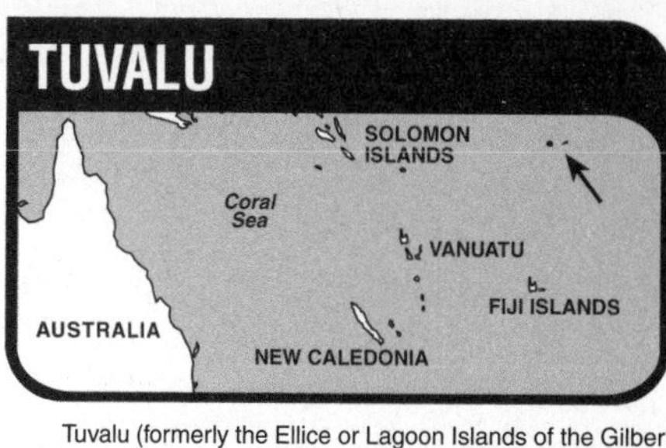


Tuvalu (formerly the Ellice or Lagoon Islands of the Gilbert and Ellice Islands), located in the South Pacific north of the Fiji Islands, has an area of 10 sq. mi. (26 sq.km.) and a population of *9,000. Capital: Funafuti. The independent state includes the islands of Nanumanga, Nanumea, Nui, Niutao, Viatupa, Funafuti, Nukufetau, Nukulailai and Nurakita. The latter four islands were claimed by the United States until relinquished by the Feb. 7, 1979, Treaty of Friendship signed by the United States and Tuvalu. The principal industries are copra production and phosphate mining.

Tuvalu is a member of the Commonwealth of Nations. Elizabeth II is Head of State as Queen of Tuvalu.

**RULER**
British, until 1978

**MONETARY SYSTEM**
100 Cents = 1 Dollar

# CONSTITUTIONAL MONARCHY WITHIN THE COMMONWEALTH

## STANDARD COINAGE

**KM# 237 50 CENTS**
20.00 g., Aluminum-Bronze, 38.74 mm. **Ruler:** Elizabeth II **Subject:** Sumo-Wrestling Tournament Hawaii 2007

| Date | Mintage | VF20 | XF40 | MS60 | MS63 | MS65 |
|---|---|---|---|---|---|---|
| 2007 | — | — | — | — | — | 20.00 |

**KM# 168 50 CENTS**
15.59 g., 0.999 Silver 0.5007 oz. ASW, 36.6 mm. **Ruler:** Elizabeth II **Rev:** Two doves tying pink ribbon heart

| Date | Mintage | VF20 | XF40 | MS60 | MS63 | MS65 |
|---|---|---|---|---|---|---|
| 2011 | 2,500 | PF65 50.00 | | | | |

**KM# 191 50 CENTS**
15.59 g., 0.9999 Silver 0.5012 oz. ASW, 36.6 mm. **Ruler:** Elizabeth II **Subject:** Forever Love **Rev:** Two koalas framed by heart shaped gum leaves and blossoms

| Date | Mintage | VF20 | XF40 | MS60 | MS63 | MS65 |
|---|---|---|---|---|---|---|
| 2012 P | 7,500 | PF65 60.00 | | | | |

**KM# 193 50 CENTS**
15.55 g., 0.999 Silver 0.4994 oz. ASW, 30.6 mm. **Ruler:** Elizabeth II **Rev:** Baby dragon in color

| Date | Mintage | VF20 | XF40 | MS60 | MS63 | MS65 |
|---|---|---|---|---|---|---|
| 2012 P | — | PF65 90.00 | | | | |

**KM# 213 50 CENTS**
15.59 g., 0.999 Silver 0.5008 oz. ASW, 36.6 mm. **Ruler:** Elizabeth II **Subject:** Forest Babies - Grey Wolf

| Date | Mintage | VF20 | XF40 | MS60 | MS63 | MS65 |
|---|---|---|---|---|---|---|
| 2013 | Est. 10000 | PF65 30.00 | | | | |

**KM# 214 50 CENTS**
15.59 g., 0.999 Silver 0.5008 oz. ASW, 36.6 mm. **Ruler:** Elizabeth II **Subject:** Forest Babies - Red Squirrel

| Date | Mintage | VF20 | XF40 | MS60 | MS63 | MS65 |
|---|---|---|---|---|---|---|
| 2013 | Est. 10000 | PF65 30.00 | | | | |

**KM# 215 50 CENTS**
15.59 g., 0.999 Silver 0.5008 oz. ASW, 36.6 mm. **Ruler:** Elizabeth II **Subject:** Forest Babies - Brown Bear

| Date | Mintage | VF20 | XF40 | MS60 | MS63 | MS65 |
|---|---|---|---|---|---|---|
| 2013 | Est. 10000 | PF65 30.00 | | | | |

**KM# 40 DOLLAR**
20.00 g., Brass, 38.7 mm. **Ruler:** Elizabeth II **Subject:** Dinosaurs **Obv:** Crowned head right **Rev:** Giganotosaurus **Edge:** Reeded **Note:** See KM#49.

| Date | Mintage | VF20 | XF40 | MS60 | MS63 | MS65 |
|---|---|---|---|---|---|---|
| 2002 | 50,000 | — | — | — | 18.00 | 22.00 |

**KM# 41 DOLLAR**
20.00 g., Brass, 38.7 mm. **Ruler:** Elizabeth II **Subject:** Dinosaurs **Obv:** Crowned head right **Rev:** Dromaeosaurus **Edge:** Reeded **Note:** See KM#50.

| Date | Mintage | VF20 | XF40 | MS60 | MS63 | MS65 |
|---|---|---|---|---|---|---|
| 2002 | 50,000 | — | — | — | 18.00 | 22.00 |

**KM# 42 DOLLAR**
20.00 g., Brass, 38.7 mm. **Ruler:** Elizabeth II **Subject:** Dinosaurs **Obv:** Crowned head right **Rev:** Seismosaurus **Edge:** Reeded **Note:** See KM#52.

| Date | Mintage | VF20 | XF40 | MS60 | MS63 | MS65 |
|---|---|---|---|---|---|---|
| 2002 | 50,000 | — | — | — | 18.00 | 22.00 |

**KM# 43 DOLLAR**
20.00 g., Brass, 38.7 mm. **Ruler:** Elizabeth II **Subject:** Dinosaurs **Obv:** Crowned head right **Rev:** Stegosaurus **Edge:** Reeded **Note:** See KM#51.

| Date | Mintage | VF20 | XF40 | MS60 | MS63 | MS65 |
|---|---|---|---|---|---|---|
| 2002 | 50,000 | — | — | — | 18.00 | 22.00 |

**KM# 149 DOLLAR**
31.10 g., 0.999 Silver 0.999 oz. ASW, 40.7 mm. **Ruler:** Elizabeth II **Subject:** Harry Potter **Rev:** Multicolor dementor

| Date | Mintage | VF20 | XF40 | MS60 | MS63 | MS65 |
|---|---|---|---|---|---|---|
| 2004 | — | — | — | — | — | 45.00 |

**KM# 150 DOLLAR**
31.10 g., 0.999 Silver 0.999 oz. ASW, 40.7 mm. **Ruler:** Elizabeth II **Subject:** Harry Potter **Rev:** Multicolor owl

| Date | Mintage | VF20 | XF40 | MS60 | MS63 | MS65 |
|---|---|---|---|---|---|---|
| 2004 | — | — | — | — | — | 45.00 |

**KM# 151 DOLLAR**
31.10 g., 0.999 Silver 0.999 oz. ASW, 40.7 mm. **Ruler:** Elizabeth II **Subject:** Harry Potter **Rev:** Multicolor color Harry Potter chasing snitch

| Date | Mintage | VF20 | XF40 | MS60 | MS63 | MS65 |
|---|---|---|---|---|---|---|
| 2004 | — | — | — | — | — | 45.00 |

**KM# 222 DOLLAR**
31.64 g., 0.999 Silver Plated Copper 1.0161 oz. **Ruler:** Elizabeth II **Subject:** Australian Penny

| Date | Mintage | VF20 | XF40 | MS60 | MS63 | MS65 |
|---|---|---|---|---|---|---|
| 2005 | — | PF65 52.00 | | | | |

**KM# 53 DOLLAR**
Silver **Ruler:** Elizabeth II **Obv:** Crowned head right **Rev:** 1955 Mercedes Benz 300 SL Gullwing

| Date | Mintage | VF20 | XF40 | MS60 | MS63 | MS65 |
|---|---|---|---|---|---|---|
| 2006 | — | PF65 55.00 | | | | |

**KM# 54 DOLLAR**
Silver **Ruler:** Elizabeth II **Obv:** Crowned head right **Rev:** 1963 Jaguar E-Type colorized

| Date | Mintage | VF20 | XF40 | MS60 | MS63 | MS65 |
|---|---|---|---|---|---|---|
| 2006 | — | PF65 55.00 | | | | |

**KM# 55 DOLLAR**
Silver **Ruler:** Elizabeth II **Obv:** Crowned head right **Rev:** 1969 Datsun 240Z

| Date | Mintage | VF20 | XF40 | MS60 | MS63 | MS65 |
|---|---|---|---|---|---|---|
| 2006 | — | PF65 65.00 | | | | |

**KM# 58 DOLLAR**
31.31 g., 0.999 Silver 1.0056 oz. ASW enameled, 40.51 mm. **Ruler:** Elizabeth II **Subject:** 400th Anniversary of First European Sighting of Australia **Obv:** Crowned bust right **Obv. Legend:** QUEEN ELIZABETH II **Rev:** Bust of Captain James Cook at left, his ship; "H.M.S. Endeavor" within ship's wheel **Rev. Inscription:** 1770 DISCOVERY - EASTERN AUSTRALIA **Edge:** Reeded

| Date | Mintage | VF20 | XF40 | MS60 | MS63 | MS65 |
|---|---|---|---|---|---|---|
| 2006 | — | PF65 85.00 | | | | |

**KM# 59 DOLLAR**
31.31 g., 0.999 Silver 1.0056 oz. ASW enameled, 40 mm. **Ruler:** Elizabeth II **Subject:** 400th Anniversary of First European Sighting of Australia **Obv:** Crowned bust right **Obv. Legend:** QUEEN ELIZABETH II **Rev:** Bust of Abel Jansoon Tasman at left, his Dutch ship within compass rose **Rev. Legend:** 1642 DISCOVERY OF VAN DIEMAN'S LAND **Edge:** Reeded

| Date | Mintage | VF20 | XF40 | MS60 | MS63 | MS65 |
|---|---|---|---|---|---|---|
| 2006 | — | PF65 85.00 | | | | |

**KM# 60 DOLLAR**
31.11 g., 0.999 Silver 0.999 oz. ASW enameled, 40 mm. **Ruler:** Elizabeth II **Subject:** 400th Anniversary of First European Sighting of Australia **Obv:** Crowned bust right **Obv. Legend:** QUEEN ELIZABETH II **Rev:** Bust of William Dampier at right, his ship within wreath **Rev. Legend:** 1688 BRITISH DISCOVERY OF AUSTRALIA **Edge:** Reeded

| Date | Mintage | VF20 | XF40 | MS60 | MS63 | MS65 |
|---|---|---|---|---|---|---|
| 2006 | — | PF65 85.00 | | | | |

**KM# 61 DOLLAR**
31.31 g., 0.999 Silver 1.0056 oz. ASW enameled, 40 mm. **Ruler:** Elizabeth II **Subject:** 400th Anniversary of First European Sighting of Australia **Obv:** Crowned bust right **Obv. Legend:** QUEEN ELIZABETH II **Rev:** Dutch ship"Duyfken" within compas rose **Rev. Legend:** 1606 FIRST EUROPEAN DISCOVERY AUSTRALIA **Edge:** Reeded

| Date | Mintage | VF20 | XF40 | MS60 | MS63 | MS65 |
|---|---|---|---|---|---|---|
| 2006 | — | PF65 85.00 | | | | |

**KM# 68 DOLLAR**
31.10 g., 0.999 Silver 0.999 oz. ASW, 40 mm. **Ruler:** Elizabeth II **Obv:** Crowned bust right **Obv. Legend:** QUEEN ELIZABETH II - TUVALU **Rev:** Red-back Spider, multicolor

| Date | Mintage | VF20 | XF40 | MS60 | MS63 | MS65 |
|---|---|---|---|---|---|---|
| 2006 | 5,000 | PF65 285 | | | | |

**KM# 170 DOLLAR**

31.11 g., 0.999 Silver 0.999 oz. ASW, 40.6 mm. **Ruler:** Elizabeth II **Rev:** Lamborghini in color

| Date | Mintage | VF20 | XF40 | MS60 | MS63 | MS65 |
|---|---|---|---|---|---|---|
| 2006 | — | PF65 65.00 | | | | |

**KM# 171 DOLLAR**

31.11 g., 0.999 Copper Plated Silver 0.999 oz., 40.6 mm. **Ruler:** Elizabeth II **Rev:** 1923 1/2 Penny of Australia, reverse

| Date | Mintage | VF20 | XF40 | MS60 | MS63 | MS65 |
|---|---|---|---|---|---|---|
| 2006 | — | PF65 90.00 | | | | |

**KM# 224 DOLLAR**

31.10 g., 0.999 Silver and Gold 0.9989 oz. **Ruler:** Elizabeth II **Subject:** War Planes **Rev:** Fokker in color

| Date | Mintage | VF20 | XF40 | MS60 | MS63 | MS65 |
|---|---|---|---|---|---|---|
| 2006 | Est. 500 | PF65 52.00 | | | | |

**KM# 225 DOLLAR**

31.10 g., Silver and Gold **Ruler:** Elizabeth II **Subject:** War Planes **Rev:** Spitfire in Color

| Date | Mintage | VF20 | XF40 | MS60 | MS63 | MS65 |
|---|---|---|---|---|---|---|
| 2006 | — | PF65 52.00 | | | | |

**KM# 226 DOLLAR**

31.10 g., 0.999 Silver and Gold 0.9989 oz. **Ruler:** Elizabeth II **Subject:** War Planes **Rev:** MIG 15 in color

| Date | Mintage | VF20 | XF40 | MS60 | MS63 | MS65 |
|---|---|---|---|---|---|---|
| 2006 | Est. 500 | PF65 52.00 | | | | |

**KM# 227 DOLLAR**

31.10 g., Silver and Gold **Ruler:** Elizabeth II **Subject:** War Planes **Rev:** Sea Harrier in color

| Date | Mintage | VF20 | XF40 | MS60 | MS63 | MS65 |
|---|---|---|---|---|---|---|
| 2006 | Est. 500 | PF65 53.00 | | | | |

**KM# 228 DOLLAR**

31.10 g., Silver and Gold **Ruler:** Elizabeth II **Subject:** War Planes **Rev:** Lockheed FA-22 Raptor

| Date | Mintage | VF20 | XF40 | MS60 | MS63 | MS65 |
|---|---|---|---|---|---|---|
| 2006 | Est. 500 | PF65 53.00 | | | | |

**KM# 229 DOLLAR**

31.64 g., 0.999 Silver Plated Copper 1.0161 oz., 40 mm. **Ruler:** Elizabeth II **Subject:** Australian Money **Rev:** Australian 1/2 penny

| Date | Mintage | VF20 | XF40 | MS60 | MS63 | MS65 |
|---|---|---|---|---|---|---|
| 2006 | Est. 5000 | PF65 52.00 | | | | |

**KM# 230 DOLLAR**

31.64 g., 0.999 Silver 1.0161 oz. ASW, 40 mm. **Ruler:** Elizabeth II **Subject:** Cars of the World **Rev:** Corvette Sting Ray in color

| Date | Mintage | VF20 | XF40 | MS60 | MS63 | MS65 |
|---|---|---|---|---|---|---|
| 2006 | Est. 1500 | PF65 52.00 | | | | |

**KM# 231 DOLLAR**

31.64 g., 0.999 Silver 1.0161 oz. ASW, 40 mm. **Ruler:** Elizabeth II **Subject:** Cars of the World **Rev:** Lamborghini Countach in color

| Date | Mintage | VF20 | XF40 | MS60 | MS63 | MS65 |
|---|---|---|---|---|---|---|
| 2006 | Est. 1500 | PF65 52.00 | | | | |

**KM# 62 DOLLAR**

31.10 g., 0.999 Silver 0.999 oz. ASW, 40.51 mm. **Ruler:** Elizabeth II **Obv:** Crowned bust right **Obv. Legend:** ELIZABETH II **Rev:** Multicolor Great White Shark **Edge:** Reeded

| Date | Mintage | VF20 | XF40 | MS60 | MS63 | MS65 |
|---|---|---|---|---|---|---|
| 2007 | 5,000 | PF65 200 | | | | |

**KM# 63 DOLLAR**

0.999 Silver, 40 mm. **Ruler:** Elizabeth II **Series:** Fighting Ships of WW II **Obv:** Crowned bust right **Obv. Legend:** QUEEN ELIZABETH II - TUVALU **Rev:** USSR Sevastopol, multicolor water

| Date | Mintage | VF20 | XF40 | MS60 | MS63 | MS65 |
|---|---|---|---|---|---|---|
| 2007 | 1,500 | PF65 75.00 | | | | |

**KM# 64 DOLLAR**

0.999 Silver, 40 mm. **Ruler:** Elizabeth II **Series:** Fighting Ships of WW II **Obv:** Crowned bust right **Obv. Legend:** QUEEN ELIZABETH II - TUVALU **Rev:** HMS Hood, multicolor water and smoke

| Date | Mintage | VF20 | XF40 | MS60 | MS63 | MS65 |
|---|---|---|---|---|---|---|
| 2007 | 1,500 | PF65 75.00 | | | | |

**KM# 65 DOLLAR**

0.999 Silver, 40 mm. **Ruler:** Elizabeth II **Series:** Fighting Ships of WW II **Obv:** Crowned bust right **Obv. Legend:** QUEEN ELIZABETH II - TUVALU **Rev:** Bismarck, multicolor water and gun flashes

| Date | Mintage | VF20 | XF40 | MS60 | MS63 | MS65 |
|---|---|---|---|---|---|---|
| 2007 | 1,500 | PF65 75.00 | | | | |

**KM# 66 DOLLAR**

0.999 Silver, 40 mm. **Ruler:** Elizabeth II **Series:** Fighting Ships of WW II **Obv. Legend:** QUEEN ELIZABETH II - TUVALU **Rev:** IJN Yamato, multicolor water and rising sun

| Date | Mintage | VF20 | XF40 | MS60 | MS63 | MS65 |
|---|---|---|---|---|---|---|
| 2007 | 1,500 | PF65 75.00 | | | | |

**KM# 67 DOLLAR**

0.999 Silver, 40 mm. **Ruler:** Elizabeth II **Series:** Fighting Ships of WW II **Obv:** Crowned bust right **Obv. Legend:** QUEEN ELIZABETH II - TUVALU **Rev:** USS Missouri

| Date | Mintage | VF20 | XF40 | MS60 | MS63 | MS65 |
|---|---|---|---|---|---|---|
| 2007 | 1,500 | PF65 75.00 | | | | |

**KM# 71 DOLLAR**

31.10 g., 0.999 Silver 0.999 oz. ASW, 40.6 mm. **Ruler:** Elizabeth II **Subject:** Early Governors of Austrialia **Obv:** Head right **Rev:** Multicolor Arthur Phillip **Edge:** Reeded

| Date | Mintage | VF20 | XF40 | MS60 | MS63 | MS65 |
|---|---|---|---|---|---|---|
| 2008 | 1,808 | PF65 90.00 | | | | |

**KM# 72 DOLLAR**

31.10 g., 0.999 Silver 0.999 oz. ASW, 40.6 mm. **Ruler:** Elizabeth II **Subject:** Early Governors of Australia **Obv:** Head right **Rev:** Multicolor John Hunter **Edge:** Reeded

| Date | Mintage | VF20 | XF40 | MS60 | MS63 | MS65 |
|---|---|---|---|---|---|---|
| 2008 | 1,808 | PF65 90.00 | | | | |

**KM# 73 DOLLAR**

31.10 g., 0.999 Silver 0.999 oz. ASW, 40.6 mm. **Ruler:** Elizabeth II **Subject:** Early Governors of Australia **Obv:** Head right **Rev:** Multicolor Philip G. King

| Date | Mintage | VF20 | XF40 | MS60 | MS63 | MS65 |
|---|---|---|---|---|---|---|
| 2008 | 1,808 | PF65 90.00 | | | | |

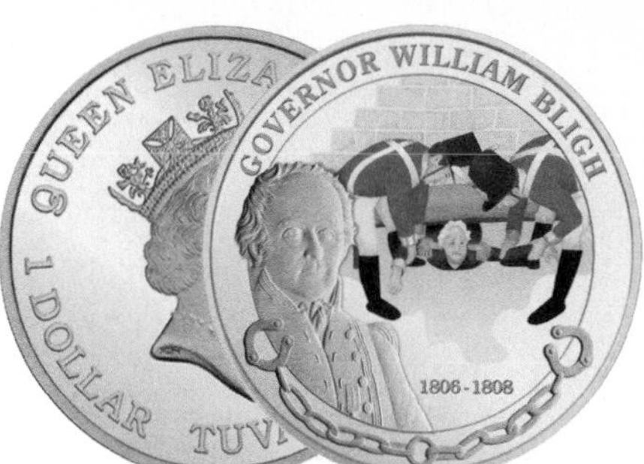


**KM# 74 DOLLAR**

31.10 g., 0.999 Silver 0.999 oz. ASW, 40.6 mm. **Ruler:** Elizabeth II **Subject:** Early Governors of Australia **Obv:** Head right **Rev:** Multicolor William Bligh **Edge:** Reeded

| Date | Mintage | VF20 | XF40 | MS60 | MS63 | MS65 |
|---|---|---|---|---|---|---|
| 2008 | 1,808 | PF65 90.00 | | | | |

**KM# 75 DOLLAR**

31.10 g., 0.999 Silver 0.999 oz. ASW, 40.6 mm. **Ruler:** Elizabeth II **Subject:** Early Governors of Australia **Obv:** Head right **Rev:** Multicolor Lahlan Macquarie

| Date | Mintage | VF20 | XF40 | MS60 | MS63 | MS65 |
|---|---|---|---|---|---|---|
| 2008 | 1,808 | PF65 90.00 | | | | |

**KM# 76 DOLLAR**

37.11 g., 0.999 Silver 1.1919 oz. ASW, 40.6 mm. **Ruler:** Elizabeth II **Obv:** Head right **Rev:** Multicolor Australian Lesser Blue-ringed Octopus **Edge:** Reeded

| Date | Mintage | VF20 | XF40 | MS60 | MS63 | MS65 |
|---|---|---|---|---|---|---|
| 2008 | 5,000 | PF65 220 | | | | |

**KM# 81 DOLLAR**

31.11 g., 0.999 Silver 0.999 oz. ASW **Ruler:** Elizabeth II **Subject:** Motorcycles **Rev:** Indian Chief

| Date | Mintage | VF20 | XF40 | MS60 | MS63 | MS65 |
|---|---|---|---|---|---|---|
| 2008 Proff | — | PF65 80.00 | | | | |

**KM# 82 DOLLAR**
31.11 g., 0.999 Silver 0.999 oz. ASW **Ruler:** Elizabeth II **Subject:** Motorcycles **Rev:** BMW R12

| Date | Mintage | VF20 | XF40 | MS60 | MS63 | MS65 |
|---|---|---|---|---|---|---|
| 2008 | — | **PF65** 80.00 | | | | |

**KM# 83 DOLLAR**
31.11 g., 0.999 Silver 0.999 oz. ASW **Ruler:** Elizabeth II **Subject:** Motorcycles **Rev:** BSA Gold Star DBD34

| Date | Mintage | VF20 | XF40 | MS60 | MS63 | MS65 |
|---|---|---|---|---|---|---|
| 2008 | — | **PF65** 80.00 | | | | |

**KM# 84 DOLLAR**
31.11 g., 0.999 Silver 0.999 oz. ASW **Ruler:** Elizabeth II **Subject:** Motorcycles **Rev:** Norton - Commando 750

| Date | Mintage | VF20 | XF40 | MS60 | MS63 | MS65 |
|---|---|---|---|---|---|---|
| 2008 | — | **PF65** 80.00 | | | | |

**KM# 85 DOLLAR**
31.11 g., 0.999 Silver 0.999 oz. ASW **Ruler:** Elizabeth II **Subject:** Motorcycles **Rev:** Honda CB760

| Date | Mintage | VF20 | XF40 | MS60 | MS63 | MS65 |
|---|---|---|---|---|---|---|
| 2008 | — | **PF65** 80.00 | | | | |

**KM# 240 DOLLAR**
31.64 g., 0.999 Silver 1.0161 oz. ASW, 40 mm. **Ruler:** Elizabeth II **Subject:** Christmas **Rev:** Christmas tree in color

| Date | Mintage | VF20 | XF40 | MS60 | MS63 | MS65 |
|---|---|---|---|---|---|---|
| 2008 | Est. 5000 | **PF65** 52.00 | | | | |

**KM# 80 DOLLAR**
31.11 g., 0.999 Silver 0.999 oz. ASW **Ruler:** Elizabeth II **Subject:** Barbie, 50th Anniversary **Rev:** Barbie doll and drawing

| Date | Mintage | VF20 | XF40 | MS60 | MS63 | MS65 |
|---|---|---|---|---|---|---|
| 2009 | 20,000 | **PF65** 60.00 | | | | |

**KM# 87 DOLLAR**
31.11 g., 0.999 Silver 0.999 oz. ASW, 40 mm. **Ruler:** Elizabeth II **Rev:** Saltwater Crocodile

| Date | Mintage | VF20 | XF40 | MS60 | MS63 | MS65 |
|---|---|---|---|---|---|---|
| 2009 | — | **PF65** 175 | | | | |

**KM# 88 DOLLAR**
31.11 g., 0.999 Silver 0.999 oz. ASW **Ruler:** Elizabeth II **Subject:** Battle of Hastings **Rev:** Battle scene in multicolor

| Date | Mintage | VF20 | XF40 | MS60 | MS63 | MS65 |
|---|---|---|---|---|---|---|
| 2009 | — | **PF65** 70.00 | | | | |

**KM# 89 DOLLAR**
31.11 g., 0.999 Silver 0.999 oz. ASW, 40.6 mm. **Ruler:** Elizabeth II **Subject:** Battle of Cannae, 216 BC **Rev:** Battlefield scene, multicolor

| Date | Mintage | VF20 | XF40 | MS60 | MS63 | MS65 |
|---|---|---|---|---|---|---|
| 2009 | 5,000 | **PF65** 70.00 | | | | |

**KM# 90 DOLLAR**
31.11 g., 0.999 Silver 0.999 oz. ASW **Ruler:** Elizabeth II **Subject:** Battle of Gettysburg **Rev:** Battlefield scene, multicolor

| Date | Mintage | VF20 | XF40 | MS60 | MS63 | MS65 |
|---|---|---|---|---|---|---|
| 2009 | — | **PF65** 70.00 | | | | |

**KM# 91 DOLLAR**
31.11 g., 0.999 Silver 0.999 oz. ASW **Ruler:** Elizabeth II **Subject:** Battle of Balaklava, 1854 **Rev:** Battle scene, multicolor

| Date | Mintage | VF20 | XF40 | MS60 | MS63 | MS65 |
|---|---|---|---|---|---|---|
| 2009 | — | **PF65** 70.00 | | | | |

**KM# 92 DOLLAR**
31.11 g., 0.999 Silver 0.999 oz. ASW **Ruler:** Elizabeth II **Subject:** Poltava, Peter the Great's 300th Anniversary **Rev:** Statue of Peter on horseback, multicolor battle scene

| Date | Mintage | VF20 | XF40 | MS60 | MS63 | MS65 |
|---|---|---|---|---|---|---|
| 2009 | — | **PF65** 70.00 | | | | |

**KM# 94 DOLLAR**
31.11 g., 0.999 Silver 0.999 oz. ASW, 40.6 mm. **Ruler:** Elizabeth II **Subject:** Transformers **Rev:** Optimus Prime, multicolor

| Date | Mintage | VF20 | XF40 | MS60 | MS63 | MS65 |
|---|---|---|---|---|---|---|
| 2009 | 5,000 | **PF65** 75.00 | | | | |

**KM# 95 DOLLAR**
31.11 g., 0.999 Silver 0.999 oz. ASW, 40.6 mm. **Ruler:** Elizabeth II **Subject:** Transformers **Rev:** Megatron, multicolor

| Date | Mintage | VF20 | XF40 | MS60 | MS63 | MS65 |
|---|---|---|---|---|---|---|
| 2009 | 5,000 | **PF65** 75.00 | | | | |

**KM# 96 DOLLAR**
31.11 g., 0.999 Silver 0.999 oz. ASW, 40.6 mm. **Ruler:** Elizabeth II **Subject:** Fall of the Berlin Wall, 20th Anniversary **Rev:** Brandenburg gate, multicolor

| Date | Mintage | VF20 | XF40 | MS60 | MS63 | MS65 |
|---|---|---|---|---|---|---|
| 2009 | 5,000 | **PF65** 65.00 | | | | |

**KM# 97 DOLLAR**
31.11 g., 0.999 Silver 0.999 oz. ASW, 40.6 mm. **Ruler:** Elizabeth II **Subject:** Golden Age of Piracy - Black Bart **Obv:** Head right **Rev:** Black Bart at left, multicolor treasure items at right

| Date | Mintage | VF20 | XF40 | MS60 | MS63 | MS65 |
|---|---|---|---|---|---|---|
| 2009 | 1,500 | **PF65** 80.00 | | | | |

**KM# 98 DOLLAR**
31.11 g., 0.999 Silver 0.999 oz. ASW, 40.6 mm. **Ruler:** Elizabeth II **Subject:** Golden Age of Piracy - Black Beard **Obv:** Head right **Rev:** Black Beard at left, multicolor treasure chest at right

| Date | Mintage | VF20 | XF40 | MS60 | MS63 | MS65 |
|---|---|---|---|---|---|---|
| 2009 | 1,500 | **PF65** 80.00 | | | | |

**KM# 99 DOLLAR**
31.11 g., 0.999 Silver 0.999 oz. ASW, 40.6 mm. **Ruler:** Elizabeth II **Subject:** Golden Age of Piracy - William Kidd **Obv:** Head right **Rev:** William Kidd at left, multicolor pistol and treasure map at right

| Date | Mintage | VF20 | XF40 | MS60 | MS63 | MS65 |
|---|---|---|---|---|---|---|
| 2009 | 1,500 | **PF65** 80.00 | | | | |

**KM# 100 DOLLAR**
31.11 g., 0.999 Silver 0.999 oz. ASW, 40.6 mm. **Ruler:** Elizabeth II **Subject:** Golden Age of Piracy - Henry Morgan **Obv:** Head right **Rev:** Henry Morgan at left, multicolor kegs at right

| Date | Mintage | VF20 | XF40 | MS60 | MS63 | MS65 |
|---|---|---|---|---|---|---|
| 2009 | 1,500 | **PF65** 80.00 | | | | |

**KM# 101 DOLLAR**
31.11 g., 0.999 Silver 0.999 oz. ASW, 40.6 mm. **Ruler:** Elizabeth II **Subject:** Golden Age of Piracy - Calico Jack **Obv:** Head right **Rev:** Calico jack at left, multicolor pirate flag at right

| Date | Mintage | VF20 | XF40 | MS60 | MS63 | MS65 |
|---|---|---|---|---|---|---|
| 2009 | 1,500 | **PF65** 80.00 | | | | |

**KM# 102 DOLLAR**
31.11 g., 0.999 Silver 0.999 oz. ASW, 40.6 mm. **Ruler:** Elizabeth II **Subject:** Nikolai Gogol, 200th Anniversary of Birth **Obv:** Head right **Rev:** Bust at left, multicolor

| Date | Mintage | VF20 | XF40 | MS60 | MS63 | MS65 |
|---|---|---|---|---|---|---|
| 2009 | 6,000 | **PF65** 60.00 | | | | |

**KM# 122 DOLLAR**
31.14 g., 0.999 Silver 1.000 oz. ASW, 40.6 mm. **Ruler:** Elizabeth II **Subject:** Mendelssohn

| Date | Mintage | VF20 | XF40 | MS60 | MS63 | MS65 |
|---|---|---|---|---|---|---|
| 2009 P | 5,000 | **PF65** 70.00 | | | | |

**KM# 123 DOLLAR**
31.14 g., 0.999 Silver 1.000 oz. ASW, 40.6 mm. **Ruler:** Elizabeth II **Subject:** Chopin

| Date | Mintage | VF20 | XF40 | MS60 | MS63 | MS65 |
|---|---|---|---|---|---|---|
| 2009 P | 5,000 | **PF65** 70.00 | | | | |

## KM# 133 DOLLAR

31.14 g., 0.999 Silver 1.000 oz. ASW, 40.6 mm. **Ruler:** Elizabeth II **Subject:** Battle fo Poltava, 300th Anniversary **Rev:** Rearing horse

| Date | Mintage | VF20 | XF40 | MS60 | MS63 | MS65 |
|---|---|---|---|---|---|---|
| 2009 P | — | PF65 75.00 | | | | |

## KM# 162 DOLLAR

31.11 g., 0.999 Silver 0.999 oz. ASW, 40 mm. **Ruler:** Elizabeth II **Rev:** Charles Darwin, youthful multicolor portrait, older man portrait, ship Beagle.

| Date | Mintage | VF20 | XF40 | MS60 | MS63 | MS65 |
|---|---|---|---|---|---|---|
| 2009 | — | PF65 75.00 | | | | |

## KM# 242 DOLLAR

20.00 g., 0.999 Silver 0.6424 oz. ASW, 40 mm. **Ruler:** Elizabeth II **Subject:** 200th Birthday of Charles Darwin **Rev:** Evolutionary theory

| Date | Mintage | VF20 | XF40 | MS60 | MS63 | MS65 |
|---|---|---|---|---|---|---|
| 2009 | Est. 5000 | — | — | — | — | 32.00 |

## KM# 243 DOLLAR

20.00 g., 0.999 Silver 0.6424 oz. ASW, 40 mm. **Ruler:** Elizabeth II **Subject:** 200th Birthday of Charles Darwin **Rev:** Open book "On the Origin of Species" and portrait of Darwin

| Date | Mintage | VF20 | XF40 | MS60 | MS63 | MS65 |
|---|---|---|---|---|---|---|
| 2009 | Est. 5000 | — | — | — | — | 32.00 |

## KM# 93 DOLLAR

62.21 g., 0.999 Silver 1.9981 oz. ASW **Ruler:** Elizabeth II **Subject:** Battle of Marathon **Rev:** Pheidippides' run

| Date | Mintage | VF20 | XF40 | MS60 | MS63 | MS65 |
|---|---|---|---|---|---|---|
| 2010 | 5,000 | PF65 95.00 | | | | |

## KM# 103 DOLLAR

31.11 g., 0.999 Silver 0.999 oz. ASW, 40.6 mm. **Ruler:** Elizabeth II **Subject:** Anton Chekhov, 150th Anniversary of Birth **Obv:** Head right **Rev:** Chekhov multicolor portrait at left, comedy and tragedy masks at right

| Date | Mintage | VF20 | XF40 | MS60 | MS63 | MS65 |
|---|---|---|---|---|---|---|
| 2010 | 6,000 | PF65 60.00 | | | | |

## KM# 104 DOLLAR

31.11 g., 0.999 Silver 0.999 oz. ASW, 40 mm. **Ruler:** Elizabeth II **Subject:** Great River Journeys - The Rhine **Obv:** Head right **Rev:** Tour boat, color castle in background

| Date | Mintage | VF20 | XF40 | MS60 | MS63 | MS65 |
|---|---|---|---|---|---|---|
| 2010 | 1,500 | PF65 90.00 | | | | |

## KM# 105 DOLLAR

31.11 g., 0.999 Silver 0.999 oz. ASW, 40 mm. **Ruler:** Elizabeth II **Subject:** Great River Journeys - Volga **Obv:** Head right **Rev:** Tour boat and color river front view

| Date | Mintage | VF20 | XF40 | MS60 | MS63 | MS65 |
|---|---|---|---|---|---|---|
| 2010 | 1,500 | PF65 90.00 | | | | |

## KM# 106 DOLLAR

31.11 g., 0.999 Silver 0.999 oz. ASW, 40 mm. **Ruler:** Elizabeth II **Subject:** Great River Journeys - Yangtzee **Obv:** Head right **Rev:** Sail boat and color river gorge

| Date | Mintage | VF20 | XF40 | MS60 | MS63 | MS65 |
|---|---|---|---|---|---|---|
| 2010 | 1,500 | PF65 90.00 | | | | |

## KM# 107 DOLLAR

31.11 g., 0.999 Silver 0.999 oz. ASW, 40 mm. **Ruler:** Elizabeth II **Subject:** Great River Journeys - Mississippi **Obv:** Head right **Rev:** Delta Queen and multicolor New Orleans skyline

| Date | Mintage | VF20 | XF40 | MS60 | MS63 | MS65 |
|---|---|---|---|---|---|---|
| 2010 | 1,500 | PF65 90.00 | | | | |

## KM# 108 DOLLAR

31.11 g., 0.999 Silver 0.999 oz. ASW, 40 mm. **Ruler:** Elizabeth II **Subject:** Great River Journeys - The Nile **Obv:** Head right **Rev:** Dhow, classical sculpture, multicolor sandscape

| Date | Mintage | VF20 | XF40 | MS60 | MS63 | MS65 |
|---|---|---|---|---|---|---|
| 2010 | 1,500 | PF65 90.00 | | | | |

## KM# 109 DOLLAR

31.11 g., 0.999 Silver 0.999 oz. ASW, 40 mm. **Ruler:** Elizabeth II **Subject:** Ned Kelly - Outlaw **Obv:** Head right **Rev:** Ned Kelly multicolor - Reward Poster

| Date | Mintage | VF20 | XF40 | MS60 | MS63 | MS65 |
|---|---|---|---|---|---|---|
| 2010 | 1,880 | PF65 90.00 | | | | |

## KM# 110 DOLLAR

31.11 g., 0.999 Silver 0.999 oz. ASW, 40 mm. **Ruler:** Elizabeth II **Subject:** Ned Kelly - Armour **Obv:** Head right **Rev:** Ned Kelley's helmet in multicolor

| Date | Mintage | VF20 | XF40 | MS60 | MS63 | MS65 |
|---|---|---|---|---|---|---|
| 2010 | 1,880 | PF65 90.00 | | | | |

## KM# 111 DOLLAR

31.11 g., 0.999 Silver 0.999 oz. ASW, 40 mm. **Ruler:** Elizabeth II **Subject:** Ned Kelly - Siege **Obv:** Head right **Rev:** Ned Kelly in shoutout, multicolor

| Date | Mintage | VF20 | XF40 | MS60 | MS63 | MS65 |
|---|---|---|---|---|---|---|
| 2010 | 1,880 | PF65 90.00 | | | | |

## KM# 112 DOLLAR

31.11 g., 0.999 Silver 0.999 oz. ASW, 40 mm. **Ruler:** Elizabeth II **Subject:** Ned Kelly - Gallows **Obv:** Head right **Rev:** Ned Kelly standing at the gallows, multicolor

| Date | Mintage | VF20 | XF40 | MS60 | MS63 | MS65 |
|---|---|---|---|---|---|---|
| 2010 | 1,880 | PF65 90.00 | | | | |

## KM# 113 DOLLAR

25.00 g., 0.925 Silver 0.7435 oz. ASW **Ruler:** Elizabeth II **Rev:** Sea horse facing left, Swarovski crystal chip eye **Shape:** 38.61

| Date | Mintage | VF20 | XF40 | MS60 | MS63 | MS65 |
|---|---|---|---|---|---|---|
| 2010 | 2,500 | PF65 65.00 | | | | |

## KM# 114 DOLLAR

0.50 g., 0.999 Gold 0.0161 oz. AGW, 11 mm. **Ruler:** Elizabeth II **Rev:** Sea horse facing right

| Date | Mintage | VF20 | XF40 | MS60 | MS63 | MS65 |
|---|---|---|---|---|---|---|
| 2010 | 15,000 | PF65 50.00 | | | | |

## KM# 115 DOLLAR

25.00 g., 0.925 Silver 0.7435 oz. ASW, 38.6 mm. **Ruler:** Elizabeth II **Subject:** Marine Life **Rev:** Hawksbill sea turtle, multicolor

| Date | Mintage | VF20 | XF40 | MS60 | MS63 | MS65 |
|---|---|---|---|---|---|---|
| 2010 | 2,500 | PF65 50.00 | | | | |

**KM# 117 DOLLAR**
31.14 g., 0.999 Silver 1.000 oz. ASW, 40.6 mm. **Ruler:** Elizabeth II **Subject:** Ballet - Don Quixote **Rev:** Multicolor windmill scene

| Date | Mintage | VF20 | XF40 | MS60 | MS63 | MS65 |
|---|---|---|---|---|---|---|
| 2010 P | 2,500 | PF65 80.00 | | | | |

**KM# 118 DOLLAR**
31.14 g., 0.999 Silver 1.000 oz. ASW, 40.6 mm. **Ruler:** Elizabeth II **Subject:** Ballet - Sleeping Beauty **Rev:** Multicolor castle scene

| Date | Mintage | VF20 | XF40 | MS60 | MS63 | MS65 |
|---|---|---|---|---|---|---|
| 2010 P | 2,500 | PF65 80.00 | | | | |

**KM# 119 DOLLAR**
31.14 g., 0.999 Silver 1.000 oz. ASW, 40.6 mm. **Ruler:** Elizabeth II **Subject:** Ballet - Nutcracker **Rev:** Multicolor snow scene

| Date | Mintage | VF20 | XF40 | MS60 | MS63 | MS65 |
|---|---|---|---|---|---|---|
| 2010 P | 2,500 | PF65 80.00 | | | | |

**KM# 120 DOLLAR**
31.14 g., 0.999 Silver 1.000 oz. ASW, 40.6 mm. **Ruler:** Elizabeth II **Subject:** Ballet - Swan Lake **Rev:** Multicolor swan and lake scene

| Date | Mintage | VF20 | XF40 | MS60 | MS63 | MS65 |
|---|---|---|---|---|---|---|
| 2010 P | 2,500 | PF65 80.00 | | | | |

**KM# 121 DOLLAR**
31.14 g., 0.999 Silver 1.000 oz. ASW, 40.6 mm. **Ruler:** Elizabeth II **Subject:** Ballet - Cinderella **Rev:** Multicolor pumpkin coach scene

| Date | Mintage | VF20 | XF40 | MS60 | MS63 | MS65 |
|---|---|---|---|---|---|---|
| 2010 P | 2,500 | PF65 80.00 | | | | |

**KM# 124 DOLLAR**
31.14 g., 0.999 Silver 1.000 oz. ASW, 40.6 mm. **Ruler:** Elizabeth II **Subject:** Robert Schumann **Rev:** Bust, G-cleff and score

| Date | Mintage | VF20 | XF40 | MS60 | MS63 | MS65 |
|---|---|---|---|---|---|---|
| 2010 P | 5,000 | PF65 70.00 | | | | |

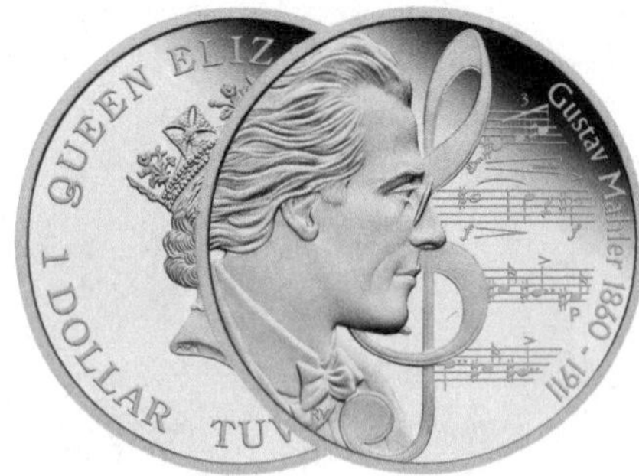


**KM# 125 DOLLAR**
31.14 g., 0.999 Silver 1.000 oz. ASW, 40.6 mm. **Ruler:** Elizabeth II **Subject:** Gustav Mahler

| Date | Mintage | VF20 | XF40 | MS60 | MS63 | MS65 |
|---|---|---|---|---|---|---|
| 2010 P | 5,000 | PF65 70.00 | | | | |

**KM# 127 DOLLAR**
31.14 g., 0.999 Silver 1.000 oz. ASW, 40.6 mm. **Ruler:** Elizabeth II **Subject:** Warrior - Legionary **Rev:** Multicolor Roman Legionary soldier standing

| Date | Mintage | VF20 | XF40 | MS60 | MS63 | MS65 |
|---|---|---|---|---|---|---|
| 2010 P | — | PF65 80.00 | | | | |

**KM# 128 DOLLAR**
31.14 g., 0.999 Silver 1.000 oz. ASW, 40.6 mm. **Ruler:** Elizabeth II **Subject:** Warrior - Viking **Rev:** Multicolor Viking

| Date | Mintage | VF20 | XF40 | MS60 | MS63 | MS65 |
|---|---|---|---|---|---|---|
| 2010 P | — | PF65 80.00 | | | | |

**KM# 129 DOLLAR**
31.14 g., 0.999 Silver 1.000 oz. ASW, 40.6 mm. **Ruler:** Elizabeth II **Subject:** Warrior - Knight **Rev:** Multicolor Knight

| Date | Mintage | VF20 | XF40 | MS60 | MS63 | MS65 |
|---|---|---|---|---|---|---|
| 2010 P | — | PF65 80.00 | | | | |

**KM# 130 DOLLAR**
31.14 g., 0.999 Silver 1.000 oz. ASW, 40.6 mm. **Ruler:** Elizabeth II **Subject:** Warrior - Samurai **Rev:** Multicolor Samurai

| Date | Mintage | VF20 | XF40 | MS60 | MS63 | MS65 |
|---|---|---|---|---|---|---|
| 2010 P | — | PF65 80.00 | | | | |

**KM# 131 DOLLAR**
31.14 g., 0.999 Silver 1.000 oz. ASW, 40 mm. **Ruler:** Elizabeth II **Subject:** Banjo" Paterson Ballard - Man from Snowy River **Rev:** Multicolor cowboy chasing two horses

| Date | Mintage | VF20 | XF40 | MS60 | MS63 | MS65 |
|---|---|---|---|---|---|---|
| 2010 P | — | PF65 80.00 | | | | |

**KM# 134 DOLLAR**
31.14 g., 0.999 Silver 1.000 oz. ASW, 40.6 mm. **Ruler:** Elizabeth II **Rev:** Multicolor brown snake

| Date | Mintage | VF20 | XF40 | MS60 | MS63 | MS65 |
|---|---|---|---|---|---|---|
| 2010 P | — | PF65 185 | | | | |

**KM# 135 DOLLAR**
31.14 g., 0.999 Silver 1.000 oz. ASW, 40.6 mm. **Ruler:** Elizabeth II **Subject:** German Unification, 20th Anniversary **Rev:** Large 20, statues on Brandenburg gate

| Date | Mintage | VF20 | XF40 | MS60 | MS63 | MS65 |
|---|---|---|---|---|---|---|
| 2010 P | 5,000 | PF65 75.00 | | | | |

**KM# 136 DOLLAR**
31.14 g., 0.999 Silver 1.000 oz. ASW, 40.6 mm. **Ruler:** Elizabeth II **Subject:** Sir Charles Kingsford

| Date | Mintage | VF20 | XF40 | MS60 | MS63 | MS65 |
|---|---|---|---|---|---|---|
| 2010 P | — | PF65 75.00 | | | | |

**KM# 137 DOLLAR**
31.14 g., 0.999 Silver 1.000 oz. ASW, 40.6 mm. **Ruler:** Elizabeth II **Subject:** Working dogs **Rev:** Multicolor golden retreiver pups

| Date | Mintage | VF20 | XF40 | MS60 | MS63 | MS65 |
|---|---|---|---|---|---|---|
| 2010 P | — | PF65 85.00 | | | | |

**KM# 138 DOLLAR**
31.14 g., 0.999 Silver 1.000 oz. ASW, 40.6 mm. **Ruler:** Elizabeth II **Subject:** Man from Snowy River **Rev:** Multicolor group of horsemen

| Date | Mintage | VF20 | XF40 | MS60 | MS63 | MS65 |
|---|---|---|---|---|---|---|
| 2010 P | — | PF65 75.00 | | | | |

**KM# 139 DOLLAR**
31.14 g., 0.999 Silver 1.000 oz. ASW, 40.7 mm. **Ruler:** Elizabeth II **Subject:** Trucks - W900 **Rev:** Truck cab

| Date | Mintage | VF20 | XF40 | MS60 | MS63 | MS65 |
|---|---|---|---|---|---|---|
| 2010 P | — | **PF65** 75.00 | | | | |

**KM# 140 DOLLAR**
31.14 g., 0.999 Silver 1.000 oz. ASW, 40.6 mm. **Ruler:** Elizabeth II **Subject:** Trucks - Cascadia **Rev:** Multicolor truck cab

| Date | Mintage | VF20 | XF40 | MS60 | MS63 | MS65 |
|---|---|---|---|---|---|---|
| 2010 P | — | **PF65** 75.00 | | | | |

**KM# 141 DOLLAR**
31.14 g., 0.999 Silver 1.000 oz. ASW, 40.6 mm. **Ruler:** Elizabeth II **Subject:** Trucks - R500 **Rev:** Multicolor truck cab

| Date | Mintage | VF20 | XF40 | MS60 | MS63 | MS65 |
|---|---|---|---|---|---|---|
| 2010 P | — | **PF65** 75.00 | | | | |

**KM# 142 DOLLAR**
31.14 g., 0.999 Silver 1.000 oz. ASW, 40.6 mm. **Ruler:** Elizabeth II **Subject:** Trucks - GiGamax **Rev:** Multicolor truck cab

| Date | Mintage | VF20 | XF40 | MS60 | MS63 | MS65 |
|---|---|---|---|---|---|---|
| 2010 P | — | **PF65** 75.00 | | | | |

**KM# 143 DOLLAR**
31.14 g., 0.999 Silver 1.000 oz. ASW, 40.7 mm. **Ruler:** Elizabeth II **Subject:** Tanks - A22 Churchill **Rev:** Multicolor tank

| Date | Mintage | VF20 | XF40 | MS60 | MS63 | MS65 |
|---|---|---|---|---|---|---|
| 2010 P | — | **PF65** 75.00 | | | | |

**KM# 144 DOLLAR**
31.14 g., 0.999 Silver 1.000 oz. ASW **Ruler:** Elizabeth II **Subject:** Tanks - M-4 Sherman **Rev:** Multicolor tank **Shape:** 40.6

| Date | Mintage | VF20 | XF40 | MS60 | MS63 | MS65 |
|---|---|---|---|---|---|---|
| 2010 P | — | **PF65** 75.00 | | | | |

**KM# 145 DOLLAR**
31.14 g., 0.999 Silver 1.000 oz. ASW, 40.6 mm. **Ruler:** Elizabeth II **Subject:** Tanks - Type 97 Chi-Ha **Rev:** Multicolor tank

| Date | Mintage | VF20 | XF40 | MS60 | MS63 | MS65 |
|---|---|---|---|---|---|---|
| 2010 P | — | **PF65** 75.00 | | | | |

**KM# 146 DOLLAR**
31.14 g., 0.999 Silver 1.000 oz. ASW, 40.6 mm. **Ruler:** Elizabeth II **Subject:** Tanks - T-34 **Rev:** Multicolor tank

| Date | Mintage | VF20 | XF40 | MS60 | MS63 | MS65 |
|---|---|---|---|---|---|---|
| 2010 P | — | **PF65** 75.00 | | | | |

**KM# 147 DOLLAR**
31.14 g., 0.999 Silver 1.000 oz. ASW, 40.6 mm. **Ruler:** Elizabeth II **Subject:** Tanks - PzK pfw VI Tiger 1 **Rev:** Multicolor tank

| Date | Mintage | VF20 | XF40 | MS60 | MS63 | MS65 |
|---|---|---|---|---|---|---|
| 2010 P | — | **PF65** 75.00 | | | | |

**KM# 148 DOLLAR**
13.90 g., Aluminum-Bronze, 30.6 mm. **Ruler:** Elizabeth II **Rev:** Blackbeard standing, treasure chest at right

| Date | Mintage | VF20 | XF40 | MS60 | MS63 | MS65 |
|---|---|---|---|---|---|---|
| 2010 P | — | — | — | — | — | 15.00 |

**KM# 126 DOLLAR**
31.14 g., 0.999 Silver 1.000 oz. ASW, 40.6 mm. **Ruler:** Elizabeth II **Subject:** Franz List

| Date | Mintage | VF20 | XF40 | MS60 | MS63 | MS65 |
|---|---|---|---|---|---|---|
| 2011 P | 5,000 | **PF65** 70.00 | | | | |

**KM# 163 DOLLAR**
31.14 g., 0.999 Silver 1.000 oz. ASW, 40.6 mm. **Ruler:** Elizabeth II **Subject:** Australia's extinct animals - Thylacine **Obv:** Head in diadem right **Rev:** Thylacine - Tasmanian tiger in multicolor

| Date | Mintage | VF20 | XF40 | MS60 | MS63 | MS65 |
|---|---|---|---|---|---|---|
| 2011 P | 5,000 | **PF65** 250 | | | | |

**KM# 165 DOLLAR**
31.11 g., 0.999 Silver 0.999 oz. ASW, 40.6 mm. **Ruler:** Elizabeth II **Obv:** Head with tiara right **Rev:** Australia's Box Jellyfish in color **Edge:** Reeded

| Date | Mintage | VF20 | XF40 | MS60 | MS63 | MS65 |
|---|---|---|---|---|---|---|
| 2011 | 5,000 | PF65 120 | | | | |

**KM# 172 DOLLAR**
31.11 g., 0.999 Silver 0.999 oz. ASW, 40.6 mm. **Ruler:** Elizabeth II **Subject:** Franz Lizst, 200th anniversary of birth **Rev:** Lizst at left, G-cleft, 4 lines of score

| Date | Mintage | VF20 | XF40 | MS60 | MS63 | MS65 |
|---|---|---|---|---|---|---|
| 2011 | — | PF65 80.00 | | | | |

**KM# 177 DOLLAR**
13.80 g., Aluminum-Bronze, 30.6 mm. **Ruler:** Elizabeth II **Subject:** Henry Morgan **Rev:** Morgan, ship, chest and barrels

| Date | Mintage | VF20 | XF40 | MS60 | MS63 | MS65 |
|---|---|---|---|---|---|---|
| 2011 P | — | — | — | — | — | 15.00 |

**KM# 178 DOLLAR**
13.80 g., Aluminum-Bronze, 30.8 mm. **Ruler:** Elizabeth II **Subject:** Calico Jack **Rev:** Jack standing, ship, Skull and crossed-swords flag

| Date | Mintage | VF20 | XF40 | MS60 | MS63 | MS65 |
|---|---|---|---|---|---|---|
| 2011 P | — | — | — | — | — | 15.00 |

**KM# 179 DOLLAR**
13.80 g., Aluminum-Bronze, 30.8 mm. **Ruler:** Elizabeth II **Subject:** Black Bart **Rev:** Bart at left, ship and cross

| Date | Mintage | VF20 | XF40 | MS60 | MS63 | MS65 |
|---|---|---|---|---|---|---|
| 2011 P | — | — | — | — | — | 15.00 |

**KM# 180 DOLLAR**
13.80 g., Aluminum-Bronze, 30.8 mm. **Ruler:** Elizabeth II **Subject:** William Kidd **Rev:** Bust at left, ship, pistol and map

| Date | Mintage | VF20 | XF40 | MS60 | MS63 | MS65 |
|---|---|---|---|---|---|---|
| 2011 P | — | — | — | — | — | 15.00 |

**KM# 181 DOLLAR**
31.14 g., 0.999 Silver 1.000 oz. ASW, 40.6 mm. **Ruler:** Elizabeth II **Subject:** Ships that changed the World **Rev:** Santa Maria under sail

| Date | Mintage | VF20 | XF40 | MS60 | MS63 | MS65 |
|---|---|---|---|---|---|---|
| 2011 P | 5,000 | PF65 75.00 | | | | |

**KM# 182 DOLLAR**
31.14 g., 0.999 Silver 1.000 oz. ASW, 40.6 mm. **Ruler:** Elizabeth II **Subject:** Ships that changed the World **Rev:** Golden Hind under sail

| Date | Mintage | VF20 | XF40 | MS60 | MS63 | MS65 |
|---|---|---|---|---|---|---|
| 2011 P | 5,000 | PF65 75.00 | | | | |

**KM# 183 DOLLAR**
31.14 g., 0.999 Silver 1.000 oz. ASW, 40.6 mm. **Ruler:** Elizabeth II **Subject:** Heroes and Villians **Rev:** Holmes and Moriarty

| Date | Mintage | VF20 | XF40 | MS60 | MS63 | MS65 |
|---|---|---|---|---|---|---|
| 2011 P | 1,500 | PF65 80.00 | | | | |

**KM# 184 DOLLAR**
31.14 g., 0.999 Silver 1.000 oz. ASW, 40.6 mm. **Ruler:** Elizabeth II **Subject:** Heroes and Villains **Rev:** van Helsing and Dracula

| Date | Mintage | VF20 | XF40 | MS60 | MS63 | MS65 |
|---|---|---|---|---|---|---|
| 2011 P | 1,500 | PF65 80.00 | | | | |

**KM# 185 DOLLAR**
31.14 g., 0.999 Silver 1.000 oz. ASW, 40.6 mm. **Ruler:** Elizabeth II **Subject:** Heroes and Villains **Rev:** Robin Hood and the Sherif

| Date | Mintage | VF20 | XF40 | MS60 | MS63 | MS65 |
|---|---|---|---|---|---|---|
| 2011 P | 1,500 | PF65 80.00 | | | | |

**KM# 186 DOLLAR**
31.14 g., 0.999 Silver 1.000 oz. ASW, 40.6 mm. **Ruler:** Elizabeth II **Subject:** Heros and Villains **Rev:** Peter Pan and Captain Hook

| Date | Mintage | VF20 | XF40 | MS60 | MS63 | MS65 |
|---|---|---|---|---|---|---|
| 2011 P | 1,500 | PF65 80.00 | | | | |

**KM# 187 DOLLAR**
31.14 g., 0.999 Silver 1.000 oz. ASW, 40.6 mm. **Ruler:** Elizabeth II **Subject:** Heroes and Villains **Rev:** Dr. Jeckel and Mr. Hyde

| Date | Mintage | VF20 | XF40 | MS60 | MS63 | MS65 |
|---|---|---|---|---|---|---|
| 2011 P | 1,500 | PF65 80.00 | | | | |

**KM# 195 DOLLAR**
31.14 g., 0.999 Silver 1.000 oz. ASW, 40.6 mm. **Ruler:** Elizabeth II **Subject:** Working dogs - Beagle

| Date | Mintage | VF20 | XF40 | MS60 | MS63 | MS65 |
|---|---|---|---|---|---|---|
| 2011 | — | PF65 95.00 | | | | |

**KM# 196 DOLLAR**
31.14 g., 0.999 Silver 1.000 oz. ASW, 40.6 mm. **Ruler:** Elizabeth II **Subject:** Working dogs - Border Collie

| Date | Mintage | VF20 | XF40 | MS60 | MS63 | MS65 |
|---|---|---|---|---|---|---|
| 2011 | — | PF65 75.00 | | | | |

**KM# 197 DOLLAR**
31.14 g., 0.999 Silver 1.000 oz. ASW, 40.6 mm. **Ruler:** Elizabeth II **Subject:** Working dogs - German Shepard

| Date | Mintage | VF20 | XF40 | MS60 | MS63 | MS65 |
|---|---|---|---|---|---|---|
| 2011 | — | PF65 95.00 | | | | |

**KM# 198 DOLLAR**
31.14 g., 0.999 Silver 1.000 oz. ASW, 40.6 mm. **Ruler:** Elizabeth II **Subject:** Working dogs - Australian Cattle Dog

| Date | Mintage | VF20 | XF40 | MS60 | MS63 | MS65 |
|---|---|---|---|---|---|---|
| 2011 | — | PF65 85.00 | | | | |

**KM# 202 DOLLAR**
15.50 g., 0.925 Silver 0.461 oz. ASW, 35 mm. **Ruler:** Elizabeth II **Subject:** Coral Protection **Rev:** Dendrocyra Cylindriclus, coral in color

| Date | Mintage | VF20 | XF40 | MS60 | MS63 | MS65 |
|---|---|---|---|---|---|---|
| 2011 | 1,000 | PF65 65.00 | | | | |

**KM# 188 DOLLAR**
31.14 g., 0.999 Silver 1.000 oz. ASW, 40.6 mm. **Ruler:** Elizabeth II **Subject:** Ships that changed the World **Rev:** Mayflower at sail

| Date | Mintage | VF20 | XF40 | MS60 | MS63 | MS65 |
|---|---|---|---|---|---|---|
| 2012 P | 5,000 | PF65 100 | | | | |

**KM# 189 DOLLAR**
31.14 g., 0.999 Silver 1.000 oz. ASW, 40.6 mm. **Ruler:** Elizabeth II **Subject:** Ships that changed the World **Rev:** U.S.S. Constitution in sea battle

| Date | Mintage | VF20 | XF40 | MS60 | MS63 | MS65 |
|---|---|---|---|---|---|---|
| 2012 P | 5,000 | PF65 100 | | | | |

**KM# 190 DOLLAR**
13.80 g., Aluminum-Bronze, 30.6 mm. **Ruler:** Elizabeth II **Subject:** Year of the Dragon **Rev:** Baby Dragon in color

| Date | Mintage | VF20 | XF40 | MS60 | MS63 | MS65 |
|---|---|---|---|---|---|---|
| 2012 P | 10,000 | — | — | — | — | 15.00 |

**KM# 192 DOLLAR**
31.14 g., 0.999 Silver 1.000 oz. ASW, 40.6 mm. **Ruler:** Elizabeth II **Rev:** R.M.S. Titanic sailing forward, tug at side

| Date | Mintage | VF20 | XF40 | MS60 | MS63 | MS65 |
|---|---|---|---|---|---|---|
| 2012 P | 5,000 | PF65 100 | | | | |

**KM# 194 DOLLAR**
31.14 g., 0.999 Silver 1.000 oz. ASW **Ruler:** Elizabeth II **Subject:** Wildlife in Need **Obv:** Head with tiara right **Rev:** Black rhinoceros and calf in color **Edge:** Reeded

| Date | Mintage | VF20 | XF40 | MS60 | MS63 | MS65 |
|---|---|---|---|---|---|---|
| 2012 P | 5,000 | PF65 100 | | | | |

**KM# 203 DOLLAR**
31.11 g., 0.999 Silver 0.999 oz. ASW, 40.6 mm. **Ruler:** Elizabeth II **Subject:** Wildlife in Need: Polar Bear **Rev:** Polar Bear family in color

| Date | Mintage | VF20 | XF40 | MS60 | MS63 | MS65 |
|---|---|---|---|---|---|---|
| 2012 | Est. 5000 | PF65 80.00 | | | | |

**KM# 204 DOLLAR**
31.11 g., 0.999 Silver 0.999 oz. ASW, 40.6 mm. **Ruler:** Elizabeth II **Subject:** Wildlife in Need: Black Rhinocerous **Rev:** Rhino in color

| Date | Mintage | VF20 | XF40 | MS60 | MS63 | MS65 |
|---|---|---|---|---|---|---|
| 2012 | Est. 5000 | PF65 80.00 | | | | |

**KM# 205 DOLLAR**
31.11 g., 0.999 Silver 0.999 oz. ASW, 40.6 mm. **Ruler:** Elizabeth II **Subject:** Wildlife in Need: Siberian Tiger

| Date | Mintage | VF20 | XF40 | MS60 | MS63 | MS65 |
|---|---|---|---|---|---|---|
| 2012 | — | PF65 80.00 | | | | |

**KM# 206 DOLLAR**
31.11 g., 0.999 Silver 0.999 oz. ASW, 40.6 mm. **Ruler:** Elizabeth II **Subject:** Deadly and Dangerous: Funnel Web Spider

| Date | Mintage | VF20 | XF40 | MS60 | MS63 | MS65 |
|---|---|---|---|---|---|---|
| 2012 | 5,000 | PF65 125 | | | | |

**KM# 207 DOLLAR**
31.11 g., 0.999 Silver 0.999 oz. ASW, 40.6 mm. **Ruler:** Elizabeth II **Subject:** Wildlife in Need: Orangutan **Rev:** Orangutan in color

| Date | Mintage | VF20 | XF40 | MS60 | MS63 | MS65 |
|---|---|---|---|---|---|---|
| 2012 | Est. 5000 | PF65 80.00 | | | | |

**KM# 208 DOLLAR**
31.14 g., 0.999 Silver 1.000 oz. ASW, 40.6 mm. **Ruler:** Elizabeth II **Subject:** Marilyn Monroe

| Date | Mintage | VF20 | XF40 | MS60 | MS63 | MS65 |
|---|---|---|---|---|---|---|
| 2012 | Est. 12500 | PF65 75.00 | | | | |

**KM# 209 DOLLAR**
31.10 g., 0.999 Silver 0.9989 oz. ASW, 40.6 mm. **Ruler:** Elizabeth II **Subject:** St. George and the Dragon **Rev:** St. George and the Dragon colorized

| Date | Mintage | VF20 | XF40 | MS60 | MS63 | MS65 |
|---|---|---|---|---|---|---|
| 2012 | Est. 5000 | PF65 100 | | | | |

**KM# 210 DOLLAR**
31.11 g., 0.999 Silver 0.999 oz. ASW, 40.6 mm. **Ruler:** Elizabeth II **Subject:** Dragons of Legend: Red Welsh Dragon

| Date | Mintage | VF20 | XF40 | MS60 | MS63 | MS65 |
|---|---|---|---|---|---|---|
| 2012 | Est. 5000 | PF65 135 | | | | |

**KM# 212 DOLLAR**
31.11 g., 0.999 Silver 0.999 oz. ASW, 40.6 mm. **Ruler:** Elizabeth II **Subject:** Dragons of Legend: Chinese Dragon

| Date | Mintage | VF20 | XF40 | MS60 | MS63 | MS65 |
|---|---|---|---|---|---|---|
| 2012 | 5,000 | PF65 135 | | | | |

**KM# 173 2 DOLLARS**
Silver, 38.6 mm. **Ruler:** Elizabeth II **Subject:** Year of the Goat **Obv:** Head crowned right **Rev:** Two goats

| Date | Mintage | VF20 | XF40 | MS60 | MS63 | MS65 |
|---|---|---|---|---|---|---|
| 2003 | — | PF65 50.00 | | | | |

**KM# 175 2 DOLLARS**
31.11 g., 0.999 Silver 0.999 oz. ASW, 38.6 mm. **Ruler:** Elizabeth II **Obv:** Head crowned right **Rev:** Harry Potter with wand raised, being followed by Dementor **Edge:** Reeded

| Date | Mintage | VF20 | XF40 | MS60 | MS63 | MS65 |
|---|---|---|---|---|---|---|
| 2004 | — | PF65 50.00 | | | | |

**KM# 218 2 DOLLARS**
31.10 g., 0.999 Silver 0.9989 oz. ASW, 38 mm. **Ruler:** Elizabeth II **Subject:** Chinese Lunar Year of the Monkey

| Date | Mintage | VF20 | XF40 | MS60 | MS63 | MS65 |
|---|---|---|---|---|---|---|
| 2004 | Est. 47500 | PF65 50.00 | | | | |

**KM# 219 2 DOLLARS**
31.10 g., 0.999 Silver 0.9989 oz. ASW, 38.7 mm. **Ruler:** Elizabeth II **Subject:** Harry Potter - Film by JK Rowling

| Date | Mintage | VF20 | XF40 | MS60 | MS63 | MS65 |
|---|---|---|---|---|---|---|
| 2004 | — | PF65 50.00 | | | | |

**KM# 220 2 DOLLARS**
31.10 g., 0.999 Silver 0.9989 oz. ASW, 38.7 mm. **Ruler:** Elizabeth II **Subject:** Harry Potter the Movie **Rev:** Harry Potter with the Golden Snitch

| Date | Mintage | VF20 | XF40 | MS60 | MS63 | MS65 |
|---|---|---|---|---|---|---|
| 2004 | — | PF65 50.00 | | | | |

**KM# 221 2 DOLLARS**
31.10 g., 0.999 Silver 0.9989 oz. ASW **Ruler:** Elizabeth II **Subject:** Chinese Lunar Year of the Rooster **Rev:** Two Roosters

| Date | Mintage | VF20 | XF40 | MS60 | MS63 | MS65 |
|---|---|---|---|---|---|---|
| 2005 | Est. 47500 | PF65 40.00 | | | | |

**KM# 223 2 DOLLARS**
31.10 g., 0.999 Silver 0.9989 oz. ASW, 38 mm. **Ruler:** Elizabeth II **Subject:** Chinese Lunar Year of the Dog

| Date | Mintage | VF20 | XF40 | MS60 | MS63 | MS65 |
|---|---|---|---|---|---|---|
| 2006 | Est. 47500 | PF65 50.00 | | | | |

**KM# 236 2 DOLLARS**
31.10 g., 0.999 Silver 0.9989 oz. ASW, 38 mm. **Ruler:** Elizabeth II **Subject:** Lunar Year of the Pig

| Date | Mintage | VF20 | XF40 | MS60 | MS63 | MS65 |
|---|---|---|---|---|---|---|
| 2007 | Est. 47500 | PF65 50.00 | | | | |

**KM# 238 2 DOLLARS**
31.10 g., 0.999 Silver 0.9989 oz. ASW, 38 mm. **Ruler:** Elizabeth II **Subject:** Chinese Lunar Year of the Rat

| Date | Mintage | VF20 | XF40 | MS60 | MS63 | MS65 |
|---|---|---|---|---|---|---|
| 2008 | — | PF65 50.00 | | | | |

**KM# 241 2 DOLLARS**
31.10 g., 0.999 Silver 0.9989 oz. ASW, 38 mm. **Ruler:** Elizabeth II **Subject:** Chinese Lunar Year of the Buffalo **Rev:** Water Buffalo

| Date | Mintage | VF20 | XF40 | MS60 | MS63 | MS65 |
|---|---|---|---|---|---|---|
| 2009 | Est. 47500 | PF65 50.00 | | | | |

**KM# 116 2 DOLLARS**
1.24 g., 0.999 Gold 0.0398 oz. AGW, 13.92 mm. **Ruler:** Elizabeth II **Rev:** Los Reyes sailing ship

| Date | Mintage | VF20 | XF40 | MS60 | MS63 | MS65 |
|---|---|---|---|---|---|---|
| 2010 | 15,000 | PF65 85.00 | | | | |

**KM# 169 2 DOLLARS**
Gold, 13.9 mm. **Ruler:** Elizabeth II **Subject:** Marine life **Rev:** Sea horse

| Date | Mintage | VF20 | XF40 | MS60 | MS63 | MS65 |
|---|---|---|---|---|---|---|
| 2010 | — | PF65 80.00 | | | | |

**KM# 244 2 DOLLARS**
31.10 g., 0.999 Silver 0.9989 oz. ASW, 38 mm. **Ruler:** Elizabeth II **Subject:** Chinese Lunar Year of the Tiger

| Date | Mintage | VF20 | XF40 | MS60 | MS63 | MS65 |
|---|---|---|---|---|---|---|
| 2010 | Est. 47500 | PF65 50.00 | | | | |

**KM# 245 2 DOLLARS**
31.10 g., 0.999 Silver 0.9989 oz. ASW, 38 mm. **Ruler:** Elizabeth II **Subject:** Chinese Lunar Year of the Rabbit **Rev:** Two rabbits

| Date | Mintage | VF20 | XF40 | MS60 | MS63 | MS65 |
|---|---|---|---|---|---|---|
| 2011 | Est. 47500 | PF65 50.00 | | | | |

**KM# 174 3 DOLLARS**
1.22 g., 0.999 Gold 0.0393 oz. AGW, 13.9 mm. **Ruler:** Elizabeth II **Subject:** Year of the Horse **Rev:** Horse galloping right

| Date | Mintage | VF20 | XF40 | MS60 | MS63 | MS65 |
|---|---|---|---|---|---|---|
| 2002 | — | PF65 115 | | | | |
| 2008 | — | PF65 115 | | | | |

**KM# 217 3 DOLLARS**
1.24 g., 0.9999 Gold 0.0399 oz. AGW, 13.92 mm. **Ruler:** Elizabeth II **Subject:** Gold Bullion Coin **Rev:** Chinese lunar year of the horse

| Date | Mintage | VF20 | XF40 | MS60 | MS63 | MS65 |
|---|---|---|---|---|---|---|
| 2002 | — | PF65 75.00 | | | | |
| 2002 | — | PF65 75.00 | | | | |
| 2002 | — | PF65 75.00 | | | | |

**KM# 158 3 DOLLARS**
1.22 g., 0.999 Gold 0.0393 oz. AGW, 13.9 mm. **Ruler:** Elizabeth II **Rev:** Australian owl

| Date | Mintage | VF20 | XF40 | MS60 | MS63 | MS65 |
|---|---|---|---|---|---|---|
| 2005 | — | PF65 100 | | | | |
| 2006 | — | PF65 100 | | | | |
| 2007 | — | PF65 100 | | | | |

**KM# 232 3 DOLLARS**
1.24 g., 0.9999 Gold 0.0399 oz. AGW, 13.92 mm. **Ruler:** Elizabeth II **Subject:** Gold Bullion coin

| Date | Mintage | VF20 | XF40 | MS60 | MS63 | MS65 |
|---|---|---|---|---|---|---|
| 2006 | — | PF65 75.00 | | | | |

**KM# 152 3 DOLLARS**
1.22 g., 0.999 Gold 0.0393 oz. AGW, 13.9 mm. **Ruler:** Elizabeth II **Rev:** Multicolor mouse with heart

| Date | Mintage | VF20 | XF40 | MS60 | MS63 | MS65 |
|---|---|---|---|---|---|---|
| 2008 | — | — | — | — | — | 95.00 |

**KM# 199 3 DOLLARS**
1.24 g., 0.9999 Gold 0.0399 oz. AGW, 14.5 mm. **Ruler:** Elizabeth II **Subject:** Lucky waving cat

| Date | Mintage | VF20 | XF40 | MS60 | MS63 | MS65 |
|---|---|---|---|---|---|---|
| 2011 | 2,000 | PF65 125 | | | | |

**KM# 200 3 DOLLARS**
1.24 g., 0.9999 Gold 0.0399 oz. AGW, 14.5 mm. **Ruler:** Elizabeth II **Subject:** Lucky waving cats

| Date | Mintage | VF20 | XF40 | MS60 | MS63 | MS65 |
|---|---|---|---|---|---|---|
| 2011 | 2,000 | PF65 125 | | | | |

**KM# 246 3 DOLLARS**
1.24 g., 0.9999 Gold 0.0399 oz. AGW, 13.92 mm. **Ruler:** Elizabeth II **Subject:** Gold Bullion Coin - Maneki Neko

| Date | Mintage | VF20 | XF40 | MS60 | MS63 | MS65 |
|---|---|---|---|---|---|---|
| 2011 | — | — | — | — | — | 80.00 |

**KM# 246a 3 DOLLARS**
1.24 g., 0.9999 Gold 0.0399 oz. AGW, 13.92 mm. **Ruler:** Elizabeth II **Subject:** Gold Bullion Coin - Maneki Neko **Rev:** Cat in white and green

| Date | Mintage | VF20 | XF40 | MS60 | MS63 | MS65 |
|---|---|---|---|---|---|---|
| 2011 | — | — | — | — | — | 80.00 |

**KM# 246b 3 DOLLARS**
1.24 g., 0.9999 Gold 0.0399 oz. AGW, 13.92 mm. **Ruler:** Elizabeth II **Subject:** Gold Bullion Coin - Maneki Neko **Rev:** Cats in white and purple

| Date | Mintage | VF20 | XF40 | MS60 | MS63 | MS65 |
|---|---|---|---|---|---|---|
| 2011 | — | — | — | — | — | 80.00 |

**KM# 49 5 DOLLARS**
62.50 g., 0.999 Silver 2.0074 oz. ASW, 49.9 mm. **Ruler:** Elizabeth II **Subject:** Dinosaurs **Obv:** Crowned head right **Rev:** Giganotosaurus **Edge:** Reeded

| Date | Mintage | VF20 | XF40 | MS60 | MS63 | MS65 |
|---|---|---|---|---|---|---|
| 2002 | 1,000 | PF65 90.00 | | | | |

**KM# 50 5 DOLLARS**
62.50 g., 0.999 Silver 2.0074 oz. ASW, 49.9 mm. **Ruler:** Elizabeth II **Subject:** Dinosaurs **Obv:** Crowned head right **Rev:** Dromaeosaurus **Edge:** Reeded

| Date | Mintage | VF20 | XF40 | MS60 | MS63 | MS65 |
|---|---|---|---|---|---|---|
| 2002 | 1,000 | PF65 90.00 | | | | |

**KM# 51 5 DOLLARS**
62.50 g., 0.999 Silver 2.0074 oz. ASW, 49.9 mm. **Ruler:** Elizabeth II **Subject:** Dinosaurs **Obv:** Crowned head right **Rev:** Stegosaurus **Edge:** Reeded

| Date | Mintage | VF20 | XF40 | MS60 | MS63 | MS65 |
|---|---|---|---|---|---|---|
| 2002 | 1,000 | PF65 90.00 | | | | |

**KM# 52 5 DOLLARS**
62.50 g., 0.999 Silver 2.0074 oz. ASW, 49.9 mm. **Ruler:** Elizabeth II **Subject:** Dinosaurs **Obv:** Crowned head right **Rev:** Seismosaurus **Edge:** Reeded

| Date | Mintage | VF20 | XF40 | MS60 | MS63 | MS65 |
|---|---|---|---|---|---|---|
| 2002 | 1,000 | PF65 90.00 | | | | |

**KM# 211 5 DOLLARS**
156.67 g., 0.999 Silver 5.0321 oz. ASW, 65.6 mm. **Ruler:** Elizabeth II **Subject:** Dragons of Legend: Yin and Yang Year of the Dragon **Obv:** Gold and Purple dragons

| Date | Mintage | VF20 | XF40 | MS60 | MS63 | MS65 |
|---|---|---|---|---|---|---|
| 2012 | Est. 1000 | PF65 450 | | | | |

**KM# 159 15 DOLLARS**
3.11 g., 0.999 Gold 0.0999 oz. AGW, 17.95 mm. **Ruler:** Elizabeth II **Rev:** Australian owl

| Date | Mintage | VF20 | XF40 | MS60 | MS63 | MS65 |
|---|---|---|---|---|---|---|
| 2005 | — | PF65 195 | | | | |
| 2006 | — | PF65 195 | | | | |
| 2007 | — | PF65 195 | | | | |

**KM# 233 15 DOLLARS**
3.13 g., 0.9999 Gold 0.1006 oz. AGW, 13.92 mm. **Ruler:** Elizabeth II **Subject:** Gold Bullion Coin

| Date | Mintage | VF20 | XF40 | MS60 | MS63 | MS65 |
|---|---|---|---|---|---|---|
| 2006 | — | PF65 200 | | | | |

**KM# 153 15 DOLLARS**
3.11 g., 0.999 Gold 0.0999 oz. AGW, 17.95 mm. **Ruler:** Elizabeth II **Rev:** Multicolor mouse and golden egg

| Date | Mintage | VF20 | XF40 | MS60 | MS63 | MS65 |
|---|---|---|---|---|---|---|
| 2008 | — | — | — | — | — | 235 |

**KM# 201 15 DOLLARS**
3.11 g., 0.9999 Gold 0.100 oz. AGW, 18 mm. **Ruler:** Elizabeth II **Subject:** Lucky waving cat

| Date | Mintage | VF20 | XF40 | MS60 | MS63 | MS65 |
|---|---|---|---|---|---|---|
| 2011 | 2,000 | PF65 225 | | | | |

**KM# 247 15 DOLLARS**
3.13 g., 0.9999 Gold 0.1006 oz. AGW, 13.92 mm. **Ruler:** Elizabeth II **Subject:** Gold Bullion Coin - Maneki Neko

| Date | Mintage | VF20 | XF40 | MS60 | MS63 | MS65 |
|---|---|---|---|---|---|---|
| 2011 | — | PF65 195 | | | | |

**KM# 132 25 DOLLARS**
7.77 g., 0.999 Gold 0.2496 oz. AGW, 22.6 mm. **Ruler:** Elizabeth II **Subject:** Ned Kelly **Rev:** Multicolor gun slinger and steel helmet

| Date | Mintage | VF20 | XF40 | MS60 | MS63 | MS65 |
|---|---|---|---|---|---|---|
| 2010 P | 1,000 | PF65 600 | | | | |

**KM# 239 28 DOLLARS**
8.88 g., 0.9999 Gold 0.2855 oz. AGW, 19.94 mm. **Ruler:** Elizabeth II **Subject:** Chinese Blessing Sign

| Date | Mintage | VF20 | XF40 | MS60 | MS63 | MS65 |
|---|---|---|---|---|---|---|
| 2008 | — | PF65 580 | | | | |

**KM# 160 30 DOLLARS**
6.22 g., 0.999 Gold 0.1998 oz. AGW, 21.95 mm. **Ruler:** Elizabeth II **Rev:** Australian owl

| Date | Mintage | VF20 | XF40 | MS60 | MS63 | MS65 |
|---|---|---|---|---|---|---|
| 2005 | — | PF65 375 | | | | |
| 2006 | — | PF65 375 | | | | |
| 2007 | — | PF65 375 | | | | |

**KM# 234 30 DOLLARS**
6.26 g., 0.9999 Gold 0.2012 oz. AGW, 13.92 mm. **Ruler:** Elizabeth II **Subject:** Gold Bullion Coin

| Date | Mintage | VF20 | XF40 | MS60 | MS63 | MS65 |
|---|---|---|---|---|---|---|
| 2006 | — | PF65 385 | | | | |

**KM# 154 30 DOLLARS**
15.55 g., 0.999 Gold 0.4996 oz. AGW, 21.95 mm. **Ruler:** Elizabeth II **Rev:** Multicolor mouse and money bag

| Date | Mintage | VF20 | XF40 | MS60 | MS63 | MS65 |
|---|---|---|---|---|---|---|
| 2008 | — | — | — | — | — | 975 |

**KM# 167 30 DOLLARS**
6.22 g., 0.9995 Platinum 0.1999 oz. APW **Ruler:** Elizabeth II **Rev:** Horse galloping right

| Date | Mintage | VF20 | XF40 | MS60 | MS63 | MS65 |
|---|---|---|---|---|---|---|
| 2008 | — | PF65 500 | | | | |

**KM# 176 30 DOLLARS**
6.22 g., 0.999 Platinum 0.1998 oz. APW, 21.95 mm. **Ruler:** Elizabeth II **Subject:** Year of the Horse **Obv:** Head crowned right **Rev:** Horse galloping right

| Date | Mintage | VF20 | XF40 | MS60 | MS63 | MS65 |
|---|---|---|---|---|---|---|
| 2008 | — | PF65 400 | | | | |

**KM# 155 30 DOLLARS**
6.22 g., 0.999 Gold 0.1998 oz. AGW, 21.95 mm. **Ruler:** Elizabeth II **Rev:** Cow seated with fans above

| Date | Mintage | VF20 | XF40 | MS60 | MS63 | MS65 |
|---|---|---|---|---|---|---|
| 2009 | — | — | — | — | — | 375 |

**KM# 156 30 DOLLARS**
6.22 g., 0.999 Gold 0.1998 oz. AGW, 21.95 mm. **Ruler:** Elizabeth II **Rev:** Cow standing with success symbol

| Date | Mintage | VF20 | XF40 | MS60 | MS63 | MS65 |
|---|---|---|---|---|---|---|
| 2009 | — | — | — | — | — | 375 |

**KM# 157 30 DOLLARS**
6.22 g., 0.999 Gold 0.1998 oz. AGW, 21.95 mm. **Ruler:** Elizabeth II **Rev:** Cow standing next to money bag

| Date | Mintage | VF20 | XF40 | MS60 | MS63 | MS65 |
|---|---|---|---|---|---|---|
| 2009 | — | — | — | — | — | 375 |

**KM# 164 30 DOLLARS**
6.22 g., 0.999 Gold 0.1998 oz. AGW **Ruler:** Elizabeth II **Obv:** Head crowned right **Rev:** Horse running right

| Date | Mintage | VF20 | XF40 | MS60 | MS63 | MS65 |
|---|---|---|---|---|---|---|
| 2010 | — | PF65 400 | | | | |

### KM# 166 30 DOLLARS

6.22 g., 0.9995 Gold 0.1999 oz. AGW **Ruler:** Elizabeth II **Rev:** Horse galloping right

| Date | Mintage | VF20 | XF40 | MS60 | MS63 | MS65 |
|---|---|---|---|---|---|---|
| 2010 | — | PF65 400 | | | | |

### KM# 161 50 DOLLARS

15.55 g., 0.999 Gold 0.4996 oz. AGW, 30 mm. **Ruler:** Elizabeth II **Rev:** Australiam owl

| Date | Mintage | VF20 | XF40 | MS60 | MS63 | MS65 |
|---|---|---|---|---|---|---|
| 2005 | — | PF65 925 | | | | |
| 2006 | — | PF65 925 | | | | |
| 2007 | — | PF65 925 | | | | |

### KM# 235 50 DOLLARS

15.59 g., 0.9999 Gold 0.5012 oz. AGW, 13.92 mm. **Ruler:** Elizabeth II **Subject:** Gold Bullion Coin

| Date | Mintage | VF20 | XF40 | MS60 | MS63 | MS65 |
|---|---|---|---|---|---|---|
| 2006 | — | PF65 950 | | | | |

### KM# 69 100 DOLLARS

Gold **Ruler:** Elizabeth II **Obv:** Crowned head right **Rev:** Red 1963 Corvette Sting Ray

| Date | Mintage | VF20 | XF40 | MS60 | MS63 | MS65 |
|---|---|---|---|---|---|---|
| 2006 | 250 | PF65 1,850 | | | | |

# UGANDA

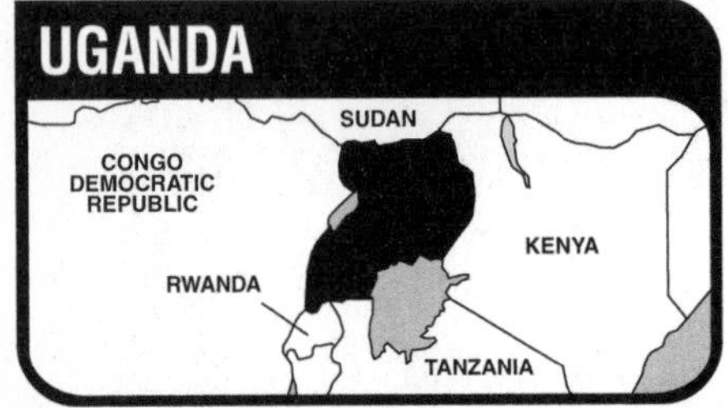


The Republic of Uganda, a former British protectorate located astride the equator in east-central Africa, has an area of 91,134 sq. mi. (236,040 sq. km.) and a population of *17 million. Capital: Kampala. Agriculture, including livestock, is the basis of the economy; there is some mining of copper, tin, gold and lead. Coffee, cotton, copper and tea are exported.

Uganda is a member of the Commonwealth of Nations. The president is Chief of State and Head of Government.

For earlier coinage refer to East Africa.

**MONETARY SYSTEM**

100 Cents = 1 Shilling

## REPUBLIC

## STANDARD COINAGE

### KM# 66 50 SHILLINGS

4.00 g., Nickel Plated Steel **Obv:** National arms **Rev:** Antelope head facing

| Date | Mintage | VF20 | XF40 | MS60 | MS63 | MS65 |
|---|---|---|---|---|---|---|
| 2003 | — | — | — | — | 1.00 | 1.25 |
| 2007 | — | — | — | — | 1.00 | 1.25 |

### KM# 67 100 SHILLINGS

7.00 g., Copper-Nickel, 26.9 mm. **Obv:** National arms **Rev:** African bull **Edge:** Reeded

| Date | Mintage | VF20 | XF40 | MS60 | MS63 | MS65 |
|---|---|---|---|---|---|---|
| 2003 | — | — | — | 1.00 | 1.50 | 1.75 |
| 2007 | — | — | — | 1.00 | 1.50 | 1.75 |
| 2008 | — | — | — | 1.00 | 1.50 | 1.75 |

### KM# 129 100 SHILLINGS

3.54 g., Stainless Steel, 23.98 mm. **Series:** Zodiac **Obv:** National arms **Rev:** Monkey with elf-like ears **Edge:** Plain

| Date | Mintage | VF20 | XF40 | MS60 | MS63 | MS65 |
|---|---|---|---|---|---|---|
| 2004 | — | — | — | 1.00 | 1.50 | 2.50 |

### KM# 130 100 SHILLINGS

Steel, 23 mm. **Rev:** Type I of five different monkeys

| Date | Mintage | VF20 | XF40 | MS60 | MS63 | MS65 |
|---|---|---|---|---|---|---|
| 2004 | — | — | — | 1.25 | 1.75 | 2.75 |

### KM# 131 100 SHILLINGS

Steel, 23 mm. **Rev:** Type II of five different monkeys

| Date | Mintage | VF20 | XF40 | MS60 | MS63 | MS65 |
|---|---|---|---|---|---|---|
| 2004 | — | — | — | 1.25 | 1.75 | 2.75 |

### KM# 132 100 SHILLINGS

Steel, 23 mm. **Rev:** Type III of five different monkeys

| Date | Mintage | VF20 | XF40 | MS60 | MS63 | MS65 |
|---|---|---|---|---|---|---|
| 2004 | — | — | — | 1.25 | 1.75 | 2.75 |

### KM# 133 100 SHILLINGS

Steel, 23 mm. **Rev:** Type IV of five different monkys

| Date | Mintage | VF20 | XF40 | MS60 | MS63 | MS65 |
|---|---|---|---|---|---|---|
| 2004 | — | — | — | 1.00 | 1.50 | 2.75 |

### KM# 134 100 SHILLINGS

Steel, 23 mm. **Rev:** Type V of five different monkeys

| Date | Mintage | VF20 | XF40 | MS60 | MS63 | MS65 |
|---|---|---|---|---|---|---|
| 2004 | — | — | — | 1.25 | 1.75 | 2.75 |

### KM# 135 100 SHILLINGS

3.54 g., Steel, 23.98 mm. **Series:** Zodiac **Obv:** National arms **Rev:** Ox **Edge:** Plain

| Date | Mintage | VF20 | XF40 | MS60 | MS63 | MS65 |
|---|---|---|---|---|---|---|
| 2004 | — | — | — | 1.00 | 1.50 | 2.50 |

### KM# 136 100 SHILLINGS

3.54 g., Steel, 23.98 mm. **Series:** Zodiac **Obv:** National arms **Rev:** Goat **Edge:** Plain

| Date | Mintage | VF20 | XF40 | MS60 | MS63 | MS65 |
|---|---|---|---|---|---|---|
| 2004 | — | — | — | 1.00 | 1.50 | 2.50 |

### KM# 137 100 SHILLINGS

3.54 g., Steel, 23.98 mm. **Series:** Zodiac **Obv:** National arms **Rev:** Horse **Edge:** Plain

| Date | Mintage | VF20 | XF40 | MS60 | MS63 | MS65 |
|---|---|---|---|---|---|---|
| 2004 | — | — | — | 1.00 | 1.50 | 2.50 |

### KM# 138 100 SHILLINGS

3.54 g., Steel, 23.98 mm. **Series:** Zodiac **Obv:** National arms **Rev:** Dragon **Edge:** Plain

| Date | Mintage | VF20 | XF40 | MS60 | MS63 | MS65 |
|---|---|---|---|---|---|---|
| 2004 | — | — | — | 1.00 | 1.50 | 2.50 |

### KM# 139 100 SHILLINGS

3.54 g., Steel, 23.98 mm. **Series:** Zodiac **Obv:** National arms **Rev:** Dog **Edge:** Plain

| Date | Mintage | VF20 | XF40 | MS60 | MS63 | MS65 |
|---|---|---|---|---|---|---|
| 2004 | — | — | — | 1.00 | 1.50 | 2.50 |

### KM# 140 100 SHILLINGS

3.54 g., Steel, 23.98 mm. **Series:** Zodiac **Obv:** National arms **Rev:** Tiger **Edge:** Plain

| Date | Mintage | VF20 | XF40 | MS60 | MS63 | MS65 |
|---|---|---|---|---|---|---|
| 2004 | — | — | — | 1.00 | 1.50 | 2.50 |

### KM# 141 100 SHILLINGS

3.54 g., Steel, 23.98 mm. **Series:** Zodiac **Obv:** National arms **Rev:** Snake **Edge:** Plain

| Date | Mintage | VF20 | XF40 | MS60 | MS63 | MS65 |
|---|---|---|---|---|---|---|
| 2004 | — | — | — | 1.00 | 1.50 | 2.50 |

### KM# 142 100 SHILLINGS

3.54 g., Steel, 23.98 mm. **Series:** Zodiac **Obv:** National arms **Rev:** Rooster **Edge:** Plain

| Date | Mintage | VF20 | XF40 | MS60 | MS63 | MS65 |
|---|---|---|---|---|---|---|
| 2004 | — | — | — | 1.00 | 1.50 | 2.50 |

### KM# 143 100 SHILLINGS

3.54 g., Steel, 23.98 mm. **Series:** Zodiac **Obv:** National arms **Rev:** Rabbit **Edge:** Plain

| Date | Mintage | VF20 | XF40 | MS60 | MS63 | MS65 |
|---|---|---|---|---|---|---|
| 2004 | — | — | — | 1.00 | 1.50 | 2.50 |

### KM# 144 100 SHILLINGS

3.54 g., Steel, 23.98 mm. **Series:** Zodiac **Obv:** National arms **Rev:** Rat **Edge:** Plain

| Date | Mintage | VF20 | XF40 | MS60 | MS63 | MS65 |
|---|---|---|---|---|---|---|
| 2004 | — | — | — | 1.00 | 1.50 | 2.50 |

### KM# 145 100 SHILLINGS

3.54 g., Steel, 23.98 mm. **Series:** Zodiac **Obv:** National arms **Rev:** Pig **Edge:** Plain

| Date | Mintage | VF20 | XF40 | MS60 | MS63 | MS65 |
|---|---|---|---|---|---|---|
| 2004 | — | — | — | 1.00 | 1.50 | 2.50 |

### KM# 188 100 SHILLINGS

3.53 g., Nickel Plated Steel, 24 mm. **Series:** Zodiac **Obv:** National arms **Obv. Legend:** BANK OF UGANDA **Rev:** Head of a rat **Rev. Legend:** BANK OF UGANDA **Edge:** Plain

| Date | Mintage | VF20 | XF40 | MS60 | MS63 | MS65 |
|---|---|---|---|---|---|---|
| 2004 | — | — | — | 1.25 | 1.75 | 2.75 |

### KM# 189 100 SHILLINGS

3.53 g., Nickel Plated Steel, 24 mm. **Series:** Zodiac **Obv:** National arms **Obv. Legend:** BANK OF UGANDA **Rev:** Head of an ox **Rev. Legend:** BANK OF UGANDA **Edge:** Plain

| Date | Mintage | VF20 | XF40 | MS60 | MS63 | MS65 |
|---|---|---|---|---|---|---|
| 2004 | — | — | — | 1.25 | 1.75 | 2.75 |

### KM# 190 100 SHILLINGS

3.53 g., Nickel Plated Steel, 24 mm. **Series:** Zodiac **Obv:** National arms **Obv. Legend:** BANK OF UGANDA **Rev:** Head of a tiger **Rev. Legend:** BANK OF UGANDA **Edge:** Plain

| Date | Mintage | VF20 | XF40 | MS60 | MS63 | MS65 |
|---|---|---|---|---|---|---|
| 2004 | — | — | — | 1.25 | 1.75 | 2.75 |

### KM# 191 100 SHILLINGS

3.53 g., Nickel Plated Steel, 24 mm. **Series:** Zodiac **Obv:** National arms **Obv. Legend:** BANK OF UGANDA **Rev:** Head of a rabbit **Rev. Legend:** BANK OF UGANDA **Edge:** Plain

| Date | Mintage | VF20 | XF40 | MS60 | MS63 | MS65 |
|---|---|---|---|---|---|---|
| 2004 | — | — | — | 1.25 | 1.75 | 2.75 |

### KM# 192 100 SHILLINGS

3.53 g., Nickel Plated Steel, 24 mm. **Series:** Zodiac **Obv:** National arms **Obv. Legend:** BANK OF UGANDA **Rev:** Head of a dragon **Rev. Legend:** BANK OF UGANDA **Edge:** Plain

| Date | Mintage | VF20 | XF40 | MS60 | MS63 | MS65 |
|---|---|---|---|---|---|---|
| 2004 | — | — | — | 1.25 | 1.75 | 2.75 |

### KM# 193 100 SHILLINGS

3.53 g., Nickel Plated Steel, 24 mm. **Series:** Zodiac **Obv:** National arms **Obv. Legend:** BANK OF UGANDA **Rev:** Head and hood of Cobra snake **Rev. Legend:** BANK OF UGANDA **Edge:** Plain

| Date | Mintage | VF20 | XF40 | MS60 | MS63 | MS65 |
|---|---|---|---|---|---|---|
| 2004 | — | — | — | 1.25 | 1.75 | 2.75 |

### KM# 194 100 SHILLINGS

3.53 g., Nickel Plated Steel, 24 mm. **Series:** Zodiac **Obv:** National arms **Obv. Legend:** BANK OF UGANDA **Rev:** Head of a horse **Rev. Legend:** BANK OF UGANDA **Edge:** Plain

| Date | Mintage | VF20 | XF40 | MS60 | MS63 | MS65 |
|---|---|---|---|---|---|---|
| 2004 | — | — | — | 1.25 | 1.75 | 2.75 |

### KM# 195 100 SHILLINGS

3.53 g., Nickel Plated Steel, 24 mm. **Series:** Zodiac **Obv:** National arms **Obv. Legend:** BANK OF UGANDA **Rev:** Head of a goat **Rev. Legend:** BANK OF UGANDA **Edge:** Plain

| Date | Mintage | VF20 | XF40 | MS60 | MS63 | MS65 |
|---|---|---|---|---|---|---|
| 2004 | — | — | — | 1.25 | 1.75 | 2.75 |

### KM# 196 100 SHILLINGS

3.53 g., Nickel Plated Steel, 24 mm. **Series:** Zodiac **Obv:** National arms **Obv. Legend:** BANK OF UGANDA **Rev:** Head of a monkey **Rev. Legend:** BANK OF UGANDA **Edge:** Plain

| Date | Mintage | VF20 | XF40 | MS60 | MS63 | MS65 |
|---|---|---|---|---|---|---|
| 2004 | — | — | — | 1.25 | 1.75 | 2.75 |

### KM# 197 100 SHILLINGS

3.53 g., Nickel Plated Steel, 24 mm. **Series:** Zodiac **Obv:** National arms **Obv. Legend:** BANK OF UGANDA **Rev:** Forepart of a rooster **Rev. Legend:** BANK OF UGANDA **Edge:** Plain

| Date | Mintage | VF20 | XF40 | MS60 | MS63 | MS65 |
|---|---|---|---|---|---|---|
| 2004 | — | — | — | 1.25 | 1.75 | 2.75 |

### KM# 198 100 SHILLINGS

3.53 g., Nickel Plated Steel, 24 mm. **Series:** Zodiac **Obv:** National arms **Obv. Legend:** BANK OF UGANDA **Rev:** Head of a dog **Rev. Legend:** BANK OF UGANDA **Edge:** Plain

| Date | Mintage | VF20 | XF40 | MS60 | MS63 | MS65 |
|---|---|---|---|---|---|---|
| 2004 | — | — | — | 1.25 | 1.75 | 2.75 |

### KM# 199 100 SHILLINGS

3.53 g., Nickel Plated Steel, 24 mm. **Series:** Zodiac **Obv:** National arms **Obv. Legend:** BANK OF UGANDA **Rev:** Head of a pig **Rev. Legend:** BANK OF UGANDA **Edge:** Plain

| Date | Mintage | VF20 | XF40 | MS60 | MS63 | MS65 |
|---|---|---|---|---|---|---|
| 2004 | — | — | — | 1.25 | 1.75 | 2.75 |

### KM# 200 100 SHILLINGS

Copper-Nickel **Subject:** Year of the Monkey **Obv. Legend:** BANK OF UGANDA **Rev:** Monkey swingging right

| Date | Mintage | VF20 | XF40 | MS60 | MS63 | MS65 |
|---|---|---|---|---|---|---|
| 2004 | — | — | — | 1.50 | 2.00 | 3.00 |

**KM# 201 100 SHILLINGS**
Copper-Nickel **Subject:** Year of the Monkey **Obv. Legend:** BANK OF UGANDA

| Date | Mintage | VF20 | XF40 | MS60 | MS63 | MS65 |
|---|---|---|---|---|---|---|
| 2004 | — | — | — | 1.50 | 2.00 | 3.00 |

**KM# 202 100 SHILLINGS**
Copper-Nickel **Subject:** Year of the Monkey **Obv. Legend:** BANK OF UGANDA **Rev:** Diana Monkey right on all fours

| Date | Mintage | VF20 | XF40 | MS60 | MS63 | MS65 |
|---|---|---|---|---|---|---|
| 2004 | — | — | — | 1.50 | 2.00 | 3.00 |

**KM# 203 100 SHILLINGS**
Copper-Nickel **Subject:** Year of the Monkey **Obv. Legend:** BANK OF UGANDA **Rev:** Monkey seated left

| Date | Mintage | VF20 | XF40 | MS60 | MS63 | MS65 |
|---|---|---|---|---|---|---|
| 2004 | — | — | — | 1.50 | 2.00 | 3.00 |

**KM# 204 100 SHILLINGS**
Copper-Nickel **Subject:** Year of the Monkey **Obv. Legend:** BANK OF UGANDA **Rev:** Monkeys seated right, looking left over his shoulder

| Date | Mintage | VF20 | XF40 | MS60 | MS63 | MS65 |
|---|---|---|---|---|---|---|
| 2004 | — | — | — | 1.50 | 2.00 | 3.00 |

**KM# 67a 100 SHILLINGS**
7.00 g., Nickel Plated Steel, 26.9 mm. **Obv:** National arms **Rev:** African bull **Edge:** Reeded

| Date | Mintage | VF20 | XF40 | MS60 | MS63 | MS65 |
|---|---|---|---|---|---|---|
| 2007 | — | — | — | 1.00 | 1.50 | 1.75 |
| 2008 | — | — | — | 1.00 | 1.50 | 1.75 |

**KM# 68 200 SHILLINGS**
8.05 g., Copper-Nickel, 24.9 mm. **Obv:** National arms **Rev:** Cichlid fish above value and date **Edge:** Plain

| Date | Mintage | VF20 | XF40 | MS60 | MS63 | MS65 |
|---|---|---|---|---|---|---|
| 2003 | — | — | — | 1.50 | 2.00 | 3.00 |
| 2008 | — | — | — | 1.50 | 2.00 | 3.00 |

**KM# 68a 200 SHILLINGS**
8.05 g., Nickel Plated Steel, 24.9 mm. **Obv:** National arms **Rev:** Cichlid fish above value and date

| Date | Mintage | VF20 | XF40 | MS60 | MS63 | MS65 |
|---|---|---|---|---|---|---|
| 2007 | — | — | — | 1.50 | 2.00 | 3.00 |
| 2008 | — | — | — | 1.50 | 2.00 | 3.00 |

**KM# 69 500 SHILLINGS**
9.00 g., Nickel-Brass, 23.5 mm. **Obv:** National arms **Rev:** East African crowned crane head left **Edge:** Reeded

| Date | Mintage | VF20 | XF40 | MS60 | MS63 | MS65 |
|---|---|---|---|---|---|---|
| 2003 | — | — | — | 1.75 | 2.50 | 4.00 |
| 2008 | — | — | — | 1.75 | 2.50 | 4.00 |

**KM# 77 1000 SHILLINGS**
19.84 g., Copper-Nickel, 38.6 mm. **Subject:** Colourful Big Five of Africa **Obv:** Arms with supporters **Rev:** Multicolor rhinocerous within stamp design in front of outlined African map **Edge:** Reeded

| Date | Mintage | VF20 | XF40 | MS60 | MS63 | MS65 |
|---|---|---|---|---|---|---|
| 2001 | — | **PF65** 17.50 | | | | |

**KM# 78 1000 SHILLINGS**
19.84 g., Copper-Nickel, 38.6 mm. **Subject:** Colourful Big Five of Africa **Obv:** Arms with supporters **Rev:** Multicolor lion within stamp design in front of outlined African map **Edge:** Reeded

| Date | Mintage | VF20 | XF40 | MS60 | MS63 | MS65 |
|---|---|---|---|---|---|---|
| 2001 | — | **PF65** 17.50 | | | | |

**KM# 79 1000 SHILLINGS**
19.84 g., Copper-Nickel, 38.6 mm. **Subject:** Coulourful Big Five of Africa **Obv:** Arms with supporters **Rev:** Multicolor water buffalo within stamp design in front of outlined African map **Edge:** Reeded

| Date | Mintage | VF20 | XF40 | MS60 | MS63 | MS65 |
|---|---|---|---|---|---|---|
| 2001 | — | **PF65** 17.50 | | | | |

**KM# 80 1000 SHILLINGS**
19.84 g., Copper-Nickel, 38.6 mm. **Subject:** Colourful Big Five of Africa **Obv:** Arms with supporters **Rev:** Multicolor leopard within stamp design in front of outlined map **Edge:** Reeded

| Date | Mintage | VF20 | XF40 | MS60 | MS63 | MS65 |
|---|---|---|---|---|---|---|
| 2001 | — | **PF65** 17.50 | | | | |

**KM# 81 1000 SHILLINGS**
19.84 g., Copper-Nickel, 38.6 mm. **Subject:** Colourful Big Five of Africa **Obv:** Arms with supporters **Rev:** Multicolor elephant within stamp design in front of outlined map **Edge:** Reeded

| Date | Mintage | VF20 | XF40 | MS60 | MS63 | MS65 |
|---|---|---|---|---|---|---|
| 2001 | — | **PF65** 17.50 | | | | |

**KM# 173 1000 SHILLINGS**
Silver **Subject:** XVII World Football Championship Games - Korea and Japan **Obv. Legend:** BANK OF UGANDA **Rev:** Football - gilt

| Date | Mintage | VF20 | XF40 | MS60 | MS63 | MS65 |
|---|---|---|---|---|---|---|
| 2001 | — | **PF63** 23.00 | **PF65** 27.00 | | | |

**KM# 82 1000 SHILLINGS**
24.83 g., 0.999 Silver 0.7975 oz. ASW, 38.6 mm. **Subject:** World of Football **Obv:** Arms with supporters **Rev:** Soccer ball globe **Edge:** Reeded

| Date | Mintage | VF20 | XF40 | MS60 | MS63 | MS65 |
|---|---|---|---|---|---|---|
| 2002 | — | **PF63** 30.00 | **PF65** 35.00 | | | |

**KM# 83 1000 SHILLINGS**
24.83 g., 0.999 Silver 0.7975 oz. ASW, 38.6 mm. **Subject:** World of Football **Obv:** Arms with supporters **Rev:** Soccer ball in net **Edge:** Reeded

| Date | Mintage | VF20 | XF40 | MS60 | MS63 | MS65 |
|---|---|---|---|---|---|---|
| 2002 | — | **PF65** 27.50 | | | | |

**KM# 84 1000 SHILLINGS**
24.83 g., 0.999 Silver 0.7975 oz. ASW, 38.6 mm. **Subject:** World of Football **Obv:** Arms with supporters **Rev:** Goalie catching ball, red kicker insert at right **Edge:** Reeded

| Date | Mintage | VF20 | XF40 | MS60 | MS63 | MS65 |
|---|---|---|---|---|---|---|
| 2002 | — | **PF65** 27.50 | | | | |

**KM# 85 1000 SHILLINGS**
24.83 g., 0.999 Silver 0.7975 oz. ASW, 38.6 mm. **Subject:** World of Football **Obv:** Arms with supporters **Rev:** Two players going after the ball, red runner insert at left **Edge:** Reeded

| Date | Mintage | VF20 | XF40 | MS60 | MS63 | MS65 |
|---|---|---|---|---|---|---|
| 2002 | — | **PF65** 27.50 | | | | |

**KM# 86 1000 SHILLINGS**
24.83 g., 0.999 Silver 0.7975 oz. ASW, 38.6 mm. **Subject:** World of Football **Obv:** Arms with supporters **Rev:** Player kicking ball, blue kicker insert at right **Edge:** Reeded

| Date | Mintage | VF20 | XF40 | MS60 | MS63 | MS65 |
|---|---|---|---|---|---|---|
| 2002 | — | PF65 27.50 | | | | |

**KM# 101 1000 SHILLINGS**
29.44 g., Silver Plated Bronze (Specific gravity 8.8675), 38.5 mm. **Series:** Gorillas of Africa **Obv:** National arms **Rev:** Seated gorilla **Edge:** Reeded

| Date | Mintage | VF20 | XF40 | MS60 | MS63 | MS65 |
|---|---|---|---|---|---|---|
| 2002 | — | PF65 6.50 | | | | |
| 2003 | — | PF65 6.00 | | | | |

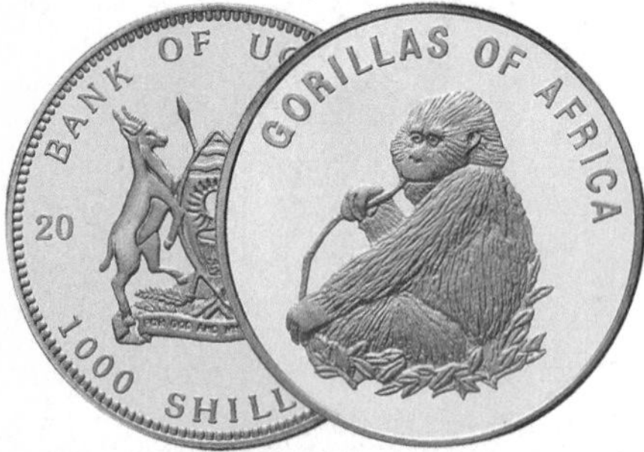


**KM# 102 1000 SHILLINGS**
29.44 g., Silver Plated Bronze (Specific gravity 8.8675), 38.5 mm. **Series:** Gorillas of Africa **Obv:** National arms **Rev:** Gorilla eating **Edge:** Reeded

| Date | Mintage | VF20 | XF40 | MS60 | MS63 | MS65 |
|---|---|---|---|---|---|---|
| 2002 | — | PF65 6.50 | | | | |
| 2003 | — | PF65 6.00 | | | | |

**KM# 103 1000 SHILLINGS**
29.44 g., Silver Plated Bronze (Specific gravity 8.8675), 38.5 mm. **Series:** Gorillas of Africa **Obv:** National arms **Rev:** Gorilla on all fours **Edge:** Reeded

| Date | Mintage | VF20 | XF40 | MS60 | MS63 | MS65 |
|---|---|---|---|---|---|---|
| 2002 | — | PF65 6.50 | | | | |
| 2003 | — | PF65 6.00 | | | | |

**KM# 104 1000 SHILLINGS**
29.44 g., Silver Plated Bronze (Specific gravity 8.8675), 38.5 mm. **Series:** Gorillas of Africa **Obv:** National arms **Rev:** Gorilla female with infant **Edge:** Reeded

| Date | Mintage | VF20 | XF40 | MS60 | MS63 | MS65 |
|---|---|---|---|---|---|---|
| 2002 | — | PF65 6.50 | | | | |
| 2003 | — | PF65 10.00 | | | | |

**KM# 106 1000 SHILLINGS**
29.16 g., Silver Plated Bronze (Specific gravity 8.8096), 38.6 mm. **Subject:** Marine Life **Obv:** Arms with supporters **Rev:** Multicolor sea horses **Edge:** Reeded

| Date | Mintage | VF20 | XF40 | MS60 | MS63 | MS65 |
|---|---|---|---|---|---|---|
| 2002 | — | PF65 10.00 | | | | |

**KM# 107 1000 SHILLINGS**
29.16 g., Silver Plated Bronze (Specific gravity 8.8096), 38.6 mm. **Subject:** Marine Life **Obv:** Arms with supporters **Rev:** Multicolor Hammerhead sharks **Edge:** Reeded

| Date | Mintage | VF20 | XF40 | MS60 | MS63 | MS65 |
|---|---|---|---|---|---|---|
| 2002 | — | PF65 10.00 | | | | |

**KM# 108 1000 SHILLINGS**
29.16 g., Silver Plated Bronze (Specific gravity 8.8096), 38.6 mm. **Subject:** Marine Life **Obv:** Arms with supporters **Rev:** Multicolor Stingray **Edge:** Reeded

| Date | Mintage | VF20 | XF40 | MS60 | MS63 | MS65 |
|---|---|---|---|---|---|---|
| 2002 | — | PF65 10.00 | | | | |

**KM# 109 1000 SHILLINGS**
29.16 g., Silver Plated Bronze (Specific gravity 8.8096), 38.6 mm. **Subject:** Marine Life **Obv:** Arms with supporters **Rev:** Multicolor Seal **Edge:** Reeded

| Date | Mintage | VF20 | XF40 | MS60 | MS63 | MS65 |
|---|---|---|---|---|---|---|
| 2002 | — | PF65 10.00 | | | | |

**KM# 110 1000 SHILLINGS**
29.16 g., Silver Plated Bronze (Specific gravity 8.8096), 38.6 mm. **Subject:** Marine Life **Obv:** Arms with supporters **Rev:** Multicolor sea turtle **Edge:** Reeded

| Date | Mintage | VF20 | XF40 | MS60 | MS63 | MS65 |
|---|---|---|---|---|---|---|
| 2002 | — | PF65 10.00 | | | | |

**KM# 111 1000 SHILLINGS**
29.16 g., Silver Plated Bronze (Specific gravity 8.8096), 38.6 mm. **Subject:** Marine Life **Obv:** Arms with supporters **Rev:** Multicolor dolphins **Edge:** Reeded

| Date | Mintage | VF20 | XF40 | MS60 | MS63 | MS65 |
|---|---|---|---|---|---|---|
| 2002 | — | PF65 10.00 | | | | |

**KM# 112 1000 SHILLINGS**
29.16 g., Silver Plated Bronze (Specific gravity 8.8096), 38.6 mm. **Subject:** Marine Life **Obv:** Arms with supporters **Rev:** Multicolor octopus **Edge:** Reeded

| Date | Mintage | VF20 | XF40 | MS60 | MS63 | MS65 |
|---|---|---|---|---|---|---|
| 2002 | — | PF65 10.00 | | | | |

**KM# 113 1000 SHILLINGS**
29.16 g., Silver Plated Bronze (Specific gravity 8.8096), 38.6 mm. **Subject:** Marine Life **Obv:** Arms with supporters **Rev:** Multicolor red fish **Edge:** Reeded

| Date | Mintage | VF20 | XF40 | MS60 | MS63 | MS65 |
|---|---|---|---|---|---|---|
| 2002 | — | PF65 10.00 | | | | |

**KM# 114 1000 SHILLINGS**
29.16 g., Silver Plated Bronze (Specific gravity 8.8096), 38.6 mm. **Subject:** Marine Life **Obv:** Arms with supporters **Rev:** Multicolor black fish with white dots **Edge:** Reeded

| Date | Mintage | VF20 | XF40 | MS60 | MS63 | MS65 |
|---|---|---|---|---|---|---|
| 2002 | — | PF65 10.00 | | | | |

**KM# 115 1000 SHILLINGS**
29.16 g., Silver Plated Bronze (Specific gravity 8.8096), 38.6 mm. **Subject:** Marine Life **Obv:** Arms with supporters **Rev:** Multicolor yellow and black striped fish **Edge:** Reeded

| Date | Mintage | VF20 | XF40 | MS60 | MS63 | MS65 |
|---|---|---|---|---|---|---|
| 2002 | — | PF65 10.00 | | | | |

**KM# 105 1000 SHILLINGS**
29.20 g., Silver Plated Bronze (Specific gravity 9.0123), 38.6 mm. **Subject:** Pope John Paul II **Obv:** Arms with supporters **Rev:** Pope saying mass, design of Zambian 1000 Kwacha KM-160 **Edge:** Reeded **Note:** Muling error

| Date | Mintage | VF20 | XF40 | MS60 | MS63 | MS65 |
|---|---|---|---|---|---|---|
| 2003 | — | PF63 300 | PF65 325 | | | |

**KM# 240 1000 SHILLINGS**
Silver Gilt, 38.6 mm. **Obv:** Arms **Rev:** Pope John Paul II bust facing

| Date | Mintage | VF20 | XF40 | MS60 | MS63 | MS65 |
|---|---|---|---|---|---|---|
| 2003 | — | PF63 75.00 | PF65 85.00 | | | |

**KM# 216 1000 SHILLINGS**
Bronze **Subject:** Christmas **Obv. Legend:** BANK OF UGANDA **Rev:** Peace on Earth

| Date | Mintage | VF20 | XF40 | MS60 | MS63 | MS65 |
|---|---|---|---|---|---|---|
| 2004 | 500 | — | — | — | — | 50.00 |

**KM# 278 1000 SHILLINGS**
10.25 g., Bi-Metallic Brass center in Copper-Nickel ring, 27 mm. **Subject:** Independence, 50th Anniversary **Obv:** Coat of Arms **Rev:** Crested crane **Edge:** Reeded **Edge Lettering:** Incised in middle with: BOU 1000

| Date | Mintage | VF20 | XF40 | MS60 | MS63 | MS65 |
|---|---|---|---|---|---|---|
| 2012 | — | — | — | — | 4.50 | 6.00 |

**KM# 75 2000 SHILLINGS**
49.90 g., 0.999 Silver 1.6027 oz. ASW, 50 mm. **Subject:** Illusion: "Spirit of the Mountain **Obv:** Crowned head right divides date above arms with supporters **Rev:** Landscape and tree that looks like a male portrait **Edge:** Reeded

| Date | Mintage | VF20 | XF40 | MS60 | MS63 | MS65 |
|---|---|---|---|---|---|---|
| 2001 | — | PF63 80.00 | PF65 90.00 | | | |

**KM# 121 2000 SHILLINGS**
25.00 g., 0.925 Silver 0.7435 oz. ASW, 38.6 mm. **Subject:** Queen Elizabeth's 75th Birthday **Obv:** Arms with supporters above crowned head right **Rev:** Queen accepting flowers from children **Edge:** Reeded

| Date | Mintage | VF20 | XF40 | MS60 | MS63 | MS65 |
|---|---|---|---|---|---|---|
| 2001 | 2,000 | PF63 32.00 | PF65 37.00 | | | |

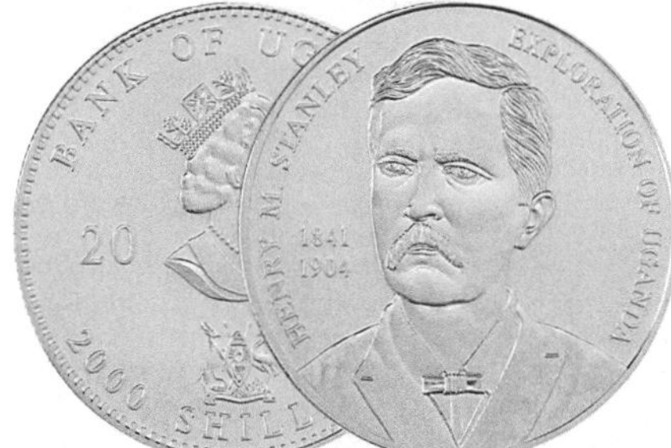


**KM# 100 2000 SHILLINGS**
31.40 g., 0.999 Silver 1.0085 oz. ASW, 38.8 mm. **Obv:** Crowned head right divides date above arms with supporters **Rev:** Bust of Henry M. Stanley facing **Edge:** Reeded

| Date | Mintage | VF20 | XF40 | MS60 | MS63 | MS65 |
|---|---|---|---|---|---|---|
| 2002 | — | — | — | — | 32.00 | 37.00 |

**KM# 175 2000 SHILLINGS**
15.55 g., 0.999 Silver 0.4994 oz. ASW **Series:** Famous Places in China **Subject:** Yugan Garden - Shanghai **Obv:** Two dragons **Obv. Legend:** BANK OF UGANDA

| Date | Mintage | VF20 | XF40 | MS60 | MS63 | MS65 |
|---|---|---|---|---|---|---|
| 2003 | 3,000 | PF63 35.00 | PF65 40.00 | | | |

**KM# 176 2000 SHILLINGS**
15.55 g., 0.999 Silver 0.4994 oz. ASW **Series:** Famous Places in China **Subject:** Tiger Hill Pagoda - Jiangsu **Obv:** Two dragons **Obv. Legend:** BANK OF UGANDA

| Date | Mintage | VF20 | XF40 | MS60 | MS63 | MS65 |
|---|---|---|---|---|---|---|
| 2003 | 3,000 | PF63 35.00 | PF65 40.00 | | | |

**KM# 177 2000 SHILLINGS**
15.55 g., 0.999 Silver 0.4994 oz. ASW **Series:** Famous Places in China **Subject:** Mount Huangshan - Anhwei **Obv:** Two dragons **Obv. Legend:** BANK OF UGANDA

| Date | Mintage | VF20 | XF40 | MS60 | MS63 | MS65 |
|---|---|---|---|---|---|---|
| 2003 | 3,000 | PF63 35.00 | PF65 40.00 | | | |

**KM# 178 2000 SHILLINGS**
15.55 g., 0.999 Silver 0.4994 oz. ASW **Series:** Famous Places in China **Subject:** Zhangjiajie - Hunan **Obv:** Two dragons **Obv. Legend:** BANK OF UGANDA

| Date | Mintage | VF20 | XF40 | MS60 | MS63 | MS65 |
|---|---|---|---|---|---|---|
| 2003 | 3,000 | PF63 35.00 | PF65 40.00 | | | |

**KM# 179 2000 SHILLINGS**
15.55 g., 0.999 Silver 0.4994 oz. ASW **Series:** Famous Places in China **Subject:** Stone Forest - Yunnan **Obv:** Two dragons **Obv. Legend:** BANK OF UGANDA

| Date | Mintage | VF20 | XF40 | MS60 | MS63 | MS65 |
|---|---|---|---|---|---|---|
| 2003 | 3,000 | PF63 35.00 | PF65 40.00 | | | |

**KM# 180 2000 SHILLINGS**
15.55 g., 0.999 Silver 0.4994 oz. ASW **Series:** Famous Places in China **Subject:** Potala Palace - Lhasa, Tibet **Obv:** Two dragons **Obv. Legend:** BANK OF UGANDA

| Date | Mintage | VF20 | XF40 | MS60 | MS63 | MS65 |
|---|---|---|---|---|---|---|
| 2003 | 3,000 | PF63 35.00 | PF65 40.00 | | | |

**KM# 181 2000 SHILLINGS**
15.55 g., 0.999 Silver 0.4994 oz. ASW **Series:** Famous Places inChina **Subject:** Yangtse River Gorges **Obv:** Two dragons **Obv. Legend:** BANK OF UGANDA

| Date | Mintage | VF20 | XF40 | MS60 | MS63 | MS65 |
|---|---|---|---|---|---|---|
| 2003 | 3,000 | PF63 35.00 | PF65 40.00 | | | |

**KM# 182 2000 SHILLINGS**
31.10 g., 0.999 Silver 0.9989 oz. ASW **Series:** Chinese symbolism **Subject:** Harmony **Obv. Legend:** BANK OF UGANDA **Rev:** Dragon and phoenix

| Date | Mintage | VF20 | XF40 | MS60 | MS63 | MS65 |
|---|---|---|---|---|---|---|
| 2003 | 3,000 | PF63 60.00 | PF65 65.00 | | | |

**KM# 183 2000 SHILLINGS**
31.10 g., 0.999 Silver 0.9989 oz. ASW **Series:** Chinese symbolism **Subject:** Happiness **Obv. Legend:** BANK OF UGANDA **Rev:** Unicorn

| Date | Mintage | VF20 | XF40 | MS60 | MS63 | MS65 |
|---|---|---|---|---|---|---|
| 2003 | 3,000 | PF63 60.00 | PF65 65.00 | | | |

**KM# 184 2000 SHILLINGS**
31.10 g., 0.999 Silver 0.9989 oz. ASW **Series:** Chinese symbolism **Subject:** Health and long life **Obv. Legend:** BANK OF UGANDA **Rev:** Two cranes

| Date | Mintage | VF20 | XF40 | MS60 | MS63 | MS65 |
|---|---|---|---|---|---|---|
| 2003 | 3,000 | PF63 60.00 | PF65 65.00 | | | |

**KM# 185 2000 SHILLINGS**
31.10 g., 0.999 Silver 0.9989 oz. ASW **Series:** Chinese symbolism **Subject:** Success **Obv. Legend:** BANK OF UGANDA **Rev:** Carp

| Date | Mintage | VF20 | XF40 | MS60 | MS63 | MS65 |
|---|---|---|---|---|---|---|
| 2003 | 3,000 | PF63 60.00 | PF65 65.00 | | | |

**KM# 186 2000 SHILLINGS**
31.10 g., 0.999 Silver 0.9989 oz. ASW **Series:** Chinese symbolism **Subject:** Wealth **Obv. Legend:** BANK OF UGANDA **Rev:** Toad

| Date | Mintage | VF20 | XF40 | MS60 | MS63 | MS65 |
|---|---|---|---|---|---|---|
| 2003 | 3,000 | PF63 60.00 | PF65 65.00 | | | |

**KM# 187 2000 SHILLINGS**
4.00 g., 0.9999 Gold 0.1286 oz. AGW **Series:** Guanyin **Subject:** Fulun **Obv:** Lotus blossom **Obv. Legend:** BANK OF UGANDA

| Date | Mintage | VF20 | XF40 | MS60 | MS63 | MS65 |
|---|---|---|---|---|---|---|
| 2003 | — | PF63 245 | PF65 265 | | | |

**KM# 205 2000 SHILLINGS**
Silver **Subject:** XXVIII Summer Olympics - Athens 2004 **Obv. Legend:** BANK OF UGANDA **Rev:** Sprinter

| Date | Mintage | VF20 | XF40 | MS60 | MS63 | MS65 |
|---|---|---|---|---|---|---|
| 2003 | 500 | PF63 60.00 | PF65 65.00 | | | |

**KM# 206 2000 SHILLINGS**
31.10 g., 0.999 Silver 0.9989 oz. ASW **Series:** Chinese symbolic floral New Year paintings **Obv. Legend:** BANK OF UGANDA **Rev:** Carp and Lotus blossom - multicolor

| Date | Mintage | VF20 | XF40 | MS60 | MS63 | MS65 |
|---|---|---|---|---|---|---|
| 2004 | 2,000 | PF63 60.00 | PF65 65.00 | | | |

**KM# 207 2000 SHILLINGS**
31.10 g., 0.999 Silver 0.9989 oz. ASW **Series:** Chinese symbolic floral New Year paintings **Obv. Legend:** BANK OF UGANDA **Rev:** Deer - multicolor

| Date | Mintage | VF20 | XF40 | MS60 | MS63 | MS65 |
|---|---|---|---|---|---|---|
| 2004 | 2,000 | PF63 60.00 | PF65 65.00 | | | |

**KM# 208 2000 SHILLINGS**
31.10 g., 0.999 Silver 0.9989 oz. ASW **Series:** Chinese symbolic floral New Year paintings **Subject:** Abundance **Obv. Legend:** BANK OF UGANDA **Rev:** Fruit - multicolor

| Date | Mintage | VF20 | XF40 | MS60 | MS63 | MS65 |
|---|---|---|---|---|---|---|
| 2004 | 2,000 | PF63 60.00 | PF65 65.00 | | | |

**KM# 209 2000 SHILLINGS**
31.10 g., 0.999 Silver 0.9989 oz. ASW **Series:** Chinese symbolic floral New Year paintings **Subject:** Peace and prosperity **Obv. Legend:** BANK OF UGANDA **Rev:** Multicolor

| Date | Mintage | VF20 | XF40 | MS60 | MS63 | MS65 |
|---|---|---|---|---|---|---|
| 2004 | 2,000 | PF63 60.00 | PF65 65.00 | | | |

**KM# 210 2000 SHILLINGS**
31.10 g., 0.999 Silver 0.9989 oz. ASW **Series:** Chinese symbolic floral New Year paintings **Subject:** Happiness **Obv. Legend:** BANK OF UGANDA **Rev:** Multicolor

| Date | Mintage | VF20 | XF40 | MS60 | MS63 | MS65 |
|---|---|---|---|---|---|---|
| 2004 | 2,000 | PF63 60.00 | PF65 65.00 | | | |

**KM# 211 2000 SHILLINGS**
31.10 g., 0.999 Silver 0.9989 oz. ASW **Series:** Chinese Dieties **Subject:** Happiness **Obv. Legend:** BANK OF UGANDA **Rev:** Fú - multicolor

| Date | Mintage | VF20 | XF40 | MS60 | MS63 | MS65 |
|---|---|---|---|---|---|---|
| 2004 | 2,000 | PF63 60.00 | PF65 65.00 | | | |

**KM# 212 2000 SHILLINGS**
31.10 g., 0.999 Silver 0.9989 oz. ASW **Series:** Chinese Deities **Subject:** Prosperity **Obv. Legend:** BANK OF UGANDA **Rev:** Lù - multicolor

| Date | Mintage | VF20 | XF40 | MS60 | MS63 | MS65 |
|---|---|---|---|---|---|---|
| 2004 | 2,000 | PF63 60.00 | PF65 65.00 | | | |

**KM# 213 2000 SHILLINGS**
31.10 g., 0.999 Silver 0.9989 oz. ASW **Series:** Chinese Dieties **Subject:** Health and Long Life **Obv. Legend:** BANK OF UGANDA **Rev:** Shòu - multicolor

| Date | Mintage | VF20 | XF40 | MS60 | MS63 | MS65 |
|---|---|---|---|---|---|---|
| 2004 | 2,000 | PF63 60.00 | PF65 65.00 | | | |

**KM# 217 2000 SHILLINGS**
31.10 g., 0.999 Silver 0.9989 oz. ASW **Obv:** Lotus blossom **Obv. Legend:** BANK OF UGANDA **Rev:** Guanyin - multicolor

| Date | Mintage | VF20 | XF40 | MS60 | MS63 | MS65 |
|---|---|---|---|---|---|---|
| 2005 | 2,000 | PF63 75.00 | PF65 85.00 | | | |

**KM# 221 2000 SHILLINGS**
Silver Plated Bronze **Series:** XIX World Football Championship - South Africa 2010 **Obv:** National arms **Obv. Legend:** BANK OF UGANDA **Rev:** Player about to kick

| Date | Mintage | VF20 | XF40 | MS60 | MS63 | MS65 |
|---|---|---|---|---|---|---|
| 2005 | 10,000 | PF63 15.00 | PF65 17.00 | | | |

**KM# 222 2000 SHILLINGS**
Silver Plated Bronze **Series:** XIX World Football Championship - South Afrika 2010 **Obv:** National arms **Obv. Legend:** BANK OF UGANDA **Rev:** Ball in net

| Date | Mintage | VF20 | XF40 | MS60 | MS63 | MS65 |
|---|---|---|---|---|---|---|
| 2005 | 10,000 | PF63 15.00 | PF65 17.00 | | | |

**KM# 223 2000 SHILLINGS**
Silver Plated Bronze **Series:** XIX World Football Championship - South Afrika 2010 **Obv:** National arms **Obv. Legend:** BANK OF UGANDA **Rev:** Player, map of Afrika

| Date | Mintage | VF20 | XF40 | MS60 | MS63 | MS65 |
|---|---|---|---|---|---|---|
| 2005 | 10,000 | PF63 15.00 | PF65 17.00 | | | |

**KM# 224 2000 SHILLINGS**
Silver Plated Bronze **Series:** XIX World Football Championship - South Afrika 2010 **Obv:** National arms **Obv. Legend:** BANK OF UGANDA **Rev:** Goalkeeper with ball

| Date | Mintage | VF20 | XF40 | MS60 | MS63 | MS65 |
|---|---|---|---|---|---|---|
| 2005 | 10,000 | PF63 15.00 | PF65 17.00 | | | |

**KM# 225 2000 SHILLINGS**
Silver Plated Bronze **Series:** XIX World Football Championship - South Afrika 2010 **Obv:** National arms **Obv. Legend:** BANK OF UGANDA **Rev:** Player and ball

| Date | Mintage | VF20 | XF40 | MS60 | MS63 | MS65 |
|---|---|---|---|---|---|---|
| 2005 | 10,000 | PF63 15.00 | PF65 17.00 | | | |

**KM# 226 2000 SHILLINGS**
40.00 g., Bronze Gilt **Series:** Zodiac **Subject:** Year of the Dog **Obv:** Two dragons **Obv. Legend:** BANK OF UGANDA **Rev:** Three dogs - multicolor

| Date | Mintage | VF20 | XF40 | MS60 | MS63 | MS65 |
|---|---|---|---|---|---|---|
| 2006 | — | PF63 45.00 | PF65 50.00 | | | |

**KM# 227 2000 SHILLINGS**
40.00 g., Bronze Gilt **Series:** Zodiac **Subject:** Year of the Dog **Obv:** Archaic Chinese characters **Obv. Legend:** BANK OF UGANDA **Rev:** Two dogs - multicolor

| Date | Mintage | VF20 | XF40 | MS60 | MS63 | MS65 |
|---|---|---|---|---|---|---|
| 2006 | — | PF63 45.00 | PF65 50.00 | | | |

**KM# 227a 2000 SHILLINGS**
31.10 g., 0.999 Silver 0.9989 oz. ASW **Series:** Zodiac **Subject:** Year of the Dog **Obv:** Archaic Chinese characters **Obv. Legend:** BANK OF UGANDA **Rev:** Two dogs - multicolor

| Date | Mintage | VF20 | XF40 | MS60 | MS63 | MS65 |
|---|---|---|---|---|---|---|
| 2006 | 3,000 | PF63 75.00 | PF65 85.00 | | | |

**KM# 234 2000 SHILLINGS**
31.10 g., 0.999 Silver 0.9989 oz. ASW **Series:** Zodiac **Subject:** Year of the Dog **Obv. Legend:** BANK OF UGANDA **Rev:** Tibet Terrier with pup surrounded by 10 symbols

| Date | Mintage | VF20 | XF40 | MS60 | MS63 | MS65 |
|---|---|---|---|---|---|---|
| 2006 | 3,000 | PF63 75.00 | PF65 85.00 | | | |

**KM# 237 2000 SHILLINGS**
31.10 g., 0.999 Silver 0.9989 oz. ASW **Series:** Zodiac **Subject:** Year of the Dog **Obv:** National arms **Obv. Legend:** BANK OF UGANDA **Rev:** Chow-chow as watchdog, gold bars, bat and flower

| Date | Mintage | VF20 | XF40 | MS60 | MS63 | MS65 |
|---|---|---|---|---|---|---|
| 2006 | — | PF63 60.00 | PF65 65.00 | | | |

**KM# 172 5000 SHILLINGS**
4.00 g., 0.9999 Gold 0.1286 oz. AGW **Series:** Guanyin **Subject:** Chilian **Obv:** Lotus blossom **Obv. Legend:** BANK OF UGANDA

| Date | Mintage | VF20 | XF40 | MS60 | MS63 | MS65 |
|---|---|---|---|---|---|---|
| 2001 | — | PF63 245 | PF65 265 | | | |

**KM# 87 5000 SHILLINGS**
33.73 g., 0.850 Silver 0.9218 oz. ASW, 38.65 mm. **Subject:** The Big Five **Obv:** Arms with supporters **Rev:** Rhinoceros **Edge:** Reeded

| Date | Mintage | VF20 | XF40 | MS60 | MS63 | MS65 |
|---|---|---|---|---|---|---|
| 2002 | — | PF63 65.00 | PF65 70.00 | | | |

**KM# 88 5000 SHILLINGS**
33.73 g., 0.850 Silver 0.9218 oz. ASW, 38.65 mm. **Subject:** The Big Five **Obv:** Arms with supporters **Rev:** Lion **Edge:** Reeded

| Date | Mintage | VF20 | XF40 | MS60 | MS63 | MS65 |
|---|---|---|---|---|---|---|
| 2002 | — | PF63 65.00 | PF65 70.00 | | | |

**KM# 89 5000 SHILLINGS**
33.73 g., 0.850 Silver 0.9218 oz. ASW, 38.65 mm. **Subject:** The Big Five **Obv:** Arms with supporters **Rev:** Cape Buffalo **Edge:** Reeded

| Date | Mintage | VF20 | XF40 | MS60 | MS63 | MS65 |
|---|---|---|---|---|---|---|
| 2002 | — | PF63 50.00 | PF65 55.00 | | | |

**KM# 90 5000 SHILLINGS**
33.73 g., 0.850 Silver 0.9218 oz. ASW, 38.65 mm. **Subject:** The Big Five **Obv:** Arms with supporters **Rev:** Leopard **Edge:** Reeded

| Date | Mintage | VF20 | XF40 | MS60 | MS63 | MS65 |
|---|---|---|---|---|---|---|
| 2002 | — | PF63 65.00 | PF65 70.00 | | | |

**KM# 91 5000 SHILLINGS**
33.73 g., 0.850 Silver 0.9218 oz. ASW, 38.65 mm. **Subject:** The Big Five **Obv:** Arms with supporters **Rev:** Elephant **Edge:** Reeded

| Date | Mintage | VF20 | XF40 | MS60 | MS63 | MS65 |
|---|---|---|---|---|---|---|
| 2002 | — | PF63 65.00 | PF65 70.00 | | | |

**KM# 96 5000 SHILLINGS**
31.10 g., 0.999 Silver 0.999 oz. ASW, 40.6 mm. **Subject:** Matthew Flinders **Obv:** Arms with supporters below crowned head right dividing date **Rev:** Multicolor bust half left at right with ship and harbor scene at left **Edge:** Plain **Shape:** Continent of Australia

| Date | Mintage | VF20 | XF40 | MS60 | MS63 | MS65 |
|---|---|---|---|---|---|---|
| 2002 | 2,500 | PF63 55.00 | PF65 60.00 | | | |

**KM# 97 5000 SHILLINGS**
31.10 g., 0.999 Silver 0.999 oz. ASW, 40.6 mm. **Subject:** Matthew Flinders - H. M. S. Investigator **Obv:** Crowned head right divides date above arms with supporters **Rev:** Multicolor cameo at upper right of ship **Edge:** Plain **Shape:** Continent of Australia

| Date | Mintage | VF20 | XF40 | MS60 | MS63 | MS65 |
|---|---|---|---|---|---|---|
| 2002 | 2,500 | PF63 55.00 | PF65 60.00 | | | |

**KM# 98 5000 SHILLINGS**
31.10 g., 0.999 Silver 0.999 oz. ASW, 40.6 mm. **Subject:** Matthew Flinders - Meeting at Encounter Bay **Obv:** Crowned head right divides date above arms with supporters **Rev:** Date and inscription divides multicolor busts facing **Edge:** Plain **Shape:** Continent of Australia

| Date | Mintage | VF20 | XF40 | MS60 | MS63 | MS65 |
|---|---|---|---|---|---|---|
| 2002 | 2,500 | PF63 55.00 | PF65 60.00 | | | |

**KM# 99 5000 SHILLINGS**
31.10 g., 0.999 Silver 0.999 oz. ASW, 40.6 mm. **Subject:** Matthew Flinders - First Circumnavigation of Terra Australia - 1802 **Rev:** Multicolor bust right on Australian map showing his route around Australia **Edge:** Plain **Shape:** Continent of Australia

| Date | Mintage | VF20 | XF40 | MS60 | MS63 | MS65 |
|---|---|---|---|---|---|---|
| 2002 | 2,500 | PF63 55.00 | PF65 60.00 | | | |

**KM# 174 5000 SHILLINGS**
4.00 g., 0.9999 Gold 0.1286 oz. AGW **Series:** Guanyin **Subject:** Fuyu **Obv:** Lotus blossom **Obv. Legend:** BANK OF UGANDA

| Date | Mintage | VF20 | XF40 | MS60 | MS63 | MS65 |
|---|---|---|---|---|---|---|
| 2002 | — | PF63 245 | PF65 265 | | | |

**KM# 214 5000 SHILLINGS**
4.00 g., 0.9999 Gold 0.1286 oz. AGW **Series:** Guanyin **Subject:** Shile **Obv:** Lotus blossom **Obv. Legend:** BANK OF UGANDA

| Date | Mintage | VF20 | XF40 | MS60 | MS63 | MS65 |
|---|---|---|---|---|---|---|
| 2004 | — | PF63 245 | PF65 265 | | | |

**KM# 220 5000 SHILLINGS**
4.00 g., 0.9999 Gold 0.1286 oz. AGW **Series:** Guanyin **Subject:** Songjing **Obv:** Lotus blossom **Obv. Legend:** BANK OF UGANDA

| Date | Mintage | VF20 | XF40 | MS60 | MS63 | MS65 |
|---|---|---|---|---|---|---|
| 2005 | — | PF63 245 | PF65 265 | | | |

**KM# 228 6000 SHILLINGS**
4.00 g., 0.9999 Gold 0.1286 oz. AGW **Series:** Zodiac **Subject:** Year of the Dog **Obv:** Archaic Chinese characters **Obv. Legend:** BANK OF UGANDA **Rev:** Yorkshire Terrier and "Fú" - Happiness

| Date | Mintage | VF20 | XF40 | MS60 | MS63 | MS65 |
|---|---|---|---|---|---|---|
| 2006 | 14,000 | PF63 235 | PF65 250 | | | |

**KM# 229 6000 SHILLINGS**
4.00 g., 0.9999 Gold 0.1286 oz. AGW **Series:** Zodiac **Subject:** Year of the Dog **Obv:** Archaic Chinese characters **Obv. Legend:** BANK OF UGANDA **Rev:** Yorkshire Terrier and "Lù" - Prosperity

| Date | Mintage | VF20 | XF40 | MS60 | MS63 | MS65 |
|---|---|---|---|---|---|---|
| 2006 | 14,000 | PF63 235 | PF65 250 | | | |

**KM# 230 6000 SHILLINGS**
4.00 g., 0.9999 Gold 0.1286 oz. AGW **Series:** Zodiac **Subject:** Year of the Dog **Obv:** Archaic Chinese characters **Obv. Legend:** BANK OF UGANDA **Rev:** Yorkshire Terrier and "Shòu" - Health and Long Life

| Date | Mintage | VF20 | XF40 | MS60 | MS63 | MS65 |
|---|---|---|---|---|---|---|
| 2006 | 14,000 | PF63 235 | PF65 250 | | | |

**KM# 235 6000 SHILLINGS**
3.11 g., 0.9999 Gold 0.100 oz. AGW **Series:** Zodiac **Subject:** Year of the Dog **Obv. Legend:** BANK OF UGANDA **Rev:** Tibet Terrier with pup surrounded by 10 symbols

| Date | Mintage | VF20 | XF40 | MS60 | MS63 | MS65 |
|---|---|---|---|---|---|---|
| 2006 | — | PF63 175 | PF65 200 | | | |

**KM# 238 6000 SHILLINGS**
3.11 g., 0.9999 Gold 0.100 oz. AGW **Series:** Zodiac **Subject:** Year of the Dog **Obv:** National arms **Obv. Legend:** BANK OF UGANDA **Rev:** Chow-chow as watchdog, gold bars, bat and flower

| Date | Mintage | VF20 | XF40 | MS60 | MS63 | MS65 |
|---|---|---|---|---|---|---|
| 2006 | — | PF63 175 | PF65 200 | | | |

**KM# 231 8000 SHILLINGS**
8.00 g., 0.9999 Gold 0.2572 oz. AGW **Series:** Zodiac **Subject:** Year of the Dog **Obv:** Archaic Chinese characters **Obv. Legend:** BANK OF UGANDA **Rev:** Yorkshire Terrier and "Fú" - Happiness

| Date | Mintage | VF20 | XF40 | MS60 | MS63 | MS65 |
|---|---|---|---|---|---|---|
| 2006 | 1,000 | PF63 450 | PF65 475 | | | |

**KM# 232 8000 SHILLINGS**
8.00 g., 0.9999 Gold 0.2572 oz. AGW **Series:** Zodiac **Subject:** Year of the Dog **Obv:** Archaic Chinese characters **Obv. Legend:** BANK OF UGANDA **Rev:** Yorkshire Terrier and "Lù" - Prosperity

| Date | Mintage | VF20 | XF40 | MS60 | MS63 | MS65 |
|---|---|---|---|---|---|---|
| 2006 | 1,000 | PF63 450 | PF65 475 | | | |

**KM# 215 10000 SHILLINGS**
10.00 g., 0.9999 Gold 0.3215 oz. AGW **Obv:** Lotus blossom **Obv. Legend:** BANK OF UGANDA **Rev:** Buddha

| Date | Mintage | VF20 | XF40 | MS60 | MS63 | MS65 |
|---|---|---|---|---|---|---|
| 2004 | 3,000 | PF63 700 | PF65 725 | | | |

**KM# 76 12000 SHILLINGS**
6.22 g., 0.9999 Gold 0.200 oz. AGW, 22 mm. **Subject:** Illusion: "Spirit of the Mountain **Obv:** Crowned head right divides date above arms with supporters **Rev:** Landscape and tree that looks like a male portrait **Edge:** Reeded

| Date | Mintage | VF20 | XF40 | MS60 | MS63 | MS65 |
|---|---|---|---|---|---|---|
| 2001 | — | PF63 375 | PF65 400 | | | |

**KM# 236 20000 SHILLINGS**
15.55 g., 0.9999 Gold 0.4999 oz. AGW **Series:** Zodiac **Subject:** Year of the Dog **Obv. Legend:** BANK OF UGANDA **Rev:** Tibet Terrier with pup surrounded by 10 symbols

| Date | Mintage | VF20 | XF40 | MS60 | MS63 | MS65 |
|---|---|---|---|---|---|---|
| 2006 | — | PF63 900 | PF65 950 | | | |

**KM# 239 20000 SHILLINGS**
15.55 g., 0.9999 Gold 0.4999 oz. AGW **Series:** Year of the Dog **Obv:** National arms **Obv. Legend:** BANK OF UGANDA **Rev:** Chow-chow as watchdog, gold bars, bat and flower

| Date | Mintage | VF20 | XF40 | MS60 | MS63 | MS65 |
|---|---|---|---|---|---|---|
| 2006 | — | PF63 900 | PF65 950 | | | |

Ukraine (formerly the Ukrainian Soviet Socialist Republic) is bordered by Russia to the east, Russia and Belarus to the north, Poland, Slovakia and Hungary to the west, Romania and Moldova to the southwest and in the south by the Black Sea and the Sea of Azov. It has an area of 233,088 sq. mi. (603,700 sq. km.) and a population of 51.9 million. Capital: Kyiv (Kiev). Coal, grain, vegetables and heavy industrial machinery are major exports.

Ukraine is a charter member of the United Nations and has inherited the third largest nuclear arsenal in the world.

**MONETARY SYSTEM**
(1) Kopiyka
(2) Kopiyky KOÏ³ÈKH
(5 and up) Kopiyok KOÏIÈOK
100 Kopiyok = 1 Hrynia ÃPÈBEHÜ
100,000 Karbovanetsiv = 1 Hryni or Hryven)

## REPUBLIC

### REFORM COINAGE

September 2, 1996
100,000 Karbovanets = 1 Hryvnia
100 Kopiyok = 1 Hryvnia

**KM# 6 KOPIYKA**
1.50 g., Stainless Steel, 16 mm. **Obv:** National arms **Rev:** Value within wreath **Edge:** Plain

| Date | Mintage | VF20 | XF40 | MS60 | MS63 | MS65 |
|---|---|---|---|---|---|---|
| 2001 | — | — | 0.25 | 0.35 | 0.75 | 1.25 |
| 2002 | — | — | 0.25 | 0.35 | 0.75 | 1.25 |
| 2003 | — | — | 0.25 | 0.35 | 0.75 | 1.25 |
| 2004 | — | — | 0.25 | 0.35 | 0.75 | 1.25 |
| 2005 | — | — | 0.25 | 0.35 | 0.75 | 1.25 |
| 2006 | — | — | 0.25 | 0.35 | 0.75 | 1.25 |
| 2007 | — | — | 0.25 | 0.35 | 0.75 | 1.25 |
| 2008 | — | — | 0.25 | 0.35 | 0.75 | 1.25 |
| 2008 Prooflike | 5,000 | — | — | — | — | 3.00 |
| 2009 | — | — | 0.25 | 0.35 | 0.75 | 1.25 |
| 2010 | — | — | 0.25 | 0.35 | 0.75 | 1.25 |
| 2011 | — | — | 0.25 | 0.35 | 0.75 | 1.25 |
| 2011 Prooflike | 5,000 | — | — | — | — | 1.50 |
| 2012 | — | — | 0.25 | 0.35 | 0.75 | 1.25 |
| 2012 Prooflike | 5,000 | — | — | — | — | 1.50 |
| 2013 Prooflike | 5,000 | — | — | — | — | 1.50 |

**KM# 4b 2 KOPIYKY**
1.80 g., Stainless Steel, 17.3 mm. **Obv:** National arms **Rev:** Value within wreath **Edge:** Plain

| Date | Mintage | VF20 | XF40 | MS60 | MS63 | MS65 |
|---|---|---|---|---|---|---|
| 2001 | — | 0.20 | 0.30 | 0.50 | 1.00 | 1.50 |
| 2002 | — | 0.20 | 0.30 | 0.50 | 1.00 | 1.50 |
| 2003 | Est. 5000 | — | — | — | — | 300 |
| 2004 | — | 0.20 | 0.30 | 0.50 | 1.00 | 1.50 |
| 2005 | — | 0.20 | 0.30 | 0.50 | 1.00 | 1.50 |
| 2006 | — | 0.20 | 0.30 | 0.50 | 1.00 | 1.50 |
| 2007 | — | 0.20 | 0.30 | 0.50 | 1.00 | 1.50 |
| 2008 | — | 0.20 | 0.30 | 0.50 | 1.00 | 1.50 |
| 2008 Prooflike | 5,000 | — | — | — | — | 3.00 |
| 2009 | — | 0.20 | 0.30 | 0.50 | 1.00 | 1.50 |
| 2010 | — | 0.20 | 0.30 | 0.50 | 1.00 | 1.50 |
| 2011 | — | 0.20 | 0.30 | 0.50 | 1.00 | 1.50 |
| 2011 Prooflike | 5,000 | — | — | — | — | 2.00 |
| 2012 | — | 0.20 | 0.30 | 0.50 | 1.00 | 1.50 |
| 2012 Prooflike | 5,000 | — | — | — | — | 2.00 |
| 2013 | 5,000 | — | — | — | — | 2.00 |
| 2013 Prooflike | | | | | | |

**KM# 7 5 KOPIYOK**
4.30 g., Stainless Steel, 23.91 mm. **Obv:** National arms **Rev:** Value within wreath **Edge:** Reeded

| Date | Mintage | VF20 | XF40 | MS60 | MS63 | MS65 |
|---|---|---|---|---|---|---|
| 2001 Sets only | 10,000 | — | — | — | — | 25.00 |
| 2003 | — | 0.20 | 0.30 | 0.50 | 1.00 | 1.50 |
| 2004 | — | 0.20 | 0.30 | 0.50 | 1.00 | 1.50 |
| 2005 | — | 0.20 | 0.30 | 0.50 | 1.00 | 1.50 |
| 2006 | — | 0.20 | 0.30 | 0.50 | 1.00 | 1.50 |
| 2007 | — | 0.20 | 0.30 | 0.50 | 1.00 | 1.50 |
| 2008 | — | 0.20 | 0.30 | 0.50 | 1.00 | 1.50 |
| 2008 Prooflike | 5,000 | — | — | — | — | 2.50 |
| 2009 | — | 0.20 | 0.30 | 0.50 | 1.00 | 1.50 |
| 2010 | — | 0.20 | 0.30 | 0.50 | 1.00 | 1.50 |
| 2011 | — | 0.20 | 0.30 | 0.50 | 1.00 | 1.50 |
| 2011 Prooflike | 5,000 | — | — | — | — | 2.00 |
| 2012 | — | 0.20 | 0.30 | 0.50 | 1.00 | 1.50 |
| 2012 Prooflike | 5,000 | — | — | — | — | 2.00 |
| 2013 | — | 0.20 | 0.30 | 0.50 | 1.00 | 1.50 |
| 2013 Prooflike | 5,000 | — | — | — | — | 2.00 |

**KM# 1.1b 10 KOPIYOK**
1.70 g., Aluminum-Bronze, 16.24 mm. **Obv:** National arms **Rev:** Value within wreath **Edge:** Reeded

| Date | Mintage | VF20 | XF40 | MS60 | MS63 | MS65 |
|---|---|---|---|---|---|---|
| 2001 Sets only | 10,000 | — | — | — | — | 25.00 |
| 2002 | — | 0.30 | 0.60 | 1.25 | 1.75 | 2.50 |
| 2003 | — | 0.25 | 0.50 | 1.00 | 1.50 | 2.25 |
| 2004 | — | 0.25 | 0.50 | 1.00 | 1.50 | 2.25 |
| 2005 | — | 0.25 | 0.50 | 1.00 | 1.50 | 2.25 |
| 2006 | — | 0.25 | 0.50 | 1.00 | 1.50 | 2.25 |
| 2007 | — | 0.25 | 0.50 | 1.00 | 1.50 | 2.25 |
| 2008 | — | 0.25 | 0.50 | 1.00 | 1.50 | 2.25 |
| 2008 Prooflike | 5,000 | — | — | — | — | 5.00 |
| 2009 | — | 0.25 | 0.50 | 1.00 | 1.25 | 2.00 |
| 2010 | — | 0.25 | 0.50 | 1.00 | 1.25 | 2.00 |
| 2011 Prooflike | 5,000 | — | — | — | — | 5.00 |
| 2011 | — | 0.25 | 0.50 | 1.00 | 1.25 | 2.00 |
| 2012 | — | 0.25 | 0.50 | 1.00 | 1.25 | 2.00 |
| 2012 Prooflike | 5,000 | — | — | — | — | 5.00 |
| 2013 | — | 0.25 | 0.50 | 1.00 | 1.25 | 2.00 |
| 2013 Prooflike | 5,000 | — | — | — | — | 5.00 |

**KM# 2.1b 25 KOPIYOK**
2.90 g., Aluminum-Bronze, 20.8 mm. **Obv:** National arms **Rev:** Value within wreath **Edge:** Segmented reeding

| Date | Mintage | VF20 | XF40 | MS60 | MS63 | MS65 |
|---|---|---|---|---|---|---|
| 2001 | — | 0.80 | 1.75 | 3.00 | 6.00 | 25.00 |
| 2003 Prooflike | Est. 5000 | — | — | — | — | 300 |
| 2006 | — | 0.80 | 2.00 | 3.00 | 4.00 | 6.00 |
| 2007 | — | 0.80 | 2.00 | 3.00 | 4.00 | 6.00 |
| 2008 | — | — | 2.00 | 3.00 | 4.00 | 6.00 |
| 2008 Prooflike | 5,000 | — | — | — | — | 8.00 |
| 2009 | — | — | 2.00 | 2.50 | 3.50 | 5.00 |
| 2010 | — | — | 2.00 | 2.50 | 3.50 | 5.00 |
| 2011 | — | — | 2.00 | 2.50 | 3.50 | 5.00 |
| 2011 Prooflike | 5,000 | — | — | — | — | 8.00 |
| 2012 | — | — | 2.00 | 2.50 | 3.50 | 5.00 |
| 2012 Prooflike | 5,000 | — | — | — | — | 8.00 |
| 2013 | — | — | 2.00 | 2.50 | 3.50 | 5.00 |
| 2013 Prooflike | 5,000 | — | — | — | — | 8.00 |

**KM# 3.3b 50 KOPIYOK**
4.20 g., Aluminum-Bronze, 23 mm. **Obv:** National arms **Rev:** Five dots grouped in wreath to right of final letter 'K' in value **Edge:** Segmented reeding

| Date | Mintage | VF20 | XF40 | MS60 | MS63 | MS65 |
|---|---|---|---|---|---|---|
| 2001 Sets only | — | — | — | — | — | 25.00 |
| 2003 | Est. 5000 | — | — | — | 300 | — |
| 2006 | — | 1.00 | 2.00 | 3.00 | 4.00 | 6.00 |
| 2007 | — | 1.00 | 2.00 | 3.00 | 4.00 | 6.00 |
| 2008 | — | — | 2.00 | 3.00 | 4.00 | 6.00 |
| 2008 Prooflike | 5,000 | — | — | — | — | 8.00 |
| 2009 | — | — | 2.00 | 3.00 | 4.00 | 6.00 |
| 2010 | — | — | 2.00 | 3.00 | 4.00 | 6.00 |
| 2011 | — | — | 2.00 | 3.00 | 4.00 | 6.00 |
| 2011 Prooflike | 5,000 | — | — | — | — | 8.00 |
| 2012 | — | — | 2.00 | 3.00 | 4.00 | 6.00 |
| 2012 Prooflike | 5,000 | — | — | — | — | 8.00 |

**KM# 8b HRYVNIA**
6.90 g., Aluminum-Bronze, 26 mm. **Obv:** National arms **Rev:** Value, sprigs and designs **Edge:** Lettered

| Date | Mintage | VF20 | XF40 | MS60 | MS63 | MS65 |
|---|---|---|---|---|---|---|
| 2001 | — | — | 2.50 | 3.50 | 4.50 | 6.50 |

**KM# 8b.1 HRYVNIA**
7.10 g., Aluminum-Bronze, 26 mm. **Obv:** National arms **Rev:** Value, sprigs and designs **Edge:** Lettered

| Date | Mintage | VF20 | XF40 | MS60 | MS63 | MS65 |
|---|---|---|---|---|---|---|
| 2002 | — | — | 3.00 | 5.00 | 7.00 | 9.00 |
| 2003 | — | — | 2.50 | 3.50 | 4.50 | 6.50 |

**KM# 208 HRYVNIA**
6.80 g., Aluminum-Bronze, 26 mm. **Subject:** 60th Anniversary - Victory over the Nazis **Obv:** National arms above value **Rev:** Uniform lapel with Soviet military medals group **Edge:** Lettered **Edge Lettering:** Date and denomination

| Date | Mintage | VF20 | XF40 | MS60 | MS63 | MS65 |
|---|---|---|---|---|---|---|
| 2004 | 5,000,000 | — | — | — | 3.00 | 5.00 |

**KM# 209 HRYVNIA**
6.74 g., Aluminum-Bronze, 26 mm. **Obv:** National arms above value **Rev:** Half length figure of Volodymyr the Great facing holding church model building and staff **Edge:** Lettered **Edge Lettering:** Date and denomination

| Date | Mintage | VF20 | XF40 | MS60 | MS63 | MS65 |
|---|---|---|---|---|---|---|
| 2004 | 10,000,000 | — | — | — | 2.50 | 4.00 |
| 2005 | — | — | — | — | 2.00 | 3.00 |
| 2006 | — | — | — | — | 2.00 | 3.00 |
| 2008 Prooflike | 5,000 | — | — | — | — | 25.00 |
| 2010 | — | — | — | — | 2.00 | 3.00 |
| 2011 | — | — | — | — | 2.00 | 3.00 |
| 2011 Prooflike | 5,000 | — | — | — | — | 12.50 |
| 2012 | — | — | — | — | 2.50 | 4.00 |
| 2012 Prooflike | 5,000 | — | — | — | — | 12.50 |
| 2013 Prooflike | 5,000 | — | — | — | — | 12.50 |

**KM# 228 HRYVNIA**
6.80 g., Aluminum-Bronze, 26 mm. **Subject:** WW II Victory 60th Anniversary **Obv:** Value **Rev:** Soldiers in a "V" of search lights **Edge Lettering:** Value and 2010

| Date | Mintage | VF20 | XF40 | MS60 | MS63 | MS65 |
|---|---|---|---|---|---|---|
| 2005 | 5,000,000 | — | — | — | 3.50 | 6.00 |

**KM# 667 HRYVNIA**
6.80 g., Aluminum-Bronze, 26 mm. **Subject:** WWII Victory, 65th Anniversary **Obv:** Value **Rev:** Ribbon of the order of St. George and the eternal flame

| Date | Mintage | VF20 | XF40 | MS60 | MS63 | MS65 |
|---|---|---|---|---|---|---|
| 2010 | 5,000,000 | — | — | — | 3.50 | 6.00 |

**KM# 654 HRYVNIA**
31.11 g., 0.9999 Silver 0.9999 oz. ASW, 38.6 mm. **Obv:** Logo of the Ukraine National Bank **Rev:** Archangel Michael **Edge:** Reeded

| Date | Mintage | VF20 | XF40 | MS60 | MS63 | MS65 |
|---|---|---|---|---|---|---|
| 2011 | 10,000 | — | — | — | — | 24.00 |
| 2012 | 20,000 | — | — | — | — | 24.00 |
| 2013 | 10,000 | — | — | — | — | 24.00 |

**KM# 668 HRYVNIA**
6.80 g., Aluminum-Bronze, 26 mm. **Subject:** WEFA Euro 2012 Final Tournament **Obv:** Vlaue **Rev:** UEFA Euro 2012 logo

| Date | Mintage | VF20 | XF40 | MS60 | MS63 | MS65 |
|---|---|---|---|---|---|---|
| 2012 | 5,000,000 | — | — | — | 3.50 | 6.00 |

**KM# 669 HRYVNIA**
33.91 g., 0.925 Silver 1.0085 oz. ASW **Subject:** Folks Crafts **Obv:** Glassblowen products **Rev:** Glassblower **Edge:** Incuse lettering

| Date | Mintage | VF20 | XF40 | MS60 | MS63 | MS65 |
|---|---|---|---|---|---|---|
| 2012 Proof, antique finish | 7,000 | PF65 80.00 | | | | |

**KM# 106 2 HRYVNI**
12.80 g., Copper-Nickel-Zinc, 31 mm. **Series:** Olympics - Salt Lake City, 2002 **Obv:** National arms, value and designs **Rev:** Stylized ice dancing couple **Edge:** Reeded

| Date | Mintage | VF20 | XF40 | MS60 | MS63 | MS65 |
|---|---|---|---|---|---|---|
| 2001 | 30,000 | — | — | — | — | 20.00 |

**KM# 111 2 HRYVNI**
12.80 g., Copper-Nickel-Zinc, 31 mm. **Series:** Flora and Fauna **Obv:** National arms and date divides wreath, value within **Rev:** Lynx and offspring **Edge:** Reeded

| Date | Mintage | VF20 | XF40 | MS60 | MS63 | MS65 |
|---|---|---|---|---|---|---|
| 2001 | 30,000 | — | — | — | — | 40.00 |

**KM# 133 2 HRYVNI**
12.80 g., Copper-Nickel-Zinc, 31 mm. **Subject:** Kindness to Children **Obv:** National arms above value flanked by sprigs and doves **Rev:** Two children frolicking under fountain of knowledge **Edge:** Reeded

| Date | Mintage | VF20 | XF40 | MS60 | MS63 | MS65 |
|---|---|---|---|---|---|---|
| 2001 | 100,000 | — | — | — | — | 10.00 |

**KM# 134 2 HRYVNI**
12.80 g., Copper-Nickel-Zinc, 31 mm. **Subject:** 5th Anniversary of Constitution **Obv:** National arms above value flanked by sprigs **Rev:** Building above book flanked by sprigs **Edge:** Reeded

| Date | Mintage | VF20 | XF40 | MS60 | MS63 | MS65 |
|---|---|---|---|---|---|---|
| 2001 | 30,000 | — | — | — | — | 35.00 |

**KM# 136 2 HRYVNI**
12.80 g., Copper-Nickel-Zinc, 31 mm. **Subject:** Mykolaiv Zoo **Obv:** Man running alongside large cat **Rev:** Twelve animals **Edge:** Reeded

| Date | Mintage | VF20 | XF40 | MS60 | MS63 | MS65 |
|---|---|---|---|---|---|---|
| 2001 | 30,000 | — | — | — | — | 35.00 |

**KM# 137 2 HRYVNI**
12.80 g., Copper-Nickel-Zinc, 31 mm. **Subject:** Mykhailo Ostrohradskiy (Mathematician) **Obv:** National arms divides date and value divided by wavy line graph **Rev:** Head 1/4 left **Edge:** Reeded

| Date | Mintage | VF20 | XF40 | MS60 | MS63 | MS65 |
|---|---|---|---|---|---|---|
| 2001 | 30,000 | — | — | — | — | 15.00 |

**KM# 138 2 HRYVNI**
12.80 g., Copper-Nickel-Zinc, 31 mm. **Subject:** Larix Polonica **Obv:** Value within wreath **Rev:** Pine branch with cone **Edge:** Reeded

| Date | Mintage | VF20 | XF40 | MS60 | MS63 | MS65 |
|---|---|---|---|---|---|---|
| 2001 | 30,000 | — | — | — | — | 40.00 |

**KM# 139 2 HRYVNI**
12.80 g., Copper-Nickel-Zinc, 31 mm. **Subject:** Volodymyr Dal **Obv:** Books **Rev:** Head right **Edge:** Reeded

| Date | Mintage | VF20 | XF40 | MS60 | MS63 | MS65 |
|---|---|---|---|---|---|---|
| 2001 | 30,000 | — | — | — | — | 15.00 |

**KM# 147 2 HRYVNI**
12.80 g., Copper-Nickel-Zinc, 31 mm. **Series:** Olympics - Salt Lake City, 2002 **Obv:** National arms and value on ice design **Rev:** Stylized hockey player **Edge:** Reeded

| Date | Mintage | VF20 | XF40 | MS60 | MS63 | MS65 |
|---|---|---|---|---|---|---|
| 2001 | 30,000 | — | — | — | — | 15.00 |

**KM# 149 2 HRYVNI**
12.80 g., Copper-Nickel-Zinc, 31 mm. **Subject:** Mykhailo Drahomanov (Historian, Politician, etc.) **Obv:** National arms and value **Rev:** Bust right **Edge:** Reeded

| Date | Mintage | VF20 | XF40 | MS60 | MS63 | MS65 |
|---|---|---|---|---|---|---|
| 2001 | 30,000 | — | — | — | — | 15.00 |

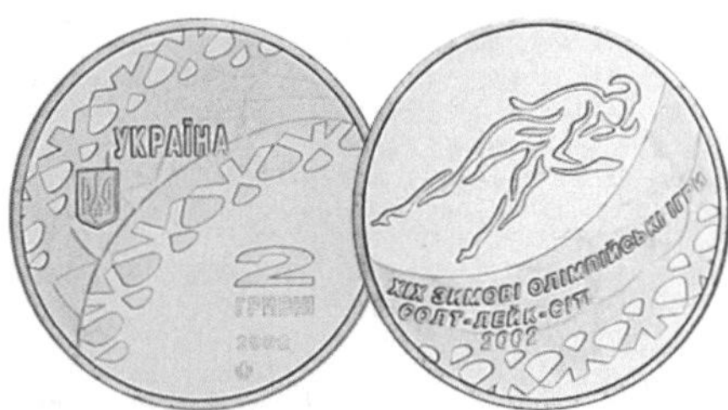


**KM# 150 2 HRYVNI**
12.80 g., Copper-Nickel-Zinc, 31 mm. **Series:** Olympics - Salt lake City, 2002 **Obv:** National arms and value on ice design **Rev:** Speed skater **Edge:** Reeded

| Date | Mintage | VF20 | XF40 | MS60 | MS63 | MS65 |
|---|---|---|---|---|---|---|
| 2002 | 30,000 | — | — | — | — | 15.00 |

**KM# 154 2 HRYVNI**
12.80 g., Copper-Nickel-Zinc, 31 mm. **Subject:** Mykola Lysenko (composer) **Obv:** Musical score and value **Rev:** Head 1/4 right **Edge:** Reeded

| Date | Mintage | VF20 | XF40 | MS60 | MS63 | MS65 |
|---|---|---|---|---|---|---|
| 2002 | 30,000 | — | — | — | — | 12.00 |

**KM# 155 2 HRYVNI**
12.80 g., Copper-Nickel-Zinc, 31 mm. **Series:** Flora and Fauna **Obv:** National arms and date divides wreath, value within **Rev:** Eurasian Eagle Owl **Edge:** Reeded

| Date | Mintage | VF20 | XF40 | MS60 | MS63 | MS65 |
|---|---|---|---|---|---|---|
| 2002 | 30,000 | — | — | — | — | 50.00 |

**KM# 156 2 HRYVNI**
12.80 g., Copper-Nickel-Zinc, 31 mm. **Subject:** Olympics - Athens, 2004 **Obv:** Two ancient figures above value **Rev:** Swimmer **Edge:** Reeded

| Date | Mintage | VF20 | XF40 | MS60 | MS63 | MS65 |
|---|---|---|---|---|---|---|
| 2002 | 30,000 | — | — | — | — | 15.00 |

**KM# 166 2 HRYVNI**
12.80 g., Copper-Nickel-Zinc, 31 mm. **Subject:** Leonid Glibov, writer (1827-1893) **Obv:** National arms and value within scroll and wreath **Rev:** 1/2-length bust right **Edge:** Reeded

| Date | Mintage | VF20 | XF40 | MS60 | MS63 | MS65 |
|---|---|---|---|---|---|---|
| 2002 | 30,000 | — | — | — | — | 15.00 |

**KM# 167 2 HRYVNI**
12.80 g., Copper-Nickel-Zinc, 31 mm. **Series:** Flora and Fauna **Obv:** National arms and date divides wreath, value within **Rev:** European Bison **Edge:** Reeded

| Date | Mintage | VF20 | XF40 | MS60 | MS63 | MS65 |
|---|---|---|---|---|---|---|
| 2003 | 50,000 | — | — | — | — | 15.00 |

**KM# 168 2 HRYVNI**
12.80 g., Copper-Nickel-Zinc, 31 mm. **Obv:** National arms and date divides wreath, value within **Rev:** Long-snouted Sea Horse **Edge:** Reeded

| Date | Mintage | VF20 | XF40 | MS60 | MS63 | MS65 |
|---|---|---|---|---|---|---|
| 2003 | 50,000 | — | — | — | — | 25.00 |

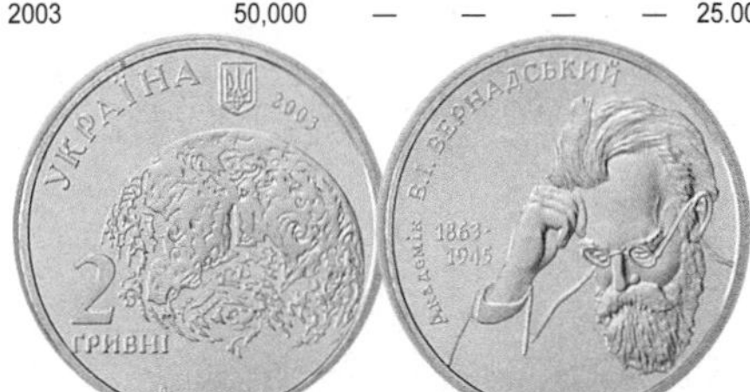

**KM# 169 2 HRYVNI**
12.80 g., Copper-Nickel-Zinc, 31 mm. **Subject:** Volodymyr Vernadskyi (academic) **Obv:** National arms, value and world globe **Rev:** Head on hand looking down **Edge:** Reeded

| Date | Mintage | VF20 | XF40 | MS60 | MS63 | MS65 |
|---|---|---|---|---|---|---|
| 2003 | 30,000 | — | — | — | — | 12.00 |

**KM# 170 2 HRYVNI**
12.80 g., Copper-Nickel-Zinc, 31 mm. **Subject:** Volodymyr Korolenko (writer) **Obv:** National arms above book and value **Rev:** Bearded head 1/4 right above dates **Edge:** Reeded

| Date | Mintage | VF20 | XF40 | MS60 | MS63 | MS65 |
|---|---|---|---|---|---|---|
| 2003 | 30,000 | — | — | — | — | 12.00 |

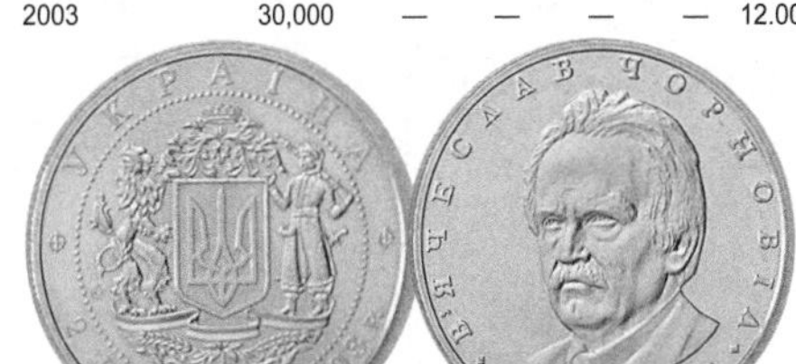

**KM# 171 2 HRYVNI**
12.80 g., Copper-Nickel-Zinc, 31 mm. **Subject:** Viacheslav Chornovil (politician) **Obv:** Arms with supporters within beaded circle **Rev:** Head 1/4 left **Edge:** Reeded

| Date | Mintage | VF20 | XF40 | MS60 | MS63 | MS65 |
|---|---|---|---|---|---|---|
| 2003 | 30,000 | — | — | — | — | 25.00 |

**KM# 178 2 HRYVNI**
1.24 g., 0.9999 Gold 0.0399 oz. AGW, 13.92 mm. **Obv:** National arms flanked by dates within beaded circle **Rev:** Spotted Salamander divides beaded circle **Edge:** Plain

| Date | Mintage | VF20 | XF40 | MS60 | MS63 | MS65 |
|---|---|---|---|---|---|---|
| 2003 | 10,000 | — | — | — | — | 125 |

**KM# 179 2 HRYVNI**
12.80 g., Copper-Nickel-Zinc, 31 mm. **Subject:** Singer Boris Gmyrya **Obv:** Value, arms ,date and musical symbol **Rev:** Head 1/4 left and dates **Edge:** Reeded

| Date | Mintage | VF20 | XF40 | MS60 | MS63 | MS65 |
|---|---|---|---|---|---|---|
| 2003 | 30,000 | — | — | — | — | 12.00 |

**KM# 180 2 HRYVNI**
12.80 g., Copper-Nickel-Zinc, 31 mm. **Subject:** 70th Anniversary National Aviation University **Obv:** World globe behind national arms, value and date **Rev:** Wright Brothers biplane **Edge:** Reeded

| Date | Mintage | VF20 | XF40 | MS60 | MS63 | MS65 |
|---|---|---|---|---|---|---|
| 2003 | 30,000 | — | — | — | — | 15.00 |

**KM# 181 2 HRYVNI**
12.80 g., Copper-Nickel-Zinc, 31 mm. **Subject:** Ostap Veresay (musician) **Obv:** Musical stringed instrument and ornamental design **Rev:** Bust facing playing stringed instrument **Edge:** Reeded

| Date | Mintage | VF20 | XF40 | MS60 | MS63 | MS65 |
|---|---|---|---|---|---|---|
| 2003 | 30,000 | — | — | — | — | 12.00 |

**KM# 182 2 HRYVNI**
12.80 g., Copper-Nickel-Zinc, 31 mm. **Subject:** Olympics **Obv:** Two ancient women with seedlings **Rev:** Boxer **Edge:** Reeded

| Date | Mintage | VF20 | XF40 | MS60 | MS63 | MS65 |
|---|---|---|---|---|---|---|
| 2003 | 30,000 | — | — | — | — | 18.00 |

**KM# 183 2 HRYVNI**
12.80 g., Copper-Nickel-Zinc, 31 mm. **Subject:** Vasyl Sukhomlynski (teacher) **Obv:** Children, books, value and national arms **Rev:** Head 1/4 right **Edge:** Reeded

| Date | Mintage | VF20 | XF40 | MS60 | MS63 | MS65 |
|---|---|---|---|---|---|---|
| 2003 | 30,000 | — | — | — | — | 12.00 |

**KM# 184 2 HRYVNI**
12.80 g., Copper-Nickel-Zinc, 31 mm. **Subject:** Andriy Malyshko (poet) **Obv:** Ornamental shawl, national arms and value **Rev:** Head 1/4 right flanked by radiant sun and tree **Edge:** Reeded

| Date | Mintage | VF20 | XF40 | MS60 | MS63 | MS65 |
|---|---|---|---|---|---|---|
| 2003 | 30,000 | — | — | — | — | 12.00 |

**KM# 201 2 HRYVNI**
12.80 g., Copper-Nickel-Zinc, 31 mm. **Subject:** Azov Dolphin **Obv:** National arms and date divides wreath, value within **Rev:** Harbor Porpoises **Edge:** Reeded

| Date | Mintage | VF20 | XF40 | MS60 | MS63 | MS65 |
|---|---|---|---|---|---|---|
| 2004 | 30,000 | — | — | — | — | 35.00 |

**KM# 202 2 HRYVNI**
12.80 g., Copper-Nickel-Zinc, 31 mm. **Subject:** Football World Cup - 2006 **Obv:** Soccer ball in net **Rev:** Two soccer players **Edge:** Reeded

| Date | Mintage | VF20 | XF40 | MS60 | MS63 | MS65 |
|---|---|---|---|---|---|---|
| 2004 | 50,000 | — | — | — | — | 15.00 |

**KM# 203 2 HRYVNI**
12.80 g., Copper-Nickel-Zinc, 31 mm. **Subject:** Serhiy Lyfar (ballet artist) **Obv:** Stylized dancer **Rev:** Head right **Edge:** Reeded

| Date | Mintage | VF20 | XF40 | MS60 | MS63 | MS65 |
|---|---|---|---|---|---|---|
| 2004 | 30,000 | — | — | — | — | 12.00 |

**KM# 210 2 HRYVNI**
12.80 g., Copper-Nickel-Zinc, 31 mm. **Subject:** 170 Years of the Kyiv National University **Obv:** National arms in center above value dividing scientific items **Rev:** University building main entrance **Edge:** Reeded

| Date | Mintage | VF20 | XF40 | MS60 | MS63 | MS65 |
|---|---|---|---|---|---|---|
| 2004 | 50,000 | — | — | — | — | 12.00 |

**KM# 211 2 HRYVNI**
12.80 g., Copper-Nickel-Zinc, 31 mm. **Subject:** Oleksander Dovzhenko (movie producer, writer) **Obv:** Boy standing in small boat **Rev:** Head facing **Edge:** Reeded

| Date | Mintage | VF20 | XF40 | MS60 | MS63 | MS65 |
|---|---|---|---|---|---|---|
| 2004 | 30,000 | — | — | — | — | 12.00 |

**KM# 212 2 HRYVNI**
12.80 g., Copper-Nickel-Zinc, 31 mm. **Subject:** Mykola Bazhan (poet, translator) **Obv:** Winged pens and value **Rev:** Head 1/4 left **Edge:** Reeded

| Date | Mintage | VF20 | XF40 | MS60 | MS63 | MS65 |
|---|---|---|---|---|---|---|
| 2004 | 30,000 | — | — | — | — | 12.00 |

**KM# 213 2 HRYVNI**
12.80 g., Copper-Nickel-Zinc, 31 mm. **Subject:** Mykhailo Kotsyubynsky (writer) **Obv:** Two reclining figures **Rev:** Head 1/4 right **Edge:** Reeded

| Date | Mintage | VF20 | XF40 | MS60 | MS63 | MS65 |
|---|---|---|---|---|---|---|
| 2004 | 30,000 | — | — | — | — | 12.00 |

**KM# 214 2 HRYVNI**
12.80 g., Copper-Nickel-Zinc, 31 mm. **Subject:** Maria Zankovetska (actress) **Obv:** National arms, value and drawn curtain **Rev:** Hooded head 1/4 left **Edge:** Reeded

| Date | Mintage | VF20 | XF40 | MS60 | MS63 | MS65 |
|---|---|---|---|---|---|---|
| 2004 | 30,000 | — | — | — | — | 12.00 |

**KM# 215 2 HRYVNI**
12.80 g., Copper-Nickel-Zinc, 31 mm. **Subject:** Mykhailo Maksymovych (historian, archaeologist) **Obv:** National arms above building and value **Rev:** Bust left **Edge:** Reeded

| Date | Mintage | VF20 | XF40 | MS60 | MS63 | MS65 |
|---|---|---|---|---|---|---|
| 2004 | 30,000 | — | — | — | — | 12.00 |

**KM# 216 2 HRYVNI**
12.80 g., Copper-Nickel-Zinc, 31 mm. **Subject:** Mykhailo Deregus (painter) **Obv:** National arms and value on artists palette **Rev:** Head right **Edge:** Reeded

| Date | Mintage | VF20 | XF40 | MS60 | MS63 | MS65 |
|---|---|---|---|---|---|---|
| 2004 | 30,000 | — | — | — | — | 12.00 |

**KM# 217 2 HRYVNI**
12.80 g., Copper-Nickel-Zinc, 31 mm. **Subject:** Nuclear Power Engineering of Ukraine **Obv:** National arms and value in atomic design **Rev:** Nuclear reactor **Edge:** Reeded

| Date | Mintage | VF20 | XF40 | MS60 | MS63 | MS65 |
|---|---|---|---|---|---|---|
| 2004 | 30,000 | — | — | — | — | 20.00 |

**KM# 227 2 HRYVNI**
1.24 g., 0.9999 Gold 0.0399 oz. AGW, 13.92 mm. **Obv:** National arms divides dates within beaded circle **Rev:** Flying White Stork divides beaded circle **Edge:** Plain

| Date | Mintage | VF20 | XF40 | MS60 | MS63 | MS65 |
|---|---|---|---|---|---|---|
| 2004 | 10,000 | — | — | — | — | 175 |

**KM# 330 2 HRYVNI**
12.80 g., Copper-Nickel-Zinc, 31 mm. **Subject:** 200th Anniversary of Kharkiv University **Obv:** National arms and atom **Rev:** University building and reflection **Edge:** Reeded

| Date | Mintage | VF20 | XF40 | MS60 | MS63 | MS65 |
|---|---|---|---|---|---|---|
| 2004 | 50,000 | — | — | — | — | 12.00 |

**KM# 331 2 HRYVNI**
12.80 g., Copper-Nickel-Zinc, 31 mm. **Subject:** Ukraine National Academy of Law named after Yaroslav the Wise **Obv:** National arms above National Academy of Law arms and date **Rev:** Building **Edge:** Reeded

| Date | Mintage | VF20 | XF40 | MS60 | MS63 | MS65 |
|---|---|---|---|---|---|---|
| 2004 | 30,000 | — | — | — | — | 20.00 |

**KM# 332 2 HRYVNI**
12.80 g., Copper-Nickel-Zinc, 31 mm. **Subject:** Yurii Fedkovych (poet, writer) **Obv:** National arms, value and man on horse **Rev:** Bust 1/4 right and dates **Edge:** Reeded

| Date | Mintage | VF20 | XF40 | MS60 | MS63 | MS65 |
|---|---|---|---|---|---|---|
| 2004 | 30,000 | — | — | — | — | 12.00 |

**KM# 346 2 HRYVNI**
12.80 g., Copper-Nickel-Zinc, 31 mm. **Subject:** Boris Liatoshynsky (composer) **Obv:** Musical G Clef symbol and value below national arms **Rev:** Head 1/4 left **Edge:** Reeded

| Date | Mintage | VF20 | XF40 | MS60 | MS63 | MS65 |
|---|---|---|---|---|---|---|
| 2005 | 20,000 | — | — | — | — | 15.00 |

**KM# 347 2 HRYVNI**
12.80 g., Copper-Nickel-Zinc, 31 mm. **Subject:** Volodymyr Filatov (surgeon) **Obv:** Light passing through the lens of an eye **Rev:** Head with cap facing **Edge:** Reeded

| Date | Mintage | VF20 | XF40 | MS60 | MS63 | MS65 |
|---|---|---|---|---|---|---|
| 2005 | 20,000 | — | — | — | — | 16.00 |

**KM# 348 2 HRYVNI**
12.80 g., Copper-Nickel-Zinc, 31 mm. **Obv:** Books between stylized horsemen **Rev:** Ulas Samchuk **Edge:** Reeded

| Date | Mintage | VF20 | XF40 | MS60 | MS63 | MS65 |
|---|---|---|---|---|---|---|
| 2005 | 20,000 | — | — | — | — | 15.00 |

**KM# 349 2 HRYVNI**
12.80 g., Copper-Nickel-Zinc, 31 mm. **Subject:** Pavlo Virsky (ballet artist) **Obv:** National arms in flower circle **Rev:** Bust right **Edge:** Reeded

| Date | Mintage | VF20 | XF40 | MS60 | MS63 | MS65 |
|---|---|---|---|---|---|---|
| 2005 | 20,000 | — | — | — | — | 15.00 |

**KM# 350 2 HRYVNI**
12.80 g., Copper-Nickel-Zinc, 31 mm. **Obv:** Roses and grapes **Rev:** Poet Maksym Rylsky **Edge:** Reeded

| Date | Mintage | VF20 | XF40 | MS60 | MS63 | MS65 |
|---|---|---|---|---|---|---|
| 2005 | 20,000 | — | — | — | — | 15.00 |

**KM# 351 2 HRYVNI**
1.24 g., 0.9999 Gold 0.0399 oz. AGW, 13.9 mm. **Obv:** National arms within beaded circle **Rev:** Scythian horseman depicted on golden plaque **Edge:** Plain

| Date | Mintage | VF20 | XF40 | MS60 | MS63 | MS65 |
|---|---|---|---|---|---|---|
| 2005 | 15,000 | — | — | — | — | 175 |

**KM# 352 2 HRYVNI**
12.80 g., Copper-Nickel-Zinc, 31 mm. **Subject:** Serhiy Vsekhsviatsky (astronomer) **Obv:** Solar Wind" depiction **Rev:** Head right **Edge:** Reeded

| Date | Mintage | VF20 | XF40 | MS60 | MS63 | MS65 |
|---|---|---|---|---|---|---|
| 2005 | 20,000 | — | — | — | — | 15.00 |

**KM# 353 2 HRYVNI**
12.80 g., Copper-Nickel-Zinc, 31 mm. **Subject:** 50 Years of Kyivmiskbud **Obv:** National arms **Rev:** Buildings **Edge:** Reeded

| Date | Mintage | VF20 | XF40 | MS60 | MS63 | MS65 |
|---|---|---|---|---|---|---|
| 2005 | 20,000 | — | — | — | — | 20.00 |

**KM# 354 2 HRYVNI**
12.80 g., Copper-Nickel-Zinc, 31 mm. **Subject:** 75 Years of Zhukovsky Aerospace University in Kharkiv **Obv:** Building divides book outline **Rev:** Airplane, computer monitor and books **Edge:** Reeded

| Date | Mintage | VF20 | XF40 | MS60 | MS63 | MS65 |
|---|---|---|---|---|---|---|
| 2005 | 30,000 | — | — | — | — | 17.00 |

**KM# 356 2 HRYVNI**
12.80 g., Copper-Nickel-Zinc, 31 mm. **Subject:** Oleksander Korniychuk (writer, playright) **Obv:** Theatrical masks and feather **Rev:** Bust 1/4 right **Edge:** Reeded

| Date | Mintage | VF20 | XF40 | MS60 | MS63 | MS65 |
|---|---|---|---|---|---|---|
| 2005 | 20,000 | — | — | — | — | 15.00 |

**KM# 357 2 HRYVNI**
12.80 g., Copper-Nickel-Zinc, 31 mm. **Obv:** National arms and date divides wreath, value within **Rev:** Sandy Mole Rat **Edge:** Reeded

| Date | Mintage | VF20 | XF40 | MS60 | MS63 | MS65 |
|---|---|---|---|---|---|---|
| 2005 | 60,000 | — | — | — | — | 10.00 |

**KM# 359 2 HRYVNI**
12.80 g., Copper-Nickel-Zinc, 31 mm. **Obv:** National arms **Rev:** Tairov Wine Institute building and cameo **Edge:** Reeded

| Date | Mintage | VF20 | XF40 | MS60 | MS63 | MS65 |
|---|---|---|---|---|---|---|
| 2005 | 20,000 | — | — | — | — | 27.50 |

**KM# 360 2 HRYVNI**
12.80 g., Copper-Nickel-Zinc, 31 mm. **Subject:** 300 Years to David Guramishvili (poet) **Obv:** Georgian and Ukrainian style ornamentation **Rev:** Head right **Edge:** Reeded

| Date | Mintage | VF20 | XF40 | MS60 | MS63 | MS65 |
|---|---|---|---|---|---|---|
| 2005 | 30,000 | — | — | — | — | 12.00 |

**KM# 361 2 HRYVNI**
12.80 g., Copper-Nickel-Zinc, 31 mm. **Subject:** Dmytro Yavornytsky (historian, archaeologist, writer) **Obv:** National arms **Rev:** Bust 3/4 right **Edge:** Reeded

| Date | Mintage | VF20 | XF40 | MS60 | MS63 | MS65 |
|---|---|---|---|---|---|---|
| 2005 | 30,000 | — | — | — | — | 15.00 |

**KM# 375 2 HRYVNI**
12.80 g., Copper-Nickel-Zinc, 31 mm. **Subject:** Oleksiy Alchevsky (banker) **Obv:** Steam train, factory, National arms and value **Rev:** Head with beard 1/4 right **Edge:** Reeded

| Date | Mintage | VF20 | XF40 | MS60 | MS63 | MS65 |
|---|---|---|---|---|---|---|
| 2005 | 20,000 | — | — | — | — | 25.00 |

**KM# 376 2 HRYVNI**
12.80 g., Copper-Nickel-Zinc, 31 mm. **Subject:** Illia Mechnikov (biologist, Nobel prize laureate) **Obv:** Amoeba and National arms **Rev:** Bust with beard facing **Edge:** Reeded

| Date | Mintage | VF20 | XF40 | MS60 | MS63 | MS65 |
|---|---|---|---|---|---|---|
| 2005 | 20,000 | — | — | — | — | 27.50 |

**KM# 377 2 HRYVNI**
12.80 g., Copper-Nickel-Zinc, 31 mm. **Subject:** Vsevolod Holubovych (politician) **Obv:** National arms **Rev:** Head 1/4 left **Edge:** Reeded

| Date | Mintage | VF20 | XF40 | MS60 | MS63 | MS65 |
|---|---|---|---|---|---|---|
| 2005 | 20,000 | — | — | — | — | 18.00 |

**KM# 378 2 HRYVNI**
12.80 g., Copper-Nickel-Zinc, 31 mm. **Subject:** Volodymyr Vynnychenko (writer, politician) **Obv:** National arms **Rev:** Head facing **Edge:** Reeded

| Date | Mintage | VF20 | XF40 | MS60 | MS63 | MS65 |
|---|---|---|---|---|---|---|
| 2005 | 20,000 | — | — | — | — | 16.00 |

**KM# 383 2 HRYVNI**
12.80 g., Copper-Nickel-Zinc, 31 mm. **Subject:** Kyiv National University of Economics **Obv:** National arms, value and graph **Rev:** University building **Edge:** Reeded

| Date | Mintage | VF20 | XF40 | MS60 | MS63 | MS65 |
|---|---|---|---|---|---|---|
| 2006 | 60,000 | — | — | — | — | 12.00 |

**KM# 384 2 HRYVNI**
12.80 g., Copper-Nickel-Zinc, 31 mm. **Subject:** Viacheslav Prokopovych (historian, publist) **Obv:** National arms **Rev:** Bust facing **Edge:** Reeded

| Date | Mintage | VF20 | XF40 | MS60 | MS63 | MS65 |
|---|---|---|---|---|---|---|
| 2006 | 30,000 | — | — | — | — | 12.00 |

**KM# 385 2 HRYVNI**
12.80 g., Copper-Nickel-Zinc, 31 mm. **Subject:** Heorhii Narbut (artist) **Obv:** Peasant couple **Rev:** Silhouette of standing figure on one leg facing right **Edge:** Reeded

| Date | Mintage | VF20 | XF40 | MS60 | MS63 | MS65 |
|---|---|---|---|---|---|---|
| 2006 | 30,000 | — | — | — | — | 12.00 |

**KM# 386 2 HRYVNI**
12.80 g., Copper-Nickel-Zinc, 31 mm. **Subject:** Oleh Antonov (aircraft engineer) **Obv:** Large jet plane **Rev:** Bust 1/4 right **Edge:** Reeded

| Date | Mintage | VF20 | XF40 | MS60 | MS63 | MS65 |
|---|---|---|---|---|---|---|
| 2006 | 45,000 | — | — | — | — | 15.00 |

**KM# 391 2 HRYVNI**
12.80 g., Copper-Nickel-Zinc, 31 mm. **Obv:** National arms above value in wreath **Rev:** Bush Katydid Grasshopper **Edge:** Reeded

| Date | Mintage | VF20 | XF40 | MS60 | MS63 | MS65 |
|---|---|---|---|---|---|---|
| 2006 | 60,000 | — | — | — | — | 10.00 |

**KM# 393 2 HRYVNI**
12.80 g., Copper-Nickel-Zinc, 31 mm. **Subject:** Mykola Strazhesko **Obv:** National arms and value **Edge:** Reeded

| Date | Mintage | VF20 | XF40 | MS60 | MS63 | MS65 |
|---|---|---|---|---|---|---|
| 2006 | 45,000 | — | — | — | — | 12.00 |

**KM# 394 2 HRYVNI**
12.80 g., Copper-Nickel-Zinc, 31 mm. **Subject:** Volodymyr Chekhivsky **Obv:** National arms and value **Edge:** Reeded

| Date | Mintage | VF20 | XF40 | MS60 | MS63 | MS65 |
|---|---|---|---|---|---|---|
| 2006 | 30,000 | — | — | — | — | 12.00 |

**KM# 395 2 HRYVNI**
12.80 g., Copper-Nickel-Zinc, 31 mm. **Subject:** Mykola Vasylenko **Obv:** National arms and value **Edge:** Reeded

| Date | Mintage | VF20 | XF40 | MS60 | MS63 | MS65 |
|---|---|---|---|---|---|---|
| 2006 | 30,000 | — | — | — | — | 12.00 |

**KM# 396 2 HRYVNI**
12.80 g., Copper-Nickel-Zinc, 31 mm. **Subject:** Ivan Franko **Obv:** National arms and value **Edge:** Reeded

| Date | Mintage | VF20 | XF40 | MS60 | MS63 | MS65 |
|---|---|---|---|---|---|---|
| 2006 | 45,000 | — | — | — | — | 12.00 |

**KM# 397 2 HRYVNI**
12.80 g., Copper-Nickel-Zinc, 31 mm. **Subject:** Dmytro Lutsenko **Obv:** National arms and value **Edge:** Reeded

| Date | Mintage | VF20 | XF40 | MS60 | MS63 | MS65 |
|---|---|---|---|---|---|---|
| 2006 | 30,000 | — | — | — | — | 12.00 |

**KM# 398 2 HRYVNI**
12.80 g., Copper-Nickel-Zinc, 31 mm. **Subject:** Mykhailo Hrushevskyi **Obv:** National arms and value **Edge:** Reeded

| Date | Mintage | VF20 | XF40 | MS60 | MS63 | MS65 |
|---|---|---|---|---|---|---|
| 2006 | 45,000 | — | — | — | — | 12.00 |

**KM# 399 2 HRYVNI**
12.80 g., Copper-Nickel-Zinc, 31 mm. **Subject:** Serhii Ostapenko **Obv:** National arms **Edge:** Reeded

| Date | Mintage | VF20 | XF40 | MS60 | MS63 | MS65 |
|---|---|---|---|---|---|---|
| 2006 | 30,000 | — | — | — | — | 12.00 |

**KM# 400 2 HRYVNI**
12.80 g., Copper-Nickel-Zinc, 31 mm. **Subject:** Mykhailo Lysenko **Obv:** National arms and value **Edge:** Reeded

| Date | Mintage | VF20 | XF40 | MS60 | MS63 | MS65 |
|---|---|---|---|---|---|---|
| 2006 | 35,000 | — | — | — | — | 12.00 |

**KM# 401 2 HRYVNI**
12.80 g., Copper-Nickel-Zinc, 31 mm. **Subject:** Economic University of Kharkiv **Edge:** Reeded

| Date | Mintage | VF20 | XF40 | MS60 | MS63 | MS65 |
|---|---|---|---|---|---|---|
| 2006 | 30,000 | — | — | — | — | 12.00 |

**KM# 403 2 HRYVNI**
1.24 g., 0.9999 Gold 0.0399 oz. AGW, 13.92 mm. **Subject:** Ram **Obv:** National arms **Edge:** Plain

| Date | Mintage | VF20 | XF40 | MS60 | MS63 | MS65 |
|---|---|---|---|---|---|---|
| 2006 | 10,000 | — | — | — | — | 150 |

**KM# 404 2 HRYVNI**
1.24 g., 0.9999 Gold 0.0399 oz. AGW, 13.92 mm. **Subject:** Bull **Obv:** National arms **Edge:** Plain

| Date | Mintage | VF20 | XF40 | MS60 | MS63 | MS65 |
|---|---|---|---|---|---|---|
| 2006 | 10,000 | — | — | — | — | 150 |

**KM# 406 2 HRYVNI**
1.24 g., 0.9999 Gold 0.0399 oz. AGW, 13.92 mm. **Subject:** The Twins **Obv:** National arms **Edge:** Plain

| Date | Mintage | VF20 | XF40 | MS60 | MS63 | MS65 |
|---|---|---|---|---|---|---|
| 2006 | 10,000 | — | — | — | — | 150 |

**KM# 408 2 HRYVNI**
1.24 g., 0.9999 Gold 0.0399 oz. AGW, 13.92 mm. **Subject:** Hedgehog **Obv:** National arms **Edge:** Plain

| Date | Mintage | VF20 | XF40 | MS60 | MS63 | MS65 |
|---|---|---|---|---|---|---|
| 2006 | 10,000 | — | — | — | — | 125 |

**KM# 428 2 HRYVNI**
12.80 g., Copper-Nickel-Zinc, 31 mm. **Subject:** Serhii Koroljov **Obv:** National arms **Edge:** Reeded

| Date | Mintage | VF20 | XF40 | MS60 | MS63 | MS65 |
|---|---|---|---|---|---|---|
| 2007 | 35,000 | — | — | — | — | 20.00 |

**KM# 429 2 HRYVNI**
12.80 g., Copper-Nickel-Zinc, 31 mm. **Subject:** Les Kurbas **Obv:** National arms **Edge:** Reeded

| Date | Mintage | VF20 | XF40 | MS60 | MS63 | MS65 |
|---|---|---|---|---|---|---|
| 2007 | 35,000 | — | — | — | — | 12.00 |

**KM# 430 2 HRYVNI**

12.80 g., Copper-Nickel-Zinc, 31 mm. **Subject:** Olexander Liapunov **Obv:** Small national arms above geometrical depiction of celestial mechanics graphics **Rev:** Large bust facing **Edge:** Reeded

| Date | Mintage | VF20 | XF40 | MS60 | MS63 | MS65 |
|---|---|---|---|---|---|---|
| 2007 | 35,000 | — | — | — | — | 12.00 |

**KM# 431 2 HRYVNI**

1.24 g., 0.9999 Gold 0.0399 oz. AGW, 13.92 mm. **Subject:** Steppe Marmot **Obv:** National arms **Edge:** Plain

| Date | Mintage | VF20 | XF40 | MS60 | MS63 | MS65 |
|---|---|---|---|---|---|---|
| 2007 | 10,000 | — | — | — | — | 150 |

**KM# 440 2 HRYVNI**

12.80 g., Copper-Nickel-Zinc, 31 mm. **Subject:** Ivan Ohienko **Obv:** Cross **Rev:** Head and hands clasped at prayer **Edge:** Reeded

| Date | Mintage | VF20 | XF40 | MS60 | MS63 | MS65 |
|---|---|---|---|---|---|---|
| 2007 | 35,000 | — | — | — | — | 12.00 |

**KM# 441 2 HRYVNI**

12.80 g., Copper-Nickel-Zinc, 31 mm. **Subject:** Oleh Olzhych **Obv:** Chestnut leaf and stone path **Rev:** Bust facing **Edge:** Reeded

| Date | Mintage | VF20 | XF40 | MS60 | MS63 | MS65 |
|---|---|---|---|---|---|---|
| 2007 | 35,000 | — | — | — | — | 12.00 |

**KM# 442 2 HRYVNI**

12.80 g., Copper-Nickel-Zinc, 31 mm. **Subject:** Donetsk Region 75th Anniversary **Obv:** Miner's lamp illuminating industrial plants **Rev:** Flag and 75 **Edge:** Reeded

| Date | Mintage | VF20 | XF40 | MS60 | MS63 | MS65 |
|---|---|---|---|---|---|---|
| 2007 | 35,000 | — | — | — | — | 20.00 |

**KM# 443 2 HRYVNI**

12.80 g., Copper-Nickel-Zinc, 31 mm. **Subject:** Olena Teliha **Obv:** Scorched cherry blossom **Rev:** Bust facing **Edge:** Reeded

| Date | Mintage | VF20 | XF40 | MS60 | MS63 | MS65 |
|---|---|---|---|---|---|---|
| 2007 | 35,000 | — | — | — | — | 12.00 |

**KM# 444 2 HRYVNI**

12.80 g., Copper-Nickel-Zinc, 31 mm. **Subject:** Orienteering **Obv:** Compass, star and benchmarks **Rev:** Runner **Edge:** Reeded

| Date | Mintage | VF20 | XF40 | MS60 | MS63 | MS65 |
|---|---|---|---|---|---|---|
| 2007 | 35,000 | — | — | — | — | 16.00 |

**KM# 445 2 HRYVNI**

12.80 g., Copper-Nickel-Zinc, 31 mm. **Subject:** Ivan Bahrianji **Obv:** Book edge **Rev:** Bust facing, book edge **Edge:** Reeded

| Date | Mintage | VF20 | XF40 | MS60 | MS63 | MS65 |
|---|---|---|---|---|---|---|
| 2007 | 35,000 | — | — | — | — | 12.00 |

**KM# 446 2 HRYVNI**

12.80 g., Copper-Nickel-Zinc, 31 mm. **Subject:** Petro Hryhorenko **Obv:** Sprout squeezing brick wall **Rev:** Head right **Edge:** Reeded

| Date | Mintage | VF20 | XF40 | MS60 | MS63 | MS65 |
|---|---|---|---|---|---|---|
| 2007 | 35,000 | — | — | — | — | 12.00 |

**KM# 447 2 HRYVNI**

12.80 g., Copper-Nickel-Zinc, 31 mm. **Subject:** 90th Anniversary of 1st Government **Obv:** Parts of early 20th century bank notes and industrial elements **Rev:** Volodymyr Vynnychenko and ornamentation **Edge:** Reeded

| Date | Mintage | VF20 | XF40 | MS60 | MS63 | MS65 |
|---|---|---|---|---|---|---|
| 2007 | 35,000 | — | — | — | — | 12.00 |

**KM# 448 2 HRYVNI**

1.24 g., 0.999 Gold 0.0398 oz. AGW, 13.9 mm. **Subject:** Capricorn **Obv:** Elements of earth, air, water and fire **Rev:** Zodiac sign

| Date | Mintage | VF20 | XF40 | MS60 | MS63 | MS65 |
|---|---|---|---|---|---|---|
| 2007 | 10,000 | — | — | — | — | 150 |

**KM# 449 2 HRYVNI**

1.24 g., 0.999 Gold 0.0398 oz. AGW, 13.9 mm. **Subject:** Aquarius **Obv:** Elements of earth, air, water and fire **Rev:** Zodiac sign, man pouring water

| Date | Mintage | VF20 | XF40 | MS60 | MS63 | MS65 |
|---|---|---|---|---|---|---|
| 2007 | 10,000 | — | — | — | — | 150 |

**KM# 450 2 HRYVNI**

1.24 g., 0.999 Gold 0.0398 oz. AGW, 13.9 mm. **Subject:** Pisces **Obv:** Elements of earth, air, water and fire **Rev:** Zodiac sign, two fish

| Date | Mintage | VF20 | XF40 | MS60 | MS63 | MS65 |
|---|---|---|---|---|---|---|
| 2007 | 10,000 | — | — | — | — | 150 |

**KM# 451 2 HRYVNI**

1.24 g., 0.999 Gold 0.0398 oz. AGW, 13.9 mm. **Subject:** Scorpion **Obv:** Elements of earth, air, water and fire **Rev:** Zodiac sign

| Date | Mintage | VF20 | XF40 | MS60 | MS63 | MS65 |
|---|---|---|---|---|---|---|
| 2007 | 10,000 | — | — | — | — | 150 |

**KM# 452 2 HRYVNI**

1.24 g., 0.999 Gold 0.0398 oz. AGW, 13.9 mm. **Subject:** Sagitarius **Obv:** Elements of earth, air, water & fire **Rev:** Zodiac sign, archer

| Date | Mintage | VF20 | XF40 | MS60 | MS63 | MS65 |
|---|---|---|---|---|---|---|
| 2007 | 10,000 | — | — | — | — | 150 |

**KM# 433 2 HRYVNI**

12.80 g., Copper-Nickel-Zinc, 31 mm. **Obv:** Small national arms at top, value in sprays with bird at left, butterfly at right **Rev:** Cinereous Vulture perched on nest with chick **Rev. Legend:** AEGYPIUS MONACHUS - ГРИФ ЧОРНИЈ **Edge:** Reeded

| Date | Mintage | VF20 | XF40 | MS60 | MS63 | MS65 |
|---|---|---|---|---|---|---|
| 2008 | 45,000 | — | — | — | — | 15.00 |

**KM# 475 2 HRYVNI**

12.80 g., Copper-Nickel-Zinc, 31 mm. **Subject:** Vasyl Stus, Poet **Edge:** Reeded

| Date | Mintage | VF20 | XF40 | MS60 | MS63 | MS65 |
|---|---|---|---|---|---|---|
| 2008 | 35,000 | — | — | — | — | 12.00 |

**KM# 476 2 HRYVNI**

12.80 g., Copper-Nickel-Zinc, 31 mm. **Subject:** Leo Landau **Edge:** Reeded

| Date | Mintage | VF20 | XF40 | MS60 | MS63 | MS65 |
|---|---|---|---|---|---|---|
| 2008 | 35,000 | — | — | — | — | 12.00 |

**KM# 477 2 HRYVNI**

12.80 g., Copper-Nickel-Zinc, 31 mm. **Subject:** Sydir Holubovych **Edge:** Reeded

| Date | Mintage | VF20 | XF40 | MS60 | MS63 | MS65 |
|---|---|---|---|---|---|---|
| 2008 | 35,000 | — | — | — | — | 12.00 |

**KM# 478 2 HRYVNI**

12.80 g., Copper-Nickel-Zinc, 31 mm. **Subject:** Kyiv Zoo, 100th Anniversary **Edge:** Reeded

| Date | Mintage | VF20 | XF40 | MS60 | MS63 | MS65 |
|---|---|---|---|---|---|---|
| 2008 | 50,000 | — | — | — | — | 15.00 |

**KM# 479 2 HRYVNI**

12.80 g., Copper-Nickel-Zinc, 31 mm. **Subject:** Yevhen Petrushevych **Edge:** Reeded

| Date | Mintage | VF20 | XF40 | MS60 | MS63 | MS65 |
|---|---|---|---|---|---|---|
| 2008 | 35,000 | — | — | — | — | 12.00 |

**KM# 481 2 HRYVNI**

12.80 g., Copper-Nickel-Zinc, 31 mm. **Subject:** Heorhii Voronyi **Edge:** Reeded

| Date | Mintage | VF20 | XF40 | MS60 | MS63 | MS65 |
|---|---|---|---|---|---|---|
| 2008 | 35,000 | — | — | — | — | 12.00 |

**KM# 482 2 HRYVNI**

1.24 g., 0.999 Gold 0.0398 oz. AGW, 13.9 mm. **Subject:** Skythian Gold (Goddess Api)

| Date | Mintage | VF20 | XF40 | MS60 | MS63 | MS65 |
|---|---|---|---|---|---|---|
| 2008 | 10,000 | — | — | — | — | 150 |

**KM# 483 2 HRYVNI**

1.24 g., 0.999 Gold 0.0398 oz. AGW, 13.9 mm. **Subject:** Zodiac **Rev:** Cancer

| Date | Mintage | VF20 | XF40 | MS60 | MS63 | MS65 |
|---|---|---|---|---|---|---|
| 2008 | 10,000 | — | — | — | — | 150 |

**KM# 484 2 HRYVNI**

1.24 g., 0.999 Gold 0.0398 oz. AGW, 13.9 mm. **Subject:** Zodiac **Rev:** Leo

| Date | Mintage | VF20 | XF40 | MS60 | MS63 | MS65 |
|---|---|---|---|---|---|---|
| 2008 | 10,000 | — | — | — | — | 150 |

**KM# 485 2 HRYVNI**

1.24 g., 0.999 Gold 0.0398 oz. AGW **Subject:** Virgo

| Date | Mintage | VF20 | XF40 | MS60 | MS63 | MS65 |
|---|---|---|---|---|---|---|
| 2008 | 10,000 | — | — | — | — | 150 |

**KM# 486 2 HRYVNI**

1.24 g., 0.999 Gold 0.0398 oz. AGW, 13.9 mm. **Subject:** Libra

| Date | Mintage | VF20 | XF40 | MS60 | MS63 | MS65 |
|---|---|---|---|---|---|---|
| 2008 | — | — | — | — | — | 150 |

**KM# 487 2 HRYVNI**

12.80 g., Copper-Nickel-Zinc, 31 mm. **Subject:** Nataliia Vzhvii **Edge:** Reeded

| Date | Mintage | VF20 | XF40 | MS60 | MS63 | MS65 |
|---|---|---|---|---|---|---|
| 2008 | 35,000 | — | — | — | — | 12.00 |

**KM# 488 2 HRYVNI**

12.80 g., Copper-Nickel-Zinc, 31 mm. **Subject:** Hryhorii Kvitka - Osnovianenko **Edge:** Reeded

| Date | Mintage | VF20 | XF40 | MS60 | MS63 | MS65 |
|---|---|---|---|---|---|---|
| 2008 | 35,000 | — | — | — | — | 12.00 |

**KM# 489 2 HRYVNI**

12.80 g., Copper-Nickel-Zinc, 31 mm. **Subject:** Western Ukraine People's Repbulic, 90th Anniversary **Edge:** Reeded

| Date | Mintage | VF20 | XF40 | MS60 | MS63 | MS65 |
|---|---|---|---|---|---|---|
| 2008 | 35,000 | — | — | — | — | 12.00 |

**KM# 490 2 HRYVNI**
12.80 g., Copper-Nickel-Zinc, 31 mm. **Subject:** Vasyl Symonenko **Edge:** Reeded

| Date | Mintage | VF20 | XF40 | MS60 | MS63 | MS65 |
|---|---|---|---|---|---|---|
| 2008 | 35,000 | — | — | — | — | 12.00 |

**KM# 533 2 HRYVNI**
12.80 g., Copper-Nickel-Zinc, 31.0 mm. **Subject:** Pavlo Chubynskyi **Obv:** Folk music instruments **Obv. Legend:** НАЦІОНАЛЬНИЈ БАНК УКРАІНИ - 2 / ГРИВНІ / 2009 **Rev:** Chubynskyi's portrait **Rev. Legend:** ПАВЛО ЧУБИНСЬКИЈ - 1839-1884 **Edge:** Reeded

| Date | Mintage | VF20 | XF40 | MS60 | MS63 | MS65 |
|---|---|---|---|---|---|---|
| 2009 | 35,000 | — | — | — | — | 12.00 |

**KM# 534 2 HRYVNI**
12.80 g., Copper-Nickel-Zinc, 31.0 mm. **Subject:** Andrii Livytskyi **Obv:** National Arms and value **Obv. Legend:** НАЦІОНАЛЬНИЈ БАНК УКРАІНИ - ДВІ ГРИВНІ **Rev:** Livytskyi's portrait **Rev. Legend:** АНДРІЈ ЛІВИЦЬКИЈ - 1879/1954 - ПРЕЗИДЕНТ УНР В ЕКЗИЛІ **Edge:** Reeded

| Date | Mintage | VF20 | XF40 | MS60 | MS63 | MS65 |
|---|---|---|---|---|---|---|
| 2009 | 35,000 | — | — | — | — | 12.00 |

**KM# 535 2 HRYVNI**
1.24 g., 0.999 Gold 0.0398 oz. AGW, 13.92 mm. **Subject:** Ukraine Fauna **Obv:** National Arms, value **Obv. Legend:** НАЦІОНАЛЬНИЈ БАНК УКРАІНИ - 2 ГРИВНІ **Rev:** Turtle **Rev. Legend:** ЧЕРЕПАХА - TESTUDINES

| Date | Mintage | VF20 | XF40 | MS60 | MS63 | MS65 |
|---|---|---|---|---|---|---|
| 2009 | 10,000 | — | — | — | — | 150 |

**KM# 536 2 HRYVNI**
12.80 g., Copper-Nickel-Zinc, 31.0 mm. **Subject:** Borys Martos **Obv:** National Arms and value **Obv. Legend:** НАЦІОНАЛЬНИЈ БАНК УКРАІНИ - ДВІ ГРИВНІ **Rev:** Martos's portrait **Rev. Legend:** БОРИС МАРТОС **Edge:** Reeded

| Date | Mintage | VF20 | XF40 | MS60 | MS63 | MS65 |
|---|---|---|---|---|---|---|
| 2009 | 35,000 | — | — | — | — | 12.00 |

**KM# 537 2 HRYVNI**
12.80 g., Copper-Nickel-Zinc, 31.0 mm. **Subject:** General Symon Petliura **Obv:** Two Military men holding wreath of a woman's profile **Obv. Legend:** НАЦІОНАЛЬНИЈ БАНК УКРАІНИ - 2 ГРИВНІ **Rev:** Petliura's portrait **Rev. Legend:** СИМОН ПЕТЛ@@НРА **Edge:** Reeded

| Date | Mintage | VF20 | XF40 | MS60 | MS63 | MS65 |
|---|---|---|---|---|---|---|
| 2009 | 35,000 | — | — | — | — | 15.00 |

**KM# 538 2 HRYVNI**
12.80 g., Copper-Nickel-Zinc, 31 mm. **Subject:** Igor Sikorskyi, 100th Anniversary of birth **Obv:** Aircraft, National Arms, value **Obv. Legend:** НАЦІОНАЛЬНИЈ БАНК УКРАІНИ - 2 ГРИВНІ **Rev:** Sikorskyi portrait as an airman, Da Vinci drawing **Rev. Legend:** ІГОР СІКОРСЬКИЈ **Edge:** Reeded

| Date | Mintage | VF20 | XF40 | MS60 | MS63 | MS65 |
|---|---|---|---|---|---|---|
| 2009 | 35,000 | — | — | — | — | 15.00 |

**KM# 539 2 HRYVNI**
12.80 g., Copper-Nickel-Zinc, 31 mm. **Subject:** Mykola Bogolijubov, physicist, 100th Anniversary of birth **Obv:** Diagram and formula, National Arms, value **Rev:** Bogolijubov's portrait **Edge:** Reeded

| Date | Mintage | VF20 | XF40 | MS60 | MS63 | MS65 |
|---|---|---|---|---|---|---|
| 2009 | 35,000 | — | — | — | — | 12.00 |

**KM# 540 2 HRYVNI**
12.80 g., Copper-Nickel-Zinc, 31 mm. **Subject:** Volodymyr Ivasiuk, poet and singer **Obv:** Flower of Chervona Ruta, electrical musical instruments **Obv. Legend:** НАЦІОНАЛЬНИЈ БАНК УКРАІНИ - 2 / ГРИВНІ / 2009 **Rev:** Ivasiuk's portrait **Rev. Legend:** ВОЛОДИМИР ІВАСЮК **Edge:** Reeded

| Date | Mintage | VF20 | XF40 | MS60 | MS63 | MS65 |
|---|---|---|---|---|---|---|
| 2009 | 35,000 | — | — | — | — | 12.00 |

**KM# 541 2 HRYVNI**
12.80 g., Copper-Nickel-Zinc, 31.0 mm. **Subject:** Bohdan-Igor Antonych, poet **Obv:** Figurative interpretation of Antonych's poetry **Obv. Legend:** НАЦІОНАЛЬНИЈ БАНК УКРАІНИ - 2 / ГРИВНІ **Rev:** Antonych's portrait **Rev. Legend:** БОГДАН-ІГОР АНТОНИЧ **Edge:** Reeded

| Date | Mintage | VF20 | XF40 | MS60 | MS63 | MS65 |
|---|---|---|---|---|---|---|
| 2009 | 35,000 | — | — | — | — | 12.00 |

**KM# 542 2 HRYVNI**
12.80 g., Copper-Nickel-Zinc, 31.0 mm. **Subject:** Kost Levytskyi **Obv:** State Coat of Arms, issue year **Obv. Legend:** НАЦІОНАЛЬНИЈ БАНК УКРАІНИ - ДВІ ГРИВНІ **Rev:** Levytskyi bust **Rev. Legend:** КОСТЬ ЛЕВИЦЬКИЈ

| Date | Mintage | VF20 | XF40 | MS60 | MS63 | MS65 |
|---|---|---|---|---|---|---|
| 2009 | 35,000 | — | — | — | — | 12.00 |

**KM# 551 2 HRYVNI**
12.80 g., Copper-Nickel-Zinc, 31.0 mm. **Subject:** Carpatho-Ukraine Republic, 70th Anniversary **Obv:** Carpathian ornamentation patterns, National Arms, value **Obv. Legend:** НАЦІОНАЛЬНИЈ БАНК УКРАІНИ - 2 / ГРИВНІ **Rev:** Transcarpathian holding flag with arms of Carpatho-Ukraine **Rev. Legend:** 70 / РОКІВ - ПРОГОЛОШЕННЯ КАРПАТСЬКОІ УКРАІНИ **Edge:** Reeded

| Date | Mintage | VF20 | XF40 | MS60 | MS63 | MS65 |
|---|---|---|---|---|---|---|
| 2009 | 35,000 | — | — | — | — | 14.00 |

**KM# 571 2 HRYVNI**
1.24 g., 0.999 Gold 0.0398 oz. AGW, 13.92 mm. **Subject:** Skythian Gold **Obv:** National Arms **Rev:** Scythian boar figure

| Date | Mintage | VF20 | XF40 | MS60 | MS63 | MS65 |
|---|---|---|---|---|---|---|
| 2009 Special Unc. | 10,000 | — | — | — | — | 150 |

**KM# 578 2 HRYVNI**
12.80 g., Copper-Nickel-Zinc, 31 mm. **Subject:** Zaporizhzhia Oblast **Obv:** Zaporizhzhia Arms **Rev:** Stone bana, Dnieper's waves and Dniporhes dam **Edge:** Reeded

| Date | Mintage | VF20 | XF40 | MS60 | MS63 | MS65 |
|---|---|---|---|---|---|---|
| 2009 | 45,000 | — | — | — | — | 13.00 |

**KM# 572 2 HRYVNI**
1.24 g., 0.999 Gold 0.0398 oz. AGW, 13.92 mm. **Obv:** National Arms **Rev:** Bee **Edge:** Plain

| Date | Mintage | VF20 | XF40 | MS60 | MS63 | MS65 |
|---|---|---|---|---|---|---|
| 2010 Special Unc. | 10,000 | — | — | — | — | 150 |

**KM# 576 2 HRYVNI**
12.80 g., Copper-Nickel-Zinc, 31 mm. **Subject:** Ukraine Ice Hockey, 100th Anniversary **Obv:** Golie before net, National Arms **Rev:** Old time and modern hockey players **Edge:** Reeded

| Date | Mintage | VF20 | XF40 | MS60 | MS63 | MS65 |
|---|---|---|---|---|---|---|
| 2010 | 35,000 | — | — | — | — | 13.00 |

**KM# 580 2 HRYVNI**
12.80 g., Copper-Nickel-Zinc, 31 mm. **Subject:** Ivan Kozhedub **Obv:** La-7 aircraft in two searchlight beams **Rev:** Kozhedub's portrait and airfield **Edge:** Reeded

| Date | Mintage | VF20 | XF40 | MS60 | MS63 | MS65 |
|---|---|---|---|---|---|---|
| 2010 | 35,000 | — | — | — | — | 14.00 |

**KM# 581 2 HRYVNI**
12.80 g., Copper-Nickel-Zinc, 31 mm. **Subject:** Lviv Polytechnic National University, 165th Anniversary **Obv:** Arts and Sciences sculptures from main building **Rev:** University building façade **Edge:** Reeded

| Date | Mintage | VF20 | XF40 | MS60 | MS63 | MS65 |
|---|---|---|---|---|---|---|
| 2010 | 45,000 | — | — | — | — | 13.00 |

**KM# 583 2 HRYVNI**
12.80 g., Copper-Nickel-Zinc, 31 mm. **Subject:** Kharkiv Polytechnic Institute, 125th Anniversary **Obv:** Radio telescope and open book **Rev:** University building at right, symbols of science at left, oval portrait of V.L. Kyrpychov **Edge:** Reeded

| Date | Mintage | VF20 | XF40 | MS60 | MS63 | MS65 |
|---|---|---|---|---|---|---|
| 2010 | 50,000 | — | — | — | — | 13.00 |

**KM# 585 2 HRYVNI**
12.80 g., Copper-Nickel, 31 mm. **Subject:** Ukraine Sovereignty, 20th Anniversary **Obv:** National flag in enamel within viburnum wreath **Rev:** Ukraine map within uneven background **Edge:** Reeded

| Date | Mintage | VF20 | XF40 | MS60 | MS63 | MS65 |
|---|---|---|---|---|---|---|
| 2010 | 35,000 | — | — | — | — | 18.00 |

**KM# 593 2 HRYVNI**
12.80 g., Copper-Nickel-Zinc, 31 mm. **Subject:** Flora and fauna **Obv:** National Arms and wreath **Rev:** Stipa Ucrainica, feather grass **Edge:** Reeded

| Date | Mintage | VF20 | XF40 | MS60 | MS63 | MS65 |
|---|---|---|---|---|---|---|
| 2010 | 35,000 | — | — | — | — | 13.00 |

**KM# 603 2 HRYVNI**
1.24 g., 0.999 Gold 0.0398 oz. AGW, 13.92 mm. **Obv:** National Arms **Rev:** Cranberry bush branch **Edge:** Plain

| Date | Mintage | VF20 | XF40 | MS60 | MS63 | MS65 |
|---|---|---|---|---|---|---|
| 2010 | 10,000 | — | — | — | — | 150 |

**KM# 608 2 HRYVNI**
12.80 g., Copper-Nickel-Zinc, 31 mm. **Subject:** Ukranian Medical Association, 100th Anniversary **Obv:** UMA Shield within wreath **Rev:** UMA in Lviv emblem (lion on cross) **Edge:** Reeded

| Date | Mintage | VF20 | XF40 | MS60 | MS63 | MS65 |
|---|---|---|---|---|---|---|
| 2010 | 35,000 | — | — | — | — | 15.00 |

**KM# 612 2 HRYVNI**
12.80 g., Copper-Nickel-Zinc, 31 mm. **Subject:** Ivan Franko National University, Lviv, 350th Anniversary **Obv:** National arms, Statuary group, value **Rev:** Main University building façade **Edge:** reeded

| Date | Mintage | VF20 | XF40 | MS60 | MS63 | MS65 |
|---|---|---|---|---|---|---|
| 2011 | 45,000 | — | — | — | — | 12.00 |

**KM# 624 2 HRYVNI**
1.24 g., 0.9999 Gold 0.0399 oz. AGW, 13.92 mm. **Subject:** Scythian Gold **Obv:** National arms **Rev:** Scythian jewlery, gilt deer

| Date | Mintage | VF20 | XF40 | MS60 | MS63 | MS65 |
|---|---|---|---|---|---|---|
| 2011 | 10,000 | — | — | — | — | 150 |

**KM# 636 2 HRYVNI**
12.80 g., Copper-Nickel-Zinc, 31 mm. **Subject:** CIS, 20th Anniversary **Obv:** National flag in color **Rev:** Commonwealth of Independent States emblem **Edge:** Reeded

| Date | Mintage | VF20 | XF40 | MS60 | MS63 | MS65 |
|---|---|---|---|---|---|---|
| 2011 | 30,000 | PF65 15.00 | | | | |

**KM# 656 2 HRYVNI**
1.24 g., 0.9999 Gold 0.0399 oz. AGW, 13.92 mm. **Obv:** National shield **Rev:** Malva flower

| Date | Mintage | VF20 | XF40 | MS60 | MS63 | MS65 |
|---|---|---|---|---|---|---|
| 2012 | Est. 8000 | PF63 120 | PF65 150 | | | |

**KM# 658 2 HRYVNI**
12.80 g., Copper-Nickel-Zinc, 31 mm. **Subject:** Sydir Kovpak WWII Soviet Hero

| Date | Mintage | VF20 | XF40 | MS60 | MS63 | MS65 |
|---|---|---|---|---|---|---|
| 2012 | Est. 15000 | — | — | — | — | 35.00 |

**KM# 661 2 HRYVNI**
12.80 g., Copper-Nickel-Zinc, 31 mm. **Subject:** 2012 London Paralympic Games **Edge:** Reeded

| Date | Mintage | VF20 | XF40 | MS60 | MS63 | MS65 |
|---|---|---|---|---|---|---|
| 2012 | Est. 30000 | — | — | — | — | 15.00 |

**KM# 675 2 HRYVNI**
12.80 g., Copper-Nickel-Zinc, 31 mm. **Subject:** XXX Summer Olympic Games - London **Obv:** London City view, National arms **Rev:** Gold State of Philip II and silhouettes of sports **Edge:** Reeded

| Date | Mintage | VF20 | XF40 | MS60 | MS63 | MS65 |
|---|---|---|---|---|---|---|
| 2012 | 30,000 | — | — | — | — | 15.00 |

**KM# 682 2 HRYVNI**
12.80 g., Copper-Nickel-Zinc, 31 mm. **Subject:** Mykhailo Kravchuk, academician **Obv:** National arms, formula, value **Rev:** Portrait of Kravchuk **Edge:** Reeded

| Date | Mintage | VF20 | XF40 | MS60 | MS63 | MS65 |
|---|---|---|---|---|---|---|
| 2012 | 15,000 | — | — | — | — | 22.00 |

**KM# 688 2 HRYVNI**
12.80 g., Copper-Nickel-Zinc, 31 mm. **Obv:** National arms, value **Rev:** The sterlet **Edge:** Reeded

| Date | Mintage | VF20 | XF40 | MS60 | MS63 | MS65 |
|---|---|---|---|---|---|---|
| 2012 | 35,000 | — | — | — | — | 18.00 |

**KM# 698 2 HRYVNI**
12.80 g., Copper-Nickel-Zinc, 31 mm. **Subject:** The Great Bustard **Obv:** National arms, date, value

| Date | Mintage | VF20 | XF40 | MS60 | MS63 | MS65 |
|---|---|---|---|---|---|---|
| 2013 | 30,000 | — | — | — | — | 17.00 |

**KM# 703 2 HRYVNI**
12.80 g., Copper-Nickel-Zinc, 31 mm. **Subject:** World Youth Championships - Athletics **Obv:** National arms, Stadium in Donetsk and value **Rev:** Girl athletes in motion **Edge:** Reeded

| Date | Mintage | VF20 | XF40 | MS60 | MS63 | MS65 |
|---|---|---|---|---|---|---|
| 2013 | 20,000 | — | — | — | — | 17.00 |

**KM# 107 5 HRYVEN**
9.40 g., Bi-Metallic Brass center in Copper-Nickel ring, 28 mm. **Subject:** New Millennium **Obv:** Spiral design within circle **Rev:** Mother and child within circle **Edge:** Segmented reeding

| Date | Mintage | VF20 | XF40 | MS60 | MS63 | MS65 |
|---|---|---|---|---|---|---|
| 2001 | 50,000 | — | — | — | — | 28.00 |

**KM# 112 5 HRYVEN**
16.54 g., Copper-Nickel-Zinc, 35 mm. **Subject:** Ostrozhska Academy **Obv:** Value, old writing and printing artifacts **Rev:** Seated figures, partial building and crowned arms with supporters **Edge:** Reeded

| Date | Mintage | VF20 | XF40 | MS60 | MS63 | MS65 |
|---|---|---|---|---|---|---|
| 2001 | 30,000 | — | — | — | — | 25.00 |

**KM# 129 5 HRYVEN**
16.54 g., Copper-Nickel-Zinc, 35 mm. **Subject:** 10th Anniversary - National Bank **Obv:** National arms between two arches **Rev:** Large building central entrance **Edge:** Reeded

| Date | Mintage | VF20 | XF40 | MS60 | MS63 | MS65 |
|---|---|---|---|---|---|---|
| 2001 | 50,000 | — | — | — | — | 12.00 |

**KM# 132 5 HRYVEN**
16.54 g., Copper-Nickel-Zinc, 35 mm. **Subject:** 10th Anniversary - National Independence **Obv:** Arms with supporters within beaded circle **Rev:** Building on map within beaded circle **Edge:** Reeded

| Date | Mintage | VF20 | XF40 | MS60 | MS63 | MS65 |
|---|---|---|---|---|---|---|
| 2001 | 100,000 | — | — | — | — | 10.00 |

**KM# 135 5 HRYVEN**
16.54 g., Copper-Nickel-Zinc, 35 mm. **Subject:** 1100th Anniversary - Poltava **Obv:** National arms above value flanked by flower sprigs **Rev:** Buildings above shield **Edge:** Reeded

| Date | Mintage | VF20 | XF40 | MS60 | MS63 | MS65 |
|---|---|---|---|---|---|---|
| 2001 | 50,000 | — | — | — | — | 15.00 |

**KM# 140 5 HRYVEN**
9.40 g., Bi-Metallic Brass center in Copper-Nickel ring, 28 mm. **Subject:** 10th Anniversary of Military forces **Obv:** Crossed maces, arms and date within wreath and circle **Rev:** Circle in center of cross within wreath and circle **Edge:** Reeded and plain sections

| Date | Mintage | VF20 | XF40 | MS60 | MS63 | MS65 |
|---|---|---|---|---|---|---|
| 2001 | 30,000 | — | — | — | — | 35.00 |

**KM# 148 5 HRYVEN**
16.54 g., Copper-Nickel-Zinc, 35 mm. **Subject:** 400 Years of Krolevets **Obv:** National arms above gateway and value **Rev:** Krolivets city arms flanked by designs **Edge:** Reeded

| Date | Mintage | VF20 | XF40 | MS60 | MS63 | MS65 |
|---|---|---|---|---|---|---|
| 2001 | 30,000 | — | — | — | — | 35.00 |

**KM# 151 5 HRYVEN**
16.54 g., Copper-Nickel-Zinc, 35 mm. **Subject:** City of Khotyn **Obv:** Value within arch above military fittings **Rev:** Castle below crowned shield **Edge:** Reeded

| Date | Mintage | VF20 | XF40 | MS60 | MS63 | MS65 |
|---|---|---|---|---|---|---|
| 2002 | 30,000 | — | — | — | — | 25.00 |

**KM# 152 5 HRYVEN**
16.54 g., Copper-Nickel-Zinc, 35 mm. **Obv:** Sun and flying geese divides beaded circle **Rev:** AN-225 Mrija" cargo jet divide beaded circle **Edge:** Reeded

| Date | Mintage | VF20 | XF40 | MS60 | MS63 | MS65 |
|---|---|---|---|---|---|---|
| 2002 | 30,000 | — | — | — | — | 75.00 |

**KM# 157 5 HRYVEN**
16.54 g., Copper-Nickel-Zinc, 35 mm. **Subject:** 1100th Anniversary - City of Romny **Obv:** Sprigs divide national arms and value **Rev:** City view **Edge:** Reeded

| Date | Mintage | VF20 | XF40 | MS60 | MS63 | MS65 |
|---|---|---|---|---|---|---|
| 2002 | 30,000 | — | — | — | — | 35.00 |

**KM# 158 5 HRYVEN**
9.43 g., Bi-Metallic Brass center in Copper-Nickel ring, 28 mm. **Subject:** 70th Anniversary of Dnipro Hydroelectric Power Station **Obv:** Turbine within circle **Rev:** Large dam within circle **Edge:** Reeded and plain sections

| Date | Mintage | VF20 | XF40 | MS60 | MS63 | MS65 |
|---|---|---|---|---|---|---|
| 2002 | 30,000 | — | — | — | — | 50.00 |

**KM# 159 5 HRYVEN**
16.54 g., Copper-Nickel-Zinc, 35 mm. **Obv:** Arms with supporters within beaded circle **Rev:** Battle scene around Batig in 1652 divides beaded circle **Edge:** Reeded

| Date | Mintage | VF20 | XF40 | MS60 | MS63 | MS65 |
|---|---|---|---|---|---|---|
| 2002 | 30,000 | — | — | — | — | 25.00 |

**KM# 163 5 HRYVEN**
16.54 g., Copper-Nickel-Zinc, 35 mm. **Subject:** Christmas **Obv:** National arms in star above value flanked by designed sprigs **Rev:** Christmas pageant scene **Edge:** Reeded

| Date | Mintage | VF20 | XF40 | MS60 | MS63 | MS65 |
|---|---|---|---|---|---|---|
| ND(2002) | 30,000 | — | — | — | — | 75.00 |

**KM# 172 5 HRYVEN**
16.54 g., Copper-Nickel-Zinc, 35 mm. **Subject:** Easter **Obv:** Circle of Easter eggs, national arms in center above value **Rev:** Religious celebration **Edge:** Reeded

| Date | Mintage | VF20 | XF40 | MS60 | MS63 | MS65 |
|---|---|---|---|---|---|---|
| 2003 | 50,000 | — | — | — | — | 35.00 |

**KM# 173 5 HRYVEN**
16.54 g., Copper-Nickel-Zinc, 35 mm. **Subject:** Antonov AN-2 Biplane **Obv:** National arms sun face and flying geese divide beaded circle **Rev:** World's largest biplane divides beaded circle **Edge:** Reeded

| Date | Mintage | VF20 | XF40 | MS60 | MS63 | MS65 |
|---|---|---|---|---|---|---|
| 2003 | 50,000 | — | — | — | — | 20.00 |

**KM# 185 5 HRYVEN**
9.40 g., Bi-Metallic Brass center in Copper-Nickel ring, 28 mm. **Subject:** 150th Anniversary of the Central Ukrainian Archives **Obv:** Value, signature and seal **Rev:** Hourglass divides books and circle **Edge:** Segmented reeding

| Date | Mintage | VF20 | XF40 | MS60 | MS63 | MS65 |
|---|---|---|---|---|---|---|
| 2003 | 30,000 | — | — | — | — | 15.00 |

**KM# 186 5 HRYVEN**
16.54 g., Copper-Nickel-Zinc, 35 mm. **Subject:** 2500th Anniversary of the City of Yevpatoria **Obv:** National arms, date and value with partial sun background **Rev:** Ancient amphora and modern city view **Edge:** Reeded

| Date | Mintage | VF20 | XF40 | MS60 | MS63 | MS65 |
|---|---|---|---|---|---|---|
| 2003 | 30,000 | — | — | — | — | 30.00 |

**KM# 187 5 HRYVEN**
16.54 g., Copper-Nickel-Zinc, 35 mm. **Subject:** 60th Anniversary - Liberation of Kiev **Obv:** Eternal flame monument **Rev:** Battle scene and map of the offense **Edge:** Reeded

| Date | Mintage | VF20 | XF40 | MS60 | MS63 | MS65 |
|---|---|---|---|---|---|---|
| 2003 | 30,000 | — | — | — | — | 20.00 |

**KM# 200 5 HRYVEN**
9.40 g., Bi-Metallic Brass center in Copper-Nickel ring, 28 mm. **Obv:** Bandura strings over ornamental design **Rev:** Bandura divides circle and wreath **Edge:** Segmented reeding

| Date | Mintage | VF20 | XF40 | MS60 | MS63 | MS65 |
|---|---|---|---|---|---|---|
| 2003 | 30,000 | — | — | — | — | 20.00 |

**KM# 204 5 HRYVEN**
16.54 g., Copper-Nickel-Zinc, 35 mm. **Subject:** 50th Anniversary - Pivdenne Space Design Office **Obv:** Satellite orbiting Earth **Rev:** Satellite above moonscape **Edge:** Reeded

| Date | Mintage | VF20 | XF40 | MS60 | MS63 | MS65 |
|---|---|---|---|---|---|---|
| 2004 | 30,000 | — | — | — | — | 17.00 |

**KM# 205 5 HRYVEN**
16.54 g., Copper-Nickel-Zinc, 35 mm. **Subject:** 2500 Anniversary City of Balaklava **Obv:** National arms between two ancient ships **Rev:** Harbor view above pillar **Edge:** Reeded

| Date | Mintage | VF20 | XF40 | MS60 | MS63 | MS65 |
|---|---|---|---|---|---|---|
| 2004 | 30,000 | — | — | — | — | 25.00 |

**KM# 218 5 HRYVEN**
16.94 g., 0.925 Silver 0.5038 oz. ASW, 33 mm. **Obv:** National arms, value and atom **Rev:** Kharkiv University building **Edge:** Reeded

| Date | Mintage | VF20 | XF40 | MS60 | MS63 | MS65 |
|---|---|---|---|---|---|---|
| 2004 | 7,000 | PF65 50.00 | | | | |

**KM# 219 5 HRYVEN**
16.94 g., 0.925 Silver 0.5038 oz. ASW, 33 mm. **Obv:** National arms above value dividing scientific items **Rev:** Kiev University building main entrance **Edge:** Reeded

| Date | Mintage | VF20 | XF40 | MS60 | MS63 | MS65 |
|---|---|---|---|---|---|---|
| 2004 | 7,000 | PF65 50.00 | | | | |

**KM# 220 5 HRYVEN**
9.43 g., Bi-Metallic BRASS center in COPPER-NICKEL ring, 28 mm. **Subject:** 50 Years of Ukraine's Membership in UNESCO **Obv:** National arms in center of sprigs and circle **Rev:** Building within sprigs and circle **Edge:** Segmented reeding

| Date | Mintage | VF20 | XF40 | MS60 | MS63 | MS65 |
|---|---|---|---|---|---|---|
| 2004 | 50,000 | — | — | — | — | 15.00 |

**KM# 221 5 HRYVEN**
16.54 g., Copper-Nickel-Zinc, 35 mm. **Subject:** Ice Breaker "Captain Belousov **Obv:** National arms on ship's wheel and anchor **Rev:** Ice breaker ship **Edge:** Reeded

| Date | Mintage | VF20 | XF40 | MS60 | MS63 | MS65 |
|---|---|---|---|---|---|---|
| 2004 | 30,000 | — | — | — | — | 16.00 |

**KM# 222 5 HRYVEN**
16.54 g., Copper-Nickel-Zinc, 35 mm. **Subject:** Whit Sunday **Obv:** National arms in flower wreath above value flanked by sprigs **Rev:** Four dancing women and child **Edge:** Reeded

| Date | Mintage | VF20 | XF40 | MS60 | MS63 | MS65 |
|---|---|---|---|---|---|---|
| 2004 | 50,000 | — | — | — | — | 20.00 |

**KM# 333 5 HRYVEN**
9.40 g., Bi-Metallic Brass center in Copper-Nickel ring, 28 mm. **Obv:** Horizontal lines across flowery design **Rev:** Cossack-style lyre within circle and wreath **Edge:** Segmented reeding

| Date | Mintage | VF20 | XF40 | MS60 | MS63 | MS65 |
|---|---|---|---|---|---|---|
| 2004 | 30,000 | — | — | — | — | 20.00 |

**KM# 334 5 HRYVEN**
16.54 g., Copper-Nickel-Zinc, 35 mm. **Subject:** 250th Anniversary of Kirovohrad **Obv:** National arms above crossed cannons and value **Rev:** Arms with supporters above city view **Edge:** Reeded

| Date | Mintage | VF20 | XF40 | MS60 | MS63 | MS65 |
|---|---|---|---|---|---|---|
| 2004 | 30,000 | — | — | — | — | 20.00 |

**KM# 335 5 HRYVEN**
16.54 g., Copper-Nickel-Zinc, 35 mm. **Subject:** 350 Years to Kharkiv **Obv:** Assumption Cathedral, value and national arms **Rev:** Kharkiv State Industrial Building complex **Edge:** Reeded

| Date | Mintage | VF20 | XF40 | MS60 | MS63 | MS65 |
|---|---|---|---|---|---|---|
| 2004 | 30,000 | — | — | — | — | 30.00 |

**KM# 336 5 HRYVEN**
9.40 g., Bi-Metallic Brass center in Copper-Nickel ring, 28 mm. **Subject:** 50th Anniversary of Crimean Union With Ukraine **Obv:** National arms on wheat sheaf on map **Rev:** Crowned lion on shield flanked by pillars within rope wreath **Edge:** Segmented reeding

| Date | Mintage | VF20 | XF40 | MS60 | MS63 | MS65 |
|---|---|---|---|---|---|---|
| 2004 | 30,000 | — | — | — | — | 20.00 |

**KM# 337 5 HRYVEN**
16.54 g., Copper-Nickel-Zinc, 35 mm. **Obv:** National arms on sun, flying geese divide beaded circle **Rev:** AN-140 Airliner divides beaded circle **Edge:** Reeded

| Date | Mintage | VF20 | XF40 | MS60 | MS63 | MS65 |
|---|---|---|---|---|---|---|
| 2004 | 50,000 | — | — | — | — | 15.00 |

**KM# 362 5 HRYVEN**
16.54 g., Copper-Nickel-Zinc, 35 mm. **Obv:** National arms on sun with flying geese divide beaded circle **Rev:** AN-124 jet divides beaded circle **Edge:** Reeded

| Date | Mintage | VF20 | XF40 | MS60 | MS63 | MS65 |
|---|---|---|---|---|---|---|
| 2005 | 60,000 | — | — | — | — | 15.00 |

**KM# 364 5 HRYVEN**
16.54 g., Copper-Nickel-Zinc, 35 mm. **Subject:** City of Korosten 1300th Anniversary **Obv:** National arms **Rev:** Ancient earring below modern building and bridge **Edge:** Reeded

| Date | Mintage | VF20 | XF40 | MS60 | MS63 | MS65 |
|---|---|---|---|---|---|---|
| 2005 | 30,000 | — | — | — | — | 18.00 |

**KM# 365 5 HRYVEN**
16.54 g., Copper-Nickel-Zinc, 35 mm. **Subject:** City of Sumy 350th Anniversary **Obv:** National arms **Rev:** City view behind city arms **Edge:** Reeded

| Date | Mintage | VF20 | XF40 | MS60 | MS63 | MS65 |
|---|---|---|---|---|---|---|
| 2005 | 30,000 | — | — | — | — | 18.00 |

**KM# 366 5 HRYVEN**
16.54 g., Copper-Nickel-Zinc, 35 mm. **Subject:** The Protection of the Virgin **Obv:** National arms on Cossack regalia **Rev:** Wedding scene **Edge:** Reeded

| Date | Mintage | VF20 | XF40 | MS60 | MS63 | MS65 |
|---|---|---|---|---|---|---|
| 2005 | 45,000 | — | — | — | — | 16.00 |

**KM# 368 5 HRYVEN**
16.54 g., Copper-Nickel-Zinc, 35 mm. **Subject:** Sorochynsky Fair **Obv:** Busts facing each other flanked by sprigs **Rev:** Farmer with family in ox cart **Edge:** Reeded

| Date | Mintage | VF20 | XF40 | MS60 | MS63 | MS65 |
|---|---|---|---|---|---|---|
| 2005 | 60,000 | — | — | — | — | 16.00 |

**KM# 379 5 HRYVEN**
16.54 g., Copper-Nickel-Zinc, 35 mm. **Subject:** 500th Anniversary - Kalmiuska Palanqua Cossack Settlement **Obv:** Cossack in ornamental frame and national arms **Rev:** Soldiers **Edge:** Reeded

| Date | Mintage | VF20 | XF40 | MS60 | MS63 | MS65 |
|---|---|---|---|---|---|---|
| 2005 | 30,000 | — | — | — | — | 18.00 |

**KM# 380 5 HRYVEN**
16.54 g., Copper-Nickel-Zinc, 35 mm. **Subject:** Sviatohirsky Assumption Monastery **Obv:** Madonna and child flanked by angels **Rev:** Hillside monastery **Edge:** Reeded

| Date | Mintage | VF20 | XF40 | MS60 | MS63 | MS65 |
|---|---|---|---|---|---|---|
| 2005 | 45,000 | — | — | — | — | 16.00 |

**KM# 387 5 HRYVEN**
16.54 g., Copper-Nickel-Zinc, 35 mm. **Subject:** Vernadsky Antarctic Station **Obv:** Flag and buildings **Rev:** Antarctica map within compass face **Edge:** Reeded

| Date | Mintage | VF20 | XF40 | MS60 | MS63 | MS65 |
|---|---|---|---|---|---|---|
| 2006 | 60,000 | — | — | — | — | 15.00 |

**KM# 388 5 HRYVEN**
16.93 g., 0.925 Silver 0.5035 oz. ASW, 33 mm. **Subject:** Year of the Dog **Obv:** Value on textile art **Rev:** Stylized dog **Edge:** Reeded

| Date | Mintage | VF20 | XF40 | MS60 | MS63 | MS65 |
|---|---|---|---|---|---|---|
| 2006 | 12,000 | PF63 200 | PF65 220 | | | |

**KM# 389 5 HRYVEN**
16.93 g., 0.925 Silver 0.5035 oz. ASW, 33 mm. **Subject:** Zodiac - Ram **Obv:** Sun face **Rev:** Ram **Edge:** Reeded

| Date | Mintage | VF20 | XF40 | MS60 | MS63 | MS65 |
|---|---|---|---|---|---|---|
| 2006 | 10,000 | PF63 90.00 | PF65 100 | | | |

**KM# 390 5 HRYVEN**
16.93 g., 0.925 Silver 0.5035 oz. ASW, 33 mm. **Subject:** Kyiv National University of Economics **Obv:** National arms, graph above value **Rev:** University building within circle **Edge:** Reeded

| Date | Mintage | VF20 | XF40 | MS60 | MS63 | MS65 |
|---|---|---|---|---|---|---|
| 2006 | 5,000 | PF63 80.00 | PF65 90.00 | | | |

**KM# 402 5 HRYVEN**
9.42 g., Bi-Metallic Brass center in Copper-Nickel ring, 28 mm. **Obv:** Symbolic sound of music **Rev:** Tsimbal stringed musical instrument **Edge:** Segmented reeding

| Date | Mintage | VF20 | XF40 | MS60 | MS63 | MS65 |
|---|---|---|---|---|---|---|
| 2006 | 100,000 | — | — | — | — | 14.00 |

**KM# 405 5 HRYVEN**
16.82 g., 0.925 Silver 0.5002 oz. ASW, 33 mm. **Subject:** Bull **Obv:** National arms

| Date | Mintage | VF20 | XF40 | MS60 | MS63 | MS65 |
|---|---|---|---|---|---|---|
| 2006 | 10,000 | PF65 90.00 | | | | |

**KM# 407 5 HRYVEN**
16.82 g., 0.925 Silver 0.5002 oz. ASW, 33 mm. **Subject:** Gemini **Obv:** National arms

| Date | Mintage | VF20 | XF40 | MS60 | MS63 | MS65 |
|---|---|---|---|---|---|---|
| 2006 | 10,000 | PF65 100 | | | | |

**KM# 409 5 HRYVEN**
16.54 g., Copper-Nickel-Zinc, 35 mm. **Subject:** 10 Years of the Constitution of Ukraine **Obv:** National arms **Edge:** Reeded

| Date | Mintage | VF20 | XF40 | MS60 | MS63 | MS65 |
|---|---|---|---|---|---|---|
| 2006 | 30,000 | — | — | — | — | 20.00 |

**KM# 411 5 HRYVEN**
16.54 g., Copper-Nickel-Zinc, 35 mm. **Subject:** 15 Years of Ukraine Independence **Obv:** National arms **Edge:** Reeded

| Date | Mintage | VF20 | XF40 | MS60 | MS63 | MS65 |
|---|---|---|---|---|---|---|
| 2006 | 75,000 | — | — | — | — | 14.00 |

**KM# 413 5 HRYVEN**
16.54 g., Copper-Nickel-Zinc, 35 mm. **Subject:** 10 Years to the Currency Reform in Ukraine **Obv:** National arms **Edge:** Reeded

| Date | Mintage | VF20 | XF40 | MS60 | MS63 | MS65 |
|---|---|---|---|---|---|---|
| 2006 | 45,000 | — | — | — | — | 15.00 |

**KM# 415 5 HRYVEN**
16.54 g., Copper-Nickel-Zinc, 35 mm. **Subject:** 750 Years of the City of L'viv **Obv:** National arms **Edge:** Reeded

| Date | Mintage | VF20 | XF40 | MS60 | MS63 | MS65 |
|---|---|---|---|---|---|---|
| 2006 | 60,000 | — | — | — | — | 15.00 |

**KM# 416 5 HRYVEN**
16.82 g., 0.925 Silver 0.5002 oz. ASW, 33 mm. **Subject:** Mykhailo Hrushevskyi **Obv:** National arms

| Date | Mintage | VF20 | XF40 | MS60 | MS63 | MS65 |
|---|---|---|---|---|---|---|
| 2006 | 5,000 | PF65 75.00 | | | | |

**KM# 417 5 HRYVEN**
16.82 g., 0.925 Silver 0.5002 oz. ASW, 33 mm. **Subject:** Dmytro Lutsenko **Obv:** National arms

| Date | Mintage | VF20 | XF40 | MS60 | MS63 | MS65 |
|---|---|---|---|---|---|---|
| 2006 | 3,000 | PF65 90.00 | | | | |

**KM# 418 5 HRYVEN**
16.82 g., 0.925 Silver 0.5002 oz. ASW, 33 mm. **Subject:** Ivan Franko **Obv:** National arms

| Date | Mintage | VF20 | XF40 | MS60 | MS63 | MS65 |
|---|---|---|---|---|---|---|
| 2006 | 5,000 | PF65 75.00 | | | | |

**KM# 420 5 HRYVEN**
16.54 g., Copper-Nickel-Zinc, 35 mm. **Subject:** Epiphany **Obv:** National arms **Edge:** Reeded

| Date | Mintage | VF20 | XF40 | MS60 | MS63 | MS65 |
|---|---|---|---|---|---|---|
| 2006 | 75,000 | — | — | — | — | 15.00 |

**KM# 422 5 HRYVEN**
16.54 g., Copper-Nickel-Zinc, 35 mm. **Subject:** Saint Kyryl Church **Obv:** National arms

| Date | Mintage | VF20 | XF40 | MS60 | MS63 | MS65 |
|---|---|---|---|---|---|---|
| 2006 | 45,000 | — | — | — | — | 15.00 |

**KM# 419 5 HRYVEN**
16.82 g., 0.925 Silver 0.5002 oz. ASW, 33 mm. **Subject:** Year of the Pig **Obv:** National arms **Edge:** Reeded

| Date | Mintage | VF20 | XF40 | MS60 | MS63 | MS65 |
|---|---|---|---|---|---|---|
| 2007 | 15,000 | PF65 145 | | | | |

**KM# 432 5 HRYVEN**
16.54 g., Copper-Nickel-Zinc, 35 mm. **Subject:** 100th Anniversary of "Motor Sich **Obv:** Small national arms above falcon in flight with two globes in background **Rev:** Jet engine **Edge:** Reeded

| Date | Mintage | VF20 | XF40 | MS60 | MS63 | MS65 |
|---|---|---|---|---|---|---|
| 2007 | 45,000 | — | — | — | — | 15.00 |

**KM# 453 5 HRYVEN**
9.40 g., Bi-Metallic Brass center in copper-nickel ring, 28 mm. **Subject:** Pure water is the source of life **Obv:** Drop of water in pond **Rev:** Man taking drink at waterfall

| Date | Mintage | VF20 | XF40 | MS60 | MS63 | MS65 |
|---|---|---|---|---|---|---|
| 2007 | 50,000 | — | — | — | — | 15.00 |

**KM# 455 5 HRYVEN**
9.40 g., Bi-Metallic Brass center in copper-nickel ring, 28 mm. **Subject:** Organization Safety and Cooperation, 16th Annual Meeting **Obv:** State emblem and ornamentation **Rev:** Parliamentary Assemby Building in Kyiv

| Date | Mintage | VF20 | XF40 | MS60 | MS63 | MS65 |
|---|---|---|---|---|---|---|
| 2007 | 35,000 | — | — | — | — | 17.00 |

**KM# 456 5 HRYVEN**
16.50 g., Copper-Nickel-Zinc, 35 mm. **Subject:** Odessa National Opera and Ballet, 120th Anniversary **Obv:** Ballet scene in oval **Rev:** Opera house in Odessa **Edge:** Reeded

| Date | Mintage | VF20 | XF40 | MS60 | MS63 | MS65 |
|---|---|---|---|---|---|---|
| 2007 | 35,000 | — | — | — | — | 15.00 |

**KM# 457 5 HRYVEN**
16.50 g., Copper-Nickel-Zinc, 35 mm. **Subject:** Chernihiv, 1100th Anniversary **Obv:** Sword hilts and slate fragment **Rev:** Town view and open book **Edge:** Reeded

| Date | Mintage | VF20 | XF40 | MS60 | MS63 | MS65 |
|---|---|---|---|---|---|---|
| 2007 | 45,000 | — | — | — | — | 16.00 |

**KM# 458 5 HRYVEN**
9.40 g., Bi-Metallic Brass center in copper-nickel ring, 28 mm. **Subject:** Buhai **Obv:** Sound waves as a baroque ornament **Rev:** Drum-like musical instrument

| Date | Mintage | VF20 | XF40 | MS60 | MS63 | MS65 |
|---|---|---|---|---|---|---|
| 2007 | 50,000 | — | — | — | — | 15.00 |

**KM# 459 5 HRYVEN**
16.54 g., Copper-Nickel-Zinc, 35 mm. **Subject:** The Famine, Genocide of the Ukranian People **Obv:** Girl standing on fallow ground **Rev:** Stork within cross, candles in background **Edge:** Reeded

| Date | Mintage | VF20 | XF40 | MS60 | MS63 | MS65 |
|---|---|---|---|---|---|---|
| 2007 | 75,000 | — | — | — | — | 15.00 |

**KM# 460 5 HRYVEN**
16.54 g., Copper-Nickel-Zinc, 35 mm. **Subject:** Crimean Resorts, 200th Anniversary **Obv:** Seaside Resort **Rev:** Felix De Searr and well **Edge:** Reeded

| Date | Mintage | VF20 | XF40 | MS60 | MS63 | MS65 |
|---|---|---|---|---|---|---|
| 2007 | 35,000 | — | — | — | — | 17.00 |

**KM# 461 5 HRYVEN**
15.55 g., 0.925 Silver 0.4624 oz. ASW, 33 mm. **Subject:** Capricorn **Obv:** Sun and seasons **Rev:** Zodiac sign

| Date | Mintage | VF20 | XF40 | MS60 | MS63 | MS65 |
|---|---|---|---|---|---|---|
| 2007 | 15,000 | PF65 75.00 | | | | |

**KM# 462 5 HRYVEN**
16.82 g., 0.925 Silver 0.5002 oz. ASW, 33 mm. **Subject:** Aquarius **Obv:** Sun and seasons **Rev:** Zodiac sign, man pouring water

| Date | Mintage | VF20 | XF40 | MS60 | MS63 | MS65 |
|---|---|---|---|---|---|---|
| 2007 | 15,000 | PF65 75.00 | | | | |

**KM# 463 5 HRYVEN**
16.82 g., 0.925 Silver 0.5002 oz. ASW, 33 mm. **Subject:** Pisces **Obv:** Sun and seasons **Rev:** Zodiac sign, two fish

| Date | Mintage | VF20 | XF40 | MS60 | MS63 | MS65 |
|---|---|---|---|---|---|---|
| 2007 | 15,000 | PF65 75.00 | | | | |

**KM# 464 5 HRYVEN**
16.82 g., 0.925 Silver 0.5002 oz. ASW, 33 mm. **Subject:** Scorpion **Obv:** Sun and seasons **Rev:** Zodiac sign, scorpion **Edge:** Reeded

| Date | Mintage | VF20 | XF40 | MS60 | MS63 | MS65 |
|---|---|---|---|---|---|---|
| 2007 | 15,000 | PF65 75.00 | | | | |

**KM# 465 5 HRYVEN**
16.82 g., 0.925 Silver 0.5002 oz. ASW, 33 mm. **Subject:** Sagittarius **Obv:** Sun and seasons **Rev:** Zodiac sign, archer

| Date | Mintage | VF20 | XF40 | MS60 | MS63 | MS65 |
|---|---|---|---|---|---|---|
| 2007 | 15,000 | PF65 75.00 | | | | |

**KM# 531 5 HRYVEN**
16.54 g., Copper-Nickel, 35 mm. **Subject:** 1100th Aniversary of Perejaslav-Khmelnytskyi **Obv:** Parchment. **Obv. Legend:** НАЦІОНАЛЬНИЈ БАНК УКРАЇНИ - 5 ГРИВЕНЬ / 2007 **Rev:** Old Rus cathedral, old Rus and Cossacks. **Rev. Legend:** ПЕРЕЯСЛАВ-ХМЕЛЬНИЦЬКИЈ - 1100

| Date | Mintage | VF20 | XF40 | MS60 | MS63 | MS65 |
|---|---|---|---|---|---|---|
| 2007 | 45,000 | — | — | — | — | 16.00 |

**KM# 500 5 HRYVEN**
16.50 g., Copper-Nickel-Zinc, 35 mm. **Subject:** The Annunciation **Edge:** Reeded

| Date | Mintage | VF20 | XF40 | MS60 | MS63 | MS65 |
|---|---|---|---|---|---|---|
| 2008 | 45,000 | — | — | — | — | 16.00 |

**KM# 501 5 HRYVEN**
16.50 g., Copper-Nickel-Zinc, 35 mm. **Subject:** Chernivtsi, 600th Anniversary **Edge:** Reeded

| Date | Mintage | VF20 | XF40 | MS60 | MS63 | MS65 |
|---|---|---|---|---|---|---|
| 2008 | 45,000 | — | — | — | — | 16.00 |

**KM# 502 5 HRYVEN**
16.50 g., Copper-Nickel-Zinc, 35 mm. **Subject:** Sniatyn, 850th Anniversary **Edge:** Reeded

| Date | Mintage | VF20 | XF40 | MS60 | MS63 | MS65 |
|---|---|---|---|---|---|---|
| 2008 | 45,000 | — | — | — | — | 16.00 |

**KM# 503 5 HRYVEN**
16.82 g., 0.925 Silver 0.5002 oz. ASW, 33 mm. **Subject:** Year of the Rat **Rev:** Rat, diamond insert eye **Edge:** Reeded

| Date | Mintage | VF20 | XF40 | MS60 | MS63 | MS65 |
|---|---|---|---|---|---|---|
| 2008 | 15,000 | PF65 90.00 | | | | |

**KM# 504 5 HRYVEN**
16.82 g., 0.925 Silver 0.5002 oz. ASW, 33 mm. **Subject:** Cancer **Edge:** Reeded

| Date | Mintage | VF20 | XF40 | MS60 | MS63 | MS65 |
|---|---|---|---|---|---|---|
| 2008 | 15,000 | PF65 75.00 | | | | |

**KM# 505 5 HRYVEN**
16.82 g., 0.925 Silver 0.5002 oz. ASW, 33 mm. **Subject:** Roman Shukhevich, General **Edge:** Reeded

| Date | Mintage | VF20 | XF40 | MS60 | MS63 | MS65 |
|---|---|---|---|---|---|---|
| 2008 | 3,000 | PF65 250 | | | | |

**KM# 506 5 HRYVEN**
16.82 g., 0.925 Silver 0.5002 oz. ASW, 33 mm. **Subject:** Leo **Edge:** Reeded

| Date | Mintage | VF20 | XF40 | MS60 | MS63 | MS65 |
|---|---|---|---|---|---|---|
| 2008 | 15,000 | PF65 75.00 | | | | |

**KM# 507 5 HRYVEN**
16.82 g., 0.925 Silver 0.5002 oz. ASW, 33 mm. **Subject:** Virgo **Edge:** Reeded

| Date | Mintage | VF20 | XF40 | MS60 | MS63 | MS65 |
|---|---|---|---|---|---|---|
| 2008 | 15,000 | PF65 75.00 | | | | |

**KM# 508 5 HRYVEN**
16.82 g., 0.925 Silver 0.5002 oz. ASW, 33 mm. **Subject:** Libra **Edge:** Reeded

| Date | Mintage | VF20 | XF40 | MS60 | MS63 | MS65 |
|---|---|---|---|---|---|---|
| 2008 | 15,000 | PF65 75.00 | | | | |

**KM# 509 5 HRYVEN**
16.54 g., Copper-Nickel-Zinc, 35 mm. **Subject:** State Arboretum "Trostianet-s", 175th Anniversary **Edge:** Reeded

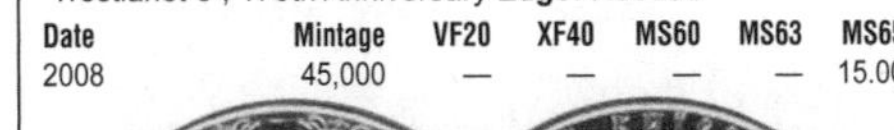

| Date | Mintage | VF20 | XF40 | MS60 | MS63 | MS65 |
|---|---|---|---|---|---|---|
| 2008 | 45,000 | — | — | — | — | 15.00 |

**KM# 510 5 HRYVEN**
16.54 g., Copper-Nickel-Zinc, 35 mm. **Subject:** Christianization of the Kievan Rus, 1020th Anniversary **Edge:** Reeded

| Date | Mintage | VF20 | XF40 | MS60 | MS63 | MS65 |
|---|---|---|---|---|---|---|
| 2008 | 45,000 | — | — | — | — | 17.00 |

**KM# 511 5 HRYVEN**
16.54 g., Copper-Nickel-Zinc, 35 mm. **Subject:** Rivne, 725th Anniversary **Edge:** Reeded

| Date | Mintage | VF20 | XF40 | MS60 | MS63 | MS65 |
|---|---|---|---|---|---|---|
| 2008 | 45,000 | — | — | — | — | 16.00 |

**KM# 512 5 HRYVEN**
16.54 g., Copper-Nickel-Zinc, 35 mm. **Subject:** Bohuslav, 975th Anniversary **Edge:** Reeded

| Date | Mintage | VF20 | XF40 | MS60 | MS63 | MS65 |
|---|---|---|---|---|---|---|
| 2008 | 45,000 | — | — | — | — | 14.00 |

**KM# 513 5 HRYVEN**
9.40 g., Bi-Metallic Brass center in copper-nickel ring, 28 mm. **Subject:** Taras Shevchenko "Prosvita Society" 140th Anniversary

| Date | Mintage | VF20 | XF40 | MS60 | MS63 | MS65 |
|---|---|---|---|---|---|---|
| 2008 | 45,000 | — | — | — | — | 14.00 |

**KM# 514 5 HRYVEN**
16.82 g., 0.925 Silver 0.5002 oz. ASW, 33 mm. **Subject:** Mariya Prymachenko

| Date | Mintage | VF20 | XF40 | MS60 | MS63 | MS65 |
|---|---|---|---|---|---|---|
| 2008 | 5,000 | PF65 75.00 | | | | |

**KM# 530 5 HRYVEN**
16.82 g., 0.925 Silver 0.5002 oz. ASW, 33 mm. **Subject:** Year of the Ox **Obv:** National Arms and value **Rev:** Ox, rubies in eyes **Edge:** Reeded

| Date | Mintage | VF20 | XF40 | MS60 | MS63 | MS65 |
|---|---|---|---|---|---|---|
| 2009 | 20,000 | PF65 75.00 | | | | |

**KM# 543 5 HRYVEN**
16.82 g., 0.925 Silver 0.5002 oz. ASW, 33.0 mm. **Subject:** Nikolai Gogol **Obv:** Compositions of two main subjects of Gogol's work, National Arms, value **Obv. Legend:** НАЦІОНАЛЬНИЈ БАНК УКРАЇНИ - 5 ГРИВЕНЬ / 2009 **Rev:** Nikolai's portrait **Rev. Legend:** МИКОЛА ГОГОЛЬ

| Date | Mintage | VF20 | XF40 | MS60 | MS63 | MS65 |
|---|---|---|---|---|---|---|
| 2009 | 5,000 | PF65 75.00 | | | | |

**KM# 544 5 HRYVEN**
16.82 g., 0.925 Silver 0.5002 oz. ASW, 33.0 mm. **Subject:** Sholem Aleichem **Obv:** Conventionalized composition, book sheets, Aleichem's signet **Obv. Legend:** НАЦІОНАЛЬНИЈ БАНК УКРАЇНИ - 5 ГРИВЕНЬ / 2009 **Rev:** Aleichem's portrait **Rev. Legend:** МИР ВАМ - ШОЛОМ-АЛЕЈХЕМ - РАБИНОВИЧ ШОЛОМ

| Date | Mintage | VF20 | XF40 | MS60 | MS63 | MS65 |
|---|---|---|---|---|---|---|
| 2009 | 5,000 | PF65 75.00 | | | | |

**KM# 545 5 HRYVEN**
16.54 g., Copper-Nickel-Zinc, 35.0 mm. **Subject:** Simferopol, 225th Anniversary **Obv:** Main railway station, National Arms **Obv. Legend:** НАЦІОНАЛЬНИЈ БАНК УКРАЇНИ - 5 ГРИВЕНЬ 2009 **Rev:** City Coat of Arms, Architectural elements **Rev. Legend:** 225 / РОКІВ - СІМФЕРОПОЛЬ **Edge:** Reeded

| Date | Mintage | VF20 | XF40 | MS60 | MS63 | MS65 |
|---|---|---|---|---|---|---|
| 2009 | 45,000 | — | — | — | — | 16.00 |

**KM# 546 5 HRYVEN**
16.82 g., 0.925 Silver 0.5002 oz. ASW, 33 mm. **Subject:** Ivan Kotljarevskyi **Obv:** National Arms, boat, column and helmet **Obv. Legend:** НАЦІОНАЛЬНИЈ БАНК УКРАЇНИ - П'ЯТЬ ГРИВЕНЬ **Rev:** Kotliarevskyi's portrait **Rev. Legend:** ...ПОКИ СОНЦЕ З НЕБА СЯЕ, ТЕБЕ НЕ ЗАБУДУТЬ! - ІВАН КОТЛЯРЕВСЬКИЈ

| Date | Mintage | VF20 | XF40 | MS60 | MS63 | MS65 |
|---|---|---|---|---|---|---|
| 2009 | 5,000 | PF65 75.00 | | | | |

**KM# 547 5 HRYVEN**
16.54 g., Copper-Nickel-Zinc, 35 mm. **Subject:** Mykolaiv, 220th Anniversary **Obv:** Varvarivskyi Bridge, gull, ship, anchor **Obv. Legend:** НАЦІОНАЛЬНИЈ БАНК УКРАЇНИ - П'ЯТЬ ГРИВЕНЬ **Rev:** Frigate Saint Nicholas, Architecture of Mykolaiv **Rev. Legend:** МИКОЛА?В - РІК ЗАСНУВАННЯ / 1789 **Edge:** Reeded

| Date | Mintage | VF20 | XF40 | MS60 | MS63 | MS65 |
|---|---|---|---|---|---|---|
| 2009 | 45,000 | — | — | — | — | 16.00 |

**KM# 548 5 HRYVEN**
9.40 g., Bi-Metallic Brass center in Copper-Nickel ring, 28 mm. **Subject:** Council of Europe, 60th Anniversary **Obv:** Stars, map of Europe **Obv. Legend:** НАЦІОНАЛЬНИЈ БАНК УКРАЇНИ - П'ЯТЬ ГРИВЕНЬ **Rev:** Council of Europe logo, stars **Rev. Legend:** COUNCIL OF EUROPE, CONSEIL DE EUROPE, РАДА ?ВРОПИ

| Date | Mintage | VF20 | XF40 | MS60 | MS63 | MS65 |
|---|---|---|---|---|---|---|
| 2009 | 45,000 | — | — | — | — | 15.00 |

### KM# 549 5 HRYVEN

16.82 g., 0.925 Silver 0.5002 oz. ASW, 33.0 mm. **Subject:** Lviv National Medical University, 225th Anniversary **Obv:** Hippocratic Oath in Latin, National Arms, value **Obv. Legend:** НАЦІОНАЛЬНИЈ БАНК УКРАІНИ - 5 / ГРИВЕНЬ **Rev:** University building **Rev. Legend:** 225 / РОКІВ - ІМЕНІ / ДАНИЛА / ГАЛИЦЬКОГО - ЛЬВІВСЬКИЈ НАЦІОНАЛЬНИЈ МЕДИЧНИЈ УНІВЕРСИТЕТ

| Date | Mintage | VF20 | XF40 | MS60 | MS63 | MS65 |
|---|---|---|---|---|---|---|
| 2009 | 7,000 | **PF65** 75.00 | | | | |

### KM# 550 5 HRYVEN

16.54 g., Copper-Nickel-Zinc, 35 mm. **Subject:** T. H. Shevchenko National Museum, 60th Anniversary **Obv:** Kateryna painting, bandura, National Arms, value **Rev:** Museum bulding and portrait **Edge:** Reeded

| Date | Mintage | VF20 | XF40 | MS60 | MS63 | MS65 |
|---|---|---|---|---|---|---|
| 2009 | 30,000 | — | — | — | — | 15.00 |

### KM# 553 5 HRYVEN

16.54 g., Copper-Nickel-Zinc, 35 mm. **Subject:** Pysanka - Easter Egg decorating **Obv:** Easter eggs, National Arms, value **Rev:** Easter bread, eggs. **Edge:** Reeded

| Date | Mintage | VF20 | XF40 | MS60 | MS63 | MS65 |
|---|---|---|---|---|---|---|
| 2009 | 50,000 | — | — | — | — | 16.00 |

### KM# 555 5 HRYVEN

16.50 g., Copper-Nickel-Zinc, 35 mm. **Subject:** Folk crafts of the Ukraine - Bokorash (Raftsmen) **Obv:** Two birds, Carpathian landscape, trees, cottages, logs **Obv. Legend:** НАЦІОНАЛЬНИЈ БАНК УКРАІНИ - 5 / ГРИВЕНЬ / 2009 **Rev:** Bokorash directing raft **Rev. Legend:** БОКОРАШ **Edge:** Reeded

| Date | Mintage | VF20 | XF40 | MS60 | MS63 | MS65 |
|---|---|---|---|---|---|---|
| 2009 | 45,000 | — | — | — | — | 15.00 |

### KM# 557 5 HRYVEN

16.54 g., Copper-Nickel-Zinc, 35.0 mm. **Subject:** International Year of Astronomy **Obv:** Urania, planets, stars, solar system, National Arms, value **Obv. Legend:** НАЦІОНАЛЬНИЈ БАНК УКРАІНИ - 5 ГРИВЕНЬ **Rev:** Yurii Drohobych, International Year of Astronomy logo, artifacts **Rev. Legend:** МІЖНАРОДНИЈ / РІК / АСТРОНОМІ? **Edge:** Reeded

| Date | Mintage | VF20 | XF40 | MS60 | MS63 | MS65 |
|---|---|---|---|---|---|---|
| 2009 | 45,000 | — | — | — | — | 15.00 |

### KM# 573 5 HRYVEN

16.50 g., Copper-Nickel-Zinc, 35 mm. **Subject:** Ukrainian Folk crafts - Cartwright **Obv:** Wood cart and wheels **Rev:** Woodcraftsman hewing wood to make cart detail **Edge:** Reeded

| Date | Mintage | VF20 | XF40 | MS60 | MS63 | MS65 |
|---|---|---|---|---|---|---|
| 2009 | 45,000 | — | — | — | — | 15.00 |

### KM# 566 5 HRYVEN

16.82 g., 0.925 Silver 0.5002 oz. ASW, 33 mm. **Subject:** Ivan Puliui **Obv:** X-ray of jewelry portrait **Rev:** Puliui portrait and text

| Date | Mintage | VF20 | XF40 | MS60 | MS63 | MS65 |
|---|---|---|---|---|---|---|
| 2010 | 5,000 | **PF65** 75.00 | | | | |

### KM# 567 5 HRYVEN

16.82 g., 0.925 Silver 0.5002 oz. ASW, 33 mm. **Subject:** Yevhen Paton **Obv:** Paton Bridge and the footbridge over Petrovska Alley **Rev:** Paton's portrait

| Date | Mintage | VF20 | XF40 | MS60 | MS63 | MS65 |
|---|---|---|---|---|---|---|
| 2010 | 5,000 | **PF65** 75.00 | | | | |

### KM# 568 5 HRYVEN

16.82 g., 0.925 Silver 0.5002 oz. ASW, 33 mm. **Subject:** Oksana Petrusenko **Obv:** Poppy flower and musical notation **Rev:** Bust facing

| Date | Mintage | VF20 | XF40 | MS60 | MS63 | MS65 |
|---|---|---|---|---|---|---|
| 2010 | 5,000 | **PF65** 75.00 | | | | |

### KM# 569 5 HRYVEN

16.82 g., 0.925 Silver 0.5002 oz. ASW, 33 mm. **Subject:** Mykola Ivanovych Pyrohov, scientist and surgeon **Obv:** Sepulchral church erected over scientist's tomb **Rev:** Half length figure in apron holding surgical instruments

| Date | Mintage | VF20 | XF40 | MS60 | MS63 | MS65 |
|---|---|---|---|---|---|---|
| 2010 | 5,000 | **PF65** 75.00 | | | | |

### KM# 577 5 HRYVEN

16.82 g., 0.925 Silver 0.5002 oz. ASW, 33 mm. **Subject:** Year of the tiger **Obv:** Vegitable ornamentation pattern, National Arms **Rev:** Stylized playful tiger **Edge:** Reeded

| Date | Mintage | VF20 | XF40 | MS60 | MS63 | MS65 |
|---|---|---|---|---|---|---|
| 2010 | 20,000 | **PF65** 75.00 | | | | |

### KM# 579 5 HRYVEN

16.54 g., Copper-Nickel-Zinc, 35 mm. **Subject:** Kyiv National University Astronomical Observatory, 165th Anniversary **Obv:** Observatory building **Rev:** Telescope and night sky **Edge:** Reeded

| Date | Mintage | VF20 | XF40 | MS60 | MS63 | MS65 |
|---|---|---|---|---|---|---|
| 2010 | 45,000 | — | — | — | — | 15.00 |

### KM# 582 5 HRYVEN

16.82 g., 0.925 Silver 0.5002 oz. ASW, 33 mm. **Subject:** Lviv Polytechnic National University, 165th Anniversary **Obv:** Arts and Science sculpture from main building **Rev:** University building façade

| Date | Mintage | VF20 | XF40 | MS60 | MS63 | MS65 |
|---|---|---|---|---|---|---|
| 2010 | 5,000 | **PF65** 75.00 | | | | |

### KM# 584 5 HRYVEN

15.55 g., 0.925 Silver 0.4624 oz. ASW, 33 mm. **Subject:** Kharkiv Polytechnic Institute, 125th Anniversary **Obv:** Radio telescope and open book **Rev:** University building and oval portrait of V.L. Kyrpychov

| Date | Mintage | VF20 | XF40 | MS60 | MS63 | MS65 |
|---|---|---|---|---|---|---|
| 2010 | 5,000 | **PF65** 75.00 | | | | |

### KM# 587 5 HRYVEN

16.50 g., Copper-Nickel-Zinc, 35 mm. **Subject:** Folk Crafts - Weaver **Obv:** Spinning wheel and weaving products **Rev:** Woman working on a loom **Edge:** Reeded

| Date | Mintage | VF20 | XF40 | MS60 | MS63 | MS65 |
|---|---|---|---|---|---|---|
| 2010 | 45,000 | — | — | — | — | 15.00 |

### KM# 589 5 HRYVEN

16.50 g., Copper-Nickel-Zinc, 35 mm. **Subject:** UKranian spas **Obv:** Two cornucopiae and the Savior's Feast **Rev:** Peasants getting food gifts blessed **Edge:** Reeded

| Date | Mintage | VF20 | XF40 | MS60 | MS63 | MS65 |
|---|---|---|---|---|---|---|
| 2010 | 45,000 | — | — | — | — | 15.00 |

### KM# 592 5 HRYVEN

16.50 g., Copper-Nickel-Zinc, 35 mm. **Subject:** Lutsk, 925th Anniversary **Obv:** Entrance tower to town's castle **Rev:** City view from tower top, city carms above **Edge:** Reeded

| Date | Mintage | VF20 | XF40 | MS60 | MS63 | MS65 |
|---|---|---|---|---|---|---|
| 2010 | 45,000 | — | — | — | — | 15.00 |

### KM# 598 5 HRYVEN

16.82 g., 0.925 Silver 0.5002 oz. ASW, 33 mm. **Subject:** Johann Georg Pinzel **Obv:** Buchach City hall **Rev:** Sculptor and angel

| Date | Mintage | VF20 | XF40 | MS60 | MS63 | MS65 |
|---|---|---|---|---|---|---|
| 2010 | 5,000 | **PF65** 75.00 | | | | |

### KM# 599 5 HRYVEN

16.82 g., 0.925 Silver 0.5002 oz. ASW, 33 mm. **Subject:** Ivan Fedorov **Obv:** Apostol book page and large quill pin **Rev:** Ivan Fedorov portrait facing

| Date | Mintage | VF20 | XF40 | MS60 | MS63 | MS65 |
|---|---|---|---|---|---|---|
| 2010 | 5,000 | PF65 75.00 | | | | |

### KM# 601 5 HRYVEN

16.54 g., Copper-Nickel-Zinc, 35 mm. **Subject:** Maritime History **Obv:** Banner seperating compas rose and seal of the Zaporohian Host **Rev:** Cossack boat of the 18th century

| Date | Mintage | VF20 | XF40 | MS60 | MS63 | MS65 |
|---|---|---|---|---|---|---|
| 2010 | 45,000 | — | — | — | — | 15.00 |

### KM# 604 5 HRYVEN

16.50 g., Copper-Nickel-Zinc, 35 mm. **Subject:** Folk Crafts - Potter **Obv:** Pottery flanking central pattern **Rev:** Potter at wheel **Edge:** Reeded

| Date | Mintage | VF20 | XF40 | MS60 | MS63 | MS65 |
|---|---|---|---|---|---|---|
| 2010 | 45,000 | — | — | — | — | 15.00 |

### KM# 610 5 HRYVEN

16.82 g., 0.925 Silver 0.5002 oz. ASW, 33 mm. **Subject:** Year of the Cat **Obv:** National arms, value and floral design **Rev:** Playful cat with green alpinites in eyes **Edge:** Reeded

| Date | Mintage | VF20 | XF40 | MS60 | MS63 | MS65 |
|---|---|---|---|---|---|---|
| 2011 | 20,000 | PF65 75.00 | | | | |

### KM# 611 5 HRYVEN

16.82 g., 0.925 Silver 0.5002 oz. ASW, 33 mm. **Subject:** Pavlo Tychyna **Obv:** View of family homestead, mallow flowers, national arms **Rev:** Portrait with books **Edge:** lettered, incuse **Edge Lettering:** .925 15.55

| Date | Mintage | VF20 | XF40 | MS60 | MS63 | MS65 |
|---|---|---|---|---|---|---|
| 2011 | 5,000 | PF65 80.00 | | | | |

### KM# 613 5 HRYVEN

16.82 g., 0.925 Silver 0.5002 oz. ASW, 33 mm. **Subject:** Ivan Franko National University, Lviv, 350th Anniversary **Obv:** National arms, statuary group, value **Rev:** Main Building façade **Edge Lettering:** .925 15.55 (Mint logo)

| Date | Mintage | VF20 | XF40 | MS60 | MS63 | MS65 |
|---|---|---|---|---|---|---|
| 2011 | 7,000 | PF65 80.00 | | | | |

### KM# 615 5 HRYVEN

16.54 g., Copper-Nickel-Zinc, 35 mm. **Obv:** Blacksmith items, two birds **Rev:** Blacksmith at work **Edge:** Reeded

| Date | Mintage | VF20 | XF40 | MS60 | MS63 | MS65 |
|---|---|---|---|---|---|---|
| 2011 | 45,000 | — | — | — | — | 15.00 |

### KM# 618 5 HRYVEN

16.82 g., 0.925 Silver 0.5002 oz. ASW, 33 mm. **Subject:** Heorhii Berehovyi **Obv:** Spacecraft launch, in orbit, sun **Rev:** Bust facing

| Date | Mintage | VF20 | XF40 | MS60 | MS63 | MS65 |
|---|---|---|---|---|---|---|
| 2011 | 5,000 | PF65 90.00 | | | | |

### KM# 619 5 HRYVEN

16.54 g., Copper-Nickel-Zinc, 35 mm. **Subject:** Taras Shevchenko, 150th Anniversary of Death **Obv:** Shevchenko's monument **Rev:** Portrait **Edge:** Reeded

| Date | Mintage | VF20 | XF40 | MS60 | MS63 | MS65 |
|---|---|---|---|---|---|---|
| 2011 | 35,000 | — | — | — | — | 15.00 |

### KM# 620 5 HRYVEN

16.82 g., 0.925 Silver 0.5002 oz. ASW, 33 mm. **Subject:** Okeksandr Bohomolets **Obv:** Hands of an adult and child **Rev:** Portrait of Bohomolets

| Date | Mintage | VF20 | XF40 | MS60 | MS63 | MS65 |
|---|---|---|---|---|---|---|
| 2011 | 5,000 | PF65 80.00 | | | | |

### KM# 621 5 HRYVEN

16.54 g., Copper-Nickel-Zinc, 35 mm. **Subject:** Taras Shevchenko National Prize of Ukraine, 50th Anniversary **Obv:** Open book, quill, palette, brushes and National Arms **Rev:** Shevchenko Portrait **Edge:** Reeded

| Date | Mintage | VF20 | XF40 | MS60 | MS63 | MS65 |
|---|---|---|---|---|---|---|
| 2011 | 35,000 | — | — | — | — | 15.00 |

### KM# 622 5 HRYVEN

16.54 g., Copper-Nickel-Zinc, 35 mm. **Subject:** Constitution, 15th Anniversary **Obv:** National flag in color within wreath **Rev:** Book of the Constitution and Verkhjovna Rada building **Edge:** Reeded

| Date | Mintage | VF20 | XF40 | MS60 | MS63 | MS65 |
|---|---|---|---|---|---|---|
| 2011 | 30,000 | — | — | — | — | 16.00 |

### KM# 623 5 HRYVEN

16.54 g., Copper-Nickel-Zinc, 35 mm. **Subject:** Zbarazh, 800th Anniversary **Obv:** Jerusalem cross on wall of Our Saviour's Transfiguration Church **Rev:** Gate of the Zbarazh Castle **Edge:** Reeded

| Date | Mintage | VF20 | XF40 | MS60 | MS63 | MS65 |
|---|---|---|---|---|---|---|
| 2011 | 35,000 | — | — | — | — | 15.00 |

### KM# 625 5 HRYVEN

16.54 g., Copper-Nickel-Zinc, 35 mm. **Obv:** Baroque design from Church **Rev:** St. Andrew's Church **Edge:** Reeded

| Date | Mintage | VF20 | XF40 | MS60 | MS63 | MS65 |
|---|---|---|---|---|---|---|
| 2011 | 45,000 | — | — | — | — | 15.00 |

### KM# 627 5 HRYVEN

16.54 g., Copper-Nickel-Zinc, 35 mm. **Obv:** Couple in a dance **Rev:** Hopak folk dance **Edge:** Reeded

| Date | Mintage | VF20 | XF40 | MS60 | MS63 | MS65 |
|---|---|---|---|---|---|---|
| 2011 | 45,000 | — | — | — | — | 15.00 |

### KM# 629 5 HRYVEN

16.54 g., Copper-Nickel-Zinc, 35 mm. **Subject:** Independence, 20th anniversary **Obv:** National arms, rushnyks and portraits **Rev:** Legend **Edge:** Reeded

| Date | Mintage | VF20 | XF40 | MS60 | MS63 | MS65 |
|---|---|---|---|---|---|---|
| 2011 | 45,000 | — | — | — | — | 17.00 |

### KM# 634 5 HRYVEN

16.82 g., 0.925 Silver 0.5002 oz. ASW, 33 mm. **Subject:** Mykhailo Yangel, 100th Anniversary of Birth **Obv:** Kosmos launch and satellite, earth in background **Rev:** Yangel portrait

| Date | Mintage | VF20 | XF40 | MS60 | MS63 | MS65 |
|---|---|---|---|---|---|---|
| 2011 | 5,000 | PF65 90.00 | | | | |

### KM# 635 5 HRYVEN

16.82 g., 0.925 Silver 0.5002 oz. ASW, 33 mm. **Subject:** Liudmyla Vasylevska, 150th Anniversary of Birth **Obv:** Girl near the sea **Rev:** Vasylevska portrait

| Date | Mintage | VF20 | XF40 | MS60 | MS63 | MS65 |
|---|---|---|---|---|---|---|
| 2011 | 5,000 | PF65 80.00 | | | | |

### KM# 638 5 HRYVEN

9.40 g., Bi-Metallic, 28 mm. **Subject:** International year of Forests **Obv:** Conceptual tree **Rev:** Tree in leaf **Edge:** Segmented reeding

| Date | Mintage | VF20 | XF40 | MS60 | MS63 | MS65 |
|---|---|---|---|---|---|---|
| 2011 | 30,000 | — | — | — | — | 16.00 |

### KM# 639 5 HRYVEN

16.82 g., 0.925 Silver 0.5002 oz. ASW, 33 mm. **Subject:** International Year of Forests **Obv:** Two birds sitting on branches **Rev:** Hand-like branches extended to the Sun

| Date | Mintage | VF20 | XF40 | MS60 | MS63 | MS65 |
|---|---|---|---|---|---|---|
| 2011 Antique finish | 3,000 | PF65 100 | | | | |

### KM# 645 5 HRYVEN

16.82 g., 0.925 Silver 0.5002 oz. ASW, 33 mm. **Subject:** Year of the Dragon **Obv:** National arms **Rev:** Dragon with orange zirconia crystals in eyes

| Date | Mintage | VF20 | XF40 | MS60 | MS63 | MS65 |
|---|---|---|---|---|---|---|
| 2011 | 20,000 | PF65 75.00 | | | | |

### KM# 647 5 HRYVEN

16.54 g., Copper-Nickel-Zinc, 35 mm. **Subject:** UEFA Euro 2012 Final Tournament **Obv:** Players superimposed on large 2012 in background **Rev:** UEFA logo and map of europe **Edge:** Reeded

| Date | Mintage | VF20 | XF40 | MS60 | MS63 | MS65 |
|---|---|---|---|---|---|---|
| 2011 | 100,000 | — | — | — | — | 15.00 |

### KM# 648 5 HRYVEN

16.54 g., 0.925 Copper-Nickel-Zinc 0.4919 oz., 35 mm. **Subject:** UEFA Euro 2012 Final Tournament **Obv:** Two players wthin stadium **Rev:** Logo and map of Ukraine **Edge:** Reeded

| Date | Mintage | VF20 | XF40 | MS60 | MS63 | MS65 |
|---|---|---|---|---|---|---|
| 2011 | 100,000 | — | — | — | — | 15.00 |

### KM# 649 5 HRYVEN

16.54 g., Copper-Nickel-Zinc, 35 mm. **Subject:** UEFA Euro 2012 Final Tournament **Obv:** UEFA logo and map of the Ukraine **Rev:** Soccer plater and Lviv stadium **Edge:** Reeded

| Date | Mintage | VF20 | XF40 | MS60 | MS63 | MS65 |
|---|---|---|---|---|---|---|
| 2011 | 100,000 | — | — | — | — | 15.00 |

### KM# 650 5 HRYVEN

16.54 g., Copper-Nickel-Zinc, 35 mm. **Subject:** UEFA Euro 2012 Final Tournament **Obv:** UEFA logo and map of the Ukraine **Rev:** Two soccer players and Metalist Stadium, Kharkiv **Edge:** Reeded

| Date | Mintage | VF20 | XF40 | MS60 | MS63 | MS65 |
|---|---|---|---|---|---|---|
| 2011 | 100,000 | — | — | — | — | 15.00 |

### KM# 651 5 HRYVEN

16.54 g., Copper-Nickel-Zinc, 35 mm. **Subject:** UEFA Euro 2012 Final Tournament **Obv:** UEFA logo and map of the Ukraine **Rev:** Soccer player and Donbass Arena, Donetsk **Edge:** Reeded

| Date | Mintage | VF20 | XF40 | MS60 | MS63 | MS65 |
|---|---|---|---|---|---|---|
| 2011 | 100,000 | — | — | — | — | 15.00 |

### KM# 653 5 HRYVEN

7.78 g., 0.9999 Gold 0.2501 oz. AGW, 20 mm. **Obv:** Logo of the Ukraine National Bank **Rev:** Archangel Michael

| Date | Mintage | VF20 | XF40 | MS60 | MS63 | MS65 |
|---|---|---|---|---|---|---|
| 2011 | 3,000 | — | — | — | — | 425 |
| 2012 | 2,000 | — | — | — | — | 450 |
| 2013 | 3,000 | — | — | — | — | 425 |

### KM# 655 5 HRYVEN

16.82 g., 0.925 Silver 0.5002 oz. ASW, 33 mm. **Subject:** Eugene Grebinka **Obv:** Cossack horseman **Rev:** Grebinka portrait

| Date | Mintage | VF20 | XF40 | MS60 | MS63 | MS65 |
|---|---|---|---|---|---|---|
| 2012 | 3,000 | PF65 85.00 | | | | |

### KM# 657 5 HRYVEN

16.54 g., Copper-Nickel-Zinc, 35 mm. **Subject:** Nikitsky Botanical Garden **Edge:** Reeded

| Date | Mintage | VF20 | XF40 | MS60 | MS63 | MS65 |
|---|---|---|---|---|---|---|
| 2012 | Est. 35000 | — | — | — | — | 15.00 |

### KM# 659 5 HRYVEN

16.50 g., Copper-Nickel, 35 mm. **Subject:** 350th Anniversary - City of Ivano-Frankivsk

| Date | Mintage | VF20 | XF40 | MS60 | MS63 | MS65 |
|---|---|---|---|---|---|---|
| 2012 | Est. 35000 | — | — | — | — | 15.00 |

### KM# 660 5 HRYVEN

16.50 g., Copper-Nickel-Zinc, 35 mm. **Subject:** Folk Craft, Kushnir (Furrier) **Edge:** Reeded

| Date | Mintage | VF20 | XF40 | MS60 | MS63 | MS65 |
|---|---|---|---|---|---|---|
| 2012 | 30,000 | — | — | — | — | 15.00 |

### KM# 663 5 HRYVEN

33.63 g., 0.925 Silver 1.0001 oz. ASW, 38.6 mm. **Subject:** Folk Music **Obv:** Wreath of periwinkle flowers covered with blue enamel with ribbons **Rev:** Couple **Edge:** Incuse lettering

| Date | Mintage | VF20 | XF40 | MS60 | MS63 | MS65 |
|---|---|---|---|---|---|---|
| 2012 | 5,000 | PF65 80.00 | | | | |

### KM# 664 5 HRYVEN

16.54 g., Copper-Nickel-Zinc, 35 mm. **Subject:** Maritime History - Ancient Navigation **Obv:** Ancient coin of the Bosporan Kingdom **Rev:** Ancient sailing ship **Edge:** Reeded

| Date | Mintage | VF20 | XF40 | MS60 | MS63 | MS65 |
|---|---|---|---|---|---|---|
| 2012 | 30,000 | — | — | — | — | 15.00 |

### KM# 670 5 HRYVEN

16.54 g., Copper-Nickel-Zinc, 35 mm. **Subject:** Folk Crafts **Obv:** Glassblown products **Rev:** Glassblower **Edge:** Reeded

| Date | Mintage | VF20 | XF40 | MS60 | MS63 | MS65 |
|---|---|---|---|---|---|---|
| 2012 | 35,000 | — | — | — | — | 15.00 |

### KM# 671 5 HRYVEN

16.93 g., 0.925 Silver 0.5035 oz. ASW, 33 mm. **Subject:** Oleksa Novakibvskyi, painter **Obv:** Value and home **Rev:** Portrait

| Date | Mintage | VF20 | XF40 | MS60 | MS63 | MS65 |
|---|---|---|---|---|---|---|
| 2012 | 3,000 | PF65 60.00 | | | | |

### KM# 678 5 HRYVEN

16.54 g., Copper-Nickel-Zinc, 35 mm. **Subject:** Yeletskyi Holy Dormition Cloister **Obv:** National arms, Main building of the cloister **Rev:** Image of the Mother of God icon **Edge:** Reeded

| Date | Mintage | VF20 | XF40 | MS60 | MS63 | MS65 |
|---|---|---|---|---|---|---|
| 2012 | 35,000 | — | — | — | — | 15.00 |

**KM# 681 5 HRYVEN**
16.54 g., Copper-Nickel-Zinc **Subject:** Town of Sudak **Obv:** National arms, St. George, value **Rev:** Town view with beach **Edge:** Reeded

| Date | Mintage | VF20 | XF40 | MS60 | MS63 | MS65 |
|---|---|---|---|---|---|---|
| 2012 | 30,000 | — | — | — | — | 15.00 |

**KM# 683 5 HRYVEN**
16.54 g., Copper-Nickel-Zinc, 35 mm. **Subject:** Chyhyryn City, 500th Anniversary **Obv:** National arms, plan of the old town, value **Rev:** Chyhyryn city view **Edge:** Reeded

| Date | Mintage | VF20 | XF40 | MS60 | MS63 | MS65 |
|---|---|---|---|---|---|---|
| 2012 | 30,000 | — | — | — | — | 15.00 |

**KM# 684 5 HRYVEN**
16.54 g., Copper-Nickel-Zinc **Subject:** Folk Music **Obv:** Wreath of Periwinkle flowers with ribbons **Rev:** Couple **Edge:** Reeded

| Date | Mintage | VF20 | XF40 | MS60 | MS63 | MS65 |
|---|---|---|---|---|---|---|
| 2012 | 30,000 | — | — | — | — | 15.00 |

**KM# 685 5 HRYVEN**
16.50 g., Copper-Nickel-Zinc, 35 mm. **Subject:** Kacha town, Aviation history **Obv:** National arms, Kacha arms and value **Rev:** Winged man holds plane

| Date | Mintage | VF20 | XF40 | MS60 | MS63 | MS65 |
|---|---|---|---|---|---|---|
| 2012 | 20,000 | — | — | — | — | 17.00 |

**KM# 686 5 HRYVEN**
16.54 g., Copper-Nickel-Zinc, 35 mm. **Subject:** Year of the Bat **Obv:** National arms, bat silhouette **Rev:** Bat in flight

| Date | Mintage | VF20 | XF40 | MS60 | MS63 | MS65 |
|---|---|---|---|---|---|---|
| 2012 | 20,000 | — | — | — | — | 17.00 |

**KM# 690 5 HRYVEN**
9.42 g., Bi-Metallic Brass center in Copper-Nickel ring **Subject:** Zhytomyr Oblast, 75th Anniversary **Obv:** Symbols of the Zhytomyr region, national arms **Rev:** Arms of the Zhytomyr Oblast **Edge:** Segmented reeding

| Date | Mintage | VF20 | XF40 | MS60 | MS63 | MS65 |
|---|---|---|---|---|---|---|
| 2012 | 15,000 | — | — | — | — | 25.00 |

**KM# 691 5 HRYVEN**
9.42 g., Bi-Metallic Brass center in Copper-Nickel ring, 28 mm. **Subject:** Mykolaiv Oblast, 75th Anniversary **Obv:** National arms and value **Rev:** Ship, amphora, ancient coin and sunflowers

| Date | Mintage | VF20 | XF40 | MS60 | MS63 | MS65 |
|---|---|---|---|---|---|---|
| 2012 | 15,000 | — | — | — | — | 25.00 |

**KM# 692 5 HRYVEN**
16.54 g., Copper-Nickel-Zinc, 35 mm. **Subject:** Year of the Bat **Obv:** National arms, silhouette of bat, value **Rev:** Bat in flight **Edge:** Reeded

| Date | Mintage | VF20 | XF40 | MS60 | MS63 | MS65 |
|---|---|---|---|---|---|---|
| 2012 | 20,000 | — | — | — | — | 17.00 |

**KM# 693 5 HRYVEN**
16.93 g., 0.925 Silver 0.5035 oz. ASW, 33 mm. **Subject:** Year of the Snake **Obv:** National arms, value **Rev:** Snake with green eye

| Date | Mintage | VF20 | XF40 | MS60 | MS63 | MS65 |
|---|---|---|---|---|---|---|
| 2012 | 20,000 | PF63 55.00 | PF65 60.00 | | | |

**KM# 696 5 HRYVEN**
16.93 g., 0.925 Silver 0.5035 oz. ASW, 33 mm. **Subject:** Volodymyr Vernadsky, first president of the Ukrainian Academy of Sciences **Obv:** National arms and value **Rev:** Portrait **Edge:** Incuse lettering

| Date | Mintage | VF20 | XF40 | MS60 | MS63 | MS65 |
|---|---|---|---|---|---|---|
| 2013 | 5,000 | PF65 60.00 | | | | |

**KM# 700 5 HRYVEN**
16.54 g., Copper-Nickel-Zinc, 35 mm. **Subject:** House of Chimeras **Obv:** National arms, Vladyslav Horodetskyi, architect, value **Rev:** Fragment of sculptural composition **Edge:** Reeded

| Date | Mintage | VF20 | XF40 | MS60 | MS63 | MS65 |
|---|---|---|---|---|---|---|
| 2013 | 30,000 | — | — | — | — | 15.00 |

**KM# 701 5 HRYVEN**
9.42 g., Bi-Metallic Brass center in Copper-Nickel ring, 28 mm. **Subject:** Luhansk Oblast, 75th Anniversary **Obv:** Industrial landscape, marmot, National arms and value **Rev:** Luhansk Oblast arms

| Date | Mintage | VF20 | XF40 | MS60 | MS63 | MS65 |
|---|---|---|---|---|---|---|
| 2013 | 20,000 | — | — | — | — | 25.00 |

**KM# 702 5 HRYVEN**
16.930 Silver ASW .925, 33 mm. **Subject:** Maternity **Obv:** National arms, baby carriage and value **Rev:** Mother holding baby **Edge:** Incuse lettering

| Date | Mintage | VF20 | XF40 | MS60 | MS63 | MS65 |
|---|---|---|---|---|---|---|
| 2013 | 5,000 | PF65 60.00 | | | | |

**KM# 705 5 HRYVEN**
16.54 g., Copper-Nickel-Zinc, 35 mm. **Subject:** Figures **Rev:** National arms, value, pectoral cross and symbols of the four Evangelists **Edge:** Reeded

| Date | Mintage | VF20 | XF40 | MS60 | MS63 | MS65 |
|---|---|---|---|---|---|---|
| 2013 | 30,000 | — | — | — | — | 17.00 |

**KM# 515 10 HRYVNI**
33.62 g., 0.925 Silver 0.9999 oz. ASW, 38.6 mm. **Subject:** The Annunciation **Edge:** Reeded

| Date | Mintage | VF20 | XF40 | MS60 | MS63 | MS65 |
|---|---|---|---|---|---|---|
| 2008 | 8,000 | PF63 85.00 | PF65 95.00 | | | |

**KM# 665 10 HRYVNI**
33.62 g., 0.925 Silver 0.9998 oz. ASW, 38.61 mm. **Subject:** Maritime History - Ancient Navigation **Obv:** Ancient coin of the Bisporan Kingdom **Rev:** Ancient sailing ship **Edge:** Lettered

| Date | Mintage | VF20 | XF40 | MS60 | MS63 | MS65 |
|---|---|---|---|---|---|---|
| 2012 | 8,000 | PF63 85.00 | PF65 95.00 | | | |

**KM# 113 10 HRYVEN**
33.62 g., 0.925 Silver 0.9999 oz. ASW, 38.61 mm. **Subject:** Ivan Mazepa (Cossack leader) **Obv:** Arms with supporters within beaded circle **Rev:** Half figure divides beaded circle flanked by palace and oval shield **Edge:** Reeded

| Date | Mintage | VF20 | XF40 | MS60 | MS63 | MS65 |
|---|---|---|---|---|---|---|
| 2001 | — | PF65 200 | | | | |

**KM# 114 10 HRYVEN**
33.62 g., 0.925 Silver 0.9999 oz. ASW, 38.61 mm. **Subject:** Great Prince Yaroslav the Wise **Obv:** Value within grape wreath **Rev:** Mosaic head facing, half length figure facing holding scroll and dome building **Edge:** Reeded

| Date | Mintage | VF20 | XF40 | MS60 | MS63 | MS65 |
|---|---|---|---|---|---|---|
| 2001 | — | PF65 1,400 | | | | |

**KM# 115 10 HRYVEN**
33.62 g., 0.925 Silver 0.9999 oz. ASW, 38.61 mm. **Series:** Ukranian Flora and Fauna **Obv:** National arms and date divides wreath, value within **Rev:** Lynx with offspring **Edge:** Reeded

| Date | Mintage | VF20 | XF40 | MS60 | MS63 | MS65 |
|---|---|---|---|---|---|---|
| 2001 | — | PF65 275 | | | | |

**KM# 130 10 HRYVEN**
33.62 g., 0.925 Silver 0.9999 oz. ASW, 38.61 mm. **Subject:** 10th Anniversary - National Bank **Obv:** National arms and value between arches **Rev:** Large building entrance **Edge:** Reeded

| Date | Mintage | VF20 | XF40 | MS60 | MS63 | MS65 |
|---|---|---|---|---|---|---|
| 2001 | 3,000 | PF65 185 | | | | |

**KM# 131 10 HRYVEN**
33.62 g., 0.925 Silver 0.9999 oz. ASW, 38.61 mm. **Series:** Olympics **Obv:** National arms and value on ice **Rev:** Stylized ice dancing couple **Edge:** Reeded

| Date | Mintage | VF20 | XF40 | MS60 | MS63 | MS65 |
|---|---|---|---|---|---|---|
| 2001 | 15,000 | PF65 55.00 | | | | |

**KM# 141 10 HRYVEN**
33.62 g., 0.925 Silver 0.9999 oz. ASW, 38.61 mm. **Subject:** Flora and Fauna **Obv:** National arms and date divides wreath, value within **Rev:** Pine branch with cone **Edge:** Reeded

| Date | Mintage | VF20 | XF40 | MS60 | MS63 | MS65 |
|---|---|---|---|---|---|---|
| 2001 | 3,000 | PF65 175 | | | | |

**KM# 142 10 HRYVEN**
33.62 g., 0.925 Silver 0.9999 oz. ASW, 38.61 mm. **Subject:** Khan Palace in Bakhchisarai **Obv:** Value in arch **Rev:** Courtyard view **Edge:** Reeded

| Date | Mintage | VF20 | XF40 | MS60 | MS63 | MS65 |
|---|---|---|---|---|---|---|
| 2001 | — | PF65 225 | | | | |

**KM# 143 10 HRYVEN**
4.31 g., 0.900 Gold 0.1247 oz. AGW, 16 mm. **Subject:** 10 Years Independence **Obv:** National arms **Rev:** Parliament building on map **Edge:** Plain

| Date | Mintage | VF20 | XF40 | MS60 | MS63 | MS65 |
|---|---|---|---|---|---|---|
| 2001 | — | PF65 1,100 | | | | |

**KM# 165 10 HRYVEN**
33.62 g., 0.925 Silver 0.9999 oz. ASW, 38.61 mm. **Subject:** Olympics **Obv:** National arms and value on ice **Rev:** Stylized hockey player **Edge:** Reeded

| Date | Mintage | VF20 | XF40 | MS60 | MS63 | MS65 |
|---|---|---|---|---|---|---|
| 2001 | 15,000 | **PF65** 55.00 | | | | |

**KM# 145 10 HRYVEN**
33.62 g., 0.925 Silver 0.9999 oz. ASW, 38.61 mm. **Subject:** Ivan Sirko **Obv:** Arms with supporters within beaded circle **Rev:** Cossack battle scene divides beaded circle **Edge:** Reeded

| Date | Mintage | VF20 | XF40 | MS60 | MS63 | MS65 |
|---|---|---|---|---|---|---|
| 2002 | 3,000 | **PF65** 275 | | | | |

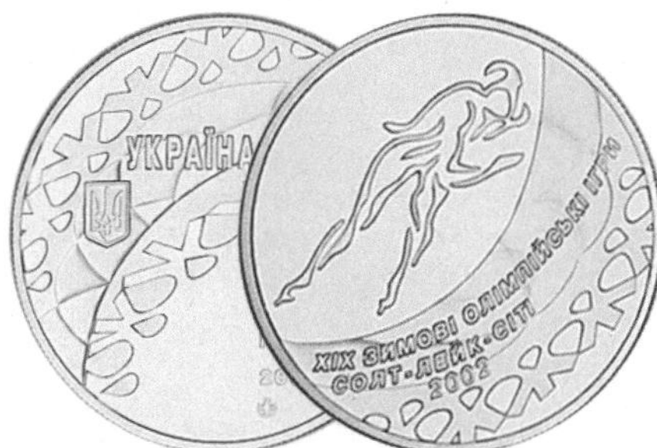

**KM# 146 10 HRYVEN**
33.62 g., 0.925 Silver 0.9999 oz. ASW, 38.61 mm. **Obv:** National arms and value on ice **Rev:** Stylized speed skater **Edge:** Reeded

| Date | Mintage | VF20 | XF40 | MS60 | MS63 | MS65 |
|---|---|---|---|---|---|---|
| 2002 | 3,000 | **PF65** 120 | | | | |

**KM# 160 10 HRYVEN**
33.95 g., 0.925 Silver 1.0097 oz. ASW, 38.61 mm. **Obv:** Value encircled by angels flanked by stars **Rev:** Steepled church and tower **Edge:** Reeded

| Date | Mintage | VF20 | XF40 | MS60 | MS63 | MS65 |
|---|---|---|---|---|---|---|
| 2002 | 3,000 | **PF65** 245 | | | | |

**KM# 161 10 HRYVEN**
33.62 g., 0.925 Silver 0.9999 oz. ASW, 38.61 mm. **Subject:** Grand Prince Vladimir Monomakh **Obv:** Value within jewelry design **Rev:** Bust holding book flanked by buildings and St. George **Edge:** Reeded

| Date | Mintage | VF20 | XF40 | MS60 | MS63 | MS65 |
|---|---|---|---|---|---|---|
| 2002 | 3,000 | **PF65** 450 | | | | |

**KM# 162 10 HRYVEN**
33.62 g., 0.925 Silver 0.9999 oz. ASW, 38.61 mm. **Subject:** Prince Svyatoslav **Obv:** Value in ornate design **Rev:** Armored half length figure facing **Edge:** Reeded

| Date | Mintage | VF20 | XF40 | MS60 | MS63 | MS65 |
|---|---|---|---|---|---|---|
| 2002 | 3,000 | **PF65** 450 | | | | |

**KM# 164 10 HRYVEN**
33.62 g., 0.925 Silver 0.9999 oz. ASW, 38.61 mm. **Subject:** Christmas **Obv:** National arms within star above value **Rev:** Christmas pageant scene **Edge:** Reeded

| Date | Mintage | VF20 | XF40 | MS60 | MS63 | MS65 |
|---|---|---|---|---|---|---|
| 2002 | 3,000 | **PF65** 550 | | | | |

**KM# 176 10 HRYVEN**
33.62 g., 0.925 Silver 0.9999 oz. ASW, 38.61 mm. **Subject:** Olympics **Obv:** Two ancient women with seedlings **Rev:** Swimmer **Edge:** Reeded

| Date | Mintage | VF20 | XF40 | MS60 | MS63 | MS65 |
|---|---|---|---|---|---|---|
| 2002 | 15,000 | **PF65** 100 | | | | |

**KM# 177 10 HRYVEN**
33.62 g., 0.925 Silver 0.9999 oz. ASW, 38.61 mm. **Subject:** Hetman Pylyp Orlik 1672-1742 **Obv:** Arms with supporters within beaded circle **Rev:** Standing figure facing holding scroll flanked by other standing figures **Edge:** Reeded

| Date | Mintage | VF20 | XF40 | MS60 | MS63 | MS65 |
|---|---|---|---|---|---|---|
| 2002 | 3,000 | **PF65** 300 | | | | |

**KM# 229 10 HRYVEN**
33.62 g., 0.925 Silver 0.9999 oz. ASW, 38.61 mm. **Obv:** National arms and date divides wreath, value within **Rev:** Eurasian Eagle Owl on branch **Edge:** Reeded

| Date | Mintage | VF20 | XF40 | MS60 | MS63 | MS65 |
|---|---|---|---|---|---|---|
| 2002 | 3,000 | **PF65** 350 | | | | |

**KM# 189 10 HRYVEN**
33.62 g., 0.925 Silver 0.9999 oz. ASW, 38.61 mm. **Subject:** Olympics **Obv:** Two ancient women with seedlings **Rev:** Boxer **Edge:** Reeded

| Date | Mintage | VF20 | XF40 | MS60 | MS63 | MS65 |
|---|---|---|---|---|---|---|
| 2003 | 15,000 | **PF65** 100 | | | | |

**KM# 190 10 HRYVEN**
33.62 g., 0.925 Silver 0.9999 oz. ASW, 38.61 mm. **Obv:** Fancy art work and sculpture **Rev:** Livadia Palace view **Edge:** Reeded

| Date | Mintage | VF20 | XF40 | MS60 | MS63 | MS65 |
|---|---|---|---|---|---|---|
| 2003 | 3,000 | **PF65** 280 | | | | |

**KM# 191 10 HRYVEN**
33.62 g., 0.925 Silver 0.9999 oz. ASW, 38.61 mm. **Obv:** National arms on sun, flying geese divides beaded circle **Rev:** Antonov AN-2 biplane divides beaded circle **Edge:** Reeded

| Date | Mintage | VF20 | XF40 | MS60 | MS63 | MS65 |
|---|---|---|---|---|---|---|
| 2003 | 3,000 | **PF65** 300 | | | | |

**KM# 192 10 HRYVEN**
33.62 g., 0.925 Silver 0.9999 oz. ASW, 38.61 mm. **Obv:** Easter eggs around arms above value **Rev:** Easter celebration **Edge:** Reeded

| Date | Mintage | VF20 | XF40 | MS60 | MS63 | MS65 |
|---|---|---|---|---|---|---|
| 2003 | 3,000 | **PF65** 425 | | | | |

**KM# 193 10 HRYVEN**
33.62 g., 0.925 Silver 0.9999 oz. ASW, 38.61 mm. **Obv:** Angels, national arms and value **Rev:** The protection of the Virgin Mary over the Pochayiv Lavra (Monastery) **Edge:** Reeded

| Date | Mintage | VF20 | XF40 | MS60 | MS63 | MS65 |
|---|---|---|---|---|---|---|
| 2003 | — | **PF65** 185 | | | | |

**KM# 194 10 HRYVEN**
33.62 g., 0.925 Silver 0.9999 oz. ASW, 38.61 mm. **Obv:** National arms and date divide wreath, value within **Rev:** Long-snouted seahorse **Edge:** Reeded

| Date | Mintage | VF20 | XF40 | MS60 | MS63 | MS65 |
|---|---|---|---|---|---|---|
| 2003 | 2,000 | **PF65** 450 | | | | |

**KM# 195 10 HRYVEN**
33.62 g., 0.925 Silver 0.9999 oz. ASW, 38.61 mm. **Subject:** Kyrylo Rozumovskyi (Cossack leader) **Obv:** Arms with supporters within beaded circle **Rev:** Half length figure 1/4 left within beaded circle **Edge:** Reeded

| Date | Mintage | VF20 | XF40 | MS60 | MS63 | MS65 |
|---|---|---|---|---|---|---|
| 2003 | 3,000 | **PF65** 240 | | | | |

**KM# 196 10 HRYVEN**
33.62 g., 0.925 Silver 0.9999 oz. ASW, 38.61 mm. **Subject:** Pavlo Polubotok (Cossack leader) **Obv:** Arms with supporters within beaded circle **Rev:** Half length figure within beaded circle **Edge:** Reeded

| Date | Mintage | VF20 | XF40 | MS60 | MS63 | MS65 |
|---|---|---|---|---|---|---|
| 2003 | 3,000 | **PF65** 325 | | | | |

**KM# 197 10 HRYVEN**
33.62 g., 0.925 Silver 0.9999 oz. ASW, 38.61 mm. **Obv:** Map, national arms and value **Rev:** Genoese Fortress in Sudak **Edge:** Reeded

| Date | Mintage | VF20 | XF40 | MS60 | MS63 | MS65 |
|---|---|---|---|---|---|---|
| 2003 | 3,000 | **PF65** 275 | | | | |

**KM# 198 10 HRYVEN**
33.62 g., 0.925 Silver 0.9999 oz. ASW, 38.61 mm. **Obv:** National arms and date divides wreath, value within **Rev:** European bison **Edge:** Reeded

| Date | Mintage | VF20 | XF40 | MS60 | MS63 | MS65 |
|---|---|---|---|---|---|---|
| 2003 | 2,000 | **PF65** 375 | | | | |

**KM# 206 10 HRYVEN**
33.91 g., 0.925 Silver 1.0085 oz. ASW, 38.61 mm. **Subject:** Azov Dolphin **Obv:** National arms and date divides wreath, value within **Rev:** Harbor Porpoises **Edge:** Reeded

| Date | Mintage | VF20 | XF40 | MS60 | MS63 | MS65 |
|---|---|---|---|---|---|---|
| 2004 | 8,000 | **PF63** 75.00 | **PF65** 100 | | | |

**KM# 207 10 HRYVEN**
33.91 g., 0.925 Silver 1.0085 oz. ASW, 38.61 mm. **Subject:** Football World Cup - 2006 **Obv:** Soccer ball in net **Rev:** Two soccer players **Edge:** Reeded

| Date | Mintage | VF20 | XF40 | MS60 | MS63 | MS65 |
|---|---|---|---|---|---|---|
| 2004 | 50,000 | **PF65** 75.00 | | | | |

**KM# 223 10 HRYVEN**
33.91 g., 0.925 Silver 1.0085 oz. ASW, 38.61 mm. **Obv:** National arms on sun, flying geese and value divides beaded circle **Rev:** AH-140 Airliner divides beaded circle **Edge:** Reeded

| Date | Mintage | VF20 | XF40 | MS60 | MS63 | MS65 |
|---|---|---|---|---|---|---|
| 2004 | 10,000 | **PF63** 125 | **PF65** 145 | | | |

**KM# 224 10 HRYVEN**
33.91 g., 0.925 Silver 1.0085 oz. ASW, 38.61 mm. **Subject:** Ice Breaker "Captain Belousov **Obv:** National arms on ship's wheel and anchor **Rev:** Ice breaker ship **Edge:** Reeded

| Date | Mintage | VF20 | XF40 | MS60 | MS63 | MS65 |
|---|---|---|---|---|---|---|
| 2004 | 10,000 | **PF63** 90.00 | **PF65** 100 | | | |

**KM# 225 10 HRYVEN**
33.62 g., 0.925 Silver 0.9999 oz. ASW, 38.61 mm. **Subject:** Whit Sunday **Obv:** National arms within wreath above value flanked by sprigs **Rev:** Four women folk dancers and child **Edge:** Reeded

| Date | Mintage | VF20 | XF40 | MS60 | MS63 | MS65 |
|---|---|---|---|---|---|---|
| 2004 | 10,000 | **PF63** 275 | **PF65** 300 | | | |

**KM# 339 10 HRYVEN**
33.62 g., 0.925 Silver 0.9999 oz. ASW, 38.61 mm. **Subject:** Ostrozhsky Family **Obv:** Our Lady of Duben and Elias Icon **Rev:** Three cameos above crowned shield **Edge:** Reeded

| Date | Mintage | VF20 | XF40 | MS60 | MS63 | MS65 |
|---|---|---|---|---|---|---|
| 2004 | 3,000 | PF65 245 | | | | |

**KM# 340 10 HRYVEN**
33.62 g., 0.925 Silver 0.9999 oz. ASW, 38.61 mm. **Subject:** St. Yura Cathedral **Obv:** Statue of St. George on horse killing dragon **Rev:** Cathedral **Edge:** Reeded

| Date | Mintage | VF20 | XF40 | MS60 | MS63 | MS65 |
|---|---|---|---|---|---|---|
| ND (2004) | 8,000 | PF63 75.00 | PF65 95.00 | | | |

**KM# 342 10 HRYVEN**
33.62 g., 0.925 Silver 0.9999 oz. ASW, 38.61 mm. **Subject:** Defense of Sevastopol 1854-56 **Obv:** National arms and value above fortifications map **Rev:** Cannon and ships **Edge:** Reeded

| Date | Mintage | VF20 | XF40 | MS60 | MS63 | MS65 |
|---|---|---|---|---|---|---|
| 2004 | 10,000 | PF63 75.00 | PF65 95.00 | | | |

**KM# 343 10 HRYVEN**
33.62 g., 0.925 Silver 0.9999 oz. ASW, 38.61 mm. **Subject:** Perejaslav Cossack Rada of 1654 **Obv:** National arms above value **Rev:** Standing figures facing **Edge:** Reeded

| Date | Mintage | VF20 | XF40 | MS60 | MS63 | MS65 |
|---|---|---|---|---|---|---|
| 2004 | 8,000 | PF63 115 | PF65 135 | | | |

**KM# 358 10 HRYVEN**
33.62 g., 0.925 Silver 0.9999 oz. ASW, 38.61 mm. **Subject:** Spalax Arenarius Reshetnik **Obv:** National arms and date divides wreath, value within **Rev:** Sandy mole rat **Edge:** Reeded

| Date | Mintage | VF20 | XF40 | MS60 | MS63 | MS65 |
|---|---|---|---|---|---|---|
| 2005 | 8,000 | PF63 50.00 | PF65 65.00 | | | |

**KM# 367 10 HRYVEN**
33.62 g., 0.925 Silver 0.9999 oz. ASW, 38.61 mm. **Subject:** The Protection of the Virgin **Obv:** National arms on Cossack regalia **Rev:** Wedding scene **Edge:** Reeded

| Date | Mintage | VF20 | XF40 | MS60 | MS63 | MS65 |
|---|---|---|---|---|---|---|
| 2005 | 8,000 | PF63 100 | PF65 125 | | | |

**KM# 370 10 HRYVEN**
33.62 g., 0.925 Silver 0.9999 oz. ASW, 38.61 mm. **Subject:** 60 Years UN Membership **Obv:** National arms, value and olive branch **Rev:** UN logo above partial globe **Edge:** Reeded

| Date | Mintage | VF20 | XF40 | MS60 | MS63 | MS65 |
|---|---|---|---|---|---|---|
| 2005 | 5,000 | PF65 75.00 | | | | |

**KM# 371 10 HRYVEN**
33.62 g., 0.925 Silver 0.9999 oz. ASW, 38.61 mm. **Subject:** National Anthem **Obv:** Musical score, national arms, value and date **Rev:** Coiled legend around holographic flower **Edge:** Reeded

| Date | Mintage | VF20 | XF40 | MS60 | MS63 | MS65 |
|---|---|---|---|---|---|---|
| 2005 | 3,000 | PF65 300 | | | | |

**KM# 372 10 HRYVEN**
33.62 g., 0.925 Silver 0.9999 oz. ASW, 38.61 mm. **Subject:** 100 Years of Olga Kobylianska Music and Drama Theatre in Chernivtsi **Obv:** Statue **Rev:** Theater **Edge:** Reeded

| Date | Mintage | VF20 | XF40 | MS60 | MS63 | MS65 |
|---|---|---|---|---|---|---|
| 2005 | 5,000 | PF65 100 | | | | |

**KM# 373 10 HRYVEN**
33.62 g., 0.925 Silver 0.9999 oz. ASW, 38.61 mm. **Subject:** Sviatohirsky Lavra Monastery **Obv:** Madonna and child flanked by angels **Rev:** Monastery on river bank **Edge:** Reeded

| Date | Mintage | VF20 | XF40 | MS60 | MS63 | MS65 |
|---|---|---|---|---|---|---|
| 2005 | 8,000 | PF65 120 | | | | |

**KM# 381 10 HRYVEN**
33.86 g., 0.925 Silver 1.007 oz. ASW, 38.61 mm. **Subject:** Baturyn Hetman Capital City **Obv:** National arms within sun rays, value flanked by standing figures **Rev:** Four cameos and banner above city view **Edge:** Reeded

| Date | Mintage | VF20 | XF40 | MS60 | MS63 | MS65 |
|---|---|---|---|---|---|---|
| 2005 | 5,000 | PF65 125 | | | | |

**KM# 382 10 HRYVEN**
33.86 g., 0.925 Silver 1.007 oz. ASW, 38.61 mm. **Subject:** Symyrenko Family **Obv:** Country name below national arms within sprigs **Rev:** Family tree **Edge:** Reeded

| Date | Mintage | VF20 | XF40 | MS60 | MS63 | MS65 |
|---|---|---|---|---|---|---|
| 2005 | 5,000 | PF65 100 | | | | |

**KM# 392 10 HRYVEN**
33.62 g., 0.925 Silver 0.9999 oz. ASW, 38.61 mm. **Obv:** National arms above value in wreath **Rev:** Grasshopper **Edge:** Reeded

| Date | Mintage | VF20 | XF40 | MS60 | MS63 | MS65 |
|---|---|---|---|---|---|---|
| 2006 | 8,000 | PF65 135 | | | | |

**KM# 410 10 HRYVEN**
33.62 g., 0.925 Silver 0.9999 oz. ASW, 38.61 mm. **Subject:** 10 Years of the Constitution of Ukraine **Obv:** National arms **Edge:** Reeded

| Date | Mintage | VF20 | XF40 | MS60 | MS63 | MS65 |
|---|---|---|---|---|---|---|
| 2006 | 5,000 | PF65 85.00 | | | | |

**KM# 421 10 HRYVEN**
33.62 g., 0.925 Silver 0.9998 oz. ASW, 38.61 mm. **Subject:** Epiphany **Obv:** National arms **Edge:** Reeded

| Date | Mintage | VF20 | XF40 | MS60 | MS63 | MS65 |
|---|---|---|---|---|---|---|
| 2006 | 10,000 | PF65 75.00 | | | | |

**KM# 423 10 HRYVEN**
33.62 g., 0.925 Silver 0.9999 oz. ASW, 38.61 mm. **Subject:** Saint Kyryl Church **Obv:** National arms **Edge:** Reeded

| Date | Mintage | VF20 | XF40 | MS60 | MS63 | MS65 |
|---|---|---|---|---|---|---|
| 2006 | 8,000 | PF65 75.00 | | | | |

**KM# 424 10 HRYVEN**
33.62 g., 0.925 Silver 0.9999 oz. ASW, 38.61 mm. **Subject:** Chyhyryn **Obv:** National arms **Edge:** Reeded

| Date | Mintage | VF20 | XF40 | MS60 | MS63 | MS65 |
|---|---|---|---|---|---|---|
| 2006 | 5,000 | PF65 120 | | | | |

**KM# 425 10 HRYVEN**
33.62 g., 0.925 Silver 0.9999 oz. ASW, 38.61 mm. **Subject:** Clearing House, 10th Anniversary **Obv:** National arms **Edge:** Reeded

| Date | Mintage | VF20 | XF40 | MS60 | MS63 | MS65 |
|---|---|---|---|---|---|---|
| 2006 | 5,000 | PF65 100 | | | | |

**KM# 427 10 HRYVEN**
33.62 g., 0.925 Silver 0.9999 oz. ASW, 38.61 mm. **Subject:** Twentieth Winter Olympic Games of 2006 **Obv:** National arms **Edge:** Reeded

| Date | Mintage | VF20 | XF40 | MS60 | MS63 | MS65 |
|---|---|---|---|---|---|---|
| 2006 | 5,000 | PF65 85.00 | | | | |

**KM# 466 10 HRYVEN**
33.62 g., 0.925 Silver 0.9999 oz. ASW, 38.6 mm. **Subject:** Odessa National Opera and Ballet, 120th Anniversary **Obv:** Interior view from stage **Rev:** Opera house in Odessa **Edge:** Reeded

| Date | Mintage | VF20 | XF40 | MS60 | MS63 | MS65 |
|---|---|---|---|---|---|---|
| 2007 | 5,000 | PF65 85.00 | | | | |

**KM# 467 10 HRYVEN**
33.62 g., 0.925 Silver 0.9999 oz. ASW, 38.61 mm. **Subject:** Ivan Bohun **Edge:** Reeded

| Date | Mintage | VF20 | XF40 | MS60 | MS63 | MS65 |
|---|---|---|---|---|---|---|
| 2007 | 5,000 | PF65 95.00 | | | | |

**KM# 516 10 HRYVEN**
33.62 g., 0.925 Silver 0.9999 oz. ASW, 38.61 mm. **Subject:** Black Griffin **Edge:** Reeded

| Date | Mintage | VF20 | XF40 | MS60 | MS63 | MS65 |
|---|---|---|---|---|---|---|
| 2008 | 7,000 | PF63 80.00 | PF65 95.00 | | | |

**KM# 517 10 HRYVEN**
33.62 g., 0.925 Silver 0.9999 oz. ASW, 38.61 mm. **Subject:** Sevastopol, 225th Anniversary **Edge:** Reeded

| Date | Mintage | VF20 | XF40 | MS60 | MS63 | MS65 |
|---|---|---|---|---|---|---|
| 2008 | 5,000 | PF65 85.00 | | | | |

**KM# 518 10 HRYVEN**
33.62 g., 0.925 Silver 0.9999 oz. ASW, 38.61 mm. **Subject:** Swallow's Nest **Edge:** Reeded

| Date | Mintage | VF20 | XF40 | MS60 | MS63 | MS65 |
|---|---|---|---|---|---|---|
| 2008 | 5,000 | PF65 95.00 | | | | |

**KM# 519 10 HRYVEN**
33.62 g., 0.925 Silver 0.9999 oz. ASW, 38.61 mm. **Subject:** Tereschenko Family **Edge:** Reeded

| Date | Mintage | VF20 | XF40 | MS60 | MS63 | MS65 |
|---|---|---|---|---|---|---|
| 2008 | 7,000 | PF63 80.00 | PF65 90.00 | | | |

**KM# 520 10 HRYVEN**
33.62 g., 0.925 Silver 0.9999 oz. ASW, 38.61 mm. **Subject:** Ukranian Swedish Alliances XVII-XVIII Century **Edge:** Reeded

| Date | Mintage | VF20 | XF40 | MS60 | MS63 | MS65 |
|---|---|---|---|---|---|---|
| 2008 | 5,000 | PF65 100 | | | | |

**KM# 521 10 HRYVEN**
33.62 g., 0.925 Silver 0.9999 oz. ASW, 38.61 mm. **Subject:** Hlukhiv **Edge:** Reeded

| Date | Mintage | VF20 | XF40 | MS60 | MS63 | MS65 |
|---|---|---|---|---|---|---|
| 2008 | 7,000 | PF63 80.00 | PF65 90.00 | | | |

**KM# 522 10 HRYVEN**
33.62 g., 0.925 Silver 0.9999 oz. ASW, 38.61 mm. **Subject:** UNESCO World Heritage Site - LVIV **Edge:** Reeded

| Date | Mintage | VF20 | XF40 | MS60 | MS63 | MS65 |
|---|---|---|---|---|---|---|
| 2008 | 5,000 | PF65 120 | | | | |

**KM# 523 10 HRYVEN**
33.62 g., 0.925 Silver 0.9999 oz. ASW, 38.61 mm. **Subject:** Cathedral in Buky Village **Edge:** Reeded

| Date | Mintage | VF20 | XF40 | MS60 | MS63 | MS65 |
|---|---|---|---|---|---|---|
| 2008 | 5,000 | PF65 150 | | | | |

**KM# 532 10 HRYVEN**
33.62 g., 0.925 Silver 0.9999 oz. ASW, 38.61 mm. **Subject:** Annunciation **Obv:** Conventionalized setting of the Gospel, lilies. **Obv. Legend:** НАЦІОНАЛЬНИЈ БАНК УКРАІНИ - 10 ГРИВЕНЬ **Rev:** Annunciation scene. **Rev. Legend:** БЛАГОВІЩЕННЯ **Edge:** Reeded

| Date | Mintage | VF20 | XF40 | MS60 | MS63 | MS65 |
|---|---|---|---|---|---|---|
| 2008 | 8,000 | PF63 90.00 | PF65 100 | | | |

**KM# 556 10 HRYVEN**
33.62 g., 0.925 Silver 0.9999 oz. ASW, 38.61 mm. **Subject:** Folk Crafts of the Ukraine - Bokorash (Raftsmen) **Obv:** Two birds, Carpathian landscape, trees, cottages, logs **Obv. Legend:** НАЦІОНАЛЬНИЈ БАНК УКРАІНИ - 10 / ГРИВЕНЬ / 2009 **Rev:** Bokorash directing raft **Rev. Legend:** БОКОРАШ

| Date | Mintage | VF20 | XF40 | MS60 | MS63 | MS65 |
|---|---|---|---|---|---|---|
| 2009 Antique patina | Est. 10000 | — | — | — | — | 65.00 |

**KM# 559 10 HRYVEN**
33.62 g., 0.925 Silver 0.9999 oz. ASW, 38.61 mm. **Subject:** Surb Khach Monastery **Obv:** National Arms, vegitation ornament pattern **Obv. Legend:** НАЦІОНАЛЬНИЈ БАНК УКРАІНИ - ДЕСЯТЬ ГРИВЕНЬ **Rev:** Monastery buildings **Rev. Legend:** СТАРИЈ КРИМ - ВІРМЕНСЬКИЈ МОНАСТИР Х PV СТ. - СУРБ ХАЧ **Edge:** Segmented reeding

| Date | Mintage | VF20 | XF40 | MS60 | MS63 | MS65 |
|---|---|---|---|---|---|---|
| 2009 | Est. 10000 | PF63 85.00 | PF65 95.00 | | | |

**KM# 560 10 HRYVEN**
33.62 g., 0.925 Silver 0.9999 oz. ASW, 38.61 mm. **Subject:** Battle of Konotop, 350th Anniversary **Obv:** Hetman's Insignia, Cossack arms and bandura, National Arms. **Obv. Legend:** НАЦІОНАЛЬНИЈ БАНК УКРАІНИ - 10 / ГРИВНЬ **Rev:** Ivan Vyhovskyi with sabre, Cossacks, Konotop fortifications, banners. **Rev. Legend:** ПЕРЕМОГА В КОНОТОПСЬКІЈ БИТВІ - 350 РОКІВ

| Date | Mintage | VF20 | XF40 | MS60 | MS63 | MS65 |
|---|---|---|---|---|---|---|
| 2009 | 8,000 | PF63 90.00 | PF65 100 | | | |

**KM# 561 10 HRYVEN**
33.62 g., 0.925 Silver 0.9999 oz. ASW, 38.61 mm. **Subject:** Church of the Holy Spirit in Rogatyn **Obv:** Church Icon with candelabra flanking, National Arms **Rev:** Church facade

| Date | Mintage | VF20 | XF40 | MS60 | MS63 | MS65 |
|---|---|---|---|---|---|---|
| 2009 | Est. 10000 | PF63 90.00 | PF65 100 | | | |

**KM# 562 10 HRYVEN**
33.62 g., 0.925 Silver 0.9999 oz. ASW, 38.61 mm. **Subject:** Famous Ukranian Families - Galagan Family **Obv:** The family estate, National Arms, value **Rev:** Galagan's College building and three portraits

| Date | Mintage | VF20 | XF40 | MS60 | MS63 | MS65 |
|---|---|---|---|---|---|---|
| 2009 | 7,000 | PF63 85.00 | PF65 95.00 | | | |

**KM# 563 10 HRYVEN**
33.62 g., 0.925 Silver 0.9999 oz. ASW, 38.61 mm. **Subject:** Kiev Academy of Operatta Theater, 75th Anniversary **Obv:** Dance scene, National Arms, value **Obv. Legend:** НАЦІОНАЛЬНИЈ БАНК УКРАІНИ - 10 / ГРИВНЬ / 2009 **Rev:** Theater building, operetta character silhouettes. **Rev. Legend:** КИІВСЬКИЈ АКАДЕМІЧНИЈ ТЕАТР ОПЕРЕТИ - 75/РОКІВ

| Date | Mintage | VF20 | XF40 | MS60 | MS63 | MS65 |
|---|---|---|---|---|---|---|
| 2009 | 5,000 | PF65 95.00 | | | | |

**KM# 574 10 HRYVEN**
33.62 g., 0.925 Silver 0.9999 oz. ASW, 38.61 mm. **Subject:** Ukrainian folk craft - Cartwright **Obv:** Wagon and wheels **Rev:** Woodcraftsman hewing wood to make a cart detail **Edge:** Reeded

| Date | Mintage | VF20 | XF40 | MS60 | MS63 | MS65 |
|---|---|---|---|---|---|---|
| 2009 | 10,000 | — | — | — | — | 65.00 |

**KM# 570 10 HRYVEN**
33.62 g., 0.925 Silver 0.9999 oz. ASW, 38.6 mm. **Subject:** Pulyp Oriyk Constitution, 300th Anniversary **Obv:** Hetman and Cossack officials **Rev:** Pylyp Orlyk, quill pen and constitution

| Date | Mintage | VF20 | XF40 | MS60 | MS63 | MS65 |
|---|---|---|---|---|---|---|
| 2010 | 7,000 | PF63 85.00 | PF65 95.00 | | | |

**KM# 575 10 HRYVEN**
33.62 g., 0.925 Silver 0.9998 oz. ASW, 38.61 mm. **Subject:** Vancouver Winter Olympics **Obv:** Winter scene **Rev:** Snowflake, sport figures, downhill skier at left

| Date | Mintage | VF20 | XF40 | MS60 | MS63 | MS65 |
|---|---|---|---|---|---|---|
| 2010 | 8,000 | PF63 85.00 | PF65 95.00 | | | |

**KM# 586 10 HRYVEN**
33.62 g., 0.925 Silver 0.9998 oz. ASW, 38.61 mm. **Obv:** Icon of Our Lady of Zarvanytsia **Rev:** Cathedral of Our Lady of Zarvanytsia

| Date | Mintage | VF20 | XF40 | MS60 | MS63 | MS65 |
|---|---|---|---|---|---|---|
| 2010 | 7,000 | PF65 95.00 | | | | |

**KM# 588 10 HRYVEN**
3362.00 g., 0.925 Silver 99.9839 oz. ASW, 38.61 mm. **Subject:** Folk Crafts - Weaving **Obv:** Spinning wheel and weaving products **Rev:** Woman working at a loom

| Date | Mintage | VF20 | XF40 | MS60 | MS63 | MS65 |
|---|---|---|---|---|---|---|
| 2010 Proof, Antique finish | 10,000 | PF65 100 | | | | |

**KM# 590 10 HRYVEN**
33.62 g., 0.925 Silver 0.9998 oz. ASW, 38.61 mm. **Subject:** Ukraine Spas **Obv:** Two cornucopiae and Savior's fest **Rev:** Peasants getting food gifts blessed

| Date | Mintage | VF20 | XF40 | MS60 | MS63 | MS65 |
|---|---|---|---|---|---|---|
| 2010 | 10,000 | PF63 90.00 | PF65 100 | | | |

**KM# 594 10 HRYVEN**
33.62 g., 0.925 Silver 0.9998 oz. ASW, 38.61 mm. **Subject:** Flora and Fauna **Obv:** National Arms and wreath **Rev:** Stipa Ucrainica, feather grass

| Date | Mintage | VF20 | XF40 | MS60 | MS63 | MS65 |
|---|---|---|---|---|---|---|
| 2010 | 8,000 | PF63 85.00 | PF65 95.00 | | | |

**KM# 600 10 HRYVEN**
33.62 g., 0.925 Silver 0.9998 oz. ASW, 38.61 mm. **Subject:** Hetman Danylo Apostol **Obv:** National arms, Archangel Michael and Crowned lion (Symbols of Kyiv and Lviv) **Rev:** Danylo Apostol half length figure holding scep-tre

| Date | Mintage | VF20 | XF40 | MS60 | MS63 | MS65 |
|---|---|---|---|---|---|---|
| 2010 | 8,000 | PF63 85.00 | PF65 95.00 | | | |

**KM# 605 10 HRYVEN**
32.62 g., 0.925 Silver 0.9701 oz. ASW, 38.61 mm. **Subject:** Folk Crafts - Potter **Obv:** Pottery flanking central design **Rev:** Potter at wheel

| Date | Mintage | VF20 | XF40 | MS60 | MS63 | MS65 |
|---|---|---|---|---|---|---|
| 2010 Proof, Antique finish | 10,000 | PF65 65.00 | | | | |

### KM# 606 10 HRYVEN

33.62 g., 0.925 Silver 0.9998 oz. ASW, 38.6 mm. **Subject:** Tarnovskyi Family **Obv:** Mansion in Kachanivka, Chernihiv oblast **Rev:** Vasyl Tarnovskyi standing and oval portraits of Hryhorii and Vasyl.

| Date | Mintage | VF20 | XF40 | MS60 | MS63 | MS65 |
|---|---|---|---|---|---|---|
| 2010 | 10,000 | PF63 85.00 | PF65 95.00 | | | |

### KM# 616 10 HRYVEN

33.62 g., 0.925 Silver 0.9999 oz. ASW, 38.61 mm. **Obv:** Blacksmith items, two little birds **Rev:** Blacksmith at work

| Date | Mintage | VF20 | XF40 | MS60 | MS63 | MS65 |
|---|---|---|---|---|---|---|
| 2011 Antique finish | 10,000 | — | — | — | — | 65.00 |

### KM# 626 10 HRYVEN

33.62 g., 0.925 Silver 0.9999 oz. ASW, 38.61 mm. **Obv:** Baroque element from the Church **Rev:** St. Andrew's Church

| Date | Mintage | VF20 | XF40 | MS60 | MS63 | MS65 |
|---|---|---|---|---|---|---|
| 2011 | 8,000 | PF63 85.00 | PF65 95.00 | | | |

### KM# 628 10 HRYVEN

33.62 g., 0.925 Silver 0.9999 oz. ASW, 38.61 mm. **Obv:** Hopak dance **Rev:** Dancing Cossack

| Date | Mintage | VF20 | XF40 | MS60 | MS63 | MS65 |
|---|---|---|---|---|---|---|
| 2011 | 7,000 | PF63 85.00 | PF65 95.00 | | | |

### KM# 632 10 HRYVEN

33.62 g., 0.925 Silver 0.9999 oz. ASW, 38.61 mm. **Subject:** Hryhorovych-Barskyi family **Obv:** Samson fountain in Kyiv **Rev:** Arms of the family

| Date | Mintage | VF20 | XF40 | MS60 | MS63 | MS65 |
|---|---|---|---|---|---|---|
| 2011 | 5,000 | PF65 95.00 | | | | |

### KM# 641 10 HRYVEN

33.62 g., 0.925 Silver 0.9999 oz. ASW, 38.61 mm. **Subject:** UEFA Euro 2012 Final Tournament **Obv:** UEFA logo hologram and map of the Ukraine **Rev:** Two players, Olympic Stadium, Kyiv and city view

| Date | Mintage | VF20 | XF40 | MS60 | MS63 | MS65 |
|---|---|---|---|---|---|---|
| 2011 | 15,000 | PF63 85.00 | PF65 95.00 | | | |

### KM# 642 10 HRYVEN

33.62 g., 0.925 Silver 0.9999 oz. ASW, 38.61 mm. **Subject:** UEFA Euro 2012 Final Tornament **Obv:** UEFA Euro 2012 Logo and map **Rev:** Player, city view and Livi Stadium

| Date | Mintage | VF20 | XF40 | MS60 | MS63 | MS65 |
|---|---|---|---|---|---|---|
| 2011 | 15,000 | PF63 85.00 | PF65 95.00 | | | |

### KM# 643 10 HRYVEN

33.62 g., 0.925 Silver 0.9999 oz. ASW, 38.61 mm. **Subject:** UEFA Euro 2012 Final Tournament **Obv:** UEFA logo hologram and Map of Ukraine **Rev:** City view with two players

| Date | Mintage | VF20 | XF40 | MS60 | MS63 | MS65 |
|---|---|---|---|---|---|---|
| 2011 | 15,000 | PF63 85.00 | PF65 95.00 | | | |

### KM# 644 10 HRYVEN

33.62 g., 0.925 Silver 0.9999 oz. ASW, 38.61 mm. **Subject:** UEFA Euro 2012 Final Tournament **Obv:** UEFA logo hologram and map of Ukraine **Rev:** Player with ball, Donbass Arena

| Date | Mintage | VF20 | XF40 | MS60 | MS63 | MS65 |
|---|---|---|---|---|---|---|
| 2011 | 15,000 | PF63 85.00 | PF65 95.00 | | | |

### KM# 662 10 HRYVEN

32.62 g., 0.925 Silver 0.9701 oz. ASW, 38.6 mm. **Subject:** 80 Years of the formation of Donetsk region

| Date | Mintage | VF20 | XF40 | MS60 | MS63 | MS65 |
|---|---|---|---|---|---|---|
| 2012 | Est. 5000 | PF65 90.00 | | | | |

### KM# 666 10 HRYVEN

33.62 g., 0.925 Silver 0.9998 oz. ASW, 50 mm. **Subject:** UEFA EURO 2012 Championship **Obv:** UEFA Championship cup **Rev:** Soccer player and part of ball **Note:** Pairs up with a Polish 10 Zl.

| Date | Mintage | VF20 | XF40 | MS60 | MS63 | MS65 |
|---|---|---|---|---|---|---|
| 2012 | 10,000 | PF65 150 | | | | |

### KM# 672 10 HRYVEN

33.63 g., 0.925 Silver 1.0001 oz. ASW, 38.61 mm. **Subject:** Petro Kalnyshevski, Cossack military leader **Obv:** Archangel Michael, crowned lion (symbols of Kyiv and Lviv) and National arms **Edge:** Incuse lettering

| Date | Mintage | VF20 | XF40 | MS60 | MS63 | MS65 |
|---|---|---|---|---|---|---|
| 2012 | 5,000 | PF65 85.00 | | | | |

### KM# 673 10 HRYVEN

33.63 g., 0.925 Silver 1.0001 oz. ASW, 38.6 mm. **Subject:** Ivano-Frankvsk City, 350 Anniversary **Obv:** National arms, Ratusha building **Rev:** Church of the Virgin Mary **Edge:** Incuse lettering

| Date | Mintage | VF20 | XF40 | MS60 | MS63 | MS65 |
|---|---|---|---|---|---|---|
| 2012 | 3,000 | PF65 80.00 | | | | |

### KM# 676 10 HRYVEN

33.63 g., 0.925 Silver 1.0001 oz. ASW, 38.6 mm. **Subject:** XXX Summer Olympics - London **Obv:** London city view, National arms **Rev:** Stater of Philip II and silhouettes of sports **Edge:** Incuse lettering

| Date | Mintage | VF20 | XF40 | MS60 | MS63 | MS65 |
|---|---|---|---|---|---|---|
| 2012 | 5,000 | PF65 85.00 | | | | |

### KM# 677 10 HRYVEN

33.63 g., 0.925 Silver 1.0001 oz. ASW, 38.6 mm. **Subject:** Yeletskyi Holy Dormition Cloister **Obv:** National arms, Main building of the cloister **Rev:** Image of the Mother of God icon **Edge:** Incuse lettering

| Date | Mintage | VF20 | XF40 | MS60 | MS63 | MS65 |
|---|---|---|---|---|---|---|
| 2012 | 7,000 | PF63 70.00 | PF65 80.00 | | | |

### KM# 679 10 HRYVEN

33.63 g., 0.925 Silver 1.0001 oz. ASW, 38.6 mm. **Subject:** Folk Crafts **Obv:** Traditional Ukranian clothing **Rev:** Furrier **Edge:** Incuse lettering

| Date | Mintage | VF20 | XF40 | MS60 | MS63 | MS65 |
|---|---|---|---|---|---|---|
| 2012 Proof, antique finish | 5,000 | PF65 80.00 | | | | |

### KM# 680 10 HRYVEN

33.63 g., 0.925 Silver 1.0001 oz. ASW, 38.6 mm. **Subject:** Town of Sudak, 1800th Anniversary **Obv:** National arms, St. George, value **Rev:** Town view with beach **Edge:** Incuse lettering

| Date | Mintage | VF20 | XF40 | MS60 | MS63 | MS65 |
|---|---|---|---|---|---|---|
| 2012 | 3,000 | PF65 85.00 | | | | |

### KM# 687 10 HRYVEN

33.63 g., 0.925 Silver 1.0001 oz. ASW, 38.6 mm. **Subject:** Zhovkva Synagogue **Obv:** National arms, fragment of building façade **Rev:** Synagogue building **Edge:** Incuse lettering

| Date | Mintage | VF20 | XF40 | MS60 | MS63 | MS65 |
|---|---|---|---|---|---|---|
| 2012 | 7,000 | PF63 70.00 | PF65 80.00 | | | |

### KM# 689 10 HRYVEN

33.63 g., 0.925 Silver 1.0001 oz. ASW **Obv:** National arms and value **Rev:** The Sterlet **Edge:** Reeded

| Date | Mintage | VF20 | XF40 | MS60 | MS63 | MS65 |
|---|---|---|---|---|---|---|
| 2012 | 7,000 | PF63 70.00 | PF65 80.00 | | | |

### KM# 697 10 HRYVEN

33.63 g., 0.925 Silver 1.0001 oz. ASW, 38.6 mm. **Subject:** The Great Bustard **Obv:** National arms, value **Edge:** Reeded

| Date | Mintage | VF20 | XF40 | MS60 | MS63 | MS65 |
|---|---|---|---|---|---|---|
| 2013 | 5,000 | PF65 80.00 | | | | |

### KM# 699 10 HRYVEN

33.63 g., 0.925 Silver 1.0001 oz. ASW, 38.6 mm. **Subject:** House with Chimeras **Obv:** National arms, Vladyslav Horodetskyi, architect and value **Rev:** Fragment of Sculptural composition

| Date | Mintage | VF20 | XF40 | MS60 | MS63 | MS65 |
|---|---|---|---|---|---|---|
| 2013 | 5,000 | PF65 80.00 | | | | |

### KM# 144 20 HRYVEN

67.24 g., 0.925 Silver 1.9997 oz. ASW, 50 mm. **Subject:** 10 Years Independence **Obv:** National arms **Rev:** Parliament building on map within beaded circle **Edge:** Segmented reeding

| Date | Mintage | VF20 | XF40 | MS60 | MS63 | MS65 |
|---|---|---|---|---|---|---|
| 2001 | 1,000 | PF65 4,000 | | | | |

### KM# 174 20 HRYVEN

14.70 g., Bi-Metallic .916 Gold center in .925 silver ring, 31 mm. **Subject:** Kyiv Rus" Culture **Obv:** Old arms of Ukraine, Prince and a cathedral model in his hand and princess **Rev:** Old Rus earring **Edge:** Reeded and plain sections

| Date | Mintage | VF20 | XF40 | MS60 | MS63 | MS65 |
|---|---|---|---|---|---|---|
| 2001 | 2,000 | PF65 1,000 | | | | |

### KM# 175 20 HRYVEN

14.70 g., Bi-Metallic .916 Gold center in .925 Silver ring, 31 mm. **Subject:** Scythian Culture **Obv:** Warrior with a bowl in his hand and to the right, a Queen of Scythia **Rev:** Stylized horse flanked by pegasists **Edge:** Reeded and plain sections

| Date | Mintage | VF20 | XF40 | MS60 | MS63 | MS65 |
|---|---|---|---|---|---|---|
| 2001 | 2,000 | PF65 1,200 | | | | |

**KM# 153 20 HRYVEN**

67.24 g., 0.925 Silver 1.9997 oz. ASW, 50 mm. **Obv:** National arms on sun and flying geese divides beaded circle **Rev:** AN-225 Mrija" cargo jet divides beaded circle **Edge:** Reeded and plain sections

| Date | Mintage | VF20 | XF40 | MS60 | MS63 | MS65 |
|---|---|---|---|---|---|---|
| 2002 | 2,002 | PF65 1,200 | | | | |

**KM# 188 20 HRYVEN**

67.24 g., 0.925 Silver 1.9997 oz. ASW, 50 mm. **Subject:** 60th Anniversary - Liberation of Kiev **Obv:** Eternal flame monument **Rev:** Map and battle scene **Edge:** Segmented reeding

| Date | Mintage | VF20 | XF40 | MS60 | MS63 | MS65 |
|---|---|---|---|---|---|---|
| 2003 | 2,000 | PF65 400 | | | | |

**KM# 226 20 HRYVEN**

67.24 g., 0.925 Silver 1.9998 oz. ASW, 50 mm. **Subject:** Our Souls Do Not Die **Obv:** National arms above value **Rev:** Bust of Taras Shevchenko facing flanked by standing figures **Edge:** Segmented reeding

| Date | Mintage | VF20 | XF40 | MS60 | MS63 | MS65 |
|---|---|---|---|---|---|---|
| 2004 | 4,000 | PF65 250 | | | | |

**KM# 344 20 HRYVEN**

67.24 g., 0.925 Silver 1.9998 oz. ASW, 50 mm. **Subject:** 2006 Olympic Games **Obv:** Woman holding flame and branch **Rev:** Six athletes around flame within square design **Edge:** Segmented reeding

| Date | Mintage | VF20 | XF40 | MS60 | MS63 | MS65 |
|---|---|---|---|---|---|---|
| 2004 | 5,000 | PF65 200 | | | | |

**KM# 363 20 HRYVEN**

67.24 g., 0.925 Silver 1.9998 oz. ASW, 50 mm. **Obv:** National arms on sun with flying geese divides beaded circle **Rev:** AN-124 jet plane divides beaded circle **Edge:** Segmented reeding

| Date | Mintage | VF20 | XF40 | MS60 | MS63 | MS65 |
|---|---|---|---|---|---|---|
| 2005 | 5,000 | PF65 200 | | | | |

**KM# 369 20 HRYVEN**

67.24 g., 0.925 Silver 1.9998 oz. ASW, 50 mm. **Subject:** Sorochynsky Fair **Obv:** Busts facing each other flanked by flower sprigs **Rev:** Farmer leading family in ox cart **Edge:** Segmented reeding

| Date | Mintage | VF20 | XF40 | MS60 | MS63 | MS65 |
|---|---|---|---|---|---|---|
| 2005 | 5,000 | PF65 250 | | | | |

**KM# 374 20 HRYVEN**

67.24 g., 0.925 Silver 1.9998 oz. ASW, 50 mm. **Subject:** 60th Anniversary of Victory in WWII **Obv:** Flying cranes divides value, date and national arms **Rev:** V-shaped searchlight beams filled with soldiers, order of the Patriotic War at bottom left **Edge:** Segmented reeding

| Date | Mintage | VF20 | XF40 | MS60 | MS63 | MS65 |
|---|---|---|---|---|---|---|
| 2005 | 5,000 | PF65 200 | | | | |

**KM# 412 20 HRYVEN**

67.25 g., 0.925 Silver 2.000 oz. ASW, 50 mm. **Subject:** 15 Years of Ukraine Independency **Obv:** National arms

| Date | Mintage | VF20 | XF40 | MS60 | MS63 | MS65 |
|---|---|---|---|---|---|---|
| 2006 | 7,000 | PF65 200 | | | | |

**KM# 468 20 HRYVEN**

14.23 g., Silver, 31 mm. **Subject:** Pure water is source of life **Obv:** Drop of water in pond **Rev:** Man taking drink from waterfall **Edge:** Segmented reeding

| Date | Mintage | VF20 | XF40 | MS60 | MS63 | MS65 |
|---|---|---|---|---|---|---|
| 2007 Prooflike | 3,000 | — | — | — | — | 600 |

**KM# 469 20 HRYVEN**
67.26 g., 0.925 Silver 2.0003 oz. ASW, 50 mm. **Subject:** Chumaky's Way **Obv:** Hologram wheel at center of fiery spiral **Rev:** Merchant's carts under night sky

| Date | Mintage | VF20 | XF40 | MS60 | MS63 | MS65 |
|---|---|---|---|---|---|---|
| 2007 | 5,000 | PF65 350 | | | | |

**KM# 470 20 HRYVEN**
67.25 g., 0.925 Silver 2.000 oz. ASW, 50 mm. **Subject:** The Famine, Genocide of the Ukranina People **Obv:** Girl standing on fallow ground, small green plant at left **Rev:** Swan at center of cross, candles in background

| Date | Mintage | VF20 | XF40 | MS60 | MS63 | MS65 |
|---|---|---|---|---|---|---|
| 2007 Antique finish | 10,000 | — | — | — | 200 | — |

**KM# 524 20 HRYVEN**
67.25 g., 0.925 Silver 2.000 oz. ASW, 50 mm. **Subject:** Kyiv, 1000th Anniversary of minting

| Date | Mintage | VF20 | XF40 | MS60 | MS63 | MS65 |
|---|---|---|---|---|---|---|
| 2008 | 5,000 | PF65 250 | | | | |

**KM# 552 20 HRYVEN**
67.25 g., 0.925 Silver 2.000 oz. ASW, 50.0 mm. **Subject:** Republic of Carpatho-Ukraine - 70th Anniversary of proclamation **Obv:** Carpathian ornament patterns, National Arms, value **Obv. Legend:** НАЦІОНАЛЬНИЈ БАНК УКРАЇНИ - 20 / ГРИВНЬ **Rev:** Transcarpathian holding flag with the arms of the Carpatho-Ukraine **Rev. Legend:** 70 / РОКІВ - ПРОГОЛОШЕННЯ КАРПАТСЬКОЇ УКРАЇНИ

| Date | Mintage | VF20 | XF40 | MS60 | MS63 | MS65 |
|---|---|---|---|---|---|---|
| 2009 | 3,000 | PF65 300 | | | | |

**KM# 554 20 HRYVEN**
67.25 g., 0.925 Silver 2.000 oz. ASW, 50 mm. **Subject:** Pysanka - Easter Egg decorating **Obv:** Ukrainian embroidered towels, eggs, Naitonal Arms, value **Rev:** Female pysanka maker ornamenting egg, young girl watching

| Date | Mintage | VF20 | XF40 | MS60 | MS63 | MS65 |
|---|---|---|---|---|---|---|
| 2009 | 8,000 | PF63 230 | PF65 250 | | | |

**KM# 591 20 HRYVEN**
67.26 g., 0.925 Silver 2.0003 oz. ASW partially gilt, 50 mm. **Subject:** Zymne Cloister **Obv:** Madonna icon partially gilt **Rev:** Zymne Cloister

| Date | Mintage | VF20 | XF40 | MS60 | MS63 | MS65 |
|---|---|---|---|---|---|---|
| 2010 | 5,000 | PF65 400 | | | | |

**KM# 596 20 HRYVEN**
67.26 g., 0.925 Silver 2.0003 oz. ASW, 50 mm. **Subject:** Battle of Grunwald, 600th Anniversary **Obv:** Value within wreath, three armored hands holding horizontal sword **Rev:** Knights with spears on horseback in battle

| Date | Mintage | VF20 | XF40 | MS60 | MS63 | MS65 |
|---|---|---|---|---|---|---|
| 2010 | 5,000 | PF65 175 | | | | |

**KM# 602 20 HRYVEN**
67.25 g., 0.925 Silver 2.000 oz. ASW, 50 mm. **Subject:** Maritime History **Obv:** Banner, compass rose and seal of Zaporozhin host **Rev:** Cossack boat of the 18th century

| Date | Mintage | VF20 | XF40 | MS60 | MS63 | MS65 |
|---|---|---|---|---|---|---|
| 2010 | 5,000 | PF65 150 | | | | |

**KM# 614 20 HRYVEN**
67.25 g., 0.925 Silver 2.000 oz. ASW, 50 mm. **Subject:** Lesya Ukrainka's "The Forest Song" **Obv:** Portrait **Rev:** Girl holding willow branch, boy in distance

| Date | Mintage | VF20 | XF40 | MS60 | MS63 | MS65 |
|---|---|---|---|---|---|---|
| 2011 | 4,000 | PF65 200 | | | | |

**KM# 617 20 HRYVEN**
67.25 g., 0.925 Silver 2.000 oz. ASW, 50 mm. **Subject:** Peresopnytsia Gospels **Obv:** Gospel maker icon **Rev:** Four miniatures of the initial illustrations of each Gospel

| Date | Mintage | VF20 | XF40 | MS60 | MS63 | MS65 |
|---|---|---|---|---|---|---|
| 2011 Antique finish | 4,000 | — | — | — | — | 230 |

**KM# 637 20 HRYVEN**
67.28 g., 0.925 Silver 2.0009 oz. ASW, 50 mm. **Subject:** Ukrainian Railroads, 150th Anniversary **Obv:** Modern high-speed train **Rev:** Ukrainian railways logo, gilt

| Date | Mintage | VF20 | XF40 | MS60 | MS63 | MS65 |
|---|---|---|---|---|---|---|
| 2011 | 4,000 | PF65 220 | | | | |

**KM# 640 20 HRYVEN**
67.28 g., 0.925 Silver 2.0009 oz. ASW, 62.2 mm. **Subject:** UEFA Euro 2012 Final Tournament **Obv:** Holographic images of UEFA Euro 2012 logo **Rev:** Stadium

| Date | Mintage | VF20 | XF40 | MS60 | MS63 | MS65 |
|---|---|---|---|---|---|---|
| 2011 | 15,000 | PF63 200 | PF65 220 | | | |

**KM# 652 20 HRYVEN**
31.11 g., 0.9999 Gold 0.9999 oz. AGW, 32 mm. **Subject:** Archangel Michael **Obv:** Logo of the Ukraine National Bank **Rev:** Archangel Michael **Edge:** Segmented reeding

| Date | Mintage | VF20 | XF40 | MS60 | MS63 | MS65 |
|---|---|---|---|---|---|---|
| 2011 | 1,500 | — | — | — | — | 2,200 |
| 2012 | 5,000 | — | — | — | — | 2,000 |
| 2013 | 2,500 | — | — | — | — | 1,700 |

**KM# 694 20 HRYVEN**
67.26 g., 0.925 Silver 2.0003 oz. ASW, 50 mm. **Subject:** Semen Hulak-Artemovsky, 200th Annversary **Obv:** National arms and value **Rev:** Portrait **Edge:** Incuse lettering

| Date | Mintage | VF20 | XF40 | MS60 | MS63 | MS65 |
|---|---|---|---|---|---|---|
| 2013 | 4,000 | PF65 150 | | | | |

**KM# 695 20 HRYVEN**
67.26 g., 0.925 Silver 2.0003 oz. ASW, 50 mm. **Subject:** Liadova Cave Monastery, 1000th Anniversary **Obv:** National arms, value, St. Antony of the Caves **Rev:** Stylized fragment of the Cave Monastery **Edge:** Incuse lettering

| Date | Mintage | VF20 | XF40 | MS60 | MS63 | MS65 |
|---|---|---|---|---|---|---|
| 2013 | 3,000 | PF65 150 | | | | |

**KM# 704 20 HRYVEN**
67.26 g., 0.925 Silver 2.0004 oz. ASW, 50 mm. **Subject:** Christianization of Kyivan Rus, 1025th Anniversary **Obv:** National arms, value, pectoral cross and symbols of the four evangelists **Rev:** Figures **Edge:** Incuse lettering

| Date | Mintage | VF20 | XF40 | MS60 | MS63 | MS65 |
|---|---|---|---|---|---|---|
| 2013 | 3,500 | PF65 350 | | | | |

**KM# 426 50 HRYVEN**
17.63 g., 0.900 Gold 0.5101 oz. AGW, 25 mm. **Subject:** Nestor - The Chronicler **Obv:** National arms

| Date | Mintage | VF20 | XF40 | MS60 | MS63 | MS65 |
|---|---|---|---|---|---|---|
| 2006 | 5,000 | PF65 1,400 | | | | |

**KM# 525 50 HRYVEN**
17.63 g., 0.900 Gold 0.5101 oz. AGW, 25 mm. **Subject:** Swallow's Nest Castle **Edge:** Plain

| Date | Mintage | VF20 | XF40 | MS60 | MS63 | MS65 |
|---|---|---|---|---|---|---|
| 2008 | 4,000 | PF65 1,400 | | | | |

**KM# 526 50 HRYVEN**
500.00 g., 0.9999 Silver 16.0738 oz. ASW **Subject:** Visit of Ecumenical Patriarch Bartholomew I

| Date | Mintage | VF20 | XF40 | MS60 | MS63 | MS65 |
|---|---|---|---|---|---|---|
| 2008 | 1,000 | PF65 2,200 | | | | |

**KM# 564 50 HRYVEN**
500.00 g., 0.999 Silver 16.0593 oz. ASW, 85 mm. **Subject:** Mykola Hohol's stories - Evenings on a farm near Dykanka **Obv:** Hohol's portrait with quill, National arms, value **Rev:** Christmas star with yellow sapphire

| Date | Mintage | VF20 | XF40 | MS60 | MS63 | MS65 |
|---|---|---|---|---|---|---|
| 2009 | Est. 1500 | PF65 2,500 | | | | |

**KM# 595 50 HRYVEN**
17.63 g., 0.900 Gold 0.5101 oz. AGW, 25 mm. **Subject:** Ukrainian ballet **Obv:** Ballet shoes **Rev:** Ballet couple **Edge:** Plain

| Date | Mintage | VF20 | XF40 | MS60 | MS63 | MS65 |
|---|---|---|---|---|---|---|
| 2010 | 4,000 | PF65 1,400 | | | | |

**KM# 609 50 HRYVEN**
500.00 g., 0.999 Silver 16.0593 oz. ASW, 85 mm. **Subject:** Cradle of the Ukrainian Cossacks **Obv:** Zaporizka Sich, historic site, shield and swords below **Rev:** Dovbysh (Cossack drummer) beating kettle drums, ornamental pattern

| Date | Mintage | VF20 | XF40 | MS60 | MS63 | MS65 |
|---|---|---|---|---|---|---|
| 2010 | Est. 1500 | PF65 2,500 | | | | |

**KM# 631 50 HRYVEN**
500.00 g., 0.999 Silver 16.0593 oz. ASW, 85 mm. **Subject:** Independence, 20th Anniversary **Obv:** National arms, rushnyks, portraits **Rev:** Legend within wreath

| Date | Mintage | VF20 | XF40 | MS60 | MS63 | MS65 |
|---|---|---|---|---|---|---|
| 2011 | 1,000 | — | — | — | — | 2,500 |

**KM# 633 50 HRYVEN**
500.00 g., 0.999 Silver 16.0593 oz. ASW, 85 mm. **Subject:** St. Sophia Cathedral, 1000th Anniversary **Obv:** St. Sophia Cathedral cupolas, model of XI century design **Rev:** Altar mural mosaics

| Date | Mintage | VF20 | XF40 | MS60 | MS63 | MS65 |
|---|---|---|---|---|---|---|
| 2011 | 1,000 | — | — | — | — | 2,500 |

**KM# 674 50 HRYVEN**
500.00 g., 0.999 Silver 16.0593 oz. ASW, 85 mm. **Subject:** Nikitsky Botanical Garden, 200th Anniversary **Obv:** National Arms, Christian Steven portrait **Rev:** Legend **Edge Lettering:** Incuse lettering

| Date | Mintage | VF20 | XF40 | MS60 | MS63 | MS65 |
|---|---|---|---|---|---|---|
| 2012 | 1,000 | — | — | — | — | 1,000 |

**KM# 199 100 HRYVEN**
34.56 g., 0.900 Gold 1.000 oz. AGW, 32 mm. **Subject:** Ancient Scythian Culture **Obv:** National arms above ornamental design and value within rope wreath **Rev:** Ancient craftsmen and jewelry **Edge:** Reeded

| Date | Mintage | VF20 | XF40 | MS60 | MS63 | MS65 |
|---|---|---|---|---|---|---|
| 2003 | 1,500 | PF65 7,500 | | | | |

**KM# 345 100 HRYVEN**
34.56 g., 0.900 Gold 1.000 oz. AGW, 32 mm. **Subject:** The Golden Gate **Obv:** National arms above value between two stylized cranes **Rev:** Riders approaching castle gate **Edge:** Segmented reeding

| Date | Mintage | VF20 | XF40 | MS60 | MS63 | MS65 |
|---|---|---|---|---|---|---|
| 2004 | 2,000 | PF65 5,000 | | | | |

**KM# 414 100 HRYVEN**
1000.00 g., 0.999 Silver 32.1186 oz. ASW, 100 mm. **Subject:** 10 Years to the Currency Reform in Ukraine **Obv:** National arms **Note:** Illustration reduced.

| Date | Mintage | VF20 | XF40 | MS60 | MS63 | MS65 |
|---|---|---|---|---|---|---|
| 2006 | 1,501 | PF65 6,500 | | | | |

**KM# 471 100 HRYVEN**
34.56 g., 0.900 Gold 1.000 oz. AGW, 32 mm. **Subject:** The Ostroh Bible **Obv:** Part of illumination on page **Rev:** Ivan Fedorov and Kostiantyn of Ostroth holding open bible

| Date | Mintage | VF20 | XF40 | MS60 | MS63 | MS65 |
|---|---|---|---|---|---|---|
| 2007 | 4,000 | PF65 3,000 | | | | |

**KM# 527 100 HRYVEN**
1000.00 g., 0.999 Silver 32.1186 oz. ASW **Subject:** Kievan Rus

| Date | Mintage | VF20 | XF40 | MS60 | MS63 | MS65 |
|---|---|---|---|---|---|---|
| 2008 | 800 | PF65 4,500 | | | | |

**KM# 558 100 HRYVEN**
1000.00 g., 0.999 Silver 32.1186 oz. ASW, 100 mm. **Subject:** International Year of Astronomy **Obv:** Solar System, armillary sphere, stars. **Obv. Legend:** НАЦІОНАЛЬНИЈ БАНК УКРАІНИ - 100 / ГРИВНЬ **Rev:** Galileo, stars, telescope, galaxies, observatory, Saturn (as the letter O). **Rev. Legend:** МІЖНАРОДНИЈ РІК АСТРОНОМІР

| Date | Mintage | VF20 | XF40 | MS60 | MS63 | MS65 |
|---|---|---|---|---|---|---|
| 2009 | Est. 700 | PF65 4,500 | | | | |

**KM# 565 100 HRYVEN**
34.57 g., 0.900 Gold 1.0003 oz. AGW, 32 mm. **Subject:** Ancient Site - Chersonesos Taurica **Obv:** Ancient ruins, coins, Naitonal Arms **Rev:** Ruins of ancient Chersonesos **Edge:** Segmented reeding

| Date | Mintage | VF20 | XF40 | MS60 | MS63 | MS65 |
|---|---|---|---|---|---|---|
| 2009 | 4,000 | PF65 3,000 | | | | |

**KM# 597 100 HRYVEN**
34.56 g., 0.900 Gold 1.000 oz. AGW, 32 mm. **Subject:** Bosporan Kingdom **Obv:** Panticapaeum runins: classical columns, winged animals **Rev:** Panticapaeum stater, buildings, ancient sailing vessel

| Date | Mintage | VF20 | XF40 | MS60 | MS63 | MS65 |
|---|---|---|---|---|---|---|
| 2010 | 3,000 | PF65 3,000 | | | | |

**KM# 630 100 HRYVEN**
34.56 g., 0.900 Gold 1.000 oz. AGW, 32 mm. **Subject:** Independence, 20th Anniversary **Obv:** National arms in center of rushnyks, Portraits around **Rev:** Legend within wreath

| Date | Mintage | VF20 | XF40 | MS60 | MS63 | MS65 |
|---|---|---|---|---|---|---|
| 2011 | 1,000 | PF65 4,500 | | | | |

**KM# 706 100 HRYVEN**
34.57 g., 0.900 Gold 1.0003 oz. AGW, 32 mm. **Obv:** National arms, value, pectoral cross and symbolic figures of the four Evangelists **Rev:** Figures **Edge:** Incuse lettering

| Date | Mintage | VF20 | XF40 | MS60 | MS63 | MS65 |
|---|---|---|---|---|---|---|
| 2013 | 1,025 | PF65 3,000 | | | | |

**KM# 646 500 HRYVEN**
500.00 g., 0.9999 Gold 16.0738 oz. AGW, 80 mm. **Subject:** UEFA Euro 2012 Final Tournament **Obv:** Map of Europe, logo, tournament cities around **Rev:** Large and smaller images of players

| Date | Mintage | VF20 | XF40 | MS60 | MS63 | MS65 |
|---|---|---|---|---|---|---|
| 2011 | Est. 500 | — | — | — | — | 47,000 |

## MINT SETS

| KM# | Date | Mintage | Identification | Issue Price | Mkt Val |
|---|---|---|---|---|---|
| MS2 | 2001 (8) | 5,000 | KM#1.1b, 2.1b, 3.3b, 4b, 6, 7, 8b, 129 | — | 150 |
| MS3 | 2006 (8) | 5,000 | KM#1.1b, 2.1b, 3.3b, 4b, 6, 7, 8b, 411 | — | 30.00 |
| MS4 | 2008 (7) | 5,000 | KM#1.1b, 2.1b, 3.3b, 4b, 6, 7, 209, prooflike | — | 100 |
| MS5 | 2011 (7) | 5,000 | KM#1.1b, 2.1b, 3.3b, 4b, 6, 7, 209. Prooflike | — | 45.00 |
| MS6 | 2012 (7) | 5,000 | KM#1.1b, 2.1b, 3.3b, 4b, 6, 7, 209. Prooflike | — | 50.00 |

# UNITED ARAB EMIRATES

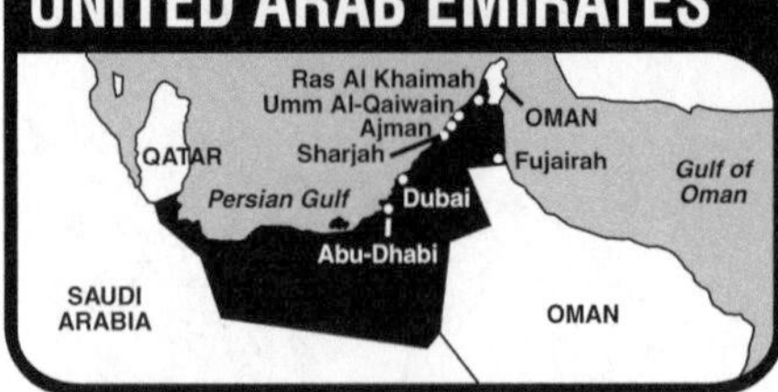


The seven United Arab Emirates (formerly known as the Trucial Sheikhdoms or States), located along the southern shore of the Persian Gulf, are comprised of the Sheikhdoms of Abu Dhabi, Dubai, al-Sharjah, Ajman, Umm al Qaiwain, Ras al-Khaimah and al-Fujairah. They have a combined area of about 32,000 sq. mi. (83,600 sq. km.) and a population of *2.1 million. Capital: Abu Zaby (Abu Dhabi). Since the oil strikes of 1958-60, the economy has centered about petroleum.

TITLES

الامارات العربية المتحدة

al-Imara(t) al-Arabiya(t) al-Muttahida(t)

## UNITED EMIRATES

### STANDARD COINAGE

**KM# 2.2 5 FILS**
Bronze **Series:** F.A.O. **Obv:** Value **Rev:** Fish above dates **Note:** Reduced size.

| Date | Mintage | VF20 | XF40 | MS60 | MS63 | MS65 |
|---|---|---|---|---|---|---|
| AH1422-2001 | — | — | 0.15 | 0.25 | 0.30 | 1.50 |
| AH1426-2005 | — | — | 0.15 | 0.25 | 0.30 | 1.50 |

**KM# 3.2 10 FILS**
Bronze, 19 mm. **Obv:** Value **Rev:** Arab dhow above dates **Note:** Reduced size.

| Date | Mintage | VF20 | XF40 | MS60 | MS63 | MS65 |
|---|---|---|---|---|---|---|
| AH1422-2001 | — | 0.30 | 0.50 | 0.70 | 1.25 | 1.75 |
| AH1425-2005 | — | 0.20 | 0.35 | 0.50 | 0.80 | 1.20 |

**KM# 4 25 FILS**
3.50 g., Copper-Nickel, 20 mm. **Obv:** Value **Rev:** Gazelle above dates **Edge:** Reeded

| Date | Mintage | VF20 | XF40 | MS60 | MS63 | MS65 |
|---|---|---|---|---|---|---|
| AH1425-2005 | — | — | 0.40 | 0.60 | 1.00 | 1.50 |
| AH1428-2007 | — | — | 0.40 | 0.60 | 1.00 | 1.50 |
| AH1428-2008 | — | — | 0.40 | 0.50 | 0.75 | 1.50 |
| AH1432-2011 | — | — | 0.40 | 0.50 | 0.75 | 1.50 |

**KM# 16 50 FILS**
4.30 g., Copper-Nickel, 21 mm. **Obv:** Value **Rev:** Oil derricks above dates **Shape:** 7-sided **Note:** Reduced size.

| Date | Mintage | VF20 | XF40 | MS60 | MS63 | MS65 |
|---|---|---|---|---|---|---|
| AH1425-2005 | — | — | 0.70 | 1.25 | 2.00 | 2.50 |
| AH1428-2007 | — | — | 0.50 | 1.00 | 1.50 | 2.00 |
| AH1428-2008 | — | — | 0.50 | 1.00 | 1.50 | 2.00 |

**KM# 6.2 DIRHAM**
6.40 g., Copper-Nickel, 24 mm. **Obv:** Value **Rev:** Jug above dates **Edge:** Reeded **Note:** Reduced size.

| Date | Mintage | VF20 | XF40 | MS60 | MS63 | MS65 |
|---|---|---|---|---|---|---|
| AH1425-2005 | — | 0.35 | 0.65 | 1.25 | 2.50 | 4.00 |
| AH1426-2006 | — | 0.35 | 0.65 | 1.00 | 2.00 | 4.00 |
| AH1428-2007 | — | 0.35 | 0.65 | 1.00 | 2.00 | 4.00 |
| AH1433-2012 | — | — | — | 1.25 | 1.85 | 2.25 |

**KM# 6.2a DIRHAM**
6.40 g., Nickel Plated Stainless Steel, 24 mm. **Rev:** Jug above dates

| Date | Mintage | F12 | VF20 | XF40 | MS60 | MS63 |
|---|---|---|---|---|---|---|
| AH1435-2014 | — | — | — | — | 1.25 | 1.85 |

**KM# 49 DIRHAM**
6.40 g., Copper-Nickel, 24 mm. **Subject:** 25th Anniversary - Armed Forces Unification **Obv:** Value **Rev:** Heraldic eagle within rope wreath **Edge:** Reeded

| Date | Mintage | VF20 | XF40 | MS60 | MS63 | MS65 |
|---|---|---|---|---|---|---|
| ND-2001 | 250,000 | — | 2.00 | 5.00 | 7.00 | 8.00 |

**KM# 51 DIRHAM**
6.33 g., Copper-Nickel, 24 mm. **Subject:** 50 Years of Formal Education **Obv:** Value **Rev:** Symbolic design **Edge:** Reeded

| Date | Mintage | VF20 | XF40 | MS60 | MS63 | MS65 |
|---|---|---|---|---|---|---|
| ND (2003) | — | — | 2.00 | 5.00 | 7.00 | 8.00 |

**KM# 52 DIRHAM**
6.40 g., Copper-Nickel, 24 mm. **Subject:** Abu Dhabi National Bank 35th Anniversary **Obv:** Value **Rev:** Bank building tower divide dates within circle **Edge:** Reeded

| Date | Mintage | VF20 | XF40 | MS60 | MS63 | MS65 |
|---|---|---|---|---|---|---|
| ND (2003) | — | — | 1.50 | 3.00 | 5.00 | 7.00 |

**KM# 54 DIRHAM**
6.40 g., Copper-Nickel, 24 mm. **Subject:** 40th Anniversary of Crude Oil Exports **Obv:** Value **Rev:** ADCO" logo **Edge:** Reeded

| Date | Mintage | VF20 | XF40 | MS60 | MS63 | MS65 |
|---|---|---|---|---|---|---|
| ND (2003) | — | — | 2.00 | 4.00 | 6.00 | 8.00 |

**KM# 73 DIRHAM**
6.40 g., Copper-Nickel, 23.93 mm. **Subject:** WBG & IMF meeting in Dubai 2003 **Obv:** Denomination **Rev:** Mosaic arc **Edge:** Reeded

| Date | Mintage | VF20 | XF40 | MS60 | MS63 | MS65 |
|---|---|---|---|---|---|---|
| 2003 | 250,000 | — | 2.00 | 6.00 | 9.00 | 11.00 |

**KM# 74 DIRHAM**
6.40 g., Copper-Nickel, 24 mm. **Subject:** First Gulf Bank 25th Anniversary **Obv:** Value **Rev:** Bank logo **Edge:** Reeded

| Date | Mintage | VF20 | XF40 | MS60 | MS63 | MS65 |
|---|---|---|---|---|---|---|
| ND-2004 | — | — | 2.00 | 4.00 | 6.00 | 8.00 |

**KM# 83 DIRHAM**
6.47 g., Copper-Nickel, 24.02 mm. **Subject:** Honoring Mother of Nations **Obv:** Large value **Rev:** Inscription in flower bud at center **Rev. Legend:** Sheikha Fatima Bint Mubarak **Edge:** Reeded

| Date | Mintage | VF20 | XF40 | MS60 | MS63 | MS65 |
|---|---|---|---|---|---|---|
| 2005 | — | — | 1.50 | 3.50 | 5.00 | 7.00 |

**KM# 78 DIRHAM**
6.40 g., Copper-Nickel, 24 mm. **Obv:** Value **Obv. Legend:** UNITED ARAB EMIRATES **Rev:** Police badge in center **Rev. Legend:** DUABI POLICE GOLDEN JUBILEE **Edge:** Reeded

| Date | Mintage | VF20 | XF40 | MS60 | MS63 | MS65 |
|---|---|---|---|---|---|---|
| ND-2006 | — | — | 1.50 | 4.00 | 6.00 | 8.00 |

**KM# 76 DIRHAM**
6.40 g., Copper-Nickel, 24 mm. **Subject:** Sharjah International Airport, 75th Anniversary **Obv:** Value **Obv. Legend:** UNITED ARAB EMIRATES **Rev:** Three birds in flight under arc **Edge:** Reeded

| Date | Mintage | VF20 | XF40 | MS60 | MS63 | MS65 |
|---|---|---|---|---|---|---|
| 2007 | — | — | 1.50 | 3.50 | 5.00 | 7.00 |

**KM# 77 DIRHAM**
6.30 g., Copper-Nickel, 24 mm. **Obv:** Value **Rev:** Zakum Development Co. logo **Edge:** Reeded

| Date | Mintage | VF20 | XF40 | MS60 | MS63 | MS65 |
|---|---|---|---|---|---|---|
| ND-2007 | — | — | 1.50 | 4.00 | 6.00 | 8.00 |

**KM# 79 DIRHAM**
6.43 g., Copper-Nickel, 24.03 mm. **Obv:** Value **Obv. Legend:** UNITED ARAB EMIRATES **Rev:** Large "30" and logo **Rev. Legend:** 30TH ANNIVERSARY OF THE 1ST LNG SHIPMENT **Rev. Inscription:** ADGAS **Edge:** Reeded

| Date | Mintage | VF20 | XF40 | MS60 | MS63 | MS65 |
|---|---|---|---|---|---|---|
| ND-2007 | — | — | 1.50 | 4.00 | 6.00 | 8.00 |

**KM# 84 DIRHAM**
6.40 g., Copper-Nickel, 24 mm. **Subject:** 10th Anniversary of the Hamdan Bin Rashed Award for Distinguished Academic Performance **Obv:** Large value **Rev:** 10 below pen with tip touching star **Edge:** Reeded

| Date | Mintage | VF20 | XF40 | MS60 | MS63 | MS65 |
|---|---|---|---|---|---|---|
| ND-2007 | — | — | 1.50 | 3.50 | 5.00 | 7.00 |

**KM# 96 DIRHAM**
6.40 g., Copper-Nickel, 24 mm. **Subject:** U.A.E. Boy Scouts, 50th Anniversary **Obv:** Value at center **Rev:** Scout Fleur-de-lis within rope circle

| Date | Mintage | VF20 | XF40 | MS60 | MS63 | MS65 |
|---|---|---|---|---|---|---|
| 2007 | — | — | 1.50 | 4.00 | 6.00 | 8.00 |

**KM# 85 DIRHAM**
6.40 g., Copper-Nickel **Subject:** National Bank of Abu Dhabi, 40th Anniversary **Obv:** Large value **Obv. Legend:** UNITED ARAB EMIRATES **Rev:** Large stylized "40 **Edge:** Reeded

| Date | Mintage | VF20 | XF40 | MS60 | MS63 | MS65 |
|---|---|---|---|---|---|---|
| ND-2008 | — | — | — | 2.50 | 3.50 | 5.00 |

**KM# 99 DIRHAM**
6.40 g., Copper-Nickel **Subject:** I Love UAE **Obv:** Large value **Rev:** Heart shaped **Rev. Legend:** UNITED ARAB EMRITES **Edge:** Reeded

| Date | Mintage | VF20 | XF40 | MS60 | MS63 | MS65 |
|---|---|---|---|---|---|---|
| ND-2009 | — | — | — | 2.50 | 3.50 | 5.00 |

**KM# 100 DIRHAM**
6.40 g., Copper-Nickel, 24 mm. **Obv:** Large value **Obv. Legend:** UNITED ARAB EMIRATES **Rev:** DIFC (Dubai International Financial Centre) **Edge:** Reeded

| Date | Mintage | VF20 | XF40 | MS60 | MS63 | MS65 |
|---|---|---|---|---|---|---|
| 2009 | — | — | — | 2.50 | 3.50 | 5.00 |

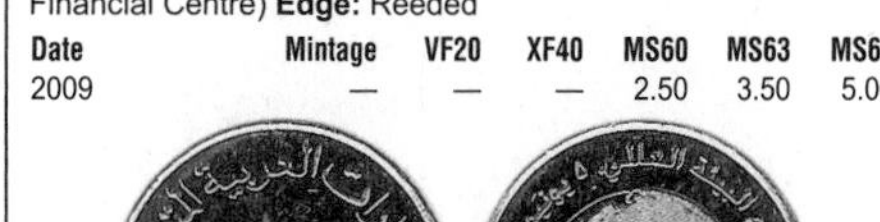

**KM# 101 DIRHAM**
6.40 g., Copper-Nickel **Subject:** World Environment Day **Obv:** Large value **Obv. Legend:** UNITED ARAB EMIRATES **Rev:** Map of the Mid East and Africa regions **Edge:** Reeded

| Date | Mintage | VF20 | XF40 | MS60 | MS63 | MS65 |
|---|---|---|---|---|---|---|
| 2009 | — | — | — | 2.50 | 3.50 | 5.00 |

**KM# 109 DIRHAM**
6.40 g., Copper-Nickel, 24 mm. **Subject:** I Love UAE

| Date | Mintage | VF20 | XF40 | MS60 | MS63 | MS65 |
|---|---|---|---|---|---|---|
| 2009 | — | — | — | 2.50 | 3.50 | 5.00 |

**KM# 6.3 DIRHAM**
6.10 g., Nickel Plated Steel, 24 mm. **Obv:** Value **Rev:** Jug above date **Edge:** Reeded

| Date | Mintage | VF20 | XF40 | MS60 | MS63 | MS65 |
|---|---|---|---|---|---|---|
| AH1433-2012 | — | 0.35 | 0.65 | 1.25 | 2.00 | 4.00 |

**KM# 102 DIRHAM**
6.40 g., Copper-Nickel, 24 mm. **Subject:** 50th Anniversary of Oil Exports **Obv:** Large value **Rev:** Anniversary logo

| Date | Mintage | F12 | VF20 | XF40 | MS60 | MS63 |
|---|---|---|---|---|---|---|
| 2012 | — | — | — | — | 2.50 | 3.50 |

**KM# 103 DIRHAM**
6.40 g., Copper-Nickel, 24 mm. **Obv:** World Environment Day logo

| Date | Mintage | VF20 | XF40 | MS60 | MS63 | MS65 |
|---|---|---|---|---|---|---|
| 2012 | — | — | — | 2.50 | 3.50 | 5.00 |

**KM# 47 50 DIRHAMS**
40.22 g., 0.925 Silver 1.1961 oz. ASW, 40 mm. **Subject:** 25th Anniversary - Women's Union (1975-2000) **Obv:** Bust of President H. H. Sheikh Zayed bin Sultan Al Nahyan 7/8 right **Rev:** Stylized gazelle **Edge:** Reeded

| Date | Mintage | VF20 | XF40 | MS60 | MS63 | MS65 |
|---|---|---|---|---|---|---|
| ND-2001 | — | PF63 100 | PF65 120 | | | |

**KM# 59 50 DIRHAMS**
40.00 g., 0.925 Silver 1.1896 oz. ASW, 40 mm. **Subject:** 25th Anniversary - Arab Bank of Investment and Foreign Trade **Edge:** Reeded

| Date | Mintage | VF20 | XF40 | MS60 | MS63 | MS65 |
|---|---|---|---|---|---|---|
| ND-2001 | 2,000 | PF63 125 | PF65 140 | | | |

**KM# 60 50 DIRHAMS**
40.00 g., 0.925 Silver 1.1896 oz. ASW, 40 mm. **Subject:** 25th Anniversary - Armed Forces Unification **Edge:** Reeded

| Date | Mintage | VF20 | XF40 | MS60 | MS63 | MS65 |
|---|---|---|---|---|---|---|
| ND-2001 | 10,000 | PF63 90.00 | PF65 110 | | | |

**KM# 61 50 DIRHAMS**
40.00 g., 0.925 Silver 1.1896 oz. ASW, 40 mm. **Subject:** 30th Anniversary - Al-Ain National Museum **Edge:** Reeded

| Date | Mintage | VF20 | XF40 | MS60 | MS63 | MS65 |
|---|---|---|---|---|---|---|
| ND-2001 | 5,000 | PF63 85.00 | PF65 100 | | | |

**KM# 62 50 DIRHAMS**
40.00 g., 0.925 Silver 1.1896 oz. ASW, 40 mm. **Subject:** 25th Anniversary - University of the U.A.E. **Obv:** Bust of President H. H. Sheikh Zayed bin Sultan Al Nahyan 7/8 right **Rev:** Inscriptions **Edge:** Reeded

| Date | Mintage | VF20 | XF40 | MS60 | MS63 | MS65 |
|---|---|---|---|---|---|---|
| ND-2002 | 5,000 | PF63 85.00 | PF65 100 | | | |

**KM# 63 50 DIRHAMS**
40.00 g., 0.925 Silver 1.1896 oz. ASW, 40 mm. **Subject:** Etisalat - Emirates Telecommunications, 25th Anniversary **Obv:** Value **Rev:** Stylized 25 **Edge:** Reeded

| Date | Mintage | VF20 | XF40 | MS60 | MS63 | MS65 |
|---|---|---|---|---|---|---|
| ND-2002 | 5,000 | PF63 100 | PF65 120 | | | |

**KM# 64 50 DIRHAMS**
40.00 g., 0.925 Silver 1.1896 oz. ASW, 40 mm. **Subject:** Sheikh Hamdan bin Rashid al Maktoum Award for Medical Sciences **Obv:** Value **Rev:** Sheikh Hamdan bin Rashid al Maktoum bust 3/4 left **Edge:** Reeded

| Date | Mintage | VF20 | XF40 | MS60 | MS63 | MS65 |
|---|---|---|---|---|---|---|
| ND-2002 | 2,000 | PF63 250 | PF65 350 | | | |

**KM# 65 50 DIRHAMS**
40.00 g., 0.925 Silver 1.1896 oz. ASW, 40 mm. **Subject:** Al Ahmadia School, 90th Anniversary **Obv:** Sheikh Rashid bin Saaed al Maktoum 3/4 left **Rev:** School building **Edge:** Reeded

| Date | Mintage | VF20 | XF40 | MS60 | MS63 | MS65 |
|---|---|---|---|---|---|---|
| ND-2002 | 5,000 | PF63 100 | PF65 120 | | | |

**KM# 67 50 DIRHAMS**
40.00 g., 0.925 Silver 1.1896 oz. ASW, 40 mm. **Subject:** Administrative Development Institute, 20th Anniversary **Obv:** Sheikh Zayed bin Sultan al Nahyan bust 3/4 right **Rev:** Eagle **Edge:** Reeded

| Date | Mintage | VF20 | XF40 | MS60 | MS63 | MS65 |
|---|---|---|---|---|---|---|
| ND-2002 | 2,000 | PF63 160 | PF65 180 | | | |

**KM# 50 50 DIRHAMS**
40.00 g., 0.925 Silver 1.1896 oz. ASW, 40 mm. **Obv:** Value **Rev:** FIFA 2003 World Youth Soccer Championship **Edge:** Reeded

| Date | Mintage | VF20 | XF40 | MS60 | MS63 | MS65 |
|---|---|---|---|---|---|---|
| ND-2003 | — | PF65 95.00 | | | | |

**KM# 66 50 DIRHAMS**
40.00 g., 0.925 Silver 1.1896 oz. ASW, 40 mm. **Subject:** Ministry of Finance and Industry ISO Certification **Obv:** Value **Rev:** Eagle at center **Edge:** Reeded

| Date | Mintage | VF20 | XF40 | MS60 | MS63 | MS65 |
|---|---|---|---|---|---|---|
| ND-2003 | 3,000 | PF65 110 | | | | |

**KM# 68 50 DIRHAMS**
40.00 g., 0.925 Silver 1.1896 oz. ASW, 40 mm. **Subject:** U.A.E. Central Bank, 30th Anniversary **Obv:** Sheikh Zayed bin Sultan al Nahyan bust 3/4 right **Rev:** Sheikh Maktoum bin Rashid al Maktoum bust 3/4 right **Edge:** Reeded

| Date | Mintage | VF20 | XF40 | MS60 | MS63 | MS65 |
|---|---|---|---|---|---|---|
| ND-2003 | 5,000 | PF63 130 | PF65 150 | | | |

**KM# 69 50 DIRHAMS**
40.00 g., 0.925 Silver 1.1896 oz. ASW, 40 mm. **Subject:** 58th Annual Meeting of the World Bank Group and the Int'l Money Fund **Obv:** Colored dots **Edge:** Reeded

| Date | Mintage | VF20 | XF40 | MS60 | MS63 | MS65 |
|---|---|---|---|---|---|---|
| ND-2003 | 10,000 | PF63 100 | PF65 120 | | | |

**KM# 70 50 DIRHAMS**
40.00 g., 0.925 Silver 1.1896 oz. ASW, 40 mm. **Subject:** 40th Anniversary - First Oil Export from Abu Dhabi Onshore Oil Fields (ADCO) **Obv:** Bust of President H. H. Sheikh Zayed bin Sultan Al Nayhan 3/4 right **Rev:** Logo **Edge:** Reeded

| Date | Mintage | VF20 | XF40 | MS60 | MS63 | MS65 |
|---|---|---|---|---|---|---|
| ND-2004 | — | PF63 550 | PF65 600 | | | |

**KM# 71 50 DIRHAMS**
40.00 g., 0.925 Silver 1.1896 oz. ASW, 40 mm. **Subject:** 25th Anniversary - Sharjah City for Humanitarian Services (SCHS) **Edge:** Reeded

| Date | Mintage | VF20 | XF40 | MS60 | MS63 | MS65 |
|---|---|---|---|---|---|---|
| ND-2005 | — | PF63 150 | PF65 175 | | | |

**KM# 98 50 DIRHAMS**
40.00 g., 0.925 Silver 1.1896 oz. ASW, 40 mm. **Subject:** Sheikha Fatima Birt Mubarak, Mother of the Nation

| Date | Mintage | VF20 | XF40 | MS60 | MS63 | MS65 |
|---|---|---|---|---|---|---|
| 2005 | — | PF63 120 | PF65 140 | | | |

**KM# 82 50 DIRHAMS**
40.00 g., 0.925 Silver 1.1896 oz. ASW, 40 mm. **Subject:** 25th Anniversary Emirates Banks Association **Obv:** Value **Obv. Legend:** UNITED ARAB EMIRATES **Rev:** Logo **Edge:** Reeded

| Date | Mintage | VF20 | XF40 | MS60 | MS63 | MS65 |
|---|---|---|---|---|---|---|
| ND-2007 | — | PF63 140 | PF65 180 | | | |

**KM# 95 50 DIRHAMS**
40.00 g., 0.925 Silver 1.1896 oz. ASW, 40 mm. **Subject:** Hamdan Bin Rashed Award for Distinguished Academic Performance **Obv:** Denomination, legend above **Rev:** Pen with tip touching star, legend above **Edge:** Reeded **Note:** Issued 10th Anniversary of the Award

| Date | Mintage | VF20 | XF40 | MS60 | MS63 | MS65 |
|---|---|---|---|---|---|---|
| ND(2008) | — | PF63 1,000 | PF65 1,100 | | | |

**KM# 107 50 DIRHAMS**
60.00 g., 0.916 Gold 1.767 oz. AGW, 42.45 mm. **Subject:** World Energy Forum, Dubai **Obv:** Double portraits **Rev:** Logo

| Date | Mintage | VF20 | XF40 | MS60 | MS63 | MS65 |
|---|---|---|---|---|---|---|
| 2012 | — | PF65 3,000 | | | | |

**KM# 80 100 DIRHAMS**
60.00 g., 0.925 Silver 1.7844 oz. ASW, 50 mm. **Obv:** Sheikh Zayed bin Sultan **Rev:** Sheikh Zayed Mosque

| Date | Mintage | VF20 | XF40 | MS60 | MS63 | MS65 |
|---|---|---|---|---|---|---|
| 2004 | — | PF63 180 | PF65 200 | | | |

**KM# 97 100 DIRHAMS**
60.00 g., 0.925 Silver 1.7844 oz. ASW, 50 mm. **Subject:** Sheikh Khalifa Ben Zayed, 1st Anniversary **Rev:** Emir's Palace

| Date | Mintage | VF20 | XF40 | MS60 | MS63 | MS65 |
|---|---|---|---|---|---|---|
| 2005 | — | PF63 180 | PF65 200 | | | |

**KM# 104 100 DIRHAMS**
0.925 Silver, 40 mm. **Subject:** 5th Anniversary of Date Palm Award

| Date | Mintage | VF20 | XF40 | MS60 | MS63 | MS65 |
|---|---|---|---|---|---|---|
| 2012 | Est. 2000 | PF63 150 | PF65 170 | | | |

**KM# 105 100 DIRHAMS**
40.00 g., 0.925 Silver 1.1896 oz. ASW **Subject:** 25th National Day

| Date | Mintage | VF20 | XF40 | MS60 | MS63 | MS65 |
|---|---|---|---|---|---|---|
| 2012 | — | PF63 150 | PF65 170 | | | |

# UNITED STATES OF AMERICA

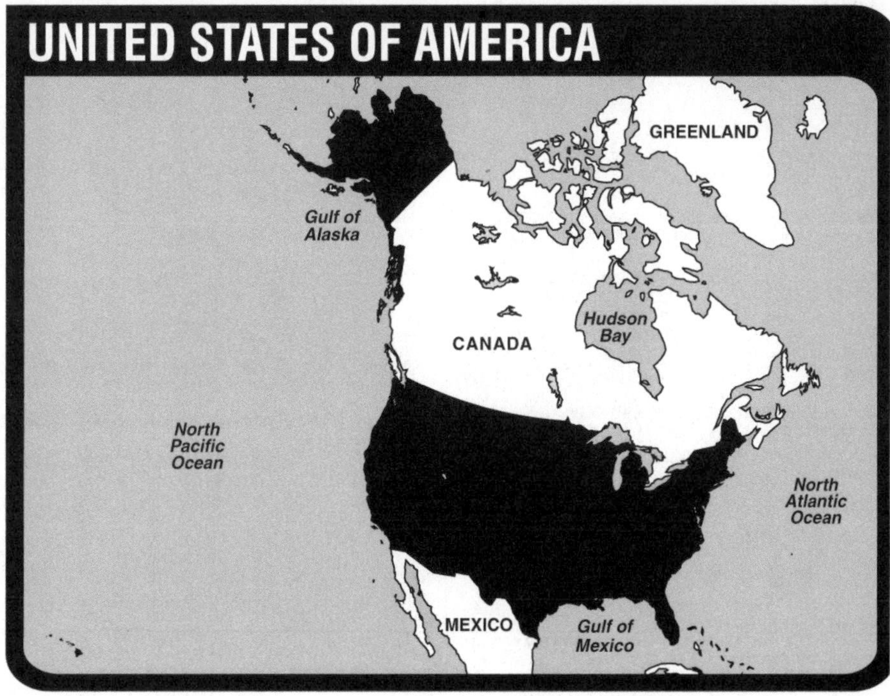


The United States of America as politically organized, under the Articles of Confederation consisted of the 13 original British-American colonies; New Hampshire, Massachusetts, Rhode Island, Connecticut, New York, New Jersey, Pennsylvania, Delaware, Virginia, North Carolina, South Carolina, Georgia and Maryland. Clustered along the eastern seaboard of North America between the forests of Maine and the marshes of Georgia. Under the Article of Confederation, the United States had no national capital: Philadelphia, where the "United States in Congress Assembled", was the "seat of government". The population during this political phase of America's history (1781-1789) was about 3 million, most of whom lived on self-sufficient family farms. Fishing, lumbering and the production of grains for export were major economic endeavors. Rapid strides were also being made in industry and manufacturing by 1775, the (then) colonies were accounting for one-seventh of the world's production of raw iron.

On the basis of the voyage of John Cabot to the North American mainland in 1497, England claimed the entire continent. The first permanent English settlement was established at Jamestown, Virginia, in 1607. France and Spain also claimed extensive territory in North America. At the end of the French and Indian Wars (1763), England acquired all of the territory east of the Mississippi River, including East and West Florida. From 1776 to 1781, the States were governed by the Continental Congress. From 1781 to 1789, they were organized under the Articles of Confederation, during which period the individual States had the right to issue money. Independence from Great Britain was attained with the American Revolution in 1776. The Constitution organized and governs the present United States. It was ratified on Nov. 21, 1788.

**MINT MARKS**

C – Charlotte, N.C., 1838-61
CC – Carson City, NV, 1870-93
D – Dahlonega, GA, 1838-61
D – Denver, CO, 1906-present
O – New Orleans, LA, 1838-1909
P – Philadelphia, PA, 1793-present
S – San Francisco, CA, 1854-present
W – West Point, NY, 1984-present

**BULLION COINS**

Silver Eagle = $1.00
Gold 1/10 Ounce = $5.00
Gold ¼ Ounce = $10.00
Gold ½ Ounce = $25.00
Gold Ounce = $50.00
Platinum 1/10 Ounce = $10.00
Platinum ¼ Ounce = $25.00
Platinum ½ Ounce = $50.00
Platinum Ounce = $100.00

## CIRCULATION COINAGE

## CENT

### Lincoln Cent

Lincoln Memorial reverse

**KM# 201b • Copper Plated Zinc,** 19 mm. • **Note:** MS60 prices are for brown coins and MS65 prices are for coins that are at least 90% original red.

| Date | Mintage | XF40 | MS65 | Prf65 |
|---|---|---|---|---|
| 2001 | 4,959,600,000 | — | 3.00 | — |
| 2001D | 5,374,990,000 | — | 3.00 | — |
| 2001S | 3,099,096 | — | — | 3.50 |
| 2002 | 3,260,800,000 | — | 3.00 | — |
| 2002D | 4,028,055,000 | — | 3.00 | — |
| 2002S | 3,157,739 | — | — | 3.50 |
| 2003 | 3,300,000,000 | — | 3.50 | — |
| 2003D | 3,548,000,000 | — | 3.50 | — |
| 2003S | 3,116,590 | — | — | 3.50 |
| 2004 | 3,379,600,000 | — | 3.50 | — |
| 2004D | 3,456,400,000 | — | 3.50 | — |
| 2004S | 2,992,069 | — | — | 3.50 |
| 2005 | 3,935,600,000 | — | 2.50 | — |
| 2005 Satin Finish | 1,160,000 | — | 4.00 | — |
| 2005D | 3,764,450,000 | — | 2.50 | — |
| 2005D Satin Finish | 1,160,000 | — | 4.00 | — |
| 2005S | 3,273,000 | — | — | 3.50 |
| 2006 | 4,290,000,000 | — | 2.00 | — |
| 2006 Satin Finish | 847,361 | — | 4.00 | — |
| 2006D | 3,944,000,000 | — | 2.50 | — |
| 2006D Satin Finish | 847,361 | — | 4.00 | — |
| 2006S | 2,923,105 | — | — | 3.50 |
| 2007 | 3,762,400,000 | — | 2.00 | — |
| 2007 Satin Finish | 895,628 | — | 4.00 | — |
| 2007D | 3,638,800,000 | — | 2.00 | — |
| 2007D Satin Finish | 895,628 | — | 4.00 | — |
| 2007S | 2,577,166 | — | — | 3.50 |
| 2008 | 2,558,800,000 | — | 2.25 | — |
| 2008 Satin Finish | 745,464 | — | 4.00 | — |
| 2008D | 2,849,600,000 | — | 2.25 | — |
| 2008D Satin Finish | 745,464 | — | 4.00 | — |
| 2008S | 2,169,561 | — | — | 4.50 |

### Lincoln Bicentennial

Bust right obverse Log cabin reverse

**KM# 441** • 2.50 g., **Copper Plated Zinc**, 19 mm. • **Subject:** Early Childhood in Kentucky **Rev. Designer:** Richard Masters and James Licaretz

| Date | Mintage | XF40 | MS65 | Prf65 |
|---|---|---|---|---|
| 2009P | 284,400,000 | — | 1.50 | — |
| 2009D | 350,400,000 | — | 1.50 | — |

**KM# 441a** • 3.31 g., **Brass**, 19 mm. • **Subject:** Early childhood in Kentucky **Rev. Designer:** Richard Masters and James Licaretz

| Date | Mintage | XF40 | MS65 | Prf65 |
|---|---|---|---|---|
| 2009P Satin finish | 784,614 | — | 4.00 | — |
| 2009D Satin finish | 784,614 | — | 4.00 | — |
| 2009S | 2,995,615 | — | — | 4.00 |

Lincoln seated on log reverse

**KM# 442** • 2.50 g., **Copper Plated Zinc**, 19 mm. • **Subject:** Formative years in Indiana **Rev. Designer:** Charles Vickers

| Date | Mintage | XF40 | MS65 | Prf65 |
|---|---|---|---|---|
| 2009P | 376,000,000 | — | 1.50 | — |
| 2009D | 363,600,000 | — | 1.50 | — |

**KM# 442a** • 3.11 g., **Brass**, 19 mm. • **Subject:** Formative years in Indiana **Rev. Designer:** Charles Vickers

| Date | Mintage | XF40 | MS65 | Prf65 |
|---|---|---|---|---|
| 2009P Satin finish | 784,614 | — | 4.00 | — |
| 2009D Satin finish | 784,614 | — | 4.00 | — |
| 2009S | 2,995,615 | — | — | 4.00 |

Lincoln standing before Illinois Statehouse reverse

**KM# 443** • 2.50 g., **Copper Plated Zinc**, 19 mm. • **Subject:** Professional life in Illinois **Rev. Designer:** Joel Iskowitz and Don Everhart

| Date | Mintage | XF40 | MS65 | Prf65 |
|---|---|---|---|---|
| 2009P | 316,000,000 | — | 1.50 | — |
| 2009D | 336,000,000 | — | 1.50 | — |

**KM# 443a** • 3.11 g., **Brass**, 19 mm. • **Subject:** Professional life in Illinois **Rev. Designer:** Joel Iskowitz and Don Everhart

| Date | Mintage | XF40 | MS65 | Prf65 |
|---|---|---|---|---|
| 2009P Satin finish | 784,614 | — | 4.00 | — |
| 2009D Satin finish | 784,614 | — | 4.00 | — |
| 2009S | 2,995,615 | — | — | 4.00 |

Capitol Building reverse

**KM# 444** • 2.50 g., **Copper Plated Zinc Subject:** Presidency in Washington, DC **Rev. Designer:** Susan Gamble and Joseph Menna **Shape:** 19

| Date | Mintage | XF40 | MS65 | Prf65 |
|---|---|---|---|---|
| 2009P | 129,600,000 | — | 1.50 | — |
| 2009D | 198,000,000 | — | 1.50 | — |

**KM# 444a** • 3.11 g., **Brass**, 19 mm. • **Subject:** Presidency in Washington, DC **Rev. Designer:** Susan Ganmble and Joseph Menna

| Date | Mintage | XF40 | MS65 | Prf65 |
|---|---|---|---|---|
| 2009P Satin finish | 784,614 | — | 4.00 | — |
| 2009D Satin finish | 784,614 | — | 4.00 | — |
| 2009S | 2,995,615 | — | — | 4.00 |

## Lincoln - Shield Reverse

Lincoln bust right obverse
Shield reverse

**KM# 468** • 2.50 g., **Copper Plated Zinc**, 19 mm. • **Obv. Designer:** Victor D. Brenner **Rev. Designer:** Lyndall Bass and Joseph Menna

| Date | Mintage | XF40 | MS65 | Prf65 |
|---|---|---|---|---|
| 2010P | 1,963,630,000 | — | 1.50 | — |
| 2010P Satin finish | 583,912 | — | — | — |
| 2010D | 2,047,200,000 | — | 1.50 | — |
| 2010D Satin finish | 583,912 | — | — | — |
| 2010S | 1,689,364 | — | — | 4.00 |
| 2011P | 2,006,800,000 | — | 1.50 | — |
| 2011D | 2147483647 | — | 1.50 | — |
| 2011S | 1,673,010 | — | — | 4.00 |
| 2012P | 3,132,000,000 | — | 1.50 | — |
| 2012D | 2,883,200,000 | — | 1.50 | — |
| 2012S | 1,237,415 | — | — | 4.00 |
| 2013P | 3,750,400,000 | — | 1.50 | — |
| 2013D | 3,319,600,000 | — | 1.50 | — |
| 2013S | 1,237,926 | — | — | 4.00 |
| 2014P | — | — | 1.50 | — |
| 2014D | — | — | 1.50 | — |
| 2014S | — | — | — | 4.00 |
| 2015P | — | — | — | — |
| 2015D | — | — | — | — |
| 2015S | — | — | — | — |

# 5 CENTS

## Jefferson Nickel

Pre-war design resumed reverse

**KM# A192** • 5.00 g., **Copper-Nickel**, 21.2 mm. • **Edge:** Plain **Designer:** Felix Schlag

| Date | Mintage | XF40 | MS65 | Prf65 |
|---|---|---|---|---|
| 2001P | 675,704,000 | — | 3.75 | — |
| 2001D | 627,680,000 | — | 3.75 | — |
| 2001S | 3,099,096 | — | — | 1.00 |
| 2002P | 539,280,000 | — | 3.75 | — |
| 2002D | 691,200,000 | — | 3.75 | — |
| 2002S | 3,157,739 | — | — | 1.00 |
| 2003P | 441,840,000 | — | 3.75 | — |
| 2003D | 383,040,000 | — | 3.75 | — |
| 2003S | 3,116,590 | — | — | 1.00 |

## Jefferson - Westward Expansion - Lewis & Clark Bicentennial

Jefferson era peace medal design: two clasped hands, pipe and hatchet reverse

**KM# 360** • 5.00 g., **Copper-Nickel**, 21.2 mm. • **Obv. Designer:** Felix Schlag **Rev. Designer:** Norman E. Nemeth

| Date | Mintage | MS65 | Prf65 |
|---|---|---|---|
| 2004P | 361,440,000 | 1.50 | — |
| 2004D | 372,000,000 | 1.50 | — |
| 2004S | 2,992,069 | — | 5.00 |

Lewis and Clark's Keelboat reverse

**KM# 361** • 5.00 g., **Copper-Nickel**, 21.2 mm. • **Obv. Designer:** Felix Schlag **Rev. Designer:** Al Maletsky

| Date | Mintage | MS65 | Prf65 |
|---|---|---|---|
| 2004P | 366,720,000 | 1.50 | — |
| 2004D | 344,880,000 | 1.50 | — |
| 2004S | 2,965,422 | — | 5.00 |

Thomas Jefferson large profile right obverse
American Bison right reverse

**KM# 368** • 5.00 g., **Copper-Nickel**, 21.2 mm. • **Obv. Designer:** Joe Fitzgerald and Don Everhart II **Rev. Designer:** Jamie Franki and Norman E. Nemeth

| Date | Mintage | MS65 | Prf65 |
|---|---|---|---|
| 2005P | 448,320,000 | 1.50 | — |
| 2005P Satin Finish | 1,160,000 | 4.00 | — |
| 2005D | 487,680,000 | 1.50 | — |
| 2005D Satin Finish | 1,160,000 | 4.00 | — |
| 2005S | 3,344,679 | — | 6.50 |

Jefferson, large profile obverse
Pacific coastline reverse

**KM# 369** • 5.00 g., **Copper-Nickel**, 21.2 mm. • **Subject:** Ocean in View!, oh the joy! **Obv. Designer:** Joe Fitzgerald and Don Everhart **Rev. Designer:** Joe Fitzgerald and Donna Weaver

| Date | Mintage | MS65 | Prf65 |
|---|---|---|---|
| 2005P | 394,080,000 | 1.25 | — |
| 2005P Satin Finish | 1,160,000 | 4.00 | — |
| 2005D | 411,120,000 | 1.25 | — |
| 2005D Satin Finish | 1,160,000 | 4.00 | — |
| 2005S | 3,344,679 | — | 5.50 |

## Jefferson large facing portrait - Enhanced Monticello Reverse

**KM# 381** • 5.00 g., **Copper-Nickel**, 21.2 mm. • **Subject:** Jefferson facing head **Obv. Designer:** Jamie N. Franki and Donna Weaver **Rev. Designer:** Felix Schlag and John Mercanti

| Date | Mintage | MS65 | Prf65 |
|---|---|---|---|
| 2006P | 693,120,000 | 2.50 | — |
| 2006P Satin finish | 847,361 | 4.00 | — |
| 2006D | 809,280,000 | 2.50 | — |
| 2006D Satin finish | 847,361 | 4.00 | — |
| 2006S | 3,054,436 | — | 5.00 |
| 2007P | 571,680,000 | 2.50 | — |
| 2007P Satin finish | 895,628 | 4.00 | — |
| 2007D | 626,160,000 | 2.50 | — |
| 2007D Satin finish | 895,628 | 4.00 | — |
| 2007S | 2,577,166 | — | 4.00 |
| 2008P | 279,840,000 | 2.50 | — |
| 2008P Satin finish | 745,464 | 4.00 | — |
| 2008D | 345,600,000 | 2.50 | — |
| 2008D Satin finish | 745,464 | 4.00 | — |
| 2008S | 2,169,561 | — | 4.00 |
| 2009P | 39,840,000 | 3.50 | — |
| 2009P Satin finish | 784,614 | 4.00 | — |
| 2009D | 46,800,000 | 1.75 | — |
| 2009D Satin finish | 784,614 | 4.00 | — |
| 2009S | 2,179,867 | — | 3.00 |
| 2010P | 260,640,000 | 1.50 | — |
| 2010P Satin finish | — | 4.00 | — |
| 2010D | 229,920,000 | 1.50 | — |
| 2010D Satin finish | — | 4.00 | — |
| 2010S | 1,689,216 | — | 3.00 |
| 2011P | 450,000,000 | 1.50 | — |
| 2011D | 540,240,000 | 1.50 | — |
| 2011S | 1,673,010 | — | 4.00 |
| 2012P | 464,640,000 | 1.50 | — |
| 2012D | 558,960,000 | 1.50 | — |
| 2012S | 1,237,415 | — | 4.00 |
| 2013P | 607,440,000 | 1.50 | — |
| 2013D | 615,600,000 | 1.50 | — |
| 2013S | 1,237,926 | — | 3.00 |
| 2014P | — | 1.50 | — |
| 2014D | — | 1.50 | — |
| 2014S | — | — | 3.00 |
| 2015P | — | 2.50 | — |
| 2015D | — | 2.50 | — |
| 2015S | — | — | 3.00 |

# DIME

## Roosevelt Dime

Mint mark 1968- present

**KM# 195a** • 2.27 g., **Copper-Nickel Clad Copper**, 17.91 mm. • **Designer:** John R. Sinnock **Note:** The 1979-S and 1981-S Type II proofs have clearer mint marks than the Type I proofs of those years. On the 1982 no-mint-mark variety, the mint mark was inadvertently left off.

| Date | Mintage | MS65 | Prf65 |
|---|---|---|---|
| 2001P | 1,369,590,000 | 2.75 | — |
| 2001D | 1,412,800,000 | 2.75 | — |
| 2001S | 2,249,496 | — | 3.75 |
| 2002P | 1,187,500,000 | 2.75 | — |
| 2002D | 1,379,500,000 | 3.00 | — |
| 2002S | 2,268,913 | — | 2.50 |
| 2003P | 1,085,500,000 | 3.00 | — |
| 2003D | 986,500,000 | 3.00 | — |
| 2003S | 2,076,165 | — | 2.60 |
| 2004P | 1,328,000,000 | 3.00 | — |
| 2004D | 1,159,500,000 | 3.00 | — |
| 2004S | 1,804,396 | — | 4.75 |
| 2005P | 1,412,000,000 | 2.75 | — |
| 2005P Satin Finish | — | 4.00 | — |
| 2005D | 1,423,500,000 | 2.75 | — |
| 2005D Satin Finish | — | 4.00 | — |
| 2005S | 2,275,000 | — | 2.60 |
| 2006P | 1,381,000,000 | 2.50 | — |
| 2006P Satin Finish | — | 4.00 | — |
| 2006D | 1,447,000,000 | 2.50 | — |
| 2006D Satin Finish | — | 4.00 | — |
| 2006S | 2,000,428 | — | 2.50 |
| 2007P | 1,047,500,000 | 2.00 | — |
| 2007P Satin Finish | — | 3.00 | — |
| 2007D | 1,042,000,000 | 2.00 | — |
| 2007D Satin Finish | — | 3.00 | — |
| 2007S | 1,702,116 | — | 2.50 |
| 2008P | 391,000,000 | 1.25 | — |
| 2008 Satin Finish | — | 2.50 | — |
| 2008D | 624,500,000 | 1.25 | — |
| 2008D Satin Finish | — | 2.50 | — |
| 2008S | 1,405,674 | — | 2.50 |
| 2009P | 96,500,000 | 1.25 | — |
| 2009P Satin Finish | — | 1.00 | — |
| 2009D | 49,500,000 | 1.25 | — |
| 2009D Satin Finish | — | 1.00 | — |
| 2009S | 1,482,502 | — | 2.50 |
| 2010P | 557,000,000 | 4.00 | — |
| 2010P Satin Finish | — | 2.00 | — |
| 2010D | 562,000,000 | 4.00 | — |
| 2010D Satin Finish | — | 2.00 | — |
| 2010S | 1,103,815 | — | 2.50 |
| 2011P | 748,000,000 | 4.00 | — |
| 2011D | 754,000,000 | 4.00 | — |
| 2011S | 1,098,835 | — | 2.50 |
| 2012P | 808,000,000 | 4.00 | — |
| 2012D | 868,000,000 | 4.00 | — |
| 2012S | 841,972 | — | 2.50 |
| 2013P | 1,086,500,000 | 4.00 | — |
| 2013D | 1,025,500,000 | 4.00 | — |
| 2013S | 821,031 | — | 2.50 |
| 2014P | — | 2.00 | — |
| 2014D | — | 2.00 | — |
| 2014S | — | — | 2.50 |
| 2015P | — | 2.00 | — |
| 2015D | — | 2.00 | — |
| 2015S | — | — | 2.50 |

**KM# 195b** • 2.50 g., 0.900 **Silver** 0.0723 oz. ASW, 17.9 mm. • **Designer:** John R. Sinnock

| Date | Mintage | Prf65 |
|---|---|---|
| 2001S | 849,600 | 5.00 |
| 2002S | 888,826 | 5.00 |
| 2003S | 1,090,425 | 4.75 |
| 2004S | 1,175,934 | 5.00 |
| 2005S | 1,069,679 | 5.00 |
| 2006S | 1,054,008 | 4.50 |
| 2007S | 875,050 | 6.00 |
| 2008S | 763,887 | 6.50 |
| 2009S | 697,365 | 6.75 |
| 2010S | 585,401 | 6.75 |
| 2011S | 574,175 | 6.75 |
| 2012S | 395,443 | 6.75 |
| 2013S | 821,031 | 6.75 |

# QUARTER

## 50 State Quarters

### New York

**KM# 318** • 5.67 g., **Copper-Nickel Clad Copper**, 24.3 mm.

| Date | Mintage | MS63 | MS65 | Prf65 |
|---|---|---|---|---|
| 2001P | 655,400,000 | 0.80 | 5.50 | — |
| 2001D | 619,640,000 | 0.80 | 5.50 | — |
| 2001S | 3,094,140 | — | — | 4.00 |

**KM# 318a** • 6.25 g., 0.900 **Silver**, 0.1808 oz. ASW 24.3 mm.

| Date | Mintage | MS63 | MS65 | Prf65 |
|---|---|---|---|---|
| 2001S | 889,697 | — | — | 9.50 |

### North Carolina

**KM# 319** • 5.67 g., **Copper-Nickel Clad Copper**, 24.3 mm.

| Date | Mintage | MS63 | MS65 | Prf65 |
|---|---|---|---|---|
| 2001P | 627,600,000 | 1.00 | 5.50 | — |
| 2001D | 427,876,000 | 1.00 | 6.50 | — |
| 2001S | 3,094,140 | — | — | 4.00 |

**KM# 319a** • 6.25 g., 0.900 **Silver**, 0.1808 oz. ASW 24.3 mm.

| Date | Mintage | MS63 | MS65 | Prf65 |
|---|---|---|---|---|
| 2001S | 889,697 | — | — | 9.50 |

### Rhode Island

**KM# 320** • 5.67 g., **Copper-Nickel Clad Copper**, 24.3 mm.

| Date | Mintage | MS63 | MS65 | Prf65 |
|---|---|---|---|---|
| 2001P | 423,000,000 | 0.80 | 5.50 | — |
| 2001D | 447,100,000 | 0.80 | 6.00 | — |
| 2001S | 3,094,140 | — | — | 4.00 |

**KM# 320a** • 6.25 g., 0.900 **Silver**, 0.1808 oz. ASW 24.3 mm.

| Date | Mintage | MS63 | MS65 | Prf65 |
|---|---|---|---|---|
| 2001S | 889,697 | — | — | 9.50 |

### Vermont

**KM# 321** • 5.67 g., **Copper-Nickel Clad Copper**, 24.3 mm.

| Date | Mintage | MS63 | MS65 | Prf65 |
|---|---|---|---|---|
| 2001P | 423,400,000 | 0.80 | 6.50 | — |
| 2001D | 459,404,000 | 0.80 | 6.50 | — |
| 2001S | 3,094,140 | — | — | 4.00 |

**KM# 321a** • 6.25 g., 0.900 **Silver**, 0.1808 oz. ASW 24.3 mm.

| Date | Mintage | MS63 | MS65 | Prf65 |
|---|---|---|---|---|
| 2001S | 889,697 | — | — | 9.50 |

### Kentucky

**KM# 322** • 5.67 g., **Copper-Nickel Clad Copper**, 24.3 mm.

| Date | Mintage | MS63 | MS65 | Prf65 |
|---|---|---|---|---|
| 2001P | 353,000,000 | 1.00 | 6.50 | — |
| 2001D | 370,564,000 | 1.00 | 7.00 | — |
| 2001S | 3,094,140 | — | — | 4.00 |

**KM# 322a** • 6.25 g., 0.900 **Silver**, 0.1808 oz. ASW 24.3 mm.

| Date | Mintage | MS63 | MS65 | Prf65 |
|---|---|---|---|---|
| 2001S | 889,697 | — | — | 9.50 |

### Tennessee

**KM# 331** • 5.67 g., **Copper-Nickel Clad Copper**, 24.3 mm.

| Date | Mintage | MS63 | MS65 | Prf65 |
|---|---|---|---|---|
| 2002P | 361,600,000 | 1.40 | 6.50 | — |
| 2002D | 286,468,000 | 1.40 | 7.00 | — |
| 2002S | 3,084,245 | — | — | 2.30 |

**KM# 331a** • 6.25 g., 0.900 **Silver**, 0.1808 oz. ASW 24.3 mm.

| Date | Mintage | MS63 | MS65 | Prf65 |
|---|---|---|---|---|
| 2002S | 892,229 | — | — | 8.50 |

### Ohio

**KM# 332** • 5.67 g., **Copper-Nickel Clad Copper**, 24.3 mm.

| Date | Mintage | MS63 | MS65 | Prf65 |
|---|---|---|---|---|
| 2002P | 217,200,000 | 0.80 | 5.50 | — |
| 2002D | 414,832,000 | 0.80 | 5.50 | — |
| 2002S | 3,084,245 | — | — | 2.30 |

**KM# 332a** • 6.25 g., 0.900 **Silver**, 0.1808 oz. ASW 24.3 mm.

| Date | Mintage | MS63 | MS65 | Prf65 |
|---|---|---|---|---|
| 2002S | 892,229 | — | — | 8.50 |

### Louisiana

**KM# 333** • 5.67 g., **Copper-Nickel Clad Copper**, 24.3 mm.

| Date | Mintage | MS63 | MS65 | Prf65 |
|---|---|---|---|---|
| 2002P | 362,000,000 | 0.80 | 5.50 | — |
| 2002D | 402,204,000 | 0.80 | 6.00 | — |
| 2002S | 3,084,245 | — | — | 2.30 |

**KM# 333a** • 6.25 g., 0.900 **Silver**, 0.1808 oz. ASW 24.3 mm.

| Date | Mintage | MS63 | MS65 | Prf65 |
|---|---|---|---|---|
| 2002S | 892,229 | — | — | 8.50 |

### Indiana

**KM# 334** • 5.67 g., **Copper-Nickel Clad Copper**, 24.3 mm.

| Date | Mintage | MS63 | MS65 | Prf65 |
|---|---|---|---|---|
| 2002P | 362,600,000 | 0.80 | 5.00 | — |
| 2002D | 327,200,000 | 0.80 | 5.00 | — |
| 2002S | 3,084,245 | — | — | 2.30 |

**KM# 334a** • 6.25 g., 0.900 **Silver**, 0.1808 oz. ASW 24.3 mm.

| Date | Mintage | MS63 | MS65 | Prf65 |
|---|---|---|---|---|
| 2002S | 892,229 | — | — | 8.50 |

### Mississippi

**KM# 335** • 5.67 g., **Copper-Nickel Clad Copper**, 24.3 mm.

| Date | Mintage | MS63 | MS65 | Prf65 |
|---|---|---|---|---|
| 2002P | 290,000,000 | 0.80 | 5.00 | — |
| 2002D | 289,600,000 | 0.80 | 5.00 | — |
| 2002S | 3,084,245 | — | — | 2.30 |

**KM# 335a** • 6.25 g., 0.900 **Silver**, 0.1808 oz. ASW 24.3 mm.

| Date | Mintage | MS63 | MS65 | Prf65 |
|---|---|---|---|---|
| 2002S | 892,229 | — | — | 8.50 |

### Illinois

**KM# 343** • 5.67 g., **Copper-Nickel Clad Copper**, 24.3 mm.

| Date | Mintage | MS63 | MS65 | Prf65 |
|---|---|---|---|---|
| 2003P | 225,800,000 | 1.10 | 5.00 | — |
| 2003D | 237,400,000 | 1.10 | 5.00 | — |
| 2003S | 3,408,516 | — | — | 2.30 |

**KM# 343a** • 6.25 g., 0.900 **Silver**, 0.1808 oz. ASW 24.3 mm.

| Date | Mintage | MS63 | MS65 | Prf65 |
|---|---|---|---|---|
| 2003S | 1,257,555 | — | — | 8.50 |

### Alabama

**KM# 344** • 5.67 g., **Copper-Nickel Clad Copper**, 24.3 mm.

| Date | Mintage | MS63 | MS65 | Prf65 |
|---|---|---|---|---|
| 2003P | 225,000,000 | 0.65 | 5.00 | — |
| 2003D | 232,400,000 | 0.65 | 5.00 | — |
| 2003S | 3,408,516 | — | — | 2.30 |

**KM# 344a** • 6.25 g., 0.900 **Silver**, 0.1808 oz. ASW 24.3 mm.

| Date | Mintage | MS63 | MS65 | Prf65 |
|---|---|---|---|---|
| 2003S | 1,257,555 | — | — | 8.50 |

### Maine

**KM# 345** • 5.67 g., **Copper-Nickel Clad Copper**, 24.3 mm.

| Date | Mintage | MS63 | MS65 | Prf65 |
|---|---|---|---|---|
| 2003P | 217,400,000 | 0.65 | 5.00 | — |
| 2003D | 213,400,000 | 0.65 | 5.00 | — |
| 2003S | 3,408,516 | — | — | 2.30 |

**KM# 345a** • 6.25 g., 0.900 **Silver**, 0.1808 oz. ASW 24.3 mm.

| Date | Mintage | MS63 | MS65 | Prf65 |
|---|---|---|---|---|
| 2003S | 1,257,555 | — | — | 8.50 |

### Missouri

**KM# 346** • 5.67 g., **Copper-Nickel Clad Copper**, 24.3 mm.

| Date | Mintage | MS63 | MS65 | Prf65 |
|---|---|---|---|---|
| 2003P | 225,000,000 | 0.65 | 5.00 | — |
| 2003D | 228,200,000 | 0.65 | 5.00 | — |
| 2003S | 3,408,516 | — | — | 2.30 |

**KM# 346a** • 6.25 g., 0.900 **Silver**, 0.1808 oz. ASW 24.3 mm.

| Date | Mintage | MS63 | MS65 | Prf65 |
|---|---|---|---|---|
| 2003S | 1,257,555 | — | — | 8.50 |

### Arkansas

**KM# 347** • 5.67 g., **Copper-Nickel Clad Copper**, 24.3 mm.

| Date | Mintage | MS63 | MS65 | Prf65 |
|---|---|---|---|---|
| 2003P | 228,000,000 | 0.65 | 5.00 | — |
| 2003D | 229,800,000 | 0.65 | 5.00 | — |
| 2003S | 3,408,516 | — | — | 2.30 |

**KM# 347a** • 6.25 g., 0.900 **Silver**, 0.1808 oz. ASW 24.3 mm.

| Date | Mintage | MS63 | MS65 | Prf65 |
|---|---|---|---|---|
| 2003S | 1,257,555 | — | — | 8.50 |

## Michigan

**KM# 355** • 5.67 g., **Copper-Nickel Clad Copper**, 24.3 mm.

| Date | Mintage | MS63 | MS65 | Prf65 |
|---|---|---|---|---|
| 2004P | 233,800,000 | 0.65 | 5.00 | — |
| 2004D | 225,800,000 | 0.65 | 5.00 | — |
| 2004S | 2,740,684 | — | — | 2.30 |

**KM# 355a** • 6.25 g., 0.900 **Silver**, 0.1808 oz. ASW 24.3 mm.

| Date | Mintage | MS63 | MS65 | Prf65 |
|---|---|---|---|---|
| 2004S | 1,775,370 | — | — | 8.50 |

## Florida

**KM# 356** • 5.67 g., **Copper-Nickel Clad Copper**, 24.3 mm.

| Date | Mintage | MS63 | MS65 | Prf65 |
|---|---|---|---|---|
| 2004P | 240,200,000 | 0.65 | 5.00 | — |
| 2004D | 241,600,000 | 0.65 | 5.00 | — |
| 2004S | 2,740,684 | — | — | 2.30 |

**KM# 356a** • 6.25 g., 0.900 **Silver**, 0.1808 oz. ASW 24.3 mm.

| Date | Mintage | MS63 | MS65 | Prf65 |
|---|---|---|---|---|
| 2004S | 1,775,370 | — | — | 8.50 |

## Texas

**KM# 357** • 5.67 g., **Copper-Nickel Clad Copper**, 24.3 mm.

| Date | Mintage | MS63 | MS65 | Prf65 |
|---|---|---|---|---|
| 2004P | 278,800,000 | 0.65 | 5.00 | — |
| 2004D | 263,000,000 | 0.65 | 5.00 | — |
| 2004S | 2,740,684 | — | — | 2.30 |

**KM# 357a** • 6.25 g., 0.900 **Silver**, 0.1808 oz. ASW 24.3 mm.

| Date | Mintage | MS63 | MS65 | Prf65 |
|---|---|---|---|---|
| 2004S | 1,775,370 | — | — | 8.50 |

## Iowa

**KM# 358** • 5.67 g., **Copper-Nickel Clad Copper**, 24.3 mm.

| Date | Mintage | MS63 | MS65 | Prf65 |
|---|---|---|---|---|
| 2004P | 213,800,000 | 0.65 | 5.00 | — |
| 2004D | 251,800,000 | 0.65 | 5.00 | — |
| 2004S | 2,740,684 | — | — | 2.30 |

**KM# 358a** • 6.25 g., 0.900 **Silver**, 0.1808 oz. ASW 24.3 mm.

| Date | Mintage | MS63 | MS65 | Prf65 |
|---|---|---|---|---|
| 2004S | — | — | — | 8.50 |

## Wisconsin

**KM# 359** • 5.67 g., **Copper-Nickel Clad Copper**, 24.3 mm.

| Date | Mintage | MS63 | MS65 | Prf65 |
|---|---|---|---|---|
| 2004P | 226,400,000 | 0.65 | 5.00 | — |
| 2004D | 226,800,000 | 0.65 | 5.00 | — |
| 2004D Extra Leaf Low | Est. 9000 | 135 | 190 | — |
| 2004D Extra Leaf High | Est. 3000 | 175 | 285 | — |
| 2004S | — | — | — | 2.30 |

**KM# 359a** • 6.25 g., 0.900 **Silver**, 0.1808 oz. ASW 24.3 mm.

| Date | Mintage | MS63 | MS65 | Prf65 |
|---|---|---|---|---|
| 2004S | 1,775,370 | — | — | 8.50 |

## California

**KM# 370** • 5.67 g., **Copper-Nickel Clad Copper**, 24.3 mm.

| Date | Mintage | MS63 | MS65 | Prf65 |
|---|---|---|---|---|
| 2005P | 257,200,000 | 0.65 | 5.00 | — |
| 2005P Satin Finish | Inc. above | 1.50 | 4.50 | — |
| 2005D | 263,200,000 | 0.65 | 5.00 | — |
| 2005D Satin Finish | Inc. above | 1.50 | 4.50 | — |
| 2005S | 3,262,960 | — | — | 2.30 |

**KM# 370a** • 6.25 g., 0.900 **Silver**, 0.1808 oz. ASW 24.3 mm.

| Date | Mintage | MS63 | MS65 | Prf65 |
|---|---|---|---|---|
| 2005S | 1,679,600 | — | — | 8.50 |

## Minnesota

**KM# 371** • 5.67 g., **Copper-Nickel Clad Copper**, 24.3 mm.

| Date | Mintage | MS63 | MS65 | Prf65 |
|---|---|---|---|---|
| 2005P | 226,400,000 | 0.65 | 5.00 | — |
| 2005P Satin Finish | Inc. above | 1.50 | 4.50 | — |
| 2005D | 226,800,000 | 0.65 | 5.00 | — |
| 2005D Satin Finish | Inc. above | 1.50 | 4.50 | — |
| 2005S | 3,262,960 | — | — | 2.30 |

**KM# 371a** • 6.25 g., 0.900 **Silver**, 0.1808 oz. ASW 24.3 mm.

| Date | Mintage | MS63 | MS65 | Prf65 |
|---|---|---|---|---|
| 2005S | 1,679,600 | — | — | 8.50 |

## Oregon

**KM# 372** • 5.67 g., **Copper-Nickel Clad Copper**, 24.3 mm.

| Date | Mintage | MS63 | MS65 | Prf65 |
|---|---|---|---|---|
| 2005P | 316,200,000 | 0.65 | 5.00 | — |
| 2005P Satin Finish | Inc. above | 1.50 | 4.50 | — |
| 2005D | 404,000,000 | 0.65 | 5.00 | — |
| 2005D Satin Finish | Inc. above | 1.50 | 4.50 | — |
| 2005S | 3,262,960 | — | — | 2.30 |

**KM# 372a** • 6.25 g., 0.900 **Silver**, 0.1808 oz. ASW 24.3 mm.

| Date | Mintage | MS63 | MS65 | Prf65 |
|---|---|---|---|---|
| 2005S | 1,679,600 | — | — | 8.50 |

## Kansas

**KM# 373** • 5.67 g., **Copper-Nickel Clad Copper**, 24.3 mm.

| Date | Mintage | MS63 | MS65 | Prf65 |
|---|---|---|---|---|
| 2005P | 263,400,000 | 0.65 | 5.00 | — |
| 2005P Satin Finish | Inc. above | 1.50 | 4.50 | — |
| 2005D | 300,000,000 | 0.65 | 5.00 | — |
| 2005D Satin Finish | Inc. above | 1.50 | 4.50 | — |
| 2005S | 3,262,960 | — | — | 2.30 |

**KM# 373a** • 6.25 g., 0.900 **Silver**, 0.1808 oz. ASW 24.3 mm.

| Date | Mintage | MS63 | MS65 | Prf65 |
|---|---|---|---|---|
| 2005S | 1,679,600 | — | — | 8.50 |

## West Virginia

**KM# 374** • 5.67 g., **Copper-Nickel Clad Copper**, 24.3 mm.

| Date | Mintage | MS63 | MS65 | Prf65 |
|---|---|---|---|---|
| 2005P | 365,400,000 | 0.65 | 5.00 | — |
| 2005P Satin Finish | Inc. above | 1.50 | 4.50 | — |
| 2005D | 356,200,000 | 0.65 | 5.00 | — |
| 2005D Satin Finish | Inc. above | 1.50 | 4.50 | — |
| 2005S | 3,262,960 | — | — | 2.30 |

**KM# 374a** • 6.25 g., 0.900 **Silver**, 0.1808 oz. ASW 24.3 mm.

| Date | Mintage | MS63 | MS65 | Prf65 |
|---|---|---|---|---|
| 2005S | 1,679,600 | — | — | 8.50 |

## Nevada

**KM# 382** • 5.67 g., **Copper-Nickel Clad Copper**, 24.3 mm.

| Date | Mintage | MS63 | MS65 | Prf65 |
|---|---|---|---|---|
| 2006P | 277,000,000 | 0.65 | 5.00 | — |
| 2006P Satin Finish | Inc. above | 1.50 | 4.50 | — |
| 2006D | 312,800,000 | 0.65 | 5.00 | — |
| 2006D Satin Finish | Inc. above | 1.50 | 4.50 | — |
| 2006S | 2,862,078 | — | — | 2.30 |

**KM# 382a** • 6.25 g., 0.900 **Silver**, 0.1808 oz. ASW 24.3 mm.

| Date | Mintage | MS63 | MS65 | Prf65 |
|---|---|---|---|---|
| 2006S | 1,571,839 | — | — | 8.50 |

## Nebraska

**KM# 383** • 5.67 g., **Copper-Nickel Clad Copper**, 24.3 mm.

| Date | Mintage | MS63 | MS65 | Prf65 |
|---|---|---|---|---|
| 2006P | 318,000,000 | 0.65 | 5.00 | — |
| 2006P Satin Finish | Inc. above | 1.50 | 4.50 | — |
| 2006D | 273,000,000 | 0.65 | 5.00 | — |
| 2006D Satin Finish | Inc. above | 1.50 | 4.50 | — |
| 2006S | 2,862,078 | — | — | 2.30 |

**KM# 383a** • 6.25 g., 0.900 **Silver**, 0.1808 oz. ASW 24.3 mm.

| Date | Mintage | MS63 | MS65 | Prf65 |
|---|---|---|---|---|
| 2006S | 1,571,839 | — | — | 8.50 |

## Colorado

**KM# 384** • 5.67 g., **Copper-Nickel Clad Copper**, 24.3 mm.

| Date | Mintage | MS63 | MS65 | Prf65 |
|---|---|---|---|---|
| 2006P | 274,800,000 | 0.65 | 5.00 | — |
| 2006P Satin Finish | Inc. above | 1.50 | 4.50 | — |
| 2006D | 294,200,000 | 0.65 | 5.00 | — |
| 2006D Satin Finish | Inc. above | 1.50 | 4.50 | — |
| 2006S | 2,862,078 | — | — | 2.30 |

**KM# 384a** • 6.25 g., 0.900 **Silver**, 0.1808 oz. ASW 24.3 mm.

| Date | Mintage | MS63 | MS65 | Prf65 |
|---|---|---|---|---|
| 2006S | 1,571,839 | — | — | 8.50 |

## North Dakota

**KM# 385** • 5.67 g., **Copper-Nickel Clad Copper**, 24.3 mm.

| Date | Mintage | MS63 | MS65 | Prf65 |
|---|---|---|---|---|
| 2006P | 305,800,000 | 0.65 | 5.00 | — |
| 2006P Satin Finish | Inc. above | 1.50 | 4.50 | — |
| 2006D | 359,000,000 | 0.65 | 5.00 | — |
| 2006D Satin Finish | Inc. above | 1.50 | 4.50 | — |
| 2006S | 2,862,078 | — | — | 2.30 |

**KM# 385a** • 6.25 g., 0.900 **Silver**, 0.1808 oz. ASW 24.3 mm.

| Date | Mintage | MS63 | MS65 | Prf65 |
|---|---|---|---|---|
| 2006S | 1,571,839 | — | — | 8.50 |

## South Dakota

**KM# 386** • 5.67 g., **Copper-Nickel Clad Copper**, 24.3 mm.

| Date | Mintage | MS63 | MS65 | Prf65 |
|---|---|---|---|---|
| 2006P | 245,000,000 | 0.65 | 5.00 | — |
| 2006P Satin Finish | Inc. above | 1.50 | 4.50 | — |
| 2006D | 265,800,000 | 0.65 | 5.00 | — |
| 2006D Satin Finish | Inc. above | 1.50 | 4.50 | — |
| 2006S | 2,862,078 | — | — | 2.30 |

**KM# 386a** • 6.25 g., 0.900 **Silver**, 0.1808 oz. ASW 24.3 mm.

| Date | Mintage | MS63 | MS65 | Prf65 |
|---|---|---|---|---|
| 2006S | 1,571,839 | — | — | 8.50 |

## Montana

**KM# 396** • 5.67 g., **Copper-Nickel Clad Copper**, 24.3 mm.

| Date | Mintage | MS63 | MS65 | Prf65 |
|---|---|---|---|---|
| 2007P | 257,000,000 | 0.65 | 5.00 | — |
| 2007P Satin Finish | — | 1.50 | 4.50 | — |
| 2007D | 256,240,000 | 0.65 | 5.00 | — |
| 2007D Satin Finish | — | 1.50 | 4.50 | — |
| 2007S | 2,374,778 | — | — | 2.30 |

**KM# 396a** • 6.25 g., 0.900 **Silver**, 0.1808 oz. ASW 24.3 mm.

| Date | Mintage | MS63 | MS65 | Prf65 |
|---|---|---|---|---|
| 2007S | 1,299,878 | — | — | 8.50 |

## Washington

**KM# 397** • 5.67 g., **Copper-Nickel Clad Copper**, 24.3 mm.

| Date | Mintage | MS63 | MS65 | Prf65 |
|---|---|---|---|---|
| 2007P | 265,200,000 | 0.65 | 5.00 | — |
| 2007P Satin Finish | — | 1.50 | 4.50 | — |
| 2007D | 280,000,000 | 0.65 | 5.00 | — |
| 2007D Satin Finish | — | 1.50 | 4.50 | — |
| 2007S | 2,374,778 | — | — | 2.30 |

**KM# 397a** • 6.25 g., 0.900 **Silver**, 0.1808 oz. ASW 24.3 mm.

| Date | Mintage | MS63 | MS65 | Prf65 |
|---|---|---|---|---|
| 2007S | 1,299,878 | — | — | 8.50 |

## Idaho

**KM# 398** • 5.67 g., **Copper-Nickel Clad Copper**, 24.3 mm.

| Date | Mintage | MS63 | MS65 | Prf65 |
|---|---|---|---|---|
| 2007P | 294,600,000 | 0.65 | 5.00 | — |
| 2007P Satin finish | — | 1.50 | 4.50 | — |
| 2007D | 286,800,000 | 0.65 | 5.00 | — |
| 2007D Satin finish | — | 1.50 | 4.50 | — |
| 2007S | 2,374,778 | — | — | 2.30 |

**KM# 398a** • 6.25 g., 0.900 **Silver**, 0.1808 oz. ASW 24.3 mm.

| Date | Mintage | MS63 | MS65 | Prf65 |
|---|---|---|---|---|
| 2007S | 1,299,878 | — | — | 8.50 |

## Wyoming

**KM# 399** • 5.67 g., **Copper-Nickel Clad Copper**, 24.3 mm.

| Date | Mintage | MS63 | MS65 | Prf65 |
|---|---|---|---|---|
| 2007P | 243,600,000 | 0.65 | 5.00 | — |
| 2007P Satin finish | — | 1.50 | 4.50 | — |
| 2007D | 320,800,000 | 0.65 | 5.00 | — |
| 2007 Satin finish | — | 1.50 | 4.50 | — |
| 2007S | 2,374,778 | — | — | 2.30 |

**KM# 399a** • 6.25 g., 0.900 **Silver**, 0.1808 oz. ASW 24.3 mm.

| Date | Mintage | MS63 | MS65 | Prf65 |
|---|---|---|---|---|
| 2007S | 1,299,878 | — | — | 8.50 |

## Utah

**KM# 400** • 5.67 g., **Copper-Nickel Clad Copper**, 24.3 mm.

| Date | Mintage | MS63 | MS65 | Prf65 |
|---|---|---|---|---|
| 2007P | 255,000,000 | 0.65 | 5.00 | — |
| 2007P Satin finish | — | 1.50 | 4.50 | — |
| 2007D | 253,200,000 | 0.65 | 5.00 | — |
| 2007D Satin finish | — | 1.50 | 4.50 | — |
| 2007S | 2,374,778 | — | — | 2.30 |

**KM# 400a** • 6.25 g., 0.900 **Silver**, 0.1808 oz. ASW

| Date | Mintage | MS63 | MS65 | Prf65 |
|---|---|---|---|---|
| 2007S | 1,299,878 | — | — | 8.50 |

## Oklahoma

**KM# 421** • 5.67 g., **Copper-Nickel Clad Copper**, 24.3 mm.

| Date | Mintage | MS63 | MS65 | Prf65 |
|---|---|---|---|---|
| 2008P | 222,000,000 | 0.65 | 5.00 | — |
| 2008P Satin finish | — | 1.50 | 4.50 | — |
| 2008D | 194,600,000 | 0.65 | 5.00 | — |
| 2008D Satin finish | — | 1.50 | 4.50 | — |
| 2008S | 2,100,000 | — | — | 2.30 |

**KM# 421a** • 6.25 g., 0.900 **Silver**, 0.1808 oz. ASW 24.3 mm.

| Date | Mintage | MS63 | MS65 | Prf65 |
|---|---|---|---|---|
| 2008S | 1,200,000 | — | — | 8.50 |

## New Mexico

**KM# 422** • 5.67 g., **Copper-Nickel Clad Copper**, 24.3 mm.

| Date | Mintage | MS63 | MS65 | Prf65 |
|---|---|---|---|---|
| 2008P | 244,200,000 | 0.65 | 5.00 | — |
| 2008P Satin finish | — | 1.50 | 4.50 | — |
| 2008D | 244,400,000 | 0.65 | 5.00 | — |
| 2008D Satin finish | — | 1.50 | 4.50 | — |
| 2008S | 2,100,000 | — | — | 2.30 |

**KM# 422a** • 6.25 g., 0.900 **Silver**, 0.1808 oz. ASW 24.3 mm.

| Date | Mintage | MS63 | MS65 | Prf65 |
|---|---|---|---|---|
| 2008S | 1,200,000 | — | — | 8.50 |

## Arizona

**KM# 423** • 5.67 g., **Copper-Nickel Clad Copper**, 24.3 mm.

| Date | Mintage | MS63 | MS65 | Prf65 |
|---|---|---|---|---|
| 2008P | 244,600,000 | 0.65 | 5.00 | — |
| 2008P Satin finish | — | 1.50 | 4.50 | — |
| 2008D | 265,000,000 | 0.65 | 5.00 | — |
| 2008D Satin finish | — | 1.50 | 4.50 | — |
| 2008S | 2,100,000 | — | — | 2.30 |

**KM# 423a** • 6.25 g., 0.900 **Silver**, 0.1808 oz. ASW 24.3 mm.

| Date | Mintage | MS63 | MS65 | Prf65 |
|---|---|---|---|---|
| 2008S | 1,200,000 | — | — | 8.50 |

## Alaska

**KM# 424** • 5.67 g., **Copper-Nickel Clad Copper**, 24.3 mm.

| Date | Mintage | MS63 | MS65 | Prf65 |
|---|---|---|---|---|
| 2008P | 251,800,000 | 0.65 | 5.00 | — |
| 2008P Satin finish | — | 1.50 | 4.50 | — |
| 2008D | 254,000,000 | 0.65 | 5.00 | — |
| 2008D Satin finish | — | 1.50 | 4.50 | — |
| 2008S | 2,100,000 | — | — | 2.30 |

**KM# 424a** • 6.25 g., 0.900 **Silver**, 0.1808 oz. ASW 24.3 mm.

| Date | Mintage | MS63 | MS65 | Prf65 |
|---|---|---|---|---|
| 2008S | 1,200,000 | — | — | 8.50 |

## Hawaii

**KM# 425** • 5.67 g., **Copper-Nickel Clad Copper**, 24.3 mm.

| Date | Mintage | MS63 | MS65 | Prf65 |
|---|---|---|---|---|
| 2008P | 254,000,000 | 0.65 | 5.00 | — |
| 2008P Satin finish | — | 1.50 | 4.50 | — |
| 2008D | 263,600,000 | 0.65 | 5.00 | — |
| 2008D Satin finish | — | 1.50 | 4.50 | — |
| 2008S | 2,100,000 | — | — | 2.30 |

**KM# 425a** • 6.25 g., 0.900 **Silver**, 0.1808 oz. ASW 24.3 mm.

| Date | Mintage | MS63 | MS65 | Prf65 |
|---|---|---|---|---|
| 2008S | 1,200,000 | — | — | 8.50 |

## DC and Territories

## District of Columbia

**KM# 445** • 5.67 g., **Copper-Nickel Clad Copper**, 24.3 mm. **Rev. Designer:** Don Everhart

| Date | Mintage | MS63 | MS65 | Prf65 |
|---|---|---|---|---|
| 2009P | 83,600,000 | 0.75 | 5.00 | — |
| 2009D | 88,800,000 | 0.75 | 5.00 | — |
| 2009S | 2,113,478 | — | — | 3.75 |

**KM# 445a** • 6.25 g., 0.900 **Silver**, 0.1808 oz. ASW 24.3 mm.

| Date | Mintage | MS63 | MS65 | Prf65 |
|---|---|---|---|---|
| 2009S | 996,548 | — | — | 7.75 |

## Puerto Rico

**KM# 446** • 5.67 g., **Copper-Nickel Clad Copper**, 24.3 mm. **Rev. Designer:** Joseph Menna

| Date | Mintage | MS63 | MS65 | Prf65 |
|---|---|---|---|---|
| 2009P | 53,200,000 | 0.75 | 5.00 | — |
| 2009D | 86,000,000 | 0.75 | 5.00 | — |
| 2009S | 2,113,478 | — | — | 3.75 |

**KM# 446a** • 6.25 g., 0.900 **Silver**, 0.1808 oz. ASW 24.3 mm.

| Date | Mintage | MS63 | MS65 | Prf65 |
|---|---|---|---|---|
| 2009S | 996,548 | — | — | 7.75 |

## Guam

**KM# 447** • 5.67 g., **Copper-Nickel Clad Copper**, 24.3 mm. **Rev. Designer:** James Licaretz

| Date | Mintage | MS63 | MS65 | Prf65 |
|---|---|---|---|---|
| 2009P | 45,000,000 | 0.75 | 5.00 | — |
| 2009D | 42,600,000 | 0.75 | 5.00 | — |
| 2009S | 2,113,478 | — | — | 3.75 |

**KM# 447a** • 6.25 g., 0.900 **Silver**, 0.1808 oz. ASW 24.3 mm.

| Date | Mintage | MS63 | MS65 | Prf65 |
|---|---|---|---|---|
| 2009S | 996,548 | — | — | 7.75 |

## American Samoa

**KM# 448** • 5.67 g., **Copper-Nickel Clad Copper**, 24.3 mm. **Rev. Designer:** Charles Vickers

| Date | Mintage | MS63 | MS65 | Prf65 |
|---|---|---|---|---|
| 2009P | 42,600,000 | 0.75 | 5.00 | — |
| 2009D | 39,600,000 | 0.75 | 5.00 | — |
| 2009S | 2,113,478 | — | — | 3.75 |

**KM# 448a** • 6.25 g., 0.900 **Silver**, 0.1808 oz. ASW 24.3 mm.

| Date | Mintage | MS63 | MS65 | Prf65 |
|---|---|---|---|---|
| 2009S | 996,548 | — | — | 7.75 |

## US Virgin Islands

**KM# 449** • 5.67 g., **Copper-Nickel Clad Copper**, 24.3 mm. **Rev. Designer:** Joseph Menna

| Date | Mintage | MS63 | MS65 | Prf65 |
|---|---|---|---|---|
| 2009P | 41,000,000 | 0.75 | 5.00 | — |
| 2009D | 41,000,000 | 0.75 | 5.00 | — |
| 2009S | 2,113,478 | — | — | 3.75 |

**KM# 449a** • 6.25 g., 0.900 **Silver**, 0.1808 oz. ASW 24.3 mm.

| Date | Mintage | MS63 | MS65 | Prf65 |
|---|---|---|---|---|
| 2009S | 996,548 | — | — | 7.75 |

## Northern Mariana Islands

**KM# 466** • 5.67 g., **Copper-Nickel Clad Copper**, **Rev. Designer:** Pheve Hemphill

| Date | Mintage | MS63 | MS65 | Prf65 |
|---|---|---|---|---|
| 2009P | 35,200,000 | 0.75 | 5.00 | — |
| 2009D | 37,600,000 | 0.75 | 5.00 | — |
| 2009S | 2,113,478 | — | — | 3.75 |

**KM# 466a** • 6.25 g., 0.900 **Silver**, 0.1808 oz. ASW

| Date | Mintage | MS63 | MS65 | Prf65 |
|---|---|---|---|---|
| 2009S | 996,548 | — | — | 7.75 |

## America the Beautiful

## Hot Springs, Ark.

**KM# 469** • 5.67 g., **Copper-Nickel Clad Copper**, 24.3 mm.

| Date | Mintage | MS63 | MS65 | Prf65 |
|---|---|---|---|---|
| 2010P | 35,600,000 | 0.75 | 5.00 | — |
| 2010D | 34,000,000 | 0.75 | 5.00 | — |
| 2010S | 1,401,903 | — | — | 3.75 |

**KM# 469a** • 6.25 g., 0.900 **Silver**, 0.1808 oz. ASW

| Date | Mintage | MS63 | MS65 | Prf65 |
|---|---|---|---|---|
| 2010S | 859,435 | — | — | 7.75 |

## Yellowstone National Park

**KM# 470** • 5.67 g., **Copper-Nickel Clad Copper**, 24.3 mm. **Rev. Designer:** Don Everhart

| Date | Mintage | MS63 | MS65 | Prf65 |
|---|---|---|---|---|
| 2010P | 33,600,000 | 0.75 | 5.00 | — |
| 2010D | 34,800,000 | 0.75 | 5.00 | — |
| 2010S | 1,402,756 | — | — | 3.75 |

**KM# 470a** • 6.25 g., 0.900 **Silver**, 0.1808 oz. ASW

| Date | Mintage | MS63 | MS65 | Prf65 |
|---|---|---|---|---|
| 2010 | 859,435 | — | — | 7.75 |

## Yosemite National Park

**KM# 471** • 5.67 g., **Copper-Nickel Clad Copper**, 24.3 mm. **Rev. Designer:** Joseph Menna and Phebe Hemphill

| Date | Mintage | MS63 | MS65 | Prf65 |
|---|---|---|---|---|
| 2010P | 35,200,000 | 0.75 | 5.00 | — |
| 2010D | 34,800,000 | 0.75 | 5.00 | — |
| 2010S | 1,400,215 | — | — | 3.75 |

**KM# 471a** • 6.25 g., 0.900 **Silver**, 0.1808 oz. ASW

| Date | Mintage | MS63 | MS65 | Prf65 |
|---|---|---|---|---|
| 2010 | 859,435 | — | — | 7.75 |

## Grand Canyon National Park

**KM# 472** • 5.67 g., **Copper-Nickel Clad Copper**, 24.3 mm. **Rev. Designer:** Phebe Hemphill

| Date | Mintage | MS63 | MS65 | Prf65 |
|---|---|---|---|---|
| 2010P | 34,800,000 | 0.75 | 5.00 | — |
| 2010D | 35,400,000 | 0.75 | 5.00 | — |
| 2010S | 1,399,970 | — | — | 3.75 |

**KM# 472a** • 6.25 g., 0.900 **Silver**, 0.1808 oz. ASW

| Date | Mintage | MS63 | MS65 | Prf65 |
|---|---|---|---|---|
| 2010 | 859,435 | — | — | 7.75 |

## Mount Hood National Park

**KM# 473** • 5.67 g., **Copper-Nickel Clad Copper**, 24.3 mm. **Rev. Designer:** Phebe Hemphill

| Date | Mintage | MS63 | MS65 | Prf65 |
|---|---|---|---|---|
| 2010P | 34,400,000 | 0.75 | 5.00 | — |
| 2010D | 34,400,000 | 0.75 | 5.00 | — |
| 2010S | 1,397,101 | — | — | 3.75 |

**KM# 473a** • 6.25 g., 0.900 **Silver**, 0.1808 oz. ASW

| Date | Mintage | MS63 | MS65 | Prf65 |
|---|---|---|---|---|
| 2010S | 859,435 | — | — | 7.75 |

## Gettysburg National Military Park

**KM# 494** • 5.67 g., **Copper-Nickel Clad Copper**, 24 mm. **Rev. Designer:** Joel Iskowitz and Phebe Hemphill

| Date | Mintage | MS63 | MS65 | Prf65 |
|---|---|---|---|---|
| 2011P | 30,800,000 | 0.75 | 5.00 | — |
| 2011D | 30,400,000 | 0.75 | 5.00 | — |
| 2011S | 1,271,553 | — | — | 3.75 |

**KM# 494a** • 6.25 g., 0.900 **Silver**, 0.1808 oz. ASW

| Date | Mintage | MS63 | MS65 | Prf65 |
|---|---|---|---|---|
| 2011S | 722,076 | — | — | 7.75 |

## Glacier National Park

**KM# 495** • 5.67 g., **Copper-Nickel Clad Copper**, 24 mm. **Rev. Designer:** Barbara Fox and Charles L. Vickers

| Date | Mintage | MS63 | MS65 | Prf65 |
|---|---|---|---|---|
| 2011P | 30,400,000 | 0.75 | 5.00 | — |
| 2011D | 31,200,000 | 0.75 | 5.00 | — |
| 2011S | 1,268,452 | — | — | 3.75 |

**KM# 495a** • 6.25 g., 0.900 **Silver**, 0.1808 oz. ASW

| Date | Mintage | MS63 | MS65 | Prf65 |
|---|---|---|---|---|
| 2011S | 722,076 | — | — | 7.75 |

## Olympic National Park

**KM# 496** • 5.67 g., **Copper-Nickel Clad Copper**, 24 mm.

| Date | Mintage | MS63 | MS65 | Prf65 |
|---|---|---|---|---|
| 2011P | 30,400,000 | 0.75 | 5.00 | — |
| 2011D | 30,600,000 | 0.75 | 5.00 | — |
| 2011S | 1,267,361 | — | — | 3.75 |

**KM# 496a** • 6.25 g., 0.900 **Silver**, 0.1808 oz. ASW

| Date | Mintage | MS63 | MS65 | Prf65 |
|---|---|---|---|---|
| 2011S | 722,076 | — | — | 7.75 |

## Vicksburg National Military Park

**KM# 497** • 5.67 g., **Copper-Nickel Clad Copper**, 24 mm. **Rev. Designer:** Thomas Cleveland and Joseph Menna

| Date | Mintage | MS63 | MS65 | Prf65 |
|---|---|---|---|---|
| 2011P | 30,800,000 | 0.75 | 5.00 | — |
| 2011D | 33,400,000 | 0.75 | 5.00 | — |
| 2011S | 1,267,691 | — | — | 3.75 |

**KM# 497a** • 6.25 g., 0.900 **Silver**, 0.1808 oz. ASW

| Date | Mintage | MS63 | MS65 | Prf65 |
|---|---|---|---|---|
| 2011S | 722,076 | — | — | 7.75 |

## Chickasaw National Recreation Area

**KM# 498** • 5.67 g., **Copper-Nickel Clad Copper**, 24 mm. **Rev. Designer:** Donna Weaver and Jim Licaretz

| Date | Mintage | MS63 | MS65 | Prf65 |
|---|---|---|---|---|
| 2011P | 73,800,000 | 0.75 | 5.00 | — |
| 2011D | 69,400,000 | 0.75 | 5.00 | — |
| 2011S | 1,266,010 | — | — | 3.75 |

**KM# 498a** • 6.25 g., 0.900 **Silver**, 0.1808 oz. ASW

| Date | Mintage | MS63 | MS65 | Prf65 |
|---|---|---|---|---|
| 2011S | 722,076 | — | — | 7.75 |

## El Yunque National Forest

**KM# 519** • 5.67 g., **Copper-Nickel Clad Copper**, 24.3 mm. **Rev. Designer:** Gary Whitley and Michael Gaudioso

| Date | Mintage | MS63 | MS65 | Prf65 |
|---|---|---|---|---|
| 2012P | 25,800,000 | 0.75 | 5.00 | — |
| 2012D | 25,800,000 | 0.75 | 5.00 | — |
| 2012S | 1,010,361 | — | 7.50 | — |
| 2012S | 1,679,240 | — | — | 3.75 |

**KM# 519a** • 6.25 g., 0.900 **Silver**, 0.1808 oz. ASW 24.3 mm.

| Date | Mintage | MS63 | MS65 | Prf65 |
|---|---|---|---|---|
| 2012S | 557,891 | — | — | 7.75 |

## Chaco Culture National Historic Park

**KM# 520** • 5.71 g., **Copper-Nickel Clad Copper**, 24.3 mm.

| Date | Mintage | MS63 | MS65 | Prf65 |
|---|---|---|---|---|
| 2012P | 22,000,000 | 0.75 | 8.00 | — |
| 2012D | 22,000,000 | 0.75 | 8.00 | — |
| 2012S | 960,049 | — | 10.00 | — |
| 2012S | 1,389,020 | — | — | 4.00 |

**KM# 520a** • 6.25 g., 0.900 **Silver**, 0.1808 oz. ASW 24.3 mm.

| Date | Mintage | MS63 | MS65 | Prf65 |
|---|---|---|---|---|
| 2012S | 557,891 | — | — | 7.75 |

## Acadia National Park

**KM# 521** • 5.67 g., **Copper-Nickel Clad Copper**, 24.3 mm. **Rev. Designer:** Barbara Fox and Joseph Menna

| Date | Mintage | MS63 | MS65 | Prf65 |
|---|---|---|---|---|
| 2012P | 24,800,000 | 0.75 | 5.00 | — |
| 2012D | 21,606,000 | 0.75 | 5.00 | — |
| 2012S | 960,409 | — | 7.50 | — |
| 2012S | 1,409,120 | — | — | 3.75 |

**KM# 521a** • 6.25 g., 0.900 **Silver**, 0.1808 oz. ASW 24.3 mm.

| Date | Mintage | MS63 | MS65 | Prf65 |
|---|---|---|---|---|
| 2012S | 557,891 | — | — | 7.75 |

## Hawai'i Volcanoes National Park

**KM# 522** • 5.67 g., **Copper-Nickel Clad Copper**, 24.3 mm. **Rev. Designer:** Charles L. Vickers

| Date | Mintage | MS63 | MS65 | Prf65 |
|---|---|---|---|---|
| 2012P | 46,200,000 | 0.75 | 5.00 | — |
| 2012D | 78,600,000 | 0.75 | 5.00 | — |
| 2012S | 961,272 | — | 7.50 | — |
| 2012S | 1,407,520 | — | — | 3.75 |

**KM# 522a** • 6.25 g., 0.900 **Silver**, 0.1808 oz. ASW 24.3 mm.

| Date | Mintage | MS63 | MS65 | Prf65 |
|---|---|---|---|---|
| 2012S | 557,891 | — | — | 7.75 |

## Denali National Park

**KM# 523** • 5.67 g., **Copper-Nickel Clad Copper**, 24.3 mm.

| Date | Mintage | MS63 | MS65 | Prf65 |
|---|---|---|---|---|
| 2012P | 135,400,000 | 0.75 | 5.00 | — |
| 2012D | 166,600,000 | 0.75 | 5.00 | — |
| 2012S | 957,856 | — | 7.50 | — |
| 2012S | 1,401,920 | — | — | 3.75 |

**KM# 523a** • 6.25 g., 0.900 **Silver**, 0.1808 oz. ASW 24.3 mm.

| Date | Mintage | MS63 | MS65 | Prf65 |
|---|---|---|---|---|
| 2012S | 557,891 | — | — | 7.75 |

## White Mountain National Forest

**KM# 542** • 5.67 g., **Copper-Nickel Clad Copper**, 24.3 mm.

| Date | Mintage | MS63 | MS65 | Prf65 |
|---|---|---|---|---|
| 2013P | 68,800,000 | 0.75 | 5.00 | — |
| 2013D | 107,600,000 | 0.75 | 5.00 | — |
| 2013S | 950,080 | — | 7.50 | — |
| 2013S | — | — | — | 3.75 |

**KM# 542a** • 6.25 g., 0.900 **Silver**, 0.1808 oz. ASW 24.3 mm.

| Date | Mintage | MS63 | MS65 | Prf65 |
|---|---|---|---|---|
| 2013S | 579,409 | — | — | 7.75 |

## Perry's Victory and International Peace Memorial

**KM# 543** • 5.67 g., **Copper-Nickel Clad Copper**, 24.3 mm. **Rev. Designer:** Don Everhart

| Date | Mintage | MS63 | MS65 | Prf65 |
|---|---|---|---|---|
| 2013P | 107,800,000 | 0.75 | 5.00 | — |
| 2013D | 131,600,000 | 0.75 | 5.00 | — |
| 2013S | 913,563 | — | 7.50 | — |
| 2013S | — | — | — | 3.75 |

**KM# 543a** • 6.25 g., 0.900 **Silver**, 0.1808 oz. ASW 24.3 mm.

| Date | Mintage | MS63 | MS65 | Prf65 |
|---|---|---|---|---|
| 2013S | 579,409 | — | — | 7.75 |

## Great Basin National Park

**KM# 544** • 5.67 g., **Copper-Nickel Clad Copper**, 24.3 mm. **Rev. Designer:** Ronald D. Sanders and Renata Gordon

| Date | Mintage | MS63 | MS65 | Prf65 |
|---|---|---|---|---|
| 2013P | 122,400,000 | 0.75 | 5.00 | — |
| 2013D | 141,400,000 | 0.75 | 5.00 | — |
| 2013S | 911,525 | — | 7.50 | — |
| 2013S | — | — | — | 3.75 |

**KM# 544a** • 6.25 g., 0.900 **Silver**, 0.1808 oz. ASW 24.3 mm.

| Date | Mintage | MS63 | MS65 | Prf65 |
|---|---|---|---|---|
| 2013S | 579,409 | — | — | 7.75 |

## Fort McHenry National Monument and Historic Shrine

**KM# 545** • 5.67 g., **Copper-Nickel Clad Copper**, 24.3 mm. **Rev. Designer:** Joseph Menna

| Date | Mintage | MS63 | MS65 | Prf65 |
|---|---|---|---|---|
| 2013P | 120,000,000 | 0.75 | 5.00 | — |
| 2013D | 151,400,000 | 0.75 | 5.00 | — |
| 2013S | 911,451 | — | 7.50 | — |
| 2013S | — | — | — | 3.75 |

**KM# 545a** • 6.25 g., 0.900 **Silver**, 0.1808 oz. ASW 24.3 mm.

| Date | Mintage | MS63 | MS65 | Prf65 |
|---|---|---|---|---|
| 2013S | 579,409 | — | — | 7.75 |

## Mount Rushmore National Memorial

**KM# 546** • 5.67 g., **Copper-Nickel Clad Copper**, 24.3 mm. **Rev. Designer:** Joseph Menna

| Date | Mintage | MS63 | MS65 | Prf65 |
|---|---|---|---|---|
| 2013P | 231,800,000 | 0.75 | 5.00 | — |
| 2013D | 272,400,000 | 0.75 | 5.00 | — |
| 2013S | 920,695 | — | 7.50 | — |
| 2013S | — | — | — | 3.75 |

**KM# 546a** • 6.25 g., 0.900 **Silver**, 0.1808 oz. ASW 24.3 mm.

| Date | Mintage | MS63 | MS65 | Prf65 |
|---|---|---|---|---|
| 2013S | 579,409 | — | — | 7.75 |

## Great Smokey Mountains National Park

**KM# 566** • 5.67 g., **Copper-Nickel Clad Copper**, 24.3 mm.

| Date | Mintage | MS63 | MS65 | Prf65 |
|---|---|---|---|---|
| 2014P | — | 0.75 | 5.00 | — |
| 2014D | — | 0.75 | 5.00 | — |
| 2014S | — | — | — | 3.75 |

**KM# 566a** • 6.25 g., 0.900 **Silver**, 0.1808 oz. ASW 24.3 mm.

| Date | Mintage | MS63 | MS65 | Prf65 |
|---|---|---|---|---|
| 2014S | — | — | — | 7.75 |

## Shenandoah National Park

**KM# 567** • 5.67 g., **Copper-Nickel Clad Copper**, 24.3 mm.

| Date | Mintage | MS63 | MS65 | Prf65 |
|---|---|---|---|---|
| 2014P | — | 0.75 | 5.00 | — |
| 2014D | — | 0.75 | 5.00 | — |
| 2014S | — | — | — | 3.75 |

**KM# 567a** • 6.25 g., 0.900 **Silver**, 0.1808 oz. ASW 24.3 mm.

| Date | Mintage | MS63 | MS65 | Prf65 |
|---|---|---|---|---|
| 2014S | — | — | — | 7.75 |

## Arches National Park

**KM# 568** • 5.67 g., **Copper-Nickel Clad Copper**, 24.3 mm.

| Date | Mintage | MS63 | MS65 | Prf65 |
|---|---|---|---|---|
| 2014P | — | 0.75 | 5.00 | — |
| 2014D | — | 0.75 | 5.00 | — |
| 2014S | — | — | — | 3.75 |

**KM# 568a** • 6.25 g., 0.900 **Silver**, 0.1808 oz. ASW 24.3 mm.

| Date | Mintage | MS63 | MS65 | Prf65 |
|---|---|---|---|---|
| 2014S | — | — | — | 7.75 |

## Great Sand Dunes National Park

**KM# 569** • 5.67 g., **Copper-Nickel Clad Copper**, 24.3 mm.

| Date | Mintage | MS63 | MS65 | Prf65 |
|---|---|---|---|---|
| 2014P | — | 0.75 | 5.00 | — |
| 2014D | — | 0.75 | 5.00 | — |
| 2014S | — | — | — | 3.75 |

**KM# 569a** • 6.25 g., 0.900 **Silver**, 0.1808 oz. ASW 24.3 mm.

| Date | Mintage | MS63 | MS65 | Prf65 |
|---|---|---|---|---|
| 2014S | — | — | — | 7.75 |

## Everglades National Park

**KM# 570** • 5.67 g., **Copper-Nickel Clad Copper**, 24.3 mm.

| Date | Mintage | MS63 | MS65 | Prf65 |
|---|---|---|---|---|
| 2014P | — | 0.75 | 5.00 | — |
| 2014D | — | 0.75 | 5.00 | — |
| 2014S | — | — | — | 3.75 |

**KM# 570a** • 6.25 g., 0.900 **Silver**, 0.1808 oz. ASW 24.3 mm.

| Date | Mintage | MS63 | MS65 | Prf65 |
|---|---|---|---|---|
| 2014S | — | — | — | 7.75 |

# HALF DOLLAR

## Kennedy Half Dollar

**KM# A202b** • 11.34 g., **Copper-Nickel Clad Copper**, 30.61 mm. • **Edge:** Reeded **Note:** KM#202b design and composition resumed. The 1979-S and 1981-S Type II proofs have clearer mint marks than the Type I proofs of those years.

| Date | Mintage | MS65 | Prf65 |
|---|---|---|---|
| 2001P | 21,200,000 | 10.00 | — |
| 2001D | 19,504,000 | 9.00 | — |
| 2001S | 2,235,000 | — | 5.00 |
| 2002P | 3,100,000 | 10.00 | — |
| 2002D | 2,500,000 | 10.50 | — |
| 2002S | 2,268,913 | — | 5.00 |
| 2003P | 2,500,000 | 6.00 | — |
| 2003D | 2,500,000 | 6.00 | — |
| 2003S | 2,076,165 | — | 5.00 |
| 2004P | 2,900,000 | 4.50 | — |
| 2004D | 2,900,000 | 4.50 | — |
| 2004S | 1,789,488 | — | 6.00 |
| 2005P | 3,800,000 | 6.00 | — |
| 2005P Satin finish | 1,160,000 | 8.00 | — |
| 2005D | 3,500,000 | 5.00 | — |
| 2005D Satin finish | 1,160,000 | 10.00 | — |
| 2005S | 2,275,000 | — | 5.00 |
| 2006P | 2,400,000 | 4.50 | — |
| 2006P Satin finish | 847,361 | 12.00 | — |
| 2006D | 2,000,000 | 4.50 | — |
| 2006D Satin finish | 847,361 | 14.00 | — |
| 2006S | 1,934,965 | — | 6.00 |
| 2007P | 2,400,000 | 4.50 | — |
| 2007P Satin finish | — | 8.00 | — |
| 2007D | 2,400,000 | 4.50 | — |
| 2007D Satin finish | — | 8.00 | — |
| 2007S | 1,702,116 | — | 6.00 |
| 2008P | 1,700,000 | 4.50 | — |
| 2008P Satin finish | — | 8.50 | — |
| 2008D | 1,700,000 | 4.50 | — |
| 2008D Satin finish | — | 8.50 | — |
| 2008S | 1,405,674 | — | 9.00 |
| 2009P | 1,900,000 | 4.50 | — |
| 2009P Satin finish | — | 8.50 | — |
| 2009D | 1,900,000 | 4.50 | — |
| 2009D Satin finish | — | 8.50 | — |
| 2009S | 1,482,502 | — | 6.00 |
| 2010P | 1,800,000 | 4.50 | — |
| 2010P Satin finish | — | 8.50 | — |
| 2010D | 1,700,000 | 4.50 | — |
| 2010D Satin finish | — | 8.50 | — |
| 2010S | 1,103,815 | — | 13.00 |
| 2011P | 1,750,000 | 4.50 | — |
| 2011D | 1,700,000 | 4.50 | — |
| 2011S | 1,098,835 | — | 9.00 |
| 2012P | 1,800,000 | 4.50 | — |
| 2012D | 1,700,000 | 4.50 | — |
| 2012S | 841,972 | — | 9.00 |
| 2013P | 5,000,000 | 4.50 | — |
| 2013D | 4,600,000 | 4.50 | — |
| 2013S | 821,031 | — | 9.00 |
| 2014D | — | 4.50 | — |
| 2014P | — | 4.50 | — |
| 2014S | — | — | 9.00 |
| 2015D | — | 4.50 | — |
| 2015P | — | 4.50 | — |
| 2015S | — | — | 9.00 |

**KM# A202c** • 12.50 g., 0.900 **Silver** 0.3617 oz. ASW, 30.6 • **Designer:** Gilroy Roberts

| Date | Mintage | MS65 | Prf65 |
|---|---|---|---|
| 2001S | 849,600 | — | 13.20 |
| 2002S | 888,816 | — | 13.20 |
| 2003S | 1,040,425 | — | 13.20 |
| 2004S | 1,175,935 | — | 13.20 |
| 2005S | 1,069,679 | — | 14.20 |
| 2006S | 988,140 | — | 14.20 |
| 2007S | 1,384,797 | — | 15.70 |
| 2008S | 620,684 | — | 14.20 |
| 2009S | 697,365 | — | 13.20 |
| 2010S | 585,401 | — | 14.20 |
| 2011S | 574,175 | — | 14.20 |
| 2012S | 395,443 | — | 14.20 |
| 2013S | 451,342 | — | 14.20 |
| 2014S | — | — | 12.00 |
| 2015S | — | — | 9.00 |

# DOLLAR

## Sacagawea Dollar

Sacagawea bust right, with baby on back obverse Eagle in flight left reverse

**KM# 310** • 8.07 g., **Copper-Zinc-Manganese-Nickel Clad Copper**, 26.5 mm. • **Obv. Designer:** Glenda Goodacre **Rev. Designer:** Thomas D. Rodgers

| Date | Mintage | MS63 | MS65 | Prf65 |
|---|---|---|---|---|
| 2001P | 62,468,000 | 2.25 | 6.00 | — |
| 2001D | 70,909,500 | 2.25 | 8.00 | — |
| 2001S | 3,084,000 | — | — | 16.00 |
| 2002P | 3,865,610 | 3.00 | 9.00 | — |
| 2002D | 3,732,000 | 2.75 | 10.00 | — |
| 2002S | 3,157,739 | — | — | 10.00 |
| 2003P | 3,090,000 | 4.50 | 10.00 | — |
| 2003D | 3,090,000 | 4.75 | 12.00 | — |
| 2003S | 3,116,590 | — | — | 8.00 |
| 2004P | 2,660,000 | 3.50 | 6.00 | — |
| 2004D | 2,660,000 | 4.00 | 8.00 | — |
| 2004S | 2,992,069 | — | — | 7.50 |
| 2005P | 2,520,000 | 3.00 | 9.00 | — |
| 2005P Satin Finish | 1,160,000 | 5.00 | 9.00 | — |
| 2005D | 2,520,000 | 3.00 | 10.00 | — |
| 2005D Satin Finish | 1,160,000 | 5.00 | 9.00 | — |
| 2005S | 3,273,000 | — | — | 6.00 |
| 2006P | 4,900,000 | 3.25 | 6.00 | — |
| 2006P Satin Finish | 847,361 | 4.50 | 9.00 | — |
| 2006D | 2,800,000 | 3.50 | 10.00 | — |
| 2006D Satin Finish | 847,361 | 4.00 | 6.00 | — |
| 2006S | 3,054,436 | — | — | 9.00 |
| 2007P | 3,640,000 | 2.25 | 5.50 | — |
| 2007P Satin Finish | 895,628 | 4.00 | 6.00 | — |
| 2007D | 3,920,000 | 2.25 | 7.50 | — |
| 2007D Satin Finish | 895,628 | 4.00 | 6.00 | — |
| 2007S | 2,577,166 | — | — | 6.50 |
| 2008P | 1,820,000 | 2.00 | 7.00 | — |
| 2008P Satin Finish | 745,464 | 4.00 | 6.00 | — |
| 2008D | 1,820,000 | 3.50 | 10.00 | — |
| 2008D Satin Finish | 745,464 | 4.00 | 6.00 | — |
| 2008S | 2,169,561 | — | — | 16.00 |

## Native American Dollar - Planting crops reverse

**KM# 467 •** 8.07 g., **Copper-Zinc-Manganese-Nickel Clad Copper**, 26.5 mm. • **Obv. Designer:** Glenda Goodacre **Rev. Designer:** Norm Nemeth **Edge Lettering:** E PLURIBUS UNUM, date, mint mark **Note:** Date and mint mark on edge

| Date | Mintage | MS63 | MS65 | Prf65 |
|---|---|---|---|---|
| 2009P | 37,380,000 | 2.00 | 5.00 | — |
| 2009P Satin finish | 784,614 | 4.00 | 7.00 | — |
| 2009D | 33,880,000 | 2.00 | 5.00 | — |
| 2009D Satin finish | 784,614 | 4.00 | 7.00 | — |
| 2009S | 2,179,867 | — | — | 6.00 |

## Hiawatha belt reverse

**KM# 474 •** 8.07 g., **Copper-Zinc-Manganese-Nickel Clad Copper**, 26.5 mm. • **Obv. Designer:** Glenda Goodacre **Rev. Designer:** Thomas Cleveland and Charles L. Vickers **Edge Lettering:** E PLURIBUS UNUM, date, mint mark **Note:** Date and mint mark on edge

| Date | Mintage | MS63 | MS65 | Prf65 |
|---|---|---|---|---|
| 2010P | 32,060,000 | 2.00 | 5.00 | — |
| 2010P Satin Finish | 583,897 | 4.00 | 7.00 | — |
| 2010D | 48,720,000 | 2.00 | 5.00 | — |
| 2010D Satin Finish | 583,897 | 4.00 | 7.00 | — |
| 2010S | 1,689,364 | — | — | 12.50 |

## Peace Pipe reverse

**KM# 503 •** 8.07 g., **Copper-Zinc-Manganese-Nickel Clad Copper**, 26.5 mm. • **Obv. Designer:** Glenna Goodacre **Rev. Designer:** Richard Masters and Joseph Menna **Edge Lettering:** E PLURIBUS UNUM, date, mint mark **Note:** Date and mint mark on edge

| Date | Mintage | MS63 | MS65 | Prf65 |
|---|---|---|---|---|
| 2011P | 29,400,000 | 2.00 | 5.50 | — |
| 2011D | 48,160,000 | 2.00 | 5.00 | — |
| 2011S | 1,453,276 | — | — | 8.00 |

## Horse reverse

**KM# 528 •** 8.07 g., **Copper-Zinc-Manganese-Nickel Clad Copper**, 26.5 mm. • **Obv. Designer:** Glenda Goodacre **Rev. Designer:** Thomas Cleveland and Phebe Hemphill **Edge Lettering:** E PLURIBUS UNUM, date, mint mark **Note:** Date and mint mark on edge

| Date | Mintage | MS63 | MS65 | Prf65 |
|---|---|---|---|---|
| 2012P | 2,800,000 | 2.00 | 7.00 | — |
| 2012D | 3,080,000 | 2.00 | 7.00 | — |
| 2012S | 1,189,445 | — | — | 12.50 |

## Delaware Treaty of 1778

**KM# 551 •** 8.07 g., **Copper-Zinc-Manganese-Nickel Clad Copper**, 26.5 mm. • **Edge:** E PLURIBUS UNUM, date, mint mark **Note:** Date and mint mark on edge.

| Date | Mintage | MS63 | MS65 | Prf65 |
|---|---|---|---|---|
| 2013P | 1,820,000 | 2.00 | 7.00 | — |
| 2013D | 1,820,000 | 2.00 | 7.00 | — |
| 2013S | 1,192,690 | — | — | 12.50 |

## Native Hospitality

**KM# 575 •** 8.07 g., **Copper-Zinc-Manganese-Nickel Clad Copper**, 26.5 mm. •

| Date | Mintage | MS63 | MS65 | Prf65 |
|---|---|---|---|---|
| 2014P | — | 2.00 | 7.00 | — |
| 2014D | — | 2.00 | 7.00 | — |
| 2014S | — | — | — | 12.50 |

# PRESIDENTS

## George Washington

**KM# 401 •** 8.07 g., **Copper-Zinc-Manganese-Nickel Clad Copper**, 26.5 mm. **Obv. Designer:** Joseph Menna **Rev. Designer:** Don Everhart **Edge Lettering:** IN GOD WE TRUST date, mint mark E PLURIBUS UNUM **Note:** Date and mint mark incuse on edge.

| Date | Mintage | MS63 | MS65 | Prf65 |
|---|---|---|---|---|
| 2007P | 176,680,000 | 2.00 | 3.00 | — |
| 2007P Satin Finish | 895,628 | 2.00 | 4.00 | — |
| (2007) Plain edge error | Inc. above | 175 | 275 | — |
| 2007D | 163,680,000 | 2.00 | 3.00 | — |
| 2007D Satin Finish | 895,628 | 2.00 | 4.00 | — |
| 2007S | 3,883,103 | — | — | 3.00 |

## John Adams

**KM# 402 •** 8.07 g., **Copper-Zinc-Manganese-Nickel Clad Copper**, 26.5 mm. **Obv. Designer:** Joel Iskowitz and Charles Vickers **Rev. Designer:** Don Everhart **Edge Lettering:** IN GOD WE TRUST date, mint mark E PLURIBUS UNUM **Note:** Date and mint mark incuse on edge.

| Date | Mintage | MS63 | MS65 | Prf65 |
|---|---|---|---|---|
| 2007P | 112,420,000 | 2.00 | 4.00 | — |
| 2007S Double edge lettering | Inc. above | — | — | 3.00 |
| 2007D Satin Finish | 895,628 | 2.00 | 4.00 | — |
| 2007D | 112,140,000 | 60.00 | 70.00 | — |
| 2007P Plain edge error | Inc. above | 45.00 | 65.00 | — |
| 2007D Satin Finish | 895,628 | 2.00 | 3.00 | — |
| 2007P | 3,877,409 | 2.00 | 3.00 | — |

## Thomas Jefferson

**KM# 403 •** 8.07 g., **Copper-Zinc-Manganese-Nickel Clad Copper**, 26.5 mm. **Obv. Designer:** Joseph Menna **Rev. Designer:** Don Everhart **Edge Lettering:** IN GOD WE TRUST date, mint mark E PLURIBUS UNUM **Note:** Date and mint mark incuse on edge.

| Date | Mintage | MS63 | MS65 | Prf65 |
|---|---|---|---|---|
| 2007P | 100,800,000 | 2.00 | 3.00 | — |
| 2007P Satin Finish | 895,628 | 2.00 | 4.00 | — |
| 2007D | 102,810,000 | 2.00 | 3.00 | — |
| 2007D Satin Finish | 895,628 | 2.00 | 4.00 | — |
| 2007S | 3,877,573 | — | — | 3.00 |

## James Madison

**KM# 404 •** 8.07 g., **Copper-Zinc-Manganese-Nickel Clad Copper**, 26.5 mm. **Obv. Designer:** Joel Iskowitz and Don Everhart **Rev. Designer:** Don Everhart **Edge Lettering:** IN GOD WE TRUST date, mint mark E PLURIBUS UNUM **Note:** Date and mint mark incuse on edge.

| Date | Mintage | MS63 | MS65 | Prf65 |
|---|---|---|---|---|
| 2007P | 84,560,000 | 2.00 | 3.00 | — |
| 2007P Satin Finish | 895,628 | 2.00 | 4.00 | — |
| 2007D | 87,780,000 | 2.00 | 3.00 | — |
| 2007D Satin Finish | 895,628 | 2.00 | 4.00 | — |
| 2007S | 3,876,829 | — | — | 3.00 |

## James Monroe

**KM# 426 •** 8.07 g., **Copper-Zinc-Manganese-Nickel Clad Copper**, 26.5 mm. **Obv. Designer:** Joseph Menna **Rev. Designer:** Don Everhart **Edge Lettering:** IN GOD WE TRUST date, mint mark E PLURIBUS UNUM

| Date | Mintage | MS63 | MS65 | Prf65 |
|---|---|---|---|---|
| 2008P | 64,260,000 | 2.00 | 3.00 | — |
| 2008P Satin Finish | 745,464 | 2.00 | 4.00 | — |
| 2008D | 60,230,000 | 2.00 | 3.00 | — |
| 2008D Satin Finish | 745,464 | 2.00 | 4.00 | — |
| 2008S | 3,000,000 | — | — | 4.00 |

## John Quincy Adams

**KM# 427 •** 8.07 g., **Copper-Zinc-Manganese-Nickel Clad Copper**, 26.5 mm. **Obv. Designer:** Don Everhart **Rev. Designer:** Don Everhart **Edge Lettering:** IN GOD WE TRUST date, mint mark E PLURIBUS UNUM **Note:** Date and mint mark incuse on edge.

| Date | Mintage | MS63 | MS65 | Prf65 |
|---|---|---|---|---|
| 2008P | 57,540,000 | 2.00 | 3.00 | — |
| 2008P Satin Finish | 745,464 | 2.00 | 4.00 | — |
| 2008D | 57,720,000 | 2.00 | 3.00 | — |
| 2008D Satin Finish | 745,464 | 2.00 | 4.00 | — |
| 2008S | 3,000,000 | — | — | 4.00 |

## Andrew Jackson

**KM# 428** • 8.07 g., **Copper-Zinc-Manganese-Nickel Clad Copper**, 26.5 mm. **Obv. Designer:** Joel Iskowitz and Jim Licaretz **Rev. Designer:** Don Everhart **Edge Lettering:** IN GOD WE TRUST date, mint mark E PLURIBUS UNUM **Note:** Date and mint mark incuse on edge.

| Date | Mintage | MS63 | MS65 | Prf65 |
|---|---|---|---|---|
| 2008P | 61,180,000 | 2.00 | 3.00 | — |
| 2008P Satin Finish | 745,464 | 2.00 | 4.00 | — |
| 2008D | 61,070,000 | 2.00 | 3.00 | — |
| 2008D Satin Finish | 745,464 | 2.00 | 4.00 | — |
| 2008S | 3,000,000 | — | — | 4.00 |

## Martin van Buren

**KM# 429** • 8.07 g., **Copper-Zinc-Manganese-Nickel Clad Copper**, 26.5 mm. **Obv. Designer:** Joel Iskowitz and Phebe Hemphill **Rev. Designer:** Don Everhart **Edge Lettering:** IN GOD WE TRUST date, mint mark E PLURIBUS UNUM **Note:** Date and mint mark incuse on edge.

| Date | Mintage | MS63 | MS65 | Prf65 |
|---|---|---|---|---|
| 2008P | 51,520,000 | 2.00 | 3.00 | — |
| 2008P Satin Finish | 745,464 | 2.00 | 4.00 | — |
| 2008D | 50,960,000 | 2.00 | 3.00 | — |
| 2008D Satin Finish | 745,464 | 2.00 | 4.00 | — |
| 2008S | 3,000,000 | — | — | 4.00 |

## William Henry Harrison

**KM# 450** • 8.07 g., **Copper-Zinc-Manganese-Nickel Clad Copper**, 26.5 mm. **Obv. Designer:** Joseph Menna **Rev. Designer:** Don Everhart **Edge Lettering:** E PLURIBUS UNUM, date, mint mark **Note:** Date and mint mark on edge

| Date | Mintage | MS63 | MS65 | Prf65 |
|---|---|---|---|---|
| 2009P | 43,260,000 | 2.00 | 3.00 | — |
| 2009P Satin Finish | 784,614 | 2.00 | 4.00 | — |
| 2009D | 55,160,000 | 2.00 | 3.00 | — |
| 2009P Satin Finish | 784,614 | 2.00 | 4.00 | — |
| 2009S | 2,224,827 | — | — | 3.00 |

## John Tyler

**KM# 451** • 8.07 g., **Copper-Zinc-Manganese-Nickel Clad Copper**, 26.5 mm. **Obv. Designer:** Phebe Hemphill **Rev. Designer:** Don Everhart **Edge Lettering:** E PLURIBUS UNUM, date, mint mark **Note:** Date and mint mark on edge.

| Date | Mintage | MS63 | MS65 | Prf65 |
|---|---|---|---|---|
| 2009P | 43,540,000 | 2.00 | 3.00 | — |
| 2009P Satin Finish | 784,614 | 2.00 | 4.00 | — |
| 2009D | 43,540,000 | 2.00 | 3.00 | — |
| 2009D Satin Finish | 784,614 | 2.00 | 4.00 | — |
| 2009S | 2,224,827 | — | — | 3.00 |

## James K. Polk

**KM# 452** • 8.07 g., **Copper-Zinc-Manganese-Nickel Clad Copper**, 26.5 mm. **Obv. Designer:** Susan Gamble and Charles Vickers **Rev. Designer:** Don Everhart **Edge Lettering:** E PLURIBUS UNUM, date, mint mark **Note:** Date and mint mark on edge

| Date | Mintage | MS63 | MS65 | Prf65 |
|---|---|---|---|---|
| 2009P | 46,620,000 | 2.00 | 3.00 | — |
| 2009P Satin Finish | 784,614 | 2.00 | 4.00 | — |
| 2009D | 41,720,000 | 2.00 | 3.00 | — |
| 2009D Satin Finish | 784,614 | 2.00 | 4.00 | — |
| 2009S | 2,224,827 | — | — | 3.00 |

## Zachary Taylor

**KM# 453** • 8.07 g., **Copper-Zinc-Manganese-Nickel Clad Copper**, 26.5 mm. **Obv. Designer:** Don Everhart **Rev. Designer:** Don Everhart **Edge Lettering:** E PLURIBUS UNUM, date, mint mark **Note:** Date and mint mark on edge.

| Date | Mintage | MS63 | MS65 | Prf65 |
|---|---|---|---|---|
| 2009P | 41,580,000 | 2.00 | 3.00 | — |
| 2009P Satin Finish | 784,614 | 2.00 | 4.00 | — |
| 2009D | 36,680,000 | 2.00 | 3.00 | — |
| 2009D Satin Finish | 784,614 | 2.00 | 4.00 | — |
| 2009S | 2,224,827 | — | — | 3.00 |

## Millard Filmore

**KM# 475** • 8.07 g., **Copper-Zinc-Manganese-Nickel Clad Copper**, 26.5 mm. **Obv. Designer:** Don Everhart **Rev. Designer:** Don Everhart **Edge Lettering:** E PLURIBUS UNUM, date, mint mark **Note:** Date and mint mark on edge.

| Date | Mintage | MS63 | MS65 | Prf65 |
|---|---|---|---|---|
| 2010P | 37,520,000 | 2.00 | 3.00 | — |
| 2010P Satin Finish | 583,897 | 2.00 | 4.00 | — |
| 2010D | 36,960,000 | 2.00 | 3.00 | — |
| 2010D Satin Finish | 583,897 | 2.00 | 4.00 | — |
| 2010S | 2,224,827 | — | — | 4.00 |

## Franklin Pierce

**KM# 476** • 8.07 g., **Copper-Zinc-Manganese-Nickel Clad Copper**, 26.5 mm. **Obv. Designer:** Susan Gamble and Charles L. Vickers **Rev. Designer:** Don Everhart **Edge Lettering:** E PLURIBUS UNUM, date, mint mark **Note:** Date and mint mark on edge.

| Date | Mintage | MS63 | MS65 | Prf65 |
|---|---|---|---|---|
| 2010P | 38,220,000 | 2.00 | 3.00 | — |
| 2010P Satin Finish | 583,897 | 2.00 | 4.00 | — |
| 2010D | 38,360,000 | 2.00 | 3.00 | — |
| 2010D Satin Finish | 583,897 | 2.00 | 4.00 | — |
| 2010S | 2,224,827 | — | — | 4.00 |

## James Buchanan

**KM# 477** • 8.07 g., **Copper-Zinc-Manganese-Nickel Clad Copper**, 26.5 mm. **Obv. Designer:** Phebe Hemphill **Rev. Designer:** Don Everhart **Edge Lettering:** E PLURIBUS UNUM, date, mint mark **Note:** Date and mint mark on edge.

| Date | Mintage | MS63 | MS65 | Prf65 |
|---|---|---|---|---|
| 2010P | 36,820,000 | 2.00 | 3.00 | — |
| 2010P Satin Finish | 583,897 | 2.00 | 4.00 | — |
| 2010D | 36,540,000 | 2.00 | 3.00 | — |
| 2010D Satin Finish | 583,897 | 2.00 | 4.00 | — |
| 2010S | 2,224,827 | — | — | 4.00 |

## Abraham Lincoln

**KM# 478** • 8.07 g., **Copper-Zinc-Manganese-Nickel Clad Copper**, 26.5 mm. **Obv. Designer:** Don Everhart **Rev. Designer:** Don Everhart **Edge Lettering:** E PLURIBUS UNUM, date, mint mark **Note:** Date and mint mark on edge.

| Date | Mintage | MS63 | MS65 | Prf65 |
|---|---|---|---|---|
| 2010P | 49,000,000 | 2.00 | 3.00 | — |
| 2010P Satin Finish | 583,897 | 2.00 | 4.00 | — |
| 2010D | 48,020,000 | 2.00 | 3.00 | — |
| 2010D Satin Finish | 583,897 | 2.00 | 4.00 | — |
| 2010S | 2,224,827 | — | — | 4.00 |

## Andrew Johnson

**KM# 499** • 8.07 g., **Copper-Zinc-Manganese-Nickel Clad Copper**, 26.5 mm. **Obv. Designer:** Don Everhart **Rev. Designer:** Don Everhart **Edge Lettering:** E PLURIBUS UNUM, date, mint mark **Note:** Date and mint mark on edge.

| Date | Mintage | MS63 | MS65 | Prf65 |
|---|---|---|---|---|
| 2011P | 35,560,000 | 2.00 | 3.00 | — |
| 2011D | 37,100,000 | 2.00 | 3.00 | — |
| 2011S | 1,706,916 | — | — | 4.00 |

## Ulysses S. Grant

**KM# 500** • 8.07 g., **Copper-Zinc-Manganese-Nickel Clad Copper**, 26.5 mm. **Obv. Designer:** Don Everhart **Rev. Designer:** Don Everhart **Edge Lettering:** E PLURIBUS UNUM, date, mint mark **Note:** Date and mint mark on edge.

| Date | Mintage | MS63 | MS65 | Prf65 |
|---|---|---|---|---|
| 2011P | 38,080,000 | 2.00 | 3.00 | — |
| 2011D | 37,940,000 | 2.00 | 3.00 | — |
| 2011S | 1,706,916 | — | — | 4.00 |

## Rutherford B. Hayes

**KM# 501** • 8.07 g., **Copper-Zinc-Manganese-Nickel Clad Copper**, 26.5 mm. **Obv. Designer:** Don Everhart **Rev. Designer:** Don Everhart **Edge Lettering:** E PLURIBUS UNUM, date, mint mark **Note:** Date and mint mark on edge.

| Date | Mintage | MS63 | MS65 | Prf65 |
|---|---|---|---|---|
| 2011P | 37,660,000 | 2.00 | 3.00 | — |
| 2011D | 36,820,000 | 2.00 | 3.00 | — |
| 2011S | 1,706,916 | — | — | 4.00 |

## James Garfield

**KM# 502 •** 8.07 g., **Copper-Zinc-Manganese-Nickel Clad Copper**, 26.5 mm. **Obv. Designer:** Phebe Hemphill **Rev. Designer:** Don Everhart **Edge Lettering:** E PLURIBUS UNUM, date, mint mark **Note:** Date and mint mark on edge.

| Date | Mintage | MS63 | MS65 | Prf65 |
|---|---|---|---|---|
| 2011P | 37,100,000 | 2.00 | 3.00 | — |
| 2011D | 37,100,000 | 2.00 | 3.00 | — |
| 2011S | 1,706,916 | — | — | 4.00 |

## Chester A. Arthur

**KM# 524 •** 8.07 g., **Copper-Zinc-Manganese-Nickel Clad Copper**, 26.5 mm. **Obv. Designer:** Don Everhart **Rev. Designer:** Don Everhart **Edge Lettering:** E PLURIBUS UNUM, date, mintmark **Note:** Date and mintmark on edge

| Date | Mintage | MS63 | MS65 | Prf65 |
|---|---|---|---|---|
| 2012P | 6,020,000 | 2.00 | 3.00 | — |
| 2012D | 4,060,000 | 2.00 | 3.00 | — |
| 2012S | — | — | — | 5.00 |

## Grover Cleveland, first term

**KM# 525 •** 8.07 g., **Copper-Zinc-Manganese-Nickel Clad Copper**, 26.5 mm. **Obv. Designer:** Don Everhart **Rev. Designer:** Don Everhart **Edge Lettering:** E PLURIBUS UNUM, date, mintmark **Note:** Date and mintmark on edge

| Date | Mintage | MS63 | MS65 | Prf65 |
|---|---|---|---|---|
| 2012P | 5,460,000 | 2.00 | 3.00 | — |
| 2012D | 4,060,000 | 2.00 | 3.00 | — |
| 2012S | 1,438,710 | — | — | 5.00 |

## Benjamin Harrison

**KM# 526 •** 8.07 g., **Copper-Zinc-Manganese-Nickel Clad Copper**, 26.5 mm. **Obv. Designer:** Phebe Hemphill **Rev. Designer:** Don Everhart **Edge Lettering:** E PLURIBUS UNUM, date, mintmark **Note:** Date at mint mark on edge

| Date | Mintage | MS63 | MS65 | Prf65 |
|---|---|---|---|---|
| 2012P | 5,640,001 | 2.00 | 3.00 | — |
| 2012D | 4,200,000 | 2.00 | 3.00 | — |
| 2012S | 1,438,710 | — | — | 5.00 |

## Grover Cleveland, second term

**KM# 527 •** 8.07 g., **Copper-Zinc-Manganese-Nickel Clad Copper**, 26.5 mm. **Obv. Designer:** Don Everhart **Rev. Designer:** Don Everhart **Edge Lettering:** E PLURIBUS UNUM, date, mintmark **Note:** Date and mintmark on edge

| Date | Mintage | MS63 | MS65 | Prf65 |
|---|---|---|---|---|
| 2012P | 10,680,000 | 2.00 | 3.00 | — |
| 2012D | 3,920,000 | 2.00 | 3.00 | — |
| 2012S | 1,438,710 | — | — | 5.00 |

## William McKinley

**KM# 547 •** 8.07 g., **Copper-Zinc-Manganese-Nickel Clad Copper**, 26.5 mm. **Edge:** E PLURIBUS UNUM, date, mint mark **Note:** Date and mint mark on edge.

| Date | Mintage | MS63 | MS65 | Prf65 |
|---|---|---|---|---|
| 2013P | 4,760,000 | 2.00 | 3.00 | — |
| 2013D | 3,365,100 | 2.00 | 3.00 | — |
| 2013S | 1,449,415 | — | — | 5.00 |

## Theodore Roosevelt

**KM# 548 •** 8.07 g., **Copper-Zinc-Manganese-Nickel Clad Copper**, 26.5 mm. **Edge:** E PLURIBUS UNUM, date, mint mark **Note:** Date and mint mark on edge.

| Date | Mintage | MS63 | MS65 | Prf65 |
|---|---|---|---|---|
| 2013P | 5,310,700 | 2.00 | 3.00 | — |
| 2013D | 3,920,000 | 2.00 | 3.00 | — |
| 2013S | 1,449,415 | — | — | 5.00 |

## William Howard Taft

**KM# 549 •** 8.07 g., **Copper-Zinc-Manganese-Nickel Clad Copper**, 26.5 mm. **Edge:** E PLURIBUS UNUM, date, mint mark **Note:** Date and mint mark on edge.

| Date | Mintage | MS63 | MS65 | Prf65 |
|---|---|---|---|---|
| 2013P | 4,760,000 | 2.00 | 3.00 | — |
| 2013D | 3,360,000 | 2.00 | 3.00 | — |
| 2013S | 1,449,415 | — | — | 5.00 |

## Woodrow Wilson

**KM# 550 •** 8.07 g., **Copper-Zinc-Manganese-Nickel Clad Copper**, 26.5 mm. **Edge:** E PLURIBUS UNUM, date, mint mark **Note:** Date and mint mark on edge.

| Date | Mintage | MS63 | MS65 | Prf65 |
|---|---|---|---|---|
| 2013P | 4,620,000 | 2.00 | 3.00 | — |
| 2013D | 3,360,000 | 2.00 | 3.00 | — |
| 2013S | 1,449,415 | — | — | 5.00 |

## Warren G. Harding

**KM# 571 •** 8.07 g., **Copper-Zinc-Manganese-Nickel Clad Copper**, 26.5 mm. **Note:** Date and mint mark on edge.

| Date | Mintage | MS63 | MS65 | Prf65 |
|---|---|---|---|---|
| 2014P | — | 2.00 | 3.00 | — |
| 2014D | — | 2.00 | 3.00 | — |
| 2014S | — | — | — | 5.00 |

## Calvin Coolidge

**KM# 572 •** 8.07 g., **Copper-Zinc-Manganese-Nickel Clad Copper**, 26.5 mm. **Note:** Date and mint mark on edge.

| Date | Mintage | MS63 | MS65 | Prf65 |
|---|---|---|---|---|
| 2014P | — | 2.00 | 5.00 | — |
| 2014D | — | 2.00 | 5.00 | — |
| 2014S | — | — | — | 5.00 |

## Herbert Hoover

**KM# 573 •** 8.07 g., **Copper-Zinc-Manganese-Nickel Clad Copper**, 26.5 mm. **Note:** Date and mint mark on edge.

| Date | Mintage | MS63 | MS65 | Prf65 |
|---|---|---|---|---|
| 2014P | — | 2.00 | 3.00 | — |
| 2014D | — | 2.00 | 3.00 | — |
| 2014S | — | — | — | 5.00 |

## Franklin D. Roosevelt

**KM# 574 •** 8.07 g., **Copper-Zinc-Manganese-Nickel Clad Copper**, 26.5 mm. **Note:** Date and mint mark on edge.

| Date | Mintage | MS63 | MS65 | Prf65 |
|---|---|---|---|---|
| 2014P | — | 2.00 | 3.00 | — |
| 2014D | — | 2.00 | 3.00 | — |
| 2014S | — | — | — | 5.00 |

# COMMEMORATIVE COINAGE

## HALF DOLLAR

**U. S. CAPITOL VISITOR CENTER. KM# 323 Obv. Designer:** Dean McMullen **Obv.** Capitol sillouete, 1800 structure in detail **Rev. Designer:** Alex Shagin and Marcel Jovine **Rev:** Legend within circle of stars

| Date | Mintage | MS63 | MS65 | Prf65 |
|---|---|---|---|---|
| 2001P | 99,157 | — | 14.50 | — |
| 2001P | 77,962 | — | — | 15.50 |

**FIRST FLIGHT CENTENNIAL. KM# 348 Obv. Designer:** John Mercanti **Obv.** Wright Monument at Kitty Hawk **Rev. Designer:** Donna Weaver **Rev:** Wright Flyer in flight

| Date | Mintage | MS63 | MS65 | Prf65 |
|---|---|---|---|---|
| 2003P | 57,726 | — | 15.00 | — |
| 2003P | 111,569 | — | — | 17.00 |

**AMERICAN BALD EAGLE. KM# 438 Obv. Designer:** Susan Gamble and Joseph Menna **Obv.** Two eaglets in nest with egg **Rev. Designer:** Donna Weaver and Charles Vickers **Rev:** Eagle Challenger facing right, American Flag in background

| Date | Mintage | MS63 | MS65 | Prf65 |
|---|---|---|---|---|
| 2008S | 120,180 | — | 12.50 | — |
| 2008S | 222,577 | — | — | 14.00 |

**U.S. ARMY. KM# 506 Obv. Designer:** Donna Weaver and Charles L. Vickers **Obv.** Army contributions during peacetime, surveying, building a flood wall and space exploration **Rev. Designer:** Thomas Cleveland and Joseph Menna **Rev:** Continental soldier with musket **Edge:** Reeded

| Date | Mintage | MS63 | MS65 | Prf65 |
|---|---|---|---|---|
| 2011D | 39,461 | — | 69.00 | — |
| 2011S | 68,349 | — | — | 35.00 |

**FIVE-STAR GENERALS - HENRY "HAP" ARNOLD AND OMAR N. BRADLEY. KM# 554 Obv.** Two portraits facing **Rev:** Shield

| Date | Mintage | MS63 | MS65 | Prf65 |
|---|---|---|---|---|
| 2013P | 38,097 | — | 50.00 | — |
| 2013S | 47,337 | — | — | 60.00 |

**BASEBALL HALL OF FAME. KM# 576 Obv.** Glove **Rev:** Baseball

| Date | Mintage | MS63 | MS65 | Prf65 |
|---|---|---|---|---|
| 2014D | — | — | 50.00 | — |
| 2014S | — | — | — | 60.00 |

## DOLLAR

**CAPITOL VISITOR CENTER. KM# 324 Obv. Designer:** Marika Somogyi **Obv.** Original and current Capital facades **Rev. Designer:** John Mercanti **Rev:** Eagle with sheild and ribbon

| Date | Mintage | MS63 | MS65 | Prf65 |
|---|---|---|---|---|
| 2001P | 66,636 | — | 40.80 | — |
| 2001P | 143,793 | — | — | 40.80 |

**NATIVE AMERICAN - BISON. KM# 325 Designer:** James E. Fraser **Obv.** Native American bust right **Rev:** Bison standing left

| Date | Mintage | MS63 | MS65 | Prf65 |
|---|---|---|---|---|
| 2001D | 197,131 | — | 165 | — |
| 2001P | 272,869 | — | — | 169 |

**2002 WINTER OLYMPICS - SALT LAKE CITY. KM# 336 Obv. Designer:** John Mercanti **Obv.** Salt Lake City Olympic logo **Rev. Designer:** Donna Weaver **Rev:** Stylized skyline with mountains in background

| Date | Mintage | MS63 | MS65 | Prf65 |
|---|---|---|---|---|
| 2002P | 35,388 | — | 40.80 | — |
| 2002P | 142,873 | — | — | 38.30 |

**U.S. MILITARY ACADEMY AT WEST POINT -BICENTENNIAL. KM# 338 Obv. Designer:** T. James Ferrell **Obv.** Cadet Review flagbearers, Academy buildings in background **Rev. Designer:** John Mercanti **Rev:** Academy emblems - Corinthian helmet and sword

| Date | Mintage | MS63 | MS65 | Prf65 |
|---|---|---|---|---|
| 2002W | 103,201 | — | 38.30 | — |
| 2002W | 288,293 | — | — | 39.80 |

**FIRST FLIGHT CENTENNIAL. KM# 349 Obv. Designer:** T. James Ferrell **Obv.** Orville and Wilbur Wright busts left **Rev. Designer:** Norman E. Nemeth **Rev:** Wright Flyer over dunes **Edge:** Reeded

| Date | Mintage | MS63 | MS65 | Prf65 |
|---|---|---|---|---|
| 2003P | 53,761 | — | 40.80 | — |
| 2003P | 193,086 | — | — | 46.80 |

**THOMAS A. EDISON - ELECTRIC LIGHT 125TH ANNIVERSARY. KM# 362 Obv. Designer:** Donna Weaver **Obv.** Edison half-length figure facing holding light bulb **Rev. Designer:** John Mercanti **Rev:** Light bulb and rays

| Date | Mintage | MS63 | MS65 | Prf65 |
|---|---|---|---|---|
| 2004P | 68,031 | — | 40.80 | — |
| 2004P | 213,409 | — | — | 41.80 |

**LEWIS AND CLARK CORPS OF DISCOVERY BICENTENNIAL. KM# 363 Designer:** Donna Weaver **Obv.** Lewis and Clark standing **Rev:** Jefferson era clasped hands peace medal

| Date | Mintage | MS63 | MS65 | Prf65 |
|---|---|---|---|---|
| 2004P | 90,323 | — | 40.80 | — |
| 2004P | 288,492 | — | — | 46.80 |

**JOHN MARSHALL, 250TH BIRTH ANNIVERSARY. KM# 375 Obv. Designer:** John Mercanti **Obv.** Marshall bust left **Rev. Designer:** Donna Weaver **Rev:** Marshall era Supreme Court Chamber

| Date | Mintage | MS63 | MS65 | Prf65 |
|---|---|---|---|---|
| 2005P | 48,953 | — | 37.30 | — |
| 2005P | 141,993 | — | — | 35.80 |

**U.S. MARINE CORPS, 230TH ANNIVERSARY. KM# 376 Obv. Designer:** Norman E. Nemeth **Obv.** Flag Raising at Mt. Suribachi on Iwo Jima **Rev. Designer:** Charles Vickers **Rev:** Marine Corps emblem

| Date | Mintage | MS63 | MS65 | Prf65 |
|---|---|---|---|---|
| 2005P | 130,000 | — | 48.00 | — |
| 2005P | 370,000 | — | — | 52.50 |

**BENJAMIN FRANKLIN, 300TH BIRTH ANNIVERSARY. KM# 387 Obv. Designer:** Norman E. Nemeth **Obv.** Youthful Franklin flying kite **Rev. Designer:** Charles Vickers **Rev:** Revolutionary era "JOIN, or DIE" snake cartoon illustration

| Date | Mintage | MS63 | MS65 | Prf65 |
|---|---|---|---|---|
| 2006P | 58,000 | — | 40.80 | — |
| 2006P | 142,000 | — | — | 45.00 |

**BENJAMIN FRANKLIN, 300TH BIRTH ANNIVERSARY. KM# 388 Obv. Designer:** Don Everhart II **Obv.** Bust 3/4 right, signature in oval below **Rev. Designer:** Donna Weaver **Rev:** Continental Dollar of 1776 in center

| Date | Mintage | MS63 | MS65 | Prf65 |
|---|---|---|---|---|
| 2006P | 58,000 | — | 40.80 | — |
| 2006P | 142,000 | — | — | 51.00 |

**SAN FRANCISCO MINT MUSEUM. KM# 394 Obv. Designer:** Sherl J. Winter **Obv.** 3/4 view of building **Rev. Designer:** George T. Morgan **Rev:** Reverse of 1880s Morgan silver dollar

| Date | Mintage | MS63 | MS65 | Prf65 |
|---|---|---|---|---|
| 2006S | 65,609 | — | 40.80 | — |
| 2006S | 255,700 | — | — | 40.80 |

**JAMESTOWN - 400TH ANNIVERSARY. KM# 405 Obv. Designer:** Donna Weaver and Don Everhart II **Obv.** Two settlers and Native American **Rev. Designer:** Susan Gamble and Charles Vickers **Rev:** Three ships

| Date | Mintage | MS63 | MS65 | Prf65 |
|---|---|---|---|---|
| 2007P | 79,801 | — | 40.80 | — |
| 2007P | 258,802 | — | — | 38.30 |

**CENTRAL HIGH SCHOOL DESEGREGATION. KM# 418 Obv. Designer:** Richard Masters and Charles Vickers **Obv.** Children's feet walking left with adult feet in military boots **Rev. Designer:** Don Everhart II **Rev:** Little Rock's Central High School

| Date | Mintage | MS63 | MS65 | Prf65 |
|---|---|---|---|---|
| 2007P | 66,093 | — | 40.80 | — |
| 2007P | 124,618 | — | — | 43.00 |

**AMERICAN BALD EAGLE. KM# 439 Obv. Designer:** Joel Iskowitz and Don Everhart II **Obv.** Eagle with flight, mountain in background at right **Rev. Designer:** James Licaretz **Rev:** Great Seal of the United States

| Date | Mintage | MS63 | MS65 | Prf65 |
|---|---|---|---|---|
| 2008P | 110,073 | — | 44.00 | — |
| 2008P | 243,558 | — | — | 38.30 |

**LINCOLN BICENTENNIAL. KM# 454 Obv. Designer:** Justin Kunz and Don Everhart II **Obv.** 3/4 portrait facing right **Rev. Designer:** Phebe Hemphill **Rev:** Part of Gettysburg Address within wreath

| Date | Mintage | MS63 | MS65 | Prf65 |
|---|---|---|---|---|
| 2009P | 125,000 | — | 55.00 | — |
| 2009P | 375,000 | — | — | 55.00 |

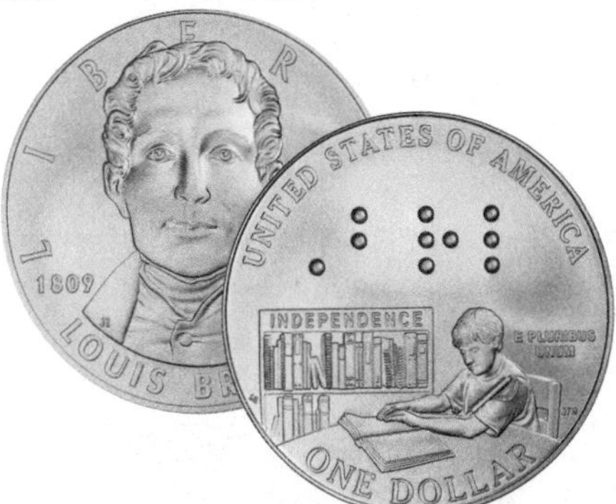


**LOUIS BRAILLE BIRTH BICENTENNIAL. KM# 455 Obv. Designer:** Joel Iskowitz and Phebe Hemphill **Obv.** Louis Braille bust facing **Rev. Designer:** Susan Gamble and Joseph Menna **Rev:** School child reading book in Braille, BRL in Braille code above

| Date | Mintage | MS63 | MS65 | Prf65 |
|---|---|---|---|---|
| 2009P | 82,639 | — | 38.50 | — |
| 2009P | 135,235 | — | — | 38.30 |

**AMERICAN VETERANS DISABLED FOR LIFE. KM# 479 Obv. Designer:** Don Everhart II **Obv.** Soldier's feet, crutches **Rev. Designer:** Thomas Cleveland and Joseph Menna **Rev:** Legend within wreath

| Date | Mintage | MS63 | MS65 | Prf65 |
|---|---|---|---|---|
| 2010W | 77,859 | — | 40.80 | — |
| 2010W | 189,881 | — | — | 42.30 |

**BOY SCOUTS OF AMERICA, 100TH ANNIVERSARY. KM# 480 Obv. Designer:** Donna Weaver **Obv.** Cub Scout, Boy Scout and Venturer saluting **Rev. Designer:** Jim Licaretz **Rev:** Boy Scouts of America logo

| Date | Mintage | MS63 | MS65 | Prf65 |
|---|---|---|---|---|
| 2010P | 105,020 | — | 38.50 | — |
| 2010P | 244,963 | — | — | 42.00 |

**MEDAL OF HONOR. KM# 504 Obv. Designer:** James Licaretz **Obv.** Medal of Honor designs for Army, Navy and Air Force awards **Rev. Designer:** Richard Masters and Phebe Hemphill **Rev:** Army infantry doldier carrying another to safety **Edge:** Reeded

| Date | Mintage | MS63 | MS65 | Prf65 |
|---|---|---|---|---|
| 2011S | 44,769 | — | 46.50 | — |
| 2011S | 112,850 | — | — | 43.50 |

**U.S. ARMY. KM# 507 Obv. Designer:** Richard Masters and Michael Gaudioso **Obv.** Male and femlae soldier heads looking outward **Rev. Designer:** Susan Gamble and Don Everhart, II **Rev:** Seven core values of the Army, Eagle from the great seal **Edge:** Reeded

| Date | Mintage | MS63 | MS65 | Prf65 |
|---|---|---|---|---|
| 2011S | 43,512 | — | 45.00 | — |
| 2011S | 119,829 | — | — | 43.50 |

**NATIONAL INFANTRY MUSEUM AND SOLDIER CENTER. KM# 529 Obv. Designer:** Joel Iskowitz and Michael Gaudioso **Obv.** Infantry soldier advancing left **Rev. Designer:** Ronald D. Sanders and Norman E. Nemeth **Rev:** Crossed rifles insignia

| Date | Mintage | MS63 | MS65 | Prf65 |
|---|---|---|---|---|
| 2012 | — | — | 50.00 | — |
| 2012 | — | — | — | 60.00 |

**STAR-SPANGLED BANNER. KM# 530 Obv. Designer:** Joel Iskowitz and Phebe Hemphill **Obv.** Liberty waving 15 star and stripe flag, Ft. McHenry in background **Rev. Designer:** William C Burgard III and Don Everhart **Rev:** Modern American Flag

| Date | Mintage | MS63 | MS65 | Prf65 |
|---|---|---|---|---|
| 2012 | — | — | 50.00 | — |
| 2012 | — | — | — | 60.00 |

**GIRL SCOUTS OF THE USA, 100TH ANNIVERSARY. KM# 552 Obv.** Three busts right **Rev:** Trefoil logo

| Date | Mintage | MS63 | MS65 | Prf65 |
|---|---|---|---|---|
| 2013W | 37,461 | — | 50.00 | — |
| 2013W | 86,353 | — | — | 60.00 |

**FIVE-STAR GENERALS - GEORGE C. MARSHALL AND DWIGHT D. EISENHOWER. KM# 553 Obv.** Two busts facing, strips from flag in background **Rev:** Lamp from U.S. Army Command and General Staff College

| Date | Mintage | MS63 | MS65 | Prf65 |
|---|---|---|---|---|
| 2013W | 34,639 | — | 50.00 | — |
| 2013S | 69,290 | — | — | 60.00 |

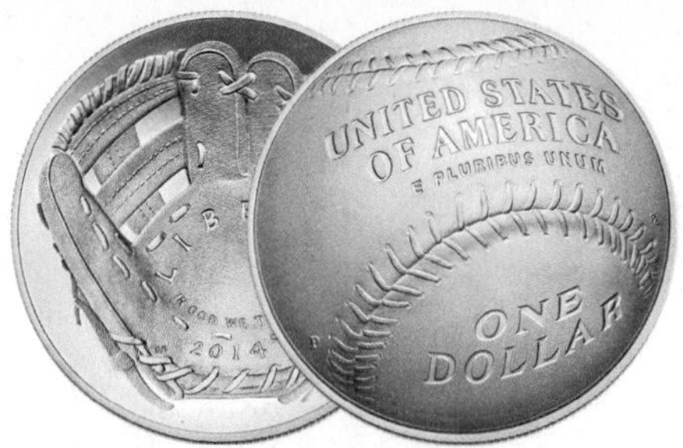


**BASEBALL HALL OF FAME. KM# 577 Obv.** Baseball glove **Rev:** Baseball

| Date | Mintage | MS63 | MS65 | Prf65 |
|---|---|---|---|---|
| 2014P | — | — | 50.00 | — |
| 2014P | — | — | — | 60.00 |

**CIVIL RIGHTS ACT OF 1964. KM# 579 Obv.** Three Civil Rights marchers **Rev:** Torch

| Date | Mintage | MS63 | MS65 | Prf65 |
|---|---|---|---|---|
| 2014P | — | — | 50.00 | — |
| 2014P | — | — | — | 60.00 |

## $5 (HALF EAGLE)

**CAPITOL VISITOR CENTER. KM# 326 Designer:** Elizabeth Jones **Obv.** Column at right **Rev:** First Capital building

| Date | Mintage | MS63 | MS65 | Prf65 |
|---|---|---|---|---|
| 2001W | 6,761 | — | 1,750 | — |
| 2001W | 27,652 | — | — | 442 |

**2002 WINTER OLYMPICS. KM# 337 Designer:** Donna Weaver **Obv.** Salt Lake City Olympics logo **Rev:** Stylized cauldron

| Date | Mintage | MS63 | MS65 | Prf65 |
|---|---|---|---|---|
| 2002W | 10,585 | — | 452 | — |
| 2002W | 32,877 | — | — | 442 |

**SAN FRANCISCO MINT MUSEUM. KM# 395 Obv. Designer:** Charles Vickers and Joseph Menna **Obv.** Front entrance façade **Rev. Designer:** Christian Gobrecht **Rev:** Eagle as on 1860's $5. Gold

| Date | Mintage | MS63 | MS65 | Prf65 |
|---|---|---|---|---|
| 2006S | 16,230 | — | 442 | — |
| 2006S | 41,517 | — | — | 442 |

**JAMESTOWN - 400TH ANNIVERSARY. KM# 406 Obv. Designer:** John Mercanti **Obv.** Settler and Native American **Rev. Designer:** Susan Gamble and Norman Nemeth **Rev:** Jamestown Memorial Church ruins

| Date | Mintage | MS63 | MS65 | Prf65 |
|---|---|---|---|---|
| 2007W | 18,843 | — | 442 | — |
| 2007W | 47,050 | — | — | 442 |

**AMERICAN BALD EAGLE. KM# 440 Obv. Designer:** Susan Gamble adn Phebe Hemphill **Obv.** Two eagles on branch **Rev. Designer:** Don Everhart II **Rev:** Eagle with shield

| Date | Mintage | MS63 | MS65 | Prf65 |
|---|---|---|---|---|
| 2008W | 13,467 | — | 457 | — |
| 2008W | 59,269 | — | — | 442 |

**MEDAL OF HONOR. KM# 505 Obv. Designer:** Joseph Menna **Obv.** 1861 Medal of Honor design for the Navy **Rev. Designer:** Joel Iskowitz and Michael Gaudioso **Rev:** Minerva standing with shield and Union flag, field artillery canon flanking **Edge:** Reeded

| Date | Mintage | MS63 | MS65 | Prf65 |
|---|---|---|---|---|
| 2011S | 18,012 | — | — | 500 |
| 2011S | 8,251 | — | 585 | — |

**U.S. ARMY. KM# 508 Obv. Designer:** Joel Iskowitz and Phebe Hemphill **Obv.** Five Soldiers of different eras **Rev. Designer:** Joseph Menna **Rev:** Elements from the Army's emblem **Edge:** Reeded

| Date | Mintage | MS63 | MS65 | Prf65 |
|---|---|---|---|---|
| 2011P | 8,062 | — | 585 | — |
| 2011W | 17,173 | — | — | 495 |

**STAR-SPANGLED BANNER. KM# 531 Obv. Designer:** Donna Weaver **Obv.** Naval battle scene from the War of 1812. American ship in foreground, damaged British ship in background **Rev. Designer:** Joseph Menna **Rev:** 15 stars and 15 stripes, opening words to the Star-Spangled Banner: O say can you see.

| Date | Mintage | MS63 | MS65 | Prf65 |
|---|---|---|---|---|
| 2012 | — | — | 585 | — |
| 2012 | — | — | — | 600 |

**FIVE-STAR GENERALS - DOUGLAS MACARTHUR. KM# 555 Obv.** Head facing at left **Rev:** Lamp

| Date | Mintage | MS63 | MS65 | Prf65 |
|---|---|---|---|---|
| 2013P | 5,658 | — | — | — |
| 2013S | 15,843 | — | — | — |

**BASEBALL HALL OF FAME. KM# 578 Obv.** Baseball glove **Rev:** Baseball

| Date | Mintage | MS63 | MS65 | Prf65 |
|---|---|---|---|---|
| 2014W | — | — | — | — |
| 2014W | — | — | — | — |

## $10 (EAGLE)

**FIRST FLIGHT CENTENNIAL. KM# 350 Obv. Designer:** Donna Weaver **Obv.** Orvile and Wilbur Wright busts facing **Rev. Designer:** Norman Nemeth **Rev:** Wright flyer and eagle

| Date | Mintage | MS63 | MS65 | Prf65 |
|---|---|---|---|---|
| 2003P | 10,129 | — | 1,050 | — |
| 2003W | 21,846 | — | — | 893 |

## $20 (DOUBLE EAGLE)

**KM# 464 Designer:** Augustus Saint-Gaudens **Obv.** Ultra high relief Liberty holding torch, walking forward **Rev:** Eagle in flight left, sunrise in background

| Date | Mintage | MS63 | MS65 | Prf65 |
|---|---|---|---|---|
| 2009 | 115,178 | — | 1,950 | — |

# AMERICA THE BEAUTIFUL SILVER BULLION

## SILVER QUARTER

**KM# 489 • RevDesc:** Park Headquarters and fountain • 155.55 g., 0.999 **Silver** 4.996 oz. ASW • **Rev. Designer:** Don Everhart II and Joseph Menna

| Date | Mintage | MS65 | MS69 |
|---|---|---|---|
| 2010 | 33,000 | 290 | 360 |
| 2010P Vapor Blast finish | 27,000 | 250 | 375 |

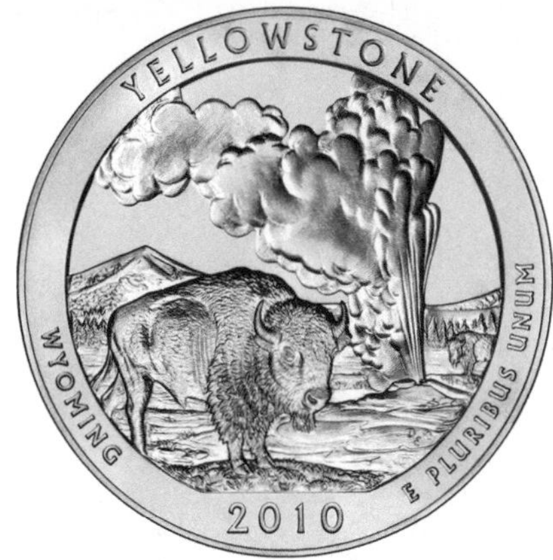

**KM# 490 • RevDesc:** Old Faithful geyser and bison • 155.55 g., 0.999 **Silver** 4.996 oz. ASW • **Rev. Designer:** Don Everhart II

| Date | Mintage | MS65 | MS69 |
|---|---|---|---|
| 2010 | 33,000 | 275 | 360 |
| 2010P Vapor Blast finish | 27,000 | 240 | 325 |

**KM# 491 • RevDesc:** El Capitan, largest monolith of granite in the world • 155.55 g., 0.999 **Silver** 4.996 oz. ASW • **Rev. Designer:** Joseph Menna and Phebe Hemphill

| Date | Mintage | MS65 | MS69 |
|---|---|---|---|
| 2010 | 33,000 | 275 | 385 |
| 2010P Vapor blast finish | 27,000 | 225 | 260 |

**KM# 492 • RevDesc:** Grabarues above the Nankoweap Delta in Marble Canyon near the Colorado River • 155.55 g., 0.999 **Silver** 4.996 oz. ASW • **Rev. Designer:** Phebe Hemphill

| Date | Mintage | MS65 | MS69 |
|---|---|---|---|
| 2010 | 33,000 | 250 | 325 |
| 2010P Vapor blast finish | 26,019 | 225 | 325 |

**KM# 493 • RevDesc:** Mt. Hood with Lost Lake in the foreground • 155.55 g., 0.999 **Silver** 4.996 oz. ASW • **Rev. Designer:** Phebe Hemphill

| Date | Mintage | MS65 | MS69 |
|---|---|---|---|
| 2010 | 33,000 | 275 | 360 |
| 2010P Vapor blast finish | 25,318 | 200 | 260 |

**KM# 513 • RevDesc:** 72nd Pennsylvania Infantry Monumnet on the battle line of the Union Army at Cemetery Ridge • 155.55 g., 0.999 **Silver** 4.996 oz. ASW • **Rev. Designer:** Joel Iskowitz and Phebe Hemphill

| Date | Mintage | MS65 | MS69 |
|---|---|---|---|
| 2011 | 126,700 | 200 | 260 |
| 2011P Vapor blast finish | 24,625 | 190 | 240 |

**KM# 514 • RevDesc:** Northeast slope of Mount Reynolds • 155.55 g., 0.999 **Silver** 4.996 oz. ASW • **Rev. Designer:** Barbara Fox and Charles L. Vickers

| Date | Mintage | MS65 | MS69 |
|---|---|---|---|
| 2011 | 126,700 | 200 | 260 |
| 2011P Vapor blast finish | 20,503 | 190 | 240 |

**KM# 515 • RevDesc:** Roosevelt elk on a gravel river bar along the Hoh River, Mount Olympus in the background • 155.55 g., 0.999 **Silver** 4.996 oz. ASW • **Rev. Designer:** Susan Gambel and Michael Gaudioso

| Date | Mintage | MS65 | MS69 |
|---|---|---|---|
| 2011 | 85,900 | 200 | 260 |
| 2011P Vapor blast finish | 17,988 | 190 | 240 |

**KM# 516 • RevDesc:** U.S.S. Cairo on the Yazoo River • 155.55 g., 0.999 **Silver** 4.996 oz. ASW • **Rev. Designer:** Thomas Cleveland and Joseph menna

| Date | Mintage | MS65 | MS69 |
|---|---|---|---|
| 2011 | 39,500 | 200 | 260 |
| 2011P Vapor blast finish | 18,181 | 190 | 240 |

**KM# 517 • RevDesc:** Limestone Lincoln Bridge • 155.55 g., 0.999 **Silver** 4.996 oz. ASW • **Rev. Designer:** Donna Weaver and James Licaretz

| Date | Mintage | MS65 | MS69 |
|---|---|---|---|
| 2011 | 29,700 | 200 | 260 |
| 2011P Vapor blast finish | 16,386 | 190 | 240 |

**KM# 536 • RevDesc:** Coquin tree frog and Puerto Rico parrot • 155.55 g., 0.999 **Silver** 4.996 oz. ASW

| Date | Mintage | MS65 | MS69 |
|---|---|---|---|
| 2012 | 21,900 | 200 | 260 |
| 2012P Vapor blast finish | 15,271 | 190 | 240 |

**KM# 537 • RevDesc:** Two elevated kivas at Chetro Ketl complex • 155.52 g., 0.999 **Silver** 4.9951 oz. ASW

| Date | Mintage | MS65 | MS69 |
|---|---|---|---|
| 2012 | 20,000 | 200 | 260 |
| 2012P Vapor blast finish | 12,679 | 190 | 240 |

**KM# 538 • RevDesc:** Bass Harbor Head Lighthouse • 155.52 g., 0.999 **Silver** 4.9951 oz. ASW

| Date | Mintage | MS65 | MS69 |
|---|---|---|---|
| 2012 | 25,400 | 200 | 260 |
| 2012P Vapor blast finish | 13,196 | 190 | 240 |

**KM# 539 • RevDesc:** Volcano erupting • 155.52 g., 0.999 **Silver** 4.9951 oz. ASW

| Date | Mintage | MS65 | MS69 |
|---|---|---|---|
| 2012 | 20,000 | 200 | 260 |
| 2012P Vapor blast finish | 13,789 | 190 | 240 |

**KM# 540 • RevDesc:** Dall sheep and Mount McKinley • 155.55 g., 0.999 **Silver** 4.9961 oz. ASW

| Date | Mintage | MS65 | MS69 |
|---|---|---|---|
| 2012 | 20,000 | 200 | 260 |
| 2012P Vapor blast finish | 10,180 | 190 | 240 |

**KM# 556 • RevDesc:** Mountain vista • 155.55 g., 0.999 **Silver** 4.996 oz. ASW

| Date | Mintage | MS65 | MS69 |
|---|---|---|---|
| 2013 | 35,000 | 200 | 260 |
| 2013P Vapor blast finish | 20,530 | 190 | 240 |

**KM# 557** • **RevDesc:** Perry standing and Memorial column • 155.55 g., 0.999 **Silver** 4.996 oz. ASW

| Date | Mintage | MS65 | MS69 |
|---|---|---|---|
| 2013 | 30,000 | 200 | 260 |
| 2013P Vapor blast finsih | 17,707 | 190 | 240 |

**KM# 558** • **RevDesc:** Ancient weatherworn tree • 155.55 g., 0.999 **Silver** 4.996 oz. ASW

| Date | Mintage | MS65 | MS69 |
|---|---|---|---|
| 2013 | 30,000 | 190 | 240 |
| 2013P Vapor blast finish | 17,792 | 200 | 260 |

**KM# 559** • **RevDesc:** Fort McHenry and flag • 155.55 g., 0.999 **Silver** 4.996 oz. ASW

| Date | Mintage | MS65 | MS69 |
|---|---|---|---|
| 2013 | 30,000 | 200 | 260 |
| 2013 Vapor blast finish | 19,802 | 190 | 240 |

**KM# 560** • **RevDesc:** Presidential head sculpture on Mt. Rushmore • 155.55 g., 0.999 **Silver** 4.996 oz. ASW

| Date | Mintage | MS65 | MS69 |
|---|---|---|---|
| 2013 | 35,000 | 190 | 240 |
| 2013P Vapor blast finish | 23,547 | 200 | 260 |

**KM# 580**155.550 **Silver** ASW

| Date | Mintage | MS65 | MS69 |
|---|---|---|---|
| 2014 | 29,500 | 200 | 260 |
| 2014P Vapor blast finish | 24,705 | 190 | 240 |

**KM# 581** • 155.55 g., 0.999 **Silver** 4.996 oz. ASW

| Date | Mintage | MS65 | MS69 |
|---|---|---|---|
| 2014 | — | — | 260 |
| 2014P Vapor blast finish | — | — | 240 |

**KM# 582** • 155.55 g., 0.999 **Silver** 4.996 oz. ASW

| Date | Mintage | MS65 | MS69 |
|---|---|---|---|
| 2014 | — | 200 | 260 |
| 2014P Vapor blast finish | — | 190 | 240 |

**KM# 583** • 155.55 g., 0.999 **Silver** 4.996 oz. ASW

| Date | Mintage | MS65 | MS69 |
|---|---|---|---|
| 2014 | — | 200 | 260 |
| 2014P Vapor blast finish | — | 190 | 240 |

**KM# 584** • 155.55 g., 0.999 **Silver** 4.996 oz. ASW

| Date | Mintage | MS65 | MS69 |
|---|---|---|---|
| 2014 | — | 200 | 260 |
| 2014P Vapor blast finish | — | 190 | 240 |

# AMERICAN EAGLE BULLION COINS

## SILVER DOLLAR

**KM# 273 • ObvDesc:** Liberty walking left • **RevDesc:** Eagle with shield • 31.11 g., 0.9993 **Silver** 0.9993 oz. ASW, 40.6 • **Obv. Designer:** Adolph A. Weinman • **Rev. Designer:** John Mercanti

| Date | Mintage | MS65 | Prf65 |
|---|---|---|---|
| 2001 | 9,001,711 | 26.80 | — |
| 2001W | 746,398 | — | 38.00 |
| 2002W | 10,539,026 | 26.80 | — |
| 2002 | 647,342 | — | 48.00 |
| 2003W | 8,495,008 | 23.30 | — |
| 2003 | 747,831 | — | 48.00 |
| 2004 | 8,882,754 | — | 48.00 |
| 2004W | 801,602 | 23.30 | — |
| 2005 | 8,891,025 | 23.30 | — |
| 2005W | 816,663 | — | 38.00 |
| 2006 | 10,676,522 | 23.30 | — |
| 2006P Burnished Unc. | 468,000 | 70.00 | — |
| 2006W | 1,093,600 | — | 38.00 |
| 2006W Reverse Proof | Est. 250000 | — | 215 |
| 2006 20th Aniv. 3 pc. set | — | — | 345 |
| 2007W | 9,028,036 | 23.30 | — |
| 2007W Burnished Unc. | 690,891 | 23.30 | — |
| 2007 | 821,759 | — | 38.00 |
| 2008W | 20,583,000 | 23.30 | — |
| 2008 Burnished Unc. | Est. 550000 | 60.00 | — |
| 2008 Reverse of '07, U in United with rounded bottom. | Est. 47000 | 525 | — |
| 2008W | 713,353 | — | 38.00 |
| 2009 | 30,459,000 | 23.30 | — |
| 2010 | 34,764,500 | 23.30 | — |
| 2010 | — | — | 38.00 |
| 2011W | 39,764,500 | 22.30 | — |
| 2011P Reverse Proof | 100,000 | — | 280 |
| 2011 Burnished Unc. | 100,000 | 45.00 | — |
| 2011S Burnished Unc. | — | 265 | — |
| 2011W | 850,000 | — | 45.00 |
| 2012 | — | 20.30 | — |
| 2012S Reverse Proof | — | — | 110 |
| 2012 | 60,203 | — | 41.00 |
| 2012W Burnished Unc. | 33,742,500 | 62.00 | — |
| 2013W | 178,941 | 20.30 | — |
| 2013W Enhanced Finish | — | 93.50 | — |
| 2013 | — | — | 42.00 |
| 2013 Enhanced Finish | — | 26.00 | — |
| 2013W Enhanced Finish Reverse Proof | — | — | 65.00 |
| 2014 | — | 20.30 | — |
| 2014 | — | — | 42.00 |

## GOLD $5

**KM# 216 •** 3.39 g., 0.9167 **Gold** 0.100 oz. AGW, 16.5 • **Obv. Designer:** Augustus Saint-Gaudens • **Rev. Designer:** Miley Busiek

| Date | Mintage | MS65 | Prf65 |
|---|---|---|---|
| 2001 | 269,147 | 145 | — |
| 2001W | 37,530 | — | 147 |
| 2002 | 230,027 | 175 | — |
| 2002W | 40,864 | — | 147 |
| 2003W | 245,029 | 175 | — |
| 2003 | 40,027 | — | 147 |
| 2004W | 250,016 | 195 | — |
| 2004 | 35,131 | — | 225 |
| 2005W | 300,043 | 145 | — |
| 2005 | 49,265 | — | 225 |
| 2006W | 285,006 | 175 | — |
| 2006 Burnished Unc. | 20,643 | 175 | — |
| 2006W | 47,277 | — | 147 |
| 2007 | 190,010 | 175 | — |
| 2007W Burnished Unc. | 22,501 | 190 | — |
| 2007W | 58,553 | — | 147 |
| 2008W | 305,000 | 145 | — |
| 2008 Burnished Unc. | 12,657 | 325 | — |
| 2008W | Est. 29000 | — | 147 |
| 2009 | 27,000 | 143 | — |
| 2010 | 435,000 | 151 | — |
| 2010W | 54,285 | — | 147 |
| 2011 | 350,000 | 185 | — |
| 2011W | 42,697 | — | 147 |
| 2012W | — | 149 | — |
| 2012W | 20,740 | — | 225 |
| 2013W | — | 165 | — |
| 2013 | 21,879 | — | 200 |
| 2014 | — | 165 | — |
| 2014 | — | — | 200 |

## GOLD $10

**KM# 217 •** 8.48 g., 0.9167 **Gold** 0.250 oz. AGW, 22 • **Obv. Designer:** Augustus Saint-Gaudens • **Rev. Designer:** Miley Busiek

| Date | Mintage | MS65 | Prf65 |
|---|---|---|---|
| 2001 | 71,280 | — | 345 |
| 2001W | 25,613 | 605 | — |
| 2002 | 62,027 | — | 345 |
| 2002W | 29,242 | 605 | — |
| 2003 | 74,029 | 353 | — |
| 2003W | 30,292 | — | 345 |
| 2004 | 72,014 | — | 345 |
| 2004W | 28,839 | 353 | — |
| 2005 | 72,015 | 353 | — |
| 2005W | 37,207 | — | 345 |
| 2006 | 60,004 | 353 | — |
| 2006W Burnished Unc. | 15,188 | — | 345 |
| 2006W | 36,127 | 600 | — |
| 2007 | 34,004 | 610 | — |
| 2007W Burnished Unc. | 12,786 | — | 345 |
| 2007W | 46,189 | — | 610 |
| 2008 | Est. 58000 | 625 | — |
| 2008W Burnished Unc. | 8,883 | — | 715 |
| 2008W | 28,000 | 336 | — |
| 2009 | 110,000 | 353 | — |
| 2010 | 86,000 | 353 | — |
| 2010W | 44,507 | — | 345 |
| 2011 | 80,000 | — | 345 |
| 2011W | 28,782 | 353 | — |
| 2012 | — | 353 | — |
| 2012W | 13,375 | — | 345 |
| 2013 | — | 353 | — |
| 2013 | 12,642 | — | 475 |
| 2014 | — | 353 | — |
| 2014 | — | — | 475 |

## GOLD $25

**KM# 218 •** 16.97 g., 0.9167 **Gold** 0.500 oz. AGW, 27 • **Obv. Designer:** Augustus Saint-Gaudens • **Rev. Designer:** Miley Busiek

| Date | Mintage | MS65 | Prf65 |
|---|---|---|---|
| 2001 | 48,047 | — | 700 |
| 2001W | 23,240 | 1,550 | — |
| 2002 | 70,027 | 1,050 | — |
| 2002W | 26,646 | — | 700 |
| 2003 | 79,029 | — | 700 |
| 2003W | 28,270 | 666 | — |
| 2004 | 98,040 | 666 | — |
| 2004W | 27,330 | — | 700 |
| 2005 | 80,023 | — | 700 |
| 2005W | 34,311 | 666 | — |
| 2006 | 66,004 | — | 700 |
| 2006W Burnished Unc. | 15,164 | 1,000 | — |
| 2006W | 34,322 | 669 | — |
| 2007 | 47,002 | 1,115 | — |
| 2007W Burnished Unc. | 11,458 | — | 700 |
| 2007W | 44,025 | 1,025 | — |
| 2008 | 61,000 | 1,550 | — |
| 2008W Burnished Unc. | 15,683 | — | 860 |
| 2008W | 27,800 | 669 | — |
| 2009 | 55,000 | 669 | — |
| 2010 | 81,000 | 666 | — |
| 2010W | 44,527 | — | 700 |
| 2011 | 70,000 | — | 700 |
| 2011W | 26,781 | 666 | — |
| 2012W | — | 666 | — |
| 2013W | 12,570 | — | 975 |
| 2013 | — | 666 | — |
| 2014 | — | 666 | — |
| 2014 | — | — | 975 |

## GOLD $50

**KM# 219 •** 33.93 g., 0.9167 **Gold** 1.000 oz. AGW, 32.7 • **Obv. Designer:** Augustus Saint-Gaudens • **Rev. Designer:** Miley Busiek

| Date | Mintage | MS65 | Prf65 |
|---|---|---|---|
| 2001 | 143,605 | 1,273 | — |
| 2001W | 24,555 | — | 1,295 |
| 2002 | 222,029 | 1,273 | — |
| 2002W | 27,499 | — | 1,295 |
| 2003 | 416,032 | 1,273 | — |
| 2003W | 28,344 | — | 1,295 |
| 2004 | 417,149 | 1,273 | — |
| 2004W | 28,215 | — | 1,295 |
| 2005W | 356,555 | 1,273 | — |
| 2005 | 35,246 | — | 1,295 |
| 2006 | 237,510 | 1,273 | — |
| 2006W Burnished Unc. | 45,912 | 1,340 | — |
| 2006W | 47,000 | — | 1,295 |
| 2006W Reverse Proof | 10,000 | — | 2,600 |
| 2007W | 140,016 | 1,285 | — |
| 2007W Burnished Unc. | 18,609 | 1,675 | — |
| 2007 | 51,810 | — | 1,295 |
| 2008W | 710,000 | 1,273 | — |
| 2008W Burnished Unc. | 11,908 | 2,200 | — |
| 2008W Reverse of '07 | — | — | |
| 2008W | 29,000 | — | 2,150 |
| 2009 | 122,000 | 1,273 | — |
| 2010W | 1,125,000 | 1,273 | — |
| 2010 | 59,480 | — | 1,295 |
| 2011 | 857,000 | 1,273 | — |
| 2011 Burnished Unc. | 8,729 | 2,350 | — |
| 2011W | 48,306 | — | 1,295 |
| 2012W | — | 1,273 | — |
| 2012 Burnished Unc. | 5,829 | 2,800 | — |
| 2013W | 24,753 | 1,273 | — |
| 2013 | — | — | 1,850 |
| 2014 | — | — | 1,850 |
| 2014 | — | 1,273 | — |

## PLATINUM $10

**KM# 283 • RevDesc:** Eagle flying right over sunrise • 3.11 g., 0.9995 **Platinum** 0.0999 oz. APW, 17 • **Obv. Designer:** John Mercanti • **Rev. Designer:** Thomas D. Rogers Sr

| Date | Mintage | MS65 | Prf65 |
|---|---|---|---|
| 2001 | 52,017 | 156 | — |
| 2002 | 23,005 | 156 | — |
| 2003 | 22,007 | 156 | — |
| 2004 | 15,010 | 156 | — |
| 2005 | 14,013 | 156 | — |
| 2006 | 11,001 | 425 | — |
| 2006W Burnished Unc. | — | 156 | — |
| 2007 | 13,003 | 590 | — |
| 2007W Burnished Unc. | — | 364 | — |
| 2008 | 17,000 | 156 | — |
| 2008 Burnished Unc. | — | 310 | — |

**KM# 327 • RevDesc:** Eagle in flight over Southwestern cactus desert • 3.11 g., 0.9995 **Platinum** 0.0999 oz. APW, 17 • **Obv. Designer:** John Mercanti

| Date | Mintage | MS65 | Prf65 |
|---|---|---|---|
| 2001W | 12,174 | — | 180 |

**KM# 339 • RevDesc:** Eagle fishing in America's Northwest • 3.11 g., 0.9995 **Platinum** 0.0999 oz. APW, 17 • **Obv. Designer:** John Mercanti

| Date | Mintage | MS65 | Prf65 |
|---|---|---|---|
| 2002W | 12,365 | — | 180 |

**KM# 351 • RevDesc:** Eagle pearched on a Rocky Mountain Pine branch against a flag backdrop • 3.11 g., 0.9995 **Platinum** 0.0999 oz. APW, 17 • **Obv. Designer:** John Mercanti • **Rev. Designer:** Al Maletsky

| Date | Mintage | MS65 | Prf65 |
|---|---|---|---|
| 2003W | 9,534 | — | 368 |

**KM# 364 • RevDesc:** Chester French, 1907. The sculpture is outside the N.Y. Customs House, now part of the Smithsonian's Museum of the American Indian • 3.11 g., 0.9995 **Platinum** 0.0999 oz. APW, 17 • **Obv. Designer:** John Mercanti

| Date | Mintage | MS65 | Prf65 |
|---|---|---|---|
| 2004W | 7,161 | — | 445 |

**KM# 377 • RevDesc:** Eagle with cornucopiae • 3.11 g., 0.9995 **Platinum** 0.0999 oz. APW, 17 • **Obv. Designer:** John Mercanti • **Rev. Designer:** Donna Weaver

| Date | Mintage | MS65 | Prf65 |
|---|---|---|---|
| 2005W | 8,104 | — | 265 |

**KM# 389 • RevDesc:** Liberty seated writing between two columns • 3.11 g., 0.9995 **Platinum** 0.0999 oz. APW, 17 • **Obv. Designer:** John Mercanti

| Date | Mintage | MS65 | Prf65 |
|---|---|---|---|
| 2006W | 10,205 | — | 180 |

**KM# 414 • RevDesc:** Eagle with shield • 3.11 g., 0.9995 **Platinum** 0.0999 oz. APW, 17 • **Obv. Designer:** John Mercanti

| Date | Mintage | MS65 | Prf65 |
|---|---|---|---|
| 2007W | 8,176 | — | 180 |

**KM# 434 • RevDesc:** Justice standing before eagle • 3.11 g., 0.9995 **Platinum** 0.0999 oz. APW, 17 • **Obv. Designer:** John Mercanti

| Date | Mintage | MS65 | Prf65 |
|---|---|---|---|
| 2008W | 8,176 | — | 495 |

**KM# 460** • 3.11 g., 0.9995 **Platinum** 0.0999 oz. APW, 17 • **Obv. Designer:** John Mercanti

| Date | Mintage | MS65 | Prf65 |
|---|---|---|---|
| 2009W | 5,600 | — | — |

## PLATINUM $25

**KM# 284 • RevDesc:** Eagle in flight over sunrise • 7.79 g., 0.9995 **Platinum** 0.2502 oz. APW, 22 • **Obv. Designer:** John Mercanti • **Rev. Designer:** Thomas D. Rogers Sr

| Date | Mintage | MS65 | Prf65 |
|---|---|---|---|
| 2001 | 21,815 | 364 | — |
| 2002 | 27,405 | 364 | — |
| 2003 | 25,207 | 364 | — |
| 2004 | 18,010 | 364 | — |
| 2005 | 12,013 | 364 | — |
| 2006 | 12,001 | 375 | — |
| 2006W Burnished Unc. | — | 590 | — |
| 2007 | 8,402 | 364 | — |
| 2007W Burnished Unc. | — | 590 | — |
| 2008 | — | 336 | — |
| 2008 Burnished Unc. | 22,800 | 625 | — |

**KM# 328 • RevDesc:** Eagle in flight over Southwestern cactus desert • 7.79 g., 0.9995 **Platinum** 0.2502 oz. APW, 22 • **Obv. Designer:** John Mercanti

| Date | Mintage | MS65 | Prf65 |
|---|---|---|---|
| 2001W | 8,847 | — | 368 |

**KM# 340 • RevDesc:** Eagle fishing in America's Northwest • 7.79 g., 0.9995 **Platinum** 0.2502 oz. APW, 22 • **Obv. Designer:** John Mercanti

| Date | Mintage | MS65 | Prf65 |
|---|---|---|---|
| 2002W | 9,282 | — | 368 |

**KM# 352 • RevDesc:** Eagle pearched on a Rocky Mountain Pine branch against a flag backdrop. • 7.79 g., 0.9995 **Platinum** 0.2502 oz. APW, 22 • **Obv. Designer:** John Mercanti • **Rev. Designer:** Al Maletsky

| Date | Mintage | MS65 | Prf65 |
|---|---|---|---|
| 2003W | 7,044 | — | 368 |

**KM# 365 • RevDesc:** Chester French, 1907. The sculpture is outside the N.Y. Customs House, now part of the Smithsonian's Museum of the American Indian • 7.79 g., 0.9995 **Platinum** 0.2502 oz. APW, 22 • **Obv. Designer:** John Mercanti

| Date | Mintage | MS65 | Prf65 |
|---|---|---|---|
| 2004W | 5,193 | — | 1,000 |

**KM# 378 • RevDesc:** Eagle with cornucopiae • 7.79 g., 0.9995 **Platinum** 0.2502 oz. APW, 22 • **Obv. Designer:** John Mercanti • **Rev. Designer:** Donna Weaver

| Date | Mintage | MS65 | Prf65 |
|---|---|---|---|
| 2005W | 6,592 | — | 610 |

**KM# 390 • RevDesc:** Liberty seated writing between two columns • 7.79 g., 0.9995 **Platinum** 0.2502 oz. APW, 22 • **Obv. Designer:** John Mercanti

| Date | Mintage | MS65 | Prf65 |
|---|---|---|---|
| 2006W | 7,813 | — | 368 |

**KM# 415 • RevDesc:** Eagle with shield • 7.79 g., 0.9995 **Platinum** 0.2502 oz. APW, 22 • **Obv. Designer:** John Mercanti

| Date | Mintage | MS65 | Prf65 |
|---|---|---|---|
| 2007W Polished Freedom | 6,017 | — | 368 |
| 2007W Frosted Freedom, Rare | — | — | — |

**KM# 435 • RevDesc:** Justice holding scales, standing before eagle • 7.79 g., 0.9995 **Platinum** 0.2502 oz. APW, 22 • **Obv. Designer:** John Mercanti

| Date | Mintage | MS65 | Prf65 |
|---|---|---|---|
| 2008W | 6,017 | — | 715 |

**KM# 461** • 7.79 g., 0.9995 **Platinum** 0.2502 oz. APW, 22 • **Obv. Designer:** John Mercanti

| Date | Mintage | MS65 | Prf65 |
|---|---|---|---|
| 2009W | 3,800 | — | 374 |

## PLATINUM $50

**KM# 285 • RevDesc:** Eagle flying right over sunrise • 15.55 g., 0.9995 **Platinum** 0.4998 oz. APW, 27 • **Obv. Designer:** John Mercanti • **Rev. Designer:** Thomas D. Rogers Sr

| Date | Mintage | MS65 | Prf65 |
|---|---|---|---|
| 2001 | 12,815 | 732 | — |
| 2002 | 24,005 | 732 | — |
| 2003 | 17,409 | 732 | — |
| 2004 | 13,236 | 732 | — |
| 2005 | 9,013 | 732 | — |
| 2006W | 9,602 | 844 | — |
| 2006 Burnished Unc. | — | 844 | — |
| 2007W | 7,001 | 732 | — |
| 2007 Burnished Unc. | — | 844 | — |
| 2008 | 14,000 | 732 | — |
| 2008W Burnished Unc. | — | 1,100 | — |

**KM# 329 • RevDesc:** Eagle in flight over Southwestern cactus desert • 15.55 g., 0.9995 **Platinum** 0.4998 oz. APW, 27 • **Obv. Designer:** John Mercanti

| Date | Mintage | MS65 | Prf65 |
|---|---|---|---|
| 2001W | 8,254 | — | 730 |

**KM# 341 • RevDesc:** Eagle fishing in America's Northwest • 15.55 g., 0.9995 **Platinum** 0.4998 oz. APW, 27 • **Obv. Designer:** John Mercanti

| Date | Mintage | MS65 | Prf65 |
|---|---|---|---|
| 2002W | 8,772 | — | 730 |

**KM# 353 • RevDesc:** Eagle pearched on a Rocky Mountain Pine branch against a flag backdrop • 15.55 g., 0.9995 **Platinum** 0.4998 oz. APW, 27 • **Obv. Designer:** John Mercanti • **Rev. Designer:** Al Maletsky

| Date | Mintage | MS65 | Prf65 |
|---|---|---|---|
| 2003W | 7,131 | — | 730 |

**KM# 366 • RevDesc:** Chester French, 1907. The sculpture is outside the N.Y. Customs House, now part of the Smithsonian's Museum of the American Indian • 15.55 g., 0.9995 **Platinum** 0.4998 oz. APW, 27 • **Obv. Designer:** John Mercanti

| Date | Mintage | MS65 | Prf65 |
|---|---|---|---|
| 2004W | 5,063 | — | 1,550 |

**KM# 379 • RevDesc:** Eagle with cornucopiae • 15.55 g., 0.9995 **Platinum** 0.4998 oz. APW, 27 • **Obv. Designer:** John Mercanti • **Rev. Designer:** Donna Weaver

| Date | Mintage | MS65 | Prf65 |
|---|---|---|---|
| 2005W | 5,942 | — | 1,175 |

**KM# 391 • RevDesc:** Liberty seated writing between two columns • 15.55 g., 0.9995 **Platinum** 0.4998 oz. APW, 27 • **Obv. Designer:** John Mercanti

| Date | Mintage | MS65 | Prf65 |
|---|---|---|---|
| 2006W | 7,649 | — | 730 |

**KM# 416 • RevDesc:** Eagle with shield • 15.55 g., 0.9995 **Platinum** 0.4998 oz. APW, 27 • **Obv. Designer:** John Mercanti

| Date | Mintage | MS65 | Prf65 |
|---|---|---|---|
| 2007W Reverse Proof | 22,873 | — | 730 |
| 2007W Frosted Freedom, Rare | — | — | — |

**KM# 436 • RevDesc:** Justice standing before eagle • 15.55 g., 0.9995 **Platinum** 0.4998 oz. APW, 27 • **Obv. Designer:** John Mercanti

| Date | Mintage | MS65 | Prf65 |
|---|---|---|---|
| 2008W | 22,873 | — | 1,225 |

**KM# 462 •** 15.55 g., 0.9995 **Platinum** 0.4998 oz. APW, 27 • **Obv. Designer:** John Mercanti

| Date | Mintage | MS65 | Prf65 |
|---|---|---|---|
| 2009 | 3,600 | — | — |

## PLATINUM $100

**KM# 286 • ObvDesc:** Statue of Liberty • **RevDesc:** Eagle in flight over sun rise • 31.11 g., 0.9995 **Platinum** 0.9995 oz. APW, 33 • **Obv. Designer:** John Mercanti • **Rev. Designer:** Thomas D. Rogers Sr

| Date | Mintage | MS65 | Prf65 |
|---|---|---|---|
| 2001 | 14,070 | 1,344 | — |
| 2002 | 11,502 | 1,344 | — |
| 2003 | 8,007 | 1,344 | — |
| 2004 | 7,009 | 1,344 | — |
| 2005 | 6,310 | 1,344 | — |
| 2006 | 6,000 | 1,344 | — |
| 2006W Burnished Unc. | — | 2,200 | — |
| 2007W | — | 1,380 | — |
| 2007 Burnished Unc. | 7,202 | 2,100 | — |
| 2008 | 21,800 | 1,350 | — |
| 2008W Burnished Unc. | — | 2,500 | — |
| 2011 | — | — | — |

**KM# 330 • RevDesc:** Eagle in flight over Southwestern cactus desert • 31.11 g., 0.9995 **Platinum** 0.9995 oz. APW, 33 • **Obv. Designer:** John Mercanti

| Date | Mintage | MS65 | Prf65 |
|---|---|---|---|
| 2001W | 8,969 | — | 1,350 |

**KM# 342 • RevDesc:** Eagle fishing in America's Northwest • 31.11 g., 0.9995 **Platinum** 0.9995 oz. APW, 33 • **Obv. Designer:** John Mercanti

| Date | Mintage | MS65 | Prf65 |
|---|---|---|---|
| 2002W | 9,834 | — | 1,350 |

**KM# 354 • RevDesc:** Eagle pearched on a Rocky Mountain Pine branch against a flag backdrop • 31.11 g., 0.9995 **Platinum** 0.9995 oz. APW, 33 • **Obv. Designer:** John Mercanti • **Rev. Designer:** Al Maletsky

| Date | Mintage | MS65 | Prf65 |
|---|---|---|---|
| 2003W | 8,246 | — | 1,363 |

**KM# 367 • RevDesc:** Inspired by the sculpture "America" by Daniel Chester French, 1907. The sculpture is outside the N.Y. Customs House, now part of the Smithsonian's Museum of the American Indian • 31.11 g., 0.9995 **Platinum** 0.9995 oz. APW, 33 • **Obv. Designer:** John Mercanti • **Rev. Designer:** Donna Weaver

| Date | Mintage | MS65 | Prf65 |
|---|---|---|---|
| 2004W | 6,007 | — | 1,625 |

**KM# 380 • RevDesc:** Eagle with cornucopiae • 31.11 g., 0.9995 **Platinum** 0.9995 oz. APW, 33 • **Obv. Designer:** John Mercanti • **Rev. Designer:** Donna Weaver

| Date | Mintage | MS65 | Prf65 |
|---|---|---|---|
| 2005W | 6,602 | — | 2,400 |

**KM# 392 • RevDesc:** Liberty seated writing between two columns • 31.11 g., 0.9995 **Platinum** 0.9995 oz. APW, 33 • **Obv. Designer:** John Mercanti

| Date | Mintage | MS65 | Prf65 |
|---|---|---|---|
| 2006W | 9,152 | — | 1,350 |

**KM# 417 • RevDesc:** Eagle with shield • 31.11 g., 0.9995 **Platinum** 0.9995 oz. APW, 33 • **Obv. Designer:** John Mercanti

| Date | Mintage | MS65 | Prf65 |
|---|---|---|---|
| 2007W Freedom Frosted | 8,363 | — | 1,375 |
| 2007W Freedom Polished | — | — | 50,000 |

**KM# 437 • RevDesc:** Justice standing before eagle • 31.11 g., 0.9995 **Platinum** 0.9995 oz. APW, 33 • **Obv. Designer:** John Mercanti

| Date | Mintage | MS65 | Prf65 |
|---|---|---|---|
| 2008W | 8,363 | — | 3,000 |

**KM# 463** • **RevDesc:** Four portraits • 31.10 g., 0.9995 **Platinum** 0.9995 oz. APW, 33 • **Obv. Designer:** John Mercanti

| Date | Mintage | MS65 | Prf65 |
|---|---|---|---|
| 2009W Proof | 4,900 | — | 2,260 |

**KM# 488** • **RevDesc:** Statue of Justice holding scales • 31.11 g., 0.999 **Platinum** 0.999 oz. APW, 33 • **Obv. Designer:** John Mercanti

| Date | Mintage | MS65 | Prf65 |
|---|---|---|---|
| 2010W | — | — | 2,175 |

**KM# 518** • **RevDesc:** Female with dove, walking in field • 31.11 g., 0.9995 **Platinum** 0.9995 oz. APW, 33

| Date | Mintage | MS65 | Prf65 |
|---|---|---|---|
| 2011W | 10,299 | — | 1,650 |

**KM# 541** • **RevDesc:** Colonial soldier and flag • 31.11 g., 0.9995 **Platinum** 0.9995 oz. APW, 33

| Date | Mintage | MS65 | Prf65 |
|---|---|---|---|
| 2012 | — | — | 1,400 |

**KM# 585** • **RevDesc:** Female and gears of industry • 31.11 g., 0.9995 **Platinum** 0.9995 oz. APW, 33

| Date | Mintage | MS65 | Prf65 |
|---|---|---|---|
| 2013 | — | — | 1,538 |

**KM# 586** • 31.11 g., 0.9995 **Platinum** 0.9995 oz. APW, 33

| Date | Mintage | MS65 | Prf65 |
|---|---|---|---|
| 2014W | — | — | 1,620 |

# BISON BULLION COINAGE

## GOLD $5

**KM# 411** • **ObvDesc:** Indian Head right • **RevDesc:** Bison • 3.11 g., 0.9999 **Gold** 0.100 oz. AGW

| Date | Mintage | MS65 | Prf65 |
|---|---|---|---|
| 2008W | 17,429 | 600 | — |
| 2008W | 18,884 | — | 660 |

## GOLD $10

**KM# 412** • **ObvDesc:** Indian Head right • **RevDesc:** Bison • 7.79 g., 0.9999 **Gold** 0.2503 oz. AGW

| Date | Mintage | MS65 | Prf65 |
|---|---|---|---|
| 2008W | 9,949 | 1,375 | — |
| 2008W | 13,125 | — | 1,550 |

## GOLD $25

**KM# 413** • **ObvDesc:** Indian Head right • **RevDesc:** Bison • 15.55 g., 0.999 **Gold** 0.4995 oz. AGW

| Date | Mintage | MS65 | Prf65 |
|---|---|---|---|
| 2008W | 16,908 | 1,350 | — |
| 2008W | 12,169 | — | 1,850 |

## GOLD $50

**KM# 393** • **ObvDesc:** Indian head right • **RevDesc:** Bison standing left on mound • 31.11 g., 0.9999 **Gold** 0.9999 oz. AGW, 32 • **Designer:** James E. Fraser

| Date | Mintage | MS65 | Prf65 |
|---|---|---|---|
| 2006 | 337,012 | 1,273 | — |
| 2006W Proof | 246,267 | — | 1,435 |
| 2007 | 136,503 | 1,273 | — |
| 2007W Proof | 58,998 | — | 1,435 |
| 2008 | 189,500 | 1,273 | — |
| 2008W Burnished | 18,863 | — | 3,200 |
| 2008W Moy Family Chop, Proof | — | — | 3,950 |
| 2009 | 200,000 | 1,273 | — |
| 2009W Proof | 49,306 | — | 1,405 |
| 2010 | 209,000 | 1,273 | — |
| 2010W Proof | 49,263 | — | 1,435 |
| 2011W | 174,500 | 1,273 | — |
| 2011 Proof | 28,693 | — | 1,435 |
| 2012 | 132,000 | 1,273 | — |
| 2012W Proof | 19,765 | — | 2,000 |
| 2013W | — | 1,273 | — |
| 2013 Reverse Proof | 47,836 | 1,950 | |
| 2014 | — | 1,273 | — |
| 2014 | — | — | 1,950 |

# FIRST SPOUSE GOLD COINAGE

## GOLD $10

**KM# 407** • **ObvDesc:** Bust 3/4 facing • **RevDesc:** Martha Washington seated sewing • 15.55 g., 0.9999 **Gold** 0.500 oz. AGW, 26.5 • **Obv. Designer:** Joseph Menna • **Rev. Designer:** Susan Gamble and Don Everhart

| Date | Mintage | MS65 | Prf65 |
|---|---|---|---|
| 2007W | 17,661 | 654 | — |
| 2007W | 19,169 | — | 654 |

**KM# 408** • **ObvDesc:** Bust 3/4 facing • **RevDesc:** Abigail Adams seated at desk writing to John during the Revolutionary War • 15.55 g., 0.9999 **Gold** 0.500 oz. AGW, 26.5 • **Obv. Designer:** Joseph Menna • **Rev. Designer:** Thomas Cleveland and Phebe Hemphill

| Date | Mintage | MS65 | Prf65 |
|---|---|---|---|
| 2007W | 17,142 | — | 654 |
| 2007W | 17,149 | 654 | — |

**KM# 409** • **ObvDesc:** Bust design from coinage • **RevDesc:** Jefferson's tombstone • 15.55 g., 0.9999 **Gold** 0.500 oz. AGW, 26.5 • **Obv. Designer:** Robert Scot and Phebe Hemphill • **Rev. Designer:** Charles Vickers

| Date | Mintage | MS65 | Prf65 |
|---|---|---|---|
| 2007W | 19,823 | — | 654 |
| 2007W | 19,815 | 654 | — |

**KM# 410** • **ObvDesc:** Bust 3/4 facing • **RevDesc:** Dolley standing before painting of Washington, which she saved from the White House • 15.55 g., 0.9999 **Gold** 0.500 oz. AGW, 26.5 • **Obv. Designer:** Don Everhart • **Rev. Designer:** Joel Iskowitz and Don Everhart

| Date | Mintage | MS65 | Prf65 |
|---|---|---|---|
| 2007W | 11,813 | 654 | — |
| 2007W | 17,661 | — | 654 |

**KM# 430** • **ObvDesc:** Bust 3/4 facing right • **RevDesc:** Elizabeth standing before mirror • 15.55 g., 0.999 **Gold** 0.4995 oz. AGW, 26.5 • **Obv. Designer:** Joel Iskowitz and Don Everhart • **Rev. Designer:** Donna Weaver and Charles Vickers

| Date | Mintage | MS65 | Prf65 |
|---|---|---|---|
| 2008W | 4,519 | 695 | — |
| 2008W | 7,933 | — | 725 |

**KM# 431** • **ObvDesc:** Bust 3/4 facing right • **RevDesc:** Lousia and son Charles before entrance • 15.55 g., 0.999 **Gold** 0.4995 oz. AGW, 26.5 • **Obv. Designer:** Susan Gamble and Phebe Hemphill • **Rev. Designer:** Joseph Menna

| Date | Mintage | MS65 | Prf65 |
|---|---|---|---|
| 2008W | 4,223 | 735 | — |
| 2008W | 7,454 | — | 765 |

**KM# 432** • **ObvDesc:** Capped and draped bust left • **RevDesc:** Andrew Jackson on horseback right • 15.55 g., 0.999 **Gold** 0.4995 oz. AGW, 26.5 • **Obv. Designer:** John Reich • **Rev. Designer:** Justin Kunz and Don Everhart

| Date | Mintage | MS65 | Prf65 |
|---|---|---|---|
| 2008W | 4,281 | 900 | — |
| 2008W | 7,454 | — | 935 |

**KM# 433** • **ObvDesc:** Seated Liberty with shiled • **RevDesc:** Youthful van Buren seated under tree, family tavern in distance • 15.55 g., 0.999 **Gold** 0.4995 oz. AGW, 26.5 • **Obv. Designer:** Christian Gobrecht • **Rev. Designer:** Thomas Cleveland and James Licaretz

| Date | Mintage | MS65 | Prf65 |
|---|---|---|---|
| 2008W | 3,443 | 995 | — |
| 2008W | 6,187 | — | 1,035 |

**KM# 456** • **ObvDesc:** Bust 3/4 left • **RevDesc:** Anna reading to her three children • 15.55 g., 0.999 **Gold** 0.4995 oz. AGW, 26.5 • **Obv. Designer:** Donna Weaver and Joseph Menna • **Rev. Designer:** Thomas Cleveland and Charles Vickers

| Date | Mintage | MS65 | Prf65 |
|---|---|---|---|
| 2009W | 2,993 | 1,050 | — |
| 2009W | 5,801 | — | 1,090 |

**KM# 457** • **ObvDesc:** Bust facing • **RevDesc:** Letitia and two children playing outside of Cedar Grove Plantation • 15.55 g., 0.999 **Gold** 0.4995 oz. AGW, 26.5 • **Obv. Designer:** Phebe Hemphill • **Rev. Designer:** Susan Gamble and Norm Nemeth

| Date | Mintage | MS65 | Prf65 |
|---|---|---|---|
| 2009W | 2,381 | 950 | — |
| 2009W | 4,341 | — | 987 |

**KM# 458** • **ObvDesc:** Bust facing • **RevDesc:** Julia and John Tyler dancing • 15.55 g., 0.999 **Gold** 0.4995 oz. AGW • **Designer:** Joel Iskowitz and Don Everhart • **Rev. Designer:** 26.5

| Date | Mintage | MS65 | Prf65 |
|---|---|---|---|
| 2009W | 2,188 | 1,000 | — |
| 2009W | 3,878 | — | 1,040 |

**KM# 459** • **ObvDesc:** Bust 3/4 right • **RevDesc:** Sarah seated at desk as personal secretary to James Polk • 15.55 g., 0.999 **Gold** 0.4995 oz. AGW, 26.5 • **Designer:** Phebe Hemphill

| Date | Mintage | MS65 | Prf65 |
|---|---|---|---|
| 2009W | 1,893 | 715 | — |
| 2009W | 3,512 | — | 744 |

**KM# 465** • **ObvDesc:** Bust 3/4 left • **RevDesc:** Margaret Taylor nurses wounded soldier during the Seminole War • 15.55 g., 0.999 **Gold** 0.4995 oz. AGW, 26.5 • **Obv. Designer:** Phebe Hemphill and Charles Vickers • **Rev. Designer:** Mary Beth Zeitz and James Licaretz

| Date | Mintage | MS65 | Prf65 |
|---|---|---|---|
| 2009W | 3,430 | 734 | — |
| 2009W | 4,787 | — | 734 |

**KM# 481** • **RevDesc:** Abigail Filmore placing books on library shelf • 15.52 g., 0.999 **Gold** 0.4985 oz. AGW, 26.5 • **Obv. Designer:** Phebe Hemphill • **Rev. Designer:** Susan Gamble and Joseph Menna

| Date | Mintage | MS65 | Prf65 |
|---|---|---|---|
| 2010W | 3,482 | 745 | — |
| 2010W | 6,130 | — | 765 |

**KM# 482** • **RevDesc:** Jane Pierce seated on porch • 15.52 g., 0.999 **Gold** 0.4985 oz. AGW, 26.5 • **Obv. Designer:** Donna Weaver and Don Everhart • **Rev. Designer:** Donna Weaver and Charles Vickers

| Date | Mintage | MS65 | Prf65 |
|---|---|---|---|
| 2010W | 3,338 | 725 | — |
| 2010W | 4,775 | — | 755 |

**KM# 483** • **RevDesc:** Buchanan as clerk • 15.52 g., 0.999 **Gold** 0.4985 oz. AGW, 26.5 • **Obv. Designer:** Christian Gobrecht • **Rev. Designer:** Joseph Menna

| Date | Mintage | MS65 | Prf65 |
|---|---|---|---|
| 2010W | 5,162 | 770 | — |
| 2010W | 7,110 | — | 801 |

**KM# 484** • **RevDesc:** Mary Lincoln visiting soldiers at hospital • 15.52 g., 0.999 **Gold** 0.4985 oz. AGW, 26.5 • **Obv. Designer:** Phebe Hemphill • **Rev. Designer:** Joel Iskowitz and Pheve Hemphill

| Date | Mintage | MS65 | Prf65 |
|---|---|---|---|
| 2010W | 3,965 | 900 | — |
| 2010W | 6,861 | — | 940 |

**KM# 509** • **ObvDesc:** Bust of Eliza Johnson • 15.55 g., 0.999 **Gold** 0.4994 oz. AGW, 26.5

| Date | Mintage | MS65 | Prf65 |
|---|---|---|---|
| 2011W | 2,915 | 735 | — |
| 2011W | 3,907 | — | 765 |

**KM# 510** • **ObvDesc:** Bust of Julia Grant • 15.55 g., 0.999 **Gold** 0.4995 oz. AGW, 26.5

| Date | Mintage | MS65 | Prf65 |
|---|---|---|---|
| 2011W | 2,952 | 705 | — |
| 2011W | 3,969 | — | 734 |

**KM# 511** • **ObvDesc:** Bust of Lucy Hayes • 15.55 g., 0.999 **Gold** 0.4995 oz. AGW, 26.5

| Date | Mintage | MS65 | Prf65 |
|---|---|---|---|
| 2011W | 2,263 | 1,429 | — |
| 2011W | 3,885 | — | 1,486 |

**KM# 512** • **ObvDesc:** Bust of Lucretia Garfield • 15.55 g., 0.999 **Gold** 0.4995 oz. AGW, 26.5

| Date | Mintage | MS65 | Prf65 |
|---|---|---|---|
| 2011W | 2,498 | 1,150 | — |
| 2011W | 3,652 | — | 1,196 |

**KM# 532** • 15.55 g., 0.999 **Gold** 0.4995 oz. AGW, 26.5

| Date | Mintage | MS65 | Prf65 |
|---|---|---|---|
| 2012W | 2,798 | 720 | — |
| 2012W | 3,506 | — | 740 |

**KM# 533** • **ObvDesc:** Frances Cleveland • 15.55 g., 0.999 **Gold** 0.4995 oz. AGW, 26.5

| Date | Mintage | MS65 | Prf65 |
|---|---|---|---|
| 2012W | 2,454 | 695 | — |
| 2012W | 3,158 | — | 695 |

**KM# 534** • **ObvDesc:** Caroline Harrison • 15.55 g., 0.999 **Gold** 0.4995 oz. AGW, 26.5

| Date | Mintage | MS65 | Prf65 |
|---|---|---|---|
| 2012W | 2,436 | 745 | — |
| 2012W | 3,046 | — | 745 |

**KM# 535** • **ObvDesc:** Frances Cleveland • 15.55 g., 0.999 **Gold** 0.4995 oz. AGW, 26.5

| Date | Mintage | MS65 | Prf65 |
|---|---|---|---|
| 2012W | 2,425 | 1,050 | — |
| 2012W | 3,104 | — | 1,075 |

**KM# 561** • **ObvDesc:** Bust of Ida McKinley • 15.55 g., 0.999 **Gold** 0.4995 oz. AGW, 26.5

| Date | Mintage | MS65 | Prf65 |
|---|---|---|---|
| 2013W | — | 755 | — |
| 2013W | — | — | 755 |

**KM# 562 • ObvDesc:** Bust of Edith Roosevelt • 15.55 g., 0.999 **Gold** 0.4995 oz. AGW, 26.5

| Date | Mintage | MS65 | Prf65 |
|---|---|---|---|
| 2013W | — | 750 | — |
| 2013W | — | — | 750 |

**KM# 563 • ObvDesc:** Bust of Helen Taft • 15.55 g., 0.999 **Gold** 0.4995 oz. AGW, 26.5

| Date | Mintage | MS65 | Prf65 |
|---|---|---|---|
| 2013W | — | 755 | — |
| 2013W | — | — | 755 |

**KM# 564 • ObvDesc:** Bust of Ellen Wilson • 15.55 g., 0.999 **Gold** 0.4995 oz. AGW, 26.5

| Date | Mintage | MS65 | Prf65 |
|---|---|---|---|
| 2013W | — | 755 | — |
| 2013W | — | — | 755 |

**KM# 565 • ObvDesc:** Bust of Edith Wilson • 15.55 g., 0.999 **Gold** 0.4995 oz. AGW, 26.5

| Date | Mintage | MS65 | Prf65 |
|---|---|---|---|
| 2013W | — | 755 | — |
| 2013W | — | — | 755 |

# UNCIRCULATED ROLLS

Listings are for rolls containing uncirculated coins. Large date and small date varieties for 1960 and 1970 apply to the one cent coins.

| Date | Cents | Nickels | Dimes | Quarters | Halves |
|---|---|---|---|---|---|
| 2001P | 3.75 | 4.75 | 7.75 | — | 16.50 |
| 2001D | 2.00 | 6.50 | 7.25 | — | 16.00 |
| 2002P | 2.00 | 4.00 | 7.25 | — | 20.00 |
| 2002D | 3.25 | 4.10 | 7.25 | — | 20.00 |
| 2003P | 3.35 | 7.50 | 7.00 | — | 22.50 |
| 2003D | 2.00 | 3.50 | 7.00 | — | 19.50 |
| 2004P Peace Medal Nickel | 1.75 | 6.75 | 7.00 | — | 30.00 |
| 2004D Peace Medal Nickel | 2.50 | 7.00 | 7.00 | — | 30.00 |
| 2004P Keelboat Nickel | — | 4.00 | — | — | — |
| 2004D Keelboat Nickel | — | 3.50 | — | — | — |
| 2005P Bison Nickel | 1.75 | 3.25 | 7.00 | — | 21.00 |
| 2005D Bison Nickel | 2.75 | 3.25 | 7.00 | — | 21.00 |
| 2005P Ocean in view Nickel | — | 3.25 | — | — | — |
| 2005D Ocean in view Nickel | — | 3.25 | — | — | — |
| 2006P | 2.75 | 3.25 | 8.50 | — | 29.00 |
| 2006D | 1.75 | 3.25 | 8.50 | — | 29.00 |
| 2007P | 1.75 | 3.50 | 8.00 | — | 21.00 |
| 2007D | 1.75 | 3.50 | 7.75 | — | 21.00 |
| 2008P | 1.75 | 3.75 | 8.00 | — | 24.50 |
| 2008D | 1.75 | 3.75 | 7.50 | — | 25.50 |
| 2009P Log Cabin | 2.00 | 23.00 | 13.50 | — | 18.50 |
| 2009D Log Cabin | 2.15 | 13.50 | 13.50 | — | 18.50 |
| 2009P Log Splitter | 1.75 | — | — | — | — |
| 2009D Log Splitter | 1.75 | — | — | — | — |
| 2009P Professional | 1.75 | — | — | — | — |
| 2009D Professional | 1.75 | — | — | — | — |
| 2009P President | 2.00 | — | — | — | — |
| 2009D President | 2.00 | — | — | — | — |

# 50 STATE QUARTERS

Listings are for rolls containing uncirculated coins.

| Date | Philadelphia | Denver |
|---|---|---|
| 2001 New York | 14.00 | 14.00 |
| 2001 North Carolina | 14.50 | 15.00 |
| 2001 Rhode Island | 14.00 | 15.50 |
| 2001 Vermont | 14.50 | 14.50 |
| 2001 Kentucky | 16.50 | 18.50 |
| 2002 Tennessee | 30.00 | 39.50 |
| 2002 Ohio | 21.50 | 21.50 |
| 2002 Louisiana | 14.00 | 14.00 |
| 2002 Indiana | 14.50 | 15.50 |
| 2002 Mississippi | 16.50 | 16.50 |
| 2003 Illinois | 39.00 | 45.00 |
| 2003 Alabama | 17.00 | 18.50 |
| 2003 Maine | 14.50 | 15.50 |
| 2003 Missouri | 14.50 | 14.75 |
| 2003 Arkansas | 14.50 | 15.50 |
| 2004 Michigan | 13.75 | 14.50 |
| 2004 Florida | 13.75 | 14.50 |
| 2004 Texas | 14.00 | 15.00 |
| 2004 Iowa | 14.00 | 14.50 |
| 2004 Wisconsin | 15.50 | 16.50 |
| 2005 California | 21.00 | 22.50 |
| 2005 Minnesota | 17.50 | 17.50 |
| 2005 Oregon | 13.75 | 13.75 |
| 2005 Kansas | 13.75 | 14.50 |
| 2005 West Virginia | 13.50 | 13.75 |
| 2006 Nevada | 13.75 | 13.75 |
| 2006 Nebraska | 13.75 | 14.00 |
| 2006 Colorado | 13.75 | 14.00 |
| 2006 North Dakota | 13.75 | 14.50 |
| 2006 South Dakota | 13.75 | 13.75 |
| 2007 Montana | 14.00 | 17.00 |
| 2007 Washington | 18.00 | 18.75 |
| 2007 Idaho | 15.50 | 15.50 |
| 2007 Wyoming | 14.75 | 15.00 |
| 2007 Utah | 15.00 | 14.50 |
| 2008 Oklahoma | 13.75 | 13.75 |
| 2008 New Mexico | 14.00 | 15.50 |
| 2008 Arizona | 15.50 | 13.75 |
| 2008 Alaska | 13.50 | 13.75 |
| 2008 Hawaii | 13.50 | 13.50 |

# MINT SETS

| Date | Sets Sold | Issue Price | Value |
|---|---|---|---|
| 2001 | 1,066,900 | 14.95 | 7.20 |
| 2002 | 1,139,388 | 14.95 | 7.05 |
| 2003 | 1,002,555 | 14.95 | 8.25 |
| 2004 | 844,484 | 16.95 | 8.00 |
| 2005 | — | 16.95 | 7.20 |
| 2006 | — | 16.95 | 7.25 |
| 2007 | — | — | 17.25 |
| 2008 | — | — | 45.00 |
| 2009 18 piece clad set | — | — | 19.50 |
| 2010 28 piece clad set | — | — | 29.70 |
| 2010 14 piece clad set | — | — | 22.50 |
| 2011 14 piece clad set | 532,059 | — | 23.50 |
| 2012 14 piece clad set | 365,298 | — | 74.00 |

# MODERN COMMEMORATIVE COIN SETS

## American Buffalo

| Date | Price |
|---|---|
| 2001 2001 2 coin set: 90% silver unc. & proof $1.; KM325. | 330 |

## Capitol Visitor Center

| Date | Price |
|---|---|
| 2001 2001 3 coin set: proof half, silver dollar, gold $5; KM323, 324, 326. | 495 |

## Winter Olympics - Salt Lake City

| Date | Price |
|---|---|
| 2002 2002 2 coin set: proof 90% silver dollar KM336 & $5.00 Gold KM337. | 465 |
| 2002 2002 4 coin set: 90% silver unc. & proof $1, KM336 & unc. & proof gold $5, KM337. | 925 |

## Thomas Alva Edison

| Date | Price |
|---|---|
| 2004 2004 Uncirculated silver dollar and light bulb. | 55.00 |

## Lewis and Clark Bicentennial

| Date | Price |
|---|---|
| 2004 2004 Coin and pouch set. | 65.00 |
| 2004 2004 coin and currency set: Uncirculated silver dollar, two 2005 nickels, replica 1901 $10 Bison note, silver plated peace medal, three stamps & two booklets. | 58.00 |
| 2004 2004 Westward Journey Nickel series coin and medal set: Proof Sacagawea dollar, two 2005 proof nickels and silver plated peace medal. | 40.00 |

## Chief Justice John Marshall

| Date | Price |
|---|---|
| 2005 2005 Coin and Chronicles set: Uncirculated silver dollar, booklet and BEP intaglio portrait. | 57.00 |

## U.S. Marine Corps

| Date | Price |
|---|---|
| 2005 2005 Uncirculated silver dollar and stamp set. | 63.00 |

## Benjamin Franklin Tercentennary

| Date | Price |
|---|---|
| 2006 2006 Coin and Chronicles set: Uncirculated "Scientist" silver dollar, four stamps, Poor Richards Almanac and intaglio print. | 49.00 |

## Central High School Desegregation

| Date | Price |
|---|---|
| 2007 2007 Little Rock Dollar and medal set, KM#418 | 47.80 |

## American Bald Eagle

| Date | Price |
|---|---|
| 2008 2008 Proof half dollar, dollar and $5 gold, KM438, KM439, KM440 | 490 |
| 2008 2008 Bald Eagle young collector's set; Half Dollar, KM#438 | 23.00 |

## Louis Braille

| Date | Price |
|---|---|
| 2009 Braille Education set, KM#455 | 43.50 |

# PROOF SETS

| Date | Sets Sold | Issue Price | Value |
|---|---|---|---|
| 2001S 10 piece | 2,249,498 | 19.95 | 11.00 |
| 2001S 5 quarter set | 774,800 | 13.95 | 5.00 |
| 2001S Silver | 849,600 | 31.95 | 44.50 |
| 2002S 10 piece | 2,319,766 | 19.95 | 6.10 |
| 2002S 5 quarter set | 764,419 | 13.95 | 3.05 |
| 2002S Silver | 892,229 | 31.95 | 30.50 |
| 2003S 10 piece | 2,175,684 | 16.75 | 5.80 |
| 2003S 5 quarter set | 1,225,507 | 13.95 | 2.25 |
| 2003S Silver | 1,142,858 | 31.95 | 32.50 |
| 2004S 11 piece | 1,804,396 | 22.95 | 9.10 |
| 2004S 5 quarter set | 987,960 | 23.95 | 2.50 |
| 2004S Silver 11 piece | 1,187,673 | 37.95 | 28.50 |
| 2004S Silver 5 quarter set | 594,137 | — | 19.00 |
| 2005S American Legacy | — | — | 84.50 |
| 2005S American Legacy | — | — | 77.50 |
| 2005S 11 piece | — | 22.95 | 10.50 |
| 2005S 5 quarter set | — | 15.95 | 2.25 |
| 2005S Silver 11 piece | — | 37.95 | 31.50 |
| 2005S Silver 5 quarter set | — | 23.95 | 18.75 |
| 2006S 10 piece clad | — | 22.95 | 8.25 |
| 2006S 5 quarter set | — | 15.95 | 2.80 |
| 2006S Silver 10 piece | — | 37.95 | 33.50 |
| 2006S Silver 5 quarter set | — | 23.95 | 21.75 |
| 2006S American Legacy | — | — | 77.50 |
| 2007S 5 quarter set | — | 13.95 | 4.40 |
| 2007S Silver 5 quarter set | — | 22.95 | 19.00 |
| 2007S 14 piece clad | — | — | 15.75 |
| 2007S Silver 14 piece | — | — | 37.00 |
| 2007S Presidential $ set | — | — | 5.35 |
| 2007S American Legacy | — | — | 93.50 |
| 2008S 5 quarter clad set | — | 22.95 | 41.50 |
| 2008S 5 quarter silver set | — | — | 20.80 |
| 2008S 14 piece silver set | 734,045 | — | 42.25 |
| 2008 14 piece clad set | — | — | 38.50 |
| 2008S Presidential $ set | — | — | 11.75 |
| 2008S American Legacy | — | — | 93.50 |
| 2009S 18 piece clad set | 1,477,967 | — | 23.25 |
| 2009S 18 piece silver set | 694,406 | — | 52.00 |
| 2009S Presidential $ set | 627,925 | — | 10.50 |
| 2009S Lincoln Chronicle | — | — | 107 |
| 2009S Lincoln 4 piece | — | — | 10.00 |
| 2009S 6 quarter clad set | — | — | 5.60 |
| 2009S 6 quarter silver set | — | — | 22.00 |
| 2010S 14 piece clad set | 1,103,950 | — | 45.50 |
| 2010S 14 piece silver set | 583,912 | — | 50.00 |
| 2010S Presidential $ set | 535,463 | — | 20.50 |
| 2010S 6 quarter set | 276,335 | — | 15.25 |
| 2010S 5 quarter silver set | 274,003 | — | 21.00 |
| 2011S 5 quarter silver set | 147,005 | — | 28.00 |
| 2011S 14 piece silver set | 572,247 | — | 72.00 |
| 2011S 5 quarter clad set | 151,434 | — | 14.50 |
| 2011S Presidential $ set | 299,161 | — | 28.25 |
| 2011S 14 piece clad set | 1,095,318 | — | 38.50 |
| 2011S 6 quarter set | — | — | 15.00 |
| 2012S 5 quarter silver set | — | — | 35.25 |
| 2012S 14 piece silver set | — | — | 212 |
| 2012S 6 quarter set | — | — | 14.50 |
| 2012S 14 piece clad set | — | — | 105 |
| 2012S Presidential $ set | — | — | 72.00 |
| 2012 8 piece Limited Edition | — | — | 225 |

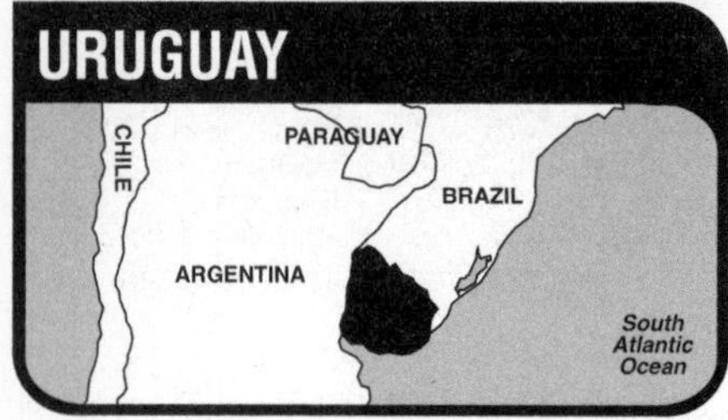


The Oriental Republic of Uruguay (so called because of its location on the east bank of the Uruguay River) is situated on the Atlantic coast of South America between Argentina and Brazil. This South American country has an area of 68,536 sq. mi. (176,220 sq. km.) and a population of *3 million. Capital: Montevideo. Uruguay's chief economic asset is the rich, rolling grassy plains. Meat, wool, hides and skins are exported.

**MINT MARKS**

(ba) – Buenos Aires
(br) – Acunaciones Espanolas S.A., Barcelona
(k) – Kremnica (Slovakia)
(m) - Madrid
Mo, (mo) and Mx - Mexico City
(p) – thunderbolt: Poissy, France
(rcm) – Royal Canadian Mint
(rj) – Rio de Janeiro
(sa) – Pretoria, South Africa
So, (so) – Santiago (Small o above S); (except 2007 2 Pesos Uruguayos)

# REPUBLIC

## REFORM COINAGE

1,000 Nuevos Pesos = 1 Uruguayan Peso;
100 Centesimos = 1 Uruguayan Peso (UYP)
March 1993

### KM# 106 50 CENTESIMOS

3.00 g., Stainless Steel, 21 mm. **Obv:** Bust of Artigas right **Obv. Legend:** REPUBLICA ORIENTAL DEL URUGUAY **Rev:** Value, date and sprig **Edge:** Plain **Note:** Coin rotation.

| Date | Mintage | VF20 | XF40 | MS60 | MS63 | MS65 |
|---|---|---|---|---|---|---|
| 2002 (sa) | 10,000,000 | — | — | 0.30 | 0.70 | 0.80 |
| 2005 (m) | 15,000,000 | — | — | 0.30 | 0.70 | 0.80 |
| 2008 (k) | 35,000,000 | — | — | 0.30 | 0.70 | 0.80 |

### KM# 103.2 UN PESO URUGUAYO

3.50 g., Aluminum-Bronze, 20 mm. **Obv:** Bust of Artigas right **Obv. Legend:** REPUBLICA ORIENTAL DEL URUGUAY **Rev:** Value and date **Edge:** Plain **Note:** Medal rotation; left point of bust shoulder points at "P" in Republic.

| Date | Mintage | VF20 | XF40 | MS60 | MS63 | MS65 |
|---|---|---|---|---|---|---|
| 2005 So | 40,000,000 | — | — | 0.20 | 0.40 | 0.60 |
| 2007 So | 25,000,000 | — | — | 0.20 | 0.40 | 0.60 |

### KM# 135 UN PESO URUGUAYO

3.50 g., Brass Plated Steel, 20 mm. **Obv:** Arms in circle, date below **Obv. Legend:** REPUBLICA ORIENTAL DEL URUGUAY **Rev:** Mulita (armadillo) **Edge:** Plain

| Date | Mintage | VF20 | XF40 | MS60 | MS63 | MS65 |
|---|---|---|---|---|---|---|
| 2011 (m) | 40,000,000 | — | — | — | 0.25 | 0.50 |
| 2012 (a) | 160,000,000 | — | — | — | 0.25 | 0.50 |

### KM# 104.2 2 PESOS URUGUAYOS

4.50 g., Aluminum-Bronze, 23 mm. **Obv:** Bust of Artigas right **Obv. Legend:** REPUBLICA ORIENTAL DEL URUGUAY **Rev:** Value and date **Edge:** Plain **Note:** Medal rotation. Left point of bust shoulder points at "P" in "Republic".

| Date | Mintage | VF20 | XF40 | MS60 | MS63 | MS65 |
|---|---|---|---|---|---|---|
| 2007 So | 25,000,000 | — | — | 0.50 | 0.75 | 1.00 |

Note: Minted at Paris with the So mintmark.

### KM# 136 2 PESOS URUGUAYOS

4.50 g., Brass Plated Steel, 23 mm. **Obv:** Arms in circle, date below **Obv. Legend:** REPUBLICA ORIENTAL DEL URUGUAY **Rev:** Carpincho **Edge:** Plain

| Date | Mintage | VF20 | XF40 | MS60 | MS63 | MS65 |
|---|---|---|---|---|---|---|
| 2011 (m) | 40,000,000 | — | — | — | 0.50 | 0.75 |
| 2012 (a) | 80,000,000 | — | — | — | 0.50 | 0.75 |

### KM# 120.1 5 PESOS URUGUAYOS

6.30 g., Aluminum-Bronze, 26 mm. **Obv:** Bust of Antigas right **Obv. Legend:** REPUBLICA ORIENTAL DEL URUGUAY **Rev:** Value **Edge:** Plain **Note:** Left point of bust shoulder points at "U" in "Republic".

| Date | Mintage | VF20 | XF40 | MS60 | MS63 | MS65 |
|---|---|---|---|---|---|---|
| 2003 (ba) | 15,150,000 | — | — | — | 1.50 | 2.00 |

### KM# 120.2 5 PESOS URUGUAYOS

6.30 g., Aluminum-Bronze, 26 mm. **Obv:** Bust of Artigas right **Obv. Legend:** REPUBLICA ORIENTAL DEL URUGUAY • **Rev:** Value, date **Note:** Left point of bust shoulder points at "P" in "Republic".

| Date | Mintage | VF20 | XF40 | MS60 | MS63 | MS65 |
|---|---|---|---|---|---|---|
| 2005 So | 30,000,000 | — | — | — | 1.50 | 2.00 |
| 2008 So | 20,000,000 | — | — | — | 1.50 | 2.00 |

### KM# 137 5 PESOS URUGUAYOS

6.40 g., Brass Plated Steel, 25.5 mm. **Obv:** Arms in circle, date below **Obv. Legend:** REPUBLICA ORIENTAL DEL URUGUAY **Rev:** Nandu **Edge:** Palin

| Date | Mintage | VF20 | XF40 | MS60 | MS63 | MS65 |
|---|---|---|---|---|---|---|
| 2011 (l) | 10,000,000 | — | — | — | 0.75 | 1.00 |

### KM# 121 10 PESOS URUGUAYOS

10.40 g., Bi-Metallic Aluminum-Bronze center in Stainless Steel ring, 28 mm. **Obv:** Artigas head right within circle **Rev:** Value above signature within circle **Edge:** Plain

| Date | Mintage | VF20 | XF40 | MS60 | MS63 | MS65 |
|---|---|---|---|---|---|---|
| 2000 (rcm) | 40,000,000 | — | — | 1.50 | 1.75 | 3.00 |

Note: 5-pointed star on each side of date, issued 2006

### KM# 134 10 PESOS URUGUAYOS

10.40 g., Bi-Metallic Brass center in Copper-Nickel ring, 28 mm. **Obv:** Oval arms, country name and date **Rev:** Puma walking left, sunrise in background and value

| Date | Mintage | VF20 | XF40 | MS60 | MS63 | MS65 |
|---|---|---|---|---|---|---|
| 2011 (l) | 20,000,000 | — | — | — | 1.00 | 1.25 |

### KM# 139 50 PESOS URUGUAYOS

10.40 g., Copper Plated Steel, 28 mm. **Subject:** Bicentennial of Uruguayan Independence **Obv:** Portrait of General Jose Artigas, country name and value **Rev:** Sun and rays and inscriptions "BICENTENARIO DE LOS HECHOS HISTORICOS" and "1811-2011" **Edge:** Reeded

| Date | Mintage | VF20 | XF40 | MS60 | MS63 | MS65 |
|---|---|---|---|---|---|---|
| 2011 (k) | 10,000,000 | — | — | — | 4.00 | 4.50 |

### KM# 133 500 PESOS URUGAUAYOS

12.50 g., 0.900 Silver 0.3617 oz. ASW, 33 mm. **Subject:** Salto, 250th Anniversary **Obv:** Uruguay map with City of Salto location **Rev:** Emblem of the Department of Salto

| Date | Mintage | VF20 | XF40 | MS60 | MS63 | MS65 |
|---|---|---|---|---|---|---|
| 2006 (u) | 10,000 | PF63 22.00 | PF65 25.00 | | | |

### KM# 122 1000 PESOS URUGUAYOS

27.00 g., 0.925 Silver 0.803 oz. ASW, 40 mm. **Subject:** XVIII World Championship Football - Germany 2006 **Obv:** National arms **Obv. Legend:** REPUBLICA ORIENTAL DEL URUGUAY **Rev:** Soccer player and value **Edge:** Reeded

| Date | Mintage | VF20 | XF40 | MS60 | MS63 | MS65 |
|---|---|---|---|---|---|---|
| 2003 (m) | — | PF63 45.00 | PF65 50.00 | | | |

### KM# 123 1000 PESOS URUGUAYOS

27.00 g., 0.925 Silver 0.803 oz. ASW, 40 mm. **Subject:** XVIII World Championship Football - Germany 2006 **Obv:** National arms above date **Obv. Legend:** REPUBLICA ORIENTAL DEL URUGUAY **Rev:** Stylized soccer player and value **Edge:** Reeded

| Date | Mintage | VF20 | XF40 | MS60 | MS63 | MS65 |
|---|---|---|---|---|---|---|
| 2004 (m) | — | PF63 45.00 | PF65 50.00 | | | |

**KM# 125 1000 PESOS URUGUAYOS**
27.00 g., 0.925 Silver 0.803 oz. ASW, 40 mm. **Subject:** 100th Anniversary FIFA - 1930 Championship **Obv:** Football before net **Obv. Legend:** REPUBLICA ORIENTAL DEL URUGUAY **Rev:** Sun of national flag **Edge:** Reeded

| Date | Mintage | VF20 | XF40 | MS60 | MS63 | MS65 |
|---|---|---|---|---|---|---|
| 2004 (m) | — | PF63 40.00 | PF65 45.00 | | | |

**KM# 124 1000 PESOS URUGUAYOS**
27.00 g., 0.925 Silver 0.803 oz. ASW, 40 mm. **Subject:** XVIII World Championship Football - Germany 2006 **Obv:** National arms above date **Obv. Legend:** REPUBLICA ORIENTAL DEL URUGUAY **Rev:** FIFA trophy **Edge:** Reeded

| Date | Mintage | VF20 | XF40 | MS60 | MS63 | MS65 |
|---|---|---|---|---|---|---|
| 2005 (m) | — | PF63 45.00 | PF65 50.00 | | | |

**KM# 140 1000 PESOS URUGUAYOS**
25.00 g., 0.900 Silver 0.7234 oz. ASW, 37 mm. **Subject:** Bicentennial of Uruguayan Independence **Obv:** Painting by Juan Luis Blanes of the surrender of Posadas at the battle of Las Piedras on May 18, 1811, country name and value **Rev:** Sun and rays and inscription "BICENTENARIO DE LOS HECHOS HISTORICOS" and "1811-2011 **Edge:** Reeded

| Date | Mintage | VF20 | XF40 | MS60 | MS63 | MS65 |
|---|---|---|---|---|---|---|
| 2011 (k) | 5,000 | PF63 70.00 | PF65 80.00 | | | |

**KM# 126 5000 PESOS URUGUAYOS**
6.75 g., 0.925 Gold 0.2007 oz. AGW, 23 mm. **Subject:** 100th Anniversary FIFA - 1930 Championship **Obv:** Football **Obv. Legend:** REPUBLICA ORIENTAL DEL URUGUAY **Rev:** Tower of Homage in Montevideo **Edge:** Reeded

| Date | Mintage | VF20 | XF40 | MS60 | MS63 | MS65 |
|---|---|---|---|---|---|---|
| 2004 (m) | — | PF65 400 | | | | |

**KM# 127 5000 PESOS URUGUAYOS**
6.75 g., 0.925 Gold 0.2007 oz. AGW, 23 mm. **Subject:** XVIII World Championship Football - Germany 2006 **Obv:** National arms **Obv. Legend:** REPUBLICA ORIENTAL DEL URUGUAY **Rev:** Stylized player and value **Edge:** Reeded

| Date | Mintage | VF20 | XF40 | MS60 | MS63 | MS65 |
|---|---|---|---|---|---|---|
| 2004 (m) | — | PF65 475 | | | | |

## MINT SETS

| KM# | Date | Mintage | Identification | Issue Price | Mkt Val |
|---|---|---|---|---|---|
| MS5 | 1994-2003 (7) | — | KM#102, 105 (1994), 103.2, 104.2 (1998), 106 (2002), 120.1 (2003), 121 (2000) (ba) | — | 15.00 |

# UZBEKISTAN

The Republic of Uzbekistan (formerly the Uzbek S.S.R.), is bordered on the north by Kazakhstan, to the east by Kirghizia and Tajikistan, on the south by Afghanistan and on the west by Turkmenistan. The republic is comprised of the regions of Andizhan, Bukhara, Dzhizak, Ferghana, Kashkadar, Khorezm (Khiva), Namangan, Navoi, Samarkand, Surkhan-Darya, Syr-Darya, Tashkent and the Karakalpak Autonomous Republic. It has an area of 172,741 sq. mi. (447,400 sq. km.) and a population of 20.3 million. Capital: Tashkent. Crude oil, natural gas, coal, copper, and gold deposits make up the chief resources, while intensive farming, based on artificial irrigation, provides an abundance of cotton.

**MONETARY SYSTEM**
100 Tiyin = 1 Som

## REPUBLIC

### STANDARD COINAGE

**KM# 13 5 SOM**
3.35 g., Brass Plated Steel, 21.2 mm. **Obv:** National arms **Rev:** Value and map **Edge:** Plain

| Date | Mintage | VF20 | XF40 | MS60 | MS63 | MS65 |
|---|---|---|---|---|---|---|
| 2001 | — | — | — | 0.75 | 1.35 | 1.75 |

Note: 2 reverse map varieties known

**KM# 14 10 SOM**
2.71 g., Nickel Clad Steel, 19.75 mm. **Obv:** National arms **Rev:** Value and map **Edge:** Plain

| Date | Mintage | VF20 | XF40 | MS60 | MS63 | MS65 |
|---|---|---|---|---|---|---|
| 2001 | — | — | — | 1.00 | 1.50 | 2.50 |

Note: 2 reverse map varieties exist

**KM# 15 50 SOM**
8.00 g., Nickel Clad Steel, 26.2 mm. **Obv:** National arms **Rev:** Value and map **Edge:** Segmented reeding

| Date | Mintage | VF20 | XF40 | MS60 | MS63 | MS65 |
|---|---|---|---|---|---|---|
| 2001 | — | — | 1.20 | 2.50 | 4.00 | 7.00 |

**KM# 16 50 SOM**
7.90 g., Nickel Clad Steel, 26.3 mm. **Subject:** 2700th Anniversary of Shahrisabz Town **Obv:** National arms **Rev:** Statue and ruins above value **Edge:** Segmented reeding

| Date | Mintage | VF20 | XF40 | MS60 | MS63 | MS65 |
|---|---|---|---|---|---|---|
| 2002 | — | — | 1.00 | 2.50 | 3.50 | 6.00 |

**KM# 18 100 SOM**
Bronze, 38.61 mm. **Subject:** Alisher Novoiy, 500th Anniversary of Death **Obv:** National arms **Obv. Legend:** O'ZBEKISTON MARKAZIY BANKI **Rev:** Alisher Navoiy

| Date | Mintage | VF20 | XF40 | MS60 | MS63 | MS65 |
|---|---|---|---|---|---|---|
| 2001 | — | — | — | 15.00 | 18.00 | 20.00 |

**KM# 19 100 SOM**
31.10 g., 0.999 Silver 0.9989 oz. ASW **Obv:** National arms **Obv. Legend:** O'ZBEKISTON MARKAZIY BANKI **Rev:** Parliament building in Toskent

| Date | Mintage | VF20 | XF40 | MS60 | MS63 | MS65 |
|---|---|---|---|---|---|---|
| 2001 | 1,000 | PF63 225 | PF65 245 | | | |

**KM# 20 100 SOM**
31.10 g., 0.999 Silver 0.9989 oz. ASW **Obv:** National arms **Obv. Legend:** O'ZBEKISTON MARKAZIY BANKI **Rev:** Amir-Timur Museum

| Date | Mintage | VF20 | XF40 | MS60 | MS63 | MS65 |
|---|---|---|---|---|---|---|
| 2001 | 1,000 | PF63 225 | PF65 245 | | | |

**KM# 21 100 SOM**
31.10 g., 0.999 Silver 0.9989 oz. ASW **Obv:** National Arms **Obv. Legend:** O'BEKISTON MARKAZY BANKI **Rev:** Toskent town hall

| Date | Mintage | VF20 | XF40 | MS60 | MS63 | MS65 |
|---|---|---|---|---|---|---|
| 2001 | 1,000 | PF63 225 | PF65 245 | | | |

**KM# 22 100 SOM**
31.10 g., 0.999 Silver 0.9989 oz. ASW **Obv:** National arms **Obv. Legend:** O'ZBEKISTON MARKAZIY BANKI **Rev:** World

| Date | Mintage | VF20 | XF40 | MS60 | MS63 | MS65 |
|---|---|---|---|---|---|---|
| 2001 | 1,000 | PF63 225 | PF65 245 | | | |

**KM# 23 100 SOM**
31.10 g., 0.999 Silver 0.9989 oz. ASW **Obv:** National arms **Obv. Legend:** O'ZBEKISTON MARKAZIY BANKI **Rev:** Football player

| Date | Mintage | VF20 | XF40 | MS60 | MS63 | MS65 |
|---|---|---|---|---|---|---|
| 2001 | 1,000 | PF63 225 | PF65 245 | | | |

**KM# 24 100 SOM**
31.10 g., 0.999 Silver 0.9989 oz. ASW **Obv:** National arms **Obv. Legend:** O'BEKISTON MARKAZIY BANKI **Rev:** Track runner

| Date | Mintage | VF20 | XF40 | MS60 | MS63 | MS65 |
|---|---|---|---|---|---|---|
| 2001 | 1,000 | PF63 225 | PF65 245 | | | |

**KM# 25 100 SOM**
31.10 g., 0.999 Silver 0.9989 oz. ASW **Obv:** National arms **Obv. Legend:** O'ZBEKISTON MARKAZIY BANKI **Rev:** Judo expert

| Date | Mintage | VF20 | XF40 | MS60 | MS63 | MS65 |
|---|---|---|---|---|---|---|
| 2001 | 1,000 | PF63 225 | PF65 245 | | | |

**KM# 26 100 SOM**
31.10 g., 0.999 Silver 0.9989 oz. ASW **Obv:** National arms **Obv. Legend:** O'ZBEKISTON MARKAZIY BANKI **Rev:** Tennis player

| Date | Mintage | VF20 | XF40 | MS60 | MS63 | MS65 |
|---|---|---|---|---|---|---|
| 2001 | 1,000 | PF63 225 | PF65 245 | | | |

**KM# 27 100 SOM**
31.10 g., 0.999 Silver 0.9989 oz. ASW **Obv:** National arms **Obv. Legend:** O'ZBEKISTON MARKAZIY BANKI **Rev:** Lenk monument in Timur

| Date | Mintage | VF20 | XF40 | MS60 | MS63 | MS65 |
|---|---|---|---|---|---|---|
| 2001 | 1,000 | PF63 225 | PF65 245 | | | |

**KM# 28 100 SOM**
31.10 g., 0.999 Silver 0.9989 oz. ASW **Obv:** National arms **Obv. Legend:** O'ZBEKISTON MARKAZIY BANKI **Rev:** Aliser Navoi monument

| Date | Mintage | VF20 | XF40 | MS60 | MS63 | MS65 |
|---|---|---|---|---|---|---|
| 2001 | 1,000 | PF63 225 | PF65 245 | | | |

**KM# 29 100 SOM**
31.10 g., 0.999 Silver 0.9989 oz. ASW **Obv:** National arms **Obv. Legend:** O'ZBEKISTON MARKAZIY BANKI **Rev:** Registan in Samarkand

| Date | Mintage | VF20 | XF40 | MS60 | MS63 | MS65 |
|---|---|---|---|---|---|---|
| 2001 | 1,000 | PF63 225 | PF65 245 | | | |

**KM# 30 100 SOM**
31.10 g., 0.999 Silver 0.9989 oz. ASW **Obv:** National arms **Obv. Legend:** O'BEKISTON MARKAZIY BANKI **Rev:** Bell tower in Toskent

| Date | Mintage | VF20 | XF40 | MS60 | MS63 | MS65 |
|---|---|---|---|---|---|---|
| 2001 | 1,000 | PF63 225 | PF65 245 | | | |

**KM# 17 100 SOM**
7.92 g., Nickel Plated Steel, 26.95 mm. **Subject:** 10th Annniversary State Currency **Obv:** National arms **Obv. Legend:** O'ZBEKISTON MARKAZIV BANKI **Rev:** Sun rays over outlined map and value **Rev. Legend:** O'BEKISTON MILLIY VALYUTASIGA **Edge:** Lettered

| Date | Mintage | VF20 | XF40 | MS60 | MS63 | MS65 |
|---|---|---|---|---|---|---|
| 2004 | — | — | — | 12.50 | 15.00 | 18.00 |

**KM# 31 100 SOM**
7.92 g., Nickel Plated Steel, 27 mm. **Subject:** Tashkent, 2200th Anniversary of settlement **Obv:** National arms **Rev:** Linear archway and monument in background

| Date | Mintage | VF20 | XF40 | MS60 | MS63 | MS65 |
|---|---|---|---|---|---|---|
| 2009 | — | — | — | 3.50 | 5.00 | 8.00 |

**KM# 32 100 SOM**
7.92 g., Nickel Plated Steel, 27 mm. **Subject:** Tashkent, 2200th Anniversary of settlement **Obv:** National arms **Rev:** Monument

| Date | Mintage | VF20 | XF40 | MS60 | MS63 | MS65 |
|---|---|---|---|---|---|---|
| 2009 | — | — | — | 3.50 | 5.00 | 8.00 |

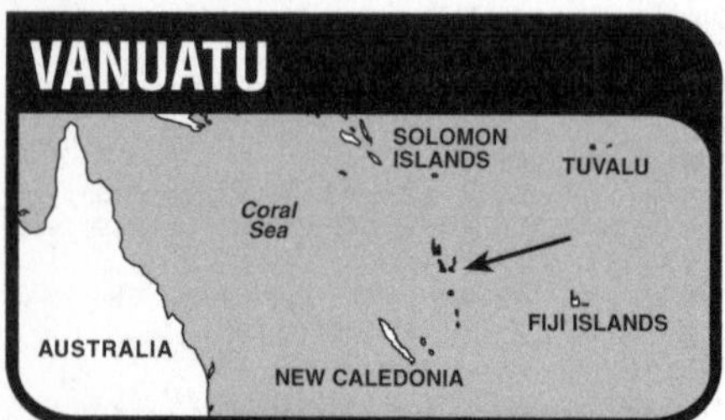

**KM# 34.1 500 SOM**
Copper-Nickel, 25 mm. **Subject:** Independence, 20th Anniversary **Obv:** National emblem, sun disc behind eagle's head **Rev:** Building

| Date | Mintage | VF20 | XF40 | MS60 | MS63 | MS65 |
|---|---|---|---|---|---|---|
| 2011 | — | — | — | — | 15.00 | 18.00 |

**KM# 34.2 500 SOM**
Copper-Nickel, 25 mm. **Subject:** Independence, 20th Anniversary **Obv:** National emblem, without sun disc behind eagle's head **Rev:** Building

| Date | Mintage | VF20 | XF40 | MS60 | MS63 | MS65 |
|---|---|---|---|---|---|---|
| 2011 | — | — | — | — | 15.00 | 18.00 |

# VANUATU

SOLOMON ISLANDS
TUVALU
Coral Sea
FIJI ISLANDS
AUSTRALIA
NEW CALEDONIA

The Republic of Vanuatu, formerly New Hebrides Condominium, a group of islands located in the South Pacific 500 miles (800 km.) west of Fiji, were under the joint sovereignty of Great Britain and France. The islands have an area of 5,700 sq. mi. (14,760 sq. km.) and a population of 165,000, mainly Melanesians of mixed blood. Capital: Port-Vila. The volcanic and coral islands, while malarial land subject to frequent earthquakes, are extremely fertile, and produce copra, coffee, tropical fruits and timber for export.

The New Hebrides were discovered by Portuguese navigator Pedro de Quiros (sailing under orders by the King of Spain) in 1606, visited by French explorer Bougainville in 1768, and named by British navigator Capt. James Cook in 1774. Ships of all nations converged on the islands to trade for sandalwood, prompting France and Britain to relinquish their individual claims and declare the islands a neutral zone in 1878. The New Hebrides were placed under the control of a mixed Anglo-French commission of naval officers during the native uprisings of 1887, and established as a condominium under the joint sovereignty of France and Great Britain in 1906.

Vanuatu became an independent republic within the Commonwealth in July 1980. A president is Head of State and the Prime Minister is Head of Government.

**MONETARY SYSTEM**
Vatu to Present

# REPUBLIC

## STANDARD COINAGE

**KM# 3 VATU**
1.99 g., Nickel-Brass, 16.95 mm. **Obv:** National arms **Rev:** Shell and value **Edge:** Plain

| Date | Mintage | VF20 | XF40 | MS60 | MS63 | MS65 |
|---|---|---|---|---|---|---|
| 2002 | — | — | 0.15 | 0.25 | 0.50 | 0.75 |

**KM# 4 2 VATU**
3.00 g., Nickel-Brass, 20 mm. **Obv:** National arms **Rev:** Shell and value **Edge:** Plain

| Date | Mintage | VF20 | XF40 | MS60 | MS63 | MS65 |
|---|---|---|---|---|---|---|
| 2002 | — | — | 0.25 | 0.45 | 0.85 | 1.50 |

**KM# 5 5 VATU**
4.10 g., Nickel-Brass, 23.5 mm. **Obv:** National arms **Rev:** Shell and value **Edge:** Plain

| Date | Mintage | VF20 | XF40 | MS60 | MS63 | MS65 |
|---|---|---|---|---|---|---|
| 2002 | — | — | 0.30 | 0.50 | 1.00 | 1.75 |
| 2009 | — | — | 0.30 | 0.50 | 1.00 | 1.75 |

**KM# 6 10 VATU**
6.10 g., Copper-Nickel, 23.95 mm. **Obv:** National arms **Rev:** Crab and value, palm trees **Edge:** Plain

| Date | Mintage | VF20 | XF40 | MS60 | MS63 | MS65 |
|---|---|---|---|---|---|---|
| 2009 | — | — | 0.35 | 0.65 | 1.25 | 2.00 |

**KM# 45 10 VATU**
Copper-Nickel silver plated **Obv:** Arms **Rev:** Multicolor butterfly (Papilio Toboroi)

| Date | Mintage | VF20 | XF40 | MS60 | MS63 | MS65 |
|---|---|---|---|---|---|---|
| 2006 | 2,500 | — | — | — | — | 32.00 |

**KM# 46 10 VATU**
Copper-Nickel silver plated **Obv:** Arms **Rev:** Multicolor butterfly (Taenaris Catops)

| Date | Mintage | VF20 | XF40 | MS60 | MS63 | MS65 |
|---|---|---|---|---|---|---|
| 2006 | 2,500 | — | — | — | — | 32.00 |

**KM# 47 10 VATU**
Copper-Nickel silver plated **Obv:** Arms **Rev:** Multicolor Butterfly (Ornithoptera Priamus Urvillianus)

| Date | Mintage | VF20 | XF40 | MS60 | MS63 | MS65 |
|---|---|---|---|---|---|---|
| 2006 | 2,500 | — | — | — | — | 32.00 |

**KM# 48 10 VATU**
Copper-Nickel silver plated **Obv:** Arms **Rev:** Multicolor butterfly (Ornithoptera Paradisea)

| Date | Mintage | VF20 | XF40 | MS60 | MS63 | MS65 |
|---|---|---|---|---|---|---|
| 2006 | 2,500 | — | — | — | — | 32.00 |

**KM# 49 10 VATU**
Copper-Nickel silver plated **Obv:** Arms **Rev:** Multicolor butterfly (Cethosia Cydippe)

| Date | Mintage | VF20 | XF40 | MS60 | MS63 | MS65 |
|---|---|---|---|---|---|---|
| 2006 | 2,500 | — | — | — | — | 32.00 |

**KM# 50 10 VATU**
Copper-Nickel silver plated **Obv:** Arms **Rev:** Multicolor butterfly (Delias Sagessa)

| Date | Mintage | VF20 | XF40 | MS60 | MS63 | MS65 |
|---|---|---|---|---|---|---|
| 2006 | 2,500 | — | — | — | — | 32.00 |

**KM# 51 10 VATU**
Copper-Nickel, 38.61 mm. **Subject:** Barack Obama **Obv:** National arms **Rev:** Profile right

| Date | Mintage | VF20 | XF40 | MS60 | MS63 | MS65 |
|---|---|---|---|---|---|---|
| 2009 | — | — | — | — | — | 14.00 |

**KM# 59 10 VATU**
26.03 g., Silver Plated Copper-Nickel, 38.61 mm. **Subject:** Beach Volleyball **Obv:** National arms **Rev:** Two players going for ball at net

| Date | Mintage | VF20 | XF40 | MS60 | MS63 | MS65 |
|---|---|---|---|---|---|---|
| 2009 | 30,000 | PF63 22.00 | PF65 25.00 | | | |

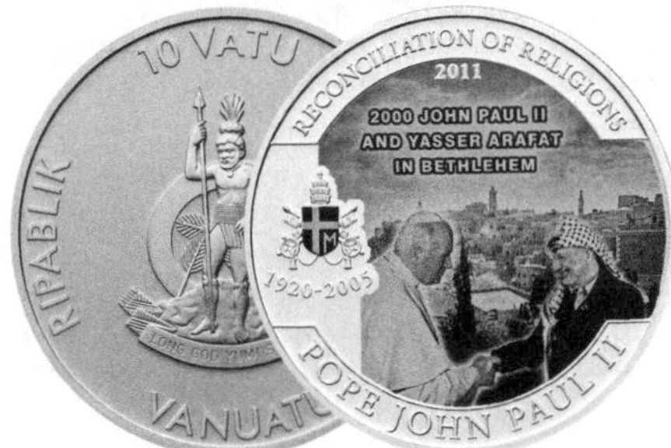


**KM# 65 10 VATU**
27.00 g., Silver Plated Copper, 38.61 mm. **Obv:** National arms **Rev:** Color image of John Paul II and Yaser Arafat

| Date | Mintage | VF20 | XF40 | MS60 | MS63 | MS65 |
|---|---|---|---|---|---|---|
| 2011 | 1,500 | PF65 28.00 | | | | |

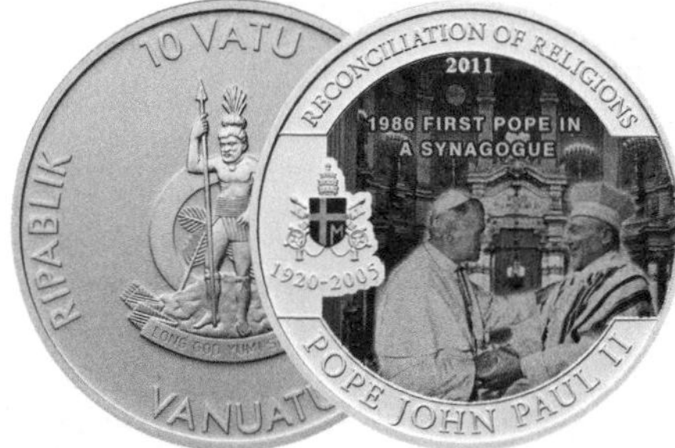


**KM# 66 10 VATU**
27.00 g., Silver Plated Copper, 38.61 mm. **Obv:** National arms **Rev:** Color image of John Paul II and Rabbi of Rome

| Date | Mintage | VF20 | XF40 | MS60 | MS63 | MS65 |
|---|---|---|---|---|---|---|
| 2011 | 1,500 | PF65 28.00 | | | | |

**KM# 77 10 VATU**
0.50 g., 0.585 Gold 0.0094 oz. AGW with 24Kt plating, 11 mm. **Subject:** Pierre de Coubertin

| Date | Mintage | VF20 | XF40 | MS60 | MS63 | MS65 |
|---|---|---|---|---|---|---|
| 2013 | Est. 5000 | PF63 50.00 | PF65 55.00 | | | |

**KM# 79 10 VATU**
0.50 g., 0.585 Gold 0.0094 oz. AGW, 11 mm. **Subject:** Leonardo da Vinci - Vitruvian Man

| Date | Mintage | VF20 | XF40 | MS60 | MS63 | MS65 |
|---|---|---|---|---|---|---|
| 2013 | Est. 5000 | PF63 50.00 | PF65 55.00 | | | |

**KM# 81 10 VATU**
0.50 g., 0.585 Gold 0.0094 oz. AGW with 24Kt plating, 11 mm. **Subject:** Eiffel Tower

| Date | Mintage | VF20 | XF40 | MS60 | MS63 | MS65 |
|---|---|---|---|---|---|---|
| 2013 | Est. 7500 | PF63 50.00 | PF65 55.00 | | | |

**KM# 93 10 VATU**
27.00 g., Silver Plated Copper, 38.61 mm. **Obv:** National arms **Rev:** Apollo capsule, moon in color

| Date | Mintage | VF20 | XF40 | MS60 | MS63 | MS65 |
|---|---|---|---|---|---|---|
| 2013 Black proof | 972 | PF65 25.00 | | | | |

**KM# 56 20 VATU**
0.50 g., 0.999 Gold 0.0161 oz. AGW, 11 mm. **Obv:** National arms **Rev:** SMS Europa under full sail

| Date | Mintage | VF20 | XF40 | MS60 | MS63 | MS65 |
|---|---|---|---|---|---|---|
| 2008 | 10,000 | PF63 65.00 | PF65 75.00 | | | |

**KM# 57 20 VATU**
0.50 g., 0.999 Gold 0.0161 oz. AGW, 11 mm. **Obv:** National arms **Rev:** Sokrates head

| Date | Mintage | VF20 | XF40 | MS60 | MS63 | MS65 |
|---|---|---|---|---|---|---|
| 2009 | 10,000 | PF63 65.00 | PF65 75.00 | | | |

**KM# 60 20 VATU**
0.50 g., 0.999 Gold 0.0161 oz. AGW, 11 mm. **Obv:** National arms **Rev:** Pantheon

| Date | Mintage | VF20 | XF40 | MS60 | MS63 | MS65 |
|---|---|---|---|---|---|---|
| 2009 | 10,000 | PF63 65.00 | PF65 75.00 | | | |

**KM# 67 20 VATU**
0.50 g., 0.999 Gold 0.0161 oz. AGW, 11 mm. **Obv:** National arms **Rev:** Turtle drawn in sand

| Date | Mintage | VF20 | XF40 | MS60 | MS63 | MS65 |
|---|---|---|---|---|---|---|
| 2011 | 10,000 | PF63 65.00 | PF65 75.00 | | | |

**KM# 78 20 VATU**
0.50 g., 0.999 Gold 0.0161 oz. AGW, 11 mm. **Subject:** Leonardo da Vinci - Vitruvian Man

| Date | Mintage | VF20 | XF40 | MS60 | MS63 | MS65 |
|---|---|---|---|---|---|---|
| 2013 | Est. 5000 | PF63 50.00 | PF65 55.00 | | | |

**KM# 80 20 VATU**
0.50 g., 0.999 Gold 0.0161 oz. AGW, 11 mm. **Subject:** Eifel Tower

| Date | Mintage | VF20 | XF40 | MS60 | MS63 | MS65 |
|---|---|---|---|---|---|---|
| 2013 | Est. 7500 | PF63 50.00 | PF65 55.00 | | | |

**KM# 82 20 VATU**
0.50 g., 0.585 Gold 0.0094 oz. AGW with 24Kt plating, 11 mm. **Subject:** Canals of Venice

| Date | Mintage | VF20 | XF40 | MS60 | MS63 | MS65 |
|---|---|---|---|---|---|---|
| 2013 | Est. 10000 | PF63 45.00 | PF65 50.00 | | | |

**KM# 83 20 VATU**
0.50 g., 0.585 Gold 0.0094 oz. AGW with 24Kt plating, 11 mm. **Subject:** Stonehedge

| Date | Mintage | VF20 | XF40 | MS60 | MS63 | MS65 |
|---|---|---|---|---|---|---|
| 2013 | Est. 10000 | PF63 45.00 | PF65 50.00 | | | |

**KM# 84 20 VATU**
0.50 g., 0.585 Gold 0.0094 oz. AGW with 24Kt plating, 11 mm. **Subject:** Pantheon

| Date | Mintage | VF20 | XF40 | MS60 | MS63 | MS65 |
|---|---|---|---|---|---|---|
| 2013 | Est. 10000 | PF63 45.00 | PF65 50.00 | | | |

**KM# 85 20 VATU**
0.50 g., 0.585 Gold 0.0094 oz. AGW with 24Kt plating, 11 mm. **Subject:** Kaaba

| Date | Mintage | VF20 | XF40 | MS60 | MS63 | MS65 |
|---|---|---|---|---|---|---|
| 2013 | Est. 10000 | PF63 45.00 | PF65 50.00 | | | |

**KM# 86 20 VATU**
0.50 g., 0.585 Gold 0.0094 oz. AGW with 24Kt plating, 11 mm. **Subject:** Abu Simbel

| Date | Mintage | VF20 | XF40 | MS60 | MS63 | MS65 |
|---|---|---|---|---|---|---|
| 2013 | Est. 10000 | PF63 45.00 | PF65 50.00 | | | |

**KM# 87 20 VATU**
0.50 g., 0.585 Gold 0.0094 oz. AGW with 24Kt plating, 11 mm. **Subject:** Blue Mosque

| Date | Mintage | VF20 | XF40 | MS60 | MS63 | MS65 |
|---|---|---|---|---|---|---|
| 2013 | Est. 10000 | PF63 45.00 | PF65 50.00 | | | |

**KM# 89 20 VATU**
15.55 g., 0.999 Silver 0.4994 oz. ASW, 38.61 mm. **Subject:** Raccoon with two black diamond inserts

| Date | Mintage | VF20 | XF40 | MS60 | MS63 | MS65 |
|---|---|---|---|---|---|---|
| 2013 Antique patina | Est. 1500 | PF63 50.00 | | | | |

**KM# 92 20 VATU**
15.55 g., 0.999 Silver 0.4994 oz. ASW, 38.61 mm. **Obv:** National arms **Rev:** Lunar rover, Earth in color

| Date | Mintage | VF20 | XF40 | MS60 | MS63 | MS65 |
|---|---|---|---|---|---|---|
| 2013 Antique patina | 972 | PF65 25.00 | | | | |

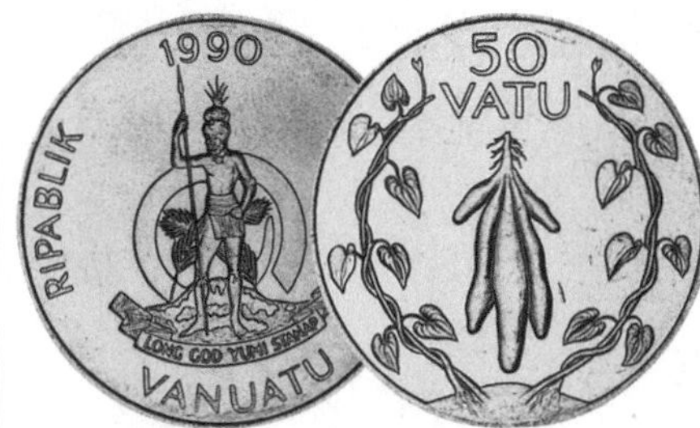


**KM# 8 50 VATU**
15.00 g., Copper-Nickel, 32.9 mm. **Series:** F.A.O. **Obv:** National arms **Rev:** Tubers encircled by leafy vines, value above

| Date | Mintage | VF20 | XF40 | MS60 | MS63 | MS65 |
|---|---|---|---|---|---|---|
| 2002 | — | — | — | 1.25 | 2.00 | 3.00 |
| 2009 | — | — | — | 1.25 | 2.00 | 3.00 |

**KM# 53 50 VATU**
Silver, 38.6 mm. **Subject:** Olympics, 2004 **Obv:** National emblem **Rev:** Athlethe with torch, large torch, fragment of ancient vase

| Date | Mintage | VF20 | XF40 | MS60 | MS63 | MS65 |
|---|---|---|---|---|---|---|
| 2003 | — | PF60 22.00 | PF63 25.00 | PF65 28.00 | | |

**KM# 38 50 VATU**
28.32 g., 0.925 Silver 0.8422 oz. ASW, 38.6 mm. **Obv:** National arms **Obv. Legend:** RIPABLIK / VANUATU **Rev:** Early sailing ship center - left, stylized compass at right **Rev. Legend:** HISTORY OF SEAFARING / PEDRO FERNANDEZ DE QUIRÓS **Edge:** Reeded

| Date | Mintage | VF20 | XF40 | MS60 | MS63 | MS65 |
|---|---|---|---|---|---|---|
| 2005 | — | PF63 42.00 | PF65 47.00 | | | |

**KM# 41 50 VATU**
25.00 g., 0.900 Silver 0.7234 oz. ASW **Series:** Protection of Marine Life **Obv:** National arms **Rev:** Tiger Shark - multicolor

| Date | Mintage | VF20 | XF40 | MS60 | MS63 | MS65 |
|---|---|---|---|---|---|---|
| 2005 | — | PF63 60.00 | PF65 70.00 | | | |

**KM# 55 50 VATU**
1.24 g., 0.999 Gold 0.0398 oz. AGW, 13.92 mm. **Obv:** National arms **Rev:** Captain Kidd

| Date | Mintage | VF20 | XF40 | MS60 | MS63 | MS65 |
|---|---|---|---|---|---|---|
| 2005 | 15,000 | PF63 65.00 | PF65 75.00 | | | |

**KM# 42 50 VATU**
25.00 g., 0.900 Silver 0.7234 oz. ASW **Series:** Protection of Marine Life **Obv:** National arms **Rev:** Sea Turtle - multicolor

| Date | Mintage | VF20 | XF40 | MS60 | MS63 | MS65 |
|---|---|---|---|---|---|---|
| 2006 | — | PF63 55.00 | PF65 65.00 | | | |

**KM# 43 50 VATU**
25.00 g., 0.900 Silver 0.7234 oz. ASW **Series:** Protection of Marine Life **Obv:** National arms **Rev:** Sea Horse - multicolor

| Date | Mintage | VF20 | XF40 | MS60 | MS63 | MS65 |
|---|---|---|---|---|---|---|
| 2006 | — | PF63 55.00 | PF65 65.00 | | | |

**KM# 52 50 VATU**
Silver **Subject:** 2006 World Cup - Germany **Obv:** National arms **Rev:** 2 soccer players and globe

| Date | Mintage | VF20 | XF40 | MS60 | MS63 | MS65 |
|---|---|---|---|---|---|---|
| 2006 | — | PF63 70.00 | PF65 80.00 | | | |

**KM# 54 50 VATU**
Silver, 38.6 mm. **Obv:** National emblem **Rev:** Two soccer players with large globe in background

| Date | Mintage | VF20 | XF40 | MS60 | MS63 | MS65 |
|---|---|---|---|---|---|---|
| 2006 | — | PF63 70.00 | PF65 80.00 | | | |

**KM# 58 50 VATU**
28.28 g., 0.925 Silver 0.841 oz. ASW, 38.61 mm. **Obv:** National Arms **Rev:** SMS Europa under full sail

| Date | Mintage | VF20 | XF40 | MS60 | MS63 | MS65 |
|---|---|---|---|---|---|---|
| 2008 | 5,000 | PF63 45.00 | PF65 50.00 | | | |

**KM# 61 50 VATU**
28.28 g., 0.925 Silver 0.841 oz. ASW, 38.61 mm. **Subject:** Beach Volleyball **Obv:** National arms **Rev:** Two players at net going for ball

| Date | Mintage | VF20 | XF40 | MS60 | MS63 | MS65 |
|---|---|---|---|---|---|---|
| 2009 | 10,000 | PF63 65.00 | PF65 75.00 | | | |

**KM# 62 50 VATU**
1.00 g., 0.999 Gold 0.0321 oz. AGW, 13.92 mm. **Obv:** National arms **Rev:** Potala Palace **Note:** The denomination does not appear on either side.

| Date | Mintage | VF20 | XF40 | MS60 | MS63 | MS65 |
|---|---|---|---|---|---|---|
| 2009 | 10,000 | PF63 85.00 | PF65 95.00 | | | |

**KM# 63 50 VATU**
28.28 g., 0.925 Silver 0.841 oz. ASW, 38.61 mm. **Obv:** National arms **Rev:** Shinkansen high speed train

| Date | Mintage | VF20 | XF40 | MS60 | MS63 | MS65 |
|---|---|---|---|---|---|---|
| 2009 | 5,000 | PF63 65.00 | PF65 75.00 | | | |

**KM# 64 50 VATU**
28.28 g., 0.925 Silver 0.841 oz. ASW **Obv:** National arms **Rev:** The Gran, trans-Australia train **Shape:** 38.61

| Date | Mintage | VF20 | XF40 | MS60 | MS63 | MS65 |
|---|---|---|---|---|---|---|
| 2010 | 5,000 | PF63 65.00 | PF65 75.00 | | | |

**KM# 68 50 VATU**
31.10 g., 0.999 Silver 0.9989 oz. ASW, 40.6 mm. **Subject:** Royal Ascot Races **Obv:** National arms **Rev:** Horse race, grandstands, Elizabeth II and Prince Philip; partially colored

| Date | Mintage | VF20 | XF40 | MS60 | MS63 | MS65 |
|---|---|---|---|---|---|---|
| 2011 | 10,000 | PF63 75.00 | PF65 85.00 | | | |

**KM# 69 50 VATU**
20.00 g., 0.925 Silver 0.5948 oz. ASW, 38.61 mm. **Obv:** National arms **Rev:** TEE VT11.5 train, map of Europe above

| Date | Mintage | VF20 | XF40 | MS60 | MS63 | MS65 |
|---|---|---|---|---|---|---|
| 2011 | 5,000 | PF63 65.00 | PF65 75.00 | | | |

**KM# 75 50 VATU**
20.00 g., 0.925 Silver 0.5948 oz. ASW, 30 x 45 mm. **Subject:** Edward Teach - Black Beard

| Date | Mintage | VF20 | XF40 | MS60 | MS63 | MS65 |
|---|---|---|---|---|---|---|
| 2012 | Est. 1000 | PF65 110 | | | | |

**KM# 70 50 VATU**
20.00 g., 0.999 Silver 0.6424 oz. ASW, 38.61 mm. **Rev:** Bust at left, Runner at race start, green ring

| Date | Mintage | VF20 | XF40 | MS60 | MS63 | MS65 |
|---|---|---|---|---|---|---|
| 2013 Reverse Proof | Est. 500 | PF63 50.00 | PF65 60.00 | | | |

**KM# 71 50 VATU**
20.00 g., 0.999 Silver 0.6424 oz. ASW, 38.61 mm. **Rev:** Bust at left - Javelin Thrower - yellow ring

| Date | Mintage | VF20 | XF40 | MS60 | MS63 | MS65 |
|---|---|---|---|---|---|---|
| 2013 Reverse Proof | Est. 500 | PF63 50.00 | PF65 60.00 | | | |

**KM# 72 50 VATU**
20.00 g., 0.999 Silver 0.6424 oz. ASW, 38.61 mm. **Rev:** Bust at left - Wrestling - Red ring

| Date | Mintage | VF20 | XF40 | MS60 | MS63 | MS65 |
|---|---|---|---|---|---|---|
| 2013 Reverse Proof | Est. 500 | PF63 50.00 | PF65 60.00 | | | |

**KM# 73 50 VATU**
20.00 g., 0.999 Silver 0.6424 oz. ASW, 38.61 mm. **Rev:** Bust at left - Long Jumper - Black ring

| Date | Mintage | VF20 | XF40 | MS60 | MS63 | MS65 |
|---|---|---|---|---|---|---|
| 2013 Reverse Proof | Est. 500 | PF63 50.00 | PF65 60.00 | | | |

**KM# 74 50 VATU**
20.00 g., 0.999 Silver 0.6424 oz. ASW, 38.61 mm. **Series:** Pierre De Coubertin - 150th Anniversary of Birth **Rev:** Bust at left, Discus Thrower, Blue ring

| Date | Mintage | VF20 | XF40 | MS60 | MS63 | MS65 |
|---|---|---|---|---|---|---|
| 2013 Reverse Proof | Est. 500 | PF63 50.00 | PF65 60.00 | | | |

**KM# 76 50 VATU**
20.00 g., 0.925 Silver 0.5948 oz. ASW, 38.61 mm. **Subject:** 2016 Olympics - Lighting of the Olympic Flame

| Date | Mintage | VF20 | XF40 | MS60 | MS63 | MS65 |
|---|---|---|---|---|---|---|
| 2013 | Est. 10000 | PF63 55.00 | PF65 65.00 | | | |

**KM# 90 50 VATU**
31.11 g., 0.999 Silver 0.999 oz. ASW, 38.61 mm. **Subject:** Raccoon with two black diamond inserts

| Date | Mintage | VF20 | XF40 | MS60 | MS63 | MS65 |
|---|---|---|---|---|---|---|
| 2013 | Est. 1000 | PF65 90.00 | | | | |

**KM# 9 100 VATU**
9.55 g., Nickel-Brass, 23.9 mm. **Obv:** National arms **Rev:** Sprouting bulbs

| Date | Mintage | VF20 | XF40 | MS60 | MS63 | MS65 |
|---|---|---|---|---|---|---|
| 2002 | — | — | — | 1.50 | 2.50 | 4.00 |
| 2008 | — | — | — | 1.50 | 2.50 | 4.00 |

**KM# 91 100 VATU**
62.20 g., 0.999 Silver 1.9978 oz. ASW, 55 mm. **Subject:** Raccoon family with six black diamond inserts

| Date | Mintage | VF20 | XF40 | MS60 | MS63 | MS65 |
|---|---|---|---|---|---|---|
| 2013 Proof, matte | Est. 500 | PF63 185 | PF65 200 | | | |

# VATICAN CITY

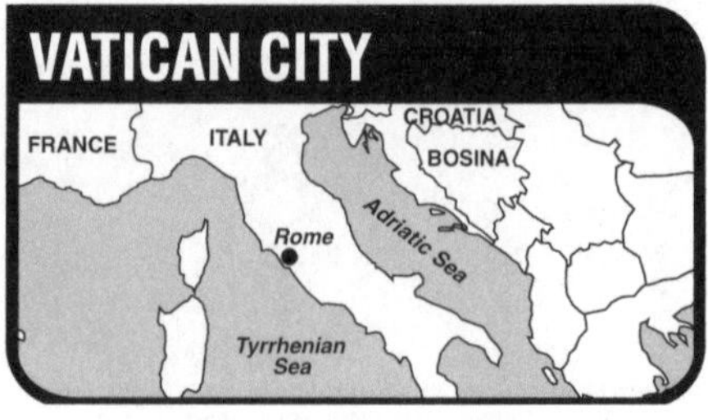


The State of the Vatican City, a papal state on the right bank of the Tiber River within the boundaries of Rome, has an area of 0.17 sq. mi. (0.44 sq. km.) and a population of *775. Capital: Vatican City.

Today the Pope exercises supreme legislative, executive and judicial power within the Vatican City, and the State of the Vatican City is recognized by many nations as an independent sovereign state under the temporal jurisdiction of the Pope, even to the extent of ambassadorial exchange. The Pope is of course, the head of the Roman Catholic Church.

**PONTIFFS**

John Paul II, 1978-2005
Sede Vacante, April 2 - 19, 2005
Benedict XVI, 2005-2013
Frances, 2013 -

**MINT MARK**

R – Rome

**MONETARY SYSTEM**

100 Centesimi = 1 Lira (thru 2002)
100 Euro Cent = 1 Euro

**DATING**

Most Vatican coins indicate the regnal year of the pope preceded by the word Anno (or an abbreviation), even if the anno domini date is omitted.

## CITY STATE
### John Paul II
### DECIMAL COINAGE

100 Centesimi = 1 Lira

**KM# 331 10 LIRE**
1.60 g., Aluminum, 23.2 mm. **Obv:** Bust left **Rev:** Papal arms **Edge:** Plain

| Date | Mintage | VF20 | XF40 | MS60 | MS63 | MS65 |
|---|---|---|---|---|---|---|
| 2001/XXIII | — | — | 1.00 | 2.50 | 3.00 | — |

**KM# 331a 10 LIRE**
Gold, 23.2 mm. **Obv:** Benedict XV bust left **Rev:** Papal arms **Note:** Struck in 2007.

| Date | Mintage | VF20 | XF40 | MS60 | MS63 | MS65 |
|---|---|---|---|---|---|---|
| 2001 R | 499 | PF63 2,000 | PF65 3,500 | | | |

**KM# 332 20 LIRE**
3.57 g., Brass, 21.2 mm. **Obv:** Bust left **Rev:** Papal arms **Edge:** Plain

| Date | Mintage | VF20 | XF40 | MS60 | MS63 | MS65 |
|---|---|---|---|---|---|---|
| 2001/XXIII | — | — | 1.00 | 2.50 | 3.00 | — |

### KM# 332a 20 LIRE

Gold, 21.2 mm. **Obv:** Pius XI bust left **Rev:** Papal arms **Note:** Struck in 2007.

| Date | Mintage | VF20 | XF40 | MS60 | MS63 | MS65 |
|---|---|---|---|---|---|---|
| 2001 R | 499 | PF63 2,000 | PF65 3,500 | | | |

### KM# 333 50 LIRE

4.50 g., Copper-Nickel, 19.2 mm. **Obv:** Pius XII bust left **Rev:** Papal arms **Edge:** Plain

| Date | Mintage | VF20 | XF40 | MS60 | MS63 | MS65 |
|---|---|---|---|---|---|---|
| 2001/XXIII | — | — | 1.00 | 2.50 | 3.00 | — |

### KM# 333a 50 LIRE

Gold, 19.2 mm. **Obv:** Pius XII bust left **Rev:** Papal arms **Note:** Struck in 2007.

| Date | Mintage | VF20 | XF40 | MS60 | MS63 | MS65 |
|---|---|---|---|---|---|---|
| 2001 R | 499 | PF63 2,500 | PF65 4,000 | | | |

### KM# 334 100 LIRE

4.50 g., Copper-Nickel, 22 mm. **Obv:** Bust left **Rev:** Papal arms within circle **Edge:** Reeded and plain sections

| Date | Mintage | VF20 | XF40 | MS60 | MS63 | MS65 |
|---|---|---|---|---|---|---|
| 2001/XXIII | — | — | 1.00 | 2.50 | 3.00 | — |

### KM# 334a 100 LIRE

Gold, 22 mm. **Obv:** John XXIII bust left **Rev:** Papal arms **Note:** Struck in 2007.

| Date | Mintage | VF20 | XF40 | MS60 | MS63 | MS65 |
|---|---|---|---|---|---|---|
| 2001 R | 499 | PF63 2,500 | PF65 4,000 | | | |

### KM# 335 200 LIRE

5.00 g., Brass, 22 mm. **Obv:** Bust right **Rev:** Papal arms within circle **Edge:** Reeded

| Date | Mintage | VF20 | XF40 | MS60 | MS63 | MS65 |
|---|---|---|---|---|---|---|
| 2001/XXIII | — | — | 1.00 | 2.50 | 3.00 | — |

### KM# 335a 200 LIRE

Gold, 22 mm. **Obv:** Paul VI bust right **Rev:** Papal arms **Note:** Struck in 2007.

| Date | Mintage | VF20 | XF40 | MS60 | MS63 | MS65 |
|---|---|---|---|---|---|---|
| 2001 R | 499 | PF63 2,500 | PF65 4,000 | | | |

### KM# 336 500 LIRE

6.77 g., Bi-Metallic Aluminum-Bronze center in Stainless steel ring, 25.7 mm. **Obv:** John Paul I head left **Rev:** Papal arms within circle **Edge:** Segmented reeding

| Date | Mintage | VF20 | XF40 | MS60 | MS63 | MS65 |
|---|---|---|---|---|---|---|
| 2001/XXIII | — | — | 3.50 | 7.00 | 8.50 | — |

### KM# 336a 500 LIRE

Gold, 25.7 mm. **Obv:** John Paul I bust left **Rev:** Papal arms

| Date | Mintage | VF20 | XF40 | MS60 | MS63 | MS65 |
|---|---|---|---|---|---|---|
| 2001 R | 499 | PF63 2,000 | PF65 3,750 | | | |

### KM# 337 1000 LIRE

8.85 g., Bi-Metallic Copper-Nickel center in Brass ring, 26.9 mm. **Obv:** John Paul II bust left **Rev:** Papal arms **Edge:** Segmented reeding

| Date | Mintage | VF20 | XF40 | MS60 | MS63 | MS65 |
|---|---|---|---|---|---|---|
| 2001/XXIII | — | — | 5.50 | 8.00 | 9.00 | — |

### KM# 337a 1000 LIRE

Gold, 26.9 mm. **Obv:** John Paul II bust left **Rev:** Papal arms

| Date | Mintage | VF20 | XF40 | MS60 | MS63 | MS65 |
|---|---|---|---|---|---|---|
| 2001 R | 499 | PF63 2,000 | PF65 3,750 | | | |

### KM# 338 1000 LIRE

14.60 g., 0.835 Silver 0.3919 oz. ASW, 31.4 mm. **Subject:** Peace **Obv:** Stylized dove in front of globe **Rev:** Crowned shield **Edge Lettering:** +++ TOTVS TVVS +++ MMI

| Date | Mintage | VF20 | XF40 | MS60 | MS63 | MS65 |
|---|---|---|---|---|---|---|
| 2001/XXIII | — | — | 20.00 | 35.00 | 40.00 | — |

### KM# 338a 1000 LIRE

Gold, 31.4 mm. **Obv:** Stylized dove in front of globe **Rev:** Crowned arms

| Date | Mintage | VF20 | XF40 | MS60 | MS63 | MS65 |
|---|---|---|---|---|---|---|
| 2001 R | 499 | PF63 2,000 | PF65 3,750 | | | |

### KM# 339 2000 LIRE

16.00 g., 0.835 Silver 0.4295 oz. ASW, 31.4 mm. **Subject:** Dialog for Peace **Obv:** Bust right holding crozier **Rev:** Dove above crowd **Edge:** Reeded

| Date | Mintage | VF20 | XF40 | MS60 | MS63 | MS65 |
|---|---|---|---|---|---|---|
| 2001/XXIII | 16,000 | — | 25.00 | 35.00 | 40.00 | — |
| 2001/XXIII | 8,000 | PF63 60.00 | PF65 70.00 | | | |

### KM# 340 5000 LIRE

18.00 g., 0.835 Silver 0.4832 oz. ASW, 32 mm. **Subject:** Easter **Obv:** Kneeling Pope praying **Rev:** Standing figure flanked by clouds below dove **Edge:** Reeded and plain sections

| Date | Mintage | VF20 | XF40 | MS60 | MS63 | MS65 |
|---|---|---|---|---|---|---|
| 2001 | — | — | 30.00 | 40.00 | 45.00 | — |
| 2001/XXIII | 16,000 | PF63 35.00 | PF65 45.00 | | | |

### KM# 390 50000 LIRE

7.50 g., 0.917 Gold 0.2211 oz. AGW, 23 mm. **Subject:** Religious symbols **Obv:** Bust right **Rev:** Cross

| Date | Mintage | VF20 | XF40 | MS60 | MS63 | MS65 |
|---|---|---|---|---|---|---|
| 2001//XXIII R | 6,000 | PF63 1,500 | PF65 2,000 | | | |

### KM# 391 100000 LIRE

15.00 g., 0.917 Gold 0.4422 oz. AGW, 28 mm. **Subject:** Religious symbols **Obv:** Bust right **Rev:** Chi rho with Alpha and Omega letters

| Date | Mintage | VF20 | XF40 | MS60 | MS63 | MS65 |
|---|---|---|---|---|---|---|
| 2001//XXIII R | 6,000 | PF63 2,000 | PF65 3,000 | | | |

## EURO COINAGE

### KM# 341 EURO CENT

2.30 g., Copper Plated Steel, 16.25 mm. **Obv:** Bust 1/4 left **Rev:** Value and globe **Edge:** Plain

| Date | Mintage | VF20 | XF40 | MS60 | MS63 | MS65 |
|---|---|---|---|---|---|---|
| 2002 R | 80,000 | — | — | — | — | 115 |
| 2002 R | — | PF65 175 | | | | |
| 2003 R Sets only | 65,000 | — | — | — | — | 55.00 |
| 2003 R | 13,000 | PF65 145 | | | | |
| 2004 R Sets only | 65,000 | — | — | — | — | 25.00 |
| 2004 R | 13,000 | PF65 145 | | | | |
| 2005 R Sets only | 85,000 | — | — | — | — | 25.00 |
| 2005 R | 16,000 | PF65 140 | | | | |

### KM# 342 2 EURO CENT

3.06 g., Copper Plated Steel, 18.75 mm. **Obv:** Bust 1/4 left **Rev:** Value and globe **Edge:** Grooved

| Date | Mintage | VF20 | XF40 | MS60 | MS63 | MS65 |
|---|---|---|---|---|---|---|
| 2002 R | 80,000 | — | — | — | — | 115 |
| 2002 R | — | PF65 175 | | | | |
| 2003 R Sets only | 65,000 | — | — | — | — | 55.00 |
| 2003 R | 13,000 | PF65 145 | | | | |
| 2004 R Sets only | 65,000 | — | — | — | — | 25.00 |
| 2004 R | 13,000 | PF65 145 | | | | |
| 2005 R Sets only | 85,000 | — | — | — | — | 25.00 |
| 2005 R | 16,000 | PF65 140 | | | | |

### KM# 343 5 EURO CENT

3.92 g., Copper Plated Steel, 21.25 mm. **Obv:** Bust 1/4 left **Rev:** Value and globe **Edge:** Plain

| Date | Mintage | VF20 | XF40 | MS60 | MS63 | MS65 |
|---|---|---|---|---|---|---|
| 2002 R | 80,000 | — | — | — | — | 115 |
| 2002 R | — | PF65 175 | | | | |
| 2003 R Sets only | 65,000 | — | — | — | — | 55.00 |
| 2003 R | 13,000 | PF65 145 | | | | |
| 2004 R Sets only | 65,000 | — | — | — | — | 28.00 |
| 2004 R | 13,000 | PF65 145 | | | | |
| 2005 R Sets only | 85,000 | — | — | — | — | 28.00 |
| 2005 R | 16,000 | PF65 140 | | | | |

### KM# 344 10 EURO CENT

4.10 g., Brass, 19.75 mm. **Obv:** Bust 1/4 left **Edge:** Reeded

| Date | Mintage | VF20 | XF40 | MS60 | MS63 | MS65 |
|---|---|---|---|---|---|---|
| 2002 R | 80,000 | — | — | — | — | 115 |
| 2002 R | — | PF65 175 | | | | |
| 2003 R Sets only | 65,000 | — | — | — | — | 55.00 |
| 2003 R | 13,000 | PF65 145 | | | | |
| 2004 R Sets only | 65,000 | — | — | — | — | 35.00 |
| 2004 R | 13,000 | PF65 145 | | | | |
| 2005 R Sets only | 85,000 | — | — | — | — | 35.00 |
| 2005 R | 16,000 | PF65 140 | | | | |

### KM# 345 20 EURO CENT

5.74 g., Brass, 22.25 mm. **Obv:** Bust 1/4 left **Rev:** Map and value **Edge:** Notched

| Date | Mintage | VF20 | XF40 | MS60 | MS63 | MS65 |
|---|---|---|---|---|---|---|
| 2002 R | 80,000 | — | — | — | — | 115 |
| 2002 R | — | PF65 175 | | | | |
| 2003 R Sets only | 65,000 | — | — | — | — | 55.00 |
| 2003 R | 13,000 | PF65 145 | | | | |
| 2004 R Sets only | 65,000 | — | — | — | — | 38.00 |
| 2004 R | 13,000 | PF65 145 | | | | |
| 2005 R Sets only | 85,000 | — | — | — | — | 38.00 |
| 2005 R | 16,000 | PF65 140 | | | | |

### KM# 346 50 EURO CENT

7.80 g., Brass, 24.25 mm. **Obv:** Bust 1/4 left **Rev:** Map and value **Edge:** Reeded

| Date | Mintage | VF20 | XF40 | MS60 | MS63 | MS65 |
|---|---|---|---|---|---|---|
| 2002 R | 80,000 | — | — | — | — | 115 |
| 2002 R | — | PF65 175 | | | | |
| 2003 R Sets only | 65,000 | — | — | — | — | 55.00 |
| 2003 R | 13,000 | PF65 145 | | | | |
| 2004 R Sets only | 65,000 | — | — | — | — | 42.00 |
| 2004 R | 13,000 | PF65 145 | | | | |
| 2005 R Sets only | 85,000 | — | — | — | — | 42.00 |
| 2005 R | 16,000 | PF65 140 | | | | |

### KM# 347 EURO

7.50 g., Bi-Metallic Copper-Nickel center in Nickel-Brass ring, 23.25 mm. **Obv:** Bust 1/4 left **Rev:** Value and map **Edge:** Segmented reeding

| Date | Mintage | VF20 | XF40 | MS60 | MS63 | MS65 |
|---|---|---|---|---|---|---|
| 2002 R | 80,000 | — | — | — | — | 100 |
| 2002 R | — | PF65 185 | | | | |
| 2003 R Sets only | 65,000 | — | — | — | — | 75.00 |
| 2003 R | 13,000 | PF65 145 | | | | |
| 2004 R Sets only | 65,000 | — | — | — | — | 60.00 |
| 2004 R | 13,000 | PF65 145 | | | | |
| 2005 R Sets only | 85,000 | — | — | — | — | 60.00 |
| 2005 R | 16,000 | PF65 140 | | | | |

### KM# 348 2 EURO

8.50 g., Bi-Metallic Nickel-Brass center in Copper-Nickel ring, 25.75 mm. **Obv:** Bust 1/4 left **Rev:** Value and map **Edge:** Reeded with 2's and stars

| Date | Mintage | VF20 | XF40 | MS60 | MS63 | MS65 |
|---|---|---|---|---|---|---|
| 2002 R | 80,000 | — | — | — | — | 165 |
| 2002 R | — | PF65 215 | | | | |
| 2003 R Sets only | 65,000 | — | — | — | — | 100 |
| 2003 R | 13,000 | PF65 185 | | | | |
| 2004 R Sets only | 65,000 | — | — | — | — | 80.00 |
| 2004 R | 13,000 | PF65 185 | | | | |
| 2005 R Sets only | 85,000 | — | — | — | — | 80.00 |
| 2005 R | 16,000 | PF65 180 | | | | |

**KM# 358 2 EURO**
8.50 g., Bi-Metallic Nickel-Brass center in Copper-Nickel ring, 25.75 mm. **Subject:** 75th Anniversary of the Founding of the Vatican City State **Obv:** St. Peter's Square within city walls, dates 1929-2004 **Rev:** Value and map **Edge:** Reeded with 2's and stars

| Date | Mintage | VF20 | XF40 | MS60 | MS63 | MS65 |
|---|---|---|---|---|---|---|
| 2004 R | 85,000 | — | — | — | — | 25.00 |

**KM# 349 5 EURO**
18.00 g., 0.835 Silver 0.4832 oz. ASW, 32 mm. **Subject:** 24th Anniversary of Reign **Obv:** Bust 1/4 left **Rev:** Allegorical female and bridge **Edge:** Lettered **Edge Lettering:** +++ TOTUS TUUS +++ MMII

| Date | Mintage | VF20 | XF40 | MS60 | MS63 | MS65 |
|---|---|---|---|---|---|---|
| 2002 R | 10,000 | PF65 125 | | | | |

**KM# 354 5 EURO**
18.00 g., 0.925 Silver 0.5353 oz. ASW, 32 mm. **Subject:** Year of the Rosary **Obv:** Pope praying the rosary **Rev:** Our Lady of Pompei" presenting rosaries to Saints Dominic and Catherine **Edge:** Reeded

| Date | Mintage | VF20 | XF40 | MS60 | MS63 | MS65 |
|---|---|---|---|---|---|---|
| 2003 R | 10,000 | PF65 65.00 | | | | |

**KM# 359 5 EURO**
18.00 g., 0.925 Silver 0.5353 oz. ASW, 32 mm. **Subject:** 150th Anniversary of the Proclamation of the Dogma of the Immaculate Conception **Obv:** Virgin Mary **Rev:** Two Papal coat of arms **Edge:** Reeded and plain sections

| Date | Mintage | VF20 | XF40 | MS60 | MS63 | MS65 |
|---|---|---|---|---|---|---|
| 2004 R | 13,000 | — | — | — | — | 60.00 |

**KM# 350 10 EURO**
22.00 g., 0.835 Silver 0.5906 oz. ASW, 34 mm. **Subject:** 24th Anniversary of Reign **Obv:** Pope holding crucifix **Rev:** Risen Christ (Message of peace) **Edge:** Reeded

| Date | Mintage | VF20 | XF40 | MS60 | MS63 | MS65 |
|---|---|---|---|---|---|---|
| 2002 R | 10,000 | PF65 80.00 | | | | |

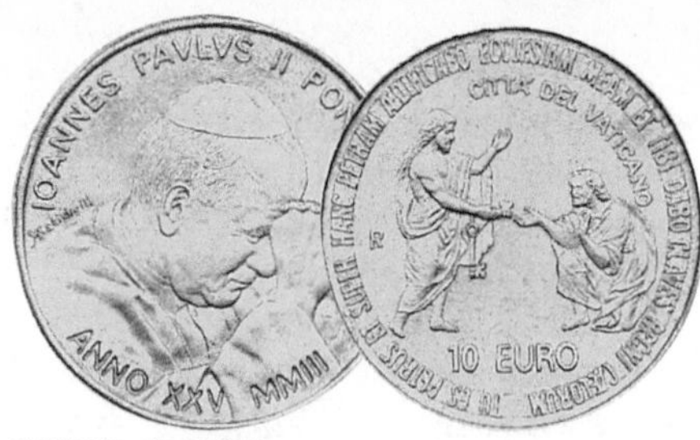

**KM# 355 10 EURO**
22.00 g., 0.925 Silver 0.6543 oz. ASW, 34 mm. **Subject:** 25th Anniversary of Reign **Obv:** Pope praying **Rev:** St. Peter receiving the keys of Earth and Heaven **Edge:** Reeded

| Date | Mintage | VF20 | XF40 | MS60 | MS63 | MS65 |
|---|---|---|---|---|---|---|
| 2003 R | 10,000 | PF65 80.00 | | | | |

**KM# 360 10 EURO**
22.00 g., 0.925 Silver 0.6543 oz. ASW, 34 mm. **Obv:** Pope praying for peace **Rev:** Tree of Life rooted in virtues **Edge:** Reeded and plain sections

| Date | Mintage | VF20 | XF40 | MS60 | MS63 | MS65 |
|---|---|---|---|---|---|---|
| 2004 R | 13,000 | — | — | — | — | 90.00 |

**KM# 361 20 EURO**
6.00 g., 0.917 Gold 0.1769 oz. AGW, 21 mm. **Subject:** Roots of Faith **Rev:** Noah's Ark

| Date | Mintage | VF20 | XF40 | MS60 | MS63 | MS65 |
|---|---|---|---|---|---|---|
| 2002 | 2,800 | PF65 1,200 | | | | |

**KM# 351 20 EURO**
6.00 g., 0.9166 Gold 0.1768 oz. AGW, 21 mm. **Rev:** Moses being found in floating basket **Edge:** Reeded

| Date | Mintage | VF20 | XF40 | MS60 | MS63 | MS65 |
|---|---|---|---|---|---|---|
| 2003 R | 2,800 | PF65 1,300 | | | | |

**KM# 363 20 EURO**
6.00 g., 0.917 Gold 0.1769 oz. AGW, 21 mm. **Rev:** David slaying Goliath

| Date | Mintage | VF20 | XF40 | MS60 | MS63 | MS65 |
|---|---|---|---|---|---|---|
| 2004/XXVII R | 3,050 | PF65 1,200 | | | | |

**KM# 362 50 EURO**
15.00 g., 0.917 Gold 0.4422 oz. AGW, 28 mm. **Subject:** Roots of Faith **Rev:** Sacrifice of Abraham

| Date | Mintage | VF20 | XF40 | MS60 | MS63 | MS65 |
|---|---|---|---|---|---|---|
| 2002 | 2,800 | PF65 2,200 | | | | |

**KM# 352 50 EURO**
15.00 g., 0.9166 Gold 0.442 oz. AGW, 28 mm. **Rev:** Moses receiving the Ten Commandments **Edge:** Reeded

| Date | Mintage | VF20 | XF40 | MS60 | MS63 | MS65 |
|---|---|---|---|---|---|---|
| 2003 R | 2,800 | PF65 2,200 | | | | |

**KM# 364 50 EURO**
15.00 g., 0.917 Gold 0.4422 oz. AGW, 28 mm. **Rev:** Judgement of Solomon

| Date | Mintage | VF20 | XF40 | MS60 | MS63 | MS65 |
|---|---|---|---|---|---|---|
| 2004/XXVII R | 3,050 | PF65 2,200 | | | | |

## Sede Vacante

**KM# 365 EURO CENT**
2.30 g., Copper Plated Steel, 16.25 mm. **Obv:** Arms of Cardinal Eduardo Martinez Somalo **Rev:** Value and globe

| Date | Mintage | VF20 | XF40 | MS60 | MS63 | MS65 |
|---|---|---|---|---|---|---|
| MMV (2005) R Sets only | 60,000 | — | — | — | — | 45.00 |

**KM# 366 2 EURO CENT**
3.06 g., Copper Plated Steel, 18.75 mm. **Obv:** Arms of Cardinal Eduardo Martinez Somalo **Rev:** Value and globe **Edge:** Grooved

| Date | Mintage | VF20 | XF40 | MS60 | MS63 | MS65 |
|---|---|---|---|---|---|---|
| MMV (2005) R Sets only | 60,000 | — | — | — | — | 42.00 |

**KM# 367 5 EURO CENT**
3.92 g., Copper Plated Steel, 21.25 mm. **Obv:** Arms of Cardinal Eduardo Martinez Somalo **Rev:** Value and globe

| Date | Mintage | VF20 | XF40 | MS60 | MS63 | MS65 |
|---|---|---|---|---|---|---|
| MMV (2005) R Sets only | 60,000 | — | — | — | — | 45.00 |

**KM# 368 10 EURO CENT**
4.10 g., Brass, 19.75 mm. **Obv:** Arms of Cardinal Eduardo Martinez Somalo **Rev:** Map and value **Edge:** Reeded

| Date | Mintage | VF20 | XF40 | MS60 | MS63 | MS65 |
|---|---|---|---|---|---|---|
| MMV (2005) R Sets only | 60,000 | — | — | — | — | 48.00 |

**KM# 369 20 EURO CENT**
5.74 g., Brass, 22.25 mm. **Obv:** Arms of Cardinal Eduardo Martinez Somalo **Rev:** Map and value **Edge:** Notched

| Date | Mintage | VF20 | XF40 | MS60 | MS63 | MS65 |
|---|---|---|---|---|---|---|
| MMV (2005) R Sets only | 60,000 | — | — | — | — | 50.00 |

**KM# 370 50 EURO CENT**
7.80 g., Brass, 24.25 mm. **Obv:** Arms of Cardinal Eduardo Martinez Somalo **Rev:** Map and value **Edge:** Reeded

| Date | Mintage | VF20 | XF40 | MS60 | MS63 | MS65 |
|---|---|---|---|---|---|---|
| MMV (2005) R Sets only | 60,000 | — | — | — | — | 55.00 |

**KM# 371 EURO**
7.50 g., Bi-Metallic Copper-Nickel center in Nickel-Brass ring, 23.25 mm. **Obv:** Arms of Cardinal Eduardo Martinez Somalo **Rev:** Value and map **Edge:** Segmented reeding

| Date | Mintage | VF20 | XF40 | MS60 | MS63 | MS65 |
|---|---|---|---|---|---|---|
| MMV (2005) R Sets only | 60,000 | — | — | — | — | 70.00 |

**KM# 372 2 EURO**
8.50 g., Bi-Metallic Nickel-Brass center in Copper-Nickel ring, 25.75 mm. **Obv:** Arms of Cardinal Eduardo Martinez Somalo **Rev:** Map and value **Edge:** Reeded with 2's and stars

| Date | Mintage | VF20 | XF40 | MS60 | MS63 | MS65 |
|---|---|---|---|---|---|---|
| MMV (2005) R Sets only | 60,000 | — | — | — | — | 75.00 |

**KM# 373 5 EURO**
18.00 g., 0.925 Silver 0.5353 oz. ASW, 32 mm. **Obv:** Dove within square **Rev:** Arms of Cardinal Eduardo Martinez Somalo **Edge:** Reeded

| Date | Mintage | VF20 | XF40 | MS60 | MS63 | MS65 |
|---|---|---|---|---|---|---|
| MMV (2005) R | 13,440 | PF65 200 | | | | |

## Benedict XVI

**KM# 375 EURO CENT**
2.30 g., Copper Plated Steel, 16.25 mm. **Obv:** Pope's bust facing 3/4 right **Obv. Legend:** CITTA' DEL VATICANO **Rev:** Value and globe **Edge:** Plain

| Date | Mintage | VF20 | XF40 | MS60 | MS63 | MS65 |
|---|---|---|---|---|---|---|
| 2006 R Sets only | 85,000 | — | — | — | — | 12.00 |
| 2006 R | 16,000 | PF65 18.00 | | | | |
| 2007 R Sets only | 85,000 | — | — | — | — | 12.00 |
| 2007 R | 16,000 | PF65 18.00 | | | | |
| MMVIII (2008) R Sets only | 85,000 | — | — | — | — | 12.00 |
| MMVIII (2008) R | 16,000 | PF65 18.00 | | | | |
| 2009 R Sets only | 85,000 | — | — | — | — | 12.00 |
| 2009 R | 16,000 | PF65 18.00 | | | | |
| 2010 R Sets only | 94,000 | — | — | — | — | 12.00 |
| 2010 R | 15,000 | PF65 18.00 | | | | |
| 2011 R | 94,000 | — | — | — | — | 12.00 |
| 2011 R | 15,000 | PF65 18.00 | | | | |
| 2012 R | 84,000 | — | — | — | — | 12.00 |
| 2012 R | 15,000 | PF65 18.00 | | | | |
| 2013 R | 85,000 | — | — | — | — | 12.00 |
| 2013 R | 15,000 | PF65 18.00 | | | | |

**KM# 376 2 EURO CENT**
3.06 g., Copper Plated Steel, 18.75 mm. **Obv:** Pope's bust facing 3/4 right **Obv. Legend:** CITTA' DEL VATICANO **Rev:** Value and globe **Edge:** Grooved

| Date | Mintage | VF20 | XF40 | MS60 | MS63 | MS65 |
|---|---|---|---|---|---|---|
| 2006 R Sets only | 85,000 | — | — | — | — | 15.00 |
| 2006 R | 16,000 | PF65 20.00 | | | | |
| 2007 R Sets only | 85,000 | — | — | — | — | 15.00 |

| Date | Mintage | VF20 | XF40 | MS60 | MS63 | MS65 |
|---|---|---|---|---|---|---|
| 2007 R | 16,000 | PF65 20.00 | | | | |
| MDVIII (2008) R Sets only | 85,000 | — | — | — | — | 15.00 |
| MDVIII (2008) R | 16,000 | PF65 20.00 | | | | |
| 2009 R Sets only | 85,000 | — | — | — | — | 15.00 |
| 2009 R | 16,000 | PF65 20.00 | | | | |
| 2010 R Sets only | 94,000 | — | — | — | — | 15.00 |
| 2010 R | 15,000 | PF65 20.00 | | | | |
| 2011 R | 94,000 | — | — | — | — | 15.00 |
| 2011 R | 15,000 | PF65 20.00 | | | | |
| 2012 R | 84,000 | — | — | — | — | 15.00 |
| 2012 R | 15,000 | PF65 20.00 | | | | |
| 2013 R | 85,000 | — | — | — | — | 15.00 |
| 2013 R | 15,000 | PF65 20.00 | | | | |

**KM# 377 5 EURO CENT**
3.92 g., Copper Plated Steel, 21.25 mm. **Obv:** Pope's bust facing 3/4 right **Obv. Legend:** CITTA' DEL VATICANO **Rev:** Value and globe **Edge:** Plain

| Date | Mintage | VF20 | XF40 | MS60 | MS63 | MS65 |
|---|---|---|---|---|---|---|
| 2006 R Sets only | 85,000 | — | — | — | — | 16.50 |
| 2006 R | 16,000 | PF65 22.50 | | | | |
| 2007 R Sets only | 85,000 | — | — | — | — | 16.50 |
| 2007 R | 16,000 | PF65 22.50 | | | | |
| MDVIII (2008) R Sets only | 85,000 | — | — | — | — | 16.50 |
| MDVIII (2008) R | 16,000 | PF65 22.50 | | | | |
| 2009 R Sets only | 85,000 | — | — | — | — | 16.50 |
| 2009 R | 16,000 | PF65 22.50 | | | | |
| 2010 R Sets only | 94,000 | — | — | — | — | 16.50 |
| 2010 R | 15,000 | PF65 22.50 | | | | |
| 2011 R | 94,000 | — | — | — | — | 16.50 |
| 2011 R | 15,000 | PF65 22.50 | | | | |
| 2012 R | 84,000 | — | — | — | — | 16.50 |
| 2012 R | 15,000 | PF65 22.50 | | | | |
| 2013 R | 85,000 | — | — | — | — | 16.50 |
| 2013 R | 15,000 | PF65 22.50 | | | | |

**KM# 378 10 EURO CENT**
4.10 g., Brass, 19.75 mm. **Obv:** Pope's bust facing 3/4 right **Obv. Legend:** CITTA' DEL VATICANO **Rev:** Map and value **Edge:** Reeded

| Date | Mintage | VF20 | XF40 | MS60 | MS63 | MS65 |
|---|---|---|---|---|---|---|
| 2006 R Sets only | 85,000 | — | — | — | — | 17.50 |
| 2006 R | 16,000 | PF65 25.00 | | | | |
| 2007 R Sets only | 85,000 | — | — | — | — | 17.50 |
| 2007 R | 16,000 | PF65 25.00 | | | | |

**KM# 385 10 EURO CENT**
4.10 g., Brass, 19.75 mm. **Rev:** Relief map of Western Europe, stars, lines and value **Edge:** Reeded

| Date | Mintage | VF20 | XF40 | MS60 | MS63 | MS65 |
|---|---|---|---|---|---|---|
| MMVIII (2008) R Sets only | 85,000 | — | — | — | — | 17.50 |
| MMVIII (2008) R | 16,000 | PF65 25.00 | | | | |
| 2009 R Sets only | 85,000 | — | — | — | — | 17.50 |
| 2009 R | 16,000 | PF65 25.00 | | | | |
| 2010 R Sets only | 94,000 | — | — | — | — | 17.50 |
| 2010 R | 15,000 | PF65 25.00 | | | | |
| 2011 R | 94,000 | — | — | — | — | 17.50 |
| 2011 R | 15,000 | PF65 25.00 | | | | |
| 2012 R | 84,000 | — | — | — | — | 17.50 |
| 2012 R | 15,000 | PF65 25.00 | | | | |
| 2013 R | 85,000 | — | — | — | — | 17.50 |
| 2013 R | 15,000 | PF65 25.00 | | | | |

**KM# 379 20 EURO CENT**
5.74 g., Brass, 22.25 mm. **Obv:** Pope's bust facing 3/4 right **Obv. Legend:** CITTA' DEL VATICANO **Rev:** Map and value **Edge:** Notched

| Date | Mintage | VF20 | XF40 | MS60 | MS63 | MS65 |
|---|---|---|---|---|---|---|
| 2006 R Sets only | 85,000 | — | — | — | — | 18.00 |
| 2006 R | 16,000 | PF65 28.00 | | | | |
| 2007 R Sets only | 85,000 | — | — | — | — | 18.00 |
| 2007 R | 16,000 | PF65 28.00 | | | | |

**KM# 386 20 EURO CENT**
5.74 g., Brass, 22.25 mm. **Rev:** Relief map of Western Europe, stars, lines and value **Edge:** Notched

| Date | Mintage | VF20 | XF40 | MS60 | MS63 | MS65 |
|---|---|---|---|---|---|---|
| MMVIII (2008) R Sets only | 85,000 | — | — | — | — | 18.00 |
| MMVIII (2008) R | 16,000 | PF65 28.00 | | | | |
| 2009 R Sets only | 85,000 | — | — | — | — | 18.00 |
| 2009 R | 16,000 | PF65 28.00 | | | | |
| 2010 R Sets only | 94,000 | — | — | — | — | 18.00 |
| 2010 R | 15,000 | PF65 28.00 | | | | |
| 2011 R | 94,000 | — | — | — | — | 18.00 |
| 2011 R | 15,000 | PF65 28.00 | | | | |
| 2012 R | 84,000 | — | — | — | — | 18.00 |
| 2012 R | 15,000 | PF65 28.00 | | | | |
| 2013 R | 85,000 | — | — | — | — | 18.00 |
| 2013 R | 15,000 | PF65 28.00 | | | | |

**KM# 380 50 EURO CENT**
7.80 g., Brass, 24.25 mm. **Obv:** Pope's bust facing 3/4 right **Obv. Legend:** CITTA' DEL VATICANO **Rev:** Map and value **Edge:** Reeded

| Date | Mintage | VF20 | XF40 | MS60 | MS63 | MS65 |
|---|---|---|---|---|---|---|
| 2006 R Sets only | 85,000 | — | — | — | — | 22.50 |
| 2006 R | 16,000 | PF65 35.00 | | | | |
| 2007 R Sets only | 85,000 | — | — | — | — | 22.50 |
| 2007 R | 16,000 | PF65 35.00 | | | | |

**KM# 387 50 EURO CENT**
7.80 g., Brass, 24.25 mm. **Rev:** Relief map of Western Europe, stars, lines and value **Edge:** Reeded

| Date | Mintage | VF20 | XF40 | MS60 | MS63 | MS65 |
|---|---|---|---|---|---|---|
| MMVIII (2008) R Sets only | 85,000 | — | — | — | — | 32.50 |
| MMVIII (2008) R | 16,000 | PF65 40.00 | | | | |
| 2009 R Sets only | 85,000 | — | — | — | — | 32.50 |
| 2009 R | 16,000 | PF65 40.00 | | | | |
| 2010 R Sets only | 94,000 | — | — | — | — | 32.50 |
| 2010 R | 15,000 | PF65 40.00 | | | | |
| 2011 R | 94,000 | — | — | — | — | 32.50 |
| 2011 R | 15,000 | PF65 40.00 | | | | |
| 2012 R | 94,000 | — | — | — | — | 32.50 |
| 2012 R | 15,000 | PF65 40.00 | | | | |
| 2013 R | 95,000 | — | — | — | — | 32.50 |
| 2013 R | 15,000 | PF65 40.00 | | | | |

**KM# 381 EURO**
7.50 g., Bi-Metallic Copper-Nickel center in Nickel-Brass ring., 23.25 mm. **Obv:** Pope's bust facing 3/4 right **Obv. Legend:** CITTA' - DEL VATICANO **Rev:** Value and map **Edge:** Segmented reeding

| Date | Mintage | VF20 | XF40 | MS60 | MS63 | MS65 |
|---|---|---|---|---|---|---|
| 2006 R Sets only | 85,000 | — | — | — | — | 25.00 |
| 2006 R | 16,000 | PF65 40.00 | | | | |
| 2007 R Sets only | 85,000 | — | — | — | — | 25.00 |
| 2007 R | 16,000 | PF65 40.00 | | | | |

**KM# 388 EURO**
7.50 g., Bi-Metallic Copper-Nickel center in Nickel-Brass ring, 23.25 mm. **Rev:** Relief map of Western Europe, stars, lines and value **Edge:** Segmented reeding

| Date | Mintage | VF20 | XF40 | MS60 | MS63 | MS65 |
|---|---|---|---|---|---|---|
| MMVIII (2008) R Sets only | 85,000 | — | — | — | — | 25.00 |
| MMVIII (2008) R | 16,000 | PF65 40.00 | | | | |
| 2009 R Sets only | 85,000 | — | — | — | — | 25.00 |
| 2009 R | 16,000 | PF65 40.00 | | | | |
| 2010 R Sets only | 94,000 | — | — | — | — | 25.00 |
| 2010 R | 15,000 | PF65 40.00 | | | | |
| 2011 R | 94,000 | — | — | — | — | 25.00 |
| 2011 R | 15,000 | PF65 40.00 | | | | |
| 2012 R | 84,000 | — | — | — | — | 25.00 |
| 2012 R | 15,000 | PF65 40.00 | | | | |
| 2013 R | 85,000 | — | — | — | — | 25.00 |
| 2013 R | 15,000 | PF65 40.00 | | | | |

**KM# 374 2 EURO**
8.50 g., Bi-Metallic Nickel-Brass center in Copper-Nickel ring, 25.75 mm. **Subject:** World Youth Day **Obv:** Cologne Cathedral **Rev:** Value and Euro map **Edge:** Reeded with 2's and stars

| Date | Mintage | VF20 | XF40 | MS60 | MS63 | MS65 |
|---|---|---|---|---|---|---|
| 2005 R | — | — | — | — | — | 90.00 |

**KM# 382 2 EURO**
8.50 g., Bi-Metallic Nickel-Brass center in Copper-Nickel ring, 25.75 mm. **Obv:** Pope's bust facing 3/4 right **Obv. Legend:** CITTA' - DEL VATICANO **Rev:** Value and map **Edge:** Reeded with 2's and stars

| Date | Mintage | VF20 | XF40 | MS60 | MS63 | MS65 |
|---|---|---|---|---|---|---|
| 2006 R Sets only | 85,000 | — | — | — | — | 28.00 |
| 2006 R | 16,000 | PF65 50.00 | | | | |
| 2007 R Sets only | 85,000 | — | — | — | — | 28.00 |
| 2007 R | 16,000 | PF65 50.00 | | | | |

**KM# 394 2 EURO**
8.50 g., Bi-Metallic Nickel-Brass center in Copper-Nickel ring, 25.75 mm. **Subject:** Swiss guards, 500th Anniversary **Obv:** Swiss guard taking oath on flag **Rev:** Map and value **Edge:** Reeded with 2's and stars

| Date | Mintage | VF20 | XF40 | MS60 | MS63 | MS65 |
|---|---|---|---|---|---|---|
| ND (2006) R | 100,000 | — | — | — | 80.00 | 90.00 |

**KM# 399 2 EURO**
8.50 g., Bi-Metallic Nickel-Brass center in Copper-Nickel ring, 25.75 mm. **Subject:** Pope Benedict's 80th Birthday **Obv:** Bust left **Rev:** Map and value **Edge:** Reeded with 2's and stars

| Date | Mintage | VF20 | XF40 | MS60 | MS63 | MS65 |
|---|---|---|---|---|---|---|
| 2007 R | 100,000 | — | — | — | 50.00 | 60.00 |

**KM# 389 2 EURO**
8.50 g., Bi-Metallic Nickel-Brass center in Copper-Nickel ring, 25.75 mm. **Rev:** Relief map of Western Europe, stars, lines and value **Edge:** Reeded with 2's and stars

| Date | Mintage | VF20 | XF40 | MS60 | MS63 | MS65 |
|---|---|---|---|---|---|---|
| MMVIII (2008) R Sets only | 85,000 | — | — | — | — | 28.00 |
| MMVIII (2008) R | 16,000 | PF65 50.00 | | | | |
| 2009 R Sets only | 85,000 | — | — | — | — | 28.00 |
| 2009 R | 16,000 | PF65 50.00 | | | | |
| 2010 R Sets only | 94,000 | — | — | — | — | 28.00 |
| 2010 R | 15,000 | PF65 50.00 | | | | |
| 2011 R | 94,000 | — | — | — | — | 28.00 |
| 2011 R | 15,000 | PF65 50.00 | | | | |
| 2012 R | 84,000 | — | — | — | — | 25.00 |
| 2012 R | 15,000 | PF65 50.00 | | | | |
| 2013 R | 85,000 | — | — | — | — | 25.00 |
| 2013 R | 15,000 | PF65 50.00 | | | | |

**KM# 404 2 EURO**
8.50 g., Bi-Metallic Nickel-Brass center in Copper-Nickel ring, 25.75 mm. **Obv:** St. Paul being blinded on rearing horse **Rev:** Map and value **Edge:** Reeded with 2's and stars

| Date | Mintage | VF20 | XF40 | MS60 | MS63 | MS65 |
|---|---|---|---|---|---|---|
| ND (2008) R | 106,084 | — | — | — | 25.00 | 28.00 |

**KM# 410 2 EURO**
8.50 g., Bi-Metallic Nickel-Brass center in Copper-Nickel ring, 25.75 mm. **Subject:** International Year of Astronomy **Rev:** Map and value **Edge:** Reeded with 2's and stars

| Date | Mintage | VF20 | XF40 | MS60 | MS63 | MS65 |
|---|---|---|---|---|---|---|
| 2009 R | 100,000 | — | — | — | 25.00 | 28.00 |

**KM# 420 2 EURO**
8.50 g., Bi-Metallic Nickel-Brass center in Copper-Nickel ring, 25.75 mm. **Subject:** Year of the Priest **Edge:** Reeded with 2's and stars

| Date | Mintage | VF20 | XF40 | MS60 | MS63 | MS65 |
|---|---|---|---|---|---|---|
| 2010 R | 115,000 | — | — | — | 20.00 | 25.00 |

**KM# 426 2 EURO**
8.50 g., Bi-Metallic Nickel-Brass center in Copper-Nickel ring, 25.75 mm. **Subject:** 26th World Youth Day **Obv:** Youth with Vatican City flags **Edge:** Reeded with 2's and stars

| Date | Mintage | VF20 | XF40 | MS60 | MS63 | MS65 |
|---|---|---|---|---|---|---|
| 2011 R | 98,000 | — | — | — | — | 20.00 |
| 2011 R Special Unc. | 11,500 | — | — | — | — | 28.00 |

**KM# 435 2 EURO**
8.50 g., Bi-Metallic Nickel-Brass center in Copper-Nickel ring, 25.75 mm. **Subject:** 7th World Meeting of Families **Obv:** Family unit before Cathedral

| Date | Mintage | VF20 | XF40 | MS60 | MS63 | MS65 |
|---|---|---|---|---|---|---|
| 2012 R | 89,000 | — | — | — | — | 28.00 |
| 2012 R | — | PF63 40.00 | PF65 50.00 | | | |

**KM# 383 5 EURO**
18.00 g., 0.925 Silver 0.5353 oz. ASW, 32 mm. **Subject:** Life reborn **Obv:** Bust left **Rev:** Children playing among branches of an olive tree

| Date | Mintage | VF20 | XF40 | MS60 | MS63 | MS65 |
|---|---|---|---|---|---|---|
| 2005 R | 13,000 | PF65 100 | | | | |

**KM# 395 5 EURO**
18.00 g., 0.925 Silver 0.5353 oz. ASW, 32 mm. **Subject:** World Day of Peace **Obv:** Half-length figure Benedict right in vestments with crozier **Rev:** St. Benedict of Nursia seated

| Date | Mintage | VF20 | XF40 | MS60 | MS63 | MS65 |
|---|---|---|---|---|---|---|
| MMVI (2006) R | 14,160 | PF63 80.00 | PF65 90.00 | | | |

**KM# 400 5 EURO**
18.00 g., 0.925 Silver 0.5353 oz. ASW, 32 mm. **Subject:** World Day of Peace **Obv:** 1/2 length figure kneeling in prayer **Rev:** Standing St. Francis of Assissi, rays in background

| Date | Mintage | VF20 | XF40 | MS60 | MS63 | MS65 |
|---|---|---|---|---|---|---|
| MMVII (2007) R | 13,693 | PF63 45.00 | PF65 55.00 | | | |

**KM# 406 5 EURO**
18.00 g., 0.925 Silver 0.5353 oz. ASW, 32 mm. **Subject:** World Youth Day - Sydney **Obv:** Pope right, blessing **Rev:** Sydney Harbor sites

| Date | Mintage | VF20 | XF40 | MS60 | MS63 | MS65 |
|---|---|---|---|---|---|---|
| MMVIII (2008) R | 9,600 | PF63 50.00 | PF65 60.00 | | | |

**KM# 415 5 EURO**
18.00 g., 0.925 Silver 0.5353 oz. ASW, 32 mm. **Subject:** World day of Peace **Obv:** Bust right in prayer **Rev:** Candle, family

| Date | Mintage | VF20 | XF40 | MS60 | MS63 | MS65 |
|---|---|---|---|---|---|---|
| 2009 R | 9,600 | PF63 50.00 | PF65 60.00 | | | |

**KM# 421 5 EURO**
18.00 g., 0.925 Silver 0.5353 oz. ASW, 32 mm. **Subject:** Migrants and Refugees **Obv:** Benedict standing facing in vestments and mitre **Rev:** Family scene

| Date | Mintage | VF20 | XF40 | MS60 | MS63 | MS65 |
|---|---|---|---|---|---|---|
| 2010 R | 9,998 | PF63 65.00 | PF65 75.00 | | | |

**KM# 427 5 EURO**
18.00 g., 0.925 Silver 0.5353 oz. ASW, 32 mm. **Subject:** 44the World day of Peace **Obv:** Bust left **Rev:** Female standing

| Date | Mintage | VF20 | XF40 | MS60 | MS63 | MS65 |
|---|---|---|---|---|---|---|
| 2011 R | 7,998 | PF63 70.00 | PF65 80.00 | | | |

**KM# 429 5 EURO**
18.00 g., 0.925 Silver 0.5353 oz. ASW, 32 mm. **Subject:** John Paul II beautification **Obv:** Bust facing of John Paul II **Rev:** Cherubs elevating Papal Arms of John Paul II

| Date | Mintage | VF20 | XF40 | MS60 | MS63 | MS65 |
|---|---|---|---|---|---|---|
| 2011 R | 9,500 | PF63 65.00 | PF65 75.00 | | | |

**KM# 436 5 EURO**
18.00 g., 0.925 Silver 0.5353 oz. ASW, 32 mm. **Subject:** John Paul I, 100th Anniversary of Birth

| Date | Mintage | VF20 | XF40 | MS60 | MS63 | MS65 |
|---|---|---|---|---|---|---|
| 2012 R | 8,999 | PF63 80.00 | PF65 90.00 | | | |

**KM# 384 10 EURO**
22.00 g., 0.925 Silver 0.6543 oz. ASW, 34 mm. **Subject:** Disciples of Emanaus **Obv:** Bust left **Rev:** Three men seated at table

| Date | Mintage | VF20 | XF40 | MS60 | MS63 | MS65 |
|---|---|---|---|---|---|---|
| 2006 R | 13,000 | PF65 215 | | | | |

**KM# 396 10 EURO**
22.00 g., 0.925 Silver 0.6543 oz. ASW, 34 mm. **Subject:** St. Peter's Collonade, 350th Anniversary **Obv:** Collonade & Pope Benedict **Rev:** Collonade Schematics

| Date | Mintage | VF20 | XF40 | MS60 | MS63 | MS65 |
|---|---|---|---|---|---|---|
| AN II MMVI (2006) R | 14,160 | PF63 80.00 | PF65 90.00 | | | |

**KM# 401 10 EURO**
22.00 g., 0.925 Silver 0.6543 oz. ASW, 34 mm. **Subject:** World Mission Day **Obv:** Bust right in ermine cape **Rev:** Blessed Mother Theresa of Calcutta and child

| Date | Mintage | VF20 | XF40 | MS60 | MS63 | MS65 |
|---|---|---|---|---|---|---|
| AN III MMVII (2007) R | 13,694 | PF63 70.00 | PF65 80.00 | | | |

**KM# 407 10 EURO**
22.00 g., 0.925 Silver 0.6543 oz. ASW, 34 mm. **Subject:** World Day of Peace **Obv:** Pope seated on chair in full robes and miter **Rev:** The Holy Family - Jesus, Mary, Joseph

| Date | Mintage | VF20 | XF40 | MS60 | MS63 | MS65 |
|---|---|---|---|---|---|---|
| A VI MMVIII (2008) R | 9,602 | PF63 85.00 | PF65 95.00 | | | |

**KM# 417 10 EURO**
22.00 g., 0.925 Silver 0.6543 oz. ASW, 34 mm. **Subject:** Lateran Treaty, 80th Anniversary **Obv:** Bust right **Rev:** Rolled treaty with seal

| Date | Mintage | VF20 | XF40 | MS60 | MS63 | MS65 |
|---|---|---|---|---|---|---|
| 2009 R | 9,602 | PF63 85.00 | PF65 95.00 | | | |

**KM# 422 10 EURO**
22.00 g., 0.925 Silver 0.6543 oz. ASW, 34 mm. **Subject:** 43rd World day of Peace **Obv:** Bust left **Rev:** Three figures

| Date | Mintage | VF20 | XF40 | MS60 | MS63 | MS65 |
|---|---|---|---|---|---|---|
| 2010 R | 9,998 | PF63 70.00 | PF65 80.00 | | | |

**KM# 428 10 EURO**
22.00 g., 0.925 Silver 0.6543 oz. ASW, 34 mm. **Subject:** Benedict XVI's 60th Anniversary of Ordination **Obv:** Bust right **Rev:** Two fishermen hauling in net

| Date | Mintage | VF20 | XF40 | MS60 | MS63 | MS65 |
|---|---|---|---|---|---|---|
| 2011 R | 7,998 | PF63 80.00 | PF65 90.00 | | | |

**KM# 437 10 EURO**
22.00 g., 0.925 Silver 0.6543 oz. ASW, 34 mm. **Subject:** 20th World Day of the Sick

| Date | Mintage | VF20 | XF40 | MS60 | MS63 | MS65 |
|---|---|---|---|---|---|---|
| 2012 R | 8,999 | PF63 80.00 | PF65 90.00 | | | |

**KM# 392 20 EURO**
6.00 g., 0.916 Gold 0.1767 oz. AGW, 21 mm. **Subject:** Christian Initiation - Baptism **Obv:** Pope seated **Rev:** Fountain

| Date | Mintage | VF20 | XF40 | MS60 | MS63 | MS65 |
|---|---|---|---|---|---|---|
| AN I MMV (2005) R | 3,046 | PF63 550 | PF65 600 | | | |

**KM# 397 20 EURO**
6.00 g., 0.916 Gold 0.1767 oz. AGW, 21 mm. **Subject:** Christian Initiation - Confirmation **Obv:** Bust right **Rev:** Bishop confirming three

| Date | Mintage | VF20 | XF40 | MS60 | MS63 | MS65 |
|---|---|---|---|---|---|---|
| AN II MMVI (2006) R | 3,326 | PF63 550 | PF65 600 | | | |

**KM# 402 20 EURO**
6.00 g., 0.916 Gold 0.1767 oz. AGW, 21 mm. **Subject:** Christain Initiation - Eucharist **Obv:** Bust left in ermine cape **Rev:** Basket of fish and bread

| Date | Mintage | VF20 | XF40 | MS60 | MS63 | MS65 |
|---|---|---|---|---|---|---|
| AN III (2007) R | 3,426 | PF63 550 | PF65 600 | | | |

**KM# 408 20 EURO**
6.00 g., 0.917 Gold 0.1769 oz. AGW, 21 mm. **Subject:** Vatican sculpture **Obv:** Pope right in mitre **Rev:** Torso of Belvedere

| Date | Mintage | VF20 | XF40 | MS60 | MS63 | MS65 |
|---|---|---|---|---|---|---|
| AN IV MMVIII (2008) R | 2,930 | PF63 450 | PF65 500 | | | |

**KM# 416 20 EURO**
6.00 g., 0.917 Gold 0.1769 oz. AGW, 21 mm. **Subject:** Masterworks in the Vatican Collection **Rev:** John the Baptist with lamb on shoulders

| Date | Mintage | VF20 | XF40 | MS60 | MS63 | MS65 |
|---|---|---|---|---|---|---|
| 2009 R | 2,934 | **PF63** 500 | **PF65** 550 | | | |

**KM# 423 20 EURO**
6.00 g., 0.917 Gold 0.1769 oz. AGW, 21 mm. **Subject:** Vatican Sculpture - Apollo Belvedere **Obv:** Large head profile left **Rev:** Statue of Apollo Belvedere

| Date | Mintage | VF20 | XF40 | MS60 | MS63 | MS65 |
|---|---|---|---|---|---|---|
| 2010 R | 3,050 | **PF63** 450 | **PF65** 500 | | | |

**KM# 431 20 EURO**
6.00 g., 0.917 Gold 0.1769 oz. AGW, 21 mm. **Subject:** Pauline Chapel restoration **Obv:** Bust left **Rev:** Head

| Date | Mintage | VF20 | XF40 | MS60 | MS63 | MS65 |
|---|---|---|---|---|---|---|
| 2011 R | 3,050 | **PF63** 400 | **PF65** 450 | | | |

**KM# 433 20 EURO**
26.00 g., 0.925 Silver 0.7732 oz. ASW, 36 mm. **Subject:** 10th Anniversary of the Vatican Euro **Rev:** St. Peter's Basilica

| Date | Mintage | VF20 | XF40 | MS60 | MS63 | MS65 |
|---|---|---|---|---|---|---|
| 2012 R | 13,000 | **PF63** 300 | **PF65** 350 | | | |

**KM# 438 20 EURO**
6.00 g., 0.917 Gold 0.1769 oz. AGW, 21 mm. **Subject:** Restoration of the Pauline Chapel

| Date | Mintage | VF20 | XF40 | MS60 | MS63 | MS65 |
|---|---|---|---|---|---|---|
| 2012 R | 3,000 | **PF63** 350 | **PF65** 400 | | | |

**KM# 444 20 EURO**
26.00 g., 0.925 Silver 0.7732 oz. ASW, 36 mm. **Subject:** Giuseppe Verdi, 200 Anniversary of Birth **Rev:** Bust facing at left **Edge:** Reeded

| Date | Mintage | VF20 | XF40 | MS60 | MS63 | MS65 |
|---|---|---|---|---|---|---|
| 2013 R | 11,000 | **PF63** 90.00 | **PF65** 100 | | | |

**KM# 393 50 EURO**
15.00 g., 0.916 Gold 0.4418 oz. AGW, 28 mm. **Subject:** Christian Initiation - Baptism **Obv:** Pope seated **Rev:** John baptising Christ

| Date | Mintage | VF20 | XF40 | MS60 | MS63 | MS65 |
|---|---|---|---|---|---|---|
| AN I MMV (2005) R | 3,044 | **PF63** 1,400 | **PF65** 1,500 | | | |

**KM# 398 50 EURO**
15.00 g., 0.916 Gold 0.4418 oz. AGW, 28 mm. **Subject:** Christian Initiation - Confirmation **Obv:** Bust right **Rev:** Tongues of fire decending on Apostles

| Date | Mintage | VF20 | XF40 | MS60 | MS63 | MS65 |
|---|---|---|---|---|---|---|
| AN II MMVI (2006) R | 3,324 | **PF63** 1,400 | **PF65** 1,500 | | | |

**KM# 403 50 EURO**
15.00 g., 0.916 Gold 0.4418 oz. AGW, 28 mm. **Subject:** Christian Initiation - Eucharist **Obv:** Bust left in ermine cape **Rev:** Scene of the Last Supper

| Date | Mintage | VF20 | XF40 | MS60 | MS63 | MS65 |
|---|---|---|---|---|---|---|
| ANIII MMVII (2007) R | — | **PF63** 1,400 | **PF65** 1,500 | | | |

**KM# 409 50 EURO**
15.00 g., 0.917 Gold 0.4422 oz. AGW, 28 mm. **Subject:** Vatican sculpture **Obv:** Pope right in mitre **Rev:** The Pieta

| Date | Mintage | VF20 | XF40 | MS60 | MS63 | MS65 |
|---|---|---|---|---|---|---|
| AN IV MMVIII (2008) R | — | **PF63** 900 | **PF65** 1,000 | | | |

**KM# 418 50 EURO**
15.00 g., 0.917 Gold 0.4422 oz. AGW, 28 mm. **Subject:** Masterworks in the Vatican Collection **Rev:** Hercules statue group

| Date | Mintage | VF20 | XF40 | MS60 | MS63 | MS65 |
|---|---|---|---|---|---|---|
| 2009 R | 2,930 | **PF63** 1,100 | **PF65** 1,200 | | | |

**KM# 424 50 EURO**
15.00 g., 0.917 Gold 0.4422 oz. AGW, 28 mm. **Subject:** Vatican Sculpture - Augustus of Prima **Obv:** Large head profile left **Rev:** Statue of Augustus

| Date | Mintage | VF20 | XF40 | MS60 | MS63 | MS65 |
|---|---|---|---|---|---|---|
| 2010 R | 3,050 | **PF63** 1,100 | **PF65** 1,200 | | | |

**KM# 432 50 EURO**
15.00 g., 0.917 Gold 0.4422 oz. AGW, 28 mm. **Subject:** Pauline Chapel restoration **Obv:** Bust left **Rev:** Cruxifiction of St. Peter

| Date | Mintage | VF20 | XF40 | MS60 | MS63 | MS65 |
|---|---|---|---|---|---|---|
| 2011 R | 2,700 | **PF63** 850 | **PF65** 950 | | | |

**KM# 434 50 EURO**
15.00 g., 0.917 Gold 0.4422 oz. AGW, 28 mm. **Subject:** 10th Anniversary of the Vatican Euro **Rev:** St. Peter's Basilica

| Date | Mintage | VF20 | XF40 | MS60 | MS63 | MS65 |
|---|---|---|---|---|---|---|
| 2012 R | 2,000 | **PF63** 900 | **PF65** 1,000 | | | |

**KM# 439 50 EURO**
15.00 g., 0.917 Gold 0.4422 oz. AGW, 28 mm. **Subject:** Restoration of the Pauline Chapel

| Date | Mintage | VF20 | XF40 | MS60 | MS63 | MS65 |
|---|---|---|---|---|---|---|
| 2012 R | 2,500 | **PF63** 1,100 | **PF65** 1,200 | | | |

**KM# 445 50 EURO**
15.00 g., 0.917 Gold 0.4422 oz. AGW, 15 mm. **Subject:** Richard Wagner, 200th Anniversary of Birth **Rev:** Profile facing right **Edge:** Reeded

| Date | Mintage | VF20 | XF40 | MS60 | MS63 | MS65 |
|---|---|---|---|---|---|---|
| 2013 R | 2,000 | **PF63** 900 | **PF65** 1,000 | | | |

**KM# 405 100 EURO**
30.00 g., 0.917 Gold 0.8845 oz. AGW, 35 mm. **Obv:** Bust left **Rev:** The Creator from the Sistine Chapel ceiling

| Date | Mintage | VF20 | XF40 | MS60 | MS63 | MS65 |
|---|---|---|---|---|---|---|
| AN IV MMVIII (2008) R | 960 | **PF63** 1,600 | **PF65** 1,700 | | | |

**KM# 419 100 EURO**
30.00 g., 0.917 Gold 0.8845 oz. AGW, 35 mm. **Subject:** Sistine Chapel - Banishment from Eden

| Date | Mintage | VF20 | XF40 | MS60 | MS63 | MS65 |
|---|---|---|---|---|---|---|
| 2009 R | — | **PF63** 1,600 | **PF65** 1,700 | | | |

**KM# 425 100 EURO**
30.00 g., 0.917 Gold 0.8845 oz. AGW, 35 mm. **Subject:** Sistine Chapel - Last Judgement **Obv:** Bust left **Rev:** Detail of the painting

| Date | Mintage | VF20 | XF40 | MS60 | MS63 | MS65 |
|---|---|---|---|---|---|---|
| 2010 R | 1,100 | **PF63** 1,650 | **PF65** 1,750 | | | |

**KM# 430 100 EURO**
30.00 g., 0.917 Gold 0.8845 oz. AGW, 35 mm. **Subject:** Raffaell painting **Obv:** Bust left in vestments and mitre **Rev:** Horseman and captive

| Date | Mintage | VF20 | XF40 | MS60 | MS63 | MS65 |
|---|---|---|---|---|---|---|
| 2011 R | 1,100 | **PF63** 1,550 | **PF65** 1,650 | | | |

**KM# 440 100 EURO**
30.00 g., 0.917 Gold 0.8845 oz. AGW, 35 mm. **Rev:** Madonna of Foligno

| Date | Mintage | VF20 | XF40 | MS60 | MS63 | MS65 |
|---|---|---|---|---|---|---|
| 2012 R | 999 | **PF63** 2,200 | **PF65** 2,300 | | | |

**KM# 441 200 EURO**
40.00 g., 0.917 Gold 1.1793 oz. AGW, 38.5 mm. **Subject:** Theological Virtues - Faith

| Date | Mintage | VF20 | XF40 | MS60 | MS63 | MS65 |
|---|---|---|---|---|---|---|
| 2012 R | 499 | **PF63** 4,500 | **PF65** 5,500 | | | |

## Francis

**KM# 455 EURO CENT**
2.30 g., Copper Plated Steel, 16.25 mm. **Obv:** Bust left

| Date | Mintage | VF20 | XF40 | MS60 | MS63 | MS65 |
|---|---|---|---|---|---|---|
| 2014 | — | — | — | — | — | 12.00 |
| 2014 | — | **PF65** 18.00 | | | | |

**KM# 456 2 EURO CENT**
3.06 g., Copper Plated Steel, 18.75 mm. **Obv:** Bust left

| Date | Mintage | VF20 | XF40 | MS60 | MS63 | MS65 |
|---|---|---|---|---|---|---|
| 2014 | — | — | — | — | — | 25.00 |
| 2014 | — | PF65 20.00 | | | | |

**KM# 457 5 EURO CENT**
3.92 g., Copper Plated Steel, 21.25 mm. **Obv:** Bust left

| Date | Mintage | VF20 | XF40 | MS60 | MS63 | MS65 |
|---|---|---|---|---|---|---|
| 2014 | — | — | — | — | — | 16.50 |
| 2014 | — | PF65 22.50 | | | | |

**KM# 458 10 EURO CENT**
4.10 g., Brass, 19.75 mm. **Obv:** Bust facing

| Date | Mintage | VF20 | XF40 | MS60 | MS63 | MS65 |
|---|---|---|---|---|---|---|
| 2014 | — | — | — | — | — | 17.50 |
| 2014 | — | PF65 25.00 | | | | |

**KM# 459 20 EURO CENT**
5.74 g., Brass, 22.25 mm. **Obv:** Bust facing

| Date | Mintage | VF20 | XF40 | MS60 | MS63 | MS65 |
|---|---|---|---|---|---|---|
| 2014 | — | — | — | — | — | 18.00 |
| 2014 | — | PF65 28.00 | | | | |

**KM# 460 50 EURO CENT**
7.80 g., Brass, 24.25 mm. **Obv:** Bust facing

| Date | Mintage | VF20 | XF40 | MS60 | MS63 | MS65 |
|---|---|---|---|---|---|---|
| 2014 | — | — | — | — | — | 32.50 |
| 2014 | — | PF65 40.00 | | | | |

**KM# 461 EURO**
7.50 g., Bi-Metallic Copper-Nickel center in Nickel-Brass ring, 23.25 mm. **Obv:** Bust right

| Date | Mintage | VF20 | XF40 | MS60 | MS63 | MS65 |
|---|---|---|---|---|---|---|
| 2014 | — | — | — | — | — | 25.00 |
| 2014 | — | PF65 40.00 | | | | |

**KM# 446 2 EURO**
8.50 g., Bi-Metallic Brass center in Copper-Nickel ring, 25.75 mm. **Subject:** World Youth Day - Rio **Obv:** 5 youth below Christ statue

| Date | Mintage | VF20 | XF40 | MS60 | MS63 | MS65 |
|---|---|---|---|---|---|---|
| 2013 R | — | — | — | — | — | 28.00 |

**KM# 462 2 EURO**
8.50 g., Bi-Metallic, 25.75 mm. **Obv:** Bust right

| Date | Mintage | VF20 | XF40 | MS60 | MS63 | MS65 |
|---|---|---|---|---|---|---|
| 2014 | — | — | — | — | — | 25.00 |
| 2014 | — | PF65 50.00 | | | | |

**KM# 463 2 EURO**
8.50 g., Bi-Metallic, 25.75 mm. **Subject:** Fall of the Berlin Wall, 25th Anniversary

| Date | Mintage | VF20 | XF40 | MS60 | MS63 | MS65 |
|---|---|---|---|---|---|---|
| 2014 | — | — | — | — | — | 25.00 |

**KM# 448 5 EURO**
18.00 g., 0.925 Silver 0.5353 oz. ASW, 32 mm. **Obv:** Bust right in prayer **Rev:** Jesus presenting keys to Peter

| Date | Mintage | VF20 | XF40 | MS60 | MS63 | MS65 |
|---|---|---|---|---|---|---|
| MMXIII - I | — | PF65 80.00 | | | | |

**KM# 449 5 EURO**
18.00 g., 0.925 Silver 0.5353 oz. ASW, 32 mm. **Obv:** Francis holding child **Rev:** Jesus seated at right preaching

| Date | Mintage | VF20 | XF40 | MS60 | MS63 | MS65 |
|---|---|---|---|---|---|---|
| MMXIII - I | — | PF65 80.00 | | | | |

**KM# 450 5 EURO**
22.00 g., 0.925 Silver 0.6543 oz. ASW, 34 mm. **Obv:** Bust facing **Rev:** Youth harvesting wheat

| Date | Mintage | VF20 | XF40 | MS60 | MS63 | MS65 |
|---|---|---|---|---|---|---|
| MMXIII - I | — | PF65 90.00 | | | | |

**KM# 451 20 EURO**
6.00 g., 0.9167 Gold 0.1768 oz. AGW, 21 mm. **Obv:** Arms **Rev:** Pope Julius and arch

| Date | Mintage | VF20 | XF40 | MS60 | MS63 | MS65 |
|---|---|---|---|---|---|---|
| MMXIII - I | — | PF65 350 | | | | |

**KM# 452 50 EURO**
15.00 g., 0.9167 Gold 0.4421 oz. AGW, 28 mm. **Obv:** Bust right **Rev:** Pope Leo X on horseback with two cardinals

| Date | Mintage | VF20 | XF40 | MS60 | MS63 | MS65 |
|---|---|---|---|---|---|---|
| MMXIII - I | — | PF65 950 | | | | |

**KM# 453 100 EURO**
30.00 g., 0.9167 Gold 0.8842 oz. AGW, 35 mm. **Obv:** Bust right **Rev:** Mary and child, two angels below

| Date | Mintage | VF20 | XF40 | MS60 | MS63 | MS65 |
|---|---|---|---|---|---|---|
| MMXIII - I | — | PF65 1,650 | | | | |

**KM# 454 200 EURO**
40.00 g., 0.9167 Gold 1.1789 oz. AGW, 38.5 mm. **Obv:** Bust right **Rev:** Female playing lyre

| Date | Mintage | VF20 | XF40 | MS60 | MS63 | MS65 |
|---|---|---|---|---|---|---|
| MMXIII - I | — | PF65 5,500 | | | | |

## Sede Vacante

**KM# 447 2 EURO**
8.50 g., Bi-Metallic Nickel-Brass center in Copper-Nickel ring, 25.75 mm. **Obv:** Arms of Cardinal Tarciscio Bertone

| Date | Mintage | VF20 | XF40 | MS60 | MS63 | MS65 |
|---|---|---|---|---|---|---|
| 2013 | — | — | — | — | — | 100 |

**KM# 442 5 EURO**
18.00 g., 0.925 Silver 0.5353 oz. ASW, 32 mm. **Obv:** Dove in flight **Rev:** Arms of Cardinal Tarciscio Bertone

| Date | Mintage | VF20 | XF40 | MS60 | MS63 | MS65 |
|---|---|---|---|---|---|---|
| 2013 R | — | PF63 40.00 | PF65 50.00 | | | |

**KM# 443 10 EURO**
3.00 g., 0.917 Gold 0.0884 oz. AGW, 18.5 mm. **Obv:** Dove in flight **Rev:** Arms of Cardinal Tarciscio Bertone

| Date | Mintage | VF20 | XF40 | MS60 | MS63 | MS65 |
|---|---|---|---|---|---|---|
| 2013 R | 5,000 | **PF63** 450 | **PF65** 500 | | | |

## MINT SETS

| KM# | Date | Mintage | Identification | Issue Price | Mkt Val |
|---|---|---|---|---|---|
| MS107 | 2001 (8) | 26,000 | KM#331-338 | 21.25 | 200 |
| MS108 | 2002 (8) | 65,000 | KM#341-348 | 12.00 | 975 |
| MS109 | 2003 (8) | 65,000 | KM#341-348 | 15.00 | 500 |
| MS110 | 2004 (8) | 85,000 | KM#341-348 | 16.50 | 335 |
| MS111 | 2005 (8) | 85,000 | KM#341-348. | 32.50 | 335 |
| MS112 | MMV (2005) (8) | 60,000 | KM#365-372 Sede Vacante | — | 435 |
| MS113 | 2006 (8) | — | KM#375-382 | — | 210 |
| MS114 | 2007 (8) | — | KM#375-382 | — | 230 |
| MS115 | 2008 (8) | 85,000 | KM#375-377, 385-389 | 45.00 | 164 |
| MS116 | 2009 (8) | 91,400 | KM#375-377, 385-389 | 30.00 | 164 |
| MS117 | 2010 (8) | 94,000 | KM#375-377, 385-389 | 30.00 | 150 |
| MS118 | 2011 (8) | 94,000 | KM#375-377, 385-389 | — | 75.00 |
| MS119 | 2012 (8) | 85,000 | KM#375-377, 385-389 | — | 75.00 |
| MS120 | 2013 (8) | 85,000 | KM#375-377, 385-389 | — | 75.00 |

## PROOF SETS

| KM# | Date | Mintage | Identification | Issue Price | Mkt Val |
|---|---|---|---|---|---|
| PS13 | 2001 (2) | — | KM#390, 391 | — | 1,350 |
| PS15 | 2002 (8) | 9,000 | KM#341-348 | 75.00 | 1,450 |
| PS16 | 2003 (8) | 13,000 | KM#341-348 | 78.00 | 1,200 |
| PS17 | 2004 (8) | 13,000 | KM#341-348 | — | 1,200 |
| PS18 | 2005 (8) | 16,000 | KM#341-348 plus silver medal | 150 | 1,175 |
| PS19 | 2006 (8) | 16,000 | KM#375-382 plus silver medal | — | 375 |
| PS20 | 2007 (8) | 16,000 | KM#375-382 plus silver medal | — | 315 |
| PS21 | 2008 (8) | 16,000 | KM#375-377, 385-389 plus silver medal | 195 | 250 |
| PS22 | 2009 (8) | 15,000 | KM#375-377, 385-389 plus silver medal | 195 | 250 |
| PS23 | 2010 (8) | 15,000 | KM#375-377, 385-389 plus silver medal | 195 | 240 |
| PS24 | 2010 (8) | 300 | KM#375-377, 385-389 plus gold medal | 2,100 | 2,250 |
| PS25 | 2011 (9) | 14,700 | KM#375-377, 385-389 plus silver medal | — | 200 |
| PS26 | 2011 (9) | 300 | KM#375-377, 385-389 plus gold medal | — | 2,250 |
| PS27 | 2012 (9) | 13,000 | KM#375-377, 385-389, 433 | — | 200 |
| PS28 | 2012 (9) | 2,000 | KM#375-377, 385-389, 434 | — | 2,200 |
| PS29 | 2013 (9) | 11,000 | KM#375-377, 385-389, 444 | — | 200 |
| PS30 | 2013 (9) | 2,000 | KM#375-377, 385-389, 445 | — | 1,250 |

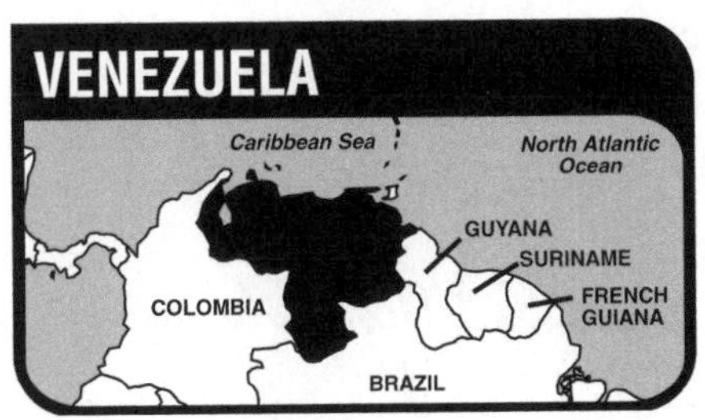


The Bolivarian Republic of Venezuela ("Little Venice"), located on the northern coast of South America between Colombia and Guyana, has an area of 352,145 sq. mi.(912,050 sq. km.) and a population of 20 million. Capital: Caracas. Petroleum and mining provide a significant portion of Venezuela's exports. Coffee, grown on 60,000 plantations, is the chief crop. Metalurgy, refining, oil, iron and steel production are the main employment industries.

**GOVERNMENT**
Republic, 1823-2000
Republic Bolivarian, 2000-

**MINT MARKS**
Maracay

# REPUBLIC

## REFORM COINAGE

1896

100 Centimos = 1 Bolivar

**Y# 80 10 BOLIVARES**
2.33 g., Nickel Clad Steel, 17 mm. **Obv:** National arms left of denomination **Obv. Legend:** REPÚBLICA BOLIVARIANA DE VENEZUELA **Rev:** Head of Bolívar left in 7-sided outline **Rev. Legend:** BOLÍVAR - LIBERTADOR **Edge:** Reeded

| Date | Mintage | VF20 | XF40 | MS60 | MS63 | MS65 |
|---|---|---|---|---|---|---|
| 2001 | — | — | — | 0.15 | 0.25 | 0.50 |
| 2002 | — | — | — | 0.15 | 0.25 | 0.50 |

**Y# 80a 10 BOLIVARES**
1.74 g., Aluminum-Zinc, 16.92 mm. **Obv:** National arms and value **Obv. Legend:** REPÚBLICA BOLIVARIANA DE VENEZUELA **Rev:** Head of Bolívar left in 7-sided outline **Rev. Legend:** BOLÍVAR - LIBERTADOR **Edge:** Reeded

| Date | Mintage | VF20 | XF40 | MS60 | MS63 | MS65 |
|---|---|---|---|---|---|---|
| 2001 | — | — | 0.15 | 0.25 | 0.45 | 0.60 |
| 2002 | — | — | 0.15 | 0.25 | 0.45 | 0.60 |
| 2004 | — | — | 0.15 | 0.25 | 0.45 | 0.60 |

**Y# 81 20 BOLIVARES**
4.32 g., Nickel Clad Steel, 20 mm. **Obv:** National arms left of denomination **Obv. Legend:** REPÚBLICA BOLIVARIANA DE VENEZUELA **Rev:** Head of Bolivar left in 7-sided outline **Rev. Legend:** BOLÍVAR - LIBERTADOR **Edge:** Plain

| Date | Mintage | VF20 | XF40 | MS60 | MS63 | MS65 |
|---|---|---|---|---|---|---|
| 2001 | — | — | — | 0.15 | 0.25 | 0.50 |
| 2002 | — | — | — | 0.15 | 0.25 | 0.50 |

**Y# 81a.1 20 BOLIVARES**
3.27 g., Aluminum-Zinc, 20 mm. **Obv:** National arms and value with wavy based "2" **Obv. Legend:** REPÚBLICA BOLÍVARIANA DE VENEZUELA **Rev:** Head of Bolívar left in 7-sided outline **Rev. Legend:** BOLÍVAR - LIBERTADOR **Edge:** Plain

| Date | Mintage | VF20 | XF40 | MS60 | MS63 | MS65 |
|---|---|---|---|---|---|---|
| 2001 | — | — | — | 0.40 | 0.65 | 1.00 |

**Y# 81a.2 20 BOLIVARES**
3.24 g., Aluminum-Zinc, 20 mm. **Obv:** National arms and value with flat based "2 **Obv. Legend:** REPÚBLICA BOLIVARIANA DE VENEZUELA **Rev:** Head of Bolívar left in 7-sided outline **Rev. Legend:** BOLÍVAR - LIBERTADOR **Edge:** Plain

| Date | Mintage | VF20 | XF40 | MS60 | MS63 | MS65 |
|---|---|---|---|---|---|---|
| 2002 | — | — | 0.25 | 0.35 | 0.60 | 0.80 |
| 2004 | — | — | 0.25 | 0.35 | 0.60 | 0.80 |

**Y# 82 50 BOLIVARES**
6.58 g., Nickel Clad Steel, 23 mm. **Obv:** National arms left of denomination **Obv. Legend:** REPÚBLICA BOLIVARIANA DE VENEZUELA **Rev:** Head of Bolivar left in 7-sided outline **Rev. Legend:** BOLÍVAR - LIBERTADOR **Edge:** Reeded

| Date | Mintage | VF20 | XF40 | MS60 | MS63 | MS65 |
|---|---|---|---|---|---|---|
| 2001 | — | — | 0.30 | 0.45 | 0.75 | 1.00 |
| 2002 | — | — | 0.30 | 0.45 | 0.75 | 1.00 |
| 2004 | — | — | 0.30 | 0.45 | 0.75 | 1.00 |

**Y# 83 100 BOLIVARES**
6.82 g., Nickel Clad Steel, 25 mm. **Obv:** National arms and value **Obv. Legend:** REPÚBUBLICA BOLIVARIANA DE VENEZUELA **Rev:** Head of Bolívar left in 7-sided ouline **Rev. Legend:** BOLÍVAR - LIBERTADO **Edge:** Plain

| Date | Mintage | VF20 | XF40 | MS60 | MS63 | MS65 |
|---|---|---|---|---|---|---|
| 2001 | — | — | 0.45 | 0.60 | 1.10 | 1.50 |
| 2002 | — | — | 0.45 | 0.60 | 1.10 | 1.50 |
| 2004 | — | — | 0.45 | 0.60 | 1.10 | 1.50 |

**Y# 94 500 BOLIVARES**
8.50 g., Nickel Plated Steel, 28.4 mm. **Obv:** National arms and denomination **Obv. Legend:** REPÚBLICA BOLIVARIANA DE VENEZUELA **Rev:** Head of Bolívar left in 7-sided outline **Rev. Legend:** BOLÍVAR - LIBERTADOR **Edge:** Segmented reeding

| Date | Mintage | VF20 | XF40 | MS60 | MS63 | MS65 |
|---|---|---|---|---|---|---|
| 2004 | — | — | 0.60 | 0.75 | 1.50 | 2.00 |

**Y# 85 1000 BOLIVARES**
8.35 g., Bi-Metallic Copper-Nickel center in Brass ring, 24 mm. **Obv:** National arms and value in center **Obv. Legend:** REPÚBLICA BOLIVARIANA DE VENEZUELA **Rev:** Head of Bolívar left **Rev. Legend:** BOLÍVAR - LIBERTADOR **Edge:** Lettered **Edge Lettering:** BCV 1000" four times

| Date | Mintage | VF20 | XF40 | MS60 | MS63 | MS65 |
|---|---|---|---|---|---|---|
| 2005 | 9,000,000 | — | 0.90 | 1.50 | 2.25 | 3.00 |

## REFORM COINAGE

2007

1000 Bolivares = 1 Bolivar Fuerte

**Y# 87 CENTIMO**
1.36 g., Copper Plated Steel, 14.9 mm. **Obv:** National arms **Obv. Legend:** REPÚBLICA BOLIVARIANA DE VENEZUELA **Rev:** Eight stars at left, large value at right **Edge:** Reeded

| Date | Mintage | VF20 | XF40 | MS60 | MS63 | MS65 |
|---|---|---|---|---|---|---|
| 2007 | — | — | — | 0.15 | 0.25 | 0.35 |
| Note: Many die rotation varieties exist. | | | | | | |
| 2009 | — | — | — | 0.15 | 0.25 | 0.35 |

**Y# 88 5 CENTIMOS**
2.03 g., Copper Plated Steel, 16.9 mm. **Obv:** National arms **Obv. Legend:** REPÚBLICA BOLIVARIANA DE VENEZUELA **Rev:** Eight stars at left, large value at right **Edge:** Plain

| Date | Mintage | VF20 | XF40 | MS60 | MS63 | MS65 |
|---|---|---|---|---|---|---|
| 2007 | — | — | — | 0.25 | 0.50 | 0.75 |
| 2009 | — | — | — | 0.25 | 0.50 | 0.75 |

**Y# 89 10 CENTIMOS**
2.62 g., Nickel Plated Steel, 18 mm. **Obv:** National arms **Obv. Legend:** REPÚBLICA BOLIVARIANA DE VENEZUELA **Rev:** Eight stars at left, large value at right **Edge:** Reeded

| Date | Mintage | VF20 | XF40 | MS60 | MS63 | MS65 |
|---|---|---|---|---|---|---|
| 2007 | — | — | — | 0.45 | 0.75 | 1.00 |
| 2009 | — | — | — | 0.45 | 0.75 | 1.00 |

**Y# 90 12-1/2 CENTIMOS**
3.93 g., Nickel Plated Steel, 23 mm. **Obv:** National arms **Obv. Legend:** REPÚBLICA BOLIVARIANA DE VENEZUELA **Rev:** Large value, eight stars below in sprays **Edge:** Plain

| Date | Mintage | VF20 | XF40 | MS60 | MS63 | MS65 |
|---|---|---|---|---|---|---|
| 2007 | — | — | — | 0.75 | 1.50 | 1.75 |

**Y# 91 25 CENTIMOS**
3.86 g., Nickel Plated Steel, 20 mm. **Obv:** National arms **Obv. Legend:** REPÚBLICA BOLIVARIANA DE VENEZUELA **Rev:** Eight stars at left, large value at center right **Edge:** Plain

| Date | Mintage | VF20 | XF40 | MS60 | MS63 | MS65 |
|---|---|---|---|---|---|---|
| 2007 | — | — | — | 1.00 | 2.00 | 2.50 |
| 2009 | — | — | — | 1.00 | 2.00 | 2.50 |

**Y# 99 25 CENTIMOS**
3.86 g., Nickel Plated Steel, 20 mm. **Subject:** Independence, 200th Anniversary **Obv:** Legend **Rev:** Large value

| Date | Mintage | VF20 | XF40 | MS60 | MS63 | MS65 |
|---|---|---|---|---|---|---|
| 2010 | — | — | — | 1.25 | 2.50 | 3.00 |

**Y# 92 50 CENTIMOS**
4.30 g., Nickel Plated Steel, 21.9 mm. **Obv:** National arms **Obv. Legend:** REPÚBLICA BOLIVARIANA DE VENEZUELA **Rev:** Eight stars at left, large value at center right **Edge:** Segmented reeding

| Date | Mintage | VF20 | XF40 | MS60 | MS63 | MS65 |
|---|---|---|---|---|---|---|
| 2007 | — | — | — | 1.50 | 3.00 | 3.50 |
| 2009 | — | — | — | 1.50 | 3.00 | 3.50 |

**Y# 100 50 CENTIMOS**
4.30 g., Nickel Plated Steel, 21.9 mm. **Subject:** Banco Central, 70th Anniversary **Obv:** Legend **Rev:** Large vlaue

| Date | Mintage | VF20 | XF40 | MS60 | MS63 | MS65 |
|---|---|---|---|---|---|---|
| 2010 | — | — | — | 1.75 | 3.50 | 4.00 |

**Y# 93 BOLIVAR**
8.04 g., Bi-Metallic Copper-Nickel center in Aluminum-Bronze ring, 24 mm. **Obv:** Eight stars at left of national arms, large value at right **Obv. Legend:** REPÚBLICA BOLIVARIANA DE VENEZUELA **Rev:** Head of Bolívar left **Edge:** Lettered **Edge Lettering:** BCV 1" repeated

| Date | Mintage | VF20 | XF40 | MS60 | MS63 | MS65 |
|---|---|---|---|---|---|---|
| 2007 | — | — | — | 2.50 | 4.50 | 6.00 |
| 2009 | — | — | — | 2.50 | 4.50 | 6.00 |

**Y# 101 50 BOLIVARES**
31.10 g., 0.999 Silver 0.9989 oz. ASW, 38.6 mm. **Subject:** Banco Central, 70th Anniversary **Obv:** Legned **Rev:** Banco Central building

| Date | Mintage | VF20 | XF40 | MS60 | MS63 | MS65 |
|---|---|---|---|---|---|---|
| 2010 | 3,000 | **PF63** 100 | **PF65** 120 | | | |

**Y# 102 50 BOLIVARES**
31.10 g., 0.999 Gold 0.9989 oz. AGW, 32 mm. **Subject:** Banco Central, 70th Anniversary **Obv:** Legend **Rev:** Banco Central building

| Date | Mintage | VF20 | XF40 | MS60 | MS63 | MS65 |
|---|---|---|---|---|---|---|
| 2010 | 1,500 | **PF65** 2,000 | | | | |

**Y# 95 200 BOLIVARES**
31.10 g., 0.999 Silver 0.999 oz. ASW, 38.61 mm. **Obv:** Flag **Rev:** Crowd outside building

| Date | Mintage | VF20 | XF40 | MS60 | MS63 | MS65 |
|---|---|---|---|---|---|---|
| 2010 | 3,000 | **PF63** 100 | **PF65** 120 | | | |

**Y# 96 200 BOLIVARES**
31.11 g., 0.999 Gold 0.999 oz. AGW, 32 mm. **Obv:** Flag **Rev:** Crowd before building

| Date | Mintage | VF20 | XF40 | MS60 | MS63 | MS65 |
|---|---|---|---|---|---|---|
| 2010 | 1,500 | **PF65** 2,000 | | | | |

**Y# 97 200 BOLIVARES**
31.11 g., 0.999 Silver 0.999 oz. ASW, 38.61 mm. **Obv:** Flag **Rev:** Francisco de Marianda

| Date | Mintage | VF20 | XF40 | MS60 | MS63 | MS65 |
|---|---|---|---|---|---|---|
| 2010 | — | **PF63** 100 | **PF65** 120 | | | |

**Y# 98 200 BOLIVARES**
31.11 g., 0.999 Gold 0.999 oz. AGW, 38.61 mm. **Obv:** Flag **Rev:** Francisco de Marianda

| Date | Mintage | VF20 | XF40 | MS60 | MS63 | MS65 |
|---|---|---|---|---|---|---|
| 2010 | — | **PF65** 2,000 | | | | |

# VIET NAM

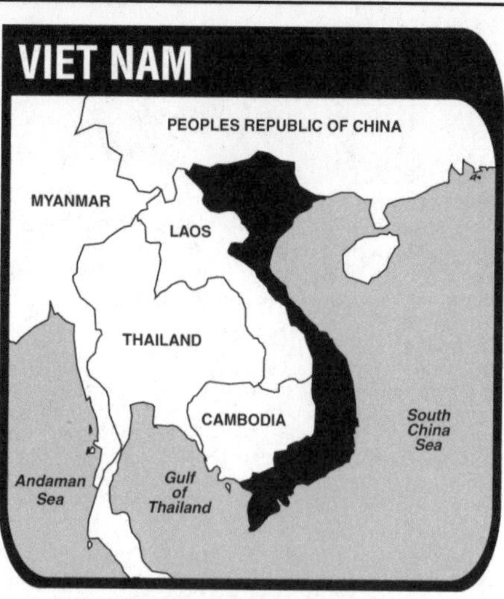


The Socialist Republic of Viet Nam, located in Southeast Asia west of the South China Sea, has an area of 127,300 sq. mi. (329,560 sq. km.) and a population of *66.8 million. Capital: Hanoi. Agricultural products, coal, and mineral ores are exported.

The activities of Communists in South Viet Nam led to the second Indochina war which came to a brief halt in 1973 (when a cease-fire was arranged and U.S. forces withdrew), but it didn't end until April 30, 1975 when South Viet Nam surrendered unconditionally. The two Viet Nams were reunited as the Socialist Republic of Viet Nam on July 2, 1976.

**NOTE:** For earlier coinage refer to French Indo-China or Tonkin.

## SOCIALIST REPUBLIC

### STANDARD COINAGE

**KM# 71 200 DONG**
3.10 g., Nickel Clad Steel, 20.75 mm. **Obv:** National emblem **Rev:** Denomination

| Date | Mintage | VF20 | XF40 | MS60 | MS63 | MS65 |
|---|---|---|---|---|---|---|
| 2003 | 125,000,000 | 0.20 | 0.35 | 0.50 | 0.75 | 1.00 |

**KM# 74 500 DONG**
4.50 g., Nickel Clad Steel, 21.86 mm. **Obv:** National emblem **Rev:** Denomination **Edge:** Segmented reeding

| Date | Mintage | VF20 | XF40 | MS60 | MS63 | MS65 |
|---|---|---|---|---|---|---|
| 2003 | 175,000,000 | 0.25 | 0.45 | 0.75 | 1.00 | 1.25 |

**KM# 72 1000 DONG**
3.70 g., Brass Plated Steel, 19 mm. **Obv:** National emblem **Rev:** Bat De Pagoda in Hanoi **Edge:** Reeded

| Date | Mintage | VF20 | XF40 | MS60 | MS63 | MS65 |
|---|---|---|---|---|---|---|
| 2003 | 250,000,000 | 0.35 | 0.50 | 0.80 | 1.25 | 1.50 |

**KM# 75 2000 DONG**
5.00 g., Brass Plated Steel, 23.5 mm. **Obv:** National emblem **Rev:** Highland Stilt House in Tay Nguyen above value **Edge:** Segmented reeding

| Date | Mintage | VF20 | XF40 | MS60 | MS63 | MS65 |
|---|---|---|---|---|---|---|
| 2003 | — | — | — | 1.75 | 2.25 | 2.75 |

### KM# 64 5000 DONG

1.24 g., 0.9999 Gold 0.040 oz. AGW, 13.92 mm. **Subject:** Year of the Snake **Obv:** State emblem **Rev:** Sea snake **Edge:** Reeded

| Date | Mintage | VF20 | XF40 | MS60 | MS63 | MS65 |
|---|---|---|---|---|---|---|
| 2001 | — | — | — | 85.00 | 100 | 120 |

### KM# 67 5000 DONG

1.24 g., 0.9999 Gold 0.040 oz. AGW, 13.9 mm. **Subject:** Year of the Horse **Obv:** State emblem **Rev:** Horse **Edge:** Reeded

| Date | Mintage | VF20 | XF40 | MS60 | MS63 | MS65 |
|---|---|---|---|---|---|---|
| 2002 | 28,000 | — | — | 75.00 | 90.00 | 110 |

### KM# 73 5000 DONG

7.60 g., Brass, 25 mm. **Obv:** National emblem **Rev:** Chua Mot Cot Pagoda in Hanoi

| Date | Mintage | VF20 | XF40 | MS60 | MS63 | MS65 |
|---|---|---|---|---|---|---|
| 2003 | 500,000,000 | 0.50 | 0.75 | 1.00 | 1.25 | 2.50 |

### KM# 57 10000 DONG

20.00 g., 0.925 Silver 0.5948 oz. ASW, 38.7 mm. **Subject:** Year of the Snake **Obv:** State emblem above value **Obv. Legend:** CONG HOA XA HOI CHU NGHIA VIET NAM **Rev:** Sea snake **Rev. Legend:** ...VIET NAM **Edge:** Reeded

| Date | Mintage | VF20 | XF40 | MS60 | MS63 | MS65 |
|---|---|---|---|---|---|---|
| 2001 (S) | — | PF65 175 | | | | |

### KM# 58 10000 DONG

20.00 g., 0.925 Silver 0.5948 oz. ASW **Subject:** Year of the Snake **Obv:** State emblem above value **Obv. Legend:** CONG HOA XA HOI CHU NGHIA VIET NAM **Rev:** Bamboo viper **Rev. Legend:** ...VIET NAM

| Date | Mintage | VF20 | XF40 | MS60 | MS63 | MS65 |
|---|---|---|---|---|---|---|
| 2001 (S) | — | PF65 175 | | | | |

### KM# 59 10000 DONG

20.00 g., 0.925 Silver 0.5948 oz. ASW **Subject:** Year of the Snake **Obv:** State emblem above value **Obv. Legend:** CONG HOA XA HOI CHU NGHIA VIET NAM **Rev:** Multicolor holographic, cobra in center **Rev. Legend:** ...VIET NAM

| Date | Mintage | VF20 | XF40 | MS60 | MS63 | MS65 |
|---|---|---|---|---|---|---|
| 2001 (S) | — | PF65 175 | | | | |

### KM# 61 10000 DONG

20.00 g., 0.999 Silver 0.6424 oz. ASW, 38.7 mm. **Subject:** Year of the Horse **Obv:** State emblem **Rev:** Horse with octagonal latent image **Edge:** Reeded

| Date | Mintage | VF20 | XF40 | MS60 | MS63 | MS65 |
|---|---|---|---|---|---|---|
| 2001 | 3,800 | PF65 175 | | | | |

Note: In proof set only

### KM# 62 10000 DONG

20.00 g., 0.999 Silver 0.6424 oz. ASW, 38.7 mm. **Subject:** Year of the Horse **Obv:** State emblem **Rev:** Horse with multicolor accoutrements **Edge:** Reeded

| Date | Mintage | VF20 | XF40 | MS60 | MS63 | MS65 |
|---|---|---|---|---|---|---|
| 2001 | 3,800 | PF65 175 | | | | |

Note: In proof set only

### KM# 63 10000 DONG

20.00 g., 0.999 Silver 0.6424 oz. ASW, 38.7 mm. **Subject:** Year of the Horse **Obv:** State emblem **Rev:** Multicolor holographic horse in center **Edge:** Reeded

| Date | Mintage | VF20 | XF40 | MS60 | MS63 | MS65 |
|---|---|---|---|---|---|---|
| 2001 | 3,800 | PF65 175 | | | | |

Note: In proof set only

### KM# 76 10000 DONG

20.00 g., 0.999 Silver 0.6424 oz. ASW, 38.7 mm. **Obv:** State emblem **Rev:** Multicolored Grey-shanked Douc Langur monkey **Edge:** Reeded

| Date | Mintage | VF20 | XF40 | MS60 | MS63 | MS65 |
|---|---|---|---|---|---|---|
| 2004 | 6,200 | PF63 100 | PF65 125 | | | |

### KM# 65 20000 DONG

7.78 g., 0.9999 Gold 0.250 oz. AGW, 22 mm. **Subject:** Year of the Snake **Obv:** State emblem **Rev:** Sea snake **Edge:** Reeded

| Date | Mintage | VF20 | XF40 | MS60 | MS63 | MS65 |
|---|---|---|---|---|---|---|
| 2001 (S) | — | PF63 550 | PF65 600 | | | |

Note: Issued in a replica Faberge egg

### KM# 68 20000 DONG

7.78 g., 0.9999 Gold 0.250 oz. AGW, 22 mm. **Subject:** Year of the Horse **Obv:** State emblem **Rev:** Horse **Edge:** Reeded

| Date | Mintage | VF20 | XF40 | MS60 | MS63 | MS65 |
|---|---|---|---|---|---|---|
| 2002 | 1,800 | PF63 550 | PF65 600 | | | |

### KM# 66 50000 DONG

15.55 g., 0.9999 Gold 0.500 oz. AGW, 27 mm. **Subject:** Year of the Snake **Obv:** State emblem **Rev:** Multicolor holographic King Cobra **Edge:** Reeded

| Date | Mintage | VF20 | XF40 | MS60 | MS63 | MS65 |
|---|---|---|---|---|---|---|
| 2001 (S) | — | PF63 1,000 | PF65 1,100 | | | |

### KM# 69 50000 DONG

15.55 g., 0.9999 Gold 0.500 oz. AGW, 27 mm. **Subject:** Year of the Horse **Obv:** State emblem **Rev:** Multicolor holographic horse **Edge:** Reeded

| Date | Mintage | VF20 | XF40 | MS60 | MS63 | MS65 |
|---|---|---|---|---|---|---|
| 2002 | 3,800 | PF63 1,000 | PF65 1,100 | | | |

## PROOF SETS

| KM# | Date | Mintage | Identification | Issue Price | Mkt Val |
|---|---|---|---|---|---|
| PS4 | 2001(S) (3) | 3,500 | KM#57-59 | 120 | 250 |
| PS5 | 2001(S) (2) | — | KM#59, 66 | — | 1,125 |
| PS6 | 2001(S) (2) | — | KM#65-66 | — | 1,575 |
| PS7 | 2002 (3) | 3,800 | KM#61-63 | — | 225 |

# WEST AFRICAN STATES

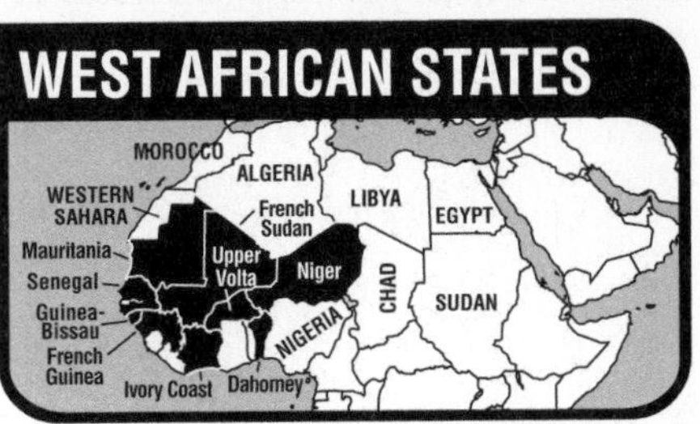


The West African States, a former federation of eight French colonial territories on the northwest coast of Africa, has an area of 1,831,079 sq. mi. (4,742,495 sq. km.) and a population of about 17 million. Capital: Dakar. The constituent territories were Mauritania, Senegal, Dahomey, French Sudan, Ivory Coast, Upper Volta, Niger and French Guinea.

The members of the federation were overseas territories within the French Union until Sept. of 1958 when all but French Guinea approved the constitution of the Fifth French Republic, thereby electing to become autonomous members of the new French Community. French Guinea voted to become the fully independent Republic of Guinea. The other seven attained independence in 1960. The French West Africa territories were provided with a common currency, a practice which was continued as the monetary union of the West African States which provides a common currency to the autonomous republics of Dahomey (now Benin), Senegal, Upper Volta (now Burkina Faso), Ivory Coast, Mali, Togo, Niger, and Guinea-Bissau.

For earlier coinage refer to Togo, and French West Africa.

**MINT MARK**

(a)- Paris, privy marks only

**MONETARY SYSTEM**

100 Centimes = 1 Franc

## FEDERATION

### STANDARD COINAGE

### KM# 8 FRANC

1.60 g., Steel **Obv:** Taku - Ashanti gold weight **Rev:** Value and date

| Date | Mintage | F12 | VF20 | XF40 | MS60 | MS63 |
|---|---|---|---|---|---|---|
| 2001 (a) | — | — | — | 0.10 | 0.35 | 0.60 |
| 2002 (a) | — | — | — | 0.10 | 0.35 | 0.60 |

### KM# 2a 5 FRANCS

3.00 g., Aluminum-Nickel-Bronze, 20 mm. **Obv:** Taku - Ashanti gold weight divides value **Rev:** Gazelle head facing

| Date | Mintage | F12 | VF20 | XF40 | MS60 | MS63 |
|---|---|---|---|---|---|---|
| 2001 (a) | — | — | 0.10 | 0.20 | 0.40 | 0.60 |
| 2002 (a) | — | — | 0.10 | 0.20 | 0.40 | 0.60 |
| 2003 (a) | — | — | 0.10 | 0.20 | 0.40 | 0.60 |
| 2004 (a) | — | — | 0.10 | 0.20 | 0.40 | 0.60 |
| 2005 (a) | — | — | 0.10 | 0.20 | 0.40 | 0.60 |
| 2006 (a) | — | — | 0.10 | 0.20 | 0.40 | 0.60 |
| 2007 (a) | — | — | — | 0.20 | 0.40 | 0.60 |
| 2008 (a) | — | — | — | 0.20 | 0.40 | 0.60 |
| 2009 (a) | — | — | — | 0.20 | 0.40 | 0.60 |
| 2010 (a) | — | — | — | 0.20 | 0.40 | 0.60 |
| 2011 (a) | — | — | — | 0.20 | 0.40 | 0.60 |

### KM# 10 10 FRANCS

4.00 g., Aluminum-Bronze, 23.4 mm. **Series:** F.A.O. **Obv:** Taku - Ashanti gold weight divides value **Rev:** People getting water

| Date | Mintage | F12 | VF20 | XF40 | MS60 | MS63 |
|---|---|---|---|---|---|---|
| 2001 (a) | — | — | 0.25 | 0.50 | 1.25 | 1.50 |
| 2002 (a) | — | — | 0.25 | 0.50 | 1.25 | 1.50 |
| 2003 (a) | — | — | 0.25 | 0.50 | 1.25 | 1.50 |
| 2004 (a) | — | — | 0.25 | 0.50 | 1.00 | 1.50 |
| 2005 (a) | — | — | 0.25 | 0.50 | 1.00 | 1.50 |
| 2006 (a) | — | — | 0.25 | 0.50 | 1.00 | 1.50 |
| 2007 (a) | — | — | — | 0.50 | 1.00 | 1.50 |
| 2008 (a) | — | — | — | 0.50 | 1.00 | 1.50 |
| 2009 (a) | — | — | — | 0.50 | 1.00 | 1.50 |

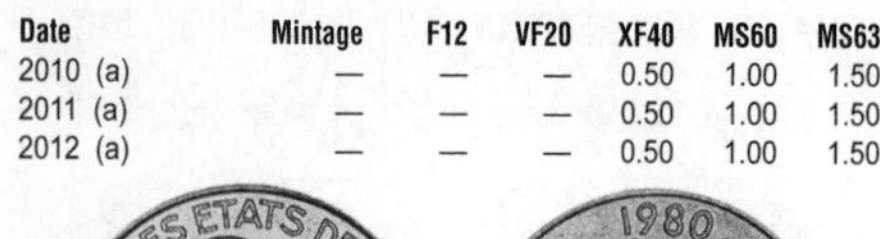

| Date | Mintage | F12 | VF20 | XF40 | MS60 | MS63 |
|---|---|---|---|---|---|---|
| 2010 (a) | — | — | — | 0.50 | 1.00 | 1.50 |
| 2011 (a) | — | — | — | 0.50 | 1.00 | 1.50 |
| 2012 (a) | — | — | — | 0.50 | 1.00 | 1.50 |

### KM# 9 25 FRANCS

7.95 g., Aluminum-Bronze, 27 mm. **Series:** F.A.O. **Obv:** Taku - Ashanti gold weight divides value **Rev:** Figure filling tube **Note:** Mint mark position varieties exist.

| Date | Mintage | F12 | VF20 | XF40 | MS60 | MS63 |
|---|---|---|---|---|---|---|
| 2001 (a) | — | — | — | 0.75 | 1.75 | 2.00 |
| 2002 (a) | — | — | — | 0.75 | 1.75 | 2.00 |
| 2003 (a) | — | — | — | 0.75 | 1.75 | 2.00 |
| 2004 (a) | — | — | — | 0.75 | 1.50 | 2.00 |
| 2005 (a) | — | — | — | 0.75 | 1.50 | 2.00 |
| 2006 (a) | — | — | — | 0.75 | 1.50 | 2.00 |
| 2007 (a) | — | — | — | 0.75 | 1.50 | 2.00 |
| 2008 (a) | — | — | — | 0.75 | 1.50 | 2.00 |
| 2009 (a) | — | — | — | 0.75 | 1.50 | 2.00 |
| 2010 (a) | — | — | — | 0.75 | 1.50 | 2.00 |
| 2011 (a) | — | — | — | 0.75 | 1.50 | 2.00 |
| 2012 (a) | — | — | — | 0.75 | 1.50 | 2.00 |

### KM# 6 50 FRANCS

5.00 g., Copper-Nickel, 22 mm. **Series:** F.A.O. **Obv:** Taku - Ashanti gold weight **Rev:** Value within mixed beans, grains and nuts

| Date | Mintage | F12 | VF20 | XF40 | MS60 | MS63 |
|---|---|---|---|---|---|---|
| 2001 (a) | — | — | 0.35 | 0.50 | 1.25 | 1.50 |
| 2002 (a) | — | — | 0.35 | 0.50 | 1.25 | 1.50 |
| 2003 (a) | — | — | 0.35 | 0.50 | 1.25 | 1.50 |
| 2004 (a) | — | — | 0.35 | 0.50 | 1.25 | 1.50 |
| 2005 (a) | — | — | 0.35 | 0.50 | 1.25 | 1.50 |
| 2006 (a) | — | — | — | 0.50 | 1.25 | 1.50 |
| 2007 (a) | — | — | — | 0.50 | 1.25 | 1.50 |
| 2009 (a) | — | — | — | 0.50 | 1.25 | 1.50 |
| 2010 (a) | — | — | — | 0.50 | 1.25 | 1.50 |
| 2011 (a) | — | — | — | 0.50 | 1.25 | 1.50 |
| 2012 (a) | — | — | — | 0.50 | 1.25 | 1.50 |

### KM# 4 100 FRANCS

7.07 g., Nickel, 26 mm. **Obv:** Taku - Ashanti gold weight **Rev:** Value within flowers **Edge:** Reeded

| Date | Mintage | F12 | VF20 | XF40 | MS60 | MS63 |
|---|---|---|---|---|---|---|
| 2001 (a) | — | — | 0.60 | 0.85 | 2.25 | 2.75 |
| 2002 (a) | — | — | 0.60 | 0.85 | 2.25 | 2.75 |
| 2003 (a) | — | — | 0.60 | 0.85 | 2.25 | 2.75 |
| 2004 (a) | — | — | 0.60 | 0.75 | 2.00 | 2.75 |
| 2005 (a) | — | — | 0.60 | 0.75 | 2.00 | 2.75 |
| 2006 (a) | — | — | 0.60 | 0.75 | 2.00 | 2.75 |
| 2009 (a) | — | — | 0.60 | 0.75 | 2.00 | 2.75 |
| 2010 (a) | — | — | 0.60 | 0.75 | 2.00 | 2.75 |
| 2012 (a) | — | — | 0.60 | 0.75 | 2.00 | 2.75 |

### KM# 14 200 FRANCS

6.90 g., Bi-Metallic Brass center in Copper-Nickel ring, 24.4 mm. **Obv:** Taku - Ashanti gold weight **Rev:** Agricultural produce and value **Edge:** Segmented reeding

| Date | Mintage | VF20 | XF40 | MS60 | MS63 | MS65 |
|---|---|---|---|---|---|---|
| 2003 | — | — | 1.60 | 4.00 | 6.00 | — |
| 2004 (a) | — | — | 1.60 | 4.00 | 6.00 | — |
| 2005 (a) | — | — | 1.60 | 4.00 | 6.00 | — |
| 2010 (a) | — | — | 1.60 | 4.00 | 6.00 | — |

### KM# 15 500 FRANCS

10.60 g., Bi-Metallic Copper-Nickel center in Brass ring, 27.9 mm. **Obv:** Taku - Ashanti gold weight **Rev:** Agricultural produce and value **Edge:** Segmented reeding

| Date | Mintage | VF20 | XF40 | MS60 | MS63 | MS65 |
|---|---|---|---|---|---|---|
| 2003 | — | 2.25 | 4.00 | 6.00 | 10.00 | 14.00 |
| 2004 (a) | — | 2.25 | 4.00 | 6.00 | 10.00 | 12.00 |
| 2005 (a) | — | 2.25 | 4.00 | 6.00 | 10.00 | 12.00 |
| 2010 (a) | — | 2.25 | 4.00 | 6.00 | 10.00 | 12.00 |

### KM# 16 1000 FRANCS

22.20 g., 0.900 Silver 0.6424 oz. ASW **Obv:** Taku - Ashanti gold weight **Rev:** Agricultural produce above sprays surrounded by names of member countries

| Date | Mintage | VF20 | XF40 | MS60 | MS63 | MS65 |
|---|---|---|---|---|---|---|
| 2002 (a) | 500 | **PF63** 150 | **PF65** 275 | | | |

### KM# 17 1000 FRANCS

22.20 g., 0.900 Silver 0.6424 oz. ASW **Subject:** FIFA World Championship Football - Germany 2006 **Obv:** Player kicking ball, tree in background **Obv. Legend:** COUPE DU MONDE DE LA FIFA - ALLEMAGNE **Rev:** Agricultural produce above sprays surrounded by names of member countries

| Date | Mintage | VF20 | XF40 | MS60 | MS63 | MS65 |
|---|---|---|---|---|---|---|
| 2004 (a) | 50,000 | **PF63** 50.00 | **PF65** 70.00 | | | |

# YEMEN REPUBLIC

The Republic of Yemen, formerly Yemen Arab Republic and Peoples Democratic Republic of Yemen, is located on the southern coast of the Arabian Peninsula. It has an area of 205,020 sq. mi. (531,000 sq. km.) and a population of 12 million. Capital: San'a. The port of Aden is the main commercial center and the area's most valuable natural resource. Recent oil and gas finds and a developing petroleum industry have improved their economic prospects. Agriculture and local handicrafts are the main industries. Cotton, fish, coffee, rock salt and hides are exported.

On May 22, 1990, the Yemen Arab Republic (North Yemen) and Peoples Democratic Republic of Yemen (South Yemen) merged into a unified Republic of Yemen. Disagreements between the two former governments simmered until civil war erupted in 1994, with the northern forces of the old Yemen Arab Republic eventually prevailing.

TITLE

المملكة المتوكلية اليمنية

al-Mamlaka(t) al-Mutawakkiliya(t) al-Yamaniya(t)

## REPUBLIC

### MILLED COINAGE

### KM# 26 5 RIYALS

4.50 g., Stainless Steel, 22.9 mm. **Obv:** Denomination within circle **Rev:** Building **Shape:** 21-sided

| Date | Mintage | VF20 | XF40 | MS60 | MS63 | MS65 |
|---|---|---|---|---|---|---|
| AH1421-2001 | — | — | — | 0.35 | 0.75 | 1.00 |
| AH1425-2004 | — | — | — | 0.35 | 0.75 | 1.00 |

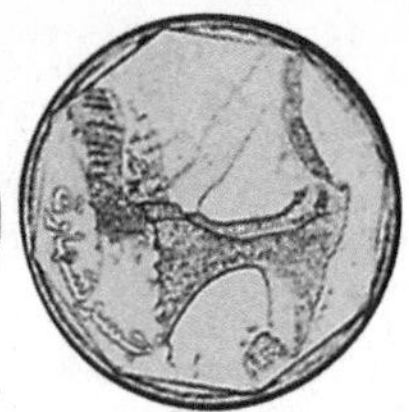

### KM# 27 10 RIYALS

6.05 g., Stainless Steel, 26 mm. **Obv:** Denomination within circle **Rev:** Bridge at Shaharah

| Date | Mintage | VF20 | XF40 | MS60 | MS63 | MS65 |
|---|---|---|---|---|---|---|
| AH1424-2003 | — | — | — | 0.50 | 1.00 | 1.50 |
| AH1430-2009 | — | — | — | 0.50 | 1.00 | 1.50 |

### KM# 29 20 RIALS

7.10 g., Bi-Metallic Brass plated Steel center in Stainless Steel ring, 29.85 mm. **Obv:** Value within circle **Rev:** Tree within circle **Edge:** Reeded

| Date | Mintage | VF20 | XF40 | MS60 | MS63 | MS65 |
|---|---|---|---|---|---|---|
| AH1425-2004 | — | — | — | 0.75 | 1.50 | 2.50 |

### KM# 29a 20 RIALS

Stainless Steel, 29.85 mm. **Obv:** Value within circle **Rev:** Tree within circle **Edge:** Reeded

| Date | Mintage | VF20 | XF40 | MS60 | MS63 | MS65 |
|---|---|---|---|---|---|---|
| AH1427-2006 | — | — | — | 0.75 | 1.50 | 2.50 |

### KM# 30 500 RIALS

21.25 g., Copper-Nickel-Zinc, 35.2 mm. **Subject:** City of San'a **Obv:** Value **Rev:** City gate below artwork **Edge:** Reeded

| Date | Mintage | VF20 | XF40 | MS60 | MS63 | MS65 |
|---|---|---|---|---|---|---|
| AH1425-2004 | — | — | — | 25.00 | 35.00 | 40.00 |

### KM# 32 500 RIALS

13.00 g., Copper-Nickel gilt, 30 mm. **Subject:** City of San'a as Arab Cultural Capital **Note:** Pin added to reverse

| Date | Mintage | VF20 | XF40 | MS60 | MS63 | MS65 |
|---|---|---|---|---|---|---|
| 2004 | — | — | — | 25.00 | 35.00 | 50.00 |

### KM# 31 1000 RIALS

73.30 g., Pewter Antique silver finish, 60.3 mm. **Subject:** City of San'a **Obv:** Value **Rev:** City gate below artwork **Edge:** Plain **Note:** Illustration reduced.

| Date | Mintage | VF20 | XF40 | MS60 | MS63 | MS65 |
|---|---|---|---|---|---|---|
| AH1425-2004 | — | — | — | 45.00 | 60.00 | 80.00 |

### KM# 33 5000 RIALS

22.20 g., 0.900 Silver 0.6424 oz. ASW, 37 mm. **Subject:** President Ali Abdullah Saleh

| Date | Mintage | VF20 | XF40 | MS60 | MS63 | MS65 |
|---|---|---|---|---|---|---|
| AH1424-2003 | — | — | — | 30.00 | 45.00 | 65.00 |

# YUGOSLAVIA

The Federal Republic of Yugoslavia, formerly the Socialist Federal Republic of Yugoslavia, a Balkan country located on the east shore of the Adriatic Sea, has an area of 39,450 sq. mi. (102,173 sq. km.) and a population of 10.5 million. Capital: Belgrade. The chief industries are agriculture, mining, manufacturing and tourism. Machinery, nonferrous metals, meat and fabrics are exported.

The name Yugoslavia appears on the coinage in letters of the Cyrillic alphabet alone until formation of the Federated Peoples Republic of Yugoslavia in 1953, after which both the Cyrillic and Latin alphabets are employed. From 1965, the coin denomination appears in the 4 different languages of the federated republics in letters of both the Cyrillic and Latin alphabets.

**MONETARY SYSTEM**

100 Para = 1 Dinar

## FEDERAL REPUBLIC

### STANDARD COINAGE

### KM# 180 DINAR

4.40 g., Copper-Nickel-Zinc, 20 mm. **Obv:** National arms within circle **Rev:** Building **Edge:** Reeded

| Date | Mintage | VF20 | XF40 | MS60 | MS63 | MS65 |
|---|---|---|---|---|---|---|
| 2002 | 60,780,000 | — | — | 0.25 | 0.45 | 0.75 |

### KM# 181 2 DINARA

5.20 g., Copper-Nickel-Zinc, 21.9 mm. **Obv:** National arms within circle **Rev:** Church **Edge:** Reeded

| Date | Mintage | VF20 | XF40 | MS60 | MS63 | MS65 |
|---|---|---|---|---|---|---|
| 2002 | 71,053,000 | — | — | 0.30 | 0.50 | 0.80 |

### KM# 182 5 DINARA

6.30 g., Copper-Nickel-Zinc, 24 mm. **Obv:** National arms **Rev:** Domed building, denomination and date at left **Edge:** Reeded

| Date | Mintage | VF20 | XF40 | MS60 | MS63 | MS65 |
|---|---|---|---|---|---|---|
| 2002 | 30,966,000 | — | — | 1.25 | 1.50 | 2.00 |

# ZAMBIA

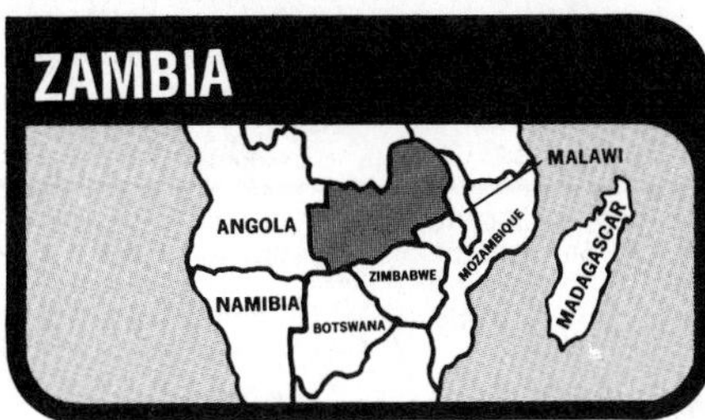


The Republic of Zambia (formerly Northern Rhodesia), a landlocked country in south-central Africa, has an area of 290,586 sq. mi. (752,610 sq. km.) and a population of*7.9 million. Capital: Lusaka. The economy of Zambia is based principally on copper, of which Zambia is the world's third largest producer. Copper, zinc, lead, cobalt and tobacco are exported. Zambia is a member of the Commonwealth of Nations. The President is the Head of State and the Head of Government.

## REPUBLIC

### DECIMAL COINAGE

100 Ngwee = 1 Kwacha

### KM# 156 500 KWACHA

15.00 g., 0.999 Silver 0.4818 oz. ASW, 34.2 mm. **Subject:** Football World Champion - 1954 Germany **Obv:** Crowned head right within circle above arms with supporters and value **Rev:** Soccer game scene in front of Berlin Wall **Edge:** Plain

| Date | Mintage | VF20 | XF40 | MS60 | MS63 | MS65 |
|---|---|---|---|---|---|---|
| 2001 | — | PF63 32.00 | PF65 35.00 | | | |

### KM# 276 500 KWACHA

15.00 g., 0.925 Silver 0.4461 oz. ASW **Subject:** World Cup games of 1954 **Rev:** Games scene from 1954

| Date | Mintage | VF20 | XF40 | MS60 | MS63 | MS65 |
|---|---|---|---|---|---|---|
| 2001 | — | PF63 22.00 | PF65 25.00 | | | |

### KM# 174 500 KWACHA

15.00 g., 0.999 Silver 0.4818 oz. ASW, 34.2 mm. **Subject:** 1972 Munich Olympics **Obv:** Crowned head right above arms with supporters **Rev:** Torch runner in stadium **Edge:** Reeded

| Date | Mintage | VF20 | XF40 | MS60 | MS63 | MS65 |
|---|---|---|---|---|---|---|
| 2002 | — | PF63 25.00 | PF65 28.00 | | | |

### KM# 74 1000 KWACHA

29.00 g., Copper-Nickel, 40 mm. **Obv:** Crowned head right above arms with supporters divides date **Rev:** Dated calendar within circular design **Shape:** 7-sided

| Date | Mintage | VF20 | XF40 | MS60 | MS63 | MS65 |
|---|---|---|---|---|---|---|
| 2002 Proof-like | — | — | — | — | 12.00 | — |
| 2003 Proof-like | — | — | — | — | 12.00 | — |
| 2004 Proof-like | — | — | — | — | 12.00 | — |

### KM# 87 1000 KWACHA

28.91 g., Copper-Nickel, 38 mm. **Series:** Patrons of the Ocean **Obv:** Arms with supporters above crowned head right within circle **Rev:** Loggerhead sea turtle **Edge:** Reeded

| Date | Mintage | VF20 | XF40 | MS60 | MS63 | MS65 |
|---|---|---|---|---|---|---|
| 2001 | — | PF65 17.00 | | | | |

### KM# 88 1000 KWACHA

28.91 g., Copper-Nickel **Series:** Patrons of the Ocean **Obv:** Arms with supporters above crowned head right within circle **Rev:** Coelacanth

| Date | Mintage | VF20 | XF40 | MS60 | MS63 | MS65 |
|---|---|---|---|---|---|---|
| 2001 | — | PF65 17.00 | | | | |

### KM# 89 1000 KWACHA

28.91 g., Copper-Nickel **Series:** Patrons of the Ocean **Obv:** Arms with supporters above crowned head right within circle **Rev:** Sea horse and fish

| Date | Mintage | VF20 | XF40 | MS60 | MS63 | MS65 |
|---|---|---|---|---|---|---|
| 2001 | — | PF65 17.00 | | | | |

### KM# 90 1000 KWACHA

28.91 g., Copper-Nickel **Series:** Patrons of the Ocean **Obv:** Arms with supporters above crowned head right within circle **Rev:** Two dolphins

| Date | Mintage | VF20 | XF40 | MS60 | MS63 | MS65 |
|---|---|---|---|---|---|---|
| 2001 | — | PF65 17.00 | | | | |

### KM# 181 1000 KWACHA

20.03 g., Silver **Subject:** 75th Birthday Queen Elizabeth II **Obv:** Crowned head of Elizabeth II in circle, national arms below **Obv. Legend:** BANK OF ZAMBIA **Rev:** Bust of Elizabeth II facing wearing tiara **Edge:** Reeded

| Date | Mintage | VF20 | XF40 | MS60 | MS63 | MS65 |
|---|---|---|---|---|---|---|
| 2001 | — | PF63 25.00 | PF65 30.00 | | | |

**KM# 277 1000 KWACHA**
20.00 g., 0.925 Silver 0.5948 oz. ASW **Subject:** Princess Diana, 4th Anniversary of Death

| Date | Mintage | VF20 | XF40 | MS60 | MS63 | MS65 |
|---|---|---|---|---|---|---|
| 2001 | — | PF63 35.00 | PF65 40.00 | | | |

**KM# 279 1000 KWACHA**
29.00 g., Copper-Nickel, 40 mm. **Rev:** 2002 Calender

| Date | Mintage | VF20 | XF40 | MS60 | MS63 | MS65 |
|---|---|---|---|---|---|---|
| 2001 | — | — | — | — | 15.00 | — |

**KM# 159 1000 KWACHA**
31.22 g., 0.999 Silver 1.0027 oz. ASW, 38.6 mm. **Obv:** Crowned head right divides date above arms with supporters **Rev:** Bust 1/4 left **Edge:** Reeded

| Date | Mintage | VF20 | XF40 | MS60 | MS63 | MS65 |
|---|---|---|---|---|---|---|
| 2002 | — | — | — | 42.50 | 45.00 | — |

**KM# 160 1000 KWACHA**
29.30 g., Silver Plated Bronze (Specific gravity 9.099), 38.6 mm. **Subject:** Pope John Paul II **Obv:** National arms **Rev:** Pope saying mass **Edge:** Reeded **Note:** Specific gravity 9.099

| Date | Mintage | VF20 | XF40 | MS60 | MS63 | MS65 |
|---|---|---|---|---|---|---|
| 2003 | — | PF63 20.00 | PF65 22.00 | | | |

**KM# 167 1000 KWACHA**
25.00 g., Copper-Nickel, 38.6 mm. **Subject:** 50th Anniversary of Elizabeth II's Coronation **Obv:** Crowned head right above arms with supporters **Rev:** Crown on pillow above crossed scepters **Edge:** Reeded

| Date | Mintage | VF20 | XF40 | MS60 | MS63 | MS65 |
|---|---|---|---|---|---|---|
| ND(2003) | — | — | — | 8.50 | 10.00 | — |

**KM# 169 1000 KWACHA**
25.00 g., Copper-Nickel, 38.6 mm. **Obv:** Crowned head right above arms with supporters **Rev:** Prince William on jet ski **Edge:** Reeded

| Date | Mintage | VF20 | XF40 | MS60 | MS63 | MS65 |
|---|---|---|---|---|---|---|
| 2003 | — | — | — | 8.50 | 10.00 | — |

**KM# 171 1000 KWACHA**
25.00 g., Copper-Nickel, 38.6 mm. **Obv:** Crowned head right above arms with supporters **Rev:** Crowned bust facing **Edge:** Reeded

| Date | Mintage | VF20 | XF40 | MS60 | MS63 | MS65 |
|---|---|---|---|---|---|---|
| ND(2003) | — | — | — | 8.50 | 10.00 | — |

**KM# 172 1000 KWACHA**
25.00 g., 0.925 Silver 0.7435 oz. ASW, 38.6 mm. **Obv:** Crowned head right above arms with supporters **Rev:** Crowned bust facing **Edge:** Reeded

| Date | Mintage | VF20 | XF40 | MS60 | MS63 | MS65 |
|---|---|---|---|---|---|---|
| ND(2003) | 5,000 | PF63 40.00 | PF65 45.00 | | | |

**KM# 183 1000 KWACHA**
7.77 g., 0.999 Silver 0.2496 oz. ASW, 26 mm. **Rev:** Elephant pair

| Date | Mintage | VF20 | XF40 | MS60 | MS63 | MS65 |
|---|---|---|---|---|---|---|
| 2003 | 2,000 | PF65 18.00 | | | | |

**KM# 285 1000 KWACHA**
29.00 g., Copper-Nickel, 40 mm. **Rev:** 2003 Calender

| Date | Mintage | VF20 | XF40 | MS60 | MS63 | MS65 |
|---|---|---|---|---|---|---|
| 2003 | — | — | — | — | 15.00 | — |

**KM# 287 1000 KWACHA**
29.00 g., Copper-Nickel, 40 mm. **Rev:** 2004 Calender

| Date | Mintage | VF20 | XF40 | MS60 | MS63 | MS65 |
|---|---|---|---|---|---|---|
| 2004 | — | — | — | — | 15.00 | — |

**KM# 290 1000 KWACHA**
7.78 g., 0.999 Silver 0.2499 oz. ASW **Rev:** Elephant

| Date | Mintage | VF20 | XF40 | MS60 | MS63 | MS65 |
|---|---|---|---|---|---|---|
| 2009 | — | PF63 20.00 | PF65 22.00 | | | |

**KM# 199 1000 KWACHA**
Silver, 38 mm. **Subject:** Deadly Bugs **Obv:** National arms **Rev:** Harvest Ant in colored insert

| Date | Mintage | VF20 | XF40 | MS60 | MS63 | MS65 |
|---|---|---|---|---|---|---|
| 2010 | — | PF63 35.00 | PF65 40.00 | | | |

**KM# 200 1000 KWACHA**
Silver, 38 mm. **Subject:** Deadly Bugs **Obv:** National arms **Rev:** Giant Hornet in colored insert

| Date | Mintage | VF20 | XF40 | MS60 | MS63 | MS65 |
|---|---|---|---|---|---|---|
| 2010 | — | PF63 35.00 | PF65 40.00 | | | |

**KM# 201 1000 KWACHA**
Silver, 38 mm. **Subject:** Deadly Bugs **Obv:** National arms **Rev:** Mosquito in multicolor insert

| Date | Mintage | VF20 | XF40 | MS60 | MS63 | MS65 |
|---|---|---|---|---|---|---|
| 2010 | — | PF63 35.00 | PF65 40.00 | | | |

**KM# 202 1000 KWACHA**
Silver, 38 mm. **Subject:** Deadly Bugs **Obv:** National arms **Rev:** Scorpion

| Date | Mintage | VF20 | XF40 | MS60 | MS63 | MS65 |
|---|---|---|---|---|---|---|
| 2010 Proof | — | — | — | — | 40.00 | 45.00 |

**KM# 203 1000 KWACHA**
Silver, 38 mm. **Subject:** Deadly Bugs **Obv:** National arms **Rev:** Tsetse Fly

| Date | Mintage | VF20 | XF40 | MS60 | MS63 | MS65 |
|---|---|---|---|---|---|---|
| 2010 | — | PF63 35.00 | PF65 40.00 | | | |

**KM# 118 2000 KWACHA**
31.10 g., 0.999 Silver 0.999 oz. ASW, 38.6 mm. **Subject:** Centennial of the Anglo-Japanese Alliance **Obv:** Queen Elizabeth **Rev:** Fantasy Japanese coin design **Edge:** Reeded

| Date | Mintage | VF20 | XF40 | MS60 | MS63 | MS65 |
|---|---|---|---|---|---|---|
| 2002 | 500 | — | — | 80.00 | 85.00 | — |

**KM# 184 2000 KWACHA**
15.15 g., 0.999 Silver 0.4866 oz. ASW **Rev:** Elephant pair

| Date | Mintage | VF20 | XF40 | MS60 | MS63 | MS65 |
|---|---|---|---|---|---|---|
| 2003 | 2,000 | PF63 25.00 | PF65 30.00 | | | |

**KM# 291 2000 KWACHA**
15.55 g., 0.999 Silver 0.4994 oz. ASW **Rev:** Elephant

| Date | Mintage | VF20 | XF40 | MS60 | MS63 | MS65 |
|---|---|---|---|---|---|---|
| 2009 | — | PF63 32.00 | PF65 35.00 | | | |

**KM# 85 4000 KWACHA**
25.10 g., 0.925 Silver 0.7465 oz. ASW, 37.9 mm. **Series:** Wildlife Protection **Obv:** Crowned head right below arms **Rev:** Lion head hologram **Edge:** Reeded **Note:** Lighter weight and smaller diameter than official specifications

| Date | Mintage | VF20 | XF40 | MS60 | MS63 | MS65 |
|---|---|---|---|---|---|---|
| 2001 | — | PF63 35.00 | PF65 40.00 | | | |

**KM# 175 4000 KWACHA**
23.00 g., 0.999 Silver 0.7387 oz. ASW, 40 mm. **Obv:** Head with tiara right divides date above arms **Rev:** Dated calendar **Shape:** Seven-sided

| Date | Mintage | VF20 | XF40 | MS60 | MS63 | MS65 |
|---|---|---|---|---|---|---|
| 2002 Prooflike | — | — | — | — | 40.00 | 45.00 |
| 2003 Prooflike | 15,000 | — | — | — | 40.00 | 45.00 |
| 2004 Prooflike | 5,000 | — | — | — | 40.00 | 45.00 |

**KM# 110 4000 KWACHA**
20.00 g., 0.999 Silver 0.6424 oz. ASW, 37.9 mm. **Series:** Patrons of the Ocean **Obv:** Crowned head right within circle below arms with supporters **Rev:** Loggerhead sea turtle **Edge:** Reeded

| Date | Mintage | VF20 | XF40 | MS60 | MS63 | MS65 |
|---|---|---|---|---|---|---|
| 2001 | — | PF63 30.00 | PF65 32.00 | | | |

**KM# 111 4000 KWACHA**
20.00 g., 0.999 Silver 0.6424 oz. ASW **Series:** Patrons of the Ocean **Obv:** Crowned head right divides date below arms with supporters **Rev:** Coelacanth fish

| Date | Mintage | VF20 | XF40 | MS60 | MS63 | MS65 |
|---|---|---|---|---|---|---|
| 2001 | — | **PF63** 35.00 | **PF65** 38.00 | | | |

**KM# 112 4000 KWACHA**
20.00 g., 0.999 Silver 0.6424 oz. ASW **Series:** Patrons of the Ocean **Obv:** Crowned head right divides date below arms with supporters **Rev:** Sea horse and fish

| Date | Mintage | VF20 | XF40 | MS60 | MS63 | MS65 |
|---|---|---|---|---|---|---|
| 2001 | — | **PF63** 32.00 | **PF65** 35.00 | | | |

**KM# 113 4000 KWACHA**
20.00 g., 0.999 Silver 0.6424 oz. ASW **Series:** Patrons of the Ocean **Obv:** Crowned head right divides date below arms with supporters **Rev:** Two dolphins

| Date | Mintage | VF20 | XF40 | MS60 | MS63 | MS65 |
|---|---|---|---|---|---|---|
| 2001 | — | **PF63** 35.00 | **PF65** 38.00 | | | |

**KM# 114 4000 KWACHA**
50.00 g., 0.999 Silver 1.6059 oz. ASW **Subject:** Illusion **Obv:** Arms with supporters below crowned head right **Rev:** Cat within window **Edge:** Plain **Note:** 50x50mm

| Date | Mintage | VF20 | XF40 | MS60 | MS63 | MS65 |
|---|---|---|---|---|---|---|
| 2001 | — | **PF63** 65.00 | **PF65** 75.00 | | | |

**KM# 166 4000 KWACHA**
25.00 g., 0.925 Silver 0.7435 oz. ASW, 38.6 mm. **Subject:** Queen Elizabeth's 75th Birthday **Obv:** Crowned head right above arms with supporters **Rev:** Bust with hat facing **Edge:** Reeded

| Date | Mintage | VF20 | XF40 | MS60 | MS63 | MS65 |
|---|---|---|---|---|---|---|
| 2001 | 2,000 | **PF63** 35.00 | **PF65** 40.00 | | | |

**KM# 275 4000 KWACHA**
50.00 g., 0.999 Silver 1.6059 oz. ASW, 50x50 mm. **Rev:** Cat in window illustration

| Date | Mintage | VF20 | XF40 | MS60 | MS63 | MS65 |
|---|---|---|---|---|---|---|
| 2001 | 5,000 | **PF63** 65.00 | **PF65** 75.00 | | | |

**KM# 280 4000 KWACHA**
23.00 g., 0.999 Silver 0.7387 oz. ASW, 40 mm. **Rev:** 2002 Calender

| Date | Mintage | VF20 | XF40 | MS60 | MS63 | MS65 |
|---|---|---|---|---|---|---|
| 2001 | — | — | — | — | — | 40.00 |

**KM# 281 4000 KWACHA**
31.10 g., 0.9999 Silver 0.9998 oz. ASW **Subject:** Japan and Great Britain relations, 100th Anniversary **Obv:** Elizabeth II and magazine **Rev:** Japanese 1 yen coin

| Date | Mintage | VF20 | XF40 | MS60 | MS63 | MS65 |
|---|---|---|---|---|---|---|
| 2002 | 1,000 | **PF63** 110 | **PF65** 125 | | | |

**KM# 282 4000 KWACHA**
Silver ASW **Subject:** Relations between Japan and Great Britain Japan and Great Britain relations, 100th Anniversary **Rev:** Victoria and Hong Kong dollar coin

| Date | Mintage | VF20 | XF40 | MS60 | MS63 | MS65 |
|---|---|---|---|---|---|---|
| 2002 | — | **PF63** 110 | **PF65** 125 | | | |

**KM# 168 4000 KWACHA**
25.00 g., 0.925 Silver 0.7435 oz. ASW, 38.6 mm. **Subject:** 50th Anniversary of Elizabeth II's Coronation **Obv:** Crowned head right above arms with supporters **Rev:** Crown on pillow above crossed scepters **Edge:** Reeded

| Date | Mintage | VF20 | XF40 | MS60 | MS63 | MS65 |
|---|---|---|---|---|---|---|
| ND(2003) | 5,000 | **PF63** 40.00 | **PF65** 45.00 | | | |

**KM# 170 4000 KWACHA**
25.00 g., 0.925 Silver 0.7435 oz. ASW, 38.6 mm. **Obv:** Crowned head right above arms with supporters **Rev:** Prince William on jet ski **Edge:** Reeded

| Date | Mintage | VF20 | XF40 | MS60 | MS63 | MS65 |
|---|---|---|---|---|---|---|
| 2003 | 5,000 | **PF63** 40.00 | **PF65** 45.00 | | | |

**KM# 286 4000 KWACHA**
23.00 g., 0.999 Silver 0.7387 oz. ASW, 40 mm. **Rev:** 2003 Calender

| Date | Mintage | VF20 | XF40 | MS60 | MS63 | MS65 |
|---|---|---|---|---|---|---|
| 2003 | 5,000 | — | — | — | — | 35.00 |

**KM# 288 4000 KWACHA**
23.00 g., 0.999 Silver 0.7387 oz. ASW, 40 mm. **Rev:** 2004 Calender

| Date | Mintage | VF20 | XF40 | MS60 | MS63 | MS65 |
|---|---|---|---|---|---|---|
| 2004 | — | — | — | — | — | 35.00 |

**KM# 117 5000 KWACHA**
31.30 g., 0.999 Silver 1.0053 oz. ASW, 38.6 mm. **Subject:** African Wildlife **Obv:** Arms with supporters **Rev:** Elephant mother and calf grazing on grass **Edge:** Reeded

| Date | Mintage | VF20 | XF40 | MS60 | MS63 | MS65 |
|---|---|---|---|---|---|---|
| 2001 Matte | — | — | — | — | 40.00 | 45.00 |
| 2001 | — | **PF63** 40.00 | **PF65** 45.00 | | | |
| Note: 50 | | | | | | |

**KM# 278 5000 KWACHA**
31.10 g., 0.999 Silver 0.9989 oz. ASW, 38.61 mm. **Rev:** Elephant

| Date | Mintage | VF20 | XF40 | MS60 | MS63 | MS65 |
|---|---|---|---|---|---|---|
| 2001 | — | — | — | — | — | 27.50 |
| 2001 | — | **PF63** 55.00 | **PF65** 60.00 | | | |

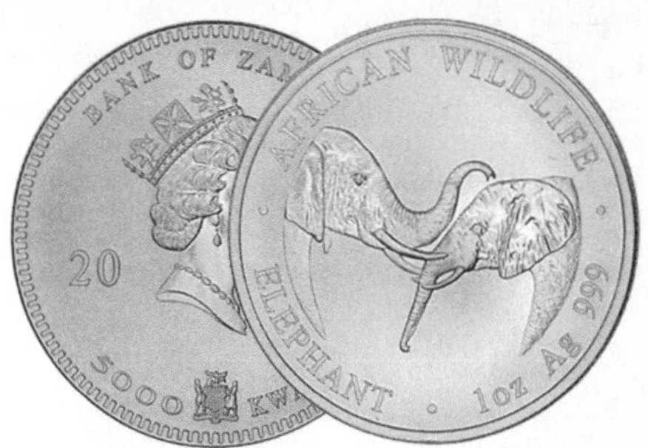


**KM# 142 5000 KWACHA**
28.64 g., 0.999 Silver 0.9199 oz. ASW, 38.5 mm. **Subject:** African Wildlife **Obv:** Queen Elizabeth's portrait above national arms and denomination **Rev:** Adult and juvenile elephants **Edge:** Reeded

| Date | Mintage | VF20 | XF40 | MS60 | MS63 | MS65 |
|---|---|---|---|---|---|---|
| 2002 | — | **PF63** 45.00 | **PF65** 50.00 | | | |
| 2002 Matte | — | — | — | — | 40.00 | 45.00 |

**KM# 143 5000 KWACHA**
28.86 g., 0.999 Silver 0.9269 oz. ASW, 38.5 mm. **Subject:** African Wildlife **Obv:** Arms with supporters **Rev:** Elephant **Edge:** Reeded

| Date | Mintage | VF20 | XF40 | MS60 | MS63 | MS65 |
|---|---|---|---|---|---|---|
| 2002 Matte | — | — | — | — | 40.00 | 45.00 |
| 2002 | — | **PF63** 45.00 | **PF65** 50.00 | | | |

**KM# 284 5000 KWACHA**
31.10 g., 0.999 Silver 0.9989 oz. ASW **Obv:** National arms **Rev:** Elephant

| Date | Mintage | VF20 | XF40 | MS60 | MS63 | MS65 |
|---|---|---|---|---|---|---|
| 2002 | — | — | — | — | — | 27.50 |
| 2002 | — | **PF63** 55.00 | **PF65** 60.00 | | | |

**KM# 165 5000 KWACHA**
31.10 g., 0.999 Silver 0.9989 oz. ASW, 38.5 mm. **Obv:** Crowned bust right divides date **Rev:** Two African elephants **Edge:** Reeded

| Date | Mintage | VF20 | XF40 | MS60 | MS63 | MS65 |
|---|---|---|---|---|---|---|
| 2003 Matte | — | — | — | — | 40.00 | 45.00 |
| 2003 | — | **PF63** 45.00 | **PF65** 50.00 | | | |

**KM# 185 5000 KWACHA**
31.11 g., 0.999 Silver 0.999 oz. ASW **Rev:** Elephant pair

| Date | Mintage | VF20 | XF40 | MS60 | MS63 | MS65 |
|---|---|---|---|---|---|---|
| 2003 | 2,000 | **PF63** 50.00 | **PF65** 55.00 | | | |

**KM# 186 5000 KWACHA**
31.11 g., 0.999 Silver 0.999 oz. ASW **Obv:** Head right **Rev:** Multicolor elephant pair

| Date | Mintage | VF20 | XF40 | MS60 | MS63 | MS65 |
|---|---|---|---|---|---|---|
| 2003 | — | PF63 38.00 | PF65 42.00 | | | |

**KM# 187 5000 KWACHA**
31.11 g., 0.999 Silver 0.999 oz. ASW partially gilt, 40 mm. **Rev:** Elephant pair, partially gilt

| Date | Mintage | VF20 | XF40 | MS60 | MS63 | MS65 |
|---|---|---|---|---|---|---|
| 2003 | — | PF63 45.00 | PF65 50.00 | | | |

**KM# 292 5000 KWACHA**
31.10 g., 0.999 Silver 0.9989 oz. ASW **Rev:** Elephant

| Date | Mintage | VF20 | XF40 | MS60 | MS63 | MS65 |
|---|---|---|---|---|---|---|
| 2009 | — | — | — | — | — | 27.50 |
| 2009 | — | PF63 55.00 | PF65 60.00 | | | |

**KM# 283 6000 KWACHA**
Gold AGW **Subject:** Elizabeth II, 50th Anniversary of Coronation **Obv:** St. George and dragon **Rev:** Elizabeth II and Buckingham Palace in color

| Date | Mintage | VF20 | XF40 | MS60 | MS63 | MS65 |
|---|---|---|---|---|---|---|
| 2002 Proof | — | — | — | — | — | — |

**KM# 188 10000 KWACHA**
62.21 g., 0.999 Silver 1.9981 oz. ASW, 50 mm. **Rev:** Two elephants

| Date | Mintage | VF20 | XF40 | MS60 | MS63 | MS65 |
|---|---|---|---|---|---|---|
| 2003 | 2,000 | PF63 125 | PF65 150 | | | |

**KM# 289 10000 KWACHA**
33.63 g., 0.925 Silver 1.000 oz. ASW, 38.72 mm. **Subject:** Bank of Zambia, 40th Anniversary **Obv:** National arms **Rev:** Hands with soil

| Date | Mintage | VF20 | XF40 | MS60 | MS63 | MS65 |
|---|---|---|---|---|---|---|
| 2004 | 1,000 | PF63 110 | PF65 125 | | | |

**KM# 293 10000 KWACHA**
62.20 g., 0.999 Silver 1.9978 oz. ASW **Rev:** Elephant

| Date | Mintage | VF20 | XF40 | MS60 | MS63 | MS65 |
|---|---|---|---|---|---|---|
| 2009 | — | PF63 110 | PF65 125 | | | |

**KM# 94 40000 KWACHA**
31.10 g., 0.9999 Gold 0.9999 oz. AGW, 37.9 mm. **Series:** Wildlife Protection **Obv:** Arms with supporters above crowned head right **Rev:** Holographic lion head **Edge:** Reeded

| Date | Mintage | VF20 | XF40 | MS60 | MS63 | MS65 |
|---|---|---|---|---|---|---|
| 2001 | — | PF65 1,750 | | | | |

**KM# 153.1 40000 KWACHA**
47.54 g., 0.9166 Gold 1.401 oz. AGW, 39 mm. **Subject:** Queen Victoria **Obv:** Crowned head right within ornate frame divides date above arms with supporters **Rev:** Crowned veiled bust of Queen Victoria left **Edge:** Reeded

| Date | Mintage | VF20 | XF40 | MS60 | MS63 | MS65 |
|---|---|---|---|---|---|---|
| 2001 Proof | 1 | — | — | — | — | — |

Note: Medallic die alignment

**KM# 153.2 40000 KWACHA**
47.54 g., 0.9166 Gold 1.401 oz. AGW, 39 mm. **Subject:** Queen Victoria **Obv:** Crowned head right within ornate frame divides date above arms with supporters **Rev:** Crowned veiled bust of Queen Victoria left **Edge:** Reeded

| Date | Mintage | VF20 | XF40 | MS60 | MS63 | MS65 |
|---|---|---|---|---|---|---|
| 2001 Matte | 1 | — | — | — | — | — |

Note: Coin die alignment

**KM# 154.1 40000 KWACHA**
47.54 g., 0.9166 Gold 1.401 oz. AGW, 39 mm. **Subject:** Edward VII **Obv:** Crowned head right within ornate frame divides date above arms with supporters **Rev:** Crowned bust of King Edward VII right **Edge:** Reeded

| Date | Mintage | VF20 | XF40 | MS60 | MS63 | MS65 |
|---|---|---|---|---|---|---|
| 2001 Proof | 1 | — | — | — | — | — |

Note: Medallic die alignment

**KM# 154.2 40000 KWACHA**
47.54 g., 0.9166 Gold 1.401 oz. AGW, 39 mm. **Subject:** Edward VII **Obv:** Crowned head right within ornate frame divides date above arms with supporters **Rev:** Crowned bust of King Edward VII right **Edge:** Reeded

| Date | Mintage | VF20 | XF40 | MS60 | MS63 | MS65 |
|---|---|---|---|---|---|---|
| 2001 Matte | 1 | — | — | — | — | — |

Note: Coin die alignment

## REFORM COINAGE

2013: 1000 old Kwacha = 1 new Kwacha

**KM# 205 5 NGWEE**
2.50 g., Nickel Plated Iron, 19 mm. **Obv:** National arms **Rev:** Zambezi Indigobird right on branch

| Date | Mintage | VF20 | XF40 | MS60 | MS63 | MS65 |
|---|---|---|---|---|---|---|
| 2012 | — | — | — | 0.30 | 0.60 | 1.00 |

**KM# 206 10 NGWEE**
3.00 g., Brass Plated Iron, 20 mm. **Obv:** National Arms **Rev:** Antelope head left

| Date | Mintage | VF20 | XF40 | MS60 | MS63 | MS65 |
|---|---|---|---|---|---|---|
| 2012 | — | — | — | 0.30 | 0.60 | 1.00 |

**KM# 208 50 NGWEE**
3.50 g., Copper Plated Iron, 21 mm. **Obv:** National arms **Rev:** Elephant head left

| Date | Mintage | VF20 | XF40 | MS60 | MS63 | MS65 |
|---|---|---|---|---|---|---|
| 2012 | — | — | — | 0.40 | 0.75 | 1.50 |

**KM# 209 KWACHA**
5.00 g., Nickel Plated Iron, 24 mm. **Obv:** National arms **Rev:** Zambian Barbet (bird) left

| Date | Mintage | VF20 | XF40 | MS60 | MS63 | MS65 |
|---|---|---|---|---|---|---|
| 2012 | — | — | — | 0.65 | 1.25 | 2.00 |

# ZIMBABWE

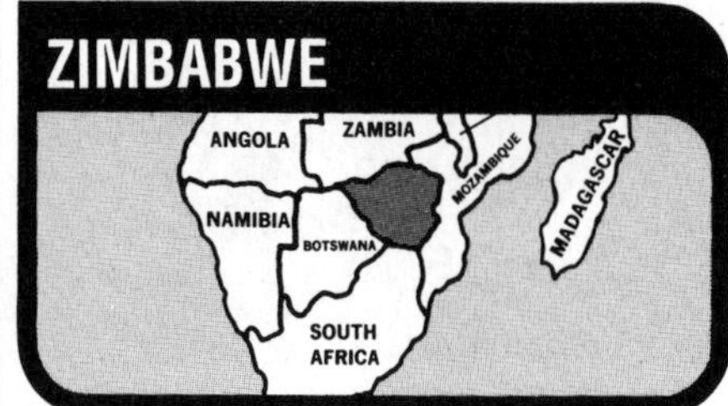


The Republic of Zimbabwe (formerly the Republic of Rhodesia or Southern Rhodesia), located in the east-central part of southern Africa, has an area of 150,804 sq. mi. (390,580 sq. km.) and a population of *10.1 million. Capital: Harare (formerly Salisbury). The economy is based on agriculture and mining. Tobacco, sugar, asbestos, copper, chrome, ore and coal are exported.

On April 18, 1980 pursuant to an act of the British Parliament, the colony of Southern Rhodesia became independent as the Republic of Zimbabwe, a member of the Commonwealth of Nations, until recently suspended.

**MONETARY SYSTEM**
100 Cents = 1 Dollar

**MINT**
Harare

## REPUBLIC

## DECIMAL COINAGE

**KM# 3a 10 CENTS**
Nickel Plated Steel, 20 mm. **Obv:** National emblem **Rev:** Baobab tree, value **Edge:** Plain

| Date | Mintage | VF20 | XF40 | MS60 | MS63 | MS65 |
|---|---|---|---|---|---|---|
| 2001 | — | 0.15 | 0.30 | 0.75 | 1.00 | 1.50 |
| 2002 | — | 0.15 | 0.30 | 0.75 | 1.00 | 1.50 |
| 2003 | — | 0.15 | 0.30 | 0.75 | 1.00 | 1.50 |

**KM# 4a 20 CENTS**
Nickel Plated Steel, 23 mm. **Obv:** National emblem **Rev:** Birchenough Bridge over the Sabi River, value below **Edge:** Plain

| Date | Mintage | VF20 | XF40 | MS60 | MS63 | MS65 |
|---|---|---|---|---|---|---|
| 2001 | — | 0.20 | 0.40 | 1.25 | 1.50 | 2.00 |
| 2002 | — | 0.20 | 0.40 | 1.25 | 1.50 | 2.00 |
| 2003 | — | 0.20 | 0.40 | 1.25 | 1.50 | 2.00 |

**KM# 5a 50 CENTS**
Nickel Plated Steel, 26 mm. **Obv:** National emblem **Rev:** Radiant sun rising, symbolic of independence, value **Edge:** Plain

| Date | Mintage | VF20 | XF40 | MS60 | MS63 | MS65 |
|---|---|---|---|---|---|---|
| 2001 | — | 0.40 | 1.00 | 1.75 | 2.00 | 2.50 |
| 2002 | — | 0.40 | 1.00 | 1.75 | 2.00 | 2.50 |
| 2003 | — | 0.40 | 1.00 | 1.75 | 2.00 | 2.50 |

**KM# 6a DOLLAR**
Nickel Plated Steel, 29 mm. **Obv:** National emblem **Rev:** Zimbabwe ruins amongst trees, value **Edge:** Reeded

| Date | Mintage | VF20 | XF40 | MS60 | MS63 | MS65 |
|---|---|---|---|---|---|---|
| 2001 | — | 1.00 | 1.25 | 1.75 | 2.50 | 3.00 |
| 2002 | — | 1.00 | 1.25 | 1.75 | 2.50 | 3.00 |
| 2003 | — | 1.00 | 1.25 | 1.75 | 2.50 | 3.00 |

**KM# 12a 2 DOLLARS**
Brass Plated Steel, 24.5 mm. **Obv:** National emblem **Rev:** Pangolin below value **Edge:** Reeded

| Date | Mintage | VF20 | XF40 | MS60 | MS63 | MS65 |
|---|---|---|---|---|---|---|
| 2001 | — | 1.25 | 2.00 | 2.50 | 4.00 | 5.00 |
| 2002 | — | 1.25 | 2.00 | 2.50 | 4.00 | 5.00 |
| 2003 | — | 1.25 | 2.00 | 2.50 | 4.00 | 5.00 |

**KM# 13 5 DOLLARS**
9.05 g., Bi-Metallic Nickel-plated-Steel center in Brass ring, 27.4 mm. **Obv:** National emblem **Rev:** Rhinoceros standing right **Edge:** Reeded

| Date | Mintage | VF20 | XF40 | MS60 | MS63 | MS65 |
|---|---|---|---|---|---|---|
| 2001 | — | — | — | 3.00 | 5.00 | 6.00 |
| 2002 | — | — | — | 3.00 | 5.00 | 6.00 |
| 2003 | — | — | — | 3.00 | 5.00 | 6.00 |

**KM# 14 10 DOLLARS**
5.20 g., Nickel Plated Steel, 21.5 mm. **Obv:** National emblem **Rev:** Water buffalo **Edge:** Reeded

| Date | Mintage | VF20 | XF40 | MS60 | MS63 | MS65 |
|---|---|---|---|---|---|---|
| 2003 | — | — | 1.50 | 2.50 | 3.50 | 5.00 |

**KM# 15 25 DOLLARS**
7.33 g., Nickel Plated Steel, 24.5 mm. **Obv:** National emblem **Rev:** Military monument **Edge:** Segmented reeding

| Date | Mintage | VF20 | XF40 | MS60 | MS63 | MS65 |
|---|---|---|---|---|---|---|
| 2003 | — | — | 1.75 | 3.00 | 4.00 | 6.00 |